THE CIA WORLD FACTBOOK 2017

THE CIA WORLD FACTBOOK 2017

CENTRAL INTELLIGENCE AGENCY

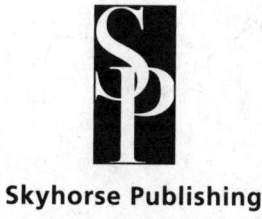

Skyhorse Publishing

Skyhorse Publishing books may be purchased in bulk at special discounts for sales promotion, corporate gifts, fund-raising, or educational purposes. Special editions can also be created to specifications. For details, contact the Special Sales Department, Skyhorse Publishing, 307 West 36th Street, 11th Floor, New York, NY 10018 or info@skyhorsepublishing.com.

Skyhorse® and Skyhorse Publishing® are registered trademarks of Skyhorse Publishing, Inc.®, a Delaware corporation.

Visit our website at www.skyhorsepublishing.com.

10 9 8 7 6 5 4 3 2 1

Library of Congress Cataloging-in-Publication Data is available on file.

Cover design by Eric Kang

Print ISBN: 978-1-5107-1288-1
Ebook ISBN: 978-1-5107-1289-8

Printed in Canada

CONTENTS

CONTENTS

INTRODUCTION

The World Factbook is prepared by the Central Intelligence Agency for the use of US Government officials, and the style, format, coverage, and content are designed to meet their specific requirements. Information is provided by Antarctic Information Program (National Science Foundation), Armed Forces Medical Intelligence Center (Department of Defense), Bureau of the Census (Department of Commerce), Bureau of Labor Statistics (Department of Labor), Central Intelligence Agency, Council of Managers of National Antarctic Programs, Defense Intelligence Agency (Department of Defense), Department of Energy, Department of State, Fish and Wildlife Service (Department of the Interior), Maritime Administration (Department of Transportation), National Geospatial-Intelligence Agency (Department of Defense), Naval Facilities Engineering Command (Department of Defense), Office of Insular Affairs (Department of the Interior), Office of Naval Intelligence (Department of Defense), US Board on Geographic Names (Department of the Interior), US Transportation Command (Department of Defense), Oil & Gas Journal, and other public and private sources.

The Factbook is in the public domain. Accordingly, it may be copied freely without permission of the Central Intelligence Agency (CIA). The official seal of the CIA, however, may **NOT** be copied without permission as required by the CIA Act of 1949 (50 U.S.C. section 403m). Misuse of the official seal of the CIA could result in civil and criminal penalties.

Citation model:
The World Factbook 2013-14. Washington, DC: Central Intelligence Agency, 2013.
https://www.cia.gov/library/publications/the-world-factbook/index.html

Comments and queries are welcome and may be addressed to:

Central Intelligence Agency
Attn: Office of Public Affairs
Washington, DC 20505
Hours: Monday-Friday 8:00 AM-4:30 PM Eastern Standard Time
Telephone: [1] (703) 482-0623
FAX: [1] (703) 482-17

A BRIEF HISTORY OF BASIC INTELLIGENCE AND *THE WORLD FACTBOOK*

The Intelligence Cycle is the process by which information is acquired, converted into intelligence, and made available to policymakers. Information is raw data from any source, data that may be fragmentary, contradictory, unreliable, ambiguous, deceptive, or wrong. Intelligence is information that has been collected, integrated, evaluated, analyzed, and interpreted. Finished intelligence is the final product of the Intelligence Cycle ready to be delivered to the policymaker.

The three types of finished intelligence are: basic, current, and estimative. Basic intelligence provides the fundamental and factual reference material on a country or issue. Current intelligence reports on new developments. Estimative intelligence judges probable outcomes. The three are mutually supportive: basic intelligence is the foundation on which the other two are constructed; current intelligence continually updates the inventory of knowledge; and estimative intelligence revises overall interpretations of country and issue prospects for guidance of basic and current intelligence. The World Factbook, The President's Daily Brief, and the National Intelligence Estimates are examples of the three types of finished intelligence.

The United States has carried on foreign intelligence activities since the days of George Washington but only since World War II have they been coordinated on a government-wide basis. Three programs have highlighted the development of coordinated basic intelligence since that time: (1) the Joint Army Navy Intelligence Studies (JANIS), (2) the National Intelligence Survey (NIS), and (3) The World Factbook.

During World War II, intelligence consumers realized that the production of basic intelligence by different components of the US Government resulted in a great duplication of effort and conflicting information. The Japanese attack on Pearl Harbor in 1941 brought home to leaders in Congress and the executive branch the need for integrating departmental reports to national policymakers. Detailed and coordinated information was needed not only on such major powers as Germany and Japan, but also on places of little previous interest. In the Pacific Theater, for example, the Navy and Marines had to launch amphibious operations against many islands about which information was unconfirmed or nonexistent. Intelligence authorities resolved that the United States should never again be caught unprepared.

In 1943, Gen. George B. Strong (G-2), Adm. H. C. Train (Office of Naval Intelligence—ONI), and Gen. William J. Donovan (Director of the Office of Strategic Services—OSS) decided that a joint effort should be initiated. A steering committee was appointed on 27 April 1943 that recommended the formation of a Joint Intelligence Study Publishing Board to assemble, edit, coordinate, and publish the Joint Army Navy Intelligence Studies (JANIS). JANIS was the first interdepartmental basic intelligence program to fulfill the needs of the US Government for an authoritative and coordinated appraisal of strategic basic intelligence. Between April 1943 and July 1947, the board published 34 JANIS studies. JANIS performed well in the war effort, and numerous letters of commendation were received, including a statement from Adm. Forrest Sherman, Chief of Staff, Pacific Ocean Areas, which said, "JANIS has become the indispensable reference work for the shore-based planners."

The need for more comprehensive basic intelligence in the post-war world was well expressed in 1946 by George S. Pettee, a noted author on national security. He wrote in The Future of American Secret Intelligence (Infantry Journal Press, 1946, page 46) that world leadership in peace requires even more elaborate intelligence than in war. "The conduct of peace involves all countries, all human activities—not just the enemy and his war production."

The Central Intelligence Agency was established on 26 July 1947 and officially began operating on 18 September 1947. Effective 1 October 1947, the Director of Central Intelligence assumed operational responsibility for JANIS. On 13 January 1948, the National Security Council issued Intelligence Directive (NSCID) No. 3, which authorized the National Intelligence Survey (NIS) program as a peacetime replacement for the wartime JANIS program. Before adequate NIS country sections could be produced, government agencies had to develop more comprehensive gazetteers and better maps. The US Board on Geographic Names (BGN) compiled the names; the Department of the Interior produced the gazetteers; and CIA produced the maps.

The Hoover Commission's Clark Committee, set up in 1954 to study the structure and administration of the CIA, reported to Congress in 1955 that: "The National Intelligence Survey is an invaluable publication which provides the essential elements of basic intelligence on all areas of the world. There will always be a continuing requirement for keeping the Survey up-to-date." The *Factbook* was created as an annual summary and update to the encyclopedic NIS studies. The first classified *Factbook* was published in August 1962, and the first unclassified version was published in June 1971. The NIS program was terminated in 1973 except for the *Factbook*, map, and gazetteer components. The 1975 *Factbook* was the first to be made available to the public with sales through the US Government Printing Office (GPO). The *Factbook* was first made available on the Internet in June 1997. The year 2010 marks the 63rd anniversary of the establishment of the Central Intelligence Agency and the 67th year of continuous basic intelligence support to the US Government by *The World Factbook* and its two predecessor programs.

The Evolution of The World Factbook

National Basic Intelligence Factbook produced semiannually until 1980. Country entries include sections on Land, Water, People, Government, Economy, Communications, and Defense Forces.

1981—Publication becomes an annual product and is renamed *The World Factbook*. A total of 165 nations are covered on 225 pages.

1983—Appendices (Conversion Factors, International Organizations) first introduced.

1984—Appendices expanded; now include: A. The United Nations, B. Selected United Nations Organizations, C. Selected International Organizations, D. Country Membership in Selected Organizations, E. Conversion Factors.

1987—A new Geography section replaces the former separate Land and Water sections. UN Organizations and Selected International Organizations appendices merged into a new International Organizations appendix. First multi-color-cover *Factbook*.

1988—More than 40 new geographic entities added to provide complete world coverage without overlap or omission. Among the new entities are Antarctica, oceans (Arctic, Atlantic, Indian, Pacific), and the World. The front-of-the-book explanatory introduction expanded and retitled to Notes, Definitions, and Abbreviations. Two new Appendices added: Weights and Measures (in place of Conversion Factors) and a Cross-Reference List of Geographic Names. *Factbook* size reaches 300 pages.

1989—Economy section completely revised and now includes an Overview briefly describing a country's economy. New entries added under People, Government, and Communications.

1990—The Government section revised and considerably expanded with new entries.

1991—A new International Organizations and Groups appendix added. *Factbook* size reaches 405 pages.

1992—Twenty new successor state entries replace those of the Soviet Union and Yugoslavia. New countries are respectively: Armenia, Azerbaijan, Belarus, Estonia, Georgia, Kazakhstan, Kyrgyzstan, Latvia, Lithuania, Moldova, Russia, Tajikistan, Turkmenistan, Ukraine, Uzbekistan; and Bosnia and Hercegovina, Croatia, Macedonia, Serbia and Montenegro, Slovenia. Number of nations in the *Factbook* rises to 188.

1993—Czechoslovakia's split necessitates new Czech Republic and Slovakia entries. New Eritrea entry added after it secedes from Ethiopia. Substantial enhancements made to Geography section.

1994—Two new appendices address Selected International Environmental Agreements. The gross domestic product (GDP) of most developing countries changed to a purchasing power parity (PPP) basis rather than an exchange rate basis. *Factbook* size up to 512 pages.

1995—The GDP of all countries now presented on a PPP basis. New appendix lists estimates of GDP on an exchange rate basis. Communications category split; Railroads, Highways, Inland waterways, Pipelines, Merchant marine, and Airports entries now make up a new Transportation category. *The World Factbook* is first produced on CD-ROM.

1996—Maps accompanying each entry now present more detail. Flags also introduced for nearly all entities. Various new entries appear under Geography and Communications. *Factbook* abbreviations consolidated into a new Appendix A. Two new appendices present a Cross-Reference List of Country Data Codes and a Cross-Reference List of Hydrogeographic Data Codes. Geographic coordinates added to Appendix H, Cross-Reference List of Geographic Names. *Factbook* size expands by 95 pages in one year to reach 652.

1997—*The World Factbook* introduced onto the Internet. A special printed edition prepared for the CIA's 50th anniversary. A schema or Guide to Country Profiles introduced. New color maps and flags now accompany each country profile. Category headings distinguished by shaded backgrounds. Number of categories expanded to nine with the addition of an Introduction (for only a few countries) and Transnational Issues (which includes Disputes-international and Illicit drugs).

1998—The Introduction category with two entries, Current issues and Historical perspective, expanded to more countries. Last year for the production of CD-ROM versions of the *Factbook*.

1999—Historical perspective and Current issues entries in the Introduction category combined into a new Background statement. Several new Economy entries introduced. A new physical map of the world added to the back-of-the-book reference maps.

2000—A new "country profile" added on the Southern Ocean. The Background statements dramatically expanded to over 200 countries and possessions. A number of new Communications entries added.

2001—Background entries completed for all 267 entities in the *Factbook*. Several new HIV/AIDS entries introduced under the People category. Revision begun on individual country maps to include elevation extremes and a partial geographic grid. Weights and Measures appendix deleted.

2002—New entry on Distribution of Family income—Gini index added. Revision of individual country maps continued (process still ongoing).

2003—In the Economy category, petroleum entries added for oil production, consumption, exports, imports, and proved reserves, as well as natural gas proved reserves.

2004—Bi-weekly updates launched on *The World Factbook* website. Additional petroleum entries included for natural gas production, consumption, exports, and imports. In the Transportation category, under Merchant marine, subfields added for foreign-owned vessels and those registered in other countries. Descriptions of the many forms of government mentioned in the Factbook incorporated into the Definitions and Notes.

2005—In the People category, a Major infectious diseases field added for countries deemed to pose a higher risk for travelers. In the Economy category, entries included for Current account balance, Investment, Public debt, and Reserves of foreign exchange and gold. The Transnational issues category expanded to include Refugees and internally displaced persons. Size of the printed *Factbook* reaches 702 pages.

2006—In the Economy category, national GDP figures now presented at Official Exchange Rates (OER) in addition to GDP at purchasing power parity (PPP). Entries in the Transportation section reordered; Highways changed to Roadways, and Ports and harbors to Ports and terminals.

2007—In the Government category, the Capital entry significantly expanded with up to four subfields, including new information having to do with time. The subfields consist of the name of the capital itself, its geographic coordinates, the time difference at the capital from coordinated universal time (UTC), and, if applicable, information on daylight saving time (DST). Where appropriate, a special note is added to highlight those countries with multiple time zones. A Trafficking in persons entry added to the Transnational issues category. A new appendix, Weights and Measures, (re)introduced to the online version of the *Factbook*.

2008—In the Geography category, two fields focus on the increasingly vital resource of water: Total renewable water resources and Freshwater withdrawal. In the Economy category, three fields added for: Stock of direct foreign investment—at home, Stock of direct foreign investment—abroad, and Market value of publicly traded shares. Concise descriptions of all major religions included in the Definitions and Notes. Responsibility for printing of *The World Factbook* turned over to the Government Printing Office.

2009—The online *Factbook* site completely redesigned with many new features. In the People category, two new fields provide information on education in terms of opportunity and resources: School Life Expectancy and Education expenditures. Additionally, the Urbanization entry expanded to include all countries. In the Economy category, five fields added: Central bank discount rate, Commercial bank prime lending rate, Stock of narrow money, Stock of broad money, and Stock of domestic credit.

2010—Weekly updates inaugurated on the *The World Factbook* website. The dissolution of the Netherlands Antilles results in two new listings: Curacao and Sint Maarten. In the Communications category, a Broadcast media field replaces the former Radio broadcast stations and TV broadcast stations entries. In the Geography section, under Natural hazards, a Volcanism subfield added for countries with historically active volcanoes. In the Government category, a new National anthems field introduced. Concise descriptions of all major Legal systems incorporated into the Definitions and Notes. In order to facilitate comparisons over time, dozens of the entries in the Economy category expanded to include two (and in some cases three) years' worth of data.

2011—The People section expanded to People and Society, incorporating ten new fields. The Economy category added Taxes and other revenues and Budget surplus (+) or deficit (−), while the Government section introduced International law organization participation and National symbols. A new African nation, South Sudan, brings the total number of countries in *The World Factbook* to 195.

2012—A new Energy category introduced with 23 energy-related fields. Several distinctive features added to *The World Factbook* website: 1) playable audio files in the Government section for the National Anthems entry, 2) online graphics in the form of a Population Pyramid feature in the People and Society category's Age Structure field, and 3) a Users Guide enabling visitors to navigate the *Factbook* more easily and efficiently. A new and distinctive Map of the World Oceans highlights an expanded array of regional and country maps. Size of the printed *Factbook*'s 50th anniversary edition reaches 847 pages.

2013—In the People and Society section five fields introduced: Demographic profile, Mother's mean age at first birth, Contraceptive prevalence rate, Dependency ratios, and Child labor—children ages 5–14. In the Transnational Issues category, a new *stateless persons* subfield embedded under the Refugees and internally displaced persons entry. In the Economy section two fields added: GDP—composition by end use and Gross national saving. In the Government category the Judicial branch entry revised and expanded to include three new subfields: *highest court(s)*, *judge selection and term of office*, and *subordinate courts*.

NOTES AND DEFINITIONS

Abbreviations This information is included in **Appendix A: Abbreviations**, which includes all abbreviations and acronyms used in the *Factbook*, with their expansions.

Acronyms An acronym is an abbreviation coined from the initial letter of each successive word in a term or phrase. In general, an acronym made up solely from the first letter of the major words in the expanded form is rendered in all capital letters (NATO from North Atlantic Treaty Organization; an exception would be ASEAN for Association of Southeast Asian Nations). In general, an acronym made up of more than the first letter of the major words in the expanded form is rendered with only an initial capital letter (Comsat from Communications Satellite Corporation; an exception would be NAM from Nonaligned Movement). Hybrid forms are sometimes used to distinguish between initially identical terms (ICC for International Chamber of Commerce and ICCt for International Criminal Court).

Administrative divisions This entry generally gives the numbers, designatory terms, and first-order administrative divisions as approved by the US Board on Geographic Names (BGN). Changes that have been reported but not yet acted on by the BGN are noted.

Age structure This entry provides the distribution of the population according to age. Information is included by sex and age group as follows: *0-14 years (children), 15-24 years (early working age), 25-54 years (prime working age), 55-64 years (mature working age), 65 years and over (elderly)*. The age structure of a population affects a nation's key socioeconomic issues. Countries with young populations (high percentage under age 15) need to invest more in schools, while countries with older populations (high percentage ages 65 and over) need to invest more in the health sector. The age structure can also be used to help predict potential political issues. For example, the rapid growth of a young adult population unable to find employment can lead to unrest.

Agriculture—products This entry is an ordered listing of major crops and products starting with the most important.

Airports This entry gives the total number of airports or airfields recognizable from the air. The runway(s) may be paved (concrete or asphalt surfaces) or unpaved (grass, earth, sand, or gravel surfaces) and may include closed or abandoned installations. Airports or airfields that are no longer recognizable (overgrown, no facilities, etc.) are not included. Note that not all airports have accommodations for refueling, maintenance, or air traffic control.

Airports—with paved runways This entry gives the total number of airports with paved runways (concrete or asphalt surfaces) by length. For airports with more than one runway, only the longest runway is included according to the following five groups—(1) *over 3,047 m* (over 10,000 ft), (2) *2,438 to 3,047 m* (8,000 to 10,000 ft), (3) *1,524 to 2,437 m* (5,000 to 8,000 ft), (4) *914 to 1,523 m* (3,000 to 5,000 ft), and (5) *under 914 m* (under 3,000 ft). Only airports with usable runways are included in this listing. Not all airports have facilities for refueling, maintenance, or air traffic control. The type aircraft capable of operating from a runway of a given length is dependent upon a number of factors including elevation of the runway, runway gradient, average maximum daily temperature at the airport, engine types, flap settings, and take-off weight of the aircraft.

Airports—with unpaved runways This entry gives the total number of airports with unpaved runways (grass, dirt, sand, or gravel surfaces) by length. For airports with more than one runway, only the longest runway is included according to the following five groups—(1) *over 3,047 m* (over 10,000 ft), (2) *2,438 to 3,047 m* (8,000 to 10,000 ft), (3) *1,524 to 2,437 m* (5,000 to 8,000 ft), (4) *914 to 1,523 m* (3,000 to 5,000 ft), and (5) *under 914 m* (under 3,000 ft). Only airports with usable runways are included in this listing. Not all airports have facilities for refueling, maintenance, or air traffic control. The type aircraft capable of operating from a runway of a given length is dependent upon a number of factors including elevation of the runway, runway gradient, average maximum daily temperature at the airport, engine types, flap settings, and take-off weight of the aircraft.

Appendixes This section includes *Factbook*-related material by topic.

Area This entry includes three subfields. *Total area* is the sum of all land and water areas delimited by international boundaries and/or coastlines. *Land area* is the aggregate of all surfaces delimited by international boundaries and/or coastlines, excluding inland water bodies (lakes, reservoirs, rivers). *Water area* is the sum of the surfaces of all inland water bodies, such as lakes, reservoirs, or rivers, as delimited by international boundaries and/or coastlines.

Area—comparative This entry provides an area comparison based on total area equivalents. Most entities are compared with the entire US or one of the 50 states based on area measurements (1990 revised) provided by the US Bureau of the Census. The smaller entities are compared with Washington, DC (178 sq km, 69 sq mi) or The Mall in Washington, DC (0.59 sq km, 0.23 sq mi, 146 acres).

Background This entry usually highlights major historic events and current issues and may include a statement about one or two key future trends.

Birth rate This entry gives the average annual number of births during a year per 1,000 persons in the population at midyear; also known as crude birth rate. The birth rate is usually the dominant factor in determining the rate of population growth. It depends on both the level of fertility and the age structure of the population.

Broadcast media This entry provides information on the approximate number of public and private TV and radio stations in a country, as well as basic information on the availability of satellite and cable TV services.

Budget This entry includes *revenues, expenditures*, and capital expenditures. These figures are calculated on an exchange rate basis, i.e., not in purchasing power parity (PPP) terms.

Budget surplus (+) or deficit (–) This entry records the difference between national government revenues and expenditures, expressed as a percent of GDP. A positive (+) number indicates that revenues exceeded expenditures (a budget surplus), while a negative (–) number indicates the reverse (a budget deficit). Normalizing the data, by dividing the budget balance by GDP, enables easy comparisons across countries and indicates whether a national government saves or borrows money. Countries with high budget deficits (relative to their GDPs) generally have more difficulty raising funds to finance expenditures, than those with lower deficits.

Capital This entry gives the *name* of the seat of government, its *geographic coordinates*, the *time difference* relative to **Coordinated Universal Time (UTC)** and the time observed in Washington, DC, and, if applicable, information on *daylight saving time* (DST). Where appropriate, a special note has been added to highlight those countries that have multiple time zones.

Carbon dioxide emissions from consumption of energy

This entry is the total amount of carbon dioxide, measured in metric tons, released by burning fossil fuels in the process of producing and consuming energy.

Central bank discount rate

This entry provides the annualized interest rate a country's central bank charges commercial, depository banks for loans to meet temporary shortages of funds.

Child labor—children ages 5-14

This entry gives the percent of children aged 5-14 (or the age range specified) engaged in child labor. We define "child labor" as work that deprives children of their childhood, their potential, and their dignity, and that is harmful to physical and mental development. It refers to work that is mentally, physically, socially, or morally dangerous and harmful to children. Such labor may deprive them of the opportunity to attend school, oblige them to leave school prematurely, or require them to combine school attendance with excessively long and heavy work. In its most extreme forms, child labor involves children being enslaved, separated from their families, exposed to serious hazards and illnesses, and/or left to fend for themselves on the streets of large cities—often a very early age.

Children under the age of 5 years underweight

This entry gives the percent of children under five considered to be underweight. Underweight means weight-for-age is approximately 2 kg below for standard at age one, 3 kg below standard for ages two and three, and 4 kg below standard for ages four and five. This statistic is an indicator of the nutritional status of a community. Children who suffer from growth retardation as a result of poor diets and/or recurrent infections tend to have a greater risk of suffering illness and death.

Climate

This entry includes a brief description of typical weather regimes throughout the year.

Coastline

This entry gives the total length of the boundary between the land area (including islands) and the sea.

Commercial bank prime lending rate

This entry provides a simple average of annualized interest rates commercial banks charge on new loans, denominated in the national currency, to their most credit-worthy customers.

Communications

This category deals with the means of exchanging information and includes the telephone, radio, television, and Internet host entries.

Communications—note

This entry includes miscellaneous communications information of significance not included elsewhere.

Constitution

This entry provides information on a country's constitution. It includes the dates of previous constitutions, the dates of the main steps in making and implementing the latest constitution, and the dates of amendments. For countries with 1-3 previous constitutions, the years are listed; for those with 4-9 previous, the entry is listed as "several previous," and for those with 10 or more, the entry is "many previous." Amendment entries are treated in the same manner, and include the date(s) of the last amendment(s).

The main steps in creating a constitution and amending it usually include drafting, legislative and/or executive branch review and approval, public referendum, and entry into law. In many countries this process is lengthy. Terms commonly used to describe constitutional changes are "amended," "revised," or "reformed." In countries such as South Korea and Turkmenistan, sources differ as to whether changes are stated as new constitutions or are amendments/ revisions to existing ones.

A few countries including Canada, Israel, and UK have no single constitution document, but have various written and unwritten acts, statutes, common laws, and practices that, when taken together, describe a body of fundamental principles or established precedents as to how their countries are governed. Countries including Hong Kong, Macau, Oman, and Saudi Arabia use the term "basic law" instead of constitution.

A number of self-governing dependencies and territories such as the Cayman Islands, Bermuda, and Gibraltar (UK), Greenland and Faroe Islands (Denmark), Aruba, Curacao, and Sint Maarten (Netherlands), and Puerto Rico and the Virgin Islands (US) have their own country-level constitutions.

Contraceptive prevalence rate

This field gives the percent of women of reproductive age (15-49) who are married or in union and are using, or whose sexual partner is using, a method of contraception according to the date of the most recent available data. The contraceptive prevalence rate is an indicator of health services, development, and women's empowerment. It is also useful in understanding, past, present, and future fertility trends, especially in developing countries.

Coordinated Universal Time (UTC)

UTC is the international atomic time scale that serves as the basis of timekeeping for most of the world. The hours, minutes, and seconds expressed by UTC represent the time of day at the Prime Meridian (0° longitude) located near Greenwich, England as reckoned from midnight. UTC is calculated by the Bureau International des Poids et Mesures (BIPM) in Sevres, France. The BIPM averages data collected from more than 200 atomic time and frequency standards located at about 50 laboratories worldwide. UTC is the basis for all civil time with the Earth divided into time zones expressed as positive or negative differences from UTC. UTC is also referred to as "Zulu time." See the Standard Time Zones of the World map included with the **Reference Maps.**

Country data codes

See **Data codes.**

Country map

Most versions of the *Factbook* provide a country map in color. The maps were produced from the best information available at the time of preparation. Names and/or boundaries may have changed subsequently.

Country name

This entry includes all forms of the country's name approved by the US Board on Geographic Names (Italy is used as an example): *conventional long form* (Italian Republic), *conventional short form* (Italy), *local long form* (Repubblica Italiana), *local short form* (Italia), *former* (Kingdom of Italy), as well as the *abbreviation.* Also see the **Terminology** note.

Crude oil—exports

This entry is the total amount of crude oil exported, in barrels per day (bbl/day).

Crude oil—imports

This entry is the total amount of crude oil imported, in barrels per day (bbl/day).

Crude oil—production

This entry is the total amount of crude oil produced, in barrels per day (bbl/day).

Crude oil—proved reserves

This entry is the stock of proved reserves of crude oil, in barrels (bbl). Proved reserves are those quantities of petroleum which, by analysis of geological and engineering data, can be estimated with a high degree of confidence to be commercially recoverable from a given date forward, from known reservoirs and under current economic conditions.

Current account balance

This entry records a country's net trade in goods and services, plus net earnings from rents, interest, profits, and dividends, and net transfer payments (such as pension funds and worker remittances) to and from the rest of the world during the period specified. These figures are calculated on an exchange rate basis, i.e., not in purchasing power parity (PPP) terms.

Data codes This information is presented in **Appendix D: Cross-Reference List of Country Data Codes** and **Appendix E: Cross-Reference List of Hydrographic Data Codes.**

Date of information In general, information available as of January in a given year is used in the preparation of the printed edition.

Daylight Saving Time (DST) This entry is included for those entities that have adopted a policy of adjusting the official local time forward, usually one hour, from Standard Time during summer months. Such policies are most common in mid-latitude regions.

Death rate This entry gives the average annual number of deaths during a year per 1,000 population at midyear; also known as crude death rate. The death rate, while only a rough indicator of the mortality situation in a country, accurately indicates the current mortality impact on population growth. This indicator is significantly affected by age distribution, and most countries will eventually show a rise in the overall death rate, in spite of continued decline in mortality at all ages, as declining fertility results in an aging population.

Debt—external This entry gives the total public and private debt owed to nonresidents repayable in internationally accepted currencies, goods, or services. These figures are calculated on an exchange rate basis, i.e., not in purchasing power parity (PPP) terms.

Demographic profile This entry describes a country's key demographic features and trends and how they vary among regional, ethnic, and socioeconomic sub-populations. Some of the topics addressed are population age structure, fertility, health, mortality, poverty, education, and migration.

Dependency ratios Dependency ratios are a measure of the age structure of a population. They relate the number of individuals that are likely to be economically "dependent" on the support of others. Dependency ratios contrast the ratio of youths (ages 0-14) and the elderly (ages 65+) to the number of those in the working-age group (ages 15-64).Changes in the dependency ratio provide an indication of potential social support requirements resulting from changes in population age structures. As fertility levels decline, the dependency ratio initially falls because the proportion of youths decreases while the proportion of the population of working age increases. As fertility levels continue to decline, dependency ratios eventually increase because the proportion of the population of working age starts to decline and the proportion of elderly persons continues to increase.

total dependency ratio—The total dependency ratio is the ratio of combined youth population (ages 0-14) and elderly population (ages 65+) per 100 people of working age (ages 15-64). A high total dependency ratio indicates that the working-age population and the overall economy face a greater burden to support and provide social services for youth and elderly persons, who are often economically dependent.

youth dependency ratio—The youth dependency ratio is the ratio of the youth population (ages 0-14) per 100 people of working age (ages 15-64). A high youth dependency ratio indicates that a greater investment needs to be made in schooling and other services for children.

elderly dependency ratio—The elderly dependency ratio is the ratio of the elderly population (ages 65+) per 100 people of working age (ages 15-64). Increases in the elderly dependency ratio put added pressure on governments to fund pensions and healthcare.

potential support ratio—The potential support ratio is the number of working-age people (ages 15-64) per one elderly person (ages 65+). As a population ages, the potential support ratio tends to fall, meaning there are fewer potential workers to support the elderly.

Dependency status This entry describes the formal relationship between a particular nonindependent entity and an independent state.

Dependent areas This entry contains an alphabetical listing of all nonindependent entities associated in some way with a particular independent state.

Diplomatic representation The US Government has diplomatic relations with 190 independent states, including 188 of the 193 UN members (excluded UN members are Bhutan, Cuba, Iran, North Korea, and the US itself). In addition, the US has diplomatic relations with 2 independent states that are not in the UN, the Holy See and Kosovo, as well as with the EU.

Diplomatic representation from the US This entry includes the *chief of mission, embassy* address, *mailing* address, *telephone* number, *FAX* number, *branch office* locations, *consulate general* locations, and *consulate* locations.

Diplomatic representation in the US This entry includes the *chief of mission, chancery address, telephone, FAX, consulate general locations,* and *consulate locations.* The use of the annotated title Appointed Ambassador refers to a new ambassador who has presented his/her credentials to the secretary of state but not the US president. Such ambassadors fulfill all diplomatic functions except meeting with or appearing at functions attended by the president until such time as they formally present their credentials at a White House ceremony.

Disputes—international This entry includes a wide variety of situations that range from traditional bilateral boundary disputes to unilateral claims of one sort or another. Information regarding disputes over international terrestrial and maritime boundaries has been reviewed by the US Department of State. References to other situations involving borders or frontiers may also be included, such as resource disputes, geopolitical questions, or irredentist issues; however, inclusion does not necessarily constitute official acceptance or recognition by the US Government.

Distribution of family income—Gini index This index measures the degree of inequality in the distribution of family income in a country. The index is calculated from the Lorenz curve, in which cumulative family income is plotted against the number of families arranged from the poorest to the richest. The index is the ratio of (a) the area between a country's Lorenz curve and the 45 degree helping line to (b) the entire triangular area under the 45 degree line. The more nearly equal a country's income distribution, the closer its Lorenz curve to the 45 degree line and the lower its Gini index, e.g., a Scandinavian country with an index of 25. The more unequal a country's income distribution, the farther its Lorenz curve from the 45 degree line and the higher its Gini index, e.g., a Sub-Saharan country with an index of 50. If income were distributed with perfect equality, the Lorenz curve would coincide with the 45 degree line and the index would be zero; if income were distributed with perfect inequality, the Lorenz curve would coincide with the horizontal axis and the right vertical axis and the index would be 100.

Drinking water source This entry provides information about access to improved or unimproved drinking water sources available to segments of the population of a country. *improved* drinking water—use of any of the following sources: piped water into dwelling, yard, or plot; public tap or standpipe; tubewell or borehole; protected dug well; protected spring; or rainwater collection. *Unimproved* drinking water—use of any of the following sources: unprotected dug well; unprotected spring; cart with small tank or drum; tanker truck; surface water, which includes rivers, dams, lakes, ponds, streams, canals or irrigation channels; or bottled water.

Economy This category includes the entries dealing with the size, development, and management of productive resources, i.e., land, labor, and capital.

Economy—overview This entry briefly describes the type of economy, including the degree of market orientation, the level of economic development, the most important natural resources, and the unique areas of specialization. It also characterizes major economic events and policy changes in the most recent 12 months and may include a statement about one or two key future macroeconomic trends.

Education expenditures This entry provides the public expenditure on education as a percent of GDP.

Electricity—consumption This entry consists of total electricity generated annually plus imports and minus exports, expressed in kilowatt-hours. The discrepancy between the amount of electricity generated and/or imported and the amount consumed and/or exported is accounted for as loss in transmission and distribution.

Electricity—exports This entry is the total exported electricity in kilowatt-hours.

Electricity—from fossil fuels This entry measures the capacity of plants that generate electricity by burning fossil fuels (such as coal, petroleum products, and natural gas), expressed as a share of the country's total generating capacity.

Electricity—from hydroelectric plants This entry measures the capacity of plants that generate electricity by water-driven turbines, expressed as a share of the country's total generating capacity.

Electricity—from nuclear fuels This entry measures the capacity of plants that generate electricity through radioactive decay of nuclear fuel, expressed as a share of the country's total generating capacity.

Electricity—from other renewable sources This entry measures the capacity of plants that generate electricity by using renewable energy sources other than hydroelectric (including, for example, wind, waves, solar, and geothermal), expressed as a share of the country's total generating capacity.

Electricity—imports This entry is the total imported electricity in kilowatt-hours.

Electricity—installed generating capacity This entry is the total capacity of currently installed generators, expressed in kilowatts (kW), to produce electricity. A 10-kilowatt (kW) generator will produce 10 kilowatt hours (kWh) of electricity, if it runs continuously for one hour.

Electricity—production This entry is the annual electricity generated expressed in kilowatt-hours. The discrepancy between the amount of electricity generated and/or imported and the amount consumed and/or exported is accounted for as loss in transmission and distribution.

Elevation extremes This entry includes both the highest point and the lowest point.

Energy This category includes entries dealing with the production, consumption, import, and export of various forms of energy including electricity, crude oil, refined petroleum products, and natural gas.

Entities Some of the independent states, dependencies, areas of special sovereignty, and governments included in this publication

are not independent, and others are not officially recognized by the US Government. "Independent state" refers to a people politically organized into a sovereign state with a definite territory. "Dependencies" and "areas of special sovereignty" refer to a broad category of political entities that are associated in some way with an independent state. "Country" names used in the table of contents or for page headings are usually the short-form names as approved by the US Board on Geographic Names and may include independent states, dependencies, and areas of special sovereignty, or other geographic entities. There are a total of 267 separate geographic entities in The World Factbook that may be categorized as follows:

INDEPENDENT STATES

195 Afghanistan, Albania, Algeria, Andorra, Angola, Antigua and Barbuda, Argentina, Armenia, Australia, Austria, Azerbaijan, The Bahamas, Bahrain, Bangladesh, Barbados, Belarus, Belgium, Belize, Benin, Bhutan, Bolivia, Bosnia and Herzegovina, Botswana, Brazil, Brunei, Bulgaria, Burkina Faso, Burma, Burundi, Cambodia, Cameroon, Canada, Cape Verde, Central African Republic, Chad, Chile, China, Colombia, Comoros, Democratic Republic of the Congo, Republic of the Congo, Costa Rica, Cote d'Ivoire, Croatia, Cuba, Cyprus, Czech Republic, Denmark, Djibouti, Dominica, Dominican Republic, Ecuador, Egypt, El Salvador, Equatorial Guinea, Eritrea, Estonia, Ethiopia, Fiji, Finland, France, Gabon, The Gambia, Georgia, Germany, Ghana, Greece, Grenada, Guatemala, Guinea, Guinea-Bissau, Guyana, Haiti, Holy See, Honduras, Hungary, Iceland, India, Indonesia, Iran, Iraq, Ireland, Israel, Italy, Jamaica, Japan, Jordan, Kazakhstan, Kenya, Kiribati, North Korea, South Korea, Kosovo, Kuwait, Kyrgyzstan, Laos, Latvia, Lebanon, Lesotho, Liberia, Libya, Liechtenstein, Lithuania, Luxembourg, Macedonia, Madagascar, Malawi, Malaysia, Maldives, Mali, Malta, Marshall Islands, Mauritania, Mauritius, Mexico, Federated States of Micronesia, Moldova, Monaco, Mongolia, Montenegro, Morocco, Mozambique, Namibia, Nauru, Nepal, Netherlands, NZ, Nicaragua, Niger, Nigeria, Norway, Oman, Pakistan, Palau, Panama, Papua New Guinea, Paraguay, Peru, Philippines, Poland, Portugal, Qatar, Romania, Russia, Rwanda, Saint Kitts and Nevis, Saint Lucia, Saint Vincent and the Grenadines, Samoa, San Marino, Sao Tome and Principe, Saudi Arabia, Senegal, Serbia, Seychelles, Sierra Leone, Singapore, Slovakia, Slovenia, Solomon Islands, Somalia, South Africa, South Sudan, Spain, Sri Lanka, Sudan, Suriname, Swaziland, Sweden, Switzerland, Syria, Tajikistan, Tanzania, Thailand, Timor-Leste, Togo, Tonga, Trinidad and Tobago, Tunisia, Turkey, Turkmenistan, Tuvalu, Uganda, Ukraine, UAE, UK, US, Uruguay, Uzbekistan, Vanuatu, Venezuela, Vietnam, Yemen, Zambia, Zimbabwe

OTHER
2 Taiwan, European Union

DEPENDENCIES AND AREAS OF SPECIAL SOVEREIGNTY
6 Australia—Ashmore and Cartier Islands, Christmas Island, Cocos (Keeling) Islands, Coral Sea Islands, Heard Island and McDonald Islands, Norfolk Island
2 China—Hong Kong, Macau
2 Denmark—Faroe Islands, Greenland
8 France—Clipperton Island, French Polynesia, French Southern and Antarctic Lands, New Caledonia, Saint Barthelemy, Saint Martin, Saint Pierre and Miquelon, Wallis and Futuna
3 Netherlands—Aruba, Curacao, Sint Maarten
3 New Zealand—Cook Islands, Niue, Tokelau
3 Norway—Bouvet Island, Jan Mayen, Svalbard
17 UK—Akrotiri, Anguilla, Bermuda, British Indian Ocean Territory, British Virgin Islands, Cayman Islands, Dhekelia, Falkland Islands, Gibraltar, Guernsey, Jersey, Isle of Man, Montserrat, Pitcairn Islands, Saint Helena, South Georgia and the South Sandwich Islands, Turks and Caicos Islands

14 US—American Samoa, Baker Island*, Guam, Howland Island*, Jarvis Island*, Johnston Atoll*, Kingman Reef*, Midway Islands*, Navassa Island, Northern Mariana Islands, Palmyra Atoll*, Puerto Rico, Virgin Islands, Wake Island (* consolidated in United States Pacific Island Wildlife Refuges entry)

MISCELLANEOUS

6 Antarctica, Gaza Strip, Paracel Islands, Spratly Islands, West Bank, Western Sahara

OTHER ENTITIES

5 oceans—Arctic Ocean, Atlantic Ocean, Indian Ocean, Pacific Ocean, Southern Ocean
1 World

267 total

Environment—current issues This entry lists the most pressing and important environmental problems. The following terms and abbreviations are used throughout the entry:

Acidification—the lowering of soil and water pH due to acid precipitation and deposition usually through precipitation; this process disrupts ecosystem nutrient flows and may kill freshwater fish and plants dependent on more neutral or alkaline conditions (see acid rain).

Acid rain—characterized as containing harmful levels of sulfur dioxide or nitrogen oxide; acid rain is damaging and potentially deadly to the earth's fragile ecosystems; acidity is measured using the pH scale where 7 is neutral, values greater than 7 are considered alkaline, and values below 5.6 are considered acid precipitation; note—a pH of 2.4 (the acidity of vinegar) has been measured in rainfall in New England.

Aerosol—a collection of airborne particles dispersed in a gas, smoke, or fog.

Afforestation—converting a bare or agricultural space by planting trees and plants; reforestation involves replanting trees on areas that have been cut or destroyed by fire.

Asbestos—a naturally occurring soft fibrous mineral commonly used in fireproofing materials and considered to be highly carcinogenic in particulate form.

Biodiversity—also biological diversity; the relative number of species, diverse in form and function, at the genetic, organism, community, and ecosystem level; loss of biodiversity reduces an ecosystem's ability to recover from natural or man-induced disruption.

Bio-indicators—a plant or animal species whose presence, abundance, and health reveal the general condition of its habitat.

Biomass—the total weight or volume of living matter in a given area or volume.

Carbon cycle—the term used to describe the exchange of carbon (in various forms, e.g., as carbon dioxide) between the atmosphere, ocean, terrestrial biosphere, and geological deposits.

Catchments—assemblages used to capture and retain rainwater and runoff; an important water management technique in areas with limited freshwater resources, such as Gibraltar.

DDT (dichloro-diphenyl-trichloro-ethane)—a colorless, odorless insecticide that has toxic effects on most animals; the use of DDT was banned in the US in 1972.

Defoliants—chemicals which cause plants to lose their leaves artificially; often used in agricultural practices for weed control, and may have detrimental impacts on human and ecosystem health.

Deforestation—the destruction of vast areas of forest (e.g., unsustainable forestry practices, agricultural and range land clearing, and the over exploitation of wood products for use as fuel) without planting new growth.

Desertification—the spread of desert-like conditions in arid or semi-arid areas, due to overgrazing, loss of agriculturally productive soils, or climate change.

Dredging—the practice of deepening an existing waterway; also, a technique used for collecting bottom-dwelling marine organisms (e.g., shellfish) or harvesting coral, often causing significant destruction of reef and ocean-floor ecosystems.

Drift-net fishing—done with a net, miles in extent, that is generally anchored to a boat and left to float with the tide; often results in an over harvesting and waste of large populations of non-commercial marine species (by-catch) by its effect of "sweeping the ocean clean."

Ecosystems—ecological units comprised of complex communities of organisms and their specific environments.

Effluents—waste materials, such as smoke, sewage, or industrial waste which are released into the environment, subsequently polluting it.

Endangered species—a species that is threatened with extinction either by direct hunting or habitat destruction.

Freshwater—water with very low soluble mineral content; sources include lakes, streams, rivers, glaciers, and underground aquifers.

Greenhouse gas—a gas that "traps" infrared radiation in the lower atmosphere causing surface warming; water vapor, carbon dioxide, nitrous oxide, methane, hydrofluorocarbons, and ozone are the primary greenhouse gases in the Earth's atmosphere.

Groundwater—water sources found below the surface of the earth often in naturally occurring reservoirs in permeable rock strata; the source for wells and natural springs.

Highlands Water Project—a series of dams constructed jointly by Lesotho and South Africa to redirect Lesotho's abundant water supply into a rapidly growing area in South Africa; while it is the largest infrastructure project in southern Africa, it is also the most costly and controversial; objections to the project include claims that it forces people from their homes, submerges farmlands, and squanders economic resources.

Inuit Circumpolar Conference (ICC)—represents the roughly 150,000 Inuits of Alaska, Canada, Greenland, and Russia in international environmental issues; a General Assembly convenes every three years to determine the focus of the ICC; the most current concerns are long-range transport of pollutants, sustainable development, and climate change.

Metallurgical plants—industries which specialize in the science, technology, and processing of metals; these plants produce highly concentrated and toxic wastes which can contribute to pollution of ground water and air when not properly disposed.

Noxious substances—injurious, very harmful to living beings.

Overgrazing—the grazing of animals on plant material faster than it can naturally regrow leading to the permanent loss of plant cover, a common effect of too many animals grazing limited range land.

Ozone shield—a layer of the atmosphere composed of ozone gas (O3) that resides approximately 25 miles above the Earth's surface and absorbs solar ultraviolet radiation that can be harmful to living organisms.

Poaching—the illegal killing of animals or fish, a great concern with respect to endangered or threatened species.

Pollution—the contamination of a healthy environment by man-made waste.

Potable water—water that is drinkable, safe to be consumed.

Salination—the process through which fresh (drinkable) water becomes salt (undrinkable) water; hence, desalination is the reverse process; also involves the accumulation of salts in topsoil caused by evaporation of excessive irrigation water, a process that can eventually render soil incapable of supporting crops.

Siltation—occurs when water channels and reservoirs become clotted with silt and mud, a side effect of deforestation and soil erosion.

Slash-and-burn agriculture—a rotating cultivation technique in which trees are cut down and burned in order to clear land for temporary agriculture; the land is used until its productivity declines at which point a new plot is selected and the process repeats; this practice is sustainable while population levels are low and time is permitted for regrowth of natural vegetation; conversely, where these conditions do not exist, the practice can have disastrous consequences for the environment.

Soil degradation—damage to the land's productive capacity because of poor agricultural practices such as the excessive use of pesticides or fertilizers, soil compaction from heavy equipment, or erosion of topsoil, eventually resulting in reduced ability to produce agricultural products.

Soil erosion—the removal of soil by the action of water or wind, compounded by poor agricultural practices, deforestation, overgrazing, and desertification.

Ultraviolet (UV) radiation—a portion of the electromagnetic energy emitted by the sun and naturally filtered in the upper atmosphere by the ozone layer; UV radiation can be harmful to living organisms and has been linked to increasing rates of skin cancer in humans.

Waterborne diseases—those in which bacteria survive in, and are transmitted through, water; always a serious threat in areas with an untreated water supply.

Environment—international agreements
This entry separates country participation in international environmental agreements into two levels—*party to* and *signed, but not ratified*. Agreements are listed in alphabetical order by the abbreviated form of the full name.

Environmental agreements
This information is presented in **Appendix C: Selected International Environmental Agreements**, which includes the name, abbreviation, date opened for signature, date entered into force, objective, and parties by category.

Ethnic groups
This entry provides an ordered listing of ethnic groups starting with the largest and normally includes the percent of total population.

Exchange rates
This entry provides the average annual price of a country's monetary unit for the time period specified, expressed in units of local currency per US dollar, as determined by international market forces or by official fiat. The International Organization for Standardization (ISO) 4217 alphabetic currency code for the national medium of exchange is presented in parenthesis. Closing daily exchange rates are not presented in *The World Factbook*, but are used to convert stock values—e.g., the market value of publicly traded shares—to US dollars as of the specified date.

Executive branch
This entry includes several subfields. *Chief of state* includes the name and title of the titular leader of the country who represents the state at official and ceremonial functions but may not be involved with the day-to-day activities of the government. *Head of government* includes the name and title of the top administrative leader who is designated to manage the day-to-day activities of the government. For example, in the UK, the monarch is the chief of state, and the prime minister is the head of government. In the US, the president is both the chief of state and the head of government. *Cabinet* includes the official name for this body of high-ranking advisers and the method for selection of members. *Elections* includes the nature of election process or accession to power, date of the last election, and date of the next election. *Election results* includes the percent of vote for each candidate in the last election.

Exports
This entry provides the total US dollar amount of merchandise exports on an f.o.b. (free on board) basis. These figures are calculated on an exchange rate basis, i.e., not in purchasing power parity (PPP) terms.

Exports—commodities
This entry provides a listing of the highest-valued exported products; it sometimes includes the percent of total dollar value.

Exports—partners
This entry provides a rank ordering of trading partners starting with the most important; it sometimes includes the percent of total dollar value.

Fiscal year
This entry identifies the beginning and ending months for a country's accounting period of 12 months, which often is the calendar year but which may begin in any month. All yearly references are for the calendar year (CY) unless indicated as a noncalendar fiscal year (FY).

Flag description
This entry provides a written flag description produced from actual flags or the best information available at the time the entry was written. The flags of independent states are used by their dependencies unless there is an officially recognized local flag. Some disputed and other areas do not have flags.

Flag graphic
Most versions of the *Factbook* include a color flag at the beginning of the country profile. The flag graphics were produced from actual flags or the best information available at the time of preparation. The flags of independent states are used by their dependencies unless there is an officially recognized local flag. Some disputed and other areas do not have flags.

Freshwater withdrawal (domestic/industrial/agricultural)
This entry provides the annual quantity of water in cubic kilometers removed from available sources for use in any purpose. Water drawn-off is not necessarily entirely consumed and some portion may be returned for further use downstream. Domestic sector use refers to water supplied by public distribution systems. Note that some of this total may be used for small industrial and/or limited agricultural purposes. Industrial sector use is the quantity of water used by self-supplied industries not connected to a public distribution system. Agricultural sector use includes water used for irrigation and livestock watering, and does not account for agriculture directly dependent on rainfall. Included are figures for *total* annual water withdrawal and *per capita* water withdrawal.

GDP (official exchange rate)
This entry gives the gross domestic product (GDP) or value of all final goods and services produced within a nation in a given year. A nation's GDP at official exchange rates (OER) is the home-currency-denominated annual GDP figure divided by the bilateral average US exchange rate with that country in that year. The measure is simple to compute and gives a precise measure of the value of output. Many economists prefer this measure when gauging the economic power an economy maintains vis-à-vis its neighbors, judging that an exchange rate captures the purchasing power a nation enjoys in the international marketplace. Official exchange rates, however, can be artificially fixed and/or subject to manipulation—resulting in claims of the country having an under- or over-valued currency—and are not necessarily the equivalent of a market-determined exchange rate. Moreover, even if the official exchange rate is market-determined, market exchange rates are frequently established by a relatively small set of goods and services (the ones the country trades) and may not capture the value of the larger set of goods the country produces. Furthermore, OER-converted GDP is not well suited to comparing domestic GDP over time, since appreciation/depreciation from one year to the next will make the OER GDP value rise/fall regardless of whether home-currency-denominated GDP changed.

GDP (purchasing power parity)
This entry gives the gross domestic product (GDP) or value of all final goods and ser-

vices produced within a nation in a given year. A nation's GDP at purchasing power parity (PPP) exchange rates is the sum value of all goods and services produced in the country valued at prices prevailing in the United States in the year noted. This is the measure most economists prefer when looking at per-capita welfare and when comparing living conditions or use of resources across countries. The measure is difficult to compute, as a US dollar value has to be assigned to all goods and services in the country regardless of whether these goods and services have a direct equivalent in the United States (for example, the value of an ox-cart or non-US military equipment); as a result, PPP estimates for some countries are based on a small and sometimes different set of goods and services. In addition, many countries do not formally participate in the World Bank's PPP project that calculates these measures, so the resulting GDP estimates for these countries may lack precision. For many developing countries, PPP-based GDP measures are multiples of the official exchange rate (OER) measure. The differences between the OER- and PPP-denominated GDP values for most of the wealthy industrialized countries are generally much smaller.

GDP—composition, by end use

This entry shows who does the spending in an economy: consumers, businesses, government, and foreigners. The distribution gives the percentage contribution to total GDP of *household consumption, government consumption, investment in fixed capital, investment in inventories, exports of goods and services,* and *imports of goods and services,* and will total 100 percent of GDP if the data are complete.

household consumption—consists of expenditures by resident households, and by nonprofit institutions that serve households, on goods and services that are consumed by individuals. This includes consumption of both domestically produced and foreign goods and services.

government consumption—consists of government expenditures on goods and services. These figures exclude government transfer payments, such as interest on debt, unemployment, and social security, since such payments are not made in exchange for goods and services supplied.

investment in fixed capital—consists of total business spending on fixed assets, such as factories, machinery, equipment, dwellings, and inventories of raw materials, which provide the basis for future production. It is measured gross of the depreciation of the assets, i.e., it includes investment that merely replaces worn-out or scrapped capital. Earlier editions of *The World Factbook* referred to this concept as Investment (gross fixed) and that data now have been moved to this new field.

investment in inventories—consists of net changes to the stock of outputs that are still held by the units that produce them, awaiting further sale to an end user, such as automobiles sitting on a dealer's lot or groceries on the store shelves. This figure may be positive or negative. If the stock of unsold output increases during the relevant time period, *investment in inventories* is positive, but, if the stock of unsold goods declines, it will be negative. *Investment in inventories* normally is an early indicator of the state of the economy. If the stock of unsold items increases unexpectedly—because people stop buying—the economy may be entering a recession;but if the stock of unsold items falls—and goods "go flying off the shelves"—businesses normally try to replace those stocks, and the economy is likely to accelerate.

exports of goods and services—consist of sales, barter, gifts, or grants of goods and services from residents to nonresidents.

imports of goods and services—consist of purchases, barter, or receipts of gifts, or grants of goods and services by residents from nonresidents. *Exports* are treated as a positive item, while imports are treated as a negative item. In a purely accounting sense, *imports* have no direct impact on GDP, which only measures output of the domestic economy. Imports are entered

as a negative item to offset the fact that the expenditure figures for consumption, investment, government, and exports also include expenditures on imports. These imports contribute directly to foreign GDP but only indirectly to domestic GDP. Because of this negative offset for imports of goods and services, the sum of the other five items, excluding imports, will always total more than 100 percent of GDP. A surplus of exports of goods and services over imports indicates an economy is investing abroad, while a deficit indicates an economy is borrowing from abroad.

GDP—composition, by sector of origin

This entry shows where production takes place in an economy. The distribution gives the percentage contribution of *agriculture, industry,* and *services* to total GDP, and will total 100 percent of GDP if the data are complete. Agriculture includes farming, fishing, and forestry. Industry includes mining, manufacturing, energy production, and construction. Services cover government activities, communications, transportation, finance, and all other private economic activities that do not produce material goods.

GDP—per capita (PPP)

This entry shows GDP on a purchasing power parity basis divided by population as of 1 July for the same year.

GDP—real growth rate

This entry gives GDP growth on an annual basis adjusted for inflation and expressed as a percent. The growth rates are year-over-year, and not compounded.

GDP methodology

In the **Economy** category, GDP dollar estimates for countries are reported both on an official exchange rate (OER) and a purchasing power parity (PPP) basis. Both measures contain information that is useful to the reader. The PPP method involves the use of standardized international dollar price weights, which are applied to the quantities of final goods and services produced in a given economy. The data derived from the PPP method probably provide the best available starting point for comparisons of economic strength and well-being between countries. In contrast, the currency exchange rate method involves a variety of international and domestic financial forces that may not capture the value of domestic output. Whereas PPP estimates for OECD countries are quite reliable, PPP estimates for developing countries are often rough approximations. In developing countries with weak currencies, the exchange rate estimate of GDP in dollars is typically one-fourth to one-half the PPP estimate. Most of the GDP estimates for developing countries are based on extrapolation of PPP numbers published by the UN International Comparison Program (UNICP) and by Professors Robert Summers and Alan Heston of the University of Pennsylvania and their colleagues. GDP derived using the OER method should be used for the purpose of calculating the share of items such as exports, imports, military expenditures, external debt, or the current account balance, because the dollar values presented in the *Factbook* for these items have been converted at official exchange rates, not at PPP. One should use the OER GDP figure to calculate the proportion of, say, Chinese defense expenditures in GDP, because that share will be the same as one calculated in local currency units. Comparison of OER GDP with PPP GDP may also indicate whether a currency is over- or under-valued. If OER GDP is smaller than PPP GDP, the official exchange rate may be undervalued, and vice versa. However, there is no strong historical evidence that market exchange rates move in the direction implied by the PPP rate, at least not in the short- or medium-term. Note: the numbers for GDP and other economic data should not be chained together from successive volumes of the *Factbook* because of changes in the US dollar measuring rod, revisions of data by statistical agencies, use of new or different sources of information, and changes in national statistical methods and practices.

Geographic coordinates This entry includes rounded latitude and longitude figures for the centroid or center point of a country expressed in degrees and minutes; it is based on the locations provided in the Geographic Names Server (GNS), maintained by the National Geospatial-Intelligence Agency on behalf of the US Board on Geographic Names.

Geographic names This information is presented in Appendix F: Cross Reference List of Geographic Names. It includes a listing of various alternate names, former names, local names, and regional names referenced to one or more related *Factbook* entries. Spellings are normally, but not always, those approved by the US Board on Geographic Names (BGN). Alternate names and additional information are included in parentheses.

Geography This category includes the entries dealing with the natural environment and the effects of human activity.

Geography—note This entry includes miscellaneous geographic information of significance not included elsewhere.

Gini index See entry for **Distribution of family income—Gini index**

GNP Gross national product (GNP) is the value of all final goods and services produced within a nation in a given year, plus income earned by its citizens abroad, minus income earned by foreigners from domestic production. The *Factbook*, following current practice, uses GDP rather than GNP to measure national production. However, the user must realize that in certain countries net remittances from citizens working abroad may be important to national well-being.

Government This category includes the entries dealing with the system for the adoption and administration of public policy.

Government—note This entry includes miscellaneous government information of significance not included elsewhere.

Government type This entry gives the basic form of government. Definitions of the major governmental terms are as follows. (Note that for some countries more than one definition applies.):

    Absolute monarchy—a form of government where the monarch rules unhindered, i.e., without any laws, constitution, or legally organized opposition.

    Anarchy—a condition of lawlessness or political disorder brought about by the absence of governmental authority.

    Authoritarian—a form of government in which state authority is imposed onto many aspects of citizens' lives.

    Commonwealth—a nation, state, or other political entity founded on law and united by a compact of the people for the common good.

    Communist—a system of government in which the state plans and controls the economy and a single—often authoritarian—party holds power; state controls are imposed with the elimination of private ownership of property or capital while claiming to make progress toward a higher social order in which all goods are equally shared by the people (i.e., a classless society).

    Confederacy (Confederation)—a union by compact or treaty between states, provinces, or territories, that creates a central government with limited powers; the constituent entities retain supreme authority over all matters except those delegated to the central government.

    Constitutional—a government by or operating under an authoritative document (constitution) that sets forth the system of fundamental laws and principles that determines the nature, functions, and limits of that government.

    Constitutional democracy—a form of government in which the sovereign power of the people is spelled out in a governing constitution.

    Constitutional monarchy—a system of government in which a monarch is guided by a constitution whereby his/her rights, duties, and responsibilities are spelled out in written law or by custom.

    Democracy—a form of government in which the supreme power is retained by the people, but which is usually exercised indirectly through a system of representation and delegated authority periodically renewed.

    Democratic republic—a state in which the supreme power rests in the body of citizens entitled to vote for officers and representatives responsible to them.

    Dictatorship—a form of government in which a ruler or small clique wield absolute power (not restricted by a constitution or laws).

    Ecclesiastical—a government administrated by a church.

    Emirate—similar to a monarchy or sultanate, but a government in which the supreme power is in the hands of an emir (the ruler of a Muslim state); the emir may be an absolute overlord or a sovereign with constitutionally limited authority.

    Federal (Federation)—a form of government in which sovereign power is formally divided—usually by means of a constitution—between a central authority and a number of constituent regions (states, colonies, or provinces) so that each region retains some management of its internal affairs; differs from a confederacy in that the central government exerts influence directly upon both individuals as well as upon the regional units.

    Federal republic—a state in which the powers of the central government are restricted and in which the component parts (states, colonies, or provinces) retain a degree of self-government; ultimate sovereign power rests with the voters who chose their governmental representatives.

    Islamic republic—a particular form of government adopted by some Muslim states; although such a state is, in theory, a theocracy, it remains a republic, but its laws are required to be compatible with the laws of Islam.

    Maoism—the theory and practice of Marxism-Leninism developed in China by Mao Zedong (Mao Tse-tung), which states that a continuous revolution is necessary if the leaders of a communist state are to keep in touch with the people.

    Marxism—the political, economic, and social principles espoused by 19th century economist Karl Marx; he viewed the struggle of workers as a progression of historical forces that would proceed from a class struggle of the proletariat (workers) exploited by capitalists (business owners), to a socialist "dictatorship of the proletariat," to, finally, a classless society—Communism.

    Marxism-Leninism—an expanded form of communism developed by Lenin from doctrines of Karl Marx; Lenin saw imperialism as the final stage of capitalism and shifted the focus of workers' struggle from developed to underdeveloped countries.

    Monarchy—a government in which the supreme power is lodged in the hands of a monarch who reigns over a state or territory, usually for life and by hereditary right; the monarch may be either a sole absolute ruler or a sovereign—such as a king, queen, or prince—with constitutionally limited authority.

    Oligarchy—a government in which control is exercised by a small group of individuals whose authority generally is based on wealth or power.

    Parliamentary democracy—a political system in which the legislature (parliament) selects the government—a prime minister, premier, or chancellor along with the cabinet ministers—according to party strength as expressed in elections; by this system, the government acquires a dual responsibility: to the people as well as to the parliament.

    Parliamentary government (Cabinet-Parliamentary government)—a government in which members of an executive branch (the cabinet and its leader—a prime minister, premier, or chancellor) are nominated to their positions by a legislature or parliament, and are directly responsible to it; this type of government can be dissolved at will by the parliament (legislature) by means of a no confidence vote or the leader of the cabinet may dissolve the parliament if it can no longer function.

Parliamentary monarchy—a state headed by a monarch who is not actively involved in policy formation or implementation (i.e., the exercise of sovereign powers by a monarch in a ceremonial capacity); true governmental leadership is carried out by a cabinet and its head—a prime minister, premier, or chancellor—who are drawn from a legislature (parliament).

Presidential—a system of government where the executive branch exists separately from a legislature (to which it is generally not accountable).

Republic—a representative democracy in which the people's elected deputies (representatives), not the people themselves, vote on legislation.

Socialism—a government in which the means of planning, producing, and distributing goods is controlled by a central government that theoretically seeks a more just and equitable distribution of property and labor; in actuality, most socialist governments have ended up being no more than dictatorships over workers by a ruling elite.

Sultanate—similar to a monarchy, but a government in which the supreme power is in the hands of a sultan (the head of a Muslim state); the sultan may be an absolute ruler or a sovereign with constitutionally limited authority.

Theocracy—a form of government in which a Deity is recognized as the supreme civil ruler, but the Deity's laws are interpreted by ecclesiastical authorities (bishops, mullahs, etc.); a government subject to religious authority.

Totalitarian—a government that seeks to subordinate the individual to the state by controlling not only all political and economic matters, but also the attitudes, values, and beliefs of its population.

Greenwich Mean Time (GMT)
The mean solar time at the Greenwich Meridian, Greenwich, England, with the hours and days, since 1925, reckoned from midnight. GMT is now a historical term having been replaced by UTC on 1 January 1972. See **Coordinated Universal Time.**

Gross domestic product See GDP

Gross national product See GNP

Gross national saving
Gross national saving is derived by deducting final consumption expenditure (household plus government) from Gross national disposable income, and consists of personal saving, plus business saving (the sum of the capital consumption allowance and retained business profits), plus government saving (the excess of tax revenues over expenditures), but excludes foreign saving (the excess of imports of goods and services over exports). The figures are presented as a percent of GDP. A negative number indicates that the economy as a whole is spending more income than it produces, thus drawing down national wealth (dissaving).

Gross world product See GWP

GWP
This entry gives the gross world product (GWP) or aggregate value of all final goods and services produced worldwide in a given year.

Health expenditures
This entry provides the total expenditure on health as a percentage of GDP. Health expenditures are broadly defined as activities performed either by institutions or individuals through the application of medical, paramedical, and/or nursing knowledge and technology, the primary purpose of which is to promote, restore, or maintain health.

Heliports
This entry gives the total number of heliports with hard-surface runways, helipads, or landing areas that support routine sustained helicopter operations exclusively and have support facilities including one or more of the following facilities: lighting, fuel, passenger handling, or maintenance. It includes former airports used exclusively for helicopter operations but excludes heliports limited to day operations and natural clearings that could support helicopter landings and takeoffs.

HIV/AIDS—adult prevalence rate
This entry gives an estimate of the percentage of adults (aged 15-49) living with HIV/AIDS. The adult prevalence rate is calculated by dividing the estimated number of adults living with HIV/AIDS at yearend by the total adult population at yearend.

HIV/AIDS—deaths
This entry gives an estimate of the number of adults and children who died of AIDS during a given calendar year.

HIV/AIDS—people living with HIV/AIDS
This entry gives an estimate of all people (adults and children) alive at yearend with HIV infection, whether or not they have developed symptoms of AIDS.

Hospital bed density
This entry provides the number of hospital beds per 1,000 people; it serves as a general measure of inpatient service availability. Hospital beds include inpatient beds available in public, private, general, and specialized hospitals and rehabilitation centers. In most cases, beds for both acute and chronic care are included. Because the level of inpatient services required for individual countries depends on several factors—such as demographic issues and the burden of disease—there is no global target for the number of hospital beds per country. So, while 2 beds per 1,000 in one country may be sufficient, 2 beds per 1,000 in another may be woefully inadequate because of the number of people hospitalized by disease.

Household income or consumption by percentage share
Data on household income or consumption come from household surveys, the results adjusted for household size. Nations use different standards and procedures in collecting and adjusting the data. Surveys based on income will normally show a more unequal distribution than surveys based on consumption. The quality of surveys is improving with time, yet caution is still necessary in making inter-country comparisons.

Hydrographic data codes See Data codes

Illicit drugs
This entry gives information on the five categories of illicit drugs—narcotics, stimulants, depressants (sedatives), hallucinogens, and cannabis. These categories include many drugs legally produced and prescribed by doctors as well as those illegally produced and sold outside of medical channels.

Cannabis (*Cannabis sativa*) is the common hemp plant, which provides hallucinogens with some sedative properties, and includes marijuana (pot, Acapulco gold, grass, reefer), tetrahydrocannabinol (THC, Marinol), hashish (hash), and hashish oil (hash oil).

Coca (mostly *Erythroxylum* coca) is a bush with leaves that contain the stimulant used to make cocaine. Coca is not to be confused with cocoa, which comes from cacao seeds and is used in making chocolate, cocoa, and cocoa butter.

Cocaine is a stimulant derived from the leaves of the coca bush.

Depressants (sedatives) are drugs that reduce tension and anxiety and include chloral hydrate, barbiturates (Amytal, Nembutal, Seconal, phenobarbital), benzodiazepines (Librium,

Valium), methaqualone (Quaalude), glutethimide (Doriden), and others (Equanil, Placidyl, Valmid).

Drugs are any chemical substances that effect a physical, mental, emotional, or behavioral change in an individual.

Drug abuse is the use of any licit or illicit chemical substance that results in physical, mental, emotional, or behavioral impairment in an individual.

Hallucinogens are drugs that affect sensation, thinking, self-awareness, and emotion. Hallucinogens include LSD (acid, microdot), mescaline and peyote (mexc, buttons, cactus), amphetamine variants (PMA, STP, DOB), phencyclidine (PCP, angel dust, hog), phencyclidine analogues (PCE, PCPy, TCP), and others (psilocybin, psilocyn).

Hashish is the resinous exudate of the cannabis or hemp plant (Cannabis sativa).

Heroin is a semisynthetic derivative of morphine.

Mandrax is a trade name for methaqualone, a pharmaceutical depressant.

Marijuana is the dried leaf of the cannabis or hemp plant (*Cannabis sativa*).

Methaqualone is a pharmaceutical depressant, referred to as mandrax in Southwest Asia and Africa.

Narcotics are drugs that relieve pain, often induce sleep, and refer to opium, opium derivatives, and synthetic substitutes. Natural narcotics include opium (paregoric, parepectolin), morphine (MS-Contin, Roxanol), codeine (Tylenol with codeine, Empirin with codeine, Robitussin AC), and thebaine. Semisynthetic narcotics include heroin (horse, smack), and hydromorphone (Dilaudid). Synthetic narcotics include meperidine or Pethidine (Demerol, Mepergan), methadone (Dolophine, Methadose), and others (Darvon, Lomotil).

Opium is the brown, gummy exudate of the incised, unripe seedpod of the opium poppy.

Opium poppy (*Papaver somniferum*) is the source for the natural and semisynthetic narcotics.

Poppy straw is the entire cut and dried opium poppy-plant material, other than the seeds. Opium is extracted from poppy straw in commercial operations that produce the drug for medical use.

Qat (kat, khat) is a stimulant from the buds or leaves of *Catha edulis* that is chewed or drunk as tea.

Quaaludes is the North American slang term for methaqualone, a pharmaceutical depressant.

Stimulants are drugs that relieve mild depression, increase energy and activity, and include cocaine (coke, snow, crack), amphetamines (Desoxyn, Dexedrine), ephedrine, ecstasy (clarity, essence, doctor, Adam), phenmetrazine (Preludin), methylphenidate (Ritalin), and others (Cylert, Sanorex, Tenuate).

Imports This entry provides the total US dollar amount of merchandise imports on a c.i.f. (cost, insurance, and freight) or f.o.b. (free on board) basis. These figures are calculated on an exchange rate basis, i.e., not in purchasing power parity (PPP) terms.

Imports—commodities This entry provides a listing of the highest-valued imported products; it sometimes includes the percent of total dollar value.

Imports—partners This entry provides a rank ordering of trading partners starting with the most important; it sometimes includes the percent of total dollar value.

Independence For most countries, this entry gives the date that sovereignty was achieved and from which nation, empire, or trusteeship. For the other countries, the date given may not represent "independence" in the strict sense, but rather some significant nationhood event such as the traditional founding date or the date of unification, federation, confederation, establishment, fundamental change in the form of government, or state succession. For a number of countries, the establishment of statehood was a lengthy evolutionary process occurring over decades or even centuries. In such cases, several significant dates are cited. Dependent areas include the notation "none" followed by the nature of their dependency status. Also see the **Terminology** note.

Industrial production growth rate This entry gives the annual percentage increase in industrial production (includes manufacturing, mining, and construction).

Industries This entry provides a rank ordering of industries starting with the largest by value of annual output.

Infant mortality rate This entry gives the number of deaths of infants under one year old in a given year per 1,000 live births in the same year. This rate is often used as an indicator of the level of health in a country.

Inflation rate (consumer prices) This entry furnishes the annual percent change in consumer prices compared with the previous year's consumer prices.

International disputes See Disputes—international

International law organization participation This entry includes information on a country's acceptance of jurisdiction of the International Court of Justice (ICJ) and of the International Criminal Court (ICCt); 55 countries have accepted ICJ jurisdiction with reservations and 11 have accepted ICJ jurisdiction without reservations; 114 countries have accepted ICCt jurisdiction. **Appendix B: International Organizations and Groups** explains the differing mandates of the ICJ and ICCt.

International organization participation This entry lists in alphabetical order by abbreviation those international organizations in which the subject country is a member or participates in some other way.

International organizations This information is presented in **Appendix B: International Organizations and Groups** which includes the name, abbreviation, date established, aim, and members by category.

Internet country code This entry includes the two-letter codes maintained by the International Organization for Standardization (ISO) in the ISO 3166 Alpha-2 list and used by the Internet Assigned Numbers Authority (IANA) to establish country-coded top-level domains (ccTLDs).

Internet hosts This entry lists the number of Internet hosts available within a country. An Internet host is a computer connected directly to the Internet; normally an Internet Service Provider's (ISP) computer is a host. Internet users may use either a hard-wired terminal, at an institution with a mainframe computer connected directly to the Internet, or may connect remotely by way of a modem via telephone line, cable, or satellite to the Internet Service Provider's host computer. The number of hosts is one indicator of the extent of Internet connectivity.

Internet users This entry gives the number of users within a country that access the Internet. Statistics vary from country to country and may include users who access the Internet at least several times a week to those who access it only once within a period of several months.

Introduction This category includes one entry, **Background**.

Investment (gross fixed) This entry records total business spending on fixed assets, such as factories, machinery, equipment, dwellings, and inventories of raw materials, which provide the basis for future production. It is measured gross of the depreciation of the assets, i.e., it includes investment that merely replaces worn-out or scrapped capital.

Irrigated land This entry gives the number of square kilometers of land area that is artificially supplied with water.

Judicial branch This entry includes three subfields. *The highest court(s)* subfield includes the name(s) of a country's highest level court(s), the number and titles of the judges, and the types of cases heard by the court, which commonly are based on civil, criminal, administrative, and constitutional law. A number of countries have separate constitutional courts. The *judge selection and term of office* subfield includes the organizations and associated officials responsible for nominating and appointing judges, and a brief description of the process. The selection process can be indicative of the independence of a country's court system from other branches of its government. Also included in this subfield are judges' tenures, which can range from a few years, to a specified retirement age, to lifelong appointments. *The subordinate courts* subfield lists the courts lower in the hierarchy of a country's court system. A few countries with federal-style governments, such as Brazil, Canada, and the US, in addition to their federal court, have separate state - or province-level court systems, though generally the two systems interact.

Labor force This entry contains the total labor force figure.

Labor force—by occupation This entry lists the percentage distribution of the labor force by sector of occupation. *Agriculture* includes farming, fishing, and forestry. *Industry* includes mining, manufacturing, energy production, and construction. *Services* cover government activities, communications, transportation, finance, and all other economic activities that do not produce material goods. The distribution will total less than 100 percent if the data are incomplete and may range from 99-101 percent due to rounding.

Land boundaries This entry contains the *total* length of all land boundaries and the individual lengths for each of the contiguous *border countries*. When available, official lengths published by national statistical agencies are used. Because surveying methods may differ, country border lengths reported by contiguous countries may differ.

Land use This entry contains the percentage shares of total land area for three different types of land use: *arable land*—land cultivated for crops like wheat, maize, and rice that are replanted after each har-

vest; *permanent crops*—land cultivated for crops like citrus, coffee, and rubber that are not replanted after each harvest; includes land under flowering shrubs, fruit trees, nut trees, and vines, but excludes land under trees grown for wood or timber; *other*—any land not arable or under permanent crops; includes permanent meadows and pastures, forests and woodlands, built-on areas, roads, barren land, etc.

Languages This entry provides a rank ordering of languages starting with the largest and sometimes includes the percent of total population speaking that language.

Legal system This entry provides the description of a country's legal system. A statement on judicial review of legislative acts is also included for a number of countries. The legal systems of nearly all countries are generally modeled upon elements of five main types: civil law (including French law, the Napoleonic Code, Roman law, Roman-Dutch law, and Spanish law); common law (including United State law); customary law; mixed or pluralistic law; and religious law (including Islamic law). An additional type of legal system—international law, which governs the conduct of independent nations in their relationships with one another—is also addressed below. The following list describes these legal systems, the countries or world regions where these systems are enforced, and a brief statement on the origins and major features of each.

Civil Law—The most widespread type of legal system in the world, applied in various forms in approximately 150 countries. Also referred to as European continental law, the civil law system is derived mainly from the Roman *Corpus Juris Civilus*, (Body of Civil Law), a collection of laws and legal interpretations compiled under the East Roman (Byzantine) Emperor Justinian I between A.D. 528 and 565. The major feature of civil law systems is that the laws are organized into systematic written codes. In civil law the sources recognized as authoritative are principally legislation—especially codifications in constitutions or statutes enacted by governments—and secondarily, custom. The civil law systems in some countries are based on more than one code.

Common Law—A type of legal system, often synonymous with "English common law," which is the system of England and Wales in the UK, and is also in force in approximately 80 countries formerly part of or influenced by the former British Empire. English common law reflects Biblical influences as well as remnants of law systems imposed by early conquerors including the Romans, Anglo-Saxons, and Normans. Some

legal scholars attribute the formation of the English common law system to King Henry II (r. 1154-1189). Until the time of his reign, laws customary among England's various manorial and ecclesiastical (church) jurisdictions were administered locally. Henry II established the king's court and designated that laws were "common" to the entire English realm. The foundation of English common law is "legal precedent"—referred to as *stare decisis*, meaning "to stand by things decided." In the English common law system, court judges are bound in their decisions in large part by the rules and other doctrines developed—and supplemented over time—by the judges of earlier English courts.

Customary Law—A type of legal system that serves as the basis of, or has influenced, the present-day laws in approximately 40 countries—mostly in Africa, but some in the Pacific islands, Europe, and the Near East. Customary law is also referred to as "primitive law," "unwritten law," "indigenous law," and "folk law." There is no single history of customary law such as that found in Roman civil law, English common law, Islamic law, or the Napoleonic Civil Code. The earliest systems of law in human society were customary, and usually developed in small agrarian and hunter-gatherer communities. As the term implies, customary law is based upon the customs of a community. Common attributes of customary legal systems are that they are seldom written down, they embody an organized set of rules regulating social relations, and they are agreed upon by members of the community. Although such law systems include sanctions for law infractions, resolution tends to be reconciliatory rather than punitive. A number of African states practiced customary law many centuries prior to colonial influences. Following colonization, such laws were written down and incorporated to varying extents into the legal systems imposed by their colonial powers.

European Union Law—A sub-discipline of international law known as "supranational law" in which the rights of sovereign nations are limited in relation to one another. Also referred to as the Law of the European Union or Community Law, it is the unique and complex legal system that operates in tandem with the laws of the 27 member states of the European Union (EU). Similar to federal states, the EU legal system ensures compliance from the member states because of the Union's decentralized political nature. The

European Court of Justice (ECJ), established in 1952 by the Treaty of Paris, has been largely responsible for the development of EU law. Fundamental principles of European Union law include: *subsidiarity*—the notion that issues be handled by the smallest, lowest, or least centralized competent authority; *proportionality*—the EU may only act to the extent needed to achieve its objectives; *conferral*—the EU is a union of member states, and all its authorities are voluntarily granted by its members; *legal certainty*—requires that legal rules be clear and precise; and *precautionary principle*—a moral and political principle stating that if an action or policy might cause severe or irreversible harm to the public or to the environment, in the absence of a scientific consensus that harm would not ensue, the burden of proof falls on those who would advocate taking the action.

French Law—A type of civil law that is the legal system of France. The French system also serves as the basis for, or is mixed with, other legal systems in approximately 50 countries, notably in North Africa, the Near East, and the French territories and dependencies. French law is primarily codified or systematic written civil law. Prior to the French Revolution (1789-1799), France had no single national legal system. Laws in the northern areas of present-day France were mostly local customs based on privileges and exemptions granted by kings and feudal lords, while in the southern areas Roman law predominated. The introduction of the Napoleonic Civil Code during the reign of Napoleon I in the first decade of the 19th century brought major reforms to the French legal system, many of which remain part of France's current legal structure, though all have been extensively amended or redrafted to address a modern nation. French law distinguishes between "public law" and "private law." Public law relates to government, the French Constitution, public administration, and criminal law. Private law covers issues between private citizens or corporations. The most recent changes to the French legal system—introduced in the 1980s—were the decentralization laws, which transferred authority from centrally appointed government representatives to locally elected representatives of the people.

International Law—The law of the international community, or the body of customary rules and treaty rules accepted as legally binding by states in their relations with each other. International law differs from other legal systems in that it primarily concerns sovereign political entities. There are three separate disciplines of international law: public international law, which governs the relationship between provinces and international entities and includes treaty law, law of the sea, international criminal law, and international humanitarian law; private international law, which addresses legal jurisdiction; and supranational law—a legal framework wherein countries are bound by regional agreements in which the laws of the member countries are held inapplicable when in conflict with supranational laws. At present the European Union is the only entity under a supranational legal system. The term "international law" was coined by Jeremy Bentham in 1780 in his *Principles of Morals and Legislation*, though laws governing relations between states have been recognized from very early times (many centuries B.C.). Modern international law developed alongside the emergence and growth of the European nation-states beginning in the early 16th century. Other factors that influenced the development of international law included the revival of legal studies, the growth of international trade, and the practice of exchanging emissaries and establishing legations. The sources of International law are set out in Article 38-1 of the Statute of the International Court of Justice within the UN Charter.

Islamic Law—The most widespread type of religious law, it is the legal system enforced in over 30 countries, particularly in the Near East, but also in Central and South Asia, Africa, and Indonesia. In many countries Islamic law operates in tandem with a civil law system. Islamic law is embodied in the sharia, an Arabic word meaning "the right path." Sharia covers all aspects of public and private life and organizes them into five categories: obligatory, recommended, permitted, disliked, and forbidden. The primary sources of sharia law are the Qur'an, believed by Muslims to be the word of God revealed to the Prophet Muhammad by the angel Gabriel, and the Sunnah, the teachings of the Prophet and his works. In addition to these two primary sources, traditional Sunni Muslims recognize the consensus of Muhammad's companions and Islamic jurists on certain issues, called ijmas, and various forms of reasoning, including analogy by legal scholars, referred to as qiyas. Shia Muslims reject ijmas and qiyas as sources of sharia law.

Mixed Law—Also referred to as pluralistic law, mixed law consists of elements of some or all of the other main types of legal systems—civil, common, customary, and religious. The mixed legal systems of a number of countries came about when colonial powers overlaid their own legal systems upon colonized regions but retained elements of the colonies' existing legal systems.

Napoleonic Civil Code—A type of civil law, referred to as the Civil Code or *Code Civil des Francais*, forms part of the legal system of France, and underpins the legal systems of Bolivia, Egypt, Lebanon, Poland, and the US state of Louisiana. The Civil Code was established under Napoleon I, enacted in 1804, and officially designated the *Code Napoleon* in 1807. This legal system combined the Teutonic civil law tradition of the northern provinces of France with the Roman law tradition of the southern and eastern regions of the country. The Civil Code bears similarities in its arrangement to the Roman *Body of Civil Law* (see Civil Law above). As enacted in 1804, the Code addressed personal status, property, and the acquisition of property. Codes added over the following six years included civil procedures, commercial law, criminal law and procedures, and a penal code.

Religious Law—A legal system which stems from the sacred texts of religious traditions and in most cases professes to cover all aspects of life as a seamless part of devotional obligations to a transcendent, imminent, or deep philosophical reality. Implied as the basis of religious law is the concept of unalterability, because the word of God cannot be amended or legislated against by judges or governments. However, a detailed legal system generally requires human elaboration. The main types of religious law are sharia in Islam, halakha in Judaism, and canon law in some Christian groups. Sharia is the most widespread religious legal system (see Islamic Law), and is the sole system of law for countries including Iran, the Maldives, and Saudi Arabia. No country is fully governed by halakha, but Jewish people may decide to settle disputes through Jewish courts and be bound by their rulings. Canon law is not a divine law as such because it is not found in revelation. It is viewed instead as human law inspired by the word of God and applying the demands of that revelation to the actual situation of the church. Canon law regulates the internal ordering of the Roman Catholic Church, the Eastern Orthodox Church, and the Anglican Communion.

Roman Law—A type of civil law developed in ancient Rome and practiced from the time of the city's founding (traditionally 753 B.C.) until the fall of the Western Empire in the 5th century A.D. Roman law remained the legal system of the Byzantine (Eastern Empire) until the fall of Constantinople in 1453. Preserved fragments of the first legal text, known as the Law of the Twelve Tables, dating from the 5th century B.C., contained specific provisions designed to change the prevailing customary law. Early Roman law was drawn from custom and statutes; later, during the time of the empire, emperors asserted their authority as the ultimate source of law. The basis for Roman laws was the idea that the exact form—not the intention—of words or of actions produced legal consequences. It was only in the late 6th century A.D. that a comprehensive Roman code of laws was published (see Civil Law above). Roman law served as the basis of law systems developed in a number of continental European countries.

Roman-Dutch Law—A type of civil law based on Roman law as applied in the Netherlands. Roman-Dutch law serves as the basis for legal systems in seven African countries, as well as Guyana, Indonesia, and Sri Lanka. This law system, which originated in the province of Holland and expanded throughout the Netherlands (to be replaced by the French Civil Code in 1809), was instituted in a number of sub-Saharan African countries during the Dutch colonial period. The Dutch jurist/philosopher Hugo Grotius was the first to attempt to reduce Roman-Dutch civil law into a system in his *Jurisprudence of Holland* (written 1619-20, commentary published 1621). The Dutch historian/lawyer Simon van Leeuwen coined the term "Roman-Dutch law" in 1652.

Spanish Law—A type of civil law, often referred to as the Spanish Civil Code, it is the present legal system of Spain and is the basis of legal systems in 12 countries mostly in Central and South America, but also in southwestern Europe, northern and western Africa, and southeastern Asia. The Spanish Civil Code reflects a complex mixture of customary, Roman, Napoleonic, local, and modern codified law. The laws of the Visigoth invaders of Spain in the 5th to 7th centuries had the earliest major influence on Spanish legal system development. The Christian Reconquest of Spain in the 11th through 15th centuries witnessed the development of customary law, which combined canon (religious) and Roman law. During several centuries of Hapsburg and Bourbon rule, systematic recompilations of the existing national legal system were attempted, but these often conflicted with local and regional customary civil laws. Legal system development for most of the 19th century concentrated on formulating a national civil law system, which was finally enacted in 1889 as the Spanish Civil Code. Several sections of the code have been revised, the most recent of which are the penal code in 1989 and the judiciary code in 2001. The Spanish Civil Code separates public and private law. Public law includes constitutional law, administrative law, criminal law, process law, financial and tax law, and international public law. Private law includes civil law, commercial law, labor law, and international private law.

United States Law—A type of common law, which is the basis of the legal system of the United States and that of its island possessions in the Caribbean and the Pacific. This legal system has several layers, more possibly than in most other countries, and is due in part to the division between federal and state law. The United States was founded not as one nation but as a union of 13 colonies, each claiming independence from the British Crown. The US Constitution, implemented in 1789, began shifting power away from the states and toward the federal government, though the states today retain substantial legal authority. US law draws its authority from four sources: *constitutional law, statutory law, administrative regulations*, and *case law*. Constitutional law is based on the US Constitution and serves as the supreme federal law. Taken together with those of the state constitutions, these documents outline the general structure of the federal and state governments and provide the rules and limits of power. US statutory law is legislation enacted by the US Congress and is codified in the United States Code.

The 50 state legislatures have similar authority to enact state statutes. Administrative law is the authority delegated to federal and state executive agencies. Case law, also referred to as common law, covers areas where constitutional or statutory law is lacking. Case law is a collection of judicial decisions, customs, and general principles that began in England centuries ago, that were adopted in America at the time of the Revolution, and that continue to develop today.

Legislative branch This entry contains information on the structure (unicameral, bicameral, tricameral), formal name, number of seats, and term of office. *Elections* includes the nature of the election process or accession to power, date of the last election, and date of the next election. *Election results* includes the percent of vote and/or number of seats held by each party in the last election.

Life expectancy at birth This entry contains the average number of years to be lived by a group of people born in the same year, if mortality at each age remains constant in the future. Life expectancy at birth is also a measure of overall quality of life in a country and summarizes the mortality at all ages. It can also be thought of as indicating the potential return on investment in human capital and is necessary for the calculation of various actuarial measures.

Literacy This entry includes a *definition* of literacy and Census Bureau percentages for the *total population, males*, and *females*. There are no universal definitions and standards of literacy. Unless otherwise specified, all rates are based on the most common definition—the ability to read and write at a specified age. Detailing the standards that individual countries use to assess the ability to read and write is beyond the scope of the *Factbook*. Information on literacy, while not a perfect measure of educational results, is probably the most easily available and valid for international comparisons. Low levels of literacy, and education in general, can impede the economic development of a country in the current rapidly changing, technology-driven world.

Location This entry identifies the country's regional location, neighboring countries, and adjacent bodies of water.

Major infectious diseases This entry lists major infectious diseases likely to be encountered in countries where the risk of such diseases is assessed to be very high as compared to the United States. These infectious diseases represent risks to US government personnel traveling to the specified country for a period of less than three years. The **degree of risk** is assessed by considering the foreign nature of these infectious diseases, their severity, and the probability of being affected by the diseases present. The diseases listed do not necessarily represent the total disease burden experienced by the local population.

The risk to an individual traveler varies considerably by the specific location, visit duration, type of activities, type of accommodations, time of year, and other factors. Consultation with a travel medicine physician is needed to evaluate individual risk and recommend appropriate preventive measures such as vaccines.

Diseases are organized into the following six exposure categories shown in italics *and listed in typical descending order of risk*. Note: The sequence of exposure categories listed in individual country entries may vary according to local conditions.

food or waterborne diseases acquired through eating or drinking on the local economy:

> **Hepatitis A**—viral disease that interferes with the functioning of the liver; spread through consumption of food or water contaminated with fecal matter, principally in areas of poor sanitation; victims exhibit fever, jaundice, and diarrhea; 15% of victims will experience prolonged symptoms over 6-9 months; vaccine available.
>
> **Hepatitis E**—water-borne viral disease that interferes with the functioning of the liver; most commonly spread through

fecal contamination of drinking water; victims exhibit jaundice, fatigue, abdominal pain, and dark colored urine.

Typhoid fever—bacterial disease spread through contact with food or water contaminated by fecal matter or sewage; victims exhibit sustained high fevers; left untreated, mortality rates can reach 20%.

vectorborne diseases acquired through the bite of an infected arthropod:

Malaria—caused by single-cell parasitic protozoa *Plasmodium*; transmitted to humans via the bite of the female Anopheles mosquito; parasites multiply in the liver attacking red blood cells resulting in cycles of fever, chills, and sweats accompanied by anemia; death due to damage to vital organs and interruption of blood supply to the brain; endemic in 100, mostly tropical, countries with 90% of cases and the majority of 1.5-2.5 million estimated annual deaths occurring in sub-Saharan Africa.

Dengue fever—mosquito-borne (*Aedes aegypti*) viral disease associated with urban environments; manifests as sudden onset of fever and severe headache; occasionally produces shock and hemorrhage leading to death in 5% of cases.

Yellow fever—mosquito-borne viral disease; severity ranges from influenza-like symptoms to severe hepatitis and hemorrhagic fever; occurs only in tropical South America and sub-Saharan Africa, where most cases are reported; fatality rate is less than 20%.

Japanese Encephalitis—mosquito-borne (*Culex tritaeniorhynchus*) viral disease associated with rural areas in Asia; acute encephalitis can progress to paralysis, coma, and death; fatality rates 30%.

African Trypanosomiasis—caused by the parasitic protozoa *Trypanosoma*; transmitted to humans via the bite of blood-sucking Tsetse flies; infection leads to malaise and irregular fevers and, in advanced cases when the parasites invade the central nervous system, coma and death; endemic in 36 countries of sub-Saharan Africa; cattle and wild animals act as reservoir hosts for the parasites.

Cutaneous Leishmaniasis—caused by the parasitic protozoa *leishmania*; transmitted to humans via the bite of sandflies; results in skin lesions that may become chronic; endemic in 88 countries; 90% of cases occur in Iran, Afghanistan, Syria, Saudi Arabia, Brazil, and Peru; wild and domesticated animals as well as humans can act as reservoirs of infection.

Plague—bacterial disease transmitted by fleas normally associated with rats; person-to-person airborne transmission also possible; recent plague epidemics occurred in areas of Asia, Africa, and South America associated with rural areas or small towns and villages; manifests as fever, headache, and painfully swollen lymph nodes; disease progresses rapidly and without antibiotic treatment leads to pneumonic form with a death rate in excess of 50%.

Crimean-Congo hemorrhagic fever—tick-borne viral disease; infection may also result from exposure to infected animal blood or tissue; geographic distribution includes Africa, Asia, the Middle East, and Eastern Europe; sudden onset of fever, headache, and muscle aches followed by hemorrhaging in the bowels, urine, nose, and gums; mortality rate is approximately 30%.

Rift Valley fever—viral disease affecting domesticated animals and humans; transmission is by mosquito and other biting insects; infection may also occur through handling of infected meat or contact with blood; geographic distribution includes eastern and southern Africa where cattle and sheep are raised; symptoms are generally mild with fever and some liver abnormalities, but the disease may progress to hemorrhagic fever, encephalitis, or ocular disease; fatality rates are low at about 1% of cases.

Chikungunya—mosquito-borne (*Aedes aegypti*) viral disease associated with urban environments, similar to Dengue Fever; characterized by sudden onset of fever, rash, and severe joint pain usually lasting 3-7 days, some cases result in persistent arthritis.

water contact diseases acquired through swimming or wading in freshwater lakes, streams, and rivers:

Leptospirosis—bacterial disease that affects animals and humans; infection occurs through contact with water, food, or soil contaminated by animal urine; symptoms include high fever, severe headache, vomiting, jaundice, and diarrhea; untreated, the disease can result in kidney damage, liver failure, meningitis, or respiratory distress; fatality rates are low but left untreated recovery can take months.

Schistosomiasis—caused by parasitic trematode flatworm *Schistosoma*; fresh water snails act as intermediate host and release larval form of parasite that penetrates the skin of people exposed to contaminated water; worms mature and reproduce in the blood vessels, liver, kidneys, and intestines releasing eggs, which become trapped in tissues triggering an immune response; may manifest as either urinary or intestinal disease resulting in decreased work or learning capacity; mortality, while generally low, may occur in advanced cases usually due to bladder cancer; endemic in 74 developing countries with 80% of infected people living in sub-Saharan Africa; humans act as the reservoir for this parasite.

aerosolized dust or soil contact disease acquired through inhalation of aerosols contaminated with rodent urine:

Lassa fever—viral disease carried by rats of the genus *Mastomys*; endemic in portions of West Africa; infection occurs through direct contact with or consumption of food contaminated by rodent urine or fecal matter containing virus particles; fatality rate can reach 50% in epidemic outbreaks.

respiratory disease acquired through close contact with an infectious person:

Meningococcal meningitis—bacterial disease causing an inflammation of the lining of the brain and spinal cord; one of the most important bacterial pathogens is *Neisseria meningitidis* because of its potential to cause epidemics; symptoms include stiff neck, high fever, headaches, and vomiting; bacteria are transmitted from person to person by respiratory droplets and facilitated by close and prolonged contact resulting from crowded living conditions, often with a seasonal distribution; death occurs in 5-15% of cases, typically within 24-48 hours of onset of symptoms; highest burden of meningococcal disease occurs in the hyperendemic region of sub-Saharan Africa known as the "Meningitis Belt" which stretches from Senegal east to Ethiopia.

animal contact disease acquired through direct contact with local animals:

Rabies—viral disease of mammals usually transmitted through the bite of an infected animal, most commonly dogs; virus affects the central nervous system causing brain alteration and death; symptoms initially are non-specific fever and headache progressing to neurological symptoms; death occurs within days of the onset of symptoms.

Major urban areas—population

This entry provides the population of the capital and up to five major cities defined as urban agglomerations with populations of at least 750,000 people. An *urban agglomeration* is defined as comprising the city or town proper and also the suburban fringe or thickly settled territory lying outside of, but adjacent to, the boundaries of the city. For smaller countries, lacking urban centers of 750,000 or more, only the population of the capital is presented.

Manpower available for military service This entry gives the number of males and females falling in the military age range for a country (defined as being ages 16-49) and assumes that every individual is fit to serve.

Manpower fit for military service This entry gives the number of males and females falling in the military age range for a country (defined as being ages 16-49) and who are not otherwise disqualified for health reasons; accounts for the health situation in the country and provides a more realistic estimate of the actual number fit to serve.

Manpower reaching militarily significant age annually This entry gives the number of males and females entering the military manpower pool (i.e., reaching age 16) in any given year and is a measure of the availability of military-age young adults.

Map references This entry includes the name of the *Factbook* reference map on which a country may be found. Note that boundary representations on these maps are not necessarily authoritative. The entry on **Geographic coordinates** may be helpful in finding some smaller countries.

Maritime claims This entry includes the following claims, the definitions of which are excerpted from the United Nations Convention on the Law of the Sea (UNCLOS), which alone contains the full and definitive descriptions:

territorial sea—the sovereignty of a coastal state extends beyond its land territory and internal waters to an adjacent belt of sea, described as the territorial sea in the UNCLOS (Part II); this sovereignty extends to the air space over the territorial sea as well as its underlying seabed and subsoil; every state has the right to establish the breadth of its territorial sea up to a limit not exceeding 12 nautical miles; the normal baseline for measuring the breadth of the territorial sea is the mean low-water line along the coast as marked on large-scale charts officially recognized by the coastal state; where the coasts of two states are opposite or adjacent to each other, neither state is entitled to extend its territorial sea beyond the median line, every point of which is equidistant from the nearest points on the baseline from which the territorial seas of both states are measured; the UNCLOS describes specific rules for archipelagic states.

contiguous zone—according to the UNCLOS (Article 33), this is a zone contiguous to a coastal state's territorial sea, over which it may exercise the control necessary to: prevent infringement of its customs, fiscal, immigration, or sanitary laws and regulations within its territory or territorial sea; punish infringement of the above laws and regulations committed within its territory or territorial sea; the contiguous zone may not extend beyond 24 nautical miles from the baselines from which the breadth of the territorial sea is measured (e.g., the US has claimed a 12-nautical mile contiguous zone in addition to its 12-nautical mile territorial sea); where the coasts of two states are opposite or adjacent to each other, neither state is entitled to extend its contiguous zone beyond the median line, every point of which is equidistant from the nearest points on the baseline from which the contiguous zone of both states are measured.

exclusive economic zone (EEZ)—the UNCLOS (Part V) defines the EEZ as a zone beyond and adjacent to the territorial sea in which a coastal state has: sovereign rights for the purpose of exploring and exploiting, conserving and managing the natural resources, whether living or non-living, of the waters superjacent to the seabed and of the seabed and its subsoil, and with regard to other activities for the economic exploitation and exploration of the zone, such as the production of energy from the water, currents, and winds; jurisdiction with regard to the establishment and use of artificial islands, installations, and structures; marine scientific research; the protection and preservation of the marine environment; the outer limit of the exclusive economic zone shall not exceed 200 nautical miles from the baselines from which the breadth of the territorial sea is measured.

continental shelf—the UNCLOS (Article 76) defines the continental shelf of a coastal state as comprising the seabed and subsoil of the submarine areas that extend beyond its territorial sea throughout the natural prolongation of its land territory to the outer edge of the continental margin, or to a distance of 200 nautical miles from the baselines from which the breadth of the territorial sea is measured where the outer edge of the continental margin does not extend up to that distance; the continental margin comprises the submerged prolongation of the landmass of the coastal state, and consists of the seabed and subsoil of the shelf, the slope and the rise; wherever the continental margin extends beyond 200 nautical miles from the baseline, coastal states may extend their claim to a distance not to exceed 350 nautical miles from the baseline or 100 nautical miles from the 2,500-meter isobath, which is a line connecting points of 2,500 meters in depth; it does not include the deep ocean floor with its oceanic ridges or the subsoil thereof.

exclusive fishing zone—while this term is not used in the UNCLOS, some states (e.g., the United Kingdom) have chosen not to claim an EEZ, but rather to claim jurisdiction over the living resources off their coast; in such cases, the term exclusive fishing zone is often used; the breadth of this zone is normally the same as the EEZ or 200 nautical miles.

Market value of publicly traded shares This entry gives the value of shares issued by publicly traded companies at a price determined in the national stock markets on the final day of the period indicated. It is simply the latest price per share multiplied by the total number of outstanding shares, cumulated over all companies listed on the particular exchange.

Maternal mortality rate The maternal mortality rate (MMR) is the annual number of female deaths per 100,000 live births from any cause related to or aggravated by pregnancy or its management (excluding accidental or incidental causes). The MMR includes deaths during pregnancy, childbirth, or within 42 days of termination of pregnancy, irrespective of the duration and site of the pregnancy, for a specified year.

Median age This entry is the age that divides a population into two numerically equal groups; that is, half the people are younger than this age and half are older. It is a single index that summarizes the age distribution of a population. Currently, the median age ranges from a low of about 15 in Uganda and Gaza Strip to 40 or more in several European countries and Japan. See the entry for "Age structure" for the importance of a young versus an older age structure and, by implication, a low versus a higher median age.

Merchant marine Merchant marine may be defined as all ships engaged in the carriage of goods; or all commercial vessels (as opposed to all nonmilitary ships), which excludes tugs, fishing vessels, offshore oil rigs, etc. This entry contains information in four fields—*total, ships by type, foreign-owned, and registered in other countries.*

Total includes the number of ships (1,000 GRT or over), total DWT for those ships, and total GRT for those ships. DWT or dead weight tonnage is the total weight of cargo, plus bunkers, stores, etc., that a ship can carry when immersed to the appropriate load line. GRT or gross register tonnage is a figure obtained by measuring the entire sheltered volume of a ship available for cargo and passengers and converting it to tons on the basis of 100 cubic feet per ton; there is no stable relationship between GRT and DWT.

Ships *by type* includes a listing of barge carriers, bulk cargo ships, cargo ships, chemical tankers, combination bulk carriers, combination ore/oil carriers, container ships, liquefied gas tankers, livestock carriers, multifunctional large-load carriers, petroleum tankers, passenger ships, passenger/cargo ships, railcar carriers, refrigerated cargo ships, roll-on/roll-off cargo ships, short-sea passenger ships, specialized tankers, and vehicle carriers.

Foreign-owned are ships that fly the flag of one country but belong to owners in another.

Registered in other countries are ships that belong to owners in one country but fly the flag of another.

Military This category includes the entries dealing with a country's military structure, manpower, and expenditures.

Military—note This entry includes miscellaneous military information of significance not included elsewhere.

Military branches This entry lists the service branches subordinate to defense ministries or the equivalent (typically ground, naval, air, and marine forces).

Military expenditures This entry gives spending on defense programs for the most recent year available as a percent of gross domestic product (GDP); the GDP is calculated on an exchange rate basis, i.e., not in terms of purchasing power parity (PPP). For countries with no military forces, this figure can include expenditures on public security and police.

Military service age and obligation This entry gives the required ages for voluntary or conscript military service and the length of service obligation.

Money figures All money figures are expressed in contemporaneous US dollars unless otherwise indicated.

Mother's mean age at first birth This entry provides the mean (average) age of mothers at the birth of their first child. It is a useful indicator for gauging the success of family planning programs aiming to reduce maternal mortality, increase contraceptive use—particularly among married and unmarried adolescents, delay age at first marriage, and improve the health of newborns.

National anthem A generally patriotic musical composition—usually in the form of a song or hymn of praise—that evokes and eulogizes the history, traditions, or struggles of a nation or its people. National anthems can be officially recognized as a national song by a country's constitution or by an enacted law, or simply by tradition. Although most anthems contain lyrics, some do not.

National holiday This entry gives the primary national day of celebration—usually independence day.

National symbol(s) A national symbol is a faunal, floral, or other abstract representation—or some distinctive object—that over time has come to be closely identified with a country or entity. Not all countries have national symbols; a few countries have more than one.

Nationality This entry provides the identifying terms for citizens—*noun* and *adjective*.

Natural gas—consumption This entry is the total natural gas consumed in cubic meters (cu m). The discrepancy between the amount of natural gas produced and/or imported and the amount consumed and/or exported is due to the omission of stock changes and other complicating factors.

Natural gas—exports This entry is the total natural gas exported in cubic meters (cu m).

Natural gas—imports This entry is the total natural gas imported in cubic meters (cu m).

Natural gas—production This entry is the total natural gas produced in cubic meters (cu m). The discrepancy between the amount of natural gas produced and/or imported and the amount consumed and/or exported is due to the omission of stock changes and other complicating factors.

Natural gas—proved reserves This entry is the stock of proved reserves of natural gas in cubic meters (cu m). Proved reserves are those quantities of natural gas, which, by analysis of geological and engineering data, can be estimated with a high degree of confidence to be commercially recoverable from a given date forward, from known reservoirs and under current economic conditions.

Natural hazards This entry lists potential natural disasters. For countries where volcanic activity is common, a *volcanism* subfield highlights historically active volcanoes.

Natural resources This entry lists a country's mineral, petroleum, hydropower, and other resources of commercial importance, such as rare earth elements (REEs). In general, products appear only if they make a significant contribution to the economy, or are likely to do so in the future.

Net migration rate This entry includes the figure for the difference between the number of persons entering and leaving a country during the year per 1,000 persons (based on midyear population). An excess of persons entering the country is referred to as net immigration (e.g., 3.56 migrants/1,000 population); an excess of persons leaving the country as net emigration (e.g., -9.26 migrants/1,000 population). The net migration rate indicates the contribution of migration to the overall level of population change. The net migration rate does not distinguish between economic migrants, refugees, and other types of migrants nor does it distinguish between lawful migrants and undocumented migrants.

Obesity—adult prevalence rate This entry gives the percent of a country's population considered to be obese. Obesity is defined as an adult having a Body Mass Index (BMI) greater to or equal to 30.0. BMI is calculated by taking a person's weight in kg and dividing it by the person's squared height in meters.

People—note This entry includes miscellaneous demographic information of significance not included elsewhere.

People and Society This category includes entries dealing with national identity (including ethnicities, languages, and religions), demography (a variety of population statistics) and societal characteristics (health and education indicators).

Personal Names—Capitalization The *Factbook* capitalizes the surname or family name of individuals for the convenience of our users who are faced with a world of different cultures and naming conventions. The need for capitalization, bold type, underlining, italics, or some other indicator of the individual's surname is apparent in the following examples: MAO Zedong, Fidel CASTRO Ruz, George W. BUSH, and TUNKU SALAHUDDIN Abdul Aziz Shah ibni Al-Marhum Sultan Hisammuddin Alam Shah. By knowing the surname, a short form without all capital letters can be used with confidence as in President Castro, Chairman Mao, President Bush, or Sultan Tunku Salahuddin. The same system of capitalization is extended to the names of leaders with surnames that are not commonly used such as Queen ELIZABETH II. For Vietnamese names, the given name is capitalized because officials are referred to by their given name rather than by their surname. For example, the president of Vietnam is Tran Duc LUONG. His surname is Tran, but he is referred to by his given name—President LUONG.

Personal Names—Spelling The romanization of personal names in the *Factbook* normally follows the same transliteration system used by the US Board on Geographic Names for spelling place names. At times, however, a foreign leader expressly indicates a preference for, or the media or official documents regularly use, a romanized spelling that differs from the transliteration derived from the US Government standard. In such cases, the Factbook uses the alternative spelling.

Personal Names—Titles The *Factbook* capitalizes any valid title (or short form of it) immediately preceding a person's name. A title standing alone is not capitalized. Examples: President PUTIN and President OBAMA are chiefs of state. In Russia, the president is chief of state and the premier is the head of the government, while in the US, the president is both chief of state and head of government.

Petroleum See entries under **Refined petroleum products**.

Petroleum products See entries under **Refined petroleum products**.

Physicians density This entry gives the number of medical doctors (physicians), including generalist and specialist medical practitioners, per 1,000 of the population. Medical doctors are defined as doctors that study, diagnose, treat, and prevent illness, disease, injury, and other physical and mental impairments in humans through the application of modern medicine. They also plan, supervise, and evaluate care and treatment plans by other health care providers. The World Health Organization estimates that fewer than 2.3 health workers (physicians, nurses, and midwives only) per 1,000 would be insufficient to achieve coverage of primary healthcare needs.

Pipelines This entry gives the lengths and types of pipelines for transporting products like natural gas, crude oil, or petroleum products.

Piracy Piracy is defined by the 1982 United Nations Convention on the Law of the Sea as any illegal act of violence, detention, or depredation directed against a ship, aircraft, persons, or property in a place outside the jurisdiction of any State. Such criminal acts committed in the territorial waters of a littoral state are generally considered to be armed robbery against ships. Information on piracy may be found, where applicable, in the **Transportation—note**.

Political parties and leaders This entry includes a listing of significant political parties, coalitions, and electoral lists as of each country's last legislative election, unless otherwise noted.

Political pressure groups and leaders This entry includes a listing of a country's political, social, labor, or religious organizations that are involved in politics, or that exert political pressure, but whose leaders do not stand for legislative election. International movements or organizations are generally not listed.

Population This entry gives an estimate from the US Bureau of the Census based on statistics from population censuses, vital statistics registration systems, or sample surveys pertaining to the recent past and on assumptions about future trends. The total population presents one overall measure of the potential impact of the country on the world and within its region. Note: Starting with the 1993 *Factbook*, demographic estimates for some countries (mostly African) have explicitly taken into account the effects of the growing impact of the HIV/AIDS epidemic. These countries are currently: The Bahamas, Benin, Botswana, Brazil, Burkina Faso, Burma, Burundi, Cambodia, Cameroon, Central African Republic, Democratic Republic of the Congo, Republic of the Congo, Cote d'Ivoire, Ethiopia, Gabon, Ghana, Guyana, Haiti, Honduras, Kenya, Lesotho, Malawi, Mozambique, Namibia, Nigeria, Rwanda, South Africa, Swaziland, Tanzania, Thailand, Togo, Uganda, Zambia, and Zimbabwe.

Population below poverty line National estimates of the percentage of the population falling below the poverty line are based on surveys of sub-groups, with the results weighted by the number of people in each group. Definitions of poverty vary considerably among nations. For example, rich nations generally employ more generous standards of poverty than poor nations.

Population growth rate The average annual percent change in the population, resulting from a surplus (or deficit) of births over deaths and the balance of migrants entering and leaving a country. The rate may be positive or negative. The growth rate is a factor in determining how great a burden would be imposed on a country by the changing needs of its people for infrastructure (e.g., schools, hospitals, housing, roads), resources (e.g., food, water, electricity), and jobs. Rapid population growth can be seen as threatening by neighboring countries.

Population pyramid A population pyramid illustrates the age and sex structure of a country's population and may provide insights about political and social stability, as well as economic development. The population is distributed along the horizontal axis, with males shown on the left and females on the right. The male and female populations are broken down into 5-year age groups represented as horizontal bars along the vertical axis, with the youngest age groups at the bottom and the oldest at the top. The shape of the population pyramid gradually evolves over time based on fertility, mortality, and international migration trends.

Some distinctive types of population pyramids are:

- A **youthful distribution** has a broad base and narrow peak and is characterized by a high proportion of children and low proportion of the elderly. This population distribution results from high fertility, high mortality, low life expectancy, and high population growth. It is typical of developing countries where female education and contraceptive use are low and health care and sanitation are poor.
- A **transitional distribution** is caused by declining fertility and mortality rates, increasing life expectancy, and slowing population growth. The population has a larger proportion of working-age people relative to children and the elderly and produces a barrel-shaped pyramid, where the mid-section bulges and the base and top are narrower. The large proportion of working-age people can create a "demographic bonus" if it is educated and productively employed.
- A **mature distribution** has fairly balanced proportions of the population in the child, working-age, and elderly age groups and will gradually form an inverted triangle population pyramid as population growth continues to fall or ceases and the proportion of older people increases. Low fertility, low mortality, and high life expectancy—made possible by the availability of advanced healthcare, family planning, sanitation, and education—lead to aging populations in industrialized countries.

Ports and terminals This entry lists major ports and terminals primarily on the basis of the amount of cargo tonnage shipped through the facilities on an annual basis. In some instances, the number of containers handled or ship visits were also considered. Most ports service multiple classes of vessels including bulk carriers (dry and liquid), break bulk cargoes (goods loaded individually in bags, boxes, crates, or drums; sometimes palletized), containers, roll-on/roll-off, and passenger ships. The listing leads off with *major seaports* handling all types of cargo. Inland *river and lake ports* are listed separately along with the river or lake name. Ports configured specifically to handle bulk cargoes are designated as *oil/gas terminals* or *dry bulk cargo ports*. As break bulk cargoes are largely transported by containers today, the entry also includes a listing of major *container ports* with the corresponding throughput measured in twenty-foot equivalent units (TEUs). Some ports are significant for handling passenger traffic and are listed as *cruise/ferry ports*. In addition to commercial traffic, many seaports also provide important military infrastructure as naval bases or dockyards.

Public debt This entry records the cumulative total of all government borrowings less repayments that are denominated in a country's home currency. Public debt should not be confused with external debt, which reflects the foreign currency liabilities of both the private and public sector and must be financed out of foreign exchange earnings.

Railways This entry states the *total* route length of the railway network and of its component parts by gauge, which is the measure of the distance between the inner sides of the load-bearing rails. The four typical types of gauges are: *broad, standard, narrow,* and *dual*. Other gauges are listed under *note*. Some 60% of the world's railways use the standard gauge of 1.4 m (4.7 ft). Gauges vary by country and sometimes within countries. The choice of gauge during initial construction was mainly in response to local conditions and the intent of the builder. Narrow-gauge railways were cheaper to build and could negotiate sharper curves, broad-gauge railways gave greater stability and permitted higher speeds. Standard-gauge railways were a compromise between narrow and broad gauges.

Rare earth elements Rare earth elements or REEs are 17 chemical elements that are critical in many of today's high-tech industries. They include lanthanum, cerium, praseodymium, neodymium, promethium, samarium, europium, gadolinium, terbium, dysprosium, holmium, erbium, thulium, ytterbium, lutetium, scandium, and yttrium. Typical applications for REEs include batteries in hybrid cars, fiber optic cables, flat panel displays, and permanent magnets, as well as some defense and medical products.

Reference maps This section includes world and regional maps.

Refined petroleum products—consumption This entry is the country's total consumption of refined petroleum products, in barrels per day (bbl/day). The discrepancy between the amount of refined petroleum products produced and/or imported and the amount consumed and/or exported is due to the omission of stock changes, refinery gains, and other complicating factors.

Refined petroleum products—exports This entry is the country's total exports of refined petroleum products, in barrels per day (bbl/day).

Refined petroleum products—imports This entry is the country's total imports of refined petroleum products, in barrels per day (bbl/day).

Refined petroleum products—production This entry is the country's total output of refined petroleum products, in barrels per day (bbl/day). The discrepancy between the amount of refined petroleum products produced and/or imported and the amount consumed and/or exported is due to the omission of stock changes, refinery gains, and other complicating factors.

Refugees and internally displaced persons This entry includes those persons residing in a country as *refugees* or internally displaced persons (IDPs). Each country's refugee entry includes only countries of origin that are the source of refugee populations of 5,000 or more. The definition of a refugee according to a United Nations Convention is "a person who is outside his/her country of nationality or habitual residence; has a well-founded fear of persecution because of his/her race, religion, nationality, membership in a particular social group or political opinion; and is unable or unwilling to avail himself/herself of the protection of that country, or to return there, for fear of persecution." The UN established the Office of the UN High Commissioner for Refugees (UNHCR) in 1950 to handle refugee matters worldwide. The UN Relief and Works Agency for Palestine Refugees in the Near East (UNRWA) has a different operational definition for a Palestinian refugee: "a person whose normal place of residence was Palestine during the period 1 June 1946 to 15 May 1948 and who lost both home and means of livelihood as a result of the 1948 conflict." However, UNHCR also assists some 400,000 Palestinian refugees not covered under the UNRWA definition. The term "internally displaced person" is not specifically covered in the UN Convention; it is used to describe people who have fled their homes for reasons similar to refugees, but who remain within their own national territory and are subject to the laws of that state.

Religions This entry is an ordered listing of religions by adherents starting with the largest group and sometimes includes the percent of total population. The core characteristics and beliefs of the world's major religions are described below.

Baha'i—Founded by Mirza Husayn-Ali (known as Baha'u'llah) in Iran in 1852, Baha'i faith emphasizes monotheism and believes in one eternal transcendent God. Its guiding focus is to encourage the unity of all peoples on the earth so that justice and peace may be achieved on earth. Baha'i revelation contends the prophets of major world religions reflect some truth or element of the divine, believes all were manifestations of God given to specific communities in specific times, and that Baha'u'llah is an additional prophet meant to call all humankind. Bahais are an open community, located worldwide, with the greatest concentration of believers in South Asia.

Buddhism—Religion or philosophy inspired by the 5th century B.C. teachings of Siddhartha Gautama (also known as Gautama Buddha "the enlightened one"). Buddhism focuses on the goal of spiritual enlightenment centered on an understanding of Gautama Buddha's Four Noble Truths on the nature of suffering, and on the Eightfold Path of spiritual and moral practice, to break the cycle of suffering of which we are a part. Buddhism ascribes to a karmic system of rebirth. Several schools and sects of Buddhism exist, differing often on the nature of the Buddha, the extent to which enlightenment can be achieved—for one or for all, and by whom—religious orders or laity.

Basic Groupings

Theravada Buddhism: The oldest Buddhist school, Theravada is practiced mostly in Sri Lanka, Cambodia, Laos, Burma, and Thailand, with minority representation elsewhere in Asia and the West. Theravadans follow the Pali Canon of Buddha's teachings, and believe that one may escape the cycle of rebirth, worldly attachment, and suffering for oneself; this process may take one or several lifetimes.

Mahayana Buddhism, including subsets Zen and Tibetan (Lamaistic) Buddhism: Forms of Mahayana Buddhism are common in East Asia and Tibet, and parts of the West. Mahayanas have additional scriptures beyond the Pali Canon and believe the Buddha is eternal and still teaching. Unlike Theravada Buddhism, Mahayana schools maintain the Buddha-nature is present in all beings and all will ultimately achieve enlightenment. Hoa Hao: a minority tradition of Buddhism practiced in Vietnam that stresses lay participation, primarily by peasant farmers; it eschews expensive ceremonies and temples and relocates the primary practices into the home.

Christianity—Descending from Judaism, Christianity's central belief maintains Jesus of Nazareth is the promised messiah of the Hebrew Scriptures, and that his life, death, and resurrection are salvific for the world. Christianity is one of the three monotheistic Abrahamic faiths, along with Islam and Judaism, which traces its spiritual lineage to Abraham of the Hebrew Scriptures. Its sacred texts include the Hebrew Bible and the New Testament (or the Christian Gospels).

Basic Groupings

Catholicism (or Roman Catholicism): This is the oldest established western Christian church and the world's largest single religious body. It is supranational, and recognizes a hierarchical structure with the Pope, or Bishop of Rome, as its head, located at the Vatican. Catholics believe the Pope is the divinely ordered head of the Church from a direct spiritual legacy of Jesus' apostle Peter. Catholicism is comprised of 23 particular Churches, or Rites—one Western (Roman or Latin-Rite) and 22 Eastern. The Latin Rite is by far the largest, making up about 98% of Catholic membership. Eastern-Rite Churches, such as the Maronite Church and the Ukrainian Catholic Church, are in communion with Rome although they preserve their own worship traditions and their immediate hierarchy consists of clergy within their own rite. The Catholic Church has a comprehensive theological and moral doctrine specified for believers in its catechism, which makes it unique among most forms of Christianity.

Mormonism (including the Church of Jesus Christ of Latter-Day Saints): Originating in 1830 in the United States under Joseph Smith, Mormonism is not characterized as a form of Protestant Christianity because it claims additional revealed Christian scriptures after the Hebrew Bible and New Testament. The Book of Mormon maintains there was an appearance of Jesus in the New World following the Christian account of his resurrection, and that the Americas are uniquely blessed continents. Mormonism believes earlier Christian traditions, such as the Roman Catholic, Orthodox, and Protestant reform faiths, are apostasies and that Joseph Smith's revelation of the Book of Mormon is a restoration of true Christianity. Mormons have a hierarchical religious leadership structure, and actively proselytize their faith; they are located primarily in the Americas and in a number of other Western countries.

Jehovah's Witnesses structure their faith on the Christian Bible, but their rejection of the Trinity is distinct from mainstream Christianity. They believe that a Kingdom of God, the Theocracy, will emerge following Armageddon and usher in a new earthly society. Adherents are required to evangelize and to follow a strict moral code.

Orthodox Christianity: The oldest established eastern form of Christianity, the Holy Orthodox Church, has a ceremonial head in the Bishop of Constantinople (Istanbul), also known as a Patriarch, but its various regional forms (e.g., Greek Orthodox, Russian Orthodox, Serbian Orthodox, Ukrainian Orthodox) are autocephalous (independent of Constantinople's authority, and have their own Patriarchs). Orthodox churches are highly nationalist and ethnic. The Orthodox Christian faith shares many theological tenets with the Roman Catholic Church, but diverges on some key premises and does not recognize the governing authority of the Pope.

Protestant Christianity: Protestant Christianity originated in the 16th century as an attempt to reform Roman Catholicism's practices, dogma, and theology. It encompasses several forms or denominations which are extremely varied in structure, beliefs, relationship to state, clergy, and governance. Many protestant theologies emphasize the primary role of scripture in their faith, advocating individual interpretation of Christian texts without the mediation of a final religious authority such as the Roman Pope. The oldest Protestant Christianities include Lutheranism, Calvinism (Presbyterians), and Anglican Christianity (Episcopalians), which have established liturgies, governing structure, and formal clergy. Other variants on Protestant Christianity, including Pentecostal movements and independent churches, may lack one or more of these elements, and their leadership and beliefs are individualized and dynamic.

Hinduism—Originating in the Vedic civilization of India (second and first millennium B.C.), Hinduism is an extremely diverse set of beliefs and practices with no single founder or religious authority. Hinduism has many scriptures; the Vedas, the Upanishads, and the Bhagavad-Gita are among some of the most important. Hindus may worship one or many deities,

usually with prayer rituals within their own home. The most common figures of devotion are the gods Vishnu, Shiva, and a mother goddess, Devi. Most Hindus believe the soul, or *atman*, is eternal, and goes through a cycle of birth, death, and rebirth (*samsara*) determined by one's positive or negative karma, or the consequences of one's actions. The goal of religious life is to learn to act so as to finally achieve liberation (*moksha*) of one's soul, escaping the rebirth cycle.

Islam—The third of the monotheistic Abrahamic faiths, Islam originated with the teachings of Muhammad in the 7th century. Muslims believe Muhammad is the final of all religious prophets (beginning with Abraham) and that the Qu'ran, which is the Islamic scripture, was revealed to him by God. Islam derives from the word submission, and obedience to God is a primary theme in this religion. In order to live an Islamic life, believers must follow the five pillars, or tenets, of Islam, which are the testimony of faith (*shahada*), daily prayer (*salah*), giving alms (*zakah*), fasting during Ramadan (*sawm*), and the pilgrimage to Mecca (*hajj*).

Basic Groupings

The two primary branches of Islam are Sunni and Shia, which split from each other over a religio-political leadership dispute about the rightful successor to Muhammad. The Shia believe Muhammad's cousin and son-in-law, Ali, was the only divinely ordained Imam (religious leader), while the Sunni maintain the first three caliphs after Muhammad were also legitimate authorities. In modern Islam, Sunnis and Shia continue to have different views of acceptable schools of Islamic jurisprudence, and who is a proper Islamic religious authority. Islam also has an active mystical branch, Sufism, with various Sunni and Shia subsets.

Sunni Islam accounts for over 75% of the world's Muslim population. It recognizes the Abu Bakr as the first caliph after Muhammad. Sunni has four schools of Islamic doctrine and law—Hanafi, Maliki, Shafi'i, and Hanbali—which uniquely interpret the *Hadith*, or recorded oral traditions of Muhammad. A Sunni Muslim may elect to follow any one of these schools, as all are considered equally valid.

Shia Islam represents 10-20% of Muslims worldwide, and its distinguishing feature is its reverence for Ali as an infallible, divinely inspired leader, and as the first Imam of the Muslim community after Muhammad. A majority of Shia are known as "Twelvers," because they believe that the 11 familial successor imams after Muhammad culminate in a 12th Imam (al-Mahdi) who is hidden in the world and will reappear at its end to redeem the righteous.

Variants

Ismaili faith: A sect of Shia Islam, its adherents are also known as "Seveners," because they believe that the rightful seventh Imam in Islamic leadership was Isma'il, the elder son of Imam Jafar al-Sadiq. Ismaili tradition awaits the return of the seventh Imam as the Mahdi, or Islamic messianic figure. Ismailis are located in various parts of the world, particularly South Asia and the Levant.

Alawi faith: Another Shia sect of Islam, the name reflects followers' devotion to the religious authority of Ali. Alawites are a closed, secretive religious group who assert they are Shia Muslims, although outside scholars speculate their beliefs may have a syncretic mix with other faiths originating in the Middle East. Alawis live mostly in Syria, Lebanon, and Turkey.

Druze faith: A highly secretive tradition and a closed community that derives from the Ismaili sect of Islam; its core beliefs are thought to emphasize a combination of Gnostic principles believing that the Fatimid caliph, al-Hakin, is the one who embodies the key aspects of goodness of the universe, which are, the intellect, the word, the soul, the preceder, and the follower. The Druze have a key presence in Syria, Lebanon, and Israel.

Jainism—Originating in India, Jain spiritual philosophy believes in an eternal human soul, the eternal universe, and a principle of "the own nature of things." It emphasizes compassion for all living things, seeks liberation of the human soul from reincarnation through enlightenment, and values personal responsibility due to the belief in the immediate consequences of one's behavior. Jain philosophy teaches non-violence and prescribes vegetarianism for monks and laity alike; its adherents are a highly influential religious minority in Indian society.

Judaism—One of the first known monotheistic religions, likely dating to between 2000-1500 B.C., Judaism is the native faith of the Jewish people, based upon the belief in a covenant of responsibility between a sole omnipotent creator God and Abraham, the patriarch of Judaism's Hebrew Bible, or *Tanakh*. Divine revelation of principles and prohibitions in the Hebrew Scriptures form the basis of Jewish law, or *halakhah*, which is a key component of the faith. While there are extensive traditions of Jewish halakhic and theological discourse, there is no final dogmatic authority in the tradition. Local communities have their own religious leadership. Modern Judaism has three basic categories of faith: Orthodox, Conservative, and Reform/Liberal. These differ in their views and observance of Jewish law, with the Orthodox representing the most traditional practice, and Reform/Liberal communities the most accommodating of individualized interpretations of Jewish identity and faith.

Shintoism—A native animist tradition of Japan, Shinto practice is based upon the premise that every being and object has its own spirit or *kami*. Shinto practitioners worship several particular *kamis*, including the *kamis* of nature, and families often have shrines to their ancestors' *kamis*. Shintoism has no fixed tradition of prayers or prescribed dogma, but is characterized by individual ritual. Respect for the *kamis* in nature is a key Shinto value. Prior to the end of World War II, Shinto was the state religion of Japan, and bolstered the cult of the Japanese emperor.

Sikhism—Founded by the Guru Nanak (born 1469), Sikhism believes in a non-anthropomorphic, supreme, eternal, creator God; centering one's devotion to God is seen as a means of escaping the cycle of rebirth. Sikhs follow the teachings of Nanak and nine subsequent gurus. Their scripture, the Guru Granth Sahib—also known as the Adi Granth—is considered the living Guru, or final authority of Sikh faith and theology. Sikhism emphasizes equality of humankind and disavows caste, class, or gender discrimination.

Taoism—Chinese philosophy or religion based upon Lao Tzu's Tao Te Ching, which centers on belief in the Tao, or the way, as the flow of the universe and the nature of things. Taoism encourages a principle of non-force, or wu-wei, as the means to live harmoniously with the Tao. Taoists believe the esoteric world is made up of a perfect harmonious balance and nature, while in the manifest world—particularly in the body—balance is distorted. The Three Jewels of the Tao—compassion, simplicity, and humility—serve as the basis for Taoist ethics. **Zoroastrianism**—Originating from the teachings of Zoroaster in about the 9th or 10th century B.C., Zoroastrianism may be the oldest continuing creedal religion. Its key beliefs center on a transcendent creator God, Ahura Mazda, and the concept of free will. The key ethical tenets of Zoroastrianism expressed in its scripture, the Avesta, are based on a dualistic worldview where one may prevent chaos if one chooses to serve God and exercises good thoughts, good words, and good deeds. Zoroastrianism is generally a closed religion and members are almost always born to Zoroastrian parents. Prior to the spread of Islam, Zoroastrianism dominated greater Iran. Today, though a minority, Zoroastrians remain primarily in Iran, India (where they are known as Parsi), and Pakistan.

Traditional beliefs

Animism: the belief that non-human entities contain souls or spirits.

Badimo: a form of ancestor worship of the Tswana people of Botswana.

Confucianism: an ideology that humans are perfectible through self-cultivation and self-creation; developed from teachings of the Chinese philosopher Confucius. Confucianism has strongly influenced the culture and beliefs of East Asian countries, including China, Japan, Korea, Singapore, Taiwan, and Vietnam.

Inuit beliefs are a form of shamanism (see below) based on animistic principles of the Inuit or Eskimo peoples.

Kirant: the belief system of the Kirat, a people who live mainly in the Himalayas of Nepal. It is primarily a form of polytheistic shamanism, but includes elements of animism and ancestor worship.

Pagan is a blanket term used to describe many unconnected belief practices throughout history, usually in reference to religions outside of the Abrahamic category (monotheistic faiths like Judaism, Christianity, and Islam).

Shamanism: beliefs and practices promoting communication with the spiritual world. Shamanistic beliefs are organized around a shaman or medicine man who—as an intermediary between the human and spirit world—is believed to be able to heal the sick (by healing their souls), communicate with the spirit world, and help souls into the afterlife through the practice of entering a trance. In shaman-based religions, the shaman is also responsible for leading sacred rites.

Spiritualism: the belief that souls and spirits communicate with the living usually through intermediaries called mediums.

Syncretic (fusion of diverse religious beliefs and practices)

Cao Dai: a nationalistic Vietnamese sect, officially established in 1926, that draws practices and precepts from Confucianism, Taoism, Buddhism, and Catholicism.

Chondogyo: or the religion of the Heavenly Way, is based on Korean shamanism, Buddhism, and Korean folk traditions, with some elements drawn from Christianity. Formulated in the 1860s, it holds that God lives in all of us and strives to convert society into a paradise on earth, populated by believers transformed into intelligent moral beings with a high social conscience.

Kimbanguist: a puritan form of the Baptist denomination founded by Simon Kimbangu in the 1920s in what is now the Democratic Republic of Congo. Adherents believe that salvation comes through Jesus' death and resurrection, like Christianity, but additionally that living a spiritually pure life following strict codes of conduct is required for salvation.

Modekngei: a hybrid of Christianity and ancient Palauan culture and oral traditions founded around 1915 on the island of Babeldaob. Adherents simultaneously worship Jesus Christ and Palauan goddesses.

Rastafarian: an afro-centrist ideology and movement based on Christianity that arose in Jamaica in the 1930s; it believes that Haile Selassie I, Emperor of Ethiopia from 1930-74, was the incarnation of the second coming of Jesus.

Santeria: practiced in Cuba, the merging of the Yoruba religion of Nigeria with Roman Catholicism and native Indian traditions. Its practitioners believe that each person has a destiny and eventually transcends to merge with the divine creator and source of all energy, Olorun.

Voodoo/Vodun: a form of spirit and ancestor worship combined with some Christian faiths, especially Catholicism. Haitian and

Louisiana Voodoo, which have included more Catholic practices, are separate from West African Vodun, which has retained a focus on spirit worship.

Non-religious

Agnosticism: the belief that most things are unknowable. In regard to religion it is usually characterized as neither a belief nor non belief in a deity.

Atheism: the belief that there are no deities of any kind.

Reserves of foreign exchange and gold This entry gives the dollar value for the stock of all financial assets that are available to the central monetary authority for use in meeting a country's balance of payments needs as of the end-date of the period specified. This category includes not only foreign currency and gold, but also a country's holdings of Special Drawing Rights in the International Monetary Fund, and its reserve position in the Fund.

Roadways This entry gives the *total* length of the road network and includes the length of the *paved* and *unpaved* portions.

Sanitation facility access This entry provides information about access to improved or unimproved sanitation facilities available to segments of the population of a country. *Improved* sanitation—use of any of the following facilities: flush or pour-flush to a piped sewer system, septic tank or pit latrine; ventilated improved pit (VIP) latrine; pit latrine with slab; or a composting toilet, *unimproved* sanitation—use of any of the following facilities: flush or pour-flush not piped to a sewer system, septic tank or pit latrine; pit latrine without a slab or open pit; bucket; hanging toilet or hanging latrine; shared facilities of any type; no facilities; or bush or field.

School life expectancy (primary to tertiary education) School life expectancy (SLE) is the total number of years of schooling (primary to tertiary) that a child can expect to receive, assuming that the probability of his or her being enrolled in school at any particular future age is equal to the current enrollment ratio at that age. Caution must be maintained when utilizing this indicator in international comparisons. For example, a year or grade completed in one country is not necessarily the same in terms of educational content or quality as a year or grade completed in another country. SLE represents the expected number of years of schooling that will be completed, including years spent repeating one or more grades.

Sex ratio This entry includes the number of males for each female in five age groups—*at birth, under 15 years, 15-64 years, 65 years and over,* and for the *total population.* Sex ratio at birth has recently emerged as an indicator of certain kinds of sex discrimination in some countries. For instance, high sex ratios at birth in some Asian countries are now attributed to sex-selective abortion and infanticide due to a strong preference for sons. This will affect future marriage patterns and fertility patterns. Eventually, it could cause unrest among young adult males who are unable to find partners.

Stateless person Statelessness is the condition whereby an individual is not considered a national by any country. Stateless people are denied basic rights, such as access to employment, housing, education, healthcare, and pensions, and they may be unable to vote, own property, open a bank account, or legally register a marriage or birth. They may also be vulnerable to arbitrary treatment and human trafficking. In at least 30 states, women cannot pass their nationality on to their children. In these countries, if a child's father is foreign, stateless, or absent, the child usually becomes stateless. Estimates of the number of stateless people are inherently imprecise because few countries have procedures to identify them; the UN approximates that there are 12 million stateless people worldwide. Stateless people are counted in a country's overall population figure if they have lived there for a year.

Stock of broad money This entry covers all of "Narrow money," plus the total quantity of time and savings deposits, credit union deposits, institutional money market funds, short-term repurchase agreements between the central bank and commercial deposit banks, and other large liquid assets held by nonbank financial institutions, state and local governments, nonfinancial public enterprises, and the private sector of the economy. National currency units have been converted to US dollars at the closing exchange rate for the date of the information. Because of exchange rate movements, changes in money stocks measured in national currency units may vary significantly from those shown in US dollars, and caution is urged when making comparisons over time in US dollars. In addition to serving as a medium of exchange, broad money includes assets that are slightly less liquid than narrow money and the assets tend to function as a "store of value"—a means of holding wealth.

Stock of direct foreign investment—abroad This entry gives the cumulative US dollar value of all investments in foreign countries made directly by residents—primarily companies—of the home country, as of the end of the time period indicated. Direct investment excludes investment through purchase of shares.

Stock of direct foreign investment—at home This entry gives the cumulative US dollar value of all investments in the home country made directly by residents—primarily companies—of other countries as of the end of the time period indicated. Direct investment excludes investment through purchase of shares.

Stock of domestic credit This entry is the total quantity of credit, denominated in the domestic currency, provided by financial institutions to the central bank, state and local governments, public non-financial corporations, and the private sector. The national currency units have been converted to US dollars at the closing exchange rate on the date of the information.

Stock of narrow money This entry, also known as "M1," comprises the total quantity of currency in circulation (notes and coins) plus demand deposits denominated in the national currency held by nonbank financial institutions, state and local governments, nonfinancial public enterprises, and the private sector of the economy, measured at a specific point in time. National currency units have been converted to US dollars at the closing exchange rate for the date of the information. Because of exchange rate movements, changes in money stocks measured in national currency units may vary significantly from those shown in US dollars, and caution is urged when making comparisons over time in US dollars. Narrow money consists of more liquid assets than broad money and the assets generally function as a "medium of exchange" for an economy.

Suffrage This entry gives the age at enfranchisement and whether the right to vote is universal or restricted.

Taxes and other revenues This entry records total taxes and other revenues received by the national government during the time period indicated, expressed as a percent of GDP. Taxes include personal and corporate income taxes, value added taxes, excise taxes, and tariffs. Other revenues include social contributions—such as payments for social security and hospital insurance—grants, and net revenues from public enterprises. Normalizing the data, by dividing total revenues by GDP, enables easy comparisons across countries, and provides an average rate at which all income (GDP) is paid to the national level government for the supply of public goods and services.

Telephone numbers All telephone numbers in *The World Factbook* consist of the country code in brackets, the city or area code (where required) in parentheses, and the local number. The one component that is not presented is the international access code, which varies from country to country. For example, an international direct dial telephone call placed from the US to Madrid, Spain, would be as follows: 011 [34] (1) 577-xxxx, where 011 is the international access code for station-to-station calls; 01 is for calls other than station-to-station calls, [34] is the country code for Spain, (1) is the city code for Madrid, 577 is the local exchange, and xxxx is the local telephone number. An international direct dial telephone call placed from another country to the US would be as follows: international access code +[1] (202) 939-xxxx, where [1] is the country code for the US, (202) is the area code for Washington, DC, 939 is the local exchange, and xxxx is the local telephone number.

Telephone system This entry includes a brief general assessment of the system with details on the domestic and international components. The following terms and abbreviations are used throughout the entry:

Arabsat—Arab Satellite Communications Organization (Riyadh, Saudi Arabia).

Autodin—Automatic Digital Network (US Department of Defense).

CB—citizen's band mobile radio communications.

Cellular telephone system—the telephones in this system are radio transceivers, with each instrument having its own private radio frequency and sufficient radiated power to reach the booster station in its area (cell), from which the telephone signal is fed to a telephone exchange.

Central American Microwave System—a trunk microwave radio relay system that links the countries of Central America and Mexico with each other.

Coaxial cable—a multichannel communication cable consisting of a central conducting wire, surrounded by and insulated from a cylindrical conducting shell; a large number of telephone channels can be made available within the insulated space by the use of a large number of carrier frequencies.

Comsat—Communications Satellite Corporation (US).

DSN—Defense Switched Network (formerly Automatic Voice Network or Autovon); basic general-purpose, switched voice network of the Defense Communications System (US Department of Defense).

Eutelsat—European Telecommunications Satellite Organization (Paris).

Fiber-optic cable—a multichannel communications cable using a thread of optical glass fibers as a transmission medium in which the signal (voice, video, etc.) is in the form of a coded pulse of light.

GSM—a global system for mobile (cellular) communications devised by the Groupe Special Mobile of the pan-European standardization organization, Conference Europeanne des Posts et Telecommunications (CEPT) in 1982.

HF—high frequency; any radio frequency in the 3,000-to 30,000-kHz range.

Inmarsat—International Maritime Satellite Organization (London); provider of global mobile satellite communications for commercial, distress, and safety applications at sea, in the air, and on land.

Intelsat—International Telecommunications Satellite Organization (Washington, DC).

Intersputnik—International Organization of Space Communications (Moscow); first established in the former Soviet Union and the East European countries, it is now marketing its services worldwide with earth stations in North America, Africa, and East Asia.

Landline—communication wire or cable of any sort that is installed on poles or buried in the ground.

Marecs—Maritime European Communications Satellite used in the Inmarsat system on lease from the European Space Agency.

Marisat—satellites of the Comsat Corporation that participate in the Inmarsat system.

Medarabtel—the Middle East Telecommunications Project of the International Telecommunications Union (ITU) providing a modern telecommunications network, primarily by microwave radio relay, linking Algeria, Djibouti, Egypt, Jordan, Libya, Morocco, Saudi Arabia, Somalia, Sudan, Syria, Tunisia, and Yemen; it was initially started in Morocco in 1970 by the Arab Telecommunications Union (ATU) and was known at that time as the Middle East Mediterranean Telecommunications Network.

Microwave radio relay—transmission of long distance telephone calls and television programs by highly directional radio microwaves that are received and sent on from one booster station to another on an optical path.

NMT—Nordic Mobile Telephone; an analog cellular telephone system that was developed jointly by the national telecommunications authorities of the Nordic countries (Denmark, Finland, Iceland, Norway, and Sweden).

Orbita—a Russian television service; also the trade name of a packet-switched digital telephone network.

Radiotelephone communications—the two-way transmission and reception of sounds by broadcast radio on authorized frequencies using telephone handsets.

PanAmSat—PanAmSat Corporation (Greenwich, CT).

SAFE—South African Far East Cable

Satellite communication system—a communication system consisting of two or more earth stations and at least one satellite that provide long distance transmission of voice, data, and television; the system usually serves as a trunk connection between telephone exchanges; if the earth stations are in the same country, it is a domestic system.

Satellite earth station—a communications facility with a microwave radio transmitting and receiving antenna and required receiving and transmitting equipment for communicating with satellites.

Satellite link—a radio connection between a satellite and an earth station permitting communication between them, either one-way (down link from satellite to earth station—television receive-only transmission) or two-way (telephone channels).

SHF—super high frequency; any radio frequency in the 3,000- to 30,000-MHz range.

Shortwave—radio frequencies (from 1.605 to 30 MHz) that fall above the commercial broadcast band and are used for communication over long distances.

Solidaridad—geosynchronous satellites in Mexico's system of international telecommunications in the Western Hemisphere.

Statsionar—Russia's geostationary system for satellite telecommunications.

Submarine cable—a cable designed for service under water.

TAT—Trans-Atlantic Telephone; any of a number of high-capacity submarine coaxial telephone cables linking Europe with North America.

Telefax—facsimile service between subscriber stations via the public switched telephone network or the international Datel network.

Telegraph—a telecommunications system designed for unmodulated electric impulse transmission.

Telex—a communication service involving teletypewriters connected by wire through automatic exchanges.

Tropospheric scatter—a form of microwave radio transmission in which the troposphere is used to scatter and reflect a fraction of the incident radio waves back to earth; powerful, highly directional antennas are used to transmit and receive the microwave signals; reliable over-the-horizon communications are

realized for distances up to 600 miles in a single hop; additional hops can extend the range of this system for very long distances.
Trunk network—a network of switching centers, connected by multichannel trunk lines.
UHF—ultra high frequency; any radio frequency in the 300-to 3,000-MHz range.
VHF—very high frequency; any radio frequency in the 30-to 300-MHz range.

Telephones—main lines in use This entry gives the total number of main telephone lines in use.

Telephones—mobile cellular This entry gives the total number of mobile cellular telephone subscribers.

Terminology Due to the highly structured nature of the *Factbook* database, some collective generic terms have to be used. For example, the word **Country** in the **Country name** entry refers to a wide variety of dependencies, areas of special sovereignty, uninhabited islands, and other entities in addition to the traditional countries or independent states. **Military** is also used as an umbrella term for various civil defense, security, and defense activities in many entries. The **Independence** entry includes the usual colonial independence dates and former ruling states as well as other significant nationhood dates such as the traditional founding date or the date of unification, federation, confederation, establishment, or state succession that are not strictly independence dates. Dependent areas have the nature of their dependency status noted in this same entry.

Terrain This entry contains a brief description of the topography.

Time difference This entry is expressed in *The World Factbook* in two ways. First, it is stated as the difference in hours between the capital of an entity and **Coordinated Universal Time (UTC)** during Standard Time. Additionally, the difference in time between the capital of an entity and that observed in Washington, D.C. is also provided. Note that the time difference assumes both locations are simultaneously observing Standard Time or Daylight Saving Time.

Time zones Ten countries (Australia, Brazil, Canada, Indonesia, Kazakhstan, Mexico, New Zealand, Russia, Spain, and the United States) and the island of Greenland observe more than one official time depending on the number of designated time zones within their boundaries. An illustration of time zones throughout the world and within countries can be seen in the Standard Time Zones of the World map included in the **Reference Maps** section of *The World Factbook*.

Total fertility rate This entry gives a figure for the average number of children that would be born per woman if all women lived to the end of their childbearing years and bore children according to a given fertility rate at each age. The total fertility rate (TFR) is a more direct measure of the level of fertility than the crude birth rate, since it refers to births per woman. This indicator shows the potential for population change in the country. A rate of two children per woman is considered the replacement rate for a population, resulting in relative stability in terms of total numbers. Rates above two children indicate populations growing in size and whose median age is declining. Higher rates may also indicate difficulties for families, in some situations, to feed and educate their children and for women to enter the labor force. Rates below two children indicate populations decreasing in size and growing older. Global fertility rates are in general decline and this trend is most pronounced in industrialized countries, especially Western Europe, where populations are projected to decline dramatically over the next 50 years.

Total renewable water resources This entry provides the long-term average water availability for a country in cubic kilo-meters of precipitation, recharged ground water, and surface inflows from surrounding countries. The values have been adjusted to account for overlap resulting from surface flow recharge of groundwater sources. Total renewable water resources provides the water total available to a country but does not include water resource totals that have been reserved for upstream or downstream countries through international agreements. Note that these values are averages and do not accurately reflect the total available in any given year. Annual available resources can vary greatly due to short-term and long-term climatic and weather variations.

Trafficking in persons Trafficking in persons is modern-day slavery, involving victims who are forced, defrauded, or coerced into labor or sexual exploitation. The International Labor Organization (ILO), the UN agency charged with addressing labor standards, employment, and social protection issues, estimates that 12.3 million people worldwide are enslaved in forced labor, bonded labor, forced child labor, sexual servitude, and involuntary servitude at any given time. Human trafficking is a multi-dimensional threat, depriving people of their human rights and freedoms, risking global health, promoting social breakdown, inhibiting development by depriving countries of their human capital, and helping fuel the growth of organized crime. In 2000, the US Congress passed the Trafficking Victims Protection Act (TVPA), reauthorized in 2003 and 2005, which provides tools for the US to combat trafficking in persons, both domestically and abroad. One of the law's key components is the creation of the US Department of State's annual *Trafficking in Persons Report*, which assesses the government response (i.e., the *current situation*) in some 150 countries with a significant number of victims trafficked across their borders who are recruited, harbored, transported, provided, or obtained for forced labor or sexual exploitation. Countries in the annual report are rated in three tiers, based on government efforts to combat trafficking. The countries identified in this entry are those listed in the *2010 Trafficking in Persons Report as Tier 2 Watch List or Tier 3* based on the following *tier rating* definitions:

> **Tier 2 Watch List** *countries do not fully comply with the minimum standards for the elimination of trafficking but are making significant efforts to do so, and meet one of the following criteria:*
> *1. they display high or significantly increasing number of victims,*
> *2. they have failed to provide evidence of increasing efforts to combat trafficking in persons, or,*
> *3. they have committed to take action over the next year.*
> **Tier 3** *countries neither satisfy the minimum standards for the elimination of trafficking nor demonstrate a significant effort to do so. Countries in this tier are subject to potential non-humanitarian and non-trade sanctions.*

Transnational issues This category includes four entries—**Disputes—international, Refugees and internally displaced persons, Trafficking in persons,** and **Illicit drugs**—that deal with current issues going beyond national boundaries.

Transportation This category includes the entries dealing with the means for movement of people and goods.

Transportation—note This entry includes miscellaneous transportation information of significance not included elsewhere.

Unemployment rate This entry contains the percent of the labor force that is without jobs. Substantial underemployment might be noted.

Unemployment, youth ages 15-24 This entry gives the percent of the total labor force ages 15-24 unemployed during a specified year.

Urbanization This entry provides two measures of the degree of urbanization of a population. The first, *urban population*, describes the percentage of the total population living in urban areas, as defined by the country. The second, *rate of urbanization*, describes the projected average rate of change of the size of the urban population over the given period of time. Additionally, the World entry includes a list of the *ten largest urban agglomerations*. An *urban agglomeration* is defined as comprising the city or town proper and also the suburban fringe or thickly settled territory lying outside of, but adjacent to, the boundaries of the city.

UTC (Coordinated Universal Time) See entry for Coordinated Universal Time.

Waterways This entry gives the total length of navigable rivers, canals, and other inland bodies of water.

Weights and Measures This information is presented in **Appendix G: Weights and Measures** and includes mathematical notations (mathematical powers and names), metric interrelationships (prefix; symbol; length, weight, or capacity; area; volume), and standard conversion factors.

Years All year references are for the calendar year (CY) unless indicated as fiscal year (FY). The calendar year is an accounting period of 12 months from 1 January to 31 December. The fiscal year is an accounting period of 12 months other than 1 January to 31 December.

GUIDE TO COUNTRY PROFILES

INTRODUCTION

Background

GEOGRAPHY

Location
Geographic coordinates
Map references
Area
total
land
water
Area—comparative
Land boundaries
total
border countries
Coastline
Maritime claims
territorial sea
contiguous zone
exclusive economic zone
continental shelf
exclusive fishing zone
Climate
Terrain
Elevation extremes
lowest point
highest point
Natural resources
Land use
arable land
permanent crops
other
Irrigated land
Total renewable water resources
Freshwater withdrawal (domestic/industrial/agricultural)
total
per capita
Natural hazards
volcanism
Environment—current issues
Environment—international agreements
party to
signed, but not ratified
Geography—note

PEOPLE AND SOCIETY

Nationality
noun
adjective
Ethnic groups
Languages
Religions
Demographic profile

Population
Age structure
0-14 years
15-24 years
25-54 years
55-64 years
65 years and over
Median Age
total
male
female
Population growth rate
Birth rate
Death rate
Net migration rate
Urbanization
urban population
rate of urbanization
Major cities—population
Sex ratio
at birth
under 15 years
15-64 years
65 years and over
total population
Maternal mortality rate
Infant mortality rate
total
male
female
Life expectancy at birth
total population
male
female
Total fertility rate
Health expenditures
Physicians density
Hospital bed density
Drinking water source
improved
unimproved
Sanitation facility access
improved
unimproved
HIV/AIDS—adult prevalence rate
HIV/AIDS—people living with HIV/AIDS
HIV/AIDS—deaths
Major infectious diseases
degree of risk
food or waterborne diseases
vectorborne diseases
water contact diseases
aerosolized dust or soil contact disease
respiratory disease
animal contact disease
Obesity—adult prevalence rate

Children under the age of 5 years underweight
Education expenditures
Literacy
definition
total population
male
female
School life expectancy (primary to tertiary)
Unemployment, youth ages 15-24
People—note

GOVERNMENT

Country name
conventional long form
conventional short form
local long form
local short form
former
abbreviation
Dependency status
Government type
Capital
name
geographic coordinates
time difference
daylight saving time
Administrative divisions
Dependent areas
Independence
National holiday
Constitution
Legal system
International law organization participation
Suffrage
Executive branch
chief of state
head of government
cabinet
elections
election results
Legislative branch
elections
election results
Judicial branch
Political parties and leaders
Political pressure groups and leaders
International organization participation
Diplomatic representation in the US
chief of mission
chancery
telephone
FAX
consulate(s) general

consulate(s)
Diplomatic representation from the US
chief of mission
embassy
mailing address
telephone
FAX
consulate(s) general
consulate(s)
branch office(s)
Flag description
National symbol(s)
National anthem
Government—note

ECONOMY

Economy—overview
GDP (purchasing power parity)
GDP (official exchange rate)
GDP—real growth rate
GDP—per capita (PPP)
GDP—composition by sector
agriculture
industry
services
Labor force
Labor force—by occupation
agriculture
industry
services
Unemployment rate
Population below poverty line
Household income or consumption by percentage share
lowest 10%
highest 10%
Distribution of family income—Gini index
Investment (gross fixed)
Budget
revenues
expenditures
Taxes and other revenues
Budget surplus (+) or deficit (−)
Public debt
Inflation rate (consumer prices)
Central bank discount rate
Commercial bank prime lending rate
Stock of narrow money
Stock of broad money
Stock of domestic credit
Market value of publicly traded shares
Agriculture—products
Industries
Industrial production growth rate
Current account balance
Exports
Exports—commodities
Exports—partners

Imports
Imports—commodities
Imports—partners
Reserves of foreign exchange and gold
Debt—external
Stock of direct foreign investment—at home
Stock of direct foreign investment—abroad
Exchange rates
Fiscal year

ENERGY

Electricity—production
Electricity—consumption
Electricity—exports
Electricity—imports
Electricity—installed generating capacity
Electricity—from fossil fuels
Electricity—from nuclear fuels
Electricity—from hydroelectric plants
Electricity—from other renewable sources
Crude oil—production
Crude oil—exports
Crude oil—imports
Crude oil—proved reserves
Refined petroleum products—production
Refined petroleum products—consumption
Refined petroleum products—exports
Refined petroleum products—imports
Natural gas—production
Natural gas—consumption
Natural gas—exports
Natural gas—imports
Natural gas—proved reserves
Carbon dioxide emissions from consumption of energy

COMMUNICATIONS

Telephones—main lines in use
Telephones—mobile cellular
Telephone system
general assessment
domestic
international
Broadcast media
Internet country code
Internet hosts
Internet users
Communications—note

TRANSPORTATION

Airports
Airports—with paved runways

total
over 3,047 m
2,438 to 3,047 m
1,524 to 2,437 m
914 to 1,523 m
under 914 m
Airports—with unpaved runways
total
over 3,047 m
2,438 to 3,047 m
1,524 to 2,437 m
914 to 1,523 m
under 914 m
Heliports
Pipelines
Railways
total
broad gauge
standard gauge
narrow gauge
dual gauge
Roadways
total
paved
unpaved
Waterways
Merchant marine
total
ships by type
foreign-owned
registered in other countries
Ports and terminals
Transportation—note

MILITARY

Military branches
Military service age and obligation
Manpower available for military service
males age 16-49
females age 16-49
Manpower fit for military service
males age 16-49
females age 16-49
Manpower reaching militarily significant age annually
males
females
Military expenditures—percent of GDP
Military—note

TRANSNATIONAL ISSUES

Disputes—international
Refugees and internally displaced persons
refugees
IDPs
Trafficking in persons
current situation
tier rating
Illicit drugs

Background: Ahmad Shah DURRANI unified the Pashtun tribes and founded Afghanistan in 1747. The country served as a buffer between the British and Russian Empires until it won independence from notional British control in 1919. A brief experiment in democracy ended in a 1973 coup and a 1978 communist countercoup. The Soviet Union invaded in 1979 to support the tottering Afghan communist regime, touching off a long and destructive war. The USSR withdrew in 1989 under relentless pressure by internationally supported anticommunist mujahidin rebels. A series of subsequent civil wars saw Kabul finally fall in 1996 to the Taliban, a hardline Pakistani sponsored movement that emerged in 1994 to end the country's civil war and anarchy. Following the 11 September 2001 terrorist attacks, a US, Allied, and anti-Taliban Northern Alliance military action toppled the Taliban for sheltering Usama BIN LADIN. A UN-sponsored Bonn Conference in 2001 established a process for political reconstruction that included the adoption of a new constitution, a presidential election in 2004, and National Assembly elections in 2005. In December 2004, Hamid KARZAI became the first democratically elected president of Afghanistan, and the National Assembly was inaugurated the following December. KARZAI was reelected in August 2009 for a second term. The 2014 presidential election was the country's first to include a runoff, which featured the top two vote getters from the first round, Abdullah ABDULLAH and Ashraf GHANI. Throughout the summer of 2014, their campaigns disputed the results and traded accusations of fraud, leading to a US led diplomatic intervention that included a full vote audit as well as political negotiations between the two camps. In September 2014, GHANI and ABDULLAH agreed to form the Government of National Unity, with GHANI inaugurated as President and ABDULLAH elevated to the newly created position of chief executive officer. The day after the inauguration, the GHANI administration signed the US-Afghan Bilateral Security Agreement and NATO Status of Forces Agreement, which provide the legal basis for the post-2014 international military presence in Afghanistan. Despite gains toward building a stable central government, the Taliban remains a serious challenge for the Afghan Government in almost every province. The Taliban still considers itself the rightful government of Afghanistan, and it remains a capable and confident insurgent force despite reports in 2015 that its founder and spiritual leader, Mullah Mohammad OMAR, died in 2013.

Location: Southern Asia, north and west of Pakistan, east of Iran

Geographic coordinates: 33 00 N, 65 00 E

Map references: Asia

Area: *total:* 652,230 sq km
land: 652,230 sq km
water: 0 sq km
country comparison to the world: 41

Area—comparative: almost six times the size of Virginia; slightly smaller than Texas

Land boundaries: *total:* 5,987 km
border countries (6): China 91 km, Iran 921 km, Pakistan 2,670 km, Tajikistan 1,357 km, Turkmenistan 804 km, Uzbekistan 144 km

Coastline: 0 km (landlocked)

Maritime claims: none (landlocked)

Climate: arid to semiarid; cold winters and hot summers

Terrain: mostly rugged mountains; plains in north and southwest

Elevation: *mean elevation:* 1,884 m

elevation extremes: *lowest point:* Amu Darya 258 m
highest point: Noshak 7,485 m

Natural resources: natural gas, petroleum, coal, copper, chromite, talc, barites, sulfur, lead, zinc, iron ore, salt, precious and semiprecious stones, arable land

Land use: *agricultural land:* 58.1%
arable land: 11.9%
permanent crops: 0.2%
permanent pasture: 46%
forest: 2.1%
other: 39.8% (2011 est.)

Irrigated land: 32,080 sq km (2012)
Total renewable water resources: 65.33 cu km (2011)

Freshwater withdrawal (domestic/industrial/agricultural): *total:* 20.28 cu km/yr (1%/1%/98%)
per capita: 823.1 cu m/yr (2005)

Natural hazards: damaging earthquakes occur in Hindu Kush mountains; flooding; droughts

Environment—current issues: limited natural freshwater resources; inadequate supplies of potable water; soil degradation; overgrazing; deforestation (much of the remaining forests are being cut down for fuel and building materials); desertification; air and water pollution

Environment—international agreements: *party to:* Biodiversity, Climate Change, Desertification, Endangered Species, Environmental Modification, Marine Dumping, Ozone Layer Protection
signed, but not ratified: Hazardous Wastes, Law of the Sea, Marine Life Conservation

Geography—note: landlocked; the Hindu Kush mountains that run northeast to southwest divide the northern provinces from the rest of the country; the highest peaks are in the northern Vakhan (Wakhan Corridor)

Nationality: *noun:* Afghan(s)
adjective: Afghan

Ethnic groups: Pashtun, Tajik, Hazara, Uzbek, other (includes smaller numbers of Baloch, Turkmen, Nuristani, Pamiri, Arab, Gujar, Brahui, Qizilbash, Aimaq, Pashai, and Kyrghyz)
note: current statistical data on the sensitive subject of ethnicity in Afghanistan is not available, and ethnicity data from small samples of respondents to opinion polls are not a reliable alternative; Afghanistan's 2004 constitution recognizes 14 ethnic groups: Pashtun, Tajik, Hazara, Uzbek, Baloch, Turkmen, Nuristani, Pamiri, Arab, Gujar, Brahui, Qizilbash, Aimaq, and Pashai (2015)

Languages: Afghan Persian or Dari (official) 50%, Pashto (official) 35%, Turkic languages (primarily Uzbek and Turkmen) 11%, 30 minor languages (primarily Balochi and Pashai) 4%, much bilingualism, but Dari functions as the lingua franca
note: the Turkic languages Uzbek and Turkmen, as well as Balochi, Pashai, Nuristani, and Pamiri are the third official languages in areas where the majority speaks them

Religions: Muslim 99.7% (Sunni 84.7–89.7%, Shia 10–15%), other 0.3% (2009 est.)

Population: 32,564,342 (July 2015 est.)
country comparison to the world: 41

Age structure: *0–14 years:* 41.47% (male 6,861,021/female 6,644,780)
15–24 years: 22.41% (male 3,716,738/female 3,579,701)
25–54 years: 29.69% (male 4,928,181/female 4,741,601)
55–64 years: 3.88% (male 621,970/female 641,307)
65 years and over: 2.55% (male 384,267/female 444,776) (2015 est.)
Dependency ratios:

Dependency ratios: *total dependency ratio:* 87%
youth dependency ratio: 82.3%
elderly dependency ratio: 4.6%
potential support ratio: 21.7% (2015 est.)

Median age: *total:* 18.4 years
male: 18.3 years
female: 18.4 years (2015 est.)
country comparison to the world: 209

Population growth rate: 2.32% (2015 est.)
country comparison to the world: 34

Birth rate: 38.57 births/1,000 population (2015 est.)
country comparison to the world: 11

Death rate: 13.89 deaths/1,000 population (2015 est.)
country comparison to the world: 9

Net migration rate: -1.51 migrant(s)/1,000 population (2015 est.)
country comparison to the world: 156

Urbanization: *urban population:* 26.7% of total population (2015)
rate of urbanization: 3.96% annual rate of change (2010–15 est.)

Major urban areas—population: KABUL (capital) 4.635 million (2015)

Sex ratio: *at birth:* 1.05 male(s)/female
0–14 years: 1.03 male(s)/female
15–24 years: 1.04 male(s)/female
25–54 years: 1.04 male(s)/female
55–64 years: 0.97 male(s)/female
65 years and over: 0.86 male(s)/female
total population: 1.03 male(s)/female (2015 est.)

Mother's mean age at first birth: 20.1
note: median age at first birth among women 25–29 (2010 est.)

Maternal mortality rate: 396 deaths/100,000 live births (2015 est.)
country comparison to the world: 22

Infant mortality rate: *total:* 115.08 deaths/1,000 live births
male: 122.64 deaths/1,000 live births
female: 107.15 deaths/1,000 live births (2015 est.)
country comparison to the world: 1

Life expectancy at birth: *total population:* 50.87 years
male: 49.52 years
female: 52.29 years (2015 est.)
country comparison to the world: 222

Total fertility rate: 5.33 children born/woman (2015 est.)
country comparison to the world: 10

Contraceptive prevalence rate: 21.2% (2010/11)

Health expenditures: 8.1% of GDP (2013)
country comparison to the world: 46

Physicians density: 0.27 physicians/1,000 population (2013)

Hospital bed density: 0.5 beds/1,000 population (2012)

Drinking water source:
improved:
urban: 78.2% of population
rural: 47% of population
total: 55.3% of population
unimproved:
urban: 21.8% of population
rural: 53% of population
total: 44.7% of population (2015 est.)

Sanitation facility access:
improved:
urban: 45.1% of population
rural: 27% of population
total: 31.9% of population

unimproved:
urban: 54.9% of population
rural: 73% of population
total: 68.1% of population (2015 est.)

HIV/AIDS—adult prevalence rate: 0.04% (2014 est.)
country comparison to the world: 122

HIV/AIDS—people living with HIV/AIDS: 6,700 (2014 est.)
country comparison to the world: 105

HIV/AIDS—deaths: 300 (2014 est.)
country comparison to the world: 97

Major infectious diseases: *degree of risk:* intermediate
food or waterborne diseases: bacterial diarrhea, hepatitis A, and typhoid fever
vectorborne disease: malaria
animal contact disease: rabies
note: highly pathogenic H5N1 avian influenza has been identified in this country; it poses a negligible riskwith extremely rare cases possible among US citizens who have close contact with birds (2013)

Obesity—adult prevalence rate: 2.4% (2014)
country comparison to the world: 182

Education expenditures: NA

Literacy: *definition:* age 15 and over can read and write
total population: 38.2%
male: 52%
female: 24.2% (2015 est.)

School life expectancy (primary to tertiary education): *total:* 11 years
male: 13 years
female: 8 years (2014)

Child labor—children ages 5–14: *total number:* 2,082,722
percentage: 25.3%
note: data on child labor in Afghanistan is uncertain and may be higher than the estimated 25.3% of children ages 5–14 derived from 2010–11 survey results; UNICEF estimated that 30% of children ages 5–14in 2011 were engaged in child labor (2010/11 est.)

GOVERNMENT

Country name: *conventional long form:* Islamic Republic of Afghanistan
conventional short form: Afghanistan
local long form: Jamhuriye Islamiye Afghanistan
local short form: Afghanistan
former: Republic of Afghanistane
etymology: the name "Afghan" originally refered to the Pashtun people (today it is understood to includeall the country's ethnic groups), while the suffix "stan" means "place of" or "country"; so Afghanistan literally means the "Land of the Afghans"

Government type: presidential Islamic republic

Capital: *name:* Kabul

Geographic coordinates: 34 31 N, 69 11 E
time difference: UTC+4.5 (9.5 hours ahead of Washington, DC, during Standard Time)

Administrative divisions: 34 provinces (welayat, singular welayat); Badakhshan, Badghis, Baghlan, Balkh, Bamyan, Daykundi, Farah, Faryab, Ghazni, Ghor, Helmand, Herat, Jowzjan, Kabul, Kandahar, Kapisa, Khost, Kunar, Kunduz, Laghman, Logar, Nangarhar, Nimroz, Nuristan, Paktika, Paktiya, Panjshir, Parwan, Samangan, Sare Pul, Takhar, Uruzgan, Wardak, Zabul

Independence: 19 August 1919 (from UK control over Afghan foreign affairs)

National holiday: Independence Day, 19 August (1919)

Constitution: several previous; latest drafted 14 December 2003—4 January 2004, signed 16 January 2004, ratified 26 January 2004 (2016)

Legal system: mixed legal system of civil, customary, and Islamic law

International law organization participation: has not submitted an ICJ jurisdiction declaration; accepts ICCt jurisdiction

Citizenship: *citizenship by birth:* no

citizenship by descent only: at least one parent must have been born in and continuously lived in Afghanistan
dual citizenship recognized: no
residency requirement for naturalization: 5 years

Suffrage: 18 years of age; universal

Executive branch: *chief of state:* President of the Islamic Republic of Afghanistan Ashraf GHANI Ahmadzai (since 29September 2014); CEO Abdullah ABDULLAH (since 29 September 2014); First Vice President Abdul Rashid DOSTAM (since 29 September 2014); Second Vice President Sarwar DANESH (since 29 September 2014); note the president is both chief of state and head of government

head of government: President of the Islamic Republic of Afghanistan Ashraf GHANI Ahmadzai (since 29 September 2014); CEO Abdullah ABDULLAH (since 29 September 2014); First Vice President Abdul Rashid DOSTAM (since 29 September 2014); Second Vice President Sarwar DANESH (since 29 September 2014)
cabinet: Cabinet consists of 25 ministers appointed by the president, approved by the National Assembly
elections/appointments: president directly elected by absolute majority popular vote in 2 rounds if needed for a 5 year term (eligible for a second term); election last held in 2 rounds on 5 April and 14 June2014 (next to be held in 2019)
election results: percent of vote in first round Abdullah ABDULLAH (National Coalition of Afghanistan) 45%, Ashraf GHANI (independent) 31.6%, Zalmai RASSOUL 11.4%, other 12%; percent of vote in secondround Ashraf GHANI 56.4%, Abdullah ABDULLAH 43.6%

Legislative branch: *description:* bicameral National Assembly consists of the Meshrano Jirga or House of Elders (102 seats; 34 members indirectly elected by district councils to serve 3 year terms, 34 indirectly elected by provincialcouncils to serve 4 year terms, and 34 nominated by the president of which 17 must be women, 2 mustrepresent the disabled, and 2 must be Kuchi nomads; members serve 5 year terms) and the Wolesi Jirga or House of People (no more than 250 seats; members directly elected in multiseat constituencies byproportional representation vote to serve 5 year terms)

note: the constitution allows the government to convene a constitutional Loya Jirga (Grand Council) onissues of independence, national sovereignty, and territorial integrity; it can amend the provisions of theconstitution and prosecute the president; it is made up of members of the National Assembly and chairpersons of the provincial and district councils; no Loya Jirga has ever been held, and district councilshave never been elected

elections: last held on 18 September 2010 (next to be held on 15 October 2016)

election results: results by party NA; note ethnicity is the main factor influencing political alliances; approximate percentage of seats by ethnic group Pashtun 39%, Hazara 24%, Tajik 21%, Uzbek 6%, other10% (including Aimak, Arab, Baloch, Nuristani, Pahhai, Turkmen, Turkic); women hold 69 seats

Judicial branch: highest court(s): Supreme Court or Stera Mahkama (consists of the Supreme Court Chief and 8 justicesorganized into criminal, public security, civil, and commercial divisions or dewans)

judge selection and term of office: court chief and justices appointed by the president with theapproval of the Wolesi Jirga; court chief and justices serve single 10year terms

subordinate courts: Appeals Courts; Primary Courts; Special Courts for issues including narcotics, security, property, family, and juveniles

Political parties and leaders: note the Ministry of Justice licensed 84 political parties as of December 2012

Political pressure groups and leaders: other: religious groups, tribal leaders, ethnically based groups, TalibanInternational organization participation: ADB, CP, ECO, EITI (candidate country), FAO, G77, IAEA, IBRD, ICAO, ICC (NGOs), ICCt, ICRM, IDA, IDB, IFAD, IFC, IFRCS, IHO, ILO, IMF, Interpol, IOC, IOM, IPU, ISO (correspondent), ITSO, ITU, MIGA, NAM, NATO (pending), OIC, OPCW, OSCE (partner), SAARC, SACEP, SCO (dialogue member), SICA (observer), UN, UNCTAD, UNESCO, UNHCR, UNIDO, UNWTO, UPU, WCO, WFTU (NGOs), WHO, WIPO, WMO, WTO

Diplomatic representation in the US: chief of mission: Ambassador Hamdullah MOHIB (since 17 September 2015)

chancery: 2341 Wyoming Avenue NW, Washington, DC 20008

telephone: [1] (202) 483-6410

FAX: [1] (202) 483-6488

consulate(s) general: Los Angeles, New York, Washington, DC

Diplomatic representation from the US: chief of mission: Ambassador P. Michael MCKINLEY (since 22 December 2014)

embassy: The Great Masood Road, Kabul

mailing address: U.S. Embassy Kabul, APO, AE 09806

telephone: [00 93] 0700-108-001

FAX: [00 93] 0700-108-564

Flag description: three equal vertical bands of black (hoist side), red, and green, with the national emblem in white centeredon the red band and slightly overlapping the other two bands; the center of the emblem features a mosquewith pulpit and flags on either side, below the mosque are numerals for the solar year 1298 (1919 in the Gregorian calendar, the year of Afghan independence from the UK); this central image is circled by aborder consisting of sheaves of wheat on the left and right, in the uppercenter is an Arabic inscription ofthe Shahada (Muslim creed) below which are rays of the rising sun over the Takbir (Arabic expression meaning "God is great"), and at bottom center is a scroll bearing the name Afghanistan; black signifies thepast, red is for the blood shed for independence, and green can represent either hope for the future, agricultural prosperity, or Islam

note: Afghanistan had more changes to its national flag in the 20th century than any other country; thecolors black, red, and green appeared on most of them

National symbol(s): lion; national colors: red, green, black

National anthem: name: "Milli Surood" (National Anthem)

lyrics/music: Abdul Bari JAHANI/Babrak WASA

note: adopted 2006; the 2004 constitution of the post-Taliban government mandated that a new nationalanthem should be written containing the phrase "Allahu Akbar" (God is Greatest) and mentioning the names of Afghanistan's ethnic groups

ECONOMY

Economy overview: Afghanistan's economy is recovering from decades of conflict. The economy has improved significantlysince the fall of the Taliban regime in 2001 largely because of the infusion of international assistance, therecovery of the agricultural sector, and service sector growth. Despite the progress of the past few years, Afghanistan is extremely poor, landlocked, and highly dependent on foreign aid. Much of the population continues to suffer from shortages of housing, clean water, electricity, medical care, and jobs. Criminality, insecurity, weak governance, lack of infrastructure, and the Afghan Government's difficulty in extendingrule of law to all parts of the country pose challenges to future economic growth. Afghanistan's livingstandards are among the lowest in the world. The international community remains committed to Afghanistan's development, pledging over $67 billion atnine donors' conferences between 2003 and 2010. In July 2012, the donors at the Tokyo conference pledged an additional $16 billion in civilian aid through 2015. Despite this help, the

Government of Afghanistan will need to overcome a number of challenges, including low revenue collection, anemic jobcreation, high levels of corruption, weak government capacity, and poor public infrastructure. Afghanistan's growth rate slowed markedly in 2014–15. The drawdown of international security forces thatstarted in 2014 has negatively affected economic growth, as a substantial portion of commerce, especiallyin the services sector, has catered to the ongoing international troop presence in the country. Afghan-President Ashraf GHANI Ahmadzai is dedicated to instituting economic reforms to include improvingrevenue collection and fighting corruption. However, the reforms will take time to implement andAfghanistan will remain dependent on international donor support over the next several years.

GDP (purchasing power parity):
$62.32 billion (2015 est.)
$61.53 billion (2014 est.)
$59.46 billion (2013 est.)
note: data are in 2015 US dollars
country comparison to the world: 104

GDP (official exchange rate): $20.84 billion (2014 est.)

GDP—real growth rate:
1.5% (2015 est.)
1.3% (2014 est.)
3.9% (2013 est.)
country comparison to the world: 156

GDP—per capita (PPP):
$1,900 (2015 est.)
$2,000 (2014 est.)
$2,000 (2013 est.)
note: data are in 2015 US dollars
country comparison to the world: 206

Gross national saving:
23.9% of GDP (2015 est.)
29.2% of GDP (2014 est.)
30.4% of GDP (2013 est.)
country comparison to the world: 56

GDP composition, by end use:
household consumption: 108.7%
government consumption: 12.8%
investment in fixed capital: 15.8%
investment in inventories: 0%
exports of goods and services: 6.5%
imports of goods and services: -43.9% (2014 est.)

GDP—composition, by sector of origin:
agriculture: 24%
industry: 21%
services: 55%
note: data exclude opium production (2014 est.)

Agriculture products: opium, wheat, fruits, nuts; wool, mutton, sheepskins, lambskins

Industries: small-scale production of bricks, textiles, soap, furniture, shoes, fertilizer, apparel, food products, nonalcoholic beverages, mineral water, cement; handwoven carpets; natural gas, coal, copper

Industrial production growth rate: 1.2% (2014 est.)
country comparison to the world: 138

Labor force: 7.983 million (2013 est.)
country comparison to the world: 60

Labor force—by occupation: *agriculture:* 78.6%
industry: 5.7%
services: 15.7% (FY08/09 est.)

Unemployment rate: 35% (2008 est.)
40% (2005 est.)
country comparison to the world: 191

Population below poverty line: 36% (FY08/09 est.)

Household income or consumption by percentage share: *lowest:* 10%: 3.8%
highest: 10%: 24% (2008)

Budget: *revenues:* $1.7 billion
expenditures: $6.639 billion (2015 est.)
Taxes and other revenues: 8.2% of GDP (2015 est.)
country comparison to the world: 212

Budget surplus (+) or deficit (–): -23.7% of GDP (2015 est.)
country comparison to the world: 217

Fiscal year: 21 December—20 December

Inflation rate (consumer prices):
-1.5% (2015 est.)
4.7% (2014 est.)
country comparison to the world: 7

Commercial bank prime lending rate: 15% (31 December 2014 est.)
15.08% (31 December 2013 est.)
country comparison to the world: 41

Stock of narrow money: $6.644 billion (31 December 2014 est.)
$6.192 billion (31 December 2013 est.)
country comparison to the world: 91

Stock of broad money: $6.945 billion (31 December 2014 est.)
$6.544 billion (31 December 2013 est.)
country comparison to the world: 119

Stock of domestic credit: -$454 million (31 December 2014 est.)
-$767.8 million (31 December 2013 est.)
country comparison to the world: 190

Market value of publicly traded shares: $NA
Current account balance: $872 million (2015 est.)
$1.604 billion (2014 est.)
country comparison to the world: 40

Exports: $2.679 billion (2013 est.)
$2.785 billion (2012 est.)
note: not including illicit exports or reexports
country comparison to the world: 131

Exports—commodities: opium, fruits and nuts, handwoven carpets, wool, cotton, hides and pelts, precious and semi-precious gems

Exports—partners: India 42.2%, Pakistan 28.9%, Tajikistan 7.6% (2015)

Imports: $12.19 billion (2013 est.)
$11.66 billion (2012 est.)
country comparison to the world: 92

Imports—commodities: machinery and other capital goods, food, textiles, petroleum products

Imports—partners: Pakistan 38.6%, India 8.9%, US 8.3%, Turkmenistan 6.2%, China 6%, Kazakhstan 5.9%, Azerbaijan 4.9% (2015)

Reserves of foreign exchange and gold: $6.681 billion (31 December 2014 est.)

$6.443 billion (31 December 2013 est.)
country comparison to the world: 89

Debt external:
$1.28 billion (FY10/11)
$2.7 billion (FY08/09)
country comparison to the world: 160

Exchange rates: afghanis (AFA) per US dollar—
63 (2015 est.)
57.25 (2014 est.)
57.25 (2013 est.)
46.75 (2011 est.)
46.45 (2010)

ENERGY

Electricity—production: 884.1 million kWh (2012 est.)
country comparison to the world: 153

Electricity—consumption: 3.893 billion kWh (2012 est.)
country comparison to the world: 126

Electricity—exports: 0 kWh (2013 est.)
country comparison to the world: 98

Electricity—imports: 3.071 billion kWh (2012 est.)
country comparison to the world: 53

Electricity—installed generating capacity: 621,000 kW (2012 est.)
country comparison to the world: 135

Electricity—from fossil fuels: 35.4% of total installed capacity (2012 est.)
country comparison to the world: 169

Electricity—from nuclear fuels: 0% of total installed capacity (2012 est.)
country comparison to the world: 37

Electricity—from hydro electric plants: 64.4% of total installed capacity (2012 est.)
country comparison to the world: 33

Electricity—from other renewable sources: 0.2% of total installed capacity (2012 est.)
country comparison to the world: 112

Crude oil—production: 0 bbl/day (2014 est.)
country comparison to the world: 104

Crude oil—exports: 0 bbl/day (2012 est.)
country comparison to the world: 94

Crude oil—imports: 0 bbl/day (2012 est.)
country comparison to the world: 153

Crude oil—proved reserves: NA bbl (1 January 2015 est.)

Refined petroleum products—production: 0 bbl/day (2012 est.)
country comparison to the world: 152

Refined petroleum products—consumption: 43,000 bbl/day (2013 est.)
country comparison to the world: 104

Refined petroleum products—exports: 0 bbl/day (2012 est.)
country comparison to the world: 151

Refined petroleum products—imports: 42,640 bbl/day (2012 est.)
country comparison to the world: 86

Natural gas—production: 159.6 million cu m (2013 est.)
country comparison to the world: 79

Natural gas—consumption: 159.6 million cu m (2013 est.)
country comparison to the world: 106

Natural gas—exports: 0 cu m (2013 est.)
country comparison to the world: 54

Natural gas—imports: 0 cu m (2013 est.)
country comparison to the world: 152

Natural gas—proved reserves: 49.55 billion cu m (1 January 2014 est.)
country comparison to the world: 64

Carbon dioxide emissions from consumption of energy: 8.552 million Mt (2012 est.)
country comparison to the world: 108

COMMUNICATIONS

Telephones—fixed lines: *total subscriptions:* 100,000
subscriptions per 100 inhabitants: less than 1 (2014 est.)
country comparison to the world: 145

Telephones—mobile cellular: *total:* 23.4 million
subscriptions per 100 inhabitants: 74 (2014 est.)
country comparison to the world: 51

Telephone system: *general assessment:* limited fixedline telephone service; an increasing number of Afghans utilize mobile-cellular phone networks
domestic: aided by the presence of multiple providers, mobilecellular telephone service continues to improve rapidly; the Afghan Ministry of Communications and Information claims that more than 90 percent of the population live in areas with access to mobilecellular services
international: country code 93; multiple VSAT's provide international and domestic voice and dataconnectivity (2012)

Broadcast media: state-owned broadcaster, Radio Television Afghanistan (RTA), operates a series of radio and televisionstations in Kabul and the provinces; an estimated 150 private radio stations, 50 TV stations, and about adozen international broadcasters are available (2007)
Radio broadcast stations: 48 (station types NA) (2009)
Television broadcast stations: 16 (1 staterun station and 15 registered private stations) (2009)

Internet country code: .af

Internet hosts: 223 (2012)
country comparison to the world: 199

Internet users: *total:* 1.9 million
percent of population: 5.9% (2014 est.)
country comparison to the world: 100

TRANSPORTATION

Airports: 52 (2013)
country comparison to the world: 91

Airports—with paved runways: *total:* 23
over 3,047 m: 4
2,438 to 3,047 m: 4
1,524 to 2,437 m: 11
914 to 1,523 m: 2

under 914 m: 2 (2013)

Airports—with unpaved runways: *total:* 29
2,438 to 3,047 m: 4
1,524 to 2,437 m: 13
914 to 1,523 m: 6
under 914 m: 6 (2013)

Heliports: 9 (2013)

Pipelines: gas 466 km (2013)

Roadways: *total:* 42,150 km
paved: 12,350 km
unpaved: 29,800 km (2006)
country comparison to the world: 84

Waterways: 1,200 km; (chiefly Amu Darya, which handles vessels up to 500 DWT) (2011)
country comparison to the world: 60

Ports and terminals: *river port(s):* Kheyrabad, Shir Khan

MILITARY AND SECURITY

Military branches: Afghan National Security Forces: Afghan National Army, Afghan Air Force, Afghan National Police, AfghanLocal Police (2016)

Military service age and obligation: 18 is the legal minimum age for voluntary military service; no conscription (2016)

Military expenditures:
28.09% of GDP (2016)
4.74% of GDP (2011)

TRANSNATIONAL ISSUES

Disputes—international: Afghan, Coalition, and Pakistan military meet periodically to clarify the alignment of the boundary on theground and on maps and since 2014 have met to discuss collaboration on the Taliban insurgency andcounter terrorism efforts; Afghan and Iranian commissioners have discussed boundary monument densification and resurvey; Iran protests Afghanistan's restricting flow of dammed Helmand Rivertributaries during drought; Pakistan has sent troops across and built fences along some remote tribalareas of its treatydefined Durand Line border with Afghanistan which serve as bases for foreign terroristsand other illegal activities; Russia remains concerned about the smuggling of poppy derivatives fromAfghanistan through Central Asian countries

Refugees and internally displaced persons:
refugees (country of origin): 241,641 (Pakistan) (2015)
IDPs: 1,174,306 (mostly Pashtuns and Kuchis displaced in the south and west due to drought and political instability) (2015)

Illicit drugs: world's largest producer of opium; poppy cultivation increased 7 percent, to a record 211,000 hectares in 2014 from 198,000 hectares in 2013, while eradication dropped sharply; relatively low opium yields due topoor weather kept potential opium production 6,300 metric tons below the record set in 2007; theTaliban and other antigovernment groups participate in and profit from the opiate trade, which is a keysource of revenue for the Taliban inside Afghanistan; widespread corruption and instability impedecounterdrug efforts; most of the heroin consumed in Europe and Eurasia is derived from Afghan opium; Afghanistan is also struggling to respond to a burgeoning domestic opiate addiction problem; vulnerable todrug money laundering through informal financial networks; illicit cultivation of cannabis and regionalsource of hashish

AKROTIRI

INTRODUCTION

Background: By terms of the 1960 Treaty of Establishment that created the independent Republic of Cyprus, the UK retained full sovereignty and jurisdiction over two areas of almost 254 square kilometers, Akrotiri and Dhekelia. The southernmost and smallest of these is the Akrotiri Sovereign Base Area, which is also referred to as the Western Sovereign Base Area.

GEOGRAPHY

Location: Eastern Mediterranean, peninsula on the southwest coast of Cyprus

Geographic coordinates: 34 37 N, 32 58 E

Map references: Middle East

Area: *total:* 123 sq km
note: includes a salt lake and wetlands
country comparison to the world: 224

Area—comparative: about 0.7 times the size of Washington, DC

Land boundaries: *total:* 48 km
border countries (1): Cyprus 48 km

Coastline: 56.3 km

Climate: temperate; Mediterranean with hot, dry summers and cool winters

Environment current issues: hunting around the salt lake; note breeding place for loggerhead and green turtles; only remaining colonyof griffon vultures is on the base

Geography—note: British extraterritorial rights also extended to several small offpost sites scattered across Cyprus; of the Sovereign Base Area (SBA) land, 60% is privately owned and farmed, 20% is owned by the Ministry of Defense, and 20% is SBA Crown land

PEOPLE AND SOCIETY

Languages: English, Greek

Population: approximately 15,700 on the Sovereign Base Areas of Akrotiri and Dhekelia including 7,700 Cypriots, 3,600 Service and UK-based contract personnel, and 4,400 dependents

GOVERNMENT

Country name: *conventional long form:* none
conventional short form: Akrotiri

etymology: named for the village that lies within the Western Sovereign Base Area on Cyprus

Dependency status: a special form of UK overseas territory; administered by an administrator who is also the Commander, British Forces Cyprus

Capital: *name:* Episkopi Cantonment (base administrative center for Akrotiri and Dhekelia)

Geographic coordinates: 34 40 N, 32 51 E
time difference: UTC+2 (7 hours ahead of Washington, DC, during Standard Time)
daylight saving time: +1hr, begins last Sunday in March; ends last Sunday in October

Constitution: presented 3 August 1960, effective 16 August 1960 (The Sovereign Base Areas of Akrotiri and Dhekelia Order in Council 1960 serves as a basic legal document); amended 1966 (2016)

Legal system: laws applicable to the Cypriot population are, as far as possible, the same as the laws of the Republic of Cyprus; note—the Sovereign Base Area Administration has its own court system to deal with civil andcriminal matters

Executive branch: *chief of state:* Queen ELIZABETH II (since 6 February 1952)

head of government: Administrator Air Vice—Marshal Michael WIGSTON (since 21 January 2015); note—administrator reports to the British Ministry of Defense; the chief officer is responsible for the day-to-day running of the civil government of the Sovereign Bases
elections/appointments: the monarchy is hereditary; administrator appointed by the monarch on the advice of the Ministry of Defense

5

Judicial branch: *highest court(s):* Senior Judges' Court (consists of several visiting judges from England and Wales)
judge selection and term of office: judge appointment and tenure NA
subordinate courts: Resident Judges' Court; Courts Martial

Diplomatic representation in the US: none (overseas territory of the UK)

Diplomatic representation from the US: none (overseas territory of the UK)

Flag description: the flag of the UK is used

National anthem: *note:* as a UK area of special sovereignty, "God Save the Queen" is official (see United Kingdom)

ECONOMY

Economy—overview: Economic activity is limited to providing services to the military and their families located in Akrotiri. Allfood and manufactured goods must be imported.
Exchange rates: note: uses the euro

COMMUNICATIONS

Broadcast media: British Forces Broadcast Service (BFBS) provides multi-channel satellite TV service as well as BFBS radio broadcasts to the Akrotiri Sovereign Base Area (2009)
Radio broadcast stations: AM NA, FM 1, shortwave NA (British Forces Broadcasting Service

(BFBS) provides Radio 1 and Radio 2 service to Akrotiri, Dhekelia, and Nicosia) (2006)
Television broadcast stations: 0 (British Forces Broadcasting Service (BFBS) provides multichannel satellite service to Akrotiri, Dhekelia, and Nicosia) (2006)

MILITARY AND SECURITY

Military—note: defense is the responsibility of the UK; Akrotiri has a full RAF base, headquarters for British Forces Cyprus, and Episkopi Support Unit

ALBANIA

INTRODUCTION

Background: Albania declared its independence from the Ottoman Empire in 1912, but was conquered by Italy in 1939 and occupied by Germany in 1943. Communist partisans took over the country in 1944. Albania allied itself first with the USSR (until 1960), and then with China (to 1978). In the early 1990s, Albania ended 46 years of xenophobic communist rule and established a multiparty democracy. The transition has proven challenging as successive governments have tried to deal with high unemployment, widespread corruption, dilapidated infrastructure, powerful organized crime networks, and combative political opponents. Albania has made progress in its democratic development since first holding multiparty elections in 1991, but deficiencies remain. International observers judged elections to be largely free and fair since ther estoration of political stability following the collapse of pyramid schemes in 1997; however, most of Albania's post-communist elections have been marred by claims of electoral fraud. Albania joined NATO in April 2009 and in June 2014 became a candidate for EU accession. Although Albania's economy continues to grow, it has slowed, and the country is still one of the

poorest in Europe. A large informal economy and an inadequate energy and transportation infrastructure remain obstacles.

Location: Southeastern Europe, bordering the Adriatic Sea and Ionian Sea, between Greece to the south and Montenegro and Kosovo to the north

Geographic coordinates: 41 00 N, 20 00 E

Map references: Europe

Area: *total:* 28,748 sq km
land: 27,398 sq km
water: 1,350 sq km
country comparison to the world: 145

Area—comparative: slightly smaller than Mary land

Land boundaries: *total:* 691 km
border countries (4): Greece 212 km, Kosovo 112 km, Macedonia 181 km, Montenegro 186 km

Coastline: 362 km

Maritime claims: *territorial sea:* 12 nm
continental shelf: 200m depth or to the depth of exploitation

Climate: mild temperate; cool, cloudy, wet winters; hot, clear, dry summers; interior is cooler and wetter

Terrain: mostly mountains and hills; small plains along coast

Elevation: *mean elevation:* 708 m

elevation extremes: *lowest point:* Adriatic Sea 0 m
highest point: Maja e Korabit (Golem Korab) 2,764 m

Natural resources: petroleum, natural gas, coal, bauxite, chromite, copper, iron ore, nickel, salt, timber, hydropower, arableland

Land use: *agricultural land:* 43.8%
arable land: 22.7%
permanent crops: 2.7%
permanent pasture: 18.4%
forest: 28.3%
other: 27.9% (2011 est.)

Irrigated land: 3,310 sq km (2012)

Total renewable water resources: 41.7 cu km (2011)

Freshwater withdrawal (domestic/industrial/agricultural): *total:* 1.31 cu km/yr (43%/18%/39%)
per capita: 413.6 cu m/yr (2006)

Natural hazards: destructive earthquakes; tsunamis occur along southwestern coast; floods; drought

Environment current issues: deforestation; soil erosion; water pollution from industrial and domestic effluents

Environment international agreements: *party to:* Air Pollution, Biodiversity, Climate Change, Climate Change-Kyoto Protocol, Desertification, Endangered Species, Hazardous Wastes, Law of the Sea, Ozone Layer Protection, Wetlands
signed, but not ratified: none of the selected agreements

Geography—note: strategic location along Strait of Otranto (links Adriatic Sea to Ionian Sea and Mediterranean Sea)

PEOPLE AND SOCIETY

Nationality: *noun:* Albanian(s)
adjective: Albanian

Ethnic groups: Albanian 82.6%, Greek 0.9%, other 1% (including Vlach, Roma (Gypsy), Macedonian, Montenegrin, and Egyptian), unspecified 15.5% (2011 est.)

Languages: Albanian 98.8% (official derived from Tosk dialect), Greek 0.5%, other 0.6% (including Macedonian, Roma, Vlach, Turkish, Italian, and SerboCroatian), unspecified 0.1% (2011 est.)

Religions: Muslim 56.7%, Roman Catholic 10%, Orthodox 6.8%, atheist 2.5%, Bektashi (a Sufi order) 2.1%, other 5.7%, unspecified 16.2%
note: all mosques and churches were closed in 1967 and religious observances prohibited; in November 1990, Albania began allowing private religious practice (2011 est.)

Population: 3,029,278 (July 2015 est.)

country comparison to the world: 137

Age structure: *0–14 years:* 18.78% (male 300,661/female 268,369)

15–24 years: 18.67% (male 291,479/female 274,019)

25–54 years: 40.39% (male 582,207/female 641,361)

55–64 years: 10.85% (male 163,003/female 165,805)

65 years and over: 11.3% (male 160,913/female 181,461) (2015 est.)

Dependency ratios: *total dependency ratio:* 44.8%

youth dependency ratio: 26.9%

elderly dependency ratio: 18%

potential support ratio: 5.6% (2015 est.)

Median age: *total:* 32 years

male: 30.8 years

female: 33.3 years (2015 est.)

country comparison to the world: 95

Population growth rate: 0.3% (2015 est.)

country comparison to the world: 175

Birth rate: 12.92 births/1,000 population (2015 est.)

country comparison to the world: 154

Death rate: 6.58 deaths/1,000 population (2015 est.)

country comparison to the world: 145

Net migration rate: -3.3 migrant(s)/1,000 population (2015 est.)

country comparison to the world: 184

Urbanization: *urban population:* 57.4% of total population (2015)

rate of urbanization: 2.21% annual rate of change (2010–15 est.)

Major urban areas population: TIRANA (capital) 454,000 (2015)

Sex ratio: *at birth:* 1.1 male(s)/female

0–14 years: 1.12 male(s)/female

15–24 years: 1.06 male(s)/female

25–54 years: 0.91 male(s)/female

55–64 years: 0.98 male(s)/female

65 years and over: 0.89 male(s)/female

total population: 0.98 male(s)/female (2015 est.)

Mother's mean age at first birth: 23.4 (2010 est.)

Maternal mortality rate: 29 deaths/100,000 live births (2015 est.)

country comparison to the world: 128

Infant mortality rate: *total:* 12.75 deaths/1,000 live births

male: 14.19 deaths/1,000 live births

female: 11.15 deaths/1,000 live births (2015 est.)

country comparison to the world: 118

Life expectancy at birth: *total population:* 78.13 years

male: 75.49 years

female: 81.04 years (2015 est.)

country comparison to the world: 60

Total fertility rate: 1.5 children born/woman (2015 est.)

country comparison to the world: 196

Contraceptive prevalence rate: 69.3% (2008/09)

Health expenditures: 5.9% of GDP (2013)

country comparison to the world: 111

Physicians density: 1.15 physicians/1,000 population (2013)

Hospital bed density: 2.6 beds/1,000 population (2012)

Drinking water source:

improved:

urban: 84.3% of population

rural: 81.8% of population

total: 83.6% of population

unimproved:

urban: 15.7% of population

rural: 18.2% of population

total: 16.4% of population (2015 est.)

Sanitation facility access:

improved:

urban: 95.5% of population

rural: 90.2% of population

total: 93.2% of population

unimproved:

urban: 4.5% of population

rural: 9.8% of population

total: 6.8% of population (2015 est.)

HIV/AIDS adult—prevalence rate: 0.04% (2013 est.)

country comparison to the world: 126

HIV/AIDS—people living with HIV/AIDS: NA

HIV/AIDS—deaths: NA

Obesity—adult prevalence rate: 18.1% (2014)

country comparison to the world: 88

Children under the age of 5 years underweight: 6.3% (2009)

country comparison to the world: 80

Education expenditures: 3.54% of GDP (2013)

country comparison to the world: 130

Literacy: *definition:* age 15 and over can read and write

total population: 97.6%

male: 98.4%

female: 96.9% (2015 est.)

School life expectancy (primary to tertiary education): *total:* 16 years

male: 16 years

female: 16 years (2014)

Child labor children—ages 514:

total number: 72,818

percentage: 12% (2005 est.)

Unemployment, youth ages 1524: *total:* 30.2%

male: 32.5%

female: 26.1% (2013 est.)

GOVERNMENT

Country name: *conventional long form:* Republic of Albania

conventional short form: Albania

local long form: Republika e Shqiperise

local short form: Shqiperia

former: People's Socialist Republic of Albania

etymology: the English-language country name seems to be derived from the ancient Illyrian tribe of the Albani; the native name "Shqiperia" is popularly interpreted to mean "Land of the eagles"

Government type: parliamentary republic

Capital: *name:* Tirana (Tirane)

Geographic coordinates: 41 19 N, 19 49 E

time difference: UTC+1 (6 hours ahead of Washington, DC, during Standard Time)

daylight saving time: +1hr, begins last Sunday in March; ends last Sunday in October

Administrative divisions: 12 counties (qarqe, singular-qark); Berat, Diber, Durres, Elbasan, Fier, Gjirokaster, Korce, Kukes, Lezhe, Shkoder, Tirane, Vlore

Independence: 28 November 1912 (from the Ottoman Empire)

National holiday: Independence Day, 28 November (1912) also known as Flag Day

Constitution: several previous; latest approved by the Assembly 21 October 1998, adopted by popular referendum 22 November 1998, promulgated 28 November 1998; amended several times, last in 2015 (2016)

Legal system: civil law system except in the northern rural areas where customary law known as the "Code of Leke" prevails

International law organization participation: has not submitted an ICJ jurisdiction declaration; accepts ICCt jurisdiction

Citizenship: *citizenship by birth:* no

citizenship by descent only: at least one parent must be a citizen of Albania

dual citizenship recognized: yes

residency requirement for naturalization: 5 years

Suffrage: 18 years of age; universal

Executive branch: *chief of state:* President of the Republic Bujar NISHANI (since 24 July 2012)

head of government: Prime Minister Edi RAMA (since 10 September 2013); Deputy Prime Minister Niko PELESHI

cabinet: Council of Ministers proposed by the prime minister, nominated by the president, and approvedby the Assembly

elections/appointments: president indirectly elected by the Assembly for a 5-year term (eligible for a second term); a candidate needs three-fifths majority vote of the Assembly in 1 of 3 rounds or a simple majority in 2 additional rounds to become president; election last held in 4 rounds during the period 30 May-11 June 2012 (next election to be held in 2017); prime minister appointed by the president on the proposal of the majority party or coalition of parties in the Assembly

election results: Bujar NISHANI elected president; Assembly vote-73 of 140 in fourth round

Legislative branch: description: unicameral Assembly or Kuvendi (140 seats; members directly elected in multi-seat constituencies by proportional representation vote to serve 4-year terms)

elections: last held on 23 June 2013 (next to be held in 2017)

election results: percent of vote by party-PS 41.36%, PD 30.63%, LSI 10.46%, PR 3.02%, PDIU 2.61%, other 11.92%; seats by party-PS 65, PD 50, LSI 16, PDIU 4, PR 3, other 2; seats by parliamentary group as of April-2015 ASHE 88, APMI 50, 2-outside of the majority and opposition groups

Judicial branch: *highest court(s):* Constitutional Court (consists of 9 judges, including a chairman); Court of Cassation (consists of 14 judges, including the chief justice)

judge selection and term of office: Constitutional Court judges appointed by the president with theconsent of the Assembly to serve single 9-year terms with onethird of the membership renewed every 3years; chairman elected by the People's Assembly for a single 3-year term; Court of Cassation judges, including the chairman, appointed by the president with the consent of the Assembly to serve single, 9-year terms)

subordinate courts: Courts of Appeal; Courts of First Instance

Political parties and leaders: Alliance for Employment, Welfare, and Integration or APMI (coalition of 24 centrist and centerrightparties) [Sali BERISHA]:

Christian Democratic Party or PDK [Nard NDOKA]

Democratic Party or PD [Lulzim BASHA]

Movement for National Development of LZHK [Dashamir SHEHI]

Republican Party or PR [Fatmir MEDIU]

Alliance for a European Albania or ASHE (coalition of 38 parties from far left to right wing) [EdiRAMA]:

Christian Democratic Party of PKD [Mark FRROKU]

Party for Justice, Integration and Unity or PDIU [Shpetim IDRIZI] (formerly part of APMI)

Socialist Movement for Integration or LSI [Ilir META]

Socialist Party or PS [Edi RAMA]

Union for Human Rights Party or PBDNJ [Vangjel DULE]

other parties: New Democratic Spirit or FRD [Bamir TOPI]

note: only the major parties of each coalition are listed

Political pressure groups and leaders: Confederation of Trade Unions of Albania or KSSH [Kol NIKOLLAJ]

Omonia [Vasil BOLLANO]

Union of Independent Trade Unions of Albania or BSPSH [Gezim KALAJA]

International organization participation: BSEC, CD, CE, CEI, EAPC, EBRD, EITI (compliant country), FAO, IAEA, IBRD, ICAO, ICC (nationalcommittees), ICCt, ICRM, IDA, IDB, IFAD, IFC, IFRCS, ILO, IMF, IMO, Interpol, IOC, IOM, IPU, ISO (correspondent), ITU, ITUC (NGOs), MIGA, NATO, OAS (observer), OIC, OIF, OPCW, OSCE, PCA, SELEC, UN, UNCTAD, UNESCO, UNIDO, UNWTO, UPU, WCO, WFTU (NGOs), WHO, WIPO, WMO, WTO

Diplomatic representation in the US: *chief of mission:* Ambassador Floreta FABER (since 18 May 2015)

chancery: 1312 18th Street NW, 4th Floor, Washington, DC 20036

telephone: [1] (202) 223-4942

FAX: [1] (202) 628-7342

consulate(s) general: New York

Diplomatic representation from the US: *chief of mission:* Ambassador Donald LU (since 13 January 2015)

embassy: Rruga e Elbasanit, 103, Tirana

mailing address: US Department of State, 9510 Tirana Place, Dulles, VA 201899510

telephone: [355] (4) 224-7285

FAX: [355] (4) 223-2222

Flag description: red with a black twoheaded eagle in the center; the design is claimed to be that of 15thcentury heroGeorge Kastrioti SKANDER-BEG, who led a successful uprising against the Ottoman Turks that resulted ina shortlived independence for some Albanian regions (144378); an unsubstantiated explanation for theeagle symbol is the tradition that Albanians see themselves as descendants of the eagle; they refer tothemselves as "Shqiptare, " which translates as "sons of the eagle"

National symbol(s): doubleheaded eagle; national colors: red, black

National anthem: name: "Hymni i Flamurit" (Hymn to the Flag)

lyrics/music: Aleksander Stavre DRENOVA/Ciprian PORUMBESCU

note: adopted 1912

ECONOMY

Economy overview: Albania, a formerly closed, centrallyplanned state, is a developing country with a modern openmarketeconomy. Albania managed to weather the first waves of the global financial crisis but, more recently, thenegative effects of the crisis have caused a significant economic slowdown. Close trade, remittance, and banking sector ties with Greece and Italy make Albania vulnerable to spillover effects of debt crises andweak growth in the euro zone. Remittances, a significant catalyst for economic growth, declined from 1215% of GDP before the 2008 financial crisis to 5.7% of GDP in 2014, mostly from Albanians residing in Greece and Italy. Theagricultural sector, which accounts for almost half of employment but only about onefifth of GDP, is limitedprimarily to small family operations and subsistence farming, because of a lack of modern equipment, unclear property rights, and the prevalence of small, inefficient plots of land. Complex tax codes andlicensing requirements, a weak judicial system, endemic corruption, poor enforcement of contracts andproperty issues, and antiquated infrastructure contribute to Albania's poor business environment, makingattracting foreign investment difficult. Albania's electricity supply is uneven despite upgraded transmission capacities with neighboring countries. Technical and nontechnical losses in electricity including theft and nonpayment continue to underminethe financial viability of the entire system, although the government has taken steps to stem nontechnicallosses and has begun to upgrade the distribution grid. Also, with help from international donors, thegovernment is taking steps to improve the poor national road and rail network, a long standing barrier tosustained economic growth. Inward FDI has increased significantly in recent years as the government has embarked on an ambitiousprogram to improve the business climate through fiscal and legislative reforms. The government isfocused on the simplification of licensing requirements and tax codes, and it entered into a newarrangement with the IMF for additional financial and technical support. Albania's IMF program may be atrisk, however, because the government has not collected sufficient tax revenue needed to reduce thebudget deficit. The country continues to face increasing public debt, exceeding its former statutory limit of60% of GDP in 2013 and reaching 73% in 2015.

GDP (purchasing power parity):
$32.65 billion (2015 est.)
$31.81 billion (2014 est.)
$31.18 billion (2013 est.)
note: data are in 2015 US dollarsunreported output may be as large as 50% of official GDP
country comparison to the world: 126

GDP (official exchange rate): $11.54 billion (2015 est.)

GDP—real growth rate:
2.6% (2015 est.)
2% (2014 est.)
1.1% (2013 est.)
country comparison to the world: 114

GDP—per capita (PPP):
$11,900 (2015 est.)
$11,400 (2014 est.)
$11,000 (2013 est.)
note: data are in 2015 US dollars
country comparison to the world: 126

Gross national saving:
16.8% of GDP (2015 est.)
15.5% of GDP (2014 est.)
18.3% of GDP (2013 est.)
country comparison to the world: 99

GDP—composition, by end use:
household consumption: 82.1%
government consumption: 11%
investment in fixed capital: 26.5%
investment in inventories: 0.2%
exports of goods and services: 36.4%
imports of goods and services: -56.2% (2015 est.)

GDP—composition, by sector of origin:
agriculture: 22.3%
industry: 15%
services: 62.6% (2015 est.)

Agriculture—products: wheat, corn, potatoes, vegetables, fruits, sugar beets, grapes; meat, dairy products; sheep

Industries: food and tobacco products; textiles and clothing; lumber, oil, cement, chemicals, mining, basic metals, hydropower

Industrial production growth rate: 3.4% (2015 est.)
country comparison to the world: 73

Labor force: 1.085 million (2015 est.)

country comparison to the world: 142

Labor force—by occupation: *agriculture:* 41.8%
industry: 11.4%
services: 46.8% (December 2014 est.)

Unemployment rate: 17.3% (2015 est.)
17.5% (2014 est.)
note: these official rates may not include those
working at nearsubsistence farming
country comparison to the world: 160

Population below poverty line: 14.3% (2012 est.)

**Household income or consumption by percentage
share:** *lowest:* 10%: 4.1%
highest: 10%: 20.5% (2012)

Distribution of family income—Gini index: 29
(2012 est.)
30 (2008 est.)
country comparison to the world: 126

Budget: *revenues:* $2.978 billion
expenditures: $3.535 billion (2015 est.)
Taxes and other revenues: 25.7% of GDP (2015
est.)
country comparison to the world: 117

Budget surplus (+) or deficit (−): 4.8% of GDP
(2015 est.)
country comparison to the world: 166

Public debt: 73.3% of GDP (2015 est.)
72.5% of GDP (2014 est.)
country comparison to the world: 41

Fiscal year: calendar year

Inflation rate (consumer prices): 1.9% (2015 est.)
1.6% (2014 est.)
country comparison to the world: 112

Central bank discount rate: 2.25% (31 December
2014)
3% (31 December 2013)
country comparison to the world: 112

Commercial bank prime lending rate: 7.6% (31
December 2015 est.)
8.66% (31 December 2014 est.)
country comparison to the world: 113

Stock of narrow money:
$2.826 billion (31 December 2015 est.)
$3.066 billion (31 December 2014 est.)
country comparison to the world: 117

Stock of broad money: $5.72 billion (31 December
2015 est.)
$6.269 billion (31 December 2014 est.)
country comparison to the world: 124

Stock of domestic credit: $7.161 billion (31
December 2015 est.)
$8.231 billion (31 December 2014 est.)
country comparison to the world: 113

Market value of publicly traded shares: $NA

Current account balance: -$1.311 billion (2015
est.)
-$1.71 billion (2014 est.)
country comparison to the world: 134

Exports: $1.011 billion (2015 est.)
$1.232 billion (2014 est.)
country comparison to the world: 160

Exports—commodities: textiles, footwear; asphalt,
metals and metallic ores, crude oil; vegetables,
fruits, tobacco

Exports—partners: Italy 42.8%, Kosovo 9.7%,
US 7.6%, China 6.1%, Greece 5.3%, Spain 4.8%
(2015)

Imports: $3.597 billion (2015 est.)
$4.057 billion (2014 est.)
country comparison to the world: 137

Imports—commodities: machinery and equipment, foodstuffs, textiles, chemicals

Imports—partners: Italy 33.4%, China 10%,
Greece 9%, Turkey 6.7%, Germany 5.2% (2015)

Reserves of foreign exchange and gold: $2.852
billion (31 December 2015 est.)
$2.665 billion (31 December 2014 est.)
country comparison to the world: 107

Debt—external:
$8.782 billion (31 December 2014 est.)
$8.209 billion (31 December 2013 est.)
country comparison to the world: 110

Stock of direct foreign investment—at home:
$5.557 billion (31 December 2013)
$4.994 billion (31 December 2012)
country comparison to the world: 97

Exchange rates: leke (ALL) per US dollar—
126.6 (2015 est.)
105.48 (2014 est.)
105.48 (2013 est.)
108.19 (2012 est.)
100.9 (2011 est.)

ENERGY

Electricity—production: 4.726 billion kWh (2014
est.)
country comparison to the world: 119

Electricity consumption: 7.793 billion kWh (2014
est.)
country comparison to the world: 99

Electricity exports: 288.5 million kWh (2014 est.)
country comparison to the world: 74

Electricity imports: 3.355 billion kWh (2014 est.)
country comparison to the world: 50

Electricity installed generating capacity: 1.878
million kW (2013 est.)
country comparison to the world: 109

Electricity from fossil fuels: 5.2% of total installed
capacity (2013 est.)
country comparison to the world: 203

Electricity from nuclear fuels: 0% of total installed
capacity (2013 est.)
country comparison to the world: 40

Electricity from hydroelectric plants: 94.8% of
total installed capacity (2013 est.)
country comparison to the world: 9

Electricity from other renewable sources: 0% of
total installed capacity (2013 est.)
country comparison to the world: 151

Crude oil—production: 20,510 bbl/day (2014 est.)
country comparison to the world: 70

Crude oil—exports: 23,320 bbl/day (2014 est.)

country comparison to the world: 57

Crude oil—imports: 3,440 bbl/day (2012 est.)
country comparison to the world: 79

Crude oil—proved reserves: 168.3 million bbl (1
January 2015 est.)
country comparison to the world: 63

Refined petroleum products—production: 2,228
bbl/day (2012 est.)
country comparison to the world: 107

Refined petroleum products—consumption:
25,000 bbl/day (2013 est.)
country comparison to the world: 120

Refined petroleum products—exports: 354 bbl/
day (2012 est.)
country comparison to the world: 117

Refined petroleum products—imports: 20,770 bbl/
day (2012 est.)
country comparison to the world: 109

Natural gas—production: 19 million cu m (2013
est.)
country comparison to the world: 89

Natural gas—consumption: 19 million cu m (2013
est.)
country comparison to the world: 112

Natural gas—exports: 0 cu m (2013 est.)
country comparison to the world: 55

Natural gas—imports: 0 cu m (2013 est.)
country comparison to the world: 155

Natural gas—proved reserves: 849.5 million cu m
(1 January 2014 est.)
country comparison to the world: 105

**Carbon dioxide emissions from consumption of
energy:** 3.962 million Mt (2012 est.)
country comparison to the world: 130

COMMUNICATIONS

Telephones—fixed lines: *total subscriptions:*
250,000
subscriptions per 100 inhabitants: 8 (2014 est.)
country comparison to the world: 123

Telephones—mobile cellular: *total:* 3.4 million
subscriptions per 100 inhabitants: 111 (2014 est.)
country comparison to the world: 133

Telephone system: *general assessment:* despite
new investment in fixed lines, teledensity remains
low with roughly 10 fixedlines per 100 people;
mobilecellular telephone use is widespread and
generally effective
domestic: offsetting the shortage of fixedline
capacity, mobilecellular phone service has been
availablesince 1996; by 2011, multiple companies
were providing mobile services, and mobile teledensity hadreached 100 per 100 persons; Internet
broadband services initiated in 2005, but growth
has been slow; Internet cafes are popular in Tirana
and have started to spread outside the capital
international: country code 355; submarine
cable provides connectivity to Italy, Croatia, and
Greece; the TransBalkan Line, a combination
submarine cable and land fiberoptic system, provides additionalconnectivity to Bulgaria, Macedonia, and Turkey; international traffic carried by

fiberoptic cable and, whennecessary, by microwave radio relay from the Tirana exchange to Italy and Greece (2011)

Broadcast media: 3 public TV networks, one of which transmits by satellite to Albanianlanguage communities in neighboringcountries; more than 60 private TV stations; many viewers can pick up Italian and Greek TV broadcastsvia terrestrial reception; cable TV service is available; 2 public radio networks and roughly 25 privateradio stations; several international broadcasters are available (2010)
Radio broadcast stations: AM 13, FM 46, short-wave 1 (2005)
Television broadcast stations: 65 (3 national, 62 local); 2 cable networks (2005)

Internet country code: .al

Internet hosts: 15,528 (2012)
country comparison to the world: 124

Internet users: *total:* 1.7 million
percent of population: 56.5% (2014 est.)
country comparison to the world: 104

TRANSPORTATION

Airports: 4 (2013)
country comparison to the world: 183

Airports—with paved runways: *total:* 4
2,438 to 3,047 m: 3

1,524 to 2,437 m: 1 (2013)
Airports—with unpaved runways: *total:* 1
914 to 1,523 m: 1 (2012)

Heliports: 1 (2013)

Pipelines: gas 331 km; oil 249 km (2013)

Railways: *total:* 677 km
standard gauge: 677 km 1.435m gauge (2014)
country comparison to the world: 104

Roadways: *total:* 18,000 km
paved: 7,020 km
unpaved: 10,980 km (2002)
country comparison to the world: 116

Waterways: 41 km (on the Bojana River) (2011)
country comparison to the world: 103

Merchant marine: *total:* 17
by type: cargo 16, roll on/roll off 1
foreign-owned: 1 (Turkey 1)
registered in other countries: 5 (Antigua and Barbuda 1, Panama 4) (2010)
country comparison to the world: 99

Ports and terminals: *major seaport(s):* Durres, Sarande, Shengjin, Vlore

MILITARY AND SECURITY

Military branches: Land Forces Command, Navy Force Command, Air Forces Command (2013)

Military service age and obligation: 19 is the legal minimum age for voluntary military service; 18 is the legal minimum age in case ofgeneral/partial compulsory mobilization (2012)

Military expenditures:
0.85% of GDP (2015)
1.04% of GDP (2014)
1.5% of GDP (2013)
1.47% of GDP (2012)
1.52% of GDP (2011)
country comparison to the world: 112

TRANSNATIONAL ISSUES

Disputes—international: none

Refugees and internally displaced persons: *stateless persons:* 7,442 (2015)

Illicit drugs: increasingly active transshipment point for Southwest Asian opiates, hashish, and cannabis transiting theBalkan route and to a lesser extent cocaine from South America destined for Western Europe; limitedopium and expanding cannabis production; ethnic Albanian narcotrafficking organizations active andexpanding in Europe; vulnerable to money laundering associated with regional trafficking in narcotics, arms, contraband, and illegal aliens

ALGERIA

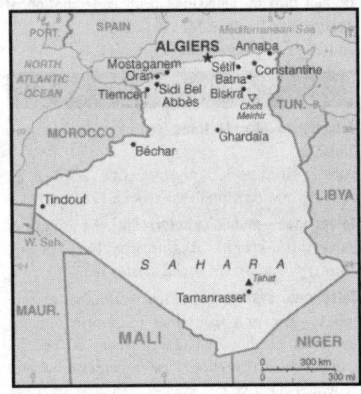

INTRODUCTION

Background: After more than a century of rule by France, Algerians fought through much of the 1950s to achieveindependence in 1962. Algeria's primary political party, the National Liberation Front (FLN), wasestablished in 1954 as part of the struggle for independence and has since largely dominated politics. The Government of Algeria in 1988 instituted a multiparty system in response to public unrest, but thesurprising first round success of the Islamic Salvation Front (FIS) in the December 1991 balloting led the Algerian army to intervene and postpone the second round of elections to prevent what the secular elitefeared would be an extremistled government from assuming power. The army began a crackdown on the FIS that spurred FIS supporters to begin attacking government targets. Fighting escalated into aninsurgency, which saw intense violence from 199298, resulting in over 100,000 deaths many attributedto indiscriminate massacres of villagers by extremists. The government gained the upper hand by the late1990s, and FIS's armed wing, the Islamic Salvation Army, disbanded in January 2000. Abdelaziz BOUTEFLIKA, with the backing of the military, won the presidency in 1999 in an election widelyviewed as fraudulent and won subsequent elections in 2004, 2009, and 2014. The government in 2011introduced some political reforms in response to the Arab Spring, including lifting the 19year-old state ofemergency restrictions and increasing women's quotas for elected assemblies, while also increasingsubsidies to the populace. Algeria's reliance on hydrocarbon revenues to finance the government andlarge subsidies for the population is under stress because of declining oil prices.

GEOGRAPHY

Location: Northern Africa, bordering the Mediterranean Sea, between Morocco and Tunisia

Geographic coordinates: 28 00 N, 3 00 E

Map references: Africa

Area: *total:* 2,381,741 sq km

land: 2,381,741 sq km
water: 0 sq km
country comparison to the world: 10

Area-comparative: slightly less than 3.5 times the size of Texas

Land boundaries: *total:* 6,734 km

PEOPLE AND SOCIETY

border countries (7): Libya 989 km, Mali 1,359 km, Mauritania 460 km, Morocco 1,900 km, Niger 951km, Tunisia 1,034 km, Western Sahara 41 km

Coastline: 998 km

Maritime claims:

territorial sea: 12 nm
exclusive fishing zone: 3252 nm

Climate: arid to semiarid; mild, wet winters with hot, dry summers along coast; drier with cold winters and hotsummers on high plateau; sirocco is a hot, dust/sand-laden wind especially common in summer

Terrain: mostly high plateau and desert; some mountains; narrow, discontinuous coastal plain

Elevation: mean elevation: 800 m

elevation extremes: *lowest point:* Chott Melrhir -40m
highest point: Tahat 3,003 m

Natural resources: petroleum, natural gas, iron ore, phosphates, uranium, lead, zinc

Land use: *agricultural land:* 17.3%
arable land: 3.1%

permanent crops: 0.4%
permanent pasture: 13.8%
forest: 0.6%
other: 82% (2011 est.)
Irrigated land: 5,700 sq km (2012)

Total renewable water resources: 11.67 cu km (2011)

Freshwater withdrawal (domestic/industrial/agricultural): *total:* 5.72 cu km/yr (26%/16%/58%)
per capita: 182 cu m/yr (2005)
Natural hazards: mountainous areas subject to severe earthquakes; mudslides and floods in rainy season

Environment-current issues: soil erosion from overgrazing and other poor farming practices; desertification; dumping of raw sewage, petroleum refining wastes, and other industrial effluents is leading to the pollution of rivers and coastalwaters; Mediterranean Sea, in particular, becoming polluted from oil wastes, soil erosion, and fertilizer-runoff; inadequate supplies of potable water

Environment-international agreements:
party to: Biodiversity, Climate Change, Climate Change Kyoto Protocol, Desertification, Endangered Species, Environmental Modification, Hazardous Wastes, Law of the Sea, Ozone Layer Protection, Ship Pollution, Wetlands
signed, but not ratified: none of the selected agreements

Geography—note: largest country in Africa

PEOPLE AND SOCIETY

Nationality: *noun:* Algerian(s)
adjective: Algerian Ethnic groups: Arab Berber 99%, European less than 1% note: although almost all Algerians are Berber in origin (not Arab), only a minority identify themselves as Berber, about 15% of the total population; these people live mostly in the mountainous region of Kabylie eastof Algiers; the Berbers are also Muslim but identify with their Berber rather than Arab cultural heritage; Berbers have long agitated, sometimes violently, for autonomy; the government is unlikely to grantautonomy but has offered to begin sponsoring teaching Berber language in schools

Languages: Arabic (official), French (lingua franca), Berber or Tamazight (official); dialects include Kabyle Berber (Taqbaylit), Shawiya Berber (Tacawit), Mzab Berber, Tuareg Berber (Tamahaq)

Religions: Muslim (official; predominantly Sunni) 99%, other (includes Christian and Jewish) <1% (2012 est.)

Population: 39,542,166 (July 2015 est.)
country comparison to the world: 34

Age structure: *0–14 years:* 28.75% (male 5,820,027/female 5,547,573)
15–24 years: 16.64% (male 3,368,415/female 3,213,185)
25–54 years: 42.84% (male 8,569,397/female 8,369,078)
55–64 years: 6.42% (male 1,289,595/female 1,248,385)
65 years and over: 5.35% (male 977,744/female 1,138,767) (2015 est.)

Dependency ratios:
total dependency ratio: 52.6%
youth dependency ratio: 43.6%
elderly dependency ratio: 9.1%
potential support ratio: 11% (2015 est.)

Median age: *total:* 27.5 years
male: 27.2 years
female: 27.8 years (2015 est.)
country comparison to the world: 133

Population growth rate: 1.84% (2015 est.)
country comparison to the world: 60

Birth rate: 23.67 births/1,000 population (2015 est.)
country comparison to the world: 63

Death rate: 4.31 deaths/1,000 population (2015 est.)
country comparison to the world: 203

Net migration rate: 0.92 migrant(s)/1,000 population (2015 est.)
country comparison to the world: 148

Urbanization: urban population: 70.7% of total population (2015)
rate of urbanization: 2.77% annual rate of change (2010–15 est.)

Major urban areas—population: ALGIERS (capital) 2.594 million; Oran 858,000 (2015)

Sex ratio: *at birth:* 1.05 male(s)/female
0–14 years: 1.05 male(s)/female
15–24 years: 1.05 male(s)/female
25–54 years: 1.02 male(s)/female
55–64 years: 1.03 male(s)/female
65 years and over: 0.86 male(s)/female
total population: 1.03 male(s)/female (2015 est.)

Maternal mortality rate: 140 deaths/100,000 live births (2015 est.)
country comparison to the world: 75
Infant mortality rate: total: 20.98 deaths/1,000 live births
male: 22.7 deaths/1,000 live births
female: 19.18 deaths/1,000 live births (2015 est.)
country comparison to the world: 83

Life expectancy at birth: *total population:* 76.59 years
male: 75.29 years
female: 77.96 years (2015 est.)
country comparison to the world: 81

Total fertility rate: 2.78 children born/woman (2015 est.)
country comparison to the world: 65

Contraceptive prevalence rate: 61.4% (2006)

Health expenditures: 6.6% of GDP (2013)
country comparison to the world: 135

Physicians density: 1.21 physicians/1,000 population (2007)

Drinking water source:
improved:
urban: 84.3% of population
rural: 81.8% of population
total: 83.6% of population
unimproved:
urban: 15.7% of population
rural: 18.2% of population
total: 16.4% of population (2015 est.)

Sanitation facility access: *improved:*
urban: 89.8% of population
rural: 82.2% of population
total: 87.6% of population
unimproved:
urban: 10.2% of population
rural: 17.8% of population
total: 12.4% of population (2015 est.)

HIV/AIDS—adult prevalence rate: 0.04% (2014 est.)
country comparison to the world: 125

HIV/AIDS—people living with HIV/AIDS: 10,500 (2014 est.)
country comparison to the world: 92

HIV/AIDS—deaths: 200 (2014 est.)
country comparison to the world: 101

Obesity—adult prevalence rate: 23.6% (2014)
country comparison to the world: 116

Children under the age of 5 years underweight: 3% (2013)
country comparison to the world: 102

Education expenditures: 4.3% of GDP (2008)
country comparison to the world: 97

Literacy: *definition:* age 15 and over can read and write
total population: 80.2%
male: 87.2%
female: 73.1% (2015 est.)

School life expectancy (primary to tertiary education): *total:* 14 years
male: 14 years
female: 15 years (2011)

Child labor—children ages 5–14: *total number:* 304,358
percentage: 5% (2006 est.)

Unemployment, youth ages 1524: *total:* 24.8%
male: 21.6%
female: 39.8% (2013 est.)
country comparison to the world: 47

GOVERNMENT

Country name: *conventional long form:* People's Democratic Republic of Algeria
conventional short form: Algeria
local long form: Al Jumhuriyah al Jaza'iriyah ad Dimuqratiyah ash Sha'biyah
local short form: Al Jaza'ir
etymology: the country name derives from the capital city of Algiers

Government type: presidential republic

Capital: *name:* Algiers

Geographic coordinates: 36 45 N, 3 03 E
time difference: UTC+1 (6 hours ahead of Washington, DC, during Standard Time)

Administrative divisions: 48 provinces (wilayas, singular wilaya); Adrar, Ain Defla, Ain Temouchent, Alger, Annaba, Batna, Bechar, Bejaia, Biskra, Blida, Bordj Bou Arreridj, Bouira, Boumerdes, Chlef, Constantine, Djelfa, El Bayadh, El Oued, El Tarf, Ghardaia, Guelma, Illizi, Jijel, Khenchela, Laghouat, Mascara, Medea, Mila, Mostaganem, M'Sila, Naama, Oran, Ouargla,

Oum el Bouaghi, Relizane, Saida, Setif, Sidi Bel Abbes, Skikda, Souk Ahras, Tamanrasset, Tebessa, Tiaret, Tindouf, Tipaza, Tissemsilt, Tizi Ouzou, Tlemcen

Independence: 5 July 1962 (from France)

National holiday: Revolution Day, 1 November (1954)

Constitution: several previous; latest approved by referendum 23 February 1989; amended several times, last in 2016 (2016)

Legal system: mixed legal system of French civil law and Islamic law; judicial review of legislative acts in ad hoc Constitutional Council composed of various public officials including several Supreme Court justices

International law organization participation: has not submitted an ICJ jurisdiction declaration; nonparty state to the ICCt

CITIZENSHIP

citizenship by birth: no
citizenship by descent only: the mother must be a citizen of Algeria
dual citizenship recognized: no
residency requirement for naturalization: 7 years

Suffrage: 18 years of age; universal

Executive branch: *chief of state:* President Abdelaziz BOUTEFLIKA (since 28 April 1999)

head of government: Prime Minister Abdelmalek SELLAL (since 28 April 2014)
cabinet: Cabinet of Ministers appointed by the president
elections/appointments: president directly elected by absolute majority popular vote in two rounds ifneeded for a 5 year term (2term limit reinstated by constitutional amendment in February 2016); electionlast held on 17 April 2014 (next to be held in April 2019); prime minister nominated by the president from themajority party in Parliament
election results: Abdelaziz BOUTEFLIKA reelected president for a fourth term; percent of vote Abdelaziz BOUTEFLIKA (FLN) 81.5%, Ali BENFLIS (FLN) 12.2%, Abdelaziz BELAID (Future Front) 3.4%, other 2.9%

Legislative branch: *description:* bicameral Parliament consists of the Council of the Nation (upper house with 144 seats; onethird of members appointed by the president, twothirds indirectly elected by simple majority vote by anelectoral college composed of local council members; members serve 6year terms with onehalf of themembership renewed every 3 years) and the National People's Assembly (lower house with 462 seatsincluding 8 seats for Algerians living abroad); members directly elected in multiseat constituencies byproportional representation vote to serve 5 year terms)
elections: Council of the Nation last held on 29 December 2012 (next to be held in December 2017); National People's Assembly last held on 10 May 2012 (next to be held on 17 May 2017)
election results: Council of the Nation percentof vote by party NA; seats by party NA; National

People's Assembly percent of vote by party NA; seats by party FLN 221, RND 70, AAV 47, FFS 21, PT17, FNA 9, El Adala 7, MPA 6, PFJ 5, FC 4, PNSD 4, other 32, independent 19

Judicial branch: *highest court(s):* Supreme Court or Cour Supreme (consists of 150 judges organized into 4 divisions: civil and commercial; social security and labor; criminal; and administrative; Constitutional Council (consists of 9 members including the court president); note Algeria's judicial system does not include sharia courtsjudge *selection and term of office:* Supreme Court judges appointed by the High Council of Magistracy, an administrative body presided over by the president of the republic, and includes the republic vicepresident and several members; judge tenure NA; Constitutional Council members 3 appointed by the president of the republic, 2 each by the 2 houses of the Parliament, 1 by the Supreme Court, and 1 by the Council of State; Council president and members appointed for single 6 year terms with half the membershiprenewed every 3 years
subordinate courts: appellate or wilaya courts; first instance or daira tribunals

Political parties and leaders: Algerian National Front or FNA [Moussa TOUATI]
Algerian Popular Movement or MPA [Amara BENYOUNES]
Algerian Rally or RA [Ali ZAGHDOUD]
Algeria's Hope Rally or TAJ [Amar GHOUL]
Dignity or El Karama [Mohamed BENHAMOU]
Ennour El Djazairi Party (Algerian Radiance Party) or PED [Badreddine BELBAZ]
Front for Change or FC [Abdelmadjid MENASRA]
Front for Justice and Development or El Adala [Abdallah DJABALLAH]
Future Front or El Mostakbel [Abdelaziz BELAID]
Green Algeria Alliance or AAV (includes Islah, Ennahda Movement, and MSP) Islamic Renaissance Movement or Ennahda Movement [Fatah RABEI] Movement of Society for Peace or MSP [Abderrazak MOKRI]
National Democratic Rally (Rassemblement National Democratique) or RND [Ahmed OUYAHIA]
National Front for Social Justice or FNJS [Khaled BOUNEDJEMA]
National Liberation Front or FLN [Amar SAIDANI] National Party for Solidarity and Development or PNSDNational Reform Movement or Islah [Djahid YOUNSI]
National Republican Alliance New Dawn Party or PFJ New Generation or Jil Jadid [Soufiane DJILALI]
Oath of 1954 or Ahd 54 [Ali Fawzi REBAINE]
Party of Justice and Liberty [Mohammed SAID]
Rally for Culture and Democracy or RCD [Mohcine BELABBAS]
Socialist Forces Front or FFS [Mustafa BOUCHACHI]
Union of Democratic and Social Forces or UFDS [Noureddine BAHBOUH]
Youth Party or PJ [Hamana BOUCHARMA]
Workers Party or PT [Louisa HANOUNE]

note: a law banning political parties based on religion was enacted in March 1997

Political pressure groups and leaders: Algerian League for the Defense of Human Rights or LADDH [Noureddine BENISSAD]
SOS Disparus [Nacera DUTOUR] Youth Action Rally or RAJ

International organization participation: ABEDA, AfDB, AFESD, AMF, AMU, AU, BIS, CAEU, CD, FAO, G-15, G-24, G-77, IAEA, IBRD, ICAO, ICC (national committees), ICRM, IDA, IDB, IFAD, IFC, IFRCS, IHO, ILO, IMF, IMO, IMSO, Interpol, IOC, IOM, IPU, ISO, ITSO, ITU, ITUC (NGOs), LAS, MIGA, MONUSCO, NAM, OAPEC, OAS (observer), OIC, OPCW, OPEC, OSCE (partner), UN, UNCTAD, UNESCO, UNHCR, UNIDO, UNITAR, UNWTO, UPU, WCO, WHO, WIPO, WMO, WTO (observer)

Diplomatic representation in the US: *chief of mission:* Ambassador Madjid BOUGUERRA (since 23 February 2015)
chancery: 2118 Kalorama Road NW, Washington, DC 20008
telephone: [1] (202) 265-2800
FAX: [1] (202) 986-5906
consulate(s) general: New York

Diplomatic representation from the US: *chief of mission:* Ambassador Joan A. POLASCHIK (since 22 September 2014)
embassy: 05 Chemin Cheikh Bachir, El-Ibrahimi, El-Biar 16030 Algiers
mailing address: B. P. 408, Alger Gare, 16030 Algiers
telephone: [213] (0) 770-08-2000
FAX: [213] (0) 770-08-2064

Flag description: two equal vertical bands of green (hoist side) and white; a red, fivepointed star within a red crescentcentered over the twocolor boundary; the colors represent Islam (green), purity and peace (white), andliberty (red); the crescent and star are also Islamic symbols, but the crescent is more closed than thoseof other Muslim countries because Algerians believe the long crescent horns bring happiness

National symbol(s): star and crescent, fennec fox; national colors: green, white, red

National anthem: name: "Kassaman" (We Pledge)
lyrics/music: Mufdi ZAKARIAH/Mohamed FAWZI
note: adopted 1962; ZAKARIAH wrote "Kassaman" as a poem while imprisoned in Algiers by Frenchcolonial forces

ECONOMY

Economy—overview: Algeria's economy remains dominated by the state, a legacy of the country's socialist post independence development model. In recent years the Algerian Government has halted the privatization of stateownedindustries and imposed restrictions on imports and foreign involvement in its economy. Hydrocarbons have long been the backbone of the economy, accounting for roughly 60% of budget revenues, 30% of

GDP, and over 95% of export earnings. Algeria has the 10th largest reserves of naturalgas in the world and is the sixth largest gas exporter. It ranks 16th in oil reserves. Hydrocarbon exports have enabled Algeria to maintain macroeconomic stability and amass large foreign currency reserves and a large budget stabilization fund available for tapping. In addition, Algeria's external debt is extremely lowat about 2% of GDP. However, Algeria has struggled to develop non hydrocarbon industries because of heavy regulation and an emphasis on state driven growth. The government's efforts have done little to reduce high youth unemployment rates or to address housing shortages. A wave of economic protests in February and March 2011 prompted the Algerian Government to offer more than $23 billion in public grants and retroactive salary and benefit increases, moves which continue to weigh on public finances. Since late 2014, declining oil prices forced the government to spend down its reserves at a high rate in order to sustain social spending on salaries and subsidies, particularly since the government has been unable to boost exports of hydrocarbons or significantly grow its nonoilsector. In 2015, the Algerian Government imposed further restrictions on imports in an effort to reduce withdrawals from its foreign exchange reserves. The Government also increased the valueadded tax onelectricity and fuel, but said it would address subsidies at a later date. Longterm economic challenges include diversifying the economy away from its reliance on hydrocarbon exports, bolstering the private sector, attracting foreign investment, and providing adequate jobs foryounger Algerians.

GDP (purchasing power parity):
$578.7 billion (2015 est.)
$557.8 billion (2014 est.)
$537.4 billion (2013 est.)
note: data are in 2015 US dollars
country comparison to the world: 34

GDP (official exchange rate):
$172.3 billion (2015 est.)

GDP—real growth rate:
3.7% (2015 est.)
3.8% (2014 est.)
2.8% (2013 est.)
country comparison to the world: 72

GDP—per capita (PPP):
$14,500 (2015 est.)
$14,300 (2014 est.)
$14,000 (2013 est.)
note: data are in 2015 US dollars
country comparison to the world: 112

Gross national saving:
34.6% of GDP (2015 est.)
43.4% of GDP (2014 est.)
45.1% of GDP (2013 est.)
country comparison to the world: 10

GDP—composition, by end use:
household consumption: 39.1%
government consumption: 21.3%
investment in fixed capital: 39.6%
investment in inventories: 7.6%

exports of goods and services: 27.4%
imports of goods and services: -35% (2015 est.)

GDP—composition, by sector of origin:
agriculture: 10.3%
industry: 46%
services: 43.7% (2015 est.)

Agriculture—products: wheat, barley, oats, grapes, olives, citrus, fruits; sheep, cattle

Industries: petroleum, natural gas, light industries, mining, electrical, petrochemical, food processing

Industrial production growth rate: 0.4% (2015 est.)
country comparison to the world: 163

Labor force: 11.77 million (2015 est.)
country comparison to the world: 48

Labor force—by occupation: *agriculture:* 10.8%, 30.9%
industry: 58.4%, 13.4%
services: (2011 est.)

Unemployment rate: 11% (2015 est.)
10.6% (2014 est.)
country comparison to the world: 123

Population below poverty line: 23% (2006 est.)

Household income or consumption by percentage share: *lowest:* 10%: 2.8%
highest: 10%: 26.8% (1995)

Distribution of family income—Gini index: 35.3 (1995)
country comparison to the world: 93

Budget: *revenues:* $49.38 billion
expenditures: $69.01 billion (2015 est.)
Taxes and other revenues: 28.2% of GDP (2015 est.)
country comparison to the world: 93

Budget surplus (+) or deficit (–): 11.2% of GDP (2015 est.)
country comparison to the world: 205

Public debt: 9.3% of GDP (2015 est.)
7.2% of GDP (2014 est.)
note: data cover central government debt as well as debt issued by subnational entities and intragovernmental debt
country comparison to the world: 169

Fiscal year: calendar year

Inflation rate (consumer prices):
4.8% (2015 est.)
2.9% (2014 est.)
country comparison to the world: 171

Central bank discount rate: 4% (31 December 2010)
4% (31 December 2009)
country comparison to the world: 97

Commercial bank prime lending rate: 8% (31 December 2015 est.)
8% (31 December 2014 est.)
country comparison to the world: 110

Stock of narrow money:
$89.89 billion (31 December 2015 est.)
$109 billion (31 December 2014 est.)
country comparison to the world: 38

Stock of broad money: $164.5 billion (31 December 2014 est.)
$152.8 billion (31 December 2013 est.)

country comparison to the world: 47

Stock of domestic credit: $57.98 billion (31 December 2015 est.)
$35.4 billion (31 December 2014 est.)
country comparison to the world: 59

Market value of publicly traded shares: $NA

Current account balance: -$27.04 billion (2015 est.)
-$9.436 billion (2014 est.)
country comparison to the world: 189

Exports: $36.3 billion (2015 est.)
$63.23 billion (2014 est.)
country comparison to the world: 59

Exports—commodities: petroleum, natural gas, and petroleum products 97% (2009 est.)

Exports partners: Spain 18.8%, France 11.2%, US 8.8%, Italy 8.7%, UK 7.1%, Brazil 5.2%, Tunisia 4.9%, Germany 4.5% (2015)

Imports: $52.65 billion (2015 est.)
$58.62 billion (2014 est.)
country comparison to the world: 50

Imports—commodities: capital goods, foodstuffs, consumer goods

Imports —partners: China 15.6%, France 14.3%, Italy 9.4%, Spain 7.4%, Germany 5.6%, Russia 4.1% (2015)

Reserves of foreign exchange and gold: $155.7 billion (31 December 2015 est.)
$179.9 billion (31 December 2014 est.)
country comparison to the world: 15

Debt external:
$4.839 billion (31 December 2014 est.)
$5.231 billion (31 December 2013 est.)
country comparison to the world: 132

Stock of direct foreign investment—at home:
$30.13 billion (31 December 2015 est.)
$28.98 billion (31 December 2014 est.)
country comparison to the world: 70

Stock of direct foreign investment—abroad:
$2.679 billion (31 December 2015 est.)
$2.589 billion (31 December 2014 est.)
country comparison to the world: 78

Exchange rates: Algerian dinars (DZD) per US dollar—
100.6 (2015 est.)
80.579 (2014 est.)
80.579 (2013 est.)
77.54 (2012 est.)
72.938 (2011 est.)

ENERGY

Electricity—production: 53.99 billion kWh (2012 est.)
country comparison to the world: 51

Electricity—consumption: 42.87 billion kWh (2012 est.)
country comparison to the world: 54

Electricity—exports: 985 million kWh (2012 est.)
country comparison to the world: 57

Electricity—imports: 936 million kWh (2012 est.)
country comparison to the world: 65

Electricity—installed generating capacity: 15.2 million kW (2013 est.)
country comparison to the world: 47

Electricity—from fossil fuels: 98% of total installed capacity (2012 est.)
country comparison to the world: 55

Electricity—from nuclear fuels: 0% of total installed capacity (2012 est.)
country comparison to the world: 38

Electricity—from hydro electric plants: 1.8% of total installed capacity (2012 est.)
country comparison to the world: 139

Electricity—from other renewable sources: 0.2% of total installed capacity (2012 est.)
country comparison to the world: 110

Crude oil—production: 1.42 million bbl/day (2014 est.)
country comparison to the world: 18

Crude oil—exports: 1.158 million bbl/day (2012 est.)
country comparison to the world: 15

Crude oil—imports: 5,900 bbl/day (2012 est.)
country comparison to the world: 77

Crude oil—proved reserves: 12.2 billion bbl (1 January 2015 est.)
country comparison to the world: 16

Refined petroleum products—production: 484,500 bbl/day (2012 est.)
country comparison to the world: 34

Refined petroleum products—consumption: 390,000 bbl/day (2013 est.)
country comparison to the world: 37

Refined petroleum products—exports: 432,700 bbl/day (2012 est.)
country comparison to the world: 17

Refined petroleum products—imports: 94,180 bbl/day (2012 est.)
country comparison to the world: 55

Natural gas—production: 79.65 billion cu m (2013 est.)
country comparison to the world: 11

Natural gas—consumption: 36.65 billion cu m (2013 est.)
country comparison to the world: 26

Natural gas—exports: 43 billion cu m (2013 est.)
country comparison to the world: 8

Natural gas—imports: 0 cu m (2013 est.)
country comparison to the world: 153

Natural gas—proved reserves: 4.505 trillion cu m (1 January 2014 est.)
country comparison to the world: 10

Carbon dioxide emissions from consumption of energy: 133.9 million Mt (2012 est.)
country comparison to the world: 35

COMMUNICATIONS

Telephones fixed lines: *total subscriptions:* 3.1 million
subscriptions per 100 inhabitants: 8 (2014 est.)
country comparison to the world: 46

Telephones mobile cellular: *total:* 37.3 million
subscriptions per 100 inhabitants: 96 (2014 est.)
country comparison to the world: 33

Telephone system: *general assessment:* privatization of Algeria's telecommunications sector began in 2000; three mobile cellular licenses have been issued and, in 2005, a consortium led by Egypt's Orascom Telecom won a 15 year license to build and operate a fixedline network in Algeria; the license will allow Orascom to develop highspeed data and other specialized services and contribute to meeting the large unfulfilled demand forbasic residential telephony; Internet broadband services began in 2003
domestic: a limited network of fixed lines with a teledensity of less than 10 telephones per 100 personshas been offset by the rapid increase in mobile cellular subscribership; in 2011, mobilecellular teledensitywas roughly 100 telephones per 100 persons
international: country code -213; landing point for the SEAMEWE4 fiberoptic submarine cablesystem that provides links to Europe, the Middle East, and Asia; microwave radio relay to Italy, France, Spain, Morocco, and Tunisia; coaxial cable to Morocco and Tunisia; participant in Medarabtel; satellite earth stations -51 (Intelsat, Intersputnik, and Arabsat) (2011)

Broadcast media: staterun Radio Television Algerienne operates the broadcast media and carries programming in Arabic, Berber dialects, and French; use of satellite dishes is widespread, providing easy access to European and Arab satellite stations; staterun radio operates several national networks and roughly 40 regional radiostations (2007)
Radio broadcast stations: AM 25, FM 1, shortwave 8 (1999)
Television broadcast stations: 46 (plus 216 repeaters) (1995)

Internet country code: .dz

Internet hosts: 676 (2012)
country comparison to the world: 178

Internet users: *total:* 6.5 million
percent of population: 16.7% (2014 est.)
country comparison to the world: 55

TRANSPORTATION

Airports: 157 (2013)
country comparison to the world: 36

Airports with—paved runways:
total: 64over 3,047 m: 12
2,438 to 3,047 m: 29
1,524 to 2,437 m: 17
914 to 1,523 m: 5
under 914 m: 1 (2013)

Airports with unpaved runways: *total:* 93
2,438 to 3,047 m: 2
1,524 to 2,437 m: 18
914 to 1,523 m: 39
under 914 m: 34 (2013)

Heliports: 3 (2013)

Pipelines: condensate 2,600 km; gas 16,415 km; liquid petroleum gas 3,447 km; oil 7,036 km; refined products 144km (2013)

Railways: *total:* 3,973 km
standard gauge: 2,888 km 1.432m gauge (283 km electrified)
narrow gauge: 1,085 km 1.055m gauge (2014)
country comparison to the world: 45

Roadways: *total:* 113,655 km
paved: 87,605 km (includes 645 km of expressways)
unpaved: 26,050 km (2010)
country comparison to the world: 42

Merchant marine: *total:* 38
by type: bulk carrier 6, cargo 8, chemical tanker 3, liquefied gas 11, passenger/cargo 3, petroleumtanker 4, roll on/roll off 3
foreignowned: 15 (UK, 15) (2010)
country comparison to the world: 78

Ports and terminals: *major seaport(s):* Algiers, Annaba, Arzew, Bejaia, Djendjene, Jijel, Mostaganem, Oran, Skikda
LNG terminal(s) (export): Arzew, Bethioua, Skikda

MILITARY AND SECURITY

Military branches: People's National Army (Armee Nationale Populaire, ANP), Land Forces (Forces Terrestres, FT), Navy ofthe Republic of Algeria (Marine de la Republique Algerienne, MRA), Air Force (AlQuwwat alJawwiya alJaza'eriya, QJJ), Territorial Air Defense Force (2009)

Military service age and obligation: 17 is the legal minimum age for voluntary military service; 19–30 years of age for compulsory service; conscript service obligation is 18 months (6 months basic training, 12 months civil projects) (2012)

Military expenditures:
4.48% of GDP (2012)
4.36% of GDP (2011)
4.48% of GDP (2010)
country comparison to the world: 8

TRANSNATIONAL ISSUES

Disputes international: Algeria and many other states reject Moroccan administration of Western Sahara; the Polisario Front, exiled in Algeria, represents the Sahrawi Arab Democratic Republic; Algeria's border with Morocco remains an irritant to bilateral relations, each nation accusing the other of harboring militants and arms smuggling; dormant disputes include Libyan claims of about 32,000 sq km still reflected on its maps of southeastern Algeria and the National Liberation Front's (FLN) assertions of a claim to Chirac Pastures in southeastern Morocco

Refugees and internally displaced persons: *refugees (country of origin):* 90,000 (Western Saharan Sahrawi, mostly living in Algerian-sponsoredcamps in the southwestern Algerian town of Tindouf) (2014)
IDPs: undetermined (civil war during 1990s) (2013)

Trafficking in persons: *current situation:* Algeria is a transit and, to a lesser extent, a destination and source country for women subjected to forced labor and sex trafficking and, to a lesser extent, men subjected to forced labor; criminal networks, sometimes extending to sub-Saharan Africa and to Europe, are involved in human smuggling and trafficking in Algeria; sub-Saharan adults enter Algeria voluntarily but illegally, often with the aid of smugglers, for onward travel to Europe, but some of the women are forced into prostitution, domestic service, and begging; some sub-Saharan men, mostly from Mali, are forced into domestic servitude; some Algerian women and children are also forced into prostitution domestically

tier rating: Tier 3—Algeria does not fully comply with the minimum standards for the elimination of trafficking and is not making significant efforts to do so: some officials denied the existence of human trafficking, hindering law enforcement efforts; the government reported its first conviction under its antitrafficking law; one potential trafficking case was investigated in 2014, but no suspected offenders were arrested; no progress was made in identifying victims among vulnerable groups or referring them to NGO run protection service, which left trafficking victims subject to arrest and detention; no anti-trafficking public awareness or educational campaigns were conducted (2015)

AMERICAN SAMOA

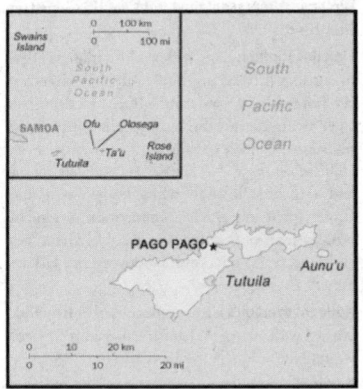

INTRODUCTION

Background: Settled as early as 1000 B.C., Samoa was not reached by European explorers until the 18th century. International rivalries in the latter half of the 19th century were settled by an 1899 treaty in which Germany and the US divided the Samoan archipelago. The US formally occupied its portion a smaller group of eastern islands with the excellent harbor of Pago Pago—the following year.

Location: Oceania, group of islands in the South Pacific Ocean, about halfway between Hawaii and New Zealand

Geographic coordinates: 14 20 S, 170 00 W

Map references: Oceania

Area: *total:* 199 sq km
land: 199 sq km
water: 0 sq km
note: includes Rose Island and Swains Island
country comparison to the world: 216

Area—comparative: slightly larger than Washington, DC

Land boundaries: 0 km

Coastline: 116 km

Maritime claims: *territorial sea:* 12 nm
exclusive economic zone: 200 nm

Climate: tropical marine, moderated by southeast trade winds; annual rainfall averages about 3 m; rainy season (November to April), dry season (May to October); little seasonal temperature variation

Terrain: five volcanic islands with rugged peaks and limited coastal plains, two coral atolls (Rose Island, Swains Island)

Elevation:

elevation extremes: *lowest point:* Pacific Ocean 0 m
highest point: Lata Mountain 964 m

Natural resources: pumice, pumicite

Land use: *agricultural land:* 21.7%
arable land: 13.3%
permanent crops: 8.4%
permanent pasture: 0%
forest: 78.3%
other: 0% (2011 est.)

Irrigated land: 0 sq km (2012)

Natural hazards: typhoons common from December to March
volcanism: limited volcanic activity on the Ofu and Olosega Islands; neither has erupted since the 19th century

Environment—current issues: limited natural freshwater resources; the water division of the government has spent substantial funds in the past few years to improve water catchments and pipelines

Geography—note: Pago Pago has one of the best natural deepwater harbors in the South Pacific Ocean, sheltered by shape from rough seas and protected by peripheral mountains from high winds; strategic location in the South Pacific Ocean

PEOPLE AND SOCIETY

Nationality: *noun:* American Samoan(s) (US nationals)
adjective: American Samoan

Ethnic groups: Pacific Islander 92.6% (includes Samoan 88.9%, Tongan 2.9%, other .8%), Asian 3.6% (includes Filipino 2.2%, other 1.4%), mixed 2.7%, other 1.2% (2010 est.)

Languages: Samoan 88.6% (closely related to Hawaiian and other Polynesian languages), English 3.9%, Tongan 2.7%, other Pacific islander 3%, other 1.8%
note: most people are bilingual (2010 est.)
Religions: Christian 98.3%, other 1%, unaffiliated 0.7% (2010 est.)

Population: 54,343 (July 2015 est.)
country comparison to the world: 208

Age structure: *0–14 years:* 24.45% (male 6,506/female 6,780)
15–24 years: 19.61% (male 5,264/female 5,395)
25–54 years: 42.1% (male 11,775/female 11,105)
55–64 years: 8.69% (male 2,326/female 2,397)
65 years and over: 5.14% (male 1,287/female 1,508) (2015 est.)

Median age: *total:* 28.8 years
male: 29.4 years
female: 28.3 years (2015 est.)
country comparison to the world: 122

Population growth rate: 0.3% (2015 est.)
country comparison to the world: 219

Birth rate: 22.89 births/1,000 population (2015 est.)
country comparison to the world: 70

Death rate: 4.75 deaths/1,000 population (2015 est.)
country comparison to the world: 197

Net migration rate: 21.13 migrant(s)/1,000 population (2015 est.)
country comparison to the world: 222

Urbanization: *urban population:* 87.2% of total population (2015)
rate of urbanization: 0.13% annual rate of change (2010–15 est.)

Major urban areas—population: PAGO PAGO (capital) 48,000 (2014)

Sex ratio: *at birth:* 1.06 male(s)/female
0–14 years: 0.96 male(s)/female
15–24 years: 0.98 male(s)/female
25–54 years: 1.06 male(s)/female
55–64 years: 0.97 male(s)/female
65 years and over: 0.85 male(s)/female
total population: 1 male(s)/female (2015 est.)

Infant mortality rate: *total:* 8.69 deaths/1,000 live births
male: 11.16 deaths/1,000 live births
female: 6.09 deaths/1,000 live births (2015 est.)
country comparison to the world: 149

Life expectancy at birth: *total population:* 75.14 years
male: 72.18 years
female: 78.28 years (2015 est.)
country comparison to the world: 105

Total fertility rate: 2.92 children born/woman (2015 est.)
country comparison to the world: 56

Drinking water source:
improved:
urban: 100% of population
rural: 100% of population
total: 100% of population
unimproved:
urban: 0% of population
rural: 0% of population
total: 0% of population (2015 est.)

Sanitation facility access:
improved:
urban: 62.5% of population
rural: 62.5% of population
total: 62.5% of population
unimproved:
urban: 37.5% of population
rural: 37.5% of population
total: 37.5% of population (2015 est.)

HIV/AIDS—adult prevalence rate: NA

HIV/AIDS people living with HIV/AIDS: NA

HIV/AIDS deaths: NA

Education expenditures: NA

GOVERNMENT

Country name: *conventional long form:* Territory of American Samoa
conventional short form: American Samoa
abbreviation: AS
etymology: the name Samoa is composed of two parts, "sa" meaning "sacred" and "moa" meaning"center, " so the name can mean "Holy Center," alternatively, it can mean "place of the sacred moa bird" of Polynesian mythology

Dependency status: unincorporated and unorganized territory of the US; administered by the Office of Insular Affairs, USDepartment of the Interior

Government type: presidential democracy; a self-governing territory of the US

Capital: *name:* Pago Pago

Geographic coordinates: 14 16 S, 170 42 W
time difference: UTC11 (6 hours behind Washington, DC, during Standard Time)

Administrative divisions:
none (territory of the US); there are no first-order administrative divisions as defined by the US Government, but there are 3 districts and 2 islands* at the second order; Eastern, Manu'a, Rose Island*, Swains Island*, Western

Independence: none (territory of the US)

National holiday: Flag Day, 17 April (1900)

Constitution: adopted 17 October 1960; revised 1 July 1967; amended several times, last in 2013 (2016)

Legal system: mixed legal system of US common law and customary law

Citizenship: see United States

Suffrage: 18 years of age; universal

Executive branch: *chief of state:* President Barack H. OBAMA (since 20 January 2009); Vice President Joseph R. BIDEN (since 20 January 2009)
head of government: Governor Lolo Matalasi MOLIGA (since 3 January 2013)
cabinet: Cabinet consists of 12 department directors appointed by the governor with the consent of the Legislative Assembly
elections/appointments: president and vice president indirectly elected on the same ballot by an Electoral College of 'electors' chosen from each state to serve a 4 year term (eligible for a second term); under the US Constitution, residents of unincorporated territories, such as American Samoa, do not vote inelections for US president and vice president; however, they may vote in Democratic and Republicanpresidential primary elections; governor and lieutenant governor directly elected on the same ballot byabsolute majority popular vote in 2 rounds if needed for a 4 year term (eligible for a second term); electionlast held on 6 November 2012 with a runoff on 20 November 2012 (next to be held in November 2016)
election results: Lolo Matalasi MOLIGA elected governor; percent of vote in second round Lolo Matalasi MOLIGA (independent) 52.9%, Faoa Aitofele SUNIA (Democratic Party) 47.1%

Legislative branch: *description:* bicameral Fono or Legislative Assembly consists of the Senate (18 seats; membersindirectly selected by regional governing councils to serve 4 year terms) and the House of Representatives (21 seats; 20 members directly elected by simple majority vote and 1 decided by public meeting on Swains Island; members serve 2year terms)
elections: House of Representatives last held on 4 November 2014 (next to be held in November 2016); Senate last held on 6 November 2012 (next to be held in November 2016)
election results: Senate percent of vote by party NA; seats by party independents 18; House of Representatives percent of vote by party NA; seats by party independents 20
note: American Samoa elects 1 member by simple majority vote to serve a 2year term as a delegate tothe US House of Representatives; the delegate can vote when serving on a committee and when the House meets as the Committee of the Whole House, but not when legislation is submitted for a "full floor" Housevote; election of delegate last held on 4 November 2014 (next to be held on November 2016)

Judicial branch: *highest court(s):* High Court of American Samoa (consists of the chief justice, associate chief justice, and 6 Samoan associate judges and organized into trial, family, drug, and appellate divisions)

*note—*American Samoa has no US federal courts
judge selection and term of office: chief justice and associate chief justice appointed by the US Secretary of the Interior to serve for life; Samoan associate judges appointed by the governor to serve for life
subordinate courts: district and village courts

Political parties and leaders: Democratic Party [Oreta M. TOGAFAU]
Republican Party[Tautai A. F. FAALEVAO]

International organization participation: AOSIS (observer), Interpol (subbureau), IOC, PIF (observer), SPC

Diplomatic representation in the US: none (territory of the US)

Diplomatic representation from the US: none (territory of the US)

Flag description: blue, with a white triangle edged in red that is based on the fly side and extends to the hoist side; a brown and white American bald eagle flying toward the hoist side is carrying two traditional Samoan symbols of authority, a war club known as a "fa'alaufa'i" (upper; left talon), and a coconut fiber fly whisk known as a "fue" (lower; right talon); the combination of symbols broadly mimics that seen on the US Great Seal and reflects the relationship between the US and American Samoa

National symbol(s): a fue (coconut fiber fly whisk) crossed with a to'oto'o (staff); national colors: red, white, blue

National anthem: *name:* "Amerika Samoa" (American Samoa)
lyrics/music: Mariota Tiumalu TUIASOSOPO/ Napoleon Andrew TUITELELEAPAGA
note: local anthem adopted 1950; as a territory of the United States, "The Star-Spangled Banner" isofficial (see United States)

ECONOMY

Economy overview: American Samoa has a traditional Polynesian economy in which more than 90% of the land is communally owned. Economic activity is strongly linked to the US with which American Samoa conducts most of its commerce. Tuna fishing and tuna processing plants are the backbone of the private sector with canned tuna the primary export. The two tuna canneries accounted for 13.1% of employment in 2013. In late September 2009, an earthquake and the resulting tsunami devastated American Samoa and nearby Samoa, disrupting transportation and power generation, and resulting in about 200 deaths. The US Federal Emergency Management Agency oversaw a relief program of nearly $25 million. Transfers from the US Government add substantially to American Samoa's economic well-being. Attempts by the government to develop a larger and broader economy are restrained by Samoa's remote location, its limited transportation, and its devastating hurricanes. Tourism is a promising developing sector. In 2015, a new fish processing company completed refurbishing the processing facilities left behind by one of the two canneries that closed in 2009 and opened a new cannery. With two operating canneries once again, fish processing and exports will rise in the coming years.

GDP (purchasing power parity):
$711 million (2013 est.)
$718 million (2012 est.)
$647 million (2012 est.)
country comparison to the world: 207

GDP—(official exchange rate): $748.6 million (2005)

GDP—real growth rate:
2.4% (2013 est.)
2.7% (2012 est.)
0.6% (2012 est.)
country comparison to the world: 208

GDP per capita (PPP):
$13,000 (2013 est.)
$13,100 (2012 est.)
$11,700 (2011 est.)
country comparison to the world: 120

GDP—composition, by end use:
household consumption: 54.6%
government consumption: 52.8%
investment if fixed capital: 2.7%
investment in inventories: 2.3%
exports of goods and services: 54.4%
imports of goods and services: -66.8% (2012)

GDP—composition, by sector of origin:
agriculture: 27.4%
industry: 12.4%
services: 60.2% (2012)

Agriculture—products: bananas, coconuts, vegetables, taro, breadfruit, yams, copra, pineapples, papayas; dairy products, livestock

Industries: tuna canneries (largely supplied by foreign fishing vessels), handicrafts

Industrial production growth rate: NA%

Labor force: 16,090 (2013)
country comparison to the world: 215

Labor force—by occupation: *agriculture:* NA
industry: 13.1%
services: 86.9% (2013)

Unemployment rate: 29.8% (2005)
country comparison to the world: 184

Population below poverty line: NA%

Household income or consumption by percentage share: *lowest:* 10%: NA%
highest: 10%: NA%

Budget: *revenues:* $241.2 million
expenditures: $243.7 million (2013 est.)
Taxes and other revenues: 32.2% of GDP (2013 est.)
country comparison to the world: 77

Budget surplus (+) or deficit (–): -0.3% of GDP (2013 est.)
country comparison to the world: 39

Fiscal year: 1 October 30 September

Inflation rate (consumer prices):
2.1% (2013)
3.5% (2012)
country comparison to the world: 117

Exports: $459 million (2013 est.)
$489 million (2012)
country comparison to the world: 175

Exports—commodities: canned tuna 93%

Exports—partners: US 100%

Imports: $564 million (2013 est.)
$508 million (2012)
country comparison to the world: 192

Imports—commodities: raw materials for canneries, food, petroleum products, machinery and parts

Debt—external: $NA

Exchange rates: the US dollar is used

ENERGY

Electricity—production: 156.4 million kWh (2013 est.)
country comparison to the world: 191

Electricity consumption: 146 million kWh (2012 est.)
country comparison to the world: 193

Electricity exports: 0 kWh (2013 est.)
country comparison to the world: 101

Electricity imports: 0 kWh (2013 est.)
country comparison to the world: 117

Electricity installed generating capacity: 45,000 kW (2012 est.)
country comparison to the world: 190

Electricity from fossil fuels: 100% of total installed capacity (2012 est.)
country comparison to the world: 36

Electricity from nuclear fuels: 0% of total installed capacity (2012 est.)
country comparison to the world: 43

Electricity from hydroelectric plants: 0% of total installed capacity (2012 est.)
country comparison to the world: 157

Electricity from other renewable sources: 0% of total installed capacity (2012 est.)
country comparison to the world: 154

Crude oil—production: 0 bbl/day (2014 est.)
country comparison to the world: 106

Crude oil—exports: 0 bbl/day (2012 est.)
country comparison to the world: 96

Crude oil—imports: 0 bbl/day (2012 est.)
country comparison to the world: 157

Crude oil—proved reserves: 0 bbl (1 January 2015 est.)
country comparison to the world: 105

Refined petroleum products—production: 0 bbl/day (2012 est.)
country comparison to the world: 154

Refined petroleum products—consumption: 2,375 bbl/day (2013 est.)
country comparison to the world: 185

Refined petroleum products—exports: 0 bbl/day (2012 est.)
country comparison to the world: 153

Refined petroleum products—imports: 2,346 bbl/day (2012 est.)
country comparison to the world: 180

Natural gas—production: 0 cu m (2013 est.)
country comparison to the world: 155

Natural gas—consumption: 0 cu m (2013 est.)
country comparison to the world: 116

Natural gas—exports: 0 cu m (2013 est.)
country comparison to the world: 58

Natural gas—imports: 0 cu m (2013 est.)
country comparison to the world: 157

Natural gas—proved reserves: 0 cu m (1 January 2014 est.)
country comparison to the world: 110

Carbon dioxide emissions from consumption of energy: 607,000 Mt (2012 est.)
country comparison to the world: 176

COMMUNICATIONS

Telephones fixed lines: *total subscriptions:* 9,900
subscriptions per 100 inhabitants: 18 (2014 est.)
country comparison to the world: 199

Telephone system: *general assessment:* good telex, telegraph, facsimile, and cellular telephone services
domestic: domestic satellite system with 1 Comsat earth station
international: country code 1684; satellite earth station 1 (IntelsatPacific Ocean)

Broadcast media: 3 TV stations; multichannel pay TV services are available; about a dozen radio stations, some of whichare repeater stations (2009)
Radio broadcast stations: AM 2, FM 3, shortwave 0 (2005)
Television broadcast stations: 1 (2006)

Internet country code: .as

Internet hosts: 2,387 (2012)
country comparison to the world: 161

Internet users: NA

TRANSPORTATION

Airports: 3 (2013)
country comparison to the world: 192

Airports—with paved runways: *total:* 3over 3,047 m:
1914 to 1,523 m: 1
under 914 m: 1 (2013)

Roadways: *total:* 241 km (2008)
country comparison to the world: 207

Ports and terminals: *major seaport(s):* Pago Pago

MILITARY AND SECURITY

Military—note: defense is the responsibility of the US

TRANSNATIONAL ISSUES

Disputes—international:
Tokelau included American Samoa's Swains Island (Olosega) in its 2006 draft independence constitution

ANDORRA

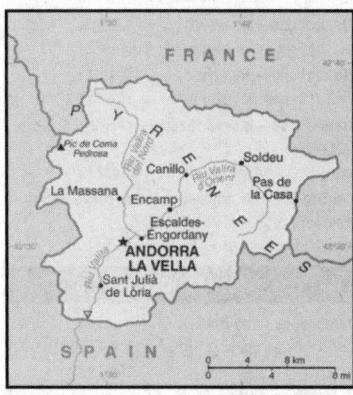

INTRODUCTION

Background: The landlocked Principality of Andorra is one of the smallest states in Europe, nestled high in the Pyrenees between the French and Spanish borders. For 715 years, from 1278 to 1993, Andorrans lived under a unique co-principality, ruled by French and Spanish leaders (from 1607 onward, the French chief of state and the Bishop of Urgell). In 1993, this feudal system was modified with the introduction of a modern, constitution; the co-princes remained as titular heads of state, but the government transformed into a parliamentary democracy. Andorra has become a popular tourist destination visited by approximately 10 million people each year drawn by the winter sports, summer climate, and duty-free shopping. Andorra has also become a wealthy international commercial center because of its mature banking sector and low taxes. As part of its effort to modernize its economy, Andorra has opened to foreign investment, and engaged in other reforms, such as advancing tax initiatives aimed at supporting a broader infrastructure. Although not a member of the EU, Andorra enjoys a special relationship with the organization and uses the euro as its national currency.

GEOGRAPHY

Location: Southwestern Europe, Pyrenees mountains, on the border between France and Spain

Geographic coordinates: 42 30 N, 1 30 E

Map references: Europe

Area: *total:* 468 sq km
land: 468 sq km
water: 0 sq km
country comparison to the world: 196

Area—comparative: 2.5 times the size of Washington, DC

Land boundaries: *total:* 118 km
border countries (2): France 55 km, Spain 63 km

Coastline: 0 km (landlocked)

Maritime claims: none (landlocked)

Climate: temperate; snowy, cold winters and warm, dry summers

Terrain: rugged mountains dissected by narrow valleys

Elevation: mean elevation: 1,996 m

elevation extremes: *lowest point:* Riu Runer 840 m
highest point: Pic de Coma Pedrosa 2,946 m

Natural resources: hydropower, mineral water, timber, iron ore, lead

Land use: *agricultural land:* 43.4%
arable land: 5.5%
permanent crops: 0%
permanent pasture: 37.9%
forest: 34%
other: 22.6% (2011 est.)

Irrigated land: 0 sq km (2012)

Natural hazards: avalanches

Environment—current issues: deforestation; overgrazing of mountain meadows contributes to soil erosion; air pollution; wastewater treatment and solid waste disposal

Environment—international agreements:
party to: Biodiversity, Desertification, Hazardous Wastes, Ozone Layer Protection
signed, but not ratified: none of the selected agreements

Geography—note: landlocked; straddles a number of important crossroads in the Pyrenees

PEOPLE AND SOCIETY

Nationality: *noun:* Andorran(s)
adjective: Andorran

Ethnic groups: Andorran 49%, Spanish 24.6%, Portuguese 14.3%, French 3.9%, other 8.2% (2012 est.)

Languages: Catalan (official), French, Castilian, Portuguese

Religions: Roman Catholic (predominant)

Population: 85,580 (July 2015 est.)
country comparison to the world: 201

Age structure: *0–14 years:* 15.04% (male 6,598/female 6,269)
15–24 years: 9.42% (male 4,182/female 3,880)
25–54 years: 47.78% (male 20,980/female 19,910)
55–64 years: 13.05% (male 5,996/female 5,176)
65 years and over: 14.71% (male 6,357/female 6,232) (2015 est.)

Median age: *total:* 43 years
male: 43.2 years
female: 42.8 years (2015 est.)
country comparison to the world: 16

Population growth rate: 0.12% (2015 est.)
country comparison to the world: 188

Birth rate: 8.13 births/1,000 population (2015 est.)
country comparison to the world: 221

Death rate: 6.96 deaths/1,000 population (2015 est.)
country comparison to the world: 134

Net migration rate: 0 migrant(s)/1,000 population (2015 est.)
country comparison to the world: 78

Urbanization: *urban population:* 85.1% of total population (2015)
rate of urbanization: 0.14% annual rate of change (2010–15 est.)

Major urban areas—population: ANDORRA LA VELLA (capital) 23,000 (2014)

Sex ratio: *at birth:* 1.07 male(s)/female
0–14 years: 1.05 male(s)/female
15–24 years: 1.08 male(s)/female
25–54 years: 1.05 male(s)/female
55–64 years: 1.16 male(s)/female
65 years and over: 1.02 male(s)/female
total population: 1.06 male(s)/female (2015 est.)

Infant mortality rate: *total:* 3.65 deaths/1,000 live births
male: 3.65 deaths/1,000 live births
female: 3.65 deaths/1,000 live births (2015 est.)
country comparison to the world: 200

Life expectancy at birth: *total population:* 82.72 years
male: 80.56 years
female: 85.02 years (2015 est.)
country comparison to the world: 8

Total fertility rate: 1.38 children born/woman (2015 est.)
country comparison to the world: 213

Health expenditures: 8.1% of GDP (2013)
country comparison to the world: 53

Physicians density: 4 physicians/1,000 population (2010)

Hospital bed density: 2.5 beds/1,000 population (2009)

Drinking water source: *improved:*
urban: 100% of population
rural: 100% of population
total: 100% of population
unimproved:
urban: 0% of population
rural: 0% of population
total: 0% of population (2015 est.)

Sanitation facility access: *improved:*
urban: 100% of population
rural: 100% of population
total: 100% of population
unimproved:
urban: 0% of population
rural: 0% of population
total: 0% of population (2015 est.)

HIV/AIDS—adult prevalence rate: NA

HIV/AIDS—people living with HIV/AIDS: NA

HIV/AIDS—deaths: NA

Obesity—adult prevalence rate: 32.1% (2014)

country comparison to the world: 58
Education expenditures: 3.1% of GDP (2014)

GOVERNMENT

Country name: *conventional long form:* Principality of Andorra
conventional short form: Andorra
local long form: Principat d'Andorra
local short form: Andorra
etymology: the origin of the country's name is obscure; since the area served as part of the Spanish March (defensive buffer zone) against the invading Moors in the 8th century, the name may derive from the Arabic "ad-darra" meaning "the forest"

Government type: parliamentary democracy (since March 1993) that retains its chiefs of state in the form of a co-principality; the two princes are the president of France and bishop of Seu d'Urgell, Spain, who arer epresented in Andorra by the co-princes' representatives

Capital: *name:* Andorra la Vella

Geographic coordinates: 42 30 N, 1 31 E
time difference: UTC+1 (6 hours ahead of Washington, DC during Standard Time)
daylight saving time: +1hr, begins last Sunday in March; ends last Sunday in October

Administrative divisions: 7 parishes (parroquies, singular—parroquia); Andorra la Vella, Canillo, Encamp, Escaldes-Engordany, La Massana, Ordino, Sant Julia de Loria

Independence: 1278 (formed under the joint sovereignty of the French Count of Foix and the Spanish Bishop of Urgell)

National holiday: Our Lady of Meritxell Day, 8 September (1278)

Constitution: drafted 1991, approved by referendum 14 March 1993, effective 28 April 1993 (2016)

Legal system: mixed legal system of civil and customary law with the influence of canon law

International law organization participation: has not submitted an ICJ jurisdiction declaration; accepts ICCt jurisdiction

Citizenship: *citizenship by birth:* no
citizenship by descent only: the mother must be an Andorran citizen or the father must have been born in Andorra and both parents maintain permanent residence in Andorra
dual citizenship recognized: no
residency requirement for naturalization: 25 years

Suffrage: 18 years of age; universal

Executive branch: *chief of state:* French Co-prince Francois HOLLANDE (since 15 May 2012); represented by Thierry LATASTE (since 5 January 2015) and Spanish Co-prince Archbishop Joan-Enric VIVES i Sicilia (since 12 May 2003); represented by Josep Maria MAUN (since 20 July 2012)

head of government: Head of Government (or Cap de Govern) Antoni MARTI PETIT (since 12 May 2011)

cabinet: Executive Council designated by head of government
elections/appointments: head of government indirectly elected by the General Council (Andorran parliament), formally appointed by the co-princes for a 4-year term; election last held on 31 March 2015 (next to be held in April 2019); the leader of the majority party in the General Council is usually elected head of government
election results: Antoni MARTI PETIT (DA) elected head of government; percent of General Council vote -79%

Legislative branch: *description:* unicameral General Council of the Valleys or Consell General de les Valls (a minimum of 28 seats; 14 members directly elected in multi-seat constituencies (parishes) by simple majority vote and 14 directly elected in a single national constituency by proportional representation vote; members serve 4-year terms); note—each voter casts two separate ballots—one for a national list and one for a parish listel
ections: last held on 1 March 2015 (next to be held in April 2019)
election results: seats by party—percent of vote by party: DA 34.5%, PLA 25.0%, PS-VA-IC-independent coalition 21.3%, SDP 9.6%, invalid votes 9.5%; seats by party: DA 15, PLA 8, PS-VA-IC-independent coalition 3, SDP 2

Judicial branch: *highest court(s):* Supreme Court of Justice of Andorra or Tribunal Superior de la Justicia d'Andorra (consists of the court president and 8 judges organized into civil, criminal, and administrative chambers); Constitutional Court or Tribunal Constitucional (consists of 4 magistrates)
judge selection and term of office: Supreme Court president and judges appointed by the Supreme Council of Justice, a 5-member judicial policy and administrative body appointed 1 each by the co-princes, 1 by the General Council, 1 by the executive council president, and 1 by the courts; judges serve 6-year renewable terms; Constitutional magistrates appointed 2 by the co-princes and 2 by the General Council; magistrates' appointments limited to 2 consecutive 8-year terms
subordinate courts: Tribunal of Judges or Tribunal de Batlles; Tribunal of the Courts or Tribunal de Corts

Political parties and leaders: Citizens' Initiative or IC [Sergi RICART] (including PS, VA, IC, and independents)
Democrats for Andorra or DA [Antoni MARTI PETIT]
Greens of Andorra or VA [Isabel LOZANO MUNOZ, Juli FERNANDEZ BLASI]
Liberal Party or PLA [Josep PINTAT FORNE]
Social Democratic Party or PS [Vincenc ALAY FERRER]
Social Democratic Progress Party or SDP [Victor NAUDI ZAMORA]
note: there are also several smaller parties at the parish level (one is Lauredian Union)

International organization participation: CE, FAO, ICAO, ICC (NGOs), ICCt, ICRM, IFRCS, Interpol, IOC, IPU, ITU, OIF, OPCW, OSCE, UN, UNCTAD, UNESCO, Union Latina, UNWTO, WCO, WHO, WIPO, WTO (observer)

Diplomatic representation in the US: *chief of mission:* Ambassador Elisenda VIVES BALMANA (since 2 March 2016)
chancery: 2 United Nations Plaza, 27th Floor, New York, NY 10017
telephone: [1] (212) 750-8064
FAX: [1] (212) 750-6630

Diplomatic representation from the US: the US does not have an embassy in Andorra; the US ambassador to Spain is accredited to Andorra; US interests in Andorra are represented by the US Consulate General's office in Barcelona (Spain); *mailing address:* Paseo Reina Elisenda de Montcada, 23,08034 Barcelona, Spain;
telephone: [34] (93) 280-2227;
FAX: [34] (93) 280-6175

Flag description: three vertical bands of blue (hoist side), yellow, and red, with the national coat of arms centered in the yellow band; the latter band is slightly wider than the other two so that the ratio of band widths is 8: 9: 8; the coat of arms features a quartered shield with the emblems of (starting in the upper left and proceeding clockwise): Urgell, Foix, Bearn, and Catalonia; the motto reads VIRTUS UNITA FORTIOR (Strength United is Stronger); the flag combines the blue and red French colors with the red and yellow of Spain to show Franco-Spanish protection
note: similar to the flags of Chad and Romania, which do not have a national coat of arms in the center, and the flag of Moldova, which does bear a national emblem

National symbol(s): national colors: blue, yellow, red

National anthem: *name:* "El Gran Carlemany" (The Great Charlemagne)
lyrics/music: Joan BENLLOCH i VIVO/Enric MARFANY BONS
note: adopted 1921; the anthem provides a brief history of Andorra in a first person narrative

ECONOMY

Economy—overview: Tourism, retail sales, and finance are the mainstays of Andorra's tiny, well-to-do economy, accounting for more than three-quarters of GDP. Andorra's duty-free status for some products and its summer and winter resorts attract millions of visitors annually, although the economic downturn in neighboring countries has curtailed the number of tourists. Agricultural production is limited—only about 5% of the land is arable—and most food has to be imported, making the economy vulnerable to changes in fuel and food prices. The principal livestock is sheep. Manufacturing output and exports consist mainly of perfumes and cosmetic products, products of the printing industry, electrical machinery and equipment, clothing, tobacco products, and furniture. Andorra is a member of the EU Customs Union and is treated as an EU member for trade in manufactured goods (no tariffs) and as a non-EU member for agricultural products. Andorra uses the euro and is effectively subject to the monetary policy of the European Central Bank. Andorra's comparative advantage as a tax haven eroded when the borders of neighboring France and Spain opened; its bank secrecy laws have been relaxed under pressure from the EU and OECD. Slower growth in Spain and France has dimmed Andorra's economic prospects. Since 2010, a drop in tourism contributed to a contraction in GDP and a sharp deterioration of public finances, prompting the government to begin implementing several austerity measures to reduce the budget deficit, including levying a special corporate tax. The Government is also planning to institute an income tax at the behest of the Organization for Economic Cooperation and Development. The new tax will apply to anyone who lives in the principality for at least 183 days in a calendar year. The first $30,000 of income will be tax free, with the next $20,000 taxed at 5%. The balance of income exceeding the initial $50,000 will be taxed at 10%, which is still less than in most West European countries. Andorra's Government also relaxed its residency and investment laws in 2012 to make the country more attractive to foreign investors. A person now must spend 90 days a year in the principality to qualify for residency, compared with the previous 180-day requirement. Foreigners now have the same property ownership rights as citizens. In addition, three new categories of residency permits were introduced. Anyone who is retired or at least not working in Andorra can obtain a permit in the first category by making a financial investment in the country of at least €400,000, which can include a property purchase.

GDP (purchasing power parity):
$3.163 billion (2012 est.)
$3.214 billion (2011 est.)
$3.227 billion (2010 est.)
note: data are in 2012 US dollars
country comparison to the world: 184

GDP (official exchange rate):
$4.8 billion (2012 est.)

GDP—real growth rate:
-1.6% (2012 est.)
-0.4% (2011 est.)
-1.9% (2010 est.)
country comparison to the world: 206

GDP—per capita (PPP):
$37,200 (2011 est.)
$37,700 (2010 est.)
$37,900 (2009 est.)
country comparison to the world: 46

GDP—composition, by sector of origin:
agriculture: 14%
industry: 79%
services: 6% (2011 est.)

Agriculture—products: small quantities of rye, wheat, barley, oats, vegetables, tobacco; sheep, cattle

Industries: tourism (particularly skiing), banking, timber, furniture

Industrial production growth rate: NA%

Labor force: 36,060 (2012)
country comparison to the world: 200

Labor force—by occupation: *agriculture:* 0.4%
industry: 4.7%
services: 94.9% (2010)

Unemployment rate: 4% (2012 est.)
1.9% (2011 est.)
country comparison to the world: 34

Population below poverty line: NA%

Household income or consumption by percentage share: *lowest:* 10%: NA%
highest: 10%: NA%

Budget: *revenues:* $1.029 billion
expenditures: $1.041 billion (2012)
Taxes and other revenues: 21.4% of GDP (2012)
country comparison to the world: 145

Budget surplus (+) or deficit (–): -0.3% of GDP (2012)
country comparison to the world: 36

Public debt: 41.1% of GDP (2012)
37.7% of GDP (2011)
country comparison to the world: 111

Fiscal year: calendar year

Inflation rate (consumer prices):
1.1% (2012 est.)
-2.5% (2011 est.)
country comparison to the world: 84

Exports: $70 million (2012 est.)
$72 million (2011 est.)
country comparison to the world: 198

Exports—commodities: tobacco products, furniture

Imports: $1.43 billion (2012 est.)
$1.501 billion (2011 est.)
country comparison to the world: 172

Imports—commodities: consumer goods, food, fuel, electricity

Debt—external: $NA

Exchange rates: euros (EUR) per US dollar—
-0.885 (2015 est.)
0.7525 (2014 est.)
0.7634 (2013 est.)
0.78 (2012 est.)
0.7185 (2011 est.)

ENERGY

Electricity—production: 91.24 million kWh (2011)
country comparison to the world: 201

Electricity—consumption: 562.4 million kWh (2012)
country comparison to the world: 169

Electricity—exports: 0 kWh (2012 est.)
country comparison to the world: 99

Electricity—imports: 0 kWh (2012 est.)

country comparison to the world: 115

Electricity—installed generating capacity: 520,000 kW (2010 est.)
country comparison to the world: 139

Electricity—from fossil fuels: 61.3% of total installed capacity (2010 est.)
country comparison to the world: 128

Electricity—from nuclear fuels: 0% of total installed capacity (2010 est.)
country comparison to the world: 41

Electricity—from hydro electric plants: 23.3% of total installed capacity (2010 est.)
country comparison to the world: 87

COMMUNICATIONS

Telephones—fixed lines: *total subscriptions:* 38,200
subscriptions per 100 inhabitants: 45 (2014 est.)
country comparison to the world: 168

Telephones—mobile cellular: *total:* 66,200
subscriptions per 100 inhabitants: 78 (2014 est.)
country comparison to the world: 198

Telephone system: *general assessment:* modern automatic telephone system
domestic: modern system with microwave radio relay connections between exchanges
international: country code—376; landline circuits to France and Spain (2012)

Broadcast media: 1 public TV station and 2 public radio stations; about 10 commercial radio stations; good reception of radio and TV broadcasts from stations in France and Spain; upgraded to terrestrial digital TV broadcasting in 2007; roughly 25 international TV channels available (2012)
Radio broadcast stations: AM 0, FM 1, shortwave 0 (easy access to radio and television broadcasts originating in France and Spain) (2009)
Television broadcast stations: 1 (2009)

Internet country code: .ad

Internet hosts: 28,383 (2012)
country comparison to the world: 109

Internet users: *total:* 76,300
percent of population: 89.3% (2014 est.)
country comparison to the world: 176

TRANSPORTATION

Roadways: *total:* 320 km (2008)
country comparison to the world: 203

MILITARY AND SECURITY

Military branches: no regular military forces, Police Service of Andorra (2011)

Military—note: defense is the responsibility of France and Spain

TRANSNATIONAL ISSUES

Disputes—international: none

ANGOLA

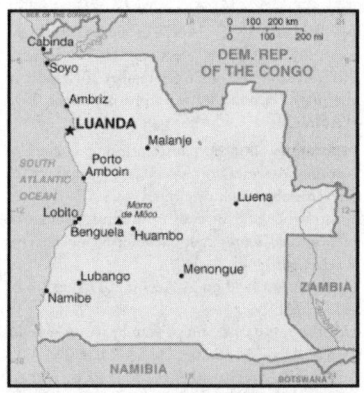

INTRODUCTION

Background: Angola is still rebuilding its country since the end of a 27year civil war in 2002. Fighting between the Popular Movement for the Liberation of Angola (MPLA), led by Jose Eduardo DOS SANTOS, and the National Union for the Total Independence of Angola (UNITA), led by Jonas SAVIMBI, followed independence from Portugal in 1975. Peace seemed imminent in 1992 when Angola held national elections, but fighting picked up again in 1993. Up to 1.5 million lives may have been lost and 4 million people displaced—during the more than a quarter century of fighting. SAVIMBI's death in 2002 ended UNITA's insurgency and cemented the MPLA's hold on power. President DOS SANTOS pushed through a newconstitution in 2010 and elections held in 2012 saw him installed as president. Angola assumed a nonpermanent seat on the UN Security Council for the 2015–16 term.

GEOGRAPHY

Location: Southern Africa, bordering the South Atlantic Ocean, between Namibia and Democratic Republic of the Congo

Geographic coordinates: 12 30 S, 18 30 E

Map references: Africa

Area: *total:* 1,246,700 sq km
land: 1,246,700 sq km
water: 0 sq km
country comparison to the world: 23

Area—comparative: slightly less than twice the size of Texas

Land boundaries: *total:* 5,369 km
border countries (4): Democratic Republic of the Congo 2,646 km (of which 225 km is the boundary of discontiguous Cabinda Province), Republic of the Congo 231 km, Namibia 1,427 km, Zambia 1,065 km

Coastline: 1,600 km

Maritime claims: *territorial sea:* 12 nm
contiguous zone: 24 nm
exclusive economic zone: 200 nm

Climate: semiarid in south and along coast to Luanda; north has cool, dry season (May to October) and hot, rainy season (November to April)

Terrain: narrow coastal plain rises abruptly to vast interior plateau

Elevation: *mean elevation:* 1,112 m

elevation extremes: *lowest point:* Atlantic Ocean 0 m
highest point: Moca 2,620 m

Natural resources: petroleum, diamonds, iron ore, phosphates, copper, feldspar, gold, bauxite, uranium

Land use: *agricultural land:* 47.3%
arable land: 3.8%
permanent crops: 0.2%
permanent pasture: 43.3%
forest: 46.8%
other: 5.9% (2011 est.)

Irrigated land: 860 sq km (2012)

Total renewable water resources: 148 cu km (2011)

Freshwater withdrawal (domestic/industrial/agricultural): *total:* 0.71 cu km/yr (45%/34%/21%)
per capita: 40.27 cu m/yr (2005)

Natural hazards: locally heavy rainfall causes periodic flooding on the plateau

Environment current issues: overuse of pastures and subsequent soil erosion attributable to population pressures; desertification; deforestation of tropical rain forest, in response to both international demand for tropical timber and to domestic use as fuel, resulting in loss of biodiversity; soil erosion contributing to water pollution and siltation of rivers and dams; inadequate supplies of potable water

Environment—international agreements: *party to:* Biodiversity, Climate Change, Climate Change-Kyoto Protocol, Desertification, Law of the Sea, Marine Dumping, Ozone Layer Protection, Ship Pollution
signed, but not ratified: none of the selected agreements

Geography—note: the province of Cabinda is an exclave, separated from the rest of the country by the Democratic Republicof the Congo

PEOPLE AND SOCIETY

Nationality: *noun:* Angolan(s)
adjective: Angolan

Ethnic groups: Ovimbundu 37%, Kimbundu 25%, Bakongo 13%, mestico (mixed European and native African) 2%, European 1%, other 22%

Languages: Portuguese 71.2% (official), Umbundu 23%, Kikongo 8.2%, Kimbundu 7.8%, Chokwe 6.5%, Nhaneca 3.4%, Nganguela 3.1%, Fiote 2.4%, Kwanhama 2.3%, Muhumbi 2.1%, Luvale 1%, other 3.6%
note: most widely spoken languages; shares sum to more than 100% because some respondents gave more than one answer on the census (2014 est.)

Religions: Roman Catholic 41.1%, Protestant 38.1%, other 8.6%, none 12.3% (2014 est.)

Population: 19,625,353
note: results from Angola's 2014 national census estimate the country's population to be 25.8 million (July 2015 est.)
country comparison to the world: 59

Age structure: *0–14 years:* 42.95% (male 4,297,988/female 4,131,037)
15–24 years: 20.65% (male 2,061,704/female 1,990,206)
25–54 years: 29.46% (male 2,916,132/female 2,865,417)
55–64 years: 3.98% (male 379,531/female 401,563)
65 years and over: 2.96% (male 269,164/female 312,611) (2015 est.)

Dependency ratios:
total dependency ratio: 99.9%
youth dependency ratio: 95.2%
elderly dependency ratio: 4.6%
potential support ratio: 21.6% (2015 est.)

Median age: *total:* 18 years
male: 17.8 years
female: 18.2 years (2015 est.)
country comparison to the world: 214

Population growth rate: 2.78% (2015 est.)
country comparison to the world: 16

Birth rate: 38.78 births/1,000 population (2015 est.)
country comparison to the world: 9

Death rate: 11.49 deaths/1,000 population (2015 est.)
country comparison to the world: 29

Net migration rate: 0.46 migrant(s)/1,000 population (2015 est.)
country comparison to the world: 71

Urbanization: *urban population:* 44% of total population (2015)
rate of urbanization: 4.97% annual rate of change (2010–15 est.)

Major urban areas—population: LUANDA (capital) 5.506 million; Huambo 1.269 million (2015)

Sex ratio: *at birth:* 1.05 male(s)/female
0–14 years: 1.04 male(s)/female
15–24 years: 1.04 male(s)/female
25–54 years: 1.02 male(s)/female
55–64 years: 0.95 male(s)/female
65 years and over: 0.86 male(s)/female
total population: 1.02 male(s)/female (2015 est.)

Mother's mean age at first birth: 18 (2008/09 est.)

Maternal mortality rate: 477 deaths/100,000 live births (2015 est.)
country comparison to the world: 25

Infant mortality rate: *total:* 78.26 deaths/1,000 live births
male: 81.96 deaths/1,000 live births
female: 74.38 deaths/1,000 live births (2015 est.)
country comparison to the world: 8

Life expectancy at birth: *total population:* 55.63 years
male: 54.49 years
female: 56.84 years (2015 est.)
country comparison to the world: 207

Total fertility rate: 5.37 children born/woman (2015 est.)
country comparison to the world: 9

Contraceptive prevalence rate: 17.7% (2008/09)

Health expenditures: 3.8% of GDP (2013)
country comparison to the world: 172

Physicians density: 0.17 physicians/1,000 population (2009)

Drinking water source: *improved:*
urban: 75.4% of population
rural: 28.2% of population
total: 49% of population
unimproved:
urban: 24.6% of population
rural: 71.8% of population
total: 51% of population (2015 est.)

Sanitation facility access: *improved:*
urban: 88.6% of population
rural: 22.5% of population
total: 51.6% of population
unimproved:
urban: 11.4% of population
rural: 77.5% of population
total: 48.4% of population (2015 est.)

HIV/AIDS adult prevalence rate: 2.41% (2014 est.)
country comparison to the world: 25

HIV/AIDS people living with HIV/AIDS: 304,400 (2014 est.)
country comparison to the world: 21

HIV/AIDS deaths: 11,770 (2014 est.)
country comparison to the world: 20

Major infectious diseases: *degree of risk:* very high
food or waterborne diseases: bacterial and protozoal diarrhea, hepatitis A, typhoid fever
vectorborne diseases: dengue fever, malaria
water contact disease: schistosomiasis
animal contact disease: rabies (2013)

Obesity adult prevalence rate: 8.5% (2014)
country comparison to the world: 147

Children under the age of 5 years underweight: 15.6% (2007)
country comparison to the world: 45

Education expenditures: 3.4% of GDP (2010)
country comparison to the world: 127

Literacy: *definition:* age 15 and over can read and write
total population: 71.1%
male: 82%

female: 60.7% (2015 est.)

School life expectancy (primary to tertiary education): *total:* 10 years
male: 13 years
female: 8 years (2011)

Child labor—children ages 5–14:
total number: 832,895
percentage: 24% (2001 est.)

GOVERNMENT

Country name: *conventional long form:* Republic of Angola
conventional short form: Angola
local long form: Republica de Angola
local short form: Angola
former: People's Republic of Angola
etymology: name derived by the Portuguese from the title "ngola" held by kings of the Ndongo (Ndongo was a kingdom in what is now northern Angola)

Government type: presidential republic

Capital: *name:* Luanda

Geographic coordinates: 8 50 S, 13 13 E
time difference: UTC+1 (6 hours ahead of Washington, DC, during Standard Time)

Administrative divisions: 18 provinces (provincias, singular provincia); Bengo, Benguela, Bie, Cabinda, Cunene, Huambo, Huila, Kwando Kubango, Kwanza Norte, Kwanza Sul, Luanda, Lunda Norte, Lunda Sul, Malanje, Moxico, Namibe, Uige, Zaire

Independence: 11 November 1975 (from Portugal)

National holiday: Independence Day, 11 November (1975)

Constitution: previous 1975, 1992; latest passed by National Assembly 21 January 2010, adopted 5 February 2010 (2016)

Legal system: civil legal system based on Portuguese civil law; no judicial review of legislation

International law organization participation: has not submitted an ICJ jurisdiction declaration; nonparty state to the ICCt

Citizenship: *citizenship by birth:* no
citizenship by descent only: at least one parent must be a citizen of Angola
dual citizenship recognized: no
residency requirement for naturalization: 10 years

Suffrage: 18 years of age; universal

Executive branch: *chief of state:* President Jose Eduardo DOS SANTOS (since 21 September 1979); Vice President Manuel Domingos VICENTE (since 26 September 2012); note—the president is both chief of state and head of government
head of government: President Jose Eduardo DOS SANTOS (since 21 September 1979); Vice President Manuel Domingos VICENTE (since 26 September 2012)
cabinet: Council of Ministers appointed by the president
elections/appointments: president indirectly elected by the National Assembly for a 5-year term

(eligible for a second consecutive or discontinuous term); note—according to the 2010 constitution, ballots are cast for parties rather than candidates, and the leader of the winning party becomes presidentelection results: NA; as leader of the MPLA, Jose Eduardo DOS SANTOS elected president following legislative elections on 31 August 2012, inaugurated on 26 September 2012 to serve the first of a possible two terms under the 2010 constitution

Legislative branch: *description:* unicameral National Assembly or Assembleia Nacional (220 seats; members directly elected in a single national constituency and in multi-seat constituencies by proportional representation vote; members serve 5-year terms)
elections: last held on 31 August 2012 (next to be held in 2017)
election results: percent of vote by party—MPLA 71.8%, UNITA 18.7%, CASA-CE 6.0%, PRS 1.7%, FNLA 1.1%, other 0.7%; seats by party—MPLA 175, UNITA 32, CASA-CE 8, PRS 3, FNLA 2

Judicial branch: *highest court(s):* Supreme Court or Tribunal da Relacao (consists of the chief justice and 16 judges; Constitutional Court or Tribunal Constitucional—legislative review (consists of 11 members)
judge selection and term of office: Supreme Court judges appointed by the president upon recommendation of the Supreme Judicial Council, an 18-member body presided over by the president; judge tenure NA; Constitutional Court judges—4 nominated by the president, 4 elected by National Assembly, 2 elected by Supreme National Council, 1 elected by competitive submission of curricula; judges serve single 7-year terms
subordinate courts: provincial and municipal courts

Political parties and leaders: Broad Convergence for the Salvation of Angola Electoral Coalition or CASA-CE [Abel CHIVUKUVUKU]
National Front for the Liberation of Angola or FNLA [Lucas NGONDA]
National Union for the Total Independence of Angola or UNITA [Isaias SAMAKUVA] (largest oppositionparty)
Popular Movement for the Liberation of Angola or MPLA [Jose Eduardo DOS SANTOS] (ruling party inpower since 1975)
Social Renewal Party or PRS [Eduardo KUANGANA]

Political pressure groups and leaders: Angolan Revolutionary Movement or ARM
Front for the Liberation of the Enclave of Cabinda or FLEC [N'zita Henriques TIAGO]
note: FLEC's small-scale armed struggle for the independence of Cabinda Province persists despite the signing of a peace accord with the government in August 2006; several factions of FLEC have broken off over the past 30 years, including the FLEC-PM [Rodrigues MINGAS], which was responsible for a deadly attack on the Togolese soccer team in 2010

International organization participation: ACP, AfDB, AU, CEMAC, CPLP, FAO, G77, IAEA, IBRD, ICAO, ICRM, IDA, IFAD, IFC, IFRCS, ILO, IMF, IMO, Interpol, IOC, IOM, IPU, ISO (correspondent), ITSO, ITU, ITUC (NGOs), MIGA, NAM, OAS (observer), OPEC, SADC, UN, UN Security Council (temporary), UNCTAD, UNESCO, UNIDO, Union Latina, UNWTO, UPU, WCO, WFTU (NGOs), WHO, WIPO, WMO, WTO

Diplomatic representation in the US: *chief of mission:* Ambassador Agostinho Tavares da Silva NETO (since 18 November 2014)
chancery: 2100–2108 16th Street NW, Washington, DC 20009
telephone: [1] (202) 785-1156
FAX: [1] (202) 822-9049
consulate(s) general: Houston, New York

Diplomatic representation from the US: *chief of mission:* Ambassador Helen Meagher LA LIME (15 May 2014)
embassy: number 32 Rua Houari Boumedienne (in the Miramar area of Luanda), Luanda
mailing address: international mail: Caixa Postal 6468, Luanda; pouch: US Embassy Luanda, US Department of State, 2550 Luanda Place, Washington, DC 20521–2550
telephone: [244] 946-44-0977
FAX: [244] (222) 641-000

Flag description: two equal horizontal bands of red (top) and black with a centered yellow emblem consisting of a five-pointed star within half a cogwheel crossed by a machete (in the style of a hammer and sickle); red represents liberty, black the African continent, the symbols characterize workers and peasants

National symbol(s): Palanca Negra Gigante (giant black sable antelope); national colors: red, black, yellow

National anthem: *name:* "Angola Avante" (Forward Angola)
lyrics/music: Manuel Rui Alves MONTEIRO/Rui Alberto Vieira Dias MINGAO
note: adopted 1975

ECONOMY

Economy overview: Angola's economy is overwhelmingly driven by its oil sector. Oil production and its supporting activities contribute about 50% of GDP, more than 70% of government revenue, and more than 90% of the country's exports. Diamonds contribute an additional 5% to exports. Subsistence agriculture provides the main livelihood for most of the people, but half of the country's food is still imported. Increased oil production supported growth averaging more than 17% per year from 2004 to 2008. A postwar reconstruction boom and resettlement of displaced persons has led to high rates of growth in construction and agriculture as well. Some of the country's infrastructure is still damaged or undeveloped from the 27-year-long civil war. However, the government since 2005 has used billions of dollars in credit lines from China, Brazil, Portugal, Germany, Spain, and the EU to help rebuild Angola's public infrastructure. Land mines left from the war still mar the countryside, and as a result, the national military, international partners, and private Angolan firms all continue to remove them. The global recession that started in 2008 stalled economic growth. In particular, lower prices for oil and diamonds during the global recession slowed GDP growth to 2.4% in 2009, and many construction projects stopped because Luanda accrued $9 billion in arrears to foreign construction companies when government revenue fell in 2008 and 2009. Angola formally abandoned its currency peg in 2009, and in November 2009 signed onto an IMF Stand-By Arrangement loan of $1.4 billion to rebuild international reserves. Consumer inflation declined from 325% in 2000 to less than 9% in 2014. Falling oil prices and slower than expected growth in non-oil GDP have reduced growth prospects for 2015. Angola has responded by reducing government subsidies and by proposing import quotas and a more restrictive licensing regime. Corruption, especially in the extractive sectors, is a major long-term challenge.

GDP (purchasing power parity):
$184.4 billion (2015 est.)
$179.1 billion (2014 est.)
$170.9 billion (2013 est.)
note: data are in 2015 US dollars
country comparison to the world: 65

GDP (official exchange rate): $103 billion (2015 est.)

GDP real growth rate:
3% (2015 est.)
4.8% (2014 est.)
6.8% (2013 est.)
country comparison to the world: 97

GDP—per capita (PPP):
$7,300 (2015 est.)
$7,300 (2014 est.)
$7,200 (2013 est.)
note: data are in 2015 US dollars
country comparison to the world: 154

Gross national saving:
0.8% of GDP (2015 est.)
12.4% of GDP (2014 est.)
21.4% of GDP (2013 est.)
country comparison to the world: 171

GDP—composition, by end use:
household consumption: 54.4%
government consumption: 20.5%
investment in fixed capital: 15.7%
investment in inventories: 0.1%
exports of goods and services: 43.8%
imports of goods and services: -34.5% (2015 est.)

GDP—composition, by sector of origin:
agriculture: 10.2%
industry: 61.4%
services: 28.4% (2011 est.)

Agriculture—products: bananas, sugarcane, coffee, sisal, corn, cotton, cassava (manioc, tapioca), tobacco, vegetables, plantains; livestock; forest products; fish

Industries: petroleum; diamonds, iron ore, phosphates, feldspar, bauxite, uranium, and gold; cement; basic metal products; fish processing; food processing, brewing, tobacco products, sugar; textiles; ship repair

Industrial production growth rate: 1.8% (2015 est.)
country comparison to the world: 120

Labor force: 10.51 million (2015 est.)
country comparison to the world: 52

Labor force—by occupation: *agriculture:* 85%
industry and services: 15% (2003 est.)

Unemployment rate: NA%

Population below poverty line: 40.5% (2006 est.)

Household income or consumption by percentage share: *lowest:* 10%: 0.6%
highest: 10%: 44.7% (2000)

Budget: *revenues:* $35.43 billion
expenditures: $41.83 billion (2015 est.)
Taxes and other revenues: 34.7% of GDP (2015 est.)
country comparison to the world: 60

Budget surplus (+) or deficit (–): -6.3% of GDP (2015 est.)
country comparison to the world: 183

Public debt: 56.7% of GDP (2015 est.)
34.9% of GDP (2014 est.)
country comparison to the world: 68

Fiscal year: calendar year

Inflation rate (consumer prices): 10.3% (2015 est.)
7.3% (2014 est.)
country comparison to the world: 212

Central bank discount rate: 9% (31 December 2014)
25% (31 December 2010)
country comparison to the world: 35

Commercial bank prime lending rate: 17.5% (31 December 2015 est.)
16.38% (31 December 2014 est.)
country comparison to the world: 22

Stock of narrow money:
$23.01 billion (31 December 2015 est.)
$30.11 billion (31 December 2014 est.)
country comparison to the world: 63

Stock of broad money: $51.71 billion (31 December 2014 est.)
$45.06 billion (31 December 2013 est.)
country comparison to the world: 68

Stock of domestic credit: $16.81 billion (31 December 2015 est.)
$23.12 billion (31 December 2014 est.)
country comparison to the world: 90

Current account balance: -$ 8.748 billion (2015 est.)
-$ 3.722 billion (2014 est.)
country comparison to the world: 177

Exports: $37.38 billion (2015 est.)
$59.98 billion (2014 est.)
country comparison to the world: 57

Exports—commodities: crude oil, diamonds, refined petroleum products, coffee, sisal, fish and fish products, timber, cotton

Exports—partners: China 43.8%, India 9.6%, US 7.7%, Spain 6.2%, South Africa 4.8%, France 4.4% (2015)

Imports: $21.93 billion (2015 est.)
$29.24 billion (2014 est.)
country comparison to the world: 71

Imports—commodities: machinery and electrical equipment, vehicles and spare parts; medicines, food, textiles, military goods

Imports—partners: China 22.1%, Portugal 13.8%, South Korea 11%, US 6.9%, South Africa 5%, UK 4.1%, France 4% (2015)

Reserves of foreign exchange and gold: $18.46 billion (31 December 2015 est.)
$27.09 billion (31 December 2014 est.)
country comparison to the world: 61

Debt—external: $28.62 billion (31 December 2014 est.)
$24 billion (31 December 2013 est.)
country comparison to the world: 75

Stock of direct foreign investment—at home: $13.01 billion (31 December 2015 est.)
$10.57 billion (31 December 2014 est.)
country comparison to the world: 89

Stock of direct foreign investment—abroad: $27.25 billion (31 December 2015 est.)
$23.44 billion (31 December 2014 est.)
country comparison to the world: 53

Exchange rates: kwanza (AOA) per US dollar—
121.9 (2015 est.)
98.303 (2014 est.)
98.303 (2013 est.)
95.47 (2012 est.)
93.741 (2011 est.)

ENERGY

Electricity production: 5.475 billion kWh (2012 est.)
country comparison to the world: 117

Electricity—consumption: 4.842 billion kWh (2012 est.)
country comparison to the world: 117

Electricity—exports: 0 kWh (2013 est.)
country comparison to the world: 100

Electricity—imports: 0 kWh (2013 est.)
country comparison to the world: 116

Electricity—installed generating capacity: 1.53 million kW (2012 est.)
country comparison to the world: 117

Electricity—from fossil fuels: 50.3% of total installed capacity (2012 est.)
country comparison to the world: 148

Electricity—from nuclear fuels: 0% of total installed capacity (2012 est.)
country comparison to the world: 42

Electricity—from hydro electric plants: 49.7% of total installed capacity (2012 est.)
country comparison to the world: 49

Electricity—from other renewable sources: 0% of total installed capacity (2012 est.)
country comparison to the world: 153

Crude oil—production: 1.742 million bbl/day (2014 est.)
country comparison to the world: 14

Crude oil—exports: 1.815 million bbl/day (2012 est.)
country comparison to the world: 8

Crude oil—imports: 0 bbl/day (2012 est.)
country comparison to the world: 156

Crude oil—proved reserves: 9.011 billion bbl (1 January 2015 est.)
country comparison to the world: 18

Refined petroleum products—production: 40,010 bbl/day (2012 est.)
country comparison to the world: 84

Refined petroleum products—consumption: 112,000 bbl/day (2013 est.)
country comparison to the world: 74

Refined petroleum products—exports: 21,740 bbl/day (2012 est.)
country comparison to the world: 71

Refined petroleum products—imports: 75,790 bbl/day (2012 est.)
country comparison to the world: 59

Natural gas—production: 925 million cu m (2013 est.)
country comparison to the world: 67

Natural gas—consumption: 495 million cu m (2013 est.)
country comparison to the world: 98

Natural gas—exports: 0 cu m (2012 est.)
country comparison to the world: 57

Natural gas—imports: 0 cu m (2013 est.)
country comparison to the world: 156

Natural gas—proved reserves: 275 billion cu m (1 January 2014 est.)
country comparison to the world: 41

Carbon dioxide emissions from consumption of energy: 31.61 million Mt (2012 est.)
country comparison to the world: 74

COMMUNICATIONS

Telephones—fixed lines: *total subscriptions:* 280,000
subscriptions per 100 inhabitants: 1 (2014 est.)
country comparison to the world: 117

Telephones—mobile cellular: *total:* 14.1 million
subscriptions per 100 inhabitants: 74 (2014 est.)
country comparison to the world: 69

Telephone system: *general assessment:* limited system; state-owned telecom had monopoly for fixed lines until 2005; demand outstripped capacity, prices were high, and services poor; Telecom Namibia, through an Angolan company, became the first private licensed operator in Angola's fixed-line telephone network; by 2010, the number of fixed-line providers had expanded to 5; Angola Telecom established mobile-cellular service in Luanda in 1993 and the network has been extended to larger towns; a privately owned, mobile-cellular service provider began operations in 2001

domestic: about two fixed lines per 100 persons; mobile-cellular teledensity about 50 telephones per 100 persons in 2011

international: country code—244; landing point for the SAT3/WASC fiber-optic submarine cable that provides connectivity to Europe and Asia; satellite earth stations—29 (2009)

Broadcast media: state controls all broadcast media with nationwide reach; state-owned Televisao Popular de Angola (TPA) provides terrestrial TV service on 2 channels; a third TPA channel is available via cable and satellite; TV subscription services are available; state-owned Radio Nacional de Angola (RNA) broadcasts on 5 stations; about a half dozen private radio stations broadcast locally (2008)

Radio broadcast stations: AM 21, FM 6, shortwave 7 (2001)
Television broadcast stations: 6 (2000)

Internet country code: .ao

Internet hosts: 20,703 (2012)
country comparison to the world: 116

Internet users: *total:* 3.7 million
percent of population: 19.4% (2014 est.)
country comparison to the world: 81

TRANSPORTATION

Airports: 176 (2013)
country comparison to the world: 32

Airports—with paved runways: *total:* 31
over 3,047 m: 7
2,438 to 3,047 m: 8
1,524 to 2,437 m: 12
914 to 1,523 m: 4 (2013)

Airports—with unpaved runways: *total:* 145
over 3,047 m: 2
2,438 to 3,047 m: 3
1,524 to 2,437 m: 31
914 to 1,523 m: 66
under 914 m: 43 (2013)

Heliports: 1 (2013)

Pipelines: gas 352 km; liquid petroleum gas 85 km; oil 1,065 km; oil/gas/water 5 km (2013)

Railways: *total:* 2,852 km
narrow gauge: 2,729 km 1.067-m gauge; 123 km 0.600-m gauge (2014)
country comparison to the world: 60

Roadways: *total:* 51,429 km
paved: 5,349 km
unpaved: 46,080 km (2001)
country comparison to the world: 75

Waterways: 1,300 km (2011)
country comparison to the world: 54

Merchant marine: *total:* 7
by type: cargo 1, chemical tanker 1, passenger/cargo 2, petroleum tanker 2, roll on/roll off 1
foreign-owned: 1 (Spain 1)
registered in other countries: 17 (Bahamas 6, Curacao 2, Cyprus 1, Liberia 1, Malta 7) (2010)
country comparison to the world: 123

Ports and terminals: *major seaport(s):* Cabinda, Lobito, Luanda, Namibe
LNG terminal(s) (export): Angola Soyo

ANGUILLA

MILITARY AND SECURITY

Military branches: Angolan Armed Forces (Forcas Armadas Angolanas, FAA): Army, Navy (Marinha de Guerra Angola, MGA), Angolan National Air Force (Forca Aerea Nacional Angolana, FANA; under operational control of the Army) (2012)

Military service age and obligation: 20–45 years of age for compulsory male and 18–45 years for voluntary male military service (registrationat age 18 is mandatory); 20–45 years of age for voluntary female service; 2-year conscript service obligation; Angolan citizenship required; the Navy (MGA) is entirely staffed with volunteers (2013)

Military expenditures:
3.63% of GDP (2012)
3.5% of GDP (2011)
3.63% of GDP (2010)
country comparison to the world: 13

TRANSNATIONAL ISSUES

Disputes—international: Democratic Republic of Congo accuses Angola of shifting monuments

Refugees and internally displaced persons: *refugees (country of origin):* 12,944 (Democratic Republic of the Congo) (2014)

Illicit drugs: used as a transshipment point for cocaine destined for Western Europe and other African states, particularly South Africa

ANGUILLA

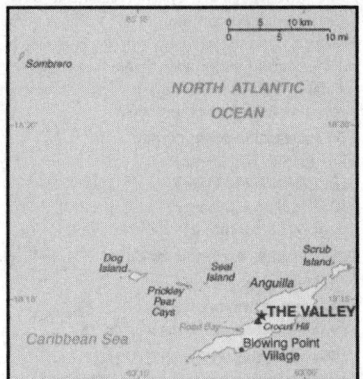

INTRODUCTION

Background: Colonized by English settlers from Saint Kitts in 1650, Anguilla was administered by Great Britain until the early 19th century, when the island—against the wishes of the inhabitants—was incorporated into a single British dependency along with Saint Kitts and Nevis. Several attempts at separation failed. In 1971, two years after a revolt, Anguilla was finally allowed to secede; this arrangement was formally recognized in 1980, with Anguilla becoming a separate British dependency.

GEOGRAPHY

Location: Caribbean, islands between the Caribbean Sea and North Atlantic Ocean, east of Puerto Rico

Geographic coordinates: 18 15 N, 63 10 W

Map references: Central America and the Caribbean

Area: *total:* 91 sq km
land: 91 sq km
water: 0 sq km
country comparison to the world: 227

Area—comparative: about one-half the size of Washington, DC

Land boundaries: 0 km

Coastline: 61 km

Maritime claims:
territorial sea: 3 nm
exclusive fishing zone: 200 nm

Climate: tropical; moderated by northeast trade winds

Terrain: flat and low-lying island of coral and limestone

Elevation: *mean elevation:* NA

elevation extremes: *lowest point:* Caribbean Sea 0 m
highest point: Crocus Hill 65 m

Natural resources: salt, fish, lobster

Land use: *agricultural land:* 0%
arable land: 0%
permanent crops: 0%
permanent pasture: 0%
forest: 61.1%
other: 38.9% (mostly rock with some commercial salt ponds) (2011 est.)

Irrigated land: 0 sq km (2012)

Natural hazards: frequent hurricanes and other tropical storms (July to October)

Environment—current issues: supplies of potable water sometimes cannot meet increasing demand largely because of poor distribution system

Geography—note: the most northerly of the Leeward Islands in the Lesser Antilles

PEOPLE AND SOCIETY

Nationality: *noun:* Anguillan(s)
adjective: Anguillan

Ethnic groups: African/black 85.3%, hispanic 4.9%, mixed 3.8%, white 3.2%, East Indian/Indian 1%, other 1.6%, unspecified 0.3% (2011 est.)

Languages: English (official)

Religions: Protestant 73.2% (includes Anglican 22.7%, Methodist 19.4%, Pentecostal 10.5%, Seventh Day Adventist 8.3%, Baptist 7.1%, Church of God 4.9%, Presbyterian 0.2%, Brethren 0.1%), Roman Catholic 6.8%, Jehovah's Witness 1.1%, other Christian 10.9%, other 3.2%, unspecified 0.3%, none 4.5% (2011 est.)

Population: 16,418 (July 2015 est.)
country comparison to the world: 221

Age structure: *0–14 years:* 22.84% (male 1,917/female 1,833)
15–24 years: 14.06% (male 1,150/female 1,159)
25–54 years: 44.73% (male 3,312/female 4,032)
55–64 years: 9.88% (male 783/female 839)
65 years and over: 8.48% (male 690/female 703) (2015 est.)

Median age: *total:* 34.3 years
male: 32.5 years
female: 36.1 years (2015 est.)
country comparison to the world: 79

Population growth rate: 2.03% (2015 est.)
country comparison to the world: 48

Birth rate: 12.67 births/1,000 population (2015 est.)
country comparison to the world: 156

Death rate: 4.57 deaths/1,000 population (2015 est.)
country comparison to the world: 199

Net migration rate: 12.18 migrant(s)/1,000 population (2015 est.)
country comparison to the world: 8

Urbanization: *urban population:* 100% of total population (2015)
rate of urbanization: 1.19% annual rate of change (2010–15 est.)

Major urban areas—population: THE VALLEY (capital) 1,000 (2014)

Sex ratio: *at birth:* 1.04 male(s)/female
0–14 years: 1.05 male(s)/female
15–24 years: 0.99 male(s)/female
25–54 years: 0.82 male(s)/female
55–64 years: 0.93 male(s)/female
65 years and over: 0.98 male(s)/female
total population: 0.92 male(s)/female (2015 est.)

Infant mortality rate: *total:* 3.37 deaths/1,000 live births
male: 3.78 deaths/1,000 live births
female: 2.95 deaths/1,000 live births (2015 est.)
country comparison to the world: 210

Life expectancy at birth: *total population:* 81.31 years
male: 78.71 years
female: 83.98 years (2015 est.)
country comparison to the world: 23

Total fertility rate: 1.75 children born/woman (2015 est.)
country comparison to the world: 163

Contraceptive prevalence rate: 43%
note: percent of women aged 15–45 (2003)

Drinking water source: *improved:*
urban: 94.6% of population
rural: NA
total: 94.6% of population
unimproved:
urban: 5.4% of population
rural: NA
total: 5.4% of population (2015 est.)

Sanitation facility access: *improved:*
urban: 97.9% of population
rural: NA
total: 97.9% of population
unimproved:
urban: 2.1% of population
rural: NA
total: 2.1% of population (2015 est.)

HIV/AIDS—adult prevalence rate: NA

HIV/AIDS—people living with HIV/AIDS: NA

HIV/AIDS—deaths: NA

Education expenditures: 2.8% of GDP (2008)
country comparison to the world: 146

GOVERNMENT

Country name: *conventional long form:* none
conventional short form: Anguilla
etymology: the name Anguilla means "eel" in various Romance languages (Spanish, Italian, Portuguese, French) and likely derives from the island's lengthy shape

Dependency status: overseas territory of the UK

Government type: parliamentary democracy (House of Assembly); self-governing overseas territory of the UK

Capital: *name:* The Valley

Geographic coordinates: 18 13 N, 63 03 W
time difference: UTC-4 (1 hour ahead of Washington, DC, during Standard Time)

Administrative divisions: none (overseas territory of the UK)

Independence: none (overseas territory of the UK)

National holiday: Anguilla Day, 30 May (1967)

Constitution: several previous; latest 1 April 1982; amended 1990 (2016)

Legal system: common law based on the English model

Citizenship: see United Kingdom

Suffrage: 18 years of age; universal

Executive branch: *chief of state:* Queen ELIZABETH II (since 6 February 1952); represented by Governor Christina SCOTT (since 23 July 2013)

head of government: Chief Minister Hubert HUGHES (since 16 February 2010)
cabinet: Executive Council appointed by the governor from among elected members of the House of Assembly
elections/appointments: the monarchy is hereditary; governor appointed by the monarch; following legislative elections, the leader of the majority party or majority coalition usually appointed chief minister by the governor

Legislative branch: *description:* unicameral House of Assembly (11 seats; seven members directly elected in single-seat constituencies by simple majority vote, two appointed by the governor, and two ex officio members—the attorney general and deputy governor; members serve five-year terms)
elections: last held on 22 April 2015 (next to be held in 2015)
election results: percent of vote by party—AUF 54.4%, AUM 38.3%, DOVE 1.4%, independent 5.9%; seats by party—AUF 6, independent 1

Judicial branch: *highest court(s):* the Eastern Caribbean Supreme Court (ECSC) is the itinerant superior court of record for the 9-member Organization of Eastern Caribbean States to include Anguilla; the ECSC—headquartered on St. Lucia—is headed by the chief justice and is comprised of the Court of Appeal with 3 justices and the High Court with 16 judges; sittings of the Court of Appeal and High Court rotate among the 9 member states; High Court judges reside in 7 member states, though none resides on Anguilla
judge selection and term of office: Eastern Caribbean Supreme Court chief justice appointed by Her Majesty, Queen ELIZABETH II; other justices and judges appointed by the Judicial and Legal Services Commission; Court of Appeal justices appointed for life with mandatory retirement at age 65; High Court judges appointed for life with mandatory retirement at age 62
subordinate courts: Magistrate's Court; Juvenile Court

Political parties and leaders: Anguilla United Front or AUF [Victor BANKS] (an alliance of the Anguilla Democratic Party or ADP and the Anguilla National Alliance or ANA)
Anguilla United Movement or AUM [Dr. Ellis WEBSTER] Democracy, Opportunity, Vision, and Empowerment Party or DOVE [Sutcliffe HODGE]

International organization participation: Caricom (associate), CDB, Interpol (subbureau), OECS, UNESCO (associate), UPU

Diplomatic representation in the US: none (overseas territory of the UK)

Diplomatic representation from the US: none (overseas territory of the UK)

Flag description: blue, with the flag of the UK in the upper hoist-side quadrant and the Anguillan coat of arms centered in the outer half of the flag; the coat of arms depicts three orange dolphins in an interlocking circular design on a white background with a turquoise-blue field below; the white in the background represents peace; the blue base symbolizes the surrounding sea, as well as faith, youth, and hope; the three dolphins stand for endurance, unity, and strength

National symbol(s): dolphin

National anthem: *name:* "God Bless Anguilla"
lyrics/music: Alex RICHARDSON
note: local anthem adopted 1981; as a territory of the United Kingdom, "God Save the Queen" is official (see United Kingdom)

ECONOMY

Economy overview: Anguilla has few natural resources, and the economy depends heavily on luxury tourism, offshore banking, lobster fishing, and remittances from emigrants. Increased activity in the tourism industry has spurred the growth of the construction sector contributing to economic growth. Anguillan officials have put substantial effort into developing the offshore financial sector, which is small but growing. In the medium term, prospects for the economy will depend largely on the tourism sector and, therefore, on revived income growth in the industrialized nations as well as on favorable weather conditions.

GDP (purchasing power parity):
$175.4 million (2009 est.)
$191.7 million (2008 est.)
$108.9 million (2004 est.)
country comparison to the world: 221

GDP (official exchange rate): $175.4 million (2009 est.)

GDP—real growth rate: -8.5% (2009 est.)
country comparison to the world: 218

GDP—per capita (PPP): $12,200 (2008 est.)
country comparison to the world: 123

GDP—composition, by end use:
household consumption: 74.9%
government consumption: 20.7%
investment in fixed capital: 20.9%
investment in inventories: 0%
exports of goods and services: 38.8%
imports of goods and services: -55.3% (2015 est.)

GDP—composition, by sector of origin:
agriculture: 2.6%
industry: 24.6%
services: 72.7% (2015 est.)

Agriculture—products: small quantities of tobacco, vegetables; cattle raising

Industries: tourism, boat building, offshore financial services

Industrial production growth rate: 2% (2015 est.)
country comparison to the world: 119

Labor force: 6,049 (2001)
country comparison to the world: 220

Labor force—by occupation: *agriculture/fishing/forestry/mining:* 4%
manufacturing: 3%
construction: 18%
transportation and utilities: 10%
commerce: 36%
services: 29% (2000 est.)

Unemployment rate: 8% (2002)
country comparison to the world: 92

Population below poverty line: 23% (2002 est.)

Household income or consumption by percentage share: *lowest:* 10%: NA%
highest: 10%: NA%

Budget: *revenues:* $64.48 million
expenditures: $71.63 million (2015 est.)
Taxes and other revenues: 36.8% of GDP (2015 est.)
country comparison to the world: 50

Budget surplus (+) or deficit (–): -4.1% of GDP (2015 est.)
country comparison to the world: 147

Public debt: 20.1% of GDP (2015 est.)
20.8% of GDP (2014 est.)
country comparison to the world: 154

Fiscal year: 1 April–31 March

Inflation rate (consumer prices):
1.3% (2015 est.)
-0.3% (2014 est.)
country comparison to the world: 91

Central bank discount rate: 6.5% (31 December 2010)
6.5% (31 December 2009)
country comparison to the world: 50

Commercial bank prime lending rate: 9% (31 December 2015 est.)
9.09% (31 December 2014 est.)
country comparison to the world: 96

Stock of narrow money:
$19.74 million (31 December 2015 est.)
$19.08 million (31 December 2014 est.)
country comparison to the world: 191

Stock of broad money: $393 million (31 December 2015 est.)
$385.3 million (31 December 2014 est.)
country comparison to the world: 186

Stock of domestic credit: $440.6 million (31 December 2015 est.)
$435.6 million (31 December 2014 est.)
country comparison to the world: 173

Current account balance: -$ 50.1 million (2015 est.)
-$ 46.9 million (2014 est.)
country comparison to the world: 63

Exports: $6 million (2015 est.)
$6.3 million (2014 est.)
country comparison to the world: 218

Exports—commodities: lobster, fish, livestock, salt, concrete blocks, rum

Imports: $128.6 million (2015 est.)
$128.7 million (2014 est.)
country comparison to the world: 215

Imports—commodities: fuels, foodstuffs, manufactures, chemicals, trucks, textiles

Debt—external:
$8.8 million (1998)
$41.04 million (31 December 2013 est.)
country comparison to the world: 201

Exchange rates: East Caribbean dollars (XCD) per US dollar—
2.7 (2015 est.)
2.7 (2014 est.)
2.7 (2013 est.)
2.7 (2012 est.)
2.7 (2011 est.)

COMMUNICATIONS

Telephones—fixed lines: *total subscriptions:* 5,900
subscriptions per 100 inhabitants: 37 (2014 est.)
country comparison to the world: 206

Telephones—mobile cellular: *total:* 26,000
subscriptions per 100 inhabitants: 162 (2014 est.)
country comparison to the world: 209

Telephone system: *general assessment:* modern internal telephone system
domestic: fixed-line teledensity is roughly 40 per 100 persons; mobile-cellular teledensity is roughly 170 per 100 persons
international: country code—1–264; landing point for the East Caribbean Fiber System submarine cable with links to 13 other islands in the eastern Caribbean extending from the British Virgin Islands to Trinidad; microwave radio relay to island of Saint Martin/Sint Maarten (2011)

Broadcast media: 1 private TV station; multi-channel cable TV subscription services are available; about 10 radio stations, one of which is government-owned (2007)
Radio broadcast stations: AM 3, FM 11, shortwave 2 (2009)
Television broadcast stations: 1 (1997)

Internet country code: .ai

Internet hosts: 269 (2012)
country comparison to the world: 192

Internet users: *total:* 3,700
percent of population: 26% (2009)
country comparison to the world: 208

TRANSPORTATION

Airports: 2 (2013)
country comparison to the world: 197

Airports—with paved runways: *total:* 1
1,524 to 2,437 m: 1 (2013)

Airports—with unpaved runways: *total:* 1
under 914 m: 1 (2013)

Roadways: *total:* 175 km
paved: 82 km
unpaved: 93 km (2004)
country comparison to the world: 211

Ports and terminals: *major seaport(s):* Blowing Point, Road Bay

MILITARY AND SECURITY

Military—note: defense is the responsibility of the UK

TRANSNATIONAL ISSUES

Disputes international: none

Illicit drugs: transshipment point for South American narcotics destined for the US and Europe

---

ANTARCTICA

INTRODUCTION

Background: Speculation over the existence of a "southern land" was not confirmed until the early 1820s when British and American commercial operators and British and Russian national expeditions began exploring the Antarctic Peninsula region and other areas south of the Antarctic Circle. Not until 1840 was it established that Antarctica was indeed a continent and not merely a group of islands or an area of ocean. Several exploration "firsts" were achieved in the early 20th century, but generally the area saw little human activity. Following World War II, however, the continent experienced an upsurge in scientific research. A number of countries have set up a range of year-round and seasonal stations, camps, and refuges to support scientific research in Antarctica. Seven have made territorial claims, but not all countries recognize these claims. In order to form a legal framework for the activities of nations on the continent, an Antarctic Treaty was negotiated that neither denies nor gives recognition to existing territorial claims; signed in 1959, it entered into force in 1961.

GEOGRAPHY

Location: continent mostly south of the Antarctic Circle

Geographic coordinates: 90 00 S, 0 00 E

Map references: Antarctic Region

Area: *total:* 14 million sq km
land: 14 million sq km (280,000 sq km ice-free, 13.72 million sq km ice-covered) (est.)
note: fifth-largest continent, following Asia, Africa, North America, and South America, but larger than Australia and the subcontinent of Europe

Area—comparative: slightly less than 1.5 times the size of the US

Land boundaries: 0 km
note: see entry on Disputes international

Coastline: 17,968 km

Maritime claims: Australia, Chile, and Argentina claim Exclusive Economic Zone (EEZ) rights or similar over 200 nm extensions seaward from their

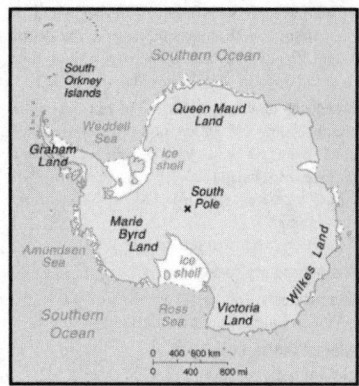

continental claims, but like the claims themselves, these zones are not Aaccepted by other countries; 22 of 29 Antarctic consultative nations have made no claims to Antarctic territory (although Russia and the US have reserved the right to do so) and do not recognize the claims of the other nations; also see the Disputes—international entry

Climate: severe low temperatures vary with latitude, elevation, and distance from the ocean; East Antarctica is colder than West Antarctica because of its higher elevation; Antarctic Peninsula has the most moderate climate; higher temperatures occur in January along the coast and average slightly below freezing

Terrain: about 98% thick continental ice sheet and 2% barren rock, with average elevations between 2,000 and 4,000 m; mountain ranges up to nearly 5,000 m; ice-free coastal areas include parts of southern Victoria Land, Wilkes Land, the Antarctic Peninsula area, and parts of Ross Island on McMurdo Sound; glaciers form ice shelves along about half of the coastline, and floating ice shelves constitute 11% of the area of the continent

Elevation: *mean elevation:* 2,300 m

elevation extremes: *lowest point:* Bentley Subglacial Trench -2,540 m
highest point: Vinson Massif 4,897 m
note: the lowest known land point in Antarctica is hidden in the Bentley Subglacial Trench; at its surface is the deepest ice yet discovered and the world's lowest elevation not under seawater

Natural resources: iron ore, chromium, copper, gold, nickel, platinum and other minerals, and coal and hydrocarbons have been found in small noncommercial quantities; none presently exploited; krill, finfish, and crab have been taken by commercial fisheries

Land use: *agricultural land:* 0%
forest: 0%
other: 100% (ice 98%, barren rock 2%) (2015 est.)

Natural hazards: katabatic (gravity-driven) winds blow coastward from the high interior; frequent blizzards form near the foot of the plateau; cyclonic storms form over the ocean and move clockwise along the coast; volcanism on Deception Island and isolated areas of West Antarctica; other seismic activity rare and weak; large icebergs may calve from ice shelf

Environment—current issues: the discovery of a large Antarctic ozone hole in the earth's stratosphere (the ozone layer)—first announced in 1985—spurred the signing of the Montreal Protocol in 1987, an international agreement phasing out the use of ozone-depleting chemicals; the ozone layer prevents most harmful wavelengths of ultra-violet (UV) light from passing through the earth's atmosphere; ozone depletion has been shown to harm a variety of Antarctic marine plants and animals (plankton); in 2002, significant areas of ice shelves disintegrated in response to regional warming; in 2016, a very gradual trend toward "healing" of the ozone hole was reported

Geography—note: the coldest, windiest, highest (on average), and driest continent; during summer, more solar radiation reaches the surface at the South Pole than is received at the Equator in an equivalent period; mostly uninhabitable, 98% of the land area is covered by the Antarctic ice sheet, the largest single mass of ice on earth

PEOPLE AND SOCIETY

Population: no indigenous inhabitants, but there are both permanent and summer-only staffed research stations
note: 53 countries have signed the 1959 Antarctic Treaty; 30 of those operate through their National Antarctic Program a number of seasonal-only (summer) and year-round research stations on the continent and its nearby islands south of 60 degrees south latitude (the region covered by the Antarctic Treaty); the population engaging in and supporting science or managing and protecting the Antarctic region varies from approximately 4,400 in summer to 1,100 in winter; in addition, approximately 1,000 personnel, including ship's crew and scientists doing onboard research, are present in the waters of the treaty region peak summer (December-February) population—4,490 total; Argentina 667, Australia 200, Australia and Romania jointly 13, Belgium 20, Brazil 40, Bulgaria 18, Chile 359, China 90, Czech Republic 20, Ecuador 26, Finland 20, France 125, France and Italy jointly 60, Germany 90, India 65, Italy 102, Japan 125, South Korea 70, NZ 85, Norway 44, Peru 28, Poland 40, Russia 429, South Africa 80, Spain 50, Sweden 20, Ukraine 24, UK 217, US 1,293, Uruguay 70 (2008–09) winter (June-August) station population—1,106 total; Argentina 176, Australia 62, Brazil 12, Chile 114, China 29, France 26, France and Italy jointly 13, Germany 9, India 25, Japan 40, South Korea 18, NZ 10, Norway 7, Poland 12, Russia 148, South Africa 10, Ukraine 12, UK 37, US 337, Uruguay 9 (2009); research stations operated within the Antarctic Treaty area (south of 60 degrees south latitude) by National Antarctic Programs year-round stations—approximately 40 total; Argentina 6, Australia 3, Brazil 1, Chile 6, China 2, France 1, France and Italy jointly 1, Germany 1, India 1, Japan 1, South Korea 1, NZ 1, Norway 1, Poland 1, Russia 5, South Africa 1, Ukraine 1, UK 2, US 3, Uruguay 1 (2009) a range of seasonal-only (summer) stations, camps, and refuges—Argentina, Australia, Belarus, Belgium, Bulgaria, Brazil, Chile, China, Czech Republic, Ecuador, Finland, France, Germany, India, Italy, Japan, South Korea, New Zealand, Norway, Peru, Poland, Russia, South Africa, Spain, Sweden, Ukraine, UK, US, and Uruguay (2008–09) in addition, during the austral summer some nations have numerous occupied locations such as tent camps, summer-long temporary facilities, and mobile traverses in support of research (May 2009 est.)

GOVERNMENT

Country name: *conventional long form:* none
conventional short form: Antarctica
etymology: name derived from two Greek words meaning "opposite to the Arctic" or "opposite to thenorth"

Government type: Antarctic Treaty Summary—the Antarctic region is governed by a system known as the Antarctic Treaty System; the system includes: 1. the Antarctic Treaty, signed on 1 December 1959 and entered into force on 23 June 1961, which establishes the legal framework for the management of Antarctica, 2. Recommendations and Measures adopted at meetings of Antarctic Treaty countries, 3. The Convention for the Conservation of Antarctic Seals (1972), 4. The Convention for the Conservation of Antarctic Marine Living Resources (1980), and 5. The Protocol on Environmental Protection to the Antarctic Treaty (1991); the 38th Antarctic Treaty Consultative Meeting was held in Sofia, Bulgaria in May 2015; at these annual meetings, decisions are made by consensus (not by vote) of all consultative member nations; by January 2016, there were 53 treaty member nations: 29 consultative and 24 non-consultative; consultative (decision-making) members include the seven nations that claim portions of Antarctica as national territory (some claims overlap) and 21 non-claimant nations; the US and Russia have reserved the right to make-claims; the US does not recognize the claims of others; Antarctica is administered through meetings of the consultative member nations; decisions from these meetings are carried out by these member nations (with respect to their own nationals and operations) in accordance with their own national laws; the years in parentheses indicate when a consultative member-nation acceded to the Treaty and when it was accepted as a consultative member, while no date indicates the country was an original 1959 treaty signatory; claimant nations are—Argentina, Australia, Chile, France, NZ, Norway, and the UK; nonclaimant consultative nations are—Belgium, Brazil (1975/1983), Bulgaria (1978/1998), China (1983/1985), Czech Republic (1962/2017), Ecuador (1987/1990), Finland (1984/1989), Germany (1979/1981), India (1983/1983), Italy (1981/1987), Japan, South Korea (1986/1989), Netherlands (1967/1990), Peru (1981/1989), Poland (1961/1977), Russia, South Africa, Spain (1982/1988), Sweden (1984/1988), Ukraine (1992/2004), Uruguay

(1980/1985), and the US; non-consultative members, with year of accession in parentheses, are—Austria (1987), Belarus (2006), Canada (1988), Colombia (1989), Cuba (1984), Denmark (1965), Estonia (2001), Greece (1987), Guatemala (1991), Hungary (1984), Iceland (2015), Kazakhstan (2015), North Korea (1987), Malaysia (2011), Monaco (2008), Mongolia (2015), Pakistan (2012), Papua New Guinea (1981), Portugal (2010), Romania (1971), Slovakia (1962/1993), Switzerland (1990), Turkey (1996), and Venezuela (1999); note—Czechoslovakia acceded to the Treaty in 1962 and separated into the Czech Republic and Slovakia in 1993; Article 1—area to be used for peaceful purposes only; military activity, such as weapons testing, is prohibited, but military personnel and equipment may be used for scientific research or any other peaceful purpose; Article 2—freedom of scientific investigation and cooperation shall continue; Article 3—free exchange of information and personnel, cooperation with the UN and other international agencies; Article 4—does not recognize, dispute, or establish territorial claims and no new claims shall be asserted while the treaty is in force; Article 5—prohibits nuclear explosions or disposal of radioactive wastes; Article 6—includes under the treaty all land and ice shelves south of 60 degrees 00 minutes south and reserves highseas rights; Article 7—treaty-state observers have free access, including aerial observation, to any area and may inspect all stations, installations, and equipment; advance notice of all expeditions and of the introduction of military personnel must be given; Article 8—allows for jurisdiction over observers and scientists by their own states; Article 9—frequent consultative meetings take place among member nations; Article 10—treaty states will discourage activities by any country in Antarctica that are contrary to the treaty; Article 11—disputes to be settled peacefully by the parties concerned or, ultimately, by the ICJ; Articles 12, 13, 14—deal with upholding, interpreting, and amending the treaty among involved nations; other agreements—some 200 recommendations adopted at treaty consultative meetings and ratified by governments; a mineral resources agreement was signed in 1988 but remains unratified; the Protocol on Environmental Protection to the Antarctic Treaty was signed 4 October 1991 and entered into force 14 January 1998; this agreement provides for the protection of the Antarctic environment through six specific annexes: 1) environmental impact assessment, 2) conservation of Antarctic fauna and flora, 3) waste disposal and waste management, 4) prevention of marine pollution, 5) area protection and management and 6) liability arising from environmental emergencies; it prohibits all activities relating to mineral resources except scientific research; a permanent Antarctic Treaty Secretariat was established in 2004 in Buenos Aires, Argentina

Legal system: Antarctica is administered through annual meetings—known as Antarctic Treaty Consultative Meetings—which include consultative member nations, non-consultative member nations, observer organizations, and expert organizations; decisions from these meetings are carried out by these member nations (with respect to their own nationals and operations) in accordance with their own national laws; more generally, access to the Antarctic Treaty area, that is to all areas between 60 and 90 degrees south latitude, is subject to a number of relevant legal instruments and authorization procedures adopted by the states party to the Antarctic Treaty; note—US law, including certain criminal offenses by or against US nationals, such as murder, may apply extraterritorially; some US laws directly apply to Antarctica; for example, the Antarctic Conservation Act, 16 U.S.C. section 2401 et seq., provides civil and criminal penalties for the following activities unless authorized by regulation of statute: the taking of native mammals or birds; the introduction of nonindigenous plants and animals; entry into specially protected areas; the discharge or disposal of pollutants; and the importation into the US of certain items from Antarctica; violation of the Antarctic Conservation Act carries penalties of up to $10,000 in fines and one year in prison; the National Science Foundation and Department of Justice share enforcement responsibilities; Public Law 95-541, the US Antarctic Conservation Act of 1978, as amended in 1996, requires expeditions from the US to Antarctica to notify, in advance, the Office of Oceans, Room 5805, Department of State, Washington, DC 20520, which reports such plans to other nations as required by the Antarctic Treaty; for more information, contact Permit Office, Office of Polar Programs, National Science Foundation, Arlington, Virginia 22230; *telephone:* (703) 292-8030, or visit its website at www.nsf.gov

ECONOMY

Economy overview: Scientific undertakings rather than commercial pursuits are the predominant human activity in Antarctica. Offshore fishing and tourism, both based abroad, account for Antarctica's limited economic activity. Antarctic fisheries, targeting three main species—Patagonian and Antarctic toothfish (Dissostichus eleginoides and D. mawsoni), mackerel icefish (Champsocephalus gunnari), and krill (Euphausia superba)—reported landing 295,000 metric tons in 2013–14 (estimated fishing is from the area covered by the Convention on the Conservation of Antarctic Marine Living Resources (CCAMLR), which extends slightly beyond the Antarctic Treaty area). Unregulated fishing, particularly of Patagonian toothfish (also known as Chilean sea bass), is an ongoing problem. The CCAMLR determines the recommended catch limits for marine species. A total of 36,702 tourists visited the Antarctic Treaty area in the 2014–15 Antarctic summer, slightly lowerthan the 37,405 visitors in 2013–14. These estimates were provided to the Antarctic Treaty by the International Association of Antarctica Tour Operators (IAATO) and do not include passengers on overflights. Nearly all of them were passengers on commercial (nongovernmental) ships and several yachts that make trips during the summer.

COMMUNICATIONS

Telephone system: *general assessment:* local systems at some research stations
domestic: commercial cellular networks operating in a small number of locations
international: country code—none allocated; via satellite (including mobile Inmarsat and Iridium systems) to and from all research stations, ships, aircraft, and most field parties (2015)

Radio broadcast stations: FM 2, shortwave 1 (information for US bases only); note—many research stations have a local FM radio station (2007)
Television broadcast stations: 1 (cable system with 6 channels; American Forces Antarctic Network-McMurdo—information for US basesonly) (2002)

Internet country code: .aq

Internet hosts: 7,764 (2012)
country comparison to the world: 139

TRANSPORTATION

Airports: 23 (2013)
country comparison to the world: 134

Airports—with unpaved runways: *total:* 23
over 3,047 m: 3
2,438 to 3,047 m: 5
1,524 to 2,437 m: 1
914 to 1,523 m: 8
under 914 m: 6 (2013)

Heliports: 53
note: all year-round and seasonal stations operated by National Antarctic Programs stations have some kind of helicopter landing facilities, prepared (helipads) or unprepared (2012)

Ports and terminals: McMurdo Station; most coastal stations have sparse and intermittent offshore anchorages; a few station shave basic wharf facilities

Transportation—note: US coastal stations include McMurdo (77 51 S, 166 40 E) and Palmer (64 43 S, 64 03 W); government use only except by permit (see Permit Office under "Legal System"); all ships at port are subject to inspection in accordance with Article 7, Antarctic Treaty; relevant legal instruments and authorization procedures adopted by the states parties to the Antarctic Treaty regulating access to the Antarctic Treaty area to all areas between 60 and 90 degrees of latitude south have to be complied with (see "Legal System"); The Hydrographic Commission on Antarctica (HCA), a commission of the International Hydrographic Organization (IHO), is responsible for hydrographic surveying and nautical charting matters in Antarctic Treaty area; it coordinates and facilitates provision of accurate and appropriate charts and other aids to navigation in support of safety of navigation in region; membership of HCA is open to any IHO Member State whose government has acceded to the Antarctic Treaty and which contributes resources or data to IHO Chart coverage of the area

MILITARY AND SECURITY

Military—note: the Antarctic Treaty prohibits any measures of a military nature, such as the establishment of military bases and fortifications, the carrying out of military maneuvers, or the testing of any type of weapon; it permits the use of military personnel or equipment for scientific research or for any other peaceful purposes

TRANSNATIONAL ISSUES

Disputes international: the Antarctic Treaty freezes, and most states do not recognize, the land and maritime territorial claims made by Argentina, Australia, Chile, France, New Zealand, Norway, and the UK (some overlapping) for three-fourths of the continent; the US and Russia reserve the right to make claims; no formal claims have been made in the sector between 90 degrees west and 150 degrees west; the International Whaling Commission created a sanctuary around the entire continent to deter catches by countries claiming to conduct scientific whaling; Australia has established a similar preserve in the waters around its territorial claim

ANTIGUA AND BARBUDA

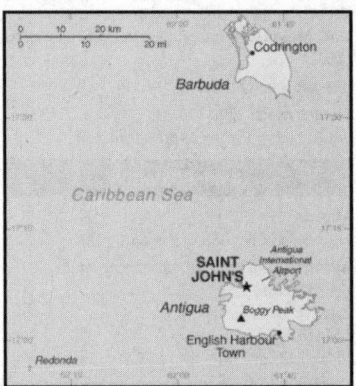

INTRODUCTION

Background: The Siboney were the first people to inhabit the islands of Antigua and Barbuda in 2400 B.C., but Arawak Indians populated the islands when COLUMBUS landed on his second voyage in 1493. Early Spanish and French settlements were succeeded by an English colony in 1667. Slavery, established to run the sugar plantations on Antigua, was abolished in 1834. The islands became an independent state within the British Commonwealth of Nations in 1981.

GEOGRAPHY

Location: Caribbean, islands between the Caribbean Sea and the North Atlantic Ocean, east-southeast of Puerto Rico

Geographic coordinates: 17 03 N, 61 48 W

Map references: Central America and the Caribbean

Area: *total:* 442.6 sq km (Antigua 280 sq km; Barbuda 161 sq km)
land: 442.6 sq km
water: 0 sq km
note: includes Redonda, 1.6 sq km
country comparison to the world: 201

Area—comparative: 2.5 times the size of Washington, DC

Land boundaries: 0 km

Coastline: 153 km

Maritime claims:
territorial sea: 12 nm
contiguous zone: 24 nm
exclusive economic zone: 200 nm
continental shelf: 200 nm or to the edge of the continental margin

Climate: tropical maritime; little seasonal temperature variation

Terrain: mostly low-lying limestone and coral islands, with some higher volcanic areas

Elevation: *mean elevation:* NA

elevation extremes: *lowest point:* Caribbean Sea 0 m
highest point: Mount Obama 402 m

Natural resources: NEGL; pleasant climate fosters tourism

Land use: *agricultural land:* 20.5%
arable land: 9.1%
permanent crops: 2.3%
permanent pasture: 9.1%
forest: 22.3%
other: 57.2% (2011 est.)

Irrigated land:
1.3 sq km (2012)

Total renewable water resources: 0.05 cu km (2011)

Freshwater withdrawal (domestic/industrial/agricultural): *total:* 0.01 cu km/yr (63%/21%/15%)
per capita: 97.67 cu m/yr (2005)

Natural hazards: hurricanes and tropical storms (July to October); periodic droughts

Environment—current issues: water management—a major concern because of limited natural freshwater resources—is further hampered by the clearing of trees to increase crop production, causing rainfall to run off quickly

Environment—international agreements: *party to:* Biodiversity, Climate Change, Climate Change-Kyoto Protocol, Desertification, Endangered Species, Environmental Modification, Hazardous Wastes, Law of the Sea, Marine Dumping, Ozone Layer Protection, Ship Pollution, Wetlands, Whaling
signed, but not ratified: none of the selected agreements

Geography—note: Antigua has a deeply indented shoreline with many natural harbors and beaches; Barbuda has a large western harbor

PEOPLE AND SOCIETY

Nationality: *noun:* Antiguan(s), Barbudan(s)
adjective: Antiguan, Barbudan

Ethnic groups: black 87.3%, mixed 4.7%, hispanic 2.7%, white 1.6%, other 2.7%, unspecified 0.9% (2011 est.)

Languages: English (official), Antiguan creole

Religions: Protestant 68.3% (Anglican 17.6%, Seventh Day Adventist 12.4%, Pentecostal 12.2%, Moravian 8.3%, Methodist 5.6%, Wesleyan Holiness 4.5%, Church of God 4.1%, Baptist 3.6%), Roman Catholic 8.2%, other 12.2%, unspecified 5.5%, none 5.9% (2011 est.)

Population: 92,436 (July 2015 est.)
country comparison to the world: 198

Age structure: *0–14 years:* 23.85% (male 11,203/female 10,847)
15–24 years: 16.89% (male 7,751/female 7,861)
25–54 years: 42.47% (male 17,939/female 21,319)
55–64 years: 9.23% (male 3,859/female 4,672)
65 years and over: 7.56% (male 3,004/female 3,981) (2015 est.)

Dependency ratios:
total dependency ratio: 45.7%
youth dependency ratio: 35.2%
elderly dependency ratio: 10.4%
potential support ratio: 9.6% (2015 est.)

Median age: *total:* 31.4 years
male: 29.6 years
female: 32.9 years (2015 est.)
country comparison to the world: 101

Population growth rate: 1.24% (2015 est.)
country comparison to the world: 95

Birth rate: 15.85 births/1,000 population (2015 est.)
country comparison to the world: 123

Death rate: 5.69 deaths/1,000 population (2015 est.)
country comparison to the world: 173

Net migration rate: 2.21 migrant(s)/1,000 population (2015 est.)
country comparison to the world: 47

Urbanization: *urban population:* 23.8% of total population (2015)
rate of urbanization: -0.95% annual rate of change (2010–15 est.)

Major urban areas—population: SAINT JOHN'S (capital) 22,000 (2014)

Sex ratio:
at birth: 1.05 male(s)/female
0–14 years: 1.03 male(s)/female
15–24 years: 0.99 male(s)/female
25–54 years: 0.84 male(s)/female
55–64 years: 0.83 male(s)/female
65 years and over: 0.76 male(s)/female
total population: 0.9 male(s)/female (2015 est.)

Infant mortality rate: *total:* 12.87 deaths/1,000 live births
male: 14.82 deaths/1,000 live births
female: 10.82 deaths/1,000 live births (2015 est.)
country comparison to the world: 117

Life expectancy at birth: *total population:* 76.33 years
male: 74.23 years
female: 78.53 years (2015 est.)
country comparison to the world: 87

Total fertility rate: 2.02 children born/woman (2015 est.)
country comparison to the world: 120

Health expenditures: 4.9% of GDP (2013)
country comparison to the world: 134

Hospital bed density: 2.1 beds/1,000 population (2011)

Drinking water source:
improved:
urban: 97.9% of population
rural: 97.9% of population
total: 97.9% of population
unimproved:
urban: 2.1% of population
rural: 2.1% of population
total: 2.1% of population (2015 est.)

Sanitation facility access:
improved:
urban: 91.4% of population
rural: 91.4% of population
total: 91.4% of population
unimproved:
urban: 8.6% of population
rural: 8.6% of population
total: 8.6% of population (2011 est.)

HIV/AIDS—adult prevalence rate: NA

HIV/AIDS—people living with HIV/AIDS: NA

HIV/AIDS—deaths: NA

Obesity—adult prevalence rate: 31% (2014)
country comparison to the world: 52

Education expenditures: 2.6% of GDP (2009)
country comparison to the world: 159

Literacy: *definition:* age 15 and over has completed five or more years of schooling
total population: 99%
male: 98.4%
female: 99.4% (2012 est.)

School life expectancy (primary to tertiary education): *total:* 14 years

male: 13 years
female: 15 years (2012)

GOVERNMENT

Country name: *conventional long form:* none
conventional short form: Antigua and Barbuda
etymology: "antiguo" is Spanish for "ancient" or "old"; the island was discovered by Christopher COLUMBUS in 1493 and, according to tradition, named by him after the church of Santa Maria la Antigua (Old Saint Mary's) in Seville; "barbuda" is Spanish for "bearded" and the adjective may refer to the alleged beards of the indigenous people or to the island's bearded-fig trees

Government type: parliamentary democracy (Parliament) under a constitutional monarchy; a Commonwealth realm

Capital: *name:* Saint John's

Geographic coordinates: 17 07 N, 61 51 W
time difference: UTC-4 (1 hour ahead of Washington, DC, during Standard Time)

Administrative divisions: 6 parishes and 2 dependencies*; Barbuda*, Redonda*, Saint George, Saint John, Saint Mary, Saint Paul, Saint Peter, Saint Philip

Independence: 1 November 1981 (from the UK)

National holiday: Independence Day (National Day), 1 November (1981)

Constitution: several previous; latest presented 31 July 1981, effective 31 October 1981 (Antigua and Barbuda Constitutional Order 1981); amended 2009, 2011 (2016)

Legal system: common law based on the English model

International law organization participation: has not submitted an ICJ jurisdiction declaration; accepts ICCt jurisdiction

Citizenship: *citizenship by birth:* yes
citizenship by descent: yes
dual citizenship recognized: yes
residency requirement for naturalization: 7 years

Suffrage: 18 years of age; universal

Executive branch: *chief of state:* Queen ELIZABETH II (since 6 February 1952); represented by Governor General Rodney WILLIAMS (since 14 August 2014)

head of government: Prime Minister Gaston BROWNE (since 13 June 2014)
cabinet: Council of Ministers appointed by the governor general on the advice of the prime minister
elections/appointments: the monarchy is hereditary; governor general appointed by the monarch on the advice of the prime minister; following legislative elections, the leader of the majority party or majority coalition usually appointed prime minister by the governor general

Legislative branch: *description:* bicameral Parliament consists of the Senate (17 seats; members appointed by the governor general) and the House of Representatives (17 seats; members directly

elected in single-seat constituencies by simple majority vote to serve 5-year terms)
elections: House of Representatives—last held on 12 June 2014 (next to be held in 2019)
election results: percent of vote by party—ALP 56.4% UPP 42%; seats by party—ALP 14, UPP 3

Judicial branch: *highest court(s):* the Eastern Caribbean Supreme Court (ECSC) is the itinerant superior court of record for the 9-member Organization of Eastern Caribbean States to include Antigua and Barbuda; the ECSC—headquartered on St. Lucia—is headed by the chief justice and is comprised of the Court of Appeal with 3 justices and the High Court with 16 judges; sittings of the Court of Appeal and High Court rotate among the 9 member states; 2 High Court judges reside on Antigua and Barbuda
judge selection and term of office: Eastern Caribbean Supreme Court Chief Justice appointed by the Her Majesty, Queen ELIZABETH II; other justices and judges appointed by the Judicial and Legal Services Commission; Court of Appeal justices appointed for life with mandatory retirement at age 65; High Court judges appointed for life with mandatory retirement at age 62
subordinate courts: Industrial Court; Magistrates' Courts

Political parties and leaders: Antigua Labor Party or ALP [Gaston BROWNE] Barbuda People's Movement or BPM [Trevor WALKER] Barbuda People's Movement for Change [Arthur NIBBS] Barbudans for a Better Barbuda [Ordrick SAMUEL] United Progressive Party or UPP [W. Baldwin SPENCER] (a coalition of three parties —Antigua Caribbean Liberation Movement or ACLM, Progressive Labor Movement or PLM, United National Democratic Party or UNDP)

Political pressure groups and leaders: Antigua Trades and Labor Union or ATLU [Wigley GEORGE] People's Democratic Movement or PDM [Hugh MARSHALL]

International organization participation: ACP, AOSIS, C, Caricom, CDB, CELAC, FAO, G-77, IBRD, ICAO, ICC (NGOs), ICCt, ICRM, IDA, IFAD, IFC, IFRCS, ILO, IMF, IMO, IMSO, Interpol, IOC, IOM, ISO (subscriber), ITU, ITUC (NGOs), MIGA, NAM (observer), OAS, OECS, OPANAL, OPCW, Petrocaribe, UN, UNCTAD, UNESCO, UPU, WFTU (NGOs), WHO, WIPO, WMO, WTO

Diplomatic representation in the US: *chief of mission:* Ambassador Sir Ronald SANDERS (since 17 September 2015)
chancery: 3216 New Mexico Avenue NW, Washington, DC 20016
telephone: [1] (202) 362-5122
FAX: [1] (202) 362-5525
consulate(s) general: Miami, New York

Diplomatic representation from the US: the US does not have an embassy in Antigua and Barbuda; the US Ambassador to Barbados is accredited to Antigua and Barbuda

Flag description: red, with an inverted isosceles triangle based on the top edge of the flag; the triangle contains three horizontal bands of black (top), light blue, and white, with a yellow rising sun in the black band; the sun symbolizes the dawn of a new era, black represents the African heritage of most of the population, blue is for hope, and red is for the dynamism of the people; the "V" stands for victory; the successive yellow, blue, and white coloring is also meant to evoke the country's tourist attractions of sun, sea, and sand

National symbol(s): fallow deer; national colors: red, white, blue, black, yellow

National anthem: *name:* "Fair Antigua, We Salute Thee"
lyrics/music: Novelle Hamilton RICHARDS/ Walter Garnet Picart CHAMBERS
note: adopted 1967; as a Commonwealth country, in addition to the national anthem, "God Save the Queen" serves as the royal anthem (see United Kingdom)

ECONOMY

Economy overview: Tourism continues to dominate Antigua and Barbuda's economy, accounting for nearly 60% of GDP and 40% of investment. The dual-island nation's agricultural production is focused on the domestic market and constrained by a limited water supply and a labor shortage stemming from the lure of higher wages in tourism and construction. Manufacturing comprises enclave-type assembly for export with major products being bedding, handicrafts, and electronic components. After taking office in 2004, the SPENCER government adopted an ambitious fiscal reform program and was successful in reducing its public debt-to-GDP ratio from approximately 130% in 2010 to 89% in 2012. In 2009, the country's economy was severely hit by the global economic crisis and suffered from the collapse of its largest private sector employer, a steep decline in tourism, a rise in debt, and a sharp economic contraction between 2009 and 2011. The country has not yet returned to its pre-crisis growth levels. Prospects for economic growth in the medium term will continue to depend on tourist arrivals from the US, Canada, and Europe and potential damages from natural disasters.

GDP (purchasing power parity):
$2.097 billion (2015 est.)
$2.053 billion (2014 est.)
$1.97 billion (2013 est.)
note: data are in 2015 US dollars
country comparison to the world: 194

GDP (official exchange rate):
$1.287 billion (2015 est.)

GDP—real growth rate:
2.2% (2015 est.)
4.2% (2014 est.)
1.5% (2013 est.)
country comparison to the world: 133

GDP—per capita (PPP):
$23,600 (2015 est.)
$23,300 (2014 est.)
$22,600 (2013 est.)
note: data are in 2015 US dollars

country comparison to the world: 79

Gross national saving:
12.8% of GDP (2015 est.)
10.6% of GDP (2014 est.)
8.8% of GDP (2013 est.)
country comparison to the world: 133

GDP—composition, by end use:
household consumption: 51.1%
government consumption: 10.2%
investment in fixed capital: 21.3%
investment in inventories: 0.1%
exports of goods and services: 47.5%
imports of goods and services: -30.2% (2015 est.)

GDP—composition, by sector of origin:
agriculture: 2.4%
industry: 17.9%
services: 79.7% (2015 est.)

Agriculture—products: cotton, fruits, vegetables, bananas, coconuts, cucumbers, mangoes, sugarcane; livestock

Industries: tourism, construction, light manufacturing (clothing, alcohol, household appliances)

Industrial production growth rate: 2% (2015 est.)
country comparison to the world: 112

Labor force: 30,000 (1991)
country comparison to the world: 205

Labor force—by occupation: *agriculture:* 7%
industry: 11%
services: 82% (1983)

Unemployment rate: 11% (2014 est.)
country comparison to the world: 126

Population below poverty line: NA%

Household income or consumption by percentage share: *lowest:* 10%: NA%
highest: 10%: NA%

Budget: *revenues:* $255.9 million
expenditures: $217 million (2015 est.)
Taxes and other revenues: 19.9% of GDP (2015 est.)
country comparison to the world: 160

Budget surplus (+) or deficit (–): 3% of GDP (2015 est.)
country comparison to the world: 13

Public debt: 89% of GDP (2012 est.)
130% of GDP (2010 est.)
country comparison to the world: 27

Fiscal year: 1 April–31 March

Inflation rate (consumer prices):
1% (2015 est.)
1.1% (2014 est.)
country comparison to the world: 80

Central bank discount rate: 6.5% (31 December 2010)
6.5% (31 December 2009)
country comparison to the world: 55

Commercial bank prime lending rate: 10% (31 December 2015 est.)
10.1% (31 December 2014 est.)
country comparison to the world: 82

Stock of narrow money:
$240.7 million (31 December 2015 est.)
$234.1 million (31 December 2014 est.)

country comparison to the world: 180

Stock of broad money: $1.127 billion (31 December 2015 est.)
$1.116 billion (31 December 2014 est.)
country comparison to the world: 168

Stock of domestic credit: $1.037 billion (31 December 2015 est.)
$1.037 billion (31 December 2014 est.)
country comparison to the world: 157

Current account balance: -$ 129 million (2015 est.)
-$ 181 million (2014 est.)
country comparison to the world: 71

Exports: $61 million (2015 est.)
$59.8 million (2014 est.)
country comparison to the world: 200

Exports—commodities: petroleum products, bedding, handicrafts, electronic components, transport equipment, food and live animals

Imports: $482.5 million (2015 est.)
$469.5 million (2014 est.)
country comparison to the world: 194

Imports—commodities: food and live animals, machinery and transport equipment, manufactures, chemicals, oil

Debt—external:
$441.2 million (31 December 2012)
$458 million (June 2010)
country comparison to the world: 182

Exchange rates: East Caribbean dollars (XCD) per US dollar—
2.7 (2015 est.)
2.7 (2014 est.)
2.7 (2013 est.)
2.7 (2012 est.)
2.7 (2011 est.)

ENERGY

Electricity—production: 315 million kWh (2012 est.)
country comparison to the world: 173

Electricity—consumption: 293 million kWh (2012 est.)
country comparison to the world: 178

Electricity—exports: 0 kWh (2013 est.)
country comparison to the world: 96

Electricity—imports: 0 kWh (2013 est.)
country comparison to the world: 113

Electricity—installed generating capacity: 55,000 kW (2012 est.)
country comparison to the world: 184

Electricity—from fossil fuels: 100% of total installed capacity (2012 est.)
country comparison to the world: 1

Electricity—from nuclear fuels: 0% of total installed capacity (2012 est.)
country comparison to the world: 35

Electricity—from hydro electric plants: 0% of total installed capacity (2012 est.)
country comparison to the world: 214

Electricity—from other renewable sources: 0% of total installed capacity (2012 est.)
country comparison to the world: 149

Crude oil—production: 0 bbl/day (2014 est.)
country comparison to the world: 103

Crude oil—exports: 0 bbl/day (2012 est.)
country comparison to the world: 93

Crude oil—imports: 0 bbl/day (2012 est.)
country comparison to the world: 151

Crude oil—proved reserves: 0 bbl (1 January 2015 est.)
country comparison to the world: 103

Refined petroleum products—production: 0 bbl/day (2012 est.)
country comparison to the world: 151

Refined petroleum products—consumption: 4,900 bbl/day (2013 est.)
country comparison to the world: 169

Refined petroleum products—exports: 175 bbl/day (2012 est.)
country comparison to the world: 119

Refined petroleum products—imports: 5,077 bbl/day (2012 est.)
country comparison to the world: 160

Natural gas—production: 0 cu m (2013 est.)
country comparison to the world: 153

Natural gas —consumption: 0 cu m (2013 est.)
country comparison to the world: 115

Natural gas—exports: 0 cu m (2013 est.)
country comparison to the world: 53

Natural gas —imports: 0 cu m (2013 est.)
country comparison to the world: 151

Natural gas—proved reserves: 0 cu m (1 January 2014 est.)
country comparison to the world: 108

Carbon dioxide emissions from consumption of energy: 586,400 Mt (2012 est.)
country comparison to the world: 178

COMMUNICATIONS

Telephones—fixed lines: *total subscriptions:* 32,400
subscriptions per 100 inhabitants: 35 (2014 est.)
country comparison to the world: 172

Telephones—mobile cellular: *total:* 109,100
subscriptions per 100 inhabitants: 120 (2014 est.)
country comparison to the world: 189

Telephone system: *general assessment:* good automatic telephone system

domestic: fixed-line teledensity roughly 40 per 100 persons; mobile-cellular teledensity is some 200 per 100 persons
international: country code—1–268; landing points for the East Caribbean Fiber System (ECFS) and the Global Caribbean Network (GCN) submarine cable systems with links to other islands in the eastern Caribbean extending from the British Virgin Islands to Trinidad; satellite earth stations—2; troposphericscatter to Saba (Netherlands) and Guadeloupe (France) (2011)

Broadcast media: state-controlled Antigua and Barbuda Broadcasting Service (ABS) operates 1 TV station; multi-channel cable TV subscription services are available; ABS operates 1 radio station; roughly 15 radio stations, some broadcasting on multiple frequencies (2007)
Radio broadcast stations: AM 3, FM 17, shortwave 0 (2008)
Television broadcast stations: 2 (1997)

Internet country code: .ag

Internet hosts: 11,532 (2012)
country comparison to the world: 130

Internet users: *total:* 81,900
percent of population: 89.7% (2014 est.)
country comparison to the world: 174

TRANSPORTATION

Airports: 3 (2013)
country comparison to the world: 193

Airports—with paved runways: *total:* 2
2,438 to 3,047 m: 1
under 914 m: 1 (2013)

Airports—with unpaved runways: *total:* 1
under 914 m: 1 (2013)

Roadways: *total:* 1,170 km
paved: 386 km
unpaved: 784 km (2011)
country comparison to the world: 183

Merchant marine: *total:* 1,257
by type: bulk carrier 49, cargo 753, carrier 6, chemical tanker 4, container 407, liquefied gas 12, refrigerated cargo 7, roll on/roll off 17, vehicle carrier 2
foreign-owned: 1,215 (Albania 1, Colombia 1, Denmark 20, Estonia 10, Germany 1094, Greece 4, Iceland 10, Latvia 16, Lithuania 3, Mexico 1, Netherlands 17, Norway 9, NZ 2, Poland 2, Russia 3, Switzerland 7, Turkey 7, UK 1, US 7) (2010)
country comparison to the world: 9

Ports and terminals: *major seaport(s):* Saint John's

MILITARY AND SECURITY

Military branches: Ministry of National Security, Royal Antigua and Barbuda Defense Force (includes Antigua and Barbuda Coast Guard) (2012)

Military service age and obligation: 18 years of age for voluntary military service; no conscription; Governor-General has powers to call upmen for national service and set the age at which they could be called up (2012)

TRANSNATIONAL ISSUES

Disputes international: none

Trafficking in persons: *current situation:* Antigua and Barbuda is a destination and transit country for adults and children subjected to sex trafficking and forced labor; forced prostitution has been reported in bars, taverns, and brothels, while forced labor occurs in domestic service and the retail sector

tier rating: Tier 2 Watch List—Antigua and Barbuda does not fully comply with the minimum standards for the elimination of trafficking; however, it is making significant efforts to do so; the government made no discernible progress in convicting traffickers in 2014 but charged two individuals in separate cases; efforts to convict traffickers have been impeded by a 2014 ruling that found the 2010 anti-trafficking act was unconstitutional because jurisdiction rests with the Magistrate's Court rather than the High Court; no new prosecutions, convictions, or punishments were recorded in 2014; credible sources have raised concerns about trafficking-related complicity among some off-duty police officers, which could hinder investigations or victims willingness to report offenses; prevention efforts were sustained, but progress in protecting victims was uneven; seven victims were assisted, which was an increase over 2013 (2015)

Illicit drugs: considered a minor transshipment point for narcotics bound for the US and Europe; more significant as an offshore financial center

ARCTIC OCEAN

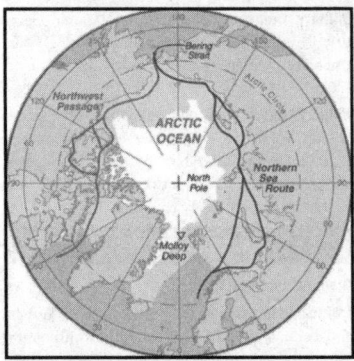

INTRODUCTION

Background: The Arctic Ocean is the smallest of the world's five oceans (after the Pacific Ocean, Atlantic Ocean, Indian Ocean, and the Southern Ocean). The Northwest Passage (US and Canada) and Northern Sea Route (Norway and Russia) are two important seasonal waterways. In recent years the polar ice pack has receded in the summer allowing for increased navigation and raising the possibility of future sovereignty and shipping disputes among the six countries bordering the Arctic Ocean (Canada, Denmark (Greenland), Iceland, Norway, Russia, US).

GEOGRAPHY

Location: body of water between Europe, Asia, and North America, mostly north of the Arctic Circle

Geographic coordinates: 90 00 N, 0 00 E

Map references: Arctic Region

Area: *total:* 14.056 million sq km
note: includes Baffin Bay, Barents Sea, Beaufort Sea, Chukchi Sea, East Siberian Sea, Greenland Sea, Hudson Bay, Hudson Strait, Kara Sea, Laptev Sea, Northwest Passage, and other tributary water bodies

Area—comparative: slightly less than 1.5 times the size of the US

Coastline: 45,389 km

Climate: polar climate characterized by persistent cold and relatively narrow annual temperature range; winters characterized by continuous darkness, cold and stable weather conditions, and clear skies; summers characterized by continuous daylight, damp and foggy weather, and weak cyclones with rain or snow

Terrain: central surface covered by a perennial drifting polar icepack that, on average, is about 3 m thick, although pressure ridges may be three times that thickness; clockwise drift pattern in the Beaufort Gyral Stream, but nearly straight-line movement from the New Siberian Islands (Russia) to Denmark Strait (between Greenland and Iceland); the icepack is surrounded by open seas during the summer, but more than doubles in size during the winter and extends to the encircling landmasses; the ocean floor is about 50% continental shelf (highest percentage of any ocean) with the remainder a central basin interrupted by three submarine ridges (Alpha Cordillera, Nansen Cordillera, and Lomonosov Ridge)

Elevation: *mean depth:* -1,205 m

elevation extremes: *lowest point:* Molloy Deep -5,607 m
highest point: sea level 0 m

Natural resources: sand and gravel aggregates, placer deposits, polymetallic nodules, oil and gas fields, fish, marine mammals (seals and whales)

Natural hazards: ice islands occasionally break away from northern Ellesmere Island; icebergs calved from glaciers in western Greenland and extreme northeastern Canada; permafrost in islands; virtually ice locked from October to June; ships subject to superstructure icing from October to May

Environment—current issues: endangered marine species include walruses and whales; fragile ecosystem slow to change and slow to recover from disruptions or damage; thinning polar icepack

Geography—note: major chokepoint is the southern Chukchi Sea (northern access to the Pacific Ocean via the Bering Strait); strategic location between North America and Russia; shortest marine link between the extremes of eastern and western Russia; floating research stations operated by the US and Russia; maximum snow cover in March or April about 20 to 50 centimeters over the frozen ocean; snow cover lasts about 10 months

GOVERNMENT

Country name: *etymology:* the name Arctic comes from the Greek word "arktikos" meaning "near the bear" or" northern, " and that word derives from "arktos, " meaning "bear"; the name refers either to the constellation Ursa Major, the "Great Bear, " which is prominent in the northern celestial sphere, or to the constellation Ursa Minor, the "Little Bear, " which contains Polaris, the North (Pole) Star

ECONOMY

Economy—overview: Economic activity is limited to the exploitation of natural resources, including petroleum, natural gas, fish, and seals.

TRANSPORTATION

Ports and terminals: *major seaport(s):* Churchill (Canada), Murmansk (Russia), Prudhoe Bay (US)

Transportation—note: sparse network of air, ocean, river, and land routes; the Northwest Passage (North America) and Northern Sea Route (Eurasia) are important seasonal waterways

TRANSNATIONAL ISSUES

Disputes—international: Canada and the US dispute how to divide the Beaufort Sea and the status of the Northwest Passage but continue to work cooperatively to survey the Arctic continental shelf; Denmark (Greenland) and Norway have made submissions to the Commission on the Limits of the Continental shelf (CLCS) and Russia is collecting additional data to augment its 2001 CLCS submission; record summer melting of sea ice in the Arctic has renewed interest in maritime shipping lanes and sea floor exploration; Norway and Russia signed a comprehensive maritime boundary agreement in 2010

ARGENTINA

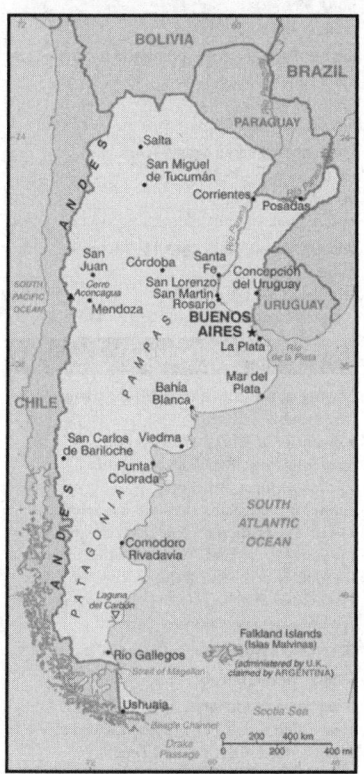

INTRODUCTION

Background: In 1816, the United Provinces of the Rio Plata declared their independence from Spain. After Bolivia, Paraguay, and Uruguay went their separate ways, the area that remained became Argentina. The country's population and culture were heavily shaped by immigrants from throughout Europe, with Italy and Spain providing the largest percentage of newcomers from 1860 to 1930. Up until about the mid-20th century, much of Argentina's history was dominated by periods of internal political conflict between Federalists and Unitarians and between civilian and military factions. After World War II, an era of Peronist populism and direct and indirect military interference in subsequent governments was followed by a military junta that took power in 1976. Democracy returned in 1983 after a failed bid to seize the Falkland Islands (Islas Malvinas) by force, and has persisted despite numerous challenges, the most formidable of which was a severe economic crisis in 2001–02 that led to violent public protests and the successive resignations of several presidents.

GEOGRAPHY

Location: Southern South America, bordering the South Atlantic Ocean, between Chile and Uruguay

Geographic coordinates: 34 00 S, 64 00 W

Map references: South America

Land boundaries: *total:* 2,780,400 sq km
land: 2,736,690 sq km
water: 43,710 sq km
country comparison to the world: 8

Area—comparative: slightly less than three-tenths the size of the US
total: 11,968 km
border countries (5): Bolivia 942 km, Brazil 1,263 km, Chile 6,691 km, Paraguay 2,531 km, Uruguay 541km

Coastline: 4,989 km

Maritime claims: *territorial sea:* 12 nm
contiguous zone: 24 nm
exclusive economic zone: 200 nm
continental shelf: 200 nm or to the edge of the continental margin

Climate: mostly temperate; arid in southeast; sub-antarctic in southwest

Terrain: rich plains of the Pampas in northern half, flat to rolling plateau of Patagonia in south, rugged Andes along western border

Elevation: *mean elevation:* 595 m

elevation extremes: *lowest point:* Laguna del Carbon 105 m (located between Puerto San Julian and Comandante Luis Piedra Buena in the province of Santa Cruz)
highest point: Cerro Aconcagua 6,960 m (located in the northwestern corner of the province of Mendoza; highest point in South America)

Natural resources: fertile plains of the pampas, lead, zinc, tin, copper, iron ore, manganese, petroleum, uranium, arable land

Land use: *agricultural land:* 53.9%
arable land: 13.9%
permanent crops: 0.4%
permanent pasture: 39.6%
forest: 10.7%
other: 35.4% (2011 est.)

Irrigated land: 23,600 sq km (2012)

Total renewable water resources: 814 cu km (2011)

Freshwater withdrawal (domestic/industrial/agricultural): *total:* 32.57 cu km/yr (23%/13%/64%)
per capita: 864.9 cu m/yr (2005)

Natural hazards: San Miguel de Tucuman and Mendoza areas in the Andes subject to earthquakes; pamperos are violent windstorms that can strike the pampas and northeast; heavy flooding in some areas
volcanism: volcanic activity in the Andes Mountains along the Chilean border; Copahue (elev.

2,997 m) last erupted in 2000; other historically active volcanoes include Llullaillaco, Maipo, Planchon-Peteroa, SanJose, Tromen, Tupungatito, and Viedma

Environment current issues: environmental problems (urban and rural) typical of an industrializing economy such as deforestation, soil degradation, desertification, air pollution, and water pollution
note: Argentina is a world leader in setting voluntary greenhouse gas targets

Environment international agreements:
party to: Antarctic-Environmental Protocol, Antarctic-Marine Living Resources, Antarctic Seals, Antarctic Treaty, Biodiversity, Climate Change, Climate Change-Kyoto Protocol, Desertification, Endangered Species, Environmental Modification, Hazardous Wastes, Law of the Sea, Marine Dumping, Ozone Layer Protection, Ship Pollution, Wetlands, Whaling
signed, but not ratified: Marine Life Conservation

Geography—note: second-largest country in South America (after Brazil); strategic location relative to sea lanes between the South Atlantic and the South Pacific Oceans (Strait of Magellan, Beagle Channel, Drake Passage); diverse geophysical landscapes range from tropical climates in the north to tundra in the far south; Cerro-Aconcagua is the Western Hemisphere's tallest mountain, while Laguna del Carbon is the lowest point in the Western Hemisphere

PEOPLE AND SOCIETY

Nationality: *noun:* Argentine(s)
adjective: Argentine

Ethnic groups: white (mostly Spanish and Italian) 97%, mestizo (mixed white and Amerindian ancestry), Amerindian, or other nonwhite groups 3%

Languages: Spanish (official), Italian, English, German, French, indigenous (Mapudungun, Quechua)

Religions: nominally Roman Catholic 92% (less than 20% practicing), Protestant 2%, Jewish 2%, other 4%

Demographic profile: Argentina's population continues to grow but at a slower rate because of its steadily declining birth rate. Argentina's fertility decline began earlier than in the rest of Latin America, occurring most rapidly between the early 20th century and the 1950s and then becoming more gradual. Life expectancy has been improving, most notably among the young and the poor. While the population under age 15 is shrinking, the youth cohort—ages 15–24 is the largest in Argentina's history and will continue to bolster the working-age population. If this large working-age population is well-educated and gainfully employed, Argentina is likely to experience an economic boost and possibly higher per capita savings and investment. Although literacy and primary school enrollment are nearly universal, grade repetition is problematic and secondary school completion is low. Both of these issues vary widely by region and socioeconomic group. Argentina has been primarily a country of immigration for most of its history, welcoming European immigrants after its independence in the 19th century and attracting especially large numbers from Spain and Italy. European immigration diminished in the 1950s, when Argentina's military dictatorships tightened immigration rules and European economies rebounded. Regional migration, however, continued to supply low-skilled workers and today it accounts for three-quarters of Argentina's immigrant population. The first waves of highly skilled Argentine emigrant workers headed mainly to the United States and Spain in the 1960s and 1970s. The ongoing European economic crisis is driving the return migration of some Argentinean and other Latin American nationals, as well as the immigration of Europeans to South America, where Argentina is a key recipient.

Population: 43,431,886 (July 2015 est.)
country comparison to the world: 33

Age structure: *0–14 years:* 24.74% (male 5,498,766/female 5,244,55)
15–24 years: 15.59% (male 3,458,318/female 3,311,765)
25–54 years: 39.01% (male 8,452,645/female 8,489,476)
55–64 years: 9.11% (male 1,917,317/female 2,040,750)
65 years and over: 11.55% (male 2,088,160/female 2,930,134) (2015 est.)

Dependency ratios:
total dependency ratio: 56.5%
youth dependency ratio: 39.4%
elderly dependency ratio: 17.1%
potential support ratio: 5.8% (2015 est.)

Median age: *total:* 31.4 years
male: 30.3 years
female: 32.6 years (2015 est.)
country comparison to the world: 102

Population growth rate: 0.93% (2015 est.)
country comparison to the world: 124

Birth rate: 16.64 births/1,000 population (2015 est.)
country comparison to the world: 111

Death rate:
7.33 deaths/1,000 population (2015 est.)
country comparison to the world: 117

Net migration rate: 0 migrant(s)/1,000 population (2015 est.)
country comparison to the world: 110

Urbanization: *urban population:* 91.8% of total population (2015)
rate of urbanization: 1.04% annual rate of change (2010–15 est.)

Major urban areas population: BUENOS AIRES (capital) 15.18 million; Cordoba 1.511 million; Rosario 1.381 million; Mendoza 1.009 million; San Miguel de Tucuman 910,000; La Plata 846,000 (2015)

Sex ratio: *at birth:* 1.05 male(s)/female
0–14 years: 1.05 male(s)/female
15–24 years: 1.04 male(s)/female
25–54 years: 1 male(s)/female
55–64 years: 0.94 male(s)/female
65 years and over: 0.71 male(s)/female
total population: 0.97 male(s)/female (2015 est.)

Maternal mortality rate: 52 deaths/100,000 live births (2015 est.)
country comparison to the world: 84

Infant mortality rate: *total:* 9.69 deaths/1,000 live births
male: 10.86 deaths/1,000 live births
female: 8.47 deaths/1,000 live births (2015 est.)
country comparison to the world: 140

Life expectancy at birth: *total population:* 77.69 years
male: 74.46 years
female: 81.09 years (2015 est.)
country comparison to the world: 66

Total fertility rate: 2.23 children born/woman (2015 est.)
country comparison to the world: 97

Contraceptive prevalence rate: 78.9% (2004/05)

Health expenditures: 7.3% of GDP (2013)
country comparison to the world: 52

Physicians density: 3.86 physicians/1,000 population (2013)

Hospital bed density: 4.7 beds/1,000 population (2012)

Drinking water source:
improved:
urban: 99% of population
rural: 100% of population
total: 99.1% of population
unimproved:
urban: 1% of population
rural: 0% of population
total: 0.9% of population (2015 est.)

Sanitation facility access:
improved:
urban: 96.2% of population
rural: 98.3% of population
total: 96.4% of population
unimproved:
urban: 3.8% of population
rural: 1.7% of population
total: 3.6% of population (2015 est.)

HIV/AIDS adult prevalence rate: 0.47% (2014 est.)
country comparison to the world: 69

HIV/AIDS people living with HIV/AIDS: 126,600 (2014 est.)
country comparison to the world: 37

HIV/AIDS—deaths: 1,500 (2014 est.)
country comparison to the world: 60

Obesity—adult prevalence rate: 26.5% (2014)
country comparison to the world: 29

Children under the age of 5 years underweight: 2.3% (2005)
country comparison to the world: 119

Education expenditures: 5.3% of GDP (2013)
country comparison to the world: 32

Literacy: *definition:* age 10 and over can read and write
total population: 98.1%
male: 98%
female: 98.1% (2015 est.)

School life expectancy (primary to tertiary education): *total:* 17 years
male: 16 years
female: 18 years (2013)

Child labor-children ages 5–14:
total number: 435,252
percentage: 7%
note: data represent children ages 513 (2003 est.)

Unemployment, youth ages 15–24: *total:* 19.4%
male: 17%
female: 23.5% (2013 est.)
country comparison to the world: 63

GOVERNMENT

Country name: *conventional long form:* Argentine Republic
conventional short form: Argentina
local long form: Republica Argentina
local short form: Argentina
etymology: originally the area was referred to as Tierra Argentina, i.e., "Land beside the Silvery River"or "silvery land, " which referred to the massive estuary in the east of the country, the Rio de la Plata (Riverof Silver); over time the name shortened to simply Argentina or "silvery"

Government type: presidential republic

Capital: *name:* Buenos Aires

Geographic coordinates: 34 36 S, 58 22 W
time difference: UTC-3 (2 hours ahead of Washington, DC, during Standard Time)

Administrative divisions: 23 provinces (provincias, singular—provincia) and 1 autonomous city*; Buenos Aires, Catamarca, Chaco, Chubut, Ciudad Autonoma de Buenos Aires*, Cordoba, Corrientes, Entre Rios, Formosa, Jujuy, La Pampa, La Rioja, Mendoza, Misiones, Neuquen, Rio Negro, Salta, San Juan, San Luis, Santa Cruz, Santa Fe, Santiago del Estero, Tierra del Fuego Antartida e Islas del Atlantico Sur (Tierra del Fuego), Tucuman
note: the US does not recognize any claims to Antarctica

Independence: 9 July 1816 (from Spain)

National holiday: Revolution Day, 25 May (1810)

Constitution: several previous; latest effective 11 May 1853; amended many times, last in 1994 (2016)

Legal system: civil law system based on West European legal systems; note—in 2014, Congress passed government-backed reform to the civil code that will go into effect in 2016

International law organization participation: has not submitted an ICJ jurisdiction declaration; accepts ICCt jurisdiction

Citizenship: *citizenship by birth:* yes
citizenship by descent: yes
dual citizenship recognized: yes

residency requirement for naturalization: 2 years

Suffrage: 18–70 years of age; universal and compulsory; 16–17 years of age optional for national elections

Executive branch: *chief of state:* President Mauricio MACRI (since 10 December 2015); Vice President Gabriela MICHETTI (since 10 December 2015); note-the president is both chief of state and head of government

head of government: President Mauricio MACRI (since 10 December 2015); Vice President Gabriela MICHETTI (since 10 December 2015)
cabinet: Cabinet appointed by the president
elections/appointments: president and vice president directly elected on the same ballot by qualified majority popular vote for a 4-year term (eligible for a second consecutive term); election last held in 2 rounds on 25 October and 22 November 2015 (next to be held in October 2019)
election results: Mauricio MACRI elected president; percent of vote: first-round results—Daniel SCIOLI (PJ) 37.1%, Mauricio MACRI (PRO) 34.2%, Sergio MASSA (FR/PJ) 21.4%, other 7.3%; second-round results—Mauricio MACRI (PRO) 51.4%, Daniel SCIOLI (PJ) 48.6%

Legislative branch: *description:* bicameral National Congress or Congreso Nacional consists of the Senate (72 seats; members directly elected in multi-seat constituencies by simple majority vote to serve 6-year terms with one-third of the membership elected every 2 years) and the Chamber of Deputies (257 seats; members directly elected in multi-seat constituencies by proportional representation vote; members serve 4-year terms with one-half of the membership renewed every 2 years)
elections: Senate last—held on 25 October 2015 (next to be held October 2017); Chamber of Deputies—last held on 25 October 2015 (next to be held October 2017)
election results: Senate—percent of vote by bloc or party—NA; seats by bloc or party—Cambiemos 12, FpV 8, PF 2, Progresistas 2; Chamber of Deputies—percent of vote by bloc or party—NA; seats by bloc or party—FpV 84, Cambiemos 21, FR and allies 8, Progresistas 9, Federal Peronism 3, PP 3, other 2; note—as of 1 February 2016, the total seats per party of bloc in the legislature is as follows: Senate FpV 117, UCR/CC 50, Pro 41, PJ 36, PS/GEN 9, other 4; Chamber of Deputies FpV 42, UCR/CC 11, PJ 10, Pro 4, PS/GEN 2, other 3

Judicial branch: *highest court(s):* Supreme Court or Corte Suprema (consists of the court president, vice-president, and 5 judges)
judge selection and term of office: judges nominated by the president and approved by the Senate; judges have a mandatory retirement age of 75
subordinate courts: federal level appellate, district, and territorial courts; provincial level supreme, appellate, and first instance courts

Political parties and leaders: Cambiemos (a coalition composed of CC, PRO, and UCR) [Mauricio MACRI]

Civic Coalition or CC (a coalition loosely affiliated with Elisa CARRIO)
Dissident Peronists (PJ Disidente) or Federal Peronism (a right-wing faction of the Justicialist Party opposed to the Kirchners) [Ramon PUERTA]
Front for Victory or FpV (left-wing faction of PJ) [Cristina FERNANDEZ DE KIRCHNER]
Peronist (or Justicialist) Party or PJ [Eduardo FELLNER]
Popular Path or PP
Progresistas [Margarita STOLBIZER]
Radical Civic Union or UCR [Ernesto SANZ]
Republican Proposal or PRO [Mauricio MACRI]
Socialist Party or PS [Hermes BINNER]
Renewal Front (Frente Renovador) or FR [Sergio MASSA]
numerous provincial parties

Political pressure groups and leaders: Argentine Association of Pharmaceutical Labs or CILFA
Argentine Industrial Union (manufacturers' association)
Argentine Rural Confederation or CRA (small to medium landowners' association)
Argentine Rural Society (large landowners' association)
Blue and White CGT (dissident CGT labor confederation)
Central of Argentine Workers or CTA (a union for employed and unemployed workers)
General Confederation of Labor or CGT (Peronist-leaning umbrella labor organization)
Roman Catholic Church
other: business organizations; Peronist-dominated labor movement; Piquetero groups (popular protest organizations that can be either pro or anti-government); students

International organization participation: AfDB (nonregional member), Australia Group, BCIE, BIS, CAN (associate), CD, CELAC, FAO, FATF, G-15, G-20, G-24, G-77, IADB, IAEA, IBRD, ICAO, ICC (national committees), ICCt, ICRM, IDA, IFAD, IFC, IFRCS, IHO, ILO, IMF, IMO, IMSO, Interpol, IOC, IOM, IPU, ISO, ITSO, ITU, ITUC (NGOs), LAES, LAIA, Mercosur, MIGA, MINURSO, MINUSTAH, NAM (observer), NSG, OAS, OPANAL, OPCW, Paris Club (associate), PCA, SICA (observer), UN, UN Security Council (temporary), UNASUR, UNCTAD, UNESCO, UNFICYP, UNHCR, UNIDO, Union Latina (observer), UNTSO, UNWTO, UPU, WCO, WFTU (NGOs), WHO, WIPO, WMO, WTO, ZC

Diplomatic representation in the US: *chief of mission:* Ambassador Martin LOUSTEAU (since 28 January 2016)
chancery: 1600 New Hampshire Avenue NW, Washington, DC 20009
telephone: [1] (202) 238-6400
FAX: [1] (202) 332-3171
consulate(s) general: Atlanta, Chicago, Houston, Los Angeles, Miami, New York, Washington, DC

Diplomatic representation from the US: *chief of mission:* Ambassador Noah Bryson MAMET (since 16 January 2015)

embassy: Avenida Colombia 4300, C1425GMN Buenos Aires
mailing address: international mail: use embassy street address; APO address: US Embassy Buenos Aires, Unit 4334, APO AA 34034
telephone: [54] (11) 5777-4533
FAX: [54] (11) 5777-4240

Flag description: three equal horizontal bands of light blue (top), white, and light blue; centered in the white band is a radiant yellow sun with a human face known as the Sun of May; the colors represent the clear skies and snow of the Andes; the sun symbol commemorates the appearance of the sun through cloudy skies on 25 May 1810 during the first mass demonstration in favor of independence; the sun features are those of Inti, the Inca god of the sun

National symbol(s): Sun of May (a sun with face symbol); national colors: light blue, white

National anthem: *name:* "Himno Nacional Argentino" (Argentine National Anthem)
lyrics/music: Vicente LOPEZ y PLANES/Jose Blas PARERA
note: adopted 1813; Vicente LOPEZ was inspired to write the anthem after watching a play about the 1810 May Revolution against Spain

ECONOMY

Economy overview: Argentina benefits from rich natural resources, a highly literate population, an export-oriented agricultural sector, and a diversified industrial base. Although one of the world's wealthiest countries 100 years ago, Argentina suffered during most of the 20th century from recurring economic crises, persistent fiscal and current account deficits, high inflation, mounting external debt, and capital flight. A severe depression, growing public and external indebtedness, and an unprecedented bank run culminated in 2001 in the most serious economic, social, and political crisis in the country's turbulent history. Interim President Adolfo RODRIGUEZ SAA declared a default-at the time the largest ever-on the government's foreign debt in December of that year, and abruptly resigned only a few days after taking office. His successor, Eduardo DUHALDE, announced an end to the peso's decade-long 1-to-1 peg to the US dollar in early 2002. The economy bottomed out that year, with real GDP 18% smaller than in 1998 and almost 60% of Argentines below the poverty line. Real GDP rebounded to grow by an average 8.5% annually over the subsequent six years, taking advantage of previously idled industrial capacity and labor, an audacious debt restructuring and reduced debt burden, excellent international financial conditions, and expansionary monetary and fiscal policies. Inflation also increased, however, during the administration of President Nestor KIRCHNER, which responded with price restraints on businesses, as well as export taxes and restraints, and beginning in 2007, with understating inflation data.

Cristina FERNANDEZ DE KIRCHNER succeeded her husband as president in late 2007, and the rapid economic growth of previous years began to slow sharply the following year as government policies held back exports and the world economy fell into recession. The economy in 2010 rebounded strongly from the 2009 recession, but has slowed since late 2011 even as the government continued to rely on expansionary fiscal and monetary policies, which have kept inflation in the double digits.

The government has taken multiple steps in recent years to deal with these problems. It expanded state intervention in the economy throughout 2012. In May 2012 the Congress approved the nationalization of the oil company YPF from Spain's Repsol. The government expanded formal and informal measures to restrict imports during the year, including a requirement for pre-registration and pre-approval of all imports. In July 2012, the government also further tightened currency controls in an effort to bolster foreign reserves and stem capital flight. In October 2013, the government settled long standing international arbitral disputes dating to before and following the 2001 Argentine financial crisis. During 2014, the government continued its expansionary fiscal and monetary policies and foreign exchange and imports controls. Between 2011 and 2013, Central Bank foreign reserves had dropped $21.3 billion from a high of $52.7 billion. In July 2014, Argentina and China agreed on an $11 billion currency swap; the Argentine Central Bank has received the equivalent of $3.2 billion in Chinese yuan, which it counts as international reserves.

In 2014, the government also took some measures to mend ties with the international financial community, including engaging with the IMF to improve its economic data reporting, reaching a compensation agreement with Repsol for the expropriation of YPF, and agreeing to pay $9.7 billion in arrears to the Paris Club over five years, including $606 million owed to the US. In July 2014, Argentina made its first payment to Paris Club creditors. At the same time, the Argentine Government in July 2014 entered a technical default on its external debt after it failed to reach an agreement with holdout creditors in the US. The FERNANDEZ DE KIRCHNER government rejected repeated attempts by the court to encourage a negotiated solution with holdouts. Throughout much of 2015, negotiations to repay holdout creditors stalled. The government's delay in reaching a settlement and the continuation of interventionist policies contributed to high inflation and a prolonged recession.

After being elected into office on December 10, President MACRI has taken significant steps to liberalize the Argentine economy. His administration lifted capital controls; floated the peso, negotiated debt payments with holdout bond creditors, and removed export controls on some commodities.

GDP (purchasing power parity):
$972 billion (2015 est.)
$960.4 billion (2014 est.)
$956.1 billion (2013 est.)
note: data are in 2015 US dollars
country comparison to the world: 26

GDP (official exchange rate):
$585.6 billion (2015 est.) GDP real

GDP—real growth rate:
1.2% (2015 est.)
0.5% (2014 est.)
2.9% (2013 est.)
country comparison to the world: 166

GDP—per capita (PPP):
$22,600 (2015 est.)
$22,500 (2014 est.)
$22,700 (2013 est.)
note: data are in 2015 US dollars
country comparison to the world: 81

Gross national saving:
15.6% of GDP (2015 est.)
18.2% of GDP (2014 est.)
17.9% of GDP (2013 est.)
country comparison to the world: 108

GDP—composition, by end use:
household consumption: 64.6%
government consumption: 16.7%
investment in fixed capital: 17.3%
investment in inventories: 1.6%
exports of goods and services: 12.9%
imports of goods and services: 13.1% (2015 est.)

GDP—composition, by sector of origin:
agriculture: 10.5%
industry: 29.1%
services: 60.4% (2015 est.)

Agriculture—products: sunflower seeds, lemons, soybeans, grapes, corn, tobacco, peanuts, tea, wheat; livestock

Industries: food processing, motor vehicles, consumer durables, textiles, chemicals and petrochemicals, printing, metallurgy, steel

Industrial production growth rate: 0.3%
note: based on private sector estimates (2015 est.)
country comparison to the world: 164

Labor force: 17.47 million
note: urban areas only (2015 est.)
country comparison to the world: 36

Labor force—by occupation: agriculture: 5%
industry: 23%
services: 72% (2009 est.)

Unemployment rate: 7.6% (2015 est.)
7.3% (2014 est.)
country comparison to the world: 89

Population below poverty line: 30%
note: data are based on private estimates (2010 est.)

Household income or consumption by percentage share: lowest: 10%: 1.5%
highest: 10%: 32.3% (2010 est.)

Distribution of family income—Gini index: 45.8 (2009)
country comparison to the world: 39

Budget: revenues: $143.4 billion
expenditures: $170.4 billion (2015 est.)
Taxes and other revenues: 24.8% of GDP (2015 est.)
country comparison to the world: 122

Budget surplus (+) or deficit (–):

-4.7% of GDP (2015 est.)
country comparison to the world: 164

Public debt: 45.8% of GDP (2015 est.)
42.7% of GDP (2014 est.)
country comparison to the world: 95

Fiscal year: calendar year

Inflation rate (consumer prices):
27.6% (2015 est.)
37.6% (2014 est.)
note: data are derived from private estimates
country comparison to the world: 221

Central bank discount rate: NA%

Commercial bank prime lending rate: 23.6% (31 December 2015 est.)
24.01% (31 December 2014 est.)
country comparison to the world: 7

Stock of narrow money:
$69.37 billion (31 December 2015 est.)
$62.87 billion (31 December 2014 est.)
country comparison to the world: 43

Stock of broad money: $150.3 billion (31 December 2015 est.)
$138.6 billion (31 December 2014 est.)
country comparison to the world: 51

Stock of domestic credit: $208.2 billion (31 December 2015 est.)
$183.3 billion (31 December 2014 est.)
country comparison to the world: 43

Market value of publicly traded shares:
$34.24 billion (31 December 2012 est.)
$43.58 billion (31 December 2011)
$63.91 billion (31 December 2010 est.)
country comparison to the world: 59

Current account balance: -$16.11 billion (2015 est.)
-$7.441 billion (2014 est.)
country comparison to the world: 183

Exports: $65.95 billion (2015 est.)
$67.42 billion (2014 est.)
country comparison to the world: 43

Exports commodities: soybeans and derivatives, petroleum and gas, vehicles, corn, wheat

Exports partners: Brazil 17%, China 8.6%, US 5.9% (2015)

Imports: $60.56 billion (2015 est.)
$65.25 billion (2014 est.)
country comparison to the world: 43

Imports commodities: machinery, motor vehicles, petroleum and natural gas, organic chemicals, plastics

Imports partners: Brazil 22.1%, US 16.1%, China 15.4%, Germany 5.1% (2015)

Reserves of foreign exchange and gold: $28.22 billion (31 December 2015 est.)
$31.4 billion (31 December 2014 est.)
country comparison to the world: 52

Debt external:
$147 billion (31 December 2014 est.)
$143.7 billion (31 December 2013 est.)
country comparison to the world: 41

Stock of direct foreign investment—at home:
$125.9 billion (31 December 2015 est.)

$116.5 billion (31 December 2014 est.)
country comparison to the world: 42

Stock of direct foreign investment—abroad:
$37.66 billion (31 December 2015 est.)
$36.44 billion (31 December 2014 est.)
country comparison to the world: 48

Exchange rates: Argentine pesos (ARS) per US dollar—
9.2 (2015 est.)
8.0753 (2014 est.)
8.0753 (2013 est.) 4.54 (2012 est.)
4.1101 (2011 est.)

ENERGY

Electricity—production: 127.9 billion kWh (2012 est.)
country comparison to the world: 29

Electricity—consumption: 117.1 billion kWh (2012 est.)
country comparison to the world: 30

Electricity—exports: 506 million kWh (2012 est.)
country comparison to the world: 67

Electricity—imports: 8.116 billion kWh (2012 est.)
country comparison to the world: 27

Electricity—installed generating capacity: 34.95 million kW (2012 est.)
country comparison to the world: 27

Electricity—from fossil fuels: 68.1% of total installed capacity (2012 est.)
country comparison to the world: 114

Electricity—from nuclear fuels: 2.7% of total installed capacity (2012 est.)
country comparison to the world: 27

Electricity—from hydro electric plants: 26% of total installed capacity (2012 est.)
country comparison to the world: 85

Electricity—from other renewable sources: 0.4% of total installed capacity (2012 est.)
country comparison to the world: 104

Crude oil—production: 532,100 bbl/day (2014 est.)
country comparison to the world: 28

Crude oil—exports: 59,630 bbl/day (2012 est.)
country comparison to the world: 42

Crude oil—imports: 100 bbl/day (2012 est.)
country comparison to the world: 83

Crude oil—proved reserves: 2.354 billion bbl (1 January 2015 est.)
country comparison to the world: 35

Refined petroleum products—production: 678,700 bbl/day (2012 est.)
country comparison to the world: 26

Refined petroleum products—consumption: 770,000 bbl/day (2013 est.)
country comparison to the world: 24

Refined petroleum products—exports: 59,470 bbl/day (2012 est.)
country comparison to the world: 54

Refined petroleum products—imports: 99,930 bbl/day (2012 est.)

country comparison to the world: 53

Natural gas—production: 36.89 billion cu m (2013 est.)
country comparison to the world: 25

Natural gas—consumption: 47.99 billion cu m (2013 est.)
country comparison to the world: 18

Natural gas—exports: 100 million cu m (2013 est.)
country comparison to the world: 45

Natural gas—imports: 11.2 billion cu m (2013 est.)
country comparison to the world: 24

Natural gas—proved reserves: 378.8 billion cu m (1 January 2014 est.)
country comparison to the world: 36

Carbon dioxide emissions from consumption of energy: 196 million Mt (2012 est.)
country comparison to the world: 31

COMMUNICATIONS

Telephones fixed—lines: *total subscriptions:* 9.4 million
subscriptions per 100 inhabitants: 22 (2014 est.)
country comparison to the world: 21

Telephones—mobile cellular: *total:* 66.4 million
subscriptions per 100 inhabitants: 154 (2014 est.)
country comparison to the world: 23

Telephone system: *general assessment:* in 1998 Argentina opened its telecommunications market to competition and foreign investment encouraging the growth of modern telecommunications technology; fiber-optic cable trunk lines are being installed between all major cities; major networks are entirely digital and the availability of telephone service is improving
domestic: microwave radio relay, fiber-optic cable, and a domestic satellite system with 40 earth stations serve the trunk network; fixed-line teledensity is increasing gradually and mobile-cellular subscribership is increasing rapidly; broadband Internet services are gaining ground
international: country code—54; landing point for the Atlantis-2, UNISUR, South America-1, and South American Crossing/Latin American Nautilus submarine cable systems that provide links to Europe, Africa, South and Central America, and US; satellite earth stations—112; 2 international gateways near Buenos Aires (2011)

Broadcast media: government owns a TV station and a radio network; more than 2 dozen TV stations and hundreds of privately owned radio stations; high rate of cable TV subscription usage (2007)
Radio broadcast stations: AM 260, FM (probably more than 1,000, mostly unlicensed), shortwave 6 (1998)
Television broadcast stations: 42 (plus 444 repeaters) (1997)

Internet country code: .ar

Internet hosts: 11.232 million (2012)
country comparison to the world: 13

Internet users: *total:* 25.7 million

percent of population: 59.7% (2014 est.)
country comparison to the world: 23

TRANSPORTATION

Airports: 1,138 (2013)
country comparison to the world: 6

Airports with—paved runways: *total:* 161
over 3,047 m: 4
2,438 to 3,047 m: 29
1,524 to 2,437 m: 65
914 to 1,523 m: 53
under 914 m: 10 (2013)

Airports with—unpaved runways: *total:* 977
over 3,047 m: 1
2,438 to 3,047 m: 1
1,524 to 2,437 m: 43
914 to 1,523 m: 484
under 914 m: 448 (2013)

Heliports: 2 (2013)

Pipelines: gas 29,930 km; liquid petroleum gas 41 km; oil 6,248 km; refined products 3,631 km (2013)

Railways: *total:* 36,917.4 km
broad gauge: 26,391 km 1.676-m gauge (149 km electrified)
standard gauge: 2,745.1 km 1.435-m gauge (41.1 km electrified)
narrow gauge: 7,523.3 km 1.000-m gauge; 258 km 0.750-m gauge (2014)
country comparison to the world: 8

Roadways: *total:* 231,374 km
paved: 69,412 km (includes 734 km of expressways)
unpaved: 161,962 km (2004)
country comparison to the world: 21

Waterways: 11,000 km (2012)
country comparison to the world: 12

Merchant marine: *total:* 36
by type: bulk carrier 1, cargo 5, chemical tanker 6, container 1, passenger/cargo 1, petroleum tanker 18, refrigerated cargo 4
foreign—owned: 14 (Brazil 1, Chile 6, Spain 3, Taiwan 2, UK 2)
registered in other countries: 15 (Liberia 1, Panama 5, Paraguay 5, Uruguay 1, unknown 3) (2010)
country comparison to the world: 80

Ports and terminals: *major seaport(s):* Bahia Blanca, Buenos Aires, La Plata, Punta Colorada, Ushuaia
river port(s): Arroyo Seco, Rosario, San Lorenzo San Martin (Parana)
container port(s) (TEUs): Buenos Aires (1,851,701)
LNG terminal(s) (import): Bahia Blanca

MILITARY AND SECURITY

Military branches: Argentine Army (Ejercito Argentino), Navy of the Argentine Republic (Armada Republica; includes naval aviation and naval infantry), Argentine Air Force (Fuerza Aerea Argentina, FAA) (2013)

Military service age and obligation: 18–24 years of age for voluntary military service (18–21 requires parental consent); no conscription; if the number of volunteers fails to meet the quota of recruits for a particular year, Congress can authorize the conscription of citizens turning 18 that year for a period not exceeding one year (2012)

Military expenditures:
0.91% of GDP (2012)
0.9% of GDP (2011)
0.91% of GDP (2010)
country comparison to the world: 106

Military—note: the Argentine military is a well-organized force constrained by the country's prolonged economic hardship; the country has recently experienced a strong recovery, and the military is implementing a modernization plan aimed at making the ground forces lighter and more responsive (2008)

TRANSNATIONAL ISSUES

Disputes international: Argentina continues to assert its claims to the UK-administered Falkland Islands (Islas Malvinas), South Georgia, and the South Sandwich Islands in its constitution, forcibly occupying the Falklands in 1982, but in 1995 agreed to no longer seek settlement by force; UK continues to reject Argentine requests for sovereignty talks; territorial claim in Antarctica partially overlaps UK and Chilean claims; uncontested dispute between Brazil and Uruguay over Braziliera/Brasiliera Island in the Quarai/Cuareim River leaves the tripoint with Argentina in question; in 2010, the ICJ ruled in favor of Uruguay's operation of two paper mills on the Uruguay River, which forms the border with Argentina; the two

countries formed a joint pollution monitoring regime; the joint boundary commission, established by Chile and Argentina in 2001 has yet to map and demarcate the delimited boundary in the inhospitable Andean Southern Ice Field (Campo de Hielo Sur); contraband smuggling, human trafficking, and illegal narcotic trafficking are problems in theporous areas of the border with Bolivia

Illicit drugs: a transshipment country for cocaine headed for Europe, heroin headed for the US, and ephedrine and pseudoephedrine headed for Mexico; some money-laundering activity, especially in the Tri-Border Area; law enforcement corruption; a source for precursor chemicals; increasing domestic consumption of drugs in urban centers, especially cocaine base and synthetic drugs (2008)

ARMENIA

INTRODUCTION

Background: Armenia prides itself on being the first nation to formally adopt Christianity (early 4th century). Despite periods of autonomy, over the centuries Armenia came under the sway of various empires including the Roman, Byzantine, Arab, Persian, and Ottoman. During World War I in the western portion of Armenia, the Ottoman Empire instituted a policy of forced resettlement coupled with other harsh practices that resulted in at least 1 million Armenian deaths. The eastern area of Armenia was ceded by the Ottomans to Russia in 1828; this portion declared its independence in 1918, but was conquered by the Soviet Red Army in 1920.

Armenian leaders remain preoccupied by the long conflict with Azerbaijan over Nagorno-Karabakh, a primarily Armenian-populated region, assigned to Soviet Azerbaijan in the 1920s by Moscow. Armenia and Azerbaijan began fighting over the area in 1988; the struggle escalated after both

countries attained independence from the Soviet Union in 1991. By May 1994, when a ceasefire took hold, ethnic Armenian forces held not only Nagorno-Karabakh but also seven surrounding regions, approximately 14 percent of Azerbaijan's territory. The economies of both sides have been hurt by their inability to make substantial progress toward a peaceful resolution.

Turkey closed the common border with Armenia in 1993 in support of Azerbaijan in its conflict with Armenia over control of Nagorno-Karabakh and surrounding areas, further hampering Armenian economic growth. In 2009, senior Armenian leaders began pursuing rapprochement with Turkey, aiming to secure an opening of the border, but Turkey has not yet ratified the Protocols normalizing relations between the two countries. In January 2015, Armenia joined Russia, Belarus, and Kazakhstan as a member of the Eurasian Economic Union.

GEOGRAPHY

Location: Southwestern Asia, between Turkey (to the west) and Azerbaijan

Geographic coordinates: 40 00 N, 45 00 E

Map references: Asia

Area: *total:* 29,743 sq km
land: 28,203 sq km
water: 1,540 sq km
country comparison to the world: 143

Area—comparative: slightly smaller than Maryland

Land boundaries: *total:* 1,570 km
border countries (4): Azerbaijan 996 km, Georgia 219 km, Iran 44 km, Turkey 311 km

Coastline: 0 km (landlocked)

Maritime claims: none (landlocked)

Climate: highland continental, hot summers, cold winters

Terrain: Armenian Highland with mountains; little forest land; fast flowing rivers; good soil in Aras River valley

Elevation: *mean elevation:* 1,792 m

elevation extremes: *lowest point:* Debed River 400 m
highest point: Aragats Lerrnagagat' 4,090 m

Natural resources: small deposits of gold, copper, molybdenum, zinc, bauxite

Land use: *agricultural land:* 59.7%
arable land: 15.8%
permanent crops: 1.9%
permanent pasture: 42%
forest: 9.1%
other: 31.2% (2011 est.)

Irrigated land: 2,740 sq km (2012)

Total renewable water resources: 7.77 cu km (2011)

Freshwater withdrawal (domestic/industrial/agricultural): *total:* 2.86 cu km/yr (40%/6%/54%) per capita: 929.7 cu m/yr (2010)

Natural hazards: occasionally severe earthquakes; droughts

Environment current—issues: soil pollution from toxic chemicals such as DDT; the energy crisis of the 1990s led to deforestation when citizens scavenged for firewood; pollution of Hrazdan (Razdan) and Aras Rivers; the draining of Sevana Lich (Lake Sevan), a result of its use as a source for hydropower, threatens drinking water supplies; restart of Metsamor nuclear power plant in spite of its location in a seismically active zone

Environment—international agreements: *party to:* Air Pollution, Biodiversity, Climate Change, Climate Change-Kyoto Protocol, Desertification, Environmental Modification, Hazardous Wastes, Law of the Sea, Ozone Layer Protection, Wetlands *signed, but not ratified:* Air Pollution-Persistent Organic Pollutants

Geography—note: landlocked in the Lesser Caucasus Mountains; Sevana Lich (Lake Sevan) is the largest lake in thismountain range

PEOPLE AND SOCIETY

Nationality: *noun:* Armenian(s)
adjective: Armenian

Ethnic groups: Armenian 98.1%, Yezidi (Kurd) 1.1%, other 0.7% (2011 est.)

Languages: Armenian (official) 97.9%, Kurdish (spoken by Yezidi minority) 1%, other 1% (2011 est.)

Religions: Armenian Apostolic 92.6%, Evangelical 1%, other 2.4%, none 1.1%, unspecified 2.9% (2011 est.)

Population: 3,056,382 (July 2015 est.)
country comparison to the world: 136

Age structure: *0–14 years:* 19.05% (male 310,893/female 271,479)
15–24 years: 14.42% (male 225,029/female 215,700)
25–54 years: 43.47% (male 638,983/female 689,519)
55–64 years: 12.35% (male 171,584/female 205,751)
65 years and over: 10.71% (male 130,804/female 196,640) (2015 est.)

Dependency ratios:
total dependency ratio: 41.3%
youth dependency ratio: 26%
elderly dependency ratio: 15.3%
potential support ratio: 6.5% (2015 est.)

Median age: *total:* 34.2 years
male: 32.3 years
female: 36.1 years (2015 est.)
country comparison to the world: 80

Population growth rate: -0.15% (2015 est.)
country comparison to the world: 211

Birth rate: 13.61 births/1,000 population (2015 est.)
country comparison to the world: 145

Death rate: 9.34 deaths/1,000 population (2015 est.)
country comparison to the world: 61

Net migration rate: -5.8 migrant(s)/1,000 population (2015 est.)
country comparison to the world: 196

Urbanization: *urban population:* 62.7% of total population (2015)
rate of urbanization: -0.11% annual rate of change (2010–15 est.)

Major urban areas—population: YEREVAN (capital) 1,044 (2015)

Sex ratio: *at birth:* 1.13 male(s)/female
0–14 years: 1.15 male(s)/female
15–24 years: 1.04 male(s)/female
25–54 years: 0.93 male(s)/female
55–64 years: 0.83 male(s)/female
65 years and over: 0.67 male(s)/female
total population: 0.94 male(s)/female (2015 est.)

Mother's mean age at first birth: 23.5 (2011 est.)

Maternal mortality rate: 25 deaths/100,000 live births (2015 est.)
country comparison to the world: 123

Infant mortality rate: *total:* 13.51 deaths/1,000 live births
male: 14.95 deaths/1,000 live births
female: 11.88 deaths/1,000 live births (2015 est.)
country comparison to the world: 111

Life expectancy at birth: *total population:* 74.37 years
male: 71.13 years
female: 78.03 years (2015 est.)
country comparison to the world: 121

Total fertility rate: 1.64 children born/woman (2015 est.)
country comparison to the world: 177

Contraceptive prevalence rate: 54.9% (2010)

Health expenditures: 4.5% of GDP (2013)
country comparison to the world: 152

Physicians density: 2.7 physicians/1,000 population (2013)

Hospital bed density: 3.9 beds/1,000 population (2012)

Drinking water source:
improved:
urban: 100% of population
rural: 100% of population
total: 100% of population
unimproved:
urban: 0% of population
rural: 0% of population
total: 0% of population (2015 est.)

Sanitation facility access:
improved:
urban: 96.2% of population
rural: 78.2% of population
total: 89.5% of population
unimproved:
urban: 3.8% of population
rural: 21.8% of population
total: 10.5% of population (2015 est.)

HIV/AIDS—adult prevalence rate: 0.22% (2014 est.)
country comparison to the world: 96

HIV/AIDS—people living with HIV/AIDS: 4,000 (2014 est.)
country comparison to the world: 109

HIV/AIDS—deaths: 200 (2014 est.)
country comparison to the world: 102

Obesity—adult prevalence rate: 19.9% (2014)
country comparison to the world: 68

Children under the age of 5 years underweight: 5.3% (2010)
country comparison to the world: 89

Education expenditures: 2.2% of GDP (2014)
country comparison to the world: 132

Literacy: *definition:* age 15 and over can read and write
total population: 99.7%
male: 99.7%
female: 99.6% (2015 est.)

School life expectancy (primary to tertiary education): *total:* 12 years
male: 11 years
female: 14 years (2009)

Child labor—children ages 5–14:
total number: 19,596
percentage: 4%
note: data represent children ages 7–17 (2007 est.)

Unemployment, youth ages 15–24: *total:* 36.1%
male: 31.8%
female: 41.5% (2013 est.)
country comparison to the world: 13

GOVERNMENT

Country name: *conventional long form:* Republic of Armenia
conventional short form: Armenia
local long form: Hayastani Hanrapetut'yunlocal short form: Hayastan
former: Armenian Soviet Socialist Republic, Armenian Republic
etymology: the eetymology of the country's name remains obscure; according to tradition, the country is named after Hayk, the legendary patriarch of the Armenians and the great-great-grandson of Noah; Hayk's descendant, Aram, purportedly is the source of the name Armenia

Government type: semi-presidential republic
note: a constituional referendum approved in December 2015 will change the government type to a parliamentary system, replacing the semi-presidential system and becoming effective for the 2017–18 electoral cycle

Capital: *name:* Yerevan

Geographic coordinates: 40 10 N, 44 30 E
time difference: UTC+4 (9 hours ahead of Washington, DC, during Standard Time)

Administrative divisions: 11 provinces (marzer, singular-marz); Aragatsotn, Ararat, Armavir, Geghark'unik', Kotayk', Lorri, Shirak, Syunik', Tavush, Vayots' Dzor, Yerevan

Independence: 21 September 1991 (from the Soviet Union)

National holiday: Independence Day, 21 September (1991)

Constitution: previous 1915, 1978; latest adopted 5 July 1995; amended 2005, 2015; note—the 2015 amendment, approved in December 2015 by a public referendum and effective for the 2017–18 electoral cycle, changes the government type from the current semi-presidential system to a parliamentary system (2016)
note: the 2015 amendment, approved in December 2015 by a public referendum and effective for the 2017–18 electoral cycle, changes the government type from the current semi-presidential system to a parliamentary system (2016)

Legal system: civil law system

International law organization participation: has not submitted an ICJ jurisdiction declaration; non-party state to the ICCt

Citizenship: *citizenship by birth:* no

citizenship by descent only: at least one parent must be a citizen of Armenia

dual citizenship recognized: yes

residency requirement for naturalization: 3 years

Suffrage: 18 years of age; universal

Executive branch: *chief of state:* President Serzh SARGSIAN (since 9 April 2008)

head of government: Prime Minister Hovik ABRAHAMYAN (since 13 April 2014)

cabinet: Council of Ministers appointed by the prime minist

erelections/appointments: president directly elected by absolute majority popular vote in two rounds if needed for a 5-year term (eligible for a second term); election last held on 18 February 2013 (next to be held in February 2018); prime minister appointed by the president based on majority support in the National Congress; the prime minister and Council of Ministers must resign if the National Congress refuses to accept their program

election results: Serzh SARGSIAN reelected president in one round; percent of vote—Serzh SARGSIAN (RPA) 58.6%, Raffi HOVHANNISIAN (Heritage Party) 36.7%, Hrant BAGRATIAN (ANM) 2.2%, other 2.5%

note: constitutional changes adopted in December 2015 will transform the government to a parliamentary system by 2018; for the scheduled February 2018 election, the president will be indirectly elected by parliament and will serve a single 7-year term; following the 2018 election, the prime minister will be elected based on majority support of the National Assembly

Legislative branch: *description:* unicameral National Assembly (Parliament) or Azgayin Zhoghov (131 seats; 90 members directly elected in single-seat constituencies by proportional representation vote and 41 directly elected by simple majority vote; members serve 5-year terms)

elections: last held on 6 May 2012 (next to be held in the spring of 2017)

election results: percent of vote by party—RPA 44%, Prosperous Armenia 30.1%, ANC 7.1%, Heritage Party 5.8%, ARF (Dashnak) 5.7%, Rule of Law 5.5%, other 1.8%; seats by party—RPA 69, Prosperous Armenia 37, ANC 7, Rule of Law 6, Heritage Party 5, ARF (Dashnak) 5, independent 2

Judicial branch: *highest court(s):* Court of Cassation (consists of the court chairman and organized into a criminal chamber and a civil and administrative chamber, each with a court chairman and 2 judges); Constitutional Court (consists of 9 judges)

judge selection and term of office: Court of Cassation judges nominated by the Judicial Council, a 9-member body of selected judges and legal scholars; judges appointed by the president; Constitutional Court judges—4 appointed by the president, and 5 elected by National Assembly; judges of both courts can serve until retirement at age 65

subordinate courts: 2 Courts of Appeal (for civil cases and for criminal and military cases); district courts; Administrative Court

Political parties and leaders: Armenian National Congress or ANC (bloc of independent and opposition parties) [Levon TERPETROSSIAN]

Armenian National Movement or ANM [Ararat ZURABIAN]

Armenian Revolutionary Federation or ARF ("Dashnak" Party) [Hrant MARKARIAN]

Heritage Party [Raffi HOVHANNISIAN]

People's Party of Armenia [Stepan DEMIRCHIAN]

Prosperous Armenia [Naira ZOHRABYAN]

Republican Party of Armenia or RPA [Serzh SARGSIAN]

Rule of Law Party (Orinats Yerkir) [Artur BAGHDASARIAN]

Political pressure groups and leaders: Aylentrank (Impeachment Alliance) [Nikol PASHINIAN] Yerkrapah Union [Manvel GRIGORIAN]

International organization participation: ADB, BSEC, CD, CE, CIS, CSTO, EAEC (observer), EAEU, EAPC, EBRD, FAO, GCTU, IAEA, IBRD, ICAO, ICC (NGOs), ICRM, IDA, IFAD, IFC, IFRCS, ILO, IMF, Interpol, IOC, IOM, IPU, ISO, ITSO, ITU, MIGA, NAM (observer), OAS (observer), OIF, OPCW, OSCE, PFP, UN, UNCTAD, UNESCO, UNIDO, UNIFIL, UNWTO, UPU, WCO, WFTU (NGOs), WHO, WIPO, WMO, WTO

Diplomatic representation in the US: *chief of mission:* Ambassador Grigor HOVHANNISSIAN (since 28 January 2016)

chancery: 2225 R Street NW, Washington, DC 20008

telephone: [1] (202) 319-1976

FAX: [1] (202) 319-2982

consulate(s) general: Glendale (CA)

Diplomatic representation from the US: *chief of mission:* Ambassador Richard MILLS (since 13 February 2015)

embassy: 1 American Ave., Yerevan 0082

mailing address: American Embassy Yerevan, US Department of State, 7020 Yerevan Place, Washington, DC 20521–7020

telephone: [374] (10) 464-700

FAX: [374] (10) 464-742

Flag description: three equal horizontal bands of red (top), blue, and orange; the color red recalls the blood shed for liberty, blue the Armenian skies as well as hope, and orange the land and the courage of the workers who farm it

National symbol(s): Mount Ararat, eagle, lion; national colors: red, blue, orange

National anthem: *name:* "Mer Hayrenik" (Our Fatherland)

lyrics/music: Mikael NALBANDIAN/Barsegh KANACHYA

N*note:* adopted 1991; based on the anthem of the Democratic Republic of Armenia (1918–1922) but with different lyrics

ECONOMY

Economy overview: Under the old Soviet central planning system, Armenia developed a modern industrial sector, supplying machine tools, textiles, and other manufactured goods to sister republics, in exchange for raw materials and energy. Armenia has since switched to smalls-cale agriculture and away from the large agroindustrial complexes of the Soviet era. Armenia has only two open trade borders—Iran and Georgia—because its borders with Azerbaijan and Turkey have been closed since 1991 and 1993, respectively, as a result of Armenia's ongoing conflict with Azerbaijan over the separatist Nagorno-Karabakh region.

Armenia joined the WTO in January 2003. The government has made some improvements in tax and customs administration in recent years, but anti-corruption measures have been ineffective. Armenia will need to pursue additional economic reforms and strengthen the rule of law in order to regain economic growth and improve economic competitiveness and employment opportunities, especially given its economic isolation from two of its nearest neighbors, Turkey and Azerbaijan.

Armenia's geographic isolation, a narrow export base, and pervasive monopolies in important business sectors have made it particularly vulnerable to the sharp deterioration in the global economy and the economic downturn in Russia. Armenia is particularly dependent on Russian commercial and governmental support and most key Armenian infrastructure is Russian-owned and/or managed, especially in the energy sector, including electricity and natural gas. Remittances from expatriates working in Russia are equivalent to about 20% of GDP and partly offset the country's severe trade imbalance. Armenia joined Russia in the Eurasian Economic Union upon the bloc's launch in January 2015, even though the ruble's sharp depreciation in December 2014 led to currency instability, inflation, and a significant decrease in exports from Armenia to Russia.

GDP (purchasing power parity):
$25.32 billion (2015 est.)
$24.58 billion (2014 est.)
$23.75 billion (2013 est.)
note: data are in 2015 US dollars
country comparison to the world: 136

GDP (official exchange rate):
$10.57 billion (2015 est.)

GDP—real growth rate:
3% (2015 est.)
3.5% (2014 est.)
3.3% (2013 est.)
country comparison to the world: 98

GDP—per capita (PPP):
$8,500 (2015 est.)
$8,200 (2014 est.)
$8,000 (2013 est.)
note: data are in 2015 US dollars
country comparison to the world: 144

Gross national saving:
16.4% of GDP (2015 est.)
13.8% of GDP (2014 est.)
14.7% of GDP (2013 est.)
country comparison to the world: 103

GDP—composition, by end use:
household consumption: 82.8%
government consumption: 12.6%

investment in fixed capital: 20%
investment in inventories: -0.5%
exports of goods and services: 29.5%
imports of goods and services: -44.4% (2015 est.)

GDP—composition, by sector of origin:
agriculture: 23.3%
industry: 30.1%
services: 46.7% (2015 est.)

Agriculture—products: fruit (especially grapes), vegetables; livestock

Industries: diamond processing, metal-cutting machine tools, forging and pressing machines, electric motors, knitted wear, hosiery, shoes, silk fabric, chemicals, trucks, instruments, microelectronics, jewelry, software, food processing, brandy, mining

Industrial production growth rate: 0.3% (2015 est.)
country comparison to the world: 165

Labor force: 1.508 million (2015 est.)
country comparison to the world: 131

Labor force—by occupation: *agriculture:* 39%
industry: 17%
services: 44% (2011 est.)

Unemployment rate: 17.8% (2014 est.)
country comparison to the world: 163

Population below poverty line: 32% (2013 est.)

Household income or consumption by percentage share: *lowest:* 10%: 3.7%
highest: 10%: 24.8% (2012)

Distribution of family income—Gini index: 30.3 (2012)
31.3 (2011)
country comparison to the world: 120

Budget: *revenues:* $2.541 billion
expenditures: $2.849 billion (2015 est.)
Taxes and other revenues: 24% of GDP (2015 est.)
country comparison to the world: 130

Budget surplus (+) or deficit (–): -2.9% of GDP (2015 est.)
country comparison to the world: 109

Public debt: 47.5% of GDP (2015 est.)
43.5% of GDP (2014 est.)
country comparison to the world: 88

Fiscal year: calendar year

Inflation rate (consumer prices):
3.7% (2015 est.)
3% (2014 est.)
country comparison to the world: 150

Central bank discount rate: 10.5% (10 February 2015) 8% (11 January 2012)
note: this is the Refinancing Rate, the key monetary policy instrument of the Armenian National Bank
country comparison to the world: 21

Commercial bank prime lending rate: 17.3% (31 December 2015 est.)
16.41% (31 December 2014 est.)
note: average lending rate on loans up to one year
country comparison to the world: 25

Stock of narrow money:
$1.127 billion (31 December 2015 est.)

$1.118 billion (31 December 2014 est.)
country comparison to the world: 149

Stock of broad money: $2.038 billion (31 December 2015 est.)
$1.723 billion (31 December 2014 est.)
country comparison to the world: 153

Stock of domestic credit: $6.212 billion (31 December 2015 est.)
$5.219 billion (31 December 2014 est.)
country comparison to the world: 116

Market value of publicly traded shares:
$132.1 million (31 December 2012 est.)
$139.6 million (31 December 2011)
$144.8 million (31 December 2010 est.)
country comparison to the world: 119

Current account balance: -$335 million (2015 est.) $
-849 million (2014 est.)
country comparison to the world: 90

Exports: $1.496 billion (2015 est.)
$1.665 billion (2014 est.)
country comparison to the world: 150

Exports—commodities: pig iron, unwrought copper, nonferrous metals, gold, diamonds, mineral products, foodstuffs, energy

Exports—partners: Russia 15.2%, China 11.1%, Germany 9.8%, Iraq 8.8%, Georgia 7.8%, Canada 7.6%, Bulgaria 5.3%, Iran 5.3% (2015)

Imports: $3.117 billion (2015 est.)
$3.734 billion (2014 est.)
country comparison to the world: 144

Imports—commodities: natural gas, petroleum, tobacco products, foodstuffs, diamonds, pharmaceuticals, cars

Imports—partners: Russia 29.1%, China 9.7%, Germany 6.2%, Iran 6.1%, Italy 4.6%, Turkey 4.2% (2015)

Reserves of foreign exchange and gold: $1.209 billion (31 December 2015 est.)
$1.489 billion (31 December 2014 est.)
country comparison to the world: 126

Debt—external:
$8.537 billion (31 December 2014 est.)
$8.695 billion (31 December 2013 est.)
country comparison to the world: 111

Stock of direct foreign investment—at home: $4.817 billion (2013)
country comparison to the world: 98

Exchange rates: drams (AMD) per US dollar—
480.9 (2015 est.)
415.92 (2014 est.)
415.92 (2013 est.)
401.76 (2012 est.)
372.5 (2011 est.)

ENERGY

Electricity—production: 7.622 billion kWh (2012 est.)
country comparison to the world: 105

Electricity—consumption: 5.043 billion kWh (2012 est.)
country comparison to the world: 115

Electricity—exports: 1.696 billion kWh (2012 est.)
country comparison to the world: 47

Electricity—imports: 98 million kWh (2012 est.)
country comparison to the world: 93

Electricity—installed generating capacity: 4.021 million kW (2012 est.)
country comparison to the world: 82

Electricity—from fossil fuels: 32.2% of total installed capacity (2011 est.)
country comparison to the world: 177

Electricity—from nuclear fuels: 34.3% of total installed capacity (2011 est.)
country comparison to the world: 3

Electricity—from hydro electric plants: 33.5% of total installed capacity (2011 est.)
country comparison to the world: 66

Electricity—from other renewable sources: 0% of total installed capacity (2011 est.)
country comparison to the world: 152

Crude oil—production: 0 bbl/day (2014 est.)
country comparison to the world: 105

Crude oil—exports: 0 bbl/day (2013 est.)
country comparison to the world: 95

Crude oil—imports: 0 bbl/day (2013 est.)
country comparison to the world: 155

Crude oil—proved reserves: 0 bbl (1 January 2015 est.)
country comparison to the world: 104

Refined petroleum products—production: 0 bbl/day (2012 est.)
country comparison to the world: 153

Refined petroleum products—consumption: 8,700 bbl/day (2013 est.)
country comparison to the world: 157

Refined petroleum products—exports: 0 bbl/day (2012 est.)
country comparison to the world: 152

Refined petroleum products—imports: 8,722 bbl/day (2012 est.)
country comparison to the world: 141

Natural gas—production: 0 cu m (2013 est.)
country comparison to the world: 154

Natural gas—consumption: 2.01 billion cu m (2014 est.)
country comparison to the world: 80

Natural gas—exports: 0 cu m (2013 est.)
country comparison to the world: 56

Natural gas—imports: 2.061 billion cu m (2014 est.)
country comparison to the world: 48

Natural gas—proved reserves: 0 cu m (1 January 2014 est.)
country comparison to the world: 109

Carbon dioxide emissions from consumption of energy: 12.12 million Mt (2012 est.)
country comparison to the world: 97

COMMUNICATIONS

Telephones—fixed lines: *total subscriptions:* 560,000

43

subscriptions per 100 inhabitants: 18 (2014 est.)
country comparison to the world: 94

Telephones—mobile cellular: *total:* 3.5 million
subscriptions per 100 inhabitants: 113 (2014 est.)
country comparison to the world: 130

Telephone system: *general assessment:* telecommunications investments have made major inroads in modernizing and upgrading the outdated telecommunications network inherited from the Soviet era; now 100% privately owned and undergoing modernization and expansion; mobile-cellular services monopoly terminated in late 2004, and a second and third provider began operations in 2005 and 2009 respectively
domestic: reliable modern fixe-dline and mobile-cellular services are available across Yerevan and in major cities and towns; significant but ever-shrinking gaps remain in mobile-cellular coverage in rural areas
international: country code—374; Yerevan is connected to the Trans-Asia-Europe fiber-optic cable through Iran; additional international service is available by microwave radio relay and landline connections to the other countries of the Commonwealth of Independent States, through the Moscow international switch, and by satellite to the rest of the world; satellite earth stations—3 (2008)

Broadcast media: 2 public TV networks operating alongside about 40 privately owned TV stations that provide local to near nationwide coverage; major Russian broadcast stations are widely available; subscription cable TV services are available in most regions; Public Radio of Armenia is a national, state-run broadcast network that operates alongside 21 privately owned radio stations; several major international broadcasters are available (2015)
Radio broadcast stations: AM 9, FM 16, shortwave 1 (2006)

Television broadcast stations: 48 (private television stations alongside 2 public networks; major Russian channels widely available) (2006)

Internet country code: .am

Internet hosts: 194,142 (2012)
country comparison to the world: 73

Internet users: *total:* 1.3 million
percent of population: 43.6% (2014 est.)
country comparison to the world: 117

TRANSPORTATION

Airports: 11 (2013)
country comparison to the world: 154

Airports—with paved runways: *total:* 10
over 3,047 m: 2
2,438 to 3,047 m: 2
1,524 to 2,437 m: 4
914 to 1,523 m: 2 (2013)

Airports—with unpaved runways: *total:* 1
914 to 1,523 m: 1 (2013)

Pipelines: gas 2,233 km (2013)

Railways: *total:* 780 km
broad gauge: 780 km 1.520-m gauge (780 km electrified)
note: 726 km operational (2014)
country comparison to the world: 97

Roadways: *total:* 7,792 km (2013)
country comparison to the world: 143

MILITARY AND SECURITY

Military branches: Armenian Armed Forces: Ground Forces, Air Force and Air Defense; "Nagorno-Karabakh Republic": Nagorno-Karabakh Self-Defense Force (NKSDF) (2011)

Military service age and obligation: 18–27 years of age for voluntary or compulsory military service; 2-year conscript service obligation; 17 year olds are eligible to become cadets at military higher

education institutes, where they are classified as military personnel (2012)

Military expenditures: 4.29% of GDP (2014)
4.1% of GDP (2013)
3.92% of GDP (2012)
3.87% of GDP (2011)
3.92% of GDP (2010)
country comparison to the world: 10

TRANSNATIONAL ISSUES

Disputes—international: the dispute over the break-away Nagorno-Karabakh region and the Armenian military occupation of surrounding lands in Azerbaijan remains the primary focus of regional instability; residents hav eevacuated the former Soviet-era small ethnic enclaves in Armenia and Azerbaijan; Turkish authorities have complained that blasting from quarries in Armenia might be damaging the medieval ruins of Ani, on the other side of the Arpacay valley; in 2009, Swiss mediators facilitated an accord reestablishing diplomatic ties between Armenia and Turkey, but neither side has ratified the agreement and the rapprochement effort has faltered; local border forces struggle to control the illegal transit of goods and people across the porous, undemarcated Armenian, Azerbaijani, and Georgian borders; ethnic Armenian groups in the Javakheti region of Georgia seek greater autonomy from the Georgian Government

Refugees and internally displaced persons: *refugees (country of origin):* 14,994 (Syria ethnic Armenians) (2014)
IDPs: 8,400 (conflict with Azerbaijan over Nagorno-Karabakh) (2015)
stateless persons: 311 (2015)

Illicit drugs: illicit cultivation of small amount of cannabis for domestic consumption; minor transit point for illicit drugs—mostly opium and hashish moving—from Southwest Asia to Russia and to a lesser extent the rest of Europe

ARUBA

INTRODUCTION

Background: Discovered and claimed for Spain in 1499, Aruba was acquired by the Dutch in 1636. The island's economy has been dominated by three main industries. A 19th century gold rush was followed by prosperity brought on by the opening in 1924 of an oil refinery. The last decades of the 20th century saw a boom in the tourism industry. Aruba seceded from the Netherlands Antilles in 1986 and became a separate, autonomous member of the Kingdom of the Netherlands. Movement toward full independence was halted at Aruba's request in 1990.

GEOGRAPHY

Location: Caribbean, island in the Caribbean Sea, north of Venezuela

Geographic coordinates: 12 30 N, 69 58 W

Map references: Central America and the Caribbean

Area: *total:* 180 sq km
land: 180 sq km
water: 0 sq km
country comparison to the world: 218

Area—comparative: slightly larger than Washington, DC

Land boundaries: 0 km

Coastline: 68.5 km

Maritime claims: *territorial sea:* 12 nm

Climate: tropical marine; little seasonal temperature variation

Terrain: flat with a few hills; scant vegetation

Elevation: *mean elevation:* NA

elevation extremes: *lowest point:* Caribbean Sea 0 m

highest point: Ceru Jamanota 188 m

Natural resources: NEGL; white sandy beaches foster tourism

Land use: *agricultural land:* 11.1%
arable land: 11.1%
permanent crops: 0%
permanent pasture: 0%
forest: 2.3%
other: 86.6% (2011 est.)

Irrigated land: NA

Natural hazards: hurricanes; lies outside the Caribbean hurricane belt and is rarely threatened

Environment—current issues: NA

Geography—note: a flat, riverless island renowned for its white sand beaches; its tropical climate is moderated by constant trade winds from the Atlantic Ocean; the temperature is almost

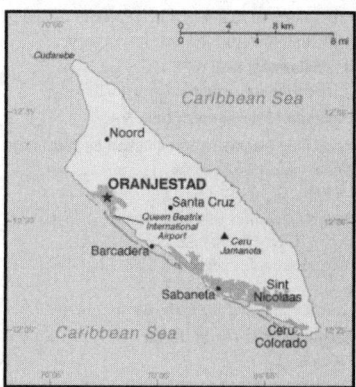

constant at about 27 degrees Celsius (81 degrees Fahrenheit)

PEOPLE AND SOCIETY

Nationality: *noun:* Aruban(s)
adjective: Aruban; Dutch

Ethnic groups: Dutch 82.1%, Colombian 6.6%, Venezuelan 2.2%, Dominican 2.2%, Haitian 1.2%, other 5.5%, unspecified 0.1% (2010 est.)

Languages: Papiamento (official) (a creole language that is a mixture of Portuguese, Spanish, Dutch, English, and, to a lesser extent, French, as well as elements of African languages and the language of the Arawak) 69.4%, Spanish 13.7%, English (widely spoken) 7.1%, Dutch (official) 6.1%, Chinese 1.5%, other 1.7%, unspecified 0.4% (2010 est.)

Religions: Roman Catholic 75.3%, Protestant 4.9% (includes Methodist 0.9%, Adventist 0.9%, Anglican 0.4%, other Protestant 2.7%), Jehovah's Witness 1.7%, other 12%, none 5.5%, unspecified 0.5% (2010 est.)

Population: 112,162 (July 2015 est.)
country comparison to the world: 190

Age structure: *0–14 years:* 17.69% (male 9,953/female 9,888)
15–24 years: 13.27% (male 7,470/female 7,417)
25–54 years: 42.59% (male 23,015/female 24,750)
55–64 years: 13.73% (male 7,114/female 8,287)
65 years and over: 12.72% (male 5,591/female 8,677) (2015 est.)

Dependency ratios:
total dependency ratio: 44%
youth dependency ratio: 26.4%
elderly dependency ratio: 17.6%
potential support ratio: 5.7% (2015 est.)

Median age: *total:* 39 years
male: 37.1 years
female: 40.8 years (2015 est.)
country comparison to the world: 56

Population growth rate: 1.33% (2015 est.)
country comparison to the world: 89

Birth rate: 12.56 births/1,000 population (2015 est.)
country comparison to the world: 157

Death rate: 8.18 deaths/1,000 population (2015 est.)
country comparison to the world: 92

Net migration rate: 8.92 migrant(s)/1,000 population (2015 est.)
country comparison to the world: 12

Urbanization: *urban population:* 41.5% of total population (2015)
rate of urbanization: -0.28% annual rate of change (2010–15 est.)

Major urban areas—population: ORANJESTAD (capital) 29,000 (2014)

Sex ratio: *at birth:* 1.02 male(s)/female
0–14 years: 1.01 male(s)/female
15–24 years: 1.01 male(s)/female
25–54 years: 0.93 male(s)/female
55–64 years: 0.86 male(s)/female
65 years and over: 0.64 male(s)/female
total population: 0.9 male(s)/female (2015 est.)

Infant mortality rate: *total:* 11.37 deaths/1,000 live births
male: 14.94 deaths/1,000 live births
female: 7.74 deaths/1,000 live births (2015 est.)
country comparison to the world: 127

Life expectancy at birth: *total population:* 76.56 years
male: 73.5 years
female: 79.68 years (2015 est.)
country comparison to the world: 83

Total fertility rate: 1.84 children born/woman (2015 est.)
country comparison to the world: 146

Drinking water source:
improved:
urban: 98.1% of population
rural: 98.1% of population
total: 98.1% of population
unimproved:
urban: 1.9% of population
rural: 1.9% of population
total: 1.9% of population (2015 est.)

Sanitation facility access:
improved:
urban: 97.7% of population
rural: 97.7% of population
total: 97.7% of population
unimproved:
urban: 2.3% of population
rural: 2.3% of population
total: 2.3% of population (2015 est.)

HIV/AIDS—adult prevalence rate: NA

HIV/AIDS—people living with HIV/AIDS: NA

HIV/AIDS—deaths: NA

Education expenditures: 6% of GDP (2011)
country comparison to the world: 41

Literacy: *definition:* age 15 and over can read and write
total population: 97.5%
male: 97.5%
female: 97.5% (2015 est.)

School life expectancy (primary to tertiary education): *total:* 14 years
male: 13 years

female: 14 years (2012)

Unemployment, youth ages 15–24:
total: 28.9%
male: 29.9%
female: 27.5% (2010 est.)
country comparison to the world: 43

GOVERNMENT

Country name: *conventional long form:* none
conventional short form: Aruba
etymology: the origin of the island's name is unclear; according to tradition, the name comes from the Spanish phrase "oro huba" (there was gold), but in fact no gold was ever found on the island; another possibility is the native word "oruba, " which means "well situated"

Dependency status: constituent country of the Kingdom of the Netherlands; full autonomy in internal affairs obtained in 1986 upon separation from the Netherlands Antilles; Dutch Government responsible for defense and foreign affairs

Government type: parliamentary democracy (Legislature); part of the Kingdom of the Netherlands

Capital: *name:* Oranjestad

Geographic coordinates: 12 31 N, 70 02 W
time difference: UTC-4 (1 hour ahead of Washington, DC, during Standard Time)

Administrative divisions: none (part of the Kingdom of the Netherlands)
note: Aruba is one of four constituent parts (countries) of the Kingdom of the Netherlands; the other three parts are the Netherlands, Curacao, and Sint Maarten

Independence: none (part of the Kingdom of the Netherlands)

National holiday: Flag Day, 18 March (1976)

Constitution: previous 1947, 1955; latest drafted and approved August 1985, enacted 1 January 1986 (regulates governance of Aruba, but is subordinate to the Charter for the Kingdom of the Netherlands); note—in October 2010, following dissolution of the Netherlands Antilles, Aruba became a constituent country within the Kingdom of the Netherlands (2016)

Legal system: civil law system based on the Dutch civil code

Citizenship: see the Netherlands

Suffrage: 18 years of age; universal

Executive branch: *chief of state:* King WILLEM-ALEXANDER of the Netherlands (since 30 April 2013); represented by Governor General Fredis REFUNJOL (since 11 May 2004)

head of government: Prime Minister Michiel "Mike" Godfried EMAN (since 30 October 2009)
cabinet: Council of Ministers elected by the Legislature (Staten) elections/appointments: the monarchy is hereditary; governor general appointed by the monarch for a 6-year term; prime minister and deputy prime minister indirectly elected by the Staten for 4-year term; election last held on 25 September 2009 (next to be held by September 2013)

election results: Michiel "Mike" Godfried EMAN (AVP) elected prime minister; percent of legislative vote—NA

Legislative branch: *description:* unicameral Legislature or Staten (21 seats; members directly elected in a single nationwideconstituency by proportional representation vote; members serve 4-year terms)
elections: last held on 27 September 2013 (next to be held in 2017)
election results: percent of vote by party—NA
seats by party—AVP 13, MEP 8

Judicial branch: *highest court(s):* Joint Court of Justice of Aruba, Curacao, Sint Maarten, and of Bonaire, Sint Eustatitus and Saba or "Joint Court of Justice" (consists of the presiding judge, NA members, and NA substitutes); final appeals heard by the Supreme Court, in The Hague, Netherlands
note—prior to 2010, the Joint Court of Justice was the Common Court of Justice of the Netherlands Antilles and Aruba
judge selection and term of office: Joint Court judges appointed by the monarch for life
subordinate courts: Courts in First Instance

Political parties and leaders: Aruban People's Party or AVP [Michiel "Mike" EMAN]
People's Electoral Movement Party or MEP [Evelyn WEVERCROES]
Real Democracy or PDR [Andin BIKKER]

Political pressure groups and leaders: other: environmental groups

International organization participation: Caricom (observer), FATF, ILO, IMF, Interpol, IOC, ITUC (NGOs), UNESCO (associate), UNWTO (associate), UPU

Diplomatic representation in the US: none (represented by the Kingdom of the Netherlands); note - there is a Minister Plenipotentiary for Aruba at the Embassy of the Kingdom of the Netherlands

Diplomatic representation from the US: the US does not have an embassy in Aruba; the Consul General to Curacao is accredited to Aruba

Flag description: blue, with two narrow, horizontal, yellow stripes across the lower portion and a red, four-pointed star outlined in white in the upper hoist-side corner; the star represents Aruba and its red soil and white beaches, its four points the four major languages (Papiamento, Dutch, Spanish, English) as well as the four points of a compass, to indicate that its inhabitants come from all over the world; the blue symbolizes Caribbean waters and skies; the stripes represent the island's two main "industries": the flow of tourists to the sun-drenched beaches and the flow of minerals from the earth

National symbol(s): Hooiberg (Haystack) Hill; national colors: blue, yellow, red, white

National anthem: *name:* "Aruba Deshi Tera" (Aruba Precious Country)
lyrics/music: Juan Chabaya 'Padu' LAMPE/Rufo Inocencio WEVER
note: local anthem adopted 1986; as part of the Kingdom of the Netherlands, "Het Wilhelmus" is official (see Netherlands)

ECONOMY

Economy overview: Tourism, petroleum bunkering, hospitality, and financial and business services are the mainstays of the small open Aruban economy.
Tourist arrivals have rebounded strongly following a dip after the 2008 global financial crisis. Tourism now accounts for a majority of economic activity. Over 1 million tourists per year visit Aruba, with the large majority of those from the US. The rapid growth of the tourism sector has resulted in a substantial expansion of other activities. Construction continues to boom with hotel capacity five times the 1985 level. Aruba is heavily dependent on imports and is making efforts to expand exports to achieve a more desirable trade balance. Almost all consumer and capital goods are imported, with the US, the Netherlands, and Panama being the major suppliers.
Aruba weathered two major shocks in recent years: fallout from the global financial crisis, which had its largest impact on tourism, and the closure of its oil refinery in 2009. However, tourism and related industries have continued to grow, and the Aruban government is working to attract more diverse industries. Aruba's banking sector withstood the recession well, and unemployment has significantly decreased.

GDP (purchasing power parity):
$2.516 billion (2009 est.)
$2.258 billion (2005 est.)
$2.205 billion (2004 est.)
country comparison to the world: 190

GDP (official exchange rate):
$2.516 billion (2009 est.)

GDP—real growth rate: 2.4% (2005 est.)
country comparison to the world: 129

GDP—per capita (PPP): $25,300 (2011 est.)
country comparison to the world: 74

GDP—composition, by end use:
household consumption: 63.3%
government consumption: 28.3%
investment in fixed capital: 22.9%
investment in inventories: 0%
exports of goods and services: 68.1%
imports of goods and services: -82.6% (2015 est.)

GDP—composition, by sector of origin:
agriculture: 0.4%
industry: 33.3%
services: 66.3% (2002 est.)

Agriculture—products: aloes; livestock; fish

Industries: tourism, petroleum transshipment facilities, banking

Industrial production growth rate: NA%

Labor force: 51,610
note: of the 51,610 workers aged 15 and over in the labor force, 32,252 were born in Aruba and 19,353 came from abroad; foreign workers are 38% of the employed population (2007 est.)
country comparison to the world: 192

Labor force—by occupation: *agriculture:* NA%
industry: NA%
services: NA%

note: most employment is in wholesale and retail trade, followed by hotels and restaurants

Unemployment rate: 6.9% (2005 est.)
country comparison to the world: 81

Population below poverty line: NA%

Household income or consumption by percentage share: *lowest:* 10%: NA%
highest: 10%: NA%

Budget: *revenues:* $648.1 million
expenditures: $838.3 million (2015 est.)
Taxes and other revenues: 25.8% of GDP (2015 est.)
country comparison to the world: 114

Budget surplus (+) or deficit (–): -7.6% of GDP (2015 est.)
country comparison to the world: 196
Public debt: 67% of GDP (2013)
55% of GDP (2012)
country comparison to the world: 52

Fiscal year: calendar year

Inflation rate (consumer prices):
1% (2015 est.)
0.4% (2014 est.)
country comparison to the world: 81

Central bank discount rate: 1% (31 December 2010)
3% (31 December 2009)
country comparison to the world: 123

Commercial bank prime lending rate: 9% (31 December 2015 est.)
7.3% (31 December 2014 est.)
country comparison to the world: 95

Stock of narrow money:
$990.2 million (31 December 2015 est.)
country comparison to the world: 154

Stock of broad money: $1.942 billion (31 December 2014 est.)
$1.838 billion (31 December 2013 est.)
country comparison to the world: 158

Stock of domestic credit: $1.754 billion (31 December 2014 est.)
$1.754 billion (31 December 2014 est.)
country comparison to the world: 142

Exports: $189.2 million (2015 est.)
$236.5 million (2014 est.)
country comparison to the world: 189

Exports—commodities: live animals and animal products, art and collectibles, machinery and electrical equipment, transport equipment

Exports—partners: Colombia 28.2%, Netherlands Antilles 18.1%, US 14.3%, Netherlands 10.1%, Mexico 6.5%, Venezuela 6.3%, Panama 4.1% (2015)

Imports: $1.329 billion (2015 est.)
$1.35 billion (2014 est.)
country comparison to the world: 173

Imports—commodities: machinery and electrical equipment, refined oil for bunkering and reexport, chemicals; foodstuffs

Imports—partners: US 55.4%, Netherlands 11.2% (2015)

Debt external:

$693.2 million (31 December 2014 est.)
$666.4 million (31 December 2013 est.)
country comparison to the world: 172

Exchange rates: Aruban guilders/florins per US dollar—
1.79 (2015 est.) 1.79 (2014 est.)
1.79 (2013 est.)
1.79 (2012 est.)
1.79 (2011 est.)

ENERGY

Electricity—production: 990 million kWh (2012 est.)
country comparison to the world: 149

Electricity—consumption: 920.7 million kWh (2012 est.)
country comparison to the world: 156

Electricity—exports: 0 kWh (2013 est.)
country comparison to the world: 95

Electricity—imports: 0 kWh (2013 est.)
country comparison to the world: 112

Electricity—installed generating capacity: 320,000 kW (2012 est.)
country comparison to the world: 148

Electricity—from fossil fuels: 90.6% of total installed capacity (2012 est.)
country comparison to the world: 73

Electricity—from nuclear fuels: 0% of total installed capacity (2012 est.)
country comparison to the world: 34

Electricity—from hydro electric plants: 0% of total installed capacity (2012 est.)
country comparison to the world: 154

Electricity—from other renewable sources: 9.4% of total installed capacity (2012 est.)
country comparison to the world: 39

Crude oil—production: 0 bbl/day (2014 est.)
country comparison to the world: 102

Crude oil—exports: 0 bbl/day (2012 est.)
country comparison to the world: 92

Crude oil—imports: 229,000 bbl/day (2012 est.)
country comparison to the world: 32

Crude oil—proved 0reserves: 0 bbl (1 January 2015 est.)
country comparison to the world: 102

Refined petroleum products—production: 234,600 bbl/day (2012 est.)
country comparison to the world: 48

Refined petroleum products—consumption: 6,400 bbl/day (2013 est.)
country comparison to the world: 163

Refined petroleum products—exports: 234,600 bbl/day (2012 est.)
country comparison to the world: 30

Refined petroleum products—imports: 6,341 bbl/day (2012 est.)
country comparison to the world: 150

Natural gas—production: 01 cu m (2013 est.)
country comparison to the world: 96

Natural gas—consumption: 1 cu m (2013 est.)
country comparison to the world: 114

Natural gas—exports: 1 cu m (2013 est.)
country comparison to the world: 52

Natural gas—imports: 1 cu m (2013 est.)
country comparison to the world: 75

Natural gas—proved reserves: 0 cu m (1 January 2014 est.)
country comparison to the world: 107

Carbon dioxide emissions from consumption of energy: 876,400 Mt (2012 est.)
country comparison to the world: 168

COMMUNICATIONS

Telephones—fixed lines: *total subscriptions:* 35,000
subscriptions per 100 inhabitants: 32 (2014 est.)
country comparison to the world: 169

Telephones—mobile cellular: *total:* 139,700
subscriptions per 100 inhabitants: 126 (2014 est.)
country comparison to the world: 185

Telephone system: *general assessment:* modern fully automatic telecommunications system
domestic: increased competition through privatization; 3 mobile-cellular service providers are now licensed

international: country code—297; landing site for the PAN-AM submarine telecommunications cable system that extends from the US Virgin Islands through Aruba to Venezuela, Colombia, Panama, and the west coast of South America; extensive interisland microwave radio relay links (2007)

Broadcast media: 2 commercial TV stations; cable TV subscription service provides access to foreign channels; about 20 commercial radio stations broadcast (2007)
Radio broadcast stations: AM 2, FM 16, shortwave 0 (2004)
Television broadcast stations: 1 (1997)

Internet country code: .aw

Internet hosts: 40,560 (2012)
country comparison to the world: 101

Internet users: *total:* 87,700
percent of population: 79.2% (2014 est.)
country comparison to the world: 172

TRANSPORTATION

Airports: 1 (2013)
country comparison to the world: 210

Airports—with paved runways: *total:* 1
2,438 to 3,047 m: 1 (2013)

Ports and terminals: *major seaport(s):* Barcadera, Oranjestad
oil terminal(s): Sint Nicolaas
cruise port(s): Oranjestad

MILITARY AND SECURITY

Military branches: no regular military forces (2011)

Military—note: defense is the responsibility of the Netherlands; the Aruba security services focus on organized crime and terrorism

TRANSNATIONAL ISSUES

Disputes—international: none

Illicit drugs: transit point for US- and Europe-bound narcotics with some accompanying money-laundering activity; relatively high percentage of population consumes cocaine

ASHMORE AND CARTIER ISLANDS

INTRODUCTION

Background: These uninhabited islands came under Australian authority in 1931; formal administration began two years later. Ashmore Reef supports a rich and diverse avian and marine habitat; in 1983, it became a National Nature Reserve. Cartier Island, a former bombing range, became a marine reserve in 2000.

GEOGRAPHY

Location: Southeastern Asia, islands in the Indian Ocean, midway between northwestern Australia and Timor island

Geographic coordinates: 12 14 S, 123 05 E

Map references: Southeast Asia

Area: *total:* 5 sq km
land: 5 sq km
water: 0 sq km
note: includes Ashmore Reef (West, Middle, and East Islets) and Cartier Island
country comparison to the world: 250

Area—comparative: about eight times the size of the National Mall in Washington, DC

Land boundaries: 0 km

Coastline: 74.1 km

Maritime claims: *territorial sea:* 12 nm
contiguous zone: 12 nm
exclusive fishing zone: 200 nm
continental shelf: 200-m depth or to the depth of exploitation

Climate: tropical

Terrain: low with sand and coral

Elevation: *mean elevation:* NA

elevation extremes: *lowest point:* Indian Ocean 0 m
highest point: unnamed location 3 m

Natural resources: fish

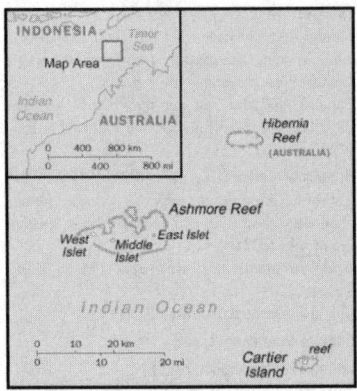

Land use: *agricultural land:* 0%
forest: 0%
other: 100% (all grass and sand) (2011 est.)

Natural hazards: surrounded by shoals and reefs that can pose maritime hazards

Environment—current issues: illegal killing of protected wildlife by traditional Indonesian fisherman, as well as fishing by non-traditional Indonesian vessels, are ongoing problems

Geography—note: Ashmore Reef National Nature Reserve established in August 1983; Cartier Island Marine Reserve established in 2000

PEOPLE AND SOCIETY

Population: no indigenous inhabitants
note: Indonesian fishermen are allowed access to the lagoon and fresh water at Ashmore Reef's West Island; access to East and Middle Islands is by permit only

GOVERNMENT

Country name: *conventional long form:* Territory of Ashmore and Cartier Islands
conventional short form: Ashmore and Cartier Islands
etymology: named after British Captain Samuel ASHMORE, who first sighted his namesake island in 1811, and after the ship Cartier, from which the second island was discovered in 1800

Dependency status: territory of Australia; administered from Canberra by the Department of Regional Australia, Local Government, Arts and Sport

Legal system: the laws of the Commonwealth of Australia and the laws of the Northern Territory of Australia, where applicable, apply

Citizenship: see Australia

Diplomatic representation in the US: none (territory of Australia)

Diplomatic representation from the US: none (territory of Australia)

Flag description: the flag of Australia is used

ECONOMY

Economy overview: no economic activity

TRANSPORTATION

Ports and terminals: *none; offshore anchorage only*

MILITARY AND SECURITY

Military note: defense is the responsibility of Australia; periodic visits by the Royal Australian Navy and Royal Australian Air Force

TRANSNATIONAL ISSUES

Disputes—international: Australia has closed parts of the Ashmore and Cartier reserve to Indonesian traditional fishing; Indonesian groups challenge Australia's claim to Ashmore Reef

ATLANTIC OCEAN

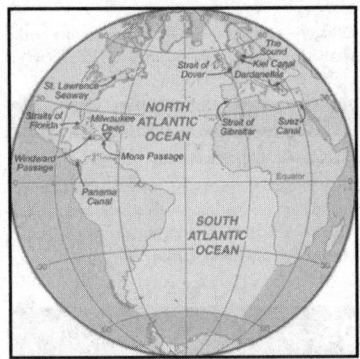

INTRODUCTION

Background: The Atlantic Ocean is the second largest of the world's five oceans (after the Pacific Ocean, but larger than the Indian Ocean, Southern Ocean, and Arctic Ocean). The Kiel Canal (Germany), Oresund (Denmark-Sweden), Bosporus (Turkey), Strait of Gibraltar (Morocco-Spain), and the Saint Lawrence Seaway (Canada-US) are important strategic access waterways. The decision by the International Hydrographic Organization in the spring of 2000 to delimit a fifth world ocean, the Southern Ocean, removed the portion of the Atlantic Ocean south of 60 degrees south latitude.

GEOGRAPHY

Location: body of water between Africa, Europe, the Arctic Ocean, the Americas, and the Southern Ocean

Geographic coordinates: 0 00 N, 25 00 W

Map references: Political Map of the World

Area: *total:* 76.762 million sq km
note: includes Baltic Sea, Black Sea, Caribbean Sea, Davis Strait, Denmark Strait, part of the Drake Passage, Gulf of Mexico, Labrador Sea, Mediterranean Sea, North Sea, Norwegian Sea, almost all of the Scotia Sea, and other tributary water bodies

Area—comparative: about 7.5 times the size of the US

Coastline: 111,866 km

Climate: tropical cyclones (hurricanes) develop off the coast of Africa near Cabo Verde and move westward into the Caribbean Sea; hurricanes can occur from May to December but are most frequent from August to November

Terrain: surface usually covered with sea ice in Labrador Sea, Denmark Strait, and coastal portions of the Baltic Sea from October to June; clockwise warm-water gyre (broad, circular system of currents) in the northern Atlantic, counterclockwise warm-water gyre in the southern Atlantic; the ocean floor is dominated by the Mid-Atlantic Ridge, a rugged north-south centerline for the entire Atlantic basin

Elevation: mean depth: -3,646 m

elevation extremes: *lowest point:* Milwaukee Deep in the Puerto Rico Trench -8,605m
highest point: sea level 0 m

Natural resources: oil and gas fields, fish, marine mammals (seals and whales), sand and gravel aggregates, placer deposits, polymetallic nodules, precious stones

Natural hazards: icebergs common in Davis Strait, Denmark Strait, and the northwestern Atlantic Ocean from February to August and have been spotted as far south as Bermuda and the Madeira Islands; ships subject to superstructure icing in extreme northern Atlantic from October to May; persistent fog can be a maritime hazard from May to September; hurricanes (May to December)

Environment—current issues: endangered marine species include the manatee, seals, sea lions, turtles, and whales; drift net fishing is hastening the decline of fish stocks and contributing to international disputes; municipal sludge pollution off eastern US, southern Brazil, and eastern Argentina; oil pollution in Caribbean Sea, Gulf of Mexico, Lake Maracaibo, Mediterranean Sea, and North Sea; industrial waste and municipal sewage pollution in Baltic Sea, North Sea, and Mediterranean Sea

Geography—note: major chokepoints include the Dardanelles, Strait of Gibraltar, access to the Panama and Suez Canals; strategic straits include the Strait of Dover, Straits of Florida, Mona Passage, The Sound (Oresund), and Windward Passage; the Equator divides the Atlantic Ocean into the North Atlantic Ocean and South Atlantic Ocean

GOVERNMENT

Country name: *etymology:* name derives from the Greek description of the waters beyond the Strait of Gibraltar, Atlantis thalassa, meaning "Sea of Atlas"

ECONOMY

Economy—overview: The Atlantic Ocean provides some of the world's most heavily trafficked sea routes, between and within the Eastern and Western Hemispheres. Other economic activity includes the exploitation of natural resources, e.g., fishing, dredging of aragonite sands (The Bahamas), and production of crude oil and natural gas (Caribbean Sea, Gulf of Mexico, and North Sea).

TRANSPORTATION

Ports and terminals: *major seaport(s):* Alexandria (Egypt), Algiers (Algeria), Antwerp (Belgium), Barcelona (Spain), Buenos Aires (Argentina), Casablanca (Morocco), Colon (Panama), Copenhagen (Denmark), Dakar (Senegal), Gdansk (Poland), Hamburg (Germany), Helsinki (Finland), Las Palmas (Canary Islands, Spain), Le Havre (France), Lisbon (Portugal), London (UK), Marseille (France), Montevideo (Uruguay), Montreal (Canada), Naples (Italy), New Orleans (US), New York (US), Oran (Algeria), Oslo (Norway), Peiraiefs or Piraeus (Greece), Rio de Janeiro (Brazil), Rotterdam (Netherlands), Saint Petersburg (Russia), Stockholm (Sweden)

Transportation—note: Kiel Canal and Saint Lawrence Seaway are two important waterways; significant domestic commercial and recreational use of Intracoastal Waterway on central and south Atlantic seaboard and Gulf of Mexico coast of US; the International Maritime Bureau reports the territorial waters of littoral states and offshore Atlantic waters as high risk for piracy and armed robbery against ships, particularly in the Gulf of Guinea off West Africa; in 2014, 41 commercial vessels were attacked in the Gulf of Guinea with 5 hijacked and 144 crew members taken hostage; hijacked vessels are often disguised and cargoes stolen; crews have been robbed and stores or cargoes stolen

TRANSNATIONAL ISSUES

Disputes—international: some maritime disputes (see littoral states)

AUSTRALIA

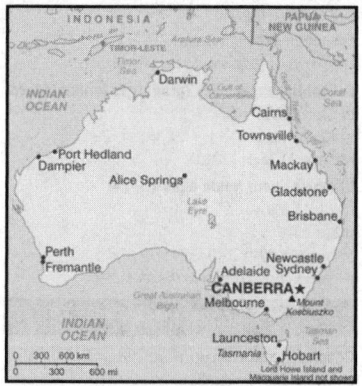

INTRODUCTION

Background: Prehistoric settlers arrived on the continent from Southeast Asia at least 40,000 years before the first Europeans began exploration in the 17th century. No formal territorial claims were made until 1770, when Capt. James COOK took possession of the east coast in the name of Great Britain (all of Australia was claimed as British territory in 1829 with the creation of the colony of Western Australia). Six colonies were created in the late 18th and 19th centuries; they federated and became the Commonwealth of Australia in 1901. The new country took advantage of its natural resources to rapidly develop agricultural and manufacturing industries and to make a major contribution to the Allied effort in World Wars I and II. In recent decades, Australia has become an internationally competitive, advanced market economy due in large part to economic reforms adopted in the 1980s and its location in one of the fastest growing regions of the world economy. Long-term concerns include an aging population, pressure on infrastructure, and environmental issues such as floods, droughts, and bushfires. Australia is the driest inhabited continent on earth, making it particularly vulnerable to the challenges of climate change. Australia is home to 10 percent of the world's biodiversity, and a great number of its flora and fauna exist nowhere else in the world.

GEOGRAPHY

Location: Oceania, continent between the Indian Ocean and the South Pacific Ocean

Geographic coordinates: 27 00 S, 133 00 E

Map references: Oceania

Area: *total:* 7,741,220 sq km
land: 7,682,300 sq km
water: 58,920 sq km
note: includes Lord Howe Island and Macquarie Island
country comparison to the world: 6

Area—comparative: slightly smaller than the US contiguous 48 states

Land boundaries: 0 km

Coastline: 25,760 km

Maritime claims: *territorial sea:* 12 nm
contiguous zone: 24 nm
exclusive economic zone: 200 nm
continental shelf: 200 nm or to the edge of the continental margin

Climate: generally arid to semiarid; temperate in south and east; tropical in north

Terrain: mostly low plateau with deserts; fertile plain in southeast

Elevation: *mean elevation:* 330 m

elevation extremes: *lowest point:* Lake Eyre - 15 m
highest point: Mount Kosciuszko 2,229 m

Natural resources: bauxite, coal, iron ore, copper, tin, gold, silver, uranium, nickel, tungsten, rare earth elements, mineral sands, lead, zinc, diamonds, natural gas, petroleum
note: Australia is the world's largest net exporter of coal accounting for 29% of global coal exports

Land use: *agricultural land:* 53.4%
arable land: 6.2%
permanent crops: 0.1%
permanent pasture: 47.1%
forest: 19.3%
other: 27.3% (2011 est.)

Irrigated land: 25,500 sq km (2012)

Total renewable water resources: 492 cu km (2011)

Freshwater withdrawal (domestic/industrial/agricultural): *total:* 22.58 cu km/yr (27%/18%/55%)
per capita: 1,152 cu m/yr (2010)

Natural hazards: cyclones along the coast; severe droughts; forest fires
volcanism: volcanic activity on Heard and McDonald Islands

Environment—current issues: soil erosion from overgrazing, industrial development, urbanization, and poor farming practices; soil salinity rising due to the use of poor quality water; desertification; clearing for agricultural purposes threatens the natural habitat of many unique animal and plant species; the Great Barrier Reef off the northeast coast, the largest coral reef in the world, is threatened by increased shipping and its popularity as a tourist site; limited natural freshwater resources

Environment—international agreements: *party to:* Antarctic-Environmental Protocol, Antarctic-Marine Living Resources, Antarctic Seals, Antarctic Treaty, Biodiversity, Climate Change, Climate Change-Kyoto Protocol, Desertification, Endangered Species, Environmental Modification, Hazardous Wastes, Law of the Sea, Marine Dumping, Marine Life Conservation, Ozone Layer Protection, Ship Pollution, Tropical Timber 83, Tropical Timber 94, Wetlands, Whaling
signed, but not ratified: none of the selected agreements

Geography—note: world's smallest continent but sixth largest country; the largest country in Oceania, the largest country entirely in the Southern Hemisphere, and the largest country without land borders; the only continent without glaciers; population concentrated along the eastern and southeastern coasts; the invigorating sea breeze known as the "Fremantle Doctor" affects the city of Perth on the west coast and is one of the most consistent winds in the world

PEOPLE AND SOCIETY

Nationality: *noun:* Australian(s)
adjective: Australian

Ethnic groups: English 25.9%, Australian 25.4%, Irish 7.5%, Scottish 6.4%, Italian 3.3%, German 3.2%, Chinese 3.1%, Indian 1.4%, Greek 1.4%, Dutch 1.2%, other 15.8% (includes Australian aboriginal .5%), unspecified 5.4%
note: data represents self-identified ancestry, over a third of respondents reported two ancestries (2011 est.)

Languages: English 76.8%, Mandarin 1.6%, Italian 1.4%, Arabic 1.3%, Greek 1.2%, Cantonese 1.2%, Vietnamese 1.1%, other 10.4%, unspecified 5% (2011 est.)

Religions: Protestant 30.1% (Anglican 17.1%, Uniting Church 5.0%, Presbyterian and Reformed 2.8%, Baptist, 1.6%, Lutheran 1.2%, Pentecostal 1.1%, other Protestant 1.3%), Catholic 25.3% (Roman Catholic 25.1%, other Catholic 0.2%), other Christian 2.9%, Orthodox 2.8%, Buddhist 2.5%, Muslim 2.2%, Hindu 1.3%, other 1.3%, none 22.3%, unspecified 9.3% (2011 est.)

Population: 22,751,014 (July 2015 est.)
country comparison to the world: 56

Age structure: *0–14 years:* 17.9% (male 2,089,561/female 1,982,719)
15–24 years: 13.14% (male 1,533,526/female 1,455,870)
25–54 years: 41.67% (male 4,822,083/female 4,658,371)
55–64 years: 11.82% (male 1,333,924/female 1,355,347)
65 years and over: 15.47% (male 1,628,108/female 1,891,505) (2015 est.)

Dependency ratios: *total dependency ratio:* 50.9%
youth dependency ratio: 28.2%
elderly dependency ratio: 22.7%
potential support ratio: 4.4% (2015 est.)

Median age: *total:* 38.4 years
male: 37.7 years
female: 39.2 years (2015 est.)
country comparison to the world: 58

Population growth rate: 1.07% (2015 est.)
country comparison to the world: 114

Birth rate: 12.15 births/1,000 population (2015 est.)
country comparison to the world: 162

Death rate: 7.14 deaths/1,000 population (2015 est.)
country comparison to the world: 126

Net migration rate: 5.65 migrant(s)/1,000 population (2015 est.)
country comparison to the world: 23

Urbanization: *urban population:* 89.4% of total population (2015)
rate of urbanization: 1.47% annual rate of change (2010–15 est.)

Major urban areas—population: Sydney 4.505 million; Melbourne 4.203 million; Brisbane 2.202 million; Perth 1.861 million; Adelaide 1.256 million; CANBERRA (capital) 423,000 (2015)

Sex ratio: *at birth:* 1.06 male(s)/female
0–14 years: 1.05 male(s)/female
15–24 years: 1.05 male(s)/female
25–54 years: 1.04 male(s)/female
55–64 years: 0.98 male(s)/female
65 years and over: 0.86 male(s)/female
total population: 1.01 male(s)/female (2015 est.)

Mother's mean age at first birth: 30.5 (2006 est.)

Maternal mortality rate: 6 deaths/100,000 live births (2015 est.)
country comparison to the world: 164

Infant mortality rate: *total:* 4.37 deaths/1,000 live births
male: 4.67 deaths/1,000 live births
female: 4.04 deaths/1,000 live births (2015 est.)
country comparison to the world: 188

Life expectancy at birth: *total population:* 82.15 years
male: 79.7 years
female: 84.74 years (2015 est.)
country comparison to the world: 13

Total fertility rate: 1.77 children born/woman (2015 est.)
country comparison to the world: 159

Contraceptive prevalence rate: 72.3%
note: percent of women aged 18–44 (2005)

Health expenditures: 9.4% of GDP (2013)
country comparison to the world: 37

Physicians density: 3.27 physicians/1,000 population (2011)

Hospital bed density: 3.9 beds/1,000 population (2010)

Drinking water source:
improved:

urban: 100% of population
rural: 100% of population
total: 100% of population
unimproved:
urban: 0% of population
rural: 0% of population
total: 0% of population (2015 est.)

Sanitation facility access:
improved:
urban: 100% of population
rural: 100% of population
total: 100% of population
unimproved:
urban: 0% of population
rural: 0% of population
total: 0% of population (2015 est.)

HIV/AIDS—adult prevalence rate: 0.17% (2013 est.)
country comparison to the world: 100

HIV/AIDS—people living with HIV/AIDS: 28,200 (2013 est.)
country comparison to the world: 74

HIV/AIDS—deaths: fewer than 100 (2013 est.)
country comparison to the world: 105

Obesity—adult prevalence rate: 29.9% (2014)
country comparison to the world: 44

Children under the age of 5 years underweight: 0.2% (2007)
country comparison to the world: 138

Education expenditures: 5.3% of GDP (2013)
country comparison to the world: 56

School life expectancy (primary to tertiary education): *total:* 20 years
male: 20 years
female: 21 years (2013)

Unemployment, youth ages 15–24:
total: 12.2%
male: 13%
female: 11.3% (2013 est.)
country comparison to the world: 93

GOVERNMENT

Country name: *conventional long form:* Commonwealth of Australia
conventional short form: Australia
etymology: the name Australia derives from the Latin "australis" meaning "southern"; the Australian landmass was long referred to as "Terra Australis" or the Southern Land

Government type: parliamentary democracy (Federal Parliament) under a constitutional monarchy; a Commonwealth realm

Capital: *name:* Canberra

Geographic coordinates: 35 16 S, 149 08 E
time difference: UTC+10 (15 hours ahead of Washington, DC, during Standard Time)
daylight saving time: +1hr, begins first Sunday in October; ends first Sunday in April
note: Australia has three time zones

Administrative divisions: 6 states and 2 territories*; Australian Capital Territory*, New South

Wales, Northern Territory*, Queensland, South Australia, Tasmania, Victoria, Western Australia

Dependent areas: Ashmore and Cartier Islands, Christmas Island, Cocos (Keeling) Islands, Coral Sea Islands, Heard Islandand and McDonald Islands, Norfolk Island

Independence: 1 January 1901 (from the federation of UK colonies)

National holiday: Australia Day (commemorates the arrival of the First Fleet of Australian settlers), 26 January (1788); ANZAC Day (commemorates the anniversary of the landing of troops of the Australian and New Zealand Army Corps during World War I at Gallipoli, Turkey), 25 April (1915)

Constitution: 9 July 1900; effective 1 January 1901; amended several times, last in 1977; note—a referendum to amend the constitution to reflect the Aboriginal and Torres Strait Islander Peoples Recognition Act 2013 is planned for early 2017 (2016)

Legal system: common law system based on the English model

International law organization participation: accepts compulsory ICJ jurisdiction with reservations; accepts ICCt jurisdiction

Citizenship: *citizenship by birth:* no
citizenship by descent only: at least one parent must be a citizen or permanent resident of Australia
dual citizenship recognized: yes
residency requirement for naturalization: 4 years

Suffrage: 18 years of age; universal and compulsory

Executive branch: *chief of state:* Queen of Australia ELIZABETH II (since 6 February 1952); represented by Governor General Sir Peter COSGROVE (since 28 March 2014)

head of government: Prime Minister Malcolm TURNBULL (since 15 September 2015); Deputy Prime Minister Barnaby JOYCE (since 18 February 2016)

cabinet: Cabinet nominated by the prime minister from among members of Parliament and sworn in by the governor general

elections/appointments: the monarchy is hereditary; governor general appointed by the monarch on the recommendation of the prime minister; following legislative elections, the leader of the majority party or majority coalition is sworn in as prime minister by the governor general

Legislative branch: *description:* bicameral Federal Parliament consists of the Senate (76 seats; 12 members from each of the 6 states and 2 each from the 2 mainland territories; members directly elected in multi-seat constituencies by proportional representation vote; members serve 6-year terms with one-half of state membership renewed every 3 years and territory membership renewed every 3 years) and the House of Representatives (150 seats; members directly elected in single-seat constituencies by majority preferential vote; members serve terms of up to 3 years)

elections: Senate—last held on 2 July 2016; House of Representatives—last held on 2 July 2016; this election represents a rare double dissolution where all 226 seats in both the Senate and House of Representatives are up for reelection

election results: Senate—percent of vote by party NA awaiting final results; seats by party NA—awaiting final results; House of Representatives—percent of vote by party Liberal/National Coalition 42.14%, ALP 34.91%, The Greens 9.93%, Katter's Australian Party 0.55%, Nick Xenophon Team 1.86%, independents 2.85%; seats by party Liberal/National Coalition 77, ALP 68, The Greens 1, Katter's Australian Party 1, Nick Xenophon Team 1, independents 2

Judicial branch: *highest court(s):* High Court of Australia (consists of 7 justices, including the chief justice); note—each of the 6 states, 2 territories, and Norfolk Island has a Supreme Court; the High Court is the final appellate court beyond the state and territory supreme courts

judge selection and term of office: justices appointed by the governor-general in council for life withmandatory retirement at age 70

subordinate courts: subordinate courts at the federal level: Federal Court; Federal Magistrates' Courts of Australia; Family Court; subordinate courts at the state and territory level: Local Court—New South Wales; Magistrates' Courts—Victoria, Queensland, South Australia, Western Australia, Tasmania, Northern Territory, Australian Capital Territory; District Courts—New South Wales, Queensland, South Australia, Western Australia; County Court—Victoria; Family Court—Western Australia; Court of Petty Sessions—Norfolk Island

Political parties and leaders: Australian Greens Party [Richard DI NATALE]
Australian Labor Party [Bill SHORTEN]
Country Liberal Party or CLP [Adam GILES]
Family First Party [Bob DAY]
Katter's Australian Party [Bob KATTER]
Liberal National Party of Queensland or LNP [Lawrence SPRINGBORG]
Liberal Party [Malcolm TURNBULL]
National Party of Australia [Warren TRUSS]
Palmer United Party or PUP [Clive PALMER]

Political pressure groups and leaders: *other:* business groups, environmental groups, social groups, trade unions

International organization participation: ADB, ANZUS, APEC, ARF, ASEAN (dialogue partner), Australia Group, BIS, C, CD, CP, EAS, EBRD, EITI (implementing country), FAO, FATF, G-20, IAEA, IBRD, ICAO, ICC (national committees), ICCt, ICRM, IDA, IEA, IFC, IFRCS, IHO, ILO, IMF, IMO, IMSO, Interpol, IOC, IOM, IPU, ISO, ITSO, ITU, ITUC (NGOs), MIGA, NEA, NSG, OECD, OPCW, OSCE (partner), Pacific Alliance (observer), Paris Club, PCA, PIF, SAARC (observer), SICA (observer), Sparteca, SPC, UN, UN Security Council (temporary), UNCTAD, UNESCO, UNHCR, UNMISS, UNMIT, UNRWA, UNTSO, UNWTO, UPU, WCO, WFTU (NGOs), WHO, WIPO, WMO, WTO, ZC

Diplomatic representation in the US: *chief of mission:* Ambassador Joseph Benedict HOCKEY (since 28 January 2016)
chancery: 1601 Massachusetts Avenue NW, Washington, DC 20036
telephone: [1] (202) 797-3000
FAX: [1] (202) 797-3168
consulate(s) general: Atlanta, Chicago, Honolulu, Houston, Los Angeles, New York, San Francisco

Diplomatic representation from the US: *chief of mission:* Ambassador Morrell John BERRY (since 25 September 2013)
embassy: Moonah Place, Yarralumla, Canberra, Australian Capital Territory 2600
mailing address: APO AP 96549
telephone: [61] (02) 6214-5600
FAX: [61] (02) 6214-5970
consulate(s) general: Melbourne, Perth, Sydney

Flag description: blue with the flag of the UK in the upper hoist-side quadrant and a large seven-pointed star in the lower hoist-side quadrant known as the Commonwealth or Federation Star, representing the federation of the colonies of Australia in 1901; the star depicts one point for each of the six original states and one representing all of Australia's internal and external territories; on the fly half is a representation of the Southern Cross constellation in white with one small, five-pointed star and four larger, seven-pointed stars

National symbol(s): Southern Cross constellation (five, seven-pointed stars), kangaroo, emu; national colors: green, gold

National anthem: *name:* "Advance Australia Fair"
lyrics/music: Peter Dodds McCORMICK
note: adopted 1984; although originally written in the late 19th century, the anthem was not used for all official occasions until 1984; as a Commonwealth country, in addition to the national anthem, "God Save the Queen" is also played at Royal functions (see United Kingdom)

GOVERNMENT

Economy—overview: Following two decades of continuous growth, low unemployment, contained inflation, very low public debt, and a strong and stable financial system, Australia enters 2016 facing a range of growth constraints, principally driven by a sharp fall in global prices of key export commodities. Demand for resources and energy from Asia and especially China has stalled and sharp drops in current prices have impacted growth.

The services sector is the largest part of the Australian economy, accounting for about 70% of GDP and 75% of jobs. Australia was comparatively unaffected by the global financial crisis as the banking system has remained strong and inflation is under control.

Australia benefited from a dramatic surge in its terms of trade in recent years, although this trend has reversed due to falling global commodity prices. Australia is a significant exporter of natural resources, energy, and food. Australia's abundant and diverse natural resources attract high levels of foreign investment and include extensive reserves of coal, iron, copper, gold, natural gas, uranium, and renewable energy sources. A series of major investments, such as the US$40 billion Gorgon Liquid Natural Gas project, will significantly expand the resources sector.

Australia is an open market with minimal restrictions on imports of goods and services. The process of opening up has increased productivity, stimulated growth, and made the economy more flexible and dynamic. Australia plays an active role in the World Trade Organization, APEC, the G-20, and other trade forums. Australia's free trade agreement (FTA) with China entered into force in 2015, adding to existing FTAs with the Republic of Korea, Japan, Chile, Malaysia, New Zealand, Singapore, Thailand, and the US, and a regional FTA with ASEAN and New Zealand. Australia continues to negotiate bilateral agreements with India and Indonesia, as well as larger agreements with its Pacific neighbors and the Gulf Cooperation Council countries, and an Asia-wide Regional Comprehensive Economic Partnership that includes the ten ASEAN countries and China, Japan, Korea, New Zealand and India. Australia is also working on the Trans-Pacific Partnership Agreement with Brunei, Canada, Chile, Japan, Malaysia, Mexico, New Zealand, Peru, Singapore, the US, and Vietnam.

GDP (purchasing power parity):
$1.489 trillion (2015 est.)
$1.454 trillion (2014 est.)
$1.56 trillion (2013 est.)
note: data are in 2015 US dollars
country comparison to the world: 19

GDP (official exchange rate): $1.224 trillion (2015 est.)

GDP—real growth rate:
2.5% (2015 est.)
2.6% (2014 est.)
2% (2013 est.)
country comparison to the world: 123

GDP—per capita (PPP):
$65,400 (2015 est.)
$64,700 (2014 est.)
$65,400 (2013 est.)
note: data are in 2015 US dollars
country comparison to the world: 14

Gross national saving:
22.2% of GDP (2015 est.)
23.7% of GDP (2014 est.)
24.2% of GDP (2013 est.)
country comparison to the world: 66

GDP—composition, by end use:
household consumption: 57%
government consumption: 17.9%
investment in fixed capital: 25.7%
investment in inventories: 0%
exports of goods and services: 18.5%
imports of goods and services: -19.1% (2015 est.)

GDP—composition, by sector of origin:

agriculture: 3.7%
industry: 28.9%
services: 67.4% (2015 est.)

Agriculture—products: wheat, barley, sugarcane, fruits; cattle, sheep, poultry

Industries: mining, industrial and transportation equipment, food processing, chemicals, steel

Industrial production growth rate: 2.7% (2015 est.)
country comparison to the world: 95

Labor force: 12.5 million (2015 est.)
country comparison to the world: 45

Labor force—by occupation: *agriculture:* 3.6%
industry: 21.1%
services: 75.3% (2009 est.)

Unemployment rate: 6.2% (2015 est.)
6.1% (2014 est.)
country comparison to the world: 70

Population below poverty line: NA%

Household income or consumption by percentage share: *lowest:* 10%: 2%
highest: 10%: 25.4% (1994)

Distribution of family income—Gini index: 30.3 (2008) 35.2 (1994)
country comparison to the world: 119

Budget: *revenues:* $425.7 billion
expenditures: $451.4 billion (2015 est.)
Taxes and other revenues: 34.3% of GDP (2015 est.)
country comparison to the world: 65

Budget surplus (+) or deficit (–): -2.1% of GDP (2015 est.)
country comparison to the world: 76

Public debt: 44.3% of GDP (2015 est.)
42.4% of GDP (2014 est.)
country comparison to the world: 103

Fiscal year: 1 July 30 June

Inflation rate (consumer prices):
1.5% (2015 est.)
2.5% (2014 est.)
country comparison to the world: 99

Central bank discount rate: 3% (28 February 2013)
4.35% (31 December 2010)
note: this is the Reserve Bank of Australia's "cash rate target, " or policy rate
country comparison to the world: 106

Commercial bank prime lending rate: 5.6% (31 December 2015 est.)
5.95% (31 December 2014 est.)
country comparison to the world: 135

Stock of narrow money:
$222.3 billion (31 December 2015 est.)
$227.2 billion (31 December 2014 est.)
country comparison to the world: 19

Stock of broad money: $1.661 trillion (31 December 2013 est.)
$1.648 trillion (31 December 2012 est.)
country comparison to the world: 11

Stock of domestic credit: $1.932 trillion (31 December 2015 est.)
$2.097 trillion (31 December 2014 est.)
country comparison to the world: 12

Market value of publicly traded shares:
$1.286 trillion (31 December 2012 est.)
$1.198 trillion (31 December 2011)
$1.455 trillion (31 December 2010 est.)
country comparison to the world: 10

Current account balance: -$56.2 billion (2015 est.)
-$43.83 billion (2014 est.)
country comparison to the world: 194

Exports: $184.4 billion (2015 est.)
$240.8 billion (2014 est.)
country comparison to the world: 27

Exports—commodities: coal, iron ore, gold, meat, wool, alumina, wheat, machinery and transport equipment

Exports—partners: China 32.2%, Japan 15.9%, South Korea 7.1%, US 5.4%, India 4.2% (2015)

Imports: $208.4 billion (2015 est.)
$240.5 billion (2014 est.)
country comparison to the world: 21

Imports—commodities: machinery and transport equipment, computers and office machines, telecommunication equipment andparts; crude oil and petroleum—products

Imports partners: China 23%, US 11.2%, Japan 7.4%, South Korea 5.5%, Thailand 5.1%, Germany 4.6% (2015)

Reserves of foreign exchange and gold: $55 billion (31 December 2015 est.)
$53.89 billion (31 December 2014 est.)
country comparison to the world: 38

Debt—external:
$1.381 trillion (31 December 2014 est.)
$1.374 trillion (31 December 2013 est.)
country comparison to the world: 14

Stock of direct foreign investment—at home:
$642.2 billion (31 December 2015 est.)
$593.8 billion (31 December 2014 est.)
country comparison to the world: 15

Stock of direct foreign investment—abroad:
$475.7 billion (31 December 2015 est.)
$473.3 billion (31 December 2014 est.)
country comparison to the world: 18

Exchange rates: Australian dollars (AUD) per US dollar—
1.33 (2015 est.)
1.1094 (2014 est.)
1.1094 (2013 est.)
0.97 (2012 est.)
0.9695 (2011 est.)

ENERGY

Electricity—production: 235.2 billion kWh (2012 est.)
country comparison to the world: 20

Electricity—consumption: 222.6 billion kWh (2012 est.)
country comparison to the world: 18

Electricity—exports: 0 kWh (2013 est.)
country comparison to the world: 102

Electricity—imports: 0 kWh (2013 est.)
country comparison to the world: 118

Electricity—installed generating capacity: 63.25 million kW (2012 est.)
country comparison to the world: 16

Electricity—from fossil fuels: 78.5% of total installed capacity (2012 est.)
country comparison to the world: 95

Electricity—from nuclear fuels: 0% of total installed capacity (2012 est.)
country comparison to the world: 44

Electricity—from hydro electric plants: 12.7% of total installed capacity (2012 est.)
country comparison to the world: 108

Electricity—from other renewable sources: 7.6% of total installed capacity (2012 est.)
country comparison to the world: 49

Crude oil—production: 354,300 bbl/day (2014 est.)
country comparison to the world: 31

Crude oil—exports: 235,400 bbl/day (2013 est.)
country comparison to the world: 29

Crude oil—imports: 461,900 bbl/day (2013 est.)
country comparison to the world: 20

Crude oil—proved reserves: 1.193 billion bbl (1 January 2015 est.)
country comparison to the world: 40

Refined petroleum products—production: 630,600 bbl/day (2013 est.)
country comparison to the world: 28

Refined petroleum products—consumption: 1.082 million bbl/day (2014 est.)
country comparison to the world: 21

Refined petroleum products—exports: 53,600 bbl/day (2013 est.)
country comparison to the world: 55

Refined petroleum products—imports: 424,000 bbl/day (2013 est.)
country comparison to the world: 17

Natural gas—production: 62.72 billion cu m (2014 est.)
country comparison to the world: 15

Natural gas—consumption: 38.79 billion cu m (2014 est.)
country comparison to the world: 24

Natural gas—exports: 31.62 billion cu m (2014 est.)
country comparison to the world: 11

Natural gas—imports: 6.937 billion cu m (2014 est.)
country comparison to the world: 30

Natural gas—proved reserves: 1.219 trillion cu m (1 January 2014 est.)
country comparison to the world: 24

Carbon dioxide emissions from consumption of energy: 420.6 million Mt (2012 est.)
country comparison to the world: 17

COMMUNICATIONS

Telephones—fixed lines: *total subscriptions:* 9.19 million
subscriptions per 100 inhabitants: 41 (2014 est.)
country comparison to the world: 22

Telephones—mobile cellular: *total:* 31 million
subscriptions per 100 inhabitants: 138 (2014 est.)
country comparison to the world: 39

Telephone system: *general assessment:* excellent domestic and international service

domestic: domestic satellite system; significant use of radiotelephone in areas of low population density; rapid growth of mobile telephones
international: country code—61; landing point for the SEA-ME-WE-3 optical telecommunications submarine cable with links to Asia, the Middle East, and Europe; the Southern Cross fiber optic submarine cable provides links to New Zealand and the United States; satellite earth stations—10 Intelsat (4 IndianOcean and 6 Pacific Ocean), 2 Inmarsat, 2 Globalstar, 5 other) (2007)

Broadcast media: the Australian Broadcasting Corporation (ABC) runs multiple national and local radio networks and TV stations, as well as Australia Network, a TV service that broadcasts throughout the Asia-Pacific region and is the main public broadcaster; Special Broadcasting Service (SBS), a second large public broadcaster, operates radio and TV networks broadcasting in multiple languages; several large national commercial TV networks, a large number of local commercial TV stations, and hundreds of commercial radio stations are accessible; cable and satellite systems are available (2008)
Radio broadcast stations: AM 262, FM 345, shortwave 1 (1998)
Television broadcast stations: 104 (1997)

Internet country code: .au

Internet hosts: 17.081 million (2012)
country comparison to the world: 8

Internet users: *total:* 20.2 million
percent of population: 89.6% (2014 est.)
country comparison to the world: 28

TRANSPORTATION

Airports: 480 (2013)
country comparison to the world: 16

Airports—with paved runways: *total:* 349
over 3,047 m: 11
2,438 to 3,047 m: 14
1,524 to 2,437 m: 155
914 to 1,523 m: 155
under 914 m: 14 (2013)

Airports—with unpaved runways: *total:* 131
1,524 to 2,437 m: 16
914 to 1,523 m: 101
under 914 m: 14 (2013)

Heliports: 1 (2013)

Pipelines: condensate/gas 637 km; gas 30,054 km; liquid petroleum gas 240 km; oil 3,609 km; oil/gas/water 110 km; refined products 72 km (2013)

Railways: *total:* 36,967.5 km
broad gauge: 3,727 km 1.600-m gauge (372 km electrified)
standard gauge: 18,727 km 1.435-m gauge (650 km electrified)
narrow gauge: 14,513.5 km 1.067-m gauge (2,075.5 km electrified) (2014)
country comparison to the world: 7

Roadways: *total:* 823,217 km
paved: 356,343 km
unpaved: 466,874 km (2011)
country comparison to the world: 9

Waterways: 2,000 km (mainly used for recreation on Murray and Murray-Darling river systems) (2011)
country comparison to the world: 42

Merchant marine: *total:* 41

by type: bulk carrier 8, cargo 7, liquefied gas 4, passenger 6, passenger/cargo 6, petroleum tanker 5, roll on/roll off 5
foreign-owned: 17 (Canada 5, Germany 2, Singapore 2, South Africa 1, UK 5, US 2)
registered in other countries: 25 (Bahamas 1, Dominica 1, Fiji 2, Liberia 1, Netherlands 1, Panama 4, Singapore 12, Tonga 1, UK 1, US 1) (2010)
country comparison to the world: 75

Ports and terminals: *major seaport(s):* Brisbane, Cairns, Darwin, Fremantle, Geelong, Gladstone, Hobart, Melbourne, Newcastle, Port Adelaide, Port Kembla, Sydney
dry bulk cargo port(s): Dampier (iron ore), Dalrymple Bay (coal), Hay Point (coal), Port Hedland (iron ore), Port Walcott (iron ore)
container port(s) (TEUs): Brisbane (1,004,983), Melbourne (2,467,967), Sydney (2,028,074) (2011)
LNG terminal(s) (export): Darwin, Karratha, Burrup, Curtis Island

MILITARY AND SECURITY

Military branches: Australian Defense Force (ADF): Australian Army, Royal Australian Navy (includes Naval Aviation Force), Royal Australian Air Force, Joint Operations Command (JOC) (2013)

Military service age and obligation: 17 years of age for voluntary military service (with parental consent); no conscription; women allowed to serve in most combat roles, except the Army special forces (2013)

Military expenditures:
1.71% of GDP (2012)
1.84% of GDP (2011)
1.71% of GDP (2010)
country comparison to the world: 50

TRANSNATIONAL ISSUES

Disputes—international: In 2007, Australia and Timor-Leste agreed to a 50-year development zone and revenue sharing arrangement and deferred a maritime boundary; Australia asserts land and maritime claims to Antarctica; Australia's 2004 submission to the Commission on the Limits of the Continental Shelf extends its continental margins over 3.37 million square kilometers, expanding its seabed roughly 30 percent beyond its claimed EEZ; all borders between Indonesia and Australia have been agreed upon bilaterally, but a 1997 treaty that would settle the last of their maritime and EEZ boundary has yet to be ratified by Indonesia's legislature; Indonesian groups challenge Australia's claim to Ashmore Reef; Australia closed parts of the Ashmore and Cartier reserve to Indonesian traditional fishing

Refugees and internally displaced persons: *refugees (country of origin):* 7,675 (Afghanistan) (2014)

Illicit drugs: Tasmania is one of the world's major suppliers of licit opiate products; government maintains strictcontrols over areas of opium poppy cultivation and output of poppy straw concentrate; major consumer ofcocaine and amphetamines

53

AUSTRIA

INTRODUCTION

Background: Once the center of power for the large Austro-Hungarian Empire, Austria was reduced to a small republic after its defeat in World War I. Following annexation by Nazi Germany in 1938 and subsequent occupation by the victorious Allies in 1945, Austria's status remained unclear for a decade. A State Treaty signed in 1955 ended the occupation, recognized Austria's independence, and forbade unification with Germany. A constitutional law that same year declared the country's "perpetual neutrality" as a condition for Soviet military withdrawal. The Soviet Union's collapse in 1991 and Austria's entry into the EU in 1995 have altered the meaning of this neutrality. A prosperous, democratic country, Austria entered the EU Economic and Monetary Union in 1999.

GEOGRAPHY

Location: Central Europe, north of Italy and Slovenia

Geographic coordinates: 47 20 N, 13 20 E

Map references: Europe

Area: *total:* 83,871 sq km
land: 82,445 sq km
water: 1,426 sq km
country comparison to the world: 114

Area—comparative: about the size of South Carolina; slightly more than two-thirds the size of Pennsylvania

Land boundaries: *total:* 2,524 km
border countries (8): Czech Republic 402 km, Germany 801 km, Hungary 321 km, Italy 404 km, Liechtenstein 34 km, Slovakia 105 km, Slovenia 299 km, Switzerland 158 km

Coastline: 0 km (landlocked)

Maritime claims: none (landlocked)

Climate: temperate; continental, cloudy; cold winters with frequent rain and some snow in lowlands and snow in mountains; moderate summers with occasional showers

Terrain: mostly mountains (Alps) in the west and south; mostly flat or gently sloping along the eastern and northern margins

Elevation: *mean elevation:* 910 m

elevation extremes: *lowest point:* Neusiedler See 115 m
highest point: Grossglockner 3,798 m

Natural resources: oil, coal, lignite, timber, iron ore, copper, zinc, antimony, magnesite, tungsten, graphite, salt, hydropower

Land use: *agricultural land:* 38.4%
arable land: 16.5%
permanent crops: 0.8%
permanent pasture: 21.1%
forest: 47.2%
other: 14.4% (2011 est.)

Irrigated land: 1,170 sq km (2012)

Total renewable water resources: 77.7 cu km (2011)

Freshwater withdrawal (domestic/industrial/agricultural): *total:* 3.66 cu km/yr (18%/79%/3%)
per capita: 452.4 cu m/yr (2008)

Natural hazards: landslides; avalanches; earthquakes

Environment—current issues: some forest degradation caused by air and soil pollution; soil pollution results from the use of agricultural chemicals; air pollution results from emissions by coal- and oil-fired power stations and industrial plants and from trucks transiting Austria between northern and southern Europe

Environment—international agreements: *party to:* Air Pollution, Air Pollution-Nitrogen Oxides, Air Pollution-Persistent Organic Pollutants, Air Pollution-Sulfur 85, Air Pollution-Sulphur 94, Air Pollution-Volatile Organic Compounds, Antarctic Treaty, Biodiversity, Climate Change, Climate Change-Kyoto Protocol, Desertification, Endangered Species, Environmental Modification, Hazardous Wastes, Law of the Sea, Ozone Layer Protection, Ship Pollution, Tropical Timber 83, Tropical Timber 94, Wetlands, Whaling
signed, but not ratified: none of the selected agreements

Geography—note: landlocked; strategic location at the crossroads of central Europe with many easily traversable Alpine passes and valleys; major river is the Danube; population is concentrated on eastern lowlands because of steep slopes, poor soils, and low temperatures elsewhere

PEOPLE AND SOCIETY

Nationality: *noun:* Austrian(s)
adjective: Austrian

Ethnic groups: Austrians 91.1%, former Yugoslavs 4% (includes Croatians, Slovenes, Serbs, and Bosniaks), Turks 1.6%, Germans 0.9%, other or unspecified 2.4% (2001 census)

Languages: German (official nationwide) 88.6%, Turkish 2.3%, Serbian 2.2%, Croatian (official in Burgenland) 1.6%, other (includes Slovene, official in South Carinthia, and Hungarian, official in Burgenland) 5.3% (2001 est.)

Religions: Catholic 73.8% (includes Roman Catholic 73.6%, other Catholic 0.2%), Protestant 4.9%, Muslim 4.2%, Orthodox 2.2%, other 0.8% (includes other Christian), none 12%, unspecified 2% (2001 est.)

Population: 8,665,550 (July 2015 est.)
country comparison to the world: 95

Age structure: *0–14 years:* 14.05% (male 622,856/female 594,349)
15–24 years: 11.55% (male 510,614/female 490,90)
25–54 years: 42.98% (male 1,861,777/female 1,862,705)
55–64 years: 12.51% (male 535,691/female 548,022)
65 years and over: 18.92% (male 706,288/female 932,858) (2015 est.)

Dependency ratios:
total dependency ratio: 49.2%
youth dependency ratio: 21.2%
elderly dependency ratio: 28%
potential support ratio: 3.6% (2015 est.)

Median age: *total:* 43.6 years
male: 42.5 years
female: 44.6 years (2015 est.)
country comparison to the world: 11

Population growth rate: 0.55% (2015 est.)
country comparison to the world: 153

Birth rate: 9.41 births/1,000 population (2015 est.)
country comparison to the world: 204

Death rate: 9.42 deaths/1,000 population (2015 est.)
country comparison to the world: 58

Net migration rate: 5.56 migrant(s)/1,000 population (2015 est.)
country comparison to the world: 24
Urbanization: urban population: 66% of total population (2015)
rate of urbanization: 0.4% annual rate of change (2010–15 est.)

Major urban areas population: VIENNA (capital) 1.753 million (2015)

Sex ratio: *at birth:* 1.05 male(s)/female
0–14 years: 1.05 male(s)/female
15–24 years: 1.04 male(s)/female
25–54 years: 1 male(s)/female
55–64 years: 0.98 male(s)/female
65 years and over: 0.76 male(s)/female
total population: 0.96 male(s)/female (2015 est.)

Mother's mean age at first birth: 28.5 (2011 est.)

Maternal mortality rate: 4 deaths/100,000 live births (2015 est.)
country comparison to the world: 178

Infant mortality rate: *total:* 3.45 deaths/1,000 live births

male: 3.82 deaths/1,000 live births

female: 3.06 deaths/1,000 live births (2015 est.)

country comparison to the world: 206

Life expectancy at birth: *total population:* 81.39 years

male: 78.76 years

female: 84.15 years (2015 est.)

country comparison to the world: 22

Total fertility rate: 1.46 children born/woman (2015 est.)

country comparison to the world: 203

Contraceptive prevalence rate: 69.6%

note: percent of women aged 18–46 (2008/09)

Health expenditures: 11% of GDP (2013)

country comparison to the world: 11

Physicians density: 4.83 physicians/1,000 population (2011)

Hospital bed density: 7.6 beds/1,000 population (2011)

Drinking water source:

improved:

urban: 100% of population

rural: 100% of population

total: 100% of population

unimproved:

urban: 0% of population

rural: 0% of population

total: 0% of population (2015 est.)

Sanitation facility access:

improved:

urban: 100% of population

rural: 100% of population

total: 100% of population

unimproved:

urban: 0% of population

rural: 0% of population

total: 0% of population (2015 est.)

HIV/AIDS—adult prevalence rate: NA

HIV/AIDS—people living with HIV/AIDS: NA

HIV/AIDS—deaths: NA

Obesity—adult prevalence rate: 20.1% (2014)

country comparison to the world: 93

Education expenditures: 5.6% of GDP (2013)

country comparison to the world: 44

School life expectancy (primary to tertiary education): *total:* 16 years

male: 16 years

female: 16 years (2014)

Unemployment, youth ages 15–24: *total:* 9.2%

male: 8.9%

female: 9.4% (2013 est.)

country comparison to the world: 108

GOVERNMENT

Country name: *conventional long form:* Republic of Austria

conventional short form: Austria

local long form: Republik Oesterreich

local short form: Oesterreich

etymology: the name Oesterreich means "eastern realm" or "eastern march" and dates to the 10th century; the designation refers to the fact that Austria was the easternmost extension of Bavaria, and in fact of all the Germans; the word Austria is a Latinization of the German name

Government type: federal parliamentary republic

Capital: *name:* Vienna

Geographic coordinates: 48 12 N, 16 22 E

time difference: UTC+1 (6 hours ahead of Washington, DC, during Standard Time)

daylight saving time: +1hr, begins last Sunday in March; ends last Sunday in October

Administrative divisions: 9 states (Bundeslaender, singular—Bundesland); Burgenland, Kaernten (Carinthia), Niederoesterreich (Lower Austria), Oberoesterreich (Upper Austria), Salzburg, Steiermark (Styria), Tirol (Tyrol), Vorarlberg, Wien (Vienna)

Independence: 12 November 1918 (republic proclaimed); notable earlier dates: 976 (Margravate of Austria established); 17 September 1156 (Duchy of Austria founded); 11 August 1804 (Austrian Empire proclaimed)

National holiday: National Day, 26 October (1955); note—commemorates the passage of the law on permanent neutrality

Constitution: several previous; latest adopted 1 October 1920, revised 1929, replaced May 1934 (authoritarian-corporate constitution), replaced by German Weimar constitution in 1938 following German annexation; latest reinstated 1 May 1945 (1920 constitution with 1929 revisions); amended many times, last in 2014 (2016)

Legal system: civil law system; judicial review of legislative acts by the Constitutional Court

International law organization participation: accepts compulsory ICJ jurisdiction; accepts ICCt jurisdiction

Citizenship: *citizenship by birth:* no

citizenship by descent only: at least one parent must be a citizen of Austria

dual citizenship recognized: no

residency requirement for naturalization: 10 years

Suffrage: 16 years of age; universal

Executive branch: *chief of state:* Acting President Doris BURES (since 8 July 2016)

head of government: Chancellor Christian KERN (SPOe) (since 17 May 2016); Vice Chancellor Reinhold MITTERLEHNER (OeVP) (since 1 September 2014)

cabinet: Council of Ministers chosen by the president on the advice of the chancellor

elections/appointments: president directly elected by absolute majority popular vote in 2 rounds if needed for a 6-year term (eligible for a second term); elections last held on 24 April 2016 (first round) and 22 May 2016 (second round), the latter was ruled invalid and a re-vote will be held 2 October 2016; next presidential elections to be held in April 2022; chancellor appointed by the president but determined by the majority coalition

parties in the Federal Assembly; vice chancellor appointed by the president on the advice of the chancellor

election results: percent of vote: first-round results—Norbet HOFER (FPO) 35.1%, Alexander van der BELLIEN (independent, allied with the Greens) 21.3%, Irmgard GRISS (independent) 18.9%, Rudolf HUNDSTORFER (SPOe) 11.3%, Andreas KHOL (OeVP) 11.1%, Richard LUGNER (independent) 2.3%; second round results—Alexander van der BELLIEN 50.3%, Norbet HOFER 49.7%; on 1 July 2016, theConstitutional Court ordered a rerun of the 22 May 2016 runoff election to be held 2 October 2016; former President Heinz FISCHER's term ended July 8; his functions were replaced by the three Presidents of the National Council Doris BURES, Karlheinz KOPF, and Norbert HOFER

Legislative branch: *description:* bicameral Federal Assembly or Bundesversammlung consists of the Federal Council or Bundesrat (62 seats; members appointed by state parliaments with each state receiving 3 to 12 seats in proportion to its population; members serve 5- or 6-year terms) and the National Council or Nationalrat (183 seats; members directly elected in single-seat constituencies by proportional representation vote; members serve 5-year terms)

elections: National Council—last held on 29 September 2013 (next to be held by September 2018)

election results: National Council—percent of vote by party—SPOe 26.8%, OeVP 24.0%, FPOe 20.5%, Greens 12.4%, Team Stronach 5.7%, NEOS 5.0%, other 5.6%; seats by party—SPOe 52, OeVP 47, FPOe40, Greens 24, Team Stronach 11, NEOS 9; note—currently: SPOe 52, OeVP 50, FPOe 38, Greens 24, NEOS 9, Team Stronach 6, without faction 4

Judicial branch: *highest court(s):* Supreme Court of Justice or Oberster Gerichtshof (consists of 85 judges organized into 17 senates or panels of 5 judges each); Constitutional Court or Verfassungsgerichtshof (consists of 20 judges including 6 substitutes; Administrative Court or Verwaltungsgerichtshof—2 judges plus other members depending on the importance of the case)

judge selection and term of office: Supreme Court judges nominated by executive branch departments and appointed by the president; judges serve for life; Constitutional Court judges nominated by several executive branch departments and approved by the president; judges serve for life; Administrative Court judges recommended by executive branch departments and appointed by the president; terms of judges and members determined by the president

subordinate courts: Courts of Appeal (4); Regional Courts (20); district courts (120); county courts

Political parties and leaders: Austrian People's Party or OeVP [Reinhold MITTERLEHNER] Communist Party of Austria or KPOe [Mirko MESSNER]

Freedom Party of Austria or FPOe [Heinz Christian STRACHE]

The Greens [Eva GLAWISCHNIG]
NEOS The
New Austria [Matthias STROLZ]
Social Democratic Party of Austria or SPOe [Christian KERN]
"Team Stronach" [Frank STRONACH]

Political pressure groups and leaders: Austrian Trade Union Federation or OeGB (nominally independent but primarily Social Democratic)
Federal Agriculture Chamber (OeVP-dominated)
Federal Economic Chamber (OeVP-dominated)
Labor Chamber or AK (Social Democratic-leaning think tank)
OeVP-oriented Association of Austrian Industrialists or IV
Roman Catholic Church, including its chief lay organization, Catholic Action
other: three composite leagues of the Austrian People's Party or OeVP representing business, labor, farmers, and other nongovernment organizations in the areas of environment and human rights

International organization participation: ADB (nonregional member), AfDB (nonregional member), Australia Group, BIS, BSEC (observer), CD, CE, CEI, CERN, EAPC, EBRD, ECB, EIB, EMU, ESA, EU, FAO, FATF, G-9, IADB, IAEA, IBRD, ICAO, ICC (national committees), ICCt, ICRM, IDA, IEA, IFAD, IFC, IFRCS, IGAD (partners), ILO, IMF, IMO, Interpol, IOC, IOM, IPU, ISO, ITSO, ITU, ITUC (NGOs), MIGA, MINURSO, NEA, NSG, OAS (observer), OECD, OIF (observer), OPCW, OSCE, Paris Club, PCA, PFP, Schengen Convention, SELEC (observer), UN, UNCTAD, UNESCO, UNFICYP, UNHCR, UNIDO, UNIFIL, UNTSO, UNWTO, UPU, WCO, WFTU (NGOs), WHO, WIPO, WMO, WTO, ZC

Diplomatic representation in the US: *chief of mission:* Ambassador Wolfgang WALDNER (since 28 January 2016)
chancery: 3524 International Court NW, Washington, DC 20008–3035
telephone: [1] (202) 895-6700
FAX: [1] (202) 895-6750
consulate(s) general: Los Angeles, New York
consulate(s): Chicago

Diplomatic representation from the US: *chief of mission:* Ambassador Alexa Lange WESNER (since 22 October 2013)
embassy: Boltzmanngasse 16, A-1090, Vienna
mailing address: use embassy street address
telephone: [43] (1) 31339-0
FAX: [43] (1) 3100682

Flag description: three equal horizontal bands of red (top), white, and red; the flag design is certainly one of the oldest—if not the oldest—national banners in the world; according to tradition, in 1191, following a fierce battle in the Third Crusade, Duke Leopold V of Austria's white tunic became completely blood-spattered; upon removal of his wide belt or sash, a white band was revealed; the red-white-red color combination was subsequently adopted as his banner

National symbol(s): golden eagle, edelweiss, Alpine gentian; national colors: red, white

National anthem: *name:* "Bundeshymne" (Federal Hymn)
lyrics/music: Paula von PRERADOVIC/Wolfgang Amadeus MOZART or Johann HOLZER (disputed)
note: adopted 1947; the anthem is also known as "Land der Berge, Land am Strome" (Land of the Mountains, Land by the River); Austria adopted a new national anthem after World War II to replace the former imperial anthem composed by Franz Josef HAYDN, which had been appropriated by Germany in 1922 and was thereafter associated with the Nazi regime; a gendered version of the lyrics was adopted by the Austrian Federal Assembly in fall 2011 and became effective 1 January 2012

ECONOMY

Economy—overview: Austria, with its well-developed market economy, skilled labor force, and high standard of living, is closely tied to other EU economies, especially Germany's. Its economy features a large service sector, a relatively sound industrial sector, and a small, but highly developed agricultural sector.

Economic growth has been relatively weak in recent years, approaching 0.9% in 2015. Austria's 5.8% unemployment rate, while low by European standards, is at its highest rate since the end of World War II, driven by an increased number of refugees and EU migrants entering the labor market. Without extensive vocational training programs and generous early retirement, the unemployment rate would be even higher. Although Austria's fiscal position compares favorably with other euro-zone countries, it faces several external risks, such as unexpectedly weak world economic growth threatening the export market, Austrian banks' continued exposure to Central and Eastern Europe, repercussions from the Hypo Alpe Adria bank collapse, political and economic uncertainties caused by the European sovereign debt crisis, the currentre fugee crisis, and continued unrest in Russia/Ukraine. Early signs point towards a slight improvement in 2016, driven by low interest rates on government debt. Currently, the budget deficit stands at 2.7% of GDP and public debt has reached a post-war high of 84.2% of the GDP.

GDP (purchasing power parity):
$404.3 billion (2015 est.)
$400.8 billion (2014 est.)
$399.4 billion (2013 est.)
note: data are in 2015 US dollars
country comparison to the world: 47

GDP (official exchange rate):
$374.1 billion (2015 est.)

GDP—real growth rate:
0.9% (2015 est.)
0.4% (2014 est.)
0.3% (2013 est.)
country comparison to the world: 181

GDP—per capita (PPP):
$47,300 (2015 est.)

$47,100 (2014 est.)
$47,300 (2013 est.)
note: data are in 2015 US dollars
country comparison to the world: 27

Gross national saving: 25.8% of GDP (2015 est.)
23.5% of GDP (2014 est.)
25.1% of GDP (2013 est.)
country comparison to the world: 46

GDP—composition, by end use:
household consumption: 53.2%
government consumption: 19.6%
investment in fixed capital: 22.1%
investment in inventories: 0.8%
exports of goods and services: 52.2%
imports of goods and services: -47.9% (2015 est.)

GDP—composition, by sector of origin:
agriculture: 1.4%
industry: 27.9%
services: 70.7% (2015 est.)

Agriculture—products: grains, potatoes, wine, fruit; dairy products, cattle, pigs, poultry; lumber and other forestry products

Industries: construction, machinery, vehicles and parts, food, metals, chemicals, lumber, paper and paperboard, communications equipment, tourism

Industrial production growth rate: 1.1% (2015 est.)
country comparison to the world: 143

Labor force: 3.448 million (2015 est.)
country comparison to the world: 100

Labor force—by occupation: *agriculture:* 0.7%
industry: 25.3%
services: 74% (2015 est.)

Unemployment rate: 5.8% (2015 est.)
5.6% (2014 est.)
country comparison to the world: 64

Population below poverty line: 4% (2014 est.)

Household income or consumption by percentage share: *lowest:* 10%: 2.8%
highest: 10%: 23.5% (2012 est.)

Distribution of family income—Gini index: 29.2 (2013)
26.3 (2007)
country comparison to the world: 125

Budget: *revenues:* $189.2 billion
expenditures: $196.8 billion (2015 est.)
Taxes and other revenues: 50.6% of GDP (2015 est.)
country comparison to the world: 13

Budget surplus (+) or deficit (–): -2.1% of GDP (2015 est.)
country comparison to the world: 77

Public debt: 83.4% of GDP (2015 est.)
84.6% of GDP (2014 est.)
note: this is general government gross debt, defined in the Maastricht Treaty as consolidated general government gross debt at nominal value, outstanding at the end of the year; it covers the following categories of government liabilities (as defined in ESA95): currency and deposits (AF.2), securities other than shares excluding financial derivatives (AF.3, excluding AF.34), and loans (AF.4); the general government sector comprises the sub-sectors of central government, state

government, local governmentand social security funds; as a percentage of GDP, the GDP used as a denominator is the gross domestic product in current year prices
country comparison to the world: 29

Fiscal year: calendar year

Inflation rate (consumer prices):
0.8% (2015 est.)
1.5% (2014 est.)
country comparison to the world: 73

Commercial bank prime lending rate: 1.9% (31 December 2015 est.)
2.15% (31 December 2014 est.)
country comparison to the world: 181

Stock of narrow money:
$185.8 billion (31 December 2015 est.)
$191.8 billion (31 December 2014 est.)
note: see entry for the European Union for money supply for the entire euro area; the European Central Bank (ECB) controls monetary policy for the 18 members of the Economic and Monetary Union (EMU); individual members of the EMU do not control the quantity of money circulating within their own borders
country comparison to the world: 22

Stock of broad money: $428.9 billion (31 December 2014 est.)
$439.3 billion (31 December 2013 est.)
country comparison to the world: 26

Stock of domestic credit: $474.9 billion (31 December 2015 est.)
$507.3 billion (31 December 2014 est.)
country comparison to the world: 27

Market value of publicly traded shares:
$106 billion (31 December 2012 est.)
$82.37 billion (31 December 2011)
$67.68 billion (31 December 2010 est.)
country comparison to the world: 43

Current account balance: $13.46 billion (2015 est.)
$8.437 billion (2014 est.)
country comparison to the world: 19

Exports: $141.4 billion (2015 est.)
$164.3 billion (2014 est.)
country comparison to the world: 32

Exports—commodities: machinery and equipment, motor vehicles and parts, paper and paperboard, metal goods, chemicals, ironand steel, textiles, foodstuffs

Exports—partners: Germany 29.4%, US 6.4%, Italy 6.1%, Switzerland 5.7%, France 4.4%, Slovakia 4.2% (2015)

Imports: $139.8 billion (2015 est.)
$167.5 billion (2014 est.)
country comparison to the world: 30

Imports—commodities: machinery and equipment, motor vehicles, chemicals, metal goods, oil and oil products, natural gas; foodstuffs

Imports—partners: Germany 41.5%, Italy 6.3%, Switzerland 6%, Czech Republic 4.2% (2015)

Reserves of foreign exchange and gold: $22.24 billion (31 December 2015 est.)
$24.94 billion (31 December 2014 est.)

country comparison to the world: 57

Debt external:
$675 billion (30 September 2015 est.)
$740.1 billion (31 December 2014 est.)
country comparison to the world: 21

Stock of direct foreign investment—at home:
$327.9 billion (31 December 2015 est.)
$318.4 billion (31 December 2014 est.)
country comparison to the world: 21

Stock of direct foreign investment abroad:
$375.5 billion (31 December 2015 est.)
$366.3 billion (31 December 2014 est.)
country comparison to the world: 20

Exchange rates: euros (EUR) per US dollar—
0.885 (2015 est.)
0.7525 (2014 est.)
0.7634 (2013 est.)
0.78 (2012 est.)
0.7185 (2011 est.)

ENERGY

Electricity—production: 64.74 billion kWh (2015 est.)
country comparison to the world: 43

Electricity—consumption: 69.75 billion kWh (2015 est.)
country comparison to the world: 40

Electricity—exports: 19.31 billion kWh (2015 est.)
country comparison to the world: 10

Electricity—imports: 29.37 billion kWh (2015 est.)
country comparison to the world: 8

Electricity—installed generating capacity: 24.22 million kW (2014 est.)
country comparison to the world: 35

Electricity—from fossil fuels: 32.8% of total installed capacity (2014 est.)
country comparison to the world: 175

Electricity—from nuclear fuels: 0% of total installed capacity (2014 est.)
country comparison to the world: 45

Electricity—from hydro electric plants: 56% of total installed capacity (2014 est.)
country comparison to the world: 39

Electricity—from other renewable sources: 11.1% of total installed capacity (2014 est.)
country comparison to the world: 32

Crude oil—production: 21,760 bbl/day (2014 est.)
country comparison to the world: 67

Crude oil—exports: 0 bbl/day (2014 est.)
country comparison to the world: 97

Crude oil—imports: 173,900 bbl/day (2014 est.)
country comparison to the world: 36

Crude oil—proved reserves: 61.69 million bbl (1 January 2015 est.)
country comparison to the world: 79

Refined petroleum products—production: 194,600 bbl/day (2013 est.)
country comparison to the world: 55

Refined petroleum products—consumption: 260,700 bbl/day (2014 est.)
country comparison to the world: 46

Refined petroleum products—exports: 48,820 bbl/day (2013 est.)
country comparison to the world: 57

Refined petroleum products—imports: 121,300 bbl/day (2013 est.)
country comparison to the world: 46

Natural gas—production: 1.244 billion cu m (2014 est.)
country comparison to the world: 62

Natural gas—consumption: 7.764 billion cu m (2014 est.)
country comparison to the world: 50

Natural gas—exports: 2.373 billion cu m (2014 est.)
country comparison to the world: 36

Natural gas—imports: 10.17 billion cu m (2014 est.)
country comparison to the world: 26

Natural gas—proved reserves: 11.1 billion cu m (1 January 2014 est.)
country comparison to the world: 80

Carbon dioxide emissions from consumption of energy: 76.2 million Mt (2014 est.)

COMMUNICATIONS

Telephones—fixed lines: *total subscriptions:* 3.27 million
subscriptions per 100 inhabitants: 38 (2014 est.)
country comparison to the world: 45

Telephones—mobile cellular: *total:* 13 million
subscriptions per 100 inhabitants: 150 (2014 est.)
country comparison to the world: 71

Telephone system: *general assessment:* highly developed and efficient
domestic: fixed-line subscribership has been in decline since the mid-1990s with mobile-cellular subscribership eclipsing it by the late 1990s; the fiber-optic net is very extensive; all telephone applications and Internet services are available; broadband is available in major cities
international: country code—43; earth stations available in the Intelsat, Eutelsat satellite systems (2016)

Broadcast media: worldwide cable and satellite TV are available; the public incumbent ORF competes with three other major, several regional domestic, and up to 400 international TV stations; TV coverage is in principle 100%, but only 90% use broadcast media; Internet streaming not only complements, but increasingly replaces regular TV stations (2016)
Radio broadcast stations: FM 65 (plus several hundred repeaters), shortwave 1 (2009)
Television broadcast stations: 9 (2010)

Internet country code: .at

Internet hosts: 3.512 million (2012)
country comparison to the world: 30

Internet users: *total:* 7.2 million
percent of population: 83.7% (2014 est.)

country comparison to the world: 53

TRANSPORTATION

Airports: 52 (2013)
country comparison to the world: 90

Airports—with paved runways: *total:* 24
over 3,047 m: 1
2,438 to 3,047 m: 5
1,524 to 2,437 m: 1
914 to 1,523 m: 4
under 914 m: 13 (2013)

Airports—with unpaved runways: *total:* 28
1,524 to 2,437 m: 1
914 to 1,523 m: 3
under 914 m: 24 (2013)

Heliports: 1 (2013)

Pipelines: gas 4,736 km; oil 663 km; refined products 157 km (2013)

Railways: *total:* 5,267.7 km
standard gauge: 5,267.7 km 1.435m gauge (3,556.4 km electrified) (2014)
country comparison to the world: 35

Roadways: *total:* 133,597 km
paved: 133,597 km (includes 2,207 km of expressways) (2016)
country comparison to the world: 39

Waterways: 358 km (2011)
country comparison to the world: 89

Merchant marine: *registered in other countries:* 3 (Cyprus 1, Kazakhstan 1, Saint Vincent and the Grenadines 1) (2010)
country comparison to the world: 134

Ports and terminals: *river port(s):* Enns, Krems, Linz, Vienna (Danube)

MILITARY AND SECURITY

Military branches: Land Forces (KdoLdSK), Air Forces (KdoLuSK)

Military service age and obligation: registration requirement at age 17, the legal minimum age for voluntary military service; 18 is the legal minimum age for compulsory military service (6 months), or optionally, alternative civil/community service (9 months); males 18 to 50 years old in the militia or inactive reserve are subject to compulsory service; in a January 2012 referendum, a majority of Austrians voted in favor of retaining the system of compulsory military service (with the option of alternative/non-military service) instead of switching to a professional army system (2015)

Military expenditures:
0.55% of GDP (2015 est.)
0.62% of GDP (2014)
0.63% of GDP (2013)
0.68% of GDP (2012)
0.7% of GDP (2011)
country comparison to the world: 115

Disputes—international: none

Refugees and internally displaced persons: *refugees (country of origin):* 11,906 (Afghanistan); 19,577 (Russia) (2014)
stateless persons: 828 (2015)

Illicit drugs: transshipment point for Southwest Asian heroin and South American cocaine destined for Western Europe; increasing consumption of European-produced synthetic drugs

AZERBAIJAN

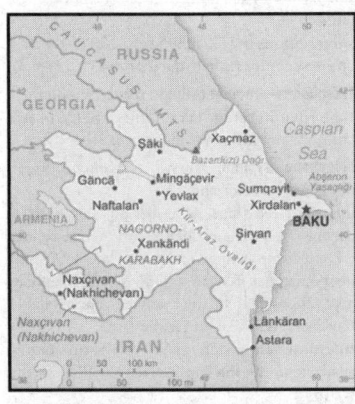

INTRODUCTION

Background: Azerbaijan a nation with a majority-Turkic and majority-Shia Muslim population—was briefly independent (from 1918 to 1920) following the collapse of the Russian Empire; it was subsequently incorporated intothe Soviet Union for seven decades. Azerbaijan has yet to resolve its conflict with Armenia over Nagorno-Karabakh, a primarily ethnic Armenian populated region that Moscow recognized in 1923 as anautonomous republic within Soviet Azerbaijan after Armenia and Azerbaijan disputed the territory's status. Armenia and Azerbaijan began fighting over the area in 1988; the struggle escalated after both countriesattained independence from the Soviet Union in 1991. By May 1994, when a ceasefire took hold, ethnicArmenian forces held not only Nagorno Karabakh but also seven surrounding provinces in the territory ofAzerbaijan. The OSCE Minsk Group, cochaired by the US, France, and Russia, is the frameworkestablished to mediate a peaceful resolution of the conflict. Corruption in the country is widespread, and the government, which eliminated presidential term limits in a2009 referendum, has been accused of authoritarianism. Although the poverty rate has been reduced andinfrastructure investment has increased substantially in recent years due to revenue from oil and gasproduction, reforms have not adequately addressed weaknesses in most government institutions, particularly in the education and health sectors, as well as the court system.

Location: Southwestern Asia, bordering the Caspian Sea, between Iran and Russia, with a small European portionnorth of the Caucasus range

Geographic coordinates: 40 30 N, 47 30 E

Map references: Asia

Area: *total:* 86,600 sq km

Land boundaries: *land:* 82,629 sq km
water: 3,971 sq km
note: includes the exclave of Naxcivan Autonomous Republic and the Nagorno Karabakh region; theregion's autonomy was abolished by Azerbaijani Supreme Soviet on 26 November 1991
country comparison to the world: 113

Area—comparative: slightly smaller than Maine
total: 2,468 km

border countries (5): Armenia 996 km, Georgia 428 km, Iran 689 km, Russia 338 km, Turkey 17 km

Coastline: 0 km (landlocked); note Azerbaijan borders the Caspian Sea (713 km)

Maritime claims: none (landlocked)

Climate: dry, semiarid steppe

Terrain: large, flat KurAraz Ovaligi (KuraAraks Lowland, much of it below sea level) with Great CaucasusMountains to the north, Qarabag Yaylasi (Karabakh Upland) to the west; Baku lies on Abseron Yasaqligi (Apsheron Peninsula) that juts into Caspian Sea

Elevation: *mean elevation:* 384 m

elevation extremes: *lowest point:* Caspian Sea -28m
highest point: Bazarduzu Dagi 4,485 m

Natural resources: petroleum, natural gas, iron ore, nonferrous metals, bauxite

Land use: *agricultural land:* 57.6%
arable land: 22.8%
permanent crops: 2.7%
permanent pasture: 32.1%
forest: 11.3%
other: 31.1% (2011 est.)

Irrigated land: 14,277 sq km (2012)

Total renewable water resources: 34.68 cu km (2011)

Freshwater withdrawal (domestic/industrial/agricultural): *total:* 12.21 cu km/yr (4%/18%/78%)
per capita: 1,384 cu m/yr (2010)

Natural hazards: droughts

Environment—current issues: local scientists consider the Abseron Yasaqligi (Apsheron Peninsula) (including Baku and Sumqayit) andthe Caspian Sea to be the ecologically most devastated area in the world because of severe air, soil, andwater pollution; soil pollution results from oil spills, from the use of DDT pesticide, and from toxicdefoliants used in the production of cotton

Environment—international agreements: *party to:* Air Pollution, Biodiversity, Climate Change, Climate Change-Kyoto Protocol, Desertification, Endangered Species, Hazardous Wastes, Marine Dumping, Ozone Layer Protection, Ship Pollution, Wetlands

signed, but not ratified: none of the selected agreements

Geography—note: both the main area of the country and the Naxcivan exclave are landlocked

PEOPLE AND SOCIETY

Nationality: *noun:* Azerbaijani(s)
adjective: Azerbaijani

Ethnic groups: Azerbaijani 91.6%, Lezgian 2%, Russian 1.3%, Armenian 1.3%, Talysh 1.3%, other 2.4%
note: the separatist Nagorno-Karabakh region is populated almost entirely by ethnic Armenians (2009 est.)

Languages: Azerbaijani (Azeri) (official) 92.5%, Russian 1.4%, Armenian 1.4%, other 4.7% (2009 est.)

Religions: Muslim 96.9% (predominantly Shia), Christian 3%, other <0.1, unaffiliated <0.1 (2010 est.)
note: religious affiliation is still nominal in Azerbaijan; percentages for actual practicing adherents aremuch lower

Population: 9,780,780 (July 2015 est.)
country comparison to the world: 92

Age structure: *0–14 years:* 22.72% (male 1,190,101/female 1,031,632)
15–24 years: 16.69% (male 847,738/female 784,379)
25–54 years: 45.17% (male 2,158,226/female 2,259,284)
55–64 years: 9.06% (male 409,137/female 477,078)
65 years and over: 6.37% (male 237,547/female 385,658) (2015 est.)

Dependency ratios: *total dependency ratio:* 38%
youth dependency ratio: 30.3%
elderly dependency ratio: 7.8%
potential support ratio: 12.9% (2015 est.)

Median age: *total:* 30.5 years
male: 28.9 years
female: 32.2 years (2015 est.)
country comparison to the world: 107

Population growth rate: 0.96% (2015 est.)
country comparison to the world: 121

Birth rate: 16.64 births/1,000 population (2015 est.)
country comparison to the world: 112

Death rate: 7.07 deaths/1,000 population (2015 est.)
country comparison to the world: 132

Net migration rate: 0 migrant(s)/1,000 population (2015 est.)
country comparison to the world: 109

Urbanization: *urban population:* 54.6% of total population (2015)
rate of urbanization: 1.56% annual rate of change (2010–15 est.)

Major urban areas population: BAKU (capital) 2.374 million (2015)

Sex ratio: *at birth:* 1.11 male(s)/female
0–14 years: 1.15 male(s)/female
15–24 years: 1.08 male(s)/female
25–54 years: 0.96 male(s)/female
55–64 years: 0.86 male(s)/female
65 years and over: 0.62 male(s)/female
total population: 0.98 male(s)/female (2015 est.)

Mother's mean age at first birth: 23.4 (2011 est.)

Maternal mortality rate: 25 deaths/100,000 live births (2015 est.)
country comparison to the world: 113

Infant mortality rate: *total:* 25.68 deaths/1,000 live births
male: 26.52 deaths/1,000 live births
female: 24.74 deaths/1,000 live births (2015 est.)
country comparison to the world: 70

Life expectancy at birth: *total population:* 72.2 years
male: 69.19 years
female: 75.54 years (2015 est.)
country comparison to the world: 143

Total fertility rate: 1.91 children born/woman (2015 est.)
country comparison to the world: 135

Contraceptive prevalence rate: 51.1% (2006)

Health expenditures: 5.6% of GDP (2013)
country comparison to the world: 128

Physicians density: 3.4 physicians/1,000 population (2013)

Hospital bed density: 4.7 beds/1,000 population (2012)

Drinking water source: *improved:*
urban: 94.7% of population
rural: 77.8% of population
total: 87% of population
unimproved:
urban: 5.3% of population
rural: 22.2% of population
total: 13% of population (2015 est.)

Sanitation facility access: *improved:*
urban: 91.6% of population
rural: 86.6% of population
total: 89.3% of population
unimproved:
urban: 8.4% of population
rural: 13.4% of population
total: 10.7% of population (2015 est.)

HIV/AIDS—adult prevalence rate: 0.14% (2014 est.)
country comparison to the world: 106

HIV/AIDS—people living with HIV/AIDS: 8,400 (2014 est.)
country comparison to the world: 100

HIV/AIDS—deaths: 400 (2014 est.)
country comparison to the world: 92

Obesity—adult prevalence rate: 22.2% (2014)
country comparison to the world: 71

Children under the age of 5 years underweight: 4.9% (2013)
country comparison to the world: 75

Education expenditures: 2.5% of GDP (2013)
country comparison to the world: 158

Literacy: *definition:* age 15 and over can read and write
total population: 99.8%
male: 99.9%
female: 99.8% (2015 est.)

School life expectancy (primary to tertiary education): *total:* 13 years
male: 13 years
female: 13 years (2014)

Child labor—children ages 5–14: *total number:* 144,397
percentage: 7%
note: data represent children ages 5–17 (2005 est.)

Unemployment, youth ages 15–24:
total: 13.8%
male: 12%
female: 15.6% (2013 est.)
country comparison to the world: 83

GOVERNMENT

Country name: *conventional long form:* Republic of Azerbaijan
conventional short form: Azerbaijan
local long form: Azarbaycan Respublikasi
local short form: Azarbaycan
former: Azerbaijan Soviet Socialist Republic
etymology: the name translates as "Land of fire" and refers to naturally occurring surface fires onancient oil pools or from natural gas discharges

Government type: presidential republic

Capital: *name:* Baku (Baki, Baky)

Geographic coordinates: 40 23 N, 49 52 E
time difference: UTC+4 (9 hours ahead of Washington, DC, during Standard Time)
daylight saving time: +1hr, begins last Sunday in March; ends last Sunday in October

Administrative divisions: 66 rayons (rayonlar; rayon singular), 11 cities (saharlar; sahar singular); *rayons:* Abseron, Agcabadi, Agdam, Agdas, Agstafa, Agsu, Astara, Babak, Balakan, Barda, Beylaqan, Bilasuvar, Cabrayil, Calilabad, Culfa, Daskasan, Fuzuli, Gadabay, Goranboy, Goycay, Goygol, Haciqabul, Imisli, Ismayilli, Kalbacar, Kangarli, Kurdamir, Lacin, Lankaran, Lerik, Masalli, Neftcala, Oguz, Ordubad, Qabala, Qax, Qazax, Qobustan, Quba, Qubadli, Qusar, Saatli, Sabirabad, Sabran, Sadarak, Sahbuz, Saki, Salyan, Samaxi, Samkir, Samux, Sarur, Siyazan, Susa, Tartar, Tovuz, Ucar, Xacmaz, Xizi, Xocali, Xocavand, Yardimli, Yevlax, Zangilan, Zaqatala, Zardab *cities:* Baku, Ganca, Lankaran, Mingacevir, Naftalan, Naxcivan (Nakhichevan), Saki, Sirvan, Sumqayit, Xankandi, Yevlax

Independence: 30 August 1991 (declared from the Soviet Union); 18 October 1991 (adopted by the Supreme Council of Azerbaijan)

National holiday: Founding of the Democratic Republic of Azerbaijan, 28 May (1918)

Constitution: several previous; latest adopted 12 November 1995; amended 2002, 2009 (2016)

Legal system: civil law system

International law organization participation: has not submitted an ICJ jurisdiction declaration; nonparty state to the ICCt

Citizenship: *citizenship by birth:* yes
citizenship by descent: yes
dual citizenship recognized: no
residency requirement for naturalization: 5 years

Suffrage: 18 years of age; universal

Executive branch: *chief of state:* President Ilham ALIYEV (since 31 October 2003)

head of government: Prime Minister Artur RASIZADE (since 4 November 2003); First Deputy Prime Minister Yaqub EYYUBOV (since June 2006); note RASIZADE was previously prime minister from 20 July1996 to 4 August 2003
cabinet: Council of Ministers appointed by the president and confirmed by the National Assembly
elections/appointments: president directly elected by absolute majority popular vote in 2 rounds if needed for a 5 year term (eligible for unlimited terms); election last held on 9 October 2013 (next to be heldin October 2018); prime minister and first deputy prime minister appointed by the president and confirmedby the National Assembly
election results: Ilham ALIYEV reelected president; percent of vote Ilham ALIYEV (YAP) 84.5%, JamilHASANLI (National Council of Democratic Forces) 5.5%, other 10%
note: OSCE observers concluded that the election did not meet international standards

Legislative branch: *description:* unicameral National Assembly or Milli Mejlis (125 seats); members directly elected in single-seat constituencies by simple majority vote to serve 5-year terms)
elections: last held on 1 November 2015 (next to be held in November 2020)
election results: percent of vote by party NA; seats by party YAP 72, CSP 2, Democratic Reforms 1, Social Democratic Party 1, Social Prosperity 1, Unity Party 1, Democratic Enlightenment 1, WholeAzerbaijan Popular Front 1, Motherland 1, Civil Unity 1, Great Undertaking Party 1, independent 42

Judicial branch: *highest court(s):* Supreme Court (consists of the chairman, deputy chairman, and at least 24 judges inplenum sessions); Constitutional Court (consists of 9 judges)
judge selection and term of office: Supreme Court judges nominated by the president and appointed bythe Milli Majlis; judge tenure NA;

Constitutional Court chairman and deputy chairman appointed by the president; other court judges nominated by the president and appointed by the Milli Majlis to serve single 15 year terms
subordinate courts: Courts of Appeal (replaced the Economic Court in 2002); district and municipal courts

Political parties and leaders: Civil Solidarity Party or CSP [Sabir RUSTAMKHANLI]
Civil Unity Party or CUP [Sabir HAJIYEV]
Democratic Enlightenment [Elshan MUSAYEV]
Democratic Reforms Party [Asim MOLLAZADE]
Great Undertaking [Fazil MUSTAFA] Musavat [Arif HAJILI]
Popular Front Party [Ali KARIMLI]
Motherland Party or AVP [Fazail AGAMALI]
Social Democratic Party [Ayaz MUTALIBOV]
Social Prosperity Party [Khanhusein KAZIMLI]
Unity Party [Tahir KARIMLI]
Whole Azerbaijan Popular Front Party [Gudrat HASANGULIYEV]
Yeni (New) Azerbaijan Party or YAP [President Ilham ALIYEV]

Political pressure groups and leaders:
Club-125 [Ilhamia RZAYEVA]
Ireli Youth Movement [MirHasan SEYIDOV]
National Council of Democratic Forces [Jamil HASANLI]
NIDA Youth Movement [Turgut GAMBAR, Zaur GURBANLI]
Positive Change Youth Movement [Bakhtiyar HAJIYEV]
Republican Alternative or REAL [Ilgar MAMMADOV (in jail)]

International organization participation: ADB, BSEC, CD, CE, CICA, CIS, EAPC, EBRD, ECO, EITI (compliant country), FAO, GCTU, GUAM, IAEA, IBRD, ICAO, ICC (NGOs), ICRM, IDA, IDB, IFAD, IFC, IFRCS, ILO, IMF, IMO, Interpol, IOC, IOM, IPU, ISO, ITSO, ITU, ITUC (NGOs), MIGA, NAM, OAS (observer), OIC, OPCW, OSCE, PFP, SELEC (observer), UN, UNCTAD, UNESCO, UNHCR, UNIDO, UNWTO, UPU, WCO, WFTU (NGOs), WHO, WIPO, WMO, WTO (observer)

Diplomatic representation in the US: *chief of mission:* Ambassador Elin SULEYMANOV (since 5 December 2011)
chancery: 2741 34th Street NW, Washington, DC 20008
telephone: [1] (202) 337-3500
FAX: [1] (202) 337-5911
consulate(s) general: Los Angeles

Diplomatic representation from the US: *chief of mission:* Ambassador Robert CEKUTA (since 16 February 2015)
embassy: 111 Azadliq Prospecti, Baku AZ1007
mailing address: American Embassy Baku, US Department of State, 7050 Baku Place, Washington, DC205217050
telephone: [994] (12) 488-3300
FAX: [994] (12) 488-3320

Flag description: three equal horizontal bands of blue (top), red, and green; a crescent and eight-pointed star in white arecentered in the red band;

the blue band recalls Azerbaijan's Turkic heritage, red stands for modernizationand progress, and green refers to Islam; the crescent moon and star are a Turkic insignia; the eight starpoints represent the eight Turkic peoples of the world

National symbol(s): flames of fire; national colors: blue, red, green

National anthem: *name:* "Azerbaijan Marsi" (March of Azerbaijan)
lyrics/music: Ahmed JAVAD/Uzeyir HAJIBEYOV
note: adopted 1992; although originally written in 1919 during a brief period of independence, "Azerbaijan Marsi" did not become the official anthem until after the dissolution of the Soviet Union

ECONOMY

Economy—overview: Azerbaijan's high economic growth has been attributable to large and growing oil and gas exports, butsome nonexport sectors also featured doubledigit growth, including construction, banking, and realestate. Oil exports through the BakuTbilisi Ceyhan Pipeline, the Baku-Novorossiysk, and the Baku-Supsapipelines remain the main economic driver, but efforts to boost Azerbaijan's gas production are underway. The eventual completion of the geopolitically important Southern Gas Corridor between Azerbaijan andEurope will open up another, albeit, smaller source of revenue from gas exports. Azerbaijan has made only limited progress on instituting marketbased economic reforms. Pervasive publicand private sector corruption and structural economic inefficiencies remain a drag on longterm growth, particularly in nonenergy sectors. Several other obstacles impede Azerbaijan's economic progress, including the need for stepped up foreign investment in the nonenergy sector and the continuing conflictwith Armenia over the Nagorno-Karabakh region. Trade with Russia and the other former Soviet republicsis declining in importance, while trade is building with Turkey and the nations of Europe. Longterm prospects depend on world oil prices, Azerbaijan's ability to negotiate export routes for itsgrowing gas production, and its ability to use its energy wealth to promote growth and spur employment innonenergy sectors of the economy.

GDP (purchasing power parity):
$169.4 billion (2015 est.)
$167.6 billion (2014 est.)
$163 billion (2013 est.)
note: data are in 2015 US dollars
country comparison to the world: 68

GDP (official exchange rate): $54.05 billion (2015 est.)

GDP—real growth rate:
1.1% (2015 est.)
2.8% (2014 est.)
5.8% (2013 est.)
country comparison to the world: 170

GDP—per capita (PPP):
$18,000 (2015 est.)
$17,900 (2014 est.)
$17,600 (2013 est.)

note: data are in 2015 US dollars
country comparison to the world: 92

Gross national saving:
26.6% of GDP (2015 est.)
37.1% of GDP (2014 est.)
39.5% of GDP (2013 est.)
country comparison to the world: 40

GDP—composition, by end use:
household consumption: 50.5%
government consumption: 11.9%
investment in fixed capital: 30.4%
investment in inventories: 0.2%
exports of goods and services: 38.2%
imports of goods and services: -31.2% (2015 est.)

GDP—composition, by sector of origin:
agriculture: 6%
industry: 58%
services: 36.1% (2015 est.)

Agriculture—products: fruit, vegetables, grain, rice, grapes, tea, cotton, tobacco; cattle, pigs, sheep, goats

Industries: petroleum and petroleum products, natural gas, oilfield equipment; steel, iron ore; cement; chemicals and petrochemicals; textiles

Industrial production growth rate: 1.5% (2015 est.)
country comparison to the world: 130

Labor force: 4.899 million (2015 est.)
country comparison to the world: 86

Labor force—by occupation: *agriculture:* 38.3%
industry: 12.1%
services: 49.6% (2008)

Unemployment rate: 5.3% (2015 est.)
5.4% (2014 est.)
country comparison to the world: 57

Population below poverty line: 6% (2012 est.)

Household income or consumption by percentage share: *lowest:* 10%: 3.4%
highest: 10%: 27.4% (2008)

Distribution of family income—Gini index: 33.7 (2008) 36.5 (2001)
country comparison to the world: 101

Budget: *revenues:* $16.15 billion
expenditures: $17.88 billion (2015 est.)
Taxes and other revenues: 25.2% of GDP (2015 est.)
country comparison to the world: 119

Budget surplus (+) or deficit (–): -2.7% of GDP (2015 est.)
country comparison to the world: 99

Public debt: 11.8% of GDP (2015 est.)
8.9% of GDP (2014 est.)
country comparison to the world: 164

Fiscal year: calendar year

Inflation rate (consumer prices):
4% (2015 est.)
1.4% (2014 est.)
country comparison to the world: 158

Central bank discount rate: 5% (31 December 2012)
5.25% (31 December 2011)

note: this is the Refinancing Rate, the key policy rate for the National Bank of Azerbaijan
country comparison to the world: 78

Commercial bank prime lending rate: 14% (31 December 2015 est.)
14.19% (31 December 2014 est.)
country comparison to the world: 50

Stock of narrow money:
$9.519 billion (31 December 2015 est.)
$16.36 billion (31 December 2014 est.)
country comparison to the world: 82

Stock of broad money: $24.18 billion (31 December 2014 est.)
$20.95 billion (31 December 2013 est.)
country comparison to the world: 82

Stock of domestic credit: $24.1 billion (31 December 2015 est.)
$25.38 billion (31 December 2014 est.)
country comparison to the world: 81

Market value of publicly traded shares: $NA

Current account balance: $125 million (2015 est.)
$10.43 billion (2014 est.)
country comparison to the world: 48

Exports: $16.38 billion (2015 est.)
$28.26 billion (2014 est.)
country comparison to the world: 74

Exports—commodities: oil and gas 90%, machinery, foodstuffs, cotton

Exports—partners: Italy 26.3%, Germany 13.2%, Indonesia 7%, France 6.8%, Czech Republic 6% (2015)

Imports: $8.414 billion (2015 est.)
$9.332 billion (2014 est.)
country comparison to the world: 107

Imports—commodities: machinery and equipment, foodstuffs, metals, chemicals

Imports—partners: Russia 19.9%, Turkey 16.5%, UK 8.6%, Germany 6.6%, Italy 6.3%, US 4.1% (2015)

Reserves of foreign exchange and gold: $8.513 billion (31 December 2015 est.)
$15.55 billion (31 December 2014 est.)
country comparison to the world: 79

Debt external:
$9.833 billion (31 December 2014 est.)
$9.219 billion (31 December 2013 est.)
country comparison to the world: 107

Stock of direct foreign investment—at home:
$66.14 billion (31 December 2015 est.)
$59.02 billion (31 December 2014 est.)
country comparison to the world: 53

Stock of direct foreign investment—abroad:
$14.17 billion (31 December 2013 est.)
$11.22 billion (31 December 2014 est.)
country comparison to the world: 56

Exchange rates: Azerbaijani manats (AZN) per US dollar—
1.009 (2015 est.)
0.7844 (2014 est.)
0.7844 (2013 est.)
0.79 (2012 est.)

0.7897 (2011 est.)

ENERGY

Electricity—production:
22.99 billion kWh (2012 est.)
country comparison to the world: 72

Electricity—consumption:
17.79 billion kWh (2012 est.)
country comparison to the world: 73

Electricity—exports: 680 million kWh (2012 est.)
country comparison to the world: 62

Electricity—imports: 141 million kWh (2012 est.)
country comparison to the world: 91

Electricity—installed generating capacity: 7.114 million kW (2012 est.)
country comparison to the world: 68

Electricity—from fossil fuels: 85% of total installed capacity (2012 est.)
country comparison to the world: 90

Electricity—from nuclear fuels: 0% of total installed capacity (2012 est.)
country comparison to the world: 39

Electricity—from hydro electric plants: 14.9% of total installed capacity (2012 est.)
country comparison to the world: 102

Electricity—from other renewable sources: 0% of total installed capacity (2012 est.)
country comparison to the world: 150

Crude oil—production: 845,900 bbl/day (2014 est.)
country comparison to the world: 22

Crude oil—exports: 811,300 bbl/day (2012 est.)
country comparison to the world: 17

Crude oil—imports: 0 bbl/day (2012 est.)
country comparison to the world: 154

Crude oil—proved reserves: 7 billion bbl (1 January 2015 est.)
country comparison to the world: 20

Refined petroleum products—production: 131,600 bbl/day (2012 est.)
country comparison to the world: 67

Refined petroleum products—consumption: 99,000 bbl/day (2013 est.)
country comparison to the world: 78

Refined petroleum products—exports: 36,700 bbl/day (2012 est.)
country comparison to the world: 64

Refined petroleum products—imports: 807.1 bbl/day (2012 est.)
country comparison to the world: 201

Natural gas—production: 18.2 billion cu m (2013 est.)
country comparison to the world: 34

Natural gas—consumption:
10.91 billion cu m (2013 est.)
country comparison to the world: 46

Natural gas—exports: 7.29 billion cu m (2013 est.)
country comparison to the world: 27

Natural gas—imports: 0 cu m (2013 est.)

country comparison to the world: 154

Natural gas—proved reserves: 991.1 billion cu m (1 January 2014 est.)
country comparison to the world: 27

Carbon dioxide emissions from consumption of energy: 35.14 million Mt (2012 est.)
country comparison to the world: 72

COMMUNICATIONS

Telephones—fixed lines: *total subscriptions:* 1.8 million
subscriptions per 100 inhabitants: 19 (2014 est.)
country comparison to the world: 63

Telephones—mobile cellular: *total:* 10.6 million
subscriptions per 100 inhabitants: 109 (2014 est.)
country comparison to the world: 83

Telephone system: *general assessment:* requires considerable expansion and modernization; fixed-line telephone and abroad range of other telecom services are controlled by a stateowned telecommunications monopoly andgrowth has been stagnant; more competition exists in the mobilecellular market with four providers in 2009
domestic: teledensity of 17 fixed lines per 100 persons; mobilecellular teledensity has increased andnow exceeds 100 telephones per 100 persons; satellite service connects Baku to a modern switch in itsexclave of Naxcivan (Nakhichevan)
international: country code 994; the Trans Asia Europe (TAE) fiberoptic link transits Azerbaijanproviding international connectivity to neighboring countries; the old Soviet system of cable and microwaveis still serviceable; satellite earth stations -2 (2011)

Broadcast media: 3 staterun and 1 public TV channels; 4 domestic commercial TV stations and about 15 regional TVstations; cable TV services are available in Baku; 1 staterun and 1 public radio network operating; a smallnumber of private commercial radio stations broadcasting; local FM relays of Baku commercial stationsare available in many localities; local relays of several international broadcasters had been available untillate 2008 when their broadcasts were banned from FM frequencies (2010)
Radio broadcast stations: AM 10, FM 11, shortwave 1 (2010)

Television broadcast stations: 10 (2010)

Internet country code: .az

Internet hosts: 46,856 (2012)
country comparison to the world: 98

Internet users: *total:* 5.8 million
percent of population: 60.3% (2014 est.)
country comparison to the world: 60

TRANSPORTATION

Airports: 37 (2013)
country comparison to the world: 108

Airports—with paved runways: *total:* 30
over 3,047 m: 5
2,438 to 3,047 m: 5
1,524 to 2,437 m: 13
914 to 1,523 m: 4
under 914 m: 3 (2013)

Airports—with unpaved runways: *total:* 7
under 914 m: 7 (2013)

Heliports: 1 (2012)

Pipelines: condensate 89 km; gas 3,890 km; oil 2,446 km (2013)

Railways: *total:* 2,068 km
broad gauge: 2,068 km 1.520m gauge (1,240 km electrified) (2014)
country comparison to the world: 70

Roadways: *total:* 52,942 km
paved: 26,789 km
unpaved: 26,153 km (2006)
country comparison to the world: 74

Merchant marine: *total:* 90
by type: cargo 27, chemical tanker 1, passenger 2, passenger/cargo 8, petroleum tanker 47, roll on/rolloff 3, specialized tanker 2
foreignowned: 1 (Turkey 1)
registered in other countries: 2 (Malta 1, Saint Vincent and the Grenadines 1) (2010)
country comparison to the world: 53

Ports and terminals: *major seaport(s):* Baku (Baki) located on the Caspian Sea

MILITARY AND SECURITY

Military branches: Army, Navy, Air, and Air Defense Forces (2010)

Military service age and obligation: 1835 years of age for cumpulsory military service; service obligation 18 months or 12 months foruniversity graduates; 17 years of age for voluntary service; 17 year olds are considered to be on active service at cadet military schools (2012)

Military expenditures:
5.1% of GDP (2014)
4.7% of GDP (2013)
4.64% of GDP (2012)
4.67% of GDP (2011)
4.64% of GDP (2010)
country comparison to the world: 6

TRANSNATIONAL ISSUES

Disputes—international: Azerbaijan, Kazakhstan, and Russia ratified the Caspian seabed delimitation treaties based onequidistance, while Iran continues to insist on a onefifth slice of the sea; the dispute over the break-away Nagorno-Karabakh region and the Armenian military occupation of surrounding lands in Azerbaijan remainsthe primary focus of regional instability; residents have evacuated the former Sovietera small ethnicenclaves in Armenia and Azerbaijan; local border forces struggle to control the illegal transit of goods andpeople across the porous, undemarcated Armenian, Azerbaijani, and Georgian borders; bilateral talkscontinue with Turkmenistan on dividing the seabed and contested oilfields in the middle of the Caspian

Refugees and internally displaced persons: *IDPs:* 618,220 (conflict with Armenia over Nagorno-Karabakh; IDPs are mainly ethnic Azerbaijanis butalso include ethnic Kurds, Russians, and Turks predominantly from occupied territories around Nagorno-Karabakh; includes IDPs' descendants, returned IDPs, and people living in insecure areas and excludespeople displaced by natural disasters; around half the IDPs live in the capital Baku) (2015)
stateless persons: 3,585 (2015)

Illicit drugs: limited illicit cultivation of cannabis and opium poppy, mostly for CIS consumption; small governmente radication program; transit point for Southwest Asian opiates bound for Russia and to a lesser extent therest of Europe

BAHAMAS, THE

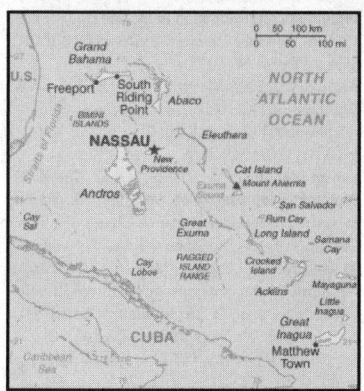

Background: Lucayan Indians inhabited the islands when Christopher COLUMBUS first set foot in the New World on San Salvador in 1492. British settlement of the islands began in 1647; the islands became a colony in 1783. Since attaining independence from the UK in 1973, The Bahamas has prospered through tourism, international banking, and investment management. Because of its location, the country is a major transshipment point for illegal drugs, particularly shipments to the US and Europe, and its territory is used for smuggling illegal migrants into the US.

GEOGRAPHY

Location: chain of islands in the North Atlantic Ocean, southeast of Florida, northeast of Cuba

Geographic coordinates: 24 15 N, 76 00 W

Map references: Central America and the Caribbean

Area: *total:* 13,880 sq km
land: 10,010 sq km
water: 3,870 sq km
country comparison to the world: 161

Area—comparative: slightly smaller than Connecticut

Land boundaries: 0 km

Coastline: 3,542 km

Maritime claims: *territorial sea:* 12 nm
exclusive economic zone: 200 nm

Climate: tropical marine; moderated by warm waters of Gulf Stream

Terrain: long, flat coral formations with some low rounded hills

Elevation: *mean elevation:* NA

elevation extremes: *lowest:* point: Atlantic Ocean 0 m
highest point: Mount Alvernia on Cat Island 63 m

Natural resources: salt, aragonite, timber, *arable land:*

Land use: *agricultural land:* 1.4%
arable land: 0.8%
permanent crops: 0.4%

permanent pasture: 0.2%
forest: 51.4%
other: 47.2% (2011 est.)

Irrigated land: 10 sq km (2012)

Total renewable water resources: 0.02 cu km (2011)

Natural hazards: hurricanes and other tropical storms cause extensive flood and wind damage

Environment—current issues: coral reef decay; solid waste disposal

Environment—international agreements: *party to:* Biodiversity, Climate Change, Climate Change-Kyoto Protocol, Desertification, Endangered Species, Hazardous Wastes, Law of the Sea, Ozone Layer Protection, Ship Pollution, Wetlands
signed, but not ratified: none of the selected agreements

Geography—note: strategic location adjacent to US and Cuba; extensive island chain of which 30 are inhabited

PEOPLE AND SOCIETY

Nationality: *noun:* Bahamian(s)
adjective: Bahamian

Ethnic groups: black 90.6%, white 4.7%, black and white 2.1%, other 1.9%, unspecified 0.7% (2010 est.)

Languages: English (official), Creole (among Haitian immigrants)

Religions: Protestant 69.9% (includes Baptist 34.9%, Anglican 13.7%, Pentecostal 8.9% Seventh Day Adventist 4.4%, Methodist 3.6%, Church of God 1.9%, Brethren 1.6%), Roman Catholic 12%, other Christian 13% (includes Jehovah's Witness 1.1%), other 0.6%, none 1.9%, unspecified 2.6% (2010 est.)

Population: 324,597

note: estimates for this country explicitly take into account the effects of excess mortality due to AIDS; this can result in lower life expectancy, higher infant mortality, higher death rates, lower population growth rates, and changes in the distribution of population by age and sex than would otherwise be expected (July 2015 est.)
country comparison to the world: 180

Age structure: *0–14 years:* 22.98% (male 37,838/female 36,747)
15–24 years: 17.15% (male 28,195/female 27,459)
25–54 years: 44.08% (male 71,528/female 71,555)
55–64 years: 8.58% (male 12,429/female 15,436)
65 years and over: 7.21% (male 8,981/female 14,429) (2015 est.)

Dependency ratios: *total dependency ratio:* 41.2%
youth dependency ratio: 29.6%
elderly dependency ratio: 11.7%
potential support ratio: 8.5% (2015 est.)

Median age: *total:* 31.5 years
male: 30.4 years
female: 32.6 years (2015 est.)
country comparison to the world: 100

Population growth rate: 0.85% (2015 est.)
country comparison to the world: 129

Birth rate: 15.5 births/1,000 population (2015 est.)
country comparison to the world: 127

Death rate: 7.05 deaths/1,000 population (2015 est.)
country comparison to the world: 133

Net migration rate: 0 migrant(s)/1,000 population (2015 est.)
country comparison to the world: 108

Urbanization: *urban population:* 82.9% of total population (2015)
rate of urbanization: 1.53% annual rate of change (2010–15 est.)

Major urban areas—population: NASSAU (capital) 267,000 (2014)

Sex ratio: *at birth:* 1.03 male(s)/female
0–14 years: 1.03 male(s)/female
15–24 years: 1.03 male(s)/female
25–54 years: 1 male(s)/female
55–64 years: 0.81 male(s)/female
65 years and over: 0.62 male(s)/female
total population: 0.96 male(s)/female (2015 est.)

Maternal mortality rate: 80 deaths/100,000 live births (2015 est.)
country comparison to the world: 111

Infant mortality rate: *total:* 11.92 deaths/1,000 live births
male: 11.75 deaths/1,000 live births
female: 12.1 deaths/1,000 live births (2015 est.)
country comparison to the world: 124

Life expectancy at birth: *total population:* 72.2 years
male: 69.77 years
female: 74.7 years (2015 est.)
country comparison to the world: 142

Total fertility rate: 1.96 children born/woman (2015 est.)
country comparison to the world: 129

Health expenditures: 7.3% of GDP (2013)
country comparison to the world: 70

Physicians density: 2.82 physicians/1,000 population (2008)

Hospital bed density: 2.9 beds/1,000 population (2011)

Drinking water source:
improved:
urban: 98.4% of population
rural: 98.4% of population
total: 98.4% of population
unimproved:
urban: 1.6% of population
rural: 1.6% of population
total: 1.6% of population (2015 est.)

Sanitation facility access:
improved:
urban: 92% of popu lation
rural: 92% of population
total: 92% of population
unimproved:
urban: 8% of population
rural: 8% of population
total: 8% of population (2015 est.)

HIV/AIDS—adult prevalence rate: 3.22% (2013 est.)

country comparison to the world: 19
HIV/AIDS—people living with HIV/AIDS: 7,700 (2013 est.)
country comparison to the world: 103
HIV/AIDS—deaths: 500 (2013 est.)
country comparison to the world: 85
Obesity—adult prevalence rate: 36.6% (2014)
country comparison to the world: 13
Education expenditures: NA
Unemployment, youth ages 15–24: *total:* 30.8%
male: 29.6%
female: 32.2% (2012 est.)
country comparison to the world: 24

GOVERNMENT

Country name: *conventional long form:* Commonwealth of The Bahamas
conventional short form: The Bahamas
etymology: name derives from the Spanish "baha mar," meaning "shallow sea," which describes the shallow waters of the Bahama Banks
Government type: parliamentary democracy (Parliament) under a constitutional monarchy; a Commonwealth realm
Capital: *name:* Nassau
Geographic coordinates: 25 05 N, 77 21 W
time difference: UTC-5 (same time as Washington, DC, during Standard Time)
daylight saving time: +1hr, begins second Sunday in March; ends first Sunday in November
Administrative divisions: 31 districts; Acklins Islands, Berry Islands, Bimini, Black Point, Cat Island, Central Abaco, Central Andros, Central Eleuthera, City of Freeport, Crooked Island and Long Cay, East Grand Bahama, Exuma, Grand Cay, Harbour Island, Hope Town, Inagua, Long Island, Mangrove Cay, Mayaguana, Moore's Island, North Abaco, North Andros, Northeleuthera, Ragged Island, Rum Cay, San Salvador, South Abaco, South Andros, Southeleuthera, Spanish Wells, West Grand Bahama
Independence: 10 July 1973 (from the UK)
National holiday: Independence Day, 10 July (1973)
Constitution: previous 1964 (preindependence); latest adopted 20 June 1973, effective 10 July 1973; amended many times, last in 2016 (2016)
Legal system: common law system based on the English model
International law organization participation: has not submitted an ICJ jurisdiction declaration; non-party state to the ICCt
Citizenship: *citizenship by birth:* no
citizenship by descent only: at least one parent must be a citizen of The Bahamas
dual citizenship recognized: no
residency requirement for naturalization: 6–9 years
Suffrage: 18 years of age; universal
Executive branch: *chief of state:* Queen ELIZABETH II (since 6 February 1952); represented by Governor General Dame Marguerite PINDLING (since 8 July 2014)
head of government: Prime Minister Perry CHRISTIE (since 8 May 2012)

cabinet: Cabinet appointed by governor general on recommendation of prime minister
elections/appointments: the monarchy is hereditary; governor general appointed by the monarch; following legislative elections, the leader of the majority party or majority coalition usually appointed prime minister by the governor general; the prime minister recommends the deputy prime minister
Legislative branch: *description:* bicameral Parliament consists of the Senate (16 seats; members appointed by the governor general upon the advice of the prime minister and the opposition leader to serve 5-year terms) and the House of Assembly (38 seats; members directly elected in single-seat constituencies by simple majority vote to serve 5-year terms); note—the government may dissolve the parliament and call elections at any time
elections: last held on 7 May 2012 (next to be held by May 2017)
election results: percent of vote by party—PLP 48.6%, FNM 42.1%, DNA 8.5%, other.8%; seats by party—PLP 29, FNM 9
Judicial branch: *highest resident court(s):* The Bahamas Court of Appeal (consists of the court president and 4 justices, organized in 3-member panels); Supreme Court (consists of the chief justice and 9 justices—as of 2015)
note: as of 2008, the Bahamas was not a party to the agreement establishing the Caribbean Court of Justice as the highest appellate court for the 15-member Caribbean Community (CARICOM); the Judicial Committee of the Privy Council (in London) serves as the final court of appeal for The Bahamas
judge selection and term of office: Court of Appeal president and Supreme Court chief justice appointed by the governor general on the advice of the prime minister after consultation with the leader of the opposition party; other Court of Appeal and Supreme Court justices appointed by the governor general upon recommendation of the Judicial and Legal Services Commission, a 5-member body headed by the chief justice; Court of Appeal justices appointed for life with mandatory retirement normally at age 68, but can be extended until age 70; Supreme Court justices appointed for life with mandatory retirement normally at age 65 but can be extended until age 67
subordinate courts: Industrial Tribunal; Stipendiary and Magistrates' Courts; Family Island Administrators
Political parties and leaders: Free National Movement or FNM [Hubert MINNIS]
Progressive Liberal Party or PLP [Perry CHRISTIE]
Democratic National Alliance [Branville MCCARTNEY]
Political pressure groups and leaders: Friends of the Environment
other: trade unions
International organization participation: ACP, AOSIS, C, Caricom, CDB, CELAC, FAO, G-77, IADB, IAEA, IBRD, ICAO, ICC (NGOs), ICRM, IDA, IFAD, IFC, IFRCS, ILO, IMF, IMO, IMSO, Interpol, IOC, IOM, ISO (correspondent), ITSO, ITU, LAES, MIGA, NAM, OAS, OPANAL,

OPCW, Petrocaribe, UN, UNCTAD, UNESCO, UNIDO, UNWTO, UPU, WCO, WHO, WIPO, WMO, WTO (observer)
Diplomatic representation in the US: *chief of mission:* Ambassador Dr. Eugene Glenwood NEWRY (since 3 December 2013)
chancery: 2220 Massachusetts Avenue NW, Washington, DC 20008
telephone: [1] (202) 319-2660
FAX: [1] (202) 319-2668
consulate(s) general: Atlanta, Miami, New York
Diplomatic representation from the US: *chief of mission:* Ambassador (vacant); Charge d' Affaires Lisa A. JOHNSON (since 9 July 2014 embassy: 42 Queen Street, Nassau, New Providence mailing address: local or express mail address: P.O. Box N-8197, Nassau; US Department of State, 3370 Nassau Place, Washington, DC 20521–3370
telephone: [1] (242) 322-1181, 328-2206 (after hours)
FAX: [1] (242) 328-2206
Flag description: three equal horizontal bands of aquamarine (top), gold, and aquamarine, with a black equilateral triangle based on the hoist side; the band colors represent the golden beaches of the islands surrounded by the aquamarine sea; black represents the vigor and force of a united people, while the pointing triangle indicates the enterprise and determination of the Bahamian people to develop the rich resources of land and sea
National symbol(s): blue marlin, flamingo, Yellow Elder flower; national colors: aquamarine, yellow, black
National anthem: *name:* "March On, Bahamaland!"
lyrics/music: Timothy GIBSON
note: adopted 1973; as a Commonwealth country, in addition to the national anthem, "God Save the Queen" serves as the royal anthem (see United Kingdom)

ECONOMY

Economy—overview: The Bahamas is one of the wealthiest Caribbean countries with an economy heavily dependent on tourism and offshore banking. Tourism together with tourism-driven construction and manufacturing accounts for approximately 60% of GDP and directly or indirectly employs half of the archipelago's labor force. Financial services constitute the second-most important sector of the Bahamian economy and, when combined with business services, account for about 35% of GDP. Manufacturing and agriculture combined contribute less than one 10th of GDP and show little growth, despite government incentives aimed at those sectors. The economy of The Bahamas shrank at an average pace of 0.8% annually between 2007 and 2011, and tourism, financial services, and construction—pillars of the national economy—remain subdued. Conditions are improving in the tourism sector, however, due to steady foreign investment led activity. New resort and marina developments are likely to provide sustained employment opportunities.

GDP (purchasing power parity): $9.166 billion (2015 est.)
$9.122 billion (2014 est.)
$9.03 billion (2013 est.)
note: data are in 2015 US dollars
country comparison to the world: 160
GDP (official exchange rate): $8.705 billion (2015 est.)
GDP—real growth rate: 0.5% (2015 est.)
1% (2014 est.) 0% (2013 est.)
country comparison to the world: 188
GDP—per capita (PPP): $25,200 (2015 est.)
$25,300 (2014 est.)
$25,400 (2013 est.)
note: data are in 2015 US dollars
country comparison to the world: 75
Gross national saving: 10.9% of GDP (2015 est.)
6.5% of GDP (2014 est.) 9.3% of GDP (2013 est.)
country comparison to the world: 148
GDP—composition, by end use:
household consumption: 70.8%
government consumption: 15.5%
investment in fixed capital: 28%
investment in inventories: 1%
exports of goods and services: 38.6%
imports of goods and services: -53.9% (2015 est.)
GDP—composition, by sector of origin:
agriculture: 2.1%
industry: 7.3%
services: 90.6% (2015 est.)
Agriculture—products: citrus, vegetables; poultry
Industries: tourism, banking, oil bunkering, maritime industries, transshipment, salt, rum, aragonite, pharmaceuticals
Industrial production growth rate: 1.5% (2015 est.)
country comparison to the world: 129
Labor force: 196,900 (2013 est.)
country comparison to the world: 171
Labor force—by occupation: *agriculture:* 3%
industry: 11%
tourism: 49%
other services: 37% (2011 est.)
Unemployment rate: 15% (2014 est.)
15.8% (2013 est.)
country comparison to the world: 151
Population below poverty line: 9.3% (2010 est.)
Household income or consumption by percentage share: *lowest:* 10%: 1%
highest: 10%: 22% (2007 est.)
Budget: *revenues:* $1.6 billion
expenditures: $1.8 billion (2015 est.)
Taxes and other *revenues:* 18% of GDP (2015 est.)
country comparison to the world: 172
Budget surplus (+) or deficit (–): -2.3% of GDP (2015 est.)
country comparison to the world: 87
Public debt: 57.6% of GDP (2013 est.)
56.1% of GDP (2012 est.)
country comparison to the world: 66
Fiscal year: 1 July—30 June
Inflation rate (consumer prices): 1.9% (2015 est.)
1.2% (2014 est.)
country comparison to the world: 113

Central bank discount rate: 4.5% (1 January 2014)
4.5% (31 December 2012)
country comparison to the world: 81
Commercial bank prime lending rate: 5.1% (31 December 2015 est.)
4.75% (31 December 2014 est.)
country comparison to the world: 146
Stock of narrow money: $2.101 billion (31 December 2015 est.)
$1.996 billion (31 December 2014 est.)
country comparison to the world: 125
Stock of broad money: $6.453 billion (31 December 2014 est.)
$6.076 billion (31 December 2013 est.)
country comparison to the world: 121
Stock of domestic credit: $9.4 billion (31 December 2015 est.)
$8.825 billion (31 December 2014 est.)
country comparison to the world: 104
Market value of publicly traded shares: $2.78 billion (31 December 2012 est.)
country comparison to the world: 96
Current account balance:
-$1.021 billion (2015 est.)
-$1.898 billion (2014 est.)
country comparison to the world: 123
Exports: $976.1 million (2015 est.)
$848.8 million (2014 est.)
country comparison to the world: 161
Exports—commodities: crawfish, aragonite, crude salt, polystyrene products
Exports—partners: Poland 26.3%, Cote dIvoire 20.9%, US 15.9%, Dominican Republic 14.3% (2015)
Imports: $2.65 billion (2015 est.)
$3.27 billion (2014 est.)
country comparison to the world: 152
Imports—commodities: machinery and transport equipment, manufactures, chemicals, mineral fuels; food and live animals
Imports—partners: US 22.3%, China 14.8%, Japan 9.5%, Poland 7.7%, South Korea 7.3%, Colombia 6.8%, Brazil 5.6%, Singapore 5.5% (2015)
Reserves of foreign exchange and gold: $950 million (31 December 2015 est.)
$874.3 million (31 December 2014 est.)
country comparison to the world: 136
Debt—external: $17.56 billion (31 December 2013 est.)
$16.35 billion (31 December 2012 est.)
country comparison to the world: 91
Exchange rates: Bahamian dollars (BSD) per US dollar—1 (2015 est.)
1 (2014 est.)
1 (2013 est.)
1 (2012 est.)
1 (2011 est.)

ENERGY

Electricity—production: 1.845 billion kWh (2012 est.)
country comparison to the world: 140
Electricity—consumption: 1.716 billion kWh (2012 est.)
country comparison to the world: 144

Electricity—exports: 0 kWh (2013 est.)
country comparison to the world: 106
Electricity—imports: 0 kWh (2013 est.)
country comparison to the world: 121
Electricity—installed generating capacity: 493,000 kW (2012 est.)
country comparison to the world: 141
Electricity—from fossil fuels: 100% of total installed capacity (2012 est.)
country comparison to the world: 5
Electricity—from nuclear fuels: 0% of total installed capacity (2012 est.)
country comparison to the world: 50
Electricity—from hydroelectric plants: 0% of total installed capacity (2012 est.)
country comparison to the world: 162
Electricity—from other renewable sources: 0% of total installed capacity (2012 est.)
country comparison to the world: 157
Crude oil—production: 0 bbl/day (2014 est.)
country comparison to the world: 110
Crude oil—exports: 0 bbl/day (2012 est.)
country comparison to the world: 100
Crude oil—imports: 0 bbl/day (2012 est.)
country comparison to the world: 161
Crude oil—proved reserves: 0 bbl (1 January 2015 est.)
country comparison to the world: 109
Refined petroleum products—production: 0 bbl/day (2012 est.)
country comparison to the world: 158
Refined petroleum products—consumption: 23,000 bbl/day (2013 est.)
country comparison to the world: 124
Refined petroleum products—exports: 41,650 bbl/day (2012 est.)
country comparison to the world: 61
Refined petroleum products—imports: 64,430 bbl/day (2012 est.)
country comparison to the world: 70
Natural gas—production: 0 cu m (2013 est.)
country comparison to the world: 159
Natural gas—consumption: 0 cu m (2013 est.)
country comparison to the world: 119
Natural gas—exports: 0 cu m (2013 est.)
country comparison to the world: 63
Natural gas—imports: 0 cu m (2013 est.)
country comparison to the world: 162
Natural gas—proved reserves: 0 cu m (1 January 2009 est.)
country comparison to the world: 114
Carbon dioxide emissions from consumption of energy: 3.836 million Mt (2012 est.)
country comparison to the world: 134

COMMUNICATIONS

Telephones—fixed lines: *total subscriptions:* 140,000
subscriptions per 100 inhabitants: 43 (2014 est.)
country comparison to the world: 140
Telephones—mobile cellular: *total:* 273,300
subscriptions per 100 inhabitants: 85 (2014 est.)
country comparison to the world: 178
Telephone system: *general assessment:* modern facilities

domestic: totally automatic system; highly developed; the Bahamas Domestic Submarine Network links 14 of the islands and is designed to satisfy increasing demand for voice and broadband Internet services

international: country code—1-242; landing point for the Americas Region Caribbean Ring System (AR CO S-1) fiber-optic submarine cable that provides links to South and Central America, parts of the Caribbean, and the US; satellite earth stations—2 (2007)

Broadcast media: 2 TV stations operated by government-owned, commercially run Broadcasting Corporation of the Bahamas (BCB); multichannel cable TV subscription service is available; about 15 radio stations operating with BCB operating a multi-channel radio broadcasting network alongside privately owned radio stations (2007)

Radio broadcast stations: AM 3, FM 11, shortwave 0 (2009)

Television broadcast stations: 2 (2006)

Internet country code: .bs

Internet hosts: 20,661 (2012)

country comparison to the world: 117

Internet users: *total:* 247,200

percent of population: 76.8% (2014 est.)

country comparison to the world: 151

TRANSPORTATION

Airports: 61 (2013)

country comparison to the world: 80

Airports—with paved runways: *total:* 24

over 3,047 m: 2

2,438 to 3,047 m: 2

1,524 to 2,437 m: 13

914 to 1,523 m: 7 (2013)

Airports—with unpaved runways: *total:* 37

1,524 to 2,437 m: 4

914 to 1,523 m: 16 *under 914 m:* 17 (2013)

Heliports: 1 (2013)

Roadways: *total:* 2,700 km

paved: 1,620 km

unpaved: 1,080 km (2011)

country comparison to the world: 171

Merchant marine: *total:* 1,160

by type: barge carrier 1, bulk carrier 238, cargo 170, carrier 2, chemical tanker 87, combination ore/oil 8, container 57, liquefied gas 71, passenger 102, passenger/cargo 26, petroleum tanker 225, refrigerated cargo 97, roll on/roll off 13, specialized tanker 2, vehicle carrier 61

foreign-owned: 1,069 (Angola 6, Australia 1, Belgium 6, Bermuda 15, Brazil 1, Canada 96, Croatia 1, Cyprus 23, Denmark 69, Finland 15, France 15, Germany 30, Greece 225, Guernsey 6, Hong Kong

3, Indonesia 2, Ireland 3, Italy 1, Japan 88, Jordan 2, Kuwait 1, Malaysia 13, Monaco 8, Montenegro 2, Netherlands 23, Nigeria 2, Norway 186, Poland 34, Saudi Arabia 16, Singapore 7, South Korea 1, Spain 6, Sweden 11, Switzerland 1, Thailand 4, Turkey 3, UAE 23, UK 18, US 109)

registered in other countries: 6 (Panama 6) (2010)

country comparison to the world: 10

Ports and terminals: *major seaport(s):* Freeport, Nassau, South Riding Point

container port(s)(TEUs): Freeport (1,116,272)(2011)

cruise port(s): Nassau

MILITARY AND SECURITY

Military branches: Royal Bahamas Defense Force: Land Force, Navy, Air Wing (2011)

Military service age and obligation: 18 years of age for voluntary male and female service; no conscription (2012)

TRANSNATIONAL ISSUES

Disputes—international: disagrees with the US on the alignment of the northern axis of a potential maritime boundary

Illicit drugs: transshipment point for cocaine and marijuana bound for US and Europe; offshore financial center

BAHRAIN

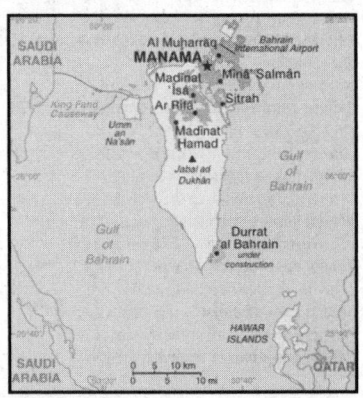

countries require it to play a delicate balancing act in foreign affairs among its larger neighbors.

The Sunni-led government has long struggled to manage relations with its large Shia-majority population. In early 2011, amid Arab uprisings elsewhere in the region, the Bahraini Government confronted similar pro-democracy and reform protests at home with police and military action, including deploying Gulf Cooperation Council security forces to Bahrain. Political talks throughout 2014 between the government and opposition and loyalist political groups failed to reach an agreement, prompting opposition political societies to boycott parliamentary and municipal council elections in late 2014. Ongoing dissatisfaction with the political status quo continues to factor into sporadic clashes between demonstrators and security forces.

INTRODUCTION

Background: In 1783, the Sunni Al-Khalifa family took power in Bahrain. In order to secure these holdings, it entered into a series of treaties with the UK during the 19th century that made Bahrain a British protectorate. The archipelago attained its independence in 1971. A steady decline in oil production and reserves since 1970 prompted Bahrain to take steps to diversify its economy, in the process developing successful petroleum processing and refining, aluminum production, and hospitality and retail sectors, and also to become a leading regional banking center, especially with respect to Islamic finance. Bahrain's small size and central location among Gulf

GEOGRAPHY

Location: Middle East, archipelago in the Persian Gulf, east of Saudi Arabia

Geographic coordinates: 26 00 N, 50 33 E

Map references: Middle East

Area: *total:* 760 sq km

land: 760 sq km

water: 0 sq km

country comparison to the world: 188

Area—comparative: 3.5 times the size of Washington, DC

Land boundaries: 0 km

Coastline: 161 km

Maritime claims: *territorial sea:* 12 nm

contiguous zone: 24 nm

continental shelf: extending to boundaries to be determined

Climate: arid; mild, pleasant winters; very hot, humid summers

Terrain: mostly low desert plain rising gently to low central escarpment

Elevation: *mean elevation:* NA

elevation extremes: *lowest:* point: Persian Gulf 0 m

highest point: Jabal ad Dukhan 122 m

Natural resources: oil, associated and nonassociated natural gas, fish, pearls

Land use: *agricultural land:* 11.3%

arable land: 2.1%

permanent crops: 3.9%

permanent pasture: 5.3%

forest: 0.7%

other: 88% (2011 est.)

Irrigated land: 40 sq km (2012)

Total renewable water resources: 0.12 cu km (2011)

Freshwater withdrawal (domestic/industrial/agricultural): *total:* 0.36 cu km/yr (50%/6%/45%)

per capita: 386 cu m/yr (2003)

Natural hazards: periodic droughts; dust storms

Environment—current issues: desertification resulting from the degradation of limited arable land, periods of drought, and dust storms; coastal degradation (damage to coastlines, coral reefs, and sea vegetation) resulting from oil spills and other discharges from large tankers, oil refineries, and distribution stations; lack of freshwater resources (groundwater and seawater are the only sources for all water needs)

Environment—international agreements: *party to:* Biodiversity, Climate Change, Climate Change-Kyoto Protocol, Desertification, Hazardous Wastes, Law of the Sea, Ozone Layer Protection, Wetlands

signed, but not ratified: none of the selected agreements

Geography—note: close to primary Middle Eastern petroleum sources; strategic location in Persian Gulf, through which much of the Western world's petroleum must transit to reach open ocean

PEOPLE AND SOCIETY

Nationality: *noun:* Bahraini(s)
adjective: Bahraini

Ethnic groups: Bahraini 46%, Asian 45.5%, other Arab 4.7%, African 1.6%, European 1%, other 1.2% (includes Gulf Cooperative country nationals, North and South Americans, and Oceanians) (2010 est.)

Languages: Arabic (official), English, Farsi, Urdu

Religions: Muslim 70.3%, Christian 14.5%, Hindu 9.8%, Buddhist 2.5%, Jewish 0.6%, folk religion <.1, unaffiliated 1.9%, other 0.2% (2010 est.)

Population: 1,346,613 (July 2015 est.)

note: immigrants make up approximately 50% of the total population, according to UN data (2015)

country comparison to the world: 156

Age structure: *0–14 years:* 19.48% (male 133,201/female 129,140)

15–24 years: 15.84% (male 120,073/female 93,182)

25–54 years: 56.13% (male 494,405/female 261,399)

55–64 years: 5.79% (male 50,466/female 27,501)

65 years and over: 2.77% (male 18,092/female 19,154) (2015 est.)

Dependency ratios: *total dependency ratio:* 31.4%

youth dependency ratio: 28.2%

elderly dependency ratio: 3.2%

potential support ratio: 31.6% (2015 est.)

Median age: *total:* 31.8 years

male: 33.3 years

female: 29.1 years (2015 est.)

country comparison to the world: 99

Population growth rate: 2.41% (2015 est.)

country comparison to the world: 31

Birth rate: 13.66 births/1,000 population (2015 est.)

country comparison to the world: 144

Death rate: 2.69 deaths/1,000 population (2015 est.)

country comparison to the world: 222

Net migration rate: 13.09 migrant(s)/1,000 population (2015 est.)

country comparison to the world: 6

Urbanization: *urban population:* 88.8% of total population (2015)

rate of urbanization: 1.71% annual rate of change (2010–15 est.)

Major urban areas—population: MANAMA (capital) 411,000 (2015)

Sex ratio: *at birth:* 1.03 male(s)/female

0–14 years: 1.03 male(s)/female

15–24 years: 1.29 male(s)/female

25–54 years: 1.89 male(s)/female

55–64 years: 1.84 male(s)/female

65 years and over: 0.95 male(s)/female

total population: 1.54 male(s)/female (2015 est.)

Maternal mortality rate: 15 deaths/100,000 live births (2015 est.)

country comparison to the world: 138

Infant mortality rate: *total:* 9.35 deaths/1,000 live births

male: 10.4 deaths/1,000 live births

female: 8.26 deaths/1,000 live births (2015 est.)

country comparison to the world: 142

Life expectancy at birth: *total population:* 78.73 years

male: 76.53 years

female: 80.98 years (2015 est.)

country comparison to the world: 51

Total fertility rate: 1.78 children born/woman (2015 est.)

country comparison to the world: 156

Health expenditures: 4.9% of GDP (2013)

country comparison to the world: 165

Physicians density: 0.92 physicians/1,000 population (2012)

Hospital bed density: 2.1 beds/1,000 population (2012)

Drinking water source:

improved:

urban: 100% of population

rural: 100% of population

total: 100% of population

unimproved:

urban: 0% of population

rural: 0% of population

total: 0% of population (2015 est.)

Sanitation facility access:

improved:

urban: 99.2% of population

rural: 99.2% of population

total: 99.2% of population

unimproved:

urban: 0.8% of population

rural: 0.8% of population

total: 0.8% of population (2015 est.)

HIV/AIDS—adult prevalence rate: NA

HIV/AIDS—people living with HIV/AIDS: NA

HIV/AIDS—deaths: NA

Obesity—adult prevalence rate: 34.1% (2014)

country comparison to the world: 20

Education expenditures: 2.6% of GDP (2012)

country comparison to the world: 153

Literacy: *definition:* age 15 and over can read and write

total population: 95.7%

male: 96.9%

female: 93.5% (2015 est.)

Unemployment, youth ages 15–24: *total:* 5.3%

male: 2.6%

female: 12.2% (2012 est.)

country comparison to the world: 127

GOVERNMENT

Country name: *conventional long form:* Kingdom of Bahrain

conventional short form: Bahrain

local long form: Mamlakat al Bahrayn

local short form: Al Bahrayn

former: Dilmun, State of Bahrain

etymology: the name means "the two seas" in Arabic and refers to the water bodies surrounding the archipelago

Government type: constitutional monarchy

Capital: *name:* Manama

Geographic coordinates: 26 14 N, 50 34 E

time difference: UTC+3 (8 hours ahead of Washington, DC, during Standard Time)

Administrative divisions: 4 governorates (muhafazat, singular—muhafazah); Asimah (Capital), Janubiyah (Southern), Muharraq, Shamaliyah (Northern)

note: each governorate administered by an appointed governor

Independence: 15 August 1971 (from the UK)

National holiday: National Day, 16 December (1971); note—15 August 1971 was the date of independence from the UK, 16 December 1971 was the date of independence from British protection

Constitution: adopted 14 February 2002; amended 2012 (2016)

Legal system: mixed legal system of Islamic law, English common law, Egyptian civil, criminal, and commercial codes; customary law

International law organization participation: has not submitted an ICJ jurisdiction declaration; non-party state to the ICCt

Citizenship: *citizenship by birth:* no

citizenship by descent only: the father must be a citizen of Bahrain

dual citizenship recognized: no

residency requirement for naturalization: 25 years; 15 years for Arab nationals

Suffrage: 20 years of age; universal; note—Bahraini Cabinet in May 2011 endorsed a draft law lowering eligibility to 18 years

Executive branch: *chief of state:* King HAMAD bin Isa Al-Khalifa (since 6 March 1999); Crown Prince SALMAN bin Hamad Al-Khalifa (son of the monarch, born 21 October 1969)

head of government: Prime Minister KHALIFA bin Salman Al-Khalifa (since 1971); First Deputy Prime Minister SALMAN bin Hamad Al Khalifa (since 11 March 2013); Deputy Prime Ministers ALI bin Khalifa bin Salman Al-Khalifa, Jawad bin Salim al-ARAIDH (since 11 December 2006), KHALID bin Abdallah Al Khalifa (since November 2010), MUHAMMAD bin Mubarak Al-Khalifa (since September 2005)

cabinet: Cabinet appointed by the monarch

elections/appointments: the monarchy is hereditary; prime minister appointed by the monarch

Legislative branch: *description:* bicameral National Assembly consists of the Consultative Council or Majlis al Shura (40 seats; members appointed by the king) and the Council of Representatives or Majlis al Nuwab (40 seats; members directly elected in single-seat constituencies by absolute majority vote in two rounds if needed; members serve 4-year renewable terms)

elections: Council of Representatives—last held in two rounds on 23 and 29 November 2014 (next to be held in November 2018)

election results: Council of Representatives—percent of vote by society—NA; seats by society—Al-Asalah (Sunni Salafi) 2, Islamic Minbar (Sunni Muslim Brotherhood) 1, independent 36, other 1; note -Bahrain has societies rather than parties

67

Judicial branch: *highest court(s):* Court of Cassation or Supreme Court of Appeal (consists of the chairman and 3 judges); Constitutional Court (consists of the president and 6 members); High Sharia Court of Appeal

note: the judiciary of Bahrain is divided into civil law courts and sharia law courts

judge selection and term of office: Court of Cassation judges appointed by royal decree and serve for a specified tenure; Constitutional Court president and members appointed by the Higher Judicial Council, a body chaired by the monarch and includes judges from the Court of Cassation, sharia law courts, and Civil High Courts of Appeal; members serve 9-year terms; High Sharia Court of Appeal member appointment and tenure NA

subordinate courts: Civil High Courts of Appeal; middle and lower civil courts; High Sharia Court of Appeal; Senior Sharia Court

Political parties and leaders: *note:* political parties are prohibited, but political societies were legalized under a July 2005 law Al-Wefaq National Islamic Society or Al-Wefeq [Ali SALMAN]

Arab Islamic Center Society [Abdulrahman AL-BAKER]

Constitutional Gathering Society [Abdulrahman AL-BAKER]

Islamic Asalah [Abd al-Halim MURAD]

Islamic Saff Society [Abdullah Khalil BUGHAMAR]

Islamic Shura Society Movement of National Justice Society [Muhi al-Din KHAN]

National Action Charter Society [Muhammad AL-BUAYNAYN]

National Democratic Action Society [Radhi AL-MOUSAWI]

National Democratic Assembly [Hasan AL-ALI]

National Dialogue Society

National Fraternity Society [Musa AL-ANSARI]

National Islamic Minbar [Ali AHMAD]

National Progressive Tribune [Abd al-Nabi SALMAN]

National Unity Gathering [Abdullatif AL-MAHMOOD]

Unitary National Democratic Assemblage [Fadhil ABBAS]

Political pressure groups and leaders: none

International organization participation: ABEDA, AFESD, AMF, CAEU, CICA, FAO, G-77, GCC, IAEA, IBRD, ICAO, ICC (national committees), ICRM, IDA, IDB, IFC, IFRCS, IHO, ILO, IMF, IMO, IMSO, Interpol, IOC, IOM (observer), IPU, ISO, ITSO, ITU, ITUC (NGOs), LAS, MIGA, NAM, OAPEC, OIC, OPCW, PCA, UN, UNCTAD, UNESCO, UNIDO, UNWTO, UPU, WCO, WFTU (NGOs), WHO, WIPO, WMO, WTO

Diplomatic representation in the US: *chief of mission:* Ambassador ABDALLAH bin Muhammad bin Rashid Al Khalifa (since 3 December 2013)

chancery: 3502 International Drive NW, Washington, DC 20008

telephone: [1] (202) 342-1111

FAX: [1] (202) 362-2192

consulate(s) general: New York

Diplomatic representation from the US: *chief of mission:* Ambassador William V. ROEBUCK (since 12 December 2014)

embassy: Building

mailing address: PSC 451, Box 660, FPO AE 09834-5100

international mail: American Embassy, Box 26431, Manama

telephone: [973] 1724-2700

FAX: [973] 1727-0547

Flag description: red, the traditional color for flags of Persian Gulf states, with a white serrated band (five white points) on the hoist side; the five points represent the five pillars of Islam

note: until 2002 the flag had eight white points, but this was reduced to five to avoid confusion with the Qatari flag

National symbol(s): a red field surmounted by a white serrated band with five white points; national colors: red, white

National anthem: *name:* "Bahrainona" (Our Bahrain)

lyrics/music: unknown

note: adopted 1971; although Mohamed Sudqi AYYASH wrote the original lyrics, they were changed in 2002 following the transformation of Bahrain from an emirate to a kingdom

ECONOMY

Economy—overview: Low oil prices have generated a budget deficit of at least a $4 billion deficit in 2015, 13% of GDP. Bahrain has few options for covering this deficit, with meager foreign assets and a constrained borrowing ability, stemming in part from a sovereign debt rating averaging just above "junk" status. Oil comprises 86% of Bahraini budget revenues, despite past efforts to diversify its economy and to build communication and transport facilities for multinational firms with business in the Gulf. As part of its diversification plans, Bahrain implemented a Free Trade Agreement (FTA) with the US in August 2006, the first FTA between the US and a Gulf state. Other major economic activities are production of aluminum—Bahrain's second biggest export after oil-finance, and construction. Bahrain continues to seek new natural gas supplies as feedstock to support its expanding petrochemical and aluminum industries. In 2011 Bahrain experienced economic setbacks as a result of domestic unrest driven by the majority Shia population, however, the economy recovered in 2012–15, partly as a result of improved tourism. In addition to addressing its current fiscal woes, Bahraini authorities face the long-term challenge of boosting Bahrain's regional competitiveness—especially regarding industry, finance, and tourism—and reconciling revenue constraints with popular pressure to maintain generous state subsidies and a large public sector.

GDP (purchasing power parity): $64.8 billion (2015 est.)

$62.82 billion (2014 est.)

$60.12 billion (2013 est.)

note: data are in 2015 US dollars

country comparison to the world: 100

GDP (official exchange rate): $30.41 billion (2015 est.)

GDP—real growth rate: 3.2% (2015 est.)

4.5% (2014 est.)

5.4% (2013 est.)

country comparison to the world: 95

GDP—per capita (PPP): $50,100 (2015 est.)

$49,500 (2014 est.)

$48,400 (2013 est.)

note: data are in 2015 US dollars

country comparison to the world: 24

Gross national saving: 12.9% of GDP (2015 est.)

31.5% of GDP (2014 est.)

34.1% of GDP (2013 est.)

country comparison to the world: 129

GDP—composition, by end use:

household consumption: 44.9%

government consumption: 16.6%

investment in fixed capital: 17.2%

investment in inventories: 1.2%

exports of goods and services: 52.3%

imports of goods and services: -32.2% (2015 est.)

GDP—composition, by sector of origin:

agriculture: 0.3%

industry: 35.3%

services: 64.4% (2015 est.)

Agriculture—products: fruit, vegetables; poultry, dairy products; shrimp, fish

Industries: petroleum processing and refining, aluminum smelting, iron pelletization, fertilizers, Islamic and offshore banking, insurance, ship repairing, tourism

Industrial production growth rate: 0.8% (2015 est.)

country comparison to the world: 152

Labor force: 759,400

note: excludes unemployed; 44% of the population in the 15–64 age group is non-national (2015 est.)

country comparison to the world: 150

Labor force—by occupation: *agriculture:* 1%

industry: 32%

services: 67% (2004 est.)

Unemployment rate: 4.1% (2014 est.)

4.3% (2013 est.)

note: official estimate; actual rate is higher

country comparison to the world: 37

Population below poverty line: NA%

Household income or consumption by percentage share: *lowest:* 10%: NA%

highest: 10%: NA%

Budget: *revenues:* $5.149 billion

expenditures: $9.257 billion (2015 est.)

Taxes and other revenues: 16.7% of GDP (2015 est.)

country comparison to the world: 181

Budget surplus (+) or deficit (−): -13.3% of GDP (2015 est.)

country comparison to the world: 211

Public debt: 66.7% of GDP (2015 est.)

43.8% of GDP (2014 est.)

country comparison to the world: 53

Fiscal year: calendar year

Inflation rate (consumer prices): 1.8% (2015 est.)

2.7% (2014 est.)

country comparison to the world: 109

Commercial bank prime lending rate: 5.9% (31 December 2015 est.)

5.88% (31 December 2014 est.)
country comparison to the world: 133
Stock of narrow money: $8.684 billion (31 December 2015 est.)
$8.232 billion (31 December 2014 est.)
country comparison to the world: 84
Stock of broad money: $27 billion (31 December 2015 est.)
$25.95 billion (31 December 2014 est.)
country comparison to the world: 78
Stock of domestic credit: $24.16 billion (31 December 2015 est.)
$25.44 billion (31 December 2014 est.)
country comparison to the world: 80
Market value of publicly traded shares: $22.1 billion (31 December 2014 est.)
$18.57 billion (31 December 2013)
$15.65 billion (31 December 2012 est.)
country comparison to the world: 64
Current account balance: -$987 million (2015 est.)
$1.523 billion (2014 est.)
country comparison to the world: 120
Exports: $14.08 billion (2015 est.)
$20.75 billion (2014 est.)
country comparison to the world: 77
Exports—commodities: petroleum and petroleum products, aluminum, textiles
Exports—partners: Saudi Arabia 3.6%, UAE 2.3%, US 2.2% (2015)
Imports: $8.791 billion (2015 est.)
$13.32 billion (2014 est.)
country comparison to the world: 104
Imports—commodities: crude oil, machinery, chemicals
Imports—partners: Saudi Arabia 28.7%, US 9.4%, China 7.4%, Japan 6.5%, Australia 5%, India 4.8% (2015)
Reserves of foreign exchange and gold: $5.051 billion (31 December 2015 est.)
$6.049 billion (31 December 2014 est.)
country comparison to the world: 93
Debt—external: $18.75 billion (31 December 2014 est.)
$17.66 billion (31 December 2013 est.)
country comparison to the world: 88
Stock of direct foreign investment—at home: $19.69 billion (31 December 2015 est.)
$18.77 billion (31 December 2014 est.)
country comparison to the world: 78
Stock of direct foreign investment—abroad: $10.82 billion (31 December 2015 est.)
$10.72 billion (31 December 2014 est.)
country comparison to the world: 58
Exchange rates: Bahraini dinars (BHD) per US dollar—
0.376 (2015 est.)
0.376 (2014 est.)
0.376 (2013 est.)
0.376 (2012 est.)
0.376 (2011 est.)

ENERGY

Electricity—production: 13.26 billion kWh (2012 est.)
country comparison to the world: 89
Electricity—consumption: 11.69 billion kWh (2012 est.)
country comparison to the world: 86
Electricity—exports: 190 million kWh (2012 est.)
country comparison to the world: 76

Electricity—imports: 35 million kWh (2012 est.)
country comparison to the world: 105
Electricity—installed generating capacity: 3.94 million kW (2012 est.)
country comparison to the world: 83
Electricity—from fossil fuels: 99.9% of total installed capacity (2012 est.)
country comparison to the world: 38
Electricity—from nuclear fuels: 0% of total installed capacity (2012 est.)
country comparison to the world: 46
Electricity—from hydroelectric plants: 0% of total installed capacity (2012 est.)
country comparison to the world: 158
Electricity—from other renewable sources: 0.1% of total installed capacity (2012 est.)
country comparison to the world: 117
Crude oil—production: 49,500 bbl/day (2014 est.)
country comparison to the world: 57
Crude oil—exports: 152,600 bbl/day (2012 est.)
country comparison to the world: 33
Crude oil—imports: 243,300 bbl/day (2012 est.)
country comparison to the world: 30
Crude oil—proved reserves: 124.6 million bbl (1 January 2015 est.)
country comparison to the world: 70
Refined petroleum products—production: 278,500 bbl/day (2012 est.)
country comparison to the world: 46
Refined petroleum products—consumption: 50,000 bbl/day (2013 est.)
country comparison to the world: 99
Refined petroleum products—exports: 242,900 bbl/day (2012 est.)
country comparison to the world: 28
Refined petroleum products—imports: 2,357 bbl/day (2012 est.)
country comparison to the world: 179
Natural gas—production: 15.7 billion cu m (2013 est.)
country comparison to the world: 36
Natural gas—consumption: 15.7 billion cu m (2013 est.)
country comparison to the world: 43
Natural gas—exports: 0 cu m (2013 est.)
country comparison to the world: 59
Natural gas—imports: 0 cu m (2013 est.)
country comparison to the world: 158
Natural gas—proved reserves: 92.03 billion cu m (1 January 2014 est.)
country comparison to the world: 55
Carbon dioxide emissions from consumption of energy: 32.2 million Mt (2012 est.)
country comparison to the world: 73

COMMUNICATIONS

Telephones—fixed lines: *total subscriptions:* 280,000
subscriptions per 100 inhabitants: 22 (2014 est.)
country comparison to the world: 118
Telephones—mobile cellular: *total:* 2.3 million
subscriptions per 100 inhabitants: 177 (2014 est.)
country comparison to the world: 148
Telephone system: *general assessment:* modern system
domestic: modern fiber-optic integrated services; digital network with rapidly growing use of mobile-cellular telephones

international: country code—973; landing point for the Fiber-Optic Link Around the Globe (FLAG) submarine cable network that provides links to Asia, Middle East, Europe, and US; tropospheric scatter to Qatar and UAE; microwave radio relay to Saudi Arabia; satellite earth station—1 (2007)
Broadcast media: state-run Bahrain Radio and Television Corporation (BRTC) operates 5 terrestrial TV networks and several radio stations; satellite TV systems provide access to international broadcasts; 1 private FM station directs broadcasts to Indian listeners; radio and TV broadcasts from countries in the region are available (2007)
Radio broadcast stations: AM 2, FM 3, shortwave 0 (1998)
Television broadcast stations: 4 (1997)
Internet country code: .bh
Internet hosts: 47,727 (2012)
country comparison to the world: 97
Internet users: *total:* 1.3 million
percent of population: 96.5% (2014 est.)
country comparison to the world: 116

TRANSPORTATION

Airports: 4 (2013)
country comparison to the world: 184
Airports—with paved runways: *total:* 4
over 3,047 m: 3
914 to 1,523 m: 1 (2013)
Heliports: 1 (2013)
Pipelines: gas 20 km; oil 54 km (2013)
Roadways: *total:* 4,122 km
paved: 3,392 km
unpaved: 730 km (2010)
country comparison to the world: 157
Merchant marine: *total:* 8
by type: bulk carrier 2, container 4, petroleum tanker 2
foreign-owned: 5 (Kuwait 5)
registered in other countries: 5 (Honduras 5) (2010)
country comparison to the world: 119
Ports and terminals: *major seaport(s):* Mina' Salman, Sitrah

MILITARY AND SECURITY

Military branches: Bahrain Defense Force (BDF): Royal Bahraini Army (RBA), Royal Bahraini Navy (RBN), Royal Bahraini Air Force (RBAF), Royal Bahraini Air Defense Force (RBADF) (2013)
Military service age and obligation: 18 years of age for voluntary military service; 15 years of age for NCOs, technicians, and cadets; no conscription (2012)
Military expenditures: 4.2% of GDP (2014)
4.1% of GDP (2013)
3.9% of GDP (2010)
country comparison to the world: 19

TRANSNATIONAL ISSUES

Disputes—international: none

BANGLADESH

INTRODUCTION

Background: Muslim conversions and settlement in the region now referred to as Bangladesh began in the 10th century, primarily from Arab and Persian traders and preachers. Europeans established trading posts in the area in the 16th century. Eventually the area known as Bengal, primarily Hindu in the western section and mostly Muslim in the eastern half, became part of British India. Partition in 1947 resulted in an eastern wing of Pakistan in the Muslim-majority area, which became East Pakistan. Calls for greater autonomy and animosity between the eastern and western wings of Pakistan led to a Bengali independence movement. That movement, led by the Awami League (AL) and supported by India, won the independence war for Bangladesh in 1971, during which at least 300,000 civilians died.

The post-independence AL government faced daunting challenges and in 1975 was overthrown by the military, triggering a series of military coups that resulted in a military-backed government and subsequent creation of the Bangladesh Nationalist Party (BNP) in 1978. That government also ended in a coup in 1981, followed by military-backed rule until democratic elections occurred in 1991. The BNP and AL alternated in power between 1991 and 2013, with the exception of a military-backed, emergency caretaker regime that suspended parliamentary elections planned for January 2007 in an effort to reform the political system and root out corruption. That government returned the country to fully democratic rule in December 2008 with the election of the AL and Prime Minister Sheikh HASINA. In January 2014, the incumbent AL won the national election by an overwhelming majority after the BNP boycotted, extending HASINA's term as prime minister. With the help of international development assistance, Bangladesh has reduced the poverty rate from over half of the population to less than a third, achieved Millennium Development Goals for maternal and child health, and made great progress in food security since independence. The economy has grown at an annual average of about 6% over the last two decades and the country reached World Bank lower-middle income status in 2015.

GEOGRAPHY

Location: Southern Asia, bordering the Bay of Bengal, between Burma and India

Geographic coordinates: 24 00 N, 90 00 E

Map references: Asia

Area: *total:* 148,460 sq km
land: 130,170 sq km
water: 18,290 sq km
country comparison to the world: 95

Area—comparative: slightly smaller than Iowa

Land boundaries: *total:* 4,413 km
border countries (2): Burma 271 km, India 4,142 km

Coastline: 580 km

Maritime claims: *territorial sea:* 12 nm
contiguous zone: 18 nm exclusive
economic zone: 200 nm
continental shelf: to the outer limits of the continental margin

Climate: tropical; mild winter (October to March); hot, humid summer (March to June); humid, warm rainy monsoon (June to October)

Terrain: mostly flat alluvial plain; hilly in southeast

Elevation: *mean elevation:* 85 m

elevation extremes: *lowest:* point: Indian Ocean 0 m
highest point: Keokradong 1,230 m

Natural resources: natural gas, arable land, timber, coal

Land use: *agricultural land:* 70.1%
arable land: 59%
permanent crops: 6.5%
permanent pasture: 4.6%
forest: 11.1%
other: 18.8% (2011 est.)

Irrigated land: 53,000 sq km (2012)

Total renewable water resources: 1,227 cu km (2011)

Freshwater withdrawal (domestic/industrial/agricultural): *total:* 35.87 cu km/yr (10%/2%/88%)
per capita: 238.3 cu m/yr (2008)

Natural hazards: droughts; cyclones; much of the country routinely inundated during the summer monsoon season

Environment—current issues: many people are landless and forced to live on and cultivate flood-prone land; waterborne diseases prevalent in surface water; water pollution, especially of fishing areas, results from the use of commercial pesticides; ground water contaminated by naturally occurring arsenic; intermittent water shortages because of falling water tables in the northern and central parts of the country; soil degradation and erosion; deforestation; severe overpopulation

Environment—international agreements: *party to:* Biodiversity, Climate Change, Climate Change-Kyoto Protocol, Desertification, Endangered Species, Environmental Modification, Hazardous Wastes, Law of the Sea, Ozone Layer Protection, Ship Pollution, Wetlands
signed, but not ratified: none of the selected agreements

Geography—note: most of the country is situated on deltas of large rivers flowing from the Himalayas: the Ganges unites with the Jamuna (main channel of the Brahmaputra) and later joins the Meghna to eventually empty into the Bay of Bengal

PEOPLE AND SOCIETY

Nationality: *noun:* Bangladeshi(s)
adjective: Bangladeshi

Ethnic groups: Bengali at least 98%, ethnic groups 1.1%
note: Bangladesh's government recognizes 27 ethnic groups under the 2010 Cultural Institution for Small Anthropological Groups Act; other sources estimate there are about 75 ethnic groups; critics of the 2011 census claim that it underestimates the size of Bangladesh's ethnic population (2011 est.)

Languages: Bangla 98.8% (official, also known as Bengali), other 1.2% (2011 est.)

Religions: Muslim 89.1%, Hindu 10%, other 0.9% (includes Buddhist, Christian) (2013 est.)

Population: 168,957,745 (July 2015 est.)
country comparison to the world: 9

Age structure: *0–14 years:* 31.62% (male 27,115,731/female 26,311,130)
15–24 years: 18.86% (male 14,976,910/female 16,880,807)
25–54 years: 38.27% (male 30,608,224/female 34,053,744)
55–64 years: 6.12% (male 5,196,932/female 5,150,199)
65 years and over: 5.13% (male 4,258,664/female 4,405,404) (2015 est.)

Dependency ratios: *total dependency ratio:* 52.5%
youth dependency ratio: 44.9%
elderly dependency ratio: 7.6%
potential support ratio: 13.2% (2015 est.)

Median age: *total:* 24.7 years
male: 24.2 years
female: 25.1 years (2015 est.)
country comparison to the world: 155

Population growth rate: 1.6% (2015 est.)
country comparison to the world: 75

Birth rate: 21.14 births/1,000 population (2015 est.)
country comparison to the world: 76

Death rate: 5.61 deaths/1,000 population (2015 est.)
country comparison to the world: 174

Net migration rate: 0.46 migrant(s)/1,000 population (2015 est.)
country comparison to the world: 72

Urbanization: *urban population:* 34.3% of total population (2015)

rate of urbanization: 3.55% annual rate of change (2010–15 est.)

Major urban areas—population: DHAKA (capital) 17.598 million; Chittagong 4.539 million; Khulna 1.022 million; Rajshahi 844,000 (2015)

Sex ratio: *at birth:* 1.04 male(s)/female

0–14 years: 1.03 male(s)/female

15–24 years: 0.89 male(s)/female

25–54 years: 0.9 male(s)/female

55–64 years: 1.01 male(s)/female

65 years and over: 0.97 male(s)/female

total population: 0.95 male(s)/female (2015 est.)

Mother's mean age at first birth: 18.1

note: median age at first birth among women 25–29 (2011 est.)

Maternal mortality rate: 176 deaths/100,000 live births (2015 est.)

country comparison to the world: 49

Infant mortality rate: *total:* 44.09 deaths/1,000 live births

male: 46.56 deaths/1,000 live births

female: 41.53 deaths/1,000 live births (2015 est.)

country comparison to the world: 46

Life expectancy at birth: *total population:* 70.94 years

male: 69.02 years

female: 72.94 years (2015 est.)

country comparison to the world: 151

Total fertility rate: 2.4 children born/woman (2015 est.)

country comparison to the world: 82

Contraceptive prevalence rate: 61.2% (2011)

Health expenditures: 3.7% of GDP (2013)

country comparison to the world: 169

Physicians density: 0.36 physicians/1,000 population (2011)

Hospital bed density: 0.6 beds/1,000 population (2011)

Drinking water source:

improved:

urban: 86.5% of population

rural: 87% of population

total: 86.9% of population

unimproved:

urban: 13.5% of population

rural: 13% of population

total: 13.1% of population (2015 est.)

Sanitation facility access:

improved:

urban: 57.7% of population

rural: 62.1% of population

total: 60.6% of population

unimproved:

urban: 42.3% of population

rural: 37.9% of population

total: 39.4% of population (2015 est.)

HIV/AIDS—adult prevalence rate: 0.01% (2014 est.)

country comparison to the world: 130

HIV/AIDS—people living with HIV/AIDS: 8,900 (2014 est.)

country comparison to the world: 96

HIV/AIDS—deaths: 700 (2014 est.)

country comparison to the world: 75

Major infectious diseases: *degree of risk:* high

food or waterborne diseases: bacterial and protozoal diarrhea, hepatitis A and E, and typhoid fever

vectorborne diseases: dengue fever and malaria are high risks in some locations

water contact disease: leptospirosis

animal contact disease: rabies

note: highly pathogenic H5N1 avian influenza has been identified in this country; it poses a negligible risk with extremely rare cases possible among US citizens who have close contact with birds (2013)

Obesity—adult prevalence rate: 3.3% (2014)

country comparison to the world: 190

Children under the age of 5 years underweight: 32.6% (2014)

country comparison to the world: 5

Education expenditures: 2% of GDP (2013)

country comparison to the world: 161

Literacy: *definition:* age 15 and over can read and write

total population: 61.5%

male: 64.6%

female: 58.5% (2015 est.)

School life expectancy (primary to tertiary education): *total:* 10 years

male: 10 years

female: 10 years (2011)

Child labor—children ages 5–14: *total number:* 4,485,497

percentage: 13% (2006 est.)

Unemployment, youth ages 15–24: *total:* 8.7%

male: 8.3%

female: 9.2% (2010 est.)

country comparison to the world: 105

GOVERNMENT

Country name: *conventional long form:* People's Republic of Bangladesh

conventional short form: Bangladesh

local long form: Gana Prajatantri Bangladesh

local short form: Bangladesh former: East Bengal, East Pakistan

etymology: the name—a compound of the Bengali words "Bangla" (Bengal) and "desh" (country)—means "Country of Bengal"

Government type: parliamentary republic

Capital: *name:* Dhaka

Geographic coordinates: 23 43 N, 90 24 E

time difference: UTC+6 (11 hours ahead of Washington, DC, during Standard Time)

Administrative divisions: 8 divisions; Barisal, Chittagong, Dhaka, Khulna, Mymensingh, Rajshahi, Rangpur, Sylhet

Independence: 16 December 1971 (from West Pakistan)

National holiday: Independence Day, 26 March (1971); Victory Day, 16 December (1971); note—26 March 1971 is the date of the Awami League's declaration of an independent Bangladesh, and 16 December, known as Victory Day, memorializes the military victory over Pakistan and the official creation of the state of Bangladesh

Constitution: previous 1935, 1956, 1962 (preindependence); latest enacted 4 November 1972, effective 16 December 1972, suspended March 1982,

restored November 1986; amended many times, last in 2014 (2016)

Legal system: mixed legal system of mostly English common law and Islamic law

International law organization participation: has not submitted an ICJ jurisdiction declaration; accepts ICCt jurisdiction

Citizenship: *citizenship by birth:* no

citizenship by descent only: at least one parent must be a citizen of Bangladesh

dual citizenship recognized: yes, but limited to select countries

residency requirement for naturalization: 5 years

Suffrage: 18 years of age; universal

Executive branch: *chief of state:* President Abdul HAMID (since 24 April 2013); note—Abdul HAMID served as acting president following the death of Zillur RAHMAN in March 2013; HAMID was subsequently indirectly elected by the National Parliament and sworn in 24 April 2013

head of government: Prime Minister Sheikh HASINA (since 6 January 2009)

cabinet: Cabinet selected by the prime minister, appointed by the president

elections/appointments: president indirectly elected by the National Parliament for a 5-year term (eligible for a second term); election last held on 22 April 2013 (next to be held by 2018); the president appoints as prime minister the majority party leader in the National Parliament

election results: President Abdul HAMID (AL) elected by the National Parliament unopposed; Sheikh HASINA reappointed prime minister as leader of the majority AL party

Legislative branch: *description:* unicameral House of the Nation or Jatiya Sangsad (350 seats; 300 members in single-seat territorial constituencies directly elected by simple majority popular vote; 50 members—reserved for women only—indirectly elected by the elected members by proportional respresentation vote using the single transferable vote method; all members serve 5-year terms)

elections: last held on 5 January 2014 (next to be held by January 2019); note—the 5 January 2014 poll was marred by widespread violence, boycotts, general strikes, and low voter turnout

election results: percent of vote by party—AL-led Alliance 79%, JP (Ershad) 11.3%, WP 2.1%, JSD 1.8%, other parties 1.0%, independent 4.8%; seats by party—AL 234, JP 34, WP 6, JSD 5, other 5, independent 15; 1 seat repolled

Judicial branch: *highest court(s):* Supreme Court of Bangladesh (organized into the Appellate Division with 7 justices and the High Court Division with 99 justices)

judge selection and term of office: chief justice and justices appointed by the president; justices serve until retirement at age 67

subordinate courts: civil courts include: Assistant Judge's Court; Joint District Judge's Court; Additional District Judge's Court; District Judge's Court; criminal courts include: Court of Sessions; Court of Metropolitan Sessions; special courts/

tribunals; Metropolitan Magistrate Courts; Magistrate Court

Political parties and leaders: Awami League or AL [Sheikh HASINA]

Bangladesh Nationalist Front or BNF [Abdul Kalam AZADI]

Bangladesh Nationalist Party or BNP [Khaleda ZIA]

Bangladesh Tariqat Federation or BTF [Syed Nozibul Bashar MAIZBHANDARI]

Jatiya Party or JP (Ershad faction) [Hussain Mohammad ERSHAD]

Jatiya Party or JP (Manju faction) [Anwar Hossain MANJU]

Liberal Democratic Party or LDP [Oli AHMED]

National Socialist Party or JSD [KHALEQUZZAMAN]

Workers Party or WP [Rashed Khan MENON]

Political pressure groups and leaders: Aino Salish Kendro (Centre for Law and Mediation) or ASK (legal aid and civil rights)

Bangladesh Cen ter for Worker Solidarity

Bangladesh Rural Advancement Committee or BRAC

Federation of Bangladesh Chambers of Commerce and Industry M inistry of Women's and Children's Affairs or MoWCA (advocacy group to end gender-based violence) Odikhar (human rights group) *other:* associations of madrassa teachers; business associations, including those intended to promote international trade; development and advocacy NGOs associated with the Grameen Bank; environmentalists; Islamist groups; labor rights advocacy groups; NGOs focused on poverty alleviation, and international trade; religious leaders; tribal groups and advocacy organizations; union leaders

International organization participation: ADB, ARF, BIMSTEC, C, CD, CICA (observer), CP, D-8, FAO, G-77, IAEA, IBRD, ICAO, ICC (national committees), ICRM, IDA, IDB, IFAD, IFC, IFRCS, IHO, ILO, IMF, IMO, IMSO, Interpol, IOC, IOM, IPU, ISO, ITSO, ITU, ITUC (NGOs), MIGA, MINURSO, MINUSMA, MONUSCO, NAM, OIC, OPCW, PCA, SAARC, SACEP, UN, UNAMID, UNCTAD, UNESCO, UNHCR, UNIDO, UNIFIL, UNMIL, UNMISS, UNOCI, UNWTO, UPU, WCO, WFTU (NGOs), WHO, WIPO, WMO, WTO

Diplomatic representation in the US: *chief of mission:* Ambassador Mohammad ZIAUDDIN (since 18 September 2014)

chancery: 3510 International Drive NW, Washington, DC 20008

telephone: [1] (202) 244-0183

FAX: [1] (202) 244-2771

consulate(s) general: Los Angeles, New York

Diplomatic representation from the US: *chief of mission:* Ambassador Marcia BERNICAT (since 12 January 2015)

embassy: Madani Avenue, Baridhara, Dhaka 1212

mailing address: G. P.O. Box 323, Dhaka 1000

telephone: [880] (2) 5566-2000

FAX: [880] (2) 5566-2915

Flag description: green field with a large red disk shifted slightly to the hoist side of center; the red disk represents the rising sun and the sacrifice to achieve independence; the green field symbolizes the lush vegetation of Bangladesh

National symbol(s): Bengal tiger, water lily; national colors: green, red

National anthem: *name:* "Amar Shonar Bangla" (My Golden Bengal)

lyrics/music: Rabindranath TAGORE

note: adopted 1971; Rabindranath TAGORE, a Nobel laureate, also wrote India's national anthem

ECONOMY

Economy—overview: Bangladesh's economy has grown roughly 6% per year since 1996 despite political instability, poor infrastructure, corruption, insufficient power supplies, slow implementation of economic reforms, and the 2008–09 global financial crisis and recession. Although more than half of GDP is generated through the services sector, almost half of Bangladeshis are employed in the agriculture sector, with rice as the single-most-important product. Garment exports, the backbone of Bangladesh's industrial sector, accounted for more than 80% of total exports and surpassed $25 billion in 2015. The sector continues to grow, despite a series of factory accidents that have killed more than 1,000 workers, and crippling strikes, including a nationwide transportation blockade implemented by the political opposition during the first several months of 2015. Steady garment export growth combined with remittances from overseas Bangladeshis—which *totaled* about $15 billion and 8% of GDP in 2015—are the largest contributors to Bangladesh's sustained economic growth and rising foreign exchange reserves.

GDP (purchasing power parity): $577 billion (2015 est.)

$536.5 billion (2014 est.)

$496.6 billion (2013 est.)

note: data are in 2015 US dollars

country comparison to the world: 35

GDP (official exchange rate): $202.3 billion (2015 est.)

GDP—real growth rate: 6.4% (2015 est.)

6.3% (2014 est.)

6% (2013 est.)

country comparison to the world: 25

GDP—per capita (PPP): $3,600 (2015 est.)

$3,400 (2014 est.)

$3,300 (2013 est.)

note: data are in 2015 US dollars

country comparison to the world: 179

Gross national saving: 28.4% of GDP (2015 est.)

29.2% of GDP (2014 est.)

29.8% of GDP (2013 est.)

country comparison to the world: 29

GDP—composition, by end use:

household consumption: 72.3%

government consumption: 5.4%

investment in fixed capital: 29%

investment in inventories: 1.9%

exports of goods and services: 17.2%

imports of goods and services: -25.8% (2015 est.)

GDP—composition, by sector of origin:

agriculture: 16%

industry: 30.4%

services: 53.6% (2015 est.)

Agriculture—products: rice, jute, tea, wheat, sugarcane, potatoes, tobacco, pulses, oilseeds, spices, fruit; beef, milk, poultry

Industries: jute, cotton, garments, paper, leather, fertilizer, iron and steel, cement, petroleum products, tobacco, pharmaceuticals, ceramics, tea, salt, sugar, edible oils, soap and detergent, fabricated metal products, electricity, natural gas

Industrial production growth rate: 9.4% (2015 est.)

country comparison to the world: 10

Labor force: 81.95 million

note: extensive export of labor to Saudi Arabia, Kuwait, UAE, Oman, Qatar, and Malaysia; workers' remittances were $10.9 billion in FY09/10 (2015 est.)

country comparison to the world: 7

Labor force—by occupation: *agriculture:* 47%

industry: 13%

services: 40% (2010 est.)

Unemployment rate: 4.9% (2015 est.)

5% (2014 est.)

note: about 40% of the population is underemployed; many persons counted as employed work only a few hours a week and at low wages

country comparison to the world: 50

Population below poverty line: 31.5% (2010 est.)

Household income or consumption by percentage share: *lowest:* 10%: 4%

highest: 10%: 27% (2010 est.)

Distribution of family income—Gini index: 32.1 (2010) 33.6 (1996)

country comparison to the world: 111

Budget: *revenues:* $21.28 billion

expenditures: $27.45 billion (2015 est.)

Taxes and other revenues: 11% of GDP (2015 est.)

country comparison to the world: 209

Budget surplus (+) or deficit (–): -3% of GDP (2015 est.)

country comparison to the world: 111

Public debt: 31.9% of GDP (2015 est.)

28.8% of GDP (2014 est.)

country comparison to the world: 139

Fiscal year: 1 July–30 June

Inflation rate (consumer prices): 6.4% (2015 est.)

7% (2014 est.)

country comparison to the world: 187

Central bank discount rate: 5% (31 December 2010)

5% (31 December 2009)

country comparison to the world: 77

Commercial bank prime lending rate: 11.2% (31 December 2015 est.)

13% (31 December 2014 est.)

country comparison to the world: 72

Stock of narrow money: $21.69 billion (31 December 2015 est.)

$19.01 billion (31 December 2014 est.)

country comparison to the world: 64

Stock of broad money: $107.5 billion (31 December 2015 est.)

$95.2 billion (31 December 2014 est.)

country comparison to the world: 53

Stock of domestic credit: $113.4 billion (31 December 2015 est.)

$101.2 billion (31 December 2014 est.)

country comparison to the world: 50

Market value of publicly traded shares: $50.98 billion (31 December 2015 est.)
$41.73 billion (31 December 2014)
$23.55 billion (31 December 2011 est.)
country comparison to the world: 53
Current account balance: -$2.176 billion (2015 est.)
-$120 million (2014 est.)
country comparison to the world: 149
Exports: $29.93 billion (2015 est.)
$29.93 billion (2014 est.)
country comparison to the world: 63
Exports—commodities: garments, knitwear, agricultural products, frozen food (fish and seafood), jute and jute goods, leather
Exports—partners: US 13.9%, Germany 12.9%, UK 8.9%, France 5%, Spain 4.7% (2015)
Imports: $38.22 billion (2015 est.)
$40.1 billion (2014 est.)
country comparison to the world: 57
Imports—commodities: cotton, machinery and equipment, chemicals, iron and steel, foodstuffs
Imports—partners: China 22.4%, India 14.1%, Singapore 5.2% (2015)
Reserves of foreign exchange and gold: $26.41 billion (30 November 2015 est.)
$22.31 billion (31 December 2014 est.)
country comparison to the world: 53
Debt—external: $24.47 billion (31 December 2014 est.)
$27.8 billion (31 December 2013 est.)
country comparison to the world: 81
Stock of direct foreign investment—at home: $9.355 billion (31 December 2014 est.)
$8.593 billion (31 December 2013 est.)
country comparison to the world: 93
Stock of direct foreign investment—abroad: $134.1 million (31 December 2015 est.)
$130 million (31 December 2014 est.)
country comparison to the world: 93
Exchange rates: taka (BDT) per US dollar—77.42 (2015 est.)
77.57 (2014 est.)
77.614 (2013 est.)
81.86 (2012 est.)
74.152 (2011 est.)

ENERGY

Electricity—production: 47.31 billion kWh (2012 est.)
country comparison to the world: 56
Electricity—consumption: 41.52 billion kWh (2012 est.)
country comparison to the world: 55
Electricity—exports: 0 kWh (2013 est.)
country comparison to the world: 107
Electricity—imports: 0 kWh (2013 est.)
country comparison to the world: 122
Electricity—installed generating capacity: 6.36 million kW (2013 est.)
country comparison to the world: 70
Electricity—from fossil fuels: 97.7% of total installed capacity (2013 est.)
country comparison to the world: 56
Electricity—from nuclear fuels: 0% of total installed capacity (2013 est.)

country comparison to the world: 51
Electricity—from hydroelectric plants: 2.3% of total installed capacity (2013 est.)
country comparison to the world: 136
Electricity—from other renewable sources: 0% of total installed capacity (2013 est.)
country comparison to the world: 158
Crude oil—production: 4,000 bbl/day (2014 est.)
country comparison to the world: 85
Crude oil—exports: 313 bbl/day (2012 est.)
country comparison to the world: 88
Crude oil—imports: 25,320 bbl/day (2012 est.)
country comparison to the world: 65
Crude oil—proved reserves: 28 million bbl (1 January 2015 est.)
country comparison to the world: 83
Refined petroleum products—production: 26,110 bbl/day (2012 est.)
country comparison to the world: 89
Refined petroleum products—consumption: 109,000 bbl/day (2013 est.)
country comparison to the world: 76
Refined petroleum products—exports: 2,560 bbl/day (2012 est.)
country comparison to the world: 102
Refined petroleum products 75,830 bbl/day (2012 est.)
country comparison to the world: 58
Natural gas—production: 22.86 billion cu m (2013 est.)
country comparison to the world: 28
Natural gas—consumption: 22.86 billion cu m (2013 est.)
country comparison to the world: 34
Natural gas—exports: 0 cu m (2013 est.)
country comparison to the world: 64
Natural gas—imports: 0 cu m (2013 est.)
country comparison to the world: 163
Natural gas—proved reserves: 264.6 billioncum (1 January 2014 est.)
country comparison to the world: 42
Carbon dioxide emissions from consumption of energy: 63.5 million Mt (2012 est.)
country comparison to the world: 52

COMMUNICATIONS

Telephones—fixed lines: *total subscriptions:* 1.09 million
subscriptions per 100 inhabitants: 1 (2014 est.)
country comparison to the world: 74
Telephones—mobile cellular: *total:* 120.4 million subscriptions per 100 inhabitants: 72 (2014 est.)
country comparison to the world: 12
Telephone system: *general assessment:* inadequate for a modern country; introducing digital systems; trunk systems include VHF and UHF microwave radio relay links, and some fiber-optic cable in cities
domestic: fixed-line teledensity remains only about 1 per 100 persons; mobile-cellular telephone subscribership has been increasing rapidly and now exceeds 67 telephones per 100 persons
international: country code—880; landing point for the SEA-ME-WE-4 fiber-optic submarine cable system that provides links to Europe, the Middle East, and Asia; satellite earth stations—6;

international radiotelephone communications and landline service to neighboring countries (2011)
Broadcast media: state-owned Bangladesh Television (BTV) operates 1 terrestrial TV station, 3 radio networks, and about 10 local stations; 8 private satellite TV stations and 3 private radio stations also broadcasting; foreign satellite TV stations are gaining audience share in the large cities; several international radio broadcasters are available (2007)
Radio broadcast stations: AM 17, FM 19, shortwave 2 (2009)
Television broadcast stations: 17 (2009)
Internet country code: .bd
Internet hosts: 71,164 (2012)
country comparison to the world: 87
Internet users:
total: 11.4 million percent of population: 6.9% (2014 est.)
country comparison to the world: 42

TRANSPORTATION

Airports: 18 (2013)
country comparison to the world: 139
Airports—with paved runways: *total:* 16
over 3,047 m: 2
2,438 to 3,047 m: 2
1,524 to 2,437 m: 6
914 to 1,523 m: 1
under 914 m: 5 (2013)
Airports—with unpaved runways: *total:* 2
1,524 to 2,437 m: 1
under 914 m: 1 (2013)
Heliports: 3 (2013)
Pipelines: gas 2,950 km (2013)
Railways: *total:* 2,460 km
broad gauge: 659 km 1.676-m gauge
narrow gauge: 1,801 km 1.000-m gauge (2014)
country comparison to the world: 65
Roadways: *total:* 21,269 km
paved: 2,021 km
unpaved: 19,248 km (2010)
country comparison to the world: 106
Waterways: 8,370 km (includes up to 3,060 km of main cargo routes; network reduced to 5,200 km in the dry season) (2011)
country comparison to the world: 16
Merchant marine: *total:* 62
by type: bulk carrier 25, cargo 28, chemical tanker 1, container 5, petroleum tanker 3
foreign-owned: 8 (China 1, Singapore 7)
registered in other countries: 10 (Comoros 1, Hong Kong 1, Panama 5, Saint Vincent and the Grenadines 1, Sierra Leone 1, Singapore 1) (2010)
country comparison to the world: 64
Ports and terminals: *major seaport(s):* Chittagong
river port(s): Mongla Port (Sela River)
container port(s): Chittagong (1,392,104) (2011)
Transportation—note: the International Maritime Bureau reports the territorial waters of Bangladesh remain a risk for armed robbery against ships; in 2014, attacks against commercial vessels increased to 21 over 12 such incidents in 2013

MILITARY AND SECURITY

Military branches: *Bangladesh Defense Force:* Bangladesh Army (Sena Bahini), Bangladesh Navy (Noh Bahini, BN), Bangladesh Air Force (Biman Bahini, BAF) (2013)
Military service age and obligation: 16–19 years of age for voluntary military service; Bangladeshi birth and 10th grade education required; initial obligation 15 years (2012)
Military expenditures: 1.09% of GDP (2014)
1.15% of GDP (2013)
1.35% of GDP (2012)
1.44% of GDP (2011)

1.35% of GDP (2010)
country comparison to the world: 86

TRANSNATIONAL ISSUES

Disputes—international: Bangladesh referred its maritime boundary claims with Burma and India to the International Tribunal on the Law of the Sea; Indian Prime Minister Singh's September 2011 visit to Bangladesh resulted in the signing of a Protocol to the 1974 Land Boundary Agreement between India and Bangladesh, which had called for the settlement of longstanding boundary disputes over undemarcated areas and the exchange of territorial enclaves, but which had never been

implemented; Bangladesh struggles to accommodate 32,000 Rohingya, Burmese Muslim minority from Arakan State, livingas refugees in Cox's Bazar; Burmese border authorities are constructing a 200 km (124 mi) wire fence designed to deter illegal cross-border transit and tensions from the military build-up along border

Refugees and internally displaced persons: *refugees (country of origin):* 232,462 (Burma) (2014)
IDPs: 426,000 (violence, human rights violations, religious persecution, natural disasters) (2015)

Illicit drugs: transit country for illegal drugs produced in neighboring countries

BARBADOS

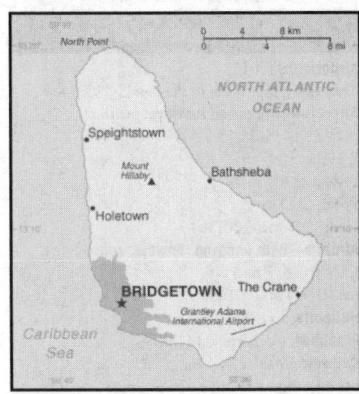

INTRODUCTION

Background: The island was uninhabited when first settled by the British in 1627. African slaves worked the sugar plantations established on the island until 1834 when slavery was abolished. The economy remained heavily dependent on sugar, rum, and molasses production through most of the 20th century. The gradual introduction of social and political reforms in the 1940s and 1950s led to complete independence from the UK in 1966. In the 1990s, tourism and manufacturing surpassed the sugar industry in economic importance.

GEOGRAPHY

Location: Caribbean, island in the North Atlantic Ocean, northeast of Venezuela
Geographic coordinates: 13 10 N, 59 32 W
Map references: Central America and the Caribbean
Area: *total:* 430 sq km
land: 430 sq km
water: 0 sq km
country comparison to the world: 202
Area—comparative: 2.5 times the size of Washington, DC
Land boundaries: 0 km

Coastline: 97 km
Maritime claims: *territorial sea:* 12 nm exclusive
economic zone: 200 nm
Climate: tropical; rainy season (June to October)
Terrain: relatively flat; rises gently to central highland region
Elevation: *mean elevation:* NA
elevation extremes: lowest: point: Atlantic Ocean 0 m
highest point: Mount Hillaby 336 m
Natural resources: petroleum, fish, natural gas
Land use: *agricultural land:* 32.6%
arable land: 25.6%
permanent crops: 2.3%
permanent pasture: 4.7%
forest: 19.4%
other: 48% (2011 est.)
Irrigated land: 50 sq km (2012)
Total renewable water resources: 0.08 cu km (2011)
Freshwater withdrawal (domestic/industrial/agricultural): *total:* 0.1 cu km/yr (20%/26%/54%)
per capita: 371.3 cu m/yr (2009)
Natural hazards: infrequent hurricanes; periodic landslides
Environment—current issues: pollution of coastal waters from waste disposal by ships; soil erosion; illegal solid waste disposal threatens contamination of aquifers
Environment—international agreements: *party to:* Biodiversity, Climate Change, Climate Change-Kyoto Protocol, Desertification, Endangered Species, Hazardous Wastes, Law of the Sea, Marine Dumping, Ozone Layer Protection, Ship Pollution, Wetlands
signed, but not ratified: none of the selected agreements
Geography—note: easternmost Caribbean island

PEOPLE AND SOCIETY

Nationality: *noun:* Barbadian(s) or Bajan (colloquial)
adjective: Barbadian or Bajan (colloquial)

Ethnic groups: black 92.4%, white 2.7%, mixed 3.1%, East Indian 1.3%, other 0.2%, unspecified 0.2% (2010 est.)
Languages: English (official), Bajan (English-based creole language, widely spoken in informal settings)
Religions: Protestant 66.4% (includes Anglican 23.9%, other Pentecostal 19.5%, Adventist 5.9%, Methodist 4.2%, Wesleyan 3.4%, Nazarene 3.2%, Church of God 2.4%, Baptist 1.8%, Moravian 1.2%, other Protestant 0.9%), Roman Catholic 3.8%, other Christian 5.4% (includes Jehovah's Witness 2.0%, other 3.4%), Rastafarian 1%, other 1.5%, none 20.6%, unspecified 1.2% (2010 est.)
Population: 290,604 (July 2015 est.)
country comparison to the world: 181
Age structure: *0–14 years:* 18.29% (male 26,570/female 26,583)
15–24 years: 13.35% (male 19,323/female 19,461)
25–54 years: 44.62% (male 64,604/female 65,069)
55–64 years: 12.87% (male 17,483/female 19,907)
65 years and over: 10.88% (male 12,596/female 19,008) (2015 est.)
Dependency ratios: *total dependency ratio:* 50.4%
youth dependency ratio: 29.1%
elderly dependency ratio: 21.3%
potential support ratio: 4.7% (2015 est.)
Median age: *total:* 38 years
male: 36.9 years
female: 39.1 years (2015 est.)
country comparison to the world: 60
Population growth rate: 0.31% (2015 est.)
country comparison to the world: 173
Birth rate: 11.87 births/1,000 population (2015 est.)
country comparison to the world: 168
Death rate: 8.44 deaths/1,000 population (2015 est.)
country comparison to the world: 80
Net migration rate: -0.3 migrant(s)/1,000 population (2015 est.)
country comparison to the world: 128
Urbanization: *urban population:* 31.5% of total population (2015)

rate of urbanization: 0.13% annual rate of change (2010–15 est.)

Major urban areas—population: BRIDGETOWN (capital) 90,000 (2014)

Sex ratio: *at birth:* 1.01 male(s)/female

0–14 years: 1 male(s)/female

15–24 years: 0.99 male(s)/female

25–54 years: 0.99 male(s)/female

55–64 years: 0.88 male(s)/female

65 years and over: 0.66 male(s)/female

total population: 0.94 male/female (2015 est.)

Maternal mortality rate: 27 deaths/100,000 live births (2015 est.)

country comparison to the world: 106

Infant mortality rate: *total:* 10.42 deaths/1,000 live births

male: 11.52 deaths/1,000 live births

female: 9.31 deaths/1,000 live births (2015 est.)

country comparison to the world: 133

Life expectancy at birth: *total population:* 75.18 years

male: 72.82 years

female: 77.56 years (2015 est.)

country comparison to the world: 104

Total fertility rate: 1.68 children born/woman (2015 est.)

country comparison to the world: 174

Health expenditures: 6.8% of GDP (2013)

country comparison to the world: 104

Physicians density: 1.81 physicians/1,000 population (2005)

Hospital bed density: 6.2 beds/1,000 population (2012)

Drinking water source:

improved:

urban: 99.7% of population

rural: 99.7% of population

total: 99.7% of population

unimproved:

urban: 0.3% of population

rural: 0.3% of population

total: 0.3% of population (2015 est.)

Sanitation facility access:

improved:

urban: 96.2% of population

rural: 96.2% of population

total: 96.2% of population

unimproved:

urban: 3.8% of population

rural: 3.8% of population

total: 3.8% of population (2015 est.)

HIV/AIDS—adult prevalence rate: 0.88% (2013 est.)

country comparison to the world: 50

HIV/AIDS—people living with HIV/AIDS: 1,500 (2012 est.)

country comparison to the world: 118

HIV/AIDS—deaths: NA

Obesity—adult prevalence rate: 33.2% (2014)

country comparison to the world: 14

Children under the age of 5 years underweight: 3.5% (2012)

Education expenditures: 6.7% of GDP (2014)

country comparison to the world: 54

School life expectancy (primary to tertiary education): *total:* 15 years

male: 14 years

female: 17 years (2011)

Unemployment, youth ages 15–24: *total:* 29.6%

male: 27.7%

female: 31.9% (2013 est.)

GOVERNMENT

Country name: *conventional long form:* none

conventional short form: Barbados

etymology: the name derives from the Portuguese "as barbadas," which means "the bearded ones" and can refer either to the long, hanging roots of the island's bearded-fig trees or to the alleged beards of the native Carib inhabitants

Government type: parliamentary democracy (Parliament) under a constitutional monarchy; a Commonwealth realm

Capital: *name:* Bridgetown

Geographic coordinates: 13 06 N, 59 37 W

time difference: UTC-4 (1 hour ahead of Washington, DC, during Standard Time)

Administrative divisions: 11 parishes and 1 city*; Bridgetown*, Christ Church, Saint Andrew, Saint George, Saint James, Saint John, Saint Joseph, Saint Lucy, Saint Michael, Saint Peter, Saint Philip, Saint Thomas

Independence: 30 November 1966 (from the UK)

National holiday: Independence Day, 30 November (1966)

Constitution: adopted 22 November 1966, effective 30 November 1966; amended several times, last in 2007 (2016)

Legal system: English common law; no judicial review of legislative acts

International law organization participation: accepts compulsory ICJ jurisdiction with reservations; accepts ICCt jurisdiction

Citizenship: *citizenship by birth:* yes

citizenship by descent: yes

dual citizenship recognized: yes

residency requirement for naturalization: 5 years

Suffrage: 18 years of age; universal

Executive branch: *chief of state:* Queen ELIZABETH II (since 6 February 1952); represented by Governor General Elliot BELGRAVE (since 1 June 2012)

head of government: Prime Minister Freundel STUART (since 23 October 2010)

cabinet: Cabinet appointed by the governor general on the advice of the prime minister

elections/appointments: the monarchy is hereditary; governor general appointed by the monarch; following legislative elections, the leader of the majority party or leader of the majority coalition usually appointed prime minister by the governor general; the prime minister recommends the deputy prime minister

Legislative branch: *description:* bicameral Parliament consists of the Senate (21 seats; members appointed by the governor general—12 on the advice of the Prime Minister, 2 on the advice of the opposition leader, and 7 at the discretion of the governor general) and the House of Assembly (30 seats; members directly elected in single-seat constituencies by simple majority vote to serve 5-year terms)

elections: House of Assembly—last held on 21 February 2013 (next to be called in 2018)

election results: House of Assembly—percent of vote by party—DLP 51.3%, BLP 48.3%, other 0.4%; seats by party—DLP 16, BLP 14

Judicial branch: *highest court(s):* Supreme Court (consists of the High Court with 8 justices) and the Court of Appeal (consists of the chief Justice and president of the court and 4 justices; note—Barbados, a member of the Caribbean Court of Justice, replaced the Judicial Committee of the Privy Council (in London) as the final court of appeal

judge selection and term of office: Supreme Court chief justice appointed by the governor-general on the recommendation of the prime minister and opposition leader of Parliament; other justices appointed by the governor-general on the recommendation of the Judicial and Legal Service Commission, a 5-member independent body consisting of the Supreme Court chief justice, the commission head, and governor-general appointees recommended by the prime minister; justices serve until mandatory retirement at age 65

subordinate courts: Magistrates' Courts

Political parties and leaders: Barbados Labor Party or BLP [Mia MOTTLEY]

Democratic Labor Party or DLP [Freundel STUART]

People's Empowerment Party or PEP [David COMISSIONG]

Political pressure groups and leaders: Barbados Secondary Teachers' Union or BSTU [Mary REDMAN]

Barbados Union of Teachers or BUT [Karen BEST]

Barbados Workers Union or BWU [Linda BROOKS]

Clement Payne Labor Union [David COMISSIONG]

Congress of Trade Unions and Staff Associations of Barbados or CTUSAB, (includes the BWU, NUPW, BUT, and BSTU) [Leroy TROTMAN]

National Union of Public Workers or NUPW [Walter MALONEY]

International organization participation: ACP, AOSIS, C, Caricom, CDB, CELAC, FAO, G-77, IADB, IBRD, ICAO, ICCt, ICRM, IDA, IFAD, IFC, IFRCS, ILO, IMF, IMO, Interpol, IOC, ISO, ITSO, ITU, ITUC (NGOs), LAES, MIGA, NAM, OAS, OPANAL, OPCW, UN, UNCTAD, UNESCO, UNHCR, UNIDO, UPU, WCO, WFTU (NGOs), WHO, WIPO, WMO, WTO

Diplomatic representation in the US: *chief of mission:* Ambassador John E. BEALE (since 29 January 2009)

chancery: 2144 Wyoming Avenue NW, Washington, DC 20008

telephone: [1] (202) 939-9200

FAX: [1] (202) 332-7467

consulate(s) general: Miami, New York

consulate(s): Los Angeles

Diplomatic representation from the US: *chief of mission:* Ambassador Linda S. TAGLIALATELA (since 1 February 2016) note—also accredited to Antigua and Barbuda, Dominica, Grenada, Saint

Kitts and Nevis, Saint Lucia, and Saint Vincent and the Grenadines

embassy: U.S. Embassy, Wildey Business Park, Wildey, St. Michael BB 14006

mailing address: P.O. Box 302, Bridgetown BB 11000; (Department Name) Unit 3120, DPO AA 34055

telephone: [1] (246) 227-4000

FAX: [1] (246) 431-0179

Flag description: three equal vertical bands of blue (hoist side), gold, and blue with the head of a black trident centered on the gold band; the band colors represent the blue of the sea and sky and the gold of the beaches; the trident head represents independence and a break with the past (the colonial coat of arms contained a complete trident)

National symbol(s): Neptune's trident, pelican, Red Bird of Paradise flower (also known as Pride of Barbados); national colors: blue, yellow, black

National anthem: name: "The National Anthem of Barbados"

lyrics/music: Irving BURGIE/C. Van Roland EDWARDS

note: adopted 1966; the anthem is also known as "In Plenty and In Time of Need"

ECONOMY

Economy—overview: Barbados is the wealthiest and most developed country in the Eastern Caribbean and enjoys one of the highest per capita incomes in the region. Historically, the Barbadian economy was dependent on sugarcane cultivation and related activities. However, in recent years the economy has diversified into light industry and tourism with about four-fifths of GDP and of exports being attributed to services. Offshore finance and information services are important foreign exchange earners and thrive from having the same time zone as eastern US financial centers and a relatively highly educated workforce. Barbados' tourism, financial services, and construction industries have been hard hit since the onset of the global economic crisis in 2008. Barbados' public debt-to-GDP ratio rose from 56% in 2008 to 101% in 2015. Growth prospects are limited because of a weak tourism outlook and planned austerity measures.

GDP (purchasing power parity): $4.636 billion (2015 est.)

$4.614 billion (2014 est.)

$4.604 billion (2013 est.)

note: data are in 2015 US dollars

country comparison to the world: 176

GDP (official exchange rate): $4.412 billion (2015 est.)

GDP—real growth rate: 0.5% (2015 est.)

0.2% (2014 est.)

0% (2013 est.)

country comparison to the world: 189

GDP—per capita (PPP): $16,600 (2015 est.)

$16,500 (2014 est.)

$16,600 (2013 est.)

note: data are in 2015 US dollars

country comparison to the world: 97

Gross national saving: 8.4% of GDP (2015 est.)

4.1% of GDP (2014 est.)

4% of GDP (2013 est.)

country comparison to the world: 158

GDP—composition, by end use:

household consumption: 83%

government consumption: 14.5%

investment in fixed capital: 14.5%

investment in inventories: -0.6%

exports of goods and services: 36.7%

imports of goods and services: -48.1% (2015 est.)

GDP—composition, by sector of origin:

agriculture: 3.1%

industry: 11.3%

services: 85.7% (2015 est.)

Agriculture—products: sugarcane, vegetables, cotton

Industries: tourism, sugar, light manufacturing, component assembly for export

Industrial production growth rate: -3.6% (2015 est.)

country comparison to the world: 186

Labor force: 142,000 (2015 est.)

country comparison to the world: 179

Labor force—by occupation: *agriculture:* 10%

industry: 15%

services: 75% (1996 est.)

Unemployment rate: 10.8% (2015 est.) 11.5% (2014 est.)

country comparison to the world: 122

Population below poverty line: NA%

Household income or consumption by percentage share: *lowest:* 10%: NA%

highest: 10%: NA%

Budget: *revenues:* $1.3 billion (2013 est.)

expenditures: $1.55 billion (2015 est.)

Taxes and other revenues: 29.2% of GDP (2015 est.)

country comparison to the world: 86

Budget surplus (+) or deficit (–): -5.6% of GDP (2015 est.)

country comparison to the world: 177

Public debt: 101% of GDP (2015 est.)

99.2% of GDP (2014 est.)

country comparison to the world: 16

Fiscal year: 1 April–31 March

Inflation rate (consumer prices): 0.5% (2015 est.)

1.9% (2014 est.)

country comparison to the world: 62

Central bank discount rate: 7% (31 December 2010)

7% (31 December 2009)

country comparison to the world: 49

Commercial bank prime lending rate: 8.1% (31 December 2015 est.)

8.38% (31 December 2014 est.)

country comparison to the world: 107

Stock of narrow money: $1.903 billion (31 December 2015 est.)

$1.82 billion (31 December 2014 est.)

country comparison to the world: 128

Stock of broad money: $4.481 billion (31 December 2015 est.)

$4.342 billion (31 December 2014 est.)

country comparison to the world: 135

Stock of domestic credit: $5.587 billion (31 December 2015 est.)

$5.293 billion (31 December 2014 est.)

country comparison to the world: 120

Market value of publicly traded shares: $4.495 billion (31 December 2012 est.)

$4.571 billion (31 December 2011)

$4.366 billion (31 December 2010 est.)

country comparison to the world: 88

Current account balance: -$231 million (2015 est.)

-$388 million (2014 est.)

country comparison to the world: 84

Exports: $471.6 million (2015 est.)

$474.4 million (2014 est.)

country comparison to the world: 174

Exports—commodities: manufactures, sugar, molasses, rum, other foodstuffs and beverages, chemicals, electrical components

Exports—partners: Trinidad and Tobago 22.5%, US 11.8%, St. Lucia 9.2%, St. Vincent and the Grenadines 5.7%, Antigua and Barbuda 4.7%, St. Kitts and Nevis 4.4%, Guyana 4.2% (2015)

Imports: $1.628 billion (2015 est.)

$1.652 billion (2014 est.)

country comparison to the world: 170

Imports—commodities: consumer goods, machinery, foodstuffs, construction materials, chemicals, fuel, electrical components

Imports—partners: Trinidad and Tobago 39%, US 31.1% (2015)

Reserves of foreign exchange and gold: $662.6 million (31 December 2015 est.)

$632.3 million (31 December 2014 est.)

country comparison to the world: 141

Debt—external: $4.49 billion (2010 est.)

$668 million (2003 est.)

country comparison to the world: 134

Exchange rates: Barbadian dollars (BBD) per US dollar—

2 (2015 est.)

2 (2014 est.)

2 (2013 est.)

2 (2012 est.)

2 (2011 est.)

note: the Barbadian dollar is pegged to the US dollar

ENERGY

Electricity—production: 981 million kWh (2012 est.)

country comparison to the world: 150

Electricity—consumption: 938 million kWh (2012 est.)

country comparison to the world: 154

Electricity—exports: 0 kWh (2013 est.)

country comparison to the world: 103

Electricity—imports: 0 kWh (2013 est.)

country comparison to the world: 119

Electricity—installed generating capacity: 239,000 kW (2012 est.)

country comparison to the world: 156

Electricity—from fossil fuels: 100% of total installed capacity (2012 est.)

country comparison to the world: 3

Electricity—from nuclear fuels: 0% of total installed capacity (2012 est.)

country comparison to the world: 47

Electricity—from hydroelectric plants: 0% of total installed capacity (2012 est.)
country comparison to the world: 159
Electricity—from other renewable sources: 0% of total installed capacity (2012 est.)
country comparison to the world: 155
Crude oil—production: 1,000 bbl/day (2014 est.)
country comparison to the world: 91
Crude oil—exports: 764.5 bbl/day (2012 est.)
country comparison to the world: 84
Crude oil—imports: 0 bbl/day (2012 est.)
country comparison to the world: 158
Crude oil—proved reserves: 2.53 million bbl (1 January 2015 est.)
country comparison to the world: 97
Refined petroleum products—production: 0 bbl/day (2012 est.)
country comparison to the world: 155
Refined petroleum products—consumption: 9,000 bbl/day (2013 est.)
country comparison to the world: 155
Refined petroleum products—exports: 0 bbl/day (2012 est.)
country comparison to the world: 154
Refined petroleum products—imports: 9,276 bbl/day (2012 est.)
country comparison to the world: 138
Natural gas—production: 20 million cu m (2013 est.)
country comparison to the world: 87
Natural gas—consumption: 20 million cu m (2013 est.)
country comparison to the world: 111
Natural gas—exports: 0 cu m (2013 est.)
country comparison to the world: 60
Natural gas—imports: 0 cu m (2013 est.)
country comparison to the world: 159
Natural gas—proved reserves: 141.6 million cu m (1 January 2014 est.)
country comparison to the world: 106
Carbon dioxide emissions from consumption of energy: 1.312 million Mt (2012 est.)
country comparison to the world: 162

COMMUNICATIONS

Telephones—fixed lines: *total subscriptions:* 150,000
subscriptions per 100 inhabitants: 52 (2014 est.)
country comparison to the world: 138
Telephones—mobile cellular: *total:* 305,500
subscriptions per 100 inhabitants: 105 (2014 est.)
country comparison to the world: 176
Telephone system: *general assessment:* island-wide automatic telephone system
domestic: fixed-line teledensity of roughly 50 per 100 persons; mobile-cellular telephone density approaching 125 per 100 persons
international: country code—1 -246; landing point for the East Caribbean Fiber System (ECFS) submarine cable with links to 13 other islands in the eastern Caribbean extending from the British Virgin Islands to Trinidad; satellite earth stations—1 (Intelsat—Atlantic Ocean); tropospheric scatter to Trinidad and Saint Lucia (2009)
Broadcast media: government-owned Caribbean Broadcasting Corporation (CBC) operates the lone terrestrial TV station; CBC also operates a multi-channel cable TV subscription service; roughly a dozen radio stations, consisting of a CBC-operated network operating alongside privately owned radio stations (2007)
Radio broadcast stations: AM 2, FM 13, shortwave 0 (2009)
Television broadcast stations: 1 (plus 2 cable channels) (2004)
Internet country code: .bb
Internet hosts: 1,524 (2012)
country comparison to the world: 167
Internet users: *total:* 227,400
percent of population: 78.5% (2014 est.)
country comparison to the world: 152

TRANSPORTATION

Airports: 1 (2013)
country comparison to the world: 236
Airports—with paved runways: *total:* 1 over 3,047 m: 1 (2013)
Pipelines: gas 33 km; oil 64 km; refined products 6 km (2013)
Roadways: *total:* 1,600 km

paved: 1,600 km (2011)
country comparison to the world: 177
Merchant marine: *total:* 109
by type: bulk carrier 23, cargo 52, chemical tanker 13, container 6, passenger 1, passenger/cargo 1, petroleum tanker 8, refrigerated cargo 4, roll on/roll off 1
foreign-owned: 83 (Canada 11, Greece 14, Iran 5, Lebanon 2, Norway 38, Sweden 4, Syria 1, Turkey 1, UAE 1, UK 6) (2010)
country comparison to the world: 49
Ports and terminals: *major seaport(s):* Bridgetown

MILITARY AND SECURITY

Military branches: Royal Barbados Defense Force: Troops Command, Barbados Coast Guard (2011)
Military service age and obligation: 18 years of age for voluntary military service, or earlier with parental consent; no conscription (2013)
Military—note: the Royal Barbados Defense Force includes a land-based Troop Command and a small Coast Guard; the primary role of the land element is island defense against external aggression; the Command consists of a single, part-time battalion with a small regular cadre deployed throughout the island; the cadre increasingly supports the police in patrolling the coastline for smuggling and other illicit activities

TRANSNATIONAL ISSUES

Disputes—international: Barbados and Trinidad and Tobago abide by the April 2006 Permanent Court of Arbitration decision delimiting a maritime boundary and limiting catches of flying fish in Trinidad and Tobago's exclusive economic zone; joins other Caribbean states to counter Venezuela's claim that Aves Island sustains human habitation, a criterion under the UN Convention on the Law of the Sea, which permits Venezuela to extend its Economic Exclusion Zone/continental shelf over a large portion of the eastern Caribbean Sea
Illicit drugs: one of many Caribbean transshipment points for narcotics bound for Europe and the US; offshore financial center

BELARUS

INTRODUCTION

Background: After seven decades as a constituent republic of the USSR, Belarus attained its independence in 1991. It has retained closer political and economic ties to Russia than have any of the other former Soviet republics. Belarus and Russia signed a treaty on a two-state union on 8 December 1999 envisioning greater political and economic integration. Although Belarus agreed to a framework to carry out the accord, serious implementation has yet to take place. Since his election in July 1994 as the country's first and only directly elected president, Aleksandr LUKASHENKO has steadily consolidated his power through authoritarian means and a centralized economic system. Government restrictions on political and civil freedoms, freedom of speech and the press, peaceful assembly, and religion have remained in place. The situation was somewhat aggravated after security services cracked down on mass protests challenging election results in the capital, Minsk, following the 2010 presidential election, but little protest occurred after the 2015 election.

GEOGRAPHY

Location: Eastern Europe, east of Poland
Geographic coordinates: 53 00 N, 28 00 E
Map references: Europe

Area: *total:* 207,600 sq km
land: 202,900 sq km
water: 4,700 sq km
country comparison to the world: 86
Area—comparative: slightly less than twice the size of Kentucky; slightly smaller than Kansas
Land boundaries: *total:* 3,642 km
border countries (5): Latvia 161 km, Lithuania 640 km, Poland 418 km, Russia 1,312 km, Ukraine 1,111 km
Coastline: 0 km (landlocked)
Maritime claims: none (landlocked)
Climate: cold winters, cool and moist summers; transitional between continental and maritime
Terrain: generally flat with much marshland
Elevation: *mean elevation:* 160 m

elevation extremes: *lowest:* point: Nyoman River 90 m
highest point: Dzyarzhynskaya Hara 346 m
Natural resources: timber, peat deposits, small quantities of oil and natural gas, granite, dolomitic limestone, marl, chalk, sand, gravel, clay
Land use: *agricultural land:* 43.7%
arable land: 27.2%
permanent crops: 0.6%
permanent pasture: 15.9%
forest: 42.7%
other: 13.6% (2011 est.)
Irrigated land: 1,140 sq km (2012)
Total renewable water resources: 58 cu km (2011)
Freshwater withdrawal (domestic/industrial/agricultural): *total:* 4.34 cu km/yr (32%/65%/3%) per capita: 435.4 m/yr (2009)
Natural hazards: NA
Environment—current issues: soil pollution from pesticide use; southern part of the country contaminated with fallout from 1986 nuclear reactor accident at Chornobyl' in northern Ukraine
Environment—international agreements: *party to:* Air Pollution, Air Pollution-Nitrogen Oxides, Air Pollution-Sulfur 85, Biodiversity, Climate Change, Climate Change-Kyoto Protocol, Desertification, Endangered Species, Environmental Modification, Hazardous Wastes, Law of the Sea, Marine Dumping, Ozone Layer Protection, Ship Pollution, Wetlands
signed, but not ratified: none of the selected agreements
Geography—note: landlocked; glacial scouring accounts for the flatness of Belarusian terrain and for its 11,000 lakes

PEOPLE AND SOCIETY

Nationality: *noun:* Belarusian(s)
adjective: Belarusian
Ethnic groups: Belarusian 83.7%, Russian 8.3%, Polish 3.1%, Ukrainian 1.7%, other 2.4%, unspecified 0.9% (2009 est.)
Languages: Russian (official) 70.2%, Belarusian (official) 23.4%, other 3.1% (includes small Polish- and Ukrainian-speaking minorities), unspecified 3.3% (2009 est.)
Religions: Orthodox 48.3%, Catholic 7.1%, other 3.5%, non-believers 41.1% (2011 est.)
Population: 9,589,689 (July 2015 est.)

country comparison to the world: 93
Age structure: *0–14 years:* 15.51% (male 765,070/female 722,540)
15–24 years: 11.12% (male 548,487/female 517,840)
25–54 years: 45.3% (male 2,132,051/female 2,212,223)
55–64 years: 13.62% (male 575,816/female 730,432)
65 years and over: 14.44% (male 439,257/female 945,973) (2015 est.)
Dependency ratios: *total dependency ratio:* 43%
youth dependency ratio: 23%
elderly dependency ratio: 20%
potential support ratio: 5% (2015 est.)
Median age: *total:* 39.6 years
male: 36.5 years
female: 42.6 years (2015 est.)
country comparison to the world: 50
Population growth rate: -0.2% (2015 est.)
country comparison to the world: 215
Birth rate: 10.7 births/1,000 population (2015 est.)
country comparison to the world: 184
Death rate: 13.36 deaths/1,000 population (2015 est.)
country comparison to the world: 16
Net migration rate: 0.7 migrant(s)/1,000 population (2015 est.)
country comparison to the world: 69
Urbanization: *urban population:* 76.7% of total population (2015)
rate of urbanization: 0.05% annual rate of change (2010–15 est.)
Major urban areas—population: MINSK (capital) 1.915 million (2015)
Sex ratio: *at birth:* 1.06 male(s)/female
0–14 years: 1.06 male(s)/female
15–24 years: 1.06 male(s)/female
25–54 years: 0.96 male(s)/female
55–64 years: 0.79 male(s)/female
65 years and over: 0.46 male(s)/female
total population: 0.87 male(s)/female (2015 est.)
Mother's mean age at first birth: 25.1 (2011 est.)
Maternal mortality rate: 4 deaths/100,000 live births (2015 est.)
country comparison to the world: 181
Infant mortality rate: *total:* 3.62 deaths/1,000 live births
male: 4.04 deaths/1,000 live births
female: 3.17 deaths/1,000 live births (2015 est.)
country comparison to the world: 202
Life expectancy at birth: *total population:* 72.48 years
male: 66.91 years
female: 78.38 years (2015 est.)
country comparison to the world: 139
Total fertility rate: 1.47 children born/woman (2015 est.)
country comparison to the world: 199
Contraceptive prevalence rate: 63.1% (2012)
Health expenditures: 6.1% of GDP (2013)
country comparison to the world: 143
Physicians density: 3.93 physicians/1,000 population (2013)
Hospital bed density: 11.3 beds/1,000 population (2011)

Drinking water source:
improved:
urban: 99.9% of population
rural: 99.1% of population
total: 99.7% of population
unimproved:
urban: 0.1% of population
rural: 0.9% of population
total: 0.3% of population (2015 est.)
Sanitation facility access:
improved:
urban: 94.1% of population
rural: 95.2% of population
total: 94.3% of population
unimproved:
urban: 5.9% of population
rural: 4.8% of population
total: 5.7% of population (2015 est.)
HIV/AIDS—adult prevalence rate: 0.52% (2014 est.)
country comparison to the world: 67
HIV/AIDS—people living with HIV/AIDS: 29,400 (2014 est.)
country comparison to the world: 72
HIV/AIDS—deaths: 1,000 (2014 est.)
country comparison to the world: 67
Obesity—adult prevalence rate: 25.2% (2014)
country comparison to the world: 65
Children under the age of 5 years underweight: 1.3% (2005)
country comparison to the world: 129
Education expenditures: 5% of GDP (2014)
country comparison to the world: 71
Literacy: *definition:* age 15 and over can read and write
total population: 99.7%
male: 99.8%
female: 99.7% (2015 est.)
School life expectancy (primary to tertiary education):
total: 16 years
male: 15 years
female: 16 years (2014)
Child labor—children ages 5–14: *total number:* 54,218
percentage: 5% (2005 est.)
Unemployment, youth ages 15–24:
total: 12.5%
male: 12.4%
female: 12.6% (2009 est.)
country comparison to the world: 88

GOVERNMENT

Country name: *conventional long form:* Republic of Belarus
conventional short form: Belarus
local long form: Respublika Byelarus'/Respublika Belarus
local short form: Byelarus'/Belarus'
former: Belorussian (Byelorussian) Soviet Socialist Republic
etymology: the name is a compound of the Belarusian words "bel" (white) and "Rus" (the Old East Slavic ethnic designation) to form the meaning White Rusian or White Ruthenian

Government type: presidential republic in name, although in fact a dictatorship

Capital: *name:* Minsk

Geographic coordinates: 53 54 N, 27 34 E

time difference: UTC+2 (7 hours ahead of Washington, DC, during Standard Time)

Administrative divisions: 6 provinces (voblastsi, singular—voblasts') and 1 municipality* (horad); Brest, Homyel' (Gomel'), Horad Minsk* (Minsk City), Hrodna (Grodno), Mahilyow (Mogilev), Minsk, Vitsyebsk (Vitebsk)

note: administrative divisions have the same names as their administrative centers; Russian spelling provided for reference when different from Belarusian

Independence: 25 August 1991 (from the Soviet Union)

National holiday: Independence Day, 3 July (1944); note—3 July 1944 was the date Minsk was liberated from German troops, 25 August 1991 was the date of independence from the Soviet Union

Constitution: several previous; latest drafted between late 1991 and early 1994, signed 15 March 1994; amended 1996, 2004 (2016)

Legal system: civil law system; note—nearly all major codes (civil, civil procedure, criminal, criminal procedure, family, and labor) have been revised and came into force in 1999 or 2000

International law organization participation: has not submitted an ICJ jurisdiction declaration; non-party state to the ICCt

Citizenship: *citizenship by birth:* no

citizenship by descent only: at least one parent must be a citizen of Belarus

dual citizenship recognized: no

residency requirement for naturalization: 7 years

Suffrage: 18 years of age; universal

Executive branch: *chief of state:* president Aleksandr LUKASHENKO (since 20 July 1994)

head of government: prime minister Andrey KABYAKOV (since 27 December 2014); first deputy prime minister Vasily MATYUSHEVSKIY (since 27 December 2014)

cabinet: Council of Ministers appointed by the president

elections/appointments: president directly elected by absolute majority popular vote in 2 rounds if needed for a 5-year term (no term limits); first election took place on 23 June and 10 July 1994; according to the 1994 constitution, the next election should have been held in 1999, however, Aleksandr LUKASHENKO extended his term to 2001 via a November 1996 referendum; subsequent election held on 9 September 2001; an October 2004 referendum ended presidential term limits and allowed the president to run in a third (19 March 2006), fourth (19 December 2010), and fifth election (11 October 2015); next election in 2020; prime minister and deputy prime ministers appointed by the president and approved by the National Assembly

election results: Aleksandr LUKASHENKO reelected president; percent of vote—Aleksandr LUKASHENKO (independent) 83.5%, Tatsiana KARATKEVICH (Tell the Truth) 4.4%,

Sergey GAYDUKEVICH (LDP) 3.3%, other 8.8%; note—election marred by electoral fraud

Legislative branch: *description:* bicameral National Assembly or Natsionalnoye Sobraniye consists of the Council of the Republic or Sovet Respubliki (64 seats; 56 members indirectly elected by regional and Minsk city councils and 8 members appointed by the president; members serve 4-year terms) and the Chamber of Representatives or Palata Predstaviteley (110 seats; members directly elected in single-seat constituencies by absolute majority vote with a second round if needed; members serve 4-year terms); note—the US does not recognize the legitimacy of the National Assembly

elections: Palata Predstaviteley—last held on 23 September 2012 (next to be held in 2016); OSCE observers determined that the election was neither free nor impartial and that vote counting was problematic in a number of polling stations; pro-LUKASHENKO candidates won every seat with no opposition representation in the chamber; international observers determined that the previous election, on 28 September 2008, despite minor improvements, also fell short of democratic standards, with pro-LUKASHENKO candidates winning every seat

election results: Sovet Respubliki—percent of vote by party—NA; seats by party—NA; Palata Predstaviteley—percent of vote by party—NA; seats by party—KPB 3, AP 1, Republican Party of Labor and Justice 1, no affiliation 104, vacant 1

Judicial branch: *highest court(s):* Supreme Court (consists of the chairman, deputy chairman, and NA judges); Constitutional Court (consists of 12 judges including a chairman and deputy chairman)

judge selection and term of office: Supreme Court judges appointed by the president with the consent of the Council of the Republic; judges initially appointed for 5 years and evaluated for life appointment; Constitutional Court judges—6 appointed by the president and 6 elected by the Chamber of Representatives; judges can serve for 11 years with an age limit of 70

subordinate courts: provincial (including Minsk city) courts; first instance (district) courts; economic courts; military courts

Political parties and leaders: pro-government parties: Belarusian Agrarian Party or AP [Mikhail SHIMANSKIY]

Belarusian Patriotic Party [Nikolai ULAKHOVICH]

Belarusian Socialist Sporting Party [Vladimir ALEKSANDROVICH]

Communist Party of Belarus or KPB [Igor KARPENKO]

Liberal Democratic Party or LDP [Sergey GAYDUKEVICH]

Republican Party [Vladimir BELOZOR]

Republican Party of Labor and Justice [Vasiliy ZADNEPRYANIY]

opposition parties: Belarusian Christian Democracy Party [Pavel SEVERINETS]

(unregistered) Belarusian Liberal Party of Freedom and Progress [Vladimir NOVOSYAD]

(unregistered) Belarusian Party of the Green [Anastasiya DOROFEYEVA]

Belarusian Party of the Left "Fair World" [Sergey KALYAKIN]

Belarusian Popular Front or BPF [Aleksey YANUKEVICH]

Belarusian Social-Democratic Assembly [Stanislav SHUSHKEVICH]

Belarusian Social Democratic Party ("Assembly") or BSDPH [Irina VESHTARD]

Belarusian Social Democratic Party (People's Assembly) [Nikolay STATKEVICH]

(unregistered) Christian Conservative Party or BPF [Zyanon PAZNYAK]

United Civic Party or UCP [Anatoliy LEBEDKO]

Political pressure groups and leaders: Assembly of Pro-Democratic NGOs [Sergey MATSKEVICH]

(unregistered) Belarusian Association of Journalists [Andrei BASTUNETS]

Belarusian Congress of Democratic Trade Unions [Aleksandr YAROSHUK]

Belarusian Helsinki Committee [Aleh HULAK]

F or Freedom M ovement [Aleksandr Milinkevich]

Malady Front (Young Front) [Zmitser DASHKEVICH]

(unregistered) Vyasna (Spring) human rights center [Ales BELYATSKIY]

(unregistered) Perspektiva [Anatoliy SHUMCHENKO]

(small business association) "Tell the Truth" Movement [Tatsiana KARATKEVICH]

(unregistered) Women's Independent Democratic Movement [Ludmila PETINA]

International organization participation: BSEC (observer), CBSS (observer), CEI, CIS, CSTO, EAEC, EAEU, EAPC, EBRD, FAO, GCTU, IAEA, IBRD, ICAO, ICC (NGOs), ICRM, IDA, IFC, IFRCS, ILO, IMF, IMSO, Interpol, IOC, IOM, IPU, ISO, ITU, ITUC (NGOs), MIGA, NAM, NSG, OPCW, OSCE, PCA, PFP, SCO (dialogue member), UN, UNCTAD, UNESCO, UNIDO, UNIFIL, UNWTO, UPU, WCO, WFTU (NGOs), WHO, WIPO, WMO, WTO (observer), ZC

Diplomatic representation in the US: *chief of mission:* Ambassador (vacant; recalled by Belarus in 2008); Charge d'Affaires Pavel SHIDLOVSKIY (since 23 April 2014)

chancery: 1619 New Hampshire Avenue NW, Washington, DC 20009

telephone: [1] (202) 986-1606

FAX: [1] (202) 986-1805

consulate(s) general: New York

Diplomatic representation from the US: *chief of mission:* Ambassador (vacant; left in 2008 upon insistence of Belarusian Government); Charge d'Affaires Scott RAULAND (since 30 June 2014)

embassy: 46 Starovilenskaya Street, Minsk 220002

mailing address: Unit 7010 Box 100, DPO AE 09769

telephone: [375] (17) 210-12–83

FAX: [375] (17) 334-7853

Flag description: red horizontal band (top) and green horizontal band one-half the width of the red band; a white vertical stripe on the hoist side bears Belarusian national ornamentation in red; the red band color recalls past struggles from oppression, the green band represents hope and the many forests of the country

National symbol(s): no clearly defined current national symbol; the mounted knight known as Pahonia (the Chaser) is the traditional Belarusian symbol; national colors: green, red, white

National anthem: *name:* "My, Bielarusy" (We Belarusians)

lyrics/music: Mikhas KLIMKOVICH and Uladzimir KARYZNA/Nester SAKALOUSKI

note: music adopted 1955, lyrics adopted 2002; after the fall of the Soviet Union, Belarus kept the music of its Soviet-era anthem but adopted new lyrics; also known as "Dziarzauny himn Respubliki Bielarus" (State Anthem of the Republic of Belarus)

ECONOMY

Economy—overview: As part of the former Soviet Union, Belarus had a relatively well-developed, though aging industrial base; it retained this industrial base—which is now outdated, energy inefficient, and dependent on subsidized Russian energy and preferential access to Russian markets—following the breakup of the USSR. The country also has a broad agricultural base which is largely inefficient and dependent on government subsidies. After an initial burst of capitalist reform from 1991–94, including privatization of smaller state enterprises and some service sector businesses, creation of institutions of private property, and development of entrepreneurship, Belarus' economic development greatly slowed. About 80% of all industry remains in state hands, and foreign investment has been hindered by a climate hostile to business. A few banks, which had been privatized after independence, were renationalized. State banks account for 75% of the banking sector.

Economic output, which had declined for several years following the collapse of the Soviet Union, revived in the mid-2000s due to the boom in oil prices. Belarus has only small reserves of crude oil, though it imports most of its crude oil and natural gas from Russia at prices substantially below the world market. Belarus exported refined oil products at market prices produced from Russian crude oil purchased at a steep discount. In late 2006, Russia began a process of rolling back its subsidies on oil and gas to Belarus. Tensions over Russian energy reached a peak in 2010, when Russia stopped the export of all subsidized oil to Belarus save for domestic needs. In December 2010, Russia and Belarus reached a deal to restart the export of discounted oil to Belarus. In 2015, Belarus continued to import Russian crude oil at a discounted price. However, the plunge in global oil prices heavily reduced revenues.

Little new foreign investment has occurred in recent years. In 2011, a financial crisis began, triggered by government directed salary hikes unsupported by commensurate productivity increases. The crisis was compounded by an increased cost in Russian energy inputs and an overvalued Belarusian ruble, and eventually led to a near three-fold devaluation of the Belarusian ruble in 2011.

In November 2011, Belarus agreed to sell to Russia its remaining shares in Beltransgaz, the Belarusian natural gas pipeline operator, in exchange for reduced prices for Russian natural gas. Receiving part of a $3 billion loan from the Russian-dominated Eurasian Economic Community (EurAsEC) Bail-out Fund, a $1 billion loan from the Russian state-owned bank Sberbank, and the $2.5 billion sale of Beltransgaz to Russian state-owned Gazprom helped stabilize the situation in 2012; nevertheless, the Belarusian currency lost more than 60% of its value, as the rate of inflation reached new highs in 2011 and 2012, before calming in 2013. In December 2013, Russia announced a new loan for Belarus of up to $2 billion for 2014. Notwithstanding foreign assistance, the Belarusian economy continued to struggle under the weight of high external debt servicing payments and trade deficit. In mid-December 2014, structural economic shortcomings were aggravated by the devaluation of the Russian ruble and triggered a near 40% devaluation of the Belarusian ruble. Belarus entered 2015 with stagnant economic growth and reduced hard currency reserves, with under one month of import cover.

GDP (purchasing power parity): $167.7 billion (2015 est.)

$174.5 billion (2014 est.)

$171.8 billion (2013 est.)

note: data are in 2015 US dollars

country comparison to the world: 70

GDP (official exchange rate): $54.61 billion (2015 est.)

GDP—real growth rate: -3.9% (2015 est.)

1.6% (2014 est.)

1% (2013 est.)

country comparison to the world: 212

GDP—per capita (PPP): $17,700 (2015 est.)

$18,400 (2014 est.)

$18,100 (2013 est.)

note: data are in 2015 US dollars

country comparison to the world: 93

Gross national saving: 33.9% of GDP (2015 est.)

28.6% of GDP (2014 est.)

29.2% of GDP (2013 est.)

country comparison to the world: 11

GDP—composition, by end use:

household consumption: 53.9%

government consumption: 15.2%

investment in fixed capital: 31.2%

investment in inventories: 1.7%

exports of goods and services: 59.4%

imports of goods and services: -61.4% (2015 est.)

GDP—composition, by sector of origin:

agriculture: 9.3%

industry: 41.3%

services: 49.4% (2015 est.)

Agriculture—products: grain, potatoes, vegetables, sugar beets, flax; beef, milk

Industries: metal-cutting machine tools, tractors, trucks, earthmovers, motorcycles, televisions, synthetic fibers, fertilizer, textiles, radios, refrigerators

Industrial production growth rate: -7% (2015 est.)

country comparison to the world: 194

Labor force: 4.546 million (2013 est.)

country comparison to the world: 89

Labor force—by occupation: *agriculture:* 9.3%

industry: 32.7%

services: 58% (2014 est.)

Unemployment rate: 0.7% (2014 est.) 0.5% (2013 est.)

note: official registered unemployed; large number of underemployed workers

country comparison to the world: 3

Population below poverty line: 6.3% (2012 est.)

Household income or consumption by percentage share: *lowest:* 10%: 3.8%

highest: 10%: 21.9% (2008)

Distribution of family income—Gini index: 26.5 (2011)

21.7 (1998)

country comparison to the world: 136

Budget: *revenues:* $21.85 billion

expenditures: $22.04 billion (2015 est.)

Taxes and other revenues: 35.2% of GDP (2015 est.)

country comparison to the world: 56

Budget surplus (+) or deficit (–): -0.3% of GDP (2015 est.)

country comparison to the world: 37

Public debt: 36.4% of GDP (2015 est.)

34.1% of GDP (2014 est.)

country comparison to the world: 126

Fiscal year: calendar year

Inflation rate (consumer prices): 13.5% (2015 est.)

18.1% (2014 est.)

country comparison to the world: 216

Central bank discount rate: 20% (13 August 2014)

10.5% (31 December 2010)

country comparison to the world: 6

Commercial bank prime lending rate: 19% (31 December 2015 est.)

18.74% (31 December 2014 est.)

country comparison to the world: 16

Stock of narrow money: $2.518 billion (31 December 2015 est.)

$3.524 billion (31 December 2014 est.)

country comparison to the world: 119

Stock of broad money: $5.651 billion (31 December 2015 est.)

$7.608 billion (31 December 2014 est.)

country comparison to the world: 126

Stock of domestic credit: $21.47 billion (31 December 2015 est.)

$27.3 billion (31 December 2014 est.)

country comparison to the world: 83

Market value of publicly traded shares: $NA

Current account balance: -$1.064 billion (2015 est.)

-$5.197 billion (2014 est.)

country comparison to the world: 125

Exports: $28.63 billion (2015 est.)

$35.74 billion (2014 est.)

country comparison to the world: 64

Exports—commodities: machinery and equipment, mineral products, chemicals, metals, textiles, foodstuffs

Exports—partners: Russia 39%, UK 11.2%, Ukraine 9.5%, Netherlands 4.3%, Germany 4.1% (2015)

Imports: $29.72 billion (2015 est.)

$38.33 billion (2014 est.)
country comparison to the world: 65
Imports—commodities: mineral products, machinery and equipment, chemicals, foodstuffs, metals
Imports—partners: Russia 56.6%, China 7.9%, Germany 4.6% (2015)
Reserves of foreign exchange and gold: $4.41 billion (31 December 2015 est.)
$5.059 billion (31 December 2014 est.)
country comparison to the world: 97
Debt—external: $40.02 billion (31 December 2014 est.)
$39.62 billion (31 December 2013 est.)
country comparison to the world: 69
Stock of direct foreign investment—at home: $10.17 billion (31 December 2014 est.)
country comparison to the world: 91
Stock of direct foreign investment—abroad: $6 billion (31 December 2014 est.)
country comparison to the world: 68
Exchange rates: Belarusian rubles (BYB/BYR) per US dollar—
15,712.8 (2015 est.)
10,224.1 (2014 est.)
10,224.1 (2013 est.)
8,336.9 (2012 est.)
4,974.6 (2011 est.)

ENERGY

Electricity—production: 31.5 billion kWh (2013 est.)
country comparison to the world: 63
Electricity—consumption: 37.88 billion kWh (2013 est.)
country comparison to the world: 58
Electricity—exports: 2.797 billion kWh (2012 est.)
country comparison to the world: 39
Electricity—imports: 6.716 billion kWh (2013 est.)
country comparison to the world: 36
Electricity—installed generating capacity: 7.751 million kW (2012 est.)
country comparison to the world: 64
Electricity—from fossil fuels: 99.7% of total installed capacity (2012 est.)
country comparison to the world: 43
Electricity—from nuclear fuels: 0% of total installed capacity (2012 est.)
country comparison to the world: 57
Electricity—from hydroelectric plants: 0.2% of total installed capacity (2012 est.)
country comparison to the world: 150
Electricity—from other renewable sources: 0.1% of total installed capacity (2012 est.)
country comparison to the world: 116
Crude oil—production: 30.000 bbl/day (2014 est.)
country comparison to the world: 64
Crude oil—exports: 32,320 bbl/day (2012 est.)
country comparison to the world: 50
Crude oil—imports: 433,400 bbl/day (2012 est.)
country comparison to the world: 21
Crude oil—proved reserves: 198 million bbl (1 January 2015 est.)
country comparison to the world: 60

Refined petroleum products—production: 440,000 bbl/day (2012 est.)
country comparison to the world: 38
Refined petroleum products—consumption: 171,000 bbl/day (2013 est.)
country comparison to the world: 62
Refined petroleum products—exports: 357,300 bbl/day (2012 est.)
country comparison to the world: 23
Refined petroleum products—imports: 90,420 bbl/day (2012 est.)
country comparison to the world: 56
Natural gas—production: 210 million cu m (2013 est.)
country comparison to the world: 77
Natural gas—consumption: 22.28 billion cu m (2013 est.)
country comparison to the world: 35
Natural gas—exports: 0 cu m (2013 est.)
country comparison to the world: 68
Natural gas—imports: 20.1billion cu m (2014 est.)
country comparison to the world: 16
Natural gas—proved reserves: 2.832 billion cu m (1 January 2014 est.)
country comparison to the world: 97
Carbon dioxide emissions from consumption of energy: 67.13 million Mt (2012 est.)
country comparison to the world: 50

COMMUNICATIONS

Telephones—fixed lines: *total subscriptions:* 4.5 million
subscriptions per 100 inhabitants: 47 (2014 est.)
country comparison to the world: 35
Telephones—mobile cellular: *total:* 11.4 million
subscriptions per 100 inhabitants: 119 (2014 est.)
country comparison to the world: 80
Telephone system: *general assessment:* Belarus lags behind its neighbors in upgrading telecommunications infrastructure; modernization of the network progressing with roughly two-thirds of switching equipment now digital
domestic: state-owned Beltelcom is the sole provider of fixed-line local and long distance service; fixed-line teledensity is improving although rural areas continue to be underserved; multiple GSM mobile-cellular networks are experiencing rapid growth; mobile-cellular teledensity now exceeds 100 telephones per 100 persons
international: country code—375; Belarus is a member of the Trans-European Line (TEL), Trans-Asia-Europe (TAE) fiber-optic line, and has access to the Trans-Siberia Line (TSL); 3 fiber-optic segments provide connectivity to Latvia, Poland, Russia, and Ukraine; worldwide service is available to Belarus through this infrastructure; additional analog lines to Russia; Intelsat, Eutelsat, and Intersputnik earth stations (2008)
Broadcast media: 4 state-controlled national TV channels; Polish and Russian TV broadcasts are available in some areas; state-run Belarusian Radio operates 3 national networks and an external service; Russian and Polish radio broadcasts are available (2007)
Radio broadcast stations: AM 28, FM 37, shortwave 11 (1998)

Television broadcast stations: 47 (plus 27 repeaters) (1995)
Internet country code: .by
Internet hosts: 295,217 (2012)
country comparison to the world: 64
Internet users: *total:* 5 million
percent of population: 52.2% (2014 est.)
country comparison to the world: 66

TRANSPORTATION

Airports: 65 (2013)
country comparison to the world: 75
Airports—with paved runways: *total:* 33
over 3,047 m: 1
2,438 to 3,047 m: 20
1,524 to 2,437 m: 4
914 to 1,523 m: 1
under 914 m: 7 (2013)
Airports—with unpaved runways: *total:* 32
over 3,047 m: 1
1,524 to 2,437 m: 1
914 to 1,523 m: 2
under 914 m: 28 (2013)
Heliports: 1 (2013)
Pipelines: gas 5,386 km; oil 1,589 km; refined products 1,730 km (2013)
Railways: *total:* 5,528 km
broad gauge: 5,503 km 1.520-m gauge (874 km electrified)
standard gauge: 25 km 1.435-m gauge (2014)
country comparison to the world: 34
Roadways: *total:* 86,392 km
paved: 74,651 km
unpaved: 11,741 km (2010)
country comparison to the world: 54
Waterways: 2,500 km (major rivers are the west-flowing Western Dvina and Neman rivers and the south-flowing Dnepr River and its tributaries, the Berezina, Sozh, and Pripyat rivers) (2011)
country comparison to the world: 35

Ports and terminals: *river port(s):* Mazyr (Prypyats')

MILITARY AND SECURITY

Military branches: Belarus Armed Forces: Land Force, Air and Air Defense Force, Special Operations Force (2013)
Military service age and obligation: 18–27 years of age for compulsory military service; conscript service obligation is 12–18 months, depending on academic qualifications; 17 year olds are eligible to become cadets at military higher education institutes, where they are classified as military personnel (2012)
Military expenditures: 1.3% of GDP (2014)
1.3% of GDP (2013)
1.2% of GDP (2012)
1.27% of GDP (2011)
country comparison to the world: 82

TRANSNATIONAL ISSUES

Disputes—international: boundary demarcated with Latvia and Lithuania; as a member state that forms part of the EU's external border, Poland has implemented strict Schengen border rules to restrict illegal immigration and trade along its border with Belarus

Refugees and internally displaced persons: *refugees (country of origin):* 126,407 applicants for forms of legal stay other than asylum (Ukraine) (2015)

stateless persons: 5,635 (2015)

Trafficking in persons: *current situation:* Belarus is a source, transit, and destination country for women, men, and children subjected to sex trafficking and forced labor; more victims are exploited within Belarus than abroad; Belarusians exploited abroad are primarily trafficked to Germany, Poland, Russian, and Turkey but also other European countries, the Middle East, Japan, Kazakhstan, and Mexico; Moldovans, Russians, Ukrainians, and Vietnamese are exploited in

Belarus; state-sponsored forced labor is a continuing problem; students are forced to do farm labor without pay and military conscripts are forced to perform unpaid non-military work; the government has retained a decree forbidding workers in state-owned wood processing factories from leaving their jobs without their employers' permission

tier rating: Tier 3—Belarus does not fully comply with the minimum standards for the elimination of trafficking and was placed on Tier 3 after being on the Tier 2 Watch List for two consecutive years without making progress; government efforts to repeal state-sponsored forced labor policies and domestic trafficking were inadequate; no trafficking offenders were convicted in 2014, and the number of investigations progressively declined

from 2005–2014; efforts to protect trafficking victims remain insufficient, with no identification and referral mechanism in place; care facilities were not trafficking-specific and were poorly equipped, leading most victims to seek assistance from private shelters (2015)

Illicit drugs: limited cultivation of opium poppy and cannabis, mostly for the domestic market; transshipment point for illicit drugs to and via Russia, and to the Baltics and Western Europe; a small and lightly regulated financial center; anti-money-laundering legislation does not meet international standards and was weakened further when know-your-customer requirements were curtailed in 2008; few investigations or prosecutions of money-laundering activities (2008)

BELGIUM

INTRODUCTION

Background: Belgium became independent from the Netherlands in 1830; it was occupied by Germany during World Wars I and II. The country prospered in the past half century as a modern, technologically advanced European state and member of NATO and the EU. Political divisions between the Dutch-speaking Flemings of the north and the French-speaking Walloons of the south have led in recent years to constitutional amendments granting these regions formal recognition and autonomy. Its capital, Brussels, is home to numerous international organizations including the EU and NATO.

GEOGRAPHY

Location: Western Europe, bordering the North Sea, between France and the Netherlands

Geographic coordinates: 50 50 N, 4 00 E

Map references: Europe

Area: *total:* 30,528 sq km
land: 30,278 sq km
water: 250 sq km

country comparison to the world: 141

Area—comparative: about the size of Maryland

Land boundaries: *total:* 1,297 km border countries (4): France 556 km, Germany 133 km, Luxembourg 130 km, Netherlands 478 km

Coastline: 66.5 km

Maritime claims: *territorial sea:* 12 nm

contiguous zone: 24 nm

exclusive economic zone: geographic coordinates define outer limit

continental shelf: median line with neighbors

Climate: temperate; mild winters, cool summers; rainy, humid, cloudy

Terrain: flat coastal plains in northwest, central rolling hills, rugged mountains of Ardennes Forest in southeast

Elevation: *mean elevation:* 181 m

elevation extremes: lowest: point: North Sea 0 m *highest point:* Botrange 694 m

Natural resources: construction materials, silica sand, carbonates, arable land

Land use: *agricultural land:* 44.1%
arable land: 27.2%
permanent crops: 0.8%
permanent pasture: 16.1%
forest: 22.4%
other: 33.5% (2011 est.)

Irrigated land: 230 sq km (2012)

Total renewable water resources: 18.3 cu km (2011)

Freshwater withdrawal (domestic/industrial/agricultural): *total:* 6.22 cu km/yr (12%/88%/1%)
per capita: 589.8 cu m/yr (2007)

Natural hazards: flooding is a threat along rivers and in areas of reclaimed coastal land, protected from the sea by concrete dikes

Environment—current issues: intense pressures from human activities: urbanization, dense transportation network, industry, extensive animal breeding and crop cultivation; air and water pollution also have repercussions for neighboring countries

Environment—international agreements: *party to:* Air Pollution, Air Pollution-Nitrogen Oxides, Air

Pollution-Persistent Organic Pollutants, Air Pollution-Sulfur 85, Air Pollution-Sulfur 94, Air Pollution-Volatile Organic Compounds, Antarctic-Environmental Protocol, Antarctic-Marine Living Resources, Antarctic Seals, Antarctic Treaty, Biodiversity, Climate Change, Climate Change-Kyoto Protocol, Desertification, Endangered Species, Environmental Modification, Hazardous Wastes, Law of the Sea, Marine Dumping, Marine Life Conservation, Ozone Layer Protection, Ship Pollution, Tropical Timber 83, Tropical Timber 94, Wetlands, Whaling

signed, but not ratified: none of the selected agreements

Geography—note: crossroads of Western Europe; most West European capitals are within 1,000 km of Brussels, the seat of both the European Union and NATO

PEOPLE AND SOCIETY

Nationality: *noun:* Belgian(s)
adjective: Belgian

Ethnic groups: Flemish 58%, Walloon 31%, mixed or other 11%

Languages: Dutch (official) 60%, French (official) 40%, German (official) less than 1%

Religions: R oman Catholic 75%, other (includes Protestant) 25%

Population: 11,323,973 (July 2015 est.)
country comparison to the world: 78

Age structure: *0–14 years:* 17.08% (male 990,272/female 943,363)

15–24 years: 11.59% (male 669,540/female 642,486)

25–54 years: 40.45% (male 2,308,285/female 2,272,085)

55–64 years: 12.65% (male 709,347/female 723,696)

65 years and over: 18.23% (male 893,096/female 1,171,803) (2015 est.)

Dependency ratios:
total dependency ratio: 54.2%
youth dependency ratio: 26.1%
elderly dependency ratio: 28.1%

potential support ratio: 3.6% (2015 est.)

Median age: *total:* 41.4 years
male: 40.2 years
female: 42.6 years (2015 est.)
country comparison to the world: 32
Population growth rate: 0.76% (2015 est.)
country comparison to the world: 143
Birth rate: 11.41 births/1,000 population (2015 est.)
country comparison to the world: 171
Death rate: 9.63 deaths/1,000 population (2015 est.)
country comparison to the world: 52
Net migration rate: 5.87 migrant(s)/1,000 population (2015 est.)
country comparison to the world: 21
Urbanization: *urban population:* 97.9% of total population (2015)
rate of urbanization: 0.48% annual rate of change (2010–15 est.)
Major urban areas—population: BRUSSELS (capital) 2.045 million; Antwerp 994,000 (2015)
Sex ratio: *at birth:* 1.05 male(s)/female
0–14 years: 1.05 male(s)/female
15–24 years: 1.04 male(s)/female
25–54 years: 1.02 male(s)/female
55–64 years: 0.98 male(s)/female
65 years and over: 0.76 male(s)/female
total population: 0.97 male(s)/female (2015 est.)
Mother's mean age at first birth: 28.2 (2010 est.)
Maternal mortality rate: 7 deaths/100,000 live births (2015 est.)
country comparison to the world: 156
Infant mortality rate:
total: 3.41 deaths/1,000 live births
male: 3.81 deaths/1,000 live births
female: 3 deaths/1,000 live births (2015 est.)
country comparison to the world: 209
Life expectancy at birth:
total population: 80.88 years
male: 78.3 years
female: 83.58 years (2015 est.)
country comparison to the world: 29
Total fertility rate: 1.78 children born/woman (2015 est.)
country comparison to the world: 157
Contraceptive prevalence rate: 70.4%
note: percent of women aged 18–49 (2008/10)
Health expenditures: 11.2% of GDP (2013)
country comparison to the world: 16
Physicians density: 3.78 physicians/1,000 population (2010)
Hospital bed density: 6.5 beds/1,000 population (2012)
Drinking water source:
improved:
urban: 100% of population
rural: 100% of population
total: 100% of population
unimproved:
urban: 0% of population
rural: 0% of population
total: 0% of population (2015 est.)
Sanitation facility access:
improved:
urban: 99.5% of population

rural: 99.4% of population
total: 99.5% of population
unimproved:
urban: 0.5% of population
rural: 0.6% of population
total: 0.5% of population (2015 est.)
HIV/AIDS—adult prevalence rate: NA
HIV/AIDS—people living with HIV/AIDS: NA
HIV/AIDS—deaths: NA
Obesity—adult prevalence rate: 22.1% (2014)
country comparison to the world: 83
Education expenditures: 6.4% of GDP (2011)
country comparison to the world: 30
School life expectancy (primary to tertiary education): *total:* 20 years
male: 19 years
female: 21 years (2014)
Unemployment, youth ages 15–24: *total:* 23.2%
male: 24%
female: 22.3% (2013 est.)
country comparison to the world: 55

GOVERNMENT

Country *name: conventional long form:* Kingdom of Belgium
conventional short form: Belgium
local long form: Royaume de Belgique (French)/Koninkrijk Belgie (Dutch)/Koenigreich Belgien (German)
local short form: Belgique/Belgie/Belgien
etymology: the name derives from the Belgae, an ancient Celtic tribal confederation that inhabited an area between the English Channel and the west bank of the Rhine in the first centuries B.C.
Government type: federal parliamentary democracy under a constitutional monarchy
Capital: *name:* Brussels
Geographic coordinates: 50 50 N, 4 20 E
time difference: UTC + 1 (6 hours ahead of Washington, DC, during Standard Time)
daylight saving time: +1hr, begins last Sunday in March; ends last Sunday in October
Administrative divisions: 3 regions (French: regions, singular—region; Dutch: gewesten, singular—gewest); Brussels-Capital Region, also known as Brussels Hoofdstedelijk Gewest (Dutch), Region de Bruxelles-Capitale (French long form), Bruxelles-Capitale (French short form); Flemish Region (Flanders), also known as Vlaams Gewest (Dutch long form), Vlaanderen (Dutch short form), Region Flamande (French long form), Flandre (French short form); Walloon Region (Wallonia), also known as Region Wallone (French long form), Wallonie (French short form), Waals Gewest (Dutch long form), Wallonie (Dutch short form)
note: as a result of the 1993 constitutional revision that furthered devolution into a federal state, there are now three levels of government (federal, regional, and linguistic community) with a complex division of responsibilities; the 2012 sixth state reform transferred additional competencies from the federal state to the regions and linguistic communities

Independence: 4 October 1830 (a provisional government declared independence from the Netherlands); 21 July 1831 (King LEOPOLD I ascended to the throne)
National holiday: 21 July (1831) Ascension Day (ascension to the throne of King LEOPOLD I)
Constitution: drafted 25 November 1830, approved 7 February 1831, entered into force 26 July 1831, revised 14 July 1993 (creating a federal state); amended many times, last in 2014 (2016)
Legal system: civil law system based on the French Civil Code; note—Belgian law continues to be modified in conformance with the legislative norms mandated by the European Union; judicial review of legislative acts
International law organization participation: accepts compulsory ICJ jurisdiction with reservations; accepts ICCt jurisdiction
Citizenship: *citizenship by birth:* no
citizenship by descent only: at least one parent must be a citizen of Belgium
dual citizenship recognized: yes
residency requirement for naturalization: 5 years
Suffrage: 18 years of age; universal and compulsory
Executive branch: *chief of state:* King PHILIPPE (since 21 July 2013); Heir Apparent Princess ELISABETH, daughter of the monarch

head of government: Prime Minister Charles MICHEL (since 11 October 2014); Deputy Prime Ministers Alexander DE CROO (since 22 October 2012), Jan JAMBON (since 11 October 2014), Kris PEETERS, Didier REYNDERS (since 30 December 2008)
cabinet: Council of Ministers formally appointed by the monarch
elections/appointments: the monarchy is hereditary and constitutional; following legislative elections, the leader of the majority party or majority coalition usually appointed prime minister by the monarch and approved by Parliament
Legislative branch: *description:* bicameral Parliament consists of the Senate or Senaat in Dutch, Senat in French (71 seats; 40 members directly elected in multi-seat constituencies by proportional representation vote and 31 indirectly elected by Community Parliaments; members serve 4-year terms) and the Chamber of Representatives or Kamer van Volksvertegenwoordigers in Dutch, Chambre des Representants in French (150 seats; members directly elected in multi-seat constituencies by proportional representation vote; members serve 4-year terms)
note: the 1993 constitutional revision that further devolved Belgium into a federal state created three levels of government (federal, regional, and linguistic community) with a complex division of responsibilities; this reality leaves six governments, each with its own legislative assembly; changes above occurred since the sixth state reform
elections: Chamber of Deputies—last held on 23 May 2014 (next to be held in May 2019); note -elections will coincide with the EU's elections
election results: Chamber of Deputies—percent of vote by party—N-VA 20.3%, PS 11.7%, CD&V 11.6%, Open VLD 9.8%, MR 9.6%, SP.A 8.8%,

Groen! 5.3%, CDH 5.0% Workers' Party 3.7%, VB 3.7%, Ecolo 3.3%, Defi 1.8%, PP 1.5%, other 3.9%; seats by party—N-VA 33, PS 23, CD&V 18, Open VLD 14, MR 20, SP.A 13, Groen! 6, CDH 9, Workers' Party 2, VB 3, Ecolo 6, Defi 2, PP 1

Judicial branch: *highest court(s):* Constitutional Court or Grondwettelijk Hof in Dutch and Cour constitutionelle in French (consists of 12 judges—6 Dutch-speaking and 6 French-speaking); Supreme Court of Justice or Hof van Cassatie in Dutch and Cour de Cassation in French (court organized into 3 chambers: civil and commercial; criminal; social, fiscal, and armed forces; each chamber includes a Dutch division and a French division, each with a chairperson and 5–6 judges) *judge selection and term of office:* Constitutional Court judges appointed by the monarch from candidates submitted by Parliament; judges appointed for life with mandatory retirement at age 70; Supreme Court judges appointed by the monarch from candidates submitted by the High Council of Justice, a 44-member independent body of judicial and non-judicial members; judges appointed for life

subordinate courts: Courts of Appeal; regional courts; specialized courts for administrative, commercial, labor, and audit issues; magistrate's courts; justices of the peace

Political parties and leaders: *Flemish parties:*
Christian Democratic and Flemish or CD&V [Wouter BEKE]
Flemish Liberals and Democrats or Open VLD [Gwendolyn RUTTEN]
Groen! [Meyrem ALMACI]
(formerly AGALEV, Flemish Greens) New Flemish Alliance or N-VA [Bart DE WEVER]
Social Progressive Alternative or SP.A [John CROMBEZ]
Vlaams Belang (Flemish Interest) or VB [Tom VAN GRIEKEN]
Francophone parties:
Ecolo (Francophone Greens) [Patrick DUPRIEZ and Zakia KHATTABI]
Francophone Federalist Democrats or Defi [Olivier MAINGAIN]
Humanist and Democratic Center or CDH [Benoit LUTGEN]
People's Party or PP [Mischael MODRIKAMEN]
Reform Movement or MR [Olivier CHASTEL]
Socialist Party or PS [Elio DI RUPO]
Workers' Party [Peter MERTENS]
other minor parties

Political pressure groups and leaders:
Belgian General Federation of Labor [Rudy DE LEEUW, Marc GOBLET]
Confederation of Christan Trade Unions [Marc LEEMANS, Marie-Helene SKA]
Federation of Enterprises in Belgium [Pieter TIMMERMANS, Michele SIOEN]
other: numerous other associations representing bankers, manufacturers, middle-class artisans, and the legal and medical professions; trade unions; various organizations representing the cultural interests of Flanders and Wallonia; various peace groups such as Pax Christi and groups representing immigrants

International organization participation: ADB (nonregional members), AfDB (nonregional members), Australia Group, Benelux, BIS, CD, CE, CERN, EAPC, EBRD, ECB, EIB, EITI (implementing country), EMU, ESA, EU, FAO, FATF, G-9, G-10, IADB, IAEA, IBRD, ICAO, ICC (national committees), ICCt, ICRM, IDA, IEA, IFAD, IFC, IFRCS, IGAD (partners), IHO, ILO, IMF, IMO, IMSO, Interpol, IOC, IOM, IPU, ISO, ITSO, ITU, ITUC (NGOs), MIGA, MONUSCO, NATO, NEA, NSG, OAS (observer), OECD, OIF, OPCW, OSCE, Pacific Alliance (observer), Paris Club, PCA, Schengen Convention, SELEC (observer), UN, UNCTAD, UNESCO, UNHCR, UNIDO, UNIFIL, UNRWA, UNTSO, UPU, WCO, WHO, WIPO, WMO, WTO, ZC

Diplomatic representation in the US: *chief of mission:* Ambassador Johan VERBEKE (since 10 March 2014)
chancery: 3330 Garfield Street NW, Washington, DC 20008
telephone: [1] (202) 333-6900
FAX: [1] (202) 333-3079
consulate(s) general: Atlanta, Los Angeles, New York

Diplomatic representation from the US: *chief of mission:* Ambassador Denise Campbell BAUER (since 26 September 2013)
embassy: 27 Boulevard du Regent [Regentlaan], B-1000 Brussels
mailing address: PSC 82, Box 002, APO AE 09710
telephone: [32] (2) 811-4000
FAX: [32] (2) 811-4500

Flag description: three equal vertical bands of black (hoist side), yellow, and red; the vertical design was based on the flag of France; the colors are those of the arms of the duchy of Brabant (yellow lion with red claws and tongue on a black field)

National symbol(s): lion; national colors: red, black, yellow

National anthem: *name:* "La Brabanconne" (The Song of Brabant)
lyrics/music: Louis-Alexandre DECHET[French] Victor CEULEMANS [Dutch]/Francois VAN CAMPENHOUT
note: adopted 1830; according to legend, Louis-Alexandre DECHET, an actor at the theater in which the revolution against the Netherlands began, wrote the lyrics with a group of young people in a Brussels cafe

ECONOMY

Economy—overview: This modern, open, and private-enterprise-based economy has capitalized on its central geographic location, highly developed transport network, and diversified industrial and commercial base. Industry is concentrated mainly in the more heavily-populated region of Flanders in the north. With few natural resources, Belgium imports substantial quantities of raw materials and exports a large volume of manufactures, making its economy vulnerable to shifts in foreign demand, particularly with Belgium's EU trade partners.

Roughly three-quarters of Belgium's trade is with other EU countries. In 2015, Belgian GDP grew by 1.4%, the unemployment rate stabilized at 8.6%, and the budget deficit was 2.7% of GDP. Prime Minister Charles MICHEL's center-right government has pledged to further reduce the deficit in response to EU pressure to reduce Belgium's high public debt, which remains above 100% of GDP, but such efforts could also dampen economic growth. In addition to restrained public spending, low wage growth and high unemployment promise to curtail a more robust recovery in private consumption. The government has pledged to pursue a reform program to improve Belgium's competitiveness, including changes to tax policy, labor market rules, and welfare benefits. These changes risk worsening tensions with trade unions and triggering extended strikes.

GDP (purchasing power parity):
$494.1 billion (2015 est.)
$487.4 billion (2014 est.)
$481 billion (2013 est.)
note: data are in 2015 US dollars
country comparison to the world: 39

GDP (official exchange rate): $454.7 billion (2015 est.)

GDP—real growth rate: 1.4% (2015 est.) 1.3% (2014 est.) 0% (2013 est.)
country comparison to the world: 159

GDP—per capita (PPP): $43,600 (2015 est.)
$43,500 (2014 est.)
$43,100 (2013 est.)
note: data are in 2015 US dollars
country comparison to the world: 35

Gross national saving: 23.3% of GDP (2015 est.) 22.8% of GDP (2014 est.) 21.9% of GDP (2013 est.)
country comparison to the world: 63

GDP—composition, by end use:
household consumption: 51.8%
government consumption: 24.1%
investment in fixed capital: 23%
investment in inventories: -0.9%
exports of goods and services: 82%
imports of goods and services: -80% (2015 est.)

GDP—composition, by sector of origin:
agriculture: 0.7%
industry: 22.3%
services: 77% (2015 est.)

Agriculture—products: sugar beets, fresh vegetables, fruits, grain, tobacco; beef, veal, pork, milk

Industries: engineering and metal products, motor vehicle assembly, transportation equipment, scientific instruments, processed food and beverages, chemicals, base metals, textiles, glass, petroleum

Industrial production growth rate: -0.6% (2015 est.)
country comparison to the world: 169

Labor force: 5.279 million (2015 est.)
country comparison to the world: 75

Labor force—by occupation: *agriculture:* 1.3%
industry: 18.6%
services: 80.1% (2013 est.)

Unemployment rate: 8.6% (2015 est.) 8.5% (2014 est.)
country comparison to the world: 98

Population below poverty line: 15.1% (2013 est.)

Household income or consumption by percentage share: *lowest:* 10%: 3.4%
highest: 10%: 28.4% (2006)

Distribution of family income—Gini index: 25.9 (2013 est.) 28.7 (1996)
country comparison to the world: 139

Budget: *revenues:* $226.8 billion
expenditures: $239.4 billion (2015 est.)
Taxes and other revenues: 49.5% of GDP (2015 est.)
country comparison to the world: 16

Budget surplus (+) or deficit (–): -2.7% of GDP (2015 est.)
country comparison to the world: 101

Public debt: 107% of GDP (2015 est.) 106.3% of GDP (2014 est.)

note: data cover general government debt and include debt instruments issued (or owned) by government entities other than the treasury; the data include treasury debt held by foreign entities; the data include debt issued by subnational entities, as well as intra-governmental debt; intra-governmental debt consists of treasury borrowings from surpluses in the social funds, such as for retirement, medical care, and unemployment; debt instruments for the social funds are not sold at public auctions; general government debt is defined by the Maastricht definition and calculated by the National Bank of Belgium as consolidated gross debt; the debt is defined in European Regulation EC479/2009 concerning the implementation of the protocol on the excessive deficit procedure annexed to the Treaty on European Union (Treaty of Maastricht) of 7 February 1992; the sub-sectors of consolidated gross debt are: federal government, communities and regions, local government, and social security funds
country comparison to the world: 12

Fiscal year: calendar year

Inflation rate (consumer prices): 0.6% (2015 est.) 0.5% (2014 est.)
country comparison to the world: 67

Central bank discount rate: 0.05% (31 December 2013) 0.3% (31 December 2010)

note: this is the European Central Bank's rate on the marginal lending facility, which offers overnight credit to banks in the euro area
country comparison to the world: 151

Commercial bank prime lending rate: 2.5% (31 December 2015 est.) 3.23% (31 December 2014 est.)
country comparison to the world: 175

Stock of narrow money: $188 billion (31 December 2015 est.)
$182.5 billion (31 December 2014 est.)

note: see entry for the European Union for money supply for the entire euro area; the European Central Bank (ECB) controls monetary policy for the 18 members of the Economic and Monetary Union (EMU); individual members of the EMU do not control the quantity of money circulating within their own borders
country comparison to the world: 21

Stock of broad money: $606.9 billion (31 December 2014 est.)

$630.9 billion (31 December 2013 est.)
country comparison to the world: 21

Stock of domestic credit: $526.1 billion (31 December 2015 est.)
$564.1 billion (31 December 2014 est.)
country comparison to the world: 24

Market value of publicly traded shares: $300.1 billion (31 December 2012 est.)
$229.9 billion (31 December 2011)
$269.3 billion (31 December 2010 est.)
country comparison to the world: 30

Current account balance: $2.359 billion (2015 est.) -$1.147 billion (2014 est.)
country comparison to the world: 31

Exports: $281.7 billion (2015 est.)
$326 billion (2014 est.)
country comparison to the world: 19

Exports—commodities: chemicals, machinery and equipment, finished diamonds, metals and metal products, foodstuffs

Exports—partners: Germany 16.9%, France 15.5%, Netherlands 11.4%, UK 8.8%, US 6%, Italy 5% (2015)

Imports: $280.3 billion (2015 est.)
$330.8 billion (2014 est.)
country comparison to the world: 17

Imports—commodities: raw materials, machinery and equipment, chemicals, raw diamonds, pharmaceuticals, foodstuffs, transportation equipment, oil products

Imports—partners: Netherlands 16.7%, Germany 12.7%, France 9.6%, US 8.7%, UK 5.1%, Ireland 4.7%, China 4.3% (2015)

Reserves of foreign exchange and gold: $25.4 billion (31 December 2014 est.)
$26.92 billion (31 December 2013 est.)
country comparison to the world: 54

Debt—external: $1.312 trillion (31 December 2014 est.)
$1.285 trillion (31 December 2013 est.)
country comparison to the world: 16

Stock of direct foreign investment—at home: $1.24 trillion (31 December 2015 est.)
$1.206 trillion (31 December 2014 est.)
country comparison to the world: 7

Stock of direct foreign investment—abroad: $1.144 trillion (31 December 2015 est.)
$1.118 trillion (31 December 2013 est.)
country comparison to the world: 10

Exchange rates: euros (EUR) per US dollar—
0.885 (2015 est.)
0.7525 (2014 est.)
0.7634 (2013 est.)
0.78 (2012 est.)
0.7185 (2011 est.)

ENERGY

Electricity—production: 76.09 billion kWh (2012 est.)
country comparison to the world: 38

Electricity—consumption: 81.89 billion kWh (2012 est.)
country comparison to the world: 36

Electricity—exports: 7.603 billion kWh (2013 est.)
country comparison to the world: 26

Electricity—imports: 17.24 billion kWh (2013 est.)
country comparison to the world: 12

Electricity—installed generating capacity: 20.98 million kW (2012 est.)
country comparison to the world: 38

Electricity—from fossil fuels: 39.3% of total installed capacity (2012 est.)
country comparison to the world: 165

Electricity—from nuclear fuels: 28.2% of total installed capacity (2012 est.)
country comparison to the world: 5

Electricity—from hydroelectric plants: 0.6% of total installed capacity (2012 est.)
country comparison to the world: 146

Electricity—from other renewable sources: 25.7% of total installed capacity (2012 est.)
country comparison to the world: 8

Crude oil—production: 0 bbl/day (2014 est.)
country comparison to the world: 109

Crude oil—exports: 54,900 bbl/day (2013 est.)
country comparison to the world: 44

Crude oil—imports: 618,400 bbl/day (2013 est.)
country comparison to the world: 17

Crude oil—proved reserves: 0 bbl (1 January 2015 est.)
country comparison to the world: 108

Refined petroleum products—production: 666,900 bbl/day (2013 est.)
country comparison to the world: 27

Refined petroleum products—consumption: 618,700 bbl/day (2014 est.)
country comparison to the world: 31

Refined petroleum products—exports: 497,500 bbl/day (2013 est.)
country comparison to the world: 14

Refined petroleum products—imports: 548.000 bbl/day (2013 est.)
country comparison to the world: 14

Natural gas—production: 0 cu m (2014 est.)
country comparison to the world: 158

Natural gas—consumption: 15.8 billion cu m (2014 est.)
country comparison to the world: 41

Natural gas—exports: 845 million cu m (2014 est.)
country comparison to the world: 38

Natural gas—imports: 16.85 billion cu m (2014 est.)
country comparison to the world: 21

Natural gas—proved reserves: 0 cu m (1 January 2014 est.)
country comparison to the world: 113

Carbon dioxide emissions from consumption of energy: 139.1 million Mt (2012 est.)
country comparison to the world: 34

COMMUNICATIONS

Telephones—fixed lines: *total subscriptions:* 4.7 million subscriptions per 100 inhabitants:
country comparison to the world: 32

Telephones—mobile cellular: *total:* 12.7 million subscriptions per 100 inhabitants: 113 (2014 est.)
country comparison to the world: 73

Telephone system: *general assessment:* highly developed, technologically advanced, and

85

completely automated domestic and international telephone and telegraph facilities

domestic: nationwide mobile-cellular telephone system; extensive cable network; limited microwave radio relay network

international: country code—32; landing point for a number of submarine cables that provide links to Europe, the Middle East, and Asia; satellite earth stations—7 (Intelsat—3) (2007)

Broadcast media: a segmented market with the three major communities (Flemish, French, and German-speaking) each having responsibility for their own broadcast media; multiple TV channels exist for each community; additionally, in excess of 90% of households are connected to cable and can access broadcasts of TV stations from neighboring countries; each community has a public radio network coexisting with private broadcasters (2007)

Radio broadcast stations: AM 7, FM 79, shortwave 1 (1998)

Television broadcast stations: 25 (plus 10 repeaters) (1997)

Internet country code: .be

Internet hosts: 5.192 million (2012)

country comparison to the world: 21

Internet users: *total:* 9.5 million percent of population: 84.7% (2014 est.)

country comparison to the world: 46

TRANSPORTATION

Airports: 41 (2013)

country comparison to the world: 102

Airports—with paved runways: *total:* 26

over 3,047 m: 6

2,438 to 3,047 m: 9

1,524 to 2,437 m: 2

914 to 1,523 m: 1

under 914 m: 8 (2013)

Airports—with unpaved runways: *total:* 15

under 914 m: 15 (2013)

Heliports: 1 (2013)

Pipelines: gas 3,139 km; oil 154 km; refined products 535 km (2013)

Railways: *total:* 3,592 km

standard gauge: 3,592 km 1.435-m gauge (2,960 km electrified) (2014)

country comparison to the world: 50

Roadways: *total:* 154,012 km

paved: 120,514 km (includes 1,756 km of expressways)

unpaved: 33,498 km (2010)

country comparison to the world: 31

Waterways: 2,043 km (1,528 km in regular commercial use) (2012)

country comparison to the world: 41

Merchant marine: total: 87

by type: bulk carrier 23, cargo 15, chemical tanker 5, container 4, liquefied gas 23, passenger 2, petroleum tanker 8, roll on/roll off 7

foreign-owned: 15 (Denmark 4, France 7, Russia 1, UK 2, US 1)

registered in other countries: 107 (Bahamas 6, Cambodia 1, Cyprus 3, France 7, Gibraltar 1, Greece 17, Hong Kong 26, Liberia 1, Luxembourg 11, Malta 7, Marshall Islands 1, Mozambique 2, North Korea 1, Panama 1, Portugal 8, Russia 4, Saint Kitts and Nevis 1, Saint Vincent and the Grenadines 7, Singapore 1, Vanuatu 1) (2010)

country comparison to the world: 56

Ports and terminals: *major seaport(s):* Oostende, Zeebrugge river port(s): Antwerp, Gent (Schelde River); Brussels (Senne River); Liege (Meuse River)

container port(s) (TEUs): Antwerp (8,664,243), Zeebrugge (2,207,257) (2011)

LNG terminal(s) (import): Zeebrugge

MILITARY AND SECURITY

Military branches: Belgian Armed Forces: Land Operations Command, Naval Operations Command, Air Operations Command (2012)

Military service age and obligation: 18 years of age for male and female voluntary military service; conscription abolished in 1994 (2012)

Military expenditures: 0.97% of GDP (2014) 1.01% of GDP (2013) 1.05% of GDP (2012) 1.05% of GDP (2011) 1.08% of GDP (2010)

country comparison to the world: 97

TRANSNATIONAL ISSUES

Disputes—international: none

Refugees and internally displaced persons: *refugees (country of origin):* 5,038 (Afghanistan) (2014) stateless persons: 5,776 (2015)

Illicit drugs: growing producer of synthetic drugs and cannabis; transit point for US-bound ecstasy; source of precursor chemicals for South American cocaine processors; transshipment point for cocaine, heroin, hashish, and marijuana entering Western Europe; despite a strengthening of legislation, the country remains vulnerable to money laundering related to narcotics, automobiles, alcohol, and tobacco; significant domestic consumption of ecstasy

BELIZE

INTRODUCTION

Background: Belize was the site of several Mayan city states until their decline at the end of the first millennium A.D. The British and Spanish disputed the region in the 17th and 18th centuries;

it formally became the colony of British Honduras in 1854. Territorial disputes between the UK and Guatemala delayed the independence of Belize until 1981. Guatemala refused to recognize the new nation until 1992 and the two countries are involved in an ongoing border dispute. Tourism has become the mainstay of the economy. Current concerns include the country's heavy foreign debt burden, high unemployment, growing involvement in the Mexican and South American drug trade, high crime rates, and one of the highest HIV/AIDS prevalence rates in Central America.

GEOGRAPHY

Location: Central America, bordering the Caribbean Sea, between Guatemala and Mexico

Geographic coordinates: 17 15 N, 88 45 W

Map references: Central America and the Caribbean

Area: *total:* 22,966 sq km

land: 22,806 sq km

water: 160 sq km

country comparison to the world: 152

Area—comparative: slightly smaller than Massachusetts

Land boundaries: *total:* 542 km

border countries (2): Guatemala 266 km, Mexico 276 km

Coastline: 386 km

Maritime claims: *territorial sea:* 12 nm in the north, 3 nm in the south; note—from the mouth of the Sarstoon River to Ranguana Cay, Belize's territorial sea is 3 nm; according to Belize's Maritime Areas Act, 1992, the purpose of this limitation is to provide a framework for negotiating a definitive agreement on territorial differences with Guatemala

exclusive economic zone: 200 nm

Climate: tropical; very hot and humid; rainy season (May to November); dry season (February to May)

Terrain: flat, swampy coastal plain; low mountains in south

Elevation: *mean elevation:* 173 m

elevation extremes: *lowest:* point: Caribbean Sea 0 m

highest point: Doyle's Delight 1,160 m

Natural resources: *arable land:* potential, timber, fish, hydropower
Land use: *agricultural land:* 6.9%
arable land: 3.3%
permanent crops: 1.4%
permanent pasture: 2.2%
forest: 60.6%
other: 32.5% (2011 est.)
Irrigated land: 35 sq km (2012)
Total renewable water resources: 18.55 cu km (2011)
Freshwater withdrawal (domestic/industrial/agricultural): *total:* 0.22 cu km/yr (4%/49%/46%)
per capita: 845.2 cu m/yr (2000)
Natural hazards: frequent, devastating hurricanes (June to November) and coastal flooding (especially in south)
Environment—current issues: deforestation; water pollution from sewage, industrial effluents, agricultural runoff; solid and sewage waste disposal
Environment—international agreements: *party to:* Biodiversity, Climate Change, Climate Change-Kyoto Protocol, Desertification, Endangered Species, Hazardous Wastes, Law of the Sea, Ozone Layer Protection, Ship Pollution, Wetlands, Whaling
signed, but not ratified: none of the selected agreements
Geography—note: only country in Central America without a coastline on the North Pacific Ocean

PEOPLE AND SOCIETY

Nationality: *noun:* Belizean(s)
adjective: Belizean
Ethnic groups: mestizo 52.9%, Creole 25.9%, Maya 11.3%, Garifuna 6.1%, East Indian 3.9%, Mennonite 3.6%, white 1.2%, Asian 1%, other 1.2%, unknown 0.3%
note: percentages add up to more than 100% because respondents were able to identify more than one ethnic origin (2010 est.)
Languages: English 62.9% (official), Spanish 56.6%, Creole 44.6%, Maya 10.5%, German 3.2%, Garifuna 2.9%, other 1.8%, unknown 0.3%, none 0.2% (cannot speak)
note: shares sum to more than 100% because some respondents gave more than one answer on the census (2010 est.)
Religions: Roman Catholic 40.1%, Protestant 31.5% (includes Pentecostal 8.4%, Seventh Day Adventist 5.4%, Anglican 4.7%, Mennonite 3.7%, Baptist 3.6%, Methodist 2.9%, Nazarene 2.8%), Jehovah's Witness 1.7%, other 10.5% (includes Baha'i, Buddhist, Hindu, Morman, Muslim, Rastafarian), unknown 0.6%, none 15.5% (2010 est.)
Demographic profile: Migration continues to transform Belize's population. About 16% of Belizeans live abroad, while immigrants constitute approximately 15% of Belize's population. Belizeans seeking job and educational opportunities have preferred to emigrate to the United States rather than former colonizer Great Britain because of the United States' closer proximity and stronger trade ties with Belize. Belizeans also emigrate to Canada, Mexico, and English-speaking

Caribbean countries. The emigration of a large share of Creoles (Afro-Belizeans) and the influx of Central American immigrants, mainly Guatemalans, Salvadorans, and Hondurans, has changed Belize's ethnic composition. Mestizos have become the largest ethnic group, and Belize now has more native Spanish speakers than English or Creole speakers, despite English being the official language. In addition, Central American immigrants are establishing new communities in rural areas, which contrasts with the urbanization trend seen in neighboring countries. Recently, Chinese, European, and North American immigrants have become more frequent.

Immigration accounts for an increasing share of Belize's population growth rate, which is steadily falling due to fertility decline. Belize's declining birth rate and its increased life expectancy are creating an aging population. As the elderly population grows and nuclear families replace extended households, Belize's government will be challenged to balance a rising demand for pensions, social services, and healthcare for its senior citizens with the need to reduce poverty and social inequality and to improve sanitation.

Population: 347,369 (July 2015 est.)
country comparison to the world: 178
Age structure: *0–14 years:* 34.87% (male 61,822/female 59,312)
15–24 years: 20.86% (male 36,897/female 35,547)
25–54 years: 35.88% (male 63,048/female 61,587)
55–64 years: 4.69% (male 8,072/female 8,224)
65 years and over: 3.7% (male 6,056/female 6,804) (2015 est.)
Dependency ratios:
total dependency ratio: 56.8%
youth dependency ratio: 50.9%
elderly dependency ratio: 5.9%
potential support ratio: 17% (2015 est.)
Median age: *total:* 22.1 years
male: 21.9 years
female: 22.3 years (2015 est.)
country comparison to the world: 178
Population growth rate: 1.87% (2015 est.)
country comparison to the world: 59
Birth rate: 24.68 births/1,000 population (2015 est.)
country comparison to the world: 54
Death rate: 5.97 deaths/1,000 population (2015 est.)
country comparison to the world: 167
Net migration rate: 0 migrant(s)/1,000 population (2015 est.)
country comparison to the world: 107
Urbanization: *urban population:* 44% of total population (2015)
rate of urbanization: 1.93% annual rate of change (2010–15 est.)
Major urban areas—population: BELMOPAN (capital) 17,000 (2014)
Sex ratio: *at birth:* 1.05 male(s)/female
0–14 years: 1.04 male(s)/female
15–24 years: 1.04 male(s)/female
25–54 years: 1.02 male(s)/female
55–64 years: 0.98 male(s)/female
65 years and over: 0.89 male(s)/female

total population: 1.03 male(s)/female (2015 est.)
Maternal mortality rate: 28 deaths/100,000 live births (2015 est.)
country comparison to the world: 105
Infant mortality rate: *total:* 19.82 deaths/1,000 live births
male: 22.08 deaths/1,000 live births
female: 17.44 deaths/1,000 live births (2015 est.)
country comparison to the world: 87
Life expectancy at birth: *total* population: 68.59 years
male: 67.01 years
female: 70.25 years (2015 est.)
country comparison to the world: 162
Total fertility rate: 2.95 children born/woman (2015 est.)
country comparison to the world: 55
Contraceptive prevalence rate: 55.2% (2011)
Health expenditures: 5.4% of GDP (2013)
country comparison to the world: 121
Physicians density: 0.83 physicians/1,000 population (2009)
Hospital bed density: 1.1 beds/1,000 population (2012)
Drinking water source:
improved:
urban: 98.9% of population
rural: 100% of population
total: 99.5% of population
unimproved:
urban: 1.1% of population
rural: 0% of population
total: 0.5% of population (2015 est.)
Sanitation facility access:
improved:
urban: 93.5% of population
rural: 88.2% of population
total: 90.5% of population
unimproved:
urban: 6.5% of population
rural: 11.8% of population
total: 9.5% of population (2015 est.)
HIV/AIDS—adult prevalence rate: 1.18% (2014 est.)
country comparison to the world: 38
HIV/AIDS—people living with HIV/AIDS: 2,700 (2014 est.)
country comparison to the world: 114
HIV/AIDS—deaths: 100 (2014 est.)
country comparison to the world: 128
Major infectious diseases: *degree of risk:* high
food or waterborne diseases: bacterial diarrhea, hepatitis A, and typhoid fever
vectorborne diseases: dengue fever and malaria (2013)
Obesity—adult prevalence rate: 20.6% (2014)
country comparison to the world: 15
Children under the age of 5 years underweight: 6.2% (2011)
country comparison to the world: 81
Education expenditures: 6.2% of GDP (2013)
country comparison to the world: 29
School life expectancy (primary to tertiary education): *total:* 13 years
male: 13 years
female: 13 years (2013)

Child labor—children ages 5–14: *total number:* 27,751

percentage: 40% (2001 est.)

Unemployment, youth ages 15–24: total: 25%

male: 18%

female: 35.6% (2012 est.)

country comparison to the world: 56

GOVERNMENT

Country name: *conventional long form:* none

conventional short form: Belize former: British Honduras

etymology: may be named for the Belize River, whose name possibly derives from the Maya word "belix," meaning "muddy-watered"

Government type: parliamentary democracy (National Assembly) under a constitutional monarchy; a Commonwealth realm

Capital: *name:* Belmopan

Geographic coordinates: 17 15 N, 88 46 W

time difference: UTC-6 (1 hour behind Washington, DC, during Standard Time)

Administrative divisions: 6 districts; Belize, Cayo, Corozal, Orange Walk, Stann Creek, Toledo

Independence: 21 September 1981 (from the UK)

National holiday: Battle of St. George's Caye Day (National Day), September 10, 1798; Independence Day, 21 September (1981)

Constitution: previous 1954, 1963 (preindependence); latest signed and entered into force 21 September 1981; amended several times, last in 2012 (2016)

Legal system: English common law

International law organization participation: has not submitted an ICJ jurisdiction declaration; accepts ICCt jurisdiction

Citizenship: *citizenship by birth:* yes

citizenship by descent: yes

dual citizenship recognized: yes

residency requirement for naturalization: 5 years

Suffrage: 18 years of age; universal

Executive branch: *chief of state:* Queen ELIZABETH II (since 6 February 1952); represented by Governor General Sir Colville YOUNG, Sr. (since 17 November 1993)

head of government: Prime Minister Dean Oliver BARROW (since 8 February 2008); Deputy Prime Minister Gaspar VEGA (since 12 February 2008)

cabinet: Cabinet appointed by the governor general on the advice of the prime minister from among members of the National Assembly

elections/appointments: the monarchy is hereditary; governor general appointed by the monarch; following legislative elections, the leader of the majority party or majority coalition usually appointed prime minister by the governor general; prime minister recommends the deputy prime minister

Legislative branch: *description:* bicameral National Assembly consists of the Senate (12 seats; members appointed by the governor general—6 on the advice of the prime minister, 3 on the advice of the leader of the opposition, and 1 each on the advice of the Belize Council of Churches and Evangelical Association of Churches, the Belize Chamber of Commerce and Industry and the Belize Better Business Bureau, and the National Trade Union Congress and the Civil Society Steering Committee; members serve 5-year terms) and the House of Representatives (31 seats; members directly elected in single-seat constituencies by simple majority vote to serve 5-year terms)

elections: House of Representatives—last held on 4 November 2015 (next to be held in or before 2020)

election results: percent of vote by party—UDP 50.52%, PUP 47.77%, other 1.71%; seats by party -UDP 19, PUP 12

Judicial branch: *highest court(s):* Supreme Court of Judicature (consists of the Court of Appeal with the court president and 3 justices, and the Supreme Court with the chief justice and 2 judges); in 2005, Belize ceased final appeals in civil and criminal cases to the Judicial Committee of the Privy Council (in London), replacing it with the Caribbean Court of Justice, the judicial organ of the Caribbean Community

judge selection and term of office: Court of Appeal president and justices appointed by the governor general upon advice of the prime minister after consultation with the National Assembly opposition leader; justices' tenures vary by terms of appointment; Supreme Court chief justice appointed by the governor-general upon the advice of the prime minister and the National Assembly opposition leader; other judges appointed by the governor-general upon the advice of the Judicial and Legal Services Section of the Public Services Commission and with the concurrence of the prime minister after consultation with the National Assembly opposition leader; judges can be appointed beyond age 65 but must retire by age 75; in 2013, the Supreme Court chief justice overturned a constitutional amendment that had restricted Court of Appeal judge appointments to as short as 1 year

subordinate courts: Summary Jurisdiction Courts (criminal) and District Courts (civil)

Political parties and leaders: Belize Progressive Party or BPP [Patrick ROGERS] (formed in 2015 from a merger of the People's National Party, elements of the VIP, and other smaller political groups)

People's United Party or PUP [vacant]

United Democratic Party or UDP [Dean Oliver BARROW]

Political pressure groups and leaders: National Trade Union Congress of Belize or NTUC/B [Marvin MORA]

International organization participation: ACP, AOSIS, C, Caricom, CD, CDB, CELAC, FAO, G-77, IADB, IAEA, IBRD, ICAO, ICC (NGOs), ICRM, IDA, IFAD, IFC, IFRCS, ILO, IMF, IMO, Interpol, IOC, IOM, ITU, LAES, MIGA, NAM, OAS, OPANAL, OPCW, PCA, Petrocaribe, SICA, UN, UNCTAD, UNESCO, UNIDO, UPU, WCO, WHO, WIPO, WMO, WTO

Diplomatic representation in the US: *chief of mission:* Ambassador Patrick ANDREWS (since 17 September 2015)

chancery: 2535 Massachusetts Avenue NW, Washington, DC 20008

telephone: [1] (202) 332-9636

FAX: [1] (202) 332-6888

consulate(s) general: Los Angeles

Diplomatic representation from the US: *chief of mission:* Ambassador Carlos Roberto MORENO (since 24 June 2014)

embassy: Floral Park Road, Belmopan City, Cayo District

mailing address: P.O. Box 497, Belmopan City, Cayo District, Belize

telephone: [501] 822-4011

FAX: [501] 822-4012

Flag description: blue with a narrow red stripe along the top and the bottom edges; centered is a large white disk bearing the coat of arms; the coat of arms features a shield flanked by two workers in front of a mahogany tree with the related motto SUB UMBRA FLOREO (I Flourish in the Shade) on a scroll at the bottom, all encircled by a green garland of 50 mahogany leaves; the colors are those of the two main political parties: blue for the PUP and red for the UDP; various elements of the coat of arms—the figures, the tools, the mahogany tree, and the garland of leaves—recall the logging industry that led to British settlement of Belize

note: Belize's flag is the only national flag that depicts human beings; two British overseas territories, Montserrat and the British Virgin Islands, also depict humans

National symbol(s): Baird's tapir (a large, browsing, forest-dwelling mammal), keel-billed toucan, Black Orchid; national colors: red, blue

National anthem: *name:* "Land of the Free"

lyrics/music: Samuel Alfred HAYNES/Selwyn Walford YOUNG

note: adopted 1981; as a Commonwealth country, in addition to the national anthem, "God Save the Queen" serves as the royal anthem (see United Kingdom)

ECONOMY

Economy—overview: Tourism is the number one foreign exchange earner in this small economy, followed by exports of crude oil, marine products, sugar, citrus, and bananas. The government's expansionary monetary and fiscal policies, initiated in September 1998, led to GDP growth averaging nearly 4% in 1999–2007. Oil discoveries in 2006 bolstered this growth and oil exploration continues, but production has fallen in recent years and future oil revenues remain uncertain. Growth slipped to 0% in 2009, due to the global economic slowdown, natural disasters, and a temporary drop in the price of oil, but growth grew to 2.2% in 2015. Although Belize has the third highest per capita income in Central America, the average income figure masks a huge income disparity between rich and poor, and a key government objective remains reducing poverty and inequality with the help of international donors. High unemployment, a growing trade deficit and heavy foreign debt burden continue to be major concerns.

GDP (purchasing power parity): $3.049 billion (2015 est.)

$3.005 billion (2014 est.)

$2.901 billion (2013 est.)

note: data are in 2015 US dollars

country comparison to the world: 187

GDP (official exchange rate): $1.763 billion (2015 est.)

GDP—real growth rate: 1.5% (2015 est.) 3.6% (2014 est.) 1.5% (2013 est.)

country comparison to the world: 154

GDP—per capita (PPP): $8,400 (2015 est.)

$8,400 (2014 est.)

$8,300 (2013 est.)

note: data are in 2015 US dollars

country comparison to the world: 145

Gross national saving:

5.6% of GDP (2015 est.)

8.5% of GDP (2014 est.)

11% of GDP (2013 est.)

country comparison to the world: 162

GDP—composition, by end use: household consumption: 72%

government consumption: 17.6%

investment in fixed capital: 17.9%

investment in inventories: 0.4%

exports of goods and services: 56.5%

imports of goods and services: -64.4% (2015 est.)

GDP—composition, by sector of origin:

agriculture: 12.7%

industry: 15.5%

services: 71.8% (2015 est.)

Agriculture—products: bananas, cacao, citrus, sugar; fish, cultured shrimp; lumber

Industries: garment production, food processing, tourism, construction, oil

Industrial production growth rate: 0.5% (2015 est.)

country comparison to the world: 160

Labor force: 120,500

note: shortage of skilled labor and all types of technical personnel (2008 est.)

country comparison to the world: 180

Labor force—by occupation: agriculture: 10.2%

industry: 18.1%

services: 71.7% (2007 est.)

Unemployment rate: 12.9% (2014 est.) 14.1% (2013 est.)

country comparison to the world: 139

Population below poverty line: 41% (2013 est.)

Household income or consumption by percentage share: lowest: 10%: NA%

highest: 10%: NA%

Budget: revenues: $500 million

expenditures: $550 million (2015 est.)

Taxes and other revenues: 28.4% of GDP (2015 est.)

country comparison to the world: 89

Budget surplus (+) or deficit (–): -2.8% of GDP (2015 est.)

country comparison to the world: 102

Public debt: 81.3% of GDP (2015 est.) 77.6% of GDP (2014 est.)

country comparison to the world: 32

Fiscal year: 1 April–31 March

Inflation rate (consumer prices): -0.6% (2015 est.)

1.2% (2014 est.)

country comparison to the world: 22

Central bank discount rate: 18% (31 December 2010) 12% (31 December 2009)

country comparison to the world: 8

Commercial bank prime lending rate: 10.6% (31 December 2015 est.) 10.8% (31 December 2014 est.)

country comparison to the world: 77

Stock of narrow money: $659 million (31 December 2015 est.)

$657 million (31 December 2014 est.)

country comparison to the world: 161

Stock of broad money: $1.539 billion (31 December 2015 est.)

$1.336 billion (31 December 2014 est.)

country comparison to the world: 162

Stock of domestic credit: $1.15 billion (31 December 2015 est.)

$1 billion (31 December 2014 est.)

country comparison to the world: 155

Market value of publicly traded shares: $NA

Current account balance: -$181 million (2015 est.) -$130 million (2014 est.)

country comparison to the world: 78

Exports: $580.7 million (2015 est.)

$588.6 million (2014 est.)

country comparison to the world: 169

Exports—commodities: sugar, bananas, citrus, clothing, fish products, molasses, wood, crude oil

Exports—partners: UK 30.8%, US 18.7%, Nigeria 6.7%, Trinidad and Tobago 4.8%, Ireland 4.2%, Jamaica 4.2% (2015)

Imports: $964.4 million (2015 est.)

$925.5 million (2014 est.)

country comparison to the world: 181

Imports—commodities: machinery and transport equipment, manufactured goods; fuels, chemicals, pharmaceuticals; food, beverages, tobacco

Imports—partners: US 26.6%, Mexico 11.7%, Cuba 10.2%, Guatemala 9%, China 7.5%, Trinidad and Tobago 5.6% (2015)

Reserves of foreign exchange and gold: $634.1 million (31 December 2015 est.)

$486.9 million (31 December 2014 est.)

country comparison to the world: 142

Debt—external: $1.348 billion (31 December 2014 est.)

$1.249 billion (31 December 2013 est.)

country comparison to the world: 158

Exchange rates: Belizean dollars (BZD) per US dollar—

2 (2015 est.)

2 (2014 est.)

2 (2013 est.)

2 (2012 est.)

2 (2011 est.)

ENERGY

Electricity—production: 423 million kWh (2012 est.)

country comparison to the world: 165

Electricity—consumption: 605 million kWh (2012 est.)

country comparison to the world: 168

Electricity—exports: 0 kWh (2013 est.)

country comparison to the world: 108

Electricity—imports: 234 million kWh (2013 est.)

country comparison to the world: 87

Electricity—installed generating capacity: 194,100 kW (2012 est.)

country comparison to the world: 160

Electricity—from fossil fuels: 46.9% of total installed capacity (2012 est.)

country comparison to the world: 153

Electricity—from nuclear fuels: 0% of total installed capacity (2012 est.)

country comparison to the world: 52

Electricity—from hydroelectric plants: 27.3% of total installed capacity (2012 est.)

country comparison to the world: 84

Electricity—from other renewable sources: 25.8% of total installed capacity (2012 est.)

country comparison to the world: 7

Crude oil—production: 1,818 bbl/day (2014 est.)

country comparison to the world: 89

Crude oil—exports: 3,240 bbl/day (2012 est.)

country comparison to the world: 76

Crude oil—imports: 0 bbl/day (2012 est.)

country comparison to the world: 162

Crude oil—proved reserves: 6.7 million bbl (1 January 2015 est.)

country comparison to the world: 96

Refined petroleum products—production: 0 bbl/day (2012 est.)

country comparison to the world: 159

Refined petroleum products—comsumption: 3,500 bbl/day (2013 est.)

country comparison to the world: 179

Refined petroleum products—exports: 0 bbl/day (2012 est.)

country comparison to the world: 157

Refined petroleum products—imports: 3,486 bbl/day (2012 est.)

country comparison to the world: 171

Natural gas—production: 0 cu m (2013 est.)

country comparison to the world: 160

Natural gas—consumption: 0 cu m (2013 est.)

country comparison to the world: 120

Natural gas—exports: 0 cu m (2013 est.)

country comparison to the world: 65

Natural gas—imports: 0 cu m (2013 est.)

country comparison to the world: 164

Natural gas—proved reserves: 0 cu m (1 January 2014 est.)

country comparison to the world: 115

Carbon dioxide emissions from consumption of energy: 675,200 Mt (2012 est.)

country comparison to the world: 174

COMMUNICATIONS

Telephones—fixed lines: total subscriptions: 22,700

subscriptions per 100 inhabitants: 7 (2014 est.)

country comparison to the world: 180

Telephones—mobile cellular: total: 172,300

subscriptions per 100 inhabitants: 51 (2014 est.)

country comparison to the world: 182

Telephone system: general assessment: above-average system; trunk network depends primarily on microwave radio relay

domestic: fixed-line teledensity of slightly less than 10 per 100 persons; mobile-cellular teledensity approaching 70 per 100 persons *international:* country code—501; landing point for the Americas Region Caribbean Ring System (ARCOS-1) fiber-optic telecommunications submarine cable that provides links to South and Central America, parts of the Caribbean, and the US; satellite earth station—8 (Intelsat—2, unknown—6) (2011)

Broadcast media: 8 privately owned TV stations; multi-channel cable TV provides access to foreign stations; about 25 radio stations broadcasting on roughly 50 different frequencies; state-run radio was privatized in 1998 (2007)

Radio broadcast stations: AM 1, FM 16, short-wave 0 (2006)

Television broadcast stations: 7 (2008)

Internet country code: .bz

Internet hosts: 3,392 (2012)

country comparison to the world: 152

Internet users: *total:* 91,200

percent of population: 26.8% (2014 est.)

country comparison to the world: 170

TRANSPORTATION

Airports: 47 (2013)

country comparison to the world: 92

Airports—with paved runways: *total:* 62,438 to 3,047 m: 1

914 to 1,523 m: 2

under 914 m: 3 (2013)

Airports—with unpaved runways: *total:* 412,438 to 3,047 m: 1

914 to 1,523 m: 11

under 914 m: 29 (2013)

Roadways: *total:* 2,870 km

paved: 488 km

unpaved: 2,382 km (2011)

country comparison to the world: 170

Waterways: 825 km (navigable only by small craft) (2011)

country comparison to the world: 70

Merchant marine: *total:* 247

by type: barge carrier 1, bulk carrier 33, cargo 156, chemical tanker 2, liquefied gas 1, passenger/cargo 4, petroleum tanker 9, refrigerated cargo 30, roll on/roll off 10, specialized tanker 1

foreign-owned: 152 (Bulgaria 1, China 61, Croatia 1, Estonia 1, Greece 2, Iceland 1, Italy 3, Latvia 9, Lithuania 1, Netherlands 1, Norway 2, Russia 30, Singapore 4, Switzerland 1, Syria 4, Thailand 1, Turkey 16, UAE 3, UK 4, Ukraine 6) (2010)

country comparison to the world: 33

Ports and terminals: *major seaport(s):* Belize City, Big Creek

MILITARY AND SECURITY

Military branches: Belize Defense Force (BDF): Army, BDF Air Wing (includes Special Boat Unit), BDF Volunteer Guard (2011)

Military service age and obligation: 18 years of age for voluntary military service; laws allow for conscription only if volunteers are insufficient; conscription has never been implemented; volunteers typically outnumber available positions by 3: 1; initial service obligation 12 years (2012)

Military expenditures: NA% (2012) 1.08% of GDP (2011) NA% (2010)

TRANSNATIONAL ISSUES

Disputes—international: Guatemala persists in its territorial claim to half of Belize, but agrees to the Line of Adjacency to keep Guatemalan squatters out of Belize's forested interior; both countries agreed in April 2012 to hold simultaneous referenda, scheduled for 6 October 2013, to decide whether to refer the dispute to the ICJ for binding

resolution, but this vote was suspended indefinitely; Belize and Mexico are working to solve minor border demarcation discrepancies arising from inaccuracies in the 1898 border treaty

Trafficking in persons: *current situation:* Belize is a source, destination, and transit country for men, women, and children subjected to forced labor and sex trafficking; the coerced prostitution of women and children by family members has not led to arrests; child sex tourism, involving primarily US citizens, is on the rise; sex trafficking and forced labor of Belizean and foreign women and LGBT individuals occurs in bars, nightclubs, brothels, and domestic service; workers from Central America, Mexico, and Asia may fall victim to forced labor in restaurants, shops, agriculture, and fishing

tier rating: Tier 3—Belize does not comply fully with the minimum standards for the elimination of human trafficking and is not making significant efforts to do so; authorities did not initiate any new trafficking investigations of prosecutions, and cases from previous years remain pending; law enforcement efforts to use informal means to identify and refer victims were ineffective and draft procedures for referring victims to services are still not finalized; trafficking victims were more commonly arrested, detained, or deported based on immigration violations than provided with assistance; the government did not make progress in implementing the 2012–2014 anti-trafficking national strategic plan (2015)

Illicit drugs: transshipment point for cocaine; small-scale illicit producer of cannabis, primarily for local consumption; offshore sector money-laundering activity related to narcotics trafficking and other crimes (2008)

BENIN

INTRODUCTION

Background: Present day Benin was the site of Dahomey, a West African kingdom that rose to prominence in about 1600 and over the next two and a half centuries became a regional power, largely based on its slave trade. Coastal areas of Dahomey began to be controlled by the French in the second half of the 19th century; the entire kingdom was conquered by 1894. French Dahomey achieved independence in 1960; it changed its name to the Republic of Benin in 1975.

A succession of military governments ended in 1972 with the rise to power of Mathieu KERE-KOU and the establishment of a government based on Marxist-Leninist principles. A move to representative government began in 1989. Two years later, free elections ushered in former Prime Minister Nicephore SOGLO as president, marking the first successful transfer of power in Africa from a dictatorship to a democracy. KEREKOU was returned to power by elections held in 1996

and 2001, though some irregularities were alleged. KEREKOU stepped down at the end of his second term in 2006 and was succeeded by Thomas YAYI Boni, a political outsider and independent. YAYI, who won a second five-year term in March 2011, has attempted to stem corruption and has strongly promoted accelerating Benin's economic growth.

GEOGRAPHY

Location: Western Africa, bordering the Bight of Benin, between Nigeria and Togo

Geographic coordinates: 9 30 N, 2 15 E

Map references: Africa

Area: *total:* 112,622 sq km

land: 110,622 sq km

water: 2,000 sq km

country comparison to the world: 102

Area—comparative: slightly smaller than Pennsylvania

Land boundaries: *total:* 2,123 km

border countries (4): Burkina Faso 386 km, Niger 277 km, Nigeria 809 km, Togo 651 km

Coastline: 121 km

Maritime claims: *territorial sea:* 200 nm

Climate: tropical; hot, humid in south; semiarid in north

Terrain: mostly flat to undulating plain; some hills and low mountains

Elevation: *mean elevation:* 273 m

elevation extremes: *lowest point:* Atlantic Ocean 0 m

highest point: Mont Sokbaro 658 m

Natural resources: small offshore oil deposits, limestone, marble, timber

Land use: *agricultural land:* 31.3%

arable land: 22.9%

permanent crops: 3.5%

permanent pasture: 4.9%

forest: 40%

other: 28.7% (2011 est.)

Irrigated land: 230 sq km (2012)

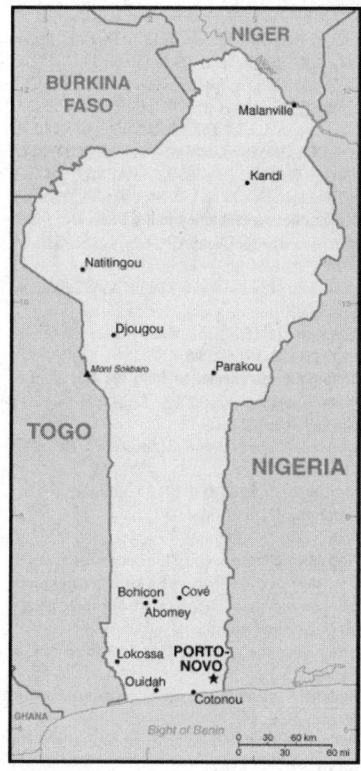

Total renewable water resources: 26.39 cu km (2011)

Freshwater withdrawal (domestic/industrial/agricultural): *total:* 0.13 cu km/yr (32%/23%/45%) *per capita:* 18.74 cu m/yr (2001)

Natural hazards: hot, dry, dusty harmattan wind may affect north from December to March

Environment—current issues: inadequate supplies of potable water; poaching threatens wildlife populations; deforestation; desertification

Environment—international agreements: *party to:* Biodiversity, Climate Change, Climate Change-Kyoto Protocol, Desertification, Endangered Species, Environmental Modification, Hazardous Wastes, Law of the Sea, Ozone Layer Protection, Ship Pollution, Wetlands, Whaling *signed, but not ratified:* none of the selected agreements

Geography—note: sandbanks create difficult access to a coast with no natural harbors, river mouths, or islands

PEOPLE AND SOCIETY

Nationality: *noun:* Beninese (singular and plural) *adjective:* Beninese

Ethnic groups: Fon and related 39.2%, Adja and related 15.2%, Yoruba and related 12.3%, Bariba and related 9.2%, Fulani and related 7%, Ottamari and related 6.1%, Yoa-Lokpa and related 4%, Dendi and related 2.5%, other 1.6%, unspecified 2.9% (2002 est.)

Languages: French (official), Fon and Yoruba (most common vernaculars in south), tribal languages (at least six major ones in north)

Religions: Catholic 27.1%, Muslim 24.4%, Vodoun 17.3%, Protestant 10.4% (Celestial 5%, Methodist 3.2%, other Protestant 2.2%), other traditional religions 6%, other Christian 5.3%, other 1.9%, none 6.5%, unspecified 1.1% (2002 est.)

Population: 10,448,647

note: estimates for this country explicitly take into account the effects of excess mortality due to AIDS; this can result in lower life expectancy, higher infant mortality, higher death rates, lower population growth rates, and changes in the distribution of population by age and sex than would otherwise be expected (July 2015 est.) *country comparison to the world:* 88

Age structure: 0–14 years: 43.42% (male 2,314,981/female 2,222,185) *15–24 years:* 20.19% (male 1,073,356/female 1,036,459) *25–54 years:* 30.04% (male 1,585,098/female 1,553,965) *55–64 years:* 3.53% (male 157,171/female 211,292) *65 years and over:* 2.82% (male 116,693/female 177,447) (2015 est.)

Dependency ratios: *total* dependency ratio: 82% *youth dependency ratio:* 76.7% *elderly dependency ratio:* 5.3% *potential support ratio:* 19% (2015 est.)

Median age: *total:* 17.9 years *male:* 17.5 years *female:* 18.3 years (2015 est.) *country comparison to the world:* 216

Population growth rate: 2.78% (2015 est.) *country comparison to the world:* 15

Birth rate: 36.02 births/1,000 population (2015 est.) *country comparison to the world:* 19

Death rate: 8.21 deaths/1,000 population (2015 est.) *country comparison to the world:* 87

Net migration rate: 0 migrant(s)/1,000 population (2015 est.) *country comparison to the world:* 106

Urbanization: *urban population:* 44% of total population (2015) *rate of urbanization:* 3.67% annual rate of change (2010–15 est.)

Major urban areas—population: PORTO-NOVO (capital) 268,000 (2014); COTONOU (seat of government) 682,000; Abomey-Calavi 757,000 (2015)

Sex ratio: *at birth:* 1.05 male(s)/female *0–14 years:* 1.04 male(s)/female *15–24 years:* 1.04 male(s)/female *25–54 years:* 1.02 male(s)/female *55–64 years:* 0.74 male(s)/female *65 years and over:* 0.66 male(s)/female *total population:* 1.01 male(s)/female (2015 est.)

Mother's mean age at first birth: 20.3

note: median age at first birth among women 25–29 (2011/12 est.)

Maternal mortality rate: 405 deaths/100,000 live births (2015 est.)

country comparison to the world: 34

Infant mortality rate: *total:* 55.68 deaths/1,000 live births *male:* 58.8 deaths/1,000 live births *female:* 52.4 deaths/1,000 live births (2015 est.) *country comparison to the world:* 25

Life expectancy at birth: *total* population: 61.47 years *male:* 60.11 years *female:* 62.9 years (2015 est.) *country comparison to the world:* 194

Total fertility rate: 4.95 children born/woman (2015 est.)

country comparison to the world: 16

Contraceptive prevalence rate: 12.9% (2011/12)

Health expenditures: 4.6% of GDP (2013)

country comparison to the world: 154

Physicians density: 0.06 physicians/1,000 population (2008)

Hospital bed density: 0.5 beds/1,000 population (2010)

Drinking water source:

improved:

urban: 85.2% of population

rural: 72.1% of population

total: 77.9% of population

unimproved:

urban: 14.8% of population

rural: 27.9% of population

total: 22.1% of population (2015 est.)

Sanitation facility access:

improved:

urban: 35.6% of population

rural: 7.3% of population

total: 19.7% of population

unimproved:

urban: 64.4% of population

rural: 92.7% of population

total: 80.3% of population (2015 est.)

HIV/AIDS—adult prevalence rate: 1.14% (2014 est.)

country comparison to the world: 41

HIV/AIDS—people living with HIV/AIDS: 77,900 (2014 est.)

country comparison to the world: 47

HIV/AIDS—deaths: 2,400 (2014 est.)

country comparison to the world: 53

Major infectious diseases: *degree of risk:* very high

food or waterborne diseases: bacterial and protozoal diarrhea, hepatitis A, and typhoid fever *vectorborne diseases:* dengue fever, malaria, and yellow fever *respiratory disease:* meningococcal meningitis *animal contact disease:* rabies (2013)

Obesity—adult prevalence rate: 8.1% (2014)

country comparison to the world: 151

Children under the age of 5 years underweight: 18% (2014)

country comparison to the world: 30

Education expenditures: 4.4% of GDP (2014)

country comparison to the world: 64

Literacy: *definition:* age 15 and over can read and write *total population:* 38.4%

male: 49.9%

female: 27.3% (2015 est.)

School life expectancy (primary to tertiary education): *total:* 12 years

male: 14 years

female: 11 years (2013)

Child labor—children ages 5–14: *total number:* 1,020,981

percentage: 46% (2006 est.)

Unemployment, youth ages 15–24: *total:* 2.4%

male: 1.5%

female: 3.1% (2010 est.)

GOVERNMENT

Country name: *conventional long form:* Republic of Benin

conventional short form: Benin

local long form: Republique du Benin

local short form: Benin former: Dahomey

etymology: named for the Bight of Benin, the body of water on which the country lies

Government type: presidential republic

Capital: *name:* Porto-Novo (official capital); note—Cotonou (seat of government)

Geographic coordinates: 6 29 N, 2 37 E

time difference: UTC + 1 (6 hours ahead of Washington, DC, during Standard Time)

Administrative divisions: 12 departments; Alibori, Atacora, Atlantique, Borgou, Collines, Couffo, Donga, Littoral, Mono, Oueme, Plateau, Zou

Independence: 1 August 1960 (from France)

National holiday: National Day, 1 August (1960)

Constitution: previous 1946, 1958 (preindependence); latest adopted by referendum 2 December 1990, promulgated 11 December 1990 (2016)

Legal system: civil law system modeled largely on the French system and some customary law

International law organization participation: has not submitted an ICJ jurisdiction declaration; accepts ICCt jurisdiction

Citizenship: *citizenship by birth:* no

citizenship by descent only: at least one parent must be a citizen of Benin

dual citizenship recognized: yes

residency requirement for naturalization: 10 years

Suffrage: 18 years of age; universal

Executive branch: *chief of state:* President Patrice TALON (since 6 April 2016); note—the president is both chief of state and head of government

head of government: President Patrice TALON (since 6 April 2016); Prime Minister (vacant)

cabinet: Council of Ministers appointed by the president

elections/appointments: president directly elected by absolute majority popular vote in 2 rounds if needed for a 5-year term (eligible for a second term); last held on 6 March and 20 March 2016 (next to be held in 2021)

election results: Patrice TALON elected president; first round percent of vote—Lionel ZINSOU (FCBE) 28.4%, Patrice TALON (independent) 24.8%, Sebastien AJAVON (independent) 23.0%, Abdoulaye Bio TCHANE (ABT) 8.8%, Pascal

KOUPAKI (NC) 5.9%, other 9.1%; second round percent of vote—Patrice TALON (independent) 65.4%, Lionel ZINSOU (FCBE) 34.6%

Legislative branch: *description:* unicameral National Assembly or Assemblee Nationale (83 seats; members directly elected in multi-seat constituencies by proportional representation vote; members serve 4-year terms)

elections: last held on 26 April 2015 (next to be held in April 2019)

election results: percent of vote by party—FCBE 30.2%, UN 14.4%, PRD 10.6%, AND 7.6%, RB-RP 7.1%, other 30.1%; seats by party—FCBE 33, UN 13, PRD 10, AND 5, RB-RP 7, other 15

Judicial branch: *highest court(s):* Supreme Court or Cour Supreme (consists of the court president and 3 chamber presidents organized into an administrative division, judicial chamber, and chamber of accounts); Constitutional Court or Cour Constitutionnelle (consists of 7 members including the court president); High Court of Justice (consists of the Constitutional Court members, 6 members appointed by the National Assembly, and the Supreme Court president); note—jurisdiction of the High Court of Justice is limited to cases of high treason by the national president or members of the government

judge selection and term of office: Supreme Court president and judges appointed by the national president upon the advice of the National Assembly; judges appointed for single renewable 5-year terms; Constitutional Court members—4 appointed by the National Assembly and 3 by the national president; members appointed for single renewable 5-year terms; High Court of Justice "other" members elected by the National Assembly; member tenure NA

subordinate courts: Court of Appeal or Cour d'Appel; district courts; village courts; Assize courts

Political parties and leaders: Alliance for a Triumphant Benin or ABT [Abdoulaye BIO TCHANE]

African Movement for Development and Progress or MADEP [Sefou FAGBOHOUN]

Benin Renaissance or RB [Lehady SOGLO]

Cowrie Force for an Emerging Benin or FCBE [Yayi BONI]

Democratic Renewal Party or PRD [Adrien HOUNGBEDJI]

New Consciousness Rally or NC [Pascal KOUPAKI]

Patriotic Awakening or RP [Janvier YAHOUEDEOU]

Social Democrat Party or PSD [Emmanuel GOLOU]

Sun Alliance or AS [Sacca LAFIA]

Union Makes the Nation or UN [Adrien HOUNGBEDJI] (alliance superceded Alliance for Dynamic Democracyor ADD)

United Democratic Forces or FDU [Mathurin NAGO]

note: approximately 20 additional minor parties

Political pressure groups and leaders: *other:* economic groups; environmentalists; political groups; teachers' unions and other educational groups

International organization participation: ACP, AfDB, AU, CD, ECOWAS, Entente, FAO, FZ,

G-77, IAEA, IBRD, ICAO, ICCt, ICRM, IDA, IDB, IFAD, IFC, IFRCS, ILO, IMF, IMO, Interpol, IOC, IOM, IPU, ISO, ITSO, ITU, ITUC (NGOs), MIGA, MINUSMA, MONUSCO, NAM, OAS (observer), OIC, OIF, OPCW, PCA, UN, UNAMID, UNCTAD, UNESCO, UNHCR, UNIDO, UNMIL, UNMISS, UNOCI, UNWTO, UPU, WADB (regional), WAEMU, WCO, WFTU (NGOs), WHO, WIPO, WMO, WTO

Diplomatic representation in the US: *chief of mission:* Ambassador Omar AROUNA (since 21 May 2014)

chancery: 2124 Kalorama Road NW, Washington, DC 20008

telephone: [1] (202) 232-6656

FAX: [1] (202) 265-1996

Diplomatic representation from the US: *chief of mission:* Ambassador Lucy TAMLYN (since 8 November 2015)

embassy: Caporal Bernard Anani, 01 BP 2012, Cotonou

mailing address: 01 B. P.2012, Cotonou

telephone: [229] 21-30-06-50

FAX: [229] 21-30-66-82

Flag description: two equal horizontal bands of yellow (top) and red (bottom) with a vertical green band on the hoist side; green symbolizes hope and revival, yellow wealth, and red courage

note: uses the popular Pan-African colors of Ethiopia

National symbol(s): leopard; national colors: green, yellow, red

National anthem: *name:* "L'Aube Nouvelle" (The Dawn of a New Day)

lyrics/music: Gilbert Jean DAGNON

note: adopted 1960

ECONOMY

Economy—overview: The free market economy of Benin remains underdeveloped and dependent on subsistence agriculture, cotton production, and regional trade. Cotton is a key export commodity; high prices supported export earnings. Growth in real output has averaged 6.5% since 2014. Inflation has subsided and remained 1% over the past several years.

An insufficient electrical supply continues to hamper Benin's economic growth though the government recently has taken steps to increase domestic power production. Private foreign direct investment is small, and foreign aid accounts for the majority of investment in infrastructure projects. Benin's 2001 privatization policy continues in telecommunications, water, electricity, and agriculture. Benin has appealed for international assistance to mitigate piracy against commercial shipping in its territory. Though security remains a problem, the Port of Cotonou has made progress towards implementing the International Ship and Port Facility Security (ISPS) Code in an effort to remain competitive. Projects included in Benin's $307 million Millennium Challenge Corporation (MCC) compact (2006–2011) were designed to increase investment and private sector activity by improving key institutional and physical infrastructure. The four projects focused on access to land, access to financial services, access to justice, and access to markets (including modernization of the port). The Port of Cotonou is the largest component of Benin's economy with revenues projected to account for more than 40% of Benin's national budget. Realizing its economic potential requires further efforts to infrastructure upgrades, stemming corruption, and expanding access to foreign markets in Nigeria and neighboring land-locked countries. In September 2015, Benin signed a MCC second Compact for $375 million that is designed to strengthen the national utility service provider, attract private sector investment, fund infrastructure investments in electricity genera-tion and distribution, and develop off-grid electri-fication for poor and unserved households. In order to raise growth, Benin plans to attract more for-eign investment, place more emphasis on tourism, facilitate the development of new food processing systems and agricultural products, encourage new information and communication technology, and establish Independent Power Producers (IPP).

GDP (purchasing power parity): $22.95 billion (2015 est.)
$21.81 billion (2014 est.)
$20.47 billion (2013 est.)
note: data are in 2015 US dollars
country comparison to the world: 141
GDP (official exchange rate): $8.471 billion (2015 est.)
GDP—real growth rate: 5.2% (2015 est.) 6.5% (2014 est.) 6.9% (2013 est.)
country comparison to the world: 39
GDP—per capita (PPP): $2,100 (2015 est.)
$2,100 (2014 est.)
$2,000 (2013 est.)
note: data are in 2015 US dollars
country comparison to the world: 201
Gross national saving:
16.7% of GDP (2015 est.)
15.6% of GDP (2014 est.)
19% of GDP (2013 est.)
country comparison to the world: 100
GDP—composition, by end use:
household consumption: 77.9%
government consumption: 11.6%
investment in fixed capital: 27.8%
investment in inventories: 0.6%
exports of goods and services: 20.1%
imports of goods and services: -38% (2015 est.)
GDP—composition, by sector of origin:
agriculture: 36.3%
industry: 13.5%
services: 50.2% (2015 est.)
Agriculture—products: cotton, corn, cassava (manioc, tapioca), yams, beans, palm oil, peanuts, cashews; livestock
Industries: textiles, food processing, construction materials, cement
Industrial production growth rate: 3.2% (2015 est.)
country comparison to the world: 80
Labor force: 3.662 million (2007 est.)
country comparison to the world: 96
Unemployment rate: NA%
Population below poverty line: 37.4% (2007 est.)

Household income or consumption by percentage share: *lowest:* 10%: 3.1%
highest: 10%: 29% (2003)
Distribution of family income—Gini index: 36.5 (2003)
country comparison to the world: 85
Budget: *revenues:* $1.762 billion
expenditures: $1.895 billion (2015 est.)
Taxes and other revenues: 22.9% of GDP (2015 est.)
country comparison to the world: 136
Budget surplus (+) or deficit (–): -1.7% of GDP (2015 est.)
country comparison to the world: 65
Public debt: 35% of GDP (2015 est.) 33.8% of GDP (2014 est.)
country comparison to the world: 127
Fiscal year: calendar year
Inflation rate (consumer prices): 0.3% (2015 est.) -1.1% (2014 est.)
country comparison to the world: 59
Central bank discount rate: 4.25% (31 December 2010) 4.25% (31 December 2009)
country comparison to the world: 91
Commercial bank prime lending rate: NA%
Stock of narrow money: $2.388 billion (31 December 2015 est.)
$2.336 billion (31 December 2014 est.)
country comparison to the world: 121
Stock of broad money: $4.165 billion (31 December 2014 est.)
$3.61 billion (31 December 2013 est.)
country comparison to the world: 139
Stock of domestic credit: $1.697 billion (31 December 2015 est.)
$1.792 billion (31 December 2014 est.)
country comparison to the world: 143
Market value of publicly traded shares: $NA
Current account balance: -$937 million (2015 est.) -$896 million (2014 est.)
country comparison to the world: 118
Exports: $2.047 billion (2015 est.)
$2.147 billion (2014 est.)
country comparison to the world: 137
Exports—commodities: cotton, cashews, shea but-ter, textiles, palm products, seafood
Exports—partners: India 24.8%, Gabon 15%, China 7.3%, Niger 6.1%, Bangladesh 5.1%, Nige-ria 5%, Vietnam 4.3% (2015)
Imports: $2.646 billion (2015 est.)
$2.736 billion (2014 est.)
country comparison to the world: 153
Imports—commodities: foodstuffs, capital goods, petroleum products
Imports—partners: China 42.2%, US 8.9%, India 5.7%, Malaysia 4.8%, Thailand 4.3%, France 4% (2015)
Reserves of foreign exchange and gold: $808.5 million (31 December 2015 est.)
$726 million (31 December 2014 est.)
country comparison to the world: 139
Debt—external: $2.635 billion (31 December 2014 est.)
$2.367 billion (31 December 2013 est.)
country comparison to the world: 146

Exchange rates: Communaute Financiere Afric-aine francs (XOF) per US dollar—
580.5 (2015 est.)
494.42 (2014 est.)
494.42 (2013 est.)
510.53 (2012 est.)
471.87 (2011 est.)

ENERGY

Electricity—production: 154 million kWh (2012 est.)
country comparison to the world: 192
Electricity—consumption: 911 million kWh (2012 est.)
country comparison to the world: 157
Electricity—exports: 0 kWh (2013 est.)
country comparison to the world: 111
Electricity—imports: 983 million kWh (2012 est.)
country comparison to the world: 63
Electricity—installed generating capacity: 163,000 kW (2015 est.)
country comparison to the world: 161
Electricity—from fossil fuels: 99.4% of total installed capacity (2012 est.)
country comparison to the world: 47
Electricity—from nuclear fuels: 0% of total installed capacity (2012 est.)
country comparison to the world: 56
Electricity—from hydroelectric plants: 0.6% of total installed capacity (2012 est.)
country comparison to the world: 145
Electricity—from other renewable sources: 0% of total installed capacity (2012 est.)
country comparison to the world: 160
Crude oil—production: 0 bbl/day (2014 est.)
country comparison to the world: 112
Crude oil—exports: 0 bbl/day (2012 est.)
country comparison to the world: 102
Crude oil—imports: 0 bbl/day (2012 est.)
country comparison to the world: 164
Crude oil—proved reserves: 8 million bbl (1 Janu-ary 2015 est.)
country comparison to the world: 95
Refined petroleum products—production: 0 bbl/day (2012 est.)
country comparison to the world: 160
Refined petroleum products—consumption: 31,000 bbl/day (2013 est.)
country comparison to the world: 115
Refined petroleum products—exports: 0 bbl/day (2012 est.)
country comparison to the world: 160
Refined petroleum products—imports: 30,930 bbl/day (2012 est.)
country comparison to the world: 97
Natural gas—production: 0 cu m (2013 est.)
country comparison to the world: 162
Natural gas—consumption: 0 cu m (2013 est.)
country comparison to the world: 121
Natural gas—exports: 0 cu m (2013 est.)
country comparison to the world: 67
Natural gas—imports: 0 cu m (2013 est.)
country comparison to the world: 167
Natural gas—proved reserves: 1.133 billion cu m (1 January 2014 est.)
country comparison to the world: 102

Carbon dioxide emissions from consumption of energy: 4.581 million Mt (2012 est.)
country comparison to the world: 129

COMMUNICATIONS

Telephones—fixed lines: *total subscriptions:* 200,000
subscriptions per 100 inhabitants: 2 (2014 est.)
country comparison to the world: 127
Telephones—mobile cellular: *total:* 10.8 million
subscriptions per 100 inhabitants: 106 (2014 est.)
country comparison to the world: 82
Telephone system: *general assessment:* inadequate system of open-wire, microwave radio relay, and cellular connections; fixed-line network characterized by aging, deteriorating equipment
domestic: fixed-line teledensity only about 2 per 100 persons; spurred by the presence of multiple mobile-cellular providers, cellular telephone subscribership has been increasing rapidly
international: country code—229; landing point for the SAT-3/WASC fiber-optic submarine cable that provides connectivity to Europe and Asia; long distance fiber-optic links with Togo, Burkina Faso, Niger, and Nigeria; satellite earth stations—7 (Intelsat-Atlantic Ocean) (2008)
Broadcast media: state-run Office de Radiodiffusion et de Television du Benin (ORTB) operates a TV station with multiple channels providing a wide broadcast reach; several privately owned TV stations broadcast from Cotonou; satellite TV subscription service is available; state-owned radio, under ORTB control, includes a national station supplemented by a number of regional stations; substantial number of privately owned radio broadcast stations; transmissions of a few international broadcasters are available on FM in Cotonou (2007)
Radio broadcast stations: AM 1, FM 34, short-wave 1 (2007)
Television broadcast stations: 6 (2007)
Internet country code: .bj
Internet hosts: 491 (2012)
country comparison to the world: 183
Internet users: *total:* 441,000
percent of population: 4.3% (2014 est.)
country comparison to the world: 132

TRANSPORTATION

Airports: 6 (2013)
country comparison to the world: 171
Airports—with paved runways: *total:* 11,524 to 2,437 m: 1 (2013)
Airports—with unpaved runways: *total:* 5
2,438 to 3,047 m: 2
1,524 to 2,437 m: 1
914 to 1,523 m: 2 (2013)
Railways: *total:* 438 km
narrow gauge: 438 km 1.000-m gauge (2014)
country comparison to the world: 118
Roadways: *total:* 16,000 km
paved: 1,400 km
unpaved: 14,600 km (2006)
country comparison to the world: 119

Waterways: 150 km (seasonal navigation on River Niger along northern border) (2011)
country comparison to the world: 101
Ports and terminals: *major seaport(s):* Cotonou
LNG terminal(s) (import): Cotonou

MILITARY AND SECURITY

Military branches: Benin Armed Forces (Forces Armees Beninoises, FAB): Army (l'Arme de Terre), Benin Navy (Forces Navales Beninois, FNB), Benin Air Force (Force Aerienne du Benin, FAB) (2013)
Military service age and obligation: 18–35 years of age for selective compulsory and voluntary military service; a higher education diploma is required; both sexes are eligible for military service; conscript tour of duty—18 months (2013)
Military expenditures: 1.03% of GDP (2012) NA% (2011) 1.03% of GDP (2010)
country comparison to the world: 99

TRANSNATIONAL ISSUES

Disputes—international: talks continue between Benin and Togo on funding the Adjrala hydroelectric dam on the Mona River; Benin retains a border dispute with Burkina Faso near the town of Koualou; location of Benin-Niger-Nigeria tripoint is unresolved

Illicit drugs: transshipment point used by traffickers for cocaine destined for Western Europe; vulnerable to money laundering due to poorly enforced financial regulations (2008)

BERMUDA

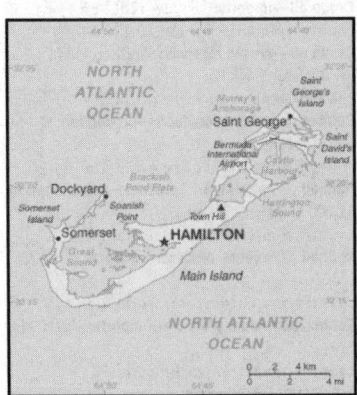

INTRODUCTION

Background: Bermuda was first settled in 1609 by shipwrecked English colonists heading for Virginia. Self-governing since 1620, Bermuda is the oldest and most populous of the British overseas territories. Vacationing to the island to escape North American winters first developed in Victorian times. Tourism continues to be important to the island's economy, although international business has overtaken it in recent years. Bermuda has also developed into a highly successful offshore financial center. A referendum on independence from the UK was soundly defeated in 1995.

GEOGRAPHY

Location: North America, group of islands in the North Atlantic Ocean, east of South Carolina (US)
Geographic coordinates: 32 20 N, 64 45 W
Map references: North America
Area: *total:* 54 sq km
land: 54 sq km
water: 0 sq km
country comparison to the world: 232
Area—comparative: about one-third the size of Washington, DC
Land boundaries: 0 km
Coastline: 103 km
Maritime claims: *territorial sea:* 12 nm
exclusive fishing zone: 200 nm
Climate: subtropical; mild, humid; gales, strong winds common in winter
Terrain: low hills separated by fertile depressions
Elevation: *mean elevation:* NA

elevation extremes: *lowest:* point: Atlantic Ocean 0 m
highest point: Town Hill 76 m
Natural resources: limestone, pleasant climate fostering tourism
Land use: *agricultural land:* 14.8%
arable land: 14.8%
permanent crops: 0%
permanent pasture: 0%
forest: 20%
other: 65.2% (2011 est.)
Irrigated land: NA
Natural hazards: hurricanes (June to November)
Environment—current issues: sustainable development
Geography—note: consists of about 138 coral islands and islets with ample rainfall, but no rivers or freshwater lakes; some land was leased by the US Government from 1941 to 1995

PEOPLE AND SOCIETY

Nationality: *noun:* Bermudian(s)
adjective: Bermudian
Ethnic groups: black 53.8%, white 31%, mixed 7.5%, other 7.1%, unspecified 0.6% (2010 est.)
Languages: English (official), Portuguese

Religions: Protestant 46.2% (includes Anglican 15.8%, African Methodist Episcopal 8.6%, Seventh Day Adventist 6.7, Pentecostal 3.5%, Methodist 2.7%, Presbyterian 2.0%, Church of God 1.6%, Baptist 1.2%, Salvation Army 1.1%, Brethren 1.0%, other Protestant 2.0%), Roman Catholic 14.5%, Jehovah's Witness 1.3%, other Christian 9.1%, Muslim 1%, other 3.9%, none 17.8%, unspecified 6.2% (2010 est.)

Population: 70,196 (July 2015 est.)

country comparison to the world: 204

Age structure: 0–14 years: 17.31% (male 6,144/ female 6,009)

15–24 years: 12.21% (male 4,302/female 4,269)

25–54 years: 38.56% (male 13,541/female 13,526)

55–64 years: 15% (male 4,963/female 5,568)

65 years and over: 16.92% (male 5,002/female 6,872) (2015 est.)

Median age: *total:* 43.1 years

male: 41.2 years

female: 44.9 years (2015 est.)

country comparison to the world: 15

Population growth rate: 0.5% (2015 est.)

country comparison to the world: 159

Birth rate: 11.33 births/1,000 population (2015 est.)

country comparison to the world: 174

Death rate: 8.23 deaths/1,000 population (2015 est.)

country comparison to the world: 85

Net migration rate: 1.88 migrant(s)/1,000 population (2015 est.)

country comparison to the world: 53

Urbanization: *urban population:* 100% of total population (2015)

rate of urbanization: 0.19% annual rate of change (2010–15 est.)

Major urban areas—population: HAMILTON (capital) 10,000 (2014)

Sex ratio: *at birth:* 1.02 male(s)/female

0–14 years: 1.02 male(s)/female

15–24 years: 1.01 male(s)/female

25–54 years: 1 male(s)/female

55–64 years: 0.89 male(s)/female

65 years and over: 0.73 male(s)/female

total population: 0.94 male(s)/female (2015 est.)

Infant mortality rate: *total:* 2.48 deaths/1,000 live births

male: 2.58 deaths/1,000 live births

female: 2.37 deaths/1,000 live births (2015 est.)

country comparison to the world: 219

Life expectancy at birth: *total population:* 81.15 years

male: 77.94 years

female: 84.42 years (2015 est.)

country comparison to the world: 25

Total fertility rate: 1.95 children born/woman (2015 est.)

country comparison to the world: 130

HIV/AIDS—adult prevalence rate: NA

HIV/AIDS—people living with HIV/AIDS: NA

HIV/AIDS—deaths: NA

Education expenditures: 1.8% of GDP (2014)

country comparison to the world: 151

School life expectancy (primary to tertiary education): *total:* 12 years

male: 11 years

female: 12 years (2014)

Unemployment, youth ages 15–24: *total:* 35.7%

male: 34.8%

female: 36.5% (2012 est.)

GOVERNMENT

Country name: *conventional long form:* none

conventional short form: Bermuda former: Somers Islands

etymology: the islands making up Bermuda are named after Juan de BERMUDEZ, a nearly 16th century Spanish sea captain and the first European explorer of the archipelago

Dependency status: overseas territory of the UK

Government type: parliamentary democracy (Parliament); self-governing overseas territory of the UK

Capital: *name:* Hamilton

Geographic coordinates: 32 17 N, 64 47 W

time difference: UTC-4 (1 hour ahead of Washington, DC, during Standard Time)

daylight saving time: +1hr, begins second Sunday in March; ends first Sunday in November

Administrative divisions: 9 parishes and 2 municipalities*; Devonshire, Hamilton, Hamilton*, Paget, Pembroke, Saint George*, Saint George's, Sandys, Smith's, Southampton, Warwick

Independence: none (overseas territory of the UK)

National holiday: Bermuda Day, 24 May

Constitution: several previous (dating to 1684); latest entered into force 8 June 1968; amended several times, last in 2012 (2016)

Legal system: English common law

International law organization participation: has not submitted an ICJ jurisdiction declaration; non-party state to the ICCt

Citizenship: *citizenship by birth:* no

citizenship by descent only: at least one parent must be a citizen of the UK

dual citizenship recognized: yes

residency requirement for naturalization: 10 years

Suffrage: 18 years of age; universal

Executive branch: *chief of state:* Queen ELIZABETH II (since 6 February 1952); represented by Governor George FERGUSSON (since 23 May 2012)

head of government: Premier Michael DUNKLEY (since 20 May 2014)

cabinet: Cabinet nominated by the premier, appointed by the governor

elections/appointments: the monarchy is hereditary; governor appointed by the monarch; following legislative elections, the leader of the majority party or majority coalition usually appointed premier by the governor

Legislative branch: *description:* bicameral Parliament consists of the Senate (11 seats; members appointed—3 by the governor, 5 by the premier, and 3 by the opposition party; members serve 5-year terms) and the House of Assembly (36 seats; members directly elected in single-seat constituencies by simple majority vote to serve up to 5-year terms)

elections: last held on 17 December 2012 (next to be held not later than 2017)

election results: percent of vote by party—OBA 51.7%, PLP 46.1%, other 2.2%; seats by party—OBA 19, PLP 17

Judicial branch: highest resident court (s): Court of Appeal (consists of the court president and 4 justices); Supreme Court (consists of the chief justice, 4 puisne judges, and 1 associate justice); note—the Judicial Committee of the Privy Council, in London, is the court of final appeal

judge selection and term of office: Court of Appeal justice appointed by the governor; justice tenure by individual appointment; Supreme Court judges nominated by the Judicial and Legal Services Commission and appointed by the governor; judge tenure NA

subordinate courts: commercial court (began in 2006); magistrates' courts

Political parties and leaders: One Bermuda Alliance or OBA [Thad HOLLIS]

Progressive Labor Party or PLP [Marc BEAN]

Political pressure groups and leaders: Association of Bermuda Insurers and Reinsurers or ABIR [Bradley KADING]

Association of Bermuda International Companies or ABIC [George HUTCHINGS]

Bermuda Employer's Council [Keith JENSEN]

Bermuda Industrial Union or BIU [Chris Furbert]

Bermuda Public Services Union or BPSU [Kevin GRANT and Ed BALL]

Bermuda Union of Teachers [Michael CHARLES]

International organization participation: Caricom (associate), ICC (NGOs), Interpol (subbureau), IOC, ITUC (NGOs), UPU, WCO

Diplomatic representation in the US: none (overseas territory of the UK)

Diplomatic representation from the US: *chief of mission:* Consul General Robert SETTJE (since August 2012)

consulate(s) general: Crown Hill, 16 Middle Road, Devonshire DVO3

mailing address: P.O. Box HM325, Hamilton HMBX; American Consulate General Hamilton, US Department of State, 5300 Hamilton Place, Washington, DC 20520–5300

telephone: [1] (441) 295-1342

FAX: [1] (441) 295-1592, 296-9233

Flag description: red, with the flag of the UK in the upper hoist-side quadrant and the Bermudian coat of arms (a white shield with a red lion standing on a green grassy field holding a scrolled shield showing the sinking of the ship Sea Venture off Bermuda in 1609) centered on the outer half of the flag; it was the shipwreck of the vessel, filled with english colonists originally bound for Virginia, that led to the settling of Bermuda

note: the flag is unusual in that it is only British overseas territory that uses a red ensign, all others use blue

National symbol(s): red lion

National anthem: *name:* "Hail to Bermuda"

lyrics/music: Bette JOHNS

note: serves as a local anthem; as a territory of the United Kingdom, "God Save the Queen" is official (see United Kingdom)

ECONOMY

Economy—overview: Tourism accounts for about 5% of Bermuda's GDP, but a much larger share of employment. Over 80% of its visitors come from the US. The sector struggled in the wake of the global recession of 2008–09. International business, which consists primarily of reinsurance and other financial services, is the real bedrock of Bermuda's economy, consistently accounting for about 85% of the island's GDP. Even this sector, however, has lost roughly 5,000 high-paying expatriate jobs since 2008, weighing heavily on household consumption and retail sales. Bermuda must import almost everything. Agriculture and industry are limited due to the small size of the island. Bermuda's economy entered its seventh straight year of recession in 2015. Unemployment is 9%, public debt is growing and exceeds $2.3 billion, the government pension fund faces a $2.4 billion shortfall, and the economy has not attracted significant amounts of new foreign investment. Bermuda's FY 2015–16 budget projects a 12% larger deficit than FY14/15. The government announced it would borrow $125 million in 2015 to meet current operating expenses. Still, Bermuda enjoys the fourth highest per capita income in the world, about 70% higher than that of the US.

GDP (purchasing power parity): $5.198 billion (2013 est.)
$5.331 billion (2012 est.)
$5.6 billion (2011 est.)
country comparison to the world: 173

GDP (official exchange rate): $5.198 billion (2013 est.)

GDP—real growth rate: -2.5% (2013 est.) -4.8% (2012) -3.5% (2011 est.)
country comparison to the world: 209

GDP—per capita (PPP): $85,700 (2013 est.)
$85,400 (2012 est.)
$86,000 (2011 est.)
country comparison to the world: 5

GDP—composition, by end use:
household consumption: 55.1%
government consumption: 17.3%
investment in fixed capital: 10.9%
investment in inventories: -0.1%
exports of goods and services: 47.3%
imports of goods and services: -30.5% (2015 est.)

GDP—composition, by sector of origin:
agriculture: 0.8%
industry: 5.9%
services: 93.3% (2015 est.)

Agriculture—products: bananas, vegetables, citrus, flowers; dairy products, honey

Industries: international business, tourism, light manufacturing

Industrial production growth rate: 1.8% (2015 est.)
country comparison to the world: 122

Labor force: 33,490 (2014 est.)
country comparison to the world: 203

Labor force—by occupation: *agriculture:* 2%
industry: 15%
services: 83% (2013 est.)

Unemployment rate: 9% (2014 est.) 7% (2013)
country comparison to the world: 107

Population below poverty line: 11% (2008 est.)

Household income or consumption by percentage share: *lowest:* 10%: NA%
highest: 10%: NA%

Budget: *revenues:* $895.6 million
expenditures: $1.106 billion (2015 est.)
Taxes and other revenues: 17.2% of GDP (2015 est.)
country comparison to the world: 176

Budget surplus (+) or deficit (–): -4% of GDP (2015 est.)
country comparison to the world: 145

Public debt: 43% of GDP (FY14/15)
country comparison to the world: 106

Fiscal year: 1 April—31 March

Inflation rate (consumer prices): 1.6% (2015 est.) 2% (2014 est.)
country comparison to the world: 102

Stock of narrow money: $3.374 billion (30 September 2014 est.)
$3.422 billion (31 December 2013 est.)
note: figures do not include US dollars, which also circulate freely
country comparison to the world: 111

Stock of broad money: $22.1 billion (30 September 2014 est.)
$25.1 billion (31 December 2013 est.)
country comparison to the world: 87

Stock of domestic credit: $NA

Market value of publicly traded shares: $1.487 billion (31 December 2012 est.)
$1.436 billion (31 December 2011)
$1.535 billion (31 December 2010 est.)
country comparison to the world: 103

Exports: $12 million (2015 est.)
$11 million (2014 est.)
country comparison to the world: 216

Exports—commodities: reexports of pharmaceuticals

Exports—partners: US 14.4%, Iceland 13.7%, Spain 6.8%, UK 5.8%, Mauritius 5.6% (2015)

Imports: $958 million (2015 est.)
$968 million (2014 est.)
country comparison to the world: 182

Imports—commodities: clothing, fuels, machinery and transport equipment, construction materials, chemicals, food and live animals

Imports—partners: South Korea 49.5%, US 14.6%, Germany 11.4%, China 9%, Turkmenistan 5.2% (2015)

Debt—external: $2.435 billion (2015 est.)
$1.4 billion (2012 est.)
country comparison to the world: 147

Stock of direct foreign investment—at home: $2.641 billion (2014 est.)
$2.664 billion (2013 est.)
country comparison to the world: 106

Stock of direct foreign investment—abroad: $889 million (2014 est.)
$NA (2013 est.)
country comparison to the world: 84

Exchange rates: Bermudian dollars (BMD) per US dollar—
1 (2015 est.)
1 (2014 est.)
1 (2013 est.)

1 (2012 est.)

ENERGY

Electricity—production: 648.9 million kWh (2014 est.)
country comparison to the world: 159

Electricity—consumption: 664.2 million kWh (2013 est.)
country comparison to the world: 165

Electricity—exports: 0 kWh (2013 est.)
country comparison to the world: 105

Electricity—imports: 0 kWh (2013 est.)
country comparison to the world: 120

Electricity—installed generating capacity: 167,400 kW (2014 est.)
country comparison to the world: 162

Electricity—from fossil fuels: 98.2% of total installed capacity (2014 est.)
country comparison to the world: 54

Electricity—from nuclear fuels: 0% of total installed capacity (2014 est.)
country comparison to the world: 49

Electricity—from hydroelectric plants: 0% of total installed capacity (2014 est.)
country comparison to the world: 161

Electricity—from other renewable sources: 1.8% of total installed capacity
note: the Tynes Bay Waste Treatment Facility turns waste to electric energy (2014 est.)
country comparison to the world: 84

Crude oil—production: 0 bbl/day (2014 est.)
country comparison to the world: 108

Crude oil—exports: 0 bbl/day (2015 est.)
country comparison to the world: 99

Crude oil—imports: 0 bbl/day (2014 est.)
country comparison to the world: 160

Crude oil—proved reserves: 0 bbl (1 January 2015 est.)
country comparison to the world: 107

Refined petroleum products—production: 0 bbl/day (2012 est.)
country comparison to the world: 157

Refined petroleum products—consumption: 4,600 bbl/day (2013 est.)
country comparison to the world: 174

Refined petroleum products—exports: 0 bbl/day (2014 est.)
country comparison to the world: 156

Refined petroleum products—imports: 889.3 bbl/day (2015 est.)
country comparison to the world: 200

Natural gas—production: 0 cu m (2014 est.)
country comparison to the world: 157

Natural gas—consumption: 0 cu m (2013 est.)
country comparison to the world: 118

Natural gas—exports: 0 cu m (2013 est.)
country comparison to the world: 62

Natural gas—imports: 0 cu m (2014 est.)
country comparison to the world: 161

Natural gas—proved reserves: 0 cu m (1 January 2014 est.)
country comparison to the world: 112

Carbon dioxide emissions from consumption of energy: 614,200 Mt (2012 est.)
country comparison to the world: 175

COMMUNICATIONS

Telephones—fixed lines: *total subscriptions:* 29,200
subscriptions per 100 inhabitants: 42 (2014 est.)
country comparison to the world: 173
Telephones—mobile cellular: *total:* 59,500
subscriptions per 100 inhabitants: 85 (2014 est.)
country comparison to the world: 201
Telephone system: *general assessment:* a good, fully automatic digital telephone system with fiber-optic trunk lines
domestic: the system has a high fixed-line teledensity coupled with a mobile-cellular teledensity of roughly 125 per 100 persons
international: country code—1 -441; landing points for the GlobeNet, Gemini Bermuda, CBUS, and the Challenger Bermuda-1 (CB-1) submarine cables; satellite earth stations—3 (2010)
Broadcast media: 3 TV stations; cable and satellite TV subscription services are available; roughly 13 radio stations operating (2012)
Radio broadcast stations: AM 5, FM 4, shortwave 1 (2009)

Television broadcast stations: 3 (2005)
Internet country code: .bm
Internet hosts: 20,040 (2012)
country comparison to the world: 119
Internet users: *total:* 68,300
percent of population: 97.8% (2014 est.)
country comparison to the world: 179

TRANSPORTATION

Airports: 1 (2013)
country comparison to the world: 212
Airports—with paved runways: *total:* 12,438 to 3,047 m: 1 (2013)
Roadways: *total:* 447 km
paved: 447 km
note: 225 km public roads; 222 km private roads (2010)
country comparison to the world: 198
Merchant marine: *total:* 139
by type: bulk carrier 22, chemical tanker 3, container 14, liquefied gas 43, passenger 27, passenger/cargo 2, petroleum tanker 19, refrigerated cargo 9
foreign-owned: 105 (France 1, Germany 14, Greece 8, Hong Kong 4, Ireland 1, Israel 3, Japan

2, Monaco 2, Nigeria 11, Norway 5, Sweden 14, UK 14, US 26)
registered in other countries: 241 (Bahamas 15, Cyprus 1, France 5, Greece 3, Hong Kong 20, Isle of Man 7, Liberia 4, Malta 15, Marshall Islands 35, Netherlands 1, Norway 24, Panama 27, Philippines 47, Saint Vincent and the Grenadines 1, Singapore 25, UK 6, US 5) (2010)
country comparison to the world: 41
Ports and terminals: *major seaport(s):* Hamilton, Ireland Island, Saint George

MILITARY AND SECURITY

Military branches: Bermuda Regiment (2012)
Military service age and obligation: 18–45 years of age for voluntary male or female enlistment in the Bermuda Regiment; males must register at age 18 and may be subject to conscription; term of service is 38 months for volunteers or conscripts (2012)
Military—note: defense is the responsibility of the UK

TRANSNATIONAL ISSUES

Disputes—international: none

BHUTAN

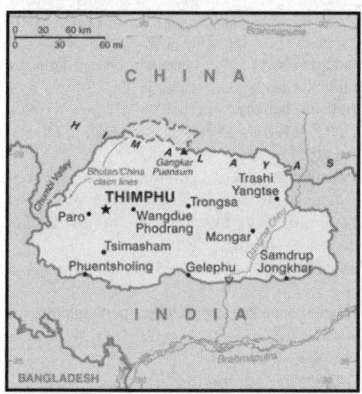

INTRODUCTION

Background: Following Britain's victory in the 1865 Duar War, Britain and Bhutan signed the Treaty of Sinchulu, under which Bhutan would receive an annual subsidy in exchange for ceding land to British India. Ugyen WANGCHUCK—who had served as the de facto ruler of an increasingly unified Bhutan and had improved relations with the British toward the end of the 19th century—was named king in 1907. Three years later, a treaty was signed whereby the British agreed not to interfere in Bhutanese internal affairs, and Bhutan allowed Britain to direct its foreign affairs. Bhutan negotiated a similar arrangement with independent India after 1947. Two years later, a formal Indo-Bhutanese accord returned to Bhutan

a small piece of the territory annexed by the British, formalized the annual subsidies the country received, and defined India's responsibilities in defense and foreign relations. Under a succession of modernizing monarchs beginning in the 1950s, Bhutan joined the UN in 1971 and slowly continued its engagement beyond its borders. In March 2005, King Jigme Singye WANGCHUCK unveiled the government's draft constitution—which introduced major democratic reforms—and held a national referendum for its approval. In December 2006, the King abdicated the throne in favor of his son, Jigme Khesar Namgyel WANGCHUCK. In early 2007, India and Bhutan renegotiated their treaty, eliminating the clause that stated that Bhutan would be "guided by" India in conducting its foreign policy, although Thimphu continues to coordinate closely with New Delhi. Elections for seating the country's first parliament were completed in March 2008; the king ratified the country's first constitution in July 2008. Bhutan experienced a peaceful turnover of power following parliamentary elections in 2013, which resulted in the defeat of the incumbent party. The disposition of some 18,000 refugees of the roughly 100,000 who fled or were forced out of Bhutan in the 1990s—and who are housed in two UN refugee camps in Nepal—remains unresolved.

GEOGRAPHY

Location: Southern Asia, between China and India
Geographic coordinates: 27 30 N, 90 30 E
Map references: Asia
Area: *total:* 38,394 sq km
land: 38,394 sq km
water: 0 sq km

country comparison to the world: 137
Area—comparative: about one-half the size of Indiana
Land boundaries: *total:* 1,136 km
border countries (2): China 477 km, India 659 km
Coastline: 0 km (landlocked)
Maritime claims: none (landlocked)
Climate: varies; tropical in southern plains; cool winters and hot summers in central valleys; severe winters and cool summers in Himalayas
Terrain: mostly mountainous with some fertile valleys and savanna
Elevation: *mean elevation:* 2,220 m
elevation extremes: *lowest:* point: Drangeme Chhu 97 m
highest point: Gangkar Puensum 7,570 m
Natural resources: timber, hydropower, gypsum, calcium carbonate
Land use: *agricultural land:* 13.6%
arable land: 2.6%
permanent crops: 0.3%
permanent pasture: 10.7%
forest: 85.5%
other: 0.9% (2011 est.)
Irrigated land: 320 sq km (2012)
Total renewable water resources: 78 cu km (2011)
Freshwater withdrawal (domestic/industrial/agricultural): *total:* 0.34 cu km/yr (5%/1%/94%)
per capita: 458 cu m/yr (2008)
Natural hazards: violent storms from the Himalayas are the source of the country's Bhutanese name, which translates as Land of the Thunder Dragon; frequent landslides during the rainy season
Environment—current issues: soil erosion; limited access to potable water

97

Environment—international agreements: *party to:* Biodiversity, Climate Change, Climate Change-Kyoto Protocol, Desertification, Endangered Species, Hazardous Wastes, Ozone Layer Protection *signed, but not ratified:* Law of the Sea

Geography—note: landlocked; strategic location between China and India; controls several key Himalayan mountain passes

PEOPLE AND SOCIETY

Nationality: *noun:* Bhutanese (singular and plural) *adjective:* Bhutanese

Ethnic groups: Ngalop (also known as Bhote) 50%, ethnic Nepalese 35% (includes Lhotsampas—one of several Nepalese ethnic groups), indigenous or migrant tribes 15%

Languages: Sharchhopka 28%, Dzongkha (official) 24%, Lhotshamkha 22%, other 26% (includes foreign languages) (2005 est.)

Religions: Lamaistic Buddhist 75.3%, Indian- and Nepalese-influenced Hinduism 22.1%, other 2.6% (2005 est.)

Population: 741,919 (July 2015 est.)
country comparison to the world: 165

Age structure: 0–14 years: 26.76% (male 101,418/female 97,132)
15–24 years: 19.68% (male 74,373/female 71,600)
25–54 years: 41.6% (male 164,520/female 144,089)
55–64 years: 5.85% (male 23,271/female 20,144)
65 years and over: 6.12% (male 23,754/female 21,618) (2015 est.)

Dependency ratios:
total dependency ratio: 46.9%
youth dependency ratio: 39.5%
elderly dependency ratio: 7.4%
potential support ratio: 13.4% (2015 est.)

Median age:
total: 26.7 years
male: 27.2 years
female: 26.1 years (2015 est.)
country comparison to the world: 144

Population growth rate: 1.11% (2015 est.)
country comparison to the world: 112

Birth rate: 17.78 births/1,000 population (2015 est.)
country comparison to the world: 106

Death rate: 6.69 deaths/1,000 population (2015 est.)
country comparison to the world: 141

Net migration rate: 0 migrant(s)/1,000 population (2015 est.)
country comparison to the world: 105

Urbanization: *urban population:* 38.6% of total population (2015)
rate of urbanization: 3.69% annual rate of change (2010–15 est.)

Major urban areas—population: THIMPHU (capital) 152,000 (2014)

Sex ratio: *at birth:* 1.05 male(s)/female
0–14 years: 1.04 male(s)/female
15–24 years: 1.04 male(s)/female
25–54 years: 1.14 male(s)/female
55–64 years: 1.16 male(s)/female
65 years and over: 1.1 male(s)/female
total population: 1.09 male(s)/female (2015 est.)

Maternal mortality rate: 148 deaths/100,000 live births (2015 est.)
country comparison to the world: 59

Infant mortality rate: *total:* 35.91 deaths/1,000 live births
male: 36.27 deaths/1,000 live births
female: 35.53 deaths/1,000 live births (2015 est.)
country comparison to the world: 61

Life expectancy at birth: *total population:* 69.51 years
male: 68.56 years
female: 70.51 years (2015 est.)
country comparison to the world: 158

Total fertility rate: 1.97 children born/woman (2015 est.)
country comparison to the world: 128

Contraceptive prevalence rate: 65.6% (2010)

Health expenditures: 3.6% of GDP (2013)
country comparison to the world: 167

Physicians density: 0.26 physicians/1,000 population (2012)

Hospital bed density: 1.8 beds/1,000 population (2012)

Drinking water source:
improved:
urban: 100% of population
rural: 100% of population
total: 100% of population
unimproved:
urban: 0% of population
rural: 0% of population
total: 0% of population (2015 est.)

Sanitation facility access:
improved:
urban: 77.9% of population
rural: 33.1% of population
total: 50.4% of population
unimproved:
urban: 22.1% of population
rural: 66.9% of population
total: 49.6% of population (2015 est.)

HIV/AIDS—adult prevalence rate: 0.13% (2013 est.)
country comparison to the world: 110

HIV/AIDS—people living with HIV/AIDS: 600 (2013 est.)
country comparison to the world: 123

HIV/AIDS—deaths: NA

Major infectious diseases: *degree of risk:* high food or waterborne
diseases: bacterial and protozoal diarrhea, hepatitis A, and typhoid fever
vectorborne diseases: dengue fever and malaria (2013)

Obesity—adult prevalence rate: 5.9% (2014)
country comparison to the world: 154

Children under the age of 5 years underweight: 12.8% (2010)
country comparison to the world: 59

Education expenditures: 5.9% of GDP (2014)
country comparison to the world: 86

Literacy: *definition:* age 15 and over can read and write
total population: 64.9%
male: 73.1%
female: 55% (2015 est.)

School life expectancy (primary to tertiary education): *total:* 13 years
male: 12 years
female: 13 years (2013)

Child labor—children ages 5–14: *total number:* 25,801
percentage: 18% (2010 est.)

Unemployment, youth ages 15–24: *total:* 9.6%
male: 9.2%
female: 9.9% (2013 est.)
country comparison to the world: 119

GOVERNMENT

Country name: *conventional long form:* Kingdom of Bhutan
conventional short form: Bhutan
local long form: Druk Gyalkhap
local short form: Druk Yul
etymology: named after the Bhotia, the ethnic Tibetans who migrated from Tibet to Bhutan; Bod is the Tibetan name for their land; the Bhutanese name "Druk Yul" means "Land of the Thunder Dragon"

Government type: constitutional monarchy

Capital: *name:* Thimphu

Geographic coordinates: 27 28 N, 89 38 E
time difference: UTC+6 (11 hours ahead of Washington, DC, during Standard Time)

Administrative divisions: 20 districts (dzongkhag, singular and plural); Bumthang, Chhukha, Chirang, Daga, Gasa, Geylegphug, Ha, Lhuntshi, Mongar, Paro, Pemagatsel, Punakha, Samchi, Samdrup Jongkhar, Shemgang, Tashigang, Tashi Yangtse, Thimphu, Tongsa, Wangdi Phodrang

Independence: 1907 (became a unified kingdom under its first hereditary king)

National holiday: National Day (Ugyen WANGCHUCK became first hereditary king), 17 December (1907)

Constitution: previous governing documents were various royal decrees; first constitution drafted November 2001-March 2005, ratified 18 July 2008; amended 2011 (2016)

Legal system: civil law based on Buddhist religious law

International law organization participation: has not submitted an ICJ jurisdiction declaration; non-party state to the ICCt

Citizenship: *citizenship by birth:* no
citizenship by descent only: the father must be a citizen of Bhutan
dual citizenship recognized: no
residency requirement for naturalization: 10 years

Suffrage: 18 years of age; universal

Executive branch: *chief of state:* King Jigme Khesar Namgyel WANGCHUCK (since 14 December 2006); note—King Jigme Singye WANGCHUCK abdicated the throne on 14 December 2006 to his son

head of government: Prime Minister Tshering TOBGAY (since July 2013)
cabinet: Council of Ministers or Lhengye Zhungtshog members nominated by the monarch in consultation with the prime minister and approved by the National Assembly; members serve 5-year terms

elections/appointments: the monarchy is hereditary but can be removed by a two-third vote of Parliament; leader of the majority party in Parliament is nominated as the prime minister, appointed by the monarch

Legislative branch: *description:* bicameral Parliament or Chi Tshog consists of the non-partisan National Council or Gyelyong Tshogde (25 seats; 20 members directly elected in single-seat constituencies by simple majority vote and 5 members appointed by the king; members serve 5-year terms) and the National Assembly or Tshogdu (47 seats; members directly elected in single-seat constituencies by proportional representation vote to serve 5-year terms)

elections: National Council election last held on 23 April 2013 (next to be held in 2018); National Assembly election first round held on 31 May 2013 and second round on 13 July 2013

election results: National Council—seats by party—independent 20 (all candidates required to run as independents; National Assembly—first round—percent of vote by party—DPT 44.5%; PDP 32.5%; DNT 17.0%; DCT 5.9%; second round—percent of vote by party—PDP 54.9%, DPT 45.1%; seats by party—PDP 32, DPT 15

Judicial branch: *highest court(s):* Supreme Court (consists of 5 justices including the chief justice); note—the Supreme Court has sole jurisdiction in constitutional matters

judge selection and term of office: Supreme Court chief justice appointed by the monarch upon the advice of the National Judicial Commission, a 4-member body to include the Legislative Committee of the National Assembly, the attorney general, the Chief Justice of Bhutan and the senior Associate Justice of the Supreme Court; other judges (drangpons) appointed by the monarch from among the High Court judges selected by the National Judicial Commission; chief justice serves a 5-year term or until reaching age 65 years, whichever is earlier; the 4 other judges serve 10-year terms or until age 65, whichever is earlier

subordinate courts: High Court (first appellate court); District or Dzongkhag Courts; sub-district or Dung khag Courts

Political parties and leaders: Bhutan Kuen-Nyam Party or BKP [Sonam TOBGAY]
Bhutan Peace and Prosperity Party (Druk Phuensum Tshogpa) or DPT [Pema GYAMTSHO]
Druck Chirwang Tshogpa or DCT
Druk Nymrub Tshogpa or DNT
People's Democratic Party or PDP [Tshering TOBGAY]

Political pressure groups and leaders: Druk National Congress (exiled)
United Front for Democracy (exiled)
other: Buddhist clergy; ethnic Nepali-Bhutanese organizations (exiled)

International organization participation: ADB, BIMSTEC, CP, FAO, G-77, IBRD, ICAO, IDA, IFAD, IFC, IMF, Interpol, IOC, IOM (observer), IPU, ISO (correspondent), ITSO, ITU, MIGA, NAM, OPCW, SAARC, SACEP, UN, UNCTAD, UNESCO, UNIDO, UNTSO, UNWTO, UPU, WCO, WHO, WIPO, WMO, WTO (observer)

Diplomatic representation in the US: none; note—the Permanent Mission to the UN for Bhutan has consular jurisdiction in the US; the permanent representative to the UN is Kunzang C. NAMGYEL (since February 2014); address: 343 East 43rd Street, New York, NY 10017
telephone: [1] (212) 682–2268
FAX: [1] (212) 661–0551
consulate(s) general: New York

Diplomatic representation from the US: the US and Bhutan have no formal diplomatic relations, although frequent informal contact is maintained via the US embassy in New Delhi (India) and Bhutan's Permanent Mission to the UN

Flag description: divided diagonally from the lower hoist-side corner; the upper triangle is yellow and the lower triangle is orange; centered along the dividing line is a large black and white dragon facing away from the hoist side; the dragon, called the Druk (Thunder Dragon), is the emblem of the nation; its white color stands for purity and the jewels in its claws symbolize wealth; the background colors represent spiritual and secular powers within Bhutan: the orange is associated with Buddhism, while the yellow denotes the ruling dynasty

National symbol(s): thunder dragon known as Druk Gyalpo; national colors: orange, yellow

National anthem: *name:* "Druk tsendhen" (The Thunder Dragon Kingdom)
lyrics/music: Gyaldun Dasho Thinley DORJI/Aku TONGMI
note: adopted 1953

ECONOMY

Economy—overview: Bhutan's economy, small and less developed, is based largely on hydropower, agriculture, and forestry, which provide the main livelihood for more than half of the population. Because rugged mountains dominate the terrain and make the building of roads and other infrastructure difficult and expensive, industrial production is primarily of the cottage industry type. The economy is closely aligned with India's through strong trade and monetary links and is dependent on India for financial assistance and migrant laborers for development projects, especially for road construction. Bhutan inked a pact in December 2014 to expand duty-free trade with Bangladesh, the only trade partner with which Bhutan enjoys a surplus. Multilateral development organizations administer most educational, social, and environment programs, and take into account the government's desire to protect the country's environment and cultural traditions. For example, the government, in its cautious expansion of the tourist sector, encourages visits by upscale, environmentally conscientious tourists. Complicated controls and uncertain policies in areas such as industrial licensing, trade, labor, and finance continue to hamper foreign investment. Bhutan's largest export—hydropower to India—could spur sustainable growth in the coming years if Bhutan resolves chronic delays in construction. Bhutan currently taps only 5% of its 30,000-megawatt hydropower potential and is behind schedule in building 12 new hydropower dams with a combined capacity of 10,000 megawatts by 2020 in accordance with a deal signed in 2008 with India. The high volume of imported materials to build hydropower plants has expanded Bhutan's trade and current account deficits. However, Bhutan and India in April 2014 agreed to begin four additional hydropower projects, which would generate 2,120 megawatts in total. Bhutan also is exploring energy exports to Bangladesh.

GDP (purchasing power parity): $6.385 billion (2015 est.)
$5.93 billion (2014 est.)
$5.573 billion (2013 est.)
note: data are in 2015 US dollars
country comparison to the world: 168

GDP (official exchange rate): $2.214 billion (2015 est.)

GDP—real growth rate: 7.7% (2015 est.)
6.4% (2014 est.)
4.9% (2013 est.)
country comparison to the world: 11

GDP—per capita (PPP): $8,200 (2015 est.)
$7,700 (2014 est.)
$7,400 (2013 est.)
note: data are in 2015 US dollars
country comparison to the world: 148

Gross national saving: 21.6% of GDP (2015 est.)
22.3% of GDP (2014 est.)
28.6% of GDP (2013 est.)
country comparison to the world: 71

GDP—composition, by end use:
household consumption: 68.4%
government consumption: 21.5%
investment in fixed capital: 47.1%
investment in inventories: 0%
exports of goods and services: 37.3%
imports of goods and services: -74.3% (2015 est.)

GDP—composition, by sector of origin:
agriculture: 16.8%
industry: 40.5%
services: 42.7% (2014 est.)

Agriculture—products: rice, corn, root crops, citrus; dairy products, eggs

Industries: cement, wood products, processed fruits, alcoholic beverages, calcium carbide, tourism

Industrial production growth rate: 6% (2015 est.)
country comparison to the world: 21

Labor force: 348,800
note: major shortage of skilled labor (2015 est.)
country comparison to the world: 161

Labor force—by occupation: *agriculture:* 57%
industry: 21%
services: 22% (2014 est.)

Unemployment rate: 2.6% (2014 est.)
2.9% (2013 est.)
country comparison to the world: 17

Population below poverty line: 12% (2012 est.)

Household income or consumption by percentage share: *lowest:* 10%: 2.8%
highest: 10%: 30.6% (2012)

Distribution of family income—Gini index: 38.7 (2012)
38.1 (2007)
country comparison to the world: 73

Budget: *revenues:* $608 million
expenditures: $692.7 million

note: the government of India finances nearly one-quarter of Bhutan's budget expenditures (2015 est.)

Taxes and other revenues: 26.9% of GDP (2015 est.)

country comparison to the world: 103

Budget surplus (+) or deficit (–): -3.2% of GDP (2015 est.)

country comparison to the world: 122

Public debt: 98.5% of GDP (2015 est.)

91.2% of GDP (2014 est.)

country comparison to the world: 18

Fiscal year: 1 July—30 June

Inflation rate (consumer prices): 7.2% (2015 est.)

9.6% (2014 est.)

country comparison to the world: 195

Central bank discount rate: NA%

Commercial bank prime lending rate: 14.2% (31 December 2015 est.)

14.2% (31 December 2014 est.)

country comparison to the world: 48

Stock of narrow money: $738.7 million (31 December 2015 est.)

$683.7 million (31 December 2014 est.)

country comparison to the world: 159

Stock of broad money: $1.305 billion (31 December 2015 est.)

$1.184 billion (31 December 2014 est.)

country comparison to the world: 167

Stock of domestic credit: $1.018 billion (31 December 2015 est.)

$1.01 billion (31 December 2014 est.)

country comparison to the world: 159

Market value of publicly traded shares: $320 million (31 December 2013)

$283.4 million (31 December 2012)

country comparison to the world: 115

Current account balance: -$591 million (2015 est.)

-$459 million (2014 est.)

country comparison to the world: 106

Exports: $375 million (2015 est.)

$409.2 million (2014 est.)

country comparison to the world: 179

Exports—commodities: electricity (to India), ferrosilicon, cement, calcium carbide, copper wire, manganese, vegetable oil

Exports—partners: India 83.8%, Hong Kong 10.8% (2013 est.)

Imports: $965 million (2015 est.)

$927.6 million (2014 est.)

country comparison to the world: 180

Imports—commodities: fuel and lubricants, passenger cars, machinery and parts, fabrics, rice

Imports—partners: India 72.3%, South Korea 6% (2013 est.)

Debt—external: $1.855 billion (31 December 2014 est.)

$1.844 billion (31 December 2014 est.)

country comparison to the world: 152

Stock of direct foreign investment—at home: $173.8 million (31 December 2015 est.)

$145.4 million (31 December 2014 est.)

country comparison to the world: 116

Exchange rates: ngultrum (BTN) per US dollar— 63.9 (2015 est.)

60.98 (2014 est.)

61.03 (2013 est.)

53.44 (2012 est.)

46.67 (2011 est.)

ENERGY

Electricity—production: 7.147 billion kWh (2014 est.)

country comparison to the world: 109

Electricity—consumption: 2.085 billion kWh (2014 est.)

country comparison to the world: 141

Electricity—exports: 5.147 billion kWh (2014 est.)

country comparison to the world: 31

Electricity—imports: 159 million kWh (2014 est.)

country comparison to the world: 90

Electricity—installed generating capacity: 1.499 million kW (2014 est.)

country comparison to the world: 120

Electricity—from fossil fuels: 0.7% of total installed capacity (2013 est.)

country comparison to the world: 210

Electricity—from nuclear fuels: 0% of total installed capacity (2013 est.)

country comparison to the world: 59

Electricity—from hydroelectric plants: 99.3% of total installed capacity (2013 est.)

country comparison to the world: 4

Electricity—from other renewable sources: 0% of total installed capacity (2013 est.)

country comparison to the world: 162

Crude oil—production: 0 bbl/day (2014 est.)

country comparison to the world: 114

Crude oil—exports: 0 bbl/day (2013 est.)

country comparison to the world: 10

Crude oil—imports: 0 bbl/day (2013 est.)

country comparison to the world: 166

Crude oil—proved reserves: 0 bbl (1 January 2015 est.)

country comparison to the world: 112

Refined petroleum products—production: 0 bbl/day (2012 est.)

country comparison to the world: 162

Refined petroleum products—consumption: 2,000 bbl/day (2013 est.)

country comparison to the world: 188

Refined petroleum products—exports: 0 bbl/day (2013 est.)

country comparison to the world: 162

Refined petroleum products—imports: 1,870 bbl/day (2013 est.)

country comparison to the world: 183

Natural gas—production: 0 cu m (2013 est.)

country comparison to the world: 164

Natural gas—consumption: 0 cu m (2013 est.)

country comparison to the world: 123

Natural gas—exports: 0 cu m (2013 est.)

country comparison to the world: 70

Natural gas—imports: 0 cu m (2013 est.)

country comparison to the world: 169

Natural gas—proved reserves: 0 cu m (1 January 2014 est.)

country comparison to the world: 118

Carbon dioxide emissions from consumption of energy: 320,800 Mt (2012 est.)

country comparison to the world: 188

COMMUNICATIONS

Telephones—fixed lines: *total subscriptions:* 23,800

subscriptions per 100 inhabitants: 3 (2014 est.)

country comparison to the world: 176

Telephones—mobile cellular: *total:* 628,300

subscriptions per 100 inhabitants: 86 (2014 est.)

country comparison to the world: 165

Telephone system: *general assessment:* urban towns and district headquarters have telecommunications services

domestic: low teledensity; domestic service is poor especially in rural areas; mobile-cellular service, started in 2003, is now widely available

international: country code—975; international telephone and telegraph service via landline and microwave relay through India; satellite earth station—1 Intelsat (2012)

Broadcast media: state-owned TV station established in 1999; cable TV service offers dozens of Indian and other international channels; first radio station, privately launched in 1973, is now state-owned; 5 private radio stations are currently broadcasting (2012)

Radio broadcast stations: AM 0, FM 9, shortwave 1 (2007)

Television broadcast stations: 1 (2007)

Internet country code: .bt

Internet hosts: 14,590 (2012)

country comparison to the world: 126

Internet users: *total:* 203,100

percent of population: 27.7% (2014 est.)

country comparison to the world: 155

TRANSPORTATION

Airports: 2 (2013)

country comparison to the world: 198

Airports—with paved runways: *total:* 2

1,524 to 2,437 m: 1

914 to 1,523 m: 1 (2013)

Airports—with unpaved runways: *total:* 1

914 to 1,523 m: 1 (2012)

Roadways: *total:* 10,578 km

paved: 2,975 km (includes 2,180 km of natonal highways)

unpaved: 7,603 km (2013)

country comparison to the world: 135

MILITARY AND SECURITY

Military branches: Royal Bhutan Army (includes Royal Bodyguard and Royal Bhutan Police) (2009)

Military service age and obligation: 18 years of age for voluntary military service; no conscription; militia training is compulsory for males aged 20–25, over a 3-year period (2012)

TRANSNATIONAL ISSUES

Disputes—international: lacking any treaty describing the boundary, Bhutan and China continue negotiations to establish a common boundary alignment to resolve territorial disputes arising from substantial cartographic discrepancies, the largest of which lie in Bhutan's northwest and along the Chumbi salient

BOLIVIA

INTRODUCTION

Background: Bolivia, named after independence fighter Simon BOLIVAR, broke away from Spanish rule in 1825; much of its subsequent history has consisted of a series of nearly 200 coups and countercoups. Democratic civilian rule was established in 1982, but leaders have faced difficult problems of deep-seated poverty, social unrest, and illegal drug production.

In December 2005, Bolivians elected Movement Toward Socialism leader Evo MORALES president—by the widest margin of any leader since the restoration of civilian rule in 1982—after he ran on a promise to change the country's traditional political class and empower the nation's poor, indigenous majority. In December 2009 and October 2014, President MORALES easily won reelection. His party maintained control of the legislative branch of the government, which has allowed him to continue his process of change. In October 2011, the country held its first judicial elections to select judges for the four highest courts. MORALES has publicly described the elected judiciary as a failed experiment that has not resolved judicial backlogs or extended pre-trial detention. He has called for a public referendum on the judicial system.

GEOGRAPHY

Location: Central South America, southwest of Brazil

Geographic coordinates: 17 00 S, 65 00 W

Map references: South America

Area: *total:* 1,098,581 sq km
land: 1,083,301 sq km
water: 15,280 sq km
country comparison to the world: 28

Area—comparative: slightly less than three times the size of Montana

Land boundaries: *total:* 7,252 km
border countries (5): Argentina 942 km, Brazil 3,403 km, Chile 942 km, Paraguay 753 km, Peru 1,212 km

Coastline: 0 km (landlocked)

Maritime claims: none (landlocked)

Climate: varies with altitude; humid and tropical to cold and semiarid

Terrain: rugged Andes Mountains with a highland plateau (Altiplano), hills, lowland plains of the Amazon Basin

Elevation: *mean elevation:* 1,192 m

elevation extremes: *lowest:* point: Rio Paraguay 90 m
highest point: Nevado Sajama 6,542 m

Natural resources: tin, natural gas, petroleum, zinc, tungsten, antimony, silver, iron, lead, gold, timber, hydropower

Land use: *agricultural land:* 34.3%
arable land: 3.6%
permanent crops: 0.2%
permanent pasture: 30.5%
forest: 52.5%
other: 13.2% (2011 est.)

Irrigated land: 3,000 sq km (2012)

Total renewable water resources: 622.5 cu km (2011)

Freshwater withdrawal (domestic/industrial/agricultural): *total:* 2.64 cu km/yr (25%/14%/61%)
per capita: 305.8 cu m/yr (2005)

Natural hazards: flooding in the northeast (March to April)
volcanism: volcanic activity in Andes Mountains on the border with Chile; historically active volcanoes in this region are Irruputuncu (elev.5,163 m), which last erupted in 1995, and Olca-Paruma

Environment—current issues: the clearing of land for agricultural purposes and the international demand for tropical timber are contributing to deforestation; soil erosion from overgrazing and poor cultivation methods (including slash-and-burn agriculture); desertification; loss of biodiversity; industrial pollution of water supplies used for drinking and irrigation

Environment—international agreements: *party to:* Biodiversity, Climate Change, Climate Change-Kyoto Protocol, Desertification, Endangered Species, Hazardous Wastes, Law of the Sea, Marine Dumping, Ozone Layer Protection, Ship Pollution, Tropical Timber 83, Tropical Timber 94, Wetlands
signed, but not ratified: Environmental Modification, Marine Life Conservation

Geography—note: landlocked; shares control of Lago Titicaca, world's highest navigable lake (elevation 3,805 m), with Peru

PEOPLE AND SOCIETY

Nationality: *noun:* Bolivian(s)
adjective: Bolivian

Ethnic groups: mestizo (mixed white and Amerindian ancestry) 68%, indigenous 20%, white 5%, cholo/chola 2%, black 1%, other 1%, unspecified 3%; 44% of respondents indicated feeling part of some indigenous group, predominantly Quechua or Aymara
note: results among surveys vary based on the wording of the ethnicity question and the available

response choices; the 2001 national census did not provide "mestizo" as a response choice, resulting in a much higher proportion of respondents identifying themselves as belonging to one of the available indigenous ethnicity choices; the use of "mestizo" and "cholo" varies among response choices in surveys, with surveys using the terms interchangeably, providing one or the other as a response choice, or providing the two as separate response choices (2009 est.)

Languages: Spanish (official) 60.7%, Quechua (official) 21.2%, Aymara (official) 14.6%, foreign languages 2.4%, Guarani (official) 0.6%, other native languages 0.4%, none 0.1%
note: Bolivia's 2009 constitution designates Spanish and all indigenous languages as official; 36 indigenous languages are specified, including some that are extinct (2001 est.)

Religions: Roman Catholic 76.8%, Evangelical and Pentecostal 8.1%, Protestant 7.9%, other 1.7%, none 5.5% (2012 est.)

Demographic profile: Bolivia ranks at or near the bottom among Latin American countries in several areas of health and development, including poverty, education, fertility, malnutrition, mortality, and life expectancy. On the positive side, more children are being vaccinated and more pregnant women are getting prenatal care and having skilled health practitioners attend their births. Bolivia's income inequality is the highest in Latin America and one of the highest in the world. Public education is of poor quality, and educational opportunities are among the most unevenly distributed in Latin America, with girls and indigenous and rural children less likely to be literate or to complete primary school. The lack of access to education and family planning services helps to sustain Bolivia's high fertility rate—approximately three children per woman. Bolivia's lack of clean water and basic sanitation, especially in rural areas, contributes to health problems. Almost 7% of Bolivia's population lives abroad, primarily to work in Argentina, Brazil, Spain, and the United States. In recent years, more restrictive immigration policies in Europe and the United States have increased the flow of Bolivian emigrants to neighboring Argentina and Brazil.

Population: 10,800,882 (July 2015 est.)
country comparison to the world: 82

Age structure: 0–14 years: 32.85% (male 1,807,779/female 1,740,188)
15–24 years: 19.65% (male 1,074,697/female 1,047,575)
25–54 years: 36.69% (male 1,932,183/female 2,030,485)
55–64 years: 5.75% (male 288,621/female 332,824)
65 years and over: 5.06% (male 241,447/female 305,083) (2015 est.)

Dependency ratios:
total dependency ratio: 63.7%
youth dependency ratio: 53.1%

elderly dependency ratio: 10.6%
potential support ratio: 9.4% (2015 est.)

Median age: *total:* 23.7 years
male: 22.9 years
female: 24.4 years (2015 est.)
country comparison to the world: 163

Population growth rate: 1.56% (2015 est.)
country comparison to the world: 77

Birth rate: 22.76 births/1,000 population (2015 est.)
country comparison to the world: 71

Death rate: 6.52 deaths/1,000 population (2015 est.)
country comparison to the world: 148

Net migration rate: -0.62 migrant(s)/1,000 population (2015 est.)
country comparison to the world: 139

Urbanization: *urban population:* 68.5% of total population (2015)
rate of urbanization: 2.26% annual rate of change (2010–15 est.)

Major urban areas—population: Santa Cruz 2.107 million; LA PAZ (capital) 1.816 million; Cochabamba 1.24 million; Sucre (constitutional capital) 372,000 (2015)

Sex ratio: *at birth:* 1.05 male(s)/female
0–14 years: 1.04 male(s)/female
15–24 years: 1.03 male(s)/female
25–54 years: 0.95 male(s)/female
55–64 years: 0.87 male(s)/female
65 years and over: 0.79 male(s)/female
total population: 0.98 male(s)/female (2015 est.)

Mother's mean age at first birth: 21.2
note: median age at first birth among women 25–29 (2008 est.)

Maternal mortality rate: 206 deaths/100,000 live births (2015 est.)
country comparison to the world: 58

Infant mortality rate: *total:* 37.49 deaths/1,000 live births
male: 41.06 deaths/1,000 live births
female: 33.75 deaths/1,000 live births (2015 est.)
country comparison to the world: 58

Life expectancy at birth: *total* population: 68.86 years
male: 66.08 years
female: 71.78 years (2015 est.)
country comparison to the world: 161

Total fertility rate: 2.73 children born/woman (2015 est.)
country comparison to the world: 68

Contraceptive prevalence rate: 60.5% (2008)

Health expenditures: 6.1% of GDP (2013)
country comparison to the world: 122

Physicians density: 0.47 physicians/1,000 population (2011)

Hospital bed density: 1.1 beds/1,000 population (2012)

Drinking water source:
improved:
urban: 96.7% of population
rural: 75.6% of population
total: 90% of population
unimproved:
urban: 3.3% of population
rural: 24.4% of population

total: 10% of population (2015 est.)

Sanitation facility access:
improved:
urban: 60.8% of population
rural: 27.5% of population
total: 50.3% of population
unimproved:
urban: 39.2% of population
rural: 72.5% of population
total: 49.7% of population (2015 est.)

HIV/AIDS—adult prevalence rate: 0.29% (2014 est.)
country comparison to the world: 83

HIV/AIDS—people living with HIV/AIDS: 17,900 (2014 est.)
country comparison to the world: 80

HIV/AIDS—deaths: 700 (2014 est.)
country comparison to the world: 77

Major infectious diseases: *degree of risk:* very high
food or waterborne diseases: bacterial diarrhea and hepatitis A
vectorborne diseases: dengue fever, malaria, and yellow fever (2013)

Obesity—adult prevalence rate: 15.8% (2014)
country comparison to the world: 109

Children under the age of 5 years underweight: 4.5% (2008)
country comparison to the world: 95

Education expenditures: 7.3% of GDP (2014)
country comparison to the world: 24

Literacy: *definition:* age 15 and over can read and write
total population: 95.7%
male: 97.8%
female: 93.6% (2015 est.)

School life expectancy (primary to tertiary education): *total:* 14 years
male: 14 years
female: 14 years (2007)

Child labor—children ages 5–14: *total number:* 757,352
percentage: 26.4%
note: data represent children ages 5–17 (2008 est.)

Unemployment, youth ages 15–24: *total:* 6.2%
male: 5.1%
female: 7.8% (2011 est.)
country comparison to the world: 122

GOVERNMENT

Country name: *conventional long form:* Plurinational State of Bolivia
conventional short form: Bolivia local long form: Estado Plurinacional de Bolivia local short form: Bolivia
etymology: the country is named after Simon BOLIVAR, a 19th-century leader in the South American wars for independence

Government type: presidential republic

Capital: *name:* La Paz (administrative capital); Sucre (constitutional capital)

Geographic coordinates: 16 30 S, 68 09 W
time difference: UTC-4 (1 hour ahead of Washington, DC, during Standard Time)

Administrative divisions: 9 departments (departamentos, singular—departamento); Beni,

Chuquisaca, Cochabamba, La Paz, Oruro, Pando, Potosi, Santa Cruz, Tarija

Independence: 6 August 1825 (from Spain)

National holiday: Independence Day, 6 August (1825)

Constitution: many previous; latest drafted 6 August 2006—9 December 2008, approved by referendum 25 January 2009, effective 7 February 2009; amended 2013; note—inearly 2016, a proposed amendment allowing the president and vice-president to run for a third term was defeated in a referendum (2016)

Legal system: civil law system with influences from Roman, Spanish, canon (religious), French, and indigenous law

International law organization participation: has not submitted an ICJ jurisdiction declaration; accepts ICCt jurisdiction

Citizenship: *citizenship by birth:* yes
citizenship by descent: yes
dual citizenship recognized: yes
residency requirement for naturalization: 3 years

Suffrage: 18 years of age, universal and compulsory

Executive branch: *chief of state:* President Juan Evo MORALES Ayma (since 22 January 2006); Vice President Alvaro GARCIA Linera (since 22 January 2006); note—the president is both chief of state and head of government

head of government: President Juan Evo MORALES Ayma (since 22 January 2006); Vice President Alvaro GARCIA Linera (since 22 January 2006)
cabinet: Cabinet appointed by the president
elections/appointments: president and vice president directly elected on the same ballot by absolute majority popular vote in 2 rounds if needed for a 5-year term (eligible for a second term); election last held on 12 October 2014 (next to be held in 2019); note—a presidential candidate wins an election one of 3 ways
election results: Juan Evo MORALES Ayma reelected president; percent of vote—Juan Evo MORALES Ayma 61%; Samuel DORIA MEDINA Arana 24.5%; Jorge QUIROGA 9.1%; other 5.4%

Legislative branch: *description:* bicameral Plurinational Legislative Assembly or Asamblea Legislativa Plurinacional consists of the Chamber of Senators or Camara de Senadores (36 seats; members directly elected in multi-seat constituencies by proportional representation vote; members serve 5-year terms) and the Chamber of Deputies or Camara de Diputados (130 seats; 70 members directly elected in single-seat constituencies by simple majority vote, 53 indirectly elected in single-seat constituencies by proportional representation vote, and 7—apportioned to non-contiguous, rural areas in 7 of the 9 states—directly elected in single-seat constituencies by simple majority vote; members serve 5-year terms)
elections: Chamber of Senators and Chamber of Deputies—last held on 12 October 2014 (next to be held in 2019)
election results: Chamber of Senators—percent of vote by party—NA; seats by party—MAS 25,

UD 9, PDC 2; Chamber of Deputies—percent of vote by party—NA; seats by party—MAS 88, UD 32, PDC 10

Judicial branch: *highest court(s):* Supreme Court or Tribunal Supremo de Justicia (consists of 12 judges); Plurinational Constitutional Tribunal (consists of 7 primary and 7 alternate magistrates); Plurinational Electoral Organ (consists of 7 members)

judge selection and term of office: Supreme Court and Plurinational Constitutional Tribunal judges elected by popular vote from list of candidates pre-selected by Plurinational Legislative Assembly for 6-year terms); Plurinational Electoral Organ members—6 judges elected by the Assembly and 1 appointed by the president; judges and members serve 6-year terms; note—the 2009 constitution reformed the procedure for selecting judicial officials for the Supreme Court, Constitutional Tribunal, and the Plurinational Electoral Organ by direct national vote, which occurred in October 2011

subordinate courts: Agro-Environmental Court; Council of the Judiciary; District Courts (in each of the 9 administrative departments)

Political parties and leaders: Christian Democratic Party or PDC [Jorge Fernando QUIROGA Ramirez]

Movement Toward Socialism or MAS [Juan Evo MORALES Ayma]

United Democrats or UD [Samuel DORIA MEDINA Arana]

Political pressure groups and leaders: Bolivian Workers Central or COB

Federation of Neighborhood Councils of El Alto or FEJUVE

Landless Movement or MST

National Coordinator for Change or CONALCAM

Sole Confederation of Campesino Workers of Bolivia or CSUTCB

other: Cocalero groups; indigenous organizations (including Confederation of Indigenous Peoples of Eastern Bolivia or CIDOB and National Council of Ayullus and Markas of Quollasuyu or CONAMAQ); Interculturales union or CSCIB; labor unions (including the Central Bolivian Workers' Union or COB and Cooperative Miners Federation or FENCOMIN)

International organization participation: CAN, CD, CELAC, FAO, G-77, IADB, IAEA, IBRD, ICAO, ICC (national committees); ICCt, ICRM, IDA, IFAD, IFC, IFRCS, ILO, IMF, IMO, Interpol, IOC, IOM, IPU, ISO (correspondent), ITSO, ITU, LAES, LAIA, Mercosur (associate), MIGA, MINUSTAH, MONUSCO, NAM, OAS, OPANAL, OPCW, PCA, UN, UNAMID, UNASUR, UNCTAD, UNESCO, UNIDO, Union Latina, UNMIL, UNMISS, UNOCI, UNWTO, UPU, WCO, WFTU (NGOs), WHO, WIPO, WMO, WTO

Diplomatic representation in the US: *chief of mission:* Ambassador (vacant); Charge d'Affaires Freddy BERSATTI Tudela

chancery: 3014 Massachusetts Avenue NW, Washington, DC 20008

telephone: [1] (202) 328-4155

FAX: [1] (202) 328-3712

consulate(s) general: Houston, Los Angeles, Miami, New York, Washington, DC

note: as of September 2008, the US expelled the Bolivian ambassador to the US

Diplomatic representation from the US: *chief of mission:* Ambassador (vacant); Charge d'Affaires Peter Brennan (since June 2014

embassy: Avenida Arce 2780, Casilla 425, La Paz

mailing address: P.O . Box 425, La Paz; APO AA 34032

telephone: [591] (2) 216-8000

FAX: [591] (2) 216-8111

note: in September 2008, the Bolivian Government expelled the US Ambassador to Bolivia, and the countries have yet to reinstate ambassadors

Flag description: three equal horizontal bands of red (top), yellow, and green with the coat of arms centered on the yellow band; red stands for bravery and the blood of national heroes, yellow for the nation's mineral resources, and green for the fertility of the land

note: similar to the flag of Ghana, which has a large black five-pointed star centered in the yellow band; in 2009, a presidential decree made it mandatory for a so-called wiphala—a square, multicolored flag representing the country's indigenous peoples—to be used alongside the traditional flag

National symbol(s): llama, Andean condor; national colors: red, yellow, green

National anthem: *name:* "Cancion Patriotica" (Patriotic Song)

lyrics/music: Jose Ignacio de SANJINES/Leopoldo Benedetto VINCENTI

note: adopted 1852

ECONOMY

Economy—overview: Bolivia is a resource rich country with strong growth attributed to captive markets for natural gas exports—to Brazil and Argentina. Gas accounts for roughly 50% of Bolivia's *total* exports and will fund more than half of its 2015 budget. However, the country remains one of the least developed countries in Latin America because of state-oriented policies that deter investment and growth.

Following a disastrous economic crisis during the early 1980s, reforms spurred private investment, stimulated economic growth, and cut poverty rates in the 1990s. The period 2003–05 was characterized by political instability, racial tensions, and violent protests against plans—subsequently abandoned—to export Bolivia's newly discovered natural gas reserves to large Northern Hemisphere markets. In 2005, the government passed a controversial hydrocarbons law that imposed significantly higher royalties and required foreign firms then operating under risk-sharing contracts to surrender all production to the state energy company in exchange for a predetermined service fee. The global recession slowed growth, but Bolivia recorded the highest growth rate in South America during 2009 and has averaged 5.3% growth each year since 2009. High commodity prices between 2010 and 2013 sustained rapid growth and large trade surpluses. The global decline in oil prices in late 2014 exerted downward pressure on the price

Bolivia receives for exported gas and resulted in lower GDP growth rates and losses in government revenue in 2015. A lack of foreign investment in the key sectors of mining and hydrocarbons, along with conflict among social groups, pose challenges for the Bolivian economy. In 2015, President Evo MORALES expanded efforts to court international investment and boost Bolivia's energy production capacity. MORALES passed an investment law and promised not to nationalize additional industries in an effort to improve the investment climate.

GDP (purchasing power parity): $74.39 billion (2015 est.)

$70.98 billion (2014 est.)

$67.31 billion (2013 est.)

note: data are in 2015 US dollars

country comparison to the world: 95

GDP (official exchange rate): $33.21 billion (2015 est.)

GDP—real growth rate: 4.8% (2015 est.) 5.5% (2014 est.) 6.8% (2013 est.)

country comparison to the world: 44

GDP—per capita (PPP): $6,500 (2015 est.)

$6,300 (2014 est.)

$6,100 (2013 est.)

note: data are in 2015 US dollars

country comparison to the world: 156

Gross national saving: 13% of GDP (2015 est.)

20.5% of GDP (2014 est.)

23.9% of GDP (2013 est.)

country comparison to the world: 128

GDP—composition, by end use: *household consumption:* 63.2%

government consumption: 15%

investment in fixed capital: 19.9%

investment in inventories: 0.9%

exports of goods and services: 41.5%

imports of goods and services: -40.5% (2015 est.)

GDP—composition, by sector of origin:

agriculture: 13.2%

industry: 38.3%

services: 48.5% (2014 est.)

Agriculture—products: soybeans, quinoa, Brazil nuts, sugarcane, coffee, corn, rice, potatoes, chia, coca

Industries: mining, smelting, petroleum, food and beverages, tobacco, handicrafts, clothing, jewelry

Industrial production growth rate: 3.6% (2015 est.)

country comparison to the world: 68

Labor force: 4.962 million (2015 est.)

country comparison to the world: 83

Labor force—by occupation: *agriculture:* 32%

industry: 20%

services: 47.9% (2009 est.)

Unemployment rate: 7.4% (2015 est.)

7.3% (2014 est.)

note: data are for urban areas; widespread underemployment

country comparison to the world: 87

Population below poverty line: 45%

note: based on percent of population living on less than the international standard of $2/day (2011 est.)

Household income or consumption by percentage share: *lowest:* 10%: 0.8%

highest: 10%: 33.6% (2012 est.)
Distribution of family income—Gini index: 46.6 (2012)
57.9 (1999)
country comparison to the world: 32
Budget: *revenues:* $16.28 billion
expenditures: $18.04 billion (2015 est.)
Taxes and other revenues: 48.6% of GDP (2015 est.)
country comparison to the world: 17
Budget surplus (+) or deficit (–): -5.2% of GDP (2015 est.)
country comparison to the world: 174
Public debt: 37.5% of GDP (2015 est.)
35.8% of GDP (2014 est.)
note: data cover general government debt, and includes debt instruments issued by government entities other than the treasury; the data include treasury debt held by foreign entities; the data include debt issued by subnational entities
country comparison to the world: 123
Fiscal year: calendar year
Inflation rate (consumer prices): 4.1% (2015 est.)
5.8% (2014 est.)
country comparison to the world: 160
Central bank discount rate: 4.5% (31 December 2013)
4% (31 december 2012)
country comparison to the world: 84
Commercial bank prime lending rate: 8.5% (31 December 2015 est.)
9.69% (31 December 2014 est.)
country comparison to the world: 102
Stock of narrow money: $9.727 billion (31 December 2015 est.)
$8.386 billion (31 December 2014 est.)
country comparison to the world: 81
Stock of broad money: $20.19 billion (31 December 2015 est.)
$17.4 billion (31 December 2014 est.)
country comparison to the world: 89
Stock of domestic credit: $18.46 billion (31 December 2015 est.)
$14.55 billion (31 December 2014 est.)
country comparison to the world: 88
Market value of publicly traded shares: $9.684 billion (31 December 2013)
$7.689 billion (31 December 2012)
$6.089 billion (31 December 2011)
country comparison to the world: 75
Current account balance: -$2.286 billion (2015 est.)
$61 million (2014 est.)
country comparison to the world: 152
Exports: $9.591 billion (2015 est.)
$12.15 billion (2014 est.)
country comparison to the world: 92
Exports—commodities: natural gas, mineral ores, gold, soybeans and soy products, tin
Exports—partners: Brazil 28.1%, Argentina 16.9%, US 12.1%, Colombia 6.3%, China 5.3%, Japan 4.7%, South Korea 4.3% (2015)
Imports: $10.43 billion (2015 est.)
$9.935 billion (2014 est.)
country comparison to the world: 98

Imports—commodities: machinery, petroleum products, vehicles, iron and steel, plastics
Imports—partners: China 17.9%, Brazil 16.5%, Argentina 11.8%, US 10.6%, Peru 6.2%, Japan 5.2%, Chile 4.6% (2015)
Reserves of foreign exchange and gold: $14.68 billion (31 December 2015 est.)
$15.12 billion (31 December 2014 est.)
country comparison to the world: 70
Debt—external: $8.228 billion (31 December 2014 est.)
$7.895 billion (31 December 2013 est.)
country comparison to the world: 112
Stock of direct foreign investment—at home: $10.56 billion (31 December 2013)
$8.809 billion (31 December 2012)
country comparison to the world: 90
Stock of direct foreign investment—abroad: $0 (31 December 2013 est.)
$0 (31 December 2012 est.)
country comparison to the world: 104
Exchange rates: bolivianos (BOB) per US dollar—
6.91 (2015 est.)
6.91 (2014 est.)
6.91 (2013 est.)
6.94 (2012 est.)
6.9875 (2011 est.)

ENERGY

Electricity—production: 7.375 billion kWh (2013 est.)
country comparison to the world: 106
Electricity—consumption: 6.456 billion kWh (2012 est.)
country comparison to the world: 108
Electricity—exports: 0 kWh (2013 est.)
country comparison to the world: 109
Electricity—imports: 0 kWh (2013 est.)
country comparison to the world: 123
Electricity—installed generating capacity: 1.649 million kW (2012 est.)
country comparison to the world: 114
Electricity—from fossil fuels: 68.8% of total installed capacity (2012 est.)
country comparison to the world: 111
Electricity—from nuclear fuels: 0% of total installed capacity (2012 est.)
country comparison to the world: 54
Electricity—from hydroelectric plants: 30% of total installed capacity (2012 est.)
country comparison to the world: 76
Electricity—from other renewable sources: 1.3% of total installed capacity (2012 est.)
country comparison to the world: 90
Crude oil—production: 51,130 bbl/day (2014 est.)
country comparison to the world: 55
Crude oil—exports: 60.71 bbl/day (2013 est.)
country comparison to the world: 91
Crude oil—imports: 0 bbl/day (2013 est.)
country comparison to the world: 163
Crude oil—proved reserves: 209.8 million bbl (1 January 2015 est.)
country comparison to the world: 58
Refined petroleum products—production: 48,990 bbl/day (2012 est.)

country comparison to the world: 81
Refined petroleum products—consumption: 71,000 bbl/day (2013 est.)
country comparison to the world: 89
Refined petroleum products—exports: 0 bbl/day (2013 est.)
country comparison to the world: 158
Refined petroleum products—imports: 15,560 bbl/day (2013 est.)
country comparison to the world: 123
Natural gas—production: 20.8 billion cu m (2013 est.)
country comparison to the world: 31
Natural gas—consumption: 3.2 billion cu m (2013 est.)
country comparison to the world: 70
Natural gas—exports: 17.6 billion cu m (2013 est.)
country comparison to the world: 16
Natural gas—imports: 0 cu m (2013 est.)
country comparison to the world: 165
Natural gas—proved reserves: 281.5 billion cu m (1 January 2014 est.)
country comparison to the world: 40
Carbon dioxide emissions from consumption of energy: 17.28 million Mt (2012 est.)
country comparison to the world: 84

COMMUNICATIONS

Telephones—fixed lines: *total subscriptions:* 880,000
subscriptions per 100 inhabitants: 8 (2014 est.)
country comparison to the world: 83
Telephones—mobile cellular: *total:* 10.5 million
subscriptions per 100 inhabitants: 98 (2014 est.)
country comparison to the world: 84
Telephone system: *general assessment:* Bolivian National Telecommunications Company was privatized in 1995 but re-nationalized in 2007; the primary trunk system is being expanded and employs digital microwave radio relay; some areas are served by fiber-optic cable; system operations, reliability, and coverage have steadily improved
domestic: most telephones are concentrated in La Paz, Santa Cruz, and other capital cities; mobile-cellular telephone use expanding rapidly and, in 2011, teledensity reached about 80 per 100 persons
international: country code—591; satellite earth station—1 Intelsat (Atlantic Ocean) (2011)
Broadcast media: large number of radio and TV stations broadcasting with private media outlets dominating; state-owned and private radio and TV stations generally operating freely, although both pro-government and anti-government groups have attacked media outlets in response to their reporting (2010)
Radio broadcast stations: AM 171, FM 73, short-wave 77 (1999)
Television broadcast stations: 48 (1997)
Internet country code: .bo
Internet hosts: 180,988 (2012)
country comparison to the world: 75
Internet users: *total:* 3.9 million percent of population: 36.6% (2014 est.)
country comparison to the world: 78

TRANSPORTATION

Airports: 855 (2013)
country comparison to the world: 7
Airports—with paved runways: *total:* 21
over 3,047 m: 5
2,438 to 3,047 m: 4
1,524 to 2,437 m: 6
914 to 1,523 m: 6 (2013)
Airports—with unpaved runways: *total:* 834
over 3,047 m: 1
2,438 to 3,047 m: 4
1,524 to 2,437 m: 47
914 to 1,523 m: 151
under 914 m: 631 (2013)
Pipelines: gas 5,457 km; liquid petroleum gas 51 km; oil 2,511 km; refined products 1,627 km (2013)
Railways: *total:* 3,504 km
narrow gauge: 3,504 km 1.000-m gauge (2014)
country comparison to the world: 51
Roadways: *total:* 80,488 km
paved: 6,850 km
unpaved: 73,638 km (2010)
country comparison to the world: 59
Waterways: 10,000 km (commercially navigable almost exclusively in the northern and eastern parts of the country) (2012)
country comparison to the world: 13
Merchant marine: *total:* 18
by type: bulk carrier 1, cargo 14, petroleum tanker 1, roll on/roll off 2
foreign-owned: 5 (Syria 4, UK 1, (2010)
country comparison to the world: 98
Ports and terminals: *river port(s):* Puerto Aguirre (Paraguay/Parana)
note: Bolivia has free port privileges in maritime ports in Argentina, Brazil, Chile, and Paraguay

MILITARY AND SECURITY

Military branches: Bolivian Armed Forces: Bolivian Army (Ejercito Boliviano, EB), Bolivian Naval Force (Fuerza Naval Boliviana, FNB; includes Marines), Bolivian Air Force (Fuerza Aerea Boliviana, FAB) (2013)
Military service age and obligation: 18–49 years of age for 12-month compulsory male and female military service; Bolivian citizenship required; 17 years of age for voluntary service; when annual number of volunteers falls short of goal, compulsory recruitment is effected, including conscription of boys as young as 14; 15–19 years of age for voluntary premilitary service, provides exemption from further military service (2013)
Military expenditures: 1.47% of GDP (2012)
1.47% of GDP (2011)
1.47% of GDP (2010)
country comparison to the world: 64

TRANSNATIONAL ISSUES

Disputes—international: Chile and Peru rebuff Bolivia's reactivated claim to restore the Atacama corridor, ceded to Chile in 1884, but Chile offers instead unrestricted but not sovereign maritime access through Chile for Bolivian natural gas; contraband smuggling, human trafficking, and illegal narcotic trafficking are problems in the porous areas of the border with Argentina
Trafficking in persons: *current situation:* Bolivia is a source country for men, women, and children subjected to forced labor and sex trafficking domestically and abroad; indigenous children are particularly vulnerable; Bolivia is a source country for men, women, and children subjected to forced labor and sex trafficking domestically and abroad; rural and poor Bolivians, most of whom are indigenous, and LGBT youth are particularly vulnerable;

Bolivians perform forced labor domestically in mining, ranching, agriculture, and domestic service, and a significant number are in forced labor abroad in sweatshops, agriculture, domestic service, and the informal sector; women and girls are sex trafficked within Bolivia and in neighboring countries, such as Argentina, Peru, and Chile; a limited number of women from nearby countries are sex trafficked in Bolivia

tier rating: Tier 2 Watch List—Bolivia does not comply fully with the minimum standards for the elimination of human trafficking; however, it is making significant efforts to do so; the government did not demonstrate overall increasing anti-trafficking efforts, and poor data collection made it difficult to assess the number of investigations, prosecutions, and victim identifications and referrals to care services; authorities did not adequately differentiate between human trafficking and other crimes, such as domestic violence and child abuse; law enforcement failed to implement a nearly detection protocol for identifying trafficking cases and lacked a formal process for identifying trafficking victims among vulnerable populations; specialized victim services were inadequately funded and virtually non-existent for adult women and male victims (2015)

Illicit drugs: world's third-largest cultivator of coca (after Colombia and Peru) with an estimated 30,000 hectares under cultivation in 2011, a decrease of 13 percent over 2010; third largest producer of cocaine, estimated at 265 metric tons potential pure cocaine in 2011, a 29 percent increase over 2010; transit country for Peruvian and Colombian cocaine destined for Brazil, Argentina, Chile, Paraguay, and Europe; weak border controls; some money-laundering activity related to narcotics trade; major cocaine consumption (2013)

BOSNIA AND HERZEGOVINA

INTRODUCTION

Background: Bosnia and Herzegovina declared sovereignty in October 1991 and independence from the former Yugoslavia on 3 March 1992 after a referendum boycotted by ethnic Serbs. The Bosnian Serbs -supported by neighboring Serbia and Montenegro—responded with armed resistance aimed at partitioning the republic along ethnic lines and joining Serb-held areas to form a "Greater Serbia." In March 1994, Bosniaks and Croats reduced the number of warring factions from three to two by signing an agreement creating a joint Bosniak-Croat Federation of Bosnia and Herzegovina. On 21 November 1995, in Dayton, Ohio, the warring parties initialed a peace agreement that ended three years of interethnic civil strife (the final agreement was signed in Paris on 14 December 1995).
The Dayton Peace Accords retained Bosnia and Herzegovina's international boundaries and created a multiethnic and democratic government

charged with conducting foreign, diplomatic, and fiscal policy. Also recognized was a second tier of government composed of two entities roughly equal in size: the predominantly Bosniak-Bosnian Croat Federation of Bosnia and Herzegovina and the predominantly Bosnian Serb-led Republika Srpska (RS). The Federation and RS governments are responsible for overseeing most government functions. Additionally, the Dayton Accords established the Office of the High Representative to oversee the implementation of the civilian aspects of the agreement. The Peace Implementation Council at its conference in Bonn in 1997 also gave the High Representative the authority to impose legislation and remove officials, the so-called "Bonn Powers." An original NATO-led international peacekeeping force (IFOR) of 60,000 troops assembled in 1995 was succeeded over time by a smaller, NATO-led Stabilization Force (SFOR). In 2004, European Union peacekeeping troops (EUFOR) replaced SFOR. Currently,

EUFOR deploys around 600 troops in theater in a security assistance and training capacity.

GEOGRAPHY

Location: Southeastern Europe, bordering the Adriatic Sea and Croatia

Geographic coordinates: 44 00 N, 18 00 E

Map references: Europe

Area: *total:* 51,197 sq km
land: 51,187 sq km
water: 10 sq km
country comparison to the world: 129

Area—comparative: slightly smaller than West Virginia

Land boundaries: *total:* 1,543 km
border countries (3): Croatia 956 km, Montenegro 242 km, Serbia 345 km

Coastline: 20 km

Maritime claims: NA

Climate: hot summers and cold winters; areas of high elevation have short, cool summers and long, severe winters; mild, rainy winters along coast

Terrain: mountains and valleys

Elevation: *mean elevation:* 500 m

elevation extremes: *lowest:* point: Adriatic Sea 0 m
highest point: Maglic 2,386 m

Natural resources: coal, iron ore, bauxite, copper, lead, zinc, chromite, cobalt, manganese, nickel, clay, gypsum, salt, sand, timber, hydropower

Land use: *agricultural land:* 42.2%
arable land: 19.7%
permanent crops: 2%
permanent pasture: 20.5%
forest: 42.8%
other: 15% (2011 est.)

Irrigated land: 30 sq km (2012)

Total renewable water resources: 37.5 cu km (2011)

Natural hazards: destructive earthquakes

Environment—current issues: air pollution from metallurgical plants; sites for disposing of urban waste are limited; water shortages and destruction of infrastructure because of the 1992–95 civil strife; deforestation

Environment—international agreements: *party to:* Air Pollution, Biodiversity, Climate Change, Climate Change-Kyoto Protocol, Desertification, Hazardous Wastes, Law of the Sea, Marine Life Conservation, Ozone Layer Protection, Wetlands
signed, but not ratified: none of the selected agreements

Geography—note: within Bosnia and Herzegovina's recognized borders, the country is divided into a joint Bosniak/Croat Federation (about 51% of the territory) and the Bosnian Serb-led Republika Srpska or RS (about 49% of the territory); the region called Herzegovina is contiguous to Croatia and Montenegro, and traditionally has been settled by an ethnic Croat majority in the west and an ethnic Serb majority in the east

PEOPLE AND SOCIETY

Nationality: *noun:* Bosnian(s), Herzegovinian(s)
adjective: Bosnian, Herzegovinian

Ethnic groups: Bosniak 50.1%, Serb 30.8%, Croat 15.4%, other 2.7%
note: the methodology remains disputed and Republika Srspka authorities refuse to recognize the results; Bosniak has replaced Muslim as an ethnic term in part to avoid confusion with the religious term Muslim—an adherent of Islam (2013 est.)

Languages: Bosnian (official), Croatian (official), Serbian (official)

Religions: Muslim 40%, Orthodox 31%, Roman Catholic 15%, other 14%

Population: 3,867,055 (July 2015 est.)
country comparison to the world: 129

Age structure: *0–14 years:* 13.48% (male 269,086/female 252,189)
15–24 years: 12.36% (male 246,849/female 231,007)
25–54 years: 46.48% (male 902,704/female 894,787)
55–64 years: 14.01% (male 259,579/female 282,371)
65 years and over: 13.67% (male 206,288/female 322,195) (2015 est.)

Dependency ratios: *total* dependency ratio: 40.7%
youth dependency ratio: 19%
elderly dependency ratio: 21.7%
potential support ratio: 4.6% (2015 est.)

Median age: *total:* 41.2 years
male: 39.8 years
female: 42.6 years (2015 est.)
country comparison to the world: 35

Population growth rate: -0.13% (2015 est.)
country comparison to the world: 207

Birth rate: 8.87 births/1,000 population (2015 est.)
country comparison to the world: 212

Death rate: 9.75 deaths/1,000 population (2015 est.)
country comparison to the world: 48

Net migration rate: -0.38 migrant(s)/1,000 population (2015 est.)
country comparison to the world: 131

Urbanization: *urban population:* 39.8% of *total* population (2015)
rate of urbanization: 0.14% annual rate of change (2010–15 est.)

Major urban areas—population: SARAJEVO (capital) 318,000 (2015)

Sex ratio: *at birth:* 1.07 male(s)/female
0–14 years: 1.07 male(s)/female
15–24 years: 1.07 male(s)/female
25–54 years: 1.01 male(s)/female
55–64 years: 0.92 male(s)/female
65 years and over: 0.64 male(s)/female
total population: 0.95 male(s)/female (2015 est.)

Mother's mean age at first birth: 26.3 (2011 est.)

Maternal mortality rate: 11 deaths/100,000 live births (2015 est.)
country comparison to the world: 157

Infant mortality rate: *total:* 5.72 deaths/1,000 live births
male: 5.79 deaths/1,000 live births
female: 5.64 deaths/1,000 live births (2015 est.)
country comparison to the world: 169

Life expectancy at birth: *total population:* 76.55 years

male: 73.54 years
female: 79.77 years (2015 est.)
country comparison to the world: 85

Total fertility rate: 1.27 children born/woman (2015 est.)
country comparison to the world: 218

Contraceptive prevalence rate: 45.8% (2011/12)

Health expenditures: 9.6% of GDP (2013)
country comparison to the world: 24

Physicians density: 1.93 physicians/1,000 population (2013)

Hospital bed density: 3.5 beds/1,000 population (2010)

Drinking water source:
improved:
urban: 99.7% of population
rural: 100% of population
total: 99.9% of population
unimproved:
urban: 0.3% of population
rural: 0% of population
total: 0.1% of population (2015 est.)

Sanitation facility access:
improved:
urban: 98.9% of population
rural: 92% of population
total: 94.8% of population
unimproved:
urban: 1.1% of population
rural: 8% of population
total: 5.2% of population (2015 est.)

HIV/AIDS—adult prevalence rate: NA

HIV/AIDS—people living with HIV/AIDS: NA

HIV/AIDS—deaths: NA

Obesity—adult prevalence rate: 19.2% (2014)
country comparison to the world: 47

Children under the age of 5 years underweight: 1.5% (2012)
country comparison to the world: 127

Education expenditures: NA

Literacy: *definition:* age 15 and over can read and write
total population: 98.5%
male: 99.5%
female: 97.5% (2015 est.)

School life expectancy (primary to tertiary education): *total:* 14 years
male: 14 years
female: 15 years (2014)

Child labor—children ages 5–14: *total number:* 24,722
percentage: 5% (2006 est.)

Unemployment, youth ages 15–24: *total:* 62.8%
male: 62.8%
female: 62.8% (2012 est.)
country comparison to the world: 1

GOVERNMENT

Country name: *conventional long form:* none
conventional short form: Bosnia and Herzegovina
local long form: none
local short form: Bosna i Hercegovina
former: People's Republic of Bosnia and Herzegovina, Socialist Republic of Bosnia and Herzegovina
abbreviation: BiH
etymology: the larger northern territory is named for the Bosna River; the smaller southern section

takes its name from the German word "herzog," meaning "duke," and the ending "-ovina," meaning "land," forming the combination denoting "dukedom"

Government type: parliamentary republic

Capital: *name:* Sarajevo

Geographic coordinates: 43 52 N, 18 25 E

time difference: UTC + 1 (6 hours ahead of Washington, DC, during Standard Time)

daylight saving time: +1hr, begins last Sunday in March; ends last Sunday in October

Administrative divisions: 2 first-order administrative divisions and 1 internationally supervised district*—the Federation of Bosnia and Herzegovina (Federacija Bosne i Hercegovine) (predominantly Bosniak-Croat), the Republika Srpska (predominately Serb), Brcko District (Brcko Distrikt)*; note—Brcko District is in northeastern Bosnia and is a self-governing administrative unit under the sovereignty of Bosnia and Herzegovina and formally held in condominium between the two entities

Independence: 1 March 1992 (from Yugoslavia); note—referendum for independence completed on 1 March 1992; independence declared on 3 March 1992

National holiday: National Day (Statehood Day), 25 November (1943); Independence Day, 1 March (1992); note—observed only in the Federation of Bosnia and Herzegovina Dayton Agreement Day, 21 November (2007); note—observed only in the Republika Srpska

note: there is no national-level holiday

Constitution: 14 December 1995 (constitution included as part of the Dayton Peace Accords); amended several times, last in 2009; note—each of the entities has its own constitution (2016)

Legal system: civil law system; Constitutional Court review of legislative acts

International law organization participation: has not submitted an ICJ jurisdiction declaration; accepts ICCt jurisdiction

Citizenship: *citizenship by birth:* no

citizenship by descent only: at least one parent must be a citizen of Bosnia and Herzegovina

dual citizenship recognized: yes, provided there is a bilateral agreement with the other state

residency requirement for naturalization: 8 years

Suffrage: 18 years of age, 16 if employed; universal

Executive branch: *chief of state:* Chairman of the Presidency Bakir IZETBEGOVIC (chairman since 17 March 2016, presidency member since 10 November 2010—Bosniak); Dragan COVIC (presidency member since 17 November 2014—Croat); Mladen IVANIC (presidency member since 17 November 2014—Serb)

head of government: Chairman of the Council of Ministers Denis ZVIZDIC (since 11 February 2015)

cabinet: Council of Ministers nominated by the council chairman, approved by the state-level House of Representatives

elections/appointments: 3-member presidency (1 Bosniak and 1 Croat elected from the Federation of Bosnia and Herzegovina and 1 Serb elected from

the Republika Srpska) directly elected by simple majority popular vote for a 4-year term (eligible for a second term, but then ineligible for 4 years); the presidency chairpersonship rotates every 8 months and resumes where it left off following each general election; election last held on 12 October 2014 (next to be held in October 2018); the chairman of the Council of Ministers appointed by the presidency and confirmed by the state-level House of Representatives

election results: percent of vote—Mladen IVANIC 48.7%—Serb seat; Dragan COVIC 52.2%—Croat seat; Bakir IZETBEGOVIC 32.9%—Bosniak seat

note: President of the Federation of Bosnia and Herzegovina Marinko CAVARA (since 11 February 2015); Vice Presidents Melika MAHMUT-BEGOVIC (since 11 February 2015), Milan DUNOVIC (since 11 February 2015); President of the Republika Srpska Milorad DODIK (since 15 November 2010); Vice Presidents Ramiz SAL-KIC (since 24 November 2014), Josip JERKOVIC (since 24 November 2014)

Legislative branch: *description:* bicameral Parliamentary Assembly or Skupstina consists of the House of Peoples or Dom Naroda (15 seats—5 Bosniak, 5 Croat, 5 Serb; members designated by the Federation of Bosnia and Herzegovina's House of Peoples and the Republika Srpska's National Assembly to serve 4-year terms) and the state-level House of Representatives or Predstavnicki Dom (42 seats to include 28 seats allocated to the Federation of Bosnia and Herzegovina and 14 to the Republika Srpska; members directly elected by proportional representation vote to serve 4-year terms); note—the Federation of Bosnia and Herzegovina has a bicameral legislature that consists of the House of Peoples (58 seats—17 Bosniak, 17 Croat, 17 Serb, 7 other) and the House of Representatives (98 seats; members directly elected by proportional representation vote to serve 4-year terms); Republika Srpska's unicameral legislature is the National Assembly (83 directly elected delegates serve 4-year terms)

elections: House of Peoples—last constituted in 11 February 2015 (next likely to be constituted in 2019); state-level House of Representatives—election last held on 12 October 2014 (next to be held in October 2018)

election results: House of Peoples—percent of vote by party/coalition—NA; seats by party/coalition-NA; state-level House of Representatives—percent of vote by party/coalition—Federation votes: SDA 27.9%, DF 15.3%, SBB BiH 14.4%, Croat People's Assembly coalition or HNS (HDZ BiH-HSS-NHI-HKDU-HSP BiH-HSP HB) 12.2%, SDP 9.5%, HDZ-1990 4.1%, BPS-Sefer Halilovic 3.7%, A-SDA 2.3%, other 10.6%; Republika Srpska votes: SNSD 38.5%, SDS 32.6%, PDP-NDP 7.8%, DNS 5.7%, SDA 4.9%, other 10.5%; seats by party/coalition—SDA 10, SNSD 6, SDS 5, DF 5, SBB BiH 4, Croat People's Assembly coalition or HNS (HDZ BiH-HSS-NHI-HKDU-HSP BiH-HSP HB) 4, SDP 3, PDP-NDP 1, HDZ-1990 1, BPS-Sefer Halilovic 1, DNS 1, A-SDA 1

Judicial branch: *highest court(s):* BiH Constitutional Court (consists of 9 members); Court of BiH

(consists of 44 national judges and 7 international judges organized into 3 divisions—Administrative, Appellate, and Criminal, which includes a War Crimes Chamber)

judge selection and term of office: BiH Constitutional Court judges—4 selected by the Bosniak/Croat Federation's House of Representatives, 2 selected by the Republika Srpska's National Assembly, and 3 non-Bosnian judges selected by the president of the European Court of Human Rights; Court of BiH president and national judges appointed by the High Judicial and Prosecutorial Council; Court of BiH president appointed for renewable 6-year term; other national judges appointed to serve until age 70; international judges recommended by the president of the Court of BiH and appointed by the High Representative for Bosnia and Herzegovina; international judges appointed to serve until age 70

subordinate courts: the Federation has 10 cantonal courts plus a number of municipal courts; the Republika Srpska has a supreme court, 5 district courts, and a number of municipal courts

Political parties and leaders: Alliance for a Better Future of BiH or SBB BiH [Fahrudin RADONCIC]
Alliance of Independent Social Democrats or SNSD [Milorad DODIK]
Alternative Party for Democratic Activity or A-SDA [Nermin OGRESEVIC]
Bosnian-Herzegovinian Patriotic Party-Sefer Halilovic or BPS-Sefer Halilovic [Sefer HALILOVIC]
Croat Peasants' Party or HSS [Mario KARAMATIC]
Croatian Christian Democratic Union of Bosnia and Herzegovina or HKDU [Ivan MUSA]
Croatian Democratic Union of Bosnia and Herzegovina or HDZ-BiH [Dragan COVIC]
Croatian Democratic Union 1990 or HDZ-1990 [acting president Ilija CVITANOVIC]
Croatian Party of Rights or HSP BiH [Stanko PRIMORAC]
Croatian Party of Rights of Herceg-Bosne or HSP HB [Vesna PINJUH]
Croatian People's Party-Liberal Democrats or HNS [Ivan VRDOLJAK]
Democratic Front of DF [Zeljko KOMSIC]
Democratic Peoples' Alliance or DNS [Marko PAVIC]
Party for Democratic Action or SDA [Bakir IZETBEGOVIC]
Party of Democratic Progress or PDP [Branislav BORENOVIC]
People's Democratic Movement or NDP [Dragan CAVIC]
Serb Democratic Party or SDS [Mladen BOSIC]
Social Democratic Party or SDP [Nermin NIKSIC]

Political pressure groups and leaders:

other: war veterans; displaced persons associations; family associations of missing persons; private media

International organization participation: BIS, CD, CE, CEI, EAPC, EBRD, FAO, G-77, IAEA, IBRD, ICAO, ICC (NGOs), ICCt, ICRM, IDA, IFAD, IFC, IFRCS, ILO, IMF, IMO, IMSO, Interpol, IOC, IOM, IPU, ISO, ITSO, ITU, ITUC (NGOs), MIGA, MINUSMA, MONUSCO, NAM (observer), OAS (observer), OIC (observer), OIF (observer), OPCW, OSCE, PFP, SELEC, UN, UNCTAD, UNESCO, UNIDO, UNWTO, UPU, WCO, WHO, WIPO, WMO, WTO (observer)

Diplomatic representation in the US: *chief of mission:* Ambassador Haris HRLE (since 23 October 2015)

chancery: 2109 E Street NW, Washington, DC 20037

telephone: [1] (202) 337-1500

FAX: [1] (202) 337-1502

consulate(s) general: Chicago, New York

Diplomatic representation from the US: *chief of mission:* Ambassador Maureen CORMACK (since 16 January 2015)

embassy: 1 Robert C. Frasure Street, 71000 Sarajevo

mailing address: use embassy street address

telephone: [387] (33) 704-000

FAX: [387] (33) 659-722

branch office(s): Banja Luka, Mostar

Flag description: a wide medium blue vertical band on the fly side with a yellow isosceles triangle abutting the band and the top of the flag; the remainder of the flag is medium blue with seven full five-pointed white stars and two half stars top and bottom along the hypotenuse of the triangle; the triangle approximates the shape of the country and its three points stand for the constituent peoples—Bosniaks, Croats, and Serbs; the stars represent Europe and are meant to be continuous (thus the half stars at top and bottom); the colors (white, blue, and yellow) are often associated with neutrality and peace, and traditionally are linked with Bosnia

note: one of several flags where a prominent component of the design reflects the shape of the country; other such flags are those of Brazil, Eritrea, and Vanuatu

National symbol(s): golden lily; national colors: blue, yellow, white

National anthem: *name:* "Drzavna himna Bosne i Hercegovine" (The National Anthem of Bosnia and Herzegovina)

lyrics/music: none officially; Dusan SESTIC and Benjamin ISOVIC/Dusan SESTIC

note: music adopted 1999; lyrics accepted 2009 but not yet approved

ECONOMY

Economy—overview: Bosnia has a transitional economy with limited market reforms. The economy relies heavily on the export of metals, energy, textiles, and furniture as well as on remittances and foreign aid. A highly decentralized government hampers economic policy coordination and reform, while excessive bureaucracy and a segmented market discourage foreign investment. Foreign banks, primarily from Austria and Italy, now control most of the banking sector. The konvertibilna marka (convertible mark or BAM)—the national currency introduced in 1998—is pegged to the euro, and confidence in the currency and the banking sector has remained stable. Interethnic warfare in Bosnia and Herzegovina caused production to plummet by 80% from 1992 to 1995

and unemployment to soar, but the economy made progress until 2008, when the global economic crisis caused a downturn. Bosnia and Herzegovina became a full member of the Central European Free Trade Agreement in September 2007.

Bosnia's private sector is growing slowly, but foreign investment has dropped sharply since 2007. Government spending—including transfer payments—remains high, at roughly 40% of GDP, because of redundant government offices at the national, sub-national, and municipal level. High unemployment remains the most serious macroeconomic problem. Successful implementation of a value-added tax in 2006 provided a steady source of revenue for the government and helped rein in gray-market activity. National-level statistics have also improved over time but a large share of economic activity remains un official and unrecorded. Bosnia and Herzegovina's top economic priorities are: acceleration of integration into the EU; strengthening the fiscal system; public administration reform; World Trade Organization membership; and securing economic growth by fostering a dynamic, competitive private sector.

GDP (purchasing power parity): $40.53 billion (2015 est.)

$39.43 billion (2014 est.)

$39.01 billion (2013 est.)

note: data are in 2015 US dollars

country comparison to the world: 113

GDP (official exchange rate): $15.79 billion (2015 est.)

GDP—real growth rate: 2.8% (2015 est.)

1.1% (2014 est.)

2.4% (2013 est.)

country comparison to the world: 107

GDP—per capita (PPP): $10,500 (2015 est.)

$10,200 (2014 est.)

$10,100 (2013 est.)

note: data are in 2015 US dollars

country comparison to the world: 136

Gross national saving: 10.4% of GDP (2015 est.)

10% of GDP (2014 est.)

11.5% of GDP (2013 est.)

country comparison to the world: 150

GDP—composition, by end use:

household consumption: 81.2%

government consumption: 21.6%

investment in fixed capital: 18.3%

investment in inventories: 1.3%

exports of goods and services: 32.8%

imports of goods and services: -55.1% (2014 est.)

GDP—composition, by sector of origin:

agriculture: 7.9%

indu try: 26.5%

services: 65.6% (2014 est.)

Agriculture—products: wheat, corn, fruits, vegetables; livestock

Industries: steel, coal, iron ore, lead, zinc, manganese, bauxite, aluminum, motor vehicle assembly, textiles, tobacco products, wooden furniture, ammunition, domestic appliances, oil refining

Industrial production growth rate: 2.6% (2015 est.)

country comparison to the world: 99

Labor force: 1.47 million (2015 est.)

country comparison to the world: 132

Labor force—by occupation: *agriculture:* 19%

industry: 30%

services: 51% (2013)

Unemployment rate: 43.9% (2014 est.)

43.9% (2014 est.)

note: official rate; actual rate is lower as many technically unemployed persons work in the gray economy

country comparison to the world: 198

Population below poverty line: 17.2% (2011 est.)

Household income or consumption by percentage share: *lowest:* 10%: 2.7%

highest: 10%: 27.3% (2007)

Distribution of family income—Gini index: 36.2 (2007)

country comparison to the world: 87

Budget: *revenues:* $7.204 billion

expenditures: $7.565 billion (2015 est.)

Taxes and other revenues: 46.3% of GDP (2015 est.)

country comparison to the world: 21

Budget surplus (+) or deficit (–): -2.3% of GDP (2015 est.)

country comparison to the world: 85

Public debt: 46.1% of GDP (2015 est.)

44.8% of GDP (2014 est.)

note: data cover general government debt and include debt instruments issued (or owned) by government entities other than the treasury; the data include treasury debt held by foreign entities; the data include debt issued by subnational entities, as well as intra-governmental debt; intra-governmental debt consists of treasury borrowings from surpluses in the social funds, such as for retirement, medical care, and unemployment; debt instruments for the social funds are not sold at public auctions

country comparison to the world: 93

Fiscal year: calendar year

Inflation rate (consumer prices): -1% (2015 est.)

-0.9% (2014 est.)

country comparison to the world: 12

Commercial bank prime lending rate: 5.9% (31 December 2015 est.)

6.64% (31 December 2014 est.)

country comparison to the world: 134

Stock of narrow money: $3.948 billion (31 December 2015 est.)

$4.538 billion (31 December 2014 est.)

country comparison to the world: 109

Stock of broad money: $9.223 billion (31 December 2015 est.)

$10.72 billion (31 December 2014 est.)

country comparison to the world: 109

Stock of domestic credit: $8.717 billion (31 December 2015 est.)

$10.48 billion (31 December 2014 est.)

country comparison to the world: 107

Market value of publicly traded shares: $NA

Current account balance: -$1.078 billion (2015 est.)

-$1.45 billion (2014 est.)

country comparison to the world: 126

Exports: $3.942 billion (2015 est.)

$4.49 billion (2014 est.)

country comparison to the world: 119

Exports—commodities: metals, clothing, wood products

Exports—partners: Slovenia 16.5%, Italy 15.9%, Germany 12.1%, Croatia 11.5%, Austria 11.1%, Turkey 5.2% (2015)

Imports: $8.784 billion (2015 est.)
$9.982 billion (2014 est.)
country comparison to the world: 105

Imports—commodities: machinery and equipment, chemicals, fuels, foodstuffs

Imports—partners: Croatia 19.2%, Germany 13.8%, Slovenia 13.8%, Italy 10.9%, Austria 5.7%, Hungary 5.2%, Turkey 4.5% (2015)

Reserves of foreign exchange and gold: $4.625 billion (31 December 2015 est.)
$4.744 billion (31 December 2014 est.)
country comparison to the world: 96

Debt—external: $11.2 billion (31 December 2014 est.)
$11.08 billion (31 December 2013 est.)
country comparison to the world: 103

Stock of direct foreign investment—at home: $7.92 billion (2014 est.)
$7.721 billion (2013 est.)
country comparison to the world: 94

Stock of direct foreign investment—abroad: $0 (2014)
country comparison to the world: 105

Exchange rates: konvertibilna markas (BAM) per US dollar—
1.823 (2015 est.)
1.4718 (2014 est.)
1.4718 (2013 est.)
1.52 (2012 est.)
1.407 (2011 est.)

ENERGY

Electricity—production: 16.3 billion kWh (2013 est.)
country comparison to the world: 81

Electricity—consumption: 12.56 billion kWh (2013 est.)
country comparison to the world: 84

Electricity—exports: 5.097 billion kWh (2013 est.)
country comparison to the world: 32

Electricity—imports: 1.353 billion kWh (2013 est.)
country comparison to the world: 57

Electricity—installed generating capacity: 4.3 million kW (2013 est.)
country comparison to the world: 78

Electricity—from fossil fuels: 54.8% of total installed capacity (2013 est.)
country comparison to the world: 142

Electricity—from nuclear fuels: 0% of total installed capacity (2013 est.)
country comparison to the world: 53

Electricity—from hydroelectric plants: 43.6% of total installed capacity (2013 est.)
country comparison to the world: 55

Electricity—from other renewable sources: 1.5% of total installed capacity (2013 est.)
country comparison to the world: 86

Crude oil—production: 0 bbl/day (2014 est.)
country comparison to the world: 111

Crude oil—exports: 0 bbl/day (2013 est.)
country comparison to the world: 101

Crude oil—imports: 20,040 bbl/day (2012 est.)
country comparison to the world: 69

Crude oil—proved reserves: 0 bbl (1 January 2015 est.)
country comparison to the world: 110

Refined petroleum products—production: 22,690 bbl/day (2012 est.)
country comparison to the world: 92

Refined petroleum products—consumption: 34,000 bbl/day (2013 est.)
country comparison to the world: 112

Refined petroleum products—exports: 4,255 bbl/day (2012 est.)
country comparison to the world: 98

Refined petroleum products—imports: 15,250 bbl/day (2012 est.)
country comparison to the world: 124

Natural gas—production: 0 cu m (2014 est.)
country comparison to the world: 161

Natural gas—consumption: 275 million cu m (2014 est.)
country comparison to the world: 103

Natural gas—exports: 0 cu m (2014 est.)
country comparison to the world: 66

Natural gas—imports: 275 million cu m (2014 est.)
country comparison to the world: 69

Natural gas—proved reserves: 0 cu m (1 January 2014 est.)
country comparison to the world: 116

Carbon dioxide emissions from consumption of energy: 26 million Mt (2012 est.)
country comparison to the world: 77

COMMUNICATIONS

Telephones—fixed lines: *total subscriptions:* 850,000
subscriptions per 100 inhabitants: 22 (2014 est.)
country comparison to the world: 84

Telephones—mobile cellular: *total:* 3.5 million
subscriptions per 100 inhabitants: 90 (2014 est.)
country comparison to the world: 129

Telephone system: *general assessment:* postwar reconstruction of the telecommunications network, aided by an internationally sponsored program, resulted in sharp increases in fixed-line telephone availability
domestic: fixed-line teledensity roughly 25 per 100 persons; mobile-cellular subscribership has been increasing rapidly and stands at roughly 80 telephones per 100 persons
international: country code—387; no satellite earth stations (2011)

Broadcast media: 3 public TV broadcasters: Radio and TV of Bosnia and Herzegovina, Federation TV (operating 2 networks), and Republika Srpska Radio-TV; a local commercial network of 5 TV stations; 3 private, near-national TV stations and dozens of small independent TV broadcasting stations; 3 large public radio broadcasters and many private radio stations (2010)
Radio broadcast stations: AM 8, FM 16, shortwave 1 (1998)
Television broadcast stations: 33 (1995)

Internet country code: .ba

Internet hosts: 155,252 (2012)
country comparison to the world: 77

Internet users: *total:* 2.6 million

percent of population: 67.5% (2014 est.)
country comparison to the world: 89

TRANSPORTATION

Airports: 24 (2013)
country comparison to the world: 130

Airports—with paved runways: *total:* 7
2,438 to 3,047 m: 4
1,524 to 2,437 m: 1
under 914 m: 2 (2013)

Airports—with unpaved runways: *total:* 17
1,524 to 2,437 m: 1
914 to 1,523 m: 5
under 914 m: 11 (2013)

Heliports: 6 (2013)

Pipelines: gas 147 km; oil 9 km (2013)

Railways: *total:* 965 km
standard gauge: 965 km 1.435-m gauge (565 km electrified) (2014)
country comparison to the world: 88

Roadways: *total:* 22,926 km
paved: 19,426 km (4,652 km of interurban roads)
unpaved: 3,500 km (2010)
country comparison to the world: 102

Waterways: (Sava River on northern border; open to shipping but use limited) (2011)

Ports and terminals: *river port(s):* Bosanska Gradiska, Bosanski Brod, Bosanski Samac, Brcko, Orasje (Sava River)

MILITARY AND SECURITY

Military branches: Armed Forces of Bosnia and Herzegovina (Oruzanih Snaga Bosne i Hercegovine, OSBiH): Army of Bosnia and Herzegovina, Air Force and Air Defense (Brigada Zracnih Snaga i Protuzracne Odbrane, br ZSiPZO), Tactical Support Brigade (Brigada Takticke Podrske, br TP) (2015)

Military service age and obligation: 18 years of age for voluntary military service; mandatory retirement at age 35 or after 15 years of service for E-1 through E-4, mandatory retirement at age 50 and 30 years of service for E-5 through E-9, mandatory retirement at age 55 and 30 years of service for all officers (2014)

Military expenditures: 0.98% of GDP (2014)
1.04% of GDP (2013)
1.35% of GDP (2012)
1.15% of GDP (2011)
1.35% of GDP (2010)
country comparison to the world: 75

TRANSNATIONAL ISSUES

Disputes—international: Serbia delimited about half of the boundary with Bosnia and Herzegovina, but sections along the Drina River remain in dispute

Refugees and internally displaced persons: *refugees (country of origin):* 6,703 (Croatia) (2014)
IDPs: 98,324 (Bosnian Croats, Serbs, and Bosniaks displaced by inter-ethnic violence, human rights violations, and armed conflict during the 1992–1995 war) (2015)
stateless persons: 58 (2015)

Illicit drugs: increasingly a transit point for heroin being trafficked to Western Europe; minor transit point for marijuana; remains highly vulnerable to money-laundering activity given a primarily cash-based and unregulated economy, weak law enforcement, and instances of corruption

BOTSWANA

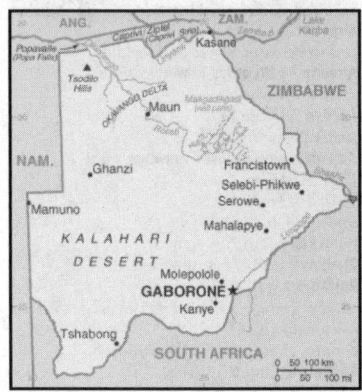

INTRODUCTION

Background: Formerly the British protectorate of Bechuanaland, Botswana adopted its new name at independence in 1966. More than four decades of uninterrupted civilian leadership, progressive social policies, and significant capital investment have created one of the most stable economies in Africa. The ruling Botswana Democratic Party has won every election since independence; President Ian KHAMA was reelected for a second term in 2014. Mineral extraction, principally diamond mining, dominates economic activity, though tourism is a growing sector due to the country's conservation practices and extensive nature preserves. Botswana has one of the world's highest known rates of HIV/AIDS infection, but also one of Africa's most progressive and comprehensive programs for dealing with the disease.

GEOGRAPHY

Location: Southern Africa, north of South Africa

Geographic coordinates: 22 00 S, 24 00 E

Map references: Africa

Area: *total:* 581,730 sq km
land: 566,730 sq km
water: 15,000 sq km
country comparison to the world: 48

Area—comparative: slightly smaller than Texas

Land boundaries: *total:* 4,347.15 km
border countries (4): Namibia 1,544 km, South Africa 1,969 km, Zambia 0.15 km, Zimbabwe 834 km

Coastline: 0 km (landlocked)

Maritime claims: none (landlocked)

Climate: semiarid; warm winters and hot summers

Terrain: predominantly flat to gently rolling tableland; Kalahari Desert in southwest

Elevation: *mean elevation:* 1,013 m

elevation extremes: *lowest:* point: junction of the Limpopo and Shashe Rivers 513 m
highest point: Tsodilo Hills 1,489 m

Natural resources: diamonds, copper, nickel, salt, soda ash, potash, coal, iron ore, silver

Land use: *agricultural land:* 45.8%
arable land: 0.6%
permanent crops: 0%
permanent pasture: 45.2%
forest: 19.8%
other: 34.4% (2011 est.)

Irrigated land: 20 sq km (2012)

Total renewable water resources: 12.24 cu km (2011)

Freshwater withdrawal (domestic/industrial/agricultural): *total:* 0.19 cu km/yr (42%/19%/39%)
per capita: 107.3 cu m/yr (2005)

Natural hazards: periodic droughts; seasonal August winds blow from the west, carrying sand and dust across the country, which can obscure visibility

Environment—current issues: overgrazing; desertification; limited freshwater resources

Environment—international agreements: *party to:* Biodiversity, Climate Change, Climate Change-Kyoto Protocol, Desertification, Endangered Species, Hazardous Wastes, Law of the Sea, Ozone Layer Protection, Wetlands
signed, but not ratified: none of the selected agreements

Geography—note: landlocked; population concentrated in eastern part of the country

PEOPLE AND SOCIETY

Nationality: *noun:* Motswana (singular), Batswana (plural)
adjective: Motswana (singular), Batswana (plural)

Ethnic groups: Tswana (or Setswana) 79%, Kalanga 11%, Basarwa 3%, other, including Kgalagadi and white 7%

Languages: Setswana 77.3%, Sekalanga 7.4%, Shekgalagadi 3.4%, English (official) 2.8%, Zezuru/Shona 2%, Sesarwa 1.7%, Sembukushu 1.6%, Ndebele 1%, other 2.8% (2011 est.)

Religions: Christian 79.1%, Badimo 4.1%, other 1.4% (includes Baha'i, Hindu, Muslim, Rastafarian), none 15.2%, unspecified 0.3% (2011 est.)

Population: 2,182,719
note: estimates for this country explicitly take into account the effects of excess mortality due to AIDS; this can result in lower life expectancy, higher infant mortality, higher death rates, lower population growth rates, and changes in the distribution of population by age and sex than would otherwise be expected (July 2015 est.)
country comparison to the world: 145

Age structure: *0–14 years:* 32.66% (male 363,264/female 349,517)
15–24 years: 21.49% (male 233,090/female 235,894)
25–54 years: 37.31% (male 433,246/female 381,151)
55–64 years: 4.48% (male 43,604/female 54,261)
65 years and over: 4.06% (male 35,346/female 53,346) (2015 est.)

Dependency ratios: *total dependency ratio:* 55.3%
youth dependency ratio: 49.7%
elderly dependency ratio: 5.6%
potential support ratio: 17.9% (2015 est.)

Median age: *total:* 23.1 years m ale: 23.1 years
female: 23 years (2015 est.)
country comparison to the world: 168

Population growth rate: 1.21% (2015 est.)
country comparison to the world: 99

Birth rate: 20.96 births/1,000 population (2015 est.)
country comparison to the world: 77

Death rate: 13.39 deaths/1,000 population (2015 est.)
country comparison to the world: 15

Net migration rate: 4.56 migrant(s)/1,000 population (2015 est.)
country comparison to the world: 28

Urbanization: *urban population:* 57.4% of total population (2015)
rate of urbanization: 1.29% annual rate of change (2010–15 est.)

Major urban areas—population: GABORONE (capital) 247,000 (2014)

Sex ratio: *at birth:* 1.03 male(s)/female
0–14 years: 1.04 male(s)/female
15–24 years: 0.99 male(s)/female
25–54 years: 1.14 male(s)/female
55–64 years: 0.8 male(s)/female
65 years and over: 0.66 male(s)/female
total population: 1.03 male(s)/female (2015 est.)

Mother's mean age at first birth: 19 (2007 est.)

Maternal mortality rate: 129 deaths/100,000 live births (2015 est.)
country comparison to the world: 61

Infant mortality rate: *total:* 8.93 deaths/1,000 live births
male: 9.26 deaths/1,000 live births
female: 8.59 deaths/1,000 live births (2015 est.)
country comparison to the world: 145

Life expectancy at birth: *total population:* 54.18 years
male: 55.97 years
female: 52.33 years (2015 est.)
country comparison to the world: 212

Total fertility rate: 2.33 children born/woman (2015 est.)
country comparison to the world: 90

Contraceptive prevalence rate: 52.8%
note: percent of women aged 12–49 (2007/08)

Health expenditures: 5.4% of GDP (2013)
country comparison to the world: 132

Physicians density: 0.4 physicians/1,000 population (2009)

Hospital bed density: 1.8 beds/1,000 population (2010)

Drinking water source:
improved:
urban: 99.2% of population
rural: 92.3% of population
total: 96.2% of population
unimproved:

urban: 0.8% of population
rural: 7.7% of population
total: 3.8% of population (2015 est.)
Sanitation facility access:
improved:
urban: 78.5% of population
rural: 43.1% of population
total: 63.4% of population
unimproved:
urban: 21.5% of population
rural: 56.9% of population
total: 36.6% of population (2015 est.)
HIV/AIDS—adult prevalence rate: 25.16% (2014 est.)
country comparison to the world: 2
HIV/AIDS—people living with HIV/AIDS: 392,400 (2014 est.)
country comparison to the world: 19
HIV/AIDS—deaths: 5,100 (2014 est.)
country comparison to the world: 30
Major infectious diseases: *degree of risk:* high
food or waterborne diseases: bacterial diarrhea, hepatitis A, and typhoid fever
vectorborne disease: malaria (2013)
Obesity—adult prevalence rate: 19.5% (2014)
country comparison to the world: 128
Children under the age of 5 years underweight: 11.2% (2008)
country comparison to the world: 66
Education expenditures: 9.6% of GDP (2009)
country comparison to the world: 5
Literacy: *definition:* age 15 and over can read and write
total population: 88.5%
male: 88%
female: 88.9% (2015 est.)
School life expectancy (primary to tertiary education): *total:* 13 years
male: 13 years
female: 13 years (2013)

Child labor—children ages 5–14: *total number:* 45,036
percentage: 9%
note: data represent children ages 7–17 (2006 est.)
Unemployment, youth ages 15–24: *total:* 36%
male: 29.6%
female: 43.5% (2010 est.)

GOVERNMENT

Country name: *conventional long form:* Republic of Botswana
conventional short form: Botswana
local long form: Republic of Botswana
local short form: Botswana
former: Bechuanaland
etymology: the name Botswana means "Land of the Tswana"—referring to the country's major ethnic group
Government type: parliamentary republic
Capital: *name:* Gaborone
Geographic coordinates: 24 38 S, 25 54 E
time difference: UTC+2 (7 hours ahead of Washington, DC, during Standard Time)
Administrative divisions: 10 districts and 6 town councils*; Central, Chobe, Francistown*,

Gaborone*, Ghanzi, Jwaneng*, Kgalagadi, Kgatleng, Kweneng, Lobatse*, Northeast, North West, Selebi-Phikwe*, Southeast, Southern, Sowa Town*
Independence: 30 September 1966 (from the UK)
National holiday: Independence Day (Botswana Day), 30 September (1966)
Constitution: previous 1960 (preindependence); latest adopted March 1965, effective 30 September 1966; amended several times, last in 2006 (2016)
Legal system: mixed legal system of civil law influenced by the Roman-Dutch model and also customary and common law
International law organization participation: accepts compulsory ICJ jurisdiction with reservations; accepts ICCt jurisdiction
Citizenship: *citizenship by birth:* no
citizenship by descent only: at least one parent must be a citizen of Botswana
dual citizenship recognized: no
residency requirement for naturalization: 10 years
Suffrage: 18 years of age; universal
Executive branch: *chief of state:* President Seretse Khama Ian KHAMA (since 1 April 2008); Vice President Ponatshego KEDIKILWE (since 2 August 2012); note—the president is both chief of state and head of government

head of government: President Seretse Khama Ian KHAMA (since 1 April 2008); Vice President Ponatshego KEDIKILWE (since 2 August 2012)
cabinet: Cabinet appointed by the president
elections/appointments: president indirectly elected by the National Assembly for a 5-year term (eligible for a second term); election last held on 24 October 2014 (next to be held in October 2019); vice president appointed by the president
election results: Seretse Khama Ian KHAMA elected president; percent of National Assembly vote—NA
Legislative branch: *description:* unicameral Parliament consists of the National Assembly (63 seats; 57 members directly elected in single-seat constituencies by simple majority vote, 4 nominated by the president and indirectly elected by simple majority vote by the rest of the National Assembly, and 2 ex-officio members—the president and attorney general; elected members serve 5-year terms); note—the House of Chiefs (Ntlo ya Dikgosi), an advisory body to the National Assembly, consists of 35 members—8 hereditary chiefs from Botswana's principal tribes, 22 indirectly elected by the chiefs, and 5 appointed by the president; the House of Chiefs consults on issues including powers of chiefs, customary courts, customary law, tribal property, and constitutional amendments
elections: National Assembly elections last held on 24 October 2014 (next to be held in October 2019)
election results: percent of vote by party—BDP 46.5%, UDC 30.0%, BCP 20.4%, independent 3.1%; seats by party—BDP 37, UDC 17, BCP 3
Judicial branch: *highest court(s):* Court of Appeal, High Court (each consists of a chief justice and a number of other judges as prescribed by the Parliament)

judge selection and term of office: Court of Appeal and High Court chief justices appointed by the president and other judges appointed by the president upon the advice of the Judicial Service Commission; all judges appointed to serve until age 70
subordinate courts: Industrial Court (with circuits scheduled monthly in the capital city and in 3 districts); Magistrates Courts (1 in each district); Customary Court of Appeal; Paramount Chief's Court/Urban Customary Court; Senior Chief's Representative's Court; Chief's Representative's Court; Headman's Court
Political parties and leaders: Botswana Alliance Movement or BAM [Ephraim Lepetu SETSHWAELO]
Botswana Congress Party or BCP [Dumelang SALESHANDO]
Botswana Democratic Party or BDP [Ian KHAMA]
Botswana Movement for Democracy or BMD [Ndaba GAOLATLHE]
Botswana National Front or BNF [Duma BOKO]
Botswana Peoples Party or BPP [Motlatsi MOLAPISI]
Umbrella for Democratic Change or UDC [Duma BOKO] (includes BMD, BPP, and BNF)
Political pressure groups and leaders: First People of the Kalahari (Bushman organization)
Pitso Ya Ba Tswana
Society for the Promotion of Ikalanga Language (Kalanga elites)
other: diamond mining companies
International organization participation: ACP, AfDB, AU, C, CD, FAO, G-77, IAEA, IBRD, ICAO, ICCt, ICRM, IDA, IFAD, IFC, IFRCS, ILO, IMF, Interpol, IOC, IOM, IPU, ISO, ITSO, ITU, ITUC (NGOs), MIGA, NAM, OPCW, SACU, SADC, UN, UNCTAD, UNESCO, UNIDO, UNWTO, UPU, WCO, WFTU (NGOs), WHO, WIPO, WMO, WTO
Diplomatic representation in the US: *chief of mission:* Ambassador David John NEWMAN (since 3 August 2015)
chancery: 1531–1533 New Hampshire Avenue NW, Washington, DC 20036
telephone: [1] (202) 244-4990
FAX: [1] (202) 244-4164
consulate(s) general: Atlanta
Diplomatic representation from the US: *chief of mission:* Ambassador Earl R. MILLER (since 30 January 2015)
embassy: Embassy Drive, Government Enclave (off Khama Crescent), Gaborone
mailing address: Embassy Enclave, P.O. Box 90, Gaborone
telephone: [267] 395-3982
FAX: [267] 318-0232
Flag description: light blue with a horizontal white-edged black stripe in the center; the blue symbolizes water in the form of rain, while the black and white bands represent racial harmony
National symbol(s): zebra; national colors: blue, white, black
National anthem: *name:* "Fatshe leno la rona" (Our Land)
lyrics/music: Kgalemang Tumedisco MOTSETE

111

note: adopted 1966

ECONOMY

Economy—overview: Botswana has maintained one of the world's highest economic growth rates since independence in 1966. Diamond mining has fueled much of the expansion and currently accounts for one quarter of GDP, approximately 85% of export earnings, and about one-third of the government's revenues. Tourism is the secondary earner of foreign exchange and many Batswana engage in subsistence farming and cattle raising. Through fiscal discipline and sound management, Botswana transformed itself from one of the poorest countries in the world to a middle-income country with a per capita GDP of $17,700 in 2015. Two major investment services rank Botswana as the best credit risk in Africa. Botswana's economy is highly correlated with global economic trends because of its heavy reliance on a single luxury export. According to official government statistics, unemployment is 19.5%, but unofficial estimates run much higher. De Beers, a major international diamond company, signed a 10-year deal with Botswana in 2012 and moved its rough stone sorting and trading division from London to Gaborone in 2013. The move was geared to support the development of Botswana's nascent downstream diamond industry.

Following the 2008 global recession Botswana's economy recovered in 2010. However, the Government of Botswana estimates the economy grew by only 1% in 2015. This was primarily due to the downturn in the global diamond market; water and power shortages also played a role. In October 2015 President Ian KHAMA announced a stimulus plan to boost the economy through projects in agricultural production, construction, manufacturing, and tourism development. In 2016, Botswana entered its fourth year of drought, detrimental to Botswana's small, but vital agriculture sector. The prevalence of HIV/AIDS is second highest in the world and threatens the country's impressive economic gains.

GDP (purchasing power parity): $34.84 billion (2015 est.)
$34.96 billion (2014 est.)
$33.88 billion (2013 est.)
note: data are in 2015 US dollars
country comparison to the world: 122
GDP (official exchange rate): $12.86 billion (2015 est.)
GDP—real growth rate: -0.3% (2015 est.)
3.2% (2014 est.)
9.9% (2013 est.)
country comparison to the world: 202
GDP—per capita (PPP): $16,400 (2015 est.)
$16,600 (2014 est.)
$16,300 (2013 est.)
note: data are in 2015 US dollars
country comparison to the world: 98
Gross national saving: 37.1% of GDP (2015 est.)
46.3% of GDP (2014 est.)
41.8% of GDP (2013 est.)
country comparison to the world: 6
GDP—composition, by end use:
household consumption: 48.2%

government consumption: 16.8%
investment in fixed capital: 31%
investment in inventories: -1.6%
exports of goods and services: 60.7%
imports of goods and services: -55.1% (2015 est.)
GDP—composition, by sector of origin:
agriculture: 1.8%
industry: 32.9%
services: 65.3% (2015 est.)
Agriculture—products: livestock, sorghum, maize, millet, beans, sunflowers, groundnuts
Industries: diamonds, copper, nickel, salt, soda ash, potash, coal, iron ore, silver; livestock processing; textiles
Industrial production growth rate: -1.2% (2015 est.)
country comparison to the world: 175
Labor force: 1.155 million (2015 est.)
country comparison to the world: 140
Labor force—by occupation: *agriculture:* NA%
industry: NA%
services: NA%
Unemployment rate: 20% (2013 est.)
17.8% (2009 est.)
country comparison to the world: 164
Population below poverty line: 30.3% (2003 est.)
Household income or consumption by percentage share: *lowest:* 10%: NA%
highest: 10%: NA%
Distribution of family income—Gini index: 60.5 (2009)
country comparison to the world: 2
Budget: *revenues:* $5.078 billion
expenditures: $5.55 billion (2015 est.)
Taxes and other revenues: 38.8% of GDP (2015 est.)
country comparison to the world: 44
Budget surplus (+) or deficit (−): -3.6% of GDP (2015 est.)
country comparison to the world: 133
Public debt: 17% of GDP (2015 est.) 15.5% of GDP (2014 est.)
country comparison to the world: 159
Fiscal year: 1 April—31 March
Inflation rate (consumer prices): 3% (2015 est.)
4.4% (2014 est.)
country comparison to the world: 138
Central bank discount rate: 6% (31 December 2015)
7.5% (31 December 2014)
country comparison to the world: 44
Commercial bank prime lending rate: 7.5% (31 December 2015 est.)
9% (31 December 2014 est.)
country comparison to the world: 114
Stock of narrow money: $1.569 billion (31 December 2015 est.)
$1.388 billion (31 December 2014 est.)
country comparison to the world: 138
Stock of broad money: $8.293 billion (31 December 2013 est.)
$7.635 billion (31 December 2012 est.)
country comparison to the world: 112
Stock of domestic credit: $1.634 billion (31 December 2015 est.)
$1.272 billion (31 December 2014 est.)

country comparison to the world: 146
Market value of publicly traded shares: $4.588 billion (31 December 2012 est.)
$4.107 billion (31 December 2011)
$4.076 billion (31 December 2010 est.)
country comparison to the world: 87
Current account balance: $1.202 billion (2015 est.)
$2.496 billion (2014 est.)
country comparison to the world: 35
Exports: $6.66 billion (2015 est.)
$8.516 billion (2014 est.)
country comparison to the world: 102
Exports—commodities: diamonds, copper, nickel, soda ash, meat, textiles
Imports: $7.331 billion (2015 est.)
$7.989 billion (2014 est.)
country comparison to the world: 111
Imports—commodities: foodstuffs, machinery, electrical goods, transport equipment, textiles, fuel and petroleum products, wood and paper products, metal and metal products
Reserves of foreign exchange and gold: $7.99 billion (31 December 2015 est.)
$8.323 billion (31 December 2014 est.)
country comparison to the world: 80
Debt—external: $2.256 billion (31 December 2014 est.)
$2.43 billion (31 December 2013 est.)
country comparison to the world: 149
Exchange rates: pulas (BWP) per US dollar—
10.04 (2015 est.)
8.9761 (2014 est.)
8.9761 (2013 est.)
7.62 (2012 est.)
6.8382 (2011 est.)

ENERGY

Electricity—production: 235 million kWh (2012 est.)
country comparison to the world: 182
Electricity—consumption: 3.213 billion kWh (2012 est.)
country comparison to the world: 132
Electricity—exports: 0 kWh (2013 est.)
country comparison to the world: 104
Electricity—imports: 3.371 billion kWh (2012 est.)
country comparison to the world: 49
Electricity—installed generating capacity: 132,000 kW (2012 est.)
country comparison to the world: 169
Electricity—from fossil fuels: 100% of total installed capacity (2012 est.)
country comparison to the world: 4
Electricity—from nuclear fuels: 0% of total installed capacity (2012 est.)
country comparison to the world: 48
Electricity—from hydroelectric plants: 0% of total installed capacity (2012 est.)
country comparison to the world: 160
Electricity—from other renewable sources: 0% of total installed capacity (2012 est.)
country comparison to the world: 156
Crude oil—production: 0 bbl/day (2014 est.)
country comparison to the world: 107

Crude oil—exports: 0 bbl/day (2012 est.)
country comparison to the world: 98
Crude oil—imports: 0 bbl/day (2012 est.)
country comparison to the world: 159
Crude oil—proved reserves: 0 bbl (1 January 2015 est.)
country comparison to the world: 106
Refined petroleum products—production: 0 bbl/day (2012 est.)
country comparison to the world: 156
Refined petroleum products—consumption: 18,000 bbl/day (2013 est.)
country comparison to the world: 134
Refined petroleum products—exports: 0 bbl/day (2012 est.)
country comparison to the world: 155
Refined petroleum products—imports: 18,320 bbl/day (2012 est.)
country comparison to the world: 115
Natural gas—production: 0 cu m (2013 est.)
country comparison to the world: 156
Natural gas—consumption: 0 cu m (2013 est.)
country comparison to the world: 117
Natural gas—exports: 0 cu m (2013 est.)
country comparison to the world: 61
Natural gas—imports: 0 cu m (2013 est.)
country comparison to the world: 160
Natural gas—proved reserves: 0 cu m (1 January 2014 est.)
country comparison to the world: 111
Carbon dioxide emissions from consumption of energy: 3.919 million Mt (2012 est.)
country comparison to the world: 132

COMMUNICATIONS

Telephones—fixed lines: *total subscriptions:* 170,000
subscriptions per 100 inhabitants: 8 (2014 est.)
country comparison to the world: 132
Telephones—mobile cellular: *total:* 3.4 million
subscriptions per 100 inhabitants: 158 (2014 est.)
country comparison to the world: 131
Telephone system: *general assessment:* Botswana is participating in regional development efforts; expanding fully digital system with fiber-optic cables linking the major population centers in the east as well as a system of open-wire lines, microwave radio relays links, and radiotelephone communication stations
domestic: fixed-line teledensity has declined in recent years and now stands at roughly 7 telephones per 100 persons; mobile-cellular teledensity now pushing 140 telephones per 100 persons
international: country code—267; international calls are made via satellite, using international direct dialing; 2 international exchanges; digital microwave radio relay links to Namibia, Zambia, Zimbabwe, and South Africa; satellite earth station—1 Intelsat (Indian Ocean) (2011)
Broadcast media: 2 TV stations—1 state-owned and 1 privately owned; privately owned satellite TV subscription service is available; 2 state-owned national radio stations; 3 privately owned radio stations broadcast locally (2007)
Radio broadcast stations: AM 8, FM 13, shortwave 4 (2001)
Television broadcast stations: 2 (1 state-owned, 1 private) (2007)
Internet country code: .bw
Internet hosts: 1,806 (2012)
country comparison to the world: 163
Internet users: *total:* 283,500 percent of population: 13.2% (2014 est.)
country comparison to the world: 144

TRANSPORTATION

Airports: 74 (2013)
country comparison to the world: 70
Airports—with paved runways: *total:* 10
over 3,047 m: 2
2,438 to 3,047 m: 1
1,524 to 2,437 m: 6
914 to 1,523 m: 1 (2013)
Airports—with unpaved runways: *total:* 64
1,524 to 2,437 m: 5
914 to 1,523 m: 46
under 914 m: 13 (2013)
Railways: *total:* 888 km
narrow gauge: 888 km 1.067-m gauge (2014)
country comparison to the world: 93
Roadways: *total:* 17,916 km

note: includes 8,916 km of Public Highway Network roads (6,116 km paved and 2,800 km unpaved) and 9,000 km of District Council roads (2011)
country comparison to the world: 117

MILITARY AND SECURITY

Military branches: Botswana Defense Force (BDF): Ground Forces Command, Air Wing Command, Defense Logistics Command, Special Forces Group (2013)
Military service age and obligation: 18 is the legal minimum age for voluntary military service; no conscription (2012)
Military expenditures: 2% of GDP (2013)
2.31% of GDP (2012)
2.43% of GDP (2011)
2.31% of GDP (2010)
country comparison to the world: 34

TRANSNATIONAL ISSUES

Disputes—international: none

Trafficking in persons: *current situation:* Botswana is a source, transit, and destination country for women and children subjected to sex trafficking and forced labor; young Batswana servingas domestic workers, sometimes sent by their parents, may be denied education and basic necessities or experience confinement and abuse indicative of forced labor; Batswana girls and women also are forced into prostitution domestically; adults and children of San ethnicity were reported to be in forced labor on farms and at cattle posts in the country's rural west

tier rating: Tier 2 Watch List—Botswana does not fully comply with the minimum standards for the elimination of trafficking; however, it is making significant efforts to do so; an anti-trafficking act was passed at the beginning of 2014, but authorities did not investigate, prosecute, or convict any offenders or government officials complicit in trafficking or operationalize victim identification and referral procedures based on the new law; the government sponsored a radio campaign to familiarize the public with the issue of human trafficking (2015)

BOUVET ISLAND

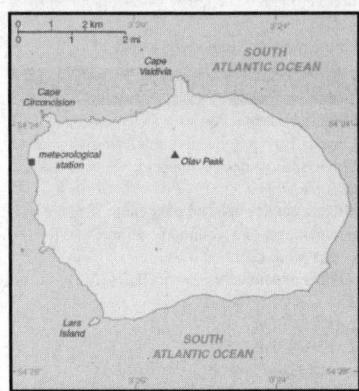

INTRODUCTION

Background: This uninhabited, volcanic, Antarctic island is almost entirely covered by glaciers making it difficult to approach; it is recognized as the most remote island on Earth. Bouvet Island was discovered in 1739 by a French naval officer after whom it is named. No claim was made until 1825, when the British flag was raised. In 1928, the UK waived its claim in favor of Norway, which had occupied the island the previous year. In 1971, Norway designated Bouvet Island and the adjacent territorial waters a nature reserve. Since 1977, Norway has run an automated meteorological station and studied foraging strategies and distribution of fur seals and penguins on the island. In February 2006, an earthquake weakened the station's foundation causing it to be blown out to sea in a winter storm. Norway erected a new research station in 2014 that can hold six people for periods of two to four months.

GEOGRAPHY

Location: island in the South Atlantic Ocean, southwest of the Cape of Good Hope (South Africa)

Geographic coordinates: 54 26 S, 3 24 E

Map references: Antarctic Region

Area: *total:* 49 sq km

land: 49 sq km

water: 0 sq km

country comparison to the world: 233

Area—comparative: about 0.3 times the size of Washington, DC

Land boundaries: 0 km

Coastline: 29.6 km

Maritime claims: *territorial sea:* 4 nm

Climate: antarctic

Terrain: volcanic; coast is mostly inaccessible

Elevation: *mean elevation:* NA

elevation extremes: *lowest:* point: South Atlantic Ocean 0 m

highest point: Olav Peak 935 m

Natural resources: none

Land use: *agricultural land:* 0%

arable land: 0%

permanent crops: 0%

permanent pasture: 0%

forest: 0%

other: 100% (93% ice) (2011 est.)

Natural hazards: NA

Environment—current issues: NA

Geography—note: covered by glacial ice; declared a nature reserve by Norway

PEOPLE AND SOCIETY

Population: uninhabited

GOVERNMENT

Country name: *conventional long form:* none

conventional short form: Bouvet Island

etymology: named after the French naval officer Jean-Baptiste Charles BOUVET who discovered the island in 1739

Dependency status: territory of Norway; administered by the Polar Department of the Ministry of Justice and Oslo Police

Legal system: the laws of Norway, where applicable, apply

Flag description: the flag of Norway is used

ECONOMY

Economy—overview: no economic activity; declared a nature reserve

COMMUNICATIONS

Internet country code: .bv

Internet hosts: 6 (2012)

country comparison to the world: 230

Communications—note: has an automated meteorological station

TRANSPORTATION

Portsand terminals: none; offshore anchorage only

MILITARY AND SECURITY

Military—note: defense is the responsibility of Norway

TRANSNATIONAL ISSUES

Disputes—international: none

BRAZIL

INTRODUCTION

Background: Following more than three centuries under Portuguese rule, Brazil gained its independence in 1822, maintaining a monarchical system of government until the abolition of slavery in 1888 and the subsequent proclamation of a republic by the military in 1889. Brazilian coffee exporters politically dominated the country until populist leader Getulio VARGAS rose to power in 1930. By far the largest and most populous country in South America, Brazil underwent more than a half century of populist and military government until 1985, when the military regime peacefully ceded power to civilian rulers. Brazil continues to pursue industrial and agricultural growth and development of its interior. Having successfully weathered a period of global financial difficulty in the late 20th century, Brazil was seen as one of the world's strongest emerging markets and a contributor to global growth. The awarding of the 2014 FIFA World Cup and 2016 Summer Olympic Games, the first ever to be held in South America, was seen as symbolic of the country's rise. However, since about 2013, Brazil has been plagued by a shrinking economy, growing unemployment, and rising inflation. Political scandal resulted in the impeachment of President Dilma ROUSSEFF in May 2016; her vice president, Michel TEMER, is currently acting president.

GEOGRAPHY

Location: Eastern South America, bordering the Atlantic Ocean

Geographic coordinates: 10 00 S, 55 00 W

Map references: South America

Area: *total:* 8,515,770 sq km
land: 8,358,140 sq km
water: 157,630 sq km
note: includes Arquipelago de Fernando de Noronha, Atol das Rocas, Ilha da Trindade, Ilhas Martin Vaz, and Penedos de Sao Pedro e Sao Paulo
country comparison to the world: 5

Area—comparative: slightly smaller than the US

Land boundaries: *total:* 16,145 km

border countries (10): Argentina 1,263 km, Bolivia 3,403 km, Colombia 1,790 km, French Guiana 649 km, Guyana 1,308 km, Paraguay 1,371 km, Peru 2,659 km, Suriname 515 km, Uruguay 1,050 km, Venezuela 2,137 km

Coastline: 7,491 km

Maritime claims: *territorial sea:* 12 nm contiguous zone: 24 nm exclusive

economic zone: 200 nm continental shelf: 200 nm or to edge of the continental margin

Climate: mostly tropical, but temperate in south

Terrain: mostly flat to rolling lowlands in north; some plains, hills, mountains, and narrow coastal belt

Elevation: *mean elevation:* 320 m

elevation extremes: *lowest point:* Atlantic Ocean 0 m

highest point: Pico da Neblina 2,994 m

Natural resources: bauxite, gold, iron ore, manganese, nickel, phosphates, platinum, tin, rare earth-elements, uranium, petroleum, hydropower, timber

Land use: *agricultural land:* 32.9%
arable land: 8.6%
permanent crops: 0.8%
permanent pasture: 23.5%
forest: 61.9%
other: 5.2% (2011 est.)

Irrigated land: 54,000 sq km (2012)

Total renewable water resources: 8,233 cu km (2011)

Freshwater withdrawal (domestic/industrial/agricultural): *total:* 58.07 cu km/yr (28%/17%/55%)
per capita: 306 cu m/yr (2006)

Natural hazards: recurring droughts in northeast; floods and occasional frost in south

Environment—current issues: deforestation in Amazon Basin destroys the habitat and endangers a multitude of plant and animal species indigenous to the area; there is a lucrative illegal wildlife trade; air and water pollution in Rio de Janeiro, Sao Paulo, and several other large cities; land degradation and water pollution caused by improper mining activities; wetland degradation; severe oil spills

Environment—international agreements: *party to:* Antarctic-Environmental Protocol, Antarctic-Marine Living Resources, Antarctic Seals, Antarctic Treaty, Biodiversity, Climate Change, Climate Change-Kyoto Protocol, Desertification, Endangered Species, Environmental Modification, Hazardous Wastes, Law of the Sea, Marine Dumping, Ozone Layer Protection, Ship Pollution, Tropical Timber 83, Tropical Timber 94, Wetlands, Whaling

signed, but not ratified: none of the selected agreements

Geography—note: largest country in South America and in the Southern Hemisphere; shares common boundaries with every South American country except Chile and Ecuador

PEOPLE AND SOCIETY

Nationality: *noun:* Brazilian(s)
adjective: Brazilian

Ethnic groups: white 47.7%, mulatto (mixed white and black) 43.1%, black 7.6%, Asian 1.1%, indigenous 0.4% (2010 est.)

Languages: Portuguese (official and most widely spoken language)
note: less common languages include Spanish (border areas and schools), German, Italian, Japanese, English, and a large number of minor Amerindian languages

Religions: Roman Catholic 64.6%, other Catholic 0.4%, Protestant 22.2% (includes Adventist 6.5%, Assembly of God 2.0%, Christian Congregation of Brazil 1.2%, Universal Kingdom of God 1.0%, other Protestant 11.5%), other Christian 0.7%, Spiritist 2.2%, other 1.4%, none 8%, unspecified 0.4% (2010 est.)

Demographic profile: Brazil's rapid fertility decline since the 1960s is the main factor behind the country's slowing population growth rate, aging population, and fast-paced demographic transition. Brasilia has not taken full advantage of its large working-age population to develop its human capital and strengthen its social and economic institutions but is funding a study abroad program to bring advanced skills back to the country. The current favorable age structure will begin to shift around 2025, with the labor force shrinking and the elderly starting to compose an increasing share of the total population. Well-funded public pensions have nearly wiped out poverty among the elderly, and Bolsa Familia and other social programs have lifted tens of millions out of poverty. More than half of Brazil's population is considered middle class, but poverty and income inequality levels remain high; the Northeast, North, and Center-West, women, and black, mixed race, and indigenous populations are disproportionately affected. Disparities in opportunities foster social exclusion and contribute to Brazil's high crime rate, particularly violent crime in cities and favelas. Brazil has traditionally been a net recipient of immigrants, with its southeast being the prime destination. After the importation of African slaves was outlawed in the mid-19th century, Brazil sought Europeans (Italians, Portuguese, Spaniards, and Germans) and later Asians (Japanese) to work in agriculture, especially coffee cultivation. Recent immigrants come mainly from Argentina, Chile, and Andean countries (many are unskilled illegal migrants) or are returning Brazilian nationals. Since Brazil's economic downturn in the 1980s, emigration to the United States, Europe, and Japan has been rising but is negligible relative to Brazil's total population. The majority of these emigrants are well-educated and middle-class. Fewer Brazilian peasants are emigrating to neighboring countries to take up agricultural work.

Population: 204,259,812 (July 2015 est.)
country comparison to the world: 6

Age structure: 0–14 years: 23.27% (male 24,223,817/female 23,304,372)

15–24 years: 16.47% (male 17,058,031/female 16,579,678)

25–54 years: 43.8% (male 44,358,524/female 45,111,178)

55–64 years: 8.66% (male 8,348,783/female 9,343,347)

65 years and over: 7.8% (male 6,776,742/female 9,155,340) (2015 est.)

Dependency ratios: total dependency ratio: 44.7% youth dependency ratio: 33.3% elderly dependency ratio: 11.3% potential support ratio: 8.8% (2015 est.)

Median age: total: 31.1 years

male: 30.3 years

female: 31.9 years (2015 est.)

country comparison to the world: 104

Population growth rate: 0.77% (2015 est.)

country comparison to the world: 142

Birth rate: 14.46 births/1,000 population (2015 est.)

country comparison to the world: 136

Death rate: 6.58 deaths/1,000 population (2015 est.)

country comparison to the world: 144

Net migration rate: -0.14 migrant(s)/1,000 population (2015 est.)

country comparison to the world: 116

Urbanization: urban population: 85.7% of total population (2015)

rate of urbanization: 1.17% annual rate of change (2010–15 est.)

Major urban areas—population: Sao Paulo 21.066 million; Rio de Janeiro 12.902 million; Belo Horizonte 5.716 million; BRASILIA (capital) 4.155 million; Fortaleza 3.88 million; Recife 3.739 million (2015)

Sex ratio: at birth: 1.05 male(s)/female

0–14 years: 1.04 male(s)/female

15–24 years: 1.03 male(s)/female

25–54 years: 0.98 male(s)/female

55–64 years: 0.89 male(s)/female

65 years and over: 0.74 male(s)/female

total population: 0.97 male(s)/female (2015 est.)

Maternal mortality rate: 44 deaths/100,000 live births (2015 est.)

country comparison to the world: 103

Infant mortality rate: total: 18.6 deaths/1,000 live births

male: 21.8 deaths/1,000 live births

female: 15.23 deaths/1,000 live births (2015 est.)

country comparison to the world: 95

Life expectancy at birth: total population: 73.53 years

male: 69.99 years

female: 77.25 years (2015 est.)

country comparison to the world: 129

Total fertility rate: 1.77 children born/woman (2015 est.)

country comparison to the world: 158

Contraceptive prevalence rate: 80.3% (2006)

Health expenditures: 9.7% of GDP (2013)

country comparison to the world: 31

Physicians density: 1.89 physicians/1,000 population (2013)

Hospital bed density: 2.3 beds/1,000 population (2012)

Drinking water source:

improved:

urban: 100% of population

rural: 87% of population

total: 98.1% of population

unimproved:

urban: 0% of population

rural: 13% of population

total: 1.9% of population (2015 est.)

Sanitation facility access:

improved:

urban: 88% of population

rural: 51.5% of population

total: 82.8% of population

unimproved:

urban: 12% of population

rural: 48.5% of population

total: 17.2% of population (2015 est.)

HIV/AIDS—adult prevalence rate: 0.55% (2013 est.)

country comparison to the world: 62

HIV/AIDS—people living with HIV/AIDS: 726,000 (2013 est.)

country comparison to the world: 13

HIV/AIDS—deaths: 15,800 (2013 est.)

country comparison to the world: 17

Major infectious diseases: degree of risk: very high

food or waterborne diseases: bacterial diarrhea and hepatitis A

vectorborne diseases: dengue fever and malaria

water contact disease: schistosomiasis

Obesity—adult prevalence rate: 20.1% (2014)

country comparison to the world: 102

Children under the age of 5 years underweight: 2.2% (2007)

country comparison to the world: 121

Education expenditures: 5.9% of GDP (2012)

country comparison to the world: 49

Literacy: definition: age 15 and over can read and write

total population: 92.6%

male: 92.2%

female: 92.9% (2015 est.)

School life expectancy (primary to tertiary education): total: 15 years

male: 15 years

female: 16 years (2013)

Child labor—children ages 5–14: total number: 959,942

percentage: 3%

note: data represent children ages 5–13 (2009 est.)

Unemployment, youth ages 15–24: total: 15%

male: 12.3%

female: 18.7% (2013 est.)

country comparison to the world: 76

GOVERNMENT

Country name: conventional long form: Federative Republic of Brazil

conventional short form: Brazil

local long form: Republica Federativa do Brasil

local short form: Brasil

etymology: the country name derives from the brazilwood tree that used to grow plentifully along the coast of Brazil and that was used to produce a deep red dye

Government type: federal presiden tial republic

Capital: name: Brasilia

Geographic coordinates: 15 47 S, 47 55 W

time difference: UTC-3 (2 hours ahead of Washington, DC, during Standard Time)

daylight saving time: +1hr, begins third Sunday in October; ends third Sunday in February

note: Brazil has three time zones, including one for the Fernando de Noronha Islands

Administrative divisions: 26 states (estados, singular—estado) and 1 federal district* (distrito federal); Acre, Alagoas, Amapa, Amazonas, Bahia, Ceara, Distrito Federal*, Espirito Santo, Goias, Maranhao, Mato Grosso, Mato Grosso do Sul, Minas Gerais, Para, Paraiba, Parana, Pernambuco, Piaui, Rio de Janeiro, Rio Grande do Norte, Rio Grande do Sul, Rondonia, Roraima, Santa Catarina, Sao Paulo, Sergipe, Tocantins

Independence: 7 September 1822 (from Portugal)

National holiday: Independence Day, 7 September (1822)

Constitution: several previous; latest ratified 5 October 1988; amended many times, last in 2016 (2016)

Legal system: civil law; note—a new civil law code was enacted in 2002 replacing the 1916 code

International law organization participation: has not submitted an ICJ jurisdiction declaration; accepts ICCt jurisdiction

Citizenship: citizenship by birth: yes

citizenship by descent: yes

dual citizenship recognized: yes

residency requirement for naturalization: 4 years

Suffrage: voluntary between 16 to 18 years of age and over 70; compulsory between 18 to 70 years of age; note -military conscripts by law cannot vote

Executive branch: chief of state: Acting President Michel Miguel Elias TEMER Lulia (since 12 May 2016); Vice President (vacant); note—the president is both chief of state and head of government

head of government: Acting President Michel Miguel Elias TEMER Lulia (since 12 May 2016); Vice President (vacant)

cabinet: Cabinet appointed by the president

elections/appointments: president and vice president directly elected on the same ballot by absolute majority popular vote in 2 rounds if needed for a single 4-year term (eligible for a second term); election last held on 5 October 2014 with runoff on 26 October 2014 (next to be held October 2018)

election results: Dilma ROUSSEFF reelected president in a runoff election; percent of vote—Dilma ROUSSEFF (PT) 51.6%, Aecio NEVES (PSDB) 48.4%

note: on 12 May 2016, Brazil's Senate voted to impeach President Dilma ROUSSEFF, who has now been suspended from her executive duties; Vice President Michel TEMER has taken over as acting president while she is suspended; the Senate has 180 days to conduct a trial and decide whether

ROUSSEFF should be permanently removed from office

Legislative branch: *description:* bicameral National Congress or Congresso Nacional consists of the Federal Senate or Senado Federal (81 seats; 3 members each from 26 states and 3 from the federal district directly elected in multi-seat constituencies by simple majority vote to serve 8-year terms, with one-third and two-thirds of the membership elected alternately every 4 years) and the Chamber of Deputies or Camara dos Deputados (513 seats; members directly elected in multi-seat constituencies by proportional representation vote to serve 4-year terms)

elections: Federal Senate—last held on 5 October 2014 for one-third of the Senate (next to be held in October 2018 for two-thirds of the Senate); Chamber of Deputies—last held on 5 October 2014 (next to be held in October 2018)

election results: Federal Senate—percent of vote by party—NA; seats by party—PMDB 5, PSDB 4, PDT 4, PSB 3, DEM (formerly PFL) 3, PT 2, PSD 2, PTB 2, PP 1, PR 1; Chamber of Deputies—percent of vote by party—NA; seats by party—PT 70, PMDB 66, PSDB 54, PSD 37, PP 36, PR 34, PSB 34, PTB 25, DEM (formerly PFL) 22, PRB 21, PDT 19, SD 15, PSC 12, PROS 11, PCdoB 10, PPS 10, PV 8, PHS 5, PSOL 5, PTN 4, PMN 3, PRP 3, PEN 2, PTC 2, PSDC 2, PTdoB 1, PSL 1, PRTB 1

Judicial branch: *highest court(s):* Supreme Federal Court or Supremo Tribunal Federal (consists of 11 justices)

judge selection and term of office: justices appointed by the president and approved by the Federal Senate; justices appointed to serve until mandatory retirement at age 75

subordinate courts: Tribunal of the Union, Federal Appeals Court, Superior Court of Justice, Superior Electoral Court, regional federal courts; state court system

Political parties and leaders: Brazilian Communist Party or PCB [Ivan Martins PINHEIRO]
Brazilian Democratic Movement Party or PMDB [Michel TEMER]
Brazilian Labor Party or PTB [Cristiane BRASIL]
Brazilian Renewal Labor Party or PRTB [Jose Levy FIDELIX da Cruz]
Brazilian Republican Party or PRB [Marcos Antonio PEREIRA]
Brazilian Social Democracy Party or PSDB [Aecio NEVES]
Brazilian Socialist Party or PSB [Carlos Roberto SIQUEIRA de Barros]
Christian Labor Party or PTC [Daniel TOURINHO]
Christian Social Democratic Party or PSDC [Jose Maria EYMAEL]
Communist Party of Brazil or PCdoB [Jose Renato RABELO]
Democratic Labor Party or PDT [Carlos Roberto LUPI]
The Democrats or DEM [Jose AGRIPINO] (formerly Liberal Front Party or PFL) Free Homeland Party or PPL [Sergio RUBENS]
Green Party or PV [Jose Luiz PENNA]

Humanist Party of Solidarity or PHS [Eduardo MACHADO]
Labor Party of Brazil or PTdoB [Luis Henrique de Oliveira RESENDE]
National Ecologic Party or PEN [Adilson Barroso OLIVEIRA]
National Labor Party or PTN [Jose Masci de ABREU]
National Mobilization Party or PMN [Telma RIBEIRO dos Santos]
Party of the Republic or PR [Alfredo NASCIMENTO]
Popular Socialist Party or PPS [Roberto Joao Pereira FREIRE]
Progressive Party or PP [Ciro NOGUEIRA]
Progressive Republican Party or PRP [Ovasco Roma Altimari RESENDE]
Republican Social Order Party or PROS [Euripedes JUNIOR]
Social Christian Party or PSC [Vitor Jorge Abdala NOSSEIS]
Social Democratic Party or PSD [Guilherme CAMPOS]
Social Liberal Party or PSL [Luciano Caldas BIVAR]
Socialism and Freedom Party or PSOL [Luiz ARAUJO]
Solidarity or SD [Paulo PEREIRA DA SILVA]
United Socialist Workers' Party or PSTU [Jose Maria DE ALMEIDA]
Workers' Cause Party or PCO [Rui Costa PIMENTA]
Workers' Party or PT [Rui FALCAO]

Political pressure groups and leaders: Landless Workers' Movement or MST
other: industrial federations; labor unions and federations; large farmers' associations; religious groups including evangelical Christian churches and the Catholic Church

International organization participation: AfDB (nonregional member), BIS, BRICS, CAN (associate), CD, CELAC, CPLP, FAO, FATF, G-15, G-20, G- 24, G-5, G-77, IADB, IAEA, IBRD, ICAO, ICC (national committees), ICCt, ICRM, IDA, IFAD, IFC, IFRCS, IHO, ILO, IMF, IMO, IMSO, Interpol, IOC, IOM, IPU, ISO, ITSO, ITU, ITUC (NGOs), LAES, LAIA, LAS (observer), Mercosur, MIGA, MINURSO, MINUSTAH, MONUSCO, NAM (observer), NSG, OAS, OECD (Enhanced Engagement, OPANAL, OPCW, Paris Club (associate), PCA, SICA (observer), UN, UNASUR, UNCTAD, UNESCO, UNFICYP, UNHCR, UNIDO, UNIFIL, Union Latina, UNISFA, UNITAR, UNMIL, UNMISS, UNOCI, UNRWA, UNWTO, UPU, WCO, WFTU (NGOs), WHO, WIPO, WMO, WTO

Diplomatic representation in the US: *chief of mission:* Ambassador Luiz Alberto FIGUEIREDO Machado (since 18 May 2015)
chancery: 3006 Massachusetts Avenue NW, Washington, DC 20008
telephone: [1] (202) 238-2700
FAX: [1] (202) 238-2827
consulate(s) general: Atlanta, Boston, Chicago, Hartford (CT), Houston, Los Angeles, Miami, New York, San Francisco, Washington, DC

Diplomatic representation from the US: *chief of mission:* Ambassador Liliana AYALDE (since 31 October 2013)
embassy: Avenida das Nacoes, Quadra 801, Lote 3, Distrito Federal Cep 70403–900, Brasilia
mailing address: Unit 7500, DPO, AA 34030
telephone: [55] (61) 3312-7000
FAX: [55] (61) 3225-9136
consulate(s) general: Recife, Rio de Janeiro, Sao Paulo

Flag description: green with a large yellow diamond in the center bearing a blue celestial globe with 27 white five-pointed stars; the globe has a white equatorial band with the motto ORDEME PROGRESSO (Order and Progress); the current flag was inspired by the banner of the former Empire of Brazil (1822–1889); on the imperial flag, the green represented the House of Braganza of Pedro I, the first Emperor of Brazil, while the yellow stood for the Habsburg Family of his wife; on the modern flag the green represents the forests of the country and the yellow rhombus its mineral wealth (the diamond shape roughly mirrors that of the country); the blue circle and stars, which replaced the coat of arms of the original flag, depict the sky over Rio de Janeiro on the morning of 15 November 1889—the day the Republic of Brazil was declared; the number of stars has changed with the creation of new states and has risen from an original 21 to the current 27 (one for each state and the Federal District)
note: one of several flags where a prominent component of the design reflects the shape of the country; other such flags are those of Bosnia and Herzegovina, Eritrea, and Vanuatu

National symbol(s): Southern Cross constellation; national colors: green, yellow, blue

National anthem: *name:* "Hino Nacional Brasileiro" (Brazilian National Anthem)
lyrics/music: Joaquim Osorio Duque ESTRADA/ Francisco Manoel DA SILVA
note: music adopted 1890, lyrics adopted 1922; the anthem's music, composed in 1822, was used unofficially for many years before it was adopted

ECONOMY

Economy—overview: Characterized by large and well-developed agricultural, mining, manufacturing, and service sectors, and a rapidly expanding middle class, Brazil's economy outweighs that of all other South American countries, and Brazil is expanding its presence in world markets. Since 2003, Brazil has steadily improved its macroeconomic stability, building up foreign reserves, and reducing its debt profile by shifting its debt burden toward real denominated and domestically held instruments. Since 2008, Brazil became a net external creditor and all three of the major ratings agencies awarded investment grade status to its debt. After strong growth in 2007 and 2008, the onset of the global financial crisis hit Brazil in 2008. Brazil experienced two quarters of recession, as global demand for Brazil's commodity-based exports dwindled and external credit dried up. However, Brazil was one of the first emerging markets to begin a recovery. In 2010, consumer and investor confidence revived and GDP growth reached 7.5%, the highest growth rate in the past 25 years. GDP growth has slowed since 2011, due to several factors, including overdependence on exports of raw commodities, low productivity, high operational costs, persistently high inflation, and low levels of investment. After reaching historic lows of 4.8% in 2014, the unemployment rate remains low, but is rising. Brazil's traditionally high level of income inequality has declined for the last 15 years.

Brazil's fiscal and current account balances have eroded during the past four years as the government attempted to boost economic growth through targeted tax cuts for industry and incentives to spur household consumption. After winning reelection in October 2014 by a historically narrow margin, President Dilma ROUSSEFF appointed a new economic team led by Finance Minister Joaquim LEVY, who introduced a fiscal austerity package intended to restore the primary account surplus (before interest expenditures are included) to 1.2% of GDP and preserve the country's investment-grade sovereign credit rating. LEVY encountered political headwinds and an economy facing more challenges than he anticipated. The target for the primary account surplus fell to a deficit of 2%, and two of the three main credit rating agencies downgraded Brazil to "junk" status.

Brazil seeks to strengthen its workforce and its economy over the long run by imposing local content and technology transfer requirements on foreign businesses, by investing in education through social programs such as Bolsa Familia and the Brazil Science Mobility Program, and by investing in research in the areas of space, nanotechnology, healthcare, and energy.

GDP (purchasing power parity): $3.192 trillion (2015 est.)
$3.32 trillion (2014 est.)
$3.317 trillion (2013 est.)
note: data are in 2015 US dollars
country comparison to the world: 8

GDP (official exchange rate): $1.773 trillion (2015 est.)

GDP—real growth rate: -3.8% (2015 est.) 0.1% (2014 est.) 3% (2013 est.)
country comparison to the world: 211

GDP—per capita (PPP): $15,600 (2015 est.)
$16,400 (2014 est.)
$16,500 (2013 est.)
note: data are in 2015 US dollars
country comparison to the world: 103

Gross national saving: 16.4% of GDP (2015 est.)
16.7% of GDP (2014 est.)
18.9% of GDP (2013 est.)
country comparison to the world: 102

GDP—composition, by end use:
household consumption: 63.2%
government consumption: 20.7%
investment in fixed capital: 17.6%
investment in inventories: 0%
exports of goods and services: 13.9%
imports of goods and services: -15.4% (2015 est.)

GDP—composition, by sector of origin:
agricultu re: 5.9%
industry: 22.2%

services: 71.9% (2015 est.)

Agriculture—products: coffee, soybeans, wheat, rice, corn, sugarcane, cocoa, citrus; beef

Industries: textiles, shoes, chemicals, cement, lumber, iron ore, tin, steel, aircraft, motor vehicles and parts, other machinery and equipment

Industrial production growth rate: -5% (2015 est.)
country comparison to the world: 190

Labor force: 109.2 million (2015 est.)
country comparison to the world: 6

Labor force—by occupation: *agriculture:* 15.7%
industry: 13.3%
services: 71% (2011 est.)

Unemployment rate: 6.4% (2015 est.)
4.8% (2014 est.)
country comparison to the world: 73

Population below poverty line: 21.4%
note: approximately 4% of the population are below the "extreme" poverty line (2009 est.)

Household income or consumption by percentage share: *lowest:* 10%: 0.8%
highest: 10%: 42.9% (2009 est.)

Distribution of family income—Gini index: 51.9 (2012)
55.3 (2001)
country comparison to the world: 17

Budget: *revenues:* $631 billion
expenditures: $641.2 billion (2015 est.)
Taxes and other revenues: 35.1% of GDP (2015 est.)
country comparison to the world: 57

Budget surplus (+) or deficit (–): -0.6% of GDP (2015 est.)
country comparison to the world: 48

Public debt: 67.3% of GDP (2015 est.)
58.9% of GDP (2014 est.)
country comparison to the world: 50

Fiscal year: calendar year

Inflation rate (consumer prices): 9% (2015 est.)
6.3% (2014 est.)
country comparison to the world: 208

Central bank discount rate: 10% (31 December 2013)
11% (31 December 2011)
country comparison to the world: 23

Commercial bank prime lending rate: 42.7% (31 December 2015 est.)
32.01% (31 December 2014 est.)
country comparison to the world: 2

Stock of narrow money: $90.94 billion (31 December 2015 est.)
$132.4 billion (31 December 2014 est.)
country comparison to the world: 37

Stock of broad money: $928.9 billion (31 December 2014 est.)
$835.3 billion (31 December 2013 est.)
country comparison to the world: 18

Stock of domestic credit: $1.699 trillion (31 December 2015 est.)
$2.251 trillion (31 December 2014 est.)
country comparison to the world: 14

Market value of publicly traded shares:
$1.23 trillion (31 December 2012 est.)
$1.229 trillion (31 December 2011)
$1.546 trillion (31 December 2010 est.)
country comparison to the world: 13

Current account balance: -$58.91 billion (2015 est.)
-$104.2 billion (2014 est.)
country comparison to the world: 195

Exports: $189.1 billion (2015 est.)
$225.1 billion (2014 est.)
country comparison to the world: 26

Exports—commodities: transport equipment, iron ore, soybeans, footwear, coffee, automobiles

Exports—partners: China 18.6%, US 12.7%, Argentina 6.7%, Netherlands 5.3% (2015)

Imports: $174.2 billion (2015 est.)
$229.2 billion (2014 est.)
country comparison to the world: 27

Imports—commodities: machinery, electrical and transport equipment, chemical products, oil, automotive parts, electronics

Imports—partners: China 17.9%, US 15.6%, Germany 6.1%, Argentina 6% (2015)

Reserves of foreign exchange and gold: $359.4 billion (31 December 2015 est.)
$363.6 billion (31 December 2014 est.)
country comparison to the world: 10

Debt—external: $712.5 billion (31 December 2014 est.)
$482.8 billion (31 December 2013 est.)
country comparison to the world: 20

Stock of direct foreign investment—at home:
$820.5 billion (31 December 2015 est.)
$755.5 billion (31 December 2014 est.)
country comparison to the world: 13

Stock of direct foreign investment—abroad:
$333.1 billion (31 December 2015 est.)
$313.1 billion (31 December 2014 est.)
country comparison to the world: 21

Exchange rates: reals (BRL) per US dollar—
3.419 (2015 est.)
2.3535 (2014 est.)
2.3535 (2013 est.)
1.95 (2012 est.)
1.675 (2011 est.)

ENERGY

Electricity—production: 537.6 billion kWh (2012 est.)
country comparison to the world: 10

Electricity—consumption: 483.5 billion kWh (2012 est.)
country comparison to the world: 9

Electricity—exports: 467 million kWh (2013 est.)
country comparison to the world: 69

Electricity—imports: 40.33 billion kWh (2013 est.)
country comparison to the world: 4

Electricity—installed generating capacity: 121.7 million kW (2012 est.)
country comparison to the world: 11

Electricity—from fossil fuels: 18.7% of total installed capacity (2012 est.)
country comparison to the world: 196

Electricity—from nuclear fuels: 1.5% of total installed capacity (2012 est.)
country comparison to the world: 32

Electricity—from hydroelectric plants: 69.3% of total installed capacity (2012 est.)
country comparison to the world: 24

Electricity—from other renewable sources: 10.5% of total installed capacity (2012 est.)
country comparison to the world: 34
Crude oil—production: 2.255 million bbl/day (2014 est.)
country comparison to the world: 13
Crude oil—exports: 533,300 bbl/day (2012 est.)
country comparison to the world: 22
Crude oil—imports: 344,900 bbl/day (2012 est.)
country comparison to the world: 27
Crude oil—proved reserves: 15.31 billion bbl (1 January 2015 est.)
country comparison to the world: 15
Refined petroleum products—production: 2.554 million bbl/day (2012 est.)
country comparison to the world: 8
Refined petroleum products—consumption: 3.003 million bbl/day (2013 est.)
country comparison to the world: 6
Refined petroleum products—exports: 174,700 bbl/day (2012 est.)
country comparison to the world: 36
Refined petroleum products—imports: 537,300 bbl/day (2012 est.)
country comparison to the world: 15
Natural gas—production: 21.08 billion cu m (2013 est.)
country comparison to the world: 30
Natural gas—consumption: 38.4 billion cu m (2013 est.)
country comparison to the world: 25
Natural gas—exports: 100 million cu m (2014 est.)
country comparison to the world: 44
Natural gas—imports: 19 billion cu m (2014 est.)
country comparison to the world: 18
Natural gas—proved reserves: 388.7 billion cu m (1 January 2014 est.)
country comparison to the world: 35
Carbon dioxide emissions from consumption of energy: 500.2 million Mt (2012 est.)
country comparison to the world: 13

COMMUNICATIONS

Telephones—fixed lines: *total subscriptions:* 44.1 million
subscriptions per 100 inhabitants: 22 (2014 est.)
country comparison to the world: 11
Telephones—mobile cellular: *total:* 280.7 million
subscriptions per 100 inhabitants: 139 (2014 est.)
country comparison to the world: 6
Telephone system: *general assessment:* good working system including an extensive microwave radio relay system and a domestic satellite system with 64 earth stations
domestic: fixed-line connections have remained relatively stable in recent years and stand at about 20 per 100 persons; less-expensive mobile-cellular technology has been a major driver in expanding telephone service to the lower-income segments of the population with mobile-cellular teledensity roughly 120 per 100 persons
international: country code—55; landing point for a number of submarine cables, including Americas-1, Americas-2, Atlantis-2, GlobeNet, South America-1, South American Crossing/Latin American Nautilus, and UNISUR that provide direct connectivity to South and Central America, the Caribbean, the US, Africa, and Europe; satellite earth stations—3 Intelsat (Atlantic Ocean), 1 Inmarsat (Atlantic Ocean region east), connected by microwave relay system to Mercosur Brazilsat B3 satellite earth station (2011)
Broadcast media: state-run Radiobras operates a radio and a TV network; more than 1,000 radio stations and more than 100 TV channels operating—mostly privately owned; private media ownership highly concentrated (2007)
Radio broadcast stations: AM 1, 365, FM 296, shortwave 161 (of which 91 are collocated with AM stations) (1999)
Television broadcast stations: 138 (1997)
Internet country code: .br
Internet hosts: 26.577 million (2012)
country comparison to the world: 3
Internet users: *total:* 108.2 million percent of population: 53.4% (2014 est.)
country comparison to the world: 6

TRANSPORTATION

Airports: 4,093 (2013)
country comparison to the world: 2
Airports—with paved runways: *total:* 698
over 3,047 m: 7
2,438 to 3,047 m: 27
1,524 to 2,437 m: 179
914 to 1,523 m: 436
under 914 m: 49 (2013)
Airports—with unpaved runways: *total:* 3,395
1,524 to 2,437 m: 92
914 to 1,523 m: 1,619
under 914 m: 1,684 (2013)
Heliports: 13 (2013)
Pipelines: condensate/gas 251 km; gas 17,312 km; liquid petroleum gas 352 km; oil 4,831 km; refined products 4,722 km (2013)
Railways: *total:* 28,538 km
broad gauge: 5,822.3 km 1.600-m gauge (498.3 km electrified)
dual gauge: 492 km 1.600–1.000-m gauge
standard gauge: 194 km 1.435-m gauge
narrow gauge: 23,341.6 km 1.000-m gauge (24 km electrified) (2014)
country comparison to the world: 11
Roadways: *total:* 1,580,964 km
paved: 212,798 km
unpaved: 1,368,166 km
note: does not include urban roads (2010)
country comparison to the world: 4
Waterways: 50,000 km (most in areas remote from industry and population) (2012)
country comparison to the world: 3
Merchant marine: *total:* 109
by type: bulk carrier 18, cargo 16, chemical tanker 7, container 13, liquefied gas 11, petroleum tanker 39, roll on/roll off 5
foreign-owned: 27 (Chile 1, Denmark 3, Germany 6, Greece 1, Norway 3, Spain 12, Turkey 1)
registered in other countries: 36 (Argentina 1, Bahamas 1, Ghana 1, Liberia 20, Marshall Islands 1, Panama 3, Singapore 9) (2010)
country comparison to the world: 50

Ports and terminals: *major seaport(s):* Belem, Paranagua, Rio Grande, Rio de Janeiro, Santos, Sao Sebastiao, Tubarao
river port(s): Manaus (Amazon)
dry bulk cargo port(s): Sepetiba ore terminal, Tubarao
container ports (TEUs): Santos (2,985,922), Itajai (983,985)(2011)
oil terminal(s): DTSE/Gegua oil terminal, Ilha Grande (Gebig), Guaiba Island terminal, Guamare oil terminal
LNG terminal(s)(import): Pecem, Rio de Janiero

MILITARY AND SECURITY

Military branches: Brazilian Army (Exercito Brasileiro, EB), Brazilian Navy (Marinha do Brasil (MB), includes Naval Air and Marine Corps (Corpo de Fuzileiros Navais)), Brazilian Air Force (Forca Aerea Brasileira, FAB) (2011)
Military service age and obligation: 18–45 years of age for compulsory military service; conscript service obligation is 10–12 months; 17–45 years of age for voluntary service; an increasing percentage of the ranks are "long-service" volunteer professionals; women were allowed to serve in the armed forces beginning inearly 1980s, when the Brazilian Army became the first army in South America to accept women into career ranks; women serve in Navy and Air Force only in Women's Reserve Corps (2012)
Military expenditures: 1.47% of GDP (2012)
1.49% of GDP (2011)
1.47% of GDP (2010)
country comparison to the world: 65

TRANSNATIONAL ISSUES

Disputes—international: uncontested boundary dispute between Brazil and Uruguay over Brazilera/Brasiliera Island in the Quarai/Cuareim River leaves the tripoint with Argentina in question; smuggling of firearms and narcotics continues to be an issue along the Uruguay-Brazil border; Colombian-organized illegal narcotics and paramilitary activities penetrate Brazil's border region with Venezuela

Refugees and internally displaced persons: *stateless persons:* 4 (2015)

Illicit drugs: second—largest consumer of cocaine in the world; illicit producer of cannabis; trace amounts of cocacultivation in the Amazon region, used for domestic consumption; government has a large-scale eradication program to control cannabis; important transshipment country for Bolivian, Colombian, and Peruvian cocaine headed for Europe; also used by traffickers as a way station for narcotics air trans shipments between Peru and Colombia; upsurge in drug-related violence and weapons smuggling; important market for Colombian, Bolivian, and Peruvian cocaine; illicit narcotics proceeds are often laundered through the financial system; significant illicit financial activity in the Tri-Border Area (2008)

BRITISH INDIAN OCEAN TERRITORY

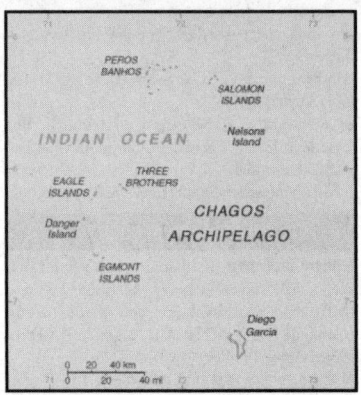

INTRODUCTION

Background: Formerly administered as part of the British Crown Colony of Mauritius, the British Indian Ocean Territory (BIOT) was established as an overseas territory of the UK in 1965. A number of the islands of the territory were later transferred to the Seychelles when it attained independence in 1976. Subsequently, BIOT has consisted only of the six main island groups comprising the Chagos Archipelago. Only Diego Garcia, the largest and most southerly of the islands, is inhabited. It contains a joint UK-US naval support facility and hosts one of four dedicated ground antennas (the others are on Ascension (Saint Helena, Ascension, and Tristan da Cunha), Kwajalein (Marshall Islands), and at Cape Canaveral, Florida (US)) that assist in the operation of the Global Positioning System (GPS) navigation system. The US Air Force also operates a telescope array on Diego Garcia as part of the Ground-Based Electro-Optical Deep Space Surveillance System (GEODSS) for tracking orbital debris, which can be a hazard to spacecraft and astronauts. Between 1967 and 1973, former agricultural workers, earlier residents in the islands, were relocated primarily to Mauritius, but also to the Seychelles. Negotiations between 1971 and 1982 resulted in the establishment of a trust fund by the British Government as compensation for the displaced islanders, known as Chagossians. Beginning in 1998, the islanders pursued a series of lawsuits against the British Government seeking further compensation and the right to return to the territory. In 2006 and 2007, British court rulings invalidated the immigration policies contained in the 2004 BIOT Constitution Order that had excluded the islanders from the archipelago, but upheld the special military status of Diego Garcia. In 2008, the House of Lords, as the final court of appeal in the UK, ruled in favor of the British Government by overturning the lower court rulings and finding no right of return for the Chagossians.

GEOGRAPHY

Location: archipelago in the Indian Ocean, south of India, about halfway between Africa and Indonesia

Geographic coordinates: 6 00 S, 71 30 E
note—Diego Garcia 7 20 S, 72 25 E

Map references: Political Map of the World

Area: *total:* 60 sq km
land: 60 sq km; Diego Garcia 44 sq km
water: 54,340 sq km
note: includes the entire Chagos Archipelago of 55 islands
country comparison to the world: 128

Area—comparative: land area is about one-third the size of Washington, DC

Land boundaries: 0 km

Coastline: 698 km

Maritime claims: *territorial sea:* 3 nm
exclusive fishing zone: 200 nm

Climate: tropical marine; hot, humid, moderated by trade winds

Terrain: flat and low (most areas do not exceed two m in elevation)

Elevation: *mean elevation:* NA

elevation extremes: *lowest:* point: Indian Ocean 0 m
highest point: unnamed location on Diego Garcia 15 m

Natural resources: coconuts, fish, sugarcane

Land use: *agricultural land:* 0%
arable land: 0%
permanent crops: 0%
permanent pasture: 0%
forest: 0%
other: 100% (2011 est.)

Natural hazards: NA

Environment—current issues: NA

Geography—note: archipelago of 55 islands; Diego Garcia, largest and southernmost island, occupies strategic location in central Indian Ocean; island is site of joint US-UK military facility

PEOPLE AND SOCIETY

Population: no indigenous inhabitants
note: approximately 1,200 former agricultural workers resident in the Chagos Archipelago, often referred to as Chagossians or Ilois, were relocated to Mauritius and the Seychelles in the 1960s and 1970s; approximately 3,000 UK and US military personnel and civilian contractors were living on the island of Diego Garcia

GOVERNMENT

Country name: *conventional long form:* British Indian Ocean Territory
conventional short form: none
abbreviation: BIOT
etymology: self-descriptive name specifying the territory's affiliation and location

Dependency status: overseas territory of the UK; administered by a commissioner, resident in the Foreign and Commonwealth Office in London

Legal system: the laws of the UK, where applicable, apply

Executive branch: *chief of state:* Queen ELIZABETH II (since 6 February 1952)

head of government: Commissioner Dr. Peter HAYES (since 17 October 2012); Administrator John MCMANUS (since April 2011); note—both reside in the UK and are represented by the officer commanding British Forces on Diego Garcia
cabinet: NA
elections/appointments: the monarchy is hereditary; commissioner and administrator appointed by the monarch

Diplomatic representation in the US: none (overseas territory of the UK)

Diplomatic representation from the US: none (overseas territory of the UK)

Flag description: white with six blue wavy horizontal stripes; the flag of the UK is in the upper hoist-side quadrant; the striped section bears a palm tree and yellow crown (the symbols of the territory) centered on the outer half of the flag; the wavy stripes represent the Indian Ocean; although not officially described, the six blue stripes may stand for the six main atolls of the archipelago

ECONOMY

Economy—overview: All economic activity is concentrated on the largest island of Diego Garcia, where a joint UK-US military facility is located. Construction projects and various services needed to support the military installation are performed by military and contract employees from the UK, Mauritius, the Philippines, and the US. Some of the natural resources found in this territory include coconuts, fish, and sugarcane. Sugarcane is still a major export for this territory. There are no industrial or agricultural activities on the islands. The territory earns foreign exchange by selling fishing licenses and postage stamps.

Exchange rates: the US dollar is used

COMMUNICATIONS

Telephone system: *general assessment:* separate facilities for military and public needs are available
domestic: all commercial telephone services are available, including connection to the Internet
international: country code (Diego Garcia)—246; international telephone service is carried by satellite (2000)

Broadcast media: Armed Forces Radio and Television Service (AFRTS) broadcasts over 3 separate frequencies for US and UK military personnel stationed on the islands (2009)

Radio broadcast stations: AM 1, FM 2, shortwave 0 (1998)

Television broadcast stations: 1 (1997)

Internet country code: .io

Internet hosts: 75,006 (2012)

country comparison to the world: 85

Airports: 1 (2013)
country comparison to the world: 213
Airports—with paved run ways: *total:* 1 over 3,047 m: 1 (2013)
Roadways: *note:* short section of paved road between port and airfield on Diego Garcia
Ports and terminals: *major seaport(s):* Diego Garcia

MILITARY AND SECURITY

Military branches: no regular military forces (2014)

Military—note: defense is the responsibility of the UK; the US lease on Diego Garcia expires in December 2016

TRANSNATIONAL ISSUES

Disputes—international: Mauritius and Seychelles claim the Chagos Islands; negotiations between 1971 and 1982 resulted in the establishment of a trust fund by the British Government as compensation for the displaced islanders, known as Chagossians, who were evicted between 1967–73; in 2001, the former inhabitants of the archipelago were granted UK citizenship and the right of return; in 2006 and 2007, British court rulings invalidated the immigration policies contained in the 2004 BIOT Constitution Order that had excluded the islanders from the archipelago; in 2008 a House of Lords' decision overturned lower court rulings, once again denying the right of return to Chagossians; in addition, the UK created the world's largest marine protection area around the Chagos islands prohibiting the extraction of any natural resources therein

BRITISH VIRGIN ISLANDS

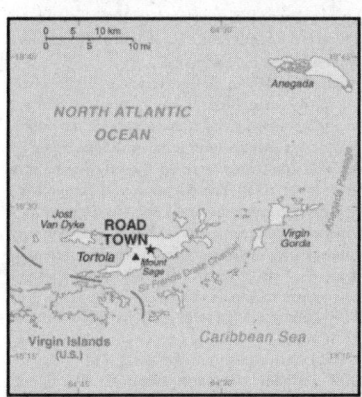

INTRODUCTION

Background: First inhabited by Arawak and later by Carib Indians, the Virgin Islands were settled by the Dutch in 1648 and then annexed by the English in 1672. The islands were part of the British colony of the Leeward Islands from 1872–1960; they were granted autonomy in 1967. The economy is closely tied to the larger and more populous US Virgin Islands to the west; the US dollar is the legal currency.

GEOGRAPHY

Location: Caribbean, between the Caribbean Sea and the North Atlantic Ocean, east of Puerto Rico
Geographic coordinates: 18 30 N, 64 30 W
Map references: Central America and the Caribbean
Area: *total:* 151 sq km
land: 151 sq km
water: 0 sq km
note: comprised of 16 in habited and more than 20 uninhabited is lands; includes the islands of Tortola, Anegada, Virgin Gorda, Jost van Dyke
country comparison to the world: 220

Area—comparative: about 0.9 times the size of Washington, DC
Land boundaries: 0 km
Coastline: 80 km
Maritime claims: *territorial sea:* 3 nm
exclusive fishing zone: 200 nm
Climate: subtropical; humid; temperatures moderated by trade winds
Terrain: coral islands relatively flat; volcanic islands steep, hilly
Elevation: *mean elevation:* NA

elevation extremes: *lowest:* point: Caribbean Sea 0 m
highest point: Mount Sage 521 m
Natural resources: NEGL; pleasant climate, beaches foster tourism
Land use: *agricultural land:* 46.7%
arable land: 6.7%
permanent crops: 6.7%
permanent pasture: 33.3%
forest: 24.3%
other: 29% (2011 est.)
Irrigated land: NA
Natural hazards: hurricanes and tropical storms (July to October)
Environment—current issues: limited natural freshwater resources except for a few seasonal streams and springs on Tortola; most of the islands' water supply comes from desalination plants
Geography—note: strong ties to nearby US Virgin Islands and Puerto Rico

PEOPLE AND SOCIETY

Nationality: *noun:* British Virgin Islander(s)
adjective: British Virgin Islander
Ethnic groups: black 82%, white 6.8%, mixed 5.9%, East Indian 3%, other 1.6%, unspecified 0.7% (2001 est.)
Languages: English (official)
Religions: Protestant 72.2% (Methodist 22.7%, Anglican 11.6%, Church of God 11.4%, Pentecostal 9.1%, Seventh Day Adventist 8.4%, Baptist 8.2%, other Protestant 0.9%), Roman Catholic 9.5%, Jehovah's Witness 2.1%, Hindu 1.9%, other 5.2%, none 6.4%, unspecified 2.7% (2001 est.)
Population: 33,454 (July 2015 est.)
country comparison to the world: 215
Age structure: *0–14 years:* 17.01% (male 2,798/female 2,891)
15–24 years: 14.14% (male 2,255/female 2,476)
25–54 years: 49.64% (male 7,840/female 8,767)
55–64 years: 10.97% (male 1,797/female 1,872)
65 years and over: 8.24% (male 1,343/female 1,415) (2015 est.)
Median age: *total:* 35.9 years
male: 35.8 years
female: 36 years (2015 est.)
country comparison to the world: 73
Population growth rate: 2.32% (2015 est.)
country comparison to the world: 33
Birth rate: 10.91 births/1,000 population (2015 est.)
country comparison to the world: 179
Death rate: 4.99 deaths/1,000 population (2015 est.)
country comparison to the world: 190
Net migration rate: 17.28 migrant(s)/1,000 population (2015 est.)
country comparison to the world: 2
Urbanization: *urban population:* 46.2% of total population (2015)
rate of urbanization: 1.8% annual rate of change (2010–15 est.)
Major urban areas—population: ROAD TOWN (capital) 13,000 (2014)
Sex ratio: *at birth:* 1.05 male(s)/female
0–14 years: 0.97 male(s)/female
15–24 years: 0.91 male(s)/female
25–54 years: 0.89 male(s)/female
55–64 years: 0.96 male(s)/female
65 years and over: 0.95 male(s)/female
total population: 0.92 male(s)/female (2015 est.)
Infant mortality rate: *total:* 12.98 deaths/1,000 live births
male: 14.79 deaths/1,000 live births
female: 11.09 deaths/1,000 live births (2015 est.)
country comparison to the world: 116

Life expectancy at birth: *total population:* 78.46 years
male: 77.12 years
female: 79.87 years (2015 est.)
country comparison to the world: 57
Total fertility rate: 1.26 children born/woman (2015 est.)
country comparison to the world: 219
Drinking water source:
improved:
urban: 98% of population
rural: 98% of population
total: 98% of population
unimproved:
urban: 2% of population
rural: 2% of population
total: 2% of population (2010 est.)
Sanitation facility access:
improved:
urban: 97.5% of population
rural: 97.5% of population
total: 97.5% of population
unimproved:
urban: 2.5% of population
rural: 2.5% of population
total: 2.5% of population (2015 est.)
HIV/AIDS—adult prevalence rate: NA
HIV/AIDS—people living with HIV/AIDS: NA
HIV/AIDS—deaths: NA
Education expenditures: 4.4% of GDP (2010)
country comparison to the world: 96
School life expectancy (primary to tertiary education): *total:* 14 years
male: NA
female: NA (2009)

GOVERNMENT

Country name: *conventional long form:* none
conventional short form: British Virgin Islands
abbreviation: BVI
etymology: the myriad islets, cays, and rocks surrounding the major islands reminded explorer Christopher COLUMBUS in 1493 of Saint Ursula and her 11,000 virgin followers (Santa Ursula y las Once Mil Virgenes), which over time shortened to the Virgins (las Virgenes)
Dependency status: overseas territory of the UK; internal self-governing
Government type: parliamentary democracy (House of Assembly); self-governing overseas territory of the UK
Capital: *name:* Road Town
Geographic coordinates: 18 25 N, 64 37 W
time difference: UTC-4 (1 hour ahead of Washington, DC, during Standard Time)
Administrative divisions: none (overseas territory of the UK)
Independence: none (overseas territory of the UK)
National holiday: Territory Day, 1 July (1956)
Constitution: several previous; latest effective 15 June 2007 (2016)
Legal system: English common law
Citizenship: see United Kingdom
Suffrage: 18 years of age; universal

Executive branch: *chief of state:* Queen ELIZABETH II (since 6 February 1952); represented by Governor John DUNCAN (since 15 August 2014)
head of government: Premier Orlando SMITH (since 9 November 2011)
cabinet: Executive Council appointed by the governor from members of the House of Assembly
elections/appointments: the monarchy is hereditary; governor appointed by the monarch; following legislative elections, the leader of the majority party or majority coalition usually appointed premier by the governor
Legislative branch: *description:* unicameral House of Assembly (13 seats; 9 members directly elected in single-seat constituencies and 4 at-large seats by simple majority vote to serve 4-year terms); note—the Assembly includes the attorney general, a non-voting ex officio member
elections: last held on 8 June 2015 (next to be held in 2019)
election results: percent of vote by party—NA; seats by party—NDP 9, VIP 3, PEP 1
Judicial branch: *highest court(s):* the Eastern Caribbean Supreme Court (ECSC) is the itinerant superior court of record for the 9-member Organization of Eastern Caribbean States to include the British Virgin Islands; the ECSC -with its headquarters on St. Lucia—is headed by the chief justice and is comprised of the Court of Appeal with 3 justices and the High Court with 16 judges; sittings of the Court of Appeal and High Court rotate among the 9 member states; 3 High Court judges reside in member states; 3 High Court judges reside on the British Virgin Islands
judge selection and term of office: Eastern Caribbean Supreme Court chief justice appointed by Her Majesty, Queen ELIZABETH II; other justices and judges appointed by the Judicial and Legal Services Commission; Court of Appeal justices appointed for life with mandatory retirement at age 65; High Court judges appointed for life with mandatory retirement at age 62
subordinate courts: Magistrates' Courts
Political parties and leaders: National Democratic Party or NDP [Orlando SMITH];; Virgin Islands Party or VIP [Julian FRASER]
Political pressure groups and leaders: Family Support Network Woman's Desk
other: environmentalists
International organization participation: Caricom (associate), CDB, Interpol (subbureau), IOC, OECS, UNESCO (associate), UPU
Diplomatic representation in the US: none (overseas territory of the UK)
Diplomatic representation from the US: none (overseas territory of the UK)
Flag description: blue with the flag of the UK in the upper hoist-side quadrant and the Virgin Islander coat of arms centered in the outer half of the flag; the coat of arms depicts a woman flanked on either side by a vertical column of six oil lamps above a scroll bearing the Latin word VIGILATE (Be Watchful); the islands were named by COLUMBUS in 1493 in honor of Saint Ursula and her 11 virgin followers (some sources say

11,000) who reputedly were martyred by the Huns in the 4th or 5th century; the figure on the banner holding a lamp represents the saint; the other lamps symbolize her followers
National symbol(s): zenaida dove, white cedar flower; national colors: yellow, green, red, white, blue
National anthem: note: as a territory of the United Kingdom, "God Save the Queen" is official (see United Kingdom)

ECONOMY

Economy—overview: The economy, one of the most stable and prosperous in the Caribbean, is highly dependent on tourism generating an estimated 45% of the national income. More than 934,000 tourists, mainly from the US, visited the islands in 2008. Because of traditionally close links with the US Virgin Islands, the British Virgin Islands has used the US dollar as its currency since 1959.
Livestock raising is the most important agricultural activity; poor soils limit the islands' ability to meet domestic food requirements.
In the mid-1980s, the government began offering offshore registration to companies wishing to incorporate in the islands, and incorporation fees now generate substantial revenues. Roughly 400,000 companies were on the offshore registry by yearend 2000. The adoption of a comprehensive insurance law in late 1994, which provides a blanket of confidentiality with regulated statutory gateways for investigation of criminal offenses, made the British Virgin Islands even more attractive to international business.
GDP (purchasing power parity): $500 million (2010 est.)
country comparison to the world: 214
GDP (official exchange rate): $1.095 billion (2008)
GDP—real growth rate: 1.3% (2010 est.)
-0.6% (2008 est.)
country comparison to the world: 161
GDP—per capita (PPP): $42,300 (2010 est.)
country comparison to the world: 37
GDP—composition, by end use:
household consumption: 36.6%
government consumption: 8.9%
investment in fixed capital: 25.7%
investment in inventories: 0%
exports of goods and services: 97.8%
imports of goods and services: -69% (2015 est.)
GDP—composition, by sector of origin:
agriculture: 1.1%
industry: 12%
services: 86.9% (2015 est.)
Agriculture—products: fruits, vegetables; livestock, poultry; fish
Industries: tourism, light industry, construction, rum, concrete block, offshore banking center
Industrial production growth rate: 2.5% (2015 est.)
country comparison to the world: 104
Labor force: 12,770 (2004)
country comparison to the world: 216
Labor force—by occupation:
agriculture: 0.6%
industry: 40%
services: 59.4% (2005)

Unemployment rate: 8.7% (2010 est.)
country comparison to the world: 100
Population below poverty line: NA%

Household income or consumption by percentage share: *lowest:* 10%: NA%
highest: 10%: NA%
Budget: *revenues:* $300 million
expenditures: $300 million (2015 est.)
Taxes and other revenues: 27.4% of GDP (2015 est.)
country comparison to the world: 100
Budget surplus (+) or deficit (–): 0% of GDP (2015 est.)
country comparison to the world: 32
Fiscal year: 1 April—31 March
Inflation rate (consumer prices): 2.3% (2015 est.) 2% (2014 est.)
country comparison to the world: 124
Current account balance: $362.6 million (2011 est.)
$279.8 million (2010 est.)
country comparison to the world: 46
Exports: $25 million (2014 est.)
$25 million (2014 est.)
country comparison to the world: 207
Exports—commodities: rum, fresh fish, fruits, animals; gravel, sand
Imports: $290 million (2014 est.)
$290 million (2014 est.)
country comparison to the world: 201
Imports—commodities: building materials, automobiles, foodstuffs, machinery
Debt—external: $36.1 million (1997)
country comparison to the world: 197
Exchange rates: the US dollar is used

ENERGY

Electricity—production: 55 million kWh (2012 est.)
country comparison to the world: 205
Electricity—consumption: 51.15 million kWh (2012 est.)
country comparison to the world: 204
Electricity—exports: 0 kWh (2013 est.)
country comparison to the world: 212
Electricity—imports: 0 kWh (2013 est.)
country comparison to the world: 215
Electricity—installed generating capacity: 44,000 kW (2012 est.)
country comparison to the world: 192
Electricity—from fossil fuels: 100% of total installed capacity (2012 est.)
country comparison to the world: 33

Electricity—from nuclear fuels: 0% of total installed capacity (2012 est.)
country comparison to the world: 204
Electricity—from hydroelectric plants: 0% of total installed capacity (2012 est.)
country comparison to the world: 210
Electricity—from other renewable sources: 0% of total installed capacity (2012 est.)
country comparison to the world: 140
Crude oil—production: 0 bbl/day (2014 est.)
country comparison to the world: 206
Crude oil—exports: 0 bbl/day (2012 est.)
country comparison to the world: 206
Crude oil—imports: 0 bbl/day (2012 est.)
country comparison to the world: 144
Crude oil—proved reserves: 0 bbl (1 January 2015 est.)
country comparison to the world: 207
Refined petroleum products—production: 0 bbl/day (2012 est.)
country comparison to the world: 144
Refined petroleum products—consumption: 800 bbl/day (2013 est.)
country comparison to the world: 205
Refined petroleum products—exports: 0 bbl/day (2012 est.)
country comparison to the world: 145
Refined petroleum products—imports: 772.6 bbl/day (2012 est.)
country comparison to the world: 202
Natural gas—production: 0 cu m (2013 est.) 140 206 206 144 207
country comparison to the world: 144
Natural gas—consumption: 0 cu m (2013 est.)
country comparison to the world: 207
Natural gas—exports: 0 cu m (2013 est.)
country comparison to the world: 206
Natural gas—imports: 0 cu m (2013 est.)
country comparison to the world: 76
Natural gas—proved reserves: 0 cu m (1 January 2014 est.)
country comparison to the world: 206
Carbon dioxide emissions from consumption of energy: 160,100 Mt (2012 est.)
country comparison to the world: 200

COMMUNICATIONS

Telephones—fixed lines: *total subscriptions:* 11,800
subscriptions per 100 inhabitants: 36 (2014 est.)
country comparison to the world: 197
Telephones—mobile cellular: *total:* 48,400
subscriptions per 100 inhabitants: 148 (2014 est.)
country comparison to the world: 202

Telephone system: *general assessment:* good overall telephone service
domestic: fixed-line connections exceed 80 per 100 persons and mobile cellular subscribership is roughly 150 per 100 persons
international: country code—1-284; connected via submarine cable to Bermuda; the East Caribbean Fiber System (ECFS) submarine cable provides connectivity to 13 other islands in the eastern Caribbean (2011)
Broadcast media: 1 private TV station; multichannel TV is available from cable and satellite subscription services; about a half dozen private radio stations (2007)
Radio broadcast stations: AM 1, FM 5, shortwave 0 (2004)
Television broadcast stations: 1 (plus 1 cable company) (1997)
Internet country code: .vg
Internet hosts: 505 (2012)
country comparison to the world: 182
Internet users: *total:* 4,000 percent of population: 16.8% (2002)
country comparison to the world: 207

TRANSPORTATION

Airports: 4 (2013)
country comparison to the world: 185
Airports—with paved run ways: *total:* 2
914 to 1,523 m: 1
under 914 m: 1 (2013)
Airports—with unpaved runways: *total:* 2
914 to 1,523 m: 2 (2013)
Roadways: *total:* 200 km
paved: 200 km (2007)
country comparison to the world: 209
Ports and terminals: *major seaport(s):* Road Harbor

MILITARY AND SECURITY

Military—note: defense is the responsibility of the UK

TRANSNATIONAL ISSUES

Disputes—international: none

Illicit drugs: transshipment point for South American narcotics destined for the US and Europe; large offshore financial center makes it vulnerable to money laundering

BRUNEI

INTRODUCTION

Background: The Sultanate of Brunei's influence peaked between the 15th and 17th centuries when its control extended over coastal areas of northwest Borneo and the southern Philippines. Brunei subsequently entered a period of decline brought on by internal strife over royal succession, colonial expansion of European powers, and piracy. In 1888, Brunei became a British protectorate; independence was achieved in 1984. The same family has ruled Brunei for over six centuries. Brunei benefits from extensive petroleum and natural gas fields, the source of one of the highest per capita GDPs in the world.

GEOGRAPHY

Location: Southeastern Asia, along the northern coast of the island of Borneo, bordering the South China Sea and Malaysia

Geographic coordinates: 4 30 N, 114 40 E

Map references: Southeast Asia

Area: *total:* 5,765 sq km

land: 5,265 sq km

water: 500 sq km

country comparison to the world: 173

Area—comparative: slightly smaller than Delaware

Land boundaries: *total:* 266 km

border countries (1): Malaysia 266 km

Coastline: 161 km

Maritime claims: *territorial sea:* 12 nm

exclusive economic zone: 200 nm or to median line

Climate: tropical; hot, humid, rainy

Terrain: flat coastal plain rises to mountains in east; hilly lowland in west

Elevation: *mean elevation:* 478 m

elevation extremes: *lowest:* point: South China Sea 0 m

highest point: Bukit Pagon 1,850 m

Natural resources: petroleum, natural gas, timber

Land use: *agricultural land:* 2.5%

arable land: 0.8%

permanent crops: 1.1%

permanent pasture: 0.6%

forest: 71.8%

other: 25.7% (2011 est.)

Irrigated land: 10 sq km (2012)

Total renewable water resources: 8.5 cu km (2011)

Freshwater withdrawal (domestic/industrial/agricultural): *total:* 0.09 cu km/yr (97%/0%/3%)

per capita: 301.6 cu m/yr (2009)

Natural hazards: typhoons, earthquakes, and severe flooding are rare

Environment—current issues: seasonal smoke/haze resulting from forest fires in Indonesia

Environment—international agreements: *party to:* Biodiversity, Climate Change, Desertification, Endangered Species, Hazardous Wastes, Law of the Sea, Ozone Layer Protection, Ship Pollution

signed, but not ratified: none of the selected agreements

Geography—note: close to vital sea lanes through South China Sea linking Indian and Pacific Oceans; two parts physically separated by Malaysia; almost an enclave within Malaysia

PEOPLE AND SOCIETY

Nationality: *noun:* Bruneian(s)

adjective: Bruneian

Ethnic groups: Malay 65.7%, Chinese 10.3%, other indigenous 3.4%, other 20.6% (2011 est.)

Languages: Malay (official), English, Chinese dialects

Religions: Muslim (official) 78.8%, Christian 8.7%, Buddhist 7.8%, other (includes indigenous beliefs) 4.7% (2011 est.)

Population: 429,646 (July 2015 est.)

country comparison to the world: 175

Age structure: *0–14 years:* 23.82% (male 52,750/female 49,579)

15–24 years: 17.13% (male 36,485/female 37,127)

25–54 years: 46.9% (male 97,228/female 104,286)

55–64 years: 7.88% (male 17,366/female 16,470)

65 years and over: 4.27% (male 8,925/female 9,430) (2015 est.)

Dependency ratios: *total* dependency ratio: 38%

youth dependency ratio: 31.9%

elderly dependency ratio: 6.1%

potential support ratio: 16.4% (2015 est.)

Median age: *total:* 29.6 years

male: 29.2 years

female: 29.9 years (2015 est.)

country comparison to the world: 114

Population growth rate: 1.62% (2015 est.)

country comparison to the world: 72

Birth rate: 17.32 births/1,000 population (2015 est.)

country comparison to the world: 107

Death rate: 3.52 deaths/1,000 population (2015 est.)

country comparison to the world: 215

Net migration rate: 2.43 migrant(s)/1,000 population (2015 est.)

country comparison to the world: 41

Urbanization: *urban population:* 77.2% of total population (2015)

rate of urbanization: -1.79% annual rate of change (2010–15 est.)

Major urban areas—population: BANDAR SERI BEGAWAN (capital) 241,000

note: the boundaries of the capital city were expanded in 2007, greatly increasing the city area; the population of the capital increased tenfold (2011)

Sex ratio: *at birth:* 1.05 male(s)/female

0–14 years: 1.06 male(s)/female

15–24 years: 0.98 male(s)/female

25–54 years: 0.93 male(s)/female

55–64 years: 1.05 male(s)/female

65 years and over: 0.95 male(s)/female

total population: 0.98 male(s)/female (2015 est.)

Maternal mortality rate: 23 deaths/100,000 live births (2015 est.)

country comparison to the world: 132

Infant mortality rate: *total:* 10.16 deaths/1,000 live births

male: 12.09 deaths/1,000 live births

female: 8.14 deaths/1,000 live births (2015 est.)

country comparison to the world: 137

Life expectancy at birth: *total population:* 76.97 years

male: 74.64 years

female: 79.41 years (2015 est.)

country comparison to the world: 76

Total fertility rate: 1.8 children born/woman (2015 est.)

country comparison to the world: 152

Health expenditures: 2.5% of GDP (2013)

country comparison to the world: 188

Physicians density: 1.44 physicians/1,000 population (2012)

Hospital bed density: 2.8 beds/1,000 population (2012)

HIV/AIDS—adult prevalence rate: NA

HIV/AIDS—people living with HIV/AIDS: NA

HIV/AIDS—deaths: NA

Obesity—adult prevalence rate: 18.6% (2014)

country comparison to the world: 141

Children under the age of 5 years underweight: 9.6% (2009)

Education expenditures: 3.8% of GDP (2014)

country comparison to the world: 126

Literacy: *definition:* age 15 and over can read and write

total population: 96%

male: 97.5%

female: 94.5% (2015 est.)

School life expectancy (primary to tertiary education): *total:* 15 years

male: 15 years

female: 15 years (2014)

GOVERNMENT

Country name: *conventional long form:* Brunei Darussalam

conventional short form: Brunei

local long form: Negara Brunei Darussalam

local short form: Brunei

etymology: derivation of the name is unclear; according to legend, MUHAMMAD SHAH, who would become the first sultan of Brunei, upon discovering what would become Brunei exclaimed "Barunah," which roughly translates as "there" or "that's it"

Government type: absolute monarchy or sultanate (locally known as Malay Islamic Monarchy)

Capital: *name:* Bandar Seri Begawan

Geographic coordinates: 4 53 N, 114 56 E

time difference: UTC+8 (13 hours ahead of Washington, DC, during Standard Time)

Administrative divisions: 4 districts (daerah-daerah, singular—daerah); Belait, Brunei-Muara, Temburong, Tutong

Independence: 1 January 1984 (from the UK)

National holiday: National Day, 23 February (1984); note—1 January 1984 was the date of independence from the UK, 23 February 1984 was the date of independence from British protection

Constitution: drafted 1954 to 1959, signed 29 September 1959; amended 1984, 2004, 2011; note—some constitutional provisions suspended since 1962 under a State of Emergency, others suspended since independence in 1984 (2016)

Legal system: mixed legal system based on English common law and Islamic law; note—in May 2014, the first phase of a sharia-based penal codes was instituted, which applies to Muslims and non-Muslims and exists in parallel to the existing common law-based code

International law organization participation: has not submitted an ICJ jurisdiction declaration; non-party state to the ICCt

Citizenship: *citizenship by birth:* no

citizenship by descent only: the father must be a citizen of Brunei

dual citizenship recognized: no

residency requirement for naturalization: 12 years

Suffrage: 18 years of age for village elections; universal

Executive branch: *chief of state:* Sultan and Prime Minister Sir HASSANAL Bolkiah (since 5 October 1967); note—the monarch is both chief of state and head of government

head of government: Sultan and Prime Minister Sir HASSANAL Bolkiah (since 5 October 1967)

cabinet: Council of Ministers appointed and presided over by the monarch; note—4 additional advisory councils appointed by the monarch are the Religious Council, Privy Council for constitutional issues, Council of Succession, and Legislative Council

elections/appointments: none; the monarchy is hereditary

Legislative branch: *description:* Legislative Council or Majlis Mesyuarat Negara Brunei (36 seats; members appointed by the sultan including 3 ex-officio members—the speaker and first and second secretaries; meets annually for approximately two weeks)

elections: last held in March 1962 (date of next election NA)

Judicial branch: *highest resident court(s):* Supreme Court (consists of Court of Appeal and High Court, each with a chief justice and 2 judges); Sharia Court of Appeal (consists of judges appointed by the monarch); note -Brunei has a dual judicial system of secular and sharia (religious) courts; the Judicial Committee of Privy Council in London serves as the final appellate court for civil cases only

judge selection and term of office: Supreme Court judges appointed by the monarch to serve until age 65, and older if approved by the monarch; Sharia Court of Appeal judges appointed by the monarch; judge tenure NA

subordinate courts: Intermediate Court; Magistrate's Courts; Juvenile Court; small claims courts; lower sharia courts

Political parties and leaders: National Development Party or NDP [YASSIN Affendi]

note: Brunei National Solidarity Party or PPKB [Abdul LATIF bin Chuchu] and People's Awareness Party or PAKAR [Awang Haji MAIDIN bin Haji Ahmad] were deregistered in 2007; parties are small and have limited activity

Political pressure groups and leaders: NA

International organization participation: ADB, APEC, ARF, ASEAN, C, CP, EAS, FAO, G-77, IAEA, IBRD, ICAO, ICC (NGOs), ICRM, IDA, IFRCS, ILO, IMF, IMO, IMSO, Interpol, IOC, ISO (correspondent), ITSO, ITU, NAM, OIC, OPCW, UN, UNCTAD, UNESCO, UNIFIL, UNWTO, UPU, WCO, WHO, WIPO, WMO, WTO

Diplomatic representation in the US: *chief of mission:* Ambassador Serbini ALI (since 28 January 2016)

chancery: 3520 International Court NW, Washington, DC 20008

telephone: [1] (202) 237-1838

FAX: [1] (202) 885-0560

consulate(s): New York

Diplomatic representation from the US: *chief of mission:* Ambassador Craig B. ALLEN (since 9 March 2015)

embassy: Simpang 336–52–16–9, Jalan Datu, Bandar Seri Begawan, BC4115

mailing address: Unit 4280, Box 40, FPO AP 96507; P.O. Box 2991, Bandar Seri Begawan BS8675, Negara Brunei Darussalam

telephone: [673] 238-4616

FAX: [673] 238-4604

Flag description: yellow with two diagonal bands of white (top, almost double width) and black starting from the upper hoist side; the national emblem in red is superimposed at the center; yellow is the color of royalty and symbolizes the sultanate; the white and black bands denote Brunei's chief ministers; the emblem includes five main components: a swallow-tailed flag, the royal umbrella representing the monarchy, the wings of four feathers symbolizing justice, tranquility, prosperity, and peace, the two upraised hands signifying the government's pledge to preserve and promote the welfare of the people, and the crescent moon denoting Islam, the state religion; the state motto "Always render service with God's

guidance" appears in yellow Arabic script on the crescent; a ribbon below the crescent reads "Brunei, the Abode of Peace"

National symbol(s): royal parasol; national colors: yellow, white, black

National anthem: *Name:* "Allah Peliharakan Sultan" (God Bless His Majesty)

lyrics/music: Pengiran Haji Mohamed YUSUF bin Pengiran Abdul Rahim/Awang Haji BESAR bin Sagap

note: adopted 1951

ECONOMY

Economy—overview: Brunei is an energy-rich sultanate on the northern coast of Borneo in Southeast Asia. Brunei boasts a well-educated, largely English-speaking population; excellent infrastructure; and a stable government intent on attracting foreign investment. Crude oil and natural gas production account for approximately 65% of GDP and 95% of exports, with Japan as the primary export market. Per capita GDP is among the highest in the world, and substantial income from overseas investment supplements income from domestic hydrocarbon production. Bruneian citizens do not pay personal income taxes, and the government provides free medical services and free education through the university level. The Bruneian Government wants to diversify its economy away from hydrocarbon exports to other industries such as information and communications technology and halal manufacturing. Brunei's trade in 2016 is set to increase following its regional economic integration in the ASEAN Economic Community, and the expected ratification of the Trans-Pacific Partnership trade agreement.

GDP (purchasing power parity): $33.22 billion (2015 est.)

$33.29 billion (2014 est.)

$34.09 billion (2013 est.)

note: data are in 2015 US dollars

country comparison to the world: 124

GDP (official exchange rate): $11.79 billion (2015 est.)

GDP—real growth rate: -0.2% (2015 est.) -2.3% (2014 est.) -2.1% (2013 est.)

country comparison to the world: 200

GDP—per capita (PPP): $79,700 (2015 est.)

$80,800 (2014 est.)

$84,000 (2013 est.)

note: data are in 2015 US dollars

country comparison to the world: 8

Gross national saving: 29% of GDP (2015 est.)

62.6% of GDP (2014 est.)

59% of GDP (2013 est.)

country comparison to the world: 28

GDP—composition, by end use:

household consumption: 15.9%

government consumption: 22%

investment in fixed capital: 32%

investment in inventories: 0%

exports of goods and services: 67.5%

imports of goods and services: -37.4% (2015 est.)

GDP—composition, by sector of origin:

agriculture: 0.9%

industry: 66.8%

services: 32.3% (2015 est.)

Agriculture—products: rice, vegetables, fruits; chickens, water buffalo, cattle, goats, eggs

Industries: petroleum, petroleum refining, liquefied natural gas, construction, agriculture, transportation

Industrial production growth rate: 0.9% (2015 est.)
country comparison to the world: 150

Labor force: 203,600 (2014 est.)
country comparison to the world: 169

Labor force—by occupation: agriculture: 4.2%
industry: 62.8%
services: 33% (2008 est.)

Unemployment rate: 6.9% (2014 est.)
9.3% (2011 est.)
country comparison to the world: 84

Population below poverty line: NA%

Household income or consumption by percentage share: *lowest:* 10%: NA%
highest: 10%: NA%

Budget: *revenues:* $4.142 billion
expenditures: $5.547 billion (2015 est.)
Taxes and other revenues: 26.9% of GDP (2015 est.)
country comparison to the world: 104

Budget surplus (+) or deficit (–): -9.1% of GDP (2015 est.)
country comparison to the world: 202

Fiscal year: 1 April—31 March

Inflation rate (consumer prices): -0.4% (2015 est.)
-0.2% (2014 est.)
country comparison to the world: 31

Commercial bank prime lending rate: 5.5% (31 December 2015 est.)
5.5% (31 December 2014 est.)
country comparison to the world: 137

Stock of narrow money: $3.32 billion (31 December 2015 est.)
$3.137 billion (31 December 2014 est.)
country comparison to the world: 113

Stock of broad money: $10.44 billion (31 December 2014 est.)
$10.11 billion (31 December 2013 est.)
country comparison to the world: 107

Stock of domestic credit: $5.788 billion (31 December 2015 est.)
$4.361 billion (31 December 2014 est.)
country comparison to the world: 119

Market value of publicly traded shares: $NA

Current account balance: $921 million (2015 est.)
$4.747 billion (2014 est.)
country comparison to the world: 38

Exports: $7.08 billion (2015 est.)
$10.51 billion (2014 est.)
country comparison to the world: 101

Exports—commodities: mineral fuels, organic chemicals

Exports—partners: Japan 35.9%, South Korea 14.8%, Thailand 10.8%, India 9.8%, NZ 5.6%, Australia 5% (2015)

Imports: $4.84 billion (2015 est.)
$3.599 billion (2014 est.)
country comparison to the world: 126

Imports—commodities: machinery and mechanical appliance parts, mineral fuels, motor vehicles, electric machinery

Imports—partners: Singapore 27.9%, China 25.3%, Malaysia 12.4%, UK 10.6%, South Korea 4.9% (2015)

Debt—external: $0 (2014)
$0 (2013)
note: public external debt only; private external debt unavailable
country comparison to the world: 204

Exchange rates: Bruneian dollars (BND) per US dollar—
1.352 (2015 est.)
1.267 (2014 est.)
1.267 (2013 est.)
1.25 (2012 est.)
1.2579 (2011 est.)

ENERGY

Electricity—production: 4.055 billion kWh (2014 est.)
country comparison to the world: 123

Electricity—consumption: 3.766 billion kWh (2014 est.)
country comparison to the world: 128

Electricity—exports: 0 kWh (2014 est.)
country comparison to the world: 113

Electricity—imports: 0 kWh (2014 est.)
country comparison to the world: 126

Electricity—installed generating capacity: 777,000 kW (2014 est.)
country comparison to the world: 130

Electricity—from fossil fuels: 100% of total installed capacity (2014 est.)
country comparison to the world: 7

Electricity—from nuclear fuels: 0% of total installed capacity (2014 est.)
country comparison to the world: 60

Electricity—from hydroelectric plants: 0% of total installed capacity (2014 est.)
country comparison to the world: 164

Electricity—from other renewable sources: 0% of total installed capacity (2014 est.)
country comparison to the world: 163

Crude oil—production: 126,500 bbl/day (2014 est.)
country comparison to the world: 41

Crude oil—exports: 117,600 bbl/day (2014 est.)
country comparison to the world: 35

Crude oil—imports: 0 bbl/day (2014 est.)
country comparison to the world: 167

Crude oil—proved reserves: 1.1 billion bbl (1 January 2015 est.)
country comparison to the world: 42

Refined petroleum products—production: 9,402 bbl/day (2012 est.)
country comparison to the world: 105

Refined petroleum products—consumption: 18,000 bbl/day (2013 est.)
country comparison to the world: 133

Refined petroleum products—exports: 254 bbl/day (2012 est.)
country comparison to the world: 118

Refined petroleum products—imports: 7,666 bbl/day (2012 est.)
country comparison to the world: 144

Natural gas—production: 12.47 billion cu m (2013 est.)

country comparison to the world: 38

Natural gas—consumption: 2.97 billion cu m (2013 est.)
country comparison to the world: 73

Natural gas—exports: 9.5 billion cu m (2013 est.)
country comparison to the world: 23

Natural gas—imports: 0 cu m (2014 est.)
country comparison to the world: 170

Natural gas—proved reserves: 390.8 billion cu m (1 January 2014 est.)
country comparison to the world: 34

Carbon dioxide emissions from consumption of energy: 8.678 million Mt (2012 est.)
country comparison to the world: 107

COMMUNICATIONS

Telephones—fixed lines: *total subscriptions:* 48,200
subscriptions per 100 inhabitants: 11 (2014 est.)
country comparison to the world: 164

Telephones—mobile cellular: *total:* 465,800
subscriptions per 100 inhabitants: 110 (2014 est.)
country comparison to the world: 171

Telephone system: *general assessment:* service throughout the country is good; international service is good to Southeast Asia, Middle East, Western Europe, and the US
domestic: every service available
international: country code—673; landing point for the SEA-ME-WE-3 optical telecommunications submarine cable that provides links to Asia, the Middle East, and Europe; the Asia-America Gateway submarine cable network provides new links to Asia and the US; satellite earth stations—2 Intelsat (1 Indian Ocean and 1 Pacific Ocean) (2011)

Broadcast media: state-controlled Radio Television Brunei (RTB) operates 5 channels; 3 Malaysian TV stations are available; foreign TV broadcasts are available via satellite and cable systems; RTB operates 5 radio networks and broadcasts on multiple frequencies; British Forces Broadcast Service (BF BS) provides radio broadcasts on 2 FM stations; some radio broadcast stations from Malaysia are available via repeaters (2009)

Radio broadcast stations: AM 1, FM 2 (transmitting on 18 different frequencies), shortwave 0 (British Forces Broadcasting Service (BFBS) station transmits two FM signals withenglish and Nepali service) (2006)

Television broadcast stations: 4 (includes 2 UHF stations broadcasting a subscription service) (2006)

Internet country code: .bn

Internet hosts: 49,457 (2012)
country comparison to the world: 96

Internet users: *total:* 277,200
percent of population: 65.6% (2014 est.)
country comparison to the world: 146

TRANSPORTATION

Airports: 1 (2013)
country comparison to the world: 214

Airports—with paved run ways: *total:* 1
over 3,047 m: 1 (2013)

Heliports: 3 (2013)
Pipelines: condensate 33 km; condensate/gas 86 km; gas 628 km; oil 492 km (2013)
Roadways: total: 3,029 km
paved: 2,425 km
unpaved: 604 km (2010)
country comparison to the world: 167
Waterways: 209 km (navigable by craft drawing less than 1.2 m; the Belait, Brunei, and Tutong rivers are major transport links) (2012)
country comparison to the world: 96
Merchant marine: total: 9
by type: chemical tanker 1, liquefied gas 8
foreign-owned: 2 (UK 2) (2010)
country comparison to the world: 115
Ports and terminals: *major seaport(s):* Muara
oil terminal(s): Lumut, Seria
LNG terminal (export): Lumut

MILITARY AND SECURITY

Military branches: Royal Brunei Armed Forces: Royal Brunei Land Forces, Royal Brunei Navy,

Royal Brunei Air Force (Tentera Udara Diraja Brunei) (2013)
Military service age and obligation: 17 years of age for voluntary military service; non-Malays are ineligible to serve; recruits from the army, navy, and air force all undergo 43-week initial training (2013)
Military expenditures: 2.43% of GDP (2012)
2.54% of GDP (2011)
2.43% of GDP (2010)
country comparison to the world: 30

TRANSNATIONAL ISSUES

Disputes—international: per Letters of Exchange signed in 2009, Malaysia in 2010 ceded two hydrocarbon concession blocks to Brunei in exchange for Brunei's sultan dropping claims to the Limbang corridor, which divides Brunei; nonetheless, Brunei claims a maritime boundary extendingas far as a median with Vietnam, thus asserting an implicit claim to Louisa Reef
Refugees and internally displaced persons: *stateless persons:* 20,524 (2015); note—thousands of

stateless persons, often ethnic Chinese, are permanent residents and their families have lived in Brunei for generations; obtaining citizenship is difficult and requires individuals to pass rigorous tests on Malay culture, customs, and language; stateless residents receive an International Certificate of Identity, which enables them to travel overseas; the government is considering changing the law prohibiting non-Bruneians, including stateless permanent residents, from owning land

Illicit drugs: drug trafficking and illegally importing controlled substances are serious offenses in Brunei and carry a mandatory death penalty

BULGARIA

INTRODUCTION

Background: The Bulgars, a Central Asian Turkic tribe, merged with the local Slavic inhabitants in the late 7th century to form the first Bulgarian state. In succeeding centuries, Bulgaria struggled with the Byzantine Empire to assert its place in the Balkans, but by the end of the 14th century the country was overrun by the Ottoman Turks. Northern Bulgaria attained autonomy in 1878 and all of Bulgaria became independent from the Ottoman Empire in 1908. Having fought on the losing side in both World Wars, Bulgaria fell within the Soviet sphere of influence and became a People's Republic in 1946. Communist domination ended in 1990, when Bulgaria held its first multiparty election since World War II and began the contentious process of moving toward political democracy and a market economy while combating inflation, unemployment, corruption, and

crime. The country joined NATO in 2004 and the EU in 2007.

GEOGRAPHY

Location: Southeastern Europe, bordering the Black Sea, between Romania and Turkey
Geographic coordinates: 43 00 N, 25 00 E
Map references: Europe
Area: *total:* 110,879 sq km
land: 108,489 sq km
water: 2,390 sq km
country comparison to the world: 105
Area—comparative: slightly larger than Tennessee
Land boundaries: *total:* 1,806 km
border countries (5): Greece 472 km, Macedonia 162 km, Romania 605 km, Serbia 344 km, Turkey 223 km
Coastline: 354 km
Maritime claims: *territorial sea:* 12 nm
contiguous zone: 24 nm
exclusive economic zone: 200 nm
Climate: temperate; cold, damp winters; hot, dry summers
Terrain: mostly mountains with lowlands in north and southeast
Elevation: *mean elevation:* 472 m
elevation extremes: *lowest:* point: Black Sea 0 m
highest point: Musala 2,925 m
Natural resources: bauxite, copper, lead, zinc, coal, timber, arable land
Land use: *agricultural land:* 46.9%
arable land: 29.9%
permanent crops: 1.5%
permanent pasture: 15.5%
forest: 36.7%
other: 16.4% (2011 est.)
Irrigated land: 1,020 sq km (2012)

Total renewable water resources: 21.3 cu km (2011)
Freshwater withdrawal (domestic/industrial/agricultural): *total:* 6.12 cu km/yr (16%/68%/16%)
per capita: 821.8 cu m/yr (2009)
Natural hazards: earthquakes; landslides
Environment—current issues: air pollution from industrial emissions; rivers polluted from raw sewage, heavy metals, detergents; deforestation; forest damage from air pollution and resulting acid rain; soil contamination from heavy metals from metallurgical plants and industrial wastes
Environment—international agreements: *party to:* Air Pollution, Air Pollution-Nitrogen Oxides, Air Pollution-Persistent Organic Pollutants, Air Pollution-Sulfur 85, Air Pollution-Sulfur 94, Air Pollution-Volatile Organic Compounds, Antarctic-Environmental Protocol, Antarctic-Marine Living Resources, Antarctic Treaty, Biodiversity, Climate Change, Climate Change-Kyoto Protocol, Desertification, Endangered Species, Environmental Modification, Hazardous Wastes, Law of the Sea, Marine Dumping, Ozone Layer Protection, Ship Pollution, Wetlands
signed, but not ratified: none of the selected agreements
Geography—note: strategic location near Turkish Straits; controls key land routes from Europe to Middle East and Asia

PEOPLE AND SOCIETY

Nationality: *noun:* Bulgarian(s)
adjective: Bulgarian
Ethnic groups: Bulgarian 76.9%, Turkish 8%, Roma 4.4%, other 0.7% (including Russian, Armenian, and Vlach), other (unknown) 10% (2011 est.)

Languages: Bulgarian (official) 76.8%, Turkish 8.2%, Roma 3.8%, other 0.7%, unspecified 10.5% (2011 est.)

Religions: Eastern Orthodox 59.4%, Muslim 7.8%, other (including Catholic, Protestant, Armenian Apostolic Orthodox, and Jewish) 1.7%, none 3.7%, unspecified 27.4% (2011 est.)

Population: 7,186,893 (July 2015 est.)
country comparison to the world: 101

Age structure: *0–14 years:* 14.53% (male 538,266/female 505,927)

15–24 years: 9.95% (male 373,340/female 341,507)

25–54 years: 43.35% (male 1,598,130/female 1,517,744)

55–64 years: 13.45% (male 451,841/female 514,696)

65 years and over: 18.72% (male 547,887/female 797,555) (2015 est.)

Dependency ratios: *total* dependency ratio: 51.9%
youth dependency ratio: 21.5%
elderly dependency ratio: 30.4%
potential support ratio: 3.3% (2015 est.)

Median age: *total:* 42.1 years
male: 40.2 years
female: 44.2 years (2015 est.)
country comparison to the world: 25

Population growth rate: -0.58% (2015 est.)
country comparison to the world: 225

Birth rate: 8.92 births/1,000 population (2015 est.)
country comparison to the world: 210

Death rate: 14.44 deaths/1,000 population (2015 est.)
country comparison to the world: 3

Net migration rate: -0.29 migrant(s)/1,000 population (2015 est.)
country comparison to the world: 126

Urbanization: *urban population:* 73.9% of *total* population (2015)
rate of urbanization: -0.31% annual rate of change (2010–15 est.)

Major urban areas—population: SOFIA (capital) 1.226 million (2015)

Sex ratio: *at birth:* 1.06 male(s)/female
0–14 years: 1.06 male(s)/female
15–24 years: 1.09 male(s)/female
25–54 years: 1.05 male(s)/female
55–64 years: 0.88 male(s)/female
65 years and over: 0.69 male(s)/female
total population: 0.95 male(s)/female (2015 est.)

Mother's mean age at first birth: 26.3 (2011 est.)

Maternal mortality rate: 11 deaths/100,000 live births (2015 est.)
country comparison to the world: 152

Infant mortality rate: *total:* 8.66 deaths/1,000 live births
male: 9.73 deaths/1,000 live births
female: 7.52 deaths/1,000 live births (2015 est.)
country comparison to the world: 150

Life expectancy at birth: *total population:* 74.39 years
male: 71.05 years
female: 77.93 years (2015 est.)
country comparison to the world: 120

Total fertility rate: 1.45 children born/woman (2015 est.)

country comparison to the world: 204

Contraceptive prevalence rate: 69.2%
note: percent of women age 20–49 (2007)

Health expenditures: 7.6% of GDP (2013)
country comparison to the world: 71

Physicians density: 3.87 physicians/1,000 population (2012)

Hospital bed density: 6.4 beds/1,000 population (2011)

Drinking water source:
improved:
urban: 99.6% of population
rural: 99% of population
total: 99.4% of population
unimproved:
urban: 0.4% of population
rural: 1% of population
total: 0.6% of population (2015 est.)

Sanitation facility access:
improved:
urban: 86.8% of population
rural: 83.7% of population
total: 86% of population
unimproved:
urban: 13.2% of population
rural: 16.3% of population
total: 14% of population (2015 est.)

HIV/AIDS—adult prevalence rate: NA

HIV/AIDS—people living with HIV/AIDS: NA

HIV/AIDS—deaths: NA

Obesity—adult prevalence rate: 25.6% (2014)
country comparison to the world: 72

Education expenditures: 3.5% of GDP (2012)
country comparison to the world: 108

Literacy: *definition:* age 15 and over can read and write
total population: 98.4%
male: 98.7%
female: 98.1% (2015 est.)

School life expectancy (primary to tertiary education): *total:* 15 years
male: 15 years
female: 15 years (2014)

Unemployment, youth ages 15–24: *total:* 28.4%
male: 30.2%
female: 25.7% (2013 est.)
country comparison to the world: 30

GOVERNMENT

Country name: *conventional long form:* Republic of Bulgaria
conventional short form: Bulgaria
local long form: Republika Bulgaria
local short form: Bulgaria
etymology: named after the Bulgar tribes who settled the lower Balkan region in the 7th century A.D.

Government type: parliamentary republic

Capital: *name:* Sofia

Geographic coordinates: 42 41 N, 23 19 E
time difference: UTC+2 (7 hours ahead of Washington, DC, during Standard Time)
daylight saving time: +1hr, begins last Sunday in March; ends last Sunday in October

Administrative divisions: 28 provinces (oblasti, singular—oblast); Blagoevgrad, Burgas, Dobrich,

Gabrovo, Haskovo, Kardzhali, Kyustendil, Lovech, Montana, Pazardzhik, Pernik, Pleven, Plovdiv, Razgrad, Ruse, Shumen, Silistra, Sliven, Smolyan, Sofia, Sofia-Grad (Sofia City), Stara Zagora, Targovishte, Varna, Veliko Tarnovo, Vidin, Vratsa, Yambol

Independence: 3 March 1878 (as an autonomous principality within the Ottoman Empire); 22 September 1908 (complete independence from the Ottoman Empire)

National holiday: Liberation Day, 3 March (1878)

Constitution: several previous; latest drafted between late 1990 and early 1991, adopted 12 July 1991; amended several times, last in 2015 (2016)

Legal system: civil law

International law organization participation: accepts compulsory ICJ jurisdiction with reservations; accepts ICCt jurisdiction

Citizenship: *citizenship by birth:* no
citizenship by descent only: at least one parent must be a citizen of Bulgaria
dual citizenship recognized: yes
residency requirement for naturalization: 5 years

Suffrage: 18 years of age; universal

Executive branch: *chief of state:* President Rosen PLEVNELIEV (since 22 January 2012); Vice President Margarita PO POVA (since 22 January 2012)

head of government: Prime Minister Boyko BORISOV (since 7 November 2014); Deputy Prime Ministers Tomislav DONCHEV (since 7 November 2014), Rumiana BACHVAROVA (since 7 November 2014), Meglena KUNEVA (since 7 November 2014); note—this is BORISOV's second term as prime minister, he first served between 27 July 2009 and 13 March 2013 cabin et: Council of M inisters nominated by the prime minister, elected by the National Assembly
elections/appointments: president and vice president elected on the same ballot by absolute majority popular vote in 2 rounds if needed for a 5-year term (eligible for a second term); election last held on 23 and 30 October 2011 (next to be held in 2016); chairman of the Council of Ministers (prime minister) elected by the National Assembly; deputy prime ministers nominated by the prime minister, elected by the National Assembly
election results: Rosen PLEVNELIEV elected president in runoff election; percent of vote— Rosen PLEVNELIEV (independent) 52.6%, Ivailo KALFIN (BSP) 47.4%

Legislative branch: *description:* unicameral National Assembly or Narodno Sabranie (240 seats; members directly elected in multi-seat constituencies by proportional representation vote to serve 4-year terms)
elections: last held on 5 October 2014 (next to be held in 2018)
election results: percent of vote by party—GERB 32.7%, CfB 15.4%, DPS 14.8%, RB 8.9%, PF 7.3%, BBTs 5.7%, Ataka 4.5%, ABV 4.2%, other 6.5%; seats by party—GERB 84, CfB 39, DPS 38, RB 23, PF 19, BBTs 15, Ataka 11, ABV 11

Judicial branch: *highest court(s):* Supreme Court of Cassation (consists of a chairman and approximately 72 judges organized into penal, civil, and commercial colleges); Supreme Administrative Court (organized in 2 colleges with various panels of 5 judges each); Constitutional Court (consists of 12 justices); note—Constitutional Court resides outside the Judiciary

judge selection and term of office: Supreme Court of Cassation and Supreme Administrative judges elected by the Supreme Judicial Council or SJC (consists of 25 members withextensive legal experience) and appointed by the president; judge tenure NA; Constitutional Court justices elected by the National Assembly and appointed by the president and the SJC; justices appointed for 9-year terms with renewal of 4 justices every 3 years

subordinate courts: appeals courts; regional and district courts; administrative courts; courts martial

Political parties and leaders: Alternative for Bulgarian Revival or ABV [Georgi PARVANOV]
Attack (Ataka) [Volen Nikolov SIDEROV]
Bulgarian Socialist Party or BSP [Mihail MIKOV]
Bulgaria of the Citizens or DBG [Meglena KUNEVA]
Bulgaria Without Censorship or BBTs [Nikolay BAREKOV]
Citizens for the European Development of Bulgaria or GERB [Boyko BORISOV]
Coalition for Bulgaria or CfB [Mikhail MIKOV] (coalition dominated by BSP) Democrats for a Strong Bulgaria or DSB [Radan KANEV]
IMRO—Bulgarian National M ovement or IMR O-BN M [Krasimir KARAKACHANOV]
Movement for Rights and Freedoms or DPS [Lyutvi MESTAN]
National Front for the Salvation of Bulgaria or NFSB [Valeri SIMEONOV]
National Movement for Stability and Progress or NDSV [Hristina HRISTOVA] (formerly National Movement Simeon II or NM S2)
Patriotic Front or PF (alliance of IMRO-BNM and NFSB)
Union of Democratic Forces or SDS [Bozhidar LUKARSKI]
Reformist Bloc or RB (a five-party alliance including the DSB, DBG, and SD S)

Political pressure groups and leaders: Confederation of Independent Trade Unions of Bulgaria or CITUB
Podkrepa Labor Confederation
other: numerous regional, ethnic, and national interest groups with various agendas

International organization participation: Australia Group, BIS, BSEC, CD, CE, CEI, CERN, EAPC, EBRD, ECB, EIB, EU, FAO, G- 9, IAEA, IBRD, ICAO, ICC (national committees), ICCt, ICRM, IDA, IF C, IFRCS, IHO (pending member), ILO, IMF, IMO, IMSO, Interpol, IOC, IOM, IPU, ISO, ITU, ITUC (NGOs), MIGA, NATO, NSG, OAS (observer), OIF, OPCW, OSCE, PCA, SELEC, UN, UNCTAD, UNESCO, UNHCR, UNIDO, UNMIL, UNWTO, UPU, WCO, WFTU (NGOs), WHO, WIPO, WMO, WTO, ZC

Diplomatic representation in the US: *chief of mission:* Ambassador Elena POPTODOROVA (since 4 August 2010)

chancery: 162122nd Street NW, Washington, DC 20008
telephone: [1] (202) 387-0174
FAX: [1] (202) 234-7973
consulate(s) general: Chicago, Los Angeles, New York

Diplomatic representation from the US: *chief of mission:* Ambassador Eric RUBIN (since February 2016)
embassy: 16 Kozyak Street, Sofia 1408
mailing address: American Embassy Sofia, US Department of State, 5740 Sofia Place, Washington, DC 20521–5740
telephone: [359] (2) 937-5100
FAX: [359] (2) 937-5320

Flag description: three equal horizontal bands of white (top), green, and red; the pan-Slavic white-blue-red colors were modified by substituting a green band (representing freedom) for the blue
note: the national emblem, formerly on the hoist side of the white stripe, has been removed

National symbol(s): lion; national colors: white, green, red

National anthem: *name:* "Mila Rodino" (Dear Homeland)
lyrics/music: Tsvetan Tsvetkov RADO SLAVOV
note: adopted 1964; composed in 1885 by a student en route to fight in the Serbo-Bulgarian War

ECONOMY

Economy—overview: Bulgaria, a former communist country that entered the EU on 1 January 2007, averaged more than 6% annual growth from 2004 to 2008, driven by significant amounts of bank lending, consumption, and foreign direct investment.

Successive governments have demonstrated a commitment to economic reforms and responsible fiscal planning, but the global downturn sharply reduced domestic demand, exports, capital inflows, and industrial production. GDP contracted by 5.5% in 2009, and has been slow to recover in the years since. Despite a favorable investment regime, including low, flat corporate income taxes, significant challenges remain. Corruption in public administration, a weak judiciary, and the presence of organized crime continue to hamper the country's investment climate and economic prospects.

GDP (purchasing power parity): $133.9 billion (2015 est.)
$130.3 billion (2014 est.)
$128.2 billion (2013 est.)
note: data are in 2015 US dollars
country comparison to the world: 77

GDP (official exchange rate): $47.17 billion (2015 est.)

GDP—real growth rate: 3% (2015 est.) 1.5% (2014 est.) 1.3% (2013 est.)
country comparison to the world: 104

GDP—per capita (PPP): $19,100 (2015 est.)
$18,500 (2014 est.)
$18,100 (2013 est.)
note: data are in 2015 US dollars
country comparison to the world: 89

Gross national saving: 23.5% of GDP (2015 est.)
22.6% of GDP (2014 est.)

23.2% of GDP (2013 est.)
country comparison to the world: 58

GDP—composition, by end use:
household consumption: 63%
government consumption: 16.2%
investment in fixed capital: 21.1%
investment in inventories: 0.1%
exports of goods and services: 66.7%
imports of goods and services: -67.1% (2015 est.)

GDP—composition, by sector of origin:
agriculture: 5.2%
industry: 27.4%
services: 67.4% (2015 est.)

Agriculture—products: vegetables, fruits, tobacco, wine, wheat, barley, sunflowers, sugar beets; livestock

Industries: electricity, gas, water; food, beverages, tobacco; machinery and equipment, base metals, chemical products, coke, refined petroleum, nuclear fuel

Industrial production growth rate: 3.5% (2015 est.)
country comparison to the world: 72

Labor force: 2.535 million
note: number of employed persons (2015 est.)
country comparison to the world: 113

Labor force—by occupation:
agriculture: 7%
industry: 30.1%
services: 62.9% (2014)

Unemployment rate: 10% (2015 est.) 10.7% (2014 est.)
country comparison to the world: 117

Population below poverty line: 21.8% (2014 est.)

Household income or consumption by percentage share: *lowest:* 10%: 2%
highest: 10%: 35.2% (2007)

Distribution of family income—Gini index: 35.4 (2013) 31.2 (2005)
country comparison to the world: 92

Budget: *revenues:* $17.81 billion
expenditures: $19.14 billion (2015 est.)
Taxes and other revenues: 37.8% of GDP (2015 est.)
country comparison to the world: 47

Budget surplus (+) or deficit (–): -2.8% of GDP (2015 est.)
country comparison to the world: 104

Public debt: 26.4% of GDP (2015 est.)
26.4% of GDP (2014 est.)
note: defined by the EU's Maastricht Treaty as consolidated general government gross debt at nominalvalue, outstanding at the end of the year in the following categories of government liabilities: currency anddeposits, securities other than shares excluding financial derivatives, and loans; general government sectorcomprises the subsectors: central government, state government, local government, and social securityfunds

Fiscal year: calendar year

Inflation rate (consumer prices): -1.1% (2015 est.) -1.6% (2014 est.)
country comparison to the world: 11

Central bank discount rate: 0.01% (31 December 2015)
0.03% (31 December 2014)

note: Bulgarian National Bank (BNB) has had no independent monetary policy since the introduction of the Currency Board regime in 1997; this is BNB's base interest rate
country comparison to the world: 154

Commercial bank prime lending rate: 7.5% (31 December 2015 est.)
8.28% (31 December 2014 est.)
country comparison to the world: 115

Stock of narrow money: $20.09 billion (31 December 2015 est.)
$17.38 billion (31 December 2014 est.)
country comparison to the world: 65

Stock of broad money: $41.32 billion (31 December 2015 est.)
$37.99 billion (31 December 2014 est.)
country comparison to the world: 73

Stock of domestic credit: $29.72 billion (31 December 2015 est.)
$29.08 billion (31 December 2014 est.)
country comparison to the world: 73

Market value of publicly traded shares: $4.797 billion (31 December 2015 est.)
$5.45 billion (31 December 2014)
$6.666 billion (31 December 2012 est.)
country comparison to the world: 85

Current account balance: $1.043 billion (2015 est.)
$658 million (2014 est.)
country comparison to the world: 37

Exports: $24.33 billion (2015 est.)
$27.91 billion (2014 est.)
country comparison to the world: 67

Exports—commodities: clothing, footwear, iron and steel, machinery and equipment, fuels

Exports—partners: Germany 12.5%, Italy 9.2%, Turkey 8.5%, Romania 8.2%, Greece 6.5%, France 4.2% (2015)

Imports: $27.66 billion (2015 est.)
$31.6 billion (2014 est.)
country comparison to the world: 66

Imports—commodities: machinery and equipment; metals and ores; chemicals and plastics; fuels, minerals, and raw materials

Imports—partners: Germany 12.9%, Russia 12%, Italy 7.6%, Romania 6.8%, Turkey 5.7%, Greece 4.8%, Spain 4.8% (2015)

Reserves of foreign exchange and gold: $22.75 billion (31 December 2015 est.)
$20.11 billion (31 December 2014 est.)
country comparison to the world: 55

Debt—external: $37.31 billion (31 December 2015 est.)
$43 billion (31 December 2014 est.)
country comparison to the world: 70

Stock of direct foreign investment—at home: $54.98 billion (31 December 2015 est.)
$52.78 billion (31 December 2014 est.)
country comparison to the world: 60

Stock of direct foreign investment—abroad: $3.26 billion (31 December 2015 est.)
$3.01 billion (31 December 2014 est.)
country comparison to the world: 74

Exchange rates: leva (BG N) per US dollar—
1.79 (2015 est.)
1.61 (2014 est.)
1.4742 (2013 est.)
1.52 (2012 est.)
1.4053 (2011 est.)

ENERGY

Electricity—production: 48.44 billion kWh (2015 est.)
country comparison to the world: 55

Electricity—consumption: 37.99 billion kWh (2015 est.)
country comparison to the world: 57

Electricity—exports: 14.7 billion kWh (2015 est.)
country comparison to the world: 14

Electricity—imports: 4.25 billion kWh (2015 est.)
country comparison to the world: 45

Electricity—installed generating capacity: 11.84 million kW (2014 est.)
country comparison to the world: 52

Electricity—from fossil fuels: 41.7% of total installed capacity (2014 est.)
country comparison to the world: 164

Electricity—from nuclear fuels: 16.9% of total installed capacity (2014 est.)
country comparison to the world: 11

Electricity—from hydroelectric plants: 8.5% of total installed capacity (2014 est.)
country comparison to the world: 119

Electricity—from other renewable sources: 32.9% of total installed capacity (2014 est.)
country comparison to the world: 4

Crude oil—production: 1,000 bbl/day (2014 est.)
country comparison to the world: 93

Crude oil—exports: 0 bbl/day (2012 est.)
country comparison to the world: 105

Crude oil—imports: 128,100 bbl/day (2012 est.)
country comparison to the world: 40

Crude oil—proved reserves: 15 million bbl (1 January 2015 est.)
country comparison to the world: 86

Refined petroleum products—prodiction: 138,500 bbl/day (2012 est.)
country comparison to the world: 65

Refined petroleum products—consumption: 89,000 bbl/day (2013 est.)
country comparison to the world: 79

Refined petroleum products- exports: 85,890 bbl/day (2012 est.)
country comparison to the world: 47

Refined petroleum products—imports: 37,280 bbl/day (2012 est.)
country comparison to the world: 88

Natural gas—production: 181 million cu m (2014 est.)
country comparison to the world: 78

Natural gas—consumption: 2.635 billion cu m (2014 est.)
country comparison to the world: 77

Natural gas—exports: 0 cu m (2013 est.)
country comparison to the world: 71

Natural gas—imports: 2.725 billion cu m (2014 est.)
country comparison to the world: 45

Natural gas—proved reserves: 5.663 billion cu m (1 January 2014 est.)
country comparison to the world: 92

Carbon dioxide emissions from consumption of energy: 43.61 million Mt (2014 est.)
country comparison to the world: 64

COMMUNICATIONS

Telephones—fixed lines: *total subscriptions:* 1.8 million
subscriptions per 100 inhabitants: 25 (2014 est.)
country comparison to the world: 64

Telephones—mobile cellular: *total:* 9.9 million
subscriptions per 100 inhabitants: 137 (2014 est.)
country comparison to the world: 87

Telephone system: *general assessment:* inherited an extensive but antiquated telecommunications network from the Soviet era; quality has improved with a modern digital trunk line now connecting switching centers in most of the regions; remaining areas are connected by digital microwave radio relay
domestic: the Bulgaria Telecommunications Company's fixed-line monopoly terminated in 2005 in an effort to upgrade fixed-line services; mobile-cellular teledensity, fostered by multiple service providers, has reached 150 telephones per 100 persons
international: country code—359; submarine cable provides connectivity to Ukraine and Russia; a combination submarine cable and land fiber-optic system provides connectivity to Italy, Albania, and Macedonia; satellite earth stations—3 (1 Intersputnik in the Atlantic Ocean region, 2 Intelsat in the Atlantic and Indian Ocean regions) (2011)

Broadcast media: 4 national terrestrial TV stations with 1 state-owned and 3 privately owned; a vast array of TV stations are available from cable and satellite TV providers; state-owned national radio broadcasts over 3 networks; large number of private radio stations broadcasting, especially in urban areas (2010)
Radio broadcast stations: AM 31, FM 63, shortwave 2 (2001)
Television broadcast stations: 39 (plus 1,242 repeaters) (2001)

Internet country code: .bg

Internet hosts: 976,277 (2012)
country comparison to the world: 47

Internet users: *total:* 4.1 million
percent of population: 57.0% (2014 est.)
country comparison to the world: 75

TRANSPORTATION

Airports: 68 (2013)
country comparison to the world: 73

Airports—with paved runways: *total:* 57
over 3,047 m: 2
2,438 to 3,047 m: 17
1,524 to 2,437 m: 12
under 914 m: 26 (2013)

Airports—with unpaved runways: *total:* 11
914 to 1,523 m: 2
under 914 m: 9 (2013)

Heliports: 1 (2013)

Pipelines: gas 2,887 km; oil 346 km; refined products 378 km (2013)

Railways: *total:* 5,114 km

standard gauge: 4,989 km 1.435-m gauge (2,880 km electrified)

narrow gauge: 125 km 0.760-m gauge (2014)

country comparison to the world: 36

Roadways: *total:* 19,512 km

paved: 19,235 km (includes 458 km of expressways)

unpaved: 277 km

note: does not include Category IV local roads (2011)

country comparison to the world: 111

Waterways: 470 km (2009)

country comparison to the world: 83

Merchant marine: *total:* 22

by type: bulk carrier 9, cargo 8, liquefied gas 2, petroleum tanker 1, roll on/roll off 2

foreign-owned: 14 (Germany 12, Russia 2)

registered in other countries: 30 (Belize 1, Comoros 4, Georgia 1, Malta 8, Moldova 1, Panama 6, Saint Vincent and the Grenadines 9) (2010)

country comparison to the world: 93

Ports and terminals: *major seaport(s):* Burgas, Varna (Black Sea)

MILITARY AND SECURITY

Military branches: Bulgarian Armed Forces: Ground Forces, Naval Forces, Bulgarian Air Forces (Bulgarski Voennovazdyshni Sily, BVVS) (2011)

Military service age and obligation: 18–27 years of age for voluntary military service; conscription ended in January 2008; service obligation 6–9 months (2012)

Military expenditures: 1.2% of GDP (2015)

1.6% of GDP (2013)

1.46% of GDP (2012)

1.55% of GDP (2011)

1.46% of GDP (2010)

country comparison to the world: 66

TRANSNATIONAL ISSUES

Disputes—international: none

Refugees and internally displaced persons: *refugees (country of origin):* 8,501 (Syria) (2014)

stateless persons: 67 (2015)

note: 35,294 estimated refugee and migrant arrivals (2015—June 2016)

Trafficking in persons: *current situation:* Bulgaria is a source and, to a lesser extent, a transit and destination country for men, women, and children subjected to sex trafficking and forced labor; Bulgaria is one of the main sources of human trafficking in the EU; women and children are increasingly sex trafficked domestically, as well as in Europe, Russia, the Middle East, and the US; adults and children become forced laborers in

agriculture, construction, and the service sector in Europe, Israel, and Zambia; Romanian girls are also subjected to sex traffic king in Bulgaria

tier rating: Tier 2 Watch List—Bulgaria does not fully comply with the minimum standards for the elimination of trafficking; however, it is making significant efforts to do so; in 2014, authorities prosecuted and convicted fewer traffickers and issued suspended sentences for the majority of those convicted; victim protection efforts declined and were minimal relative to the number of victims identified; funding for the state's two NGO-operated shelters was significantly cut, forcing them to close; specialized services for child and adult male victims were non-existent; the government took action to combat trafficking-related complicity among public officials and police officers (2015)

Illicit drugs: major European transshipment point for Southwest Asian heroin and, to a lesser degree, South American cocaine for the European market; limited producer of precursor chemicals; vulnerable to money laundering because of corruption, organized crime; some money laundering of drug-related proceeds through financial institutions (2008)

BURKINA FASO

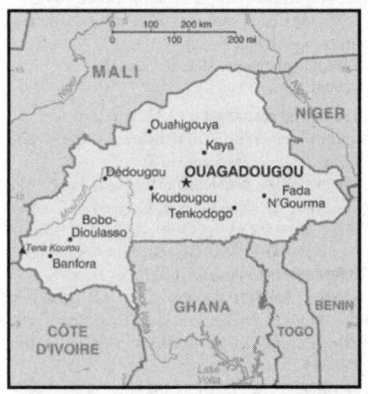

INTRODUCTION

Background: Burkina Faso (formerly Upper Volta) achieved independence from France in 1960. Repeated military coups during the 1970s and 1980s were followed by multiparty elections in the early 1990s. Former President Blaise COMPAORE (1987–2014) resigned in late October 2014 following popular protests against his efforts to amend the Constitution's two-term presidential limit. By mid-November, a framework for an interim government was adopted under the terms of the National Transition Charter. An interim administration, led by President Michel KAFANDO and

Prime Minister Yacouba Isaac ZIDA, began organizing presidential and legislative elections planned for October 2015, but these were postponed during a weeklong failed coup in September. The rescheduled elections were held on 29 November, and Roch Marc Christian KABORE was elected president in the first round. Burkina Faso's high population growth and limited natural resources result in poor economic prospects for the majority of its citizens.

GEOGRAPHY

Location: Western Africa, north of Ghana

Geographic coordinates: 13 00 N, 2 00 W

Map references: Africa

Area: *total:* 274,200 sq km

land: 273,800 sq km

water: 400 sq km

country comparison to the world: 75

Area—comparative: slightly larger than Colorado

Land boundaries: *total:* 3,611 km

border countries (6): Benin 386 km, Cote d'Ivoire 545 km, Ghana 602 km, Mali 1,325 km, Niger 622 km, Togo 131 km

Coastline: 0 km (landlocked)

Maritime claims: none (landlocked)

Climate: tropical; warm, dry winters; hot, wet summers

Terrain: mostly flat to dissected, undulating plains; hills in west and southeast

Elevation: *mean elevation:* 297 m

elevation extremes: lowest: point: Mouhoun (Black Volta) River 200 m

highest point: Tena Kourou 749 m

Natural resources: manganese, limestone, marble; small deposits of gold, phosphates, pumice, salt

Land use: *agricultural land:* 43%

arable land: 20.8%

permanent crops: 0.3%

permanent pasture: 21.9%

forest: 20.4%

other: 36.6% (2011 est.)

Irrigated land: 550 sq km (2012)

Total renewable water resources: 12.5 cu km (2011)

Freshwater withdrawal (domestic/industrial/agricultural): *total:* 0.72 cu km/yr (46%/3%/51%)

per capita: 54.99 cu m/yr (2005)

Natural hazards: recurring droughts

Environment—current issues: recent droughts and desertification severely affecting agricultural activities, population distribution, and the economy; overgrazing; soil degradation; deforestation

Environment—international agreements: *party to:* Biodiversity, Climate Change, Climate Change-Kyoto Protocol, Desertification, Endangered Species, Hazardous Wastes, Law of the Sea, Marine Life Conservation, Ozone Layer Protection, Wetlands

signed, but not ratified: none of the selected agreements

Geography—note: landlocked savanna cut by the three principal rivers of the Black, Red, and White Voltas

PEOPLE AND SOCIETY

Nationality: *noun:* Burkinabe (singular and plural) *adjective:* Burkinabe

Ethnic groups: Mossi 52.5%, Fulani 8.4%, Gurma 6.8%, Bobo 4.8%, Gurunsi 4.5%, Senufo 4.4%, Bissa 3.9%, Lobi 2.5%, Dagara 2.4%, Tuareg/Bella 1.9%, Dioula 0.8%, unspecified/no answer 0.1%, other 7% (2010 est.)

Languages: French (official), native African languages belonging to Sudanic family spoken by 90% of the population

Religions: Muslim 61.6%, Catholic 23.2%, traditional/animist 7.3%, Protestant 6.7%, other/no answer 0.2%, none 0.9% (2010 est.)

Population: 18,931,686

note: estimates for this country explicitly take into account the effects of excess mortality due to AIDS; this can result in lower life expectancy, higher infant mortality, higher death rates, lower population growth rates, and changes in the distribution of population by age and sex than would otherwise be expected (July 2015 est.)

country comparison to the world: 60

Age structure: *0–14 years:* 45.2% (male 4,286,569/female 4,270,357)

15–24 years: 20.08% (male 1,909,090/female 1,892,273)

25–54 years: 29.13% (male 2,799,042/female 2,716,439)

55–64 years: 3.14% (male 253,423/female 340,599)

65 years and over: 2.45% (male 174,647/female 289,247) (2015 est.)

Dependency ratios: *total dependency ratio:* 92.2%

youth dependency ratio: 87.6%

elderly dependency ratio: 4.6%

potential support ratio: 21.7% (2015 est.)

Median age: *total:* 17.1 years

male: 17 years

female: 17.3 years (2015 est.)

country comparison to the world: 221

Population growth rate: 3.03% (2015 est.)

country comparison to the world: 7

Birth rate: 42.03 births/1,000 population (2015 est.)

country comparison to the world: 5

Death rate: 11.72 deaths/1,000 population (2015 est.)

country comparison to the world: 28

Net migration rate: 0 migrant(s)/1,000 population (2015 est.)

country comparison to the world: 104

Urbanization: *urban population:* 29.9% of total population (2015)

rate of urbanization: 5.87% annual rate of change (2010–15 est.)

Major urban areas—population: OUAGADOU-GOU (capital) 2.741 million (2015)

Sex ratio: *at birth:* 1.03 male(s)/female

0–14 years: 1 male(s)/female

15–24 years: 1.01 male(s)/female

25–54 years: 1.03 male(s)/female

55–64 years: 0.74 male(s)/female

65 years and over: 0.6 male(s)/female

total population: 0.99 male(s)/female (2015 est.)

Mother's mean age at first birth: 19.4

note: median age at first birth among women 25–29 (2010 est.)

Maternal mortality rate: 371 deaths/100,000 live births (2015 est.)

country comparison to the world: 39

Infant mortality rate: *total:* 75.32 deaths/1,000 live births

male: 82.56 deaths/1,000 live births

female: 67.87 deaths/1,000 live births (2015 est.)

country comparison to the world: 9

Life expectancy at birth: *total population:* 55.12 years

male: 53.1 years

female: 57.21 years (2015 est.)

country comparison to the world: 210

Total fertility rate: 5.86 children born/woman (2015 est.)

country comparison to the world: 6

Contraceptive prevalence rate: 16.2% (2010/11)

Health expenditures: 6.4% of GDP (2013)

country comparison to the world: 107

Physicians density: 0.05 physicians/1,000 population (2010)

Hospital bed density: 0.4 beds/1,000 population (2010)

Drinking water source:

improved:

urban: 97.5% of population

rural: 75.8% of population

total: 82.3% of population

unimproved:

urban: 2.5% of population

rural: 24.2% of population

total: 17.7% of population (2015 est.)

Sanitation facility access:

improved:

urban: 50.4% of population

rural: 6.7% of population

total: 19.7% of population

unimproved:

urban: 49.6% of population

rural: 93.3% of population

total: 80.3% of population (2015 est.)

HIV/AIDS—adult prevalence rate: 0.94% (2014 est.)

country comparison to the world: 48

HIV/AIDS—people living with HIV/AIDS: 107,700 (2014 est.)

country comparison to the world: 42

HIV/AIDS—deaths: 3,800 (2014 est.)

country comparison to the world: 38

Major infectious diseases: *degree of risk:* very high

food or waterborne diseases: bacterial and protozoal diarrhea, hepatitis A, and typhoid fever

vectorborne disease: dengue fever, malaria, and yellow fever

water contact disease: schistosomiasis

respiratory disease: meningococcal meningitis

animal contact disease: rabies

note: highly pathogenic H5N1 avian influenza has been identified in this country; it poses a negligible risk with extremely rare cases possible among US citizens who have close contact with birds (2013)

Obesity—adult prevalence rate: 5.2% (2014)

country comparison to the world: 181

Children under the age of 5 years underweight: 26.2% (2010)

country comparison to the world: 24

Education expenditures: 4.5% of GDP (2014)

country comparison to the world: 128

Literacy: *definition:* age 15 and over can read and write

total population: 36%

male: 43%

female: 29.3% (2015 est.)

School life expectancy (primary to tertiary education): *total:* 8 years

male: 8 years

female: 7 years (2013)

Child labor—children ages 5–14: *total number:* 1,521,006

percentage: 38% (2006 est.)

Unemployment, youth ages 15–24: *total:* 3.8%

male: 4.6%

female: 2.9% (2006 est.)

country comparison to the world: 129

GOVERNMENT

Country name: *conventional long form:* none

conventional short form: Burkina Faso

local long form: none

local short form: Burkina Faso

former: Upper Volta, Republic of Upper Volta

etymology: name translates as "Land of the honest (incorruptible) men"

Government type: presidential republic

Capital: *name:* Ouagadougou

Geographic coordinates: 12 22 N, 1 31 W

time difference: UTC 0 (5 hours ahead of Washington, DC, during Standard Time)

Administrative divisions: 13 regions; Boucle du Mouhoun, Cascades, Centre, Centre-Est, Centre-Nord, Centre-Ouest, Centre-Sud, Est, Hauts-Bassins, Nord, Plateau-Central, Sahel, Sud-Ouest

Independence: 5 August 1960 (from France)

National holiday: Republic Day, 11 December (1958); note—commemorates the day that Upper Volta became an autonomous republic in the French Community

Constitution: several previous; latest approved by referendum 2 June 1991, adopted 11 June 1991; amended several times, last in 2015 for setting a two-term limit for presidents; note—constitution temporarily suspended between late October and mid-November 2014 (2016)

Legal system: civil law based on the French model and customary law

International law organization participation: has not submitted an ICJ jurisdiction declaration; accepts ICCt jurisdiction

Citizenship: *citizenship by birth:* no

citizenship by descent only: at least one parent must be a citizen of Burkina Faso

dual citizenship recognized: yes

residency requirement for naturalization: 10 years

Suffrage: 18 years of age; universal

Executive branch: *chief of state:* President Roch Marc Christian KABORE (since 29 December 2015)

head of government: Prime Minister Paul Kaba THIEBA (since 6 January 2016)

cabinet: Council of M inisters appointed by the president on the recommendation of the prime minister

elections/appointments: president elected by absolute majority popular vote in two rounds, if needed, for a 5-year term (eligible for a second); election last held on 29 November 2015 (next scheduled for November 2020); prime minister appointed by the president with consent of the National Assembly election resu lts: Roch Marc Christian KABORE elected president in one round; percent of vote—Roch Marc Christian KABORE 53.5%, Zephirin DIABRE 29.6%, Tahirou BARRY 3.1%. Benewende Stanislas SANKARA 2.8%, other 10.9%

Legislative branch: *description:* unicameral National Assembly (127 seats; members directly elected in multi-seat constituencies by proportional representation vote to serve 5-year terms)

elections: last held on 29 November 2015 (next to be held in 2020)

election results: percent of vote by party—NA; seats by party—MPP 55, UPC 33, CDP 18, Union for Rebirth/Sankarist Party 5, ADF/RDA 3, other 13

Judicial branch: *highest court(s):* Supreme Court of Appeals or Cour de Cassation (consists of NA judges); Council of State (consists of NA judges); Constitutional Council or Conseil Constitutionnel (consists of the council president and 9 members)

judge selection and term of office: Supreme Court of Appeals judges recommended by the Higher Magistrary Council (also called the Superior Court of Magistrates) and appointed by the president of Burkina Faso; judge tenure NA; Constitutional Council members appointed by the president of Burkina Faso upon the proposal of the minister of justice and the president of the National Assembly; judges appointed for 9-year terms with one-third of membership renewed every 3 years

subordinate courts: Courts of Appeal (2); first instance tribunals; district courts; specialized courts relating to issues of labor, children, and juveniles; village (customary) courts

Political parties and leaders: African Democratic Rally/Alliance for Democracy and Federation or ADF/RDA [Gilbert Noel OUEDRAOGO]

African People's Movement or MAP [Victorien TOUGOUMA]

Congress for Democracy and Progress or CDP [Achille TAPSOBA]

Le Faso Autrement [Ablasse OUEDRAOGO]

New Alliance of the Faso or NAFA [Rasmane OUEDRAOGO]

New Time for Democracy or NTD [Vincent DABILGOU]

Organization for Democracy and Work or ODT [Mahamoudou SAWADOGO]

Party for Development and Change or PDC [Saran SEREME]

Party for Democracy and Progress-Socialist Party or PDP-PS [Francois O. KABORE]

Party for Democracy and Socialism/Metba or PDS/Metba [Philippe OUEDRAOGO]

Party for National Renaissance or PAREN [Tahirou BARRY]

People's Movement for Progress or MPP [Roch March Christian KABORE]

Rally for Democracy and Socialism or RDS [Francois OUEDRAOGO]

Rally for the Development of Burkina or RDB [Celestin Saidou COMPAORE]

Rally of Ecologists of Burkina Faso or RDEB [Adama SERE]

Union for a New Burkina or UBN [Yacouba OUEDRAOGO]

Union for Progress and Change or UPC [Zephirin DIABRE]

Union for Rebirth—Sankarist Movement or UNIR-MS [Benewende Stanislas SANKARA]

Union for the Republic or UPR [Toussaint Abel COULIBALY]

Youth Alliance for the Republic and Independence or AJIR [Adama KANAZOE]

Political pressure groups and leaders: Balai Citoyen [Herve KAM]

Burkinabe General Confederation of Labor or CGTB [Bassolma BAZIE]

Burkinabe Movement for Human Rights or MBDHP [Chrysogone ZOUGMORE]

Burkinabe Society for Constitutional Law or SBDC [Abdoulaye SOMA]

Center for Democratic Governance or CGD [Thomas OUEDRAOGO]

Coalition for African Renaissance or CAR [Herve OUATTARA]

National Independent Union of Burkinabe Magistrates or SAMAB National Union for Health Workers or SYNTSHA National Union for Primary Education Teachers or SYNATEB

other: watchdog/political action groups throughout the country

International organization participation: ACP, AFDB, AU, CD, ECOWAS, EITI (compliant country), Entente, FAO, FZ, G-77, IAEA, IBRD, ICAO, ICC (NGOs), ICCt, ICRM, IDA, IDB, IFAD, IFC, IFRCS, ILO, IMF, Interpol, IOC, IOM, IPU, ISO, ITSO, ITU, ITUC (NGOs), MIGA, MINUSMA, MONUSCO, NAM, OIC, OIF, OPCW, PCA, UN, UNAMID, UNCTAD, UNESCO, UNIDO, UNISFA, UNITAR, UNWTO, UPU, WADB (regional), WAEMU, WCO, WFTU (NGOs), WHO, WIPO, WMO, WTO

Diplomatic representation in the US: *chief of mission:* Ambassador (vacant); Charge d'Affaires Seydou SINKA (since 1 November 2014)

chancery: 2340 Massachusetts Avenue NW, Washington, DC 20008

telephone: [1] (202) 332-5577

FAX: [1] (202) 667-1882

Diplomatic representation from the US: *chief of mission:* Ambassador Tulinabo Salama MUSHINGI (since 5 August 2013)

embassy: Rue 15.873, Avenue Sembene Ousmane, Ouaga 2000, Secteur 15

mailing address: 01 B. P.35, Ouagadougou 01; pouch mail—US Department of State, 2440 Ouagadougou Place, Washington, DC 20521–2440

telephone: [226] 25-49-53-00

FAX: [226] 25-49-56-28

Flag description: two equal horizontal bands of red (top) and green with a yellow five-pointed star in the center; red recalls the country's struggle for independence, green is for hope and abundance, and yellow represents the country's mineral wealth

note: uses the popular Pan-African colors of Ethiopia

National symbol(s): white stallion; national colors: red, yellow, green

National anthem: *name:* "Le Ditanye" (Anthem of Victory)

lyrics/music: Thomas SANKARA

note: adopted 1974; also known as "Une Seule Nuit" (One Single Night); written by the country's president, an avid guitar player

ECONOMY

Economy—overview: Burkina Faso is a poor, landlocked country that depends on adequate rainfall. About 80% of the population is engaged in subsistence farming and cotton is the main cash crop. The country has few natural resources and a weak industrial base. Cotton and gold are Burkina Faso's key exports—gold has accounted for about three-quarters of the country's total export revenues. Burkina Faso's economic growth and revenue depends on global prices for the two commodities. The Burkinabe economy experienced high levels of growth over the last few years, and the country has seen an upswing in gold exploration, production, and exports. Burkina Faso experienced a number of public protests over the high cost of living, corruption, and other socioeconomic issues in 2013, while the fall of the COMPAORE government in 2014 and failed coup in September 2015 disrupted economic activity and strained government finances. A new three-year IMF program was approved in 2013 to focus on improving the quality of public investment and ensuring inclusive growth. Political insecurity in neighboring Mali, unreliable energy supplies, and poor transportation links pose long-term challenges.

GDP (purchasing power parity): $30.88 billion (2015 est.)

$29.69 billion (2014 est.)

$28.55 billion (2013 est.)

note: data are in 2015 US dollars

country comparison to the world: 128

GDP (official exchange rate): $11.01 billion (2015 est.)

GDP—real growth rate: 4% (2015 est.) 4% (2014 est.) 6.6% (2013 est.)

country comparison to the world: 69

GDP—per capita (PPP): $1,700 (2015 est.)

$1,700 (2014 est.)

$1,700 (2013 est.)

note: data are in 2015 US dollars
country comparison to the world: 212
Gross national saving: 8.5% of GDP (2015 est.) 11.7% of GDP (2014 est.) 9.8% of GDP (2013 est.)
country comparison to the world: 157
GDP—composition, by end use:
household consumption: 50.5%
government consumption: 20.1%
investment in fixed capital: 29.9%
investment in inventories: 0.6%
exports of goods and services: 28.5%
imports of goods and services: -29.6% (2015 est.)
GDP—composition, by sector of origin:
agriculture: 22.9%
industry: 25.7%
services: 51.5% (2015 est.)
Agriculture—products: cotton, peanuts, shea nuts, sesame, sorghum, millet, corn, rice; livestock
Industries: cotton lint, beverages, agricultural processing, soap, cigarettes, textiles, gold
Industrial production growth rate: 3% (2015 est.)
country comparison to the world: 86
Labor force: 7.692 million
note: a large part of the male labor force migrates annually to neighboring countries for seasonal employment (2013 est.)
country comparison to the world: 63
Labor force—by occupation:
agriculture: 90%
industry and services: 10% (2000 est.)
Unemployment rate: 77% (2004)
country comparison to the world: 205
Population below poverty line: 46.7% (2009 est.)
Household income or consumption by percentage share: *lowest:* 10%: 2.9%
highest: 10%: 32.2% (2009 est.)
Distribution of family income—Gini index: 39.5 (2007) 48.2 (1994)
country comparison to the world: 66
Budget: *revenues:* $2.182 billion
expenditures: $2.475 billion (2015 est.)
Taxes and other revenues: 19.3% of GDP (2015 est.)
country comparison to the world: 163
Budget surplus (+) or deficit (–): -2.6% of GDP (2015 est.)
country comparison to the world: 94
Fiscal year: calendar year
Inflation rate (consumer prices): 0.9% (2015 est.) -0.3% (2014 est.)
country comparison to the world: 76
Central bank discount rate: 4.25% (31 December 2010) 4.25% (31 December 2009)
country comparison to the world: 92
Commercial bank prime lending rate: NA% (31 December 2014 est.)
Stock of narrow money: $1.768 billion (31 December 2015 est.)
$1.969 billion (31 December 2014 est.)
country comparison to the world: 133
Stock of broad money: $4.211 billion (31 December 2013 est.)
$3.343 billion (31 December 2012 est.)
country comparison to the world: 138

Stock of domestic credit: $3.293 billion (31 December 2015 est.)
$3.302 billion (31 December 2014 est.)
country comparison to the world: 128
Market value of publicly traded shares: $NA
Current account balance: -$622 million (2015 est.) -$1.004 billion (2014 est.)
country comparison to the world: 109
Exports: $2.194 billion (2015 est.)
$2.388 billion (2014 est.)
country comparison to the world: 135
Exports—commodities: gold, cotton, livestock
Exports—partners: Switzerland 53.3%, India 14.5% (2015)
Imports: $2.518 billion (2015 est.)
$2.631 billion (2014 est.)
country comparison to the world: 155
Imports—commodities: capital goods, foodstuffs, petroleum
Imports—partners: Cote dIvoire 23.1%, France 11.1%, Togo 7.5%, China 4.8%, Ghana 4.6% (2015)
Reserves of foreign exchange and gold: $362.5 million (31 December 2015 est.)
$297.1 million (31 December 2014 est.)
country comparison to the world: 156
Debt—external: $2.852 billion (31 December 2014 est.)
$2.564 billion (31 December 2013 est.)
country comparison to the world: 144
Exchange rates: Communaute Financiere Africaine francs (XOF) per US dollar—
580.5 (2015 est.)
494.42 (2014 est.)
494.42 (2013 est.)
510.53 (2012 est.)
471.87 (2011 est.)

Electricity—production: 522 million kWh (2012 est.)
country comparison to the world: 161
Electricity—consumption: 985.5 million kWh (2012 est.)
country comparison to the world: 150
Electricity—exports: 0 kWh (2013 est.)
country comparison to the world: 210
Electricity—imports: 500 million kWh (2012 est.)
country comparison to the world: 75
Electricity—installed generating capacity: 238,000 kW (2012 est.)
country comparison to the world: 157
Electricity—from fossil fuels: 86.6% of total installed capacity (2012 est.)
country comparison to the world: 85
Electricity—from nuclear fuels: 0% of total installed capacity (2012 est.)
country comparison to the world: 199
Electricity—from hydroelectric plants: 13.4% of total installed capacity (2012 est.)
country comparison to the world: 105
Electricity—from other renewable sources: 0% of total installed capacity (2012 est.)
country comparison to the world: 137
Crude oil—production: 0 bbl/day (2014 est.)
country comparison to the world: 203
Crude oil—exports: 0 bbl/day (2012 est.)

country comparison to the world: 203
Crude oil—imports: 0 bbl/day (2012 est.)
country comparison to the world: 141
Crude oil—proved reserves: 0 bbl (1 January 2015 est.)
country comparison to the world: 204
Refined petroleum products—production: 0 bbl/day (2012 est.)
country comparison to the world: 142
Refined petroleum products—consumption: 12,000 bbl/day (2013 est.)
country comparison to the world: 150
Refined petroleum products—exports: 0 bbl/day (2012 est.)
country comparison to the world: 143
Refined petroleum products—imports: 11,610 bbl/day (2012 est.)
country comparison to the world: 134
Natural gas—production: 0 cu m (2013 est.)
country comparison to the world: 141
Natural gas—consumption: 0 cu m (2013 est.)
country comparison to the world: 205
Natural gas—exports: 0 cu m (2013 est.)
country comparison to the world: 202
Natural gas—imports: 0 cu m (2013 est.)
country comparison to the world: 148
Natural gas—proved reserves: 0 cu m (1 January 2014 est.)
country comparison to the world: 202
Carbon dioxide emissions from consumption of energy: 1.406 million Mt (2012 est.)
country comparison to the world: 160

Telephones—fixed lines: *total subscriptions:* 120,000
subscriptions per 100 inhabitants: 1 (2014 est.)
country comparison to the world: 141
Telephones—mobile cellular: *total:* 12.5 million
subscriptions per 100 inhabitants: 68 (2014 est.)
country comparison to the world: 74
Telephone system: *general assessment:* system includes microwave radio relay, open-wire, and radiotelephone communication stations; in 2006, the government sold a 51% stake in the national telephone company and ultimately plans to retain only a 23% stake in the company
domestic: fixed-line connections stand at less than 1 per 100 persons; mobile-cellular usage, fostered by multiple providers, is increasing rapidly from a low base
international: country code—226; satellite earth station—1 Intelsat (Atlantic Ocean) (2011)
Broadcast media: 2 TV stations—1 state-owned and 1 privately owned; state-owned radio runs a national and regional network; substantial number of privately owned radio stations; transmissions of several international broadcasters available in Ouagadougou (2007)
Radio broadcast stations: AM 2, FM 26, shortwave 3 (2007)
Television broadcast stations: 3 (1 national, 2 private)
Internet country code: .bf
Internet hosts: 1,795 (2012)
country comparison to the world: 164
Internet users: *total:* 782,400

percent of population: 4.3% (2014 est.)
country comparison to the world: 125

TRANSPORTATION

Airports: 23 (2013)
country comparison to the world: 133
Airports—with paved runways: *total:* 2
over 3,047 m: 1
2,438 to 3,047 m: 1 (2013)
Airports—with unpaved runways: *total:* 21
1,524 to 2,437 m: 3
914 to 1,523 m: 13
under 914 m: 5 (2013)
Railways: *total:* 622 km
narrow gauge: 622 km 1.000-m gauge
note: another 660 km of this railway extends into
Cote d'Ivoire (2014)
country comparison to the world: 109
Roadways: *total:* 15,272 km
note: does not include urban roads (2010)
country comparison to the world: 121

MILITARY AND SECURITY

Military branches: Army, Air Force of Burkina
Faso (Force Aerienne de Burkina Faso, FABF),
National Gendarmerie (2011)

Military service age and obligation: 18 years of
age for voluntary military service; no conscription;
women may serve in supporting roles (2013)
Military expenditures: 1.39% of GDP (2012)
1.34% of GDP (2011)
1.39% of GDP (2010)
country comparison to the world: 73

TRANSNATIONAL ISSUES

Disputes—international: adding to illicit cross-
border activities, Burkina Faso has issues concerning unresolved boundary alignments with its
neighbors; demarcation is currently underway with
Mali; the dispute with Niger was referred to the
ICJ in 2010, and a dispute over several villages
with Benin persists; Benin retains a border dispute
with Burkina Faso around the town of Koualou
Refugees and internally displaced persons: refugees (country of origin): 33,069 (Mali) (2016)

Trafficking in persons: *current situation:* Burkina
Faso is a source, transit, and destination country
for women and children subjected to forced labor
and sex trafficking; Burkinabe children are forced
to work as farm hands, gold panners and washers,
street vendors, domestic servants, and beggars or in
the commercial sex trade, with some transported

to nearby countries; to a lesser extent, Burkinabe
women are recruited for legitimate jobs in the
Middle East or Europe and subsequently forced
into prostitution; women from other West African
countries are also lured to Burkina Faso for work
and subjected to forced prostitution, forced labor
in restaurants, or domestic servitude

tier rating: Tier 2 Watch List—Burkina Faso does
not fully comply with the minimum standards
for the elimination of trafficking; however, it is
making significant efforts to do so; law enforcement efforts decreased in 2014, with a significant
decline in trafficking prosecutions (none for forced
begging involving Koranic school teachers—a
prevalent form of trafficking) and no convictions,
a 2014 law criminalizing the sale of children, child
prostitution, and child pornography is undermined
by a provision allowing offenders to pay a fine in
lieu of serving prison time proportionate to the
crime; the government sustained efforts to identify
and protect a large number of child victims, relying
on support from NGOs and international organizations; nationwide awareness-raising activities
were sustained, but little was done to stop forced
begging (2015)

BURMA

INTRODUCTION

Background: Various ethnic Burmese and ethnic
minority city-states or kingdoms occupied the
present borders through the 19th century. Over a
period of 62 years (1824–1886), Britain conquered
Burma and incorporated the country into its Indian
Empire. Burma was administered as a province of
India until 1937 when it became a separate, self-
governing colony; in 1948, Burma attained independence from the British Commonwealth. Gen.
NE WIN dominated the government from 1962 to
1988, first as military ruler, then as self-appointed
president, and later as political kingpin. In response
to widespread civil unrest, NE WIN resigned in
1988, but with in months the military crush ed
student-led protests and took power.
Multiparty legislative elections in 1990 resulted in
the main opposition party—the National League
for Democracy (NLD)—winning a landslide victory. Instead of handing over power, the junta
placed NLD leader (and Nobel Peace Prize recipient) AUNG SAN SUU KYI under house arrest
from 1989 to 1995, 2000 to 2002, and from May
2003 to November 2010. In late September 2007,
the ruling junta brutally suppressed protests over in
creased fu el prices led by prodemocracy activists
and Buddhist monks, killing at least 13 people and
arresting thousands for participating in the demonstrations. I nearly May 2008, Burma was struck by
Cyclone Nargis, which left over 138,000 dead and
tens of thousands injured and homeless. Despite
this tragedy, the junta proceeded with its May constitutional referendum, the first vote in Burma since

1990. Legislative elections held in November 2010,
which the NLD boycotted and were con sidered
flawed by many in the international community,
saw the ruling Union Solidarity and Development
Party garner over 75% of the seats.
The national legislature convened in January
2011 and selected former Prime Minister THEIN
SEIN as president. Although the vast majority of
national-level appointees named by THEIN SEIN
are former or current military officers, the government initiated a series of political and economic
reforms leading to a substan tial opening of the
long-isolated country. These reforms included
releasing hundreds of political prisoners, signing a
nationwide cease-fire with several of the country's
ethnic armed groups, pursuing legal reform, and
gradually reducing restrictions on freedom of the
press, association, and civil society. At least due in
part to these reforms, AUNG SAN SUUKYI was
elected to the national legislature in April 2012
and became chair of the Committee for Rule of
Law and Tranquility. Burma served as chair of the
Association of Southeast Asian Nations (ASEAN)
for 2014. In a flawed but largely credible national
legislative election in November 2015 featuring
more than 90 political parties, the NLD again won
a landslide victory. Using its overwhelming majority in both houses of parliament, the NLD elected
HTIN KYAW, AUNG SAN SUU KYI's confi-
dant and long-time NLD supporter, as president.
Burma's first civilian government after more than
five decades of military dictatorship was sworn into
office on 30 March 2016.

GEOGRAPHY

Location: Southeastern Asia, bordering the Andaman Sea and the Bay of Bengal, between Bangladesh and Thailand

Geographic coordinates: 22 00 N, 98 00 E

Map references: Southeast Asia

Area: *total:* 676,578 sq km
land: 653,508 sq km
water: 23,070 sq km
country comparison to the world: 40

Area—comparative: slightly smaller than Texas

Land boundaries: *total:* 6,522 km
border countries (5): Bangladesh 271 km, China 2,129 km, India 1,468 km, Laos 238 km, Thailand 2,416 km

Coastline: 1,930 km

Maritime claims: *territorial sea:* 12 nm contiguous zone: 24 nm exclusive
economic zone: 200 nm continental shelf: 200 nm or to the edge of the continental margin

Climate: tropical monsoon; cloudy, rainy, hot, humid summers (southwest monsoon, June to September); less cloudy, scant rainfall, mild temperatures, lower humidity during winter (northeast monsoon, December to April)

Terrain: central lowlands ringed by steep, rugged highlands

Elevation: *mean elevation:* 702 m

elevation extremes: *lowest:* point: Andaman Sea/Bay of Bengal 0 m
highest point: Gamlang Razi 5,870 m

Natural resources: petroleum, timber, tin, antimony, zinc, copper, tungsten, lead, coal, marble, limestone, precious stones, Natural gas, hydropower, arable land:

Land use: *agricultural land:* 19.2%
arable land: 16.5%
permanent crops: 2.2%
permanent pasture: 0.5%
forest: 48.2%
other: 32.6% (2011 est.)

Irrigated land: 22,950 sq km (2012)

Total renewable water resources: 1,168 cu km (2011)

Freshwater withdrawal (domestic/industrial/agricultural): *total:* 33.23 cu km/yr (10%/1%/89%)
per capita: 728.6 cu m/yr (2005)

Natural hazards: destructive earthquakes and cyclones; flooding and landslides common during rainy season (June to September); periodic droughts

Environment—current issues: deforestation; industrial pollution of air, soil, and water; inadequate sanitation and water treatment contribute to disease

Environment—international agreements: *party to:* Biodiversity, Climate Change, Climate Change-Kyoto Protocol, Desertification, Endangered Species, Law of the Sea, Ozone Layer Protection, Ship Pollution, Tropical Timber 83, Tropical Timber 94
signed, but not ratified: none of the selected agreements

Geography—note: strategic location near major Indian Ocean shipping lanes; the north-south flowing Irrawaddy River is the country's largest and most important commercial waterway

PEOPLE AND SOCIETY

Nationality: *noun:* Burmese (singular and plural)
adjective: Burmese

Ethnic groups: Burman 68%, Shan 9%, Karen 7%, Rakhine 4%, Chinese 3%, Indian 2%, Mon 2%, other 5%

Languages: Burmese (official)
note: minority ethnic groups have their own languages

Religions: Buddhist 89%, Christian 4% (Baptist 3%, Roman Catholic 1%), Muslim 4%, Animist 1%, other 2%

Population: 56,320,206
note: estimates for this country take into account the effects of excess mortality due to AIDS; this can result in lower life expectancy, higher infant mortality, higher death rates, lower population growth rates, and changes in the distribution of population by age and sex than would otherwise be expected (July 2015 est.)
country comparison to the world: 25

Age structure: *0–14 years:* 26.07% (male 7,485,419/female 7,194,500)
15–24 years: 18.02% (male 5,138,185/female 5,009,470)
25–54 years: 43.31% (male 12,132,302/female 12,261,750)
55–64 years: 7.24% (male 1,919,725/female 2,157,789)
65 years and over: 5.36% (male 1,313,711/female 1,707,355) (2015 est.)

Dependency ratios: *total* dependency ratio: 49.1%
youth dependency ratio: 41.1%
elderly dependency ratio: 8%
potential support ratio: 12.5% (2015 est.)

Median age: *total:* 28.3 years
male: 27.7 years
female: 28.9 years (2015 est.)
country comparison to the world: 126

Population growth rate: 1.01% (2015 est.)
country comparison to the world: 116

Birth rate: 18.39 births/1,000 population (2015 est.)
country comparison to the world: 97

Death rate: 7.96 deaths/1,000 population (2015 est.)
country comparison to the world: 101

Net migration rate: -0.28 migrant(s)/1,000 population (2015 est.)
country comparison to the world: 124

Urbanization: *urban population:* 34.1% of total population (2015)
rate of urbanization: 2.49% annual rate of change (2010–15 est.)

Major urban areas—population: RANGOON (Yangon) (capital) 4.802 million; Mandalay 1.167 million; Nay Pyi Taw 1.03 million (2015)

Sex ratio: *at birth:* 1.06 male(s)/female
0–14 years: 1.04 male(s)/female
15–24 years: 1.03 male(s)/female
25–54 years: 0.99 male(s)/female
55–64 years: 0.89 male(s)/female
65 years and over: 0.77 male(s)/female

total population: 0.99 male(s)/female (2015 est.)

Mother's mean age at first birth: 21.8 (2007 est.)

Maternal mortality rate: 178 deaths/100,000 live births (2015 est.)
country comparison to the world: 54

Infant mortality rate: *total:* 43.55 deaths/1,000 live births
male: 49.84 deaths/1,000 live births
female: 36.88 deaths/1,000 live births (2015 est.)
country comparison to the world: 48

Life expectancy at birth: *total population:* 66.29 years
male: 63.89 years
female: 68.82 years (2015 est.)
country comparison to the world: 171

Total fertility rate: 2.16 children born/woman (2015 est.)
country comparison to the world: 102

Contraceptive prevalence rate: 46% (2009/10)

Health expenditures: 1.8% of GDP (2013)
country comparison to the world: 191

Physicians density: 0.61 physicians/1,000 population (2012)

Hospital bed density: 0.6 beds/1,000 population (2006)

Drinking water source:
improved:
urban: 92.7% of population
rural: 74.4% of population
total: 80.6% of population
unimproved:
urban: 7.3% of population
rural: 25.6% of population
total: 19.4% of population (2015 est.)

Sanitation facility access:
improved:
urban: 84.3% of population
rural: 73.9% of population
total: 77.4% of population
unimproved:
urban: 15.7% of population
rural: 26.1% of population
total: 22.6% of population (2012 est.)

HIV/AIDS—adult prevalence rate: 0.69% (2014 est.)
country comparison to the world: 55

HIV/AIDS—people living with HIV/AIDS: 212,600 (2014 est.)
country comparison to the world: 27

HIV/AIDS—deaths: 10,100 (2014 est.)
country comparison to the world: 23

Major infectious diseases: *degree of risk:* very high
food or waterborne diseases: bacterial and protozoal diarrhea, hepatitis A, and typhoid fever
vectorborne diseases: dengue fever, malaria, and Japanese encephalitis
water contact disease: leptospirosis
animal contact disease: rabies
note: highly pathogenic H5N1 avian influenza has been identified in this country; it poses a negligible risk withextremely rare cases possible among US citizens who have close contact with birds (2013)

Obesity—adult prevalence rate: 2.9% (2014)
country comparison to the world: 172

Children under the age of 5 years underweight: 22.6% (2010)

country comparison to the world: 27

Literacy: *definition:* age 15 and over can read and write

total population: 93.1%

male: 95.2%

female: 91.2% (2015 est.)

School life expectancy (primary to tertiary education): *total:* 8 years

male: NA

female: NA (2007)

GOVERNMENT

Country name: *conventional long form:* Union of Burma

conventional short form: Burma

local long form: Pyidaungzu Thammada Myanma Naingngandaw (translated as the Republic of the Union of Myanmar)

local short form: Myanma Naingngandaw

former: Socialist Republic of the Union of Burma, Union of Myanmar

note: since 1989 the military authorities in Burma and the current parliamentary government have promoted the name Myanmar as a conventional name for their state; the US Government has not adopted the name

etymology: both "Burma" and "Myanmar" derive from the name of the majority Burmese Bamar ethnic group

Government type: parliamentary republic

Capital: *name:* Rangoon (Yangon); note—Nay Pyi Taw is the administrative capital

Geographic coordinates: 16 48 N, 96 09 E

time difference: UTC+6.5 (11.5 hours ahead of Washington, DC, during Standard Time)

Administrative divisions: 7 regions (taing-myar, singular—taing), 7 states (pyi ne-myar, singular—pyine), 1 union territory

regions: Ayeyawady (Irrawaddy), Bago, Magway, Mandalay, Sagaing, Taninthayi, Yangon (Rangoon)

states: Chin, Kachin, Kayah, Kayin, Mon, Rakhine (Arakan),

Shan union territory: Nay Pyi Taw

Independence: 4 January 1948 (from the UK)

National holiday: Independence Day, 4 January (1948); Union Day, 12 February (1947)

Constitution: previous 1947, 1974 (suspended until 2008); latest approved by referendum 29 May 2008 (2016)

Legal system: mixed legal system of English common law (as introduced in codifications designed for colonial India) and customary law

International law organization participation: has not submitted an ICJ jurisdiction declaration; non-party state to the ICCt

Citizenship: *citizenship by birth:* no

citizenship by descent only: both parents must be citizens of Burma

dual citizenship recognized: no

residency requirement for naturalization: none

note: an applicant for naturalization must be the child or spouse of a citizen

Suffrage: 18 years of age; universal

Executive branch: *note:* the parliamentary bill creating the position of "state counsellor" was signed into law by President HTIN KYAW on 6 April 2016; the state counsellor serves the equivalent term of the president and is similar to a prime minister in that the holder acts as a link between the parliament and the executive branch *chief of state:* President HTIN KYAW (since 30 March 2016); Vice Presidents MYINT SWE (since 30 March 2016) and HENRY VAN TIO (since 30 March 2016); note—the president is both chief of state and head of government

head of government: President HTIN KYAW (since 30 March 2016); Vice Presidents MYINT SWE (since 30 March 2016) and HENRY VAN TIO (since 30 March 2016); State Counsellor AUNG SAN SUU KYI (since 6 April 2016); she concurrently serves as minister of foreign affairs and minister for the office of the president

cabinet: Cabinet appointments shared by the president and the commander-in-chief

elections/appointments: president indirectly elected by simple majority vote by the full Assembly of the Union from among 3 vice-presidential candidates nominated by the Presidential Electoral College (consists of members of the lower and upper houses and military members); the other 2 candidates become vice-presidents (president elected for a 5-year term); election last held on 15 March 2016 (next to be held in 2021)

election results: HTIN KYAW elected president; Assembly of the Union vote: HTIN KYAW 360, MYINT SWE 213, HENRY VAN TIO 79 (652 votes cast)

Legislative branch: *description:* bicameral Assembly of the Union or Pyidaungsu consists of an upper house—the House of Nationalities or Amyotha Hluttaw, (224 seats; 168 members directly elected in single-seat constituencies by absolute majority vote with a second round if needed and 56 appointed by the military; members serve 5-year terms) and a lower house—the House of Representatives or Pyithu Hluttaw, (440 seats; 330 members directly elected in single-seat constituencies by simple majority vote and 110 appointed by the military; members serve 5-year terms)

elections: last held on 8 November 2015 (next to be held in 2020)

election results: Upper House—percent of vote by party—NA; seats by party—NLD 135, USDP 11, ANP 10, SNLD 3, ZCD 2, TNP 2, independent 2, other 3, military appointees 56; Lower House—percent of vote by party—NA; seats by party—NLD 255, USDP 30, ANP 12, SNLD 12, PNO 3, TNP 3, ZCD 2, LNDP 2, independent 1, other 3, canceled due to insurgence 7, military appointees 110

Judicial branch: highest court(s): Supreme Court of the Union (consists of the chief justice and 7–11 judges)

judge selection and term of office: chief justice and judges nominated by the president, with approval of the Lower House, and appointed by the president; judges normally serve until mandatory retirement at age 70

subordinate courts: High Courts of the Region; High Courts of the State; Court of the Self-Administered Division; Court of the Self-Administered Zone; district and township courts; special courts (for juvenile, municipal, and traffic offenses); courts martial

Political parties and leaders: All Mon Region Democracy Party or AMRDP [NAING NGWE THEIN]

Arakan National Party or ANP [Dr. AYE MAUNG] (formed from the 2013 merger of the Rakhine Nationalities Development Party and the Arakan League for Democracy) National Democratic Force or NDF [KHIN MAUNG SWE]

National League for Democracy or NLD [AUNG SAN SUU KYI]

National Unity Party or NUP [THAN TIN]

Pa-O National Organization or PNO [AUNG KHAN HTI]

Shan Nationalities Democratic Party or SNDP [SAI AIK PAUNG]

Shan Nationalities League for Democracy or SNLD [KHUN HTUN OO]

Ta'ang National Party or TNP [AIK MONE]

Union Solidarity and Development Party or USDP [HTAY OO]

Zomi Congress for Democracy or ZCD [PU CIN SIAN THANG]

numerous smaller parties

Political pressure groups and leaders: *Thai border:* Ethnic Nationalities Council or ENC

Federation of Trade Unions-Burma or FTUB (exile trade union and labor advocates)

National Coalition Government of the Union of Burma or NCGUB (self-proclaimed government in exile)

["Prime Minister" Dr. SEIN WIN] consists of individuals, some legitimately elected to the People's Assembly in 1990 (the group fled to a border area and joined insurgents in December 1990 to form a parallel government in exile)

National Council-Union of Burma or NCUB (exile coalition of opposition groups)

United Nationalities Federal Council or UNFC

inside Burma: Kachin Independence Organization

Karen National Union or KNU

Karenni National People's Party or KNPP

United Wa State Army or UWSA

88 Generation Students (pro-democracy movement) several other Chin, Karen, Mon, and Shan factions

note: many restrictions on freedom of expression have been relaxed by the government; a limited number of political groups, other than parties, are approved by the government

International organization participation: ADB, ARF, ASEAN, BIMSTEC, CP, EAS, EITI (candidate country), FAO, G-77, IAEA, IBRD, ICAO, ICRM, IDA, IFAD, IFC, IFRCS, IHO, ILO, IMF, IMO, Interpol, IOC, IOM, IPU, ISO (correspondent), ITU, ITUC (NGOs), NAM, OPCW (signatory), SAARC (observer), UN, UNCTAD, UNESCO, UNIDO, UNWTO, UPU, WCO, WHO, WIPO, WMO, WTO

Diplomatic representation in the US: *chief of mission:* Ambassador KYAW MYO HTUT (since 3 December 2013)

chancery: 2300 S Street NW, Washington, DC 20008

telephone: [1] (202) 332-3344

FAX: [1] (202) 332-4351

consulate(s) general: Los Angeles, New York

Diplomatic representation from the US: *chief of mission:* Ambassador Scot MARCIEL (since 27 April 2016)

embassy: 110 University Avenue, Kamayut Township, Rangoon

mailing address: Box B, APO AP 96546

telephone: [95] (1) 536-509, 535-756, 538-038

FAX: [95] (1) 511-069

Flag description: design consists of three equal horizontal stripes of yellow (top), green, and red; centered on the green band is a large white five-pointed star that partially overlaps onto the adjacent colored stripes; the design revives the triband colors used by Burma from 1943–45, during the Japanese occupation

National symbol(s): chinthe (mythical lion); national colors: yellow, green, red, white

National anthem: *name:* "Kaba Ma Kyei" (Till the End of the World, Myanmar)

lyrics/music: SAYA TIN

note: adopted 1948; Burma is among a handful of non-European nations that have anthems rooted in indigenous traditions; the beginning portion of the anthem is a traditional Burmese anthem before transitioning into a Western-style orchestrated work

ECONOMY

Economy—overview: Since the transition to a civilian government in 2011, Burma has begun an economic overhaul aimed at attracting foreign investment and reintegrating into the global economy. Economic reforms have included establishing a managed float of the Burmese kyat in 2012, re-writing the Foreign Investment Law in 2012 to allow more foreign investment participation, granting the Central Bank operational independence in July 2013, enacting a new Anti-corruption Law in September 2013, and granting licenses to nine foreign banks in 2014 and four more foreign banks in 2016.

The government's commitment to reform, and the subsequent easing of most Western sanctions, led to accelerated growth in 2013 and 2014. In 2015, growth slowed because of political uncertainty in an election year, summer floods, and external factors, including China's slowdown and lower commodity prices. Burma's abundant natural resources, young labor force, and proximity to Asia's dynamic economies have attracted foreign investment in the energy sector, garment industry, information technology, and food and beverages. Pledged foreign direct investment grew from $4.1 billion in FY 2013 to $8.1 billion in FY 2014.

Despite these improvements, living standards have not improved for the majority of the people residing in rural areas. Burma remains one of the poorest countries in Asia—approximately 26% of the

country's 51 million people live in poverty. The previous government's isolationist policies and economic mismanagement have left Burma with poor infrastructure, endemic corruption, underdeveloped human resources, and inadequate access to capital, which will require a major commitment to reverse. The Burmese government has been slow to address impediments to economic development such as insecure land rights, a restrictive trade licensing system, an opaque revenue collection system, and an antiquated banking system. The newly elected government, led by AUNG SAN SUU KYI, will likely focus on accelerating agricultural productivity and land reforms, modernizing and opening the financial sector, and improving fiscal management.

GDP (purchasing power parity): $283.5 billion (2015 est.)

$264.9 billion (2014 est.)

$243.7 billion (2013 est.)

note: data are in 2015 US dollars

country comparison to the world: 56

GDP (official exchange rate): $66.98 billion (2015 est.)

GDP—real growth rate: 7% (2015 est.)

8.7% (2014 est.) 8.4% (2013 est.)

country comparison to the world: 15

GDP—per capita (PPP): $5,500 (2015 est.)

$5,200 (2014 est.)

$4,800 (2013 est.)

note: data are in 2015 US dollars

country comparison to the world: 164

Gross national saving: 14.9% of GDP (2015 est.)

17.9% of GDP (2014 est.)

17.2% of GDP (2013 est.)

country comparison to the world: 117

GDP—composition, by end use:

household consumption: 76.8%

government consumption: 3.9%

investment in fixed capital: 21%

investment in inventories: 0.3%

exports of goods and services: 31.7%

imports of goods and services: -33.7% (2015 est.)

GDP—composition, by sector of origin:

agriculture: 36.1%

industry: 22.3%

services: 41.6% (2015 est.)

Agriculture—products: rice, pulses, beans, sesame, groundnuts; sugarcane; fish and fish products; hardwood

Industries: agricultural processing; wood and wood products; copper, tin, tungsten, iron; cement, construction materials; pharmaceuticals; fertilizer; oil and natural gas; garments; jade and gems

Industrial production growth rate: 12.2% (2015 est.)

country comparison to the world: 3

Labor force: 36.18 million (2015 est.)

country comparison to the world: 18

Labor force—by occupation: *agriculture:* 70%

industry: 7%

services: 23% (2001 est.)

Unemployment rate: 5% (2015 est.)

5.1% (2014 est.)

country comparison to the world: 52

Population below poverty line: 32.7% (2007 est.)

Household income or consumption by percentage share: *lowest:* 10%: 2.8%

highest: 10%: 32.4% (1998)

Budget: *revenues:* $2.682 billion

expenditures: $4.471 billion (2015 est.)

Taxes and other revenues: 4.1% of GDP (2015 est.)

country comparison to the world: 215

Budget surplus (+) or deficit (–): -2.7% of GDP (2015 est.)

country comparison to the world: 100

Fiscal year: 1 April—31 March

Inflation rate (consumer prices): 11.5% (2015 est.) 5.9% (2014 est.)

country comparison to the world: 214

Central bank discount rate: 9.95% (31 December 2010) 12% (31 December 2009)

country comparison to the world: 24

Commercial bank prime lending rate: 13% (31 December 2015 est.)

13% (31 December 2014 est.)

country comparison to the world: 56

Stock of narrow money: $13.47 billion (31 December 2015 est.)

$14.07 billion (31 December 2014 est.)

country comparison to the world: 71

Stock of domestic credit: $15.41 billion (31 December 2015 est.)

$16.91 billion (31 December 2014 est.)

country comparison to the world: 91

Market value of publicly traded shares: $NA

Current account balance: -$5.943 billion (2015 est.)

-$3.683 billion (2014 est.)

country comparison to the world: 171

Exports: $9.752 billion (2015 est.)

$8.962 billion (2014 est.)

note: official export figures are grossly underestimated due to the value of timber, gems, narcotics, rice, and other products smuggled to Thailand, China, and Bangladesh

country comparison to the world: 90

Exports—commodities: natural gas; wood products; pulses and beans; fish; rice; clothing; minerals, including jade and gems

Exports—partners: China 37.7%, Thailand 25.6%, India 7.7%, Japan 6.2% (2015)

Imports: $12.64 billion (2015 est.)

$12.17 billion (2014 est.)

note: import figures are grossly underestimated due to the value of consumer goods, diesel fuel, and other products smuggled in from Thailand, China, Malaysia, and India

country comparison to the world: 90

Imports—commodities: fabric; petroleum products; fertilizer; plastics; machinery; transport equipment; cement, construction materials; food products edible oil

Imports—partners: China 42.2%, Thailand 18.5%, Singapore 11%, Japan 4.8% (2015)

Reserves of foreign exchange and gold: $9.417 billion (31 December 2015 est.)

$8.727 billion (31 December 2014 est.)

country comparison to the world: 77

Debt—external: $6.616 billion (31 December 2014 est.)

$7.367 billion (31 December 2013 est.)
country comparison to the world: 121
Exchange rates: kyats (MMK) per US dollar—
1,171.8 (2015 est.)
984.35 (2014 est.)
984.35 (2013 est.)
853.48 (2012 est.)
815 (2011 est.)

ENERGY

Electricity—production: 10.48 billion kWh (2012 est.)
country comparison to the world: 95
Electricity—consumption: 7.765 billion kWh (2012 est.)
country comparison to the world: 100
Electricity—exports: 0 kWh (2013 est.)
country comparison to the world: 110
Electricity—imports: 0 kWh (2013 est.)
country comparison to the world: 124
Electricity—installed generating capacity: 3.591 million kW (2012 est.)
country comparison to the world: 88
Electricity—from fossil fuels: 24.8% of total installed capacity (2012 est.)
country comparison to the world: 188
Electricity—from nuclear fuels: 0% of total installed capacity (2012 est.)
country comparison to the world: 55
Electricity—from hydroelectric plants: 75.2% of total installed capacity (2012 est.)
country comparison to the world: 20
Electricity—from other renewable sources: 0% of total installed capacity (2012 est.)
country comparison to the world: 159
Crude oil—production: 20,000 bbl/day (2014 est.)
country comparison to the world: 71
Crude oil—exports: 2,717 bbl/day (2012 est.)
country comparison to the world: 77
Crude oil—imports: 40 bbl/day (2012 est.)
country comparison to the world: 84
Crude oil—proved reserves: 50 million bbl (1 January 2015 est.)
country comparison to the world: 80
Refined petroleum products—production: 15,780 bbl/day (2012 est.)
country comparison to the world: 99
Refined petroleum products—consumption: 25.000 bbl/day (2013 est.)
country comparison to the world: 121
Refined petroleum products—exports: 0 bbl/day (2012 est.)
country comparison to the world: 159
Refined petroleum products—imports: 8,557 bbl/day (2012 est.)
country comparison to the world: 142
Natural gas—production: 13.1 billion cu m (2013 est.)
country comparison to the world: 37
Natural gas—consumption: 4.6 billion cu m (2013 est.)
country comparison to the world: 61
Natural gas—exports: 8.5 billion cu m (2013 est.)
country comparison to the world: 24
Natural gas—imports: 0 cu m (2013 est.)
country comparison to the world: 166

Natural gas—proved reserves: 283.2 billion cu m (1 January 2014 est.)
country comparison to the world: 39
Carbon dioxide emissions from consumption of energy: 13.34 million Mt (2012 est.)
country comparison to the world: 93

COMMUNICATIONS

Telephones—fixed lines: total subscriptions: 530,000
subscriptions per 100 inhabitants: 1 (2014 est.)
country comparison to the world: 96
Telephones—mobile cellular: *total:* 26.6 million
subscriptions per 100 inhabitants: 48 (2014 est.)
country comparison to the world: 47
Telephone system: *general assessment:* meets minimum requirements for local and intercity service for business and government
domestic: system barely capable of providing basic service; mobile-cellular phone system is grossly underdeveloped
international: country code—95; landing point for the SEA-ME-WE-3 optical telecommunications submarine cable that provides links to Asia, the Middle East, and Europe; satellite earth stations—2, Intelsat (Indian Ocean) and ShinSat (2011)
Broadcast media: government controls all domestic broadcast media; 2 state-controlled TV stations with 1 of the stations controlled by the armed forces; 2 pay-TV stations are joint state-private ventures; access to satellite TV is limited; 1 state-controlled domestic radio station and 9 FM stations that are joint state-private ventures; transmissions of several international broadcasters are available in parts of Burma; the Voice of America (VOA), Radio Free Asia (RFA), BBC Burmese service, the Democratic Voice of Burma (DVB), and Radio Australia use shortwave to broadcast in Burma; VOA, RFA, and DVB produce daily TV news programs that are transmitted by satellite to audiences in Burma
Radio broadcast stations: AM 1, FM 2, shortwave 3 (2007)
Television broadcast stations: 4 (2008)
Internet country code: .mm
Internet hosts: 1,055 (2012)
country comparison to the world: 172
Internet users: *total:* 646,700
percent of population: 1.2% (2014 est.)
country comparison to the world: 128

TRANSPORTATION

Airports: 64 (2013)
country comparison to the world: 76
Airports—with paved runways: *total:* 36
over 3,047 m: 12
2,438 to 3,047 m: 11
1,524 to 2,437 m: 12
under 914 m: 1 (2013)
Airports—with unpaved runways: *total:* 28
over 3,047 m: 1
1,524 to 2,437 m: 4
914 to 1,523 m: 10
under 914 m: 13 (2013)

Heliports: 11 (2013)
Pipelines: gas 3,739 km; oil 551 km (2013)
Railways: *total:* 5,031 km
narrow gauge: 5,031 km 1.000-m gauge (2008)
country comparison to the world: 38
Roadways: *total:* 34,377 km (includes 358 km of expressways) (2010)
country comparison to the world: 93
Waterways: 12,800 km (2011)
country comparison to the world: 10
Merchant marine: *total:* 29
by type: cargo 22, passenger 2, passenger/cargo 3, specialized tanker 1, vehicle carrier 1
foreign-owned: 2 (Germany 1, Japan 1)
registered in other countries: 3 (Panama 3) (2010)
country comparison to the world: 86
Ports and terminals: *major seaport(s):* Moulmein, Sittwe
river port(s): Rangoon (Yangon) (Rangoon River)

MILITARY AND SECURITY

Military branches: Myanmar Armed Forces (Tatmadaw): Army (Tatmadaw Kyi), Navy (Tatmadaw Yay), Air Force (Tatmadaw Lay)(2013)
Military service age and obligation: 18–35 years of age (men) and 18–27 years of age (women) for voluntary military service; no conscription (a 2010 law reintroducing conscription has not yet entered into force); 2-year service obligation; male (ages 18–45) and female (ages 18–35) professionals (including doctors, engineers, mechanics) serve up to 3 years; service terms may be stretched to 5 years in an officially declared emergency; Burma signed the Convention on the Rights of the Child (CRC) on 15 August 1991; on 27 June 2012, the regime signed a Joint Action Plan on prevention of child recruitment; in February 2013, the military formed a new task force to address forced child conscription; approximately 600 children have been released from military service since the signing of the joint action plan (2015)

TRANSNATIONAL ISSUES

Disputes—international: over half of Burma's population consists of diverse ethnic groups who have substantial numbers of kin in neighboring countries; the Naf River on the border with Bangladesh serves as a smuggling and illegal transit route; Bangladesh struggles to accommodate 29,000 Rohingya, Burmese Muslim minority from Arakan State, livingas refugees in Cox's Bazar; Burmese border authorities are constructing a 200 km (124 mi) wire fence designed to deter illegal cross-border transit and tensions from the military build-up along border with Bangladesh in 2010; Bangladesh referred its maritime boundary claims with Burma and India to the International Tribunal on the Law of the Sea; Burmese forces attempting to dig in to the largely autonomous Shan State to rout local militias tied to the drug trade, prompts local residents to periodically flee into neighboring Yunnan Province in China; fencing along the India-Burma international border at Manipur's Moreh town is in progress to check illegal drug trafficking and movement of militants; over 100,000 mostly Karen refugees and asylum seekers fleeing civil strife, political upheaval, and economic stagnation in Burma were living in remote camps in Thailand near the border as of April 2016

Refugees and internally displaced persons: *IDPs:* 644,000 (government offensives against armed ethnic minority groups near its borders with China and Thailand) (2015)

stateless persons: 938,000 (2015); note—Rohingya Muslims, living in Rakhine State, are Burma's main group of stateless people; the Burmese Government does not recognize the Rohingya as a "national race" and stripped them of their citizenship under the 1982 Citizenship law, categorizing them as "non-national" or "foreign residents"; under the Rakhine State Action Plan drafted in October 2014, the Rohingya must demonstrate their family has lived in Burma for at least 60 years to qualify for a lesser naturalized citizenship and the classification of Bengali or be put in detention camps and face deportation; native-born but non-indigenous people, such as Indians, are also stateless; the Burmese Government does not grant citizenship to children born outside of the country to Burmese parents who left the country illegally or fled persecution, such as those born in Thailand

note: estimate does not include stateless IDPs or stateless persons in IDP-like situations because they are included in estimates of IDPs (2015)

Trafficking in persons: *current situation:* Burma is a source country for men, women, and children trafficked for the purpose of forced labor and for women and children subjected to sex trafficking; Burmese adult and child labor migrants travel to East Asia, the Middle East, South Asia, and the US, where men are forced to work in the fishing, manufacturing, forestry, and construction industries and women and girls are forced into prostitution, domestic servitude, or forced labor in the garment sector; some Burmese economic migrants and Rohingya asylum seekers have become forced laborers on Thai fishing boats; some military personnel and armed ethnic groups unlawfully conscript child soldiers or coerce adults and children into forced labor; domestically, adults and children from ethnic areas are vulnerable to forced labor on plantations and in mines, while children may also be subject to forced prostitution, domestic service, and begging

tier rating: Tier 2 Watch List—Burma does not fully comply with the minimum standards for the elimination of trafficking, but it is making significant efforts to do so; the government has a written plan that, if implemented, would constitute making a significant effort toward meeting the minimum standard for eliminating human trafficking; in 2014, law enforcement continued to investigate and prosecute cross-border trafficking offenses but did little to address domestic trafficking; no civilians or government officials were prosecuted or convicted for the recruitment of child soldiers, a serious problem that is hampered by corruption and the influence of the military; victim referral and protection services remained inadequate, especially for men, and left victims vulnerable to being re-trafficked; the government coordinated anti-trafficking programs as part of its five-year national action plan (2015)

Illicit drugs: world's third largest producer of illicit opium with an estimated production in 2012 of 690 metric tons, an increase of 13% over 2011, and poppy cultivation in 2012 *totaled* 51,000 hectares, a 17% increase over 2011; production in the United Wa State Army's areas of greatest control remains low; Shan state is the source of 94.5% of Burma's poppy cultivation; lack of government will to take on major narcotrafficking groups and lack of serious commitment against money laundering continues to hinder the overall antidrug effort; major source of methamphetamine and heroin for regional consumption (2013)

BURUNDI

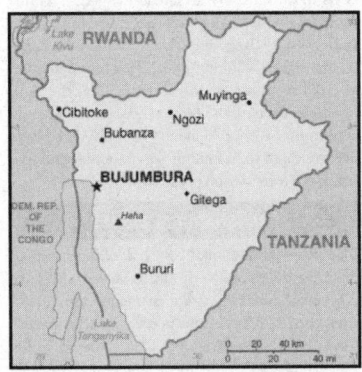

INTRODUCTION

Background: Burundi's first democratically elected president was assassinated in October 1993 after only 100 days in office, triggering widespread ethnic violence between Hutu and Tutsi factions. More than 200,000 Burundians perished during the conflict that spanned almost a dozen years. Hundreds of thousands of Burundians were internally displaced or became refugees in neighboring countries. An internationally brokered power-sharing agreement between the Tutsi-dominated government and the Hutu rebels in 2003 paved the way for a transition process that integrated defense forces, and established a new constitution

and elected a majority Hutu government in 2005. The government of President Pierre NKURUNZIZA, who was reelected in 2010 and again in a disputed election in 2015, continues to face many political and economic challenges.

GEOGRAPHY

Location: Central Africa, east of the Democratic Republic of the Congo, west of Tanzania

Geographic coordinates: 3 30 S, 30 00 E

Map references: Africa

Area: *total:* 27,830 sq km

land: 25,680 sq km

water: 2,150 sq km

country comparison to the world: 147

Area—comparative: slightly smaller than Maryland

Land boundaries: *total:* 1,140 km

border countries (3): Democratic Republic of the Congo 236 km, Rwanda 315 km, Tanzania 589 km

Coastline: 0 km (landlocked)

Maritime claims: none (landlocked)

Climate: equatorial; high plateau with considerable altitude variation (772 m to 2,670 m above sea level); average annual temperature varies with altitude from 23 to 17 degrees Celsius but is generally moderate as the average altitude is about 1,700 m; average annual rainfall is about 150 cm; two wet seasons (February to May and September to November), and two dry seasons (June to August and December to January)

Terrain: hilly and mountainous, dropping to a plateau in east, some plains

Elevation: *mean elevation:* 1,504 m

elevation extremes: *lowest:* point: Lake Tanganyika 772 m

highest point: Heha 2,670 m

Natural resources: nickel, uranium, rare earth oxides, peat, cobalt, copper, platinum, vanadium, arable land, hydropower, niobium, tantalum, gold, tin, tungsten, kaolin, limestone

Land use: *agricultural land:* 73.3%

arable land: 38.9%

permanent crops: 15.6%

permanent pasture: 18.8%

forest: 6.6%

other: 20.1% (2011 est.)

Irrigated land: 230 sq km (2012)

Total renewable water resources: 12.54 cu km (2011)

Freshwater withdrawal (domestic/industrial/agricultural): *total:* 0.29 cu km/yr (15%/5%/79%)

per capita: 43.27 cu m/yr (2005)

Natural hazards: flooding; lands lides; drought

Environment—current issues: soil erosion as a result of overgrazing and the expansion of agriculture into marginal lands; deforestation (little forested land remains because of uncontrolled cutting of trees for fuel); habitat loss threatens wildlife populations

Environment—international agreements: *party to:* Biodiversity, Climate Change, Climate Change-Kyoto Protocol, Desertification, Endangered

Species, Hazardous Wastes, Ozone Layer Protection, Wetlands

signed, but not ratified: Law of the Sea

Geography—note: landlocked; straddles crest of the Nile-Congo watershed; the Kagera, which drains into Lake Victoria, is the most remote headstream of the White Nile

PEOPLE AND SOCIETY

Nationality: *noun:* Burundian(s)
adjective: Burundian

Ethnic groups: Hutu (Bantu) 85%, Tutsi (Hamitic) 14%, Twa (Pygmy) 1%, Europeans 3,000, South Asians 2,000

Languages: Kirundi 29.7% (official), Kirundi and other language 9.1%, French (official) and French and other language 0.3%, Swahili and Swahili and other language 0.2% (along Lake Tanganyika and in the Bujumbura area), English and English and other language 0.06%, more than 2 languages 3.7%, unspecified 56.9% (2008 est.)

Religions: Catholic 62.1%, Protestant 23.9% (includes Adventist 2.3% and other Protestant 21.6%), Muslim 2.5%, other 3.6%, unspecified 7.9% (2008 est.)

Population: 10,742,276

note: estimates for this country explicitly take into account the effects of excess mortality due to AIDS; this can result in lower life expectancy, higher infant mortality, higher death rates, lower population growth rates, and changes in the distribution of population by age and sex than would otherwise be expected (July 2015 est.)

country comparison to the world: 84

Age structure: *0–14 years:* 45.64% (male 2,464,695/female 2,437,923)

15–24 years: 19.23% (male 1,030,773/female 1,035,478)

25–54 years: 28.67% (male 1,536,089/female 1,543,356)

55–64 years: 3.94% (male 198,384/female 224,563)

65 years and over: 2.52% (male 115,187/female 155,828) (2015 est.)

Dependency ratios: *total dependency ratio:* 89.7%

youth dependency ratio: 85%
elderly dependency ratio: 4.7%
potential support ratio: 21.3% (2015 est.)

Median age: *total:* 17 years
male: 16.8 years
female: 17.2 years (2015 est.)
country comparison to the world: 223

Population growth rate: 3.28% (2015 est.)
country comparison to the world: 3

Birth rate: 42.01 births/1,000 population (2015 est.)
country comparison to the world: 6

Death rate: 9.27 deaths/1,000 population (2015 est.)
country comparison to the world: 62

Net migration rate: 0 migrant(s)/1,000 population (2015 est.)
country comparison to the world: 103

Urbanization: *urban population:* 12.1% of total population (2015)

rate of urbanization: 5.66% annual rate of change (2010–15 est.)

Major urban areas—population: BUJUMBURA (capital) 751,000 (2015)

Sex ratio: *at birth:* 1.03 male(s)/female

0–1 years: 1.01 male(s)/female

15–24 years: 1 male(s)/female

25–54 years: 1 male(s)/female

55–64 years: 0.88 male(s)/female

65 years and over: 0.74 male(s)/female

total population: 0.99 male(s)/female (2015 est.)

Mother's mean age at first birth: 21.3

note: median age at first birth among women 25–29 (2010 est.)

Maternal mortality rate: 712 deaths/100,000 live births (2015 est.)

country comparison to the world: 6

Infant mortality rate: *total:* 61.89 deaths/1,000 live births

male: 68.55 deaths/1,000 live births

female: 55.04 deaths/1,000 live births (2015 est.)

country comparison to the world: 20

Life expectancy at birth: *total population:* 60.09 years

male: 58.45 years

female: 61.78 years (2015 est.)

country comparison to the world: 197

Total fertility rate: 6.09 children born/woman (2015 est.)

country comparison to the world: 2

Contraceptive prevalence rate: 21.9% (2010/11)

Health expenditures: 8% of GDP (2013)

country comparison to the world: 56

Hospital bed density: 1.9 beds/1,000 population (2011)

Drinking water source:

improved:

urban: 91.1% of population

rural: 73.8% of population

total: 75.9% of population

unimproved:

urban: 8.9% of population

rural: 26.2% of population

total: 24.1% of population (2015 est.)

Sanitation facility access:

improved:

urban: 43.8% of population

rural: 48.6% of population

total: 48% of population

unimproved:

urban: 56.2% of population

rural: 51.4% of population

total: 52% of population (2015 est.)

HIV/AIDS—adult prevalence rate: 1.11% (2014 est.)

country comparison to the world: 43

HIV/AIDS—people living with HIV/AIDS: 84,700 (2014 est.)

country comparison to the world: 45

HIV/AIDS—deaths: 3,900 (2014 est.)

country comparison to the world: 37

Major infectious diseases: *degree of risk:* very high

food or waterborne diseases: bacterial and proto-zoal diarrhea, hepatitis A, and typhoid fever

vectorborne diseases: malaria and dengue fever

water contact disease: schistosomiasis

animal contact disease: rabies (2013)

Obesity—adult prevalence rate: 2.1% (2014)
country comparison to the world: 176

Children under the age of 5 years underweight: 29.1% (2011)

country comparison to the world: 16

Education expenditures: 5.4% of GDP (2013)
country comparison to the world: 50

Literacy: *definition:* age 15 and over can read and write

total population: 85.6%
male: 88.2%
female: 83.1% (2015 est.)

School life expectancy (primary to tertiary education): *total:* 11 years

male: 11 years
female: 10 years (2013)

Child labor—children ages 5–14: *total number:* 433,187

percentage: 19% (2005 est.)

GOVERNMENT

Country name: *conventional long form:* Republic of Burundi

conventional short form: Burundi

local long form: Republique du Burundi/Republika y'u Burundi

local short form: Burundi

former: Urundi

etymology: name derived from the pre-colonial Kingdom of Burundi (17th-19th century)

Government type: presidential republic

Capital: *name:* Bujumbura

Geographic coordinates: 3 22 S, 29 21 E

time difference: UTC+2 (7 hours ahead of Washington, DC, during Standard Time)

Administrative divisions: 18 provinces; Bubanza, Bujumbura Mairie, Bujumbura Rural, Bururi, Cankuzo, Cibitoke, Gitega, Karuzi, Kayanza, Kirundo, Makamba, Muramvya, Muyinga, Mwaro, Ngozi, Rumonge, Rutana, Ruyigi

Independence: 1 July 1962 (from UN trusteeship under Belgian administration)

National holiday: Independence Day, 1 July (1962)

Constitution: several previous; latest ratified by popular referendum 28 February 2005 (2016)

Legal system: mixed legal system of Belgian civil law and customary law

International law organization participation: has not submitted an ICJ jurisdiction declaration; accepts ICCt jurisdiction

Citizenship: *citizenship by birth:* no

citizenship by descent only: the father must be a citizen of Burundi

dual citizenship recognized: no

residency requirement for naturalization: 10 years

Suffrage: 18 years of age; universal

Executive branch: *chief of state:* President Pierre NKURUNZIZA (since 26 August 2005); First Vice President Gaston SINDIMWO (since 25

August 2015); Second Vice President Joseph BUTORE (since 25 August 2015); note; the president is both chief of state and head of government

head of government: President Pierre NKURUN-ZIZA (since 26 August 2005); First Vice President Prosper BAZOMBAZA (since 13 February 2014); Second Vice President Gervais RUFYIKIRI (since 29 August 2010)

cabinet: Council of Ministers appointed by president

elections/appointments: president directly elected by absolute majority popular vote in 2 rounds if needed for a 5-year term (eligible for a second term); election last held on 21 July 2015(next to be held in 2020); vice presidents nominated by the president, endorsed by Parliament

election results: Pierre NKURUNZIZA reelected president; percent of vote—Pierre NKURUN-ZIZA (CNDD-FDD) 69.4%, Agathon RWASA (National Liberation Forces) 19%, other 11.6%

Legislative branch: *description:* bicameral Parliament or Parlement consists of the Senate or Inama Nkenguzamateka (49 seats in the July 2015 election; 34 members indirectly elected by an electoral college of provincial councils using a three-round voting system which requires a two-thirds majority vote in the first two rounds and a simple majority vote for the two leading candidates in the final round; 4 seats reserved for former heads of state, 3 seats reserved for Twas, and 8 seats for women; members serve 5-year terms) and the National Assembly or Inama Nshingamateka (121 seats in the June 2015 election; 100 members directly elected in multi-seat constituencies by proportional representation vote and 21 co-opted members—3 Twas and 18 women; members serve 5-year terms)

elections: Senate—last held on 24 July 2015 (next to be held in 2019); National Assembly—last held on 29 June 2015 (next to be held on 2020)

election results: Senate—percent of vote by party—NA; seats by party—CNDD-FDD 30, FRODEBU 3, CNDD 1, and 4 seats reserved for heads of state, 3 seats for Twas, and 8 seats for women; National Assembly—percent of vote by party (preliminary results)—CNDD-FDD 60.3%, Burundians' Hope Independent 11.2% UPRONA 2.5%, other 26%; seats by party—CNDD-FDD 77, Burundians' Hope Independent 21, U PRO NA 2, seats for women 18, seats for Twas 3

Judicial branch: highest court(s): Supreme Court (consists of 9 judges and organized into judicial, administrative, and cassation chambers)

judge selection and term of office: judges nominated by the Judicial Service Commission, a 15-member independent body of judicial and legal profession officials; judges appointed by the president with the approval of the Senate; judge tenure NA

subordinate courts: Courts of Appeal; County Courts; Courts of Residence

Political parties and leaders: Burundians' Hope Independent (also called Hope for Burundians) Front for Democracy in Burundi or FRODEBU [Leonce NGENDAKUMANA]

National Council for the Defense of Democracy— Front for the Defense of Democracy or CNDD-FDD [Pascal NYABENDA]

National Liberation Forces or FNL [Agathon RWASA]

National Council for the Defense of Democracy or CNDD [Leonard NYANGOMA]

National Resistance Movement for the Rehabilitation of the Citizen or MRC-Rurenzangemero [Epitace BANYAGANAKANDI]

Party for National Redress or PARENA [Jean-Baptiste BAGAZA]

Union for National Progress (Union pour le Progress Nationale) or UPRONA [Pierre BUYOYA]

Political pressure groups and leaders: Forum for the Strengthening of Civil Society or FORSC [Pacifique NININAHAZWE] (civil society umbrella organization)

Observatoire de lutte contre la corruption et les malversations economiques or OLUCOME [Gabriel RUFYIRI]

(anti-corruption pressure group)

other: Hutu and Tutsi militias (loosely organized)

International organization participation: ACP, AfDB, AU, CEMAC, CEPGL, CICA, COMESA, EAC, FAO, G-77, IBRD, ICAO, ICCt, ICRM, IDA, IFAD, IFC, IFRCS, ILO, IMF, Interpol, IOC, IOM, IPU, ISO (correspondent), ITU, ITUC (NGOs), MIGA, NAM, OIF, OPCW, UN, UNAMID, UNCTAD, UNESCO, UNIDO, UNISFA, UNWTO, UPU, WCO, WHO, WIPO, WMO, WTO

Diplomatic representation in the US: *chief of mission:* Ambassador Ernest NDABASHINZE (since 21 May 2014)

chancery: 2233 Wisconsin Avenue NW, Suite 408, Washington, DC 20007

telephone: [1] (202) 342-2574

FAX: [1] (202) 342-2578

Diplomatic representation from the US: *chief of mission:* Ambassador Dawn M. LIBERI (since 10 July 2012)

embassy: Avenue des Etats-Unis, Bujumbura

mailing address: B. P.1720, Bujumbura

telephone: [257] 22-207-000

FAX: [257] 22-222-926

Flag description: divided by a white diagonal cross into red panels (top and bottom) and green panels (hoist side and fly side) with a white disk superimposed at the center bearing three red six-pointed stars outlined in green arranged in a triangular design (one star above, two stars below); green symbolizes hope and optimism, white purity and peace, and red the blood shed in the struggle for independence; the three stars in the disk represent the three major ethnic groups: Hutu, Twa, Tutsi, as well as the three elements in the national motto: unity, work, progress

National symbol(s): lion; national colors: red, white, green

National anthem: *name:* "Burundi Bwacu" (Our Beloved Burundi)

lyrics/music: Jean-Baptiste NTAHOKAJA/Marc BARENGAYABO

note: adopted 1962

ECONOMY

Economy—overview: Burundi is a landlocked, resource-poor country with an underdeveloped manufacturing sector. Agriculture accounts for over 40% of GDP and employs more than 90% of the population. Burundi's primary exports are coffee and tea, which account for 90% of foreign exchange earnings. Thus, Burundi's export earnings—and its ability to pay for imports—rest primarily on weather conditions and international coffee and tea prices, although exports are a relatively small share of GDP. Burundi is heavily dependent on aid from bilateral and multilateral donors. Foreign aid in 2014 represented 42% of Burundi's national income, the second highest rate in Sub-Saharan Africa. Burundi joined the East African Community (EAC) in 2009. An ethnic war that ended in 2005 resulted in more than 200,000 deaths, forced more than 48,000 refugees into Tanzania, and displaced 140,000 others internally. Political stability, aid flows, and economic activity improved following the end of the civil war, but underlying weaknesses—a high poverty rate, poor education rates, a weak legal system, a poor transportation network, overburdened utilities, and low administrative capacity—have prevented the government from implementing planned economic reforms. Government corruption has also hindered the development of a private sector as companies have to deal withever changing rules. The purchasing power of most Burundians has decreased as wage increases have not kept pace with inflation.

In 2015, Burundi's economy suffered from political turmoil over President NKURUNZIZA's controversial third term. Blocked transportation routes disrupted the flow of agricultural goods. And donors withdrew aid, increasing Burundi's budget deficit. When the unrest ends, regional infrastructure improvements driven by the EAC and funded by the World Bank may help improve Burundi's transport connections and lower transportation costs.

GDP (purchasing power parity):

$7.711 billion (2015 est.)

$8.041 billion (2014 est.)

$7.683 billion (2013 est.)

note: data are in 2015 US dollars

country comparison to the world: 164

GDP (official exchange rate):

$2.881 billion (2015 est.)

GDP—real growth rate: -4.1% (2015 est.)

4.7% (2014 est.)

4.5% (2013 est.)

country comparison to the world: 213

GDP—per capita (PPP): $800 (2015 est.)

$900 (2014 est.)

$900 (2013 est.)

note: data are in 2015 US dollars

country comparison to the world: 227

Gross national saving: -4.4% of GDP (2015 est.)

-2.9% of GDP (2014 est.)

-4.2% of GDP (2013 est.)

country comparison to the world: 176

GDP—composition, by end use:

household consumption: 71.9%
government consumption: 21.4%
investment in fixed capital: 27.2%
investment in inventories: -2.7%
exports of goods and services: 5.5%
imports of goods and services: -23.3% (2015 est.)
GDP—composition, by sector of origin:
agriculture: 39.2%
industry: 18.1%
services: 42.7% (2015 est.)
Agriculture—products: coffee, cotton, tea, corn, sorghum, sweet potatoes, bananas, cassava (manioc, tapioca); beef, milk, hides
Industries: light consumer goods (blankets, shoes, soap, beer); assembly of imported components; public works construction; food processing
Industrial production growth rate: 5.2% (2015 est.)
country comparison to the world: 29
Labor force: 4.95 million (2015 est.)
country comparison to the world: 84
Labor force—by occupation:
agriculture: 93.6%
industry: 2.3%
services: 4.1% (2002 est.)
Unemployment rate: NA%
Population below poverty line: 68% (2002 est.)
Household income or consumption by percentage share: *lowest:* 10%: 4.1%
highest: 10%: 28% (2006)
Distribution of family income—Gini index: 42.4 (1998)
country comparison to the world: 53
Budget: *revenues:* $852 million
expenditures: $1.003 billion (2015 est.)
Taxes and other revenues: 28.7% of GDP (2015 est.)
country comparison to the world: 88
Budget surplus (+) or deficit (–): -5.1% of GDP (2015 est.)
country comparison to the world: 172
Public debt: 37.2% of GDP (2015 est.) 36.5% of GDP (2014 est.)
country comparison to the world: 124
Fiscal year: calendar year
Inflation rate (consumer prices): 5.6% (2015 est.) 4.4% (2014 est.)
country comparison to the world: 182
Central bank discount rate: 11.25% (31 December 2010) 10% (31 December 2009)
country comparison to the world: 17
Commercial bank prime lending rate: 16% (31 December 2015 est.) 15.7% (31 December 2014 est.)
country comparison to the world: 30
Stock of narrow money: $437.7 million (31 December 2015 est.)
$412.4 million (31 December 2014 est.)
country comparison to the world: 168
Stock of broad money: $594.6 million (31 December 2015 est.)
$568.6 million (31 December 2014 est.)
country comparison to the world: 177
Stock of domestic credit: $767.5 million (31 December 2015 est.)
$721.9 million (31 December 2014 est.)

country comparison to the world: 162
Market value of publicly traded shares: $NA
Current account balance: -$444 million (2015 est.) -$544 million (2014 est.)
country comparison to the world: 95
Exports: $96.6 million (2015 est.)
$122.4 million (2014 est.)
country comparison to the world: 195
Exports—commodities: coffee, tea, sugar, cotton, hides
Exports—partners: Germany 12.3%, Pakistan 10.7%, Democratic Republic of the Congo 10.7%, Uganda 8.1%, Sweden 7.8%, US 7.1%, Belgium 6.3%, Rwanda 4.6%, France 4.4% (2015)
Imports: $815.1 million (2015 est.)
$923 million (2014 est.)
country comparison to the world: 184
Imports—commodities: capital goods, petroleum products, foodstuffs
Imports—partners: Kenya 15%, Saudi Arabia 14%, Belgium 9.9%, Tanzania 8.3%, Uganda 7.3%, China 7.1%, India 4.9%, France 4% (2015)
Reserves of foreign exchange and gold: $315.7 million (31 December 2015 est.)
$317.1 million (31 December 2014 est.)
country comparison to the world: 157
Debt—external: $700.8 million (31 December 2014 est.)
$682.7 million (31 December 2013 est.)
country comparison to the world: 171
Exchange rates: Burundi francs (BIF) per US dollar—
1,578.2 (2015 est.)
1,546.7 (2014 est.)
1,546.7 (2013 est.)
1,442.51 (2012 est.)
1,261.07 (2011 est.)

ENERGY

Electricity—production: 202 million kWh (2012 est.)
country comparison to the world: 185
Electricity—consumption: 282.9 million kWh (2012 est.)
country comparison to the world: 182
Electricity—exports: 0 kWh (2013 est.)
country comparison to the world: 114
Electricity—imports: 95 million kWh (2012 est.)
country comparison to the world: 94
Electricity—installed generating capacity: 55,000 kW (2012 est.)
country comparison to the world: 185
Electricity—from fossil fuels: 1.8% of total installed capacity (2012 est.)
country comparison to the world: 207
Electricity—from nuclear fuels: 0% of total installed capacity (2012 est.)
country comparison to the world: 61
Electricity—from hydroelectric plants: 98.2% of total installed capacity (2012 est.)
country comparison to the world: 8
Electricity—from other renewable sources: 0% of total installed capacity (2012 est.)
country comparison to the world: 164
Crude oil—production: 0 bbl/day (2014 est.)

country comparison to the world: 115
Crude oil—exports: 0 bbl/day (2012 est.)
country comparison to the world: 106
Crude oil—imports: 0 bbl/day (2012 est.)
country comparison to the world: 168
Crude oil—proved reserves: 0 bbl (1 January 2015 est.)
country comparison to the world: 113
Refined petroleum products—production: 0 bbl/day (2012 est.)
country comparison to the world: 163
Refined petroleum products—consumption: 1,500 bbl/day (2013 est.)
country comparison to the world: 195
Refined petroleum products—exports: 0 bbl/day (2012 est.)
country comparison to the world: 163
Refined petroleum products—imports: 1,456 bbl/day (2012 est.)
country comparison to the world: 190
Natural gas—production: 0 cu m (2013 est.)
country comparison to the world: 165
Natural gas—consumption: 0 cu m (2013 est.)
country comparison to the world: 124
Natural gas—exports: 0 cu m (2013 est.)
country comparison to the world: 72
Natural gas—imports: 0 cu m (2013 est.)
country comparison to the world: 171
Natural gas—proved reserves: 0 cu m (1 January 2014 est.)
country comparison to the world: 119
Carbon dioxide emissions from consumption of energy: 315,100 Mt (2012 est.)
country comparison to the world: 190

COMMUNICATIONS

Telephones—fixed lines: *total subscriptions:* 21,700
subscriptions per 100 inhabitants: less than 1 (2014 est.)
country comparison to the world: 182
Telephones—mobile cellular: *total:* 3.2 million
subscriptions per 100 inhabitants: 31 (2014 est.)
country comparison to the world: 138
Telephone system: *general assessment:* sparse system of open-wire, radiotelephone communications, and low-capacity microwave radio relays
domestic: telephone density one of the lowest in the world; fixed-line connections stand at well less than 1 per 100 persons; mobile-cellular usage is increasing but remains at roughly 20 per 100 persons
international: country code—257; satellite earth station—1 Intelsat (Indian Ocean) (2011)
Broadcast media: state-controlled La Radiodiffusion et Television Nationale de Burundi (RTNB) operates the lone TV station and the only national radio network; about 10 privately owned radio stations; transmissions of several international broadcasters are available in Bujumbura (2007)
Radio broadcast stations: AM 0, FM 4, shortwave 1 (2001)
Television broadcast stations: 1 (2001)
Internet country code: .bi
Internet hosts: 229 (2012)

country comparison to the world: 198
Internet users: *total:* 144,500 percent of population: 1.4% (2014 est.)
country comparison to the world: 165

TRANSPORTATION

Airports: 7 (2013)
country comparison to the world: 165
Airports—with paved runways: *total:* 1 over 3,047 m: 1 (2013)
Airports—with unpaved runways: *total:* 6
914 to 1,523 m: 4
under 914 m: 2 (2013)
Heliports: 1 (2012)
Roadways: *total:* 12,322 km
paved: 1,286 km
unpaved: 11,036 km (2004)
country comparison to the world: 127
Waterways: (mainly on Lake Tanganyika between Bujumbura, Burundi's principal port, and lake ports in Tanzania, Zambia, and the Democratic Republic of the Congo) (2011)

Ports and terminals: *lake port(s):* Bujumbura (Lake Tanganyika)

MILITARY AND SECURITY

Military branches: National Defense Forces (Forces de Defense Nationale, FDN): Army (includes maritime wing, Air Wing), National Gendarmerie (2013)

Military service age and obligation: 18 years of age for voluntary military service; the armed forces law of 31 December 2004 did not specify a minimum age for enlistment, but the government claimed that no one younger than 18 was being recruited; mandatory retirement age 45 (enlisted), 50 (NCOs), and 55 (officers) (2012)
Military expenditures:
2.39% of GDP (2012)
NA% (2011)
2.39% of GDP (2010)
country comparison to the world: 32

TRANSNATIONAL ISSUES

Disputes—international: Burundi and Rwanda dispute two sq km (0.8 sq mi) of Sabanerwa, a farmed area in the Rukurazi Valley where the Akanyaru/Kanyaru River shifted its course southward after heavy rains in 1965; cross-border conflicts persist among Tutsi, Hutu, other ethnic groups, associated political rebels, armed gangs, and various government forces in the Great Lakes region

Refugees and internally displaced persons: *refugees (country of origin):* 52,937 (Democratic Republic of the Congo) (2016)
IDPs: undetermined (some ethnic Tutsis remain displaced from intercommunal violence that broke out after the 1993 coup and fighting between government forces and rebel groups; violence since April 2015 has caused internal displacement, but exact figures are unknown because of insecurity and fear of reprisal attacks for self-identification as an IDP) (2015)
stateless persons: 1,302 (2015)

Trafficking in persons: *current situation:* Burundi is a source country for children and possibly women subjected to forced labor and sex trafficking; business people recruit Burundian girls for prostitution domestically, as well as in Rwanda, Kenya, Uganda, and the Middle East, and recruit boys and girls for forced labor in Burundi and Tanzania; children and young adults are coerced into forced labor in farming, mining, informal commerce, fishing, or collecting river stones for construction; sometimes family, friends, and neighbors are complicit in exploiting children, at times luring them in with offers of educational or job opportunities

tier rating: Tier 3—Burundi does not comply fully with the minimum standards for the elimination of human trafficking and is not making significant efforts to do so; corruption, a lack of political will, and limited resources continue to hamper efforts to combat human trafficking; in 2014, the government did not inform judicial and law enforcement officials of the enactment of an anti-trafficking law or how to implement it and approved—but did not fund—its national anti-trafficking action plan; authorities again failed to identify trafficking victims or to provide them with adequate protective services; the government has focused on transnational child trafficking but gave little attention to its domestic child trafficking problem and adult trafficking victims (2015)

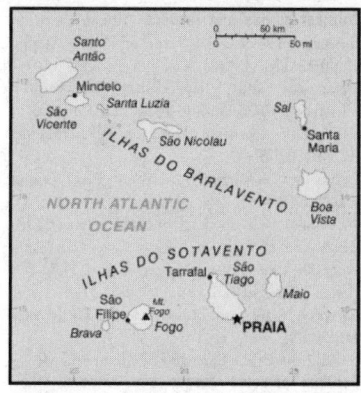

INTRODUCTION

Background: The uninhabited islands were discovered and colonized by the Portuguese in the 15th century; Cabo Verde subsequently became a trading center for African slaves and later an important coaling and resupply stop for whaling and transatlantic shipping. Following independence in 1975, and a tentative interest in unification with Guinea-Bissau, a one-party system was established and maintained until multi-party elections were held in 1990. Cabo Verde continues to exhibit one of Africa's most stable democratic governments. Repeated droughts during the second half of the 20th century caused significant hardship and prompted heavy emigration. As a result, Cabo Verde's expatriate population is greater than its domestic one. Most Cabo Verdeans have both African and Portuguese antecedents.

GEOGRAPHY

Location: Western Africa, group of islands in the North Atlantic Ocean, west of Senegal

Geographic coordinates: 16 00 N, 24 00 W

Map references: Africa

Area: *total:* 4,033 sq km
land: 4,033 sq km
water: 0 sq km
country comparison to the world: 176

Area—comparative: slightly larger than Rhode Island

Land boundaries: 0 km

Coastline: 965 km

Maritime claims: measured from claimed archipelagic baselines
territorial sea: 12 nm
contiguous zone: 24 nm
exclusive economic zone: 200 nm

Climate: temperate; warm, dry summer; precipitation meager and erratic

Terrain: steep, rugged, rocky, volcanic

Elevation: *mean elevation:* NA

elevation extremes: *lowest point:* Atlantic Ocean 0 m
highest point: Mt. Fogo 2,829 m (a volcano on Fogo Island)

Natural resources: salt, basalt rock, limestone, kaolin, fish, clay, gypsum

Land use: *agricultural land:* 18.6%
arable land: 11.7%
permanent crops: 0.7%
permanent pasture: 6.2%
forest: 21%
other: 60.4% (2011 est.)

Irrigated land: 35 sq km (2012)

Total renewable water resources: 0.3 cu km (2011)

Freshwater withdrawal (domestic/industrial/agricultural): *total:* 0.02 cu m/yr (6%/1%/93%)
per capita: 48.57 cu m/yr (2004)

Natural hazards: prolonged droughts; seasonal harmattan wind produces obscuring dust; volcanically and seismically active
volcanism: Fogo (elev. 2,829 m), which last erupted in 1995, is Cabo Verde's only active volcano

Environment—current issues: soil erosion; deforestation due to demand for firewood; water shortages; desertification; environmental damage has threatened several species of birds and reptiles; illegal beach sand extraction; overfishing

Environment—international agreements: *party to:* Biodiversity, Climate Change, Climate Change-Kyoto Protocol, Desertification, Endangered Species, Environmental Modification, Hazardous Wastes, Law of the Sea, Marine Dumping, Ozone Layer Protection, Ship Pollution, Wetlands
signed, but not ratified: none of the selected agreements

Geography—note: strategic location 500 km from west coast of Africa near major north-south sea routes; important communications station; important sea and air refueling site

PEOPLE AND SOCIETY

Nationality: *noun:* Cabo Verdean(s)
adjective: Cabo Verdean

Ethnic groups: Creole (mulatto) 71%, African 28%, European 1%

Languages: Portuguese (official), Crioulo (a blend of Portuguese and West African words)

Religions: Roman Catholic 77.3%, Protestant 3.7% (includes Church of the Nazarene 1.7%, Adventist 1.5%, Universal Kingdom of God 0.4%, and God and Love 0.1%), other Christian 4.3% (includes Christian Rationalism 1.9%, Jehovah's Witness 1%, Assembly of God 0.9%, and New Apostolic 0.5%), Muslim 1.8%, other 1.3%, none 10.8%, unspecified 0.7% (2010 est.)

Population: 545,993 (July 2015 est.)
country comparison to the world: 174

Age structure: *0–14 years:* 30.1% (male 82,623/female 81,731)

15–24 years: 20.99% (male 57,307/female 57,303)
25–54 years: 38.53% (male 102,186/female 108,177)
55–64 years: 5.29% (male 12,194/female 16,709)
65 years and over: 5.08% (male 10,466/female 17,297) (2015 est.)

Dependency ratios: *total dependency ratio:* 52%
youth dependency ratio: 45.1%
elderly dependency ratio: 7%
potential support ratio: 14.4% (2015 est.)

Median age: *total:* 24.5 years
male: 23.6 years
female: 25.3 years (2015 est.)
country comparison to the world: 157

Population growth rate: 1.36% (2015 est.)
country comparison to the world: 87

Birth rate: 20.33 births/1,000 population (2015 est.)
country comparison to the world: 82

Death rate: 6.11 deaths/1,000 population (2015 est.)
country comparison to the world: 161

Net migration rate: -0.63 migrant(s)/1,000 population (2015 est.)
country comparison to the world: 140

Urbanization: *urban population:* 65.5% of total population (2015)
rate of urbanization: 1.99% annual rate of change (2010–15 est.)

Major urban areas—population: PRAIA (capital) 145,000 (2014)

Sex ratio: *at birth:* 1.03 male(s)/female
0–14 years: 1.01 male(s)/female
15–24 years: 1 male(s)/female
25–54 years: 0.95 male(s)/female
55–64 years: 0.73 male(s)/female
65 years and over: 0.61 male(s)/female
total population: 0.94 male(s)/female (2015 est.)

Mother's mean age at first birth: 19.5
note: median age at first birth among women 25–29 (2005 est.)

Maternal mortality rate: 42 deaths/100,000 live births (2015 est.)
country comparison to the world: 83

Infant mortality rate: *total:* 23.45 deaths/1,000 live births
male: 26.89 deaths/1,000 live births
female: 19.91 deaths/1,000 live births (2015 est.)
country comparison to the world: 76

Life expectancy at birth: *total population:* 71.85 years
male: 69.58 years
female: 74.19 years (2015 est.)
country comparison to the world: 147

Total fertility rate: 2.29 children born/woman (2015 est.)
country comparison to the world: 93

Contraceptive prevalence rate: 61.3% (2005)

Health expenditures: 4.4% of GDP (2013)
country comparison to the world: 164

145

Physicians density: 0.31 physicians/1,000 population (2011)

Hospital bed density: 2.1 beds/1,000 population (2010)

Drinking water source:
improved:
urban: 94% of population
rural: 87.3% of population
total: 91.7% of population
unimproved:
urban: 6% of population
rural: 12.7% of population
total: 8.3% of population (2015 est.)

Sanitation facility access:
improved:
urban: 81.6% of population
rural: 54.3% of population
total: 72.2% of population
unimproved:
urban: 1.4% of population
rural: 45.7% of population
total: 27.8% of population (2015 est.)

HIV/AIDS—adult prevalence rate: 1.09% (2014 est.)
country comparison to the world: 44
HIV/AIDS—people living with HIV/AIDS: 3,400 (2014 est.)
country comparison to the world: 112
HIV/AIDS—deaths: 100 (2014 est.)
country comparison to the world: 125
Obesity—adult prevalence rate: 11.7% (2014)
country comparison to the world: 131
Education expenditures: 5% of GDP (2013)
country comparison to the world: 76
Literacy: *definition:* age 15 and over can read and write
total population: 87.6%
male: 92.1%
female: 83.1% (2015 est.)
School life expectancy (primary to tertiary education): *total:* 13 years
male: 13 years
female: 14 years (2014)

GOVERNMENT

Country name: *conventional long form:* Republic of Cabo Verde
conventional short form: Cabo Verde
local long form: Republica de Cabo Verde
local short form: Cabo Verde
etymology: the name derives from Cap-Vert (Green Cape) on the Senegalese coast, the westernmost point of Africa and the nearest mainland to the islands

Government type: parliamentary republic
Capital: *name:* Praia
Geographic coordinates: 14 55 N, 23 31 W
time difference: UTC-1 (4 hours ahead of Washington, DC, during Standard Time)
Administrative divisions: 22 municipalities (concelhos, singular—concelho); Boa Vista, Brava, Maio, Mosteiros, Paul, Porto Novo, Praia, Ribeira Brava, Ribeira Grande, Ribeira Grande de Santiago, Sal, Santa Catarina, Santa Catarina do

Fogo, Santa Cruz, Sao Domingos, Sao Filipe, Sao Lourenco dos Orgaos, Sao Miguel, Sao Salvador do Mundo, Sao Vicente, Tarrafal, Tarrafal de Sao Nicolau

Independence: 5 July 1975 (from Portugal)
National holiday: Independence Day, 5 July (1975)
Constitution: previous 1981; latest effective 25 September 1992; revised 1995, 1999, 2010 (2016)
Legal system: civil law system of Portugal
International law organization participation: has not submitted an ICJ jurisdiction declaration; accepts ICCt jurisdiction

Citizenship: *citizenship by birth:* no
citizenship by descent only: at least one parent must be a citizen of Cabo Verde
dual citizenship recognized: yes
residency requirement for naturalization: 5 years
Suffrage: 18 years of age; universal
Executive branch: chief of state: President Jorge Carlos FONSECA (since 9 September 2011)
head of government: Prime Minister Jose Maria Pereira NEVES (since 1 February 2001)
cabinet: Council of Ministers appointed by the president on the recommendation of the prime minister
elections/appointments: president directly elected by absolute majority popular vote in 2 rounds if needed for a 5-year term (eligible for a second term); election last held on 7 August 2011 with a second round on 21 August 2011 (next to be held in August 2016); prime minister nominated by the National Assembly and appointed by the president
election results: percent of vote in second round—Jorge Carlos FONSECA (MPD) 53.4%, Manuel Inocencio SOUSA (PAICV) 46.6%

Legislative branch: *description:* unicameral National Assembly or Assembleia Nacional (72 seats; members directly elected in multi-seat constituencies by proportional representation vote; members serve 5-year terms)
elections: last held on 20 March 2016 (next to be held in 2021)
election results: percent of vote by party (preliminary)—MPD 54.4%, PAICV 38.1%, UCID 6.9%, other 0.6%; seats by party—NA
Judicial branch: *highest court(s):* Supreme Court of Justice (consists of the chief justice and at least 5 judges)
judge selection and term of office: judges appointments—1 by the president of the republic, 1 elected by the National Assembly, and the remainder by the Supreme Council of Magistrates, a 9-member independent body presided by the chief justice and includes the high judicial inspector, 2 presidential appointees, 3 elected by the National Assembly, and 2 by their court peers; chief justice appointed by the president of the republic from among peers of the Supreme Court and in consultation with the Supreme Council of Magistrates; judge tenure NA

subordinate courts: first instance (municipal) courts; audit, military, and fiscal and customs courts

Political parties and leaders: African Party for Independence of Cabo Verde or PAICV [Janira Hopffer ALMADA]
Democratic and Independent Cabo Verdean Union or UCID [Antonio MONTEIRO]
Democratic Christian Party or PDC [Manuel RODRIGUES]
Democratic Renovation Party or PRD [Victor FIDALGO]
Movement for Democracy or MPD [Ulisses CORREIA e Silva]
Party for Democratic Convergence or PCD [Dr. Eurico MONTEIRO]
Party of Work and Solidarity or PTS [Anibal MEDINA]
Social Democratic Party or PSD [Joao ALEM]
Political pressure groups and leaders: *other:* environmentalists; political pressure groups
International organization participation: ACP, AfDB, AOSIS, AU, CD, CPLP, ECOWAS, FAO, G-77, IAEA, IBRD, ICAO, ICCt (signatory), ICRM, IDA, IFAD, IFC, IFRCS, ILO, IMF, IMO, Interpol, IOC, IOM, IPU, ITSO, ITU, ITUC (NGOs), MIGA, NAM, OIF, OPCW, UN, UNCTAD, UNESCO, UNIDO, Union Latina, UNWTO, UPU, WCO, WHO, WIPO, WMO, WTO
Diplomatic representation in the US: *chief of mission:* Ambassador Jose Luis Fialho ROCHA (since 14 July 2014)
chancery: 3415 Massachusetts Avenue NW, Washington, DC 20007
telephone: [1] (202) 965-6820
FAX: [1] (202) 965-1207
consulate(s) general: Boston
Diplomatic representation from the US: *chief of mission:* Ambassador Donald L. HEFLIN (since 29 January 2015)
embassy: Rua Abilio Macedo 6, Praia
mailing address: C. P. 201, Praia
telephone: [238] 2-60-89-00
FAX: [238] 2-61-13-55

Flag description: five unequal horizontal bands; the top-most band of blue—equal to one half the width of the flag—is followed by three bands of white, red, and white, each equal to 1/12 of the width, and a bottom stripe of blue equal to one quarter of the flag width; a circle of 10, yellow, five-pointed stars is centered on the red stripe and positioned 3/8 of the length of the flag from the hoist side; blue stands for the sea and the sky, the circle of stars represents the 10 major islands united into a nation, the stripes symbolize the road to formation of the country through peace (white) and effort (red)

National symbol(s): ten, five-pointed, yellow stars; national colors: blue, white, red, yellow
National anthem: *name:* "Cantico da Liberdade" (Song of Freedom)
lyrics/music: Amilcar Spencer LOPES/Adalberto Higino Tavares SILVA
note: adopted 1996

ECONOMY

Economy—overview: Cabo Verde's economy is vulnerable to external shocks and depends on development aid, foreign investment, remittances, and tourism. The economy is service-oriented with commerce, transport, tourism, and public services accounting for about three-fourths of GDP. Tourism is the mainstay of the economy and depends on conditions in the eurozone countries. Cabo Verde annually runs a high trade deficit financed by foreign aid and remittances from its large pool of emigrants; remittances as a share of GDP are one of the highest in Sub-Saharan Africa.

Although about 40% of the population lives in rural areas, the share of food production in GDP is low. The island economy suffers from a poor natural resource base, including serious water shortages, exacerbated by cycles of long-term drought, and poor soil for growing food on several of the islands, requiring it to import most of what it consumes. The fishing potential, mostly lobster and tuna, is not fully exploited.

Economic reforms are aimed at developing the private sector and attracting foreign investment to diversify the economy and mitigate high unemployment. The government's elevated debt levels have limited its capacity to finance any shortfalls.

GDP (purchasing power parity): $3.423 billion (2015 est.)
$3.363 billion (2014 est.)
$3.302 billion (2013 est.)
note: data are in 2015 US dollars
country comparison to the world: 181

GDP (official exchange rate): $1.595 billion (2015 est.)

GDP—real growth rate: 1.8% (2015 est.)
1.8% (2014 est.) 1% (2013 est.)
country comparison to the world: 142

GDP—per capita (PPP): $6,500 (2015 est.)
$6,500 (2014 est.)
$6,400 (2013 est.)
note: data are in 2015 US dollars
country comparison to the world: 157

Gross national saving: 31.5% of GDP (2015 est.)
29.4% of GDP (2014 est.)
34.6% of GDP (2013 est.)
country comparison to the world: 19

GDP—composition, by end use:
household consumption: 53.4%
government consumption: 14.8%
investment in fixed capital: 32.3%
investment in inventories: 0.8%
exports of goods and services: 30.6%
imports of goods and services: -31.9% (2015 est.)

GDP—composition, by sector of origin:
agriculture: 9.7%
industry: 18.3%
services: 72% (2015 est.)

Agriculture—products: bananas, corn, beans, sweet potatoes, sugarcane, coffee, peanuts; fish

Industries: food and beverages, fish processing, shoes and garments, salt mining, ship repair

Industrial production growth rate: 1.8% (2015 est.)
country comparison to the world: 124

Labor force: 196,100 (2007 est.)
country comparison to the world: 172
Unemployment rate: 12% (2014 est.)
16.4% (2013 est.)
country comparison to the world: 134
Population below poverty line: 30% (2000 est.)
Household income or consumption by percentage share: *lowest:* 10%: 1.9%
highest: 10%: 40.6% (2001)
Budget: *revenues:* $374.1 million
expenditures: $489.9 million (2015 est.)
Taxes and other revenues: 22.8% of GDP (2015 est.)
country comparison to the world: 138
Budget surplus (+) or deficit (-): -7.1% of GDP (2015 est.)
country comparison to the world: 192
Public debt: 116.2% of GDP (2015 est.)
113.7% of GDP (2014 est.)
country comparison to the world: 9
Fiscal year: calendar year
Inflation rate (consumer prices): 0.1% (2015 est.)
-0.2% (2014 est.)
country comparison to the world: 51
Central bank discount rate: 7.5% (31 December 2010)
7.5% (31 December 2009)
country comparison to the world: 43
Commercial bank prime lending rate: 10.5% (31 December 2015 est.)
10.9% (31 December 2014 est.)
country comparison to the world: 79
Stock of narrow money: $610.9 million (31 December 2015 est.)
$597.6 million (31 December 2014 est.)
country comparison to the world: 163
Stock of broad money: $1.621 billion (31 December 2015 est.)
$1.608 billion (31 December 2014 est.)
country comparison to the world: 160
Stock of domestic credit: $1.471 billion (31 December 2015 est.)
$1.449 billion (31 December 2014 est.)
country comparison to the world: 151
Current account balance: -$147 million (2015 est.)
-$150 million (2014 est.)
country comparison to the world: 76
Exports: $192.7 million (2015 est.)
$253 million (2014 est.)
country comparison to the world: 188

Exports—commodities: fuel (re-exports), shoes, garments, fish, hides

Exports—partners: Australia 83%, Spain 8.6% (2015)

Imports: $797.8 million (2015 est.) $862 million (2014 est.)
country comparison to the world: 186

Imports—commodities: foodstuffs, industrial products, transport equipment, fuels

Imports—partners: Portugal 29.9%, Australia 26.4%, Netherlands 11.2%, Spain 5.6%, China 5.6% (2015)

Reserves of foreign exchange and gold: $491.5 million (31 December 2015 est.)
$510.9 million (31 December 2014 est.)

country comparison to the world: 151
Debt—external: $1.617 billion (31 December 2014 est.)
$1.484 billion (31 December 2013 est.)
country comparison to the world: 154

Exchange rates: Cabo Verdean escudos (CVE) per US dollar—
97.58 (2015 est.)
83.114 (2014 est.)
83.114 (2013 est.)
85.82 (2012 est.)
79.32 (2011 est.)

ENERGY

Electricity—production: 307 million kWh (2012 est.)
country comparison to the world: 177
Electricity—consumption: 285.5 million kWh (2012 est.)
country comparison to the world: 180
Electricity—exports: 0 kWh (2013 est.)
country comparison to the world: 128
Electricity—imports: 0 kWh (2013 est.)
country comparison to the world: 138
Electricity—installed generating capacity: 108,500 kW (2012 est.)
country comparison to the world: 171
Electricity—from fossil fuels: 76.5% of total installed capacity (2012 est.)
country comparison to the world: 98
Electricity—from nuclear fuels: 0% of total installed capacity (2012 est.)
country comparison to the world: 75
Electricity—from hydroelectric plants: 0% of total installed capacity (2012 est.)
country comparison to the world: 167
Electricity—from other renewable sources: 23.5% of total installed capacity (2012 est.)
country comparison to the world: 10
Crude oil—production: 0 bbl/day (2014 est.)
country comparison to the world: 122
Crude oil—exports: 0 bbl/day (2012 est.)
country comparison to the world: 113
Crude oil—imports: 0 bbl/day (2012 est.)
country comparison to the world: 178
Crude oil—proved reserves: 0 bbl (1 January 2015 est.)
country comparison to the world: 121
Refined petroleum products—production: 0 bbl/day (2012 est.)
country comparison to the world: 171
Refined petroleum products—consumption: 2,600 bbl/day (2013 est.)
country comparison to the world: 184
Refined petroleum products: 0 bbl/day (2012 est.)
country comparison to the world: 172
Refined petroleum products—imports: 2,646 bbl/day (2012 est.)
country comparison to the world: 177
Natural gas—production: 0 cu m (2013 est.)
country comparison to the world: 175
Natural gas—consumption: 0 cu m (2013 est.)
country comparison to the world: 134
Natural gas—exports: 0 cu m (2013 est.)
country comparison to the world: 85

Natural gas—imports: 0 cu m (2013 est.)
country comparison to the world: 185
Natural gas—proved reserves: 0 cu m (1 January 2014 est.)
country comparison to the world: 128
Carbon dioxide emissions from consumption of energy: 385,700 Mt (2012 est.)
country comparison to the world: 187

COMMUNICATIONS

Telephones—fixed lines: *total subscriptions:* 58,500
subscriptions per 100 inhabitants: 11 (2014 est.)
country comparison to the world: 156
Telephones—mobile cellular: *total:* 613,400
subscriptions per 100 inhabitants: 114 (2014 est.)
country comparison to the world: 166
Telephone system: *general assessment:* effective system, extensive modernization from 1996–2000 following partial privatization in 1995
domestic: major service provider is Cabo Verde Telecom; fiber-optic ring, completed in 2001, links all islands providing Internet access and ISDN services; cellular service introduced in 1998; broadband services launched in 2004
international: country code—238; landing point for the Atlantis-2 fiber-optic transatlantic telephone cable that provides links to South America, Senegal, and Europe; HF radiotelephone to Senegal and Guinea-Bissau; satellite earth station—1 Intelsat (Atlantic Ocean) (2011)
Broadcast media: state-run TV and radio broadcast network plus a growing number of private broadcasters; Portuguese public TV and radio services for Africa are available; transmissions of a few international broadcasters are available (2007)
Radio broadcast stations: AM 0, FM 22 (plus 12 repeaters), shortwave 0 (2001)
Television broadcast stations: 1 (plus 7 repeaters) (2001)
Internet country code: .cv
Internet hosts: 38 (2012)
country comparison to the world: 216
Internet users: *total:* 213,900
percent of population: 39.7% (2014 est.)
country comparison to the world: 153

TRANSPORTATION

Airports: 9 (2013)
country comparison to the world: 157
Airports—with paved runways: *total:* 9
over 3,047 m: 1
1,524 to 2,437 m: 3
914 to 1,523 m: 3
under 914 m: 2 (2013)
Roadways: *total:* 1,350 km
paved: 932 km
unpaved: 418 km (2013)
country comparison to the world: 180
Merchant marine: *total:* 13
by type: cargo 3, chemical tanker 2, passenger/cargo 7, petroleum tanker 1
foreign-owned: 3 (Greece 1, Spain 1, UK 1)
registered in other countries: 1 (unknown 1) (2010)
country comparison to the world: 104
Ports and terminals: *major seaport(s):* Porto Grande

MILITARY AND SECURITY

Military branches: Armed Forces: Army (also called the National Guard, GN), Cabo Verde Coast Guard (Guardia Costeira de Cabo Verde, GCCV; includes naval infantry) (2013)
Military service age and obligation: 18–35 years of age for male and female selective compulsory military service; 2-years conscript service obligation; 17 years of age for voluntary service (with parental consent) (2013)
Military expenditures: NA% (2012)
0.51% of GDP (2011)

TRANSNATIONAL ISSUES

Disputes—international: none
Refugees and internally displaced persons: *stateless persons:* 115 (2015)
Illicit drugs: used as a transshipment point for Latin American cocaine destined for Western Europe, particularly because of Lusophone links to Brazil, Portugal, and Guinea-Bissau; has taken steps to deter drug money laundering, including a 2002 anti-money laundering reform that criminalizes laundering the proceeds of narcotics trafficking and other crimes and the establishment in 2008 of a Financial Intelligence Unit (2008)

CAMBODIA

INTRODUCTION

Background: Most Cambodians consider themselves to be Khmers, descendants of the Angkor Empire that extended over much of Southeast Asia and reached its zenith between the 10th and 13th centuries. Attacks by the Thai and Cham (from present-day Vietnam) weakened the empire, ushering in a long period of decline. The king placed the country under French protection in 1863, and it became part of French Indochina in 1887. Following Japanese occupation in World War II, Cambodia gained full independence from France in 1953. In April 1975, after a seven-year struggle, communist Khmer Rouge forces captured Phnom Penh and evacuated all cities and towns. At least 1.5 million Cambodians died from execution, forced hardships, or starvation during the Khmer Rouge regime under POL POT. A December 1978 Vietnamese invasion drove the Khmer Rouge into the countryside, began a 10-year Vietnamese occupation, and touched off almost 13 years of civil war.

The 1991 Paris Peace Accords mandated democratic elections and a cease-fire, which was not fully respected by the Khmer Rouge. UN-sponsored elections in 1993 helped restore some semblance of normalcy under a coalition government. Factional fighting in 1997 ended the first coalition government, but a second round of national elections in 1998 led to the formation of another coalition government and renewed political stability. The remaining elements of the Khmer Rouge surrendered in early 1999. Some of the surviving Khmer Rouge leaders have been tried or are awaiting trial for crimes against humanity by a hybrid UN-Cambodian tribunal supported by international assistance. Elections in July 2003 were relatively peaceful, but it took one year of negotiations between contending political parties before a coalition government was formed. In October 2004, King Norodom SIHANOUK abdicated the throne and his son, Prince Norodom SIHAMONI, was selected to succeed him. The most recent local (Commune Council) elections were held in Cambodia in 2012, with little of the preelection violence that preceded prior elections. National elections in July 2013 were disputed, with the opposition—the Cambodian National Rescue Party (CNRP)—boycotting the National Assembly. The political impasse was ended nearly a year later, with the CNRP agreeing to enter parliament in exchange for ruling party commitments to electoral and legislative reforms.

GEOGRAPHY

Location: Southeastern Asia, bordering the Gulf of Thailand, between Thailand, Vietnam, and Laos

Geographic coordinates: 13 00 N, 10 500 E

Map references: Southeast Asia

Area: *total:* 181,035 sq km
land: 176,515 sq km
water: 4,520 sq km
country comparison to the world: 90

Area—comparative: slightly smaller than Oklahoma

Land boundaries: *total:* 2,530 km
border countries (3): Laos 555 km, Thailand 817 km, Vietnam 1,158 km

Coastline: 443 km

Maritime claims: *territorial sea:* 12 nm
contiguous zone: 24 nm
exclusive economic zone: 200 nm
continental shelf: 200 nm

Climate: tropical; rainy, monsoon season (May to November); dry season (December to April); little seasonal temperature variation

Terrain: mostly low, flat plains; mountains in southwest and north

Elevation: *mean elevation:* 126 m

elevation extremes: *lowest point:* Gulf of Thailand 0 m
highest point: Phnum Aoral 1,810 m

Natural resources: oil and gas, timber, gemstones, iron ore, manganese, phosphates, hydropower potential, arable land:

Land use: *agricultural land:* 32.1%
arable land: 22.7%
permanent crops: 0.9%
permanent pasture: 8.5%
forest: 56.5%
other: 11.4% (2011 est.)

Irrigated land: 3,540 sq km (2012)

Total renewable water resources: 476.1 cu km (2011)

Freshwater withdrawal (domestic/industrial/agricultural): *total:* 2.18 cu m/yr (4%/2%/94%)
per capita: 159.8 cu m/yr (2006)

Natural hazards: monsoonal rains (June to November); flooding; occasional droughts

Environment—current issues: illegal logging activities throughout the country and strip mining for gems in the western region along the border with Thailand have resulted in habitat loss and declining biodiversity (in particular, destruction of mangrove swamps threatens natural fisheries); soil erosion; in rural areas, most of the population does not have access to potable water; declining fish stocks because of illegal fishing and overfishing

Environment—international agreements: *party to:* Biodiversity, Climate Change, Climate Change-Kyoto Protocol, Desertification, Endangered Species, Hazardous Wastes, Marine Life Conservation, Ozone Layer Protection, Ship Pollution, Tropical Timber 94, Wetlands, Whaling
signed, but not ratified: Law of the Sea

Geography—note: a land of paddies and forests dominated by the Mekong River and Tonle Sap (Southeast Asia's largest fresh water lake)

PEOPLE AND SOCIETY

Nationality: *noun:* Cambodian(s)
adjective: Cambodian

Ethnic groups: Khmer 90%, Vietnamese 5%, Chinese 1%, other 4%

Languages: Khmer (official) 96.3%, other 3.7% (2008 est.)

Religions: Buddhist (official) 96.9%, Muslim 1.9%, Christian 0.4%, other 0.8% (2008 est.)

Population: 15,708,756
note: estimates for this country take into account the effects of excess mortality due to AIDS; this can result in lower life expectancy, higher infant mortality, higher death rates, lower population growth rates, and changes in the distribution of population by age and sex than would otherwise be expected (July 2015 est.)
country comparison to the world: 69

Age structure: *0–14 years:* 31.43% (male 2,489,964/female 2,447,645)
15–24 years: 19.71% (male 1,532,016/female 1,564,240)
25–54 years: 39.61% (male 3,043,676/female 3,178,825)
55–64 years: 5.2% (male 315,741/female 501,544)
65 years and over: 4.04% (male 238,840/female 396,265) (2015 est.)

Dependency ratios: *total dependency ratio:* 55.6%
youth dependency ratio: 49.2%
elderly dependency ratio: 6.4%
potential support ratio: 15.6% (2015 est.)

Median age: *total:* 24.5 years
male: 23.8 years
female: 25.2 years (2015 est.)
country comparison to the world: 156

Population growth rate: 1.58% (2015 est.)
country comparison to the world: 76

Birth rate: 23.83 births/1,000 population (2015 est.)
country comparison to the world: 61

Death rate: 7.68 deaths/1,000 population (2015 est.)
country comparison to the world: 108

Net migration rate: -0.32 migrant(s)/1,000 population (2015 est.)
country comparison to the world: 129

Urbanization: *urban population:* 20.7% of total population (2015)
rate of urbanization: 2.65% annual rate of change (2010–15 est.)

Major urban areas—population: PHNOMPENH (capital) 1.731 million (2015)

Sex ratio: *at birth:* 1.05 male(s)/female
0–14 years: 1.02 male(s)/female
15–24 years: 0.98 male(s)/female
25–54 years: 0.96 male(s)/female
55–64 years: 0.63 male(s)/female
65 years and over: 0.6 male(s)/female
total population: 0.94 male(s)/female (2015 est.)

Mother's mean age at first birth: 22.8
note: median age at first birth among women 25–29 (2010 est.)

Maternal mortality rate: 161 deaths/100,000 live births (2015 est.)
country comparison to the world: 45

Infant mortality rate: *total:* 50.04 deaths/1,000 live births
male: 56.69 deaths/1,000 live births
female: 43.11 deaths/1,000 live births (2015 est.)
country comparison to the world: 36

Life expectancy at birth: *total population:* 64.14 years
male: 61.69 years
female: 66.7 years (2015 est.)
country comparison to the world: 180

Total fertility rate: 2.6 children born/woman (2015 est.)
country comparison to the world: 75

Contraceptive prevalence rate: 50.5% (2010/11)

Health expenditures: 7.5% of GDP (2013)
country comparison to the world: 127

Physicians density: 0.17 physicians/1,000 population (2012)

Hospital bed density: 0.7 beds/1,000 population (2011)

Drinking water source:
improved:
urban: 100% of population
rural: 69.1% of population
total: 75.5% of population
unimproved:
urban: 0% of population
rural: 30.9% of population
total: 24.5% of population (2015 est.)

Sanitation facility access:
improved:
urban: 88.1% of population
rural: 30.5% of population
total: 42.4% of population
unimproved:
urban: 11.9% of population
rural: 69.5% of population
total: 57.6% of population (2015 est.)

HIV/AIDS—adult prevalence rate: 0.64% (2014 est.)
country comparison to the world: 59

HIV/AIDS—people living with HIV/AIDS: 74,600 (2014 est.)
country comparison to the world: 49

HIV/AIDS—deaths: 2,600 (2014 est.)
country comparison to the world: 49

Major infectious diseases: *degree of risk:* very high
food or waterborne diseases: bacterial diarrhea, hepatitis A, and typhoid fever
vectorborne diseases: dengue fever, Japanese encephalitis, and malaria
note: highly pathogenic H5N1 avian influenza has been identified in this country; it poses a negligible risk with extremely rare cases possible among US citizens who have close contact with birds (2013)

Obesity—adult prevalence rate: 2.9% (2014)
country comparison to the world: 183

Children under the age of 5 years underweight: 23.9% (2014)
country comparison to the world: 18
Education expenditures: 2% of GDP (2013)
country comparison to the world: 152
Literacy: *definition:* age 15 and over can read and write
total population: 77.2%
male: 84.5%
female: 70.5% (2015 est.)
School life expectancy (primary to tertiary education): *total:* 11 years
male: 11 years
female: 10 years (2008)
Unemployment, youth ages 15–24: *total:* 0.5%
male: 0.7%
female: 0.4%
note: according to official statistics (2010 est.)
country comparison to the world: 130

GOVERNMENT

Country name: *conventional long form:* Kingdom of Cambodia
conventional short form: Cambodia
local long form: Preahreacheanachakr Kampuchea (phonetic transliteration)
local short form: Kampuchea Kampuchea
former: Khmer Republic, Democratic Kampuchea, People's Republic of Kampuchea, State of Cambodia
etymology: the English name Cambodia is an anglicization of the French Cambodge, which is the French transliteration of the native name Kampuchea
Government type: parliamentary constitutional monarchy
Capital: *name:* Phnom Penh
Geographic coordinates: 11 33 N, 104 55 E
time difference: UTC+7 (12 hours ahead of Washington, DC, during Standard Time)
Administrative divisions: 24 provinces (khett, singular and plural) and 1 municipality (krong, singular and plural)
provinces: Banteay Meanchey, Battambang, Kampong Cham, Kampong Chhnang, Kampong Speu, Kampong Thom, Kampot, Kandal, Kep, Koh Kong, Kratie, Mondolkiri, Oddar Meanchey, Pailin, Preah Vihear, Prey Veng, Pursat, Ratanakiri, Siem Reap, Sihanoukville, Stung Treng, Svay Rieng, Takeo, Tbong Khmum
municipalities: Phnom Penh (Phnum Penh)
Independence: 9 November 1953 (from France)
National holiday: Independence Day, 9 November (1953)
Constitution: previous 1947; latest promulgated 21 September 1993; amended 1999, 2008, 2014 (2016)
Legal system: civil law system (influenced by the UN Transitional Authority in Cambodia) customary law, Communist legal theory, and common law
International law organization participation: accepts compulsory ICJ jurisdiction with reservations; accepts ICCt jurisdiction
Citizenship: *citizenship by birth:* no
citizenship by descent only: at least one parent must be a citizen of Cambodia

dual citizenship recognized: yes
residency requirement for naturalization: 7 years
Suffrage: 18 years of age; universal
Executive branch: *chief of state:* King Norodom SIHAMONI (since 29 October 2004)
head of government: Prime Minister HUN SEN (since 14 January 1985); Permanent Deputy Prime Minister MEN SAM AN (since 25 September 2008); Deputy Prime Ministers SAR KHENG (since 3 February 1992), SOK AN, TEA BANH, HOR NAMHONG (all since 16 July 2004), BIN CHHIN (since 5 September 2007), KEAT CHHON, YIM CHHAI LY (since 24 September 2008), KE KIMYAN (since 12 March 2009)
cabinet: Council of Ministers named by the prime minister and appointed by the monarch
elections/appointments: monarch chosen by the 9-member, Royal Council of the Throne from among all eligible males of royal descent; following legislative elections, a member of the majority party or majority coalition named prime minister by the Chairman of the National Assembly and appointed by the monarch
Legislative branch: *description:* bicameral Parliament of Cambodia consists of the Senate (61 seats; 57 indirectly elected by parliamentarians and commune councils, 2 indirectly elected by the National Assembly, and 2 appointed by the monarch; members serve 6-year terms) and the National Assembly (123 seats; members directly elected in multi-seat constituencies by proportional representation vote; members serve 5-year terms)
note: two seats will be added to the National Assembly in 2018, for a total of 125
elections: Senate—last held on 4 February 2012 (next to be held in 2018); National Assembly—last held on 28 July 2013 (next to be held in July 2018)
election results: Senate—percent of vote by party—CPP 77.8%, SRP 22.2%; seats by party—CPP 46, SRP 11; National Assembly—percent of vote by party—CPP 48.8%, CNRP 44.5%, other 6.7%; seats by party—CPP 68, CNRP 55
Judicial branch: *highest court(s):* Supreme Court (organized into 5- and 9-judge panels and includes a court chief and deputy chief); Constitutional Court (consists of 9 members); note—in 1997, the Cambodian Government requested UN assistance in establishing trials to prosecute former Khmer Rouge senior leaders for crimes against humanity committed during the 1975-1979 Khmer Rouge regime; the Extraordinary Chambers of the Courts in Cambodia were established and began hearings for the first case in 2009
judge selection and term of office: Supreme Court and Constitutional Court judge candidates recommended by the Supreme Council of Magistracy, a 9-member body chaired by the monarch and includes other high-level judicial officers; judges of both courts appointed by the monarch; Supreme Court judge tenure NA; Constitutional Court judges appointed for 9-year terms with one-third of the court renewed every 3 years
subordinate courts: municipal and provincial courts; appellate courts; military court

Political parties and leaders: Cambodian National Rescue Party or CNRP [SAM RANGSI, also spelled SAM RAINSY] (a July 2012 merger between the Sam Rangsi Party or SRP and the former Human Rights Party or HRP [KHEM SOKHA, also spelled KEM SOKHA])
Cambodian People's Party or CPP [HUN SEN]
Political pressure groups and leaders: Partnership for Transparency Fund or PTF (anti-corruption organization)
Students Movement for Democracy
The Committee for Free and Fair Elections or Comfrel
other: human rights organizations; labor unions; youth groups
International organization participation: ADB, ARF, ASEAN, CICA, CICA (observer), EAS, FAO, G-77, IAEA, IBRD, ICAO, ICRM, IDA, IFAD, IFC, IFRCS, ILO, IMF, IMO, Interpol, IOC, IOM, IPU, ISO (correspondent), ITU, MINUSMA, MIGA, NAM, OIF, OPCW, PCA, UN, UNAMID, UNCTAD, UNESCO, UNIDO, UNIFIL, UNISFA, UNMISS, UNWTO, UPU, WCO, WFTU (NGOs), WHO, WIPO, WMO, WTO
Diplomatic representation in the US: *chief of mission:* Ambassador CHUM BUN RONG (since 3 August 2015)
chancery: 4530 16th Street NW, Washington, DC 20011
telephone: [1] (202) 726-7742
FAX: [1] (202) 726-8381
Diplomatic representation from the US: *chief of mission:* Ambassador William A. HEIDT (since 2 December 2015)
embassy:
mailing address: Unit 8166, Box P, APO AP 96546
telephone: [855] (23) 728-000
FAX: [855] (23) 728-600
Flag description: three horizontal bands of blue (top), red (double width), and blue with a white three-towered temple representing Angkor Wat outlined in black in the center of the red band; red and blue are traditional Cambodian colors
note: only national flag to incorporate an actual building into its design
National symbol(s): Angkor Wat temple, kouprey (wild ox); national colors: red, blue
National anthem: *name:* "Nokoreach" (Royal Kingdom)
lyrics/music: CHUON NAT/F. PERRUCHOT and J. JEKYLL
note: adopted 1941, restored 1993; the anthem, based on a Cambodian folk tune, was restored after the defeat of the Communist regime

ECONOMY

Economy—overview: Cambodia has experienced strong economic growth over the last decade; GDP grew at an average annual rate of over 8% between 2000 and 2010 and at least 7% since 2011. The tourism, garment, construction and real estate, and agriculture sectors accounted for the bulk of growth. Around 600,000 people, the majority of whom are women, are employed in the garment and footwear sector. An additional 500,000 Cambodians are employed in the tourism sector, and a further 50,000 people in construction. Tourism has continued to grow rapidly with foreign arrivals exceeding 2 million per year since 2007 and reaching around 4.5 million visitors in 2014. Mining also is attracting some investor interest and the government has touted opportunities for mining bauxite, gold, iron and gems.

Cambodia remains one of the poorest countries in Asia and long-term economic development remains a daunting challenge, inhibited by endemic corruption, limited human resources, high income inequality, and poor job prospects. As of 2012, approximately 2.66 million people live on less than $1.20 per Day, and 37% of Cambodian children under the age of 5 suffer from chronic malnutrition. More than 50% of the population is less than 25 years old. The population lacks education and productive skills, particularly in the impoverished countryside, which also lacks basic infrastructure.

The Cambodian Government has been working with bilateral and multilateral donors, including the Asian Development Bank, the World Bank and IMF, to address the country's many pressing needs; more than 30% of the government budget comes from donor assistance. A major economic challenge for Cambodia over the next decade will be fashioning an economic environment in which the private sector can create enough jobs to handle Cambodia's demographic imbalance.

GDP (purchasing power parity): $54.21 billion (2015 est.)
$50.7 billion (2014 est.)
$47.35 billion (2013 est.)
note: data are in 2015 US dollars
country comparison to the world: 108

GDP (official exchange rate): $18.16 billion (2015 est.)

GDP—real growth rate: 6.9% (2015 est.)
7.1% (2014 est.)
7.4% (2013 est.)
country comparison to the world: 17

GDP—per capita (PPP): $3,500 (2015 est.)
$3,300 (2014 est.)
$3,100 (2013 est.)
note: data are in 2015 US dollars
country comparison to the world: 180

Gross national saving: 11.3% of GDP (2015 est.)
11.1% of GDP (2014 est.)
11.2% of GDP (2013 est.)
country comparison to the world: 145

GDP—composition, by end use:
household consumption: 76.6%
government consumption: 5.5%
investment in fixed capital: 21.8%
investment in inventories: 1%
exports of goods and services: 63.2%
imports of goods and services: -68.1% (2015 est.)

GDP—composition, by sector of origin:
agriculture: 28.6%
industry: 27.9%
services: 43.6% (2015 est.)

Agriculture—products: rice, rubber, corn, vegetables, cashews, cassava (manioc, tapioca), silk

Industries: tourism, garments, construction, rice milling, fishing, wood and wood products, rubber, cement, gemmining, textiles

Industrial production growth rate: 9.6% (2015 est.)
country comparison to the world: 7

Labor force: 7.974 million (2013 est.)
country comparison to the world: 61

Labor force—by occupation: *agriculture:* 48.7%
industry: 19.9%
services: 31.5% (2013 est.)

Unemployment rate: 0.3% (2013 est.)
0.2% (2012 est.)
note: according to official statistics; underemployment is high
country comparison to the world: 1

Population below poverty line: 17.7% (2012 est.)

Household income or consumption by percentage share: *lowest:* 10%: 2%
highest: 10%: 28% (2013 est.)

Distribution of family income—Gini index: 37.9 (2008 est.)
41.9 (2004 est.)
country comparison to the world: 74

Budget: *revenues:* $3.334 billion
expenditures: $3.734 billion (2015 est.)
Taxes and other revenues: 18.8% of GDP (2015 est.)
country comparison to the world: 167

Budget surplus (+) or deficit (-): -2.3% of GDP (2015 est.)
country comparison to the world: 86

Public debt: 33.9% of GDP (2014 est.)
33.4% of GDP (2013 est.)
country comparison to the world: 131

Fiscal year: calendar year

Inflation rate (consumer prices): 1.2% (2015 est.)
3.9% (2014 est.)
country comparison to the world: 88

Central bank discount rate: NA% (31 December 2012)
5.25% (31 December 2007)

Commercial bank prime lending rate: 11.7% (31 December 2015 est.)
12.31% (31 December 2014 est.)
country comparison to the world: 69

Stock of narrow money: $1.655 billion (31 December 2015 est.)
$1.482 billion (31 December 2014 est.)
country comparison to the world: 135

Stock of broad money: $11.82 billion (31 December 2015 est.)
$10.47 billion (31 December 2014 est.)
country comparison to the world: 104

Stock of domestic credit: $9.903 billion (31 December 2015 est.)
$7.842 billion (31 December 2014 est.)
country comparison to the world: 102

Market value of publicly traded shares: $NA

Current account balance: -$2.042 billion (2015 est.)
-$2.032 billion (2014 est.)
country comparison to the world: 144

Exports: $7.867 billion (2015 est.)
$7.407 billion (2014 est.)
country comparison to the world: 98

Exports—commodities: clothing, timber, rubber, rice, fish, tobacco, footwear

Exports—partners: US 23.1%, UK 8.8%, Germany 8.2%, Japan 7.4%, Canada 6.7%, China 5.1%, Vietnam 5%, Thailand 4.9%, Netherlands 4.1% (2015)

Imports: $10.65 billion (2015 est.)
$10.62 billion (2014 est.)
country comparison to the world: 96

Imports—commodities: petroleum products, cigarettes, gold, construction materials, machinery, motor vehicles, pharmaceutical products

Imports—partners: Thailand 28.5%, China 22%, Vietnam 16.3%, Hong Kong 6%, Singapore 5.6% (2015)

Reserves of foreign exchange and gold: $7.091 billion (31 December 2015 est.)
$6.106 billion (31 December 2014 est.)
country comparison to the world: 86

Debt—external: $7.222 billion (31 December 2014 est.)
$6.427 billion (31 December 2013 est.)
country comparison to the world: 116

Stock of direct foreign investment—at home: $29.17 billion (2014 est.)
country comparison to the world: 72

Exchange rates: riels (KHR) per US dollar—
4,080.3 (2015 est.)
4,037.5 (2014 est.)
4,037.5 (2013 est.)
4,033 (2012 est.)
4,058.5 (2011 est.)

ENERGY

Electricity—production: 1.77 billion kWh (2013 est.)
country comparison to the world: 143

Electricity—consumption: 3.553 billion kWh (2013 est.)
country comparison to the world: 129

Electricity—exports: 0 kWh (2013 est.)
country comparison to the world: 115

Electricity—imports: 2.282 billion kWh (2013 est.)
country comparison to the world: 56

Electricity—installed generating capacity: 949,000 kW (2013 est.)
country comparison to the world: 124

Electricity—from fossil fuels: 32.7% of total installed capacity (2013 est.)
country comparison to the world: 176

Electricity—from nuclear fuels: 0% of total installed capacity (2013 est.)
country comparison to the world: 62

Electricity—from hydroelectric plants: 57.4% of total installed capacity (2013 est.)
country comparison to the world: 37

Electricity—from other renewable sources: 10% of total installed capacity (2013 est.)
country comparison to the world: 37

Crude oil—production: 0 bbl/day (2014 est.)
country comparison to the world: 116

Crude oil—exports: 0 bbl/day (2012 est.)
country comparison to the world: 107

Crude oil—imports: 0 bbl/day (2012 est.)
country comparison to the world: 169

Crude oil—proved reserves: 0 bbl (1 January 2015 est.)
country comparison to the world: 114
Refined petroleum products—production: 0 bbl/day (2012 est.)
country comparison to the world: 164
Refined petroleum products—consumption: 28,000 bbl/day (2013 est.)
country comparison to the world: 117
Refined petroleum products—exports: 0 bbl/day (2012 est.)
country comparison to the world: 164
Refined petroleum products—imports: 28,890 bbl/day (2012 est.)
country comparison to the world: 98
Natural gas—production: 0 cu m (2013 est.)
country comparison to the world: 166
Natural gas—consumption: 0 cu m (2013 est.)
country comparison to the world: 125
Natural gas—exports: 0 cu m (2013 est.)
country comparison to the world: 73
Natural gas—imports: 0 cu m (2013 est.)
country comparison to the world: 172
Natural gas—proved reserves: 0 cu m (1 January 2014 est.)
country comparison to the world: 120
Carbon dioxide emissions from consumption of energy: 6.5 million Mt (2013 est.)
country comparison to the world: 117

COMMUNICATIONS

Telephones—fixed lines: *total subscriptions:* 440,000
subscriptions per 100 inhabitants: 3 (2014 est.)
country comparison to the world: 99
Telephones—mobile cellular: *total:* 23.9 million
subscriptions per 100 inhabitants: 155 (2014 est.)
country comparison to the world: 48
Telephone system: *general assessment:* adequate fixed-line and/or cellular service in Phnom Penh and other provincial cities; mobile-cellular phone systems are widely used in urban areas to bypass deficiencies in the fixed-line network; mobile-phone coverage is rapidly expanding in rural areas
domestic: fixed-line connections stand at about 3 per 100 persons; mobile-cellular usage, aided by competition among service providers, is increasing rapidly and is over 150 per 100 persons
international: country code—855; adequate but expensive landline and cellular service available to all countries from Phnom Penh and major provincial cities; satellite earth station—1 Intersputnik (Indian Ocean region) (2011)

Broadcast media: mixture of state-owned, joint public-private, and privately owned broadcast media; 9 TV broadcast stations with most operating on multiple channels, including 1 state-operated station broadcasting from multiple locations, 6 stations either jointly operated or privately owned with some broadcasting from several locations, and 2 TV relay stations—one relaying a French TV station and the other relaying a Vietnamese TV station; multi-channel cable and satellite systems are available; roughly 50 radio broadcast stations—1 state-owned broadcaster with multiple stations and a large mixture of public and

private broadcasters; several international broadcasters are available (2009)
Radio broadcast stations: AM 1, FM 50, shortwave NA (2008)
Television broadcast stations: 9 (2009)
Internet country code: .kh
Internet hosts: 13,784 (2012)
country comparison to the world: 129
Internet users: total: 831,700
percent of population: 5.4% (2014 est.)
country comparison to the world: 124

TRANSPORTATION

Airports: 16 (2013)
country comparison to the world: 142
Airports—with paved runways: *total:* 6
2,438 to 3,047 m: 3
1,524 to 2,437 m: 2
914 to 1,523 m: 1 (2013)
Airports—with unpaved runways: *total:* 10
1,524 to 2,437 m: 2
914 to 1,523 m: 7
under 914 m: 1 (2013)
Heliports: 1 (2013)
Railways: *total:* 642 km
narrow gauge: 642 km 1.000-m gauge
note: under restoration (2014)
country comparison to the world: 108
Roadways: *total:* 44,709 km
paved: 3,607 km
unpaved: 41,102 km (2010)
country comparison to the world: 88
Waterways: 3,700 km (mainly on Mekong River) (2012)
country comparison to the world: 28
Merchant marine: *total:* 544
by type: bulk carrier 38, cargo 459, carrier 7, chemical tanker 4, container 4, liquefied gas 1, passenger 1, passenger/cargo 6, petroleum tanker 8, refrigerated cargo 11, roll on/roll off 4, vehicle carrier 1
foreign-owned: 352 (Belgium 1, Canada 2, China 177, Cyprus 4, Egypt 4, Estonia 1, French Polynesia 1, Gabon 1, Greece 2, Hong Kong 10, Indonesia 2, Ireland 1, Japan 1, Lebanon 5, Russia 50, Singapore 3, South Korea 10, Syria 22, Taiwan 1, Turkey 15, UAE 2, UK 1, Ukraine 35, Vietnam 1) (2010)
country comparison to the world: 21
Ports and terminals: *major seaport(s):* Sihanoukville (Kampong Saom)
river port(s): Phnom Penh (Mekong)

MILITARY AND SECURITY

Military branches: Royal Cambodian Armed Forces: Royal Cambodian Army, Royal Khmer Navy, Royal Cambodian Air Force; the Royal-Cambodian Gendarmerie is the military police force responsible for internal security; the National Committee for Maritime Security performs Coast Guard functions and has representation from military and civilian agencies (2016)
Military service age and obligation: 18 is the legal minimum age for compulsory and voluntary military service (2012)

Military expenditures: 2% of GDP (2015 est.)
1.8% of GDP (2014)
1.58% of GDP (2013)
1.54% of GDP (2012)
1.5% of GDP (2011)
country comparison to the world: 60

TRANSNATIONAL ISSUES

Disputes—international: Cambodia is concerned about Laos' extensive upstream dam construction; Cambodia and Thailand dispute sections of boundary; in 2011 Thailand and Cambodia resorted to arms in the dispute over the location of the boundary on the precipice surmounted by Preah Vihear Temple ruins, awarded to Cambodia by ICJ decision in 1962 and part of a UN World Heritage site; Cambodia accuses Vietnam of a wide variety of illicit cross-border activities; progress on a joint development area with Vietnam is hampered by an unresolved dispute over sovereignty of offshore islands

Trafficking in persons: *current situation:* Cambodia is a source, transit, and destination country for men, women, and children subjected to forced labor and sex trafficking; Cambodian men, women, and children migrate to countries within the region and, increasingly, the Middle East for legitimate work but are subjected to sex trafficking, domestic servitude, or forced labor in fishing, agriculture, construction, and factories; Cambodian men recruited to work on Thai-owned fishing vessels are subsequently subjected to forced labor in international waters and are kept at sea for years; poor Cambodian children are vulnerable and, often with the families' complicity, are subject to forced labor, including domestic servitude and forced begging, in Thailand and Vietnam; Cambodian and ethnic Vietnamese women and girls are trafficked from rural areas to urban centers and tourist spots for sexual exploitation; Cambodian men are the main exploiters of child prostitutes, but men from other Asian countries, and the West travel to Cambodia for child sex tourism

tier rating: Tier 2 Watch List—Cambodia does not fully comply with the minimum standards for the elimination of trafficking; however, it is making significant efforts to do so; the government has a written plan that, if implemented, would constitute making significant efforts to meet the minimum standards for the elimination of trafficking; authorities made modest progress in prosecutions and convictions of traffickers in 2014 but did not provide comprehensive data; endemic corruption continued to impede law enforcement efforts, and no complicit officials were prosecuted or convicted; the government sustained efforts to identify victims and refer them to NGOs for care, but victim protection remained inadequate, particularly for assisting male victims and victims identified abroad; a new national action plan was adopted, but guidelines for victim identification and guidance on undercover investigation techniques are still pending after several years (2015)

Illicit drugs: narcotics-related corruption reportedly involving some in the government, military, and police; limited methamphetamine production; vulnerable to money laundering due to its cash-based economy and porous borders

CAMEROON

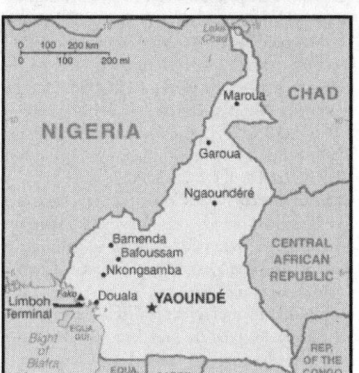

Background: French Cameroon became independent in 1960 as the Republic of Cameroon. The following year the southern portion of neighboring British Cameroon voted to merge with the new country to form the Federal Republic of Cameroon. In 1972, a new constitution replaced the federation with a unitary state, the United Republic of Cameroon. The country has generally enjoyed stability, which has enabled the development of agriculture, roads, and railways, as well as a petroleum industry. Despite slow movement toward democratic reform, political power remains firmly in the hands of President Paul BIYA.

GEOGRAPHY

Location: Central Africa, bordering the Bight of Biafra, between Equatorial Guinea and Nigeria

Geographic coordinates: 6 00 N, 12 00 E

Map references: Africa

Area: total: 475,440 sq km
land: 472,710 sq km
water: 2,730 sq km
country comparison to the world: 54

Area—comparative: slightly larger than California

Land boundaries: total: 5,018 km
border countries (6): Central African Republic 901 km, Chad 1,116 km, Republic of the Congo 494 km, Equatorial Guinea 183 km, Gabon 349 km, Nigeria 1,975 km

Coastline: 402 km

Maritime claims: territorial sea: 12 nm
contiguous zone: 24 nm

Climate: varies with terrain, from tropical along coast to semiarid and hot in north

Terrain: diverse, with coastal plain in southwest, dissected plateau in center, mountains in west, plains in north

Elevation: mean elevation: 667 m

elevation extremes: lowest point: Atlantic Ocean 0 m
highest point: Fako 4,095 m (on Cameroon Mountain)

Natural resources: petroleum, bauxite, iron ore, timber, hydropower

Land use: agricultural land: 20.6%
arable land: 13.1%
permanent crops: 3.3%
permanent pasture: 4.2%
forest: 41.7%
other: 37.7% (2011 est.)

Irrigated land: 290 sq km (2012)

Total renewable water resources: 285.5 cu km (2011)

Freshwater withdrawal (domestic/industrial/agricultural): total: 0.97 cu m/yr (23%/10%/68%)
per capita: 58.9 cu m/yr (2005)

Natural hazards: volcanic activity with periodic releases of poisonous gases from Lake Nyos and Lake Monoun volcanoes
volcanism: Mt. Cameroon (elev. 4,095 m), which last erupted in 2000, is the most frequently active volcano in West Africa; lakes in Oku volcanic field have released fatal levels of gas on occasion, killing some 1,700 people in 1986

Environment—current issues: waterborne diseases are prevalent; deforestation; overgrazing; desertification; poaching; overfishing

Environment—international agreements: party to: Biodiversity, Climate Change, Climate Change-Kyoto Protocol, Desertification, Endangered Species, Hazardous Wastes, Law of the Sea, Ozone Layer Protection, Tropical Timber 83, Tropical Timber 94, Wetlands, Whaling
signed, but not ratified: none of the selected agreements

Geography—note: sometimes referred to as the hinge of Africa; throughout the country there are areas of thermal springs and indications of current or prior volcanic activity; Mount Cameroon, the highest mountain in Sub-Saharan west Africa, is an active volcano

PEOPLE AND SOCIETY

Nationality: noun: Cameroonian(s)
adjective: Cameroonian

Ethnic groups: Cameroon Highlanders 31%, Equatorial Bantu 19%, Kirdi 11%, Fulani 10%, Northwestern Bantu 8%, Eastern Nigritic 7%, other African 13%, non-African less than 1%

Languages: 24 major African language groups, English (official), French (official)

Religions: Catholic 38.4%, Protestant 26.3%, other Christian 4.5%, Muslim 20.9%, animist 5.6%, other 1%, non- believer 3.2% (2005 est.)

Population: 23,739,218
note: estimates for this country explicitly take into account the effects of excess mortality due to AIDS; this can result in lower life expectancy, higher infant mortality, higher death rates, lower population growth rates, and changes in the distribution of population by age and sex than would otherwise be expected (July 2015 est.)
country comparison to the world: 53

Age structure: 0–14 years: 42.78% (male 5,115,958/female 5,039,122)

15–24 years: 19.58% (male 2,337,061/female 2,310,178)
25–54 years: 30.53% (male 3,644,779/female 3,603,610)
55–64 years: 3.96% (male 458,001/female 481,717)
65 years and over: 3.15% (male 348,754/female 400,038) (2015 est.)

Dependency ratios: total dependency ratio: 84.3%
youth dependency ratio: 78.4%
elderly dependency ratio: 5.9%
potential support ratio: 16.9% (2015 est.)

Median age: total: 18.4 years
male: 18.3 years
female: 18.5 years (2015 est.)
country comparison to the world: 208

Population growth rate: 2.59% (2015 est.)
country comparison to the world: 19

Birth rate: 36.17 births/1,000 population (2015 est.)
country comparison to the world: 18

Death rate: 10.11 deaths/1,000 population (2015 est.)
country comparison to the world: 42

Net migration rate: -0.15 migrant(s)/1,000 population (2015 est.)
country comparison to the world: 117

Urbanization: urban population: 54.4% of total population (2015)
rate of urbanization: 3.6% annual rate of change (2010–15 est.)

Major urban areas—population: YAOUNDE (capital) 3.066 million; Douala 2.943 million (2015)

Sex ratio: at birth: 1.03 male(s)/female
0–14 years: 1.02 male(s)/female
15–24 years: 1.01 male(s)/female
25–54 years: 1.01 male(s)/female
55–64 years: 0.95 male(s)/female
65 years and over: 0.87 male(s)/female
total population: 1.01 male(s)/female (2015 est.)

Mother's mean age at first birth: 19.7
note: median age at first birth among women 25–29 (2011 est.)

Maternal mortality rate: 596 deaths/100,000 live births (2015 est.)
country comparison to the world: 10

Infant mortality rate: total: 53.63 deaths/1,000 live births
male: 57.28 deaths/1,000 live births
female: 49.88 deaths/1,000 live births (2015 est.)
country comparison to the world: 29

Life expectancy at birth:
total population: 57.93 years
male: 56.62 years
female: 59.28 years (2015 est.)
country comparison to the world: 203

Total fertility rate: 4.76 children born/woman (2015 est.)
country comparison to the world: 20

Contraceptive prevalence rate: 23.4% (2011)

Health expenditures: 5.1% of GDP (2013)

153

country comparison to the world: 139

Physicians density: 0.08 physicians/1,000 population (2009)

Hospital bed density: 1.3 beds/1,000 population (2010)

Drinking water source:
improved:
urban: 94.8% of population
rural: 52.7% of population
total: 75.6% of population
unimproved:
urban: 5.2% of population
rural: 47.3% of population
total: 24.4% of population (2015 est.)

Sanitation facility access:
improved:
urban: 61.8% of population
rural: 26.8% of population
total: 45.8% of population
unimproved:
urban: 38.2% of population
rural: 73.2% of population
total: 54.2% of population (2015 est.)

HIV/AIDS—adult prevalence rate: 4.77% (2014 est.)
country comparison to the world: 14

HIV/AIDS—people living with HIV/AIDS: 657,500 (2014 est.)
country comparison to the world: 15

HIV/AIDS—deaths: 34,200 (2014 est.)
country comparison to the world: 7

Major infectious diseases: *degree of risk:* very high
food or waterborne diseases: bacterial and protozoal diarrhea, hepatitis A, and typhoid fever
vectorborne diseases: malaria, dengue fever, and yellow fever
water contact disease: schistosomiasis
respiratory disease: meningococcal meningitis
animal contact disease: rabies (2013)

Obesity—adult prevalence rate: 9.6% (2014)
country comparison to the world: 130

Children under the age of 5 years underweight: 14.8% (2014)
country comparison to the world: 47

Education expenditures: 3% of GDP (2013)
country comparison to the world: 133

Literacy: *definition:* age 15 and over can read and write
total population: 75%
male: 81.2%
female: 68.9% (2015 est.)

School life expectancy (primary to tertiary education): *total:* 10 years
male: 11 years
female: 10 years (2011)

Child labor—children ages 5–14: *total number:* 1,396,281
percentage: 31% (2006 est.)

Unemployment, youth ages 15–24: *total:* 6.4%
male: 5.3%
female: 7.5% (2010 est.)

GOVERNMENT

Country name: *conventional long form:* Republic of Cameroon
conventional short form: Cameroon

local long form: Republique du Cameroun/Republic of Cameroon
local short form: Cameroun/Cameroon
former: French Cameroon, British Cameroon, Federal Republic of Cameroon, United Republic of Cameroon
etymology: in the 15th century, Portuguese explorers named the area near the mouth of the Wouri River the Rio dos Camaroes (River of Prawns) after the abundant shrimp in the water; over time the designation became Cameroon in English; this is the only instance where a country is named afer a crustacean

Government type: presidential republic

Capital: *name:* Yaounde

Geographic coordinates: 3 52 N, 11 31 E
time difference: UTC + 1 (6 hours ahead of Washington, DC, during Standard Time)

Administrative divisions: 10 regions (regions, singular—region); Adamaoua, Centre, East (Est), Far North (Extreme-Nord), Littoral, North (Nord), North-West (Nord-Ouest), West (Ouest), South (Sud), South-West (Sud-Ouest)

Independence: 1 January 1960 (from French-administered UN trusteeship)

National holiday: State Unification Day (National Day), 20 May (1972)

Constitution: several previous; latest effective 18 January 1996; amended 2008 (2016)

Legal system: mixed legal system of English common law, French civil law, and customary law

International law organization participation: accepts compulsory ICJ jurisdiction; non-party state to the ICCt

Citizenship: *citizenship by birth:* no
citizenship by descent only: at least one parent must be a citizen of Cameroon
dual citizenship recognized: no
residency requirement for naturalization: 5 years

Suffrage: 20 years of age; universal

Executive branch: *chief of state:* President Paul BIYA (since 6 November 1982)

head of government: Prime Minister Philemon YANG (since 30 June 2009)
cabinet: Cabinet proposed by the prime minister, appointed by the president
elections/appointments: president directly elected by simple majority popular vote for a 7-year term (no term limits); election last held on 9 October 2011 (next to be held in October 2018); prime minister appointed by the president
election results: Paul BIYA reelected president; percent of vote—Paul BIYA (CPDM) 78.0%, John FRU NDI (SDF) 10.7%, Garga Haman ADJI 3.2%, other 8.1%

Legislative branch: *description:* bicameral Parliament or Parlement consists of the Senate or Senat (100 seats; 70 members indirectly elected by regional councils and 30 appointed by the president; members serve 5-year terms) and the National Assembly or Assemblee Nationale (180 seats; members directly elected in multi-seat constituencies by simple majority vote to serve 5-year

terms); note—the 100-member Senate was formed at the time of the April 2013 election
elections: Senate last held on 14 April 2013 (next to be held in 2018); National Assembly last held on 30 September 2013 (next to be held in 2018)
election results: Senate—percent of vote by party—NA; seats by party—CPDM 56, SDF 14; National Assembly—percent of vote by party—CPDM 73.1%, SDF 17.6%, UNDP 6.1%, UDC 2.5%, other 0.7%; seats by party—CPDM 148, SDF 18, UNDP 5, UDC 4, UPC 3, other 2

Judicial branch: *highest court(s):* Supreme Court of Cameroon (consists of 9 titular and 6 surrogate judges and organized into judicial, administrative, and audit chambers); Constitutional Council (consists of 11 members)
judge selection and term of office: Supreme Court judges appointed by the president with the advice of the Higher Judicial Council of Cameroon, a body chaired by the president and includes the minister of justice, selected magistrates, and representatives of the National Assembly; judge term NA; Constitutional Council members appointed by the president for single 9-year terms
subordinate courts: Parliamentary Court of Justice (jurisdiction limited to cases involving the president and prime minister); appellate and first instance courts; circuit and magistrate's courts

Political parties and leaders: Cameroon People's Democratic Movement or CPDM [Paul BIYA]
Cameroon People's Party or CPP [Edith Kah WALLA]
Cameroon Renaissance Movement or MRC [Maurice KAMTO]
Cameroonian Democratic Union or UDC [Adamou Ndam NJOYA]
Movement for the Defense of the Republic or MDR [Dakole DAISSALA]
Movement for the Liberation and Development of Cameroon or MLDC [Marcel YONDO]
National Union for Democracy and Progress or UNDP [Maigari BELLO BOUBA]
Progressive Movement or MP [Jean-Jacques EKINDI]
Social Democratic Front or SDF [John FRU NDI]
Union of Peoples of Cameroon or UPC [Provisionary Management Bureau]

Political pressure groups and leaders: Network of Human Rights Defenders in Central Africa or REDHAC [Maximilliene Ngo MBE]
Tribunal 53 [Patrice NGANANG]

International organization participation: ACP, AfDB, AU, BDEAC, C, CEMAC, EITI (compliant country), FAO, FZ, G-77, IAEA, IBRD, ICAO, ICRM, IDA, IDB, IFAD, IFC, IFRCS, IHO, ILO, IMF, IMO, IMSO, Interpol, IOC, IOM, IPU, ISO, ITSO, ITU, ITUC (NGOs), MIGA, MONUSCO, NAM, OIC, OIF, OPCW, PCA, UN, UNCTAD, UNESCO, UNHCR, UNIDO, UNOCI, UNWTO, UPU, WCO, WFTU (NGOs), WHO, WIPO, WMO, WTO

Diplomatic representation in the US: *chief of mission:* Ambassador Joseph FOE-ATANGANA (since 12 September 2008)
chancery: 2349 Massachusetts Avenue NW, Washington, DC 20008; current temporary

address—3400 International Drive NW, Washington, DC 20008

telephone: [1] (202) 265-8790

FAX: [1] (202) 387-3826

Diplomatic representation from the US: *chief of mission:* Ambassador Michael Stephen HOZA (since 19 September 2014) em bassy: Avenue Rosa Parks, Yaounde

mailing address: P.O. Box 817, Yaounde; pouch: American Embassy, US Department of State, Washington, DC 20521-2520

telephone: [237] 22220 15 00

Consular: [237] 22220 16 03

FAX: [237] 22220 15 00 Ext. 4531; Consular FAX: [237] 22220 17 52

branch office(s): Douala

Flag description: three equal vertical bands of green (hoist side), red, and yellow, with a yellow five-pointed star centered in the red band; the vertical tricolor recalls the flag of France; red symbolizes unity, yellow the sun, happiness, and the savannahs in the north, and green hope and the forests in the south; the star is referred to as the "star of unity"

note: uses the popular Pan-African colors of Ethiopia

National symbol(s): lion; national colors: green, red, yellow

National anthem: *name:* "O Cameroun, Berceau de nos Ancetres" (O Cameroon, Cradle of Our Forefathers)

lyrics/music: Rene Djam AFAME, Samuel Minkio BAMBA, Moise Nyatte NKO'O [French], Benard Nsokika FONLON [English]/Rene Djam AFAME

note: adopted 1957; Cameroon's anthem, also known as "Chant de Ralliement" (The Rallying Song), has been used unofficially since 1948 and officially adopted in 1957; the anthem has French and English versions whose lyrics differ

ECONOMY

Economy—overview: Modest oil resources and favorable agricultural conditions provide Cameroon with one of the best-endowed primary commodity economies in Sub-Saharan Africa. Oil remains Cameroon's main export commodity, and despite falling global oil prices, still accounts for nearly 40% of export earnings. Cameroon's economy suffers from factors that often impact underdeveloped countries, such as stagnant per capita income, a relatively inequitable distribution of income, a top-heavy civil service, endemic corruption, continuing inefficiencies of a large parastatal system in key sectors, and a generally UN favorable climate for bu siness en terprise.

Since 1990, the government has embarked on various IMF and World Bank programs designed to spur business investment, increase efficiency in agriculture, improve trade, and recapitalize the nation's banks. The IMF continues to press for economic reforms, including increased budget transparency, privatization, and poverty reduction programs. The Government of Cameroon provides subsidies for electricity, food, and fuel that have strained the federal budget and diverted funds from education, healthcare, and infrastructure projects, especially in 2015, as low oil prices have led to lower revenues. Cameroon devotes significant resources to several large infrastructure projects currently under construction, including a deep sea port in Kribi and the Lom Pangar Hydropower Project. Cameroon's energy sector continues to diversify, recently opening a natural gas powered electricity generating plant. Cameroon continues to seek foreign investment to improve its inadequate infrastructure, create jobs, and improve its economic footprint, but its unfavorable business environment remains a significant deterrent to foreign investment.

GDP (purchasing power parity): $72.64 billion (2015 est.)

$68.61 billion (2014 est.)

$64.78 billion (2013 est.)

note: data are in 2015 US dollars

country comparison to the world: 96

GDP (official exchange rate): $28.48 billion (2015 est.)

GDP—real growth rate: 5.9% (2015 est.)

5.9% (2014 est.)

5.6% (2013 est.)

country comparison to the world: 30

GDP—per capita (PPP): $3,100 (2015 est.)

$3,000 (2014 est.) $2,900 (2013 est.)

note: data are in 2015 US dollars

country comparison to the world: 188

Gross national saving: 16% of GDP (2015 est.)

17.3% of GDP (2014 est.)

17.7% of GDP (2013 est.)

country comparison to the world: 107

GDP—composition, by end use:

household consumption: 77.9%

government consumption: 11.3%

investment in fixed capital: 20.4%

investment in inventories: 0%

exports of goods and services: 16%

imports of goods and services: -25.6% (2015 est.)

GDP—composition, by sector of origin: *agriculture:* 22.3%

industry: 29.9%

services: 47.9% (2015 est.)

Agriculture—products: coffee, cocoa, cotton, rubber, bananas, oilseed, grains, cassava (manioc, tapioca); livestock; timber

Industries: petroleum production and refining, aluminum production, food processing, light consumer goods, textiles, lumber, ship repair

Industrial production growth rate: 4% (2015 est.)

country comparison to the world: 62

Labor force: 9.332 million (2015 est.)

country comparison to the world: 53

Labor force—by occupation: *agriculture:* 70%

industry: 13%

services: 17% (2001 est.)

Unemployment rate: 30% (2001 est.)

country comparison to the world: 187

Population below poverty line: 48% (2000 est.)

Household income or consumption by percentage share: *lowest:* 10%: 2.3%

highest: 10%: 35.4% (2001)

Distribution of family income—Gini index: 44.6 (2001) 47.7 (1996)

country comparison to the world: 45

Budget: *revenues:* $4.035 billion

expenditures: $5.404 billion (2015 est.)

Taxes and other revenues: 14.1% of GDP (2015 est.)

country comparison to the world: 199

Budget surplus (+) or deficit (-): -4.8% of GDP (2015 est.)

country comparison to the world: 167

Public debt: 31.7% of GDP (2015 est.)

23.7% of GDP (2014 est.)

country comparison to the world: 141

Fiscal year: 1 July—30 June

Inflation rate (consumer prices): 2.8% (2015 est.)

1.9% (2014 est.)

country comparison to the world: 134

Central bank discount rate: 4.25% (31 December 2009)

country comparison to the world: 86

Commercial bank prime lending rate: 13% (31 December 2015 est.)

13% (31 December 2014 est.)

country comparison to the world: 55

Stock of narrow money: $3.239 billion (31 December 2015 est.)

$3.65 billion (31 December 2014 est.)

country comparison to the world: 115

Stock of broad money: $5.53 billion (31 December 2015 est.)

$6.217 billion (31 December 2014 est.)

country comparison to the world: 128

Stock of domestic credit: $2.691 billion (31 December 2015 est.)

$3.127 billion (31 December 2014 est.)

country comparison to the world: 132

Market value of publicly traded shares: $230 million (31 December 2012 est.)

country comparison to the world: 116

Current account balance: -$1.647 billion (2015 est.)

-$1.396 billion (2014 est.)

country comparison to the world: 140

Exports: $5.283 billion (2015 est.)

$6.027 billion (2014 est.)

country comparison to the world: 108

Exports—commodities: crude oil and petroleum products, lumber, cocoa beans, aluminum, coffee, cotton

Exports—partners: China 16.7%, India 15.7%, Spain 6.2%, Belgium 6.1%, France 6.1%, Portugal 5.6%, Netherlands 5%, Italy 5% (2015)

Imports: $6.159 billion (2015 est.)

$6.483 billion (2014 est.)

country comparison to the world: 119

Imports—commodities: machinery, electrical equipment, transport equipment, fuel, food

Imports—partners: China 27.9%, Nigeria 13.9%, France 10.9%, Belgium 4.1% (2015)

Reserves of foreign exchange and gold: $2.51 billion (31 December 2015 est.)

$3.122 billion (31 December 2014 est.)

country comparison to the world: 114

Debt—external: $5.784 billion (31 December 2014 est.)
$4.922 billion (31 December 2013 est.)
country comparison to the world: 127

Exchange rates: Cooperation Financiere en Afrique Centrale francs (XAF) per dollar—
580.5 (2015 est.)
494.42 (2014 est.)
494.42 (2013 est.)
510.53 (2012 est.)
471.87 (2011 est.)

ENERGY

Electricity—production: 6.155 billion kWh (2012 est.)
country comparison to the world: 114
Electricity—consumption: 5.535 billion kWh (2012 est.)
country comparison to the world: 112
Electricity—exports: 0 kWh (2013 est.)
country comparison to the world: 123
Electricity—imports: 0 kWh (2013 est.)
country comparison to the world: 133
Electricity—installed generating capacity: 1.009 million kW (2012 est.)
country comparison to the world: 123
Electricity—from fossil fuels: 28.5% of total installed capacity (2012 est.)
country comparison to the world: 184
Electricity—from nuclear fuels: 0% of total installed capacity (2012 est.)
country comparison to the world: 69
Electricity—from hydroelectric plants: 71.5% of total installed capacity (2012 est.)
country comparison to the world: 21
Electricity—from other renewable sources: 0% of total installed capacity (2012 est.)
country comparison to the world: 169
Crude oil—production: 80,830 bbl/day (2014 est.)
country comparison to the world: 49
Crude oil—exports: 52,060 bbl/day (2012 est.)
country comparison to the world: 45
Crude oil—imports: 31,960 bbl/day (2012 est.)
country comparison to the world: 60
Crude oil—proved reserves: 200 million bbl (1 January 2015 est.)
country comparison to the world: 59
Refined petroleum products—production: 42,780 bbl/day (2012 est.)
country comparison to the world: 82
Refined petroleum products—consumption: 38,000 bbl/day (2013 est.)
country comparison to the world: 107
Refined petroleum products—export: 10,150 bbl/day (2012 est.)
country comparison to the world: 88
Refined petroleum products—imports: 6,061 bbl/day (2012 est.)
country comparison to the world: 152
Natural gas—production: 346 million cu m (2013 est.)
country comparison to the world: 74
Natural gas—consumption: 346 million cu m (2013 est.)
country comparison to the world: 102
Natural gas—exports: 0 cu m (2013 est.)
country comparison to the world: 80

Natural gas—imports: 0 cu m (2013 est.)
country comparison to the world: 179
Natural gas—proved reserves: 135.1 billion cu m (1 January 2014 est.)
country comparison to the world: 50
Carbon dioxide emissions from consumption of energy: 6.224 million Mt (2012 est.)
country comparison to the world: 121

COMMUNICATIONS

Telephones—fixed lines: *total subscriptions:* 1.05 million
subscriptions per 100 inhabitants: 5 (2014 est.)
country comparison to the world: 76
Telephones—mobile cellular: *total:* 17.3 million
subscriptions per 100 inhabitants: 75 (2014 est.)
country comparison to the world: 61
Telephone system: *general assessment:* system includes cable, microwave radio relay, and tropospheric scatter; Camtel, the monopoly provider of fixed-line service, provides connections for only about 3 per 100 persons; equipment is old and outdated, and connections with many parts of the country are unreliable
domestic: mobile-cellular usage, in part a reflection of the poor condition and general inadequacy of the fixed-line network, has increased sharply, reaching a subscribership base of 50 per 100 persons
international: country code—237; landing point for the SAT-3/WASC fiber-optic submarine cable that provides connectivity to Europe and Asia; satellite earth stations—2 Intelsat (Atlantic Ocean) (2011)
Broadcast media: government maintains tight control over broadcast media; state-owned Cameroon Radio Television (CRTV), broadcasting on both a TV and radio network, was the only officially recognized and fully licensed broadcaster until August 2007, when the government finally issued licenses to 2 private TV broadcasters and 1 private radio broadcaster; about 70 privately owned, unlicensed radio stations operating but are subject to closure at any time; foreign news services required to partner with state-owned national station (2007)
Radio broadcast stations: AM 2, FM 9, short-wave 3 (2001)
Television broadcast stations: 1 (2001)

Internet country code: .cm
Internet hosts: 10,207 (2012)
country comparison to the world: 134
Internet users: *total:* 1.5 million
percent of population: 6.5% (2014 est.)
country comparison to the world: 108

TRANSPORTATION

Airports: 33 (2013)
country comparison to the world: 112
Airports—with paved runways: *total:* 11
over 3,047 m: 2
2,438 to 3,047 m: 5
1,524 to 2,437 m: 3
914 to 1,523 m: 1 (2013)
Airports—with unpaved runways: *total:* 22
1,524 to 2,437 m: 4

914 to 1,523 m: 10
under 914 m: 8 (2013)

Pipelines: gas 53 km; liquid petroleum gas 5 km; oil 1,107 km; water 35 km (2013)
Railways: *total:* 987 km
narrow gauge: 987 km 1.000-m gauge
note: railway connections generally efficient but limited; rail lines connect major cities of Douala, Yaounde, Ngaoundere, and Garoua; passenger and freight service provided by CAMRAIL (2014)
country comparison to the world: 87
Roadways: *total:* 51,350 km
paved: 4,108 km
unpaved: 47,242 km
note: there are 28,857 km of national roads (2011)
country comparison to the world: 76
Waterways: (major rivers in the south, such as the Wouri and the Sanaga, are largely non-navigable; in the north, the Benue, which connects through Nigeria to the Niger River, is navigable in the rainy season only to the port of Garoua) (2010)
Ports and terminals: *river port(s):* Douala (Wouri); Garoua (Benoue)
oil terminal(s): Limboh Terminal

MILITARY AND SECURITY

Military branches: Cameroon Armed Forces (Forces Armees Camerounaises, FAC): Army (L'Armee de Terre), Navy (Marine Nationale Republique (MNR), includes naval infantry), Air Force (Armee de l'Air du Cameroun, AAC), Rapid Intervention Brigade, Fire Fighter Corps, Gendarmerie (2015)
Military service age and obligation: 18–23 years of age for male and female voluntary military service; no conscription; high school graduation required; service obligation 4 years; periodic government calls for volunteers (2012)
Military expenditures: 1.42% of GDP (2012)
1.37% of GDP (2011)
1.42% of GDP (2010)
country comparison to the world: 70

TRANSNATIONAL ISSUES

Disputes—international: Joint Border Commission with Nigeria reviewed 2002 ICJ ruling on the entire boundary and bilaterally resolved differences, including June 2006 Greentree Agreement that immediately ceded sovereignty of the Bakassi Peninsula to Cameroon with a full phase-out of Nigerian control and patriation of residents in 2008; Cameroon and Nigeria agreed on maritime delimitation in March 2008; sovereignty dispute between Equatorial Guinea and Cameroon over an island at the mouth of the Ntem River; only Nigeria and Cameroon have heeded the Lake Chad Commission's admonition to ratify the delimitation treaty, which also includes the Chad-Niger and Niger-Nigeria boundaries

Refugees and internally displaced persons: *refugees (country of origin):* 259,145 (Central African Republic); 65,103 (Nigeria) (2016)
IDPs: 190,591 (2016)

CANADA

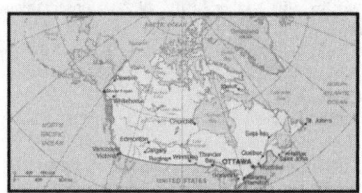

INTRODUCTION

Background: A land of vast distances and rich natural resources, Canada became a self-governing dominion in 1867, while retaining ties to the British crown. Economically and technologically, the nation has developed in parallel with the US, its neighbor to the south across the world's longest international border. Canada faces the political challenges of meeting public demands for quality improvements in health care, education, social services, and economic competitiveness, as well as responding to the particular concerns of predominantly francophone Quebec. Canada also aims to develop its diverse energy resources while maintaining its commitment to the environment.

GEOGRAPHY

Location: Northern North America, bordering the North Atlantic Ocean on the east, North Pacific Ocean on the west, and the Arctic Ocean on the north, north of the conterminous US

Geographic coordinates: 60 00 N, 95 00 W

Map references: North America
Area: *total:* 9,984,670 sq km
land: 9,093,507 sq km
water: 891,163 sq km
country comparison to the world: 2
Area—comparative: slightly larger than the US
Land boundaries: *total:* 8,893 km
border countries (1): US 8,893 km (includes 2,477 km with Alaska)
note: Canada is the world's largest country that borders only one country
Coastline: 202,080 km
Maritime claims: *territorial sea:* 12 nm
contiguous zone: 24 nm
exclusive economic zone: 200 nm
continental shelf: 200 nm or to the edge of the continental margin
Climate: varies from temperate in south to subarctic and arctic in north
Terrain: mostly plains with mountains in west, lowlands in southeast
Elevation: *mean elevation:* 487 m
elevation extremes: *lowest point:* Atlantic Ocean 0 m
highest point: Mount Logan 5,959 m
Natural resources: iron ore, nickel, zinc, copper, gold, lead, rare earth elements, molybdenum, potash, diamonds, silver, fish, timber, wildlife, coal, petroleum, natural gas, hydropower
Land use: *agricultural land:* 6.8%
arable land: 4.7%
permanent crops: 0.5%
permanent pasture: 1.6%
forest: 34.1%
other: 59.1% (2011 est.)
Irrigated land: 8,700 sq km (2012)
Total renewable water resources: 2,902 cu km (2011)
Freshwater withdrawal (domestic/industrial/agricultural): *total:* 42.2 cu m/yr (20%/70%/10%)
per capita: 1,589 cu m/yr (2010)
Natural hazards: continuous permafrost in north is a serious obstacle to development; cyclonic storms form east of the Rocky Mountains, a result of the mixing of air masses from the Arctic, Pacific, and North American interior, and produce most of the country's rain and snow east of the mountains
volcanism: the vast majority of volcanoes in Western Canada's Coast Mountains remain dormant

Environment—current issues: metal smelting, coal-burning utilities, and vehicle emissions impacting on agricultural and forest productivity; air pollution and resulting acid rain severely affecting lakes and damaging forests; ocean waters becoming contaminated due to agricultural, industrial, mining, and forestry activities
Environment—international agreements: *party to:* Air Pollution, Air Pollution-Nitrogen Oxides, Air Pollution-Persistent Organic Pollutants, Air Pollution-Sulfur 85, Air Pollution-Sulfur 94, Antarctic-Environmental Protocol, Antarctic-Marine Living Resources, Antarctic Seals, Antarctic Treaty, Biodiversity, Climate Change, Desertification, Endangered Species, Environmental Modification, Hazardous Wastes, Law of the Sea, Marine Dumping, Ozone Layer Protection, Ship Pollution, Tropical Timber 83, Tropical Timber 94, Wetlands
signed, but not ratified: Air Pollution-Volatile Organic Compounds, Marine Life Conservation

Geography—note: second-largest country in world (after Russia) and largest in the Americas; strategic location between Russia and US via north polar route; approximately 90% of the population is concentrated within 160 km (100 mi) of the US border; Canada has more fresh water than any other country and almost 9% of Canadian territory is water; Canada has at least 2 million and possibly over 3 million lakes—that is more than all other countries combined

PEOPLE AND SOCIETY

Nationality: *noun:* Canadian(s)
adjective: Canadian
Ethnic groups: Canadian 32.2%, English 19.8%, French 15.5%, Scottish 14.4%, Irish 13.8%, German 9.8%, Italian 4.5%, Chinese 4.5%, North American Indian 4.2%, other 50.9%

note: percentages add up to more than 100% because respondents were able to identify more than one ethnic origin (2011 est.)

Languages: English (official) 58.7%, French (official) 22%, Punjabi 1.4%, Italian 1.3%, Spanish 1.3%, German 1.3%, Cantonese 1.2%, Tagalog 1.2%, Arabic 1.1%, other 10.5% (2011 est.)

Religions: Catholic 39% (includes Roman Catholic 38.8%, other Catholic .2%), Protestant 20.3% (includes United Church 6.1%, Anglican 5%, Baptist 1.9%, Lutheran 1.5%, Pentecostal 1.5%, Presbyterian 1.4%, other Protestant 2.9%), Orthodox 1.6%, other Christian 6.3%, Muslim 3.2%, Hindu 1.5%, Sikh 1.4%, Buddhist 1.1%, Jewish 1%, other 0.6%, none 23.9% (2011 est.)
Population: 35,099,836 (July 2015 est.)
country comparison to the world: 39
Age structure: *0–14 years:* 15.46% (male 2,781,043/female 2,644,008)
15–24 years: 12.39% (male 2,236,425/female 2,111,681)
25–54 years: 40.69% (male 7,239,027/female 7,041,886)
55–64 years: 13.74% (male 2,389,423/female 2,433,621)
65 years and over: 17.73% (male 2,766,909/female 3,455,813) (2015 est.)
Dependency ratios: *total dependency ratio:* 47.3%
youth dependency ratio: 23.5%
elderly dependency ratio: 23.8%
potential support ratio: 4.2% (2015 est.)
Median age: *total:* 41.8 years
male: 40.6 years
female: 43.1 years (2015 est.)
country comparison to the world: 29
Population growth rate: 0.75% (2015 est.)
country comparison to the world: 146
Birth rate: 10.28 births/1,000 population (2015 est.)
country comparison to the world: 190
Death rate: 8.42 deaths/1,000 population (2015 est.)
country comparison to the world: 81
Net migration rate: 5.66 migrant(s)/1,000 population (2015 est.)
country comparison to the world: 22
Urbanization: *urban population:* 81.8% of total population (2015)
rate of urbanization: 1.22% annual rate of change (2010–15 est.)
Major urban areas—population: Toronto 5.993 million; Montreal 3.981 million; Vancouver 2.485 million; Calgary 1.337 million; OTTAWA (capital) 1.326 million; Edmonton 1.272 million (2015)
Sex ratio: *at birth:* 1.06 male(s)/female
0–14 years: 1.05 male(s)/female
15–24 years: 1.06 male(s)/female
25–54 years: 1.03 male(s)/female
55–64 years: 0.98 male(s)/female
65 years and over: 0.8 male(s)/female

total population: 0.98 male(s)/female (2015 est.)

Mother's mean age at first birth: 28.1 (2011 est.)

Maternal mortality rate: 7 deaths/100,000 live births (2015 est.)

country comparison to the world: 147

Infant mortality rate: *total:* 4.65 deaths/1,000 live births

male: 4.97 deaths/1,000 live births

female: 4.3 deaths/1,000 live births (2015 est.)

country comparison to the world: 179

Life expectancy at birth:

total population: 81.76 years

male: 79.15 years

female: 84.52 years (2015 est.)

country comparison to the world: 18

Total fertility rate: 1.59 children born/woman (2015 est.)

country comparison to the world: 184

Health expenditures: 10.9% of GDP (2013)

country comparison to the world: 15

Physicians density: 2.07 physicians/1,000 population (2010)

Hospital bed density: 2.7 beds/1,000 population (2010)

Drinking water source:

improved:

urban: 100% of population

rural: 99% of population

total: 99.8% of population

unimproved:

urban: 0% of population

rural: 1% of population

total: 0.2% of population (2015 est.)

Sanitation facility access:

improved:

urban: 100% of population

rural: 99% of population

total: 99.8% of population

unimproved:

urban: 0% of population

rural: 1% of population

total: 0.2% of population (2015 est.)

HIV/AIDS—adult prevalence rate: NA

HIV/AIDS—people living with HIV/AIDS: NA

HIV/AIDS—deaths: fewer than 400 (2013 est.)

country comparison to the world: 89

Obesity—adult prevalence rate: 30.1% (2014)

country comparison to the world: 48

Education expenditures: 5.3% of GDP (2011)

country comparison to the world: 62

Unemployment, youth ages 15–24: *total:* 13.5%

male: 15%

female: 11.9% (2014 est.)

country comparison to the world: 81

GOVERNMENT

Country name: *conventional long form:* none

conventional short form: Canada

etymology: the country name derives from the St. Lawrence Iroquoian word "kanata" meaning village or settlement

Government type: federal parliamentary democracy (Parliament of Canada) under a constitutional monarchy; a Common wealth realm

Capital: *name:* Ottawa

Geographic coordinates: 45 25 N, 75 42 W

time difference: UTC-5 (same time as Washington, DC, during Standard Time) daylight saving time: +1hr, begins second Sunday in March; ends first Sunday in November

note: Canada has six time zones

Administrative divisions: 10 provinces and 3 territories*; Alberta, British Columbia, Manitoba, New Brunswick, Newfoundland and Labrador, Northwest Territories*, Nova Scotia, Nunavut*, Ontario, Prince Edward Island, Quebec, Saskatchewan, Yukon*

Independence: 1 July 1867 (union of British North American colonies); 11 December 1931 (recognized by UK per Statute of Westminster)

National holiday: Canada Day, 1 July (1867)

Constitution: made up of unwritten and written acts, customs, judicial decisions, and traditions dating from 1763; the written part of the constitution consists of the Constitution Act of 29 March 1867, which created a federation of four provinces, and the Constitution Act of 17 April 1982; several amendments to the 1982 Constitution Act, last in 2011 (2016)

Legal system: common law system except in Quebec, where civil law based on the French civil code prevails

International law organization participation: accepts compulsory ICJ jurisdiction with reservations; accepts ICCt jurisdiction

Citizenship: *citizenship by birth:* yes

citizenship by descent: yes

dual citizenship recognized: yes

residency requirement for naturalization: 3 years

Suffrage: 18 years of age; universal

Executive branch: *head of state:* Queen ELIZABETH II (since 6 February 1952); represented by Governor General David JOHNSTON (since 1 October 2010)

head of government: Prime Minister Justin Pierre James TRUDEAU (Liberal Party) (since 4 November 2015)

cabinet: Federal Ministry chosen by the prime minister usually from among members of his own party sitting in Parliament

elections/appointments: the monarchy is hereditary; governor general appointed by the monarch on the advice of the prime minister for a 5-year term; following legislative elections, the leader of the majority party or majority coalition in the House of Commons generally designated prime minister by the governor general

Legislative branch: *description:* bicameral Parliament or Parlement consists of the Senate or Senat (105 seats; members appointed by the governor general on the advice of the prime minister and can serve until age 75) and the House of Commons or Ch ambre des Communes (338 seats; members directly elected in single-seat constituencies by simple majority vote to serve a maximum of 4-year terms)

elections: House of Commons—last held on 19 October 2015 (next to be held in 2019)

election results: House of Commons—percent of vote by party—Liberal Party 39.5%, Conservative Party 31.9%, NDP 19.7%, Bloc Quebecois 4.7%, Greens 3.4%, other .8%; seats by party—Liberal Party 184, Conservative Party 99, NDP 44, Bloc Quebecois 10, Greens 1

Judicial branch: *highest court(s):* Supreme Court of Canada (consists of the chief justice and 8 judges); note—in 1949, Canada abolished all appeals beyond its Supreme Court to the Judicial Committee of the Privy Council (in London)

judge selection and term of office: chief justice and judges appointed by the prime minister in council; all judges appointed for life with mandatory retirement at age 75

subordinate courts: federal level: Federal Court of Appeal; Federal Court; Tax Court; federal administrative tribunals; courts martial; provincial/territorial: provincial superior, appeals, first instance, and specialized courts; in 1999, the Nunavut Court—a circuit court with the power of a superior court and the territorial courts—was established to serve isolated settlements

Political parties and leaders: Bloc Quebecois [Rheal FORTIN (interim leader)]

Conservative Party of Canada or CPC [Rona AMBROSE (interim leader)]

Green Party [Elizabeth MAY]

Liberal Party [Justin TRUDEAU]

New Democratic Party or NDP [Thomas MULCAIR]

Political pressure groups and leaders: *other:* agricultural sector; automobile industry; business groups; chemical industry; commercial banks; communications sector; energy industry; environmentalists; public administration groups; steel industry; trade unions

International organization participation: ADB (nonregional member), AfDB (nonregional member), APEC, Arctic Council, ARF, ASEAN (dialogue partner), Australia Group, BIS, C, CD, CDB, CE (observer), EAPC, EBRD, EITI (implementing country), FAO, FATF, G-7, G-8, G-10, G-20, IADB, IAEA, IBRD, ICAO, ICC (national committees), ICCt, ICRM, IDA, IEA, IFAD, IFC, IFRCS, IGAD (partners), IHO, ILO, IMF, IMO, IMSO, Interpol, IOC, IOM, IPU, ISO, ITSO, ITU, ITUC (NGOs), MIGA, MINUSTAH, MONUSCO, NAFTA, NATO, NEA, NSG, OAS, OECD, OIF, OPCW, OSCE, Pacific Alliance (observer), Paris Club, PCA, PIF (partner), UN, UNCTAD, UNESCO, UNFICYP, UNHCR, UNMISS, UNRWA, UNTSO, UPU, WCO, WFTU (NGOs), WHO, WIPO, WMO, WTO, ZC

Diplomatic representation in the US: *chief of mission:* Ambassador David Brookes MACNAUGHTON (since 2 March 2016)

chancery: 501 Pennsylvania Avenue NW, Washington, DC 20001

telephone: [1] (202) 682-1740

FAX: [1] (202) 682-7726

consulate(s) general: Atlanta, Boston, Chicago, Dallas, Denver, Detroit, Los Angeles, Miami,

Minneapolis, New York, San Francisco/Silicon Valley, Seattle

trade office(s): Houston, Palo Alto (CA), San Diego; note—there are trade offices in the Consulates General

Diplomatic representation from the US: *chief of mission:* Ambassador Bruce A. HEYMAN (since 8 April 2014)

embassy: 490 Sussex Drive, Ottawa, Ontario K1N 1G8

mailing address: P.O. Box 5000, Ogdensburg, NY 13669–0430; P.O. Box 866, Station B, Ottawa, Ontario K1P 5T1

telephone: [1] (613) 688-5335

FAX: [1] (613) 688-3082

consulate(s) general: Calgary, Halifax, Montreal, Quebec City, Toronto, Vancouver

Flag description: two vertical bands of red (hoist and fly side, half width) with white square between them; an 11-pointed red maple leaf is centered in the white square; the maple leaf has long been a Canadian symbol

National symbol(s): maple leaf, beaver; national colors: red, white

National anthem: *name:* "O Canada"

lyrics/music: Adolphe-Basile ROUTHIER [French], Robert Stanley WEIR [English]/Calixa LAVALLEE

note: adopted 1980; originally written in 1880, "O Canada" served as an unofficial anthem many years before its official adoption; the anthem has French and English versions whose lyrics differ; as a Commonwealth realm, in addition to the national anthem, "God Save the Queen" serves as the royal anthem (see United Kingdom)

ECONOMY

Economy—overview: As a high-tech industrial society in the trillion-dollar class, Canada resembles the US in its market-oriented economic system, pattern of production, and high living standards. Since World War II, the impressive growth of the manufacturing, mining, and service sectors has transformed the nation from a largely rural economy into one primarily industrial and urban. In addition, the country's petroleum sector is rapidly expanding, because Alberta's oil sands significantly boosted Canada's proven oil reserves. Canada now ranks third in the world in proved oil reserves behind Venezuela and Saudi Arabia and is the world's fifth -largest oil producer.

The 1989 US-Canada Free Trade Agreement and the 1994 North American Free Trade Agreement (which includes Mexico) touched off a dramatic increase in trade and economic integration with the US, its principal trading partner. Canada enjoys a substantial trade surplus with the US, which absorbs about three-fourths of Canadian merchandise exports each year. Canada is the US's largest foreign supplier of energy, including oil, gas, and electric power, and a top source of US uranium imports. Given its abundant natural resources, highly skilled labor force, and modern capital plant, Canada enjoyed solid economic growth from 1993 through 2007. Buffeted by the

global economic crisis, the economy dropped into a sharp recession in the final months of 2008, and Ottawa posted its first fiscal deficit in 2009 after 12 years of surplus. Canada's major banks, however, emerged from the financial crisis of 2008–09 among the strongest in the world, owing to the early intervention by the Bank of Canada and the financial sector's tradition of conservative lending practices and strong capitalization. Canada achieved marginal growth in 2010–15, despite the recent drop in oil prices.

GDP (purchasing power parity): $1.632 trillion (2015 est.)

$1.613 trillion (2014 est.)

$1.574 trillion (2013 est.)

note: data are in 2015 US dollars

country comparison to the world: 16

GDP (official exchange rate): $1.552 trillion (2015 est.)

GDP—real growth rate: 1.2% (2015 est.)

2.5% (2014 est.)

2.2% (2013 est.)

country comparison to the world: 163

GDP—per capita (PPP): $45,600 (2015 est.)

$45,400 (2014 est.)

$44,800 (2013 est.)

note: data are in 2015 US dollars

country comparison to the world: 32

Gross national saving: 20.5% of GDP (2015 est.)

22% of GDP (2014 est.)

21.5% of GDP (2013 est.)

country comparison to the world: 79

GDP—composition, by end use:

household consumption: 56.7%

government consumption: 21%

investment in fixed capital: 23.3%

investment in inventories: 0.3%

exports of goods and services: 32.2%

imports of goods and services: -33.5% (2015 est.)

GDP—composition, by sector of origin: *agriculture:* 1.6%

industry: 28.9%

services: 70.5% (2015 est.)

Agriculture—products: wheat, barley, oilseed, tobacco, fruits, vegetables; dairy products; fish; forest products

Industries: transportation equipment, chemicals, processed and unprocessed minerals, food products, wood and paper products, fish products, petroleum, natural gas

Industrial production growth rate: 2.3% (2015 est.)

country comparison to the world: 105

Labor force: 19.3 million (2015 est.)

country comparison to the world: 31

Labor force—by occupation: *agriculture:* 2%

manufacturing: 13%

construction: 6%

services: 76%

other: 3% (2006 est.)

Unemployment rate: 6.9% (2015 est.)

6.9% (2014 est.)

country comparison to the world: 80

Population below poverty line: 9.4%

note: this figure is the Low Income Cut-Off, a calculation that results in higher figures than found

in many comparable economies; Canada does not have an official poverty line (2008 est.)

Household income or consumption by percentage share: *lowest:* 10%: 2.6%

highest: 10%: 24.8% (2000)

Distribution of family income—Gini index: 32.1 (2005)

31.5 (1994)

country comparison to the world: 110

Budget: *revenues:* $585 billion

expenditures: $614.1 billion (2015 est.)

Taxes and other revenues: 37.2% of GDP (2015 est.)

country comparison to the world: 48

Budget surplus (+) or deficit (-): -1.9% of GDP (2015 est.)

country comparison to the world: 70

Public debt: 95.4% of GDP (2015 est.)

94.8% of GDP (2014 est.)

note: figures are for gross general government debt, as opposed to net federal debt; gross general government debt includes both intragovernmental debt and the debt of public entities at the subnational level

country comparison to the world: 20

Fiscal year: 1 April—31 March

Inflation rate (consumer prices): 1.1% (2015 est.)

1.9% (2014 est.)

country comparison to the world: 83

Central bank discount rate: 1% (31 December 2010)

0.25% (31 December 2009)

country comparison to the world: 124

Commercial bank prime lending rate: 2.7% (31 December 2015 est.)

3% (31 December 2014 est.)

country comparison to the world: 172

Stock of narrow money: $579.9 billion (31 December 2015 est.)

$629.6 billion (31 December 2014 est.)

country comparison to the world: 9

Stock of broad money: $1.486 trillion (31 December 2014 est.)

$1.47 trillion (31 December 2013 est.)

country comparison to the world: 13

Stock of domestic credit: $2.714 trillion (31 December 2015 est.)

$2.97 trillion (31 December 2014 est.)

country comparison to the world: 9

Market value of publicly traded shares: $2.016 trillion (31 December 2012 est.)

$1.907 trillion (31 December 2011)

$2.16 trillion (31 December 2010 est.)

country comparison to the world: 7

Current account balance: -$51.38 billion (2015 est.)

-$40.59 billion (2014 est.)

country comparison to the world: 193

Exports: $428.3 billion (2015 est.)

$478.4 billion (2014 est.)

country comparison to the world: 13

Exports—commodities: motor vehicles and parts, industrial machinery, aircraft, telecommunications equipment; chemicals, plastics, fertilizers; wood pulp, timber, crude petroleum, natural gas, electricity, aluminum

Exports—partners: US 76.7% (2015)

Imports: $440.9 billion (2015 est.)
$473.8 billion (2014 est.)
country comparison to the world: 9

Imports—commodities: machinery and equipment, motor vehicles and parts, crude oil, chemicals, electricity, durable consumer goods

Imports—partners: US 53.1%, China 12.2%, Mexico 5.8% (2015)

Reserves of foreign exchange and gold: $74.7 billion (31 December 2014 est.)
$71.94 billion (31 December 2013 est.)
country comparison to the world: 30

Debt—external: $1.491 trillion (31 December 2014 est.)
$1.395 trillion (31 December 2013 est.)
country comparison to the world: 13

Stock of direct foreign investment—at home: $1.012 trillion (31 December 2015 est.)
$940.3 billion (31 December 2014 est.)
country comparison to the world: 10

Stock of direct foreign investment—abroad: $1.18 trillion (31 December 2015 est.)
$1.137 trillion (31 December 2014 est.)
country comparison to the world: 9

Exchange rates: Canadian dollars (CAD) per US dollar—
1.275 (2015 est.)
1.1047 (2014 est.)
1.0298 (2013 est.)
0.9992 (2012 est.)
0.9895 (2011 est.)

ENERGY

Electricity—production: 616.2 billion kWh (2014 est.)
country comparison to the world: 7

Electricity—consumption: 511 billion kWh (2014 est.)
country comparison to the world: 8

Electricity—exports: 58.4 billion kWh (2014 est.)
country comparison to the world: 4

Electricity—imports: 12.8 billion kWh (2014 est.)
country comparison to the world: 14

Electricity—installed generating capacity: 135 million kW (2012 est.)
country comparison to the world: 8

Electricity—from fossil fuels: 25.7% of total installed capacity (2012 est.)
country comparison to the world: 187

Electricity—from nuclear fuels: 10% of total installed capacity (2012 est.)
country comparison to the world: 19

Electricity—from hydroelectric plants: 55.8% of total installed capacity (2012 est.)
country comparison to the world: 41

Electricity—from other renewable sources: 8.3% of total installed capacity (2012 est.)
country comparison to the world: 45

Crude oil—production: 3.89 million bbl/day (2015 est.)
country comparison to the world: 5

Crude oil—exports: 2.9 million bbl/day (2014 est.)
country comparison to the world: 3

Crude oil—imports: 700,000 bbl/day (2014 est.)
country comparison to the world: 16

Crude oil—proved reserves: 171 billion bbl (1 January 2015 est.)
country comparison to the world: 3

Refined petroleum products—production: 1.894 million bbl/day (2013 est.)
country comparison to the world: 11

Refined petroleum products—consumption: 2.413 million bbl/day (2014 est.)
country comparison to the world: 9

Refined petroleum products—exports: 515,600 bbl/day (2013 est.)
country comparison to the world: 13

Refined petroleum products—imports: 230,100 bbl/day (2013 est.)
country comparison to the world: 29

Natural gas—production: 151.2 billion cu m (2014 est.)
country comparison to the world: 5

Natural gas—consumption: 104.4 billion cu m (2014 est.)
country comparison to the world: 7

Natural gas—exports: 77.96 billion cu m (2014 est.)
country comparison to the world: 5

Natural gas—imports: 21.89 billion cu m (2014 est.)
country comparison to the world: 15

Natural gas—proved reserves: 1.889 trillion cu m (1 January 2014 est.)
country comparison to the world: 18

Carbon dioxide emissions from consumption of energy: 550.8 million Mt (2012 est.)
country comparison to the world: 12

COMMUNICATIONS

Telephones—fixed lines: *total subscriptions:* 16.6 million
subscriptions per 100 inhabitants: 48 (2014 est.)
country comparison to the world: 17

Telephones—mobile cellular: *total:* 29.5 million
subscriptions per 100 inhabitants: 85 (2014 est.)
country comparison to the world: 44

Telephone system: *general assessment:* excellent service provided by modern technology
domestic: domestic satellite system with about 300 earth stations
international: country code—1; submarine cables provide links to the US and Europe; satellite earth stations—7 (5 Intelsat—4 Atlantic Ocean and 1 Pacific Ocean, and 2 Intersputnik—Atlantic Ocean region) (2011)

Broadcast media: 2 public TV broadcasting networks each with a large number of network affiliates; several private-commercial networks also with multiple network affiliates; overall, about 150 TV stations; multi-channel satellite and cable systems provide access to a wide range of stations including US stations; mix of public and commercial radio broadcasters with the Canadian Broadcasting Corporation (CBC), the public radio broadcaster, operating 4 radio networks, Radio Canada International, and radio services to indigenous populations in the north; roughly 2,000 licensed radio stations (2008)

Radio broadcast stations: AM 245, FM 582, shortwave 6 (2004)

Television broadcast stations: 148 (2007)

Internet country code: .ca

Internet hosts: 8.743 million (2012)
country comparison to the world: 14

Internet users: *total:* 32.4 million
percent of population: 92.9% (2014 est.)
country comparison to the world: 21

TRANSPORTATION

Airports: 1,467 (2013)
country comparison to the world: 4

Airports—with paved runways: *total:* 523
over 3,047 m: 21
2,438 to 3,047 m: 19
1,524 to 2,437 m: 147
914 to 1,523 m: 257
under 914 m: 79 (2013)

Airports—with unpaved runways: *total:* 944
1,524 to 2,437 m: 75
914 to 1,523 m: 385
under 914 m: 484 (2013)

Heliports: 26 (2013)

Pipelines: gas and liquid petroleum 100,000 km (2013)

Railways: *total:* 77,932 km
standard gauge: 77,932 km 1.435-m gauge (2014)
country comparison to the world: 4

Roadways: *total:* 1,042,300 km
paved: 415,600 km (includes 17,000 km of expressways)
unpaved: 626,700 km (2011)
country comparison to the world: 7

Waterways: 636 km (Saint Lawrence Seaway of 3,769 km, including the Saint Lawrence River of 3,058 km, shared with United States) (2011)
country comparison to the world: 77

Merchant marine: *total:* 181
by type: bulk carrier 62, cargo 15, carrier 1, chemical tanker 15, combination ore/oil 1, container 2, passenger 5, passenger/cargo 63, petroleum tanker 11, roll on/roll off 6
foreign-owned: 19 (Estonia 1, France 1, Netherlands 1, Norway 4, Sweden 2, US 10)
registered in other countries: 225 (Australia 5, Bahamas 96, Barbados 11, Cambodia 2, Cyprus 2, Honduras 1, Hong Kong 77, Liberia 2, Malta 5, Marshall Islands 8, Norway 1, Panama 6, Spain 4, Vanuatu 5) (2010)
country comparison to the world: 35

Ports and terminals: *major seaport(s):* Halifax, Saint John (New Brunswick), Vancouver river and lake port(s): Montreal, Quebec City, Sept-Isles (St. Lawrence); Fraser River Port (Fraser); Hamilton (Lake Ontario)
oil terminal(s): Lower Lakes terminal
dry bulk cargo port(s): Port-Cartier (iron ore and grain),
container port(s): Montreal (1,362,975), Vancouver (2,507,032)(2011)
LNG terminal(s) (import): Saint John

MILITARY AND SECURITY

Military branches: Canadian Forces: Canadian Army, Royal Canadian Navy, Royal Canadian Air Force, Canadian Joint Operations Command (2015)

Military service age and obligation: 17 years of age for voluntary male and female military service (with parental consent); 16 years of age for Reserve and Military College applicants; Canadian citizenship or permanent residence status required; maximum 34 years of age; service obligation 3–9 years (2012)

Military expenditures: 1% of GDP (2015)
1% of GDP (2014)
1% of GDP (2013)
1.24% of GDP (2012)
1.31% of GDP (2011)
country comparison to the world: 80

TRANSNATIONAL ISSUES

Disputes—international: managed maritime boundary disputes with the US at Dixon Entrance, Beaufort Sea, Strait of Juan de Fuca, and the Gulf of Maine, including the disputed Machias Seal Island and North Rock; Canada and the United States dispute how to divide the Beaufort Sea and the status of the Northwest Passage but continue to work cooperatively to survey the Arctic continental shelf; US works closely with Canada to intensify security measures for monitoring and controlling legal and illegal movement of people, transport, and commodities across the international border; sovereignty dispute with Denmark over Hans Island in the Kennedy Channel between Ellesmere Island and Greenland; commencing the collection of technical evidence for submission to the Commission on the Limits of the Continental Shelf in support of claims for continental shelf beyond 200 nm from its declared baselines in the Arctic, as stipulated in Article 76, paragraph 8, of the UN Convention on the Law of the Sea

Refugees and internally displaced persons: *refugees (country of origin):* 16,428 (Colombia); 13,231 (China); 10,745 (Sri Lanka); 8,613 (Pakistan); 8,422 (Haiti); 6,762 (Mexico) (2014)

Illicit drugs: illicit producer of cannabis for the domestic drug market and export to US; use of hydroponics technology permits growers to plant large quantities of high-quality marijuana indoors; increasing ecstasy production, some of which is destined for the US; vulnerable to narcotics money laundering because of its mature financial service sector

CAYMAN ISLANDS

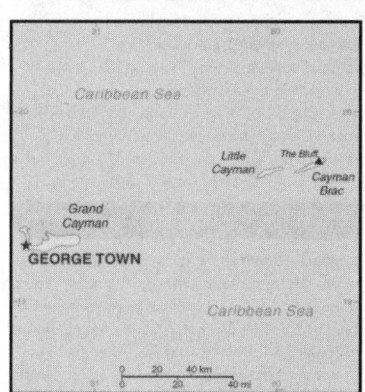

INTRODUCTION

Background: The Cayman Islands were colonized from Jamaica by the British during the 18th and 19th centuries and were administered by Jamaica after 1863. In 1959, the islands became a territory within the Federation of the West Indies. When the Federation dissolved in 1962, the Cayman Islands chose to remain a British dependency. The territory has transformed itself into a significant offshore financial center.

GEOGRAPHY

Location: Caribbean, three-island group (Grand Cayman, Cayman Brac, Little Cayman) in Caribbean Sea, 240 km south of Cuba and 268 km northwest of Jamaica

Geographic coordinates: 19 30 N, 80 30 W

Map references: Central America and the Caribbean

Area: *total:* 264 sq km
land: 264 sq km
water: 0 sq km
country comparison to the world: 211

Area—comparative: 1.5 times the size of Washington, DC

Land boundaries: 0 km

Coastline: 160 km

Maritime claims: *territorial sea:* 12 nm
exclusive fishing zone: 200 nm

Climate: tropical marine; warm, rainy summers (May to October) and cool, relatively dry winters (November to April)

Terrain: low-lying limestone base surrounded by coral reefs

Elevation: *mean elevation:* NA

elevation extremes: *lowest point:* Caribbean Sea 0 m
highest point: The Bluff on Cayman Brac 43 m

Natural resources: fish, climate and beaches that foster tourism

Land use: *agricultural land:* 11.2%
arable land: 0.8%
permanent crops: 2.1%
permanent pasture: 8.3%
forest: 52.9%
other: 35.9% (2011 est.)

Irrigated land: NA

Natural hazards: hurricanes (July to November)

Environment—current issues: no natural freshwater resources; drinking water supplies are met by reverse osmosis desalination plants

Geography—note: important location between Cuba and Central America

PEOPLE AND SOCIETY

Nationality: *noun:* Caymanian(s)
adjective: Caymanian

Ethnic groups: mixed 40%, white 20%, black 20%, expatriates of various ethnic groups 20%

Languages: English (official) 90.9%, Spanish 4%, Filipino 3.3%, other 1.7%, unspecified 0.1% (2010 est.)

Religions: Protestant 67.8% (includes Church of God 22.6%, Seventh Day Adventist 9.4%, Presbyterian/United Church 8.6%, Baptist 8.3%, Pentecostal 7.1%, non-denominational 5.3%, Anglican 4.1%, Wesleyan Holiness 2.4%), Roman Catholic 14.1%, Jehovah's Witness 1.1%, other 7%, none 9.3%, unspecified 0.7% (2010 est.)

Population: 56,092 (July 2013 est.)
note: most of the population lives on Grand Cayman (July 2015 est.)
country comparison to the world: 207

Age structure: *0–14 years:* 18.26% (male 5,158/female 5,084)
15–24 years: 12.76% (male 3,542/female 3,615)
25–54 years: 43.49% (male 11,894/female 12,500)
55–64 years: 13.93% (male 3,712/female 4,104)
65 years and over: 11.56% (male 3,047/female 3,436) (2015 est.)

Median age: *total:* 39.7 years
male: 39 years
female: 40.3 years (2015 est.)
country comparison to the world: 47

Population growth rate: 2.1% (2015 est.)
country comparison to the world: 46

Birth rate: 12.11 births/1,000 population (2015 est.)
country comparison to the world: 164

Death rate: 5.53 deaths/1,000 population (2015 est.)
country comparison to the world: 175

Net migration rate: 14.4 migrant(s)/1,000 population
note: major destination for Cubans trying to migrate to the US (2015 est.)
country comparison to the world: 4

Urbanization: *urban population:* 100% of total population (2015)
rate of urbanization: 1.54% annual rate of change (2010–15 est.)

Major urban areas—population: GEORGE TOWN (capital) 31,000 (2014)

Sex ratio: *at birth:* 1.02 male(s)/female
0–14 years: 1.02 male(s)/female

15–24 years: 0.98 male(s)/female
25–54 years: 0.95 male(s)/female
55–64 years: 0.9 male(s)/female
65 years and over: 0.89 male(s)/female
total population: 0.95 male(s)/female (2015 est.)
Infant mortality rate: *total:* 6.08 deaths/1,000 live births
male: 6.95 deaths/1,000 live births
female: 5.2 deaths/1,000 live births (2015 est.)
country comparison to the world: 165

Life expectancy at birth:
total population: 81.13 years
male: 78.43 years
female: 83.88 years (2015 est.)
country comparison to the world: 26
Total fertility rate: 1.86 children born/woman (2015 est.)
country comparison to the world: 144
Drinking water source:
improved:
urban: 97.4% of population
rural: NA
total: 97.4% of population
unimproved:
urban: 2.6% of population
rural: NA
total: 2.6% of population (2015 est.)
Sanitation facility access:
improved:
urban: 95.6% of population
total: 95.6% of population
unimproved:
urban: 4.4% of population
total: 4.4% of population (2015 est.)

HIV/AIDS—adult prevalence rate: NA

HIV/AIDS—people living with HIV/AIDS: NA

HIV/AIDS—deaths: NA
Education expenditures: NA
Literacy: *definition:* age 15 and over has ever attended school
total population: 98.9%
male: 98.7%
female: 99% (2007 est.)
Unemployment, youth ages 15–24: *total:* 24.2%
male: 32%
female: 16.6% (2013 est.)
country comparison to the world: 86

GOVERNMENT

Country name: *conventional long form:* none
conventional short form: Cayman Islands
etymology: the islands' name comes from the native Carib word "caiman," describing the marine crocodiles living there
Dependency status: overseas territory of the UK
Government type: parliamentary democracy (Legislative Assembly); self-governing overseas territory of the UK
Capital: *name:* George Town (on Grand Cayman)
Geographic coordinates: 19 18 N, 81 23 W
time difference: UTC-5 (same time as Washington, DC, during Standard Time) daylight saving time: a decision has been made to introduce DST in the archipelago for the first time beginning in 2016; a date for implementation is pending,

though it seems likely it will match the date used in the US and Canada
Administrative divisions: 6 districts; Bodden Town, Cayman Brac and Little Cayman, East End, George Town, North Side, West Bay
Independence: none (overseas territory of the UK)
National holiday: Constitution Day, first Monday in July
Constitution: several previous; latest approved 10 June 2009, entered into force 6 November 2009 (The Cayman Islands Constitution Order 2009) (2016)
Legal system: English common law and local statutes
Citizenship: see United Kingdom
Suffrage: 18 years of age; universal
Executive branch: *chief of state:* Queen ELIZABETH II (since 6 February 1952); represented by Governor Helen KILPATRICK (since 6 September 2013)
head of government: Premier Alden MCLAUGHLIN (since 29 May 2013)
cabinet: The Cabinet (6 members selected from the Legislative Assembly and appointed by the governor on the advice of the premier)
elections/appointments: the monarchy is hereditary; governor appointed by the monarch; following legislative elections, the leader of the majority party or majority coalition appointed premier by the governor
Legislative branch: *description:* unicameral Legislative Assembly (20 seats; 18 members directly elected by majority vote and 2 ex officio members—the deputy governor and attorney general—appointed by the governor; members serve 4-year terms)
elections: last held on 22 May 2013 (next to be held in 2017)
election results: percent of vote by party—PPM 36.1%, UDP 27.8%, C4C 18.6%, PNA 5.7%, independent 11.9%; seats by party—PPM 9, UDP 3, C4C 3, PNA 1, independent 2
Judicial branch: *highest resident court(s):* Court of Appeal (consists of the court president and at least 2 judges); Grand Court (consists of the court president and at least 2 judges); note—appeals beyond the Court of Appeal are heard by the Judicial Committee of the Privy Council (in London)
judge selection and term of office: Court of Appeal and Grand Court judges appointed by the governor on the advice of the Judicial and Legal Services Commission, an 8-member independent body consisting of governor appointees, Court of Appeal president, and attorneys; Court of Appeal judges' tenure based on their individual instruments of appointment; Grand Court judges normally appointed until retirement at age 65 but can be extended until age 70
subordinate courts: Summary Court
Political parties and leaders: People's Progressive Movement or PPM [Kurt TIBBETTS] United Democratic Party or UDP [McKeeva BUSH]
Political pressure groups and leaders: Coalition for Cayman or
C4C National People's Alliance or PNA
National Trust

other: environmentalists

International organization participation: Caricom (associate), CDB, Interpol (subbureau), IOC, UNESCO (associate), UPU

Diplomatic representation in the US: none (overseas territory of the UK)

Diplomatic representation from the US: none (overseas territory of the UK); consular services provided through the US Embassy in Jamaica

Flag description: a blue field with the flag of the UK in the upper hoist-side quadrant and the Caymanian coat of arms centered on the outer half of the flag; the coat of arms includes a crest with a pineapple, representing the connection with Jamaica, and a turtle, representing Cayman's seafaring tradition, above a shield bearing a golden lion, symbolizing Great Britain, below which are three green stars (representing the three islands) surmounting white and blue wavy lines representing the sea and a scroll at the bottom bearing the motto HE HATH FOUNDED IT UPON THE SEAS

National symbol(s): green sea turtle
National anthem: *name:* "Beloved Isle Cayman"
lyrics/music: Leila E. ROSS
note: adopted 1993; served as an unofficial anthem since 1930; as a territory of the United Kingdom, in addition to the local anthem, "God Save the Queen" is official (see United Kingdom)

ECONOMY

Economy—overview: With no direct taxation, the islands are a thriving offshore financial center. More than 93,000 companies were registered in the Cayman Islands as of 2008, including almost 300 banks, 800 insurers, and 10,000 mutual funds. A stock exchange was opened in 1997. Nearly 90% of the islands' food and consumer goods must be imported. The Caymanians enjoy a standard of living comparable to that of Switzerland. Tourism is also a mainstay, accounting for about 70% of GDP and 75% of foreign currency earnings. The tourist industry is aimed at the luxury market and caters mainly to visitors from North America. Total tourist arrivals exceeded 1.9 million in 2008, with about half from the US.
GDP (purchasing power parity): $2.507 billion (2014 est.)
$2.465 billion (2013 est.)
$2.435 billion (2012 est.)
country comparison to the world: 191

GDP (official exchange rate): $2.25 billion (2008 est.)
GDP—real growth rate: 1.7% (2014 est.)
1.2% (2013 est.)
1.6% (2012 est.)
country comparison to the world: 144
GDP—per capita (PPP): $43,800 (2004 est.)
country comparison to the world: 34
GDP—composition, by end use:
household consumption: 63.8%
government consumption: 14.8%
investment in fixed capital: 22.1%
investment in inventories: 0%
exports of goods and services: 49.3%

imports of goods and services: -50% (2015 est.)

GDP—composition, by sector of origin: *agriculture:* 0.3%

industry: 28.2%

services: 71.5% (2015 est.)

Agriculture—products: vegetables, fruit; livestock; turtle farming

Industries: tourism, banking, insurance and finance, construction, construction materials, furniture

Industrial production growth rate: 2% (2015 est.)

country comparison to the world: 113

Labor force: 39,000

note: nearly 55% are non-nationals (2007 est.)

country comparison to the world: 197

Labor force—by occupation: *agriculture:* 1.9%

industry: 19.1%

services: 79% (2008 est.)

Unemployment rate: 4% (2008)

4.4% (2004)

country comparison to the world: 35

Population below poverty line: NA%

Household income or consumption by percentage share: *lowest:* 10%: NA%

highest: 10%: NA%

Budget: *revenues:* $811.8 million

expenditures: $771 million (2015 est.)

Taxes and other revenues: 36.1% of GDP (2015 est.)

country comparison to the world: 52

Budget surplus (+) or deficit (-): 1.8% of GDP (2015 est.)

country comparison to the world: 16

Fiscal year: 1 April—31 March

Inflation rate (consumer prices): 1.7% (2015 est.)

1% (2014 est.)

country comparison to the world: 106

Stock of narrow money: $334.3 million (31 December 2008)

country comparison to the world: 171

Stock of broad money: $5.564 billion (31 December 2008 est.)

country comparison to the world: 127

Market value of publicly traded shares: $NA

$183.5 million (31 December 2007)

$188.4 million (31 December 2006)

Exports: $14.7 million (2015 est.) $15.2 million (2014 est.)

country comparison to the world: 215

Exports—commodities: turtle products, manufactured consumer goods

Imports: $707.4 million (2015 est.) $705.3 million (2014 est.)

country comparison to the world: 189

Imports—commodities: foodstuffs, manufactured goods, fuels

Stock of direct foreign investment—at home: $NA

Stock of direct foreign investment—abroad: $NA

Exchange rates: Caymanian dollars (KYD) per US dollar—

0.83 (2015 est.)

0.83 (2014 est.)

0.83 (2013 est.)

0.83 (2012 est.)

0.83 (2011 est.)

ENERGY

Electricity—production: 587 million kWh (2012 est.)

country comparison to the world: 160

Electricity—consumption: 545.9 million kWh (2012 est.)

country comparison to the world: 171

Electricity—exports: 0 kWh (2013 est.)

country comparison to the world: 122

Electricity—imports: 0 kWh (2013 est.)

country comparison to the world: 132

Electricity—installed generating capacity: 150,000 kW (2012 est.)

country comparison to the world: 164

Electricity—from fossil fuels: 100% of total installed capacity (2012 est.)

country comparison to the world: 9

Electricity—from nuclear fuels: 0% of total installed capacity (2012 est.)

country comparison to the world: 68

Electricity—from hydroelectric plants: 0% of total installed capacity (2012 est.)

country comparison to the world: 166

Electricity—from other renewable sources: 0% of total installed capacity (2012 est.)

country comparison to the world: 168

Crude oil—production: 0 bbl/day (2014 est.)

country comparison to the world: 118

Crude oil—exports: 0 bbl/day (2012 est.)

country comparison to the world: 110

Crude oil—imports: 0 bbl/day (2012 est.)

country comparison to the world: 173

Crude oil—proved reserves: 0 bbl (1 January 2015 est.)

country comparison to the world: 117

Refined petroleum products—production: 0 bbl/day (2012 est.)

country comparison to the world: 167

Refined petroleum products—consumption: 3,700 bbl/day (2013 est.)

country comparison to the world: 177

Refined petroleum products—exports: 0 bbl/day (2012 est.)

country comparison to the world: 168

Refined petroleum products—imports: 3,730 bbl/day (2012 est.)

country comparison to the world: 169

Natural gas—production: 0 cu m (2013 est.)

country comparison to the world: 171

Natural gas—consumption: 0 cu m (2013 est.)

country comparison to the world: 130

Natural gas—exports: 0 cu m (2013 est.)

country comparison to the world: 79

Natural gas—imports: 0 cu m (2013 est.)

country comparison to the world: 178

Natural gas—proved reserves: 0 cu m (1 January 2014 est.)

country comparison to the world: 124

Carbon dioxide emissions from consumption of energy: 473,000 Mt (2012 est.)

country comparison to the world: 181

COMMUNICATIONS

Telephones—fixed lines: *total* subscriptions: 32,900

subscriptions per 100 inhabitants: 60 (2014 est.)

country comparison to the world: 170

Telephones—mobile cellular: *total:* 91,100

subscriptions per 100 inhabitants: 166 (2014 est.)

country comparison to the world: 193

Telephone system: *general assessment:* reasonably good overall telephone system with a high fixed-line teledensity

domestic: liberalization of telecom market in 2003; introduction of competition in the mobile-cellular market in 2004

international: country code—1-345; landing points for the Maya-1, Eastern Caribbean Fiber System (ECFS), and the Cayman-Jamaica Fiber System submarine cables that provide links to the US and parts of Central and South America; satellite earth station—1 Intelsat (Atlantic Ocean) (2011)

Broadcast media: 4 TV stations; cable and satellite subscription services offer a variety of international programming; government-owned Radio Cayman operates 2 networks broadcasting on 5 stations; 10 privately owned radio stations operate alongside Radio Cayman (2007)

Radio broadcast stations: AM 1, FM 14, shortwave 0 (2009)

Television broadcast stations: 4 with cable system (2004)

Internet country code: .ky

Internet hosts: 23,472 (2012)

country comparison to the world: 114

Internet users: *total:* 43,600

percent of population: 79.4% (2014 est.)

country comparison to the world: 189

TRANSPORTATION

Airports: 3 (2013)

country comparison to the world: 196

Airports—with paved runways: *total:* 31,524 to 2,437 m: 2

914 to 1,523 m: 1 (2013)

Airports—with unpaved runways: *total:* 1914 to 1,523 m: 1 (2012)

Roadways: *total:* 785 km

paved: 785 km (2007)

country comparison to the world: 189

Merchant marine: *total:* 116

by type: bulk carrier 19, cargo 3, chemical tanker 61, liquefied gas 1, passenger 1, petroleum tanker 5, refrigerated cargo 10, vehicle carrier 16

foreign-owned: 102 (Germany 3, Greece 9, Italy 7, Japan 23, Switzerland 1, UK 2, US 57) (2010)

country comparison to the world: 46

Ports and terminals: *major seaport(s):* Cayman Brac, George Town

MILITARY AND SECURITY

Military branches: no regular military forces; Royal Cayman Islands Police Force (2012)

Military—note: defense is the responsibility of the UK

TRANSNATIONAL ISSUES

Disputes—international: none

Illicit drugs: major offshore financial center; vulnerable to drug transshipment to the US and Europe (2008)

CENTRAL AFRICAN REPUBLIC

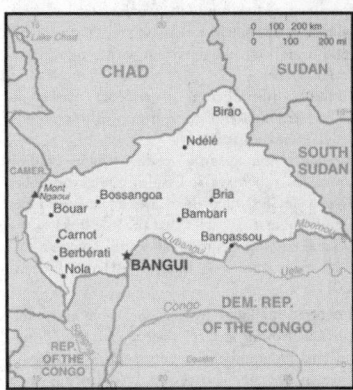

INTRODUCTION

Background: The former French colony of Ubangi-Shari became the Central African Republic upon independence in 1960. After three tumultuous decades of misrule—mostly by military governments—civilian rule was established in 1993 but lasted only a decade. In March 2003, President Ange-Felix PATASSE was deposed in a military coup led by General Francois BOZIZE, who established a transitional government. Elections held in 2005 affirmed General BOZIZE as president; he was reelected in 2011 in voting widely viewed as flawed. The government still lacks full control of the countryside, where lawlessness persists. The militant group, Lord's Resistance Army, continues to destabilize southeastern Central African Republic, and several rebel groups joined together in early December 2012 to launch a series of attacks that left them in control of numerous towns in the northern and central parts of the country. The rebels—unhappy with BOZIZE's government—participated in peace talks in early January 2013 which resulted in a coalition government including the rebellion's leadership. In March 2013, the coalition government dissolved, rebels seized the capital, and President BOZIZE fled the country. Rebel leader Michel DJOTODIA assumed the presidency and the following month established a National Transitional Council (CNT). In January 2014, the CNT elected Catherine SAMBA-PANZA as interim president. Elections completed in March 2016 installed independent candidate Faustin-Archange TOUADERA as president.

GEOGRAPHY

Location: Central Africa, north of Democratic Republic of the Congo

Geographic coordinates: 7 00 N, 21 00 E

Map references: Africa

Area: *total:* 622,984 sq km
land: 622,984 sq km
water: 0 sq km

country comparison to the world: 45

Area—comparative: slightly smaller than Texas

Land boundaries: *total:* 5,920 km
border countries (6): Cameroon 901 km, Chad 1,556 km, Democratic Republic of the Congo 1,747 km, Republic of the Congo 487 km, South Sudan 1,055 km, Sudan 174 km

Coastline: 0 km (landlocked)

Maritime claims: none (landlocked)

Climate: tropical; hot, dry winters; mild to hot, wet summers

Terrain: vast, flat to rolling plateau; scattered hills in northeast and southwest

Elevation: *mean elevation:* 635 m

elevation extremes: lowest point: Oubangui River 335 m

highest point: Mont Ngaoui 1,420 m

Natural resources: diamonds, uranium, timber, gold, oil, hydropower

Land use: *agricultural land:* 8.1%
arable land: 2.9%
permanent crops: 0.1%
permanent pasture: 5.1%
forest: 36.2%
other: 55.7% (2011 est.)

Irrigated land: 10 sq km (2012)

Total renewable water resources: 144.4 cu km (2011)

Freshwater withdrawal (domestic/industrial/agricultural): *total:* 0.07 cu m/yr (83%/17%/1%)
per capita: 17.42 cu m/yr (2005)

Natural hazards: hot, dry, dusty harmattan winds affect northern areas; floods are common

Environment—current issues: tap water is not potable; poaching has diminished the country's reputation as one of the last great wildlife refuges; desertification; deforestation

Environment—international agreements: *party to:* Biodiversity, Climate Change, Climate Change-Kyoto Protocol, Desertification, Endangered Species, Hazardous Wastes, Ozone Layer Protection, Tropical Timber 94, Wetlands
signed, but not ratified: Law of the Sea

Geography—note: landlocked; almost the precise center of Africa

PEOPLE AND SOCIETY

Nationality: *noun:* Central African(s)
adjective: Central African

Ethnic groups: Baya 33%, Banda 27%, Mandjia 13%, Sara 10%, Mboum 7%, M'Baka 4%, Yakoma 4%, other 2%

Languages: French (official), Sangho (lingua franca and national language), tribal languages

Religions: indigenous beliefs 35%, Protestant 25%, Roman Catholic 25%, Muslim 15%
note: animistic beliefs and practices strongly influence the Christian majority

Population: 5,391,539

note: estimates for this country explicitly take into account the effects of excess mortality due to AIDS; this can result in lower life expectancy, higher infant mortality, higher death rates, lower population growth rates, and changes in the distribution of population by age and sex than would otherwise be expected (July 2015 est.)

country comparison to the world: 119

Age structure: *0–14 years:* 40.43% (male 1,095,968/female 1,083,705)
15–24 years: 20.06% (male 543,491/female 537,804)
25–54 years: 32.02% (male 863,314/female 862,916)
55–64 years: 3.98% (male 96,377/female 118,278)
65 years and over: 3.52% (male 74,192/female 115,494) (2015 est.)

Dependency ratios: *total dependency ratio:* 75.2%
youth dependency ratio: 68.4%
elderly dependency ratio: 6.8%
potential support ratio: 14.8% (2015 est.)

Median age: *total:* 19.5 years
male: 19.2 years
female: 19.9 years (2015 est.)
country comparison to the world: 195

Population growth rate: 2.13% (2015 est.)
country comparison to the world: 45

Birth rate: 35.08 births/1,000 population (2015 est.)
country comparison to the world: 22

Death rate: 13.8 deaths/1,000 population (2015 est.)
country comparison to the world: 10

Net migration rate: 0 migrant(s)/1,000 population (2015 est.)
country comparison to the world: 102

Urbanization:
urban population: 40% of total population (2015)
rate of urbanization: 2.59% annual rate of change (2010–15 est.)

Major urban areas—population: BANGUI (capital) 794,000 (2015)

Sex ratio: *at birth:* 1.03 male(s)/female
0–14 years: 1.01 male(s)/female
15–24 years: 1.01 male(s)/female
25–54 years: 1 male(s)/female
55–64 years: 0.82 male(s)/female
65 years and over: 0.64 male(s)/female
total population: 0.98 male(s)/female (2015 est.)

Maternal mortality rate: 882 deaths/100,000 live births (2015 est.)
country comparison to the world: 4

Infant mortality rate: *total:* 90.63 deaths/1,000 live births
male: 98.24 deaths/1,000 live births
female: 82.79 deaths/1,000 live births (2015 est.)
country comparison to the world: 4

Life expectancy at birth:
total population: 51.81 years
male: 50.5 years

female: 53.16 years (2015 est.)
country comparison to the world: 219
Total fertility rate: 4.41 children born/woman (2015 est.)
country comparison to the world: 31
Contraceptive prevalence rate: 15.2% (2010/11)
Health expenditures: 3.9% of GDP (2013)
country comparison to the world: 168
Physicians density: 0.05 physicians/1,000 population (2009)
Hospital bed density: 1 beds/1,000 population (2011)
Drinking water source:
improved:
urban: 89.6% of population
rural: 54.4% of population
total: 68.5% of population
unimproved:
urban: 10.4% of population
rural: 45.6% of population
total: 31.5% of population (2015 est.)
Sanitation facility access:
improved:
urban: 43.6% of population
rural: 7.2% of population
total: 21.8% of population
unimproved:
urban: 56.4% of population
rural: 92.8% of population
total: 78.2% of population (2015 est.)
HIV/AIDS—adult prevalence rate: 4.25% (2014 est.)
country comparison to the world: 15
HIV/AIDS—people living with HIV/AIDS: 135,400 (2014 est.)
country comparison to the world: 34
HIV/AIDS—deaths: 9,900 (2014 est.)
country comparison to the world: 24
Major infectious diseases: *degree of risk:* very high
food or waterborne diseases: bacterial and protozoal diarrhea, hepatitis A and E, and typhoid fever
vectorborne diseases: malaria and dengue fever
respiratory disease: meningococcal meningitis
water contact disease: schistosomiasis
animal contact disease: rabies (2013)
Obesity—adult prevalence rate: 4.4% (2014)
country comparison to the world: 175
Children under the age of 5 years underweight: 23.5% (2011)
country comparison to the world: 26
Education expenditures: 1.2% of GDP (2011)
country comparison to the world: 171
Literacy: *definition:* age 15 and over can read and write
total population: 36.8%
male: 50.7%
female: 24.4% (2015 est.)
School life expectancy (primary to tertiary education): *total:* 7 years
male: 8 years
female: 6 years (2012)
Child labor—children ages 5–14: *total number:* 532,518
percentage: 47% (2006 est.)

GOVERNMENT

Country name: *conventional long form:* Central African Republic
conventional short form: none
local long form: Republique Centrafricaine
local short form: none
former: Ubangi-Shari, Central African Empire
abbreviation: CAR
etymology: self-descriptive name specifying the country's location on the continent; "Africa" is derived from the Roman designation of the area corresponding to present-day Tunisia "Africa terra, "which meant "Land of the Afri" (the tribe resident in that area), but which eventually came to mean the entire continent
Government type: presidential republic
Capital: *name:* Bangui
Geographic coordinates: 4 22 N, 18 35 E
time difference: UTC + 1 (6 hours ahead of Washington, DC, during Standard Time)
Administrative divisions: 14 prefectures (prefectures, singular—prefecture), 2 economic prefectures* (prefectures economiques, singular—prefecture economique), and 1 commune**; Bamingui-Bangoran, Bangui**, Basse-Kotto, Haute-Kotto, Haut-Mbomou, Kemo, Lobaye, Mambere-Kadei, Mbomou, Nana-Grebizi*, Nana-Mambere, Ombella-Mpoko, Ouaka, Ouham, Ouham-Pende, Sangha-Mbaere*, Vakaga
Independence: 13 August 1960 (from France)
National holiday: Republic Day, 1 December (1958)
Constitution: several previous; latest adopted by referendum in December 2015 (2016)
Legal system: civil law system based on the French model
International law organization participation: has not submitted an ICJ jurisdiction declaration; accepts ICCt jurisdiction
Citizenship: *citizenship by birth:* no
citizenship by descent only: least one parent must be a citizen of the Central African Republic
dual citizenship recognized: yes
residency requirement for naturalization: 35 years
Suffrage: 18 years of age; universal
Executive branch: *chief of state:* President Faustin-Archange TOUADERA (since 30 March 2016)
head of government: Prime Minister Simplice SARANDJI (since 2 April 2016)
cabinet: Council of Ministers appointed by the president
elections/appointments: under the new constitution, the president is elected by universal direct suffrage for a period of 5 years renewable for a second term; last election was held 20 February 2016 (next to be held April 2021)
election results: First round held on 30 December 2015, percent of vote—Anicet-Georges DOLOGUELE (URCA) 23.7%, Faustin-Archange TOUADERA (independent) 19.1%, Desire KOLINGBA (RDC) 12.0%, Martin ZIGUELE (MLPC) 11.4%, other 33.8%; second round held

on 20 February 2016, percent of vote -Faustin-Archange TOUADERA (independent) 62.7%, Anicet-Georges DOLOGUELE (URCA) 37.3%
note: rebel forces seized the capital in March 2013, forcing former President BOZIZE to flee the country; Interim President Michel DJOTODIA assumed the presidency, reinstated the prime minister, and established a National Transitional Council (CNT) in April 2013; the NTC elected Catherine SAMBA-PANZA interim president in January 2014 to serve until February 2015 when new elections were to be held; her term was extended because instability delayed new elections and the transition did not take place until the end of March 2016
Legislative branch: *description:* unicameral National Assembly or Assemblee Nationale (105 seats; members directly elected in single-seat constituencies by absolute majority vote with a second round if needed; members serve 5-year terms)
elections: last held on 23 January 2011 and 27 March 2011 (first round of elections is scheduled for 27 December 2015)
election results: percent of vote by party—NA; seats by party—KNK 61, Presidential Majority 11, independent 26, other 2; note—information on 5 seats is unavailable
Judicial branch: *highest court(s):* Supreme Court (consists of NA judges); Constitutional Court (consists of 9 judges, at least 3 of which are women)
judge selection and term of office: Supreme Court judges appointed by the president; Constitutional Court judge appointments—2 by the president, 1 by the speaker of the National Assembly, 2 elected by their peers, 2 are advocates elected by their peers, and 2 are law professors elected by their peers; judges serve 7-year non-renewable terms
subordinate courts: high courts; magistrates' courts
Political parties and leaders: Action Party for Development or PAD
Alliance for Democracy and Progress or ADP [Clement BELIBANGA]
Central African Democratic Rally or RDC [Desire Nzanga KOLINGBA]
Movement for Democracy and Development or MDD [Louis PAPENIAH]
Movement for the Liberation of the Central African People or MLPC [Martin ZIGUELE]
National Convergence (also known as Kwa Na Kwa) or KNK [Francois BOZIZE]
New Alliance for Progress or NAP [Jean-Jacques DEMAFOUTH]
Social Democratic Party or PSD [Enoch LAKOUE]
Union for Central African Renewal or URCA [Anicet-Georges DOLOGUELE]
International organization participation: ACP, AfDB, AU, BDEAC, CEMAC, EITI (compliant country) (suspended), FAO, FZ, G-77, IAEA, IBRD, ICAO, ICCt, ICRM, IDA, IFAD, IFC, IFRCS, ILO, IMF, Interpol, IOC, IOM, ITSO, ITU, ITUC (NGOs), MIGA, NAM, OIC (observer), OIF, OPCW, UN, UNCTAD,

UNESCO, UNIDO, UNWTO, UPU, WCO, WHO, WIPO, WMO, WTO

Diplomatic representation in the US: *chief of mission:* Ambassador Stanislas MOUSSA-KEMBE (since 24 August 2009)

chancery: 2704 Ontario Road NW, Washington, DC 20009

telephone: [1] (202) 483-7800

FAX: [1] (202) 332-9893

Diplomatic representation from the US: *chief of mission:* Ambassador Jeffrey HAWKINS (30 October 2015)

embassy: Avenue David Dacko, Bangui

mailing address: B. P. 924, Bangui

telephone: [236] 21 61 02 00

FAX: [236] 21 61 44 94

note: the embassy suspended operations in December, 2012; resumed limited operations on 15 Septermber 2014

Flag description: four equal horizontal bands of blue (top), white, green, and yellow with a vertical red band in center; a yellow five-pointed star to the hoist side of the blue band; banner combines the Pan-African and French flag colors; red symbolizes the blood spilled in the struggle for independence, blue represents the sky and freedom, white peace and dignity, green hope and faith, and yellow tolerance; the star represents aspiration towards a vibrant future

National symbol(s): elephant; national colors: blue, white, green, yellow, red

National anthem: *name:* "Le Renaissance" (The Renaissance)

lyrics/music: Barthelemy BOGANDA/Herbert PEPPER

note: adopted 1960; Barthelemy BOGANDA wrote the anthem's lyrics and was the first prime minister of the autonomous French territory

ECONOMY

Economy—overview: Subsistence agriculture, together with forestry and mining, remains the backbone of the economy of the Central African Republic (CAR), with about 60% of the population living in outlying areas. The agricultural sector generates more than half of GDP. Timber and diamonds account for most export earnings, followed by cotton. Important constraints to economic development include the CAR's landlocked geography, poor transportation system, largely unskilled work force, and legacy of misdirected macroeconomic policies. Factional fighting between the government and its opponents remains a drag on economic revitalization. Distribution of income is extraordinarily unequal. Grants from France and the international community can only partially meet humanitarian needs.

Since 2009, the IMF has worked closely with the government to institute reforms that have resulted in some improvement in budget transparency, but other problems remain. The government's additional spending in the run-up to the 2011 election worsened CAR's fiscal situation. In 2012, the World Bank approved $125 million in funding for transport infrastructure and regional trade,

focused on the route between CAR's capital and the port of Douala in Cameroon. After a two-year lag in donor support, the IMF's first review of CAR's extended credit facility for 2012–15 praised improvements in revenue collection but warned of weak management of spending.

Kimberley Process participants partially lifted the ban on diamond exports from the country in 2015, but persistent insecurity will prevent GDP from recovering to its pre-2013 level.

GDP (purchasing power parity): $3.018 billion (2015 est.)

$2.893 billion (2014 est.)

$2.864 billion (2013 est.)

note: data are in 2015 US dollars

country comparison to the world: 188

GDP (official exchange rate): $1.605 billion (2015 est.)

GDP—real growth rate: 4.3% (2015 est.)

1% (2014 est.)

-36% (2013 est.)

country comparison to the world: 55

GDP—per capita (PPP): $600 (2015 est.)

$600 (2014 est.)

$600 (2013 est.)

note: data are in 2015 US dollars

country comparison to the world: 228

Gross national saving: 1.7% of GDP (2015 est.)

4.7% of GDP (2014 est.)

5.7% of GDP (2013 est.)

country comparison to the world: 169

GDP—composition, by end use:

household consumption: 107.3%

government consumption: 8.2%

investment in fixed capital: 13.7%

investment in inventories: 0%

exports of goods and services: 11.3%

imports of goods and services: -40.5% (2015 est.)

GDP—composition, by sector of origin: *agriculture:* 58.3%

industry: 11.9%

services: 29.9% (2015 est.)

Agriculture—products: cotton, coffee, tobacco, cassava (manioc, tapioca), yams, millet, corn, bananas; timber

Industries: gold and diamond mining, logging, brewing, sugar refining

Industrial production growth rate: 4% (2015 est.)

country comparison to the world: 59

Labor force: 2.306 million (2015 est.)

country comparison to the world: 117

Unemployment rate: 8% (2001 est.)

note: 23% unemployment in the capital, Bangui

country comparison to the world: 91

Population below poverty line: NA%

Household income or consumption by percentage share: *lowest:* 10%: 2.1%

highest: 10%: 33% (2003)

Distribution of family income—Gini index: 61.3 (1993)

country comparison to the world: 5

Budget: *revenues:* $212 million

expenditures: $253.4 million (2015 est.)

Taxes and other revenues: 13.1% of GDP (2015 est.)

country comparison to the world: 203

Budget surplus (+) or deficit (-): -2.6% of GDP (2015 est.)

country comparison to the world: 98

Fiscal year: calendar year

Inflation rate (consumer prices): 5.4% (2015 est.)

11.6% (2014 est.)

country comparison to the world: 179

Central bank discount rate: 4.25% (31 December 2009)

4.75% (31 December 2008)

country comparison to the world: 87

Commercial bank prime lending rate: 15.5% (31 December 2015 est.)

15% (31 December 2014 est.)

country comparison to the world: 36

Stock of narrow money: $322.4 million (31 December 2015 est.)

$376.7 million (31 December 2014 est.)

country comparison to the world: 173

Stock of broad money: $410.4 million (31 December 2015 est.)

$454.7 million (31 December 2014 est.)

country comparison to the world: 185

Stock of domestic credit: $428.2 million (31 December 2015 est.)

$457.8 million (31 December 2014 est.)

country comparison to the world: 175

Market value of publicly traded shares: $NA

Current account balance: -$205 million (2015 est.)—

$95 million (2014 est.)

country comparison to the world: 81

Exports: $172.8 million (2015 est.)

$150.3 million (2014 est.)

country comparison to the world: 190

Exports—commodities: diamonds, timber, cotton, coffee

Exports—partners: Norway 52.2%, China 14.1%, Democratic Republic of the Congo 8.3% (2015)

Imports: $264.9 million (2015 est.)

$279.1 million (2014 est.)

country comparison to the world: 202

Imports—commodities: food, textiles, petroleum products, machinery, electrical equipment, motor vehicles, chemicals, pharmaceuticals

Imports—partners: Norway 39.5%, France 6.8%, US 4.6% (2015)

Debt—external: $630.1 million (31 December 2014 est.) $574.4 million (31 December 2013 est.)

country comparison to the world: 175

Exchange rates: Cooperation Financiere en Afrique Centrale francs (XAF) per US dollar—

580.5 (2015 est.)

494.42 (2014 est.)

494.42 (2013 est.)

510.53 (2012 est.)

471.87 (2011 est.)

ENERGY

Electricity—production: 181 million kWh (2012 est.)

country comparison to the world: 188

Electricity—consumption: 168.3 million kWh (2012 est.)
country comparison to the world: 190
Electricity—exports: 0 kWh (2013 est.)
country comparison to the world: 126
Electricity—imports: 0 kWh (2013 est.)
country comparison to the world: 136
Electricity—installed generating capacity: 44,000 kW (2012 est.)
country comparison to the world: 191
Electricity—from fossil fuels: 43.2% of total installed capacity (2012 est.)
country comparison to the world: 160
Electricity—from nuclear fuels: 0% of total installed capacity (2012 est.)
country comparison to the world: 73
Electricity—from hydroelectric plants: 56.8% of total installed capacity (2012 est.)
country comparison to the world: 38
Electricity—from other renewable sources: 0% of total installed capacity (2012 est.)
country comparison to the world: 171
Crude oil—production: 0 bbl/day (2014 est.)
country comparison to the world: 121
Crude oil—exports: 0 bbl/day (2012 est.)
country comparison to the world: 112
Crude oil—imports: 0 bbl/day (2012 est.)
country comparison to the world: 177
Crude oil—proved reserves: 0 bbl (1 January 2015 est.)
country comparison to the world: 120
Refined petroleum products—production: 0 bbl/day (2012 est.)
country comparison to the world: 170
Refined petroleum products—consumption: 2,300 bbl/day (2013 est.)
country comparison to the world: 186
Refined petroleum products-exports: 0 bbl/day (2012 est.)
country comparison to the world: 171
Refined petroleum products—imports: 2,318 bbl/day (2012 est.)
country comparison to the world: 181
Natural gas—production: 0 cu m (2013 est.)
country comparison to the world: 174
Natural gas—consumption: 0 cu m (2013 est.)
country comparison to the world: 133
Natural gas—exports: 0 cu m (2013 est.)
country comparison to the world: 83
Natural gas—imports: 0 cu m (2013 est.)
country comparison to the world: 183
Natural gas—proved reserves: 0 cu m (1 January 2014 est.)
country comparison to the world: 127
Carbon dioxide emissions from consumption of energy: 435,000 Mt (2012 est.)
country comparison to the world: 184

COMMUNICATIONS

Telephones—fixed lines: *total subscriptions:* 800 *subscriptions per 100 inhabitants:* less than 1 (2014 est.)

country comparison to the world: 216
Telephones—mobile cellular: *total:* 1.5 million *subscriptions per 100 inhabitants:* 28 (2014 est.)
country comparison to the world: 155
Telephone system: *general assessment:* network consists principally of microwave radio relay and low-capacity, low-powered radiotelephone communication
domestic: limited telephone service with less than 1 fixed-line connection per 100 persons; spurred by the presence of multiple mobile-cellular service providers, cellular usage is increasing from a low base; most fixed-line and mobile-cellular telephone services are concentrated in Bangui
international: country code—236; satellite earth station—1 Intelsat (Atlantic Ocean) (2011)

Broadcast media: government-owned network, Radiodiffusion Television Centrafricaine, provides domestic TV broadcasting; licenses for 2 private TV stations are pending; state-owned radio network is supplemented by a small number of privately owned broadcast stations as well as a few community radio stations; transmissions of at least 2 international broadcasters are available (2007)
Radio broadcast stations: AM 1, FM 5, shortwave 1 (2001)
Television broadcast stations: 1 (2001)

Internet country code: .cf
Internet hosts: 20 (2012)
country comparison to the world: 221
Internet users: *total:* 181,000
percent of population: 3.4% (2014 est.)
country comparison to the world: 157

TRANSPORTATION

Airports: 39 (2013)
country comparison to the world: 106
Airports—with paved runways: *total:* 2
2,438 to 3,047 m: 1
1,524 to 2,437 m: 1 (2013)
Airports—with unpaved runways: *total:* 37
2,438 to 3,047 m: 1
1,524 to 2,437 m: 11
914 to 1,523 m: 19
under 914 m: 6 (2013)
Roadways: *total:* 20,278 km
paved: 1,385 km
unpaved: 18,893 km (2010)
country comparison to the world: 107
Waterways: 2,800 km (the primary navigable river is the Ubangi, which joins the River Congo; it was the traditional route for the export of products because it connected with the Congo-Ocean railway at Brazzaville; because of the warfare on both sides of the River Congo from 1997, importers and exporters preferred routes through Cameroon) (2011)
country comparison to the world: 34
Ports and terminals: *river port(s):* Bangui (Oubangui); Nola (Sangha)

MILITARY AND SECURITY

Military branches: Central African Armed Forces (Forces Armees Centrafricaines, FACA): Ground Forces (includes Military Air Service), General Directorate of Gendarmerie Inspection (DGIG), National Police (2011)

Military service age and obligation: 18 years of age for selective military service; 2-year conscript service obligation (2012)

TRANSNATIONAL ISSUES

Disputes—international: periodic skirmishes persist over water and grazing rights among related pastoral populations along the border with southern Sudan

Refugees and internally displaced persons: *refugees (country of origin):* 5,342 (Democratic Republic of the Congo) (2015) IDPs: 415,256 (clashes between army and rebel groups since 2005; tensions between ethnic groups) (2016)

Trafficking in persons: *current situation:* Central African Republic (CAR) is a source, transit, and destination country for children subjected to forced labor and sex trafficking, women subjected to forced prostitution, and adults subjected to forced labor; most victims appear to be CAR citizens exploited within the country, with a smaller number transported back forth between the CAR and nearby countries; armed groups operating in the CAR, including those aligned with the former Seleka government and the Lord's Resistance Army, continue to recruit and re-recruit children for military activities and labor; children are also subject to domestic servitude, commercial sexual exploitation, and forced labor in agriculture, mines, shops, and street vending; women and girls are subject to domestic servitude, sexual slavery, commercial sexual exploitation, and forced marriage

tier rating: Tier 3—the Central African Republic does not fully comply with the minimum standards for the elimination of trafficking and is not making significant efforts to do so; the government conducted a limited number of investigations and prosecutions of cases of suspected human trafficking in 2014 but did not identify, provide protection to, or refer to care providers any trafficking victims; the government did not directly provide reintegration programs for demobilized child soldiers, leaving victims vulnerable to further exploitation or retrafficking by armed groups, including those affiliated with the government; in 2014, an NGO and the government began drafting a national action plan against trafficking but no efforts were reported to establish a policy against child soldiering or to raise awareness about existing laws prohibiting the use of children in the armed forces (2015)

CHAD

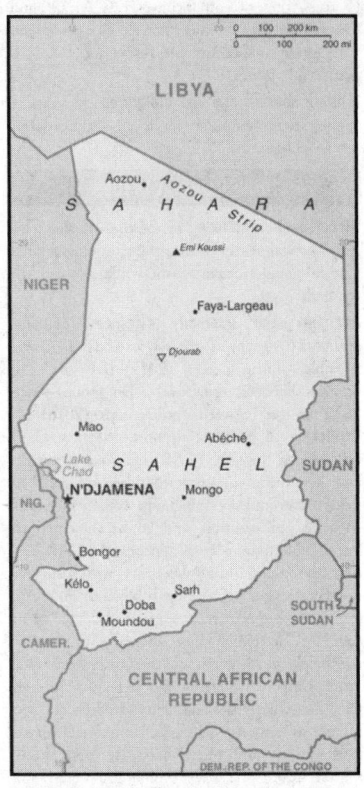

INTRODUCTION

Background: Chad, part of France's African holdings until 1960, endured three decades of civil warfare, as well as invasions by Libya, before peace was restored in 1990. The government eventually drafted a democratic constitution and held flawed presidential elections in 1996 and 2001. In 1998, a rebellion broke out in northern Chad, which has sporadically flared up despite several peace agreements between the government and insurgents. In June 2005, President Idriss DEBY held a referendum successfully removing constitutional term limits and won another controversial election in 2006. Sporadic rebel campaigns continued throughout 2006 and 2007. The capital experienced a significant insurrection in early 2008, but has had no significant rebel threats since then, in part due to Chad's 2010 rapprochement with Sudan, which previously used Chadian rebels as proxies. In late 2015, the government imposed a state of emergency in the Lake Chad region following multiple attacks by the terrorist group Boko Haram throughout the year; Boko Haram also launched several bombings in N'Djamena in mid-2015. DEBY in 2011 was reelected to his fourth term in an election that international observers

described as proceeding without incident. In January 2014, Chad began a two-year rotation on the UN Security Council.

GEOGRAPHY

Location: Central Africa, south of Libya

Geographic coordinates: 15 00 N, 19 00 E

Map references: Africa

Area: *total:* 1.284 million sq km
land: 1,259,200 sq km
water: 24,800 sq km
country comparison to the world: 21

Area—comparative: slightly more than three times the size of California

Land boundaries: *total:* 6,406 km
border countries (6): Cameroon 1,116 km, Central African Republic 1,556 km, Libya 1,050 km, Niger 1,196 km, Nigeria 85 km, Sudan 1,403 km

Coastline: 0 km (landlocked)

Maritime claims: none (landlocked)

Climate: tropical in south, desert in north

Terrain: broad, arid plains in center, desert in north, mountains in northwest, lowlands in south

Elevation: *mean elevation:* 543 m

elevation extremes: *lowest point:* Djourab 160 m
highest point: Emi Koussi 3,415 m

Natural resources: petroleum, uranium, natron, kaolin, fish (Lake Chad), gold, limestone, sand and gravel, salt

Land use: *agricultural land:* 39.6%
arable land: 3.9%
permanent crops: 0%
permanent pasture: 35.7%
forest: 9.1%
other: 51.3% (2011 est.)

Irrigated land: 300 sq km (2012)

Total renewable water resources: 43 cu km (2011)

Freshwater withdrawal (domestic/industrial/agricultural): *total:* 0.88 cu m/yr (12%/12%/76%)
per capita: 84.81 cu m/yr (2005)

Natural hazards: hot, dry, dusty harmattan winds occur in north; periodic droughts; locust plagues

Environment—current issues: inadequate supplies of potable water; improper waste disposal in rural areas contributes to soil and water pollution; desertification

Environment—international agreements: *party to:* Biodiversity, Climate Change, Desertification, Endangered Species, Hazardous Wastes, Ozone Layer Protection, Wetlands
signed, but not ratified: Law of the Sea, Marine Dumping

Geography—note: *note 1:* Chad is the largest of Africa's 16 landlocked countries
note 2: not long ago—geologically speaking—what is today the Sahara was green savannah teeming with wildlife; during the African Humid Period, roughly 11,000 to 5,000 years ago, a vibrant animal

community, including elephants, giraffes, hippos, and antelope lived there; the last remnant of the "Green Sahara" exists in the Lakes of Ounianga (oo-nee-ahn-ga) in northern Chad, a series of 18 interconnected freshwater, saline, and hypersaline lakes now protected as a World Heritage site
note 3: Lake Chad, the most significant water body in the Sahel, is a remnant of a former inland sea, paleolake Mega-Chad; at its greatest extent, sometime before 5000 B.C., Lake Mega-Chad was the largest of four Saharan paleolakes that existed during the African Humid Period; it covered an area of about 400,000 sq km (150,000 sq mi), roughly the size of today's Caspian Sea

PEOPLE AND SOCIETY

Nationality: *noun:* Chadian(s)
adjective: Chadian

Ethnic groups: Sara 27.7%, Arab 12.3%, Mayo-Kebbi 11.5%, Kanem-Bornou 9%, Ouaddai 8.7%, Hadjarai 6.7%, Tandjile 6.5%, Gorane 6.3%, Fitri-Batha 4.7%, other 6.4%, unknown 0.3% (1993 census)

Languages: French (official), Arabic (official), Sara (in south), more than 120 different languages and dialects

Religions: Muslim 58.4%, Catholic 18.5%, Protestant 16.1%, animist 4%, other 0.5%, none 2.4% (2009 est.)

Population: 11,631,456 (July 2015 est.)
country comparison to the world: 77

Age structure: *0–14 years:* 44.2% (male 2,607,314/female 2,534,163)
15–24 years: 20.9% (male 1,183,962/female 1,247,130)
25–54 years: 28.05% (male 1,479,285/female 1,783,014)
55–64 years: 3.87% (male 197,673/female 252,379)
65 years and over: 2.98% (male 143,712/female 202,824) (2015 est.)

Dependency ratios: *total dependency ratio:* 100.7%
youth dependency ratio: 95.8%
elderly dependency ratio: 4.9%
potential support ratio: 20.3% (2015 est.)

Median age: *total:* 17.4 years
male: 16.4 years
female: 18.4 years (2015 est.)
country comparison to the world: 220

Population growth rate: 1.89% (2015 est.)
country comparison to the world: 58

Birth rate: 36.6 births/1,000 population (2015 est.)
country comparison to the world: 16

Death rate: 14.28 deaths/1,000 population (2015 est.)
country comparison to the world: 6

Net migration rate: -3.45 migrant(s)/1,000 population (2015 est.)
country comparison to the world: 186

Urbanization: *urban population:* 22.5% of total population (2015)
rate of urbanization: 3.42% annual rate of change (2010–15 est.)

Major urban areas—population: N'DJAMENA (capital) 1.26 million (2015)

Sex ratio: *at birth:* 1.04 male(s)/female
0–14 years: 1.03 male(s)/female
15–24 years: 0.95 male(s)/female
25–54 years: 0.83 male(s)/female
55–64 years: 0.78 male(s)/female
65 years and over: 0.71 male(s)/female
total population: 0.93 male(s)/female (2015 est.)

Maternal mortality rate: 856 deaths/100,000 live births (2015 est.)
country comparison to the world: 2

Infant mortality rate: *total:* 88.69 deaths/1,000 live births
male: 94.23 deaths/1,000 live births
female: 82.93 deaths/1,000 live births (2015 est.)
country comparison to the world: 6

Life expectancy at birth:
total population: 49.81 years
male: 48.64 years
female: 51.03 years (2015 est.)
country comparison to the world: 224

Total fertility rate: 4.55 children born/woman (2015 est.)
country comparison to the world: 25

Contraceptive prevalence rate: 4.8% (2010)

Health expenditures: 3.6% of GDP (2013)
country comparison to the world: 174

Physicians density: 0.04 physicians/1,000 population (2006)

Drinking water source:
improved:
urban: 71.8% of population
rural: 44.8% of population
total: 50.8% of population
unimproved:
urban: 28.2% of population
rural: 55.2% of population
total: 49.2% of population (2015 est.)

Sanitation facility access:
improved:
urban: 31.4% of population
rural: 6.5% of population
total: 12.1% of population
unimproved:
urban: 68.6% of population
rural: 93.5% of population
total: 87.9% of population (2015 est.)

HIV/AIDS—adult prevalence rate: 2.53% (2014 est.)
country comparison to the world: 24

HIV/AIDS—people living with HIV/AIDS: 215,000 (2014 est.)
country comparison to the world: 25

HIV/AIDS—deaths: 11,700 (2014 est.)
country comparison to the world: 21

Major infectious diseases: *degree of risk:* very high
food or waterborne diseases: bacterial and protozoal diarrhea, hepatitis A and E, and typhoid fever
vectorborne diseases: malaria and dengue fever

water contact disease: schistosomiasis
respiratory disease: meningococcal meningitis
animal contact disease: rabies (2013)

Obesity—adult prevalence rate: 6.6% (2014)
country comparison to the world: 177

Children under the age of 5 years underweight: 28.8% (2015)
country comparison to the world: 13

Education expenditures: 2.9% of GDP (2013)
country comparison to the world: 160

Literacy: *definition:* age 15 and over can read and write French or Arabic
total population: 40.2%
male: 48.5%
female: 31.9% (2015 est.)

School life expectancy (primary to tertiary education): *total:* 7 years
male: 9 years
female: 6 years (2011)

Child labor—children ages 5–14: *total number:* 1,475,960
percentage: 48% (2010 est.)

GOVERNMENT

Country name: *conventional long form:* Republic of Chad
conventional short form: Chad
local long form: Republique du Tchad/Jumhuriyat Tshad
local short form: Tchad/Tshad
etymology: named for Lake Chad, which lies along the country's western border; the word "tsade" means "large body of water" or "lake" in several local native languages

Government type: presidential republic

Capital: *name:* N'Djamena

Geographic coordinates: 12 06 N, 15 02 E
time difference: UTC + 1 (6 hours ahead of Washington, DC, during Standard Time)

Administrative divisions: 23 regions (regions, singular—region); Barh el Gazel, Batha, Borkou, Chari-Baguirmi, Ennedi-Est, Ennedi-Ouest, Guera, Hadjer-Lamis, Kanem, Lac, Logone Occidental, Logone Oriental, Mandoul, Mayo-Kebbi Est, Mayo-Kebbi Ouest, Moyen-Chari, Ouaddai, Salamat, Sila, Tandjile, Tibesti, Ville de N'Djamena, Wadi Fira

Independence: 11 August 1960 (from France)

National holiday: Independence Day, 11 August (1960)

Constitution: several previous; latest passed by referendum 31 March 1996, entered into force 8 April 1996; amended 2005 (2016)

Legal system: mixed legal system of civil and customary law

International law organization participation: has not submitted an ICJ jurisdiction declaration; accepts ICCt jurisdiction

Citizenship: *citizenship by birth:* no
citizenship by descent only: both parents must be citizens of Chad
dual citizenship recognized: Chadian law does not address dual citizenship

residency requirement for naturalization: 15 years

Suffrage: 18 years of age; universal

Executive branch: *chief of state:* President Idriss DEBY Itno, Lt. Gen. (since 4 December 1990)

head of government: Prime Minister Albert Pahimi PADACKE (since 15 February 2016)
cabinet: Council of Ministers; members appointed by the president on the recommendation of the prime minister
elections/appointments: president directly elected by absolute majority popular vote in 2 rounds if needed for a 5-year term (no term limits); election last held on 25 April 2011 (next to be held in April 2016); prime minister appointed by the president
election results: Lt. Gen. Idriss DEBY Itno reelected president; percent of vote—Lt. Gen. Idriss DEBY (MPS) 83.6%, Albert Pahimi PADAKE (Viva RNDP) 8.6%, Nadji MADOU 7.8%

Legislative branch: *description:* unicameral National Assembly (188 seats; 118 directly elected in multi-seat constituencies by proportional representation vote and 70 directly elected in single-seat constituencies by absolute majority vote with a second round if needed; members serve 4-year terms)
elections: National Assembly—last held on 13 February and 6 May 2011 (next to be held on 30 September 2015)
election results: percent of vote by party—NA; seats by party—MPS 117, UNDR 10, RDP 9, URD 8, RNDT/Le Reveil 8, Viva-RNDP 5, FAR 4, PUR 2, UDR 2, PDSA 2, CTPD 2, other minor parties 19

Judicial branch: *highest court(s):* Supreme Court (consists of the chief justice and 15 judges or councilors and divided into 3 chambers); Constitutional Council (consists of 3 judges and 6 jurists)
judge selection and term of office: Supreme Court chief justice selected by the president; councilors -8 designated by the president and 7 by the speaker of the National Assembly; chief justice and councilors appointed for life; Constitutional Council judges—2 appointed by the president and 1 by the speaker of the National Assembly; jurists—3 each by the president and by the speaker of the National Assembly; judge term NA
subordinate courts: High Court of Justice; Courts of Appeal; tribunals; justices of the peace

Political parties and leaders: Alliance for the Renaissance of Chad or ART (includes MPS, RDP, and Viva-RNDP) Federation Action for the Republic or FAR [Ngarledjy YORONGAR]
National Rally for Development and Progress or Viva-RNDP [Dr. Nouradine Delwa Kassire COUMAKOYE]
National Union for Democracy and Renewal or UNDR [Saleh KEBZABO]
Party for Liberty and Development or PLD [Jean-Baptiste LAOKOLE]
Patriotic Salvation Movement or MPS [Idriss DEBY]
Rally for Democracy and Progress or RDP [Lol Mahamat CHOUA]

Union for Renewal and Democracy or URD [Sande NGARYIMBE]

Political pressure groups and leaders: NA

International organization participation: ACP, AfDB, AU, BDEAC, CEMAC, EITI (compliant country), FAO, FZ, G-77, IAEA, IBRD, ICAO, ICCt, ICRM, IDA, IDB, IFAD, IFC, IFRCS, ILO, IMF, Interpol, IOC, IOM, IPU, ITSO, ITU, ITUC (NGOs), MIGA, MINUSMA, NAM, OIC, OIF, OPCW, UN, UN Security Council (temporary), UNCTAD, UNESCO, UNIDO, UNOCI, UNWTO, UPU, WCO, WHO, WIPO, WMO, WTO

Diplomatic representation in the US: *chief of mission:* Ambassador Mahamat Nasser HASSANE (since 21 May 2014)
chancery: 2401 Massachusetts Avenue NW, Washington, DC 20008
telephone: [1] (202) 652-1312
FAX: [1] (202) 758-0431

Diplomatic representation from the US: *chief of mission:* Ambassador James KNIGHT (since 6 September 2013)
embassy: Avenue Felix Eboue, N'Djamena
mailing address: B. P. 413, N'Djamena
telephone: [235] 2251-70-09
FAX: [235] 2251-56-54

Flag description: three equal vertical bands of blue (hoist side), yellow, and red; the flag combines the blue and red French (former colonial) colors with the red and yellow of the Pan-African colors; blue symbolizes the sky, hope, and the south of the country, which is relatively well-watered; yellow represents the sun, as well as the desert in the north of the country; red stands for progress, unity, and sacrifice
note: similar to the flag of Romania; also similar to the flags of Andorra and Moldova, both of which have a national coat of arms centered in the yellow band; design was based on the flag of France

National symbol(s): goat (north), lion (south); national colors: blue, yellow, red

National anthem: *name:* "La Tchadienne" (The Chadian)
lyrics/music: Louis GIDROL and his students/ Paul VILLARD
note: adopted 1960

ECONOMY

Economy—overview: Chad's landlocked location results in high transportation costs for imported goods and dependence on neighboring countries. Oil and agriculture are mainstays of Chad's economy. Oil provides about 60% of export revenues, while cotton, cattle, livestock, and gum arabic provide the bulk of Chad's non-oil export earnings. The services sector contributes about one-third of GDP and has attracted foreign investment mostly through telecommunications and banking.

Nearly all of Chad's fuel is provided by one domestic refinery, and unanticipated shutdowns occasionally result in shortages. The country regulates the price of domestic fuel, providing an incentive for black market sales.

Chad's fiscal position is encumbered by declining oil prices, though high oil prices and strong local harvests supported the economy in recent years. Chad relies on foreign assistance and foreign capital for much public and private sector investment. Chad's investment climate remains challenging due to limited infrastructure, a lack of trained workers, extensive government bureaucracy, and corruption. Chad obtained a three-year extended credit facility from the IMF in 2014 and was granted debt relief under the Heavily Indebted Poor Countries Initiative in April 2015.

GDP (purchasing power parity): $30.47 billion (2015 est.)
$29.94 billion (2014 est.)
$28.01 billion (2013 est.)
note: data are in 2015 US dollars
country comparison to the world: 129

GDP (official exchange rate): $10.89 billion (2015 est.)

GDP—real growth rate: 1.8% (2015 est.)
6.9% (2014 est.)
5.7% (2013 est.)
country comparison to the world: 140

GDP—per capita (PPP): $2,600 (2015 est.)
$2,700 (2014 est.)
$2,500 (2013 est.)
note: data are in 2015 US dollars
country comparison to the world: 195

Gross national saving: 14.4% of GDP (2015 est.)
21.6% of GDP (2014 est.)
18.3% of GDP (2013 est.)
country comparison to the world: 123

GDP—composition, by end use:
household consumption: 70.8%
government consumption: 5.6%
investment in fixed capital: 32.6%
investment in inventories: 0.2%
exports of goods and services: 26.5%
imports of goods and services: -35.7% (2015 est.)

GDP—composition, by sector of origin: *agriculture:* 54.9%
industry: 14.2%
services: 30.9% (2015 est.)

Agriculture—products: cotton, sorghum, millet, peanuts, sesame, corn, rice, potatoes, onions, cassava (manioc, tapioca), cattle, sheep, goats, camels

Industries: oil, cotton textiles, brewing, natron (sodium carbonate), soap, cigarettes, construction materials

Industrial production growth rate: -1.3% (2015 est.)
country comparison to the world: 176

Labor force: 5.268 million (2015 est.)
country comparison to the world: 76

Labor force—by occupation: *agriculture:* 80%
industry and services: 20% (2006 est.)

Unemployment rate: NA%

Population below poverty line: 46.7% (2011 est.)

Household income or consumption by percentage share: *lowest:* 10%: 2.6%
highest: 10%: 30.8% (2003)

Distribution of family income—Gini index: 43.3 (2011 est.)
country comparison to the world: 50

Budget: *revenues:* $2.31 billion
expenditures: $2.739 billion (2015 est.)
Taxes and other revenues: 19.8% of GDP (2015 est.)
country comparison to the world: 161

Budget surplus (+) or deficit (-): -3.7% of GDP (2015 est.)
country comparison to the world: 135

Public debt: 31.9% of GDP (2015 est.)
30.8% of GDP (2014 est.)
country comparison to the world: 140

Fiscal year: calendar year

Inflation rate (consumer prices): 3.6% (2015 est.)
1.7% (2014 est.)
country comparison to the world: 149

Central bank discount rate: 4.25% (31 December 2009)
4.75% (31 December 2008)
country comparison to the world: 96

Commercial bank prime lending rate: 15.5% (31 December 2015 est.)
15.5% (31 December 2014 est.)
country comparison to the world: 34

Stock of narrow money: $1.633 billion (31 December 2015 est.)
$1.751 billion (31 December 2014 est.)
country comparison to the world: 136

Stock of broad money: $1.976 billion (31 December 2014 est.)
$1.751 billion (31 December 2013 est.)
country comparison to the world: 157

Stock of domestic credit: $1.266 billion (31 December 2015 est.)
$1.195 billion (31 December 2014 est.)
country comparison to the world: 154

Market value of publicly traded shares: $NA

Current account balance: -$1.392 billion (2015 est.)
-$1.242 billion (2014 est.)
country comparison to the world: 136

Exports: $4.139 billion (2015 est.)
$5.008 billion (2014 est.)
country comparison to the world: 117

Exports—commodities: oil, livestock, cotton, sesame, gum arabic, shea butter

Exports—partners: US 58.5%, India 13.3%, Japan 11.3%, China 4.1% (2015)

Imports: $3.331 billion (2015 est.)
$4.416 billion (2014 est.)
country comparison to the world: 140

Imports—commodities: machinery and transportation equipment, industrial goods, foodstuffs, textiles

Imports—partners: France 16.5%, China 14.2%, Cameroon 11%, US 6.4%, India 6%, Belgium 5.7%, Italy 4.8% (2015)

Reserves of foreign exchange and gold: $1.111 billion (31 December 2015 est.)
$1.089 billion (31 December 2014 est.)
country comparison to the world: 128

Debt—external: $3.525 billion (31 December 2014 est.)
$2.216 billion (31 December 2013 est.)
country comparison to the world: 140

Stock of direct foreign investment—at home: $NA (31 December 2010)
$4.5 billion (2006 est.)

Stock of direct foreign investment—abroad: $NA

Exchange rates: Cooperation Financiere en Afrique Centrale francs (XAF) per US dollar—
580.5 (2015 est.)
494.42 (2014 est.)
494.42 (2013 est.)
510.53 (2012 est.)
471.87 (2011 est.)

ENERGY

Electricity—production: 205 million kWh (2012 est.)
country comparison to the world: 184
Electricity—consumption: 190.7 million kWh (2012 est.)
country comparison to the world: 187
Electricity—exports: 0 kWh (2013 est.)
country comparison to the world: 117
Electricity—imports: 0 kWh (2013 est.)
country comparison to the world: 128
Electricity—installed generating capacity: 31,000 kW (2012 est.)
country comparison to the world: 197
Electricity—from fossil fuels: 100% of total installed capacity (2012 est.)
country comparison to the world: 8
Electricity—from nuclear fuels: 0% of total installed capacity (2012 est.)
country comparison to the world: 63
Electricity—from hydroelectric plants: 0% of total installed capacity (2012 est.)
country comparison to the world: 165
Electricity—from other renewable sources: 0% of total installed capacity (2012 est.)
country comparison to the world: 165
Crude oil—production: 103,400 bbl/day (2014 est.)
country comparison to the world: 45
Crude oil—exports: 104,500 bbl/day (2012 est.)
country comparison to the world: 36
Crude oil—imports: 0 bbl/day (2012 est.)
country comparison to the world: 170
Crude oil—proved reserves: 1.5 billion bbl (1 January 2015 est.)
country comparison to the world: 38
Refined petroleum products—production: 0 bbl/day (2012 est.)
country comparison to the world: 165
Refined petroleum products—consumption: 1,700 bbl/day (2013 est.)
country comparison to the world: 191
Refined petroleum products—exports: 0 bbl/day (2012 est.)
country comparison to the world: 165

Refined petroleum products—imports: 1,754 bbl/day (2012 est.)
country comparison to the world: 184
Natural gas—production: 0 cu m (2013 est.)
country comparison to the world: 168
Natural gas—consumption: 0 cu m (2013 est.)
country comparison to the world: 127
Natural gas—exports: 0 cu m (2013 est.)
country comparison to the world: 75
Natural gas—imports: 0 cu m (2013 est.)
country comparison to the world: 174
Natural gas—proved reserves: 0 cu m (1 January 2014 est.)
country comparison to the world: 122
Carbon dioxide emissions from consumption of energy: 264,300 Mt (2012 est.)
country comparison to the world: 194

COMMUNICATIONS

Telephones—fixed lines: *total subscriptions:* 23,600
subscriptions per 100 inhabitants: less than 1 (2014 est.)
country comparison to the world: 177
Telephones—mobile cellular: *total:* 5.3 million
subscriptions per 100 inhabitants: 46 (2014 est.)
country comparison to the world: 115
Telephone system: *general assessment:* inadequate system of radiotelephone communication stations with high maintenance costs and low telephone density
domestic: fixed-line connections for less than 1 per 100 persons coupled with mobile-cellular subscribership base of about 46 per 100 persons
international: country code—235; satellite earth station—1 Intelsat (Atlantic Ocean) (2011)

Broadcast media: 1 state-owned TV station; state-owned radio network, Radiodiffusion Nationale Tchadienne (RNT), operates national and regional stations; about 10 private radio stations; some stations rebroadcast programs from international broadcasters (2007)
Radio broadcast stations: AM 2, FM 4, shortwave 5 (2001)
Television broadcast stations: 1 (2001)

Internet country code: .td
Internet hosts: 6 (2012)
country comparison to the world: 229
Internet users: *total:* 273,900
percent of population: 2.4% (2014 est.)
country comparison to the world: 148

TRANSPORTATION

Airports: 59 (2013)
country comparison to the world: 82
Airports—with paved runways: *total:* 9
over 3,047 m: 2
2,438 to 3,047 m: 4

1,524 to 2,437 m: 2
under 914 m: 1 (2013)
Airports—with unpaved runways: *total:* 50
over 3,047 m: 1
2,438 to 3,047 m: 2
1,524 to 2,437 m: 14
914 to 1,523 m: 22
under 914 m: 11 (2013)
Pipelines: oil 582 km (2013)
Roadways: *total:* 40,000 km
note: consists of 25,000 km of national and regional roads and 15,000 km of local roads; 206 km of urban roads are paved (2011)
country comparison to the world: 87
Waterways: (Chari and Legone Rivers are navigable only in wet season) (2012)

MILITARY AND SECURITY

Military branches: Chadian National Army (Armee Nationale du Tchad, ANT): Ground Forces (l'Armee de Terre, AdT), Chadian Air Force (l'Armee de l'Air Tchadienne, AAT), National Gendarmerie, National and Nomadic Guard of Chad (GNNT) (2013)

Military service age and obligation: 20 is the legal minimum age for compulsory military service, with a 3-year service obligation; 18 is the legal minimum age for voluntary service; no minimum age restriction for volunteers with consent from a parent or guardian; women are subject to 1 year of compulsory military or civic service at age 21; while provisions for military service have not been repealed, they have never been fully implemented (2015)

Military expenditures: NA% (2012)
2.28% of GDP (2011)

TRANSNATIONAL ISSUES

Disputes—international: since 2003, ad hoc armed militia groups and the Sudanese military have driven hundreds of thousands of Darfur residents into Chad; Chad wishes to be a helpful mediator in resolving the Darfur conflict, and in 2010 established a joint border monitoring force with Sudan, which has helped to reduce cross-border banditry and violence; only Nigeria and Cameroon have heeded the Lake Chad Commission's admonition to ratify the delimitation treaty, which also includes the Chad-Niger and Niger-Nigeria boundaries

Refugees and internally displaced persons: *refugees (country of origin):* 297,296 (Sudan) (2015); 72,876 (Central African Republic); 7,337 (Nigeria) (2016)
IDPs: 58,748 (majority are in the east) (2016)

CHILE

INTRODUCTION

Background: Prior to the arrival of the Spanish in the 16th century, the Inca ruled northern Chile while the Mapuche inhabited central and southern Chile. Although Chile declared its independence in 1810, decisive victory over the Spanish was not achieved until 1818. In the War of the Pacific (1879–83), Chile defeated Peru and Bolivia and won its present northern regions. It was not until the 1880s that the Mapuche were brought under central government control. After a series of elected governments, the three-year-old Marxist government of Salvador ALLENDE was overthrown in 1973 by a military coup led by General Augusto PINOCHET, who ruled until a freely elected president was inaugurated in 1990. Sound economic policies, maintained consistently since the 1980s, contributed to steady growth, reduced poverty rates by over half, and helped secure the country's commitment to democratic and representative government. Chile has increasingly assumed regional and international leadership roles befitting its status as a stable, democratic nation.

GEOGRAPHY

Location: Southern South America, bordering the South Pacific Ocean, between Argentina and Peru

Geographic coordinates: 30 00 S, 71 00 W

Map references: South America

Area: *total:* 756,102 sq km
land: 743,812 sq km
water: 12,290 sq km
note: includes Easter Island (Isla de Pascua) and Isla Sala y Gomez
country comparison to the world: 38

Area—comparative: slightly smaller than twice the size of Montana

Land boundaries: *total:* 7,801 km
border countries (3): Argentina 6,691 km, Bolivia 942 km, Peru 168 km

Coastline: 6,435 km

Maritime claims: *territorial sea:* 12 nm
contiguous zone: 24 nm
exclusive economic zone: 200 nm
continental shelf: 200/350 nm

Climate: temperate; desert in north; Mediterranean in central region; cool and damp in south

Terrain: low coastal mountains; fertile central valley; rugged Andes in east

Elevation: *mean elevation:* 1,871 m

elevation extremes: *lowest point:* Pacific Ocean 0 m
highest point: Nevado Ojos del Salado 6,880 m

Natural resources: copper, timber, iron ore, nitrates, precious metals, molybdenum, hydropower

Land use: *agricultural land:* 21.1%
arable land: 1.7%
permanent crops: 0.6%
permanent pasture: 18.8%
forest: 21.9%
other: 57% (2011 est.)

Irrigated land: 11,100 sq km (2012)

Total renewable water resources: 922 cu km (2011)

Freshwater withdrawal (domestic/industrial/agricultural): *total:* 26.67 cu m/yr (4%/10%/86%)
per capita: 1,603 cu m/yr (2007)

Natural hazards: severe earthquakes; active volcanism; tsunamis
volcanism: significant volcanic activity due to more than three-dozen active volcanoes along the Andes Mountains; Lascar (elev.5,592 m), which last erupted in 2007, is the most active volcano in the northern Chilean Andes; Llaima (elev. 3,125 m) in central Chile, which last erupted in 2009, is another of the country's most active; Chaiten's 2008 eruption forced major evacuations; other notable historically active volcanoes include Cerro Hudson, Calbuco, Copahue, Guallatiri, Llullaillaco, Nevados de Chillan, Puyehue, San Pedro, and Villarrica

Environment—current issues: widespread deforestation and mining threaten natural resources; air pollution from industrial and vehicle emissions; water pollution from raw sewage

Environment—international agreements: *party to:* Antarctic-Environmental Protocol, Antarctic-Marine Living Resources, Antarctic Seals, Antarctic Treaty, Biodiversity, Climate Change, Climate Change-Kyoto Protocol, Desertification, Endangered Species, Environmental Modification, Hazardous Wastes, Law of the Sea, Marine Dumping, Ozone Layer Protection, Ship Pollution, Wetlands, Whaling
signed, but not ratified: none of the selected agreements

Geography—note: the longest north-south trending country in the world, extending across 38 degrees of latitude; strategic location relative to sea lanes between the Atlantic and Pacific Oceans (Strait of Magellan, Beagle Channel, Drake Passage); Atacama Desert—the driest desert in the world—spreads across the northern part of the country; the crater lake of Ojos del Salado is the world's highest lake (at 6,390 m)

PEOPLE AND SOCIETY

Nationality: *noun:* Chilean(s)
adjective: Chilean

Ethnic groups: white and non-indigenous 88.9%, Mapuche 9.1%, Aymara 0.7%, other indigenous groups 1% (includes Rapa Nui, Likan Antai, Quechua, Colla, Diaguita, Kawesqar, Yagan or Yamana), unspecified 0.3% (2012 est.)

Languages: Spanish 99.5% (official), English 10.2%, indigenous 1% (includes Mapudungun, Aymara, Quechua, Rapa Nui), other 2.3%, unspecified 0.2%
note: shares sum to more than 100% because some respondents gave more than one answer on the census (2012 est.)

Religions: Roman Catholic 66.7%, Evangelical or Protestant 16.4%, Jehovah's Witnesses 1%, other 3.4%, none 11.5%, unspecified 1.1% (2012 est.)

Demographic profile: Chile is in the advanced stages of demographic transition and is becoming an aging society—with fertility below replacement level, low mortality rates, and life expectancy on par with developed countries. Nevertheless, with its dependency ratio nearing its low point, Chile could benefit from its favorable age structure. It will need to keep its large working-age population productively employed, while preparing to provide for the needs of its growing proportion of elderly people, especially as women—the traditional caregivers—increasingly enter the workforce. Over the last two decades, Chile has made great strides in reducing its poverty rate, which is now lower than most Latin American countries. However, its severe income inequality ranks as the worst among members of the Organization for Economic Cooperation and Development. Unequal access to quality education perpetuates this uneven income distribution. Chile has historically been a country of emigration but has slowly become more attractive to immigrants since transitioning to democracy in 1990 and improving its economic stability (other regional destinations have concurrently experienced deteriorating economic and political conditions). Most of Chile's small but growing foreign-born population consists of transplants from other Latin American countries, especially Peru.

Population: 17,508,260 (July 2015 est.)
country comparison to the world: 64

Age structure: 0–14 years: 20.46% (male 1,827,374/female 1,754,283)
15–24 years: 15.88% (male 1,418,938/female 1,361,307)
25–54 years: 43.21% (male 3,771,003/female 3,793,655)
55–64 years: 10.24% (male 842,346/female 950,574)
65 years and over: 10.22% (male 747,930/female 1,040,850) (2015 est.)

Dependency ratios: *total dependency ratio:* 45.2%
youth dependency ratio: 29.3%
elderly dependency ratio: 16%
potential support ratio: 6.3% (2015 est.)

Median age: *total:* 33.7 years
male: 32.5 years
female: 34.9 years (2015 est.)
country comparison to the world: 84

Population growth rate: 0.82% (2015 est.)
country comparison to the world: 137

Birth rate: 13.83 births/1,000 population (2015 est.)
country comparison to the world: 141

Death rate: 6 deaths/1,000 population (2015 est.)
country comparison to the world: 165

Net migration rate: 0.34 migrant(s)/1,000 population (2015 est.)
country comparison to the world: 75

Urbanization: *urban population:* 89.5% of total population (2015)
rate of urbanization: 1.09% annual rate of change (2010–15 est.)

Major urban areas—population: SANTIAGO (capital) 6.507 million; Valparaiso 907,000; Concepcion 816,000 (2015)

Sex ratio: *at birth:* 1.04 male(s)/female
0–14 years: 1.04 male(s)/female
15–24 years: 1.04 male(s)/female
25–54 years: 0.99 male(s)/female
55–64 years: 0.89 male(s)/female
65 years and over: 0.72 male(s)/female
total population: 0.97 male(s)/female (2015 est.)

Maternal mortality rate: 22 deaths/100,000 live births (2015 est.)
country comparison to the world: 131

Infant mortality rate: *total:* 6.86 deaths/1,000 live births
male: 7.34 deaths/1,000 live births
female: 6.36 deaths/1,000 live births (2015 est.)
country comparison to the world: 160

Life expectancy at birth:
total population: 78.61 years
male: 75.58 years
female: 81.76 years (2015 est.)
country comparison to the world: 52

Total fertility rate: 1.82 children born/woman (2015 est.)
country comparison to the world: 149

Contraceptive prevalence rate: 64.2%
note: percent of women aged 15–44 (2006)

Health expenditures: 7.7% of GDP (2013)
country comparison to the world: 76

Physicians density: 1.02 physicians/1,000 population (2009)

Hospital bed density: 2.1 beds/1,000 population (2011)

Drinking water source:
improved:
urban: 99.7% of population
rural: 93.3% of population
total: 99% of population
unimproved:
urban: 0.3% of population
rural: 6.7% of population
total: 1% of population (2015 est.)

Sanitation facility access:
improved:
urban: 100% of population
rural: 90.9% of population
total: 99.1% of population
unimproved:
urban: 0% of population
rural: 9.1% of population
total: 0.9% of population (2015 est.)

HIV/AIDS—adult prevalence rate: 0.29% (2014 est.)
country comparison to the world: 84

HIV/AIDS—people living with HIV/AIDS: 39,300 (2014 est.)
country comparison to the world: 61

HIV/AIDS—deaths: 700 (2014 est.)
country comparison to the world: 76

Obesity—adult prevalence rate: 28.5% (2014)
country comparison to the world: 30

Children under the age of 5 years underweight: 0.5% (2014)
country comparison to the world: 137

Education expenditures: 4.6% of GDP (2013)
country comparison to the world: 90

Literacy: *definition:* age 15 and over can read and write
total population: 97.5%
male: 97.6%
female: 97.4% (2015 est.)

School life expectancy (primary to tertiary education): *total:* 16 years
male: 16 years
female: 17 years (2014)

Child labor—children ages 5–14: *total number:* 82,882
percentage: 3% (2003 est.)

Unemployment, youth ages 15–24: *total:* 16.1%
male: 13.9%
female: 19.2% (2013 est.)
country comparison to the world: 73

GOVERNMENT

Country name: *conventional long form:* Republic of Chile
conventional short form: Chile
local long form: Republica de Chile
local short form: Chile
etymology: derivation of the name is unclear, but it may come from the Mapuche word "chilli" meaning "limit of the earth" or from the Quechua "chiri" meaning "cold"

Government type: presidential republic

Capital: *name:* Santiago; note—Valparaiso is the seat of the national legislature
Geographic coordinates: 33 27 S, 70 40 W
time difference: UTC-3 (2 hours ahead of Washington, DC, during Standard Time)

Administrative divisions: 15 regions (regiones, singular—region); Aysen, Antofagasta, Araucania, Arica y Parinacota, Atacama, Biobio, Coquimbo, Libertador General Bernardo O'Higgins, Los Lagos, Los Rios, Magallanes y de la Antartica Chilena, Maule, Region Metropolitana (Santiago), Tarapaca, Valparaiso
note: the US does not recognize claims to Antarctica

Independence: 18 September 1810 (from Spain)

National holiday: Independence Day, 18 September (1810)

Constitution: many previous; latest adopted 11 September 1980, effective 11 March 1981; amended many times, last in 2011; note—in late 2015, the Chilean Government initiated a process to reform its constitution (2016)

Legal system: civil law system influenced by several West European civil legal systems; judicial review of legislative acts by the Constitutional Tribunal

International law organization participation: has not submitted an ICJ jurisdiction declaration; accepts ICCt jurisdiction

Citizenship: *citizenship by birth:* yes
citizenship by descent: yes
dual citizenship recognized: yes
residency requirement for naturalization: 5 years

Suffrage: 18 years of age; universal

Executive branch: *chief of state:* President Michelle BACHELET Jeria (since 11 March 2014); note—the president is both chief of state and head of government

head of government: President Michelle BACHELET Jeria (since 11 March 2014)
cabinet: Cabinet appointed by the president
elections/appointments: president directly elected by absolute majority popular vote in 2 rounds if needed for a single 4-year term; election last held on 17 November 2013 with a runoff held on 15 December 2013 (next to be held on 19 November 2017)
election results: Michelle BACHELET Jeria elected president; percent of vote—Michelle BACHELET Jeria (PS) 62.2%; Evelyn Rose MATTHEI Fornet (UDI) 37.8%

Legislative branch: *description:* bicameral National Congress or Congreso Nacional consists of the Senate or Senado (38 seats; members directly elected in multi-seat constituencies by majority vote to serve 8-year terms with one-half of the membership renewed every 4 years) and the

Chamber of Deputies or Camara de Diputados (120 seats; members directly elected in multi-seat constituencies by majority vote to serve 4-year terms); note—in both the Senate and Chamber of Deputies, the party winning at least two-thirds of the votes is entitled to 2 seats in the constituency; if it obtains less than two-thirds of the votes, it is entitled to 1 seat with the remaining seat awarded to the next highest winning party

elections: Senate—last held on 17 November 2013 (next to be held on 15 November 2017); Chamber of Deputies—last held on 17 November 2013 (next to be held on 15 November 2017)

election results: Senate—percent of vote by party—NA; seats by party—New Majority Coalition (formerly known as Concertacion) 19 (PDC 6, PS 6, PPD 6, MAS 1), Coalition for Change (formerly known as the Alianza coalition) 15 (RN 6, UDI 8, Amplitude Party 1), independents 4; Chamber of Deputies-percent of vote by party—NA; seats by party—New Majority 68 (PDC 21, PS 16, PPD 14, PC 6, PRSD 6, Citizen Left 1, independents 4), Coalition for Change 47 (UDI 29, RN 14, independents 3, EP 1), Liberal Party 1, independents 4

note: In January 2015, the Chilean Congress voted to end the binomial system that was put in place under Gen. Augusto PINOCHET; the Congress also voted to expand its size and establish rules to ensure that there is equitable gender representation; the new electoral system will be put in place in 2017

Judicial branch: *highest court(s):* Supreme Court or Corte Suprema (consists of a court president and 20 members or ministros); Constitutional Court (consists of 7 members); Electoral Court (consists of 5 members)

judge selection and term of office: Supreme Court judges appointed by the president and ratified by the Senate from lists of candidates provided by the court itself; judges appointed for life with mandatory retirement at age 70; Constitutional Court members appointed—3 by the Supreme Court, 1 by the president of the republic, 2 by the National Security Council, and 1 by the Senate; members serve 8-year terms with partial membership replacement every 4 years (the court reviews constitutionality of legislation); Electoral Court member appointments—4 by the Supreme Court and 1 a former president or vice-president of the Senate or Chamber of Deputies selected by the Supreme Court; member term NA

subordinate courts: Courts of Appeal; oral criminal tribunals; military tribunals; local police courts; specialized tribunals and courts in matters such as family, labor, customs, taxes, and electoral affairs

Political parties and leaders: Broad Social Movement or MAS [Alejandro NAVARRO Brain] Citizen Left or IC [Sergio AGUILO] Coalition for Change or CC (also known as the Alliance for Chile (Alianza) or APC) (including National Renewal or RN [Cristian MONCK-EBERG Bruner], and Independent Democratic Union or UDI [Hernan LARRAIN Fernandez] Coalition of Parties for Democracy (Concertacion) or CPD (including Christian Democratic

Party or PDC [Jorge PIZARRO Soto], Party for Democracy or PPD [Jaime Daniel QUINTANA Leal], Radical Social Democratic Party or PRSD [Ernesto VELASCO Rodriguez], and Socialist Party or PS [Isabel ALLENDE Bussi])
Communist Party of Chile (Partido Comunista de Chile) or PC [Guillermo TEILLIER del Valle]
Ecological Green Party [Felix GONZALEZ Gatica]
Equality Party [Guillermo GONZALEZ Castro]
Humanist Party or PH [Octavio GONZALEZ]
Independent Regionalist Party or PRI [Alejandra BRAVO Hidalgo]
Liberal Party (Partido Liberal de Chile) [Vlado MIROSEVIC]
Political Evolution or EP [Felipe KAST]
Progressive Party or PRO [Patricia MORALES]

Political pressure groups and leaders: Roman Catholic Church, particularly conservative groups such as Opus Dei United Labor Central or CUT (includes trade unionists from the country's five largest labor confederations)
other: university student federations at all major universities

International organization participation: APEC, BIS, CAN (associate), CD, CELAC, FAO, G-15, G-77, IADB, IAEA, IBRD, ICAO, ICC (national committees), ICCt, ICRM, IDA, IFAD, IFC, IFRCS, IHO, ILO, IMF, IMO, IMSO, Interpol, IOC, IOM, IPU, ISO, ITSO, ITU, ITUC (NGOs), LAES, LAIA, Mercosur (associate), MIGA, MINUSTAH, NAM, OAS, OECD (Enhanced Engagement, OPANAL, OPCW, Pacific Alliance, PCA, SICA (observer), UN, UN Security Council (temporary), UNASUR, UNCTAD, UNESCO, UNFICYP, UNHCR, UNIDO, Union Latina, UNMOGIP, UNTSO, UNWTO, UPU, WCO, WFTU (NGOs), WHO, WIPO, WMO, WTO

Diplomatic representation in the US: *chief of mission:* Ambassador Juan Gabriel VALDES Soublette (since 21 May 2014)
chancery: 1732 Massachusetts Avenue NW, Washington, DC 20036
telephone: [1] (202) 785-1746
FAX: [1] (202) 887-5579
consulate(s) general: Chicago, Houston, Los Angeles, Miami, New York, San Francisco

Diplomatic representation from the US: *chief of mission:* Ambassador Michael HAMMER (since April 2014)
embassy: Avenida Andres Bello 2800, Las Condes, Santiago
maiing address: APO AA 34033
telephone: [56] (2) 2330-3000
FAX: [56] (2) 2330-3710, 2330-3160

Flag description: two equal horizontal bands of white (top) and red; a blue square the same height as the white band at the hoist-side end of the white band; the square bears a white five-pointed star in the center representing a guide to progress and honor; blue symbolizes the sky, white is for the snow-covered Andes, and red represents the blood spilled to achieve independence
note: design was influenced by the US flag

National symbol(s): huemul (mountain deer), Andean condor; national colors: red, white, blue
National anthem: *name:* "Himno Nacional de Chile" (National Anthem of Chile)
lyrics/music: Eusebio LILLO Robles and Bernardo DE VERA y Pintado/Ramon CARNICER y Battle
note: music adopted 1828, original lyrics adopted 1818, adapted lyrics adopted 1847; under Augusto PINOCHET"s military rule, a verse glorifying the army was added; however, as a protest, some citizens refused to sing this verse; it was removed when democracy was restored in 1990

ECONOMY

Economy—overview: Chile has a market-oriented economy characterized by a high level of foreign trade and a reputation for strong financial institutions and sound policy that have given it the strongest sovereign bond rating in South America. Exports of goods and services account for approximately one-third of GDP, with commodities making up some 60% of total exports. Copper alone provides 20% of government revenue. From 2003 through 2013, real growth averaged almost 5% per year, despite the slight contraction in 2009 that resulted from the global financial crisis. Growth slowed to an estimated 2.3% in 2015. A continued drop in copper prices prompted Chile to experience its second consecutive year of slow growth, elevated inflation, and a depreciating currency. Chile deepened its longstanding commitment to trade liberalization with the signing of a free trade agreement with the US, which took effect on 1 January 2004. Chile has 22 trade agreements covering 60 countries including agreements with the EU, Mercosur, China, India, South Korea, and Mexico. In May 2010, Chile signed the OECD Convention, becoming the first South American country to join the OECD. In October 2015, Chile joined the US and 10 other countries and concluded negotiations on the Trans-Pacific Partnership trade agreement. The agreement will need to be ratified by the Chilean legislature. The Chilean Government has generally followed a countercyclical fiscal policy, accumulating surpluses in sovereign wealth funds during periods of high copper prices and economic growth, and generally allowing deficit spending only during periods of low copper prices and growth . As of 31 October 2015, those sovereign wealth funds—kept mostly outside the country and separate from Central Bank reserves -amounted to more than $22.4 billion. Chile used these funds to finance fiscal stimulus packages during the 2009 economic downturn. In 2014, President M ichelle BACHELET introduced tax reforms aimed at delivering her campaign promise to fight inequality and to provide access to education and health care. The reforms are expected to generate additional tax revenues equal to 3% of Chile's GDP, mostly by increasing corporate tax rates to OECD averages.

GDP (purchasing power parity): $422.4 billion (2015 est.)
$413.9 billion (2014 est.)
$406.4 billion (2013 est.)
note: data are in 2015 US dollars

country comparison to the world: 44

GDP (official exchange rate): $240.2 billion (2015 est.)

GDP—real growth rate: 2.1% (2015 est.)
1.8% (2014 est.)
4% (2013 est.)
country comparison to the world: 134

GDP—per capita (PPP): $23,500 (2015 est.)
$23,200 (2014 est.)
$23,000 (2013 est.)
note: data are in 2015 US dollars
country comparison to the world: 80

Gross national saving: 20.4% of GDP (2015 est.)
20.9% of GDP (2014 est.)
20.8% of GDP (2013 est.)
country comparison to the world: 81

GDP—composition, by end use:
household consumption: 63.7%
government consumption: 13.2%
investment in fixed capital: 20.6%
investment in inventories: 0.4%
exports of goods and services: 30.5%
imports of goods and services: -28.4% (2015 est.)

GDP—composition, by sector of origin: *agriculture:* 3.4%
industry: 35%
services: 61.6% (2015 est.)

Agriculture—products: grapes, apples, pears, onions, wheat, corn, oats, peaches, garlic, asparagus, beans; beef, poultry, wool; fish; timber

Industries: copper, lithium, other minerals, foodstuffs, fish processing, iron and steel, wood and wood products, transport equipment, cement, textiles

Industrial production growth rate: 1.7% (2015 est.)
country comparison to the world: 127

Labor force: 8.68 million (2015 est.)
country comparison to the world: 58

Labor force—by occupation: *agriculture:* 13.2%
industry: 23%
services: 63.9% (2005)

Unemployment rate: 6.4% (2015 est.) 6.3% (2014 est.)
country comparison to the world: 74

Population below poverty line: 14.4% (2013)

Household income or consumption by percentage share: *lowest:* 10%: 1.5%
highest: 10%: 42.8% (2009 est.)

Distribution of family income—Gini index: 52.1 (2009)
57.1 (2000)
country comparison to the world: 15

Budget: *revenues:* $48.4 billion
expenditures: $56.31 billion (2015 est.)
Taxes and other revenues: 20.2% of GDP (2015 est.)
country comparison to the world: 153

Budget surplus (+) or deficit (-): -3.3% of GDP (2015 est.)
country comparison to the world: 125

Public debt: 17.4% of GDP (2015 est.) 15.1% of GDP (2014 est.)
country comparison to the world: 158

Fiscal year: calendar year

Inflation rate (consumer prices): 4.3% (2015 est.)
4.4% (2014 est.)

country comparison to the world: 162

Central bank discount rate: 3.12% (31 December 2010)
0.5% (31 December 2009)
country comparison to the world: 102

Commercial bank prime lending rate: 5.5% (31 December 2015 est.)
8.1% (31 December 2014 est.)
country comparison to the world: 138

Stock of narrow money: $40.65 billion (31 December 2015 est.)
$41.97 billion (31 December 2014 est.)
country comparison to the world: 55

Stock of broad money: $154.4 billion (31 December 2014 est.)
$158 billion (31 December 2013 est.)
country comparison to the world: 49

Stock of domestic credit: $196.9 billion (31 December 2015 est.)
$197.1 billion (31 December 2014 est.)
country comparison to the world: 44

Market value of publicly traded shares: $313.3 billion (31 December 2012 est.)
$270.3 billion (31 December 2011)
$341.6 billion (31 December 2010 est.)
country comparison to the world: 28

Current account balance: -$4.765 billion (2015 est.)
-$3.317 billion (2014 est.)
country comparison to the world: 168

Exports: $61.82 billion (2015 est.)
$75.68 billion (2014 est.)
country comparison to the world: 44

Exports—commodities: copper, fruit, fish products, paper and pulp, chemicals, wine

Exports—partners: China 26.3%, US 13.2%, Japan 8.5%, South Korea 6.5%, Brazil 4.9% (2015)

Imports: $56 billion (2015 est.)
$67.91 billion (2014 est.)
country comparison to the world: 48

Imports—commodities: petroleum and petroleum products, chemicals, electrical and telecommunications equipment, industrial machinery, vehicles, natural gas

Imports—partners: China 23.4%, US 18.8%, Brazil 7.8%, Argentina 4% (2015)

Reserves of foreign exchange and gold: $38.91 billion (31 December 2015 est.)
$40.45 billion (31 December 2014 est.)
country comparison to the world: 47

Debt—external: $145.7 billion (31 December 2014 est.)
$132.6 billion (31 December 2013 est.)
country comparison to the world: 42

Stock of direct foreign investment—at home: $201.4 billion (31 December 2015 est.)
$182.9 billion (31 December 2014 est.)
country comparison to the world: 29

Stock of direct foreign investment—abroad: $92.84 billion (31 December 2015 est.)
$80.54 billion (31 December 2014 est.)
country comparison to the world: 32

Exchange rates: Chilean pesos (CLP) per US dollar—
653.6 (2015 est.)

570.37 (2014 est.)
570.37 (2013 est.)
486.49 (2012 est.)
483.67 (2011 est.)

ENERGY

Electricity—production: 66.89 billion kWh (2012 est.)
country comparison to the world: 41

Electricity—consumption: 63.39 billion kWh (2012 est.)
country comparison to the world: 41

Electricity—exports: 0 kWh (2013 est.)
country comparison to the world: 121

Electricity—imports: 0 kWh (2013 est.)
country comparison to the world: 131

Electricity—installed generating capacity: 18.16 million kW (2012 est.)
country comparison to the world: 42

Electricity—from fossil fuels: 62.1% of total installed capacity (2012 est.)
country comparison to the world: 126

Electricity—from nuclear fuels: 0% of total installed capacity (2012 est.)
country comparison to the world: 67

Electricity—from hydroelectric plants: 33% of total installed capacity (2012 est.)
country comparison to the world: 69

Electricity—from other renewable sources: 4.9% of total installed capacity (2012 est.)
country comparison to the world: 57

Crude oil—production: 6,666 bbl/day (2014 est.)
country comparison to the world: 81

Crude oil—exports: 0 bbl/day (2013 est.)
country comparison to the world: 109

Crude oil—imports: 186,900 bbl/day (2013 est.)
country comparison to the world: 34

Crude oil—proved reserves: 150 million bbl (1 January 2015 est.)
country comparison to the world: 66

Refined petroleum products—production: 205,800 bbl/day (2013 est.)
country comparison to the world: 53

Refined petroleum products—consumption: 323,300 bbl/day (2014 est.)
country comparison to the world: 40

Refined petroleum products—exports: 16,810 bbl/day (2013 est.)
country comparison to the world: 75

Refined petroleum products—imports: 139,200 bbl/day (2013 est.)
country comparison to the world: 39

Natural gas—production: 908 million cu m (2014 est.)
country comparison to the world: 69

Natural gas—consumption: 4.646 billion cu m (2014 est.)
country comparison to the world: 60

Natural gas—exports: 0 cu m (2014 est.)
country comparison to the world: 78

Natural gas—imports: 3.715 billion cu m (2014 est.)
country comparison to the world: 37

Natural gas—proved reserves: 97.97 billion cu m (1 January 2014 est.)

country comparison to the world: 54
Carbon dioxide emissions from consumption of energy: 81.51 million Mt (2012 est.)
country comparison to the world: 46

COMMUNICATIONS

Telephones—fixed lines: *total subscriptions:* 3.4 million
subscriptions per 100 inhabitants: 20 (2014 est.)
country comparison to the world: 44
Telephones—mobile cellular: *total:* 23.7 million
subscriptions per 100 inhabitants: 136 (2014 est.)
country comparison to the world: 49
Telephone system: *general assessment:* privatization began in 1988; most advanced telecommunications infrastructure in South America; modern system based on extensive microwave radio relay facilities; domestic satellite system with 3 earth stations
domestic: number of fixed-line connections have stagnated in recent years as mobile-cellular usage continues to increase, reaching 130 telephones per 100 persons
international: country code—56; landing points for the Pan American, South America-1, and South American Crossing/Latin America Nautilus submarine cables providing links to the US and to Central and South America; satellite earth stations—2 Intelsat (Atlantic Ocean) (2011)
Broadcast media: national and local terrestrial TV channels, coupled with extensive cable TV networks; the state-owned Television Nacional de Chile (TVN) network is self-financed through commercial advertising revenues and is not under direct government control; large number of privately owned TV stations; about 250 radio stations (2007)
Radio broadcast stations: AM 180, FM 64, shortwave 17 (1998)
Television broadcast stations: 63 (plus 121 repeaters) (1997)

Internet country code: .cl
Internet hosts: 2.152 million (2012)

country comparison to the world: 38
Internet users: *total:* 11.4 million
percent of population: 65.8% (2014 est.)
country comparison to the world: 43

TRANSPORTATION

Airports: 481 (2013)
country comparison to the world: 15
Airports—with paved runways: *total:* 90
over 3,047 m: 5
2,438 to 3,047 m: 7
1,524 to 2,437 m: 23
914 to 1,523 m: 31
under 914 m: 24 (2013)
Airports—with unpaved runways: *total:* 391
2,438 to 3,047 m: 5
1,524 to 2,437 m: 11
914 to 1,523 m: 56
under 914 m: 319 (2013)

Heliports: 1 (2013)

Pipelines: gas 3,160 km; liquid petroleum gas 781 km; oil 985 km; refined products 722 km (2013)
Railways: *total:* 7,281.5 km
broad gauge: 3,428 km 1.676-m gauge (1,691 km electrified)
narrow gauge: 3,853.5 km 1.000-m gauge (2014)
country comparison to the world: 30
Roadways: *total:* 77,764 km
paved: 18,119 km (includes 2,387 km of expressways)
unpaved: 59,645 km (2010)
country comparison to the world: 61
Merchant marine: *total:* 42
by type: bulk carrier 13, cargo 5, chemical tanker 7, container 2, liquefied gas 1, passenger 3, passenger/cargo 2, petroleum tanker 8, roll on/roll off 1
foreign-owned: 1 (Norway 1)
registered in other countries: 52 (Argentina 6, Brazil 1, Honduras 1, Isle of Man 9, Liberia 9, Panama 14, Peru 6, Singapore 6) (2010)
country comparison to the world: 74

Ports and terminals: *major seaport(s):* Coronel, Huasco, Lirquen, Puerto Ventanas, San Antonio, San Vicente, Valparaiso

LNG terminal(s) (import): Mejillones, Quintero

MILITARY AND SECURITY

Military branches: Chilean Army, Chilean Navy (Armada de Chile, includes Naval Aviation, Marine Corps, and Maritime Territory and Merchant Marine Directorate (Directemar)), Chilean Air Force (Fuerza Aerea de Chile, FACh) (2015)
Military service age and obligation: 18–45 years of age for voluntary male and female military service, although the right to compulsory recruitment of males 18–45 is retained; service obligation is 12 months for Army and 22 months for Navy and Air Force (2015)
Military expenditures: 2.04% of GDP (2012)
2.17% of GDP (2011)
2.04% of GDP (2010)
country comparison to the world: 38

TRANSNATIONAL ISSUES

Disputes—international: Chile and Peru rebuff Bolivia's reactivated claim to restore the Atacama corridor, ceded to Chile in 1884, but Chile has offered instead unrestricted but not sovereign maritime access through Chile to Bolivian natural gas; Chile rejects Peru's unilateral legislation to change its latitudinal maritime boundary with Chile to an equidistance line with a southwestern axis favoring Peru; in October 2007, Peru took its maritime complaint with Chile to the ICJ; territorial claim in Antarctica (Chilean Antarctic Territory) partially overlaps Argentine and British claims; the joint boundary commission, established by Chile and Argentina in 2001, has yet to map and demarcate the delimited boundary in the inhospitable Andean Southern Ice Field (Campo de Hielo Sur)

Illicit drugs: transshipment country for cocaine destined for Europe and the region; some money laundering activity, especially through the Iquique Free Trade Zone; imported precursors passed on to Bolivia; domestic cocaine consumption is rising, making Chile a significant consumer of cocaine (2008)

CHINA

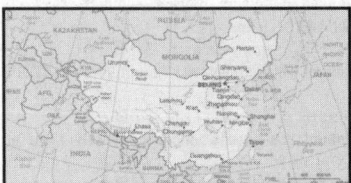

INTRODUCTION

Background: For centuries China stood as a leading civilization, outpacing the rest of the world in the arts and sciences, but in the 19th and early 20th centuries, the country was beset by civil unrest, major famines, military defeats, and foreign occupation. After World War II, the communists under MAO Zedong established an autocratic socialist system that, while ensuring China's sovereignty, imposed strict controls over everyday life and cost the lives of tens of millions of people. After 1978, MAO's successor DENG Xiaoping and other leaders focused on market-oriented economic development and by 2000 output had quadrupled. For much of the population, living standards have improved dramatically and the room for personal choice has expanded, yet political controls remain tight. Since the early 1990s, China has increased its global outreach and participation in international organizations.

GEOGRAPHY

Location: Eastern Asia, bordering the East China Sea, Korea Bay, Yellow Sea, and South China Sea, between North Korea and Vietnam
Geographic coordinates: 35 00 N, 10 500 E
Map references: Asia
Area: *total:* 9,596,960 sq km
land: 9,326,410 sq km
water: 270,550 sq km
country comparison to the world: 4

Area—comparative: slightly smaller than the US

Land boundaries: *total:* 22,457 km
border countries (14): Afghanistan 91 km, Bhutan 477 km, Burma 2,129 km, India 2,659 km,

Kazakhstan 1,765 km, North Korea 1,352 km, Kyrgyzstan 1,063 km, Laos 475 km, Mongolia 4,630 km, Nepal 1,389 km, Pakistan 438 km, Russia (northeast) 4,133 km, Russia (northwest) 46 km, Tajikistan 477 km, Vietnam 1,297 km
regional borders: Hong Kong 33 km, Macau 3 km

Coastline: 14,500 km
Maritime claims: *territorial sea:* 12 nm
contiguous zone: 24 nm
exclusive economic zone: 200 nm
continental shelf: 200 nm or to the edge of the continental margin
Climate: extremely diverse; tropical in south to subarctic in north

Terrain: mostly mountains, high plateaus, deserts in west; plains, deltas, and hills in east
Elevation: *mean elevation:* 1,840 m

elevation extremes: *lowest point:* Turpan Pendi -154 m
highest point: Mount Everest 8,850 m (highest peak in Asia and highest point on earth above sea level)
Natural resources: coal, iron ore, petroleum, natural gas, mercury, tin, tungsten, antimony, manganese, molybdenum, vanadium, magnetite, aluminum, lead, zinc, rare earth elements, uranium, hydropower potential (world's largest),
arable land:
Land use: *agricultural land:* 54.7%
arable land: 11.3%
permanent crops: 1.6%
permanent pasture: 41.8%
forest: 22.3%
other: 23% (2011 est.)
Irrigated land: 690,070 sq km (2012)

Total renewable water resources: 2,840 cu km (2011)
Freshwater withdrawal (domestic/industrial/agricultural): *total:* 554.1 cu m/yr (12%/23%/65%)
per capita: 409.9 cu m/yr (2005)

Natural hazards: frequent typhoons (about five per year along southern and eastern coasts); damaging floods; tsunamis; earthquakes; droughts; land subsidence
volcanism: China contains some historically active volcanoes including Changbaishan (also known as Baitoushan, Baegdu, or P'aektu-san), Hainan Dao, and Kunlun although most have been relatively inactive in recent centuries

Environment—current issues: air pollution (greenhouse gases, sulfur dioxide particulates) from reliance on coal produces acid rain; China is the world's largest single emitter of carbon dioxide from the burning of fossil fuels; water shortages, particularly in the north; water pollution from untreated wastes; deforestation; estimated loss of one-fifth of agricultural land since 1949 to soil erosion and economic development; desertification; trade in endangered species

Environment—international agreements: *party to:* Antarctic-Environmental Protocol, Antarctic Treaty, Biodiversity, Climate Change, Climate Change-Kyoto Protocol, Desertification, Endangered Species, Environmental Modification,

Hazardous Wastes, Law of the Sea, Marine Dumping, Ozone Layer Protection, Ship Pollution, Tropical Timber 83, Tropical Timber 94, Wetlands, Whaling
signed, but not ratified: none of the selected agreements

Geography—note: world's fourth largest country (after Russia, Canada, and US) and largest country situated entirely in Asia; Mount Everest on the border with Nepal is the world's tallest peak

PEOPLE AND SOCIETY

Nationality: *noun:* Chinese (singular and plural)
adjective: Chinese
Ethnic groups: Han Chinese 91.6%, Zhuang 1.3%, other (includes Hui, Manchu, Uighur, Miao, Yi, Tujia, Tibetan, Mongol, Dong, Buyei, Yao, Bai, Korean, Hani, Li, Kazakh, Dai and other nationalities) 7.1%
note: the Chinese Government officially recognizes 56 ethnic groups (2010 est.)
Languages: Standard Chinese or Mandarin (official; Putonghua, based on the Beijing dialect), Yue (Cantonese), Wu (Shanghainese), Minbei (Fuzhou), Minnan (Hokkien-Taiwanese), Xiang, Gan, Hakka dialects, minority languages (see Ethnic groups entry)
note: Zhuang is official in Guangxi Zhuang, Yue is official in Guangdong, Mongolian is official in Nei Mongol, Uighur is official in Xinjiang Uygur, Kyrgyz is official in Xinjiang Uygur, and Tibetan is official in Xizang (Tibet)
Religions: Buddhist 18.2%, Christian 5.1%, Muslim 1.8%, folk religion 21.9%, Hindu < 0.1%, Jewish < 0.1%, other 0.7% (includes Daoist (Taoist)), unaffiliated 52.2%
note: officially atheist (2010 est.)
Population: 1,367,485,388 (July 2015 est.)
country comparison to the world: 1
Age structure: *0–14 years:* 17.08% (male 126,146,137/female 107,410,265)
15–24 years: 13.82% (male 100,380,703/female 88,615,299)
25–54 years: 47.95% (male 334,240,795/female 321,417,301)
55–64 years: 11.14% (male 77,098,602/female 75,286,553)
65 years and over: 10.01% (male 65,573,256/female 71,316,477) (2015 est.)
Dependency ratios: *total dependency ratio:* 36.6%
youth dependency ratio: 23.5%
elderly dependency ratio: 13%
potential support ratio: 7.7% (2015 est.)
Median age: *total:* 36.8 years
male: 36 years
female: 37.7 years (2015 est.)
country comparison to the world: 66
Population growth rate: 0.45% (2015 est.)
country comparison to the world: 162
Birth rate: 12.49 births/1,000 population (2015 est.)
country comparison to the world: 159
Death rate: 7.53 deaths/1,000 population (2015 est.)
country comparison to the world: 112

Net migration rate: -0.44 migrant(s)/1,000 population (2015 est.)
country comparison to the world: 133
Urbanization: *urban population:* 55.6% of total population (2015)
rate of urbanization: 3.05% annual rate of change (2010–15 est.)

Major urban areas—population: Shanghai 23.741 million; BEIJING (capital) 20.384 million; Chongqing 13.332 million; Guangdong 12.458 m illio n; Tianjin 11.21 million; Shenzhen 10.749 million (2015)

Sex ratio: *at birth:* 1.15 male(s)/female
0–14 years: 1.17 male(s)/female
15–24 years: 1.13 male(s)/female
25–54 years: 1.04 male(s)/female
55–64 years: 1.02 male(s)/female
65 years and over: 0.92 male(s)/female
total population: 1.06 male(s)/female (2015 est.)
Maternal mortality rate: 27 deaths/100,000 live births (2015 est.)
country comparison to the world: 116
Infant mortality rate: *total:* 12.44 deaths/1,000 live births
male: 12.58 deaths/1,000 live births
female: 12.27 deaths/1,000 live births (2015 est.)
country comparison to the world: 121

Life expectancy at birth:
total population: 75.41 years
male: 73.38 years
female: 77.73 years (2015 est.)
country comparison to the world: 99
Total fertility rate: 1.6 children born/woman (2015 est.)
country comparison to the world: 181

Contraceptive prevalence rate: 84.6% (2006)
Health expenditures: 5.6% of GDP (2013)
country comparison to the world: 126

Physicians density: 1.49 physicians/1,000 population (2011)

Hospital bed density: 3.8 beds/1,000 population (2011)
Drinking water source:
improved:
urban: 97.5% of population
rural: 93% of population
total: 95.5% of population
unimproved:
urban: 2.5% of population
rural: 7% of population
total: 4.5% of population (2015 est.)
Sanitation facility access:
improved:
urban: 86.6% of population
rural: 63.7% of population
total: 76.5% of population
unimproved:
urban: 13.4% of population
rural: 36.3% of population
total: 23.5% of population (2015 est.)
HIV/AIDS—adult prevalence rate: 0.1% (2012 est.)
country comparison to the world: 112
HIV/AIDS—people living with HIV/AIDS: 780,000 (2012 est.)
country comparison to the world: 11

HIV/AIDS—deaths: NA

Major infectious diseases: *degree of risk:* intermediate

food or waterborne diseases: bacterial diarrhea, hepatitis A, and typhoid fever

vectorborne disease: Japanese encephalitis

soil contact disease: hantaviral hemorrhagic fever with renal syndrome (HFRS)

note: highly pathogenic H5N1 avian influenza has been identified in this country; it poses a negligible risk with extremely rare cases possible among US citizens who have close contact with birds (2013)

Obesity—adult prevalence rate: 7.3% (2014)
country comparison to the world: 152

Children under the age of 5 years underweight: 3.4% (2010)
country comparison to the world: 109

Education expenditures: NA

Literacy: *definition:* age 15 and over can read and write

total population: 96.4%
male: 98.2%
female: 94.5% (2015 est.)

School life expectancy (primary to tertiary education): *total:* 14 years
male: 14 years
female: 14 years (2014)

People—note: in October 2015, the Chinese Government announced that it would change its rules to allow all couples to have two children instead of just one, as mandated in 1979; the new policy was implemented on 1 January 2016 to address China's rapidly aging population and economic needs

GOVERNMENT

Country name: *conventional long form:* People's Republic of China
conventional short form: China
local long form: Zhonghua Renmin Gongheguo
local short form: Zhongguo abbreviation: PRC
etymology: English name derives from the Qin (Chin) rulers of the 3rd century B.C., who comprised the first imperial dynasty of ancient China; the Chinese name Zhongguo translates as "Central Nation"

Government type: communist state

Capital: name: Beijing

Geographic coordinates: 39 55 N, 11 623 E
time difference: UTC+8 (13 hours ahead of Washington, DC, during Standard Time)
note: despite its size, all of China falls within one time zone; many people in Xinjiang Province observe an unofficial "Xinjiang time zone" of UTC+6, two hours behind Beijing

Administrative divisions: 23 provinces (sheng, singular and plural), 5 autonomous regions (zizhiqu, singular and plural), and 4 municipalities (shi, singular and plural)
provinces: Anhui, Fujian, Gansu, Guangdong, Guizhou, Hainan, Hebei, Heilongjiang, Henan, Hubei, Hunan, Jiangsu, Jiangxi, Jilin, Liaoning, Qinghai, Shaanxi, Shandong, Shanxi, Sichuan, Yunnan, Zhejiang; (see note on Taiwan) autonomous regions: Guangxi, Nei Mongol (Inner Mongolia), Ningxia, Xinjiang Uygur, Xizang (Tibet)

m UN icipalities: Beijing, Chongqing, Shanghai, Tianjin
note: China considers Taiwan its 23rd province; see separate entries for the special administrative regions of Hong Kong and Macau

Independence: 1 October 1949 (People's Republic of China established); notable earlier dates: 221 B.C. (unification under the Qin Dynasty); 1 January 1912 (Qing Dynasty replaced by the Republic of China)

National holiday: National Day, the anniversary of the founding of the People's Republic of China, 1 October (1949)

Constitution: several previous; latest promulgated 4 December 1982; amended several times, last in 2004 (2016)

Legal system: civil law influenced by Soviet and continental European civil law systems; legislature retains power to interpret statutes; note—criminal procedure law revised in early 2012

International law organization participation: has not submitted an ICJ jurisdiction declaration; non-party state to the ICCt

Citizenship: *citizenship by birth:* no
citizenship by descent only: least one parent must be a citizen of China
dual citizenship recognized: no
residency requirement for naturalization: while naturalization is theoretically possible, in practical terms it is extremely difficult; residency is required but not specified

Suffrage: 18 years of age; universal

Executive branch: *chief of state:* President XI Jinping (since 14 March 2013); Vice President LI Yuanchao (since 14 March 2013)

head of government: Premier LI Keqiang (since 16 March 2013); Executive Vice Premiers ZHANG Gaoli (since 16 March 2013), LIU Yandong (since 16 March 2013), MA Kai (since 16 March 2013), WANG Yang (since 16 March 2013)
cabinet: State Council appointed by National People's Congress
elections/appointments: president and vice president indirectly elected by National People's Congress for a 5-year term (eligible for a second term); election last held on 5–17 March 2013 (next to be held in March 2018); premier nominated by president, confirmed by National People's Congress
election results: XI Jinping elected president; National People's Congress vote—2,952; LI Yuanchao elected vice president with 2,940 votes

Legislative branch: *description:* unicameral National People's Congress or Quanguo Renmin Daibiao Dahui (2,987 seats; members indirectly elected by municipal, regional, and provincial people's congresses, and the People's Liberation Army; members serve 5-year terms); note—in practice, only members of the Chinese Communist Party (CCP), its 8 allied parties, and CCP-approved independent candidates are elected
elections: last held in December 2012-February 2013 (next to be held in late 2017 to early 2018)
election results: percent of vote—NA; seats—2,987

Judicial branch: *highest court(s):* Supreme People's Court (consists of over 340 judges including the chief justice, 13 grand justices organized into a civil committee and tribunals for civil, economic, administrative, complaint and appeal, and communication and transportation cases)
judge selection and term of office: chief justice appointed by the People's National Congress; term limited to 2 consecutive 5-year terms; other justices and judges nominated by the chief justice and appointed by the Standing Committee of the People's National Congress; term of other justices and judges NA
subordinate courts: Higher People's Courts; Intermediate People's Courts; District and County People's Courts; Autonomous Region People's Courts; Special People's Courts for military, maritime, transportation, and forestry issues
note: in late 2014, China unveiled planned judicial reforms

Political parties and leaders: Chinese Communist Party or CCP [XI Jinping]
note: China has eight nominally independent small parties ultimately controlled by the CCP

Political pressure groups and leaders: no substantial political opposition groups exist

International organization participation: ADB, AfDB (nonregional member), APEC, Arctic Council (observer), ARF, ASEAN (dialogue partner), BIS, BRICS, CDB, CICA, EAS, FAO, FATF, G-20, G-24 (observer), G-5, G-77, IADB, IAEA, IBRD, ICAO, ICC (national committees), ICRM, IDA, IFAD, IFC, IFRCS, IHO, ILO, IMF, IMO, IMSO, Interpol, IOC, IOM (observer), IPU, ISO, ITSO, ITU, LAIA (observer), MIGA, MINURSO, MINUSMA, MONUSCO, NAM (observer), NSG, OAS (observer), OPCW, Pacific Alliance (observer), PCA, PIF (partner), SAARC (observer), SCO, SICA (observer), UN, UNAMID, UNCTAD, UNESCO, UNFICYP, UNHCR, UNIDO, UNIFIL, UNMIL, UNMISS, UNOCI, UNSC (permanent), UNTSO, UNWTO, UPU, WCO, WHO, WIPO, WMO, WTO, ZC

Diplomatic representation in the US: *chief of mission:* Ambassador CUI Tiankai (since 3 April 2013)
chancery: 3505 International Place NW, Washington, DC 20008
telephone: [1] (202) 495-2266
FAX: [1] (202) 495-2138
consulate(s) general: Chicago, Houston, Los Angeles, New York, San Francisco

Diplomatic representation from the US: *chief of mission:* Ambassador Max Sieben BAUCUS (since 18 March 2014)
embassy: 55 An Jia Lou Lu, 100600 Beijing
mailing address: PSC 461, Box 50, FPO AP 96521-0002
telephone: [86] (10) 8531-3000
FAX: [86] (10) 8531-3300
consulate(s) general: Chengdu, Guangzhou, Shanghai, Shenyang, Wuhan

Flag description: red with a large yellow five-pointed star and four smaller yellow five-pointed stars (arranged in a vertical arc toward the middle of the flag) in the upper hoist-side corner; the color red represents revolution, while the stars symbolize the four social classes—the working class, the peasantry, the urban petty bourgeoisie, and the national bourgeoisie (capitalists)—united under the Communist Party of China

National symbol(s): dragon; national colors: red, yellow

National anthem: *name:* "Yiyongjun Jinxingqu" (The March of the Volunteers)
lyrics/music: TIAN Han/NIE Er
note: adopted 1949; the anthem, though banned during the Cultural Revolution, is more commonly known as "Zhongguo Guoge" (Chinese National Song); it was originally the theme song to the 1935 Chinese movie, "Sons and Daughters in a Time of Storm"

ECONOMY

Economy—overview: Since the late 1970s, China has moved from a closed, centrally planned system to a more market-oriented one that plays a major global role; in 2010, China became the world's largest exporter. Reforms began with the phaseout of collectivized agriculture, and expanded to include the gradual liberalization of prices, fiscal decentralization, increased autonomy for state enterprises, growth of the private sector, development of stock markets and a modern banking system, and opening to foreign trade and investment. China has implemented reforms in a gradualist fashion. In recent years, China has renewed its support for state-owned enterprises in sectors considered important to "economic security," explicitly looking to foster globally competitive industries. The restructuring of the economy and resulting efficiency gains have contributed to a more than tenfold increase in GDP since 1978. Measured on a purchasing power parity (PPP) basis that adjusts for price differences, China in 2015 stood as the largest economy in the world, surpassing the US in 2014 for the first time in modern history. Still, China's per capita income is below the world average.

After keeping its currency tightly linked to the US dollar for years, China in July 2005 moved to an exchange rate system that references a basket of currencies. From mid-2005 to late 2008, cumulative appreciation of the renminbi against the US dollar was more than 20%, but the exchange rate remained virtually pegged to the dollar from the onset of the global financial crisis until June 2010, when Beijing allowed resumption of a gradual appreciation. In 2015, the People's Bank of China announced it would continue to carefully push for full convertibility of the renminbi after the currency was accepted as part of the IMF's special drawing rights basket.

The Chinese Government faces numerous economic challenges including: (a) reducing its high domestic savings rate and correspondingly low domestic consumption; (b) facilitating higher-wage job opportunities for the aspiring middle class, including rural migrants and increasing numbers of college graduates; (c) reducing

corruption and other economic crimes; and (d) containing environmental damage and social strife related to the economy's rapid transformation. Economic development has progressed further in coastal provinces than in the interior, and by 2014 more than 274 million migrant workers and their dependents had relocated to urban areas to find work. One consequence of population control policy is that China is now one of the most rapidly aging countries in the world. Deterioration in the environment—notably air pollution, soil erosion, and the steady fall of the water table, especially in the North—is another long-term problem. China continues to lose arable land: because of erosion and economic development. The Chinese government is seeking to add energy production capacity from sources other than coal and oil, focusing on nuclear and alternative energy development.

Several factors are converging to slow China's growth, including debt overhang from its credit-fueled stimulus program, industrial overcapacity, inefficient allocation of capital by state-owned banks, and the slow recovery of China's trading partners. The government's 13th Five-Year Plan, unveiled in November 2015, emphasizes continued economic reforms and the need to increase innovation and domestic consumption in order to make the economy less dependent in the future on fixed investments, exports, and heavy industry. However, China has made only marginal progress toward these rebalancing goals. The new government of President XI Jinping has signaled a greater willingness to undertake reforms that focus on China's long-term economic health, including giving the market a more decisive role in allocating resources. In 2014, China agreed to begin limiting carbon dioxide emissions by 2030.

GDP (purchasing power parity): $19.39 trillion (2015 est.)
$18.14 trillion (2014 est.)
$16.91 trillion (2013 est.)
note: data are in 2015 US dollars
country comparison to the world: 1

GDP (official exchange rate): $10.98 trillion (2015 est.)
note: because China's exchange rate is determined by fiat rather than by market forces, the official exchange rate measure of GDP is not an accurate measure of China's output; GDP at the official exchange rate substantially understates the actual level of China's output vis-a-vis the rest of the world; in China's situation, GDP at purchasing power parity provides the best measure for comparing output across countries

GDP—real growth rate: 6.9% (2015 est.)
7.3% (2014 est.)
7.7% (2013 est.)
country comparison to the world: 18

GDP—per capita (PPP): $14,100 (2015 est.)
$13,300 (2014 est.)
$12,400 (2013 est.)
note: data are in 2015 US dollars
country comparison to the world: 113

Gross national saving: 46% of GDP (2015 est.)
48% of GDP (2014 est.)

48% of GDP (2013 est.)
country comparison to the world: 3

GDP—composition, by end use:
household consumption: 38.1%
government consumption: 13.8%
investment in fixed capital: 42.4%
investment in inventories: 1%
exports of goods and services: 22.7%
imports of goods and services: -18% (2015 est.)

GDP—composition, by sector of origin: *agriculture:* 8.9%
industry: 42.7%
services: 48.4% (2015 est.)

Agriculture—products: world leader in gross value of agricultural output; rice, wheat, potatoes, corn, peanuts, tea, millet, barley, apples, cotton, oilseed; pork; fish

Industries: world leader in gross value of industrial output; mining and ore processing, iron, steel, aluminum, and other metals, coal; machine building; armaments; textiles and apparel; petroleum; cement; chemicals; fertilizers; consumer products (including footwear, toys, and electronics); food processing; transportation equipment, including automobiles, rail cars and locomotives, ships, aircraft; telecommunications equipment, commercial space launch vehicles, satellites

Industrial production growth rate: 7% (2015 est.)
country comparison to the world: 16

Labor force: 804 million
note: by the end of 2012, China's population at working age (15–64 years) was 1.004 billion (2015 est.)
country comparison to the world: 1

Labor force—by occupation: *agriculture:* 33.6%
industry: 30.3%
services: 36.1% (2012 est.)

Unemployment rate: 4.2% (2015 est.)
4.1% (2014 est.)
note: data are for registered urban unemployment, which excludes private enterprises and migrants
country comparison to the world: 40

Population below poverty line: 6.1%
note: in 2011, China set a new poverty line at RMB 2300 (approximately US $400) (2013 est.)

Household income or consumption by percentage share: *lowest:* 10%: 1.7%
highest: 10%: 30%
note: data are for urban households only (2009)

Distribution of family income—Gini index: 46.9 (2014 est.)
47.3 (2013 est.)
country comparison to the world: 29

Budget: *revenues:* $2.426 trillion
expenditures: $2.718 trillion (2015 est.)
Taxes and other revenues: 21.3% of GDP (2015 est.)
country comparison to the world: 147

Budget surplus (+) or deficit (-): -2.6% of GDP (2015 est.)
country comparison to the world: 93

Public debt: 16.7% of GDP (2015 est.)
14.9% of GDP (2014 est.)
note: official data; data cover both central government debt and local government debt, which China's National Audit Office estimated at RMB

10.72 trillion (approximately US$1.66 trillion) in 2011; data exclude policy bank bonds, Ministry of Railway debt, China Asset Management Company debt, and non-performing loans
country comparison to the world: 160

Fiscal year: calendar year
Inflation rate (consumer prices): 1.4% (2015 est.)
2% (2014 est.)
country comparison to the world: 94
Central bank discount rate: 2.25% (31 December 2014 est.)
2.25% (31 December 2013 est.)
country comparison to the world: 111
Commercial bank prime lending rate: 4.4% (31 December 2015 est.)
5.6% (31 December 2014 est.)
country comparison to the world: 156
Stock of narrow money: $5.753 trillion (31 December 2015 est.)
$5.688 trillion (31 December 2014 est.)
country comparison to the world: 2
Stock of broad money: $20.93 trillion (31 December 2015 est.)
$20.07 trillion (31 December 2014 est.)
country comparison to the world: 1
Stock of domestic credit: $18.81 trillion (31 December 2015 est.)
$17.6 trillion (31 December 2014 est.)
country comparison to the world: 3
Market value of publicly traded shares: $6.065 trillion (31 December 2014 est.)
$6.499 trillion (31 December 2013)
$5.753 trillion (31 December 2012 est.)
country comparison to the world: 3
Current account balance: $293.2 billion (2015 est.)
$219.7 billion (2014 est.)
country comparison to the world: 2
Exports: $2.27 trillion (2015 est.)
$2.244 trillion (2014 est.)
country comparison to the world: 1
Exports—commodities: electrical and other machinery, including data processing equipment, apparel, furniture, textiles, integrated circuits
Exports—partners: US 18%, Hong Kong 14.6%, Japan 6%, South Korea 4.5% (2015)
Imports: $1.596 trillion (2015 est.)
$1.808 trillion (2014 est.)
country comparison to the world: 3
Imports—commodities: electrical and other machinery, oil and mineral fuels; nuclear reactor, boiler, and machinery components; optical and medical equipment, metal ores, motor vehicles; soybeans
Imports—partners: South Korea 10.9%, US 9%, Japan 8.9%, Germany 5.5%, Australia 4.1% (2015)
Reserves of foreign exchange and gold: $3.217 trillion (31 December 2015 est.)
$3.869 trillion (31 December 2014 est.)
country comparison to the world: 1
Debt—external: $949.6 billion (31 December 2014 est.)
$874.5 billion (31 December 2013 est.)
country comparison to the world: 19

Stock of direct foreign investment—at home:
$1.723 trillion (31 December 2015 est.)
$1.334 trillion (31 December 2014 est.)
country comparison to the world: 4
Stock of direct foreign investment—abroad:
$1.111 trillion (31 December 2015 est.)
$792.3 billion (31 December 2014 est.)
country comparison to the world: 11
Exchange rates: Renminbi yuan (RMB) per US dollar—
6.243 (2015 est.)
6.1434 (2014 est.)
6.1958 (2013 est.)
6.3123 (2012 est.)
6.4615 (2011 est.)

ENERGY

Electricity—production: 5.65 trillion kWh (2014)
country comparison to the world: 1
Electricity—consumption: 5.523 trillion kWh (2014)
country comparison to the world: 1
Electricity—exports: 18.16 billion kWh (2014)
country comparison to the world: 11
Electricity—imports: 6.75 billion kWh (2014)
country comparison to the world: 35
Electricity—installed generating capacity: 1.505 billion kW (2014 est.)
country comparison to the world: 1
Electricity—from fossil fuels: 67.3% of total installed capacity (2014 est.)
country comparison to the world: 117
Electricity—from nuclear fuels: 1.5% of total installed capacity (2014 est.)
country comparison to the world: 31
Electricity—from hydroelectric plants: 22.2% of total installed capacity (2014 est.)
country comparison to the world: 89
Electricity—from other renewable sources: 9% of total installed capacity (2014 est.)
country comparison to the world: 41
Crude oil—production: 4.189 million bbl/day (2014 est.)
country comparison to the world: 4
Crude oil—exports: 12,000 bbl/day (2014 est.)
country comparison to the world: 63
Crude oil—imports: 6.167 million bbl/day (2014 est.)
country comparison to the world: 2
Crude oil—proved reserves: 24.65 billion bbl (1 January 2015 est.)
country comparison to the world: 14
Refined petroleum products—production: 9.879 million bbl/day (2012 est.)
country comparison to the world: 3
Refined petroleum products—consumption: 10.48 million bbl/day (2013 est.)
country comparison to the world: 3
Refined petroleum products—exports: 593,400 bbl/day (2014 est.)
country comparison to the world: 9
Refined petroleum products—imports: 600,000 bbl/day (2014 est.)
country comparison to the world: 12
Natural gas—production: 121.5 billion cu m (2014 est.)
country comparison to the world: 7

Natural gas—consumption: 180.4 billion cu m (2014 est.)
country comparison to the world: 4
Natural gas—exports: 2.603 billion cu m (2014 est.)
country comparison to the world: 34
Natural gas—imports: 59.7 billion cu m (2014 est.)
country comparison to the world: 5
Natural gas—proved reserves: 3.3 trillion cu m (1 January 2014 est.)
country comparison to the world: 11
Carbon dioxide emissions from consumption of energy: 10 billion Mt (2013 est.)
country comparison to the world: 1

COMMUNICATIONS

Telephones—fixed lines: *total subscriptions:* 249.4 million
subscriptions per 100 inhabitants: 18 (2014 est.)
country comparison to the world: 1
Telephones—mobile cellular: *total:* 1.3 billion
subscriptions per 100 inhabitants: 94 (2014 est.)
country comparison to the world: 1
Telephone system: *general assessment:* domestic and international services are increasingly available for private use; unevenly distributed domestic system serves principal cities, industrial centers, and many towns; China continues to develop its telecommunications infrastructure; China in the summer of 2008 began a major restructuring of its telecommunications industry, resulting in the consolidation of its six telecom service operators to three, China Telecom, China Mobile, and China Unicom, each providing both fixed-line and mobile services
domestic: interprovincial fiber-optic trunk lines and cellular telephone systems have been installed; mobile-cellular subscribership is increasing rapidly; the number of Internet users exceeded 564 million by the end of 2012; a domestic satellite system with several earth stations is in place
international: country code—86; a number of submarine cables provide connectivity to Asia, the Middle East, Europe, and the US; satellite earth stations—7 (5 Intelsat—4 Pacific Ocean and 1 Indian Ocean; 1 Intersputnik—Indian Ocean region; and 1 Inmarsat—Pacific and Indian Ocean regions) (2012)

Broadcast media: all broadcast media are owned by, or affiliated with, the Communist Party of China or a government agency; no privately owned TV or radio stations; state-run Chinese Central TV, provincial, and municipal stations offer more than 2,000 channels; the Central Propaganda Department lists subjects that are off limits to domestic broadcast media with the government maintaining authority to approve all programming; foreign-made TV programs must be approved prior to broadcast
Radio broadcast stations: AM 369, FM 259, shortwave 45 (1998)
Television broadcast stations: 3,240 (of which 209 are operated by China Central Television, 31 are provincial TV stations, and nearly 3,000 are local city stations) (1997)

Internet country code: .cn
Internet hosts: 20.602 million (2012)
country comparison to the world: 5
Internet users: *total:* 626.6 million
percent of population: 46.0% (2014 est.)
country comparison to the world: 1

TRANSPORTATION

Airports: 507 (2013)
country comparison to the world: 14
Airports—with paved runways: *total:* 463
over 3,047 m: 71
2,438 to 3,047 m: 158
1,524 to 2,437 m: 123
914 to 1,523 m: 25
under 914 m: 86 (2013)
Airports—with unpaved runways: *total:* 44
over 3,047 m: 4
2,438 to 3,047 m: 7
1,524 to 2,437 m: 6
914 to 1,523 m: 9
under 914 m: 18 (2013)
Heliports: 47 (2013)
Pipelines: condensate 9 km; gas 48,502 km; oil 23,072 km; oil/gas/water 31 km; refined products 15,298 km; water 9 km (2013)
Railways: *total:* 191,270 km
broad gauge: 100 km 1.520-m gauge
standard gauge: 190,000 km 1.435-m gauge (92,000 km electrified)
narrow gauge: 670 km 1.000-m gauge; 500 km 0.762-m gauge (2014)
country comparison to the world: 2
Roadways: *total:* 4,106,387 km
paved: 3,453,890 km (includes 84,946 km of expressways)
unpaved: 652,497 km (2011)
country comparison to the world: 3
Waterways: 110,000 km (navigable waterways) (2011)
country comparison to the world: 1
Merchant marine: *total:* 2,030
by type: barge carrier 7, bulk carrier 621, cargo 566, carrier 10, chemical tanker 140, container 206, liquefied gas 60, passenger 9, passenger/cargo 81, petroleum tanker 264, refrigerated cargo 33, roll on/roll off 8, specialized tanker 2, vehicle carrier 23
foreign-owned: 22 (Hong Kong 18, Indonesia 2, Japan 2)
registered in other countries: 1,559 (Bangladesh 1, Belize 61, Cambodia 177, Comoros 1, Cyprus 6, Georgia 10, Honduras 2, Hong Kong 500, India 1, Indonesia 1, Kiribati 26, Liberia 4, Malta 6, Marshall Islands 14, North Korea 3, Panama 534, Philippines 4, Saint Kitts and Nevis 1, Saint Vincent and the Grenadines 65, Sao Tome and Principe 1, Sierra Leone 19, Singapore 29, South Korea 6, Thailand 1, Togo 1, Tuvalu 4, UK 7, Vanuatu 1, unknown 73) (2010)
country comparison to the world: 3
Ports and terminals: *major seaport(s):* Dalian, Ningbo, Qingdao, Qinhuangdao, Shanghai, Shenzhen, Tianjin
river port(s): Guangzhou (Pearl)

container port(s) (TEUs): Dalian (6,400,300), Guangzhou (14,260,400), Ningbo (14,719,200), Qingdao (13,020,100), Shanghai (31,739,000), Shenzhen (22,570,800), Tianjin (11,587,600)(2011)
LNG terminal(s) (import): Fujian, Guangdong, Jiangsu, Shandong, Shanghai, Tangshan, Zhejiang

MILITARY AND SECURITY

Military branches: People's Liberation Army (PLA): Ground Forces, Navy (PLAN; includes marines and naval aviation), Air Force (Zhongguo Renmin Jiefangjun Kongjun, PLAAF; includes Airborne Forces), and Second Artillery Corps (strategic missile force); People's Armed Police (Renmin Wuzhuang Jingcha Budui, PAP); PLA Reserve Force (2012)
Military service age and obligation: 18–24 years of age for selective compulsory military service, with a 2-year service obligation; no minimum age for voluntary service (all officers are volunteers); 18–19 years of age for women high school graduates who meet requirements for specific military jobs; a recent military decision allows women in combat roles; the first class of women warship commanders was in 2011 (2012)
Military expenditures: 1.99% of GDP (2012)
2% of GDP (2011)
1.99% of GDP (2010)
country comparison to the world: 40

TRANSNATIONAL ISSUES

Disputes—international: continuing talks and confidence-building measures work toward reducing tensions over Kashmir that nonetheless remains militarized with portions under the de facto administration of China (Aksai Chin), India (Jammu and Kashmir), and Pakistan (Azad Kashmir and Northern Areas); India does not recognize Pakistan's ceding historic Kashmir lands to China in 1964; China and India continue their security and foreign policy dialogue started in 2005 related to the dispute over most of their rugged, militarized boundary, regional nuclear proliferation, and other matters; China claims most of India's Arunachal Pradesh to the base of the Himalayas; lacking any treaty describing the boundary, Bhutan and China continue negotiations to establish a common boundary alignment to resolve territorial disputes arising from substantial cartographic discrepancies, the largest of which lie in Bhutan's northwest and along the Chumbi salient; Burmese forces attempting to dig in to the largely autonomous Shan State to rout local militias tied to the drug trade, prompts local residents to periodically flee into neighboring Yunnan Province in China; Chinese maps show an international boundary symbol off the coasts of the littoral states of the South China Seas, where China has interrupted Vietnamese hydrocarbon exploration; China asserts sovereignty over Scarborough Reef along with the Philippines and Taiwan, and over the Spratly Islands together with Malaysia, the Philippines, Taiwan, Vietnam, and Brunei; the 2002 Declaration on the Conduct of Parties in the South China Sea eased tensions in the Spratlys but is not the legally binding code of conduct sought by some parties; Vietnam and China continue to expand

construction of facilities in the Spratlys and in March 2005, the national oil companies of China, the Philippines, and Vietnam signed a joint accord on marine seismic activities in the Spratly Islands;

China occupies some of the Paracel Islands also claimed by Vietnam and Taiwan; the Japanese-administered Senkaku Islands are also claimed by China and Taiwan; certain islands in the Yalu and Tumen rivers are in dispute with North Korea; North Korea and China seek to stem illegal migration to China by North Koreans, fleeing privations and oppression, by building a fence along portions of the border and imprisoning North Koreans deported by China; China and Russia have demarcated the once disputed islands at the Amur and Ussuri confluence and in the Argun River in accordance with their 2004 Agreement; China and Tajikistan have begun demarcating the revised boundary agreed to in the delimitation of 2002; the decade-long demarcation of the China-Vietnam land boundary was completed in 2009; citing environmental, cultural, and social concerns, China has reconsidered construction of 13 dams on the Salween River, but energy-starved Burma, with backing from Thailand, remains intent on building five hydro-electric dams downstream despite regional and international protests Chinese and Hong Kong authorities met in March 2008 to resolve ownership and use of lands recovered in Shenzhen River channelization, including 96-hectare Lok Ma Chau Loop

Refugees and internally displaced persons: *refugees (country of origin):* 300,896 (Vietnam); undetermined (North Korea) (2014) IDPs: undetermined (2014)

Trafficking in persons: *current situation:* China is a source, transit, and destination country for men, women, and children subjected to sex trafficking and forced labor; Chinese adults and children are forced into prostitution and various forms of forced labor, including begging and working in brick kilns, coal mines, and factories; women and children are recruited from rural areas and taken to urban centers for sexual exploitation, often lured by criminal syndicates or gangs with fraudulent job offers; state-sponsored forced labor, where detainees work for up to four years often with no remuneration, continues to be a serious concern; Chinese men, women, and children also may be subjected to conditions of sex trafficking and forced labor worldwide, particularly in overseas Chinese communities; women and children are trafficked to China from neighboring countries, as well as Africa and the Americas, for forced labor and prostitution

tier rating: Tier 2 Watch List—China does not fully comply with the minimum standards for the elimination of trafficking; however, it is making significant efforts to do so; official data for 2014 states that 194 alleged traffickers were arrested and at least 35 were convicted, but the government's conflation of human trafficking with other crimes makes it difficult to assess law enforcement efforts to investigate and to prosecute trafficking offenses according to international law; despite reports of complicity, no government officials were investigated, prosecuted, or convicted for their roles in trafficking offenses; authorities did not adequately protect victims and did not provide the data needed to ascertain the number of victims identified or assisted or the services provided; the National People's Congress ratified a decision to abolish "reform through labor" in 2013, but some continued to operate as state-sponsored drug detention or "custody and education" centers that force inmates to perform manual labor; some

North Korean refugees continued to be forcibly repatriated as illegal economic migrants, despite reports that some were trafficking victims (2015)

Illicit drugs: major transshipment point for heroin produced in the Golden Triangle region of Southeast Asia; growing domestic consumption of synthetic drugs, and heroin from Southeast and

Southwest Asia; source country for methamphetamine and heroin chemical precursors, despite new regulations on its large chemical industry; more people believed to be convicted and executed for drug offences than anywhere else in the world, according to NGOs (2008)

CHRISTMAS ISLAND

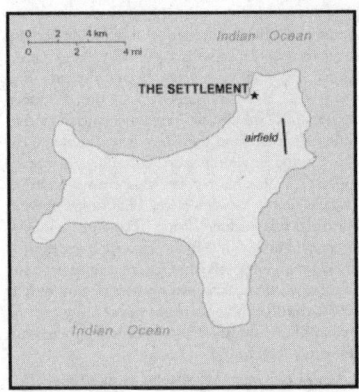

INTRODUCTION

Backg round: Named in 1643 for the day of its discovery, the island was annexed and settlement began by the UK in 1888 with the discovery of the island's phosphate deposits. Following the Second World War, Christmas Island came under the jurisdiction of the new British Colony of Singapore. The island existed as a separate Crown colony from 1 January 1958 to 1 October 1958 when its transfer to Australian jurisdiction was finalized. That date is still celebrated on the first Monday in October as Territory Day. Almost two-thirds of the island has been declared a national park.

GEOGRAPHY

Location: Southeastern Asia, island in the Indian Ocean, south of Indonesia

Geographic coordinates: 10 30 S, 105 40 E

Map references: Southeast Asia

Area: *total:* 135 sq km
land: 135 sq km
water: 0 sq km
country comparison to the world: 222

Area—comparative: about three-quarters the size of Washington, DC

Land boundaries: 0 km

Coastline: 138.9 km

Maritime claims: *territorial sea:* 12 nm
contiguous zone: 12 nm
exclusive fishing zone: 200 nm

Climate: tropical with a wet season (December to April) and dry season; heat and humidity moderated by trade winds

Terrain: steep cliffs along coast rise abruptly to central plateau

Elevation: *mean elevation:* NA

elevation extremes: *lowest point:* Indian Ocean 0 m
highest point: Murray Hill 361 m

Natural resources: phosphate, beaches

Land use: *agricultural land:* 0%
arable land: 0%
permanent crops: 0%
permanent pasture: 0%
other: 100% (mainly tropical reainforest; 63% of the island is a national park) (2011 est.)

Irrigated land: NA

Natural hazards: the narrow fringing reef surrounding the island can be a maritime hazard

Environment—current issues: loss of rainforest; impact of phosphate mining

Geography—note: located along major sea lanes of Indian Ocean

PEOPLE AND SOCIETY

Nationality: *noun:* Christmas Islander(s)
adjective: Christmas Island

Ethnic groups: Chinese 70%, European 20%, Malay 10%
note: no indigenous population (2001)

Languages: English (official), Chinese, Malay

Religions: Buddhist 16.9%, Christian 16.4%, Muslim 14.8%, other 1.3%, none 9.2%, unspecified 41.5% (2011 est.)

Population: 2,205 (July 2015 est.)
country comparison to the world: 233

Age structure: *0–14 years:* 12.79% (male 147/female 135)
15–24 years: 12.2% (male 202/female 67)
25–54 years: 57.91% (male 955/female 322)
55–64 years: 11.66% (male 172/female 85)
65 years and over: 5.44% (male 84/female 36) (2015 est.)

Population growth rate: 1.11% (2014 est.)
country comparison to the world: 110

Sex ratio: NA

Infant mortality rate: *total:* NA
male: NA
female: NA

Life expectancy at birth:

total population: NA
male: NA
female: NA

Total fertility rate: NA

HIV/AIDS—adult prevalence rate: NA

HIV/AIDS—people living with HIV/AIDS: NA

HIV/AIDS—deaths: NA

GOVERNMENT

Country name: *conventional long form:* Territory of Christmas Island
conventional short form: Christmas Island
etymology: named by English Captain William MYNORS for the day of its discovery, Christmas Day (25 December 1643)

Dependency status: non-self governing territory of Australia; administered from Canberra by the Department of Regional Australia, Local Government, Arts and Sport

Government type: non-self-governing overseas territory of Australia

Capital: *name:* The Settlement

Geographic coordinates: 10 25 S, 105 43 E
time difference: UTC+7 (12 hours ahead of Washington, DC, during Standard Time)

Administrative divisions: none (territory of Australia)

Independence: none (territory of Australia)

National holiday: Australia Day, 26 January (1788)

Constitution: 1 October 1958 (Christmas Island Act 1958); amended many times, last in 2010 (Territories Law Reform Act 2010) (2016)

Legal system: legal system is under the authority of the governor general of Australia and Australian law

Citizenship: see Australia

Suffrage: 18 years of age

Executive branch: *chief of state:* Queen ELIZABETH II (since 6 February 1952); represented by Governor General of the Commonwealth of Australia General Sir Peter COSGROVE (since 28 March 2014)

head of government: Administrator Jon STANHOPE (since 5 October 2012)
elections/appointments: the monarchy is hereditary; governor general appointed by the monarch on the recommendation of the Australian prime minister; administrator appointed by the governor

general of Australia for a 2-year term and represents the monarch and Australia

Legislative branch: *description:* unicameral Christmas Island Shire Council (9 seats; members directly elected by simple majority vote to serve 4-year terms with a portion of the membership renewed every 2 years)

elections: held every 2 years with half the members standing for election; last held In 2011 (next to be held in 2013)

election results: percent of vote—NA; seats—independents 9

Judicial branch: *highest court(s):* under the terms of the Territorial Law Reform Act 1992, Western Australia provides court services as needed for the island including the Supreme Court and subordinate courts (District Court, Magistrate Court, Family Court, Children's Court, and Coroners' Court)

Political parties and leaders: none

Political pressure groups and leaders: none

International organization participation: none

Diplomatic representation in the US: none (territory of Australia)

Diplomatic representation from the US: none (territory of Australia)

Flag description: territorial flag; divided diagonally from upper hoist to lower fly; the upper triangle is green with a yellow image of the Golden Bosun Bird superimposed; the lower triangle is blue with the Southern Cross constellation, representing Australia, superimposed; a centered yellow disk displays a green map of the island

note: the flag of Australia is used for official purposes

National symbol(s): golden bosun bird

National anthem: *note:* as a territory of Australia, "Advance Australia Fair" remains official as the national anthem, while "God Save the Queen" serves as the royal anthem (see Australia)

ECONOMY

Economy—overview: The main economic activities on Christmas Island are the mining of low grade phosphate, limited tourism, the provision of government services and more recently the construction and operation of the Immigration Detention Center. The government sector includes administration, health, education, policing, customs, quarantine, and defense.

GDP (purchasing power parity): $NA

Agriculture—products: NA

Industries: tourism, phosphate extraction (near depletion)

Labor force: NA

Budget: *revenues:* $NA
expenditures: $NA

Fiscal year: 1 July—30 June

Exports: $NA

Exports—commodities: phosphate

Imports: $NA

Imports—commodities: consumer goods

Exchange rates: Australian dollars (AUD) per US dollar—
1.33 (2015)
1.0358 (2013)
1.0358 (2013)
0.97 (2012)
0.9695 (2011)

COMMUNICATIONS

Telephone system: *general assessment:* service provided by the Australian network
domestic: GSM mobile-cellular telephone service replaced older analog system in February 2005
international: country code—61-8; satellite earth station—1 (Intelsat provides telephone and telex service) (2005)

Broadcast media: 1 community radio station; satellite broadcasts of several Australian radio and TV stations (2009)

Radio broadcast stations: AM 1, FM 2, shortwave 0 (2006)

Television broadcast stations: 0 (TV broadcasts received via satellite from mainland Australia) (2006)

Internet country code: .cx

Internet hosts: 3,028 (2012)
country comparison to the world: 155

Internet users: *total:* 464
percent of population: 16.7% (2001)
country comparison to the world: 217

TRANSPORTATION

Airports: 1 (2013)
country comparison to the world: 215

Airports—with paved runways: *total:* 1
1,524 to 2,437 m: 1 (2013)

Railways: *total:* 18 km
standard gauge: 18 km 1.435-m (not in operation) (2010)
country comparison to the world: 134

Roadways: *total:* 140 km
paved: 30 km
unpaved: 110 km (2011)
country comparison to the world: 212

Ports and terminals: *major seaport(s):* Flying Fish Cove

MILITARY AND SECURITY

Military—note: defense is the responsibility of Australia

TRANSNATIONAL ISSUES

Disputes—international: none

CLIPPERTON ISLAND

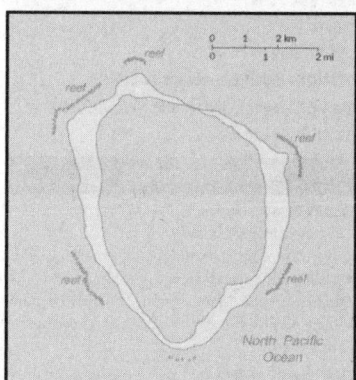

INTRODUCTION

Background: This isolated atoll was named for John CLIPPERTON, an English pirate who was rumored to have made it his hideout early in the 18th century. Annexed by France in 1855 and claimed by the US, it was seized by Mexico in 1897. Arbitration eventually awarded the island to France in 1931, which took possession in 1935.

GEOGRAPHY

Location: Middle America, atoll in the North Pacific Ocean, 1,120 km southwest of Mexico

Geographic coordinates: 10 17 N, 109 13 W

Map references: Political Map of the World

Area: *total:* 6 sq km
land: 6 sq km

water: 0 sq km
country comparison to the world: 247

Area—comparative: about 12 times the size of The Mall in Washington, DC

Land boundaries: 0 km

Coastline: 11.1 km

Maritime claims: *territorial sea:* 12 nm
exclusive economic zone: 200 nm

Climate: tropical; humid, average temperature 20–32 degrees Celsius, wet season (May to October)

Terrain: coral atoll

Elevation: *mean elevation:* NA

elevation extremes: *lowest point:* Pacific Ocean 0 m
highest point: Rocher Clipperton 29 m

Natural resources: fish
Land use: *agricultural land:* 0%
arable land: 0%
permanent crops: 0%
permanent pasture: 0%
forest: 0%
other: 100% (all coral) (2011 est.)

Natural hazards: NA

Environment—current issues: NA

Geography—note: the atoll reef is approximately 12 km (7.5 mi) in circumference; an attempt to colonize the atoll in the early 20th century ended in disaster and was abandoned in 1917

PEOPLE AND SOCIETY

Population: uninhabited

GOVERNMENT

Country name: *conventional long form:* none
conventional short form: Clipperton Island
local long form: none
local short form: Ile Clipperton
former: sometimes referred to as Ile de la Passion or Atoll Clipperton
etymology: named after an 18th-century English pirate who supposedly used the island as a base

Dependency status: possession of France; administered directly by the Minister of Overseas France

Legal system: the laws of France apply

Flag description: the flag of France is used

ECONOMY

Economy—overview: Although 115 species of fish have been identified in the territorial waters of Clipperton Island, the only economic activity is tuna fishing.

TRANSPORTATION

Ports and terminals: none; offshore anchorage only

MILITARY AND SECURITY

Military—note: defense is the responsibility of France

TRANSNATIONAL ISSUES

Disputes—international: none

COCOS (KEELING) ISLANDS

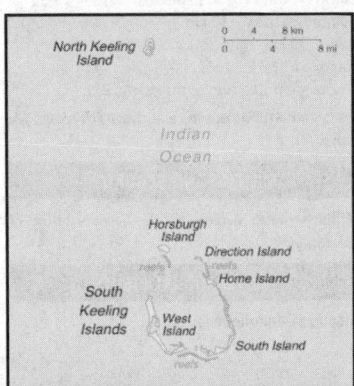

INTRODUCTION

Backg round: There are 27 coral islands in the group. Captain William KEELING discovered the islands in 1609, but they remained uninhabited until the 19th century. From the 1820s to 1978, members of the CLUNIE-ROSS family controlled the islands and the copra produced from local coconuts. Annexed by the UK in 1857, the Cocos Islands were transferred to the Australian Government in 1955. Apart from North Keeling Island, which lies 30 kilometers north of the main group, the islands form a horseshoe-shaped atoll surrounding a lagoon. North Keeling Island was declared a national park in 1995 and is administered by Parks Australia. The population on the two inhabited islands generally is split between the ethnic Europeans on West Island and the ethnic Malays on Home Island.

GEOGRAPHY

Location: Southeastern Asia, group of islands in the Indian Ocean, southwest of Indonesia, about halfway between Australia and Sri Lanka

Geographic coordinates: 12 30 S, 96 50 E
Map references: Southeast Asia
Area: *total:* 14 sq km
land: 14 sq km
water: 0 sq km
note: includes the two main islands of West Island and Home Island
country comparison to the world: 241

Area—comparative: about 24 times the size of The Mall in Washington, DC

Land boundaries: 0 km

Coastline: 26 km
Maritime claims: *territorial sea:* 12 nm
exclusive fishing zone: 200 nm

Climate: tropical with high humidity, moderated by the southeast trade winds for about nine months of the year

Terrain: flat, low-lying coral atolls
Elevation: *mean elevation:* NA

elevation extremes: *lowest point:* Indian Ocean 0 m
highest point: unnamed location 5 m

Natural resources: fish
Land use: *agricultural land:* 0%
arable land: 0%
permanent crops: 0%
permanent pasture: 0%
forest: 0%
other: 100% (2011 est.)
Irrigated land: NA

Natural hazards: cyclone season is October to April

Environment—current issues: freshwater resources are limited to rainwater accumulations in natural underground reservoirs

Geography—note: islands are thickly covered with coconut palms and other vegetation; site of a World War I naval battle in November 1914 between the Australian light cruiser HMAS

Sydney and the German raider SMS Emden; after being heavily damaged in the engagement, the Emden was beached by her captain on North Keeling Island

PEOPLE AND SOCIETY

Nationality: *noun:* Cocos Islander(s)
adjective: Cocos Islander

Ethnic groups: Europeans, Cocos Malays

Languages: Malay (Cocos dialect), English

Religions: Sunni Muslim 80%, other 20% (2002 est.)

Population: 596 (July 2014 est.)
country comparison to the world: 237
Population growth rate: 0% (2014 est.)
country comparison to the world: 197
Infant mortality rate: *total:* NA
male: NA
female: NA

Life expectancy at birth:
total population: NA
male: NA
female: NA

Total fertility rate: NA

HIV/AIDS—adult prevalence rate: NA

HIV/AIDS—people living with HIV/AIDS: NA

HIV/AIDS—deaths: NA

GOVERNMENT

Country name: *conventional long form:* Territory of Cocos (Keeling) Islands
conventional short form: Cocos (Keeling) Islands
etymology: the name refers to the abundant coconut trees on the islands and to English Captain William KEELING, the first European to sight the islands in 1609

Dependency status: non-self governing territory of Australia; administered from Canberra by the

Department of Regional Australia, Local Government, Arts and Sport

Government type: non-self-governing overseas territory of Australia

Capital: *name:* West Island

Geographic coordinates: 12 10 S, 96 50 E
time difference: UTC+6.5 (11.5 hours ahead of Washington, DC, during Standard Time)

Administrative divisions: none (territory of Australia)

Independence: none (territory of Australia)

National holiday: Australia Day, 26 January (1788)

Constitution: 23 November 1955 (Cocos (Keeling) Islands Act 1955); amended many times, last in 2010 (2016)

Legal system: common law based on the Australian model

Citizenship: see Australia

Suffrage: 18 years of age

Executive branch: *chief of state:* Queen ELIZABETH II (since 6 February 1952); represented by Governor General of the Commonwealth of Australia General Sir Peter COSGROVE (since 28 March 2014)

head of government: Administrator (nonresident) Barry HAASE (since 6 October 2014)
cabinet: NA
elections/appointments: the monarchy is hereditary; governor general appointed by the monarch on the recommendation of the Australian prime minister; administrator appointed by for a 2-year term and represents the monarch and Australia

Legislative branch: *description:* unicameral Cocos (Keeling) Islands Shire Council (7 seats; members directly elected by simple majority vote to serve 4-year terms with a portion of the membership renewed every 2 years)
elections: held every 2 years with half the members standing for election; last held in October 2011 (next to be held in October 2013)

Judicial branch: *highest court(s):* under the terms of the Territorial Law Reform Act 1992, Western Australia provides court services as needed for the island including the Supreme Court and subordinate courts (District Court, Magistrate Court,

Family Court, Children's Court, and Coroners' Court)

Political parties and leaders: none

Political pressure groups and leaders: The Cocos Islands Youth Support Centre

International organization participation: none

Diplomatic representation in the US: none (territory of Australia)

Diplomatic representation from the US: none (territory of Australia)

Flag description: the flag of Australia is used

National anthem: *note:* as a territory of Australia, "Advance Australia Fair" remains official as the national anthem, while "God Save the Queen" serves as the royal anthem (see Australia)

ECONOMY

Economy—overview: Coconuts, grown throughout the islands, are the sole cash crop. Small local gardens and fishing contribute to the food supply, but additional food and most other necessities must be imported from Australia. There is a small tourist industry.

GDP (purchasing power parity): $NA
GDP—real growth rate: 1% (2003)
country comparison to the world: 172

Agriculture—products: vegetables, bananas, pawpaws, coconuts

Industries: copra products, tourism

Labor force: NA

Labor force—by occupation: *note:* the Cocos Islands Cooperative Society Ltd. employs construction workers, stevedores, and lighterage workers; tourism is the other main source of employment

Unemployment rate: 60% (2000 est.)
country comparison to the world: 203
Budget: *revenues:* $NA
expenditures: $NA

Fiscal year: 1 July—30 June

Exports: $NA

Exports—commodities: copra

Imports: $NA

Imports—commodities: food stuffs

Exchange rates: Australian dollars (AUD) per US dollar—
1.33 (2015)
1.0358 (2013)
1.0358 (2013)
0.97 (2012)
0.9695 (2011)

COMMUNICATIONS

Telephone system: *general assessment:* telephone service is part of the Australian network; an operational local mobile-cellular network available; wireless Internet connectivity available
domestic: NA
international: country code—61; telephone, telex, and facsimile communications with Australia and elsewhere via satellite; satellite earth station—1 (Intelsat) (2001)

Broadcast media: 1 local radio station staffed by community volunteers; satellite broadcasts of several Australian radio and TV stations available (2009)
Radio broadcast stations: AM 1, FM 2, shortwave 0 (2004)
Television broadcast stations: 4 (2007)

Internet country code: .cc
Internet hosts: 42,820 (2012)
country comparison to the world: 99

TRANSPORTATION

Airports: 1 (2013)
country comparison to the world: 216
Airports—with paved runways: *total:* 1
2,438 to 3,047 m: 1 (2013)
Roadways: *total:* 22 km
paved: 10 km
unpaved: 12 km (2007)
country comparison to the world: 222

Ports and terminals: *major seaport(s):* Port Refuge

MILITARY AND SECURITY

Military—note: defense is the responsibility of Australia; the territory has a five-person police force

TRANSNATIONAL ISSUES

Disputes—international: none

COLOMBIA

INTRODUCTION

Background: Colombia was one of the three countries that emerged from the collapse of Gran Colombia in 1830 (the others are Ecuador and Venezuela). A five-decade-long conflict between government forces and antigovernment insurgent groups, principally the Revolutionary Armed Forces of Colombia (FARC) heavily funded by the drug trade, escalated during the 1990s. More than 31,000 former paramilitaries had demobilized by the end of 2006 and the United Self Defense Forces of Colombia as a formal organization had

ceased to function. In the wake of the paramilitary demobilization, emerging criminal groups arose, whose members include some former paramilitaries. The insurgents lack the military or popular support necessary to overthrow the government, but continue attacks against civilians. Large areas of the countryside are under guerrilla influence or are contested by security forces. In November 2012, the Colombian Government started formal peace negotiations with the FARC aimed at reaching a definitive bilateral cease-fire and incorporating demobilized FARC members into mainstream society and politics. The Colombian

Government has stepped up efforts to reassert government control throughout the country, and now has a presence in every one of its administrative departments. Despite decades of internal conflict and drug related security challenges, Colombia maintains relatively strong democratic institutions characterized by peaceful, transparent elections and the protection of civil liberties.

GEOGRAPHY

Location: Northern South America, bordering the Caribbean Sea, between Panama and Venezuela,

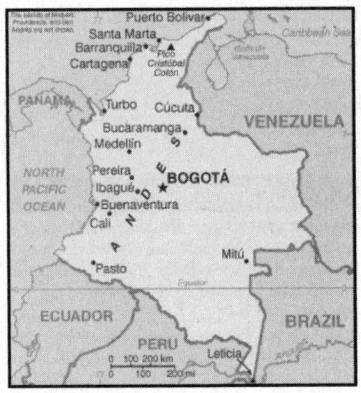

and bordering the North Pacific Ocean, between Ecuador and Panama

Geographic coordinates: 4 00 N, 72 00 W

Map references: South America

Area: *total:* 1,138,910 sq km
land: 1,038,700 sq km
water: 100,210 sq km
note: includes Isla de Malpelo, Roncador Cay, and Serrana Bank
country comparison to the world: 26

Area—comparative: slightly less than twice the size of Texas

Land boundaries: *total:* 6,672 km
border countries (5): Brazil 1,790 km, Ecuador 708 km, Panama 339 km, Peru 1,494 km, Venezuela 2,341 km

Coastline: 3,208 km (Caribbean Sea 1,760 km, North Pacific Ocean 1,448 km)

Maritime claims: *territorial sea:* 12 nm
exclusive economic zone: 200 nm
continental shelf: 200-m depth or to the depth of exploitation

Climate: tropical along coast and eastern plains; cooler in highlands

Terrain: flat coastal lowlands, central highlands, high Andes Mountains, eastern lowland plains (Llanos)

Elevation: *mean elevation:* 593 m

elevation extremes: *lowest point:* Pacific Ocean 0 m
highest point: Pico Cristobal Colon 5,775 m
note: nearby Pico Simon Bolivar also has the same elevation

Natural resources: petroleum, natural gas, coal, iron ore, nickel, gold, copper, emeralds, hydropower

Land use: *agricultural land:* 37.5%
arable land: 1.4%
permanent crops: 1.6%
permanent pasture: 34.5%
forest: 54.4%
other: 8.1% (2011 est.)

Irrigated land: 10,900 sq km (2012)

Total renewable water resources: 2,132 cu km (2011)

Freshwater withdrawal (domestic/industrial/agricultural): *total:* 12.65 cu m/yr (55%/4%/41%)
per capita: 308 cu m/yr (2010)

Natural hazards: highlands subject to volcanic eruptions; occasional earthquakes; periodic droughts
volcanism: Galeras (elev. 4,276 m) is one of Colombia's most active volcanoes, having erupted in 2009 and 2010 causing major evacuations; it has been deemed a Decade Volcano by the International Association of Volcanology and Chemistry of the Earth's Interior, worthy of study due to its explosive history and close proximity to human populations; Nevado del Ruiz (elev.5,321 m), 129 km (80 mi) west of Bogota, erupted in 1985 producing lahars (mudflows) that killed 23,000 people; the volcano last erupted in 1991; additionally, after 500 years of dormancy, Nevado del Huila reawakened in 2007 and has experienced frequent eruptions since then; other historically active volcanoes include Cumbal, Dona Juana, Nevado del Tolima, and Purace

Environment—current issues: deforestation; soil and water quality damage from overuse of pesticides; air pollution, especially in Bogota, from vehicle emissions

Environment—international agreements: *party to:* Antarctic Treaty, Biodiversity, Climate Change, Climate Change-Kyoto Protocol, Desertification, Endangered Species, Hazardous Wastes, Marine Life Conservation, Ozone Layer Protection, Ship Pollution, Tropical Timber 83, Tropical Timber 94, Wetlands
signed, but not ratified: Law of the Sea

Geography—note: only South American country with coastlines on both the North Pacific Ocean and Caribbean Sea

PEOPLE AND SOCIETY

Nationality: *noun:* Colombian(s)
adjective: Colombian

Ethnic groups: mestizo and white 84.2%, Afro-Colombian (includes multatto, Raizal, and Palenquero) 10.4%, Amerindian 3.4%, Roma <.01, unspecified 2.1% (2005 est.)

Languages: Spanish (official)

Religions: Roman Catholic 90%, other 10%

Demographic profile: Colombia is in the midst of a demographic transition resulting from steady declines in its fertility, mortality, and population growth rates. The birth rate has fallen from more than 6 children per woman in the 1960s to just above replacement level today as a result of increased literacy, family planning services, and urbanization. However, income inequality is among the worst in the world, and more than a third of the population lives below the poverty line. Colombia experiences significant legal and illegal economic emigration and refugee flows. Large-scale labor emigration dates to the 1960s; Venezuela and the United States continue to be the main host countries. Colombia is the largest source of Latin American refugees in Latin America, nearly 400,000 of whom live primarily in Venezuela and Ecuador. Forced displacement remains prevalent because of violence among guerrillas, paramilitary groups, and Colombian security forces. Afro-Colombian and indigenous populations are disproportionately affected. A leading NGO estimates that 5.2 million people have been displaced since 1985, while the Colombian Government estimates 3.6 million since 2000. These estimates may undercount actual numbers because not all internally displaced persons are registered. Historically, Colombia also has one of the world's highest levels of forced disappearances. About 30,000 cases have been recorded over the last four decades—although the number is likely to be much higher -including human rights activists, trade unionists, Afro-Colombians, indigenous people, and farmers in rural conflict zones.

Population: 46,736,728 (July 2015 est.)
country comparison to the world: 30

Age structure: *0–14 years:* 24.94% (male 5,967,860/female 5,688,106)
15–24 years: 17.81% (male 4,234,564/female 4,087,134)
25–54 years: 41.71% (male 9,653,094/female 9,841,546)
55–64 years: 8.62% (male 1,885,481/female 2,141,618)
65 years and over: 6.93% (male 1,349,613/female 1,887,712) (2015 est.)

Dependency ratios: *total dependency ratio:* 45.6%
youth dependency ratio: 35.4%
elderly dependency ratio: 10.2%
potential support ratio: 9.8% (2015 est.)

Median age: *total:* 29.3 years
male: 28.3 years
female: 30.3 years (2015 est.)
country comparison to the world: 119

Population growth rate: 1.04% (2015 est.)
country comparison to the world: 115

Birth rate: 16.47 births/1,000 population (2015 est.)
country comparison to the world: 114

Death rate: 5.4 deaths/1,000 population (2015 est.)
country comparison to the world: 177

Net migration rate: -0.64 migrant(s)/1,000 population (2015 est.)
country comparison to the world: 141

Urbanization: *urban population:* 76.4% of total population (2015)
rate of urbanization: 1.66% annual rate of change (2010–15 est.)

Major urban areas—population: BOGOTA (capital) 9.765 million; Medellin 3.911 million; Cali 2.646 million; Barranquilla 1.991 million; Bucaramanga 1.215 million; Cartagena 1.092 million (2015)

Sex ratio: *at birth:* 1.06 male(s)/female
0–14 years: 1.05 male(s)/female
15–24 years: 1.04 male(s)/female
25–54 years: 0.98 male(s)/female
55–64 years: 0.88 male(s)/female
65 years and over: 0.72 male(s)/female
total population: 0.98 male(s)/female (2015 est.)

Mother's mean age at first birth: 21.4
note: median age at first birth among women 25–29 (2010 est.)

Maternal mortality rate: 64 deaths/100,000 live births (2015 est.)

country comparison to the world: 80

Infant mortality rate: *total:* 14.58 deaths/1,000 live births

male: 17.68 deaths/1,000 live births

female: 11.3 deaths/1,000 live births (2015 est.)

country comparison to the world: 106

Life expectancy at birth:

total population: 75.48 years

male: 72.34 years

female: 78.8 years (2015 est.)

country comparison to the world: 98

Total fertility rate: 2.04 children born/woman (2015 est.)

country comparison to the world: 117

Contraceptive prevalence rate: 79.1% (2009/10)

Health expenditures: 6.8% of GDP (2013)

country comparison to the world: 85

Physicians density: 1.47 physicians/1,000 population (2010)

Hospital bed density: 1.5 beds/1,000 population (2012)

Drinking water source:

improved:

urban: 96.8% of population

rural: 73.8% of population

total: 91.4% of population

unimproved:

urban: 3.2% of population

rural: 26.2% of population

total: 8.6% of population (2015 est.)

Sanitation facility access:

improved:

urban: 85.2% of population

rural: 67.9% of population

total: 81.1% of population

unimproved:

urban: 14.8% of population

rural: 32.1% of population

total: 18.9% of population (2015 est.)

HIV/AIDS—adult prevalence rate: 0.4% (2014 est.)

country comparison to the world: 76

HIV/AIDS—people living with HIV/AIDS: 124,400 (2014 est.)

country comparison to the world: 38

HIV/AIDS—deaths: 4,700 (2014 est.)

country comparison to the world: 32

Major infectious diseases: *degree of risk:* high

food or waterborne diseases: bacterial diarrhea

vectorborne diseases: dengue fever, malaria, and yellow fever (2013)

Obesity—adult prevalence rate: 20.7% (2014)

country comparison to the world: 112

Children under the age of 5 years underweight: 3.4% (2010)

country comparison to the world: 108

Education expenditures: 4.7% of GDP (2014)

country comparison to the world: 95

Literacy: *definition:* age 15 and over can read and write

total population: 94.7%

male: 94.6%

female: 94.8% (2015 est.)

School life expectancy (primary to tertiary education): *total:* 14 years

male: 14 years

female: 15 years (2014)

Child labor—children ages 5–14: *total number:* 988,362

percentage: 9%

note: data represent children ages 5–17 (2009 est.)

Unemployment, youth ages 15–24: *total:* 19.1%

male: 14.6%

female: 25.4% (2013 est.)

country comparison to the world: 50

GOVERNMENT

Country name: *conventional long form:* Republic of Colombia

conventional short form: Colombia

local long form: Republica de Colombia

local short form: Colombia

etymology: the country is named after explorer Christopher COLUMBUS

Government type: presidential republic

Capital: *name:* Bogota

Geographic coordinates: 4 36 N, 74 05 W

time difference: UTC-5 (same time as Washington, DC, during Standard Time)

Administrative divisions: 32 departments (departamentos, singular—departamento) and 1 capital district* (distrito capital); Amazonas, Antioquia, Arauca, Atlantico, Bogota*, Bolivar, Boyaca, Caldas, Caqueta, Casanare, Cauca, Cesar, Choco, Cordoba, Cundinamarca, Guainia, Guaviare, Huila, La Guajira, Magdalena, Meta, Narino, Norte de Santander, Putumayo, Quindio, Risaralda, Archipielago de San Andres, Providencia y Santa Catalina (colloquially San Andres y Providencia), Santander, Sucre, Tolima, Valle del Cauca, Vaupes, Vichada

Independence: 20 July 1810 (from Spain)

National holiday: Independence Day, 20 July (1810)

Constitution: several previous; latest promulgated 5 July 1991; amended many times, last in 2015 (2016)

Legal system: civil law system influenced by the Spanish and French civil codes

International law organization participation: has not submitted an ICJ jurisdiction declaration; accepts ICCt jurisdiction

Citizenship: *citizenship by birth:* no

citizenship by descent only: least one parent must be a citizen or permanent resident of Colombia

dual citizenship recognized: yes

residency requirement for naturalization: 5 years

Suffrage: 18 years of age; universal

Executive branch: *chief of state:* President Juan Manuel SANTOS Calderon (since 7 August 2010); Vice President German VARGAS Lleras (since 7 August 2014); note—the president is both chief of state and head of government

head of government: President Juan Manuel SANTOS Calderon (since 7 August 2010); Vice President German VAR GAS Lleras (since 7 August 2014)

cabinet: Cabinet appointed by the president

elections/appointments: president directly elected by absolute majority vote in 2 rounds if needed for a 4-year term; election last held on 25 May 2014 with a runoff election 15 on June 2014 (next to be held on 27 May 2018); note—recent political reform eliminated presidential reelection; beginning in 2018, presidents can only serve one 4-year term

election results: Juan Manuel SANTOS Calderon reelected president in runoff; percent of vote—Juan Manuel SANTOS Calderon (U Party) 51.0%, Oscar Ivan ZULUAGA (CD) 45.0%, other 4.0%

Legislative branch: *description:* bicameral Congress or Congreso consists of the Senate or Senado (102 seats; 100 members elected nationally—not by district or state—and two elected on a special ballot for indigenous communities to serve 4-year terms) and the Chamber of Representatives or Camara de Representantes (166 seats; members elected in multi-seat constituencies by proportional representation vote to serve 4-year terms)

elections: Senate—last held on 9 March 2014 (next to be held in March 2018); Chamber of Representatives—last held on 9 March 2014 (next to be held in March 2018)

election results: Senate—percent of vote by party—NA; seats by party—U Party 21, CD 20, PC 18, PL 17, CR 9, PDA 5, Green Party 5, other 7; Chamber of Representatives—percent of vote by party—NA; seats by party—PL 39, U Party 37, PC 27, CD 19, CR 16, Green Party 6, PDA 3, other 19

Judicial branch: *highest court(s):* Supreme Court of Justice or Corte Suprema de Justicia (consists of the Civil-Agrarian and Labor Chambers each with 7 judges, and the Penal Chamber with 9 judges); Constitutional Court (consists of 9 magistrates); Council of State (consists of 31 members); Superior Judiciary Council (consists of 13 magistrates)

judge selection and term of office: Supreme Court judges appointed by the Supreme Court members from candidates submitted by the Superior Judiciary Council; judges elected for individual 8-year terms; Constitutional Court magistrates—nominated by the president, by the Supreme Court, and elected by the Senate; judges elected for individual 8-year terms; Council of State members appointed by the State Council plenary from lists nominated by the Superior Judiciary Council

subordinate courts: Superior Tribunals (appellate courts for each of the judicial districts); regional courts; civil municipal courts; Superior Military Tribunal; first instance administrative courts

Political parties and leaders: Alternative Democratic Pole or PDA [Clara LOPEZ]

Conservative Party or PC [David BARGUIL]

Democratic Center Party or CD [Alvaro URIBE Velez, Oscar Ivan ZULUAGA]

Green Alliance [Jorge LONDONO, Antonio SANGUINO, Luis AVELLANEDA, Camilo ROMERO]

Liberal Party or PL [Horacio SERPA]

Citizens Option (Opcion Ciudadana) or OC (formerly known as the National Integration Party or PIN) [Angel ALIRIO Moreno]

Radical Change or CR [Carlos Fernando GALAN]
Social National Unity Party or U Party [Roy BAR-RERAS, Jose David NAME]

note: Colombia has eight major political parties, and numerous smaller movements

Political pressure groups and leaders: Central Union of Workers or CUT
Colombian Confederation of Workers or CTC
General Confederation of Workers or CGT
National Liberation Army or ELN Revolutionary Armed Forces of Colombia or FARC

note: FARC and ELN are the two largest insurgent groups active in Colombia

International organization participation: BCIE, BIS, CAN, Caricom (observer), CD, CDB, CELAC, EITI (candidate country), FAO, G-3, G-24, G-77, IADB, IAEA, IBRD, ICAO, ICC (national committees), ICCt, ICRM, IDA, IFAD, IFC, IFRCS, IHO, ILO, IMF, IMO, IMSO, Interpol, IOC, IOM, IPU, ISO, ITSO, ITU, ITUC (NGOs), LAES, LAIA, Mercosur (associate), MIGA, NAM, OAS, OPANAL, OPCW, Pacific Alliance, PCA, UN, UNASUR, UNCTAD, UNESCO, UNHCR, UNIDO, Union Latina, UNWTO, UPU, WCO, WFTU (NGOs), WHO, WIPO, WMO, WTO

Diplomatic representation in the US: *chief of mission:* Ambassador Juan Carlos PINZON Bueno (since 3 August 2015)

chancery: 2118 Leroy Place NW, Washington, DC 20008

telephone: [1] (202) 387-8338

FAX: [1] (202) 232-8643

consulate(s) general: Atlanta, Houston, Los Angeles, Miami, New York, Newark (NJ), Orlando, San Juan (Puerto Rico)

consulate(s): Boston, Chicago, San Francisco

Diplomatic representation from the US: *chief of mission:* Ambassador Kevin WHITAKER (since 11 June 2014)

embassy: Calle 24 Bis No. 48–50, Bogota, D.C.

mailing address: Carrera 45 No. 24B-27, Bogota, D.C.

telephone: [57] (1) 275-2000

FAX: [57] (1) 275-4600

Flag description: three horizontal bands of yellow (top, double-width), blue, and red; the flag retains the three main colors of the banner of Gran Colombia, the short-lived South American republic that broke up in 1830; various interpretations of the colors exist and include: yellow for the gold in Colombia's land, blue for the seas on its shores, and red for the blood spilled in attaining freedom; alternatively, the colors have been described as representing more elemental concepts such as sovereignty and justice (yellow), loyalty and vigilance (blue), and valor and generosity (red); or simply the principles of liberty, equality, and fraternity

note: similar to the flag of Ecuador, which is longer and bears the Ecuadorian coat of arms superimposed in the center

National symbol(s): Andean condor; national colors: yellow, blue, red

National anthem: *name:* "Himno Nacional de la Republica de Colombia" (National Anthem of the Republic of Colombia)

lyrics/music: Rafael NUNEZ/Oreste SINDICI

note: adopted 1920; the anthem was created from an inspirational poem written by President Rafael NUNEZ

ECONOMY

Economy—overview: Colombia's consistently sound economic policies and aggressive promotion of free trade agreements in recent years have bolstered its ability to weather external shocks. Colombia depends heavily on energy and mining exports, making it vulnerable to a drop in commodity prices. Colombia is the world's fourth largest coal exporter and Latin America's fourth largest oil producer. Economic development is stymied by inadequate infrastructure, inequality, poverty, narcotrafficking and an uncertain security situation. Declining oil prices have resulted in a drop in government revenues. In 2014, Colombia passed a tax reform bill to offset the lost revenue from the global drop in oil prices. The SANTOS administration is also using tax reform to help finance implementation of a peace deal between FARC and the government. Colombian officials estimate a peace deal may bolster economic growth up to 2%.

Despite austerity measures put in place by the SANTOS administration, GDP and foreign direct investment fell in 2015, while the El Nino weather phenomenon caused food and energy prices to rise, with inflation spiking to 6.8%. In order to combat inflation, the Central Bank raised interest rates four times during the last four months of 2015, ending the year with a 25 basis point increase to 5.75%. Unemployment has continued to decrease and hit a record low of 8.9% in 2015, but the rate is still one of Latin America's highest. Nevertheless, Colombia's GDP growth rate makes it the region's best performer among large economies in 2015.

Real GDP growth averaged 4.8% per year from 2010–2014, continuing a decade of strong economic performance, before dropping in 2015. All three major ratings agencies upgraded Colombia's government debt to investment grade in 2013 and 2014, which helped to attract record levels of investment, mostly in the hydrocarbons sector. However, Standard & Poor's downgraded its long-term outlook from stable to negative in early 2016. The change, due largely to falling government revenues, could cause Colombia to lose its investment-grade bond status.

The SANTOS Administration's foreign policy has focused on bolstering Colombia's commercial ties and boosting investment at home. Colombia has signed or is negotiating Free Trade Agreements (FTA) with more than a dozen countries; the US-Colombia FTA went into force in May 2012. The US and Colombia have benefitted from the FTA, but Colombia's ability to take full advantage of its enhanced access to American markets continues to be constrained by lack of export diversification. Nontariff measures remain a point of contention for bilateral trade relations. Truck scrappage regulation, and restrictions on liquor, pharmaceutical, and ethanol imports are top irritants in the

bilateral trade relationship. Colombia is a founding member of the Pacific Alliance—a regional trade block formed in 2012 by Chile, Colombia, Mexico, and Peru to promote regional trade and economic integration. In 2013, Colombia began its accession process to the OECD.

GDP (purchasing power parity): $667.4 billion (2015 est.)
$647.5 billion (2014 est.)
$620.3 billion (2013 est.)
note: data are in 2015 US dollars
country comparison to the world: 32

GDP (official exchange rate): $293.2 billion (2015 est.)

GDP—real growth rate: 3.1% (2015 est.)
4.4% (2014 est.)
4.9% (2013 est.)
country comparison to the world: 96

GDP—per capita (PPP): $13,800 (2015 est.)
$13,600 (2014 est.)
$13,200 (2013 est.)
note: data are in 2015 US dollars
country comparison to the world: 115

Gross national saving: 18% of GDP (2015 est.)
20.8% of GDP (2014 est.)
20.9% of GDP (2013 est.)
country comparison to the world: 92

GDP—composition, by end use:
household consumption: 62.2%
government consumption: 18.9%
investment in fixed capital: 26%
investment in inventories: 0.4%
exports of goods and services: 17.7%
imports of goods and services: -25.2% (2015 est.)

GDP—composition, by sector of origin: *agriculture:* 6.4%
industry: 36.9%
services: 56.7% (2015 est.)

Agriculture—products: coffee, cut flowers, bananas, rice, tobacco, corn, sugarcane, cocoa beans, oilseed, vegetables; shrimp; forest products

Industries: textiles, food processing, oil, clothing and footwear, beverages, chemicals, cement; gold, coal, emeralds

Industrial production growth rate: 4% (2015 est.)
country comparison to the world: 60

Labor force: 24.34 million (2015 est.)
country comparison to the world: 28

Labor force—by occupation: *agriculture:* 17%
industry: 21%
services: 62% (2011 est.)

Unemployment rate: 8.9% (2015 est.)
9.1% (2014 est.)
country comparison to the world: 105

Population below poverty line: 27.8% (2015 est.)

Household income or consumption by percentage share: *lowest:* 10%: 1.1%
highest: 10%: 42% (2012 est.)

Distribution of family income—Gini index: 53.5 (2012) 56.9 (1996)
country comparison to the world: 12

Budget: *revenues:* $80.38 billion
expenditures: $86.79 billion (2015 est.)
Taxes and other revenues: 29.3% of GDP (2015 est.)

country comparison to the world: 85
Budget surplus (+) or deficit (-): -2.3% of GDP (2015 est.)
country comparison to the world: 84
Public debt: 46.9% of GDP (2015 est.)
46% of GDP (2014 est.)
note: data cover general government debt, and includes debt instruments issued (or owned) by government entities other than the treasury; the data include treasury debt held by foreign entities; the data include debt issued by subnational entities
country comparison to the world: 92

Fiscal year: calendar year
Inflation rate (consumer prices): 5% (2015 est.)
2.9% (2014 est.)
country comparison to the world: 175
Central bank discount rate: 5.75% (18 December 2015)
4.75% (31 December 2011)
country comparison to the world: 70
Commercial bank prime lending rate: 11.2% (31 December 2015 est.)
10.87% (31 December 2014 est.)
country comparison to the world: 73
Stock of narrow money: $33.86 billion (31 December 2015 est.)
$39.27 billion (31 December 2014 est.)
country comparison to the world: 58
Stock of broad money: $177.5 billion (31 December 2014 est.)
$161.7 billion (31 December 2013 est.)
country comparison to the world: 45
Stock of domestic credit: $155.8 billion (31 December 2015 est.)
$150.6 billion (31 December 2014 est.)
country comparison to the world: 47
Market value of publicly traded shares: $262.1 billion (31 December 2012 est.)
$201.3 billion (31 December 2011)
$208.5 billion (31 December 2010 est.)
country comparison to the world: 32
Current account balance: -$19.04 billion (2015 est.)
-$19.57 billion (2014 est.)
country comparison to the world: 187
Exports: $48.52 billion (2015 est.)
$57.03 billion (2014 est.)
country comparison to the world: 53
Exports—commodities: petroleum, coal, emeralds, coffee, nickel, cut flowers, bananas, apparel

Exports—partners: US 27.5%, Panama 7.2%, China 5.2%, Spain 4.4%, Ecuador 4% (2015)
Imports: $56.05 billion (2015 est.)
$61.61 billion (2014 est.)
country comparison to the world: 47
Imports—commodities: industrial equipment, transportation equipment, consumer goods, chemicals, paper products, fuels, electricity

Imports—partners: US 28.8%, China 18.6%, Mexico 7.1%, Germany 4.2% (2015)
Reserves of foreign exchange and gold: $45.02 billion (31 December 2015 est.)
$46.81 billion (31 December 2014 est.)
country comparison to the world: 41

Debt—external: $101.3 billion (31 December 2014 est.)
$91.98 billion (31 December 2013 est.)
country comparison to the world: 49
Stock of direct foreign investment—at home: $154.5 billion (31 December 2015 est.)
$141.7 billion (31 December 2014 est.)
country comparison to the world: 36
Stock of direct foreign investment—abroad: $45.58 billion (31 December 2015 est.)
$43.08 billion (31 December 2014 est.)
country comparison to the world: 41
Exchange rates: Colombian pesos (COP) per US dollar—
2,721.9 (2015 est.)
2,001.1 (2014 est.)
2,001.1 (2013 est.)
1,798 (2012 est.)
1,848 (2011 est.)

ENERGY

Electricity—production: 57.81 billion kWh (2012 est.)
country comparison to the world: 49
Electricity—consumption: 49.38 billion kWh (2012 est.)
country comparison to the world: 49
Electricity—exports: 715 million kWh (2012 est.)
country comparison to the world: 59
Electricity—imports: 6.5 million kWh (2012 est.)
country comparison to the world: 110
Electricity—installed generating capacity: 14.61 million kW (2012 est.)
country comparison to the world: 49
Electricity—from fossil fuels: 32.1% of total installed capacity (2012 est.)
country comparison to the world: 178
Electricity—from nuclear fuels: 0% of total installed capacity (2012 est.)
country comparison to the world: 71
Electricity—from hydroelectric plants: 67.2% of total installed capacity (2012 est.)
country comparison to the world: 27
Electricity—from other renewable sources: 0.7% of total installed capacity (2012 est.)
country comparison to the world: 100
Crude oil—production: 989,900 bbl/day (2014 est.)
country comparison to the world: 20
Crude oil—exports: 624,600 bbl/day (2012 est.)
country comparison to the world: 21
Crude oil—imports: 0 bbl/day (2012 est.)
country comparison to the world: 175
Crude oil—proved reserves: 2.445 billion bbl (1 January 2015 est.)
country comparison to the world: 34
Refined petroleum products—production: 340,400 bbl/day (2012 est.)
country comparison to the world: 41
Refined petroleum products—consumption: 324,000 bbl/day (2013 est.)
country comparison to the world: 39
Refined petroleum products—exports: 96,530 bbl/day (2012 est.)
country comparison to the world: 45

Refined petroleum products—imports: 65,110 bbl/day (2012 est.)
country comparison to the world: 69
Natural gas—production: 10.2 billion cu m (2013 est.)
country comparison to the world: 43
Natural gas—consumption: 7.609 billion cu m (2013 est.)
country comparison to the world: 51
Natural gas—exports: 2.591 billion cu m (2013 est.)
country comparison to the world: 35
Natural gas—imports: 0 cu m (2013 est.)
country comparison to the world: 181
Natural gas—proved reserves: 198.4 billion cu m (1 January 2014 est.)
country comparison to the world: 47
Carbon dioxide emissions from consumption of energy: 74.9 million Mt (2012 est.)
country comparison to the world: 48

COMMUNICATIONS

Telephones—fixed lines: *total subscriptions:* 7.2 million
subscriptions per 100 inhabitants: 16 (2014 est.)
country comparison to the world: 24
Telephones—mobile cellular: *total:* 55.3 million
subscriptions per 100 inhabitants: 120 (2014 est.)
country comparison to the world: 28
Telephone system: *general assessment:* modern system in many respects with a nationwide microwave radio relay system, a domestic satellite system with 41 earth stations, and a fiber-optic network linking 50 cities; telecommunications sector liberalized during the 1990s; multiple providers of both fixed-line and mobile-cellular services
domestic: fixed-line connections stand at about 15 per 100 persons; mobile cellular telephone subscribership is about 100 per 100 persons; competition among cellular service providers is resulting in falling local and international calling rates and contributing to the steep decline in the market share of fixed-line services
international: country code—57; multiple submarine cable systems provide links to the US, parts of the Caribbean, and Central and South America; satellite earth stations—10 (6 Intelsat, 1 Inmarsat, 3 fully digitalized international switching centers) (2011)

Broadcast media: combination of state-owned and privately owned broadcast media provide service; more than 500 radio stations and many national, regional, and local TV stations (2007)
Radio broadcast stations: AM 454, FM 34, shortwave 27 (1999)
Television broadcast stations: 60 (1997)

Internet country code: .co
Internet hosts: 4.41 million (2012)
country comparison to the world: 24
Internet users: *total:* 24.3 million
percent of population: 52.4% (2014 est.)
country comparison to the world: 25

TRANSPORTATION

Airports: 836 (2013)

country comparison to the world: 8
Airports—with paved runways: total: 121
over 3,047 m: 2
2,438 to 3,047 m: 9
1,524 to 2,437 m: 39
914 to 1,523 m: 53
under 914 m: 18 (2013)
Airports—with unpaved runways: total: 715
over 3,047 m: 1
1,524 to 2,437 m: 25
914 to 1,523 m: 201
under 914 m: 488 (2013)

Heliports: 3 (2013)

Pipelines: gas 4,991 km; oil 6,796 km; refined products 3,429 km (2013)
Railways: total: 2,141 km
standard gauge: 150 km 1.435-m gauge
narrow gauge: 1,991 km 0.914-m gauge (2015)
country comparison to the world: 94
Roadways: total: 204,855 km (2015)
country comparison to the world: 34
Waterways: 24,725 km (18,300 km navigable; the most important waterway, the River Magdalena, of which 1,488 km is navigable, is dredged regularly to ensure safe passage of cargo vessels and container barges) (2012)
country comparison to the world: 6
Merchant marine: total: 12
by type: cargo 9, chemical tanker 1, petroleum tanker 2
registered in other countries: 4 (Antigua and Barbuda 1, Panama 2, Portugal 1) (2010)

country comparison to the world: 105

Ports and terminals: major seaport(s): Atlantic Ocean (Caribbean)—Cartagena, Santa Marta, Turbo; Pacific Ocean -Buenaventura
river port(s): Barranquilla (Rio Magdalena)
oil terminal(s): Covenas offshore terminal
dry bulk cargo port(s): Puerto Bolivar (coal)
container port(s) (TEUs): Cartagena (1,853,342)

MILITARY AND SECURITY

Military branches: National Army (Ejercito Nacional), Republic of Colombia Navy (Armada Republica de Colombia, ARC, includes Naval Aviation, Naval Infantry (Infanteria de Marina, IM), and Coast Guard), Colombian Air Force (Fuerza Aerea de Colombia, FAC) (2012)

Military service age and obligation: 18–24 years of age for compulsory and voluntary military service; service obligation is 18 months (2012)
Military expenditures: 3.28% of GDP (2012)
3.06% of GDP (2011)
3.63% of GDP (2010)
country comparison to the world: 17

TRANSNATIONAL ISSUES

Disputes—international: in December 2007, ICJ allocated San Andres, Providencia, and Santa Catalina islands to Colombia under 1928 Treaty but did not rule on 82 degrees W meridian as maritime boundary with Nicaragua; managed dispute with Venezuela over maritime boundary and

Venezuelan-administered Los Monjes Islands near the Gulf of Venezuela; Colombian-organized illegal narcotics, guerrilla, and paramilitary activities penetrate all neighboring borders and have caused Colombian citizens to flee mostly into neighboring countries; Colombia, Honduras, Nicaragua, Jamaica, and the US assert various claims to Bajo Nuevo and Serranilla Bank

Refugees and internally displaced persons: IDPs: 6.3 million (conflict between government and illegal armed groups and drug traffickers since 1985; about 300,000 new IDPs each year since 2000) (2015)
stateless persons: 12 (2015)

Illicit drugs: illicit producer of coca, opium poppy, and cannabis; world's leading coca cultivator with 83,000 hectares in coca cultivation in 2011, a 17% decrease over 2010, producing a potential of 195 mt of pure cocaine; the world's largest producer of coca derivatives; supplies cocaine to nearly all of the US market and the great majority of other international drug markets; in 2012, aerial eradication dispensed herbicide to treat over 100,549 hectares combined with manual eradication of 30,486 hectares; a significant portion of narcotics proceeds are either laundered or invested in Colombia through the black market peso exchange; important supplier of heroin to the US market; opium poppy cultivation is estimated to have fallen to 1,100 hectares in 2009 while pure heroin production declined to 2.1 mt; most Colombian heroin is destined for the US market (2013)

COMOROS

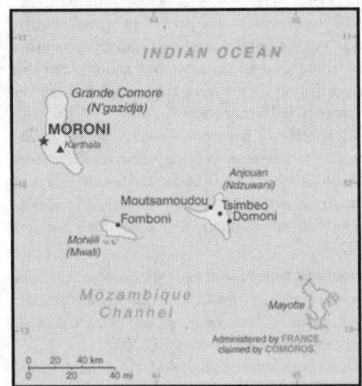

INTRODUCTION

Background: The archipelago of the Comoros in the Indian Ocean, composed of the islands of Mayotte, Anjouan, Moheli, and Grand Comore declared independence from France on 6 July 1975. France did not recognize the independence of Mayotte, which remains under French administration. Since independence, Comoros has endured political instability through realized

and attempted coups. In 1997, the islands of Anjouan and Moheli declared independence from Comoros. In 1999, military chief Col. AZALI Assoumani seized power of the entire government in a bloodless coup; he initiated the 2000 Fomboni Accords, a power-sharing agreement in which the federal presidency rotates among the three islands, and each island maintains its local government. AZALI won the 2002 federal presidential election as president from Grand Comore Island, and each island in the archipelago elected its president. AZALI stepped down in 2006 and President SAMBI was elected to office as president from Anjouan. In 2007, Mohamed BACAR effected Anjouan's de-facto secession from the Union of Comoros, refusing to step down when Comoros' other islands held legitimate elections in July. The African Union (AU) initially attempted to resolve the political crisis by applying sanctions and a naval blockade to Anjouan, but in March 2008 the AU and Comoran soldiers seized the island. The island's inhabitants generally welcomed the move. In May 2011, Ikililou DHOININE won the presidency in peaceful elections widely deemed to be free and fair. Former President AZALI Assoumani was declared the winner of the closely contested 2016 presidential election.

GEOGRAPHY

Location: Southern Africa, group of islands at the northern mouth of the Mozambique Channel, about two-thirds of the way between northern Madagascar and northern Mozambique
Geographic coordinates: 12 10 S, 44 15 E
Map references: Africa
Area: total: 2,235 sq km
land: 2,235 sq km
water: 0 sq km
country comparison to the world: 180
Area—comparative: slightly more than 12 times the size of Washington, DC
Land boundaries: 0 km
Coastline: 340 km
Maritime claims: territorial sea: 12 nm
exclusive economic zone: 200 nm
Climate: tropical marine; rainy season (November to May)
Terrain: volcanic islands, interiors vary from steep mountains to low hills
Elevation: mean elevation: NA
elevation extremes: lowest point: Indian Ocean 0 m
highest point: Karthala 2,360 m

Natural resources: fish

Land use: *agricultural land:* 84.4%
arable land: 46.7%
permanent crops: 29.6%
permanent pasture: 8.1%
forest: 1.4%
other: 14.2% (2011 est.)
Irrigated land: 1.3 sq km (2012)

Total renewable water resources: 1.2 cu km (2011)

Freshwater withdrawal (domestic/industrial/agricultural): *total:* 0.01 cu m/yr (48%/5%/47%)
per capita: 16.86 cu m/yr (1999)

Natural hazards: cyclones possible during rainy season (December to April); volcanic activity on Grand Comore
volcanism: Karthala (elev. 2,361 m) on Grand Comore Island last erupted in 2007; a 2005 eruption forced thousands of people to be evacuated and produced a large ash cloud

Environment—current issues: soil degradation and erosion results from crop cultivation on slopes without proper terracing; deforestation

Environment—international agreements: *party to:* Biodiversity, Climate Change, Climate Change-Kyoto Protocol, Desertification, Endangered Species, Hazardous Wastes, Law of the Sea, Ozone Layer Protection, Ship Pollution, Wetlands
signed, but not ratified: none of the selected agreements

Geography—note: important location at northern end of Mozambique Channel

PEOPLE AND SOCIETY

Nationality: *noun:* Comoran(s)
adjective: Comoran

Ethnic groups: Antalote, Cafre, Makoa, Oimatsaha, Sakalava

Languages: Arabic (official), French (official), Shikomoro (official; a blend of Swahili and Arabic) (Comorian)

Religions: Sunni Muslim 98%, Roman Catholic 2%
note: Islam is the state religion

Population: 780,971 (July 2015 est.)
country comparison to the world: 164

Age structure: *0–14 years:* 40.77% (male 158,654/female 159,722)
15–24 years: 18.98% (male 71,694/female 76,500)
25–54 years: 32.25% (male 119,595/female 132,299)
55–64 years: 4.17% (male 14,414/female 18,135)
65 years and over: 3.84% (male 14,018/female 15,940) (2015 est.)

Dependency ratios: *total dependency ratio:* 75.6%
youth dependency ratio: 70.7%
elderly dependency ratio: 4.9%
potential support ratio: 20.4% (2015 est.)

Median age: *total:* 19.4 years
male: 18.7 years
female: 20 years (2015 est.)
country comparison to the world: 197

Population growth rate: 1.77% (2015 est.)
country comparison to the world: 67

Birth rate: 27.84 births/1,000 population (2015 est.)
country comparison to the world: 45

Death rate: 7.57 deaths/1,000 population (2015 est.)
country comparison to the world: 111

Net migration rate: -2.53 migrant(s)/1,000 population (2015 est.)
country comparison to the world: 175

Urbanization: *urban population:* 28.3% of total population (2015)
rate of urbanization: 2.67% annual rate of change (2010–15 est.)

Major urban areas—population: MORONI (capital) 56,000 (2014)

Sex ratio: *at birth:* 1.03 male(s)/female
0–14 years: 0.99 male(s)/female
15–24 years: 0.94 male(s)/female
25–54 years: 0.9 male(s)/female
55–64 years: 0.8 male(s)/female
65 years and over: 0.88 male(s)/female
total population: 0.94 male(s)/female (2015 est.)

Mother's mean age at first birth: 24.6
note: median age at first birth among women 25–29 (2012 est.)

Maternal mortality rate: 335 deaths/100,000 live births (2015 est.)
country comparison to the world: 42

Infant mortality rate: *total:* 63.55 deaths/1,000 live births
male: 74.18 deaths/1,000 live births
female: 52.6 deaths/1,000 live births (2015 est.)
country comparison to the world: 19

Life expectancy at birth:
total population: 63.85 years
male: 61.57 years
female: 66.19 years (2015 est.)
country comparison to the world: 182

Total fertility rate: 3.6 children born/woman (2015 est.)
country comparison to the world: 43

Contraceptive prevalence rate: 19.4% (2012)

Health expenditures: 5.8% of GDP (2013)
country comparison to the world: 153

Hospital bed density: 2.2 beds/1,000 population (2006)

Drinking water source:
improved:
urban: 92.6% of population
rural: 89.1% of population
total: 90.1% of population
unimproved:
urban: 7.4% of population
rural: 10.9% of population
total: 9.9% of population (2015 est.)

Sanitation facility access:
improved:
urban: 48.3% of population
rural: 30.9% of population
total: 35.8% of population
unimproved:
urban: 51.7% of population
rural: 69.1% of population
total: 64.2% of population (2015 est.)

HIV/AIDS—adult prevalence rate: NA

HIV/AIDS—people living with HIV/AIDS: NA

HIV/AIDS—deaths: NA

Obesity—adult prevalence rate: 5.8% (2014)
country comparison to the world: 164

Children under the age of 5 years underweight: 16.9% (2012)
country comparison to the world: 39

Education expenditures: 5.1% of GDP (2012)
country comparison to the world: 15

Literacy: *definition:* age 15 and over can read and write
total population: 77.8%
male: 81.8%
female: 73.7% (2015 est.)

School life expectancy (primary to tertiary education): *total:* 11 years
male: 11 years
female: 11 years (2013)

GOVERNMENT

Country name: *conventional long form:* Union of the Comoros
conventional short form: Comoros
local long form: Udzima wa Komori (Comorian); Union des Comores (French); Jumhuriyat al Qamar al Muttahidah (Arabic)
local short form: Komori (Comorian); Comores (French); Juzur al Qamar (Arabic)
etymology: name derives from the Arabic designation "Juzur al Qamar" meaning "Islands of the Moon"

Government type: federal presidential republic
Capital: *name:* Moroni

Geographic coordinates: 11 42 S, 43 14 E
time difference: UTC+3 (8 hours ahead of Washington, DC, during Standard Time)

Administrative divisions: 3 islands and 4 municipalities*; Anjouan (Ndzuwani), Domoni*, Fomboni*, Grande Comore (N'gazidja), Moheli (Mwali), Moroni*, Moutsamoudou*

Independence: 6 July 1975 (from France)

National holiday: Independence Day, 6 July (1975)

Constitution: previous 1996; latest ratified 23 December 2001; amended 2009, 2014 (2016)

Legal system: mixed legal system of Islamic religious law, the French civil code of 1975, and customary law

International law organization participation: has not submitted an ICJ jurisdiction declaration; accepts ICCt jurisdiction

Citizenship: *citizenship by birth:* no
citizenship by descent only: at least one parent must be a citizen of the Comoros
dual citizenship recognized: no
residency requirement for naturalization: 10 years

Suffrage: 18 years of age; universal

Executive branch: *chief of state:* President Azail ASSOUMANI (since 26 May 2016); note—the president is both chief of state and head of government

head of government: President Azail ASSOUMANI (since 26 May 2016) *cabinet:* Council of Ministers appointed by the president

elections/appointments: the Union presidency rotates among the 3 islands; president directly elected by simple majority popular vote in 2 rounds for a single nonrenewable 5-year term (in the first round or primary, 3 candidates with the highest vote count by voters on the island concerned compete in the second round; second round winner determined by simple majority vote by voters on all 3 islands; election last held on 21 February 2016 and second round held 10 April 2016 (next to be held in 2021); note—in addition to the Union president, each island elects its own president

election results: Azail ASSOUMANI elected president in the second round of voting by a plurality; percent of vote in first round—Mohamed Ali SOILIHI 17.6%, Mouigni BARAKA 15.1%, Azali ASSOUMANI 15%, Fahmi Said IBRAHIM 14.5%; percent of vote in second round—Azail ASSOUMANI 41%, Mohamed Ali SOILIHI 39.9%; Mouigni BARAKA 19.1%

Legislative branch: *description:* unicameral Assembly of the Union (33 seats; 24 members elected by absolute majority vote in 2 rounds if needed and 9 members indirectly selected by island assemblies; members serve 5-year terms)

elections: last held on 25 January and 22 February 2015 (next to be held in 2020)

election results: percent of vote by party—NA; seats by party—UPDC 8, PJ 7, RDC 2, CRC 2, RADHI 1, PEC 1, independents 3; note—in addition 9 seats will be filled by nominations from the 3 island assemblies

Judicial branch: *highest court(s):* Supreme Court or Cour Supreme (consists of 7 judges); Constitutional Court (consists of 8 members)

judge selection and term of office: Supreme Court judges—2 selected by the president of the Union, 2 by the Assembly of the Union, and 1 each by the 3 island councils; judges appointed for life; Constitutional Court members appointed—1 by the president, 1 each by the 3 vice presidents, 1 by the Assembly, and 1 each by the island executives; all members serve 6-year renewable terms

subordinate courts: Court of Appeals (in Moroni); Tribunal de premiere instance; island village (community) courts; religious courts

Political parties and leaders: Convention for the Renewal of the Comoros or CRC [AZALI Assoumani]

Democratic Rally of the Comoros or RDC [Mouigni BARAKA]

Juwa Party or PJ [Ahmed Abdallah SAMBI]

Party for the Comorian Agreement (Partie Pour l'Entente Commorienne) or PEC [Fahmi Said IBRAHIM]

Rally for an Alternative of Harmonious and Integrated Development or RADHI [Abdou SOEFO]

Rally with a Development Intiiative for Enlightened Youth or RIDJA [Said Larifou]

Union for the Development of the Comoros or UPDC [Mohamed HALIFA]

Political pressure groups and leaders: Federation Comorienne des Consomateurs or FCC [Mohamed Said Abdallah MCHANGANA]

Mouvement des Entreprises comorienne or MODEC [Faharate HOUSSEIN]

Union des Chambres de Commerce et de l'Industrie et de l'Agriculture or UCCIA [Fahmy THABIT]

Confederation des Travailleurs Comoriens or CTC

other: environmentalists

International organization participation: ACP, AfDB, AMF, AOSIS, AU, CAEU (candidates), COMESA, FAO, FZ, G-77, IBRD, ICAO, ICCt, ICRM, IDA, IDB, IFAD, IFC, IFRCS, ILO, IMF, IMO, IMSO, InOC, Interpol, IOC, IOM, ITSO, ITU, ITUC (NGOs), LAS, MIGA, NAM, OIC, OIF, OPCW, UN, UNCTAD, UNESCO, UNIDO, UPU, WCO, WHO, WIPO, WMO, WTO (observer)

Diplomatic representation in the US: *chief of mission:* Ambassador Soilihi Mohamed MAMADOU (since 18 November 2014)

chancery: Mission to the US, 866 United Nations Plaza, Suite 418, New York, NY 10017

telephone: [1] (212) 750-1637

FAX: [1] (212) 750-1657

Diplomatic representation from the US: the US does not have an embassy in Comoros; the US Ambassador to Madagascar is accredited to Comoros

Flag description: four equal horizontal bands of yellow (top), white, red, and blue, with a green isosceles triangle based on the hoist; centered within the triangle is a white crescent with the convex side facing the hoist and four white, five-pointed stars placed vertically in a line between the points of the crescent; the horizontal bands and the four stars represent the four main islands of the archipelago—Mwali, N'gazidja, Ndzuwani, and Mahore (Mayotte—department of France, but claimed by Comoros)

note: the crescent, stars, and color green are traditional symbols of Islam

National symbol(s): four stars and crescent; national colors: green, white

National anthem: *name:* "Udzima wa ya Masiwa" (The Union of the Great Islands)

lyrics/music: Said Hachim SIDI ABDEREMANE/ Said Hachim SIDI ABDEREMANE and Kamildine ABDALLAH

note: adopted 1978

ECONOMY

Economy—overview: One of the world's poorest countries, Comoros is made up of three islands that are hampered by inadequate transportation links, a young and rapidly increasing population, and few natural resources. The low educational level of the labor force contributes to a subsistence level of economic activity and a heavy dependence on foreign grants and technical assistance. Agriculture, including fishing, hunting, and forestry, accounts for 50% of GDP, employs 80% of the labor force, and provides most of the exports. Export income is heavily reliant on the three main crops of vanilla, cloves, and ylang-ylang; and Comoros' export earnings are easily disrupted by disasters such as fires and extreme weather. Despite agriculture's importance to the economy, the country imports roughly 70% of its food; rice, the main staple, accounts for the bulk of imports.

Authorities are negotiating with the IMF for triennial program assistance. The government—which is racked by internal political disputes—is struggling to provide basic services, upgrade education and technical training, privatize commercial and industrial enterprises, improve health services, diversify exports, promote tourism, and reduce the high population growth rate. Recurring political instability, sometimes initiated from outside the country, has inhibited growth. Remittances from about 200,000 Comorans contribute about 25% of the country's GDP. In December 2012, IMF and the World Bank's International Development Association supported $176 million in debt relief for Comoros, resulting in a 59% reduction of its future external debt service over a period of 40 years. In late 2013, a US-based investment company invested $200 million in a project to explore for hydrocarbons in Comoran territorial waters, the largest financial investment in the country's history.

GDP (purchasing power parity): $1.214 billion (2015 est.)

$1.202 billion (2014 est.)

$1.179 billion (2013 est.)

note: data are in 2015 US dollars

country comparison to the world: 201

GDP (official exchange rate): $589 million (2015 est.)

GDP—real growth rate: 1% (2015 est.)

2% (2014 est.)

3.5% (2013 est.)

country comparison to the world: 173

GDP—per capita (PPP): $1,500 (2015 est.)

$1,500 (2014 est.)

$1,600 (2013 est.)

note: data are in 2015 US dollars

country comparison to the world: 218

Gross national saving: 14.6% of GDP (2015 est.)

12.4% of GDP (2014 est.)

12.2% of GDP (2013 est.)

country comparison to the world: 122

GDP—composition, by end use:

household consumption: 105.7%

government consumption: 29.6%

investment in fixed capital: -1.2%

investment in inventories: 9.2%

exports of goods and services: 20.8%

imports of goods and services: -64.1% (2015 est.)

GDP—composition, by sector of origin: *agriculture:* 49.7%

industry: 12.7%

services: 37.6% (2015 est.)

Agriculture—products: vanilla, cloves, ylang-ylang (perfume essence), coconuts, bananas, cassava (manioc)

Industries: fishing, tourism, perfume distillation

Industrial production growth rate: 2.5% (2015 est.)

country comparison to the world: 102

Labor force: 245,200 (2013 est.)

country comparison to the world: 168
Labor force—by occupation: *agriculture:* 80% industry and services: 20% (1996 est.)
Unemployment rate: 6.5% (2014 est.)
country comparison to the world: 75

Population below poverty line: 44.8% (2004 est.)

Household income or consumption by percentage share: *lowest:* 10%: 0.9%
highest: 10%: 55.2% (2004)
Budget: *revenues:* $129.9 million
expenditures: $147.3 million (2015 est.)
Taxes and other revenues: 22.1% of GDP (2015 est.)
country comparison to the world: 141
Budget surplus (+) or deficit (-): -3% of GDP (2015 est.)
country comparison to the world: 112
Fiscal year: calendar year
Inflation rate (consumer prices): 2% (2015 est.)
1.3% (2014 est.)
country comparison to the world: 115
Central bank discount rate: 1.93% (31 December 2010)
2.21% (31 December 2009)
country comparison to the world: 116
Commercial bank prime lending rate: 11% (31 December 2015 est.)
10.5% (31 December 2014 est.)
country comparison to the world: 74
Stock of narrow money: $114.2 million (31 December 2015 est.)
$133.3 million (31 December 2014 est.)
country comparison to the world: 186
Stock of broad money: $269.6 million (31 December 2014 est.)
$251.9 million (31 December 2013 est.)
country comparison to the world: 188
Stock of domestic credit: $144.2 million (31 December 2015 est.)
$166.6 million (31 December 2014 est.)
country comparison to the world: 182
Current account balance: -$60 million (2015 est.)
-$74 million (2014 est.)
country comparison to the world: 65
Exports: $18.6 million (2015 est.)
$18.3 million (2014 est.)
country comparison to the world: 212

Exports—commodities: vanilla, ylang-ylang (perfume essence), cloves

Exports—partners: India 28.7%, France 17%, Germany 8.7%, Saudi Arabia 7.1%, Singapore 6.6%, Netherlands 6.1%, Mauritius 5.3% (2015)
Imports: $188.2 million (2015 est.)
$216 million (2014 est.)
country comparison to the world: 206

Imports—commodities: rice and other foodstuffs, consumer goods, petroleum products, cement and construction materials, transport equipment

Imports—partners: China 18.9%, Pakistan 16.2%, France 14.7%, UAE 11.3%, India 6.4% (2015)

Debt—external: $142 million (31 December 2014 est.) $146.4 million (31 December 2013 est.)

country comparison to the world: 191
Exchange rates: Comoran francs (KMF) per US dollar—
447.3 (2015 est.)
370.81 (2014 est.)
370.81 (2013 est.)
382.9 (2012 est.)
353.9 (2011 est.)

ENERGY

Electricity—production: 43 million kWh (2012 est.)
country comparison to the world: 210
Electricity—consumption: 39.99 million kWh (2012 est.)
country comparison to the world: 209
Electricity—exports: 0 kWh (2013 est.)
country comparison to the world: 124
Electricity—imports: 0 kWh (2013 est.)
country comparison to the world: 134
Electricity—installed generating capacity: 22,000 kW (2012 est.)
country comparison to the world: 203
Electricity—from fossil fuels: 95.5% of total installed capacity (2012 est.)
country comparison to the world: 67
Electricity—from nuclear fuels: 0% of total installed capacity (2012 est.)
country comparison to the world: 70
Electricity—from hydroelectric plants: 4.5% of total installed capacity (2012 est.)
country comparison to the world: 127
Electricity—from other renewable sources: 0% of total installed capacity (2012 est.)
country comparison to the world: 170
Crude oil—production: 0 bbl/day (2014 est.)
country comparison to the world: 119
Crude oil—exports: 0 bbl/day (2012 est.)
country comparison to the world: 111
Crude oil—imports: 0 bbl/day (2012 est.)
country comparison to the world: 174
Crude oil—proved reserves: 0 bbl (1 January 2015 est.)
country comparison to the world: 118
Refined petroleum products—production: 0 bbl/day (2012 est.)
country comparison to the world: 168
Refined petroleum products—consumption: 1,000 bbl/day (2013 est.)
country comparison to the world: 202
Refined petroleum products—exports: 0 bbl/day (2012 est.)
country comparison to the world: 169
Refined petroleum products—imports: 1,009 bbl/day (2012 est.)
country comparison to the world: 197
Natural gas—production: 0 cu m (2013 est.)
country comparison to the world: 172
Natural gas—consumption: 0 cu m (2013 est.)
country comparison to the world: 131
Natural gas—exports: 0 cu m (2013 est.)
country comparison to the world: 81
Natural gas—imports: 0 cu m (2013 est.)
country comparison to the world: 180

Natural gas—proved reserves: 0 cu m (1 January 2014 est.)
country comparison to the world: 125
Carbon dioxide emissions from consumption of energy: 157,400 Mt (2012 est.)
country comparison to the world: 202

COMMUNICATIONS

Telephones—fixed lines: *total subscriptions:* 23,500
subscriptions per 100 inhabitants: 3 (2014 est.)
country comparison to the world: 178
Telephones—mobile cellular: *total:* 383,000
subscriptions per 100 inhabitants: 50 (2014 est.)
country comparison to the world: 173
Telephone system: *general assessment:* sparse system of microwave radio relay and HF radiotelephone communication stations
domestic: fixed-line connections only about 3 per 100 persons; mobile cellular usage about 30 per 100 persons
international: country code—269; landing point for the EASSy fiber-optic submarine cable system connecting East Africa with Europe and North America; HF radiotelephone communications to Madagascar and Reunion (2010)

Broadcast media: national state-owned TV station and a TV station run by Anjouan regional government; national state-owned radio; regional governments on the islands of Grande Comore and Anjouan each operate a radio station; a few independent and small community radio stations operate on the islands of Grande Comore and Moheli, and these two islands have access to Mayotte Radio and French TV (2007)
Radio broadcast stations: AM 1, FM 4, shortwave 1 (2001)
Television broadcast stations: NA

Internet country code: .km
Internet hosts: 14 (2012)
country comparison to the world: 225
Internet users: *total:* 50,200
percent of population: 6.6% (2014 est.)
country comparison to the world: 182

TRANSPORTATION

Airports: 4 (2013)
country comparison to the world: 186
Airports—with paved runways: *total:* 4
2,438 to 3,047 m: 1
914 to 1,523 m: 3 (2013)
Roadways: *total:* 880 km
paved: 673 km
unpaved: 207 km (2002)
country comparison to the world: 187
Merchant marine: *total:* 149
by type: bulk carrier 16, cargo 83, carrier 5, chemical tanker 5, container 2, passenger 2, passenger/cargo 1, petroleum tanker 17, refrigerated cargo 10, roll on/roll off 8
foreign-owned: 73 (Bangladesh 1, Bulgaria 4, China 1, Cyprus 2, Greece 4, Kenya 2, Kuwait 1, Latvia 2, Lebanon 2, Lithuania 1, Nigeria 1,

Norway 1, Pakistan 5, Russia 12, Syria 5, Turkey 8, UAE 8, UK 1, Ukraine 10, US 2) (2010)
country comparison to the world: 39

Ports and terminals: *major seaport(s):* Moroni, Mutsamudu

MILITARY AND SECURITY

Military branches: National Army for Development (l'Armee Nationale de Developpement, AND): Comoran Security Force (also called Comoran Defense Force (Force Comorienne de Defense, FCD), includes Gendarmerie), Comoran Coast Guard, Comoran Federal Police (2015)

Military service age and obligation: 18 years of age for 2-year voluntary male and female military service; no conscription (2015)

TRANSNATIONAL ISSUES

Disputes—international: claims French-administered Mayotte and challenges France's and Madagascar's claims to Banc du Geyser, a drying reef in the Mozambique Channel; in May 2008, African Union forces assisted the Comoros military recapture Anjouan Island from rebels who seized it in 2001

Trafficking in persons: *current situation:* Comoros is a source country for children subjected to forced labor and, reportedly, sex trafficking domestically, and women and children are subjected to forced labor in Mayotte; it is possibly a transit and destination country for Malagasy women and girls and a transit country for East African women and girls exploited in domestic service in the Middle East; Comoran children are forced to labor in domestic service, roadside and street vending, baking, fishing, and agriculture; some Comoran students at Koranic schools are exploited for forced agricultural or domestic labor, sometimes being subjected to physical and sexual abuse; Comoros may be particularly vulnerable to transnational trafficking because of inadequate border controls, government corruption, and the presence of international criminal networks

tier rating: Tier 3—Comoros does not fully comply with the minimum standards for the elimination of trafficking and was placed on Tier 3 after being on the Tier 2 Watch List for two consecutive years without making progress; Parliament passed revisions to the penal code in 2014, including anti-trafficking provisions and enforcement guidelines, but these amendments have not yet been passed approved by the President and put into effect; a new child labor law was passed in 2015 prohibiting child trafficking, but existing laws do not criminalize the forced prostitution of adults; authorities did not investigate, prosecute, or convict alleged trafficking offenders, including complicit officials; the government lacked victim identification and care referral procedures, did not assist any victims during 2014, and provided minimal support to NGOs offering victims psychosocial services (2015)

CONGO, DEMOCRATIC REPUBLIC OF THE

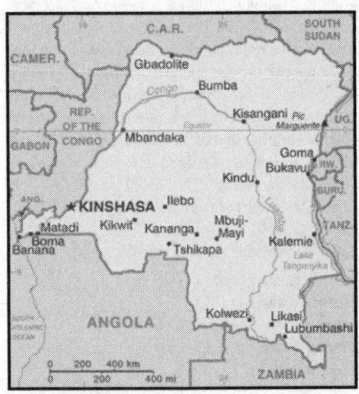

INTRODUCTION

Background: Established as an official Belgian colony in 1908, the then-Republic of the Congo gained its independence in 1960, but its early years were marred by political and social instability. Col. Joseph MOBUTU seized power and declared himself president in a November 1965 coup. He subsequently changed his name—to MOBUTU Sese Seko—as well as that of the country—to Zaire. MOBUTU retained his position for 32 years through several sham elections, as well as through brutal force. Ethnic strife and civil war, touched off by a massive inflow of refugees in 1994 from fighting in Rwanda and Burundi, led in May 1997 to the toppling of the MOBUTU regime by a rebellion backed by Rwanda and Uganda and fronted by Laurent KABILA. He renamed the country the Democratic Republic of the Congo (DRC), but in August 1998 his regime was itself challenged by a second insurrection again backed by Rwanda and Uganda. Troops from Angola, Chad, Namibia, Sudan, and Zimbabwe intervened to support KABILA's regime. In January 2001, KABILA was assassinated and his son, Joseph KABILA, was named head of state. In October 2002, the new president was successful in negotiating the withdrawal of Rwandan forces occupying the eastern DRC; two months later, the Pretoria Accord was signed by all remaining warring parties to end the fighting and establish a government of national unity. A transitional government was set up in July 2003; it held a successful constitutional referendum in December 2005 and elections for the presidency, National Assembly, and provincial legislatures took place in 2006.

In 2009, following a resurgence of conflict in the eastern DRC, the government signed a peace agreement with the National Congress for the Defense of the People (CNDP), a primarily Tutsi rebel group. An attempt to integrate CNDP members into the Congolese military failed, prompting their defection in 2012 and the formation of the M23 armed group—named after the 23 March 2009 peace agreements. Renewed conflict led to large population displacements and significant human rights abuses before the M23 was pushed out of DRC to Uganda and Rwanda in late 2013 by a joint DRC and UN offensive. In addition, the DRC continues to experience violence committed by other armed groups including the Democratic Forces for the Liberation of Rwanda, the Allied Democratic Forces, and assorted Mai Mai militias. In the most recent national elections, held in November 2011, disputed results allowed Joseph KABILA to be reelected to the presidency; the next presidential election is scheduled for late 2016.

GEOGRAPHY

Location: Central Africa, northeast of Angola

Geographic coordinates: 0 00 N, 25 00 E

Map references: Africa

Area: *total:* 2,344,858 sq km
land: 2,267,048 sq km
water: 77,810 sq km
country comparison to the world: 11

Area—comparative: slightly less than one-fourth the size of the US

Land boundaries: *total:* 10,481 km
border countries (9): Angola 2,646 km (of which 225 km is the boundary of Angola's discontiguous Cabinda Province), Burundi 236 km, Central African Republic 1,747 km, Republic of the Congo 1,229 km, Rwanda 221 km, South Sudan 714 km, Tanzania 479 km, Uganda 877 km, Zambia 2,332 km

Coastline: 37 km

Maritime claims: *territorial sea:* 12 nm
exclusive economic zone: since 2011 the DRC has a Common Interest Zone agreement with Angola for the mutual development of off-shore resources

Climate: tropical; hot and humid in equatorial river basin; cooler and drier in southern highlands; cooler and wetter in eastern highlands; north of Equator—wet season (April to October), dry season (December to February); south of Equator—wet season (November to March), dry season (April to October)

Terrain: vast central basin is a low-lying plateau; mountains in east

Elevation: *mean elevation:* 726 m

elevation extremes: *lowest point:* Atlantic Ocean 0 m
highest point: Pic Marguerite on Mont Ngaliema (Mount Stanley) 5,110 m

Natural resources: cobalt, copper, niobium, tantalum, petroleum, industrial and gem diamonds, gold, silver, zinc, manganese, tin, uranium, coal, hydropower, timber

Land use: *agricultural land:* 11.4%
arable land: 3.1%
permanent crops: 0.3%
permanent pasture: 8%
forest: 67.9%
other: 20.7% (2011 est.)

Irrigated land: 110 sq km (2012)

Total renewable water resources: 1,283 cu km (2011)

Freshwater withdrawal (domestic/industrial/agricultural): *total:* 0.68 cu m/yr (68%/21%/11%)
per capita: 11.25 cu m/yr (2005)

Natural hazards: periodic droughts in south; Congo River floods (seasonal); active volcanoes in the east along the Great Rift Valley
volcanism: Nyiragongo (elev. 3,470 m), which erupted in 2002 and is experiencing ongoing activity, poses a major threat to the city of Goma, home to a quarter million people; the volcano produces unusually fast-moving lava, known to travel up to 100 km/hr; Nyiragongo has been deemed a Decade Volcano by the International Association of Volcanology and Chemistry of the Earth's Interior, worthy of study due to its explosive history and close proximity to human populations; its neighbor, Nyamuragira, which erupted in 2010, is Africa's most active volcano; Visoke is the only other historically active volcano

Environment—current issues: poaching threatens wildlife populations; water pollution; deforestation; refugees responsible for significant deforestation, soil erosion, and wildlife poaching; mining of minerals (coltan—a mineral used in creating capacitors, diamonds, and gold) causing environmental damage

Environment—international agreements: *party to:* Biodiversity, Climate Change, Climate Change-Kyoto Protocol, Desertification, Endangered Species, Hazardous Wastes, Law of the Sea, Marine Dumping, Ozone Layer Protection, Tropical Timber 83, Tropical Timber 94, Wetlands
signed, but not ratified: Environmental Modification

Geography—note: second largest country in Africa (after Algeria) and largest country in Sub-Saharan Africa; straddles the equator; has narrow strip of land that controls the lower Congo River and is only outlet to South Atlantic Ocean; dense tropical rain forest in central river basin and eastern highlands

PEOPLE AND SOCIETY

Nationality: *noun:* Congolese (singular and plural)
adjective: Congolese or Congo

Ethnic groups: over 200 African ethnic groups of which the majority are Bantu; the four largest tribes—Mongo, Luba, Kongo (all Bantu), and the Mangbetu-Azande (Hamitic) make up about 45% of the population

Languages: French (official), Lingala (a lingua franca trade language), Kingwana (a dialect of Kiswahili or Swahili), Kikongo, Tshiluba

Religions: Roman Catholic 50%, Protestant 20%, Kimbanguist 10%, Muslim 10%, other (includes syncretic sects and indigenous beliefs) 10%

Population: 79,375,136
note: estimates for this country explicitly take into account the effects of excess mortality due to AIDS; this can result in lower life expectancy, higher infant mortality, higher death rates, lower population growth rates, and changes in the distribution of population by age and sex than would otherwise be expected (July 2015 est.)
country comparison to the world: 20

Age structure: *0–14 years:* 42.65% (male 17,061,640/female 16,793,575)
15–24 years: 21.41% (male 8,522,085/female 8,474,212)
25–54 years: 29.75% (male 11,783,887/female 11,829,078)
55–64 years: 3.56% (male 1,329,384/female 1,495,329)
65 years and over: 2.63% (male 879,823/female 1,206,123) (2015 est.)

Dependency ratios: *total dependency ratio:* 95.9%
youth dependency ratio: 90.1%
elderly dependency ratio: 5.8%
potential support ratio: 17.2% (2015 est.)

Median age: *total:* 18.1 years
male: 17.9 years
female: 18.4 years (2015 est.)
country comparison to the world: 213

Population growth rate: 2.45% (2015 est.)
country comparison to the world: 26

Birth rate: 34.88 births/1,000 population (2015 est.)
country comparison to the world: 23

Death rate: 10.07 deaths/1,000 population (2015 est.)
country comparison to the world: 43

Net migration rate: -0.27 migrant(s)/1,000 population (2015 est.)
country comparison to the world: 123

Urbanization: *urban population:* 42.5% of total population (2015)
rate of urbanization: 3.96% annual rate of change (2010–15 est.)

Major urban areas—population: KINSHASA (capital) 11.587 million; Lubumbashi 2.015 million; Mbuji-Mayi 20.007 million; Kananga 1.169 million; Kisangani 1.04 million; Bukavu 832,000 (2015)

Sex ratio: *at birth:* 1.03 male(s)/female
0–14 years: 1.02 male(s)/female
15–24 years: 1.01 male(s)/female
25–54 years: 1 male(s)/female
55–64 years: 0.89 male(s)/female
65 years and over: 0.73 male(s)/female
total population: 0.99 male(s)/female (2015 est.)

Mother's mean age at first birth: 19.9
note: median age at first birth among women 25–29 (2013/14 est.)

Maternal mortality rate: 693 deaths/100,000 live births (2015 est.)

country comparison to the world: 17

Infant mortality rate: *total:* 71.47 deaths/1,000 live births
male: 75.07 deaths/1,000 live births
female: 67.75 deaths/1,000 live births (2015 est.)
country comparison to the world: 12

Life expectancy at birth:
total population: 56.93 years
male: 55.39 years
female: 58.51 years (2015 est.)
country comparison to the world: 206

Total fertility rate: 4.66 children born/woman (2015 est.)
country comparison to the world: 23

Contraceptive prevalence rate: 17.7% (2010)

Health expenditures: 3.5% of GDP (2013)
country comparison to the world: 123

Hospital bed density: 0.8 beds/1,000 population (2006)

Drinking water source:
improved:
urban: 81.1% of population
rural: 31.2% of population
total: 52.4% of population
unimproved:
urban: 18.9% of population
rural: 68.8% of population
total: 47.6% of population (2015 est.)

Sanitation facility access:
improved:
urban: 28.5% of population
rural: 28.7% of population
total: 28.7% of population
unimproved:
urban: 71.5% of population
rural: 71.3% of population
total: 71.3% of population (2015 est.)

HIV/AIDS—adult prevalence rate: 1.04% (2014 est.)
country comparison to the world: 46

HIV/AIDS—people living with HIV/AIDS: 446,600 (2014 est.)
country comparison to the world: 17

HIV/AIDS—deaths: 24,100 (2014 est.)
country comparison to the world: 12

Major infectious diseases: *degree of risk:* very high
food or waterborne diseases: bacterial and protozoal diarrhea, hepatitis A, and typhoid fever
vectorborne diseases: malaria, dengue fever, and trypanosomiasis-gambiense (African sleeping sickness)
water contact disease: schistosomiasis
animal contact disease: rabies (2013)

Obesity—adult prevalence rate: 3.7% (2014)
country comparison to the world: 185

Children under the age of 5 years underweight: 23.4% (2014)
country comparison to the world: 25

Education expenditures: 2.2% of GDP (2013)
country comparison to the world: 157

Literacy: *definition:* age 15 and over can read and write French, Lingala, Kingwana, or Tshiluba
total population: 63.8%
male: 78.1%
female: 50% (2015 est.)

School life expectancy (primary to tertiary education): *total:* 9 years
male: 10 years
female: 8 years (2013)

Child labor—children ages 5–14: *total number:* 8,284,395
percentage: 42% (2010 est.)

GOVERNMENT

Country name: *conventional long form:* Democratic Republic of the Congo
conventional short form: DRC
local long form: Republique Democratique du Congo
local short form: RDC
former: Congo Free State, Belgian Congo, Congo/Leopoldville, Congo/Kinshasa, Zaire abbreviation: DRC
etymology: named for the Congo River, most of which lies within the DRC; the river name derives from Kongo, a Bantu kingdom that occupied its mouth at the time of Portuguese discovery in the late 15th century and whose name stems from its people the Bakongo, meaning "hunters"

Government type: semi-presidential republic

Capital: *name:* Kinshasa

Geographic coordinates: 4 19 S, 15 18 E
time difference: UTC + 1 (6 hours ahead of Washington, DC, during Standard Time)

Administrative divisions: 26 provinces (provinces, singular—province) and 1 city* (ville); Bandundu, Bas-Uele, Equateur, Haut-Katanga, Haut-Lomami, Haut-Uele, Ituri, Kasai, Kasai-Central, Kasai-Occidental (West Kasai), Kasai- Oriental, Kinshasa*, Katanga, Kongo Central, Kwango, Kwilu, Lomami, Lualaba, Mai-Ndombe, Mongala, Nord-Ubangi, Orientale, Sankuru, Sud-Ubangi, Tanganyika, Tshopo, Tshuapa

Independence: 30 June 1960 (from Belgium)

National holiday: Independence Day, 30 June (1960)

Constitution: several previous; latest adopted 13 May 2005, approved by referendum 18–19 December 2005, promulgated 18 February 2006; amended 2011 (2016)

Legal system: civil law system primarily based on Belgian law, but also customary, and tribal law

International law organization participation: accepts compulsory ICJ jurisdiction with reservations; accepts ICCt jurisdiction

Citizenship: *citizenship by birth:* no
citizenship by descent only: at least one parent must be a citizen of the Democratic Republic of the Congo
dual citizenship recognized: no
residency requirement for naturalization: 5 years

Suffrage: 18 years of age; universal and compulsory

Executive branch: *chief of state:* President Joseph KABILA (since 17 January 2001)

head of government: Prime Minister Augustin MATATA PONYO Mapon (since 18 April 2012)
cabinet: Ministers of State appointed by the president

elections/appointments: president directly elected by simple majority popular vote for a 5-year term (eligible for a second term); election last held on 28 November 2011 (next to be held on 27 November 2016); prime minister appointed by the president
election results: Joseph KABILA reelected president; percent of vote—Joseph KABILA (PPRD) 49%, Etienne TSHISEKEDI (UDPS) 32.3%, other 18.7%; note—election marred by serious voting irregularities

Legislative branch: *description:* bicameral Parliament or Parlament consists of the Senate (108 seats; members indirectly elected by provincial assemblies by proportional representation vote; members serve 5-year terms) and the National Assembly (500 seats; 439 members directly elected in multi-seat constituencies by proportional representation vote and 61 directly elected in single-seat constituencies by simple majority vote; members serve 5-year terms)
elections: Senate—last held on 19 January 2007 (follow-on elections have been delayed); National Assembly—last held on 28 November 2011 (next to be held in 2016)
election results: Senate—percent of vote by party—NA; seats by party—PPRD 22, MLC 14, FR 7, RCD 7, PDC 6, CDC 3, MSR 3, PALU 2, independent 26, other 18; National Assembly—percent of vote by party—NA; seats by party—PPRD 62, UDPS 41, PPPD 29, MSR 27, MLC 22, PALU 19, UNC 17, ARC 16, AFDC 15, ECT 11, RRC 11, independent 16, other 214 (includes numerous political parties that won 10 or fewer seats and 2 constituencies where voting was halted); note—the November 2011 election was marred by violence including the destruction of ballots in two constituencies resulting in the closure of polling sites; election results were delayed three months, strongly contested, and continue to be unresolved

Judicial branch: *highest court(s):* Supreme Court of Justice (organized into legislative and judiciary sections and consists of 26 justices); Constitutional Court (consists of 9 judges)
judge selection and term of office: Supreme Court of Justice judges nominated by the Judicial Service Council, an independent body of public prosecutors and selected judges of the lower courts; judges tenure NA; Constitutional Court judges—3 nominated by the president, 3 by the Judicial Service Council, and 3 by the legislature; judges appointed by the president to serve 9-year non-renewable terms
subordinate courts: State Security Court; Court of Appeals (organized into administrative and judiciary sections); Tribunal de Grande; magistrates' courts; customary courts

Political parties and leaders: Christian Democrat Party or PDC [Jose ENDUNDO]
Congolese Rally for Democracy or RCD [Azarias RUBERWA]
Convention of Christian Democrats or CDC
Forces of Renewal or FR [Mbusa NYAMWISI]
Movement for the Liberation of the Congo or MLC [Jean-Pierre BEMBA]

People's Party for Reconstruction and Democracy or PPRD [Henri MOVA]
Social Movement for Renewal or MSR [Pierre LUMBI]
Unified Lumumbist Party or PALU [Antoine GIZENGA]
Union for the Congolese Nation or UNC [Vital KAMERHE]
Union for Democracy and Social Progress or UDPS [Etienne TSHISEKEDI]

Political pressure groups and leaders: Allied Democratic Forces or ADF (anti-Ugandan government rebel groups)
Forces Armies de la Republique Democratique du Congor (Army of the Democratic Republic of the Congo) or FARDC
Forces Democratiques de Liberation du Rwanda or FDLR (Rwandan militia group made up of some of the perpetrators of Rwanda's genocide in 1994)

International organization participation: ACP, AfDB, AU, CEMAC, CEPGL, COMESA, EITI (compliant country), FAO, G-24, G-77, IAEA, IBRD, ICAO, ICC (NGOs), ICCt, ICRM, IDA, IFAD, IFC, IFRCS, IHO, ILO, IMF, IMO, Interpol, IOC, IOM, IPU, ISO, ITSO, ITU, ITUC (NGOs), MIGA, NAM, OIF, OPCW, PCA, SADC, UN, UNCTAD, UNESCO, UNHCR, UNIDO, UNWTO, UPU, WCO, WFTU (NGOs), WHO, WIPO, WMO, WTO

Diplomatic representation in the US: *chief of mission:* Ambassador Francois BALUMUENE (since 17 September 2015)
chancery: 1726 M Street, NW, Suite 601, Washington, DC, 20036
telephone: [1] (202) 234-7690 through 7691
FAX: [1] (202) 234-2609
representative office: New York New York

Diplomatic representation from the US: *chief of mission:* Ambassador James C. SWAN (since 6 August 2013)
embassy: 310 Avenue des Aviateurs, Kinshasa
maiing address: Unit 2220, DPO AE 09828
telephone: [243] (081) 556-0151
FAX: [243] (081) 556-0175

Flag description: sky blue field divided diagonally from the lower hoist corner to upper fly corner by a red stripe bordered by two narrow yellow stripes; a yellow, five-pointed star appears in the upper hoist corner; blue represents peace and hope, red the blood of the country's martyrs, and yellow the country's wealth and prosperity; the star symbolizes unity and the brilliant future for the country

National symbol(s): leopard; national colors: sky blue, red, yellow

National anthem: *name:* "Debout Congolaise" (Arise Congolese)
lyrics/music: Joseph LUTUMBA/Simon-Pierre BOKA di Mpasi Londi
note: adopted 1960; replaced when the country was known as Zaire; but readopted in 1997

ECONOMY

Economy—overview: The economy of the Democratic Republic of the Congo—a nation endowed with vast natural resource wealth—is slowly recovering after decades of decline.

Systemic corruption since independence in 1960, combined with countrywide instability and conflict that began in the early-90s, has dramatically reduced national output and government revenue and increased external debt. With the installation of a transitional government in 2003 after peace accords, economic conditions slowly began to improve as the transitional government reopened relations with international financial institutions and international donors, and President KABILA began implementing reforms. Progress has been slow to reach the interior of the country although clear changes are evident in Kinshasa and Lubumbashi.

Renewed activity in the mining sector, the source of most export income, has boosted Kinshasa's fiscal position and GDP growth in recent years, although recent commodity price declines threaten to erase progress. An uncertain legal framework, corruption, and a lack of transparency in government policy are long-term problems for the large mining sector and for the economy as a whole.

The country marked its thirteenth consecutive year of positive economic expansion in 2015. Much economic activity still occurs in the informal sector and is not reflected in GDP data. The DRC signed a Poverty Reduction and Growth Facility with the IMF in 2009 and received $12 billion in multilateral and bilateral debt relief in 2010, but the IMF at the end of 2012 suspended the last three payments under the loan facility—worth $240 million—because of concerns about the lack of transparency in mining contracts. In 2012, the DRC updated its business laws by adhering to OHADA, the Organization for the Harmonization of Business Law in Africa.

GDP (purchasing power parity): $62.87 billion (2015 est.)
$58.35 billion (2014 est.)
$53.45 billion (2013 est.)
note: data are in 2015 US dollars
country comparison to the world: 102

GDP (official exchange rate): $38.87 billion (2015 est.)

GDP—real growth rate: 7.7% (2015 est.)
9.2% (2014 est.) 8.5% (2013 est.)
country comparison to the world: 10

GDP—per capita (PPP): $800 (2015 est.)
$700 (2014 est.) $700 (2013 est.)
note: data are in 2015 US dollars
country comparison to the world: 226

Gross national saving: 5.5% of GDP (2015 est.)
7% of GDP (2014 est.)
10.4% of GDP (2013 est.)
country comparison to the world: 163

GDP—composition, by end use:
household consumption: 68.8%
government consumption: 13.4%
investment in fixed capital: 21.5%
investment in inventories: 0.1%
exports of goods and services: 29.6%
imports of goods and services: -33.4% (2015 est.)

GDP—composition, by sector of origin: *agriculture*: 20.3%
industry: 33.5%
services: 46.2% (2015 est.)

Agriculture—products: coffee, sugar, palm oil, rubber, tea, cotton, cocoa, quinine, cassava (manioc, tapioca), bananas, plantains, peanuts, root crops, corn, fruits; wood products

Industries: mining (copper, cobalt, gold, diamonds, coltan, zinc, tin, tungsten), mineral processing, consumer products (textiles, plastics, footwear, cigarettes), metal products, processed foods and beverages, timber, cement, commercial ship repair

Industrial production growth rate: 8.7% (2015 est.)
country comparison to the world: 13

Labor force: 28.58 million (2015 est.)
country comparison to the world: 24

Labor force—by occupation: *agriculture*: NA%
industry: NA%
services: NA%

Unemployment rate: NA%

Population below poverty line: 63% (2012 est.)

Household income or consumption by percentage share: *lowest*: 10%: 2.3%
highest: 10%: 34.7% (2006)

Budget: *revenues*: $6.084 billion
expenditures: $6.819 billion (2015 est.)
Taxes and other revenues: 15.6% of GDP (2015 est.)
country comparison to the world: 189

Budget surplus (+) or deficit (-): -1.9% of GDP (2015 est.)
country comparison to the world: 71

Public debt: 22.9% of GDP (2015 est.)
21.5% of GDP (2014 est.)
country comparison to the world: 152

Fiscal year: calendar year

Inflation rate (consumer prices): 1% (2015 est.)
1% (2014 est.)
country comparison to the world: 79

Central bank discount rate: 4% (31 December 2012)
20% (31 December 2011)
country comparison to the world: 98

Commercial bank prime lending rate: 19% (31 December 2015 est.)
18.69% (31 December 2014 est.)
country comparison to the world: 19

Stock of narrow money: $1.386 billion (31 December 2015 est.)
$1.284 billion (31 December 2014 est.)
country comparison to the world: 143

Stock of broad money: $5.018 billion (31 December 2015 est.)
$4.402 billion (31 December 2014 est.)
country comparison to the world: 131

Stock of domestic credit: $2.892 billion (31 December 2015 est.)
$2.607 billion (31 December 2014 est.)
country comparison to the world: 131

Market value of publicly traded shares: $NA

Current account balance: -$4.726 billion (2015 est.)
-$3.449 billion (2014 est.)

country comparison to the world: 167

Exports: $12.4 billion (2015 est.)
$12.98 billion (2014 est.)
country comparison to the world: 82

Exports—commodities: diamonds, copper, gold, cobalt, wood products, crude oil, coffee

Exports—partners: China 43.5%, Zambia 25%, South Korea 4.9%, Belgium 4.8% (2015)

Imports: $12.34 billion (2015 est.)
$11.98 billion (2014 est.)
country comparison to the world: 91

Imports—commodities: foodstuffs, mining and other machinery, transport equipment, fuels

Imports—partners: China 20.6%, South Africa 17.7%, Zambia 12.3%, Belgium 6.9%, Zimbabwe 5.1%, India 4.7% (2015)

Reserves of foreign exchange and gold: $1.443 billion (31 December 2015 est.)
$1.557 billion (31 December 2014 est.)
country comparison to the world: 125

Debt—external: $6.562 billion (31 December 2014 est.)
$6.082 billion (31 December 2013 est.)
country comparison to the world: 123

Exchange rates: Congolese francs (CDF) per US dollar—
927 (2015 est.)
925.23 (2014 est.)
925.23 (2013 est.)
920.25 (2012 est.)
899 (2011 est.)

ENERGY

Electricity—production: 7.885 billion kWh (2012 est.)
country comparison to the world: 103

Electricity—consumption: 7.292 billion kWh (2012 est.)
country comparison to the world: 102

Electricity—exports: 0 kWh (2012 est.)
country comparison to the world: 120

Electricity—imports: 0 kWh (2012 est.)
country comparison to the world: 130

Electricity—installed generating capacity: 2.506 million kW (2012 est.)
country comparison to the world: 98

Electricity—from fossil fuels: 1.4% of total installed capacity (2012 est.)
country comparison to the world: 209

Electricity—from nuclear fuels: 0% of total installed capacity (2012 est.)
country comparison to the world: 66

Electricity—from hydroelectric plants: 98.6% of total installed capacity (2012 est.)
country comparison to the world: 6

Electricity—from other renewable sources: 0% of total installed capacity (2012 est.)
country comparison to the world: 167

Crude oil—production: 20,000 bbl/day (2014 est.)
country comparison to the world: 72

Crude oil—exports: 20,000 bbl/day (2012 est.)
country comparison to the world: 59

Crude oil—imports: 0 bbl/day (2012 est.)
country comparison to the world: 172

Crude oil—proved reserves: 180 million bbl (1 January 2015 est.)
country comparison to the world: 61

Refined petroleum products—production: 0 bbl/day (2012 est.)
country comparison to the world: 166

Refined petroleum products—consumption: 20,000 bbl/day (2013 est.)
country comparison to the world: 129

Refined petroleum products—exports: 0 bbl/day (2012 est.)
country comparison to the world: 167

Refined petroleum products—imports: 20,620 bbl/day (2012 est.)
country comparison to the world: 110

Natural gas—production: 0 cu m (2013 est.)
country comparison to the world: 170

Natural gas—consumption: 0 cu m (2013 est.)
country comparison to the world: 129

Natu ral gas—exports: 0 cu m (2013 est.)
country comparison to the world: 77

Natural gas—imports: 0 cu m (2013 est.)
country comparison to the world: 177

Natural gas—proved reserves: 991.1 million cu m (1 January 2014 est.)
country comparison to the world: 103

Carbon dioxide emissions from consumption of energy: 2.481 million Mt (2012 est.)
country comparison to the world: 145

COMMUNICATIONS

Telephones—fixed lines: *total subscriptions:* 0
subscriptions per 100 inhabitants: less than 1 (2014 est.)
country comparison to the world: 217

Telephones—mobile cellular: *total:* 37.1 million
subscriptions per 100 inhabitants: 48 (2014 est.)
country comparison to the world: 34

Telephone system: *general assessment:* barely adequate wire and microwave radio relay service in and between urban areas; domestic satellite system with 14 earth stations; inadequate fixed-line infrastructure
domestic: state-owned operator providing less than 1 fixed-line connection per 100 persons; given the backdrop of a wholly inadequate fixed-line infrastructure, the use of mobile-cellular services has surged and mobile teledensity is roughly 20 per 100 persons
international: country code—243; satellite earth station—1 Intelsat (Atlantic Ocean) (2011)

Broadcast media: state-owned TV broadcast station with near national coverage; more than a dozen privately owned TV stations—2 with near national coverage; 2 state-owned radio stations are supplemented by more than 100 private radio stations; transmissions of at least 2 international broadcasters are available (2007)
Radio broadcast stations: AM 3, FM 11, shortwave 2 (2001)
Television broadcast stations: 4 (2001)

Internet country code: .cd
Internet hosts: 2,515 (2012)
country comparison to the world: 159
Internet users: *total:* 290,000

percent of population: less than 1% (2008)
country comparison to the world: 143

TRANSPORTATION

Airports: 198 (2013)
country comparison to the world: 27
Airports—with paved runways: *total:* 26
over 3,047 m: 3
2,438 to 3,047 m: 3
1,524 to 2,437 m: 17
914 to 1,523 m: 2
under 914 m: 1 (2013)
Airports—with unpaved runways: *total:* 172
1,524 to 2,437 m: 20
914 to 1,523 m: 87
under 914 m: 65 (2013)

Heliports: 1 (2013)

Pipelines: gas 62 km; oil 77 km; refined products 756 km (2013)
Railways: *total:* 4,007 km
narrow gauge: 3,882 km 1.067-m gauge (858 km electrified); 125 km 1.000-m gauge (2014)
country comparison to the world: 44
Roadways: *total:* 153,497 km
paved: 2,794 km
unpaved: 150,703 km (2004)
country comparison to the world: 32
Waterways: 15,000 km (including the Congo, its tributaries, and unconnected lakes) (2011)
country comparison to the world: 8
Merchant marine: *total:* 1
by type: petroleum tanker 1
foreign-owned: 1 (Republic of the Congo 1) (2010)
country comparison to the world: 147

Ports and terminals: *major seaport(s):* Banana
river or lake port(s): Boma, Bumba, Kinshasa, Kisangani, Matadi, Mbandaka (Congo); Kindu (Lualaba); Bukavu, Goma (Lake Kivu); Kalemie (Lake Tanganyika)

MILITARY AND SECURITY

Military branches: Armed Forces of the Democratic Republic of the Congo (Forces d'Armees de la Republique Democratique du Congo, FARDC): Army, National Navy (La Marine Nationale), Congolese Air Force (Force Aerienne Congolaise, FAC) (2011)

Military service age and obligation: 18–45 years of age for voluntary and compulsory military service (2012)

Military expenditures: 1.72% of GDP (2012)
1.53% of GDP (2011)
1.72% of GDP (2010)
country comparison to the world: 49

TRANSNATIONAL ISSUES

Disputes—international: heads of the Great Lakes states and UN pledged in 2004 to abate tribal, rebel, and militia fighting in the region, including northeast Congo, where the UN Organization Mission in the Democratic Republic of the Congo (MONUC), organized in 1999, maintains over 16,500 uniformed peacekeepers; members of Uganda's Lords Resistance Army forces continue to seek refuge in Congo's Garamba National Park as peace

talks with the Uganda Government evolve; the location of the boundary in the broad Congo River with the Republic of the Congo is indefinite except in the Pool Malebo/Stanley Pool area; Uganda and DRC dispute Rukwanzi Island in Lake Albert and other areas on the Semliki River with hydrocarbon potential; boundary commission continues discussions over Congolese-administered triangle of land on the right bank of the Lunkinda River claimed by Zambia near the DRC village of Pweto; DRC accuses Angola of shifting monuments

Refugees and internally displaced persons: *refugees (country of origin):* 38,028 (Rwanda) (2014); 112,775 (Central African Republic); 32,657 (Burundi) (2016)
IDPs: 1,555,112 (fighting between government forces and rebels since mid-1990s; most IDPs are in eastern provinces) (2015)

Trafficking in persons: *current situation:* The Democratic Republic of the Congo is a source, destination, and possibly a transit country for men, women, and children subjected to forced labor and sex trafficking; the majority of this trafficking is internal, and much of it is perpetrated by armed groups and rogue government forces outside official control in the country's unstable eastern provinces; Congolese adults are subjected to forced labor, including debt bondage, in unlicensed mines, and women may be forced into prostitution; Congolese women and girls are subjected to forced marriages where they are vulnerable to domestic servitude or sex trafficking, while children are forced to work in agriculture, mining, mineral smuggling, vending, portering, and begging; Congolese women and children migrate to countries in Africa, the Middle East, and Europe where some are subjected to forced prostitution, domestic servitude, and forced labor in agriculture and diamond mining; indigenous and foreign armed groups, including the Lord's Resistance Army, abduct and forcibly recruit Congolese adults and children to serve as laborers, porters, domestics, combatants, and sex slaves; some elements of the Congolese national army (FARDC) also forced adults to carry supplies, equipment, and looted goods, but no cases of the FARDC recruiting child soldiers were reported in 2014—a significant change

tier rating: Tier 2 Watch List—The Democratic Republic of the Congo does not fully comply with the minimum standards for the elimination of trafficking; however, it is making significant efforts to do so; the government took significant steps to hold military and police officials complicit in human trafficking accountable with convictions for sex slavery and arrests of armed group commanders for the recruitment and use of child soldiers; the government appears to have ceased the recruitment of child soldiers through the implementation of a UN-backed action plan; little effort was made to address labor and sex trafficking crimes committed by persons other than officials, or to identify the victims, or to provide or refer the victims to care services; awareness of various forms of trafficking is limited among law enforcement personnel and training and resources are inadequate to conduct investigations (2015)

Illicit drugs: one of Africa's biggest producers of cannabis, but mostly for domestic consumption; traffickers exploit lax shipping controls to transit pseudoephedrine through the capital; while rampant corruption and inadequate supervision leave the banking system vulnerable to money laundering, the lack of a well-developed financial system limits the country's utility as a money-laundering center (2008)

CONGO, REPUBLIC OF THE

INTRODUCTION

Background: Upon independence in 1960, the former French region of Middle Congo became the Republic of the Congo. A quarter century of experimentation with Marxism was abandoned in 1990 and a democratically elected government took office in 1992. A brief civil war in 1997 restored former Marxist President Denis SAS-SOU-Nguesso, and ushered in a period of ethnic and political unrest. Southern-based rebel groups agreed to a final peace accord in March 2003. The Republic of Congo is one of Africa's largest petroleum producers, but with declining production it will need new offshore oil finds to sustain its oil earnings over the long term.

GEOGRAPHY

Location: Central Africa, bordering the South Atlantic Ocean, between Angola and Gabon

Geographic coordinates: 1 00 S, 15 00 E

Map references: Africa

Area: *total:* 342,000 sq km
land: 341,500 sq km
water: 500 sq km
country comparison to the world: 64

Area—comparative: slightly smaller than Montana

Land boundaries: *total:* 5,008 km
border countries (5): Angola 231 km, Cameroon 494 km, Central African Republic 487 km, Democratic Republic of the Congo 1,229 km, Gabon 2,567 km

Coastline: 169 km

Maritime claims: *territorial sea:* 12 nm
contiguous zone: 24 nm
exclusive economic zone: 200 nm

Climate: tropical; rainy season (March to June); dry season (June to October); persistent high temperatures and humidity; particularly enervating climate astride the Equator

Terrain: coastal plain, southern basin, central plateau, northern basin

Elevation: *mean elevation:* 430 m

elevation extremes: *lowest point:* Atlantic Ocean 0 m
highest point: Mount Berongou 903 m

Natural resources: petroleum, timber, potash, lead, zinc, uranium, copper, phosphates, gold, magnesium, natural gas, hydropower

Land use: *agricultural land:* 31.1%
arable land: 1.6%
permanent crops: 0.2%
permanent pasture: 29.3%
forest: 65.6%
other: 3.3% (2011 est.)

Irrigated land: 20 sq km (2012)

Total renewable water resources: 832 cu km (2011)

Freshwater withdrawal (domestic/industrial/agricultural): *total:* 0.05 cu m/yr (69%/26%/4%)
per capita: 13.99 cu m/yr (2005)

Natural hazards: seasonal flooding

Environment—current issues: air pollution from vehicle emissions; water pollution from raw sewage; tap water is not potable; deforestation

Environment—international agreements: *party to:* Biodiversity, Climate Change, Climate Change-Kyoto Protocol, Desertification, Endangered Species, Hazardous Wastes, Law of the Sea, Ozone Layer Protection, Ship Pollution, Tropical Timber 83, Tropical Timber 94, Wetlands
signed, but not ratified: none of the selected agreements

Geography—note: about 70% of the population lives in Brazzaville, Pointe-Noire, or along the railroad between them

PEOPLE AND SOCIETY

Nationality: *noun:* Congolese (singular and plural)
adjective: Congolese or Congo

Ethnic groups: Kongo 48%, Sangha 20%, M'Bochi 12%, Teke 17%, Europeans and other 3%

Languages: French (official), Lingala and Monokutuba (lingua franca trade languages), many local languages and dialects (of which Kikongo is the most widespread)

Religions: Roman Catholic 33.1%, Awakening Churches/Christian Revival 22.3%, Protestant 19.9%, Salutiste 2.2%, Muslim 1.6%, Kimbanguiste 1.5%, other 8.1%, none 11.3% (2010 est.)

Population: 4,755,097
note: estimates for this country explicitly take into account the effects of excess mortality due to AIDS; this can result in lower life expectancy, higher infant mortality, higher death rates, lower population growth rates, and changes in the distribution of population by age and sex than would otherwise be expected (July 2015 est.)
country comparison to the world: 125

Age structure: *0–14 years:* 41.33% (male 991,327/female 973,745)
15–24 years: 17.48% (male 415,282/female 415,817)

25–54 years: 34.12% (male 819,204/female 803,062)
55–64 years: 4.08% (male 95,755/female 98,295)
65 years and over: 3% (male 62,332/female 80,278) (2015 est.)

Dependency ratios: *total dependency ratio:* 86.2%
youth dependency ratio: 79.4%
elderly dependency ratio: 6.8%
potential support ratio: 14.7% (2015 est.)

Median age: *total:* 19.8 years
male: 19.6 years
female: 19.9 years (2015 est.)
country comparison to the world: 191

Population growth rate: 2% (2015 est.)
country comparison to the world: 50

Birth rate: 35.85 births/1,000 population (2015 est.)
country comparison to the world: 20

Death rate: 10 deaths/1,000 population (2015 est.)
country comparison to the world: 45

Net migration rate: -5.9 migrant(s)/1,000 population (2015 est.)
country comparison to the world: 197

Urbanization: *urban population:* 65.4% of total population (2015)
rate of urbanization: 3.22% annual rate of change (2010–15 est.)

Major urban areas—population: BRAZZAVILLE (capital) 1.888 million; Pointe-Noire 969,000 (2015)

Sex ratio: *at birth:* 1.03 male(s)/female
0–14 years: 1.02 male(s)/female
15–24 years: 1 male(s)/female
25–54 years: 1.02 male(s)/female
55–64 years: 0.97 male(s)/female
65 years and over: 0.78 male(s)/female
total population: 1.01 male(s)/female (2015 est.)

Mother's mean age at first birth: 19.7
note: median age at first birth among women 20–24 (2011/12 est.)

Maternal mortality rate: 442 deaths/100,000 live births (2015 est.)
country comparison to the world: 16

Infant mortality rate: *total:* 57.92 deaths/1,000 live births
male: 62.97 deaths/1,000 live births
female: 52.71 deaths/1,000 live births (2015 est.)
country comparison to the world: 24

Life expectancy at birth:
total population: 58.79 years
male: 57.64 years
female: 59.98 years (2015 est.)
country comparison to the world: 200

Total fertility rate: 4.68 children born/woman (2015 est.)
country comparison to the world: 22

Contraceptive prevalence rate: 44.7% (2011/12)

Health expenditures: 4.1% of GDP (2013)
country comparison to the world: 179

Physicians density: 0.1 physicians/1,000 population (2007)

Drinking water source:
improved:
urban: 95.8% of population
rural: 40% of population
total: 76.5% of population
unimproved:
urban: 4.2% of population
rural: 60% of population
total: 23.5% of population (2015 est.)

Sanitation facility access:
improved:
urban: 20% of population
rural: 5.6% of population
total: 15% of population
unimproved:
urban: 80% of population
rural: 94.4% of population
total: 85% of population (2015 est.)

HIV/AIDS—adult prevalence rate: 2.75% (2014 est.)
country comparison to the world: 22

HIV/AIDS—people living with HIV/AIDS: 80,700 (2014 est.)
country comparison to the world: 46

HIV/AIDS—deaths: 4,400 (2014 est.)
country comparison to the world: 34

Major infectious diseases: *degree of risk:* very high
food or waterborne diseases: bacterial and protozoal diarrhea, hepatitis A, and typhoid fever
vectorborne disease: malaria and dengue fever
animal contact disease: rabies
water contact disease: schistosomiasis (2013)

Obesity—adult prevalence rate: 9.7% (2014)
country comparison to the world: 163

Children under the age of 5 years underweight: 12.3% (2015)
country comparison to the world: 61

Education expenditures: 6.2% of GDP (2010)
country comparison to the world: 39

Literacy: *definition:* age 15 and over can read and write
total population: 79.3%
male: 86.4%
female: 72.9% (2015 est.)

School life expectancy (primary to tertiary education): *total:* 11 years
male: 11 years
female: 11 years (2012)

Child labor—children ages 5–14: *total number:* 252,171
percentage: 25% (2005 est.)

GOVERNMENT

Country name: *conventional long form:* Republic of the Congo
conventional short form: Congo (Brazzaville)
local long form: Republique du Congo
local short form: Congo
former: French Congo, Middle Congo, People's Republic of the Congo, Congo/Brazzaville
etymology: named for the Congo River, which makes up much of the country's eastern border; the river name derives from Kongo, a Bantu kingdom

that occupied its mouth at the time of Portuguese discovery in the late 15th century and whose name stems from its people the Bakongo, meaning "hunters"

Government type: presidential republic

Capital: *name:* Brazzaville

Geographic coordinates: 4 15 S, 15 17 E
time difference: UTC + 1 (6 hours ahead of Washington, DC, during Standard Time)

Administrative divisions: 12 departments (departments, singular—department); Bouenza, Brazzaville, Cuvette, Cuvette-Ouest, Kouilou, Lekoumou, Likouala, Niari, Plateaux, Pointe-Noire, Pool, Sangha

Independence: 15 August 1960 (from France)

National holiday: Independence Day, 15 August (1960)

Constitution: previous 1992; latest approved by referendum 20 January 2002; amended 2015; note—the constitutional referendum approved in October 2015 changed the head of government from the president to the prime minister, reduced the presidential term from 7 to 5 years and limited total presidential terms to 3

Legal system: mixed legal system of French civil law and customary law

International law organization participation: has not submitted an ICJ jurisdiction declaration; accepts ICCt jurisdiction

Citizenship: *citizenship by birth:* no
citizenship by descent only: at least one parent must be a citizen of the Republic of the Congo
dual citizenship recognized: no
residency requirement for naturalization: 10 years

Suffrage: 18 years of age; universal

Executive branch: *chief of state:* President Denis SASSOU-Nguesso (since 25 October 1997)

head of government: Prime Minister Clement MOUAMBA (since 23 April 2016); note—a constitutional referendum held in 2015 approved the change of the head of government from the president to the prime minister
cabinet: Council of Ministers appointed by the president
elections/appointments: president directly elected by absolute majority popular vote in 2 rounds if needed for a 5-year term (eligible for 2 additional terms); election last held on 20 March 2016 (next to be held in 2021)
election results: Denis SASSOU-Nguesso reelected president; percent of vote—Denis SASSOU-Nguesso (PCT) 60.4%, Guy Price Parfait KOLELAS (MCDDI) 15.1%, Jean-Marie MOKOKO (independent) 13.9%, Pascal Tsaty MABIALA (UPADS) 4.4%, other 6.2%

Legislative branch: *description:* bicameral Parliament or Parlement consists of the Senate (72 seats; members indirectly elected by regional councils by simple majority vote to serve 6-year terms with one-half of membership renewed every three years) and the National Assembly (139 seats; members directly elected in single-seat

constituencies by absolute majority popular vote in two rounds if needed; members serve 5-year terms)
elections: Senate—last held on 12 October 2014 for 36 of the expiry seats (next to be held in 2020); National Assembly—last held on 15 July and 5 August 2012 (next to be held in July 2017)
election results: Senate—percent of vote by party—NA; seats by party—RMP 33, FDU 23, UPADS 2, other 7, independent 7; National Assembly—percent of vote by party—NA; seats by party—PCT 89, MCDDI 7, UPADS 7, RDPS 5, MAR 4, RC 3, MUST 2, UPDP 2, CPR 1, PRL 1, PUR 1, UFD 1, UR 1, independent 12, vacant 3

Judicial branch: *highest court(s):* Supreme Court or Cour Supreme (consists of NA judges); note—the High Court of Justice, outside the judicial authority, tries cases involving treason by the president of the republic
judge selection and term of office: judges elected by parliament and serve until retirement age
subordinate courts: courts of appeal; regional and district courts; employment tribunals; juvenile courts

Political parties and leaders: Action Movement for Renewal or MAR [Roland BOUITI-VIAUDO]
Citizen's Rally or RC
Congolese Labour Party or PCT [Denis SASSOU-NGUESSO]
Congolese Movement for Democracy and Integral Development or MCDDI [Guy Price Parfait KOLELAS]
Movement for Unity, Solidarity, and Work or MUST [Claudine MUNARI]
Pan-African Union for Social Development or UPADS [Pascal Tsaty MABIALA]
Party for the Unity of the Republic or PUR Patriotic Union for Democracy and Progress or UPDP [Auguste-Celestin GONGARD NKOUA Prospects and Realities Club or CPR
Rally for Democracy and Social Progress or RDPS [Bernard BATCHI]
Rally of the Presidential Majority or RMP
Republican and Liberal Party or PRL
Union for the Republic or UR
Union of Democratic Forces
Union for Democracy and Republicor UDR
United Democratic Forces or FDU [Sebastian EBAO]; many smaller parties

Political pressure groups and leaders: Congolese Trade Union Congress or CSC General Union of Congolese Pupils and Students or UGEEC Revolutionary Union of Congolese Women or URFC Union of Congolese Socialist Youth or UJSC

International organization participation: ACP, AfDB, AU, BDEAC, CEMAC, EITI (compliant country), FAO, FZ, G-77, IAEA, IBRD, ICAO, ICCt, ICRM, IDA, IFAD, IFC, IFRCS, ILO, IMF, IMO, Interpol, IOC, IOM, IPU, ISO (correspondent), ITSO, ITU, ITUC (NGOs), MIGA, NAM, OIF, OPCW, UN, UNCTAD, UNESCO, UNHCR, UNIDO, UNITAR, UNWTO, UPU, WCO, WFTU (NGOs), WHO, WIPO, WMO, WTO

Diplomatic representation in the US: *chief of mission:* Ambassador Serge MOMBOULI (since 31 July 2001)

chancery: 172016th Street NW, Washington, DC 20009
telephone: [1] (202) 726-5500
FAX: [1] (202) 726-1860
Diplomatic representation from the US: *chief of mission:* Ambassador Stephanie S. SULLIVAN (since 12 August 2013)
embassy: 70–83 Section D, Maya-Maya Boulevard, Brazzaville
mailing address: B.P. 1015, Brazzaville
telephone: [242] 06612-2000
Flag description: divided diagonally from the lower hoist side by a yellow band; the upper triangle (hoist side) is green and the lower triangle is red; green symbolizes agriculture and forests, yellow the friendship and nobility of the people, red is unexplained but has been associated with the struggle for independence
note: uses the popular Pan-African colors of Ethiopia
National symbol(s): lion, elephant; national colors: green, yellow, red
National anthem: *name:* "La Congolaise" (The Congolese)
lyrics/music: Jacques TONDRA and Georges KIBANGHI/Jean ROYER and Joseph SPADILIERE
note: origin ally adopted 1959, restored 1991

ECONOMY

Economy—overview: The economy is a mixture of subsistence farming and hunting, an industrial sector based largely on oil and support services, and government spending. Oil has supplanted forestry as the mainstay of the economy, providing a major share of government revenues and exports. Natural gas is increasingly being converted to electricity rather than being flared, greatly improving energy prospects. New mining projects, particularly iron ore, which entered production in late 2013, may add as much as $1 billion to annual government revenue.

Economic reform efforts have been undertaken with the support of international organizations, notably the World Bank and the IMF, including the recently concluded Article IV consultations. The current administration faces difficult economic challenges of stimulating recovery and reducing poverty. The recent drop in oil prices has constrained government spending; lower oil prices forced the government to cut more than $1 billion in planned spending. However, the government increased infrastructure spending for the September 2015 All-Africa Games and also ahead of the March 2016 presidential election, putting further pressure on the budget.

Officially the country became a net external creditor as of 2011, with external debt representing only about 16% of GDP and debt servicing less than 3% of government revenue.
GDP (purchasing power parity): $29.36 billion (2015 est.)
$28.64 billion (2014 est.)
$26.81 billion (2013 est.)
note: data are in 2015 US dollars

country comparison to the world: 130
GDP (official exchange rate): $8.878 billion (2015 est.)
GDP—real growth rate: 2.5% (2015 est.)
6.8% (2014 est.)
3.3% (2013 est.)
country comparison to the world: 122
GDP—per capita (PPP): $6,700 (2015 est.)
$6,700 (2014 est.)
$6,400 (2013 est.)
note: data are in 2015 US dollars
country comparison to the world: 155
Gross national saving: 19.1% of GDP (2015 est.)
32.7% of GDP (2014 est.)
26.5% of GDP (2013 est.)
country comparison to the world: 87
GDP—composition, by end use:
household consumption: 48.2%
government consumption: 14%
investment in fixed capital: 43.8%
investment in inventories: 0.1%
exports of goods and services: 61.6%
imports of goods and services: -67.7% (2015 est.)
GDP—composition, by sector of origin: *agriculture:* 4.9%
industry: 68.8%
services: 26.3% (2015 est.)

Agriculture—products: cassava (manioc, tapioca), sugar, rice, corn, peanuts, vegetables, coffee, cocoa; forest products
Industries: petroleum extraction, cement, lumber, brewing, sugar, palm oil, soap, flour, cigarettes
Industrial production growth rate: 1.3% (2015 est.)
country comparison to the world: 136
Labor force: 1.807 million (2013 est.)
country comparison to the world: 124
Unemployment rate: 53% (2012 est.)
country comparison to the world: 201

Population below poverty line: 46.5% (2011 est.)
Household income or consumption by percentage share: *lowest:* 10%: 2.1%
highest: 10%: 37.1% (2005)
Budget: *revenues:* $3.896 billion
expenditures: $4.747 billion (2015 est.)
Taxes and other revenues: 43.9% of GDP (2015 est.)
country comparison to the world: 28
Budget surplus (+) or deficit (-): -9.6% of GDP (2015 est.)
country comparison to the world: 203
Public debt: 47.3% of GDP (2015 est.)
36.5% of GDP (2014 est.)
country comparison to the world: 90
Fiscal year: calendar year
Inflation rate (consumer prices): 2% (2015 est.)
0.9% (2014 est.)
country comparison to the world: 114
Central bank discount rate: 4.25% (31 December 2009)
4.75% (31 December 2008)
country comparison to the world: 89
Commercial bank prime lending rate: 14.8% (31 December 2015 est.)
14.8% (31 December 2014 est.)
country comparison to the world: 43

Stock of narrow money: $4.08 billion (31 December 2015 est.)
$4.223 billion (31 December 2014 est.)
country comparison to the world: 104
Stock of broad money: $4.875 billion (31 December 2015 est.)
$4.858 billion (31 December 2014 est.)
country comparison to the world: 132
Stock of domestic credit: $362.9 million (31 December 2015 est.)
$44.13 million (31 December 2014 est.)
country comparison to the world: 177
Market value of publicly traded shares: $NA
Current account balance: -$1.264 billion (2015 est.)
-$1.281 billion (2014 est.)
country comparison to the world: 130
Exports: $5.855 billion (2015 est.)
$9.12 billion (2014 est.)
country comparison to the world: 104

Exports—commodities: petroleum, lumber, plywood, sugar, cocoa, coffee, diamonds
Exports—partners: China 42.1%, Italy 16.9%, US 4.9%, India 4.7%, Portugal 4.2% (2015)
Imports: $3.779 billion (2015 est.)
$4.939 billion (2014 est.)
country comparison to the world: 136

Imports—commodities: capital equipment, construction materials, foodstuffs
Imports—partners: China 20.3%, France 14.2%, South Korea 9.8%, US 4.9%, UK 4.4%, Italy 4.1%, India 4.1% (2015)
Reserves of foreign exchange and gold: $4.407 billion (31 December 2015 est.)
$4.939 billion (31 December 2014 est.)
country comparison to the world: 98
Debt—external: $3.763 billion (31 December 2014 est.)
$3.452 billion (31 December 2013 est.)
country comparison to the world: 136

Exchange rates: Cooperation Financiere en Afrique Centrale francs (XAF) per US dollar—
580.5 (2015 est.)
494.42 (2014 est.)
494.42 (2013 est.)
510.53 (2012 est.)
471.87 (2011 est.)

ENERGY

Electricity—production: 1.303 billion kWh (2012 est.)
country comparison to the world: 146
Electricity—consumption: 740 million kWh (2012 est.)
country comparison to the world: 161
Electricity—exports: 0 kWh (2013 est.)
country comparison to the world: 119
Electricity—imports: 55 million kWh (2012 est.)
country comparison to the world: 102
Electricity—installed generating capacity: 238,000 kW (2012 est.)
country comparison to the world: 158
Electricity—from fossil fuels: 12.2% of total installed capacity (2012 est.)

201

country comparison to the world: 197
Electricity—from nuclear fuels: 0% of total installed capacity (2012 est.)
country comparison to the world: 65
Electricity—from hydroelectric plants: 87.8% of total installed capacity (2012 est.)
country comparison to the world: 15
Electricity—from other renewable sources: 0% of total installed capacity (2012 est.)
country comparison to the world: 166
Crude oil—production: 250,000 bbl/day (2014 est.)
country comparison to the world: 33
Crude oil—exports: 278,400 bbl/day (2012 est.)
country comparison to the world: 27
Crude oil—imports: 0 bbl/day (2012 est.)
country comparison to the world: 171
Crude oil—proved reserves: 1.6 billion bbl (1 January 2015 est.)
country comparison to the world: 37
Refined petroleum products—production: 17,740 bbl/day (2012 est.)
country comparison to the world: 95
Refined petroleum products—consumption: 15,000 bbl/day (2013 est.)
country comparison to the world: 142
Refined petroleum products—exports: 5,160 bbl/day (2012 est.)
country comparison to the world: 95
Refined petroleum products—imports: 2,571 bbl/day (2012 est.)
country comparison to the world: 178
Natural gas—production: 1.65 billion cu m (2013 est.)
country comparison to the world: 59
Natural gas—consumption: 1.65 billion cu m (2013 est.)
country comparison to the world: 83
Natural gas—exports: 39 million cu m (2012 est.)
country comparison to the world: 47
Natural gas—imports: 0 cu m (2013 est.)
country comparison to the world: 176
Natural gas—proved reserves: 90.61 billion cu m (1 January 2014 est.)
country comparison to the world: 57
Carbon dioxide emissions from consumption of energy: 6.691 million Mt (2012 est.)
country comparison to the world: 116

COMMUNICATIONS

Telephones—fixed lines: *total subscriptions:* 16,300
subscriptions per 100 inhabitants: less than 1 (2014 est.)
country comparison to the world: 193
Telephones—mobile cellular: *total:* 4.9 million
subscriptions per 100 inhabitants: less than 106 (2014 est.)
country comparison to the world: 118

Telephone system: *general assessment:* primary network consists of microwave radio relay and coaxial cable with services barely adequate for government use; key exchanges are in Brazzaville, Pointe-Noire, and Loubomo; intercity lines frequently out of order
domestic: fixed-line infrastructure inadequate, providing less than 1 connection per 100 persons; in the absence of an adequate fixed-line infrastructure, mobile-cellular subscribership has surged to 90 per 100 persons
international: country code—242; satellite earth station—1 Intelsat (Atlantic Ocean) (2011)

Broadcast media: 1 state-owned TV and 3 state-owned radio stations; several privately owned TV and radio stations; satellite TV service is available; rebroadcasts of several international broadcasters are available (2007)
Radio broadcast stations: AM 1, FM 5, short-wave 3 (2001)
Television broadcast stations: 1 (2001)

Internet country code: .cg
Internet hosts: 10 (2012)
country comparison to the world: 215
Internet users: *total:* 89,500
percent of population: 1.9% (2014 est.)
country comparison to the world: 171

TRANSPORTATION

Airports: 27 (2013)
country comparison to the world: 125
Airports—with paved runways: *total:* 8
over 3,047 m: 2
2,438 to 3,047 m: 1
1,524 to 2,437 m: 5 (2013)
Airports—with unpaved runways: *total:* 19
1,524 to 2,437 m: 8
914 to 1,523 m: 9
under 914 m: 2 (2013)
Pipelines: gas 232 km; liquid petroleum gas 4 km; oil 982 km (2013)
Railways: *total:* 510 km
narrow gauge: 510 km 1.067-m gauge (2014)
country comparison to the world: 113
Roadways: *total:* 17,000 km
paved: 1,212 km
unpaved: 15,788 km (2006)
country comparison to the world: 118
Waterways: 1,120 km (commercially navigable on Congo and Oubanqui Rivers above Brazzaville; there are many ferries across the river to Kinshasa; the Congo south of Brazzaville-Kinshasa to the coast is not navigable because of rapids, necessitating a rail connection to Pointe Noire; other rivers are used for local traffic only) (2011)
country comparison to the world: 61

Merchant marine: *registered in other countries:* 1 (Democratic Republic of the Congo 1) (2010)
country comparison to the world: 148

Ports and terminals: *major seaport(s):* Pointe-Noire
river port(s): Brazzaville (Congo); Impfondo (Oubangi); Ouesso (Sangha); Oyo (Alima)
oil terminal(s): Djeno

MILITARY AND SECURITY

Military branches: Congolese Armed Forces (Forces Armees Congolaises, FAC): Army (Armee de Terre), Navy, Congolese Air Force (Armee de l'Air Congolaise); Gendarmerie; Special Presidential Security Guard (GSSP) (2013)

Military service age and obligation: 18 years of age for voluntary military service; women may serve in the Armed Forces (2012)

TRANSNATIONAL ISSUES

Disputes—international: the location of the boundary in the broad Congo River with the Democratic Republic of the Congo is undefined except in the Pool Malebo/Stanley Pool area

Refugees and internally displaced persons: *refugees (country of origin):* 9,104 (Rwanda) (2014); 28,601 (Central African Republic); 12,269 (Democratic Republic of the Congo) (2016)
IDPs: 7,800 (multiple civil wars since 1992) (2015)

Trafficking in persons: *current situation:* the Republic of the Congo is a source and destination country for children, men, and women, subjected to forced labor and sex trafficking; most trafficking victims are from Benin, the Democratic Republic of the Congo (DRC) and, to a lesser extent, other neighboring countries and are subjected to domestic servitude and market vending by West African and Congolese nationals; adults and children, the majority from the DRC, are also sex trafficked in Congo, mainly Brazzaville; internal trafficking victims, often from rural areas, are exploited as domestic servants or forced to work in quarries, bakeries, fishin g, and agriculture

tier rating: Tier 2 Watch List—the Republic of the Congo does not fully comply with the minimum standards for the elimination of trafficking; however, it is making significant efforts to do so; the country drafted an action plan based on anti-trafficking legislation, which remains pending in the Supreme Court; the government made minimal anti-trafficking law enforcement efforts in 2014, failing to prosecute or convict suspected traffickers from cases dating back to 2010; serious allegations of official complicity continue to be reported; the government lacks a systematic means of identifying victims and relies on NGOs and international organizations to identify victims and NGOs and foster families to provide care to victims; the quality of care varied widely because the foster care system was allegedly undermined by inadequate security and official complicity (2015)

COOK ISLANDS

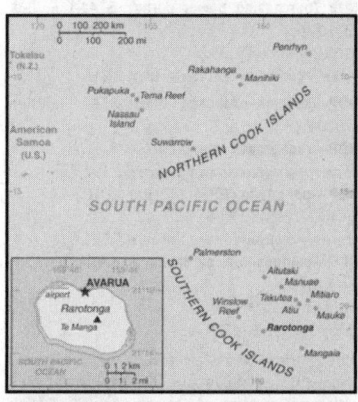

INTRODUCTION

Backg round: Named after Captain COOK, who sighted them in 1770, the islands became a British protectorate in 1888. By 1900, administrative control was transferred to New Zealand; in 1965, residents chose self-government in free association with New Zealand. The emigration of skilled workers to New Zealand, government deficits, and limited natural resources are of continuing concern.

GEOGRAPHY

Location: Oceania, group of islands in the South Pacific Ocean, about halfway between Hawaii and New Zealand

Geographic coordinates: 21 14 S, 159 46 W

Map references: Oceania

Area: *total:* 236 sq km
land: 236 sq km
water: 0 sq km
country comparison to the world: 215

Area—comparative: 1.3 times the size of Washington, DC

Land boundaries: 0 km

Coastline: 120 km

Maritime claims: territorial sea: 12 nm
exclusive economic zone: 200 nm
continental shelf: 200 nm or to the edge of the continental margin

Climate: tropical oceanic; moderated by trade winds; a dry season from April to November and a more humid season from December to March

Terrain: low coral atolls in North; volcanic, hilly islands in south

Elevation: *mean elevation:* NA

elevation extremes: *lowest point:* Pacific Ocean 0 m
highest point: Te Manga 652 m

Natural resources: coconuts (copra)
Land use: *agricultural land:* 8.4%
arable land: 4.2%

permanent crops: 4.2%
permanent pasture: 0%
forest: 64.6%
other: 27% (2011 est.)
Irrigated land: NA

Natural hazards: typhoons (November to March)

Environment—current issues: NA

Environment—international agreements: *party to:* Biodiversity, Climate Change, Climate Change-Kyoto Protocol, Desertification, Hazardous Wastes, Law of the Sea, Ozone Layer Protection

Geography—note: the northern Cook Islands are seven low-lying, sparsely populated, coral atolls; the southern Cook Islands, where most of the population lives, consist of eight elevated, fertile, volcanic isles, including the largest, Rarotonga, at 67 sq km

PEOPLE AND SOCIETY

Nationality: *noun:* Cook Islander(s)
adjective: Cook Islander

Ethnic groups: Cook Island Maori (Polynesian) 81.3%, part Cook Island Maori 6.7%, other 11.9% (2011 est.)

Languages: English (official) 86.4%, Cook Islands Maori (Rarotongan) (official) 76.2%, other 8.3%
note: shares sum to more than 100% because some respondents gave more than one answer on the census (2011 est.)

Religions: Protestant 62.8% (Cook Islands Christian Church 49.1%, Seventh Day Adventist 7.9%, Assemblies of God 3.7%, Apostolic Church 2.1%), Roman Catholic 17%, Mormon 4.4%, other 8%, none 5.6%, no response 2.2% (2011 est.)

Population: 9,838 (July 2015 est.)
note: the Cook Islands' Ministry of Finance & Economic Management estimated the resident population to have been 12,000 in December 2015
country comparison to the world: 224

Age structure: *0–14 years:* 22.15% (male 1,154/ female 1,025)
15–24 years: 17.64% (male 929/female 806)
25–54 years: 38.05% (male 1,876/female 1,867)
55–64 years: 10.81% (male 569/female 494)
65 years and over: 11.36% (male 551/female 567) (2015 est.)

Median age: *total:* 35.25 years
male: 34.6 years
female: 35.7 years (2015 est.)
country comparison to the world: 74

Population growth rate: -2.95% (2015 est.)
country comparison to the world: 233

Birth rate: 14.33 births/1,000 population (2015 est.)
country comparison to the world: 137

Death rate: 8.03 deaths/1,000 population (2015 est.)
country comparison to the world: 97

Urbanization: *urban population:* 74.5% of total population (2015)

rate of urbanization: 0.88% annual rate of change (2010–15 est.)

Sex ratio: *at birth:* 1.04 male(s)/female
0–14 years: 1.13 male(s)/female
15–24 years: 1.15 male(s)/female
25–54 years: 1.01 male(s)/female
55–64 years: 1.15 male(s)/female
65 years and over: 0.97 male(s)/female
total population: 1.07 male(s)/female (2015 est.)

Infant mortality rate: *total:* 13.87 deaths/1,000 live births
male: 16.86 deaths/1,000 live births
female: 10.73 deaths/1,000 live births (2015 est.)
country comparison to the world: 109

Life expectancy at birth:
total population: 75.6 years
male: 72.78 years
female: 78.56 years (2015 est.)
country comparison to the world: 96

Total fertility rate: 2.23 children born/woman (2015 est.)
country comparison to the world: 98

Health expenditures: 3.1% of GDP (2013)
country comparison to the world: 175

Physicians density: 1.33 physicians/1,000 population (2009)

Drinking water source:
improved:
urban: 99.9% of population
rural: 99.9% of population
total: 99.9% of population
unimproved:
urban: 0.1% of population
rural: 0.1% of population
total: 0.1% of population (2015 est.)

Sanitation facility access:
improved:
urban: 97.6% of population
rural: 97.6% of population
total: 97.6% of population
unimproved:
urban: 2.4% of population
rural: 2.4% of population
total: 2.4% of population (2015 est.)

HIV/AIDS—adult prevalence rate: NA

HIV/AIDS—people living with HIV/AIDS: NA

HIV/AIDS—deaths: NA

Obesity—adult prevalence rate: 50% (2014)
country comparison to the world: 3

Education expenditures: 3.9% of GDP (2014)
country comparison to the world: 137

School life expectancy (primary to tertiary education): *total:* 15 years
male: 14 years
female: 17 years (2014)

GOVERNMENT

Country name: *conventional long form:* none
conventional short form: Cook Islands

etymology: named after Captain James COOK, the British explorer who visited the islands in 1773 and 1777

Dependency status: self-governing in free association with New Zealand; Cook Islands is fully responsible for internal affairs; New Zealand retains responsibility for external affairs and defense in consultation with the Cook Islands

Government type: self-governing parliamentary democracy (Parliament of the Cook Islands) in free association with New Zealand

Capital: *name:* Avarua

Geographic coordinates: 21 12 S, 159 46 W

time difference: UTC-10 (5 hours behind Washington, DC, during Standard Time)

Administrative divisions: none

Independence: none (became self-governing in free association with New Zealand on 4 August 1965 and has the right at any time to move to full independence by unilateral action)

National holiday: Constitution Day, first Monday in August (1965)

Constitution: 4 August 1965 (Cook Islands Constitution Act 1964); amended many times, last in 2004 (2016)

Legal system: common law similar to New Zealand common law

International law organization participation: has not submitted an ICJ jurisdiction declaration (New Zealand normally retains responsibility for external affairs); accepts ICCt jurisdiction

Suffrage: 18 years of age; universal

Executive branch: *chief of state:* Queen ELIZABETH II (since 6 February 1952); represented by Tom J. MARSTERS (since 9 August 2013); New Zealand High Commissioner Joanna KEMPKERS (since 19 July 2013)

head of government: Prime Minister Henry PUNA (since 30 November 2010)

cabinet: Cabinet chosen by the prime minister

elections/appointments: the monarchy is hereditary; UK representative appointed by the monarch; New Zealand high commissioner appointed by the New Zealand Government; following legislative elections, the leader of the majority party or majority coalition usually becomes prime minister

Legislative branch: *description:* unicameral Parliament, formerly the Legislative Assembly (24 seats; members directly elected in single-seat constituencies by simple majority vote to serve 4-year terms); note—the House of Ariki, a 24-member parliamentary body of traditional leaders appointed by the Queen's representative serves as a consultative body to the Parliament

elections: last held on 9 July 2014 (next to be held by 2018)

election results: percent of vote by party—NA; seats by party—CIP 13, Demo 8, One Cook Islands Movement 2,1 undecided

Judicial branch: *highest resident court(s):* Court of Appeal (consists of the chief justice and 3 judges of the High Court); High Court (consists of the chief justice and at least 4 judges and organized into civil, criminal, and land divisions); note—appeals beyond the Cook Islands Court of Appeal are brought before the Judicial Committee of the Privy Council (in London)

judge selection and term of office: High Court chief justice appointed by the Queen's Representative on the advice of the Executive Council tendered by the prime minister; other judges appointed by the Queen's Representative, on the advice of the Executive Council tendered by the chief justice, High Court chief justice, and the minister of justice; chief justice and judges appointed for 3-year renewable terms

subordinate courts: justices of the peace

Political parties and leaders: Cook Islands Party or CIP [Henry PUNA]
Democratic Party or Demo [William HEATHER]
One Cook Islands Movement [Teina BISHOP]

Political pressure groups and leaders: Reform Conference (lobby for political system changes)
other: various groups lobbying for political change

International organization participation: ACP, ADB, AOSIS, FAO, ICAO, ICCt, ICRM, IFAD, IFRCS, IMO, IMSO, IOC, ITUC (NGOs), OPCW, PIF, Sparteca, SPC, UNESCO, UPU, WHO, WMO

Diplomatic representation in the US: none (self-governing in free association with New Zealand)

Diplomatic representation from the US: none (self-governing in free association with New Zealand)

Flag description: blue with the flag of the UK in the upper hoist-side quadrant and a large circle of 15 white five-pointed stars (one for every island) centered in the outer half of the flag

National symbol(s): a circle of 15, five-pointed, white stars on a blue field; national colors: blue, white

National anthem: *name:* "Te Atua Mou E" (To God Almighty)

lyrics/music: Tepaeru Te RITO/Thomas DAVIS

note: adopted 1982; as prime minister, Sir Thomas DAVIS composed the anthem; his wife, a tribal chief, wrote the lyrics

ECONOMY

Economy—overview: Like many other South Pacific island nations, the Cook Islands' economic development is hindered by the isolation of the country from foreign markets, the limited size of domestic markets, lack of natural resources, periodic devastation from natural disasters, and inadequate infrastructure. Agriculture, employing more than one-quarter of the working population, provides the economic base with major exports of copra and citrus fruit. Black pearls are the Cook Islands' leading export. Manufacturing activities are limited to fruit processing, clothing, and handicrafts. Trade deficits are offset by remittances from emigrants and by foreign aid overwhelmingly from New Zealand. In the 1980s and 1990s, the country lived beyond its means, maintaining a bloated public service and accumulating a large foreign debt. Subsequent reforms, including the sale of state assets, the strengthening of economic management, the encouragement of tourism, and a debt restructuring agreement, have rekindled investment and growth.

GDP (purchasing power parity): $244.1 million (2010 est.)
$183.2 million (2005 est.)
country comparison to the world: 218

GDP (official exchange rate): $244.1 million (2010 est.)

GDP—real growth rate: 0.1% (2005 est.)
country comparison to the world: 192

GDP—per capita (PPP): $12,300 (2010 est.)
$9,100 (2005 est.)
country comparison to the world: 121

GDP—composition, by sector of origin: *agriculture:* 5.1%
industry: 12.7%
services: 82.1% (2010 est.)

Agriculture—products: copra, citrus, pineapples, tomatoes, beans, pawpaws, bananas, yams, taro, coffee; pigs, poultry

Industries: fruit processing, tourism, fishing, clothing, handicrafts

Industrial production growth rate: 1% (2002)
country comparison to the world: 144

Labor force: 6,820 (2001)
country comparison to the world: 219

Labor force—by occupation: *agriculture:* 29%
industry: 15%
services: 56% (1995)

Unemployment rate: 13.1% (2005)
country comparison to the world: 143

Population below poverty line: NA%

Household income or consumption by percentage share: *lowest:* 10%: NA%
highest: 10%: NA%

Budget: *revenues:* $86.9 million
expenditures: $77.9 million (2010)
Taxes and other revenues: 35.6% of GDP (2010 est.)
country comparison to the world: 54

Budget surplus (+) or deficit (-): 3.7% of GDP (2010 est.)
country comparison to the world: 12

Fiscal year: 1 April—31 March

Inflation rate (consumer prices): 2.2% (2011 est.)
country comparison to the world: 123

Stock of narrow money: $38.99 million (31 December 2011 est.)
$38.99 million (31 December 2011 est.)
country comparison to the world: 190

Stock of broad money: $148.2 million (31 December 2011 est.)
$170.9 million (31 December 2010 est.)
country comparison to the world: 191

Current account balance: $26.67 million (2005)
country comparison to the world: 50

Exports: $3.125 million (2011 est.)
$5.163 million (2010 est.)
country comparison to the world: 220

Exports—commodities: copra, papayas, fresh and canned citrus fruit, coffee; fish; pearls and pearl shells; clothing

Imports: $109.3 million (2011 est.)
$90.62 million (2010 est.)

country comparison to the world: 216

Imports—commodities: foodstuffs, textiles, fuels, timber, capital goods

Debt—external: $141 million (1996 est.)
country comparison to the world: 192

Exchange rates: NZ dollars (NZD) per US dollar—
1.452 (2014 est.)
1.2187 (2013 est.)
1.2187 (2013 est.)
1.23 (2012 est.)
1.263 (2011 est.)

ENERGY

Electricity—production: 31.13 million kWh (2012 est.)
country comparison to the world: 211
Electricity—consumption: 28.95 million kWh (2012 est.)
country comparison to the world: 210
Electricity—exports: 0 kWh (2013 est.)
country comparison to the world: 129
Electricity—imports: 0 kWh (2013 est.)
country comparison to the world: 139
Electricity—installed generating capacity: 8,040 kW (2012 est.)
country comparison to the world: 209
Electricity—from fossil fuels: 99.5% of total installed capacity (2012 est.)
country comparison to the world: 46
Electricity—from nuclear fuels: 0% of total installed capacity (2012 est.)
country comparison to the world: 76
Electricity—from hydroelectric plants: 0% of total installed capacity (2012 est.)
country comparison to the world: 168
Electricity—from other renewable sources: 0.5% of total installed capacity (2012 est.)
country comparison to the world: 101
Crude oil—production: 0 bbl/day (2014 est.)
country comparison to the world: 123
Crude oil—exports: 0 bbl/day (2012 est.)
country comparison to the world: 114
Crude oil—imports: 0 bbl/day (2012 est.)
country comparison to the world: 179
Crude oil—proved reserves: 0 bbl (1 January 2015 est.)
country comparison to the world: 122
Refined petroleum products—production: 0 bbl/day (2012 est.)

country comparison to the world: 172

Refined petroleum products—consumption: 500 bbl/day (2013 est.)
country comparison to the world: 208
Refined petroleum products—exports: 0 bbl/day (2012 est.)
country comparison to the world: 173
Refined petroleum products—imports: 484.7 bbl/day (2012 est.)
country comparison to the world: 205
Natural gas—production: 0 cu m (2013 est.)
country comparison to the world: 176
Natural gas—consumption: 0 cu m (2013 est.)
country comparison to the world: 135
Natural gas—exports: 0 cu m (2013 est.)
country comparison to the world: 86
Natural gas—imports: 0 cu m (2013 est.)
country comparison to the world: 186
Natural gas—proved reserves: 0 cu m (1 January 2014 est.)
country comparison to the world: 129
Carbon dioxide emissions from consumption of energy: 150,300 Mt (2012 est.)
country comparison to the world: 204

COMMUNICATIONS

Telephones—fixed lines: total: 7,200
subscriptions per 100 inhabitants: 61 (2009)
country comparison to the world: 202
Telephones—mobile cellular: total: 7,800
subscriptions per 100 inhabitants: 66 (2009)
country comparison to the world: 213
Telephone system: *general assessment:* Telecom Cook Islands offers international direct dialing, Internet, email, fax, and Telex
domestic: individual islands are connected by a combination of satellite earth stations, microwave systems, and VHF and HF radiotelephone; within the islands, service is provided by small exchanges connected to subscribers by open-wire, cable, and fiber-optic cable
international: country code—682; satellite earth station—1 Intelsat (Pacific Ocean)
Broadcast media: 1 privately owned TV station broadcasts from Rarotonga providing a mix of local news and overseas-sourced programs; a satellite program package is available; 6 radio stations broadcast with 1 reportedly reaching all of the islands (2009)

Radio broadcast stations: AM 1, FM 1, shortwave 0 (2004)
Television broadcast stations: 1 (outer islands receive satellite broadcasts) (2004)

Internet country code: .ck
Internet hosts: 3,562 (2012)
country comparison to the world: 150
Internet users: *total:* 674
percent of population: 6.7% (2014 est.)
country comparison to the world: 216

TRANSPORTATION

Airports: 11 (2013)
country comparison to the world: 153
Airports—with paved runways: *total:* 1
1,524 to 2,437 m: 1 (2013)
Airports—with unpaved runways: *total:* 10
1,524 to 2,437 m: 2
914 to 1,523 m: 7
under 914 m: 1 (2013)
Roadways: *total:* 320 km
paved: 33 km
unpaved: 287 km (2003)
country comparison to the world: 205
Merchant marine: *total:* 35
by type: bulk carrier 2, cargo 25, passenger 1, refrigerated cargo 6, roll on/roll off 1
foreign-owned: 23 (Estonia 1, Germany 1, Lithuania 1, Norway 8, NZ 2, Russia 1, Sweden 3, Turkey 4, UK 2) (2010)
country comparison to the world: 81
Ports and terminals: *major seaport(s):* Avatiu

MILITARY AND SECURITY

Military branches: no regular military forces; National Police Department
Military—note: defense is the responsibility of New Zealand in consultation with the Cook Islands and at its request

TRANSNATIONAL ISSUES

Disputes—international: none

CORAL SEA ISLANDS

INTRODUCTION

Backg round: Scattered over more than three-quarters of a million square kilometers of ocean, the Coral Sea Islands were declared a territory of Australia in 1969. They are uninhabited except for a small meteorological staff on the Willis Islets. Automated weather stations, beacons, and a lighthouse occupy many other islands and reefs. The Coral Sea Islands Act 1969 was amended in 1997

to extend the boundaries of the Coral Sea Islands Territory around Elizabeth and Middleton Reefs.

GEOGRAPHY

Location: Oceania, islands in the Coral Sea, northeast of Australia
Geographic coordinates: 18 00 S, 152 00 E
Map references: Oceania
Area: *total:* less than 3 sq km
land: less than 3 sq km

water: 0 sq km
note: includes numerous small islands and reefs scattered over a sea area of about 780,000 sq km (300,000 sq mi) with the Willis Islets the most important
country comparison to the world: 252
Area—comparative: about four times the size of the National Mall in Washington, DC
Land boundaries: 0 km
Coastline: 3,095 km

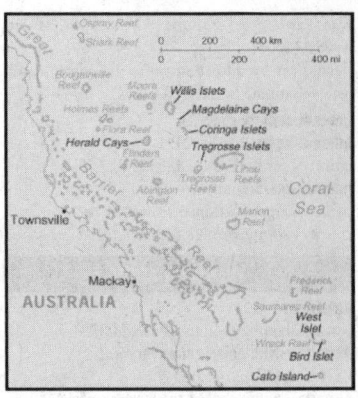

Maritime claims: *territorial sea:* 3 nm
exclusive fishing zone: 200 nm

Climate: tropical

Terrain: sand and coral reefs and islands (cays)
Elevation: *mean elevation:* NA

elevation extremes: *lowest point:* Pacific Ocean
0 m
highest point: unnamed location on Cato Island
6 m

Natural resources: NEGL
Land use: *agricultural land:* 0%
arable land: 0%

permanent crops: 0%
permanent crops: 0%
forest: 0%
other: 100% (mostly grass or scrub cover) (2011 est.)

Natural hazards: occasional tropical cyclones

Environment—current issues: no permanent freshwater resources

Geography—note: important nesting area for birds and turtles

PEOPLE AND SOCIETY

Population: no indigenous inhabitants
note: there is a staff of three to four at the meteorological station on Willis Island (July 2007 est.)

GOVERNMENT

Country name: *conventional long form:* Coral Sea Islands Territory
conventional short form: Coral Sea Islands
etymology: self-descriptive name to reflect the islands' position in the Coral Sea off the northeastern coast of Australia

Dependency status: territory of Australia; administered from Canberra by the Department of Regional Australia, Local Government, Arts and Sport

Legal system: the common law legal system of Australia, where applicable, applies

Citizenship: see Australia

Diplomatic representation in the US: none (territory of Australia)

Diplomatic representation from the US: none (territory of Australia)

Flag description: the flag of Australia is used

ECONOMY

Economy—overview: no economic activity

COMMUNICATIONS

Communications—note: automatic weather stations on many of the isles and reefs relay data to the mainland

TRANSPORTATION

Ports and terminals: none; offshore anchorage only

MILITARY AND SECURITY

Military—note: defense is the responsibility of Australia

TRANSNATIONAL ISSUES

Disputes—international: none

COSTA RICA

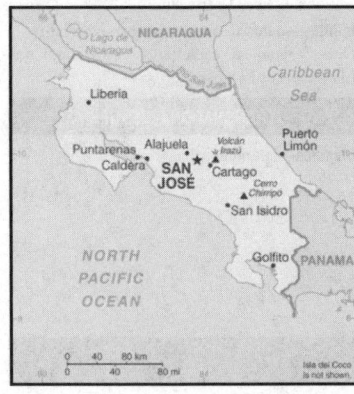

INTRODUCTION

Background: Although explored by the Spanish early in the 16th century, initial attempts at colonizing Costa Rica proved unsuccessful due to a combination of factors, including disease from mosquito-infested swamps, brutal heat, resistance by natives, and pirate raids. It was not until 1563 that a permanent settlement of Cartago was established in the cooler, fertile central highlands.

The area remained a colony for some two and a half centuries. In 1821, Costa Rica became one of several Central American provinces that jointly declared their independence from Spain. Two years later it joined the United Provinces of Central America, but this federation disintegrated in 1838, at which time Costa Rica proclaimed its sovereignty and independence. Since the late 19th century, only two brief periods of violence have marred the country's democratic development. In 1949, Costa Rica dissolved its armed forces. Although it still maintains a large agricultural sector, Costa Rica has expanded its economy to include strong technology and tourism industries. The standard of living is relatively high. Land ownership is widespread.

GEOGRAPHY

Location: Central America, bordering both the Caribbean Sea and the North Pacific Ocean, between Nicaragua and Panama

Geographic coordinates: 10 00 N, 84 00 W

Map references: Central America and the Caribbean

Area: *total:* 51,100 sq km
land: 51,060 sq km
water: 40 sq km
note: includes Isla del Coco
country comparison to the world: 130

Area—comparative: slightly smaller than West Virginia

Land boundaries: *total:* 661 km
border countries (2): Nicaragua 313 km, Panama 348 km

Coastline: 1,290 km

Maritime claims: *territorial sea:* 12 nm
exclusive economic zone: 200 nm
continental shelf: 200 nm

Climate: tropical and subtropical; dry season (December to April); rainy season (May to November); cooler in highlands

Terrain: coastal plains separated by rugged mountains including over 100 volcanic cones, of which several are major active volcanoes

Elevation: *mean elevation:* 746 m

elevation extremes: *lowest point:* Pacific Ocean
0 m
highest point: Cerro Chirripo 3,810 m

Natural resources: hydropower
Land use: *agricultural land:* 37.1%
arable land: 4.9%
permanent crops: 6.7%
permanent pasture: 25.5%
forest: 51.5%
other: 11.4% (2011 est.)
Irrigated land: 1,015 sq km (2012)

Total renewable water resources: 112.4 cu km (2011)

Freshwater withdrawal (domestic/industrial/agricultural): *total:* 5.77 cu m/yr (15%/9%/77%)
per capita: 1,582 cu m/yr (2006)

Natural hazards: occasional earthquakes, hurricanes along Atlantic coast; frequent flooding of lowlands at onset of rainy season and landslides; active volcanoes
volcanism: Arenal (elev. 1,670 m), which erupted in 2010, is the most active volcano in Costa Rica; a 1968 eruption destroyed the town of Tabacon; Irazu (elev. 3,432 m), situated just east of San Jose, has the potential to spew ash over the capital city as it did between 1963 and 1965; other historically active volcanoes include Miravalles, Poas, Rincon de la Vieja, and Turrialba

Environment—current issues: deforestation and land use change, largely a result of the clearing of land for cattle ranching and agriculture; soil erosion; coastal marine pollution; fisheries protection; solid waste management; air pollution

Environment—international agreements: *party to:* Biodiversity, Climate Change, Climate Change-Kyoto Protocol, Desertification, Endangered Species, Environmental Modification, Hazardous Wastes, Law of the Sea, Marine Dumping, Ozone Layer Protection, Wetlands, Whaling
signed, but not ratified: Marine Life Conservation

Geography—note: four volcanoes, two of them active, rise near the capital of San Jose in the center of the country; one of the volcanoes, Irazu, erupted destructively in 1963–65

PEOPLE AND SOCIETY

Nationality: *noun:* Costa Rican(s)
adjective: Costa Rican

Ethnic groups: white or mestizo 83.6%, mulato 6.7%, indigenous 2.4%, black of African descent 1.1%, other 1.1%, none 2.9%, unspecified 2.2% (2011 est.)

Languages: Spanish (official), English

Religions: Roman Catholic 76.3%, Evangelical 13.7%, Jehovah's Witnesses 1.3%, other Protestant 0.7%, other 4.8%, none 3.2%

Demographic profile: Costa Rica's political stability, high standard of living, and well-developed social benefits system set it apart from its Central American neighbors. Through the government's sustained social spending—almost 20% of GDP annually—Costa Rica has made tremendous progress toward achieving its goal of providing universal access to education, healthcare, clean water, sanitation, and electricity. Since the 1970s, expansion of these services has led to a rapid decline in infant mortality, an increase in life expectancy at birth, and a sharp decrease in the birth rate. The average number of children born per women has fallen from about 7 in the 1960s to 3.5 in the early 1980s to below replacement level today. Costa Rica's poverty rate is lower than in most Latin American countries, but it has stalled at around 20% for almost two decades.

Costa Rica is a popular regional immigration destination because of its job opportunities and social programs. Almost 9% of the population is foreign-born, with Nicaraguans comprising nearly three-quarters of the foreign population. Many Nicaraguans who perform unskilled seasonal labor enter Costa Rica illegally or overstay their visas, which continues to be a source of tension. Less than 3% of Costa Rica's population lives abroad. The overwhelming majority of expatriates have settled in the United States after completing a university degree or in order to work in a highly skilled field.

Population: 4,814,144 (July 2015 est.)
country comparison to the world: 124

Age structure: *0–14 years:* 23.12% (male 569,181/female 543,835)
15–24 years: 17.1% (male 419,712/female 403,668)
25–54 years: 43.9% (male 1,062,378/female 1,051,058)
55–64 years: 8.6% (male 202,401/female 211,709)
65 years and over: 7.27% (male 161,831/female 188,371) (2015 est.)

Dependency ratios: *total dependency ratio:* 45.4%
youth dependency ratio: 32.4%
elderly dependency ratio: 12.9%
potential support ratio: 7.7% (2015 est.)

Median age: *total:* 30.4 years
male: 30 years
female: 30.9 years (2015 est.)
country comparison to the world: 108

Population growth rate: 1.22% (2015 est.)
country comparison to the world: 97

Birth rate: 15.91 births/1,000 population (2015 est.)
country comparison to the world: 122

Death rate: 4.55 deaths/1,000 population (2015 est.)
country comparison to the world: 200

Net migration rate: 0.83 migrant(s)/1,000 population (2015 est.)
country comparison to the world: 67

Urbanization: *urban population:* 76.8% of total population (2015)
rate of urbanization: 2.74% annual rate of change (2010–15 est.)

Major urban areas—population: SAN JOSE (capital) 1.17 million (2015)

Sex ratio: *at birth:* 1.05 male(s)/female
0–14 years: 1.05 male(s)/female
15–24 years: 1.04 male(s)/female
25–54 years: 1.01 male(s)/female
55–64 years: 0.96 male(s)/female
65 years and over: 0.86 male(s)/female
total population: 1.01 male(s)/female (2015 est.)

Maternal mortality rate: 25 deaths/100,000 live births (2015 est.)
country comparison to the world: 115

Infant mortality rate: *total:* 8.46 deaths/1,000 live births
male: 9.25 deaths/1,000 live births
female: 7.64 deaths/1,000 live births (2015 est.)
country comparison to the world: 151

Life expectancy at birth:
total population: 78.4 years
male: 75.75 years
female: 81.19 years (2015 est.)
country comparison to the world: 58

Total fertility rate: 1.9 children born/woman (2015 est.)
country comparison to the world: 139

Contraceptive prevalence rate: 76.2% (2011)

Health expenditures: 9.9% of GDP (2013)
country comparison to the world: 23

Physicians density: 1.11 physicians/1,000 population (2013)

Hospital bed density: 1.2 beds/1,000 population (2012)

Drinking water source:
improved:
urban: 99.6% of population
rural: 91.9% of population
total: 97.8% of population
unimproved:
urban: 0.4% of population
rural: 8.1% of population
total: 2.2% of population (2015 est.)

Sanitation facility access:
improved:
urban: 95.2% of population
rural: 92.3% of population
total: 94.5% of population
unimproved:
urban: 4.8% of population
rural: 7.7% of population
total: 5.5% of population (2015 est.)

HIV/AIDS—adult prevalence rate: 0.26% (2014 est.)
country comparison to the world: 89

HIV/AIDS—people living with HIV/AIDS: 8,800 (2014 est.)
country comparison to the world: 97

HIV/AIDS—deaths: 200 (2014 est.)
country comparison to the world: 103

Major infectious diseases: *degree of risk:* intermediate
food or waterborne diseases: bacterial diarrhea
vectorborne diseases: dengue fever (2013)

Obesity—adult prevalence rate: 24% (2014)
country comparison to the world: 73

Children under the age of 5 years underweight: 1.1% (2009)
country comparison to the world: 130

Education expenditures: 7% of GDP (2014)
country comparison to the world: 34

Literacy: *definition:* age 15 and over can read and write
total population: 97.8%
male: 97.7%
female: 97.8% (2015 est.)

School life expectancy (primary to tertiary education): *total:* 15 years
male: 15 years
female: 16 years (2014)

Child labor—children ages 5–14: *total number:* 39,082
percentage: 5% (2002 est.)

Unemployment, youth ages 15–24: *total:* 21.8%
male: 18.8%
female: 26.8% (2013 est.)

country comparison to the world: 62

GOVERNMENT

Country name: *conventional long form:* Republic of Costa Rica
conventional short form: Costa Rica
local long form: Republica de Costa Rica
local short form: Costa Rica
etymology: the name means "rich coast" in Spanish and was first applied in the early colonial period of the 16th century

Government type: presidential republic
Capital: *name:* San Jose

Geographic coordinates: 9 56 N, 84 05 W
time difference: UTC-6 (1 hour behind Washington, DC, during Standard Time)

Administrative divisions: 7 provinces (provincias, singular—provincia); Alajuela, Cartago, Guanacaste, Heredia, Limon, Puntarenas, San Jose

Independence: 15 September 1821 (from Spain)

National holiday: Independence Day, 15 September (1821)

Constitution: previous 1825; latest effective 8 November 1949; amended many times, last in 2015 (2016)

Legal system: civil law system based on Spanish civil code; judicial review of legislative acts in the Supreme Court

International law organization participation: accepts compulsory ICJ jurisdiction; accepts ICCt jurisdiction

Citizenship: *citizenship by birth:* yes
citizenship by descent: yes
dual citizenship recognized: yes
residency requirement for naturalization: 7 years

Suffrage: 18 years of age; universal and compulsory
Executive branch: *chief of state:* President Luis Guillermo SOLIS Rivera (since 8 May 2014); First Vice President Helio FALLAS Venega (since 8 May 2014); Second Vice President Ana Helena CHACON Echeverria (since 8 May 2014); note—the president is both chief of state and head of government

head of government: President Luis Guillermo SOLIS Rivera (since 8 May 2014); First Vice President Helio FALLAS Venega (since 8 May 2014); Second Vice President Ana Helena CHACON Echeverria (since 8 May 2014)
cabinet: Cabinet selected by the president
elections/appointments: president and vice presidents directly elected on the same ballot by modified majority popular vote (40% threshold) for a 4-year term (eligible for non-consecutive terms); election last held on 2 February 2014 with a runoff on 6 April 2014 (next to be held in February 2018)
election results: Luis Guillermo SOLIS Rivera elected president; percent of vote—Luis Guillermo SOLIS Rivera (PAC) 77.8%; Johnny ARAYA (PLN) 22.2%

Legislative branch: *description:* unicameral Legislative Assembly or Asamblea Legislativa (57 seats; members directly elected in multi-seat constituencies—corresponding to the country's 7 provinces—by proportional representation vote; members serve 4-year terms)
elections: last held on 2 February 2014 (next to be held in February 2018)
election results: percent of vote by party—NA; seats by party—PLN 18, PAC 13, FA 9, PUSC 8, PML 4, other 5
Judicial branch: *highest court(s):* Supreme Court of Justice (consists of 22 judges organized into 3 cassation chambers each with 5 judges, and the Constitutional Chamber with 7 judges)
judge selection and term of office: Supreme Court of Justice judges elected by the National Assembly for 8-year terms with renewal decided by the National Assembly
subordinate courts: appellate courts; first instance and justice of the peace courts; Superior Electoral Tribunal

Political parties and leaders: Accessibility Without Exclusion or PASE [Oscar Andres LOPEZ Arias]
Broad Front (Frente Amplio) or PFA [Ana Patricia MORA]
Citizen Action Party or PAC [Olivier PEREZ Gonzalez]
Costa Rican Renovation Party or PRC [Gerardo Justo OROZCO Alvarez]
Libertarian Movement Party or ML [Victor Danilo CUBERO Corrales]
National Integration Party or PIN [Walter MUNOZ Cespedes]
National Liberation Party or PLN [Bernal JIMENEZ]
National Restoration Party or PRN [Carlos AVENDANO]
Patriotic Alliance [Jorge ARAYA Westover]
Popular Vanguard [Humber to VARGAS]
Social Christian Unity Party or PUSC [Gerardo VARGAS]

Political pressure groups and leaders: Authentic Confederation of Democratic Workers or CATD (Communist Party affiliate)
Chamber of Coffee Growers
Confederated Union of Workers or CUT (Communist Party affiliate)
Confederation of Workers Rerum Novarum or CTRN (National Libertion Party affiliate)
Costa Rican Confederation of Democratic Workers or CCTD (National Libertion Party affiliate)
Costa Rican Exporter's Chamber or CADEXCO
Costa Rican Solidarity Movement Costa Rican Union of Private Sector Enterprises or UCCAEP
Federation of Public Service Workers or FTSP
National Association for Economic Development or ANFE
National Association of Educators or ANDE
National Association of Public and Private Employees or ANEP
International organization participation: BCIE, CACM, CD, CELAC, FAO, G-77, IADB, IAEA, IBRD, ICAO, ICC (national committees), ICCt, ICRM, IDA, IFAD, IFC, IFRCS, ILO, IMF, IMO, IMSO, Interpol, IOC, IOM, IPU, ISO, ITSO, ITU, ITUC (NGOs), LAES, LAIA (observer), MIGA, NAM (observer), OAS, OIF (observer), OPANAL, OPCW, Pacific Alliance (observer), PCA, SICA, UN, UNCTAD, UNESCO, UNHCR, UNIDO, Union Latina, UNWTO, UPU, WCO, WFTU (NGOs), WHO, WIPO, WMO, WTO

Diplomatic representation in the US: *chief of mission:* Ambassador Roman MACAYA Hayes (since 18 September 2014)
chancery: 2114 S Street NW, Washington, DC 20008
telephone: [1] (202) 480-2200
FAX: [1] (202) 265-4795
consulate(s) general: Atlanta, Chicago, Houston, Los Angeles, Miami, New Orleans, New York, San Juan (Puerto Rico), Tampa (FL), Washington DC
consulate(s): San Francisco
Diplomatic representation from the US: *chief of mission:* Ambassador Stafford Fitzgerald HANEY (since 30 June 2015)
embassy: Calle 98 Via 104, Pavas, San Jose
mailing address: APO AA 34020
telephone: [506] 2519-2000
FAX: [506] 2519-2305

Flag description: five horizontal bands of blue (top), white, red (double width), white, and blue, with the coat of arms in a white elliptical disk placed toward the hoist side of the red band; Costa Rica retained the earlier blue-white-blue flag of Central America until 1848 when, in response to revolutionary activity in Europe, it was decided to incorporate the French colors into the national flag and a central red stripe was added; today the blue color is said to stand for the sky, opportunity, and perseverance, white denotes peace, happiness, and wisdom, while red represents the blood shed for freedom, as well as the generosity and vibrancy of the people
note: somewhat resembles the flag of North Korea; similar to the flag of Thailand but with the blue and red colors reversed

National symbol(s): yiguirro (clay-colored robin); national colors: blue, white, red
National anthem: *name:* "Himno Nacional de Costa Rica" (National Anthem of Costa Rica)
lyrics/music: Jose Maria ZELEDON Brenes/ Manuel Maria GUTIERREZ
note: adopted 1949; the anthem's music was originally written for an 1853 welcome ceremony for diplomatic missions from the US and UK; the lyrics were added in 1903

ECONOMY

Economy—overview: Prior to the global economic crisis, Costa Rica enjoyed stable economic growth. The economy contracted in 2009 but resumed growth at about 4% per year in 2010–15. While traditional agricultural exports of bananas, coffee, sugar, and beef are still the backbone of commodity export trade, a variety of industrial and specialized agricultural products have broadened export trade in recent years. High value-added goods and services, including medical devices, have further bolstered exports. Tourism continues to bring in foreign exchange, as Costa Rica's impressive biodiversity makes it a key destination for ecotourism.

Foreign investors remain attracted by the country's political stability and relatively high education levels, as well as the incentives offered in the free-trade zones; Costa Rica has attracted one of the highest levels of foreign direct investment per capita in Latin America. The US-Central American-Dominican Republic Free Trade Agreement (CAFTA-DR) entered into force on 1 January 2009 after significant delays within the Costa Rican legislature. CAFTA-DR has increased foreign direct investment in key sectors of the economy, including the insurance and telecommunications sectors. However, poor infrastructure, high energy costs, bureaucracy, weak investor protection, and legal uncertainty due to the difficulty of enforcing contracts and overlapping and at times conflicting responsibilities between agencies, remain impediments to greater competitiveness.

Costa Rica's economy also faces challenges due to a rising fiscal deficit, rising public debt, and relatively low levels of domestic revenue. Poverty has remained around 20–25% for nearly 20 years, and the strong social safety net that had been put into place by the government has eroded due to increased financial constraints on government expenditures. Unlike the rest of Central America, Costa Rica is not highly dependent on remittances, which in 2014 represented 1% of GDP. Immigration from Nicaragua has increasingly become a concern for the government. The estimated 300,000–500,000 Nicaraguans in Costa Rica, legally and illegally, are an important source of mostly unskilled labor, but also place heavy demands on the social welfare system.

GDP (purchasing power parity): $74.89 billion (2015 est.)
$72.23 billion (2014 est.)
$70.15 billion (2013 est.)
note: data are in 2015 US dollars
country comparison to the world: 94

GDP (official exchange rate): $52.9 billion (2015 est.)

GDP—real growth rate: 3.7% (2015 est.)
3% (2014 est.)
1.8% (2013 est.)
country comparison to the world: 75

GDP—per capita (PPP): $15,500 (2015 est.)
$15,100 (2014 est.)
$14,900 (2013 est.)
note: data are in 2015 US dollars
country comparison to the world: 105

Gross national saving: 15.1% of GDP (2015 est.)
14.9% of GDP (2014 est.)
13.8% of GDP (2013 est.)
country comparison to the world: 113

GDP—composition, by end use:
household consumption: 64.8%
government consumption: 17.5%
investment in fixed capital: 21.9%
investment in inventories: -0.6%
exports of goods and services: 30.1%
imports of goods and services: -33.7% (2015 est.)

GDP—composition, by sector of origin:
agriculture: 6%
industry: 19.7%
services: 74.3% (2015 est.)

Agriculture—products: bananas, pineapples, coffee, melons, ornamental plants, sugar, corn, rice, beans, potatoes; beef, poultry, dairy; timber

Industries: medical equipment, food processing, textiles and clothing, construction materials, fertilizer, plastic products

Industrial production growth rate: 3.6% (2015 est.)
country comparison to the world: 67

Labor force: 2.268 million
note: official estimate; excludes Nicaraguans living in Costa Rica (2015 est.)
country comparison to the world: 119

Labor force—by occupation: *agriculture:* 14%
industry: 22%
services: 64% (2006 est.)

Unemployment rate: 8.7% (2015 est.) 8.6% (2014 est.)
country comparison to the world: 102

Population below poverty line: 24.8% (2011 est.)

Household income or consumption by percentage share: *lowest:* 10%: 1.2%
highest: 10%: 39.5% (2009 est.)

Distribution of family income—Gini index: 50.3 (2009)
45.9 (1997)
country comparison to the world: 20

Budget: *revenues:* $7.5 billion
expenditures: $10.64 billion (2015 est.)
Taxes and other revenues: 14.5% of GDP (2015 est.)
country comparison to the world: 195

Budget surplus (+) or deficit (-): -6.1% of GDP (2015 est.)
country comparison to the world: 182

Public debt: 59.7% of GDP (2015 est.)
56.8% of GDP (2014 est.)
country comparison to the world: 63

Fiscal year: calendar year

Inflation rate (consumer prices): 0.8% (2015 est.)
4.5% (2014 est.)
country comparison to the world: 71

Central bank discount rate: 21.5% (31 December 2010)
23% (31 December 2009)
country comparison to the world: 3

Commercial bank prime lending rate: 16.1% (31 December 2015 est.)
14.9% (31 December 2014 est.)
country comparison to the world: 29

Stock of narrow money: $5.119 billion (31 December 2015 est.)
$4.643 billion (31 December 2014 est.)
country comparison to the world: 97

Stock of broad money: $21.55 billion (31 December 2015 est.)
$18 billion (31 December 2014 est.)
country comparison to the world: 88

Stock of domestic credit: $35.07 billion (31 December 2015 est.)
$27.25 billion (31 December 2014 est.)
country comparison to the world: 70

Market value of publicly traded shares: $2.015 billion (31 December 2012 est.)
$1.443 billion (31 December 2011)
$1.445 billion (31 December 2010 est.)
country comparison to the world: 100

Current account balance: -$2.135 billion (2015 est.)
-$2.34 billion (2014 est.)
country comparison to the world: 147

Exports: $9.756 billion (2015 est.)
$11.14 billion (2014 est.)
country comparison to the world: 89

Exports—commodities: bananas, pineapples, coffee, melons, ornamental plants, sugar; beef; seafood; electronic components, medical equipment

Exports—partners: US 33.6%, China 6.2%, Mexico 4.6%, Nicaragua 4.3%, Netherlands 4.2%, Guatemala 4% (2015)

Imports: $15.44 billion (2015 est.)
$16.35 billion (2014 est.)
country comparison to the world: 83

Imports—commodities: raw materials, consumer goods, capital equipment, petroleum, construction materials

Imports—partners: US 45.3%, China 9.8%, Mexico 7.1% (2015)

Reserves of foreign exchange and gold: $7.578 billion (31 December 2015 est.)
$7.211 billion (31 December 2014 est.)
country comparison to the world: 81

Debt—external: $19.43 billion (31 December 2014 est.)
$17.65 billion (31 December 2013 est.)
country comparison to the world: 87

Stock of direct foreign investment—at home: $27.63 billion (31 December 2015 est.)
$24.66 billion (31 December 2014 est.)
country comparison to the world: 73

Stock of direct foreign investment—abroad: $2.999 billion (31 December 2015 est.)
$2.799 billion (31 December 2014 est.)
country comparison to the world: 76

Exchange rates: Costa Rican colones (CRC) per US dollar—
535 (2015 est.)
538.32 (2014 est.)
538.32 (2013 est.)
502.9 (2012 est.)
505.66 (2011 est.)

ENERGY

Electricity—production: 10.05 billion kWh (2012 est.)
country comparison to the world: 97

Electricity—consumption: 8.987 billion kWh (2012 est.)
country comparison to the world: 93

Electricity—exports: 402 million kWh (2012 est.)
country comparison to the world: 71

Electricity—imports: 419 million kWh (2012 est.)
country comparison to the world: 77

Electricity—installed generating capacity: 3.039 million kW (2012 est.)
country comparison to the world: 94

Electricity—from fossil fuels: 30.7% of total installed capacity (2012 est.)
country comparison to the world: 182

Electricity—from nuclear fuels: 0% of total installed capacity (2012 est.)
country comparison to the world: 72

Electricity—from hydroelectric plants: 55.9% of total installed capacity (2012 est.)
country comparison to the world: 40
Electricity—from other renewable sources: 13.3% of total installed capacity (2012 est.)
country comparison to the world: 24
Crude oil—production: 0 bbl/day (2014 est.)
country comparison to the world: 120
Crude oil—exports: 1,300 bbl/day (2012 est.)
country comparison to the world: 82
Crude oil—imports: 0 bbl/day (2012 est.)
country comparison to the world: 176
Crude oil—proved reserves: 0 bbl (1 January 2015 est.)
country comparison to the world: 119
Refined petroleum products—production: 0 bbl/day (2012 est.)
country comparison to the world: 169
Refined petroleum products—consumption: 50,000 bbl/day (2013 est.)
country comparison to the world: 100
Refined petroleum products—exports: 0 bbl/day (2012 est.)
country comparison to the world: 170
Refined petroleum products—imports: 49,410 bbl/day (2012 est.)
country comparison to the world: 81
Natural gas—production: 0 cu m (2013 est.)
country comparison to the world: 173
Natural gas—consumption: 0 cu m (2013 est.)
country comparison to the world: 132
Natural gas—exports: 0 cu m (2013 est.)
country comparison to the world: 82
Natural gas—imports: 0 cu m (2013 est.)
country comparison to the world: 182
Natural gas—proved reserves: 0 cu m (1 January 2014 est.)
country comparison to the world: 126
Carbon dioxide emissions from consumption of energy: 7.29 million Mt (2012 est.)
country comparison to the world: 114

COMMUNICATIONS

Telephones—fixed lines: *total subscriptions:* 880,000
subscriptions per 100 inhabitants: 19 (2014 est.)
country comparison to the world: 82
Telephones—mobile cellular: *total:* 7.1 million
subscriptions per 100 inhabitants: 149 (2014 est.)
country comparison to the world: 104
Telephone system: *general assessment:* good domestic telephone service in terms of breadth of coverage; under the terms of CAFTA-DR, the state-run telecommunications monopoly is scheduled to be opened to competition from domestic and international firms, but has been slow to open to competition
domestic: point-to-point and point-to-multi-point microwave, fiber-optic, and coaxial cable link rural areas; Internet service is available
international: country code—506; landing points for the Americas Region Caribbean Ring System (ARCOS-1), MAYA-1, and the Pan American Crossing submarine cables that provide links to

South and Central America, parts of the Caribbean, and the US; connected to Central American Microwave System; satellite earth stations—2 Intelsat (Atlantic Ocean) (2011)
Broadcast media: multiple privately owned TV stations and 1 publicly owned TV station; cable network services are widely available; more than 100 privately owned radio stations and a public radio network (2007)
Radio broadcast stations: AM 65, FM 51, shortwave 19 (2002)
Television broadcast stations: 20 (plus 43 repeaters) (2002)

Internet country code: .cr
Internet hosts: 147,258 (2012)
country comparison to the world: 78
Internet users: *total:* 2.4 million
percent of population: 50.9% (2014 est.)
country comparison to the world: 92

TRANSPORTATION

Airports: 161 (2013)
country comparison to the world: 35
Airports—with paved runways: *total:* 47
2,438 to 3,047 m: 2
1,524 to 2,437 m: 2
914 to 1,523 m: 27
under 914 m: 16 (2013)
Airports—with unpaved runways: *total:* 114
914 to 1,523 m: 18
under 914 m: 96 (2013)
Pipelines: refined products 662 km (2013)
Railways: *total:* 278 km
narrow gauge: 278 km 1.067-m gauge
note: the entire rail network fell into disrepair and out of use at the end of the 20th century; since 2005, certain sections of rail have been rehabilitated (2014)
country comparison to the world: 124
Roadways: *total:* 39,018 km
paved: 10,133 km
unpaved: 28,885 km (2010)
country comparison to the world: 90
Waterways: 730 km (seasonally navigable by small craft) (2011)
country comparison to the world: 74
Merchant marine: *total:* 1
by type: passenger/cargo 1 (2010)
country comparison to the world: 149

Ports and terminals: *major seaport(s):* Atlantic Ocean (Caribbean)—Puerto Limon; Pacific Ocean—Caldera

MILITARY AND SECURITY

Military branches: no regular military forces; Ministry of Public Security, Government, and Police (2011)

TRANSNATIONAL ISSUES

Disputes—international: Costa Rica and Nicaragua regularly file border dispute cases over the delimitations of the San Juan River and the

northern tip of Calero Island to the International Court of Justice (ICJ); in 2009, the ICJ ruled that Costa Rican vessels carrying out police activities could not use the river, but official Costa Rican vessels providing essential services to riverside inhabitants and Costa Rican tourists could travel freely on the river; in 2011, the ICJ provisionally ruled that both countries must remove personnel from the disputed area; in 2013, the ICJ rejected Nicaragua's 2012 suit to halt Costa Rica's construction of a highway paralleling the river on the grounds of irreparable environmental damage; in 2013, the ICJ, regarding the disputed territory, ordered that Nicaragua should refrain from dredging or canal construction and refill and repair damage caused by trenches connecting the river to the Caribbean and upheld its 2010 ruling that Nicaragua must remove all personnel; in early 2014, Costa Rica brought Nicaragua to the ICJ over offshore oil concessions in the disputed region
Refugees and internally displaced persons: *refugees (country of origin):* 16,623 (Colombia) (2014) stateless persons: 1,806 (2015)
Trafficking in persons: *current situation:* Costa Rica is a source, transit, and destination country for men, women, and children subjected to sex trafficking and forced labor; Costa Rican women and children, as well as those from Nicaragua, the Dominican Republic, and other Latin American countries, are sex trafficked in Costa Rica; child sex tourism is a particular problem with offenders coming from the US and Europe; men and children from Central America, including indigenous Panamanians, and Asia are exploited in agriculture, construction, fishing, and commerce; Nicaraguans transit Costa Rica to reach Panama, where some are subjected to forced labor or sex trafficking
tier rating: Tier 2 Watch List—Costa Rica does not fully comply with the minimum standards for the elimination of trafficking; however, it is making significant efforts to do so; anti-trafficking law enforcement efforts declined in 2014, with fewer prosecutions and no convictions and no actions taken against complicit government personnel; some officials conflated trafficking with smuggling, and authorities reported the diversion of funds to combat smuggling hindered anti-trafficking efforts; the government identified more victims than the previous year but did not make progress in ensuring that victims received adequate protective services; specialized services were limited and mostly provided by NGOs without government support, even from a dedicated fund for anti-trafficking efforts; victims services were virtually non-existent outside of the capital (2015)
Illicit drugs: transshipment country for cocaine and heroin from South America; illicit production of cannabis in remote areas; domestic cocaine consumption, particularly crack cocaine, is rising; significant consumption of amphetamines; seizures of smuggled cash in Costa Rica and at the main border crossing to enter Costa Rica from Nicaraguahaverisen in recent years (2008)

COTE D'LVOIRE

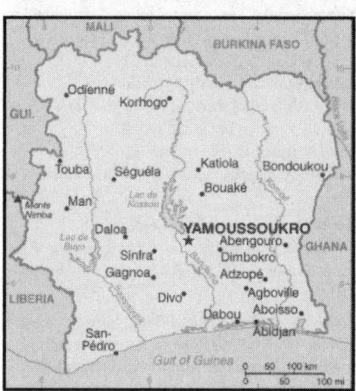

INTRODUCTION

Background: Close ties to France following independence in 1960, the development of cocoa production for export, and foreign investment all made Cote d'Ivoire one of the most prosperous of the West African states but did not protect it from political turmoil. In December 1999, a military coup—the first ever in Cote d'Ivoire's history—overthrew the government. Junta leader Robert GUEI blatantly rigged elections held in late 2000 and declared himself the winner. Popular protest forced him to step aside and brought Laurent GBAGBO into power. Ivorian dissidents and disaffected members of the military launched a failed coup attempt in September 2002 that developed into a rebellion and then a civil war. The war ended in 2003 with a cease-fire that left the country divided with the rebels holding the north, the government the south, and peacekeeping forces a buffer zone between the two. In March 2007, President GBAGBO and former New Forces rebel leader Guillaume SORO signed an agreement in which SORO joined GBAGBO's government as prime minister and the two agreed to reunite the country by dismantling the buffer zone, integrating rebel forces into the national armed forces, and holding elections. Difficulties in preparing electoral registers delayed balloting until 2010. In November 2010, Alassane Dramane OUATTARA won the presidential election over GBAGBO, but GBAGBO refused to hand over power, resulting in a five-month stand-off. In April 2011, after widespread fighting, GBAGBO was formally forced from office by armed OUATTARA supporters with the help of UN and French forces. Several thousand UN peacekeepers and several hundred French troops remain in Cote d'I voire to support the transition process. OUATTARA is focused on rebuilding the country's economy and infrastructure while rebuilding the security forces. GBAGBO is in The Hague awaiting trial for crimes against humanity.

GEOGRAPHY

Location: Western Africa, bordering the North Atlantic Ocean, between Ghana and Liberia

Geographic coordinates: 8 00 N, 5 00 W

Map references: Africa

Area: *total:* 322,463 sq km
land: 318,003 sq km
water: 4,460 sq km
country comparison to the world: 69

Area—comparative: slightly larger than New Mexico

Land boundaries: *total:* 3,458 km
border countries (5): Burkina Faso 545 km, Ghana 720 km, Guinea 816 km, Liberia 778 km, Mali 599 km

Coastline: 515 km

Maritime claims: *territorial sea:* 12 nm
exclusive economic zone: 200 nm
continental shelf: 200 nm

Climate: tropical along coast, semiarid in far north; three seasons—warm and dry (November to March), hot and dry (March to May), hot and wet (June to October)

Terrain: mostly flat to undulating plains; mountains in northwest

Elevation: *mean elevation:* 250 m

elevation extremes: *lowest point:* Gulf of Guinea 0 m
highest point: Monts Nimba 1,752 m

Natural resources: petroleum, natural gas, diamonds, manganese, iron ore, cobalt, bauxite, copper, gold, nickel, tantalum, silica sand, clay, cocoa beans, coffee, palm oil, hydropower

Land use: *agricultural land:* 64.8%
arable land: 9.1%
permanent crops: 14.2%
permanent pasture: 41.5%
forest: 32.7%
other: 2.5% (2011 est.)

Irrigated land: 730 sq km (2012)

Total renewable water resources: 81.14 cu km (2011)

Freshwater withdrawal (domestic/industrial/agricultural): *total:* 1.55 cu k/yr (41%/21%/38%)
per capita: 83.07 cu m/yr (2008)

Natural hazards: coast has heavy surf and no natural harbors; during the rainy season torrential flooding is possible

Environment—current issues: deforestation (most of the country's forests—once the largest in West Africa—have been heavily logged); water pollution from sewage and industrial and agricultural effluents

Environment—international agreements: *party to:* Biodiversity, Climate Change, Climate Change-Kyoto Protocol, Desertification, Endangered Species, Hazardous Wastes, Law of the Sea, Marine Dumping, Ozone Layer Protection, Ship Pollution, Tropical Timber 83, Tropical Timber 94, Wetlands, Whaling
signed, but not ratified: none of the selected agreements

Geography—note: most of the inhabitants live along the sandy coastal region; apart from the capital area, the forested interior is sparsely populated

PEOPLE AND SOCIETY

Nationality: *noun:* Ivoirian(s)
adjective: Ivoirian

Ethnic groups: Akan 32.1%, Voltaique or Gur 15%, Northern Mande 12.4%, Krou 9.8%, Southern Mande 9%, other 21.2% (includes European and Lebanese descent), unspecified 0.5% (2011–12 est.)

Languages: French (official), 60 native dialects of which Dioula is the most widely spoken

Religions: Muslim 40.2%, Catholic 19.4%, Evangelical 19.3%, Methodist 2.5%, other Christian 4.5%, animist or no religion 12.8%, other religion/unspecified 1.4% (2011–12 est.)
note: the majority of foreign migrant workers are Muslim (72%) and Christian (18%) (2014 est.)

Population: 23,295,302
note: estimates for this country explicitly take into account the effects of excess mortality due to AIDS; this can result in lower life expectancy, higher infant mortality, higher death rates, lower population growth rates, and changes in the distribution of population by age and sex than would otherwise be expected (July 2015 est.)
country comparison to the world: 55

Age structure: *0–14 years:* 37.94% (male 4,456,646/female 4,381,907)
15–24 years: 20.95% (male 2,459,156/female 2,420,284)
25–54 years: 33.53% (male 3,997,615/female 3,812,563)
55–64 years: 4.25% (male 495,177/female 493,854)
65 years and over: 3.34% (male 375,276/female 402,824) (2015 est.)

Dependency ratios: *total dependency ratio:* 83.5%
youth dependency ratio: 77.9%
elderly dependency ratio: 5.6%
potential support ratio: 18% (2015 est.)

Median age: *total:* 20.5 years
male: 20.6 years
female: 20.4 years (2015 est.)
country comparison to the world: 187

Population growth rate: 1.91% (2015 est.)
country comparison to the world: 55

Birth rate: 28.67 births/1,000 population (2015 est.)
country comparison to the world: 44

Death rate: 9.55 deaths/1,000 population (2015 est.)
country comparison to the world: 53

Net migration rate: 0 migrant(s)/1,000 population (2015 est.)

country comparison to the world: 101

Urbanization: *urban population:* 54.2% of total population (2015)

rate of urbanization: 3.69% annual rate of change (2010–15 est.)

Major urban areas—population: YAMOUS-SOUKRO (capital) 259,000 (2014); ABID-JAN (seat of government) 4.86 million; Bouake 762,000 (2015)

Sex ratio: *at birth:* 1.03 male(s)/female

0–14 years: 1.02 male(s)/female

15–24 years: 1.02 male(s)/female

25–54 years: 1.05 male(s)/female

55–64 years: 1 male(s)/female

65 years and over: 0.93 male(s)/female

total population: 1.02 male(s)/female (2015 est.)

Mother's mean age at first birth: 20

note: median age at first birth among women 20–24 (2011/12 est.)

Maternal mortality rate: 645 deaths/100,000 live births (2015 est.)

country comparison to the world: 27

Infant mortality rate: *total:* 58.7 deaths/1,000 live births

male: 64.77 deaths/1,000 live births

female: 52.44 deaths/1,000 live births (2015 est.)

country comparison to the world: 22

Life expectancy at birth:

total population: 58.34 years

male: 57.21 years

female: 59.51 years (2015 est.)

country comparison to the world: 202

Total fertility rate: 3.54 children born/woman (2015 est.)

country comparison to the world: 44

Contraceptive prevalence rate: 18.2% (2011/12)

Health expenditures: 5.7% of GDP (2013)

country comparison to the world: 78

Physicians density: 0.14 physicians/1,000 population (2008)

Hospital bed density: 0.4 beds/1,000 population (2006)

Drinking water source:

improved:

urban: 93.1% of population

rural: 68.8% of population

total: 81.9% of population

unimproved:

urban: 6.9% of population

rural: 31.2% of population

total: 18.1% of population (2015 est.)

Sanitation facility access:

improved:

urban: 32.8% of population

rural: 10.3% of population

total: 22.5% of population

unimproved:

urban: 67.2% of population

rural: 89.7% of population

total: 77.5% of population (2015 est.)

HIV/AIDS—adult prevalence rate: 3.46% (2014 est.)

country comparison to the world: 18

HIV/AIDS—people living with HIV/AIDS: 460,100 (2014 est.)

country comparison to the world: 16

HIV/AIDS—deaths: 21,800 (2014 est.)

country comparison to the world: 14

Major infectious diseases: *degree of risk:* very high

food or waterborne diseases: bacterial diarrhea, hepatitis A, and typhoid fever

vectorborne diseases: malaria, dengue fever, and yellow fever

water contact disease: schistosomiasis

animal contact disease: rabies

respiratory disease: meningococcal meningitis

note: highly pathogenic H5N1 avian influenza has been identified in this country; it poses a negligible risk with extremely rare cases possible among US citizens who have close contact with birds (2013)

Obesity—adult prevalence rate: 8% (2014)

country comparison to the world: 149

Children under the age of 5 years underweight: 15.7% (2012)

country comparison to the world: 43

Education expenditures: 4.7% of GDP (2014)

country comparison to the world: 89

Literacy: *definition:* age 15 and over can read and write

total population: 43.1%

male: 53.1%

female: 32.5% (2015 est.)

School life expectancy (primary to tertiary education): *total:* 9 years

male: 10 years

female: 8 years (2014)

Child labor—children ages 5–14: *total number:* 1,796,802

percentage: 35% (2006 est.)

GOVERNMENT

Country name: *conventional long form:* Republic of Cote d'Ivoire

conventional short form: Cote d'Ivoire

local long form: Republique de Cote d'Ivoire

local short form: Cote d'Ivoire

note: pronounced coat-div-whar

former: Ivory Coast

etymology: name reflects the intense ivory trade that took place in the region from the 15th to 17th centuries

Government type: presidential republic

Capital: *name:* Yamoussoukro; *note*—although Yamoussoukro has been the official capital since 1983, Abidjan remains the commercial and administrative center; the US, like other countries, maintains its Embassy in Abidjan

Geographic coordinates: 6 49 N, 5 16 W

time difference: UTC 0 (5 hours ahead of Washington, DC, during Standard Time)

Administrative divisions: 12 districts and 2 autonomous districts*; Abidjan*, Bas-Sassandra, Comoe, Denguele, Goh-Djiboua, Lacs, Lagunes, Montagnes, Sassandra-Marahoue, Savanes, Vallee du Bandama, Woroba, Yamoussoukro*, Zanzan

Independence: 7 August 1960 (from France)

National holiday: Independence Day, 7 August (1960)

Constitution: previous 1960; latest approved by referendum 23 July 2000; amended 2004, 2012 (2016)

Legal system: civil law system based on the French civil code; judicial review of legislation held in the Constitutional Chamber of the Supreme Court

International law organization participation: accepts compulsory ICJ jurisdiction with reservations; accepts ICCt jurisdiction

Citizenship: *citizenship by birth:* no

citizenship by descent only: at least one parent must be a citizen of Cote d'Ivoire

dual citizenship recognized: no

residency requirement for naturalization: 5 years

Suffrage: 18 years of age; universal

Executive branch: *chief of state:* President Alassane Dramane OUATTARA (since 4 December 2010)

head of government: Prime Minister Daniel Kablan DUNCAN (since 21 November 2012)

cabinet: Council of Ministers appointed by the president

elections/appointments: president directly elected by absolute majority popular vote in 2 rounds if needed for a 5-year term (no term limits); election last held on 25 October 2015 (next to be held in 2020); prime minister appointed by the president

election results: Alassane OUATTARA elected president; percent of vote—Alassane OUATTARA (RDR) 83.7%, Pascal Affi N'GUESSAN (ADF) 9.3%, Konan Bertin KOUADIO (independent) 3.9%, other 3.1%

Legislative branch: *description:* unicameral National Assembly or Assemblee Nationale (255 seats; members directly elected in single- and multi-seat constituencies by simple majority vote to serve 5-year terms)

elections: last held on 11 December 2011 (next to be held in 2016)

election results: percent of vote by party—RDR 42.1%, PDCI 28.6%, UDPCI 3.1%, RDP 1.7%, other 24.5%; seats by party—RDR 127, PDCI 76, UDPCI 7, RDP 4, other 2, independents 39

Judicial branch: *highest court(s):* Supreme Court or Cour Supreme (organized into Judicial, Audit, Constitutional, and Administrative Chambers; consists of the court president, 3 vice-presidents for the Judicial, Audit, and Administrative chambers, and 9 associate justices or magistrates)

judge selection and term office: judges nominated by the Superior Council of the Magistrature, a 7-member body consisting of the national president (chairman), 3 "bench" judges, and 3 public prosecutors; judges appointed for life subordinate courts: Courts of Appeal (organized into civil, criminal, and social chambers); first instance courts; peace courts

Political parties and leaders: Democratic Party of Cote d'Ivoire or PDCI [Henri Konan BEDIE]

Movement of the Future Forces or MFA [Innocent Augustin ANAKY KOBENA]

Rally of Houphouetists for Democracy and Peace Rally of the Republicans or RDR [Alassane OUATTARA]

Union for Cote d'I voire or UPCI [Gnamien KONA]

Union for Democracy and Peace in Cote d'I voire or UDPCI [Toikeuse MABRI] more than 144 smaller registered parties

Political pressure groups and leaders: Federation of University and High School Students of Cote d'I voire or FESCI [Augustin MIAN]
National Congress for the Resistance and Democracy or CNRD [Bernard DADIE]
Panafrican Congress for Justice and Peoples Equality or CO JEP [Roselin BLY]
Rally of Houphouetists for Democracy and Peace or RHDP

International organization participation: ACP, AfDB, AU, ECOWAS, EITI (compliant country), Entente, FAO, FZ, G-24, G-77, IAEA, IBRD, ICAO, ICC, ICCt, ICRM, IDA, IDB, IFAD, IFC, IFRCS, ILO, IMF, IMO, Interpol, IOC, IOM, IPU, ISO, ITSO, ITU, ITUC (NGOs), MIGA, MINUSMA, MONUSCO, NAM, OIC, OIF, OPCW, UN, UNCTAD, UNESCO, UNHCR, UNIDO, Union Latina, UN WTO, UPU, WADB (regional), WAEMU, WCO, WFTU (NGOs), WHO, WIPO, WMO, WTO

Diplomatic representation in the US: *chief of mission:* Ambassador Daouda DIABATE (since 11 February 2011)
chancery: 2424 M assachusetts Avenue NW, Washington, DC 20008
telephone: [1] (202) 797-0300
FAX: [1] (202) 462-9444

Diplomatic representation from the US: *chief of mission:* Ambassador Terence Patrick MCCULLEY (since 21 November 2013) em bassy: Cocody Riviera Golf 01, Abidjan
maiing address: B. P. 1712, Abidjan 01
telephone: [225] 22 49 40 00
FAX: [225] 22 49 42 02

Flag description: three equal vertical bands of orange (hoist side), white, and green; orange symbolizes the land (savannah) of the north and fertility, white stands for peace and unity, green represents the forests of the south and the hope for a bright future
note: similar to the flag of Ireland, which is longer and has the colors reversed—green (hoist side), white, and orange; also similar to the flag of Italy, which is green (hoist side), white, and red; design was based on the flag of France

National symbol(s): elephant; national colors: orange, white, green

National anthem: *name:* "L'Abidjanaise" (Song of Abidjan)
lyrics/music: Mathieu EKRA, Joachim BONY, and Pierre Marie COTY/Pierre Marie COTY and Pierre Michel PANG O
note: adopted 1960; although the nation's capital city moved from Abidjan to Yamoussoukro in 1983, the anthem still owes its name to the former capital

ECONOMY

Economy—overview: Cote d'I voire is heavily dependent on agriculture and related activities, which engage roughly two-thirds of the population. Cote d'I voire is the world's largest producer and exporter of cocoa beans and a significant producer and exporter of coffee and palm oil. Consequently, the economy is highly sensitive to fluctuations in international prices for these products and in climatic conditions. Cocoa, oil, and coffee are the country's top export revenue earners, but the country is also mining gold. Following the end of more than a decade of civil conflict in 2011, Cote d'Ivoire has experienced a boom in foreign investment and economic growth. In June 2012, the IMF and the World Bank announced $4.4 billion in debt relief for Cote d'I voire under the Highly Indebted Poor Countries Initiative.

GDP (purchasing power parity): $78.62 billion (2015 est.)
$72.39 billion (2014 est.)
$67.08 billion (2013 est.)
note: data are in 2015 US dollars
country comparison to the world: 92

GDP (official exchange rate): $31.17 billion (2015 est.)

GDP—real growth rate: 8.6% (2015 est.)
7.9% (2014 est.)
8.7% (2013 est.)
country comparison to the world: 6

GDP—per capita (PPP): $3,300 (2015 est.)
$3,100 (2014 est.)
$3,000 (2013 est.)
note: data are in 2015 US dollars
country comparison to the world: 183

Gross national saving: 16.4% of GDP (2015 est.)
16.1% of GDP (2014 est.)
15.7% of GDP (2013 est.)
country comparison to the world: 104

GDP—composition, by end use:
household consumption: 66.2%
government consumption: 13.7%
investment in fixed capital: 16.2%
investment in inventories: 0.8%
exports of goods and services: 43%
imports of goods and services: -39.9% (2015 est.)

GDP—composition, by sector of origin: *agriculture:* 17.4%
industry: 20.3%
services: 62.2% (2015 est.)

Agriculture—products: coffee, cocoa beans, bananas, palm kernels, corn, rice, cassava (manioc, tapioca), sweet potatoes, sugar, cotton, rubber; timber

Industries: foodstuffs, beverages; wood products, oil refining, gold mining, truck and bus assembly, textiles, fertilizer, building materials, electricity

Industrial production growth rate: 6.5% (2015 est.)
country comparison to the world: 19

Labor force: 8.31 million (2015 est.)
country comparison to the world: 59

Labor force—by occupation: *agriculture:* 68% industry and services: NA% (2007 est.)

Unemployment rate: NA%

Population below poverty line: 42% (2006 est.)

Household income or consumption by percentage share: *lowest:* 10%: 2.2%
highest: 10%: 31.8% (2008)

Distribution of family income—Gini index: 41.5 (2008) 36.7 (1995)
country comparison to the world: 56

Budget: *revenues:* $5.914 billion
expenditures: $7.067 billion (2015 est.)
Taxes and other revenues: 18.9% of GDP (2015 est.)
country comparison to the world: 166

Budget surplus (+) or deficit (-): -3.7% of GDP (2015 est.)
country comparison to the world: 137

Public debt: 52.3% of GDP (2015 est.)
45% of GDP (2014 est.)
country comparison to the world: 75

Fiscal year: calendar year

Inflation rate (consumer prices): 1.2% (2015 est.)
0.4% (2014 est.)
country comparison to the world: 85

Central bank discount rate: 4.25% (31 December 2010)
4.25% (31 December 2009)
country comparison to the world: 88

Commercial bank prime lending rate: 2.5% (31 December 2015 est.)
2.5% (31 December 2014 est.)
country comparison to the world: 174

Stock of narrow money: $7.302 billion (31 December 2015 est.) $7.785 billion (31 December 2014 est.)
country comparison to the world: 90

Stock of broad money: $12.23 billion (31 December 2014 est.)
$11.5 billion (31 December 2013 est.)
country comparison to the world: 101

Stock of domestic credit: $8.347 billion (31 December 2015 est.)
$9.138 billion (31 December 2014 est.)
country comparison to the world: 109

Market value of publicly traded shares: $7.829 billion (31 December 2012 est.)
$6.288 billion (31 December 2011)
$7.099 billion (31 December 2010 est.)
country comparison to the world: 77

Current account balance: -$542 million (2015 est.)
-$236 million (2014 est.)
country comparison to the world: 101

Exports: $11.9 billion (2015 est.)
$12.78 billion (2014 est.)
country comparison to the world: 84

Exports—commodities: cocoa, coffee, timber, petroleum, cotton, bananas, pineapples, palm oil, fish

Exports—partners: US 8.5%, Netherlands 6.2%, France 5.6%, Germany 5.6%, Nigeria 5.5%, Burkina Faso 5.5%, Belgium 5.3%, India 4.6%, Ghana 4.4%, Switzerland 4.1% (2015)

Imports: $9.154 billion (2015 est.)
$9.935 billion (2014 est.)
country comparison to the world: 103

Imports—commodities: fuel, capital equipment, foodstuffs

Imports—partners: Nigeria 21.8%, China 14.4%, France 11.3%, Bahamas, The 5% (2015)

Reserves of foreign exchange and gold: $4.882 billion (31 December 2015 est.)
$4.479 billion (31 December 2014 est.)
country comparison to the world: 95

213

Debt—external: $13.03 billion (31 December 2014 est.)
$11.29 billion (31 December 2013 est.)
country comparison to the world: 101
Stock of direct foreign investment—at home: $NA
Stock of direct foreign investment—abroad: $NA
Exchange rates: Communaute Financiere Africaine francs (XOF) per US dollar—
610.6 (2015 est.)
494.42 (2014 est.)
494.42 (2013 est.)
510.29 (2012 est.)
471.87 (2011 est.)

ENERGY

Electricity—production: 6.688 billion kWh (2012 est.)
country comparison to the world: 110
Electricity—consumption: 4.731 billion kWh (2012 est.)
country comparison to the world: 118
Electricity—exports: 645 million kWh (2012 est.)
country comparison to the world: 64
Electricity—imports: 54 million kWh (2012 est.)
country comparison to the world: 103
Electricity—installed generating capacity: 1.522 million kW (2012 est.)
country comparison to the world: 118
Electricity—from fossil fuels: 60.3% of total installed capacity (2012 est.)
country comparison to the world: 132
Electricity—from nuclear fuels: 0% of total installed capacity (2012 est.)
country comparison to the world: 114
Electricity—from hydroelectric plants: 39.7% of total installed capacity (2012 est.)
country comparison to the world: 61
Electricity—from other renewable sources: 0% of total installed capacity (2012 est.)
country comparison to the world: 184
Crude oil—production: 36,000 bbl/day (2014 est.)
country comparison to the world: 62
Crude oil—exports: 47,900 bbl/day (2012 est.)
country comparison to the world: 47
Crude oil—imports: 72,860 bbl/day (2012 est.)
country comparison to the world: 50
Crude oil—proved reserves: 100 million bbl (1 January 2015 est.)
country comparison to the world: 72
Refined petroleum products—production: 62,750 bbl/day (2012 est.)
country comparison to the world: 76
Refined petroleum products—consumption: 26,000 bbl/day (2013 est.)
country comparison to the world: 119
Refined petroleum products—exports: 39,720 bbl/day (2012 est.)
country comparison to the world: 62
Refined petroleum products—imports: 3,305 bbl/day (2012 est.)
country comparison to the world: 172
Natural gas—production: 1.78 billion cu m (2013 est.)
country comparison to the world: 58
Natural gas—consumption: 1.78 billion cu m (2013 est.)
country comparison to the world: 81
Natural gas—exports: 0 cu m (2013 est.)

country comparison to the world: 120
Natural gas—imports: 0 cu m (2013 est.)
country comparison to the world: 212
Natural gas—proved reserves: 28.32 billion cu m (1 January 2014 est.)
country comparison to the world: 71
Carbon dioxide emissions from consumption of energy: 6.403 million Mt (2012 est.)
country comparison to the world: 118

COMMUNICATIONS

Telephones—fixed lines: *total subscriptions:* 240,000
subscriptions per 100 inhabitants: 1 (2014 est.)
country comparison to the world: 124
Telephones—mobile cellular: *total:* 22.1 million
subscriptions per 100 inhabitants: 97 (2014 est.)
country comparison to the world: 54
Telephone system: *general assessment:* well-developed by African standards; telecommunications sector privatized in late 1990s and operational fixed lines have increased since that time with two fixed-line providers operating over open-wire lines, microwave radio relay, and fiber-optics; 90% digitalized
domestic: with multiple mobile-cellular service providers competing in the market, usage has increased sharply to roughly 80 per 100 persons
international: country code—225; landing point for the SAT-3/WASC fiber-optic submarine cable that provides connectivity to Europe and Asia; satellite earth stations—2 Intelsat (1 Atlantic Ocean and 1 Indian Ocean) (2011)
Broadcast media: 2 state-owned TV stations; no private terrestrial TV stations, but satellite TV subscription service is available; 2 state-owned radio stations; some private radio stations; transmissions of several international broadcasters are available (2007)
Radio broadcast stations: AM 2, FM 9, shortwave 3 (1998)
Television broadcast stations: 14 (1998)
Internet country code: .ci
Internet hosts: 9,115 (2012)
country comparison to the world: 137
Internet users: *total:* 621,500
percent of population: 2.7% (2014 est.)
country comparison to the world: 129

TRANSPORTATION

Airports: 27 (2013)
country comparison to the world: 124
Airports—with paved runways: *total:* 7
over 3,047 m: 1
2,438 to 3,047 m: 2
1,524 to 2,437 m: 4 (2013)
Airports—with unpaved runways: *total:* 20
1,524 to 2,437 m: 6
914 to 1,523 m: 11
under 914 m: 3 (2013)
Heliports: 1 (2013)
Pipelines: condensate 101 km; gas 256 km; oil 118 km; oil/gas/water 5 km; water 7 km (2013)
Railways: *total:* 660 km
narrow gauge: 660 km 1.000-m gauge

note: an additional 622 km of this railroad extends into Burkina Faso (2008)
country comparison to the world: 106
Roadways: *total:* 81,996 km
paved: 6,502 km
unpaved: 75,494 km
note: includes intercity and urban roads; another 20,000 km of dirt roads are in poor condition and 150,000 km of dirt roads are impassable (2007)
country comparison to the world: 58
Waterways: 980 km (navigable rivers, canals, and numerous coastal lagoons) (2011)
country comparison to the world: 66
Ports and terminals: *major seaport(s):* Abidjan, San-Pedro
oil terminal(s): Espoir Offshore Terminal

MILITARY AND SECURITY

Military branches: Republican Forces of Cote d'I voire (Force Republiques de Cote d'I voire, FRCI): Army, Navy, Cote d'I voire Air Force (Force Aerienne de la Cote d'I voire) (2015)
Military service age and obligation: 18–25 years of age for compulsory and voluntary male and female military service; conscription is not enforced; voluntary recruitment of former rebels into the new national army is restricted to ages 22–29 (2012)
Military expenditures: 1.65% of GDP (2012)
1.49% of GDP (2011)
1.65% of GDP (2010)
country comparison to the world: 55

TRANSNATIONAL ISSUES

Disputes—international: disputed maritime border between Cote d'I voire and Ghana
Refugees and internally displaced persons: *IDPs:* 308,272 (post-election conflict in 2010–2011, as well as civil war from 2002–2004; most pronounced in western and southwestern regions) (2015)
stateless persons: 700,000 (2015); note—many Ivoirians lack documentation proving their nationality, which prevent them from accessing education and healthcare; birth on Ivorian soil does not automatically result in citizenship; disputes over citizenship and the associated rights of the large population descended from migrants from neighboring countries is an ongoing source of tension and contributed to the country's 2002 civil war; some observers believe the government's mass naturalizations of thousands of people over the last couple of years is intended to boost its electoral support base; the government in October 2013 acceded to international conventions on statelessness and in August 2013 reformed its nationality law, key steps to clarify the nationality of thousands of residents
Illicit drugs: illicit producer of cannabis, mostly for local consumption; utility as a narcotic transshipment point to Europe reduced by ongoing political instability; while rampant corruption and inadequate supervision leave the banking system vulnerable to money laundering, the lack of a developed financial system limits the country's utility as a major money-laundering center (2008)

CROATIA

INTRODUCTION

Background: The lands that today comprise Croatia were part of the Austro-Hungarian Empire until the close of World War I. In 1918, the Croats, Serbs, and Slovenes formed a kingdom known after 1929 as Yugoslavia. Following World War II, Yugoslavia became a federal independent communist state under the strong hand of Marshal TITO. Although Croatia declared its independence from Yugoslavia in 1991, it took four years of sporadic, but often bitter, fighting before occupying Serb armies were mostly cleared from Croatian lands, along with a majority of Croatia's ethnic Serb population. Under UN supervision, the last Serb-held enclave in eastern Slavonia was returned to Croatia in 1998. The country joined NATO in April 2009 and the EU in July 2013.

GEOGRAPHY

Location: Southeastern Europe, bordering the Adriatic Sea, between Bosnia and Herzegovina and Slovenia

Geographic coordinates: 45 10 N, 15 30 E

Map references: Europe

Area: *total:* 56,594 sq km
land: 55,974 sq km
water: 620 sq km
country comparison to the world: 127

Area—comparative: slightly smaller than West Virginia

Land boundaries: *total:* 2,237 km
border countries (5): Bosnia and Herzegovina 956 km, Hungary 348 km, Montenegro 19 km, Serbia 314 km, Slovenia 600 km

Coastline: 5,835 km (mainland 1,777 km, islands 4,058 km)

Maritime claims: *territorial sea:* 12 nm
continental shelf: 200-m depth or to the depth of exploitation

Climate: Mediterranean and continental; continental climate predominant with hot summers and cold winters; mild winters, dry summers along coast

Terrain: geographically diverse; flat plains along Hungarian border, low mountains and highlands near Adriatic coastline and islands

Elevation: *mean elevation:* 331 m

elevation extremes: *lowest point:* Adriatic Sea 0 m
highest point: Dinara 1,831 m

Natural resources: oil, some coal, bauxite, low-grade iron ore, calcium, gypsum, natural asphalt, silica, mica, clays, salt, hydropower

Land use: *agricultural land:* 23.7%
arable land: 16%
permanent crops: 1.5%
permanent pasture: 6.2%
forest: 34.4%
other: 41.9% (2011 est.)

Irrigated land: 240 sq km (2012)

Total renewable water resources: 105.5 cu km (2011)

Natural hazards: destructive earthquakes

Environment—current issues: air pollution (from metallurgical plants) and resulting acid rain is damaging the forests; coastal pollution from industrial and domestic waste; landmine removal and reconstruction of infrastructure consequent to 1992–95 civil strife

Environment—international agreements: *party to:* Air Pollution, Air Pollution-Nitrogen Oxides, Air Pollution-Persistent Organic Pollutants, Air Pollution-Sulfur 94, Air Pollution-Volatile Organic Compounds, Biodiversity, Climate Change, Climate Change-Kyoto Protocol, Desertification, Endangered Species, Hazardous Wastes, Law of the Sea, Marine Dumping, Ozone Layer Protection, Ship Pollution, Wetlands, Whaling
signed, but not ratified: none of the selected agreements

Geography—note: controls most land routes from Western Europe to Aegean Sea and Turkish Straits; most Adriatic Sea islands lie off the coast of Croatia—some 1,200 islands, islets, ridges, and rocks

PEOPLE AND SOCIETY

Nationality: *noun:* Croat(s), Croatian(s)
adjective: Croatian

Ethnic groups: Croat 90.4%, Serb 4.4%, other 4.4% (including Bosniak, Hungarian, Slovene, Czech, and Roma), unspecified 0.8% (2011 est.)

Languages: Croatian (official) 95.6%, Serbian 1.2%, other 3% (including Hungarian, Czech, Slovak, and Albanian), unspecified 0.2% (2011 est.)

Religions: Roman Catholic 86.3%, Orthodox 4.4%, Muslim 1.5%, other 1.5%, unspecified 2.5%, not religious or atheist 3.8% (2011 est.)

Population: 4,464,844 (July 2015 est.)
country comparison to the world: 126

Age structure: *0–14 years:* 14.42% (male 330,355/female 313,312)
15–24 years: 11.92% (male 272,249/female 259,935)
25–54 years: 40.88% (male 903,896/female 921,337)
55–64 years: 14.55% (male 314,697/female 335,007)
65 years and over: 18.23% (male 331,889/female 482,167) (2015 est.)

Dependency ratios: *total dependency ratio:* 51.1%
youth dependency ratio: 22.5%
elderly dependency ratio: 28.6%
potential support ratio: 3.5% (2015 est.)

Median age: *total:* 42.63 years
male: 40.5 years
female: 44.1 years (2015 est.)
country comparison to the world: 20

Population growth rate: -0.13% (2015 est.)
country comparison to the world: 209

Birth rate: 9.45 births/1,000 population (2015 est.)
country comparison to the world: 203

Death rate: 12.18 deaths/1,000 population (2015 est.)
country comparison to the world: 25

Net migration rate: 1.39 migrant(s)/1,000 population (2015 est.)
country comparison to the world: 57

Urbanization: *urban population:* 59% of total population (2015)
rate of urbanization: 0.11% annual rate of change (2010–15 est.)

Major urban areas—population: ZAGREB (capital) 687,000 (2015)

Sex ratio: *at birth:* 1.06 male(s)/female
0–14 years: 1.05 male(s)/female
15–24 years: 1.05 male(s)/female
25–54 years: 0.98 male(s)/female
55–64 years: 0.94 male(s)/female
65 years and over: 0.69 male(s)/female
total population: 0.93 male(s)/female (2015 est.)

Mother's mean age at first birth: 27.9 (2011 est.)

Maternal mortality rate: 8 deaths/100,000 live births (2015 est.)
country comparison to the world: 142

Infant mortality rate: *total:* 5.77 deaths/1,000 live births
male: 5.91 deaths/1,000 live births
female: 5.62 deaths/1,000 live births (2015 est.)
country comparison to the world: 168

Life expectancy at birth:
total population: 76.61 years
male: 73.02 years
female: 80.4 years (2015 est.)
country comparison to the world: 80

Total fertility rate: 1.46 children born/woman (2015 est.)
country comparison to the world: 201

Health expenditures: 7.3% of GDP (2013)
country comparison to the world: 84

Physicians density: 2.84 physicians/1,000 population (2011)

Hospital bed density: 5.9 beds/1,000 population (2014)

Drinking water source:
improved:
urban: 99.6% of population
rural: 99.7% of population
total: 99.6% of population
unimproved:
urban: 0.4% of population
rural: 0.3% of population
total: 0.4% of population (2015 est.)

Sanitation facility access:
improved:
urban: 97.8% of population
rural: 95.8% of population
total: 97% of population
unimproved:
urban: 2.2% of population
rural: 4.2% of population
total: 3% of population (2015 est.)

HIV/AIDS—adult prevalence rate: NA

HIV/AIDS—people living with HIV/AIDS: NA

HIV/AIDS—deaths: NA

Major infectious diseases: *degree of risk:* intermediate
vectorborne diseases: tickborne encephalitis
note: highly pathogenic H5N1 avian influenza has been identified in this country; it poses a negligible risk with extremely rare cases possible among US citizens who have close contact with birds (2013)

Obesity—adult prevalence rate: 25.6% (2014)
country comparison to the world: 66

Education expenditures: 4.2% of GDP (2011)
country comparison to the world: 99

Literacy: *definition:* age 15 and over can read and write
total population: 99.3%
male: 99.7%
female: 98.9% (2015 est.)

School life expectancy (primary to tertiary education): *total:* 15 years
male: 15 years
female: 16 years (2014)

Unemployment, youth ages 15–24: *total:* 50%
male: 49.9%
female: 50.2% (2013 est.)
country comparison to the world: 9

GOVERNMENT

Country name: *conventional long form:* Republic of Croatia
conventional short form: Croatia
local long form: Republika Hrvatska
local short form: Hrvatska
former: People's Republic of Croatia, Socialist Republic of Croatia
etymology: name derives from the Croats, a Slavic tribe who migrated to the Balkans in the 7th century A.D.

Government type: parliamentary republic
Capital: *name:* Zagreb
Geographic coordinates: 45 48 N, 16 00 E

time difference: UTC + 1 (6 hours ahead of Washington, DC, during Standard Time) daylight saving time: +1hr, begins last Sunday in March; ends last Sunday in October

Administrative divisions: 20 counties (zupanije, zupanija—singular) and 1 city* (grad—singular) with special county status; Bjelovarsko-Bilogorska(Bjelovar-Bilogora), Brodsko-Posavska (Brod-Posavina), Dubrovacko-Neretvanska (Dubrovnik-Neretva), Istarska (Istria), Karlovacka (Karlovac), Koprivnicko-Krizevacka (Koprivnica-Krizevci), Krapinsko-Zagorska (Krapina-Zagorje), Licko-Senjska (Lika-Senj), Medimurska (Medimurje), Osjecko-Baranjska (Osijek-Baranja), Pozesko-Slavonska (Pozega-Slavonia), Primorsko-Goranska (Primorje-Gorski Kotar), Sibensko-Kninska (Sibenik-Knin), Sisacko-Moslavacka (Sislak-Moslavina), Splitsko-Dalmatinska (Split-Dalmatia), Varazdinska (Varazdin), Viroviticko-Podravska (Virovitica-Podravina), Vukovarsko-Srijemska (Vukovar-Syrmia), Zadarska (Zadar), Zagreb*, Zagrebacka (Zagreb county)

Independence: 25 June 1991 (from Yugoslavia)

National holiday: Independence Day, 8 October (1991) and Statehood Day, 25 June (1991); note—25 June 1991 was the day the Croatian parliament voted for independence; following a three-month moratorium to allow the European Community to solve the Yugoslav crisis peacefully, parliament adopted a decision on 8 October 1991 to sever constitutional relations with Yugoslavia

Constitution: several previous; latest adopted 22 December 1990; amended several times, last in 2014 (2016)

Legal system: civil law system influenced by legal heritage of Austria-Hungary; note—Croatian law was fully harmonized with the European Community acquis as of the June 2010 completion of EU accession negotiations

International law organization participation: has not submitted an ICJ jurisdiction declaration; accepts ICCt jurisdiction

Citizenship: *citizenship by birth:* no
citizenship by descent only: at least one parent must be a citizen of Croatia
dual citizenship recognized: yes
residency requirement for naturalization: 5 years

Suffrage: 18 years of age, 16 if employed; universal
Executive branch: *chief of state:* President Kolinda GRABAR-KITAROVIC (since 19 February 2015)

head of government: Interim Prime Minister Tihomir ORESKOVIC (since 16 June 2016); Deputy Prime Minister Bozo PETROV (since 22 January 2016); note—Deputy Prime Minister Tomislav Karamarko (since 22 January 2016) resigned 15 June 2016; Prime Minister Tihomir ORESKOVIC (since 22 January 2016) was ousted in a no-confidence vote on 16 June 2016 but remains as the interim prime minister; there is a 30-day deadline to form a new government
cabinet: Council of Ministers named by the prime minister and approved by the Assembly

elections/appointments: president directly elected by absolute majority popular vote in 2 rounds if needed for a 5-year term (eligible for a second term); election last held on 28 December 2014 and 11 January 2015 (next to be held in 2019); the leader of the majority party or majority coalition usually appointed prime minister by the president and approved by the Assembly
election results: Kolinda GRABAR-KITAROVIC elected president; percent of vote in the second round -Kolinda GRABAR-KITAROVIC (HDZ) 50.7%, Ivo JOSIPOVIC (Forward Croatia Progressive Alliance) 49.3%

Legislative branch: *description:* unicameral Assembly or Hrvatski Sabor (151 seats; members directly elected by party-list proportional representation vote using the D'Hondt method with a 5% threshold: 14 seats in each of 10 districts; 8 seats in a single nationwide district for minorities; 3 seats in a single special district for the Croatian diaspora, members serve for 4-year terms)
elections: last held on 8 November 2015 (next likely to be held in mid-September)—Assembly voted on 20 June 2016 to dissolve on 15 July 2016, resulting in snap elections
election results: percent of vote by party/coalition—NA; number of seats by party/coalition—Patriotic Coalition (included HDZ, HSP AS, HSS) 59, Croatia is Growing (included SDP, HNS, Croatian Laborists -Labor Party, HSU) 56, Most-NL 19, Our Own Right (included IDS) 3, Labor and Solidarity Coalition (included New Wave) 2, HDSSB 2, Human Blockade 1, Successful Croatia (included People's Party—Reformists Party, Forward Croatia!, Progressive Alliance) 1, minorities 8 (included SDSS 3)
note: seats by party as of 8 March 2016—HDZ 51, SDP 42, Most-NL 16, HNS 9, minorities 8 (includes SDSS 3), IDS 3, HSP AS 3, Croatian Laborists—Labor Party 3, HDSSB 2, HSLS 2, HSU 2, BM365-SRS 2, HRID 2, People's Party—Reformists Party 1, BUZ 1, HDS 1, HRAST 1 Human Blockade 1, Independent List Petrina 1

Judicial branch: *highest court(s):* Supreme Court (consists of the court president and vice president, 25 civil department justices, and 16 criminal department justices)
judge selection and term of office: president of Supreme Court nominated by president of Croatia and elected by Croatian Sabor for a 4-year term; other Supreme Court justices appointed by National Judicial Council; all judges serve until age 70
subordinate courts: Administrative Court; county, municipal, and specialized courts; note—there is an 11-member Constitutional Court with jurisdiction limited to constitutional issues but is outside Croatia's judical system

Political parties and leaders: Bloc of Pensioners Together or BUZ [Milivoj SPIKA]
Bridge of Independent Lists or Most-NL [Bozo PETROV]
Croatia is Growing [Zoran MILANOVIC] (coalition including SDP, HNS, Croatian

Laborists—Labor Party, HSU) Croatian Christian Democratic Party or HDS [Goran DODIG]

Croatian Democratic Congress of Slavonia and Baranja or HDSSB [Dragan VULIN]

Croatian Democratic Union or HDZ (vacant)

Croatian Initiative for Dialogue or HRID [Drago PRGOMET]

Croatian Laborists—Labor Party [Nansi TIRELI]

Croatian Party of Rights—dr. Ante Starcevic or HSP AS [Ivan TEPES]

Croatian Peasant Party or HSS [Branko HRG]

Croatian Pensioner Party or HSU [Silvano HRELJA]

Croatian People's Party—Liberal Democrats or HNS [Vesna PUSIC]

Croatian Social Liberal Party or HSLS [Darinko KOSOR]

Forward Croatia Progressive Alliance [Ivo JOSIPOVIC]

Human Blockade [Ivan SINCIC]

Independent Democratic Serb Party or SDSS [Vojislav STANIMIROVIC]

Independent List Petrina [Stipe PETRINA]

Istrian Democratic Assembly or IDS [Boris MILETIC]

Istrian Democrats [Damir KAJIN]

Milan Bandic 365—Party of Labor and Solidarity or BM365-SRS [Milan BANDIC]

Movement for Successful Croatia or HRAST [Ladislav ILCIC]

Patriotic Coalition [Tomislav KARAMARKO] (including HDZ, HSP AS, HSS, BUZ, HDS, HSLS, HRAST)

People's Party—Reformists Party [Radimir CACIC]

Social Democratic Party of Croatia or SDP [Zoran MILANOVIC]

Political pressure groups and leaders: *other:* human rights groups

International organization participation: Australia Group, BIS, BSEC (observer), CD, CE, CEI, EAPC, EBRD, ECB, EMU, EU, FAO, G-11, IADB, IAEA, IBRD, ICAO, ICC (national committees), ICCt, ICRM, IDA, IFAD, IFC, IFRCS, IHO, ILO, IMF, IMO, IMSO, Interpol, IOC, IOM, IPU, ISO, ITSO, ITU, ITUC (NGOs), MIGA, MINURSO, NAM (observer), NATO, NSG, OAS (observer), OIF (observer), OPCW, OSCE, PCA, SELEC, UN, UNCTAD, UNESCO, UNFICYP, UNHCR, UNIDO, UNIFIL, UNMIL, UNMOGIP, UNWTO, UPU, WCO, WHO, WIPO, WMO, WTO, ZC

Diplomatic representation in the US: *chief of mission:* Ambassador Josip "Josko" PARO (since 20 April 2012)

chancery: 2343 Massachusetts Avenue NW, Washington, DC 20008

telephone: [1] (202) 588-5899

FAX: [1] (202) 588-8936

consulate(s) general: Chicago, Los Angeles, New York

Diplomatic representation from the US: *chief of mission:* Ambassador Julieta Valls NOYES (since 5 October 2015)

embassy: 2 Thomas Jefferson Street, 10010 Zagreb

mailing address: use embassy street address

telephone: [385] (1) 661-2200

FAX: [385] (1) 661-2373

Flag description: three equal horizontal bands of red (top), white, and blue—the Pan-Slav colors—superimposed by the Croatian coat of arms; the coat of arms consists of one main shield (a checkerboard of 13 red and 12 silver (white) fields) surmounted by five smaller shields that form a crown over the main shield; the five small shields represent five historic regions (from left to right): Croatia, Dubrovnik, Dalmatia, Istria, and Slavonia

note: the Pan-Slav colors were inspired by the 19th-century flag of Russia

National symbol(s): red-white checkerboard; national colors: red, white, blue

National anthem: *name:* "Lijepanasa domovino" (Our Beautiful Homeland)

lyrics/music: Antun MIHANOVIC/Josip RUNJANIN

note: adopted 1972; "Lijepa nasa domovino," whose lyrics were written in 1835, served as an unofficial anthem beginning in 1891

ECONOMY

Economy—overview: Though still one of the wealthiest of the former Yugoslav republics, Croatia's economy suffered badly during the 1991-95 war. The country's output during that time collapsed, and Croatia missed the early waves of investment in Central and Eastern Europe that followed the fall of the Berlin Wall. Between 2000 and 2007, however, Croatia's economic fortunes began to improve with moderate but steady GDP growth between 4% and 6% led by a rebound in tourism and credit-driven consumer spending. Inflation over the same period remained tame and the currency, the kuna, stable.

Croatia experienced an abrupt slowdown in the economy in 2008 and has yet to recover; economic growth was stagnant or negative in each year since 2009. Difficult problems still remain including a stubbornly high unemployment rate, uneven regional development, and a challenging investment climate. Croatia continues to face reduced foreign investment.

On 1 July 2013, Croatia joined the EU, following a decade-long application process. Croatia will be a member of the European Exchange Rate Mechanism until it meets the criteria for joining the Economic and Monetary Union and adopts the euro as its currency. EU accession has increased pressure on the government to reduce Croatia's relatively high public debt, which triggered the EU's excessive deficit procedure for fiscal consolidation. Zagreb has cut spending since 2012, and the government also raised additional revenues through more stringent tax collection and by raising the value-added tax. The government has also sought to accelerate privatization of non-strategic assets, with mixed success.

GDP (purchasing power parity): $91.1 billion (2015 est.)

$89.62 billion (2014 est.)

$89.95 billion (2013 est.)

note: data are in 2015 US dollars

country comparison to the world: 85

GDP (official exchange rate): $48.85 billion (2015 est.)

GDP—real growth rate: 1.6% (2015 est.)

-0.4% (2014 est.)

-1.1% (2013 est.)

country comparison to the world: 151

GDP—per capita (PPP): $21,600 (2015 est.)

$21,100 (2014 est.)

$21,100 (2013 est.)

note: data are in 2015 US dollars

country comparison to the world: 83

Gross national saving: 22.7% of GDP (2015 est.)

18.9% of GDP (2014 est.)

19.9% of GDP (2013 est.)

country comparison to the world: 64

GDP—composition, by end use:

household consumption: 59.6%

government consumption: 19.8%

investment in fixed capital: 18.7%

investment in inventories: -0.3%

exports of goods and services: 49%

imports of goods and services: -46.8% (2015 est.)

GDP—composition, by sector of origin: *agriculture:* 4.3%

industry: 26.7%

services: 69.1% (2015 est.)

Agriculture—products: arable crops (wheat, corn, barley, sugar beet, sunflower, rapeseed, alfalfa, clover); vegetables (potatoes, cabbage, onion, tomato, pepper); fruits (apples, plum, mandarins, olives), grapes for wine; livestock (cattle, cows, pigs); dairy products

Industries: chemicals and plastics, machine tools, fabricated metal, electronics, pig iron and rolled steel products, aluminum, paper, wood products, construction materials, textiles, shipbuilding, petroleum and petroleum refining, food and beverages, tourism

Industrial production growth rate: 2.6% (2015 est.)

country comparison to the world: 100

Labor force: 1.708 million (2015 est.)

country comparison to the world: 126

Labor force—by occupation: *agriculture:* 1.9%

industry: 27.6%

services: 70.4% (2014)

Unemployment rate: 19.3% (2015 est.)

20.3% (2014 est.)

country comparison to the world: 168

Population below poverty line: 19.5% (2014 est.)

Household income or consumption by percentage share: *lowest:* 10%: 3.3%

highest: 10%: 27.5% (2008 est.)

Distribution of family income—Gini index: 32 (2010)

29 (1998)

country comparison to the world: 112

Budget: *revenues:* $20.49 billion

expenditures: $22.91 billion (2015 est.)

Taxes and other revenues: 41.9% of GDP (2015 est.)

country comparison to the world: 31

Budget surplus (+) or deficit (-): -5% of GDP (2015 est.)

country comparison to the world: 171

Public debt: 89.5% of GDP (2015 est.)

85.1% of GDP (2014 est.)

country comparison to the world: 26

Fiscal year: calendar year

Inflation rate (consumer prices): -0.5% (2015 est.)
-0.2% (2014 est.)
country comparison to the world: 25

Central bank discount rate: 7% (31 December 2013)
7% (31 December 2012)
country comparison to the world: 46

Commercial bank prime lending rate: 7.8% (31 December 2015 est.)
7.8% (31 December 2014 est.)
country comparison to the world: 111

Stock of narrow money: $8.822 billion (31 December 2015 est.)
$10.07 billion (31 December 2014 est.)
country comparison to the world: 83

Stock of broad money: $49.38 billion (31 December 2014 est.)
$49.24 billion (31 December 2013 est.)
country comparison to the world: 69

Stock of domestic credit: $38.42 billion (31 December 2015 est.)
$47.3 billion (31 December 2014 est.)
country comparison to the world: 67

Market value of publicly traded shares: $36.29 billion (31 December 2014 est.)
$33.75 billion (31 December 2013)
$33.44 billion (31 December 2012 est.)
country comparison to the world: 58

Current account balance: $2.143 billion (2015 est.)
$380 million (2014 est.)
country comparison to the world: 32

Exports: $12.23 billion (2015 est.)
$12.95 billion (2014 est.)
country comparison to the world: 83

Exports—commodities: transport equipment, machinery, textiles, chemicals, foodstuffs, fuels

Exports—partners: Italy 13.4%, Slovenia 12.5%, Germany 11.4%, Bosnia and Herzegovina 9.9%, Austria 6.6%, Serbia 4.9% (2015)

Imports: $19.28 billion (2015 est.) $21.39 billion (2014 est.)
country comparison to the world: 76

Imports—commodities: machinery, transport and electrical equipment; chemicals, fuels and lubricants; foodstuffs

Imports—partners: Germany 15.5%, Italy 13.1%, Slovenia 10.7%, Austria 9.2%, Hungary 7.8% (2015)

Reserves of foreign exchange and gold: $13.94 billion (31 December 2015 est.)
$15.42 billion (31 December 2014 est.)
country comparison to the world: 71

Debt—external: $62.09 billion (31 December 2014 est.)
$61.04 billion (31 December 2013 est.)
country comparison to the world: 59

Stock of direct foreign investment—at home: $42 billion (31 December 2015 est.)
$40.19 billion (31 December 2014 est.)
country comparison to the world: 63

Stock of direct foreign investment—abroad: $7.712 billion (31 December 2015 est.)

$7.792 billion (31 December 2014 est.)
country comparison to the world: 64

Exchange rates: kuna (HRK) per US dollar—
6.927 (2015 est.)
5.7482 (2014 est.)
5.7482 (2013 est.)
5.85 (2012 est.)
5.3439 (2011 est.)

ENERGY

Electricity—production: 13.38 billion kWh (2014 est.)
country comparison to the world: 88

Electricity—consumption: 16.97 billion kWh (2014 est.)
country comparison to the world: 74

Electricity—exports: 2.866 billion kWh (2014 est.)
country comparison to the world: 38

Electricity—imports: 6.592 billion kWh (2014 est.)
country comparison to the world: 37

Electricity—installed generating capacity: 4.22 million kW (2012 est.)
country comparison to the world: 80

Electricity—from fossil fuels: 37.1% of total installed capacity (2013 est.)
country comparison to the world: 168

Electricity—from nuclear fuels: 7.7% of total installed capacity (2013 est.)
country comparison to the world: 21

Electricity—from hydroelectric plants: 48.5% of total installed capacity (2013 est.)
country comparison to the world: 50

Electricity—from other renewable sources: 6.6% of total installed capacity (2013 est.)
country comparison to the world: 53

Crude oil—production: 10,070 bbl/day (2014 est.)
country comparison to the world: 79

Crude oil—exports: 0 bbl/day (2014 est.)
country comparison to the world: 138

Crude oil—imports: 37,300 bbl/day (2014 est.)
country comparison to the world: 56

Crude oil—proved reserves: 71 million bbl (1 January 2015 est.)
country comparison to the world: 77

Refined petroleum products—production: 56,650 bbl/day (2014 est.)
country comparison to the world: 80

Refined petroleum products—consumption: 75,000 bbl/day (2013 est.)
country comparison to the world: 86

Refined petroleum products—exports: 29,060 bbl/day (2014 est.)
country comparison to the world: 69

Refined petroleum products—imports: 32,890 bbl/day (2014 est.)
country comparison to the world: 94

Natural gas—production: 1.805 billion cu m (2014 est.)
country comparison to the world: 57

Natural gas—consumption: 2.81 billion cu m (2014 est.)
country comparison to the world: 75

Natural gas—exports: 422 million cu m (2014 est.)

country comparison to the world: 40

Natural gas—imports: 1.079 billion cu m (2014 est.)
country comparison to the world: 57

Natural gas—proved reserves: 24.92 billion cu m (1 January 2014 est.)
country comparison to the world: 72

Carbon dioxide emissions from consumption of energy: 5.598 million Mt (2012 est.)
country comparison to the world: 124

COMMUNICATIONS

Telephones—fixed lines: *total subscriptions:* 1.57 million
subscriptions per 100 inhabitants: 35 (2014 est.)
country comparison to the world: 66

Telephones—mobile cellular: *total:* 4.5 million
subscriptions per 100 inhabitants: 100 (2014 est.)
country comparison to the world: 123

Telephone system: *general assessment:* the telecommunications network has improved steadily since the mid-1990s, covering much of what were once inaccessible areas; local lines are digital
domestic: fixed-line teledensity holding steady at about 40 per 100 persons; mobile-cellular telephone subscriptions exceed the population
international: country code—385; digital international service is provided through the main switch in Zagreb; Croatia participates in the Trans-Asia-Europe fiber-optic project, which consists of 2 fiber-optic trunk connections with Slovenia and a fiber-optic trunk line from Rijeka to Split and Dubrovnik; the ADRIA-1 submarine cable provides connectivity to Albania and Greece (2011)

Broadcast media: the national state-owned public broadcaster, Croatian Radiotelevision, operates 4 terrestrial TV networks, a satellite channel that rebroadcasts programs for Croatians living abroad, and 6 regional TV centers; 2 private broadcasters operate national terrestrial networks; roughly 25 privately owned regional TV stations; multi-channel cable and satellite TV subscription services are available; state-owned public broadcaster operates 3 national radio networks and 9 regional radio stations; 2 privately owned national radio networks and more than 170 regional, county, city, and community radio stations (2012)
Radio broadcast stations: AM 16, FM 98, shortwave 5 (1999)
Television broadcast stations: 36 (plus 321 repeaters) (1995)

Internet country code: .hr
Internet hosts: 729,420 (2012)
country comparison to the world: 50
Internet users: *total:* 2.9 million
percent of population: 65.1% (2014 est.)
country comparison to the world: 86

TRANSPORTATION

Airports: 69 (2013)
country comparison to the world: 72
Airports—with paved runways: *total:* 24
over 3,047 m: 2
2,438 to 3,047 m: 6

1,524 to 2,437 m: 3
914 to 1,523 m: 3
under 914 m: 10 (2013)
Airports—with unpaved runways: *total:* 45
1,524 to 2,437 m: 1
914 to 1,523 m: 6
under 914 m: 38 (2013)
Heliports: 1 (2013)
Pipelines: gas 2,410 km; oil 610 km (2011)
Railways: *total:* 2,722 km
standard gauge: 2,722 km 1.435-m gauge (985 km electrified) (2014)
country comparison to the world: 61
Roadways: *total:* 26,958 km (includes 1,416 km of expressways) (2015)
country comparison to the world: 97
Waterways: 785 km (2009)
country comparison to the world: 73
Merchant marine: *total:* 77
by type: bulk carrier 24, cargo 7, chemical tanker 8, passenger/cargo 27, petroleum tanker 10, refrigerated cargo 1
foreign-owned: 2 (Norway 2)
registered in other countries: 31 (Bahamas 1, Belize 1, Liberia 1, Malta 6, Marshall Islands 12, Panama 2, Saint Vincent and the Grenadines 8) (2010)
country comparison to the world: 57

Ports and terminals: *major seaport(s):* Ploce, Rijeka, Sibernik, Split
river port(s): Vukovar (Danube)
oil terminal(s): Omisalj

MILITARY AND SECURITY

Military branches: Armed Forces of the Republic of Croatia (Oruzane Snage Republike Hrvatske, OSRH) consists of five major commands directly subordinate to a General Staff: Ground Forces (Hrvatska Kopnena Vojska, HKoV), Naval Forces (Hrvatska Ratna Mornarica, HRM; includes coast guard), Air Force and Air Defense Command (Hrvatsko Ratno Zrakoplovstvo I Protuzracna Obrana), Joint Education and Training Command, Logistics Command; Military Police Force supports each of the three Croatian military forces (2012)

Military service age and obligation: 18–27 years of age for voluntary military service; 6-month service obligation (2012)
Military expenditures: 1.38% of GDP (2015)
1.41% of GDP (2014)
1.47% of GDP (2013)
1.7% of GDP (2012)
1.77% of GDP (2011)
country comparison to the world: 51

TRANSNATIONAL ISSUES

Disputes—international: dispute remains with Bosnia and Herzegovina over several small sections of the boundary related to maritime access that hinders ratification of the 1999 border agreement; since the breakup of Yugoslavia in the early 1990s, Croatia and Slovenia have each claimed sovereignty over Pirin Bay and four villages, and Slovenia has objected to Croatia's claim of an exclusive economic zone in the Adriatic Sea; in 2009, however Croatia and Slovenia signed a binding international arbitration agreement to define their disputed land and maritime borders, which led to Slovenia lifting its objections to Croatia joining the EU; Slovenia continues to impose a hard border Schengen regime with Croatia, which joined the EU in 2013 but has not yet fulfilled Schengen requirements

Refugees and internally displaced persons: *stateless persons:* 2,873 (2015)
note: 658,036 estimated refugee and migrant arrivals (2015—March 2016)

Illicit drugs: transit point along the Balkan route for Southwest Asian heroin to Western Europe; has been used as a transit point for maritime shipments of South American cocaine bound for Western Europe (2008)

CUBA

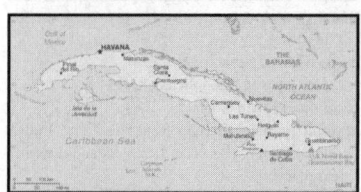

INTRODUCTION

Background: The native Amerindian population of Cuba began to decline after the European discovery of the island by Christopher COLUMBUS in 1492 and following its development as a Spanish colony during the next several centuries. Large numbers of African slaves were imported to work the coffee and sugar plantations, and Havana became the launching point for the annual treasure fleets bound for Spain from Mexico and Peru. Spanish rule eventually provoked an independence movement and occasional rebellions that were harshly suppressed. US intervention during the Spanish-American War in 1898 assisted the Cubans in overthrowing Spanish ru le. The Treaty of Paris established Cuban in dependence from Spain in 1898 and, following three-and-a-half years of subsequent US military rule, Cuba became an independent republic in 1902 after which the island experienced a string of governments mostly dominated by the military and corrupt politicians. Fidel CASTRO led a rebel army to victory in 1959; his authoritarian rule held the

subsequent regime together for nearly five decades. He stepped down as president in February 2008 in favor of his younger brother Raul CASTRO. Cuba's communist revolution, with Soviet support, was exported throughout Latin America and Africa during the 1960s, 1970s, and 1980s.
The country faced as evere economic downtu rn in 1990 following the with drawal of former Soviet subsidies worth $4–6 billion annually. Cuba at times portrays the US embargo, in place since 1961, as the source of its difficulties. Illicit migration to the US—using homemade rafts, alien smugglers, air flights, or via the US's southern border—is a continuing problem. In FY 2014, the US Coast Guard interdicted 2,111 Cuban nationals at sea, the highest number since FY 2008. Also in FY 2014, 24,289 Cuban migrants presented themselves at various land border ports of entry through out the US. As a result of efforts begun in December 2014 by President OBAMA to re-establishment diplomatic relations with the Cuban government, which were severed in January 1961, the US and Cuba reopened embassies in their respective countries on 20 July 2015. Over the past decade, there has been growing communication with the Cuban Government to address national interests .

GEOGRAPHY

Location: Caribbean, island between the Caribbean Sea and the North Atlantic Ocean, 150 km south of Key West, Florida

Geographic coordinates: 21 30 N, 80 00 W
Map references: Central America and the Caribbean
Area: *total:* 110,860 sq km
land: 109,820 sq km
water: 1,040 sq km
country comparison to the world: 106
Area—comparative: slightly smaller than Pennsylvania
Land boundaries: *total:* 28.5 km border countries: US Naval Base at Guantanamo Bay 28.5 km
note: Guantanamo Naval Base is leased by the US and remains part of Cuba
Coastline: 3,735 km
Maritime claims: *territorial sea:* 12 nm
contiguous zone: 24 nm
exclusive economic zone: 200 nm
Climate: tropical; moderated by trade winds; dry season (November to April); rainy season (May to October)
Terrain: mostly flat to rolling plains, with rugged hills and mountains in the southeast
Elevation: mean elevati on: 108 m
elevation extremes: lowest point: Caribbean Sea 0 m
highest point: Pico Turquino 2,005 m
Natural resources: cobalt, nickel, iron ore, chromium, copper, salt, timber, silica, petroleum, arable land:
Land use: *agricultural land:* 60.3%
arable land: 33.8%

permanent crops: 3.6%
permanent pasture: 22.9%
forest: 27.3%
other: 12.4% (2011 est.)
Irrigated land: 8,700 sq km (2012)

Total renewable water resources: 38.12 cu km (2011)

Freshwater withdrawal (domestic/industrial/agricultural): *total:* 4.42 cu m/yr (22%/14%/65%)
per capita: 392.6 cu m/yr (2010)

Natural hazards: the east coast is subject to hurricanes from August to November (in general, the country averages about one hurricane every other year); droughts are common

Environment—current issues: air and water pollution; biodiversity loss; deforestation

Environment—international agreements: *party to:* Antarctic Treaty, Biodiversity, Climate Change, Climate Change-Kyoto Protocol, Desertification, Endangered Species, Environmental Modification, Hazardous Wastes, Law of the Sea, Marine Dumping, Ozone Layer Protection, Ship Pollution, Wetlands
signed, but not ratified: Marine Life Conservation

Geography—note: largest country in Caribbean and westernmost island of the Greater Antilles

PEOPLE AND SOCIETY

Nationality: noun: Cuban(s)
adjective: Cuban

Ethnic groups: white 64.1%, mestizo 26.6%, black 9.3% (2012 est.)

Languages: Spanish (official)

Religions: nominally Roman Catholic 85%, Protestant, Jehovah's Witnesses, Jewish, Santeria
note: prior to CASTRO assuming power

Population: 11,031,433 (July 2015 est.)
country comparison to the world: 80

Age structure: *0–14 years:* 15.96% (male 904,800/female 855,309)
15–24 years: 13.29% (male 752,160/female 714,384)
25–54 years: 47.16% (male 2,620,536/female 2,581,344)
55–64 years: 10.65% (male 562,207/female 612,438)
65 years and over: 12.95% (male 639,515/female 788,740) (2015 est.)

Dependency ratios: *total dependency ratio:* 43.4%
youth dependency ratio: 23.4%
elderly dependency ratio: 20%
potential support ratio: 5% (2015 est.)

Median age: *total:* 40.4 years
male: 39.5 years
female: 41.3 years (2015 est.)
country comparison to the world: 41

Population growth rate: -0.15% (2015 est.)
country comparison to the world: 210

Birth rate: 9.9 births/1,000 population (2015 est.)
country comparison to the world: 196

Death rate: 7.72 deaths/1,000 population (2015 est.)
country comparison to the world: 106

Net migration rate: -3.66 migrant(s)/1,000 population (2015 est.)
country comparison to the world: 188

Urbanization: *urban population:* 77.1% of total population (2015)
rate of urbanization: 0.07% annual rate of change (2010–15 est.)

Major urban areas—population: HAVANA (capital) 2.137 million (2015)

Sex ratio: *at birth:* 1.06 male(s)/female
0–14 years: 1.06 male(s)/female
15–24 years: 1.05 male(s)/female
25–54 years: 1.02 male(s)/female
55–64 years: 0.92 male(s)/female
65 years and over: 0.81 male(s)/female
total population: 0.99 male(s)/female (2015 est.)

Maternal mortality rate: 39 deaths/100,000 live births (2015 est.)
country comparison to the world: 85

Infant mortality rate: *total:* 4.63 deaths/1,000 live births
male: 4.97 deaths/1,000 live births
female: 4.27 deaths/1,000 live births (2015 est.)
country comparison to the world: 180

Life expectancy at birth:
total population: 78.39 years
male: 76.08 years
female: 80.84 years (2015 est.)
country comparison to the world: 59

Total fertility rate: 1.47 children born/woman (2015 est.)
country comparison to the world: 200

Contraceptive prevalence rate: 74.3% (2010/11)

Health expenditures: 8.8% of GDP (2013)
country comparison to the world: 47

Physicians density: 6.72 physicians/1,000 population (2010)

Hospital bed density: 5.3 beds/1,000 population (2012)

Drinking water source:
improved:
urban: 96.4% of population
rural: 89.8% of population
total: 94.9% of population
unimproved:
urban: 3.6% of population
rural: 10.2% of population
total: 5.1% of population (2015 est.)

Sanitation facility access:
improved:
urban: 94.4% of population
rural: 89.1% of population
total: 93.2% of population
unimproved:
urban: 5.6% of population
rural: 10.9% of population
total: 6.8% of population (2015 est.)

HIV/AIDS—adult prevalence rate: 0.25% (2014 est.)
country comparison to the world: 94

HIV/AIDS—people living with HIV/AIDS: 17,100 (2014 est.)
country comparison to the world: 82

HIV/AIDS—deaths: 100 (2014 est.)
country comparison to the world: 126

Major infectious diseases: *degree of risk:* intermediate
food or waterborne diseases: bacterial diarrhea and hepatitis A
vectorborne diseases: dengue fever (2013)

Obesity—adult prevalence rate: 27.2% (2014)
country comparison to the world: 85

Education expenditures: 12.8% of GDP (2010)
country comparison to the world: 2

Literacy: *definition:* age 15 and over can read and write
total population: 99.8%
male: 99.9%
female: 99.8% (2015 est.)

School life expectancy (primary to tertiary education): *total:* 14 years
male: 14 years
female: 14 years (2014)

Unemployment, youth ages 15–24: *total:* 6.1%
male: 6.4%
female: 5.6% (2010 est.)
country comparison to the world: 131

People—note: illicit emigration is a continuing problem; Cubans attempt to depart the island and enter the US using homemade rafts, alien smugglers, direct flights, or falsified visas; Cubans also use non-maritime routes to enter the US including direct flights to Miami and overland via the southwest border; the number of Cubans migrating to the US has surged since the beginning of improved US-Cuban relations in late December 2014

GOVERNMENT

Country name: *conventional long form:* Republic of Cuba
conventional short form: Cuba
local long form: Republica de Cuba
local short form: Cuba
etymology: name derives from the Taino Indian designation for the island "coabana" meaning "great place"

Government type: communist state

Capital: *name:* Havana

Geographic coordinates: 23 07 N, 82 21 W
time difference: UTC-5 (same time as Washington, DC, during Standard Time)
daylight saving time: +1hr, begins second Sunday in March; ends first Sunday in November; note -Cuba has been known to alter the schedule of DST on short notice in an attempt to conserve electricity for lighting

Administrative divisions: 15 provinces (provincias, singular—provincia) and 1 special municipality* (municipio especial); Artemisa, Camaguey, Ciego de Avila, Cienfuegos, Granma, Guantanamo, Holguin, Isla de la Juventud*, La Habana, Las Tunas, Matanzas, Mayabeque, Pinar del Rio, Sancti Spiritus, Santiago de Cuba, Villa Clara

Independence: 20 May 1902 (from Spain 10 December 1898; administered by the US from 1898 to 1902); not acknowledged by the Cuban Government as a day of independence

National holiday: Triumph of the Revolution (Liberation Day), 1 January (1959)

Constitution: several previous; latest adopted by referendum 15 February 1976, effective 24 February 1976; amended 1978, 1992, 2002 (2016)

Legal system: civil law system based on Spanish civil code

International law organization participation: has not submitted an ICJ jurisdiction declaration; non-party state to the ICCt

Citizenship: *citizenship by birth:* yes
citizenship by descent: yes
dual citizenship recognized: no
residency requirement for naturalization: unknown

Suffrage: 16 years of age; universal

Executive branch: *chief of state:* President of the Council of State and President of the Council of Ministers Gen. Raul CASTRO Ruz (president since 24 February 2008); First Vice President of the Council of State and First Vice President of the Council of Ministers Miguel DIAZ-CANEL Bermudez (since 24 February 2013); note—the president is both chief of state and head of government

head of government: President of the Council of State and President of the Council of Ministers Gen. Raul CASTRO Ruz (president since 24 February 2008); First Vice President of the Council of State and First Vice President of the Council of Ministers Miguel DIAZ-CANEL Bermudez (since 24 February 2013)

cabinet: Council of Ministers proposed by the president of the Council of State, appointed by the National Assembly or the 28-member Council of State, and elected by the assembly to act on its behalf when it is not in session

elections/appointments: president and vice presidents indirectly elected by the National Assembly for a 5-year term (no term limit); election last held on 24 February 2013 (next to be held in 2018)

election results: Gen. Raul CASTRO Ruz (PCC) reelected president; percent of National Assembly vote—100%; Miguel DIAZ-CANEL (PCC) Bermudez elected vice president; percent of National Assembly vote-100%

Legislative branch: *description:* unicameral National Assembly of People's Power or Asemblea Nacional del Poder Popular (614 seats; members directly elected by absolute majority in a modified two-round vote; members serve 5-year terms); note—the National Candidature Commission submits a slate of approved candidates who must obtain 50-percent of valid votes to be elected; if not, a byelection may be held or the seat remains vacant

elections: last held on 3 February 2013 (next to be held in 2018)

election results: Cuba's Communist Party is the only legal party, and officially sanctioned candidates run unopposed

Judicial branch: *highest court(s):* People's Supreme Court (consists of court president, vice president, 41 professional justices, and NA lay judges; organized into the "Whole," State Council, and criminal, civil, administrative, labor, crimes against the state, and military courts)

judge selection and term of office: professional judges elected by the National Assembly to serve

2.5-year terms; lay judges nominated by workplace collectives and neighborhood associations and elected by municipal or provincial assemblies; lay judges appointed for 5-year terms and serve up to 30 days per year

subordinate courts: People's Provincial Courts; People's Regional Courts; People's Courts

Political parties and leaders: Cuban Communist Party or PCC [Raul CASTRO Ruz, first secretary]

Political pressure groups and leaders: Cuban Commission for Human Rights and National Reconciliation
Damas de Blanco (Ladies in White) National Association of Small Farmers
Patriotic Union of Cuba
other: political dissidents and bloggers

International organization participation: ACP, ALBA, AOSIS, CELAC, FAO, G-77, IAEA, ICAO, ICC (national committees), ICRM, IFAD, IFRCS, IHO, ILO, IMO, IMSO, Interpol, IOC, IOM (observer), IPU, ISO, ITSO, ITU, LAES, LAIA, NAM, OAS (excluded from formal participation since 1962), OPANAL, OPCW, PCA, Petrocaribe, PIF (partner), UN, UNCTAD, UNESCO, UNIDO, Union Latina, UNWTO, UPU, WCO, WFTU (NGOs), WHO, WIPO, WMO, WTO

Diplomatic representation in the US: *chief of mission:* Ambassador Jose Ramon CABANAS Rodriguez (since 17 September 2015)
chancery: 2630 16th Street NW, Washington, DC 20009
telephone: [1] (202) 797-8518
FAX: NA
consulate(s) general: NA

Diplomatic representation from the US: *chief of mission:* Ambassador (vacant); Charge d'Affaires Jeffrey DELAURENTIS (since 20 July 2015)
embassy: Calzada between L&M Streets, Vedado, Havana mailing address: use embassy street address
telephone: [53] (7) 839-4100
FAX: NA

Flag description: five equal horizontal bands of blue (top, center, and bottom) alternating with white; a red equilateral triangle based on the hoist side bears a white, five-pointed star in the center; the blue bands refer to the three old divisions of the island: central, occidental, and oriental; the white bands describe the purity of the independence ideal; the triangle symbolizes liberty, equality, and fraternity, while the red color stands for the blood shed in the independence struggle; the white star, called La Estrella Solitaria (the Lone Star) lights the way to freedom and was taken from the flag of Texas
note: design similar to the Puerto Rican flag, with the colors of the bands and triangle reversed

National symbol(s): royal palm; national colors: red, white, blue

National anthem: *name:* "La Bayamesa" (The Bayamo Song)
lyrics/music: Pedro FIGUEREDO
note: adopted 1940; Pedro FIGUEREDO first performed "La Bayamesa" in 1868 during the Ten Years War against the Spanish; a leading figure in the uprising, FIGUEREDO was captured in 1870 and executed by a firing squad; just prior to the fusillade he is reputed to have shouted, "Morir por

la Patria es vivir" (To die for the country is to live), a line from the anthem

ECONOMY

Economy—overview: The government continues to balance the need for loosening its socialist economic system against a desire for firm political control. In April 2011, the government held the first Cuban Communist Party Congress in almost 13 years, during which leaders approved a plan for wide-ranging economic changes. Since then, the government has slowly and incrementally implemented limited economic reforms, including allowing Cubans to buy electronic appliances and cell phones, stay in hotels, and buy and sell used cars. The government has cut state sector jobs as part of the reform process, and it has opened up some retail services to "self-employment," leading to the rise of so-called "cuentapropistas" or entrepreneurs.

Approximately 476,000 Cuban workers are currently registered as self-employed.

The Cuban regime has updated its economic model to include permitting the private ownership and sale of real estate and new vehicles, allowing private farmers to sell agricultural goods directly to hotels, allowing the creation of non-agricultural cooperatives, adopting a new foreign investment law, and launching a "Special Development Zone" around the Mariel port.

Since late 2000, Venezuela has provided petroleum products to Cuba on preferential terms, supplying nearly 100,000 barrels per day. Cuba has been paying for the oil, in part, with the services of Cuban personnel in Venezuela, including some 30,000 medical professionals.

GDP (purchasing power parity): $128.5 billion (2014 est.)
$126.9 billion (2013 est.)
$123.5 billion (2012 est.)
note: data are in 2012 US dollars
country comparison to the world: 79

GDP (official exchange rate): $77.15 billion (2013 est.)
note: data are in Cuban Pesos at CUP 1 = US$ Official Exchange Rate

GDP—real growth rate: 1.3% (2014 est.)
2.7% (2013 est.)
3% (2012 est.)
country comparison to the world: 160

GDP—per capita (PPP): $10,200 (2010 est.)
$10,000 (2009 est.)
$10,000 (2008 est.)
note: data are in 2010 US dollars
country comparison to the world: 137

Gross national saving: 12.3% of GDP (2015 est.)
13.2% of GDP (2014 est.)
12.8% of GDP (2013 est.)
country comparison to the world: 137

GDP—composition, by end use:
household consumption: 55.8%
government consumption: 31.8%
investment in fixed capital: 10.9%
investment in inventories: 0.1%
exports of goods and services: 21.2%
imports of goods and services: -19.8% (2015 est.)

GDP—composition, by sector of origin:
agriculture: 4%

industry: 23.5%
services: 72.7% (2015 est.)

Agriculture—products: sugar, tobacco, citrus, coffee, rice, potatoes, beans; livestock

Industries: petroleum, nickel, cobalt, pharmaceuticals, tobacco, construction, steel, cement, agricultural machinery, sugar

Industrial production growth rate: 9.6% (2015 est.)
country comparison to the world: 9

Labor force: 5.111 million
note: state sector 72.3%, non-state sector 27.7% (2015 est.)
country comparison to the world: 81

Labor force—by occupation: *agriculture:* 18%
industry: 10%
services: 72% (2013 est.)

Unemployment rate: 3% (2015 est.)
2.7% (2014 est.)
note: these are official rates; unofficial estimates are about double the official figures
country comparison to the world: 26

Population below poverty line: NA%

Household income or consumption by percentage share: *lowest:* 10%: NA%
highest: 10%: NA%

Budget: *revenues:* $2.721 billion
expenditures: $2.919 billion (2015 est.)
Taxes and other revenues: 3.5% of GDP (2015 est.)
country comparison to the world: 216

Budget surplus (+) or deficit (-): -0.3% of GDP (2015 est.)
country comparison to the world: 38

Public debt: 31.6% of GDP (2015 est.)
32.1% of GDP (2014 est.)
country comparison to the world: 142

Fiscal year: calendar year

Inflation rate (consumer prices): 4.4% (2015 est.)
5.3% (2014 est.)
country comparison to the world: 163

Central bank discount rate: NA%

Commercial bank prime lending rate: NA%

Stock of narrow money: $1.307 billion (31 December 2015 est.)
$965.2 million (31 December 2014 est.)
country comparison to the world: 145

Stock of broad money: $24.63 billion (31 December 2013 est.)
$24.08 billion (31 December 2012 est.)
country comparison to the world: 81

Stock of domestic credit: $NA

Current account balance: -$145.7 million (2015 est.)
$1.996 billion (2014 est.)
country comparison to the world: 75

Exports: $4.41 billion (2015 est.)
$5.187 billion (2014 est.)
country comparison to the world: 113

Exports—commodities: petroleum, nickel, medical products, sugar, tobacco, fish, citrus, coffee

Exports—partners: Canada 17.8%, Venezuela 13.9%, China 13.1%, Netherlands 6.4%, Spain 5.4%, Belize 4.8% (2015)

Imports: $15.24 billion (2015 est.)

$13.11 billion (2014 est.)
country comparison to the world: 85

Imports—commodities: petroleum, food, machinery and equipment, chemicals

Imports—partners: Venezuela 31.8%, China 17.6%, Spain 10%, Brazil 4.8% (2015)

Reserves of foreign exchange and gold: $11.6 billion (31 December 2015 est.)
$11.1 billion (31 December 2014 est.)
country comparison to the world: 75

Debt—external: $25.21 billion (31 December 2014 est.)
$24.65 billion (31 December 2013 est.)
country comparison to the world: 78

Stock of direct foreign investment—at home: $NA
Stock of direct foreign investment—abroad: $4.138 billion (2006 est.)
country comparison to the world: 71

Exchange rates: Cuban pesos (CUP) per US dollar—
18.43 (2015 est.)
22.7 (2014 est.)
22.7 (2013 est.)
1 (2012 est.)
0.9847 (2011 est.)

ENERGY

Electricity—production: 19.14 billion kWh (2013 est.)
country comparison to the world: 76

Electricity—consumption: 16.2 billion kWh (2013 est.)
country comparison to the world: 76

Electricity—exports: 0 kWh (2013 est.)
country comparison to the world: 127

Electricity—imports: 0 kWh (2013 est.)
country comparison to the world: 137

Electricity—installed generating capacity: 6.055 million kW (2013 est.)
country comparison to the world: 72

Electricity—from fossil fuels: 99.3% of total installed capacity (2013 est.)
country comparison to the world: 48

Electricity—from nuclear fuels: 0% of total installed capacity (2013 est.)
country comparison to the world: 74

Electricity—from hydroelectric plants: 0.7% of total installed capacity (2013 est.)
country comparison to the world: 144

Electricity—from other renewable sources: 0.1% of total installed capacity (2013 est.)
country comparison to the world: 120

Crude oil—production: 50,000 bbl/day (2014 est.)
country comparison to the world: 56

Crude oil—exports: 74,000 bbl/day (2013 est.)
country comparison to the world: 40

Crude oil—imports: 160,000 bbl/day (2013 est.)
country comparison to the world: 37

Crude oil—proved reserves: 124 million bbl (1 January 2015 est.)
country comparison to the world: 71

Refined petroleum products—production: 92,660 bbl/day (2012 est.)
country comparison to the world: 74

Refined petroleum products—consumption: 170,000 bbl/day (2013 est.)
country comparison to the world: 63

Refined petroleum products—exports: 15,080 bbl/day (2012 est.)
country comparison to the world: 78

Refined petroleum products—imports: 24,640 bbl/day (2012 est.)
country comparison to the world: 101

Natural gas—production: 1.034 billion cu m (2013 est.)
country comparison to the world: 65

Natural gas—consumption: 1.034 billion cu m (2013 est.)
country comparison to the world: 89

Natural gas—exports: 0 cu m (2013 est.)
country comparison to the world: 84

Natural gas—imports: 0 cu m (2013 est.)
country comparison to the world: 184

Natural gas—proved reserves: 70.79 billion cu m (1 January 2014 est.)
country comparison to the world: 58

Carbon dioxide emissions from consumption of energy: 25.99 million Mt (2012 est.)
country comparison to the world: 78

COMMUNICATIONS

Telephones—fixed lines: *total subscriptions:* 1.26 million
subscriptions per 100 inhabitants: 11 (2014 est.)
country comparison to the world: 67

Telephones—mobile cellular: *total:* 2.5 million
subscriptions per 100 inhabitants: 23 (2014 est.)
country comparison to the world: 144

Telephone system: *general assessment:* greater investment beginning in 1994 and the establishment of a new Ministry of Information Technology and Communications in 2000 has resulted in improvements in the system; national fiber-optic system under development; 95% of switches digitized by end of 2006; mobile-cellular telephone service is expensive and must be paid in convertible pesos; around 1.3 million Cubans owned cell phones in 2011; state communications started service of email to cell phones through nauta.cu accounts; Cuban Government has opened Internet cafes around the island, which are expensive and offer slow-speed connections
domestic: fixed-line density remains low at 10 per 100 inhabitants; mobile-cellular service expanding but remains only about 10 per 100 persons
international: country code—53; the ALBA-1 fiber-optic submarine cable links Cuba, Jamaica, and Venezuela; fiber-optic cable laid to but not linked to US network; satellite earth station—1 Intersputnik (Atlantic Ocean region) (2011)

Broadcast media: government owns and controls all broadcast media with private ownership of electronic media prohibited; government operates 4 national TV networks and many local TV stations; government operates 6 national radio networks, an international station, and many local radio stations; Radio-TV Marti is beamed from the US (2007)

Radio broadcast stations: AM 169, FM 55, shortwave 1 (1998)
Television broadcast stations: 58 (1997)
Internet country code: .cu
Internet hosts: 3,244 (2012)
country comparison to the world: 154
Internet users: *total:* 3 million
percent of population: 27.5%
note: private citizens are prohibited from buying computers or accessing the Internet without special authorization; foreigners may access the Internet in large hotels but are subject to firewalls; some Cubans buy illegal passwords on the black market or take advantage of public outlets to access limited email and the government-controlled "intranet" (2014 est.)
country comparison to the world: 85

TRANSPORTATION

Airports: 133 (2013)
country comparison to the world: 43
Airports—with paved runways: *total:* 64
over 3,047 m: 7
2,438 to 3,047 m: 10
1,524 to 2,437 m: 16
914 to 1,523 m: 4
under 914 m: 27 (2013)
Airports—with unpaved runways: *total:* 69
914 to 1,523 m: 11
under 914 m: 58 (2013)
Pipelines: gas 41 km; oil 230 km (2013)
Railways: *total:* 8,285 km
standard gauge: 8,125 km 1.435-m gauge (105 km electrified)
narrow gauge: 160 km 1.000-m gauge
note: 82 km of standard gauge track is not for public use (2014)
country comparison to the world: 25
Roadways: *total:* 60,858 km

paved: 29,820 km (includes 639 km of expressways)
unpaved: 31,038 km (2001)
country comparison to the world: 68
Waterways: 240 km (almost all navigable inland waterways are near the mouths of rivers) (2011)
country comparison to the world: 94
Merchant marine: *total:* 3
by type: cargo 1, passen ger 1, refrigerated cargo 1
registered in other countries: 5 (Curacao 1, Panama 2, unknown 2) (2010)
country comparison to the world: 135
Ports and terminals: *major seaport(s):* Antilla, Cienfuegos, Guantanamo, Havana, Matanzas, Mariel, Nuevitas Bay, Santiago de Cuba

MILITARY AND SECURITY

Military branches: Revolutionary Armed Forces (Fuerzas Armadas Revolucionarias, FAR): Revolutionary Army (Ejercito Revolucionario, ER, includes Territorial Militia Troops (Milicia de Tropas de Territoriales, MTT)), Revolutionary Navy (Marina de Guerra Revolucionaria, MGR, includes Marine Corps), Revolutionary Air and Air Defense Forces (Defensas Anti-Aereas y Fuerza Aerea Revolucionaria, DAAFAR); Youth Labor Army (Ejercito Juvenil del Trabajo, EJT) (2013)
Military service age and obligation: 17–28 years of age for compulsory military service; 2-year service obligation; both sexes subject to military service (2012)
Military—note: the collapse of the Soviet Union deprived the Cuban military of its major economic and logistic support and had a significant impact on the state of Cuban equipment; the army remains well trained and professional in nature; the lack of replacement parts for its existing equipment has increasingly affected operational capabilities (2013)

TRANSNATIONAL ISSUES

Disputes—international: US Naval Base at Guantanamo Bay is leased to US and only mutual agreement or US abandonment of the facility can terminate the lease
Trafficking in persons: *current situation:* Cuba is a source country for adults and children subjected to sex trafficking and forced labor; child sex trafficking and child sex tourism occur in Cuba, while some Cubans are forced into prostitution in South America and the Caribbean; allegations have been made that some Cubans have been forced or coerced to work at Cuban medical missions abroad; assessing the scope of trafficking within Cuba is difficult because of the lack of information
tier rating: Tier 2 Watch List—Cuba does not fully comply with the minimum standards for the elimination of trafficking; however, it is making significant efforts to do so; Cuba's penal code does not criminalize all forms of human trafficking, but the government reported that it is in the process of amending its criminal code to comply with the 2000 UN TIP Protocol, to which it acceded in 2013; the government in 2014 prosecuted and convicted 13 sex traffickers and provided services to the victims in those cases but does not have shelters specifically for trafficking victims; the government did not recognize forced labor as a problem and took no action to address it; state media produced newspaper articles and TV and radio programs to raise public awareness about sex trafficking (2015)
Illicit drugs: territorial waters and air space serve as transshipment zone for US- and European-bound drugs; established the death penalty for certain drug-related crimes in 1999 (2008)

CURACAO

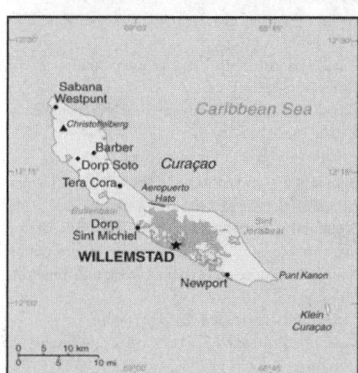

INTRODUCTION

Background: Originally settled by Arawak Indians, Curacao was seized by the Dutch in 1634 along with the neighboring island of Bonaire. Once the center of the Caribbean slave trade, Curacao was hard hit economically by the abolition of slavery in 1863. Its prosperity (and that of neighboring Aruba) was restored in the early 20th century with the construction of the Isla Refineria to service the newly discovered Venezuelan oil fields. In 1954, Curacao and several other Dutch Caribbean possessions were reorganized as the Netherlands Antilles, part of the Kingdom of the Netherlands. In referenda in 2005 and 2009, the citizens of Curacao voted to become a self-governing country within the Kingdom of the Netherlands. The change in status became effective in October 2010 with the dissolution of the Netherlands Antilles.

GEOGRAPHY

Location: Caribbean, an island in the Caribbean Sea, 30 nm off the coast of Venezuela
Geographic coordinates: 12 10 N, 69 00 W

Map references: Central America and the Caribbean
Area: *total:* 444 sq km
land: 444 sq km
water: 0 sq km
country comparison to the world: 200
Area—comparative: more than twice the size of Washington, DC
Land boundaries: 0 km
Coastline: 364 km
Maritime claims: *territorial sea:* 12 nm
exclusive fishing zone: 12 nm
Climate: tropical marine climate, ameliorated by northeast trade winds, results in mild temperatures; semiarid with average rainfall of 60 cm/year
Terrain: generally low, hilly terrain
Elevation: *mean elevation:* NA
elevation extremes: *lowest point:* Caribbean Sea 0 m
highest point: Mt. Christoffel 372 m

Natural resources: calcium phosphates, aloes, sorghum, peanuts, vegetables, tropical fruit

Land use: *agricultural land:* 10%
arable land: 10%
permanent crops: 0%
permanent pasture: 0%
forest: 0%
other: 90% (2011 est.)

Irrigated land: NA

Total renewable water resources: NA

Natural hazards: Curacao is south of the Caribbean hurricane belt and is rarely threatened

Environment—current issues: NA

Geography—note: Curacao is a part of the Windward Islands (southern) group

PEOPLE AND SOCIETY

Nationality: *noun:* Curacaoan
adjective: Curacaoan; Dutch

Ethnic groups: Afro-Caribbean majority; Dutch, French, Latin American, East Asian, South Asian, Jewish minorities

Languages: Papiamento (official) (a creole language that is a mixture of Portuguese, Spanish, Dutch, English, and, to a lesser extent, French, as well as elements of African languages and the language of the Arawak) 81.2%, Dutch (official) 8%, Spanish 4%, English (official) 2.9%, other 3.9% (2001 census)

Religions: Roman Catholic 72.8%, Pentecostal 6.6%, Protestant 3.2%, Adventist 3%, Jehovah's Witness 2%, Evangelical 1.9%, other 3.8%, none 6%, unspecified 0.6% (2011 est.)

Population: 148,406 (July 2015 est.)
country comparison to the world: 189

Age structure: *0–14 years:* 20.3% (male 15,334/female 14,739)
15–24 years: 14.7% (male 11,356/female 10,448)
25–54 years: 37.6% (male 27,125/female 28,716)
55–64 years: 13.2% (male 8,545/female 11,150)
65 years and over: 14.2% (male 8,698/female 12,340) (2015 est.)

Dependency ratios: *total dependency ratio:* 51.1%
youth dependency ratio: 28.7%
elderly dependency ratio: 22.4%
potential support ratio: 4.5% (2015 est.)

Median age: *total:* 36.1 years
male: 33 years
female: 39.9 years (2015 est.)
country comparison to the world: 69

Population growth rate: 0.43% (2015 est.)

Birth rate: 13.8 births/1,000 population (2015 est.)

Death rate: 8.2 deaths/1,000 population (2015 est.)
country comparison to the world: 98

Net migration rate: -1.4 migrant(s)/1,000 population (2015 est.)
country comparison to the world: 59

Urbanization: *urban population:* 89.3% of total population (2015)
rate of urbanization: 2.04% annual rate of change (2010–15 est.)

Major urban areas—population: WILLEMSTAD (capital) 145,000 (2014)

Sex ratio: *at birth:* 1.05 male(s)/female
0–14 years: 1.04 male(s)/female
15–24 years: 1.09 male(s)/female
25–54 years: 0.94 male(s)/female
55–64 years: 0.77 male(s)/female
65 years and over: 0.7 male(s)/female
total population: 0.92 male(s)/female (2015 est.)

Infant mortality rate: *total:* 7.9 deaths/1,000 live births
male: 8.5 deaths/1,000 live births
female: 7.3 deaths/1,000 live births (2015 est.)

Life expectancy at birth:
total population: 78.2 years
male: 75.9 years
female: 80.6 years (2015 est.)
country comparison to the world: 62

Total fertility rate: 2.07 children born/woman (2015 est.)
country comparison to the world: 107

HIV/AIDS—adult prevalence rate: NA

HIV/AIDS—people living with HIV/AIDS: NA

HIV/AIDS—deaths: NA

Education expenditures: 4.9% of GDP (2013)

School life expectancy (primary to tertiary education): *total:* 18 years
male: 18 years
female: 19 years (2013)

GOVERNMENT

Country name: *Dutch long form:* Land Curacao
Dutch short form: Curacao Papiamentu
long form: Pais Korsou Papiamentu
short form: Korsou
former: Netherlands Antilles; Curacao and Dependencies
etymology: the most plausible name derivation is that the island was designated Isla de la Curacion (Spanish meaning "Island of the Cure" or "Island of Healing") or Ilha da Curacao (Portuguese meaning the same) to reflect the locale's function as a recovery stop for sick crewmen

Dependency status: constituent country within the Kingdom of the Netherlands; full autonomy in internal affairs granted in 2010; Dutch Government responsible for defense and foreign affairs

Government type: parliamentary

Capital: *name:* Willemstad

Geographic coordinates: 12 06 N, 68 55 W
time difference: UTC-4 (1 hour ahead of Washington, DC, during Standard Time)

Administrative divisions: none (part of the Kingdom of the Netherlands)
note: Curacao is one of four constituent parts (countries) of the Kingdom of the Netherlands; the other three parts are the Netherlands, Aruba, and Sint Maarten

Independence: none (part of the Kingdom of the Netherlands)

National holiday: King's Day, 27 April 1967

Constitution: previous 1947, 1955; latest adopted 5 September 2010, entered into force 10 October 2010 (regulates governance of Curacao but is subordinate to the Charter for the Kingdom of the Netherlands); note—in October 2010, with the dissolution of the Netherlands Antilles, Curacao became a constituent country within the Kingdom of the Netherlands

Legal system: based on Dutch civil law system with some English common law influence

Citizenship: see the Netherlands

Suffrage: 18 years of age; universal

Executive branch: *chief of state:* King WILLEM-ALEXANDER of the Netherlands (since 30 April 2013); represented by Governor Lucille A. GEORGE-WOUT (since 4 November 2013)
head of government: Prime Minister Bernard WHITEMAN (1 September 2015); Prime Minister Ivar ASJES resigned 31 August 2015
cabinet: Cabinet appointed by the governor
elections: the monarch is hereditary; governor general appointed by the monarch; following legislative elections, the leader of the majority party is usually elected prime minister by the parliament; next election is scheduled for 2016

Legislative branch: *description:* unicameral Estates of Curacao or Staten van Curacao (21 seats; members directly elected by proportional representation vote to serve 4-year terms)
elections: last held 19 October 2012 (next to be held in 2016)
election results: percent of vote by party—PS 22.6%, MFK 21.2%, PAR 19.7%, PAIS 17.7%, MAN 9.5%, PNP 5.9%, other 3.4%; seats by party—PS 5, MFK 5, PAR 4, PAIS 4, MAN 2, PNP 1

Judicial branch: *highest court(s):* Common Court of Justice of Aruba, Curacao, Sint Maarten, Bonaire, Sint Eustatius and Saba (consists of judges from the subordinate courts) judge selection and terms of office: NA
subordinate courts: first instance courts, appeals court; specialized courts

Political parties and leaders: Movementu Futuro Korsou or MFK [Gerrit SCHOTTE]
Movishon Antia Nobo or MAN [Hensley KOEIMAN]
Partido Antia Restruktura or PAR [Zita JESUS-LEITO]
Partido pa Adelanto I Inovashon Soshal or PAIS [Alex ROSARIA]
Partido Nashonal di Pueblo or PNP [Humphrey DAVELAAR]
Pueblo Soberano or PS [Ivar ASJES]

Diplomatic representation in the US: none (represented by the Kingdom of the Netherlands)

Diplomatic representation from the US: *chief of mission:* Consul General James R. Moore (since June 2013); note—also accredited to Aruba and Sint Martin
consulate(s) general: J. B. Gorsiraweg
mailing address: P.O. Box 158, Willemstad, Curacao
telephone: [599] (9) 4613066
FAX: [599] (9) 4616489

Flag description: on a blue field a horizontal yellow band somewhat below the center divides the flag into proportions of 5:1:2; two five-pointed white stars—the smaller above and to the left of the larger—appear in the canton; the blue of the upper and lower sections symbolizes the sky and sea respectively; yellow represents the sun; the stars symbolize Curacao and its uninhabited smaller sister island of Klein Curacao; the five star points signify the five continents from which Curacao's people derive

National symbol(s): laraha (citrus tree); national colors: blue, yellow, white

National anthem: *name:* Himmo di Korsou (Anthem of Curacao)
lyrics/music: Guillermo ROSARIO, Mae HENRIQUEZ, Enrique MULLER, Betty DORAN/Frater Candidus NOWENS, Errol "El Toro" COLINA
note: adapted 1978; the lyrics, originally written in 1899, were rewritten in 1978 to make them less colonial in nature

ECONOMY

Economy—overview: Most of Curacao's GDP results from services. Tourism, petroleum refining and bunkering, offshore finance, and transportation and communications are the mainstays of this small island economy, which is closely tied to the outside world. Curacao has limited natural resources, poor soil, and inadequate water supplies, and budgetary problems complicate reform of the health and education systems. Although GDP grew only slightly during the past decade, Curacao enjoys a high per capita income and a well-developed infrastructure compared with other countries in the region.

Curacao has an excellent natural harbor that can accommodate large oil tankers, and the port of Willemstad hosts a free trade zone and a dry dock. Venezuelan state oil company PdVSA, under a contract in effect until 2019, leases the single refinery on the island from the government, directly employing some 1,000 people; most of the oil for the refinery is imported from Venezuela; most of the refined products are exported to the US and Asia. Almost all consumer and capital goods are imported, with the US, the Netherlands and Venezuela being the major suppliers.

The government is attempting to diversify its industry and trade and has signed an Association Agreement with the EU to expand business there. In 2013, the government implemented changes to the sales tax and reformed the public pension and health care systems, including increasing the sales tax from 5% to as high as 9% on some products, raising the age for public pension withdrawals to 65, and requiring citizens to pay higher premiums.

GDP (purchasing power parity): $3.128 billion (2012 est.)
$3.02 billion (2011 est.)
$2.96 billion (2010 est.)
note: data are in 2012 US dollars
country comparison to the world: 185

GDP (official exchange rate): $5.6 billion (2012 est.)

GDP—real growth rate: 3.6% (2012 est.)
2% (2011 est.)
0.1% (2010 est.)
country comparison to the world: 77

GDP—per capita (PPP): $15,000 (2004 est.)
country comparison to the world: 107

GDP—composition, by sector of origin: *agriculture:* 0.7%
industry: 15.5%
services: 83.8% (2012 est.)

Agriculture—products: aloe, sorghum, peanuts, vegetables, tropical fruit

Industries: tourism, petroleum refining, petroleum transshipment, light manufacturing, financial and business services

Industrial production growth rate: NA%

Labor force: 73,010 (2013)
country comparison to the world: 185

Labor force—by occupation: *agriculture:* 1.2%
industry: 16.9%
services: 81.8% (2008 est.)

Unemployment rate: 13% (2013 est.)
9.8% (2011 est.)
country comparison to the world: 141

Taxes and other revenues: 16.6% of GDP (2012 est.)
country comparison to the world: 182

Budget surplus (+) or deficit (-): -0.4% of GDP (2012 est.)
country comparison to the world: 44

Public debt: 33.2% of GDP (2012 est.)
40.6% of GDP (2011 est.)
country comparison to the world: 134

Inflation rate (consumer prices): 2.6% (2013 est.)
2.8% (2012 est.)
country comparison to the world: 131

Exports: $1.607 billion (2011 est.)
$1.44 billion (2010 est.)
country comparison to the world: 147

Exports—commodities: petroleum products

Imports: $1.285 billion (2011 est.)
$1.275 billion (2010 est.)
country comparison to the world: 174

Imports—commodities: crude petroleum, food, manufactures

Exchange rates: Netherlands Antillean guilders (ANG) per US dollar—
1.79 (2014)
1.79 (2013)
1.79 (2012 est.)
1.79 (2011 est.)

ENERGY

Electricity—producti on: 1.785 billion kWh (2012 est.)
country comparison to the world: 142

Electricity—consumption: 968 million kWh (2008 est.)
country comparison to the world: 152

Electricity—exports: 0 kWh (2009 est.)
country comparison to the world: 116

Electricity—imports: 0 kWh (2009 est.)
country comparison to the world: 127

Crude oil—proved reserves: 0 bbl (1 January 2011 est.)
country comparison to the world: 115

Refined petroleum products—production: 531 bbl/day (2010 est.)
country comparison to the world: 110

Refined petroleum products—consumption: 72,000 bbl/day (2010 est.)
country comparison to the world: 88

Refined petroleum products—exports: 211,100 bbl/day (2009 est.)
country comparison to the world: 33

Refined petroleum products—imports: 291,700 bbl/day (2009 est.)
country comparison to the world: 25

Natural gas—production: 0 cu m (2009 est.)
country comparison to the world: 167

Natural gas—consumption: 0 cu m (2009 est.)
country comparison to the world: 126

Natural gas—exports: 0 cu m (2009 est.)
country comparison to the world: 74

Natural gas—imports: 0 cu m (2009 est.)
country comparison to the world: 173

Natural gas—proved reserves: 0 cu m (1 January 2011 est.)
country comparison to the world: 121

COMMUNICATIONS

Telephone system: *international:* country code—599

Broadcast media: government-run Telecuracao operates a TV station and a radio station; several privately owned radio stations

Internet country code: .cw

Internet hosts: NA

Internet users: NA

TRANSPORTATION

Roadways: *total:* 550 km
country comparison to the world: 193

Ports and terminals: *major seaport(s):* Willemstad
oil terminal(s): Bullen Baai (Curacao Terminal)
bulk cargo port(s): Fuik Bay (phosphate rock)

MILITARY AND SECURITY

Military branches: no regular military forces; the Dutch Government controls foreign and defense policy (2012)

Military service age and obligation: no conscription (2010)

Military—note: defense is the responsibility of the Kingdom of the Netherlands

CYPRUS

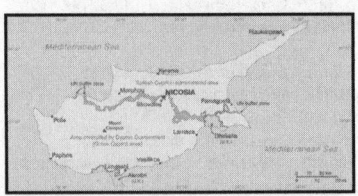

INTRODUCTION

Background: A former British colony, Cyprus became independent in 1960 following years of resistance to British rule. Tensions between the Greek Cypriot majority and Turkish Cypriot minority came to a head in December when violence broke out in the capital of Nicosia. Despite the deployment of UN peacekeepers in sporadic intercommunal violence continued, forcing most Turkish Cypriots into enclaves throughout the island. In 1974, a Greek Government-sponsored attempt to overthrow the elected president of Cyprus was met by military intervention from Turkey, which soon controlled more than a third of the island. In 1983, the Turkish Cypriot administered area declared itself the "Turkish Republic of Northern Cyprus" ("TRNC"), but it is recognized only by Turkey. A UN-mediated agreement, the Annan Plan, failed to win approval by both communities in 2004. In February 2014, after a hiatus of nearly two years, the leaders of the two communities resumed formal discussions under UN auspices aimed at reuniting the divided island. Talks were suspended in October 2014, but resumed in earnest in May 2015 following the election of a new Turkish Cypriot "president." The entire island entered the EU on 1 May 2004, although the EU acquis—the body of common rights and obligations—applies only to the areas under the internationally recognized government, and is suspended in the area administered by Turkish Cypriots. However, individual Turkish Cypriots able to document their eligibility for Republic of Cyprus citizenship legally enjoy the same rights accorded to other citizens of EU states.

GEOGRAPHY

Location: Middle East, island in the Mediterranean Sea, south of Turkey

Geographic coordinates: 35 00 N, 33 00 E

Map references: Middle East

Area: *total:* 9,251 sq km (of which 3,355 sq km are in north Cyprus)
land: 9,241 sq km
water: 10 sq km
country comparison to the world: 171

Area—comparative: about 0.6 times the size of Connecticut

Land boundaries: *total:* 156 km

border sovereign base areas: Akrotiri 48 km, Dhekelia 108 km

Coastline: 648 km

Maritime claims: *territorial sea:* 12 nm
contiguous zone: 24 nm
continental shelf: 200-m depth or to the depth of exploitation

Climate: temperate; Mediterranean with hot, dry summers and cool winters

Terrain: central plain with mountains to north and south; scattered but significant plains along southern coast

Elevation: *mean elevation:* 91 m

elevation extremes: *lowest point:* Mediterranean Sea 0 m
highest point: Mount Olympus 1,951 m

Natural resources: copper, pyrites, asbestos, gypsum, timber, salt, marble, clay earth pigment

Land use: *agricultural land:* 13.4%
arable land: 9.8%
permanent crops: 3.2%
permanent pasture: 0.4%
forest: 18.8%
other: 67.8% (2011 est.)

Irrigated land: 460 sq km (2012)

Total renewable water resources: 0.78 cu km (2011)

Freshwater withdrawal (domestic/industrial/agricultural): *total:* 0.18 cu m/yr (10%/3%/86%)
per capita: 164.7 cu m/yr (2009)

Natural hazards: moderate earthquake activity; droughts

Environment—current issues: water resource problems (no natural reservoir catchments, seasonal disparity in rainfall, sea water intrusion to island's largest aquifer, increased salination in the north); water pollution from sewage and industrial wastes; coastal degradation; loss of wildlife habitats from urbanization

Environment—international agreements: *party to:* Air Pollution, Air Pollution-Nitrogen Oxides, Air Pollution-Persistent Organic Pollutants, Air Pollution-Sulfur 94, Biodiversity, Climate Change, Climate Change-Kyoto Protocol, Desertification, Endangered Species, Environmental Modification, Hazardous Wastes, Law of the Sea, Marine Dumping, Ozone Layer Protection, Ship Pollution, Wetlands
signed, but not ratified: none of the selected agreements

Geography—note: the third largest island in the Mediterranean Sea (after Sicily and Sardinia)

PEOPLE AND SOCIETY

Nationality: *noun:* Cypriot(s)
adjective: Cypriot

Ethnic groups: Greek 98.8%, other 1% (includes Maronite, Armenian, Turkish-Cypriot), unspecified 0.2%

note: data represent only the government-controlled area of Cyprus (2011 est.)

Languages: Greek (official) 80.9%, Turkish (official) 0.2%, English 4.1%, Romanian 2.9%, Russian 2.5%, Bulgarian 2.2%, Arabic 1.2%, Filipino 1.1%, other 4.3%, unspecified 0.6%

note: data represent only the government-controlled area of Cyprus (2011 est.)

Religions: Orthodox Christian 89.1%, Roman Catholic 2.9%, Protestant/Anglican 2%, Muslim 1.8%, Buddhist 1%, other (includes Maronite, Armenian Church, Hindu) 1.4%, unknown 1.1%, none/atheist 0.6%

note: data represent only the government-controlled area of Cyprus (2011 est.)

Population: 1,189,197 (July 2015 est.)
country comparison to the world: 161

Age structure: *0–14 years:* 15.61% (male 95,431/female 90,159)
15–24 years: 14.87% (male 96,152/female 80,633)
25–54 years: 46.97% (male 293,582/female 264,935)
55–64 years: 11.05% (male 62,826/female 68,551)
65 years and over: 11.51% (male 59,363/female 77,565) (2015 est.)

Dependency ratios: *total dependency ratio:* 41.6%
youth dependency ratio: 23.4%
elderly dependency ratio: 18.2%
potential support ratio: 5.5% (2015 est.)

Median age: *total:* 36.1 years
male: 34.7 years
female: 37.7 years (2015 est.)
country comparison to the world: 68

Population growth rate: 1.43% (2015 est.)
country comparison to the world: 84

Birth rate: 11.41 births/1,000 population (2015 est.)
country comparison to the world: 172

Death rate: 6.62 deaths/1,000 population (2015 est.)
country comparison to the world: 143

Net migration rate: 9.48 migrant(s)/1,000 population (2015 est.)
country comparison to the world: 11

Urbanization: *urban population:* 66.9% of total population (2015)
rate of urbanization: 0.89% annual rate of change (2010–15 est.)

Major urban areas—population: NICOSIA (capital) 251,000 (2014)

Sex ratio: *at birth:* 1.05 male(s)/female
0–14 years: 1.06 male(s)/female
15–24 years: 1.19 male(s)/female
25–54 years: 1.11 male(s)/female
55–64 years: 0.92 male(s)/female
65 years and over: 0.77 male(s)/female
total population: 1.04 male(s)/female (2015 est.)

Mother's mean age at first birth: 28.5
note: data represent only government-controlled areas (2010 est.)

Maternal mortality rate: 7 deaths/100,000 live births (2015 est.)
country comparison to the world: 154
Infant mortality rate: *total:* 8.36 deaths/1,000 live births
male: 9.97 deaths/1,000 live births
female: 6.68 deaths/1,000 live births (2015 est.)
country comparison to the world: 152

Life expectancy at birth:
total population: 78.51 years
male: 75.7 years
female: 81.46 years (2015 est.)
country comparison to the world: 54
Total fertility rate: 1.46 children born/woman (2015 est.)
country comparison to the world: 202
Health expenditures: 7.4% of GDP (2013)
country comparison to the world: 72
Physicians density: 2.33 physicians/1,000 population (2012)
Hospital bed density: 3.5 beds/1,000 population (2011)
Drinking water source:
improved:
urban: 100% of population
rural: 100% of population
total: 100% of population
unimproved:
urban: 0% of population
rural: 0% of population
total: 0% of population (2015 est.)
Sanitation facility access:
improved:
urban: 100% of population
rural: 100% of population
total: 100% of population
unimproved:
urban: 0% of population
rural: 0% of population
total: 0% of population (2015 est.)
HIV/AIDS—adult prevalence rate: 0.06% (2013 est.)
country comparison to the world: 117
HIV/AIDS—people living with HIV/AIDS: 400 (2013 est.)
country comparison to the world: 125
HIV/AIDS—deaths: fewer than 100 (2013 est.)
country comparison to the world: 124
Obesity—adult prevalence rate: 24.5% (2014)
country comparison to the world: 53
Education expenditures: 6.6% of GDP (2011)
country comparison to the world: 19
Literacy: *definition:* age 15 and over can read and write
total population: 99.1%
male: 99.5%
female: 98.7% (2015 est.)
School life expectancy (primary to tertiary education): *total:* 14 years
male: 14 years
female: 15 years (2014)
Unemployment, youth ages 15–24: *total:* 38.9%
male: 41.1%
female: 36.8% (2013 est.)
country comparison to the world: 32

People—note: demographic data for Cyprus represent the population of the government-controlled area and the area administered by Turkish Cypriots, unless otherwise indicated

GOVERNMENT

Country name: *conventional long form:* Republic of Cyprus
conventional short form: Cyprus
local long form: Kypriaki Dimokratia/Kibris Cumhuriyeti
local short form: Kypros/Kibris
note: the Turkish Cypriot community, which administers the northern part of the island, refers to itself as the "Turkish Republic of Northern Cyprus" or "TRNC" ("Kuzey Kibris Turk Cumhuriyeti" or "KKTC")
etymology: the derivation of the name "Cyprus" is unknown, but the extensive mining of copper metal on the island in antiquity gave rise to the Latin word "cuprum" for copper
Government type: Republic of Cyprus—presidential democracy; Turkish Republic of Northern Cyprus (self-declared)—semi-presidential democracy
note: a separation of the two main ethnic communities inhabiting the island began following the outbreak of communal strife in 1963; this separation was further solidified when a Greek military-junta-supported coup attempt prompted the Turkish intervention in July 1974 that gave the Turkish Cypriots de facto control in the north; Greek Cypriots control the only internationally recognized government on the island; on 15 November 1983, then Turkish Cypriot "President" Rauf DENKTAS declared independence and the formation of a "Turkish Republic of Northern Cyprus" ("TRNC"), which is recognized only by Turkey
Capital: *name:* Nicosia (Lefkosia/Lefkosa)
Geographic coordinates: 35 10 N, 33 22 E
time difference: UTC+2 (7 hours ahead of Washington, DC, during Standard Time) daylight saving time: +1hr, begins last Sunday in March; ends last Sunday in October
Administrative divisions: 6 districts; Ammochostos (Famagusta); (all but a small part located in the Turkish Cypriot community), Keryneia (Kyrenia; the only district located entirely in the Turkish Cypriot community), Larnaka (Larnaca; with a small part located in the Turkish Cypriot community), Lefkosia (Nicosia; a small part administered by Turkish Cypriots), Lemesos (Limassol), Pafos (Paphos); note—the 5 "districts" of the "TRNC" are Gazimagusa (Famagusta), Girne (Kyrenia), Guzelyurt (Morphou), Iskele (Trikomo), Lefkosia (Nicosia)
Independence: 16 August 1960 (from the UK); note—Turkish Cypriots proclaimed self-rule on 13 February 1975 and independence in 1983, but these proclamations are recognized only by Turkey
National holiday: Independence Day, 1 October (1960); note—Turkish Cypriots celebrate 15 November (1983) as "Republic Day"
Constitution: ratified 16 August 1960; amended 1996, 2013; note—in 1963, the constitution was partly suspended as Turkish Cypriots withdrew from the government; Turkish-held territory in 1983 was declared the "Turkish Republic of Northern Cyprus" ("TRNC"); in 1985, the "TRNC" approved its own constitution (2016)
Legal system: mixed legal system of English common law and civil law with European law supremacy
International law organization participation: accepts compulsory ICJ jurisdiction with reservations; accepts ICCt jurisdiction
Citizenship: *citizenship by birth:* no
citizenship by descent only: at least one parent must be a citizen of Cyprus
dual citizenship recognized: yes
residency requirement for naturalization: 7 years
Suffrage: 18 years of age; universal
Executive branch: *chief of state:* President Nicos ANASTASIADES (since 28 February 2013); note—the president is both chief of state and head of government; vice president (vacant); note—vice presidency reserved for Turkish Cy priot
head of government: President Nicos ANASTASIADES (since 28 February 2013)
cabinet: Council of Ministers appointed by the president; note—under the 1960 constitution, 3 of the ministerial posts reserved for Turkish Cypriots, appointed by the vice president; positions currently filled by Greek Cypriots
elections/appointments: president directly elected by absolute majority popular vote in 2 rounds if needed for a 5-year term; election last held on 17 and 24 February 2013 (next to be held in February 2018)
election results: Nicos ANASTASIADES elected president; percent of vote in first round—Nicos ANASTASIADES (DISY) 45.5%, Stavros MALAS (AKEL) 26.9%, Giorgos LILLIKAS (SP) 24.9%, other 2.7%; percent of vote in second round—Nicos ANASTASIADES 57.5%, Savros MALAS 42.5%
note: Mustafa AKINCI elected "president" of the "TRNC" on 30 April 2015; percent of vote in first round (19 April 2015)—Dervis EROGLU (UBP) 28.2%, Mustafa AKINCI (TDP) 26.9%, other 44.9%; percent of vote in runoff (26 April 2015)—AKINCI 60.5%, EROGLU 39.5%; Huseyin OZGURGUN is "TRNC prime minister" since 8 April 2016
Legislative branch: *description:* area under government control: unicameral House of Representatives or Vouli Antiprosopon (80 seats; 56 assigned to Greek Cypriots, 24 to Turkish Cypriots, but only those assigned to Greek Cypriots are filled; members directly elected by both proportional representation and preferential vote; members serve 5-year terms); area administered by Turkish Cypriots: unicameral Assembly of the Republic or Cumhuriyet Meclisi (50 seats; members directly elected by proportional representation vote to serve 5-year terms)
elections: area under government control: last held on 22 May 2016 (next to be held in May 2021); area administered by Turkish Cypriots: last held on 28 July 2013 (next to be held on July 2018)
election results: area under government control: House of Representatives—percent of vote by

227

party -DISY 30.7%, AKEL 25.7%, DIKO 14.5%, KS-EDEK 6.2%, Citizen's Alliance 5.0% Solidarity Movement 5.2%, other 11.7%; seats by party— DISY 18, AKEL 16, DIKO 9, KS-EDEK 3, Citizen's Alliance 3, Solidarity Movement 3, other 7; area administered by Turkish Cypriots: "Assembly of the Republic"—percent of vote by party—CTP-BG 38.4%, UBP 27.3%, DP-UG 23.2%, TDP 7.4%, other 3.7%; seats by party—CTP-BG 21, UBP 14, DP-UG 12, TDP 3

Judicial branch: *highest court(s):* Supreme Court of Cyprus (consists of 13 judges including the court president); note -the highest court in the "Turkish Republic of Northern Cyprus" ("TRNC") is the "Supreme Court" (consists of 8 "judges" including the "court president")

judge selection and term of office: Republic of Cyprus Supreme Court judges appointed by the president of the republic upon the recommendation of the Supreme Court judges; judge tenure until age 68; "TRNC Supreme Court" judges appointed by the "Supreme Council of Judicature," a 12-member body of judges, the attorney general, appointees—1 each by the president of the "TRNC" and by the Legislative Assembly, and 1 member elected by the Bar Association; judge tenure NA

subordinate courts: Republic of Cyprus district courts; Assize Courts; specialized courts for issues relating to family, industrial disputes, military, and rent control; "TRNC Assize Courts"; "district and family courts"

Political parties and leaders: *area under government control:* Citizens' Alliance or SP [Giorgos LILLIKAS]

Democratic Party or DIKO [Nikolas PAPADOPOULOS]

Democratic Rally or DISY [Averof NEOPHYTOU (of Neofytou)]

Ecological and Environmental Movement or KOP (Green Party) [Giorgos PERDIKIS]

European Party or EVROKO [Dimitris SYLLOURIS]

Movement of Social Democrats or KS-EDEK [Marinos SIZOPOULOS]

National Popular Front or ELAM [Christos CHRISTOU]

Progressive Party of the Working People or AKEL (Communist Party) [Andros KYPRIANOU]

Solidarity Movement [Eleni THEOCHAROUS]

United Democrats or EDI [Praxoula ANTONIADOU]

area administered by Turkish Cypriots: Communal Democracy Party or TDP [Cemal OZYIGIT]

Cyprus Socialist Party or KSP [Mehmet BIRINCI]

Democrat Party-National Forces or DP-UG [Serdar DENKTAS]

National Justice Party or UAP [Fatma SOLMAZ]

National Unity Party or UBP [Huseyin OZGURGUN]

New Cyprus Party or YKP [Murat KANATLI]

People's Party or HP [Kudret OZERSAY]

Republican Turkish Party-United Forces or CTP-BG [Mehmet Ali TALAT]

Social Democratic Party or SDP [Tozun TUNALI]

United Cyprus Party or BKP [Izzet IZCAN]

Political pressure groups and leaders: Confederation of Cypriot Workers or SEK [Nikos MOYSEOS] (pro-West)

Pan-Cyprian Labor Federation or PEO [Pambis KYRITSIS] (Communist controlled) area administered by Turkish Cypriots: Confederation of Revolutionary Labor Unions or Dev-Is Federation of Turkish Cypriot Labor Unions or Turk-Sen [Asian BICAKLI]

International organization participation: Australia Group, C, CD, CE, EBRD, ECB, EIB, EMU, EU, FAO, IAEA, IBRD, ICAO, ICC (national committees), ICCt, ICRM, IDA, IFAD, IFC, IFRCS, IHO, ILO, IMF, IMO, IMSO, Interpol, IOC, IOM, IPU, ISO, ITSO, ITU, ITUC (NGOs), MIGA, NAM, NSG, OAS (observer), OIF, OPCW, OSCE, PCA, UN, UNCTAD, UNESCO, UNHCR, UNIDO, UNIFIL, UNWTO, UPU, WCO, WFTU (NGOs), WHO, WIPO, WMO, WTO

Diplomatic representation in the US: *chief of mission:* Ambassador George CHACALLI (since 30 May 2013)

chancery: 2211 R Street NW, Washington, DC 20008

telephone: [1] (202) 462-5772, 462-0873

FAX: [1] (202) 483-6710

consulate(s) general: New York

note: representative of the Turkish Cypriot community in the US is Ismet KORUKOGLU; office at 1667 K Street NW, Washington, DC; telephone [1] (202) 887-6198

Diplomatic representation from the US: *chief of mission:* Ambassador Kathleen Ann DOHERTY (since 7 October 2015)

embassy: corner of Metochiou and Ploutarchou Streets, 2407 Engomi, Nicosia

mailing address: P.O. Box 24536, 1385 Nicosia

telephone: [357] (22) 393939

FAX: [357] (22) 780944

Flag description: white with a copper-colored silhouette of the island (the island has long been famous for its copper deposits) above two green crossed olive branches in the center of the flag; the branches symbolize the hope for peace and reconciliation between the Greek and Turkish communities

note: the "Turkish Republic of Northern Cyprus" flag retains the white field of the Cyprus national flag but displays narrow horizontal red stripes positioned a small distance from the top and bottom edges between which are centered a red crescent and a red five-pointed star; the banner is modeled after the Turkish national flag but with the colors reversed

National symbol(s): Cypriot mouflon (wild sheep), white dove; national colors: blue, white

National anthem: *name:* "Ymnos eis tin Eleftherian" (Hymn to Liberty)

lyrics/music: Dionysios SOLOMOS/Nikolaos MANTZAROS

note: adopted 1960; Cyprus adopted the Greek national anthem as its own; the Turkish Cypriot community in Cyprus uses the anthem of Turkey

ECONOMY

Economy—overview: The area of the Republic of Cyprus under government control has a market economy dominated by the service sector, which accounts for more than four-fifths of GDP. Tourism, financial services, shipping, and real estate have traditionally been the most important sectors. Cyprus has been a member of the EU since May 2004 and adopted the euro as its national currency in January 2008. During the first five years of EU membership, the Cyprus economy grew at an average rate of about 4%, with unemployment between 2004 and 2008 averaging about 4%. However, the economy tipped into recession in 2009 as the ongoing global financial crisis and resulting low demand hit the tourism and construction sectors. An overextended banking sector with excessive exposure to Greek debt added to the contraction. Cyprus' biggest two banks were among the largest holders of Greek bonds in Europe and had a substantial presence in Greece through bank branches and subsidiaries. Following numerous downgrades of its credit rating, Cyprus lost access to international capital markets in May 2011. In July 2012, Cyprus became the fifth euro-zone government to request an economic bailout program from the European Commission, European Central Bank and the International Monetary Fund—known collectively as the "Troika."

Shortly after the election of President Nikos ANASTASIADES in February 2013, Cyprus reached an agreement with the Troika on a $13 billion bailout that resulted in losses on uninsured bank deposits. The bailout triggered a two-week bank closure and the imposition of capital controls that remained partially in place until April 2015. Cyprus' two largest banks merged and the combined entity was recapitalized through conversion of some large bank deposits to shares and imposition of losses on bank bondholders. As with other EU countries, the Troika conditioned the bailout on passing financial and structural reforms and privatizing state-owned enterprises. Despite downsizing and restructuring, the Cypriot financial sector throughout 2015 remained burdened by the largest stock of non-performing loans in the eurozone, equal to nearly half of all loans. Since the bailout, Cyprus has received positive appraisals by the Troika and outperformed fiscal targets but has struggled to overcome political opposition to bailout-mandated legislation, particularly regarding privatizations. Cyprus emerged from recession in 2015 and its economy grew an estimated 1.6% for the year, setting a positive tone for the scheduled end of the bailout program in March 2016.

In October 2013, a US-Israeli consortium completed preliminary appraisals of hydrocarbon deposits in Cyprus' exclusive economic zone (EEZ), which revealed an estimated gross mean reserve of about 130 billion cubic meters. Though exploration continues in Cyprus' EEZ, no additional commercially exploitable reserves were identified during the exploratory drilling in 2014/2015. Developing offshore hydrocarbon resources remains a critical component of the government's economic recovery efforts, but development has been delayed as a result of regional developments and disagreements about exploitation methods.

Economy—overview: Even though the whole of the island is part of the EU, implementation of the EU "acquis communautaire" has been suspended in the area administered by Turkish Cypriots, known locally as the "Turkish Republic of Northern Cyprus" ("TRNC"), until political conditions permit the reunification of the island. The market-based economy of the "TRNC" is roughly one-fifth the size of its southern neighbor and is likewise dominated by the service sector with a large portion of the population employed by the government. In 2012—the latest year for which data are available—the services sector, which includes the public sector, trade, tourism, and education, contributed 58.7% to economic output. In the same year, light manufacturing and agriculture contributed 2.7% and 6.2%, respectively. Manufacturing is limited mainly to food and beverages, furniture and fixtures, construction materials, metal and non-metal products, textiles and clothing. The "TRNC" maintains few economic ties with the Republic of Cyprus outside of trade in construction materials. Since its creation, the "TRNC" has heavily relied on financial assistance from Turkey, which supports the "TRN C" defense, telecommunications, water and postal services. The Turkish Lira is the preferred currency, though foreign currencies are widely accepted in business transactions. The "TRNC" remains vulnerable to the Turkish market and monetary policy because of its use of the Turkish Lira. The "TRNC" weathered the European financial crisis relatively unscathed—compared to the Republic of Cyprus—because of the lack of financial sector development, the health of the Turkish economy, and its separation from the rest of the island. The "TRN C" economy experienced growth estimated at 2.8% in 2013 and 2.3% in 2014 and is projected to grow 3.8% in 2015.

GDP (purchasing power parity): $28.06 billion (2015 est.)
$27.62 billion (2014 est.)
$28.33 billion (2013 est.)
note: data are in 2015 US dollars
GDP (purchasing power parity): $1.829 billion (2007 est.)
country comparison to the world: 133

GDP (official exchange rate): $19.33 billion (2015 est.)
GDP—real growth rate: 1.6% (2015 est.)
-2.5% (2014 est.)
-5.9% (2013 est.)
GDP—real growth rate: 2.3% (2014 est.)
country comparison to the world: 150
GDP—per capita (PPP): $32,800 (2015 est.)
$32,600 (2014 est.)
$33,000 (2013 est.)
note: data are in 2015 US dollars
country comparison to the world: 56
Gross national saving: 10.2% of GDP (2015 est.)
8.6% of GDP (2014 est.)
8.7% of GDP (2013 est.)
country comparison to the world: 152
GDP—composition, by end use:
household consumption: 69.4%
government consumption: 14.7%

investment in fixed capital: 10.7%
investment in inventories: 1%
exports of goods and services: 55.9%
imports of goods and services: -51.7% (2015 est.)
GDP—composition, by sector of origin: *agriculture:* 2.1%
industry: 10.3%
services: 87.4% (2014 est.)

Agriculture—products: citrus, vegetables, barley, grapes, olives, vegetables; poultry, pork, lamb; dairy, cheese Agriculture—products: citrus fruit, dairy, potatoes, grapes, olives, poultry, lamb

Industries: tourism, food and beverage processing, cement and gypsum, ship repair and refurbishment, textiles, light chemicals, metal products, wood, paper, stone and clay products Industries: foodstuffs, textiles, clothing, ship repair, clay, gypsum, copper, furniture
Industrial production growth rate: -2.3% (2015 est.)
Industrial production growth rate: -0.3% (2007 est.)
country comparison to the world: 181
Labor force: 349,700 (2014 est.)
Labor force: 95,030 (2007 est.)
country comparison to the world: 160
Labor force—by occupation: *agriculture:* 3.8%
industry: 15.2%
services: 81% (2014 est.)
Labor force—by occupation:
agriculture: 14.5%,
industry: 29%,
services: 56.5% (2004)
Unemployment rate: 15.5% (2015 est.)
16.1% (2014 est.)
Unemployment rate: 9.4% (2005 est.)
country comparison to the world: 154
Population below poverty line: NA%
Household income or consumption by percentage share: *lowest:* 10%: 3.3%
highest: 10%: 28.8% (2014)
Distribution of family income—Gini index: 34.8 (2014 est.)
32.4 (2013 est.)
country comparison to the world: 96
Budget: revenues:: $7.743 billion
expenditures:: $7.857 billion (2015 est.)
Budget: *revenues:* $2.5 billion,
expenditures: $2.5 billion (2006)
Taxes and other revenues: 39.9% of GDP (2015 est.)
country comparison to the world: 40
Budget surplus (+) or deficit (-): -1% of GDP (2015 est.)
country comparison to the world: 54
Public debt: 108.4% of GDP (2015 est.)
108.2% of GDP (2014 est.)
note: data cover general government debt and include debt instruments issued (or owned) by government entities other than the treasury; the data include treasury debt held by foreign entities; the data exclude debt issued by subnational entities, as well as intra-governmental debt; intra-governmental debt consists of treasury borrowings

from surpluses in the social funds, such as for retirement, medical care, and unemployment
country comparison to the world: 11
Fiscal year: calendar year
Inflation rate (consumer prices): -1.5% (2015 est.)
-0.3% (2014 est.)
country comparison to the world: 6
Central bank discount rate: 0.05% (31 December 2013)
0.3% (31 December 2010)
note: this is the European Central Bank's rate on the marginal lending facility, which offers overnight credit to banks in the euro area
country comparison to the world: 153
Commercial bank prime lending rate: 4.7% (31 December 2015 est.)
5.88% (31 December 2014 est.)
country comparison to the world: 150
Stock of narrow money: $3.44 billion (31 December 2015 est.)
$4.382 billion (31 December 2014 est.)
note: see entry for the European Union for money supply for the entire euro area; the European Central Bank (ECB) controls monetary policy for the 18 members of the Economic and Monetary Union (EMU); individual members of the EMU do not control the quantity of money circulating within their own borders
country comparison to the world: 110
Stock of broad money: $43.41 billion (31 December 2014 est.)
$47.99 billion (31 December 2013 est.)
country comparison to the world: 72
Stock of domestic credit: $50.49 billion (31 December 2015 est.)
$65.42 billion (31 December 2014 est.)
country comparison to the world: 61
Market value of publicly traded shares: $1.996 billion (31 December 2012 est.)
$2.853 billion (31 December 2011)
$6.834 billion (31 December 2010 est.)
country comparison to the world: 101
Current account balance: -$992 million (2015 est.)
-$1.052 billion (2014 est.)
country comparison to the world: 121
Exports: $1.818 billion (2014 est.)
$2.018 billion (2013 est.)

Exports: $68.1 million, f.o.b. (2007 est.)
country comparison to the world: 143

Exports—commodities: citrus, potatoes, pharmaceuticals, cement, clothing

Exports—partners: Greece 10.9%, Ireland 10.2%, UK 7.2%, Israel 6% (2015)
Imports: $6.755 billion (2014 est.)
$6.32 billion (2013 est.)

Imports: $1.2 billion, f.o.b. (2007 est.)
country comparison to the world: 115

Imports—commodities: consumer goods, petroleum and lubricants, machinery, transport equipment
Imports—partners: Greece 25.7%, UK 9.1%, Italy 8%, Germany 7.5%, Israel 5.5%, China 4.8%, Netherlands 4.1% (2015)
Reserves of foreign exchange and gold: $864 million (31 December 2015 est.)

$890.9 million (31 December 2014 est.)
Reserves of foreign exchange and gold: $NA
country comparison to the world: 138
Debt—external: $95.28 billion (31 December 2013 est.)
$103.5 billion (31 December 2012 est.)
Debt—external: $NA
country comparison to the world: 54
Stock of direct foreign investment—at home: $60.35 billion (31 December 2015 est.)
$59.1 billion (31 December 2014 est.)
country comparison to the world: 56
Stock of direct foreign investment—abroad: $43.82 billion (31 December 2015 est.)
$42.87 billion (31 December 2014 est.)
country comparison to the world: 43

Exchange rates: euros (EUR) per US dollar—
0.885 (2015 est.)
0.7525 (2014 est.)
0.7634 (2013 est.)
0.78 (2012 est.)
0.7185 (2011 est.)

Exchange rates: Turkish new lira per US dollar: 1.9 (2013) 1.8 (2012) 1.668 (2011) 1.5026 (2010) 1.55 (2009)

Economy of the area administered by Turkish Cypriots: Economy—overview: Even though the whole of the island is part of the EU, implementation of the EU "acquis communautaire" has been suspended in the area administered by Turkish Cypriots, known locally as the "Turkish Republic of Northern Cyprus" ("TRNC"), until political conditions permit the reunification of the island. The market-based economy of the "TRNC" is roughly one-fifth the size of its southern neighbor and is likewise dominated by the service sector with a large portion of the population employed by the government. In 2012—the latest year for which data are available—the services sector, which includes the public sector, trade, tourism, and education, contributed 58.7% to economic output. In the same year, light manufacturing and agriculture contributed 2.7% and 6.2%, respectively. Manufacturing is limited mainly to food and beverages, furniture and fixtures, construction materials, metal and non-metal products, textiles and clothing. The "TRNC" maintains few economic ties with the Republic of Cyprus outside of trade in construction materials. Since its creation, the "TRNC" has heavily relied on financial assistance from Turkey, which supports the "TRNC" defense, telecommunications, water and postal services. The Turkish Lira is the preferred currency, though foreign currencies are widely accepted in business transactions. The "TRNC" remains vulnerable to the Turkish market and monetary policy because of its use of the Turkish Lira. The "TRNC" weathered the European financial crisis relatively unscathed—compared to the Republic of Cyprus—because of the lack of financial sector development, the health of the Turkish economy, and its separation from the rest of the island. The "TRNC" economy experienced growth estimated at 2.8% in 2013 and 2.3% in 2014 and is projected to grow 3.8% in 2015.

GDP (purchasing power parity): $1.829 billion (2007 est.)

GDP—real growth rate: 2.3% (2014 est.)
2.8% (2013 est.)

GDP—per capita: $11,700 (2007 est.)

GDP—composition by sector:
agriculture: 6.2%,
industry: 35.1%,
services: 58.7% (2012 est.)
Labor force: 95,030 (2007 est.)

Labor force—by occupation:
agriculture: 14.5%,
industry: 29%,
services: 56.5% (2004)

Unemployment rate: 9.4% (2005 est.)

Population below poverty line: %NA

Inflation rate: 11.4% (2006)

Budget: *revenues:* $2.5 billion,
expenditures: $2.5 billion (2006)

Agriculture—products: citrus fruit, dairy, potatoes, grapes, olives, poultry, lamb Industries: foodstuffs, textiles, clothing, ship repair, clay, gypsum, copper, furniture

Industrial production growth rate: -0.3% (2007 est.)

Electricity production: 998.9 million kWh (2005)

Electricity consumption: 797.9 million kWh (2005)

Exports: $68.1 million, f.o.b. (2007 est.)

Export—commodities: citrus, dairy, potatoes, textiles

Export—partners: Turkey 40%; direct trade between the area administered by Turkish Cypriots and the area under government control remains limited

Imports: $1.2 billion, f.o.b. (2007 est.)

Import—commodities: vehicles, fuel, cigarettes, food, minerals, chemicals, machinery

Import—partners: Turkey 60%; direct trade between the area administered by Turkish Cypriots and the area under government control remains limited

Reserves of foreign exchange and gold: $NA

Debt—external: $NA

Currency (code): Turkish new lira (YTL)

Exchange rates: Turkish new lira per US dollar:
1.9 (2013)
1.8 (2012)
1.668 (2011)
1.5026 (2010)
1.55 (2009)

ENERGY

Electricity—production: 3.942 billion kWh (2013 est.)
country comparison to the world: 125
Electricity—consumption: 4.296 billion kWh (2012 est.)
country comparison to the world: 122
Electricity—exports: 0 kWh (2013 est.)
country comparison to the world: 130
Electricity—imports: 0 kWh (2013 est.)
country comparison to the world: 140
Electricity—installed generating capacity: 1.658 million kW (2012 est.)

country comparison to the world: 113
Electricity—from fossil fuels: 90% of total installed capacity (2012 est.)
country comparison to the world: 77
Electricity—from nuclear fuels: 0% of total installed capacity (2012 est.)
country comparison to the world: 77
Electricity—from hydroelectric plants: 0% of total installed capacity (2012 est.)
country comparison to the world: 169
Electricity—from other renewable sources: 10% of total installed capacity (2012 est.)
country comparison to the world: 38
Crude oil—production: 0 bbl/day (2014 est.)
country comparison to the world: 124
Crude oil—exports: 0 bbl/day (2012 est.)
country comparison to the world: 115
Crude oil—imports: 0 bbl/day (2012 est.)
country comparison to the world: 180
Crude oil—proved reserves: 0 bbl (1 January 2015 est.)
country comparison to the world: 123
Refined petroleum products—production: 0 bbl/day (2012 est.)
country comparison to the world: 173
Refined petroleum products—consumption: 53,000 bbl/day (2013 est.)
country comparison to the world: 97
Refined petroleum products—exports: 0 bbl/day (2012 est.)
country comparison to the world: 174
Refined petroleum products—imports: 52,480 bbl/day (2012 est.)
country comparison to the world: 78
Natural gas—production: 0 cu m (2013 est.)
country comparison to the world: 177
Natural gas—consumption: 0 cu m (2013 est.)
country comparison to the world: 136
Natural gas—exports: 0 cu m (2013 est.)
country comparison to the world: 87
Natural gas—imports: 0 cu m (2013 est.)
country comparison to the world: 187
Natural gas—proved reserves: 141.6 billion cu m (1 January 2014 est.)
country comparison to the world: 49
Carbon dioxide emissions from consumption of energy: 8.801 million Mt (2012 est.)
country comparison to the world: 106

COMMUNICATIONS

Telephones—fixed lines: *total subscriptions:* 330,000
subscriptions per 100 inhabitants: 28 (2014 est.)
country comparison to the world: 112
Telephones—mobile cellular: *total:* 1.1 million
subscriptions per 100 inhabitants: 95 (2014 est.)
country comparison to the world: 157
Telephone system: *general assessment:* excellent in both area under government control and area administered by Turkish Cypriots
domestic: open-wire, fiber-optic cable, and microwave radio relay
international: country code—357 (area administered by Turkish Cypriots uses the country code of Turkey—90); a number of submarine cables,

including the SEA-ME-WE-3, combine to provide connectivity to Western Europe, the Middle East, and Asia; tropospheric scatter; satellite earth stations—8 (3 Intelsat—1 Atlantic Ocean and 2 Indian Ocean, 2 Eutelsat, 2 Intersputnik, and 1 Arabsat)

Broadcast media: mixture of state and privately run TV and radio services; the public broadcaster operates 2 TV channels and 4 radio stations; 6 private TV broadcasters, satellite and cable TV services including telecasts from Greece and Turkey, and a number of private radio stations are available; in areas administered by Turkish Cypriots, th ere are 2 public TV stations, 4 public radio stations, and privately owned TV and radio broadcast stations (2007)
Radio broadcast stations: area under *government control:* AM 5, FM 76, shortwave 0 *area administered by Turkish Cypriots:* AM 1, FM 20, shortwave 1 (2004)
Television broadcast stations: area under government control: 8 area administered by Turkish Cypriots: 2 (plus 4 relay) (2004)

Internet country code: .cy
Internet hosts: 252,013 (2012)
country comparison to the world: 67
Internet users: total: 738,900
percent of population: 63.0% (2014 est.)
country comparison to the world: 127

Airports: 15 (2013)
country comparison to the world: 145
Airports—with paved runways: total: 13
2,438 to 3,047 m: 7
1,524 to 2,437 m: 2
914 to 1,523 m: 3
under 914 m: 1 (2013)

Airports—with unpaved runways: total: 2
under 914 m: 2 (2013)
Heliports: 9 (2013)
Roadways: total: 20,006 km government control: 13,006 km (includes 2,277 km of expressways)
paved: 8,564 km
unpaved: 4,442 km
Turkish Cypriot control: 7,000 km (2011)
country comparison to the world: 108
Merchant marine: total: 838
by type: bulk carrier 278, cargo 163, chemical tanker 77, container 201, liquefied gas 11, passenger 3, passenger/cargo 25, petroleum tanker 62, refrigerated cargo 5, roll on/roll off 9, vehicle carrier 4
foreign-owned: 622 (Angola 1, Austria 1, Belgium 3, Bermuda 1, Canada 2, China 6, Denmark 6, Estonia 6, France 16, Germany 192, Greece 201, Hong Kong 2, India 4, Iran 10, Ireland 3, Italy 6, Japan 16, Netherlands 23, Norway 14, Philippines 1, Poland 24, Portugal 2, Russia 46, Singapore 1, Slovenia 5, Spain 6, Sweden 5, Turkey 1, UAE 3, UK 7, Ukraine 3, US 5)
registered in other countries: 152 (Bahamas 23, Cambodia 4, Comoros 2, Finland 1, Gibraltar 1, Greece 3, Hong Kong 3, Liberia 9, Malta 32, Marshall Islands 40, Norway 1, Panama 5, Russia 13, Saint Vincent and the Grenadines 3, Sierra Leone 2, Singapore 6, unknown 4) (2010)
country comparison to the world: 13

Ports and terminals: *major seaport(s):* area under government control: Larnaca, Limassol, Vasilikos; area administered by Turkish Cypriots: Famagusta, Kyrenia

Military branches: *Republic of Cyprus:* Cypriot National Guard (Ethniki Froura, EF; includes naval and air elements); Northern Cyprus: Turkish Cypriot Security Force (GKK) (2014)

Military service age and obligation: *Cypriot National Guard (CNG):* 18–50 years of age for compulsory military service for all Greek Cypriot males; 17 years of age for voluntary service; 14-month service obligation (2016)
Military expenditures: 2.1% of GDP (2013)
2.05% of GDP (2012)
2.14% of GDP (2011)
2.05% of GDP (2010)
country comparison to the world: 37

Disputes—international: hostilities in 1974 divided the island into two de facto autonomous entities, the internationally recognized Cypriot Government and a Turkish-Cypriot community (north Cyprus); the 1,000-strong UN Peacekeeping Force in Cyprus (UNFICYP) has served in Cyprus since 1964 and maintains the buffer zone between north and south; on 1 May 2004, Cyprus entered the EU still divided, with the EU's body of legislation and standards (acquis communitaire) suspended in the north; Turkey protests Cypriot Government creating hydrocarbon blocks and maritime boundary with Lebanon in March 2007

Refugees and internally displaced persons: *IDPs:* 272,000 (both Turkish and Greek Cypriots; many displaced since 1974) (2015)

Illicit drugs: minor transit point for heroin and hashish via air routes and container traffic to Europe, especially from Lebanon and Turkey; some cocaine transits as well; despite a strengthening of anti-money-laundering legislation, remains vulnerable to money laundering; reporting of suspicious transactions in offshore sector remains weak (2008)

CZECHIA

Background: At the close of World War I, the Czechs and Slovaks of the former Austro-Hungarian Empire merged to form Czechoslovakia. During the interwar years, having rejected a federal system, the new country's predominantly Czech leaders were frequently preoccupied with meeting the increasingly strident demands of other ethnic minorities within the republic, most notably the Slovaks, the Sudeten Germans, and the Ruthenians (Ukrainians). On the eve of World War II, Nazi Germany occupied the territory that today comprises Czechia, and Slovakia became an independent state allied with Germany. After the war, a reunited but truncated Czechoslovakia (less Ruthenia) fell within the Soviet sphere of influence. In 1968, an invasion by Warsaw Pact troops ended the efforts of the country's leaders to liberalize communist rule and create "socialism with a human face," ushering in a period of repression known as "normalization." The peaceful "Velvet Revolution" swept the Communist Party from power at the end of 1989 and inaugurated a return to democratic rule and a market economy. On 1 January 1993, the country underwent a nonviolent "velvet divorce" into its two national components, the Czech Republic and Slovakia. The Czech Republic joined NATO in 1999 and the European Union in 2004. The country changed its short-form name to Czechia in 2016.

Location: Central Europe, between Germany, Poland, Slovakia, and Austria

Geographic coordinates: 49 45 N, 15 30 E

Map references: Europe
Area: *total:* 78,867 sq km
land: 77,247 sq km
water: 1,620 sq km
country comparison to the world: 116

Area—comparative: slightly smaller than South Carolina

Land boundaries: *total:* 2,143 km
border countries (4): Austria 402 km, Germany 704 km, Poland 796 km, Slovakia 241 km
Coastline: 0 km (landlocked)
Maritime claims: none (landlocked)

Climate: temperate; cool summers; cold, cloudy, humid winters

Terrain: Bohemia in the west consists of rolling plains, hills, and plateaus surrounded by low mountains; Moravia in the east consists of very hilly country

Elevation: *mean elevation:* 433 m

elevation extremes: *lowest point:* Labe (Elbe) River 115 m

highest point: Snezka 1,602 m

Natural resources: hard coal, soft coal, kaolin, clay, graphite, timber, arable land:

Land use: *agricultural land:* 54.8%

arable land: 41%

permanent crops: 1%

permanent pasture: 12.8%

forest: 34.4%

other: 10.8% (2011 est.)

Irrigated land: 320 sq km (2012)

Total renewable water resources: 13.15 cu km (2011)

Freshwater withdrawal (domestic/industrial/agricultural): *total:* 1.7 cu m/yr (41%/56%/2%)

per capita: 164.7 cu m/yr (2009)

Natural hazards: flooding

Environment—current issues: air and water pollution in areas of northwest Bohemia and in northern Moravia around Ostrava present health risks; acid rain damaging forests; efforts to bring industry up to EU code should improve domestic pollution

Environment—international agreements: *party to:* Air Pollution, Air Pollution-Nitrogen Oxides, Air Pollution-Persistent Organic Pollutants, Air Pollution-Sulfur 85, Air Pollution-Sulfur 94, Air Pollution-Volatile Organic Compounds, Antarctic-Environmental Protocol, Antarctic Treaty, Biodiversity, Climate Change, Climate Change-Kyoto Protocol, Desertification, Endangered Species, Environmental Modification, Hazardous Wastes, Law of the Sea, Ozone Layer Protection, Ship Pollution, Wetlands, Whaling

signed, but not ratified: none of the selected agreements

Geography—note: landlocked; strategically located astride some of oldest and most significant land routes in Europe; Moravian Gate is a traditional military corridor between the North European Plain and the Danube in central Europe

PEOPLE AND SOCIETY

Nationality: *noun:* Czech(s)

adjective: Czech

Ethnic groups: Czech 64.3%, Moravian 5%, Slovak 1.4%, other 1.8%, unspecified 27.5% (2011 est.)

Languages: Czech (official) 95.4%, Slovak 1.6%, other 3% (2011 census)

Religions: Roman Catholic 10.4%, Protestant (includes Czech Brethren and Hussite) 1.1%, other and unspecified 54%, none 34.5% (2011 est.)

Population: 10,644,842 (July 2015 est.)

country comparison to the world: 85

Age structure: *0–14 years:* 15% (male 819,864/female 776,639)

15–24 years: 10.23% (male 559,108/female 529,598)

25–54 years: 43.7% (male 2,387,303/female 2,264,774)

55–64 years: 13.06% (male 673,060/female 717,296)

65 years and over: 18.01% (male 791,823/female 1,125,377) (2015 est.)

Dependency ratios: *total dependency ratio:* 49.5%

youth dependency ratio: 22.5%

elderly dependency ratio: 27%

potential support ratio: 3.7% (2015 est.)

Median age: *total:* 41.3 years

male: 40 years

female: 42.6 years (2015 est.)

country comparison to the world: 34

Population growth rate: 0.16% (2015 est.)

country comparison to the world: 185

Birth rate: 9.63 births/1,000 population (2015 est.)

country comparison to the world: 202

Death rate: 10.34 deaths/1,000 population (2015 est.)

country comparison to the world: 37

Net migration rate: 2.33 migrant(s)/1,000 population (2015 est.)

country comparison to the world: 43

Urbanization: *urban population:* 73% of total population (2015)

rate of urbanization: 0.35% annual rate of change (2010–15 est.)

Major urban areas—population: PRAGUE (capital) 1.314 million (2015)

Sex ratio: *at birth:* 1.06 male(s)/female

0–14 years: 1.06 male(s)/female

15–24 years: 1.06 male(s)/female

25–54 years: 1.05 male(s)/female

55–64 years: 0.94 male(s)/female

65 years and over: 0.7 male(s)/female

total population: 0.97 male(s)/female (2015 est.)

Mother's mean age at first birth: 27.8 (2011 est.)

Maternal mortality rate: 4 deaths/100,000 live births (2015 est.)

country comparison to the world: 173

Infant mortality rate: *total:* 2.63 deaths/1,000 live births

male: 2.76 deaths/1,000 live births

female: 2.49 deaths/1,000 live births (2015 est.)

country comparison to the world: 216

Life expectancy at birth:

total population: 78.48 years

male: 75.5 years

female: 81.62 years (2015 est.)

country comparison to the world: 55

Total fertility rate: 1.44 children born/woman (2015 est.)

country comparison to the world: 205

Contraceptive prevalence rate: 86.3%

note: percent of women aged 18–49 (2008)

Health expenditures: 7.2% of GDP (2013)

country comparison to the world: 63

Physicians density: 3.71 physicians/1,000 population (2010)

Hospital bed density: 6.8 beds/1,000 population (2011)

Drinking water source:

improved:

urban: 100% of population

rural: 100% of population

total: 100% of population

unimproved:

urban: 0% of population

rural: 0% of population

total: 0% of population (2015 est.)

Sanitation facility access:

improved:

urban: 99.1% of population

rural: 99.2% of population

total: 99.1% of population

unimproved:

urban: 0.9% of population

rural: 0.8% of population

total: 0.9% of population (2015 est.)

HIV/AIDS—adult prevalence rate: 0.05% (2013 est.)

country comparison to the world: 120

HIV/AIDS—people living with HIV/AIDS: 3,400 (2013 est.)

country comparison to the world: 111

HIV/AIDS—deaths: fewer than 100 (2013 est.)

country comparison to the world: 121

Obesity—adult prevalence rate: 29.1% (2014)

country comparison to the world: 21

Education expenditures: 4.3% of GDP (2012)

country comparison to the world: 106

Literacy: *definition:* NA

total population: 99%

male: 99%

female: 99% (2011 est.)

School life expectancy (primary to tertiary education): *total:* 17 years

male: 16 years

female: 18 years (2014)

Unemployment, youth ages 15–24: *total:* 19%

male: 18.6%

female: 19.4% (2013 est.)

country comparison to the world: 57

GOVERNMENT

Country name: *conventional long form:* Czech Republic

conventional short form: Czechia

local long form: Ceska republika

local short form: Cesko

etymology: name derives from the Czechs, a West Slavic tribe who rose to prominence in the late 9th century A.D.

Government type: parliamentary republic

Capital: *name:* Prague

Geographic coordinates: 50 05 N, 14 28 E

time difference: UTC + 1 (6 hours ahead of Washington, DC, during Standard Time) daylight saving time: +1hr, begins last Sunday in March; ends last Sunday in October

Administrative divisions: 13 regions (kraje, singular—kraj) and 1 capital city* (hlavni mesto); Jihocesky (South Bohemia), Jihomoravsky (South Moravia), Karlovarsky (Karlovy Vary),

Kralovehradecky (Hradec Kralove), Liberecky (Liberec), Moravskoslezsky (Moravia-Silesia), Olomoucky (Olomouc), Pardubicky (Pardubice), Plzensky (Pilsen), Praha (Prague)*, Stredocesky (Central Bohemia), Ustecky (Usti), Vysocina (Highlands), Zlinsky (Zlin)

Independence: 1 January 1993 (Czechoslovakia split into the Czech Republic and Slovakia); note—although 1 January is the day the Czech Republic came into being, the Czechs commemorate 28 October 1918, the day the former Czechoslovakia declared its independence from the Austro-Hungarian Empire, as their independence day

National holiday: Czechoslovak Founding Day, 28 October (1918)

Constitution: previous 1960; latest ratified 16 December 1992, effective 1 January 1993; amended several times, last in 2013 (2016)

Legal system: new civil code enacted in 2014, replacing civil code of 1964—based on former Austro-Hungarian civil codes and socialist theory—and reintroducing former Czech legal terminology

International law organization participation: has not submitted an ICJ jurisdiction declaration; accepts ICCt jurisdiction

Citizenship: *citizenship by birth:* no
citizenship by descent only: at least one parent must be a citizen of the Czech Republic
dual citizenship recognized: no
residency requirement for naturalization: 5 years

Suffrage: 18 years of age; universal

Executive branch: *chief of state:* President Milos ZEMAN (since 8 March 2013)

head of government: Prime Minister Bohuslav SOBOTKA (since 17 January 2014); First Deputy Prime Minister Andrej BABIS and Deputy Prime Minister Pavel BELOBRADEK (both since 29 January 2014)

cabinet: Cabinet appointed by the president on the recommendation of the prime minister
elections/appointments: president directly elected by absolute majority popular vote in 2 rounds if needed for a 5-year term (limited to 2 consecutive terms); elections last held on 11–12 January 2013 with a runoff on 25–26 January 2013 (next to be held in January 2018); prime minister appointed by the president for a 4-year term
election results: Milos ZEMAN elected president; percent of popular vote—Milos ZEMAN (SPO) 54.8%, Karel SCHWARZENBERG (TOP 09) 45.2%

Legislative branch: *description:* bicameral Parliament or Parlament consists of the Senate or Senat (81 seats; members directly elected in single-seat constituencies by absolute majority vote in two rounds if needed; members serve 6-year terms with one-third of the membership renewed every 2 years) and the Chamber of Deputies or Poslanecka Snemovna (200 seats; members directly elected in multi-seat constituencies by proportional representation vote; members serve 4-year terms)

elections: Senate—last held in two rounds on 10–11 and 17–18 October 2014 (next to be held in October 2016); Chamber of Deputies—last held on 25–26 October 2013 (next to be held in 2017)
election results: Senate—percent of vote by party—NA; seats by party/caucus as of 15 December 2015—CSSD 33, ODS 14, KDU-CSL 11, STAN+TOP 096, KSCM+SPO+S.cz 6, ANO+S.cz 5, independent 6; Chamber of Deputies—percent of vote by party—CSSD 20.5%, ANO 201118.7%, KSCM 14.9%, TOP 0912%, ODS 7.7%, Usvit 6.9%, KDU-CSL 6.8% other 12.5%; seats by party—CSSD 50, ANO 201147, KSCM 33, TOP 09 + STAN 26, ODS 16, KDU-CSL 14, Usvit 8, independent 6

Judicial branch: *highest court(s):* Supreme Court (organized into Civil Law and Commercial Division, and Criminal Division each with a court chief justice, vice justice, and several judges); Constitutional Court (consists of 15 justices); Supreme Administrative Court (consists of 28 judges)
judge selection and term of office: Supreme Court judges proposed by the Chamber of Deputies and appointed by the president; judges appointed for life; Constitutional Court judges appointed by the president and confirmed by the Senate; judges appointed for 10-year, renewable terms; Supreme Administrative Court judges selected by the president of the Court; judge term NA
subordinate courts: High Court; superior, regional, and district courts

Political parties and leaders: *parties in parliament:* ANO 2011 or ANO [Andrej BABIS]
Christian Democratic Union-Czechoslovak People's Party or KDU-CSL [Pavel BELOBRADEK]
Civic Democratic Party or ODS [Petr FIALA]
Communist Party of Bohemia and Moravia or KSCM [Vojtech FILIP]
Czech Social Democratic Party or CSSD [Bohuslav SOBOTKA]
Dawn—National Coalition or Usvit [Miroslav LIDINSKY]
Freedom and Direct Democracy or SPD [Tomio O KAMURA]
Mayors and Independents or STAN [Martin PUTA] (allied with TOP 09)
Tradition Responsibility Prosperity 09 or TOP 09 [Miroslav KALO USEK]
parties outside parliament: Czech Pirate Party [Lukas CERNOHORSKY]
Free Citizens Party or Svobodni [Petr MACH]
Green Party or SZ [Jana DRAPALOVA]
Liberal Reform Party or Ostravak [Eva SCHWARZOVA]
Mayors for Liberec Region or SLK [Marek PIETER]
North Bohemians or S. cz [Bronislav SCH WARZ]
Party of Civic Rights or SPO [Jan VELEBA]

Political pressure groups and leaders: Czech-Moravian Confederation of Trade Unions or CMKOS [Josef STREDULA]

International organization participation: Australia Group, BIS, BSEC (observer), CD, CE, CEI, CERN, EAPC, EBRD, ECB, EIB, ESA, EU, FAO, IAEA, IBRD, ICAO, ICC (national committees), ICCt, ICRM, IDA, IEA, IFC, IFRCS, ILO, IMF, IMO, IMSO, Interpol, IOC, IOM, IPU, ISO, ITSO, ITU, ITUC (NGOs), MIGA, MON USCO, NATO, NEA, NSG, OAS (observer), OECD, OIF (observer), OPCW, OSCE, PCA, Schengen Convention, SELEC, UN, UNCTAD, UNESCO, UNHCR, UNIDO, UN WTO, UPU, WCO, WFTU (NGOs), WHO, WIPO, WMO, WTO, ZC

Diplomatic representation in the US:
chief of mission: Ambassador Petr GAN DALOVIC (since 23 May 2011)
chancery: 3900 Spring of Freedom Street NW, Washington, DC 20008
telephone: [1] (202) 274-9100
FAX: [1] (202) 966-8540
consulate(s) general: Chicago, Los Angeles, New York

Diplomatic representation from the US: *chief of mission:* Ambassador Andrew H. SCHAPIRO (since 30 September 2014)
em bassy: Trziste 15,11801 Prague 1—Mala Strana
mailing address: use embassy street address
telephon e: [420] 257022000
FAX: [420] 257022809

Flag description: two equal horizontal bands of white (top) and red with a blue isosceles triangle based on the hoist side
note: is identical to the flag of the former Czechoslovakia

National symbol(s): double-tailed lion; national colors: white, red, blue

National anthem: *name:* "Kde domov muj?" (Where is My Home?)
lyrics/music: Josef Kajetan TYL/Frantisek Jan SKROUP
note: adopted 1993; the anthem was originally written as incidental music to the play "Fidlovacka" (1834), it soon became very popular as an unofficial anthem of the Czech nation; its first verse served as the official Czechoslovak anthem beginning in 1918, while the second verse (Slovak) was dropped after the split of Czechoslovakia in 1993

ECONOMY

Economy—overview: Czechia is a stable and prosperous market economy that is closely integrated with the EU, especially since the country's EU accession in 2004. The auto industry is the largest single industry, and, together with its upstream suppliers, accounts for nearly 24% of Czech manufacturing. Czechia produced more than a million cars for the first time in 2010, over 80% of which were exported. While the conservative, inward-looking Czech financial system has remained relatively healthy, the small, open, export-driven Czech economy remains sensitive to changes in the economic performance of its main export markets, especially Germany. When Western Europe and Germany fell into recession in late 2008, demand for Czech goods plunged, leading to double digit drops in industrial production and exports. As a result, real GDP fell sharply in 2009. The economy slowly recovered in the second half of 2009 and registered weak growth in the next two years. In 2012 and 2013, however, the economy fell into a recession again, due both to a slump in external demand in the EU and to the government's austerity measures, returning to weak growth in 2014, and stronger growth in 2015. Foreign and domestic businesses alike voice concerns about corruption, especially in public procurement. Other long term challenges include dealing with a rapidly aging population, funding an unsustainable pension and health care system, and diversifying away from manufacturing and toward a more high-tech, services-based, knowledge economy.

GDP (purchasing power parity): $332.5 billion (2015 est.)
$319 billion (2014 est.)
$312.8 billion (2013 est.)
note: data are in 2015 US dollars
country comparison to the world: 51

GDP (official exchange rate): $181.9 billion (2015 est.)

GDP—real growth rate: 4.2% (2015 est.)
2% (2014 est.)
-0.5% (2013 est.)
country comparison to the world: 57

GDP—per capita (PPP): $31,600 (2015 est.)
$30,300 (2014 est.)
$29,700 (2013 est.)
note: data are in 2015 US dollars
country comparison to the world: 59

Gross national saving: 27.5% of GDP (2015 est.)
25.4% of GDP (2014 est.)
24.2% of GDP (2013 est.)
country comparison to the world: 34

GDP—composition, by end use:
household consumption: 47.7%
government consumption: 19%
investment in fixed capital: 25.1%
investment in inventories: -0.1%
exports of goods and services: 85.5%
imports of goods and services: -77.2% (2015 est.)

GDP—composition, by sector of origin: *agriculture:* 2.7%
industry: 38.2%
services: 59.2% (2015 est.)

Agriculture—products: wheat, potatoes, sugar beets, hops, fruit; pigs, poultry

Industries: motor vehicles, metallurgy, machinery and equipment, glass, armaments

Industrial production growth rate: 5% (2015 est.)
country comparison to the world: 33

Labor force: 5.479 million (2015 est.)
country comparison to the world: 74

Labor force—by occupation: *agriculture:* 2.6%
industry: 37.4%
services: 60% (2012)

Unemployment rate: 6.5% (2015 est.)
7.7% (2014 est.)
country comparison to the world: 77

Population below poverty line: 8.6% (2012 est.)

Household income or consumption by percentage share: *lowest:* 10%: 1.5%
highest: 10%: 29.1% (2012 est.)

Distribution of family income—Gini index: 24.9 (2012)
25.4 (1996)
country comparison to the world: 141

Budget: *revenues:* $72.21 billion
expenditures: $75.56 billion (2015 est.)
Taxes and other revenues: 39.6% of GDP (2015 est.)
country comparison to the world: 41

Budget surplus (+) or deficit (-): -1.8% of GDP (2015 est.)
country comparison to the world: 69

Public debt: 41.4% of GDP (2015 est.)
42.1% of GDP (2014 est.)
country comparison to the world: 109

Fiscal year: calendar year

Inflation rate (consumer prices): 0.3% (2015 est.)
0.4% (2014 est.)
country comparison to the world: 57

Central bank discount rate: 0.05% (31 December 2013)
0.05% (31 December 2012)
note: this is the two-week repo, the main rate CNB uses
country comparison to the world: 147

Commercial bank prime lending rate: 4.5% (31 December 2015 est.)
4.64% (31 December 2014 est.)
country comparison to the world: 154

Stock of narrow money: $126.1 billion (31 December 2015 est.)
$122.8 billion (31 December 2014 est.)
country comparison to the world: 29

Stock of broad money: $152.9 billion (31 December 2014 est.)
$155.7 billion (31 December 2013 est.)
country comparison to the world: 50

Stock of domestic credit: $148.5 billion (31 December 2015 est.)
$137.1 billion (31 December 2014 est.)
country comparison to the world: 48

Market value of publicly traded shares: $54.92 billion (30 December 3013 est.)
$59.88 billion (28 December 2012)
$53.2 billion (30 December 2011 est.)
country comparison to the world: 51

Current account balance: $1.648 billion (2015 est.)
$366 million (2014 est.)
country comparison to the world: 33

Exports: $133.8 billion (2015 est.)
$110.5 billion (2014 est.)
country comparison to the world: 34

Exports—commodities: machinery and transport equipment, raw materials, fuel, chemicals

Exports—partners: Germany 32.4%, Slovakia 9%, Poland 5.8%, UK 5.3%, France 5.1%, Austria 4.1% (2015)

Imports: $124 billion (2015 est.)
$101.9 billion (2014 est.)
country comparison to the world: 33

Imports—commodities: machinery and transport equipment, raw materials and fuels, chemicals

Imports—partners: Germany 30%, Poland 9%, China 8.3%, Slovakia 6.6%, Netherlands 5%, Austria 4.1% (2015)

Reserves of foreign exchange and gold: $73.5 billion (31 December 2015 est.)
$54.49 billion (31 December 2014 est.)
country comparison to the world: 31

Debt—external: $125.1 billion (31 December 2014 est.)
$137.4 billion (31 December 2013 est.)
country comparison to the world: 47

Stock of direct foreign investment—at home: $147.6 billion (31 December 2015 est.)
$142.6 billion (31 December 2014 est.)
country comparison to the world: 37

Stock of direct foreign investment—abroad: $41.14 billion (31 December 2015 est.)
$40.14 billion (31 December 2014 est.)
country comparison to the world: 44

Exchange rates: koruny (CZK) per US dollar—
24.19 (2015 est.)
20.758 (2014 est.)
20.758 (2013 est.)
19.59 (2012 est.)
17.696 (2011 est.)

ENERGY

Electricity—production: 81.86 billion kWh (2012 est.)
country comparison to the world: 37

Electricity—consumption: 60.55 billion kWh (2012 est.)
country comparison to the world: 42

Electricity—exports: 27.46 billion kWh (2013 est.)
country comparison to the world: 7

Electricity—imports: 10.57 billion kWh (2013 est.)
country comparison to the world: 21

Electricity—installed generating capacity: 20.21 million kW (2012 est.)
country comparison to the world: 40

Electricity—from fossil fuels: 55.6% of total installed capacity (2012 est.)
country comparison to the world: 141

Electricity—from nuclear fuels: 18.8% of total installed capacity (2012 est.)
country comparison to the world: 10

Electricity—from hydroelectric plants: 5.3% of total installed capacity (2012 est.)
country comparison to the world: 125

Electricity—from other renewable sources: 14.6% of total installed capacity (2012 est.)
country comparison to the world: 21

Crude oil—production: 3,000 bbl/day (2014 est.)
country comparison to the world: 86

Crude oil—exports: 464.4 bbl/day (2013 est.)
country comparison to the world: 87

Crude oil—imports: 131,300 bbl/day (2013 est.)
country comparison to the world: 39

Crude oil—proved reserves: 15 million bbl (1 January 2015 est.)
country comparison to the world: 88

Refined petroleum products—production: 152,600 bbl/day (2013 est.)
country comparison to the world: 63

Refined petroleum products—consumption: 201,000 bbl/day (2014 est.)
country comparison to the world: 58
Refined petroleum products—exports: 37,680 bbl/day (2013 est.)
country comparison to the world: 63
Refined petroleum products—imports: 70,010 bbl/day (2013 est.)
country comparison to the world: 63
Natural gas—production: 245 million cu m (2014 est.)
country comparison to the world: 76
Natural gas—consumption: 7.508 billion cu m (2014 est.)
country comparison to the world: 53
Natural gas—exports: 1 million cu m (2014 est.)
country comparison to the world: 50
Natural gas—imports: 7.249 billion cu m (2014 est.)
country comparison to the world: 29
Natural gas—proved reserves: 4.276 billion cu m (1 January 2014 est.)
country comparison to the world: 95
Carbon dioxide emissions from consumption of energy: 91.15 million Mt (2012 est.)
country comparison to the world: 41

COMMUNICATIONS

Telephones—fixed lines: *total subscriptions:* 1.89 million
subscriptions per 100 inhabitants: 18 (2014 est.)
country comparison to the world: 60
Telephones—mobile cellular: *total:* 14 million
subscriptions per 100 inhabitants: 131 (2014 est.)
country comparison to the world: 70
Telephone system: *general assessment:* privatization and modernization of the Czech telecommunication system got a late start but is advancing steadily; virtually all exchanges now digital; existing copper subscriber systems enhanced with Asymmetric Digital Subscriber Line (ADSL) equipment to accommodate Internet and other digital signals; trunk systems include fiber-optic cable and microwave radio relay
domestic: access to the fixed-line telephone network expanded throughout the 1990s, but the number of fixed line connections has been dropping since then; mobile telephone usage increased sharply beginning in the mid-1990s, and the number of cellular telephone subscriptions now greatly exceeds the population
international: country code—420; satellite earth stations—6 (2 Intersputnik—Atlantic and Indian Ocean regions, 1 Intelsat, 1 Eutelsat, 1 Inmarsat, 1 Globalstar) (2011)
Broadcast media: roughly 130 TV broadcasters operating some 350 channels with 4 publicly operated and the remainder in private hands; 16 TV stations have national coverage with 4 being publicly operated; cable and satellite TV subscription services are available; 63 radio broadcasters are registered operating roughly 80 radio stations with 15 stations publicly operated; 10 radio stations provide national coverage with the remainder local or regional (2008)
Radio broadcast stations: AM 31, FM 304, shortwave 17 (2000)
Television broadcast stations: 71 (2008)
Internet country code: .cz
Internet hosts: 4.148 million (2012)
country comparison to the world: 27
Internet users: *total:* 8.2 million
percent of population: 77.5% (2014 est.)
country comparison to the world: 49

TRANSPORTATION

Airports: 128 (2013)
country comparison to the world: 46
Airports—with paved runways: *total:* 41
over 3,047 m: 2
2,438 to 3,047 m: 9
1,524 to 2,437 m: 12
914 to 1,523 m: 2
under 914 m: 16 (2013)
Airports—with unpaved runways: *total:* 87
1,524 to 2,437 m: 1
914 to 1,523 m: 25
under 914 m: 61 (2013)
Heliports: 1 (2013)
Pipelines: gas 7,160 km; oil 536 km; refined products 94 km (2013)
Railways: *total:* 9,621.5 km
standard gauge: 9,519.5 km 1.435-m gauge (3,240.5 km electrified)
narrow gauge: 102 km 0.760-m gauge (2014)
country comparison to the world: 23

Roadways: *total:* 130,661 km (includes urban roads)
paved: 130,661 km (includes 730 km of expressways) (2011)
country comparison to the world: 38
Waterways: 664 km (principally on Elbe, Vltava, Oder, and other navigable rivers, lakes, and canals) (2010)
country comparison to the world: 76
Merchant marine: *registered in other countries:* 1 (Saint Vincent and the Grenadines 1) (2010)
country comparison to the world: 150
Ports and terminals: *river port(s):* Prague (Vltava); Decin, Usti nad Labem (Elbe)

MILITARY AND SECURITY

Military branches: Army of the Czech Republic (Armada Ceske Republiky): General Staff (Generalni Stab; includes Land Forces (Pozemni Sily) and Air Forces (Vzdusne Sily)) (2015)
Military service age and obligation: 18–28 years of age for male and female voluntary military service; no conscription (2012)
Military expenditures: 1.04% of GDP (2015)
1.08% of GDP (2014)
1.06% of GDP (2013)
1.13% of GDP (2012)
1.15% of GDP (2011)
country comparison to the world: 94

TRANSNATIONAL ISSUES

Disputes—international: while threats of international legal action never materialized in 2007, 915, 220 Austrians, with the support of the popular Freedom Party, signed a petition in January 2008, demanding that Austria block the Czech Republic's accession to the EU unless Prague closes its controversial Soviet-style nuclear plant in Temelin, bordering Austria

Refugees and internally displaced persons: *stateless persons:* 1,502 (2015)

Illicit drugs: transshipment point for Southwest Asian heroin and minor transit point for Latin American cocaine to Western Europe; producer of synthetic drugs for local and regional markets; susceptible to money laundering related to drug trafficking, organized crime; significant consumer of ecstasy (2008)

D

INTRODUCTION

Background: Once the seat of Viking raiders and later a major north European power, Denmark has evolved into a modern, prosperous nation that is participating in the general political and economic integration of Europe. It joined NATO in 1949 and the EEC (now the EU) in 1973. However, the country has opted out of certain elements of the EU's Maastricht Treaty, including the European Economic and Monetary Union, European defense cooperation, and issues concerning certain justice and home affairs.

GEOGRAPHY

Location: Northern Europe, bordering the Baltic Sea and the North Sea, on a peninsula north of Germany (Jutland); also includes several major islands (Sjaelland, Fyn, and Bornholm)

Geographic coordinates: 56 00 N, 10 00 E

Map references: Europe

Area: *total:* 43,094 sq km
land: 42,434 sq km
water: 660 sq km
note: includes the island of Bornholm in the Baltic Sea and the rest of metropolitan Denmark (the Jutland Peninsula, and the major islands of Sjaelland and Fyn), but excludes the Faroe Islands and Greenland
country comparison to the world: 134

Area—comparative: slightly less than twice the size of Massachusetts

Land boundaries: *total:* 140 km
border countries (1): Germany 140 km

Coastline: 7,314 km

Maritime claims: *territorial sea:* 12 nm
contiguous zone: 24 nm
exclusive economic zone: 200 nm
continental shelf: 200-m depth or to the depth of exploitation

Climate: temperate; humid and overcast; mild, windy winters and cool summers

Terrain: low and flat to gently rolling plains

Elevation: *mean elevation:* 34 m

elevation extremes: *lowest point:* Lammefjord -7 m
highest point: Mollehoj/Ejer Bavnehoj 171 m

Natural resources: petroleum, natural gas, fish, arable land:, salt, limestone, chalk, stone, gravel and sand

Land use: *agricultural land:* 63.4%
arable land: 58.9%
permanent crops: 0.1%
permanent pasture: 4.4%
forest: 12.9%
other: 23.7%
note: highest percentage of arable land: for any country in the world (2011 est.)

Irrigated land: 4,350 sq km (2012)

Total renewable water resources: 6 cu km (2011)

Freshwater withdrawal (domestic/industrial/agricultural): *total:* 0.66 cu km/yr (58%/5%/36%)
per capita: 118.4 cu m/yr (2009)

Natural hazards: flooding is a threat in some areas of the country (e.g., parts of Jutland, along the southern coast of the island of Lolland) that are protected from the sea by a system of dikes

Environment—current issues: air pollution, principally from vehicle and power plant emissions; nitrogen and phosphorus pollution of the North Sea; drinking and surface water becoming polluted from animal wastes and pesticides

Environment—international agreements: *party to:* Air Pollution, Air Pollution-Nitrogen Oxides, Air Pollution-Persistent Organic Pollutants, Air Pollution-Sulfur 85, Air Pollution-Sulfur 94, Air Pollution-Volatile Organic Compounds, Antarctic Treaty, Biodiversity, Climate Change, Climate Change-Kyoto Protocol, Desertification, Endangered Species, Environmental Modification, Hazardous Wastes, Law of the Sea, Marine Dumping, Marine Life Conservation, Ozone Layer Protection, Ship Pollution, Tropical Timber 83, Tropical Timber 94, Wetlands, Whaling
signed, but not ratified: none of the selected agreements

Geography—note: controls Danish Straits (Skagerrak and Kattegat) linking Baltic and North Seas; about one-quarter of the population lives in greater Copenhagen

PEOPLE AND SOCIETY

Nationality: *noun:* Dane(s)
adjective: Danish

Ethnic groups: Scandinavian, Inuit, Faroese, German, Turkish, Iranian, Somali

Languages: Danish, Faroese, Greenlandic (an Inuit dialect), German (small minority)
note: English is the predominant second language

Religions: Evangelical Lutheran (official) 80%, Muslim 4%, other (denominations of less than 1% each, includes Roman Catholic, Jehovah's Witness, Serbian Orthodox Christian, Jewish, Baptist, and Buddhist) 16% (2012 est.)

Population: 5,581,503 (July 2015 est.)
country comparison to the world: 116

Age structure: *0–14 years:* 16.77% (male 480,267/female 455,946)
15–24 years: 13.11% (male 373,547/female 358,150)
25–54 years: 39.03% (male 1,085,130/female 1,093,162)
55–64 years: 12.41% (male 344,509/female 348,201)
65 years and over: 18.68% (male 466,566/female 576,025) (2015 est.)

Dependency ratios:
total dependency ratio: 55.9%
youth dependency ratio: 26.3%
elderly dependency ratio: 29.6%
potential support ratio: 3.4% (2015 est.)

Median age: *total:* 41.8 years
male: 40.9 years
female: 42.8 years (2015 est.)
country comparison to the world: 30

Population growth rate: 0.22% (2015 est.)
country comparison to the world: 182

Birth rate: 10.27 births/1,000 population (2015 est.)
country comparison to the world: 191

Death rate: 10.25 deaths/1,000 population (2015 est.)
country comparison to the world: 38

Net migration rate: 2.2 migrant(s)/1,000 population (2015 est.)
country comparison to the world: 49

Urbanization: *urban population:* 87.7% of total population (2015)
rate of urbanization: 0.6% annual rate of change (2010-15 est.)

Major urban areas—population: COPENHAGEN (capital) 1.268 million (2015)

Sex ratio: *at birth:* 1.06 male(s)/female
0–14 years: 1.05 male(s)/female
15–24 years: 1.04 male(s)/female
25–54 years: 0.99 male(s)/female
55–64 years: 0.99 male(s)/female
65 years and over: 0.81 male(s)/female
total population: 0.97 male(s)/female (2015 est.)

Mother's mean age at first birth: 29.1 (2012 est.)

Maternal mortality rate: 6 deaths/100,000 live births (2015 est.)
country comparison to the world: 151

Infant mortality rate: *total:* 4.05 deaths/1,000 live births
male: 4.12 deaths/1,000 live births
female: 3.97 deaths/1,000 live births (2015 est.)
country comparison to the world: 191

Life expectancy at birth: *total population:* 79.25 years

male: 76.82 years
female: 81.81 years (2015 est.)
country comparison to the world: 47

Total fertility rate: 1.73 children born/woman (2015 est.)
country comparison to the world: 168

Health expenditures: 10.6% of GDP (2013)
country comparison to the world: 14

Physicians density: 3.49 physicians/1,000 population (2010)

Hospital bed density: 3.5 beds/1,000 population (2010)

Drinking water source:
improved:
urban: 100% of population
rural: 100% of population
total: 100% of population
unimproved:
urban: 0% of population
rural: 0% of population
total: 0% of population (2015 est.)

Sanitation facility access:
improved:
urban: 99.6% of population
rural: 99.6% of population
total: 99.6% of population
unimproved:
urban: 0.4% of population
rural: 0.4% of population
total: 0.4% of population (2015 est.)

HIV/AIDS—adult prevalence rate: 0.16% (2014 est.)
country comparison to the world: 102

HIV/AIDS—people living with HIV/AIDS: 6,000 (2014 est.)
country comparison to the world: 108

HIV/AIDS—deaths: fewer than 100 (2014 est.)
country comparison to the world: 123

Obesity—adult prevalence rate: 21% (2014)
country comparison to the world: 107

Education expenditures: 8.5% of GDP (2011)
country comparison to the world: 8

School life expectancy (primary to tertiary education): *total:* 19 years
male: 18 years
female: 20 years (2014)

Unemployment, youth ages 15–24:
total: 12.6%
male: 13.7%
female: 11.5% (2014 est.)
country comparison to the world: 84

GOVERNMENT

Country name: *conventional long form:* Kingdom of Denmark
conventional short form: Denmark
local long form: Kongeriget Danmark
local short form: Danmark
etymology: the name derives from the words "Dane(s)" and "mark"; the latter referring to a march (borderland) or forest

Government type: parliamentary constitutional monarchy

Capital: *name:* Copenhagen
Geographic coordinates: 55 40 N, 12 35 E
time difference: UTC + 1 (6 hours ahead of Washington, DC, during Standard Time)
daylight saving time: +1hr, begins last Sunday in March; ends last Sunday in October
note: applies to continental Denmark only, not to its North Atlantic components

Administrative divisions: metropolitan Denmark—5 regions (regioner, singular-region); Hovedstaden (Capital), Midtjylland (Central Jutland), Nordjylland (North Jutland), Sjaelland (Zealand), Syddanmark (Southern Denmark)
note: an extensive local government reform merged 271 municipalities into 98 and 13 counties into five regions, effective 1 January 2007

Independence: ca. 965 (unified and Christianized under HARALDI Gormson); 5 June 1849 (became a parliamentary constitutional monarchy)

National holiday: none designated; Constitution Day, 5 June (1849) is generally viewed as National Day

Constitution: several previous; latest adopted 5 June 1953; changed several times, last in 2009 (Danish Act of Succession) (2016)

Legal system: civil law; judicial review of legislative acts

International law organization participation: accepts compulsory ICJ jurisdiction with reservations; accepts ICCt jurisdiction

Citizenship: *citizenship by birth:* no
citizenship by descent only: at least one parent must be a citizen of Denmark
dual citizenship recognized: yes
residency requirement for naturalization: 7 years

Suffrage: 18 years of age; universal

Executive branch: *chief of state:* Queen MARGRETHE II (since 14 January 1972); Heir Apparent Crown Prince FREDERIK, elder son of the monarch (born on 26 May 1968)

head of government: Prime Minister Lars LOEKKE RASMUSSEN (since 28 June 2015)
cabinet: Council of State appointed by the monarch
elections/appointments: the monarchy is hereditary; following legislative elections, the leader of the majority party or majority coalition usually appointed prime minister by the monarch

Legislative branch: *description:* unicameral People's Assembly or Folketing (179 seats, including 2 representing Greenland and 2 representing the Faroe Islands; members directly elected in multi-seat constituencies by proportional representation vote; members serve 4-year terms unless the Folketing is dissolved earlier)
elections: last held on 18 June 2015 (next to be held by June 2019)
election results: percent of vote by party—SDP 26.3%, DF 21.1%, V 19.5%, EL 7.8%, LA 7.5%, AP 4.8%, SLP 4.6%, SF 4.2%, C 3.4%, other

0.9%; seats by party—SDP 47, DF 37, V 34, EL 14, LA 13, AP 9, SLP 8, SF 7, C 6; note—does not include each of the two seats from Greenland and the Faroe Islands

Judicial branch: *highest court(s):* Supreme Court (consists of the court president and 18 judges)
judge selection and term of office: judges appointed by the monarch upon the recommendation of the Minister of Justice with the advice of the Judicial Appointments Council, a 6-member independent body of lawyers and judges; judges appointed for life with retirement at age 70
subordinate court(s): Special Court of Indictment and Revision; 2 High Courts; Maritime and Commercial Court; county courts

Political parties and leaders: Alternative Party or AP [Uffe ELBAEK]
Conservative People's Party or C [Soren PAPE POULSEN]
Danish People's Party or DF [Kristian THULESEN DAHL]
Liberal Alliance or LA [Anders SAMUELSEN]
Liberal Party or V [Lars LOEKKE RASMUSSEN]
Red-Green Alliance (Unity List) or EL [collective leadership, spokesperson Johanne SCHMIDT-NIELSEN]
Social Democratic Party or SDP [Mette FREDERIKSEN]
Social Liberal Party or SLP [Morten OSTERGAARD]
Socialist People's Party or SF [Pia OLSEN DYHR]

Political pressure groups and leaders: Confederation of Danish Employers or DA [CEO Jacob HOLBRAAD]
Confederation of Danish Industries or DI [CEO Karsten DYBVAD]
Confederation of Danish Labor Unions (Landsorganisationen) or LO [President Lizette RISGAARD] Dane Age Association [President Bjarne HASTRUP]
Danish Shipowners' Association [Director General and CEO Anne STEFFENSEN]]
Danish Bankers Association [CEO Ulrik NODGAARD]
Danish Society for Nature Conservation or DN [President Ella Maria BISSCHOP-LARSEN]
other: environmental groups; humanitarian relief; development assistance; human rights NGOs

International organization participation: ADB (nonregional member), AfDB (nonregional member), Arctic Council, Australia Group, BIS, CBSS, CD, CE, CERN, EAPC, EBRD, ECB, EIB, EITI (implementing country), ESA, EU, FAO, FATF, G-9, IADB, IAEA, IBRD, ICAO, ICC (national committees), ICCt, ICRM, IDA, IEA, IFAD, IFC, IFRCS, IGAD (partners), IHO, ILO, IMF, IMO, IMSO, Interpol, IOC, IOM, IPU, ISO, ITSO, ITU, ITUC (NGOs), MIGA, MINUSMA, NATO, NC, NEA, NIB, NSG, OAS (observer), OECD, OPCW, OSCE, Paris Club, PCA, Schengen Convention, UN, UNCTAD, UNESCO, UNHCR, UNIDO, UNMIL, UNMISS, UNRWA, UNTSO, UPU, WCO, WHO, WIPO, WMO, WTO, ZC

Diplomatic representation in the US: *chief of mission:* Ambassador Lars Gert LOSE (since 17 September 2015)
chancery: 3200 Whitehaven Street NW, Washington, DC 20008
telephone: [1] (202) 234-4300
FAX: [1] (202) 328-1470
consulate(s) general: Chicago, New York

Diplomatic representation from the US: *chief of mission:* Ambassador Rufus GIFFORD (since 13 September 2013)
embassy: Dag Hammarskjolds Alle 24,2100 Copenhagen 0
mailing address: Unit 5280, DPO, AE 09716
telephone: [45] 33 41 71 00
FAX: [45] 35 43 02 23

Flag description: red with a white cross that extends to the edges of the flag; the vertical part of the cross is shifted to the hoist side; the banner is referred to as the Dannebrog (Danish flag) and is one of the oldest national flags in the world; traditions as to the origin of the flag design vary, but the best known is a legend that the banner fell from the sky during an early-13th century battle; caught up by the Danish king before it ever touched the earth, this heavenly talisman inspired the royal army to victory; in actuality, the flag may derive from a crusa de banner or ensign
note: the shifted cross design element was subsequently adopted by the other Nordic countries of Finland, Iceland, Norway, and Sweden

National symbol(s): lion, mute swan; national colors: red, white

National anthem: *name:* "Der er et yndigt land" (There is a Lovely Land); "Kong Christian" (King Christian)
lyrics/music: Adam Gottlob OEHLEN-SCHLAGER/Hans Ernst KROYER; Johannes EWALD/unknown
note: Denmark has two national anthems with equal status; "Der er et yndigt land, "adopted 1844, is a national anthem, while "Kong Christian, "adopted 1780, serves as both a national and royal anthem; "Kong Christian" is also known as "Kong Christian stod ved hojen mast" (King Christian Stood by the Lofty Mast) and "Kongesangen" (The King's Anthem); within Denmark, the royal anthem is played only when royalty is present and is usually followed by the national anthem; when royalty is not present, only the national anthem is performed; outside Denmark, the royal anthem is played, unless the national anthem is requested

ECONOMY

Economy—overview: This thoroughly modern market economy features a high-tech agricultural sector, advanced industry with world-leading firms in pharmaceuticals, maritime shipping and renewable energy, and a high dependence on foreign trade. Denmark is a net exporter of food, oil, and gas and enjoys a comfortable balance of payments surplus, but depends on imports of raw materials for the manufacturing sector. Danes en joy a high standard of living and the Danish economy is characterized by extensive government welfare

measures and an equitable distribution of income. An aging population will be a major long-term issue. Denmark is a member of the EU; Danish legislation and regulations conform to EU standards on almost all issues. Despite previously meeting the criteria to join the European Economic and Monetary Union, Denmark has negotiated an opt-out with the EU and is not required to adopt the euro. Within the EU, Denmark is among the strongest supporters of trade liberalization.
After a long consumption-driven upswing, Denmark's economy began slowing in 2007 with the end of a housing boom. Housing prices dropped markedly in 2008–09 but, with significant regional differences, have since recovered. Household indebtedness is still relatively high at more than 305% of net disposable income in 2014, while household net worth—from private pension schemes and other assets—amounted to 546% of net disposable income. The global financial crisis exacerbated this cyclical slowdown by increasing domestic borrowing costs and lowering foreign demand for Danish exports. Denmark maintained a healthy budget surplus for many years up to 2008, but the budget balance swung into deficit in 2009. The structural budget deficit has remained below 1% and is estimated at -0.4% in 2016. Denmark is experiencing a lackluster economic recovery, having still not regained the GDP level of 2008. GDP contracted in 2012 and 2013, followed by real growth of 1.3% in 2014, and 1.2% in 2015. The government projects 1.9% growth in 2016, while private sector estimates are about 1% growth. A historically low level of unemployment rose with the economic downturn but the labor market has strengthened since 2013, and unemployment stood at about 4.5% in early 2016, based on the national measure. Productivity growth was significantly below the OECD average in 2012–2014.

GDP (purchasing power parity):
$258.7 billion (2015 est.)
$255.7 billion (2014 est.)
$252.5 billion (2013 est.)
note: data are in 2015 US dollars
country comparison to the world: 59

GDP (official exchange rate):
$295 billion (2015 est.)

GDP—real growth rate:
1.2% (2015 est.)
1.3% (2014 est.)
-0.2% (2013 est.)
country comparison to the world: 164

GDP—per capita (PPP): $45,700 (2015 est.)
$45,400 (2014 est.)
$45,100 (2013 est.)
note: data are in 2015 US dollars
country comparison to the world: 31

Gross national saving: 26.3% of GDP (2015 est.)
27.6% of GDP (2014 est.)
26.6% of GDP (2013 est.)
country comparison to the world: 43

GDP—composition, by end use:
household consumption: 48.1%
government consumption: 26.4%
investment in fixed capital: 18.3%

investment in inventories: 0.4%
exports of goods and services: 51.9%
imports of goods and services: -45.1% (2015 est.)

GDP—composition, by sector of origin:
agriculture: 1.3%
industry: 22.4%
services: 76.3% (2015 est.)

Agriculture—products: barley, wheat, potatoes, sugar beets; pork, dairy products; fish

Industries: iron, steel, nonferrous metals, chemicals, food processing, machinery and transportation equipment, textiles and cloth ing, electronics, construction, furniture and other wood products, sh ipbuilding and refurbish ment, windmills, ph armaceuticals, medical equipment

Industrial production growth rate: 0.7% (2015 est.)
country comparison to the world: 155

Labor force: 2.774 million (2015 est.)
country comparison to the world: 107

Labor force—by occupation: *agriculture:* 2.6%
industry: 20.3%
services: 77.1% (2011 est.)

Unemployment rate: 4.7% (2015 est.)
4.9% (2014 est.)
country comparison to the world: 46

Population below poverty line: 13.4% (2011 est.)

Household income or consumption by percentage share: *lowest:* 10%: 1.9%
highest: 10%: 28.7% (2007)

Distribution of family income—Gini index:
24.8 (2011 est.)
24.7 (1992)
country comparison to the world: 143

Budget: *revenues:* $161.7 billion
expenditures: $170.9 billion (2015 est.)
Taxes and other revenues: 55.6% of GDP (2015 est.)
country comparison to the world: 9

Budget surplus (+) or deficit (-):
-3.2% of GDP (2015 est.)
country comparison to the world: 118

Public debt:
47.2% of GDP (2015 est.)
45.1% of GDP (2014 est.)
note: data cover general government debt and include debt instruments issued (or owned) by government entities other than the treasury; the data include treasury debt held by foreign entities; the data include debt issued by subnational entities, as well as intra-governmental debt; intra-governmental debt consists of treasury borrowings from surpluses in the social funds, such as for retirement, medical care, and unemployment; debt instruments for the social funds are not sold at public auctions
country comparison to the world: 91

Fiscal year: calendar year

Inflation rate (consumer prices):
0.5% (2015 est.)
0.6% (2014 est.)
country comparison to the world: 61

Central bank discount rate: 0.75% (31 December 2011)

0.75% (31 December 2010)
country comparison to the world: 126

Commercial bank prime lending rate:
2.9% (31 December 2015 est.)
3.62% (31 December 2014 est.)
country comparison to the world: 170

Stock of narrow money:
$157.3 billion (31 December 2015 est.)
$154.7 billion (31 December 2014 est.)
country comparison to the world: 26

Stock of broad money:
$181.1 billion (31 December 2014 est.)
$189.2 billion (31 December 2013 est.)
country comparison to the world: 42

Stock of domestic credit:
$631.7 billion (31 December 2015 est.)
$705.9 billion (31 December 2014 est.)
country comparison to the world: 21

Market value of publicly traded shares:
$224.9 billion (31 December 2015 est.)
$179.5 billion (31 December 2011)
$231.7 billion (31 December 2010 est.)
country comparison to the world: 34

Current account balance:
$20.28 billion (2015 est.)
$26.71 billion (2014 est.)
country comparison to the world: 15

Exports: $94.1 billion (2015 est.)
$111.4 billion (2014 est.)
country comparison to the world: 37

Exports—commodities: machinery and instruments, meat and meat products, dairy products, fish, pharmaceuticals, furniture, windmills

Exports—partners: Germany 17.8%, Sweden 11.6%, US 8.4%, Norway 6.3%, UK 6.3%, Netherlands 4.4%, China 4.2% (2015)

Imports: $83.81 billion (2015 est.)
$101.3 billion (2014 est.)
country comparison to the world: 36

Imports—commodities: machinery and equipment, raw materials and semimanufactures for industry, chemicals, grain and foodstuffs, consumer goods

Imports—partners: Germany 20.4%, Sweden 12.3%, Netherlands 8.1%, China 7.3%, Norway 6.1%, UK 4.4% (2015)

Reserves of foreign exchange and gold:
$102.5 billion (31 December 2015 est.)
$75.38 billion (31 December 2014 est.)
country comparison to the world: 23

Debt—external: $534.6 billion (31 December 2014 est.)
$609.8 billion (31 December 2013 est.)
country comparison to the world: 25

Stock of direct foreign investment—at home:
$145.1 billion (31 December 2015 est.)
$144.5 billion (31 December 2014 est.)
country comparison to the world: 38

Stock of direct foreign investment—abroad:
$252.3 billion (31 December 2015 est.)
$249.8 billion (31 December 2014 est.)
country comparison to the world: 25

Exchange rates: Danish kroner (DKK) per US dollar—
6.588 (2015 est.)
5.6125 (2014 est.)
5.6125 (2013 est.)
5.79 (2012 est.)
5.3687 (2011 est.)

ENERGY

Electricity—production: 28.93 billion kWh (2012 est.)
country comparison to the world: 65

Electricity—consumption: 31.96 billion kWh (2012 est.)
country comparison to the world: 60

Electricity—exports: 10.38 billion kWh (2013 est.)
country comparison to the world: 21

Electricity—imports: 11.46 billion kWh (2013 est.)
country comparison to the world: 19

Electricity—installed generating capacity:
14.05 million kW (2012 est.)
country comparison to the world: 50

Electricity—from fossil fuels: 56.8% of total installed capacity (2012 est.)
country comparison to the world: 140

Electricity—from nuclear fuels: 0% of total installed capacity (2012 est.)
country comparison to the world: 78

Electricity—from hydroelectric plants: 0.1% of total installed capacity (2012 est.)
country comparison to the world: 153

Electricity—from other renewable sources:
43.1% of total installed capacity (2012 est.)
country comparison to the world: 1

Crude oil—production: 165,200 bbl/day (2014 est.)
country comparison to the world: 40

Crude oil—exports: 136,600 bbl/day (2013 est.)
country comparison to the world: 34

Crude oil—imports: 99,690 bbl/day (2013 est.)
country comparison to the world: 48

Crude oil—proved reserves: 611 million bbl (1 January 2015 est.)
country comparison to the world: 46

Refined petroleum products—production:
177,800 bbl/day (2013 est.)
country comparison to the world: 57

Refined petroleum products—consumption:
153,900 bbl/day (2014 est.)
country comparison to the world: 65

Refined petroleum products—exports:
129,500 bbl/day (2013 est.)
country comparison to the world: 42

Refined petroleum products—imports:
141,100 bbl/day (2013 est.)
country comparison to the world: 38

Natural gas—production: 4.612 billion cu m (2014 est.)
country comparison to the world: 53

Natural gas—consumption: 3.16 billion cu m (2014 est.)
country comparison to the world: 71

Natural gas—exports: 2.093 billion cu m (2014 est.)
country comparison to the world: 37

Natural gas -imports: 625 million cu m (2014 est.)
country comparison to the world: 62

Natural gas—proved reserves: 43.01 billion cu m (1 January 2014 est.)
country comparison to the world: 66

Carbon dioxide emissions from consumption of energy: 40.51 million Mt (2012 est.)
country comparison to the world: 67

COMMUNICATIONS

Telephones—fixed lines: *total subscriptions:* 1.88 million
subscriptions per 100 inhabitants: 34 (2014 est.)
country comparison to the world: 61

Telephones—mobile cellular: *total:* 7.1 million
subscriptions per 100 inhabitants: 128 (2014 est.)
country comparison to the world: 106

Telephone system: *general assessment:* excellent telephone and telegraph services
domestic: buried and submarine cables and microwave radio relay form trunk network, multiple mobile-cellular communications systems
international: country code—45; a series of fiber-optic submarine cables link Denmark with Canada, Faroe Islands, Germany, Iceland, Netherlands, Norway, Poland, Russia, Sweden, and UK; satellite earth stations—18 (6 Intelsat, 10 Eutelsat, 1 Orion, 1 Inmarsat (Blaavand-Atlantic-East)); note—the Nordic countries (Denmark, Finland, Iceland, Norway, and Sweden) share the Danish earth station and the Eik, Norway, station for worldwide Inmarsat access (2011)

Broadcast media: strong public-sector TV presence with state-owned Danmarks Radio (DR) operating 6 channels and publicly owned TV2 operating roughly a half dozen channels; broadcasts of privately owned stations are available via satellite and cable feed; DR operates 4 nationwide FM radio stations, 10 digital audio broadcasting stations, and 14 web-based radio stations; in 2010, there were 140 commercial and 187 community (non-commercial) radio stations
Radio broadcast stations: AM 1, FM 355, shortwave 0 (1998)
Television broadcast stations: 172 (2008)

Internet country code: .dk

Internet hosts: 4.297 million (2012)
country comparison to the world: 25

Internet users: *total:* 5.4 million
percent of population: 96.1% (2014 est.)
country comparison to the world: 62

TRANSPORTATION

Airports: 80 (2013)
country comparison to the world: 68
Airports—with paved runways: *total:* 28

over 3,047 m: 2
2,438 to 3,047 m: 7
1,524 to 2,437 m: 5
914 to 1,523 m: 12
under 914 m: 2 (2013)

Airports—with unpaved runways: *total:* 52
914 to 1,523 m: 5
under 914 m: 47 (2013)

Pipelines: condensate 11 km; gas 4,377 km; oil 647 km; oil/gas/water 2 km (2013)

Railways: *total:* 2,633 km
standard gauge: 2,633 km 1.435-m gauge (642 km electrified) (2015)
country comparison to the world: 66

Roadways: *total:* 74,497 km
paved: 74,497 km (includes 1,188 km of expressways) (2016)
country comparison to the world: 63

Waterways: 400 km (2010)
country comparison to the world: 87

Merchant marine: *total:* 367
by type: bulk carrier 4, cargo 48, carrier 1, chemical tanker 125, container 94, liquefied gas 4, passenger 1, passenger/cargo 40, petroleum tanker 36, refrigerated cargo 3, roll on/roll off 8, specialized tanker 3
foreign-owned: 27 (Germany 9, Greenland 1, Norway 2, Sweden 15)
registered in other countries: 582 (Antigua and Barbuda 20, Bahamas 69, Belgium 4, Brazil 3,

Curacao 1, Cyprus 6, Egypt 1, France 11, Gibraltar 7, Hong Kong 42, Isle of Man 30, Italy 4, Jamaica 1, Liberia 8, Lithuania 8, Luxembourg 1, Malaysia 1, Malta 34, Marshall Islands 7, Moldova 1, Netherlands 27, Norway 7, Panama 41, Philippines 2, Portugal 4, Saint Vincent and the Grenadines 9, Singapore 149, Sweden 4, UK 43, Uruguay 1, US 31, Venezuela 1, unknown 4) (2010)
country comparison to the world: 27

Ports and terminals: *major seaport(s):* Baltic Sea—Aarhus, Copenhagen, Fredericia, Kalundborg; North Sea—Esbjerg,
river port(s): Aalborg (Lan gerak)
dry bulk cargo port(s): Ensted (coal)
cruise port(s): Copen hagen

MILITARY AND SECURITY

Military branches: Defense Command: Army Operational Command, Admiral Danish Fleet, Arctic Command, Tactical Air Command, Home Guard (2010)

Military service age and obligation: 18 years of age for compulsory and voluntary military service; conscripts serve an initial training period that varies from 4 to 12 months according to specialization; reservists are assigned to mobilization units following completion of their conscript service; women eligible to volunteer for military service (2012)

Military expenditures: 1.2% of GDP (2015)

1.17% of GDP (2014)
1.37% of GDP (2013)
1.41% of GDP (2012)
1.35% of GDP (2011)
country comparison to the world: 71

TRANSNATIONAL ISSUES

Disputes—international: Iceland, the UK, and Ireland dispute Denmark's claim that the Faroe Islands' continental shelf extends beyond 200 nm; sovereignty dispute with Canada over Hans Island in the Kennedy Channel between Ellesmere Island and Greenland; Denmark (Greenland) and Norway have made submissions to the Commission on the Limits of the Continental Shelf (CLCS) and Russia is collecting additional data to augment its 2001 CLCS submission

Refugees and internally displaced persons: *refugees (country of origin):* 7,253 (Afghanistan) (2014)
stateless persons: 6,580 (2015)

DHEKELIA

INTRODUCTION

Background: By terms of the 1960 Treaty of Establishment that created the independent Republic of Cyprus, the UK retained full sovereignty and jurisdiction over two areas of almost 254 square kilometers—Akrotiri and Dhekelia. The larger of these is the Dhekelia Sovereign Base Area, which is also referred to as the Eastern Sovereign Base Area.

GEOGRAPHY

Location: Eastern Mediterranean, on the southeast coast of Cyprus near Famagusta

Geographic coordinates: 34 59 N, 33 45 E

Map references: Middle East

Area: *total:* 130.8 sq km
note: area surrounds three Cypriot enclaves
country comparison to the world: 223

Area—comparative: about three-quarters the size of Washington, DC

Land boundaries: *total:* 108 km
border countries (1): Cyprus 108 km

Coastline: 27.5 km

Climate: temperate; Mediterranean with hot, dry summers and cool winters

Environment—current issues: netting and trapping of small migrant songbirds in the spring and autumn

Geography—note: British extraterritorial rights also extended to several small off-post sites scattered across Cyprus; of the Sovereign Base Area (SBA) land, 60% is privately owned and farmed, 20% is owned by the Ministry of Defense, and 20% is SBA Crown land

PEOPLE AND SOCIETY

Languages: English, Greek

Population: approximately 15,700 live on the Sovereign Base Areas of Akrotiri and Dhekelia including 7,700 Cypriots, 3,600 service and UK based contract personnel, and 4,400 dependents

GOVERNMENT

Country name: *conventional long form:* none
conventional short form: Dhekelia

Dependency status: a special form of UK overseas territory; administered by an administrator who is also the Commander, British Forces Cyprus

Capital: *name:* Episkopi Cantonment (base administrative center for Akrotiri and Dhekelia); located in Akrotiri

Geographic coordinates: 34 40 N, 32 51 E
time difference: UTC+2 (7 hours ahead of Washington, DC, during Standard Time)
daylight saving time: +1hr, begins last Sunday in March; ends last Sunday in October

Constitution: presented 3 August 1960, effective 16 August 1960 (The Sovereign Base Areas of Akrotiri and Dhekelia Order in Council 1960, serves as a basic legal document); amended 1966 (2016)

Legal system: laws applicable to the Cypriot population are, as far as possible, the same as the laws of the Republic of Cyprus; note—the Sovereign Base Area Administration has its own court system to deal with civil and criminal matters

Executive branch: *chief of state:* Queen ELIZABETH II (since 6 February 1952)

head of government: Administrator Air Vice-Marshall Michael WIGSTON (since 21 January 2015); note—reports to the British Ministry of Defense

elections/appointments: the monarchy is hereditary; administrator appointed by the monarch on the advice of the Ministry of Defense

Judicial branch: *highest court(s):* Senior Judges' Court (consists of several visiting judges from England and Wales)

judge selection and term of office: judges appointment and tenure NA

subordinate court(s): Resident Judges' Court; Courts Martial

Diplomatic representation in the US: none (overseas territory of the UK)

Diplomatic representation from the US: none (overseas territory of the UK)

Flag description: the flag of the UK is used

National anthem: *note:* as a United Kingdom area of special sovereignty, "God Save the Queen" is official (see United Kingdom)

ECONOMY

Economy—overview: Economic activity is limited to providing services to the military and their families located in Dhekelia. All food and manufactured goods must be imported.

Industries: none

Exchange rates: *note:* uses the euro

COMMUNICATIONS

Broadcast media: British Forces Broadcast Service (BFBS) provides multi-channel satellite TV

service as well as BFBS radio broadcasts to the Dhekelia Sovereign Base (2009)

Radio broadcast stations: AM NA, FM 1 (located in Akrotiri), shortwave NA (British Forces Broadcasting Service (BFBS) provides Radio 1 and Radio 2 service to Akrotiri, Dhekelia, and Nicosia) (2006)

Television broadcast stations: 0 (British Forces Broadcasting Service (BF BS) provides multi-channel satellite service to Akrotiri, Dhekelia, and Nicosia) (2006)

MILITARY AND SECURITY

Military—note: defense is the responsibility of the UK; includes Dhekelia Garrison and Ayios Nikolaos Station connected by a roadway

---

DJIBOUTI

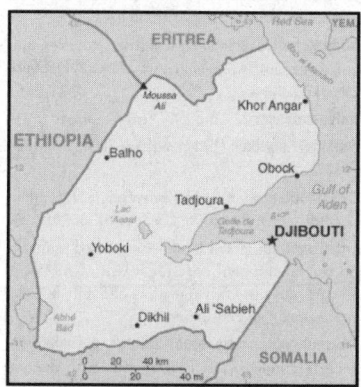

INTRODUCTION

Background: The French Territory of the Afars and the Issas became Djibouti in 1977. Hassan Gouled APTIDON installed an authoritarian one-party state and proceeded to serve as president until 1999. Unrest among the Afar minority during the 1990s led to a civil war that ended in 2001 with a peace accord between Afar rebels and the Somali Issa-dominated government. In 1999, Djibouti's first multiparty presidential election resulted in the election of Ismail Omar GUELLEH as president; he was reelected to a second term in 2005 and extended his tenure in office via a constitutional amendment, which allowed him to begin a

third term in 2011. Djibouti occupies a strategic geographic location at the intersection of the Red Sea and the Gulf of Aden and serves as an important shipping portal for goods entering and leaving the east African highlands and transshipments between Europe, the Middle East, and Asia. The government holds longstanding ties to France, which maintains a significant military presence in the country, and has strong ties with the US. Djibouti hosts several thousand members of US armed services at US-run Camp Lemonnier.

GEOGRAPHY

Location: Eastern Africa, bordering the Gulf of Aden and the Red Sea, between Eritrea and Somalia

Geographic coordinates: 11 30 N, 43 00 E

Map references: Africa

Area: *total:* 23,200 sq km
land: 23,180 sq km
water: 20 sq km
country comparison to the world: 151

Area—comparative: slightly smaller than New Jersey

Land boundaries: *total:* 528 km
border countries (3): Eritrea 125 km, Ethiopia 342 km, Somalia 61 km

Coastline: 314 km

Maritime claims: *territorial sea:* 12 nm
contiguous zone: 24 nm
exclusive economic zone: 200 nm

Climate: desert; torrid, dry

Terrain: coastal plain and plateau separated by central mountains

Elevation: *mean elevation:* 430 m

elevation extremes: *lowest point:* Lac Assal -155 m
highest point: Moussa Ali 2,028 m

Natural resources: potential geothermal power, gold, clay, granite, lim estone, m arble, salt, diatomite, gypsum, pum ice, petroleum

Land use: *agricultural land:* 73.4%
arable land: 0.1%
permanent crops: 0%
permanent pasture: 73.3%
forest: 0.2%
other: 26.4% (2011 est.)

Irrigated land: 10 sq km (2012)

Total renewable water resources: 0.3 cu km (2011)

Freshwater withdrawal (domestic/industrial/agricultural): *total:* 0.02 cu km/yr (84%/0%/16%)
per capita: 24.84 cu m/yr (2000)

Natural hazards: earthquakes; droughts; occasional cyclonic disturbances from the Indian Ocean bring heavy rains and flash floods

volcanism: experiences limited volcanic activity; Ardoukoba (elev. 298 m) last erupted in 1978; Manda-Inakir, located along the Ethiopian border, is also historically active

Environment—current issues: inadequate supplies of potable water; limited arable land; desertification; endangered species

Environment—international agreements: *party to:* Biodiversity, Climate Change, Climate Change-Kyoto Protocol, Desertification, Endangered Species, Hazardous Wastes, Law of the Sea, Ozone Layer Protection, Ship Pollution, Wetlands *signed, but not ratified:* none of the selected agreements

Geography—note: strategic location near world's busiest shipping lanes and close to Arabian oilfields; terminus of rail traffic into Ethiopia; mostly wasteland; Lac Assal (Lake Assal) is the lowest point in Africa and the saltiest lake in the world

PEOPLE AND SOCIETY

Nationality: *noun:* Djiboutian(s)
adjective: Djiboutian

Ethnic groups: Somali 60%, Afar 35%, other 5% (includes French, Arab, Ethiopian, and Italian)

Languages: French (official), Arabic (official), Somali, Afar

Religions: Muslim 94%, Christian 6%

Population: 828,324 (July 2015 est.)
country comparison to the world: 163

Age structure: *0–14 years:* 32.31% (male 134,166/female 133,479)
15–24 years: 21.82% (male 85,021/female 95,706)
25–54 years: 37.59% (male 129,382/female 182,021)
55–64 years: 4.67% (male 17,970/female 20,689)
65 *years and over:* 3.61% (male 13,422/female 16,468) (2015 est.)

Dependency ratios: *total dependency ratio:* 58.5%
youth dependency ratio: 51.9%
elderly dependency ratio: 6.6%
potential support ratio: 15.1% (2015 est.)

Median age: *total:* 23.2 years
male: 21.5 years
female: 24.5 years (2015 est.)
country comparison to the world: 167

Population growth rate: 2.2% (2015 est.)
country comparison to the world: 40

Birth rate: 23.65 births/1,000 population (2015 est.)
country comparison to the world: 64

Death rate: 7.73 deaths/1,000 population (2015 est.)
country comparison to the world: 105

Net migration rate: 6.06 migrant(s)/1,000 population (2015 est.)
country comparison to the world: 20

Urbanization: *urban population:* 77.3% of total population (2015)
rate of urbanization: 1.6% annual rate of change (2010–15 est.)

Major urban areas—population: DJIBOUTI (capital) 529,000 (2015)

Sex ratio: *at birth:* 1.03 male(s)/female
0–14 years: 1.01 male(s)/female
15–24 years: 0.89 male(s)/female
25–54 years: 0.71 male(s)/female

55–64 years: 0.87 male(s)/female
65 years and over: 0.82 male(s)/female
total populati on: 0.85 male(s)/female (2015 est.)

Maternal mortality rate: 229 deaths/100,000 live births (2015 est.)
country comparison to the world: 56

Infant mortality rate: *total:* 48.7 deaths/1,000 live births
male: 55.79 deaths/1,000 live births
female: 41.39 deaths/1,000 live births (2015 est.)
country comparison to the world: 39

Life expectancy at birth: *total population:* 62.79 years
male: 60.28 years
female: 65.37 years (2015 est.)
country comparison to the world: 188

Total fertility rate: 2.39 children born/woman (2015 est.)
country comparison to the world: 83

Contraceptive prevalence rate: 19% (2012)

Health expenditures: 8.9% of GDP (2013)
country comparison to the world: 44

Physicians density: 0.23 physicians/1,000 population (2006)

Hospital bed density: 1.4 beds/1,000 population (2012)

Drinking water source:
improved:
urban: 97.4% of population
rural: 64.7% of population
total: 90% of population
unimproved:
urban: 2.6% of population
rural: 35.3% of population
total: 10% of population (2015 est.)

Sanitation facility access:
improved:
urban: 59.8% of population
rural: 5.1% of population
total: 47.4% of population
unimproved:
urban: 40.2% of population
rural: 94.9% of population
total: 52.6% of population (2015 est.)

HIV/AIDS—adult prevalence rate: 1.59% (2014 est.)
country comparison to the world: 32

HIV/AIDS—people living with HIV/AIDS: 9,900 (2014 est.)
country comparison to the world: 93

HIV/AIDS—deaths: 600 (2014 est.)
country comparison to the world: 80

Major infectious diseases: *degree of risk:* high
food or waterborne diseases: bacterial and protozoal diarrhea, hepatitis A, and typhoid fever
vectorborne disease: dengue fever
note: highly pathogenic H5N1 avian influenza has been identified in this country; it poses a negligible risk with extremely rare cases possible among US citizens who have close contact with birds (2013)

Obesity—adult prevalence rate: 8.5% (2014)

country comparison to the world: 134

Children under the age of 5 years underweight: 29.8% (2012)
country comparison to the world: 14

Education expenditures: 4.5% of GDP (2010)
country comparison to the world: 11

School life expectancy (primary to tertiary education): *total:* 6 years
male: 7 years
female: 6 years (2011)

Child labor—children ages 5–14:
total number: 13,176
percentage: 8% (2006 est.)

GOVERNMENT

Country name: *conventional long form:* Republic of Djibouti
conventional short form: Djibouti
local long form: Republique de Djibouti/Jumhuriyat Jibuti
local short form: Djibouti/Jibuti
former: French Territory of the Afars and Issas, French Somaliland
etymology: the country name derives from the capital city of Djibouti

Government type: semi-presidential republic

Capital: *name:* Djibouti
Geographic coordinates: 11 35 N, 43 09 E
time difference: UTC+3 (8 hours ahead of Washington, DC, during Standard Time)

Administrative divisions: 6 districts (cercles, singular—cercle); Ali Sabieh, Arta, Dikhil, Djibouti, Obock, Tadjourah

Independence: 27 June 1977 (from France)

National holiday: Independence Day, 27 June (1977)

Constitution: approved by referendum 4 September 1992; amended 2006, 2008, 2010 (2016)

Legal system: mixed legal system based primarily on the French civil code (as it existed in 1997), Islamic religious law (in matters of family law and successions), and customary law

International law organization participation: accepts compulsory ICJ jurisdiction with reservations; accepts ICCt jurisdiction

Citizenship: *citizenship by birth:* no
citizenship by descent only: the mother must be a citizen of Djibouti
dual citizenship recognized: no
residency requirement for naturalization: 10 years

Suffrage: 18 years of age; universal

Executive branch: *chief of state:* President Ismail Omar GUELLEH (since 8 May 1999)
head of government: Prime Minister Abdoulkader Kamil MOHAMED (since 1 April 2013)
cabinet: Council of Ministers appointed by the prime minister
elections/appointments: president directly elected by absolute majority popular vote in 2

rounds if needed for a 5-year term; (constitution amended in 2010 to allow a third term); election last held on 8 April 2016 (next to be held by 2021); prime minister appointed by the president
election results: Ismail Omar GUELLEH reelected president for a fourth term; percent of vote-Ismail Omar GUELLEH (RPP) 87%, Omar Elmi KHAIREH (represented the USN) 7.3%, other 5.6%

Legislative branch: *description:* unicameral National Assembly or Assemblee Nationale, formerly the Chamber of Deputies (65 seats; 52 members directly elected in multi-seat constituencies by simple majority vote and 13 directly elected in multi-seat constituencies by proportional representation vote; members serve 5-year terms)
elections: last held on 22 February 2013 (next to be held in 2018)
election results: percent of vote by party—UMP 61.5%, USN 35.6%, CDU 3.0%; seats by party—UMP 43, USN 21, CDU 1

Judicial branch: *highest court(s):* Supreme Court or Cour Supreme (consists of NA magistrates); Constitutional Council (consists of 6 magistrates)
judge selection and term of office: Supreme Court magistrates appointed by the president with the advice of the Superior Council of the M agistracy; magistrates appointed for life with retirement at age 65; Constitutional magistrates—2 appointed by the president, 2 by the president of the National Assembly, and 2 by High Council of the Judiciary; magistrates appointed for 8-year, non-renewable terms
subordinate courts: High Court of Appeal; 5 Courts of First Instance; customary courts

Political parties and leaders: Democratic National Party or PND [ADEN Robleh Awaleh] Democratic Renewal Party or PRD [Abdillahi HAMARITEH]
Djibouti Development Party or PDD [Mohamed Daoud CHEHEM]
Front pour la Restauration de l'Unite Democratique or FRUD [Ali Mohamed DAOUD]
Movement for Development and Liberty or MODEL [Sheikh Guirreh MEIDAL]
People's Rally for Progress or RPP [Ismail O mar GUELLEH] (governing party)
Peoples Social Democratic Party or PPSD [Moumin Bahdon FARAH]
Republican Alliance for Democracy or ARD [Ahmed YOUSSOUF]
Union for a Presidential Majority or UMP (a coalition of parties including RPP, FRUD, PND, and PPSD)
Union for Democracy and Justice or UDJ [Ismail GUEDI Hared]
Union for National Salvation or USN (an umbrella coalition comprising PRD, PDD, MO DEL, ARD, and UDJ) [Ahmed Youssouf HOUMER]

International organization participation: ACP, AfDB, AFESD, AMF, AU, CAEU (candidates), COMESA, FAO, G-77, IBRD, ICAO, ICCt, ICRM, IDA, IDB, IFAD, IFC, IFRCS, IGAD, ILO, IMF, IMO, Interpol, IOC, IOM, IPU, ITU, ITUC (NGOs), LAS, MIGA, MINURSO, NAM,

OIC, OIF, OPCW, UN, UNCTAD, UNESCO, UNHCR, UNIDO, UNWTO, UPU, WCO, WFTU (NGOs), WHO, WIPO, WMO, WTO

Diplomatic representation in the US: *chief of mission:* Ambassador Siad DOUALEH (since 28 January 2016)
chancery: 1156 15th Street NW, Suite 515, Washington, DC 20005
telephone: [1] (202) 331-0270
FAX: [1] (202) 331-0302

Diplomatic representation from the US: *chief of mission:* Ambassador Thomas P. KELLY III (since 13 October 2014)
embassy: Lot 350-B, Haramouss, Djibouti
mailing address: B. P. 185, Djibouti
telephone: [253] 21 45 30 00
FAX: [253] 21 45 31 29

Flag description: two equal horizontal bands of light blue (top) and light green with a white isosceles triangle based on the hoist side bearing a red five-pointed star in the center; blue stands for sea and sky and the Issa Somali people; green symbolizes earth and the Afar people; white represents peace; the red star recalls the struggle for independence and stands for unity

National symbol(s): red star; national colors: light blue, green, white, red

National anthem: *name:* "Jabuuti" (Djibouti)
lyrics/music: Aden ELMI/Abdi ROBLEH
note: adopted 1977

ECONOMY

Economy—overview: Djibouti's economy is based on service activities connected with the country's strategic location as a deepwater port on the Red Sea. Three-fourths of Djibouti's inhabitants live in the capital city; the remainder are mostly nomadic herders. Scant rainfall and less than 4% arable land: limits crop production to small quantities of fruits and vegetables, and most food must be imported. Djibouti provides services as both a transit port for the region and an international transshipment and refueling center. Imports, exports, and re-exports—primarily of coffee from landlocked neighbor Ethiopia—represent 70% of port activity at Djibouti's container terminal. Djibouti has few natural resources and little industry. The nation is, therefore, heavily dependent on foreign assistance to help support its balance of payments and to finance development projects. An official unemployment rate of nearly 50%—with youth unemployment near 80%—continues to be a major problem. Inflation declined to 3% in 2014 due to low international food prices and a decline in electricity tariffs. Djibouti's reliance on diesel-generated electricity and imported food and water leave average consumers vulnerable to global price shocks, though in mid-2015 Djibouti passed new legislation to liberalize the energy sector. The government has emphasized infrastructure development for transportation and energy and Djibouti—with the help of foreign partners—has begun to increase and modernize its port capacity.

GDP (purchasing power parity):

$3.094 billion (2015 est.)
$2.905 billion (2014 est.)
$2.741 billion (2013 est.)
note: data are in 2015 US dollars
country comparison to the world: 186

GDP (official exchange rate): $1.727 billion (2015 est.)

GDP—real growth rate: 6.5% (2015 est.)
6% (2014 est.)
5% (2013 est.)
country comparison to the world: 23

GDP—per capita (PPP): $3,200 (2015 est.)
$3,100 (2014 est.)
$3,000 (2013 est.)
note: data are in 2015 US dollars
country comparison to the world: 187

Gross national saving: 31.2% of GDP (2015 est.)
18.5% of GDP (2014 est.)
17.2% of GDP (2013 est.)
country comparison to the world: 21

GDP—composition, by end use:
household consumption: 63.4%
government consumption: 33.6%
investment in fixed capital: 36.1%
investment in inventories: 0.4%
exports of goods and services: 40.1%
imports of goods and services: -73.6% (2015 est.)

GDP—composition, by sector of origin:
agriculture: 2.8%
industry: 16.4%
services: 80.8% (2015 est.)

Agriculture—products: fruits, vegetables; goats, sheep, camels, animal hides

Industries: construction, agricultural processing, shipping

Industrial production growth rate: 4.5% (2015 est.)
country comparison to the world: 38

Labor force: 294,600 (2012)
country comparison to the world: 164

Labor force—by occupation: *agriculture:* NA%
industry: NA%
services: NA%

Unemployment rate: 60% (2014 est.)
59% (2007 est.)
country comparison to the world: 204

Population below poverty line: 23%
note: percent of population below $1.25 per day at purchasing power parity (2015 est.)

Household income or consumption by percentage share: *lowest:* 10%: 2.4%
highest: 10%: 30.9% (2002)

Distribution of family income—Gini index: 40.9 (2002)
country comparison to the world: 57

Budget: *revenues:* $587.5 million
expenditures: $792.9 million (2015 est.)
Taxes and other revenues: 33.7% of GDP (2015 est.)
country comparison to the world: 69

Budget surplus (+) or deficit (-):
-11.8% of GDP (2015 est.)
country comparison to the world: 206

Public debt: 38.6% of GDP (2012 est.)
country comparison to the world: 121

Fiscal year: calendar year

Inflation rate (consumer prices): 2.1% (2015 est.)
2.9% (2014 est.)
country comparison to the world: 118

Commercial bank prime lending rate: 12% (31 December 2015 est.)
12.69% (31 December 2014 est.)
country comparison to the world: 67

Stock of narrow money: $1.007 billion (31 December 2015 est.)
$963.4 million (31 December 2014 est.)
country comparison to the world: 153

Stock of broad money: $1.43 billion (31 December 2014 est.)
$1.24 billion (31 December 2013 est.)
country comparison to the world: 165

Stock of domestic credit: $560.1 million (31 December 2015 est.)
$527.9 million (31 December 2014 est.)
country comparison to the world: 167

Current account balance: -$504 million (2015 est.)
-$407 million (2014 est.)
country comparison to the world: 96

Exports: $141.6 million (2015 est.)
$130.1 million (2014 est.)
country comparison to the world: 191

Exports—commodities: reexports, hides and skins, coffee (in transit), scrap metal

Exports—partners: Somalia 79.5%, US 5.4%, Yemen 4.6%, UAE 4% (2015)

Imports: $983.9 million (2015 est.)
$969.7 million (2014 est.)
country comparison to the world: 179

Imports—commodities: foods, beverages, transport equipmen t, chemicals, petroleum products, clothing

Imports—partners: China 42.1%, Saudi Arabia 14.3%, Indonesia 5.9%, India 4.4% (2015)

Debt—external: $905.5 million (31 December 2014 est.)
$832.8 million (31 December 2013 est.)
country comparison to the world: 166

Stock of direct foreign investment—at home:
$1.367 billion (31 December 2015 est.)
$1.102 billion (31 December 2014 est.)
country comparison to the world: 108

Exchange rates: Djiboutian francs (DJF) per US dollar—
177.7 (2015 est.)
177.72 (2014 est.)
177.72 (2013 est.)
177.72 (2012 est.)
177.72 (2011 est.)

ENERGY

Electricity—production: 335 million kWh (2012 est.)
country comparison to the world: 171

Electricity—consumption: 311.6 million kWh (2012 est.)
country comparison to the world: 175

Electricity—exports: 0 kWh (2013 est.)
country comparison to the world: 131

Electricity—imports: 0 kWh (2013 est.)
country comparison to the world: 141

Electricity—installed generating capacity: 131,400 kW (2012 est.)
country comparison to the world: 170

Electricity—from fossil fuels: 98.9% of total installed capacity (2012 est.)
country comparison to the world: 50

Electricity—from nuclear fuels: 0% of total installed capacity (2012 est.)
country comparison to the world: 79

Electricity—from hydroelectric plants: 0% of total installed capacity (2012 est.)
country comparison to the world: 170

Electricity—from other renewable sources: 1.1% of total installed capacity (2012 est.)
country comparison to the world: 93

Crude oil—production: 0 bbl/day (2014 est.)
country comparison to the world: 125

Crude oil—exports: 0 bbl/day (2012 est.)
country comparison to the world: 116

Crude oil—imports: 0 bbl/day (2012 est.)
country comparison to the world: 181

Crude oil—proved reserves: 0 bbl (1 January 2015 est.)
country comparison to the world: 124

Refined petroleum products—production: 0 bbl/day (2012 est.)
country comparison to the world: 174

Refined petroleum products—consumption: 8,000 bbl/day (2013 est.)
country comparison to the world: 158

Refined petroleum products—exports: 19.18 bbl/day (2012 est.)
country comparison to the world: 125

Refined petroleum products—imports: 8,089 bbl/day (2012 est.)
country comparison to the world: 143

Natural gas—production: 0 cu m (2013 est.)
country comparison to the world: 178

Natural gas—consumption: 0 cu m (2013 est.)
country comparison to the world: 137

Natural gas—exports: 0 cu m (2013 est.)
country comparison to the world: 88

Natural gas—imports: 0 cu m (2013 est.)
country comparison to the world: 188

Natural gas—proved reserves: 0 cu m (1 January 2014 est.)
country comparison to the world: 130

Carbon dioxide emissions from consumption of energy: 1.796 million Mt (2012 est.)
country comparison to the world: 151

COMMUNICATIONS

Telephones—fixed lines: *total subscriptions:* 21,900

subscriptions per 100 inhabitants: 3 (2014 est.)
country comparison to the world: 181

Telephones—mobile cellular: total: 287,000
subscriptions per 100 inhabitants: 35 (2014 est.)
country comparison to the world: 177

Telephone system: *general assessment:* telephone facilities in the city of Djibouti are adequate, as are the microwave radio relay connections to outlying areas of the country
domestic: Djibouti Telecom is the sole provider of telecommunications services and utilizes mostly a microwave radio relay network; fiber-optic cable is installed in the capital; rural areas connected via wireless local loop radio systems; mobile cellular coverage is primarily limited to the area in and around Djibouti city
international: country code—253; landing point for the SEA-ME-WE-3 and EASSy fiber-optic submarine cable systems providing links to Asia, the Middle East, Europe and North America; satellite earth stations—2 (1 Intelsat—Indian Ocean and 1 Arabsat); Medarabtel regional microwave radio relay telephone network (2009)

Broadcast media: state-owned Radiodiffusion-Television de Djibouti operates the sole terrestrial TV station, as well as the only 2 domestic radio networks; no private TV or radio stations; transmissions of several international broadcasters are available (2007)
Radio broadcast stations: AM 1, FM 2, shortwave 0 (2001)
Television broadcast stations: 1 (2001)

Internet country code: .dj

Internet hosts: 215 (2012)
country comparison to the world: 200

Internet users: *total:* 73,500
percent of population: 9.1% (2014 est.)
country comparison to the world: 178

TRANSPORTATION

Airports: 13 (2013)
country comparison to the world: 152

Airports—with paved runways: *total:* 3
over 3,047 m: 1
2,438 to 3,047 m: 1
1,524 to 2,437 m: 1 (2013)

Airports—with unpaved runways: *total:* 10
1,524 to 2,437 m: 1
914 to 1,523 m: 7
under 914 m: 2 (2013)

Railways: *total:* 100 km (Djibouti segment of the 781 km Addis Ababa-Djibouti railway)
narrow gauge: 100 km 1.000-m gauge
note: railway is under joint con trol of Djibouti and Ethiopia but is largely inoperable (2008)
country comparison to the world: 128

Roadways: *total:* 3,065 km
paved: 1,379 km
unpaved: 1,686 km (2000)
country comparison to the world: 166

Ports and terminals: *major seaport(s):* Djibouti

Transportation—note: while attacks continued to decrease, with only 4 in 2014, the International

Maritime Bureau reports offshore waters in the Gulf of Aden remain a high risk for piracy; the presence of several naval task forces in the Gulf of Aden and additional anti-piracy measures on the part of ship operators, including the use of on-board armed security teams, contributed to the drop in incidents

MILITARY AND SECURITY

Military branches: Djibouti Armed Forces (Forces Armees Djiboutiennes, FAD): Djibouti National Army (includes Navy, Djiboutian Air Force (Force Aerienne Djiboutienne, FAD), National Gendarmerie (GN)) (2013)

Military service age and obligation: 18 years of age for voluntary military service; 16–25 years of age for voluntary military training; no conscription (2012)

TRANSNATIONAL ISSUES

Disputes—international: Djibouti maintains economic ties and border accords with "Somaliland"

leadership while maintaining some political ties to various factions in Somalia; Kuwait is chief investor in the 2008 restoration and upgrade of the Ethiopian-Djibouti rail link; in 2008, Eritrean troops moved across the border on Ras Doumera peninsula and occupied Doumera Island with undefined sovereignty in the Red Sea

Refugees and internally displaced persons: *refugees (country of origin):* 12,363 (Somalia) (2015); 19,636 (Yemen) (2016)

Trafficking in persons: *current situation:* Djibouti is a transit, source, and destination country for men, women, and children subjected to forced labor and sex trafficking; economic migrants from East Africa en route to Yemen and other Middle East locations are vulnerable to exploitation in Djibouti; some women and girls may be forced into domestic servitude or prostitution after reaching Djibouti City, the Ethiopia-Djibouti trucking corridor, or Obock—the main crossing point into Yemen; Djiboutian and foreign children may be forced to beg, to work as domestic servants, or to commit theft and other petty crimes

tier rating: Tier 2 Watch List—Djibouti does not fully comply with the minimum standards for the elimination of trafficking; however, it is making significant efforts to do so; in 2014, Djibouti was granted a waiver from an otherwise required downgrade to Tier 3 because its government has a written plan that, if implemented would constitute making significant efforts to bring itself into compliance with the minimum standards for the elimination of trafficking; one forced labor trafficker was convicted in 2014 but received a suspended sentence inadequate to deter trafficking; authorities did not investigate or prosecute any other forced labor crimes, any sex trafficking offenses, or any officials complicit in human trafficking, and remained limited in their ability to recognize or protect trafficking victims; official round-ups, detentions, and deportations of non-Djiboutian residents, including children without screening for trafficking victims remained routine; the government did not provide care to victims but supported local NGOs operating centers that assisted victims (2015)

DOMINICA

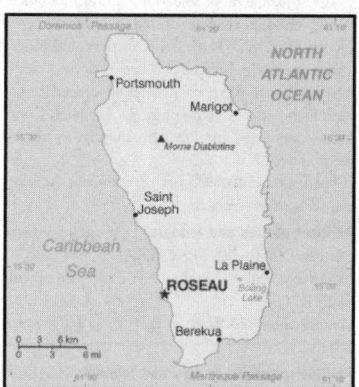

INTRODUCTION

Background: Dominica was the last of the Caribbean islands to be colonized by Europeans due chiefly to the fierce resistance of the native Caribs. France ceded possession to Great Britain in 1763, which colonized the island in 1805. In 1980, two years after independence, Dominica's fortunes improved when a corrupt and tyrannical administration was replaced by that of Mary Eugenia CHARLES, the first female prime minister in the Caribbean, who remained in office for 15 years. Some 3,000 Carib Indians still living on Dominica are the only pre-Columbian population remaining in the eastern Caribbean.

GEOGRAPHY

Location: Caribbean, island between the Caribbean Sea and the North Atlantic Ocean, about

halfway between Puerto Rico and Trinidad and Tobago

Geographic coordinates: 15 25 N, 61 20 W

Map references: Central America and the Caribbean

Area: *total:* 751 sq km
land: 751 sq km
water: 0 sq km
country comparison to the world: 189

Area—comparative: slightly more than four times the size of Washington, DC

Land boundaries: 0 km

Coastline: 148 km

Maritime claims: *territorial sea:* 12 nm
contiguous zone: 24 nm
exclusive economic zone: 200 nm

Climate: tropical; moderated by northeast trade winds; heavy rainfall

Terrain: rugged mountains of volcanic origin

Elevation: *mean elevation:* NA

elevation extremes: *lowest point:* Caribbean Sea 0 m
highest point: Morne Diablotins 1,447 m

Natural resources: timber, hydropower, arable land

Land use: *agricultural land:* 34.7%
arable land: 8%
permanent crops: 24%
permanent pasture: 2.7%
forest: 59.2%
other: 6.1% (2011 est.)

Irrigated land: NA

Total renewable water resources: NA

Freshwater withdrawal (domestic/industrial/agricultural): *total:* 0.02 cu km/yr
per capita: 244.1 cu m/yr (2004)

Natural hazards: flash floods are a constant threat; destructive hurricanes can be expected during the late summer months

Environment—current issues: NA

Environment—international agreements: *party to:* Biodiversity, Climate Change, Climate Change-Kyoto Protocol, Desertification, Endangered Species, Environmental Modification, Hazardous Wastes, Law of the Sea, Ozone Layer Protection, Ship Pollution, Whaling
signed, but not ratified: none of the selected agreements

Geography—note: known as "The Nature Island of the Caribbean" due to its spectacular, lush, and varied flora and fauna, which are protected by an extensive natural park system; the most mountainous of the Lesser Antilles, its volcanic peaks are cones of lava craters and include Boiling Lake, the second-largest, thermally active lake in the world

PEOPLE AND SOCIETY

Nationality: *noun:* Dominican(s)
adjective: Dominican

Ethnic groups: black 86.6%, mixed 9.1%, indigenous 2.9%, other 1.3%, unspecified 0.2% (2001 est.)

Languages: English (official), French patois

Religions: Roman Catholic 61.4%, Protestant 28.6% (includes Evangelical 6.7%, Seventh Day Adventist 6.1%, Pentecostal 5.6%, Baptist 4.1%, Methodist 3.7%, Church of God 1.2%, other 1.2%), Rastafarian 1.3%, Jehovah's Witnesses

245

1.2%, other 0.3%, none 6.1%, unspecified 1.1% (2001 est.)

Population: 73,607 (July 2015 est.)
country comparison to the world: 202

Age structure: *0–14 years:* 21.96% (male 8,265/female 7,902)
15–24 years: 16.14% (male 6,117/female 5,762)
25–54 years: 41.83% (male 15,617/female 15,170)
55–64 years: 9.39% (male 3,696/female 3,213)
65 years and over: 10.69% (male 3,463/female 4,402) (2015 est.)

Median age: *total:* 32.6 years
male: 32.1 years
female: 33 years (2015 est.)
country comparison to the world: 90

Population growth rate: 0.21% (2015 est.)
country comparison to the world: 183

Birth rate: 15.41 births/1,000 population (2015 est.)
country comparison to the world: 129

Death rate: 7.91 deaths/1,000 population (2015 est.)
country comparison to the world: 102

Net migration rate: -5.38 migrant(s)/1,000 population (2015 est.)
country comparison to the world: 195

Urbanization: *urban population:* 69.5% of total population (2015)
rate of urbanization: 0.84% annual rate of change (2010–15 est.)

Major urban areas—population: ROSEAU (capital) 15,000 (2014)

Sex ratio: *at birth:* 1.05 male(s)/female
0–14 years: 1.05 male(s)/female
15–24 years: 1.06 male(s)/female
25–54 years: 1.03 male(s)/female
55–64 years: 1.15 male(s)/female
65 years and over: 0.79 male(s)/female
total population: 1.02 male(s)/female (2015 est.)

Infant mortality rate: *total:* 11.25 deaths/1,000 live births
male: 14.94 deaths/1,000 live births
female: 7.36 deaths/1,000 live births (2015 est.)
country comparison to the world: 128

Life expectancy at birth: *total population:* 76.79 years
male: 73.82 years
female: 79.91 years (2015 est.)
country comparison to the world: 78

Total fertility rate: 2.04 children born/woman (2015 est.)
country comparison to the world: 116

Health expenditures: 6% of GDP (2013)
country comparison to the world: 112

Hospital bed density: 3.8 beds/1,000 population (2012)

Drinking water source:
improved:
urban: 95.7% of population
unimproved:
urban: 4.3% of population (2015 est.)

Sanitation facility access:
improved:
urban: 79.6% of population
rural: 84.3% of population
total: 81.1% of population
unimproved:
urban: 20.4% of population
rural: 15.7% of population
total: 18.9% of population (2007 est.)

HIV/AIDS—adult prevalence rate: NA

HIV/AIDS—people living with HIV/AIDS: NA

HIV/AIDS—deaths: NA

Obesity—adult prevalence rate: 25.9% (2014)
country comparison to the world: 61

GOVERNMENT

Country name: *conventional long form:* Commonwealth of Dominica
conventional short form: Dominica
etymology: the island was named by explorer Christopher COLUMBUS for the day of the week on which he spotted it, Sunday ("Domingo" in Latin), 3 November 1493

Government type: parliamentary republic

Capital: *name:* Roseau

Geographic coordinates: 15 18 N, 61 24 W
time difference: UTC-4 (1 hour ah ead of Wash ington, DC, during Standard Time)

Administrative divisions: 10 parishes; Saint Andrew, Saint David, Saint George, Saint John, Saint Joseph, Saint Luke, Saint Mark, Saint Patrick, Saint Paul, Saint Peter

Independence: 3 November 1978 (from the UK)

National holiday: Independence Day, 3 November (1978)

Constitution: previous 1967 (preindependence); latest presented 25 July 1978, entered into force 3 November 1978; amended several times, last in 2015 (2016)

Legal system: common law based on the English model

International law organization participation: accepts compulsory ICJ jurisdiction; accepts ICCt jurisdiction

Citizenship: *citizenship by birth:* yes
citizenship by descent: yes
dual citizenship recognized: yes
residency requirement for naturalization: 5 years

Suffrage: 18 years of age; universal

Executive branch: *chief of state:* President Charles A. SAVARIN (since 2 October 2013)

head of government: Prime Minister Roosevelt SKERRIT (since 8 January 2004)
cabinet: Cabinet appointed by the president on the advice of the prime minister
elections/appointments: president nominated by the prime minister and leader of the opposition party and elected by the House of Assembly for a 5-year term (eligible for a second term); election last held on 30 September 2013 (next to be held in October 2018); prime minister appointed by the president

election results: Charles A. SAVARIN (DLP) elected president by a vote of 19–0 on 30 September 2013

Legislative branch: *description:* unicameral House of Assembly (32 seats; 21 representatives directly elected in single-seat constituencies by simple majority vote, 9 senators appointed by the Assembly, and 2 ex-officio members -the House Speaker and the Clerk of the House; members serve 5-year terms)
elections: last held on 8 December 2014 (next to be held in 2019); note—tradition dictates that the election is held within five years of the last election, but technically it is five years from the first seating of parliament plus a 90-day grace period
election results: percent of vote by party—NA; seats by party—DLP 15, UWP 6

Judicial branch: *highest court(s):* The Eastern Caribbean Supreme Court (ECSC) is the itinerant superior court of record for the 9-member Organization of Eastern Caribbean States to include Dominica; the ECSC—based on St. Lucia—is headed by the chief justice and is comprised of the Court of Appeal with 3 justices and the High Court with 16 judges; sittings of the Court of Appeal and High Court rotate among the 9 member states; 2 High Court judges reside in Dominica; note—Dominica is a member of the Caribbean Court of Justice judge selection and term of office: ECSC chief justice appointed by Her Majesty, Queen ELIZABETH II; other justices and judges appointed by the Judicial and Legal Services Commission; Court of Appeal justices appointed for life with mandatory retirement at age 65; High Court judges appointed for life with mandatory retirement at age 62
subordinate courts: Court of Summary Jurisdiction; magistrates' courts

Political parties and leaders: Dominica Freedom Party or DFP [Judith PESTAINA]
Dominica Labor Party or DLP [Roosevelt SKERRIT]
Dominica United Workers Party or UWP [Hector JOHN]

Political pressure groups and leaders: Dominica Liberation Movement or DLM (a small leftist party)

International organization participation: ACP, AOSIS, C, Caricom, CD, CDB, CELAC, Commonwealth of Nations, ECCU, FAO, G-77, IAEA, IBRD, ICCt, ICRM, IDA, IFAD, IFC, IFRCS, ILO, IMF, IMO, Interpol, IOC, ISO (correspondent), ITU, ITUC (NGOs), MIGA, NAM, OAS, OECS, OIF, OPANAL, OPCW, Petrocaribe, UN, UNCTAD, UNESCO, UNIDO, UPU, WF TU, WH O, WIPO, WMO, WTO

Diplomatic representation in the US: *chief of mission:* Ambassador Hubert J. CHARLES (since 16 July 2010)
chancery: 3216 New Mexico Avenue NW, Washington, DC 20016
telephone: [1] (202) 364-6781
FAX: [1] (202) 364-6791
consulate(s) general: New York

Diplomatic representation from the US: the US does not have an embassy in Dominica; the US Ambassador to Barbados is accredited to Dominica

Flag description: green with a centered cross of three equal bands—the vertical part is yellow (hoist side), black, and white and the horizontal part is yellow (top), black, and white; superimposed in the center of the cross is a red disk bearing a Sisserou parrot, unique to Dominica, encircled by 10 green, five-pointed stars edged in yellow; the 10 stars represent the 10 administrative divisions (parishes); green symbolizes the island's lush vegetation; the triple-colored cross represents the Christian Trinity; the yellow color denotes sunshine, the main agricultural products (citrus and bananas), and the native Carib Indians; black is for the rich soil and the African heritage of most citizens; white signifies rivers, waterfalls, and the purity of aspirations; the red disc stands for social justice

National symbol(s): Sisserou parrot, Carib Wood flower; national colors: green, yellow, black, white, red

National anthem: *name:* "Isle of Beauty"
lyrics/music: Wilfred Oscar Morgan POND/Lemuel McPherson CHRISTIAN
note: adopted 1967

ECONOMY

Economy—overview: The Dominican economy has been dependent on agriculture—primarily bananas—in years past, but increasingly has been driven by tourism as the government seeks to promote Dominica as an "ecotourism" destination. Moreover, Dominica has an offshore medical education sector. In order to diversify the island's economy, the government is also attempting to foster an offshore financial industry and plans to sign agreements with the private sector to develop geothermal energy resources. In 2003, the government began a comprehensive restructuring of the economy—including the elimination of price controls, privatization of the state banana company, and tax increases—to address an economic and financial crisis and to meet IMF requirements. In 2009 and 2013, the economy contracted as a result of the global recession; growth remains anemic. Although public debt levels continue to exceed pre-recession levels, the debt burden declined from 78% of GDP in 2011 to approximately 70% in 2012.

GDP (purchasing power parity):
$763 million (2015 est.)
$797.4 million (2014 est.)
$767.6 million (2013 est.)
note: data are in 2015 US dollars
country comparison to the world: 206

GDP (official exchange rate):
$497 million (2015 est.)

GDP—real growth rate: -4.3% (2015 est.)
3.9% (2014 est.)

0.6% (2013 est.)
country comparison to the world: 214

GDP—per capita (PPP): $10,700 (2015 est.)
$11,200 (2014 est.)
$10,800 (2013 est.)
note: data are in 2015 US dollars
country comparison to the world: 134

Gross national saving: 1.7% of GDP (2015 est.)
1.7% of GDP (2014 est.)
0.4% of GDP (2013 est.)
country comparison to the world: 168

GDP—composition, by end use:
household consumption: 51.8%
government consumption: 23.3%
investment in fixed capital: 27.9%
investment in inventories: 0.1%
exports of goods and services: 66.9%
imports of goods and services: -70% (2015 est.)

GDP—composition, by sector of origin:
agriculture: 15%
industry: 14.2%
services: 70.8% (2015 est.)

Agriculture—products: bananas, citrus, mangos, root crops, coconuts, cocoa
note: forest and fishery potential not exploited

Industries: soap, coconut oil, tourism, copra, furniture, cement blocks, shoes

Industrial production growth rate: 1.5% (2015 est.)
country comparison to the world: 135

Labor force: 25,000 (2000 est.)
country comparison to the world: 208

Labor force—by occupation: *agriculture:* 40%
industry: 32%
services: 28% (2002 est.)

Unemployment rate: 23% (2000 est.)
country comparison to the world: 174

Population below poverty line: 29% (2009 est.)

Household income or consumption by percentage share: *lowest:* 10%: NA%
highest: 10%: NA%

Budget: *revenues:* $148.1 million
expenditures: $148.1 million (2015 est.)
Taxes and other revenues: 27.5% of GDP (2015 est.)
country comparison to the world: 98

Budget surplus (+) or deficit (-): 0% of GDP (2015 est.)
country comparison to the world: 29

Public debt: 70% of GDP (2012 est.)
78% of GDP (2009 est.)
country comparison to the world: 46

Fiscal year: 1 July—30 June

Inflation rate (consumer prices):
-0.8% (2015 est.)
0.8% (2014 est.)
country comparison to the world: 17

Central bank discount rate:
6.5% (31 December 2010)
6.5% (31 December 2009)

country comparison to the world: 53

Commercial bank prime lending rate:
8.8% (31 December 2015 est.)
8.94% (31 December 2014 est.)
country comparison to the world: 99

Stock of narrow money:
$95.11 million (31 December 2015 est.)
$86.92 million (31 December 2014 est.)
country comparison to the world: 187

Stock of broad money:
$499.6 million (31 December 2015 est.)
$462.6 million (31 December 2014 est.)
country comparison to the world: 182

Stock of domestic credit:
$333.3 million (31 December 2015 est.)
$314.8 million (31 December 2014 est.)
country comparison to the world: 178

Current account balance: -$70 million (2015 est.)
-$68 million (2014 est.)
country comparison to the world: 66

Exports: $39.4 million (2015 est.)
$38.6 million (2014 est.)
country comparison to the world: 204

Exports—commodities: bananas, soap, bay oil, vegetables, grapefruit, oranges

Exports—partners: Japan 38.1%, Jamaica 19%, Antigua and Barbuda 10.4%, Trinidad and Tobago 6.2%, St. Lucia 4.8%, St. Kitts and Nevis 4.2% (2015)

Imports: $182.9 million (2015 est.)
$186.9 million (2014 est.)
country comparison to the world: 207

Imports—commodities: manufactured goods, machinery and equipment, food, chemicals

Imports—partners: Japan 42%, Trinidad and Tobago 17%, US 11.9%, China 6% (2015)

Reserves of foreign exchange and gold:
$100 million (31 December 2015 est.)
$103 million (31 December 2014 est.)
country comparison to the world: 165

Debt—external: $292.9 million (31 December 2014 est.)
$292.9 million (31 December 2013 est.)
country comparison to the world: 186

Exchange rates: East Caribbean dollars (XCD) per US dollar—
-2.7 (2015 est.)
2.7 (2014 est.)
2.7 (2013 est.)
2.7 (2012 est.)
2.7 (2011 est.)

ENERGY

Electricity—production: 96.5 million kWh (2012 est.)
country comparison to the world: 200

Electricity—consumption: 89.75 million kWh (2012 est.)
country comparison to the world: 200

Electricity—exports: 0 kWh (2013 est.)
country comparison to the world: 132

Electricity -imports: 0 kWh (2013 est.)
country comparison to the world: 142

Electricity—installed generating capacity: 33,200 kW (2012 est.)
country comparison to the world: 196

Electricity—from fossil fuels: 60.2% of total installed capacity (2012 est.)
country comparison to the world: 133

Electricity—from nuclear fuels: 0% of total installed capacity (2012 est.)
country comparison to the world: 80

Electricity—from hydroelectric plants: 18.1% of total installed capacity (2012 est.)
country comparison to the world: 97

Electricity—from other renewable sources: 21.7% of total installed capacity (2012 est.)
country comparison to the world: 15

Crude oil—production: 0 bbl/day (2014 est.)
country comparison to the world: 126

Crude oil—exports: 0 bbl/day (2012 est.)
country comparison to the world: 117

Crude oil—imports: 0 bbl/day (2012 est.)
country comparison to the world: 182

Crude oil—proved reserves: 0 bbl (1 January 2015 est.)
country comparison to the world: 125

Refined petroleum products—production: 0 bbl/day (2012 est.)
country comparison to the world: 175

Refined petroleum products—consumption: 900 bbl/day (2013 est.)
country comparison to the world: 204

Refined petroleum products—exports: 0 bbl/day (2012 est.)
country comparison to the world: 175

Refined petroleum products—imports: 915.9 bbl/day (2012 est.)
country comparison to the world: 198

Natural gas—production: 0 cu m (2013 est.)
country comparison to the world: 179

Natural gas—consumption: 0 cu m (2013 est.)
country comparison to the world: 138

Natural gas—exports: 0 cu m (2013 est.)
country comparison to the world: 89

Natural gas—imports: 0 cu m (2013 est.)
country comparison to the world: 189

Natural gas—proved reserves: 0 cu m (1 January 2014 est.)
country comparison to the world: 131

Carbon dioxide emissions from consumption of energy: 132,100 Mt (2012 est.)
country comparison to the world: 206

COMMUNICATIONS

Telephones—fixed lines: *total subscriptions:* 17,600
subscriptions per 100 inhabitants: 24 (2014 est.)
country comparison to the world: 188

Telephones—mobile cellular: *total:* 92,200
subscriptions per 100 inhabitants: 126 (2014 est.)
country comparison to the world: 192

Telephone system: *general assessment:* fully automatic network
domestic: fixed-line connections continued to decline slowly with the two active operators providing about 20 fixed-line connections per 100 persons; subscribership among the three mobile-cellular providers continued to increase with teledensity reaching 150 per 100 persons
international: country code—1–767; landing points for the East Caribbean Fiber Optic System (ECFS) and the Global Caribbean Network (GCN) submarine cables providing connectivity to other islands in the eastern Caribbean extending from the British Virgin Islands to Trinidad; microwave radio relay and SHF radiotelephone links to Martinique and Guadeloupe; VHF and UHF radiotelephone links to Saint Lucia (2010)

Broadcast media: no terrestrial TV service available; subscription cable TV provider offers some locally produced programming plus channels from the US, Latin America, and the Caribbean; state-operated radio roadcasts on 6 stations; privately owned radio broadcasts on about 15 stations (2007)
Radio broadcast stations: AM 4, FM 18, shortwave 0 (2009)
Television broadcast stations: 1 (2004)

Internet country code: .dm

Internet hosts: 723 (2012)
country comparison to the world: 175

Internet users: *total:* 43,400

percent of population: 59.1% (2014 est.)
country comparison to the world: 190

TRANSPORTATION

Airports: 2 (2013)
country comparison to the world: 199

Airports—with paved runways: *total:* 2
1,524 to 2,437 m: 1
914 to 1,523 m: 1 (2013)

Roadways: *total:* 1,512 km
paved: 762 km
unpaved: 750 km (2010)
country comparison to the world: 178

Merchant marine: *total:* 43
by type: bulk carrier 11, cargo 22, chemical tanker 2, petroleum tanker 4, refrigerated cargo 3, roll on/roll off 1
foreign-owned: 32 (Australia 1, Estonia 6, Germany 5, Greece 4, India 2, Latvia 2, Norway 1, Russia 3, Saudi Arabia 2, Syria 4, Turkey 1, Ukraine 1)
registered in other countries: 1 (Saint Vincent and the Grenadines 1) (2010)
country comparison to the world: 73

Ports and terminals: *major seaport(s):* Portsmouth, Roseau

MILITARY AND SECURITY

Military branches: no regular military forces; Commonwealth of Dominica Police Force (includes Coast Guard) (2012)

TRANSNATIONAL ISSUES

Disputes—international: Dominica is the only Caribbean state to challenge Venezuela's sovereignty claim over Aves Island and joins the other island nations in challenging whether the feature sustains human habitation, a criterion under the UN Convention on the Law of the Sea, which permits Venezuela to extend its EEZ and continental shelf claims over a large portion of the eastern Caribbean Sea

Illicit drugs: transshipment point for narcotics bound for the US and Europe; minor cannabis producer (2008)

DOMINICAN REPUBLIC

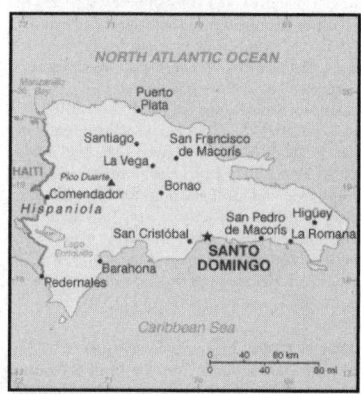

INTRODUCTION

Background: The Taino—indigenous inhabitants of Hispaniola prior to the arrival of the Europeans—divided the island into five chiefdoms and territories. Christopher COLUMBUS explored and claimed the island on his first voyage in 1492; it became a springboard for Spanish conquest of the Caribbean and the American mainland. In 1697, Spain recognized French dominion over the western third of the island, which in 1804 became Haiti. The remainder of the island, by then known as Santo Domingo, sought to gain its own independence in 1821 but was conquered and ruled by the Haitians for 22 years; it finally attained independence as the Dominican Republic in 1844. In 1861, the Dominicans voluntarily returned to the Spanish Empire, but two years later they launched a war that restored independence in 1865. A legacy of unsettled, mostly non-representative rule followed, capped by the dictatorship of Rafael Leonidas TRUJILLO from 1930 to 1961. Juan BOSCH was elected president in 1962 but was deposed in a military coup in 1963. In 1965, the US led an intervention in the midst of a civil war sparked by an uprising to restore BOSCH. In 1966, Joaquin BALAGUER defeated BOSCH in the presidential election. BALAGUER maintained a tight grip on power for most of the next 30 years when international reaction to flawed elections forced him to curtail his term in 1996. Since then, regular competitive elections have been held in which opposition candidates have won the presidency. Former President Leonel FERNANDEZ Reyna (first term 1996–2000) won election to a new term in 2004 following a constitutional amendment allowing presidents to serve more than one term, and was later reelected to a second consecutive term. In 2012, Danilo M EDINA Sanchez became president; he was reelected in 2016.

GEOGRAPHY

Location: Caribbean, eastern two-thirds of the island of Hispaniola, between the Caribbean Sea and the North Atlantic Ocean, east of Haiti

Geographic coordinates: 19 00 N, 70 40 W

Map references: Central America and the Caribbean

Area: *total:* 48,670 sq km
land: 48,320 sq km
water: 350 sq km
country comparison to the world: 132

Area—comparative: slightly more than twice the size of New Hampshire

Land boundaries: *total:* 376 km
border countries (1): Haiti 376 km

Coastline: 1,288 km

Maritime claims: measured from claimed archipelagic straight baselines
territorial sea: 12 nm
contiguous zone: 24 nm
exclusive economic zone: 200 nm
continental shelf: 200 nm or to the edge of the continental margin

Climate: tropical maritime; little seasonal temperature variation; seasonal variation in rainfall

Terrain: rugged highlands and mountains interspersed with fertile valleys

Elevation: *mean elevation:* 424 m

elevation extremes: *lowest point:* Lago Enriquillo -46 m
highest point: Pico Duarte 3,175 m

Natural resources: nickel, bauxite, gold, silver, arable land:

Land use: *agricultural land:* 51.5%
arable land: 16.6%
permanent crops: 10.1%
permanent pasture: 24.8%
forest: 40.8%
other: 7.7% (2011 est.)

Irrigated land: 3,070 sq km (2012)

Total renewable water resources: 21 cu km (2011)

Freshwater withdrawal (domestic/industrial/agricultural): *total:* 5.47 cu km/yr (26%/1%/72%)
per capita: 574.2 cu m/yr (2005)

Natural hazards: lies in the middle of the hurricane belt and subject to severe storms from June to October; occasional flooding; periodic droughts

Environment—current issues: water shortages; soil eroding into the sea damages coral reefs; deforestation

Environment—international agreements:
party to: Biodiversity, Climate Change, Climate Change-Kyoto Protocol, Desertification, Endangered Species, Hazardous Wastes, Marine Dumping, Marine Life Conservation, Ozone Layer Protection, Ship Pollution, Wetlands
signed, but not ratified: Law of the Sea

Geography—note: shares island of Hispaniola with Haiti (eastern two-thirds makes up the Dominican Republic, western one-third is Haiti)

PEOPLE AND SOCIETY

Nationality: *noun:* Dom inican(s)

adjective: Dominican

Ethnic groups: mixed 73%, white 16%, black 11%

Languages: Spanish (official)

Religions: Roman Catholic 95%, other 5%

Population: 10,478,756 (July 2015 est.)
country comparison to the world: 87

Age structure: 0–14 years: 27.53% (male 1,467,374/female 1,416,998)
15–24 years: 18.39% (male 982,191/female 945,087)
25–54 years: 39.41% (male 2,113,028/female 2,016,733)
55–64 years: 7.44% (male 392,230/female 387,052)
65 years and over: 7.23% (male 349,983/female 408,080) (2015 est.)

Dependency ratios: *total dependency ratio:* 57.8%
youth dependency ratio: 47.3%
elderly dependency ratio: 10.5%
potential support ratio: 9.5% (2015 est.)

Median age: *total:* 27.4
years male: 27.2
years female: 27.6 years (2015 est.)
country comparison to the world: 136

Population growth rate: 1.23% (2015 est.)
country comparison to the world: 96

Birth rate: 18.73 births/1,000 population (2015 est.)
country comparison to the world: 93

Death rate: 4.55 deaths/1,000 population (2015 est.)
country comparison to the world: 201

Net migration rate: -1.91 migrant(s)/1,000 population (2015 est.)
country comparison to the world: 164

Urbanization: *urban population:* 79% of total population (2015)
rate of urbanization: 2.6% annual rate of change (2010–15 est.)

Major urban areas—population: SANTO DOMINGO (capital) 2.945 million (2015)

Sex ratio: *at birth:* 1.04 male(s)/female
0–14 years: 1.04 male(s)/female
15–24 years: 1.04 male(s)/female
25–54 years: 1.05 male(s)/female
55–64 years: 1.01 male(s)/female
65 years and over: 0.86 male(s)/female
total population: 1.03 male(s)/female (2015 est.)

Mother's mean age at first birth: 21.3
note: median age at first birth among women 25–29 (2013 est.)

Maternal mortality rate: 92 deaths/100,000 live births (2015 est.)
country comparison to the world: 62

Infant mortality rate: *total:* 18.84 deaths/1,000 live births
male: 20.75 deaths/1,000 live births
female: 16.86 deaths/1,000 live births (2015 est.)
country comparison to the world: 94

Life expectancy at birth: *total population:* 77.97 years
male: 75.76 years
female: 80.28 years (2015 est.)
country comparison to the world: 63

Total fertility rate: 2.33 children born/woman (2015 est.)
country comparison to the world: 89

Contraceptive prevalence rate: 73% (2009/10)

Health expenditures: 5.4% of GDP (2013)
country comparison to the world: 130

Physicians density: 1.49 physicians/1,000 population (2011)

Hospital bed density: 1.7 beds/1,000 population (2011)

Drinking water source:
improved:
urban: 85.4% of population
rural: 81.9% of population
total: 84.7% of population
unimproved:
urban: 14.6% of population
rural: 18.1% of population
total: 15.3% of population (2015 est.)

Sanitation facility access:
improved:
urban: 86.2% of population
rural: 75.7% of population
total: 84% of population
unimproved:
urban: 13.8% of population
rural: 24.3% of population
total: 16% of population (2015 est.)

HIV/AIDS—adult prevalence rate: 1.04% (2014 est.)
country comparison to the world: 45

HIV/AIDS—people living with HIV/AIDS: 69,300 (2014 est.)
country comparison to the world: 52

HIV/AIDS—deaths: 3,100 (2014 est.)
country comparison to the world: 44

Major infectious diseases: *degree of risk:* high
food or waterborne diseases: bacterial diarrhea, hepatitis A, and typhoid fever
vectorborne disease: dengue fever (2013)

Obesity—adult prevalence rate: 23% (2014)
country comparison to the world: 90

Children under the age of 5 years underweight: 4% (2013)
country comparison to the world: 106

Education expenditures: 2.1% of GDP (2007)
country comparison to the world: 163

Literacy: *definition:* age 15 and over can read and write
total population: 91.8%
male: 91.2%
female: 92.3% (2015 est.)

School life expectancy (primary to tertiary education): *total:* 13 years
male: 13 years
female: 14 years (2014)

Unemployment, youth ages 15–24: *total:* 31.4%

male: 22.2%
female: 46.7% (2013 est.)
country comparison to the world: 26

GOVERNMENT

Country name: *conventional long form:* Dominican Republic
conventional short form: The Dominican
local long form: Republica Dominicana
local short form: La Dominicana
etymology: the country name derives from the capital city of Santo Domingo (Saint Dominic)

Government type: presidential republic

Capital: *name:* Santo Domingo

Geographic coordinates: 18 28 N, 69 54 W
time difference: UTC-4 (1 hour ahead of Washington, DC, during Standard Time)

Administrative divisions: 10 regions (regiones, singular—region); Cibao Nordeste, Cibao Noroeste, Cibao Norte, Cibao Sur, El Valle, Enriquillo, Higuamo, Ozama, Valdesia, Yuma

Independence: 27 February 1844 (from Haiti)

National holiday: Independence Day, 27 February (1844)

Constitution: many previous (38 total); latest proclaimed 26 January 2010; note—the Dominican Republic Government has a practice of promulgating a "new" constitution whenever an amendment is ratified (2016)

Legal system: civil law system based on the French civil code; Criminal Procedures Code modified in 2004 to include important elements of an accusatory system

International law organization participation: accepts compulsory ICJ jurisdiction; accepts ICCt jurisdiction

Citizenship: *citizenship by birth:* no
citizenship by descent only: at least one parent must be a citizen of the Dominican Republic
dual citizenship recognized: yes
residency requirement for naturalization: 2 years

Suffrage: 18 years of age, universal and compulsory; married persons regardless of age can vote; note—members of the armed forces and national police by law cannot vote

Executive branch: *chief of state:* President Danilo MEDINA Sanchez (since 16 August 2012); Vice President Margarita CEDENO DE FERNANDEZ (since 16 August 2012); note—the president is both chief of state and head of government

head of government: President Danilo MEDINA Sanchez (since 16 August 2012); Vice President Margarita CEDENO DE FERNANDEZ (since 16 August 2012)
cabinet: Cabinet nominated by the president
elections/appointments: president and vice president directly elected on the same ballot by absolute vote in 2 rounds if needed for a 4-year term (eligible for consecutive terms); election last held on 20 May 2012 (next to be held in 2016)
election results: Danilo MEDINA Sanchez elected president; percent of vote—Danilo MEDINA Sanchez (PLD) 51.2%, Hipolito MEJIA (PRD) 47%, other 1.8%; Margarita CEDENO DE FERNANDEZ (PLD) elected vice president

Legislative branch: *description:* bicameral National Congress or Congreso Nacional consists of the Senate or Senado (32 seats; members directly elected in single-seat constituencies by simple majority vote to serve 4-year terms) and the House of Representatives or Camara de Diputados (195 seats; members directly elected in multi-seat constituencies by proportional representation vote; members serve 4-year terms)
elections: Senate—last held on 16 May 2010 (next to be held in May 2016); House of Representatives-last held on 16 May 2010 (next to be held in May 2016); note—in order to synchronize presidential, legislative, and local elections for 2016, members elected in 2010 will actually serve six-year terms
election results: Senate—percent of vote by party—NA; seats by party—PLD 31, PRSC 1; House of Representatives—percent of vote by party—NA; seats by party—PLD 105, PRD 75, PRSC 3

Judicial branch: *highest court(s):* Supreme Court of Justice or Suprema Corte de Justicia (consists of a minimum of 16 magistrates); Constitutional Court or Tribunal Constitucional (consists of 13 judges); note—the Constitutional Court was established in 2010 by constitutional amendment
judge selection and term of office: Supreme Court and Constitutional Court judges appointed by the National Council of the Judiciary comprised of the president, the leaders of both chambers of congress, the president of the Supreme Court, and a non-governing party congressional representative; Supreme Court judges appointed for 7-year terms; Constitutional Court judges appointed for 9-year terms
subordinate court(s): courts of appeal; courts of first instance; justices of the peace; special courts for juvenile, labor, and land cases; Contentious Administrative Court for cases filed against the government

Political parties and leaders:
Dominican Liberation Party or PLD [Leonel FERNANDEZ Reyna]
Dominican Revolutionary Party or PRD [Miguel VARGAS Maldonado]
National Progressive Front [Vinicio CASTILLO, Pelegrin CASTILLO]
Social Christian Reformist Party or PRSC [Carlos MORALES Troncoso]

Political pressure groups and leaders:
Citizen Participation Group (Participacion Ciudadania)
Collective of Popular Organizations or COP
Foundation for Institution-Building and Justice or FINJUS

International organization participation: ACP, AO SIS, BCIE, Caricom (observer), CD, CELAC, FAO, G-77, IADB, IAEA, IBRD, ICAO, ICC (national committees), ICCt, ICRM, IDA, IFAD, IFC, IFRCS, IHO, ILO, IMF, IMO, Interpol, IOC, IO M, IPU, ISO (correspondent), ITSO, ITU, ITUC (NGOs), LAES, LAIA, MIGA, MINU SMA, NAM, OAS, OIF (observer), OPA-NAL, OPCW, Pacific Alliance (observer), PCA, Petrocaribe, SICA (associated member), UN, UNCTAD, UNESCO, UNIDO, Union Latina, UNWTO, UPU, WCO, WFTU (NGOs), WHO, WIPO, WMO, WTO

Diplomatic representation in the US: *chief of mission:* Ambassador Jose Tomas PEREZ (since 23 February 2015)
chancery: 1715 22nd Street NW, Washington, DC 20008
telephone: [1] (202) 332-6280
FAX: [1] (202) 265-8057
consulate(s) general: Boston, Chicago, Los Angeles, Mayaguez (Puerto Rico), Miami, New Orleans, New York, San Juan (Puerto Rico)
consulate(s): San Francisco

Diplomatic representation from the US: *chief of mission:* Ambassador James Walter BREWSTER, Jr. (since 9 December 2013)
embassy: Av. Republica de Colombia
mailing address: Unit 5500, APO AA 34041-5500
telephone: [1] (809) 567-7775
FAX: [1] (809) 686-7437

Flag description: a centered white cross that extends to the edges divides the flag into four rectangles—the top on es are blue (hoist side) and red, and the bottom ones are red (hoist side) and blue; a small coat of arms featuring a shield supported by a laurel branch (left) and a palm branch (right) is at the center of the cross; above the shield a blue ribbon displays the motto, DIOS, PATRIA, LIBERTAD (God, Fatherland, Liberty), and below the shield, REPUBLICA DOMINICANA appears on a red ribbon; in the shield a bible is opened to a verse that reads "Y la verdad nos hara libre" (And the truth shall set you free); blue stands for liberty, white for salvation, and red for the blood of heroes

National symbol(s): palmchat (bird); national colors: red, white, blue

National anthem: *name:* "Himno Nacional" (National Anthem)
lyrics/music: Emilio PRUD'HOMME/Jose REYES
note: adopted 1934; also known as "Quisqueyanos valientes" (Valient Sons of Quisqueye); the anthem never refers to the people as Dominican but rather calls them "Quisqueyanos," a reference to the indigenous name of the island

ECONOMY

Economy—overview: The Dominican Republic has long been viewed primarily as an exporter of sugar, coffee, and tobacco, but in recent years the service sector has overtaken agriculture as the economy's largest employer, due to growth in construction, tourism, and free trade zones. The mining sector has also played a greater role in the export market since late 2012 with the commencement of the extraction phase of the Pueblo Viejo Gold and Silver mine. The country suffers from marked income inequality; the poorest half of the population receives less than one-fifth of GDP, while the richest 10% enjoys nearly 40% of GDP. High unemployment, a large informal sector, and underemployment remain important long-term challenges. The economy is highly dependent upon the US, the destination for approximately half of exports. Remittances from the US amount to about 7% of GDP, equivalent to about a third of exports and two-thirds of tourism receipts. The Central America-Dominican Republic Free Trade Agreement (CAFTA-DR) came into force

in March 2007, boosting investment and exports and reducing losses to the Asian garment industry. The Dominican Republic's economy rebounded from the global recession in 2010–15, and the fiscal situation is improving. A tax reform package passed in November 2012, a reduction in government spending, and lower energy costs helped to narrow the central government budget deficit from 6.6% of GDP in 2012 to 2.6% in 2015. A liability management operation in January 2015, in which the government paid down over $4 billion of the country's Petrocaribe debt at a discount of 52% with proceeds from the sale of $2.5 billion in global bonds, reduced the country's debt load by approximately by 4% of GDP. Analysts project 6% GDP growth in 2016 and inflation within the Central Bank's target of 4.0% 1.0%, due to low oil prices, increased remittances, and continued expansion in the services sector based on growth in construction.

GDP (purchasing power parity): $149.7 billion (2015 est.)
$139.9 billion (2014 est.)
$130.3 billion (2013 est.)
note: data are in 2015 US dollars
country comparison to the world: 74

GDP (official exchange rate): $67.49 billion (2015 est.)

GDP—real growth rate: 7% (2015 est.)
7.3% (2014 est.)
4.8% (2013 est.)
country comparison to the world: 16

GDP—per capita (PPP): $15,000 (2015 est.)
$14,200 (2014 est.)
$13,300 (2013 est.)
note: data are in 2015 US dollars
country comparison to the world: 108

GDP—composition, by end use:
household consumption: 68.2%
government consumption: 10.7%
investment in fixed capital: 21%
investment in inventories: 1%
exports of goods and services: 23.4%
imports of goods and services: -24.3% (2015 est.)

GDP—composition, by sector of origin:
agriculture: 5.6%
industry: 31.4%
services: 63% (2015 est.)

Agriculture—products: cocoa, tobacco, sugarcane, coffee, cotton, rice, beans, potatoes, corn, bananas; cattle, pigs, dairy products, beef, eggs

Industries: tourism, sugar processing, gold mining, textiles, cement, tobacco, electrical components, medical devices

Industrial production growth rate: 5% (2015 est.)
country comparison to the world: 34

Labor force: 4.93 million (2015 est.)
country comparison to the world: 85

Labor force—by occupation: *agriculture:* 14.4%
industry: 20.8%
services: 64.7% (2014 est.)

Unemployment rate: 14% (2015 est.)
14.5% (2014 est.)
country comparison to the world: 148

Population below poverty line: 41.1% (2013 est.)

Household income or consumption by percentage share: *lowest:* 10%: 1.9%

highest: 10%: 37.4% (2013 est.)

Distribution of family income—Gini index:
47.1 (2013 est.)
45.7 (2012 est.)
country comparison to the world: 28

Budget: *revenues:* $10.68 billion
expenditures: $11.71 billion (2015 est.)
Taxes and other revenues: 16% of GDP (2015 est.)
country comparison to the world: 183

Budget surplus (+) or deficit (-): -1.6% of GDP (2015 est.)
country comparison to the world: 63

Public debt: 44.7% of GDP (2015 est.)
45.4% of GDP (2014 est.)
country comparison to the world: 102

Fiscal year: calendar year

Inflation rate (consumer prices): 0.8% (2015 est.)
3% (2014 est.)
country comparison to the world: 72

Commercial bank prime lending rate:
14.7% (31 December 2015 est.)
13.9% (31 December 2014 est.)
country comparison to the world: 44

Stock of narrow money:
$6.005 billion (31 December 2015 est.)
$5.488 billion (31 December 2014 est.)
country comparison to the world: 94

Stock of broad money:
$18.74 billion (31 December 2015 est.)
$16.99 billion (31 December 2014 est.)
country comparison to the world: 90

Stock of domestic credit:
$28.87 billion (31 December 2015 est.)
$27.16 billion (31 December 2014 est.)
country comparison to the world: 74

Market value of publicly traded shares: $NA

Current account balance:
-$1.299 billion (2015 est.)
-$2.026 billion (2014 est.)
country comparison to the world: 133

Exports: $9.617 billion (2015 est.)
$9.92 billion (2014 est.)
country comparison to the world: 91

Exports—commodities: gold, silver, cocoa, sugar, coffee, tobacco, meats, consumer goods

Exports—partners: US 42.5%, Haiti 16.5%, Canada 8.1%, India 4.8% (2015)

Imports: $15.26 billion (2015 est.)
$17.29 billion (2014 est.)
country comparison to the world: 84

Imports—commodities: petroleum, foodstuffs, cotton and fabrics, chemicals and pharmaceuticals

Imports—partners: US 41.9%, China 9.2%, Venezuela 5.6%, Trinidad and Tobago 4.5%, Mexico 4.4% (2015)

Reserves of foreign exchange and gold:
$4.962 billion (31 December 2015 est.)
$4.862 billion (31 December 2014 est.)
country comparison to the world: 94

Debt—external:
$24.31 billion (31 December 2014 est.)
$23.83 billion (31 December 2013 est.)
country comparison to the world: 82

Stock of direct foreign investment—at home:

$30.3 billion (31 December 2015 est.)
$28.31 billion (31 December 2014 est.)
country comparison to the world: 69

Stock of direct foreign investment—abroad:
$347.2 million (31 December 2015 est.)
$127.2 million (31 December 2014 est.)
country comparison to the world: 89

Exchange rates: Dominican pesos (DOP) per US dollar—
45.02 (2015 est.)
43.556 (2014 est.)
43.556 (2013 est.)
39.34 (2012 est.)
38.232 (2011 est.)

ENERGY

Electricity—production: 17.97 billion kWh (2014 est.)
country comparison to the world: 78

Electricity—consumption: 15.14 billion kWh (2014 est.)
country comparison to the world: 78

Electricity—exports: 0 kWh (2014 est.)
country comparison to the world: 133

Electricity—imports: 0 kWh (2014 est.)
country comparison to the world: 143

Electricity—installed generating capacity: 3.702 million kW (2013 est.)
country comparison to the world: 87

Electricity—from fossil fuels: 85.2% of total installed capacity (2013 est.)
country comparison to the world: 88

Electricity—from nuclear fuels: 0% of total installed capacity (2013 est.)
country comparison to the world: 81

Electricity—from hydroelectric plants: 13.2% of total installed capacity (2013 est.)
country comparison to the world: 106

Electricity—from other renewable sources: 1.6% of total installed capacity (2013 est.)
country comparison to the world: 85

Crude oil—production: 0 bbl/day (2014 est.)
country comparison to the world: 127

Crude oil—exports: 0 bbl/day (2014 est.)
country comparison to the world: 118

Crude oil—imports: 26,500 bbl/day (2014 est.)
country comparison to the world: 64

Crude oil—proved reserves: 0 bbl (1 January 2015 est.)
country comparison to the world: 126

Refined petroleum products—production: 25,390 bbl/day (2014 est.)
country comparison to the world: 90

Refined petroleum products—consumption: 80,820 bbl/day (2014 est.)
country comparison to the world: 83

Refined petroleum products—exports: 0 bbl/day (2014 est.)
country comparison to the world: 176

Refined petroleum products—imports: 54,920 bbl/day (2012 est.)
country comparison to the world: 75

Natural gas—production: 0 cu m (2013 est.)
country comparison to the world: 180

Natural gas—consumption: 1.45 billion cu m (2013 est.)

country comparison to the world: 85

Natural gas—exports: 0 cu m (2013 est.)
country comparison to the world: 90

Natural gas—imports: 1.45 billion cu m (2013 est.)
country comparison to the world: 54

Natural gas—proved reserves: 0 cu m (1 January 2014 est.)
country comparison to the world: 132

Carbon dioxide emissions from consumption of energy: 20.8 million Mt (2012 est.)
country comparison to the world: 81

COMMUNICATIONS

Telephones—fixed lines: *total subscriptions:* 1.23 million (2014 est.)
subscriptions per 100 inhabitants: 10 (2015)
country comparison to the world: 68

Telephones—mobile cellular: *total:* 8.3 million
subscriptions per 100 in habitants: 90 (2015)
country comparison to the world: 94

Telephone system: *general assessment:* relatively efficient system based on island-wide microwave radio relay network
domestic: fixed-line teledensity is about 10 per 100 persons; multiple providers of mobile-cellular service with a subscribership of nearly 90 per 100 persons
international: country code—1–809; 1–829; 1–849; landing point for the Americas Region Caribbean Ring System (ARCOS-1), Antillas 1, AMX-1, and the Fibralink submarine cables that provide links to South and Central America, parts of the Caribbean, and US; satellite earth station—1 Intelsat (Atlantic Ocean) (2015)

Broadcast media: combination of state-owned and privately owned broadcast media; 1 state-owned TV network and a number of private TV networks; networks operate repeaters to extend signals throughout country; combination of state-owned and privately owned radio stations with more than 300 radio stations operating (2015)
Radio broadcast stations: AM 120, FM 56, shortwave 4 (1998)
Television broadcast stations: 25 (2003)

Internet country code: .do

Internet hosts: 404,500 (2012)
country comparison to the world: 55

Internet users: *total:* 5 million
percent of population: 48.2% (2014 est.)
country comparison to the world: 69

TRANSPORTATION

Airports: 36 (2013)
country comparison to the world: 110

Airports—with paved runways: *total:* 16
over 3,047 m: 3
2,438 to 3,047 m: 4
1,524 to 2,437 m: 4
914 to 1,523 m: 4
under 914 m: 1 (2013)

Airports—with unpaved runways: *total:* 20
1,524 to 2,437 m: 1
914 to 1,523 m: 1
under 914 m: 18 (2013)

Heliports: 1 (2013)

Pipelines: gas 27 km; oil 103 km (2013)

Rail ways: *total:* 496 km
standard gauge: 354 km 1.435-m gauge
narrow gauge: 142 km 0.762-m gauge (2014)
country comparison to the world: 115

Roadways: *total:* 19,705 km
paved: 9,872 km
un paved: 9,833 km (2002)
country comparison to the world: 110

Ports and terminals: *major seaport(s):* Puerto Haina, Puerto Plata, Santo Domingo
oil terminal(s): Punta Nizao oil terminal
LNG terminal(s) (import): Andres LNG terminal (Boca Chica)

MILITARY AND SECURITY

Military branches: Army (Ejercito Nacional, EN), Navy (Marina de Guerra, MdG; includes naval infantry), Dominican Air Force (Fuerza Aerea Dominicana, FAD) (2013)

Military service age and obligation: 17–21 years of age for voluntary military service; recruits must have completed primary school and be Dominican Republic citizens; women may volunteer (2012)

Military expenditures: 0.61% of GDP (2012)
0.63% of GDP (2011)
0.61% of GDP (2010)
country comparison to the world: 121

TRANSNATIONAL ISSUES

Disputes—international: Haitian migrants cross the porous border into the Dominican Republic to find work; illegal migrants from the Dominican Republic cross the Mona Passage each year to Puerto Rico to find better work

Refugees and internally displaced persons: *stateless persons:* 133,770 (2015); note—a September 2013 Constitutional Court ruling revoked the citizenship of those born after 1929 to immigrants without proper documentation, even though the constitution at the time automatically granted citizenship to children born in the Dominican Republic and the 2010 constitution provides that constitutional provisions cannot be applied retroactively; the decision overwhelmingly affected people of Haitian descent whose relatives had come to the Dominican Republic since the 1940s as a cheap source of labor for sugar plantations; a May 2014 law passed by the Dominican Congress will regularize the status of those with birth certificates but will require those without them to prove they were born in the Dominican Republic and to apply for naturalization
note: revised estimate includes only individuals born to parents who were both born abroad; it does not include individuals born in the country to one Dominican-born and one foreign-born parent or subsequent generations of individuals of foreign descent; the estimate, as such, does not include all stateless persons (2015)

Illicit drugs: transshipment point for South American drugs destined for the US and Europe; has become a transshipment point for ecstasy from the Netherlands and Belgium destined for US and Canada; substantial money laundering activity in particular by Colombian narcotics traffickers; significant amphetamine consumption (2008)

INTRODUCTION

Background: What is now Ecuador formed part of the northern Inca Empire until the Spanish conquest in 1533. Quito became a seat of Spanish colonial government in 1563 and part of the Viceroyalty of New Granada in 1717. The territories of the Viceroyalty—New Granada (Colombia), Venezuela, and Quito—gained their independence between 1819 and 1822 and formed a federation known as Gran Colombia. When Quito withdrew in 1830, the traditional name was changed in favor of the "Republic of the Equator." Between 1904 and 1942, Ecuador lost territories in a series of conflicts with its neighbors. A border war with Peru that flared in 1995 was resolved in 1999. Although Ecuador marked 30 years of civilian governance in 2004, the period was marred by political instability. Protests in Quito contributed to the mid-term ouster of three of Ecuador's last four democratically elected presidents. In late 2008, voters approved a new constitution, Ecuador's 20th since gaining independence. General elections were held in February 2013, and voters reelected President Rafael CORREA.

GEOGRAPHY

Location: Western South America, bordering the Pacific Ocean at the Equator, between Colombia and Peru

Geographic coordinates: 2 00 S, 77 30 W

Map references: South America

Area: *total:* 283,561 sq km
land: 276,841 sq km
water: 6,720 sq km
note: includes Galapagos Islands
country comparison to the world: 74

Area—comparative: slightly smaller than Nevada

Land boundaries: *total:* 2,237 km
border countries (2): Colombia 708 km, Peru 1,529 km Coastline: 2,237 km

Maritime claims: *territorial sea:* 200 nm
continental shelf: 100 nm from 2,500-m isobath

Climate: tropical along coast, becoming cooler inland at higher elevations; tropical in Amazonian jungle lowlands

Terrain: coastal plain (costa), inter-Andean central highlands (sierra), and flat to rolling eastern jungle (oriente)

Elevation: *mean elevation:* 1,117 m

elevation extremes: *lowest point:* Pacific Ocean 0 m
highest point: Chimborazo 6,267 m
note: because the earth is not a perfect sphere and has an equatorial bulge, the highest point on the planet furthest from its center is Mount Chimborazo not Mount Everest, which is merely the highest peak above sea level

Natural resources: petroleum, fish, timber, hydropower

Land use: *agricultural land:* 29.7%
arable land: 4.7%;
permanent crops: 5.6%;
permanent pasture: 19.4%
forest: 38.9%
other: 31.4% (2011 est.)

Irrigated land: 15,000 sq km (2012)

Total renewable water resources: 424.4 cu km (2011)

Freshwater withdrawal (domestic/industrial/agricultural): *total:* 9.92 cu km/yr (13%/6%/81%)
per capita: 716.1 cu m/yr (2005)

Natural hazards: frequent earth quakes; landslides; volcanic activity; floods; periodic droughts
volcanism: volcanic activity concentrated along the Andes Mountains; Sangay (elev.5,230 m), which erupted in 2010, is mainland Ecuador's most active volcano; other historically active volcanoes in the Andes include Antisana, Cayambe, Chacana, Cotopaxi, Guagua Pichincha, Reventador, Sumaco, and Tungurahua; Fernandina (elev.1,476 m), a shield volcano that last erupted in 2009, is the most active of the many Galapagos volcanoes; other historically active Galapagos volcanoes include Wolf, Sierra Negra, Cerro Azul, Pinta, March ena, and Santiago

Environment—current issues: deforestation; soil erosion; desertification; water pollution; pollution from oil production wastes in ecologically sensitive areas of the Amazon Basin and Galapagos Islands

Environment—international agreements: *party to:* Antarctic-Environmental Protocol, Antarctic Treaty, Biodiversity, Climate Change, Climate Change-Kyoto Protocol, Desertification, Endangered Species, Hazardous Wastes, Ozone Layer Protection, Sh ip Pollution, Tropical Timber 83, Tropical Timber 94, Wetlands
signed, but not ratified: none of the selected agreements

Geography—note: Cotopaxi in Andes is highest active volcano in world

PEOPLE AND SOCIETY

Nationality: *noun:* Ecuadorian(s)

adjective: Ecuadorian

Ethnic groups: mestizo (mixed Amerindian and white) 71.9%, Montubio 7.4%, Amerindian 7%, white 6.1%, Afroecuadorian 4.3%, mulato 1.9%, black 1%, other 0.4% (2010 est.)

Languages: Spanish (Castilian) 93% (official), Quechua 4.1%, other indigenous 0.7%, foreign 2.2%
note: (Quechua and Shuar are official languages of intercultural relations; other indigenous languages are in official use by indigenous peoples in the areas they inhabit) (2010 est.)

Religions: Roman Catholic 74%, Evangelical 10.4%, Jehovah's Witness 1.2%, other 6.4% (includes Mormon Buddhist, Jewish, Spiritualist, Muslim, Hindu, indigenous religions, African American religions, Pentecostal), atheist 7.9%, agnostic 0.1%
note: data represents persons at least 16 years of age from five Ecuadoran cities (2012 est.)

Demographic profile: Ecuador's high poverty and income inequality most affect indigenous, mixed race, and rural populations. The government has increased its social spending to ameliorate these problems, but critics question the efficiency and implementation of its national development plan. Nevertheless, the conditional cash transfer program, which requires participants' children to attend school and have medical check-ups, has helped improve educational attainment and healthcare among poor children. Ecuador is stalled at above replacement level fertility and the population most likely will keep growing rather than stabilize. An estimated 2 to 3 million Ecuadorians live abroad, but increased unemployment in key receiving countries—Spain, the United States, and Italy—is slowing emigration and increasing the likelihood of returnees to Ecuador. The first large-scale emigration of Ecuadorians occurred between 1980 and 2000, when an economic crisis drove Ecuadorians from southern provinces to New York City, where they had trade contacts. A second, nationwide wave of emigration in the late 1990s was caused by another economic downturn, political instability, and a currency crisis. Spain was the logical destination because of its shared language and the wide availability of low-skilled, informal jobs at a time when increased border surveillance made illegal migration to the US difficult. Ecuador has a small but growing immigrant population and is Latin America's top recipient of refugees; 98% are neighboring Colombians fleeing violence in their country.

Population: 15,868,396 (July 2015 est.)
country comparison to the world: 68

Age structure: *0–14 years:* 27.99% (male 2,265,935/female 2,175,864)
15–24 years: 18.56% (male 1,494,206/female 1,451,152)
25–54 years: 39.16% (male 3,027,989/female 3,185,924)

55–64 years: 7.23% (male 563,259/female 584,730)
65 years and over: 7.05% (male 533,796/female 585,541) (2015 est.)

Dependency ratios: *total dependency ratio:* 55.6%
youth dependency ratio: 45.1%
elderly dependency ratio: 10.4%
potential support ratio: 9.6% (2015 est.)

Median age: *total:* 27 years
male: 26.3 years
female: 27.7 years (2015 est.)
country comparison to the world: 142

Population growth rate: 1.35% (2015 est.)
country comparison to the world: 88

Birth rate: 18.51 births/1,000 population (2015 est.)
country comparison to the world: 95

Death rate: 5.06 deaths/1,000 population (2015 est.)
country comparison to the world: 186

Net migration rate: 0 migrant(s)/1,000 population (2015 est.)
country comparison to the world: 100

Urbanization: *urban population:* 63.7% of total population (2015)
rate of urbanization: 1.9% annual rate of change (2010–15 est.)

Major urban areas—population: Guayaquil 2.709 million; QUITO (capital) 1.726 million (2015)

Sex ratio: *at birth:* 1.05 male(s)/female
0–14 years: 1.04 male(s)/female
15–24 years: 1.03 male(s)/female
25–54 years: 0.95 male(s)/female
55–64 years: 0.96 male(s)/female
65 years and over: 0.91 male(s)/female
total population: 0.99 male(s)/female (2015 est.)

Maternal mortality rate: 64 deaths/100,000 live births (2015 est.)
country comparison to the world: 67

Infant mortality rate: *total:* 17.38 deaths/1,000 births
male: 20.51 deaths/1,000 live births
female: 14.1 deaths/1,000 live births (2015 est.)
country comparison to the world: 99

Life expectancy at birth: *total population:* 76.56 years
male: 73.6 years
female: 79.67 years (2015 est.)
country comparison to the world: 82

Total fertility rate: 2.25 children born/woman (2015 est.)
country comparison to the world: 95

Health expenditures: 7.5% of GDP (2013)
country comparison to the world: 98

Physicians density: 1.72 physicians/1,000 population (2011)

Hospital bed density: 1.6 beds/1,000 population (2011)

Drinking water source:
improved:
urban: 93.4% of population
rural: 75.5% of population

total: 86.9% of population
unimproved:
urban: 6.6% of population
rural: 24.5% of population
total: 13.1% of population (2015 est.)

Sanitation facility access:
improved:
urban: 87% of population
rural: 80.7% of population
total: 84.7% of population
unimproved:
urban: 13% of population
rural: 19.3% of population
total: 15.3% of population (2015 est.)

HIV/AIDS—adult prevalence rate: 0.34% (2014 est.)
country comparison to the world: 80

HIV/AIDS—people living with HIV/AIDS: 32,700 (2014 est.)
country comparison to the world: 67

HIV/AIDS—deaths: 1,200 (2014 est.)
country comparison to the world: 63

Major infectious diseases: *degree of risk:* high
food or waterborne diseases: bacterial diarrhea, hepatitis A, and typhoid fever
vectorborne diseases: dengue fever and malaria (2013)

Obesity—adult prevalence rate: 18% (2014)
country comparison to the world: 86

Children under the age of 5 years underweight: 6.4% (2013)
country comparison to the world: 82

Education expenditures: 4.2% of GDP (2012)
country comparison to the world: 94

Literacy: *definition:* age 15 and over can read and write
total population: 94.5%
male: 95.4%
female: 93.5% (2015 est.)

School life expectancy (primary to tertiary education): *total:* 14 years
male: 14 years
female: 15 years (2012)

Child labor—children ages 5–14: *total number:* 227,599
percentage: 8% (2008 est.)

Unemployment, youth ages 15–24: *total:* 10.9%
male: 8.4%
female: 15.7% (2013 est.)
country comparison to the world: 96

GOVERNMENT

Country name: *conventional long form:* Republic of Ecuador
conventional short form: Ecuador
local long form: Republica del Ecuador
local short form: Ecuador
etymology: the country's position on the globe, straddling the Equator, accounts for its Spanish name

Government type: presidential republic

Capital: *name:* Quito

Geographic coordinates: 0 13 S, 78 30 W

time difference: UTC-5 (same time as Washington, DC, during Standard Time)

Administrative divisions: 24 provinces (provincias, singular—provincia); Azuay, Bolivar, Canar, Carchi, Chimborazo, Cotopaxi, El Oro, Esmeraldas, Galapagos, Guayas, Imbabura, Loja, Los Rios, Manabi, Morona-Santiago, Napo, Orellana, Pastaza, Pichincha, Santa Elena, Santo Domingo de los Tsachilas, Sucumbios, Tungurahua, Zamora-Chinchipe

Independence: 24 May 1822 (from Spain)

National holiday: Independence Day (independence of Quito), 10 August (1809)

Constitution: many previous; latest approved 20 October 2008; amended 2011; note—a 2015 constitutional amendment lifting presidential term limits becomes effective in 2021 (2016)

Legal system: civil law based on the Chilean civil code with modifications; traditional law in indigenous communities

International law organization participation: has not submitted an ICJ jurisdiction declaration; accepts ICCt jurisdiction

Citizenship: *citizenship by birth:* yes
citizenship by descent: yes
dual citizenship recognized: no
residency requirement for naturalization: 3 years

Suffrage: 18–65 years of age, universal and compulsory; 16–18, over 65, and other eligible voters, voluntary

Executive branch: *chief of state:* President Rafael CORREA Delgado (since 15 January 2007); Vice President Jorge GLAS Espinel (since 24 May 2013); note—the president is both chief of state and head of government

head of government: President Rafael CORREA Delgado (since 15 January 2007); Vice President Jorge GLAS Espinel (since 24 May 2013)
cabinet: Cabinet appointed by the president
elections/appointments: president and vice president directly elected on the same ballot by absolute majority popular vote in 2 rounds if needed for a 4-year term (eligible for a second term); election last held on 17 February 2013 (next to be held in 2017)
election results: President Rafael CORREA Delgado reelected president; percent of vote—Rafael CORREA Delgado (Alianza PAIS Movement) 57.2%, Guillermo LASSO (CREO) 22.7%, Lucio GUTIERREZ (PSP) 6.8%, Mauricio RODAS (SUMA) 3.9%, other 9.4%

Legislative branch: *description:* unicameral National Assembly or Asamblea Nacional (137 seats; 116 members directly elected in single-seat constituencies by simple majority vote, 15 members directly elected in a single nationwide constituency by proportional representation vote, and 6 directly elected in multi-seat constituencies for Ecuadorians living abroad by simple majority vote; members serve 4-year terms)
elections: last held on 17 February 2013 (next to be held in 2017)

election results: percent of vote by party—NA; seats by party—PAIS 100, CREO 11, PSC 6, AVANZA 5, MUPP 5, PSP 5, other 5; note—defections by members of National Assembly are commonplace, resulting in frequent changes in the numbers of seats held by the various parties

Judicial branch: *highest court(s):* National Court of Justice or Corte Nacional de Justicia (consists of 21 judges including the chief justice and organized into 5 specialized chambers); Constitutional Court or Corte Constitucional (con sists of 9 judges)

judge selection and term of office: justices of National Court of Justice elected by the Judiciary Council, a 9-member independent body of law professionals; judges elected for 9-year, non-renewable terms, with one-third of the membership renewed every 3 years; Constitutional Court judges appointed by the executive, legislative, and Citizen Participation branches of government; judges appointed for 9-year non-renewable terms with one-third of the membership renewed every 3 years

subordinate court(s): Fiscal Tribunal; Election Dispute Settlement Courts, provincial courts (one for each province); cantonal courts

Political parties and leaders: Alianza PAIS movement [Rafael Vicente CORREA Delgado]

Avanza Party or AVANZA [Ramiro GONZALEZ]

Creating Opportunities Movement or CREO [Guillermo LASSO]

Institutional Renewal and National Action Party or PRIAN [Alvaro NOBOA]

Pachakutik Plurinational Unity Movement or MUPP [Rafael ANTUNI]

Patriotic Society Party or PSP [Lucio GUTIERREZ Borbua]

Popular Democracy Movement or MPD [Luis VILLACIS]

Roldosist Party or PRE

Social Christian Party or PSC [Pascual DELCIO PPO] Socialist Party [Fabian SOLANO]

Society United for More Action or SUMA [Mauricio RODAS]

Warrior's Spirit Movement [Jaime NEBOT]

Political pressure groups and leaders: Confederation of Indigenous Nationalities of Ecuador or CONAIE [Humberto CHOLANGO]

Federation of Indigenous Evangelists of Ecuador or FEINE [Manuel CHUGCHILAN, president]

National Federation of Indigenous Afro-Ecuatorianos and Peasants or FENOCIN

National Teacher's Union or UNE [Mariana PALLASCO]

International organization participation: CAN, CD, CELAC, FAO, G-11, G-77, IADB, IAEA, IBRD, ICAO, ICC (national committees), ICCt, ICRM, IDA, IFAD, IFC, IFRCS, IHO, ILO, IMF, IMO, Interpol, IOC, IOM, IPU, ISO, ITSO, ITU, ITUC (NGO s), LAES, LAIA, Mercosur (associate), MIGA, MINUSTAH, NAM, OAS, OPANAL, OPCW, OPEC, Pacific Alliance (observer), PCA, SICA (observer), UN, UNAMID, UNASUR, UNCTAD, UNESCO, UNHCR, UNIDO, Union Latina, UNISFA, UNMIL, UNMISS, UNOCI, UNWTO, UPU, WCO, WFTU(NGOs), WHO, WIPO, WMO, WTO

Diplomatic representation in the US: *chief of mission:* Ambassador Jose Francisco BORJA Cevallos (since 18 May 2015)

chancery: 2535 15th Street NW, Washington, DC 20009

telephone: [1] (202) 234–7200

FAX: [1] (202) 667–3482

consulate(s) general: Atlanta, Chicago, Houston, Los Angeles, Miami, Minneapolis, New Haven (CT), New Or leans, New York, Newark (NJ), Phoenix, San Francisco

Diplomatic representation from the US: *chief of mission:* Ambassador Adam E. NAMM (since 26 April 2012)

embassy: Avenida Avigiras E12–170 y Avenida Eloy Alfaro, Quito

mailing address: Avenida Guayacanes N 52–205 y Avenida Avigiras

telephone: [593] (2) 398-5000

FAX: [593] (2) 398-5100

consulate(s) general: Guayaquil

Flag description: three horizontal bands of yellow (top, double width), blue, and red with the coat of arms superimposed at the center of the flag; the flag retains the three main colors of the banner of Gran Colombia, the South American republic that broke up in 1830; the yellow color represents sunshine, grain, and mineral wealth, blue the sky, sea, and rivers, and red the blood of patriots spilled in the struggle for freedom and justice

note: similar to the flag of Colombia, which is shorter and does not bear a coat of arms

National symbol(s): Andean condor; national colors: yellow, blue, red

National anthem: *name:* "Salve, Oh Patria!" (We Salute You, Our Homeland)

lyrics/music: Juan Leon MERA/Antonio NEUMANE

note: adopted 1948; Juan Leon MERA wrote the lyrics in 1865; only the chorus and second verse are sung

ECONOMY

Economy—overview: Ecuador is substantially dependent on its petroleum resources, which have accounted for more than half of the country's export earnings and approximately 25% of public sector revenues in recent years. In 1999/2000, Ecuador's economy suffered from a banking crisis, with GDP contracting by 5.3% and poverty increasing significantly. In March 2000, the Congress approved a series of structural reforms that also provided for the adoption of the US dollar as legal tender. Dollarization stabilized the economy, and positive growth returned in the years that followed, helped by high oil prices, remittances, and increased non-traditional exports. The economy grew an average of 4.3% per year from 2002 to 2006, the highest five-year average in 25 years. After moderate growth in 2007, the economy reached a growth rate of 6.4% in 2008, buoyed by high global petroleum prices and increased public sector investment. President Rafael CORREA Delgado, who took office in January 2007, defaulted in December 2008 on Ecuador's sovereign debt, which, with a total face value of approximately US$3.2 billion, represented about 30% of Ecuador's public external debt. In May 2009, Ecuador bought back 91% of its "defaulted" bonds via an international reverse auction. Economic policies under the CORREA administration—for example, an announcement in late 2009 of its intention to terminate 13 bilateral investment treaties, including one with the US—have generated economic uncertainty and discouraged private investment. China has become Ecuador's largest foreign lender since Quito defaulted in 2008, allowing the government to maintain a high rate of social spending; Ecuador contracted with the Chinese government for more than $9.9 billion in forward oil sales, project financing, and-bud get support loan sas of December 2013. The level of foreign investment in Ecuador continues to be one of the lowest in the region as a result of an unstable regulatory environment, weak rule of law, and the crowding-out effect of public investments. Faced with a 2013 trade deficit of $1.1 billion, Ecuador erected technical barriers to trade in December 2013, causing tensions with its largest trading partners. Ecuador also decriminalized intellectual property rights violations in February 2014. In March, 2015 Ecuador imposed tariff surcharges for 15 months from 5% to 45% on an estimated 32% of imports. In 2014, oil output increased slightly and production remained steady in 2015. In 2015, however, lower oil prices forced CORREA to cut the budget twice, and the government has considered further budget and subsidy cuts for 2016.

GDP (purchasing power parity): $183.4 billion (2015 est.)

$183.3 billion (2014 est.)

$176.8 billion (2013 est.)

note: data are in 2015 US dollars

country comparison to the world: 66

GDP (official exchange rate): $98.83 billion (2015 est.)

GDP—real growth rate: 0% (2015 est.)

3.7% (2014 est.)

4.6% (2013 est.)

country comparison to the world: 194

GDP—per capita (PPP): $11,300 (2015 est.)

$11,400 (2014 est.)

$11,200 (2013 est.)

note: data are in 2015 US dollars country comparison to the world: 131

Gross national saving: 21.2% of GDP (2015 est.)

28.1% of GDP (2014 est.)

27.7% of GDP (2013 est.)

country comparison to the world: 77

GDP—composition, by end use:

household consumption: 60.5%

government consumption: 13.9%

investment in fixed capital: 26.7%

investment in inventories: 0.5%

exports of goods and services: 23.9%

imports of goods and services: -25.5% (2015 est.)

GDP—composition, by sector of origin: *agriculture:* 6.1%
industry: 34.2%
services: 59.7% (2015 est.)

Agriculture—products: bananas, coffee, cocoa, rice, potatoes, cassava (manioc, tapioca), plantains, sugarcane; cattle, sheep, pigs, beef, pork, dairy products; fish, shrimp; balsa wood

Industries: petroleum, food processing, textiles, wood products, chemicals

Industrial production growth rate: -1%
note: excludes oil refining (2015 est.)
country comparison to the world: 173

Labor force: 7.336 million (2015 est.)
country comparison to the world: 64

Labor force—by occupation: *agriculture:* 27.8%
industry: 17.8%
services: 54.4% (2012 est.)

Unemployment rate: 4.8% (2015 est.)
4.3% (2014 est.)
country comparison to the world: 49

Population below poverty line: 25.6% (December 2013 est.)

Household income or consumption by percentage share: *lowest 10%:* 1.4%
highest: 10%: 35.4%
note: data for urban households only (2012 est.)

Distribution of family income—Gini index: 48.5 (December 2013)
50.5 (December 2010)
note: data are for urban households
country comparison to the world: 24

Budget: *revenues:* $35.1 billion
expenditures: $39.8 billion (2015 est.)

Taxes and other revenues: 35.5% of GDP (2015 est.)
country comparison to the world: 55

Budget surplus (+) or deficit (–): -4.8% of GDP (2015 est.)
country comparison to the world: 168

Public debt: 32.4% of GDP (2015 est.) 27.7% of GDP (2014 est.)
country comparison to the world: 137

Fiscal year: calendar year

Inflation rate (consumer prices): 4% (2015 est.)
3.6% (2014 est.)
country comparison to the world: 152

Central bank discount rate: 8.17% (31 December 2011)
8.68% (31 December 2010)
country comparison to the world: 39

Commercial bank prime lending rate: 8.8% (31 December 2015 est.)
8.12% (31 December 2014 est.)
country comparison to the world: 98

Stock of narrow money: $9.748 billion (31 December 2015 est.)
$9.531 billion (31 December 2014 est.)
country comparison to the world: 80

Stock of broad money: $34.53 billion (31 December 2014 est.)
$28.44 billion (31 December 2013 est.)

country comparison to the world: 76

Stock of domestic credit: $34.2 billion (31 December 2015 est.)
$31.97 billion (31 December 2014 est.)
country comparison to the world: 72

Market value of publicly traded shares:
$5.911 billion (31 December 2012 est.)
$5.779 billion (31 December 2011)
$5.263 billion (31 December 2010 est.)
country comparison to the world: 84

Current account balance: -$2.819 billion (2015 est.)
-$567 million (2014 est.)
country comparison to the world: 155

Exports: $18.36 billion (2015 est.)
$26.6 billion (2014 est.)
country comparison to the world: 73

Exports—commodities: petroleum, bananas, cut flowers, shrimp, cacao, coffee, wood, fish

Exports—partners: US 39.5%, Chile 6.2%, Peru 5.1%, Vietnam 4.3%, Colombia 4.3% (2015)

Imports: $20.93 billion (2015 est.)
$26.67 billion (2014 est.)
country comparison to the world: 73

Imports—commodities: industrial materials, fuels and lubricants, nondurable consumer goods

Imports—partners: US 27.1%, China 15.3%, Colombia 8.3%, Panama 4.9% (2015)

Reserves of foreign exchange and gold: $3.128 billion (31 December 2015 est.)
$3.949 billion (31 December 2014 est.)
country comparison to the world: 105

Debt—external: $25.03 billion (31 December 2014 est.)
$20.28 billion (31 December 2013 est.)
country comparison to the world: 79

Stock of direct foreign investment—at home:
$14.91 billion (31 December 2015 est.)
$14.41 billion (31 December 2014 est.)
country comparison to the world: 87

Stock of direct foreign investment—abroad: $6.33 billion (31 December 2012 est.)
$6.33 billion (31 December 2011 est.)
country comparison to the world: 67

Exchange rates: the US dollar became Ecuador's currency in 2001

ENERGY

Electricity—production: 22.11 billion kWh (2012 est.)
country comparison to the world: 74

Electricity—consumption: 19.02 billion kWh (2012 est.)
country comparison to the world: 71

Electricity—exports: 12 million kWh (2012 est.)
country comparison to the world: 90

Electricity—imports: 238 million kWh (2012 est.)
country comparison to the world: 86

Electricity—installed generating capacity: 5.384 million kW (2012 est.)
country comparison to the world: 75

Electricity—from fossil fuels: 57.3% of total installed capacity (2012 est.)
country comparison to the world: 139

Electricity—from nuclear fuels: 0% of total installed capacity (2012 est.)
country comparison to the world: 82

Electricity—from hydroelectric plants: 41.5% of total installed capacity (2012 est.)
country comparison to the world: 57

Electricity—from other renewable sources:
1.1% of total installed capacity (2012 est.)
country comparison to the world: 92

Crude oil—production: 556,400 bbl/day (2014 est.)
country comparison to the world: 27

Crude oil—exports: 413,000 bbl/day (2013 est.)
country comparison to the world: 23

Crude oil—imports: 0 bbl/day (2012 est.)
country comparison to the world: 183

Crude oil—proved reserves: 8.832 billion bbl (1 January 2015 est.)
country comparison to the world: 19

Refined petroleum products—production: 207,300 bbl/day (2013 est.)
country comparison to the world: 52

Refined petroleum products—consumption: 254,000 bbl/day (2013 est.)
country comparison to the world: 48

Refined petroleum products—exports: 31,530 bbl/day (2013 est.)
country comparison to the world: 68

Refined petroleum products—imports: 135,500 bbl/day (2012 est.)
country comparison to the world: 41

Natural gas—production: 515 million cu m (2013 est.)
country comparison to the world: 71

Natural gas—consumption: 515 million cu m (2013 est.)
country comparison to the world: 97

Natural gas—exports: 0 cu m (2013 est.)
country comparison to the world: 91

Natural gas—imports: 0 cu m (2013 est.)
country comparison to the world: 190

Natural gas—proved reserves: 6.003 billion cu m (1 January 2014 est.)
country comparison to the world: 89

Carbon dioxide emissions from consumption of energy: 37.23 million Mt (2012 est.)
country comparison to the world: 70

COMMUNICATIONS

Telephones—fixed lines: *total subscriptions:* 2.44 million
subscriptions per 100 inhabitants: 16 (2014 est.)
country comparison to the world: 55

Telephones—mobile cellular: *total:* 16.6 million
subscriptions per 100 inhabitants: 106 (2014 est.)
country comparison to the world: 65

Telephone system: *general assessment:* elementary fixed-line service but increasingly sophisticated mobile-cellular network

domestic: fixed-line services provided by multiple telecommunications operators; fixed-line teledensity stands at about 15 per 100 persons; mobile-cellular use has surged and subscribership has reached 100 per 100 persons

international: country code—593; landing points for the PAN-AM and South America-1 submarine cables that provide links to the west coast of South America, Panama, Colombia, Venezuela, and extending onward to Aruba and the US Virgin Islands in the Caribbean; satellite earth station—1 Intelsat (Atlantic Ocean) (2011)

Broadcast media: multiple TV networks and many local channels, as well as more than 300 radio stations; many TV and radio stations are privately owned; the government owns or controls 5 national TV stations and multiple radio stations; broadcast media required by law to give the government free air time to broadcast programs produced by the state (2007)

Radio broadcast stations: AM 392, FM 35, shortwave 29 (2001)

Television broadcast stations: 7 (plus 14 repeaters) (2000)

Internet country code: .ec

Internet hosts: 170,538 (2012)
country comparison to the world: 76

Internet users: *total:* 5.9 million
percent of population: 37.6% (2014 est.)
country comparison to the world: 59

Airports: 432 (2013)
country comparison to the world: 20

Airports—with paved runways: *total:* 104
over 3,047 m: 4

2,438 to 3,047 m: 5
1,524 to 2,437 m: 18
914 to 1,523 m: 26
under 914 m: 51 (2013)

Airports—with unpaved runways: *total:* 328
914 to 1,523 m: 37
under 914 m: 291 (2013)

Heliports: 2 (2013)

Pipelines: extra heavy crude 527 km; gas 71 km; oil 2,131 km; refined products 1,526 km (2013)

Railways: *total:* 965 km
narrow gauge: 965 km 1.067-m gauge (2014)
country comparison to the world: 89

Roadways: *total:* 43,670 km
paved: 6,472 km
unpaved: 37,198 km (2007)
country comparison to the world: 83

Waterways: 1,500 km (most inaccessible) (2012)
country comparison to the world: 52

Merchant marine: *total:* 44
by type: cargo 1, chemical tanker 4, liquefied gas 1, passenger 9, petroleum tanker 28, refrigerated cargo 1
registered in other countries: 4 (Panama 3, Peru 1) (2010)
country comparison to the world: 72

Ports and terminals: *major seaport(s):* Esm eraldas, Manta, Puerto Bolivar
river port(s): Guayaquil (Guayas)
container port(s) (TEUs): Guayaquil (1,405,762)

Transportation—note: the International Maritime Bureau continues to report the territorial and offshore waters as at risk for piracy and armed robbery against ships; vessels, including commercial shipping and pleasure craft, have been attacked and hijacked both at anchor and while underway; crews have been robbed and stores or cargoes stolen

Military branches: Ecuadorian Armed Forces: Ecuadorian Land Force (Fuerza Terrestre Ecuatoriana, FTE), Ecuadorian Navy (Fuerza Naval del Ecuador (FNE), includes Naval Infantry, Naval Aviation, Coast Guard), Ecuadorian Air Force (Fuerza Aerea Ecuatoriana, FAE) (2012)

Military service age and obligation: 18 years of age for selective conscript m ilitary service; conscription has been suspended; 18 years of age for voluntary military service; Air Force 18–22 years of age, Ecadorian birth requirement; 1-year service obligation (2012)

Military expenditures: 2.83% of GDP (2012) 3.2% of GDP (2011) 2.83% of GDP (2010)
country comparison to the world: 24

Disputes—international: organized illegal narcotics operations in Colombia penetrate across Ecuador's shared border, which thousands of Colombians also cross to escape the violence in their home country

Refugees and internally displaced persons: *refugees (country of origin):* 121,317 (Colombia) (2014)
IDPs: 28,775 (earthquake April 2016) (2016)

Illicit drugs: significant transit country for cocaine originating in Colombia and Peru, with much of the US-bound cocaine passing through Ecuadorian Pacific waters; im porter of precursor chem icals used in production of illicit narcotics; attractive location for cash-placement by drug traffickers laundering money because of dollarization and weak anti-money-laundering regime; increased activity on the northern frontier by trafficking groups and Colombian insu rgents (2008)

EGYPT

Background: The regularity and richness of the annual Nile River flood, coupled with semi-isolation provided by deserts to the east and west, allowed for the development of one of the world's great civilizations. A unified kingdom arose circa 3200 B.C., and a series of dynasties ruled in Egypt for the next three millennia. The last native dynasty fell to the Persians in 341 B.C., who in turn were replaced by the Greeks, Romans, and Byzantines. It was the Arabs who introduced Islam and the Arabic language in the 7th century and who ruled for the next six centuries. A local military caste, the Mamluks took control about 1250 and continued to govern after the conquest of Egypt by the Ottoman Turks in 1517. Completion of the Suez Canal in 1869 elevated Egypt as an important world transportation hub. Ostensibly to protect its investments, Britain seized control of Egypt's government in 1882, but nominal allegiance to the Ottoman Empire continued until 1914. Partially independent from the UK in 1922, Egypt acquired full sovereignty from Britain in 1952. The completion of the Aswan High Dam in 1971 and the resultant Lake Nasser have altered the time-honored place of the Nile River in the agriculture and ecology of Egypt. A rapidly growing population (the largest in the Arab world), limited arable land, and dependence on the Nile all continue to overtax resources and stress society. The government has struggled to meet the demands of Egypt's population through economic reform and massive investment in communications and physical infrastructure. Inspired by the 2010 Tunisian revolution, Egyptian opposition groups led demonstrations and labor strikes countrywide, culminating in President Hosni MUBARAK's ouster. Egypt's military assumed national leadership until a new parliament was in place in early 2012; later that same year, Mohammed MORSI won the presidential election. Following often violent protests throughout the spring of 2013 against MORSI's government and the Muslim Brotherhood, the Egyptian Armed Forces intervened and removed MORSI from power in July 2013 and replaced him with interim president Adly MANSOUR. In January 2014, voters approved a new constitution by referendum and in May 2014 elected Abdel Fattah EL SISI president. Egypt elected a new legislature in December 2015, the first parliament since 2012.

Location: Northern Africa, bordering the Mediterranean Sea, between Libya and the Gaza Strip,

257

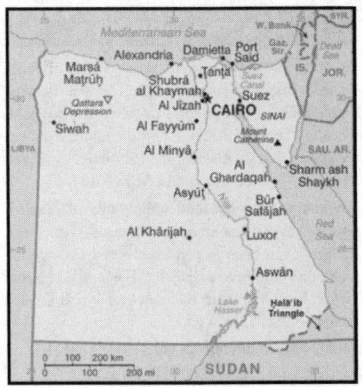

and the Red Sea north of Sudan, and includes the Asian Sinai Peninsula

Geographic coordinates: 27 00 N, 30 00 E

Map references: Africa

Area: *total:* 1,001,450 sq km
land: 995,450 sq km
water: 6,000 sq km
country comparison to the world: 30

Area—comparative: more than eight times the size of Ohio; slightly more than three times the size of New Mexico

Land boundaries: *total:* 2,612 km
border countries (4): Gaza Strip 13 km, Israel 208 km, Libya 1,115 km, Sudan 1,276 km

Coastline: 2,450 km

Maritime claims: *territorial sea:* 12 nm
contiguous zone: 24 nm
exclusive economic zone: 200 nm or the equidistant median line with Cyprus
continental shelf: 200 nm

Climate: desert; hot, dry summers with moderate winters

Terrain: vast desert plateau interrupted by Nile valley and delta

Elevation: mean elevation: 321 m

elevation extremes: *lowest point:* Qattara Depression -133 m
highest point: Mount Catherine 2,629 m

Natural resources: petroleum, natural gas, iron ore, phosphates, manganese, limestone, gypsum, talc, asbestos, lead, rare earth elements, zinc

Land use: *agricultural land:* 3.6%
arable land: 2.8%;
permanent crops: 0.8%;
permanent pasture: 0%
forest: 0.1%
other: 96.3% (2011 est.)

Irrigated land: 36,500 sq km (2012)

Total renewable water resources: 57.3 cu km (2011)

Freshwater withdrawal (domestic/industrial/agricultural): *total:* 68.3 cu km/yr (8%/6%/86%)
per capita: 973.3 cu m/yr (2000)

Natural hazards: periodic droughts; frequent earthquakes; flash floods; landslides; hot, driving windstorms called khamsin occur in spring; dust storms; sandstorms

Environment—current issues: agricultural land being lost to urbanization and windblown sands; increasing soil salination below Aswan High Dam; desertification; oil pollution threatening coral reefs, beaches, and marine habitats; other water pollution from agricultural pesticides, raw sewage, and industrial effluents; limited natural freshwater resources away from the Nile, which is the only perennial water source; rapid growth in population overstraining the Nile and natural resources

Environment—international agreements: party to: Biodiversity, Climate Change, Climate Change-Kyoto Protocol, Desertification, Endangered Species, Environmental Modification, Hazardous Wastes, Law of the Sea, Marine Dumping, Ozone Layer Protection, Ship Pollution, Tropical Timber 83, Tropical Timber 94, Wetlands
signed, but not ratified: none of the selected agreements

Geography—note: controls Sinai Peninsula, only land bridge between Africa and remainder of Eastern Hemisphere; controls Suez Canal, a sea link between Indian Ocean and Mediterranean Sea; size, and juxtaposition to Israel, establish its major role in Middle Eastern geopolitics; dependence on upstream neighbors; dominance of Nile basin issues; prone to influxes of refugees from Sudan and the Palestinian territories

PEOPLE AND SOCIETY

Nationality: *noun:* Egyptian(s)
adjective: Egyptian

Ethnic groups: Egyptian 99.6%, other 0.4% (2006 census)

Languages: Arabic (official), English and French widely understood by educated classes

Religions: Muslim (predominantly Sunni) 90%, Christian (majority Coptic Orthodox, other Christians include Armenian Apostolic, Catholic, Maronite, Orthodox, and Anglican) 10% (2012 est.)

Population: 88,487,396 (July 2015 est.)
country comparison to the world: 16

Age structure: *0–14 years:* 31.89% (male 14,430,312/female 13,790,448)
15–24 years: 17.64% (male 7,985,589/female 7,620,404)
25–54 years: 38.45% (male 17,307,230/female 16,715,153)
55–64 years: 6.86% (male 2,971,475/female 3,100,747)
65 years and over: 5.16% (male 2,058,911/female 2,507,127) (2015 est.)

Dependency ratios: *total dependency ratio:* 62.3%
youth dependency ratio: 53.8%
elderly dependency ratio: 8.5%
potential support ratio: 11.8% (2015 est.)

Median age: *total:* 25.3 years
male: 24.9 years
female: 25.6 years (2015 est.)
country comparison to the world: 150

Population growth rate: 1.79% (2015 est.)
country comparison to the world: 65

Birth rate: 22.9 births/1,000 population (2015 est.)
country comparison to the world: 69

Death rate: 4.77 deaths/1,000 population (2015 est.)
country comparison to the world: 195

Net migration rate: -0.19 migrant(s)/1,000 population (2015 est.)
country comparison to the world: 118

Urbanization: *urban population:* 43.1% of total population (2015)
rate of urbanization: 1.68% annual rate of change (2010–15 est.)

Major urban areas—population: CAIRO (capital) 18.772 million; Alexandria 4.778 million (2015)

Sex ratio: *at birth:* 1.05 male(s)/female
0–14 years: 1.05 male(s)/female
15–24 years: 1.05 male(s)/female
25–54 years: 1.04 male(s)/female
55–64 years: 0.96 male(s)/female
65 years and over: 0.82 male(s)/female
total population: 1.02 male(s)/female (2015 est.)

Mother's mean age at first birth: 22.7
note: median age at first birth among women 25–29 (2014 est.)

Maternal mortality rate: 33 deaths/100,000 live births (2015 est.)
country comparison to the world: 92

Infant mortality rate: *total:* 21.55 deaths/1,000 live births
male: 23 deaths/1,000 live births
female: 20.02 deaths/1,000 live births (2015 est.)
country comparison to the world: 81

Life expectancy at birth: *total population:* 73.7 years
male: 71.06 years
female: 76.47 years (2015 est.)
country comparison to the world: 126

Total fertility rate: 2.83 children born/woman (2015 est.)
country comparison to the world: 61

Contraceptive prevalence rate: 60.3% (2008)

Health expenditures: 5.1% of GDP (2013)
country comparison to the world: 142

Physicians density: 2.83 physicians/1,000 population (2009)

Hospital bed density: 0.5 beds/1,000 population (2012)

Drinking water source: *improved:*
urban: 100% of population
rural: 99% of population
total: 99.4% of population
unimproved:
urban: 0% of population
rural: 1% of population
total: 0.6% of population (2015 est.)

Sanitation facility access: *improved:*
urban: 96.8% of population
rural: 93.1% of population

total: 94.7% of population
unimproved:
urban: 3.2% of population
rural: 6.9% of population
total: 5.3% of population (2015 est.)

HIV/AIDS—adult prevalence rate: 0.02% (2014 est.)
country comparison to the world: 128

HIV/AIDS—people living with HIV/AIDS: 8,800 (2014 est.)
country comparison to the world: 98

HIV/AIDS—deaths: 300 (2014 est.)
country comparison to the world: 98

Major infectious diseases: *degree of risk:* intermediate
food or waterborne diseases: bacterial diarrhea, hepatitis A, and typhoid fever
water contact disease: schistosomiasis
note: highly pathogenic H5N1 avian influenza has been identified in this country; it poses a negligible risk with extremely rare cases possible among US citizens who have close contact with birds (2013)

Obesity—adult prevalence rate: 27.7% (2014)
country comparison to the world: 17

Children under the age of 5 years underweight: 7% (2014)
country comparison to the world: 77

Education expenditures: 3.8% of GDP (2008)
country comparison to the world: 117

Literacy: *definition:* age 15 and over can read and write
total population: 73.8%
male: 82.2%
female: 65.4% (2015 est.)

School life expectancy (primary to tertiary education): *total:* 13 years
male: 13 years
female: 13 years (2014)

Unemployment, youth ages 15–24: *total:* 34.3%
male: 28.7%
female: 52.2% (2013 est.)
country comparison to the world: 37

GOVERNMENT

Country name: *conventional long form:* Arab Republic of Egypt
conventional short form: Egypt
local long form: Jumhuriyat Misr al-Arabiyah
local short form: Misr
former: United Arab Republic (with Syria)
etymology: the English name "Egypt" derives from the ancient Greek name for the country "Aigyptos"; the Arabic name "Misr" can be traced to the ancient Akkadian "misru" meaning border or frontier

Government type: presidential republic

Capital: *name:* Cairo

Geographic coordinates: 30 03 N, 31 15 E
time difference: UTC+2 (7 hours ahead of Washington, DC, during Standard Time)

Administrative divisions: governorates (muhafazat, singular—muhafazat); Ad Daqahliyah, Al Bahr

al Ahmar (Red Sea), Al Buhayrah, Al Fayyum, Al Gharbiyah, Al Iskandariyah (Alexandria), Al Isma'iliyah (Ismailia), Al Jizah (Giza), Al Minufiyah, Al Minya, Al Qahirah (Cairo), Al Qalyubiyah, Al Uqsur (Luxor), Al Wadi al Jadid (New Valley), As Suways (Suez), Ash Sharqiyah, Aswan, Asyut, Bani Suwayf, Bur Sa'id (Port Said), Dumyat (D amietta), Janub Sina' (South Sinai), Kafr ash Shaykh, Matruh, Qina, Shamal Sina' (North Sinai), Suhaj

Independence: February 1922 (from UK protectorate status; the revolution that began on 23 July 1952 led to a republic being declared on 18 June 1953 and all British troops withdrawn on 18 June 1956); note—it was ca.3200 B. C. that the Two Lands of Upper (southern) and Lower (northern) Egypt were first united politically

National holiday: Revolution Day, 23 July (1952)

Constitution: several previous; latest approved by a constitutional committee in December 2013, approved by referendum held on 14–15 January 2014, ratified by interim president on 19 January 2014 (2016)

Legal system: mixed legal system based on napoleonic civil and penal law, Islamic religious law, and vestiges of colonialera laws; judicial review of the constitutionality of laws by the Supreme Constitutional Court

International law organization participation: accepts compulsory ICJ jurisdiction with reservations; non-party state to the ICCt

Citizenship: *citizenship by birth:* no
citizenship by descent only: if the father was born in Egypt
dual citizenship recognized: only with prior permission from the government
residency requirement for naturalization: 10 years

Suffrage: 18 years of age; universal and compulsory

Executive branch: *Chief of state:* President Abdelfattah Said ELSISI (since 8 June 2014)

head of government: Prime Minister Sherif ISMAIL (since 12 September 2015); note—Prime Minister Ibrahim MEHLAB resigned 12 September 2015
cabinet: Cabinet sworn in 19 September 2015
elections/appointments: president elected by absolute majority popular vote in 2 rounds if needed for a 4-year term (eligible for a second term); election last held on 26–28 May 2014 (next to be held in May 2018); prime minister appointed by the president, approved by the House of Representatives
election resul ts: Abdelfattah Said ELSISI elected president; percent of vote in 1 round—Abdelfattah Said ELSISI (independent) 96.6%, Hamdeen SABAHI (Egyptian Current Party) 3.4%

Legislative branch: *description:* unicameral House of Representatives (Majlis Al-Nowaab); 596 seats; 448 members directly elected by individual candidacy system, 120 members—with quotas for women, youth, Christians and workers—elected in party-list constituencies by simple majority popular vote, and 28 members selected by the president;

member term NA; note—inaugural session held on 10 January 2016
elections: multi-phase election completed on 16 December 2015 (next election NA)
election results: percent of vote by party—NA; seats by party—NA

Judicial branch: *highest court(s):* Supreme Constitutional Court or SCC (consists of the court president and 10 justices); the SCC serves as the final court of arbitration on the constitutionality of laws and conflicts between lower courts regarding jurisdiction and rulings; Court of Cassation (CC) (consists of the court president and 550 judges organized in circuits with cases heard by panels of 5 judges); the CC is the highest appeals body for civil and criminal cases, also known as "ordinary justices"; Supreme Administrative Court (SAC)—consists of the court president and organized in circuits with cases heard by panels of 5 judges); the SAC is the highest court of the State Council
judge selection and term of office: under the 2014 constitution, all judges and justices selected by the Supreme Judiciary Council and appointed by the president of the Republic; tenure NA
subordinate courts: Courts of Appeal; Courts of First Instance; courts of limited jurisdiction; Family Court (established in 2004)

Political parties and leaders: officially recognized: Al-Dustour (Constitution) Party [Tamer GOMAA]
Al-Karama Party [Mohamed SAMY]
Al-Nour [Yunis MAKHYUN]
Al-Wasat Party [Mohamad Abdel LATIF]
Al-Watan [Imad Abd al-GHAFUR]
Building and Development Party or BDP [Yomna EL-H AM AKI]
Conference Party [Omar EL-MOKHTAR]
Congress Party [Omar Mokhtar SEMEIDA]
Egyptian National Movement Party [Ahmed SHAFIK]
Egyptian Social Democratic Party [Mervat TALAWAY]
El Tagamu'u Party [Sayed Abdel AAL]
F ree Egyptians Party [Essam KHALIL]
Future of Homeland Party [Qadry ABU HUSSEIN]
Knights of Egypt Party [General Abdel Rafe DARWISH]
Mostaqbal Watan Party [M ohamed BADRAN]
N ew Wafd Party [Sayed al-BAD ADWI]
Popular Current Party [Ahmed Kamel AL-BEHERI]
Reform and Development Party [Mohamad Anwar al-SADAT]
Socialist Popular Alliance [Abu Al-Izz AL-HARIRI]
Strong Egypt Party [Abdel Moneim Aboul FOTOUH]

Political pressure groups and leaders: NA

International organization participation: ABEDA, AfDB, AFESD, AMF, AU, BSEC (observer), CAEU, CD, CICA, COMESA, D-8, EBRD, FAO, G-15, G-24, G-77, IAEA, IBRD, ICAO, ICC (national committees), ICRM, IDA, IDB,

259

IFAD, IFC, IFRCS, IHO, ILO, IMF, IMO, IMSO, Interpol, IOC, IOM, IPU, ISO, ITSO, ITU, LAS, MIGA, MINURSO, MINUSMA, MONUSCO, NAM, OAPEC, OAS (observer), OIC, OIF, OSCE (partner), PCA, UN, UNAMID, UNC-TAD, UNESCO, UNHCR, UNIDO, UNMISS, UNOCI, UNRWA, UNWTO, UPU, WCO, WFTU (NGOs), WHO, WIPO, WMO, WTO

Diplomatic representation in the US: *chief of mission:* Ambassador Yasser REDA (since 17 September 2015)
chancery: 3521 International Court NW, Washington, DC 20008
telephone: [1] (202) 895-5400
FAX: [1] (202) 244-4319
consulate(s) general: Chicago, Houston, Los Angeles, New York

Diplomatic representation from the US: *chief of mission:* Ambassador R. Stephen BEECROFT (since 18 December 2014)
embassy: 5 Tawfik Diab St., Garden City, Cairo
mailing address: Unit 64900, Box 15, APOAE 09839–4900; 5 Tawfik Diab Street, Garden City, Cairo
telephone: [20] (2) 2797-3300
FAX: [20] (2) 2797-3200

Flag description: three equal horizontal bands of red (top), white, and black; the national emblem (a gold Eagle of Saladin facing the hoist side with a shield superimposed on its chest above a scroll bearing the name of the country in Arabic) centered in the white band; the band colors derive from the Arab Liberation flag and represent oppression (black), overcome through bloody struggle (red), to be replaced by a bright future (white)
note: similar to the flag of Syria, which has two green stars in the white band, Iraq, which has an Arabic inscription centered in the white band, and Yemen, which has a plain white band

National symbol(s): golden eagle, white lotus; national colors: red, white, black

National anthem: *name:* "Bilady, Bilady, Bilady" (My Homeland, My Homeland, My Homeland)
lyrics/music: Younis-al QADI/Sayed DARWISH
note: adopted 1979; the current anthem, less militaristic than the previous one, was created after the signing of the 1979 peace treaty with Israel; Sayed DARWISH, commonly considered the father of modern Egyptian music, composed the anthem

ECONOMY

Economy—overview: Occupying the northeast corner of the African continent, Egypt is bisected by the highly fertile Nile valley, where most economic activity takes place. Egypt's economy was highly centralized during the rule of former President Gamal Abdel NASSER but opened up considerably under former Presidents Anwar EL-SADAT and Mohamed Hosni MUBARAK. Cairo from 2004 to 2008 pursued business clim ate reforms to attract foreign investment and facilitate growth. Poor living conditions and limited job opportunities for the average Egyptian contribute

to public discontent, a major factor leading to the January 2011 revolution that ousted MUBARAK. The uncertain political, security, and policy environment since 2011 caused economic growth to slow significantly, hurting tourism, manufacturing, and other sectors and pushing up unemployment. Weak growth and limited foreign exchange earnings have made public finances unsustainable, leaving authorities dependent on expensive borrowing for deficit finance and on Gulf allies to help cover the import bill. In 2015, higher levels of foreign investment contributed to a slight rebound in GDP growth after a particularly depressed post-revolution period.

GDP (purchasing power parity): $1.048 trillion (2015 est.)
$1.006 trillion (2014 est.)
$984 billion (2013 est.)
note: data are in 2015 US dollars
country comparison to the world: 24

GDP (official exchange rate): $330.8 billion (2015 est.)

GDP—real growth rate: 4.2% (2015 est.) 2.2% (2014 est.) 2.1% (2013 est.)
country comparison to the world: 58

GDP—per capita (PPP): $11,800 (2015 est.)
$11,600 (2014 est.)
$11,600 (2013 est.)
note: data are in 2015 US dollars
country comparison to the world: 127

Gross national saving: 10.9% of GDP (2015 est.)
13% of GDP (2014 est.)
12.1% of GDP (2013 est.)
country comparison to the world: 147

GDP—composition, by end use:
household consumption: 80.8%
government consumption: 11.7%
investment in fixed capital: 12.1%
investm ent in inventories: 0.5%
exports of goods and services: 14%
imports of goods and services: -19.1% (2015 est.)

GDP—composition, by sector of origin:
agriculture: 14.3%
industry: 39.6%
services: 46.1% (2015 est.)

Agriculture—products: cotton, rice, corn, wheat, beans, fruits, vegetables; cattle, water buffalo, sheep, goats

Industries: textiles, food processing, tourism, chemicals, pharmaceuticals, hydrocarbons, construction, cement, metals, light manufactures

Industrial production growth rate: 3.3% (2015 est.)
country comparison to the world: 77

Labor force: 28.87 million (2015 est.)
country comparison to the world: 23

Labor force—by occupation: *agriculture:* 29.2%
industry: 23.5%
services: 47.3% (2013 est.)

Unemployment rate: 12.8% (2015 est.)
13% (2014 est.)
country comparison to the world: 138

Population below poverty line: 25.2% (2011 est.)

Household income or consumption by percentage share: lowest 10%: 4%
highest: 10%: 26.6% (2008)

Distribution of family income—Gini index: 30.8 (2008)
32.1 (2005)
country comparison to the world: 116

Budget: *revenues:* $76.61 billion
expenditures: $111.5 billion (2015 est.)

Taxes and other revenues: 26.7% of GDP (2015 est.)
country comparison to the world: 109

Budget surplus (+) or deficit (–): -12.2% of GDP (2015 est.)
country comparison to the world: 208

Public debt: 91.7% of GDP (2015 est.)
93.7% of GDP (2014 est.)
note: data cover central government debt and includes debt instruments issued (or owned) by government entities other than the treasury; the data include treasury debt held by foreign entities; the data include debt issued by subnational entities, as well as intra-governmental debt; intra-governmental debt consists of treasury borrowings from surpluses in the social funds, such as for retirement, medical care, and unemployment; debt instruments for the social funds are sold at public auctions
country comparison to the world: 24

Fiscal year: 1 July—30 June

Inflation rate (consumer prices): 11% (2015 est.)
10.1% (2014 est.)
country comparison to the world: 213

Central bank discount rate: 9.75% (30 October 2014)
8.75% (5 December 2013)
country comparison to the world: 25

Commercial bank prime lending rate: 11.7% (31 December 2015 est.)
11.71% (31 December 2014 est.)
country comparison to the world: 70

Stock of narrow money: $66.67 billion (31 December 2015 est.)
$62.34 billion (31 December 2014 est.)
country comparison to the world: 45

Stock of broad money: $245.5 billion (31 December 2015 est.)
$224.7 billion (31 December 2014 est.)
country comparison to the world: 41

Stock of domestic credit: $271 billion (31 December 2015 est.)
$259.3 billion (31 December 2014 est.)
country comparison to the world: 37

Market value of publicly traded shares: $73.04 billion (30 November 2014 est.)
$58.01 billion (31 December 2012)
$48.68 billion (31 December 2011 est.)
country comparison to the world: 47

Current account balance: -$12.18 billion (2015 est.)
-$2.356 billion (2014 est.)
country comparison to the world: 180

Exports: $20.88 billion (2015 est.)
$26.15 billion (2014 est.)
country comparison to the world: 72

Exports—commodities: crude oil and petroleum products, fruits and vegetables, cotton, textiles, metal products, chemicals, processed food

Exports—partners: Saudi Arabia 9.1%, Italy 7.5%, Turkey 5.8%, UAE 5.1%, US 5.1%, UK 4.4%, India 4.1% (2015)

Imports: $57.91 billion (2015 est.)
$70.46 billion (2014 est.)
country comparison to the world: 46

Imports—commodities: machinery and equipment, foodstuffs, chemicals, wood products, fuels

Imports—partners: China 13%, Germany 7.7%, US 5.9%, Turkey 4.5%, Russia 4.4%, Italy 4.4%, Saudi Arabia 4.1% (2015)

Reserves of foreign exchange and gold: $17.05 billion (31 December 2015 est.) $14.45 billion (31 December 2014 est.)
country comparison to the world: 65

Debt—external: $41.32 billion (31 December 2014 est.)
$45.75 billion (31 December 2013 est.)
country comparison to the world: 67

Stock of direct foreign investment—at home: $89.65 billion (31 December 2015 est.)
$84.39 billion (31 December 2014 est.)
country comparison to the world: 48

Stock of direct foreign investment—abroad: $7.362 billion (31 December 2015 est.)
$6.839 billion (31 December 2014 est.)
country comparison to the world: 66

Exchange rates: Egyptian pounds (EGP) per US dollar—
7.72 (2015 est.)
7.08 (2014 est.)
7.08 (2013 est.)
6.06 (2012 est.)
5.9358 (2011 est.)

ENERGY

Electricity—production: 155.3 billion kWh (2012 est.)
country comparison to the world: 26

Electricity—consumption: 135.6 billion kWh (2012 est.)
country comparison to the world: 26

Electricity—exports: 1.474 billion kWh (2012 est.)
country comparison to the world: 49

Electricity—imports: 77 million kWh (2012 est.)
country comparison to the world: 97

Electricity—installed generating capacity: 27 million kW (2013 est.)
country comparison to the world: 32

Electricity—from fossil fuels: 87.7% of total installed capacity (2012 est.)
country comparison to the world: 81

Electricity—from nuclear fuels: 0% of total installed capacity (2012 est.)
country comparison to the world: 83

Electricity—from hydroelectric plants: 9.5% of total installed capacity (2012 est.)
country comparison to the world: 118

Electricity—from other renewable sources: 2.8% of total installed capacity (2012 est.)
country comparison to the world: 74

Crude oil—production: 478,400 bbl/day (2014 est.)
country comparison to the world: 29

Crude oil—exports: 189,000 bbl/day (2013 est.)
country comparison to the world: 31

Crude oil—imports: 80,000 bbl/day (2013 est.)
country comparison to the world: 49

Crude oil—proved reserves: 4.4 billion bbl (1 January 2015 est.)
country comparison to the world: 26

Refined petroleum products—production: 445,000 bbl/day (2013 est.)
country comparison to the world: 37

Refined petroleum products—consumption: 752,000 bbl/day (2013 est.)
country comparison to the world: 25

Refined petroleum products—exports: 83,000 bbl/day (2013 est.)
country comparison to the world: 49

Refined petroleum products—imports: 170,000 bbl/day (2013 est.)
country comparison to the world: 33

Natural gas—production: 57.6 billion cu m (2013 est.)
country comparison to the world: 17

Natural gas—consumption: 52.72 billion cu m (2013 est.)
country comparison to the world: 14

Natural gas—exports: 3.823 billion cu m (2013 est.)
country comparison to the world: 32

Natural gas—imports: 2.832 billion cu m (2013 est.)
country comparison to the world: 43

Natural gas—proved reserves: 2.18 trillion cu m (1 January 2014 est.)
country comparison to the world: 17

Carbon dioxide emissions from consumption of energy: 206.3 million Mt (2012 est.)
country comparison to the world: 29

COMMUNICATIONS

Telephones—fixed lines: *total subscriptions:* 6.32 million
subscriptions per 100 inhabitants: 7 (2014 est.)
country comparison to the world: 26

Telephones—mobile cellular: *total:* 95.3 million
subscriptions per 100 inhabitants: 110 (2014 est.)
country comparison to the world: 17

Telephone system: *general assessment:* underwent extensive upgrading during 1990s; principal centers at Alexandria, Cairo, Al Mansurah, Ismailia, Suez, and Tanta are connected by coaxial cable and microwave radio relay

domestic: largest fixed-line system in the region; multiple mobile-cellular networks with a near 100-percent penetration of the market
international: country code—20; landing point for Aletar, the SEA-ME-WE-3 and SEA-ME-WE-4 submarine cable networks, Link Around the Globe (FLAG) Falcon and FLAG FEA; satellite earth stations—4 (2 Intelsat—Atlantic Ocean and Indian Ocean, 1 Arabsat, and 1 Inmarsat); tropospheric scatter to Sudan; microwave radio relay to Israel; a participant in Medarabtel (2015)

Broadcast media: mix of state-run and private broadcast media; state-run TV operates 2 national and 6 regional terrestrial networks, as well as a few satellite channels; about 20 private satellite channels and a large number of Arabic satellite channels are available via subscription; state-run radio operates about 70 stations belonging to 8 networks; 2 privately owned radio stations operational (2008)
Radio broadcast stations: AM 42 (plus 15 repeaters), FM 22, shortwave 1 (2010)
Television broadcast stations: 64 (2010)

Internet country code: .eg

Internet hosts: 200,430 (2012)
country comparison to the world: 71

Internet users: *total:* 42 million
percent of population: 48.3% (2014 est.)
country comparison to the world: 15

TRANSPORTATION

Airports: 83 (2013)
country comparison to the world: 66

Airports—with paved runways: *total:* 72
over 3,047 m: 15
2,438 to 3,047 m: 36
1,524 to 2,437 m: 15
under 914 m: 6 (2013)

Airports—with unpaved runways: *total:* 11
2,438 to 3,047 m: 1
1,524 to 2,437 m: 3
914 to 1,523 m: 4
under 914 m: 3 (2013)

Heliports: 7 (2013)

Pipelines: condensate 486 km; condensate/gas 74 km; gas 7,986 km; liquid petroleum gas 957 km; oil 5,225 km; oil/gas/water 37 km; refined products 895 km; water 65 km (2013)

Railways: *total:* 5,085 km
standard gauge: 5,085 km 1.435-m gauge (62 km electrified) (2014)
country comparison to the world: 37

Roadways: *total:* 137,430 km
paved: 126,742 km (includes 838 km of expressways)
unpaved: 10,688 km (2010)
country comparison to the world: 37

Waterways: 3,500 km (includes the Nile River, Lake Nasser, Alexandria-Cairo Waterway, and numerous smaller canals in Nile Delta; the Suez Canal (193.5 km including approaches) is navigable by oceangoing vessels drawing up to 17.68 m) (2011)

country comparison to the world: 29

Merchant marine: *total:* 67

by type: bulk carrier 16, cargo 20, container 3, passenger/cargo 7, petroleum tanker 12, roll on/roll off 9

foreign-owned: 13 (Denmark 1, France 1, Greece 8, Jordan 2, Lebanon 1)

registered in other countries: 42 (Cambodia 4, Georgia 7, Honduras 2, Liberia 3, Malta 1, Marshall Islands 1, Moldova 5, Panama 11, Saint Kitts and Nevis 1, Saint Vincent and the Grenadines 2, Saudi Arabia 1, Sierra Leone 3, unknown 1) (2010)

country comparison to the world: 62

Ports and terminals: *major seaport(s):* Mediterranean Sea—Alexandria, Damietta, El Dekheila, Port Said; Gulf of Suez—Suez

oil terminal(s): Ain Sukhna terminal, Sidi Kerir terminal

container port(s) (TEUs): Alexandria (1,108,826), Port Said (East) (2,617,043), Port Said (West) (1,138,753)

LNG terminal(s) (export): Damietta, Idku (Abu Qir Bay)

MILITARY AND SECURITY

Military branches: Army, Navy, Air Force, Air Defense Forces (2015)

Military service age and obligation: 18–30 years of age for male conscript military service; service obligation—18–36 months, followed by a 9-year reserve obligation; voluntary enlistment possible from age 16 (2012)

Military expenditures: 1.76% of GDP (2014)
1.67% of GDP (2013)

1.72% of GDP (2012)
1.86% of GDP (2011)
1.72% of GDP (2010)
country comparison to the world: 53

TRANSNATIONAL ISSUES

Disputes—international: Sudan claims but Egypt de facto administers security and economic development of Halaib region north of the 22nd parallel boundary; Egypt no longer shows its administration of the Bir Tawil trapezoid in Sudan on its maps; Gazan breaches in the security wall with Egypt in January 2008 highlight difficulties in monitoring the Sinai border; Saudi Arabia claims Egyptian-adm inistered islands of Tiran and Sanafir

Refugees and internally displaced persons: *refugees (country of origin):* 70,023 (West Bank and Gaza Strip); 12,730 (Sudan); 5,149 (Iraq) (2014); 117,168 (Syria); 6,231 (Somalia) (2016)
IDPs: 78,000 (2015)
stateless persons: 22 (2015)

Trafficking in persons: *current situation:* Egypt is a source, transit, and destination country for men, wom en, and children subjected to sex trafficking and forced labor; Egyptian children, including the large population of street children are vulnerable to forced labor in domestic service, begging and agriculture or may be victims of sex trafficking or child sex tourism, which occurs in Cairo, Alexandria, and Luxor; some Egyptian wom en and girls are sold into "temporary" or "summer" marriages with Gulf men, through the complicity of their parents or marriage brokers, and are exploited for prostitution or forced labor; Egyptian men are subject to forced labor in neighboring countries,

while adults from South and Southeast Asia and East Africa—and increasingly Syrian refugees—are forced to work in domestic service, construction, cleaning, and begging in Egypt; women and girls, including migrants and refugees, from Asia, sub-Saharan Africa, and the Middle East are sex trafficked in Egypt; the Egyptian military cracked down on criminal group's smuggling, abducting, trafficking, and extorting African migrants in the Sinai Peninsula, but the practice has reemerged in along Egypt's western border with Libya

tier rating: Tier 2 Watch List—Egypt does not fully comply with the minimum standards for the elimination of trafficking; however, it is making significant efforts to do so; the government gathered data nationwide on trafficking cases to better allocated and prioritize anti-trafficking efforts, but overall it did not demonstrate increased progress; prosecutions increased in 2014, but no offenders were convicted for the second consecutive year; fewer trafficking victims were identified in 2014, which represents a significant and ongoing decrease from the previous two reporting periods; the government relied on NGOs and international organizations to identify and refer victims to protective services, and focused on EgyptiaNVictims and refused to provide some services to foreigN-Victims, at times including shelter (2015)

Illicit drugs: transit point for cannabis, heroin, and opium moving to Europe, Israel, and North Africa; transit stop for Nigerian drug couriers; concern as money laundering site due to lax enforcement of financial regulations

EL SALVADOR

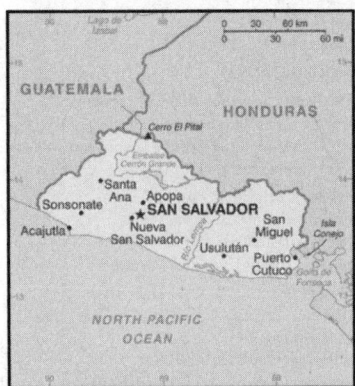

INTRODUCTION

Background: El Salvador achieved independence from Spain in 1821 and from the Central American Federation in 1839. A 12-year civil war, which cost about 75,000 lives, was brought to a close

in 1992 when the government and leftist rebels signed a treaty that provided for military and political reforms.

GEOGRAPHY

Location: Central America, bordering the North Pacific Ocean, between Guatemala and Honduras

Geographic coordinates: 1350 N, 8855 W

Map references: Central America and the Caribbean

Area: *total:* 21,041 sq km
land: 20,721 sq km
water: 320 sq km
country comparison to the world: 153

Area—comparative: about the same size as New Jersey

Land boundaries: *total:* 590 km
border countries (2): Guatemala 199 km, Honduras 391 km

Coastline: 307 km

Maritime claims: *territorial sea:* 12 nm
contiguous zone: 24 nm
exclusive economic zone: 200 nm

Climate: tropical; rainy season (May to October); dry season (November to April); tropical on coast; temperate in uplands

Terrain: mostly mountains with narrow coastal belt and central plateau

Elevation: *mean elevation:* 442 m

elevation extremes: *lowest point:* Pacific Ocean 0 m
highest point: Cerro El Pital 2,730 m

Natural resources: hydropower, geotherm al power, petroleum, arable land:

Land use: *agricultural land:* 74.7%
arable land: 33.1%;
permanent crops: 10.9%;
permanent pasture: 30.7%
forest: 13.6%
other: 11.7% (2011 est.)

Irrigated land: 452 sq km (2012)

Total renewable water resources: 25.23 cu km (2011)

Freshwater withdrawal (domestic/industrial/agricultural): *total:* 1.84 cu km/yr (22%/14%/64%)
per capita: 301.9 cu m/yr (2007)

Natural hazards: known as the Land of Volcanoes; frequent and sometimes destructive earthquakes and volcanic activity; extremely susceptible to hurricanes

volcanism: significant volcanic activity; San Salvador (elev.1,893 m), which last erupted in 1917, has the potential to cause major harm to the country's capital, which lies just below the volcano's slopes; San Miguel (elev. 2,130 m), which last erupted in 2002, is one of the most active volcanoes in the country; other historically active volcanoes include Conchaguita, Ilopango, Izalco, and Santa Ana

Environment—current issues: deforestation; soil erosion; water pollution; contamination of soils from disposal of toxic wastes

Environment—international agreements: *party to:* Biodiversity, Climate Change, Climate Change-Kyoto Protocol, Desertification, Endangered Species, Hazardous Wastes, Ozone Layer Protection, Wetlands

signed, but not ratified: Law of the Sea

Geography—note: smallest Central American country and only one without a coastline on Caribbean Sea

PEOPLE AND SOCIETY

Nationality: *noun:* Salvadoran(s)
adjective: Salvadoran

Ethnic groups: mestizo 86.3%, white 12.7%, Amerindian 0.2% (includes Lenca, Kakawira, Nahua-Pipil), black 0.1%, other 0.6% (2007 est.)

Languages: Spanish (official), Nawat (among some Amerindians)

Religions: Roman Catholic 57.1%, Protestant 21.2%, Jehovah's Witnesses 1.9%, Mormon 0.7%, other religions 2.3%, none 16.8% (2003 est.)

Demographic profile: El Salvador is the smallest and most densely populated country in Central America. It is well into its dem ographic transition, experiencing slower population growth, a decline in its num ber of youths, and the gradual aging of its population. The increased use of family planning has substantially lowered El Salvador's fertility rate, from approxim ately 6 children per wom an in the 1970s to replacem ent level today. A 2008 national fam ily planning survey showed that female sterilization rem ained the most comm on contraception method in El Salvador—its sterilization rate is among the highest in Latinamerica and the Caribbean—but that the use of injectable contraceptives is growing. Fertility differences between rich and poor and urban and rural wom en are narrowing. Salvadorans fled during the 1979 to 1992 civil war mainly to the United States but also to Canada and to neighboring Mexico, Guatemala, Honduras, Nicaragua, and Costa Rica. Emigration to the United States increased again in the 1990s and 2000s as a result of deteriorating economic conditions, natural disasters (Hurricane Mitch in 1998 and earthquakes in 2001), and family reunification. At least 20% of El Salvador's population lives abroad. The remittances they send home account for close to 20% of GDP, are the second largest source of external income after exports, and have helped reduce poverty.

Population: 6,141,350 (July 2015 est.)
country comparison to the world: 110

Age structure: *0–14 years:* 27.31% (male 860,122/female 816,855)
15–24 years: 20.71% (male 638,989/female 632,741)
25–54 years: 38.1% (male 1,077,378/female 1,262,585)
55–64 years: 6.8% (male 186,570/female 230,839)
65 years and over: 7.09% (male 192,713/female 242,558) (2015 est.)

Dependency ratios: *total dependency ratio:* 54.3%
youth dependency ratio: 41.7%
elderly dependency ratio: 12.6%
potential support ratio: 7.9% (2015 est.)

Median age: *total:* 26.1 years
male: 24.6 years
female: 27.6 years (2015 est.)
country comparison to the world: 146

Population growth rate: 0.25% (2015 est.)
country comparison to the world: 178

Birth rate: 16.46 births/1,000 population (2015 est.)
country comparison to the world: 115

Death rate: 5.69 deaths/1,000 population (2015 est.)
country comparison to the world: 172

Net migration rate: -8.28 migrant(s)/1,000 population (2015 est.)
country comparison to the world: 209

Urbanization: *urban population:* 66.7% of total population (2015)
rate of urbanization: 1.4% annual rate of change (2010–15 est.)

Major urban areas—population: SAN SALVADOR (capital) 1.098 million (2015)

Sex ratio: *at birth:* 1.05 male(s)/female
0–14 years: 1.05 male(s)/female
15–24 years: 1.01 male(s)/female
25–54 years: 0.85 male(s)/female
55–64 years: 0.81 male(s)/female
65 years and over: 0.8 male(s)/female
total population: 0.93 male(s)/female (2015 est.)

Mother's mean age at first birth: 20.8
note: median age at first birth among women 25–29 (2008 est.)

Maternal mortality rate: 54 deaths/100,000 live births (2015 est.)
country comparison to the world: 81

Infant mortality rate: *total:* 17.86 deaths/1,000 live births
male: 19.94 deaths/1,000 live births
female: 15.68 deaths/1,000 live births (2015 est.)
country comparison to the world: 98

Life expectan cyatbirth: *total population:* 74.42 years
male: 71.14 years
female: 77.86 years (2015 est.)
country comparison to the world: 119

Total fertility rate: 1.91 children born/woman (2015 est.)
country comparison to the world: 138

Contraceptive prevalence rate: 72.3%
note: percent of women aged 15–44 (2008)

Health *expenditures:* 6.9% of GDP (2013)

country comparison to the world: 91

Physicians density: 1.6 physicians/1,000 population (2008)

Hospital bed density: 1.1 beds/1,000 population (2012)

Drinking water source:
improved:
urban: 97.5% of population
rural: 86.5% of population
total: 93.8% of population
unimproved:
urban: 2.5% of population
rural: 13.5% of population
total: 6.2% of population (2015 est.)

Sanitation facility access:
improved:
urban: 82.4% of population rural: 60% of population *total:* 75% of population
unimproved:
urban: 17.6% of population rural: 40% of population *total:* 25% of population (2015 est.)

HIV/AIDS—adult prevalence rate: 0.53% (2014 est.)
country comparison to the world: 65

HIV/AIDS—people living with HIV/AIDS: 20,900 (2014 est.)
country comparison to the world: 76

HIV/AIDS—deaths: 400 (2014 est.)
country comparison to the world: 94

Major infectious diseases: *degree of risk:* high
food or waterborne diseases: bacterial and protozoal diarrhea
vectorborne diseases: dengue fever (2013)

Obesity—adult prevalence rate: 20.1% (2014)
country comparison to the world: 51

Children under the age of 5 years underweight: 5% (2014)
country comparison to the world: 78

Education *expenditures:* 3.4% of GDP (2011)
country comparison to the world: 129

Literacy: *definition:* age 15 and over can read and write
total population: 88%
male: 90.4%
female: 86% (2015 est.)

School life expectancy (primary to tertiary education): *total:* 13 years
male: 13 years
female: 13 years (2014)

Child labor—children ages 5–14: *total number:* 179,303
percentage: 4%
note: data represent children ages 5–17 (2007 est.)

Unemployment, youth ages 15–24: *total:* 12.4%
male: 11.8%
female: 13.6% (2013 est.)
country comparison to the world: 89

GOVERNMENT

Country name: *conventional long form:* Republic of El Salvador
conventional short form: El Salvador
local long form: Republica de El Salvador
local short form: El Salvador
etymology: name is an abbreviation of the original Spanish conquistador designation for the area

"Provincia de Nuestro Senor Jesus Cristo, el Salvador del Mundo" (Province of Our Lord Jesus Christ, the Saviour of the World), which became simply "El Salvador" (The Savior)

Government type: presidential republic

Capital: *name:* San Salvador

Geographic coordinates: 1342 N, 8912 W

time difference: UTC-6 (1 hour behind Washington, DC, during Standard Time)

Administrative divisions: 14 departments (departamentos, singular—departamento); Ahuachapan, Cabanas, Chalatenango, Cuscatlan, La Libertad, La Paz, La Union, Morazan, San Miguel, San Salvador, San Vicente, Santa Ana, Sonsonate, Usulutan

Independence: 15 September 1821 (from Spain)

National holiday: Independence Day, 15 September (1821)

Constitution: many previous; latest drafted 16 December 1983, enacted 23 December 1983; amended many times, last in 2014 (2016)

Legal system: civil law system with minor common law influence; judicial review of legislative acts in the Supreme Court

International law organization participation: has not submitted an ICJ jurisdiction declaration; non-party state to the ICCt

Citizenship: *citizenship by birth:* yes

citizenship by descent: yes

dual citizenship recognized: yes

residency requirement for naturalization: 5 years

Suffrage: 18 years of age; universal

Executive branch: *chief of state:* President Salvador SANCHEZ CEREN (since 1 June 2014); Vice President Salvador Oscar ORTIZ (since 1 June 2014); note—the president is both chief of state and head of government

head of government: President Salvador SANCHEZ CEREN (since 1 June 2014); Vice President Salvador Oscar ORTIZ (since 1 June 2014)

cabinet: Council of Ministers selected by the president

elections/appointments: president and vice president directly elected on the same ballot by absolute majority popular vote in 2 rounds if needed for a single 5-year term; election last held on 2 February 2014, with a runoff on 9 March 2014 (next to be held in February 2019)

election results: Salvador SANCHEZ CEREN elected president; percent of vote: first-round results -Salvador SANCHEZ CEREN (FMLN) 48.9%, Norman QUIJANO (ARENA) 39%, Antonio SACA (CN) 11.4%, other 0.7%; second-round results—Salvador SANCHEZ CEREN 50.1%, Norman QUIJANO 49.9%

Legislative branch: *description:* unicameral Legislative Assembly or Asamblea Legislativa (84 seats; members directly elected in multi-seat constituencies and a single nationwide constituency by proportional representation vote to serve 3-year terms)

elections: last held on 1 March 2015 (next to be held in March 2018)

election results: percent of vote by party—NA; seats by party—ARENA 35, FMLN 31, GANA 11, PCN 6, PDC 1

Judicial branch: *highest court(s):* Supreme Court or Corte Suprema de Justicia (CSJ) (consists of 15 judges assigned to constitutional, civil, penal, and administrative conflict divisions)

judge selection and term of office: judges elected by the Legislative Assembly on the recommendation of the National Council of the Judicature, an independent body elected by the Legislative Assembly; judges elected for a 9-year term, with renewal of one-third of judges every 3 years; consecutive re-election is allowed

subordinate court(s): Appellate Courts; Courts of First Instance; Courts of Peace

Political parties and leaders: Christian Democratic Party or PDC [Rodolfo Antonio PARKER Soto]

Democratic Change (Cambio Democratico) or CD [Douglas AVILES] (formerly United Democratic Center or CDU)

Farabundo Marti National Liberation Front or FMLN [Medardo GONZALEZ]

Great Alliance for National Unity or GANA [Jose Andres ROVIRA Caneles]

National Conciliation Party or PCN [Manuel RODRIGUEZ]

Nationalist Republican Alliance or ARENA [Jorge VELADO]

Political pressure groups and leaders: *labor organizations:* Electrical Industry Union of El Salvador or SI ES Federation of the Construction Industry, Similar Transport and other activities, or FESINCONTRANS National Confederation of Salvadoran Workers or CNTS National Trade Union Federation of Salvadoran Workers or FENASTRAS National Union of Salvadoran Workers or UNTS Port Industry Union of El Salvador or SIPES Salvadoran Workers Central or CTS Union of Judiciary Workers or SITTOJ Union of Workers of the Ministry of Treasury or SITRAMI Workers Union of Electrical Corporation or STCEL

business organizations: American Chamber of Commerce in El Salvador National Association of Private Enterprise or AN EP Salvadoran Chamber of Commerce Salvadoran Chamber of the Construction Industry or CASALCO Salvadoran Industrial Association or ASI

International organization participation: BCIE, CACM, CD, CELAC, FAO, G-11, G-77, IADB, IAEA, IBRD, ICAO, ICC (national committees), ICRM, IDA, IFAD, IFC, IFRCS, ILO, IMF, IMO, Interpol, IOC, IOM, IPU, ISO (correspondent), ITSO, ITU, ITUC (NGOs), LAES, LAIA (observer), MIGA, MINURSO, MINUSTAH, NAM (observer), OAS, OPANAL, OPCW, Pacific Alliance (observer), PCA, Petrocaribe, SICA, UN, UNCTAD, UNESCO, UNIDO, UNIFIL, Union Latina, UNISFA, UNMISS, UNOCI, UNWTO, UPU, WCO, WFTU (NGOs), WHO, WIPO, WMO, WTO

Diplomatic representation in the US: *chief of mission:* Ambassador Francisco Roberto ALTSCHUL Fuentes (since 18 September 2014)

chancery: 140016th Street NW, Suite 100, Washington, DC 20036

telephone: [1] (202) 595-7517

FAX: [1] (202) 232-1928

consulate(s) general: Atlanta, Boston, Brentwood (NY), Chicago, Coral Gables (FL), Dallas, Houston, Las Vegas (NV), Los Angeles, McAllen (TX), New York, Nogales (AZ), San Francisco, Seattle, Tucson (AZ), Washington, DC, Woodbridge (VA), Woodstock (GA)

consulate(s): Elizabeth (NJ), Newark (NJ)

Diplomatic representation from the US: *chief of mission:* Ambassador Jean MAN ES (since January 2016)

embassy: Final Boulevard Santa Elena Sur, Antiguo Cuscatlan, La Libertad, San Salvador

mailing address: Unit 3450, APO AA 34023; 3450 San Salvador Place, Washington, DC 20521–3450

telephone: [503] 2501–2999

FAX: [503] 2501–2150

Flag description: three equal horizontal bands of blue (top), white, and blue with the national coat of arms centered in the white band; the coat of arms features a round emblem encircled by the words REPUBLICA DE EN LA AMERICA CENTRAL; the banner is based on the former blue-white-blue flag of the Federal Republic of Central America; the blue bands symbolize the Pacific Ocean and the Caribbean Sea, while the white band represents the land between the two bodies of water, as well as peace and prosperity

note: similar to the flag of Nicaragua, which has a different coat of arms centered in the white band—it features a triangle encircled by the words REPUBLICA DENICARAGUA on top and AMERICA CENTRAL on the bottom; also similar to the flag of Honduras, which has five blue stars arranged in an X pattern centered in the white band

National symbol(s): turquoise-browed motmot (bird); national colors: blue, white

National anthem: *name:* "Himno Nacional de El Salvador" (National Anthem of El Salvador)

lyrics/music: Juan Jose CANAS/Juan ABERLE

note: officially adopted 1953, in use since 1879; at 4: 20 minutes the anthem of El Salvador is one of the world's longest

ECONOMY

Economy—overvie: The smallest country in Central America geographically, El Salvador has the fourth largest economy in the region. With the global recession, real GDP contracted in 2009 and economic growth has since remained low, averaging less than 2% from 2010 to 2014, but recovered somewhat in 2015. Remittances accounted for 17% of GDP in 2014 and were received by about a third of all households. In 2006, El Salvador was the first country to ratify the Dominican Republic-Central American Free Trade Agreement, which has bolstered the export of processed foods, sugar, and ethanol, and supported investment in the apparel sector amid increased Asian competition. In September 2015, El Salvador kicked off a five-year $277 million second compact with the Millennium Challenge Corporation—a US Government agency aimed at stimulating economic growth and reducing poverty—to improve El Salvador's competitiveness and productivity in international markets. . The Salvadoran Government maintained fiscal discipline during post-war reconstruction and rebuilding following earthquakes in 2001 and hurricanes in 1998 and 2005, but El Salvador's public debt, estimated at 65% of GDP in 2015, has been growing over the last several years. Total external debt was nearly 60% of GDP in 2015.

GDP (purchasing power parity): $52.95 billion (2015 est.)
$51.71 billion (2014 est.)
$50.72 billion (2013 est.)
note: data are in 2015 US dollars
country comparison to the world: 109
GDP (official exchange rate): $25.77 billion (2015 est.)
GDP—real growth rate: 2.4% (2015 est.) 2% (2014 est.) 1.8% (2013 est.)
country comparison to the world: 126
GDP—per capita (PPP): $8,300 (2015 est.)
$8,100 (2014 est.)
$8,000 (2013 est.)
note: data are in 2015 US dollars
country comparison to the world: 146
Gross national saving: 10.6% of GDP (2015 est.)
8.8% of GDP (2014 est.)
8.5% of GDP (2013 est.)
country comparison to the world: 149
GDP—composition, by end use: *household consumption:* 92.3%
government consumption: 11.9%
investment in fixed capital: 12.6%
investment in inventories: 0.1%
exports of goods and services: 27%
imports of goods and services: -43.9% (2015 est.)
GDP—composition, by sector of origin: *agriculture:* 10.7%
industry: 25.5%
services: 63.8% (2015 est.)
Agriculture—products: coffee, sugar, corn, rice, beans, oilseed, cotton, sorghum; beef, dairy products
Industries: food processing, beverages, petroleum, chemicals, fertilizer, textiles, furniture, light metals
Industrial production growth rate: 2.2% (2015 est.)
country comparison to the world: 110
Labor force: 2.774 million (2015 est.)
country comparison to the world: 108
Labor force—by occupation: *agriculture:* 21%
industry: 20%
services: 58% (2011 est.)
Unemployment rate: 6.1% (2015 est.)
6.2% (2014 est.)
note: data are official rates; but underemployment is high
country comparison to the world: 67
Population below poverty line: 36.5% (2010 est.)
Household income or consumption by percentage share: *lowest:* 10%: 1%
highest: 10%: 37% (2009 est.)
Distribution of family income—Gini index:

46.9 (2007)
52.5 (2001)
country comparison to the world: 30
Budget: *revenues:* $5.133 billion
expenditures: $5.938 billion (2015 est.)
Taxes and other revenues: 20% of GDP (2015 est.)
country comparison to the world: 157
Budget surplus (+) or deficit (–): -3.1% of GDP (2015 est.)
country comparison to the world: 117
Public debt: 64.9% of GDP (2015 est.)
62.4% of GDP (2014 est.)
note: El Salvador's total public debt includes nonfinancial public sector debt, financial public sector debt, and central bank debt
country comparison to the world: 54
Fiscal year: calendar year
Inflation rate (consumer prices): -0.7% (2015 est.)
1.1% (2014 est.)
country comparison to the world: 20
Commercial bank prime lending rate: 6.1% (31 December 2015 est.)
5.99% (31 December 2014 est.)
country comparison to the world: 127
Stock of narrow money: $3.017 billion (31 December 2015 est.)
$2.92 billion (31 December 2014 est.)
country comparison to the world: 116
Stock of broad money: $11.45 billion (31 December 2014 est.)
$10.87 billion (31 December 2013 est.)
country comparison to the world: 105
Stock of domestic credit: $13.22 billion (31 December 2015 est.)
$12.26 billion (31 December 2014 est.)
country comparison to the world: 94
Market value of publicly traded shares: $10.74 billion (31 December 2012 est.)
$5.474 billion (31 December 2011)
$4.227 billion (31 December 2010 est.)
country comparison to the world: 73
Current account balance: -$826 million (2015 est.)
-$1.194 billion (2014 est.)
country comparison to the world: 115
Exports: $4.489 billion (2015 est.)
$4.256 billion (2014 est.)
country comparison to the world: 112
Exports—commodities: offshore assembly exports, coffee, sugar, textiles and apparel, gold, ethanol, chemicals, electricity, iron and steel manufactures
Exports—partners: US 47.1%, Honduras 13.9%, Guatemala 13.6%, Nicaragua 6.6%, Costa Rica 4.5% (2015)
Imports: $9.213 billion (2015 est.)
$9.463 billion (2014 est.)
country comparison to the world: 102
Imports—commodities: raw materials, consumer goods, capital goods, fuels, foodstuffs, petroleum, electricity
Imports—partners: US 39.4%, Guatemala 9.6%, China 8.1%, Mexico 7.4%, Honduras 5.7% (2015)
Reserves of foreign exchange and gold: $2.66 billion (31 December 2015 est.)
$2.693 billion (31 December 2014 est.)
country comparison to the world: 110

Debt—external: $15.14 billion (31 December 2014 est.)
$14.05 billion (31 December 2013 est.)
country comparison to the world: 97
Stock of direct foreign investment—at home: $9.708 billion (31 December 2015 est.)
$9.358 billion (31 December 2014 est.)
country comparison to the world: 92
Stock of direct foreign investment—abroad: $727.3 million (31 December 2015 est.)
$857.3 million (31 December 2014 est.)
country comparison to the world: 85
Exchange rates: *note:* the US dollar is used as a medium of exchange and circulates freely in the economy

ENERGY

Electricity—production: 6.18 billion kWh (2012 est.)
country comparison to the world: 113
Electricity—consumption: 5.665 billion kWh (2012 est.)
country comparison to the world: 111
Electricity—exports: 78 million kWh (2012 est.)
country comparison to the world: 81
Electricity—imports: 163 million kWh (2012 est.)
country comparison to the world: 89
Electricity—installed generating capacity: 1.507 million kW (2012 est.)
country comparison to the world: 119
Electricity—from fossil fuels: 53.1% of total installed capacity (2012 est.)
country comparison to the world: 145
Electricity—from nuclear fuels: 0% of total installed capacity (2012 est.)
country comparison to the world: 88
Electricity—from hydroelectric plants: 31.3% of total installed capacity (2012 est.)
country comparison to the world: 73
Electricity—from other renewable sources: 15.5% of total installed capacity (2012 est.)
country comparison to the world: 19
Crude oil—production: 0 bbl/day (2014 est.)
country comparison to the world: 131
Crude oil—exports: 0 bbl/day (2012 est.)
country comparison to the world: 120
Crude oil—imports: 9,940 bbl/day (2012 est.)
country comparison to the world: 75
Crude oil—proved reserves: 0 bbl (1 January 2015 est.)
country comparison to the world: 130
Refined petroleum products—production: 11,600 bbl/day (2012 est.)
country comparison to the world: 101
Refined petroleum products—consumption: 45,000 bbl/day (2013 est.)
country comparison to the world: 103
Refined petroleum products—exports: 2,939 bbl/day (2012 est.)
country comparison to the world: 100
Refined petroleum products—imports: 36,510 bbl/day (2012 est.)
country comparison to the world: 90
Natural gas—production: 0 cu m (2013 est.)
country comparison to the world: 183
Natural gas—consumption: 0 cu m (2013 est.)

country comparison to the world: 140
Natural gas—exports: 0 cu m (2013 est.)
country comparison to the world: 95
Natural gas—imports: 0 cu m (2013 est.)
country comparison to the world: 193
Natural gas—proved reserves: 0 cu m (1 January 2014 est.)
country comparison to the world: 135
Carbon dioxide emissions from consumption of energy:
6.375 million Mt (2012 est.)
country comparison to the world: 119

COMMUNICATIONS

Telephones—fixed lines: *total subscriptions:* 950,000
subscriptions per 100 inhabitants: 15 (2014 est.)
country comparison to the world: 79
Telephones—mobile cellular: *total:* 9.2 million
subscriptions per 100 inhabitants: 150 (2014 est.)
country comparison to the world: 90
Telephone system: *general assessment:* multiple mobile-cellular providers are expanding services rapidly and in 2011 teledensity exceeded 135 per 100 persons; growth in fixed-line services has slowed in the face of mobile-cellular competition
domestic: nationwide microwave radio relay system
international: country code—503; satellite earth station—1 Intelsat (Atlantic Ocean); connected to Central American Microwave System (2011)
Broadcast media: multiple privately owned national terrestrial TV networks, supplemented by cable TV networks that carry international channels; hundreds of commercial radio broadcast stations and 1 government-owned radio broadcast station (2007)
Radio broadcast stations: AM 52, FM 144, shortwave 0 (2005)
Television broadcast stations: 5 (1997)
Internet country code: .sv
Internet hosts: 24,070 (2012)
country comparison to the world: 113
Internet users: *total:* 1.7 million
percent of population: 27.3% (2014 est.)
country comparison to the world: 102

TRANSPORTATION

Airports: 68 (2013)
country comparison to the world: 74
Airports—with paved runways: *total:* 5
over 3,047 m: 1
1,524 to 2,437 m: 1
914 to 1,523 m: 2
under 914 m: 1 (2013)
Airports—with unpaved runways: *total:* 63
1,524 to 2,437 m: 1
914 to 1,523 m: 11
under 914 m: 51 (2013)
Heliports: 2 (2013)
Railways: *total:* 12.5 km
narrow gauge: 12.5 km 0.914-m gauge (2014)
country comparison to the world: 135
Roadways: *total:* 6,918 km
paved: 3,247 km (in cludes 341 km of expressways)
unpaved: 3,671 km (2010)
country comparison to the world: 148
Waterways: (Rio Lempa is partially navigable by small craft) (2011)
Ports and terminals: *major seaport(s):* Puerto Cutuco
oil terminal(s): Acajutla offshore terminal

MILITARY AND SECURITY

Military branches: Salvadoran Armed Forces (Fuerza Armada de El Salvador, FAES): Salvadoran Army (Ejercito de El Salvador, ES), Salvadoran Navy (Fuerza Naval de El Slavador, FNES), Salvadoran Air Force (Fuerza Aerea Salvadorena, FAS) (2013)
Military service age and obligation: 18 years of age for selective compulsory military service; 16–22 years of age for voluntary male or female service; service obligation is 12 months, with 11 months for officers and NCOs (2012)
Military *expenditures:* 0.99% of GDP (2012)
1.11% of GDP (2011)
0.99% of GDP (2010)
country comparison to the world: 101

TRANSNATIONAL ISSUES

Disputes—*international:* International Court of Justice (ICJ) ruled on the delimitation of "bolsones" (disputed areas) along the El Salvador-Honduras boundary, in 1992, with final agreement by the parties in 2006 after an Organization of American States survey and a further ICJ ruling in 2003; the 1992 ICJ ruling advised a tripartite resolution to a maritime boundary in the Gulf of Fonseca advocating Honduran access to the Pacific; El Salvador continues to claim tiny Conejo Island, not identified in the ICJ decision, off Honduras in the Gulf of Fonseca
Refugees and internally displaced persons: *IDPs:* 289,000 (2015)
Illicit drugs: transshipment point for cocaine; small amounts of marijuana produced for local consumption; significant use of cocaine

EQUATORIAL GUINEA

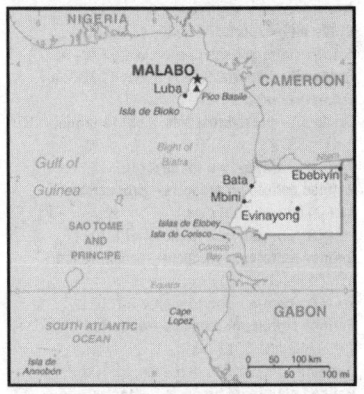

INTRODUCTION

Background: Equatorial Guinea gained independence in 1968 after 190 years of Spanish rule; it is one of the smallest countries in Africa consisting of a mainland territory and five inhabited islands. The capital of Malabo is located on the island of Bioko, approximately 25 km from the Cameroonian coastline in the Gulf of Guinea. Between 1968 and 1979, autocratic President Francisco MACIAS NGUEMA virtually destroyed all of the country's political, economic, and social institutions before being deposed by his nephew Teodoro OBIANG NGUEMA MBASOGO in a coup. President OBIANG has ruled since October 1979 and was reelected in 2016. Although nominally a constitutional democracy since 1991, presidential and legislative elections since 1996 have generally been labeled as flawed. The president exerts almost total control over the political system and has placed legal and bureaucratic barriers that prevent political opposition. Equatorial Guinea has experienced rapid economic growth due to the discovery of large offshore oil reserves, and in the last decade has become Sub-Saharan Africa's third largest oil exporter. Despite the country's economic windfall from oil production, resulting in a massive increase in government revenue in recent years, the drop in global oil prices has placed significant strain on the state budget. Equatorial Guinea continues to seek to diversify its economy and to increase foreign investment despite limited improvements in the population's living standards. Equatorial Guinea is the host of major regional and international conferences and continues to seek a greater role in regional affairs.

GEOGRAPHY

Location: Central Africa, bordering the Bight of Biafra, between Cameroon and Gabon
Geographic coordinates: 200 N, 1000 E
Map references: Africa
Area: *total:* 28,051 sq km
land: 28,051 sq km
water: 0 sq km
country comparison to the world: 146

Area—comparative: slightly smaller than Maryland

Land boundaries: *total:* 528 km

border countries (2): Cameroon 183 km, Gabon 345 km

Coastline: 296 km

Maritime claims: *territorial sea:* 12 nm

exclusive economic zone: 200 nm

Climate: tropical; always hot, humid

Terrain: coastal plains rise to interior hills; islands are volcanic

Elevation: *mean elevation:* 577 m

elevation extremes: *lowest point:* Atlantic Ocean 0 m

highest point: Pico Basile 3,008 m

Natural resources: petroleum, natural gas, timber, gold, bauxite, diam onds, tantalum, sand and gravel, clay

Land use: *agricultural land:* 10.1%

arable land: 4.3%;

permanent crops: 2.1%;

permanent pasture: 3.7%

forest: 57.5%

other: 32.4% (2011 est.)

Irrigated land: NA

Total renewable water resources: 26 cu km (2011)

Freshwater withdrawal (domestic/industrial/agricultural): *total:* 0.02 cu km/yr (80%/15%/5%)

per capita: 31.41 cu m/yr (2005)

Natural hazards: violent windstorms; flash floods

volcanism: Santa Isabel (elev. 3,007 m), which last erupted in 1923, is the country's only historically active volcano; Santa Isabel, along with two dormant volcanoes, form Bioko Island in the Gulf of Guinea

Environment—current issues: tap water is non-potable; deforestation

Environment—international agreements: *party to:* Biodiversity, Climate Change, Climate Change-Kyoto Protocol, Desertification, Endangered Species, Hazardous Wastes, Law of the Sea, Marine Dumping, Ozone Layer Protection, Ship Pollution, Wetlands

signed, but not ratified: none of the selected agreements

Geography—note: insular and continental regions widely separated

PEOPLE AND SOCIETY

Nationality: *noun:* Equatorial Guinean(s) or Equatoguinean(s)

adjective: Equatorial Guinean or Equatoguinean

Ethnic groups: Fang 85.7%, Bubi 6.5%, Mdowe 3.6%, Annobon 1.6%, Bujeba 1.1%, other 1.4% (1994 census)

Languages: Spanish (official) 67.6%, other (includes French (official), Fang, Bubi) 32.4% (1994 census)

Religions: nominally Christian and predominantly Roman Catholic, pagan practices

Population: 740,743 (July 2015 est.)

country comparison to the world: 166

Age structure: *0–14 years:* 40.47% (male 152,305/female 147,454)

15–24 years: 19.55% (male 73,728/female 71,086)

25–54 years: 31.74% (male 116,937/female 118,148)

55–64 years: 4.24% (male 13,519/female 17,884)

65 years and over: 4.01% (male 12,462/female 17,220) (2015 est.)

Dependency ratios: *total dependency ratio:* 72.9%

youth dependency ratio: 67.9%

elderly dependency ratio: 5%

poten tial support ratio: 20% (2015 est.)

Median age: *total:* 19.5 years

male: 19 years

female: 20 years (2015 est.)

country comparison to the world: 194

Population growth rate: 2.51% (2015 est.)

country comparison to the world: 23

Birth rate: 33.31 births/1,000 population (2015 est.)

country comparison to the world: 32

Death rate: 8.19 deaths/1,000 population (2015 est.)

country comparison to the world: 89

Net migration rate: 0 migrant(s)/1,000 population (2015 est.)

country comparison to the world: 99

Urbanization: *urban population:* 39.9% of total population (2015)

rate of urbanization: 3.12% annual rate of change (2010–15 est.)

Major urban areas—population: MALABO (capital) 145,000 (2014)

Sex ratio: *at birth:* 1.03 male(s)/female

0–14 years: 1.03 male(s)/female

15–24 years: 1.04 male(s)/female

25–54 years: 0.99 male(s)/female

55–64 years: 0.76 male(s)/female

65 years and over: 0.72 male(s)/female

total population: 0.99 male(s)/female (2015 est.)

Maternal mortality rate: 342 deaths/100,000 live births (2015 est.)

country comparison to the world: 47

Infant mortality rate: *total:* 69.17 deaths/1,000 live births

male: 70.21 deaths/1,000 live births

female: 68.09 deaths/1,000 live births (2015 est.)

country comparison to the world: 14

Life expectancy at birth: *total population:* 63.85 years

male: 62.76 years

female: 64.97 years (2015 est.)

country comparison to the world: 183

Total fertility rate: 4.57 children born/woman (2015 est.)

country comparison to the world: 24

Contraceptive prevalence rate: 12.6% (2011)

Health *expenditures:* 3.5% of GDP (2013)

country comparison to the world: 149

Hospital bed density: 2.1 beds/1,000 population (2010)

Drinking water source: improved:

urban: 72.5% of population

rural: 31.5% of population

total: 47.9% of population

unimproved:

urban: 27.5% of population

rural: 68.5% of population

total: 52.1% of population (2015 est.)

Sanitation facility access: improved:

urban: 79.9% of population

rural: 71% of population

total: 74.5% of population

unimproved:

urban: 20.1% of population

rural: 29% of population

total: 25.5% of population (2015 est.)

HIV/AIDS—adult prevalence rate: 6.16% (2014 est.)

country comparison to the world: 11

HIV/AIDS—people living with HIV/AIDS: 31,600 (2014 est.)

country comparison to the world: 70

HIV/AIDS—deaths: 800 (2014 est.)

country comparison to the world: 71

Major infectious diseases: *degree of risk:* very high

food or waterborne diseases: bacterial and protozoal diarrhea, hepatitis A, and typhoid fever

vectorborne disease: malaria and dengue fever

animal contact disease: rabies (2013)

Obesity—adult prevalence rate: 16.2% (2014)

country comparison to the world: 129

Children under the age of 5 years underweight: 5.6% (2010)

country comparison to the world: 87

Literacy: *definition:* age 15 and over can read and write

total population: 95.3%

male: 97.4%

female: 93% (2015 est.)

GOVERNMENT

Country name: *conventional long form:* Republic of Equatorial Guinea

conventional short form: Equatorial Guinea

local long form: Republica de Guinea Ecuatorial/ Republique de Guinee Equatoriale

local short form: Guinea Ecuatorial/Guinee Equatoriale

former: Spanish Guinea

etymology: the country is named for the Guinea region of West Africa th at lies along the Gulf of Guinea and stretches north to the Sahel; the "equatorial" refers to the fact that the country lies just north of the Equator

Government type: presidential republic

Capital: *name:* Malabo

Geographic coordinates: 3 45 N, 8 47 E

time difference: UTC + 1 (6 hours ahead of Washington, DC, during Standard Time)

Administrative divisions: 7 provinces (provincias, singular—provincia); Annobon, Bioko Norte, Bioko Sur, Centro Sur, Kie-Ntem, Litoral, Wele-Nzas

Independence: 12 October 1968 (from Spain)

National holiday: Independence Day, 12 October (1968)

Constitution: approved by referendum 17 November 1991; amended several times, last in 2012 (2016)

Legal system: mixed system of civil and customary law

International law organization participation: has not submitted an ICJ jurisdiction declaration; non-party state to the ICCt

Citizenship: *citizenship by birth:* no
citizenship by descent only: at least one parent must be a citizen of Equatorial Guinea
dual citizenship recognized: no
residency requirement for naturalization: 10 years

Suffrage: 18 years of age; universal

Executive branch: *chief of state:* President Brig. Gen. (Ret.) Teodoro Obiang NGUEMA MGAS-OGO (since 3 August 1979 when he seized power in a military coup)

head of government: Prime Minister Vicente EHATE TOMI (since 22 May 2012); First Deputy Prime Minister Clemente ENGONG NGUEMA ONGUENE; Second Deputy Prime Minister Francisco Pascual OBAMA ASUE; Third Deputy Prime Minister Alfonso NSUE MOKUY

cabinet: Council of Ministers appointed by the president

elections/appointments: president directly elected by simple majority popular vote for a 7-year term (eligible for a second term); election last held on 14 April 2016 (next to be held in 2023); prime minister and deputy prime ministers appointed by the president

election results: Teodoro Obiang NGUEMA MBASOGO reelected president; percent of vote—Teodoro Obiang NGUEMA MBASOGO (PDGE) 93.7%

Legislative branch: *description:* bicameral National Assembly or Asemblea Nacional, formerly the unicameral Parliament, consists of the Senate or Senado (70 seats; 55 members directly elected by simple majority vote and 15 appointed by the president) and the House of People's Representatives or Camara de Representantes del Pueblo (100 seats; members directly elected in multi-seat constituencies by proportional representation vote to serve 5-year terms);

note—the constitutional referendum of 2011 established the Senate and was implemented at the time of the May 2013 elections

elections: last held on 26 May 2013 (next to be held in 2018)

election results: Senate—percent of vote by party—NA; seats by party—PDGE 54, CPDS 1; Chamber of Deputies—percent of vote by party—NA; seats by party—PDGE 99, CPDS 1

Judicial branch: *highest court(s):* Supreme Court of Justice (consists of the chief justice—who is also chief of state -and 9 judges); Constitutional Court (consists of the court president and 4 members)

judge selection and term of office: Supreme Court judges appointed by the president for 5-year terms; Constitutional Court members appointed by the president, 2 of which are nominated by the Chamber of Deputies

subordinate court(s): Court of Guarantees; military courts; Courts of Appeal; first instance tribunals; district and county tribunals

Political parties and leaders: Convergence Party for Social Democracy or CPDS [Andres ESONOONDO]

Democratic Party for Equatorial Guinea or PDGE [Jeronimo OSA OSA ECORO] (ruling party)
Electoral Coalition or EC
Popular Action of Equatorial Guinea or APGE [Carmelo MBA BACALE]
Popular Union or UP [Daniel MARTINEZ AYECABA]
not officially registered parties: Democratic Republican Force or FDR [Guillermo NGUEMA ELA] Independent Candidacy or CI [Gabriel NSE OBIANG OBONO]
Party for Progress of Equatorial Guinea or PPGE [Severo MOTO]
Union for the Center Right or UDC [Avelino MOCACHE MEAENGA]

note: in November 2014, the government hosted a National Dialogue process to engage with the political opposition; the opposition participated with limited attendance and engagement; on March 18,2015, the CPDS, FDR, and UP formed a coalition called the Front of Democratic Opposition or FOD

Political pressure groups and leaders: ASODE-GUE (Madrid-based pressure group for democratic reform)
Coalicion CEIBA (group formed by diverse, exiled political parties)
C.O.R.E.D. (originally led by Raimundo Ela Nsang; based in Paris)
EG Justice (US-based anti-corruption group)

International organization participation: ACP, AfDB, AU, BDEAC, CEMAC, CPLP (associate), FAO, FZ, G-77, IBRD, ICAO, ICRM, IDA, IFAD, IFC, IFRCS, ILO, IMF, IMO, Interpol, IOC, IPU, ITSO, ITU, MIGA, NAM, OAS (observer), OIF, OPCW, UN, UNCTAD, UNESCO, UNIDO, UNWTO, UPU, WHO, WIPO, WTO (observer)

Diplomatic representation in the US: *chief of mission:* Ambassador Miguel Ntutumu EVUNA ANDEME (since 23 February 2015)
chancery: 202016th Street NW, Washington, DC 20009
telephone: [1] (202) 518-5700
FAX: [1] (202) 518-5252
consul general(s): Houston

Diplomatic representation from the US: *chief of mission:* Ambassador Mark L. ASQUINO (since 4 October 2012)
embassy: Carretera Malabo II, Malabo, Guinea Ecuatorial
mailing address: US Embassy Malabo, US Department of State, Washington, DC 20521-2520
telephone: [240] 333 09 57 41

Flag description: three equal horizontal bands of green (top), white, and red, with a blue isosceles triangle based on the hoist side and the coat of arms centered in the white band; the coat of arms has six yellow six-pointed stars (representing the mainland and five offshore islands) above a gray shield bearing a silk-cotton tree and below which is a scroll with the motto UNIDAD, PAZ, JUSTICIA (Unity, Peace, Justice); green symbolizes the jungle and natural resources, blue represents the sea that connects the mainland to the islands, white stands for peace, and red recalls the fight for independence

National symbol(s): silk cotton tree; national colors: green, white, red, blue

National anthem: *name:* "Caminemos pisando la senda" (Let Us Tread the Path)
lyrics/music: Atanasio Ndongo MIYONO/Atanasio Ndongo MIYONO or Ramiro Sanchez LOPEZ (disputed)
note: adopted 1968

ECONOMY

Economy—overvie: Exploitation of oil and gas deposits, beginning in the 1990s, has driven economic growth in Equatorial Guinea, allowing per capita GDP to rise to over $29,000 in 2014. Forestry and farming are minor components of GDP. Although preindependence Equatorial Guinea counted on cocoa production for hard currency earnings, the neglect of the rural economy since independence has diminished the potential for agriculture-led growth. Subsistence farming is the dominant form of livelihood. Declining revenue from hydrocarbon production, high levels of infrastructure expenditures, lack of economic diversification, and corruption have pushed the economy into decline in recent years and led to limited improvements in the general population's living conditions.

Foreign assistance programs by the World Bank and the IMF have been cut since 1993 because of corruption and mismanagement, and as a middle income country Equatorial Guinea is now ineligible for most donor assistance. The government has been widely criticized for its lack of transparency and misuse of oil revenues and has attempted to address this issue by working towards compliance with the Extractive Industries Transparency Initiative. US foreign assistance to Equatorial Guinea is limited in part because of US restrictions pursuant to the Trafficking Victims Protection Act. Equatorial Guinea hosted two economic diversification symposia in 2014 that focused on attracting investment in five sectors: agriculture and animal ranching, fishing, mining and petrochemicals, tourism, and financial services. Undeveloped mineral resources include gold, zinc, diamonds, columbite-tantalite, and other base metals.

GDP (purchasing power parity): $25.39 billion (2015 est.)
$28.91 billion (2014 est.)
$28.99 billion (2013 est.)
note: data are in 2015 US dollars
country comparison to the world: 134

GDP (official exchange rate): $9.403 billion (2015 est.)

GDP—real growth rate: -12.2% (2015 est.)
-0.3% (2014 est.)
-6.5% (2013 est.)
country comparison to the world: 221

GDP—per capita (PPP): $31,800 (2015 est.)
$37,200 (2014 est.)
$38,300 (2013 est.)
note: data are in 2015 US dollars
country comparison to the world: 58

Gross national saving: 23.9% of GDP (2015 est.)
25.3% of GDP (2014 est.)
29.4% of GDP (2013 est.)

country comparison to the world: 55
GDP—composition, by end use: *household consumption:* 19.8%
government consumption: 6.4%
investment in fixed capital: 62.4%
investment in inventories: 0.1%
exports of goods and services: 61%
imports of goods and services: -49.7% (2015 est.)
GDP—composition, by sector of origin: *agriculture:* 5.1%
industry: 85.7%
services: 9.2% (2014 est.)
Agriculture—products: coffee, cocoa, rice, yams, cassava (manioc, tapioca), bananas, palm oil nuts; livestock; timber
Industries: petroleum, natural gas, sawmilling
Industrial production growth rate: -10.8% (2015 est.)
country comparison to the world: 197
Labor force: 195,200 (2007 est.)
country comparison to the world: 173
Unemployment rate: 22.3% (2009 est.)
country comparison to the world: 172
Population below poverty line: NA%
Household income or consumption by percentage share: *lowest 10%:* NA%
highest 10%: NA%

Budget: *revenues:* $2.99 billion
expenditures: $3.58 billion (2015 est.)
Taxes and other revenues: 29.8% of GDP (2015 est.)
country comparison to the world: 82
Budget surplus (+) or deficit (–): -5.9% of GDP (2015 est.)
country comparison to the world: 179
Public debt: 15.8% of GDP (2015 est.)
13% of GDP (2014 est.)
country comparison to the world: 161
Fiscal year: calendar year
Inflation rate (consumer prices): 3.2% (2015 est.)
4.3% (2014 est.)
country comparison to the world: 141
Central bank discount rate: 8.5% (31 December 2010)
4.25% (31 December 2009)
country comparison to the world: 37
Commercial bank prime lending rate: 14% (31 December 2015 est.)
15% (31 December 2014 est.)
country comparison to the world: 49
Stock of narrow money: $2.001 billion (31 December 2015 est.)
$2.504 billion (31 December 2014 est.)
country comparison to the world: 127
Stock of broad money: $3.788 billion (31 December 2014 est.)
$3.841 billion (31 December 2013 est.)
country comparison to the world: 142
Stock of domestic credit: $940.8 million (31 December 2015 est.)
$655.2 million (31 December 2014 est.)
country comparison to the world: 160
Current account balance: -$617 million (2015 est.)
-$1.493 billion (2014 est.)
country comparison to the world: 108
Exports: $9.169 billion (2015 est.)

$14.76 billion (2014 est.)
country comparison to the world: 93
Exports—commodities: petroleum products, timber
Exports—partners: China 16.6%, South Korea 15.1%, Spain 9%, Brazil 8.2%, Netherlands 6.8%, South Africa 6.6%, India 5.8%, UK 5.7%, France 5.7% (2015)
Imports: $4.143 billion (2015 est.)
$5.475 billion (2014 est.)
country comparison to the world: 132
Imports—commodities: petroleum sector equipment, other equipment, construction materials, vehicles
Imports—partners: Netherlands 16.9%, Spain 16.3%, China 14.9%, US 8.9%, Cote divoire 6%, France 4.8% (2015)
Reserves of foreign exchange and gold: $1.903 billion (31 December 2015 est.)
$2.907 billion (31 December 2014 est.)
country comparison to the world: 120
Debt—external: $1.416 billion (31 December 2014 est.)
$1.562 billion (31 December 2013 est.)
country comparison to the world: 156
Exchange rates: Cooperation Financiere en Afrique Centrale francs (XAF) per US dollar—
580.5 (2015 est.)
494.42 (2014 est.)
494.42 (2013 est.)
510.53 (2012 est.)
471.87 (2011 est.)

ENERGY

Electricity—production: 100 million kWh (2012 est.)
country comparison to the world: 198
Electricity—consumption: 93 million kWh (2012 est.)
country comparison to the world: 198
Electricity—exports: 0 kWh (2013 est.)
country comparison to the world: 134
Electricity—imports: 0 kWh (2013 est.)
country comparison to the world: 144
Electricity—installed generating capacity: 164,000 kW (2012 est.)
country comparison to the world: 163
Electricity—from fossil fuels: 22.6% of total installed capacity (2012 est.)
country comparison to the world: 190
Electricity—from nuclear fuels: 0% of total installed capacity (2012 est.)
country comparison to the world: 85
Electricity—from hydroelectric plants: 77.4% of total installed capacity (2012 est.)
country comparison to the world: 18
Electricity—from other renewable sources: 0% of total installed capacity (2012 est.)
country comparison to the world: 172
Crude oil—production: 248,000 bbl/day (2014 est.)
country comparison to the world: 34
Crude oil—exports: 318,100 bbl/day (2012 est.)
country comparison to the world: 24
Crude oil—imports: 0 bbl/day (2012 est.)
country comparison to the world: 184

Crude oil—proved reserves: 1.1 billion bbl (1 January 2015 est.)
country comparison to the world: 41
Refined petroleum products—production: 0 bbl/day (2012 est.)
country comparison to the world: 176
Refined petroleum products—consumption: 4,900 bbl/day (2013 est.)
country comparison to the world: 171
Refined petroleum products—exports: 0 bbl/day (2012 est.)
country comparison to the world: 177
Refined petroleum products—imports: 4,863 bbl/day (2012 est.)
country comparison to the world: 163
Natural gas—production: 6.29 billion cu m (2013 est.)
country comparison to the world: 48
Natural gas—consumption: 1.49 billion cu m (2013 est.)
country comparison to the world: 84
Natural gas—exports: 4.8 billion cu m (2013 est.)
country comparison to the world: 30
Natural gas—imports: 0 cu m (2013 est.)
country comparison to the world: 191
Natural gas—proved reserves: 36.81 billion cu m (1 January 2014 est.)
country comparison to the world: 67
Carbon dioxide emissions from consumption of energy: 5.614 million Mt (2012 est.)
country comparison to the world: 123

COMMUNICATIONS

Telephones—fixed lines: *total subscriptions:* 15,100
subscriptions per 100 inhabitants: 2 (2014 est.)
country comparison to the world: 194
Telephones—mobile cellular: *total:* 516,500
subscriptions per 100 inhabitants: 72 (2014 est.)
country comparison to the world: 170
Telephone system: *general assessment:* digital fixed-line network in most major urban areas and good mobile cellular coverage
domestic: fixed-line density is about 2 per 100 persons; mobile-cellular subscribership has been increasing and in 2011 stood at about 60 percent of the population
international: country code—240; international communications from Bata and Malabo to African and European countries; satellite earth station—1 Intelsat (Indian Ocean) (2011)
Broadcast media: state maintains control of broadcast media with domestic broadcast media limited to 1 state-owned TV station, 1 private TV station owned by the president's eldest son, 1 state-owned radio station, and 1 private radio station owned by the president's eldest son; satellite TV service is available; transmissions of multiple international broadcasters are accessible (2013)
Radio broadcast stations: AM 0, FM 3, shortwave 5 (2001)
Television broadcast stations: 1 (2001)
Internet country code: gq
Internet hosts: 7 (2012)
country comparison to the world: 227

Internet users: *total:* 115,100
percent of population: 15.9% (2014 est.)
country comparison to the world: 167

TRANSPORTATION

Airports: 7 (2013)
country comparison to the world: 166
Airports—with paved runways: *total:* 6
over 3,047 m: 1
2,438 to 3,047 m: 2
1,524 to 2,437 m: 1
under 914 m: 2 (2013)
Airports—with unpaved runways: *total:* 1
2,438 to 3,047 m: 1 (2013)
Pipelines: condensate 42 km; condensate/gas 5 km; gas 79 km; oil 71 km (2013)
Roadways: *total:* 2,880 km (2000)
country comparison to the world: 169
Merchant marine: *total:* 5
by type: cargo 1, chemical tanker 1, petroleum tanker 3
foreign-owned: 1 (Norway 1) (2010)
country comparison to the world: 124
Ports and terminals: *major seaport(s):* Bata, Luba, Malabo
LNG terminal(s) (export): Bioko Island

MILITARY AND SECURITY

Military branches: Equatorial Guinea Armed Forces (FAGE): Equatorial Guinea National Guard (Guardia Nacional de Guinea Ecuatorial, GNGE (Army), Navy, Air Force (2013)
Military service age and obligation: 18 years of age for selective compulsory military service, although conscription is rare in practice; 2-year service obligation; women hold only administrative positions in the Navy (2013)

TRANSNATIONAL ISSUES

Disputes—international: in 2002, ICJ ruled on an equidistance settlement of Cameroon-Equatorial Guinea-Nigeria maritime boundary in the Gulf of Guinea, but a dispute between Equatorial Guinea and Cameroon over an island at the mouth of the Ntem River and imprecisely defined maritime coordinates in the ICJ decision delayed final delimitation; UN urged Equatorial Guinea and Gabon to resolve the sovereignty dispute over Gabon occupied Mbane and lesser islands and to create a maritime boundary in the hydrocarbon-rich Corisco Bay
Trafficking in persons: *current situation:* Equatorial Guinea is a source country for children

subjected to sex trafficking and destination country for men, women, and children subjected to forced labor; Equatorial Guinean girls may be encouraged by their parents to engage in the sex trade in urban centers to receive groceries, gifts, housing, and money; children are also trafficked from nearby countries for work as domestic servants, market laborers, ambulant vendors, and launderers; women are trafficked to Equatorial Guinea from Cameroon, Benin, other neighboring countries, and China for forced labor or prostitution
tier rating: Tier 3—Equatorial Guinea does not fully comply with the minimum standards on the elimination of trafficking and is not making significant efforts to do so; in 2014, the government made no efforts to investigate or prosecute any suspected trafficking offenders or to identify or protect victims, despite its 2004 law prohibiting all forms of trafficking and mandating the provision of services to victims; undocumented migrants continued to be deported without being screened to assess whether any were trafficking victims; authorities did not undertake any trafficking awareness campaigns, implement any programs to address forced child labor, or make any other efforts to prevent trafficking (2015)

ERITREA

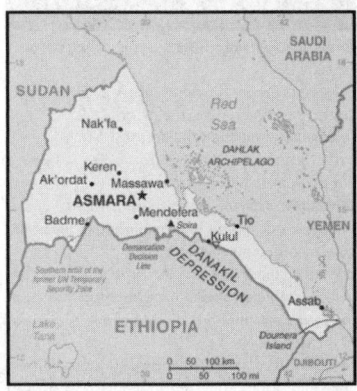

INTRODUCTION

Background: After independence from Italian colonial control in 1941 and 10 years of British administrative control, the UN established Eritrea as an autonomous region within the Ethiopian federation in 1952. Ethiopia's full annexation of Eritrea as a province 10 years later sparked a violent 30-year struggle for independence that ended in 1991 with Eritrean rebels defeating government forces. Eritreans overwhelmingly approved independence in a 1993 referendum. ISAIAS Afworki has been Eritrea's only president since independence; his rule, particularly since 2001, has been highly autocratic and repressive. His government

has created a highly militarized society by pursuing an unpopular program of mandatory conscription into national service, sometimes of indefinite length. A two-and-a-half-year border war with Ethiopia that erupted in 1998 ended under UN auspices in December 2000. A UN peacekeeping operation was established that monitored a 25 km-wide Temporary Security Zone. The Eritrea-Ethiopia Boundary Commission (EEBC) created in April 2003 was tasked "to delimit and demarcate the colonial treaty border based on pertinent colonial treaties (1900, 1902, and 1908) and applicable international law." The EEBC on 30 November 2007 remotely demarcated the border, assigning the town of Badme to Eritrea, despite Ethiopia's maintaining forces there from the time of the 1998–2000 war. Eritrea insisted that the UN terminate its peacekeeping mission on 31 July 2008. Eritrea has accepted the EEBC's "virtual demarcation" decision and repeatedly called on Ethiopia to remove its troops. Ethiopia has not accepted the demarcation decision, and neither party has entered into meaningful dialogue to resolve the impasse. Eritrea is subject to several UN Security Council Resolutions (from 2009, 2011, and 2012) imposing various military and economic sanctions, iNView of evidence that it has supported armed opposition groups in the region.

GEOGRAPHY

Location: Eastern Africa, bordering the Red Sea, between Djibouti and Sudan

Geographic coordinates: 1500 N, 3900 E
Map references: Africa
Area: *total:* 117,600 sq km
land: 101,000 sq km
water: 16,600 sq km
country comparison to the world: 101
Area—comparative: slightly larger than Pennsylvania
Land boundaries: *total:* 1,840 km
border countries (3): Djibouti 125 km, Ethiopia 1,033 km, Sudan 682 km
Coastline: 2,234 km (mainland on Red Sea 1,151 km, islands in Red Sea 1,083 km)
Maritime claims: *territorial sea:* 12 nm
Climate: hot, dry desert strip along Red Sea coast; cooler and wetter in the central highlands (up to 61 cm of rainfall annually, heaviest June to September); semiarid in western hills and lowlands
Terrain: dominated by extension of Ethiopian north-south trending highlands, descending on the east to a coastal desert plain, on the northwest to hilly terrain and on the southwest to flat-to-rolling plains
Elevation: *mean elevation:* 853 m
elevation extremes: *lowest point:* near Kulul within the Danakil Depression -75 m
highest point: Soira 3,018 m
Natural resources: gold, potash, zinc, copper, salt, possibly oil and natural gas, fish
Land use: *agricultural land:* 75.1%
arable land: 6.8%;
permanent crops: 0%;
permanent pasture: 68.3%

forest: 15.1%
other: 9.8% (2011 est.)

Irrigated land: 210 sq km (2012)
Total renewable water resources: 6.3 cu km (2011)
Freshwater withdrawal (domestic/industrial/agricultural): *total:* 0.58 cu km/yr (5%/0%/95%)
per capita: 121.3 cu m/yr (2004)
Natural hazards: frequent droughts, rare earthquakes and volcanoes; locust swarms
volcanism: Dubbi (elev. 1,625 m), which last erupted in 1861, was the country's only historically active volcano until Nabro (2,218 m) came to life on 12 June 2011
Environment—current issues: deforestation; desertification; soil erosion; overgrazing; loss of infrastructure from civil warfare
Environment—international agreements: *party to:* Biodiversity, Climate Change, Climate Change-Kyoto Protocol, Desertification, Endangered Species, Hazardous Wastes, Ozone Layer Protection
signed, but not ratified: none of the selected agreements
Geography—note: strategic geopolitical position along world's busiest shipping lanes; Eritrea retained the entire coastline of Ethiopia along the Red Sea upon de jure independence from Ethiopia on 24 May 1993

PEOPLE AND SOCIETY

Nationality: *noun:* Eritrean(s)
adjective: Eritrean
Ethnic groups: nine recognized ethnic groups: Tigrinya 55%, Tigre 30%, Saho 4%, Kunama 2%, Rashaida 2%, Bilen 2%, other (Afar, Beni Amir, Nera) 5% (2010 est.)
Languages: Tigrinya (official), Arabic (official), English (official), Tigre, Kunama, Afar, other Cushitic languages
Religions: Muslim, Coptic Christian, Roman Catholic, Protestant
Population: 6,527,689 (July 2015 est.)
country comparison to the world: 107
Age structure: *0–14 years:* 40.25% (male 1,320,752/female 1,306,357)
15–24 years: 20.43% (male 665,900/female 667,509)
25–54 years: 31.86% (male 1,031,391/female 1,048,303)
55–64 years: 3.73% (male 104,004/female 139,637)
65 years and over: 3.74% (male 104,513/female 139,323) (2015 est.)
Dependency ratios: *total dependency ratio:* 83.2%
youth dependency ratio: 78.4%
elderly dependency ratio: 4.8%
potential support ratio: 20.7% (2015 est.)
Median age: *total:* 19.3 years
male: 19 years
female: 19.7 years (2015 est.)
country comparison to the world: 199
Population growth rate: 2.25% (2015 est.)
country comparison to the world: 36
Birth rate: 30 births/1,000 population (2015 est.)
country comparison to the world: 41

Death rate: 7.52 deaths/1,000 population (2015 est.)
country comparison to the world: 113
Net migration rate: 0 migrant(s)/1,000 population (2015 est.)
country comparison to the world: 98
Urbanization: *urban population:* 22.6% of total population (2015)
rate of urbanization: 5.11% annual rate of change (2010–15 est.)
Major urban areas—population: ASMARA (capital) 804,000 (2015)
Sex ratio: *at birth:* 1.03 male(s)/female
0–14 years: 1.01 male(s)/female
15–24 years: 1 male(s)/female
25–54 years: 0.98 male(s)/female
55–64 years: 0.75 male(s)/female
65 years and over: 0.75 male(s)/female
total population: 0.98 male(s)/female (2015 est.)
Mother's mean age at first birth: 21.3
note: median age at first birth among women 25–29 (2010 est.)
Maternal mortality rate: 501 deaths/100,000 live births (2015 est.)
country comparison to the world: 46
Infant mortality rate: *total:* 37.53 deaths/1,000 live births
male: 42.59 deaths/1,000 live births
female: 32.31 deaths/1,000 live births (2015 est.)
country comparison to the world: 56
Life expectancy at birth: *total population:* 63.81 years
male: 61.65 years
female: 66.03 years (2015 est.)
country comparison to the world: 184
Total fertility rate: 4.02 children born/woman (2015 est.)
country comparison to the world: 37
Health expenditures: 3% of GDP (2013)
country comparison to the world: 184
Hospital bed density: 0.7 beds/1,000 population (2011)
Drinking water source: improved:
urban: 73.2% of population
rural: 53.3% of population
total: 57.8% of population
unimproved:
urban: 26.8% of population
rural: 46.7% of population
total: 42.2% of population (2015 est.)
Sanitation facility access: improved:
urban: 44.5% of population
rural: 7.3% of population
total: 15.7% of population
unimproved:
urban: 55.5% of population
rural: 92.7% of population
total: 84.3% of population (2015 est.)
HIV/AIDS—adult prevalence rate: 0.68% (2014 est.)
country comparison to the world: 56
HIV/AIDS—people living with HIV/AIDS: 16,100 (2014 est.)
country comparison to the world: 86
HIV/AIDS—deaths: 700 (2014 est.)
country comparison to the world: 78

Major infectious diseases: *degree of risk:* high
food or waterborne diseases: bacterial diarrhea, hepatitis A, and typhoid fever *vectorborne diseases:* malaria and dengue fever (2013)
Obesity—adult prevalence rate: 3.4% (2014)
country comparison to the world: 188
Children under the age of 5 years underweight: 38.8% (2010)
country comparison to the world: 7
Education expenditures: 2.1% of GDP (2006)
country comparison to the world: 165
Literacy: *definition:* age 15 and over can read and write
total population: 73.8%
male: 82.4%
female: 65.5% (2015 est.)
School life expectancy (primary to tertiary education): *total:* 5 years
male: 6 years
female: 4 years (2010)

GOVERNMENT

Country name: *conventional long form:* State of Eritrea
conventional short form: Eritrea
local long form: Hagere Ertra
local short form: Ertra
former: Eritrea Autonomous Region in Ethiopia
etymology: the country name derives from the ancient Greek appellation "Erythra Thalassa" meaning Red Sea, which is the major water body bordering the country
Government type: presidential republic
Capital: *name:* Asmara (Asmera)
Geographic coordinates: 1520 N, 3856 E
time difference: UTC+3 (8 hours ahead of Washington, DC, during Standard Time)
Administrative divisions: 6 regions (zobatat, singular—zoba); Anseba, Debub (South), Debubawi K'eyih Bahri (Southern Red Sea), Gash Barka, Ma'akel (Central), Semenawi Keyih Bahri (Northern Red Sea)
Independence: 24 May 1993 (from Ethiopia)
National holiday: Independence Day, 24 May (1991)
Constitution: adopted 23 May 1997 (not fully implemented); note—drafting of a new constitution, which began in 2014, continued into 2016 (2016)
Legal system: mixed legal system of civil, customary, and Islamic religious law
International law organization participation: has not submitted an ICJ jurisdiction declaration; non-party state to the ICCt
Citizenship: *citizenship by birth:* no
citizenship by descent only: at least one parent must be a citizen of Eritrea
dual citizenship recognized: no
residency requirement for naturalization: 20 years
Suffrage: 18 years of age; universal
Executive branch: *chief of state:* President ISAIAS Afworki (since 8 June 1993); note—the president is both chief of state and head of government and is head of the State Council and National Assembly

271

head of government: President ISAIAS Afworki (since 8 June 1993) *cabinet:* State Council appointed by the president

elections/appointments: president indirectly elected by the National Assembly for a 5-year term (eligible for a second term); the only election was held on 8 June 1993, following independence from Ethiopia (next election postponed indefinitely)

election results: ISAIAS Afworki elected president by the transitional National Assembly; percent of National Assembly vote—ISAIAS Afworki (PFDJ) 95%, other 5%

Legislative branch: description: unicameral National Assembly or Hagerawi Baito (150 seats; 75 members indirectly elected by the ruling party and 75 directly elected by simple majority vote; members serve 5-year terms)

elections: in May 1997, following the adoption of the new constitution, 75 members of the PFDJ Central Committee (the old Central Committee of the EPLF), 60 members of the 527-member Constituent Assembly, which had been established in 1997 to discuss and ratify the new constitution, and 15 representatives of Eritreans living abroad were formed into a Transitional National Assembly to serve as the country's legislative body until countrywide elections to form a National Assembly were held; although only 75 of 150 members of the Transitional National Assembly were elected, the constitution stipulates that once past the transition stage, all members of the National Assembly will be elected by secret ballot of all eligible voters; National Assembly elections scheduled for December 2001 were postponed indefinitely due to the war with Ethiopia

Judicial branch: *highest court(s):* High Court (consists of 20 judges and organized into civil, commercial, criminal, labor, administrative, and customary sections)

judge selection and term of office: High Court judges appointed by the president

subordinate courts: regional/zonal courts; community courts; special courts; sharia courts (for issues dealing with Muslim marriage, inheritance, and family); military courts

Political parties and leaders: People's Front for Democracy and Justice or PFDJ [ISAIAS Afworki] (the only party recognized by the government)

note: a National Assembly committee drafted a law on political parties in January 2001, but the full National Assembly never debated or voted on it

Political pressure groups and leaders: Democratic Movement for the Liberation of Eritrean Kunama or DMLEK Eritrean Democratic Alliance or EDA Eritrean Islamic Party for Justice and Development or EIPJD (includes the Eritrean Islamic Jihad (EIJ), Eritrean Islamic Jihad Movement (EIJM), Eritrean Islamic Salvation, and the Eritrean Islamic Foundation)

Eritrean National Congress for Democratic Change or ENCDC

Eritrean National Salvation Front or ENSF
Eritrean People's Democratic Party or EPDP
Red Sea Afar Democratic Organization or RSADO

International organization participation: ACP, AfDB, AU, COMESA, FAO, G-77, IAEA, IBRD, ICAO, ICC (NGOs), IDA, IFAD, IFC, IFRCS (observer), ILO, IMF, IMO, Interpol, IOC, ISO (correspondent), ITU, ITUC (NGOs), LAS (observer), MIGA, NAM, OPCW, PCA, UN, UNCTAD, UNESCO, UNIDO, UNWTO, UPU, WCO, WFTU (NGOs), WHO, WIPO, WMO

Diplomatic representation in the US: *chief of mission:* Ambassador (vacant); Charge d'Affaires BERHANE Gebrehiwet Solomon (since 15 March 2011)

chancery: 1708 New Hampshire Avenue NW, Washington, DC 20009

telephone: [1] (202) 319–1991
FAX: [1] (202) 319-1304

Diplomatic representation from the US: *chief of mission:* Ambassador (vacant); Charge d'Affaires Louis MAZEL (since 10 July 2014)

embassy: 179 Ala Street, Asmara

mailing address: P. O. Box 211, Asmara

telephone: [291] (1) 120004

FAX: [291] (1) 127584

Flag description: red isosceles triangle (based on the hoist side) dividing the flag into two right triangles; the upper triangle is green, the lower one is blue; a gold wreath encircling a gold olive branch is centered on the hoist side of the red triangle; green stands for the country's agriculture economy, red signifies the blood shed in the fight for freedom, and blue symbolizes the bounty of the sea; the wreath-olive branch symbol is similar to that on the first flag of Eritrea from 1952; the shape of the red triangle broadly mimics the shape of the country

note: one of several flags where a prominent component of the design reflects the shape of the country; other such flags are those of Bosnia and Herzegovina, Brazil, and Vanuatu

National symbol(s): camel; national colors: green, red, blue

National anthem: *name:* "Ertra, Ertra, Ertra" (Eritrea, Eritrea, Eritrea)

lyrics/music: SOLOMON Tsehaye Beraki/Isaac Abraham MEHAREZGI and ARON Tekle Tesfatsion

note: adopted 1993; upon independence from Ethiopia

ECONOMY

Economy—overview: Since formal independence from Ethiopia in 1993, Eritrea has faced many economic problems, including lack of financial resources and chronic drought, which have been exacerbated by restrictive economic policies. Eritrea has a command economy under the control of the sole political party, the People's Front for Democracy and Justice. Like the economies of many African nations, a large share of the population -nearly 80% in Eritrea—is engaged in subsistence agriculture, but the sector only produces a small share of the country's total output.

Since the conclusion of the Ethiopia-Eritrea war in 2000, the government has expanded use of military and party-owned businesses to complete President ISAIAS's development agenda. The government

has strictly controlled the use of foreign currency by limiting access and availability; new regulations in 2013 aimed at relaxing currency controls have had little economic effect. Few large private enterprises exist in Eritrea and most operate in conjunction with government partners, including a number of large international mining ventures, which began production in 2013. In late 2015, the government of Eritrea introduced a new currency, retaining the name nakfa, and restricted the amount of hard currency individuals could withdraw from banks per month. The changeover has resulted in exchange fluctuations and the scarcity of hard currency available in the market.

While reliable statistics on food security are difficult to obtain, erratic rainfall and the percentage of the labor force tied up in national service continue to interfere with agricultural production and economic development. Eritrea's harvests generally cannot meet the food needs of the country without supplemental grain purchases. Copper, potash, and gold production is likely to drive economic growth and government revenue over the next few years, but military spending will continue to compete with development and investment plans. Eritrea's economic future will depend on market reform, international sanctions, global food prices, and success at addressing social problems suchas refugee emigration.

GDP (purchasing power parity): $8.713 billion (2015 est.)

$8.316 billion (2014 est.)
$7.921 billion (2013 est.)
note: data are in 2015 US dollars
country comparison to the world: 162

GDP (official exchange rate): $4.666 billion (2015 est.)

GDP—real growth rate: 4.8% (2015 est.)
5% (2014 est.)
3.1% (2013 est.)
country comparison to the world: 45

GDP—per capita (PPP): $1,300 (2015 est.)
$1,300 (2014 est.)
$1,300 (2013 est.)
note: data are in 2015 US dollars; estimates for the size of the Eritrean population vary widely from 3 to 6 million
country comparison to the world: 219

Gross national saving: 1.3% of GDP (2015 est.)
4% of GDP (2014 est.)
3.6% of GDP (2013 est.)
country comparison to the world: 170

GDP—composition, by end use:
household consumption: 76.9%
government consumption: 21.1%
investment in fixed capital: 13.6%
investmen tininventories: -0.1%
exports of goods and services: 7.6%
imports of goods and services: -19.1% (2015 est.)

GDP—composition, by sector of origin: *agriculture:* 12.3%
industry: 29.4%
services: 58.3% (2015 est.)

Agriculture—products: sorghum, lentils, vegetables, corn, cotton, tobacco, sisal; livestock, goats; fish

Industries: food processing, beverages, clothing and textiles, light manufacturing, salt, cement
Industrial production growth rate: 5% (2015 est.)
country comparison to the world: 30
Labor force: 3.263 million (2015 est.)
country comparison to the world: 101
Labor force—by occupation: *agriculture:* 80%
industry and services: 20% (2004 est.)
Unemployment rate: 8.6% (2013 est.)
10% (2012 est.)
country comparison to the world: 99
Population below poverty line: 50% (2004 est.)

Household income or consumption by percentage share: *lowest:* 10%: NA%
highest: 10%: NA%

Budget: *revenues:* $1.443 billion
expenditures: $2.016 billion (2015 est.)
Taxes and other revenues: 33.9% of GDP (2015 est.)
country comparison to the world: 66
Budget surplus (+) or deficit (–): -13.4% of GDP (2015 est.)
country comparison to the world: 212
Public debt: 122.6% of GDP (2015 est.)
125.3% of GDP (2014 est.)
country comparison to the world: 7
Fiscal year: calendar year
Inflation rate (consumer prices): 9% (2015 est.)
10% (2014 est.)
country comparison to the world: 207
Commercial bank prime lending rate: NA%
Stock of narrow money: $2.516 billion (31 December 2015 est.)
$2.129 billion (31 December 2014 est.)
country comparison to the world: 120
Stock of broad money: $5.523 billion (31 December 2015 est.)
$4.494 billion (31 December 2014 est.)
country comparison to the world: 129
Stock of domestic credit: $4.974 billion (31 December 2015 est.)
$4.052 billion (31 December 2014 est.)
country comparison to the world: 124
Current account balance: -$102 million (2015 est.)
$23 million (2014 est.)
country comparison to the world: 68
Exports: $510.9 million (2015 est.)
$504.9 million (2014 est.)
country comparison to the world: 172
Exports—commodities: gold and other minerals, livestock, sorghum, textiles, food, small manufactures
Imports: $1.157 billion (2015 est.)
$1.15 billion (2014 est.)
country comparison to the world: 177
Imports—commodities: machinery, petroleum products, food, manufactured goods
Reserves of foreign exchange and gold: $247.8 million (31 December 2015 est.)
$218.9 million (31 December 2014 est.)
country comparison to the world: 159
Debt—external: $955.6 million (31 December 2014 est.)
$945.2 million (31 December 2013 est.)
country comparison to the world: 165
Exchange rates: nakfa (ERN) per US dollar—

15.38 (2015 est.)
15.375 (2014 est.)
15.375 (2013 est.)
15.375 (2012 est.)
15.375 (2011 est.)

ENERGY

Electricity—production: 338 million kWh (2012 est.)
country comparison to the world: 170
Electricity—consumption: 284 million kWh (2012 est.)
country comparison to the world: 181
Electricity—exports: 0 kWh (2013 est.)
country comparison to the world: 135
Electricity—imports: 0 kWh (2013 est.)
country comparison to the world: 145
Electricity—installed generating capacity: 140,800 kW (2012 est.)
country comparison to the world: 166
Electricity—from fossil fuels: 98.7% of total installed capacity (2012 est.)
country comparison to the world: 51
Electricity—from nuclear fuels: 0% of total installed capacity (2012 est.)
country comparison to the world: 87
Electricity—from hydroelectric plants: 0% of total installed capacity (2012 est.)
country comparison to the world: 171
Electricity—from other renewable sources: 1.3% of total installed capacity (2012 est.)
country comparison to the world: 91
Crude oil—production: 0 bbl/day (2014 est.)
country comparison to the world: 130
Crude oil—exports: 0 bbl/day (2012 est.)
country comparison to the world: 119
Crude oil—imports: 0 bbl/day (2012 est.)
country comparison to the world: 186
Crude oil—proved reserves: 0 bbl (1 January 2015 est.)
country comparison to the world: 129
Refined petroleum products—production: 0 bbl/day (2012 est.)
country comparison to the world: 178
Refined petroleum products—consumption: 3,500 bbl/day (2013 est.)
country comparison to the world: 178
Refined petroleum products—exports: 0 bbl/day (2012 est.)
country comparison to the world: 178
Refined petroleum products—imports: 3,500 bbl/day (2012 est.)
country comparison to the world: 170
Natural gas—production: 0 cu m (2013 est.)
country comparison to the world: 182
Natural gas—consumption: 0 cu m (2013 est.)
country comparison to the world: 139
Natural gas—exports: 0 cu m (2013 est.)
country comparison to the world: 94
Natural gas—imports: 0 cu m (2013 est.)
country comparison to the world: 192
Natural gas—proved reserves: 0 cu m (1 January 2014 est.)
country comparison to the world: 134
Carbon dioxide emissions from consumption of energy: 739,500 Mt (2012 est.)

country comparison to the world: 173

COMMUNICATIONS

Telephones—fixed lines: *total subscriptions:* 64,000
subscriptions per 100 inhabitants: 1 (2014 est.)
country comparison to the world: 154
Telephones—mobile cellular: *total:* 417,400
subscriptions per 100 inhabitants: 7 (2014 est.)
country comparison to the world: 172
Telephone system: *general assessment:* inadequate; most fixed-line telephones are in Asmara; government is seeking international tenders to improve the system; cell phones in increasing use throughout the country
domestic: combined fixed-line and mobile-cellular subscribership is less than 5 per 100 persons
international: country code—291 (2011)
Broadcast media: government controls broadcast media with private ownership prohibited; 1 state-owned TV station; state-owned radio operates 2 networks; purchases of satellite dishes and subscriptions to international broadcast media are permitted (2007)
Radio broadcast stations: AM 2, FM NA, shortwave 2 (2000)
Television broadcast stations: 2 (2006)
Internet country code: .er
Internet hosts: 701 (2012)
country comparison to the world: 177
Internet users: *total:* 58,100
percent of population: 0.91% (2014 est.)
country comparison to the world: 180

TRANSPORTATION

Airports: 13 (2013)
country comparison to the world: 151
Airports—with paved runways: *total:* 4
over 3,047 m: 2
2,438 to 3,047 m: 2 (2013)
Airports—with unpaved runways: *total:* 9
over 3,047 m: 1
2,438 to 3,047 m: 1
1,524 to 2,437 m: 5
914 to 1,523 m: 2 (2013)
Heliports: 1 (2013)
Railways: *total:* 306 km
narrow gauge: 306 km 0.950-m gauge (2014)
country comparison to the world: 122
Roadways: *total:* 4,010 km
paved: 874 km
unpaved: 3,136 km (2000)
country comparison to the world: 159
Merchant marine: *total:* 4
by type: cargo 2, petroleum tanker 1, roll on/roll off 1 (2010)
country comparison to the world: 129
Ports and terminals: *major seaport(s):* Assab, Massawa

MILITARY AND SECURITY

Military branches: Eritrean Armed Forces: Eritrean Ground Forces, Eritrean Navy, Eritrean Air Force (includes Air Defense Force) (2011)

273

Military service age and obligation: 18–40 years of age for male and female voluntary and compulsory military service; 16-month conscript service obligation (2012)

TRANSNATIONAL ISSUES

Disputes—international: Eritrea and Ethiopia agreed to abide by 2002 Ethiopia-Eritrea Boundary Commission's (EEBC) delimitation decision, but neither party responded to the revised line detailed in the November 2006 EEBC Demarcation Statement; Sudan accuses Eritrea of supporting eastern Sudanese rebel groups; in 2008, Eritrean troops moved across the border on Ras Doumera peninsula and occupied Doumera Island with undefined sovereignty in the Red Sea

Trafficking in persons: *current situation:* Eritrea is a source country for men, women, and children trafficked for the purposes of forced labor domestically and, to a lesser extent, sex and labor trafficking abroad; the country's national service program is often abused, with conscripts detained indefinitely and subjected to forced labor; Eritrean migrants, often fleeing national service, face strict exit control procedures and limited access to passports and visas, making them vulnerable to trafficking; Eritrean secondary school children are required to take part in public works projects during their summer breaks and must attend military and educational camp in their final year to obtain a high school graduation certificate and to gain access to higher education and some jobs; some Eritreans living in or near refugee camps, particularly in Sudan, are kidnapped by criminal groups and held for ransom in the Sinai Peninsula and Libya, where they are subjected to forced labor and abuse

tier rating: Tier 3—Eritrea does not fully comply with the minimum standards for the elimination of trafficking and is not making significant efforts to do so; the government failed to investigate or prosecute any trafficking offenses or to identify or protect any victims; while the government continued to warn citizens of the dangers of human trafficking through awareness-raising events and poster campaigns, authorities lacked an understanding of the crime, conflating trafficking with transnational migration; Eritrea is not a party to the 2000 UN TIP Protocol (2015)

ESTONIA

INTRODUCTION

Background: After centuries of Danish, Swedish, German, and Russian rule, Estonia attained independence in 1918. Forcibly incorporated into the USSR in 1940—an action never recognized by the US—it regained its freedom in 1991 with the collapse of the Soviet Union. Since the last Russian troops left in 1994, Estonia has been free to promote economic and political ties with the West. It joined both NATO and the EU in the spring of 2004, formally joined the OECD in late 2010, and adopted the eurOAS its official currency on 1 January 2011.

GEOGRAPHY

Location: Eastern Europe, bordering the Baltic Sea and Gulf of Finland, between Latvia and Russia
Geographic coordinates: 5900 N, 2600 E
Map references: Europe
Area: *total:* 45,228 sq km
land: 42,388 sq km
water: 2,840 sq km
note: includes 1,520 islands in the Baltic Sea
country comparison to the world: 133
Area—comparative: about twice the size of New Jersey

Land boundaries: *total:* 657 km
border countries (2): Latvia 333 km, Russia 324 km
Coastline: 3,794 km
Maritime claims: *territorial sea:* 12 nm
exclusive economic zone: limits as agreed to by Estonia, Finland, Latvia, Sweden, and Russia
Climate: maritime; wet, moderate winters, cool summers
Terrain: marshy, lowlands; flat in the north, hilly in the south
Elevation: *mean elevation:* 61 m
elevation extremes: *lowest point:* Baltic Sea 0 m
highest point: Suur Munamagi 318 m
Natural resources: oil shale, peat, rare earth elements, phosphorite, clay, limestone, sand, dolomite, arable land, sea mud
Land use: *agricultural land:* 22.2%;
arable land: 14.9%;
permanent crops: 0.1%;
permanent pasture: 7.2%
forest: 52.1%
other: 25.7% (2011 est.)
Irrigated land: 40 sq km (2012)
Total renewable water resources: 12.81 cu km (2011)
Freshwater withdrawal (domestic/industrial/agricultural): *total:* 1.8 cu km/yr (3%/97%/0%)
per capita: 1,337 cu m/yr (2009)
Natural hazards: sometimes flooding occurs in the spring
Environment—current issues: air polluted with sulfur dioxide from oil-shale burning power plants in northeast; however, the amounts of pollutants emitted to the air have fallen dramatically; the pollution load of wastewater at purification plants has decreased substantially; Estonia has more than 1,400 natural and manmade lakes, the smaller of which in agricultural areas need to be monitored; coastal seawater is polluted in certain locations
Environment—international agreements: *party to:* Air Pollution, Air Pollution-Nitrogen Oxides, Air Pollution-Persistent Organic Pollutants, Air Pollution-Sulfur 85, Air Pollution-Volatile Organic Compounds, Antarctic Treaty, Biodiversity, Climate Change, Climate Change-Kyoto Protocol, Endangered Species, Hazardous Wastes, Law of the Sea, Ozone Layer Protection, Ship Pollution, Wetlands
signed, but not ratified: none of the selected agreements
Geography—note: the mainland terrain is flat, boggy, and partly wooded; offshore lie more than 1,500 islands

PEOPLE AND SOCIETY

Nationality: *noun:* Estonian(s)
adjective: Estonian
Ethnic groups: Estonian 68.7%, Russian 24.8%, Ukrainian 1.7%, Belarusian 1%, Finn 0.6%, other 1.6%, unspecified 1.6% (2011 est.)
Languages: Estonian (official) 68.5%, Russian 29.6%, Ukrainian 0.6%, other 1.2%, unspecified 0.1% (2011 est.)
Religions: Lutheran 9.9%, Orthodox 16.2%, other Christian (including Methodist, Seventh-Day Adventist, Roman Catholic, Pentecostal) 2.2%, other 0.9%, none 54.1%, unspecified 16.7% (2011 est.)
Population: 1,265,420 (July 2015 est.)
country comparison to the world: 158
Age structure: *0–14 years:* 15.99% (male 103,855/female 98,478)
15–24 years: 9.74% (male 63,840/female 59,425)
25–54 years: 41.83% (male 265,496/female 263,873)
55–64 years: 13.32% (male 75,279/female 93,264)
65 years and over: 19.12% (male 81,525/female 160,385) (2015 est.)
Dependency ratios: *total dependency ratio:* 53.5%
youth dependency ratio: 24.7%
elderly dependency ratio: 28.8%
potential support ratio: 3.5% (2015 est.)
Median age: *total:* 42.1 years
male: 38.7 years
female: 45.5 years (2015 est.)
country comparison to the world: 26
Population growth rate: -0.55% (2015 est.)
country comparison to the world: 224

Birth rate: 10.51 births/1,000 population (2015 est.)
country comparison to the world: 185
Death rate: 12.4 deaths/1,000 population (2015 est.)
country comparison to the world: 24
Net migration rate: -3.6 migrant(s)/1,000 population (2015 est.)
country comparison to the world: 187
Urbanization: *urban population:* 67.5% of total population (2015)
rate of urbanization: -0.45% annual rate of change (2010–15 est.)
Major urban areas—population: TALLINN (capital) 391,000 (2015)
Sex ratio: *at birth:* 1.05 male(s)/female
0–14 years: 1.06 male(s)/female
15–24 years: 1.07 male(s)/female
25–54 years: 1.01 male(s)/female
55–64 years: 0.81 male(s)/female
65 years and over: 0.51 male(s)/female
total population: 0.87 male(s)/female (2015 est.)
Mother's mean age at first birth: 26.4 (2011 est.)
Maternal mortality rate: 9 deaths/100,000 live births (2015 est.)
country comparison to the world: 184
Infant mortality rate: *total:* 3.85 deaths/1,000 live births
male: 3.73 deaths/1,000 live births
female: 3.98 deaths/1,000 live births (2015 est.)
country comparison to the world: 195
Life expectancy at birth: *total population:* 76.47 years
male: 71.64 years
female: 81.53 years (2015 est.)
country comparison to the world: 86
Total fertility rate: 1.59 children born/woman (2015 est.)
country comparison to the world: 183
Contraceptive prevalence rate: 63.4%
note: percent of women aged 18–49 (2004/05)
Health expenditures: 5.7% of GDP (2013)
country comparison to the world: 113
Physicians density: 3.24 physicians/1,000 population (2012)
Hospital bed density: 5.3 beds/1,000 population (2011)
Drinking water source: improved:
urban: 100% of population
rural: 99% of population
total: 99.6% of population
unimproved:
urban: 0% of population
rural: 1% of population
total: 0.4% of population (2015 est.)
Sanitation facility access: improved:
urban: 97.5% of population
rural: 96.6% of population
total: 97.2% of population
unimproved:
urban: 2.5% of population
rural: 3.4% of population
total: 2.8% of population (2015 est.)
HIV/AIDS—adult prevalence rate: 1.3% (2013 est.)
country comparison to the world: 37

HIV/AIDS—people living with HIV/AIDS: 8,600 (2013 est.)
country comparison to the world: 99
HIV/AIDS—deaths: NA
Major infectious diseases: *degree of risk:* intermediate
vectorborne disease: tickborne encephalitis (2013)
Obesity—adult prevalence rate: 24.5% (2014)
country comparison to the world: 95
Education *expenditures:* 4.7% of GDP (2012)
country comparison to the world: 52
Literacy: *definition:* age 15 and over can read and write
total population: 99.8%
male: 99.8%
female: 99.8% (2015 est.)
School life expectancy (primary to tertiary education): *total:* 17 years
male: 16 years
female: 17 years (2013)
Unemployment, youth ages 15–24: *total:* 18.7%
male: 17.8%
female: 19.7% (2013 est.)
country comparison to the world: 53

GOVERNMENT

Country name: *conventional long form:* Republic of Estonia
conventional short form: Estonia
local long form: Eesti Vabariik
local short form: Eesti
former: Estonian Soviet Socialist Republic
etymology: the country name may be derived from the Aesti, an ancient people who lived along the eastern Baltic Sea in the first centuries A.D.
Government type: parliamentary republic
Capital: *name:* Tallinn
Geographic coordinates: 5926 N, 2443 E
time difference: UTC+2 (7 hours ahead of Washington, DC, during Standard Time)
daylight saving time: +1hr, begins last Sunday in March; ends last Sunday in October
Administrative divisions: 15 counties (maakonnad, singular—maakond); Harjumaa (Tallinn), Hiiumaa (Kardla), Ida-Virumaa (Johvi), Jarvamaa (Paide), Jogevamaa (Jogeva), Laanemaa (Haapsalu), Laane-Virumaa (Rakvere), Parnumaa (Parnu), Polvamaa (Polva), Raplamaa (Rapla), Saaremaa (Kuressaare), Tartumaa (Tartu), Valgamaa (Valga), Viljandimaa (Viljandi), Vorumaa (Voru)
note: counties have the administrative center name following in parentheses
Independence: 20 August 1991 (declared); 6 September 1991 (recognized by the Soviet Union)
National holiday: Independence Day, 24 February (1918); note—24 February 1918 was the date Estonia declared its independence from Soviet Russia and established its statehood; 20 August 1991 was the date it declared its independence from the Soviet Union
Constitution: several previous; latest adopted 28 June 1992; amended several times, last in 2015 (2016)
Legal system: civil law system

International law organization participation: accepts compulsory ICJ jurisdiction with reservations; accepts ICCt jurisdiction
Citizenship: *citizenship by birth:* no
citizenship by descent only: at least one parent must be a citizen of Estonia
dual citizenship recognized: no
residency requirement for naturalization: 5 years
Suffrage: 18 years of age; universal for all Estonian citizens
Executive branch: *chief of state:* President Toomas Hendrik ILVES (since 9 October 2006)
head of government: Taavi ROIVAS (since 26 March 2014)
cabinet: Cabinet appointed by the prime minister, approved by Parliament
elections/appointments: president indirectly elected by Parliament for a 5-year term (eligible for a second term); if a candidate does not secure two-thirds of the votes after 3 rounds of balloting, then an electoral assembly of Parliament and local council members elects the president, choosing between the 2 candidates with the highest number of votes; election last held on 29 August 2011 (next to be held in the fall of 2016); prime minister nominated by the president and approved by Parliament
election results: Toomas Hendrik ILVES reelected president; Parliament vote—Toomas Hendrik ILVES (independent) 73, Indrek TAR and (independent) 25
Legislative branch: *description:* unicameral Parliament or Riigikogu (101 seats; members directly elected in multi-seat constituencies by proportional representation vote to serve 4-year terms)
elections: last held on 1 March 2015 (next to be held in March 2019)
election results: percent of vote by party—RE 27.7%, K 24.8%, SDE 15.2%, IRL 13.7%, EV 8.7%, EKRE 8.1%, other 1.8%; seats by party—RE 30, K 27, SDE 15, IRL 14, EV 8, EKRE 7
Judicial branch: *highest court(s):* Supreme Court (consists of the chief justice and organized into the Civil Chamber with a chamber chairman and 6 justices, the Criminal Chamber with a chamber chairman and 5 justices, the Administrative Law Chamber with a chamber chairman and 4 justices, and the Constitutional Review Chamber with 9 members—the chief justice and 2 justices from the Civil Chamber, 3 from the Criminal Chamber and 3 from the Administrative chamber)
judge selection and term of office: the chief justice is proposed by the president and appointed by the Riigikogu; other justices proposed by the chief justice and appointed by the Riigikogu; justices appointed for life
subordinate courts: circuit (appellate) courts; administrative, county, city, and specialized courts
Political parties and leaders: Center Party of Estonia (Keskerakond) or K [Edgar SAVISAAR]
Estonian Conservative People's Party (Konservatiivne Rahvaerakond) or EKRE [Mart HELME]
Estonian Reform Party (Reformierakond) or RE [Taavi ROIVAS] Free Party or EV [Andres HERKEL]

275

Social Democratic Party or SDE [Jevgeni OSSINOVSKI]

Union of Pro Patria and Res Publica (Isamaa je Res Publica Liit) or IRL [Margus TSAHKNA]

International organization participation: Australia Group, BA, BIS, CBSS, CD, CE, EAPC, EBRD, ECB, EIB, EMU, ESA (cooperating state), EU, FAO, IAEA, IBRD, ICAO, ICC (national committees), ICCt, ICRM, IDA, IEA, IFAD, IFC, IFRCS, IHO, ILO, IMF, IMO, Interpol, IOC, IOM, IPU, ISO, ITSO, ITU, ITUC (NGOs), MIGA, MINUSMA, NATO, NIB, NSG, OAS (observer), OECD, OIF (observer), OPCW, OSCE, PCA, Schengen Convention, UN, UNCTAD, UNESCO, UNHCR, UNTSO, UPU, WCO, WHO, WIPO, WMO, WTO

Diplomatic representation in the US: *chief of mission:* Ambassador Eerik MARMEI (since 18 September 2014)

chancery: 2131 Massachusetts Avenue NW, Washington, DC 20008

telephone: [1] (202) 588–0101

FAX: [1] (202) 588–0108

consulate(s) general: New York

Diplomatic representation from the US: *chief of mission:* Ambassador James D. MELVILLE Jr. (since 8 December 2015)

embassy: Kentmanni 20,15099 Tallinn

mailing address: use embassy street address

telephone: [372] 668–8100

FAX: [372] 668–8134

Flag description: three equal horizontal bands of blue (top), black, and white; various interpretations are linked to the flag colors; blue represents faith, loyalty, and devotion, while also reminiscent of the sky, sea, and lakes of the country; black symbolizes the soil of the country and the dark past and suffering endured by the Estonian people; white refers to the striving towards enlightenment and virtue, and is the color of birch bark and snow, as well as summer nights illuminated by the midnight sun

National symbol(s): barn swallow, cornflower; national colors: blue, black, white

National anthem: *name:* "Mu isamaa, mu onNJa room" (My Native Land, My Pride and Joy)

lyrics/music: Johann Voldemar JANNSEN/Fredrik PACIUS

note: adopted 1920, though banned between 1940 and 1990 under Soviet occupation; the anthem, used in Estonia since 1869, shares the same melody as Finland's but has different lyrics

ECONOMY

Economy—overview: Estonia, a member of the EUsince 2004 and the eurozone since 2011, has a modern market-based economy and one of the higher per capita income levels in Central Europe and the Baltic region. Estonia's successive governments have pursued a free market, pro-business economic agenda, and sound fiscal policies that have resulted in balanced budgets and low public debt.

The economy benefi ts from strong electronics and telecommunications sectors and strong trade ties with Finland, Sweden, and Germany. After two years of robust recovery in 2011 and 2012, the Estonian economy faltered in 2013 with only 1.6% GDP growth, mainly due to continuing recession in much of the EU. GDP growth in 2014 was 2.9% but dropped to 1.2% in 2015 due to lower demand in key Scandinavian export markets. GDP growth is expected to be about 2.2% in 2016.

Estonia is challenged by a shortage of labor, both skilled and unskilled, although the government has amended its immigration law to allow easier hiring of highly qualified foreign workers.

GDP (purchasing power parity): $37.55 billion (2015 est.)

$37.15 billion (2014 est.)

$36.1 billion (2013 est.)

note: data are in 2015 US dollars

country comparison to the world: 115

GDP (official exchange rate): $22.7 billion (2015 est.)

GDP—real growth rate: 1.1% (2015 est.)

2.9% (2014 est.)

1.6% (2013 est.)

country comparison to the world: 169

GDP—per capita (PPP): $28,600 (2015 est.)

$28,200 (2014 est.)

$27,400 (2013 est.)

note: data are in 2015 US dollars

country comparison to the world: 64

Gross national saving: 25.9% of GDP (2015 est.)

27.5% of GDP (2014 est.)

27.7% of GDP (2013 est.)

country comparison to the world: 44

GDP—composition, by end use: *household consumption:* 50.6%

government consumption: 20.5%

investment in fixed capital: 26.2%

investm entininventories: -0.4%

exports of goods and services: 89.9%

imports of goods and services: -86.8% (2015 est.)

GDP—composition, by sector of origin: *agriculture:* 3.7%

industry: 28.4%

services: 67.9% (2015 est.)

Agriculture—products: grain, potatoes, vegetables; livestock and dairy products; fish

Industries: food, engineering, electronics, wood and wood products, textiles; information technology, telecommunications

Industrial production growth rate: 3.2% (2015 est.)

country comparison to the world: 79

Labor force: 669,400 (2015 est.)

country comparison to the world: 151

Labor force—by occupation: *agriculture:* 3.9%

industry: 28.4%

services: 67.7% (2014)

Unemployment rate: 6.2% (2015 est.) 7.3% (2014 est.)

country comparison to the world: 71

Population below poverty line: 21.6% (2014 est.)

Household income or consumption by percentage share: *lowest:* 10%: 2.7%

highest: 10%: 27.7% (2004)

Distribution of family income—Gini index: 35.6 (2014) 37 (1999)

country comparison to the world: 90

Budget: *revenues:* $8.757 billion

expenditures: $8.734 billion (2015 est.)

Taxes and other revenues: 38.2% of GDP (2015 est.)

country comparison to the world: 46

Budget surplus (+) or deficit (–): 0.1% of GDP (2015 est.)

country comparison to the world: 28

Public debt: 10.2% of GDP (2015 est.)

10.6% of GDP (2014 est.)

note: data cover general government debt, and includes debt instruments issued (or owned) by government entities, in cluding sub-sectors of cen tral government, state government, local govern-ment, and social security funds

country comparison to the world: 167

Fiscal year: calendar year

Inflation rate (consumer prices): 0.1% (2015 est.)

0.5% (2014 est.)

country comparison to the world: 49

Central bank discount rate: 0.05% (31 December 2013) 0.3% (31 December 2012)

country comparison to the world: 144

Commercial bank prime lending rate: 5.1% (31 December 2015 est.)

4.76% (31 December 2014 est.)

country comparison to the world: 144

Stock of narrow money: $10.09 billion (31 December 2015 est.)

$10.19 billion (31 December 2014 est.)

note: see entry for the European Union for money supply for the entire euro area; the European Central Bank (ECB) controls monetary policy for the 18 members of the Economic and Monetary Union (EMU); individual members of the EMU do not control the quantity of money circulating within their own borders

country comparison to the world: 77

Stock of broad money: $14.71 billion (31 December 2014 est.)

$14.05 billion (31 December 2013 est.)

country comparison to the world: 97

Stock of domestic credit: $18.54 billion (31 December 2015 est.)

$20.47 billion (31 December 2014 est.)

country comparison to the world: 87

Market value of publicly traded shares: $2.034 billion (31 December 2014 est.)

$2.591 billion (31 December 2013)

$2.332 billion (31 December 2012 est.)

country comparison to the world: 99

Current account balance: $437 million (2015 est.)

$272 million (2014 est.)

country comparison to the world: 43

Exports: $13.44 billion (2015 est.)

$14.96 billion (2014 est.)

country comparison to the world: 79

Exports—commodities: machinery and electrical equipment 34%, food products and beverages 9%, mineral fuels 9%, wood and wood products 10%, metals 7%, furniture 9%, vehicles and parts 6%, chemicals 5% (2015 est.)

Exports—partners: Sweden 18.8%, Finland 16%, Latvia 10.4%, Russia 6.7%, Lithuania 5.9%, Germany 5.2%, Norway 4.1% (2015)

Imports: $14.43 billion (2015 est.)

$16.39 billion (2014 est.)

country comparison to the world: 87

Imports—commodities: machinery and electrical equipment 28%, mineral fuels 11%, food and food products 10%, vehicles 9%, chemical products 8%, metals 8% (2015 est.)

Imports—partners: Finland 14.5%, Germany 11%, Lithuania 9%, Sweden 8.5%, Latvia 8.3%, Poland 7.4%, Russia 6.1%, Netherlands 5.5%, China 4.8% (2015)

Reserves of foreign exchange and gold: $509.8 million (31 December 2015 est.)

$436.8 million (31 December 2014 est.)

country comparison to the world: 149

Debt—external: $22.95 billion (31 December 2014 est.)

$24.15 billion (31 December 2013 est.)

country comparison to the world: 84

Stock of direct foreign investment—at home: $26.34 billion (31 December 2015 est.)

$24.99 billion (31 December 2014 est.)

country comparison to the world: 74

Stock of direct foreign investment—abroad: $9.262 billion (31 December 2015 est.)

$9.012 billion (31 December 2014 est.)

country comparison to the world: 61

Exchange rates: kroon (EEK) per US dollar— 0.9227 (2015 est.)

0.7525 (2014 est.)

0.7525 (2013 est.)

0.72 (2011 est.)

ENERGY

Electricity—production: 12.44 billion kWh (2014 est.)

country comparison to the world: 91

Electricity—consumption: 7.417 billion kWh (2014 est.)

country comparison to the world: 101

Electricity—exports: 6.484 billion kWh (2014 est.)

country comparison to the world: 27

Electricity—imports: 3.73 billion kWh (2014 est.)

country comparison to the world: 48

Electricity—installed generating capacity: 3.138 million kW (2014 est.)

country comparison to the world: 93

Electricity—from fossil fuels: 87% of total installed capacity (2014 est.)

country comparison to the world: 84

Electricity—from nuclear fuels: 0% of total installed capacity (2014 est.)

country comparison to the world: 86

Electricity—from hydroelectric plants: 0.2% of total installed capacity (2014 est.)

country comparison to the world: 151

Electricity—from other renewable sources: 12% of total installed capacity (2014 est.)

country comparison to the world: 28

Crude oil—production: 0 bbl/day (2014 est.)

country comparison to the world: 129

Crude oil—exports: 11,680 bbl/day (2013 est.)

country comparison to the world: 64

Crude oil—imports: 0 bbl/day (2013 est.)

country comparison to the world: 185

Crude oil—proved reserves: 0 bbl (1 January 2015 est.)

country comparison to the world: 128

Refined petroleum products—production: 0 bbl/day (2013 est.)

country comparison to the world: 177

Refined petroleum products—consumption: 32,100 bbl/day (2014 est.)

country comparison to the world: 114

Refined petroleum products—exports: 6,738 bbl/day (2013 est.)

country comparison to the world: 91

Refined petroleum products—imports: 31,140 bbl/day (2013 est.)

country comparison to the world: 96

Natural gas—production: 0 cu m (2015 est.)

country comparison to the world: 181

Natural gas—consumption: 530 million cu m (2014 est.)

country comparison to the world: 96

Natural gas—exports: 0 cu m (2015 est.)

country comparison to the world: 93

Natural gas—imports: 530 million cu m (2014 est.)

country comparison to the world: 64

Natural gas—proved reserves: 0 cu m (1 January 2014 est.)

country comparison to the world: 133

Carbon dioxide emissions from consumption of energy: 5.686 million Mt (2012 est.)

country comparison to the world: 122

COMMUNICATIONS

Telephones—fixed lines: *total subscriptions:* 410,000

subscriptions per 100 inhabitants: 32 (2014 est.)

country comparison to the world: 103

Telephones—mobile cellular: *total:* 2.1 million

subscriptions per 100 inhabitants: 162 (2014 est.)

country comparison to the world: 150

Telephone system: *general assessment:* foreign investment in the form of joint business ventures greatly improved telephone service with a wide range of high-quality voice, data, and Internet services available

domestic: substantial fiber-optic cable systems carry telephone, TV, and radio traffic in the digital mode; Internet services are widely available; schools and libraries are connected to the Internet, a large percentage of the population files income tax returns online, and online voting was used for the first time in the 2005 local elections

international: country code—372; fiber-optic cables to Finland, Sweden, Latvia, and Russia provide worldwide packet-switched service; 2 international switches are located in Tallinn (2011)

Broadcast media: the publicly owned broadcaster, Eesti Rahvusringhaaling (ERR), operates 2 TV channels and 5 radio networks; growing number of private commercial radio stations broadcasting nationally, regionally, and locally; fully transitioned to digital television in 2010; national private TV channels expanding service; a range of channels are aimed at Russian-speaking viewers; high penetration rate for cable TV services with more than half of Estonian households connected (2008)

Radio broadcast stations: AM 0, FM 34, shortwave 0 (2009)

Television broadcast stations: 15 (2008)

Internet country code: .ee

Internet hosts: 865,494 (2012)

country comparison to the world: 49

Internet users: *total:* 1 million

percent of population: 81.6% (2014 est.)

country comparison to the world: 122

TRANSPORTATION

Airports: 18 (2013)

country comparison to the world: 141

Airports—with paved runways: *total:* 13

over 3,047 m: 2

2,438 to 3,047 m: 8

1,524 to 2,437 m: 2

914 to 1,523 m: 1 (2013)

Airports—with unpaved runways: *total:* 5

1,524 to 2,437 m: 1

914 to 1,523 m: 1

under 914 m: 3 (2013)

Heliports: 1 (2012)

Pipelines: gas 868 km (2013)

Railways: *total:* 1,196 km

broad gauge: 1,196 km 1.520-m and 1.524-m gauge (133 km electrified)

note: includes 277 km of private rail (2014)

country comparison to the world: 85

Roadways: *total:* 58,412 km (includes urban roads)

paved: 10,427 km (includes 115 km of expressways)

unpaved: 47,985 km (2011)

country comparison to the world: 72

Waterways: 335 km (320 km are navigable year round) (2011)

country comparison to the world: 90

Merchant marine: *total:* 25

by type: cargo 4, chemical tanker 1, passenger/cargo 18, petroleum tanker 2

foreign-owned: 3 (Germany 1, Norway 2)

registered in other countries: 63 (Antigua and Barbuda 10, Belize 1, Cambodia 1, Canada 1, Cook Islands 1, Cyprus 6, Dominica 6, Finland 2, Latvia 3, Malta 16, Russia 1, Saint Vincent and the Grenadines 8, Sierra Leone 2, Sweden 3, Venezuela 1, unknown 1) (2010)

country comparison to the world: 89

Ports and terminals: *major seaport(s):* Kuivastu, Kunda, Muuga, Parnu Reid, Sillamae, Tallinn

MILITARY AND SECURITY

Military branches: Estonian Defense Forces (Eesti Kaitsevagi): Land Force (Maavagi), Navy (Merevagi), Air Force (Ohuvagi), Defense League (Kaitseliit) (2012)

Military service age and obligation: 18–27 for compulsory military or governmental service, conscript service requirement 8–11 months depending on education; NCOs, reserve officers, and specialists serve 11 months (2013)

Military *expenditures:* 2% of GDP (2015)

2% of GDP (2014)

2% of GDP (2013)

1.92% of GDP (2012)

1.69% of GDP (2011)
1.92% of GDP (2010)
country comparison to the world: 39

TRANSNATIONAL ISSUES

Disputes—internationan: Russia and Estonia in May 2005 signed a technical border agreement, but Russia in June2005 recalled its signature after the Estonian parliament added to its domestic ratification act a historical preamble referencing the Soviet occupation and Estonia's pre-war borders under the 1920 Treaty of Tartu; Russia contends that the preamble allows Estonia to make territorial claims on Russia in the future, while Estonian officials deny that the preamble has any legal

impact on the treaty text; Russia demands better treatment of the Russian-speaking population in Estonia; as a member state that forms part of the EU's external border, Estonia implements strict Schengen border rules with Russia

Refugees and internally displaced persons: *stateless persons:* 85,301 (2015); note—following independence in 1991, automatic citizenship was restricted to those who were Estonian citizens prior to the 1940 Soviet occupation and their descendants; thousands of ethnic Russians remained stateless when forced to choose between passing Estonian language and citizenship tests or applying for Russian citizenship; one reason for demurring on Estonian citizenship was to retain the right of

visa-free travel to Russia; stateless residents can vote in local elections but not general elections; stateless parents who have been lawful residents of Estonia for at least five years can apply for citizenship for their children before they turn 15 years old

Illicit drugs: growing producer of synthetic drugs; increasingly important transshipment zone for cannabis, cocaine, opiates, and synthetic drugs since joining the European Union and the Schengen Accord; potential money laundering related to organized crime and drug trafficking is a concern, as is possible use of the gambling sector to launder funds; major use of opiates and ecstasy

ETHIOPIA

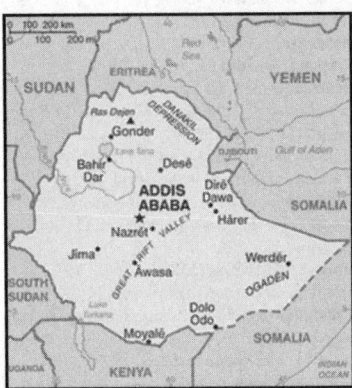

INTRODUCTION

Background: Unique among African countries, the ancient Ethiopian monarchy maintained its freedom from colonial rule with the exception of a short-lived Italian occupation from 1936–41. In 1974, a military junta, the Derg, deposed Emperor Haile SELASSIE (who had ruled since 1930) and established a socialist state. Torn by bloody coups, uprisings, wide-scale drought, and massive refugee problems, the regime was finally toppled in 1991 by a coalition of rebel forces, the Ethiopian People's Revolutionary Democratic Front. A constitution was adopted in 1994, and Ethiopia's first multiparty elections were held in 1995. A border war with Eritrea in the late 1990s ended with a peace treaty in December 2000. In November 2007, the Eritrea-Ethiopia Border Commission (EEBC) issued specific coordinates as virtually demarcating the border and pronounced its work finished. Alleging that the EEBC acted beyond its mandate in issuing the coordinates, Ethiopia has not accepted them and has not withdrawn troops from previously contested areas pronounced by the EEBC as belonging to Eritrea. In August 2012, longtime leader Prime Minister MELES Zenawi died in office and was replaced

by his Deputy Prime Minister HAILEMARIAM Desalegn, marking the first peaceful transition of power in decades.

GEOGRAPHY

Location: Eastern Africa, west of Somalia
Geographic coordinates: 800 N, 3800 E
Map references: Africa
Area: *total:* 1,104,300 sq km
land: 1 million sq km
water: 104,300 sq km
country comparison to the world: 27
Area—comparative: slightly less than twice the size of Texas
Land boundaries: *total:* 5,925 km
border countries (6): Djibouti 342 km, Eritrea 1,033 km, Kenya 867 km, Somalia 1,640 km, South Sudan 1,299 km, Sudan 744 km
Coastline: 0 km (landlocked)
Maritime claims: none (landlocked)
Climate: tropical monsoon with wide topographic-induced variation
Terrain: high plateau with central mountain range divided by Great Rift Valley
Elevation: *mean elevation:* 1,330 m
elevation extremes: *lowest point:* Danakil Depression -125 m
highest point: Ras Dejen 4,533 m
Natural resources: small reserves of gold, platinum, copper, potash, natural gas, hydropower
Land use: *agricultural land:* 36.3%
arable land: 15.2%;
permanent crops: 1.1%;
permanent pasture: 20%
forest: 12.2%
other: 51.5% (2011 est.)
Irrigated land: 2,900 sq km (2012)
Total renewable water resources: 122 cu km (2011)
Freshwater withdrawal (domestic/industrial/agricultural): *total:* 5.56 cu km/yr (13%/1%/86%)
per capita: 80.5 cu m/yr (2005)

Natural hazards: geologically active Great Rift Valley susceptible to earthquakes, volcanic eruptions; frequent droughts
volcanism: volcanic activity in the Great Rift Valley; Erta Ale (elev.613 m), which has caused frequent lava flows in recent years, is the country's most active volcano; Dabbahu became active in 2005, forcing evacuations; other historically active volcanoes include Alayta, Dalaffilla, Dallol, Dama Ali, Fentale, Kone, Manda Hararo, and Manda-Inakir
Environment—current issues: deforestation; overgrazing; soil erosion; desertification; water shortages in some areas from water-intensive farming and poor management
Environment—international agreements: *party to:* Biodiversity, Climate Change, Climate Change-Kyoto Protocol, Desertification, Endangered Species, Hazardous Wastes, Ozone Layer Protection
signed, but not ratified: Environmental Modification, Law of the Sea
Geography—note: landlocked—entire coastline along the Red Sea was lost with the de jure independence of Eritrea on 24 May 1993; Ethiopia is, therefore, the most populous landlocked country in the world; the Blue Nile, the chief headstream of the Nile by water volume, rises in T'ana Hayk (Lake Tana) in northwest Ethiopia; three major crops are believed to have originated in Ethiopia: coffee, grain sorghum, and castor bean

PEOPLE AND SOCIETY

Nationality: *noun:* Ethiopian(s)
adjective: Ethiopian
Ethnic groups: Oromo 34.4%, Amhara (Amara) 27%, Somali (Somalie) 6.2%, Tigray (Tigrinya) 6.1%, Sidama 4%, Gurage 2.5%, Welaita 2.3%, Hadiya 1.7%, Afar (Affar) 1.7%, Gamo 1.5%, Gedeo 1.3%, Silte 1.3%, Keficho 1.2%, other 8.8% (2007 est.)
Languages: Oromo (official working language in the State of Oromiya) 33.8%, Amharic (official national language) 29.3%, Somali (official working language of the State of Sumale) 6.2%, Tigrigna (Tigrinya) (official working language of

the State of Tigray) 5.9%, Sidamo 4%, Wolaytta 2.2%, Gurage 2%, Afar (official working language of the State of Afar) 1.7%, Hadiyya 1.7%, Gamo 1.5%, Gedeo 1.3%, Opuuo 1.2%, Kafa 1.1%, other 8.1%, English (major foreign language taught in schools), Arabic (2007 est.)

Religions: EthiopiaNorthodox 43.5%, Muslim 33.9%, Protestant 18.5%, traditional 2.7%, Catholic 0.7%, other 0.6% (2007 est.)

Population: 99,465,819

note: estimates for this country explicitly take into account the effects of excess mortality due to AIDS; this can result in lower life expectancy, higher infant mortality, higher death rates, lower population growth rates, and changes in the distribution of population by age and sex than would otherwise be expected (July 2015 est.)

country comparison to the world: 14

Age structure: *0–14 years:* 43.94% (male 21,900,571/female 21,809,643)

15–24 years: 19.98% (male 9,865,976/female 10,009,596)

25–54 years: 29.31% (male 14,487,280/female 14,667,179)

55–64 years: 3.88% (male 1,882,315/female 1,981,762)

65 years and over: 2.88% (male 1,289,336/female 1,572,161) (2015 est.)

Dependency ratios: *total dependency ratio:* 81.6%

youth dependency ratio: 75.2%

elderly dependency ratio: 6.3%

potential support ratio: 15.8% (2015 est.)

Median age: *total:* 17.7 years

male: 17.5 years

female: 17.8 years (2015 est.)

country comparison to the world: 218

Population growth rate: 2.89% (2015 est.)

country comparison to the world: 10

Birth rate: 37.27 births/1,000 population (2015 est.)

country comparison to the world: 13

Death rate: 8.19 deaths/1,000 population (2015 est.)

country comparison to the world: 90

Net migration rate: -0.22 migrant(s)/1,000 population (2015 est.)

country comparison to the world: 119

Urbanization: *urban population:* 19.5% of total population (2015)

rate of urbanization: 4.89% annual rate of change (2010–15 est.)

Major urban areas—population: ADDIS ABABA (capital) 3.238 million (2015)

Sex ratio: *at birth:* 1.03 male(s)/female

0–14 years: 1 male(s)/female

15–24 years: 0.99 male(s)/female

25–54 years: 0.99 male(s)/female

55–64 years: 0.95 male(s)/female

65 years and over: 0.82 male(s)/female

total population: 0.99 male(s)/female (2015 est.)

Mother's mean age at first birth: 19.6

note: median age at first birth among women 25–29 (2011 est.)

Maternal mortality rate: 353 deaths/100,000 live births (2015 est.)

country comparison to the world: 33

Infant mortality rate: *total:* 53.37 deaths/1,000 live births

male: 61.08 deaths/1,000 live births

female: 45.43 deaths/1,000 live births (2015 est.)

country comparison to the world: 31

Life expectancy at birth: *total population:* 61.48 years

male: 59.11 years

female: 63.93 years (2015 est.)

country comparison to the world: 193

Total fertility rate: 5.15 children born/woman (2015 est.)

country comparison to the world: 14

Contraceptive prevalence rate: 28.6% (2010/11)

Health expenditures: 5.1% of GDP (2013)

country comparison to the world: 166

Physicians density: 0.03 physicians/1,000 population (2009)

Hospital bed density: 6.3 beds/1,000 population (2011)

Drinking water source: improved:

urban: 93.1% of population

rural: 48.6% of population

total: 57.3% of population

unimproved:

urban: 6.9% of population

rural: 51.4% of population

total: 42.7% of population (2015 est.)

Sanitation facility access: improved:

urban: 27.2% of population

rural: 28.2% of population

total: 28% of population

unimproved:

urban: 72.8% of population

rural: 71.8% of population

total: 72% of population (2015 est.)

HIV/AIDS—adult prevalence rate: 1.15% (2014 est.)

country comparison to the world: 40

HIV/AIDS—people living with HIV/AIDS: 730,300 (2014 est.)

country comparison to the world: 12

HIV/AIDS—deaths: 23,400 (2014 est.)

country comparison to the world: 13

Major infectious diseases: *degree of risk:* very high

food or waterborne diseases: bacterial and protozoal diarrhea, hepatitis A, and typhoid fever

vectorb orne diseases: malaria and den gue fever

respiratory disease: menin gococcal men in gitis

animal contact disease: rabies

water contact disease: schistosomiasis (2013)

Obesity—adult prevalence rate: 3.3% (2014)

country comparison to the world: 191

Children under the age of 5 years underweight: 25.2% (2014)

country comparison to the world: 15

Education expenditures: 4.5% of GDP (2013)

country comparison to the world: 85

Literacy: *definition:* age 15 and over can read and write

total population: 49.1%

male: 57.2%

female: 41.1% (2015 est.)

School life expectancy (primary to tertiary education): *total:* 8 years

male: 9 years

female: 8 years (2012)

Child labor—children ages 5–14: *total number:* 10,693,164

percentage: 53% (2005 est.)

Unemployment, youth ages 15–24: *total:* 7.3%

male: 5%

female: 9.6% (2013 est.)

country comparison to the world: 36

GOVERNMENT

Country name: *conventional long form:* Federal Democratic Republic of Ethiopia

conventional short form: Ethiopia

local long form: Ityop'iya Federalawi Demokrasiyawi Ripeblik

local short form: Ityop'iya

former: Abyssinia, Italian East Africa

abbrevi ation: FDRE

etymology: the country name derives from the Greek word "Aethiopia, "which in classical times referred to lands south of Egypt in the Upper Nile region

Government type: federal parliamentary republic

Capital: *name:* Addis Ababa

Geographic coordinates: 902 N, 3842 E

time difference: UTC+3 (8 hours ahead of Washington, DC, during Standard Time)

Administrative divisions: 9 ethnically based states (kililoch, singular—kilil) and 2 self-governing administrations* (astedaderoch, singular—astedader); Adis Abeba* (Addis Ababa), Afar, Amara (Amhara), Binshangul Gumuz, Dire Dawa*, Gambela Hizboch (Gambela Peoples), Hareri Hizb (Harari People), Oromiya (Oromia), Sumale (Somali), Tigray, Ye Debub Biheroch Bihereseboch na Hizboch (Southern Nations, Nationalities, and Peoples)

Independence: oldest independent country in Africa and one of the oldest in the world—at least 2,000 years (may be traced to the Aksumite Kingdom, which coalesced in the first century B.C.)

National holiday: National Day (defeat of MENGISTU regime), 28 May (1991)

Constitution: several previous; latest drafted June 1994, adopted 8 December 1994, entered into force 21 August 1995 (2016)

Legal system: civil law system

International law organization participation: has not submitted an ICJ jurisdiction declaration; non-party state to the ICCt

Citizenship: *citizenship by birth:* no

citizenship by descent only: at least one parent must be a citizen of Ethiopia

dual citizenship recognized: no

residency requirement for naturalization: 4 years

Suffrage: 18 years of age; universal

Executive branch: *chief of state:* President MULATU Teshome Wirtu (since 7 October 2013)

head of government: Prime Minister HAILEMARIAM Desalegn (since 21 September 2012);

Deputy Prime Ministers DEMEKE Mekonnen Hassen and DEBRETSION Gebre-Michael

cabinet: Council of Ministers selected by the prime minister and approved by the House of People's Representatives

elections/appointments: president indirectly elected by both chambers of Parliament for a 6-year term (eligible for a second term); election last held on 7 October 2013 (next to be held in October 2019); prime minister designated by the majority party following legislative elections

election results: MULATU Teshome Wirtu (OPDO) elected president by acclamation

Legislative branch: bicameral Parliament consists of the House of Federation or Yefedereshein Mikir Bete (108 seats; members indirectly elected by state assemblies to serve 5-year terms) and the House of People's Representatives or Yehizb Tewokayoch Mekir Bete (547 seats; members directly elected in single-seat constituencies by simple majority vote to serve 5-year terms; note—the House of Federation is responsible for interpreting the constitution and federal-regional issues and the House of People's Representatives is responsible for passing legislation

elections: last held on 24 May 2015 (next to be held in 2020)

election results: House of Representatives percent of vote—NA; seats by party—EPRDF 500, SPDP 24, BGPDP 9, ANDP 8, GPUDM 3, APDO 1, HNL 1, independent 1

Judicial branch: *highest court(s):* Federal Supreme Court or Supreme Imperial Court (consists of 11 judges); note—the Federal Supreme Court has jurisdiction for all constitutional issues

judge selection and term of office: president and vice president of Federal Supreme Court nominated by the prime minister and appointed by the House of People's Representatives; other Supreme Court judges nominated by the Federal Judicial Administrative Council and appointed by the House of People's Representatives; judges serve until retirement at age 60

subordinate court(s): federal high courts and federal courts of first instance; state court systems (mirror structure of federal system); sharia courts and customary and traditional courts

Political parties and leaders: Afar National Democratic Party or ANDP [Mohammed KEDIR]

Argoba People's Democratic Organization or APDO

Benishangul Gumuz People's Democratic Party or BGPDP Blue Party (Semayawi Party) [Yanatan TESFAYE, spokesman]

Ethiopian Federal Democratic Forum or FORUM [Dr. Moga FRISSA] (a UDJ-led 6-party alliance established for the 2010 parliamentary elections)

Ethiopian People's Revolutionary Democratic Front or EPRDF [Hailemarian DESALEGN] (including the following organizations: Amhara National Democratic Movement or ANDM; Oromo People's Democratic Organization or OPDO; Southern Ethiopian People's Democratic Movement or SEPDM; Tigray People's Liberation Front or TPLF)

Gambella Peoples Unity Democratic Movement or GPUDMH arari National League or HNL [YASIN Husein] Somali People's Democratic Party or SPDP

Political pressure groups and leaders: Ethiopian People's Patriotic Front or EPPF Ogaden National Liberation Front or ONLF Oromo Liberation Front or OLF [DAOUD Ibsa]

International organization participation: ACP, AfDB, AU, COMESA, EITI (candidate country), FAO, G-24, G-77, IAEA, IBRD, ICAO, ICRM, IDA, IFAD, IFC, IFRCS, IGAD, ILO, IMF, IMO, Interpol, IOC, IOM, IPU, ISO, ITSO, ITU, ITUC (NGOs), MIGA, NAM, OPCW, PCA, UN, UNAMID, UNCTAD, UNESCO, UNHCR, UNIDO, UNISFA, UNMIL, UNOCI, UNWTO, UPU, WCO, WFTU (NGOs), WHO, WIPO, WMO, WTO (observer)

Diplomatic representation in the US: *chief of mission:* Ambassador GIRMA Birru Geda (since 6 January 2011)

chancery: 3506 International Drive NW, Washington, DC 20008

telephone: [1] (202) 364–1200

FAX: [1] (202) 587–0195

consulate(s) general: Los Angeles, Seattle

consulate(s): Houston, New York

Diplomatic representation from the US: *chief of mission:* Ambassador Patricia Marie HASLACH (since 25 September 2013)

embassy: Entoto Street, Addis Ababa

mailing address: P.O . Box 1014, Addis Ababa

telephone: 130-6000

FAX: 124-2401 130-6000

Flag description: three equal horizontal bands of green (top), yellow, and red, with a yellow pentagram and single yellow rays emanating from the angles between the points on a light blue disk centered on the three bands; green represents hope and the fertility of the land, yellow symbolizes justice and harmony, while red stands for sacrifice and heroism in the defense of the land; the blue of the disk symbolizes peace and the pentagram represents the unity and equality of the nationalities and peoples of Ethiopia

note: Ethiopia is the oldest independent country in Africa, and the three main colors of her flag (adopted ca.1895) were so often appropriated by other African countries upon independence that they became known as the Pan-African colors; the emblem in the center of the current flag was added in 1996

National symbol(s): Abyssinian lion (traditional), yellow pentagram with five rays of light on a blue field (promoted by current government); national colors: green, yellow, red

National anthem: *name:* "Whedefit Gesgeshi Woud Enat Ethiopia" (March Forward, Dear Mother Ethiopia)

lyrics/music: DEREJE Melaku Mengesha/SOLOMON Lulu

note: adopted 1992

ECONOMY

Economy—overview: Ethiopia has grown at a rate between 8% and 11% annually for more than a decade and the country is the fifth-fastest growing economy among the 188 IMF member countries. This growth has been driven by sustained progress in the agricultural and service sectors. Ethiopia has

the lowest level of income-inequality in Africa and one of the lowest in the world, with a Gini coefficient comparable to that of the Scandanavian countries. Yet despite progress toward eliminating extreme poverty, Ethiopia remains one of the poorest countries in the world, due both to rapid population growth and a low starting base. Changes in rainfall associated with world-wide weather patterns resulted in the worst drought in thirty years in 2015/2016, creating food insecurity for millions of Ethiopians.

Almost 80% of Ethiopia's population is still employed in the agricultural sector, but services have surpassed agriculture as the principal source of GDP. Under Ethiopia's constitution, the state owns all land and provides long-term leases to tenants. Since 2005, the Ethiopian government has introduced a system to register traditional land use rights and provide certificates documenting these rights. Initial surveys show that land-use certificates have significantly increased the willingness of farmers to invest in improvements on their land, from terracing to irrigation. However, title rights in urban areas, particularly Addis Ababa, are poorly regulated, and subject to corruption.

Ethiopia's export earnings are led by the services sector—primarily Ethiopian airlines—followed by several commodities. While coffee remains the largest foreign exchange earner, Ethiopia is diversifying exports and commodities suchas gold, sesame, khat, livestock and horticulture products are becoming increasingly important. Manufacturing represents less than 8% of total exports. The banking, insurance, telecommunications, and micro-credit industries are restricted to domestic investors, but Ethiopia has attracted significant foreign investment in textiles, leather, commercial agriculture, and light manufacturing. Ethiopia remains a one-party state with a planned economy. In the fall of 2015, the government finalized and published the current 2016–2020 five year plan, known as the Growth and Transformation Plan (GTP II). GTP II emphasizes developing manufactures in sectors where Ethiopia has a comparative advantage in exporting, including textiles and garments, leather goods, and processed agricultural products. New infrastructure projects are to include power production and distribution, roads, rails, airports and industrial parks. To support industrialization, Ethiopia plans to increase power generation by 8,320 MW, up from an installed capacity of 2,000 MW, by building three more major dams and expanding to other sources of renewable energy. Construction is underway on an electric railway network that will connect Ethiopia to all its neighbors, with a link to the Port of Djibouti already finished and partially functioning. A tripling of capacity at the international airport in Addis Ababa to 25 million passengers will be completed in 2017, while construction of a completely new airport is being planned by 2025. Meanwhile, the domestic airport network has expanded to nineteen airports in a country where mountains and deserts make developing and maintaining a road network challenging. Despite difficult topography, more than a hundred thousand kilometers of roads have been built, connecting previously isolated regions.

GDP (purchasing power parity): $161.6 billion (2015 est.)
$146.7 billion (2014 est.)
$133 billion (2013 est.)
note: data are in 2015 US dollars
country comparison to the world: 72
GDP (official exchange rate): $61.63 billion (2015 est.)
GDP—real growth rate: 10.2% (2015 est.)
10.3% (2014 est.)
9.9% (2013 est.)
country comparison to the world: 2
GDP—per capita (PPP): $1,800 (2015 est.)
$1,700 (2014 est.)
$1,500 (2013 est.)
note: data are in 2015 US dollars
country comparison to the world: 208
Gross national saving: 27% of GDP (2015 est.)
26.7% of GDP (2014 est.)
28.1% of GDP (2013 est.)
country comparison to the world: 39
GDP—composition, by end use:
household consumption: 68.6%
government consumption: 8.3%
investment in fixed capital: 39%
investment in inventories: 0%
exports of goods and services: 10.3%
imports of goods and services: -26.2% (2015 est.)
GDP—composition, by sector of origin:
agriculture: 41.4%
industry: 15.6%
services: 43% (2015 est.)
Agriculture—products: cereals, coffee, oilseed, cotton, sugarcane, vegetables, khat, cut flowers; hides, cattle, sheep, goats; fish
Industries: food processing, beverages, textiles, leather, garments, chemicals, metals processing, cement
Industrial production growth rate: 8.5% (2015 est.)
country comparison to the world: 14
Labor force: 49.27 million (2015 est.)
country comparison to the world: 14
Labor force—by occupation: *agriculture:* 85%
industry: 5%
services: 10% (2009 est.)
Unemployment rate: 17.5% (2012 est.)
18% (2011 est.)
country comparison to the world: 161
Population below poverty line: 29.6% (2014 est.)
Household income or consumption by percentage share: *lowest:* 10%: 4.1%
highest: 10%: 25.6% (2005)
Distribution of family income—Gini index: 33 (2011) 30 (2000)
country comparison to the world: 105
Budget: *revenues:* $9.114 billion
expenditures: $11 billion (2015 est.)
Taxes and other revenues: 15.8% of GDP (2015 est.)
country comparison to the world: 187
Budget surplus (+) or deficit (–): -3.3% of GDP (2015 est.)
country comparison to the world: 124
Public debt: 45.8% of GDP (2015 est.)

47.5% of GDP (2014 est.)
note: official data cover central government debt, including debt instruments issued (or owned) by government entities other than the treasury and treasury debt owned by foreign entities; the data exclude debt issued by subnational entities, as well as intragovernmental debt; debt instruments for the social funds are not sold at public auctions
country comparison to the world: 96
Fiscal year: 8 July—7 July
Inflation rate (consumer prices): 10.1% (2015 est.)
7.4% (2014 est.)
country comparison to the world: 211
Central bank discount rate: NA%
Commercial bank prime lending rate: 11.5% (31 December 2015 est.)
11% (31 December 2014 est.)
country comparison to the world: 71
Stock of narrow money: $11.53 billion (31 December 2015 est.)
$9.981 billion (31 December 2014 est.)
country comparison to the world: 75
Stock of broad money: $23.77 billion (31 December 2015 est.)
$20.75 billion (31 December 2014 est.)
country comparison to the world: 84
Stock of domestic credit: $27.75 billion (31 December 2015 est.)
$22.58 billion (31 December 2014 est.)
country comparison to the world: 77
Market value of publicly traded shares: $NA
Current account balance: -$7.893 billion (2015 est.) -$4.407 billion (2014 est.)
country comparison to the world: 175
Exports: $3.761 billion (2015 est.)
$3.721 billion (2014 est.)
country comparison to the world: 123
Exports—commodities: coffee (27%, by value), oilseeds (17%), edible vegetables including khat (17%), gold (13%), flowers (7%), live animals (7%), raw leather products (3%), meat products (3%)
Exports—partners: Switzerland 14.3%, China 11.7%, US 9.5%, Netherlands 8.8%, Saudi Arabia 5.9%, Germany 5.7% (2015)
Imports: $10.69 billion (2015 est.)
$11.57 billion (2014 est.)
country comparison to the world: 95
Imports—commodities: machinery and aircraft (14%, by value), metal and metal products, (14%), electrical materials, (13%), petroleum products (12%), motor vehicles, (10%), chemicals and fertilizers (4%)
Imports—partners: China 20.4%, US 9.2%, Saudi Arabia 6.5%, India 4.5% (2015)
Reserves of foreign exchange and gold: $3.589 billion (31 December 2015 est.)
$3.483 billion (31 December 2014 est.)
country comparison to the world: 103
Debt—external: $15.55 billion (31 December 2014 est.)
$12.56 billion (31 December 2013 est.)
country comparison to the world: 95
Exchange rates: birr (ETB) per US dollar—
21.55 (2015 est.)

19.8 (2014 est.)
19.8 (2013 est.)
17.71 (2012 est.)
16.899 (2011 est.)

ENERGY

Electricity—production: 6.632 billion kWh (2012 est.)
country comparison to the world: 111
Electricity—consumption: 5.227 billion kWh (2012 est.)
country comparison to the world: 114
Electricity—exports: 400 million kWh (2012 est.)
country comparison to the world: 72
Electricity—imports: 0 kWh (2013 est.)
country comparison to the world: 146
Electricity—installed generating capacity: 2.47 million kW (2012 est.)
country comparison to the world: 99
Electricity—from fossil fuels: 8.3% of total installed capacity (2012 est.)
country comparison to the world: 201
Electricity—from nuclear fuels: 0% of total installed capacity (2012 est.)
country comparison to the world: 89
Electricity—from hydroelectric plants: 88.2% of total installed capacity (2012 est.)
country comparison to the world: 14
Electricity—from other renewable sources: 3.6% of total installed capacity (2012 est.)
country comparison to the world: 66
Crude oil—production: 0 bbl/day (2014 est.)
country comparison to the world: 132
Crude oil—exports: 0 bbl/day (2012 est.)
country comparison to the world: 121
Crude oil—imports: 0 bbl/day (2012 est.)
country comparison to the world: 187
Crude oil—proved reserves: 430,000 bbl (1 January 2015 est.)
country comparison to the world: 101
Refined petroleum products—production: 0 bbl/day (2012 est.)
country comparison to the world: 179
Refined petroleum products—consumption: 51,000 bbl/day (2013 est.)
country comparison to the world: 98
Refined petroleum products—exports: 0 bbl/day (2012 est.)
country comparison to the world: 179
Refined petroleum products—imports: 51,960 bbl/day (2012 est.)
country comparison to the world: 79
Natural gas—production: 0 cu m (2013 est.)
country comparison to the world: 184
Natural gas—consumption: 0 cu m (2013 est.)
country comparison to the world: 141
Natural gas—exports: 0 cu m (2013 est.)
country comparison to the world: 96
Natural gas—imports: 0 cu m (2013 est.)
country comparison to the world: 194
Natural gas—proved reserves: 24.92 billion cu m (1 January 2014 est.)
country comparison to the world: 73
Carbon dioxide emissions from consumption of energy: 8.213 million Mt (2012 est.)
country comparison to the world: 109

281

COMMUNICATIONS

Telephones—fixed lines: *total subscriptions:* 820,000
subscriptions per 100 inhabitants: 1 (2014 est.)
country comparison to the world: 87
Telephones—mobile cellular: *total:* 30.5 million
subscriptions per 100 inhabitants: 32 (2014 est.)
country comparison to the world: 41
Telephone system: *general assessment:* inadequate telephone system with the Ethio Telecom maintaining a monopoly over telecommunication services; open-wire, microwave radio relay; radio communication in the HF, VHF, and UHF frequencies; 2 domestic satellites provide the national trunk service
domestic: the number of fixed lines and mobile telephones is increasing from a small base; combined fixed-line and mobile-cellular teledensity is roughly 15 per 100 persons
international: country code—251; open-wire to Sudan and Djibouti; microwave radio relay to Kenya and Djibouti; satellite earth stations—3 Intelsat (1 Atlantic Ocean and 2 Pacific Ocean) (2011)
Broadcast media: 6 public TV stations broadcasting nationally and 10 public radio broadcasters; 7 private radio stations and 18 commun ity radio stations (2015)
Radio broadcast stations: AM 8, FM 0, shortwave 1 (2001)
Television broadcast stations: 1 (plus 24 repeaters) (2001)
Internet country code: .et
Internet hosts: 179 (2012)
country comparison to the world: 203
Internet users: *total:* 1.6 million
percent of population: 1.7% (2014 est.)
country comparison to the world: 107

TRANSPORTATION

Airports: 57 (2013)

country comparison to the world: 83
Airports—with paved runways: *total:* 17
over 3,047 m: 3
2,438 to 3,047 m: 8
1,524 to 2,437 m: 4
under 914 m: 2 (2013)
Airports—with unpaved runways: *total:* 40
2,438 to 3,047 m: 3
1,524 to 2,437 m: 9
914 to 1,523 m: 20
under 914 m: 8 (2013)
Railways: *total:* 681 km (Ethiopian segment of the 781 km Addis Ababa-Djibouti railroad)
narrow gauge: 681 km 1.000-m gauge
note: railway is under joint control of Djibouti and Ethiopia (2015)
country comparison to the world: 102
Roadways: *total:* 110,414 km
paved: 14,354 km
unpaved: 96,060 km (2015)
country comparison to the world: 78
Merchant marine: *total:* 8
by type: cargo 8 (2010)
country comparison to the world: 121
Ports and terminals: Ethiopia is landlocked and uses the ports of Djibouti in Djibouti and Berbera in Somalia

MILITARY AND SECURITY

Military branches: Ethiopian National Defense Force (ENDF): Ground Forces, Ethiopian Air Force (Ye Ityopya Ayer Hayl, ETAF) (2013)
Military service age and obligation: 18 years of age for voluntary military service; no compulsory military service, but the military can conduct callups when necessary and compliance is compulsory (2012)
Military expenditures: 0.91% of GDP (2012)
1.1% of GDP (2011)
0.91% of GDP (2010)
country comparison to the world: 107

TRANSNATIONAL ISSUES

Disputes—international: Eritrea and Ethiopia agreed to abide by the 2002 Eritrea-Ethiopia Boundary Commission's (EEBC) delimitation decision, but neither party responded to the revised line detailed in the November 2006 EEBC Demarcation Statement; the undemarcated former British administrative line has little meaning as a political separation to rival clans within Ethiopia's Ogaden and southern Somalia's Oromo region; Ethiopian forces invaded southern Somalia and routed Islamist courts from Mogadishu in January 2007; "Somaliland" secessionists provide port facilities in Berbera and trade ties to landlocked Ethiopia; civil unrest in eastern Sudan has hampered efforts to demarcate the porous boundary with Ethiopia
Refugees and internally displaced persons: *refugees (country of origin):* 286,001 (South Sudan) (refugees and asylum seekers); 250,988 (Somalia) (refugees and asylum seekers); 155,276 (Eritrea) (refugees and asylum seekers); 37,959 (Sudan) (refugees and asylum seekers) (2016)
IDPs: 450,000 (border war with Eritrea from 1998–2000; ethnic clashes; and ongoing fighting between the Ethiopian military and separatist rebel groups in the Sumale and Oromiya regions; natural disasters; intercommunal violence; most IDPs live in Sumale state) (2015)
Illicit drugs: transit hub for heroin originating in Southwest and Southeast Asia and destined for Europe, as well as cocaine destined for markets in southern Africa; cultivates qat (khat) for local use and regional export, principally to Djibouti and Somalia (legal in all three countries); the lack of a well-developed financial system limits the country's utility as a money laundering center

EUROPEAN UNION

INTRODUCTION

Preliminary statement: The evolution of what is today the European Union (EU) from a regional economic agreement among six neighboring states in 1951 to today's hybrid intergovernmental and supranational organization of 28 countries across the European continent stands as an unprecedented phenomenon in the annals of history. Dynastic unions for territorial consolidation were long the norm in Europe; on a few occasions even country-level unions were arranged—the Polish-Lithuanian Commonwealth and the Austro-Hungarian Empire were examples. But for such a large number of nation-states to cede some of their sovereignty to an overarching entity is unique. Although the EU is not a federation in the strict sense, it is far more than a free-trade association such as ASEAN, NAFTA, or Mercosur, and it has certain attributes associated with independent nations: its own flag, currency (for some members), and law-making abilities, as well as diplomatic representation and a common foreign and security policy in its dealings with external partners.

Thus, inclusion of basic intelligence on the EU has been deemed appropriate as a new, separate entity in The World Factbook. However, because of the EU's special status, this description is placed after the regular country entries.

Background: Following the two devastating World Wars in the first half of the 20th century, a number of far-sighted European leaders in the late 1940s sought a response to the overwhelming desire for peace and reconciliation on the continent. In 1950, the French Foreign Minister Robert SCHUMAN proposed pooling the production of coal and steel in Western Europe and setting up an organization for that purpose that would bring France and the Federal Republic of

Germany together and would be open to other countries as well. The following year, the European Coal and Steel Community (ECSC) was set up when six members—Belgium, France, West Germany, Italy, Luxembourg, and the Netherlands—signed the Treaty of Paris.

The ECSC was so successful that within a few years the decision was made to integrate other elements of the countries' economies. In 1957, envisioning an "ever closer union," the Treaties of Rome created the European Economic Community (EEC) and the European Atomic Energy Community (Euratom), and the six member states undertook to eliminate trade barriers among themselves by forming a common market. In 1967, the institutions of all three communities were formally merged into the European Community (EC), creating a single Commission, a single Council of Ministers, and the body known today as the European Parliament. Members of the European Parliament were initially selected by national parliaments, but in 1979 the first direct elections were undertaken and have been held every five years since.

In 1973, the first enlargement of the EC took place with the addition of Denmark, Ireland, and the UK. The 1980s saw further membership expansion with Greece joining in 1981 and Spain and Portugal in 1986. The 1992 Treaty of Maastricht laid the basis for further forms of cooperation in foreign and defense policy, in judicial and internal affairs, and in the creation of an economic and monetary union—including a common currency. This further integration created the European Union (EU), at the time standing alongside the EC. In 1995, Austria, Finland, and Sweden joined the EU/EC, raising the membership total to 15.

A new currency, the euro, was launched in world money markets on 1 January 1999; it became the unit of exchange for all EU member states except Denmark, Sweden, and the UK. In 2002, citizens of those 12 countries began using euro banknotes and coins. Ten new countries joined the EU in 2004—Cyprus, the Czech Republic, Estonia, Hungary, Latvia, Lithuania, Malta, Poland, Slovakia, and Slovenia. Bulgaria and Romania joined in 2007 and Croatia in 2013, bringing the current membership to 28. (Seven of these new countries—Cyprus, Estonia, Latvia, Lithuania, Malta, Slovakia, and Slovenia—have now adopted the euro, bringing total eurozone membership to 19.)

In an effort to ensure that the EU could function efficiently with an expanded membership, the Treaty of Nice (concluded in 2000; entered into force in 2003) set forth rules to streamline the size and procedures of EU institutions. An effort to establish a "Constitution for Europe," growing out of a Convention held in 2002–2003, foundered when it was rejected in referenda in France and the Netherlands in 2005. A subsequent effort in 2007 incorporated many of the features of the rejected draft Constitutional Treaty while also making a number of substantive and symbolic changes. The new treaty, referred tOAS

the Treaty of Lisbon, sought to amend existing treaties rather than replace them. The treaty was approved at the EU intergovernmental conference of the then 27 member states held in Lisbon in December 2007, after which the process of national ratifications began. In October 2009, an Irish referendum approved the Lisbon Treaty (overturning a previous rejection) and cleared the way for an ultimate unanimous endorsement. Poland and the Czech Republic ratified soon after. The Lisbon Treaty came into force on 1 December 2009 and the EU officially replaced and succeeded the EC. The Treaty's provisions are part of the basic consolidated versions of the Treaty on European Union (TUE) and the Treaty on the Functioning of the European Union (TFUE) now governing what remains a very specific integration project. Frustrated by a remote bureaucracy in Brussels and massive migration into the country, UK citizens on 23 June 2016 narrowly voted to leave the EU. The so-called "Brexit" will take years to carry out, but could be the signal for referenda in other EU countries where skepticism of EU membership benefits is strong.

GEOGRAPHY

Location: Europe between the North Atlantic Ocean in the west and Russia, Belarus, and Ukraine to the east

Map references: Europe

Area: *total:* 4,324,782 sq km

Area—comparative: less than one-half the size of the US

Land boundaries: *total:* 13,271 km
border countries (17): Albania 212 km, Andorra 118 km, Belarus 1,176 km, Bosnia and Herzegovina 956 km, HolySee 3 km, Liechtenstein 34 km, Macedonia 396 km, Moldova 683 km, Monaco 6 km, Montenegro 19 km, Norway 2,375 km, Russia 2,435 km, San Marino 37 km, Serbia 1,353 km, Switzerland 1,729 km, Turkey 415 km, Ukraine 1,324 km
note: data for European continent only

Coastline: 65,992.9 km

Climate: cold temperate; potentially subarctic in the north to temperate; mild wet winters; hot dry summers in the south

Terrain: fairly flat along Baltic and Atlantic coasts; mountainous in the central and southern areas

Elevation: *mean elevation:* about 300 m
elevation extremes: lowest point: Lammefjord, Denmark -7 m; Zuidplaspolder, Netherlands -7 m
highest point: Mont Blanc 4,807 m

Natural resources: iron ore, natural gas, petroleum, coal, copper, lead, zinc, bauxite, uranium, potash, salt, hydropower, arable land, timber, fish

Irrigated land: 154,539.82 sq km (2011 est.)

Total renewable water resources: 2,057.76 cu km (2011)

Natural hazards: flooding along coasts; avalanches in mountainous area; earthquakes in the south; volcanic eruptions in Italy; periodic droughts in Spain; ice floes in the Baltic

Environment—current issues: various forms of air, soil, and water pollution; see individual country entries

Environment—international agreements: *party to:* Air Pollution, Air Pollution-Nitrogen Oxides, Air Pollution-Persistent Organic Pollutants, Air Pollution-Sulphur 94, Antarctic-Marine Living Resources, Biodiversity, Climate Change, Climate Change-Kyoto Protocol, Desertification, Hazardous Wastes, Law of the Sea, Ozone Layer Protection, Tropical Timber 83, Tropical Timber 94
signed but not ratified: Air Pollution-Volatile Organic Compounds

PEOPLE AND SOCIETY

Languages: Bulgarian, Croatian, Czech, Danish, Dutch, English, Estonian, Finnish, French, German, Greek, Hungarian, Irish, Italian, Latvian, Lithuanian, Maltese, Polish, Portuguese, Romanian, Slovak, Slovene, Spanish, Swedish
note: only the 24 official languages are listed; German, the major language of Germany, Austria, and Switzerland, is the most widely spoken mother tongue—about 16% of the EU population; English is the most widely spoken foreign language—about 38% of the EU population is conversant with it (2012)

Religions: Roman Catholic 48%, Protestant 12%, Orthodox 8%, other Christian 4%, Muslim 2%, other 1% (includes Jewish, Sikh, Buddhist, Hindu), atheist 7%, non-believer/agnostic 16%, unspecified 2% (2012 est.)

Population: 513,949,445 (July 2015 est.)
country comparison to the world: 3

Age structure: *0–14 years:* 15.5% (male 40,819,985/female 38,752,319)
15–24 years: 11% (male 29,022,494/female 27,724,216)
25–54 years: 41.9% (male 108,625,856/female 106,777,338)
55–64 years: 12.8% (male 31,915,689/female 33,797,415)
65 years and over: 18.8% (male 41,266,149/female 55,247,984) (2015 est.)

Median age: *total:* 42.5 years
male: 41 years
female: 43.9 years (2015 est.)
country comparison to the world: 21

Population growth rate: 0.25% (2015 est.)

Birth rate: 10.2 births/1,000 population (2015 est.)

Death rate: 10.2 deaths/1,000 population (2015 est.)

Net migration rate: 2.5 migrant(s)/1,000 population (2015 est.)

Sex ratio: *at birth:* 1.06 male(s)/female
0–14 years: 1.05 male(s)/female
15–24 years: 1.05 male(s)/female
25–54 years: 1.02 male(s)/female
55–64 years: 0.94 male(s)/female
65 years and over: 0.75 male(s)/female
total population: 0.96 male(s)/female (2015 est.)

Infant mortality rate: *total:* 4 deaths/1,000 live births
male: 4.4 deaths/1,000 live births
female: 3.6 deaths/1,000 live births (2015 est.)
country comparison to the world: 193

Life expectancy at birth: *total population:* 80.2 years
male: 77.4 years

female: 83.2 years (2015 est.)
country comparison to the world: 38
Total fertility rate: 1.61 children born/woman (2015 est.)
Hospital bed density: 5.4 beds/1,000 population (2011)
HIV/AIDS—adult prevalence rate: note—see individual entries of member states
HIV/AIDS—people living with HIV/AIDS: note—see individual entries of member states
HIV/AIDS—deaths: note—see individual entries of member states

GOVERNMENT

Union name: *conventional long form:* European Union
abbreviation: EU
Political structure: a hybrid and unique intergovernmental and supranational organization
Capital: *name:* Brussels (Belgium), Strasbourg (France), Luxembourg; note—the European Council, a gathering of the EU heads of state and/or government, and the Council of the European Union, a ministerial-level body of ten formations, meet in Brussels, Belgium, except for Council meetings held in Luxembourg in April, June, and October; the European Parliament meets in Brussels and Strasbourg, France, and has administrative offices in Luxembourg; the Court of Justice of the European Union is located in Luxembourg; and the European Central Bank is located in Frankfurt, Germany

Geographic coordinates: (Brussels) 5050 N, 420 E
time difference: UTC + 1 (6 hours ahead of Washington, DC, during Standard Time)
daylight saving time: +1hr, begins last Sunday in March; ends last Sunday in October
Member states: 28 countries: Austria, Belgium, Bulgaria, Croatia, Cyprus, Czech Republic, Denmark, Estonia, Finland, France, Germany, Greece, Hungary, Ireland, Italy, Latvia, Lithuania, Luxembourg, Malta, Netherlands, Poland, Portugal, Romania, Slovakia, Slovenia, Spain, Sweden, UK; note—candidate countries: Iceland, Macedonia, Montenegro, Serbia, Turkey

note: there are non-European overseas countries and territories (OCTs) having special relations with Denmark, France, the Netherlands, and the UK (list is annexed to the Treaty on the Functioning of the European Union), that are associated with the Union to promote their economic and social development; member states apply to their trade with OCTs the same treatment as they accord each other pursuant to the treaties; OCT nationals are in principle EU citizens, but these countries are neither part of the EU, nor subject to the EU there are 25 OCTs (1 with Denmark [Greenland], 6 with France [French Polynesia; French Southern and Antarctic Lands; New Caledonia; Saint Barthelemy; Saint Pierre and Miquelon; Wallis and Futuna], 6 with the Netherlands [Aruba, Bonaire, Curacao, Saba, Sint Eustatius, Sint Maarten], and 12 with the UK [Anguilla; Bermuda; British Antarctic Territory; British Indian Ocean Territory; British Virgin Islands; Cayman Islands; Falkland Islands; Montserrat; Pitcairn Islands; Saint Helena, Ascension, and Tristan da Cunha; South Georgia and the South Sandwich Islands; Turks and Caicos Islands]), of which 22 have joined the Overseas Countries and Territories Association (OCTA); the 3 OCTs that are not part of OCTA (British Antarctic Territory, British Indian Ocean Territory, South Georgia and the South Sandwich Islands) do not have a permanent population

Independence: 7 February 1992 (Maastricht Treaty signed establishing the European Union); 1 November 1993 (Maastricht Treaty entered into force)
note: the Treaties of Rome, signed on 25 March 1957 and subsequently entered into force on 1 January 1958, created the European Economic Community and the European Atomic Energy Community; a series of subsequent treaties have been adopted to increase efficiency and transparency, to prepare for new member states, and to introduce new areas of cooperation—suchas a single currency; the Treaty of Lisbon, signed on 13 December 2007 and entered into force on 1 December 2009 is the most recent of these treaties and is intended to make the EU more democratic, more efficient, and better able to address global problems with one voice
National holiday: Europe Day (also known as Schuman Day) 9 May (1950); note—the day in 1950 that Robert SCHUMAN proposed the creation of what became the European Coal and Steel Community, the progenitor of today's European Union, with the aim of achieving a united Europe
Constitution: none; note—the EU legal order relies primarily on two consolidated texts encompassing all provisions as amended from a series of past treaties: the Treaty on European Union (TEU), as modified by the Lisbon Treaty, states in Article 1 that "the HIGH CONTRACTING PARTIES establish among themselves a EUROPEAN UNION . . . on which the Member States confer competences to attain objectives they have in common"; Article 1 of the TEU states further that the EU is "founded on the present Treaty and on the Treaty on the Functioning of the European Union (hereinafter referred to as 'the Treaties'), "both possessing the same legal value; Article 6 of the TEU provides that a separately adopted Charter of Fundamental Rights of the European Union "shall have the same legal value as the Treaties" (2016)
Legal system: unique supranational law system in which, according to an interpretive declaration of member-state governments appended to the Treaty of Lisbon, "the Treaties and the law adopted by the Union on the basis of the Treaties have primacy over the law of Member States" under conditions laid down in the case law of the Court of Justice; key principles of EU law include fundamental rights as guaranteed by the Charter of Fundamental Rights and as resulting from constitutional traditions common to the EU's states; EU law is divided into 'primary' and 'secondary' legislation; primary legislation is derived from the consolidated versions of the Treaty on European Union and the Treaty on the Functioning of the European

Union) and are the basis for all EU action; secondary legislation—which includes directives, regulations, and decisions—is derived from the principles and objectives set out in the treaties
Suffrage: 18 years of age (16 years in Austria); universal; voting for the European Parliament is permitted in each member state
Executive branch: under the EU treaties there are three distinct institutions, each of which conducts functions that may be regarded as executive in nature:
the European Council: brings together heads of state and government, along with the president of the European Commission, and meets at least four times a year; its aim is to provide the impetus for the development of the Union and to issue general policy guidelines; the Treaty of Lisbon established the position of "permanent" (full-time) president of the European Council; leaders of the EU member states appoint the president for a 21/2 year term, renewable once; the president's responsibilities include chairing the EU Summits and providing policy and organizational continuity; the current president is Donald TUSK (Poland), since 1 December 2014, succeeding Herman VAN ROMPUY (Belgian; 2009–14)
the Council of the European Union: consists of ministers of each EU member state and meets regularly in 10 different configurations depending on the subject matter; it conducts policymaking and coordinating functions as well as legislative functions; ministers of EU member states chair meetings of the Council of the EU based on a 6-month rotating presidency except for the meetings of EU Foreign Ministers in the Foreign Affairs Council that are chaired by the High Represntative for Foreign Affairs and Security Policy
the European Commission: headed by a College of Commissioners comprised of 28 members -including the president), one from each member country; each commissioner is responsible for one or more policy areas; the Commission's main responsibilities include the sole right to initiate EU legislation (except for foreign and security/defense policy), promoting the general interest of the EU, acting as "guardian of the Treaties" by monitoring the application of EU law, implementing/executing the EU budget, managing programs, negotiating on the EU's behalf in core policy areas suchas trade, and ensuring the Union's external representation in some policy areas; its current president is Jean-Claude JUNCKER (Luxembourg) elected on 15 July 2014 (took office on 1 November 2014); the president of the European Commission is nominated by the European Council and formally "elected" by the European Parliament; the Commission president allocates specific responsibilities among the members of the "college" (appointed by common accord of the member state governments in consultation with the president-elect); the European Parliament confirms the entire Commission for a 5-year term; President JUNCKER reorganized the structure of the College around clusters or project teams coordinated by 7 vice presidents in line with the current Commission's main political priorities and

appointed Frans TIMMERMANS (Netherlands) to act as his first vice president; the confirmation process for the next Commission expected be held in the fall of 2019

note: for external representation and foreign policy making, leaders of the EU member states appointed Federica MOGHERINI (Italy) as the High Representative of the European Union for Foreign Affairs and Security Policy; MOGHERINI took office on 1 November 2014, succeeding Cahrerine ASHTON (UK) (200914); the High Representative's concurrent appointment as Vice President of the European Commission endows her position with the policymaking influence of the Council of the EU and the budgetary influence (subject to Council's approval) of the Council of the EU and the budgetary/management influence of the European Commission; the High Representative helps develop and implement the EU's Common Foreign and Security Policy and Common Security and Defense Policy component, chairs the Foreign Affairs Council, represents and acts for the Union in many international contexts, and oversees the European External Action Service, the diplomatic corps of the EU, established on 1 December 2010

Legislative branch: *description:* two legislative bodies consisting of the Council of the European Union (28 seats; ministers representing the 28 member states and the European Parliament (751 seats; seats allocated among member states roughly in proportion to population size; members elected by proportional representation to serve 5-year terms); note—the European Parliament President, currently Martin SCHULZ (German Socialist) is elected by a majority of fellow members (MEPs) of the European Parliament and represents the Parliament within the EU and internationally; the Council of the EU and the MEPs share responsibilities for adopting the bulk of EU legislation, normally acting in co-decision on Commission proposals (but not in the area of Common Foreign and Security Policy, which is governed by consensus of the EU member state governments)

elections: last held on 22–25 May 2014 (next to be held May-June 2019)

election results: percent of vote—EPP 29.4%, S&D 25.4%, ECR 9.3%, ALDE 8.9%, GUE/NGL 6.9%, Greens/EFA 6.7%, EFD 6.4%, independent 6.9%; seats by party—EPP 221, S&D 191, ECR 70, ALDE 67, GUE/NGL 52, Greens/EFA 50, EFD 48, independent 52

Judicial branch: *note:* the European Court of Justice (ECJ) ensures that EU law is interpreted and applied uniformly throughout the EU, resolves disputed issues among the EU institutions and with member states, issues opinions on questions of EU law referred by member state courts

highest court(s): ECJ (consists of 28 judges—1 from each member state); the court may sit as a full court, in a "G rand Chamber" of 13 judges in special cases but usually in chambers of 3 to 5 judges

judge selection and term of office: judges appointed by the common consent of the member states to serve 6-year renewable terms

subordinate court(s): General Court; Civil Service Tribunal

Political parties and leaders: European United Left-Nordic Green Left or GUE/NGL [Gabriele ZIMMER]

Europe of Freedom and Direct Democracy or EFD [Nigel FARAGE and David BORRELLI]

European Conservatives and Reformists or ECR [Syed KAMALL]

European Greens/European Free Alliance or Greens/EFA [Rebecca HARMS and Philippe LAM BERTS]

Alliance of Liberals and Democrats for Europe or ALDE [Guy VERH OF STADT]

Group of the European People's Party or EPP [Manfred WEBER]

Group of the Alliance of Socialists and Democrats or S&D [Gianni PITELLA]

International organization participation: ARF, ASEAN (dialogue member), Australian Group, BIS, BSEC (observer), CBSS, CERN, EBRD, FAO, FATF, G-8, G-10, G-20, IDA, IEA, IGAD (partners), LAIA (observer), NSG (observer), OAS (observer), OECD, PIF (partner), SAARC (observer), SICA (observer), UN (observer), UNRWA (observer), WCO, WTO, ZC (observer)

Diplomatic representation in the US: *chief of mission:* Ambassador David O'SULLIVAN (since 18 November 2014)

chancery: 2175 K Street, NW, Suite 800, Washington, DC 20037

telephone: [1] (202) 862-9500

FAX: [1] (202) 429-1766

Diplomatic representation from the US: *chief of mission:* Ambassador Anthony Luzzatto GARDNER (since 18 March 2014)

embassy: 13 Zinnerstraat/Rue Zinner, B-1000 Brussels

mailing address: use embassy street address

telephone: [32] (2) 811–4100

FAX: [32] (2) 811–5154

Flag description: a blue field with 12 five-pointed gold stars arranged in a circle in the center; blue represents the sky of the Western world, the stars are the peoples of Europe in a circle, a symbol of unity; the number of stars is fixed

National symbol(s): a circle of 12, five-pointed, golden yellow stars on a blue field; union colors: blue, yellow

National anthem: *name:* "Ode to Joy"

lyrics/music: no lyrics/Ludwig VON BEETHOVEN, arranged by Herbert VON KARAJAN

note: adopted 1972; official EU anthem since 1985; the song is meant to represent all of Europe rather than just the organization, conveying ideas of peace, freedom, and unity; the song also serves as the anthem for the Council of Europe

ECONOMY

Economy—overview: Internally, the 28 EU member states have adopted the framework of a single market with free movement of goods, services and capital. Internationally, the EU aims to bolster Europe's trade position and its political and economic weight.

Despite great differences in per capita income among member states (from $13,000 to $82,000) and in national attitudes toward issues like inflation, debt, and foreign trade, the EU has achieved a high degree of coordination of monetary and fiscal policies. A common currency—the euro—circulates among 19 of the member states, under the auspices of the European Economic and Monetary Union (EMU). Eleven member states introduced the euroOAS their common currency on 1 January 1999 (Greece did so two years later). Since 2004, 13 states acceded to the EU. Of the 13, Slovenia (2007), Cyprus and Malta (2008), Slovakia (2009), Estonia (2011), Latvia (2014), and Lithuania (2015) have adopted the euro; 7 other member states—not including the UK nor Denmark, which have formal opt-outs—are required by EU treaties to adopt the common currency upon meeting fiscal and monetary convergence criteria. The EU economy is slowly recovering from the 2008–09 global economic crisis and the ensuing sovereign debt crisis in the euro zone in 2011. The bloc posted moderate GDP growth in 2014 and 2015, but the recovery has been uneven. Some EU member states (Czech Republic, Ireland and Spain) have recorded strong growth while others (Finland, Greece) are struggling to shake off recession. The recovery has been buoyed by lower commodities prices and accommodative monetary policy, which has lowered interest rates and the euro's foreign exchange value. Despite EU/IMF rescue programs in Greece, Ireland, Portugal, Spain and Cyprus, significant drags on growth remain, including high public and private debt loads, low domestic demand that discourages investment, aging populations, onerous regulations, and high unemployment. These factors—in combination with low oil prices—have subdued inflation in the euro zone despite the European Central Bank's (ECB) efforts to spur more lending and investment through its asset-buying program and negative interest rates. The ECB in December 2015 stated it would widen its asset-buying program and extend it until March 2017 to fend off deflation and improve borrowing conditions in the euro zone.

Beyond the risk of deflation, the EU economy is vulnerable to a slowdown of global trade that would shrink the EU's ample external trade surplus. Another round of financial market turmoil because of disagreements between bailed-out Greece and its euro-zone creditor could also be detrimental to a stronger EU recovery if it hurts consumer and investor confidence. To bolster economic growth and create jobs, EU leaders have moved forward with plans to use $28 (€21) billion in public money as seed capital to attract private investors to fund $421 [€315] billion in infrastructure projects from 2015 to 2017, focusing on energy, broadband, transport, education, and research and innovation. They also are forging ahead on creating a capital markets union to ease the burdens of cross-border investment in the bloc. Externally, the EU continues to negotiate an ambitious and comprehensive free trade agreement with the US, the goal of which is to expand already large trade and investment flows.

GDP (purchasing power parity): $19.18 trillion (2015 est.)

$18.64 trillion (2014 est.)

$18.08 trillion (2013 est.)

note: data are in 2015 US dollars

country comparison to the world: 2

GDP (official exchange rate): $16.27 trillion (2015 est.)

GDP—real growth rate: 1.9% (2015 est.)

1.4% (2014 est.)

0.2% (2013 est.)

country comparison to the world: 137

GDP—per capita (PPP): $37,800 (2015 est.)

$36,900 (2014 est.)

$35,900 (2013 est.)

note: data are in 2015 US dollars

country comparison to the world: 45

Gross national saving: 21.4% of GDP (2015 est.)

21.1% of GDP (2014 est.)

21% of GDP (2013 est.)

country comparison to the world: 74

GDP—composition, by end use:

household consumption: 58.2%

government consumption: 21.6%

investment in fixed capital: 17.3%

investment in inventories: 0.1%

exports of goods and services: 44.9%

imports of goods and services: -42.1% (2013 est.)

GDP—composition, by sector of origin:

agriculture: 1.6%

industry: 24.4%

services: 71.3% (2015 est.)

Agriculture—products: wheat, barley, oilseeds, sugar beets, wine, grapes; dairy products, cattle, sheep, pigs, poultry; fish

Industries: among the world's largest and most technologically advanced regions, the EU industrial base includes: ferrous and non-ferrous metal production and processing, metal products, petroleum, coal, cement, chemicals, pharmaceuticals, aerospace, rail transportation equipment, passenger and commercial vehicles, construction equipment, industrial equipment, shipbuilding, electrical power equipment, machine tools and automated manufacturing systems, electronics and telecommunications equipment, fishing, food and beverages, furniture, paper, textiles

Industrial production growth rate: 1.5% (2015 est.)

country comparison to the world: 134

Labor force: 231.6 million (2015 est.)

country comparison to the world: 3

Labor force—by occupation: *agriculture:* 5%

industry: 21.9%

services: 73.1% (2014 est.)

Unemployment rate: 9.5% (2015 est.)

9.8% (2014)

country comparison to the world: 112

Population below poverty line: 9.8% note—see individual country entries of member states

Household income or consumption by percentage share: *lowest 10%:* 2.8%

highest 10%: 23.9% (2014 est.)

Distribution of family income—Gini index: 30.9 (2014 est.)

30.5 (2013 est.)

country comparison to the world: 115

Taxes and other revenues: 45.2% of GDP (2014 est.)

country comparison to the world: 23

Budget surplus (+) or deficit (–): -3% of GDP

country comparison to the world: 113

Public debt: 86.8% of GDP (2014)

85.5% of GDP (2013)

country comparison to the world: 28

Fiscal year: NA

Inflation rate (consumer prices): 0.1% (2015 est.)

0.5% (2014 est.)

country comparison to the world: 50

Central bank discount rate: 0.05% (31 December 2013)

0.3% (31 December 2012)

note: this is the European Central Bank's rate on the marginal lending facility, which offers overnight credit to banks in the euro area

country comparison to the world: 138

Commercial bank prime lending rate: 0.32% (31 December 2014 est.)

0.56% (31 December 2013 est.)

country comparison to the world: 184

Stock of narrow money: $7.165 trillion (31 December 2013)

$7.422 trillion (31 December 2012)

note: this is the quantity of money, M1, for the euro area, converted into US dollars at the exchange rate for the date indicated; it excludes the stock of money carried by non-euro-area members of the European Union, e.g., UK pounds, Danish kroner, and Czech koruny

country comparison to the world: 1

Stock of broad money: $12.49 trillion (31 December 2012 est.)

$12.29 trillion (31 December 2011 est.)

note: this is the quantity of broad money for the euro area, converted into US dollars at the exchange rate for the date indicated; it excludes the stock of broad money carried by non-euro-area members of the European Union

country comparison to the world: 2

Stock of domestic credit: $21.71 trillion (31 December 2012 est.)

$21.29 trillion (31 December 2011 est.)

note: this figure refers to the euro area only; it excludes credit data for non-euro-area members of the EU

country comparison to the world: 1

Market value of publicly traded shares: $10.4 trillion (31 December 2012 est.)

$9.36 trillion (31 December 2011)

$10.56 trillion (31 December 2010 est.)

country comparison to the world: 2

Current account balance: $351.9 billion (2015 est.)

$88.12 billion (2014 est.)

country comparison to the world: 1

Exports: $2.259 trillion (2014 est.)

$2.306 trillion (2013 est.)

note: external exports, excluding intra-EU trade

country comparison to the world: 2

Exports—commodities: machinery, motor vehicles, pharmaceuticals and other chemicals, fuels, aircraft, plastics, iron and steel, wood pulp and paper products, alcoholic beverages, furniture

Exports—partners: United States 17.1%, China 8.5%, Switzerland 7.8%, Russia 7.2%, Turkey 4.4% (2013 est.)

Imports: $2.244 trillion (2014 est.) $2.238 trillion (2013 est.)

note: external imports, excluding intra-EU trade

country comparison to the world: 2

Imports—commodities: fuels and crude oil, machinery, vehicles, pharmaceuticals and other chemicals, precious gemstones, textiles, aircraft, plastics, metals, ships

Imports—partners: China 16.1%, United States 11.4%, Russia 11%, Switzerland 5.9%, Norway 4.3% (2013 est.)

Reserves of foreign exchange and gold: $740.9 billion (31 December 2014 est.)

note: $746.9 billion (31 December 2013)

country comparison to the world: 3

Debt—external: $13.05 trillion (31 December 2014 est.)

$14.14 trillion (31 December 2013)

country comparison to the world: 2

Stock of direct foreign investment—at home: $NA

$5.148 trillion (2012)

$4.828 trillion (2011)

country comparison to the world: 1

Stock of direct foreign investment—abroad: $9.121 trillion (2012)

$8.721 trillion (2011)

country comparison to the world: 1

Exchange rates: euros per US dollar—

0.885 (2015 est.)

0.7525 (2014 est.)

0.7634 (2013 est.)

0.7752 (2012 est.)

0.7185 (2011 est.)

ENERGY

Electricity—production: 3.166 trillion kWh (2014 est.)

country comparison to the world: 3

Electricity—consumption: 2.771 trillion kWh (2013 est.)

country comparison to the world: 3

Electricity—exports: 336.2 billion kWh (2013 est.)

country comparison to the world: 1

Electricity—imports: 349.5 billion kWh (2013 est.)

country comparison to the world: 1

Electricity—installed generating capacity: 947 million kW (2012 est.)

country comparison to the world: 3

Electricity—from fossil fuels: 49% of total installed capacity (2012 est.)

country comparison to the world: 149

Electricity—from nuclear fuels: 12.9% of total installed capacity (2012 est.)

country comparison to the world: 15

Electricity—from hydroelectric plants: 10.7% of total installed capacity (2012 est.)

country comparison to the world: 114

Electricity—from other renewable sources: 22.9% of total installed capacity (2012 est.)

country comparison to the world: 13
Crude oil—production: 1.411 million bbl/day (2014 est.)
country comparison to the world: 19
Crude oil—proved reserves: 5.789 billion bbl (1 January 2015 est.)
country comparison to the world: 22
Refined petroleum products—production: 11.12 million bbl/day (2014 est.)
country comparison to the world: 2
Refined petroleum products—consumption: 12.53 million bbl/day (2014 est.)
country comparison to the world: 2
Refined petroleum products—exports: 2.196 million bbl/day (2013 est.)
country comparison to the world: 3
Refined petroleum products—imports: 8.613 million bbl/day (2013 est.)
country comparison to the world: 1
Natural gas—production: 132.3 billion cu m (2014 est.)
country comparison to the world: 6
Natural gas—consumption: 386.9 billion cu m (2014 est.)
country comparison to the world: 3
Natural gas—exports: 93.75 billion cu m (2010 est.)
country comparison to the world: 4
Natural gas—imports: 420.6 billion cu m (2010 est.)
country comparison to the world: 1
Natural gas—proved reserves: 1.492 billion cu m (1 January 2015 est.)
country comparison to the world: 100
Carbon dioxide emissions from consumption of energy: 3.705 billion Mt (2014 est.)
country comparison to the world: 3

COMMUNICATIONS

Telephones—fixed lines: *total:* 213.8 million (2014 est.)
country comparison to the world: 2
Telephones—mobile cellular: *total:* 632.5 million (2014 est.)
country comparison to the world: 3
Telephone system: note—see individual country entries of member states
Radio broadcast stations: AM 930, FM 13,655, shortwave 71 (1998); note—sum of individual country radio broadcast stations; there is also a European-wide station (Euroradio)

Television broadcast stations: 2,700 (1995); note—sum of individual country television broadcast stations excluding repeaters; there is also a European-wide station (Eurovision)
Internet country code: .eu; note—see country entries of member states for individual country codes
Internet hosts: 201,116; note—this sum reflects the number of Internet hosts assigned the .eu Internet country code (2012)
Internet users: *total:* 398.1 million (2014 est.)
country comparison to the world: 2

TRANSPORTATION

Airports: 3,102 (2013)
Airports—with paved runways: *total:* 1,882
over 3,047 m: 120
2,438 to 3,047 m: 341
1,524 to 2,437 m: 507
914 to 1,523 m: 425
under 914 m: 489 (2015)
Airports—with unpaved runways: *total:* 1,244
over 3,047 m: 1
2,437 to 3,047 m: 1
1,524 to 2,437 m: 15
914 to 1,523 m: 245
under 914 m: 982 (2013)
Heliports: 90 (2013)
Railways: *total:* 230,548 km (2013)
Roadways: *total:* 10,582,653 km (2013)
Waterways: 53,384 km (2013)
Ports and terminals: major port(s): Antwerp (Belgium), Barcelona (Spain), Braila (Romania), Bremen (Germany), Burgas (Bulgaria), Constanta (Romania), Copenhagen (Denmark), Galati (Romania), Gdansk (Poland), Hamburg (Germany), Helsinki (Finland), Las Palmas (Canary Islands, Spain), Le Havre (France), Lisbon (Portugal), London (UK), Marseille (France), Naples (Italy), Peiraiefs or Piraeus (Greece), Riga (Latvia), Rotterdam (Netherlands), Split (Croatia), Stockholm (Sweden), Talinn (Estonia), Tulcea (Romania), Varna (Bulgaria)

MILITARY AND SECURITY

Military expenditures: 1.65% of GDP (2012)
1.66% of GDP (2011)
1.65% of GDP (2010)
country comparison to the world: 56
Military—note: the five-nation Eurocorps—created in 1992 by France, Germany, Belgium, Spain,

and Luxembourg—has deployed troops and police on peacekeeping missions to Bosnia-Herzegovina, Macedonia, and the Democratic Republic of the Congo and assumed command of the ISAF in Afghanistan in August 2004; Eurocorps directly commands the 5,000-man Franco-German Brigade, the Multinational Command Support Brigade, and EUFOR in Bosnia and Herzegovina; in November 2004, the EU Council of Ministers formally committed to creating 131,500-man battle groups by the end of 2007, to respond to international crises on a rotating basis; 22 of the EU's 28 nations have agreed to supply troops; France, Italy, and the UK formed the first of three battle groups in 2005; Norway, Sweden, Estonia, and Finland established the Nordic Battle Group effective 1 January 2008; nine other groups are to be formed; a rapid-reaction naval EU Maritime Task Group was stood up in March 2007 (2007)

TRANSNATIONAL ISSUES

Disputes—international: as a political union, the EU has no border disputes with neighboring countries, but Estonia has no land boundary agreements with Russia, Slovenia disputes its land and maritime boundaries with Croatia, and Spain has territorial and maritime disputes with Morocco and with the UK over Gibraltar; the EU has set up a Schengen area—consisting of 22 EU member states that have signed the convention implementing the Schengen agreements or "acquis" (1985 and 1990) on the free movement of persons and the harmonization of border controls in Europe; these agreements became incorporated into EU law with the implementation of the 1997 Treaty of Amsterdam on 1 May 1999; in addition, non-EU States Iceland and Norway (as part of the Nordic Union) have been included in the Schengen area since 1996 (full members in 2001), Switzerland since 2008, and Liechtenstein since 2011 bringing the total current membership to 26; the UK (since 2000) and Ireland (since 2002) take part in only some aspects of the Schengen area, especially with respect to police and criminal matters; nine of the 13 new member states that joined the EU since 2004 joined Schengen on 21 December 2007; of the four remaining EU states, Romania, Bulgaria, and Croatia are obligated to eventually join, while Cyprus' entry is held up by the ongoing Cyprus dispute

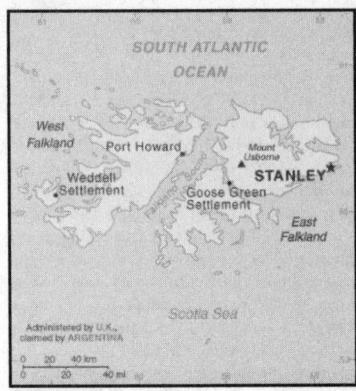

INTRODUCTION

Background: Although first sighted by an English navigator in 1592, the first landing (English) did not occur until almost a century later in 1690, and the first settlement (French) was not established until 1764. The colony was turned over to Spain two years later and the islands have since been the subject of a territorial dispute, first between Britain and Spain, then between Britain and Argentina. The UK asserted its claim to the islands by establishing a naval garrison there in 1833. Argentina invaded the islands on 2 April 1982. The British responded with an expeditionary force that landed seven weeks later and after fierce fighting forced an Argentine surrender on 14 June 1982. With hostilities ended and Argentine forces withdrawn, UK administration resumed. In response to renewed calls from Argentina for Britain to relinquish control of the islands, a referendum was held in March 2013, which resulted in 99.8% of the population voting to remain a part of the UK.

GEOGRAPHY

Location: Southern South America, islands in the South Atlantic Ocean, about 500 km east of southern Argentina

Geographic coordinates: 51 45 S, 59 00 W

Map references: South America

Area: *total:* 12,173 sq km
land: 12,173 sq km
water: 0 sq km
note: includes the two main islands of East and West Falkland and about 200 small islands
country comparison to the world: 165

Area—comparative: slightly smaller than Connecticut

Land boundaries: 0 km

Coastline: 1,288 km

Maritime claims: *territorial sea:* 12 nm
continental shelf: 200 nm
exclusive fishing zone: 200 nm

Climate: cold marine; strong westerly winds, cloudy, humid; rain occurs on more than half of days in year; average annual rainfall is 60 cm in Stanley; occasional snow all year, except in January and February, but typically does not accumulate

Terrain: rocky, hilly, mountainous with some boggy, undulating plains

Elevation: *mean elevation:* NA

elevation extremes: *lowest point:* Atlantic Ocean 0 m
highest point: Mount Usborne 705 m

Natural resources: fish, squid, wildlife, calcified seaweed, sphagnum moss

Land use: *agricultural land:* 92.4%
arable land: 0%
permanent crops: 0%
permanent pasture: 92.4%
forest: 0%
other: 7.6% (2011 est.)

Irrigated land: NA

Natural hazards: strong winds persist throughout the year

Environment—current issues: overfishing by unlicensed vessels is a problem; reindeer—introduced to the islands in 2001 from South Georgia—are part of a farming effort to produce specialty meat and diversify the islands' economy; this is the only commercial reindeer herd in the world unaffected by the 1986 Chornobyl disaster

Geography—note: deeply indented coast provides good natural harbors; short growing season

PEOPLE AND SOCIETY

Nationality: *noun:* Falkland Islander(s)
adjective: Falkland Island

Ethnic groups: Falkland Islander 57%, British 24.6%, St. Helenian 9.8%, Chilean 5.3%, other 3.4% (2012 est.)

Languages: English 89%, Spanish 7.7%, other 3.3% (2006 est.)

Religions: Christian 66%, none 32%, other 2% (2012 est.)

Population: 2,931 (2014 est.)
country comparison to the world: 230

Population growth rate: 0.01% (2014 est.)
country comparison to the world: 193

Birth rate: 10.9 births/1,000 population (2012 est.)

Death rate: 4.9 deaths/1,000 population (2012 est.)

Net migration rate: NA

Urbanization: *urban population:* 76.2% of total population (2015)
rate of urbanization: 0.96% annual rate of change (2010–15 est.)

Major urban areas—population: STANLEY (capital) 2,000 (2014)

Sex ratio: *total population:* 1.11 male(s)/female

note: sex ratio is somewhat skewed by the high proportion of males at the Royal Air Force station, Mount Pleasant Airport (MPA); excluding MPA, the sex ratio of the total population would be 1.01 (2012 est.)

Infant mortality rate: *total:* NA
male: NA
female: NA

Life expectancy at birth: *total population:* 77.9
male: 75.6
female: 79.6 (2012 est.)

Total fertility rate: NA

HIV/AIDS—adult prevalence rate: NA

HIV/AIDS—people living with HIV/AIDS: NA

HIV/AIDS—deaths: NA

GOVERNMENT

Country name: *conventional long form:* none
conventional short form: Falkland Islands (Islas Malvinas)
etymology: the archipelago takes its name from the Falkland Sound, the strait separating the two main islands; the channel itself was named after the Viscount of Falkland who sponsored an expedition to the islands in 1690; the Spanish name for the archipelago derives from the French "Iles Malouines," the name applied to the islands by French explorer Louis-Antoine de BOUGAINVILLE in 1764

Dependency status: overseas territory of the UK; also claimed by Argentina

Government type: parliamentary democracy (Legislative Assembly); self-governing overseas territory of the UK

Capital: *name:* Stanley

Geographic coordinates: 51 42 S, 57 51 W
time difference: UTC-4 (1 hour ahead of Washington, DC, during Standard Time)

Administrative divisions: none (overseas territory of the UK; also claimed by Argentina)

Independence: none (overseas territory of the UK; also claimed by Argentina)

National holiday: Liberation Day, 14 June (1982)

Constitution: previous 1985; latest entered into force 1 January 2009 (2016)

Legal system: English common law and local statutes

Citizenship: see United Kingdom

Suffrage: 18 years of age; universal

Executive branch: *chief of state:* Queen ELIZABETH II (since 6 February 1952); represented by Governor Colin ROBERTS (since 28 April 2014)

head of government: Chief Executive Keith PADGETT (since 1 February 2012)
cabinet: Executive Council elected by the Legislative Council

elections/appointments: the monarchy is hereditary; governor appointed by the monarch; chief executive appointed by the governor

Legislative branch: *description:* unicameral Legislative Assembly, formerly the Legislative Council (10 seats; 8 members directly elected by majority vote and 2 appointed ex officio members—the chief executive, appointed by the governor, and the financial secretary; members serve 4-year terms)
elections: last held on 7 November 2013 (next to be held in November 2017)
election results: percent of vote—NA; seats—independent 8

Judicial branch: *highest resident court(s):* Court of Appeal (consists of the court president, the chief justice as an ex officio, non-resident member, and 2 justices of appeal); Supreme Court (consists of the chief justice); note—appeals beyond the Court of Appeal are referred to the Judicial Committee of the Privy Council (in London) judge selection and term of office: all justices appointed by the governor; tenure specified in each justice's instrument of appointment
subordinate courts: Magistrate's Court (senior magistrate presides over civil and criminal divisions); Court of Summary Jurisdiction

Political parties and leaders: *none:* all independents

Political pressure groups and leaders: Falkland Islands Association (supports freedom of the people from external causes)

International organization participation: UPU

Diplomatic representation in the US: none (overseas territory of the UK)

Diplomatic representation from the US: none (overseas territory of the UK; also claimed by Argentina)

Flag description: blue with the flag of the UK in the upper hoist-side quadrant and the Falkland Island coat of arms centered on the outer half of the flag; the coat of arms contains a white ram (sheep raising was once the major economic activity) above the sailing ship Desire (whose crew discovered the islands) with a scroll at the bottom bearing the motto DESIRE THE RIGHT

National symbol(s): ram

National anthem: *name:* "Song of the Falklands""
lyrics/m u sic: Christopher LANHAM
note: adopted 1930s; the song is the local unofficial anthem; as a territory of the United Kingdom, "God Save the Queen" is official (see United Kingdom)

ECONOMY

Economy—overview: The economy was formerly based on agriculture, mainly sheep farming, but fishing and tourism currently comprise the bulk of economic activity. In 1987, the government began selling fishing licenses to foreign trawlers operating within the Falkland Islands' exclusive fishing zone. These license fees net more than $40 million per year, which help support the island's health,

education, and welfare system. The waters around the Falkland Islands are known for their squid, which account for around 75% of the annual 200,000 ton catch.
Dairy farming supports domestic consumption; crops furnish winter fodder. Foreign exchange earnings come from shipments of high-grade wool to the UK and from the sale of postage stamps and coins. In 2001, the government purchased 100 reindeer with the intent to increase the number to 10,000 over the following 20 years so that venison could be exported to Scandinavia and Chile.
Tourism, especially ecotourism, is increasing rapidly, with about 69,000 visitors in 2009. The British military presence also provides a sizable economic boost. The islands are now self-financing except for defense.
In 1993, the British Geological Survey announced a 200-mile oil exploration zone around the islands, and early seismic surveys suggest substantial reserves capable of producing 500,000 barrels per day. Political tensions between the UK and Argentina remain high following the start of oil drilling activities in the waters. In September 2011, a British exploration firm announced that it plans to commence oil production in 2016.

GDP (purchasing power parity):
$164.5 million (2007 est.)
$105.1 million (2002 est.)
country comparison to the world: 223

GDP (official exchange rate): $164.5 million (2007 est.)

GDP—per capita (PPP): $55,400 (2002 est.)
country comparison to the world: 21

GDP—composition, by sector of origin:
agriculture: 95%
industry: NA%
services: NA% (1996)

Agriculture—products: fodder and vegetable crops; venison, sheep, dairy products; fish, squid

Industries: fish and wool processing; tourism

Industrial production growth rate: NA%

Labor force: 1,944 (2012 est.)
country comparison to the world: 228

Labor force—by occupation: *agriculture:* 95% (mostly sheepherding and fishing)
industry and services: 5% (1996)

Unemployment rate: 4.1% (2010)
country comparison to the world: 36

Population below poverty line: NA%

Household income or consumption by percentage share: *lowest:* 10%: NA%
highest: 10%: NA%

Budget: *revenues:* $67.1 million
expenditures: $75.3 million (FY09/10)
Taxes and other revenues: 40.8% of GDP (FY09/10)
country comparison to the world: 34

Budget surplus (+) or deficit (–): -5% of GDP (FY09/10)
country comparison to the world: 170

Fiscal year: 1 April—31 March

Inflation rate (consumer prices): 1.2% (2003)
country comparison to the world: 87

Exports: $125 million (2004 est.)
country comparison to the world: 193

Exports—commodities: wool, hides, meat, venison, fish, squid

Imports: $90 million (2004 est.)
country comparison to the world: 218

Imports—commodities: fuel, food and drink, building materials, clothing

Debt—external: $NA

Exchange rates: Falkland pounds (FKP) per US dollar—
0.6528 (2015)
0.6391 (2013)
0.6391 (2013)
0.63 (2012)
0.624 (2011)

ENERGY

Electricity—production: 12 million kWh (2012 est.)
country comparison to the world: 215

Electricity—consumption: 11.16 million kWh (2012 est.)
country comparison to the world: 214

Electricity—exports: 0 kWh (2013 est.)
country comparison to the world: 137

Electricity—imports: 0 kWh (2013 est.)
country comparison to the world: 148

Electricity—installed generating capacity: 10,000 kW (2012 est.)
country comparison to the world: 208

Electricity—from fossil fuels: 90% of total installed capacity (2012 est.)
country comparison to the world: 78

Electricity—from nuclear fuels: 0% of total installed capacity (2012 est.)
country comparison to the world: 91

Electricity—from hydroelectric plants: 0% of total installed capacity (2012 est.)
country comparison to the world: 172

Electricity—from other renewable sources: 10% of total installed capacity (2012 est.)
country comparison to the world: 36

Crude oil—production: 0 bbl/day (2014 est.)
country comparison to the world: 135

Crude oil—exports: 0 bbl/day (2012 est.)
country comparison to the world: 124

Crude oil—imports: 0 bbl/day (2012 est.)
country comparison to the world: 189

Crude oil—proved reserves: 0 bbl (1 January 2015 est.)
country comparison to the world: 133

Refined petroleum products—production: 0 bbl/day (2012 est.)
country comparison to the world: 181

Refined petroleum products—consumption: 300 bbl/day (2013 est.)
country comparison to the world: 210

Refined petroleum products—exports: 0 bbl/day (2012 est.)
country comparison to the world: 180

Refined petroleum products—imports: 312.5 bbl/day (2012 est.)
country comparison to the world: 207

Natural gas—production: 0 cu m (2013 est.)
country comparison to the world: 186

Natural gas—consumption: 0 cu m (2013 est.)
country comparison to the world: 143

Natural gas—exports: 0 cu m (2013 est.)
country comparison to the world: 99

Natural gas—imports: 0 cu m (2013 est.)
country comparison to the world: 196

Natural gas—proved reserves: 0 cu m (1 January 2014 est.)
country comparison to the world: 138

Carbon dioxide emissions from consumption of energy: 45,570 Mt (2012 est.)
country comparison to the world: 209

COMMUNICATIONS

Telephones—fixed lines: *total subscriptions:* 2,100
subscriptions per 100 inhabitants: 66 (2014 est.)
country comparison to the world: 214

Telephones—mobile cellular: *total:* 4,200

subscriptions per 100 in habitants: 133 (2014 est.)
country comparison to the world: 216

Telephone system: *domestic:* government-operated radiotelephone and private VHF/CB radiotelephone networks provide effective service to almost all points on both islands
international: country code—500; satellite earth station—1 Intelsat (Atlantic Ocean) with links through London to other countries (2011)

Broadcast media: TV service provided by a multi-channel service provider; radio services provided by the public broadcaster, Falkland Islands Radio Service, broadcasting on both AM and FM frequencies, and by the British Forces Broadcasting Service (BFBS) (2007)
Radio broadcast stations: AM 1, F M 7, short-wave 0 (British F orces Broadcasting Service (BF BS) provides Radio 1 and R adio 2 service) (2006)
Television broadcast stations:
2 (British Forces Broadcasting Service (BFBS) provides multi-channel satellite service to members of UK F orces as well as islanders); cable television is available in Stanley (2006)

Internet country code: .fk
Internet hosts: 110 (2012)
country comparison to the world: 206
Internet users: *total:* 2,900
percent of population: 92.4% (2009)

country comparison to the world: 209

TRANSPORTATION

Airports: 7 (2013)
country comparison to the world: 170

Airports—with paved runways: *total:* 2
2,438 to 3,047 m: 1
914 to 1,523 m: 1 (2013)

Airports—with unpaved runways: *total:* 5
under 914 m: 5 (2013)

Roadways: *total:* 440 km
paved: 50 km
unpaved: 390 km (2008)
country comparison to the world: 199

Ports and terminals: *major seaport(s):* Stanley

MILITARY AND SECURITY

Military branches: no regular military forces
Military—note: defense is the responsibility of the UK

TRANSNATIONAL ISSUES

Disputes—international: Argentina, which claims the islands in its constitution and briefly occupied them by force in 1982, agreed in 1995 to no longer seek settlement by force; UK continues to reject Argentine requests for sovereignty talks

FAROE ISLANDS

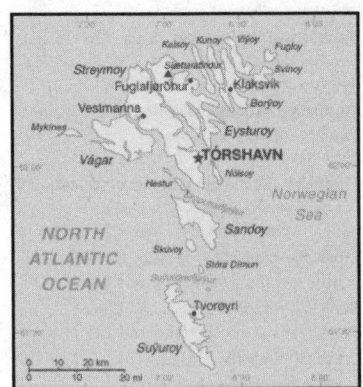

INTRODUCTION

Background: The population of the Faroe Islands is largely descended from Viking settlers who arrived in the 9th century. The islands have been connected politically to Denmark since the 14th century. A high degree of self-government was granted the Faroese in 1948, who have autonomy over most internal affairs while Denmark is responsible

for justice, defense, and foreign affairs. The Faroe Islands are not part of the European Union.

GEOGRAPHY

Location: Northern Europe, island group between the Norwegian Sea and the North Atlantic Ocean, about halfway between I celand and Norway

Geographic coordinates: 62 00 N, 7 00 W

Map references: Europe

Area: *total:* 1,393 sq km
land: 1,393 sq km
water: 0 sq km (some lakes and streams)
country comparison to the world: 183

Area—comparative: eight times the size of Washington, DC

Land boundaries: 0 km

Coastline: 1,117 km

Maritime claims: *territorial sea:* 3 nm
continental shelf: 200 nm or agreed boundaries or median line
exclusive fishing zone: 200 nm or agreed boundaries or median line

Climate: mild winters, cool summers; usually overcast; foggy, windy

Terrain: rugged, rocky, some low peaks; cliffs along most of coast

Elevation: *mean elevation:* NA

elevation extremes: *lowest point:* Atlantic Ocean 0 m
highest point: Slaettaratindur 882 m

Natural resources: fish, whales, hydropower, possible oil and gas

Land use: *agricultural land:* 2.1%
arable land: 2.1%
permanent crops: 0%
permanent pasture: 0%
forest: 0.1%
other: 97.8% (2011 est.)

Natural hazards: NA

Environment—current issues: NA

Environment—international agreements: *party to:* Marine Dumping—associate member to the London Convention and Ship Pollution

Geography—note: archipelago of 17 inhabited islands and one uninhabited island, and a few uninhabited islets; strategically located along important sea lanes in northeastern Atlantic; precipitous terrain limits habitation to small coastal lowlands

PEOPLE AND SOCIETY

Nationality: *noun:* Faroese (singular and plural)

adjective: Faroese

Ethnic groups: Faroese 89.2% (Scandinavian and Anglo-Saxon descent), Danish 7.1%, other 3.7% (includes Icelander, Norwegian, Greenlander, Filipino, Thai, British)
note: data represent respondents by country of birth (2011 est.)

Languages: Faroese 93.8% (derived from Old Norse), Danish 3.2%, other 3% (2011 est.)

Religions: Christian 89.3% (predominantly Evangelical Lutheran), other 0.7%, more than one religion 0.2%, none 3.8%, unspecified 6% (2011 est.)

Population: 50,196 (July 2015 est.)
country comparison to the world: 212

Age structure: *0–14 years:* 20.1% (male 5,224/female 4,866)
15–24 years: 14.96% (male 3,848/female 3,662)
25–54 years: 37.04% (male 10,090/female 8,502)
55–64 years: 11.73% (male 3,033/female 2,854)
65 years and over: 16.17% (male 3,926/female 4,191) (2015 est.)

Median age: *total:* 37.7 years
male: 37.1 years
female: 38.4 years (2015 est.)
country comparison to the world: 63

Population growth rate: 0.51% (2015 est.)
country comparison to the world: 158

Birth rate: 13.77 births/1,000 population (2015 est.)
country comparison to the world: 142

Death rate: 8.71 deaths/1,000 population (2015 est.)
country comparison to the world: 72

Net migration rate: 0 migrant(s)/1,000 population (2015 est.)
country comparison to the world: 97

Urbanization: *urban population:* 42% of total population (2015)
rate of urbanization: 0.47% annual rate of change (2010–15 est.)

Major urban areas—population: TORSHAVN (capital) 21,000 (2014)

Sex ratio: *at birth:* 1.07 male(s)/female
0–14 years: 1.07 male(s)/female
15–24 years: 1.05 male/female
25–54 years: 1.19 male/female
55–64 years: 1.06 male/female
65 years and over: 0.94 male/female
total population: 1.09 male(s)/female (2015 est.)

Infant mortality rate: *total:* 5.6 deaths/1,000 live births
male: 5.86 deaths/1,000 live births
female: 5.32 deaths/1,000 live births (2015 est.)
country comparison to the world: 170

Life expectancy at birth: *total population:* 80.24 years
male: 77.73 years
female: 82.93 years (2015 est.)
country comparison to the world: 37

Total fertility rate: 2.37 children born/woman (2015 est.)
country comparison to the world: 84

Hospital bed density: 4.7 beds/1,000 population (2012)

HIV/AIDS—adult prevalence rate: NA

HIV/AIDS—people living with HIV/AIDS: NA

HIV/AIDS—deaths: NA

GOVERNMENT

Country name: *conventional long form:* none
conventional short form: Faroe Islands
local long form: none
local short form: Foroyar
etymology: the archipelgo's name may derive from the Old Norse word "faer, " meaning sheep

Dependency status: part of the Kingdom of Denmark; self-governing overseas administrative division of Denmark since 1948

Government type: parliamentary democracy (Faroese Parliament); part of the Kingdom of Denmark

Capital: *name:* Torshavn

Geographic coordinates: 62 00 N, 6 46 W
time difference: UTC 0 (5 hours ahead of Washington, DC, during Standard Time)
daylight saving time: +1hr, begins last Sunday in March; ends last Sunday in October

Administrative divisions: none (part of the Kingdom of Denmark; self-governing overseas administrative division of Denmark); there are no first-order administrative divisions as defined by the US Government, but there are 30 municipalities

Independence: none (part of the Kingdom of Denmark; self-governing overseas administrative division of Denmark)

National holiday: Olaifest (Olavsoka),29 July

Constitution: 5 June 1953 (Danish Constitution), 23 March 1948 (Home Rule Act), and 24 June 2005 (Takeover Act) serve as the Faroe Islands constitutional position in the Unity of the Realm (2016)

Legal system: the laws of Denmark, where applicable, apply

Citizenship: see Denmark

Suffrage: 18 years of age; universal

Executive branch: *chief of state:* Queen MARGRETHE II of Denmark (since 14 January 1972), represented by High Commissioner Dan Michael KNUDSEN, chief administrative officer (since 2008)

head of government: Prime Minister Aksel V. JOHANNESEN (since 15 September 2015)
cabinet: Landsstyri appointed by the prime minister
elections/appointments: the monarchy is hereditary; high commissioner appointed by the monarch; following legislative elections, the leader of the majority party or majority coalition usually elected prime minister by the F aroese Parliament; election last held on 1 September 2015
election results: Aksel V. JOHANNESEN elected prime minister; Parliament vote—NA

Legislative branch: *description:* unicameral F aroese Parliament or Logting (33 seats; members directly elected in a single nationwide constituency by proportional representation vote; members serve 4-year terms)
note: election of 2 seats to the Danish Parliament was last held on 18 June 2015 (next to be held no later than J une 2019); percent of vote by party—NA; seats by party—Social Democratic Party 1, Republic 1
elections: last held on 1 September 2015 (next to be held no later than October 2019)
election results: percent of vote by party—Social Democratic Party 25.1%, Republic 20.7%, People's Party, 18.9%, Union Party 18.7%, Progressive Party 7.0%, Center Party 5.5%, Self-Government Party 4.1%; seats by party—Social Democratic Party 8, Republic 7, People's Party 6, Union Party 6, Center Party 2, Progressive Party 2, Self-Government Party 2

Judicial branch: the Faroese Court or Raett (Ret—Danish) decides both civil and criminal cases; the Court is part of the Danish legal system

Political parties and leaders:
Center Party (Midflokkurin) [Jenis av RANA]
Independence (or Self-Govenment) Party (Sjalvstyrisflokkurin) [Jogvan SKORHEIM]
People's Party (Folkaflokkurin) [Jorgen NICLASEN]
Progressive Party (Framsokn) [Poul MICHELSEN]
Republic (Tjodveldi) (formerly the Republican Party) [Hogni HOYDAL]
Social Democratic Party (Javnadarflokkurin) [Aksel V. JOHANNESEN]
Union Party (Sambandsflokkurin) [Bardur a STEIG NIELSEN]

Political pressure groups and leaders:
other: conservationists

International organization participation: Arctic Council, IMO (associate), NC, NIB, UNESCO (associate), UPU

Diplomatic representation in the US: none (self-governing overseas administrative division of Denmark)

Diplomatic representation from the US: none (self-governing overseas administrative division of Denmark)

Flag description: white with a red cross outlined in blue extending to the edges of the flag; the vertical part of the cross is shifted toward the hoist side in the style of the Dannebrog (Danish flag); referred to as Merkid, meaning "the banner" or "the mark," the flag resembles those of neighboring Iceland and Norway, and uses the same three colors—but in a different sequence; white represents the clear Faroese sky as well as the foam of the waves; red and blue are traditional F aroese colors

National symbol(s): ram; national colors: red, white, blue

National anthem: *name:* "Mitt alfagra land" (My Fairest Land)
lyrics/music: Simun av SKAROI/Peter ALBERG
note: adopted 1948; the anthem is also known as "Tu alfagra land mitt" (Thou Fairest Land of Mine); as a self-governing overseas administrative division of Denmark, the Faroe Islands are permitted their own national anthem

ECONOMY

Economy—overview: The Faroese economy has experienced a period of significant growth since 2011, due to increases in fish prices, salmon farming, and catches in the pelagic fisheries. Nominal GDP growth was an estimated 7.5% in 2013 and 5.9% in 2014. The fisheries sector accounts for about 95% of exports and half of GDP. Unemployment is low, estimated at 2.9% in mid-2015.
The public budget has exhibited deficits since 2008, which were financed through increased borrowing. Public debt reached 38% of GDP in 2015. Aided by an annual subsidy from Denmark amounting to about 4% of Faroese GDP, the Faroese have a standard of living equal to that of Denmark. Dependence on fishing makes the economy vulnerable to price fluctuations. Projections for fish prices are favorable and increasing public infrastructure investments are likely to lead to continued growth in the short term.

GDP (purchasing power parity):
$1.831 billion (2014 est.)
$1.729 billion (2013 est.)
$1.471 billion (2013 est.)
country comparison to the world: 198

GDP (official exchange rate): $2.32 billion (2010 est.)

GDP—real growth rate: 5.9% (2014 est.)
7.5% (2013 est.)
2.9% (2013 est.)
country comparison to the world: 31

GDP—per capita (PPP): $36,600 (2014 est.)
country comparison to the world: 47

GDP—composition, by sector of origin:
agriculture: 16%
industry: 29%
services: 55% (2007 est.)

Agriculture—products: milk, potatoes, vegetables; sheep; salmon, herring, mackerel and other fish

Industries: fishing, fish processing, tourism, small ship repair and refurbishment, handicrafts

Industrial production growth rate: 3.4% (2009 est.)
country comparison to the world: 74

Labor force: 25,000 (2015 est.)
country comparison to the world: 209

Labor force—by occupation: *agriculture:* 10.7%
industry: 18.9%
services: 70.3% (November 2010)

Unemployment rate: 2.9% (2015 est.)
3.1% (2014)
country comparison to the world: 21

Population below poverty line: NA%

Household income or consumption by percentage share: *lowest:* 10%: NA%
highest: 10%: NA%

Budget: *revenues:* $1.025 billion
expenditures: $1.301 billion
note: Denmark supplies the Faroe Islands with almost one-third of their public funds (2010 est.)
Taxes and other revenues: 44.2% of GDP (2010 est.)
country comparison to the world: 27

Budget surplus (+) or deficit (–): -11.9% of GDP (2010 est.)
country comparison to the world: 207

Fiscal year: calendar year

Inflation rate (consumer prices): 2.3% (2011)
0.4% (2010)
country comparison to the world: 125

Exports: $824 million (2010)
$767 million (2009)
country comparison to the world: 165

Exports—commodities: fish and fish products 95%, ships (2009 est.)

Exports—partners: Russia 20.2%, UK 16.6%, Denmark 16.3%, Nigeria 11.6%, China 9.3%, US 7.2%, Netherlands 5.6%, Norway 4% (2015)

Imports: $776 million (2010)
$786 million (2009)
country comparison to the world: 187

Imports—commodities: goods for household consumption, machinery and tran sport equipment, fuels, raw materials and semi-man ufactures, cars

Imports—partners: Denmark 43.9%, Turkey 12.3%, Norway 10%, China 6.2%, Netherlands 4.9%, Germany 4.4% (2015)

Debt—external: $888.8 million (2010)
$68.1 million (2006)
country comparison to the world: 168

Exchange rates: Danish kroner (DKK) per US dollar—
6.588 (2011)
5.3687 (2011)
5.3687 (2011)
5.79 (2012 est.)
5.3687 (2011 est.)

ENERGY

Electricity—production: 281 million kWh (2012 est.)
country comparison to the world: 181

Electricity—consumption: 261.3 million kWh (2012 est.)
country comparison to the world: 185

Electricity—exports: 0 kWh (2013 est.)
country comparison to the world: 139

Electricity—imports: 0 kWh (2013 est.)
country comparison to the world: 150

Electricity—installed generating capacity: 108,100 kW (2012 est.)
country comparison to the world: 172

Electricity—from fossil fuels: 60.1% of total installed capacity (2012 est.)
country comparison to the world: 134

Electricity—from nuclear fuels: 0% of total installed capacity (2012 est.)
country comparison to the world: 93

Electricity—from hydroelectric plants: 36.1% of total installed capacity (2012 est.)
country comparison to the world: 63

Electricity—from other renewable sources: 3.8% of total installed capacity (2012 est.)
country comparison to the world: 64

Crude oil—production: 0 bbl/day (2014 est.)
country comparison to the world: 137

Crude oil—exports: 0 bbl/day (2012 est.)
country comparison to the world: 126

Crude oil—imports: 0 bbl/day (2012 est.)
country comparison to the world: 191

Crude oil—proved reserves: 0 bbl (1 January 2015 est.)
country comparison to the world: 135

Refined petroleum products—production: 0 bbl/day (2012 est.)
country comparison to the world: 183

Refined petroleum products—consumption: 4,900 bbl/day (2013 est.)
country comparison to the world: 170

Refined petroleum products—exports: 0 bbl/day (2012 est.)
country comparison to the world: 182

Refined petroleum products—imports: 4,879 bbl/day (2012 est.)
country comparison to the world: 162

Natural gas—production: 0 cu m (2013 est.)
country comparison to the world: 188

Natural gas—consumption: 0 cu m (2013 est.)
country comparison to the world: 144

Natural gas—exports: 0 cu m (2013 est.)
country comparison to the world: 100

Natural gas—imports: 0 cu m (2013 est.)
country comparison to the world: 197

Natural gas—proved reserves: 0 cu m (1 January 2014 est.)
country comparison to the world: 140

Carbon dioxide emissions from consumption of energy: 753,400 Mt (2012 est.)
country comparison to the world: 172

COMMUNICATIONS

Telephones—fixed lines: *total subscriptions:* 17,300
subscriptions per 100 inhabitants: 35 (2014 est.)
country comparison to the world: 189

Telephones—mobile cellular: *total:* 61,400
subscriptions per 100 inhabitants: 123 (2014 est.)
country comparison to the world: 199

Telephone system: *general assessment:* good international communications; good domestic facilities
domestic: conversion to digital system completed in 1998; both NMT (analog) and GSM (digital) mobile telephone systems are installed
international: country code—298; satellite earth stations—1 Orion; 1 fiber-optic submarine cable to the Shetland Islands, linking the Faroe Islands with Denmark and Iceland; fiber-optic submarine cable connection to Canada-Europe cable (2011)

Broadcast media: 1 publicly owned TV station; the Faroese telecommunications company distributes local and international channels through its digital terrestrial network; publicly owned radio station supplemented by 3 privately owned stations broadcasting over multiple frequencies (2015)

Radio broadcast stations: AM 1, FM 13, shortwave 0 (1998)

Television broadcast stations: 3 (plus 43 repeaters) (September 1995)

Internet country code: .fo

Internet hosts: 7,575 (2012)
country comparison to the world: 140

Internet users: *total:* 44,000
percent of population: 88.2% (2014 est.)
country comparison to the world: 188

TRANSPORTATION

Airports: 1 (2013)
country comparison to the world: 217

Airports—with paved runways: *total:* 1

1,524 to 2,437 m: 1 (2013)

Roadways: *total:* 960 km (2015)
country comparison to the world: 197

Merchant marine: *total:* 37
by type: cargo 20, chemical tanker 7, container 2, passenger/cargo 3, refrigerated cargo 3, roll on/roll off 2
foreign-owned: 28 (Iceland 4, Norway 13, Sweden 11) (2010)
country comparison to the world: 79

Ports and terminals: *major seaport(s):* Fuglafjordur, Torshavn, Vagur

MILITARY AND SECURITY

Military branches: no regular military forces; the Government of Denmark has responsibility for defense; as such, the Danish military's Joint Arctic

---

Command is responsible for territorial defense of the Faroe Islands (2016)

Military—note: defense is the responsibility of Denmark

TRANSNATIONAL ISSUES

Disputes—international: because anticipated offshore hydrocarbon resources have not been realized, earlier Faroese proposals for full independence have been deferred; Iceland, the UK, and Ireland dispute Denmark's claim that the Faroe Islands' continental shelf extends beyond 200 nm

---

FIJI

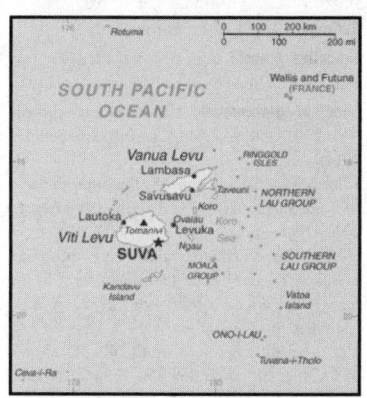

INTRODUCTION

Background: Fiji became independent in 1970 after nearly a century as a British colony. Democratic rule was interrupted by two military coups in 1987 caused by concern over a government perceived as dominated by the Indian community (descendants of contract laborers brought to the islands by the British in the 19th century). The coups and a 1990 constitution that cemented native Melanesian control of Fiji led to heavy Indian emigration; the population loss resulted in economic difficulties, but ensured that Melanesians became the majority. A new constitution enacted in 1997 was more equitable. Free and peaceful elections in 1999 resulted in a government led by an Indo-Fijian, but a civilian-led coup in 2000 ushered in a prolonged period of political turmoil. Parliamentary elections held in 2001 provided Fiji with a democratically elected government led by Prime Minister Laisenia QARASE. Reelected in May 2006, QARASE was ousted in a December 2006 military coup led by Commodore Voreqe BAINIMARAMA, who

---

initially appointed himself acting president but in January 2007 became interim prime minister. Following years of political turmoil, long-delayed legislative elections were held in September 2014 that were deemed "credible" by international observers and that resulted in BAINIMARAMA being reelected.

GEOGRAPHY

Location: Oceania, island group in the South Pacific Ocean, about two-thirds of the way from Hawaii to New Zealand

Geographic coordinates: 18 00 S, 175 00 E

Map references: Oceania

Area: *total:* 18,274 sq km
land: 18,274 sq km
water: 0 sq km
country comparison to the world: 157

Area—comparative: slightly smaller than New Jersey

Land boundaries: 0 km

Coastline: 1,129 km

Maritime claims: measured from claimed archipelagic straight baselines
territorial sea: 12 nm
exclusive economic zone: 200 nm
continental shelf: 200-m depth or to the depth of exploitation; rectilinear shelf claim added

Climate: tropical marine; only slight seasonal temperature variation

Terrain: mostly mountains of volcanic origin

Elevation: *mean elevation:* NA

elevation extremes: *lowest point:* Pacific Ocean 0 m
highest point: Tomanivi 1,324 m

Natural resources: timber, fish, gold, copper, offshore oil potential, hydropower

---

Land use:
agricultural land: 23.3%
arable land: 9%
permanent crops: 4.7%
permanent pasture: 9.6%
forest: 55.7%
other: 21% (2011 est.)

Irrigated land: 40 sq km (2012)

Total renewable water resources: 28.55 cu km (2011)

Freshwater withdrawal (domestic/industrial/agricultural): *total:* 0.08 cu km/yr (30%/11%/59%)
per capita: 100.1 cu m/yr (2005)

Natural hazards: cyclonic storms can occur from November to January

Environment—current issues: deforestation; soil erosion

Environment—international agreements: *party to:* Biodiversity, Climate Change, Climate Change-Kyoto Protocol, Desertification, Endangered Species, Law of the Sea, Marine Life Conservation, Ozone Layer Protection, Tropical Timber 83, Tropical Timber 94, Wetlands
signed, but not ratified: none of the selected agreements

Geography—note: includes 332 islands; approximately 110 are inhabited

PEOPLE AND SOCIETY

Nationality: *noun:* Fijian(s)
adjective: Fijian

Ethnic groups: iTaukei 56.8% (predominantly Melanesian with a Polynesian admixture), Indian 37.5%, Rotuman 1.2%, other 4.5% (European, part European, other Pacific Islanders, Chinese)
note: a 2010 law replaces 'Fijian' with 'iTuakei' when referring to the original and native settlers of Fiji (2007 est.)

Languages: English (official), Fijian (official), Hindustani

Religions: Protestant 45% (Methodist 34.6%, Assembly of God 5.7%, Seventh Day Adventist 3.9%, and Anglican 0.8%), Hindu 27.9%, other Christian 10.4%, Roman Catholic 9.1%, Muslim 6.3%, Sikh 0.3%, other 0.3%, none 0.8% (2007 est.)

Population: 909,389 (July 2015 est.)
country comparison to the world: 162

Age structure: *0–14 years:* 28.03% (male 130,251/female 124,633)
15–24 years: 16.73% (male 77,716/female 74,449)
25–54 years: 41.12% (male 191,393/female 182,571)
55–64 years: 8.04% (male 37,019/female 36,141)
65 years and over: 6.07% (male 25,386/female 29,830) (2015 est.)

Dependency ratios: *total dependency ratio:* 52.8%
youth dependency ratio: 43.9%
elderly dependency ratio: 8.9%
potential support ratio: 11.2% (2015 est.)

Median age: *total:* 28.2 years
male: 28 years
female: 28.4 years (2015 est.)
country comparison to the world: 127

Population growth rate: 0.67% (2015 est.)
country comparison to the world: 149

Birth rate: 19.43 births/1,000 population (2015 est.)
country comparison to the world: 88

Death rate: 6.04 deaths/1,000 population (2015 est.)
country comparison to the world: 163

Net migration rate: -6.75 migrant(s)/1,000 population (2015 est.)
country comparison to the world: 203

Urbanization: *urban population:* 53.7% of total population (2015)
rate of urbanization: 1.45% annual rate of change (2010–15 est.)

Major urban areas—population: SUVA (capital) 176,000 (2014)

Sex ratio: *at birth:* 1.05 male(s)/female
0–14 years: 1.05 male(s)/female
15–24 years: 1.04 male(s)/female
25–54 years: 1.05 male(s)/female
55–64 years: 1.02 male(s)/female
65 years and over: 0.85 male(s)/female
total population: 1.03 male(s)/female (2015 est.)

Maternal mortality rate: 30 deaths/100,000 live births (2015 est.)
country comparison to the world: 129

Infant mortality rate: *total:* 9.94 deaths/1,000 live births
male: 10.97 deaths/1,000 live births
female: 8.87 deaths/1,000 live births (2015 est.)
country comparison to the world: 138

Life expectancy at birth: *total population:* 72.43 years
male: 69.79 years
female: 75.2 years (2015 est.)

country comparison to the world: 141

Total fertility rate: 2.47 children born/woman (2015 est.)
country comparison to the world: 81

Health expenditures: 4.1% of GDP (2013)
country comparison to the world: 160

Physicians density: 0.43 physicians/1,000 population (2009)

Hospital bed density: 2 beds/1,000 population (2009)

Drinking water source:
improved:
urban: 99.5% of population
rural: 91.2% of population
total: 95.7% of population
unimproved:
urban: 0.5% of population
rural: 8.8% of population
total: 4.3% of population (2015 est.)

Sanitation facility access:
improved:
urban: 93.4% of population
rural: 88.4% of population
total: 91.1% of population
unimproved:
urban: 6.6% of population
rural: 11.6% of population
total: 8.9% of population (2015 est.)

HIV/AIDS—adult prevalence rate: 0.13% (2014 est.)
country comparison to the world: 109

HIV/AIDS—people living with HIV/AIDS: 700 (2014 est.)
country comparison to the world: 122

HIV/AIDS—deaths: fewer than 100 (2014 est.)
country comparison to the world: 120

Obesity—adult prevalence rate: 35.9% (2014)
country comparison to the world: 25

Education expenditures: 3.9% of GDP (2013)
country comparison to the world: 102

Unemployment, youth ages 15–24: *total:* 18.7%
male: 14.8%
female: 25.4% (2007 est.)

GOVERNMENT

Country name: *conventional long form:* Republic of Fiji
conventional short form: Fiji
local long form: Republic of Fiji/Matanitu ko Viti
local short form: Fiji/Viti
etymology: the Fijians called their home Viti, but the neighboring Tongans called it Fisi, and in the Anglicized spelling of the Tongan pronunciation—promulgated by explorer Captain James COOK—the designation became Fiji

Government type: parliamentary republic

Capital: *name:* Suva (on Viti Levu)

Geographic coordinates: 18 08 S, 178 25 E
time difference: UTC + 12 (17 hours ahead of Washington, DC, during Standard Time)

daylight saving time: +1hr, begins fourth Sunday in October; ends third Sunday in January

Administrative divisions: 14 provinces and 1 dependency*; Ba, Bua, Cakaudrove, Kadavu, Lau, Lomaiviti, Macuata, Nadroga and Navosa, Naitasiri, Namosi, Ra, Rewa, Rotuma*, Serua, Tailevu

Independence: 10 October 1970 (from the UK)

National holiday: Fiji Independence Day, 10 October (1970)

Constitution: several previous; latest signed into law September 2013 (2016)

Legal system: common law system based on the English model

International law organization participation: has not submitted an ICJ jurisdiction declaration; accepts ICCt jurisdiction

Citizenship: *citizenship by birth:* no
citizenship by descent only: at least one parent must be a citizen of Fiji
dual citizenship recognized: yes
residency requirement for naturalization: 5 years

Suffrage: 18 years of age; universal

Executive branch: *chief of state:* President Jioji Konousi KONROTE (since 12 November 2015)

head of government: Prime Minister Voreqe "Frank" BAINIMARAMA (since 22 September 2014)
cabinet: Cabinet appointed by the prime minister from among members of Parliament and is responsible to Parliament
elections/appointments: under the constitution, president elected by the Parliament for a 5-year term (eligible for a second term); prime minister appointed by the president
election results: Jioji Konousi KONROTE elected 12 October 2015 defeating Ratu Epeli GANILAU 31 to 14

Legislative branch: *description:* unicameral Parliament (50 seats; members directly elected in a nationwide, multi-seat constituency by open-list proportional representation vote to serve 4-year terms; the new constitution of 2013 restructured Parliament from bicameral to unicameral
elections: last held on 17 September 2014 (next to be held in 2019)
election results: percent of vote by party—Fiji First 59.2%, SDL 28.2%, National Federation Party 5.5%, other 7.1%; seats by party—Fiji First 32, SDL 15, National Federation Party 3

Judicial branch: *highest court(s):* Supreme Court (consists of the chief justice, all justices of the Court of Appeal, and judges appointed specifically as Supreme Court judges); Court of Appeal (consists of the court president, all puisne judges of the High Court, and judges specifically appointed to the Court of Appeal); High Court (chaired by the chief justice and includes a minimum of 10 puisne judges; High Court organized into civil, criminal, family, employment, and tax divisions); note—in

1987, the Supreme Court assumed functions formerly performed by the Judicial Committee of the Privy Council (in London)

judge selection and term of office: chief justice appointed by the president of Fiji on the advice of the prime minister following consultation with the parliamentary leader of the opposition; judges of the Supreme Court, the president of the Court of Appeal, the justices of the Court of Appeal, and puisne judges of the High Court appointed by the president of Fiji upon the nomination of the Judicial Service Commission after consulting with the cabinet minister and the committee of the House of Representatives responsible for the administration of justice; the chief justice, Supreme Court judges and justices of Appeal generally required to retire at age 70 but may be waived for one or more sessions of the court; puisne judges appointed for not less than 4 years nor more than 7 years with mandatory retirement at age 65

subordinate courts: Magistrates' Court (organized into civil, criminal, juvenile, and small claims divisions)

Political parties and leaders: FijiFirst [Aiyaz SAYED-KHAIYUM]
Fiji Labor Party or FLP [Mahendra CHAUDHRY]
Fiji United Freedon Party or FUFP [Jagath KARUNARATNE]
National Federation Party or NFP [Dalip KUMAR] (primarily Indian)
Peoples Democratic Party or PDP [Adi Sivia QORO]
Social Democratic Liberal Party or SODELPA [Pio TABAIWALU]

Political pressure groups and leaders: Group Against Racial Discrimination or GARD [Dr. Anirudk SINGH] (suports restoration of a democratic government)
Viti Landowners Association

International organization participation: ACP, ADB, AOSIS, C, CP, FAO, G-77, IAEA, IBRD, ICAO, ICCt, ICRM, IDA, IFAD, IFC, IFRCS, IHO, ILO, IMF, IMO, Interpol, IOC, IO , ISO, ITSO, ITU, ITUC (NGOs), MIGA, OPCW, PCA, PIF, Sparteca (suspended), SPC, UN, UNCTAD, UNDOF, UNESCO, UNIDO, UNMISS, UNWTO, UPU, WCO, WFTU (NGOs), WHO, WIPO, WMO, WTO

Diplomatic representation in the US: *chief of mission:* Ambassador Solo MARA (since 28 January 2016)
chancery: 2000 M Street NW, Suite 710, Washington, DC 20036
telephone: [1] (202) 466-8320
FAX: [1] (202) 466-8325

Diplomatic representation from the US: *chief of mission:* Ambassador Judith CEFKIN (since 3 February 2015); note—also accredited to Kiribati, Nauru, Tonga, and Tuvalu
embassy: 158 Princes Rd, Tamavua
mailing address: P.O. Box 218, Suva

telephone: [679] 331-4466
FAX: [679] 330-8685

Flag description: light blue with the flag of the UK in the upper hoist-side quadrant and the Fijian shield centered on the outer half of the flag; the blue symbolizes the Pacific ocean and the Union Jack reflects the links with Great Britain; the shield—taken from Fiji's coat of arms—depicts a yellow lion above a white field quartered by the cross of Saint George; the four quarters depict stalks of sugarcane, a palm tree, bananas, and a white dove

National symbol(s): Fijian canoe; national color: light blue

National anthem: *name:* "God Bless Fiji"
lyrics/music: Michael Francis Alexander PRESCOTT/C. Austin MILES (adapted by Michael Francis Alexander PR ESCO TT)
note: adopted 1970; known in Fijian as "Meda Dau Doka" (Let US Show Pride); adapted from the hymn, "Dwelling in Beulah Land, " the anthem's English lyrics are generally sung, although they differ in meaning from the official Fijian lyrics

ECONOMY

Economy—overview: Fiji, endowed with forest, mineral, and fish resources, is one of the most developed and connected of the Pacific island economies. Earnings from the tourism industry, with an estimated 755,000 tourists visiting in 2015, and remittances from Fijian's working abroad are the country's largest foreign exchange earners. Fiji's sugar remains a significant industry and a major export. The sugar industry reforms since 2010 have improved productivity and returns, but the industry faces the complete withdrawal of European Union preferential prices by 2017. Fiji's trade imbalance continues to widen with increased imports and sluggish performan ce of dom estic exports.

The return to parliamentary democracy and successful elections in September 2014 have boosted investor confidence. Private sector investment in 2015 exceeded 20% of GDP, compared to 13% in 2013.

GDP (purchasing power parity): $8.048 billion (2015 est.)
$7.716 billion (2014 est.)
$7.329 billion (2013 est.)
note: data are in 2015 US dollars
country comparison to the world: 163

GDP (official exchange rate): $4.782 billion (2015 est.)

GDP—real growth rate: 4.3% (2015 est.)
5.3% (2014 est.)
4.7% (2013 est.)
country comparison to the world: 54

GDP—per capita (PPP): $9,000 (2015 est.)
$8,700 (2014 est.)
$8,300 (2013 est.)
note: data are in 2015 US dollars
country comparison to the world: 139

Gross national saving: 13.6% of GDP (2015 est.)
10.5% of GDP (2014 est.)
7.6% of GDP (2013 est.)
country comparison to the world: 127

GDP—composition, by end use:
household consumption: 72%
government consumption: 13.5%
investment in fixed capital: 20.4%
investment in inventories: -0.1%
exports of goods and services: 56.7%
imports of goods and services: -62.5% (2015 est.)

GDP—composition, by sector of origin: *agriculture:* 11.9%
industry: 19.6%
services: 68.4% (2015 est.)

Agriculture—products: sugarcane, coconuts, cassava (manioc, tapioca), rice, sweet potatoes, bananas; cattle, pigs, horses, goats; fish

Industries: tourism, sugar, clothing, copra, gold, silver, lumber, small cottage industries

Industrial production growth rate: 2.2% (2015 est.)
country comparison to the world: 109

Labor force: 347,700 (2015 est.)
country comparison to the world: 162

Labor force—by occupation: *agriculture:* 70%
industry and services: 30% (2001 est.)

Unemployment rate: 8.8% (2014 est.)
8.7% (2013 est.)
country comparison to the world: 104

Population below poverty line: 31% (2009 est.)

Household income or consumption by percentage share: *lowest:* 10%: 2.6%
highest: 10%: 34.9% (2009 est.)

Budget: *revenues:* $1.087 billion
expenditures: $1.182 billion (2015 est.)
Taxes and other revenues: 24% of GDP (2015 est.)
country comparison to the world: 131

Budget surplus (+) or deficit (−): -2.1% of GDP (2015 est.)
country comparison to the world: 79

Public debt: 49.5% of GDP (2015 est.)
51.8% of GDP (2014 est.)
country comparison to the world: 82

Fiscal year: calendar year

Inflation rate (consumer prices):
2.8% (2015 est.)
0.5% (2014 est.)
country comparison to the world: 133

Central bank discount rate:
1.75% (31 December 2010)
3% (31 December 2009)
country comparison to the world: 117

Commercial bank prime lending rate:
6.1% (31 December 2015 est.)
5.76% (31 December 2014 est.)
country comparison to the world: 128

Stock of narrow money:
$1.85 billion (31 December 2015 est.)
$1.823 billion (31 December 2014 est.)
country comparison to the world: 131

Stock of broad money:
$3.165 billion (31 December 2015 est.)
$3.118 billion (31 December 2014 est.)
country comparison to the world: 145

Stock of domestic credit:
$2.979 billion (31 December 2015 est.)
$2.896 billion (31 December 2014 est.)
country comparison to the world: 130

Market value of publicly traded shares:
$452.5 million (31 December 2012 est.)
$392.2 million (31 December 2011)
$418.8 million (31 December 2010 est.)
country comparison to the world: 114

Current account balance:
-$257 million (2015 est.)
-$326 million (2014 est.)
country comparison to the world: 86

Exports: $1.244 billion (2015 est.)
$1.152 billion (2014 est.)
country comparison to the world: 153

Exports—commodities: sugar, garments, gold, timber, fish, molasses, coconut oil, mineral water

Exports—partners: US 13.4%, Australia 10.2%, Samoa 6.7%, Tonga 5.9% (2015)

Imports: $2.283 billion (2015 est.) $2.403 billion (2014 est.)
country comparison to the world: 158

Imports—commodities: manufactured goods, machinery and transport equipment, petroleum products, food, chemicals

Imports—partners: China 16.2%, South Korea 15.7%, NZ 14%, Australia 13.4%, Singapore 8.7%, France 7% (2015)

Reserves of foreign exchange and gold:
$903 million (31 December 2015 est.)
$916.2 million (31 December 2014 est.)
country comparison to the world: 137

Debt—external:
$769.1 million (31 December 2014 est.)
$797.5 million (31 December 2013 est.)
country comparison to the world: 169

Stock of direct foreign investment—at home:
$4.193 billion (31 December 2015 est.)
$3.893 billion (31 December 2014 est.)
country comparison to the world: 100

Stock of direct foreign investment—abroad:
$50.08 million (31 December 2014 est.)
$50.2 million (31 December 2012 est.)
country comparison to the world: 98

Exchange rates: Fijian dollars (FJD) per US dollar—
2.115 (2015 est.)
1.8874 (2014 est.)
1.8874 (2013 est.)
1.79 (2012 est.)
1.7932 (2011 est.)

ENERGY

Electricity—production: 857.5 million kWh (2013 est.)
country comparison to the world: 155

Electricity—consumption: 777.6 million kWh (2012 est.)
country comparison to the world: 160

Electricity—exports: 0 kWh (2013 est.)
country comparison to the world: 136

Electricity—imports: 0 kWh (2013 est.)
country comparison to the world: 147

Electricity—installed generating capacity: 259,000 kW (2012 est.)
country comparison to the world: 154

Electricity—from fossil fuels: 46.3% of total installed capacity (2012 est.)
country comparison to the world: 154

Electricity—from nuclear fuels: 0% of total installed capacity (2012 est.)
country comparison to the world: 90

Electricity—from hydroelectric plants: 48.3% of total installed capacity (2012 est.)
country comparison to the world: 51

Electricity—from other renewable sources: 5.4% of total installed capacity (2012 est.)
country comparison to the world: 56

Crude oil—production: 0 bbl/day (2014 est.)
country comparison to the world: 134

Crude oil—exports: 0 bbl/day (2012 est.)
country comparison to the world: 123

Crude oil—imports: 0 bbl/day (2012 est.)
country comparison to the world: 188

Crude oil—proved reserves: 0 bbl (1 January 2015 est.)
country comparison to the world: 132

Refined petroleum products—production: 0 bbl/day (2012 est.)
country comparison to the world: 180

Refined petroleum products—consumption: 9,400 bbl/day (2013 est.)
country comparison to the world: 154

Refined petroleum products—exports: 690.3 bbl/day (2012 est.)
country comparison to the world: 112

Refined petroleum products—imports: 10,130 bbl/day (2012 est.)
country comparison to the world: 136

Natural gas—production: 0 cu m (2013 est.)
country comparison to the world: 185

Natural gas—consumption: 0 cu m (2013 est.)
country comparison to the world: 142

Natural gas—exports: 0 cu m (2013 est.)
country comparison to the world: 98

Natural gas—imports: 0 cu m (2013 est.)
country comparison to the world: 195

Natural gas—proved reserves: 0 cu m (1 January 2014 est.)
country comparison to the world: 137

Carbon dioxide emissions from consumption of energy: 1.543 million Mt (2012 est.)
country comparison to the world: 157

COMMUNICATIONS

Telephones—fixed lines: *total subscriptions:* 74,700

subscriptions per 100 inhabitants: 8 (2014 est.)
country comparison to the world: 150

Telephones—mobile cellular: *total:* 876,200
subscriptions per 100 inhabitants: 97 (2014 est.)
country comparison to the world: 161

Telephone system: *general assessment:* modern local, interisland, and international (wire/radio integrated) public and special-purpose telephone, telegraph, and teleprinter facilities; regional radio communications center
domestic: telephone or radio telephone links to almost all inhabited islands; most towns and large villages have automatic telephone exchanges and direct dialing; combined fixed-line and mobile-cellular teledensity roughly 100 per 100 persons
international: country code—679; access to important cable links between US and Canada, as well as between NZ and Australia; satellite earth stations—2 Inmarsat (Pacific Ocean) (2011)

Broadcast media: Fiji TV, a publicly traded company, operates a free-to-air channel, as well as Sky Fiji and Sky Pacific multichannel pay-TV services; state-owned commercial company, Fiji Broadcasting Corporation, Ltd, operates 6 radio stations—2 public broadcasters and 4 commercial broadcasters with multiple repeaters; 5 radio stations with repeaters operated by Communications Fiji, Ltd; transmissions of multiple international broadcasters are available (2009)
Radio broadcast stations: AM 13, FM 40, short-wave 0 (1998)
Television broadcast stations: NA

Internet country code: .fj

Internet hosts: 21,739 (2012)
country comparison to the world: 115

Internet users: total: 331,700

percent of population: 36.7% (2014 est.)
country comparison to the world: 139

TRANSPORTATION

Airports: 28 (2013)
country comparison to the world: 121

Airports—with paved runways: *total:* 4
over 3,047 m: 1
1,524 to 2,437 m: 1
914 to 1,523 m: 2 (2013)

Airports—with unpaved runways: *total:* 24
914 to 1,523 m: 5
under 914 m: 19 (2013)

Railways: *total:* 597 km
narrow gauge: 597 km 0.600-m gauge
note: belongs to the government-owned Fiji Sugar Corporation; used to haul sugarcane during the harvest season, which runs from May to December (2008)
country comparison to the world: 110

Roadways: *total:* 3,440 km
paved: 1,686 km
unpaved: 1,754 km (2011)
country comparison to the world: 163

Waterways: 203 km (122 km are navigable by motorized craft and 200-metric-ton barges) (2012)
country comparison to the world: 97

Merchant marine: *total:* 11
by type: passenger 4, passenger/cargo 4, refrigerated cargo 1, roll on/roll off 2
foreign-owned: 2 (Australia 2) (2010)
country comparison to the world: 108

Ports and terminals: *major seaport(s):* Lautoka, Levuka, Suva

Military branches: Republic of Fiji Military Forces (RFMF): Land Forces, Naval Forces (2011)

Military service age and obligation: 18 years of age for voluntary military service; mandatory retirement at age 55 (2013)

Military expenditures: 1.47% of GDP (2012)
1.44% of GDP (2011)
1.47% of GDP (2010)
country comparison to the world: 61

TRANSNATIONAL ISSUES

Disputes—international: none

FINLAND

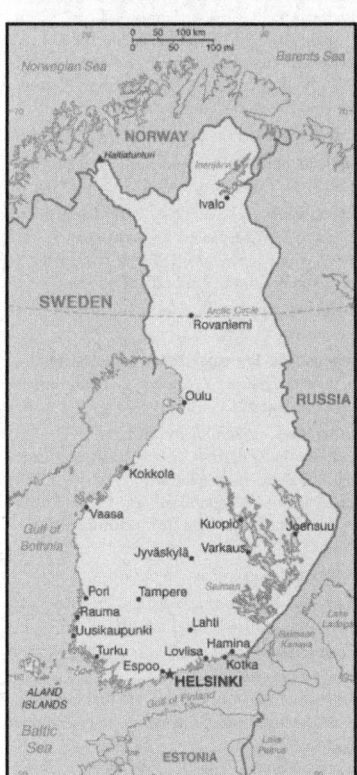

INTRODUCTION

Background: Finland was a province and then a grand duchy under Sweden from the 12th to the 19th centuries, and an autonomous grand duchy of Russia after 1809. It gained complete independence in 1917. During World War II, Finland successfully defended its in dependence through cooperation with Germany and resisted subsequent invasions by the Soviet Union—albeit with some loss of territory. In the subsequent h alf century, Finland transformed from a farm/forest economy to a diversified modern industrial economy; per capita income is among the highest in Western Europe. A member of the EU since 1995, Finland

was the only Nordic state to join the euro single currency at its initiation in January 1999. In the 21st century, the key features of Finland's modern welfare state are high quality education, promotion of equality, and a national social welfare system—currently challenged by an aging population and the fluctuations of an export-driven economy.

GEOGRAPHY

Location: Northern Europe, bordering the Baltic Sea, Gulf of Bothnia, and Gulf of Finland, between Sweden and Russia

Geographic coordinates: 64 00 N, 26 00 E

Map references: Europe

Area: *total:* 338,145 sq km
land: 303,815 sq km
water: 34,330 sq km
country comparison to the worl d: 65

Area—comparative: slightly more than two times the size of Georgia; slightly smaller than Montana

Land boundaries: *total:* 2,563 k m
border countries (3): Norway 709 km, Sweden 545 km, Russia 1,309 km

Coastline: 1,250 km

Maritime claims: *territorial sea:* 12 nm (in the Gulf of Finland—3 nm)
contiguous zone: 24 nm
exclusive fishing zone: 12 nm; extends to continental shelf boundary with Sweden, Estonia, and Russia
continental shelf: 200 m depth or to the depth of exploitation

Climate: cold temperate; potentially subarctic but comparatively mild because of moderating influence of the North Atlantic Current, Baltic Sea, and more than 60,000 lakes

Terrain: mostly low, flat to rolling plains interspersed with lakes and low hills

Elevation: *mean elevation:* 164 m

elevation extremes: *lowest point:* Baltic Sea 0 m
highest point: Halti (alternatively Haltia, Haltitunturi, Haltiatunturi) 1,328 m

Natural resources: timber, iron ore, copper, lead, zinc, chromite, nickel, gold, silver, limestone

Land use: *agricultural land:* 7.5%
arable land: 7.4%
permanent crops: 0%

permanent pasture: 0.1%
forest: 72.9%
other: 19.6% (2011 est.)

Irrigated land: 690 sq km (2012)

Total renewable water resources: 110 cu km (2011)

Freshwater withdrawal (domestic/industrial/agricultural):
total: 1.63 cu km/yr (25%/72%/3%)
per capita: 308.9 cu m/yr (2005)

Natural hazards: NA

Environment—current issues: air pollution from manufacturing and power plants contributing to acid rain; water pollution from industrial wastes, agricultural chemicals; habitat loss threatens wildlife populations

Environment—international agreements: *party to:* Air Pollution, Air Pollution-Nitrogen Oxides, Air Pollution-Persistent Organic Pollutants, Air Pollution-Sulfur 85, Air Pollution-Sulfur 94, Air Pollution-Volatile Organic Compounds, Antarctic-Environmental Protocol, Antarctic-Marine Living Resources, Antarctic Treaty, Biodiversity, Climate Change, Climate Change-Kyoto Protocol, Desertification, Endangered Species, Environmental Modification, Hazardous Wastes, Law of the Sea, Marine Dumping, Marine Life Conservation, Ozone Layer Protection, Ship Pollution, Tropical Timber 83, Tropical Timber 94, Wetlands, Whaling
signed, but not ratified: none of the selected agreements

Geography—note: long boundary with Russia; H elsinki is northernmost national capital on European continent; population concentrated on small southwestern coastal plain

PEOPLE AND SOCIETY

Nationality: *noun:* Finn(s)
adjective: Finnish

Ethnic groups: Finn 93.4%, Swede 5.6%, Russian 0.5%, Estonian 0.3%, Roma 0.1%, Sami 0.1% (2006)

Languages: Finnish (official) 89%, Swedish (official) 5.3%, Russian 1.3%, other 4.4% (2014 est.) \

Religions: Lutheran 73.8%, Orthodox 1.1%, other or none 25.1% (2014 est.)

Population: 5,476,922 (July 2015 est.)

country comparison to the world: 117

Age structure: *0–14 years:* 16.41% (male 459,560/female 439,343)

15–24 years: 11.79% (male 329,815/female 316,130)

25–54 years: 38.03% (male 1,062,429/female 1,020,216)

55–64 years: 13.56% (male 365,383/female 377,390)

65 years and over: 20.21% (male 477,024/female 629,632) (2015 est.)

Dependency ratios: *total dependency ratio:* 58.3%
youth dependency ratio: 25.9%
elderly dependency ratio: 32.4%
potential support ratio: 3.1% (2015 est.)

Median age: *total:* 42.4 years
male: 40.7 years
female: 44.3 years (2015 est.)
country comparison to the world: 22

Population growth rate: 0.4% (2015 est.)
country comparison to the world: 165

Birth rate: 10.72 births/1,000 population (2015 est.)
country comparison to the world: 183

Death rate: 9.83 deaths/1,000 population (2015 est.)
country comparison to the world: 47

Net migration rate: 3.1 migrant(s)/1,000 population (2015 est.)
country comparison to the world: 38

Urbanization: *urban population:* 84.2% of total population (2015)
rate of urbanization: 0.5% annual rate of change (2010–15 est.)

Major urban areas—population: HELSINKI (capital) 1.18 million (2015)

Sex ratio: *at birth:* 1.05 male(s)/female
0–14 years: 1.05 male(s)/female
15–24 years: 1.04 male(s)/female
25–54 years: 1.04 male(s)/female
55–64 years: 0.97 male(s)/female
65 years and over: 0.76 male(s)/female
total population: 0.97 male(s)/female (2015 est.)

Mother's mean age at first birth: 28.5 (2012 est.)

Maternal mortality rate: 3 deaths/100,000 live births (2015 est.)
country comparison to the world: 174

Infant mortality rate: *total:* 2.52 deaths/1,000 live births
male: 2.65 deaths/1,000 live births
female: 2.39 deaths/1,000 live births (2015 est.)
country comparison to the world: 218

Life expectancy at birth: *total population:* 80.77 years
male: 77.82 years
female: 83.86 years (2015 est.)
country comparison to the world: 30

Total fertility rate: 1.75 children born/woman (2015 est.)
country comparison to the world: 164

Health expenditures: 9.4% of GDP (2013)
country comparison to the world: 39

Physicians density: 2.91 physicians/1,000 population (2009)

Hospital bed density: 5.5 beds/1,000 population (2011)

Drinking water source:
improved:
urban: 100% of population
rural: 100% of population
total: 100% of population
unimproved:
urban: 0% of population
rural: 0% of population
total: 0% of population (2015 est.)

Sanitation facility access:
improved:
urban: 99.4% of population
rural: 88% of population
total: 97.6% of population
unimproved:
urban: 0.6% of population
rural: 12% of population
total: 2.4% of population (2015 est.)

HIV/AIDS—adult prevalence rate: NA

HIV/AIDS—people living with HIV/AIDS: NA

HIV/AIDS—deaths: NA

Obesity—adult prevalence rate: 22.8% (2014)
country comparison to the world: 77

Education expenditures: 7.2% of GDP (2013)
country comparison to the world: 27

School life expectancy (primary to tertiary education): *total:* 19 years
male: 18 years
female: 20 years (2014)

Unemployment, youth ages 15–24: *total:* 20%
male: 23%
female: 17.2% (2013 est.)
country comparison to the world: 65

GOVERNMENT

Country name: *conventional long form:* Republic of Finland
conventional short form: Finland
local long form: Suomen tasavalta/Republiken Finland
local short form: Suomi/Finland
etymology: name may derive from the ancient Fenni peoples who are first described as living in northeastern Europe in the first centuries A.D.

Government type: parliamentary republic

Capital: *name:* Helsinki

Geographic coordinates: 60 10 N, 24 56 E
time difference: UTC+2 (7 hours ahead of Washington, DC, during Standard Time)
daylight saving time: +1hr, begins last Sunday in March; ends last Sunday in October

Administrative divisions: 19 regions (maakunnat, singular—maakunta (Finnish); landskapen, singular—landskapet (Swedish)); Aland (Swedish), Ahvenanmaa (Finnish); Etela-Karjala (Finnish), Sodra Karelen (Swedish) [South Karelia]; Etela-Pohjanmaa (Finnish), Sodra Osterbotten (Swedish) [South Ostrobothnia]; Etela-Savo

(Finnish), Sodra Savolax (Swedish) [South Savo]; Kanta-Hame (Finnish), Egentliga Tavastland (Swedish); Kainuu (Finnish), Kajanaland (Swedish); Keski-Pohjanmaa (Finnish), Mellersta Osterbotten (Swedish) [Central Ostrobothnia]; Keski-Suomi (Finnish), Mellersta Finland (Swedish) [Central Finland]; Kymenlaakso (Finnish), Kymmenedalen (Swedish); Lappi (Finnish), Lappland (Swedish); Paijat-Hame (Finnish), Paijanne-Tavastland (Swedish); Pirkanmaa (Finnish), Birkaland (Swedish) [Tampere]; Pohjanmaa (Finnish), Osterbotten (Swedish) [Ostrobothnia]; Pohjois-Karjala (Finnish), Norra Karelen (Swedish) [North Karelia]; Pohjois-Pohjanmaa (Finnish), Norra Osterbotten (Swedish) [North Ostrobothnia]; Pohjois-Savo (Finnish), Norra Savolax (Swedish) [North Savo]; Satakunta (Finnish and Swedish); Uusimaa (Finnish), Nyland (Swedish) [Newland]; Varsinais-Suomi (Finnish), Egentliga Finland (Swedish) [Southwest Finland]

Independence: 6 December 1917 (from Russia)

National holiday: Independence Day, 6 December (1917)

Constitution: previous 1906, 1919; latest drafted 17 June 1997, approved by Parliament 11 June 1999, entered into force 1 March 2000; amended several times, last in 2012 (2016)

Legal system: civil law system based on the Swedish model

International law organization participation: accepts compulsory ICJ jurisdiction with reservations; accepts ICCt jurisdiction

Citizenship: *citizenship by birth:* no
citizenship by descent only: at least one parent must be a citizen of Finland
dual citizenship recognized: yes
residency requirement for naturalization: 6 years

Suffrage: 18 years of age; universal

Executive branch: *chief of state:* President Sauli NIINISTO (since 1 March 2012)

head of government: Prime Minister Juha SIPILA (since 29 May 2015)
cabinet: Council of State or Valtioneuvosto appointed by the president, responsible to Parliament
elections/appointments: president directly elected by absolute m ajority popular vote in 2 rounds if needed for a 6-year term (eligible for a second term); election last held on 5 February 2012 (next to be held in February 2018); prime minister appointed by Parliament in 2015
election results: percent of vote in first round— Sauli NIINISTO (Kok) 37%, Pekka HAAVISTO (Vihr) 18.8%, Paavo VAYRYNEN (Kesk) 17.5%, Timo SOINI (TF) 9.4%, Paavo LIPPONEN (SDP) 6.7%, Paavo ARHINMAKI (Vas) 5.5%, Eva BIAUDET (SFP) 2.7%, Sari ESSAYAH (KD) 2.5%; Sauli NIINISTO elected president in second round held on 5 February 2012—NIINISTO 62.6%, HAAVISTO 37.4%; Juha SIPILA appointed prime minister

Legislative branch: *description:* unicameral Parliament or Eduskunta (200 seats; 199 members directly elected in single-and multi-seat constituencies by proportional representation vote and 1 member in the province of a land directly elected by simple majority vote; members serve 4-year terms)

elections: last held on 19 April 2015 (next to be held by April 2019)

election results: percent of vote by party—Kesk 21.1%, PS 17.6%, Kok 18.2%, SDP 16.5%, Vihr 8.5%, Vas 7.1%, SFP 4.9%, KD 3.5%, other 2.6%; seats by party—Kesk 49, PS 38, Kok 37, SDP 34, Vihr 15, Vas 12, SF P 9, KD 5, other 1 (Aland Coalition)

Judicial branch: *highest court(s):* Supreme Court or Korkein Oikeus (consists of the court president and 18 judges); Supreme Administrative Court (consists of 21 judges including the court president and organized into 3 chambers); note—Finland has a dual judicial system—courts with civil and criminal jurisdiction, and administrative courts with jurisdiction for litigation between individuals and administrative organs of the state and communities

judge selection and term of office: Supreme Court and Supreme Administrative Court judges appointed by the president of the republic; judges serve until mandatory retirement at age 65

subordinate courts: 6 Courts of Appeal; 8 regional administrative courts; 27 district courts; special courts for issues relating to markets, labor, insurance, impeachment, land, tenancy, and water rights

Political parties and leaders: Center Party or Kesk [Juha SIPILA]
Christian Democrats or KD [Sari ESSAYAH]
Finns Party or PS [Timo SOINI]
Green League or Vihr [Ville NIINISTO] Left Alliance or Vas [Paavo ARHINMAKI]
National Coalition Party or Kok [Alexander STUBB]
Social Democratic Party or SDP [Antti RINNE]
Swedish People's Party or SFP [Carl HAGLUND]

International organization participation:
ADB (nonregional member), AfDB (nonregional member), Arctic Council, Australia Group, BIS, CBSS, CD, CE, CERN, EAPC, EBRD, ECB, EIB, EITI (implementing country), EMU, ESA, EU, FAO, FATF, G-9, IADB, IAEA, IBRD, ICAO, ICC (national committees), ICCt, ICRM, IDA, IEA, IFAD, IFC, IFRCS, IHO, ILO, IMF, IMO, IMSO, Interpol, IOC, IOM, IPU, ISO, ITSO, ITU, ITUC (NGOs), MIGA, MINUSMA, NC, NEA, NIB, NSG, OAS (observer), OECD, OPCW, OSCE, Pacific Alliance (observer), Paris Club, PCA, PFP, Schengen Convention, UN, UNCTAD, UNESCO, UNHCR, UNIDO, UNIFIL, UNMIL, UNMOGIP, UNRWA, UNTSO, UPU, WCO, WFTU (NGOs), WHO, WIPO, WMO, WTO, ZC

Diplomatic representation in the US: *chief of mission:* Ambassador Kirsti KAUPPI (since 17 September 2015)

chancery: 3301 Massachusetts Avenue NW, Washington, DC 20008

telephone: [1] (202) 298-5800

FAX: [1] (202) 298-6030

consulate(s) general: Los Angeles, New York

Diplomatic representation from the US: *chief of mission:* Ambassador Charles C. ADAMS, Jr. (since 3 August 2015)

embassy: Itainen Puistotie 14B, 00140 Helsinki

mailing address: APO AE 09723

telephone: [358] (9) 616250

FAX: [358] (9) 6162 5800

Flag description: white with a blue cross extending to the edges of the flag; the vertical part of the cross is shifted to the hoist side in the style of the Dannebrog (Danish flag); the blue represents the thousands of lakes scattered across the country, while the white is for the snow that covers the land in winter

National symbol(s): lion; national colors: blue, white

National anthem: *name:* "Maamme" (Our Land)

lyrics/music: Johan Ludvig RUNEBERG/Fredrik PACIUS

note: in use since 1848; although never officially adopted by law, the anthem has been popular since it was first sung by a student group in 1848; Estonia's anthem uses the same melody as that of Finland

ECONOMY

Economy—overview: Finland has a highly industrialized, largely free-market economy with per capita GDP almost as high as that of Austria, Belgium, the Netherlands, or Sweden. Trade is important, with exports accounting for over one-third of GDP in recent years. Finland is historically competitive in manufacturing—principally the wood, metals, engineering, telecommunications, and electronics industries. Finland excels in export of technology for mobile phones as well as promotion of startups in the information and communications technology (ICT), gaming, cleantech, and biotechnology sectors. Except for timber and several minerals, Finland depends on imports of raw materials, energy, and some components for manufactured goods. Because of the cold climate, agricultural development is limited to maintaining self-sufficiency in basic products. Forestry, an important export industry, provides a secondary occupation for the rural population. Finland had been one of the best performing economies within the EU before 2009 and its banks and financial markets avoided the worst of global financial crisis. However, the world slowdown hit exports and domestic demand hard in that year, causing Finland's economy to contract from 2012–14. The recession affected general government finances and the debt ratio. Finland's main challenges will be reducing high labor costs and boosting demand for its exports. In the long term, Finland must address a rapidly aging population and decreasing productivity in traditional industries that threaten competitiveness, fiscal sustainability, and economic growth. The depreciating ruble and Russia's general economic slowdown will dampen exports to Russia.

GDP (purchasing power parity):
$225 billion (2015 est.)
$224 billion (2014 est.)
$225.6 billion (2013 est.)
note: data are in 2015 US dollars
country comparison to the world: 62

GDP (official exchange rate): $229.7 billion (2015 est.)

GDP—real growth rate: 0.4% (2015 est.)
-0.7% (2014 est.)
-0.8% (2013 est.)
country comparison to the world: 190

GDP—per capita (PPP): $41,100 (2015 est.)
$41,100 (2014 est.)
$41,600 (2013 est.)
note: data are in 2015 US dollars
country comparison to the world: 40

Gross national saving: 19% of GDP (2015 est.)
19.8% of GDP (2014 est.)
19.7% of GDP (2013 est.)
country comparison to the world: 88

GDP—composition, by end use:
household consumption: 53.8%
government consumption: 23.9%
investment in fixed capital: 19.7%
in vestment in inventories: 1.4%
exports of goods and services: 36.1%
imports of goods and services: -34.9% (2015 est.)

GDP—composition, by sector of origin:
agriculture: 2.9%
industry: 26.9%
services: 70.2% (2015 est.)

Agriculture—products: barley, wheat, sugar beets, potatoes; dairy cattle; fish

Industries: metals and metal products, electronics, machinery and scientific instruments, shipbuilding, pulp and paper, foodstuffs, chemicals, textiles, clothing

Industrial production growth rate: 1.6% (2015 est.)
country comparison to the world: 128

Labor force: 2.673 million (2015 est.)
country comparison to the world: 110

Labor force—by occupation:
agriculture and forestry: 4.4%
industry: 15.5%
construction: 7.1%
commerce: 21.3%
finance, insurance, and business services: 13.3%
transport and communications: 9.9%
public services: 28.5% (2011)

Unemployment rate: 9.4% (2015 est.)
8.7% (2014 est.)
country comparison to the world: 110

Population below poverty line: NA%

Household income or consumption by percentage share: *lowest:* 10%: 3.6%
highest: 10%: 24.7% (2007)

Distribution of family income—Gini index:
26.8 (2008)
25.6 (1991)
country comparison to the world: 135

Budget: *revenues:* $131.4 billion

expenditures: $137.3 billion
note: Central Government Budget (2015 est.)
Taxes and other revenues: 57% of GDP (2015 est.)
country comparison to the world: 8

Budget surplus (+) or deficit (–): -2.5% of GDP (2015 est.)
country comparison to the world: 91

Public debt: 61.2% of GDP (2015 est.)
59.3% of GDP (2014 est.)
note: data cover general govern men t debt and in clude debt in strumen ts issued (or own ed) by government entities other than the treasury; the data include treasury debt held by foreign enti-ties; the data include debt issued by subnational entities, as well as intra-governmental debt; intra-governmental debt consists of treasury bor-rowings from surpluses in the social funds, such as for retirement, medical care, and unemployment; debt instruments for the social funds are not sold at public auctions
country comparison to the world: 58

Fiscal year: calendar year

Inflation rate (consumer prices):
-0.2% (2015 est.)
1.2% (2014 est.)
country comparison to the world: 35

Central bank discount rate:
0.05% (31 December 2013)
0.3% (31 December 2010)
note: this is the European Central Bank's rate on the marginal lending facility, which offers over-night credit to banks in the euro area
country comparison to the world: 148

Commercial bank prime lending rate:
1.9% (31 December 2015 est.)
2.21% (31 December 2014 est.)
country comparison to the world: 180

Stock of narrow money:
$121.3 billion (31 December 2015 est.)
$118.8 billion (31 December 2014 est.)
note: see entry for the European Union for money supply for the entire euro area; the European Cen-tral Bank (ECB) controls monetary policy for the 18 members of the Economic and Monetary Union (EMU); individual members of the EMU do not control the quantity of money circulating within their own borders
country comparison to the world: 30

Stock of broad money:
$179.8 billion (31 December 2014 est.)
$195.3 billion (31 December 2013 est.)
country comparison to the world: 43

Stock of domestic credit:
$404.7 billion (31 December 2015 est.)
$410.1 billion (31 December 2014 est.)
country comparison to the world: 28

Market value of publicly traded shares:
$158.7 billion (31 December 2012 est.)
$143.1 billion (31 December 2011)
$118.2 billion (31 December 2010 est.)
country comparison to the world: 38

Current account balance: $272 million (2015 est.)

-$2.566 billion (2014 est.)
country comparison to the world: 47

Exports: $66.9 billion (2015 est.)
$79.2 billion (2014 est.)
country comparison to the world: 42

Exports—commodities: electrical and optical equipment, machinery, transport equipment, paper and pulp, chemicals, basic metals; timber

Exports—partners: Germany 13.9%, Sweden 10.1%, US 7%, Netherlands 6.6%, Russia 5.9%, UK 5.2%, China 4.7% (2015)

Imports: $58.05 billion (2015 est.)
$72.94 billion (2014 est.)
country comparison to the world: 45

Imports—commodities: foodstuffs, petroleum and petroleum products, chemicals, transport equip-ment, iron and steel, machinery, computers, elec-tronic industry products, textile yarn and fabrics, grains

Imports—partners: Germany 17%, Sweden 16%, Russia 11%, Netherlands 9.1%, Denmark 4.1% (2015)

Reserves of foreign exchange and gold:
$11.1 billion (31 December 2015 est.)
$10.67 billion (31 December 2014 est.)
country comparison to the world: 76

Debt—external:
$547.5 billion (31 December 2014 est.)
$571.8 billion (31 December 2013 est.)
country comparison to the world: 24

Stock of direct foreign investment—at home:
$139.7 billion (31 December 2015 est.)
$138 billion (31 December 2014 est.)
country comparison to the world: 40

Stock of direct foreign investment—abroad:
$208.3 billion (31 December 2015 est.)
$202.2 billion (31 December 2014 est.)
country comparison to the world: 26

Exchange rates: euros (EUR) per US dollar—
0.885 (2015 est.)
0.7525 (2014 est.)
0.7634 (2013 est.)
0.78 (2012 est.)
0.7185 (2011 est.)

ENERGY

Electricity—production: 67.51 billion kWh (2012 est.)
country comparison to the world: 40

Electricity—consumption: 82.04 billion kWh (2012 est.)
country comparison to the world: 35

Electricity—exports: 1.876 billion kWh (2013 est.)
country comparison to the world: 45

Electricity—imports: 17.59 billion kWh (2013 est.)
country comparison to the world: 11

Electricity—installed generating capacity: 16.94 million kW (2012 est.)
country comparison to the world: 45

Electricity—from fossil fuels: 51.6% of total installed capacity (2012 est.)
country comparison to the world: 146

Electricity—from nuclear fuels: 16.2% of total installed capacity (2012 est.)
country comparison to the world: 12

Electricity—from hydroelectric plants: 18.9% of total installed capacity (2012 est.)
country comparison to the world: 95

Electricity—from other renewable sources: 13.3% of total installed capacity (2012 est.)
country comparison to the world: 25

Crude oil—production: 0 bbl/day (2014 est.)
country comparison to the world: 133

Crude oil—exports: 0 bbl/day (2013 est.)
country comparison to the world: 122

Crude oil—imports: 236,000 bbl/day (2013 est.)
country comparison to the world: 31

Crude oil—proved reserves: 0 bbl (1 January 2015 est.)
country comparison to the world: 131

Refined petroleum products—production: 300,200 bbl/day (2013 est.)
country comparison to the world: 43

Refined petroleum products—consumption: 196,300 bbl/day (2014 est.)
country comparison to the world: 59

Refined petroleum products—exports: 182,400 bbl/day (2013 est.)
country comparison to the world: 35

Refined petroleum products—imports: 127,300 bbl/day (2013 est.)
country comparison to the world: 44

Natural gas—production: 3 million cu m (2014 est.)
country comparison to the world: 94

Natural gas—consumption: 3.082 billion cu m (2014 est.)
country comparison to the world: 72

Natural gas—exports: 0 cu m (2014 est.)
country comparison to the world: 97

Natural gas—imports: 3.08 billion cu m (2014 est.)
country comparison to the world: 41

Natural gas—proved reserves: 0 cu m (1 January 2014 est.)
country comparison to the world: 136

Carbon dioxide emissions from consumption of energy: 46.81 million Mt (2012 est.)
country comparison to the world: 61

COMMUNICATIONS

Telephones—fixed lines: total subscriptions: 640,000
subscriptions per 100 inhabitants: 12 (2014 est.)
country comparison to the world: 90

Telephones—mobile cellular: total: 7.6 million
subscriptions per 100 inhabitants: 139 (2014 est.)
country comparison to the world: 99

Telephone system: general assessment: modern system with excellent service *domestic:* digital fiber-optic, fixed-line network and an extensive mobile-cellular network provide domestic needs

international: country code—358; submarine cables provide links to Estonia and Sweden; satellite earth stations—access to Intelsat transmission service via a Swedish satellite earth station, 1 Inmarsat (Atlantic and Indian Ocean regions); note—Finland shares the Inmarsat earth station with the other Nordic countries (Denmark, Iceland, Norway, and Sweden) (2011)

Broadcast media: a mix of publicly operated TV stations and privately owned TV stations; in 2008, the 2 publicly owned TV stations expanded services and the largest private TV station has introduced several special-interest pay-TV channels; cable and satellite multi-channel subscription services are available; all TV signals have been broadcast digitally since September 2007; analog broadcasts via cable networks were terminated in February 2008; public broadcasting maintains a network of 13 national and 25 regional radio stations; a large number of private radio broadcasters (2008)

Radio broadcast stations: AM 2, FM 59, shortwave 2 (2008)

Television broadcast stations: 120 (plus 431 repeaters) (1999); note—on 1 September 2007, Finland began broadcasting all television signals digitally; analog broadcasts via cable networks were discontinued 29 February 2008

Internet country code: .fi;

note—Aland Islands assigned .ax

Internet hosts: 4.763 million (2012)
country comparison to the world: 22

Internet users: *total:* 5.1 million
percent of population: 94.0% (2014 est.)
country comparison to the world: 64

Airports: 148 (2013)
country comparison to the world: 39

Airports—with paved runways: *total:* 74 over 3,047 m: 3
2,438 to 3,047 m: 26
1,524 to 2,437 m: 10
914 to 1,523 m: 21
under 914 m: 14 (2013)

Airports—with unpaved runways: *total:* 74
914 to 1,523 m: 3
under 914 m: 71 (2013)

Pipelines: gas 1,689 km (2010)

Railways: *total:* 5,919 km
broad gauge: 5,919 km 1.524-m gauge (3,067 km electrified) (2014)
country comparison to the world: 32

Roadways: *total:* 454,000 km
highways: 78,000 km (50,000 paved, including 700 km of expressways; 28,000 unpaved)
urban roads: 26,000 km
private and forest roads: 350,000 km (2012)
country comparison to the world: 60

Waterways: 8,000 km (includes Saimaa Canal system of 3,577 km; southern part leased from Russia; water transport used frequently in the summer and widely replaced with sledges on the ice in winter; there are 187,888 lakes in Finland that cover 31,500 km); Finland also maintains 8,200 km of coastal fairways (2013)
country comparison to the world: 17

Merchant marine: *total:* 97
by type: bulk carrier 2, cargo 25, carrier 1, chemical tanker 6, container 3, passenger 5, passenger/cargo 16, petroleum tanker 5, roll on/roll off 31, vehicle carrier 3

foreign-owned: 5 (Cyprus 1, Estonia 2, Iceland 1, Sweden 1)
registered in other countries: 47 (Bahamas 8, Germany 3, Gibraltar 2, Malta 3, Netherlands 13, Panama 2, Sweden 16) (2010)
country comparison to the world: 51

Ports and terminals: *major seaport(s):* Helsinki, Kotka, Naantali, Porvoo, Raahe, Rauma

Military branches: Finnish Defense Forces (FDF): Army (Puolustusvoimat), Navy (Merivoimat; includes Coastal Defense Forces), Air Force (Ilmavoimat) (2013)

Military service age and obligation: 18 years of age for male voluntary and compulsory—and female voluntary—national military and nonmilitary service; service obligation 6–12 months; military obligation to age 60 (2012)

Military expenditures: 1.37% of GDP (2016 est.)
1.29% of GDP (2015)
1.3% of GDP (2014)
1.41% of GDP (2013)
1.47% of GDP (2012)
1.42% of GDP (2011)
country comparison to the world: 62

Disputes—international: various groups in Finland advocate restoration of Karelia and other areas ceded to the former Soviet Union, but the Finnish Government asserts no territorial demands

Refugees and internally displaced persons: *stateless persons:* 2,427 (2015)

FRANCE

Background: France today is one of the most modern countries in the world and is a leader among European nations. It plays an influential global role as a permanent member of the United Nations Security Council, NATO, the G-8, the G-20, the EU, and other multilateral organizations. France rejoined NATO's integrated military command structure in 2009, reversing DE GAULLE's 1966 decision to withdraw French forces from NATO. Since 1958, it has constructed a hybrid presidential-parliamentary governing system resistant to the instabilities experienced in earlier, more purely parliamentary administrations. In recent decades, its reconciliation and cooperation with Germany have proved central to the economic integration of Europe, including the introduction of a common currency, the euro, in January 1999. In the early 21st century, five French overseas entities—French Guiana, Guadeloupe, Martinique, Mayotte, and Reunion—became French regions and were made part of France proper.

Location: *metropolitan France:* Western Europe, bordering the Bay of Biscay and English Channel, between Belgium and Spain, southeast of the UK; bordering the Mediterranean Sea, between Italy and Spain

French Guiana: Northern South America, bordering the North Atlantic Ocean, between Brazil and Suriname

Guadeloupe: Caribbean, islands between the Caribbean Sea and the North Atlantic Ocean, southeast of Puerto Rico

Martinique: Caribbean, island between the Caribbean Sea and North Atlantic Ocean, north of Trinidad and Tobago

Mayotte: Southern Indian Ocean, island in the Mozambique Channel, about halfway between northern Madagascar and northern Mozambique

Reunion: Southern Africa, island in the Indian Ocean, east of Madagascar

Geographic coordinates: metropolitan France: 46 00 N, 2 00 E

French Guiana: 4 00 N, 53 00 W

Guadeloupe: 16 15 N, 61 35 W

Martinique: 14 40 N, 6100 W

Mayotte: 12 50 S, 45 10 E

Reunion: 21 06 S, 55 36 E

Map references: *metropolitan France:* Europe

French Guiana: South America

Guadeloupe: Central America and the Caribbean

Martinique: Central America and the Caribbean

Mayotte: Africa

Reunion: World

Area: *total:* 643,801 sq km; 551,500 sq km (metropolitan France)

land: 640,427 sq km; 549,970 sq km (metropolitan France)

water: 3,374 sq km; 1,530 sq km (metropolitan France)

note: the first numbers include the overseas regions of French Guiana, Guadeloupe, Martinique, Mayotte, and Reunion

country comparison to the world: 43

Area—comparative: slightly more than four times the size of Georgia; slightly less than the size of Texas

Land boundaries: *metropolitan France—total:* 2,751 km

border countries (8): Andorra 55 km, Belgium 556 km, Germany 418 km, Italy 476 km, Luxembourg 69 km, Monaco 6 km, Spain 646 km, Switzerland 525 km

French Guiana—total: 1,205 km

border countries (2): Brazil 649 km, Suriname 556 km

Coastline: *total:* 4,853 km

metropolitan France: 3,427 km

Maritime claims: *territorial sea:* 12 nm

contiguous zone: 24 nm

exclusive economic zone: 200 nm (does not apply to the M editerranean Sea)

continental shelf: 200-m depth or to the depth of exploitation

Climate: *metropolitan France:* generally cool winters and mild summers, but mild winters and hot summers along the Mediterranean; occasional strong, cold, dry, north-to-northwesterly wind known as mistral

French Guiana: tropical; hot, humid; little seasonal temperature variation

Guadeloupe and Martinique: subtropical tempered by trade winds; moderately high humidity; rainy season (June to October); vulnerable to devastating cyclones (hurricanes) every eight years on average

Mayotte: tropical; marine; hot, humid, rainy season during northeastern monsoon (November to May); dry season is cooler (May to November)

Reunion: tropical, but temperature moderates with elevation; cool and dry (May to November), hot and rainy (November to April)

Terrain: *metropolitan France:* mostly flat plains or gently rolling hills in north and west; remainder is mountainous, especially Pyrenees in south, Alps in east

French Guiana: low-lying coastal plains rising to hills and small mountains

Guadeloupe: Basse-Terre is volcanic in origin with interior mountains; Grande-Terre is low limestone formation; most of the seven other islands are volcanic in origin

Martinique: mountainous with indented coastline; dormant volcano

Mayotte: generally undulating, with deep ravines and ancient volcanic peaks

Reunion: mostly rugged and mountainous; fertile lowlands along coast

Elevation: *mean elevation:* 375 m

elevation extremes: *lowest point:* Rhone River delta -2 m

highest point: Mont Blanc 4,807 m

note: to assess the possible effects of climate change on the ice and snow cap of Mont Blanc, its surface and peak have been extensively measured in recent years; these new peak measurements have exceeded the traditional height of 4,807 m and have varied between 4,808 m and 4,811 m; the actual rock summit is 4,792 m and is 40 m away from the ice-covered summit

Natural resources: *metropolitan France:* coal, iron ore, bauxite, zinc, uranium, antimony, arsenic, potash, feldspar, fluorspar, gypsum, timber, arable land, fish

French Guiana: gold deposits, petroleum, kaolin, niobium, tantalum, clay

Land use: *agricultural land:* 52.7%

arable land: 33.4%

permanent crops: 1.8%

permanent pasture: 17.5%

forest: 29.2%

other: 18.1% (2011 est.)

Irrigated land: *total:* 26,420 sq km 26,950 sq km

metropolitan France: 26,000 sq km (2012)

Total renewable water resources: 211 cu km (2011)

Freshwater withdrawal (domestic/industrial/agricultural): *total:* 31.62 cu km/yr (19%/71%/10%)

per capita: 512.1 cu m/yr (2009)

Natural hazards: *metropolitan France:* flooding; avalanches; midwinter windstorms; drought; forest fires in south near the Mediterranean

overseas departments: hurricanes (cyclones); flooding; volcanic activity (Guadeloupe, Martinique, Reunion)

Environment—current issues: some forest damage from acid rain; air pollution from industrial and vehicle emissions; water pollution from urban wastes, agricultural runoff

Environment—international agreements:

party to: Air Pollution, Air Pollution-Nitrogen Oxides, Air Pollution-Persistent Organic Pollutants, Air Pollution-Sulfur 85, Air Pollution-Sulfur 94, Air Pollution-Volatile Organic Compounds, Antarctic-Environmental Protocol, Antarctic-Marine Living Resources, Antarctic Seals, Antarctic Treaty, Biodiversity, Climate Change, Climate Change-Kyoto Protocol, Desertification, Endangered Species, Hazardous Wastes, Law of the Sea, Marine Dumping, Marine Life Conservation, Ozone Layer Protection, Ship Pollution, Tropical Timber 83, Tropical Timber 94, Wetlands, Whaling

signed, but not ratified: none of the selected agreements

Geography—note: largest West European nation; most major French rivers—the Meuse, Seine, Loire, Charente, Dordogne, and Garonne—flow northward or westward into the Atlantic Ocean, only the Rhone flows southward into the M editerranean Sea

PEOPLE AND SOCIETY

Nationality: *noun:* Frenchman(men), French woman(women)

adjective: French

Ethnic groups: Celtic and Latin with Teutonic, Slavic, North African, Indochinese, Basque minorities

overseas departments: black, white, mulatto, East Indian, Chinese, Amerindian

Languages: French (official) 100%, rapidly declining regional dialects and languages (Provencal, Breton, Alsatian, Corsican, Catalan, Basque, Flemish)

overseas departments: French, Creole patois, Mahorian (a Swahili dialect)

Religions: Christian (overwhelmingly Roman Catholic) 63–66%, Muslim 7–9%, Buddhist 0.5–0.75%, Jewish 0.5–0.75%, other 0.5–1.0%, none 23–28%

note: France maintains a tradition of secularism and has not officially collected data on religious affiliation since the 1872 national census, which complicates assessments of France's religious composition; an 1872 law prohibiting state authorities from collecting data on individuals' ethnicity or religious beliefs was reaffirmed by a 1978 law emphasizing the prohibition of the collection or exploitation of personal data revealing an individual's race, ethnicity, or political, philosophical, or religious opinions; a 1905 law codified France's separation of church and state (2015 est.)

Population: 66,553,766

note: the above figure is for metropolitan France and five overseas regions; the metropolitan France population is 62,814,233 (July 2015 est.)

country comparison to the world: 22

Age structure: *0–14 years:* 18.66% (male 6,350,008/female 6,066,407)

15–24 years: 11.82% (male 4,025,283/female 3,842,989)

25–54 years: 38.31% (male 12,823,675/female 12,671,013)

55–64 years: 12.48% (male 4,008,672/female 4,294,218)

65 years and over: 18.74% (male 5,360,078/ female 7,111,423) (2015 est.)

Dependency ratios: *total dependency ratio:* 60.3%

youth dependency ratio: 29.6%

elderly dependency ratio: 30.6%

potential support ratio: 3.3% (2015 est.)

Median age: *total:* 41.1 years

male: 39.4 years

female: 42.6 years (2015 est.)

country comparison to the world: 38

Population growth rate: 0.43% (2015 est.)

country comparison to the world: 163

Birth rate: 12.38 births/1,000 population (2015 est.)

country comparison to the world: 160

Death rate: 9.16 deaths/1,000 population (2015 est.)

country comparison to the world: 65

Net migration rate:

1.09 migrant(s)/1,000 population (2015 est.)

country comparison to the world: 62

Urbanization: *urban population:* 79.5% of total population (2015)

rate of urbanization: 0.84% annual rate of change (2010–15 est.)

Major urban areas—population: PARIS (capital) 10.843 million; Lyon 1.609 million; Marseille-Aix-en-Provence 1.605 million; Lille 1.027 million; Nice-Cannes 967,000; Toulouse 938,000 (2015)

Sex ratio: *at birth:* 1.05 male(s)/female

0–14 years: 1.05 male(s)/female

15–24 years: 1.05 male(s)/female

25–54 years: 1.01 male(s)/female

55–64 years: 0.93 male(s)/female

65 years and over: 0.75 male(s)/female

total population: 0.96 male(s)/female (2015 est.)

Mother's mean age at first birth: 28.1 (2010 est.)

Maternal mortality rate: 8 deaths/100,000 live births (2015 est.)

country comparison to the world: 158

Infant mortality rate: *total:* 3.28 deaths/1,000 live births

male: 3.6 deaths/1,000 live births

female: 2.94 deaths/1,000 live births (2015 est.)

country comparison to the world: 213

Life expectancy at birth: *total population:* 81.75 years

male: 78.65 years

female: 85.01 years (2015 est.)

country comparison to the world: 19

Total fertility rate: 2.08 children born/woman (2015 est.) country comparison to the world: 110

Contraceptive prevalence rate: 76.4%

note: percent of women aged 20–49 (2008)

Health expenditures: 11.7% of GDP (2013)

country comparison to the world: 9

Physicians density: 3.19 physicians/1,000 population (2013)

Hospital bed density: 6.4 beds/1,000 population (2011)

Drinking water source:

improved:

urban: 100% o f population

rural: 100% of population

total: 100% of population

unimproved:

urban: 0% of population

rural: 0% of population

total: 0% of population (2015 est.)

Sanitation facility access:

improved:

urban: 98.6% of population

rural: 98.9% of population

total: 98.7% of population

unimproved:

urban: 1.4% of population

rural: 1.1% of population

total: 1.3% of population (2015 est.)

HIV/AIDS—adult prevalence rate: NA

HIV/AIDS—people living with HIV/AIDS: NA

HIV/AIDS—deaths: 1,500 (2013 est.)

country comparison to the world: 59

Obesity—adult prevalence rate: 25.7% (2014)

country comparison to the world: 108

Education expenditures: 5.5% of GDP (2012)

country comparison to the world: 43

School life expectancy (primary to tertiary education): *total:* 16 years

male: 16 years

female: 17 years (2014)

Unemployment, youth ages 15–24: *total:* 23.9%

male: 23.7%

female: 24.2% (2013 est.)

country comparison to the world: 39

GOVERNMENT

Country name: *conventional long form:* French Republic

conventional short form: France

local long form: Republique francaise

local short form: France

etymology: name derives from the Latin "Francia" meaning "Land of the Franks"; the Franks were a group of Germanic tribes located along the middle and lower Rhine River in the 3rd century A.D. who merged with Gallic-Roman populations in succeeding centuries and to whom they passed on their name

Government type: semi-presidential republic

Capital: *name:* Paris

Geographic coordinates: 48 52 N, 2 20 E

time difference: UTC + 1 (6 hours ahead of Washington, DC, during Standard Time)

daylight saving time: +1hr, begins last Sunday in March; ends last Sunday in October note: applies to metropolitan France only, not to its overseas departments, collectivities, or territories

Administrative divisions: 27 regions (regions, singular—region); Alsace, Aquitaine, Auvergne, Basse-Normandie (Lower Normandy), Bourgogne (Burgundy), Bretagne (Brittany), Centre-Val de Loire, Champagne-Ardenne, Corse (Corsica), Franche-Comte, Guadeloupe, Guyane (French Guiana), Haute-Normandie (Upper Normandy), Ile-de-France, Languedoc-Roussillon, Limousin, Lorraine, Martinique, Mayotte, Midi-Pyrenees, Nord-Pas-de-Calais, Pays de la Loire, Picardie, Poitou-Charentes, Provence-Alpes-Cote d'Azur, Reunion, Rhone-Alpes note 1: France is divided into 22 metropolitan regions (including the "territorial collectivity" of Corse or Corsica) and 5 overseas regions (French Guiana, Guadeloupe, Martinique, Mayotte, and Reunion) and is subdivided into 96 metropolitan departments and 5 overseas departments (which are the same as the overseas regions); on 1 January 2016 the number of metropolitan regions was reduced from 22 to 13 through amalgamation, but the names of many of the new regions have not been finalized note 2: on 1 January 2016 the number of metropolitan regions was reduced from 22 to 13 through amalgamation, but the names of many of the new regions have not been finalized; new permanent names are due to be confirmed by 1 J uly 2016

Dependent areas: Clipperton Island, French Polynesia, French Southern and Antarctic Lands, New Caledonia, Saint Barthelemy, Saint Martin, Saint Pierre and Miquelon, Wallis and Futuna

note: the US does not recognize claims to Antarctica; New Caledonia has been considered a "sui generis" collectivity of France since 1998, a unique status falling between that of an independent country and a French overseas department

Independence: no official date of independence: 486 (Frankish tribes unified under Merovingian kingship); 10 August 843 (Western Francia established from the division of the Carolingian Empire); 14 July 1789 (French monarchy overthrown); 22 September 1792 (First French Republic founded); 4 October 1958 (Fifth French Republic established)

National holiday: Fetedela Federation, 14 July (1790); note—although often incorrectly referred to as Bastille Day, the celebration actually commemorates the holiday held on the first anniversary of the storming of the Bastille (on 14 July 1789) and the establishment of a constitutional monarchy; other names for the holiday are Fete Nationale (National Holiday) and quatorze juillet (14th of July)

Constitution: many previous; latest effective 4 October 1958; amended many times, last in 2008 (2016)

Legal system: civil law; review of administrative but not legislative acts

International law organization participation: has not submitted an ICJ jurisdiction declaration; accepts ICCt jurisdiction

Citizenship: *citizenship by birth:* no

citizenship by descent only: at least one parent must be a citizen of France

dual citizenship recognized: yes
residency requirement for naturalization: 5 years

Suffrage: 18 years of age; universal

Executive branch: *chief of state:* President Francois HOLLANDE (since 15 May 2012)

head of government: Prime Minister Manuel VALLS (since 1 April 2014)

cabinet: Council of Ministers appointed by the president at the suggestion of the prime minister
elections/appointments: president directly elected by absolute majority popular vote in 2 rounds if needed for a 5-year term (eligible for a second term); election last held on 22 April and 6 May 2012 (next to be held in the spring of 2017); prime minister appointed by the president

election results: Francois HOLLANDE elected president; percent of vote in first round—Francois HOLLANDE (PS) 28.6%, Nicolas SARKOZY (UMP) 27.2%, Marine LEPEN (FN) 17.9%, Jean-Luc MELENCHON (PG) 11.1%, Francois BAYROU (moDem) 9.1%, other 6.1%; percent of vote in second round -HOLLANDE 51.6%, SARKOZY 48.4%

Legislative branch: *description:* bicameral Parliament or Parlement consists of the Senate or Senat (348 seats—328 for metropolitan France and overseas departments and regions of Guadeloupe, Martinque, French Guiana, Reunion, and Mayotte, 2 for New Caledonia, 2 for French Polynesia, 1 for Saint-Pierre and Miquelon, 1 for Saint-Barthelemy, 1 for Saint-Martin, 1 for Wallis and Futuna, and 12 for French nationals abroad; members indirectly elected by departmental electoral colleges using absolute majority vote in two rounds if needed for departments with 1-3 members and proportional representation vote in departments with 4 or more members; members serve 6-year terms with one-half of the membership renewed every 3 years) and the National Assembly or Assemblee Nationale (577 seats—556 for metropolitan France, 10 for overseas departments, and 11 for citizens abroad; members directly elected by absolute majority vote in two rounds if n eeded to serve 5-year terms)

elections: Senate—last held on 28 September 2014 (next to be held in September 2017); National Assembly—last held on 10 and 17 June 2012 (next to be held in June 2017)

election results: Senate—percent of vote by party—NA; seats by party—UMP 187, PS 152, other 9; National Assembly—percent of vote by party—PS 48.5%, UMP 33.6%, miscellaneous left wing parties 3.8%, Greens 3.0%, miscellaneous right wing parties 2.6%, NC 2.1%, PRG 2.1%, FDG 1.7%, other 2.6%; seats by party—PS 280, UMP 194, miscellaneous left wing parties 22, Greens 17, miscellaneous right wing parties 15, NC 12, PRG 12, FDG 10, other 15

Judicial branch:

highest court(s): Court of Cassation or Cour de Cassation (consists of the court president, 6 divisional presiding judges, 120 trial judges, and 70 deputy judges organized into 6 divisions—3 civil,

1 commercial, 1 labor, and 1 criminal); Constitutional Council (consists of 9 members)

judge selection and term of office: Court of Cassation judges appointed by the president of the republic from nominations from the High Council of the Judiciary, presided by the Court of Cassation and 15 appointed members; judge term of appointment NA; Constitutional Council members appointed—3 by the president of the republic and 3 each by the National Assembly and Senate presidents; members serve 9-year, non-renewable terms with one third of the membership renewed every 3 years

subordinate courts: appellate courts or Cour d'Appel; regional courts or Tribunal de Grande Instance; first instance courts or Tribunal' d'instance

Political parties and leaders: Europe Ecology—The Greens or EELV [Emmanuelle COSSE]
French Communist Party or PCF [Pierre LAURENT]
Left Front Coalition or FDG [Jean-Luc MELENCHON]
Left Party or PG [Jean-Luc MELENCHON and Martine BILLARD]
Left Radical Party or PRG [Jean-Michel BAYLET] (previously Radical Socialist Party or PRS and the Left Radical Movement or MRG)
Movement for France or MPF [Philippe DE VILLIERS]
National Front or FN [Marine LE PEN]
New Anticapitalist Party or NPA [collective leadership; main spokesperson Christine POUPIN]
New Center or NC [Herve MORIN]
Radical Party [Jean-Louis BORLOO]
Rally for France or RPF [Charles PASQUA]
Republican and Citizen Movement or MRC [Jean-Luc LAURENT]
Socialist Party or PS [Haerlem DESIR]
The Republicans (formerly Union for a Popular Movement or UMP) [Nicolas SARKOZY]
Union des Democrates et Independants or UDI [Jean-Louis BORLOO] and Democratic Movement or MoDem [Francois BAYROU] (previously Union for French Democracy or UDF); together known as UDI-Modem
United Republic or RS [Dominique DE VILLEPIN]
Worker's Struggle (Lutte Ouvriere) or LO [collective leadership; spokespersons Nathalie ARTHAUD and Arlette LAQUILLER]

Political pressure groups and leaders: Confederation francaise de l'encadrement—Confederation generale des cadres (French Confederation of Management—General Confederation of Executives) or CFE-CGC [Carole COUVERT, president] (independent white-collar union with 140,000 members) Confederation Francaise Democratique du Travail (French Democratic Confederation of Labor) or CFDT [Laurent BERGER, secretary general] (left-leaning labor union with approximately 875,000 members) Confederation francaise des travailleurs chretiens (French Confederation of Christian Workers) or CFTC [Philippe LOUIS, president] (independent labor union founded by Catholic workers that claims 142,000 members)

Confederation generale du travail (General Confederation of Labor) or CGT [Bernard TH I BAU LT, secretary general] (historically com m unist labor union with approximately 710,000 members) Confederation generale du travail—Force ouvriere (General Confederation of Labor—Worker's Force) or FO [Jean-Claude MAILLY, secretary general] (independent labor union with an estimated 300,000 members) Mouvement des entreprises de France or MEDEF [Pierre GATTAZ, president] (employers' union with claim ed 750,000 companies as members)
French Guiana: conservationists; gold mining pressure groups; hunting pressure groups
Guadeloupe: Christian Movement for the Liberation of Guadeloupe or KLPG
General Federation of Guadeloupe Workers or CGT-G
General Union of Guadeloupe Workers or UGTG
Movement for an Independent Guadeloupe or MPGI
The Socialist Renewal Movement
Martinique: Caribbean Revolutionary Alliance or ARC
Central Union for Martinique Workers or CSTM
Frantz Fanon Circle
League of Workers and Peasants
Proletarian Action Group or GAP
Reunion: NA

International organization participation: ADB (nonregional member), AfDB (nonregional member), Arctic Council (observer), Australia Group, BDEAC, BIS, BSEC (observer), CBSS (observer), CE, CERN, EAPC, EBRD, ECB, EIB, EITI (implementing country), EMU, ESA, EU, FAO, FATF, FZ, G-5, G-7, G-8, G-10, G-20, IADB, IAEA, IBRD, ICAO, ICC (national committees), ICCt, ICRM, IDA, IEA, IFAD, IFC, IFRCS, IGAD (partners), IHO, ILO, IMF, IMO, IMSO, InOC, Interpol, IOC, IOM, IPU, ISO, ITSO, ITU, ITUC (NGOs), MIGA, MINURSO, MINUSMA, MINUSTAH, MONUSCO, NATO, NEA, NSG, OAS (observer), OECD, OIF, OPCW, OSCE, Pacific Alliance (observer), Paris Club, PCA, PI F (partner), Schengen Convention, SELEC (observer), SPC, UN, UNCTAD, UNESCO, UNHCR, UNIDO, UNIF IL, Union Latina, UNMIL, UNOCI, UNRWA, UNSC (permanent), UNTSO, UNWTO, UPU, WCO, WFTU (NGOs), WHO, WIPO, WMO, WTO, ZC

Diplomatic representation in the US:

chief of mission: Ambassador Gerard ARAUD (since 18 September 2014)
chancery: 4101 Reservoir Road NW, Washington, DC 20007
telephone: [1] (202) 944–6000
FAX: [1] (202) 944–6166
consu late(s) general: Atlanta, Boston, Chicago, Houston, Los Angeles, Miami, New Orleans, New York, San F rancisco, Washington DC

Diplomatic representation from the US:

chief of mission: Ambassador Jane D. HARTLEY (since 31 October 2014); note—also accredited to Monaco

embassy: 2 Avenue Gabriel, 75382 Paris Cedex 08

mailing address: PSC 116, APO AE 09777

telephone: [33] (1) 43-12-22-22

FAX: [33] (1) 42 66 97 83

consulate(s) general: Marseille, Strasbourg

Flag description: three equal vertical bands of blue (hoist side), white, and red; known as the "Le drapeau tricolore" (French Tricolor), the origin of the flag dates to 1790 and the French Revolution when the "ancient French color" of white was combined with the blue and red colors of the Parisian militia; the official flag for all French dependent areas

note: the design and/or colors are similar to a number of other flags, including those of Belgium, Chad, Cote d'Ivoire, Ireland, Italy, Luxembourg, and Netherlands

National symbol(s): Gallic rooster, fleur-de-lis, Marianne (female personification); national colors: blue, white, red

National anthem: *name:* "La Marseillaise" (The Song of Marseille)

lyrics/music: Claude-Joseph ROUGET de Lisle

note: adopted 1795, restored 1870; originally known as "Chant de Guerre pour l'Armee du Rhin" (War Song for the Army of the Rhine), the National Guard of Marseille made the song famous by singing it while marching into Paris in 1792 during the French Revolutionary Wars

ECONOMY

Economy—overview: The French economy is diversified across all sectors. The government has partially or fully privatized many large companies, including Air France, France Telecom, Renault, and Thales. However, the government maintains a strong presence in some sectors, particularly power, public transport, and defense industries. With more than 84 million foreign tourists per year, France is the most visited country in the world and maintains the third largest income in the world from tourism. France's leaders remain committed to a capitalism in which they maintain social equity by means of laws, tax policies, and social spending that mitigate economic inequality. France's real GDP increased by 1.1% in 2015. The unemployment rate (including overseas territories) increased from 7.8% in 2008 to 9.9% in the fourth quarter of 2014. Youth unemployment in metropolitan France decreased from a high of 25.4% in the fourth quarter of 2012 to 24.3% in the fourth quarter of 2014. Lower-than-expected growth and high spending have strained France's public finances. The budget deficit rose sharply from 3.3% of GDP in 2008 to 7.5% of GDP in 2009 before improving to 4% of GDP in 2014 and 2015, while France's public debt rose from 68% of GDP to more than 98% in 2015, and may hit 100% in 2016. Elected on a conventionally leftist platform, President Francois HOLLANDE surprised and angered many supporters with a January 2014 speech announcing a sharp change in his economic policy, recasting himself as a liberalizing reformer. The government's budget for 2014 shifted the balance of fiscal consolidation from taxes to a total of $24 billion in spending cuts. In December 2014, HOLLANDE announced additional reforms, including a plan to extend commercial business hours, liberalize professional services, and sell off $6.2–12.4 billion in state owned assets. France's tax burden remains well above the EU average and income tax cuts over the past decade are being partly reversed, particularly for higher earners. The top rate of income tax is 41%. The government is allowing a 75% payroll tax on salaries over $1.24 million to lapse.

GDP (purchasing power parity): $2.647 trillion (2015 est.)

$2.617 trillion (2014 est.)

$2.612 trillion (2013 est.)

note: data are in 2015 US dollars country comparison to the world: 11

GDP (official exchange rate): $2.422 trillion (2015 est.)

GDP—real growth rate: 1.1% (2015 est.)

0.2% (2014 est.)

0.7% (2013 est.)

country comparison to the world: 168

GDP—per capita (PPP): $41,200 (2015 est.)

$40,900 (2014 est.)

$41,000 (2013 est.)

note: data are in 2015 US dollars

country comparison to the world: 38

Gross national saving: 21.4% of GDP (2015 est.)

21.2% of GDP (2014 est.)

21.5% of GDP (2013 est.)

country comparison to the world: 73

GDP—composition, by end use:

household consumption: 55.6%

government consumption: 24.3%

investment in fixed capital: 21.2%

investment in inventories: 0.3%

exports of goods and services: 29.3%

imports of goods and services: -30.7% (2015 est.)

GDP—composition, by sector of origin:

agriculture: 1.7%

industry: 19.3%

services: 79% (2015 est.)

Agriculture—products: wheat, cereals, sugar beets, potatoes, wine grapes; beef, dairy products; fish

Industries: machinery, chemicals, automobiles, metallurgy, aircraft, electronics; textiles, food processing; tourism

Industrial production growth rate: 0.5% (2015 est.)

country comparison to the world: 161

Labor force: 29.84 million (2015 est.)

country comparison to the world: 20

Labor force—by occupation: *agriculture:* 3%

industry: 21.3%

services: 75.7% (2013 est.)

Unemployment rate: 9.9% (2015 est.)

9.9% (2014 est.)

note: includes overseas territories

country comparison to the world: 114

Population below poverty line: 8.1% (2012 est.)

Household income or consumption by percentage share: *lowest:* 10%: 3.6%

highest: 10%: 25.4% (2013)

Distribution of family income—Gini index: 30.1 (2013) 30.5 (2012)

country comparison to the world: 122

Budget: *revenues:* $1.253 trillion

expenditures: $1.351 trillion (2015 est.)

Taxes and other revenues: 51.7% of GDP (2015 est.)

country comparison to the world: 12

Budget surplus (+) or deficit (–): -4% of GDP (2015 est.)

country comparison to the world: 143

Public debt: 98.2% of GDP (2015 est.)

95.5% of GDP (2014 est.)

note: data cover general government debt and include debt instruments issued (or owned) by government entities other than the treasury; the data include treasury debt held by foreign entities; the data include debt issued by subnational entities, as well as intra-governmental debt; intra-governmental debt consists of treasury borrowings from surpluses in the social funds, such as for retirement, medical care, and unemployment; debt instruments for the social funds are not sold at public auctions

country comparison to the world: 19

Fiscal year: calendar year

Inflation rate (consumer prices):

0.1% (2015 est.)

0.6% (2014 est.)

country comparison to the world: 48

Central bank discount rate:

0.05% (31 December 2014)

0.25% (31 December 2013)

note: this is the European Central Bank's rate on the marginal lending facility, which offers overnight credit to banks in the euro area

country comparison to the world: 145

Commercial bank prime lending rate:

2.1% (31 December 2015 est.)

2.6% (31 December 2014 est.)

country comparison to the world: 177

Stock of narrow money:

$981.9 billion (31 December 2015 est.)

$989.7 billion (31 December 2014 est.)

note: see entry for the European Union for money supply for the entire euro area; the European Central Bank (ECB) controls monetary policy for the 18 members of the Economic and Monetary Union (EMU); individual members of the EMU do not control the quantity of money circulating within their own borders

country comparison to the world: 7

Stock of broad money:

$2.541 trillion (31 December 2014 est.)

$2.771 trillion (31 December 2013 est.)

country comparison to the world: 7

Stock of domestic credit:

$3.593 trillion (31 December 2015 est.)

$3.831 trillion (31 December 2014 est.)

country comparison to the world: 6

Market value of publicly traded shares:
$1.762 trillion (31 December 2012 est.)
$1.538 trillion (31 December 2011)
$1.983 trillion (31 December 2010 est.)
country comparison to the world: 8

Current account balance: -$3.041 billion (2015 est.)
-$26.24 billion (2014 est.)
country comparison to the world: 159

Exports: $509.1 billion (2015 est.)
$584.5 billion (2014 est.)
country comparison to the world: 7

Exports—commodities: machinery and transportation equipment, aircraft, plastics, chemicals, pharmaceutical products, iron and steel, beverages

Exports—partners: Germany 15.9%, Spain 7.3%, US 7.2%, Italy 7.1%, UK 7.1%, Belgium 6.8% (2015)

Imports: $539 billion (2015 est.)
$631.1 billion (2014 est.)
country comparison to the world: 7

Imports—commodities: machinery and equipment, vehicles, crude oil, aircraft, plastics, chemicals

Imports—partners: Germany 19.5%, Belgium 10.7%, Italy 7.7%, Netherlands 7.5%, Spain 6.8%, US 5.5%, China 5.4%, UK 4.3% (2015)

Reserves of foreign exchange and gold:
$143.5 billion (31 December 2014 est.)
$144.9 billion (31 December 2013 est.)
country comparison to the world: 17

Debt—external: $5.496 trillion (31 December 2014 est.)
$5.549 trillion (31 December 2013 est.)
country comparison to the world: 5

Stock of direct foreign investment—at home:
$1.124 trillion (31 December 2015 est.)
$1.103 trillion (31 December 2014 est.)
country comparison to the world: 9

Stock of direct foreign investment—abroad:
$1.542 trillion (31 December 2015 est.)
$1.532 trillion (31 December 2014 est.)
country comparison to the world: 6

Exchange rates: euros (EUR) per US dollar—
0.885 (2015 est.)
0.7525 (2014 est.)
0.7634 (2013 est.)
0.7752 (2012 est.)
0.7185 (2011 est.)

ENERGY

Electricity—production: 568 billion kWh (2013 est.)
country comparison to the world: 9

Electricity—consumption: 451.1 billion kWh (2012 est.)
country comparison to the world: 11

Electricity—exports: 60.15 billion kWh (2013 est.)
country comparison to the world: 3

Electricity—imports: 11.69 billion kWh (2013 est.)

country comparison to the world: 18

Electricity—installed generating capacity: 129.3 million kW (2012 est.)
country comparison to the world: 9

Electricity—from fossil fuels: 20.3% of total installed capacity (2012 est.)
country comparison to the world: 195

Electricity—from nuclear fuels: 48.8% of total installed capacity (2012 est.)
country comparison to the world: 2

Electricity—from hydroelectric plants: 14.2% of total installed capacity (2012 est.)
country comparison to the world: 103

Electricity—from other renewable sources: 11.2% of total installed capacity (2012 est.)
country comparison to the world: 29

Crude oil—production: 15,340 bbl/day (2014 est.)
country comparison to the world: 76

Crude oil—exports: 3,664 bbl/day (2013 est.)
country comparison to the world: 75

Crude oil—imports: 1.129 million bbl/day (2013 est.)

country comparison to the world: 12

Crude oil—proved reserves: 84.08 million bbl (1 January 2015 est.)
country comparison to the world: 74

Refined petroleum products—production: 1.27 million bbl/day (2013 est.)
country comparison to the world: 18

Refined petroleum products—consumption: 1.706 million bbl/day (2014 est.)
country comparison to the world: 15

Refined petroleum products—exports: 411,100 bbl/day (2013 est.)
country comparison to the world: 18

Refined petroleum products—imports: 888,800 bbl/day (2013 est.)
country comparison to the world: 7

Natural gas—production: 18 million cu m (2014 est.)
country comparison to the world: 90

Natural gas—consumption: 35.76 billion cu m (2014 est.)
country comparison to the world: 27

Natural gas—exports: 3.544 billion cu m (2014 est.)
country comparison to the world: 33

Natural gas—imports: 41.18 billion cu m (2014 est.)
country comparison to the world: 10

Natural gas—proved reserves: 9.656 billion cu m (1 January 2014 est.)
country comparison to the world: 82

Carbon dioxide emissions from consumption of energy: 385.6 million Mt (2013 est.)
country comparison to the world: 19

COMMUNICATIONS

Telephones—fixed lines: *total subscriptions:* 38.81 million

subscriptions per 100 inhabitants: 59 (2014 est.)
country comparison to the world: 8

Telephones—mobile cellular: *total:* 64.9 million
subscriptions per 100 inhabitants: 98 (2014 est.)
country comparison to the world: 24

Telephone system: *general assessment:* highly developed
domestic: extensive cable and microwave radio relay; extensive use of fiber-optic cable; domestic satellite system
international: country code—33; numerous submarine cables provide links throughout Europe, Asia, Australia, the Middle East, and US; satellite earth stations—more than 3 (2 Intelsat (with total of 5 antennas—2 for Indian Ocean and 3 for Atlantic Ocean), NA Eutelsat, 1 Inmarsat—Atlantic Ocean region); HF radiotelephone communications with more than 20 countries
overseas departments: country codes: French Guiana—594; Guadeloupe—590; Martinique—596; Mayotte—262; Reunion—262 (2011)

Broadcast media: a mix of both publicly operated and privately owned TV stations; state-owned France television stations operate 4 networks, one of which is a network of regional stations, and has part-interest in several thematic cable/satellite channels and international channels; a large number of privately owned regional and local TV stations; multi-channel satellite and cable services provide a large number of channels; public broadcaster Radio France operates 7 national networks, a series of regional networks, and operates services for overseas territories and foreign audiences; Radio France Internationale, under the Ministry of Foreign Affairs, is a leading international broadcaster; a large number of commercial FM stations, with many of them consolidating into commercial networks (2008)
Radio broadcast stations: AM 41, FM about 3,500 (this figure is an approximation and includes many repeaters), shortwave 2 (1998)
Television broadcast stations: 584 (plus 9,676 repeaters) (1995)

Internet country code: metropolitan France—.fr; French Guiana—.gf; Guadeloupe—.gp; Martinique—.mq; Mayotte—.yt; Reunion .re

Internet hosts: 17.266 million (2012)
country comparison to the world: 7

Internet users: *total:* 56.8 million
percent of population: 85.8% (2014 est.)
country comparison to the world: 11

TRANSPORTATION

Airports: 464 (2013)
country comparison to the world: 17

Airports—with paved runways: *total:* 294
over 3,047 m: 14
2,438 to 3,047 m: 25
1,524 to 2,437 m: 97
914 to 1,523 m: 83
under 914 m: 75 (2013)

Airports—with unpaved runways: *total:* 170
1,524 to 2,437 m: 1
914 to 1,523 m: 64

under 914 m: 105 (2013)

Heliports: 1 (2013)

Pipelines: gas 15,322 km; oil 2,939 km; refined products 5,084 km (2013)

Railways: *total:* 29,640 km
standard gauge: 29,473 km 1.435-m gauge (15,561 km electrified)
narrow gauge: 167 km 1.000-m gauge (63 km electrified) (2014)
country comparison to the world: 10

Roadways: *total:* 1,028,446 km (metropolitan France)
paved: 1,028,446 km (includes 11,416 km of expressways)
note: not included are 5,100 km of roadways in overseas departments (2010)
country comparison to the world: 8

Waterways: metropolitan France: 8,501 km (1,621 km navigable by craft up to 3,000 metric tons) (2010)

Merchant marine: *total:* 162
by type: bulk carrier 3, cargo 7, chemical tanker 34, container 27, liquefied gas 12, passenger 10, passenger/cargo 41, petroleum tanker 16, refrigerated cargo 1, roll on/roll off 11
foreign-owned: 50 (Belgium 7, Bermuda 5, Denmark 11, French Polynesia 11, Germany 1, New Caledonia 3, Singapore 3, Sweden 4, Switzerland 5)
registered in other countries: 151 (Bahamas 15, Belgium 7, Bermuda 1, Canada 1, Cyprus 16, Egypt 1, Hong Kong 4, Indonesia 1, Ireland 2, Italy 2, Luxembourg 15, Malta 8, Marshall Islands 7,

Mexico 1, Morocco 3, Netherlands 2, Norway 5, Panama 7, Saint Vincent and the Grenadines 2, Singapore 3, South Korea 2, Taiwan 2, UK 39, US 4, unknown 1) (2010)
country comparison to the world: 36

Ports and terminals: *major seaport(s):* Brest, Calais, Dunkerque, Le Havre, Marseille, Nantes,
river port(s): Paris, Rouen (Seine); Strasbourg (Rhine); Bordeaux (Garronne)
container port(s): Le Havre (2,215,262)(2011)
cruise/ferry port(s): Calais, Cherbourg, Le Havre
LNG terminal(s) (import): Fos Cavaou, Fos Tonkin, Montoir de Bretagne

MILITARY AND SECURITY

Military branches: Army (Armee de Terre; includes Marines, Foreign Legion, Army Light Aviation), Navy (Marine Nationale), Air Force (Armee de l'Air (AdlA); includes Air Defense) (2011)

Military service age and obligation: 18–25 years of age for male and female voluntary military service; no conscription; 1-year service obligation; women serve in noncombat posts (2013)

Military expenditures: 1.8% of GDP (2014)
1.9% of GDP (2013)
1.9% of GDP (2012)
country comparison to the world: 47

TRANSNATIONAL ISSUES

Disputes—international: Madagascar claims the French territories of Bassas da India, Europa Island, Glorioso Islands, and Juan de Nova Island;

Comoros claims Mayotte; Mauritius claims Tromelin Island; territorial dispute between Suriname and the French overseas department of French Guiana; France asserts a territorial claim in Antarctica (Adelie Land); France and Vanuatu claim Matthew and Hunter Islands, east of New Caledonia

Refugees and internally displaced persons: *refugees (country of origin):* 23,966 (Sri Lanka); 13,727 (Democratic Republic of the Congo); 13,644 (Russia); 12,003 (Cambodia); 12,119 (Serbia and Kosovo); 10,699 (Turkey); 8,281 (Vietnam); 7,036 (Laos); 5,201 (Guinea); 5,058 (Mauritania) (2014)
stateless persons: 1,326 (2015)

Illicit drugs: *metropolitan France:* transshipment point for South American cocaine, Southwest Asian heroin, and European synthetics
French Guiana: small amount of marijuana grown for local consumption; minor transshipment point to Europe
Martinique: transshipment point for cocaine and marijuana bound for the US and Europe

FRENCH POLYNESIA

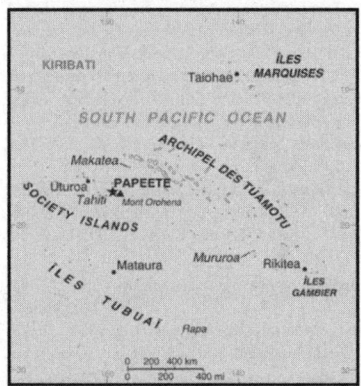

INTRODUCTION

Background: The French annexed various Polynesian island groups during the 19th century. In September 1995, France stirred up widespread protests by resuming nuclear testing on the Mururoa Atoll after a three-year moratorium. The tests

were halted in January 1996. In recent years, French Polynesia's autonomy has been considerably expanded.

GEOGRAPHY

Location: Oceania, five archipelagoes (Archipel des Tuamotu, Iles Gambier, Iles Marquises, Iles Tubuai, Society Islands) in the South Pacific Ocean about halfway between South America and Australia

Geographic coordinates: 15 00 S, 140 00 W

Map references: Oceania

Area: *total:* 4,167 sq km (118 islands and atolls; 67 are inhabited)
land: 3,827 sq km
water: 340 sq km
country comparison to the world: 175

Area—comparative: slightly less than one-third the size of Connecticut

Land boundaries: 0 km

Coastline: 2,525 km

Maritime claims: *territorial sea:* 12 nm
exclusive economic zone: 200 nm

Climate: tropical, but moderate

Terrain: mixture of rugged high islands and low islands with reefs

Elevation: *mean elevation:* NA

elevation extremes: *lowest point:* Pacific Ocean 0 m
highest point: Mont Orohena 2,241 m

Natural resources: timber, fish, cobalt, hydropower

Land use: *agricultural land:* 12.5%
arable land: 0.7%
permanent crops: 6.3%
permanent pasture: 5.5%
forest: 43.7%
other: 43.8% (2011 est.)

Irrigated land: 10 sq km (2012)

Natural hazards: occasional cyclonic storms in January

Environment—current issues: NA

Geography—note: includes five archipelagoes: four volcanic (Iles Gambier, Iles Marquises, Iles Tubuai, Society Islands) and one coral (Archipel des Tuamotu); Makatea in French Polynesia is one of the three great phosphate rock islands in the Pacific Ocean—the others are Banaba (Ocean Island) in Kiribati and Nauru

PEOPLE AND SOCIETY

Nationality: *noun:* French Polynesian(s)
adjective: French Polynesian

Ethnic groups: Polynesian 78%, Chinese 12%, local French 6%, metropolitan French 4%

Languages: French (official) 61.1%, Polynesian (official) 31.4%, Asian languages 1.2%, other 0.3%, unspecified 6% (2002 census)

Religions: Protestant 54%, Roman Catholic 30%, other 10%, no religion 6%

Population: 282,703 (July 2015 est.)
country comparison to the world: 182

Age structure: *0–14 years:* 23.31% (male 33,894/ female 32,005)
15–24 years: 16.36% (male 23,980/female 22,270)
25–54 years: 44.1% (male 63,931/female 60,749)
55–64 years: 8.83% (male 12,847/female 12,120)
65 years and over: 7.4% (male 10,142/female 10,765) (2015 est.)

Dependency ratios: *total dependency ratio:* 42.2%
youth dependency ratio: 31.5%
elderly dependency ratio: 10.7%
poten tial support ratio: 9.3% (2015 est.)

Median age: *total:* 31 years
male: 30.9 years
female: 31.2 years (2015 est.)
country comparison to the world: 105

Population growth rate: 0.94% (2015 est.)
country comparison to the world: 122

Birth rate: 15.22 births/1,000 population (2015 est.)
country comparison to the world: 131

Death rate: 5.02 deaths/1,000 population (2015 est.)
country comparison to the world: 189

Net migration rate: -0.84 migrant(s)/1,000 population (2015 est.)
country comparison to the world: 145

Urbanization: *urban population:* 55.9% of total population (2015)
rate of urbanization: 0.85% annual rate of change (2010–15 est.)

Major urban areas—population: PAPEETE (capital) 133,000 (2014)

Sex ratio: *at birth:* 1.05 male(s)/female
0–14 years: 1.06 male(s)/female
15–24 years: 1.08 male(s)/female
25–54 years: 1.05 male(s)/female
55–64 years: 1.06 male(s)/female
65 years and over: 0.94 male(s)/female
total population: 1.05 male(s)/female (2015 est.)

Infant mortality rate: *total:* 4.73 deaths/1,000 live births
male: 5.25 deaths/1,000 live births
female: 4.18 deaths/1,000 live births (2015 est.)
country comparison to the world: 177

Life expectancy at birth: *total population:* 76.98 years

male: 74.72 years
female: 79.36 years (2015 est.)
country comparison to the world: 75

Total fertility rate: 1.92 children born/woman (2015 est.)
country comparison to the world: 133

Drinking water source:
improved:
urban: 100% of population
rural: 100% of population
total: 100% of population
unimproved:
urban: 0% of population
rural: 0% of population
total: 0% of population (2015 est.)

Sanitation facility access:
improved:
urban: 98.5% of population
rural: 98.5% of population
total: 98.5% of population
unimproved:
urban: 1.5% of population
rural: 1.5% of population
total: 1.5% of population (2015 est.)

HIV/AIDS—adult prevalence rate: NA

HIV/AIDS—people living with HIV/AIDS: NA

HIV/AIDS—deaths: NA

Unemployment, youth ages 15–24: *total:* 34.2%
male: 31.4%
female: 38.5% (2007 est.)

GOVERNMENT

Country name: *conventional long form:* Overseas Lands of French Polynesia
conventional short form: French Polynesia
local long form: Pays d'outre-mer de la Polynesie Francaise
local short form: Polynesie Francaise
former: French Colony of Oceania
etymology: the term "Polynesia" is an 18th-century construct composed of two Greek words, "poly" (many) and "nesoi" (islands), and refers to the more than 1,000 islands scattered over the central and southern Pacific Ocean

Dependency status: overseas lands of France; overseas territory of France from 1946–2003; overseas collectivity of France since 2003, though it is often referred to as an overseas country due to its degree of autonomy

Government type: parliamentary democracy (Assembly of French Polynesia); an overseas collectivity of France

Capital: *name:* Papeete (located on Tahiti)

Geographic coordinates: 17 32 S, 149 34 W
time difference: UTC-10 (5 hours behind Washington, DC, during Standard Time)

Administrative divisions: none (overseas lands of France); there are no first-order administrative divisions as defined by the US Government, but there are 5 second order administrative units named Iles Australes, Iles du Vent, Iles Marquises, Iles Sous le Vent, Iles Tuamotu et Gambier

Independence: none (overseas lands of France)

National holiday: Fete de la Federation, 14 July (1789); note—the local holiday is Internal Autonomy Day, 29 June (1880)

Constitution: 4 October 1958 (French Constitution)

Legal system: the laws of France, where applicable, apply

Citizenship: see France

Suffrage: 18 years of age; universal

Executive branch: *chief of state:* President Francois HOLLANDE (since 15 May 2012), represented by Acting High Commissioner of the Republic Marc TSCHIGGFREY (since 25 May 2016)

head of government: President of French Polynesia Edouard FRITCH (since 12 September 2014)
cabinet: Council of Ministers approved by the Assembly from a list of its members submitted by the president
elections/appointments: French president directly elected by absolute majority popular vote in 2 rounds if needed for a 5-year term (eligible for a second term); high commissioner appointed by the French president on the advice of the French Ministry of Interior; French Polynesia president indirectly elected by Assembly of French Polynesia for a 5-year term (no term limits)

Legislative branch: *description:* unicameral Assembly of French Polynesia or Assemblee de la Polynesie Francaise (57 seats; elections held in two rounds; in the second round, 38 members directly elected in multi-seat constituencies by proportional representation vote; the party receiving the most votes gets an additional 19 seats; members serve 5-year terms)
note: two seats were elected to the French Senate for a 6-year term on 20 September 2014 (next to be held in September 2022); results—percent of vote by party—NA; seats by party—Popular Rally 1, People's Servant Party 1; two seats were elected to the French National Assembly for a 5-year term on 17 June 2012 (next to be held by June 2017); results—percent of vote by party—NA; seats by party—UMP 2; note—the UMP is France's ruling pary, the Union for a Popular Movement
elections: last held on 21 April 2013 and 5 May 2013 (next to be held in 2018)
election results: percent of vote by party—Popular Rally 45.1%, UPD 29.3%, A Tia Porinetia 25.6%; seats by party—Popular Rally 38, UPD 11, A Tia Porinetia 8

Judicial branch: *highest court(s):* Court of Appeal or Cour d'Appel (composition NA); note—appeals beyond the French Polynesia Court of Appeal are heard by the Court of Cassation (in Paris)
judge selection and term of office: NA
subordinate courts: Court of the First Instance or Tribunal de Premiere Instance; Court of Administrative Law or Tribunal Administratif

Political parties and leaders: A Tia Porinetia [Teva ROHFRITSCH]

Alliance for a New Democracy or ADN (includes the parties The New Star and This Country is Yours)

New Fatherland Party (Ai'a Api) [Emile VERNAUDON]

Our Home alliance

People's Servant Party (Tavini Huiraatira) [Oscar TEMARU]

Popular Rally (Tahoeraa Huiraatira) [Gaston FLOSSE]

Union for Democracy alliance or UPD [Oscar TEMARU]

International organization participation: ITUC (NGOs), PIF (associate member), SPC, UPU, WMO

Diplomatic representation in the US: none (overseas lands of France)

Diplomatic representation from the US: none (overseas lands of France)

Flag description: two red horizontal bands encase a wide white band in a 1: 2: 1 ratio; centered on the white band is a disk with a blue and white wave pattern depicting the sea on the lower half and a gold and white ray pattern depicting the sun on the upper half; a Polynesian canoe rides on the wave pattern; the canoe has a crew of five represented by five stars that symbolize the five island groups; red and white are traditional Polynesian colors

note: similar to the red-wh ite-red flag of Tah iti, the largest of the islands in French Polynesia, which has no emblem in the white band; the flag of France is used for official occasions

National symbol(s): outrigger canoe; national colors: red, wh ite

National anthem: *name:* "Ia Ora 'O Tahiti Nui" (Long Live Tahiti Nui)

lyrics/music: Maeva BOUGES, Irmine TEHEI, Angele TEROROTUA, Johanna NOUVEAU, Patrick AMARU, Louis MAMATUI, and Jean-Pierre CELESTIN (the compositional group created both the lyrics and music)

note: adopted 1993; serves as a local anth em; as a territory of France, "La M arseillaise" is official (see France)

Government—note: under certain acts of France, French Polynesia has acquired autonomy in all areas except those relating to police, monetary policy, tertiary education, immigration, and defense and foreign affairs; the duties of its president are fash ioned after those of the French prime minister

ECONOMY

Economy—overview: Since 1962, when France stationed military personnel in the region, French Polynesia has ch anged from a subsistence agricultural economy to one in which a high proportion of the work force is eith er employed by the military or supports the tourist industry. With the halt of French nuclear testing in 1996, the military contribution to the economy fell sharply. After growing at an average yearly rate of 4.2% from 1997–2007, GDP stagnated in 2008 and fell by 4.2% in 2009, marking French Polynesia's entry into recession.

GDP growth was positive in 2010–12. Following steady employment level increases between 2002 and 2007 that averaged 2.4% yearly, the number of workers fell by an annual average of 2.2% between 2008 and 2013, due in part to decreased tourism (down an average of 4% per year) in th at time period. French Polynesia's tourism-dominated service sector accounted for 85% of total value added for the economy in 2009, employing 80% of the workforce. A small manufacturing sector predominantly processes products from French Polynesia's primary sector—3% of total economy—including agriculture, pearl farming, and fishing.

GDP (purchasing power parity):
$7.15 billion (2012 est.)
$6.982 billion (2011 est.)
$6.963 billion (2010 est.)
country comparison to the world: 165

GDP (official exchange rate):
$7.15 billion (2012 est.)

GDP—real growth rate:
2.4% (2012 est.)
0.3% (2011 est.)
2.2% (2010 est.)
country comparison to the world: 125

GDP—per capita (PPP):
$26,100 (2012 est.)
$26,000 (2010 est.)
country comparison to the world: 72

GDP—composition, by sector of origin:
agriculture: 2.5%
industry: 13%
services: 84.5% (2009)

Agriculture—products: coconuts, vanilla, vegetables, fruits, coffee; poultry, beef, dairy products; fish

Industries: tourism, pearls, agricultural processing, handicrafts, phosphates

Industrial production growth rate: NA%

Labor force: 114,300 (2012 est.)
country comparison to the world: 182

Labor force—by occupation: *agriculture:* 13%
industry: 19%
services: 68% (2013)

Unemployment rate: 21.8% (2012)
11.7% (2010)
country comparison to the world: 171

Population below poverty line: 19.7% (2009 est.)

Household income or consumption by percentage share: *lowest:* 10%: NA%
highest: 10%: NA%

Budget: *revenues:* $1.891 billion
expenditures: $1.833 billion (2012)
Taxes and other revenues: 26.4% of GDP (2012)
country comparison to the world: 112

Budget surplus (+) or deficit (−): 0.8% of GDP (2012)
country comparison to the world: 21

Fiscal year: calendar year

Inflation rate (consumer prices):
1.1% (2013 est.)
1.5% (2011 est.)
country comparison to the world: 82

Market value of publicly traded shares: $NA

Exports:
$230 million (2013 est.)
$211 million (2005 est.)
country comparison to the world: 185

Exports—commodities: cultured pearls, coconut products, mother-of-pearl, vanilla, shark meat

Exports—partners: Japan 35%, US 24%, Hong Kong 17%, France 9.1%, China 4.2% (2014)

Imports: $1.72 billion (2013 est.)
$1.706 billion (2005 est.)
country comparison to the world: 167

Imports—commodities: fuels, foodstuffs, machinery and equipment

Imports—partners: France 24%, South Korea 10%, China 9.6%, USA 9.3%, New Zealand 8.5%, Singapore 8.2%, Australia 4% (2014)

Debt—external: $NA

Exchange rates: Comptoirs Francais du Pacifique francs (XPF) per US dollar—
89.85 (2013 est.)
90.56 (2012 est.)
85.74 (2011 est.)

ENERGY

Electricity—production: 702 million kWh (2012 est.)
country comparison to the world: 158

Electricity—consumption: 652.9 million kWh (2012 est.)
country comparison to the world: 166

Electricity—exports: 0 kWh (2013 est.)
country comparison to the world: 140

Electricity—imports: 0 kWh (2013 est.)
country comparison to the world: 151

Electricity—installed generating capacity: 224,000 kW (2012 est.)
country comparison to the world: 159

Electricity—from fossil fuels: 79% of total installed capacity (2012 est.)
country comparison to the world: 94

Electricity—from nuclear fuels: 0% of total installed capacity (2012 est.)
country comparison to the world: 94

Electricity—from hydroelectric plants: 21% of total installed capacity (2012 est.)
country comparison to the world: 90

Electricity—from other renewable sources: 0% of total installed capacity (2012 est.)
country comparison to the world: 173

Crude oil—production: 0 bbl/day (2014 est.)
country comparison to the world: 138

Crude oil—exports: 0 bbl/day (2012 est.)
country comparison to the world: 127

Crude oil—imports: 0 bbl/day (2012 est.)
country comparison to the world: 192

Crude oil—proved reserves: 0 bbl (1 January 2015 est.)
country comparison to the world: 136

Refined petroleum products—production: 0 bbl/day (2012 est.)

309

country comparison to the world: 184

Refined petroleum products—consumption: 7,000 bbl/day (2013 est.)
country comparison to the world: 159

Refined petroleum products—exports: 0 bbl/day (2012 est.)
country comparison to the world: 183

Refined petroleum products—imports: 6,994 bbl/day (2012 est.)
country comparison to the world: 145

Natural gas—production: 0 cu m (2013 est.)
country comparison to the world: 189

Natural gas—consumption: 0 cu m (2013 est.)
country comparison to the world: 145

Natural gas—exports: 0 cu m (2013 est.)
country comparison to the world: 101

Natural gas—imports: 0 cu m (2013 est.)
country comparison to the world: 198

Natural gas—proved reserves: 0 cu m (1 January 2014 est.)
country comparison to the world: 141

Carbon dioxide emissions from consumption of energy: 1.071 million Mt (2012 est.)
country comparison to the world: 166

COMMUNICATIONS

Telephones—fixed lines: *total subscriptions:* 55,000
subscriptions per 100 inhabitants: 20 (2014 est.)
country comparison to the world: 159

Telephones—mobilecellular: *total:* 239,700
subscriptions per 100 inhabitants: 86 (2014 est.)
country comparison to the world: 180

Telephone system: *domestic:* combined fixed-line and mobile-cellular density is roughly 100 per 100 persons
international: country code—689; satellite earth station—1 intelsat (Pacific Ocean) (2011)

Broadcast media: the publicly owned French Overseas Network (RFO), which operates in France's overseas departments and territories, broadcasts on 2 TV channels and 1 radio station; 1 government-owned TV station; a small number of privately owned radio stations (2008)
Radio broadcast stations: AM 2, FM 14, shortwave 2 (1998)
Television broadcast stations: 7 (plus 17 repeaters) (1997)

Internet country code: .pf

Internet hosts: 37,949 (2012)
country comparison to the world: 103

Internet users: *total:* 161,100
percent of population: 57.5% (2014 est.)
country comparison to the world: 163

TRANSPORTATION

Airports: 54 (2013)
country comparison to the world: 87

Airports—with paved runways: *total:* 45
over 3,047 m: 2

1,524 to 2,437 m: 5
914 to 1,523 m: 33
under 914 m: 5 (2013)

Airports—with unpaved runways: *total:* 9
914 to 1,523 m: 4
under 914 m: 5 (2013)

Heliports: 1 (2013)

Roadways: *total:* 2,590 km
paved: 1,735 km
unpaved: 855 km (1999)
country comparison to the world: 172

Merchant marine:
registered in other countries: 12 (Cambodia 1, France 11) (2010)
country comparison to the world: 107

Ports and terminals:
major seaport(s): Papeete

MILITARY AND SECURITY

Military branches: no regular military forces (2011)

Military—note: defense is the responsibility of France

TRANSNATIONAL ISSUES

Disputes—international: none

FRENCH SOUTHERN AND ANTARCTIC LANDS

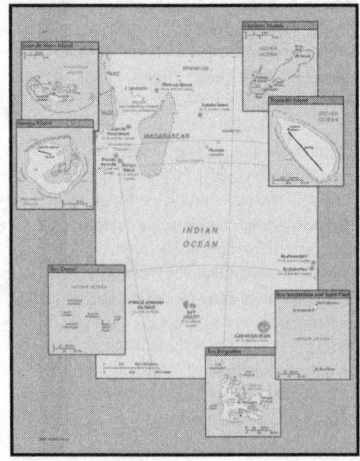

INTRODUCTION

Background: In February 2007, the Iles Eparses became an integral part of the French Southern and Antarctic Lands (TAAF). The Southern Lands are now divided into five administrative districts, two of which are archipelagos, Iles Crozet and Iles Kerguelen; the third is a district composed of two volcanic islands, Ile Saint-Paul and Ile Amsterdam; the fourth, Iles Eparses, consists of five scattered tropical islands around Madagascar. They contain no permanent inhabitants and are visited only by researchers studying the native fauna, scientists at the various scientific stations, fishermen, and military personnel. The fifth district is the Antarctic portion, which consists of "Adelie Land," a thin slice of the Antarctic continent discovered and claimed by the French in 1840.

Ile Amsterdam: Discovered but not named in 1522 by the Spanish, the island subsequently received the appellation of Nieuw Amsterdam from a Dutchman; it was claimed by France in 1843. A short-lived attempt at cattle farming began in 1871. A French meteorological station established on the island in 1949 is still in use.

Ile Saint Paul: Claimed by France since 1893, the island was a fishing industry center from 1843 to 1914. In 1928, a spiny lobster cannery was established, but when the company went bankrupt in 1931, seven workers were abandoned. Only two survived until 1934 when rescue finally arrived.

Iles Crozet: A large archipelago formed from the Crozet Plateau, Iles Crozet is divided into two

main groups: L'Occidental (the West), which includes Ile aux Cochons, Ilots des Apotres, Ile des Pingouins, and the reefs Brisants de l'Heroine; and L'Oriental (the East), which includes Ile d'Est and Ile de la Possession (the largest island of the Crozets). Discovered and claimed by France in 1772, the islands were used for seal hunting and as a base for whaling. Originally administered as a dependency of Madagascar, they became part of the TAAF in 1955.

Iles Kerguelen: This island group, discovered in 1772, consists of one large island (Ile Kerguelen) and about 300 smaller islands. A permanent group of 50 to 100 scientists resides at the main base at Port-aux-Francais.

Adelie Land: The only non-insular district of the TAAF is the Antarctic claim known as "Adelie Land." The US Government does not recognize it as a French dependency.

Bassas da India: A French possession since 1897, this atoll is a volcanic rock surrounded by reefs and is awash at high tide.

Europa Island: This heavily wooded island has been a French possession since 1897; it is the site of a small military garrison that staffs a weather station.

Glorioso Islands: A French possession since 1892, the Glorioso Islands are composed of two lushly vegetated coral islands (Ile Glorieuse and Ile du Lys) and three rock islets. A military garrison operates a weather and radio station on Ile Glorieuse.

Juan de Nova Island: Named after a famous 15th-century Spanish navigator and explorer, the island has been a French possession since 1897. It has been exploited for its guano and phosphate. Presently a small military garrison oversees a meteorological station.

Tromelin Island: First explored by the French in 1776, the island came under the jurisdiction of Reunion in 1814. At present, it serves as a sea turtle sanctuary and is the site of an important meteorological station.

GEOGRAPHY

Location: southeast and east of Africa, islands in the southern Indian Ocean, some near Madagascar and others about equidistant between Africa, Antarctica, and Australia; note—French Southern and Antarctic Lands include Ile Amsterdam, Ile Saint-Paul, Iles Crozet, Iles Kerguelen, Bassas da India, Europa Island, Glorioso Islands, Juan de Nova Island, and Tromelin Island in the southern Indian Ocean, along with the French-claimed sector of Antarctica, "Adelie Land"; the US does not recognize the French claim to "Adelie Land"

Geographic coordinates:
Ile Amsterdam (Ile Amsterdam et Ile Saint-Paul): 37 50 S, 77 32 E
Ile Saint-Paul (Ile Amsterdam et Ile Saint-Paul): 38 72 S, 77 53 E
Iles Crozet: 46 25 S, 5100 E
Iles Kerguelen: 49 15 S, 69 35 E
Bassas da India (Iles Eparses): 21 30 S, 39 50 E
Europa Island (Iles Eparses): 22 20 S, 40 22 E
Glorioso Islands (Iles Eparses): 11 30 S, 47 20 E
Juan de Nova Island (Iles Eparses): 17 03 S, 42 45 E
Tromelin Island (Iles Eparses): 1 5 52 S, 54 25 E

Map references: Antarctic Region, Africa

Area: *Ile Amsterdam (Ile Amsterdam et Ile Saint-Paul):* total—55 sq km; land—55 sq km; water—0 sq km
Ile Saint-Paul (Ile Amsterdam et Ile Saint-Paul): total—7 sq km; land—7 sq km; water—0 sq km
Iles Crozet: total—352 sq km; land—352 sq km; water—0 sq km
Iles Kerguelen: total—7,215 sq km; land—7,215 sq km; water—0 sq km
Bassas da India (Iles Eparses): total—80 sq km; land—0.2 sq km; water—79.8 sq km (lagoon)
Europa Island (Iles Eparses): total—28 sq km; land—28 sq km; water—0 sq km
Glorioso Islands (Iles Eparses): total—5 sq km; land—5 sq km; water—0 sq km
Juan de Nova Island (Iles Eparses): total—4.4 sq km; land—4.4 sq km; water—0 sq km
Tromelin Island (Iles Eparses): total—1 sq km; land—1 sq km; water—0 sq km
note: excludes "Adelie Land" claim of about 500,000 sq km in Antarctica that is not recognized by the US
country comparison to the world: 230

Area—comparative: *Ile Amsterdam (Ile Amsterdam et Ile Saint-Paul):* less than one-half the size of Washington, DC
Ile Saint-Paul (Ile Amsterdam et Ile Saint-Paul): more than 10 times the size of The Mall in Washington, DC
Iles Crozet: about twice the size of Washington, DC
Iles Kerguelen: slightly larger than Delaware
Bassas da India (Iles Eparses): land area about one-third the size of The Mall in Washington, DC
Europa Island (Iles Eparses): about one-sixth the size of Washington, DC
Glorioso Islands (Iles Eparses): about eight times the size of The Mall in Washington, DC
Juan de Nova Island (Iles Eparses): about seven times the size of The Mall in Washington, DC
Tromelin Island (Iles Eparses): about 1.7 times the size of The Mall in Washington, DC

Land boundaries: 0 km

Coastline: *Ile Amsterdam (Ile Amsterdam et Ile Saint-Paul):* 28 km
Ile Saint-Paul (Ile Amsterdam et Ile Saint-Paul):
Iles Kerguelen: 2,800 km
Bassas da India (Iles Eparses): 35.2 km
Europa Island (Iles Eparses): 22.2 km
Glorioso Islands (Iles Eparses): 35.2 km
Juan de Nova Island (Iles Eparses): 24.1 km
Tromelin Island (Iles Eparses): 3.7 km

Maritime claims: *territorial sea:* 12 nm
exclusive economic zone: 200 nm from Iles Kerguelen and Iles Eparses (does not include the rest of French Southern and Antarctic Lands); Juan de Nova Island and Tromelin Island claim a continental shelf of 200-m depth or to the depth of exploitation

Climate: *Ile Amsterdam et Ile Saint-Paul:* oceanic with persistent westerly winds and high humidity
Iles Crozet: windy, cold, wet, and cloudy
Iles Kerguelen: oceanic, cold, overcast, windy
Iles Eparses: tropical

Terrain: *Ile Amsterdam (Ile Amsterdam et Ile Saint-Paul):* a volcanic island with steep coastal cliffs; the center floor of the volcano is a large plateau
Ile Saint-Paul (Ile Amsterdam et Ile Saint-Paul): triangular in shape, the island is the top of a volcano, rocky with steep cliffs on the eastern side; has active thermal springs
Iles Crozet: a large archipelago formed from the Crozet Plateau is divided into two groups of islands
Iles Kerguelen: the interior of the large island of Ile Kerguelen is composed of high mountains, hills, valleys, and plains with peninsulas stretching off its coasts
Bassas da India (Iles Eparses): atoll, awash at high tide; shallow (15 m) lagoon
Europa Island, Glorioso Islands, Juan de Nova Island: low, flat, and sandy
Tromelin Island (Iles Eparses): low, flat, sandy; likely volcanic seamount

Elevation: *mean elevation:* NA

elevation extremes: *lowest point:* Indian Ocean 0 m
highest point: Mont de la Dives on Ile Amsterdam (Ile Amsterdam et Ile Saint-Paul) 867 m; unnamed location on Ile Saint-Paul (Ile Amsterdam et Ile Saint-Paul) 272 m; Pic Marion-Dufresne in Iles Crozet 1,090 m; Mont Ross in Iles Kerguelen 1,850 m; unnamed location on Bassas de India (Iles Eparses) 2.4 m; unnamed location on Europa Island (Iles Eparses) 24 m; unnamed location on Glorioso Islands (Iles Eparses) 12 m; unnamed location on Juan de Nova Island (Iles Eparses) 10 m; unnamed location on Tromelin Island (Iles Eparses) 7 m

Natural resources: fish, crayfish
note: Glorioso Islands and Tromelin Island (Iles Eparses) have guano, phosphates, and coconuts

Natural hazards: Ile Amsterdam and Ile Saint-Paul are inactive volcanoes; Iles Eparses subject to periodic cyclones; Bassas da India is a maritime hazard since it is under water for a period of three hours prior to and following the high tide and surrounded by reefs
volcanism: Reunion Island—Piton de la Fournaise (elev. 2,632 m.), which has erupted many times in recent years including 2010, is one of the world's most active volcanoes; although rare, eruptions outside the volcano's caldera could threaten nearby cities

Environment—current issues: introduction of foreign species on Iles Crozet has caused severe damage to the original ecosystem; overfishing of Patagonian toothfish around Iles Crozet and Iles Kerguelen

Geography—note: islands' component is widely scattered across remote locations in the southern Indian Ocean
Bassas da India (Iles Eparses): atoll is a circular reef atop a long-extinct, submerged volcano
Europa Island and Juan de Nova Island (Iles Eparses): wildlife sanctuary for seabirds and sea turtles
Glorioso Island (Iles Eparses): islands and rocks are surrounded by an extensive reef system
Tromelin Island (Iles Eparses): climatologically important location for forecasting cyclones in the western Indian Ocean; wildlife sanctuary (seabirds, tortoises)

PEOPLE AND SOCIETY

Population: no indigenous inhabitants
Ile Amsterdam (Ile Amsterdam et Ile Saint-Paul): no permanent residents but has a meteorological station
Ile Saint-Paul (Ile Amsterdam et Ile Saint-Paul): uninhabited but is frequently visited by fishermen and has a scientific research cabin for short stays
Iles Crozet: uninhabited except for 18 to 30 people staffing the Alfred Faure research station on Ile del la Possession
Iles Kerguelen: 50 to 100 scientists are located at the main base at Port-aux-Francais on Ile Kerguelen
Bassas da India (Iles Eparses): uninhabitable

Europa Island, Glorioso Islands, Juan de Nova Islan d (I les Eparses): a small French military garrison and a few meteorologists on each possession; visited by scientists

Tromelin Island (Iles Eparses): uninhabited, except for visits by scientists

GOVERNMENT

Country name: *conventional long form:* Territory of the French Southern and Antarctic Lands
conventional short form: French Southern and Antarctic Lands
local long form: Territoire des Terres Australes et An tarctiques Francaises
local short form: Terres Australes et An tarctiques Francaises
abbreviation: TAAF
etymology: self-descriptive name specifying the territories' affiliation and location in the Southern Hemisphere

Dependency status: overseas territory of France since 1955

Administrative divisions: none (overseas territory of France); there are no first-order administrative divisions as defined by the US Government, but there are five administrative districts named Iles Crozet, Iles Eparses, Iles Kerguelen, Ile Saint-Paul et Ile Amsterdam; the fifth district is the "Adelie Land" claim in Antarctica that is not recognized by the US

Legal system: the laws of France, where applicable, apply

Citizenship: see France

Executive branch: *chief of state:* President Francois HOLLANDE (since 15 May 2012), represented by Senior Administrator Cecile POGGO DI BORGO (since 13 October 2014)

International organization participation: UPU

Diplomatic representation in the US: none (overseas territory of France)

Diplomatic representation from the US: none (overseas territory of France)

Flag description: the flag of France is used

National anthem: note: as a territory of France, "La Marseillaise" is official (see France)

ECONOMY

Economy—overview: Economic activity is limited to servicin g meteorological and geophysical research station s, military bases, and French and other fishing fleets. The fish catches landed on Iles Kerguelen by foreign ships are exported to France and Reunion.

COMMUNICATIONS

Internet country code: .tf

Internet hosts: 53 (2012)
country comparison to the world: 214

Communications—note: has one or more meteorological stations on each possession

TRANSPORTATION

Airports: 4; note—one each on Europa Island, Glorioso Islands, Juan de Nova Island, and Tromelin Island in the Iles Eparses district (2013) country comparison to the world: 191

Ports and terminals: none; offshore anchorage only

MILITARY AND SECURITY

Military—note: defense is the responsibility of France

TRANSNATIONAL ISSUES

Disputes—international: French claim to "Adelie Land" in Antarctica is not recognized by the US
Bassas da India, Europa Island, Glorioso Islands, Juan de Nova Island (Iles Eparses): claimed by Madagascar; the vegetated drying cays of Banc du Geyser, which were claimed by Madagascar in 1976, also fall within the EEZ claims of the Comoros and France (Glorioso Islands)
Trom elin Islan d (I les Eparses): claimed by Mauritius

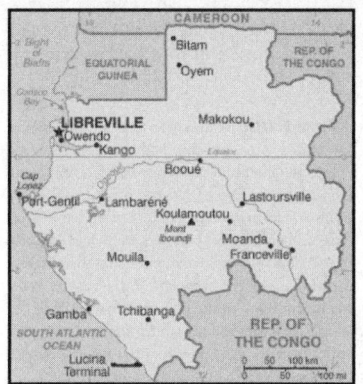

INTRODUCTION

Background: El Hadj Omar BONGO Ondimba—one of the longest-serving heads of state in the world—dominated the country's political scene for four decades (1967–2009) following independence from France in 1960. President BONGO introduced a nominal multiparty system and a new constitution in the early 1990s. However, allegations of electoral fraud during local elections in December 2002 and the presidential election in 2005 exposed the weaknesses of formal political structures in Gabon. Following President BONGO's death in 2009, a new election brought Ali BONGO Ondimba, son of the former president, to power. Despite constrained political conditions, Gabon's small population, abundant natural resources, and considerable foreign support have helped make it one of the more stable African countries.

GEOGRAPHY

Location: Central Africa, bordering the Atlantic Ocean at the Equator, between Republic of the Congo and Equatorial Guinea

Geographic coordinates: 1 00 S, 11 45 E

Map references: Africa

Area: *total:* 267,667 sq km
land: 257,667 sq km
water: 10,000 sq km
country comparison to the world: 77

Area—comparative: slightly smaller than Colorado

Land boundaries: *total:* 3,261 km
border countries (3): Cameroon 349 km, Republic of the Congo 2,567 km, Equatorial Guinea 345 km

Coastline: 885 km

Maritime claims: *territorial sea:* 12 nm
contiguous zone: 24 nm
exclusive economic zone: 200 nm

Climate: tropical; always hot, humid

Terrain: narrow coastal plain; hilly interior; savanna in east and south

Elevation: *mean elevation:* 377 m

elevation extremes: *lowest point:* Atlantic Ocean 0 m
highest point: Mont Iboundji 1,575 m

Natural resources: petroleum, natural gas, diamond, niobium, manganese, uranium, gold, timber, iron ore, hydropower

Land use: *agricultural land:* 19%
arable land: 1.2%
permanent crops: 0.6%
permanent pasture: 17.2%
forest: 81%
other: 0% (2011 est.)

Irrigated land: 40 sq km (2012)

Total renewable water resources: 164 cu km (2011)

Freshwater withdrawal (domestic/industrial/agricultural): *total:* 0.14 cu km/yr (61%/10%/29%)
per capita: 97.68 cu m/yr (2005)

Natural hazards: NA

Environment—current issues: deforestation; poaching

Environment—international agreements: *party to:* Biodiversity, Climate Change, Climate Change-Kyoto Protocol, Desertification, Endangered Species, Hazardous Wastes, Law of the Sea, Marine Dumping, Ozone Layer Protection, Ship Pollution, Tropical Timber 83, Tropical Timber 94, Wetlands, Whaling
signed, but not ratified: none of the selected agreements

Geography—note: a small population and oil and mineral reserves have helped Gabon become one of Africa's wealthier countries; in general, these circum stances have allowed the country to maintain and conserve its pristine rain forest and rich biodiversity

PEOPLE AND SOCIETY

Nationality: *noun:* Gabonese (singular and plural)
adjective: Gabonese

Ethnic groups: Bantu tribes, including four major tribal groupings (Fang, Bapounou, Nzebi, Obamba); other Africans and Europeans, 154,000, including 10,700 French and 11,000 persons of dual nationality

Languages: French (official), Fang, Myene, Nzebi, Bapounou/Eschira, Bandjabi

Religions: Catholic 41.9%, Protestant 13.7%, other Christian 32.4%, Muslim 6.4%, animist 0.3%, other 0.3%, none/no answer 5% (2012 est.)

Population: 1,705,336
note: estimates for this country explicitly take into account the effects of excess mortality due to AIDS; this can result in lower life expectancy, higher infant mortality, higher death rates, lower population growth rates, and changes in the distribution of population by age and sex than would otherwise be expected (July 2015 est.)
country comparison to the world: 154

Age structure: *0–14 years:* 42.06% (male 360,412/female 356,787)
15–24 years: 20.29% (male 173,395/female 172,678)
25–54 years: 29.66% (male 253,304/female 252,493)
55–64 years: 4.2% (male 34,561/female 37,108)
65 years and over: 3.79% (male 27,621/female 36,977) (2015 est.)

Dependency ratios: *total dependency ratio:* 73.1%
youth dependency ratio: 64.3%
elderly dependency ratio: 8.8%
potential support ratio: 11.3% (2015 est.)

Median age: *total:* 18.6 years
male: 18.4 years
female: 18.8 years (2015 est.)
country comparison to the world: 206

Population growth rate: 1.93% (2015 est.)
country comparison to the world: 53

Birth rate: 34.49 births/1,000 population (2015 est.)
country comparison to the world: 25

Death rate: 13.12 deaths/1,000 population (2015 est.)
country comparison to the world: 17

Net migration rate: -2.03 migrant(s)/1,000 population (2015 est.)
country comparison to the world: 168

Urbanization: *urban population:* 87.2% of total population (2015)
rate of urbanization: 2.7% annual rate of change (2010–15 est.)

Major urban areas—population: LIBREVILLE (capital) 707,000 (2015)

Sex ratio: *at birth:* 1.03 male(s)/female
0–14 years: 1.01 male(s)/female
15–24 years: 1 male(s)/female
25–54 years: 1 male(s)/female
55–64 years: 0.93 male(s)/female
65 years and over: 0.75 male(s)/female
total population: 0.99 male(s)/female (2015 est.)

Mother's mean age at first birth: 20.3
note: median age at first birth among women 25–29 (2012 est.)

Maternal mortality rate: 291 deaths/100,000 live births (2015 est.)
country comparison to the world: 50

Infant mortality rate: *total:* 46.07 deaths/1,000 live births
male: 53.11 deaths/1,000 live births
female: 38.81 deaths/1,000 live births (2015 est.)
country comparison to the world: 43

Life expectancy at birth: *total population:* 52.04 years
male: 51.56 years
female: 52.53 years (2015 est.)

country comparison to the world: 217

Total fertility rate: 4.46 children born/woman (2015 est.)
country comparison to the world: 29

Contraceptive prevalence rate: 31.1% (2012)
Health expenditures: 3.8% of GDP (2013)
country comparison to the world: 173

Hospital bed density: 6.3 beds/1,000 population (2010)

Drinking water source:
improved:
urban: 97.2% of population
rural: 66.7% of population
total: 93.2% of population
unimproved:
urban: urban: 2.8% of population
rural: 33.3% of population
total: 6.8% of population (2015 est.)

Sanitation facility access:
improved:
urban: 43.4% of population
rural: 31.5% of population
total: 41.9% of population
unimproved:
urban: 56.6% of population
rural: 68.5% of population
total: 58.1% of population (2015 est.)

HIV/AIDS—adult prevalence rate: 3.91% (2014 est.)
country comparison to the world: 16

HIV/AIDS—people living with HIV/AIDS: 47,500 (2014 est.)
country comparison to the world: 57

HIV/AIDS—deaths: 1,500 (2014 est.)
country comparison to the world: 61

Major infectious diseases: *degree of risk:* very high
food or waterborne diseases: bacterial diarrhea, hepatitis A, and typhoid fever
vectorborne disease: malaria and dengue fever
water contact disease: schistosomiasis
animal contact disease: rabies (2013)

Obesity—adult prevalence rate: 15.8% (2014)
country comparison to the world: 124

Children under the age of 5 years underweight: 6.5% (2012)
country comparison to the world: 79

Education expenditures: NA

Literacy: *definition:* age 15 and over can read and write
total population: 83.2%
male: 85.3%
female: 81% (2015 est.)

Unemployment, youth ages 15–24: *total:* 35.7%
male: 30.6%
female: 41.9% (2010 est.)

GOVERNMENT

Country name: *conventional long form:* Gabonese Republic
conventional short form: Gabon
local long form: Republique Gabonaise

local short form: Gabon
etymology: name originates from the Portuguese word "gabao" meaning "cloak," which is roughly the shape that the early explorers gave to the estuary of the Komo River by the capital of Libreville

Government type: presidential republic

Capital: *name:* Libreville

Geographic coordinates: 0 23 N, 9 27 E
time difference: UTC + 1 (6 hours ahead of Washington, DC, during Standard Time)

Administrative divisions: 9 provinces; Estuaire, Haut-Ogooue, Moyen-Ogooue, Ngounie, Nyanga, Ogooue-Ivindo, Ogooue-Lolo, Ogooue-Maritime, Woleu-Ntem

Independence: 17 August 1960 (from France)

National holiday: Independence Day, 17 August (1960)

Constitution: previous 1961; latest drafted May 1990, adopted 15 March 1991, promulgated 26 March 1991; amended several times, last in 2011 (2016)

Legal system: mixed legal system of French civil law and custom ary law

International law organization participation: has not submitted an ICJ jurisdiction declaration; accepts ICCt jurisdiction

Citizenship: *citizenship by birth:* no
citizenship by descent only: at least one parent must be a citizen of Gabon
dual citizenship recognized: no
residency requirement for naturalization: 10 years

Suffrage: 18 years of age; universal

Executive branch: *chief of state:* President Ali BONGO Ondimba (since 16 October 2009)

head of government: Prime Minister Daniel ONAONDO (since 27 January 2014)
cabinet: Council of Ministers appointed by the prime minister in consultation with the president
elections/appointments: president directly elected by simple majority popular vote for a 7-year term (no term limits); election last held on 30 August 2009 (next to be held in 2016); prime m inister appointed by the president
election results: Ali BONGO Ondim ba elected president; percent of vote—Ali BONGO Ondim ba (PDG) 41.7%, Andre MBA OBAME (independent) 25.9%, Pierre MAMBOUNDOU (UPG) 25.2%, Zacharie MYBOTO (UGDD) 3.9%, other 3.3%

Legislative branch: *description:* bicam eral Parliam ent or Parlement consists of the Senate or Senat (102 seats; m embers indirectly elected by municipal councils and departmental assem blies by absolute majority vote in two rounds; m embers serve 6-year terms) and the National Assembly or Assem blee Nationale (120 seats; mem bers elected in single-seat constituencies by absolute majority vote in two rounds if needed; m embers serve 5-year terms)
elections: Senate—last held on 18 January 2009 (next to be held in January 2015); National

Assembly -last held on 17 December 2011 (next to be held in December 2016)
election results: Senate—percent of vote by party—NA; seats by party—PDG 75, RPG 6, UGDD 3, CLR 2, PGCI 2, PSD 2, UPG 2, ADERE 1, independent 9; National Assembly—percent of vote by party—NA; seats by party—PDG 114, RPG 3, other 3

Judicial branch: *highest court(s):* Suprem e Court (organized into Judicial, Adm inistrative, and Accounts chambers and consists of NA judges); Constitutional Court (consists of 9 judges)
judge selection and term of office: Supreme Court judges appointment and tenure NA; Constitutional Court judges appointed—3 by the national president, 3 by the president of the Senate, and 3 by the president of the National Assembly; judges serve 7-year, single renewable terms
subordinate courts: Courts of Appeal; Court of State Security; county courts; military courts

Political parties and leaders: Circle of Liberal Reformers or CLR [General Jean-Boniface ASSELE]
Democratic and Republican Alliance or ADERE [DIDJOB Divungui di Ndinge]
Gabonese Democratic Party or PDG [Ali BONGO Ondimba]
Independent Center Party of Gabon or PGCI [Luccheri GAHILA]
National Rally of Woodcutters-Democratic or RNB-D [Pierre Andre KOMBILA]
Social Democratic Party or PSD [Pierre Claver MAGANGA-MOUSSAVOU]
Union for the New Republic or UPRN [Louis Gaston MAYILA]
Union of Gabonese People or UPG [Richard MOULOMBA]

Political parties and leaders: NA

International organization participation: ACP, AfDB, AU, BDEAC, CEMAC, FAO, FZ, G-24, G-77, IAEA, IBRD, ICAO, ICCt, ICRM, IDA, IDB, IFAD, IFC, IFRCS, ILO, IMF, IMO, IMSO, Interpol, IOC, IOM, IPU, ISO, ITSO, ITU, ITUC (NGOs), MIGA, NAM, OIC, OIF, OPCW, UN, UNCTAD, UNESCO, UNIDO, UNWTO, UPU, WCO, WHO, WIPO, WMO, WTO

Diplomatic representation in the US: *chief of mission:* Ambassador Baudelaire Ndong ELLA (since 31 July 2015)
chancery: 203420th Street NW, Suite 200, Washington, DC 20009
telephone: [1] (202) 797-1000
FAX: [1] (301) 332-0668

Diplomatic representation from the US: *chief of mission:* Ambassador Cythia AKUETTEH (since 13 August 2014); note—also accredited to Sao Tome and Principe
embassy: Boulevard du Bord de Mer, Libreville
mailing address: Centre Ville, B. P.4000, Libreville; pouch: 2270 Libreville Place, Washington, DC 20521–2270
telephone: [241] 01-45-71-00, after hours—07380171
FAX: [241] 74 55 07

Flag description: three equal horizontal bands of green (top), yellow, and blue; green represents the country's forests and natural resources, gold represents the equator (which transects Gabon) as well as the sun, blue represents the sea

National symbol(s): black panther; national colors: green, yellow, blue

National anthem: *name:* "La Concorde" (The Concorde)
lyrics/music: Georges Aleka DAMAS
note: adopted 1960

ECONOMY

Economy—overview: Gabon enjoys a per capita income four times that of most sub-Saharan African nations, but because of high income inequality, a large proportion of the population remains poor. Gabon relied on timber and manganese exports until oil was discovered offshore in the early 1970s. From 2010 to 2014, oil accounted for approximately 80% of Gabon's exports, 45% of its GDP, and 60% of its state budget revenues. Gabon faces fluctuating prices for its oil, timber, and manganese exports. A rebound of oil prices from 2001 to 2013 helped growth, but declining production, as some fields passed their peak production, has hampered Gabon from fully realizing potential gains. GDP grew nearly 6% per year over the 2010–14 period, but slowed significantly in 2015 as oil prices declined. Low oil prices also weakened government revenue and negatively affected the trade and current account balances.

Despite an abundance of natural wealth, poor fiscal management and over-reliance on oil has stifled the economy. There are frequent power cuts and water shortages. However, President BONGO has made efforts to increase transparency and is taking steps to make Gabon a more attractive investment destination to diversify the economy. BONGO has attempted to boost growth by increasing government investment in human resources and infrastructure.

GDP (purchasing power parity):
$34.58 billion (2015 est.)
$33.24 billion (2014 est.)
$31.87 billion (2013 est.)
note: data are in 2015 US dollars
country comparison to the world: 123

GDP (official exchange rate): $14.35 billion (2015 est.)

GDP—real growth rate: 4% (2015 est.)
4.3% (2014 est.)
5.6% (2013 est.)
country comparison to the world: 67

GDP—per capita (PPP): $18,600 (2015 est.)
$18,200 (2014 est.)
$17,700 (2013 est.)
note: data are in 2015 US dollars
country comparison to the world: 90

Gross national saving: 34.8% of GDP (2015 est.)
42.9% of GDP (2014 est.)
41% of GDP (2013 est.)
country comparison to the world: 9

GDP—composition, by end use:

household consumption: 43.8%
government consumption: 21%
investment in fixed capital: 27.2%
investment in inventories: 3%
exports of goods and services: 38%
imports of goods and services: -33% (2015 est.)

GDP—composition, by sector of origin:
agriculture: 3.7%
industry: 39.1%
services: 57.2% (2015 est.)

Agriculture—products: cocoa, coffee, sugar, palm oil, rubber; cattle; okoume (a tropical softwood); fish

Industries: petroleum extraction and refining; manganese, gold; chemicals, ship repair, food and beverages, textiles, lumbering and plywood, cement

Industrial production growth rate: -8% (2015 est.)
country comparison to the world: 195

Labor force: 653,700 (2015 est.)
country comparison to the world: 152

Labor force—by occupation: *agriculture:* 60%
industry: 15%
services: 25% (2000 est.)

Unemployment rate: 21% (2006 est.)
country comparison to the world: 170

Population below poverty line: NA%

Household income or consumption by percentage share: *lowest:* 10%: 2.5%
highest: 10%: 32.7% (2005)

Budget: *revenues:* $3.563 billion
expenditures: $3.944 billion (2015 est.)
Taxes and other revenues: 25.8% of GDP (2015 est.)
country comparison to the world: 115

Budget surplus (+) or deficit (–): -2.8% of GDP (2015 est.)
country comparison to the world: 103

Public debt: 44.8% of GDP (2015 est.)
28.5% of GDP (2014 est.)
country comparison to the world: 100

Fiscal year: calendar year

Inflation rate (consumer prices): 0.1% (2015 est.)
4.5% (2014 est.)
country comparison to the world: 47

Central bank discount rate: 3% (31 December 2010)
4.25% (31 December 2009)
country comparison to the world: 103

Commercial bank prime lending rate: 15.3% (31 December 2015 est.)
15% (31 December 2014 est.)
country comparison to the world: 38

Stock of narrow money: $1.872 billion (31 December 2015 est.)
$2.448 billion (31 December 2014 est.)
country comparison to the world: 130

Stock of broad money: $4.545 billion (31 December 2014 est.)
$4.421 billion (31 December 2013 est.)
country comparison to the world: 134

Stock of domestic credit: $1.594 billion (31 December 2015 est.)
$2.3 billion (31 December 2014 est.)
country comparison to the world: 147

Market value of publicly traded shares: $NA

Current account balance: -$409 million (2015 est.)
$1.467 billion (2014 est.)
country comparison to the world: 92

Exports: $5.561 billion (2015 est.)
$8.872 billion (2014 est.)
country comparison to the world: 106

Exports—commodities: crude oil, timber, manganese, uranium

Exports—partners: China 15.5%, Italy 7.3%, Trinidad and Tobago 7.2%, Australia 7%, Spain 6.3%, South Korea 5.4%, Netherlands 5%, US 4.7% (2015)

Imports: $2.429 billion (2015 est.)
$3.089 billion (2014 est.)
country comparison to the world: 157

Imports—commodities: machinery and equipment, foodstuffs, chemicals, construction materials

Imports—partners: China 21.4%, France 19.6%, US 6.5%, Benin 4.7% (2015)

Reserves of foreign exchange and gold: $1.825 billion (31 December 2015 est.)
$2.495 billion (31 December 2014 est.)
country comparison to the world: 121

Debt—external: $4.736 billion (31 December 2014 est.)
$4.316 billion (31 December 2013 est.)
country comparison to the world: 133

Exchange rates: Cooperation Financiere en Afrique Centrale francs (XAF) per US dollar—
596.3 (2015 est.)
494.42 (2014 est.)
494.42 (2013 est.)
510.53 (2012 est.)
471.87 (2011 est.)

ENERGY

Electricity—production: 2.111 billion kWh (2012 est.)
country comparison to the world: 138

Electricity—consumption: 1.68 billion kWh (2012 est.)
country comparison to the world: 145

Electricity—exports: 0 kWh (2013 est.)
country comparison to the world: 142

Electricity—imports: 0 kWh (2013 est.)
country comparison to the world: 153

Electricity—installed generating capacity: 415,000 kW (2012 est.)
country comparison to the world: 144

Electricity—from fossil fuels: 59% of total installed capacity (2012 est.)
country comparison to the world: 137

Electricity—from nuclear fuels: 0% of total installed capacity (2012 est.)
country comparison to the world: 96

Electricity—from hydroelectric plants: 41% of total installed capacity (2012 est.)
country comparison to the world: 58

Electricity—from other renewable sources: 0% of total installed capacity (2012 est.)
country comparison to the world: 175

Crude oil—production: 240,000 bbl/day (2014 est.)
country comparison to the world: 36

Crude oil—exports: 226,800 bbl/day (2012 est.)
country comparison to the world: 30

Crude oil—imports: 0 bbl/day (2012 est.)
country comparison to the world: 194

Crude oil—proved reserves: 2 billion bbl (1 January 2015 est.)
country comparison to the world: 36

Refined petroleum products—production: 18,750 bbl/day (2012 est.)
country comparison to the world: 94

Refined petroleum products—consumption: 18,000 bbl/day (2013 est.)
country comparison to the world: 132

Refined petroleum products—exports: 5,678 bbl/day (2012 est.)
country comparison to the world: 92

Refined petroleum products—imports: 5,042 bbl/day (2012 est.)
country comparison to the world: 161

Natural gas—production: 384 million cu m (2013 est.)
country comparison to the world: 73

Natural gas—consumption: 384 million cu m (2013 est.)
country comparison to the world: 101

Natural gas—exports: 0 cu m (2013 est.)
country comparison to the world: 103

Natural gas—imports: 0 cu m (2013 est.)
country comparison to the world: 200

Natural gas—proved reserves: 28.32 billion cu m (1 January 2014 est.)
country comparison to the world: 69

Carbon dioxide emissions from consumption of energy: 5.437 million Mt (2012 est.)
country comparison to the world: 125

COMMUNICATIONS

Telephones—fixed lines: *total subscriptions:* 17,200
subscriptions per 100 inhabitants: 1 (2014 est.)
country comparison to the world: 190

Telephones—mobile cellular: *total:* 3.6 million
subscriptions per 100 inhabitants: 215 (2014 est.)
country comparison to the world: 128

Telephone system: *general assessment:* adequate system of cable, microwave radio relay, tropospheric scatter, radiotelephone communication stations, and a domestic satellite system with 12 earth stations
domestic: a growing mobile cellular network with multiple providers is making telephone service more widely available with mobile cellular tel-edensity exceeding 100 per 100 persons
international: country code—241; landing point for the SAT-3/WASC fiber-optic submarine cable that provides connectivity to Europe and Asia; satellite earth stations—3 Intelsat (Atlantic Ocean) (2011)

Broadcast media: state owns and operates 2 TV stations and 2 radio broadcast stations; a few private radio and TV stations; transmissions of at least 2 international broadcasters are accessible; satellite service subscriptions are available (2007)
Radio broadcast stations: AM 6, FM 7 (plus 11 repeaters), shortwave 4 (2001)
Television broadcast stations: 4 (plus 4 repeaters) (2001)

Internet country code: .ga

Internet hosts: 127 (2012)
country comparison to the world: 205

Internet users: *total:* 164,800
percent of population: 9.9% (2014 est.)
country comparison to the world: 161

TRANSPORTATION

Airports: 44 (2013)
country comparison to the world: 99

Airports—with paved runways: *total:* 14
over 3,047 m: 1
2,438 to 3,047 m: 2
1,524 to 2,437 m: 9
914 to 1,523 m: 1
under 914 m: 1 (2013)

Airports—with unpaved runways: *total:* 30
1,524 to 2,437 m: 7
914 to 1,523 m: 9
under 914 m: 14 (2013)

Pipelines: gas 807 km; oil 1,639 km; water 3 km (2013)

Railways: *total:* 649 km
standard gauge: 649 km 1.435-m gauge (2014)
country comparison to the world: 107

Roadways: *total:* 9,170 km
paved: 1,097 km
unpaved: 8,073 km (2007)
country comparison to the world: 139

Waterways: 1,600 km (310 km on Ogooue River) (2010)
country comparison to the world: 49

Merchant marine: *registered in other countries:* 2 (Cambodia 1, Panama 1) (2010)
country comparison to the world: 140

Ports and terminals: *major seaport(s):* Libreville, Owendo, Port-Gentil
oil terminal(s): Gamba, Lucina

MILITARY AND SECURITY

Military branches: Gabonese Defense Forces (Forces de Defense Gabonaise): Land Force (Force Terrestre), Gabonese Navy (Marine Gabonaise), Gabonese Air Forces (Forces Aerienne Gabonaises, FAG) (2012)

Military service age and obligation: 20 years of age for voluntary military service; no conscription (2012)

Military expenditures: 1.34% of GDP (2012)
NA% (2011)
1.34% of GDP (2010)
country comparison to the world: 76

TRANSNATIONAL ISSUES

Disputes—international: UN urges Equatorial Guinea and Gabon to resolve the sovereignty dispute over Gabon-occupied Mbane Island and lesser islands and to establish a maritime boundary in hydrocarbon-rich Corisco Bay

Trafficking in persons: *current situation:* Gabon is primarily a destination and transit country for adults and children from West and Central African countries subjected to forced labor and sex trafficking; boys are forced to work as street vendors, mechanics, or in the fishing sector, while girls are subjected to domestic servitude or forced to work in markets or roadside restaurants; West African women are forced into domestic servitude or prostitution; men are reportedly forced to work on cattle farms; some foreign adults end up in forced labor in Gabon after initially seeking the help of human smugglers to help them migrate clandestinely; traffickers operate in loose, ethnic-based criminal networks, with female traffickers recruiting and facilitating the transport of victims from source countries; in some cases, families turn child victims over to traffickers, who promise paid jobs in Gabon

tier rating: Tier 2 Watch List—Gabon does not fully comply with the minimum standards for the elimination of trafficking; however, it is making significant efforts to do so; Gabon's existing laws do not prohibit all forms of trafficking, and the government failed to pass a legal amendment drafted in 2013 to criminalize the trafficking of adults; anti-trafficking law enforcement decreased in 2014, dropping from 50 investigations to 16, and the only defendant to face prosecution fled the country; government efforts to identify and refer victims to protective services declined from 50 child victims in 2013 to just 3 in 2014, none of whom was referred to a care facility; the government provided support to four centers offering services to orphans and vulnerable children—14 child victims identified by an NGO received government assistance; no adult victims have been identified since 2009 (2015)

GAMBIA, THE

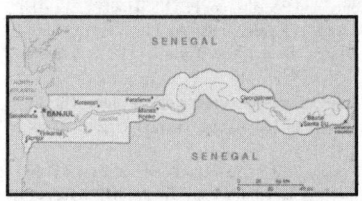

INTRODUCTION

Background: The Gambia gained its independence from the UK in 1965. Geographically surrounded by Senegal, it formed a short-lived Confederation of Senegambia between 1982 and 1989. In 1991 the two nations signed a friendship and cooperation treaty, but tensions have flared up intermittently since then. Yahya JAMMEH led a military coup in 1994 that overthrew the president and banned political activity. A new constitution and presidential election in 1996, followed by parliamentary balloting in 1997, completed a nominal return to civilian rule. JAMMEH was elected president in all subsequent elections including most recently in late 2011. A presidential election is scheduled for December 2016

GEOGRAPHY

Location: Western Africa, bordering the North Atlantic Ocean and Senegal

Geographic coordinates: 13 28 N, 16 34 W

Map references: Africa

Area: *total:* 11,300 sq km
land: 10,120 sq km
water: 1,180 sq km
country comparison to the world: 167

Area—comparative: slightly less than twice the size of Delaware

Land boundaries: *total:* 749 km
border countries (1): Senegal 749 km

Coastline: 80 km

Maritime claims: *territorial sea:* 12 nm
contiguous zone: 18 nm
exclusive fishing zone: 200 nm
continental shelf: extent not specified

Climate: tropical; hot, rainy season (June to November); cooler, dry season (November to May)

Terrain: flood plain of the Gambia River flanked by some low hills

Elevation: *mean elevation:* 34 m

elevation extremes: *lowest point:* Atlantic Ocean 0 m
highest point: unnamed elevation 53 m

Natural resources: fish, clay, silica sand, titanium (rutile and ilmenite), tin, zircon

Land use: *agricultural land:* 56.1%
arable land: 41%

permanent crops: 0.5%
permanent pasture: 14.6%
forest: 43.9%
other: 0% (2011 est.)

Irrigated land: 50 sq km (2012)

Total renewable water resources: 8 cu km (2011)

Freshwater withdrawal (domestic/industrial/agricultural): *total:* 0.09 cu km/yr (41%/21%/39%)
per capita: 65.77 cu m/yr (2005)

Natural hazards: drought (rainfall has dropped by 30% in the last 30 years)

Environment—current issues: deforestation; desertification; water-borne diseases prevalent

Environment—international agreements: *party to:* Biodiversity, Climate Change, Climate Change-Kyoto Protocol, Desertification, Endangered Species, Hazardous Wastes, Law of the Sea, Ozone Layer Protection, Ship Pollution, Wetlands, Whaling
signed, but not ratified: none of the selected agreements

Geography—note: almost an enclave of Senegal; smallest country in Africa

PEOPLE AND SOCIETY

Nationality: *noun:* Gambian(s)
adjective: Gambian

Ethnic groups: Mandinka/Jahanka 33.8%, Fulani/Tukulur/Lorobo 22.1%, Wollof 12.2%, Jola/Karoninka 10.9%, Serahuleh 7%, Serere 3.2%, Manjago 2.1%, Bambara 1%, Creole/Aku Marabout 0.8%, other 0.9%, non-Gambian 5.2%, no answer 0.7% (2013 est.)

Languages: English (official), Mandinka, Wolof, Fula, other indigenous vernaculars

Religions: Muslim 95.7%, Christian 4.2%, none 0.1%, no answer 0.1% (2013 est.)

Population: 1,967,709 (July 2015 est.)
country comparison to the world: 149

Age structure: *0–14 years:* 38.31% (male 378,449/female 375,417)
15–24 years: 20.81% (male 202,218/female 207,194)
25–54 years: 33.45% (male 322,250/female 335,860)
55–64 years: 4.08% (male 38,717/female 41,532)
65 years and over: 3.36% (male 30,886/female 35,186) (2015 est.)

Dependency ratios: *total dependency ratio:* 94.2%
youth dependency ratio: 89.7%
elderly dependency ratio: 4.5%
potential support ratio: 22.3% (2015 est.)

Median age: *total:* 20.5 years
male: 20.2 years
female: 20.8 years (2015 est.)
country comparison to the world: 186

Population growth rate: 2.16% (2015 est.)

country comparison to the world: 43

Birth rate: 30.86 births/1,000 population (2015 est.)
country comparison to the world: 39

Death rate: 7.15 deaths/1,000 population (2015 est.)
country comparison to the world: 125

Net migration rate: -2.12 migrant(s)/1,000 population (2015 est.)
country comparison to the world: 170

Urbanization: *urban population:* 59.6% of total population (2015)
rate of urbanization: 4.33% annual rate of change (2010–15 est.)

Major urban areas—population: BANJUL (capital) 504,000 (2015)

Sex ratio: *at birth:* 1.03 male(s)/female
0–14 years: 1.01 male(s)/female
15–24 years: 0.98 male(s)/female
25–54 years: 0.96 male(s)/female
55–64 years: 0.93 male(s)/female
65 years and over: 0.88 male(s)/female
total population: 0.98 male(s)/female (2015 est.)

Mother's mean age at first birth: 20.9
note: median age at first birth among women 25–29 (2013 est.)

Maternal mortality rate: 706 deaths/100,000 live births (2015 est.)
country comparison to the world: 29

Infant mortality rate: *total:* 63.9 deaths/1,000 live births
male: 69.33 deaths/1,000 live births
female: 58.3 deaths/1,000 live births (2015 est.)
country comparison to the world: 18

Life expectancy at birth: *total population:* 64.6 years
male: 62.27 years
female: 67 years (2015 est.)
country comparison to the world: 177

Total fertility rate: 3.73 children born/woman (2015 est.)
country comparison to the world: 42

Contraceptive prevalence rate: 9% (2013)

Health expenditures: 6% of GDP (2013)
country comparison to the world: 144

Physicians density: 0.11 physicians/1,000 population (2008)

Hospital bed density: 1.1 beds/1,000 population (2011)

Drinking water source:
improved:
urban: 94.2% of population
rural: 84.4% of population
total: 90.2% of population
unimproved:
urban: urban: 5.8% of population
rural: 15.6% of population
total: 9.8% of population (2015 est.)

Sanitation facility access:
improved:
urban: 61.5% of population
rural: 55% of population
total: 58.9% of population
unimproved:
urban: urban: 38.5% of population
rural: 45% of population
total: 41.1% of population (2015 est.)

HIV/AIDS—adult prevalence rate: 1.82% (2014 est.)
country comparison to the world: 28

HIV/AIDS—people living with HIV/AIDS: 20,300 (2014 est.)
country comparison to the world: 77

HIV/AIDS—deaths: 900 (2014 est.)
country comparison to the world: 68

Major infectious diseases: *degree of risk:* very high
food or waterborne diseases: bacterial and proto-zoal diarrhea, hepatitis A, and typhoid fever
vectorborne diseases: malaria and dengue fever
water contact disease: schistosomiasis
respiratory disease: meningococcal meningitis
animal contact disease: rabies (2013)

Obesity—adult prevalence rate: 9.1% (2014)
country comparison to the world: 138

Children under the age of 5 years underweight: 16.4% (2013)
country comparison to the world: 38

Education expenditures: 2.8% of GDP (2013)
country comparison to the world: 109

Literacy: *definition:* age 15 and over can read and write
total population: 55.5%
male: 63.9%
female: 47.6% (2015 est.)

School life expectancy (primary to tertiary education): *total:* 9 years
male: 9 years
female: 9 years (2010)

Child labor—children ages 5–14: *total number:* 103,389
percentage: 25% (2006 est.)

GOVERNMENT

Country name: *conventional long form:* Republic of The Gambia
conventional short form: The Gambia
etymology: named for the Gambia River that flows through the heart of the country

Government type: presidential republic

Capital: *name:* Banjul

Geographic coordinates: 13 27 N, 16 34 W
time difference: UTC 0 (5 hours ahead of Washington, DC, during Standard Time)

Administrative divisions: 5 divisions and 1 city*; Banjul*, Central River, Lower River, North Bank, Upper River, Western

Independence: 18 February 1965 (from the UK)

National holiday: Independence Day, 18 February (1965)

Constitution: previous 1970; latest adopted 8 April 1996, approved by referendum 8 August 1996, effective 16 January 1997; amended several times, last in 2010 (2016)

Legal system: mixed legal system of English common law, Islamic law, and customary law

International law organization participation: accepts compulsory ICJ jurisdiction with reservations; accepts ICCt jurisdiction

Citizenship: *citizenship by birth:* yes
citizenship by descent: yes
dual citizenship recognized: no
residency requirement for naturalization: 5 years

Suffrage: 18 years of age; universal

Executive branch: *chief of state:* President Yahya JAMMEH (since 18 October 1996); Vice President Isatou NJIE-SAIDY (since 20 March 1997); note—the president is both chief of state and head of government

head of government: President Yahya JAMMEH (since 18 October 1996); Vice President Isatou NJIE-SAIDY (since 20 March 1997)
cabinet: Cabinet appointed by the president
elections/appointments: president directly elected by simple majority popular vote for a 5-year term (no term limits); election last held on 24 November 2011 (next to be held in 2016)
election results: Yahya JAMMEH reelected president; percent of vote—Yahya JAMMEH (APRC) 71.5%, Ousainou DARBOE (UDP) 17.4%, Hamat BAH (NRP) 11.1%

Legislative branch: *description:* unicameral National Assembly (53 seats; 48 members directly elected in single-seat constituencies by simple majority vote and 5 appointed by the president; members serve 5-year terms)
elections: last held on 29 March 2012 (next to be held in 2017)
election results: percent of vote by party—APRC 51.8%, NRP 9.4%, independent 38.8%; seats by party—APRC 42, NRP2, independent 4

Judicial branch: *highest court(s):* Supreme Court of The Gambia (consists of the chief justice and 6 other justices; court sessions held with 5 justices)
judge selection and term of office: justices appointed by the president after consultation with the Judicial Service Commission, a 6-member independent body o f high—level judicial officials, a presidential appointee, and a National Assembly appointee; justices appointed for life or until mandatory retirement age
subordinate courts: Court of Appeal; High Court; Special Criminal Court; Khadis or Muslim courts; district tribunals; magistrates courts

Political parties and leaders: Alliance for Patriotic Reorientation and Construction or APRC [Yahya JAMMEH]
Gambia Moral Congress or GMC [Mai FATTY]
Gambia Party for Democracy and Progress or GPDP [Henry GOMEZ]
National Reconciliation Party or NRP [Hamat BAH]

National Convention Party or NCP [Ebrima Janko SANYANG]
People's Democratic Organization for Independence and Socialism or PDOIS [Halifa SALLAH]
People's Progressive Party or PPP [Omar JALLOW]
United Democratic Party or UDP [Ousainou DARBOE]

Political pressure groups and leaders: The Association of Non-Governmental Organizations or TANGO
Female Lawyers Association of Gambia or FLAG
Gambia Committee on Traditional Practices or GAMCOTRAP
Gambia Press Union or GPU
West African Peace Building Network-Gambian Chapter or WANEB-GAMBIA
Youth Employment Network Gambia or YEN Gambia
other: special needs group advocates; teachers and principals

International organization participation: ACP, AfDB, AU, ECOWAS, FAO, G-77, IBRD, ICAO, ICCt, ICRM, IDA, IDB, IFAD, IFC, IFRCS, ILO, IMF, IMO, Interpol, IOC, IOM, IPU, ISO (correspondent), ITSO, ITU, ITUC (NGOs), MIGA, MINUSMA, NAM, OIC, OPCW, UN, UNAMID, UNCTAD, UNESCO, UNIDO, UNMIL, UNOCI, UNWTO, UPU, WCO, WFTU (NGOs), WHO, WIPO, WMO, WTO

Diplomatic representation in the US: *chief of mission:* Ambassador Omar FAYE (since 3 August 2015)
chancery: 2233 Wisconsin Avenue NW, Georgetown Plaza, Suite 240, Washington, DC 20007
telephone: [1] (202) 785-1379, 1399, 1425 [1] (202) 785-1379, 1399, 1425
FAX: [1] (202) 342-0240

Diplomatic representation from the US: *chief of mission:* Ambassador C. Patricia ALSUP (since 11 January 2016)
embassy: Kairaba Avenue, Fajara, Banjul
mailing address: P. M. B. No.19, Banjul
telephone: [220] 439-2856, 437-6169, 437-6170
FAX: [220] 439-2475

Flag description: three equal horizontal bands of red (top), blue with white edges, and green; red stands for the sun and the savannah, blue represents the Gambia River, and green symbolizes forests and agriculture; the white stripes denote unity and peace

National symbol(s): lion; national colors: red, blue, green, white

National anthem: *name:* "For The Gambia, Our Homeland"
lyrics/music: Virginia Julie HOWE/adapted by Jeremy Frederick HOWE
note: adopted 1965; the music is an adaptation of the traditional Mandinka song "Foday Kaba Dumbuya"

ECONOMY

Economy—overview: The government has invested strongly in the agriculture sector because three-quarters of the population depends on the sector for its livelihood and agriculture provides for another one-fifth of GDP. The agricultural sector has untapped potential—less than half of arable land is cultivated. Small-scale manufacturing activity features the processing of peanuts, fish, and hides. The Gambia's re-export trade accounts for almost 80% of goods exports and China has been its largest trade partner for both exports and imports for several years.

The Gambia has sparse natural resource deposits and a limited agricultural base. It relies heavily on remittances from workers overseas and tourist receipts. Remittance inflows to The Gambia amount to about one-fifth of the country's GDP. The Gambia's natural beauty and proximity to Europe has made it one of the larger tourist destinations in West Africa, boosted by government and private sector investments in eco-tourism and upscale facilities. Tourism normally brings in about 20% of GDP, but suffered in 2014 from tourists' fears of Ebola virus in neighboring West African countries. Unemployment and underemployment remain high.

Economic progress depends on sustained bilateral and multilateral aid, on responsible government economic management, and on continued technical assistance from multilateral and bilateral donors. International donors and lenders continue to be concerned about the quality of fiscal management. The IMF provided $10.8 million in emergency financial assistance to The Gambia in April 2015 to shore up the country's finances. Relations with international donors have been tarnished by the country's human rights record.

GDP (purchasing power parity):
$3.261 billion (2015 est.)
$3.124 billion (2014 est.)
$3.131 billion (2013 est.)
note: data are in 2015 US dollars
country comparison to the world: 182

GDP (official exchange rate): $893 million (2015 est.)

GDP—real growth rate: 4.4% (2015 est.)
-0.2% (2014 est.)
4.8% (2013 est.)
country comparison to the world: 53

GDP—per capita (PPP): $1,600 (2015 est.)
$1,600 (2014 est.)
$1,700 (2013 est.)
note: data are in 2015 US dollars
country comparison to the world: 213

Gross national saving: 4.6% of GDP (2015 est.)
14.3% of GDP (2014 est.)
9.8% of GDP (2013 est.)
country comparison to the world: 164

GDP—composition, by end use:
household consumption: 81.7%
government consumption: 9.6%
investment in fixed capital: 19.8%
investment in inventories: 0%
exports of good s and services: 34.7%
imports of goods and services: -45.8% (2015 est.)

GDP—composition, by sector of origin:
agricu ltu re: 19.9%

industry: 13.2%
services: 66.9% (2015 est.)

Agriculture—products: rice, millet, sorghum, peanuts, corn, sesame, cassava (manioc, tapioca), palm kernels; cattle, sheep, goats

Industries: peanuts, fish, hides, tourism, beverages, agricultural machinery assembly, woodworking, metalworking, clothing

Industrial production growth rate: 4.4% (2015 est.)
country comparison to the world: 44

Labor force: 777,100 (2007 est.)
country comparison to the world: 149

Labor force—by occupation: agriculture: 75%
industry: 19%
services: 6% (1996)

Unemployment rate: NA%

Population below poverty line: 48.4% (2010 est.)

Household income or consumption by percentage share: lowest: 10%: 2%
highest: 10%: 36.9% (2003)

Distribution of family income—Gini index: 50.2 (1998)
country comparison to the world: 21

Budget: revenues: $226.8 million
expenditures: $324.4 million (2015 est.)
Taxes and other revenues: 29.8% of GDP (2015 est.)
country comparison to the world: 83

Budget surplus (+) or deficit (–): -12.8% of GDP (2015 est.)
country comparison to the world: 210

Fiscal year: calendar year

Inflation rate (consumer prices): 6.8% (2015 est.)
6.2% (2014 est.)
country comparison to the world: 192

Central bank discount rate: 9% (31 December 2009)
11% (31 December 2008)
country comparison to the world: 34

Commercial bank prime lending rate: 30.8% (31 December 2015 est.)
28.5% (31 December 2014 est.)
country comparison to the world: 4

Stock of narrow money: $243.5 million (31 December 2015 est.)
$186.2 million (31 December 2014 est.)
country comparison to the world: 179

Stock of broad money: $534.7 million (31 December 2014 est.)
$511.5 million (31 December 2013 est.)
country comparison to the world: 181

Stock of domestic credit: $482.1 million (31 December 2015 est.)
$357.8 million (31 December 2014 est.)
country comparison to the world: 170

Market value of publicly traded shares: $NA

Current account balance: -$136 million (2015 est.)
-$90 million (2014 est.)
country comparison to the world: 72

Exports: $102.5 million (2015 est.)

$123.5 million (2014 est.)
country comparison to the world: 194

Exports—commodities: peanut products, fish, cotton lint, palm kernels

Exports—partners: China 47.5%, India 27.2%, France 5.9%, UK 4.9% (2015)

Imports: $310 million (2015 est.)
$335 million (2014 est.)
country comparison to the world: 200

Imports—commodities: foodstuffs, manufactures, fuel, machinery and transport equipment

Imports—partners: China 34.2%, Brazil 8.1%, Senegal 6.9%, India 5.7%, Netherlands 4.8% (2015)

Reserves of foreign exchange and gold:
$82.5 million (31 December 2015 est.)
$159.3 million (31 December 2014 est.)
country comparison to the world: 166

Debt—external: g: $546.6 million (31 December 2014 est.)
$522.7 million (31 December 2013 est.)
country comparison to the world: 177

Exchange rates: dalasis (GMD) per US dollar—
41 (2015 est.)
41.733 (2014 est.)
41.733 (2013 est.)
32.08 (2012 est.)
29.4615 (2011 est.)

ENERGY

Electricity—production: 235 million kWh (2012 est.)
country comparison to the world: 183

Electricity—consumption: 218.6 million kWh (2012 est.)
country comparison to the world: 186

Electricity—exports: 0 kWh (2013 est.)
country comparison to the world: 141

Electricity—imports: 0 kWh (2013 est.)
country comparison to the world: 152

Electricity—installed generating capacity: 62,000 kW (2012 est.)
country comparison to the world: 182

Electricity—from fossil fuels: 100% of total installed capacity (2012 est.)
country comparison to the world: 10

Electricity—from nuclear fuels: 0% of total installed capacity (2012 est.)
country comparison to the world: 95

Electricity—from hydroelectric plants: 0% of total installed capacity (2012 est.)
country comparison to the world: 173

Electricity—from other renewable sources: 0% of total installed capacity (2012 est.)
country comparison to the world: 174

Crude oil—production: 0 bbl/day (2014 est.)
country comparison to the world: 139

Crude oil—exports: 0 bbl/day (2012 est.)
country comparison to the world: 128

Crude oil—imports: 0 bbl/day (2012 est.)
country comparison to the world: 193

Crude oil—proved reserves: 0 bbl (1 January 2015 est.)
country comparison to the world: 137

Refined petroleum products—production: 0 bbl/day (2012 est.)
country comparison to the world: 185

Refined petroleum products—consumption: 3,100 bbl/day (2013 est.)
country comparison to the world: 181

Refined petroleum products—exports: 41.62 bbl/day (2012 est.)
country comparison to the world: 122

Refined petroleum products—imports: 3,159 bbl/day (2012 est.)
country comparison to the world: 174

Natural gas—production: 0 cu m (2013 est.)
country comparison to the world: 190

Natural gas—consumption: 0 cu m (2013 est.)
country comparison to the world: 146

Natural gas—exports: 0 cu m (2013 est.)
country comparison to the world: 102

Natural gas—imports: 0 cu m (2013 est.)
country comparison to the world: 199

Natural gas—proved reserves: 0 cu m (1 January 2014 est.)
country comparison to the world: 142

Carbon dioxide emissions from consumption of energy: 472,200 Mt (2012 est.)
country comparison to the world: 182

COMMUNICATIONS

Telephones—fixed lines: *total subscriptions:* 55,800
subscriptions per 100 inhabitants: 3 (2014 est.)
country comparison to the world: 158

Telephones—mobile cellular: *total:* 2.3 million
subscriptions per 100 inhabitants: 119 (2014 est.)
country comparison to the world: 146

Telephone system: *general assessment:* adequate microwave radio relay and open-wire network; state-owned Gambia Telecommunications partially privatized in 2007
domestic: combined fixed-line and mobile-cellular teledensity, aided by multiple mobile-cellular providers, is roughly 80 per 100 persons

international: country code—220; microwave radio relay links to Senegal and Guinea-Bissau; a landing station for the Africa Coast to Europe (ACE) undersea fiber-optic cable completed in 2011 and launched in 2012; satellite earth station—1 Intelsat (Atlantic Ocean) (2015)

Broadcast media: state-owned, single-channel TV service; state-owned radio station and 15 privately owned radio stations; 6 community radio stations; transmissions of multiple international broadcasters are available, some via shortwave radio; cable and satellite TV subscription services are obtainable in some parts of the country (2015)
Radio broadcast stations: AM 3, FM 2, shortwave 0 (2001)
Television broadcast stations: 1 (government-owned) (1997)

Internet country code: .gm

Internet hosts: 656 (2012)
country comparison to the world: 179

Internet users: *total:* 274,000
percent of population: 14.2% (2014 est.)
country comparison to the world: 147

TRANSPORTATION

Airports: 1 (2013)
country comparison to the world: 218

Airports—with paved runways: *total:* 1
over 3,047 m: 1 (2013)

Roadways: *total:* 3,740 km
paved: 711 km
unpaved: 3,029 km (2011)
country comparison to the world: 160

Waterways: 390 km (on River Gambia; small oceangoing vessels can reach 190 km) (2010)
country comparison to the world: 88

Merchant marine: *total:* 4
by type: passenger/cargo 3, petroleum tanker 1 (2010)
country comparison to the world: 130

Ports and terminals: *major seaport(s):* Banjul

MILITARY AND SECURITY

Military branches: Office of the Chief of Defense Staff: Gambian National Army (GNA), Gambian

Navy (GN), Republican National Guard (RNG) (2010)

Military service age and obligation: 18 years of age for male and female voluntary military service; no conscription; service obligation 6 months (2012)

TRANSNATIONAL ISSUES

Disputes—international: attempts to stem refugees, cross-border raids, arms smuggling, and other illegal activities by separatists from southern Senegal's Casamance region, as well as from conflicts in other west African states

Refugees and internally displaced persons: *refugees (country of origin):* 11,036 (Senegal) (2014)

Trafficking in persons: *current situation:* The Gambia is a source and destination country for women and children subjected to forced labor and sex trafficking; Gambian women, girls, and, to a lesser extent, boys are exploited for prostitution and domestic servitude; women, girls, and boys from West African countries are trafficked to The Gambia for commercial sexual exploitation, particularly by European sex tourists; boys in some Koranic schools are forced into street vending or begging; some Gambian children have been identified as victims of forced labor in neighboring West African countries

tier rating: Tier 3—The Gambia does not fully comply with the minimum standards for the elimination of trafficking and is not making significant efforts to do so; the government demonstrated minimal anti-trafficking law enforcement efforts, investigating one trafficking case but not prosecuting or convicting any offenders in 2014; authorities did not investigate, prosecute, or convict any government employees complicit in trafficking, although corruption was a serious problem; the government identified and repatriated 19 Gambian girls subjected to domestic servitude in Lebanon but did not identify or provide protective services to any trafficking victims in The Gambia; a government program continued to provide resources and financial support to 12 Koranic schools on the condition that their students were not forced to beg (2015)

GAZA STRIP

INTRODUCTION

Background: Inhabited since at least the 15th century B.C., Gaza has been dominated by many different peoples and empires throughout its history; it was incorporated into the Ottoman Empire in the early 16th century. Gaza fell to British forces during World War I, becoming a part of the British Mandate of Palestine. Following the 1948 Arab-Israeli War, Egypt administered the newly formed Gaza Strip; it was captured by Israel in the Six-Day War in 1967. Under a series of agreements known

as the Oslo accords signed between 1994 and 1999, Israel transferred to the newly-created Palestinian Authority (PA) security and civilian responsibility for many Palestinian-populated areas of the Gaza Strip as well as the West Bank. Negotiations to determine the permanent status of the West Bank and Gaza Strip stalled in 2001, after which the area witnessed a violent intifada or uprising.

In early 2003, the "Quartet" of the US, EU, UN, and Russia presented a roadmap to a final peace settlement by 2005, calling for two states. Following PA President Yasir ARAFAT's death in late

2004 and the subsequent election of Mahmud ABBAS (head of the Fatah political faction) as the PA president in 2005, Israel and the Palestinians agreed to move the peace process forward. Israel by late 2005 unilaterally withdrew all of its settlers and soldiers and dismantled its military facilities in the Gaza Strip, but continues to control the Gaza Strip's land and maritime borders and airspace. In early 2006, the Islamic Resistance Movement (HAMAS) won a majority in the Palestinian Legislative Council election. Attempts to form a unity government between Fatah and

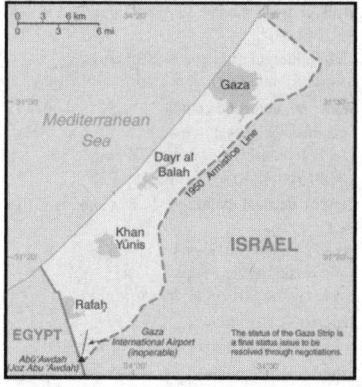

HAMAS failed and violent clashes between their respective supporters ensued, culminating in HAMAS's violent seizure of all military and governmental institutions in the Gaza Strip in June 2007. Since HAMAS's takeover, Israel and Egypt have enforced tight restrictions on movement and access of goods and individuals into and out of the territory. Fatah and HAMAS have since reached a series of agreements aimed at restoring political unity between the Gaza Strip and the West Bank but have struggled to implement them. In April 2014, the two factions signed an agreement and two months later President ABBAS formed an interim government of independent technocrats, none of whom were affiliated with HAMAS. The factions, however, continue to disagree over how to implement the deal and HAMAS remains in de facto control of the Gaza Strip.

In July 2014, HAMAS and other Gaza-based militant groups engaged in a 51-day conflict with Israel—the third conflict since HAMAS's takeover in 2007—culminating in late August with an open-ended truce that continues to hold despite the absence of a negotiated cease-fire and occasional violations by both sides. Reconstruction efforts since the end of the conflict have been hampered by Israeli restrictions on goods entering the Gaza Strip and inadequate donor aid. The UN in 2015 published a study assessing that the Gaza Strip could become uninhabitable by 2020 absent a substantial easing on border restrictions. In an attempt to reenergize peace talks between the Israelis and Palestinians, France in June 2016 hosted a ministerial meeting that included participants from 29 countries, although not Israel or the Palestinians, to lay the groundwork for an envisioned "multilateral peace conference" later in the year.

GEOGRAPHY

Location: Middle East, bordering the Mediterranean Sea, between Egypt and Israel

Geographic coordinates: 31 25 N, 34 20 E

Map references: Middle East

Area: *total:* 360 sq km
land: 360 sq km
water: 0 sq km

country comparison to the world: 206

Area—comparative: slightly more than twice the size of Washington, DC

Land boundaries: *total:* 72 km
border countries (2): Egypt 13 km, Israel 59 km

Coastline: 40 km

Maritime claims: see entry for Israel
note: effective 3 January 2009, the Gaza maritime area is closed to all maritime traffic and is under blockade imposed by Israeli Navy until further notice

Climate: temperate, mild winters, dry and warm to hot summers

Terrain: flat to rolling, sand- and dune-covered coastal plain

Elevation: *mean elevation:* NA

elevation extremes: *lowest point:* Mediterranean Sea 0 m
highest point: Abu 'Awdah (Joz Abu 'Awdah) 105 m

Natural resources: arable land, natural gas

Irrigated land: 240 sq km; note—includes West Bank (2012)

Natural hazards: droughts

Environment—current issues: desertification; salination of fresh water; sewage treatment; waterborne disease; soil degradation; depletion and contamination of underground water resources

Geography—note: strategic strip of land along Mideast-North African trade routes has experienced an incredibly turbulent history; the town of Gaza itself has been besieged countless times in its history; there are no Israeli settlements in the Gaza Strip; the Gaza Strip settlements were evacuated in 2005 (2014)

PEOPLE AND SOCIETY

Nationality: *noun:* NA
adjective: NA

Ethnic groups: Palestinian Arab

Languages: Arabic, Hebrew (spoken by many Palestinians), English (widely understood)

Religions: Muslim 98.0—99.0% (predominantly Sunni), Christian <1.0%, other, unaffiliated, unspecified <1.0%
note: dismantlement of Israeli settlements was completed in September 2005; Gaza has had no Jewish population since then (2012 est.)

Population: 1,869,055 (July 2015 est.)
country comparison to the world: 152

Age structure: *0–14 years:* 42.75% (male 410,599/female 388,473)
15–24 years: 20.34% (male 194,798/female 185,295)
25–54 years: 30.66% (male 293,556/female 279,471)
55–64 years: 3.59% (male 33,843/female 33,198)
65 years and over: 2.67% (male 20,667/female 29,155) (2015 est.)

Dependency ratios: *total dependency ratio:* 76%
youth dependency ratio: 70.8%

elderly dependency ratio: 5.2%
potential support ratio: 19.2%
note: data represent Gaza Strip and the West Bank (2015 est.)

Median age: *total:* 18.4 years
male: 18.2 years
female: 18.6 years (2015 est.)
country comparison to the world: 210

Population growth rate: 2.81% (2015 est.)
country comparison to the world: 13

Birth rate: 31.11 births/1,000 population (2015 est.)
country comparison to the world: 37

Death rate: 3.04 deaths/1,000 population (2015 est.)
country comparison to the world: 221

Net migration rate: 0 migrant(s)/1,000 population (2015 est.)
country comparison to the world: 96

Urbanization: *urban population:* 75.3% of total population (2015)
rate of urbanization: 2.81% annual rate of change (2010–15 est.)
note: data represent Gaza Strip and West Bank

Sex ratio: *at birth:* 1.06 male(s)/female
0–14 years: 1.06 male(s)/female
15–24 years: 1.05 male(s)/female
25–54 years: 1.05 male(s)/female
55–64 years: 1.02 male(s)/female
65 years and over: 0.71 male(s)/female
total population: 1.04 male(s)/female (2015 est.)

Mother's mean age at first birth: 19
note: median age at first birth among women 25–29 (2004 est.)

Maternal mortality rate: 45 deaths/100,000 live births
note: data represent Gaza Strip and West Bank (2015 est.)
country comparison to the world: 94

Infant mortality rate: *total:* 14.94 deaths/1,000 live births
male: 15.97 deaths/1,000 live births
female: 13.86 deaths/1,000 live births (2015 est.)
country comparison to the world: 105

Life expectancy at birth: *total population:* 74.87 years
male: 73.11 years
female: 76.74 years (2015 est.)
country comparison to the world: 110

Total fertility rate: 4.08 children born/woman (2015 est.)
country comparison to the world: 35

Contraceptive prevalence rate: 52.5% (includes Gaza Strip and West Bank) (2010)

Physicians density: 2.1 physicians/1,000 population (2013)

Hospital bed density: 1.3 beds/1,000 population (2010)

Drinking water source:
improved:
urban: 50.7% of population
rural: 81.5% of population

total: 58.4% of population
unimproved:
urban: urban: 49.3% of population
rural: 18.5% of population
total: 41.6% of population
note: includes Gaza Strip and the West Bank
(2015 est.)

Sanitation facility access:
improved:
urban: 93% of population
rural: 90.2% of population
total: 92.3% of population
unimproved:
urban: 7% of popu lation
rural: 9.8% of population
total: 7.7% of population
note: includes Gaza Strip and the West Bank
(2015 est.)

HIV/AIDS—adult prevalence rate: NA

HIV/AIDS—people living with HIV/AIDS: NA

HIV/AIDS—deaths: NA

Literacy: *definition:* age 15 and over can read and
write
total population: 96.5%
male: 98.4%
female: 94.5%
note: estimates are for Gaza and the West Bank
(2015 est.)

**School life expectancy (primary to tertiary educa-
tion):** *total:* 13 years
male: 12 years
female: 14 years
note: data represent Gaza and West Bank (2014)

Unemployment, youth ages 15–24: *total:* 41%
male: 37%
female: 64.7%
note: includes West Bank (2013 est.)
country comparison to the world: 14

GOVERNMENT

Country name: *conventional long form:* none
conventional short form: Gaza Strip
local lon g form: none
local short form: Qita' Ghazzah
etymology: named for the largest city in the
region, Gaza, whose settlement can be traced back
to at least the 15th century B.C. (as "Ghazzat")

ECONOMY

Economy—overview: Israeli security measures and
Israeli-Palestinian violence continue to degrade
economic conditions in the Gaza Strip, the smaller
of the two areas comprising the Palestinian territories. Israeli-imposed border controls became more
restrictive after HAMAS seized control of the
territory in June 2007. They have produced high
unemployment, elevated poverty rates, and a sh
arp contraction of the private sector, which had
relied primarily on export markets.
Egypt's ongoing crackdown on the Gaza Strip's
extensive tunnel-based smuggling network has
exacerbated fuel, construction material, and consumer goods shortages in the territory. The 51-day

conflict in July 2014 that HAMAS and other
Gaza-based militant groups fought with Israel further depressed the Gaza Strip's already aid-depend-
ent economy. Donor support for reconstruction
and relaxed Israeli import restrictions in 2014 and
2015 h ave fallen short of postconflict needs, with
almost 100,000 people remaining internally displaced because their homes have yet to be rebuilt
or repaired.

GDP (purchasing power parity): see entry for West
Bank

GDP (official exchange rate): $2.938 billion (2014
est.)
note: excludes West Bank

GDP—real growth rate:
-15.2% (2014 est.)
5.6% (2013 est.)
7% (2012)
note: excludes West Bank
country comparison to the world: 222

GDP—per capita (PPP): see entry for West Bank

GDP—composition, by end use:
household consumption: 99%
government consumption: 45.6%
investment in fixed capital: 9%
investment in inventories: -21%
exports of goods and services: 5.1%
imports of goods and services: -38.3%
note: data exclude West Bank (2014 est.)

GDP—composition, by sector of origin: 4.7%
13.7%
81.6%
note: data exclude West Bank (2014 est.)

Agriculture—products: olives, fruit, vegetables,
flowers; beef, dairy products

Industries: textiles, food processing, furniture

Industrial production growth rate: 3.1% see entry
for West Bank
country comparison to the world: 82

Labor force: 471,000
note: excludes West Bank (2015 est.)
country comparison to the world: 157

Labor force—by occupation: *agriculture:* 5.2%
industry: 10%
services: 84.8%
note: data exclude West Bank (2015 est.)

Unemployment rate: 43.9% (2014 est.)
32.6% (2013 est.)
note: data exclude West Bank
country comparison to the world: 197

Population below poverty line: 30%
note: data exclude West Bank (2011 est.)
Budget: see entry for West Bank

Fiscal year: calendar year

Inflation rate (consumer prices): 2.9% (2014 est.)
-0.8% (2013 est.)
note: 2.9% excludes West Bank
country comparison to the world: 137

Commercial bank prime lending rate: see entry for
West Bank

Stock of narrow money: see entry for West Bank

Stock of broad money: $2.356 billion (31 Decem-
ber 2014 est.)
$2.16 billion (31 December 2013 est.)
country comparison to the world: 149

Stock of domestic credit: $1.274 billion (31
December 2015 est.)
$1.147 billion (31 December 2014 est.)
country comparison to the world: 153

Current account balance: -$2.894 billion (2014
est.)
-$1.412 billion (2013 est.)
note: excludes Wes t Bank
country comparison to the world: 156

Exports: $1.692 billion (2013 est.)
country comparison to the world: 146

Exports—commodities: strawberries, carnations,
vegetables, fish (small Israeli-controlled Kerem
Shalom crossing)

Imports: see entry for West Bank

Imports—commodities: food, consumer goods, fuel

Debt—external: see entry for West Bank

Exchange rates: see entry for West Bank
and irregular shipments, as permitted to transit the

ENERGY

Electricity—production: 51,000 kWh (2011 est.)
country comparison to the world: 220

Electricity—consumption: 202,000 kWh (2009)
country comparison to the world: 217

Electricity—exports: 0 kWh (2011 est.)
country comparison to the world: 149

Electricity—imports: 193,000 kWh (2011 est.)
country comparison to the world: 111

Crude oil—proved reserves: 0 bbl (1 January 2010
est.)
country comparison to the world: 144

COMMUNICATIONS

Telephones—fixed lines: 403,118 (includes the
West Bank) (2014 est.)

Telephones—mobile cellular: *total:* 3,197,550
(includes the West Bank)
subscriptions per 100 inhabitants: 117 (includes
the West Bank) (2014 est.)

Telephone system: *general assessment:* Gaza continues to repair the damage to its telecommunications infrastructure caused by fighting in 2009
domestic: Israeli company BEZEK and the Palestinian company PALTEL are responsible for fixed-
line services; the Palestinian JAWWAL company
provides cellular services
international: country code—970 (2009)

Broadcast media: 1 TV station and about 10 radio
stations; satellite TV accessible (2008)
Radio broadcast stations: AM 0, FM 10, shortwave 0 (2008)
Television broadcast stations: 1 (2008)

Internet country code: .ps; note—same as the West
Bank

Internet users: *total:* 1,379,000 (includes the West
Bank)

percent of population: 34.4% (includes the West Bank) (2009)

TRANSPORTATION

Airports: 1 (2013)
country comparison to the world: 219
Airports—with paved runways: *total:* 1
over 3,047 m: 1 (2013)
Heliports: 1 (2013)
Roadways: *note:* see entry for the West Bank
Ports and terminals: *major seaport(s):* Gaza

MILITARY AND SECURITY

Military branches: HAMAS does not have a conventional military in the Gaza Strip but maintains security forces in addition to its military wing, the 'Izz al-Din al-Qassam Brigades; the military wing reports to the Hamas Political Bureau leadership, which remains scattered throughout the region since relocating from its Damascus headquarters in early 2012 (2015)

TRANSNATIONAL ISSUES

Disputes—international: the status of the Gaza Strip is a final status issue to be resolved through negotiations; Israel removed settlers and military personnel from Gaza Strip in September 2005

Refugees and internally displaced persons: *refugees (country of origin):* 1,258,559 (Palestinian refugees) (2014)
IDPs: 221,000 (includes persons displaced within the Gaza strip due to the intensification of the Israeli-Palestinian conflict since June 2014 and other Palestinian IDPs in the Gaza Strip and West Bank who fled as long ago as 1967, although confirmed cumulative data do not go back beyond 2006) (2015)

GEORGIA

INTRODUCTION

Background: The region of present day Georgia contained the ancient kingdoms of Colchis and Kartli-1beria. The area came under Roman influence in the first centuries A.D., and Christianity became the state religion in the 330s. Domination by Persians, Arabs, and Turks was followed by a Georgian golden age (11th-13th centuries) that was cut short by the Mongol invasion of 1236. Subsequently, the Ottoman and Persian empires competed for influence in the region. Georgia was absorbed into the Russian Empire in the 19th century. Independent for three years (1918–1921) following the Russian revolution, it was forcibly incorporated into the USSR in 1921 and regained its independence when the Soviet Union dissolved in 1991.

Mounting public discontent over rampant corruption and ineffective government services, followed by an attempt by the incumbent Georgian Government to manipulate parliamentary elections in November 2003, touched off widespread protests that led to the resignation of Eduard SHEVARDNADZE, president since 1995. In the aftermath of that popular movement, which became known as the "Rose Revolution," new elections in early 2004 swept Mikheil SAAKASHVILI into power along with his United National Movement (UNM) party. Progress on market reforms and democratization has been made in the years since independence, but this progress has been complicated by Russian assistance and support to the separatist

regions of Abkhazia and South Ossetia. Periodic flare-ups in tension and violence culminated in a five-day conflict in August 2008 between Russia and Georgia, including the invasion of large portions of undisputed Georgian territory. Russian troops pledged to pull back from most occupied Georgian territory, but in late August 2008 Russia unilaterally recognized the independence of Abkhazia and South Ossetia, and Russian military forces remain in those regions.

Billionaire philanthropist Bidzina IVANISHVILI's unexpected entry into politics in October 2011 brought the divided opposition together under his Georgian Dream coalition, which won a majority of seats in the October 2012 parliamentary elections and removed UNM from power. Conceding defeat, SAAKASHVILI named IVANISHVILI as prime minister and allowed Georgian Dream to create a new government. Georgian Dream's Giorgi MARG VELASHVILI was inaugurated as president on 17 November 2013, ending a tense year of power-sharing between SAAKASHVILI and IVANISHVILI. IVANISHVILI voluntarily resigned from office after the presidential succession, and Georgia's legislature on 20 November 2013 confirmed Irakli GARIBASHVILI as his replacement. These changes in leadership represent unique examples of a former Soviet state that emerged to conduct democratic and peaceful government transitions of power. Popular and government support for integration with the West is high in Georgia. Joining the EU and NATO are among the country's top foreign policy goals.

GEOGRAPHY

Location: Southwestern Asia, bordering the Black Sea, between Turkey and Russia, with a sliver of land north of theCaucasus extending into Europe; note—Georgia views itself as part of Europe
Geographic coordinates: 42 00 N, 43 30 E
Map references: Asia
Area: *total:* 69,700 sq km

land: 69,700 sq km
water: 0 sq km
country comparison to the world: 121
Area—comparative: slightly smaller than South Carolina; slightly larger than West Virginia
Land boundaries: *total:* 1,814 km
border countries (4): Armenia 219 km, Azerbaijan 428 km, Russia 894 km, Turkey 273 km
Coastline: 310 km
Maritime claims: *territorial sea:* 12 nm
exclusive economic zone: 200 nm
Climate: warm and pleasant; Mediterranean-like on Black Sea coast
Terrain: largely mountainous with Great Caucasus Mountains in the north and Lesser Caucasus Mountains in the south; Kolkhet'is Dablobi (Kolkhida Lowland) opens to the Black Sea in the west; Mtkvari River Basin in the east; fertile soils in river valley flood plains and foothills of Kolkhida Lowland
Elevation: *mean elevation:* 1,432 m
elevation extremes: *lowest point:* Black Sea 0 m
highest point: Mt'a Shkhara 5,201 m
Natural resources: timber, hydropower, manganese deposits, iron ore, copper, minor coal and oil deposits; coastal climate and soils allow for important tea and citrus growth
Land use: *agricultural land:* 35.5%
arable land: 5.8%
permanent crops: 1.8%
permanent pasture: 27.9%
forest: 39.4%
other: 25.1% (2011 est.)
Irrigated land: 4,330 sq km (2012)
Total renewable water resources: 63.33 cu km (2011)
Freshwater withdrawal (domestic/industrial/agricultural): *total:* 1.81 cu km/yr (20%/22%/58%)
per capita: 410.6 cu m/yr (2005)
Natural hazards: earthquakes

Environment—current issues: air pollution, particularly in Rust'avi; heavy pollution of Mtkvari River and the Black Sea; inadequate
supplies of potable water; soil pollution from toxic chemicals

Environment—international agreements: *party to:* Air Pollution, Biodiversity, Climate Change, Climate Change-Kyoto Protocol, Desertification, Endangered Species, Hazardous Wastes, Law of the Sea, Ozone Layer Protection, Ship Pollution, Wetlands
signed, but not ratified: none of the selected agreements

Geography—note: strategically located east of the Black Sea; Georgia controls much of the Caucasus Mountains and the routes through them

PEOPLE AND SOCIETY

Nationality: *noun:* Georgian(s)
adjective: Georgian

Ethnic groups: Georgian 83.8%, Azeri 6.5%, Armenian 5.7%, Russian 1.5%, other 2.5% (2002 est.)

Languages: Georgian (official) 71%, Russian 9%, Armenian 7%, Azeri 6%, other 7%
note: Abkhaz is the official language in Abkhazia

Religions: Orthodox Christian (official) 83.9%, Muslim 9.9%, Armenian-G regorian 3.9%, Catholic 0.8%, other 0.8%, none 0.7% (2002 census)

Population: 4,931,226 (July 2015 est.)
country comparison to the world: 122

Age structure: *0–14 years:* 17.73% (male 460,376/female 414,028)
15–24 years: 13.35% (male 344,179/female 314,321)
25–54 years: 40.93% (male 978,151/female 1,040,364)
55–64 years: 12.45% (male 275,586/female 338,524)
65 years and over: 15.53% (male 299,876/female 465,821) (2015 est.)

Dependency ratios: *total dependency ratio:* 45.7% you th dependency ratio: 25.2%
elderly dependency ratio: 20.4%
potential support ratio: 4.9% (2015 est.)

Median age: *total:* 37.9 years
male: 35 years
female: 40.5 years (2015 est.)
country comparison to the world: 61

Population growth rate: -0.08% (2015 est.)
country comparison to the world: 204

Birth rate: 12.74 births/1,000 population (2015 est.)
country comparison to the world: 155

Death rate: 10.82 deaths/1,000 population (2015 est.)
country comparison to the world: 34

Net migration rate: -2.7 migrant(s)/1,000 population (2015 est.)
country comparison to the world: 176

Urbanization: *urban population:* 53.6% of total population (2015)

rate of urbanization: -0.1% annual rate of change (2010–15 est.)

Major urban areas—population: TBILISI (capital) 1.147 million (2015)

Sex ratio: *at birth:* 1.08 male(s)/female
0–14 years: 1.11 male(s)/female
15–24 years: 1.1 male(s)/female
25–54 years: 0.94 male(s)/female
55–64 years: 0.81 male(s)/female
65 years and over: 0.64 male(s)/female
total population: 0.92 male(s)/female (2015 est.)

Mother's mean age at first birth: 24
note: data do not cover Abkhazia and South Ossetia (2011 est.)

Maternal mortality rate: 36 deaths/100,000 live births (2015 est.)
country comparison to the world: 91

Infant mortality rate: *total:* 16.15 deaths/1,000 live births
male: 18.31 deaths/1,000 live births
female: 13.82 deaths/1,000 live births (2015 est.)
country comparison to the world: 100

Life expectancy at birth: *total population:* 75.95 years
male: 71.85 years
female: 80.36 years (2015 est.)
country comparison to the world: 91

Total fertility rate: 1.76 children born/woman (2015 est.)
country comparison to the world: 161

Contraceptive prevalence rate: 53.4%
note: percent of women aged 15–44 (2010)

Health expenditures: 9.4% of GDP (2013)
country comparison to the world: 34

Physicians density: 4.27 physicians/1,000 population (2013)

Hospital bed density: 2.6 beds/1,000 population (2012)

Drinking water source:
improved:
urban: 100% of popu lation
rural: 100% of population
total: 100% of population
unimproved:
urban: urban: 0% of population
rural: 0% of population
total: 0% of population (2015 est.)

Sanitation facility access:
improved:
urban: 95.2% of population
rural: 75.9% of population
total: 86.3% of population
unimproved:
urban: urban: 4.8% of population
rural: 24.1% of population
total: 13.7% of population
(2015 est.)

HIV/AIDS—adult prevalence rate: 0.28% (2014 est.)
country comparison to the world: 86

HIV/AIDS—people living with HIV/AIDS: 6,600 (2014 est.)

country comparison to the world: 106

HIV/AIDS—deaths: 100 (2014 est.)
country comparison to the world: 119

Obesity—adult prevalence rate: 22.1% (2014)
country comparison to the world: 82

Children under the age of 5 years underweight: 1.1% (2009)
country comparison to the world: 131

Education expenditures: 2% of GDP (2012)
country comparison to the world: 167

Literacy: *definition:* age 15 and over can read and write
total population: 99.8%
male: 99.8%
female: 99.7% (2015 est.)

School life expectancy (primary to tertiary education): *total:* 15 years
male: 15 years
female: 15 years (2014)

Child labor—children ages 5–14: *total number:* 121,659
percentage: 18% (2005 est.)

Unemployment, youth ages 15–24: *total:* 35.6%
male: 35.3%
female: 36.4% (2013 est.)
country comparison to the world: 23

GOVERNMENT

Country name: *conventional long form:* none
conventional short form: Georgia
local long form: none
local short form: Sak'art'velo
former: Georgian Soviet Socialist Republic
etymology: the Western name may derive from the Persian designation "gurgan" meaning "Land of the wolves"; the native name "Sak'art'velo" means "Land of the Kartvelians" and refers to the core central Georgian region of Kartli

Government type: semi-presidential republic

Capital: *name:* Tbilisi

Geographic coordinates: 41 41 N, 44 50 E
time difference: UTC+4 (9 hours ahead of Washington, DC, during Standard Time)

Administrative divisions: 9 regions (mkharebi, singular—mkhare), 1 city (kalaki), and 2 autonomous republics (avtomnoy respubliki, singular—avtom respublika)
regions: Guria, Imereti, Kakheti, Kvemo Kartli, Mtskheta Mtianeti, Racha-Lechkhumi and Kvemo Svaneti, Samegrelo and Zemo Svaneti, Samtskhe-Javakheti, Shida Kartli; note—the breakaway region of South Ossetia consists of the northern part of Shida Kartli, eastern slivers of the Imereti region and Racha-Lechkhumi and Kvemo Svaneti, and part of western Mtskheta-Mtianeti
city: Tbilisi
autonomous republics: Abkhazia or Ap'khazet'is Avtonomiuri Respublika (Sokhumi), Ajaria or Acharis Avtonomiuri Respublika (Bat'umi)
note 1: the administrative centers of the two autonomous republics are shown in parentheses

note 2: the United States recognizes the breakaway regions of Abkhazia and South Ossetia to be part of Georgia

Independence: 9 April 1991 (from the Soviet Union); notable earlier date: A.D.1008 (Georgia unified under King BAGRAT III)

National holiday: Independence Day, 26 May (1918); note—26 May 1918 was the date of independence from Soviet Russia, 9 April 1991 was the date of independence from the Soviet Union

Constitution: previous 1921, 1978 (based on 1977 Soviet Union constitution); latest approved 24 August 1995, effective 17 October 1995; amended several times, last in 2013 (2016)

Legal system: civil law system

International law organization participation: accepts compulsory ICJ jurisdiction; accepts ICCt jurisdiction

Citizenship: *citizenship by birth:* no
citizenship by descent only: at least one parent must be a citizen of Georgia
dual citizenship recognized: no
residency requirement for naturalization: 10 years

Suffrage: 18 years of age; universal

Executive branch: *chief of state:* President Giorgi MARGVELASHVILI (since 17 November 2013)

head of government: Prime Minister Giorgi KVIRIKASHVILI (since 30 December 2015); First Deputy Prime Minister Dimitry KUMSISHVILI
cabinet: Cabinet of Ministers
elections/appointments: president directly elected by absolute majority popular vote in 2 rounds if needed for a 5-year term (eligible for a second term); election last held on 27 October 2013 (next to be held in October 2018); prime minister nominated by Parliament, appointed by the president
election results: Giorgi MARGVELASHVILI elected president; percent of vote—Giorgi MARGVELASHVILI (Georgian Dream) 62.1%, Davit BAKRADZE (UNM) 21.7%, Nino BURJANADZE 10.2%, other 6%

Legislative branch: *description:* unicameral Parliament or Sakartvelos Parlamenti (150 seats; 77 members directly elected in a single nationwide constituency by proportional representation vote and 73 directly elected in single-seat constituencies by simple majority vote; members serve 4-year terms)
elections: last held on 1 October 2012 (next to be held in 2016)
election results: percent of vote by party—Georgian Dream-led coalition 55%, United National Movement 40.3%, other 4.7%; seats by party—Georgian Dream 85, United National Movement 65

Judicial branch: *highest court(s):* Supreme Court (organized into several specialized judicial chambers; number of judges determined by the president of Georgia); Constitutional Court (consists of 9 judges)

note—the Abkhazian and Ajarian Autonomous republics each have a supreme court and a hierarchy of lower courts
judge selection and term of office: Supreme Court judges nominated by the president and appointed by the Parliament; judges serve not less than 10-year terms; Constitutional Court judges appointed by the president following candidate selection by the Justice Council of Georgia, a 12-member consultative body of high-level judges, and presidential and parliamentary appointees; judges appointed for 10-year terms
subordinate courts: Courts of Appeal; regional (town) and district courts

Political parties and leaders: Alliance of Patriots [Irma INASHVILI]
Conservative Party [Zviad DZIDZIGURI]
European Democrats [Paata DAVITAIA]
Free Georgia [Kak ha KUKAVA]
Georgian Dream (a five-party coalition composed of Georgian Dream-Democratic Georgia, Republican Party, National Forum, Conservative Party, and Industry Will Save Georgia)
Georgian Dream-Democratic Georgia [Irakli GARIBASHVILI]
Green Party of Georgia [Gia GACHECHILADZE]
Industry Will Save Georgia (Industrialists) or IWSG [Giorgi TOPADZE]
National Democratic Party or NDP [Bachuki KARDAVA]
National Forum [Kakhaber SHARTAVA]
New Rights [Pikria CHIKHRADZE]
Our Georgia-Free Democrats (OGFD) [Irakli ALASANIA]
Republican Party [Khatuna SAMNIDZE]
United Democratic Movement [Nino BURJANADZE]
United National Movement or UNM [vacant]

Political pressure groups and leaders: *other:* separatists in the Russian-occupied regions of Abkhazia and South Ossetia

International organization participation: ADB, BSEC, CD, CE, CPLP (associate), EAPC, EBRD, FAO, G-11, GCTU, GUAM, IAEA, IBRD, ICAO, ICC (national committees), ICCt, ICRM, IDA, IFAD, IFC, IFRCS, ILO, IMF, IMO, Interpol, IOC, IOM, IPU, ISO (correspondent), ITSO, ITU, ITUC (NGOs), MIGA, OAS (observer), OIF (observer), OPCW, OSCE, PFP, SELEC (observer), UN, UNCTAD, UNESCO, UNIDO, UNWTO, UPU, WCO, WHO, WIPO, WMO, WTO

Diplomatic representation in the US: *chief of mission:* Ambassador Archil GEGESHIDZE (since 12 April 2013)
chancery: 1824 R Street NW, Washington, DC 20009
telephone: [1] (202) 387-2390
FAX: [1] (202) 387-0864
consulate(s) general: New York

Diplomatic representation from the US: *chief of mission:* Ambassador Ian C. KELLY (since 17 September 2015)
embassy: 11 George Balanchine Street, T'bilisi 0131

mailing address: 7060 T'bilisi Place, Washington, DC 20521 -7060
telephone: [995] (32) 227-70-00
FAX: [995] (32) 253-23-10

Flag description: white rectangle with a central red cross extending to all four sides of the flag; each of the four quadrants displays a small red bolnur-katskhuri cross; sometimes referred to as the Five-Cross Flag; although adopted as the official Georgian flag in 2004, the five-cross design appears to date back to the 14th century

National symbol(s): Saint George, lion; national colors: red, white

National anthem: *name:* "Tavisupleba" (Liberty)
lyrics/music: Davit MAGRADSE/Zakaria PALIASHVILI (adapted by Joseb KETSCHAKMADSE)
note: adopted 2004; after the Rose Revolution, a new anthem with music based on the operas "Abesalom da Eteri" and "Daisi" was adopted

ECONOMY

Economy—overview: Georgia's main economic activities include cultivation of agricultural products such as grapes, citrus fruits, and hazelnuts; mining of manganese, copper, and gold; and producing alcoholic and nonalcoholic beverages, metals, machinery, and chemicals in small-scale industries. The country imports nearly all of its needed supplies of natural gas and oil products. It has sizeable hydropower capacity that now provides most of its energy needs.

Georgia has overcome the chronic energy shortages and gas supply interruptions of the past by renovating hydropower plants and by increasingly relying on natural gas imports from Azerbaijan instead of from Russia. Construction of the Baku-T'bilisi-C eyhan oil pipeline, the South Caucasus gas pipeline, and the Kars-Akhalkalaki railroad are part of a strategy to capitalize on Georgia's strategic location between Europe and Asia and develop its role as a transit point for gas, oil, and other goods. The expansion of the South Caucasus pipeline, as part of the Shah Deniz II Southern Gas Corridor project, will result in a $2 billion foreign investment in Georgia, the largest ever in the country. gas from Shah Deniz II is expected to begin flowing in 2019.

Georgia's economy sustained GDP growth of more than 10% in 2006–07, based on strong inflows of foreign investment and robust government spending. However, GDP growth slowed following the August 2008 conflict with Russia, and sunk to negative 4% in 2009 as foreign direct investment and workers' remittances declined in the wake of the global financial crisis. The economy rebounded in 2010–13, but FDI inflows, the engine of Georgian economic growth prior to the 2008 conflict, have not recovered fully. Unemployment has also remained high.

The country is pinning its hopes for renewed growth on a determined effort to continue to liberalize the economy by reducing regulation, taxes, and corruption in order to attract foreign investment, with a focus on hydropower, agriculture, tourism, and textiles production. Georgia has historically suffered from a chronic failure to collect tax revenues; however, since 2004 the government has simplified the tax code, improved tax administration, increased tax enforcement, and cracked down on petty corruption, leading to higher revenues. The government has received high marks from the World Bank for its anti-corruption efforts. Since 2012, the Georgian Dream-led government has continued the previous administration's low-regulation, low-tax, free market policies, while modestly increasing social spending, strengthening antitrust policy, and amending the labor code to comply with International Labor Standards. The government published its 2020 Economic Development Strategy in early 2014 and former Prime Minister Bidzina IVANISHVILI launched the Georgian Co-Investment Fund, a $6 billion private equity fund that will invest in tourism, agriculture, logistics, energy, infrastructure, and manufacturing. In mid-2014, Georgia signed an association agreement with the EU, paving the way to free trade and visa-free travel.

GDP (purchasing power parity):
$35.6 billion (2015 est.)
$34.65 billion (2014 est.)
$33.12 billion (2013 est.)
note: data are in 2015 US dollars
country comparison to the world: 120

GDP (official exchange rate): $14.01 billion (2015 est.)

GDP—real growth rate:
2.8% (2015 est.)
4.6% (2014 est.)
3.4% (2013 est.)
country comparison to the world: 109

GDP—per capita (PPP):
$9,600 (2015 est.)
$9,300 (2014 est.)
$8,800 (2013 est.)
note: data are in 2015 US dollars
country comparison to the world: 138

Gross national saving:
21.7% of GDP (2015 est.)
19.2% of GDP (2014 est.)
19.5% of GDP (2013 est.)
country comparison to the world: 69

GDP—composition, by end use:
household consumption: 70%
government consumption: 17.1%
investment in fixed capital: 26%
investment in inventories: 4%
exports of goods and services: 45%
imports of goods and services: -62.1% (2015 est.)

GDP—composition, by sector of origin:
agriculture: 9.2%
industry: 22.1%
services: 68.7% (2015 est.)

Agriculture—products: citrus, grapes, tea, hazelnuts, vegetables; livestock

Industries: steel, machine tools, electrical appliances, mining (manganese, copper, gold), chemicals, wood products, wine

Industrial production growth rate: 4.3% (2015 est.)

country comparison to the world: 50

Labor force: 1.959 million (2011 est.)
country comparison to the world: 123

Labor force—by occupation: agriculture: 55.6%
industry: 8.9%
services: 35.5% (2006 est.)

Unemployment rate: 16.7% (2015 est.)
12.4% (2014 est.)
country comparison to the world: 157

Population below poverty line: 9.2% (2010 est.)

Household income or consumption by percentage share: lowest: 10%: 2%
highest: 10%: 31.3% (2008)

Distribution of family income—Gini index: 46 (2011)
37.1 (1996)
country comparison to the world: 36

Budget: revenues: $3.874 billion
expenditures: $4.319 billion (2015 est.)
Taxes and other revenues: 28.2% of GDP (2015 est.)
country comparison to the world: 94

Budget surplus (+) or deficit (–): -3.2% of GDP (2015 est.)
country comparison to the world: 123

Public debt: 38.8% of GDP (2015 est.)
35.3% of GDP (2014 est.)
note: data cover general government debt, and includes debt instruments issued (or owned) by government entities other than the treasury; the data include treasury debt held by foreign entities; the data include debt issued by subnational entities; Georgia does not maintain intra-governmental debt or social funds
country comparison to the world: 119

Fiscal year: calendar year

Inflation rate (consumer prices): 4% (2015 est.)
3.1% (2014 est.)
country comparison to the world: 157

Central bank discount rate: 3.75% (15 January 2013)
5.25% (31 December 2012)
note: this is the Refinancing Rate, the key monetary policy rate of the National Bank of Georgia
country comparison to the world: 99

Commercial bank prime lending rate: 12.1% (31 December 2015 est.)
11.91% (31 December 2014 est.)
country comparison to the world: 66

Stock of narrow money: $2.061 billion (31 December 2015 est.)
$2.415 billion (31 December 2014 est.)
country comparison to the world: 126

Stock of broad money: $4.72 billion (31 September 2012 est.)
$4.249 billion (31 December 2011 est.)
country comparison to the world: 133

Stock of domestic credit: $7.298 billion (31 December 2015 est.)
$7.596 billion (31 December 2014 est.)
country comparison to the world: 112

Market value of publicly traded shares: $943.4 million (31 December 2012 est.)

$795.7 million (31 December 2011)
$1.06 billion (31 December 2010 est.)
country comparison to the world: 108

Current account balance: -$1.627 billion (2015 est.)
-$1.745 billion (2014 est.)
country comparison to the world: 139

Exports: $3.535 billion (2015 est.)
$3.995 billion (2014 est.)
country comparison to the world: 125

Exports—commodities: vehicles, ferro-alloys, fertilizers, nuts, scrap metal, gold, copper ores

Exports—partners: Azerbaijan 10.9%, Bulgaria 9.7%, Turkey 8.4%, Armenia 8.2%, Russia 7.4%, China 5.7%, US 4.7%, Uzbekistan 4.4% (2015)

Imports: $7.466 billion (2015 est.)
$8.235 billion (2014 est.)
country comparison to the world: 110

Imports—commodities: fuels, vehicles, machinery and parts, grain and other foods, pharmaceuticals

Imports—partners: Turkey 17.2%, Russia 8.1%, China 7.6%, Azerbaijan 7%, Ireland 5.9%, Ukraine 5.9%, Germany 5.6% (2015)

Reserves of foreign exchange and gold: $2.422 billion (31 December 2015 est.)
$2.699 billion (31 December 2014 est.)
country comparison to the world: 115

Debt—external: $13.56 billion (31 December 2014 est.)
$13.17 billion (31 December 2013 est.)
country comparison to the world: 100

Stock of direct foreign investment—at home: $13.25 billion (31 December 2015 est.)
$12.4 billion (31 December 2014 est.)
country comparison to the world: 88

Stock of direct foreign investment—abroad: $1.839 billion (31 December 2015 est.)
$1.643 billion (31 December 2014 est.)
country comparison to the world: 80

Exchange rates: laris (GEL) per US dollar—
2.246 (2015 est.)
1.7657 (2014 est.)
1.7657 (2013 est.)
1.65 (2012 est.)
1.6865 (2011 est.)

ENERGY

Electricity—production: 9.475 billion kWh (2012 est.)
country comparison to the world: 99

Electricity—consumption: 8.468 billion kWh (2012 est.)
country comparison to the world: 95

Electricity—exports: 528 million kWh (2012 est.)
country comparison to the world: 66

Electricity—imports: 615 million kWh (2012 est.)
country comparison to the world: 72

Electricity—installed generating capacity: 4.308 million kW (2012 est.)
country comparison to the world: 77

Electricity—from fossil fuels: 39.2% of total installed capacity (2012 est.)

country comparison to the world: 166

Electricity—from nuclear fuels: 0% of total installed capacity (2012 est.)
country comparison to the world: 97

Electricity—from hydroelectric plants: 60.8% of total installed capacity (2012 est.)
country comparison to the world: 35

Electricity—from other renewable sources: 0% of total installed capacity (2012 est.)
country comparison to the world: 176

Crude oil—production: 1,000 bbl/day (2014 est.)
country comparison to the world: 94

Crude oil—exports: 727 bbl/day (2012 est.)
country comparison to the world: 85

Crude oil—imports: 0 bbl/day (2013 est.)
country comparison to the world: 195

Crude oil—proved reserves: 35 million bbl (1 January 2015 est.)
country comparison to the world: 82

Refined petroleum products—production: 0 bbl/day (2013 est.)
country comparison to the world: 186

Refined petroleum products—consumption: 21,000 bbl/day (2013 est.)
country comparison to the world: 127

Refined petroleum products—exports: 40.88 bbl/day (2012 est.)
country comparison to the world: 123

Refined petroleum products—imports: 21,770 bbl/day (2012 est.)
country comparison to the world: 108

Natural gas—production: 0 cu m (2013 est.)
country comparison to the world: 191

Natural gas—consumption: 2.03 billion cu m (2013 est.)
country comparison to the world: 79

Natural gas—exports: 0 cu m (2013 est.)
country comparison to the world: 104

Natural gas—imports: 2.03 billion cu m (2013 est.)
country comparison to the world: 49

Natural gas—proved reserves: 8.495 billion cu m (1 January 2014 est.)
country comparison to the world: 83

Carbon dioxide emissions from consumption of energy: 6.258 million Mt (2012 est.)
country comparison to the world: 120

COMMUNICATIONS

Telephones—fixed lines: total subscriptions: 1.1 million
subscriptions per 100 inhabitants: 22 (2014 est.)
country comparison to the world: 73

Telephones—mobile cellular: total: 5.4 million
subscriptions per 100 inhabitants: 109 (2014 est.)
country comparison to the world: 114

Telephone system: general assessment: fixed-line telecommunications network has limited coverage outside Tbilisi; multiple mobile-cellular providers provide services to an increasing subscribership throughout the country
domestic: cellular telephone networks cover the entire country; mobile-cellular teledensity roughly 100 per 100 people; intercity facilities include a fiber-optic line between T'bilisi and K'ut'aisi
international: country code—995; the Georgia-Russia fiber-optic submarine cable provides connectivity to Russia; international service is available by microwave, landline, and satellite through the Moscow switch; international electronic mail and telex service are available (2011)

Broadcast media: 1 public broadcaster in Tbilisi, 1 state-owned broadcaster in Ajaria Autonomous Republic; 8 privately owned TV stations; state run public broadcaster operates 2 TV stations; dozens of cable TV operators, several major commercial TV stations, and several dozen private radio stations; state run public broadcaster operates 2 radio stations (2012)
Radio broadcast stations: AM 7, FM 12, short-wave 4 (1998)
Television broadcast stations: 12 (plus repeaters) (1998)

Internet country code: .ge

Internet hosts: 357,864 (2012)
country comparison to the world: 59

Internet users: total: 2.5 million
percent of population: 50.6% (2014 est.)
country comparison to the world: 91

TRANSPORTATION

Airports: 22 (2013)
country comparison to the world: 135

Airports—with paved runways: total: 18
over 3,047 m: 1
2,438 to 3,047 m: 7
1,524 to 2,437 m: 3
914 to 1,523 m: 5
under 914 m: 2 (2013)

Airports—with unpaved runways: total: 4
1,524 to 2,437 m: 1
914 to 1,523 m: 2
under 914 m: 1 (2013)

Heliports: 2 (2013)

Pipelines: gas 1,596 km; oil 1,175 km (2013)

Railways: total: 1,363 km
broad gauge: 1,326 km 1.520-m gauge (1,251 km electrified)
narrow gauge: 37 km 0.912-m gauge (37 km electrified) (2014)
country comparison to the world: 81

Roadways: total: 19,109 km
paved: 19,109 km (includes 69 km of expressways) (2010)
country comparison to the world: 113

Merchant marine: total: 142
by type: bulk carrier 13, cargo 114, chemical tanker 1, container 1, liquefied gas 1, passenger/cargo 1, petroleum tanker 3, refrigerated cargo 1, roll on/roll off 5, vehicle carrier 2
foreign-owned: 95 (Bulgaria 1, China 10, Egypt 7, Hong Kong 3, Israel 1, Italy 2, Latvia 1, Lebanon 1, Romania 7, Russia 6, Syria 24, Turkey 14, UAE 2, UK 5, Ukraine 10, US 1)
registered in other countries: 1 (unknown 1) (2010)
country comparison to the world: 40

Ports and terminals: major seaport(s): Black Sea—Bat'umi, P'ot'i

MILITARY AND SECURITY

Military branches: Georgian Armed Forces: Land Forces (include Air and Air Defense Forces); separatist Abkhazia Armed Forces: Ground Forces, Air Forces; separatist South Ossetia Armed Forces
note: Georgian naval forces have been incorporated into the Coast Guard, which is part of the Ministry of Internal Affairs rather than the Ministry of Defense (2015)

Military service age and obligation: 18 to 34 years of age for compulsory and voluntary active duty military service; conscript service obligation is 18 months (2012)

Military expenditures: 26% of GDP (2014)
2.7% of GDP (2013)
2.88% of GDP (2012)
3.25% of GDP (2011)
2.88% of GDP (2010)
country comparison to the world: 27

TRANSNATIONAL ISSUES

Disputes—international: Russia's military support and subsequent recognition of Abkhazia and South Ossetia independence in 2008 continue to sour relations with Georgia

Refugees and internally displaced persons: IDPs: 268,416 (displaced in the 1990s as a result of armed conflict in the breakaway republics of Abkhazia and South Ossetia; displaced in 2008 by fighting between Georgia and Russia over South Ossetia) (2015)
stateless persons: 627 (2015)

Illicit drugs: limited cultivation of cannabis and opium poppy, mostly for domestic consumption; used as transshipment point for opiates via Central Asia to Western Europe and Russia

GERMANY

INTRODUCTION

Background: As Europe's largest economy and second most populous nation (after Russia), Germany is a key member of the continent's economic, political, and defense organizations. European power struggles immersed Germany in two devastating World Wars in the first half of the 20th century and left the country occupied by the victorious Allied powers of the US, UK, France, and the Soviet Union in 1945. With the advent of the Cold War, two German states were formed in 1949: the western Federal Republic of Germany (FRG) and the eastern German Democratic Republic (GDR). The democratic FRG embedded itself in key western economic and security organizations, the EC, which became the EU, and NATO, while the communist GDR was on the front line of the Soviet-led Warsaw Pact. The decline of the USSR and the end of the Cold War allowed for German unification in 1990. Since then, Germany has expended considerable funds to bring eastern productivity and wages up to western standards. In January 1999, Germany and 10 other EU countries introduced a common European exchange currency, the euro.

GEOGRAPHY

Location: Central Europe, bordering the Baltic Sea and the North Sea, between the Netherlands and Poland, south of Denmark

Geographic coordinates: 51 00 N, 9 00 E

Map references: Europe

Area: *total:* 357,022 sq km
land: 348,672 sq km
water: 8,350 sq km
country comparison to the world: 63

Area—comparative: three times the size of Pennsylvania; slightly smaller than Montana

Land boundaries: *total:* 3,714 km
border countries (9): Austria 801 km, Belgium 133 km, Czech Republic 704 km, Denmark 140 km, France 418 km, Luxembourg 128 km, Netherlands 575 km, Poland 467 km, Switzerland 348 km

Coastline: 2,389 km

Maritime claims: *territorial sea:* 12 nm
exclusive economic zone: 200 nm
continental shelf: 200-m depth or to the depth of exploitation

Climate: temperate and marine; cool, cloudy, wet winters and summers; occasional warm mountain (foehn) wind

Terrain: lowlands in north, uplands in center, Bavarian Alps in south

Elevation: *mean elevation:* 263 m

elevation extremes: *lowest point:* Neuendorf bei Wilster -3.54 m
highest point: Zugspitze 2,963 m

Natural resources: coal, lignite, natural gas, iron ore, copper, nickel, uranium, potash, salt, construction materials, timber, arable land

Land use: *agricultural land:* 48%
arable land: 34.1%
permanent crops: 0.6%
permanent pasture: 13.3%
forest: 31.8%
other: 20.2% (2011 est.)

Irrigated land: 6,500 sq km (2012)

Total renewable water resources: 154 cu km (2011)

Freshwater withdrawal (domestic/industrial/agricultural): *total:* 32.3 cu km/yr (16%/84%/0%)
per capita: 391.4 cu m/yr (2007)

Natural hazards: flooding

Environment—current issues: emissions from coal-burning utilities and industries contribute to air pollution; acid rain, resulting from sulfur dioxide emissions, is damaging forests; pollution in the Baltic Sea from raw sewage and industrial effluents from rivers in eastern Germany; hazardous waste disposal; government established a mechanism for ending the use of nuclear power by 2022; government working to meet EU commitment to identify nature preservation areas in line with the EU's Flora, Fauna, and Habitat directive

Environment—international agreements: *party to:* Air Pollution, Air Pollution-Nitrogen Oxides, Air Pollution-Persistent Organic Pollutants, Air Pollution-Sulfur 85, Air Pollution-Sulfur 94, Air Pollution-Volatile Organic Compounds, Antarctic-Environmental Protocol, Antarctic-Marine Living Resources, Antarctic Seals, Antarctic Treaty, Biodiversity, Climate Change, Climate Change-Kyoto Protocol, Desertification, Endangered Species, Environmental Modification, Hazardous Wastes, Law of the Sea, Marine Dumping, Ozone Layer Protection, Ship Pollution, Tropical Timber 83, Tropical Timber 94, Wetlands, Whaling
signed, but not ratified: none of the selected agreements

Geography—note: strategic location on North European Plain and along the entrance to the Baltic Sea; most major rivers in Germany—the Rhine, Weser, Oder, Elbe—flow northward; the Danube, which originates in the German Alps, flows eastward

PEOPLE AND SOCIETY

Nationality: *noun:* German(s)
adjective: German

Ethnic groups: German 91.5%, Turkish 2.4%, other 6.1% (made up largely of Greek, Italian, Polish, Russian, Serbo-Croatian, Spanish)

Languages: German (official)
note: Danish, Frisian, Sorbian, and Romany are official minority languages; Low German, Danish, North Frisian, Sater Frisian, Lower Sorbian, Upper Sorbian, and Romany are recognized as regional languages under the European Charter for Regional or Minority Languages

Religions: Protestant 34%, Roman Catholic 34%, Muslim 3.7%, unaffiliated or other 28.3%
Population: 80,854,408 (July 2015 est.)
country comparison to the world: 18

Age structure: *0–14 years:* 12.88% (male 5,346,086/female 5,068,071)
15–24 years: 10.38% (male 4,279,962/female 4,113,746)
25–54 years: 41.38% (male 16,934,180/female 16,519,932)
55–64 years: 13.91% (male 5,571,694/female 5,675,104)
65 years and over: 21.45% (male 7,591,298/female 9,754,335) (2015 est.)

Dependency ratios: *total dependency ratio:* 51.8%
youth dependency ratio: 19.6%
elderly dependency ratio: 32.2%
potential support ratio: 3.1% (2015 est.)

Median age: *total:* 46.5 years
male: 45.4 years
female: 47.5 years (2015 est.)
country comparison to the world: 3

Population growth rate: -0.17% (2015 est.)
country comparison to the world: 214

Birth rate: 8.47 births/1,000 population (2015 est.)
country comparison to the world: 217

Death rate: 11.42 deaths/1,000 population (2015 est.)
country comparison to the world: 30

Net migration rate: 1.24 migrant(s)/1,000 population (2015 est.)
country comparison to the world: 60

Urbanization: *urban population:* 75.3% of total population (2015)
rate of urbanization: 0.16% annual rate of change (2010–15 est.)

Major urban areas—population: BERLIN (capital) 3.563 million; Hamburg 1.831 million;

Munich 1.438 million; Cologne 1.037 million (2015)

Sex ratio: *at birth:* 1.06 male(s)/female
0–14 years: 1.06 male(s)/female
15–24 years: 1.04 male(s)/female
25–54 years: 1.03 male(s)/female
55–64 years: 0.98 male(s)/female
65 years and over: 0.78 male(s)/female
total population: 0.97 male(s)/female (2015 est.)

Mother's mean age at first birth: 29.2 (2012 est.)

Maternal mortality rate: 6 deaths/100,000 live births (2015 est.)
country comparison to the world: 165

Infant mortality rate: *total:* 3.43 deaths/1,000 live births
male: 3.72 deaths/1,000 live births
female: 3.12 deaths/1,000 live births (2015 est.)
country comparison to the world: 208

Life expectancy at birth: *total population:* 80.57 years
male: 78.26 years
female: 83 years (2015 est.)
country comparison to the world: 32

Total fertility rate: 1.44 children born/woman (2015 est.)
country comparison to the world: 206

Contraceptive prevalence rate: 66.2%
note: percent of women aged 18–49 (2005)

Health expenditures: 11.3% of GDP (2013)
country comparison to the world: 13

Physicians density: 3.89 physicians/1,000 population (2012)

Hospital bed density: 8.2 beds/1,000 population (2011)

Drinking water source:
improved:
urban: 100% of population
rural: 100% of population
total: 100% of population
unimproved:
urban: 0% o f p op u lation
rural: 0% of population
total: 0% of population (2015 est.)

Sanitation facility access:
improved:
urban: 99.3% of population
rural: 99% of population
total: 99.2% of population
unimproved:
urban: urban: 0.7% of population
rural: 1% of population
total: 0.8% of population (2015 est.)

HIV/AIDS—adult prevalence rate: 0.15% (2013 est.)
country comparison to the world: 103

HIV/AIDS—people living with HIV/AIDS: 77,500 (2013 est.)
country comparison to the world: 48

HIV/AIDS—deaths: 400 (2013 est.)
country comparison to the world: 93

Obesity—adult prevalence rate: 22.7% (2014)
country comparison to the world: 59

Children under the age of 5 years underweight: 1.1% (2006)
country comparison to the world: 132

Education expenditures: 4.9% of GDP (2012)
country comparison to the world: 74

School life expectancy (primary to tertiary education): *total:* 17 years
male: 17 years
female: 17 years (2014)

Unemployment, youth ages 15–24: *total:* 7.9%
male: 8.6%
female: 7.1% (2013 est.)
country comparison to the world: 112

GOVERNMENT

Country name: *conventional long form:* Federal Republic of Germany
conventional short form: Germany
local long form: Bundesrepublik Deutschland
local short form: Deutschland
former: German Empire, German Republic, German Reich
etymology: the Gauls (Celts) of Western Europe may have referred to the newly arriving Germanic tribes who settled in neighboring areas east of the Rhine during the first centuries B. C. as "Germani," a term the Romans adopted as "Germania"; the native designation "Deutsch" comes from the Old High German "diutisc" meaning "of the people"

Government type: federal parliamentary republic

Capital: *name:* Berlin

Geographic coordinates: 52 31 N, 13 24 E
time difference: UTC + 1 (6 hours ahead of Washington, DC, during Standard Time)
daylight saving time: +1hr, begins last Sunday in March; ends last Sunday in October

Administrative divisions: 16 states (Laender, singular—Land); Baden-Wuerttemberg, Bayern (Bavaria), Berlin, Brandenburg, Bremen, Hamburg, Hessen (Hesse), Mecklenburg-Vorpommern (Mecklenburg-Western Pomerania), Niedersachsen (Lower Saxony), Nordrhein-Westfalen (North Rhine-Westphalia), Rheinland-Pfalz (Rhineland-Palatinate), Saarland, Sachsen (Saxony), Sachsen-Anhalt (Saxony-Anhalt), Schleswig-Holstein, Thueringen (Thuringia); note—Bayern, Sachsen, and Thueringen refer to themselves as free states (F reistaaten, singular—Freistaat), while Hamburg prides itself on being a Free and Hanseatic City (Freie und Hansestadt)

Independence: 18 January 1871 (establishment of the German Empire); divided into four zones of occupation (UK, US, USSR, and France) in 1945 following World War II; Federal Republic of Germany (FRG or West Germany) proclaimed on 23 May 1949 and included the former UK, US, and French zones; German Democratic Republic (GDR or East Germany) proclaimed on 7 October 1949 and included the former USSR zone; West Germany and East Germany unified on 3 October 1990; all four powers formally relinquished rights on 15 March 1991; notable earlier dates: 10 August 843 (Eastern Francia established from the

division of the Carolingian Empire); 2 February 962 (crowning of OTTOI, recognized as the first Holy Roman Emperor)

National holiday: Unity Day, 3 October (1990)

Constitution: previous 1919 (Weimar Constitution); latest drafted 10 to 23 August 1948, approved 12 May 1949, promulgated 23 May 1949, entered into force 24 May 1949; amended many times, last in 2012 (2016)

Legal system: civil law system

International law organization participation: accepts compulsory ICJ jurisdiction with reservations; accepts ICCt jurisdiction

Citizenship: *citizenship by birth:* no
citizenship by descent only: at least one parent must be a German citizen or a resident alien who has lived in Germany at least 8 years
dual citizenship recognized: yes, but requires prior permission from government
residency requirement for naturalization: 8 years

Suffrage: 18 years of age; universal

Executive branch: *chief of state:* President Joachim GAUCK (since 23 March 2012)

head of government: *Chancellor Angela MERKEL (since 22 November 2005)*
cabinet: Cabinet or Bundesminister (Federal Ministers) recommended by the chancellor, appointed by the president
elections/appointments: president indirectly elected for a 5-year term (eligible for a second term) by a Federal Convention consisting of the 630-member Federal Parliament (Bundestag) and 630 delegates indirectly elected by the state parliaments; election last held on 19 February 2012 (next to be held by June 2017); chancellor indirectly elected by absolute majority by the Federal Parliament for a 4-year term; Federal Parliament vote for chancellor last held on 17 December 2013 (next to be held following the general election, no later than autumn 2017)
election results: Joachim GAUCK elected president; Federal Convention vote count—Joachim GAUCK (independent) 991, Beate KLARSFELD (independent) 126, Olaf ROSE (National People's Union) 3; Angela MERKEL (CDU) reelected chancellor; Federal Parliament vote—462 for, 150 against, 49 abstentions

Legislative branch: *description:* bicameral Parliament or Parlament consists of the Federal Council or Bundesrat (69 seats; members appointed by each of the 16 state governments or landtags) and the Federal Diet or Bundestag (631 seats—total seats can vary each electoral term; approximately one-half of members directly elected in multi-seat constituencies by proportional representation vote and approximately one-half directly elected in single-seat constituencies by simple majority vote; members serve 4-year terms)
elections: Bundestag—last held on 22 September 2013 (next to be held no later than autumn 2017); most all postwar German governments have been coalitions; note—there are no elections for the Bundesrat; composition is determined by the

composition of the state-level governments; the composition of the Bundesrat has the potential to change any time one of the 16 states holds an election

election results: Bundestag—percent of vote by party—CDU/CSU 41.5%, SPD 25.7%, Left 8.6%, Greens 8.4%, FDP 4.8%, other 10.9%; seats by party—CDU/CSU 311, SPD 193, Left 64, Greens 63

Judicial branch: *highest court(s):* Federal Court of Justice (court consists of 127 judges including the court president, vice-presidents, presiding judges, and other judges, and organized into 25 Senates subdivided into 12 civil panels, 5 criminal panels, and 8 special panels; Federal Constitutional Court or Bundesverfassungsgericht (consists of 2 Senates each subdivided into 3 chambers, each with a chairman and 8 members)

judge selection and term of office: Federal Court of Justice judges selected by the Judges Election Committee, which consists of the Secretaries of Justice from each of the 16 federated States and 16 members appointed by the Federal Parliament; judges appointed by the president of Germany; judges serve until mandatory retirement at age 65; Federal Constitutional Court judges—one-half elected by the House of Representatives and one-half by the Senate; judges appointed for 12-year terms with mandatory retirement at age 68

subordinate courts: Federal Administrative Court; Federal Finance Court; Federal Labor Court; Federal Social Court; each of the 16 German states or Land has its own constitutional court and a hierarchy of ordinary (civil, criminal, family) and specialized (administrative, finance, labor, social) courts

Political parties and leaders: Alliance '90/Greens [Cem OEZDEMIR and Simone PETER]

Alternative for Germany or AFD [Frauke PETRY and Jorg MEUTHEN]

Christian Democratic Union or CDU [Angela MERKEL]

Christian Social Union or CSU [Horst SEEHOFER]

Free Democratic Party or FDP [Christian LINDNER]

Left Party or Die Linke [Katia KIPPING and Bernd RIEXINGER]

Social Democratic Party or SPD [Sigmar GABRIEL]

Political pressure groups and leaders: *other:* business associations and employers' organizations trade unions; religious, immigrant, expellee, and veterans groups

International organization participation: ADB (nonregional member), AfDB (nonregional member), Arctic Council (observer), Australia Group, BIS, BSEC (observer), CBSS, CD, CDB, CE, CERN, EAPC, EBRD, ECB, EIB, EITI (implementing country), EMU, ESA, EU, FAO, FATF, G-5, G-7, G-8, G-10, G-20, IADB, IAEA, IBRD, ICAO, ICC (national committees), ICCt, ICRM, IDA, IEA, IFAD, IFC, IFRCS, IGAD (partners), IHO, ILO, IMF, IMO, IMSO, Interpol, IOC, IOM, IPU, ISO, ITSO, ITU, ITUC (NGOs), MIGA,

MINURSO, MINUSMA, NATO, NEA, NSG, OAS (observer), OECD, OPCW, OSCE, Pacific Alliance (observer), Paris Club, PCA, Schengen Convention, SELEC (observer), SICA (observer), UN, UNAMID, UNCTAD, UNESCO, UNHCR, UNIDO, UNIFIL, UNMISS, UNRWA, UNWTO, UPU, WCO, WHO, WIPO, WMO, WTO, ZC

Diplomatic representation in the US: *chief of mission:* Ambassador Hans Peter WITTIG (since 21 May 2014)

chancery: 4645 Reservoir Road NW, Washington, DC 20007

telephone: [1] (202) 298-4000

FAX: [1] (202) 298-4249

consulate(s) general: Atlanta, Boston, Chicago, Houston, Los Angeles, Miami, New York, San Francisco

Diplomatic representation from the US: *chief of mission:* Ambassador John B. EMERSON (since 26 August 2013)

embassy: Pariser Platz 2

mailing address: Clayallee 170, 14191 Berlin

telephone: [49] (30) 8305-0

FAX: [49] (30) 8305-1215

consulate(s) general: Duesseldorf, Frankfurt am Main, Hamburg, Leipzig, Munich

Flag description: three equal horizontal bands of black (top), red, and gold; these colors have played an important role in German history and can be traced back to the medieval banner of the Holy Roman Emperor—a black eagle with red claws and beak on a gold field

National symbol(s): golden eagle; national colors: black, red, yellow

National anthem: *name:* "Das Lied der Deutschen" (Song of the Germans)

lyrics/music: August Heinrich HOFFMANN VON FALLERSLEBEN/Franz Joseph HAYDN

note: adopted 1922; the anthem, also known as "Deutschlandlied" (Song of Germany), was originally adopted for its connection to the March 1848 liberal revolution; following appropriation by the Nazis of the first verse, specifically the phrase, "Deutschland, Deutschland ueber alles" (Germany, Germany above all) to promote nationalism, it was banned after 1945; in 1952, its third verse was adopted by West Germany as its national anthem; in 1990, it became the national anthem for the reunited Germany

ECONOMY

Economy—overview: The German economy—the fifth largest economy in the world in PPP terms and Europe's largest—is a leading exporter of machinery, vehicles, chemicals, and household equipment and benefits from a highly skilled labor force. Like its Western European neighbors, Germany faces significant demographic challenges to sustained long-term growth. Low fertility rates and a large increase in net immigration are increasing pressure on the country's social welfare system and necessitate structural reforms. Reforms launched by the government of Chancellor Gerhard SCHROEDER (1998–2005), deemed necessary

to address chronically high unemployment and low average growth, contributed to strong growth and falling unemployment. These advances, as well as a government subsidized, reduced working hou r scheme, help explain the relatively modest increase in unemployment during the 2008–09 recession -the deepest since World War II. The new German Government introduced a minimum wage of about $11.60 (8.50 euros) per hour that took effect in 2015.

Stimulus and stabilization efforts initiated in 2008 and 2009 and tax cuts introduced in Chancellor Angela MERKEL's second term increased Germany's total budget deficit—including federal, state, and municipal -to 4.1% in 2010, but slower spending and higher tax revenues reduced the deficit to 0.8% in 2011 and in 2015 Germany reached a budget surplus of 0.9%. Aconstitutional amendment approved in 2009 limits the federal government to structural deficits of no more than 0.35% of GDP per annum as of 2016, though the target was already reached in 2012.

The German economy suffers from low levels of investment, and a government plan to invest 15 billion euros during 2016–18, largely in infrastructure, is intended to spur needed private investment. Following the March 2011 Fukushima nuclear disaster, Chancellor Angela MERKEL announced in May 2011 that eight of the country's 17 nuclear reactors would be shut down immediately and the remaining plants would close by 2022. Germany plans to replace nuclear power largely with renewable energy, which accounted for 27.8% of gross electricity consumption in 2014, up from 9% in 2000. Before the shutdown of the eight reactors, Germany relied on nuclear power for 23% of its electricity generating capacity and 46% of its base-load electricity production. Domestic consumption, bolstered by low energy prices and a weak euro, are likely to drive German GDP growth again in 2016.

GDP (purchasing power parity): $3.841 trillion (2015 est.)
$3.786 trillion (2014 est.)
$3.727 trillion (2013 est.)
note: data are in 2015 US dollars
country comparison to the world: 6

GDP (official exchange rate): $3.358 trillion (2015 est.)

GDP—real growth rate: 1.5% (2015 est.)
1.6% (2014 est.)
0.4% (2013 est.)
country comparison to the world: 153

GDP—per capita (PPP): $46,900 (2015 est.)
$46,600 (2014 est.)
$46,100 (2013 est.)
note: data are in 2015 US dollars
country comparison to the world: 28

Gross national saving: 27.3% of GDP (2015 est.)
26.6% of GDP (2014 est.)
26.1% of GDP (2013 est.)
country comparison to the world: 36

GDP—composition, by end use:
household consumption: 54.2%
government consumption: 19.1%

investment in fixed capital: 20.2%
investment in inventories: -0.7%
exports of goods and services: 46.1%
imports of goods and services: -38.9% (2015 est.)

GDP—composition, by sector of origin:
agriculture: 0.7%
industry: 30.2%
services: 69.1% (2015 est.)

Agriculture—products: potatoes, wheat, barley, sugar beets, fruit, cabbages; milk products; cattle, pigs, poultry

Industries: among the world's largest and most technologically advanced producers of iron, steel, coal, cement, chemicals, machinery, vehicles, machine tools, electronics, automobiles, food and beverages, shipbuilding, textiles

Industrial production growth rate: 1.5% (2015 est.)
country comparison to the world: 133

Labor force: 45.04 million (2015 est.)
country comparison to the world: 15

Labor force—by occupation: *agriculture:* 1.6%
industry: 24.6%
services: 73.8% (2011)

Unemployment rate: 4.8% (2015 est.)
5% (2014 est.)
country comparison to the world: 48

Population below poverty line: 15.5% (2010 est.)

Household income or consumption by percentage share: *lowest:* 10%: 3.6%
highest: 10%: 24% (2000)

Distribution of family income—Gini index: 27 (2006)
30 (1994)
country comparison to the world: 133

Budget: *revenues:* $1.515 trillion
expenditures: $1.484 trillion (2015 est.)
Taxes and other revenues: 45% of GDP (2015 est.)
country comparison to the world: 24

Budget surplus (+) or deficit (–): 0.9% of GDP (2015 est.)
country comparison to the world: 20

Public debt: 71.7% of GDP (2015 est.)
74.3% of GDP (2014 est.)

note: general government gross debt is defined in the Maastricht Treaty as consolidated general government gross debt at nominal value, outstanding at the end of the year in the following categories of government liabilities (as defined in ESA95): currency and deposits (AF.2), securities other than shares excluding financial derivatives (AF.3, excluding AF.34), and loans (AF.4); the general government sector comprises the sub-sectors of central government, state government, local government and social security funds; the series are presented as a percentage of GDP and in millions of euros; GDP used as a denominator is the gross domestic product at current market prices; data expressed in national currency are converted into euros using end-of-year exchange rates provided by the European Central Bank
country comparison to the world: 45

Fiscal year: calendar year

Inflation rate (consumer prices): 0.1% (2015 est.)
0.8% (2014 est.)
country comparison to the world: 46

Central bank discount rate: 0.05%
(31 December 2013) 0.3% (31 December 2010)
note: this is the European Central Bank's rate on the marginal lending facility, which offers overnight credit to banks in the euro area
country comparison to the world: 146

Commercial bank prime lending rate: 1.7% (31 December 2015 est.)
2.47% (31 December 2014 est.)
country comparison to the world: 182

Stock of narrow money: $1.936 trillion (31 December 2015 est.)
$1.841 trillion (31 December 2014 est.)
note: see entry for the European Union for money supply for the entire euro area; the European Central Bank (ECB) controls monetary policy for the 18 members of the Economic and Monetary Union (EMU); individual members of the EMU do not control the quantity of money circulating within their own borders
country comparison to the world: 5

Stock of broad money: $4.347 trillion (31 December 2014 est.)
$4.451 trillion (31 December 2013 est.)
country comparison to the world: 5

Stock of domestic credit: $5.036 trillion (31 December 2015 est.)
$4.976 trillion (31 December 2014 est.)
country comparison to the world: 5

Market value of publicly traded shares: $1.486 trillion (31 December 2012 est.)
$1.184 trillion (31 December 2011)
$1.43 trillion (31 December 2010 est.)
country comparison to the world: 9

Current account balance: $285.2 billion (2015 est.)
$282.9 billion (2014 est.)
country comparison to the world: 3

Exports: $1.292 trillion (2015 est.)
$1.492 trillion (2014 est.)
country comparison to the world: 4

Exports—commodities: motor vehicles, machinery, chemicals, computer and electronic products, electrical equipment, pharmaceuticals, metals, transport equipment, foodstuffs, textiles, rubber and plastic products

Exports—partners: US 9.6%, France 8.6%, UK 7.5%, Netherlands 6.6%, China 6%, Italy 4.9%, Austria 4.8%, Poland 4.4%, Switzerland 4.2% (2015)

Imports: $983.9 billion (2015 est.)
$1.188 trillion (2014 est.)
country comparison to the world: 4

Imports—commodities: machinery, data processing equipment, vehicles, chemicals, oil and gas, metals, electric equipment, pharmaceuticals, foodstuffs, agricultural products

Imports—partners: Netherlands 13.7%, France 7.6%, China 7.3%, Belgium 6%, Italy 5.2%,

Poland 5%, US 4.7%, Czech Republic 4.5%, UK 4.2%, Austria 4.2%, Switzerland 4.2% (2015)

Reserves of foreign exchange and gold: $192.8 billion (31 December 2014 est.)
$198.2 billion (31 December 2013 est.)
country comparison to the world: 14

Debt—external: $5.597 trillion (31 December 2014 est.)
$5.998 trillion (31 December 2013 est.)
country comparison to the world: 4

Stock of direct foreign investment—at home: $1.442 trillion (31 December 2015 est.)
$1.416 trillion (31 December 2014 est.)
country comparison to the world: 6

Stock of direct foreign investment—abroad: $2.068 trillion (31 December 2015 est.)
$1.986 trillion (31 December 2014 est.)
country comparison to the world: 3

Exchange rates: euros (EUR) per US dollar—
0.885 (2015 est.)
0.7525 (2014 est.)
0.7634 (2013 est.)
0.7752 (2012 est.)
0.7185 (2011 est.)

ENERGY

Electricity—production: 585.2 billion kWh (2012 est.)
country comparison to the world: 8

Electricity—consumption: 540.1 billion kWh (2012 est.)
country comparison to the world: 7

Electricity—exports: 71.43 billion kWh (2013 est.)
country comparison to the world: 2

Electricity—imports: 39.16 billion kWh (2013 est.)
country comparison to the world: 5

Electricity—installed generating capacity: 177.1 million kW (2012 est.)
country comparison to the world: 7

Electricity—from fossil fuels: 45.7% of total installed capacity (2012 est.)
country comparison to the world: 155

Electricity—from nuclear fuels: 6.8% of total installed capacity (2012 est.)
country comparison to the world: 23

Electricity—from hydroelectric plants: 2.5% of total installed capacity (2012 est.)
country comparison to the world: 135

Electricity—from other renewable sources: 41.2% of total installed capacity (2012 est.)
country comparison to the world: 2

Crude oil—production: 48,830 bbl/day (2014 est.)
country comparison to the world: 58

Crude oil—exports: 670.7 bbl/day (2013 est.)
country comparison to the world: 86

Crude oil—imports: 1.83 million bbl/day (2013 est.)
country comparison to the world: 6

Crude oil—proved reserves: 226.8 million bbl (1 January 2015 est.)

country comparison to the world: 57

Refined petroleum products—production: 2.15 million bbl/day (2013 est.)
country comparison to the world: 9

Refined petroleum products—consumption: 2.399 million bbl/day (2014 est.)
country comparison to the world: 10

Refined petroleum products—exports: 407,300 bbl/day (2013 est.)
country comparison to the world: 19

Refined petroleum products—imports: 734,800 bbl/day (2013 est.)
country comparison to the world: 9

Natural gas—production: 10.06 billion cu m (2014 est.)
country comparison to the world: 44

Natural gas—consumption: 77.48 billion cu m (2014 est.)
country comparison to the world: 9

Natural gas—Exports: 19.24 billion cu m (2014 est.)
country comparison to the world: 15

Natural gas—imports: 86.84 billion cu m (2014 est.)
country comparison to the world: 3

Natural gas—proved reserves: 116 billion cu m (1 January 2014 est.)
country comparison to the world: 51

Carbon dioxide emissions from consumption of energy: 788.3 million Mt (2012 est.)
country comparison to the world: 7

COMMUNICATIONS

Telephones—fixed lines: *total subscriptions:* 47.02 million
subscriptions per 100 inhabitants: 58 (2014 est.)
country comparison to the world: 5

Telephones—mobile cellular: *total:* 99.5 million
subscriptions per 100 inhabitants: 123 (2014 est.)
country comparison to the world: 15

Telephone system: *general assessment:* one of the world's most technologically advanced telecommunications systems; as a result of intensive capital expenditures since reunification, the formerly backward system of the eastern part of the country, dating back to World War II, has been modernized and integrated with that of the western part
domestic: extensive system of automatic telephone exchanges connected by modern networks of fiber-optic cable, coaxial cable, microwave radio relay, and a domestic satellite system; cellular telephone service is widely available, expanding rapidly, and includes roaming service to many foreign countries
international: country code—49; Germany's international service is excellent worldwide, consisting of extensive land and undersea cable facilities as well as earth stations in the Inmarsat, Intelsat, Eutelsat, and Intersputnik satellite systems (2011)

Broadcast media: a mixture of publicly operated and privately owned TV and radio stations; national and regional public broadcasters compete with nearly 400 privately owned national and regional TV stations; more than 90% of households have cable or satellite TV; hundreds of radio stations including multiple national radio networks, regional radio networks, and a large number of local radio stations (2008)
Radio broadcast stations: AM 51, FM 787, shortwave 4 (1998)
Television broadcast stations: 373 (plus 8,042 repeaters) (1995)

Internet country code: .de

Internet hosts: 20.043 million (2012)
country comparison to the world: 6

Internet users: *total:* 70.3 million
percent of population: 86.8% (2014 est.)
country comparison to the world: 8

TRANSPORTATION

Airports: 539 (2013)
country comparison to the world: 13

Airports—with paved runways: *total:* 318
over 3,047 m: 14
2,438 to 3,047 m: 49
1,524 to 2,437 m: 60
914 to 1,523 m: 70
under 914 m: 125 (2013)

Airports—with unpaved runways: *total:* 221
1,524 to 2,437 m: 1
914 to 1,523 m: 35
under 914 m: 185 (2013)

Heliports: 23 (2013)

Pipelines: condensate 37 km; gas 26,985 km; oil 2,826 km; refined products 4,479 km; water 8 km (2013)

Railways: *total:* 43,468.3 km
standard gauge: 43,209.3 km 1.435-m gauge (19,973 km electrified)
narrow gauge: 220 km 1.000-m gauge (79 km electrified); 15 km 0.900-m gauge; 24 km 0.750-m gauge (2014)
country comparison to the world: 6

Roadways: *total:* 645,000 km
paved: 645,000 km (includes 12,800 km of expressways)
note: includes local roads (2010)
country comparison to the world: 12

Waterways: 7,467 km (Rhine River carries most goods; Main-Danube Canal links North Sea and Black Sea) (2012)
country comparison to the world: 18

Merchant marine: *total:* 427
by type: barge carrier 2, bulk carrier 6, cargo 51, carrier 1, chemical tanker 15, container 298, liquefied gas 6, passenger 4, passenger/cargo 24, petroleum tanker 10, refrigerated cargo 3, roll on/roll off 6, vehicle carrier 1
foreign-owned: 6 (Finland 3, Netherlands 1, Switzerland 2)
registered in other countries: 3,420 (Antigua and Barbuda 1094, Australia 2, Bahamas 30, Bermuda 14, Brazil 6, Bulgaria 12, Burma 1, Cayman Islands 3, Cook Islands 1, Curacao 25, Cyprus 192, Denmark 9, Dominica 5, Estonia 1, France 1, Gibraltar 123, Hong Kong 10, Isle of Man 56, Jamaica 10, Liberia 1185, Luxembourg 9, Malta 135, Marshall Islands 248, Morocco 1, Netherlands 86, NZ 2, Panama 24, Papua New Guinea 1, Philippines 2, Portugal 14, Saint Vincent and the Grenadines 3, Singapore 32, Slovakia 3, Spain 4, Sri Lanka 8, Sweden 3, UK 59, US 5, Venezuela 1) (2010)
country comparison to the world: 24

Ports and terminals: *major seaport(s):* Baltic Sea—Rostock; North Sea—Wilhelmshaven
river port(s): Bremen (Weser); Bremerhaven (Geeste); Duisburg, Karlsruhe, Neuss-Dusseldorf (Rhine); Brunsbuttel, Hamburg (Elbe); Lubeck (Wakenitz)
oil terminal(s): Brunsbuttel Canal terminals
container port(s): Bremen/Bremerhaven (5,915,487), Hamburg (9,014,165) (2011)
LNG terminal(s) (import): Hamburg

MILITARY AND SECURITY

Military branches: Federal Armed Forces (Bundeswehr): Army (Heer), Navy (Deutsche Marine, includes naval air arm), Air Force (Luftwaffe), Joint Support Services (Streitkraeftebasis, SKB), Central Medical Service (Zentraler Sanitaetsdienst, ZSanDstBw) (2013)

Military service age and obligation: 17–23 years of age for male and female voluntary military service; conscription ended 1 July 2011; service obligation 8–23 months or 12 years; women have been eligible for voluntary service in all military branches and positions since 2001 (2013)

Military expenditures: 1.18% of GDP (2015)
1.35% of GDP (2012)
1.34% of GDP (2011)
1.35% of GDP (2010)
country comparison to the world: 74

TRANSNATIONAL ISSUES

Disputes—international: none

Refugees and internally displaced persons: *refugees (country of origin):* 41,167 (Iraq); 40,994 (Syria); 27,814 (Afghanistan); 22,242 (Turkey); 18,814 (Iran); 9,294 (Serbia and Kosovo) (2014)
stateless persons: 12,569 (2015)

Illicit drugs: source of precursor chemicals for South American cocaine processors; transshipment point for and consumer of Southwest Asian heroin, Latin American cocaine, and European-produced synthetic drugs; major financial center

GHANA

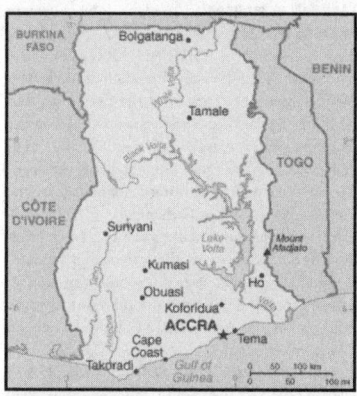

INTRODUCTION

Background: Formed from the merger of the British colony of the Gold Coast and the Togoland trust territory, Ghana in 1957 became the first sub-Saharan country in colonial Africa to gain its independence. Ghana endured a long series of coups before Lt. Jerry RAWLINGS took power in 1981 and banned political parties. After approving a new constitution and restoring multiparty politics in 1992, RAWLINGS won presidential elections in 1992 and 1996 but was constitutionally prevented from running for a third term in 2000. John KUFUOR succeeded him and was reelected in 2004. John Atta MILLS won the 2008 presidential election and took over as head of state, but he died in July 2012 and was constitutionally succeeded by his vice president, John Dramani MAHAMA, who subsequently won the December 2012 presidential election.

GEOGRAPHY

Location: Western Africa, bordering the Gulf of Guinea, between Cote d'I voire and Togo

Geographic coordinates: 8 00 N, 2 00 W

Map references: Africa

Area: *total:* 238,533 sq km
land: 227,533 sq km
water: 11,000 sq km
country comparison to the world: 82

Area—comparative: slightly smaller than Oregon

Land boundaries: *total:* 2,420 km
border countries (3): Burkina Faso 602 km, Cote d'Ivoire 720 km, Togo 1,098 km

Coastline: 539 km

Maritime claims: *territorial sea:* 12 nm
contiguous zone: 24 nm
exclusive economic zone: 200 nm
continental shelf: 200 nm

Climate: tropical; warm and comparatively dry along southeast coast; hot and humid in southwest; hot and dry in north

Terrain: mostly low plains with dissected plateau in south-central area

Elevation: *mean elevation:* 190 m

elevation extremes: *lowest point:* Atlantic Ocean 0 m
highest point: Mount Afadjato 885 m

Natural resources: gold, timber, industrial diamonds, bauxite, manganese, fish, rubber, hydropower, petroleum, silver, salt, limestone

Land use: *agricultural land:* 69.1%
arable land: 20.7%
permanent crops: 11.9%
permanent pasture: 36.5%
forest: 21.2%
other: 9.7% (2011 est.)

Irrigated land: 340 sq km (2012)

Total renewable water resources: 53.2 cu km (2011)

Freshwater withdrawal (domestic/industrial/agricultural): *total:* 0.98 cu km/yr (24%/10%/66%)
per capita: 48.82 cu m/yr (2000)

Natural hazards: dry, dusty, northeastern harmattan winds from January to March; droughts

Environment—current issues: recurrent drought in north severely affects agricultural activities; deforestation; overgrazing; soil erosion; poaching and habitat destruction threatens wildlife populations; water pollution; inadequate supplies of potable water

Environment—international agreements: *party to:* Biodiversity, Climate Change, Climate Change-Kyoto Protocol, Desertification, Endangered Species, Environmental Modification, Hazardous Wastes, Law of the Sea, Ozone Layer Protection, Ship Pollution, Tropical Timber 83, Tropical Timber 94, Wetlands
signed, but not ratified: Marine Life Conservation

Geography—note: Lake Volta is the world's largest artificial lake (manmade reservoir) by surface area (8,482 sq km; 3,275 sq mi); the lake was created following the completion of the Akosombo Dam in 1965, which holds back the White Volta and Black Volta Rivers

PEOPLE AND SOCIETY

Nationality: *noun:* Ghanaian(s)
adjective: Ghanaian

Ethnic groups: Akan 47.5%, Mole-Dagbon 16.6%, Ewe 13.9%, Ga-Dangme 7.4%, Gurma 5.7%, Guan 3.7%, Grusi 2.5%, Mande 1.1%, other 1.4% (2010 est.)

Languages: Asante 16%, Ewe 14%, Fante 11.6%, Boron (Brong) 4.9%, Dagomba 4.4%, Dangme 4.2%, Dagarte (Dagaba) 3.9%, Kokomba 3.5%, Akyem 3.2%, Ga 3.1%, other 31.2%
note: English is the official language (2010 est.)

Religions: Christian 71.2% (Pentecostal/Charismatic 28.3%, Protestant 18.4%, Catholic 13.1%, other 11.4%), Muslim 17.6%, traditional 5.2%, other 0.8%, none 5.2% (2010 est.)

Population: 26,327,649
note: estimates for this country explicitly take into account the effects of excess mortality due to AIDS; this can result in lower life expectancy, higher infant mortality, higher death rates, lower population growth rates, and changes in the distribution of population by age and sex than would otherwise be expected (July 2015 est.)
country comparison to the world: 49

Age structure: *0–14 years:* 38.38% (male 5,076,131/female 5,027,960)
15–24 years: 18.69% (male 2,449,026/female 2,472,756)
25–54 years: 33.95% (male 4,338,197/female 4,598,796)
55–64 years: 4.84% (male 619,516/female 654,720)
65 years and over: 4.14% (male 505,056/female 585,491) (2015 est.)

Dependency ratios: *total dependency ratio:* 73%
youth dependency ratio: 67.2%
elderly dependency ratio: 5.9%
potential support ratio: 17% (2015 est.)

Median age: *total:* 20.9 years
male: 20.5 years
female: 21.4 years (2015 est.)
country comparison to the world: 185

Population growth rate: 2.18% (2015 est.)
country comparison to the world: 41

Birth rate: 31.09 births/1,000 population (2015 est.)
country comparison to the world: 38

Death rate: 7.22 deaths/1,000 population (2015 est.)
country comparison to the world: 123

Net migration rate: -2.02 migrant(s)/1,000 population (2015 est.)
country comparison to the world: 167

Urbanization: *urban population:* 54% of total population (2015)
rate of urbanization: 3.4% annual rate of change (2010–15 est.)

Major urban areas—population: Kumasi 2.599 million; ACCRA (capital) 2.277 million (2015)

Sex ratio: *at birth:* 1.03 male(s)/female
0–14 years: 1.01 male(s)/female
15–24 years: 0.99 male(s)/female
25–54 years: 0.94 male(s)/female
55–64 years: 0.95 male(s)/female
65 years and over: 0.86 male(s)/female
total population: 0.97 male(s)/female (2015 est.)

Mother's mean age at first birth: 22.6
note: median age at first birth among women 25–29 (2014 est.)

Maternal mortality rate: 319 deaths/100,000 live births (2015 est.)
country comparison to the world: 32

Infant mortality rate: *total:* 37.37 deaths/1,000 live births
male: 41.39 deaths/1,000 live births
female: 33.23 deaths/1,000 live births (2015 est.)
country comparison to the world: 59

Life expectancy at birth: *total population:* 66.18 years
male: 63.76 years
female: 68.66 years (2015 est.)
country comparison to the world: 172

Total fertility rate: 4.06 children born/woman (2015 est.)
country comparison to the world: 36

Contraceptive prevalence rate: 19.5% (2013)

Health expenditures: 5.4% of GDP (2013)
country comparison to the world: 133

Physicians density: 0.1 physicians/1,000 population (2010)

Hospital bed density: 0.9 beds/1,000 population (2011)

Drinking water source:
improved:
urban: 92.6% of population
rural: 84% of population
total: 88.7% of population
unimproved:
urban: urban: 7.4% of population
rural: 16% of population
total: 11.3% of population (2015 est.)

Sanitation facility access:
improved:
urban: 20.2% of population
rural: 8.6% of population
total: 14.9% of population
unimproved:
urban: urban: 79.8% of population
rural: 91.4% of population
total: 85.1% of population(2015 est.)

HIV/AIDS—adult prevalence rate: 1.47% (2014 est.)
country comparison to the world: 34

HIV/AIDS—people living with HIV/AIDS: 250,200 (2014 est.)
country comparison to the world: 23

HIV/AIDS—deaths: 9,200 (2014 est.)
country comparison to the world: 26

Major infectious diseases: *degree of risk:* very high
food or waterborne diseases: bacterial and protozoal diarrhea, hepatitis A, and typhoid fever
vectorborne diseases: malaria, dengue fever, and yellow fever
water contact disease: schistosomiasis respiratory disease: meningococcal meningitis
animal contact disease: rabies
note: highly pathogenic H5N1 avian influenza has been identified in this country; it poses a negligible risk with extremely rare cases possible among US citizens who have close contact with birds (2013)
Obesity—adult prevalence rate: 10.9% (2014)
country comparison to the world: 140

Children under the age of 5 years underweight: 11% (2014)

country comparison to the world: 55

Education expenditures: 6% of GDP (2013)
country comparison to the world: 13

Literacy: *definition:* age 15 and over can read and write
total population: 76.6%
male: 82%
female: 71.4% (2015 est.)

School life expectancy (primary to tertiary education): *total:* 11 years
male: 12 years
female: 11 years (2014)

Child labor—children ages 5–14: *total number:* 1,806,750
percentage: 34% (2006 est.)

Unemployment, youth ages 15–24: *total:* 11.2%
male: 10.2%
female: 12% (2010 est.)

GOVERNMENT

Country name: *conventional long form:* Republic of Ghana
conventional short form: Ghana
former: Gold Coast
etymology: named for the medieval West African kingdom of the same name, but whose location was actually further north than the modern country

Government type: presidential republic

Capital: *name:* Accra
geographic coordinates: 5 33 N, 0 13 W
time difference: UTC 0 (5 hours ahead of Washington, DC, during Standard Time)

Administrative divisions: 10 regions; Ashanti, Brong-Ahafo, Central, Eastern, Greater Accra, Northern, Upper East, Upper West, Volta, Western

Independence: 6 March 1957 (from the UK)

National holiday: Independence Day, 6 March (1957)

Constitution: several previous; latest drafted 31 March 1992, approved and promulgated 28 April 1992, entered into force 7 January 1993; amended 1996 (2016)

Legal system: mixed system of English common law and customary law

International law organization participation: has not submitted an ICJ jurisdiction declaration; accepts ICCt jurisdiction

Citizenship: *citizenship by birth:* no
citizenship by descent only: at least one parent or grandparent must be a citizen of Ghana
dual citizenship recognized: yes
residency requirement for naturalization: 5 years

Suffrage: 18 years of age; universal

Executive branch: *chief of state:* President John Dramani MAHAMA (since 24 July 2012); Vice President Kwesi Bekoe AMISSAH-ARTHUR (since 6 August 2012); note—President MAHAMA assumed the presidency after the death of President John Atta MILLS and

subsequently won the December 2012 presidential election; the president is both chief of state and head of government

head of government: President John Dramani MAHAMA (since 24 July 2012); Vice President Kwesi Bekoe AMISSAH-ARTHUR (since 6 August 2012); note—President MAHAMA assumed the presidency after the death of President John Atta MILLS and subsequently won the December 2012 presidential election; the president is both chief of state and head of government
cabinet: Council of Ministers; nominated by the president, approved by Parliament
elections/appointments: president and vice president directly elected on the same ballot by absolute majority popular vote in 2 rounds if needed for a 4-year term (eligible for a second term); election last held on 8 December 2012 (next to be held on 7 November 2016)
election results: John Dramani MAHAMA elected president; percent of vote—John Dramani MAHAMA (NDC) 50.7%, Nana Addo Dankwa AKUFO-ADDO (NPP) 47.7%, other 1.6%

Legislative branch: *description:* unicameral Parliament (275 seats; members directly elected in single-seat constituencies by simple majority vote to serve 4-year terms)
elections: last held on 7–8 December 2012 (next to be held on 7 November 2016)
election results: percent of vote by party—NPP 47.5%, NDC 46.4%, PNC 0.6%, independent 2.5%, other 3.0%; seats by party—NDC 150, NPP 120, PNC 1, independent 3, other 1

Judicial branch: *highest court(s):* Supreme Court (consists of a chief justice and 12 justices)
judge selection and term of office: chief justice appointed by the president in consultation with the Council of State (a small advisory body of prominent citizens) and with the approval of Parliament; other justices appointed by the president upon the advice of the Judicial Council (an 18-member independent body of judicial, military and police officials, and presidential nominees) and on the advice of the Council of State; justices can retire at age 60, with compulsory retirement at age 70
subordinate courts: Court of Appeal; High Court; Circuit Court; District Court; regional tribunals

Political parties and leaders: Convention People's Party or CPP [Samia NKRUMAH]
National Democratic Congress or NDC [John Dramani MAHAMA]
New Patriotic Party or NPP [Nana AFUKO-ADDO]
People's National Convention or PNC [Hassan AYARIGA]
note: listed are four of the more popular political parties as of December 2012; there are more than 20 registered parties

Political pressure groups and leaders: Christian Aid (water rights)
Committee for Joint Action or CJA (social and economic issues)

National Coalition Against the Privatization of Water or CAP (water rights) Oxfam (water rights) Public Citizen (water rights)

Students Coalition Against EPA [Kwabena Ososukene OKAI] (education reform)

Third World Network (social and economic issues)

International organization participation: ACP, AfDB, AU, C, ECOWAS, EITI (compliant country), FAO, G-24, G-77, IAEA, IBRD, ICAO, ICC (national committees), ICCt, ICRM, IDA, IFAD, IFC, IFRCS, ILO, IMF, IMO, IMSO, Interpol, IOC, IOM, IPU, ISO, ITSO, ITU, ITUC (NGOs), MIGA, MINURSO, MINUSMA, MONUSCO, NAM, OAS (observer), OIF, OPCW, UN, UNAMID, UNCTAD, UNESCO, UNHCR, UNIDO, UNIFIL, UNISFA, UNMIL, UNMISS, UNOCI, UNWTO, UPU, WCO, WFT U (NGO s), WHO, WIPO, WMO, WTO

Diplomatic representation in the US: *chief of mission:* Ambassador Martha Ama Akyaa POBEE (since 31 July 2015)

chancery: 3512 International Drive NW, Washington, DC 20008

telephone: [1] (202) 686-4520

FAX: [1] (202) 686-4527

consulate(s) general: New York

Diplomatic representation from the US: *chief of mission:* Ambassador Robert P. JACKSON (since 4 February 2016)

embassy: 24 Fourth Circular Rd., Cantonments, Accra

mailing address: P.O. Box 194, Accra

telephone: [233] 30-2741-000

FAX: [233] 30-2741-389

Flag description: three equal horizontal bands of red (top), yellow, and green, with a large black five-pointed star centered in the yellow band; red symbolizes the blood shed for independence, yellow represents the country's mineral wealth, while green stands for its forests and natural wealth; the black star is said to be the lodestar of African freedom

note: uses the popular Pan-African colors of Ethiopia; similar to the flag of Bolivia, which has a coat of arms centered in the yellow band

National symbol(s): black star, golden eagle; national colors: red, yellow, green, black

National anthem: *name:* "God Bless Our Homeland Ghana"

lyrics/music: unknown/Philip GBEHO

note: music adopted 1957, lyrics adopted 1966; the lyrics were changed twice, in 1966 when a republic was declared and after a 1966 coup

ECONOMY

Economy—overview: Ghana's economy was strengthened by a quarter century of relatively sound management, a competitive business enironment, and sustained reductions in poverty levels, but in recent years has suffered the consequences of loose fiscal policy, high budget and current account deficits, and a depreciating currency. Ghana has a market-based economy with relatively few policy barriers to trade and investment in comparison with other countries in the region, and Ghana is well-endowed with natural resources. Agriculture accounts for nearly one-quarter of GDP and employs more than half of the workforce, mainly small landholders. The services sector accounts for about half of GDP. Gold and cocoa exports, and individual remittances, are major sources of foreign exchange. Expansion of Ghana's nascent oil industry has boosted economic growth, but the recent oil price crash has reduced by half Ghana's 2015 anticipated oil revenue. Production at Jubilee, Ghana's offshore oilfield, began in mid-December 2010 and currently produces roughly 110,000 barrels per day. The country's first gas processing plant at Atubao is also producing natural gas from the Jubilee field, providing power to several of Ghana's thermal power plants. As of 2015, the biggest single economic issue facing Ghana is the lack of consistent electricity. While the MAHAMA administration is taking steps to improve the situation, little progress has been made. Ghana signed a $920 million extended credit facility with the IMF in April 2015 to help it address its growing economic crisis. The IMF fiscal targets will require Ghana to reduce the fiscal deficit by cutting subsidies, decreasing the bloated public sector wage bill, strengthening revenue administration, and increasing revenues. The challenge for Ghana will come as the MAHAMA Administration approaches the 2016 election cycle facing public dissatisfaction in the midst of econom ic austerity.

GDP (purchasing power parity): $114.7 billion (2015 est.)

$110.8 billion (2014 est.)

$106.6 billion (2013 est.)

note: data are in 2015 US dollars

country comparison to the world: 82

GDP (official exchange rate): $36.04 billion (2015 est.)

GDP—real growth rate: 3.5% (2015 est.)

4% (2014 est.)

7.3% (2013 est.)

country comparison to the world: 85

GDP—per capita (PPP): $4,300 (2015 est.)

$4,200 (2014 est.)

$4,200 (2013 est.)

note: data are in 2015 US dollars

country comparison to the world: 175

Gross national saving: 15.6% of GDP (2015 est.)

15.2% of GDP (2014 est.)

13.5% of GDP (2013 est.)

country comparison to the world: 111

GDP—composition, by end use:

household consumption: 65.4%

government consumption: 18%

investment in fixed capital: 26.2%

investment in inventories: 0.9%

exports of goods and services: 35%

imports of goods and services: -45.5% (2015 est.)

GDP—composition, by sector of origin:

agriculture: 20.7%

industry: 27.7%

services: 51.6% (2015 est.)

Agriculture—products: cocoa, rice, cassava (manioc, tapioca), peanuts, corn, shea nuts, bananas; timber

Industries: mining, lumbering, light manufacturing, aluminum smelting, food processing, cement, small commercial ship building, petroleum

Industrial production growth rate: 4.5% (2015 est.)

country comparison to the world: 42

Labor force: 11.54 million (2015 est.)

country comparison to the world: 51

Labor force—by occupation: *agriculture:* 44.7%

industry: 14.4%

services: 40.9% (2013 est.)

Unemployment rate: 5.2% (2013 est.)

country comparison to the world: 56

Population below poverty line: 24.2% (2013 est.)

Household income or consumption by percentage share: *lowest:* 10%: 2%

highest: 10%: 32.8% (2006)

Distribution of family income—Gini index: 42.3 (2012–13)

41.9 (2005–06)

country comparison to the world: 54

Budget: *revenues:* $8.123 billion

expenditures: $10.83 billion (2015 est.)

Taxes and other revenues: 21.6% of GDP (2015 est.)

country comparison to the world: 144

Budget surplus (+) or deficit (–): -7.2% of GDP (2015 est.)

country comparison to the world: 193

Public debt: 76% of GDP (2015 est.)

70.9% of GDP (2014 est.)

country comparison to the world: 35

Fiscal year: calendar year

Inflation rate (consumer prices): 17.2% (2015 est.)

15.5% (2014 est.)

country comparison to the world: 219

Central bank discount rate: 21% (31 December 2014)

16% (31 December 2013)

country comparison to the world: 4

Commercial bank prime lending rate: 28.9% (31 December 2015 est.)

27% (31 December 2014 est.)

country comparison to the world: 5

Stock of narrow money: $5.751 billion (31 December 2015 est.)

$5.64 billion (31 December 2014 est.)

country comparison to the world: 95

Stock of broad money: $12.2 billion (31 December 2015 est.)

$11.69 billion (31 December 2014 est.)

country comparison to the world: 103

Stock of domestic credit: $12.91 billion (31 December 2015 est.)

$13.82 billion (31 December 2014 est.)

country comparison to the world: 96

Market value of publicly traded shares: $3.465 billion (31 December 2012 est.)
$3.097 billion (31 December 2011)
$3.531 billion (31 December 2010 est.)
country comparison to the world: 93

Current account balance: -$2.99 billion (2015 est.)
-$3.698 billion (2014 est.)
country comparison to the world: 158

Exports: $10.75 billion (2015 est.)
$13.22 billion (2014 est.)
country comparison to the world: 86

Exports—commodities: oil, gold, cocoa, timber, tuna, bauxite, aluminum, manganese ore, diamonds, horticultural products

Exports—partners: India 25.2%, Switzerland 12.2%, China 10.6%, France 5.7% (2015)

Imports: $13.42 billion (2015 est.)
$14.57 billion (2014 est.)
country comparison to the world: 89

Imports—commodities: capital equipment, refined petroleum, foodstuffs

Imports—partners: China 32.6%, Nigeria 14%, Netherlands 5.5%, US 5.4% (2015)

Reserves of foreign exchange and gold: $5.617 billion (31 December 2015 est.)
$5.324 billion (31 December 2014 est.)
country comparison to the world: 91

Debt—external: $17.2 billion (31 December 2014 est.)
$15.83 billion (31 December 2013 est.)
country comparison to the world: 93

Stock of direct foreign investment—at home: $19.85 billion (31 December 2013 est.)
$118 million (31 December 2012 est.)
country comparison to the world: 77

Stock of direct foreign investment—abroad: $16.62 billion (31 December 2013 est.)
$109 million (31 December 2012 est.)
country comparison to the world: 55

Exchange rates: cedis (GHC) per US dollar—
3.73 (2015 est.)
2.895 (2014 est.)
2.895 (2013 est.)
1.8 (2012 est.)
1.512 (2011 est.)

ENERGY

Electricity—production: 12.87 billion kWh (2013 est.)
country comparison to the world: 90

Electricity—consumption: 10.58 billion kWh (2013 est.)
country comparison to the world: 88

Electricity—exports: 122 million kWh (2013 est.)
country comparison to the world: 77

Electricity—imports: 27 million kWh (2013 est.)
country comparison to the world: 106

Electricity—installed generating capacity: 2.847 million kW (2015 est.)
country comparison to the world: 96

Electricity—from fossil fuels: 45.4% of total installed capacity (2012 est.)
country comparison to the world: 156

Electricity—from nuclear fuels: 0% of total installed capacity (2012 est.)
country comparison to the world: 98

Electricity—from hydroelectric plants: 54.6% of total installed capacity (2012 est.)
country comparison to the world: 44

Electricity—from other renewable sources: 0% of total installed capacity (2012 est.)
country comparison to the world: 177

Crude oil—production: 105,000 bbl/day (2014 est.)
country comparison to the world: 44

Crude oil—exports: 83,870 bbl/day (2012 est.)
country comparison to the world: 37

Crude oil—imports: 24,200 bbl/day (2012 est.)
country comparison to the world: 66

Crude oil—proved reserves: 660 million bbl (1 January 2015 est.)
country comparison to the world: 45

Refined petroleum products—production: 11,490 bbl/day (2012 est.)
country comparison to the world: 102

Refined petroleum products—consumption: 75,000 bbl/day (2013 est.)
country comparison to the world: 85

Refined petroleum products—exports
Exports: 8,107 bbl/day (2012 est.)
country comparison to the world: 90

Refined petroleum products—imports: 74,550 bbl/day (2012 est.)
country comparison to the world: 60

Natural gas—production: 0 cu m (2014 est.)
country comparison to the world: 192

Natural gas—consumption: 430 million cu m (2013 est.)
country comparison to the world: 99

Natural gas—exports: 0 cu m (2013 est.)
country comparison to the world: 105

Natural gas—imports: 430 million cu m (2013 est.)
country comparison to the world: 65

Natural gas—proved reserves: 22.65 billion cu m (1 January 2014 est.)
country comparison to the world: 74

Carbon dioxide emissions from consumption of energy: 9.098 million Mt (2012 est.)
country comparison to the world: 105

COMMUNICATIONS

Telephones—fixed lines: *total subscriptions:* 260,000
subscriptions per 100 inhabitants: 1 (2014 est.)
country comparison to the world: 120

Telephones—mobile cellular: *total:* 30.4 million
subscriptions per 100 inhabitants: 118 (2014 est.)
country comparison to the world: 42

Telephone system: *general assessment:* primarily microwave radio relay; wireless local loop has been installed; outdated and unreliable fixed-line infrastructure heavily concentrated in Accra
domestic: competition among multiple mobile-cellular providers has spurred growth with a subscribership of more than 80 per 100 persons and rising
international: country code—233; landing point for the SAT-3/WASC, Main One, and GLO-1 fiber-optic submarine cables that provide connectivity to South Africa, Europe, and Asia; satellite earth stations—4 Intelsat (Atlantic Ocean); microwave radio relay link to Panaftel system connects Ghana to its neighbors (2009)

Broadcast media: state-owned TV station, 2 state-owned radio networks; several privately owned TV stations and a large number of privately owned radio stations; transmissions of multiple international broadcasters are accessible; several cable and satellite TV subscription services are obtainable (2007)
Radio broadcast stations: AM 0, FM 86, shortwave 3 (2007)
Television broadcast stations: 7 (2007)

Internet country code: .gh

Internet hosts: 59,086 (2012)
country comparison to the world: 93

Internet users: *total:* 5 million
percent of population: 19.6% (2014 est.)
country comparison to the world: 68

TRANSPORTATION

Airports: 10 (2013)
country comparison to the world: 156

Airports—with paved runways: *total:* 7
over 3,047 m: 1
2,438 to 3,047 m: 1
1,524 to 2,437 m: 3
914 to 1,523 m: 2 (2013)

Airports—with unpaved runways: *total:* 3
914 to 1,523 m: 3 (2013)

Pipelines: gas 394 km; oil 20 km; refined products 361 km (2013)

Railways: *total:* 947 km
narrow gauge: 947 km 1.067-m gauge (2014)
country comparison to the world: 90

Roadways: *total:* 109,515 km
paved: 13,787 km
unpaved: 95,728 km (2009)
country comparison to the world: 43

Waterways: 1,293 km (168 km for launches and lighters on Volta, Ankobra, and Tano Rivers; 1,125 km of arterial and feeder waterways on Lake Volta) (2011)
country comparison to the world: 56

Merchant marine: *total:* 4
by type: petroleum tan ker 1, refrigerated cargo 3
foreign-owned: 2 (Brazil 1, South Korea 1) (2010)
country comparison to the world: 133

Ports and terminals: *major seaport(s):* Takoradi, Tema

MILITARY AND SECURITY

Military branches: Ghana Army, Ghana Navy, Ghana Air Force (2012)

Military service age and obligation: 18–26 years of age for voluntary military service, with basic education certificate; no conscription; must be HIV/AIDS negative (2012)

Military expenditures: 0.56% of GDP (2014)
0.61% of GDP (2013)
0.27% of GDP (2012)
country comparison to the world: 125

TRANSNATIONAL ISSUES

Disputes—international: disputed maritime border between Ghana and Cote d'Ivoire

Refugees and internally displaced persons: *refugees (country of origin):* 9,779 (Cote d'Ivoire; flight from 2010 post-election fighting); 5,262 (Liberia) (2014)

Trafficking in persons: *current situation:* Ghana is a source, transit, and destination country for men, women, and children subjected to forced labor and sex trafficking; the trafficking of Ghanians, particularly children, internally is more common than the trafficking of foreign nationals;

Ghanian children are subjected to forced labor in fishing, domestic service, street hawking, begging, portering, mining, quarrying, herding, and agriculture, with girls, and to a lesser extent boys, forced into prostitution; Ghanian women, sometimes lured with legitimate job offers, and girls are sex trafficked in West Africa, the Middle East, and Europe; Ghanian men fraudulently recruited for work in the Middle East are subjected to forced labor or prostitution, and a few Ghanian adults have been identified as victims of false labor in the US; women and girls from Vietnam, China, and neighboring West African countries are sex trafficked in Ghana; the country is also a transit point for sex trafficking from West Africa to Europe

tier rating: Tier 2 Watch List—Ghana does not fully comply with the minimum standards for the elimination of trafficking; however, it is making significant efforts to do so; Ghana continued to investigate and prosecute trafficking offenses but was unable to ramp up its anti-trafficking efforts in 2014 because the government failed to provide law enforcement or protection agencies with operating

budgets; victim protection efforts decreased in 2014, with significantly fewer victims identified; most child victims were referred to NGO-run facilities, but care for adults was lacking because the government did not provide any support to the country's Human Trafficking Fund for victim services or its two shelters; anti-trafficking prevention measures increased modestly, including reconvening of the Human Trafficking Management Board, public awareness campaigns on child labor and trafficking, and anti-trafficking TV and radio programs (2015)

Illicit drugs: illicit producer of cannabis for the international drug trade; major transit hub for Southwest and Southeast Asian heroin and, to a lesser extent, South American cocaine destined for Europe and the US; widespread crime and money-laundering problem, but the lack of a well-developed financial infrastructure limits the country's utility as a money-laundering center; significant domestic cocaine and cannabis use

GIBRALTAR

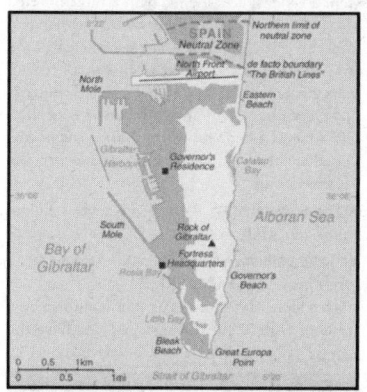

INTRODUCTION

Background: Strategically important, Gibraltar was reluctantly ceded to Great Britain by Spain in the 1713 Treaty of Utrecht; the British garrison was formally declared a colony in 1830. In a referendum held in 1967, Gibraltarians voted overwhelmingly to remain a British dependency. The subsequent granting of autonomy in 1969 by the UK led Spain to close the border and sever all communication links. Between 1997 and 2002, the UK and Spain held a series of talks on establishing temporary joint sovereignty over Gibraltar. In response to these talks, the Gibraltar Government called a referendum in late 2002 in which the majority of citizens voted overwhelmingly against any sharing of sovereignty with Spain. Since late 2004, Spain, the UK, and Gibraltar have held tripartite talks with the aim of cooperatively resolving problems

that affect the local population, and work continues on cooperation agreements in areas such as taxation and financial services; communications and maritime security; policy, legal and customs services; environmental protection; and education and visa services. Throughout 2009, a dispute over Gibraltar's claim to territorial waters extending out three miles gave rise to periodic non-violent maritime confrontations between Spanish and UK naval patrols and in 2013, the British reported a record number of entries by Spanish vessels into waters claimed by Gibraltar following a dispute over Gibraltar's creation of an artificial reef in those waters. A new noncolonial constitution came into effect in 2007, and the European Court of First Instance recognized Gibraltar's right to regulate its own tax regime in December 2008. The UK retains responsibility for defense, foreign relations, internal security, and financial stability.

GEOGRAPHY

Location: Southwestern Europe, bordering the Strait of Gibraltar, which links the Mediterranean Sea and the North Atlantic Ocean, on the southern coast of Spain

Geographic coordinates: 36 08 N, 5 21 W

Map references: Europe

Area: *total:* 6.5 sq km
land: 6.5 sq km
water: 0 sq km
country comparison to the world: 244

Area—comparative: more than 10 times the size of The National Mall in Washington, D.C.

Land boundaries: *total:* 1.2 km
border countries (1): Spain 1.2 km

Coastline: 12 km

Maritime claims: *territorial sea:* 3 nm

Climate: Mediterranean with mild winters and warm summers

Terrain: a narrow coastal lowland borders the Rock of Gibraltar

Elevation: *mean elevation:* NA

elevation extremes: *lowest point:* Mediterranean Sea 0 m
highest point: Rock of Gibraltar 426 m

Natural resources: none

Land use: *agricultural land:* 0%
arable land: 0%
permanent crops: 0%
permanent pasture: 0%
forest: 0%
other: 100% (2011 est.)

Irrigated land: NA

Natural hazards: NA

Environment—current issues: limited natural freshwater resources: large concrete or natural rock water catchments collect rainwater (no longer used for drinking water) and adequate desalination plant

Geography—note: strategic location on Strait of Gibraltar that links the North Atlantic Ocean and Mediterranean Sea

PEOPLE AND SOCIETY

Nationality: *noun:* Gibraltarian(s) adjective: Gibraltar

Ethnic groups: Spanish, Italian, English, Maltese, Portuguese, German, North Africans

Languages: English (used in schools and for official purposes), Spanish, Italian, Portuguese

337

Religions: Roman Catholic 78.1%, Church of England 7%, Muslim 4%, other Christian 3.2%, Jewish 2.1%, Hindu 1.8%, other 0.9%, none 2.9% (2001 est.)

Population: 29,258 (July 2015 est.)
country comparison to the world: 219

Age structure: *0–14 years:* 20.11% (male 3,014/female 2,870)
15–24 years: 15.58% (male 2,383/female 2,174)
25–54 years: 38.44% (male 5,678/female 5,569)
55–64 years: 10.47% (male 1,418/female 1,644)
65 years and over: 15.41% (male 2,216/female 2,292) (2015 est.)

Median age: *total:* 34.2 years
male: 33.3 years
female: 35.2 years (2015 est.)
country comparison to the world: 81

Population growth rate: 0.24% (2015 est.)
country comparison to the world: 180

Birth rate: 14.08 births/1,000 population (2015 est.)
country comparison to the world: 139

Death rate: 8.37 deaths/1,000 population (2015 est.)
country comparison to the world: 83

Net migration rate: -3.28 migrant(s)/1,000 population (2015 est.)
country comparison to the world: 183

Urbanization: *urban population:* 100% of total population (2015)
rate of urbanization: 0.07% annual rate of change (2010–15 est.)

Major urban areas—population: GIBRALTAR (capital) 29,000 (2014)

Sex ratio: *at birth:* 1.07 male(s)/female
0–14 years: 1.05 male(s)/female
15–24 years: 1.1 male(s)/female
25–54 years: 1.02 male(s)/female
55–64 years: 0.86 male(s)/female
65 years and over: 0.97 male(s)/female
total population: 1.01 male(s)/female (2015 est.)

Infant mortality rate: *total:* 6.16 deaths/1,000 live births
male: 6.85 deaths/1,000 live births
female: 5.42 deaths/1,000 live births (2015 est.)
country comparison to the world: 164

Life expectancy at birth: *total population:* 79.28 years
male: 76.43 years
female: 82.34 years (2015 est.)
country comparison to the world: 46

Total fertility rate: 1.91 children born/woman (2015 est.)
country comparison to the world: 134

HIV/AIDS—adult prevalence rate: NA

HIV/AIDS—people living with HIV/AIDS: NA

HIV/AIDS—deaths: NA

Education expenditures: NA

GOVERNMENT

Country name: *conventional long form:* none
conventional short form: Gibraltar

etymology: from the Spanish derivation of the Arabic "Jabal Tariq, "which means "Mountain of Tariq" and which refers to the Rock of Gibraltar

Dependency status: overseas territory of the UK

Government type: parliamentary democracy (Parliament); self-governing overseas territory of the UK

Capital: *name:* Gibraltar

Geographic coordinates: 36 08 N, 5 21 W
time difference: UTC + 1 (6 hours ahead of Washington, DC, during Standard Time)
daylight saving time: +1hr, begins last Sunday in March; ends last Sunday in October

Administrative divisions: none (overseas territory of the UK)

Independence: none (overseas territory of the UK)

National holiday: National Day, 10 September (1967); note—day of the national referendum to decide whether to remain with the UK or join Spain

Constitution: previous 1969; latest passed by referendum 30 November 2006, entered into effect 14 December 2006, entered into force 2 January 2007 (2016)

Legal system: the laws of the UK, where applicable, apply
Citizenship: see United Kingdom

Suffrage: 18 years of age; universal; and British citizens with six months residence or more

Executive branch: *chief of state:* Queen ELIZABETH II (since 6 February 1952); represented by Governor Lt. Gen. Edward DAVIS (since 19 January 2016)

head of government: Chief Minister Fabian PICARDO (since 9 December 2011)
cabinet: Council of Ministers appointed from among the 17 elected members of the Parliament by the governor in consultation with the chief minister
elections/appointments: the monarchy is hereditary; governor appointed by the monarch; following legislative elections, the leader of the majority party or majority coalition usually appointed chief minister by the governor

Legislative branch: *description:* unicameral Parliament (18 seats; 17 members directly elected in a single nationwide constituency by majority vote and 1 appointed by Parliament as speaker; members serve 4-year terms)
elections: last held on 26 November 2015 (next to be held not later than December 2019)
election results: percent of vote by party—GSLP 68.4%, GSD 31.6%; seats by party—GSLP 10, GSD 7

Judicial branch: *highest resident court(s):* Court of Appeal (consists of at least 3 judges, including the court president); Supreme Court of Gibraltar (consists of the chief justice and 3 judges); note—appeals beyond the Court of Appeal are heard by the Judicial Committee of the Privy Council (in London)
judge selection and term of office: Court of Appeal and Supreme Court judges appointed by the governor upon the advice of the Judicial

Service Commission, a 7-member body of judges and appointees of the governor; tenure of the Court of Appeal president based on terms of appointment; Supreme Court chief justice and judge normally appointed until retirement at age 67, but can be extended 3 years
subordinate courts: Court of First Instance; Magistrates' Court; specialized tribunals for issues relating to social security, taxes, and employment

Political parties and leaders: Gibraltar Liberal Party [Joseph GARCIA]
Gibraltar Social Democrats or GSD [Daniel FEETHAM]
Gibraltar Socialist Labor Party or GSLP [Fabian PICARDO]
Progressive Democratic Party [Nick CRUZ]

Political pressure groups and leaders: Chamber of Commerce
Gibraltar Representatives Organization
Women's Association

International organization participation: ICC (NGOs), Interpol (subbureau), UPU

Diplomatic representation in the US: none (overseas territory of the UK)

Diplomatic representation from the US: none (overseas territory of the UK)

Flag description: two horizontal bands of white (top, double width) and red with a three-towered red castle in the center of the white band; hanging from the castle gate is a gold key centered in the red band; the design is that of Gibraltar's coat of arms granted on 10 July 1502 by King Ferdinand and Queen Isabella of Spain; the castle symbolizes Gibraltar as a fortress, while the key represents Gibraltar's strategic importance—the key to the Mediterranean

National symbol(s): Barbary macaque; national colors: red, white, yellow

National anthem: *name:* "Gibraltar Anthem"
lyrics/music: Peter EMBERLEY
note: adopted 1994; serves as a local anthem; as a territory of the United Kingdom, "God Save the Queen" remains official (see United Kingdom)

ECONOMY

Economy—overview: Self-sufficient Gibraltar benefits from an extensive shipping trade, offshore banking, and its position as an international conference center. Tax rates are low to attract foreign investment. The British military presence has been sharply reduced and now contributes about 7% to the local economy, compared with 60% in 1984. In recent years, Gibraltar has seen major structural change from a public to a private sector economy, but changes in government spending still have a major impact on the level of employment. The financial sector, tourism (over 11 million visitors in 2012), gaming revenues, shipping services fees, and duties on consumer goods also generate revenue. The financial sector, tourism, and the shipping sector contribute 30%, 30%, and 25%, respectively, of GDP. Telecommunications, e-commerce, and e-gaming account for the remaining 15%.

GDP (purchasing power parity): $1.85 billion (2013 est.)
$2 billion (2012 est.)
$1.106 billion (2006 est.)
country comparison to the world: 197

GDP (official exchange rate): $1.85 billion (2013 est.)

GDP—real growth rate: 6% (2008 est.)
8.8% (2007 est.)
0% (2006 est.)
country comparison to the world: 29

GDP—per capita (PPP): $43,000 (2008 est.)
$41,200 (2007 est.)
$38,400 (2006 est.)
country comparison to the world: 36

GDP—composition, by sector of origin:
agriculture: 0%
industry: 0%
services: 100% (2008 est.)

Agriculture—products: none

Industries: tourism, banking and finance, ship repairing, tobacco

Industrial production growth rate: NA%

Labor force: 22,910 (2013 est.)
country comparison to the world: 211

Labor force—by occupation: *agriculture:* NEGL
industry: 40%
services: 60% (2001)

Unemployment rate: 3% (2005 est.)
country comparison to the world: 24

Population below poverty line: NA%

Household income or consumption by percentage share: *lowest:* 10%: NA%
highest: 10%: NA%

Budget: *revenues:* $475.8 million
expenditures: $452.3 million (2008 est.)
Taxes and other revenues: 25.7% of GDP (2008 est.)
country comparison to the world: 116

Budget surplus (+) or deficit (–): 1.3% of GDP (2008 est.)
country comparison to the world: 18

Public debt: 7.5% of GDP (2008 est.)
9.3% of GDP (2006 est.)
country comparison to the world: 173

Fiscal year: 1 July–30 June

Inflation rate (consumer prices): 2.5% (2013 est.)
2.2% (2012 est.)
country comparison to the world: 128

Exports: $271 million (2004 est.)
country comparison to the world: 184

Exports—commodities: (principally reexports) petroleum 51%, manufactured goods (2010 est.)

Imports: $2.967 billion (2004 est.)
country comparison to the world: 147

Imports—commodities: fuels, man ufactured goods, foodstuffs

Debt—external: $NA

Exchange rates: Gibraltar poun ds (GIP) per US dollar—
0.885 (2015 est.)

0.7525 (2014 est.)
0.7634 (2013 est.)
0.64 (2012)
0.624 (2011)

ENERGY

Electricity—production: 165 million kWh (2012 est.)
country comparison to the world: 190

Electricity—consumption: 160 million kWh (2012 est.)
country comparison to the world: 192

Electricity—exports: 0 kWh (2013 est.)
country comparison to the world: 143

Electricity—imports: 0 kWh (2013 est.)
country comparison to the world: 154

Electricity—installed generating capacity: 43,000 kW (2012 est.)
country comparison to the world: 193

Electricity—from fossil fuels: 100% of total installed capacity (2012 est.)
country comparison to the world: 11

Electricity—from nuclear fuels: 0% of total installed capacity (2012 est.)
country comparison to the world: 99

Electricity—from hydroelectric plants: 0% of total installed capacity (2012 est.)
country comparison to the world: 174

Electricity—from other renewable sources: 0% of total installed capacity (2012 est.)
country comparison to the world: 178

Crude oil—production: 0 bbl/day (2014 est.)
country comparison to the world: 140

Crude oil—exports: 0 bbl/day (2012 est.)
country comparison to the world: 129

Crude oil—imports: 0 bbl/day (2012 est.)
country comparison to the world: 196

Crude oil—proved reserves: 0 bbl (1 January 2015 est.)
country comparison to the world: 138

Refined petroleum products—production: 0 bbl/day (2012 est.)
country comparison to the world: 187

Refined petroleum products—consumption: 53,000 bbl/day (2013 est.)
country comparison to the world: 95

Refined petroleum products—exports: 0 bbl/day (2012 est.)
country comparison to the world: 184

Refined petroleum products—imports: 53,970 bbl/day (2012 est.)
country comparison to the world: 76

Natu ral gas—production: 0 cu m (2013 est.)
country comparison to the world: 193

Natural gas—consumption: 0 cu m (2013 est.)
country comparison to the world: 147

Natural gas—exports: 0 cu m (2013 est.)
country comparison to the world: 106

Natural gas—imports: 0 cu m (2013 est.)
country comparison to the world: 201

Natural gas—proved reserves:

0 cu m (1 January 2014 est.)
country comparison to the world: 143

Carbon dioxide emissions from consumption of energy: 3.946 million Mt (2012 est.)
country comparison to the world: 131

COMMUNICATIONS

Telephones—fixed lines: *total subscriptions:* 23,400
subscriptions per 100 inhabitants: 80 (2014 est.)
country comparison to the world: 179

Telephones—mobile cellular: *total:* 38,000
subscriptions per 100 inhabitants: 130 (2014 est.)
country comparison to the world: 205

Telephone system: *general assessment:* adequate, automatic domestic system and adequate international facilities
domestic: automatic exchange facilities
international: country code—350; radiotelephone; microwave radio relay; satellite earth station—1 Intelsat (Atlantic Ocean)

Broadcast media: Gibraltar Broadcasting Corporation (GBC) provides TV and radio broadcasting services via 1 TV station and 4 radio stations; British Forces Broadcasting Service (BFBS) operates 1 radio station; broadcasts from Spanish radio and TV stations are accessible (2008)
Radio broadcast stations: AM 1, FM 5, shortwave 0 (1998)
Television broadcast stations: 1 (plus 3 repeaters) (1997)

Internet country code: .gi

Internet hosts: 3,509 (2012)
country comparison to the world: 151

Internet users: *total:* 20,200
percent of population: 70.14% (2009)
country comparison to the world: 200

TRANSPORTATION

Airports: 1 (2013)
country comparison to the world: 220

Airports—with paved runways: *total:* 1
1,524 to 2,437 m: 1 (2013)

Roadways: *total:* 29 km
paved: 29 km (2007)
country comparison to the world: 221

Merchant marine: *total:* 267
by type: bulk carrier 3, cargo 146, chemical tanker 64, container 28, liquefied gas 2, petroleum tanker 14, roll on/roll off 2, vehicle carrier 8
foreign-owned: 254 (Belgium 1, Cyprus 1, Denmark 7, Finland 2, Germany 123, Greece 8, Iceland 1, Italy 4, Jersey 1, Morocco 4, Netherlands 34, Norway 46, Sweden 11, UAE 5, UK 6)
registered in other countries: 6 (Liberia 5, Panama 1) (2010)
country comparison to the world: 32

Ports and terminals: *major seaport(s):* Gibraltar

MILITARY AND SECURITY

Military branches: Royal Gibraltar Regiment (2013)

Military—note: defense is the responsibility of the UK; the Royal Gibraltar Regiment replaced the last British regular infantry forces in 1992

TRANSNATIONAL ISSUES

Disputes—international: in 2002, Gibraltar residents voted overwhelmingly by referendum to reject any "shared sovereignty" arrangement; the Government of Gibraltar insists on equal participation in talks between the UK and Spain; Spain disapproves of UK plans to grant Gibraltar even greater autonomy

GREECE

INTRODUCTION

Background: Greece achieved independence from the Ottoman Empire in 1830. During the second half of the 19th century and the first half of the 20th century, it gradually added neighboring islands and territories, most with Greek-speaking populations. In World War II, Greece was first invaded by Italy (1940) and subsequently occupied by Germany (1941–44); fighting endured in a protracted civil war between supporters of the king and other anti-communist and communist rebels. Following the latter's defeat in 1949, Greece joined NATO in 1952. In 1967, a group of military officers seized power, establishing a military dictatorship that suspended many political liberties and forced the king to flee the country. In 1974 following the collapse of the dictatorship, democratic elections and a referendum created a parliamentary republic and abolished the monarchy. In 1981, Greece joined the EC (now the EU); it became the 12th member of the European Economic and Monetary Union (EMU) in 2001. Greece has suffered a

GEOGRAPHY

Location: Southern Europe, bordering the Aegean Sea, Ionian Sea, and the Mediterranean Sea, between Albania and Turkey

Geographic coordinates: 39 00 N, 22 00 E

Map references: Europe

Area: *total:* 131,957 sq km

land: 130,647 sq km
water: 1,310 sq km
country comparison to the world: 97

Area—comparative: slightly smaller than Alabama

Land boundaries: *total:* 1,110 km
border countries (4): Albania 212 km, Bulgaria 472 km, Macedonia 234 km, Turkey 192 km

Coastline: 13,676 km

Maritime claims: *territorial sea:* 12 nm
continental shelf: 200-m depth or to the depth of exploitation

Climate: temperate; mild, wet winters; hot, dry summers

Terrain: mountainous with ranges extending into the sea as peninsulas or chains of islands

Elevation: *mean elevation:* 498 m

elevation extremes: *lowest point:* Mediterranean Sea 0 m
highest point: Mount Olympus 2,917 m

Natural resources: lignite, petroleum, iron ore, bauxite, lead, zinc, nickel, magnesite, marble, salt, hydropower potential

Land use: *agricultural land:* 63.4%
arable land: 19.7%
permanent crops: 8.9%
permanent pasture: 34.8%
forest: 30.5%
other: 6.1% (2011 est.)

Irrigated land: 15,550 sq km (2012)

Total renewable water resources: 74.25 cu km (2011)

Freshwater withdrawal (domestic/industrial/agricultural): *total:* 9.47 cu km/yr (9%/2%/89%)
per capita: 841.4 cu m/yr (2007)

Natural hazards: severe earthquakes
volcanism: Santorini (elev.367 m) has been deemed a Decade Volcano by the International Association of Volcanology and Chemistry of the Earth's Interior, worthy of study due to its explosive history and close proximity to human populations; although there have been very few eruptions in recent centuries, Methana and Nisyros in the Aegean are classified as historically active

Environment—current issues: air pollution; water pollution

Environment—international agreements: *party to:* Air Pollution, Air Pollution-Nitrogen Oxides, Air Pollution-Sulfur 94, Antarctic-Environmental Protocol, Antarctic-Marine Living Resources, Antarctic Treaty, Biodiversity, Climate Change, Climate Change-Kyoto Protocol, Desertification, Endangered Species, Environmental Modification, Hazardous Wastes, Law of the Sea, Marine Dumping, Ozone Layer Protection, Ship Pollution, Tropical Timber 83, Tropical Timber 94, Wetlands
signed, but not ratified: Air Pollution-Persistent Organic Pollutants, Air Pollution-Volatile Organic Compounds

Geography—note: strategic location dominating the Aegean Sea and southern approach to Turkish Straits; a peninsular country, possessing an archipelago of about 2,000 islands

PEOPLE AND SOCIETY

Nationality: *noun:* Greek(s)
adjective: Greek

Ethnic groups: population: Greek 93%, other (foreign citizens) 7% (2001 census)
note: data represent citizenship, since Greece does not collect data on ethnicity

Languages: Greek (official) 99%, other (includes English and French) 1%

Religions: Greek Orthodox (official) 98%, Muslim 1.3%, other 0.7%

Population: 10,775,643 (July 2015 est.)
country comparison to the world: 83

Age structure: *0–14 years:* 14.01% (male 777,647/female 732,137)
15–24 years: 9.72% (male 534,855/female 512,183)
25–54 years: 42.97% (male 2,306,832/female 2,323,787)
55–64 years: 12.84% (male 679,033/female 704,833)
65 years and over: 20.46% (male 964,736/female 1,239,600) (2015 est.)

Dependency ratios: *total dependency ratio:* 56.2%
youth dependency ratio: 22.8%
elderly dependency ratio: 33.4%
potential support ratio: 3% (2015 est.)

Median age: *total:* 43.8 years
male: 42.8 years
female: 44.9 years (2015 est.)
country comparison to the world: 8

Population growth rate: -0.01% (2015 est.)
country comparison to the world: 199

Birth rate: 8.66 births/1,000 population (2015 est.)
country comparison to the world: 214

Death rate: 11.09 deaths/1,000 population (2015 est.)
country comparison to the world: 32

Net migration rate: 2.32 migrant(s)/1,000 population (2015 est.)
country comparison to the world: 44

Urbanization: *urban population:* 78% of total population (2015)
rate of urbanization: 0.47% annual rate of change (2010–15 est.)

Major urban areas—population: ATHENS (capital) 3.052 million (2015)

Sex ratio: *at birth:* 1.06 male(s)/female
0–14 years: 1.06 male(s)/female
15–24 years: 1.04 male(s)/female
25–54 years: 0.99 male(s)/female
55–64 years: 0.96 male(s)/female
65 years and over: 0.78 male(s)/female
total population: 0.96 male(s)/female (2015 est.)

Mother's mean age at first birth: 31.2 (2010 est.)

Maternal mortality rate: 3 deaths/100,000 live births (2015 est.)
country comparison to the world: 183

Infant mortality rate: *total:* 4.7 deaths/1,000 live births
male: 5.16 deaths/1,000 live births
female: 4.22 deaths/1,000 live births (2015 est.)
country comparison to the world: 178

Life expectancy at birth: *total population:* 80.43 years
male: 77.83 years
female: 83.2 years (2015 est.)
country comparison to the world: 34

Total fertility rate: 1.42 children born/woman (2015 est.)
country comparison to the world: 210

Health expenditures: 9.8% of GDP (2013)
country comparison to the world: 32

Hospital bed density: 4.8 beds/1,000 population (2009)

Drinking water source:
improved:
urban: 100% of population
rural: 100% of population
total: 100% of population
unimproved:
urban: 0% o f population
rural: 0% of population
total: 0% of population(2015 est.)

Sanitation facility access:
improved:
urban: 99.2% of population
rural: 98.1% of population
total: 99% of population
unimproved:
urban: urban: 0.8% of population
rural: 1.9% of population
total: 1% of population (2015 est.)

HIV/AIDS—adult prevalence rate: NA

HIV/AIDS—people living with HIV/AIDS: NA

HIV/AIDS—deaths: NA

Obesity—adult prevalence rate: 25.1% (2014)
country comparison to the world: 96

Education expenditures: 4.1% of GDP (2005)
country comparison to the world: 111

Literacy: *definition:* age 15 and over can read and write
total population: 97.7%
male: 98.5%
female: 96.9% (2015 est.)

School life expectancy (primary to tertiary education): *total:* 17 years
male: 17 years
female: 17 years (2013)

Unemployment, youth ages 15–24: *total:* 58.3%
male: 53.6%
female: 64.2% (2013 est.)
country comparison to the world: 3

GOVERNMENT

Country name: *conventional long form:* Hellenic Republic
conventional short form: Greece
local long form: Elliniki Dimokratia
local short form: Ellas or Ellada
former: Hellenic State, Kingdom of Greece
etymology: the English name derives from the Roman (Latin) designation "Graecia," meaning "Land of the Greeks"; the Greeks call their country "Hellas" or "Ellada"

Government type: parliamentary republic

Capital: *name:* Athens

Geographic coordinates: 37 59 N, 23 44 E
time difference: UTC+2 (7 hours ahead of Washington, DC, during Standard Time)
daylight saving time: +1hr, begins last Sunday in March; ends last Sunday in October

Administrative divisions: 13 regions (perifereies, singular—perifereia) and 1 autonomous monastic state* (aftonomi monastiki politeia); Agion Oros* (Mount Athos), Anatoliki Makedonia kai Thraki (East Macedonia and Thrace), Attiki (Attica), Dytiki Ellada (West Greece), Dytiki Makedonia (West Macedonia), Ionia Nisia (Ionian Islands), Ipeiros (Epirus), Kentriki Makedonia (Central Macedonia), Kriti (Crete), Notio Aigaio (South Aegean), Peloponnisos (Peloponnese), Sterea Ellada (Central Greece), Thessalia (Thessaly), Voreio Aigaio (North Aegean)

Independence: 3 February 1830 (from the Ottoman Empire); note—25 March 1821, outbreak of the national revolt against the Ottomans; 3 February 1830, signing of the London Protocol recognizing Greek independence by Great Britain, France, and Russia

National holiday: Independence Day, 25 March (1821)

Constitution: many previous; latest entered into force 11 June 1975; amended 1986, 2001, 2008 (2016)

Legal system: civil legal system based on Roman law

International law organization participation: accepts compulsory ICJ jurisdiction with reservations; accepts ICCt jurisdiction

Citizenship: *citizenship by birth:* no
citizenship by descent only: at least one parent must be a citizen of Greece
dual citizenship recognized: yes
residency requirement for naturalization: 10 years

Suffrage: 18 years of age; universal and compulsory

Executive branch: *chief of state:* President Prokopis PAVLOPOULOS (since 13 March 2015)

head of government: Prime Minister Alexis TSIPRAS (since 21 September 2015); note—Vassiliki THANOU-CHRISTOFILOU served as interim prime minister beginning on 27 August 2015 after the resignation of Alexis TSIPRAS on 20 August 2015; she was Greece's first female prime minister
cabinet: Cabinet appointed by the president on the recommendation of the prime minister
elections/appointments: president elected by Hellenic Parliament for a 5-year term (eligible for a second term); election last held on 18 February 2015 (next to be held by February 2020); president appoints as prime minister the leader of the majority party or coalition in the Hellenic Parliament
election results: Prokopios PAVLOPOULOS (ND) elected president by Parliament—233 of 300 votes

Legislative branch: *description:* unicameral Hellenic Parliament or Vouli ton Ellinon (300 seats; 288 members directly elected in single- and multi-seat constituencies by proportional representation vote and 12 seats are filled from nationwide party lists; 50 seats allocated to the party with the highest total valid vote count and remaining seats are apportioned according to each party's or coalition's vote percentage; members serve up to 4 years)
elections: last held on 20 September 2015 (next to be held by 2019); note—snap elections were called because of upheaval in the governing SYRIZA party over a new bailout deal with international creditors
election results: percent of vote by party—SYRIZA 35.5%, ND 28.1%, Golden Dawn 7.0%, PASOK-DIMAR 6.3%, KKE 5.6%, To Potami 4.1%, ANEL 3.7%, EK 3.4%, other 6.3%; seats by party—SYRIZA 145, ND 75, Golden Dawn 18, PASOK-DIMAR 17, KKE 15, To Potami 11, ANEL 10, EK 9; note—only parties surpassing a 3% threshold are entitled to parliamentary seats; parties need 10 seats to become formal parliamentary groups but can retain that status if the party participated in the last election and received the minimum 3% threshold

Judicial branch: *highest court(s):* Hellenic Supreme Court of Civil and Penal Law (consists of 56 judges)
judge selection and term of office: judges selected by the Supreme Judicial Council which includes the president of the Supreme Court, other judges, and the prosecutor of the Supreme Court; judges appointed for life following a 2-year probationary period

subordinate courts: Supreme Administrative Court; Courts of Appeal; Courts of First Instance; Court of Auditors

Political parties and leaders: Anticapitalist Left Cooperation for the Overthrow or ANTARSYA [collective leadership]
Coalition of the Radical Left or SYRIZA [Alexios (Alexis) TSIPRAS]
Communist Party of Greece or KKE [Dimitrios KOUTSOUMBAS]
Democratic Left or DIMAR [Athanasios (Thanassis) THEOCHAROPOULOS]
Golden Dawn [Nikolaos MICHALOLIAKOS]
Independent Greeks or ANEL [Panagiotis (Panos) KAMMENOS]
Movement of Democratic Socialists or KIDISO [Georgiose PAPANDREOU]
N ew Democracy or ND [Kyriakos MITSOTAKIS]
Panhellenic Socialist Movement or PASOK [Fofi GENIMMATA]
Popular Unity [Panagiotis LAFAZANIS]
To Potami (The River) [Stavros THEODORAKIS]
Union of Centrists or EK [Vassilis LEVENTIS]

Political pressure groups and leaders: Supreme Administration of Civil Servants Unions or ADEDY [Spyros PAPASPYROS]
Federation of Greek Industries or SEV [Dimitris DASKALOPOU LOS]
General Confederation of Greek Workers or GSEE [Ioannis PANAGOPOULOS]

International organization participation: Australia Group, BIS, BSEC, CD, CE, CERN, EAPC, EBRD, ECB, EIB, EMU, ESA, EU, FAO, FATF, IAEA, IBRD, ICAO, ICC (national committees), ICCt, ICRM, IDA, IEA, IFAD, IFC, IFR CS, IGAD (partners), IHO, ILO, IMF, IMO, IMSO, Interpol, IOC, IOM, IPU, ISO, ITSO, ITU, ITUC (NGOs), MIGA, NATO, NEA, NSG, OAS (observer), OECD, OIF, OPCW, OSCE, PCA, Schengen Convention, SELEC, UN, UNCTAD, UN ESCO, UNHCR, UNIDO, UNIFIL, UNWTO, UPU, WCO, WFTU (NGOs), WHO, WIPO, WMO, WTO, ZC

Diplomatic representation in the US: *chief of mission:* Ambassador Christos P. PANAGOPOULOS (since 17 September 2012)
chancery: 2217 Massachusetts Avenue NW, Washington, DC 20008
telephone: [1] (202) 939-1300
FAX: [1] (202) 939-1324
consulate(s) general: Boston, Chicago, Los Angeles, New York, Tampa (FL), San Francisco
consulate(s): Atlanta, Houston

Diplomatic representation from the US: chief of mission: Ambassador David D. PEARCE (since 18 October 2013)
embassy: 91 Vasillisis Sophias Avenue, 10160 Athens
mailing address: PSC 108, APOAE 09842–0108
telephone: [30] (210) 721-2951
FAX: [30] (210) 645-6282
consulate(s) general: Thessaloniki (2012)

Flag description: nine equal horizontal stripes of blue alternating with white; a blue square bearing a white cross appears in the upper hoist-side corner; the cross symbolizes Greek Orthodoxy, the established religion of the country; there is no agreed upon meaning for the nine stripes or for the colors; the exact shade of blue has never been set by law and has varied from a light to a dark blue over time

National symbol(s): Greek cross (white cross on blue field, arms equal length); national colors: blue, white

National anthem: *name:* "Ymnos eis tin Eleftherian" (Hymn to Liberty)
lyrics/music: Dionysios SOLOMOS/Nikolaos MANTZAROS
note: adopted 1864; the anthem is based on a 158-stanza poem by the same name, which was inspired by the Greek Revolution of 1821 against the Ottomans (only the first two stanzas are used); Cyprus also uses "Hymn to Liberty" as its anthem

ECONOMY

Economy—overview: Greece has a capitalist economy with a public sector accounting for about 40% of GDP and with per capita GDP about two-thirds that of the leading euro-zone economies. Tourism provides 18% of GDP. Immigrants make up nearly one-fifth of the work force, mainly in agricultural and unskilled jobs. Greece is a major beneficiary of EU aid, equal to about 3.3% of annual GDP.
The Greek economy averaged growth of about 4% per year between 2003 and 2007, but the economy went into recession in 2009 as a result of the world financial crisis, tightening credit conditions, and Athens' failure to address a growing budget deficit. By 2013 the economy had contracted 26%, compared with the pre-crisis level of 2007. Greece met the EU's Growth and Stability Pact budget deficit criterion of no more than 3% of GDP in 2007–08, but violated it in 2009, with the deficit reaching 15% of GDP. Deteriorating public finances, inaccurate and misreported statistics, and consistent underperformance on reforms prompted major credit rating agencies to downgrade Greece's international debt rating in late 2009 and led the country into a financial crisis. Under intense pressure from the EU and international market participants, the government accepted a bailout program that called on Athens to cut government spending, decrease tax evasion, overhaul the civil-service, health-care, and pension systems, and reform the labor and product markets. Austerity measures reduced the deficit to 3% in 2015. Successive Greek governments, however, failed to push through many of the most unpopular reforms in the face of widespread political opposition, including from the country's powerful labor unions and the general public. In April 2010, a leading credit agency assigned Greek debt its lowest possible credit rating, and in May 2010, the International Monetary Fund and euro-zone governments provided Greece emergency short-and medium-term loans worth $147 billion so that the country could make debt repayments to creditors. In exchange for the largest bailout ever assembled, the government announced combined spending cuts and tax increases totaling $40 billion over three years, on top of the tough austerity measures already taken. Greece, however, struggled to meet the targets set by the EU and the IMF, especially after Eurostat—the EU's statistical office—revised upward Greece's deficit and debt numbers for 2009 and 2010. European leaders and the IMF agreed in October 2011 to provide Athens a second bailout package of $169 billion. The second deal called for holders of Greek government bonds to write down a significant portion of their holdings to try to alleviate Greece's government debt burden. However, Greek banks, saddled with a significant portion of sovereign debt, were adversely affected by the write down and $60 billion of the second bailout package was set aside to ensure the banking system was adequately capitalized. In exchange for the second bailout, Greece promised to step up efforts to increase tax collection, to reduce the size of government, and to rein in health spending. These austerity measures were designed to generate $7.8 billion in savings during 2013–15, but in fact prolonged Greece's economic recession and depressed tax revenues.
In 2014, the Greek economy began to turn the corner on the recession. Greece achieved three significant milestones: balancing the budget—not including debt repayments; issuing government debt in financial markets for the first time since 2010; and generating 0.7% GDP growth—the first economic expansion since 2007.
Despite the nascent recovery, widespread discontent with austerity measures helped propel the far-left Coalition of the Radical Left (SYRIZA) party into government in national legislative elections in January 2015. Between January and July 2015, frustrations between the SYRIZA-led government and Greece's EU and IMF creditors over the implementation of bailout measures and disbursement of funds led the Greek government to run up significant arrears to suppliers and Greek banks to rely on emergency lending, and also called into question Greece's future in the euro zone. To stave off a collapse of the banking system, Greece imposed capital controls in June 2015 shortly before rattling international financial markets by becoming the first developed nation to miss a loan payment to the IMF. Unable to reach an agreement with creditors, Prime Minister Alexios TSIPRAS held a nation-wide referendum on 5 July on whether to accept the terms of Greece's bailout, campaigning for the ultimately successful "no" vote. The TSIPRAS government subsequently agreed, however, to a new $96 billion bailout in order to avert Greece's exit from the monetary bloc. On 20 August, Greece signed its third bailout which allowed it to cover significant debt payments to its EU and IMF creditors and ensure the banking sector retained access to emergency liquidity. The TSIPRAS government—which retook office on 20 September after calling new elections in late August—successfully secured disbursal of two delayed tranches of bailout funds. Despite the economic turmoil, Greek GDP did not contract as sharply as feared, with official source estimates of a -0.2% contraction in 2015, boosted in part by a strong tourist season.

GDP (purchasing power parity): $286 billion (2015 est.)

$286.6 billion (2014 est.)
$284.8 billion (2013 est.)
note: data are in 2015 US dollars
country comparison to the world: 55

GDP (official exchange rate): $195.3 billion (2015 est.)

GDP—real growth rate: -0.2% (2015 est.)
0.7% (2014 est.)
-3.2% (2013 est.)
country comparison to the world: 197

GDP—per capita (PPP): $26,400 (2015 est.)
$26,200 (2014 est.)
$25,900 (2013 est.)
note: data are in 2015 US dollars
country comparison to the world: 68

Gross national saving: 9.8% of GDP (2015 est.)
10.1% of GDP (2014 est.)
9.4% of GDP (2013 est.)
country comparison to the world: 153

GDP—composition, by end use:
household consumption: 70.3%
government consumption: 20%
investment in fixed capital: 11.7%
investment in inventories: -1.8%
exports of goods and services: 30.1%
imports of goods and services: -30.3% (2015 est.)

GDP—composition, by sector of origin:
agriculture: 3.9%
industry: 13.3%
services: 82.8% (2015 est.)

Agriculture—products: wheat, corn, barley, sugar beets, olives, tomatoes, wine, tobacco, potatoes; beef, dairy products

Industries: tourism, food and tobacco processing, textiles, chemicals, metal products; mining, petroleum

Industrial production growth rate: 0.6% (2015 est.)
country comparison to the world: 157

Labor force: 4.832 million (2015 est.)
country comparison to the world: 87

Labor force—by occupation: *agriculture:* 12.6%
industry: 15%
services: 72.4% (30 October 2015 est.)

Unemployment rate: 25% (30 October 2015 est.)
26.5% (2014 est.)
country comparison to the world: 177

Population below poverty line: 36% (2014 est.)

Household income or consumption by percentage share: *lowest:* 10%: 1.7%
highest: 10%: 26.7% (2015 est.)

Distribution of family income—Gini index: 36.7 (2012 est.)
35.7 (2011)
country comparison to the world: 82

Budget: *revenues:* $56.33 billion
expenditures: $60.19 billion (2015 est.)
Taxes and other revenues: 27.7% of GDP (2015 est.)
country comparison to the world: 96

Budget surplus (+) or deficit (–): -1.9% of GDP (2015 est.)
country comparison to the world: 72

Public debt: 171.3% of GDP (2015 est.)
178.6% of GDP (2014 est.)
country comparison to the world: 3

Fiscal year: calendar year

Inflation rate (consumer prices): -1.1% (2015 est.)
-1.4% (2014 est.)
country comparison to the world: 9

Central bank discount rate: 0.05% (31 March 2016)
0.15% (11 June 2014)
note: this is the European Central Bank's rate on the marginal lending facility, which offers overn ight credit to banks in the euro area
country comparison to the world: 143

Commercial bank prime lending rate: 6% (31 December 2015 est.)
6.52% (31 December 2014 est.)
country comparison to the world: 130

Stock of narrow money: $118.4 billion (31 December 2015 est.)
$115.7 billion (31 December 2014 est.)
note: see entry for the European Union for money supply for the entire euro area; the European Central Bank (ECB) controls monetary policy for the 18 members of the Economic and Monetary Union (EMU); individual members of the EMU do not control the quantity of money circulating within their own borders
country comparison to the world: 31

Stock of broad money: $260.9 billion (31 December 2014 est.)
$264.6 billion (31 December 2013 est.)
country comparison to the world: 38

Stock of domestic credit: $267.3 billion (31 December 2015 est.)
$298.9 billion (31 December 2014 est.)
country comparison to the world: 38

Market value of publicly traded shares:
$44.58 billion (31 December 2012 est.)
$33.65 billion (31 December 2011)
$72.64 billion (31 December 2010 est.)
country comparison to the world: 54

Current account balance: -$8 million (2015 est.)
-$5.006 billion (2014 est.)
country comparison to the world: 56

Exports: $25.31 billion (2015 est.)
$35.6 billion (2014 est.)
country comparison to the world: 66

Exports—commodities: food and beverages, manufactured goods, petroleum products, chemicals, textiles

Exports—partners: Italy 11.2%, Germany 7.3%, Turkey 6.6%, Cyprus 5.9%, Bulgaria 5.2%, US 4.8%, UK 4.2%, Egypt 4% (2015)

Imports: $47.21 billion (2015 est.)
$63.76 billion (2014 est.)
country comparison to the world: 53

Imports—commodities: machinery, transport equipment, fuels, chemicals

Imports—partners: Germany 10.7%, Italy 8.4%, Russia 7.9%, Iraq 7%, China 5.9%, Netherlands 5.5%, France 4.5% (2015)

Reserves of foreign exchange and gold: $6.433 billion (February 2015 est.)
$6.212 billion (31 December 2014 est.)
country comparison to the world: 90

Debt—external: $514.4 billion (31 December 2014 est.)
$575.4 billion (31 December 2013 est.)
country comparison to the world: 26

Stock of direct foreign investment—at home:
$31.24 billion (31 December 2015 est.)
$30.15 billion (31 December 2014 est.)
country comparison to the world: 66

Stock of direct foreign investment—abroad: $40.1 billion (31 December 2015 est.)
$40.96 billion (31 December 2014 est.)
country comparison to the world: 45

Exchange rates: euros (EUR) per US dollar—
0.885 (2015 est.)
0.7525 (2014 est.)
0.7634 (2013 est.)
0.78 (2012 est.)
0.7185 (2011 est.)

ENERGY

Electricity—production: 57.55 billion kWh (2012 est.)
country comparison to the world: 50

Electricity—consumption: 57.73 billion kWh (2012 est.)
country comparison to the world: 45

Electricity—exports: 2.602 billion kWh (2013 est.)
country comparison to the world: 41

Electricity—imports: 4.705 billion kWh (2013 est.)
country comparison to the world: 43

Electricity—installed generating capacity: 22.3 million kW (2012 est.)
country comparison to the world: 37

Electricity—from fossil fuels:
70.4% of total installed capacity (2012 est.)
country comparison to the world: 106

Electricity—from nuclear fuels: 0% of total installed capacity (2012 est.)
country comparison to the world: 103

Electricity—from hydroelectric plants: 11.4% of total installed capacity (2012 est.)
country comparison to the world: 112

Electricity—from other renewable sources: 15.1% of total installed capacity (2012 est.)
country comparison to the world: 20

Crude oil—production: 1,162 bbl/day (2014 est.)
country comparison to the world: 90

Crude oil—exports: 1,863 bbl/day (2013 est.)
country comparison to the world: 79

Crude oil—imports: 468,000 bbl/day (2013 est.)
country comparison to the world: 18

Crude oil—proved reserves: 10 million bbl (1 January 2015 est.)
country comparison to the world: 93

Refined petroleum products—production: 518.000 bbl/day (2013 est.)

country comparison to the world: 32

Refined petroleum products—consumption: 282,600 bbl/day (2014 est.)
country comparison to the world: 44

Refined petroleum products—exports: 265,400 bbl/day (2013 est.)
country comparison to the world: 27

Refined petroleum products—imports: 73,720 bbl/day (2013 est.)
country comparison to the world: 61

Natural gas—production: 5 million cu m (2014 est.)
country com p arison to the world: 92

Natural gas—consumption: 2.924 billion cu m (2014 est.)
country comparison to the world: 74

Natural gas—exports: 0 cu m (2014 est.)
country comparison to the world: 110

Natural gas—imports: 2.931 billion cu m (2014 est.)
country comparison to the world: 42

Natural gas—proved reserves: 991.1 million cu m (1 January 2014 est.)
country comparison to the world: 104

Carbon dioxide emissions from consumption of energy: 78.8 million Mt (2013 est.)
country comparison to the world: 47

COMMUNICATIONS

Telephones—fixed lines: *total subscriptions:* 5.22 million
subscriptions per 100 inhabitants: 48 (2014 est.)
country comparison to the world: 29

Telephones—mobile cellular: *total:* 12.8 million
subscriptions per 100 inhabitan ts: 119 (2014 est.)
country comparison to the world: 72

Telephone system: *general assessment:* adequate, modern networks reach all areas; good mobile telephone and international service
domestic: microwave radio relay trunk system; extensive open-wire connections; submarine cable to offshore islands
international: country code—30; landing point for the SEA-ME-WE-3 optical telecommunications submarine cable that provides links to Europe, Middle East, and Asia; a number of smaller submarine cables provide connectivity to various parts of Europe, the Middle East, and Cyprus; tropospheric scatter; satellite earth stations—4 (2 Intelsat—1 Atlantic Ocean and 1 Indian Ocean, 1 Eutelsat, and 1 Inmarsat—Indian Ocean region)

Broadcast media: Broadcast media dominated by the private sector; roughly 150 private TV channels, about ten of which broadcast nationwide; 1 government-owned terrestrial TV channel with national coverage; 3 privately owned satellite channels; multi-channel satellite and cable TV services available; upwards of 1,500 radio station

s, all of them privately owned; government-owned broadcaster has 2 National radio stations (2014)
Radio broadcast stations: AM 26, FM 88, short-wave 4 (1998)
Television broadcast stations: 36 (plus 1,341 repeaters); also 2 stations in the American Armed Forces Radio and Television Service (1995)

Internet country code: .gr

Internet hosts: 3.201 million (2012)
country comparison to the world: 32

Internet users: *total:* 6.2 million
percent of population: 57.9% (2014 est.)
country comparison to the world: 56

TRANSPORTATION

Airports: 77 (2013)
country comparison to the world: 69

Airports—with paved runways: *total:* 68
over 3,047 m: 6
2,438 to 3,047 m: 15
1,524 to 2,437 m: 19
914 to 1,523 m: 18
under 914 m: 10 (2013)

Airports—with unpaved runways: *total:* 9
914 to 1,523 m: 2
under 914 m: 7 (2013)

Heliports: 9 (2013)

Pipelines: gas 1,329 km; oil 94 km (2013)

Railways: *total:* 2,548 km
standard gauge: 1,565 km 1.435-m gauge (764 km electrified)
narrow gauge: 961 km 1.000-m gauge; 22 km 0.750-m gauge (2014)
country comparison to the world: 64

Roadways: *total:* 116,960 km
paved: 41,357 km (includes 1,091 km of expressways)
unpaved: 75,603 km (2010)
country comparison to the world: 40

Waterways: 6 km (the 6-km-long Corinth Canal crosses the Isthmus of Corinth; it shortens a sea voyage by 325 km) (2012)
country comparison to the world: 106

Merchant marine: *total:* 860
by type: bulk carrier 262, cargo 49, carrier 1, chemical tanker 68, container 35, liquefied gas 13, passenger 7, passenger/cargo 109, petroleum tanker 302, roll on/roll off 14
foreign-owned: 42 (Belgium 17, Bermuda 3, Cyprus 3, Italy 5, UK 6, US 8)
registered in other countries: 2,459 (Antigua and Barbuda 4, Bahamas 225, Barbados 14, Belize 2, Bermuda 8, Brazil 1, Cabo Verde 1, Cambodia 2, Cayman Islands 9, Comoros 4, Curacao 1, Cyprus 201, Dominica 4, Egypt 8, Gibraltar 8, Honduras 4, Hong Kong 27, Indonesia 1, Isle of Man 62, Italy 7, Jamaica 3, Liberia 505, Malta 469, Marshall Islands 408, Mexico 2, Moldova 1, Panama 379, Philippines 5, Portugal 2, Saint Kitts and Nevis 2, Saint Vincent and the Grenadines 42, Sao

Tome and Principe 1, Saudi Arabia 4, Singapore 22, UAE 3, Uruguay 1, Vanuatu 3, Venezuela 4, unknown 10) (2010)
country comparison to the world: 12

Ports and terminals: *major seaport(s):* Aspropyrgos, Pachi, Piraeus, Thessaloniki
oil terminal(s): Agioi Theodoroi
LNG terminal(s) (import): Revithoussa

MILITARY AND SECURITY

Military branches: Hellenic Army (Ellinikos Stratos, ES), Hellenic Navy (Elliniko Polemiko Navtiko, EPN), Hellenic Air Force (Elliniki Polemiki Aeroporia, EPA) (2013)

Military service age and obligation: 19–45 years of age for compulsory military service; during wartime the law allows for recruitment beginning January of the year of inductee's 18th birthday, thus including 17 year olds; 18 years of age for volunteers; conscript service obligation is 1 year for the Army and 9 months for the Air Force and Navy; women are eligible for voluntary military service (2014)

Military expenditures: 2.46% of GDP (2015 est.)
2.2% of GDP (2014)
2.19% of GDP (2013)
2.26% of GDP (2012)
note: based on 2010 prices
country comparison to the world: 48

TRANSNATIONAL ISSUES

Disputes—international: Greece and Turkey continue discussions to resolve their complex maritime, air, territorial, and boundary disputes in the Aegean Sea; Greece rejects the use of the name Macedonia or Republic of Macedonia; the mass migration of unemployed Albanians still remains a problem for developed countries, chiefly Greece and Italy

Refugees and internally displaced persons: *stateless persons:* 198 (2015)
note: 1,017,669 estimated refugee and migrant arrivals by sea (2015—June 2016)

Illicit drugs: a gateway to Europe for traffickers smuggling cannabis and heroin from the Middle East and Southwest Asia to the West and precursor chemicals to the East; some South American cocaine transits or is consumed in Greece; money laundering related to drug trafficking and organized crime

GREENLAND

INTRODUCTION

Background: Greenland, the world's largest island, is about 81% ice-capped. Vikings reached the island in the 10th century from Iceland; Danish colonization began in the 18th century, and Greenland became an integral part of the Danish Realm in 1953. It joined the European Community (now the EU) with Denmark in 1973 but withdrew in 1985 over a dispute centered on stringent fishing quotas. Greenland remains a member of the Overseas Countries and Territories Association of the EU. Green land was granted self-government in 1979 by the Danish parliament; the law went into effect the following year. Greenland voted in favor of increased self-rule in November 2008 and acquired greater responsibility for internal affairs when the Act on Greenland Self-Government was signed into law in June 2009. Denmark, however, continues to exercise control over several policy areas on behalf of Greenland, including foreign affairs, security, and financial policy in consultation with Green land's Self-Rule Government.

GEOGRAPHY

Location: Northern North America, island between the Arctic Ocean and the North Atlantic Ocean, northeast of Canada

Geographic coordinates: 72 00 N, 40 00 W

Map references: *Arctic Region*

Area: *total:* 2,166,086 sq km
land: 2,166,086 sq km (410,449 sq km ice-free, 1,755,637 sq km ice-covered)
country comparison to the world: 12

Area—comparative: slightly more than three times the size of Texas

Land boundaries: 0 km

Coastline: 44,087 km

Maritime claims: *territorial sea:* 3 n m
exclusive fishing zone: 200 nm or agreed boundaries or median line
continental shelf: 200 nm or agreed boundaries or median line

Climate: arctic to subarctic; cool summers, cold winters

Terrain: flat to gradually sloping icecap covers all but a narrow, mountainous, barren, rocky coast

Elevation: *mean elevation:* 1,792 m

elevation extremes: *lowest point:* Atlantic Ocean 0 m
highest point: Gunnbjorn Fjeld 3,700 m

Natural resources: coal, iron ore, lead, zinc, molybdenum, diamonds, gold, platinum, niobium, tantalite, uranium, fish, seals, whales, hydropower, possible oil and gas

Land use: *agricultural land:* 0.6%
arable land: 0%
permanent crops: 0%
permanent pasture: 0.6%
forest: 0%
other: 99.4% (2011 est.)

Irrigated land: NA

Natural hazards: continuous permafrost over northern two-thirds of the island

Environment—current issues: protection of the arctic environment; preservation of the Inuit traditional way of life, including whaling and seal hunting

Geography—note: dominates North Atlantic Ocean between North America and Europe; sparse population confined to small settlements along coast; close to one-quarter of the population lives in the capital, Nuuk; world's second largest ice sheet after that of Antarctica

PEOPLE AND SOCIETY

Nationality: *noun:* Greenlander(s)
adjective: Greenlandic

Ethnic groups: Inuit 88%, Danish and other 12% (2010 est.)

Languages: Greenlandic (East Inuit) (official), Danish (official), English

Religions: Evangelical Lutheran, traditional Inuit spiritual beliefs

Population: 57,733 (July 2015 est.)
country comparison to the world: 206

Age structure: *0–14 years:* 21.35% (male 6,263/female 6,064)
15–24 years: 16.2% (male 4,736/female 4,615)
25–54 years: 42.03% (male 12,751/female 11,516)
55–64 years: 11.87% (male 3,858/female 2,996)
65 years and over: 8.55% (male 2,640/female 2,294) (2015 est.)

Median age: *total:* 33.7 years
male: 34.9 years
female: 32.5 years (2015 est.)
country comparison to the world: 85

Population growth rate: 0% (2015 est.)
country comparison to the world: 196

Birth rate: 14.48 births/1,000 population (2015 est.)
country comparison to the world: 135

Death rate: 8.49 deaths/1,000 population (2015 est.)
country comparison to the world: 77

Net migration rate: -5.98 migrant(s)/1,000 population (2015 est.)
country comparison to the world: 198

Urbanization: *urban population:* 86.4% of total population (2015)
rate of urbanization: 0.74% annual rate of change (2010–15 est.)

Major urban areas—population: NUUK (capital) 17,000 (2014)

Sex ratio: *at birth:* 1.05 male(s)/female
0–14 years: 1.03 male(s)/female
15–24 years: 1.03 male(s)/female
25–54 years: 1.11 male(s)/female
55–64 years: 1.29 male(s)/female
65 years and over: 1.15 male(s)/female
total population: 1.1 male(s)/female (2015 est.)

Infant mortality rate: *total:* 9.23 deaths/1,000 live births
male: 10.54 deaths/1,000 live births
female: 7.85 deaths/1,000 live births (2015 est.)
country comparison to the world: 143

Life expectancy at birth: *total population:* 72.1 years
male: 69.41 years
female: 74.92 years (2015 est.)
country comparison to the world: 144

Total fertility rate: 2.03 children born/woman (2015 est.)
country comparison to the world: 118

Physicians density: 1.67 physicians/1,000 population (2009)

Hospital bed density: 5.8 beds/1,000 population (2009)

Drinking water source:
improved:
urban: 100% of population
rural: 100% of population
total: 100% of population
unimproved:
urban: 0% of population
rural: 0% of population

total: 0% of population (2015 est.)

Sanitation facility access:
improved:
urban: 100% of population
rural: 100% of population
total: 100% of population
unimproved:
urban: 0% of population
rural: 0% of population
total: 0% of population (2015 est.)

HIV/AIDS—adult prevalence rate: NA

HIV/AIDS—people living with HIV/AIDS: NA

HIV/AIDS—deaths: NA

GOVERNMENT

Country name: *conventional long form:* none
conventional short form: Greenland
local long form: none
local short form: Kalaallit Nunaat
note: named by Norwegian adventurer Erik THORVALDSSON (Erik the Red) in 985 in order to entice settlers to the island

Dependency status: part of the Kingdom of Denmark; self-governing overseas administrative division of Denmark since 1979

Government type: parliamentary democracy (Parliament of Greenland); part of the Kingdom of Denmark

Capital: *name:* Nuuk (Godthaab)

Geographic coordinates: 64 11 N, 51 45 W
time difference: UTC-3 (2 hours ahead of Washington, DC, during Standard Time)
daylight saving time: +1hr, begins last Sunday in March; ends last Sunday in October
note: Greenland has four time zones

Administrative divisions: 4 municipalities (kommuner, singular kommune); Kujalleq, Qaasuitsup, Qeqqata, Sermersooq
note: the North and East Greenland National Park (Avannaarsuani Tunumilu Nuna Allanngutsaaliugaq) and the Thule Air Base in Pituffik (in northwest Greenland) are two unincorporated areas; the national park's 972,000 sq km—about 46% of the island—makes it the largest national park in the world and also the most northerly

Independence: none (extensive self-rule as part of the Kingdom of Denmark; foreign affairs is the responsibility of Denmark, but Greenland actively participates in international agreements relating to Greenland)

National holiday: June 21 (longest day)

Constitution: previous 1953 (Greenland established as a constituency in the Danish constitution), 1979 (Greenland Home Rule Act); latest 21 June 2009 (Greenland Self-G overnment Act) (2016)

Legal system: the laws of Denmark apply where applicable and Greenlandic law applies to other areas

Citizenship: see Denmark

Suffrage: 18 years of age; universal

Executive branch: *chief of state:* Queen MARGRETHE II of Denmark (since 14 January 1972), represented by High Commissioner Mikaela ENGELL (since April 2011)

head of government: Premier Kim KIELSEN (since 30 September 2014)
cabinet: Home Rule Government elected by the Parliament (Landsting) on the basis of the strength of parties
elections/appointments: the monarchy is hereditary; high commissioner appointed by the monarch; premier indirectly elected by Parliament
election results: Kim KIELSEN elected premier; Parliament vote—Kim KIELSEN (S) 34.3%, Sara OLSVIG (IA) 33.2%, Anda ULDUM (D) 11.8%, other 20.7%

Legislative branch: *description:* unicameral Parliament or Inatsisartut (Landsting) (31 seats; members directly elected in multi-seat constituencies by proportional representation vote to serve 4-year terms)
note: two representatives were elected to the Danish Parliament or Folketing on 18 June 2015 (next to be held by June 2019); percent of vote by party—NA; seats by party—Siumut 1, Inuit Ataqatiigit 1
elections: last held on 28 November 2014 (next to be held by 2018)
election results: percent of vote by party—S 34.6%, IA 33.5%, D 11.9%, PN 11.7%, A 6.6%, other 1.7%; seats by party—S 11, IA 11, D 4, PN 3, A 2 (2013)

Judicial branch: *highest court(s):* High Court of Greenland (consists of the presiding professional judge and 2 lay assessors); note—appeals beyond the High Court of Greenland can be heard by the Supreme Court (in Copenhagen)
judge selection and term of office: judges appointed by the monarch upon the recommendation of the Judicial Appointments Council, a 6-member independent body of judges and lawyers; judges appointed for life with retirement at age 70
subordinate courts: Court of Greenland; 18 district or magistrates' courts

Political parties and leaders:
Democrats Party or D (Demokraatit) [Randi VESTERGAARD]
Forward Party or S (Siumut) [Kim KIELSEN]
Inuit Community or IA (Inuit Ataqatiigit) [Sara OLSVIG]
Inuit Party or PI (Partii Inuit) [Nikku OLSEN]
Partii Naleraq or PN [H ans ENOKSEN]
Solidarity Party or A (Atassut) [Knud KRISTIANSEN]

Political pressure groups and leaders: *other:* conservationists; environmentalists; those wanting independence

International organization participation: Arctic Council, ICC, NC, NIB, UPU

Diplomatic representation in the US: none (self-governing overseas administrative division of Denmark): note—Greenland has an office in the Danish Embassy to the US; it also has offices in the Danish consulates of Chicago and New York

Diplomatic representation from the US: none (self-governing overseas administrative division of Denmark); note—the U Sembassy in Copenhagen has an office devoted to Greenland

Flag description: two equal horizontal bands of white (top) and red with a large disk slightly to the hoist side of center—the top half of the disk is red, the bottom half is white; the design represents the sun reflecting off a field of ice; the colors are the same as those of the Danish flag and symbolize Greenland's links to the Kingdom of Denmark

National symbol(s): polar bear; national colors: red, white

National anthem: *name:* "Nunarput utoqqarsuanngoravit" ("Our Country, Who's Become So Old" also translated as "You Our Ancient Land")
lyrics/music: Henrik LUND/Jonathan PETERSEN
note: adopted 1916; the government also recognizes "Nunaasiilasooq" as a secondary anthem

ECONOMY

Economy—overview: The economy remains critically dependent on exports of shrimp and fish, income from resource exploration and extraction, and on a substantial subsidy from the Danish Government. The subsidy was budgeted to be about $535 million in 2015, approximately 56% of government revenues that year. The public sector, including publicly owned enterprises and the municipalities, plays the dominant role in Greenland's economy. Greenland's real GDP contracted about 5% from 2012 to 2014. Real growth is projected for 2015 and 2016 due to increasing world prices for fish and shellfish, public construction activities, and to a small degree from increased revenues from small-scale mining.

During the last decade the Greenland Home Rule Government pursued conservative fiscal and monetary policies, bu t public pressure has increased for better schools, health care, and retirement systems. The public budget exhibited a deficit of 2% of GDP in 2014, but public debt remains low at about 5% of GDP. The Greenlandic economy has benefited from increasing catches and exports of shrimp, Greenland halibut and, more recently, mackerel. Due to Greenland's continued dependence on exports of fish—which accounted for 91% of exports in 2015—the economy remains very sensitive to external demand and price fluctuations.

The Greenlandic economy is expected to expand in 2016, but significant challenges face the island. High unemployment, structural challenges stemming from low levels of qualified labor, geographic dispersion, an undiversified economy, the long-termsustainability of the public budget, and a declining population due to emigration. Catches in fisheries have been declining in recent years and a reversal in prices will quickly lead to vulnerabilities. Hydrocarbon exploration has ceased with declining oil prices and currently only three mines are under development. The island has potential for natural resource exploitation with rare-earth, uranium, and iron ore mineral projects proposed.

Tourism offers another avenue of economic growth for Greenland, with increasing numbers of cruise lines now operating in Greenland's western and southern waters during the peak summer tourism season.

GDP (purchasing power parity):
$2.173 billion (2014 est.)
$2.154 billion (2013 est.)
$2.165 billion (2012 est.)
note: data are in 2011 US dollars
country comparison to the world: 193

GDP (official exchange rate): $2.16 billion (2011 est.)

GDP—real growth rate: 0.9% (2014 est.)
-0.5% (2013 est.)
1.5% (2012 est.)
country comparison to the world: 179

GDP—per capita (PPP): $37,900 (2008 est.)
$38,100 (2007 est.)
country comparison to the world: 44

GDP—composition, by sector of origin:
agriculture: 13.9%
industry: 19.2%
services: 67% (2012 est.)

Agriculture—products: sheep, cow, rein deer, fish

Industries: fish processing (mainly shrimp and Greenland halibut); gold, zinc, anorthosite and ruby mining; handicrafts, hides and skins, small shipyards

Industrial production growth rate: NA%

Labor force: 26,990 (2012 est.)
country comparison to the world: 207

Labor force—by occupation: *agriculture:* 13.9%
industry: 19.2%
services: 67% (2012 est.)

Unemployment rate: 9.4% (2013 est.)
4.2% (2010 est.)
country comparison to the world: 108

Population below poverty line: 9.2% (2007 est.)

Household income or consumption by percentage share: *lowest:* 10%: NA%
highest: 10%: NA%

Budget: *revenues:* $1.72 billion
expenditures: $1.68 billion (2010)
Taxes and other revenues: 79.6% of GDP (2010)
country comparison to the world: 4

Budget surplus (+) or deficit (−): 1.9% of GDP (2010)
country comparison to the world: 15

Fiscal year: calendar year

Inflation rate (consumer prices): 1.8% (2012 est.)
2.8% (2011 est.)
country comparison to the world: 111

Exports: $384.3 million (2010)
$358 million (2009)
country comparison to the world: 178

Exports—commodities: fish and fish products, 91% (2015 est.)

Exports—partners: Denmark 51.6%, China 11.1%, Japan 9.1%, Russia 7.2% (2015)

Imports: $814.2 million (2010)

$726 million (2009)
country comparison to the world: 185

Imports—commodities: machinery and transport equipment, manufactured goods, food, petroleum products

Imports—partners: Denmark 67.1%, Sweden 14.1%, Iceland 5.1% (2015)

Debt—external: $36.4 million (2010)
$58 million (2009)
country comparison to the world: 196

Exchange rates: Danish kroner (DKK) per US dollar—
6.588 (2015 est.)
5.6125 (2014 est.)
5.3687 (2013 est.)
5.79 (2012 est.)
5.3687 (2011 est.)

ENERGY

Electricity—production: 314 million kWh (2012 est.)
country comparison to the world: 175

Electricity—consumption: 292 million kWh (2012 est.)
country comparison to the world: 179

Electricity—exports: 0 kWh (2013 est.)
country comparison to the world: 145

Electricity—imports: 0 kWh (2013 est.)
country comparison to the world: 156

Electricity—installed generating capacity: 106,000 kW (2012 est.)
country comparison to the world: 173

Electricity—from fossil fuels: 100% of total installed capacity (2012 est.)
country comparison to the world: 12

Electricity—from nuclear fuels:
0% of total installed capacity (2012 est.)
country comparison to the world: 101

Electricity—from hydroelectric plants: 0% of total installed capacity (2012 est.)
country comparison to the world: 176

Electricity—from other renewable sources: 0% of total installed capacity (2012 est.)
country comparison to the world: 179

Crude oil—production: 0 bbl/day (2014 est.)
country comparison to the world: 142

Crude oil—exports: 0 bbl/day (2012 est.)
country comparison to the world: 131

Crude oil—imports: 0 bbl/day (2012 est.)
country comparison to the world: 198

Crude oil—proved reserves: 0 bbl (1 January 2015 est.)
country comparison to the world: 140

Refined petroleum products—production: 0 bbl/day (2012 est.)
country comparison to the world: 189

Refined petroleum products—consumption: 7,000 bbl/day (2013 est.)
country comparison to the world: 160

Refined petroleum products—exports: 0 bbl/day (2012 est.)
country comparison to the world: 186

Refined petroleum products—imports: 6,971 bbl/day (2012 est.)
country comparison to the world: 146

Natural gas—production: 0 cu m (2013 est.)
country comparison to the world: 195

Natural gas—consumption: 0 cu m (2013 est.)
country comparison to the world: 149

Natural gas—exports: 0 cu m (2013 est.)
country comparison to the world: 108

Natural gas—imports: 0 cu m (2013 est.)
country comparison to the world: 203

Natural gas—proved reserves: 0 cu m (1 January 2014 est.)
country comparison to the world: 145

Carbon dioxide emissions from consumption of energy: 604,900 Mt (2012 est.)
country comparison to the world: 177

COMMUNICATIONS

Telephones—fixed lines: *total subscriptions:* 17,200
subscriptions per 100 inhabitants: 30 (2014 est.)
country comparison to the world: 191

Telephones—mobile cellular: *total:* 60,800
subscriptions per 100 inhabitants: 105 (2014 est.)
country comparison to the world: 200

Telephone system: *general assessment:* adequate domestic and international service provided by satellite, cables, and microwave radio relay; totally digital since 1995
domestic: microwave radio relay and satellite; the fundamental telecommunications infrastructure consists of a digital radio link from Nanortalik in south Greenland to Uummannaq in north Greenland; satellites cover north and east Greenland, both in terms of domestic and foreign telecommunications; a marine cable connects south and west Greenland to the rest of the world, extending from Nuuk and Qaqortoq to Canada and Iceland
international: country code—299; satellite earth stations—15 (12 Intelsat, 1 Eutelsat, 2 Americom GE-2 (all Atlantic Ocean)) (2015)

Broadcast media: the Greenland Broadcasting Company provides public radio and TV services throughout the island with a broadcast station and a series of repeaters; a few private local TV and radio stations; Danish public radio rebroadcasts are available (2015)
Radio broadcast stations: AM 5, FM 14, shortwave 0 (2008)
Television broadcast stations: 1 (plus some local low-power stations, and 3 American Forces Radio and Television Service (AFRTS) stations (1997)

Internet country code: .gl

Internet hosts: 15,645 (2012)
country comparison to the world: 123

Internet users: *total:* 40,100
percent of population: 69.5% (2014 est.)
country comparison to the world: 192

TRANSPORTATION

Airports: 15 (2013)

country comparison to the world: 147

Airports—with paved runways: *total:* 10
2,438 to 3,047 m: 2
1,524 to 2,437 m: 1
914 to 1,523 m: 1
under 914 m: 6 (2013)

Airports—with unpaved runways: *total:* 5
1,524 to 2,437 m: 1
914 to 1,523 m: 1
under 914 m: 2 (2013)

Roadways: *note:* although there are short roads in towns, there are no roads between towns; inter-urban transport is either by sea or by air (2015)

Merchant marine: *registered in other countries:* 1 (Denmark 1) (2010)
country comparison to the world: 156

Ports and terminals: *major seaport(s):* Sisimiut

MILITARY AND SECURITY

Military branches: no regular military forces; the Government of Denmark has responsibility for defense, as such the Danish military's Joint Arctic Command is responsible for territorial defense of Greenland (2016)

Military—note: defense is the responsibility of Denmark

TRANSNATIONAL ISSUES

Disputes—international: managed dispute between Canada and Denmark over Hans Island in the Kennedy Channel between Canada's Elles-mere Island and Greenland; Denmark (Green-land) and Norway have made submissions to the Commission on the Limits of the Continental Shelf (CLCS) and Russia is collecting additional data to augment its 2001 CLCS submission

GRENADA

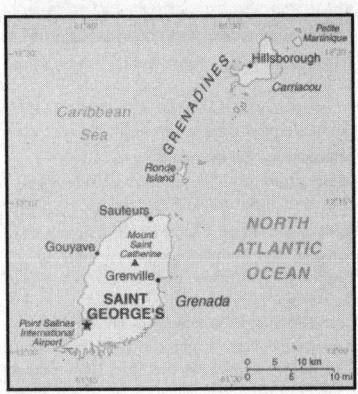

INTRODUCTION

Background: Carib Indians inhabited Grenada when Christopher COLUMBUS discovered the island in 1498, but it remained uncolonized for more than a century. The French settled Grenada in the 17th century, established sugar estates, and imported large numbers of African slaves. Britain took the island in 1762 and vigorously expanded sugar production. In the 19th century, cacao even-tually surpassed sugar as the main export crop; in the 20th century, nutmeg became the leading export. In 1967, Britain gave Grenada autonomy over its in ternal affairs. Full independence was attain ed in 1974 mak in g Grenada one of the smallest independent countries in the Western Hemisphere. Grenada was seized by a Marxist mili-tary council on 19 October 1983. Six days later the island was invaded by US forces and those of six other Caribbean nations, which quickly captured the ringleaders and their hundreds of Cuban advis-ers. Free elections were rein s tituted the following year and have continu ed since then.

GEOGRAPHY

Location: Caribbean, is land between the Carib-bean Sea and Atlantic Ocean, north of Trinidad and Tobago

Geographic coordinates: 12 07 N, 61 40 W

Map references: Central America and the Caribbean

Area: *total:* 344 sq km
land: 344 sq km
water: 0 sq km
country comparison to the world: 207

Area—comparative: twice the size of Washington, DC

Land boundaries: 0 km

Coastline: 121 km

Maritime claims: *territorial sea:* 12 nm
exclusive economic zone: 200 nm

Climate: tropical; tempered by north east trade winds

Terrain: volcanic in origin with central mountains

Elevation: *mean elevation:* NA

elevation extremes: *lowest point:* Caribbean Sea 0 m
highest point: Mount Saint Catherine 840 m

Natural resources: timber, tropical fruit, deepwater harbors

Land use: *agricultural land:* 32.3%
arable land: 8.8%
permanent crops: 20.6%
permanent pasture: 2.9%
forest: 50%
other: 17.7% (2011 est.)

Irrigated land: 20 sq km (2012)

Total renewable water resources: NA

Natural hazards: lies on edge of hurricane belt; hurricane season lasts from June to November

Environment—current issues: NA

Environment—international agreements: *party to:* Biodiversity, Climate Change, Climate Change-Kyoto Protocol, Desertification, Endangered Species, Law of the Sea, Ozone Layer Protection, Whaling
signed, but not ratified: none of the selected agreements

Geography—note: the administration of the islands of the Grenadines group is divided between Saint Vincent and the Grenadines and Grenada

PEOPLE AND SOCIETY

Nationality: *noun:* Grenadian(s)
adjective: Grenadian

Ethnic groups: African descent 89.4%, mixed 8.2%, East Indian 1.6%, other 0.9% (includes indigenous) (2001 est.)

Languages: English (official), French patois

Religions: Roman Catholic 44.6%, Protestant 43.5% (includes Anglican 11.5%, Pentecostal 11.3%, Seventh Day Adventist 10.5%, Baptist 2.9%, Church of God 2.6%, Methodist 1.8%, Evangelical 1.6%, other 1.3%), Jehovah's Witness 1.1%, Rastafarian 1.1%, other 6.2%, none 3.6%

Population: 110,694 (July 2015 est.)
country comparison to the world: 191

Age structure: *0–14 years:* 24.35% (male 13,958/female 12,998)
15–24 years: 16.02% (male 8,830/female 8,906)
25–54 years: 40.35% (male 22,891/female 21,771)
55–64 years: 9.65% (male 5,482/female 5,204)
65 years and over: 9.62% (male 4,888/female 5,766) (2015 est.)

Dependency ratios: *total dependency ratio:* 50.7%
youth dependency ratio: 39.9%
elderly dependency ratio: 10.8%
potential support ratio: 9.3% (2015 est.)

Median age: *total:* 30.4 years
male: 30.4 years
female: 30.4 years (2015 est.)
country comparison to the world: 109

Population growth rate: 0.48% (2015 est.)
country comparison to the world: 161

Birth rate: 16.03 births/1,000 population (2015 est.)
country comparison to the world: 120

Death rate: 8.08 deaths/1,000 population (2015 est.)
country comparison to the world: 96

Net migration rate: -3.13 migrant(s)/1,000 popula-tion (2015 est.)
country comparison to the world: 182

Urbanization: *urban population:* 35.6% of total population (2015)
rate of urbanization: 0.33% annual rate of change (2010–15 est.)

Major urban areas—population: SAINT-GEORGE'S (capital) 38,000 (2014)

Sex ratio: *at birth:* 1.1 male(s)/female
0–14 years: 1.07 male(s)/female
15–24 years: 0.99 male(s)/female
25–54 years: 1.05 male(s)/female
55–64 years: 1.05 male(s)/female
65 years and over: 0.85 male(s)/female
total population: 1.03 male(s)/female (2015 est.)

Maternal mortality rate: 27 deaths/100,000 live births (2015 est.)
country comparison to the world: 134

Infant mortality rate: *total:* 10.21 deaths/1,000 live births
male: 9.59 deaths/1,000 live births
female: 10.9 deaths/1,000 live births (2015 est.)
country comparison to the world: 136

Life expectancy at birth: *total population:* 74.05 years
male: 71.47 years
female: 76.88 years (2015 est.)
country comparison to the world: 125

Total fertility rate: 2.06 children born/woman (2015 est.)
country comparison to the world: 112

Health expenditures: 6.3% of GDP (2013)
country comparison to the world: 97

Physicians density: 0.66 physicians/1,000 population (2006)

Hospital bed density: 3.5 beds/1,000 population (2012)
Drinking water source:
improved:
urban: 99% of population
rural: 95.3% of population
total: 96.6% of population unimproved:
urban: 1% of population
rural: 4.7% of population
total: 3.4% of population (2015 est.)

Sanitation facility access:
improved:
urban: 97.5% of population
rural: 98.3% of population
total: 98% of population
unimproved:
urban: urban: 2.5% of population
rural: 1.7% of population
total: 2% of population (2015 est.)

HIV/AIDS—adult prevalence rate: NA

HIV/AIDS—people living with HIV/AIDS: NA

HIV/AIDS—deaths: NA

Obesity—adult prevalence rate: 24.6% (2014)
country comparison to the world: 78

School life expectancy (primary to tertiary education): *total:* 16 years
male: 15 years
female: 16 years (2009)

GOVERNMENT

Country name: *conventional long form:* none
conventional short form: Grenada
etymology: probably named for the Spanish city of Granada; in Spanish "granada" means "pomegranate"

Government type: parliamentary democracy (Parliament); a Commonwealth realm

Capital: *name:* Saint George's

Geographic coordinates: 12 03 N, 61 45 W
time difference: UTC-4 (1 hour ahead of Washington, DC, during Standard Time)

Administrative divisions: 6 parishes and 1 dependency*; Carriacou and Petite Martinique*, Saint Andrew, Saint David, Saint George, Saint John, Saint Mark, Saint Patrick

Independence: 7 February 1974 (from the UK)

National holiday: Independence Day, 7 February (1974)

Constitution: previous 1967; latest presen ted 19 December 1973, effective 7 February 1974, suspended 1979 following a revolution, but restored in 1983; amen ded 1991 (Con stitution al Judica-ture Act, 1991); n ote—in late 2015, as part of con stitution al reform, Parliamen t completed its first reading of a package of amen dmen ts (2016)

Legal system: common law based on English model

International law organization participation: has not submitted an ICJ jurisdiction declaration; accepts ICCt jurisdiction

Citizenship: *citizenship by birth:* yes
citizenship by descent: yes
dual citizenship recogn ized: yes
residency requirement for naturalization: 7 years for persons from a non-Caribbean state and 4 years for apers on from a Caribbean state

Suffrage: 18 years of age; universal

Executive branch: *chief of state:* Queen ELIZA-BETH II (since 6 February 1952); represented by Governor General Cecile LA GRENADE (since 7 May 2013)

head of government: Prime Minister Keith MITCHELL (since 20 February 2013)
cabinet: Cabinet appointed by the governor general on the advice of the prime minister
elections/appointments: the monarchy is hereditary; governor general appointed by the monarch; following legislative elections, the leader of the majority party or majority coalition usually appointed prime minister by the governor general

Legislative branch: *description:* bicameral Parliament consists of the Senate (13 seats; members appointed by the governor general—10 on the advice of the prime minister and 3 on the advice of the opposition party leader; members serve 5-year terms) and the House of Representatives (15 seats; members directly elected in single-seat constituencies by simple majority vote to serve 5-year terms)
elections: last held on 19 February 2013 (next to be held in 2018)

election results: House of Representatives—percent of vote by party—NNP 59%, NDC 41%; seats by party—NNP 15

Judicial branch: *highest court(s):* Supreme Court of Grenada (consists of the High Court with 3 justices and a 2-tier Court of Appeal with NA justices); note—the Eastern Caribbean Supreme Court (ECSC) is the itinerant superior court of record for the 9-member Organization of Eastern Caribbean States to include Grenada; the ECSC—with its headquarters on St. Lucia—is headed by the chief justice and is comprised of the Court of Appeal with 3 justices and the High Court with 16 judges; sittings of the Court of Appeal and High Court rotate among the member states
judge selection and term of office: justice selection and tenure NA
subordinate courts: magistrates' courts; Court of Magisterial Appeals

Political parties and leaders: Grenada United Labor Party or GULP [Wilfred HAYES]
National Democratic Congress or NDC [Tillman THOMAS]
New National Party or NNP [Keith MITCHELL]

Political pressure groups and leaders: Committee for Human Rights in Grenada or CHRG
New Jewel Movement Support Group
The British Grenada Friendship Society
The New Jewel 19 Committee

International organization participation: ACP, AOSIS, C, Caricom, CDB, CELAC, FAO, G-77, IBRD, ICAO, ICCt (signatory), ICRM, IDA, IFAD, IFC, IFRCS, ILO, IMF, IMO, Interpol, IOC, ITU, ITUC, LAES, MIGA, NAM, OAS, OECS, OPANAL, OPCW, Petrocaribe, UN, UNCTAD, UNESCO, UNIDO, UPU, WHO, WIPO, WTO

Diplomatic representation in the US: *chief of mission:* Ambassador Ethelstan A. FRIDAY (since 3 September 2013)
chancery: 1701 New Hampshire Avenue NW, Washington, DC 20009
telephone: [1] (202) 265-2561
FAX: [1] (202) 265-2468
consulate(s) general: Miami

Diplomatic representation from the US: *chief of mission:* the US does not have an embassy in Grenada; the US Ambassador to Barbados is accredited to Grenada
embassy: Lance-aux-Epines Stretch, Saint George's
mailing address: P.O. Box 54, Saint George's
telephone: [1] (473) 444-1173 through 1176
FAX: [1] (473) 444-4820

Flag description: a rectangle divided diagonally into yellow triangles (top and bottom) and green triangles (hoist side and outer side), with a red border around the flag; there are seven yellow, five-pointed stars with three centered in the top red border, three centered in the bottom red border, and one on a red disk superimposed at the center of the flag; there is also a symbolic nutmeg pod on the hoist-side triangle (Grenada is the world's second-largest producer of nutmeg, after Indonesia);

349

the seven stars stand for the seven administrative divisions, with the central star denoting the capital, St. George; yellow represents the sun and the warmth of the people, green stands for vegetation and agriculture, and red symbolizes harmony, unity, and courage

National symbol(s): Grenada dove, Bougainvillea flower; national colors: red, yellow, green

National anthem: *name:* "Hail Grenada"
lyrics/music: Irva Merle BAPTISTE/Louis Arnold MASANTO
note: adopted 1974

ECONOMY

Economy—overview: Grenada relies on tourism as its main source of foreign exchange especially since the construction of an international airport in 1985. Strong performances in construction and manufacturing, together with the development of tourism and higher education—especially in medicine—contributed to growth in national output; however, economic growth remained stagnant in 2010–14, after a sizable contraction in 2009, because of the global economic slowdown's effects on tourism and remittances. Gross national saving -and wealth—has been declining since 2010. Hurricanes Ivan (2004) and Emily (2005) severely damaged the agricultural sector—particularly nutmeg and cocoa cultivation—which had been a key driver of economic growth. Grenada has rebounded from the devastating effects of the hurricanes but is now saddled with the debt burden from the rebuilding process. Public debt-to-GDP is about 110%, leaving the MITCHELL administration limited room to engage in public investments and social spending. MITCHELL in 2013 announced a structural adjustment program that includes a plan to increase tax revenue.

GDP (purchasing power parity): $1.401 billion (2015 est.)
$1.34 billion (2014 est.)
$1.268 billion (2013 est.)
note: data are in 2015 US dollars
country comparison to the world: 199

GDP (official exchange rate): $954 million (2015 est.)

GDP—real growth rate: 4.6% (2015 est.)
5.7% (2014 est.)
2.4% (2013 est.)
country comparison to the world: 46

GDP—per capita (PPP): $13,100 (2015 est.)
$12,600 (2014 est.)
$12,000 (2013 est.)
note: data are in 2015 US dollars
country comparison to the world: 119

Gross national saving: 3.8% of GDP (2015 est.)
1.4% of GDP (2014 est.)
-3.2% of GDP (2013 est.)
country comparison to the world: 167

GDP—composition, by end use:
household consumption: 93%
government consumption: 15.2%
investment in fixed capital: 16.1%
investment in inventories: -0.1%

exports of good s and services: 16.9%
imports of goods and services: -41.1% (2015 est.)

GDP—composition, by sector of origin:
agriculture: 6.2%
industry: 14.3%
services: 79.5% (2015 est.)

Agriculture—products: bananas, cocoa, nutmeg, mace, citrus, avocados, root crops, sugarcane, corn, vegetables

Industries: food and beverages, textiles, light assembly operations, tourism, construction

Industrial production growth rate: -1% (2015 est.)
country comparison to the world: 172

Labor force: 59,900 (2013 est.)
country comparison to the world: 188

Labor force—by occupation: *agriculture:* 11%
industry: 20%
services: 69% (2008 est.)

Unemployment rate: 33.5% (2013)
25% (2008)
country comparison to the world: 190

Population below poverty line: 38% (2008 est.)

Household income or consumption by percentage share: *lowest:* 10%: NA%
highest: 10%: NA%

Budget: *revenues:* $191.8 million
expenditures: $230.9 million (2012 est.)
Taxes and other revenues: 20.1% of GDP (2012 est.)
country comparison to the world: 155

Budget surplus (+) or deficit (–): -4.1% of GDP (2012 est.)
country comparison to the world: 148

Public debt: 110% of GDP (2012 est.)
country comparison to the world: 10

Fiscal year: calendar year

Inflation rate (consumer prices): -1.3% (2015 est.)
-0.8% (2014 est.)
country comparison to the world: 8

Central bank discount rate: 6.5% (31 December 2009)
6.5% (31 December 2008)
country comparison to the world: 54

Commercial bank prime lending rate: 9.2% (31 December 2015 est.)
9.19% (31 December 2014 est.)
country comparison to the world: 92

Stock of narrow money: $183.3 million (31 December 2015 est.)
$172.8 million (31 December 2014 est.)
country comparison to the world: 183

Stock of broad money: $773.7 million (31 December 2015 est.)
$747.4 million (31 December 2014 est.)
country comparison to the world: 174

Stock of domestic credit: $627.1 million (31 December 2015 est.)
$623.8 million (31 December 2014 est.)
country comparison to the world: 164

Market value of publicly traded shares: $NA

Current account balance: -$144 million (2015 est.)
-$142 million (2014 est.)
country comparison to the world: 74

Exports: $43.8 million (2015 est.)
$42.2 million (2014 est.)
country comparison to the world: 203

Exports—commodities: nutmeg, bananas, cocoa, fruit and vegetables, clothing, mace

Exports—partners: Nigeria 44.7%, St. Lucia 10.8%, Antigua and Barbuda 7.3%, St. Kitts and Nevis 6.6%, Dominica 6.6%, US 5.8% (2015)

Imports: $310.4 million (2015 est.)
$306.6 million (2014 est.)
country comparison to the world: 199

Imports—commodities: food, manufactured goods, machinery, chemicals, fuel

Imports—partners: Trinidad and Tobago 49.6%, US 16.4% (2015)

Debt—external: $679 million (2013 est.)
$538 million (2010 est.)
country comparison to the world: 173

Exchange rates: East Caribbean dollars (XCD) per US dollar—
2.7 (2015 est.)
2.7 (2014 est.)
2.7 (2013 est.)
2.7 (2012 est.)
2.7 (2011 est.)

ENERGY

Electricity—production: 193 million kWh (2012 est.)
country comparison to the world: 186

Electricity—consumption: 178 million kWh (2012 est.)
country comparison to the world: 189

Electricity—exports: 0 kWh (2013 est.)
country comparison to the world: 144

Electricity—imports: 0 kWh (2013 est.)
country comparison to the world: 155

Electricity—installed generating capacity: 48,700 kW (2012 est.)
country comparison to the world: 186

Electricity—from fossil fuels: 98.6% of total installed capacity (2012 est.)
country comparison to the world: 52

Electricity—from nuclear fuels: 0% of total installed capacity (2012 est.)
country comparison to the world: 100

Electricity—from hydroelectric plants: 0% of total installed capacity (2012 est.)
country comparison to the world: 175

Electricity—from other renewable sources: 1.4% of total installed capacity (2012 est.)
country comparison to the world: 89

Crude oil—production: 0 bbl/day (2014 est.)
country comparison to the world: 141

Crude oil—exports: 0 bbl/day (2012 est.)
country comparison to the world: 130

Crude oil—imports: 0 bbl/day (2012 est.)

country comparison to the world: 197

Crude oil—proved reserves: 0 bbl (1 January 2015 est.)
country comparison to the world: 139

Refined petroleum products—production: 0 bbl/day (2012 est.)
country comparison to the world: 188

Refined petroleum products—consumption: 2,000 bbl/day (2013 est.)
country comparison to the world: 187

Refined petroleum products—exports: 0 bbl/day (2012 est.)
country comparison to the world: 185

Refined petroleum products—imports: 2,012 bbl/day (2012 est.)
country comparison to the world: 182

Natural gas—production: 0 cu m (2013 est.)
country comparison to the world: 194

Natural gas—consumption: 0 cu m (2013 est.)
country comparison to the world: 148

Natural gas—exports: 0 cu m (2013 est.)
country comparison to the world: 107

Natural gas—imports: 0 cu m (2013 est.)
country comparison to the world: 202

Natural gas—proved reserves: 0 cu m (1 January 2014 est.)
country comparison to the world: 144

Carbon dioxide emissions from consumption of energy: 431,300 Mt (2012 est.)
country comparison to the world: 185

COMMUNICATIONS

Telephones—fixed lines: *total subscriptions:* 28,600
subscriptions per 100 inhabitants: 26 (2014 est.)
country comparison to the world: 174

Telephones—mobile cellular: *total:* 134,500
subscriptions per 100 inhabitants: 122 (2014 est.)
country comparison to the world: 186

Telephone system: *general assessment:* automatic, island-wide telephone system
domestic: interisland VHF and UHF radiotelephone links
international: country code—1–473; landing point for the East Caribbean Fiber Optic System (ECFS) submarine cable with links to 13 other islands in the eastern Caribbean extending from the British Virgin Islands to Trinidad; SHF radiotelephone links to Trinidad and Tobago and Saint Vincent; VHF and UHF radio links to Trinidad (2009)

Broadcast media: the Grenada Broadcasting Network, jointly owned by the government and the Caribbean Communications Network of Trinidad and Tobago, operates a TV station and 2 radio stations; multi-channel cable TV subscription service is available; a dozen private radio stations also broadcast (2007)
Radio broadcast stations: AM 2, FM 12, shortwave 0 (2009)
Television broadcast stations: 2 (2009)

Internet country code: .gd

Internet hosts: 80 (2012)
country comparison to the world: 212

Internet users: *total:* 49,600
percent of population: 45.1% (2014 est.)
country comparison to the world: 183

TRANSPORTATION

Airports: 3 (2013)
country comparison to the world: 195

Airports—with paved runways: *total:* 3
2,438 to 3,047 m: 1
1,524 to 2,437 m: 1
under 914 m: 1 (2013)

Roadways: *total:* 1,127 km
paved: 687 km
unpaved: 440 km (2001)
country comparison to the world: 184

Ports and terminals: *major seaport(s):* Saint George's

MILITARY AND SECURITY

Military branches: no regular military forces; Royal Grenada Police Force (includes Coast Guard) (2010)

TRANSNATIONAL ISSUES

Disputes—international: none

Illicit drugs: small-scale cannabis cultivation; lesser transshipment point for marijuana and cocaine to US

GUAM

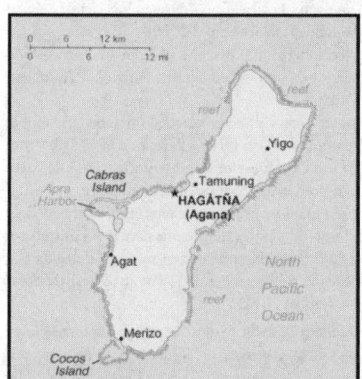

INTRODUCTION

Backg round: Spain ceded Guam to the US in 1898. Captured by the Japanese in 1941, it was retaken by the US three years later. The military installations on the island are some of the most strategically important US bases in the Pacific.

GEOGRAPHY

Location: Ocean ia, island in the North Pacific Ocean, about three-quarters of the way from Hawaii to the Philippines

Geographic coordinates: 13 28 N, 144 47 E

Map references: Oceania

Area: *total:* 544 sq km
land: 544 sq km
water: 0 sq km
country comparison to the world: 195

Area—comparative: three times the s ize of Was hin gton, DC

Land boundaries: 0 km

Coastline: 125.5 km

Maritime claims: *terri tori al sea:* 12 nm
exclusive economic zone: 200 nm

Climate: tropical marine; generally warm and humid, moderated by northeast trade winds; dry season (January to June), rainy season (July to December); little seasonal temperature variation

Terrain: volcanic origin, surrounded by coral reefs; relatively flat coralline limestone plateau (source of most fresh water), with steep coastal cliffs and narrow coastal plains in north, low hills in center, mountains in south

Elevation: *mean elevation:* NA

elevation extremes: *lowest point:* Pacific Ocean 0 m
highest point: Mount Lamlam 406 m

Natural resources: aquatic wildlife (supporting tourism), fishing (largely undeveloped)

Land use: *agricultural land:* 33.4%
arable land: 1.9%
permanent crops: 16.7%
permanent pasture: 14.8%
forest: 47.9%
other: 18.7% (2011 est.)

Irrigated land: 2 sq km (2012)

Natural hazards: frequent squalls during rainy season; relatively rare but potentially destructive typhoons (June to December)

Environment—current issues: extirpation of native bird population by the rapid proliferation of the brown tree snake, an exotic, invasive species

Geography—note: largest and southernmost island in the Mariana Islands archipelago; strategic location in western North Pacific Ocean

351

PEOPLE AND SOCIETY

Nationality: *noun:* Guamanian(s) (US citizens)
adjective: Guamanian

Ethnic groups: Chamorro 37.3%, Filipino 26.3%, white 7.1%, Chuukese 7%, Korean 2.2%, other Pacific Islander 2%, other Asian 2%, Chinese 1.6%, Palauan 1.6%, Japanese 1.5%, Pohnpeian 1.4%, mixed 9.4%, other 0.6% (2010 est.)

Languages: English 43.6%, Filipino 21.2%, Chamorro 17.8%, other Pacific island languages 10%, Asian languages 6.3%, other 1.1% (2010 est.)

Religions: Roman Catholic 85%, other 15% (1999 est.)

Population: 161,785 (July 2015 est.)
country comparison to the world: 188

Age structure: *0–14 years:* 25.47% (male 21,189/ female 20,017)
15–24 years: 17% (male 14,267/female 13,241)
25–54 years: 39.23% (male 32,315/female 31,159)
55–64 years: 9.4% (male 7,655/female 7,560)
65 years and over: 8.89% (male 6,552/female 7,830) (2015 est.)

Dependency ratios: *total dependency ratio:* 52%
youth dependency ratio: 38.7%
elderly dependency ratio: 13.3%
potential support ratio: 7.5% (2015 est.)

Median age: *total:* 30.1 years
male: 29.6 years
female: 30.7 years (2015 est.)
country comparison to the world: 111

Population growth rate: 0.54% (2015 est.)
country comparison to the world: 156

Birth rate: 16.82 births/1,000 population (2015 est.)
country comparison to the world: 109

Death rate: 5.12 deaths/1,000 population (2015 est.)
country comparison to the world: 184

Net migration rate: -6.34 migrant(s)/1,000 population (2015 est.)
country comparison to the world: 202

Urbanization: *urban population:* 94.5% of total population (2015)
rate of urbanization: 1.36% annual rate of change (2010–15 est.)

Major urban areas—population: HAGATNA (capital) 143,000 (2014)

Sex ratio: *at birth:* 1.06 male(s)/female
0–14 years: 1.06 male(s)/female
15–24 years: 1.08 male(s)/female
25–54 years: 1.04 male(s)/female
55–64 years: 1.01 male(s)/female
65 years and over: 0.84 male(s)/female
total population: 1.03 male(s)/female (2015 est.)

Infant mortality rate: *total:* 5.41 deaths/1,000 live births
male: 5.81 deaths/1,000 live births
female: 4.99 deaths/1,000 live births (2015 est.)
country comparison to the world: 171

Life expectancy at birth: *total population:* 78.98 years

male: 75.94 years
female: 82.21 years (2015 est.)
country comparison to the world: 50

Total fertility rate: 2.34 children born/woman (2015 est.)
country comparison to the world: 87

Drinking water source:
improved:
urban: 99 .5% of population
rural: 99.5% of population
total: 99.5% of population
unimproved:
urban: 0.5% of population
rural: 0.5% of population
total: 0.5% of population (2015 est.)

Sanitation facility access:
improved:
urban: 89.8% of population
rural: 89.8% of population
total: 89.8% of population
unimproved:
urban: 10.2% of population
rural: 10.2% of population
total: 10.2% of population (2015 est.)

HIV/AIDS—adult prevalence rate: NA

HIV/AIDS—people living with HIV/AIDS: NA

HIV/AIDS—deaths: NA

Unemployment, youth ages 15–24: *total:* 29.4%
male: 29.7%
female: 28.9% (2011 est.)
country comparison to the world: 25

GOVERNMENT

Country name: *conventional long form:* Territory of Guam
conventional short form: Guam
local long form: Guahan
local short form: Guahan
etymology: the native Chamorro name for the island "Guahan" (meaning "we have" or "ours") was changed to Guam in the 1898 Treaty of Paris whereby Spain relinquished Guam, Cuba, Puerto Rico, and the Philippines to the US

Dependency status: organized, unincorporated territory of the US with policy relations between Guam and the US under the jurisdiction of the Office of Insular Affairs, US Department of the Interior

Government type: presidential democracy; a self-governing unincorporated territory of the US

Capital: *name:* Hagatna (Agana)

Geographic coordinates: 13 28 N, 144 44 E
time difference: UTC + 10 (15 hours ahead of Washington, DC, during Standard Time)

Administrative divisions: none (territory of the US)

Independence: none (territory of the US)

National holiday: Discovery Day (or Magellan Day), first Monday in March (1521)

Constitution: effective 1 July 1950 (Guam Act of 1950 serves as a constitution); amended many times, last in 2015 (2016)

Legal system: common law modeled on US system; US federal laws apply

Citizenship: see United States

Suffrage: 18 years of age; universal; note—Guamanians are US citizens but do not vote in US presidential elections

Executive branch: *chief of state:* President Barack H. OBAMA (since 20 January 2009); Vice President Joseph R. BIDEN (since 20 January 2009)

head of government: Governor Eddie CALVO (since 3 January 2011); Lieutenant Governor Ray TENORIO (since 3 January 2011)
cabinet: Cabinet appointed by the governor with the consent of the Legislature
elections/appointments: president and vice president indirectly elected on the same ballot by an Electoral College of 'electors' chosen from each state to serve a 4-year term (eligible for a second term); under the US Constitution, residents of unincorporated territories, such as Guam, do not vote in elections for US president and vice president; however, they may vote in Democratic and Republican presidential primary elections; governor and lieutenant governor elected on the same ballot by absolute majority vote in 2 rounds if needed for a 4-year term (eligible for 2 consecutive terms); election last held on 4 November 2014 (next to be held in November 2018)
election results: Eddie CALVO reelected governor; percent of vote—E ddie CALVO (Republican Party) 64%, Carl GUTIERREZ (Democratic Party) 36%; Ray TENORIO elected lieutenant governor

Legislative branch: *description:* unicameral Legislature of Guam or Liheslaturan Guahan (15 seats; members elected in a single countrywide constituency by simple majority vote to serve 2-year terms)
elections: last held on 4 November 2014 (next to be held on 8 November 2016)
election results: percent of vote by party—NA; seats by party—Democratic Party 9, Republican Party 6
note: Guam directly elects 1 member by simple majority vote to serve a 2-year term as a delegate to the US House of Representatives; the delegate can vote when serving on a committee and when the House meets as the Committee of the Whole House, but not when legislation is submitted for a "full floor" House vote; election of delegate last held on 6 November 2012 (next to be held on 8 November 2014)

Judicial branch: *highest court(s):* Supreme Court of Guam (consists of 3 justices); note—appeals beyond the Supreme Court of Guam are heard by the US Supreme Court
judge selection and term of office: justices appointed by the governor and confirmed by the Guam legislature; justices appointed for life subject to retention election every 10 years
subordinate courts: Superior Court of Guam—includes several divisions; US Federal District Court for the District of Guam (a US territorial court; appeals beyond this court are heard before the US Court of Appeals for the Ninth Circuit)

Political parties and leaders: Democratic Party [Carlo BRANCH]
Republican Party [Mike BENITO]

Political pressure groups and leaders: Guam Commission on Decolonization
Guam Federation of Teachers' Union
Guam Waterworks Authority Workers
We Are Guahan

International organization participation: AOSIS (observer), IOC, PIF (observer), SPC, UPU

Diplomatic representation in the US: none (territory of the US)

Diplomatic representation from the US: none (territory of the US)

Flag description: territorial flag is dark blue with a narrow red border on all four sides; centered is a red-bordered, pointed, vertical ellipse containing a beach scene, a proa or outrigger canoe with sail, and a palm tree with the word GUAM superimposed in bold red letters; the proa is sailing in Agana Bay with the promontory of Punta Dos Amantes, near the capital, in the background; the shape of the central emblem is that of a Chamorro sling stone, used as a weapon for defense or hunting; blue represents the sea and red the blood shed in the struggle against oppression
note: the US flag is the national flag

National symbol(s): coconut tree; national colors: deep blue, red

National anthem: *name:* "Fanohge Chamoru" (Stand Ye Guamanians)
lyrics/music: Ramon Manalisay SABLAN [English], Lagrimas UNTALAN [Chamoru]/Ramon Manalisay SABLAN
note: adopted 1919; the local anthem is also known as "Guam Hymn"; as a territory of the United States, "The Star-Spangled Banner," which generally follows the playing of "Stand Ye Guamanians," is official (see United States)

ECONOMY

Economy—overview: US national defense spending is the main driver of Guam's economy, followed by tourism and other services. Total federal spending (defense and non-defense) amounted to $1.973 billion in 2014, or 40.4% of GDP. Service exports, mainly spending by foreign tourists while on Guam, amounted to $651 million in 2013, or 13.3% of GDP. In 2013, Guam's economy grew 0.6%. Despite slow growth, Guam's economy has been stable over the last decade. National defense spending cushions the island's economy against fluctuations in tourism. Guam serves as a forward US base for the Western Pacific and is home to thousands of American military personnel. Federal grants amounted to $373.3 million in 2013, or 32.6% of Guam's total revenues for the fiscal year.

GDP (purchasing power parity):
$4.882 billion (2013 est.)
$4.756 billion (2012 est.)
$4.562 billion (2011 est.)
country comparison to the world: 175

GDP (official exchange rate): $4.6 billion (2010 est.)

GDP—real growth rate: 0.6% (2013 est.)
1.8% (2012)
-0.3% (2011)
country comparison to the world: 186

GDP—per capita (PPP): $30,500 (2013 est.)
$29,800 (2012 est.)
$28,600 (2011 est.)
country comparison to the world: 61

GDP—composition, by end use:
household consumption: 63.7%
government consumption: 64.9%
investment in fixed assets: 5.8%
in vestmen t in in ven tori es: NA
exports of goods and services: 17%
imports of goods and services: -51.2% (2013)

GDP—composition, by sector of origin:
agriculture: NA%
industry: NA%
services: NA%

Agriculture—products: fruits, copra, vegetables; eggs, pork, poultry, beef

Industries: national defense, tourism, construction, transshipment services, concrete products, printing and publishing, food processing, textiles

Industrial production growth rate: NA%

Labor force: 70,490
note: this number is for the civilian labor force only (2013 est.)
country comparison to the world: 186

Labor force—by occupation: *agriculture:* 0.3%
industry: 21.6%
services: 78.1% (2013)

Unemployment rate: 8.4% (2013 est.)
8.2% (2010 est.)
country comparison to the world: 97

Population below poverty line: 23% (2001 est.)

Household income or consumption by percentage share: *lowest:* 10%: NA%
highest: 10%: NA%

Budget: *revenues:* $1.147 billion
expenditures: $1.188 billion (2013 est.)
Taxes and other revenues: 24.9% of GDP (2013 est.)
country comparison to the world: 121

Budget surplus (+) or deficit (–): -0.9% of GDP (2013 est.)
country comparison to the world: 52

Public debt: 32.1% of GDP (2013)
35.8% of GDP (2012)
country comparison to the world: 138

Fiscal year: 1 October–30 September

Inflation rate (consumer prices): 1.8% (2014 est.)
4% (2011 est.)
country comparison to the world: 110

Exports: $828 million (2013 est.)
$795 million (2012)
country comparison to the world: 164

Exports—commodities: transshipments of refined petroleum products, construction materials, fish, foodstuffs and beverages

Imports: $2.501 billion (2013 est.)
$2.438 billion (2012)
country comparison to the world: 156

Imports—commodities: petroleum and petroleum products, food, manufactured goods

Debt—external: $NA

Exchange rates: the US dollar is used

ENERGY

Electricity—production: 1.566 billion kWh (2013 est.)
country comparison to the world: 145

Electricity—consumption: 1.566 billion kWh (2012 est.)
country comparison to the world: 147

Electricity—exports: 0 kWh (2013 est.)
country comparison to the world: 146

Electricity—imports: 0 k Wh (2013 es t.)
country comparison to the world: 157

Electricity—installed generating capacity: 552,000 kW (2012 est.)
country comparison to the world: 137

Electricity—from fossil fuels: 100% of total installed capacity (2012 est.)
country comparison to the world: 13

Electricity—from nuclear fuels: 0% of total installed capacity (2012 est.)
country comparison to the world: 102

Electricity—from hydroelectric plants: 0% of total installed capacity (2012 est.)
country comparison to the world: 177

Electricity—from other renewable sources: 0% of total installed capacity (2012 est.)
country comparison to the world: 180

Crude oil—production:
0 bbl/day (2014 est.)
country comparison to the world: 143

Crude oil—exports: 0 bbl/day (2012 est.)
country comparison to the world: 132

Crude oil—imports: 0 bbl/day (2012 est.)
country comparison to the world: 199

Crude oil—proved reserves: 0 bbl (1 January 2015 est.)
country comparison to the world: 141

Refined petroleum products—production: 0 bbl/day (2012 est.)
country comparison to the world: 190

Refined petroleum products—consumption: 12,510 bbl/day (2014 est.)
country comparison to the world: 148

Refined petroleum products—exports: 0 bbl/day (2012 est.)
country comparison to the world: 187

Refined petroleum products—imports: 15,620 bbl/day (2012 est.)
country comparison to the world: 122

Natural gas—production: 0 cu m (2014 est.)
country comparison to the world: 196

Natural gas—consumption: 0 cu m (2014 est.)
country comparison to the world: 150

Natural gas—exports: 0 cu m (2014 est.)
country comparison to the world: 109

Natural gas—imports: 0 cu m (2014 est.)
country comparison to the world: 204

Natural gas—proved reserves: 0 cu m (1 January 2014 est.)
country comparison to the world: 146

Carbon dioxide emissions from consumption of energy: 1.775 million Mt (2012 est.)
country comparison to the world: 152

COMMUNICATIONS

Telephones—fixed lines: *total subscriptions:* 67,400
subscriptions per 100 inhabitants: 42 (2014 est.)
country comparison to the world: 152

Telephones—mobile cellular: *total:* 98,000
subscriptions per 100 inhabitants: 62 (2004)
country comparison to the world: 191

Telephone system: *general assessment:* modern system, integrated with US facilities for direct dialing, including free use of 800 numbers
domestic: digital system, including mobile-cellular service and local access to the Internet
international: country code—1–671; major landing point for submarine cables between Asia and the US (Guam is a transpacific communications hub for major carriers linking the US and Asia); satellite earth stations—2 Intelsat (Pacific Ocean) (2011)

Broadcast media: about a dozen TV channels, including digital channels; multi-channel cable TV services are available; roughly 20 radio stations (2009)
Radio broadcast stations: AM 3, FM 11, shortwave 2 (2005)
Television broadcast stations: 3 (2006)

Internet country code: .gu

Internet hosts: 23 (2012)
country comparison to the world: 219

Internet users: *total:* 107,800
percent of population: 67.0% (2014 est.)
country comparison to the world: 168

TRANSPORTATION

Airports: 5 (2013)
country comparison to the world: 179

Airports—with paved runways: *total:* 4
over 3,047 m: 2
2,438 to 3,047 m: 1
914 to 1,523 m: 1 (2013)

Airports—with unpaved runways: *total:* 1
under 914 m: 1 (2013)

Roadways: *total:* 1,045 km (2008)
country comparison to the world: 186

Ports and terminals: *major seaport(s):* Apra Harbor

MILITARY AND SECURITY

Military—note: defense is the responsibility of the US

TRANSNATIONAL ISSUES

Disputes—international: none

GUATEMALA

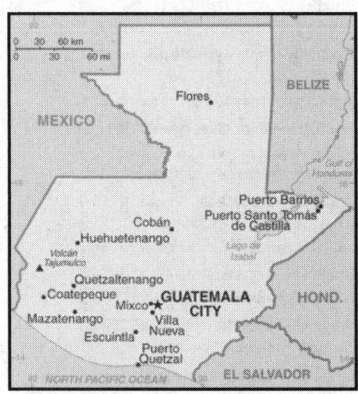

INTRODUCTION

Background: The Maya civilization flourished in Guatemala and surrounding regions during the first millennium A.D. After almost three centuries as a Spanish colony, Guatemala won its independence in 1821. During the second half of the 20th century, it experienced a variety of military and civilian governments, as well as a 36-year guerrilla war. In 1996, the government signed a peace agreement formally ending the internal conflict, which had left more than 200,000 people dead and had created, by some estimates, about 1 million refugees.

GEOGRAPHY

Location: Central America, bordering the North Pacific Ocean, between El Salvador and Mexico, and bordering the Gulf of Honduras (Caribbean Sea) between Honduras and Belize

Geographic coordinates: 15 30 N, 90 15 W

Map references: Central America and the Caribbean

Area: *total:* 108,889 sq km
land: 107,159 sq km
water: 1,730 sq km
country comparison to the world: 107

Area—comparative: slightly smaller than Pennsylvania

Land boundaries: *total:* 1,667 km
border countries (4): Belize 266 km, El Salvador 199 km, Honduras 244 km, Mexico 958 km

Coastline: 400 km

Maritime claims: *territorial sea:* 12 nm
exclusive economic zone: 200 nm
continental shelf: 200-m depth or to the depth of exploitation

Climate: tropical; hot, humid in lowlands; cooler in highlands

Terrain: mostly mountains with narrow coastal plains and rolling limestone plateau

Elevation: *mean elevation:* 759 m

elevation extremes: *lowest point:* Pacific Ocean 0 m
highest point: Volcan Tajumulco 4,211 m (highest point in Central America)

Natural resources: petroleum, nickel, rare woods, fish, chicle, hydropower

Land use: *agricultural land:* 41.2%
arable land: 14.2%
permanent crops: 8.8%
permanent pasture: 18.2%
forest: 33.6%

other: 25.2% (2011 est.)

Irrigated land: 3,375 sq km (2012)

Total renewable water resources: 111.3 cu m (2011)

Freshwater withdrawal (domestic/industrial/agricultural): *total:* 3.46 cu km/yr (15%/31%/54%)
per capita: 259.1 cu m/yr (2006)

Natural hazards: numerous volcanoes in mountains, with occasional violent earthquakes; Caribbean coast extremely susceptible to hurricanes and other tropical storms
volcanism: significant volcanic activity in the Sierra Madre range; Santa Maria (elev.3,772 m) has been deemed a Decade Volcano by the International Association of Volcanology and Chemistry of the Earth's Interior, worthy of study due to its explosive history and close proximity to human populations; Pacaya (elev.2,552 m), which erupted in May 2010 causing an ashfall on Guatemala City and prompting evacuations, is one of the country's most active volcanoes with frequ ent eruptions since 1965; other historically active volcanoes include Acatenango, Almolonga, Atitlan, Fuego, and Tacana

Environment—current issues: deforestation in the Peten rainforest; soil erosion; water pollution

Environment—international agreements: *party to:* Antarctic Treaty, Biodiversity, Climate Change, Climate Change-Kyoto Protocol, Desertification, Endangered Species, Environmental Modification, Hazardous Wastes, Law of the Sea, Marine Dumping, Ozone Layer Protection, Ship Pollution, Wetlands, Whaling
signed, but not ratified: none of the selected agreements

Geography—note: no natural harbors on west coast

PEOPLE AND SOCIETY

Nationality: *noun:* Guatemalan(s)
adjective: Guatemalan

Ethnic groups: Mestizo (mixed Amerindian-Spanish—in local Spanish called Ladino) and European 59.4%, K'iche 9.1%, Kaqchikel 8.4%, Mam 7.9%, Q'eqchi 6.3%, other Mayan 8.6%, indigenous non-Mayan 0.2%, other 0.1% (2001 census)

Languages: Spanish (official) 60%, Amerindian languages 40%
note: there are 23 officially recognized Amerindian languages, inclu ding Quiche, Cakchiquel, Kekchi, Mam, Garifuna, and Xinca

Religions: Roman Catholic, Protestant, indigenous Mayan beliefs

Demographic profile: Guatemala is a predominantly poor country that struggles in several areas of health and development, including infant, child, and maternal mortality, malnutrition, literacy, and contraceptive awareness and use. The country's large indigenous population is disproportionately affected. Guatemala is the most populous country in Central America and has the highest fertility rate in Latin America. It also has the highest population growth rate in Latin America, which is likely to continue because of its large reproductive-age population and high birth rate. Almost half of Guatemala's population is under age 19, making it the youngest population in Latin America. Guatemala's total fertility rate has slowly declined during the last few decades due in part to limited government-funded health programs. However, the birth rate is still more than three children per woman and is markedly higher among its rural and indigenous populations. Guatemalans have a history of emigrating legally and illegally to Mexico, the United States, and Canada because of a lack of economic opportunity, political instability, and natural disasters. Emigration, primarily to the United States, escalated during the 1960 to 1996 civil war and accelerated after a peace agreement was signed. Thousands of Guatemalans who fled to Mexico returned after the war, but labor migration to southern Mexico continues.

Population: 14,918,999 (July 2015 est.)
country comparison to the world: 71

Age structure: *0–14 years:* 35.57% (male 2,704,784/female 2,602,397)
15–24 years: 21.99% (male 1,646,350/female 1,633,666)
25–54 years: 32.93% (male 2,337,192/female 2,575,674)
55–64 years: 5.2% (male 370,456/female 405,496)
65 years and over: 4.31% (male 298,319/female 344,665) (2015 est.)

Dependency ratios: *total dependency ratio:* 70.9%
youth dependency ratio: 62.6%
elderly dependency rati o: 8.3%
potential support ratio: 12.1% (2015 est.)

Median age: *total:* 21.4 years

male: 20.7 years
female: 22 years (2015 est.)
country comparison to the world: 181

Population growth rate: 1.82% (2015 est.)
country comparison to the world: 63

Birth rate: 24.89 births/1,000 population (2015 est.)
country comparison to the world: 53

Death rate: 4.77 deaths/1,000 population (2015 est.)
country comparison to the world: 196

Net migration rate: -1.97 migrant(s)/1,000 population (2015 est.)
country comparison to the world: 165

Urbanization: *urban population:* 51.6% of total population (2015)
rate of urbanization: 3.4% annual rate of change (2010–15 est.)

Major urban areas—population: GUATE-MALACITY (capital) 2.918 million (2015)

Sex ratio: *at birth:* 1.05 male(s)/female
0–14 years: 1.04 male(s)/female
15–24 years: 1.01 male(s)/female
25–54 years: 0.91 male(s)/female
55–64 years: 0.91 male(s)/female
65 years and over: 0.87 male(s)/female
total population: 0.97 male(s)/female (2015 est.)

Mother's mean age at first birth: 20.3
note: median age at first birth among women 25–29 (2008/09 est.)

Maternal mortality rate: 88 deaths/100,000 live births (2015 est.)
country comparison to the world: 64

Infant mortality rate: *total:* 22.73 deaths/1,000 live births
male: 24.73 deaths/1,000 live births
female: 20.62 deaths/1,000 live births (2015 est.)
country comparison to the world: 77

Life expectancy at birth: *total population:* 72.02 years
male: 70.07 years
female: 74.06 years (2015 est.)
country comparison to the world: 145

Total fertility rate: 2.9 children born/woman (2015 est.)
country comparison to the world: 57

Health expenditures: 6.5% of GDP (2013)
country comparison to the world: 88

Physicians density: 0.93 physicians/1,000 population (2009)

Hospital bed density: 0.6 beds/1,000 population (2011)

Drinking water source:
improved:
urban: 98.4% of population
rural: 86.8% of population
total: 92.8% of population
unimproved:
urban: urban: 1.6% of population
rural: 13.2% of population
total: 7.2% of population (2015 est.)

Sanitation facility access:

improved:
urban: 77.5% of population
rural: 49.3% of population
total: 63.9% of population
unimproved:
urban: 22.5% of population
rural: 50.7% of population
total: 36.1% of population (2015 est.)

HIV/AIDS—adult prevalence rate: 0.54% (2014 est.)
country comparison to the world: 64

HIV/AIDS—people living with HIV/AIDS: 49,100 (2014 est.)
country comparison to the world: 56

HIV/AIDS—deaths: 1,700 (2014 est.)
country comparison to the world: 58

Major infectious diseases: *degree of risk:* high
food or waterborne diseases: bacterial diarrhea, hepatitis A, and typhoid fever
vectorborne disease: dengue fever and malaria (2013)

Obesity—adult prevalence rate: 16.4% (2014)
country comparison to the world: 100

Children under the age of 5 years underweight: 12.6% (2015)
country comparison to the world: 57

Education expenditures: 2.8% of GDP (2013)
country comparison to the world: 139

Literacy: *definition:* age 15 and over can read and write
total population: 81.5%
male: 87.4%
female: 76.3% (2015 est.)

School life expectancy (primary to tertiary education): *total:* 11 years
male: 11 years
female: 10 years (2013)

Child labor—children ages 5–14: *total number:* 929,852
percentage: 21%
note: data represent children ages 5–17 (2006 est.)

Unemployment, youth ages 15–24: *total:* 6.3%
male: 6.5%
female: 5.8% (2013 est.)
country comparison to the world: 117

GOVERNMENT

Country name: *conventional long form:* Republic of Guatemala
conventional short form: Guatemala
local long form: Republica de Guatemala
local short form: Guatemala
etymology: name derives from the Mayan word meaning "land of trees"

Government type: presidential republic

Capital: *name:* Guatemala City

Geographic coordinates: 14 37 N, 90 31 W
time difference: UTC-6 (1 hour behind Washington, DC, during Standard Time)

Administrative divisions: 22 departments (departamentos, singular—departamento); Alta Verapaz, Baja Verapaz, Chimaltenango, Chiquimula, El

Progreso, Escuintla, Guatemala, Huehuetenango, Izabal, Jalapa, Jutiapa, Peten, Quetzaltenango, Quiche, Retalhuleu, Sacatepequez, San Marcos, Santa Rosa, Solola, Suchitepequez, Totonicapan, Zacapa

Independence: 15 September 1821 (from Spain)

National holiday: Independence Day, 15 September (1821)

Constitution: several previous; latest adopted 31 May 1985, effective 14 January 1986; suspended, reinstated, and amended in 1994 (2016)

Legal system: civil law system; judicial review of legislative acts

International law organization participation: has not submitted an ICJ jurisdiction declaration; accepts ICCt jurisdiction

Citizenship: *citizenship by birth:* yes
citizenship by descent: yes
du alcitizenship recognized: yes
residency requirement for naturalization: 5 years with no absences of six consecutive months or longer or absences totaling more than a year

Suffrage: 18 years of age; universal; note—active duty members of the armed forces and police by law cannot vote and are restricted to their barracks on election day

Executive branch: *chief of state:* President Jimmy Ernesto MORALES Cabrera (since 14 January 2016); Vice President Jafeth CABRERA Franco (since 14 January 2016); note—the president is both chief of state and head of government

head of government: President Jimmy Ernesto MORALES Cabrera (since 14 January 2016); Vice President Jafeth CABRERA Franco (since 14 January 2016)

cabinet: Council of Ministers appointed by the president

elections/appointments: president and vice president directly elected on the same ballot by absolute majority popular vote in 2 rounds if needed for a 4-year term (not eligible for consecutive terms); election last held in 2 rounds on 6 September and 25 October 2015 (next to be held in September 2019)

election results: Jimmy Ernesto MORALES Cabrera (FNC) elected president; percent of vote in first round—Jimmy Ernesto MORALES Cabrera (FNC) 23.8%, Sandra TORRES (UNE) 19.8%, Manuel BALDIZON (LIDER) 19.6%; percent of vote in second round—Jimmy Ernesto MORALES Cabrera (FNC) 67.4%, Sandra TORRES (UNE) 32.6%

Legislative branch: *description:* unicameral Congress of the Republic or Congreso de la Republica (158 seats; 127 members directly elected in multiseat constituencies within each of the country's 22 departments by simple majority vote and 31 directly elected in a single nationwide constituency by proportional representation vote; members serve 4-year terms)

elections: last held on 6 September 2015 (next to be held in September 2019)

election results: percent of vote by party—LIDER 19.10%, UNE 14.83%, TODOS 9.74%, PP 9.43%,

FCN 8.75%, EG 6.24%, PU 5.69%, UCN 5.43%, Winaq-URNG-MAIZ 4.32%, Convergence 3.84%, VIVA 3.66%, PAN 3.42, FUERZA 2.07%, other 3.48%; seats by party—LIDER 44, UNE 36, TODOS 18, PP 17, FCN 11, EG 7, UCN 6, PU 5, Winaq-URNG-MAIZ 3, Convergence 3, VIVA 3, PAN 3, FUERZA 2

Judicial branch: *highest court(s):* Supreme Court of Justice or Corte Suprema de Justicia (consists of 13 magistrates including the court president and organized into 3 chambers); note—the court president also supervises trial judges countrywide; Constitutional Court or Corte de Constitucionalidad (consists of 5 judges and 5 alternates)

judge selection and term of office: Supreme Court magistrates elected by the Congress of the Republic from candidates proposed by the Postulation Committee, an independent body of deans of the country's university law schools, representatives of the country's law associations, and representatives of the Courts of Appeal; magistrates elected for concurrent, renewable 5-year terms; Constitutional Court judges—1 elected by the Congress of the Republic, 1 by the Supreme Court, 1 by the president of the republic, 1 by the (public) University of San Carlos, and 1 by the lawyers bar association; judges elected for concurrent, renewable 5-year terms; the presidency of the court rotates among the magistrates for a single 1-year term

subordinate courts: numerous first instance and appellate courts

Political parties and leaders: Commitment, Renewal, and Order or CREO [Roberto GONZALEZ Diaz-Duran]
Convergence
Democratic Union or UD [Edwin Armando MARTINEZ Herrera]
Encounter for Guatemala or EG [N ineth MONTENEGRO Cottom]
Everyone Together for Guatemala or TODOS [Felipe ALEJOS]
FUERZA [Maurico REDFORD]
Grand National Alliance or GANA [Jaime Antonio MARTINEZ Lohayza]
Guatemalan National Revolutionary Unity or Winaq-URNG [Angel SANCHEZ Viesca]
Institutional Republican Party (formerly the Guatemalan Republican Front) or PRI [Luis Fernando PEREZ]
National Advancement Party or PAN [Juan GUTIERREZ Strauss]
National Unity for Hope or UNE [Sandra TORRES]
Nationalist Change Union or UCN [Mario ESTRADA]
National Convergence Front or FCN [Edgar Justino OVALLE Maldonado]
New National Alternative or ANN [Pablo MONSANTO]
Patriot Party or PP [Ingrid Roxana BALDETTI Elias]
Renewed Democratic Liberty or LIDER [Manuel BALDIZON]
Unionista Party or PU [Alvaro ARZU Irigoyen]
Victoria (Victory) [Amilcar RIVERA]
Vision with Values or VIVA [Harold CABALLEROS] (part of a coalition with EG during the last legislative election)

Political pressure groups and leaders: Alliance Against Impunity or AI (includes among others Center for Legal Action on Human Rights (CALDH), Family and Friends of the Disappeared of Guatemala (FAMDEGUA))
Civic and Political Convergence of Women
Committee for Campesino Unity or CUC
Coordinating Committee of Agricultural, Commercial, Industrial, and Financial Associations or CACIF
Foundation for the Development of Guatemala or FUNDESA
Guatemala Visible
Mutual Support Group or GAM
Movimiento PRO-Justicia
National Union of Agriculture Workers or UNAGRO

International organization participation: BCIE, CACM, CD, CELAC, EITI (compliant country), FAO, G-24, G-77, IADB, IAEA, IBRD, ICAO, ICC (national committees), ICCt (signatory), ICRM, IDA, IFAD, IFC, IFRCS, IHO, ILO, IMF, IMO, Interpol, IOC, IOM, IPU, ISO (correspondent), ITSO, ITU, ITUC (NGOs), LAES, LAIA (observer), MIGA, MINUSTAH, MONUSCO, NAM, OAS, OPANAL, OPCW, Pacific Alliance (observer), PCA, Petrocaribe, SICA, UN, UNCTAD, UNESCO, UNIDO, UNIFIL, Union Latina, UNISFA, UNITAR, UNMISS, UNOCI, UNWTO, UPU, WCO, WFTU (NGOs), WHO, WIPO, WMO, WTO

Diplomatic representation in the US: *chief of mission:* Ambassador (vacant)
chancery: 2220 R Street NW, Washington, DC 20008
telephone: [1] (202) 745-4952
FAX: [1] (202) 745-1908
consulate(s): Del Rio (TX), San Bernadino (CA), Silver Spring (MD), Tucson (AZ)
consulate(s) general: Atlanta, Chicago, Denver, Houston, Los Angeles, McAllen (TX), Miami, New York, Phoenix, Providence (RI), San Francisco, Silver Spring (MD), Tucson (AZ)

Diplomatic representation from the US: *chief of mission:* Ambassador Todd D. ROBINSON (since 10 October 2014)
embassy: 7–01 Avenida Reforma, Zone 10, Guatemala City
mailing address: DPO AA 34024
telephone: [502] 2326-4000
FAX: [502] 2326-4654

Flag description: three equal vertical bands of light blue (hoist side), white, and light blue, with the coat of arms centered in the white band; the coat of arms includes a green and red quetzal (the national bird) representing liberty and a scroll bearing the inscription LIBERTAD 15 DE SEPTIEMBRE DE 1821 (the original date of independence from Spain) all superimposed on a pair of crossed rifles signifying Guatemala's willingness to defend itself and a pair of crossed swords representing honor and framed by a laurel wreath symbolizing victory; the blue bands represent the Pacific Ocean and Caribbean Sea; the white band denotes peace and purity

National symbol(s): quetzal (bird); national colors: blue, white

National anthem: *name:* "Himno Nacional de Guatemala" (National Anthem of Guatemala) *lyrics/music:* Jose Joaquin PALMA/Rafael Alvarez OVALLE *note:* adopted 1897, modified lyrics adopted 1934; Cuban poet Jose Joaquin PALMA anonymously submitted lyrics to a public contest calling for a national anthem; his authorship was not discovered until 1911

ECONOMY

Economy—overview: Guatemala is the most populous country in Central America with a GDP per capita roughly half the average for Latin America and the Caribbean. The agricultural sector accounts for 13.6% of GDP and 31% of the labor force; key agricultural exports include sugar, coffee, bananas, and vegetables. Guatemala is the top remittance recipient in Central America as a result of Guatemala's large expatriate community in the US. These inflows are a primary source of foreign income, equivalent to over one-half of the country's exports or one-tenth of its GDP.

The 1996 peace accords, which ended 36 years of civil war, removed a major obstacle to foreign investment, and since then Guatemala has pursued important reforms and macroeconomic stabilization. The Dominican Republic-Central America Free Trade Agreement (CAFTA-DR) entered into force in July 2006, spurring increased investment and diversification of exports, with the largest increases in ethanol and non-traditional agricultural exports. While CAFTA-DR has helped improve the investment climate, concerns over security, the lack of skilled workers, and poor infrastructure continue to hamper foreign direct investment.

The distribution of income remains highly unequal with the richest 20% of the population accounting for more than 51% of Guatemala's overall consumption. More than half of the population is below the national poverty line, and 23% of the population lives in extreme poverty. Poverty among indigenous groups, which make up more than 40% of the population, averages 79%, with 39.8% of the indigenous population living in extreme poverty. Nearly one-half of Guatemala's children under age five are chronically malnourished, one of the highest malnutrition rates in the world.

Guatemala is facing growing fiscal pressures exacerbated by multiple corruption scandals in 2015 that led to the resignation of the president, vice president, and numerous high-level economic officials.

GDP (purchasing power parity): $125.9 billion (2015 est.)
$121 billion (2014 est.)
$116.1 billion (2013 est.)
note: data are in 2015 US dollars
country comparison to the world: 81

GDP (official exchange rate): $63.91 billion (2015 est.)

GDP—real growth rate: 4.1% (2015 est.)
4.3% (2014 est.)
3.7% (2013 est.)
country comparison to the world: 64

GDP—per capita (PPP): $7,700 (2015 est.)
$7,600 (2014 est.)
$7,500 (2013 est.)
note: data are in 2015 U Sdollars
country comparison to the world: 150

Gross national saving: 11.7% of GDP (2015 est.)
11.5% of GDP (2014 est.)
11.5% of GDP (2013 est.)
country comparison to the world: 141

GDP—composition, by end use:
household consumption: 85.9%
government consumption: 10.7%
investment in fixed capital: 13.9%
investment in in ven tori es: 0.6%
exports of goods and services: 22.8%
imports of goods and services: -33.9% (2015 est.)

GDP—composition, by sector of origin:
agriculture: 13.4%
industry: 23.8%
services: 62.7% (2015 est.)

Agriculture—products: sugarcane, corn, bananas, coffee, beans, cardamom; cattle, sheep, pigs, chickens

Industries: sugar, textiles and clothing, furniture, chemicals, petroleum, metals, rubber, tourism

Industrial production growth rate: 4% (2015 est.)
country comparison to the world: 57

Labor force: 6.316 million (2014 est.)
country comparison to the world: 68

Labor force—by occupation: *agriculture:* 31.2%
industry: 14.4%
services: 54.4% (2014 est.)

Unemployment rate: 2.9% (2014 est.)
3% (2013 est.)
country comparison to the world: 19

Population below poverty line: 59.3% (2014 est.)

Household income or consumption by percentage share: *lowest:* 10%: 1.3%
highest: 10%: 42.4% (2006)

Distribution of family income—Gini index: 53 (2014 est.)
56 (2011)
country comparison to the world: 14

Budget: *revenues:* $7.243 billion
expenditures: $8.724 billion (2015 est.)
Taxes and other revenues: 11.5% of GDP (2015 est.)
country comparison to the world: 207

Budget surplus (+) or deficit (–): -2.3% of GDP (2015 est.)
country comparison to the world: 82

Public debt: 24.2% of GDP (2015 est.)
24.4% of GDP (2014 est.)
country comparison to the world: 151

Fiscal year: calendar year

Inflation rate (consumer prices): 2.4% (2015 est.)
3.4% (2014 est.)
country comparison to the world: 126

Central bank discount rate: 6.5% (31 December 2010)
country comparison to the world: 57

Commercial bank prime lending rate: 13.2% (31 December 2015 est.)
13.77% (31 December 2014 est.)
country comparison to the world: 53

Stock of narrow money: $10.24 billion (31 December 2015 est.)
$9.19 billion (31 December 2014 est.)
country comparison to the world: 76

Stock of broad money: $23.19 billion (31 December 2015 est.)
$21.17 billion (31 December 2014 est.)
country comparison to the world: 85

Stock of domestic credit: $28.06 billion (31 December 2015 est.)
$26.3 billion (31 December 2014 est.)
country comparison to the world: 76

Market value of publicly traded shares: $NA

Current account balance: -$315 million (2015 est.)
-$1.23 billion (2014 est.)
country comparison to the world: 88

Exports: $10.73 billion (2015 est.)
$10.8 billion (2014 est.)
country comparison to the world: 87

Exports—commodities: sugar, coffee, petroleum, apparel, bananas, fruits and vegetables, cardamom, manufacturing products, precious stones and metals, electricity

Exports—partners: US 34.9%, El Salvador 8.4%, Honduras 7.3%, Nicaragua 5%, Canada 4.6%, Mexico 4.3%, Costa Rica 4.1% (2015)

Imports: $17.64 billion (2015 est.)
$18.28 billion (2014 est.)
country comparison to the world: 78

Imports—commodities: fuels, machinery and transport equipment, construction materials, grain, fertilizers, electricity, mineral products, chemical products, plastic materials and products

Imports—partners: US 38.3%, China 13.4%, Mexico 11.8%, El Salvador 4.9% (2015)

Reserves of foreign exchange and gold: $7.473 billion (31 December 2015 est.)
$7.329 billion (31 December 2014 est.)
country comparison to the world: 83

Debt—external: $18.33 billion (31 December 2014 est.)
$16.82 billion (31 December 2013 est.)
country comparison to the world: 90

Exchange rates: quetzales (GTQ) per US dollar—
7.671 (2015 est.)
7.7322 (2014 est.)
7.7322 (2013 est.)
7.83 (2012 est.)
7.7854 (2011 est.)

ENERGY

Electricity—production: 9.781 billion kWh (2014 est.)
country comparison to the world: 98

Electricity—consumption: 8.915 billion kWh (2014 est.)
country comparison to the world: 94

Electricity—exports: 1.025 billion kWh (2014 est.)
country comparison to the world: 55

Electricity—imports: 664 million kWh (2014 est.)
country comparison to the world: 71

Electricity—installed generating capacity: 3.73 million kW (2015 est.)
country comparison to the world: 85

Electricity—from fossil fuels: 61.9% of total installed capacity (2015 est.)
country comparison to the world: 127

Electricity—from nuclear fuels: 0% of total installed capacity (2015 est.)
country comparison to the world: 104

Electricity—from hydroelectric plants: 29.1% of total installed capacity (2015 est.)
country comparison to the world: 80

Electricity—from other renewable sources: 8.9% of total installed capacity (2015 est.)
country comparison to the world: 42

Crude oil—production: 10,040 bbl/day (2015 est.)
country comparison to the world: 80

Crude oil—exports: 8,711 bbl/day (2015 est.)
country comparison to the world: 67

Crude oil—imports: 0 bbl/day (2015 est.)
country comparison to the world: 200

Crude oil—proved reserves: 83.07 million bbl (1 January 2015 est.)
country comparison to the world: 75

Refined petroleum products—production: 1,228 bbl/day (2015 est.)
country comparison to the world: 109

Refined petroleum products—consumption: 87,840 bbl/day (2015 est.)
country comparison to the world: 80

Refined petroleum products—exports: 12,960 bbl/day (2015 est.)
country comparison to the world: 82

Refined petroleum products—imports: 100,400 bbl/day (2015 est.)
country comparison to the world: 52

Natural gas—production: 0 cu m (2013 est.)
country comparison to the world: 197

Natural gas—consumption: 0 cu m (2013 est.)
country comparison to the world: 151

Natural gas—exports: 0 cu m (2013 est.)
country comparison to the world: 111

Natural gas—imports: 0 cu m (2013 est.)
country comparison to the world: 205

Natural gas—proved reserves: 2.96 billion cu m (1 January 2006 est.)
country comparison to the world: 96

Carbon dioxide emissions from consumption of energy: 13.07 million Mt (2012 est.)
country comparison to the world: 94

COMMUNICATIONS

Telephones—fixed lines: *total subscriptions:* 1.72 million

subscriptions per 100 inhabitants: 12 (2014 est.)
country comparison to the world: 65

Telephones—mobile cellular: *total:* 16.9 million
subscriptions per 100 inhabitants: 115 (2014 est.)
country comparison to the world: 63

Telephone system: *general assessment:* fairly modern network centered in the city of Guatemala
domestic: state-owned telecommunications company privatized in the late 1990s opening the way for competition; fixed-line teledensity roughly 10 per 100 persons; fixed-line investments are being concentrated on improving rural connectivity; mobile-cellular teledensity approaching 140 per 100 persons
international: country code—502; landing point for both the Americas Region Caribbean Ring System (ARCOS-1) and the SAM-1 fiber optic submarine cable system that, together, provide connectivity to South and Central America, parts of the Caribbean, and the US; connected to Central American Microwave System; satellite earth station—1 Intelsat (Atlantic Ocean) (2013)

Broadcast media: 4 privately owned national terrestrial TV channels dominate TV broadcasting; multi-channel satellite and cable services are available; 1 government-owned radio station and hundreds of privately owned radio station s (2007)
Radio broadcast stations: AM 130, FM 487, shortwave 15 (2000)
Television broadcast stations: 26 (plus 27 repeaters) (1997)

Internet country code: .gt

Internet hosts: 357,552 (2012)
country comparison to the world: 60

Internet users: *total:* 2.5 million
percent of population: 17.1% (2014 est.)
country comparison to the world: 90

TRANSPORTATION

Airports: 291 (2013)
country comparison to the world: 23

Airports—with paved runways: *total:* 16
2,438 to 3,047 m: 2
1,524 to 2,437 m: 4
914 to 1,523 m: 6
under 914 m: 4 (2013)

Airports—with unpaved runways: *total:* 275
2,438 to 3,047 m: 1
1,524 to 2,437 m: 2
914 to 1,523 m: 77
under 914 m: 195 (2013)

Heliports: 1 (2013)

Pipelines: oil 480 km (2013)

Railways: *total:* 800 km
narrow gauge: 800 km 0.914-m gauge (2014)
country comparison to the world: 96

Roadways: *total:* 17,332 km
paved: 7,483 km
unpaved: 9,849 km (includes 4,795 km of rural roads) (2015)

country comparison to the world: 130

Waterways: 990 km (260 km navigable year round; additional 730 km navigable during high-water season) (2012)
country comparison to the world: 65

Ports and terminals: *major seaport(s):* Puerto Quetzal, Santo Tomas de Castilla

MILITARY AND SECURITY

Military branches: National Army of Guatemala (Ejercito Nacional de Guatemala, ENG; includes Guatemalan Navy (Fuerza de Mar, including Marines) and Guatemalan Air Force (Fuerza Aerea Guatemalteca, FAG)) (2013)

Military service age and obligation: all male citizens between the ages of 18 and 50 are eligible for military service; in practice, most of the force is volunteer, however, a selective draft system is employed, resulting in a small portion of 17–21 year-olds conscripted; conscript service obligation varies from 1 to 2 years; women can serve as officers (2013)

Military expenditures: 0.42% of GDP (2014)
0.46% of GDP (2013)
0.44% of GDP (2012)
0.41% of GDP (2011)
0.42% of GDP (2010)
country comparison to the world: 129

TRANSNATIONAL ISSUES

Disputes—international: annual ministerial meetings under the Organization of American States-initiated Agreement on the Framework for Negotiations and Confidence Building Measures continue to address Guatemalan land and maritime claims in Belize and the Caribbean Sea; Guatemala persists in its territorial claim to half of Belize, but agrees to Line of Adjacency to keep Guatemalan squatters out of Belize's forested interior; both countries agreed in April 2012 to hold simultaneous referenda, scheduled for 6 October 2013, to decide whether to refer the dispute to the ICJ for binding resolution, but this vote was suspended indefinitely; Mexico must deal with thousands of impoverished Guatemalans and other Central Americans who cross the porous border looking for work in Mexico and the US

Refugees and internally displaced persons: *IDPs:* 251,000 (more than three decades of internal conflict that ended in 1996 displaced mainly the indigenous Maya population and rural peasants; ongoing drug cartel and gang violence) (2015)

Illicit drugs: major transit country for cocaine and heroin; in 2005, cultivated 100 hectares of opium poppy after reemerging as a potential source of opium in 2004; potential production of less than 1 metric ton of pure heroin; marijuana cultivation for mostly domestic consumption; proximity to Mexico makes Guatemala a major staging area for drugs (particularly for cocaine); money laundering is a serious problem; corruption is a major problem

GUERNSEY

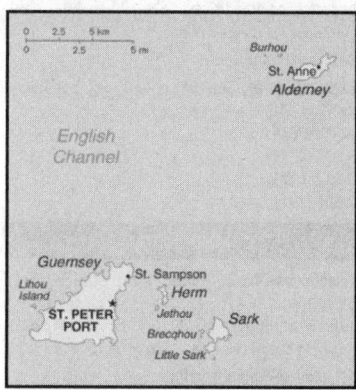

INTRODUCTION

Background: Guernsey and the other Channel Islands represent the last remnants of the medieval Dukedom of Normandy, which held sway in both France and England. The islands were the only British soil occupied by German troops in World War II. Guernsey is a British crown dependency but is not part of the UK or of the EU. However, the UK Government is constitutionally responsible for its defense and international representation.

GEOGRAPHY

Location: Western Europe, islands in the English Channel, northwest of France

Geographic coordinates: 49 28 N, 2 35 W

Map references: Europe

Area: *total:* 78 sq km
land: 78 sq km
water: 0 sq km
note: includes Alderney, Guernsey, Herm, Sark, and some other smaller islands
country comparison to the world: 228

Area—comparative: about one-half the size of Washington, DC

Land boundaries: 0 km

Coastline: 50 km

Maritime claims: *territorial sea:* 3 nm
exclusive fishing zone: 12 nm

Climate: temperate with mild winters and cool summers; about 50% of days are overcast

Terrain: mostly flat with low hills in southwest

Elevation: *mean elevation:* NA

elevation extremes: *lowest point:* Atlantic Ocean 0 m
highest point: unnamed elevation on Sark 114 m

Natural resources: cropland

Irrigated land: NA

Natural hazards: NA

Environment—current issues: NA

Geography—note: large, deepwater harbor at Saint Peter Port

PEOPLE AND SOCIETY

Nationality: *noun:* Channel Islander(s)
adjective: Channel Islander

Ethnic groups: British and Norm an-French descent with small percentages from other European countries

Languages: English, French, Norman-French dialect spoken in country districts

Religions: Protestant (Anglican, Presbyterian, Baptist, Congregational, Methodist), Rom an Catholic

Population: 66,080 (July 2015 est.)
country comparison to the world: 205

Age structure: *0–14 years:* 14.49% (male 4,956/female 4,619)
15–24 years: 11.71% (male 3,940/female 3,798)
25–54 years: 42.05% (male 14,007/female 13,782)
55–64 years: 12.86% (male 4,237/female 4,260)
65 years and over: 18.89% (male 5,643/female 6,838) (2015 est.)

Dependency ratios: *total dependency ratio:* 47%
youth dependency ratio: 21.6%
elderly dependency ratio: 25.4%
potential support ratio: 3.9%
note: data represents the Channel Islands (2015 est.)

Median age: *total:* 43.4 years
male: 42.1 years
female: 44.5 years (2015 est.)
country comparison to the world: 13

Population growth rate: 0.34% (2015 est.)
country comparison to the world: 169

Birth rate: 9.84 births/1,000 population (2015 est.)
country comparison to the world: 198

Death rate: 8.78 deaths/1,000 population (2015 est.)
country comparison to the world: 70

Net migration rate: 2.32 migrant(s)/1,000 population (2015 est.)
country comparison to the world: 45

Urbanization: *urban population:* 31.4% of total population (2014)
rate of urbanization: 0.76% annual rate of change (2010–15 est.)
note: data is for the Channel Islands

Sex ratio: *at birth:* 1.05 male(s)/female
0–14 years: 1.07 male(s)/female
15–24 years: 1.04 male(s)/female
25–54 years: 1.02 male(s)/female
55–64 years: 1 male(s)/female
65 years and over: 0.83 male(s)/female
total population: 0.99 male(s)/female (2015 est.)

Infant mortality rate: *total:* 3.44 deaths/1,000 live births
male: 3.74 deaths/1,000 live births
female: 3.13 deaths/1,000 live births (2015 est.)

country comparison to the world: 207

Life expectancy at birth: *total population:* 82.47 years
male: 79.79 years
female: 85.29 years (2015 est.)
country comparison to the world: 10

Total fertility rate: 1.55 children born/woman (2015 est.)
country comparison to the world: 189

HIV/AIDS—adult prevalence rate: NA

HIV/AIDS—people living with HIV/AIDS: NA

HIV/AIDS—deaths: NA

GOVERNMENT

Country name: *conventional long form:* Bailiwick of Guernsey
conventional short form: Guernsey
etymology: the name is of Old Norse origin, but the meaning of the root "Guern(s)" is uncertain; the "-ey" ending means "island"

Dependency status: British crown dependency

Government type: parliamentary democracy (States of Deliberation); a Crown dependency of the UK

Capital: *name:* Saint Peter Port

Geographic coordinates: 49 27 N, 2 32 W
time difference: UTC 0 (5 hours ahead of Washington, DC, during Standard Time)
daylight saving time: +1hr, begins last Sunday in March; ends last Sunday in October

Administrative divisions: none (British crown dependency); there are no first-order administrative divisions as defined by the US Government, but there are 10 parishes: Castel, Forest, Saint Andrew, Saint Martin, Saint Peter Port, Saint Pierre du Bois, Saint Sampson, Saint Saviour, Torteval, Vale

Independence: none (British crown dependency)

National holiday: Liberation Day, 9 May (1945)

Constitution: unwritten; includes royal charters, statutes, and common law and practice

Legal system: customary legal system based on Norman customary law, and includes elements of the French Civil Code and English common law

Citizenship: see United Kingdom

Suffrage: 16 years of age; universal

Executive branch: *chief of state:* Queen ELIZABETH II (since 6 February 1952); represented by Lieutenant Governor (vacant); note—Lieutenant Governor Air Marshall Peter WALKER died 6 September 2015; Bailiff Sir Richard COLLAS becomes acting lieutenant governor

head of government: Chief Minister Jonathan LETOCQ (since 12 March 2014); Bailiff Sir Richard COLLAS (since 23 March 2012)
cabinet: none; note—the Policy Council, elected by the States of Deliberation, functions mainly as policy coordination body

elections/appointments: the monarchy is hereditary; lieutenant governor and bailiff appointed
by the monarch; chief minister indirectly elected
by States of Deliberation election last held on 12
March 2014 (next to be held May 2016)
election results: Jonathan LETOCQ (independent) elected chief minister; States of Deliberation
vote -22 of 42 votes

Legislative branch: *description:* unicameral States
of Deliberation (47 seats—45 People's Deputies
and 2 representatives of the States of Alderney;
members directly elected by majority vote to serve
4-year terms); note—non-voting members include
the bailiff (presiding officer), attorney-general,
and solicitor-general
elections: last held on 27 April 2016 (next to be
held in 2020)
election results: percent of vote—NA; seats—all
independent

Judicial branch: *highest resident court(s):* Guernsey Court of Appeal (consists of the Bailiff of
Guernsey, who is the ex-officio president of the
Guernsey Court of Appeal, and at least 12 judges);
Royal Court (organized into 3 divisions—F ull
Court sits with 1 judge and 7 to 12 jurats acting as
judges of fact, Ordinary Court sits with 1 judge and
normally 3 jurats, and Matrimonial Causes Division sits with a 1 judge and 4 jurats); note -appeals
beyond Guernsey courts are heard by the Judicial
Committee of the Privy Council (in London)
judge selection and term of office: Royal Court
Bailiff, Deputy Bailiff and Court of Appeal justices
appointed by the British Crown and hold office at
Her Majesty's pleasure; jurats elected by the States
of Election, a body chaired by the Bailiff and a
number of jurats
subordinate courts: Court of Alderney; Court
of the Seneschal of Sark; Magistrate's Court
(includes Juvenile Court); Contracts Court; Ecclesiastical Court; Court of Chief Pleas

Political parties and leaders: none; all
independents

Political pressure groups and leaders: No More
Masts [Colin FALLAIZE]
Stop Traffic Endangering Pedestrian Safety or
STEPS

International organization participation: UPU

Diplomatic representation in the US: none (British
crown dependency)

Diplomatic representation from the US: none
(British crown dependency)

Flag description: white with the red cross of Saint
George (patron saint of England) extending to the
edges of the flag and a yellow equal-armed cross of
William the Conqueror superimposed on the Saint
George cross; the red cross represents the old ties
with England and the fact that Guernsey is a British Crown dependency; the gold cross is a replica
of the one used by Duke William of Normandy at
the Battle of Hastings

National symbol(s): Guernsey cow, donkey;
national colors: red, white, yellow

National anthem: *name:* "Sarnia Cherie" (Guernsey Dear)

lyrics/music: George DEIGHTON/Domencio
SANTANGELO
note: adopted 1911; serves as a local anthem; as a
British crown dependency, "God Save the Queen"
remains official (see United Kingdom)

ECONOMY

Economy—overview: Financial services account
for about 40% of employment and about 55%
of total income in this tiny, prosperous Channel
Island economy. Tourism, manufacturing, and horticulture, mainly tomatoes and cut flowers, have
been declining. Financial services, construction,
retail, and the public sector have been growing.
Light tax and death duties make Guernsey a popular tax haven. In October 2014, Guernsey signed
an OECD agreement to automatically exchange
some financial account information to limit tax
avoidance and evasion.

GDP (purchasing power parity): $3.451 billion
(2014 est.)
$3.42 billion (2013 est.)
$3.36 billion (2012 est.)
country comparison to the world: 180

GDP (official exchange rate): $2.742 billion (2005
est.)

GDP—real growth rate: 0.9% (2014 est.)
1.2% (2013 est.)
4.2% (2012 est.)
country comparison to the world: 180

GDP—per capita (PPP): $52,300 (2014 est.)
country comparison to the world: 23

GDP—composition, by sector of origin:
agriculture: 3%
industry: 10%
services: 87% (2000)

Agriculture—products: tomatoes, greenhouse
flowers, sweet peppers, eggplant, fruit; Guernsey
cattle

Industries: tourism, banking

Industrial production growth rate: NA%

Labor force: 31,470 (March 2006)
country comparison to the world: 204

Unemployment rate: 0.9% (March 2006 est.)
country comparison to the world: 4

Population below poverty line: NA%

**Household income or consumption by percentage
share:** *lowest:* 10%: NA%
highest: 10%: NA%

Budget: *revenues:* $563.6 million
expenditures: $530.9 million (2005)
Taxes and other revenues: 20.6% of GDP (2005)
country comparison to the world: 151

Budget surplus (+) or deficit (–): 1.2% of GDP
(2005)
country comparison to the world: 19

Fiscal year: calendar year

Inflation rate (consumer prices): 3.4% (June 2006
est.)
country comparison to the world: 145

Exports: $NA

Exports—commodities: tomatoes, flowers and
ferns, sweet peppers, eggplant, other vegetables

Imports: $NA

Imports—commodities: coal, gasoline, oil,
machinery and equipment

Debt—external: $NA

Exchange rates: Guernsey pound per US dollar—
0.6528 (2015)
0.607 (2014)
0.607 (2013)
0.63 (2012)
0.624 (2011)

COMMUNICATIONS

Telephones—fixed lines: *total subscriptions:*
45,100
subscriptions per 100 inhabitants: 70 (2014 est.)
country comparison to the world: 165

Telephones—mobile cellular: *total:* 43,800
subscriptions per 100 inhabitants: 70 (2004)
country comparison to the world: 203

Telephone system: *domestic:* fixed-line and
mobile-cellular services widely available; combined fixed-line and mobile-cellular teledensity
exceeds 100 per 100 persons
international: country code—44; 1 submarine
cable (2011)

Broadcast media: multiple UK terrestrial TV
broadcasts are received via a transmitter in Jersey
with relays in Jersey, Guernsey, and Alderney; satellite packages are available; BBC Radio Guernsey
and 1 other radio station operating (2009)
Radio broadcast stations: AM 1, FM 1, shortwave 0 (1998)
Television broadcast stations: 1 (1997)

Internet country code: .gg

Internet hosts: 239 (2012)
country comparison to the world: 196

Internet users: *total:* 48,300
percent of population: 74.94% (2009)
country comparison to the world: 185

TRANSPORTATION

Airports: 2 (2013)
country comparison to the world: 200

Airports—with paved runways: *total:* 2
1,524 to 2,437 m: 1
under 914 m: 1 (2013)

Ports and terminals: *major seaport(s):* Braye Bay,
Saint Peter Port

MILITARY AND SECURITY

Military—note: defense is the responsibility of the
UK

TRANSNATIONAL ISSUES

Disputes—international: none

GUINEA

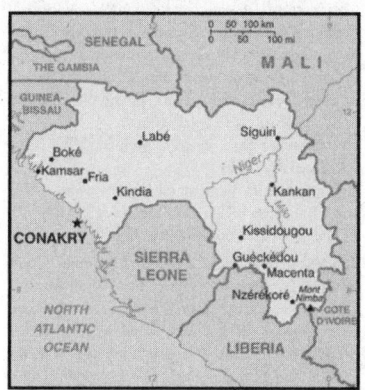

INTRODUCTION

Background: Guinea is at a turning point after decades of authoritarian rule since gaining its independence from France in 1958. Guinea held its first free and competitive democratic presidential and legislative elections in 2010 and 2013 respectively, and in October 2015 held a second consecutive presidential election. Alpha CONDE was reelected to a second five-year term as president in 2015, and the National Assembly was seated in January 2014. CONDE's first cabinet is the first all-civilian government in Guinea. Previously, Sekou TOURE ruled the country as president from independence to his death in 1984. Lansana CONTE came to power in 1984 when the military seized the government after TOURE's death. Gen. CONTE organized and won presidential elections in 1993, 1998, and 2003, though all the polls were rigged. Upon CONTE's death in December 2008, Capt. Moussa Dadis CAMARA led a military coup, seizing power and suspending the constitution. His unwillingness to yield to domestic and international pressure to step down led to heightened political tensions that culminated in September 2009 when presidential guards opened fire on an opposition rally killing more than 150 people, and in early December 2009 when CAMARA was wounded in an assassination attempt and exiled to Burkina Faso. A transitional government led by Gen. Sekouba KONATE paved the way for Guinea's transition to a fledgling democracy.

GEOGRAPHY

Location: Western Africa, bordering the North Atlantic Ocean, between Guinea-Bissau and Sierra Leone

Geographic coordinates: 11 00 N, 10 00 W

Map references: Africa

Area: total: 245,857 sq km
land: 245,717 sq km
water: 140 sq km
country comparison to the world: 79

Area—comparative: slightly smaller than Oregon

Land boundaries: total: 4,046 km
border countries (6): Cote d'Ivoire 816 km, Guinea-Bissau 421 km, Liberia 590 km, Mali 1,062 km, Senegal 363 km, Sierra Leone 794 km

Coastline: 320 km

Maritime claims: territorial sea: 12 nm
exclusive economic zone: 200 nm

Climate: generally hot and humid; monsoonal-type rainy season (June to November) with southwesterly winds; dry season (December to May) with northeasterly harmattan winds

Terrain: generally flat coastal plain, hilly to mountainous interior

Elevation: mean elevation: 472 m

elevation extremes: lowest point: Atlantic Ocean 0 m
highest point: Mont Nimba 1,752 m

Natural resources: bauxite, iron ore, diamonds, gold, uranium, hydropower, fish, salt

Land use: agricultural land: 58.1%
arable land: 11.8%
permanent crops: 2.8%
permanent pasture: 43.5%
forest: 26.5%
other: 15.4% (2011 est.)

Irrigated land: 950 sq km (2012)

Total renewable water resources: 226 cu km (2011)

Freshwater withdrawal (domestic/industrial/agricultural): total: 0.55 cu km/yr (39%/10%/51%)
per capita: 64.3 cu m/yr (2005)

Natural hazards: hot, dry, dusty harmattan haze may reduce visibility during dry season

Environment—current issues: deforestation; inadequate potable water; desertification; soil contamination and erosion; overfishing, overpopulation in forest region; poor mining practices have led to environmental damage

Environment—international agreements: party to: Biodiversity, Climate Change, Climate Change-Kyoto Protocol, Desertification, Endangered Species, Hazardous Wastes, Law of the Sea, Ozone Layer Protection, Ship Pollution, Wetlands, Whaling
signed, but not ratified: none of the selected agreements

Geography—note: the Niger and its important tributary the Milo River have their sources in the Guinean highlands

PEOPLE AND SOCIETY

Nationality: noun: Guinean(s)
adjective: Guinean

Ethnic groups: Fulani (Peul) 33.9%, Malinke 31.1%, Soussou 19.1%, Guerze 6%, Kissi 4.7%, Toma 2.6%, other/no answer 2.7% (2012 est.)

Languages: French (official)

note: each ethnic group has its own language

Religions: Muslim 86.7%, Christian 8.9%, animist/other/none 4.4% (2012 est.)

Population: 11,780,162 (July 2015 est.)
country comparison to the world: 76

Age structure: 0–14 years: 41.87% (male 2,491,593/female 2,440,933)
15–24 years: 19.6% (male 1,165,462/female 1,143,022)
25–54 years: 30.46% (male 1,799,050/female 1,789,062)
55–64 years: 4.45% (male 250,531/female 273,756)
65 years and over: 3.62% (male 188,469/female 238,284) (2015 est.)

Dependency ratios: total dependency ratio: 83.8%
youth dependency ratio: 78.2%
elderly dependency ratio: 5.6%
potential support ratio: 17.8% (2015 est.)

Median age: total: 18.8 years
male: 18.5 years
female: 19 years (2015 est.)
country comparison to the world: 204

Population growth rate: 2.63% (2015 est.)
country comparison to the world: 18

Birth rate: 35.74 births/1,000 population (2015 est.)
country comparison to the world: 21

Death rate: 9.46 deaths/1,000 population (2015 est.)
country comparison to the world: 55

Net migration rate: 0 migrant(s)/1,000 population (2015 est.)
country comparison to the world: 95

Urbanization: urban population: 37.2% of total population (2015)
rate of urbanization: 3.82% annual rate of change (2010–15 est.)

Major urban areas—population: CONAKRY (capital) 1.936 million (2015)

Sex ratio: at birth: 1.03 male(s)/female
0–14 years: 1.02 male(s)/female
15–24 years: 1.02 male(s)/female
25–54 years: 1.01 male(s)/female
55–64 years: 0.92 male(s)/female
65 years and over: 0.79 male(s)/female
total population: 1 male(s)/female (2015 est.)

Mother's mean age at first birth: 19
note: median age at first birth among women 20–24 (2012 est.)

Maternal mortality rate: 679 deaths/100,000 live births (2015 est.)
country comparison to the world: 13

Infant mortality rate: total: 53.43 deaths/1,000 live births
male: 56.26 deaths/1,000 live births
female: 50.52 deaths/1,000 live births (2015 est.)
country comparison to the world: 30

Life expectancy at birth: *total population:* 60.08 years
male: 58.55 years
female: 61.66 years (2015 est.)
country comparison to the world: 198

Total fertility rate: 4.88 children born/woman (2015 est.)
country comparison to the world: 18

Contraceptive prevalence rate:
5.6% (2012)

Health expenditures: 4.7% of GDP (2013)
country comparison to the world: 102

Physicians density: 0.1 physicians/1,000 population (2005)

Hospital bed density: 0.3 beds/1,000 population (2011)

Drinking water source:
improved:
urban: 92.7% of population
rural: 67.4% of population
total: 76.8% of population
unimproved:
urban: urban: 7.3% of population
rural: 32.6% of population
total: 23.2% of population (2015 est.)

Sanitation facility access:
improved:
urban: 34.1% of population
rural: 11.8% of population
total: 20.1% of population
unimproved:
urban: urban: 65.9% of population
rural: 88.2% of population
total: 79.9% of population (2015 est.)

HIV/AIDS—adult prevalence rate: 1.55% (2014)
country comparison to the world: 33

HIV/AIDS—people living with HIV/AIDS: 118,000 (2014 est.)
country comparison to the world: 40

HIV/AIDS—deaths: 3,800 (2014 est.)
country comparison to the world: 39

Major infectious diseases: *degree of risk:* very high
food or waterborne diseases: bacterial and protozoal diarrhea, hepatitis A, and typhoid fever
vector borne diseases: malaria, dengue fever, and yellow fever
water contact disease: schistosomiasis
aerosolized dust or soil contact disease: Lassa fever
animal contact disease: rabies (2013)

Obesity—adult prevalence rate: 5.9% (2014)
country comparison to the world: 165

Children under the age of 5 years underweight: 18.7% (2012)
country comparison to the world: 33

Education expenditures: 3.5% of GDP (2013)
country comparison to the world: 156

Literacy: *definition:* age 15 and over can read and write
total population: 30.4%
male: 38.1%
female: 22.8% (2015 est.)

School life expectancy (primary to tertiary education): *total:* 9 years
male: 10 years
female: 8 years (2014)

Child labor—children ages 5–14: *total number:* 571,774
percentage: 25% (2003 est.)

Unemployment, youth ages 15–24: *total:* 1%
male: 1.5%
female: 0.6% (2012 est.)

GOVERNMENT

Country name: *conventional long form:* Republic of Guinea
conventional short form: Guinea
local long form: Republique de Guinee
local short form: Guinee
former: French Guinea
note: the country is named after the Guinea region of West Africa that lies along the Gulf of Guinea and stretches north to the Sahel

Government type: presidential republic

Capital: *name:* Conakry

Geographic coordinates: 9 30 N, 13 42 W
time difference: UTC 0 (5 hours ahead of Washington, DC, during Standard Time)

Administrative divisions: 7 regions administrative and 1 gouvenorat*; Boke, Conakry*, Faranah, Kankan, Kindia, Labe, Mamou, N'Zerekore

Independence: 2 October 1958 (from France)

National holiday: Independence Day, 2 October (1958)

Constitution: previous 1958, 1990; latest promulgated 19 April 2010, approved 7 May 2010 (2016)

Legal system: civil law system based on the French model

International law organization participation: accepts compulsory ICJ jurisdiction with reservations; accepts ICCt jurisdiction

Citizenship: *citizenship by birth:* no
citizenship by descent only: at least one parent must be a citizen of Guinea
dual citizenship recognized: no
residency requirement for naturalization: na

Suffrage: 18 years of age; universal

Executive branch: *chief of state:* President Alpha CONDE (since 21 December 2010)

head of government: Prime Minister Mamady YOULA (since 26 December 2015); Prime Minister Mohamed Said FOFANA (since 24 December 2010) resigned 12/23/15
cabinet: Council of Ministers appointed by the president
elections/appointments: president directly elected by absolute majority popular vote in 2 rounds if needed for a 5-year term (eligible for a second term); election last held on 11 October 2015 (next scheduled for 2020); prime minister appointed by the president
election results: Alpha CONDE reelected president; percent of vote—Alpha CONDE (RPG)

57.8%, Cellou Dalein DIALLO (UFDG) 31.4%, other 10.8%

Legislative branch: *description:* unicameral People's National Assembly or Assemblee Nationale Populaire (114 seats; 76 members directly elected in a single nationwide constituency by proportional representation vote and 38 directly elected in single-seat constituencies by simple majority vote; members serve 4-year terms)
elections: last held on 28 September 2013 (next scheduled for 2018)
election results: percent of vote by party—NA; seats by party—RPG 53, UFDG 37, UFR 10, PEDN 2, UPG 2, other parties 10

Judicial branch: *highest court(s):* Supreme Court or Cour Supreme (organized into Administrative Chamber and Civil, Penal, and Social Chamber; court consists of the first president, 2 chamber presidents, at least 4 councillors, the solicitor general and NA deputies); Constitutional Court (consists of 9 members)
judge selection and term of office: Supreme Court first president appointed by the national president after consultation with the National Assembly; other members appointed by presidential decree; member tenure NA; Constitutional Court member appointments—2 by the National Assembly and the president of the republic, 3 experienced judges designated by their peers, 1 experienced lawyer, 1 university professor with expertise in public law designated by peers, and 2 experienced representatives of the Independent National Institution of Human Rights; members serve single 9-year terms
subordinate courts: includes Court of Appeal or Cour d'Appel; courts of first instance or Tribunal de Premiere Instance; High Court of Justice or Cour d'Assises; labor court; military tribunal; justices of the peace; specialized courts

Political parties and leaders: National Party for Hope and Development or PEDN [Lansana KOUYATE]
Rally for the Guinean People or RPG [Alpha CONDE]
Union for the Progress of Guinea or UPG [Jean Marie DORE]
Union of Democratic Forces of Guinea or UFDG [Cellou Dalein DIALLO]
Union of Republican Forces or UFR [Sidya TOURE]
note: listed are the five most popular parties as of December 2015

Political pressure groups and leaders: National Confederation of Guinean Workers-Labor Union of Guinean Workers or CNTG-USTG Alliance (includes National Confederation of Guinean Workers or CNTG, Labor Union of Guinean Workers or USTG)
Syndicate of Guinean Teachers and Researchers or SLECG

International organization participation: ACP, AfDB, AU, ECOWAS, EITI (compliant country), FAO, G-77, IBRD, ICAO, ICCt, ICRM, IDA, IDB, IFAD, IFC, IFRCS, ILO, IMF, IMO, Interpol, IOC, IOM, IPU, ISO (correspondent), ITSO, ITU, ITUC (NGOs), MIGA,

MINURSO, MINUSMA, MONUSCO, NAM, OIC, OIF, OPCW, UN, UNCTAD, UNESCO, UNHCR, UNIDO, UNISFA, UNMISS, UNOCI, UNWTO, UPU, WCO, WFTU (NGOs), WHO, WIPO, WMO, WTO

Diplomatic representation in the US: *chief of mission:* Ambassador Mamady CONDE (since 14 July 2014)
chancery: 2112 Leroy Place NW, Washington, DC 20008
telephone: [1] (202) 986-4300
FAX: [1] (202) 986-3800

Diplomatic representation from the US: *chief of mission:* Ambassador Dennis B. HANKINS (since December 2015)
embassy: Koloma, Conakry, east of Hamdallaye Circle
mailing address: B. P.603, Transversale No.2, Centre Administratif de Koloma, Commune de Ratoma, Conakry
telephone: [224] 655-10-40-00
FAX: [224] 655-10-42-97

Flag description: three equal vertical bands of red (hoist side), yellow, and green; red represents the people's sacrifice for liberation and work; yellow stands for the sun, for the riches of the earth, and for justice; green symbolizes the country's vegetation and unity
note: uses the popular Pan-African colors of Ethiopia; the colors from left to right are the reverse of those on the flags of neighboring Mali and Senegal

National symbol(s): *national colors:* red, yellow, green

National anthem: *name:* "Liberte" (Liberty)
lyrics/music: unknown/Fodeba KEITA
note: adopted 1958

ECONOMY

Economy—overview: Guinea is a poor country of approximately 11.7 million people that possesses the world's largest reserves of bauxite and largest untapped high-grade iron ore reserves (Simandou), as well as gold and diamonds. In addition, Guinea has fertile soil, ample rainfall, and is the source of several West African rivers, including the Senegal, Niger, and Gambia. Guinea's hydro potential is enormous and the country could be a major exporter of electricity. The country also has tremendous agriculture potential. Gold, bauxite, and diamonds are Guinea's main mineral exports. International investors have shown interest in Guinea's unexplored mineral reserves, which have the potential to propel Guinea's future growth. Following the death of long-term President Lansana CONTE in 2008 and the coup that followed, international donors, including the G-8, the IMF, and the World Bank, significantly curtailed their development programs in Guinea. However, the IMF approved a new 3-year Extended Credit Facility arrangement in 2012, following the December 2010 presidential elections. In September 2012, Guinea achieved Heavily Indebted Poor Countries completion point status. Future access to international assistance and investment will depend on

the government's ability to be transparent, combat corruption, reform its banking system, improve its business environment, and build infrastructure. In April 2013, the government amended its mining code to reduce taxes and royalties. In 2014, Guinea also complied with requirements of the Extractive Industries Transparency Initiative by publishing its mining contracts and was found to be compliant.

The biggest threats to Guinea's economy are political instability, the continuation of the Ebola-virus epidemic, and low international commodity prices. Rising international donor support and reduced government investment spending will lessen fiscal strains created by the Ebolavirus epidemic, but economic recovery will be a long process while the government continues to fight the disease. The economic toll of Ebolavirus on the Guinean economy is considerable. Ebola stalled promising economic growth in 2014–15, and the economy will continue to stagnate in 2016, unless Ebolavirus is eradicated. Several projects have stalled, such as offshore oil exploration and the giant Simandou iron ore project. The 240 megawatt Kaleta Dam, which was inaugurated in September 2015, has expanded access to electricity for residents of Conakry. Although the recent political stability has brought renewed interest in Guinea from the private sector, an enduring legacy of corruption, inefficiency, and lack of government transparency, combined with fears of Ebolavirus, continue to undermine Guinea's economic viability. Successive governments have failed to address the country's crumbling infrastructure, which is needed for economic development. Guinea suffers from chronic electricity shortages; poor roads, rail lines and bridges; and a lack of access to clean water—all of which continue to plague economic development. The present government, led by President Alpha CONDE, is working to create an economy to attract foreign investment and hopes to have greater participation from western countries and firms in Guinea's economic development.

GDP (purchasing power parity): $14.98 billion (2015 est.)
$14.96 billion (2014 est.)
$14.8 billion (2013 est.)
note: data are in 2015 US dollars
country comparison to the world: 154

GDP (official exchange rate): $6.696 billion (2015 est.)

GDP—real growth rate: 0.1% (2015 est.)
1.1% (2014 est.)
2.3% (2013 est.)
country comparison to the world: 191

GDP—per capita (PPP): $1,200 (2015 est.)
$1,200 (2014 est.)
$1,300 (2013 est.)
note: data are in 2015 US dollars
country comparison to the world: 221

Gross national saving: -12.3% of GDP (2015 est.)
-16.4% of GDP (2014 est.)
-6.5% of GDP (2013 est.)
country comparison to the world: 177

GDP—composition, by end use:

household consumption: 96.6%
government consumption: 8.9%
investment in fixed capital: 13.2%
investment in inventories: 0.1%
exports of good s and services: 23.6%
imports of goods and services: -42.4% (2015 est.)

GDP—composition, by sector of origin:
agriculture: 19.7%
industry: 37.2%
services: 43.1% (2015 est.)

Agriculture—products: rice, coffee, pineapples, mangoes, palm kernels, cocoa, cassava (manioc, tapioca), bananas, potatoes, sweet potatoes; cattle, sheep, goats; timber

Industries: bauxite, gold, diamonds, iron ore; light manufacturing, agricultural processing

Industrial production growth rate: -2% (2015 est.)
country comparison to the world: 179

Labor force: 5.24 million (2015 est.)
country comparison to the world: 77

Labor force—by occupation: *agriculture:* 76%
industry and services: 24% (2006 est.)

Unemployment rate: NA%

Population below poverty line: 47% (2006 est.)

Household income or consumption by percentage share: *lowest:* 10%: 2.7%
highest: 10%: 30.3% (2007)

Distribution of family income—Gini index: 39.4 (2007)
40.3 (1994)
country comparison to the world: 68

Budget: *revenues:* $1.546 billion
expenditures: $2.104 billion (2015 est.)
Taxes and other revenues: 23% of GDP (2015 est.)
country comparison to the world: 134

Budget surplus (+) or deficit (–): -8.3% of GDP (2015 est.)
country comparison to the world: 200

Fiscal year: calendar year

Inflation rate (consumer prices): 8.2% (2015 est.)
9.7% (2014 est.)
country comparison to the world: 202

Central bank discount rate: NA% (31 December 2010)
22.25% (31 December 2005)

Commercial bank prime lending rate: 23% (31 December 2015 est.)
23% (31 December 2014 est.)
country comparison to the world: 8

Stock of narrow money: $1.758 billion (31 December 2015 est.)
$1.84 billion (31 December 2014 est.)
country comparison to the world: 134

Stock of broad money: $2.093 billion (31 December 2015 est.)
$2.175 billion (31 December 2014 est.)
country comparison to the world: 151

Stock of domestic credit: $2.005 billion (31 December 2015 est.)
$2.226 billion (31 December 2014 est.)
country comparison to the world: 140

363

Market value of publicly traded shares: $NA

Current account balance: -$1.503 billion (2015 est.)
-$1.718 billion (2014 est.)
country comparison to the world: 138

Exports: $1.81 billion (2015 est.)
$1.763 billion (2014 est.)
country comparison to the world: 144

Exports—commodities: bauxite, gold, diamonds, coffee, fish, agricultural products

Exports—partners: India 22.5%, Spain 8.2%, Ireland 7.3%, Germany 6.2%, Belgium 5.5%, Ukraine 5.3%, France 4.1% (2015)

Imports: $1.94 billion (2015 est.)
$2.175 billion (2014 est.)
country comparison to the world: 165

Imports—commodities: petroleum products, metals, machinery, transport equipment, textiles, grain and other foodstuffs

Imports—partners: China 20.3%, Netherlands 5.4%, India 4.4% (2015)

Reserves of foreign exchange and gold: $302.8 million (31 December 2015 est.)
$302.4 million (31 December 2014 est.)
country comparison to the world: 158

Debt—external: $1.283 billion (31 December 2014 est.)
$1.198 billion (31 December 2013 est.)
country comparison to the world: 159

Stock of direct foreign investment—abroad: $67.3 million (31 December 2015 est.)
$67.3 million (31 December 2014 est.)
country comparison to the world: 97

Exchange rates: Guinean francs (GNF) per US dollar—
7,305 (2015 est.)
7,014.1 (2014 est.)
7,014.1 (2013 est.)
6,986 (2012 est.)
6,658 (2011 est.)

ENERGY

Electricity—production: 971 million kWh (2012 est.)
country comparison to the world: 151

Electricity—consumption: 903 million kWh (2012 est.)
country comparison to the world: 158

Electricity—exports: 0 kWh (2013 est.)
country comparison to the world: 147

Electricity—imports: 0 kWh (2013 est.)
country comparison to the world: 158

Electricity—installed generating capacity: 398,000 kW (2012 est.)
country comparison to the world: 146

Electricity—from fossil fuels: 67.8% of total installed capacity (2012 est.)
country comparison to the world: 116

Electricity—from nuclear fuels: 0% of total installed capacity (2012 est.)
country comparison to the world: 105

Electricity—from hydroelectric plants: 32.2% of total installed capacity (2012 est.)
country comparison to the world: 71

Electricity—from other renewable sources: 0% of total installed capacity (2012 est.)
country comparison to the world: 181

Crude oil—production: 0 bbl/day (2014 est.)
country comparison to the world: 144

Crude oil—exports: 0 bbl/day (2012 est.)
country comparison to the world: 133

Crude oil—imports: 0 bbl/day (2012 est.)
country comparison to the world: 201

Crude oil—proved reserves: 0 bbl (1 January 2015 est.)
country comparison to the world: 142

Refined petroleum products—production: 0 bbl/day (2012 est.)
country comparison to the world: 191

Refined petroleum products—consumption: 9,000 bbl/day (2013 est.)
country comparison to the world: 156

Refined petroleum products—exports: 0 bbl/day (2012 est.)
country comparison to the world: 188

Refined petroleum products—imports: 9,089 bbl/day (2012 est.)
country comparison to the world: 139

Natural gas—production: 0 cu m (2013 est.)
country comparison to the world: 198

Natural gas—consumption: 0 cu m (2013 est.)
country comparison to the world: 152

Natural gas—exports: 0 cu m (2013 est.)
country comparison to the world: 112

Natural gas—imports: 0 cu m (2013 est.)
country comparison to the world: 206

Natural gas—proved reserves: 0 cu m (1 January 2014 est.)
country comparison to the world: 147

Carbon dioxide emissions from consumption of energy: 1.388 million Mt (2012 est.)
country comparison to the world: 161

COMMUNICATIONS

Telephones—fixed lines: *total subscriptions:* 0
subscriptions per 100 inhabitants: less than 1 (2014 est.)
country comparison to the world: 219

Telephones—mobile cellular: *total:* 8.7 million
subscriptions per 100 inhabitants: 76 (2014 est.)
country comparison to the world: 93

Telephone system: *general assessment:* inadequate system of open-wire lines, small radiotelephone communication stations, and new microwave radio relay system
domestic: Conakry reasonably well-served; coverage elsewhere remains inadequate and large companies tend to rely on their own systems for nationwide links; fixed-line teledensity less than 1 per 100 persons; mobile-cellular subscribership is expanding and exceeds 40 per 100 persons
international: country code—224; satellite earth station—1 Intelsat (Atlantic Ocean) (2011)

Broadcast media: government maintains marginal control over broadcast media; single state-run TV station; state-run radio broadcast station also operates several stations in rural areas; a steadily increasing number of privately owned radio stations, nearly all in Conakry, and about a dozen community radio stations; foreign TV programming available via satellite and cable subscription services (2011)
Radio broadcast stations: AM 0, FM 5, shortwave 3 (2006)
Television broadcast stations: 6 (2001)

Internet country code: .gn

Internet hosts: 15 (2012)
country comparison to the world: 223

Internet users: *total:* 195,100
percent of population: 1.7% (2014 est.)
country comparison to the world: 156

TRANSPORTATION

Airports: 16 (2013)
country comparison to the world: 144

Airports—with paved runways: *total:* 4
over 3,047 m: 1
1,524 to 2,437 m: 3 (2013)

Airports—with unpaved runways: *total:* 12
1,524 to 2,437 m: 7
914 to 1,523 m: 3
under 914 m: 2 (2013)

Railways: *total:* 662 km
narrow gauge: 662 km 1.000-m gauge (20014)
country comparison to the world: 105

Roadways: *total:* 44,348 km
paved: 4,342 km
npaved: 40,006 km (2003)
country comparison to the world: 79

Waterways: 1,300 km (navigable by shallow-draft native craft in the northern part of the Niger River system) (2011)
country comparison to the world: 53

Ports and terminals: *major seap ort(s):* Conakry, Kamsar

MILITARY AND SECURITY

Military branches: National Armed Forces: Army, Guinean Navy (Armee de Mer or Marine Guineenne, includes Marines), Guinean Air Force (Force Aerienne de Guinee) (2009)

Military service age and obligation: 18–25 years of age for compulsory and voluntary military service; 18-month conscript service obligation (2012)

TRANSNATIONAL ISSUES

Disputes—international: conflicts among rebel groups, warlords, and youth gangs in neighboring states have spilled over into Guinea resulting in domestic instability; Sierra Leone considers Guinea's definition of the flood plain limits to define the left bank boundary of the Makona and Moa Rivers excessive and protests Guinea's continued occupation of these lands, including the hamlet of Yenga, occupied since 1998

Refugees and internally displaced persons: *refugees (country of origin):* 6,580 (Cote d'Ivoire) (2014)

Trafficking in persons: *current situation:* Guinea is a source, transit, and, to a lesser extent, a destination country for men, women, and children subjected to forced labor and sex trafficking; the majority of trafficking victims are Guinean children, and trafficking is more prevalent among Guineans than foreign national migrants; Guinean girls are subjected to domestic servitude and commercial sexual exploitation, while boys are forced to beg or to work as street vendors, shoe shiners, or miners; Guinea is a source country and transit point for West African children forced to work as miners in the region; Guinean women and girls are subjected to domestic servitude and sex trafficking in West Africa, the Middle East, the US, and increasingly Europe, while Thai, Chinese, and Vietnamese women are forced into prostitution and some West Africans are forced into domestic servitude in Guinea

tier rating: Tier 2 Watch List—Guinea does not fully comply with the minimum standards for the elimination of trafficking; however, it is making significant efforts to do so; in 2014, Guinea was granted a waiver from an otherwise required downgrade to Tier 3 because its government has a written plan that, if implemented would constitute making significant efforts to bring itself into compliance with the minimum standards for the elimination of trafficking; no new investigations were conducted in 2014, and the one ongoing case led to the prosecution of four offenders for forced child labor, three of whom were convicted but given inadequate sentences for the crime; the government did not identify or provide protective services to victims and did not support NGOs that assisted victims but continued to refer child victims to NGOs on an ad hoc basis; Guinean law does not prohibit all forms of trafficking, excluding, for example, debt bondage; the 2014 ebola outbreak negatively affected Guinea's ability to address human trafficking (2015)

GUINEA-BISSAU

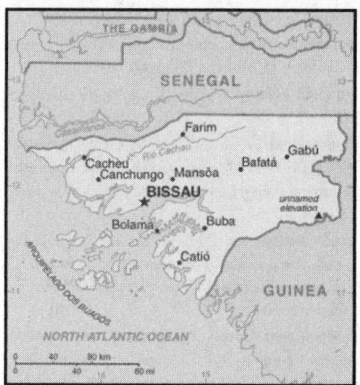

INTRODUCTION

Background: Since independence from Portugal in 1974, Guinea-Bissau has experienced considerable political and military upheaval. In 1980, a military coup established authoritarian dictator Joao Bernardo 'Nino' VIEIRA as president. Despite setting a path to a market economy and multiparty system, VIEIRA's regime was characterized by the suppression of political opposition and the purging of political rivals. Several coup attempts through the 1980s and early 1990s failed to unseat him. In 1994 VIEIRA was elected president in the country's first free, multiparty election. A military mutiny and resulting civil war in 1998 eventually led to VIEIRA's ouster in May 1999. In February 2000, a transitional government turned over power to opposition leader Kumba YALA after he was elected president in transparent polling. In September 2003, after only three years in office, YALA was overthrown in a bloodless military coup, and businessman Henrique ROSA was sworn in as interim president. In 2005, former President VIEIRA was reelected, pledging to pursue economic development and national reconciliation; he was assassinated in March 2009. Malam Bacai SANHA was elected in an emergency election held in June 2009, but he passed away in January 2012 from a long-term illness. A military coup in April 2012 prevented Guinea-Bissau's second-round presidential election—to determine SANHA's successor—from taking place. Following mediation by the Economic Community of Western African States, a civilian transitional government assumed power in 2012 and remained until Jose Mario VAZ won free and fair election in 2014.

GEOGRAPHY

Location: Western Africa, bordering the North Atlantic Ocean, between Guinea and Senegal

Geographic coordinates: 12 00 N, 15 00 W

Map references: Africa

Area: *total:* 36,125 sq km
land: 28,120 sq km
water: 8,005 sq km
country comparison to the world: 138

Area—comparative: slightly less than three times the size of Connecticut

Land boundaries: *total:* 762 km
border countries (2): Guinea 421 km, Senegal 341 km

Coastline: 350 km

Maritime claims: *territorial sea:* 12 nm
exclusive economic zone: 200 nm

Climate: tropical; generally hot and humid; monsoonal-type rainy season (June to November) with southwesterly winds; dry season (December to May) with northeasterly harmattan winds

Terrain: mostly low-lying coastal plain with a deeply indented estuarine coastline rising to savanna in east; numerous off-shore islands including the Arquipelago Dos Bijagos consisting of 18 main islands and many small islets

Elevation: *mean elevation:* 70 m

elevation extremes: *lowest point:* Atlantic Ocean 0 m

highest point: unnamed elevation in the eastern part of the country 300 m

Natural resources: fish, timber, phosphates, bauxite, clay, granite, limestone, unexploited deposits of petroleum

Land use: *agricultural land:* 44.8%
arable land: 8.2%
permanent crops: 6.9%
permanent pasture: 29.7%
forest: 55.2%
other: 0% (2011 est.)

Irrigated land: 250 sq km (2012)

Total renewable water resources: 31 cu km (2011)

Freshwater withdrawal (domestic/industrial/agricultural): *total:* 0.18 cu km/yr (18%/6%/76%)
per capita: 135.7 cu m/yr (2005)

Natural hazards: hot, dry, dusty harmattan haze may reduce visibility during dry season; brush fires

Environment—current issues: deforestation; soil erosion; overgrazing; overfishing

Environment—international agreements: *party to:* Biodiversity, Climate Change, Climate Change-Kyoto Protocol, Desertification, Endangered Species, Hazardous Wastes, Law of the Sea, Ozone Layer Protection, Wetlands
signed, but not ratified: none of the selected agreements

Geography—note: this small country is swampy along its western coast and low-lying inland

PEOPLE AND SOCIETY

Nationality: *noun:* Bissau-Guinean(s)
adjective: Bissau-Guinean

Ethnic groups: Fulani 28.5%, Balanta 22.5%, Mandinga 14.7%, Papel 9.1%, Manjaco 8.3%, Beafada 3.5%, Mancanha 3.1%, Bijago 2.1%, Felupe 1.7%, Mansoanca 1.4%, Balanta Mane 1%, other 1.8%, none 2.2% (2008 est.)

Languages: Crioulo 90.4%, Portuguese 27.1% (official), French 5.1%, English 2.9%, other 2.4%

note: shares sum to more than 100% because some respondents gave more than one answer on the census (2008 est.)

Religions: Muslim 45.1%, Christian 22.1%, animist 14.9%, none 2%, unspecified 15.9% (2008 est.)

Population: 1,726,170 (July 2015 est.)
country comparison to the world: 153

Age structure: *0–14 years:* 39.53% (male 340,575/female 341,747)
15–24 years: 20.18% (male 172,787/female 175,511)
25–54 years: 32.3% (male 277,820/female 279,762)
55–64 years: 4.66% (male 30,010/female 50,354)
65 years and over: 3.34% (male 21,671/female 35,933) (2015 est.)

Dependency ratios: *total dependency ratio:* 78.4%
youth dependency ratio: 72.8%
elderly dependency ratio: 5.7%
potential support ratio: 17.7% (2015 est.)

Median age: *total:* 19.9 years
male: 19.4 years
female: 20.4 years (2015 est.)
country comparison to the world: 190

Population growth rate: 1.91% (2015 est.)
country comparison to the world: 56

Birth rate: 33.38 births/1,000 population (2015 est.)
country comparison to the world: 31

Death rate: 14.33 deaths/1,000 population (2015 est.)
country comparison to the world: 4

Net migration rate: 0 migrant(s)/1,000 population (2015 est.)
country comparison to the world: 94

Urbanization: *urban population:* 49.3% of total population (2015)
rate of urbanization: 4.13% annual rate of change (2010–15 est.)

Major urban areas—population: BISSAU (capital) 492,000 (2015)

Sex ratio: *at birth:* 1.03 male(s)/female
0–14 years: 1 male(s)/female
15–24 years: 0.98 male(s)/female
25–54 years: 0.99 male(s)/female
55–64 years: 0.6 male(s)/female
65 years and over: 0.6 male(s)/female
total population: 0.95 male(s)/female (2015 est.)

Maternal mortality rate: 549 deaths/100,000 live births (2015 est.)
country comparison to the world: 7

Infant mortality rate: *total:* 89.21 deaths/1,000 live births
male: 98.8 deaths/1,000 live births
female: 79.33 deaths/1,000 live births (2015 est.)
country comparison to the world: 5

Life expectancy at birth: *total population:* 50.23 years
male: 48.21 years
female: 52.31 years (2015 est.)

country comparison to the world: 223

Total fertility rate: 4.23 children born/woman (2015 est.)
country comparison to the world: 32

Contraceptive prevalence rate: 14.2% (2010)

Health expenditures: 5.5% of GDP (2013)
country comparison to the world: 116

Physicians density: 0.1 physicians/1,000 population (2009)

Hospital bed density: 1 beds/1,000 population (2009)

Drinking water source:
improved:
urban: 98.8% of population
rural: 60.3% of population
total: 79.3% of population
unimproved:
urban: urban: 1.2% of population
rural: 39.7% of population
total: 20.7% of population (2015 est.)

Sanitation facility access:
improved:
urban: 33.5% of population
rural: 8.5% of population
total: 20.8% of population
unimproved:
urban: 66.5% of population
rural: 91.5% of population
total: 79.2% of population (2015 est.)

HIV/AIDS—adult prevalence rate: 3.69% (2014 est.)
country comparison to the world: 17

HIV/AIDS—people living with HIV/AIDS: 42,000 (2014 est.)
country comparison to the world: 59

HIV/AIDS—deaths: 1,900 (2014 est.)
country comparison to the world: 57

Major infectious diseases: *degree of risk:* very high
food or waterborne diseases: bacterial and protozoal diarrhea, hepatitis A, and typhoid fever
vectorborne diseases: malaria, dengue fever, and yellow fever
water contact disease: schistosomiasis
animal contact disease: rabies (2013)

Obesity—adult prevalence rate: 6.3% (2014)
country comparison to the world: 159

Children under the age of 5 years underweight: 17% (2014)
country comparison to the world: 35

Education expenditures: 2.4% of GDP (2013)

Literacy: *definition:* age 15 and over can read and write
total population: 59.9%
male: 71.8%
female: 48.3% (2015 est.)

School life expectancy (primary to tertiary education): *total:* 9 years
male: NA
female: NA (2006)

Child labor—children ages 5–14: *total number:* 226,316

percentage: 57% (2010 est.)

GOVERNMENT

Country name: *conventional long form:* Republic of Guinea-Bissau
conventional short form: Guinea-Bissau
local long form: Republica da Guine-Bissau
local short form: Guine-Bissau
former: Portuguese Guinea
note: the country is named after the Guinea region of West Africa that lies along the Gulf of Guinea and stretches north to the Sahel; "Bissau" distinguishes the country from neighboring Guinea

Government type: semi-presidential republic

Capital: *name:* Bissau

Geographic coordinates: 11 51 N, 15 35 W
time difference: UTC 0 (5 hours ahead of Washington, DC, during Standard Time)

Administrative divisions: 9 regions (regioes, singular—regiao); Bafata, Biombo, Bissau, Bolama/Bijagos, Cacheu, Gabu, Oio, Quinara, Tombali

Independence: 24 September 1973 (declared); 10 September 1974 (from Portugal)

National holiday: Independence Day, 24 September (1973)

Constitution: promulgated 16 May 1984; amended 1991, 1993, 1996; note—constitution suspended following military coup in April 2012 and restored in 2014 (2016)

Legal system: mixed legal system of civil law which incorporated Portuguese law at independence and influenced by early French civil code and customary law

International law organization participation: accepts compulsory ICJ jurisdiction; non-party state to the ICCt

Citizenship: *citizenship by birth:* yes
citizenship by descent: yes
dual citizen shiprecognized: no
residency requirement for naturalization: 5 years

Suffrage: 18 years of age; universal

Executive branch: *chief of state:* President Jose Mario VAZ (since 17 June 2014)

head of government: Prime Minister Baciro DJA (since 27 May 2016); the initial appointment of Baciro DJA in August 2015 was nullified by the Supreme Court and he resigned; Prime Minister Carlos CORREIA (since 17 September 2015) was dismissed by President VAZ on 12 May 2016
cabinet: Cabinet nominated by the prime minister, appointed by the president
elections/appointments: president directly elected by absolute majority popular vote in two rounds if needed for a 5-year term (no term limits); election last held on 13 April 2014 with a runoff on 18 May 2014 (next to be held in 2019); prime minister appointed by the president after consultation with party leaders in the National People's Assembly
election results: first round—Jose Mario VAZ (PAIGC) 41%, Nuno Gomez NABIAM

(independent) 25.1%, other 33.9%; Jose Mario VAZ elected president in second round—Jose Mario VAZ 61.9%, Nuno Gomez NABIAM 38.1%

Legislative branch: *description:* unicameral National People's Assembly or Assembleia Nacional Popular (102 seats; members directly elected in 2 single- and 27 multi-seat constituencies by closed party-list proportional representation vote to serve 4-year terms)

elections: last held on 13 April 2014 (next to be held in 2018)

election results: percent of vote by party—PAIGC 48.0%, PRS 30.8%, other parties 21.2%; seats by party—PAIGC 57, PRS 41, other 4

Judicial branch: *highest court(s):* Supreme Court or Suprema Tribunal de Justica (consists of 9 judges and organized into Civil, Criminal, and Social and Administrative Disputes Chambers); note—the Supreme Court has both appellate and constitutional jurisdiction

judge selection and term of office: judges nominated by the Higher Council of the Magistrate, a major government organ responsible for judge appointments, dismissals, and judiciary discipline; judges appointed by the president with life tenure

subordinate courts: Appeal Court; regional (first instance) courts; military court

Political parties and leaders: African Party for the Independence of Guinea-Bissau and Cabo Verde or PAIGC [Domingos Simoes PEREIRA]
Democratic Convergence Party or PCD [Vicente FERNANDES]
New Democracy Party or PND [Mamadu Iaia DJALO]
Party for Social Renewal or PRS [Alberto NAMBEIA]
Republican Party for Independence and Development or PRID [Aristides GOMES]
Union for Change or UM [Agnelo REGALA]

Political pressure groups and leaders: Chamber of Commerce of Agriculture, Industry, and Services

International organization participation: ACP, AfDB, AOSIS, AU, CPLP, ECOWAS, FAO, FZ, G-77, IBRD, ICAO, ICRM, IDA, IDB, IFAD, IFC, IFRCS, ILO, IMF, IMO, Interpol, IOC, IOM, IPU, ITSO, ITU, ITUC (NGOs), MIGA, MINUSMA, NAM, OIC, OIF, OPCW, UN, UNCTAD, UNESCO, UNIDO, UNWTO, UPU, WADB (regional), WAEMU, WCO, WFTU (NGOs), WHO, WIPO, WMO, WTO

Diplomatic representation in the US: *chief of mission:* none; note—Guinea-Bissau does not have official representation in Washington, DC

Diplomatic representation from the US: the US Embassy suspended operations on 14 June 1998 in the midst of violent conflict between forces loyal to then President VIEIRA and military-led junta; the US Ambassador to Senegal, currently Ambassador James P. ZUMWALT, is accredited to Guinea-Bissau

Flag description: two equal horizontal bands of yellow (top) and green with a vertical red band on the hoist side; there is a black five-pointed star centered in the red band; yellow symbolizes the

sun; green denotes hope; red represents blood shed during the struggle for independence; the black star stands for African unity

note: uses the popular Pan-African colors of Ethiopia; the flag design was heavily influenced by the Ghanaian flag

National symbol(s): black star; national colors: red, yellow, green, black

National anthem: *name:* "Esta e a Nossa Patria Bem Amada" (This Is Our Beloved Country)

lyrics/music: Amilcar Lopes CABRAL/XIAO He

note: adopted 1974; a delegation from then Portuguese Guinea visited China in 1963 and heard music by XIAO He; Amilcar Lopes CABRAL, the leader of Guinea-Bissau's independence movement, asked the composer to create a piece that would inspire his people to struggle for independence

ECONOMY

Economy—overview: Guinea-Bissau is highly dependent on subsistence agriculture, cashew nut exports, and foreign assistance. Two out of three Bissau-Guineans remain below the absolute poverty line. The legal economy is based on farming and fishing, but illegal logging and trafficking in narcotics are also important economic activities. The combination of limited economic prospects, weak institutions, and favorable geography have made this West African country a way station for drugs bound for Europe while trade in illegal logging, food, and fishing is also significant.

Guinea-Bissau has substantial potential for development of mineral resources including phosphates, bauxite, and mineral sands. The country's climate and soil make it feasible to grow a wide range of cash crops, fruit, vegetables, and tubers; however, cashews generate more than 80% of export receipts and are the main source of income for many rural communities.

With renewed donor support following elections in April-May 2014 and a successful regional bond issuance, the government of Guinea-Bissau made progress paying salaries, settling domestic arrears, and gaining more control over revenues and expenditures, but was deposed by the President in August 2015. A political stalement since th en has resulted in weak governance.

GDP (purchasing power parity): $2.68 billion (2015 est.)
$2.557 billion (2014 est.)
$2.494 billion (2013 est.)
note: data are in 2015 US dollars
country comparison to the world: 189

GDP (official exchange rate): $1.057 billion (2015 est.)

GDP—real growth rate: 4.8% (2015 est.)
2.5% (2014 est.)
0.8% (2013 est.)
country comparison to the world: 42

GDP—per capita (PPP): $1,500 (2015 est.)
$1,500 (2014 est.)
$1,500 (2013 est.)
note: data are in 2015 US dollars

country comparison to the world: 216

Gross national saving: 10.3% of GDP (2015 est.)
7.4% of GDP (2014 est.)
2.6% of GDP (2013 est.)
country comparison to the world: 151

GDP—composition, by end use:
household consumption: 93.2%
government consumption: 12.5%
investment in fixed capital: 5.5%
investment in inventories: 0.1%
exports of goods and services: 18.3%
imports of goods and services: -29.6% (2015 est.)

GDP—composition, by sector of origin:
agriculture: 44.7%
industry: 13.4%
services: 41.9% (2015 est.)

Agriculture—products: rice, corn, beans, cassava (manioc, tapioca), cash ew nuts, peanuts, palm kernels, cotton; timber; fish

Industries: agricultural products processing, beer, soft drinks

Industrial production growth rate: 2.3% (2015 est.)
country comparison to the world: 106

Labor force: 731,300 (2013 est.)
country comparison to the world: 153

Labor force—by occupation: *agriculture:* 82%
industry and services: 18% (2000 est.)

Unemployment rate: NA%
Population below poverty line: 67% (2015 est.)

Household income or consumption by percentage share: *lowest:* 10%: 2.9%
highest: 10%: 28% (2002)

Budget: *revenues:* $155.3 million
expenditures: $185.2 million (2015 est.)
Taxes and other revenues: 15% of GDP (2015 est.)
country comparison to the world: 192

Budget surplus (+) or deficit (−): -2.9% of GDP (2015 est.)
country comparison to the world: 106

Fiscal year: calendar year

Inflation rate (consumer prices): 1.5% (2015 est.)
-1% (2014 est.)
country comparison to the world: 101

Central bank discount rate: 4.25% (31 December 2009)
4.75% (31 December 2008)
country comparison to the world: 95

Commercial bank prime lending rate: 15% (31 December 2015 est.)
15% (31 December 2014 est.)
country comparison to the world: 42

Stock of narrow money: $433.1 million (31 December 2015 est.)
$392.5 million (31 December 2014 est.)
country comparison to the world: 169

Stock of broad money: $489.4 million (31 December 2015 est.)
$452.1 million (31 December 2014 est.)
country comparison to the world: 183

Stock of domestic credit: $163.5 million (31 December 2015 est.)

$160.1 million (31 December 2014 est.)
country comparison to the world: 181

Market value of publicly traded shares: $NA

Current account balance: -$10 million (2015 est.)
-$38 million (2014 est.)
country comparison to the world: 58

Exports: $198.2 million (2015 est.)
$171.9 million (2014 est.)
country comparison to the world: 187

Exports—commodities: fish, shrimp; cashews, peanuts, palm kernels, raw and sawn lumber

Exports—partners: India 63.5%, Nigeria 20.3%, China 5.7%, Togo 5.6% (2015)

Imports: $218.2 million (2015 est.)
$227.5 million (2014 est.)
country comparison to the world: 205

Imports—commodities: foodstuffs, machinery and transport equipment, petroleum products

Imports—partners: Portugal 27.1%, Senegal 12.8%, China 6.5%, Spain 5.5%, Cuba 4.8% (2015)

Debt—external: $1.095 billion (31 December 2010 est.)
$941.5 million (31 December 2000 est.)
country comparison to the world: 161

Exchange rates: Communaute Financiere Africaine francs (XOF) per US dollar—
580.5 (2015 est.)
494.42 (2014 est.)
494.42 (2013 est.)
510.53 (2012 est.)
471.87 (2011 est.)

ENERGY

Electricity—production: 50 million kWh (2012 est.)
country comparison to the world: 207

Electricity—consumption: 46.5 million kWh (2012 est.)
country comparison to the world: 206

Electricity—exports: 0 kWh (2013 est.)
country comparison to the world: 185

Electricity—imports: 0 kWh (2013 est.)
country comparison to the world: 191

Electricity—installed generating capacity: 39,000 kW (2015 est.)
country comparison to the world: 200

Electricity—from fossil fuels: 99% of total installed capacity (2015 est.)
country comparison to the world: 25

Electricity—from nuclear fuels: 0% of total installed capacity (2015 est.)
country comparison to the world: 168

Electricity—from hydroelectric plants: 0% of total installed capacity (2015 est.)
country comparison to the world: 194

Electricity—from other renewable sources: 1 % of total installed capacity (2015 est.)
country comparison to the world: 123

Crude oil—production: 0 bbl/day (2014 est.)
country comparison to the world: 182

Crude oil—exports: 0 bbl/day (2012 est.)
country comparison to the world: 178

Crude oil—imports: 0 bbl/day (2012 est.)
country comparison to the world: 115

Crude oil—proved reserves: 0 bbl (1 January 2015 est.)
country comparison to the world: 181

Refined petroleum products—production: 0 bbl/day (2012 est.)
country comparison to the world: 123

Refined petroleum products—consumption: 2,700 bbl/day (2013 est.)
country comparison to the world: 183

Refined petroleum products—exports: 0 bbl/day (2012 est.)
country comparison to the world: 214

Refined petroleum products—imports: 2,661 bbl/day (2012 est.)
country comparison to the world: 176

Natural gas—production: 0 cu m (2013 est.)
country comparison to the world: 120

Natural gas—consumption: 0 cu m (2013 est.)
country comparison to the world: 187

Natural gas—exports: 0 cu m (2013 est.)
country comparison to the world: 167

Natural gas—imports: 0 cu m (2013 est.)
country comparison to the world: 123

Natural gas—proved reserves: 0 cu m (1 January 2014 est.)
country comparison to the world: 186

Carbon dioxide emissions from consumption of energy: 460,100 Mt (2012 est.)
country comparison to the world: 183

COMMUNICATIONS

Telephones—fixed lines: *total subscriptions:* 5,000
subscriptions per 100 inhabitants: less than 1 (2014 est.)
country comparison to the world: 208

Telephones—mobile cellular: *total:* 1.1 million
subscriptions per 100 inhabitants: 65 (2014 est.)
country comparison to the world: 156

Telephone system: *general assessment:* small system including a combination of microwave radio relay, open-wire lines, radiotelephone, and mobile cellular communications
domestic: fixed-line teledensity less than 1 per 100 persons; mobile cellular teledensity is roughly 50 per 100 persons
international: country code—245 (2011)

Broadcast media: 1 state-owned TV station and a second station, Radio e Televisao de Portugal (RTP) Africa, is operated by Portuguese public broadcaster (RTP); 1 state-owned radio station, several private radio stations, and some community radio stations; multiple international broadcasters are available (2007)
Radio broadcast stations: AM 1 (transmitter out of service), FM 4, shortwave 0 (2001)
Television broadcast stations: 1 (2007)

Internet country code: .gw

Internet hosts: 90 (2012)
country comparison to the world: 211

Internet users: *total:* 56,100
percent of population: 3.3% (2014 est.)
country comparison to the world: 181

TRANSPORTATION

Airports: 8 (2013)
country comparison to the world: 160

Airports—with paved runways: *total:* 2
over 3,047 m: 1
1,524 to 2,437 m: 1 (2013)

Airports—with unpaved runways: *total:* 6
1,524 to 2,437 m: 1
914 to 1,523 m: 2
under 914 m: 3 (2013)

Roadways: *total:* 3,455 km
paved: 965 km
unpaved: 2,490 km (2002)
country comparison to the world: 162

Waterways: (rivers are partially navigable; many inlets and creeks provide shallow-water access to much of interior)
(2012)

Ports and terminals: *major seaport(s):* Bissau, Buba, Cacheu, Farim

MILITARY AND SECURITY

Military branches: People's Revolutionary Armed Force (FARP): Army, Navy, National Air Force (Forca Aerea Nacional); Presidential Guard (2012)

Military service age and obligation: 18–25 years of age for selective compulsory military service (Air Force service is voluntary); 16 years of age or younger, with parental consent, for voluntary service (2013)

Military expenditures: 1.85% of GDP (2012)
1.81% of GDP (2011)
1.85% of GDP (2010)
country comparison to the world: 45

TRANSNATIONAL ISSUES

Disputes—international: in 2006, political instability within Senegal's Casamance region resulted in thousands of Senegalese refugees, cross-border raids, and arms smuggling into Guinea-Bissau

Refugees and internally displaced persons: *refugees (country of origin):* 8,601 (Senegal) (2014)

Trafficking in persons: *current situation:* Guinea-Bissau is a source country for children subjected to forced labor and sex trafficking; the extent to which adults are trafficked for forced labor or forced prostitution is unclear; boys are forced into street vending in Guinea-Bissau and manual labor, agriculture, and mining in Senegal, while girls may be forced into street vending, domestic service, and, to a lesser extent, prostitution in Guinea and Senegal; some Bissau-Guinean boys at Koranic schools are forced into begging by religious teachers

tier rating: Tier 3—Guinea-Bissau does not fully comply with the minimum standards for the elimination of trafficking and is not making significant efforts to do so; despite enacting an anti-trafficking law and adopting a national action plan in 2011, the country failed to demonstrate any notable anti-trafficking efforts for the third consecutive year; existing laws prohibiting all forms of trafficking were not used to prosecute any trafficking offenders in 2014, and only one case of potential child labor trafficking was under investigation; authorities continued to rely entirely on NGOs and international organizations to provide victims with protective services; no trafficking prevention activities were conducted (2015)

Illicit drugs: increasingly important transit country for South American cocaine en route to Europe; enabling environment for trafficker operations due to pervasive corruption; archipelago-like geography near the capital facilitates drug smuggling

GUYANA

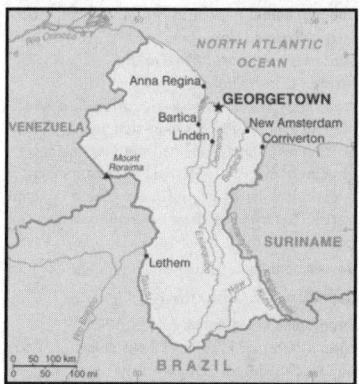

INTRODUCTION

Background: Originally a Dutch colony in the 17th century, by 1815 Guyana had become a British possession. The abolition of slavery led to settlement of urban areas by former slaves and the importation of indentured servants from India to work the sugar plantations. The resulting ethnocultural divide has persisted and has led to turbulent politics. Guyana achieved independence from the UK in 1966, and since then it has been ruled mostly by socialist-oriented governments. In 1992, Cheddi JAGAN was elected president in what is considered the country's first free and fair electionsince independence. After his death five years later, his wife, Janet JAGAN, became president but resigned in 1999 due to poor health. Her successor, Bharrat JAGDEO, was reelected in 2001 and again in 2006. Early elections held in May 2015 resulted in the replacement of President Donald RAMO TAR by David GRANGER.

GEOGRAPHY

Location: Northern South America, bordering the North Atlantic Ocean, between Suriname and Venezuela

Geographic coordinates: 5 00 N, 59 00 W

Map references: South America

Area: *total:* 214,969 sq km
land: 196,849 sq km
water: 18,120 sq km
country comparison to the world: 85

Area—comparative: slightly smaller than Idaho

Land boundaries: *total:* 2,933 km
border countries (3): Brazil 1,308 km, Suriname 836 km, Venezuela 789 km

Coastline: 459 km

Maritime claims: *territorial sea:* 12 nm
exclusive economic zone: 200 nm
continental shelf: 200 nm or to the outer edge of the continental margin

Climate: tropical; hot, humid, moderated by northeast trade winds; two rainy seasons (May to August, November to January)

Terrain: mostly rolling highlands; low coastal plain; savanna in south

Elevation: *mean elevation:* 207 m

elevation extremes: *lowest point:* Atlantic Ocean 0 m
highest point: Mount Roraima 2,835 m

Natural resources: bauxite, gold, diamonds, hardwood timber, shrimp, fish

Land use: *agricultural land:* 8.4%
arable land: 2.1%
permanent crops: 0.1%
permanent pasture: 6.2%
forest: 77.4%
other: 14.2% (2011 est.)

Irrigated land: 1,430 sq km (2012)

Total renewable water resources: 241 cu km (2011)

Freshwater withdrawal (domestic/industrial/agricultural): *total:* 1.64 cu km/yr (4%/1%/94%)
per capita: 2,222 cu m/yr (2010)
Natural hazards: flash flood threat during rainy seasons

Environment—current issues: water pollution from sewage and agricultural and industrial chemicals; deforestation

Environment—international agreements: *party to:* Biodiversity, Climate Change, Climate Change-Kyoto Protocol, Desertification, Endangered Species, Hazardous Wastes, Law of the Sea, Ozone Layer Protection, Ship Pollution, Tropical Timber 83, Tropical Timber 94
signed, but not ratified: none of the selected agreements

Geography—note: the third-smallest country in South America after Suriname and Uruguay; substantial portions of its western and eastern territories are claimed by Venezuela and Suriname respectively

PEOPLE AND SOCIETY

Nationality: *noun:* Guyanese (singular and plural)
adjective: Guyanese

Ethnic groups: East Indian 43.5%, black (African) 30.2%, mixed 16.7%, Amerindian 9.1%, other 0.5% (includes Portuguese, Chinese, white) (2002 est.)

Languages: English (official), Guyanese Creole, Amerindian languages (including Caribbean and Arawak languages), Indian languages (including Caribbean Hindustani, a dialect of Hindi), Chinese (2014 est.)

Religions: Protestant 30.5% (Pentecostal 16.9%, Anglican 6.9%, Seventh Day Adventist 5%, Methodist 1.7%), Hindu 28.4%, Roman Catholic 8.1%, Muslim 7.2%, Jehovah's Witness 1.1%, other Christian 17.7%, other 1.9%, none 4.3%, unspecified 0.9% (2002 est.)

Demographic profile: Guyana is the only English-speaking country in South America and shares cultural and historical bonds with the Anglophone Caribbean. Guyana's two largest ethnic groups are the Afro-Guyanese (descendants of African slaves) and the Indo-Guyanese (descendants of Indian indentured laborers), which together comprise about three quarters of Guyana's population. Tensions periodically have boiled over between the two groups, which back ethnically based political parties and vote along ethnic lines. Poverty reduction has stagnated since the late 1990s. About one-third of the Guyanese population lives below the poverty line; indigenous people are disproportionately affected. Although Guyana's literacy rate is reported to be among the highest in the Western Hemisphere, the level of functional literacy is considerably lower, which has been attributed to poor education quality, teacher training, and infrastructure. Guyana's emigration rate is among the highest in the world—more than 55% of its citizens reside abroad -and it is one of the largest recipients of remittances relative to GDP among Latin American and Caribbean counties. Although remittances are a vital source of income for most citizens, the pervasive emigration of skilled workers deprives Guyana of professionals in healthcare and other key sectors. More than 80% of Guyanese nationals with tertiary level educations have emigrated. Brain drain and the concentration of limited medical resources in Georgetown hamper Guyana's ability to meet the health needs of its predominantly rural population. Guyana has one of the highest HIV prevalence rates in the region and continues to rely on international support for its HIV treatment and prevention programs.

Population: 735,222

note: estimates for this country explicitly take into account the effects of excess mortality due to AIDS; this can result in lower life expectancy, higher infant mortality, higher death rates, lower population growth rates, and changes in the distribution of population by age and sex than would otherwise be expected (July 2015 est.)
country comparison to the world: 167

Age structure: 0–14 years: 28.07% (male 105,078/female 101,296)
15–24 years: 21.26% (male 80,303/female 76,022)
25–54 years: 37.42% (male 143,490/female 131,644)
55–64 years: 7.72% (male 25,426/female 31,304)
65 years and over: 5.53% (male 16,877/female 23,782) (2015 est.)

Dependency ratios: total dependency ratio: 51.1%
youth dependency ratio: 43.5%
elderly dependency ratio: 7.6%
potential support ratio: 13.2% (2015 est.)

Median age: total: 25.4 years
male: 25 years
female: 25.8 years (2015 est.)
country comparison to the world: 149

Population growth rate: 0.02% (2015 est.)
country comparison to the world: 192

Birth rate: 15.59 births/1,000 population (2015 est.)
country comparison to the world: 126

Death rate: 7.32 deaths/1,000 population (2015 est.)
country comparison to the world: 119

Net migration rate: -8.06 migrant(s)/1,000 population (2015 est.)
country comparison to the world: 207

Urbanization: urban population: 28.6% of total population (2015)
rate of urbanization: 0.76% annual rate of change (2010–15 est.)

Major urban areas—population: GEORGETOWN (capital) 124,000 (2014)

Sex ratio: at birth: 1.05 male(s)/female
0–14 years: 1.04 male(s)/female
15–24 years: 1.06 male(s)/female
25–54 years: 1.09 male(s)/female
55–64 years: 0.81 male(s)/female
65 years and over: 0.71 male(s)/female
total population: 1.02 male(s)/female (2015 est.)

Mother's mean age at first birth: 20.8
note: median age at first birth among women 25–29 (2009 est.)

Maternal mortality rate: 229 deaths/100,000 live births (2015 est.)
country comparison to the world: 43

Infant mortality rate: total: 32.56 deaths/1,000 live births
male: 36.52 deaths/1,000 live births
female: 28.4 deaths/1,000 live births (2015 est.)
country comparison to the world: 65

Life expectancy at birth: total population: 68.09 years
male: 65.1 years
female: 71.24 years (2015 est.)
country comparison to the world: 164

Total fertility rate: 2.08 children born/woman (2015 est.)
country comparison to the world: 111

Contraceptive prevalence rate: 42.5% (2009)

Health expenditures: 6.5% of GDP (2013)
country comparison to the world: 93

Physicians density: 0.21 physicians/1,000 population (2010)

Hospital bed density: 2 beds/1,000 population (2009)

Drinking water source:
improved:
urban: 98.2% of population
rural: 98.3% of population
total: 98.3% of population
unimproved:
urban: urban: 1.8% of population
rural: 1.7% of population
total: 1.7% of population (2015 est.)

Sanitation facility access:
improved:
urban: 87.9% of population
rural: 82% of population
total: 83.7% of population
unimproved:
urban: urban: 12.1% of population
rural: 18% of population
total: 16.3% of population (2015 est.)

HIV/AIDS—adult prevalence rate: 1.81% (2014 est.)
country comparison to the world: 29

HIV/AIDS—people living with HIV/AIDS: 9,700 (2014 est.)
country comparison to the world: 94

HIV/AIDS—deaths: 100 (2014 est.)
country comparison to the world: 118

Major infectious diseases: degree of risk: very high
food or waterborne diseases: bacterial and protozoal diarrhea, hepatitis A, and typhoid fever
vectorborne diseases: dengue fever and malaria (2013)

Obesity—adult prevalence rate: 21.9% (2014)
country comparison to the world: 113

Children under the age of 5 years underweight: 8.5% (2014)
country comparison to the world: 67

Education expenditures: 3.2% of GDP (2012)
country comparison to the world: 136

Literacy: definition: age 15 and over has ever attended school

total population: 88.5%
male: 87.2%
female: 89.8% (2015 est.)

School life expectancy (primary to tertiary education): total: 10 years
male: 10 years
female: 10 years (2012)

Child labor—children ages 5–14: total number: 30,255
percentage: 16% (2006 est.)

GOVERNMENT

Country name: conventional long form: Cooperative Republic of Guyana
conventional short form: Guyana
former: British Guiana
etymology: the name is derived from Guiana, the original name for the region that included British Guiana, Dutch Guiana, and French Guiana; ultimately the word is derived from an indigenous Amerindian language and means "land of many waters" (referring to the area's multitude of rivers and streams)

Government type: parliamentary republic

Capital: name: Georgetown
Geographic coordinates: 6 48 N, 58 09 W
time difference: UTC-4 (1 hour ahead of Washington, DC, during Standard Time)

Administrative divisions: 10 regions; Barima-Waini, Cuyuni-Mazaruni, Demerara-Mahaica, East Berbice-Corentyne, Essequibo Islands-West Demerara, Mahaica-Berbice, Pomeroon-Supenaam, Potaro-Siparuni, Upper Demerara-Berbice, Upper Takutu-Upper Essequibo

Independence: 26 May 1966 (from the UK)

National holiday: Republic Day, 23 February (1970)

Constitution: several previous; latest promulgated 6 October 1980; amended many times, last in 2009; note—in 2015, Guinea's High Court reversed the constitutional two-term presidential limit (2016)

Legal system: common law system, based on the English model, with some Roman-Dutch civil law influence

International law organization participation: has not submitted an ICJ jurisdiction declaration; accepts ICCt jurisdiction

Citizenship: citizenship by birth: yes
citizenship by descent: yes
dual citizenship recognized: no
residency requirement for natu ralization: na

Suffrage: 18 years of age; universal

Executive branch: chief of state: President David GRANGER (since 16 May 2015)

head of government: Prime Minister Moses NAG-AMOOTOO (since 20 May 2015)
cabinet: Cabinet of Ministers appointed by the president, responsible to the National Assembly
elections/appointments: president indirectly elected by the National Assembly from party lists to serve a 5-year term (no term limits); election

last held on 11 May 2015 (next to be held in 2020); prime minister appointed by the president
election results: David GRANGER (APNU-AFC) elected president by National Assembly; percent of vote—50.3%

Legislative branch: *description:* unicameral National Assembly (65 seats; members directly elected in multi-seat constituencies and a single nationwide constituency by proportional representation vote; members serve 5-year terms)
elections: last held on 11 May 2015 (next to be held by May 2020)
election results: percent of vote by party—APNU 50.3%, PPP/C 49.19%, other 0.51%; seats by party -APNU 33, PPP/C 32

Judicial branch: *highest court(s):* Supreme Court of Judicature (consists of the Court of Appeal with a chief justice and 3 justices, and the High Court with a chief justice and 10 justices organized into 3- or 5-judge panels); note -in 2009, Guyana ceased final appeals in civil and criminal cases to the Judicial Committee of the Privy Council (in London), replacing it with the Caribbean Court of Justice, the judicial organ of the Caribbean Community
judge selection and term of office: Court of Appeal and High Court chief justices appointed by the president; other judges of both courts appointed by the Judicial Service Commission, a body appointed by the president; judges appointed for life with retirement at age 65
subordinate courts: Land Court; magistrates' courts

Political parties and leaders: A Partnership for National Unity or APNU [David A. GRANGER]
Alliance for Change or AFC [Khemraj RAMJATTAN]
Justice for All Party [C.N. SHARMA]
People's Progressive Party/Civic or PPP/C [D on ald RAMOTAR]
Rise, Organize, and Rebuild or ROAR [Ravi DEV]
The United Force or TUF [Manzoor NADIR]
The Unity Party [Joey JAGAN]
Vision Guyana [Peter RAMSAROOP]

Political pressure groups and leaders:
Amerindian People's Association
Guyana Bar Association
Guyana Citizens Initiative
Guyana Human Rights Association
Guyana Public Service Union or GPSU
Private Sector Commission
Trades Union Congress

International organization participation: ACP, AOSIS, C, Caricom, CD, CDB, CELAC, FAO, G-77, IADB, IBRD, ICAO, ICCt, ICRM, IDA, IFAD, IFC, IFRCS, ILO, IMF, IMO, Interpol, IOC, IOM, ISO (correspondent), ITU, LAES, MIGA, NAM, OAS, OIC, OPANAL, OPCW, PCA, Petrocaribe, UN, UNASUR, UNCTAD, UNESCO, UNIDO, UPU, WCO, WFTU (NGOs), WHO, WIPO, WMO, WTO

Diplomatic representation in the US: chief of mission: Ambassador Bayney KARRAN (since 4 December 2003)

chancery: 2490 Tracy Place NW, Washington, DC 20008
telephone: [1] (202) 265-6900
FAX: [1] (202) 232-1297
consulate(s) general: New York

Diplomatic representation from the US: *chief of mission:* Ambassador Perry L. HOLLOWAY (since 2 October 2015)
embassy: US Embassy, 100 Young and Duke Streets, Kingston, Georgetown
mailing address: P.O. Box 10507, Georgetown; US Embassy, 3170 Georgetown Place, Washington DC 20521–3170
telephone: [592] 225-4900 through 4909
FAX: [592] 225-8497

Flag description: green with a red isosceles triangle (based on the hoist side) superimposed on a long, yellow arrowhead; there is a narrow, black border between the red and yellow, and a narrow, white border between the yellow and the green; green represents forest and foliage; yellow stands for mineral resources and a bright future; white symbolizes Guyana's rivers; red signifies zeal and the sacrifice of the people; black indicates perseverance

National symbol(s): Canje pheasant (hoatzin), jaguar, Victoria Regia water lily; national colors: red, yellow, green, black, white

National anthem: *name:* "Dear Land of Guyana, of Rivers and Plains"
lyrics/music: Archibald Leonard LUKERL/Robert Cyril Gladstone POTTER
note: adopted 1966

ECONOMY

Economy—overview: The Guyanese economy exhibited moderate economic growth in recent years and is based largely on agriculture and extractive industries. The economy is heavily dependent upon the export of six commodities—sugar, gold, bauxite, shrimp, timber, and rice—which represent nearly 60% of the country's GDP and are highly susceptible to adverse weather conditions and fluctuations in commodity prices. Much of Guyana's growth in recent years has come from a surge in gold production in response to global prices, although downward trends in gold prices may threaten future growth. In 2014, production of sugar dropped to a 24-year low.
Guyana's entrance into the Caricom Single Market and Economy in January 2006 has broadened the country's export market, primarily in the raw materials sector. Guyana has experienced positive growth almost every year over the past decade. Inflation has been kept under control. Recent years have seen the government's stock of debt reduced significantly—with external debt now less than half of what it was in the early 1990s. Despite recent improvements, the government is still juggling a sizable external debt against the urgent need for expanded public investment. In March 2007, the Inter-American Development Bank, Guyana's principal donor, canceled Guyana's nearly $470 million debt, equivalent to 21% of GDP, which along with other Highly Indebted Poor Country debt forgiveness, brought the debt-to-GDP ratio

down from 183% in 2006 to 67% in 2015. Guyana had become heavily indebted as a result of the inward-looking, state-led development model pursued in the 1970s and 1980s.
Chronic problems include a shortage of skilled labor and a deficient infrastructure.

GDP (purchasing power parity): $5.759 billion (2015 est.)
$5.59 billion (2014 est.)
$5.383 billion (2013 est.)
note: data are in 2015 US dollars
country comparison to the world: 172

GDP (official exchange rate): $3.164 billion (2015 est.)

GDP—real growth rate: 3% (2015 est.)
3.8% (2014 est.)
5.2% (2013 est.)
country comparison to the world: 102

GDP—per capita (PPP): $7,500 (2015 est.)
$7,300 (2014 est.)
$7,100 (2013 est.)
note: data are in 2015 US dollars
country comparison to the world: 151

Gross national saving: 9.3% of GDP (2015 est.)
5.6% of GDP (2014 est.)
3.4% of GDP (2013 est.)
country comparison to the world: 155

GDP—composition, by end use:
household consumption: 90.7%
government consumption: 13.3%
investment in fixed capital: 22.3%
investment in inventories: -13.4%
exports of goods and services: 48.4%
imports of goods and services: -61.3% (2015 est.)

GDP—composition, by sector of origin:
agriculture: 21.8%
industry: 25.3%
services: 52.9% (2015 est.)

Agriculture—products: sugarcane, rice, edible oils; beef, pork, poultry; shrimp, fish

Industries: bauxite, sugar, rice milling, timber, textiles, gold mining

Industrial production growth rate: -10% (2015 est.)
country comparison to the world: 196

Labor force: 313,800 (2013 est.)
country comparison to the world: 163

Labor force—by occupation: *agriculture:* NA%
industry: NA%
services: NA%

Unemployment rate: 11.1% (2013)
11.3% (2012)
country comparison to the world: 127

Population below poverty line: 35% (2006 est.)

Household income or consumption by percentage share: *lowest:* 10%: 1.3%
highest: 10%: 33.8% (1999)

Distribution of family income—Gini index: 44.6 (2007)
43.2 (1999)
country comparison to the world: 46

Budget: *revenues:* $805.8 million

expenditures: $940 million (2015 est.)
Taxes and other revenues: 25.2% of GDP (2015 est.)
country comparison to the world: 120

Budget surplus (+) or deficit (–): -4.2% of GDP (2015 est.)
country comparison to the world: 151

Public debt: 67.4% of GDP (2015 est.)
63.1% of GDP (2014 est.)
country comparison to the world: 49

Fiscal year: calendar year

Inflation rate (consumer prices): -0.3% (2015 est.)
1% (2014 est.)
country comparison to the world: 33

Central bank discount rate: 5.5% (31 December 2011)
4.25% (31 December 2010)
country comparison to the world: 71

Commercial bank prime lending rate: 12.8% (31 December 2015 est.)
12.83% (31 December 2014 est.)
country comparison to the world: 60

Stock of narrow money: $705.8 million (31 December 2015 est.)
$635.3 million (31 December 2014 est.)
country comparison to the world: 160

Stock of broad money: $1.68 billion (31 December 2015 est.)
$1.596 billion (31 December 2014 est.)
country comparison to the world: 159

Stock of domestic credit:
$1.68 billion (31 December 2015 est.)
$1.551 billion (31 December 2014 est.)
country comparison to the world: 144

Market value of publicly traded shares:
$610.9 million (31 December 2012 est.)
$440.4 million (31 December 2011)
$339.8 million (31 December 2010 est.)
country comparison to the world: 111

Current account balance: -$151 million (2015 est.)
-$388 million (2014 est.)
country comparison to the world: 77

Exports: $1.096 billion (2015 est.)
$1.251 billion (2014 est.)
country comparison to the world: 158

Exports—commodities: sugar, gold, bauxite, alumina, rice, shrimp, molasses, rum, timber

Exports—partners: US 33.5%, Canada 17.9%, UK 6.7%, Ukraine 4.3%, Jamaica 4% (2015)

Imports: $1.708 billion (2015 est.)
$1.834 billion (2014 est.)
country comparison to the world: 168

Imports—commodities: manufactures, machinery, petroleum, food

Imports—partners: US 24.6%, Trinidad and Tobago 24.1%, China 10.8%, Suriname 9.5% (2015)

Reserves of foreign exchange and gold:
$614.3 million (31 December 2015 est.)
$667.9 million (31 December 2014 est.)
country comparison to the world: 145

Debt—external: $2.303 billion (31 December 2013 est.)
$1.974 billion (31 December 2012 est.)
country comparison to the world: 148

Exchange rates: Guyanese dollars (GYD) per US dollar—
206.5 (2015 est.)
206.45 (2014 est.)
206.45 (2013 est.)
204.36 (2012 est.)
204.02 (2011 est.)

ENERGY

Electricity—production: 800 million kWh (2012 est.)
country comparison to the world: 156

Electricity—consumption: 558 million kWh (2012 est.)
country comparison to the world: 170

Electricity—exports: 0 kWh (2013 est.)
country comparison to the world: 148

Electricity—imports: 0 kWh (2013 est.)
country comparison to the world: 159

Electricity—installed generating capacity: 376,500 kW (2012 est.)
country comparison to the world: 147

Electricity—from fossil fuels: 96.1% of total installed capacity (2012 est.)
country comparison to the world: 63

Electricity—from nuclear fuels: 0% of total installed capacity (2012 est.)
country comparison to the world: 106

Electricity—from hydroelectric plants: 0.3% of total installed capacity (2012 est.)
country comparison to the world: 149

Electricity—from other renewable sources: 3.6% of total installed capacity (2012 est.)
country comparison to the world: 67
Crude oil—production: 0 bbl/day (2014 est.)
country comparison to the world: 145

Crude oil—exports: 0 bbl/day (2012 est.)
country comparison to the world: 134

Crude oil—imports: 0 bbl/day (2012 est.)
country comparison to the world: 202

Crude oil—proved reserves: 0 bbl (1 January 2015 est.)
country comparison to the world: 143

Refined petroleum products—production: 0 bbl/day (2012 est.)
country comparison to the world: 192

Refined petroleum products—consumption: 10,800 bbl/day (2013 est.)
country comparison to the world: 152

Refined petroleum products—exports: 0 bbl/day (2012 est.)
country comparison to the world: 189

Refined petroleum products—imports: 10,810 bbl/day (2012 est.)
country comparison to the world: 135

Natural gas—production: 0 cu m (2013 est.)
country comparison to the world: 199

Natural gas—consumption: 0 cu m (2013 est.)
country comparison to the world: 153

Natural gas—exports: 0 cu m (2013 est.)
country comparison to the world: 113

Natural gas—imports: 0 cu m (2013 est.)
country comparison to the world: 207

Natural gas—proved reserves: 0 cu m (1 January 2014 est.)
country comparison to the world: 148

Carbon dioxide emissions from consumption of energy: 1.661 million Mt (2012 est.)
country comparison to the world: 154

COMMUNICATIONS

Telephones—fixed lines: *total subscriptions:* 160,000
subscriptions per 100 inhabitants: 22 (2014 est.)
country comparison to the world: 134

Telephones—mobile cellular: *total:* 566,900
subscriptions per 100 inhabitants: 77 (2014 est.)
country comparison to the world: 167

Telephone system: *general assessment:* fair system for long-distance service; microwave radio relay network for trunk lines; many areas still lack fixed-line telephone services
domestic: fixed-line teledensity is about 20 per 100 persons; mobile-cellular teledensity about 70 per 100 persons in 2011
international: country code—592; tropospheric scatter to Trinidad; satellite earth station—1 Intelsat (Atlantic Ocean) (2011)

Broadcast media: government-dominated broadcast media; the National Communications Network (NCN) TV is state-owned; a few private TV stations relay satellite services; the state owns and operates 2 radio stations broadcasting on multiple frequencies capable of reaching the entire country; government limits on licensing of new private radio stations continue to constrain competition in broadcast media (2007)
Radio broadcast stations: AM 3, FM 3, shortwave 1 (2009)
Television broadcast stations: 3 (1 public station; 2 private stations which relay US satellite services) (1997)

Internet country code: .gy

Internet hosts: 24,936 (2012)
country comparison to the world: 112

Internet users: *total:* 270,200
percent of population: 36.7% (2014 est.)
country comparison to the world: 149

TRANSPORTATION

Airports: 117 (2013)
country comparison to the world: 50

Airports—with paved runways: *total:* 11
1,524 to 2,437 m: 2
914 to 1,523 m: 1
under 914 m: 8 (2013)

Airports—with unpaved runways: *total:* 106
1,524 to 2,437 m: 1
914 to 1,523 m: 16

under 914 m: 89 (2013)

Roadways: *total:* 7,970 km
paved: 590 km
unpaved: 7,380 km (2001)
country comparison to the world: 141

Waterways: 330 km (the Berbice, Demerara, and Essequibo Rivers are navigable by oceangoing vessels for 150 km, 100 km, and 80 km respectively) (2012)
country comparison to the world: 91

Merchant marine: *total:* 10
by type: cargo 7, petroleum tanker 2, refrigerated cargo 1
registered in other countries: 3 (Saint Vincent and the Grenadines 2, unknown 1) (2010)
country comparison to the world: 114

Ports and terminals: *major seaport(s):* Georgetown

MILITARY AND SECURITY

Military branches: Guyana Defense Force: Army (includes Air Corps, Coast Guard) (2012)

Military service age and obligation: 18 years of age or older for voluntary military service; no conscription (2014)

Military expenditures: 1.09% of GDP (2012)
1.17% of GDP (2011)
1.09% of GDP (2010)
country comparison to the world: 93

TRANSNATIONAL ISSUES

Disputes—international: all of the area west of the Essequibo River is claimed by Venezuela preventing any discussion of a maritime boundary; Guyana has expressed its intention to join Barbados in asserting claims before UN Convention on the Law of the Sea (UNCLOS) that Trinidad and Tobago's maritime boundary with Venezuela extends into their waters; Suriname claims a triangle of land between the New and Kutari/Koetari rivers in a historic dispute over the headwaters of the Courantyne; Guyana seeks arbitration under provisions of the UNCLOS to resolve the long-standing dispute with Suriname over the axis of the territorial sea boundary in potentially oil-rich waters

Trafficking in persons: *current situation:* Guyana is a source and destination country for men, women, and children subjected to sex trafficking and forced labor—children are particularly vulnerable; women and girls from Guyana, Venezuela, Suriname, Brazil, and the Dominican Republic are forced into prostitution in Guyana's interior mining communities and urban areas; forced labor is reported in mining, agriculture, forestry, domestic service, and shops; Guyanese nationals are also trafficked to Suriname, Jamaica, and other Caribbean countries for sexual exploitation and forced labor

tier rating: Tier 2 Watch List—Guyana does not fully comply with the minimum standards for the elimination of trafficking; however, it is making significant efforts to do so; in 2014, Guyana was granted a waiver from an otherwise required downgrade to Tier 3 because its government has a written plan that, if implemented would constitute making significant efforts to bring itself into compliance with the minimum standards for the elimination of trafficking; the government released its anti-trafficking action plan in June 2014 but made uneven efforts to implement it; law enforcement was weak, investigating seven trafficking cases, prosecuting four alleged traffickers, and convicting one trafficker—a police officer—who was released on bail pending appeal; in 2014, as in previous years, Guyanese courts dismissed the majority of ongoing trafficking prosecutions; the government referred some victims to care services, which were provided by NGOs with little or no government support (2015)

Illicit drugs: transshipment point for narcotics from South America—primarily Venezuela—to Europe and the US; producer of cannabis; rising money laundering related to drug trafficking and human smuggling

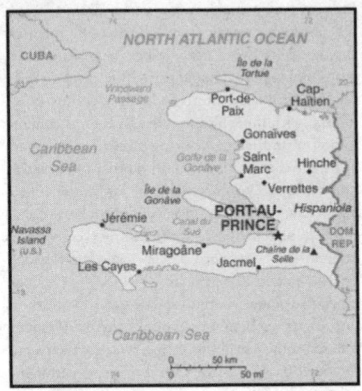

INTRODUCTION

Background: The native Taino—who inhabited the island of Hispaniola when it was discovered by Christopher COLUMBUS in 1492—were virtually annihilated by Spanish settlers within 25 years. In the early 17th century, the French established a presence on Hispaniola. In 1697, Spain ceded to the French the western third of the island, which later became Haiti. The French colony, based on forestry and sugar-related industries, became one of the wealthiest in the Caribbean but only through the heavy importation of African slaves and considerable environmental degradation. In the late 18th century, Haiti's nearly half million slaves revolted under Toussaint L'OUVERTU RE. After a prolonged struggle, Haiti became the first post-colonial black-led nation in the world, declaring its independence in 1804. Currently the poorest country in the Western Hemisphere, Haiti has experienced political instability for most of its history. A massive magnitude 7.0 earthquake struck HaitIin January 2010 with an epicenter about 25 km (15 mi) west of the capital, Port-au-Prince. Estimates are that over 300,000 people were killed and some 1.5 million left homeless. The earthquake was assessed as the worst in this region over the last 200 years. President Michel MARTELLY resigned in February 2016 and was replaced by Interim President Jocelerme PRI VERT who will lead until new elections take place later in the year.

GEOGRAPHY

Location: Caribbean, western one-third of the island of Hispaniola, between the Caribbean Sea and the North Atlantic
Ocean, west of the Dominican Republic
Geographic coordinates: 19 00 N, 72 25 W
Map references: Central America and the Caribbean
Area: total: 27,750 sq km
land: 27,560 sq km
water: 190 sq km

country comparison to the world: 148
Area—comparative: slightly smaller than Maryland
Land boundaries: total: 376 km
border countries (1): Dominican Republic 376 km
Coastline: 1,771 km
Maritime claims: territorial sea: 12 nm
contiguous zone: 24 nm
exclusive economic zone: 200 nm
continental shelf: to depth of exploitation
Climate: tropical; semiarid where mountains in east cut off trade winds
Terrain: mostly rough and mountainous
Elevation: mean elevation: 470 m
elevation extremes: lowest point: Caribbean Sea 0 m
highest point: Chaine de la Selle 2,680 m
Natural resources: bauxite, copper, calcium carbonate, gold, marble, hydropower, arable land:
Land use: agricultural land: 66.4%
arable land: 38.5%
permanent crops: 10.2%
permanent pasture: 17.7%
forest: 3.6%
other: 30% (2011 est.)
Irrigated land: 970 sq km (2012)
Total renewable water resources: 14.03 cu km (2011)
Freshwater withdrawal (domestic/industrial/agricultural): total: 1.2 cu km/yr (17%/3%/80%)
per capita: 134.3 cu m/yr (2009)
Natural hazards: lies in the middle of the hurricane belt and subject to severe storms from June to October; occasional flooding and earthquakes; periodic droughts
Environment—current issues: extensive deforestation (much of the remaining forested land is being cleared for agriculture and used as fu el); soil erosion; inadequate su pplies of potable water
Environment—international agreements: party to: Biodiversity, Climate Change, Climate Change-Kyoto Protocol, Desertification, Law of the Sea, Marine Dumping, Marine Life Conservation, Ozone Layer Protection
signed, but not ratified: Hazardous Wastes
Geography—note: shares island of Hispaniola with Dominican Republic (western one-third is Haiti, eastern two-thirds is the Dominican Republic)

PEOPLE AND SOCIETY

Nationality: noun: Haitian(s)
adjective: Haitian
Ethnic groups: black 95%, mulatto and white 5%
Languages: French (official), Creole (official)
Religions: Roman Catholic (official) 54.7%, Protestant 28.5% (Baptist 15.4%, Pentecostal 7.9%, Adventist 3%, Methodist 1.5%, other 0.7%), voodoo (official) 2.1%, other 4.6%, none 10.2%
note: many Haitians practice elements of voodoo in addition to another religion, most often Roman Catholicism; voodoo was recognized as an official religion in 2003

Population: 10,110,019
note: estimates for this country explicitly take into account the effects of excess mortality due to AIDS; this can result in lower life expectancy, higher infant mortality, higher death rates, lower population growth rates, and changes in the distribution of population by age and sex than would otherwise be expected (July 2015 est.)
country comparison to the world: 89
Age structure: 0–14 years: 33.28% (male 1,686,647/female 1,678,156)
15–24 years: 21.64% (male 1,093,024/female 1,094,591)
25–54 years: 35.78% (male 1,801,988/female 1,815,819)
55–64 years: 5.11% (male 247,588/female 269,103)
65 years and over: 4.18% (male 188,952/female 234,151) (2015 est.)
Dependency ratios: total dependency ratio: 62.3%
youth dependency ratio: 54.8%
elderly dependency ratio: 7.5%
potential support ratio: 13.3% (2015 est.)
Median age: total: 22.5 years
male: 22.3 years
female: 22.7 years (2015 est.)
country comparison to the world: 174
Population growth rate: 1.172% (2015 est.)
country comparison to the world: 103
Birth rate: 22.31 births/1,000 population (2015 est.)
country comparison to the world: 73
Death rate: 7.83 deaths/1,000 population (2015 est.)
country comparison to the world: 103
Net migration rate: -2.76 migrant(s)/1,000 population (2015 est.)
country comparison to the world: 177
Urbanization: urban Population: 58.6% of total population (2015)
rate of urbanization: 3.78% annual rate of change (2010–15 est.)
Major urban areas—Population: PORT-AU-PRINCE (capital) 2.44 million (2015)
Sex ratio: at birth: 1.01 male(s)/female
0–14 years: 1.01 male(s)/female
15–24 years: 1 male(s)/female
25–54 years: 0.99 male(s)/female
55–64 years: 0.92 male(s)/female
65 years and over: 0.81 male(s)/female
total population: 0.99 male(s)/female (2015 est.)
Mother's mean age at first birth: 22.7
note: median age at first birth among women 25–29 (2012)
Maternal mortality rate: 359 deaths/100,000 live births (2015 est.)
country comparison to the world: 31
Infant mortality rate: total: 47.98 deaths/1,000 live births
male: 51.71 deaths/1,000 live births
female: 44.21 deaths/1,000 live births (2015 est.)
country comparison to the world: 40

Life expectancy at birth: *total Population:* 63.51 years

male: 62.07 years

female: 64.95 years (2015 est.)

country comparison to the world: 187

Total fertility rate: 2.69 children born/woman (2015 est.)

country comparison to the world: 71

Contraceptive prevalence rate: 34.5% (2012)

Health expenditures: 9.4% of GDP (2013)

country comparison to the world: 96

Hospital bed density: 1.3 beds/1,000 population (2007)

Drinking water source:

improved:

urban: 64.9% of population

rural: 47.6% of population

total: 57.7% of population

unimproved:

urban: 35.1% of population

rural: 52.4% of population

total: 42.3% of population (2015 est.)

Sanitation facility access:

improved:

urban: 33.6% of population

rural: 19.2% of population

total: 27.6% of population

unimproved:

urban: 66.4% of population

rural: 80.8% of population

total: 72.4% of population (2015 est.)

HIV/AIDS—adult prevalence rate: 1.93% (2014 est.)

country comparison to the world: 27

HIV/AIDS—people living with HIV/AIDS: 141,300 (2014 est.)

country comparison to the world: 33

HIV/AIDS—deaths: 3,800 (2014 est.)

country comparison to the world: 40

Major infectious diseases: *degree of risk:* very high

food or waterborne diseases: bacterial and protozoal diarrhea, hepatitis A and E, and typhoid fever

vectorborne diseases: dengue fever and malaria (2013)

Obesity—adult prevalence rate: 10.7% (2014)

country comparison to the world: 137

Children under the age of 5 years underweight: 11.6% (2012)

country comparison to the world: 64

Education expenditures: NA

Literacy: *definition:* age 15 and over can read and write

total Population: 60.7%

male: 64.3%

female: 57.3% (2015 est.)

Child labor—children ages 5–14: *total number:* 2,587,205

percentage: 21% (2006 est.)

GOVERNMENT

Country name: *conventional long form:* Republic of Haiti

conventional short form: Haiti

local long form: Republique d'Haiti/Repiblik d Ayiti

local short form: Haiti/Ayiti

etymology: the native Taino name means "land of high mountains" and was originally applied to the entire island of Hispaniola

Government type: semi-presidential republic

Capital: *name:* Port-au-Prince

Geographic coordinates: 18 32 N, 72 20 W

time difference: UTC-5 (same time as Washington, DC, during Standard Time)

daylight saving time: +1hr, begins second Sunday in March; ends first Sunday in November

Administrative divisions: 10 departments (departements, singular—departement); Artibonite, Centre, Grand'Anse, Nippes, Nord, Nord-Est, Nord-Ouest, Ouest, Sud, Sud-Est

Independence: 1 January 1804 (from France)

National holiday: Independence Day, 1 January (1804)

Constitution: many previous (23 total); latest adopted 10 March 1987; amended 2012 (2016)

Legal system: civil law system strongly influenced by Napoleonic Code

International law organization participation: accepts compulsory ICJ jurisdiction; non-party state to the ICCt

Citizenship: *citizenship by birth:* no

citizenship by descent only: at least one parent must be a native-born citizen of Haiti

dual citizenship recognized: no

residency requirement for naturalization: 5 years

Suffrage: 18 years of age; universal

Executive branch: *chief of state:* Interim President Jocelerme PRIVERT (since 14 February 2016); note—parliament elected Interim President PRIVERT after President Michel MARTELLY stepped down from office 7 February 2016

head of government: Prime Minister Enex JEAN-CHARLES (since 25 March 2016)

cabinet: Cabinet chosen by the prime minister in consultation with the president; parliament must ratify the Cabinet and Prime Minister's governing policy

elections/appointments: president directly elected by absolute majority popular vote in 2 rounds if needed for a 5-year term (eligible for a single non-consecutive term); election last held on 25 October 2015, but a runoff scheduled for 24 April 2016 was postponed; on 6 June 2016, the Provisional Electoral Council announced that it had accepted a recommendation by an independent commission, which had found that fraud had marred the October 2015 vote, to formally annul the results; a repeat of the first round of the presidential election will now take place 9 October 2016, with a second round to be held on 8 January 2017

election results: 2010 election—Michel MARTELLY elected president in runoff; percent of vote—Michel MARTELLY (Peasant's Response) 68%, Mirlande MANIGAT (RDNP) 32%

Legislative branch: *description:* bicameral legislature or "le Corps Legislatif ou parlement" consists of le Senat or Senate (30 seats; members directly elected in multi-seat constituencies by absolute majority vote in two rounds if needed; members

serve 6-year terms with one-third of the membership renewed every 2 years) and la Chambre de deputes or Chamber of Deputies (118 seats; members directly elected in single-seat constituencies by absolute majority vote in two rounds if needed; members serve 4-year terms); note -when the two chambers meet collectively it is known as L'Assemblee Nationale or the National Assembly that is convened for specific purposes spelled out in the constitution

elections: Senate—last held on 9 August 2015 with run-off election on 25 October 2015 (next possible election in 2017); Chamber of Deputies—last held on 9 August 2015 with run-off election on 25 October 2015 (next regular election may be held in 2017)

election results: 2015 Senate—percent of vote by party—NA; seats by party—NA; 2015 Chamber of Deputies—percent of vote by party—N A; seats by party—N A; note—official results pending

Judicial branch: *highest court(s):* Supreme Court or Cour de Cassation (consists of a chief judge and other judges); note—HaitIIs a member of the Caribbean Court of Justice

judge selection and term of office: judges appointed by the president from candidate lists submitted by the Senate of the National Assembly; note—Article 174 of the Haiti Constitution states "Judges of the Supreme Court . . . are appointed for 10 years." whereas Article 177 states "Judges of the Supreme Court are appointed for life."

subordinate courts: Courts of Appeal; Courts of First Instance; magistrates' courts; special courts

Political parties and leaders: Assembly of Progressive National Democrats or RDNP [Mirlande MANIGAT]

Christian and Citizen For Haiti's Reconstruction or ACCRHA [Chavannes JEUNE]

Christian Movement for a New Haiti or MCNH [Luc MESADIEU]

Convention for Democratic Unity or KID [Evans PAUL]

Cooperative Action to Rebuild Haiti or KONBA [Jean William JEANTY]

December 16 Platform or Platfom 16 Desanm [Dr. Gerard BLOT]

Democratic Alliance or ALYAN S [Evans PAU L] (coalition composed of KID and PPRH)

Democratic Centers's National Council or CON-ACED [Osner FEVRY]

Democratic Movement for the Liberation of Haiti-Revolutionary Party of Haiti or MODELH -PRDH

Effort and Solidarity to Create an Alternative for the People or ESKAM P [Joseph JASME] Fanmi Lavalas or FL [Jean-Bertrand ARISTIDE]

For Us All or PONT [Jean-Marie CHERESTAL]

Fusion of Haitian Social Democrats or FHSD [Edmonde Supplice BEAUZILE]

Grouping of Citizens for HOPE or RESPE [Charles-Henri BAKER]

Haiti Action or AAA [Youri LATORTUE]

Haitian Tet Kale Party or PHTK [Ann Valerie Timothee MILFORT]

Haitians for Haiti [Yvon NEPTUNE]

Independent Movement for National Reconstruction or MIRN [Luc FLEURINORD]

Konbit Pou refe Ayiti or KONBIT

Lavni Organization or LAVN I [Yves CRISTALIN]

Liberal Party of Haiti or PLH [Jean Andre VICTOR]

Liberation Platform or PLATF OR MELIBERATION

Love Haiti or Renmen Ayiti [Jean-Henry CEANT and Camille LEBLANC]

Merging of Haitian Social Democrats or FUSION [Edmonde Supplice BEAUZILE] (coalition of Ayiti Capable, Haitian National Revolutionary Party, and National Congress of Democratic Movements)

Mobilization for National Development or MDN [Hubert de RONCERAY]

National Front for the Reconstruction of Haiti or FRN [Guy PHILIPPE]

New Christian Movement for a New Haiti or MOCHRENA [Luc MESADIEU]

Patriotic Movement of the Democratic Opposition or MOPOD

Patriotic Unity or IP [Marie Denise CLAUDE]

Peasant Platform or PP

Peasant's Response or Repons Peyizan [Michel MARTELLY]

Platform Alternative for Progress and Democracy or ALTENATIV [Victor BENOIT and Evans PAUL]

Platform of Haitian Patriots or PLAPH [Dejean BELISAIRE and Himmler REBU]

Platform Pitit Dessalines or PPD [Moise JEAN -CHARLES] Pont

Popular Party for the Renewal of Haiti or PPRH [Claude ROMAIN]

PPG18

Rally or RASAMBLE

Renmen Ayiti or RA [Jean-Henry CEANT]

Respect or RESPE

Socialist Action Movement or MAS

Strength in Unity or Ansanm Nou Fo [Leslie VOLTAIRE]

Struggling People's Organization or OPL [Sauveur PIERRE-ETIENNE]

Truth (Verite)

Union [Chavannes JEUNE]

Union of Haitian Citizens for Democracy, Development, and Education or UCADDE [Jeantel JOSEPH]

Union of Nationalist and Progressive Haitians or UNPH [Edouard FRANCISQUE]

Unity or Inite [Levaillant LOUIS-JEUNE] (coalition that includes Front for Hope or L'ESPWA)

Vigilance or Veye Yo [Lavarice GAUDIN]

Youth for People's Power or JPP [Rene CIVIL]

Political pressure groups and leaders: Autonomous Organizations of Haitian Workers or CATH [Fignole ST-CYR]

Confederation of Haitian Workers or CTH

Economic Forum of the Private Sector or EF [Reginald BOULOS]

Federation of Workers Trade Unions or FOS

General Organization of Independent Haitian Workers [Patrick NUMAS]

Grand-Anse Resistance Committee or KOREGA

Haitian Association of Industries or ADIH [Georges SASSINE]

National Popular Assembly or APN

Papaye Peasants Movement or MPP [Chavannes JEAN-BAPTISTE]

Popular Organizations Gathering Power or PROP

Protestant Federation of Haiti

Roman Catholic Church

International organization participation: ACP, AOSIS, Caricom, CD, CDB, CELAC, FAO, G-77, IADB, IAEA, IBRD, ICAO, ICC (NGOs), ICRM, IDA, IFAD, IFC, IFRCS, ILO, IMF, IMO, Interpol, IOC, IOM, IPU, ITSO, ITU, ITUC (NGOs), LAES, MIGA, NAM, OAS, OIF, OPANAL, OPCW, PCA, Petrocaribe, UN, UNCTAD, UNESCO, UNIDO, Union Latina, UNWTO, UPU, WCO, WFTU (NGOs), WHO, WIPO, WMO, WTO

Diplomatic representation in the US: *chief of mission:* Ambassador Paul Getty ALTIDOR (since 17 April 2012)

chancery: 2311 Massachusetts Avenue NW, Washington, DC 20008

telephone: [1] (202) 332-4090

FAX: [1] (202) 745-7215

consulate(s) general: Atlanta, Boston, Chicago, Miami, Orlando (FL), New York, San Juan (Puerto Rico)

Diplomatic representation from the US: *chief of mission:* Ambassador Peter MULREAN (since 6 October 2015)

embassy: Tabarre 41, Route de Tabarre, Port-au-Prince

mailing address: (in Haiti) P.O. Box 1634, Port-au-Prince, Haiti; (from abroad) 3400 Port-au-Prince, State Department, Washington, DC 20521-3400

telephone: [509] 2229-8000

FAX: [509] 229-8028

Flag description: two equal horizontal bands of blue (top) and red with a centered white rectangle bearing the coat of arms, which contains a palm tree flanked by flags and two cannons above a scroll bearing the motto L'UNION FAITLA FORCE (Union Makes Strength); the colors are taken from the French Tricolor and represent the Union of blacks and mulattoes

National symbol(s): Hispaniolan trogon (bird), hibiscus flower; national colors: blue, red

National anthem: *name:* "La Dessalinienne" (The Dessalines Song)

lyrics/music: Justin LHERISSON/Nicolas GEFFRARD

note: adopted 1904; named for Jean-Jacques DESSALINES, a leader in the Haitian Revolution and first ruler of an independent Haiti

ECONOMY

Economy—overview: Haiti's economy suffered a severe setback in January 2010 when a 7.0 magnitude earthquake destroyed much of its capital city, Port-au-Prince, and neighboring areas. Currently the poorest country in the Western Hemisphere, with 80% of the population living under the poverty line and 54% in abject poverty, the earthquake further inflicted $7.8 billion in damage and caused the country's GDP to contract. In 2011, GDP growth rose to 5.5% as the Haitian economy began recovering from the earthquake. However, growth slowed in 2015 to 2% as political uncertainty, drought conditions, and the depreciation of the national currency took a toll on investment and economic growth. HaitIIs a free market economy with low labor costs and tariff-free access to the US for many of its exports. Two-fifths of all Haitians depend on the agricultural sector, mainly small-scale subsistence farming, which remains vulnerable to damage from frequent natural disasters, exacerbated by the country's widespread deforestation. Poverty, corruption, vulnerability to natural disasters, and low levels of education for much of the population are among Haiti's most serious impediments to economic growth. Remittances are the primary source of foreign exchange, in 2015 equaling over one-fifth of GDP, and nearly double the combined value of Haitian exports and foreign direct investment. US economic engagement under the Caribbean Basin Trade Partnership Act (CBTPA) and the 2008 Haitian Hemispheric Opportunity through Partnership Encouragement Act (HOPE II) helped increase apparel exports and investment by providing duty-free access to the US. The Haiti Economic Lift Program (HELP) Act of 2010 extended the CBTPA and HOPE II until 2020, while the Trade Preferences Extension Act of 2015 extended trade benefits provided to HaitIIn the HOPE and HELP Acts through September 2025. Apparel sector exports in 2015 reached $904 million and account for about 90% of Haitian exports and more than 10% of the GDP. Investment in HaitIIs hampered by the difficulty of doing business and weak infrastructure, including access to electricity. Haiti's outstanding external debt was cancelled by donor countries following the 2010 earthquake, but has since risen to nearly $2 billion as of December 2015, the majority of which is owed to Venezuela under the PetroCaribe program. Although the government has increased its revenue collection, it continues to rely on formal international economic assistance for fiscal sustainability, with over 20% of its annual budget coming from foreign aid or direct budget support.

GDP (purchasing power parity): $18.75 billion (2015 est.)

$18.56 billion (2014 est.)

$18.06 billion (2013 est.)

note: data are in 2015 US dollars

country comparison to the world: 148

GDP (official exchange rate): $8.618 billion (2015 est.)

GDP—real growth rate: 1% (2015 est.)

2.8% (2014 est.)

4.2% (2013 est.)

country comparison to the world: 176

GDP—per capita (PPP): $1,800 (2015 est.)

$1,800 (2014 est.)

$1,700 (2013 est.)

note: data are in 2015 US dollars

country comparison to the world: 211

Gross national saving: 26.5% of GDP (2015 est.)

24.8% of GDP (2014 est.)

23.7% of GDP (2013 est.)

country comparison to the world: 42

GDP—composition, by end use:

household consumption: 103.9%
government consumption: 0%
investment in fixed capital: 29.5%
investment in inventories: -5.3%
exports of goods and services: 14%
imports of goods and services: -42.1%
note: figure for household consumption also includes government consumption (2015 est.)
GDP—composition, by sector of origin:
agriculture: 23.6%
industry: 20.1%
services: 56.3% (2015 est.)
Agriculture—products: coffee, mangoes, cocoa, sugarcane, rice, corn, sorghum; wood, vetiver
Industries: textiles, sugar refining, flour milling, cement, light assembly using imported parts
Industrial production growth rate: 5% (2015 est.)
country comparison to the world: 32
Labor force: 4.594 million
note: shortage of skilled labor, unskilled labor abundant (2014 est.)
country comparison to the world: 88
Labor force—by occupation: *agriculture:* 38.1%
industry: 11.5%
services: 50.4% (2010)
Unemployment rate: 40.6% (2010 est.)
note: widespread unemployment and underemployment; more than two-thirds of the labor force do not have formal jobs
country comparison to the world: 196
Population below poverty line: 58.5% (2012 est.)
Household income or consumption by percentage share: *lowest:* 10%: 0.7%
highest: 10%: 47.7% (2001)
Distribution of family income—Gini Index: 60.8 (2012)
59.2 (2001)
country comparison to the world: 7
Budget: *revenues:* $1.814 billion
expenditures: $2.185 billion (2015 est.)
Taxes and other revenues: 20.6% of GDP (2015 est.)
country comparison to the world: 152
Budget surplus (+) or deficit (–): -4.3% of GDP (2015 est.)
country comparison to the world: 152
Public debt: 26.5% of GDP (2015 est.)
26.6% of GDP (2014 est.)
country comparison to the world: 147
Fiscal year: 1 October—30 September
Inflation rate (consumer prices): 7.5% (2015 est.)
3.9% (2014 est.)
country comparison to the world: 197
Commercial bank prime lending rate: 12.3% (31 December 2015 est.)
10.8% (31 December 2014 est.)
country comparison to the world: 64
Stock of narrow money: $1.095 billion (31 December 2015 est.)
$1.271 billion (31 December 2014 est.)
country comparison to the world: 150
Stock of broad money: $3.818 billion (31 December 2015 est.)
$3.793 billion (31 December 2014 est.)
country comparison to the world: 141

Stock of domestic credit: $2.302 billion (31 December 2015 est.)
$2.175 billion (31 December 2014 est.)
country comparison to the world: 135
Market value of publicly traded shares: $NA
Current account balance: -$206 million (2015 est.)
-$551 million (2014 est.)
country comparison to the world: 82
Exports: $1.029 billion (2015 est.)
$961 million (2014 est.)
country comparison to the world: 159
Exports—commodities: apparel, manufactures, oils, cocoa, mangoes, coffee
Exports—partners: US 85.3% (2015)
Imports: $3.436 billion (2015 est.)
$3.666 billion (2014 est.)
country comparison to the world: 139
Imports—commodities: food, manufactured goods, machinery and transport equipment, fuels, raw materials
Imports—partners: Dominican Republic 35.3%, US 24.5%, Netherlands Antilles 9.4%, China 9.4% (2015)
Reserves of foreign exchange and gold: $1.803 billion (31 December 2015 est.)
$1.99 billion (31 December 2014 est.)
country comparison to the world: 122
Debt—external: $1.9 billion (31 December 2015 est.)
$1.366 billion (31 December 2014 est.)
country comparison to the world: 150
Stock of direct foreign investment—at home: $1.299 billion (31 December 2015 est.)
$1.185 billion (31 December 2014 est.)
country comparison to the world: 109
Exchange rates: gourdes (HTG) per US dollar—
47.63 (2015 est.)
45.22 (2014 est.)
45.22 (2013 est.)
41.95 (2012 est.)
40.52 (2011 est.)

ENERGY

Electricity—production: 1.089 billion kWh (2012 est.)
country comparison to the world: 147
Electricity—consumption: 452 million kWh (2012 est.)
country comparison to the world: 172
Electricity—exports: 0 kWh (2013 est.)
country comparison to the world: 150
Electricity—imports: 0 kWh (2013 est.)
country comparison to the world: 160
Electricity—installed generating capacity: 267,800 kW (2012 est.)
country comparison to the world: 153
Electricity—from fossil fuels: 77.3% of total installed capacity (2012 est.)
country comparison to the world: 96
Electricity—from nuclear fuels: 0% of total installed capacity (2012 est.)
country comparison to the world: 107
Electricity—from hydroelectric plants: 22.7% of total installed capacity (2012 est.)
country comparison to the world: 88

Electricity—from other renewable sources: 0% of total installed capacity (2012 est.)
country comparison to the world: 182
Crude oil—production: 0 bbl/day (2014 est.)
country comparison to the world: 146
Crude oil—exports: 0 bbl/day (2012 est.)
country comparison to the world: 135
Crude oil—imports: 0 bbl/day (2012 est.)
country comparison to the world: 203
Crude oil—proved reserves: 0 bbl (1 January 2015 est.)
country comparison to the world: 145
Refined petroleum products—production: 0 bbl/day (2012 est.)
country comparison to the world: 193
Refined petroleum products—consumption: 15,000 bbl/day (2013 est.)
country comparison to the world: 143
Refined petroleum products—exports: 0 bbl/day (2012 est.)
country comparison to the world: 190
Refined petroleum products—imports: 14,720 bbl/day (2012 est.)
country comparison to the world: 127
Natural gas—production: 0 cu m (2013 est.)
country comparison to the world: 200
Natural gas—consumption: 0 cu m (2013 est.)
country comparison to the world: 154
Natural gas—exports: 0 cu m (2013 est.)
country comparison to the world: 114
Natural gas—imports: 0 cu m (2013 est.)
country comparison to the world: 208
Natural gas—proved reserves: 0 cu m (1 January 2014 est.)
country comparison to the world: 149
Carbon dioxide emissions from consumption of energy: 2.094 million Mt (2012 est.)
country comparison to the world: 148

COMMUNICATIONS

Telephones—fixed lines: *total subscriptions:* 41,000
subscriptions per 100 inhabitants: less than 1 (2014 est.)
country comparison to the world: 167
Telephones—mobile cellular: *total:* 6.8 million
subscriptions per 100 inhabitants: 68 (2014 est.)
country comparison to the world: 107
Telephone system: *general assessment:* telecommunications infrastructure is among the least-developed in Latin America and the Caribbean; domestic cell service is functional
domestic: mobile-cellular telephone services have expanded greatly in the last five years due to low-cost GSM phones and pay-as-you-go plans; mobile-cellular teledensity is about 60 per 100 persons
international: country code—509; satellite earth station—1 Intelsat (Atlantic Ocean) (2015)
Broadcast media: 130 television stations throughout the country, including 1 government-owned; cable TV subscription service available; 495 radio stations (of them, only 135 are licensed), including 1 government-owned; more than 250 private and community radio stations; over 50 FM stations in Port-au-Prince alone (2015)

Radio broadcast stations: AM 41, FM 53, short-wave 0 (2009)
Television broadcast stations: 2 (plus a cable TV service) (1997)
Internet country code: .ht
Internet hosts: 555 (2012)
country comparison to the world: 181
Internet users: *total:* 1.2 million
percent of Population: 11.6% (2014 est.)
country comparison to the world: 119

TRANSPORTATION

Airports: 14 (2013)
country comparison to the world: 148
Airports—with paved runways: *total:* 4
2,438 to 3,047 m: 2
914 to 1,523 m: 2 (2013)
Airports—with unpaved runways: *total:* 10
914 to 1,523 m: 2
under 914 m: 8 (2013)
Road ways: *total:* 4,266 km
paved: 768 km
unpaved: 3,498 km (2009)
country comparison to the world: 156
Ports and terminals: *major seaport(s):* Cap-Haitien, Gonaives, Jacmel, Port-au-Prince

MILITARY AND SECURITY

Military branches: no regular military forces—small Coast Guard; a Ministry of National Defense established May 2012; the regular Haitian Armed Forces (FAdH)—Army, Navy, and Air Force—have been demobilized but still exist on paper

until or unless they are constitutionally abolished (2011)

TRANSNATIONAL ISSUES

Disputes—international: since 2004, peacekeepers from the UN Stabilization Mission in Haiti have assisted in maintaining civil order in Haiti; the mission currently includes 6,685 military, 2,607 police, and 443 civilian personnel; despite efforts to control illegal migration, Haitians cross into the Dominican Republic and sail to neighboring countries; Haiti claims US-administered Navassa Island
Refugees and internally displaced persons: *IDPs:* 62,590 (includes only IDPs from the 2010 earthquake living in camps or camp-like situations; information is lacking about IDPs living outside camps or who have left camps) (2016)
stateless persons: 977 (2015)
note: stateless persons are individuals without a nationality who were born in the Dominican Republic prior to January 2010
Trafficking in persons: *current situation:* HaitIIs a source, transit, and destination country for men, women, and children subjected to forced labor and sex trafficking; most of Haiti's trafficking cases involve children in domestic servitude vulnerable to physical and sexual abuse; dismissed and runaway child domestic servants often end up in prostitution, begging, or street crime; other exploited populations included low-income Haitians, child laborers, and women and children living in IDP camps dating to the 2010 earthquake; Haitian adults are vulnerable to fraudulent labor recruitment abroad and, along with children, may be subjected to forced labor in the Dominican Republic,

elsewhere in the Caribbean, South America, and the US; Dominicans are exploited in sex trafficking and forced labor in Haiti
tier rating: Tier 2 Watch List—Haiti does not fully comply with the minimum standards for the elimination of trafficking; however, it is making significant efforts to do so; in 2014, Haiti was granted a waiver from an otherwise required downgrade to Tier 3 because its government has a written plan that, if implemented would constitute making significant efforts to bring itself into compliance with the minimum standards for the elimination of trafficking; in 2014, Haiti developed a national anti-trafficking action plan and enacted a law prohibiting all forms of human trafficking, although judicial corruption hampered its implementation; progress was made in investigating and prosecuting suspected traffickers, but no convictions were made; the government sustained limited efforts to identify and refer victims to protective services, which were provided mostly by NGOs without government support; campaigns to raise awareness about child labor and child trafficking continued (2015)
Illicit drugs: Caribbean transshipment point for cocaine en route to the US and Europe; substantial bulk cash smuggling activity; Colombian narcotics traffickers favor Haiti for illicit financial transactions; pervasive corruption; significant consumer of cannabis

HEARD ISLAND AND MCDONALD ISLANDS

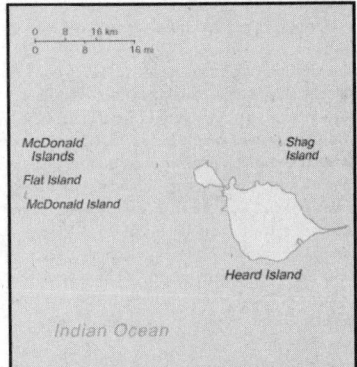

INTRODUCTION

Background: The UK transferred these uninhabited, barren, sub-Antarctic islands to Australia in 1947. Populated by large numbers of seal and bird species, the islands have been designated a nature preserve.

GEOGRAPHY

Location: islands in the Indian Ocean, about two-thirds of the way from Madagascar to Antarctica
Geographic coordinates: 53 06 S, 72 31 E
Map references: Antarctic Region
Area: *total:* 412 sq km
land: 412 sq km
water: 0 sq km
country comparison to the world: 203
Area—comparative: slightly more than two times the size of Washington, DC
Land boundaries: 0 km
Coastline: 101.9 km
Maritime claims: *territorial sea:* 12 nm
exclusive fishing zone: 200 nm
Climate: antarctic
Terrain: Heard Island—80% ice-covered, bleak and mountainous, dominated by a large massif (Big Ben) and an active volcano (Mawson Peak); McDonald Islands—small and rocky
Elevation: *mean elevation:* NA

elevation extremes: *lowest point:* Indian Ocean 0 m
highest point: Mawson Peak on Big Ben volcano 2,745 m

Natural resources: fish
Land use: *agricultural land:* 0%
arable land: 0%
permanent crops: 0%
permanent pasture: 0%
forest: 0%
other: 100% (2011 est.)
Natural hazards: Mawson Peak, an active volcano, is on Heard Island
Environment—current issues: NA
Geography—note: Mawson Peak on Heard Island is the highest Australian mountain (at 2,745 meters, it is taller than Mt. Kosciuszko in Australia proper), and one of only two active volcanoes located in Australian territory, the other being McDonald Island; in 1992, McDonald Island broke its dormancy and began erupting; it has erupted several times since, most recently in 2005

PEOPLE AND SOCIETY

Population: uninhabited

GOVERNMENT

Country name: *conventional long form:* Territory of Heard Island and McDonald Islands *conventional short form:* Heard Island and McDonald Islands

abbreviation: HIMI

etymology: named after American Captain John HEARD, who sighted the island on 25 November 1853, and American Captain William McDONALD, who discovered the islands on 4 January 1854

Dependency status: territory of Australia; administered from Canberra by the Department of Sustainability, Environment, Water, Population and Communities (Australian Antarctic Division)

Legal system: the laws of Australia, where applicable, apply

Diplomatic representation in the US: none (territory of Australia)

Diplomatic representation from the US: none (territory of Australia)

Flag description: the flag of Australia is used

ECONOMY

Economy—overview: The islands have no indigenous economic activity, but the Australian Government allows limited fishing in the surrounding waters. Visits to Heard Island typically focus on terrestrial and marine research and infrequent private expeditions.

COMMUNICATIONS

Internet country code: .hm

Internet hosts: 102 (2012)
country comparison to the world: 208

TRANSPORTATION

Ports and terminals: none; offshore anchorage only

MILITARY AND SECURITY

Military—note: defense is the responsibility of Australia; Australia conducts fisheries patrols

TRANSNATIONAL ISSUES

Disputes—international: none

HOLY SEE (VATICAN CITY)

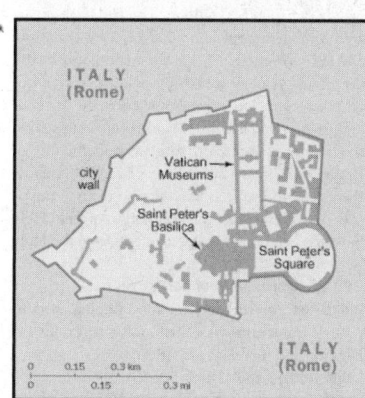

INTRODUCTION

Background: Popes in their secular role ruled portions of the Italian peninsula for more than a thousand years until the mid-19th century, when many of the Papal States were seized by the newly united Kingdom of Italy. In 1870, the pope's holdings were further circumscribed when Rome itself was annexed. Disputes between a series of "prisoner" popes and Italy were resolved in 1929 by three Lateran Treaties, which established the independent state of Vatican City and granted Roman Catholicism special status in Italy. In 1984, a concordat between the Holy See and Italy modified certain of the earlier treaty provisions, including the primacy of Roman Catholicism as the Italian state religion. Present concerns of the Holy See include religious freedom, threats against minority Christian communities in Africa and the Middle East, sexual misconduct by clergy, international development, interreligious dialogue and reconciliation, and the application of church doctrine in an era of rapid change and globalization. About 1.2 billion people worldwide profess Catholicism—the world's largest Christian faith.

GEOGRAPHY

Location: Southern Europe, an enclave of Rome (Italy)

Geographic coordinates: 41 54 N, 12 27 E

Map references: Europe

Area: *total:* 0.44 sq km
land: 0.44 sq km
water: 0 sq km
country comparison to the world: 257

Area—comparative: about 0.7 times the size of the National Mall in Washington, DC

Land boundaries: *total:* 3.4 km
border countries (1): Italy 3.4 km

Coastline: 0 km (landlocked)

Maritime claims: none (landlocked)

Climate: temperate; mild, rainy winters (September to May) with hot, dry summers (May to September)

Terrain: urban; low hill

Elevation: *mean elevation:* NA

elevation extremes: *lowest point:* Saint Peter's Square 19 m
highest point: Vatican Gardens (Vatican Hill) 77 m

Natural resources: none

Land use: *agricultural land:* 0%
arable land: 0%
permanent crops: 0%
permanent pasture: 0%
forest: 0%
other: 100% (urban area) (2011 est.)

Natural hazards: NA

Environment—current issues: NA

Environment—international agreements: *party to:* Ozone Layer Protection
signed, but not ratified: Air Pollution, Environmental Modification

Geography—note: landlocked; enclave in Rome, Italy; world's smallest state; beyond the territorial boundary of Vatican City, the Lateran Treaty of 1929 grants the Holy See extra territorial authority over 23 sites in Rome and five outside of Rome, including the Pontifical Palace at Castel Gandolfo (the Pope's summer residence)

PEOPLE AND SOCIETY

Nationality: *noun:* none
adjective: none

Ethnic groups: Italians, Swiss, other

Languages: Italian, Latin, French, various other languages

Religions: Roman Catholic

Population: 1,000 (2015 est.)
country comparison to the world: 236

Population growth rate: 0% (2014 est.)
country comparison to the world: 195

Urbanization: *urban Population:* 100% of total population (2015)
rate of urbanization: 0.03% annual rate of change (2010–15 est.)

Major urban areas—Population: VATICAN CITY (capital) 1,000 (2014)

HIV/AIDS—adult prevalence rate: NA

HIV/AIDS—people living with HIV/AIDS: NA

HIV/AIDS—deaths: NA

Education expenditures: NA

GOVERNMENT

Country name: *conventional long form:* The Holy See (Vatican City State)
conventional short form: Holy See (Vatican City)
local long form: La Santa Sede (Stato della Citta del Vaticano)
local short form: Santa Sede (Citta del Vaticano)
etymology: "holy" comes from the Greek word "hera" meaning "sacred"; "see" comes from the Latin word "sedes" meaning "seat," and refers to the episcopal chair; the term "Vatican" derives from the hill Mons Vaticanus on which the Vatican is located and which comes from the Latin "vaticinari" (to prophecy), referring to the fortune tellers and soothsayers who frequented the area in Roman times

Government type: ecclesiastical elective monarchy; self described as an "absolute monarchy"

Capital: *name:* Vatican City

Geographic coordinates: 41 54 N, 12 27 E

time difference: UTC + 1 (6 hours ahead of Washington, DC, during Standard Time)

daylight saving time: +1hr, begins last Sunday in March; ends last Sunday in October

Administrative divisions: none

Independence: 11 February 1929; note—the three treaties signed with Italy on 11 February 1929 acknowledged, among other things, the full sovereignty of the Holy See and established its territorial extent; however, the origin of the Papal States, which over centuries varied considerably in extent, may be traced back to 754

National holiday: Election Day of Pope FRANCIS, 13 March (2013)

Constitution: previous 1929, 1963; latest adopted 26 November 2000, effective 22 February 2001 (Fundamental Law of Vatican City State); note—in October 2013, Pope Francis instituted a 9-member Council of Cardinal Advisors to reform the administrative apparatus of the Holy See (Roman Curia) to include writing a new constitution (2016)

Legal system: religious legal system based on canon (religious) law

International law organization participation: has not submitted an ICJ jurisdiction declaration; non-party state to the ICCt

Citizenship: *citizenship by birth:* no

citizenship by descent: no

dual citizenship recognized: no

residency requirement for naturalization: not applicable

note: in the Holy See, citizenship is acquired by law, ex iure, or by adminstrative decision; in the first instance citizenship is a function of holding office within the Holy See as in the case of cardinals resident in Vatican City or diplomats of the Holy See; in the second instance, citizenship may be requested in a limited set of circumstances for those who reside within Vatican City under papal authorization, as a function of their office or service, or as the spouses and children of current citizens; citizenship is lost once an individual no longer permanently resides in Vatican City, normally reverting to the citizenship previously held

Suffrage: election of the pope is limited to cardinals less than 80 years old

Executive branch: *chief of state:* Pope FRANCIS (since 13 March 2013)

head of government: Secretary of State Cardinal Pietro PAROLIN (since 15 October 2013)

cabinet: Pontifical Commission for the State of Vatican City appointed by the pope

elections/appointments: pope elected by the College of Cardinals, usually for life or until voluntary resignation; election last held on 13 March 2013 (next to be held after the death or resignation of the current pope); Secretary of State appointed by the pope

election results: Jorge Mario BERGOGLIO, former Archbishop of Buenos Aires, elected Pope FRANCIS

Legislative branch: *description:* unicameral Pontifical Commission for Vatican City State or Pontificia Commissione per lo Stato della Citta del Vaticano (7 seats; members appointed by the pope to serve 5-year terms)

Judicial branch: *highest court(s):* Supreme Court or Supreme Tribunal of the Apostolic Signatura (consists of the cardinal prefect, who serves as ex-officio president of the court, and 2 other cardinals); note—judicial duties were established by the Motu Proprio, papal directive, of Pope PIUS XII on 1 May 1946; many Vatican City criminal matters are handled by the Republic of Italy courts

judge selection and term of office: cardinal prefect appointed by the Pope; the other 2 cardinals of the court appointed by the cardinal prefect on a yearly basis

subordinate courts: Appellate Court of Vatican City; Tribunal of Vatican City

Political parties and leaders: none

Political pressure groups and leaders: none (exclusive of influence exercised by church officers)

International organization participation: CE (observer), IAEA, Interpol, IOM, ITSO, ITU, ITUC (NGOs), OAS (observer), OPCW, OSCE, Schengen Convention (de facto member), SICA (observer), UN (observer), UNCTAD, UNHCR, Union Latina (observer), UNWTO (observer), UPU, WIPO, WTO (observer)

Diplomatic representation in the US: *chief of mission:* Apostolic Nuncio Archbishop Christophe PIERRE (since 25 April 2016) 2016

chancery: 3339 Massachusetts Avenue NW, Washington, DC 20008

telephone: [1] (202) 333-7121

FAX: [1] (202) 337-4036

Diplomatic representation from the US: *chief of mission:* Ambassador Kenneth Francis HACKETT (since 21 October 2013)

embassy: American Embassy to the Holy See, Via Sallustiana, 49,00187 Rome, Italy

mailing address: Unit 5660, Box 66, DPO AE 09624–0066

telephone: [39] (06) 4674-3428

FAX: [39] (06) 575-8346

Flag description: two vertical bands of yellow (hoist side) and white with the arms of the Holy See, consisting of the crossed keys of Saint Peter surmounted by the three-tiered papal tiara, centered in the white band; the yellow color represents the pope's spiritual power, the white his worldly power

National symbol(s): crossed keys beneath a papal tiara; national colors: yellow, white

National anthem: *name:* "Inno e Marcia Pontificale" (Hymn and Pontifical March); often called The Pontifical Hymn

lyrics/music: Raffaello LAVAGNA/Charles-Francois GOUNOD

note: adopted 1950

ECONOMY

Economy—overview: The Holy See is supported financially by a variety of sources, including investments, real estate income, and donations from Catholic individuals, dioceses, and institutions; these help fund the Roman Curia (Vatican bureaucracy), diplomatic missions, and media outlets. Moreover, an annual collection taken up in dioceses and from direct donations go to a nonbudgetary fund, known as Peter's Pence, which is used directly by the Pope for charity, disaster relief, and aid to churches in developing nations. Donations increased between 2010 and 2011.

The separate Vatican City State budget includes the Vatican museums and post office and is supported financially by the sale of stamps, coins, medals, and tourist mementos; by fees for admission to museums; and by publication sales. Its revenues increased between 2010 and 2011 because of expanded opening hours and a growing number of visitors. However, the Holy See has not escaped the financial difficulties engulfing other European countries; in 2012, it started a spending review to determine where to cut costs to reverse its 2011 budget deficit of $20 million. The Holy See generated a modest surplus in 2012 before recording a $32 million deficit in 2013, driven primarily by the decreasing value of gold. Most public expenditures go to wages and other personnel costs; the incomes and living standards of lay workers are comparable to those of counterparts who work in the city of Rome. in February 2014, Pope FRANCIS created the Secretariat of the Economy to oversee financial and administrative operations of the Holy See, part of a broader campaign to reform the Holy See's finances.

GDP (purchasing power parity): $NA

Industries: printing; production of coins, medals, postage stamps; mosaics, staff uniforms; worldwide banking and financial activities

Labor force: 2,885 (December 2011)

country comparison to the world: 226

Labor force—by occupation: *note:* essentially services with a small amount of industry; nearly all dignitaries, priests, nuns, guards, and the approximately 3,000 lay workers live outside the Vatican

Population below poverty line: NA%

Budget: *revenues:* $308 million

expenditures: $326.4 million (2011)

Taxes and other revenues: NA%

Budget surplus (+) or deficit (−): NA%

Fiscal year: calendar year

Exchange rates: euros (EUR) per US dollar—

-0.885 (2015 est.)

0.7525 (2014 est.)

0.7634 (2013 est.)

0.78 (2012 est.)

0.7185 (2011 est.)

COMMUNICATIONS

Telephone system: *general assessment:* automatic digital exchange

domestic: connected via fiber optic cable to Telecom Italia network

international: country code—39; uses Italian system (2012)

Broadcast media: the Vatican Television Center (CTV) transmits live broadcasts of the Pope's Sunday and Wednesday audiences, as well as the Pope's public celebrations; CTV also produces

documentaries; Vatican Radio is the Holy See's official broadcasting service broadcasting via shortwave, AM and FM frequencies, and via satellite and Internet connections (2008)
Radio broadcast stations: AM 5, FM 3, shortwave 5 (2008)
Television broadcast stations: 1 (2008)
Internet country code: .va
Internet hosts: 107 (2012)

country comparison to the world: 207

MILITARY AND SECURITY

Military branches: Pontifical Swiss Guard Corps (Corpo della Guardia Svizzera Pontificia) (2013)
Military service age and obligation: Pontifical Swiss Guard Corps (Corpo della Guardia Svizzera Pontificia): 19–30 years of age for voluntary

military service; no conscription; must be Roman Catholic, a Swiss citizen, with a secondary education (2013)
Military—note: defense is the responsibility of Italy; ceremonial and limited security duties performed by Pontifical Swiss Guard

TRANSNATIONAL ISSUES

Disputes—international: none

HONDURAS

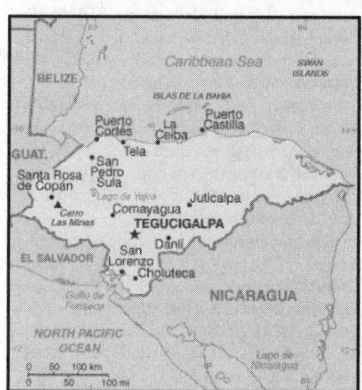

INTRODUCTION

Background: Once part of Spain's vast empire in the New World, Honduras became an independent nation in 1821. After two and a half decades of mostly military rule, a freely elected civilian government came to power in 1982. During the 1980s, Honduras proved a haven for anti-Sandinista contras fighting the Marxist Nicaraguan Government and an ally to Salvadoran Government forces fighting leftist guerrillas. The country was devastated by Hurricane Mitch in 1998, which killed about 5,600 people and caused approximately $2 billion in damage. Since then, the economy has slowly rebounded.

GEOGRAPHY

Location: Central America, bordering the Caribbean Sea, between Guatemala and Nicaragua and bordering the Gulf of Fonseca (North Pacific Ocean), between El Salvador and Nicaragua
Geographic coordinates: 15 00 N, 86 30 W
Map references: Central America and the Caribbean
Area: *total:* 112,090 sq km
land: 111,890 sq km
water: 200 sq km
country comparison to the world: 103
Area—comparative: slightly larger than Tennessee
Land boundaries: *total:* 1,575 km
border countries (3): Guatemala 244 km, El Salvador 391 km, Nicaragua 940 km

Coastline: 823 km (Caribbean Sea 669 km, Gulf of Fonseca 163 km)
Maritime claims: *territorial sea:* 12 nm
contiguous zone: 24 nm
exclusive economic zone: 200 nm
continental shelf: natural extension of territory or to 200 nm
Climate: subtropical in lowlands, temperate in mountains
Terrain: mostly mountains in interior, narrow coastal plains
Elevation: *mean elevation:* 684 m
elevation extremes: *lowest point:* Caribbean Sea 0 m
highest point: Cerro Las Minas 2,870 m
Natural resources: timber, gold, silver, copper, lead, zinc, iron ore, antimony, coal, fish, hydropower
Land use: *agricultural land:* 28.8%
arable land: 9.1%
permanent crops: 4%
permanent pasture: 15.7%
forest: 45.3%
other: 25.9% (2011 est.)
Irrigated land: 900 sq km (2012)
Total renewable water resources: 95.93 cu km (2011)
Freshwater withdrawal (domestic/industrial/agricultural): *total:* 2.12 cu km/yr (16%/23%/61%)
per capita: 295.6 cu m/yr (2006)
Natural hazards: frequent, but generally mild, earthquakes; extremely susceptible to damaging hurricanes and floods along the Caribbean coast
Environment—current issues: urban population expanding; deforestation results from logging and the clearing of land for agricultural purposes; further land degradation and soil erosion hastened by uncontrolled development and improper land use practices such as farming of marginal lands; mining activities polluting Lago de Yojoa (the country's largest source of fresh water), as well as several rivers and streams, with heavy metals
Environment—international agreements: *party to:* Biodiversity, Climate Change, Climate Change-Kyoto Protocol, Desertification, Endangered Species, Hazardous Wastes, Law of the Sea, Marine Dumping, Ozone Layer Protection, Ship Pollution, Tropical Timber 83, Tropical Timber 94, Wetlands
signed, but not ratified: none of the selected agreements

Geography—note: has only a short Pacific coast but a long Caribbean shoreline, including the virtually uninhabited eastern Mosquito Coast

PEOPLE AND SOCIETY

Nationality: *noun:* Honduran(s)
adjective: Honduran
Ethnic groups: mestizo (mixed Amerindian and European) 90%, Amerindian 7%, black 2%, white 1%
Languages: Spanish (official), Amerindian dialects
Religions: Roman Catholic 97%, Protestant 3%
Demographic profile: Honduras is one of the poorest countries in Latin America and has the world's highest murder rate. More than half of the population lives in poverty and per capita income is one of the lowest in the region. Poverty rates are higher among rural and indigenous people and in the south, west, and along the eastern border than in the north and central areas where most of Honduras' industries and infrastructure are concentrated. The increased productivity needed to break Honduras' persistent high poverty rate depends, in part, on further improvements in educational attainment. Although primary-school enrollment is near 100%, educational quality is poor, the dropout rate and grade repetition remain high, and teacher and school accountability is low.
Honduras' population growth rate has slowed since the 1990s, but it remains high at nearly 2% annually because the birth rate averages approximately three children per woman and more among rural, indigenous, and poor women. Consequently, Honduras' young adult population—ages 15 to 29—is projected to continue growing rapidly for the next three decades and then stabilize or slowly shrink. Population growth and limited job prospects outside of agriculture will continue to drive emigration. Remittances represent about a fifth of GDP.
Population: 8,746,673
note: estimates for this country explicitly take into account the effects of excess mortality due to AIDS; this can result in lower life expectancy, higher infant mortality, higher death rates, lower population growth rates, and changes in the distribution of population by age and sex than would otherwise be expected (July 2015 est.)
country comparison to the world: 94
Age structure: *0–14 years:* 34.18% (male 1,527,234/female 1,462,763)

15–24 years: 21.14% (male 943,039/female 906,273)

25–54 years: 35.73% (male 1,578,654/female 1,546,902)

55–64 years: 4.85% (male 197,602/female 226,294)

65 years and over: 4.09% (male 156,023/female 201,889) (2015 est.)

Dependency ratios: *total dependency ratio:* 57.8%

youth dependency ratio: 50.1%

elderly dependency ratio: 7.7%

potential support ratio: 13.1% (2015 est.)

Median age: *total:* 22.3 years

male: 21.9 years

female: 22.7 years (2015 est.)

country comparison to the world: 175

Population growth rate: 1.68% (2015 est.)

country comparison to the world: 70

Birth rate: 23.14 births/1,000 population (2015 est.)

country comparison to the world: 65

Death rate: 5.17 deaths/1,000 population (2015 est.)

country comparison to the world: 182

Net migration rate: -1.16 migrant(s)/1,000 population (2015 est.)

country comparison to the world: 153

Urbanization: *urban Population:* 54.7% of total population (2015)

rate of urbanization: 3.14% annual rate of change (2010–15 est.)

Major urban areas—Population: TEGUCIGALPA (capital) 1.123 million; San Pedro Sula 852,000 (2015)

Sex ratio: *at birth:* 1.05 male(s)/female

0–14 years: 1.04 male(s)/female

15–24 years: 1.04 male(s)/female

25–54 years: 1.02 male(s)/female

55–64 years: 0.87 male(s)/female

65 years and over: 0.77 male(s)/female

total population: 1.01 male(s)/female (2015 est.)

Mother's mean age at first birth: 20.4

note: median age a first birth among women 25–29 (2011–12 est.)

Maternal mortality rate: 129 deaths/100,000 live births (2015 est.)

country comparison to the world: 69

Infant mortality rate: *total:* 18.18 deaths/1,000 live births

male: 20.59 deaths/1,000 live births

female: 15.66 deaths/1,000 live births (2015 est.)

country comparison to the world: 97

Life expectancy at birth: *total population:* 71 years

male: 69.34 years

female: 72.74 years (2015 est.)

country comparison to the world: 150

Total fertility rate: 2.78 children born/woman (2015 est.)

country comparison to the world: 64

Contraceptive prevalence rate: 73.2% (2011/12)

Health expenditures: 8.7% of GDP (2013)

country comparison to the world: 48

Physicians density: 0.37 physicians/1,000 population (2005)

Hospital bed density: 0.7 beds/1,000 population (2012)

Drinking water source:

improved:

urban: 97.4% of population

rural: 83.8% of population

total: 91.2% of population

unimproved:

urban: 2.6% of population

rural: 16.2% of population

total: 8.8% of population (2015 est.)

Sanitation facility access:

improved:

urban: 86.7% of population

rural: 77.7% of population

total: 82.6% of population

unimproved:

urban: 13.3% of population

rural: 22.3% of population

total: 17.4% of population (2015 est.)

HIV/AIDS—adult prevalence rate: 0.42% (2014 est.)

country comparison to the world: 74

HIV/AIDS—people living with HIV/AIDS: 23,000 (2014 est.)

country comparison to the world: 75

HIV/AIDS—deaths: 1,200 (2014 est.)

country comparison to the world: 64

Major infectious diseases: *degree of risk:* high

food or waterborne diseases: bacterial diarrhea, hepatitis A, and typhoid fever

vectorborne diseases: dengue fever and malaria (2013)

Obesity—adult prevalence rate: 16.3% (2014)

country comparison to the world: 106

Children under the age of 5 years underweight: 7.1% (2012)

country comparison to the world: 76

Education expenditures: 5.9% of GDP (2013)

Literacy: *definition:* age 15 and over can read and write

total population: 88.5%

male: 88.4%

female: 88.6% (2015 est.)

School life expectancy (primary to tertiary education): *total:* 11 years

male: 11 years

female: 12 years (2014)

Child labor—children ages 5–14: *total number:* 280,809

percentage: 16% (2002 est.)

Unemployment, youth ages 15–24: *total:* 8%

male: 5.5%

female: 13.8% (2011 est.)

country comparison to the world: 113

GOVERNMENT

Country name: *conventional long form:* Republic of Honduras

conventional short form: Honduras

local long form: Republica de Honduras

local short form: Honduras

etymology: the name means "depths" in Spanish and refers to the deep anchorage in the northern Bay of Trujillo

Government type: presidential republic

Capital: *name:* Tegucigalpa

Geographic coordinates: 14 06 N, 87 13 W

time difference: UTC-6 (1 hour behind Washington, DC during Standard Time)

daylight saving time: none scheduled for 2013

Administrative divisions: 18 departments (departamentos, singular—departamento); Atlantida, Choluteca, Colon, Comayagua, Copan, Cortes, El Paraiso, Francisco Morazan, Gracias a Dios, Intibuca, Islas de la Bahia, La Paz, Lempira, Ocotepeque, Olancho, Santa Barbara, Valle, Yoro

Independence: 15 September 1821 (from Spain)

National holiday: Independence Day, 15 September (1821)

Constitution: several previous; latest approved 11 January 1982, effective 20 January 1982; amended many times, last in 2012; note—in 2015, the Honduran Supreme Court struck down several constitutional articles on presidential term limits (2016)

Legal system: civil law system

International law organization participation: accepts compulsory ICJ jurisdiction with reservations; accepts ICCt jurisdiction

Citizenship: *citizenship by birth:* yes

citizenship by descent: yes

dual citizenship recognized: yes

residency requirement for naturalization: 1 to 3 years

Suffrage: 18 years of age; universal and compulsory

Executive branch: *chief of state:* President Juan Orlando HERNANDEZ Alvarado (since 27 January 2014); Vice Presidents Ricardo ALVAREZ, Rossana GUEVARA, and Lorena HERRERA (since 27 January 2014); note—the president is both chief of state and head of government

head of government: President Juan Orlando HERNANDEZ Alvarado (since 27 January 2014); Vice Presidents Ricardo ALVAREZ, Rossana GUEVARA, and Lorena HERRERA (since 27 January 2014)

cabinet: Cabinet appointed by president

elections/appointments: president directly elected by simple majority popular vote for a single 4-year term; election last held on 24 November 2013 (next to be held in November 2017)

election results: Juan Orlando HERNANDEZ Alvarado elected president; percent of vote—Juan Orlando HERNANDEZ Alvarado (PNH) 36.9%, Xiomara CASTRO (LIBRE) 28.8%, Mauricio VILLEDA (PL) 20.3%, Salvador NASRALLA (PAC) 13.4%, other 0.6%

Legislative branch: *description:* unicameral National Congress or Congreso Nacional (128 seats; members directly elected in multi-seat constituencies by proportional representation vote; members serve 4-year terms)

elections: last held on 24 November 2013 (next to be held in November 2017)

election results: percent of vote by party—PNH 33.6%, LIBRE 27.5%, PL 17.0%, PAC 15.2%, PINU 1.9%, UD 1.7%, DC 1.6%, other 1.5%; seats by party—PNH 48, LIBRE 37, PL 27, PAC 13, PINU 1, UD 1, DC 1

Judicial branch: *highest court(s):* Supreme Court of Justice or Corte Suprema de Justicia (15 principal judges—including the court president—and 7 alternates; court organized into civil, criminal, and labor chambers); note—the court has both judicial and constitutional jurisdiction

judge selection and term of office: court president elected by his peers; judges elected by the National Congress from candidates proposed by the Nominating Board, a diverse 7-member group of judicial officials, other government and non-government officials selected by each of their organizations; judges elected by Congress for renewable, 7-year terms

subordinate courts: courts of appeal; courts of first instance; peace courts

Political parties and leaders: Anti-Corruption Party or PAC [Salvador NASRALLA]

Christian Democratic Party or DC [Felicito AVILA Ordonez]

Democratic Unification Party or UD [Cesar HAM]

Freedom and Refounding Party or LIBRE [Jose Manuel ZELAYA Rosales]

Liberal Party or PL [Mauricio VILLEDA Bermudez]

National Party of Honduras or PNH [Gladys Aurora LOPEZ]

Social Democratic Innovation and Unity Party or PI NU [Jorge Rafael AGUI LAR Paredes]

Political pressure groups and leaders: Beverage and Related Industries Syndicate or STIBYS

Committee for the Defense of Human Rights in Honduras or CODEH

Commiittee of the Relatives of the Disappeared in Honduras or COFADEH

Confederation of Honduran Workers or CTH

Coordinating Committee of Popular Organizations or CCOP

General Workers Confederation or CGT

Honduran Council of Private Enterprise or COHEP

National Association of Honduran Campesinos or ANACH

National Union of Campesinos or UNC

Popular Bloc or BP

United Confederation of Honduran Workers or CUTH

United Farm Workers' Movement of the Aguan OR MUCA

International organization participation: BCIE, CACM, CD, CELAC, EITI (candidate country), FAO, G-11, G-77, IADB, IAEA, IBRD, ICAO, ICCt, ICRM, IDA, IFAD, IFC, IFRCS, ILO, IMF, IMO, Interpol, IOC (suspended), IOM, IPU, ISO (subscriber), ITSO, ITU, ITUC (NGOs), LAES, LAIA (observer), MIGA, MINURSO, MINUS-TAH, NAM, OAS, OPANAL, OPCW, Pacific Alliance (observer), PCA, Petrocaribe, SICA, UN, UNCTAD, UNESCO, UNIDO, Union Latina, UNWTO, UPU, WCO (suspended), WFTU (NGOs), WHO, WIPO, WMO, WTO

Diplomatic representation in the US: *chief of mission:* Ambassador Jorge Alberto MILLA Reyes (since 21 May 2014)

chancery: Suite 4-M, 3007 Tilden Street NW, Washington, DC 20008

telephone: [1] (202) 966-2604

FAX: [1] (202) 966-9751

consulate(s): Dallas, McAllen (TX0

consulate(s) general: Atlanta, Chicago, Houston, Los Angeles, Miami, New Orleans, New York, San Francisco

Diplomatic representation from the US: *chief of mission:* Ambassador James D. NEALON (since 21 August 2014)

embassy: Avenida La Paz, Apartado Postal No.3453, Tegucigalpa

mailing address: American Embassy, APO AA 34022, Tegucigalpa

telephone: [504] 2236-9320, 2238-5114

FAX: [504] 2236-9037

Flag description: three equal horizontal bands of blue (top), white, and blue, with five blue, five-pointed stars arranged in an X pattern centered in the white band; the stars represent the members of the former Federal Republic of Central America: Costa Rica, El Salvador, Guatemala, Honduras, and Nicaragua; the blue bands symbolize the Pacific Ocean and the Caribbean Sea; the white band represents the land between the two bodies of water and the peace and prosperity of its people

note: similar to the flag of El Salvador, which features a round emblem encircled by the words REPUBLICA DE EL SALVADOR EN LA AMERICA CENTRAL centered in the white band; also similar to the flag of Nicaragua, which features a triangle encircled by the words REPUB-LICA DE NICARAGUA on top and AMERICA CENTRAL on the bottom, centered in the white band

National symbol(s): scarlet macaw, white-tailed deer; national colors: blue, white

National anthem: *name:* "Himno Nacional de Honduras" (National Anthem of Honduras)

lyrics/music: Augusto Constancio COELLO/Carlos HARTLING

note: adopted 1915; the anthem's seven verses chronicle Honduran history; on official occasions, only the chorus and last verse are sung

ECONOMY

Economy—Overview: Honduras, the second poorest country in Central America, suffers from extraordinarily unequal distribution of income, as well as high underemployment. While historically dependent on the export of bananas and coffee, Honduras has diversified its export base to include apparel and automobile wire harnessing. Honduras's economy depends heavily on US trade and remittances. The US-Central America-Dominican Republic Free Trade Agreement came into force in 2006 and has helped foster foreign direct investment, but physical and political insecurity, as well as crime and perceptions of corruption, may deter potential investors; about 15% of foreign direct investment is from US firms.

The economy registered modest economic growth of 2.6%-4.0% from 2010 to 2015, insufficient to improve living standards for the nearly 65% of the population in poverty. in 2015, Honduras faced rising public debt but its economy has performed better than expected due to low oil prices and improved investor confidence. The IMF continues to monitor the three-year standby arrangement

signed in December 2014, aimed at easing Honduras's poor fiscal position.

GDP (purchasing power parity): $41.06 billion (2015 est.)

$39.62 billion (2014 est.)

$38.43 billion (2013 est.)

note: data are in 2015 US dollars

country comparison to the world: 112

GDP (official exchange rate): $20.3 billion (2015 est.)

GDP—real growth rate: 3.6% (2015 est.)

3.1% (2014 est.)

2.8% (2013 est.)

country comparison to the world: 78

GDP—per capita (PPP): $4,900 (2015 est.)

$4,800 (2014 est.)

$4,700 (2013 est.)

note: data are in 2015 US dollars

country comparison to the world: 172

Gross national saving: 18.8% of GDP (2015 est.)

14.4% of GDP (2014 est.)

10.4% of GDP (2013 est.)

country comparison to the world: 90

GDP—composition, by end use:

household consumption: 81.6%

government consumption: 15.7%

investment in fixed capital: 23.5%

investment in inventories: -0.2%

exports of goods and services: 44.4%

imports of goods and services: -65% (2015 est.)

GDP—composition, by sector of origin:

agriculture: 13.9%

industry: 26.4%

services: 59.7% (2015 est.)

Agriculture—products: bananas, coffee, citrus, corn, African palm; beef; timber; shrimp, tilapia, lobster, sugar, oriental vegetables

Industries: sugar, coffee, woven and knit apparel, wood products, cigars

Industrial production growth rate: 3.3% (2015 est.)

country comparison to the world: 76

Labor force: 3.647 million (2015 est.)

country comparison to the world: 97

Labor force—by occupation: *agriculture:* 39.2%

industry: 20.9%

services: 39.8% (2005 est.)

Unemployment rate: 4.1% (2015 est.)

4.3% (2014 est.)

note: about one-third of the people are underemployed

country comparison to the world: 38

Population below poverty line: 60% (2010 est.)

Household income or consumption by percentage share: *lowest:* 10%: 0.4%

highest: 10%: 42.4% (2009 est.)

Distribution of family income—Gini Index:

57.7 (2007)

53.8 (2003)

country comparison to the world: 9

Budget: *revenues:* $3.434 billion

expenditures: $4.188 billion (2015 est.)

Taxes and other revenues: 17.2% of GDP (2015 est.)

country comparison to the world: 177

Budget surplus (+) or deficit (–): -3.8% of GDP (2015 est.)

country comparison to the world: 140

Public debt: 47.4% of GDP (2015 est.) 43.4% of GDP (2014 est.)

country comparison to the world: 89

Fiscal year: calendar year

Inflation rate (consumer prices): 3.2% (2015 est.) 6.1% (2014 est.)

country comparison to the world: 142

Central bank discount rate: 6.25% (31 December 2010)

country comparison to the world: 62

Commercial bank prime lending rate: 17.3% (31 December 2015 est.) 20.61% (31 December 2014 est.)

country comparison to the world: 26

Stock of narrow money: $2.167 billion (31 December 2015 est.) $2.105 billion (31 December 2014 est.)

country comparison to the world: 124

Stock of broad money: $8.087 billion (31 December 2015 est.) $7.538 billion (31 December 2014 est.)

country comparison to the world: 113

Stock of domestic credit: $12.24 billion (31 December 2015 est.) $11.41 billion (31 December 2014 est.)

country comparison to the world: 100

Market value of publicly traded shares: $NA

Current account balance: -$1.291 billion (2015 est.) -$1.444 billion (2014 est.)

country comparison to the world: 132

Exports: $7.759 billion (2015 est.) $8.072 billion (2014 est.)

country comparison to the world: 99

Exports—commodities: coffee, apparel, coffee, shrimp, automobile wire harnesses, cigars, bananas, gold, palm oil, fruit, lobster, lumber

Exports—partners: US 36%, Germany 8.7%, El Salvador 8.5%, Guatemala 6%, Nicaragua 5.6%, Netherlands 4.1% (2015)

Imports: $10.9 billion (2015 est.) $11.07 billion (2014 est.)

country comparison to the world: 94

Imports—commodities: communications equipment, machinery and transport, industrial raw materials, chemical products, fuels, foods tuffs

Imports—partners: US 35.2%, China 13.6%, Guatemala 9.2%, Mexico 6.6%, El Salvador 5.1% (2015)

Reserves of foreign exchange and gold: $3.543 billion (31 December 2015 est.) $3.458 billion (31 December 2014 est.)

country comparison to the world: 104

Debt—external: $7.041 billion (31 December 2014 est.) $6.831 billion (31 December 2013 est.)

country comparison to the world: 118

Exchange rates: lempiras (HNL) per US dollar— 22.28 (2015 est.) 21.137 (2014 est.) 21.137 (2013 est.) 19.64 (2012 est.) 18.895 (2011 est.)

ENERGY

Electricity—production: 7.309 billion kWh (2012 est.)

country comparison to the world: 107

Electricity—consumption: 5.036 billion kWh (2012 est.)

country comparison to the world: 116

Electricity—exports: 79 million kWh (2012 est.)

country comparison to the world: 80

Electricity—imports: 76 million kWh (2012 est.)

country comparison to the world: 98

Electricity—installed generating capacity: 1.877 million kW (2012 est.)

country comparison to the world: 110

Electricity—from fossil fuels: 60.9% of total installed capacity (2012 est.)

country comparison to the world: 131

Electricity—from nuclear fuels: 0% of total installed capacity (2012 est.)

country comparison to the world: 109

Electricity—from hydroelectric plants: 28.7% of total installed capacity (2012 est.)

country comparison to the world: 81

Electricity—from other renewable sources: 10.4% of total installed capacity (2012 est.)

country comparison to the world: 35

Crude oil—production: 0 bbl/day (2014 est.)

country comparison to the world: 148

Crude oil—exports: 0 bbl/day (2012 est.)

country comparison to the world: 137

Crude oil—imports: 0 bbl/day (2012 est.)

country comparison to the world: 205

Crude oil—proved reserves: 0 bbl (1 January 2015 est.)

country comparison to the world: 147

Refined petroleum products—production: 0 bbl/day (2012 est.)

country comparison to the world: 195

Refined petroleum products—consumption: 49,000 bbl/day (2013 est.)

country comparison to the world: 102

Refined petroleum products—Exports: 11,600 bbl/day (2012 est.)

country comparison to the world: 85

Refined petroleum products—imports: 62,760 bbl/day (2012 est.)

country comparison to the world: 72

Natural gas—production: 0 cu m (2013 est.)

country comparison to the world: 202

Natural gas—consumption: 0 cu m (2013 est.)

country comparison to the world: 155

Natural gas—exports: 0 cu m (2013 est.)

country comparison to the world: 116

Natural gas—imports: 0 cu m (2013 est.)

country comparison to the world: 209

Natural gas—proved reserves: 0 cu m (1 January 2014 est.)

country comparison to the world: 151

Carbon dioxide emissions from consumption of energy: 10.33 million Mt (2012 est.)

country comparison to the world: 100

COMMUNICATIONS

Telephones—fixed lines: *total subscriptions:* 530,000

subscriptions per 100 inhabitants: 6 (2014 est.)

country comparison to the world: 95

Telephones—mobile cellular: *total:* 7.7 million

subscriptions per 100 inhabitants: 90 (2014 est.)

country comparison to the world: 97

Telephone system: *general assessment:* fixed-line connections are increasing but still limited; competition among multiple providers of mobile-cellular services is contributing to a sharp increase in subscribership

domestic: beginning in 2003, private sub-operators allowed to provide fixed lines in order to expand telephone coverage contributing to a small increase in fixed-line teledensity; mobile-cellular subscribership is roughly 100 per 100 persons

international: country code—504; landing point for both the Americas Region Caribbean Ring System (ARCOS-1) and the MAYA-1 fiber-optic submarine cable system that together provide connectivity to South and Central America, parts of the Caribbean, and the US; satellite earth stations—2 Intelsat (Atlantic Ocean); connected to Central American Microwave System (2011)

Broadcast media: multiple privately owned terrestrial TV networks, supplemented by multiple cable TV networks; Radio Honduras is the lone government-owned radio network; roughly 300 privately owned radio stations (2007)

Radio broadcast stations: AM 241, FM 53, shortwave 12 (1998)

Television broadcast stations: 11 (plus 17 repeaters) (1997)

Internet country code: .hn

Internet hosts: 30,955 (2012)

country comparison to the world: 107

Internet users: *total:* 1.7 million

percent of Population: 19.4% (2014 est.)

country comparison to the world: 103

TRANSPORTATION

Airports: 103 (2013)

country comparison to the world: 54

Airports—with paved runways: *total:* 13 2,438 to 3,047 m: 3 1,524 to 2,437 m: 3 914 to 1,523 m: 4 under 914 m: 3 (2013)

Airports—with unpaved runways: total: 90 1,524 to 2,437 m: 1 914 to 1,523 m: 16 under 914 m: 73 (2013)

Railways: *total:* 699 km

narrow gauge: 164 km 1.067-m gauge; 115 km 1.057-m gauge; 420 km 0.914-m gauge (2014)

country comparison to the world: 100

Roadways: total: 14,742 km

paved: 3,367 km

unpaved: 11,375 km (1,543 km summer only)

note: an additional 8,951 km of non-official roads used by the coffee industry (2012)

country comparison to the world: 123

Waterways: 465 km (most navigable only by small craft) (2012)

country comparison to the world: 84

Merchant marine: *total:* 88

by type: bulk carrier 5, cargo 39, carrier 2, chemical tanker 5, container 1, passenger 4, passenger/cargo 1, petroleum tanker 21, refrigerated cargo 7, roll on/roll off 3

foreign-owned: 47 (Bahrain 5, Canada 1, Chile 1, China 2, Egypt 2, Greece 4, Israel 1, Japan 4,

Lebanon 2, Montenegro 1, Panama 1, Singapore 11, South Korea 6, Taiwan 1, Thailand 2, UAE 1, UK 1, US 1) (2010)
country comparison to the world: 55
Ports and terminals: *major seaport(s):* La Ceiba, Puerto Cortes, San Lorenzo, Tela

MILITARY AND SECURITY

Military branches: Honduran Armed Forces (Fuerzas Armadas de Honduras, FFAA): Army, Navy (includes Naval Infantry), Honduran Air Force (Fuerza Aerea Hondurena, FAH) (2012)
Military service age and obligation: 18 years of age for voluntary 2- to 3-year military service; no conscription (2012)
Military expenditures:
1.05% of GDP (2012)
1.13% of GDP (2011)

1.05% of GDP (2010)
country comparison to the world: 96

TRANSNATIONAL ISSUES

Disputes—international: International Court of Justice (ICJ) ruled on the delimitation of "bolsones" (disputed areas) along the El Salvador-Honduras border in 1992 with final settlement by the parties in 2006 after an Organization of American States survey and a further ICJ ruling in 2003; the 1992 ICJ ruling advised a tripartite resolution to a maritime boundary in the Gulf of Fonseca with consideration of Honduran access to the Pacific; El Salvador continues to claim tiny Conejo Island, not mentioned in the ICJ ruling, off Honduras in the Gulf of Fonseca; Honduras claims the Belizean-administered Sapodilla Cays off the coast of Belize in its constitution, but

agreed to a joint ecological park around the cays should Guatemala consent to a maritime corridor in the Caribbean under the OAS-sponsored 2002 Belize-Guatemala Differendum
Refugees and internally displaced persons: *IDPs:* 174,000 (violence, extortion, threats, forced recruitment by urban gangs) (2015)
Illicit drugs: transshipment point for drugs and narcotics; illicit producer of cannabis, cultivated on small plots and used principally for local consumption; corruption is a major problem; some money-laundering activity

HONG KONG

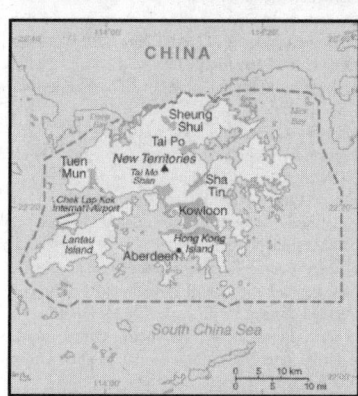

INTRODUCTION

Background: Occupied by the UK in 1841, Hong Kong was formally ceded by China the following year; various adjacent lands were added later in the 19th century. Pursuant to an agreement signed by China and the UK on 19 December 1984, Hong Kong became the Hong Kong Special Administrative Region of the People's Republic of China on 1 July 1997. In this agreement, China promised that, under its "one country, two systems" formula, China's socialist economic system would not be imposed on Hong Kong and that Hong Kong would enjoy a "high degree of autonomy" in all matters except foreign and defense affairs for the subsequent 50 years.

GEOGRAPHY

Location: Eastern Asia, bordering the South China Sea and China
Geographic coordinates: 22 15 N, 114 10 E
Map references: Southeast Asia
Area: *total:* 1,108 sq km
land: 1,073 sq km

water: 35 sq km
country comparison to the world: 184
Area—comparative: six times the size of Washington, DC
Land boundaries: *total:* 33 km
regional border: China 33 km
Coastline: 733 km
Maritime claims: *territorial sea:* 3 nm
Climate: subtropical monsoon; cool and humid in winter, hot and rainy from spring through summer, warm and sunny in fall
Terrain: hilly to mountainous with steep slopes; lowlands in north
Elevation: *mean elevation:* NA
elevation extremes: lowest point: South China Sea 0 m
highest point: Tai Mo Shan 958 m
Natural resources: outstanding deepwater harbor, feldspar
Land use: *agricultural land:* 5%
arable land: 3.2%
permanent crops: 0.9%
permanent pasture: 0.9%
forest: 0%
other: 95% (2011 est.)
Irrigated land: 10 sq km (2012)
Natural hazards: occasional typhoons
Environment—current issues: air and water pollution from rapid urbanization
Environment—international agreements: *party to:* Marine Dumping (associate member), Ship Pollution (associate member)
Geography—note: composed of more than 200 islands

PEOPLE AND SOCIETY

Nationality: *noun:* Chinese/Hong Konger
adjective: Chinese/Hong Kong
Ethnic groups: Chinese 93.1%, Indonesian 1.9%, Filipino 1.9%, other 3% (2011 est.)

Languages: Cantonese (official) 89.5%, English (official) 3.5%, Putonghua (Mandarin) 1.4%, other Chinese dialects 4%, other 1.6% (2011 est.)
Religions: eclectic mixture of local religions 90%, Christian 10%
Population: 7,141,106 (July 2015 est.)
country comparison to the world: 103
Age structure: *0–14 years:* 12.11% (male 458,458/female 406,506)
15–24 years: 11.13% (male 410,701/female 383,902)
25–54 years: 46.16% (male 1,408,524/female 1,887,927)
55–64 years: 15.26% (male 531,684/female 557,904)
65 years and over: 15.34% (male 516,255/female 579,245) (2015 est.)
Dependency ratios: *total dependency ratio:* 37%
youth dependency ratio: 16.4%
elderly dependency ratio: 20.6%
potential support ratio: 4.8% (2015 est.)
Median age: *total:* 43.6 years
male: 43 years
female: 44 years (2015 est.)
country comparison to the world: 12
Population growth rate: 0.38% (2015 est.)
country comparison to the world: 166
Birth rate: 9.23 births/1,000 population (2015 est.)
country comparison to the world: 206
Death rate: 7.07 deaths/1,000 population (2015 est.)
country comparison to the world: 131
Net migration rate: 1.68 migrant(s)/1,000 population (2015 est.)
country comparison to the world: 55
Urbanization: *urban Population:* 100% of total population (2015)
rate of urbanization: 0.74% annual rate of change (2010–15 est.)
Major urban areas—Population: Hong Kong 7.26 million (2014)
Sex ratio: *at birth:* 1.12 male(s)/female

0–14 years: 1.13 male(s)/female
15–24 years: 1.07 male(s)/female
25–54 years: 0.75 male(s)/female
55–64 years: 0.95 male(s)/female
65 years and over: 0.89 male(s)/female
total population: 0.87 male(s)/female (2015 est.)
Mother's mean age at first birth: 29.8 (2008 est.)
Infant mortality rate: *total:* 2.73 deaths/1,000 live births
male: 2.96 deaths/1,000 live births
female: 2.46 deaths/1,000 live births (2015 est.)
country comparison to the world: 215
Life expectancy at birth: *total population:* 82.86 years
male: 80.24 years
female: 85.78 years (2015 est.)
country comparison to the world: 7
Total fertility rate: 1.18 children born/woman (2015 est.)
country comparison to the world: 221
Contraceptive prevalence rate: 79.5% (2007)
HIV/AIDS—people living with HIV/AIDS: NA
HIV/AIDS—deaths: NA
Education expenditures: 3.6% of GDP (2014)
country comparison to the world: 124
School life expectancy (primary to tertiary education): *total:* 16 years
male: 16 years
female: 16 years (2014)
Unemployment, youth ages 15–24: *total:* 9.4%
male: 11.3%
female: 7.8% (2013 est.)
country comparison to the world: 106

GOVERNMENT

Country name: *conventional long form:* Hong Kong Special Administrative Region
conventional short form: Hong Kong
local long form: Heung Kong Takpit Hangching Ku (Eitel/Dyer-Ball); Xianggang Tebie Xingzhengqu (Hanyu Pinyin)
local short form: Heung Kong (Eitel/Dyer-Ball); Xianggang (Hanyu Pinyin)
abbreviation: HK
etymology: probably an imprecise phonetic rendering of the Cantonese name meaning "fragrant harbor"
Dependency status: special administrative region of China
Government type: presidential limited democracy; a special administrative region of the PRC
Administrative divisions: none (special administrative region of China)
Independence: none (special administrative region of China)
National holiday: National Day (Anniversary of the Founding of the People's Republic of China), 1 October (1949); note—1 July 1997 is celebrated as Hong Kong Special Administrative Region Establishment Day
Constitution: several previous (governance documents while under British authority); latest drafted April 1988 to February 1989, approved March 1990, effective 1 July 1997 (Basic Law of the Hong Kong Special Administrative Region of the People's Republic of China serves as the constitution);

note—since 1990, China's National People's Congress has interpreted specific articles of the Basic Law (2016)
Legal system: mixed legal system of common law based on the English model and Chinese customary law (in matters of family and land tenure)
Citizenship: see China
Suffrage: 18 years of age in direct elections for half of the Legislative Council seats and all of the seats in 18 district councils; universal for permanent residents living in the territory of Hong Kong for the past 7 years; note -in indirect elections, suffrage is limited to about 220,000 members of functional constituencies for the other half of the legislature and a 1,200-member election committee for the chief executive drawn from broad sectoral groupings, central government bodies, municipal organizations, and elected Hong Kong officials
Executive branch: *chief of state:* President of China XI Jinping (since 14 March 2013)
head of government: Chief Executive LEUNG Chun-ying [C.Y. LEUNG] (since 1 July 2012)
cabinet: Executive Council or ExCo appointed by the chief executive
elections/appointments: president indirectly elected by National People's Congress for a 5-year term (eligible for a second term); election last held on 5–17 March 2013 (next to be held in March 2018); chief executive indirectly elected by the Election Committee and appointed by the Central People's Government for a 5-year term (eligible for a second term); LEUNG Chun-ying [C. Y. LEUNG] elected chief executive on 25 March 2012 and took office on 1 July 2012 (next to be held in March 2017)
election results: LEUNG Chun-ying elected chief executive; Election Committee vote—LEUNG Chun-ying 689, Henry TANG 285, Albert HO 76
note: the Legislative Council voted in June 2010 to expand the electoral committee to 1,200 seats for the 2012 election
Legislative branch: *description:* unicameral Legislative Council or LegCo (70 seats; 35 members directly elected in multi-seat constituencies by party-list proportional representation vote; 30 members indirectly elected by the approximately 220,000 members of various functional constituencies based on a variety of methods; five at large "super-seat" members directed elected by all of Hong Kong's eligible voters who do not participate in a functional constituency; members serve 4-year terms)
elections: last held on 9 September 2012; by-election to fill a vacancy held on 28 February 2016; (next general election to be held on 4 September 2016)
election results: percent of vote by block—pro-democracy 56.2%; pro-Beijing 42.7%, independent 1.1%; seats by block/party—pro-Beijing 43 (DAB 13, BPA 7, FTU 6, Liberal Party 5, NPP 2, other 10); pro-democracy 27 (Democratic Party 6, Civic Party 6, Labor Party 4, PP 3, LSD 1, ADPL 1, PTU 1, Neo Democrats 1, NWSC 1, independent democrats 3)
Judicial branch: *highest court(s):* Court of Final Appeal (consists of the chief justice, 3 permanent

judges and 20 non-permanent judges); note—a sitting bench consists of the chief justice and 3 permanent and 1 non-permanent judges
judge selection and term of office: all judges appointed by the Hong Kong Chief Executive upon the recommendation of the Judicial Officers Recommendation Commission, an independent body consisting of the Secretary for Justice and other judges, judicial and legal professionals; permanent judges appointed until normal retirement at age 65, but can be extended; non-permanent judges appointed for renewable 3-year terms without age limit
subordinate courts: High Court (consists of the Court of Appeal and Court of First Instance); District Courts (includes Family and Land Courts); magistrates' courts; specialized tribunals
Political parties and leaders: *parties:* Association for Democracy and People's Livelihood or ADPL [Rosanda MOK Ka-han]
Business and Professional Alliance or BPA [Andrew LEUNG Kwan-yuen]
Civic Party [Audrey EU]
Democratic Alliance for the Betterment and Progress of Hong Kong or DAB [Starry LEE Wai-king]
Democratic Party [Emily LAU]
Federation of Trade Unions or FTU [Stanley NG Chau-pei]
Labor Party [Suzanne WU Shui-shan]
League of Social Democrats or LSD [Avery NGMan-yuen]
Liberal Party [Felix CHUN G Kwok-pan]
Neighborhood and Workers Service Center or NWSC [LEUNG Yui-chung]
Neo Dem ocrats [collective leadership]
New People's Party or NPP [Regina I P Lau Su-yee]
People Power or PP [Erica YUEN Mi-ming]
others: Professional Commons (think tank) [Charles Peter MOK] Professional Teachers Union or PTU
note: political blocks include: pro-democracy—ADPL, Civic Party, Democratic Party, Labor Party, LSD, PP, Professional Commons; pro-Beijing—DAB, FTU, Liberal Party, NPP, BPA; there is no political party ordinance, so there are no registered political parties; politically active groups register as societies or companies
Political pressure groups and leaders: Chinese General Chamber of Commerce (pro-China)
Chinese Manufacturers' Association of Hong Kong
Civic Act-up [Cyd HO Sau-lan, Legislative Council of Hong Kong member] (pro-democracy)
Federation of Hong Kong Industries
Hong Kong Alliance in Support of the Patriotic Democratic Movement in China [Albert HO, chairman]
Hong Kong and Kowloon Trade Union Council (pro-Taiwan)
Hong Kong General Chamber of Commerce
Hong Kong Professional Teachers' Union [FUNG Wai-wah, president]
International organization participation: ADB, APEC, BIS, FATF, ICC (national committees), IHO, IMF, IMO (associate), Interpol (subbureau),

IOC, ISO (correspondent), ITUC (NGOs), UN WTO (associate), UPU, WCO, WMO, WTO

Diplomatic representation in the US: none (Special Administrative Region of China); Hong Kong Economic and Trade Office (HKETO) carries out normal liaison and communication with the US Government and other US entities

commissioner: Clement C.M. LEUNG

office: 1520 18th Street NW, Washington, DC 20036

telephone: [1] 202 331-8947

FAX: [1] 202 331-8958

HKETO offices: New York, San Francisco

Diplomatic representation from the US: *chief of mission:* Consul General Clifford A. HART Jr. (since 30 July 2013); note—also accredited to Macau

consulate(s) general: 26 Garden Road, Hong Kong

mailing address: Unit 8000, Box 1, DPO AP 96521–0006

telephone: [852] 2523-9011

FAX: [852] 2845-1598

Flag description: red with a stylized, white, five-petal Bauhinia flower in the center; each petal contains a small, red, five-pointed star in its middle; the red color is the same as that on the Chinese flag and represents the motherland; the fragrant Bauhinia—developed in Hong Kong the late 19th century—has come to symbolize the region; the five stars echo those on the flag of China

National symbol(s): orchid tree flower; national colors: red, white

National anthem: *note:* as a Special Administrative Region of China, "Yiyongjun Jinxingqu" is the official anthem (see China)

ECONOMY

Economy—overview: Hong Kong has a free market economy, highly dependent on international trade and finance—the value of goods and services trade, including the sizable share of re-exports, is about four times GDP. Hong Kong has no tariffs on imported goods, and it levies excise duties on only four commodities, whether imported or produced locally: hard alcohol, tobacco, hydrocarbon oil, and methyl alcohol. There are no quotas or dumping laws. Hong Kong continues to link its currency closely to the US dollar, maintaining an arrangement established in 1983.

Hong Kong's open economy left it exposed to the global economic slowdown that began in 2008. Although increasing integration with China through trade, tourism, and financial links helped it to make an initial recovery more quickly than many observers anticipated, its continued reliance on foreign trade and investment leaves it vulnerable to renewed global financial market volatility or a slowdown in the global economy.

The Hong Kong Government is promoting the Special Administrative Region (SAR) as the site for Chinese renminbi (RMB) internationalization. Hong Kong residents are allowed to establish RMB-denominated savings accounts; RMB-denominated corporate and Chinese government bonds have been issued in Hong Kong; and RMBtrade settlement is allowed. The territory far exceeded the RMBconversion quota set by Beijing for trade settlements in 2010 due to the growth of earnings from exports to the mainland. RMB deposits grew to roughly 9.4% of total system deposits in Hong Kong by the end of 2015. The government is pursuing efforts to introduce additional use of RMB in Hong Kong financial markets and is seeking to expand the RMB quota.

The mainland has long been Hong Kong's largest trading partner, accounting for about half of Hong Kong's total trade by value. Hong Kong's natural resources are limited, and food and raw materials must be imported. As a result of China's easing of travel restrictions, the number of mainland tourists to the territory has surged from 4.5 million in 2001 to 47.3 million in 2014, outnumbering visitors from all other countries combined. Mainland visitors to Hong Kong declined 3% in 2015 to approximately 45.7 million, reflecting an overall drop of 2.5% in total visitors to Hong Kong. Hong Kong has also established itself as the premier stock market for Chinese firms seeking to list abroad. In 2015, mainland Chinese companies constituted about 51% of the firms listed on the Hong Kong Stock Exchange and accounted for about 62.1% of the Exchange's market capitalization. During the past decade, as Hong Kong's manufacturing industry moved to the mainland, its service industry has grown rapidly. in 2014, Hong Kong and China signed a new agreement on achieving basic liberalization of trade in services in Guangdong Province under the Closer Economic Partnership Agreement, adopted in 2003 to forge closer ties between Hong Kong and the mainland. The new measures, effective from March 2015, cover a negative list and a most-favored treatment provision, and will improve access to the mainland's service sector for Hong Kong-based companies. Credit expansion and a tight housing supply have caused Hong Kong property prices to rise rapidly; consumer prices increased 4.4% in 2014, but slowed to 2.9% in 2015. Lower- and middle-income segments of the population are increasingly unable to afford adequate housing. Hong Kong's economic integration with the mainland continues to be most evident in the banking and finance sector. Initiatives like the Hong Kong-Shanghai Stock Connect, the Mutual Recognition of Funds, and The Hong Kong Shanghai Gold Connect are all important steps towards opening up the Mainland's capital markets and has reinforced Hong Kong's leading role as China's offshore RMB market. Additional connect schemes from bonds to commodities and other investment products are also under exploration by Hong Kong authorities.

GDP (purchasing power parity): $414.6 billion (2015 est.)

$405 billion (2014 est.)

$394.6 billion (2013 est.)

note: data are in 2015 US dollars

country comparison to the world: 45

GDP (official exchange rate): $309.9 billion (2015 est.)

GDP—real growth rate: 2.4% (2015 est.)

2.6% (2014 est.)

3.1% (2013 est.)

country comparison to the world: 124

GDP—per capita (PPP): $56,700 (2015 est.)

$55,700 (2014 est.)

$54,600 (2013 est.)

note: data are in 2015 US dollars

country comparison to the world: 18

Gross national saving: 24.8% of GDP (2015 est.)

25.1% of GDP (2014 est.)

25.5% of GDP (2013 est.)

country comparison to the world: 49

GDP—composition, by end use:

household consumption: 65.7%

government consumption: 9.5%

investment in fixed capital: 22.9%

investment in inventories: 0.2%

exports of goods and services: 201.6%

imports of goods and services: -199.9% (2015 est.)

GDP—composition, by sector of origin:

agriculture: 0.1%

industry: 7.2%

services: 92.8% (2015 est.)

Agriculture—products: fresh vegetables and fruit; poultry, pork; fish

Industries: textiles, clothing, tourism, banking, shipping, electronics, plastics, toys, watches, clocks

Industrial production growth rate: 1.2% (2015 est.)

country comparison to the world: 137

Labor force: 3.883 million (2015 est.)

country comparison to the world: 93

Labor force—by occupation: *manufacturing:* 3.8%

construction: 2.8%

wholesale and retail trade, restaurants, and hotels: 53.3%

financing, insurance, and real estate: 12.5%

transport and communications: 10.1%

community and social services: 17.1%

note: above data exclude public sector (2013 est.)

Unemployment rate: 2.9% (2015 est.)

3.2% (2014 est.)

country comparison to the world: 20

Population below poverty line: 19.6% (2012 est.)

Household income or consumption by percentage share: *lowest:* 10%: NA%

highest: 10%: NA%

Distribution of family income—Gini Index: 53.7 (2011)

53.3 (2007)

country comparison to the world: 11

Budget: *revenues:* $63.72 billion

expenditures: $62.7 billion (2015 est.)

Taxes and other revenues: 20.7% of GDP (2015 est.)

country comparison to the world: 150

Budget surplus (+) or deficit (–): 0.3% of GDP (2015 est.)

country comparison to the world: 23

Public debt: 39.5% of GDP (2015 est.)

39.5% of GDP (2014 est.)

country comparison to the world: 116

Fiscal year: 1 April—31 March

Inflation rate (consumer prices): 3% (2015 est.)

4.4% (2014 est.)

country comparison to the world: 139
Central bank discount rate: 0.5% (31 December 2013)
0.5% (31 December 2012)
country comparison to the world: 130
Commercial bank prime lending rate: 5.1% (31 December 2015 est.)
5% (31 December 2014 est.)
country comparison to the world: 147
Stock of narrow money: $252.1 billion (31 December 2015 est.)
$220.3 billion (31 December 2014 est.)
country comparison to the world: 18
Stock of broad money: $1.576 trillion (31 December 2015 est.)
$1.42 trillion (31 December 2014 est.)
country comparison to the world: 12
Stock of domestic credit: $749.3 billion (31 December 2015 est.)
$687.7 billion (31 December 2014 est.)
country comparison to the world: 19
Market value of publicly traded shares: $3.082 trillion (31 December 2013 est.)
$2.814 trillion (31 December 2012)
$2.248 trillion (31 December 2011 est.)
country comparison to the world: 5
Current account balance: $9.395 billion (2015 est.)
$3.787 billion (2014 est.)
country comparison to the world: 23
Exports: $499.4 billion (2015 est.)
$519.3 billion (2014 est.)
country comparison to the world: 8
Exports—commodities: electrical machinery and appliances, textiles, apparel, footwear, watches and clocks, toys, plastics, precious stones, printed material
Exports—partners: China 53.7%, US 9.5% (2015)
Imports: $524.3 billion (2015 est.)
$549.5 billion (2014 est.)
country comparison to the world: 8
Imports—commodities: raw materials and semimanufactures, consumer goods, capital goods, foodstuffs, fuel (most is reexported)
Imports—partners: China 49%, Japan 6.4%, Singapore 6.1%, US 5.2%, South Korea 4.3% (2015)
Reserves of foreign exchange and gold: $341.3 billion (31 December 2015 est.)
$328.5 billion (31 December 2014 est.)
country comparison to the world: 11
Debt—external: $1.29 trillion (31 December 2014 est.)
$1.161 trillion (31 December 2013 est.)
country comparison to the world: 17
Stock of direct foreign investment—at home: $1.838 trillion (31 December 2015 est.)
$1.686 trillion (31 December 2014 est.)
country comparison to the world: 3
Stock of direct foreign investment—abroad: $1.72 trillion (31 December 2015 est.)
$1.597 trillion (31 December 2014 est.)
country comparison to the world: 5
Exchange rates: Hong Kong dollars (HKD) per US dollar—
7.764 (2015 est.)
7.754 (2014 est.)
7.754 (2013 est.)
7.756 (2012 est.)
7.784 (2011 est.)

ENERGY

Electricity—production: 39.97 billion kWh (2013 est.)
country comparison to the world: 58

Electricity—consumption: 44.21 billion kWh (2013 est.)
country comparison to the world: 53
Electricity—exports: 1.65 billion kWh (2013 est.)
country comparison to the world: 48
Electricity—imports: 10.71 billion kWh (2013 est.)
country comparison to the world: 20
Electricity—installed generating capacity: 10.67 million kW (2013 est.)
country comparison to the world: 55
Electricity—from fossil fuels: 100% of total installed capacity (2013 est.)
country comparison to the world: 14
Electricity—from nuclear fuels: 0% of total installed capacity (2013 est.)
country comparison to the world: 108
Electricity—from hydroelectric plants: 0% of total installed capacity (2013 est.)
country comparison to the world: 178
Electricity—from other renewable sources: 0% of total installed capacity (2013 est.)
country comparison to the world: 183
Crude oil—production: 0 bbl/day (2014 est.)
country comparison to the world: 147
Crude oil—exports:
0 bbl/day (2013 est.)
country comparison to the world: 136
Crude oil—imports:
0 bbl/day (2013 est.)
country comparison to the world: 204
Crude oil—proved reserves:
0 bbl (1 January 2015 est.)
country comparison to the world: 146
Refined petroleum products—production: 0 bbl/day (2013 est.)
country comparison to the world: 194
Refined petroleum products—consumption: 360,000 bbl/day (2013 est.)
country comparison to the world: 38
Refined petroleum products—exports: 12,010 bbl/day (2013 est.)
country comparison to the world: 84
Refined petroleum products imports: 345,900 bbl/day (2013 est.)
country comparison to the world: 19
Natural gas—production: 0 cu m (2013 est.)
country comparison to the world: 201
Natural gas—consumption: 2.743 billion cu m (2013 est.)
country comparison to the world: 76
Natural gas—exports: 0 cu m (2013 est.)
country comparison to the world: 115
Natural gas—imports: 2.743 billion cu m (2013 est.)
country comparison to the world: 44
Natural gas—proved reserves: 0 cu m (1 January 2014 est.)
country comparison to the world: 150
Carbon dioxide emissions from consumption of energy: 88.63 million Mt (2012 est.)
country comparison to the world: 42

COMMUNICATIONS

Telephones—fixed lines: *total subscriptions:* 4.43 million

subscriptions per 100 inhabitants: 62 (2014 est.)
country comparison to the world: 36
Telephones—mobile cellular: *total:* 17.4 million
subscriptions per 100 inhabitants: 244 (2014 est.)
country comparison to the world: 60
Telephone system: *general assessment:* modern facilities provide excellent domestic and international services
domestic: microwave radio relay links and extensive fiber-optic network
international: country code—852; multiple international submarine cables provide connections to Asia, US, Australia, the Middle East, and Western Europe; satellite earth stations—3 Intelsat (1 Pacific Ocean and 2 Indian Ocean); coaxial cable to Guangzhou, China (2012)
Broadcast media: 2 commercial terrestrial TV networks each with multiple stations; multi-channel satellite and cable TV systems available; 3 radio networks, one of which is government funded, operate about 15 radio stations (2012)
Radio broadcast stations: AM 6, FM 10, shortwave 0 (2009)
Television broadcast stations: 2 (2 TV networks, each broadcasting on 2 chann els) (2009)
Internet country code: .hk
Internet hosts: 870,041 (2012)
country comparison to the world: 48
Internet users: *total:* 5.6 million
percent of Population: 79.2% (2014 est.)
country comparison to the world: 61

TRANSPORTATION

Airports: 2 (2013)
country comparison to the world: 201
Airports—with paved runways: *total:* 2
over 3,047 m: 1
1,524 to 2,437 m: 1 (2013)
Heliports: 9 (2013)
Roadways: *total:* 2,100 km
paved: 2,100 km (2015)
country comparison to the world: 175
Merchant marine: *total:* 1,644
by type: barge carrier 2, bulk carrier 785, cargo 198, carrier 10, chemical tanker 149, container 288, liquefied gas 31, passenger 4, passenger/cargo 9, petroleum tanker 156, roll on/roll off 5, vehicle carrier 7
foreign-owned: 976 (Bangladesh 1, Belgium 26, Bermuda 20, Canada 77, China 500, Cyprus 3, Denmark 42, France 4, Germany 10, Greece 27, Indonesia 10, Iran 3, Japan 79, Libya 1, Norway 48, Russia 1, Singapore 13, South Korea 3, Switzerland 5, Taiwan 25, UAE 1, UK 33, US 44)
registered in other countries: 341 (Bahamas 3, Bermuda 4, Cambodia 10, Chin a 18, Curacao 1, Cyprus 2, Georgia 3, India 2, Kiribati 2, Liberia 48, Malaysia 8, Malta 4, Marshall Islands 3, NZ 1, Panama 144, Saint Vincent and the Grenadin es 5, Seychelles 1, Sierra Leone 7, Singapore 46, Thailand 1, UK 12, unknown 16) (2010)
country comparison to the world: 5
Ports and terminals: *major seaport(s):* Hong Kong

HUNGARY

INTRODUCTION

Background: Hungary became a Christian kingdom in A.D.1000 and for many centuries served as a bulwark against Ottoman Turkish expansion in Europe. The kingdom eventually became part of the polyglot Austro-Hungarian Empire, which collapsed during World War I. The country fell under communist rule following World War II. In 1956, a revolt and an announced withdrawal from the Warsaw Pact were met with a massive military intervention by Moscow. Under the leadership of Janos KADAR in 1968, Hungary began liberalizing its economy, introducing so-called "Goulash Communism." Hungary held its first multiparty elections in 1990 and initiated a free market economy. It joined NATO in 1999 and the EU five years later.

GEOGRAPHY

Location: Central Europe, northwest of Romania

Geographic coordinates: 47 00 N, 20 00 E

Map references: Europe

Area: *total:* 93,028 sq km
land: 89,608 sq km
water: 3,420 sq km
country comparison to the world: 110

Area—comparative: slightly smaller than Virginia; about the same size as Indiana

Land boundaries: *total:* 2,106 km
border countries (7): Austria 321 km, Croatia 348 km, Romania 424 km, Serbia 164 km, Slovakia 627 km, Slovenia 94 km, Ukraine 128 km

Coastline: 0 km (landlocked)

Maritime claims: none (landlocked)

Climate: temperate; cold, cloudy, humid winters; warm summers

Terrain: mostly flat to rolling plains; hills and low mountains on the Slovakian border

Elevation: *mean elevation:* 143 m

elevation extremes: *lowest point:* Tisza River 78 m

highest point: Kekes 1,014 m

Natural resources: bauxite, coal, natural gas, fertile soils, arable land;

Land use: *agricultural land:* 58.9%
arable land: 48.5%
permanent crops: 2%
permanent pasture: 8.4%
forest: 22.5%
other: 18.6% (2011 est.)

Irrigated land: 1,721 sq km (2012)

Total renewable water resources: 104 cu km (2011)

Freshwater withdrawal (domestic/industrial/agricultural): *total:* 5.58 cu km/yr (12%/83%/5%)
per capita: 555.9 cu m/yr (2007)

Environment—current issues: the upgrading of Hungary's standards in waste management, energy efficiency, and air, soil, and water pollution to meet EU requirements will require large investments

Environment—international agreements: *party to:* Air Pollution, Air Pollution-Nitrogen Oxides, Air Pollution-Persistent Organic Pollutants, Air Pollution-Sulfur 85, Air Pollution-Sulfur 94, Air Pollution-Volatile Organic Compounds, Antarctic Treaty, Biodiversity, Climate Change, Climate Change-Kyoto Protocol, Desertification, Endangered Species, Environmental Modification, Hazardous Wastes, Law of the Sea, Marine Dumping, Ozone Layer Protection, Ship Pollution, Wetlands, Whaling

signed, but not ratified: none of the selected agreements

Geography—note: landlocked; strategic location astride main land routes between Western Europe and Balkan Peninsula as well as between Ukraine and Mediterranean basin; the north-south flowing Duna (Danube) and Tisza Rivers divide the country into three large regions

PEOPLE AND SOCIETY

Nationality: *noun:* Hungarian(s)
adjective: Hungarian

Ethnic groups: Hungarian 85.6%, Roma 3.2%, German 1.9%, other 2.6%, unspecified 14.1%
note: percentages add up to more than 100% because respondents were able to identify more than one ethnic group (2011 est.)

Languages: Hungarian (official) 99.6%, English 16%, German 11.2%, Russian 1.6%, Romanian 1.3%, French 1.2%, other 4.2%

note: shares sum to more than 100% because some respondents gave more than one answer on the census; Hungarian is the mother tongue of 98.9% of Hungarian speakers (2011 est.)

Religions: Roman Catholic 37.2%, Calvinist 11.6%, Lutheran 2.2%, Greek Catholic 1.8%, other 1.9%, none 18.2%, unspecified 27.2% (2011 est.)

Population: 9,897,541 (July 2015 est.)
country comparison to the world: 90

Age structure: *0–14 years:* 14.8% (male 754,729/female 710,394)
15–24 years: 11.44% (male 583,320/female 548,520)
25–54 years: 41.65% (male 2,070,725/female 2,051,695)
55–64 years: 13.87% (male 630,426/female 742,657)
65 years and over: 18.24% (male 677,420/female 1,127,655) (2015 est.)

Dependency ratios: *total dependency ratio:* 47.9%
youth dependency ratio: 21.5%
elderly dependency ratio: 26.3%
potential support ratio: 3.8% (2015 est.)

Median age: *total:* 41.4 years
male: 39.5 years
female: 43.8 years (2015 est.)
country comparison to the world: 33

Population growth rate: -0.22% (2015 est.)
country comparison to the world: 216

Birth rate: 9.16 births/1,000 population (2015 est.)
country comparison to the world: 207

Death rate: 12.73 deaths/1,000 population (2015 est.)
country comparison to the world: 20

Net migration rate: 1.33 migrant(s)/1,000 population (2015 est.)
country comparison to the world: 58

Urbanization: *urban Population:* 71.2% of total population (2015)
rate of urbanization: 0.47% annual rate of change (2010–15 est.)

Major urban areas—Population: BUDAPEST (capital) 1.714 million (2015)

Sex ratio: *at birth:* 1.06 male(s)/female
0–14 years: 1.06 male(s)/female
15–24 years: 1.06 male(s)/female
25–54 years: 1.01 male(s)/female
55–64 years: 0.85 male(s)/female
65 years and over: 0.6 male(s)/female

total Population: 0.91 male(s)/female (2015 est.)
Mother's mean age at first birth: 28.3 (2011 est.)
Maternal mortality rate: 17 deaths/100,000 live births (2015 est.)
country comparison to the world: 135
Infant mortality rate: *total:* 5.02 deaths/1,000 live births
male: 5.3 deaths/1,000 live births
female: 4.74 deaths/1,000 live births (2015 est.)
country comparison to the world: 176
Life expectancy at birth: *total Population:* 75.69 years
male: 71.96 years
female: 79.62 years (2015 est.)
country comparison to the world: 94
Total fertility rate: 1.43 children born/woman (2015 est.)
country comparison to the world: 207
Health expenditures: 8% of GDP (2013)
country comparison to the world: 61

Physicians density: 3.1 physicians/1,000 population (2012)

Hospital bed density: 7.2 beds/1,000 population (2011)

Drinking water source:
improved:
urban: 100% of population
rural: 100% of population
total: 100% of population
unimproved:
urban: 0% of popu lation
rural: 0% of population
total: 0% of population (2015 est.)
Sanitation facility access:
improved:
urban: 97.8% of population
rural: 98.6% of population
total: 98% of population
unimproved:
urban: 2.2% of population
rural: 1.4% of population
total: 2% of population (2015 est.)
HIV/AIDS—adult prevalence rate: NA
HIV/AIDS—people living with HIV/AIDS: NA
HIV/AIDS—deaths: 100 (2013 est.)
country comparison to the world: 107
Major infectious diseases: *degree of risk:* intermediate
vectorborne diseases: tickborne encephalitis (2013)
Obesity—adult prevalence rate: 26% (2014)
country comparison to the world: 37
Education expenditures: 4.6% of GDP (2011)
country comparison to the world: 81
Literacy: *definition:* age 15 and over can read and write
total population: 99.1%
male: 99.1%
female: 99% (2015 est.)
School life expectancy (primary to tertiary education): *total:* 16 years
male: 15 years
female: 16 years (2014)
Unemployment, youth ages 15–24: *total:* 27.2%
male: 26.3%
female: 28.4% (2013 est.)
country comparison to the world: 31

GOVERNMENT

Country name: *conventional long form:* none
conventional short form: Hungary
local long form: none
local short form: Magyarorszag
etymology: the Byzantine Greeks refered to the tribes that arrived on the steppes of Eastern Europe in the 9th century as the "Oungroi," a name that was later Latinized to "Ungri" and which became "Hungari"; the name originally meant an "[alliance of] ten tribes"; the Hungarian name "Magyarorszag" means "Land of the Magyars"; the term may derive from the most prominent of the Hungarian tribes, the Megyer
Government type: parliamentary republic
Capital: *name:* Budapest
Geographic coordinates: 47 30 N, 19 05 E
time difference: UTC + 1 (6 hours ahead of Washington, DC, during Standard Time)
daylight saving time: +1hr, begins last Sunday in March; ends last Sunday in October
Administrative divisions: 19 counties (megyek, singular—megye), 23 cities with county rights (megyei jogu varosok, singular-megyei jogu varos), and 1 capital city (fovaros)
counties: Bacs-Kiskun, Baranya, Bekes, Borsod-Abauj-Zemplen, Csongrad, Fejer, Gyor-Moson-Sopron, Hajdu-Bihar, Heves, Jasz-Nagy kun-Szolnok, Komarom-Esztergom, Nograd, Pest, Somogy, Szabolcs-Szatmar-Bereg, Tolna, Vas, Veszprem, Zala
cities with county rights: Bekescsaba, Debrecen, Dunaujvaros, Eger, Erd, Gyor, Hodmezovasarhely, Kaposvar, Kecskemet, Miskolc, Nagykanizsa, Nyiregyhaza, Pecs, Salgotarjan, Sopron, Szeged, Szekesfehervar, Szekszard, Szolnok, Szombathely, Tatabanya, Veszprem, Zalaegerszeg
capital city: Budapest
Independence: 16 November 1918 (republic proclaimed); notable earlier dates: 25 December 1000 (crowning of King STEPHEN I, traditional founding date); 30 March 1867 (Austro-Hungarian dual monarchy established)
National holiday: Saint Stephen's Day, 20 August; note—commemorates the date when his remains were transferred to Buda (now Budapest)
Constitution: previous 1949 (heavily amended in 1989 following collapse of communism); latest approved 18 April 2011, signed 25 April 2011, effective 1 January 2012; amended several times, last in 2013 (2016)
Legal system: civil legal system influenced by the German model
International law organization participation: accepts compulsory ICJ jurisdiction with reservations; accepts ICCt jurisdiction
Citizenship: *citizenship by birth:* no
citizenship by descent only: at least one parent must be a citizen of Hungary
dual citizenship recognized: yes
residency requirement for naturalization: 8 years
Suffrage: 18 years of age, 16 if married; universal
Executive branch: *chief of state:* Janos ADER (since 10 May 2012)

head of government: Prime Minister Viktor ORBAN (since 29 May 2010)
cabinet: Cabinet of Ministers proposed by the prime minister and appointed by the president
elections/appointments: president indirectly elected by the National Assembly with two-thirds majority vote in first round or simple majority vote in second round for a 5-year term (eligible for a second term); election last held on 2 May 2012 (next to be held by May 2017); prime minister elected by the National Assembly on the recommendation of the president
election results: Janos ADER (Fidesz) elected president; National Assembly vote—262 to 40; Viktor ORBAN (Fidesz) elected prime minister; National Assembly vote—130 to 57 (in 2014)
Legislative branch: *description:* unicameral National Assembly or Orszaggyules (199 seats; 106 members directly elected in single-member constituencies by simple majority vote and 93 members directly elected in a single nationwide constituency by party list proportional representation vote; members serve 4-year terms)
elections: last held on 6 April 2014 (next to be held by April 2018)
election results: percent of vote by party—Fidesz-KDNP 44.5%, Unity 26%, Jobbik 20.5%, LMP 5.3%, other 3.7%; seats by party—Fidesz-KDNP 133, Unity 38, Jobbik 23, LMP 5
Judicial branch: *highest court(s):* Curia or Supreme Judicial Court (consists of the Curia president, vice president, and approximately 76 judges organized into 16 civil chambers, 3 criminal chambers, and 4 administrative chambers); Constitutional Court (consists of 15 judges including the court president and 2 vice-presidents)
judge selection and term of office: Curia president elected from among its members for 9 years by the National Assembly on the recommendation of the president of the republic; other Curia judges appointed by the president upon the recommendation of the National Judicial Council, a separate 15-member administrative body; judge tenure based on interim evaluations until normal retirement age; Constitutional Court judges elected by two-thirds vote of the National Assembly; members serve single renewable 12-year terms with mandatory retirement at age 70
subordinate courts: 5 regional courts of appeal; 19 regional or county courts (including Budapest Metropolitan Court); 20 administrative and labor courts; 111 district or local courts
Political parties and leaders: Christian Democratic People's Party or KDNP [Zsolt SEMJEN]
Democratic Coalition or DK [Ferenc GYURCSANY]
Dialogue for Hungary or PM [Javor BENEDEK, Timea SZABO, co-chairs]
Fidesz-Hungarian Civic Alliance or Fidesz [Viktor ORBAN]
Hungarian Liberal Party or MLP [Gabor FODOR]
Hungarian Socialist Party or MSZP [Jozsef TOBIAS]
Movement for a Better Hungary or Jobbik [Gabor VONA]

Politics Can Be Different or LMP [Andras SCHIFFER, Bernadett SZEL]

Together 2014 or Egyutt [Peter JUHASZ, Peter KONYA, Viktor SZIGETVARI]

Political pressure groups and leaders: Civil Osszefogas Forum ("Civil Unity Forum," nominally independent organization that serves as the steering committee for the pro-government mass organization Bekemenet (Peace March), supporting ORBAN government's policies)

Hungarian Civil Liberties Union (Tarsasag a Szabadsagjogokert) or TASZ (freedom of expression, information privacy)

Hungarian Helsinki Committee (asylum seekers' rights, human rights in law enforcement and the judicial system)

MigSzol (Migrant Solidarity Group of Hungary) (independent advocacy group on migration crisis)

MostMi ("Now Us") [Bori TAKACS, Zsolt VARADY] (Facebook group that was a major participant at anti-government demonstrations in late 2014-early 2015; pro-Europe, anti-establishment movement that blames Fidesz for the state of the country, but also blames all established political parties for perceived political and economic failures since the fall of communism) Okotars (empowerment of civil society in Hungary)

other: Energy Club (Energia Klub)

Greenpeace Hungary (Greenpeace Magyarorszag)

International organization participation: Australia Group, BIS, CD, CE, CEI, CERN, EAPC, EBRD, ECB, EIB, ESA (cooperating state), EU, FAO, G-9, IAEA, IBRD, ICAO, ICC (national committees), ICCt, ICRM, IDA, IEA, IFAD, IFC, IFRCS, ILO, IMF, IMO, IMSO, Interpol, IOC, IOM, IPU, ISO, ITSO, ITU, ITUC (NGOs), MIGA, MINURSO, NATO, NEA, NSG, OAS (observer), OECD, OIF (observer), OPCW, OSCE, PCA, Schengen Convention, SELEC, UN, UNCTAD, UNESCO, UNFICYP, UNHCR, UNIDO, UNIFIL, UNWTO, UPU, WCO, WFTU (NGOs), WHO, WIPO, WMO, WTO, ZC

Diplomatic representation in the US: *chief of mission:* Ambassador Reka SZEMERKENYI (since 23 February 2015)

chancery: 3910 Shoemaker Street NW, Washington, DC 20008

telephone: [1] (202) 362-6730

FAX: [1] (202) 966-8135

consulate(s) general: Los Angeles, New York

consulate(s): Boston

Diplomatic representation from the US: *chief of mission:* Ambassador Colleen Bradley BELL (since 21 January 2015)

embassy: Szabadsag ter 12, H-1054 Budapest

mailing address: pouch: American Embassy Budapest, 5270 Budapest Place, US Department of State,

Washington, DC 20521-5270

telephone: [36] (1) 475-4400

FAX: [36] (1) 475-4764

Flag description: three equal horizontal bands of red (top), white, and green; the flag dates to the national movement of the 18th and 19th centuries, and fuses the medieval colors of the

Hungarian coat of arms with the revolutionary tricolor form of the French flag; folklore attributes virtues to the colors: red for strength, white for faithfulness, and green for hope; alternatively, the red is seen as being for the blood spilled in defense of the land, white for freedom, and green for the pasturelands that make up so much of the country

National symbol(s): Holy Crown of Hungary (Crown of Saint Stephen); national colors: red, white, green

National anthem: *name:* "Himnusz" (Hymn) *lyrics/music:* Ferenc KOLCSEY/Ferenc ERKEL *note:* adopted 1844

ECONOMY

Economy—overview: Hungary has made the transition from a centrally planned to a market economy, with a per capita income nearly two-thirds that of the EU-28 average.

In late 2008, Hungary's impending inability to service its short-term debt—brought on by the global financial crisis—led Budapest to obtain an IMF/EU/World Bank-arranged financial assistance package worth over $25 billion. The global economic downturn, declining exports, and low domestic consumption and investment, dampened by government austerity measures, resulted in a severe economic contraction in 2009. in 2010, the new government implemented a number of changes including cutting business and personal income taxes, but imposed "crisis taxes" on financial institutions, energy and telecom companies, and retailers. The IMF/EU bailout program lapsed at the end of 2010 and was replaced by Post Program Monitoring and Article IV Consultations on overall economic and fiscal processes. At the end of 2011 the government turned to the IMF and the EU to obtain a financial backstop to support its efforts to refinance foreign currency debt and bond obligations in 2012 and beyond, but Budapest's rejection of EU and IMF economic policy recommendations led to a breakdown in talks with the lenders in late 2012. Global demand for high yield has since helped Hungary to obtain funds on international markets. Hungary's progress reducing its deficit to under 3% of GDP led the European Commission in 2013 to permit Hungary for the first time since joining the EU in 2004 to exit the Excessive Deficit Procedure. The government remains committed to keeping the budget deficit in check and lowering public debt by using sectoral taxes, while relying on state interventionist measures to lower utility prices and boost growth and employment.

GDP (purchasing power parity): $258.4 billion (2015 est.)

$251.1 billion (2014 est.)

$242.2 billion (2013 est.)

note: data are in 2015 US dollars

country comparison to the world: 60

GDP (official exchange rate): $120.6 billion (2015 est.)

GDP—real growth rate: 2.9% (2015 est.)

3.7% (2014 est.)

1.9% (2013 est.)

country comparison to the world: 106

GDP—per capita (PPP): $26,200 (2015 est.)

$25,400 (2014 est.)

$24,400 (2013 est.)

note: data are in 2015 US dollars

country comparison to the world: 71

Gross national saving: 27.1% of GDP (2015 est.)

24.5% of GDP (2014 est.)

24.6% of GDP (2013 est.)

country comparison to the world: 37

GDP—composition, by end use:

household consumption: 49.8%

government consumption: 19.2%

investment in fixed capital: 21.8%

investment in inventories: 0.2%

exports of goods and services: 93.1%

imports of goods and services: -84.1% (2015 est.)

GDP—composition, by sector of origin:

agriculture: 4.4%

industry: 30.9%

services: 64.8% (2015 est.)

Agriculture—products: wheat, corn, sunflower seed, potatoes, sugar beets; pigs, cattle, poultry, dairy products

Industries: mining, metallurgy, construction materials, processed foods, textiles, chemicals (especially pharmaceuticals), motor vehicles

Industrial production growth rate: 3% (2015 est.)

country comparison to the world: 85

Labor force: 4.446 million (2015 est.)

country comparison to the world: 90

Labor force—by occupation: *agriculture:* 7.1%

industry: 29.7%

services: 63.2% (2011)

Unemployment rate: 6.8% (2015 est.)

7.7% (2014 est.)

country comparison to the world: 79

Population below poverty line: 14.9% (2015 est.)

Household income or consumption by percentage share: *lowest:* 10%: 3.1%

highest: 10%: 22.6% (2009)

Distribution of family income—Gini Index: 30.6 (2013 est.)

24.7 (2009)

country comparison to the world: 117

Budget: *revenues:* $56.71 billion

expenditures: $59.44 billion (2016 est.)

Taxes and other revenues: 47.9% of GDP (2016 est.)

country comparison to the world: 19

Budget surplus (+) or deficit (–): -2.3% of GDP

note: Hungary has been under the EU Excessive Deficit Procedure since it joined the EU in 2004; in March 2012 the EU elevated its Excessive Deficit Procedure against Hungary and proposed freezing 30% of the country's Cohesion Funds because 2011 deficit reductions were not achieved in a sustainable manner; in June 2012, the EU lifted the freeze, recognizing that steps had been taken to reduce the deficit; the latest EC forecasts project the Hungarian deficit to increase above 3% both in 2013 and in 2014 due to sluggish growth and the government's fiscal tightening (2016 est.)

country comparison to the world: 83

Public debt: 75.5% of GDP (2016 est.)

76.2% of GDP (2014 est.)

note: general government gross debt is defined in the Maastricht Treaty as consolidated general government gross debt at nominal value, outstanding at the end of the year in the following categories of government liabilities: currency and deposits, securities other than shares excluding financial derivatives, and government, state government, local government, and social security funds
country comparison to the world: 36
Fiscal year: calendar year
Inflation rate (consumer prices): -0.1% (2015 est.) -0.2% (2014 est.)
country comparison to the world: 39
Central bank discount rate: 1.35% (22 July 2015) 2.1% (23 July 2014)
country comparison to the world: 121
Commercial bank prime lending rate: 3% (31 December 2015 est.)
4.43% (31 December 2014 est.)
country comparison to the world: 169
Stock of narrow money: $47.18 billion (31 December 2015 est.)
$41.44 billion (31 December 2014 est.)
country comparison to the world: 52
Stock of broad money: $68.87 billion (31 December 2015 est.)
$66.91 billion (31 December 2014 est.)
country comparison to the world: 62
Stock of domestic credit: $74.85 billion (31 December 2015 est.)
$76.19 billion (31 December 2014 est.)
country comparison to the world: 57
Market value of publicly traded shares:
$25.69 billion (31 December 2015 est.)
$22.8 billion (31 December 2011)
$27.71 billion (31 December 2010 est.)
country comparison to the world: 61
Current account balance: $6.141 billion (2015 est.)
$3.13 billion (2014 est.)
country comparison to the world: 27
Exports: $97.57 billion (2015 est.)
$100 billion (2014 est.)
country comparison to the world: 36
Exports—commodities: machinery and equipment 53.5%, other manufactures 31.2%, food products 8.7%, raw materials 3.4%, fuels and electricity 3.9% (2012 est.)
Exports—partners: Germany 28%, Romania 5.4%, Slovakia 5.1%, Austria 5%, Italy 4.8%, France 4.7%, UK 4%, Czech Republic 4% (2015)
Imports: $92.92 billion (2015 est.)
$96.42 billion (2014 est.)
country comparison to the world: 34
Imports—commodities: machinery and equipment 45.4%, other manufactures 34.3%, fuels and electricity 12.6%, food products 5.3%, raw materials 2.5% (2012)
Imports—partners: Germany 25.8%, China 6.7%, Austria 6.6%, Poland 5.5%, Slovakia 5.3%, France 5%, Czech Republic 4.8%, Netherlands 4.6%, Italy 4.5% (2015)
Reserves of foreign exchange and gold: $39.39 billion (31 December 2015 est.)
$42.02 billion (31 December 2014 est.)
country comparison to the world: 46

Debt—external: $129.2 billion (31 December 2015 est.)
$202.4 billion (31 December 2013 est.)
country comparison to the world: 46
Stock of direct foreign investment—at home:
$119.8 billion (31 December 2015 est.)
$115.5 billion (31 December 2014 est.)
country comparison to the world: 43
Stock of direct foreign investment—abroad: $50.3 billion (31 December 2015 est.)
$47.74 billion (31 December 2014 est.)
country comparison to the world: 39
Exchange rates: forints (HUF) per US dollar—
273.8 (2015 est.)
232.6 (2014 est.)
232.6 (2013 est.)
225.1 (2012 est.)
201.05 (2011 est.)

ENERGY

Electricity—production: 23.46 billion kWh (2015 est.)
country comparison to the world: 71
Electricity—consumption: 21.55 billion kWh (2015 est.)
country comparison to the world: 69
Electricity—exports: 5.378 billion kWh (2015 est.)
country comparison to the world: 29
Electricity—imports: 18.15 billion kWh (2015 est.)
country comparison to the world: 10
Electricity—installed generating capacity: 9.289 million kW (2015 est.)
country comparison to the world: 58
Electricity—from fossil fuels: 22% of total installed capacity (2015 est.)
country comparison to the world: 191
Electricity—from nuclear fuels: 61% of total installed capacity (2015 est.)
country comparison to the world: 1
Electricity—from hydroelectric plants: 0.6% of total installed capacity (2015 est.)
country comparison to the world: 147
Electricity—from other renewable sources: 6.8% of total installed capacity (2014 est.)
country comparison to the world: 52
Crude oil—production: 11,410 bbl/day (2014 est.)
country comparison to the world: 78
Crude oil—exports: 1,485 bbl/day (2013 est.)
country comparison to the world: 81
Crude oil—imports: 115,300 bbl/day (2013 est.)
country comparison to the world: 43
Crude oil—proved reserves: 27.19 million bbl (1 January 2015 est.)
country comparison to the world: 84
Refined petroleum products—production: 165,000 bbl/day (2013 est.)
country comparison to the world: 61
Refined petroleum products consumption: 140,900 bbl/day (2014 est.)
country comparison to the world: 68
Refined petroleum products exports: 51,170 bbl/day (2013 est.)
country comparison to the world: 56

Refined petroleum products imports: 44,440 bbl/day (2013 est.)
country comparison to the world: 85
Natural gas—production: 1.505 billion cu m (2015 est.)
country comparison to the world: 60
Natural gas—consumption: 8.46 billion cu m (2015 est.)
country comparison to the world: 49
Natural gas—exports: 226.6 million cu m (2015 est.)
country comparison to the world: 42
Natural gas—imports: 8.167 billion cu m (2015 est.)
country comparison to the world: 28
Natural gas—proved reserves: 7.843 billion cu m (1 January 2014 est.)
country comparison to the world: 84
Carbon dioxide emissions from consumption of energy: 47.9 million Mt (2012 est.)
country comparison to the world: 60

COMMUNICATIONS

Telephones—fixed lines: *total subscriptions:* 3.01 million
subscriptions per 100 inhabitants: 30 (2014 est.)
country comparison to the world: 49
Telephones—mobile cellular: *total:* 11.7 million
subscriptions per 100 inhabitants: 118 (2014 est.)
country comparison to the world: 78
Telephone system: *general assessment:* modern telephone system is digital and highly automated; trunk services are carried by fiber-optic cable and digital microwave radio relay; a program for fiber-optic subscriber connections was initiated in 1996 *domestic:* competition among mobile-cellular service providers has led to a sharp increase in the use of mobile-cellular phones since 2000 and a decrease in the number of fixed-line connections *international:* country code—36; Hungary has fiber-optic cable connections with all neighboring countries; the international switch is in Budapest; satellite earth stations—2 Intelsat (Atlantic Ocean and Indian Ocean regions), 1 Inmarsat, 1 very small aperture terminal (VSAT) system of ground terminals (2011)
Broadcast media: mixed system of state-supported public service broadcast media and private broadcasters; the 5 publicly owned TV channels and the 2 main privately owned TV stations are the major national broadcasters; a large number of special interest channels; highly developed market for satellite and cable TV services with about two-thirds of viewers utilizing their services; 4 state-supported public-service radio networks and 1 major national commercial station; a large number of local stations including commercial, public service, non-profit, and community radio stations; digital transition completed at the end of 2013 (2016)
Radio broadcast stations: AM 5, FM 90, shortwave 1 (2008)
Television broadcast stations: 95 (2008)
Internet country code: .hu
Internet hosts: 3.145 million (2012)
country comparison to the world: 33
Internet users: *total:* 7.4 million

percent of Population: 74.4% (2014 est.)
country comparison to the world: 50

TRANSPORTATION

Airports: 41 (2013)
country comparison to the world: 104
Airports—with paved runways: *total:* 20
over 3,047 m: 2
2,438 to 3,047 m: 6
1,524 to 2,437 m: 6
914 to 1,523 m: 5
under 914 m: 1 (2013)
Airports—with unpaved runways: *total:* 21
1,524 to 2,437 m: 2
914 to 1,523 m: 8
under 914 m: 11 (2013)
Heliports: 3 (2013)
Pipelines: gas 19,028 km; oil 1,007 km; refined products 842 km (2013)
Railways: *total:* 8,049 km
broad gauge: 36 km 1.524-m gauge
standard gauge: 7,794 km 1.435-m gauge (2,889 km electrified)
narrow gauge: 219 km 0.760-m gauge (2014)
country comparison to the world: 27

Roadways: *total:* 203,601 km
paved: 77,087 km (includes 1,582 km of expressways)
unpaved: 126,514 km (2014)
country comparison to the world: 25
Waterways: 1,622 km (most on Danube River) (2011)
country comparison to the world: 47
Ports and terminals: *river port(s):* Baja, Csepel (Budapest), Dunaujvaros, Gyor-Gonyu, Mohacs (Danube)

MILITARY AND SECURITY

Military branches: Hungarian Defense Forces: Land Forces, Hungarian Air Force (Magyar Legiero, ML) (2011)
Military service age and obligation: 18–25 years of age for voluntary military service; no conscription; 6-month service obligation (2012)
Military expenditures: 0.8% of GDP (2015)
0.83% of GDP (2012)
0.99% of GDP (2011)
0.83% of GDP (2010)
country comparison to the world: 113

TRANSNATIONAL ISSUES

Disputes—international: bilateral government, legal, technical and economic working group negotiations continue in 2006 with Slovakia over Hungary's failure to complete its portion of the Gabcikovo-Nagy maros hydroelectric dam project along the Danube; as a member state that forms part of the EU's external border, Hungary has implemented the strict Schengen border rules
Refugees and internally displaced persons: *refugees (countries of origin):* 5,950 applicants for forms of legal stay oth er th an asylum (U kraine) (2015)
stateless persons: 132 (2015)
note: 406,993 estimated refugee and migrant arrivals (2015—June 2016)
Illicit drugs: transshipment point for Southwest Asian heroin and cannabis and for South American cocaine destined for Western Europe; limited producer of precursor chemicals, particularly for amphetamine and methamphetamine; efforts to counter money laundering, related to organized crime and drug trafficking are improving but remain vulnerable; significant consumer of ecstasy

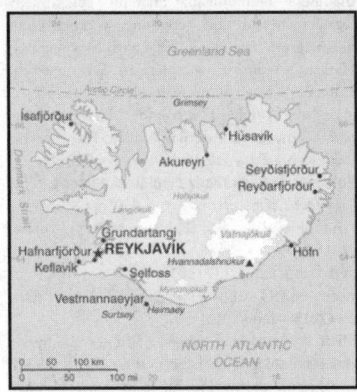

INTRODUCTION

Background: Settled by Norwegian and Celtic (Scottish and Irish) immigrants during the late 9th and 10th centuries A.D., Iceland boasts the world's oldest functioning legislative assembly, the Althingi, established in 930. Independent for over 300 years, Iceland was subsequently ruled by Norway and Denmark. Fallout from the Askja volcano of 1875 devastated the Icelandic economy and caused widespread famine. Over the next quarter century, 20% of the island's population emigrated, mostly to Canada and the US. Denmark granted limited home rule in 1874 and complete independence in 1944. The second half of the 20th century saw substantial economic growth driven primarily by the fishing industry. The economy diversified greatly after the country joined the European Economic Area in 1994, but Iceland was especially hard hit by the global financial crisis in the years following 2008. Literacy, longevity, and social cohesion are first rate by world standards.

GEOGRAPHY

Location: Northern Europe, island between the Greenland Sea and the North Atlantic Ocean, northwest of the United Kingdom
Geographic coordinates: 65 00 N, 18 00 W
Map references: Arctic Region
Area: *total:* 103,000 sq km
land: 100,250 sq km
water: 2,750 sq km
country comparison to the world: 108
Area—comparative: slightly smaller than Pennsylvania; about the same size as Kentucky
Land boundaries: 0 km
Coastline: 4,970 km
Maritime claims: *territorial sea:* 12 nm
exclusive economic zone: 200 nm
continental shelf: 200 nm or to the edge of the continental margin
Climate: temperate; moderated by North Atlantic Current; mild, windy winters; damp, cool summers

Terrain: mostly plateau interspersed with mountain peaks, icefields; coast deeply indented by bays and fiords
Elevation: *mean elevation:* 557 m
elevation extremes: *lowest point:* Atlantic Ocean 0 m
highest point: Hvannadalshnukur 2,110 m (at Vatnajokull Glacier)
Natural resources: fish, hydropower, geothermal power, diatomite
Land use: *agricultural land:* 18.7%
arable land: 1.2%
permanent crops: 0%
permanent pasture: 17.5%
forest: 0.3%
other: 81% (2011 est.)
Irrigated land: NA
Total renewable water resources: 170 cu km (2011)
Freshwater withdrawal (domestic/industrial/agricultural): *total:* 0.17 cu km/yr (49%/8%/42%)
per capita: 539.2 cu m/yr (2005)
Natural hazards: earthquakes and volcanic activity
volcanism: Iceland, situated on top of a hotspot, experiences severe volcanic activity; Eyjafjallajokull (elev.1,666 m) erupted in 2010, sendingash high into the atmosphere and seriously disrupting European air traffic; scientists continue to monitor nearby Katla (elev.1,512 m), which has a high probability of eruption in the very near future, potentially disrupting air traffic; Grimsvoetn and Hekla are Iceland's most active volcanoes; other historically active volcanoes include Askja, Bardarbunga, Brennisteinsfjoll, Esjufjoll, Hengill, Krafla, Krisuvik, Kverkfjoll, Oraefajokull, Reykjanes, Torfajokull, and Vestmannaeyjar
Environment—current issues: water pollution from fertilizer runoff; inadequate wastewater treatment
Environment—international agreements: *party to:* Air Pollution, Air Pollution-Persistent Organic Pollutants, Biodiversity, Climate Change, Climate Change-Kyoto Protocol, Desertification, Endangered Species, Hazardous Wastes, Kyoto Protocol, Law of the Sea, Marine Dumping, Ozone Layer Protection, Ship Pollution, Transboundary Air Pollution, Wetlands, Whaling
signed, but not ratified: Environmental Modification, Marine Life Conservation
Geography—note: strategic location between Greenland and Europe; westernmost European country; Reykjavik is the northernmost national capital in the world; more land covered by glaciers than in all of continental Europe

PEOPLE AND SOCIETY

Nationality: *noun:* Icelander(s)
adjective: Icelandic
Ethnic groups: homogeneous mixture of descendants of Norse and Celts 94%, population of foreign origin 6%
Languages: Icelandic, English, Nordic languages, German widely spoken

Religions: Evangelical Lutheran Church of Iceland (official) 73.8%, Roman Catholic 3.6%, Reykjavik Free Church 2.9%, Hafnarfjorour Free Church 2%, The Independent Congregation 1%, other religions 3.9% (includes Pentecostal and Asatru Association), none 5.6%, other or unspecified 7.2% (2015 est.)
Population: 331,918 (July 2015 est.)
country comparison to the world: 179
Age structure: *0–14 years:* 20.43% (male 34,653/female 33,161)
15–24 years: 14.03% (male 23,661/female 22,914)
25–54 years: 40.09% (male 67,183/female 65,871)
55–64 years: 11.67% (male 19,502/female 19,230)
65 years and over: 13.78% (male 21,344/female 24,399) (2015 est.)
Dependency ratios: *total dependency ratio:* 51.6%
youth dependency ratio: 30.8%
elderly dependen cyratio: 20.8%
potential support ratio: 4.8% (2015 est.)
Median age: *total:* 36 years
male: 35.4 years
female: 36.7 years (2015 est.)
country comparison to the world: 72
Population growth rate: 1.21% (2015 est.)
country comparison to the world: 100
Birth rate: 13.91 births/1,000 population (2015 est.)
country comparison to the world: 140
Death rate: 6.28 deaths/1,000 population (2015 est.)
country comparison to the world: 155
Net migration rate: 4.43 migrant(s)/1,000 population (2015 est.)
country comparison to the world: 29
Urbanization: *urban Population:* 94.1% of total population (2015)
rate of urbanization: 1.25% annual rate of change (2010–15 est.)
Major urban areas—Population: REYKJAVIK (capital) 184,000 (2014)
Sex ratio: *at birth:* 1.05 male(s)/female
0–14 years: 1.05 male(s)/female
15–24 years: 1.03 male(s)/female
25–54 years: 1.02 male(s)/female
55–64 years: 1.01 male(s)/female
65 years and over: 0.88 male(s)/female
total Population: 1.01 male(s)/female (2015 est.)
Mother's mean age at first birth: 27 (2011 est.)
Maternal mortality rate: 3 deaths/100,000 live births (2015 est.)
country comparison to the world: 177
Infant mortality rate: *total:* 2.06 deaths/1,000 live births
male: 2.2 deaths/1,000 live births
female: 1.91 deaths/1,000 live births (2015 est.)
country comparison to the world: 223
Life expectancy at birth: *total population:* 82.97 years
male: 80.81 years
female: 85.22 years (2015 est.)
country comparison to the world: 6

Total fertility rate: 2.02 children born/woman (2015 est.)
country comparison to the world: 119
Health expenditures: 9.1% of GDP (2013)
country comparison to the world: 38
Physicians density: 3.48 physicians/1,000 population (2012)
Hospital bed density: 3.2 beds/1,000 population (2012)
Drinking water source:
improved:
urban: 100% of population
rural: 100% of population
total: 100% of population
unimproved:
urban: 0% of population
rural: 0% of population
total: 0% of population (2015 est.)
Sanitation facility access:
improved:
urban: 98.7% of population
rural: 100% of population
total: 98.8% of population
unimproved:
urban: 1.3% of population
rural: 0% of population
total: 1.2% of population (2015 est.)
HIV/AIDS—adult prevalence rate: NA
HIV/AIDS—people living with HIV/AIDS: NA
HIV/AIDS—deaths: NA
Obesity—adult prevalence rate: 23.9% (2014)
country comparison to the world: 76
Education expenditures: 7% of GDP (2011)
country comparison to the world: 14
School life expectancy (primary to tertiary education): *total:* 19 years
male: 18 years
female: 20 years (2012)
Unemployment, youth ages 15–24: *total:* 10.7%
male: 13.6%
female: 7.8% (2013 est.)
country comparison to the world: 85

GOVERNMENT

Country name: *conventional long form:* Republic of Iceland
conventional short form: Iceland
local long form: Lydveldid Island
local short form: Island
etymology: Floki VILGERDARSON, an early explorer of the island (9th century), applied the name "land of ice" after spotting a fjord full of drift ice to the north and spending a bitter winter on the island; he eventually settled on the island, however, after he saw how it greened up in the summer and that it was in fact habitable
Government type: parliamentary republic
Capital: *name:* Reykjavik
Geographic coordinates: 64 09 N, 21 57 W
time difference: UTC 0 (5 hours ahead of Washington, DC, during Standard Time)
Administrative divisions: 8 regions; Austurland, Hofudhborgarsvaedhi, Nordhurland Eystra, Nordhurland Vestra, Sudhurland, Sudhurnes, Vestfirdhir, Vesturland

Independence: 1 December 1918 (became a sovereign state under the Danish Crown); 17 June 1944 (from Denmark; birthday of Jon SIGURDSSON-leader of Iceland's 19th Century independence movement)
National holiday: Independence Day, 17 June (1944)
Constitution: several previous; latest ratified 16 June 1944, effective 17 June 1944 (at independence); amended many times, last in 2013 (2016)
Legal system: civil law system influenced by the Danish model
International law organization participation: has not submitted an ICJ jurisdiction declaration; accepts ICCt jurisdiction
Citizenship: *citizenship by birth:* no
citizenship by descent only: at least one parent must be a citizen of Iceland
dual citizenship recognized: yes
residency requirement for naturalization: 3 to 7 years
Suffrage: 18 years of age; universal
Executive branch: *chief of state:* President Olafur Ragnar GRIMSSON (since 1 August 1996)
head of government: Acting Prime Minister Sigurdur Ingi JOHANNSSON (since 5 April 2016); becomes prime minister 7 April 2016
cabinet: Cabinet appointed by the prime minister
elections/appointments: president directly elected by simple majority popular vote for a 4-year term (no term limits); election last held on 30 June 2012 (next to be held in June 2016); following legislative elections, the leader of the majority party or majority coalition becomes prime minister
election results: Olafur Ragnar GRIMSSON-lected president; percent of vote—Olafur Ragnar GRIMSSON (independent) 52.8%, Thora ARNORSDOTTIR (independent) 33.2%, Ari Trausti GUDMUNDSSON (independent) 8.6%, others 5.4%
Legislative branch: *description:* unicameral Althingi (parliament) (63 seats; members directly elected in multi-seat constituencies by proportional representation vote to serve 4-year terms)
elections: last held on 27 April 2013 (next to be held in 2017)
election results: percent of vote by party—IP 26.7%, PP 24.4%, SDA 12.9%, LGM 10.9%, BF 8.2%, Pirate Party 5.1%, other 11.8%; seats by party—IP 19, PP 19, SDA 9, LGM 7, BF 6, Pirate Party 3
Judicial branch: *highest court(s):* Supreme Court or Haestirettur (consists of 9 judges)
judge selection and term of office: judges proposed by Ministry of Interior selection committee and appointed by the president; judges appointed for an indefinite period
subordinate courts: 8 district courts; Labor Court; Court of Impeachment
Political parties and leaders: Bright Future (Bjort framtid) or BF [Ottarr PROPPE]
Independence Party (Sjalfstaedisflokkurinn) or IP [Bjarni BENEDIKTSSON]
Left-Green Movement (Vinstrihreyfingin-graent frambod) or LGM [Katrin JAKOBSDOTTIR]

Pirate Party (Piratar) or PIP [Helgi Hafn GUNNTRSSON]
Progressive Party (Framsoknarflokkurinn) or PP [Sigmundur David GUNNLAUGSSON]
Social Democratic Alliance (Samfylkingin) or SDA [Arni Pall ARNASON]
International organization participation: Arctic Council, Australia Group, BIS, CBSS, CD, CE, EAPC, EBRD, EFTA, FAO, FATF, IAEA, IBRD, ICAO, ICC (national committees), ICCt, ICRM, IDA, IFAD, IFC, IFRCS, IHO, ILO, IMF, IMO, IMSO, Interpol, IOC, IOM, IPU, ISO, ITSO, ITU, ITUC (NGOs), MIGA, NATO, NC, NEA, NIB, NSG, OAS (observer), OECD, OPCW, OSCE, PCA, Schengen Convention, UN, UNCTAD, UNESCO, UPU, WCO, WHO, WIPO, WMO, WTO
Diplomatic representation in the US: *chief of mission:* Ambassador Geir Hilmar HAARDE (since 23 February 2015)
chancery: House of Sweden, 2900 K Street NW
telephone: [1] (202) 265-6653
FAX: [1] (202) 265-6656
consulate(s) general: New York
Diplomatic representation from the US: *chief of mission:* Ambassador Robert C. BARBER (since 23 January 2015)
embassy: Laufasvegur 21,101 Reykjavik
mailing address: US Department of State, 5640 Reykjavik Place, Washington, D.C.20521–5640
telephone: [354] 595-22-00
FAX: [354] 562-9118
Flag description: blue with a red cross outlined in white extending to the edges of the flag; the vertical part of the cross is shifted to the hoist side in the style of the Dannebrog (Danish flag); the colors represent three of the elements that make up the island: red is for the island's volcanic fires, white recalls the snow and ice fields of the island, and blue is for the surrounding ocean
National symbol(s): gyrfalcon; national colors: blue, white, red
National anthem: *name:* "Lofsongur" (Song of Praise)
lyrics/music: Matthias JOCHUMSSON/Sveinbjorn SVEINBJORNSSON
note: adopted 1944; also known as "O, Gud vors lands" (O, God of Our Land), the anthem was originally written and performed in 1874

ECONOMY

Economy—overview: Iceland's Scandinavian-type social-market economy combines a capitalist structure and free-market principles with an extensive welfare system. Except for a brief period during the 2008 crisis, Iceland has achieved high growth, low unemployment, and a remarkably even distribution of income. The economy depends heavily on the fishing industry, which provides 40% of merchandise export earnings, more than 12% of GDP, and employs nearly 5% of the work force. It remains sensitive to declining fish stocks as well as to fluctuations in world prices for its main exports: fish and fish products, aluminum, and ferrosilicon. Since 2010, tourism has become the main pillar of Icelandic economic growth, with the number of

395

tourists expected to reach or exceed 4.5 times the Icelandic population in 2016.

Iceland's economy has been diversifying into manufacturing and service industries in the last decade, particularly within the fields of tourism, software production, and biotechnology. In fall 2013, the Icelandic Government approved a joint application by Icelandic, Chinese, and Norwegian energy firms to conduct oil exploration off Iceland's northeast coast, although no exploration has yet taken place. Abundant geothermal and hydropower sources have attracted substantial foreign investment in the aluminum sector, boosted economic growth, and sparked some interest from high-tech firms looking to establish data centers using cheap green energy, although the financial crisis has put several investment projects on hold. Following the privatization of the banking sector in the early 2000s, domestic banks expanded aggressively in foreign markets, and consumers and businesses borrowed heavily in foreign currencies. Worsening global financial conditions throughout 2008 resulted in a sharp depreciation of the krona vis-avis other major currencies. The foreign exposure of Icelandic banks, whose loans and other assets totaled more than 10 times the country's GDP, became unsustainable. Iceland's three largest banks collapsed in late 2008. The country secured over $10 billion in loans from the IMF and other countries to stabilize its currency and financial sector, and to back government guarantees for foreign deposits in Icelandic banks. GDP fell 6.8% in 2009, and unemployment peaked at 9.4% in February 2009. Three new banks were established to take over the domestic assets of the collapsed banks. Two of them have majority ownership by the State, which intends to re-privatize them.

Since the collapse of Iceland's financial sector, government economic priorities have included stabilizing the krona, implementing capital controls, reducing Iceland's high budget deficit, containing inflation, addressing high household debt, restructuring the financial sector, and diversifying the economy. Iceland's financial woes prompted an initial increase in public support to join the EU and the Eurozone, with accession negotiations beginning in July 2010, but negotiations were suspended under the 2013 center-right government. Most macroeconomic indicators and employment have rebounded to pre-crisis levels, driven primarily by the unprecedented growth in tourism—averaging over 20% annually—following the well publicized volcanic eruption in 2010.

GDP (purchasing power parity): $15.15 billion (2015 est.)

$14.58 billion (2014 est.)

$14.3 billion (2013 est.)

note: data are in 2015 US dollars

country comparison to the world: 153

GDP (official exchange rate): $16.72 billion (2015 est.)

GDP—real growth rate: 4% (2015 est.)

2% (2014 est.)

4.4% (2013 est.)

country comparison to the world: 68

GDP—per capita (PPP): $46,100 (2015 est.)

$44,700 (2014 est.)

$44,400 (2013 est.)

note: data are in 2015 US dollars

country comparison to the world: 30

Gross national saving: 23.5% of GDP (2015 est.)

21% of GDP (2014 est.)

21.2% of GDP (2013 est.)

country comparison to the world: 59

GDP—composition, by end use:

household consumption: 52.1%

government consumption: 23.2%

investment in fixed capital: 18.7%

investment in inventories: 0%

exports of goods and services: 54.8%

imports of goods and services: -48.8% (2015 est.)

GDP—composition, by sector of origin:

agriculture: 5.8%

industry: 20.9%

services: 73.3% (2015 est.)

Agriculture—products: potatoes, carrots, green vegetables; mutton, chicken, pork, beef, dairy products; fish

Industries: tourism, fish processing; aluminum smelting, ferrosilicon production; geothermal power, hydropower, tourism

Industrial production growth rate: 1.5% (2015 est.)

country comparison to the world: 132

Labor force: 190,500 (2015 est.)

country comparison to the world: 175

Labor force—by occupation: *agriculture:* 4.8%

industry: 22.2%

services: 73% (2008)

Unemployment rate: 3.8% (2015 est.)

3.6% (2014 est.)

country comparison to the world: 32

Population below poverty line: NA%

note: 332,100 families (2011 est.)

Household income or consumption by percentage share: *lowest:* 10%: NA%

highest: 10%: NA%

Distribution of family income—Gini index: 28 (2006)

25 (2005)

country comparison to the world: 130

Budget: *revenues:* $6.914 billion

expenditures: $6.885 billion (2015 est.)

Taxes and other revenues: 41.3% of GDP (2015 est.)

country comparison to the world: 33

Budget surplus (+) or deficit (−): 0.2% of GDP (2015 est.)

country comparison to the world: 25

Public debt: 81.9% of GDP (2015 est.)

85.4% of GDP (2014 est.)

country comparison to the world: 31

Fiscal year: calendar year

Inflation rate (consumer prices): 1.6% (2015 est.)

2% (2014 est.)

country comparison to the world: 105

Central bank discount rate: 5.4% (31 January 2012)

5.75% (31 December 2010)

country comparison to the world: 73

Commercial bank prime lending rate: 7.4% (31 December 2015 est.)

7.74% (31 December 2014 est.)

country comparison to the world: 116

Stock of narrow money: $3.262 billion (31 December 2015 est.)

$3.213 billion (31 December 2014 est.)

country comparison to the world: 114

Stock of broad money: $8.368 billion (31 December 2013 est.)

$8.12 billion (31 December 2013 est.)

country comparison to the world: 111

Stock of domestic credit: $19.37 billion (31 December 2015 est.)

$18.36 billion (31 December 2014 est.)

country comparison to the world: 86

Market value of publicly traded shares: $2.825 billion (31 December 2012 est.)

$2.021 billion (31 December 2011)

$1.996 billion (31 December 2010 est.)

country comparison to the world: 95

Current account balance: $710 million (2015 est.)

$627 million (2014 est.)

country comparison to the world: 41

Exports: $4.4 billion (2015 est.)

$4.848 billion (2014 est.)

country comparison to the world: 115

Exports—commodities: fish and fish products 40%, aluminum, animal products, ferrosilicon, diatomite (2010 est.)

Exports—partners: Netherlands 26.1%, UK 11.6%, Spain 11.5%, Germany 7.4%, France 5.7%, US 5.7%, Norway 4.7% (2015)

Imports: $4.577 billion (2015 est.)

$4.954 billion (2014 est.)

country comparison to the world: 129

Imports—commodities: machinery and equipment, petroleum products, foodstuffs, textiles

Imports—partners: Norway 10.1%, Germany 8.6%, US 7.9%, China 7.9%, Denmark 7.1%, Netherlands 5.9%, Brazil 5.8%, UK 5% (2015)

Reserves of foreign exchange and gold: $5.289 billion (31 December 2015 est.)

$4.176 billion (31 December 2014 est.)

country comparison to the world: 92

Debt—external: $97.87 billion (31 December 2014 est.)

$107.5 billion (31 December 2013 est.)

country comparison to the world: 52

Stock of direct foreign investment—at home: $NA

$9.2 billion (31 December 2008 est.)

Stock of direct foreign investment—abroad: $NA (31 December 2011)

$8.8 billion (31 December 2008)

Exchange rates: Icelandic kronur (ISK) per US dollar—

130.1 (2015 est.)

116.77 (2014 est.)

116.77 (2013 est.)

125.08 (2012 est.)

115.95 (2011 est.)

ENERGY

Electricity—production: 17.43 billion kWh (2012 est.)

country comparison to the world: 79

Electricity—consumption: 16.94 billion kWh (2012 est.)

country comparison to the world: 75

Electricity—exports: 0 kWh (2013 est.)

country comparison to the world: 151
Electricity—imports: 0 kWh (2013 est.)
country comparison to the world: 161
Electricity—installed generating capacity: 2.658 million kW (2012 est.)
country comparison to the world: 97
Electricity—from fossil fuels: 4.3% of total installed capacity (2012 est.)
country comparison to the world: 205
Electricity—from nuclear fuels: 0% of total installed capacity (2012 est.)
country comparison to the world: 110
Electricity—from hydroelectric plants: 70.6% of total installed capacity (2012 est.)
country comparison to the world: 22
Electricity—from other renewable sources: 25.1% of total installed capacity (2012 est.)
country comparison to the world: 9
Crude oil—production: 0 bbl/day (2014 est.)
country comparison to the world: 149
Crude oil—exports: 0 bbl/day (2013 est.)
country comparison to the world: 139
Crude oil—imports: 0 bbl/day (2013 est.)
country comparison to the world: 206
Crude oil—proved reserves: 0 bbl (1 January 2015 est.)
country comparison to the world: 148
Refined petroleum products—production: 0 bbl/day (2013 est.)
country comparison to the world: 196
Refined petroleum products—consumption: 16,310 bbl/day (2014 est.)
country comparison to the world: 138
Refined petroleum products—exports: 1,831 bbl/day (2013 est.)
country comparison to the world: 107
Refined petroleum products—imports: 15,040 bbl/day (2013 est.)
country comparison to the world: 125
Natural gas—production: 0 cu m (2014 est.)
country comparison to the world: 203
Natural gas—consumption: 0 cu m (2014 est.)
country comparison to the world: 156
Natural gas—exports: 0 cu m (2014 est.)
country comparison to the world: 117
Natural gas—imports: 0 cu m (2014 est.)
country comparison to the world: 210
Natural gas—proved reserves: 0 cu m (1 January 2014 est.)
country comparison to the world: 152
Carbon dioxide emissions from consumption of energy: 3.505 million Mt (2012 est.)
country comparison to the world: 137

COMMUNICATIONS

Telephones—fixed lines: *total subscriptions:* 170,000
subscriptions per 100 inhabitants: 52 (2014 est.)
country comparison to the world: 131
Telephones—mobile cellular: *total:* 370,000
subscriptions per 100 inhabitants: 113 (2014 est.)
country comparison to the world: 175
Telephone system: *general assessment:* telecommunications infrastructure is modern and fully digitized, with satellite-earth stations, fiber-optic cables, and an extensive broadband network
domestic: liberalization of the telecommunications sector beginning in the late 1990s has led to increased competition especially in the mobile services segment of the market
international: country code—354; the CANTAT-3 and FARICE-1 submarine cable systems provide connectivity to Canada, the Faroe Islands, UK, Denmark, and Germany; a planned new section of the Hibernia-Atlantic submarine cable will provide additional connectivity to Canada, US, and Ireland; satellite earth stations—2 Intelsat (Atlantic Ocean), 1 Inmarsat (Atlantic and Indian Ocean regions); note—Iceland shares the Inmarsat earth station with the other Nordic countries (Denmark, Finland, Norway, and Sweden) (2011)
Broadcast media: state-owned public TV broadcaster operates 1 TV channel nationally; several privately owned TV stations broadcast nationally and roughly another half-dozen operate locally; about one-half the households utilize multi-channel cable or satellite TV services; state-owned public radio broadcaster operates 2 national networks and 4 regional stations; 2 privately owned radio stations operate nationally and another 15 provide more limited coverage (2007)
Radio broadcast stations: AM 3, FM about 70, shortwave 1 (2008)
Television broadcast stations: 14 (plus 156 repeaters) (1997)
Internet country code:.is
Internet hosts: 369,969 (2012)
country comparison to the world: 56
Internet users: *total:* 316,400
percent of Population: 96.5% (2014 est.)
country comparison to the world: 141

TRANSPORTATION

Airports: 96 (2013)
country comparison to the world: 60

Airports—with paved runways: *total:* 7
over 3,047 m: 1
1,524 to 2,437 m: 3
914 to 1,523 m: 3 (2013)
Airports—with unpaved runways: *total:* 89
1,524 to 2,437 m: 3
914 to 1,523 m: 26
under 914 m: 60 (2013)
Roadways: *total:* 12,890 km
paved/oiled gravel: 4,782 km (excludes urban roads)
unpaved: 8,108 km (2012)
country comparison to the world: 126
Merchant marine: *total:* 2
by type: passenger/cargo 2
registered in other countries: 19 (Antigua and Barbuda 10, Belize 1, Faroe Islands 4, Finland 1, Gibraltar 1, Norway 2) (2010)
country comparison to the world: 141
Ports and terminals: *major seaport(s):* Grundartangi, Hafnarfjordur, Reykjavik

---

MILITARY AND SECURITY

Military branches: no regular military forces; Icelandic National Police; Icelandic Coast Guard (2013)
Military expenditures: 0.13% of GDP (2012)
0.14% of GDP (2011)
0.13% of GDP (2010)
country comparison to the world: 131
Military—note: Iceland is the only NATO member that has no standing military force; all US military forces in Iceland were withdrawn as of October 2006; defense of Iceland remains a NATO commitment and NATO maintains an air policing presence in Icelandic airspace; Iceland participates in international peacekeeping missions with the civilian-manned Icelandic Crisis Response Unit (ICRU)

TRANSNATIONAL ISSUES

Disputes—international: Iceland, the UK, and Ireland dispute Denmark's claim that the Faroe Islands' continental shelf extends beyond 200 nm; the European Free Trade Association Surveillance Authority filed a suit against Iceland, claiming the country violated the European Economic Area agreement in failing to pay minimum compensation to Icesave depositors
Refugees and internally displaced persons: *stateless persons:* 131 (2015)

INDIA

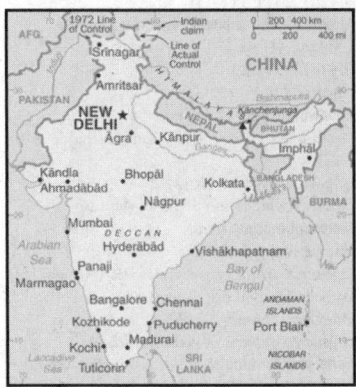

INTRODUCTION

Background: The Indus Valley civilization, one of the world's oldest, flourished during the 3rd and 2nd millennia B.C. and extended into northwestern India. Aryan tribes from the northwest infiltrated the Indian subcontinent about 1500 B.C.; their merger with the earlier Dravidian inhabitants created the classical Indian culture. The Maurya Empire of the 4th and 3rd centuries B.C.—which reached its zenith under ASHOKA—united much of South Asia. The Golden Age ushered in by the Gupta dynasty (4th to 6th centuries A.D.) saw a flowering of Indian science, art, and culture. Islam spread across the subcontinent over a period of 700 years. In the 10th and 11th centuries, Turks and Afghans invaded India and established the Delhi Sultanate. In the early 16th century, the Emperor BABUR established the Mughal Dynasty, which ruled India for more than three centuries. European explorers began establishing footholds in India during the 16th century. By the 19th century, Great Britain had become the dominant political power on the subcontinent. The British Indian Army played a vital role in both World Wars. Years of nonviolent resistance to British rule, led by Mohandas GANDHI and Jawaharlal NEHRU, eventually resulted in Indian independence, which was granted in 1947. Large-scale communal violence took place before and after the subcontinent partition into two separate states—India and Pakistan. The neighboring nations have fought three wars since independence, the last of which was in 1971 and resulted in East Pakistan becoming the separate nation of Bangladesh. India's nuclear weapons tests in 1998 emboldened Pakistan to conduct its own tests that same year. In November 2008, terrorists originating from Pakistan conducted a series of coordinated attacks in Mumbai, India's financial capital. Despite pressing problems such as significant overpopulation, environmental degradation, extensive poverty, and widespread corruption, economic growth following the launch of economic reforms in 1991 and

a massive youthful population are driving India's emergence as a regional and global power.

GEOGRAPHY

Location: Southern Asia, bordering the Arabian Sea and the Bay of Bengal, between Burma and Pakistan

Geographic coordinates: 20 00 N, 77 00 E

Map references: Asia

Area: *total:* 3,287,263 sq km
land: 2,973,193 sq km
water: 314,070 sq km
country comparison to the world: 7

Area—comparative: slightly more than one-third the size of the US

Land boundaries: *total:* 13,888 km
border countries (6): Bangladesh 4,142 km, Bhutan 659 km, Burma 1,468 km, China 2,659 km, Nepal 1,770 km, Pakistan 3,190 km

Coastline: 7,000 km

Maritime claims: *territorial sea:* 12 nm
contiguous zone: 24 nm
exclusive economic zone: 200 nm
continental shelf: 200 nm or to the edge of the continental margin

Climate: varies from tropical monsoon in south to temperate in north

Terrain: upland plain (Deccan Plateau) in south, flat to rolling plain along the Ganges, deserts in west, Himalayas in north

Elevation: *mean elevation:* 160 m

elevation extremes: *lowest point:* Indian Ocean 0 m
highest point: Kanchenjunga 8,598 m

Natural resources: coal (fourth-largest reserves in the world), iron ore, manganese, mica, bauxite, rare earth elements, titanium ore, chromite, natural gas, diamonds, petroleum, limestone, *arable land:*

Land use: *agricultural land:* 60.5%
arable land: 52.8%
permanent crops: 4.2%
permanent pasture: 3.5%
forest: 23.1%
other: 16.4% (2011 est.)

Irrigated land: 667,000 sq km (2012)

Total renewable water resources: 1,911 cu km (2011)

Freshwater withdrawal (domestic/industrial/agricultural): *total:* 761 cu km/yr (7%/2%/90%)
per capita: 613 cu m/yr (2010)

Natural hazards: droughts; flash floods, as well as widespread and destructive flooding from monsoonal rains; severe thunderstorms; earthquakes
volcanism: Barren Island (elev.354 m) in the Andaman Sea has been active in recent years

Environment—current issues: deforestation; soil erosion; overgrazing; desertification; air pollution from industrial effluents and vehicle emissions; water pollution from raw sewage and runoff of agricultural pesticides; tap water is not potable

throughout the country; huge and growing population is overstraining natural resources

Environment—international agreements: *party to:* Antarctic-Environmental Protocol, Antarctic-Marine Living Resources, Antarctic Treaty, Biodiversity, Climate Change, Climate Change-Kyoto Protocol, Desertification, Endangered Species, Environmental Modification, Hazardous Wastes, Law of the Sea, Ozone Layer Protection, Ship Pollution, Tropical Timber 83, Tropical Timber 94, Wetlands, Whaling
signed, but not ratified: none of the selected agreements

Geography—note: dominates South Asian subcontinent; near important Indian Ocean trade routes; Kanchenjunga, third tallest mountain in the world, lies on the border with Nepal

PEOPLE AND SOCIETY

Nationality: *noun:* Indian(s)
adjective: Indian

Ethnic groups: Indo-Aryan 72%, Dravidian 25%, Mongoloid and other 3% (2000)

Languages: Hindi 41%, Bengali 8.1%, Telugu 7.2%, Marathi 7%, Tamil 5.9%, Urdu 5%, Gujarati 4.5%, Kannada 3.7%, Malayalam 3.2%, Oriya 3.2%, Punjabi 2.8%, Assamese 1.3%, Maithili 1.2%, other 5.9%
note: English enjoys the status of subsidiary official language but is the most important language for national, political, and commercial communication; Hindi is the most widely spoken language and primary tongue of 41% of the people; there are 14 other official languages: Bengali, Telugu, Marathi, Tamil, Urdu, Gujarati, Malayalam, Kannada, Oriya, Punjabi, Assamese, Kashmiri, Sindhi, and Sanskrit; Hindustani is a popular variant of Hindi/Urdu Spoken widely throughout northern India but is not an official language (2001 census)

Religions: Hindu 79.8%, Muslim 14.2%, Christian 2.3%, Sikh 1.7%, other and unspecified 2% (2011 est.)

Population: 1,251,695,584 (July 2015 est.)
country comparison to the world: 2

Age structure: *0–14 years:* 28.09% (male 186,735,337/female 164,835,868)
15–24 years: 18.06% (male 119,933,717/female 106,153,113)
25–54 years: 40.74% (male 262,700,370/female 247,237,448)
55–64 years: 7.16% (male 44,993,382/female 44,620,337)
65 years and over: 5.95% (male 35,313,609/female 39,172,403) (2015 est.)

Dependency ratios: *total dependency ratio:* 52.4%
youth dependency ratio: 43.9%
elderly dependency ratio: 8.6%
potential support ratio: 11.7% (2015 est.)

Median age: *total:* 27.3 years
male: 26.7 years
female: 28 years (2015 est.)

country comparison to the world: 139
Population growth rate: 1.22% (2015 est.)
country comparison to the world: 98
Birth rate: 19.55 births/1,000 population (2015 est.)
country comparison to the world: 87
Death rate: 7.32 deaths/1,000 population (2015 est.)
country comparison to the world: 118
Net migration rate: -0.04 migrant(s)/1,000 population (2015 est.)
country comparison to the world: 112
Urbanization: *urban Population:* 32.7% of total population (2015)
rate of urbanization: 2.38% annual rate of change (2010–15 est.)
Major urban areas—Population: NEW DELHI (capital) 25.703 million; Mumbai 21.043 million; Kolkata 11.766 million; Bangalore 10.087 million; Chennai 9.62 million; Hyderabad 8.944 million (2015)
Sex ratio: *at birth:* 1.12 male(s)/female
0–14 years: 1.13 male(s)/female
15–24 years: 1.13 male(s)/female
25–54 years: 1.06 male(s)/female
55–64 years: 1.01 male(s)/female
65 years and over: 0.9 male(s)/female
total Population: 1.08 male(s)/female (2015 est.)
Mother's mean age at first birth: 19.9 (2005/06 est.)
Maternal mortality rate: 174 deaths/100,000 live births (2015 est.)
country comparison to the world: 55
Infant mortality rate: *total:* 41.81 deaths/1,000 live births
male: 40.56 deaths/1,000 live births
female: 43.22 deaths/1,000 live births (2015 est.)
country comparison to the world: 50
Life expectancy at birth: *total Population:* 68.13 years
male: 66.97 years
female: 69.42 years (2015 est.)
country comparison to the world: 163
Total fertility rate: 2.48 children born/woman (2015 est.)
country comparison to the world: 78
Contraceptive prevalence rate: 54.8% (2007/08)
Health expenditures: 4% of GDP (2013)
country comparison to the world: 159
Physicians density: 0.7 physicians/1,000 population (2012)
Hospital bed density: 0.7 beds/1,000 population (2011)
Drinking water source:
improved:
urban: 97.1% of population
rural: 92.6% of population
total: 94.1% of population
unimproved:
urban: 2.9% of population
rural: 7.4% of population
total: 5.9% of population (2015 est.)
Sanitation facility access:
improved:
urban: 62.6% of population
rural: 28.5% of population

total: 39.6% of population
unimproved:
urban: 37.4% of population
rural: 71.5% of population
total: 60.4% of population (2015 est.)
HIV/AIDS—adult prevalence rate: 0.26% (2013 est.)
country comparison to the world: 90
HIV/AIDS—people living with HIV/AIDS: 2,079,700 (2013 est.)
country comparison to the world: 3
HIV/AIDS—deaths: 127,200 (2013 est.)
country comparison to the world: 3
Major infectious diseases: *degree of risk:* very high
food or waterborne diseases: bacterial diarrhea, hepatitis A and E, and typhoid fever
vectorborne diseases: dengue fever, Japanese encephalitis, and malaria
water contact disease: leptospirosis
animal contact disease: rabies
note: highly pathogenic H5N1 avian influenza has been identified in this country; it poses a negligible risk with extremely rare cases possible among US citizens who have close contact with birds (2013)
Obesity—adult prevalence rate: 4.7% (2014)
country comparison to the world: 184
Children under the age of 5 years underweight: 43.5% (2006)
country comparison to the world: 2
Education expenditures: 3.8% of GDP (2012)
country comparison to the world: 134
Literacy: *definition:* age 15 and over can read and write
total Population: 71.2%
male: 81.3%
female: 60.6% (2015 est.)
School life expectancy (primary to tertiary education): *total:* 12 years
male: 11 years
female: 12 years (2013)
Child labor—children ages 5–14: *total number:* 26,965,074
percentage: 12% (2006 est.)
Unemployment, youth ages 15–24: *total:* 10.7%
male: 10.4%
female: 11.6% (2012 est.)
country comparison to the world: 97

GOVERNMENT

Country name: *conventional long form:* Republic of India
conventional short form: India
local long form: Republic of India/Bharatiya Ganarajya
local short form: India/Bharat
etymology: the English name derives from the Indus River; the Indian name "Bharat" may derive from the "Bharatas" tribe mentioned in the Vedas of the second millennium B.C.; the name is also associated with Emperor Bharata, the legendary conqueror of all of India
Government type: federal parliamentary republic
Capital: *name:* New Delhi
Geographic coordinates: 28 36 N, 77 12 E

time difference: UTC+5.5 (10.5 hours ahead of Washington, DC, during Standard Time)
Administrative divisions: 29 states and 7 union territories*; Andaman and Nicobar Islands*, Andhra Pradesh, Arunachal Pradesh, Assam, Bihar, Chandigarh*, Chhattisgarh, Dadra and Nagar Haveli*, Daman and Diu*, Delhi*, Goa, Gujarat, Haryana, Himachal Pradesh, Jammu and Kashmir, Jharkhand, Karnataka, Kerala, Lakshadweep*, Madhya Pradesh, Maharashtra, Manipur, Meghalaya, Mizoram, Nagaland, Odisha, Puducherry*, Punjab, Rajasthan, Sikkim, Tamil Nadu, Telangana, Tripura, Uttar Pradesh, Uttarakhand, West Bengal
note: although its status is that of a union territory, the official name of Delhi is National Capital Territory of Delhi
Independence: 15 August 1947 (from the UK)
National holiday: Republic Day, 26 January (1950)
Constitution: previous 1935 (preindependence); latest draft completed 4 November 1949, adopted 26 November 1949, effective 26 January 1950; amended many times, last in 2015 (2016)
Legal system: common law system based on the English model; separate personal law codes apply to Muslims, Christians, and Hindus; judicial review of legislative acts
International law organization participation: accepts compulsory ICJ jurisdiction with reservations; non-party state to the ICCt
Citizenship: *citizenship by birth:* no
citizenship by descent only: at least one parent must be a citizen of India
dual citizenship recognized: no
residency requirement for naturalization: 5 years
Suffrage: 18 years of age; universal
Executive branch: *chief of state:* President Pranab MUKHERJEE (since 22 July 2012); Vice President Mohammad Hamid ANSARI (since 11 August 2007)
head of government: Prime Minister Narendra MODI (since 26 May 2014)
cabinet: Union Council of Ministers recommended by the prime minister, appointed by the president
elections/appointments: president indirectly elected by an electoral college consisting of elected members of both houses of Parliament and state legislatures for a 5-year term (no term limits); election last held on 19 July 2012 (next to be held in July 2017); vice president indirectly elected by an electoral college consisting of elected members of both houses of Parliament and state legislatures for a 5-year term (no term limits); election last held on 7 August 2012 (next to be held in August 2017); following legislative elections, the prime minister is elected by parliamentary members of the majority party
election results: Pranab MUKHERJEE elected president; percent of vote—Pranab MUKHERJEE (INC prior to election) 69.3%, Purno SANGMA (independent) 30.7%; Mohammad Hamid ANSARI reelected vice president; electoral college vote—Mohammad Hamid ANSARI 490, Jaswant SINGH 238

Legislative branch: *description:* bicameral Parliament or Sansad consists of the Council of States or Rajya Sabha (245 seats; 233 members indirectly elected by state and territorial assemblies by proportional representation vote, and 12 members appointed by the president; members serve 6-year terms) and the People's Assembly or Lok Sabha (545 seats; 543 members directly elected in single-seat constituencies by simple majority vote and 2 appointed by the president; members serve 5-year terms)

elections: People's Assembly—last held April-May 2014 in 10 phases; (next to be held by May 2019)

election results: People's Assembly—percent of vote by party—BJP 31.0%, INC 19.3%, AITC 3.8%, SP 3.4%, AIADMK 3.3%, CPI(M) 3.3%, TDP 2.6%, YSRC 2.5%, AAP 2.1%, SAD 1.8%, BJD 1.7%, SS 1.7%, NCP 1.6%, RJD 1.3%, TRS 1.3%, LJP 0.4%, other 15.9%, independent 3.0%; seats by party—BJP 282, INC 44, AIADMK 37, AITC 34, BJD 20, SS 18, TDP 16, TRS 11, CPI(M) 9, YSRC 9, LJP 6, NCP 6, SP 5, AAP 4, RJD 4, SAD 4, other 33, independent 3

Judicial branch: *highest court(s):* Supreme Court (the chief justice and 25 associate justices); note—parliament approved an additional 5 judges in 2008

judge selection and term of office: justices appointed by the president to serve until age 65

subordinate courts: High Courts; District Courts; Labour Court

note: in mid-2011, India's Cabinet approved the "National Mission for Justice Delivery and Legal Reform" to eliminate judicial corruption and reduce the backlog of cases; as of mid-July 2015, the Indian Government was considering the introduction of pre-trial hearings as a method for reducing the backlog

Political parties and leaders: Aam Aadmi Party or AAP [Arvind KEJRIWAL]

All India Anna Dravida Munnetra Kazhagam or AIADMK [J. JAYALALITHAA]

All India Trinamool Congress or AITC [Mamata BANERJEE]

Bahujan Samaj Party or BSP [MAYAWATI]

Bharatiya Janata Party or BJP [Amit SHAH]

Biju Janata Dal or BJD [Naveen PATNAIK]

Communist Party of India-Marxist or CPI(M) [Prakash KARAT]

Indian National Congress or INC [Sonia GANDHI]

Lok Janshakti Party (LJP) [Ram Vilas PASWAN]

Nationalist Congress Party or NCP [Sharad PAWAR]

Rashtriya Janata Dal or RJD [Lalu Prasad YADAV]

Samajwadi Party or SP [Mulayam Singh YADAV]

Shiromani Akali Dal or SAD [Parkash Singh BADAL]

Shiv Sena or SS [Uddhav THACKERAY]

Telegana Rashtra Samithi (TRS) [K. Chandrashekar RAO]

Telugu Desam Party or TDP [Chandrabab UNAIDU]

YSR Congress (YSRC) [Jaganmohan REDDY]

note: India has dozens of national and regional political parties

Political pressure groups and leaders: All Parties Hurriyat Conference in the Kashmir Valley (separatist group)

Bajrang Dal (militant religious organization)

Jamiat Ulema-e Hind [Mahmood MADANI] (religious organization)

Rashtriya Swayamsevak Sangh [Mohan BHAGWAT] (nationalist organization)

Vishwa Hindu Parishad [Pravin TOGADIA] (militant religious organization)

other: hundreds of social reform, anti-corruption, and environmental groups at state and local level; numerous religious or militant/chauvinistic organizations; various separatist groups seeking greater communal and/or regional autonomy

International organization participation: ADB, AfDB (nonregional member), Arctic Council (observer), ARF, ASEAN (dialogue partner), BIMSTEC, BIS, BRICS, C, CD, CERN (observer), CICA, CP, EAS, FAO, FATF, G-15, G-20, G-24, G-5, G-77, IAEA, IBRD, ICAO, ICC (national committees), ICRM, IDA, IFAD, IFC, IFRCS, IHO, ILO, IMF, IMO, IMSO, Interpol, IOC, IOM, IPU, ISO, ITSO, ITU, ITUC (NGOs), LAS (observer), MIGA, MINURSO, MONUSCO, NAM, OAS (observer), OECD, OPCW, Pacific Alliance (observer), PCA, PIF (partner), SAARC, SACEP, SCO (observer), UN, UNCTAD, UNDOF, UNESCO, UNHCR, UNIDO, UNIFIL, UNISFA, UNITAR, UNMISS, UNOCI, UNWTO, UPU, WCO, WFTU (NGOs), WHO, WIPO, WMO, WTO

Diplomatic representation in the US: *chief of mission:* Ambassador Arun Kumar SINGH (since 18 May 2015)

chancery: 2107 Massachusetts Avenue NW, Washington, DC 20008; note—Consular Wing located at 2536 Massachusetts Avenue NW, Washington, DC 20008

telephone: [1](202) 939-7000

FAX: [1] (202) 265-4351

consulate(s) general: Atlanta, Chicago, Houston, New York, San Francisco

Diplomatic representation from the US: *chief of mission:* Ambassador Richard Rahul VERMA (since 16 January 2015)

embassy: Shantipath, Chanakyapuri, New Delhi 110021

mailing address: use embassy street address

telephone: [91] (11) 2419-8000

FAX: [91] (11) 2419-0017

consulate(s) general: Chennai (Madras), Hyderabad, Kolkata (Calcutta), Mumbai (Bombay)

Flag description: three equal horizontal bands of saffron (subdued orange) (top), white, and green, with a blue chakra (24-spoked wheel) centered in the white band; saffron represents courage, sacrifice, and the spirit of renunciation; white signifies purity and truth; green stands for faith and fertility; the blue chakra symbolizes the wheel of life in movement and death in stagnation

note: similar to the flag of Niger, which has a small orange disk centered in the white band

National symbol(s): the Lion Capital of Ashoka, which depicts four Asiatic lions standing back to back mounted on a circular abacus, is the official emblem; Bengal tiger; lotus flower; national colors: saffron, white, green

National anthem: *name:* "Jana-Gana-Mana" (Thou Art the Ruler of the Minds of All People) *lyrics/music:* Rabindranath TAGORE

note: adopted 1950; Rabindranath TAGORE, a Nobel laureate, also wrote Bangladesh's national anthem

ECONOMY

Economy—overview: India's diverse economy encompasses traditional village farming, modern agriculture, handicrafts, a wide range of modern industries, and a multitude of services. Slightly less than half of the work force is in agriculture, but, services are the major source of economic growth, accounting for nearly two-thirds of India's output with less than one-third of its labor force. India has capitalized on its large educated English-speaking population to become a major exporter of information technology services, business outsourcing services, and software workers.

India is developing into an open-market economy, yet traces of its past autarkic policies remain. Economic liberalization measures, including industrial deregulation, privatization of state-owned enterprises, and reduced controls on foreign trade and investment, began in the early 1990s and served to accelerate the country's growth, which averaged under 7% per year from 1997 to 2011. India's economic growth began slowing in 2011 because of a decline in investment caused by high interest rates, rising inflation, and investor pessimism about the government's commitment to further economic reforms and about slow world growth. Rising macroeconomic imbalances in India and improving economic conditions in Western countries led investors to shift capital away from India, prompting a sharp depreciation of the rupee. Growth rebounded in 2014 and 2015, with both years exceeding 7%. Investors' perceptions of India improved in early 2014, due to a reduction of the current account deficit and expectations of post-election economic reform, resulting in a surge of inbound capital flows and stabilization of the rupee. Since the election, economic reforms have focused on administrative and governance changes largely because the ruling party remains a minority in India's upper house of Parliament, which must approve most bills. Despite a high growth rate compared to the rest of the world, in 2015, India's government-owned banks faced mounting bad debt, resulting in low credit growth and restrained economic growth. The outlook for India's long-term growth is moderately positive due to a young population and corresponding low dependency ratio, healthy savings and investment rates, and increasing integration into the global economy. However, India's discrimination against women and girls, an inefficient power generation and distribution system, ineffective enforcement of intellectual property rights, decades-long civil litigation dockets, inadequate transport and agricultural infrastructure, limited non-agricultural employment opportunities, high spending and poorly-targeted subsidies, inadequate availability of quality basic and higher education, and accommodating rural-to-urban migration are significant long-term challenges.

GDP (purchasing power parity): $7.965 trillion (2015 est.)
$7.421 trillion (2014 est.)
$6.92 trillion (2013 est.)
note: data are in 2015 US dollars
country comparison to the world: 4

GDP (official exchange rate): $2.091 trillion (2015 est.)

GDP—real growth rate: 7.3% (2015 est.)
7.2% (2014 est.)
6.6% (2013 est.)
country comparison to the world: 12

GDP—per capita (PPP): $6,200 (2015 est.)
$5,800 (2014 est.)
$5,500 (2013 est.)
note: data are in 2015 US dollars
country comparison to the world: 158

Gross national saving: 32% of GDP (2015 est.)
32.7% of GDP (2014 est.)
32.9% of GDP (2013 est.)
country comparison to the world: 17

GDP—composition, by end use:
household consumption: 59.7%
government consumption: 11.7%
investment in fixed capital: 26.8%
investment in inventories: 4.4%
exports of goods and services: 19.4%
imports of goods and services: -22% (2015 est.)

GDP—composition, by sector of origin:
agriculture: 16.1%
industry: 29.5%
services: 54.4% (2015 est.)

Agriculture—products: rice, wheat, oilseed, cotton, jute, tea, sugarcane, lentils, onions, potatoes; dairy products, sheep, goats, poultry; fish

Industries: textiles, chemicals, food processing, steel, transportation equipment, cement, mining, petroleum, machinery, software, pharmaceuticals

Industrial production growth rate: 2.8% (2015 est.)
country comparison to the world: 92

Labor force: 502.1 million (2015 est.)
country comparison to the world: 2

Labor force—by occupation: *agriculture:* 49%
industry: 20%
services: 31% (2012 est.)

Unemployment rate: 7.1% (2015 est.)
7.3% (2014 est.)
country comparison to the world: 85

Population below poverty line: 29.8% (2010 est.)

Household income or consumption by percentage share: *lowest:* 10%: 3.6%
highest: 10%: 31.1% (2005)

Distribution of family income—Gini index: 33.6 (2012)
37.8 (1997)
country comparison to the world: 103

Budget: *revenues:* $236 billion
expenditures: $326.2 billion (2015 est.)
Taxes and other revenues: 10.8% of GDP (2015 est.)
country comparison to the world: 210

Budget surplus (+) or deficit (–): -4.1% of GDP (2015 est.)
country comparison to the world: 149

Public debt: 51.7% of GDP (2015 est.)
51.7% of GDP (2014 est.)
note: data cover central government debt, and exclude debt instruments issued (or owned) by government entities other than the treasury; the data include treasury debt held by foreign entities; the data exclude debt issued by subnational entities, as well as intra-governmental debt; intra-governmental debt consists of treasury borrowings from surpluses in the social funds, such as for retirement, medical care, and unemployment; debt instruments for the social funds are not sold at public auctions
country comparison to the world: 78

Fiscal year: 1 April—31 March

Inflation rate (consumer prices): 4.9% (2015 est.)
5.9% (2014 est.)
country comparison to the world: 173

Central bank discount rate: 7.75% (31 December 2014) 7.75% (31 December 2013)
note: this is the Indian central bank's policy rate—the repurchase rate
country comparison to the world: 41

Commercial bank prime lending rate: 9.9% (31 December 2015 est.)
10.25% (31 December 2014 est.)
country comparison to the world: 83

Stock of narrow money: $368.2 billion (31 December 2015 est.)
$345.6 billion (31 December 2014 est.)
country comparison to the world: 14

Stock of broad money: $1.711 trillion (31 December 2015 est.)
$1.612 trillion (31 December 2014 est.)
country comparison to the world: 10

Stock of domestic credit: $1.587 trillion (31 December 2015 est.)
$1.494 trillion (31 December 2014 est.)
country comparison to the world: 15

Market value of publicly traded shares: $1.263 trillion (31 December 2012 est.)
$1.015 trillion (31 December 2011)
$1.616 trillion (31 December 2010 est.)
country comparison to the world: 11

Current account balance: -$26.22 billion (2015 est.)
-$26.72 billion (2014 est.)
country comparison to the world: 188

Exports: $287.6 billion (2015 est.)
$329.6 billion (2014 est.)
country comparison to the world: 17

Exports—commodities: petroleum products, precious stones, vehicles, machinery, iron and steel, chemicals, pharmaceutical products, cereals, apparel

Exports—partners: US 15.2%, UAE 11.4%, Hong Kong 4.6% (2015)

Imports: $432.3 billion (2015 est.)
$472.8 billion (2014 est.)
country comparison to the world: 11

Imports—commodities: crude oil, precious stones, machinery, chemicals, fertilizer, plastics, iron and steel

Imports—partners: China 15.4%, UAE 5.5%, Saudi Arabia 5.4%, Switzerland 5.3%, US 5.1% (2015)

Reserves of foreign exchange and gold: $370.7 billion (31 December 2015 est.)
$322.8 billion (31 December 2014 est.)
country comparison to the world: 8

Debt—external: $459.1 billion (31 December 2014 est.)
$427.4 billion (31 December 2013 est.)
country comparison to the world: 28

Stock of direct foreign investment—at home: $297.1 billion (31 December 2015 est.)
$252.1 billion (31 December 2014 est.)
country comparison to the world: 22

Stock of direct foreign investment—abroad: $137.8 billion (31 December 2015 est.)
$129.8 billion (31 December 2014 est.)
country comparison to the world: 30

Exchange rates: Indian rupees (INR) per US dollar—
64.73 (2015 est.)
61.03 (2014 est.)
61.03 (2013 est.)
53.44 (2012 est.)
46.671 (2011 est.)

ENERGY

Electricity—production: 1.052 trillion kWh (2012 est.)
country comparison to the world: 5

Electricity—consumption: 864.7 billion kWh (2012 est.)
country comparison to the world: 6

Electricity—exports: 5 million kWh (2012 est.)
country comparison to the world: 91

Electricity—imports: 4.794 billion kWh (2012 est.)
country comparison to the world: 42

Electricity—installed generating capacity: 254.7 million kW (2012 est.)
country comparison to the world: 5

Electricity—from fossil fuels: 68.7% of total installed capacity (26 February 2014 est.)
country comparison to the world: 113

Electricity—from nuclear fuels: 2% of total installed capacity (26 February 2014 est.)
country comparison to the world: 29

Electricity—from hydroelectric plants: 16.9% of total installed capacity (26 February 2014 est.)
country comparison to the world: 98

Electricity—from other renewable sources: 12.4% of total installed capacity (26 February 2014 est.)
country comparison to the world: 26

Crude oil—production: 767,600 bbl/day (2014 est.)
country comparison to the world: 25

Crude oil—exports: 0 bbl/day (2013 est.)
country comparison to the world: 140

Crude oil—imports: 3.812 million bbl/day (2013 est.)
country comparison to the world: 3

Crude oil—proved reserves: 5.675 billion bbl (1 January 2015 est.)
country comparison to the world: 23

Refined petroleum products—production: 4.433 million bbl/day (2013)
country comparison to the world: 5

Refined petroleum products—consumption: 3.66 million bbl/day (2013 est.)
country comparison to the world: 5
Refined petroleum products—exports: 1.38 million bbl/day (2013 est.)
country comparison to the world: 7
Refined petroleum products—imports: 312,000 bbl/day (2013 est.)
country comparison to the world: 22
Natural gas—production: 31.7 billion cu m (2014 est.)
country comparison to the world: 27
Natural gas—consumption: 50.6 billion cu m (2014 est.)
country comparison to the world: 16
Natural gas—exports: 0 cu m (2014 est.)
country comparison to the world: 118
Natural gas—imports: 18.9 billion cu m (2014 est.)
country comparison to the world: 20
Natural gas—proved reserves: 1.427 trillion cu m (1 January 2014 est.)
country comparison to the world: 23
Carbon dioxide emissions from consumption of energy: 1.831 billion Mt (2012 est.)
country comparison to the world: 4

COMMUNICATIONS

Telephones—fixed lines: *total subscriptions:* 27 million
subscriptions per 100 inhabitants: 2 (2014 est.)
country comparison to the world: 13
Telephones—mobile cellular: *total:* 944 million
subscriptions per 100 inhabitants: 76 (2014 est.)
country comparison to the world: 2
Telephone system: *general assessment:* supported by recent deregulation and liberalization of telecommunications laws and policies, India has emerged as one of the fastest-growing telecom markets in the world; total telephone subscribership base exceeded 1 billion in 2015, an overall teledensity of roughly 81%, and subscribership is currently growing at roughly 5 million per month; urban teledensity now exceeds 100%, and rural teledensity has reached 50%
domestic: mobile cellular service introduced in 1994 and organized nationwide into four metropolitan areas and 19 telecom circles, each with multiple private service providers and one or more state-owned service providers; in recent years significant trunk capacity added in the form of fiber-optic cable and one of the world's largest domestic satellite systems, the Indian National Satellite system (INSAT), with 6 satellites supporting 33,000 very small aperture terminals (VSAT)
international: country code—91; a number of major international submarine cable systems, including SEA-ME-WE-3 with landing sites at Cochin and Mumbai (Bombay), SEA-ME-WE-4 with a landing site at Chennai, Fiber-Optic Link Around the Globe (FLAG) with a landing site at Mumbai (Bombay), South Africa -Far East (SAFE) with a landing site at Cochin, the i2i cable network linking to Singapore with landing sites at Mumbai (Bombay) and Chennai (Madras), and Tata Indicom linking Singapore and Chennai

(Madras), provide a significant increase in the bandwidth available for both voice and data traffic; satellite earth stations—8 Intelsat (Indian Ocean) and 1 Inmarsat (Indian Ocean region); 9 gateway exchanges operating from Mumbai (Bombay), New Delhi, Kolkata (Calcutta), Chennai (Madras), Jalandhar, Kanpur, Gandhinagar, Hyderabad, and Ernakulam (2015)
Broadcast media: Doordarshan, India's public TV network, operates about 20 national, regional, and local services; a large and increasing number of privately owned TV stations are distributed by cable and satellite service providers; in 2015, more than 230 million homes had access to cable and satellite TV offering more than 700 TV channels; government controls AM radio with All India Radio operating domestic and external networks; news broadcasts via radio are limited to the All India Radio Network; since 2000, privately owned FM stations have been permitted and their numbers have increased rapidly (2015)
Radio broadcast stations: AM 149, FM 171, shortwave 54 (2009)
Television broadcast stations: 1,400 (2009)
Internet country code: .in
Internet hosts: 6.746 million (2012)
country comparison to the world: 17
Internet users: *total:* 237.3 million
percent of Population: 19.2% (2014 est.)
country comparison to the world: 4

TRANSPORTATION

Airports: 346 (2013)
country comparison to the world: 21
Airports—with paved runways: *total:* 253
over 3,047 m: 22
2,438 to 3,047 m: 59
1,524 to 2,437 m: 76
914 to 1,523 m: 82
under 914 m: 14 (2013)
Airports—with unpaved runways: *total:* 93
over 3,047 m: 1
2,438 to 3,047 m: 3
1,524 to 2,437 m: 6
914 to 1,523 m: 38
under 914 m: 45 (2013)
Heliports: 45 (2013)
Pipelines: condensate/gas 9 km; gas 13,581 km; liquid petroleum gas 2,054 km; oil 8,943 km; oil/gas/water 20 km; refined products 11,069 km (2013)
Railways: *total:* 68,525 km
broad gauge: 58,404 km 1.676-m gauge (23,654 electrified)
narrow gauge: 9,499 km 1.000-m gauge; 622 km 0.762-m gauge (2014)
country comparison to the world: 5
Roadways: *total:* 4,699,024 km
note: includes 96,214 km of national highways and expressways, 147,800 km of state highways, and 4,455,010 km of other roads (2015)
country comparison to the world: 2
Waterways: 14,500 km (5,200 km on major rivers and 485 km on canals suitable for mechanized vessels) (2012)
country comparison to the world: 9

Merchant marine: *total:* 340
by type: bulk carrier 104, cargo 78, chemical tanker 22, container 14, liquefied gas 11, passenger 4, passenger/cargo 15, petroleum tanker 92
foreign-owned: 10 (China 1, Hong Kong 2, Jersey 2, Malaysia 1, UAE 4)
registered in other countries: 76 (Cyprus 4, Dominica 2, Liberia 8, Malta 3, Marshall Islands 10, Nigeria 1, Panama 24, Saint Kitts and Nevis 2, Singapore 21, unknown 1) (2010)
country comparison to the world: 29

Ports and terminals: *major seaport(s):* Chennai, Jawaharal Nehru Port, Kandla, Kolkata (Calcutta), Mumbai (Bombay), Sikka, Vishakhapatnam
container port(s) (TEUs): Chennai (1,558,343), Jawaharal Nehru Port (4,307,622)
LNG terminal (s) (import): Dabhol, Dahej, Hazira

MILITARY AND SECURITY

Military branches: Army, Navy (includes naval air arm), Air Force, Coast Guard (2011)
Military service age and obligation: 16–18 years of age for voluntary military service (Army 171/2, Air Force 17, Navy 161/2); no conscription; women may join as officers, currently serve in combat roles as pilots, and will soon be allowed in all combat roles (2016)
Military expenditures: 2.4% of GDP (2014)
2.4% of GDP (2013)
2.5% of GDP (2012)
2.6% of GDP (2011)
2.7% of GDP (2010)
country comparison to the world: 31

TRANSNATIONAL ISSUES

Disputes—international: since China and India launched a security and foreign policy dialogue in 2005, consolidated discussions related to the dispute over most of their rugged, militarized boundary, regional nuclear proliferation, Indian claims that China transferred missiles to Pakistan, and other matters continue Kashmir remains the site of the world's largest and most militarized territorial dispute with portions under the de facto administration of China (Aksai Chin), India (Jammu and Kashmir), and Pakistan (Azad Kashmir and Northern Areas) India and Pakistan resumed bilateral dialogue in February 2011 after a two-year hiatus, have maintained the 2003 cease-fire in Kashmir, and continue to have disputes over water sharing of the Indus River and its tributaries
UN Military Observer Group in India and Pakistan has maintained a small group of peacekeepers since 1949; India does not recognize Pakistan's ceding historic Kashmir lands to China in 1964; to defuse tensions and prepare for discussions on a maritime boundary, India and Pakistan seek technical resolution of the disputed boundary in Sir Creek estuary at the mouth of the Rann of Kutch in the Arabian Sea; Pakistani maps continue to show its Junagadh claim in Indian Gujarat State; Prime Minister Singh's September 2011 visit to Bangladesh resulted in the signing of a Protocol to the 1974 Land Boundary Agreement between

India and Bangladesh, which had called for the settlement of longstanding boundary disputes over undemarcated areas and the exchange of territorial enclaves, but which had never been implemented; Bangladesh referred its maritime boundary claims with Burma and India to the International Tribunal on the Law of the Sea; Joint Border Committee with Nepal continues to examine contested boundary sections, including the 400 sq km dispute over the source of the Kalapani River; India

maintains a strict border regime to keep out Maoist insurgents and control illegal cross-border activities from Nepal

Refugees and internally displaced persons: *refugees (country of origin):* 109,018 (Tibet/China); 65,057 (Sri Lanka); 14,301 (Burma); 10,395 (Afghanistan) (2014)
IDPs: 612,000 (armed conflict and intercommunal violence) (2015)

Illicit drugs: world's largest producer of licit opium for the pharmaceutical trade, but an undetermined quantity of opium is diverted to illicit international drug markets; transit point for illicit narcotics produced in neighboring countries and throughout Southwest Asia; illicit producer of methaqualone; vulnerable to narcotics money laundering through the hawala system; licit ketamine and precursor production

INDIAN OCEAN

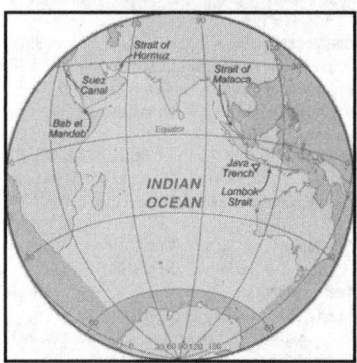

INTRODUCTION

Background: The Indian Ocean is the third largest of the world's five oceans (after the Pacific Ocean and Atlantic Ocean, but larger than the Southern Ocean and Arctic Ocean). Four critically important access waterways are the Suez Canal (Egypt), Bab el Mandeb (Djibouti-Yemen), Strait of Hormuz (Iran-Oman), and Strait of Malacca (Indonesia-Malaysia). The decision by the International Hydrographic Organization in the spring of 2000 to delimit a fifth ocean, the Southern Ocean, removed the portion of the Indian Ocean south of 60 degrees south latitude.

GEOGRAPHY

Location: body of water between Africa, the Southern Ocean, Asia, and Australia

Geographic coordinates: 20 00 S, 80 00 E
Map references: Political Map of the World
Area: *total:* 68.556 million sq km
note: includes Andaman Sea, Arabian Sea, Bay of Bengal, Flores Sea, Great Australian Bight, Gulf of Aden, Gulf of Oman, Java Sea, Mozambique Channel, Persian Gulf, Red Sea, SavUSea, Strait of Malacca, Timor Sea, and other tributary water bodies
Area—comparative: almost 7 times the size of the US
Coastline: 66,526 km
Climate: northeast monsoon (December to April), southwest monsoon (June to October); tropical cyclones occur during May/June and October/

November in the northern Indian Ocean and January/February in the southern Indian Ocean
Terrain: surface dominated by counterclockwise gyre (broad, circular system of currents) in the southern Indian Ocean; unique reversal of surface currents in the northern Indian Ocean; low atmospheric pressure over southwest Asia from hot, rising, summer air results in the southwest monsoon and southwest-to-northeast winds and currents, while high pressure over northern Asia from cold, falling, winter air results in the northeast monsoon and northeast-to-southwest winds and currents; ocean floor is dominated by the Mid-Indian Ocean Ridge and subdivided by the Southeast Indian Ocean Ridge, Southwest Indian Ocean Ridge, and Ninetyeast Ridge
Elevation: *mean depth:* -3,741 m

elevation extremes: *lowest point:* Java Trench -7,258 m
highest point: sea level 0 m
Natural resources: oil and gas fields, fish, shrimp, sand and gravel aggregates, placer deposits, polymetallic nodules
Natural hazards: occasional icebergs pose navigational hazard in southern reaches
Environment—current issues: endangered marine species include the dugong, seals, turtles, and whales; oil pollution in the Arabian Sea, Persian Gulf, and Red Sea
Geography—note: major chokepoints include Bab el Mandeb, Strait of Hormuz, Strait of Malacca, southern access to the Suez Canal, and the Lombok Strait

GOVERNMENT

Country name: *etymology:* named for the country of India, which makes up much of its northern border

ECONOMY

Economy—overview: The Indian Ocean provides major sea routes connecting the Middle East, Africa, and East Asia with Europe and the Americas. It carries a particularly heavy traffic of petroleum and petroleum products from the oilfields of the Persian Gulf and Indonesia. Its fish are of great and growing importance to the bordering countries for domestic consumption and export. Fishing fleets from Russia, Japan, South Korea, and Taiwan also exploit the Indian Ocean, mainly for shrimp

and tuna. Large reserves of hydrocarbons are being tapped in the offshore areas of Saudi Arabia, Iran, India, and western Australia. An estimated 40% of the world's offshore oil production comes from the Indian Ocean. Beach sands rich in heavy minerals and offshore placer deposits are actively exploited by bordering countries, particularly India, South Africa, Indonesia, Sri Lanka, and Thailand.

TRANSPORTATION

Ports and terminals: *major seaport(s):* Chennai (Madras, India); Colombo (Sri Lanka); Durban (South Africa); Jakarta (Indonesia); Kolkata (Calcutta, India); Melbourne (Australia); Mumbai (Bombay, India); Richards Bay (South Africa)
Transportation—note: although the number of reported incidents of piracy have dropped dramatically in 2014, the International Maritime Bureau continues to report the territorial waters of littoral states and offshore waters as high risk for piracy and armed robbery against ships, particularly in the Gulf of Aden, along the east coast of Africa, the Bay of Bengal, and the Strait of Malacca; the presence of several naval task forces in the Gulf of Aden and additional anti-piracy measures on the part of ship operators, including the use of on-board armed security teams, have reduced incidents of piracy; in response, Somali-based pirates, using hijacked fishing trawlers as "mother ships" to extend their range, shifted operations as far south as the Mozambique Channel, eastward to the vicinity of the Maldives, and northeastward to the Strait of Hormuz

TRANSNATIONAL ISSUES

Disputes—international: some maritime disputes (see littoral states)

INDONESIA

INTRODUCTION

Background: The Dutch began to colonize Indonesia in the early 17th century; Japan occupied the islands from 1942 to 1945. Indonesia declared its independence shortly before Japan's surrender, but it required four years of sometimes brutal fighting, intermittent negotiations, and UN mediation before the Netherlands agreed to transfer sovereignty in 1949. A period of sometimes unruly parliamentary democracy ended in 1957 when President SOEKARNO declared martial law and instituted "Guided Democracy. " After an abortive coup in 1965 by alleged communist sympathizers, SOEKARNO was gradually eased from power. From 1967 until 1988, President SUHARTO ruled Indonesia with his "New Order" government. After rioting toppled SUHARTO in 1998, free and fair legislative elections took place in 1999. Indonesia is now the world's third most populous democracy, the world's largest archipelagic state, and the world's largest Muslim-majority nation. Current issues include: alleviating poverty, improving education, preventing terrorism, consolidating democracy after four decades of authoritarianism, implementing economic and financial reforms, stemming corruption, reforming the criminal justice system, holding the military and police accountable for human rights violations, addressing climate change, and controlling infectious diseases, particularly those of global and regional importance. In 2005, Indonesia reached a historic peace agreement with armed separatists in Aceh, which led to democratic elections in Aceh in December 2006. Indonesia continues to face low intensity armed resistance in Papua by the separatist Free Papua Movement.

GEOGRAPHY

Location: Southeastern Asia, archipelago between the Indian Ocean and the Pacific Ocean

Geographic coordinates: 5 00 S, 120 00 E

Map references: Southeast Asia

Area: *total:* 1,904,569 sq km

land: 1,811,569 sq km

water: 93,000 sq km

country comparison to the world: 15

Area—comparative: slightly less than three times the size of Texas

Land boundaries: *total:* 2,958 km

border countries (3): Timor-Leste 253 km, Malaysia 1,881 km, Papua New Guinea 824 km

Coastline: 54,716 km

Maritime claims: measured from claimed archipelagic straight baselines

territorial sea: 12 nm

exclusive economic zone: 200 nm

Climate: tropical; hot, humid; more moderate in highlands

Terrain: mostly coastal lowlands; larger islands have interior mountains

Elevation: *mean elevation:* 367 m

elevation extremes: *lowest point:* Indian Ocean 0 m

highest point: Puncak Jaya 4,884 m

Natural resources: petroleum, tin, natural gas, nickel, timber, bauxite, copper, fertile soils, coal, gold, silver

Land use: *agricultural land:* 31.2%

arable land: 13%

permanent crops: 12.1%

permanent pasture: 6.1%

forest: 51.7%

other: 17.1% (2011 est.)

Irrigated land: 67,220 sq km (2012)

Total renewable water resources: 2,019 cu km (2011)

Freshwater withdrawal (domestic/industrial/agricultural): *total:* 113.3 cu km/yr (11%/19%/71%)

per capita: 517.3 cu m/yr (2005)

Natural hazards: occasional floods; severe droughts; tsunamis; earthquakes; volcanoes; forest fires

volcanism: Indonesia contains the most volcanoes of any country in the world—some 76 are historically active; significant volcanic activity occurs on Java, Sumatra, the Sunda Islands, Halmahera Island, Sulawesi Island, Sangihe Island, and in the Banda Sea; Merapi (elev.2,968 m), Indonesia's most active volcano and in eruption since 2010, has been deemed a Decade Volcano by the International Association of Volcanology and Chemistry of the Earth's Interior, worthy of study due to its explosive history and close proximity to human populations; other notable historically active volcanoes include Agung, Awu, Karangetang, Krakatau (Krakatoa), Makian, Raung, and Tambora

Environment—current issues: deforestation; water pollution from industrial wastes, sewage; air pollution in urban areas; smoke and haze from forest fires

Environment—international agreements: *party to:* Biodiversity, Clim ate Change, Clim ate Change-Kyoto Protocol, Desertification, Endangered Species, Hazardous Wastes, Law of the Sea, Ozone Layer Protection, Ship Pollution, Tropical Timber 83, Tropical Timber 94, Wetlands

signed, but not ratified: Marine Life Conservation

Geography—note: archipelago of 17,508 islands, some 6,000 of which are inhabited (Indonesia is the world's largest country comprised solely of islands); straddles the equator; strategic location astride or along major sea lanes from the Indian Ocean to the Pacific Ocean; despite having the fourth largest population in the world, Indonesia is the most heavily forested regiononearth after the Amazon

PEOPLE AND SOCIETY

Nationality: *noun:* Indonesian(s)

adjective: Indonesian

Ethnic groups: Javanese 40.1%, Sundanese 15.5%, Malay 3.7%, Batak 3.6%, Madurese 3%, Betawi 2.9%, Minangkabau 2.7%, Buginese 2.7%, Bantenese 2%, Banjarese 1.7%, Balinese 1.7%, Acehnese 1.4%, Dayak 1.4%, Sasak 1.3%, Chinese 1.2%, other 15% (2010 est.)

Languages: Bahasa Indonesia (official, modified form of Malay), English, Dutch, local dialects (of which the most widely spoken is Javanese)

note: more than 700 languages are used in Indonesia

Religions: Muslim 87.2%, Christian 7%, Roman Catholic 2.9%, Hindu 1.7%, other 0.9% (includes Buddhist and Confucian), unspecified 0.4% (2010 est.)

Population: 255,993,674 (July 2015 est.)

country comparison to the world: 5

Age structure: *0-14 years:* 25.82% (male 33,651,533/female 32,442,996)

15-24 years: 17.07% (male 22,238,735/female 21,454,563)

25-54 years: 42.31% (male 55,196,144/female 53,124,591)

55-64 years: 8.18% (male 9,608,548/female 11,328,421)

65 years and over: 6.62% (male 7,368,764/female 9,579,379) (2015 est.)

Dependency ratios: *total dependency ratio:* 49%

youth dependency ratio: 41.2%

elderly dependency ratio: 7.7%

potential support ratio: 13% (2015 est.)

Median age: *total:* 29.6 years

male: 29 years

female: 30.2 years (2015 est.)

country comparison to the world: 117

Population growth rate: 0.92% (2015 est.)

country comparison to the world: 125

Birth rate: 16.72 births/1,000 population (2015 est.)

country comparison to the world: 110

Death rate: 6.37 deaths/1,000 population (2015 est.)

country comparison to the world: 151

Net migration rate: -1.16 migrant(s)/1,000 population (2015 est.)

country comparison to the world: 152

Urbanization: *urban Population:* 53.7% of total population (2015)

rate of urbanization: 2.69% annual rate of change (2010-15 est.)

Major urban areas—Population: JAKARTA (capital) 10.323 million; Surabaya 2.853 million; Bandung 2.544 million; Medan 2.204 million; Semarang 1.63 million; Makassar 1.489 million (2015)

Sex ratio: *at birth:* 1.05 male(s)/female

0-14 years: 1.04 male(s)/female

15–24 years: 1.04 male(s)/female
25–54 years: 1.04 male(s)/female
55–64 years: 0.85 male(s)/female
65 years and over: 0.77 male(s)/female
total Population: 1 male(s)/female (2015 est.)
Mother's mean age at first birth: 22.8
note: median age at first birth among women 25–29 (2012 est.)
Maternal mortality rate: 126 deaths/100,000 live births (2015 est.)
country comparison to the world: 52
Infant mortality rate: *total:* 24.29 deaths/1,000 live births
male: 28.46 deaths/1,000 live births
female: 19.92 deaths/1,000 live births (2015 est.)
country comparison to the world: 71
Life expectancy at birth: *total population:* 72.45 years
male: 69.85 years
female: 75.17 years (2015 est.)
country comparison to the world: 140
Total fertility rate: 2.15 children born/woman (2015 est.)
country comparison to the world: 103
Contraceptive prevalence rate: 61.9% (2012)
Health expenditures: 3.1% of GDP (2013)
country comparison to the world: 180
Physicians density: 0.2 physicians/1,000 population (2012)
Hospital bed density: 0.9 beds/1,000 population (2012)
Drinking water source:
improved:
urban: 94.2% of population
rural: 79.5% of population
total: 87.4% of population
unimproved:
urban: 5.8% of population
rural: 20.5% of population
total: 12.6% of population (2015 est.)
Sanitation facility access:
improved:
urban: 72.3% of population
rural: 47.5% of population
total: 60.8% of population
unimproved:
urban: 27.7% of population
rural: 52.5% of population
total: 39.2% of population (2015 est.)
HIV/AIDS—adult prevalence rate: 0.47% (2014 est.)
country comparison to the world: 71
HIV/AIDS—people living with HIV/AIDS: 660,300 (2014 est.)
country comparison to the world: 14
HIV/AIDS—deaths: 33,700 (2014 est.)
country comparison to the world: 8
Major infectious diseases: *degree of risk:* very high
food or waterborne diseases: bacterial diarrhea, hepatitis A, and typhoid fever
vectorborne diseases: dengue fever and malaria
note: highly pathogenic H5N1 avian influenza has been identified in this country; it poses a negligible risk with extremely rare cases possible among US citizens who have close contact with birds (2013)

Obesity—adult prevalence rate: 5.7% (2014)
country comparison to the world: 160
Children under the age of 5 years underweight: 19.9% (2013)
country comparison to the world: 31
Education expenditures: 3.3% of GDP (2014)
country comparison to the world: 143
Literacy: *definition:* age 15 and over can read and write
total population: 93.9%
male: 96.3%
female: 91.5% (2015 est.)
School life expectancy (primary to tertiary education): *total:* 13 years
male: 13 years
female: 13 years (2014)
Child labor—children ages 5–14: *total number:* 4,026,285
percentage: 7%
note: data represent children ages 5–17 (2009 est.)
Unemployment, youth ages 15–24: *total:* 19.3%
male: 19.4%
female: 19.2% (2012 est.)
country comparison to the world: 49

GOVERNMENT

Country name: *conventional long form:* Republic of Indonesia
conventional short form: Indonesia
local long form: Republik Indonesia
local short form: Indonesia
former: Netherlands East Indies, Dutch East Indies
etymology: the name is an 18th-century construct of two Greek words, "Indos" (India) and "nesoi" (islands), meaning "Indian islands"
Government type: presidential republic
Capital: *name:* Jakarta
Geographic coordinates: 6 10 S, 106 49 E
time difference: UTC+7 (12 hours ahead of Washington, DC, during Standard Time)
note: Indonesia has three time zones
Administrative divisions: 31 provinces (provinsi-provinsi, singular—provinsi), 1 autonomous province*, 1 special region** (daerah-daerah istimewa, singular—daerah istimewa), and 1 national capital district*** (daerah khusus ibukota); Aceh*, Bali, Banten, Bengkulu, Gorontalo, Jakarta Raya***, Jambi, Jawa Barat (West Java), Jawa Tengah (Central Java), Jawa Timur (East Java), Kalimantan Barat (West Kalimantan), Kalimantan Selatan (South Kalimantan), Kalimantan Tengah (Central Kalimantan), Kalimantan Timur (East Kalimantan), Kalimantan Utara (North Kalimantan), Kepulauan Bangka Belitung (Bangka Belitung Islands), Kepulauan Riau (Riau Islands), Lampung, Maluku, Maluku Utara (North Maluku), Nusa Tenggara Barat (West Nusa Tenggara), Nusa Tenggara Timur (East Nusa Tenggara), Papua, Papua Barat (West Papua), Riau, Sulawesi Barat (West Sulawesi), Sulawesi Selatan (South Sulawesi), Sulawesi Tengah (Central Sulawesi), Sulawesi Tenggara (Southeast Sulawesi), Sulawesi Utara (North Sulawesi), Sumatera Barat (West Sumatra), Sumatera Selatan (South Sumatra), Sumatera Utara (North Sumatra), Yogyakarta**

note: following the implementation of decentralization beginning on 1 January 2001, regencies and municipalities have become the key administrative units responsible for providing most government services
Independence: 17 August 1945 (declared)
National holiday: Independence Day, 17 August (1945)
Constitution: drafted July to August 1945, effective 17 August 1945, abrogated by 1949 and 1950 constitutions, 1945 constitution restored 5 July 1959; amended several times, last in 2002; note—an amendment on "national character building and national consciousness awareness" was pending parliamentary review in early 2016 (2016)
Legal system: civil law system based on the Roman-Dutch model and influenced by customary law
International law organization participation: has not submitted an ICJ jurisdiction declaration; non-party state to the ICCt
Citizenship: *citizenship by birth:* no
citizenship by descent only: at least one parent must be a citizen of Indonesia
dual citizenship recognized: no
residency requirement for naturalization: 5 continuous years
Suffrage: 17 years of age; universal and married persons regardless of age
Executive branch: *chief of state:* President Joko WIDODO (since 20 October 2014); Vice President Jusuf KALLA (since 20 October 2014); note—the president is both chief of state and head of government

head of government: President Joko WIDODO (since 20 October 2014); Vice President Jusuf KALLA (since 20 October 2014)
cabinet: Cabinet appointed by the president
elections/appointments: president and vice president directly elected by absolute majority popular vote for a 5-year term (eligible for a second term); election last held on 9 July 2014 (next to be held in 2019)
election results: Joko WiDODO elected president; percent of vote—Joko WIDODO (PDI-P) 53.2%, PRABOWO Subianto (GERINDRA) 46.8%
Legislative branch: *description:* bicameral People's Consultative Assembly or Majelis Permusy awaratan Rakyat consists of the Regional Representative Council or Dewan Perwakilan Daerah (132 seats; non-partisan members directly elected in multi-seat constituencies by proportional representation vote to serve 5-year terms) and the House of Representatives or Dewan Perwakilan Rakyat (560 seats; members directly elected in multi-seat constituencies by single non-transferable vote to serve 5-year terms)
note: 29 other parties received less than the 2.5% vote threshold and failed to win so did not obtain any seats; because of election rules, the number of seats won does not always follow the percentage of votes received by parties
elections: last held on 9 April 2014 (next to be held in 2019)
election results: House of Representatives—percent of vote by party—PDI-P 19%, Golkar 15%,

Gerindra 12%, PD 10%, PKB 9%, PAN 8%, PKS 7%, NasDem 7%, PPP 7%, Hanura 5%; seats by party -PDI-P 109, Golkar 91, Gerindra 73, PD 61, PAN 49, PKB 47, PKS 40, NasDem 35, PPP 39, Hanura 16

Judicial branch: *highest court(s):* Supreme Court or Mahkamah Agung (51 judges divided into 8 chambers); Constitutional Court or Mahkamah Konstitusi (consists of 9 judges)

judge selection and term of office: Supreme Court judges nominated by Judicial Commission, appointed by president with concurrence of parliament; judges serve until retirement at age 65; Constitutional Court judges—3 nominated by president, 3 by Supreme Court, and 3 by parliament; judges appointed by the president; judges serve until mandatory retirement at age 70

subordinate courts: High Courts of Appeal, district courts, religious courts

Political parties and leaders: Democrat Party or PD [Susilo Bambang YUDHOYONO]

Functional Groups Party or GOLKAR [Aburizal BAKRIE]

Great Indonesia Movement Party or GERINDRA [PRABOWO Subianto Djojohadikusumo]

Indonesia Democratic Party-Struggle or PDI-P [MEGAWATI Sukarnoputri]

National Awakening Party or PKB [Muhaiman ISKANDAR]

National Mandate Party or PAN [Hatta RAJASA]

People's Conscience Party or HANURA [WIRANTO]

Prosperous Justice Party or PKS [Anis MATTA]

United Development Party or PPP [NA]

Political pressure groups and leaders: Commission for the "Disappeared" and Victims of Violence or KontraS

Indonesia Corruption Watch or ICW

Indonesian Forum for the Environment or WALHI

International organization participation: ADB, APEC, ARF, ASEAN, BIS, CD, CICA (observer), CP, D-8, EAS, EITI (compliant country), FAO, G-11, G-15, G-20, G-77, IAEA, IBRD, ICAO, ICC (national committees), ICRM, IDA, IDB, IFAD, IFC, IFRCS, IHO, ILO, IMF, IMO, IMSO, Interpol, IOC, IOM (observer), IPU, ISO, ITSO, ITU, ITUC (NGOs), MIGA, MINURSO, MINUSTAH, MONUSCO, NAM, OECD (Enhanced Engagement), OIC, OPCW, PIF (partner), UN, UNAMID, UNCTAD, UNESCO, UNIDO, UNIFIL, UNISFA, UNMIL, UNWTO, UPU, WCO, WFTU (NGOs), WHO, WIPO, WMO, WTO

Diplomatic representation in the US: *chief of mission:* Ambassador Budi BOWOLEKSONO (since 21 May 2014)

chancery: 2020 Massachusetts Avenue NW, Washington, DC 20036

telephone: [1] (202) 775-5200

FAX: [1] (202) 775-5365

consulate(s) general: Chicago, Houston, Los Angeles, New York, San Francisco

Diplomatic representation from the US: *chief of mission:* Ambassador Robert O. BLAKE, Jr. (since 30 January 2014)

embassy: Jalan Medan Merdeka Selatan 3–5, Jakarta 10110

mailing address: Unit 8129, Box 1, FPOAP 96520

telephone: [62] (21) 3435-9000

FAX: [62] (21) 386-2259

consulate general: Surabaya

consulate: Medan

consular agency: Bali

Flag description: two equal horizontal bands of red (top) and white; the colors derive from the banner of the Majapahit Empire of the 13th-15th centuries; red symbolizes courage, white represents purity

note: similar to the flag of Monaco, which is shorter; also similar to the flag of Poland, which is white (top) and red

National symbol(s): garuda (mythical bird); national colors: red, white

National anthem: *name:* "Indonesia Raya" (Great Indonesia)

lyrics/music: Wage Rudolf SOEPRATMAN

note: adopted 1945

ECONOMY

Economy—overview: Indonesia, the largest economy in Southeast Asia, has seen a slowdown in growth since 2012, mostly due to the end of the commodities export boom. During the global financial crisis, Indonesia outperformed its regional neighbors and joined China and India as the only G20 members posting growth. Indonesia's annual budget deficit is capped at 3% of GDP, and the Government of Indonesia lowered its debt-to-GDP ratio from a peak of 100% shortly after the Asian financial crisis in 1999 to less than 25% today. Fitch and Moody's upgraded Indonesia's credit rating to investment grade in December 2011. Indonesia still struggles with poverty and unemployment, inadequate infrastructure, corruption, a complex regulatory environment, and unequal resource distribution among its regions. President Joko WIDODO -elected in July 2014—seeks to develop Indonesia's maritime resources and pursue other infrastructure development, including significantly increasing its electrical power generation capacity. Fuel subsidies were significantly reduced in early 2015, a move which has helped the government redirect its spending to development priorities. Indonesia, with the nine other ASEAN members, will continue to move towards participation in the ASEAN Economic Community, though full implementation of economic integration has not yet materialized.

GDP (purchasing power parity): $2.842 trillion (2015 est.)

$2.712 trillion (2014 est.)

$2.582 trillion (2013 est.)

note: data are in 2015 US dollars

country comparison to the world: 9

GDP (official exchange rate): $859 billion (2015 est.)

GDP—real growth rate: 4.8% (2015 est.)

5% (2014 est.)

5.6% (2013 est.)

country comparison to the world: 43

GDP—per capita (PPP): $11,100 (2015 est.)

$10,800 (2014 est.)

$10,400 (2013 est.)

note: data are in 2015 US dollars

country comparison to the world: 132

Gross national saving: 32.5% of GDP (2015 est.)

31.5% of GDP (2014 est.)

30.6% of GDP (2013 est.)

country comparison to the world: 15

GDP—composition, by end use:

household consumption: 56.8%

government consumption: 9.4%

investment in fixed capital: 32.3%

investment in inventories: 1.2%

exports of goods and services: 21.7%

imports of goods and services: -21.4% (2015 est.)

GDP—composition, by sector of origin:

agriculture: 13.6%

industry: 42.8%

services: 43.6% (2015 est.)

Agriculture—products: rubber and similar products, palm oil, poultry, beef, forest products, shrimp, cocoa, coffee, medicinal herbs, essential oil, fish and its similar products, and spices

Industries: petroleum and natural gas, textiles, automotive, electrical appliances, apparel, footwear, mining, cement, medical instruments and appliances, handicrafts, chemical fertilizers, plywood, rubber, processed food, jewelry, and tourism

Industrial production growth rate: 4.5% (2015 est.)

country comparison to the world: 41

Labor force: 122.4 million (2015 est.)

country comparison to the world: 5

Labor force—by occupation: *agriculture:* 38.9%

industry: 13.2%

services: 47.9% (2012 est.)

Unemployment rate: 5.5% (2015 est.)

5.9% (2014 est.)

country comparison to the world: 61

Population below poverty line: 11.3% (2014 est.)

Household income or consumption by percentage share: *lowest:* 10%: 3.4%

highest 10%: 28.2% (2010)

Distribution of family income—Gini index: 36.8 (2009)

39.4 (2005)

country comparison to the world: 80

Budget: *revenues:* $123.3 billion

expenditures: $142.8 billion (2015 est.)

Taxes and other revenues: 14.1% of GDP (2015 est.)

country comparison to the world: 198

Budget surplus (+) or deficit (–): -2.2% of GDP (2015 est.)

country comparison to the world: 80

Public debt: 27.7% of GDP (2015 est.)

25.9% of GDP (2014 est.)

country comparison to the world: 146

Fiscal year: calendar year

Inflation rate (consumer prices): 6.4% (2015 est.)

6.4% (2014 est.)

country comparison to the world: 188

Central bank discount rate: 6.37% (31 December 2010)

6.46% (31 December 2009)

note: this figure represents the 3-month SBI rate; the Bank of Indonesia has not employed the one-month SBI since September 2010
country comparison to the world: 60
Commercial bank prime lending rate: 12.8% (31 December 2015 est.)
12.61% (31 December 2014 est.)
note: these figures represent the average annualized rate on working capital loans
country comparison to the world: 59
Stock of narrow money: $69.01 billion (31 December 2015 est.)
$75.74 billion (31 December 2014 est.)
country comparison to the world: 44
Stock of broad money: $348.6 billion (31 December 2014 est.)
$305.8 billion (31 December 2013 est.)
country comparison to the world: 29
Stock of domestic credit: $342.5 billion (31 December 2015 est.)
$360.2 billion (31 December 2014 est.)
country comparison to the world: 34
Market value of publicly traded shares: $396.8 billion (31 December 2012 est.)
$390.1 billion (31 December 2011)
$360.4 billion (31 December 2010 est.)
country comparison to the world: 25
Current account balance: -$17.76 billion (2015 est.)
-$27.52 billion (2014 est.)
country comparison to the world: 185
Exports: $152.5 billion (2015 est.)
$176 billion (2014 est.)
country comparison to the world: 30
Exports—commodities: mineral fuels, animal or vegetable fats (includes palm oil), electrical machinery, rubber, machinery and mechanical appliance parts
Exports—partners: Japan 12%, US 10.8%, China 10%, Singapore 8.4%, India 7.8%, South Korea 5.1%, Malaysia 5.1% (2015)
Imports: $138.4 billion (2015 est.)
$178.2 billion (2014 est.)
country comparison to the world: 31
Imports—commodities: mineral fuels, boilers, machinery, and mechanical parts, electric machinery, iron and steel, foodstuffs
Imports—partners: China 20.6%, Singapore 12.6%, Japan 9.3%, Malaysia 6%, South Korea 5.9%, Thailand 5.7%, US 5.3% (2015)
Reserves of foreign exchange and gold: $103.4 billion (31 December 2015 est.)
$111.9 billion (31 December 2014 est.)
country comparison to the world: 22
Debt—external: $293.2 billion (31 December 2014 est.)
$266.1 billion (31 December 2013 est.)
country comparison to the world: 33
Stock of direct foreign investment—at home: $279 billion (31 December 2015 est.)
$253.1 billion (31 December 2014 est.)
country comparison to the world: 25
Stock of direct foreign investment—abroad: $34.62 billion (31 December 2015 est.)
$24.05 billion (31 December 2014 est.)
country comparison to the world: 50

Exchange rates: Indonesian rupiah (IDR) per US dollar—
13,577.6 (2015 est.)
11,865.2 (2014 est.)
11,865.2 (2013 est.)
9,386.63 (2012 est.)
8,770.43 (2011 est.)

ENERGY

Electricity—production: 185.3 billion kWh (2012 est.)
country comparison to the world: 23
Electricity—consumption: 167.5 billion kWh (2012 est.)
country comparison to the world: 22
Electricity—exports: 0 kWh (2013 est.)
country comparison to the world: 152
Electricity—imports: 0 kWh (2013 est.)
country comparison to the world: 162
Electricity—installed generating capacity: 47.75 million kW (2012 est.)
country comparison to the world: 23
Electricity—from fossil fuels: 83.2% of total installed capacity (2012 est.)
country comparison to the world: 92
Electricity—from nuclear fuels: 0% of total installed capacity (2012 est.)
country comparison to the world: 111
Electricity—from hydroelectric plants: 11% of total installed capacity (2012 est.)
country comparison to the world: 113
Electricity—from other renewable sources: 5.8% of total installed capacity (2012 est.)
country comparison to the world: 55
Crude oil—production: 789,800 bbl/day (2014 est.)
country comparison to the world: 23
Crude oil—exports: 296,100 bbl/day (2012 est.)
country comparison to the world: 25
Crude oil—imports: 391,800 bbl/day (2012 est.)
country comparison to the world: 23
Crude oil—proved reserves: 3.693 billion bbl (1 January 2015 est.)
country comparison to the world: 29
Refined petroleum products—production: 946,500 bbl/day (2012 est.)
country comparison to the world: 24
Refined petroleum products—consumption: 1.718 million bbl/day (2013 est.)
country comparison to the world: 14
Refined petroleum products—exports: 78,690 bbl/day (2012 est.)
country comparison to the world: 51
Refined petroleum products—imports: 699,500 bbl/day (2012 est.)
country comparison to the world: 10
Natural gas—production: 70.4 billion cu m (2013 est.)
country comparison to the world: 12
Natural gas—consumption: 39.1 billion cu m (2013 est.)
country comparison to the world: 23
Natural gas—exports: 31.3 billion cu m (2013 est.)
country comparison to the world: 12
Natural gas—imports: 0 cu m (2013 est.)

country comparison to the world: 211
Natural gas—proved reserves: 2.955 trillion cu m (1 January 2014 est.)
country comparison to the world: 13
Carbon dioxide emissions from consumption of energy: 456.2 million Mt (2012 est.)
country comparison to the world: 15

COMMUNICATIONS

Telephones—fixed lines: *total subscriptions:* 29.64 million
subscriptions per 100 inhabitants: 12 (2014 est.)
country comparison to the world: 11
Telephones—mobile cellular: *total:* 319 million
subscriptions per 100 inhabitants: 126 (2014 est.)
country comparison to the world: 4
Telephone system: *general assessment:* domestic service includes an interisland microwave system, an HF radio police net, and a domestic satellite communications system; international service good
domestic: coverage provided by existing network has been expanded by use of over 200,000 telephone kiosks many located in remote areas; mobile-cellular subscribership growing rapidly
international: country code—62; landing point for both the SEA-ME-WE-3 and SEA-ME-WE-4 submarine cable networks that provide links throughout Asia, the Middle East, and Europe; satellite earth stations—2 Intelsat (1 Indian Ocean and 1 Pacific Ocean) (2011)
Broadcast media: mixture of about a dozen national TV networks—2 public broadcasters, the remainder private broadcasters—each with multiple transmitters; more than 100 local TV stations; widespread use of satellite and cable TV systems; public radio broadcaster operates 6 national networks, as well as regional and local stations; overall, more than 700 radio stations with more than 650 privately operated (2008)
Radio broadcast stations: AM 678, FM 43, shortwave 82 (1998)
Television broadcast stations: 54 local TV stations (11 National TV networks; each with its group of local transmitters) (2006)
Internet country code: .id
Internet hosts: 1.344 million (2012)
country comparison to the world: 42
Internet users: *total:* 42.4 million
percent of Population: 16.7% (2014 est.)
country comparison to the world: 14

TRANSPORTATION

Airports: 673 (2013)
country comparison to the world: 10
Airports—with paved runways: *total:* 186
over 3,047 m: 5
2,438 to 3,047 m: 21
1,524 to 2,437 m: 51
914 to 1,523 m: 72
under 914 m: 37 (2013)
Airports—with unpaved runways: *total:* 487
1,524 to 2,437 m: 4
914 to 1,523 m: 23
under 914 m: 460 (2013)

Heliports: 76 (2013)

Pipelines: condensate 1,064 km; condensate/gas 150 km; gas 11,702 km; liquid petroleum gas 119 km; oil 7,767 km; oil/gas/water 77 km; refined products 728 km; unknown 53 km; water 44 km (2013)

Railways: *total:* 8,159 km

narrow gauge: 8,159 km 1.067-m gauge (565 km electrified)

note: 4,816 km operational (2014)

country comparison to the world: 26

Roadways: *total:* 496,607 km

paved: 283,102 km

unpaved: 213,505 km (2011)

country comparison to the world: 14

Waterways: 21,579 km (2011)

country comparison to the world: 7

Merchant marine: *total:* 1,340

by type: bulk carrier 105, cargo 618, chemical tanker 69, container 120, liquefied gas 28, passenger 49, passenger/cargo 77, petroleum tanker 244, refrigerated cargo 6, roll on/roll off 12, specialized tanker 1, vehicle carrier 11

foreign-owned: 69 (China 1, France 1, Greece 1, Japan 8, Jordan 1, Malaysia 1, Singapore 46, South Korea 2, Taiwan 1, UK 2, US 2)

registered in other countries: 95 (Bahamas 2, Cambodia 2, China 2, Hong Kong 10, Liberia 4, Marshall Islands 1, Mongolia 2, Panama 10, Singapore 60, Tuvalu 1, unknown 1) (2010)

country comparison to the world: 8

Ports and terminals: *major seaport(s):* Banjarmasin, Belawan, Kotabaru, Krueg Geukueh, Palembang, Panjang, Sungai Pakning, Tanjung Perak, Tanjung Priok

container port(s) (TEUs): Tanjung Priok (5,617,562)

LNG termin al(s) (export): Bontang, Tangguh

LNG terminal(s) (import): Arun, Lampung, West Java

Transportation—note: the International Maritime Bureau continues to report the territorial and offshore waters in the Strait of Malacca and South China Sea as high risk for piracy and armed robbery against ships; attacks have increased yearly since 2009; in 2014, 100 commercial vessels were attacked and 90 crew members taken hostage; hijacked vessels are often disguised and cargo diverted to ports in East Asia; crews have been murdered or cast adrift

MILITARY AND SECURITY

Military branches: Indonesian Armed Forces (Tentara Nasional Indonesia, TNI): Army (TNI-Angkatan Darat (TNI-AD)), Navy (TNI-Angkatan Laut (TNI-AL); includes marines (Korps Marinir, KorMar), naval air arm), Air Force (TNI-Angkatan Udara (TNI-AU)), National Air Defense Command (Kommando Pertahanan Udara Nasional (Kohanudnas)) (2013)

Military service age and obligation: 18–45 years of age for voluntary military service, with selective conscription authorized; 2-year service obligation, with reserve obligation to age 45 (officers); Indonesian citizens only (2012)

Military expenditures: 0.78% of GDP (2012)

0.67% of GDP (2011)

0.78% of GDP (2010)

country comparison to the world: 116

TRANSNATIONAL ISSUES

Disputes—international: Indonesia has a stated foreign policy objective of establishing stable fixed land and maritime boundaries with all of its neighbors; three stretches of land borders with Timor-Leste have yet to be delimited, two of which are in the Oecussi exclave area, and no maritime or Exclusive Economic Zone (EEZ) boundaries have been established between the countries; many refugees from Timor-Leste who left in 2003 still reside in Indonesia and refuse repatriation; all borders between Indonesia and Australia have been agreed upon bilaterally, but a 1997 treaty that would settle the last of their maritime and EEZ boundary has yet to be ratified by Indonesia's legislature; Indonesian groups challenge Australia's claim to Ashmore Reef; Australia has closed parts of the Ashmore and Cartier Reserve to Indonesian traditional fishing and placed restrictions on certain catches; land and maritime negotiations with Malaysia are ongoing, and disputed areas include the controversial Tanjung Datu and Camar Wulan border area in Borneo and the maritime boundary in the Ambalat oil block in the Celebes Sea; Indonesia and Singapore continue to work on finalizing their 1973 maritime boundary agreement by defining unresolved areas north of Indonesia's Batam Island; Indonesian secessionists, squatters, and illegal migrants create repatriation problems for Papua New Guinea; maritime delimitation talks continue with Palau; EEZ negotiations with Vietnam are ongoing, and the two countries in Fall 2011 agreed to work together to reduce illegal fishing along their maritime boundary

Refugees and internally displaced persons: *IDPs:* 6,100 (inter-communal, inter-faith, and separatist violence between 1998 and 2004 in Aceh and Papua; religious attacks and land conflicts in 2012 and 2013; most IDPs in Aceh, Maluku, East Nusa Tengarra) (2015) (2011)

Illicit drugs: illicit producer of cannabis largely for domestic use; producer of methamphetamine and ecstasy; President WIDODO's war on drugs has led to an increase in death sentences and executions, particularly of foreign drug traffickers (2015)

IRAN

INTRODUCTION

Background: Known as Persia until 1935, Iran became an Islamic republic in 1979 after the ruling monarchy was overthrown and Shah Mohammad Reza PAHLAVI was forced into exile. Conservative clerical forces led by Ayatollah Ruhollah KHOMEINI established a theocratic system of government with ultimate political authority vested in a learned religious scholar referred to commonly as the Supreme Leader who, according to the constitution, is accountable only to the Assembly of Experts—a popularly elected 86-member body of clerics. US-Iranian relations became strained when a group of Iranian students seized the US Embassy in Tehran in November 1979 and held embassy personnel hostages until mid-January 1981. The US cut off diplomatic relations with Iran in April 1980. During the period 1980–88, Iran fought a bloody, indecisive war with Iraq that eventually expanded into the Persian Gulf and led to clashes between US Navy and Iranian military forces. Iran has been designated a state sponsor of terrorism for its activities in Lebanon and elsewhere in the world and remains subject to US, UN, and EU economic sanctions and export controls because of its continued involvement in terrorism and concerns over possible military dimensions of its nuclear program. Following the election of reformer Hojjat ol-Eslam Mohammad KHATAMI as president in 1997 and a reformist Majles (legislature) in 2000, a campaign to foster political reform in response to popular dissatisfaction was initiated. The movement floundered as conservative politicians, supported by the Supreme Leader, unelected institutions of authority like the Council of Guardians, and the security services reversed and blocked reform measures while increasing security repression. Starting with nationwide municipal elections in 2003 and continuing through Majles elections

in 2004, conservatives reestablished control over Iran's elected government institutions, which culminated with the August 2005 inauguration of hardliner Mahmud AHMADI-NEJAD as president. His controversial reelection in June 2009 sparked nationwide protests over allegations of electoral fraud. These protests were quickly suppressed, and the political opposition that arose as a consequence of AHMADI-NEJAD's election was repressed. Deteriorating economic conditions due primarily to government mismanagement and international sanctions prompted at least two major economically based protests in July and October 2012, but Iran's internal security situation remained stable. President AHMADI-NEJAD's independent streak angered regime establishment figures, including the Supreme Leader, leading to conservative opposition to his agenda for the last year of his presidency, and an alienation of his political supporters. in June 2013 Iranians elected a moderate conservative cleric Dr. Hasan Fereidun RUHANI to the presidency. He is a longtime senior member in the regime, but has made promises of reforming society and Iran's foreign policy. The UN Security Council has passed a number of resolutions calling for Iran to suspend its uranium enrichment and reprocessing activities and comply with its IAEA obligations and responsibilities, and in July 2015 Iran and the five permanent members, plus Germany (P5+1) signed the Joint Comprehensive Plan of Action (JCPOA) under which Iran agreed to restrictions on its nuclear program in exchange for sanctions relief.

GEOGRAPHY

Location: Middle East, bordering the Gulf of Oman, the Persian Gulf, and the Caspian Sea, between Iraq and Pakistan

Geographic coordinates: 32 00 N, 53 00 E

Map references: Middle East

Area: total: 1,648,195 sq km
land: 1,531,595 sq km
water: 116,600 sq km
country comparison to the world: 18

Area—comparative: almost 2.5 times the size of Texas; slightly smaller than Alaska

Land boundaries: total: 5,894 km
border countries (7): Afghanistan 921 km, Armenia 44 km, Azerbaijan 689 km, Iraq 1,599 km, Pakistan 959 km, Turkey 534 km, Turkmenistan 1,148 km

Coastline: 2,440 km
note—Iran also borders the Caspian Sea (740 km)

Maritime claims: territorial sea: 12 nm
contiguous zone: 24 nm
exclusive economic zone: bilateral agreements or median lines in the Persian Gulf
continental shelf: natural prolongation

Climate: mostly arid or semiarid, subtropical along Caspian coast

Terrain: rugged, mountainous rim; high, central basin with deserts, mountains; small, discontinuous plains along both coasts

Elevation: mean elevation: 1,305 m

elevation extremes: lowest point: Caspian Sea -28 m
highest point: Kuh-e Damavand 5,671 m

Natural resources: petroleum, natural gas, coal, chromium, copper, iron ore, lead, manganese, zinc, sulfur

Land use: agricultural land: 30.1%
arable land: 10.8%
permanent crops: 1.2%
permanent pasture: 18.1%
forest: 6.8%
other: 63.1% (2011 est.)

Irrigated land: 95,530 sq km (2012)

Total renewable water resources: 137 cu km (2011)

Freshwater withdrawal (domestic/industrial/agricultural): total: 93.3 cu km/yr (7%/1%/92%)
per capita: 1,306 cu m/yr (2004)

Natural hazards: periodic droughts, floods; dust storms, sandstorms; earthquakes

Environment—current issues: air pollution, especially in urban areas, from vehicle emissions, refinery operations, and industrial effluents; deforestation; overgrazing; desertification; oil pollution in the Persian Gulf; wetland losses from drought; soil degradation (salination); inadequate supplies of potable water; water pollution from raw sewage and industrial waste; urbanization

Environment—international agreements: party to: Biodiversity, Climate Change, Climate Change-Kyoto Protocol, Desertification, Endangered Species, Hazardous Wastes, Marine Dumping, Ozone Layer Protection, Ship Pollution, Wetlands
signed, but not ratified: Environmental Modification, Law of the Sea, Marine Life Conservation

Geography—note: strategic location on the Persian Gulf and Strait of Hormuz, which are vital maritime pathways for crude oil transport

PEOPLE AND SOCIETY

Nationality: noun: Iranian(s)
adjective: Iranian

Ethnic groups: Persian, Azeri, Kurd, Lur, Baloch, Arab, Turkmen and Turkic tribes

Languages: Persian (official), Azeri Turkic and Turkic dialects, Kurdish, Gilaki and Mazandarani, Luri, Balochi, Arabic, other

Religions: Muslim (official) 99.4% (Shia 90–95%, Sunni 5–10%), other (includes Zoroastrian, Jewish, and Christian) 0.3%, unspecified 0.4% (2011 est.)

Population: 81,824,270 (July 2015 est.)
country comparison to the world: 17

Age structure: 0–14 years: 23.69% (male 9,937,715/female 9,449,716)
15–24 years: 17.58% (male 7,386,826/female 6,998,188)
25–54 years: 46.87% (male 19,534,794/female 18,817,480)
55–64 years: 6.58% (male 2,650,049/female 2,731,997)
65 years and over: 5.28% (male 1,990,961/female 2,326,544) (2015 est.)

Dependency ratios: total dependency ratio: 40.2%
youth dependency ratio: 33.1%

elderly dependency ratio: 7.1%
potential support ratio: 14.1% (2015 est.)

Median age: total: 28.8 years
male: 28.6 years
female: 29.1 years (2015 est.)
country comparison to the world: 123

Population growth rate: 1.2% (2015 est.)
country comparison to the world: 101

Birth rate: 17.99 births/1,000 population (2015 est.)
country comparison to the world: 105

Death rate: 5.94 deaths/1,000 population (2015 est.)
country comparison to the world: 168

Net migration rate: -0.07 migrant(s)/1,000 population (2015 est.)
country comparison to the world: 114

Urbanization: urban Population: 73.4% of total population (2015)
rate of urbanization: 2.07% annual rate of change (2010–15 est.)

Major urban areas—Population: TEHRAN (capital) 8.432 million; Mashhad 3.014 million; Esfahan 1.88 million; Karaj 1.807 million; Shiraz 1.661 million; Tabriz 1.572 million (2015)

Sex ratio: at birth: 1.05 male(s)/female
0–14 years: 1.05 male(s)/female
15–24 years: 1.06 male(s)/female
25–54 years: 1.04 male(s)/female
55–64 years: 0.97 male(s)/female
65 years and over: 0.86 male(s)/female
total Population: 1.03 male(s)/female (2015 est.)

Maternal mortality rate: 25 deaths/100,000 live births (2015 est.)
country comparison to the world: 137

Infant mortality rate: total: 38.04 deaths/1,000 live births
male: 38.58 deaths/1,000 live births
female: 37.48 deaths/1,000 live births (2015 est.)
country comparison to the world: 54

Life expectancy at birth: total population: 71.15 years
male: 69.56 years
female: 72.82 years (2015 est.)
country comparison to the world: 149

Total fertility rate: 1.83 children born/woman (2015 est.)
country comparison to the world: 148

Contraceptive prevalence rate: 77.4% (2010/11)

Health expenditures: 6.7% of GDP (2013)
country comparison to the world: 86

Physicians density: 0.89 physicians/1,000 population (2005)

Hospital bed density: 0.1 beds/1,000 population (2012)

Drinking water source:
improved:
urban: 97.7% of population
rural: 92.1% of population
total: 96.2% of population
unimproved:
urban: 2.3% of population
rural: 7.9% of population
total: 3.8% of population (2015 est.)

Sanitation facility access:
improved:

urban: 92.8% of population
rural: 82.3% of population
total: 90% of population
unimproved:
urban: 7.2% of population
rural: 17.7% of population
total: 10% of population (2015 est.)
HIV/AIDS—adult prevalence rate: 0.14% (2014 est.)
country comparison to the world: 108
HIV/AIDS—people living with HIV/AIDS: 74,400 (2014 est.)
country comparison to the world: 50
HIV/AIDS—deaths: 4,100 (2014 est.)
country comparison to the world: 36
Major infectious diseases: *degree of risk:* intermediate
food or waterborne diseases: bacterial diarrhea
vectorborne diseases: Crimean-Congo hemorrhagic fever
note: highly pathogenic H5N1 avian influenza has been identified in this country; it poses a negligible risk with extremely rare cases possible among US citizens who have close contact with birds (2013)
Obesity—adult prevalence rate: 24.9% (2014)
country comparison to the world: 99
Education expenditures: 3% of GDP (2014)
country comparison to the world: 119
Literacy: *definition:* age 15 and over can read and write
total Population: 86.8%
male: 91.2%
female: 82.5% (2015 est.)
School life expectancy (primary to tertiary education): *total:* 15 years
male: 15 years
female: 15 years (2014)
Unemployment, youth ages 15–24: *total:* 28.7%
male: 25.5%
female: 41.3% (2010 est.)
country comparison to the world: 44

GOVERNMENT

Country name: *conventional long form:* Islamic Republic of Iran
conventional short form: Iran
local long form: Jomhuri-ye Eslami-ye Iran
local short form: Iran
former: Persia
etymology: name derives from the Avestan term "aryanam" meaning "Land of the noble [ones]"
Government type: theocratic republic
Capital: *name:* Tehran

Geographic coordinates: 35 42 N, 51 25 E
time difference: UTC+3.5 (8.5 hours ahead of Washington, DC, during Standard Time)
daylight saving time: +1hr, begins fourth Tuesday in March; ends fourth Thursday in September
Administrative divisions: 31 provinces (ostanha, singular—ostan); Alborz, Ardabil, Azarbayjan-e Gharbi (West Azerbaijan), Azarbayjan-e Sharqi (East Azerbaijan), Bushehr, Chahar Mahal va Bakhtiari, Esfahan, Fars, Gilan, Golestan, Hamadan, Hormozgan, Ilam, Kerman, Kermanshah, Khorasan-e Jonubi (South Khorasan), Khorasan-e

Razavi (Razavi Khorasan), Khorasan-e Shomali (North Khorasan), Khuzestan, Kohgiluyeh va Bowyer Ahmad, Kordestan, Lorestan, Markazi, Mazandaran, Qazvin, Qom, Semnan, Sistan va Baluchestan, Tehran, Yazd, Zanjan
Independence: 1 April 1979 (Islamic Republic of Iran proclaimed); notable earlier dates: ca.550 B.C. (Achaemenid (Persian) Empire established); A.D.1501 (Iran reunified under the Safavid Dynasty); 12 December 1925 (modern Iran established under the PAHLAVI Dynasty)
National holiday: Republic Day, 1 April (1979)
Constitution: previous 1906; latest adopted 24 October 1979, effective 3 December 1979; amended 1989 (2016)
Legal system: religious legal system based on secular and Islamic law
International law organization participation: has not submitted an ICJ jurisdiction declaration; non-party state to the ICCt
Citizenship: *citizenship by birth:* no
citizenship by descent only: the father must be a citizen of Iran
dual citizenship recognized: no
residency requirement for naturalization: 5 years
Suffrage: 18 years of age; universal
Executive branch: *chief of state:* Supreme Leader Ali Hoseini-KHAMENEI (since 4 June 1989)

head of government: President Hasan Fereidun RUHANI (since 3 August 2013); First Vice President Eshaq JAHANGIRI (since 5 August 2013)
cabinet: Council of Ministers selected by the president with legislative approval; the supreme leader has some control over appointments to several ministries
elections/appointments: supreme leader appointed for life by Assembly of Experts; president directly elected by absolute majority popular vote in 2 rounds if needed for a 4-year term (eligible for a second term and an additional nonconsecutive term); election last held on 14 June 2013 (next to be held in June 2017)
election results: Hasan Fereidun RUHANI elected president; percent of vote—Hasan Fereidun RUHANI Moderation and Development Party) 50.7%, Mohammad Baqer QALIBAF (Progress and Justice Population of Islamic Iran) 16.5%, Saeed JALILI (Front of Islamic Revolution Stability) 11.4%, Mohsen REZAI (Conservative) 10.6%, Ali Akber VELAYATI (Islamic Coalition Party) 6.2%, other 4.6%
note: 3 oversight bodies are also considered part of the executive branch of government
Legislative branch: *description:* unicameral Islamic Consultative Assembly or Majles-e Shura-ye Eslami or Majles (290 seats; 285 members directly elected in single- and multi-seat constituencies by two-round vote, and 1 seat each for Zoroastrians, Jews, Assyrian and Chaldean Christians, Armenians in the north of the country, and Armenians in the South; members serve 4-year terms); note—all candidates to the Majles must be approved by the Guardian Council, a 12-member group of which 6 are appointed by the supreme

leader and 6 are jurists nominated by the judiciary and elected by the Majles
elections: first round held on 26 February 2016 with second round for 68 remaining seats held on 29 April 2016; (next to be held in 2020)
election results: percent of vote by party—List of HOPE 41.7%, Principalists Grand Coalition 28.6%, People's Voice Coalition 3.8%, religious minorities 1.7%, other 1.7%, independent 22.4%,; seats by party -List of Hope 121, Principalists Grand Coalition 83, People's Voice Coalition 11, religious minorities 5, other 5, independent 65
Judicial branch: *highest court(s):* Supreme Court (consists of a president and NA judges)
judge selection and term of office: Supreme Court president appointed by the head of the Supreme Judicial Council in consultation with judges of the Supreme Court; president appointed for a 5-year term; other judge appointments and tenure NA
subordinate courts: Penal Courts I and II; Islamic Revolutionary Courts; Courts of Peace; Special Clerical Court (functions outside the judicial system and handles cases involving clerics); military courts

Political parties and leaders: List of Hope or People's Voice Coalition [Ali MOTAHARI]
Pervasive Coalition of Reformists: The Second Step [Ali SOUFI, chairman] (includes Council for Coordinating the Reforms Front, National Trust Party, Union of Islamic Iran People Party, Moderation and Development Party, Followers of Walayat [Ali LARIJANI])
Principalists Grand Coalition [Alireza ZAKANI] (includes Combatant Clergy Association and Islamic Coalition Party, Society of Devotees and Pathseekers of the Islamic Revolution, Front of Islamic Revolu tion Stability)
Progress and Justice Population of Islamic Iran [Hssein GHORBANZADEH]
Political pressure groups and leaders: *groups that support the Islamic Repu blic:* Ansar-e Hizballah
Democracy Party (Hezb-e Mardom Salari)
Executives of Construction Party (Kargozaran)
Followers of the Guardianship of the Jurisprudent (Rahrovan)
Followers of the Line of the Imam and the Leader (Peyrovan)
Islamic Iran Freedom Party (Hezb-e Azadegi)
Islamic Coalition Party (Motalefeh)
Islam ic Labor Party (Hezb-e Kar)
Militant Clerics Society or MCS (Ruhaniyun)
Moderation and Development Party (Hezb-e Etedal va Tose-eh)
Nation of Iran Unity Party (Hezb-e Etehad)
National Trust Party (Hezb-e Etemad-e Meli)
Qom Theological Lecturers Association
Reform Front Coordination Council (Shora-ye Hamahangi Eslahat) Society of Devotees (Isargaran)
Society of Modern Thinking Muslim Women of Iran (Jamiat-e Zanan-e Noandish) Steadfastness Front (Paydari)
Tehran Militant Clergy Association or MCA (Ruhaniyat) Voice of Iran ians (Neda)
Wayfarers of the Islamic Revolution (Rahpuyan)

armed political groups repressed by the government: Democratic Party of Iranian Kurdistan or KDPI

Harekat-e Ansar-e Iran (splinter faction of Jundallah)

Jaysh l-Adl (formerly known as Jundallah)

Komala

Mojahedin-e Khalq Organization or MEK (MKO)

People's Fedayeen

People's Free Life Party of Kurdistan or PJAK

International organization participation: CICA, CP, D-8, ECO, FAO, G-15, G-24, G-77, IAEA, IBRD, ICAO, ICC (national committees), ICRM, IDA, IDB, IFAD, IFC, IFRCS, IHO, ILO, IMF, IMO, IMSO, Interpol, IOC, IOM, IPU, ISO, ITSO, ITU, MIGA, NAM, OIC, OPCW, OPEC, PCA, SAARC (observer), SCO (observer), UN, UNAMID, UNCTAD, UNESCO, UNHCR, UNIDO, UNITAR, UNWTO, UPU, WCO, WFTU (NGOs), WHO, WIPO, WMO, WTO (observer)

Diplomatic representation in the US: none; note—Iran has an Interests Section in the Pakistani Embassy; address: Iranian Interests Section, Pakistani Embassy, 2209 Wisconsin Avenue NW, Washington, DC 20007

telephone: [1] (202) 965-4990

FAX: [1] (202) 965-1073

Diplomatic representation from the US: none; note—the US Interests Section is located in the Embassy of Switzerland No.39 Shahid Mousavi (Golestan 5th), Pasdaran Ave., Tehran, Iran

telephone: [98] 212254 2178/2256 5273

FAX: [98] 21 2258 0432

Flag description: three equal horizontal bands of green (top), white, and red; the national emblem (a stylized representation of the word Allah in the shape of a tulip, a symbol of martyrdom) in red is centered in the white band; ALLAH AKBAR (God is Great) in white Arabic script is repeated 11 times along the bottom edge of the green band and 11 times along the top edge of the red band; green is the color of Islam and also represents growth, white symbolizes honesty and peace, red stands for bravery and martyrdom

National symbol(s): lion; national colors: green, white, red

National anthem: *name:* "Soroud-e Melli-ye Jomhouri-ye Eslami-ye Iran" (National Anthem of the Islamic Republic of Iran)

lyrics/music: multiple authors/Hassan RIAHI

note: adopted 1990

ECONOMY

Economy—overview: Iran's economy is marked by statist policies, inefficiencies, and reliance on oil and gas exports, but Iran also possesses significant agricultural, industrial, and service sectors. The Iranian government directly owns and operates hundreds of state-owned enterprises and indirectly controls many companies affiliated with the country's security forces. Distortions—including inflation, price controls, subsidies, and a banking system holding billions of dollars of non-performing loans—weigh down the economy, undermining the potential for private-sector-led growth.

Private sector activity includes small-scale workshops, farming, some manufacturing, and services, in addition to medium-scale construction, cement production, mining, and metalworking. Significant informal market activity flourishes and corruption is widespread.

Fiscal and monetary constraints, following the expansion of international sanctions in 2012 on Iran's Central Bank and oil exports, significantly reduced Iran's oil revenue, forced government spending cuts, and sparked a sharp currency depreciation. Iran's economy contracted for the first time in two decades during both 2012 and 2013, but growth resumed in 2014. Iran continues to suffer from high unemployment and underemployment. Lack of job opportunities has prompted many educated Iranian youth to seek employment overseas, resulting in a significant "brain drain."

In June 2013, the election of President Hasan RUHANI generated widespread public expectations of economic improvement and greater international engagement. Almost two years into his term, RUHANI has achieved some success, including reining in inflation and, in July of 2015, securing the promise of sanctions relief for Iran by signing the Joint Comprehensive Plan of Action (JCPOA) with the P5 + 1. The JCPOA, which severely limits Iran's nuclear program in exchange for unfreezing Iranian assets and reopening Iran to international trade, should bolster foreign direct investment, increase trade, and stimulate growth. In spite of RUHANI's efforts, Iran's growth was tepid in 2015, and significant economic improvement resulting from sanctions relief will take months or years to materialize.

GDP (purchasing power parity): $1.371 trillion (2015 est.)

$1.371 trillion (2014 est.)

$1.314 trillion (2013 est.)

note: data are in 2015 US dollars

country comparison to the world: 20

GDP (official exchange rate): $387.6 billion (2015 est.)

GDP—real growth rate: 0% (2015 est.)

4.3% (2014 est.) -1.9% (2013 est.)

country comparison to the world: 196

GDP—per capita (PPP): $17,300 (2015 est.)

$17,500 (2014 est.)

$17,000 (2013 est.)

note: data are in 2015 US dollars

country comparison to the world: 95

Gross national saving: 30.1% of GDP (2015 est.)

34.5% of GDP (2014 est.)

39.1% of GDP (2013 est.)

country comparison to the world: 25

GDP—composition, by end use:

household consumption: 53.1%

government consumption: 10.9%

investment in fixed capital: 27.4%

investment in inventories: 6.6%

exports of goods and services: 22.8%

imports of goods and services: -20.8% (2015 est.)

GDP—composition, by sector of origin:

agriculture: 9.3%

industry: 38.4%

services: 52.3% (2015 est.)

Agriculture—products: wheat, rice, other grains, sugar beets, sugarcane, fruits, nuts, cotton; dairy products, wool; caviar

Industries: petroleum, petrochemicals, gas, fertilizers, caustic soda, textiles, cement and other construction materials, food processing (particularly sugar refining and vegetable oil production), ferrous and nonferrous metal fabrication, armaments

Industrial production growth rate: 2.9% (2015 est.)

country comparison to the world: 90

Labor force: 29.07 million

note: shortage of skilled labor (2015 est.)

country comparison to the world: 22

Labor force—by occupation: *agriculture:* 16.3%

industry: 35.1%

services: 48.6% (2013 est.)

Unemployment rate: 10.5% (2015 est.)

10.3% (2014 est.)

note: data are according to the Iranian Government

country comparison to the world: 119

Population below poverty line: 18.7% (2007 est.)

Household income or consumption by percentage share: *lowest:* 10%: 2.6%

highest: 10%: 29.6% (2005)

Distribution of family income—Gini index: 44.5 (2006)

country comparison to the world: 47

Budget: *revenues:* $56.11 billion

expenditures: $70.12 billion (2015 est.)

Taxes and other revenues: 14.1% of GDP (2015 est.)

country comparison to the world: 200

Budget surplus (+) or deficit (–): -3.5% of GDP (2015 est.)

country comparison to the world: 132

Public debt: 13.2% of GDP (2015 est.)

10.7% of GDP (2014 est.)

note: includes publicly guaran teed debt

country comparison to the world: 163

Fiscal year: 21 March—20 March

Inflation rate (consumer prices): 12% (2015 est.)

15.6% (2014 est.)

note: official Iranian estimate

country comparison to the world: 215

Central bank discount rate: NA%

Commercial bank prime lending rate: 13% (31 December 2015 est.)

14% (31 December 2014 est.)

country comparison to the world: 57

Stock of narrow money: $41.55 billion (31 December 2015 est.)

$42.59 billion (31 December 2014 est.)

country comparison to the world: 54

Stock of broad money: $282.9 billion (31 December 2015 est.)

$273.6 billion (31 December 2014 est.)

country comparison to the world: 35

Stock of domestic credit: $45.9 billion (31 December 2015 est.)

$44.83 billion (31 December 2014 est.)

country comparison to the world: 63

Market value of publicly traded shares: $172 billion (31 December 2013 est.)

$140.8 billion (31 December 2012)

$107.2 billion (31 December 2011 est.)

411

country comparison to the world: 37
Current account balance: $1.394 billion (2015 est.)
$15.89 billion (2014 est.)
country comparison to the world: 34
Exports: $78.99 billion (2015 est.)
$86.47 billion (2014 est.)
country comparison to the world: 39
Exports—commodities: petroleum 80%, chemical and petrochemical products, fruits and nuts, carpets, cement, ore
Exports—partners: China 22.2%, India 9.9%, Turkey 8.4%, Japan 4.5% (2015)
Imports: $70.63 billion (2015 est.)
$52.07 billion (2014 est.)
country comparison to the world: 39
Imports—commodities: industrial supplies, capital goods, foodstuffs and other consumer goods, technical services
Imports—partners: UAE 39.6%, China 22.4%, South Korea 4.7%, Turkey 4.6% (2015)
Reserves of foreign exchange and gold: $93.95 billion (31 December 2015 est.)
$109 billion (31 December 2014 est.)
country comparison to the world: 25
Debt—external: $6.922 billion (31 December 2014 est.)
$7.646 billion (31 December 2013 est.)
country comparison to the world: 119
Stock of direct foreign investment—at home: $44.64 billion (31 December 2015 est.)
$42.47 billion (31 December 2014 est.)
country comparison to the world: 62
Stock of direct foreign investment—abroad: $4.67 billion (31 December 2015 est.)
$4.33 billion (31 December 2014 est.)
country comparison to the world: 69
Exchange rates: Iranian rials (IRR) per US dollar—
28,944 (2015 est.)
25,912.3 (2014 est.)
25,912 (2013 est.)
12,176 (2012 est.)
10,616 (2011 est.)

ENERGY

Electricity—production: 239.2 billion kWh (2012 est.)
country comparison to the world: 18
Electricity—consumption: 195.3 billion kWh (2012 est.)
country comparison to the world: 21
Electricity—exports: 11.03 billion kWh (2012 est.)
country comparison to the world: 20
Electricity—imports: 3.897 billion kWh (2012 est.)
country comparison to the world: 46
Electricity—installed generating capacity: 78.3 million kW (2012 est.)
country comparison to the world: 15
Electricity—from fossil fuels: 85.6% of total installed capacity (2012 est.)
country comparison to the world: 87
Electricity—from nuclear fuels: 1.2% of total installed capacity (2012 est.)

country comparison to the world: 33
Electricity—from hydroelectric plants: 12.4% of total installed capacity (2012 est.)
country comparison to the world: 109
Electricity—from other renewable sources: 0.8% of total installed capacity (2012 est.)
country comparison to the world: 97
Crude oil—production: 3.614 million bbl/day (2014 est.)
country comparison to the world: 6
Crude oil—exports: 1.322 million bbl/day (2013 est.)
country comparison to the world: 11
Crude oil—imports: 28,140 bbl/day (2012 est.)
country comparison to the world: 63
Crude oil—proved reserves: 157.8 billion bbl (1 January 2015 est.)
country comparison to the world: 4
Refined petroleum products—production: 1.823 million bbl/day (2012 est.)
country comparison to the world: 12
Refined petroleum products—consumption: 1.885 million bbl/day (2013 est.)
country comparison to the world: 13
Refined petroleum products—exports: 271,800 bbl/day (2012 est.)
country comparison to the world: 26
Refined petroleum products—imports: 18,150 bbl/day (2012 est.)
country comparison to the world: 116
Natural gas—production: 172.6 billion cu m (2014 est.)
country comparison to the world: 3
Natural gas—consumption: 170.2 billion cu m (2014 est.)
country comparison to the world: 5
Natural gas—exports: 9.584 billion cu m (2014 est.)
country comparison to the world: 22
Natural gas—imports: 6.886 billion cu m (2014 est.)
country comparison to the world: 31
Natural gas—proved reserves: 34.02 trillion cu m (2014 est.)
country comparison to the world: 1
Carbon dioxide emissions from consumption of energy: 650.4 million Mt (2014 est.)
country comparison to the world: 9

COMMUNICATIONS

Telephones—fixed lines: total subscriptions: 30.59 million
subscriptions per 100 inhabitants: 38 (2014 est.)
country comparison to the world: 10
Telephones—mobile cellular: *total:* 68.9 million
subscriptions per 100 inhabitants: 85 (2014 est.)
country comparison to the world: 22
Telephone system: *general assessment:* currently being modernized and expanded with the goal of not only improving the efficiency and increasing the volume of the urban service but also bringing telephone service to several thousand villages not presently connected
domestic: the addition of new fiber cables and modern switching and exchange systems installed by Iran's state-owned telecom company have

improved and expanded the fixed-line network greatly; fixed line availability has more than doubled to more than 27 million lines since 2000; additionally, mobile-cellular service has increased dramatically serving roughly 56 million subscribers in 2011; combined fixed-line and mobile-cellular subscribership now exceeds 100 per 100 persons
international: country code—98; submarine fiber-optic cable to UAE with access to Fiber-Optic Link Around the Globe (FLAG); Trans-Asia-Europe (TAE) fiber-optic line runs from Azerbaijan through the northern portion of Iran to Turkmenistan with expansion to Georgia and Azerbaijan; HF radio and microwave radio relay to Turkey, Azerbaijan, Pakistan, Afghanistan, Turkmenistan, Syria, Kuwait, Tajikistan, and Uzbekistan; satellite earth stations—13 (9 Intelsat and 4 Inmarsat) (2011)
Broadcast media: state-run broadcast media with no private, independent broadcasters; Islamic Republic of Iran Broadcasting (IRIB), the state-run TV broadcaster, operates 5 nationwide channels, a news channel, about 30 provincial channels, and several international channels; about 20 foreign Persian-language TV stations broadcasting on satellite TV are capable of being seen in Iran; satellite dishes are illegal and, while their use had been tolerated, authorities began confiscating satellite dishes following the unrest stemming from the 2009 presidential election; IRIB operates 8 nationwide radio networks, a number of provincial stations, and an external service; most major international broadcasters transmit to Iran (2009)
Radio broadcast stations: AM 72, FM 10, shortwave 21 (2010)
Television broadcast stations: 29 (plus 450 repeaters) (1997)
Internet country code: .ir
Internet hosts: 197,804 (2012)
country comparison to the world: 72
Internet users: *total:* 22.9 million
percent of Population: 28.3% (2014 est.)
country comparison to the world: 26

TRANSPORTATION

Airports: 319 (2013)
country comparison to the world: 22
Airports—with paved runways: *total:* 140
over 3,047 m: 42
2,438 to 3,047 m: 29
1,524 to 2,437 m: 26
914 to 1,523 m: 36
under 914 m: 7 (2013)
Airports—with unpaved runways: *total:* 179
over 3,047 m: 1
2,438 to 3,047 m: 2
1,524 to 2,437 m: 9
914 to 1,523 m: 135
under 914 m: 32 (2013)
Heliports: 26 (2013)
Pipelines: condensate 7 km; condensate/gas 973 km; gas 20,794 km; liquid petroleum gas 570 km; oil 8,625 km; refined products 7,937 km (2013)
Railways: *total:* 8,483.5 km
broad gauge: 94 km 1.676-m gauge

standard gauge: 8,389.5 km 1.435-m gauge (189.5 km electrified) (2014)

country comparison to the world: 24

Roadways: *total:* 198,866 km

paved: 160,366 km (includes 1,948 km of expressways)

unpaved: 38,500 km (2010)

country comparison to the world: 26

Waterways: 850 km (on Karun River; some navigation on Lake Urmia) (2012)

country comparison to the world: 69

Merchant marine: *total:* 76

by type: bulk carrier 8, cargo 51, chemical tanker 3, container 4, liquefied gas 1, passenger/cargo 3, petroleum tanker 2, refrigerated cargo 2, roll on/roll off 2

foreign-owned: 2 (UAE 2)

registered in other countries: 71 (Barbados 5, Cyprus 10, Hong Kong 3, Malta 48, Panama 5) (2010)

country comparison to the world: 60

Ports and terminals: *major seaport(s):* Bandar-e Asaluyeh, Bandar Abbas, Bandar Emam

container port(s) (TEUs): Bandar Abbas (2,752,460)

MILITARY AND SECURITY

Military branches: Islamic Republic of Iran Regular Forces (Artesh): Ground Forces, Navy, Air Force (IRIAF), Khatemolanbia Air Defense Headquarters; Islamic Revolutionary Guard Corps (Sepah-e Pasdaran-e Enqelab-e Eslami, IRGC): Ground Resistance Forces, Navy, Aerospace Force, Qods Force (special operations); Law Enforcement Forces (2015)

Military service age and obligation: 18 years of age for compulsory military service; 16 years of age for volunteers; 17 years of age for Law Enforcement Forces; 15 years of age for Basij Forces (Popular Mobilization Army); conscript military service obligation is 18 months; women exempt from military service (2012)

TRANSNATIONAL ISSUES

Disputes—international: Iran protests Afghanistan's limiting flow of dammed Helmand River tributaries during drought; Iraq's lack of a maritime boundary with Iran prompts jurisdiction disputes beyond the mouth of the Shatt al Arab in the Persian Gulf; Iran and UAE dispute Tunb Islands and Abu Musa Island, which are occupied by Iran; Azerbaijan, Kazakhstan, and Russia ratified Caspian seabed delimitation treaties based on equidistance, while Iran continues to insist on a one-fifth slice of the sea; Afghan and Iranian commissioners have discussed boundary monument densification and resurvey

Refugees and internally displaced persons: *refugees (country of origin):* 32,000 (Iraq) (2014); 2.5—3.0 (1 million registered, 1.5—2.0 million undocumented) (Afghanistan) (2015)

Trafficking in persons: *current situation:* Iran is a source, transit, and destination country for men, women, and children subjected to sex trafficking and forced labor; organized groups sex traffic Iranian women and children in Iran and to the UAE and Europe; the transport of girls from and through Iran en route to the Gulf for sexual exploitation or forced marriages is on the rise; Iranian children are also forced to work as beggars, street vendors, and in domestic workshops; Afghan boys forced to work in construction or agriculture are vulnerable to sexual abuse by their employers; Pakistani and Afghan migrants being smuggled to Europe often are subjected to forced labor, including debt bondage

tier rating: Tier 3—Iran does not comply with the minimum standards for the elimination of trafficking, and is not making significant efforts to do so; the government does not share information on its anti-trafficking efforts, but publically available information from NGOs, the media, and international organizations indicates that Iran is not taking adequate measures to address its trafficking problems, particularly protecting victims; Iranian law does not prohibit all forms of human trafficking; female victims find it extremely difficult to get justice because Iranian courts accord women's testimony half the weight of men's, and female victims of sexual abuse, including trafficking, are likely to be prosecuted for adultery; the government did not identify or provide protection services to any victims and continued to punish victims for unlawful acts committed as a direct result of being trafficked; the government made some effort to cooperate with neighboring governments and an international organization to combat human trafficking and other crimes (2015)

Illicit drugs: despite substantial interdiction efforts and considerable control measures along the border with Afghanistan, Iran remains one of the primary transshipment routes for Southwest Asian heroin to Europe; suffers one of the highest opiate addiction rates in the world, and has an increasing problem with synthetic drugs; regularly enforces the death penalty for drug offences; lacks anti-money laundering laws; has reached out to neighboring countries to share counter-drug intelligence

IRAQ

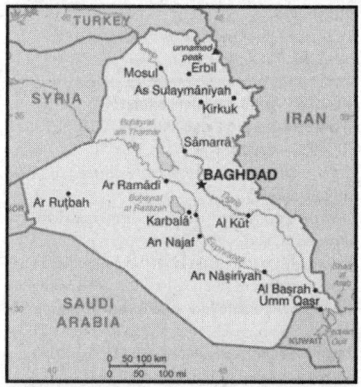

INTRODUCTION

Background: Formerly part of the Ottoman Empire, Iraq was occupied by Britain during the course of World War I; in 1920, it was declared a League of Nations mandate under UK administration. In stages over the next dozen years, Iraq attained its independence as a kingdom in 1932. A "republic" was proclaimed in 1958, but in actuality a series of strongmen ruled the country until 2003. The last was SADDAM Husayn. Territorial disputes with Iran led to an inconclusive and costly eight-year war (1980–88). in August 1990, Iraq seized Kuwait but was expelled by US-led UN coalition forces during the Gulf War of January-February 1991. Following Kuwait's liberation, the UN Security Council (UNSC) required Iraq to scrap all weapons of mass destruction and long-range missiles and to allow UN verification inspections. Continued Iraqi noncompliance with UNSC resolutions over a period of 12 years led to the US-led invasion of Iraq in March 2003 and the ouster of the SADDAM Husayn regime. US forces remained in Iraq under a UN SC mandate through 2009 and under a bilateral security agreement thereafter, helping to provide security and to train and mentor Iraqi security forces.

In October 2005, Iraqis approved a constitution in a national referendum and, pursuant to this document, elected a 275-member Council of Representatives (COR) in December 2005. The COR approved most cabinet ministers in May 2006, marking the transition to Iraq's first constitutional government in nearly a half century. Nearly nine years after the start of the Second Gulf War in Iraq, US military operations there ended in mid-December 2011. in January 2009 and April 2013, Iraq held elections for provincial councils in all governorates except for the three comprising the Kurdistan Regional Government and Kirkuk Governorate. Iraq held a national legislative election in March 2010—choosing 325 legislators in an expanded COR—and, after nine months of deadlock the COR approved the new government in December 2010. In April 2014, Iraq held a national legislative election and expanded the COR to 328 legislators. Prime Minister Nurial-MALIKI dropped his bid for a third term in office, enabling new Prime Minister Haydar al-ABADI, a Shia Muslim from Baghdad, to win parliamentary approval of his new cabinet in September 2014. Since early 2015, Iraq has been engaged in a military campaign against the Islamic State of Iraq and the Levant (ISIL) to recapture territory lost in the western and northern portion of the country.

GEOGRAPHY

Location: Middle East, bordering the Persian Gulf, between Iran and Kuwait

Geographic coordinates: 33 00 N, 44 00 E

Map references: Middle East

Area: *total:* 438,317 sq km

land: 437,367 sq km

water: 950 sq km

country comparison to the world: 59

Area—comparative: slightly more than three times the size of New York state

Land boundaries: *total:* 3,809 km

border countries (6): Iran 1,599 km, Jordan 179 km, Kuwait 254 km, Saudi Arabia 811 km, Syria 599 km, Turkey 367 km

Coastline: 58 km

Maritime claims: *territorial sea:* 12 nm

continental shelf: not specified

Climate: mostly desert; mild to cool winters with dry, hot, cloudless summers; northern mountainous regions along Iranian and Turkish borders experience cold winters with occasionally heavy snows that melt in early spring, sometimes causing extensive flooding in central and southern Iraq

Terrain: mostly broad plains; reedy marshes along Iranian border in south with large flooded areas; mountains along borders with Iran and Turkey

Elevation: *mean elevation:* 312 m

elevation extremes: *lowest point:* Persian Gulf 0 m

highest point: Cheekha Dar (Kurdish for "Black Tent") 3,611 m

Natural resources: petroleum, natural gas, phosphates, sulfur

Land use: *agricultural land:* 18.1%

arable land: 8.4%

permanent crops: 0.5%

permanent pasture: 9.2%

forest: 1.9%

other: 80% (2011 est.)

Irrigated land: 35,250 sq km (2012)

Total renewable water resources: 89.86 cu km (2011)

Freshwater withdrawal (domestic/industrial/agricultural): *total:* 66 cu km/yr (7%/15%/79%)

per capita: 2,616 cu m/yr (2000)

Natural hazards: dust storms; sandstorms; floods

Environment—current issues: government water control projects drained most of the inhabited marsh areas east of An Nasiriyah by drying up or diverting the feeder streams and rivers; a once sizable population of Marsh Arabs, who inhabited these areas for thousands of years, has been displaced; furthermore, the destruction of the natural habitat poses serious threats to the area's wildlife populations; inadequate supplies of potable water; development of the Tigris and Euphrates rivers system contingent upon agreements with upstream riparian Turkey; air and water pollution; soil degradation (salination) and erosion; desertification

Environment—international agreements: *party to:* Biodiversity, Law of the Sea, Ozone Layer Protection

signed, but not ratified: Environmental Modification

Geography—note: strategic location on Shatt al Arab waterway and at the head of the Persian Gulf

PEOPLE AND SOCIETY

Nationality: *noun:* Iraqi(s)

adjective: Iraqi

Ethnic groups: Arab 75%-80%, Kurdish 15%-20%, Turkoman, Assyrian, other 5%

Languages: Arabic (official), Kurdish (official), Turkmen (a Turkish dialect) and Assyrian (Neo-Aramaic) are official in areas where they constitute a majority of the population), Armenian

Religions: Muslim (official) 99% (Shia 60%-65%, Sunni 32%-37%), Christian 0.8%, Hindu <0.1, Buddhist <0.1, Jewish <0.1, folk religion <0.1, unafilliated 0.1, other <0.1

note: while there has been voluntary relocation of many Christian families to northern Iraq, recent reporting indicates that the overall Christian population may have dropped by as much as 50 percent since the fall of the SADDAM Husayn regime in 2003, with many fleeing to Syria, Jordan, and Lebanon (2010 est.)

Population: 37,056,169 (July 2015 est.)

country comparison to the world: 37

Age structure: *0–14 years:* 40.25% (male 7,615,835/female 7,300,957)

15–24 years: 18.98% (male 3,576,740/female 3,454,768)

25–54 years: 33.49% (male 6,276,669/female 6,132,968)

55–64 years: 3.95% (male 693,629/female 771,624)

65 years and over: 3.33% (male 549,034/female 683,945) (2015 est.)

Dependency ratios: *total dependency ratio:* 78.7%

youth dependency ratio: 73.2%

elderly dependency ratio: 5.5%

potential support ratio: 18.3% (2015 est.)

Median age: *total:* 19.7 years

male: 19.4 years

female: 20 years (2015 est.)

country comparison to the world: 192

Population growth rate: 2.93% (2015 est.)

country comparison to the world: 9

Birth rate: 31.45 births/1,000 population (2015 est.)

country comparison to the world: 35

Death rate: 3.77 deaths/1,000 population (2015 est.)

country comparison to the world: 212

Net migration rate: 1.62 migrant(s)/1,000 population (2015 est.)

country comparison to the world: 56

Urbanization: *urban Population:* 69.5% of total population (2015)

rate of urbanization: 3.01% annual rate of change (2010–15 est.)

Major urban areas—Population: BAGHDAD (capital) 6.643 million; Mosul 1.694 million; Erbil 1.166 million; Basra 1.019 million; As Sulaymaniyah 1.004 million; Najaf 889,000 (2015)

Sex ratio: *at birth:* 1.05 male(s)/female

0–14 years: 1.04 male(s)/female

15–24 years: 1.04 male(s)/female

25–54 years: 1.02 male(s)/female

55–64 years: 0.9 male(s)/female

65 years and over: 0.8 male(s)/female

total Population: 1.02 male(s)/female (2015 est.)

Maternal mortality rate: 50 deaths/100,000 live births (2015 est.)

country comparison to the world: 98

Infant mortality rate: *total:* 37.49 deaths/1,000 live births

male: 40.6 deaths/1,000 live births

female: 34.23 deaths/1,000 live births (2015 est.)

country comparison to the world: 57

Life expectancy at birth: *total population:* 74.85 years

male: 72.62 years

female: 77.19 years (2015 est.)

country comparison to the world: 111

Total fertility rate: 4.12 children born/woman (2015 est.)

country comparison to the world: 34

Contraceptive prevalence rate: 52.5% (2011)

Health expenditures: 5.2% of GDP (2013)

country comparison to the world: 170

Physicians density: 0.61 physicians/1,000 population (2010)

Hospital bed density: 1.3 beds/1,000 population (2012)

Drinking water source:

improved:

urban: 93.8% of population

rural: 70.1% of population

total: 86.6% of population

unimproved:

urban: 6.1% of population

rural: 31.5% of population

total: 14.6% of population (2015 est.)

Sanitation facility access:

improved:

urban: 86.4% of population

rural: 83.8% of population

total: 85.6% of population

unimproved:

urban: 13.6% of population

rural: 16.2% of population

total: 14.4% of population (2015 est.)

HIV/AIDS—adult prevalence rate: NA

HIV/AIDS—people living with HIV/AIDS: NA

HIV/AIDS—deaths: NA

Major infectious diseases: *degree of risk:* intermediate

food or waterborne diseases: bacterial diarrhea, hepatitis A, and typhoid fever

note: highly pathogenic H5N1 avian influenza has been identified in this country; it poses a negligible risk with extremely rare cases possible among US citizens who have close contact with birds (2013)

Obesity—adult prevalence rate: 21.2% (2014)

country comparison to the world: 42

Children under the age of 5 years underweight: 8.5% (2011)

country comparison to the world: 74

Education expenditures: NA

Literacy: *definition:* age 15 and over can read and write

total Population: 79.7%

male: 85.7%

female: 73.7% (2015 est.)

Child labor—children ages 5–14: *total number:* 715,737

percentage: 11% (2006 est.)

GOVERNMENT

Country name: *conventional long form:* Republic of Iraq

conventional short form: Iraq

local long form: Jumhuriyat al-Iraq/Komar-i Eraq

local short form: Al Iraq/Eraq

etymology: the name probably derives from "Uruk" (Biblical "Erech"), the ancient Sumerian and Babylonian city on the Euphrates River

Government type: federal parliamentary republic

Capital: *name:* Baghdad

Geographic coordinates: 33 20 N, 44 24 E

time difference: UTC+3 (8 hours ahead of Washington, DC, during Standard Time)

Administrative divisions: 18 governorates (muhafazat, singular—muhafazah (Arabic); parezgakan, singular—parezga (Kurdish)) and 1 region*; Al Anbar; Al Basrah; Al Muthanna; Al Qadisiyah (Ad Diwaniyah); An Najaf; Arbil (Erbil) (Arabic), Hewler (Kurdish); As Sulay maniyah (Arabic), Slemani (Kurdish); Babil; Baghdad; Dahuk (Arabic), Dihok (Kurdish); Dhi Qar; Diyala; Karbala'; Kirkuk; Kurdistan Regional Government*; Maysan; Ninawa; Salah ad Din; Wasit

Independence: 3 October 1932 (from League of Nations mandate under British administration); note—on 28 June 2004 the Coalition Provisional Authority transferred sovereignty to the Iraqi Interim Government

National holiday: Republic Day, July 14 (1958); note—the Government of Iraq has yet to declare an official national holiday but still observes Republic Day

Constitution: several previous; latest adopted by referendum 15 October 2005 (2016)

Legal system: mixed legal system of civil and Islamic law

International law organization participation: has not submitted an ICJ jurisdiction declaration; non-party state to the ICCt

Citizenship: *citizenship by birth:* no

citizenship by descent only: at least one parent must be a citizen of Iraq

dual citizenship recognized: yes

residency requirement for naturalization: 10 years

Suffrage: 18 years of age; universal

Executive branch: *chief of state:* President Fuad MASUM (since 24 July 2014); Vice Presidents Ayad ALLAWI (since 9 September 2014), Nuri MALIKI (since 9 September 2014), Usama al-NUJAYFI (since 9 September 2014)

head of government: Prime Minister Haydar al-ABADI (since 8 September 2014)

cabinet: Council of Ministers proposed by the prime minister, approved by Council of Representatives

elections/appointments: president indirectly elected by Council of Representatives to serve a 4-year term (eligible for a second term); election

last held on 30 April 2014 (next to be held in 2018); prime minister nominated by the president, approved by Council of Representatives

election results: Fuad MASUM elected president; Council of Representatives vote—Fuad MASUM (PUK) 211, Barham SALIH (PUK) 17; Haydar al-ABADI (Da'wa Party) approved as prime minister

Legislative branch: *description:* unicameral Council of Representatives or Majlis an-Nuwwab al-Iraqiyy (328 seats; 320 members directly elected in multi-seat constituencies by proportional representation vote and 8 seats reserved for minorities; members serve 4-year terms); note—Iraq's constitution calls for the establishment of an upper house, the Federation Council, but it has not been instituted

elections: last held on 30 April 2014 (next to be held in 2018)

election results: Council of Representatives—percent of vote by party/coalition—NA; seats by coalition/party—State of Law Coalition 95, Sadrist Movement 34, ISCI/Muwatin 30, KDP 25, United for Reform Coalition/Muttahidun 23, PUK 21, Nationalism Coalition/Watany ah 19, other Sunni coalitions/parties 15, Al-Arabiyah Coalition 10, Goran 9, other Shia parties/coalitions 9, Fadilah 6, National Reform Trend 6, Iraq Coalition 5, KIU 4, other 17

Judicial branch: *highest court(s):* Federal Supreme Court or FSC (consists of 9 judges); note—court jurisdiction limited to constitutional issues and disputes between regions or governorates and the central government); Court of Cassation (consists of a court president, 5 vice-presidents, and at least 24 judges)

judge selection and term of office: Federal Supreme Court and Court of Cassation judges appointed by the Higher Juridical Council, a 25-member committee of judicial officials that manage the judiciary and prosecutors; FSC members appointed for life; Court of Cassation judges appointed for 1-year probationary period and upon satisfactory performance may be confirmed for permanent tenure until retirement nominally at age 63

subordinate courts: Courts of Appeal (governorate level); courts of first instance; personal status, labor, criminal, juvenile, and religious courts

Political parties and leaders: Al-Arabiyah Coalition [Salih al-MUTLAQ]

Badr Organization [Hadi al-AMIRI]

Da'wa Party [Vice President Nuri al-MALIKI];;

Da'wa Tanzim [Hashim al-MUSAWI]

Fadilah Party [Muhammad al-YAQUBI]

Goran Party [Nawhirwan MUSTAFA]

Iraq Coalition [Abd al-Salam al-HAMMUDI]

Iraqi Front for National Dialogue [Salih al-MUTLAQ]

Iraqi Justice and Reform Movement [Shaykh Abdallah al-YAWR]

Islamic Supreme Council of Iraq or ISCI/Muwatin Coalition [Ammar al-HAKIM]

Kurdistan Democratic Party or KDP [Kurdistan Regional Government President Masud BARZANI]

Kurdistan Islamic Union or KIU [Mohammed FARA]

Nationalism Coalition/Wataniyah [Vice President Ayad ALLAWI]

National Movement for Reform and Development [Muhammad al-KARBULI]

National Reform Trend [Foreign Minister Ibrahim al-JAFARI]

Patriotic Union of Kurdistan or PUK [former President Jalal TALABANI]

Sadrist Movement or Ahrar Bloc [Muqtada al-SADR]

State of Law Coalition [Vice President Nuri al MALIKI]

United for Iraq/Muttahidun Party [Vice President Usama al-NUJAYFI]

United for Reform Coalition/Muttahidun [Vice President Usama al-NUJAYFI]

note: numerous smaller local, tribal, and minority parties

Political pressure groups and leaders: Sunni militias; Shia militias, some associated with political parties

International organization participation: ABEDA, AFESD, AMF, CAEU, CICA, EITI (compliant country), FAO, G-77, IAEA, IBRD, ICAO, ICRM, IDA, IDB, IFAD, IFC, IFRCS, ILO, IMF, IMO, IMSO, Interpol, IOC, IPU, ISO, ITSO, ITU, LAS, MIGA, NAM, OAPEC, OIC, OPCW, OPEC, PCA, UN, UNCTAD, UNESCO, UNIDO, UNWTO, UPU, WCO, WFTU (NGOs), WHO, WIPO, WMO, WTO (observer)

Diplomatic representation in the US: *chief of mission:* Ambassador Luqman Abd al-Rahim FAYLI (since 31 May 2013)

chancery: 3421 M assachusetts Ave, NW, Washington, DC 20007

telephone: [1] (202) 742-1600

FAX: [1] (202) 333-1129

consulate(s) general: Detroit, Los Angeles

Diplomatic representation from the US: *chief of mission:* Ambassador Stuart E. JONES (since 2 October 2014)

embassy: Al-Kindi Street, International Zone, Baghdad

mailing address: APOAE 09316

telephone: 0760-030-3000

FAX: NA

Flag description: three equal horizontal bands of red (top), white, and black; the Takbir (Arabic expression meaning "God is great") in green Arabic script is centered in the white band; the band colors derive from the Arab Liberation flag and represent oppression (black), overcome through bloody struggle (red), to be replaced by a bright future (white); the Council of Representatives approved this flag in 2008 as a compromise temporary replacement for the Ba'athist SADDAM-era flag

note: similar to the flag of Syria, which has two stars but no script; Yemen, which has a plain white band; and that of Egypt, which has a golden Eagle of Saladin centered in the white band

National symbol(s): golden eagle; national colors: red, white, black

National anthem: *name:* "Mawtini" (My Homeland)
lyrics/music: Ibrahim TOUQAN/Mohammad FLAYFEL
note: adopted 2004; following the ouster of SADDAM Husayn, Iraq adopted "Mawtini, " a popular folk song throughout the Arab world; also serves as an unofficial anthem of the Palestinian people

ECONOMY

Economy—overview: During 2015, worsening security and financial stability throughout Iraq—driven by an ongoing insurgency, decreasing oil prices, and political upheaval—decreased prospects for improving the country's economic environment and securing much-needed foreign investment. Long-term fiscal health, a strengthened investment climate, and sustained improvements in the overall standard of living still depend on a rebound in global oil prices, the central government passing major policy reforms, and finishing the conflict with ISIL.

Iraq's largely state-run economy is dominated by the oil sector, which provides more than 90% of government revenue and 80% of foreign exchange earnings. Oil exports in 2015 averaged 3.0 million barrels per day, up from 2014, but a failed revenue-and oil-sharing agreement with the Iraqi Kurdistan Region's (IKR) autonomous Kurdistan Regional Government (KRG) resulted in a loss of exports from northern oil fields. Moreover, falling global oil prices resulted in declining export revenues. Iraq's contracts with major oil companies have the potential to further expand oil exports and revenues, but Iraq will need to make significant upgrades to its oil processing, pipeline, and export infrastructure to enable these deals to reach their economic potential. The Iraqi Kurdistan Region's (IKR) autonomous Kurdistan Regional Government (KRG) passed its own oil law in 2007, and has directly signed about 50 contracts to develop IKR energy reserves. The federal government has disputed the legal authority of the KRG to conclude most of these contracts, some of which are also in areas with unresolved administrative boundaries in dispute between the federal and regional government. in December 2014, the federal government and the KRG agreed to sell oil exports from Kurdish-controlled oilfields under the federal oil ministry, in exchange for the central government paying $1 billion to the Kurdish Peshmerga forces and resuming budget transfers to the KRG that amount to 17% of Iraq's national budget. However, that deal fell apart in 2015. Iraq is making slow progress enacting laws and developing the institutions needed to implement economic policy, and political reforms are still needed to assuage investors' concerns regarding the uncertain business climate. The Government of Iraq is eager to attract additional foreign direct investment, but it faces a number of obstacles, including a tenuous political system and concerns about security and societal stability. Rampant corruption, outdated infrastructure, insufficient essential services, skilled labor shortages, and antiquated commercial laws stifle investment and continue to constrain growth of private, nonoil sectors. Under the Iraqi constitution, some competencies relevant

to the overall investment climate are either shared by the federal government and the regions or are devolved entirely to local governments. Investment in the IKR operates within the framework of the Kurdistan Region Investment Law (Law 4 of 2006) and the Kurdistan Board of Investment, which is designed to provide incentives to help economic development in areas under the authority of the KRG.

Inflation has remained under control since 2006. However, Iraqi leaders remain hard pressed to translate macroeconomic gains into an improved standard of living for the Iraqi populace. Unemployment remains a problem throughout the country despite a bloated public sector. Encouraging private enterprise through deregulation would make it easier for Iraqi citizens and foreign investors to start new businesses. Rooting out corruption and implementing reforms—such as restructuring banks and developing the private sector -would be important steps in this direction.

GDP (purchasing power parity): $544.1 billion (2015 est.)
$531.4 billion (2014 est.)
$542.9 billion (2013 est.)
note: data are in 2015 US dollars
country comparison to the world: 37
GDP (official exchange rate): $169.5 billion (2015 est.)
GDP—real growth rate: 2.4% (2015 est.) -2.1% (2014 est.) 6.6% (2013 est.)
country comparison to the world: 128
GDP—per capita (PPP): $15,500 (2015 est.)
$15,500 (2014 est.)
$16,200 (2013 est.)
note: data are in 2015 US dollars
country comparison to the world: 104
Gross national saving: 15% of GDP (2015 est.)
25.6% of GDP (2014 est.)
28.3% of GDP (2013 est.)
country comparison to the world: 115
GDP—composition, by end use:
household consumption: 55.5%
government consumption: 21.5%
investment in fixed capital: 16.5%
investment in inventories: 2%
exports of goods and services: 40.8%
imports of goods and services: -36.3%
GDP—composition, by sector of origin:
agriculture: 5.2%
industry: 49.7%
services: 45.1% (2013 est.)
Agriculture—products: wheat, barley, rice, vegetables, dates, cotton; cattle, sheep, poultry
Industries: petroleum, chemicals, textiles, leather, construction materials, food processing, fertilizer, metal fabrication/processing
Industrial production growth rate: 8.8% (2015 est.)
country comparison to the world: 12
Labor force: 8.9 million (2010 est.)
country comparison to the world: 57
Labor force—by occupation: *agriculture:* 21.6%
industry: 18.7%
services: 59.8% (2008 est.)
Unemployment rate: 16% (2012 est.)
15% (2010 est.)
country comparison to the world: 155
Population below poverty line: 25% (2008 est.)
Household income or consumption by percentage share: *lowest:* 10%: 3.6%

highest: 10%: 25.7% (2007 est.)
Budget: *revenues:* $61.09 billion
expenditures: $86.57 billion (2015 est.)
Taxes and other revenues: 37% of GDP (2015 est.)
country comparison to the world: 49
Budget surplus (+) or deficit (–): -15.4% of GDP (2015 est.)
country comparison to the world: 215
Fiscal year: calendar year
Inflation rate (consumer prices): 1.4% (2015 est.)
2.2% (2014 est.)
country comparison to the world: 95
Central bank discount rate: 6% (December 2012)
6% (December 2011)
country comparison to the world: 67
Commercial bank prime lending rate: 6% (31 December 2015 est.)
6% (31 December 2014 est.)
country comparison to the world: 129
Stock of narrow money: $61.81 billion (31 December 2015 est.)
$62.31 billion (31 December 2014 est.)
country comparison to the world: 47
Stock of broad money: $80.83 billion (31 December 2015 est.)
$78.65 billion (31 December 2014 est.)
country comparison to the world: 59
Stock of domestic credit: -$179,700 (31 December 2015 est.)
-$359,300 (31 December 2014 est.)
country comparison to the world: 189
Market value of publicly traded shares: $4 billion (9 December 2011)
$2.6 billion (31 July 2010)
$2 billion (31 July 2009 est.)
country comparison to the world: 91
Current account balance: -$10.82 billion (2015 est.)
-$1.732 billion (2014 est.)
country comparison to the world: 178
Exports: $54.65 billion (2015 est.)
$83.98 billion (2014 est.)
country comparison to the world: 50
Exports—commodities: crude oil 84%, crude materials excluding fuels, food and live animals
Exports—partners: China 22.6%, India 21.1%, South Korea 11.2%, US 7.8%, Italy 6.7%, Greece 6% (2015)
Imports: $42.94 billion (2015 est.)
$45.2 billion (2014 est.)
country comparison to the world: 55
Imports—commodities: food, medicine, manufactures
Imports—partners: Turkey 20.7%, Syria 19.6%, China 19.2%, US 4.8%, Russia 4.4% (2015)
Reserves of foreign exchange and gold: $57.07 billion (31 December 2015 est.)
$66.85 billion (31 December 2014 est.)
country comparison to the world: 37
Debt—external: $58.13 billion (31 December 2014 est.)
$59.5 billion (31 December 2013 est.)
country comparison to the world: 61
Exchange rates: Iraqi dinars (IQD) per US dollar—
1,247.6 (2015 est.)
1,213.72 (2014 est.)
1,213.72 (2013 est.)
1,166.17 (2012 est.)
1,170 (2011 est.)

ENERGY

Electricity—production: 62.3 billion kWh (2013 est.)

country comparison to the world: 45

Electricity—consumption: 53.41 billion kWh (2013 est.)

country comparison to the world: 46

Electricity—exports: 0 kWh (2013 est.)

country comparison to the world: 153

Electricity—imports: 8.201 billion kWh (2013 est.)

country comparison to the world: 26

Electricity—installed generating capacity: 11.2 million kW (2013 est.)

country comparison to the world: 53

Electricity—from fossil fuels: 92% of total installed capacity (2013 est.)

country comparison to the world: 70

Electricity—from nuclear fuels: 0% of total installed capacity (2013 est.)

country comparison to the world: 115

Electricity—from hydroelectric plants: 7.6% of total installed capacity (2013 est.)

country comparison to the world: 121

Electricity—from other renewable sources: 0% of total installed capacity (2013 est.)

country comparison to the world: 185

Crude oil—production: 3.368 million bbl/day (2014 est.)

country comparison to the world: 7

Crude oil—exports: 2.39 million bbl/day (2013 est.)

country comparison to the world: 6

Crude oil—Imports: 0 bbl/day (2013 est.)

country comparison to the world: 207

Crude oil—proved reserves: 144.2 billion bbl (1 January 2015 est.)

country comparison to the world: 5

Refined petroleum products—production: 590,400 bbl/day (2012 est.)

country comparison to the world: 29

Refined petroleum products—consumptio: 750,000 bbl/day (2013 est.)

country comparison to the world: 26

Refined petroleum products—exports: 2,153 bbl/day (2012 est.)

country comparison to the world: 105

Refined petroleum products—imports: 242,700 bbl/day (2012 est.)

country comparison to the world: 28

Natural gas—production: 1.18 billion cu m (2013 est.)

country comparison to the world: 63

Natural gas—consumption: 1.179 billion cu m (2013 est.)

country comparison to the world: 88

Natural gas—exports: 0 cu m (2013 est.)

country comparison to the world: 121

Natural gas—imports: 0 cu m (2013 est.)

country comparison to the world: 213

Natural gas—proved reserves: 3.158 trillion cu m (1 January 2014 est.)

country comparison to the world: 12

Carbon dioxide emissions from consumption of energy: 130.7 million Mt (2012 est.)

country comparison to the world: 37

COMMUNICATIONS

Telephones—fixed lines: *total subscriptions:* 1.95 million

subscriptions per 100 inhabitants: 5 (2014 est.)

country comparison to the world: 59

Telephones—mobile cellular: *total:* 33 million

subscriptions per 100 inhabitants: 92 (2014 est.)

country comparison to the world: 36

Telephone system: *general assessment:* the 2003 liberation of Iraq severely disrupted telecommunications throughout Iraq including international connections; widespread government efforts to rebuild domestic and international communications through fiber optic links are in progress; the mobile cellular market expanded rapidly to some 27 million subscribers by the end of 2012

domestic: repairs to switches and lines destroyed during 2003 continue; additional switching capacity is improving; 3 GSM operators since 2007 have expanded beyond their regional roots and offer nearly countrywide access to second-generation services; third-generation mobile services are not available nationwide; wireless local loop is available in some metropolitan areas and additional licenses have been issued with the hope of overcoming the lack of fixed-line infrastructure

international: country code—964; satellite earth stations—4 (2 Intelsat—1 Atlantic Ocean and 1 Indian Ocean, 1 Intersputnik—Atlantic Ocean region, and 1 Arabsat (inoperative)); local microwave radio relay connects border regions to Jordan, Kuwait, Syria, and Turkey; international terrestrial fiber-optic connections have been established with Saudi Arabia, Turkey, Kuwait, Jordan, and Iran; links to the Fiberoptic Link Around the Globe (FLAG) and the Gulf Bridge International (GBI) submarine fiber-optic cables have been established (2011)

Broadcast media: the number of private radio and TV stations has increased rapidly since 2003; government-owned TV and radio stations are operated by the publicly funded Iraqi Media Network; private broadcast media are mostly linked to political, ethnic, or religious groups; satellite TV is available to an estimated 70% of viewers and many of the broadcasters are based abroad; transmissions of multiple international radio broadcasters are accessible (2015)

Radio broadcast stations: 55 (station frequency types NA) (2009)

Television broadcast stations: 28 (2009)

Internet country code: iq

Internet hosts: 26 (2012)

country comparison to the world: 218

Internet users: *total:* 2.8 million

percent of Population: 7.8% (2014 est.)

country comparison to the world: 87

TRANSPORTATION

Airports: 102 (2013)

country comparison to the world: 55

Airports—with paved runways: *total:* 72

over 3,047 m: 20

2,438 to 3,047 m: 34

1,524 to 2,437 m: 4

914 to 1,523 m: 7

under 914 m: 7 (2013)

Airports—with unpaved runways: *total:* 30

over 3,047 m: 3

2,438 to 3,047 m: 5

1,524 to 2,437 m: 3

914 to 1,523 m: 13

under 914 m: 6 (2013)

Heliports: 16 (2013)

Pipelines: gas 2,455 km; liquid petroleum gas 913 km; oil 5,432 km; refined products 1,637 km (2013)

Railways: *total:* 2,272 km

standard gauge: 2,272 km 1.435-m gauge (2014)

country comparison to the world: 67

Roadways: *total:* 59,623 km

paved: 59,623 km (includes Kurdistan Region) (2012)

country comparison to the world: 70

Waterways: 5,279 km (the Euphrates River (2,815 km), Tigris River (1,899 km), and Third River (565 km) are the principal waterways) (2012)

country comparison to the world: 22

Merchant marine: *total:* 2

by type: petroleum tanker 2

registered in other countries: 2 (Marshall Islands 2) (2010)

country comparison to the world: 142

Ports and terminals: *river port(s):* Al Basrah (Shatt al-'Arab); Khawr az Zubayr, Umm Qasr (Khawr az Zubayr waterway)

MILITARY AND SECURITY

Military branches: Ministry of Defense: Iraqi Army (includes Army Aviation Directorate), Iraqi Navy, Iraqi Air Force; Counterterrorism Service (2015)

Military service age and obligation: 18–40 years of age for voluntary military service; no conscription (2013)

Military expenditures: 8.7% of GDP (2014)

3.4% of GDP (2013)

2.88% of GDP (2012)

3.27% of GDP (2011)

2.88% of GDP (2010)

country comparison to the world: 2

TRANSNATIONAL ISSUES

Disputes—international: Iraq's lack of a maritime boundary with Iran prompts jurisdiction disputes beyond the mouth of the Shatt al Arab in the Persian Gulf; Turkey has expressed concern over the autonomous status of Kurds in Iraq

Refugees and internally displaced persons: *refugees (country of origin):* 16,637 (Turkey); 11,053 (Iran); 9,246 (West Bank and Gaza Strip) (2014); 249,395 (Syria) (2016)

IDPs: 4,274,402 (since 2006 due to ethno-sectarian violence; includes 3,320,274 displaced in central and northern Iraq since January 2014) (2016)

stateless persons: 50,000 (2015); note—in the 1970s and 1980s under SADDAM Husayn's regime, thousands of Iraq's Faili Kurds, followers of Shia Islam, were stripped of their Iraqi citizenship, had their property seized by the government, and many were deported; some Faili Kurds had their citizenship reinstated under the 2006 Iraqi Nationality Law, but others lack the documentation to prove their Iraqi origins; some Palestinian refugees persecuted by the SADDAM regime remain stateless

note: estimate revised to reflect the reduction of statelessness in line with Law 26 of 2006, which allows stateless persons to apply for nationality in certain circumstances; more accurate studies of statelessness in Iraq are pending (2015)

IRELAND

INTRODUCTION

Background: Celtic tribes arrived on the island between 600 and 150 B.C. Invasions by Norsemen that began in the late 8th century were finally ended when King Brian BORU defeated the Danes in 1014. Norman invasions began in the 12th century and set off more than seven centuries of Anglo-Irish struggle marked by fierce rebellions and harsh repressions. The Irish famine of the mid-19th century saw the population of the island drop by one third through starvation and emigration. For more than a century after that the population of the island continued to fall only to begin growing again in the 1960s. Over the last 50 years, Ireland's high birthrate has made it demographically one of the youngest populations in the EU. The modern Irish state traces its origins to the failed 1916 Easter Monday Uprising that touched off several years of guerrilla warfare resulting in independence from the UK in 1921 for 26 southern counties; six northern counties remained part of the UK. UN resolved issues in Northern Ireland erupted into years of violence known as the "Troubles" that began in the 1960s. The Government of Ireland was part of a process along with the UK and US Governments that helped broker what is known as The Good Friday Agreement in Northern Ireland in 1998. This initiated a new phase of cooperation between the Irish and British Governments. Ireland was neutral in World War II and continues its policy of military neutrality. Ireland joined the European Community in 1973 and the euro zone currency union in 1999. The economic boom years of the Celtic Tiger (1995–2007) saw rapid economic growth, which came to an abrupt end in 2008 with the meltdown of the Irish banking system. Today the economy is recovering, fueled by large and growing foreign direct investment, especially from US multi-nationals.

GEOGRAPHY

Location: Western Europe, occupying five-sixths of the island of Ireland in the North Atlantic Ocean, west of Great Britain

Geographic coordinates: 53 00 N, 8 00 W
Map references: Europe
Area: *total:* 70,273 sq km
land: 68,883 sq km
water: 1,390 sq km
country comparison to the world: 120
Area—comparative: slightly larger than West Virginia
Land boundaries: *total:* 443 km
border countries (1): UK 443 km
Coastline: 1,448 km
Maritime claims: *territorial sea:* 12 nm
exclusive fishing zone: 200 nm
Climate: temperate maritime; modified by North Atlantic Current; mild winters, cool summers; consistently humid; overcast about half the time
Terrain: mostly flat to rolling interior plain surrounded by rugged hills and low mountains; sea cliffs on west coast
Elevation: *mean elevation:* 118 m
elevation extremes: lowest point: Atlantic Ocean 0 m
highest point: Carrauntoohil 1,041 m
Natural resources: natural gas, peat, copper, lead, zinc, silver, barite, gypsum, limestone, dolomite
Land use: *agricultural land:* 66.1%
arable land: 15.4%
permanent crops: 0%
permanent pasture: 50.7%
forest: 10.9%
other: 23% (2011 est.)
Irrigated land: 0 sq km (2012)
Total renewable water resources: 52 cu km (2011)
Freshwater withdrawal (domestic/industrial/agricultural): *total:* 0.79 cu km/yr (94%/6%/0%)
per capita: 226.9 cu m/yr (2007)
Natural hazards: NA
Environment—current issues: water pollution, especially of lakes, from agricultural runoff
Environment—international agreements: *party to:* Air Pollution, Air Pollution-Nitrogen Oxides, Air Pollution-Sulfur 94, Biodiversity, Climate Change, Climate Change-Kyoto Protocol, Desertification, Endangered Species, Environmental Modification, Hazardous Wastes, Law of the Sea, Marine Dumping, Ozone Layer Protection, Ship Pollution, Tropical Timber 83, Tropical Timber 94, Wetlands, Whaling
signed, but not ratified: Air Pollution-Persistent Organic Pollutants, M arine Life Conservation
Geography—note: strategic location on major air and sea routes between North America and northern Europe; over 40% of the population resides within 100 km of Dublin

PEOPLE AND SOCIETY

Nationality: *noun:* Irishman(men), Irishwoman (women), Irish (collective plural)
adjective: Irish
Ethnic groups: Irish 84.5%, other white 9.8%, Asian 1.9%, black 1.4%, mixed and other 0.9%, unspecified 1.6% (2011 est.)

Languages: English (official, the language generally used), Irish (Gaelic or Gaeilge) (official, spoken by approximately 38.7% of the population as a first or second language in 2011; mainly spoken in areas along the western coast)
Religions: Roman Catholic 84.7%, Church of Ireland 2.7%, other Christian 2.7%, Muslim 1.1%, other 1.7%, unspecified 1.5%, none 5.7% (2011 est.)
Population: 4,892,305 (July 2015 est.)
country comparison to the world: 123
Age structure: *0–14 years:* 21.5% (male 537,239/female 514,369)
15–24 years: 11.84% (male 294,771/female 284,710)
25–54 years: 43.82% (male 1,076,579/female 1,067,193)
55–64 years: 10.23% (male 250,926/female 249,453)
65 years and over: 12.61% (male 284,399/female 332,666) (2015 est.)
Dependency ratios: *total dependency ratio:* 53.7%
youth dependency ratio: 33.5%
elderly dependency ratio: 20.2%
potential support ratio: 5% (2015 est.)
Median age: *total:* 36.1 years
male: 35.8 years
female: 36.4 years (2015 est.)
country comparison to the world: 70
Population growth rate: 1.25% (2015 est.)
country comparison to the world: 94
Birth rate: 14.84 births/1,000 population (2015 est.)
country comparison to the world: 132
Death rate: 6.48 deaths/1,000 population (2015 est.)
country comparison to the world: 150
Net migration rate: 4.09 migrant(s)/1,000 population (2015 est.)
country comparison to the world: 31
Urbanization: *urban Population:* 63.2% of total population (2015)
rate of urbanization: 1.58% annual rate of change (2010–15 est.)
Major urban areas—Population: DUBLIN (capital) 1.169 million (2015)
Sex ratio: *at birth:* 1.06 male(s)/female
0–14 years: 1.04 male(s)/female
15–24 years: 1.04 male(s)/female
25–54 years: 1.01 male(s)/female
55–64 years: 1.01 male(s)/female
65 years and over: 0.86 male(s)/female
total Population: 1 male(s)/female (2015 est.)
Mother's mean age at first birth: 29.9 (2012 est.)
Maternal mortality rate: 8 deaths/100,000 live births (2015 est.)
country comparison to the world: 169
Infant mortality rate: *total:* 3.7 deaths/1,000 live births
male: 4.07 deaths/1,000 live births
female: 3.32 deaths/1,000 live births (2015 est.)
country comparison to the world: 198

Life expectancy at birth: *total population:* 80.68 years
male: 78.39 years
female: 83.11 years (2015 est.)
country comparison to the world: 31
Total fertility rate: 1.99 children born/woman (2015 est.)
country comparison to the world: 123
Contraceptive prevalence rate: 64.8%
note: percent of women aged 18–49 (2004/05)
Health expenditures: 8.9% of GDP (2013)
country comparison to the world: 57
Physicians density: 2.67 physicians/1,000 population (2013)
Hospital bed density: 2.9 beds/1,000 population (2011)
Drinking water source:
improved:
urban: 97.9% of population
rural: 97.8% of population
total: 97.9% of population
unimproved:
urban: 2.1% of population
rural: 2.2% of population
total: 2.1% of population (2015 est.)
Sanitation facility access:
improved:
urban: 89.1% of population
rural: 92.9% of population
total: 90.5% of population
unimproved:
urban: 10.9% of population
rural: 7.1% of population
total: 9.5% of population (2015 est.)
HIV/AIDS—adult prevalence rate: 0.28% (2014 est.)
country comparison to the world: 87
HIV/AIDS—people living with HIV/AIDS: 8,000 (2014 est.)
country comparison to the world: 102
HIV/AIDS—deaths: 100 (2014 est.)
country comparison to the world: 122
Obesity—adult prevalence rate: 27% (2014)
country comparison to the world: 57
Education expenditures: 5.8% of GDP (2012)
country comparison to the world: 31
School life expectancy (primary to tertiary education): *total:* 19 years
male: 19 years
female: 19 years (2012)
Unemployment, youth ages 15–24: *total:* 26.8%
male: 29.8%
female: 23.5% (2013 est.)
country comparison to the world: 38

GOVERNMENT

Country name: *conventional long form:* none
conventional short form: Ireland
local long form: none
local short form: Eire
etymology: the modern Irish name "Eire" evolved from the Gaelic "Eriu," the name of the matron goddess of Ireland (goddess of the land); the names "Ireland" in English and "Eire" in Irish are direct translations of each other
Government type: parliamentary republic

Capital: *name:* Dublin
Geographic coordinates: 53 19 N, 6 14 W
time difference: UTC 0 (5 hours ahead of Washington, DC, during Standard Time)
daylight saving time: +1hr, begins last Sunday in March; ends last Sunday in October
Administrative divisions: 28 counties and 3 cities*; Carlow, Cavan, Clare, Cork, Cork*, Donegal, Dublin*, Dun Laoghaire-Rathdown, Fingal, Galway, Galway*, Kerry, Kildare, Kilkenny, Laois, Leitrim, Limerick, Longford, Louth, Mayo, Meath, Monaghan, Offaly, Roscommon, Sligo, South Dublin, Tipperary, Waterford, Westmeath, Wexford, Wicklow
Independence: 6 December 1921 (from the UK by treaty)
National holiday: Saint Patrick's Day, 17 March
Constitution: previous 1922; latest drafted 14 June 1937, adopted by plebiscite 1 July 1937, effective 29 December 1937; amended many times, last in 2015 (2016)
Legal system: common law system based on the English model but substantially modified by customary law; judicial review of legislative acts in Supreme Court
International law organization participation: accepts compulsory ICJ jurisdiction with reservations; accepts ICCt jurisdiction
Citizenship: *citizenship by birth:* yes
citizenship by descent: yes
dual citizenship recognized: yes
residency requirement for naturalization: 4 of the previous 8 years
Suffrage: 18 years of age; universal
Executive branch: *chief of state:* President Michael D. HIGGINS (since 11 November 2011)
head of government: Taoiseach (Prime Minister) Enda KENNY (since 9 March 2011)
cabinet: Cabinet nominated by the prime minister, appointed by the president, approved by the lower house of Parliament
elections/appointments: president directly elected by majority popular vote for a 7-year term (eligible for a second term); election last held on 29 October 2011 (next to be held in October 2018); taoiseach (prime minister) nominated by the House of Representatives (Dail Eireann), appointed by the president
election results: Michael D. HIGGINS elected president; percent of vote—Michael D. HIGGINS (Labor Party) 39.6%, Sean GALLAGHER (independent) 28.5%, Martin MCGUINNESS (Sinn Fein) 13.7%, Gay MITCHELL (Fine Gael) 6.4%, David NORRIS (independent) 6.2%, other 5.6%
Legislative branch: *description:* bicameral Parliament or Oireachtas consists of the Senate or Seanad Eireann (60 seats; 43 members indirectly elected by panels of various vocational interests, 11 appointed by the prime minister, and 6 elected by graduates of the University of Dublin and the National University of Ireland; members serve 5-year terms) and the Parliament or Dail Eireann (166 seats; members directly elected in multi-seat constituencies by proportional representation vote; members serve 5-year terms)

elections: Senate—last held in 27 April 2011 (next to be held probably in 2016); House of Representatives—last held on 26 February 2016 (next to be held probably in 2021)
election results: Senate—percent of vote by party—NA; seats by party—Fine Gael 19, Fianna Fail 14, Labor Party 12, Sinn Fein 3, independent 12; House of Representatives—percent of vote by party—Fine Gael 25.5%, Fianna Fail 24.4%, Sinn Fein 13.8%, Labor Party 6.6%, AAA-PBD 4.0%, Social Democrats 3.0%, Green Party 2.7%, Renua Irland 2.2% independents 17.8%; seats by party—Fine Gael 50, Fianna Fail 44, Sinn Fein 23, Labor Party 7, AAA-PBP 6, Social Democrats 3, Green Party 2, independents 23
Judicial branch: *highest court(s):* Supreme Court of Ireland (consists of the chief justice, 9 judges, 2 ex-officio members—the presidents of the High Court and Court of Appeal—and organized in 3-, 5-, or 7-judge panels, depending on the importance or complexity of an issue of law)
judge selection and term of office: judges nominated by the prime minister and Cabinet and appointed by the president; chief justice serves in the position for 7 years; judges can serve until age 70
subordinate courts: High Court, Court of Appeal; circuit and district courts; criminal courts
Political parties and leaders: Fianna Fail [Micheal MARTIN]
Fine Gael [Enda KENNY]
Green Party [Eamon RYAN]
Labor (Labour) Party [Joan BURTON]
Renua Ireland [Lucinda CREIGHTON]
Sinn Fein [Gerry ADAMS]
Socialist Party [collective leadership]
The Workers' Party [Michael DONNELLY]
Political pressure groups and leaders: Continuity IRA (terrorist group)
Families Acting for Innocent Relatives or FAIR [Brian MCCONNELL] (seek compensation for victims of violence)
Iona Institute [David QUINN] (a conservative Catholic think tank)
Irish Anti-War Movement [Richard BOYDBARRETT] (campaigns against wars around the world) Keep Ireland Open (environmental group)
Oglaigh na hEireann (terrorist group)
Midland Railway Action Group or MRAG [Willie ALLEN] (transportation promoters)
New Irish Republican Army (terrorist group combining elements of the former Real IRA and Republican Action Against Drugs)
Peace and Neutrality Alliance [Roger COLE] (campaigns to protect Irish neutrality)
Rail USers Ireland (formerly the Platform 11—transportation promoters)
32 Country Sovereignty Movement or 32 CSM (supports unifying Northern Ireland with the rest of the island under Irish government sovereignty)
International organization participation: ADB (nonregional member), Australia Group, BIS, CD, CE, EAPC, EBRD, ECB, EIB, EMU, ESA, EU, FAO, FATF, IAEA, IBRD, ICAO, ICC (national committees), ICCt, ICRM, IDA, IEA, IFAD, IFC, IFRCS, IGAD (partners), IHO, ILO, IMF, IMO,

Interpol, IOC, IOM, IPU, ISO, ITSO, ITU, ITUC (NGOs), MIGA, MINURSO, MONUSCO, NEA, NSG, OAS (observer), OECD, OPCW, OSCE, Paris Club, PCA, PFP, UN, UNCTAD, UNDOF, UNESCO, UNHCR, UNIDO, UNIFIL, UNOCI, UNRWA, UNTSO, UPU, WCO, WHO, WIPO, WMO, WTO, ZC

Diplomatic representation in the US: *chief of mission:* Ambassador Anne Colette ANDERSON (since 28 August 2013)
chancery: 2234 Massachusetts Avenue NW, Washington, DC 20008
telephone: [1] (202) 462-3939
FAX: [1] (202) 232-5993
consulate(s) general: Atlanta, Austin (TX), Boston, Chicago, New York, San Francisco

Diplomatic representation from the US: *chief of mission:* Ambassador Kevin F. O'MALLEY (since 8 October 2014)
embassy: 42 Elgin Road, Ballsbridge, Dublin 4
mailing address: use embassy street address
telephone: [353] (1) 668-8777
FAX: [353] (1) 668-9946

Flag description: three equal vertical bands of green (hoist side), white, and orange; officially the flag colors have no meaning, but a common interpretation is that the green represents the Irish nationalist (Gaelic) tradition of Ireland; orange represents the Orange tradition (minority supporters of William of Orange); white symbolizes peace (or a lasting truce) between the green and the orange
note: similar to the flag of Cote d'Ivoire, which is shorter and has the colors reversed—orange (hoist side), white, and green; also similar to the flag of Italy, which is shorter and has colors of green (hoist side), white, and red

National symbol(s): harp, shamrock (trefoil); national colors: blue, green
National anthem: *name:* "Amhran na bhFiann" (The Soldier's Song)
lyrics/music: Peadar KEARNEY [English], Liam ORINN [Irish]/Patrick HEENEY and Peadar KEARNEY
note: adopted 1926; instead of "Amhran na bhFiann," the song "Ireland's Call" is often used at athletic events where citizens of Ireland and Northern Ireland compete as a unified team

ECONOMY

Economy—overview: Ireland is a small, modern, trade-dependent economy. Ireland was among the initial group of 12 EU Nations that began circulating the euro on 1 January 2002.
GDP growth averaged 6% in 1995–2007, but economic activity dropped sharply during the world financial crisis and the subsequent collapse of its domestic property market and construction industry. Faced with sharply reduced reven ues and a burgeoning budget deficit from efforts to stabilize its fragile banking sector, the Irish Government introduced the first in a series of draconian budgets in 2009. These measures were not sufficient to stabilize Ireland's public finances. In 2010, the budget deficit reached 32.4% of GDP—the world's largest deficit, as a percentage of GDP. In late

2010, the former COWEN government agreed to a $92 billion loan package from the EU and IMF to help Dublin recapitalize Ireland's banking sector and avoid defaulting on its sovereign debt. In March 2011, the KENNY government intensified austerity measures to meet the deficit targets under Ireland's EU-IMF bailout program. In late 2013, Ireland formally exited its EU-IMF bailout program, benefiting from its strict adherence to deficit-reduction targets and success in refinancing a large amount of banking-related debt. in 2014, the economy rapidly picked up and GDP grew by 5.2%. The recovering economy assisted lowering the deficit to 2.5% of GDP. In late 2014, the government introduced a fiscally neutral budget, marking the end of the austerity program. Continued growth of tax receipts has allowed the government to lower some taxes and increase public spending while keeping to its deficit-reduction targets. In 2015, GDP growth reached 7.8%, the highest growth in the EU for the second consecutive year.
In the wake of the collapse of the construction sector and the downturn in consumer spending and business investment, the export sector, dominated by foreign multinationals, has become an even more important component of Ireland's economy. Ireland's low corporation tax of 12.5% and a talented pool of high-tech laborers have been key factors in encouraging business investment. Loose tax residency requirements made Ireland a common destination for international firms seeking to avoid taxation. Amid growing international pressure, the government announced it would phase in more stringent tax laws, effectively closing a loophole.

GDP (purchasing power parity): $257.4 billion (2015 est.)
$238.8 billion (2014 est.)
$227 billion (2013 est.)
note: data are in 2015 US dollars
country comparison to the world: 61
GDP (official exchange rate): $238 billion (2015 est.)
GDP—real growth rate: 7.8% (2015 est.)
5.2% (2014 est.)
1.4% (2013 est.)
country comparison to the world: 9
GDP—per capita (PPP): $55,500 (2015 est.)
$51,800 (2014 est.)
$49,400 (2013 est.)
note: data are in 2015 US dollars
country comparison to the world: 20
Gross national saving: 27.7% of GDP (2015 est.)
23.9% of GDP (2014 est.)
21.2% of GDP (2013 est.)
country comparison to the world: 33
GDP—composition, by end use:
household consumption: 47%
government consumption: 13.2%
investment in fixed capital: 20.3%
investment in inventories: 0.9%
exports of goods and services: 113.5%
imports of goods and services: -94.9% (2015 est.)
GDP—composition, by sector of origin:
agriculture: 1.5%

industry: 24.9%
services: 73.5% (2015 est.)
Agriculture—products: barley, potatoes, wheat; beef, dairy products
Industries: pharmaceuticals, chemicals, computer hardware and software, food products, beverages and brewing; medical devices
Industrial production growth rate: 3% (2015 est.)
country comparison to the world: 87
Labor force: 2.176 million (2015 est.)
country comparison to the world: 121
Labor force—by occupation: *agriculture:* 5%
industry: 19%
services: 76% (2011 est.)
Unemployment rate: 9.4% (2015 est.)
11.3% (2014 est.)
country comparison to the world: 109
Population below poverty line: 5.5% (2009 est.)
Household income or consumption by percentage share: *lowest:* 10%: 2.9%
highest: 10%: 27.2% (2000)
Distribution of family income—Gini index: 33.9 (2010)
35.9 (1987)
country comparison to the world: 100
Budget: *revenues:* $78.42 billion
expenditures: $84.07 billion (2015 est.)
Taxes and other revenues: 34.5% of GDP (2015 est.)
country comparison to the world: 62
Budget surplus (+) or deficit (−): -2.5% of GDP (2015 est.)
country comparison to the world: 90
Public debt: 101.2% of GDP (2015 est.)
107.6% of GDP (2014 est.)
note: data cover general government debt, and includes debt instruments issued (or owned) by government entities other than the treasury; the data include treasury debt held by foreign entities; the data include debt issued by subnational entities, as well as intra-governmental debt; intra-governmental debt consists of treasury borrowings from surpluses in the social funds, such as for retirement, medical care, and unemployment; debt instruments for the social funds are not sold at public auctions
country comparison to the world: 15
Fiscal year: calendar year
Inflation rate (consumer prices): 0% (2015 est.)
0.3% (2014 est.)
country comparison to the world: 40
Central bank discount rate: 0.05% (31 December 2013)
0.3% (31 December 2010)
note: this is the European Central Bank's rate on the marginal lending facility, which offers overnight credit to banks in the euro area
country comparison to the world: 137
Commercial bank prime lending rate: 3.4% (31 December 2015 est.)
3.41% (31 December 2014 est.)
country comparison to the world: 166
Stock of narrow money: $140.9 billion (31 December 2015 est.)
$143.5 billion (31 December 2014 est.)
note: see entry for the European Union for money supply for the entire euro area; the European

Central Bank (ECB) controls monetary policy for the 18 members of the Economic and Monetary Union (EMU); individual members of the EMU do not control the quantity of money circulating within their own borders
country comparison to the world: 27
Stock of broad money: $255.3 billion (31 December 2014 est.)
$267.4 billion (31 December 2013 est.)
country comparison to the world: 39
Stock of domestic credit: $340.4 billion (31 December 2015 est.)
$380.3 billion (31 December 2014 est.)
country comparison to the world: 35
Market value of publicly traded shares:
$109 billion (31 December 2012 est.)
$108.1 billion (31 December 2011)
$60.45 billion (31 December 2010 est.)
country comparison to the world: 42
Current account balance: $10.6 billion (2015 est.)
$9.08 billion (2014 est.)
country comparison to the world: 22
Exports: $140.4 billion (2015 est.)
$144.8 billion (2014 est.)
country comparison to the world: 33
Exports—commodities: machinery and equipment, computers, chemicals, medical devices, pharmaceuticals; foodstuffs, animal products
Exports—partners: US 23.7%, UK 13.8%, Belgium 13.2%, Germany 6.6%, Switzerland 5.5%, Netherlands 4.4%, France 4.4% (2015)
Imports: $81.39 billion (2015 est.)
$84.38 billion (2014 est.)
country comparison to the world: 37
Imports—commodities: data processing equipment, other machinery and equipment, chemicals, petroleum and petroleum products, textiles, clothing
Imports—partners: UK 32.5%, US 14%, France 10.2%, Germany 9.3%, Netherlands 4.9%, China 4.1% (2015)
Reserves of foreign exchange and gold: $1.748 billion (31 December 2014 est.)
$1.635 billion (31 December 2013 est.)
country comparison to the world: 124
Debt—external: $1.96 trillion (31 December 2014 est.)
$2.078 trillion (31 December 2013 est.)
country comparison to the world: 11
Stock of direct foreign investment—at home:
$878.1 billion (31 December 2015 est.)
$831.9 billion (31 December 2014 est.)
country comparison to the world: 12
Stock of direct foreign investment—abroad:
$961.3 billion (31 December 2015 est.)
$939.6 billion (31 December 2014 est.)
country comparison to the world: 13
Exchange rates: euros (EUR) per US dollar—
0.885 (2015 est.)
0.7525 (2014 est.)
0.7634 (2013 est.)
0.78 (2012 est.)
0.7185 (2011 est.)

ENERGY

Electricity—production: 25.85 billion kWh (2012 est.)

country comparison to the world: 68
Electricity—consumption: 24.24 billion kWh (2012 est.)
country comparison to the world: 68
Electricity—exports: 388 million kWh (2013 est.)
country comparison to the world: 73
Electricity—imports: 2.508 billion kWh (2013 est.)
country comparison to the world: 55
Electricity—installed generating capacity: 8.759 million kW (2012 est.)
country comparison to the world: 61
Electricity—from fossil fuels: 71% of total installed capacity (2012 est.)
country comparison to the world: 105
Electricity—from nuclear fuels: 0% of total installed capacity (2012 est.)
country comparison to the world: 84
Electricity—from hydroelectric plants: 2.7% of total installed capacity (2012 est.)
country comparison to the world: 133
Electricity—from other renewable sources: 23% of total installed capacity (2012 est.)
country comparison to the world: 12
Crude oil—production: 0 bbl/day (2014 est.)
country comparison to the world: 128
Crude oil—exports: 4,866 bbl/day (2013 est.)
country comparison to the world: 73
Crude oil—imports: 66,490 bbl/day (2013 est.)
country comparison to the world: 52
Crude oil—proved reserves: 0 bbl (1 January 2015 est.)
country comparison to the world: 127
Refined petroleum products—production: 57,790 bbl/day (2013 est.)
country comparison to the world: 78
Refined petroleum products—consumption: 142,500 bbl/day (2014 est.)
country comparison to the world: 67
Refined petroleum products—exports: 23,020 bbl/day (2013 est.)
country comparison to the world: 70
Refined petroleum products—imports: 105,700 bbl/day (2013 est.)
country comparison to the world: 50
Natural gas—production: 152 million cu m (2014 est.)
country comparison to the world: 80
Natural gas—consumption: 4.408 billion cu m (2014 est.)
country comparison to the world: 62
Natural gas—exports: 0 cu m (2014 est.)
country comparison to the world: 92
Natural gas—imports: 4.246 billion cu m (2014 est.)
country comparison to the world: 33
Natural gas—proved reserves: 9.911 billion cu m (1 January 2014 est.)
country comparison to the world: 81
Carbon dioxide emissions from consumption of energy: 35.49 million Mt (2012 est.)
country comparison to the world: 71

COMMUNICATIONS

Telephones—fixed lines: *total subscriptions:* 2.02 million
subscriptions per 100 inhabitants: 42 (2014 est.)

country comparison to the world: 57
Telephones—mobile cellular: *total:* 4.9 million
subscriptions per 100 inhabitants: 101 (2014 est.)
country comparison to the world: 119
Telephone system: *general assessment:* modern digital system using cable and microwave radio relay
domestic: system privatized but dominated by former state monopoly operator; increasing levels of broadband access particularly in urban areas
international: country code—353; landing point for the Hibernia-Atlantic submarine cable with links to the US, Canada, and UK; satellite earth stations—81 (2014)
Broadcast media: publicly owned broadcaster Radio Telefis Eireann (RTE) operates 2 TV stations; commercial TV stations are available; about 75% of households utilize multi-channel satellite and TV services that provide access to a wide range of stations; RTE operates 4 national radio stations and has launched digital audio broadcasts on several stations; a number of commercial broadcast stations operate at the national, regional, and local levels (2014)
Radio broadcast stations: AM 9, FM 106, shortwave 0 (1998)
Television broadcast stations: 4 (many repeaters) (2008)
Internet country code: .ie
Internet hosts: 1.387 million (2012)
country comparison to the world: 40
Internet users: *total:* 3.9 million
percent of Population: 81.6% (2014 est.)
country comparison to the world: 79

TRANSPORTATION

Airports: 40 (2013)
country comparison to the world: 105
Airports—with paved runways: *total:* 16
over 3,047 m: 1
2,438 to 3,047 m: 1
1,524 to 2,437 m: 4
914 to 1,523 m: 5
under 914 m: 5 (2013)
Airports—with unpaved runways: *total:* 24
2,438 to 3,047 m: 1
914 to 1,523 m: 2
under 914 m: 21 (2013)
Pipelines: gas 2,147 km (2013)
Railways: *total:* 3,237 km
broad gauge: 1,872 km 1.600-m gauge (49 km electrified)
narrow gauge: 1,365 km 0.914-m gauge (operated by the Irish Peat Board to transport peat to power stations and briquetting plants) (2014)
country comparison to the world: 55
Roadways: *total:* 96,036 km
paved: 96,036 km (includes 1,224 km of expressways) (2014)
country comparison to the world: 49
Waterways: 956 km (pleasure craft only) (2010)
country comparison to the world: 67
Merchant marine: *total:* 31
by type: cargo 28, chemical tanker 2, container 1
foreign-owned: 5 (France 2, Spain 1, US 2)

421

registered in other countries: 33 (Bahamas 3, Bermuda 1, Cambodia 1, Cyprus 3, Isle of Man 1, Kazakhstan 1, Malta 4, Marshall Islands 6, Netherlands 8, Panama 1, Russia 1, Slovakia 1, Sweden 1, UK 1) (2010)

country comparison to the world: 84

Ports and terminals: major seaport(s): Dublin, Shannon Foynes

river port(s): Cork (Lee), Waterford (Suir)

container port(s) (TEUs): Dublin (1,931,001)

MILITARY AND SECURITY

Military branches: Irish Defence Forces (Oglaighnah-Eireannn), Permanent Defence Forces (PDF): Army, Naval Service, Air Corps; Reserve Defence Forces (RDF): Army, Naval Service Reserves (2014)

Military service age and obligation: 18–25 years of age for male and female voluntary military service recruits to the Permanent Defence Forces (PDF; 18–27 years of age for the Naval Service); 18–28 for cadetship (officer) applicants; 18–35 years of age for the Reserve Defence Forces (RDF); maximum obligation 12 years (PDF officers), 5 years (PDF enlisted), 3 years RDF (4 years for Naval Service Reserves); EU citizenship, refugee status, or 5-year residence in Ireland required (2014)

Military expenditures: 0.49% of GDP (2014)
0.51% of GDP (2013)
0.55% of GDP (2012)
0.59% of GDP (2011)
0.55% of GDP (2010)
country comparison to the world: 126

TRANSNATIONAL ISSUES

Disputes—international: Ireland, Iceland, and the UK dispute Denmark's claim that the Faroe Islands' continental shelf extends beyond 200 nm

Refugees and internally displaced persons: stateless persons: 99 (2015)

Illicit drugs: transshipment point for and consumer of hashish from North Africa to the UK and Netherlands and of European-produced synthetic drugs; increasing consumption of South American cocaine; minor transshipment point for heroin and cocaine destined for Western Europe; despite recent legislation, narcotics-related money laundering—using bureaux de change, trusts, and shell companies involving the offshore financial community—remains a concern

ISLE OF MAN

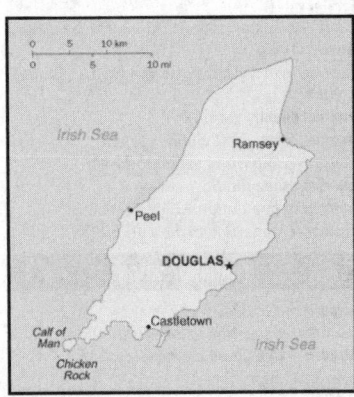

INTRODUCTION

Background: Part of the Norwegian Kingdom of the Hebrides until the 13th century when it was ceded to Scotland, the isle came under the British crown in 1765. Current concerns include reviving the almost extinct Manx Gaelic language. Isle of Man is a British crown dependency but is not part of the UK or of the European Union. However, the UK Government remains constitutionally responsible for its defense and international representation.

GEOGRAPHY

Location: Western Europe, island in the Irish Sea, between Great Britain and Ireland

Geographic coordinates: 54 15 N, 4 30 W

Map references: Europe

Area: total: 572 sq km
land: 572 sq km
water: 0 sq km
country comparison to the world: 194

Area—comparative: slightly more than three times the size of Washington, DC

Land boundaries: 0 km

Coastline: 160 km

Maritime claims: territorial sea: 12 nm
exclusive fishing zone: 12 nm

Climate: temperate; cool summers and mild winters; overcast about a third of the time

Terrain: hills in north and south bisected by central valley

Elevation: mean elevation: NA

elevation extremes: lowest point: Irish Sea 0 m
highest point: Snaefell 621 m

Natural resources: none

Land use: agricultural land: 74.7%
arable land: 43.8%
permanent crops: 0%
permanent pasture: 30.9%
forest: 6.1%
other: 19.2% (2011 est.)

Irrigated land: 0 sq km (2012)

Natural hazards: NA

Environment—current issues: waste disposal (both household and industrial); transboundary air pollution

Geography—note: one small islet, the Calf of Man, lies to the southwest and is a bird sanctuary

PEOPLE AND SOCIETY

Nationality: noun: Manxman(men), Manxwoman (women)
adjective: Manx

Ethnic groups: white 96.5%, Asian/Asian British 1.9%, other 1.5% (2011 est.)

Languages: English, Manx Gaelic (about 2% of the population has some knowledge)

Religions: Protestant (Anglican, Methodist, Baptist, Presbyterian, Society of Friends), Roman Catholic

Population: 87,545 (July 2015 est.)
country comparison to the world: 200

Age structure: 0–14 years: 16.3% (male 7,488/ female 6,778)
15–24 years: 11.81% (male 5,380/female 4,956)

25–54 years: 39.27% (male 17,153/female 17,223)
55–64 years: 12.83% (male 5,668/female 5,560)
65 years and over: 19.81% (male 8,077/female 9,262) (2015 est.)

Median age: total: 43.7 years
male: 42.9 years
female: 44.4 years (2015 est.)
country comparison to the world: 10

Population growth rate: 0.76% (2015 est.)
country comparison to the world: 145

Birth rate: 11.1 births/1,000 population (2015 est.)
country comparison to the world: 177

Death rate: 10.06 deaths/1,000 population (2015 est.)
country comparison to the world: 44

Net migration rate: 6.56 migrant(s)/1,000 population (2015 est.)
country comparison to the world: 19

Urbanization: urban Population: 52.1% of total population (2014)
rate of urbanization: 0.8% annual rate of change (2010–15 est.)

Major urban areas—population: DOUGLAS (capital) 29,000 (2014)

Sex ratio: at birth: 1.08 male(s)/female
0–14 years: 1.11 male(s)/female
15–24 years: 1.09 male(s)/female
25–54 years: 1 male(s)/female
55–64 years: 1.02 male(s)/female
65 years and over: 0.87 male(s)/female
total Population: 1 male(s)/female (2015 est.)

Infant mortality rate: total: 4.11 deaths/1,000 live births
male: 4.08 deaths/1,000 live births
female: 4.15 deaths/1,000 live births (2015 est.)
country comparison to the world: 190

Life expectancy at birth: total population: 81.09 years
male: 79.41 years
female: 82.9 years (2015 est.)
country comparison to the world: 27

Total fertility rate: 1.94 children born/woman (2015 est.)
country comparison to the world: 131
HIV/AIDS—adult prevalence rate: NA
HIV/AIDS—people living with HIV/AIDS: NA
HIV/AIDS—deaths: NA
Unemployment, youth ages 15–24: *total:* 10.1%
male: 11.8%
fem al e: 8.2% (2011 est.)
country comparison to the world: 118

GOVERNMENT

Country name: *conventional long form:* none
conventional short form: Isle of Man
abbreviation: I.O.M.
etymology: the name "man" may be derived from the Celtic word for "mountain"
Dependency status: British crown dependency
Government type: parliamentary democracy (Tynwald); a Crown dependency of the UK
Capital: *name:* Douglas

Geographic coordinates: 54 09 N, 4 29 W
time difference: UTC 0 (5 hours ahead of Washington, DC, during Standard Time)
daylight saving time: +1hr, begins last Sunday in March; ends last Sunday in October
Administrative divisions: none; there are no first-order administrative divisions as defined by the US Government, but there are 24 local authorities each with its own elections
Independence: none (British crown dependency)
National holiday: Tynwald Day, 5 July (1417, first recorded Day)
Constitution: development of the Isle of Man constitution dates to at least the 14th century; the constitution has been expanded and amended many times, last in 2015 (2016)
Legal system: the laws of the UK, where applicable, apply and include Manx statutes
Citizenship: see United Kingdom
Suffrage: 16 years of age; universal
Executive branch: *chief of state:* Lord of Mann Queen ELIZABETH II (since 6 February 1952); represented by Lieutenant Governor Adam WOOD (since 7 April 2011)

head of government: Chief Minister Allan BELL (since 11 October 2011)
cabinet: Council of Ministers appointed by the lieutenant governor
elections/appointments: the monarchy is hereditary; lieutenant governor appointed by the monarch; chief minister indirectly elected by the Tynwald for a 5-year term (eligible for second term); election last held on 11 October 2011 (next to be held in December 2016)
election results: Allan BELL (independent) elected chief minister; Tynwald vote count—27 of 30
Legislative branch: *description:* bicameral Tynwald or the High Court of Tynwald consists of the Legislative Council (11 seats; includes the President of Tynwald, 2 ex-officio members—the Lord Bishop of Sodor and Man and the attorney general—and 8 members indirectly elected by the House of Keys with renewal of 4 members every 2

years; elected members serve 4-year terms) and the House of Keys (24 seats; members directly elected by simple majority vote to serve 5-year terms)
elections: House of Keys—last held on 29 September 2011 (next to be held on 22 September 2016)
election results: House of Keys—percent of vote by party—NA; seats by party—Liberal Vannin Party 3, independent 21
Judicial branch: *highest resident court(s):* Isle of Man High Court of Justice (consists of 3 permanent judges called "deemsters" and 1 judge of appeal; organized into the Staff of Government Division or Court of Appeal and the Civil Division); the Court of General Gaol Delivery is not formally part of the High Court but is administered as though part of the High Court and deals with serious criminal cases; note—appeals beyond the Court of Appeal are referred to the Judicial Committee of the Privy Council (in London)
judge selection and term of office: judges appointed by the Lord Chancellor of England on the nomination of the lieutenant governor; judges appointed during period of good behavior
subordinate courts: Summary Court; Magistrates Court; Licensing Court; Financial Provision Court; Coroner of Inquests; Commission of Rogatoire; other specialized courts and tribunals
Political parties and leaders: Liberal Vannin Party [Kate BEECROFT]
Manx Labor Party
Mec Vannin [Bernard MOFFATT]; (sometimes referred to as the Manx Nationalist Party); advocates a sovereign state and environment policies)
note: most members sit as independents
Political pressure groups and leaders: Alliance for Progressive Government or APG (a government watchdog)
International organization participation: UPU
Diplomatic representation in the US: none (British crown dependency)
Diplomatic representation from the US: none (British crown dependency)
Flag description: red with the Three Legs of Man emblem (triskelion), in the center; the three legs are joined at the thigh and bent at the knee; in order to have the toes pointing clockwise on both sides of the flag, a two-sided emblem is used; the flag is based on the coat-of-arms of the last recognized Norse King of Mann, Magnus III (r.1252–65); the triskelion has its roots in an early Celtic sun symbol
National symbol(s): triskelion (a motif of three legs); national colors: red, white
National anthem: *name:* "Arrane Ashoonagh dy Vannin" (O Land of Our Birth)
lyrics/music: William Henry GILL [English], John J. KNEEN [Manx]/traditional
note: adopted 2003, in use since 1907; serves as a local anthem; as a British crown dependency, "God Save the Queen" is official (see United Kingdom) and is played when the sovereign, members of the royal family, or the lieutenant governor are present

ECONOMY

Economy—overview: Financial services, manufacturing, and tourism are key sectors of the economy.

The government offers low taxes and other incentives to high-technology companies and financial institutions to locate on the island; this has paid off in expanding employment opportunities in high-income industries. As a result, agriculture and fishing, once the mainstays of the economy, have declined in their contributions to GDP. The Isle of Man also attracts online gambling sites and the film industry. Online gambling sites provided about 10% of the islands income in 2014. The Isle of Man enjoys free access to EU markets and trade is mostly with the UK. In October 2014, the Isle of Man signed an OECD agreement to automatically exchange some financial account information to limit tax avoidance and evasion.
GDP (purchasing power parity): $6.298 billion (FY12/13 est.)
$5.85 billion (FY11/12 est.)
$5.621 billion (FY10/11 est.)
note: data are in 2013 US dollars
country comparison to the world: 169
GDP (official exchange rate): $4.076 billion (2007 est.)
GDP—real growth rate: 2.2% (2012)
3.4% (2011)
2.1% (2010)
country comparison to the world: 132
GDP—per capita (PPP): $83,100 (2007 est.)
$35,000 (2005 est.)
country comparison to the world: 7
GDP—composition, by sector of origin:
agriculture: 1%
industry: 13%
services: 86% (FY12/13 est.)
Agriculture—products: cereals, vegetables; cattle, sheep, pigs, poultry
Industries: financial services, light manufacturing, tourism
Labor force: 41,790 (2006)
country comparison to the world: 195
Labor force—by occupation:
agriculture, forestry, and fishing: 2%
manufacturing: 5%
construction: 8%
gas, electricity, and water: 1%
transport and communication: 9%
wholesale and retail distribution: 11%
professional and scientific services: 20%
public administration: 7%
banking and finance: 23%
tourism: 1%
entertainment and catering: 5%
miscellaneous services: 8% (2006)
Unemployment rate: 2% (April 2011 est.) 1.8% (October 2010 est.)
country comparison to the world: 14
Population below poverty line: NA%
Household income or consumption by percentage share: *lowest:* 10%: NA%
highest: 10%: NA%
Budget: *revenues:* $965 million
expenditures: $943 million (FY05/06 est.)
Taxes and other revenues: 23.7% of GDP (FY05/06 est.)
country comparison to the world: 133

423

Budget surplus (+) or deficit (–): 0.5% of GDP (FY05/06 est.)
country comparison to the world: 22
Fiscal year: 1 April—31 March
Inflation rate (consumer prices): 5% (2010 est.) 3.1% (2006)
country comparison to the world: 176
Market value of publicly traded shares: $NA
Exports: $NA
Exports—commodities: tweeds, herring, processed shellfish, beef, lamb
Imports: $NA
Imports—commodities: timber, fertilizers, fish
Debt—external: $NA
Exchange rates: Manx pounds (IMP) per US dollar—
0.6528 (2015)
0.607 (2014)
0.6472 (2013 est.)
0.6241 (2012 est.)
0.624 (2011 est.)

COMMUNICATIONS

Telephone system: *domestic:* landline, telefax, mobile cellular telephone system

international: country code—44; fiber-optic cable, microwave radio relay, satellite earth station, submarine cable
Broadcast media: national public radio broadcasts over 3 FM stations and 1 AM station; 2 commercial broadcasters operating with 1 having multiple FM stations; receives radio and TV services via relays from British TV and radio broadcasters (2008)
Radio broadcast stations: AM 1, FM 1, shortwave 0 (1998)
Television broadcast stations: 0 (receives broadcasts from the UK and satellite) (1999)
Internet country code: .im
Internet hosts: 895 (2012)
country comparison to the world: 174

TRANSPORTATION

Airports: 1 (2013)
country comparison to the world: 221
Airports—with paved runways: *total:* 1
1,524 to 2,437 m: 1 (2013)
Railways: *total:* 63 km
narrow gauge: 6 km 1.076-m gauge (6 km electrified); 57 km 0.914-m gauge (29 km electrified)

note: primarily summer tourist attractions (2008)
country comparison to the world: 130
Roadways: *total:* 500 km (2008)
country comparison to the world: 196
Merchant marine: *total:* 321
by type: bulk carrier 59, cargo 55, chemical tanker 52, container 7, liquefied gas 43, passenger/cargo 2, petroleum tanker 93, roll on/roll off 5, vehicle carrier 5
foreign-owned: 223 (Bermuda 7, Chile 9, Denmark 30, Germany 56, Greece 62, Ireland 1, Japan 19, Malaysia 6, Norway 30, South Africa 2, US 1) (2010)
country comparison to the world: 30
Ports and terminals: *major seaport(s):* Douglas, Ramsey

MILITARY AND SECURITY

Military—note: defense is the responsibility of the UK

TRANSNATIONAL ISSUES

Disputes—international: none

ISRAEL

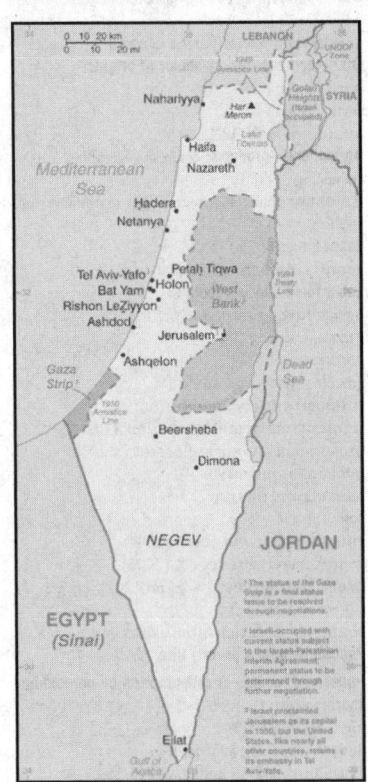

INTRODUCTION

Background: Following World War II, Britain withdrew from its mandate of Palestine, and the UN proposed partitioning the area into Arab and Jewish states, an arrangement rejected by the Arabs. Nonetheless, an Israeli state was declared in 1948, and Israel subsequently defeated the Arab armies in a series of wars that did not end deep tensions between the two sides. (The territories Israel has occupied since the 1967 war are not included in the Israel country profile, unless otherwise noted.) On 25 April 1982, Israel withdrew from the Sinai Peninsula pursuant to the 1979 Israel-Egypt Peace Treaty. In keeping with the framework established at the Madrid Conference in October 1991, Israel conducted bilateral negotiations with Palestinian representatives and Syria to achieve a permanent settlement with each. Israel and Palestinian officials on 13 September 1993 signed a Declaration of Principles (also known as the "Oslo Accords"), enshrining the idea of a two-state solution to their conflict and guiding an interim period of Palestinian self-rule. the parties achieved six additional significant interim agreements between 1994 and 1999 aimed at creating the conditions for a two-state solution, but most were never fully realized. Outstanding territorial and other disputes with Jordan were resolved in the 26 October 1994 Israel-Jordan Peace Treaty.
Progress toward a final status agreement with the Palestinians was undermined by Israeli-Palestinian violence between 2001 and February 2005. Israel in 2005 unilaterally disengaged from the Gaza Strip, evacuating settlers and its military while retaining control over most points of entry in to the Gaza Strip. The election of HAMAS to head the Palestinian Legislative Council in 2006 temporarily

froze relations between Israel and the Palestinian Authority (PA). Israel engaged in a 34-day conflict with Hizballah in Leban on from July-August 2006 and a 23-day conflict with HAMAS in the Gaza Strip from December 2008-January 2009. In November 2012, Israel engaged in a seven-day conflict with HAMAS in the Gaza Strip. Direct talks with the Palestinians most recently launched in July 2013 but were suspended in April 2014. The talks represented the fourth concerted effort to resolve final status issues between the sides since they were first discussed at Camp David in 2000. Three months later HAMAS and other militant groups launched rockets into Israel, which led to a 51-day conflict between Israel and militants in Gaza.

GEOGRAPHY

Location: Middle East, bordering the Mediterranean Sea, between Egypt and Lebanon
Geographic coordinates: 31 30 N, 34 45 E
Map referen ces: Middle East
Area: *total:* 20,770 sq km
land: 20,330 sq km
water: 440 sq km
country comparison to the world: 154
Area—comparative: slightly larger than New Jersey
Land boundaries: *total:* 1,068 km
border countries (6): Egypt 208 km, Gaza Strip 59 km, Jordan 307 km, Lebanon 81 km, Syria 83 km, West Bank 330 km
Coastline: 273 km
Maritime claims: *territorial sea:* 12 nm
continen tal shelf: to depth of exploitation
Climate: temperate; hot and dry in southern and eastern desert areas

Terrain: Negev desert in the south; low coastal plain; central mountains; Jordan Rift Valley

Elevation: *mean elevation:* 508 m

elevation extremes: *lowest point:* Dead Sea -408 m

highest point: Har Meron 1,208 m

Natural resources: timber, potash, copper ore, natural gas, phosphate rock, magnesium bromide, clays, sand

Land use: *agricultural land:* 23.8%

arable land: 13.7%

permanent crops: 3.8%

permanent pasture: 6.3%

forest: 7.1%

other: 69.1% (2011 est.)

Irrigated land: 2,250 sq km (2012)

Total renewable water resources: 1.78 cu km (2011)

Freshwater withdrawal (domestic/industrial/agricultural): *total:* 1.95 cu km/yr (39%/6%/55%)

per capita: 282.4 cu m/yr (2009)

Natural hazards: sandstorms may occur during spring and summer; droughts; periodic earthquakes

Environment—current issues: limited arable land: and natural freshwater resources pose serious constraints; desertification; air pollution from industrial and vehicle emissions; groundwater pollution from industrial and domestic waste, chemical fertilizers, and pesticides

Environment—international agreements: *party to:* Biodiversity, Climate Change, Climate Change-Kyoto Protocol, Desertification, Endangered Species, Hazardous Wastes, Ozone Layer Protection, Ship Pollution, Wetlands, Whaling

signed, but not ratified: Marine Life Conservation

Geography—note: Lake Tiberias (Sea of Galilee) is an important freshwater source; the Dead Sea is the second saltiest body of water in the world (after Lake Assal in Djibouti); in 2014, there were 423 settlements in the Israeli-occupied territories—42 settlements in the Golan Heights, 381 sites in the occupied Palestinian territories to include 212 settlements and 134 outposts in the West Bank, and 35 settlements in East Jerusalem; there are no Israeli settlements in the Gaza Strip because all were evacuated in 2005 (2014 est.)

PEOPLE AND SOCIETY

Nationality: *noun:* Israeli(s)

adjective: Israeli

Ethnic groups: Jewish 75% (of which Israel-born 74.4%, Europe/America/Oceania-born 17.4%, Africa-born 5.1%, Asia-born 3.1%), non-Jewish 25% (mostly Arab) (2013 est.)

Languages: Hebrew (official), Arabic (used officially for Arab minority), English (most commonly used foreign language)

Religions: Jewish 75%, Muslim 17.5%, Christian 2%, Druze 1.6%, other 3.9% (2013 est.)

Population: 8,049,314 (includes populations of the Golan Heights of Golan Sub-District and also East Jerusalem, which was annexed by Israel after 1967) (July 2015 est.)

note: approximately 20,500 Israeli settlers live in the Golan Heights; approximately 211,640 Israeli settlers live in East Jerusalem (2014)

country comparison to the world: 99

Age structure: *0–14 years:* 27.95% (male 1,151,247/female 1,098,632)

15–24 years: 15.5% (male 637,758/female 609,597)

25–54 years: 37.13% (male 1,528,271/female 1,460,772)

55–64 years: 8.57% (male 336,662/female 353,352)

65 years and over: 10.85% (male 389,401/female 483,622) (2015 est.)

Dependency ratios: *total dependency ratio:* 64.1%

youth dependency ratio: 45.7%

elderly dependency ratio: 18.4%

potential support ratio: 5.4% (2015 est.)

Median age: *total:* 29.6 years

male: 28.9 years

female: 30.2 years (2015 est.)

country comparison to the world: 115

Population growth rate: 1.56% (2015 est.)

country comparison to the world: 78

Birth rate: 18.48 births/1,000 population (2015 est.)

country comparison to the world: 96

Death rate: 5.15 deaths/1,000 population (2015 est.)

country comparison to the world: 183

Net migration rate: 2.24 migrant(s)/1,000 population (2015 est.)

country comparison to the world: 46

Urbanization: *urban Population:* 92.1% of total population (2015)

rate of urbanization: 1.37% annual rate of change (2010–15 est.)

Major urban areas—Population: Tel Aviv-Yafo 3.608 million; Haifa 1.097 million; JERUSALEM (proclaimed capital) 839,000 (2015)

Sex ratio: *at birth:* 1.05 male(s)/female

0–14 years: 1.05 male(s)/female

15–24 years: 1.05 male(s)/female

25–54 years: 1.05 male(s)/female

55–64 years: 0.95 male(s)/female

65 years and over: 0.81 male(s)/female

total Population: 1.01 male(s)/female (2015 est.)

Mother's mean age at first birth: 27.3 (2011 est.)

Maternal mortality rate: 5 deaths/100,000 live births (2015 est.)

country comparison to the world: 168

Infant mortality rate: *total:* 3.55 deaths/1,000 live births

male: 3.51 deaths/1,000 live births

female: 3.58 deaths/1,000 live births (2015 est.)

country comparison to the world: 204

Life expectancy at birth: *total Population:* 82.27 years

male: 80.43 years

female: 84.21 years (2015 est.)

country comparison to the world: 11

Total fertility rate: 2.68 children born/woman (2015 est.)

country comparison to the world: 72

Health expenditures: 7.2% of GDP (2013)

country comparison to the world: 68

Physicians density: 3.34 physicians/1,000 population (2012)

Hospital bed density: 3.3 beds/1,000 population (2012)

Drinking water source:

improved:

urban: 100% of population

rural: 100% of population

total: 100% of population

unimproved:

urban: 0% of population

rural: 0% of population

total: 0% of population (2015 est.)

Sanitation facility access:

improved:

urban: 100% of population

rural: 100% of population

total: 100% of population

unimproved:

urban: 0% of population

rural: 0% of population

total: 0% of population (2015 est.)

HIV/AIDS—adult prevalence rate: NA

HIV/AIDS—people living with HIV/AIDS: NA

HIV/AIDS—deaths: NA

Obesity—adult prevalence rate: 25.8% (2014)

country comparison to the world: 49

Education expenditures: 5.9% of GDP (2013)

country comparison to the world: 57

Literacy: *definition:* age 15 and over can read and write

total Population: 97.8%

male: 98.7%

female: 96.8% (2011 est.)

School life expectancy (primary to tertiary education): *total:* 16 years

male: 16 years

female: 16 years (2014)

Unemployment, youth ages 15–24: *total:* 10.5%

male: 10.4%

female: 10.7% (2013 est.)

country comparison to the world: 90

GOVERNMENT

Country name: *conventional long form:* State of Israel

conventional short form: Israel

local long form: Medinat Yisra'el

local short form: Yisra'el

etymology: named after the ancient Kingdom of Israel; according to Biblical tradition, the Jewish patriarch Jacob received the name "Israel" ("He who struggles with God") after he wrestled an entire night with an angel of the Lord; Jacob's 12 sons became the ancestors of the Israelites, also known as the Twelve Tribes of Israel, who formed the Kingdom of Israel

Government type: parliamentary democracy

Capital: *name:* Jerusalem: note—while Israel proclaimed Jerusalem as its capital in 1950, the international community does not recognize it as such; the US, like all other countries, maintains its embassy in Tel Aviv-Yafo

Geographic coordinates: 31 46 N, 35 14 E

time difference: UTC+2 (7 hours ahead of Washington, DC, during Standard Time)

daylight saving time: +1hr, Friday before the last Sunday in March; ends the last Sunday in October

Administrative divisions: 6 districts (mehozot, singular—mehoz); Central, Haifa, Jerusalem, Northern, Southern, Tel Aviv

Independence: 14 May 1948 (from League of Nations mandate under British administration)

National holiday: Independence Day, 14 May (1948); note—Israel declared independence on 14 May 1948, but the Jewish calendar is lunar and the holiday may occur in April or May

Constitution: no formal constitution; some functions of a constitution are filled mostly by the Declaration of Establishment (1948), the Basic Laws, and the Law of Return (as amended); Basic Laws amended several times, last in 2014 (2016)

Legal system: mixed legal system of English common law, British Mandate regulations, and Jewish, Christian, and Muslim religious laws

International law organization participation: has not submitted an ICJ jurisdiction declaration; withdrew acceptance of International Criminal Court jurisdiction in 2002

Citizenship: *citizenship by birth:* no

citizenship by descent only: at least one parent must be a citizen of Israel

dual citizenship recognized: yes, but naturalized citizens are not allowed to maintain dual citizenship

residency requirement for naturalization: 3 years

Suffrage: 18 years of age; universal

Executive branch: *chief of state:* President Reuven RIVLIN (since 27 July 2014)

head of government: Prime Minister Binyamin NETANYAHU (since 31 March 2009)

cabinet: Cabinet selected by prime minister and approved by the Knesset

elections/appointments: president indirectly elected by the Knesset for a 7-year term (limited to 1 term); election last held on 10 June 2014 (next to be held in 2021 but can be called earlier); following legislative elections, the president, in consultation with party leaders, tasks a Knesset member (usually the member of the largest party) with forming a government

election results: Reuven RIVLIN elected president in second round; Knesset vote—Reuven RIVLIN (Likud) 63, Meir SHEETRIT (The Movement) 53, other/invalid 4

Legislative branch: *description:* unicameral Knesset (120 seats; members directly elected in a single nationwide constituency by proportional representation vote; members serve 4-year terms)

elections: last held on 17 March 2015 (next to be held in 2019 but can be called earlier)

election results: percent of vote by party—Likud 23.4%, Zionist Camp 18.7%, Joint List 10.6%, Yesh Atid 8.8%, Kulanu 7.5%, The Jewish Home 6.7%, Shas, 5.7%, Yisrael Beitenu 5.1%, UTJ 5.0%, Meretz 3.9%, Yachad 3.0%, other 1.6%; seats by party—Likud 30, Zionist Camp 24, Joint List 13, Yesh Atid 11, Kulanu 10, The Jewish Home 8, Shas 7, Yisrael Beitenu 6, UTJ 6, Meretz 5

Judicial branch: *highest court(s):* Supreme Court (consists of the chief justice and 14 judges)

judge selection and term of office: judges selected by the Judicial Selection Committee, made up of

all 3 branches of the government and chaired by the Minister of Justice; judges can serve up to mandatory retirement at age 70

subordinate courts: district and magistrate courts; national and regional labor courts; special and religious courts

Political parties and leaders: Balad [Jamal ZAHALKA]

Democratic Front for Peace and Equality (HADASH) [ODEH]

Kulanu [Moshe KAHLON]

Labor [Yitzhak HERZOG]

Likud [Binyamin NETANYAHU]

Meretz [Zehava GALON]

SHAS [Arye DERI]

Tekumah/National Union (Ichud Leumi) [Uri ARIEL]

The Jewish Home (Habayit Hayehudi) [Naftali BENNETT]

The Movement (Hatnuah) [Tzipora "Tzipi" LIVNI]

United Arab List-Ta'al [Masud GANAIM]

United Torah Judaism or UTJ [Yaakov LITZMAN] (an alliance of three parties)

Yesh Atid [Yair LAPID]

Yisrael Beiteinu [Avigdor LIEBERMAN]

Political pressure groups and leaders: Breaking the Silence [Yehuda SHAUL, executive director] collects testimonies from soldiers who served in the West Bank and Gaza Strip

B'Tselem [Hagai EL-AD, executive director] monitors human rights abuses

Peace Now [Yariv OPPENHEIMER, secretary general] supports territorial concessions in the West Bank and Gaza Strip

YESHA Council [Avi ROEHD, chairman] promotes settler interests and opposes territorial compromise

International organization participation: BIS, BSEC (observer), CE (observer), CERN, CICA, EBRD, FAO, IADB, IAEA, IBRD, ICAO, ICC (national committees), ICRM, IDA, IFAD, IFC, IFRCS, ILO, IMF, IMO, IMSO, Interpol, IOC, IOM, IPU, ISO, ITSO, ITU, ITUC (NGOs), MIGA, OAS (observer), OECD, OPCW (signatory), OSCE (partner), Pacific Alliance (observer), Paris Club, PCA, SELEC (observer), UN, UNCTAD, UNESCO, UNHCR, UNIDO, UNWTO, UPU, WCO, WHO, WIPO, WMO, WTO

Diplomatic representation in the US: *chief of mission:* Ambassador Ron DERMER (since 3 December 2013)

chancery: 3514 International Drive NW, Washington, DC 20008

telephone: [1] (202) 364-5500

FAX: [1] (202) 364-5607

consulate(s) general: Atlanta, Boston, Chicago, Houston, Los Angeles, Miami, New York, Philadelphia, San Francisco

Diplomatic representation from the US: *chief of mission:* Ambassador Daniel B. SHAPIRO (since 29 September 2011)

embassy: 71 Hayarkon Street, Tel Aviv 6343229

telephone: [972] (3) 519-7475

FAX: [972] (3) 516-4390

consulate(s) general:

Flag description: white with a blue hexagram (six-pointed linear star) known as the Magen David (Star of David or Shield of David) centered between two equal horizontal blue bands near the top and bottom edges of the flag; the basic design resembles a traditional Jewish prayer shawl (tallit), which is white with blue stripes; the hexagram as a Jewish symbol dates back to medieval times

National symbol(s): Star of David (Magen David), menorah (seven-branched lampstand); national colors: blue, white

National anthem: *name:* "Hatikvah" (The Hope)

lyrics/music: Naftali Herz IMBER/traditional, arranged by Samuel COHEN

note: adopted 2004, unofficial since 1948; used as the anthem of the Zionist movement since 1897; the 1888 arrangement by Samuel COHEN is thought to be based on the Romanian folk song "Carul cuboi" (The Ox Driven Cart)

ECONOMY

Economy—overview: Israel has a technologically advanced free market economy. Cut diamonds, high-technology equipment, and pharmaceuticals are among its leading exports. Its major imports include crude oil, grains, raw materials, and military equipment. Israel usually posts sizable trade deficits, which are covered by tourism and other service exports, as well as significant foreign investment inflows. Between 2004 and 2013, growth averaged nearly 5% per year, led by exports. The global financial crisis of 2008–09 spurred a brief recession in Israel, but the country entered the crisis with solid fundamentals, following years of prudent fiscal policy and a resilient banking sector. Israel's economy also has weathered the Arab Spring because strong trade ties outside the Middle East have insulated the economy from spillover effects.

Slowing domestic and international demand and decreased investment resulting from Israel's uncertain security situation reduced GDP growth to an average of roughly 2.6% per year during 2014–15. Natural gas fields discovered off Israel's coast since 2009 have brightened Israel's energy security outlook. The Tamar and Leviathan fields were some of the world's largest offshore natural gas finds in the last decade. Political and regulatory issues have delayed the development of the massive Leviathan field, but production from Tamar provided a 0.8% boost to Israel's GDP in 2013 and a 0.3% boost in 2014. One of the most carbon intense OECD countries, Israel generates about 57% of its power from coal and only 2.6% from renewable sources.

Income inequality and high housing and commodity prices continue to be a concern for many Israelis. Israel's income inequality and poverty rates are among the highest of OECD countries, and there is a broad perception among the public that a small number of "tycoons" have a cartel-like grip over the major parts of the economy. Government officials have called for reforms to boost the housing supply and increase competition in the banking sector to address these public grievances. Despite calls for reforms, this restricted housing supply continues to impact the well-being of younger Israelis seeking to purchase homes. Tariffs and non-tariff barriers, coupled with guaranteed prices and customs tariffs for farmers have kept food prices high through 2015. In the long term, Israel faces structural issues, including low labor participation rates for its fastest growing social segments—the ultraorthodox and Arab-Israeli communities. Also, Israel's progressive, globally competitive, knowledge-based technology sector employs only about 8% of the workforce, with the rest mostly employed in manufacturing and services—sectors which face downward wage pressures from global competition. Expenditures on educational institutions remain low compared to most other OECD countries with similar GDP per capita.

GDP (purchasing power parity): $281.9 billion (2015 est.)
$274.8 billion (2014 est.)
$268 billion (2013 est.)
note: data are in 2015 US dollars
country comparison to the world: 57
GDP (official exchange rate): $296.1 billion (2015 est.)
GDP—real growth rate: 2.6% (2015 est.)
2.6% (2014 est.)
3.3% (2013 est.)
country comparison to the world: 115
GDP—per capita (PPP): $33,700 (2015 est.)
$33,500 (2014 est.)
$33,300 (2013 est.)
note: data are in 2015 US dollars
country comparison to the world: 55
Gross national saving: 23.5% of GDP (2015 est.)
23.7% of GDP (2014 est.)
23.3% of GDP (2013 est.)
country comparison to the world: 60
GDP—composition, by end use:
household consumption: 55.7%
government consumption: 22%
investment in fixed capital: 18.8%
investment in inventories: 0.3%
exports of goods and services: 29.7%
imports of goods and services: -26.5% (2015 est.)
GDP—composition, by sector of origin:
agriculture: 2.5%
industry: 27.3%
services: 70% (2015 est.)
Agriculture—products: citrus, vegetables, cotton; beef, poultry, dairy products
Industries: high-technology products (including aviation, communications, computer-aided design and manufactures, medical electronics, fiber optics), wood and paper products, potash and phosphates, food, beverages, and tobacco, caustic soda, cement, construction, metal products, chemical products, plastics, cut diamonds, textiles, footwear
Industrial production growth rate: 3.2% (2015 est.)
country comparison to the world: 81
Labor force: 3.86 million (2015 est.)
country comparison to the world: 94
Labor force—by occupation: *agriculture:* 1.1%
industry: 17.3%
services: 81.6% (2015 est.)

Unemployment rate: 5.6% (2015 est.)
5.9% (2014 est.)
country comparison to the world: 62
Population below poverty line: 22%
note: Israel's poverty line is $7.30 per person per day (2014 est.)
Household income or consumption by percentage share: *lowest:* 10%: 1.7%
highest: 10%: 31.3% (2010)
Distribution of family income—Gini index: 42.8 (2013)
39.2 (2008)
country comparison to the world: 51
Budget: *revenues:* $76.12 billion
expenditures: $82.12 billion (2015 est.)
Taxes and other revenues: 25.5% of GDP (2015 est.)
country comparison to the world: 118
Budget surplus (+) or deficit (−): -2% of GDP (2015 est.)
country comparison to the world: 75
Public debt: 64.4% of GDP (2015 est.)
65.9% of GDP (2014 est.)
country comparison to the world: 56
Fiscal year: calendar year
Inflation rate (consumer prices): -0.6% (2015 est.)
0.5% (2014 est.)
country comparison to the world: 23
Central bank discount rate: 0.1% (15 December 2015) 0.25% (31 December 2014)
country comparison to the world: 136
Commercial bank prime lending rate: 3.5% (31 December 2015 est.)
3.91% (31 December 2014 est.)
country comparison to the world: 164
Stock of narrow money: $59.16 billion (31 December 2015 est.)
$51.25 billion (31 December 2014 est.)
country comparison to the world: 49
Stock of broad money: $246 billion (31 December 2014 est.)
$155.6 billion (31 December 2013 est.)
country comparison to the world: 40
Stock of domestic credit: $211.4 billion (31 December 2015 est.)
$201.2 billion (31 December 2014 est.)
country comparison to the world: 42
Market value of publicly traded shares: $183.4 billion (15 December 2015 est.)
$148.8 billion (31 December 2014)
$122.9 billion (31 December 2013 est.)
country comparison to the world: 35
Current account balance: $12.27 billion (2015 est.)
$11.54 billion (2014 est.)
country comparison to the world: 20
Exports: $56.4 billion (2015 est.)
$63.34 billion (2014 est.)
country comparison to the world: 48
Exports—commodities: machinery and equipment, software, cut diamonds, agricultural products, chemicals, textiles and apparel
Exports—partners: US 27.5%, Hong Kong 8%, UK 6.1%, China 4.9% (2015)
Imports: $58.8 billion (2015 est.)
$71.2 billion (2014 est.)
country comparison to the world: 44

Imports—commodities: raw materials, military equipment, investment goods, rough diamonds, fuels, grain, consumer goods
Imports—partners: US 13%, China 9.3%, Switzerland 7.1%, Germany 6.1%, Belgium 5.3%, Italy 4% (2015)
Reserves of foreign exchange and gold: $91.61 billion (31 December 2015 est.)
$86.1 billion (31 December 2014 est.)
country comparison to the world: 26
Debt—external: $96.16 billion (31 December 2014 est.)
$95.37 billion (31 December 2013 est.)
country comparison to the world: 53
Stock of direct foreign investment—at home:
$108.5 billion (31 December 2015 est.)
$98.7 billion (31 December 2014 est.)
country comparison to the world: 44
Stock of direct foreign investment—abroad:
$83.42 billion (31 December 2015 est.)
$78.02 billion (31 December 2014 est.)
country comparison to the world: 34
Exchange rates: new Israeli shekels (ILS) per US dollar—
3.886 (2015 est.)
3.5779 (2014 est.)
3.5779 (2013 est.)
3.86 (2012 est.)
3.5781 (2011 est.)

ENERGY

Electricity—production: 64.44 billion kWh (2014 est.)
country comparison to the world: 44
Electricity—consumption: 59.83 billion kWh (2014 est.)
country comparison to the world: 43
Electricity—exports: 4.938 billion kWh (2013 est.)
country comparison to the world: 33
Electricity—imports: 0 kWh (2013 est.)
country comparison to the world: 163
Electricity—installed generating capacity: 16.25 million kW (2014 est.)
country comparison to the world: 46
Electricity—from fossil fuels: 97.4% of total installed capacity (2014 est.)
country comparison to the world: 58
Electricity—from nuclear fuels: 0% of total installed capacity (2014 est.)
country comparison to the world: 112
Electricity—from hydroelectric plants: 0% of total installed capacity (2014 est.)
country comparison to the world: 179
Electricity—from other renewable sources: 2.6% of total installed capacity (2014 est.)
country comparison to the world: 75
Crude oil—production: 390 bbl/day (2014 est.)
country comparison to the world: 96
Crude oil—exports: 5,352 bbl/day (2013 est.)
country comparison to the world: 72
Crude oil—imports: 275,600 bbl/day (2013 est.)
country comparison to the world: 29
Crude oil—proved reserves: 13.95 million bbl (1 January 2015 est.)
country comparison to the world: 89

Refined petroleum products—production: 276,300 bbl/day (2013 est.)
country comparison to the world: 47
Refined petroleum products—consumption: 234,600 bbl/day (2014 est.)
country comparison to the world: 53
Refined petroleum products—exports: 77,280 bbl/day (2013 est.)
country comparison to the world: 52
Refined petroleum products—imports: 96,590 bbl/day (2013 est.)
country comparison to the world: 54
Natural gas—production: 7.51 billion cu m (2014 est.)
country comparison to the world: 46
Natural gas—consumption: 7.57 billion cu m (2014 est.)
country comparison to the world: 52
Natural gas—exports: 0 cu m (2014 est.)
country comparison to the world: 119
Natural gas—imports: 60 million cu m (2014 est.)
country comparison to the world: 72
Natural gas—proved reserves: 285 billion cu m (1 January 2014 est.)
country comparison to the world: 38
Carbon dioxide emissions from consumption of energy: 62.5 million Mt (2014 est.)
country comparison to the world: 54

COMMUNICATIONS

Telephones—fixed lines: *total subscriptions:* 2.9 million
subscriptions per 100 inhabitants: 37 (2014 est.)
country comparison to the world: 50
Telephones—mobile cellular: *total:* 9.5 million
subscriptions per 100 inhabitants: 120 (2014 est.)
country comparison to the world: 88
Telephone system: *general assessment:* most highly developed system in the Middle East
domestic: good system of coaxial cable and microwave radio relay; all systems are digital; four privately owned mobile-cellular service providers with countrywide coverage
international: country code—972; submarine cables provide links to Europe, Cyprus, and parts of the Middle East; satellite earth stations—3 Intelsat (2 Atlantic Ocean and 1 Indian Ocean) (2011)
Broadcast media: state broadcasting network, operated by the Israel Broadcasting Authority (IBA), broadcasts on 2 channels, one in Hebrew and the other in Arabic; 5 commercial channels including a channel broadcasting in Russian, a channel broadcasting Knesset proceedings, and a music channel supervised by a public body; multi-channel satellite and cable TV packages provide access to foreign channels; IBA broadcasts on 8 radio networks with multiple repeaters and Israel Defense Forces Radio broadcasts over multiple stations; about 15 privately owned radio stations; overall more than 100 stations and repeater stations (2008)
Radio broadcast stations: AM 23, FM 15, shortwave 0 (2010)
Television broadcast stations: 7 (2009)
Internet country code: .il
Internet hosts: 2.483 million (2012)
country comparison to the world: 36
Internet users: *total:* 6 million
percent of Population: 75.8% (2014 est.)
country comparison to the world: 58

TRANSPORTATION

Airports: 47 (2013)
country comparison to the world: 94
Airports—with paved runways: *total:* 29
over 3,047 m: 2
2,438 to 3,047 m: 5
1,524 to 2,437 m: 6
914 to 1,523 m: 11
under 914 m: 5 (2013)
Airports—with unpaved runways: *total:* 18
1,524 to 2,437 m: 1
914 to 1,523 m: 3
under 914 m: 14 (2013)
Heliports: 3 (2013)
Pipelines: gas 763 km; oil 442 km; refined products 261 km (2013)
Railways: *total:* 1,250 km
standard gauge: 1,250 km 1.435-m gauge (2014)
country comparison to the world: 82
Roadways: *total:* 18,566 km
paved: 18,566 km (includes 449 km of expressways) (2011)
country comparison to the world: 115
Merchant marine: *total:* 8
by type: cargo 1, container 7
registered in other countries: 48 (Bermuda 3, Georgia 1, Honduras 1, Liberia 34, Malta 3, Moldova 2, Panama 1, Saint Vincent and the Grenadines 3) (2010)
country comparison to the world: 120
Ports and terminals: major seaport(s): Ashdod, Elat (Eilat), Hadera, Haifa
container port(s) TEUs): Ashdod (1,176,000), Haifa (1,238,000)

MILITARY AND SECURITY

Military branches: Israel Defense Forces (IDF), Israel Naval Force (IN), Israel Air Force (IAF) (2010)
Military service age and obligation: 18 years of age for compulsory (Jews, Druze) military service; 17 years of age for voluntary (Christians, Muslims, Circassians) military service; both sexes are obligated to military service; conscript service obligation—32 months for enlisted men and 24 months for enlisted women (varies based on military occupation), 48 months for officers; pilots commit to 9 years service; reserve obligation to age 41–51 (men), age 24 (women) (2015)
Military expenditures: 5.58% of GDP (2014)
5.53% of GDP (2013)
5.69% of GDP (2012)
5.87% of GDP (2011)
5.69% of GDP (2010)
country comparison to the world: 5

TRANSNATIONAL ISSUES

Disputes—international: West Bank and Gaza Strip are Israeli-occupied with current status subject to the Israeli-Palestinian Interim Agreement—permanent status to be determined through further negotiation; Israel continues construction of a "seam line" separation barrier along parts of the Green Line and within the West Bank; Israel withdrew its settlers and military from the Gaza Strip and from four settlements in the West Bank in August 2005; Golan Heights is Israeli-occupied (Lebanon claims the Shab'a Farms area of Golan Heights); since 1948, about 350 peacekeepers from the UN Truce Supervision Organization headquartered in Jerusalem monitor ceasefires, supervise armistice agreements, prevent isolated incidents from escalating, and assist other UN personnel in the region
Refugees and internally displaced persons: *refugees (country of origin):* 32,668 (Eritrea); 6,588 (Sudan) (2014)
stateless persons: 15 (2015)
Illicit drugs: increasingly concerned about ecstasy, cocaine, and heroin abuse; drugs arrive in country from Lebanon and, increasingly, from Jordan; money-laundering center

ITALY

INTRODUCTION

Background: Italy became a nation-state in 1861 when the regional states of the peninsula, along with Sardinia and Sicily, were united under King Victor EMMANUEL II. An era of parliamentary government came to a close in the early 1920s when Benito MUSSOLINI established a Fascist dictatorship. His alliance with Nazi Germany led to Italy's defeat in World War II. A democratic republic replaced the monarchy in 1946 and economic revival followed. Italy is a charter member of NATO and the European Economic Community (EEC). It has been at the forefront of European economic and political unification, joining the Economic and Monetary Union in 1999. Persistent problems include sluggish economic growth, high youth and female unemployment, organized crime, corruption, and economic disparities between southern Italy and the more prosperous north.

GEOGRAPHY

Location: Southern Europe, a peninsula extending into the central Mediterranean Sea, northeast of Tunisia

Geographic coordinates: 42 50 N, 12 50 E
Map references: Europe
Area: total: 301,340 sq km
land: 294,140 sq km
water: 7,200 sq km
note: includes Sardinia and Sicily
country comparison to the world: 72
Area—comparative: almost twice the size of Georgia; slightly larger than Arizona
Land boundaries: total: 1,836.4 km
border countries (6): Austria 404 km, France 476 km, Holy See (Vatican City) 3.4 km, San Marino 37 km, Slovenia 218 km, Switzerland 698 km
Coastline: 7,600 km
Maritime claims: territorial sea: 12 nm
continental shelf: 200-m depth or to the depth of exploitation

Climate: predominantly Mediterranean; alpine in far north; hot, dry in south
Terrain: mostly rugged and mountainous; some plains, coastal lowlands
Elevation: mean elevation: 538 m
elevation extremes: lowest point: Mediterranean Sea 0 m
highest point: Mont Blanc (Monte Bianco) de Courmayeur 4,748 m (a secondary peak of Mont Blanc)
Natural resources: coal, mercury, zinc, potash, marble, barite, asbestos, pumice, fluorspar, feldspar, pyrite (sulfur), natural gas and crude oil reserves, fish, arable land:
Land use: agricultural land: 47.1%
arable land: 22.8%
permanent crops: 8.6%
permanent pasture: 15.7%
forest: 31.4%
other: 21.5% (2011 est.)
Irrigated land: 39,500 sq km (2012)
Total renewable water resources: 191.3 cu km (2011)
Freshwater withdrawal (domestic/industrial/agricultural): total: 45.41 cu km/yr (24%/43%/34%)
per capita: 789.8 cu m/yr (2008)
Natural hazards: regional risks include landslides, mudflows, avalanches, earthquakes, volcanic eruptions, flooding; land subsidence in Venice
volcanism: significant volcanic activity; Etna (elev.3,330 m), which is in eruption as of 2010, is Europe's most active volcano; flank eruptions pose a threat to nearby Sicilian villages; Etna, along with the famous Vesuvius, which remains a threat to the millions of nearby residents in the Bay of Naples area, have both been deemed Decade Volcanoes by the International Association of Volcanology and Chemistry of the Earth's Interior, worthy of study due to their explosive history and close proximity to human populations; Stromboli, on its namesake island, has also been continuously active with moderate volcanic activity; other historically active volcanoes include Campi Flegrei, Ischia, Larderello, Pantelleria, Vulcano, and Vulsini
Environment—current issues: air pollution from industrial emissions such as sulfur dioxide; coastal and inland rivers polluted from industrial and agricultural effluents; acid rain damaging lakes; inadequate industrial waste treatment andd is posal facilities
Environment—international agreements: party to: Air Pollution, Air Pollution-Nitrogen Oxides, Air Pollution-Persistent Organic Pollutants, Air Pollution-Sulfur 85, Air Pollution-Sulfur 94, Air Pollution-Volatile Organic Compounds, Antarctic-Environmental Protocol, Antarctic-Marine Living Resources, Antarctic Seals, Antarctic Treaty, Biodiversity, Climate Change, Climate Change-Kyoto Protocol, Desertification, Endangered Species, Environmental Modification, Hazardous Wastes, Law of the Sea, Marine Dumping, Ozone

Layer Protection, Ship Pollution, Tropical Timber 83, Tropical Timber 94, Wetlands, Whaling
signed, but not ratified: none of the selected agreements
Geography—note: strategic location dominating central Mediterranean as well as southern sea and air approaches to Western Europe

PEOPLE AND SOCIETY

Nationality: noun: Italian(s)
adjective: Italian
Ethnic groups: Italian (includes small clusters of German-, French-, and Slovene-Italians in the north and Albanian-Italians and Greek-Italians in the south)
Languages: Italian (official), German (parts of Trentino-Alto Adige region are predominantly German-speaking), French (small French-speaking minority in Valle d'Aosta region), Slovene (Slovene-speaking minority in the Trieste-Gorizia area)
Religions: Christian 80% (overwhelmingly Roman Catholic with very small groups of Jehovah's Witnesses and Protestants), Muslim (about 800,000 to 1 million), Atheist and Agnostic 20%
Population: 61,855,120 (July 2015 est.)
country comparison to the world: 24
Age structure: 0–14 years: 13.73% (male 4,340,380/female 4,154,737)
15–24 years: 9.79% (male 3,035,586/female 3,020,584)
25–54 years: 42.74% (male 13,063,733/female 13,375,975)
55–64 years: 12.54% (male 3,756,546/female 3,997,190)
65 years and over: 21.2% (male 5,626,752/female 7,483,637) (2015 est.)
Dependency ratios: total dependency ratio: 56.5%
youth dependency ratio: 21.5%
elderly dependency ratio: 35.1%
potential support ratio: 2.9% (2015 est.)
Median age: total: 44.8 years
male: 43.7 years
female: 45.9 years (2015 est.)
country comparison to the world: 6
Population growth rate: 0.27% (2015 est.)
country comparison to the world: 177
Birth rate: 8.74 birth s/1,000 population (2015 est.)
country comparison to the world: 213
Death rate: 10.19 death s/1,000 population (2015 est.)
country comparison to the world: 40
Net migration rate: 4.1 migrant(s)/1,000 population (2015 est.)
country comparison to the world: 30
Urbanization: urban population: 69% of total population (2015)
rate of urbanization: 0.39% annual rate of change (2010–15 est.)
Major urban areas—Population: ROME (capital) 3.718 million; Milan 3.099 million; Naples 2.202

429

million; Turin 1.765 million; Palermo 853,000; Bergamo 840,000 (2015)

Sex ratio: *at birth:* 1.06 male(s)/female
0–14 years: 1.05 male(s)/female
15–24 years: 1.01 male(s)/female
25–54 years: 0.98 male(s)/female
55–64 years: 0.94 male(s)/female
65 years and over: 0.75 male(s)/female
total Population: 0.93 male(s)/female (2015 est.)

Mother's mean age at first birth: 30.3 (2011 est.)

Maternal mortality rate: 4 deaths/100,000 live births (2015 est.)
country comparison to the world: 180

Infant mortality rate: *total:* 3.29 deaths/1,000 live births
male: 3.49 deaths/1,000 live births
female: 3.08 deaths/1,000 live births (2015 est.)
country comparison to the world: 212

Life expectancy at birth: *total Population:* 82.12 years
male: 79.48 years
female: 84.92 years (2015 est.)
country comparison to the world: 14

Total fertility rate: 1.43 children born/woman (2015 est.)
country comparison to the world: 208

Health expenditures: 9.1% of GDP (2013)
country comparison to the world: 33

Physicians density: 3.76 physicians/1,000 population (2012)

Hospital bed density: 3.4 beds/1,000 population (2011)

Drinking water source:
improved:
urban: 100% of population
rural: 100% of population
total: 100% of population
unimproved:
urban: 0% of population
rural: 0% of population
total: 0% of population (2015 est.)

Sanitation facility access:
improved:
urban: 99.5% of population
rural: 99.6% of population
total: 99.5% of population
unimproved:
urban: 0.5% of population
rural: 0.4% of population
total: 0.5% of population (2015 est.)

HIV/AIDS—adult prevalence rate: 0.28% (2013 est.)
country comparison to the world: 85

HIV/AIDS—people living with HIV/AIDS: 122,000 (2013 est.)
country comparison to the world: 39

HIV/AIDS—deaths: NA

Obesity—adult prevalence rate: 23.7% (2014)
country comparison to the world: 97

Education expenditures: 4.1% of GDP (2011)
country comparison to the world: 93

Literacy: *definition:* age 15 and over can read and write
total Population: 99.2%
male: 99.4%
female: 99% (2015 est.)

School life expectancy (primary to tertiary education): *total:* 16 years
male: 16 years
female: 17 years (2013)

Unemployment, youth ages 15–24: *total:* 40%
male: 39%
female: 41.4% (2013 est.)
country comparison to the world: 17

GOVERNMENT

Country name: *conventional long form:* Italian Republic
conventional short form: Italy
local long form: Repubblica Italiana
local short form: Italia
former: Kingdom of Italy
etymology: derivation is unclear, but the Latin "Italia" may come from the Oscan "Viteliu" meaning "[land] of young cattle" (the bull was a symbol of southern Italic tribes)

Government type: parliamentary republic

Capital: *name:* Rome

Geographic coordinates: 41 54 N, 12 29 E
time difference: UTC + 1 (6 hours ahead of Washington, DC, during Standard Time)
daylight saving time: +1hr, begins last Sunday in March; ends last Sunday in October

Administrative divisions: 15 regions (regioni, singular—regione) and 5 autonomous regions (regioni autonome, singular—regione autonoma)
regions: Abruzzo, Basilicata, Calabria, Campania, Emilia-Romagna, Lazio (Latium), Liguria, Lombardia, Marche, Molise, Piemonte (Piedmont), Puglia (Apulia), Toscana (Tuscany), Umbria, Veneto (Venetia)
autonomous regions: Friuli-Venezia Giulia; Sardegna (Sardinia); Sicilia (Sicily); Trentino-Alto Adige (Trentino-South Tyrol) or Trentino-Suedtirol (German); Valle d'Aosta (Aosta Valley) or Vallee d'Aoste (French)

Independence: 17 March 1861 (Kingdom of Italy proclaimed; Italy was not finally unified until 1870)

National holiday: Republic Day, 2 June (1946)

Constitution: previous 1848 (originally for Kingdom of Sardinia and adopted by Kingdom of Italy in 1861); latest enacted 22 December 1947, adopted 27 December 1947, entered into force 1 January 1948; amended many times, last in 2012; note—a proposed amendment that would significantly alter the parliament is slated for a referendum in October 2016 (2016)

Legal system: civil law system; judicial review of legislation under certain conditions in Constitutional Court

International law organization participation: accepts compulsory ICJ jurisdiction with reservations; accepts ICCt jurisdiction

Citizenship: *citizenship by birth:* no
citizenship by descent only: at least one parent must be a citizen of Italy
dual citizenship recognized: yes
residency requirement for naturalization: 4 years for EUNationals, 5 years for refugees and specified exceptions, 10 years for all others

Suffrage: 18 years of age; universal except in senatorial elections, where minimum age is 25

Executive branch: *chief of state:* President Sergio MATTARELLA (3 February 2015); Giorgio NAPOLITANO resigned 14 January 2015

head of government: Prime Minister Matteo RENZI (since 22 February 2014); note—the prime minister title is President of the Council of Ministers
cabinet: Council of Ministers proposed by the prime minister and nominated by the president
elections/appointments: president indirectly elected by an electoral college consisting of both houses of Parliament and 58 regional representatives for a 7-year term (no term limits); election last held on 31 January 2015 (next scheduled for 2020); prime minister appointed by the president, confirmed by parliament
election results: Sergio MATTARELLA elected president; electoral college vote count in fourth round -665 out of 1,009 (505-vote threshold); Matteo RENZI sworn in as prime minister on 22 February 2014

Legislative branch: *description:* bicameral Parliament or Parlamento consists of the Senate or Senato della Repubblica (322 seats; 315 members directly elected in single- and multi-seat constituencies by proportional representation vote to serve 5-year terms and 7 ex-officio members appointed by the president of the Republic to serve for life) and the Chamber of Deputies or Camera dei Deputati (630 seats; 629 members directly elected in single- and multi-seat constituencies by proportional representation vote and 1 member from Valle d'Aosta elected by simple majority vote; members serve 5-year terms)
elections: Senate—last held on 24–25 February 2013 (next to be held in 2018); Chamber of Deputies -last held on 24–25 February 2013 (next to be held in 2018)
election results: Senate—percent of vote by party—NA; seats by party—center-left coalition 123 (PD 111, SEL 7, SVP 2, other 3), center-right coalition 117 (PdL 98, LN 18, other 1), M5S 54, centrist coalition 19, other 2; Chamber of Deputies—percent of vote by party—NA; seats by party—center-left coalition 345 (PD 297, SEL 37, CD 6 SVP 5), center-right coalition 125 (PdL 98, LN 18, Fdl 9), M5S 109, centrist coalition 47, other 3; note—President NAPOLITANO dissolved Parliament on 22 December 2012

Judicial branch: *highest court(s):* Supreme Court of Cassation consists of the first president (chief justice), deputy president, 54 justices presiding over 6 civil and 7 criminal divisions, and 288 judges; an additional 30 judges of lower courts serve as supporting judges; cases normally heard by 5-judge panels; more complex cases heard by 9—judge panels
judge selection and term of office: Supreme Court judges appointed by the Superior Council of the Judiciary, headed by the president of the republic, to serve NA terms; Constitutional Court judges—5 appointed by the president, 5 elected by parliament, 5 elected by select higher courts; judges serve up to 9 years)

subordinate courts: various lower civil and criminal courts (primary and secondary tribunals, courts, and courts of appeal)

Political parties and leaders: *Ruling left-center-right coalition:* Civic Choice or SC [Enrico ZANETTI]

Democratic Centre or CD [Bruno TABACCI]

Democratic Party or PD [Matteo RENZI]

The New Center-Right or NCD [Angelino ALFANO]

Union of the Center or UdC [Pier Fernando CASINI]

Center-right opposition: Brothers of Italy-National Alliance or FdI-AN [Giorgia MELONI, Ignazio LA RUSSA, and Guido CROSETTO]

Forza Italia [Silvio BERLUSCONI] (formerly PdL)

Northern League or LN [Matteo SALVINI]

other minor parties

Other parties: Civil Revolution or RC [Antonio INGROIA]

Five Star Movment or M5S [Beppe GRILLO]

South Tyrolean People's Party or SVP [Philipp ACHAMMER]

Political pressure groups and leaders: *manufacturers and merchants associations:* Confcommercio Confindustria

organized farm groups: Confcoltivatori Confagricoltura

major trade union confederations: Confederazione Generale Italiana del Lavoro or CGIL [Susanna CAMUSSO] (left wing)

Confederazione Italiana dei Sindacati Lavoratori or CISL [Raffaele BONANNI] (Roman Catholic centrist)

Unione Italiana del Lavoro or UIL [Luigi ANGELETTI] (lay centrist)

other: Roman Catholic Church

International organizati on participation: ADB (nonregional member), AfDB (nonregional member), Arctic Council (observer), Australia Group, BIS, BSEC (observer), CBSS (observer), CD, CDB, CE, CEI, CERN, EAPC, EBRD, ECB, EIB, EITI (implementing country), EMU, ESA, EU, FAO, FATF, G-7, G-8, G-10, G-20, IADB, IAEA, IBRD, ICAO, ICC (national committees), ICCt, ICRM, IDA, IEA, IFAD, IFC, IFRCS, IGAD (partners), IHO, ILO, IMF, IMO, IMSO, Interpol, IOC, IOM, IPU, ISO, ITSO, ITU, ITUC (NGOs), LAIA (observer), MIGA, MINURSO, MINUSMA, NATO, NEA, NSG, OAS (observer), OECD, OPCW, OSCE, Pacific Alliance (observer), Paris Club, PCA, PIF (partner), Schengen Convention, SELEC (observer), SICA (observer), UN, UNCTAD, UNESCO, UNHCR, UNIDO, UNIFIL, Union Latina, UNMOGIP, UNRWA, UNTSO, UNWTO, UPU, WCO, WHO, WIPO, WMO, WTO, ZC

Diplomatic representation in the US: *chief of mission:* Ambassador Armando VARRICCHIO (since 2 March 2016)

chancery: 3000 Whitehaven Street NW, Washington, DC 20008

telephone: [1] (202) 612-4400

FAX: [1] (202) 518-2151

consulate(s) general: Boston, Chicago, Detroit, Houston, Miami, New York, Los Angeles, Philadelphia, San Francisco

consulate(s): Charlotte (NC), Cleveland (OH), Detroit (MI), Hattiesburg (MS), Honolulu (HI), New Orleans, Newark (NJ), Norfolk (VA), Pittsburgh (PA), Portland (OR), Seattle

consular agency(ies): Anchorage (AL), Charleston (SC), Worcester (MA)

Diplomatic representation from the US: *chief of mission:* Ambassador John R. PHILLIPS (since 3 October 2013); note—also accredited to San Marino

embassy: Via Vittorio Veneto 121,001 87-Rome

mailing address: PSC 59, Box 100, APO AE 09624

telephone: [39] (06) 46741

FAX: [39] (06) 4674-2244

consulate(s) general: Florence, Milan, Naples

consular agency(ies): Anchorage (AL), Charleston (SC), Worcester (MA)

Flag description: three equal vertical bands of green (hoist side), white, and red; design inspired by the French flag brought to Italy by Napoleon in 1797; colors are those of Milan (red and white) combined with the green uniform color of the Milanese civic guard

note: similar to the flag of Mexico, which is longer, uses darker shades of red and green, and has its coat of arms centered on the white band; Ireland, which is longer and is green (hoist side), white, and orange; also similar to the flag of the Cote d'Ivoire, which has the colors reversed—orange (hoist side), white, and green

National symbol(s): white, five-pointed star (Stella d'Italia); national colors: red, white, green

National anthem: *name:* "Il Canto degli Italiani" (The Song of the Italians)

lyrics/music: Goffredo MAMELI/Michele NOVARO

note: adopted 1946; the anthem, originally written in 1847, is also known as "L'Inno di Mameli" (Mameli's Hymn), and "Fratelli D'Italia" (Brothers of Italy)

ECONOMY

Economy—overview: Italy has a diversified economy, which is divided into a developed industrial north, dominated by private companies, and a less-developed, highly subsidized, agricultural south, where unemployment is higher. The Italian economy is driven in large part by the manufacture of high-quality consumer goods produced by small and medium-sized enterprises, many of them family-owned.

Italy also has a sizable underground economy, which by some estimates accounts for as much as 17% of GDP. These activities are most common within the agriculture, construction, and service sectors. Italy is the third-largest economy in the eurozone, but its exceptionally high public debt and structural impediments to growth have rendered it vulnerable to scrutiny by financial markets. Public debt has increased steadily since 2007, topping 135% of GDP in 2015, but investor

concerns about Italy and the broader euro-zone crisis eased in 2013, bringing down Italy's borrowing costs on sovereign government debt from euro-era records. The government still faces pressure from investors and European partners to sustain its efforts to address Italy's long-standing structural impediments to growth, such as labor market inefficiencies and tax evasion. In 2014, economic growth and labor market conditions continued to deteriorate, with overall unemployment rising to 12.7% and youth unemployment around 40%, but Italy began to recover in 2015, with marginal growth and a slight reduction in unemployment.

GDP (purchasing power parity): $2.171 trillion (2015 est.)

$2.155 trillion (2014 est.)

$2.162 trillion (2013 est.)

note: data are in 2015 US dollars

country comparison to the world: 13

GDP (official exchange rate): $1.816 trillion (2015 est.)

GDP—real growth rate: 0.8% (2015 est.)

-0.3% (2014 est.)

-1.7% (2013 est.)

country comparison to the world: 182

GDP—per capita (PPP): $35,700 (2015 est.)

$35,400 (2014 est.)

$36,200 (2013 est.)

note: data are in 2015 US dollars

country comparison to the world: 52

Gross national saving: 18.9% of GDP (2015 est.)

18.2% of GDP (2014 est.)

17.9% of GDP (2013 est.)

country comparison to the world: 89

GDP—composition, by end use:

household consumption: 60.7%

government consumption: 19.4%

investment in fixed capital: 16.7%

investment in inventories: -0.2%

exports of goods and services: 30.1%

imports of goods and services: -26.7% (2015 est.)

GDP—composition, by sector of origin:

agriculture: 2.2%

industry: 23.6%

services: 74.2% (2015 est.)

Agriculture—products: fruits, vegetables, grapes, potatoes, sugar beets, soybeans, grain, olives; beef, dairy products; fish

Industries: tourism, machinery, iron and steel, chemicals, food processing, textiles, motor vehicles, clothing, footwear, ceramics

Industrial production growth rate: 0.6% (2015 est.)

country comparison to the world: 159

Labor force: 25.54 million (2015 est.)

country comparison to the world: 27

Labor force—by occupation:

agriculture: 3.9%

industry: 28.3%

services: 67.8% (2011)

Unemployment rate: 12.2% (2015 est.)

12.7% (2014 est.)

country comparison to the world: 135

Population below poverty line: 29.9% (2012 est.)

Household income or consumption by percentage share: *lowest:* 10%: 2.3%

highest: 10%: 26.8% (2000)

Distribution of family income—Gini index: 31.9 (2012 est.)

27.3 (1995)

country comparison to the world: 113

Budget: *revenues:* $876 billion

expenditures: $930.5 billion (2015 est.)

Taxes and other revenues: 48.2% of GDP (2015 est.)

country comparison to the world: 18

Budget surplus (+) or deficit (–): -3% of GDP (2015 est.)

country comparison to the world: 114

Public debt: 135.8% of GDP (2015 est.)

132% of GDP (2014 est.)

note: Italy reports its data on public debt according to guidelines set out in the Maastricht Treaty; general government gross debt is defined in the Maastricht Treaty as consolidated general government gross debt at nominal value, outstanding at the end of the year, in the following categories of government liabilities (as defined in ESA95): currency and deposits (A.F.2), securities other than shares excluding financial derivatives (A.F.3, excluding A.F.34), and loans (A.F.4); the general government sector comprises the central government, state government, local government and social security funds

country comparison to the world: 5

Fiscal year: calendar year

Inflation rate (consumer prices): 0.1% (2015 est.) 0.2% (2014 est.)

country comparison to the world: 52

Central bank discount rate: 0.25% (31 December 2013)

0.75% (31 December 2012)

note: this is the European Central Bank's rate on the marginal lending facility, which offers overnight credit to banks in the euro area

country comparison to the world: 134

Commercial bank prime lending rate: 4.3% (31 December 2015 est.)

4.87% (31 December 2014 est.)

country comparison to the world: 158

Stock of narrow money: $1.1 trillion (31 December 2015 est.)

$999 billion (31 December 2014 est.)

note: see entry for the European Union for money supply for the entire euro area; the European Central Bank (ECB) controls monetary policy for the 18 members of the Economic and Monetary Union (EMU); individual members of the EMU do not control the quantity of money circulating within their own borders

country comparison to the world: 6

Stock of broad money: $2.134 trillion (31 December 2014 est.)

$2.284 trillion (31 December 2013 est.)

country comparison to the world: 8

Stock of domestic credit: $3.096 trillion (31 December 2015 est.)

$3.39 trillion (31 December 2014 est.)

country comparison to the world: 8

Market value of publicly traded shares: $480.5 billion (31 December 2012 est.)

$431.5 billion (31 December 2011)

$318.1 billion (31 December 2010 est.)

country comparison to the world: 23

Current account balance: $38.74 billion (2015 est.)

$40.9 billion (2014 est.)

country comparison to the world: 11

Exports: $454.6 billion (2015 est.)

$513.7 billion (2014 est.)

country comparison to the world: 10

Exports—commodities: engineering products, textiles and clothing, production machinery, motor vehicles, transport equipment, chemicals; foodstuffs, beverages, and tobacco; minerals, nonferrous metals

Exports—partners: Germany 12.3%, France 10.3%, US 8.7%, UK 5.4%, Spain 4.8%, Switzerland 4.7% (2015)

Imports: $389.2 billion (2015 est.)

$448.4 billion (2014 est.)

country comparison to the world: 14

Imports—commodities: engineering products, chemicals, transport equipment, energy products, minerals and nonferrous metals, textiles and clothing; food, beverages, tobacco

Imports—partners: Germany 15.4%, France 8.7%, China 7.7%, Netherlands 5.6%, Spain 5%, Belgium 4.7% (2015)

Reserves of foreign exchange and gold: $142.2 billion (31 December 2014 est.)

$145.5 billion (31 December 2013 est.)

country comparison to the world: 18

Debt—external: $2.459 trillion (31 December 2014 est.)

$2.635 trillion (31 December 2013 est.)

country comparison to the world: 9

Stock of direct foreign investment—at home: $505 billion (31 December 2015 est.)

$490.2 billion (31 December 2014 est.)

country comparison to the world: 17

Stock of direct foreign investment—abroad: $692.6 billion (31 December 2015 est.)

$664.9 billion (31 December 2014 est.)

country comparison to the world: 15

Exchange rates: euros (EUR) per US dollar—

0.885 (2015 est.)

0.7525 (2014 est.)

0.7634 (2013 est.)

0.78 (2012 est.)

0.7185 (2011 est.)

ENERGY

Electricity—production: 281 billion kWh (2012 est.)

country comparison to the world: 13

Electricity—consumption: 303.1 billion kWh (2012 est.)

country comparison to the world: 13

Electricity—exports: 2.178 billion kWh (2013 est.)

country comparison to the world: 43

Electricity—imports: 44.33 billion kWh (2013 est.)

country comparison to the world: 3

Electricity—installed generating capacity: 124.2 million kW (2012 est.)

country comparison to the world: 10

Electricity—from fossil fuels: 58.9% of total installed capacity (2012 est.)

country comparison to the world: 138

Electricity—from nuclear fuels: 0% of total installed capacity (2012 est.)

country comparison to the world: 113

Electricity—from hydroelectric plants: 11.5% of total installed capacity (2012 est.)

country comparison to the world: 111

Electricity—from other renewable sources: 23.4% of total installed capacity (2012 est.)

country comparison to the world: 11

Crude oil—production: 105,700 bbl/day (2014 est.)

country comparison to the world: 43

Crude oil—exports: 28,770 bbl/day (2013 est.)

country comparison to the world: 54

Crude oil—imports: 1.346 million bbl/day (2013 est.)

country comparison to the world: 8

Crude oil—proved reserves: 544.5 million bbl (1 January 2015 est.)

country comparison to the world: 50

Refined petroleum products—production: 1.506 million bbl/day (2013 est.)

country comparison to the world: 13

Refined petroleum products—consumption: 1.235 million bbl/day (2014 est.)

country comparison to the world: 18

Refined petroleum products—export: 461,600 bbl/day (2013 est.)

country comparison to the world: 16

Refined petroleum products—imports: 260,300 bbl/day (2013 est.)

country comparison to the world: 27

Natural gas—production: 7.149 billion cu m (2014 est.)

country comparison to the world: 47

Natural gas—consumption: 61.91 billion cu m (2014 est.)

country comparison to the world: 13

Natural gas—exports: 237 million cu m (2014 est.)

country comparison to the world: 41

Natural gas—imports: 55.76 billion cu m (2014 est.)

country comparison to the world: 6

Natural gas—proved reserves: 59.43 billion cu m (1 January 2014 est.)

country comparison to the world: 62

Carbon dioxide emissions from consumption of energy: 385.8 million Mt (2012 est.)

country comparison to the world: 18

COMMUNICATIONS

Telephones—fixed lines: *total subscriptions:* 20.57 million

subscriptions per 100 inhabitants: 33 (2014 est.)

country comparison to the world: 15

Telephones—mobile cellular: *total:* 94.2 million

subscriptions per 100 inhabitants: 153 (2014 est.)

country comparison to the world: 18

Telephone system: *general assessment:* modern, well-developed, fast; fully automated telephone, telex, and data services *domestic:* high-capacity cable and microwave radio relay trunks

international: country code—39; a series of submarine cables provide links to Asia, Middle East, Europe, North Africa, and US; satellite earth stations—3 Intelsat (with a total of 5 antennas—3 for Atlantic Ocean and 2 for Indian Ocean), 1 Inmarsat (Atlantic Ocean region), and NA Eutelsat (2011)

Broadcast media: two Italian media giants dominate—the publicly owned Radiotelevisione Italiana (RAI) with 3 national terrestrial stations and privately owned Mediaset with 3 national terrestrial stations; a large number of private stations and Sky Italia—a satellite TV network; RAI operates 3 AM/FM nationwide radio stations; some 1,300 commercial radio stations (2007)

Radio broadcast stations: AM about 100, FM about 4,600, shortwave 9 (1998)

Television broadcast stations: 358 (plus 4,728 repeaters) (1995)

Internet country code: .it

Internet hosts: 25.662 million (2012)

country comparison to the world: 4

Internet users: *total:* 37 million

percent of Population: 59.9% (2014 est.)

country comparison to the world: 18

TRANSPORTATION

Airports: 129 (2013)

country comparison to the world: 45

Airports—with paved runways: *total:* 98

over 3,047 m: 9

2,438 to 3,047 m: 31

1,524 to 2,437 m: 18

914 to 1,523 m: 29

under 914 m: 11 (2013)

Airports—with unpaved runways: *total:* 31

1,524 to 2,437 m: 1

914 to 1,523 m: 10

under 914 m: 20 (2013)

Heliports: 5 (2013)

Pipelines: gas 20,223 km; oil 1,393 km; refined products 1,574 km (2013)

Railways: *total:* 20,181.7 km

standard gauge: 18,770.1 km 1.435-m gauge (12,893.6 km electrified)

narrow gauge: 122.3 km 1.000-m gauge (122.3 km electrified); 1,289.3 km 0.950-m gauge (151.3 km electrified) (2014)

country comparison to the world: 15

Roadways: *total:* 487,700 km

paved: 487,700 km (includes 6,700 km of expressways) (2007)

country comparison to the world: 15

Waterways: 2,400 km (used for commercial traffic; of limited overall value compared to road and rail) (2012)

country comparison to the world: 36

Merchant marine: *total:* 681

by type: bulk carrier 105, cargo 42, carrier 1, chemical tanker 164, container 21, liquefied gas 28, passenger 25, passenger/cargo 154, petroleum tanker 59, refrigerated cargo 4, roll on/roll off 39, specialized tanker 9, vehicle carrier 30

foreign-owned: 90 (Denmark 4, France 2, Greece 7, Luxembourg 14, Netherlands 2, Nigeria 1, Norway 6, Singapore 1, Sweden 1, Switzerland 13, Taiwan 10, Turkey 4, UK 2, US 23)

registered in other countries: 201 (Bahamas 1, Belize 3, Cayman Islands 7, Cyprus 6, Georgia 2, Gibraltar 4, Greece 5, Liberia 47, Malta 45, Marshall Islands 1, Morocco 1, Netherlands 6, Panama 25, Portugal 12, Russia 14, Saint Vincent and the Grenadines 4, Singapore 5, Slovakia 2, Spain 1, Sweden 5, Turkey 1, UK 3, unknown 1) (2010)

country comparison to the world: 17

Ports and terminals: *major seaport(s):* Augusta, Cagliari, Genoa, Livorno, Taranto, Trieste, Venice

oil terminals: Melilli (Santa Panagia) oil terminal, Sarroch oil terminal

container port(s) (TEUs): Genoa (1,847,648), Gioia Tauro (2,264,798), La Spezia (1,307,274)

LNG terminal(s) (import): La Spezia, Panigaglia, Porto Levante

MILITARY AND SECURITY

Military branches: Italian Armed Forces: Army (Esercito Italiano, EI), Navy (Marina Militare Italiana, MMI), Italian Air Force (Aeronautica Militare Italiana, AMI), Carabinieri Corps (Arma dei Carabinieri, CC), Financial Guard (Guardia di Finanza) (2015)

Military service age and obligation: 18–25 years of age for voluntary military service; women may serve in any military branch; Italian citizenship required; 1 -year service obligation (2013)

Military expenditures: 1.1% of GDP (2014)

1.2% of GDP (2013)

1.3% of GDP (2012)

country comparison to the world: 52

TRANSNATIONAL ISSUES

Disputes—international: Italy's long coastline and developed economy entices tens of thousands of illegal immigrants from southeastern Europe and northern Africa

Refugees and internally displaced persons: refugees (country of origin): 13,357 (Eritrea); 12,213 (Somalia); 8,991 (Afghanistan); 6,293 (Nigeria); 5,764 (Pakistan); 5,552 (Mali) (2014)

stateless persons: 747 (2015)

note: 208,620 estimated refugee and migrant arrivals by sea (2015—June 2016)

Illicit drugs: important gateway for and consumer of Latin American cocaine and Southwest Asian heroin entering the European market; money laundering by organized crime and from smuggling

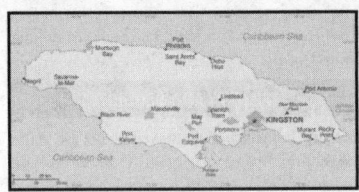

INTRODUCTION

Background: The island—discovered by Christopher COLUMBUS in 1494—was settled by the Spanish early in the 16th century. The native Taino, who had inhabited Jamaica for centuries, were gradually exterminated and replaced by African slaves. England seized the island in 1655 and established a plantation economy based on sugar, cocoa, and coffee. The abolition of slavery in 1834 freed a quarter million slaves, many of whom became small farmers. Jamaica gradually increased its independence from Britain. In 1958 it joined other British Caribbean colonies in forming the Federation of the West Indies. Jamaica gained full independence when it withdrew from the Federation in 1962. Deteriorating economic conditions during the 1970s led to recurrent violence as rival gangs affiliated with the major political parties evolved into powerful organized crime networks involved in international drug smuggling and money laundering. Violent crime, drug trafficking, and poverty pose significant challenges to the government today. Nonetheless, m any rural and resort areas remain relatively safe and contribute substantially to the economy.

GEOGRAPHY

Location: Caribbean, island in the Caribbean Sea, south of Cuba

Geographic coordinates: 18 15 N, 77 30 W

Map references: Central America and the Caribbean

Area: *total:* 10,991 sq km
land: 10,831 sq km
water: 160 sq km
country comparison to the world: 168

Area—comparative: *slightly smaller than Connecticut*

Land boundaries: 0 km

Coastline: 1,022 km

Maritime claims: measured from claimed archipelagic straight baselines
territorial sea: 12 nm
contiguous zone: 24 nm
exclusive economic zone: 200 nm
continental shelf: 200 nm or to edge of the continental margin

Climate: tropical; hot, humid; temperate interior

Terrain: mostly mountains, with narrow, discontinuous coastal plain

Elevation: *mean elevation:* 18 m

elevation extremes: *lowest point:* Caribbean Sea 0 m
highest point: Blue Mountain Peak 2,256 m

Natural resources: bauxite, gypsum, limestone

Land use: *agricultural land:* 41.4%
arable land: 11.1%
permanent crops: 9.2%
permanent pasture: 21.1%
forest: 31.1%
other: 27.5% (2011 est.)

Irrigated land: 250 sq km (2012)

Total renewable water resources: 9.4 cu km (2011)

Freshwater withdrawal (domestic/industrial/agricultural): *total:* 0.93 cu km/yr (32%/16%/52%)
per capita: 369.9 cu m/yr (2009)

Natural hazards: hurricanes (especially July to November)

Environment—current issues: heavy rates of deforestation; coastal waters polluted by industrial waste, sewage, and oil spills; damage to coral reefs; air pollution in Kingston from vehicle emissions

Environment—international agreements: party to: Biodiversity, Climate Change, Climate Change-Kyoto Protocol, Desertification, Endangered Species, Hazardous Wastes, Law of the Sea, Marine Dumping, Marine Life Conservation, Ozone Layer Protection, Ship Pollution, Wetlands
signed, but not ratified: none of the selected agreements

Geography—note: strategic location between Cayman Trench and Jamaica Channel, the main sea lanes for the Panama Canal

PEOPLE AND SOCIETY

Nationality: *noun:* Jamaican(s)
adjective: Jamaican

Ethnic groups: black 92.1%, mixed 6.1%, East Indian 0.8%, other 0.4%, unspecified 0.7% (2011 est.)

Languages: English, English patois

Religions: Protestant 64.8% (includes Seventh Day Adventist 12.0%, Pentecostal 11.0%, Other Church of God 9.2%, New Testament Church of God 7.2%, Baptist 6.7%, Church of God in Jamaica 4.8%, Church of God of Prophecy 4.5%, Anglican 2.8%, United Church 2.1%, Methodist 1.6%, Revived 1.4%, Brethren 0.9%, and Moravian 0.7%), Roman Catholic 2.2%, Jehovah's Witness 1.9%, Rastafarian 1.1%, other 6.5%, none 21.3%, unspecified 2.3% (2011 est.)

Population: 2,950,210 (July 2015 est.)
country comparison to the world: 139

Age structure: *0–14 years:* 27.97% (male 419,725/female 405,573)
15–24 years: 21.46% (male 317,873/female 315,163)
25–54 years: 37% (male 538,173/female 553,486)

55–64 years: 5.69% (male 81,281/female 86,713)
65 years and over: 7.87% (male 103,958/female 128,265) (2015 est.)

Dependency ratios: *total dependency ratio:* 48.6%
youth dependency ratio: 35%
elderly dependency ratio: 13.6%
potential support ratio: 7.4% (2015 est.)

Median Age: *total:* 25.3 years
male: 24.8 years
female: 25.8 years (2015 est.)
country comparison to the world: 151

Population growth rate: 0.68% (2015 est.)
country comparison to the world: 148

Birth rate: 18.16 births/1,000 population (2015 est.)
country comparison to the world: 102

Death rate: 6.7 deaths/1,000 population (2015 est.)
country comparison to the world: 140

Net migration rate: -4.66 migrant(s)/1,000 population (2015 est.)
country comparison to the world: 191

Urbanization: *urban population:* 54.8% of total population (2015)
rate of urbanization: 0.9% annual rate of change (2010–15 est.)

Major urban areas—population: KINGSTON (capital) 588,000 (2015)

Sex ratio: *at birth:* 1.05 male(s)/female
0–14 years: 1.04 male(s)/female
15–24 years: 1.01 male(s)/female
25–54 years: 0.97 male(s)/female
55–64 years: 0.94 male(s)/female
65 years and over: 0.81 male(s)/female
total population: 0.98 male(s)/female (2015 est.)

Mother's mean Age at first birth: 21.2
note: median Age at first birth among women 25–29 (2008 est.)

Maternal mortality rate: 89 deaths/100,000 live births (2015 est.)
country comparison to the world: 65

Infant mortality rate: *total:* 13.37 deaths/1,000 live births
male: 13.93 deaths/1,000 live births
female: 12.78 deaths/1,000 live births (2015 est.)
country comparison to the world: 112

Life expectancy at birth: *total population:* 73.55 years
male: 71.93 years
female: 75.24 years (2015 est.)
country comparison to the world: 127

Total fertility rate: 2.01 children born/woman (2015 est.)
country comparison to the world: 121

Contraceptive prevalence rate: 72.5% (2008/09)

Health expenditures: 5.9% of GDP (2013)
country comparison to the world: 114

Physicians density: 0.41 physicians/1,000 population (2008)

Hospital bed density: 1.7 beds/1,000 population (2012)

Drinking water source:
improved:
urban: 97.5% of population
rural: 89.4% of population
total: 93.8% of population
unimproved:
urban: 2.5% of population
rural: 10.6% of population
total: 6.2% of population (2015 est.)

Sanitation facility access:
improved:
urban: 79.9% of population
rural: 84.1% of population
total: 81.8% of population
unimproved:
urban: 20.1% of population
rural: 15.9% of population
total: 18.2% of population (2015 est.)

HIV/AIDS—adult prevalence rate: 1.62% (2014 est.)
country comparison to the world: 31

HIV/AIDS—people living with HIV/AIDS: 29,400 (2014 est.)
country comparison to the world: 71

HIV/AIDS—deaths: 1,300 (2014 est.)
country comparison to the world: 62

Obesity—adult prevalence rate: 26.8% (2014)
country comparison to the world: 67

Children under the age of 5 years underweight: 2.5% (2012)
country comparison to the world: 112

Education expenditures: 6% of GDP (2014)
country comparison to the world: 40

Literacy: *definition:* age 15 and over has ever attended school
total population: 88.7%
male: 84%
female: 93.1% (2015 est.)

Child labor—children Ages 5–14: *total number:* 38,516
percentage: 6% (2005 est.)

Unemployment, youth ages 15–24: *total:* 34%
male: 27.1%
female: 42.6% (2012 est.)
country comparison to the world: 20

GOVERNMENT

Country name: *conventional long form:* none
conventional short form: Jamaica
etymology: from the native Taino word "haymaca" meaning "land of wood and water" or possibly "land of springs"

Government type: parliamentary democracy (Parliament) under a constitutional monarchy; a Commonwealth realm

Capital: *name:* Kingston

Geographic coordinates: 18 00 N, 76 48 W

time difference: UTC-5 (same time as Washington, DC, during Standard Time)

Administrative divisions: 14 parishes; Clarendon, Hanover, Kingston, Manchester, Portland, Saint Andrew, Saint Ann, Saint Catherine, Saint Elizabeth, Saint James, Saint Mary, Saint Thomas, Trelawny, Westmoreland
note: for local government purposes, Kingston and Saint Andrew were amalgamated in 1923 into the present single corporate body known as the Kingston and Saint Andrew Corporation

Independence: 6 August 1962 (from the UK)

National holiday: Independence Day, 6 August(1962)

Constitution: several previous (preindependence); latest drafted 1961–62, submitted to British Parliament 24 July 1962, entered into force 6 August 1962 (at independence); amended many times, last in 2015 (2016)

Legal system: common law system based on the English model

International law organization participation: has not submitted an ICJ jurisdiction declaration; non-party state to the ICCt

Citizenship: *citizenship by birth:* yes
citizenship by descent: yes
dual citizenship recognized: yes
residency requirement for naturalization: 4 out of the previous 5 years

Suffrage: 18 years of age; universal

Executive branch: *chief of state:* Queen ELIZABETH II (since 6 February 1952); represented by Governor General Dr. Patrick L. ALLEN (since 26 February 2009)

head of government: Prime Minister Portia SIMPSON-MILLER (since 5 January 2012)
cabinet: Cabinet appointed by the governor general on the advice of the prime minister
elections/appointments: the monarchy is hereditary; governor general appointed by the monarch on the recommendation of the prime minister; following legislative elections, the leader of the majority party or majority coalition in the House of Representatives is appointed prime minister by the governor general

Legislative branch: *description:* bicameral Parliament consists of the Senate (21 seats; members appointed by the governor general on the recommendation of the prime minister and the minority party leader, 13 seats allocated to the ruling party, and 8 seats allocated to the minority party; members serve 5-year terms) and the House of Representatives (63 seats; members directly elected in single-seat constituencies by simple majority vote to serve 5-year terms)
elections: last held on 29 December 2011 (next to be held no later than December 2016)
election results: percent of vote by party—PNP 53.3%, JLP 46.6%; seats by party—PNP 41, JLP 22

Judicial branch: *highest resident court(s):* Court of Appeal (consists of president of the court and a minimum of 4 judges; Supreme Court (40 judges organized in specialized divisions); note—appeals

beyond Jamaica's highest courts are submitted to the Judicial Committee of the Privy Council (in London) rather than to the Caribbean Court of Justice (the appellate court implemented for member states of the Caribbean Community)
judge selection and term of office: chief justice of the Supreme Court and president of the Court of Appeal appointed by the governor-general on the advice of the prime minister; other judges of both courts appointed by the governor-general on the advice of the Judicial Service Commission; judges of both courts serve till age 70
subordinate courts: resident magistrate courts, district courts, and petty sessions courts

Political parties and leaders: Jamaica Labor Party or JLP [Andrew HOLNESS]
People's National Party or PNP [Portia SIMPSON-MILLER]
National Democratic Movement or NDM [Michael WILLIAMS]

Political pressure groups and leaders: New Beginnings Movementor NBM
Rastafarians

International organization participation: ACP, AOSIS, C, Caricom, CDB, CELAC, FAO, G-15, G-77, IADB, IAEA, IBRD, ICAO, ICC (NGOs), ICRM, IDA, IFAD, IFC, IFRCS, IHO, ILO, IMF, IMO, Interpol, IOC, IOM, ISO, ITSO, ITU, LAES, MIGA, NAM, OAS, OPANAL, OPCW, Petrocaribe, UN, UNCTAD, UNESCO, UNIDO, UNITAR, UNWTO, UPU, WCO, WFTU (NGOs), WHO, WIPO, WMO, WTO

Diplomatic representation in the US: *chief of mission:* Ambassador Ralph THOMAS (since 17 September 2015)
chancery: 1520 New Hampshire Avenue NW, Washington, DC 20036
telephone: [1] (202) 452-0660
FAX: [1] (202) 452-0036
consulate(s) general: Miami, New York
consulate(s): Atlanta, Boston, Chicago, Concord (MA), Houston, Los Angeles, Philadelphia (PA), Richmond (VA), San Francisco, Seattle

Diplomatic representation from the US: *chief of mission:* Ambassador Luis G. MORENO (since 13 January 2015)
embassy: 142 Old Hope Road, Kingston 6
mailing address: P.O. Box 541, Kingston 5
telephone: [1] (876) 702-6000
FAX: [1] (876) 702-6348

Flag description: diagonal yellow cross divides the flag into four triangles—green (top and bottom) and black (hoist side and fly side); green represents hope, vegetation, and agriculture, black reflects hardships overcome and to be faced, and yellow recalls golden sunshine and the island's natural resources

National symbol(s): green-and-black streamertail (bird), Guaiacum officinale (Guaiacwood); national colors: green, yellow, black

National anthem: *name:* "Jamaica, Land We Love"
lyrics/music: Hugh Braham SHERLOCK/Robert Charles LIGHTBOURNE
note: adopted 1962

435

ECONOMY

Economy—overview: The Jamaican economy is heavily dependent on services, which accounts for more than 70% of GDP. The country continues to derive most of its foreign exchange from tourism, remittances, and bauxite/alumina. Remittances and tourism each account for 30% of GDP, while bauxite/alumina exports make up roughly 5% of GDP. The bauxite/alumina sector was most affected by the global downturn while the tourism industry and remittance flow remained resilient.

Jamaica's economy faces many challenges to growth: high crime and corruption, large-scale unemployment and underemployment, and a debt-to-GDP ratio of about 130%. The attendant debt servicing cost consumes a large portion of the government's budget, limiting its ability to fund the critical infrastructure and social programs required to drive growth. Jamaica's economic growth rate in the recent past has been stagnant, averaging less than 1% per year for over 20 years.

Jamaica's onerous public debt burden is largely the result of government bailouts to ailing sectors of the economy, most notably the financial sector. In early 2010, the Jamaican Government initiated the Jamaica Debt Exchange to retire high-priced domestic bonds and reduce annual debt servicing. Despite these efforts, debt continued to be a serious concern, forcing the government to negotiate and sign a new IMF agreement in May 2013 to gain access to approximately $1 billion in additional funds. As a precursor, the government instigated a second National Debt Exchange in 2012. The IMF deal requires the government to reform its tax system, eliminate discretionary tax exemptions and waivers, and achieve an annual surplus of 7.5%, excluding debt payments, to reduce its debt below 100% of GDP by 2020. The SIMPSON-MILLER administration now faces the difficult prospect of having to achieve fiscal discipline to maintain debt payments while simultaneously attacking a serious crime problem that is hampering economic growth. High unemployment exacerbates the crime problem, including gang violence, which is fueled by the drug trade.

GDP (purchasing power parity): $24.65 billion (2015 est.)
$24.38 billion (2014 est.)
$24.25 billion (2013 est.)
note: data are in 2015 US dollars
country comparison to the world: 137

GDP (official exchange rate): $13.92 billion (2015 est.)

GDP—real growth rate: 1.1% (2015 est.)
0.5% (2014 est.) 0.2% (2013 est.)
country comparison to the world: 167

GDP—per capita (PPP): $8,800 (2015 est.)
$8,700 (2014 est.)
$8,700 (2013 est.)
note: data are in 2015 US dollars
country comparison to the world: 140

Gross national saving: 12.4% of GDP (2015 est.)
13% of GDP (2014 est.)
12% of GDP (2013 est.)

country comparison to the world: 136

GDP—composition, by end use:
household consumption: 84.8%
government consumption: 14.8%
investment in fixed capital: 22.2%
investment in inventories: 0.4%
exports of goods and services: 32.2%
imports of goods and services: -54.4% (2015 est.)

GDP—composition, by sector of origin:
agriculture: 7%
industry: 21.4%
services: 71.6% (2015 est.)

Agriculture—products: sugarcane, bananas, coffee, citrus, yams, ackees, vegetables; poultry, goats, milk; shellfish

Industries: tourism, bauxite/alumina, agricultural-processing, light manufactures, rum, cement, metal, paper, chemical products, telecommunications

Industrial production growth rate: 2% (2015 est.)
country comparison to the world: 116

Labor force: 1.308 million (2015 est.)
country comparison to the world: 135

Labor force—by occupation: agriculture: 17%
industry:19%
services: 64% (2006)

Unemployment rate: 14% (2015 est.)
14.2% (2014 est.)
country comparison to the world: 149

Population below poverty line: 16.5% (2009 est.)

Household income or consumption by percentage share: lowest: 10%: 2.1%
highest: 10%: 35.8% (2004)

Distribution of family income—Gini index: 45.5 (2004)
37.9 (2000)
country comparison to the world: 41

Budget: revenues: $3.704 billion
expenditures: $3.818 billion (2015 est.)
Taxes and other revenues: 26.8% of GDP (2015 est.)
country comparison to the world: 105

Budget surplus (+) or deficit (-): -0.8% of GDP (2015 est.)
country comparison to the world: 50

Public debt: 122.5% of GDP (2015 est.)
132.8% of GDP (2014 est.)
country comparison to the world: 8

Fiscal year: 1 April—31 March

Inflation rate (consumer prices): 4.7% (2015 est.)
8.3% (2014 est.)
country comparison to the world: 169

Central bank discount rate: 2% (31 December 2010)
country comparison to the world: 115

Commercial bank prime lending rate: 16.5% (31 December 2015 est.)
17.22% (31 December 2014 est.)
country comparison to the world: 28

Stock of narrow money: $3.328 billion (31 December 2015 est.)
$3.156 billion (31 December 2014 est.)
country comparison to the world: 112

Stock of broad money: $7.847 billion (31 December 2015 est.)
$7.519 billion (31 December 2014 est.)
country comparison to the world: 116

Stock of domestic credit: $7.397 billion (31 December 2015 est.)
$7.078 billion (31 December 2014 est.)
country comparison to the world: 111

Market value of publicly traded shares: $6.39 billion (31 December 2012 est.)
$7.223 billion (31 December 2011)
$6.626 billion (31 December 2010 est.)
country comparison to the world: 83

Current account balance: -$598 million (2015 est.)
-$980 million (2014 est.)
country comparison to the world: 107

Exports: $1.192 billion (2015 est.)
$1.482 billion (2014 est.)
country comparison to the world: 154

Exports—commodities: alumina, bauxite, sugar, rum, coffee, yams, beverages, chemicals, apparel, mineral fuels

Exports—partners: US 24.4%, Canada 16.5%, Russia 9.3%, Netherlands 8.9%, Iceland 7.2%, UK 6.5% (2015)

Imports: $4.056 billion (2015 est.)
$5.2 billion (2014 est.)
country comparison to the world: 133

Imports—commodities: food and other consumer goods, industrial supplies, fuel, parts and accessories of capital goods, machinery and transport equipment, construction materials

Imports—partners: US 32.6%, Venezuela 12.4%, China 12%, Trinidad and Tobago 11.1% (2015)

Reserves of foreign exchange and gold: $2.7 billion (31 December 2015 est.)
$2.473 billion (31 December 2014 est.)
country comparison to the world: 109

Debt—external: $17.3 billion (31 December 2014 est.)
$16.57 billion (31 December 2013 est.)
country comparison to the world: 92

Exchange rates: Jamaican dollars (JMD) per US dollar—
116.8 (2015 est.)
110.935 (2014 est.)
110.935 (2013 est.)
88.75 (2012 est.)
85.893 (2011 est.)

ENERGY

Electricity—production: 4.041 billion kWh (2012 est.)
country comparison to the world: 124

Electricity—consumption: 3.008 billion kWh (2012 est.)
country comparison to the world: 134

Electricity—exports: 0 kWh (2013 est.)
country comparison to the world: 155

Electricity—imports: 0 kWh (2013 est.)
country comparison to the world: 165

Electricity—installed generating capacity: 917,500 kW (2012 est.)
country comparison to the world: 125

Electricity—from fossil fuels: 91.7% of total installed capacity (2012 est.)
country comparison to the world: 72

Electricity—from nuclear fuels: 0% of total installed capacity (2012 est.)
country comparison to the world: 116

Electricity—from hydroelectric plants: 2.5% of total installed capacity (2012 est.)
country comparison to the world: 134

Electricity—from other renewable sources: 5.9% of total installed capacity (2012 est.)
country comparison to the world: 54

Crude oil—production: 0 bbl/day (2014 est.)
country comparison to the world: 150

Crude oil—exports: 0 bbl/day (2012 est.)
country comparison to the world: 142

Crude oil—imports: 24,160 bbl/day (2012 est.)
country comparison to the world: 67

Crude oil—proved reserves: 0 bbl (1 January 2015 est.)
country comparison to the world: 149

Refined petroleum products— production: 24,640 bbl/day (2012 est.)
country comparison to the world: 91

Refined petroleum products—consumption: 53,000 bbl/day (2013 est.)
country comparison to the world: 96

Refined petroleum products—exports: 5,480 bbl/day (2012 est.)
country comparison to the world: 93

Refined petroleum products—imports: 32,140 bbl/day (2012 est.)
country comparison to the world: 95

Natural gas—production: 0 cu m (2013 est.)
country comparison to the world: 204

Natural gas—consumption: 0 cu m (2013 est.)
country comparison to the world: 157

Natural gas—exports: 0 cu m (2013 est.)
country comparison to the world: 123

Natural gas—imports: 0 cu m (2013 est.)
country comparison to the world: 214

Natural gas—proved reserves: 0 cu m (1 January 2014 est.)
country comparison to the world: 153

Carbon dioxide emissions from consumption of energy: 12.75 million Mt (2012 est.)
country comparison to the world: 95

COMMUNICATIONS

Telephones—fixed lines: *total subscriptions:* 250,000
subscriptions per 100 inhabitants: 9 (2014 est.)
country comparison to the world: 122

Telephones—mobile cellular: *total:* 2.9 million
subscriptions per 100 inhabitants: 98 (2014 est.)
country comparison to the world: 140

Telephone system: *general assessment:* fully automatic domestic telephone network
domestic: the 1999 agreement to open the market for telecommunications services resulted in rapid growth in mobile-cellular telephone usage while the number of fixed lines in use has declined; combined mobile-cellular teledensity exceeded 110 per 100 persons in 2011
international: country code—1–876; the Fibralink submarine cable network provides enhanced delivery of business and broadband traffic and is linked to the Americas Region Caribbean Ring System (ARCOS-1) submarine cable in the Dominican Republic; the link to ARCOS-1 provides seamless connectivity to US, parts of the Caribbean, Central America, and South America; the ALBA-1 fiber-optic submarine cable links Jamaica, Cuba, and Venezuela; satellite earth stations—2 Intelsat (Atlantic Ocean) (2010)

Broadcast media: 3 free-to-air TV stations, subscription cable services, and roughly 30 radio stations (2013)
Radio broadcast stations: AM 4, FM 24, shortwave 0 (2008)
Television broadcast stations: 7 (1997)

Internet country code: .jm

Internet hosts: 3,906 (2012)
country comparison to the world: 149

Internet users: *total:* 1.5 million
percent of Population: 49.8% (2014 est.)
country comparison to the world: 109

TRANSPORTATION

Airports: 28 (2013)
country comparison to the world: 123

Airports—with paved runways: *total:* 11
2,438 to 3,047 m: 2
914 to 1,523 m: 4
under 914 m: 5 (2013)

Airports—with unpaved runways: *total:* 17
914 to 1,523 m: 1
under 914 m: 16 (2013)

Roadways: *total:* 22,121 km (includes 44 km of expressways)
paved: 16,148 km
unpaved: 5,973 km (2011)
country comparison to the world: 104

Merchant marine: *total:* 14
by type: bulk carrier 4, cargo 5, container 4, roll on/roll off 1
foreign-owned: 14 (Denmark 1, Germany 10, Greece 3) (2010)
country comparison to the world: 103

Ports and terminals: *major seaport(s):* Discovery Bay (Port Rhoades), Kingston, Montego Bay, Port Antonio, Port Esquivel, Port Kaiser, Rocky Point
container port(s) (TEUs): Kingston (1,724,928)

MILITARY AND SECURITY

Military branches: *Jamaica Defense Force:* Ground Forces, Coast Guard, Air Wing (2010)

Military service age and obligation: 17 1/2 is the legal minimum age for voluntary military service; no conscription (2012)

Military expenditures: 0.86% of GDP (2012)
0.92% of GDP (2011)
0.86% of GDP (2010)
country comparison to the world: 111

TRANSNATIONAL ISSUES

Disputes—international: none

Trafficking in persons: *current situation:* Jamaica is a source and destination country for children and adults subjected to sex trafficking and forced labor; sex trafficking of children and adults occurs on the street, in night clubs, bars, massage parlors, and private homes; child sex tourism is a problem in resort areas; Jamaicans have been subjected to sexual exploitation or forced labor in the Caribbean, Canada, the US, and the UK, while foreigners have endured conditions of forced labor in Jamaica or aboard foreign-flagged fishing vessels operating in Jamaican waters; a high number of Jamaican children are reported missing

tier rating: Tier 2 Watch List—Jamaica does not fully comply with the minimum standards for the elimination of trafficking; however, it is making significant efforts to do so; in 2014, the government made significant efforts to raise public awareness of human trafficking, and named a national trafficking-in-persons rapporteur—the first in the region; authorities initiated more new trafficking investigations than in 2013 and concluded a trafficking case in the Supreme Court, but chronic delays impeded prosecutions and no offenders were convicted for the sixth consecutive year; more adult trafficking victims were identified than in previous years, but only one child victim was identified, which was exceptionally low relative to the number of vulnerable children (2015)

Illicit drugs: transshipment point for cocaine from South America to North America and Europe; illicit cultivation and consumption of cannabis; government has an active manual cannabis eradication program; corruption is a major concern; substantial money-laundering activity; Colombian narcotics traffickers favor Jamaica for illicit financial transactions

437

JAN MAYEN

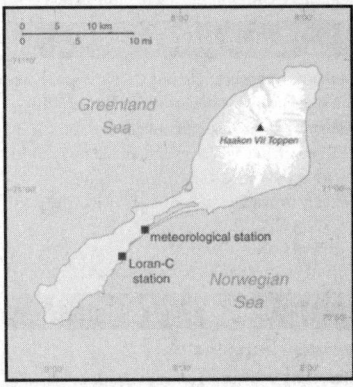

INTRODUCTION

Background: This desolate, arctic, mountainous island was named after a Dutch whaling captain who indisputably discovered it in 1614 (earlier claims are inconclusive). Visited only occasionally by seal hunters and trappers over the following centuries, the island came under Norwegian sovereignty in 1929. The long dormant Beerenberg volcano, the northernmost active volcano on earth, resumed activity in 1970 and the most recent eruption occurred in 1985.

GEOGRAPHY

Location: northern Europe, island between the Greenland Sea and the norwegian Sea, northeast of Iceland

Geographic coordinates: 71 00 N, 8 00 W

Map references: Arctic Region

Area: *total:* 377 sq km
land: 377 sq km
water: 0 sq km
country comparison to the world: 205

Area—comparative: slightly more than twice the size of Washington, DC

Land boundaries: 0 km

Coastline: 124.1 km

Maritime claims: *territorial sea:* 4 nm

contiguous zone: 10 nm
exclusive economic zone: 200 nm
continental shelf: 200-m depth or to the depth of exploitation

Climate: arctic maritime with frequent storms and persistent fog

Terrain: volcanic island, partly covered by glaciers

Elevation: *mean elevation:* NA

elevation extremes: *lowest point:* Norwegian Sea 0 m

highest point: Haakon VII Toppen on Beerenberg 2,277 m

note: Beerenberg volcano has numerous peaks; the highest point on the volcano rim is named Haakon VII Toppen, after Norway's first king following the reestablishment of Norwegian independence in 1905

Natural resources: none

Land use: *agricultural land:* 0%
arable land: 0%
permanent crops: 0%
permanent pasture: 0%
forest: 0%
other: 100% (2011 est.)

Irrigated land: 0 sq km (2012)

Natural hazards: dominated by the volcano Beerenberg

volcanism: Beerenberg (elev. 2,227 m) is norway's only active volcano; volcanic activity resumed in 1970; the most recent eruption occurred in 1985

Environment—current issues: NA

Geography—note: barren volcanic island with some moss and grass

PEOPLE AND SOCIETY

Population: no indigenous inhabitants
note: personnel operate the Long Range Navigation (Loran-C) base and the weather and coastal services radio station

GOVERNMENT

Country name: *conventional long form:* none
conventional short form: Jan Mayen

etymology: named after Dutch Captain Jan Jacobszoon MAY, one of the first explorers to reach the island in 1614

Dependency status: territory of Norway; since August 1994, administered from Oslo through the county governor (fylkesmann) of nordland; however, authority has been delegated to a station commander of the norwegian Defense Communication Service; in 2010 Norway designated the majority of Jan Mayen as a nature reserve

Legal system: the laws of norway, where applicable, apply

Flag description: the flag of norway is used

ECONOMY

Economy—overview: Jan Mayen is a volcanic island with no exploitable natural resources, although surrounding waters contain substantial fish stocks and potential untapped petroleum resources. Economic activity is limited to providing services for employees of norway's radio and meteorological stations on the island.

COMMUNICATIONS

Broad cast media: a coastal radio station has been remotely operated since 1994 (2008)
Radio broad cast stations: NA; note—there is one radio and meteorological station (1998)

TRANSPORTATION

Airports: 1 (2013)
country comparison to the world: 222

Airports—with unpaved runways: *total:* 1
1,524 to 2,437 m: 1 (2013)

Ports and terminals: none; offshore anchorage only

MILITARY AND SECURITY

Military—note: defense is the responsibility of Norway

TRANSNATIONAL ISSUES

Disputes—international: none

JAPAN

INTRODUCTION

Background: In 1603, after decades of civil warfare, the Tokugawa shogunate (a military-led, dynastic government) ushered in A long period of relative political stability and isolation from foreign influence. For more than two centuries this policy enabled Japan to enjoy a flowering of its indigenous culture. Japan opened its ports after signing the Treaty of Kanagawa with the US in 1854 and began to intensively modernize and industrialize. During the late 19th and early 20th centuries, Japan became a regional power that was able to defeat the forces of both China and Russia. It occupied Korea, Formosa (Taiwan), and southern Sakhalin Island. In 1931–32 Japan occupied Manchuria, and in 1937 it launched a full-scale invasion of China. Japan attacked US forces in 1941—triggering America's entry into World War II—and soon occupied much of East and Southeast Asia. After its defeat in World War II, Japan recovered to become an economic power and an ally of the US. While the emperor retains his throne as a symbol of national unity, elected politicians hold actual decision-making power.

Following three decades of unprecedented growth, Japan's economy experienced a major slowdown starting in the 1990s, but the country remains an economic power. In March 2011, Japan's strongest-ever earthquake, and an accompanying tsunami, devastated the northeast part of Honshu island, killed thousands, and damaged several nuclear power plants. The catastrophe hobbled the country's economy and its energy infrastructure, and tested its ability to deal with humanitarian disasters. Prime Minister Shinzo ABE was reelected to office in December 2012, and has since embarked on ambitious economic and security reforms to improve Japan's economy and bolster the country's international standing.

GEOGRAPHY

Location: Eastern Asia, island chain between the North Pacific Ocean and the Sea of Japan, east of the Korean Peninsula

Geographic coordinates: 36 00 N, 138 00 E

Map references: Asia

Area: *total:* 377,915 sq km

land: 364,485 sq km

water: 13,430 sq km

note: includes Bonin Islands (Ogasawara-gunto), Daito-shoto, Minami-jima, Okino-tori-shima, Ryukyu Islands (Nansei-shoto), and Volcano Islands (Kazan-retto)

country comparison to the world: 62

Area—comparative: slightly smaller than California

Land boundaries: 0 km

Coastline: 29,751 km

Maritime claims: *territorial sea:* 12 nm; between 3 nm and 12 nm in the international straits—La Perouse or Soya, Tsugaru, Osumi, and Eastern and Western Channels of the Korea or Tsushima Strait

contiguous zone: 24 nm

exclusive economic zone: 200 nm

Climate: varies from tropical in south to cool temperate in north

Terrain: mostly rugged and mountainous

Elevation: *mean elevation:* 438 m

elevation extremes: *lowest point:* Hachiro-gata -4 m

highest point: Mount Fuji 3,776 m

Natural resources: negligible mineral resources, fish

note: with virtually no natural energy resources, Japan is the world's largest importer of coal and liquefied natural gas, as well as the second largest importer of oil

Land use: *agricultural land:* 12.5%

arable land: 11.7%

permanent crops: 0.8%

permanent pasture: 0%

forest: 68.5%

other: 19% (2011 est.)

Irrigated land: 24,690 sq km (2012)

Total renewable water resources: 430 cu km (2011)

Freshwater withdrawal (domestic/industrial/agricultural): *total:* 90.04 cu km/yr (20%/18%/62%)

per capita: 714.3 cu m/yr (2007)

Natural hazards: many dormant and some active volcanoes; about 1,500 seismic occurrences (mostly tremors but occasional severe earthquakes) every year; tsunamis; typhoons

volcanism: both Unzen (elev. 1,500 m) and Sakura-jima (elev. 1,117 m), which lies near the densely populated city of Kagoshima, have been deemed Decade Volcanoes by the International Association of Volcanology and Chemistry of the Earth's Interior, worthy of study due to their explosive history and close proximity to human populations; other notable historically active volcanoes include Asama, Honshu Island's most active volcano, Aso, Bandai, Fuji, Iwo-Jima, Kikai, Kirishima, Komaga-take, Oshima, Suwanosejima, Tokachi, Yake-dake, and Usu

Environment—current issues: air pollution from power plant emissions results in acid rain; acidification of lakes and reservoirs degrading water quality and threatening aquatic life; Japan is one of the largest consumers of fish and tropical timber, contributing to the depletion of these resources in asia and elsewhere; following the 2011 Fukushima nuclear disaster, Japan originally planned to phase out nuclear power, but it has now implemented a new policy of seeking to restart nuclear power plants that meet strict new safety standards

Environment—international agreements: *party to:* Antarctic-Environmental Protocol, Antarctic-Marine Living Resources, Antarctic Seals, Antarctic Treaty, Biodiversity, Climate Change, Climate Change-Kyoto Protocol, Desertification, Endangered Species, Environmental Modification, Hazardous Wastes, Law of the Sea, Marine Dumping, Ozone Layer Protection, Ship Pollution, Tropical Timber 83, Tropical Timber 94, Wetlands, Whaling

signed, but not ratified: none of the selected agreements

Geography—note: strategic location in northeast Asia; composed of four main islands—from north Hokkaido, Honshu, Shikoku, and Kyushu (the "Home Islands")—and 6,848 smaller islands and islets

PEOPLE AND SOCIETY

Nationality: *noun:* Japanese (singular and plural)

adjective: Japanese

Ethnic groups: Japanese 98.5%, Koreans 0.5%, Chinese 0.4%, other 0.6%

note: up to 230,000 Brazilians of Japanese origin migrated to Japan in the 1990s to work in industries; some have returned to Brazil (2004)

Languages: Japanese

Religions: Shintoism 79.2%, Buddhism 66.8%, Christianity 1.5%, other 7.1%

note: total adherents exceeds 100% because many people practice both Shintoism and Buddhism (2012 est.)

Population: 126,919,659 (July 2015 est.)

country comparison to the world: 11

Age structure: *0–14 years:* 13.11% (male 8,582,648/female 8,051,706)

15–24 years: 9.68% (male 6,436,948/female 5,846,808)

25–54 years: 37.87% (male 23,764,421/female 24,297,773)

55–64 years: 12.76% (male 8,104,835/female 8,084,317)

65 years and over: 26.59% (male 14,693,811/female 19,056,392) (2015 est.)

Dependency ratios: *total dependency ratio:* 64.5%

youth dependency ratio: 21.1%

elderly dependency ratio: 43.3%

potential support ratio: 2.3% (2015 est.)

Median Age: *total:* 46.5 years

male: 45.2 years

female: 47.9 years (2015 est.)

country comparison to the world: 2

Population growth rate: -0.16% (2015 est.)

country comparison to the world: 212

Birth rate: 7.93 births/1,000 population (2015 est.)

country comparison to the world: 222

Death rate: 9.51 deaths/1,000 population (2015 est.)

country comparison to the world: 54

Net migration rate: 0 migrant(s)/1,000 population (2015 est.)

country comparison to the world: 93

Urbanization: *urban population:* 93.5% of total population (2015)

rate of urbanization: 0.56% annual rate of change (2010–15 est.)

Major urban areas—population: TOKYO (capital) 38.001 million; Osaka-Kobe 20.238 million; Nagoya 9.406 million; Kitakyushu-Fukuoka 5.51 million; Shizuoka-Hamamatsu 3.369 million; Sapporo 2.571 million (2015)

Sex ratio: *at birth:* 1.06 male(s)/female

0–14 years: 1.07 male(s)/female

15–24 years: 1.1 male(s)/female

25–54 years: 0.98 male(s)/female

55–64 years: 1 male(s)/female

65 years and over: 0.77 male(s)/female

total population: 0.94 male(s)/female (2015 est.)

Mother's mean Age at first birth: 30.3 (2012 est.)

Maternal mortality rate: 5 deaths/100,000 live births (2015 est.)

country comparison to the world: 176

Infant mortality rate: *total:* 2.08 deaths/1,000 live births

male: 2.31 deaths/1,000 live births

female: 1.84 deaths/1,000 live births (2015 est.)

439

country comparison to the world: 222

Life expectancy at birth: *total population:* 84.74 years

male: 81.4 years

female: 88.26 years (2015 est.)

country comparison to the world: 2

Total fertility rate: 1.4 children born/woman (2015 est.)

country comparison to the world: 211

Contraceptive prevalence rate: 54.3%

note: percent of women aged 20–49 (2005)

Health expenditures: 10.3% of GDP (2013)

country comparison to the world: 22

Physicians density: 2.3 physicians/1,000 population (2010)

Hospital bed density: 13.7 beds/1,000 population (2009)

Drinking water source:

improved:

urban: 100% of population

rural: 100% of population

total: 100% of population

unimproved:

urban: 0% of population

rural: 0% of population

total: 0% of population (2015 est.)

Sanitation facility access:

improved:

urban: 100% of population

rural: 100% of population

total: 100% of population

unimproved:

urban: 0% of population

rural: 0% of population

total: 0% of population (2015 est.)

HIV/AIDS—adult prevalence rate: NA

HIV/AIDS—people living with HIV/AIDS: NA

HIV/AIDS—deaths: NA

Obesity—adult prevalence rate: 3.5% (2014)

country comparison to the world: 157

Children under the age of 5 years underweight: 3.4% (2010)

Education expenditures: 3.8% of GDP (2014)

country comparison to the world: 115

School life expectancy (primary to tertiary education): *total:* 15 years

male: 15 years

female: 15 years (2013)

Unemployment, youth ages 15–24: *total:* 6.9%

male: 7.6%

female: 6.2% (2013 est.)

country comparison to the world: 114

GOVERNMENT

Country name: *conventional long form:* none

conventional short form: Japan

local long form: Nihon-koku/Nippon-koku

local short form: Nihon/Nippon

etymology: the English word for Japan comes via the Chinese name for the country "Cipangu"; both Nihon and Nippon mean "where the sun originates" and are frequently translated as "Land of the rising sun"

Government type: parliamentary constitutional monarchy

Capital: *name:* Tokyo

Geographic coordinates: 35 41 N, 139 45 E

time difference: UTC+9 (14 hours ahead of Washington, DC, during Standard Time)

Administrative divisions: 47 prefectures; Aichi, Akita, Aomori, Chiba, Ehime, Fukui, Fukuoka, Fukushima, Gifu, Gunma, Hiroshima, Hokkaido, Hyogo, Ibaraki, Ishikawa, Iwate, Kagawa, Kagoshima, Kanagawa, Kochi, Kumamoto, Kyoto, Mie, Miyagi, Miyazaki, Nagano, Nagasaki, Nara, Niigata, Oita, Okayama, Okinawa, Osaka, Saga, Saitama, Shiga, Shimane, Shizuoka, Tochigi, Tokushima, Tokyo, Tottori, Toyama, Wakayama, Yamagata, Yamaguchi, Yamanashi

Independence: 3 May 1947 (current constitution adopted as amendment to Meiji Constitution); notable earlier dates: 660 B.C. (traditional date of the founding of the nation by Emperor JIMMU); 29 November 1890 (Meiji Constitution provides for constitution al monarchy)

National holiday: Birth day of Emperor AKIHITO, 23 December (1933)

Constitution: previous 1890; latest approved 6 October 1946, adopted 3 November 1946, effective 3 May 1947; note -the constitution has not been amended since its enactment in 1947 (2016)

Legal system: civil law system based on German model; system also reflects Anglo-American influence and Japanese traditions; judicial review of legislative acts in the Supreme Court

International law organization participation: accepts compu lsory ICJ jurisdiction with reservations; accepts ICCt jurisdiction

Citizenship: *citizenship by birth:* no

citizenship by descent only: at least one parent must be a citizen of Japan

dual citizenship recognized: no

residency requirement for naturalization: 5 years

Suffrage: 20 years of age; u niversal

Executive branch: *chief of state:* Emperor AKIHITO (since 7 January 1989)

head of government: *Prime Minister Shinzo ABE (since 26 December 2012); Deputy Prime Minister Taro ASO (since 26 December 2012)*

cabinet: Cabinet appointed by the prime minister

elections/appointments: the monarchy is hereditary; the leader of the majority party or majority coalition in the House of Representatives usually becomes prime minister

Legislative branch: *description:* bicameral Diet or Kokkai consists of the House of Councillors or Sangi-in (242 seats; 146 members directly elected by majority vote and 96 directly elected in multiseat constituencies by proportional representation vote; members serve 6-year terms with one-half of the membership renewed every 3 years) and the House of Representatives or Shugi-in (475 seats; 295 members directly elected in single-seat constituencies by simple majority vote and 180 directly elected in multi-seat constituencies by proportional representation vote; members serve maximum 4-year terms with one-half of the membership renewed every 2 years)

elections: House of Councillors—last held on 10 July 2016 (next to be held in July 2019); House of

Representatives—last held on 14 December 2014 (next to be held by 15 December 2016)

election results: House of Councillors—percent of vote by party—NA; seats by party—LPD 121, DPJ 60, New Komeito 25, Your Party NA, JCP 14, JRP NA, SDP NA, others NA, independents 2 House of Representatives—percent of vote by party—LDP 61.26%, DPJ 15.37%, JIP 8.63%, New Komeito 7.37%, JCP 4.42%, PFG.42%, SDP.42%, PLP.42%, independents 1.68%; seats by party—LDP 291, DPJ 73, JIP 41, New Komeito 35, JCP 21, PFG 2, SDP 2, PLP 2, independents 8

note: the 2013 amended electoral law—effective for the December 2016 election—reduced to 475 the number of seats in the House of Representatives

Judicial branch: *highest court(s):* Supreme Court or Saiko saibansho (consists of the chief justice and 14 associate justices); note—the Supreme Court has jurisdiction in constitutional issues

judge selection and term of office: Supreme Court chief justice designated by the Cabinet and appointed by the monarch; associate justices appointed by the Cabinet and confirmed by the monarch; all justices are reviewed in a popular referendum at the first general election of the House of Representatives following each judge's appointment and every 10 years afterward

subordinate courts: 8 High Courts (Koto-saibansho), each with a Family Court (Katei-saiban-sho); 50 District Courts (Chiho saibansho), with 203 additional branches; 438 Summary Courts (Kani saibansho)

Political parties and leaders: Democratic Party of Japan or DPJ [Banri KAIEDA]

Japan Communist Party or JCP [Kazuo SHII]

Japan Innovation Party or JIP [Kenji EDA]

Liberal Democratic Party or LDP [Shinzo ABE]

New Komeito or NK [Natsuo YAMAGUCHI]

Party for Future Generations or PFG [Shintaro ISHIHARA]

People's Life Party or PLP [Ichiro OZAWA]

Social Democratic Party or SDP [Tadatomo YOSHIDA]

Political pressure groups and leaders: *other:* business groups; trade unions

International organization participation: ADB, AFDB (nonregional member), APEC, Arctic Council (observer), ARF, ASEAN (dialogue partner), Australia Group, BIS, CD, CE (observer), CERN (observer), CICA (observer), CP, CPLP (associate), EAS, EBRD, EITI (implementing country), FAO, FATF, G-5, G-7, G-8, G-10, G-20, IADB, IAEA, IBRD, ICAO, ICC (national committees), ICCt, ICRM, IDA, IEA, IFAD, IFC, IFRCS, IGAD (partners), IHO, ILO, IMF, IMO, IMSO, Interpol, IOC, IOM, IPU, ISO, ITSO, ITU, ITUC (NGOs), LAIA (observer), MIGA, NEA, NSG, OAS (observer), OECD, OPCW, OSCE (partner), Pacific Alliance (observer), Paris Club, PCA, PIF (partner), SAARC (observer), SELEC (observer), SICA (observer), UN, UNCTAD, UNESCO, UNHCR, UNIDO, UNMISS, UNRWA, UNWTO, UPU, WCO, WFTU (NGOs), WHO, WIPO, WMO, WTO, ZC

Diplomatic representation in the US: *chief of mission:* Ambassador Kenichiro SASAE (since 19 november 2012)

chancery: 2520 Massachusetts Avenue NW, Washington, DC 20008

telephone: [1] (202) 238-6700

FAX: [1] (202) 328-2187

consulate(s) general: Anchorage (AK), Atlanta, Boston, Chicago, Dallas, Denver (CO), Detroit (MI), Honolulu (HI), Houston, Las Vegas (NV), Los Angeles, Miami, Nashville (TN), New Orleans, New York, Oklahoma City (OK), Orlando (FL), Philadelphia (PA), Phoenix (AZ), Portland (OR), San Francisco, Seattle, Saipan (Puerto Rico), Tamuning (Guam)

Diplomatic representation from the US: *chief of mission:* Ambassador Caroline Bouvier KENNEDY (since 19 November 2013)

embassy: 1–10–5 Akasaka, Minato-ku, Tokyo 107–8420

mailing address: Unit 9800, Box 300, APO AP 96303–0300

telephone: [81] (03) 3224-5000

FAX: [81] (03) 3505-1862

consulate(s) general: Naha (Okinawa), Osaka-Kobe, Sapporo

consulate(s): Fukuoka, Nagoya

Flag description: white with a large red disk (representing the sun without rays) in the center

National symbol(s): red sun disc, chrysanthemum; national colors: red, white

National anthem: *name:* "Kimigayo" (The Emperor"s Reign)

lyrics/music: unknown/Hiromori HAYASHI

note: adopted 1999; unofficial national anthem since 1883; oldest anthem lyrics in the world, dating to the 10th century or earlier; there is some opposition to the anthem because of its association with militarism and worship of the emperor

ECONOMY

Economy—overview: Over the past 70 years, government-industry cooperation, a strong work ethic, mastery of high technology, and a comparatively small defense allocation (1% of GDP) have helped Japan develop an advanced economy. Two notable characteristics of the post-World War II economy were the close interlocking structures of manufacturers, suppliers, and distributors, known as keiretsu, and the guarantee of lifetime employment for a substantial portion of the urban labor force. Both features are now eroding under the dual pressures of global competition and domestic demographic change. Scarce in many natural resources, Japan has long been dependent on imported raw materials. Since the complete shutdown of Japan's nuclear reactors after the earthquake and tsunami disaster in 2011, Japan's industrial sector has become even more dependent than before on imported fossil fuels. A small agricultural sector is highly subsidized and protected, with crop yields among the highest in the world. While self-sufficient in rice production, Japan imports about 60% of its food on a caloric basis. For three decades, overall real economic growth had been

impressive—a 10% average in the 1960s, 5% in the 1970s, and 4% in the 1980s. Growth slowed markedly in the 1990s, averaging just 1.7%, largely because of the aftereffects of inefficient investment and an asset price bubble in the late 1980s, after which it took a considerable time for firms to reduce excess debt, capital, and labor. Modest economic growth continued after 2000, but the economy has fallen into recession four times since 2008. Government stimulus spending helped the economy recover in late 2009 and 2010, but the economy contracted again in 2011 as the massive 9.0 magnitude earthquake and the ensuing tsunami in March of that year disrupted economic activity. The economy has largely recovered in the five years since the disaster, although output in the affected areas continues to lag behind the national average. Japan enjoyed a sharp uptick in growth in 2013 on the basis of Prime Minister Shinzo ABE's "Three Arrows" economic revitalization agenda—dubbed "Abenomics"—of monetary easing, "flexible" fiscal policy, and structural reform. In 2015, ABE revised his "Three Arrows" to raise nominal GDP by 20% to 600 trillion yen by 2020, stem population decline by raising the fertility rate, and provide more support for workers with children and aging relatives. ABE's government has replaced the preceding administration's plan to phase out nuclear power with a new policy of seeking to restart nuclear power plants that meet strict new safety standards, and emphasizing nuclear energy's importance as a base-load electricity source. Japan successfully restarted two nuclear reactors at the Sendai Nuclear Power Plant in Kagoshima prefecture. In october 2015, Japan and 11 trading partners reached agreement on the TransPacific Partnership, a pact that promises to open Japan's economy to increased foreign competition and create new export opportunities for Japanese businesses.

Measured on a purchasing power parity (PPP) basis that adjusts for price differences, Japan in 2015 stood as the fourth-largest economy in the world after first-place China, which surpassed Japan in 2001, and third-place India, which edged out Japan in 2012. While seeking to stimulate and reform the economy, the government must also devise a strategy for reining in Japan's huge government debt, which amounts to more than 230% of GDP. To help raise government revenue, Japan adopted legislation in 2012 to gradually raise the consumption tax rate to 10% by 2015, beginning with a hike from 5% to 8%, implemented in April 2014. That increase had a contractionary effect on GDP, however, so PMABE in late 2014 decided to postpone the final phase of the increase until April 2017 to give the economy more time to recover. Led by the Bank of Japan's aggressive monetary easing, Japan is making progress in ending deflation, but demographic decline—a low birthrate and anaging, shrinking population—poses a major long-term challenge for the economy.

GDP (purchasing power parity): $4.83 trillion (2015 est.)

$4.807 trillion (2014 est.)

$4.809 trillion (2013 est.)

note: data are in 2015 US dollars

country comparison to the world: 5

GDP (official exchange rate): $4.123 trillion (2015 est.)

GDP—real growth rate: 0.5% (2015 est.)

0% (2014 est.)

1.4% (2013 est.)

country comparison to the world: 187

GDP—per capita (PPP): $38,100 (2015 est.)

$37,800 (2014 est.)

$37,800 (2013 est.)

note: data are in 2015 US dollars

country comparison to the world: 42

Gross national saving: 25.3% of GDP (2015 est.)

22.3% of GDP (2014 est.)

22.1% of GDP (2013 est.)

country comparison to the world: 47

GDP—composition, by end use:

household consumption: 59.6%

government consumption: 20.4%

investment in fixed capital: 21.2%

investment in inventories: -0.3%

exports of goods and services: 18.5%

imports of goods and services: -19.4% (2015 est.)

GDP—composition, by sector of origin:

agriculture: 1.2%

industry: 26.6%

services: 72.2% (2015 est.)

Agriculture—products: vegetables, rice, fish, poultry, fruit, dairy products, pork, beef, flowers, potatoes/taros/y ams, sugar cane, tea, legumes, wheat and barley

Industries: among world's largest and most technologically advanced producers of motor vehicles, electronic equipment, machine tools, steel and nonferrous metals, ships, chemicals, textiles, processed foods

Industrial production growth rate: 0.7% (2015 est.)

country comparison to the world: 156

Labor force: 64.32 million (2015 est.)

country comparison to the world: 9

Labor force—by occupation: *agriculture:* 2.9%

industry: 26.2%

services: 70.9% (February 2015 est.)

Unemployment rate: 3.3% (2015 est.)

3.6% (2014 est.)

country comparison to the world: 27

Population below poverty line: 16.1% (2013 est.)

Household income or consumption by percentage share: *lowest:* 10%: 2.7%

highest: 10%: 24.8% (2008)

Distribution of family income—Gini index: 37.9 (2011)

24.9 (1993)

country comparison to the world: 75

Budget: *revenues:* $1.439 trillion

expenditures: $1.705 trillion (2015 est.)

Taxes and other revenues: 35% of GDP (2015 est.)

country comparison to the world: 58

Budget surplus (+) or deficit (-): -6.5% of GDP (2015 est.)

country comparison to the world: 188

Public debt: 227.9% of GDP (2015 est.)

226% of GDP (2014 est.)

country comparison to the world: 1

Fiscal year: 1 April—31 March

Inflation rate (consumer prices): 0.8% (2015 est.) 2.7% (2014 est.)
country comparison to the world: 74
Central bank discount rate: 0.3% (31 December 2015)
0.3% (31 December 2014)
country comparison to the world: 131
Commercial bank prime lending rate: 1.48% (31 December 2015 est.)
1.48% (31 December 2014 est.)
country comparison to the world: 183
Stock of narrow money: $4.902 trillion (31 December 2015 est.)
$4.896 trillion (31 December 2014 est.)
country comparison to the world: 3
Stock of broad money: $8.073 trillion (31 December 2014 est.)
$8.035 trillion (31 December 2013 est.)
country comparison to the world: 4
Stock of domestic credit: $10.81 trillion (31 December 2015 est.)
$10.9 trillion (31 December 2014 est.)
country comparison to the world: 4
Market value of publicly traded shares: $4.782 trillion (31 December 2014 est.)
$4.584 trillion (31 December 2013)
$3.715 trillion (31 December 2012 est.)
country comparison to the world: 4
Current account balance: $137.5 billion (2015 est.)
$24.4 billion (2014 est.)
country comparison to the world: 4
Exports: $624 billion (2015 est.)
$699.5 billion (2014 est.)
country comparison to the world: 5
Exports—commodities: motor vehicles 14.9%; iron and steel products 5.4%; semiconductors 5%; auto parts 4.8%; power generating machinery 3.5%; plastic materials 3.3% (2014 est.)
Exports—partners: US 20.2%, China 17.5%, South Korea 7.1%, Hong Kong 5.6%, Thailand 4.5% (2015)
Imports: $625.4 billion (2015 est.)
$798.6 billion (2014 est.)
country comparison to the world: 5
Imports—commodities: petroleum 16.1%; liquid natural gas 9.1%; clothing 3.8%; semiconductors 3.3%; coal 2.4%; audio and visual apparatus 1.4% (2014 est.)
Imports—partners: China 24.8%, US 10.5%, Australia 5.4%, South Korea 4.1% (2015)
Reserves of foreign exchange and gold: $1.261 trillion (31 December 2014 est.)
$1.267 trillion (41639 est.)
country comparison to the world: 2
Debt—external: $5.18 trillion (31 December 2013 est.)
$4.026 trillion (31 December 2012)
country comparison to the world: 6
Stock of direct foreign investment—at home: $217.4 billion (31 December 2015 est.)
$193.5 billion (31 December 2014 est.)
country comparison to the world: 28
Stock of direct foreign investment—abroad: $1.313 trillion (31 December 2015 est.)
$1.193 trillion (31 December 2014 est.)

country comparison to the world: 8
Exchange rates: yen (JPY) per US dollar—
122.1 (2015 est.)
105.86 (2014 est.)
97.44 (2013 est.)
79.79 (2012 est.)
79.81 (2011 est.)

ENERGY

Electricity—production: 966.4 billion kWh (2012 est.)
country comparison to the world: 6
Electricity—consumption: 921 billion kWh (2012 est.)
country comparison to the world: 5
Electricity—exports: 0 kWh (2014 est.)
country comparison to the world: 154
Electricity—imports: 0 kWh (2014 est.)
country comparison to the world: 164
Electricity—installed generating capacity: 293.3 million kW (2012 est.)
country comparison to the world: 4
Electricity—from fossil fuels: 64.4% of total installed capacity (2012 est.)
country comparison to the world: 122
Electricity—from nuclear fuels: 15.1% of total installed capacity (2012 est.)
country comparison to the world: 14
Electricity—from hydroelectric plants: 7.6% of total installed capacity (2012 est.)
country comparison to the world: 120
Electricity—from other renewable sources: 3.8% of total installed capacity (2012 est.)
country comparison to the world: 65
Crude oil—production: 4,666 bbl/day (2014 est.)
country comparison to the world: 84
Crude oil—exports: 0 bbl/day (2014 est.)
country comparison to the world: 141
Crude oil—imports: 3.441 million bbl/day (2014 est.)
country comparison to the world: 4
Crude oil—proved reserves: 541.6 million bbl (March, 2015 est.)
country comparison to the world: 51
Refined petroleum products—production: 3.294 million bbl/day (2014 est.)
country comparison to the world: 6
Refined petroleum products—consumption: 4.297 million bbl/day (2014 est.)
country comparison to the world: 4
Refined petroleum products—exports: 324,400 bbl/day (2013 est.)
country comparison to the world: 24
Refined petroleum products—imports: 1.103 million bbl/day (2013 est.)
country comparison to the world: 5
Natural gas—production: 4.728 billion cu m (2014 est.)
country comparison to the world: 52
Natural gas—consumption: 134.3 billion cu m (2014 est.)
country comparison to the world: 6
Natural gas—exports: 0 cu m (2014 est.)
country comparison to the world: 122
Natural gas—imports: 128.3 billion cu m (2014 est.)

country comparison to the world: 2
Natural gas—proved reserves: 20.9 billion cu m (1 January 2014 est.)
country comparison to the world: 76
Carbon dioxide emissions from consumption of energy: 1.276 billion Mt (2012 est.)
country comparison to the world: 6

COMMUNICATIONS

Telephones—fixed lines: *total subscriptions:* 63.61 million
subscriptions per 100 inhabitants: 50 (2014 est.)
country comparison to the world: 4
Telephones—mobile cellular: *total:* 152.7 million
subscriptions per 100 inhabitants: 120 (2014 est.)
country comparison to the world: 8
Telephone system: *general assessment:* excellent domestic and international service
domestic: high level of modern technology and excellent service of every kind
international: country code—81; numerous submarine cables provide links throughout Asia, Australia, the Middle East, Europe, and US; satellite earth stations—7 Intelsat (Pacific and Indian Oceans), 1 Intersputnik (Indian Ocean region), 2 Inmarsat (Pacific and Indian Ocean regions), and 8 SkyPerfect JSAT (2012)
Broadcast media: a mixture of public and commercial broadcast TV and radio stations; 6 national terrestrial TV networks including 1 public broadcaster; the large number of radio and TV stations available provide a wide range of choices; satellite and cable services provide access to international channels (2012)
Radio broadcast stations: AM 215 (plus 370 repeaters), FM 89 (plus 485 repeaters), shortwave 21 (2001)
Television broadcast stations: 211; note—in addition, US Forces are served by 3 TV stations and 2 TV cable services (1999)
Internet country code: .jp
Internet hosts: 64.453 million (2012)
country comparison to the world: 2
Internet users: *total:* 109.3 million
percent of Population: 86.0% (2014 est.)
country comparison to the world: 5

TRANSPORTATION

Airports: 175 (2013)
country comparison to the world: 33
Airports—with paved runways: *total:* 142
over 3,047 m: 6
2,438 to 3,047 m: 45
1,524 to 2,437 m: 38
914 to 1,523 m: 28
under 914 m: 25 (2013)
Airports—with unpaved runways: *total:* 33
914 to 1,523 m: 5
under 914 m: 28 (2013)
Heliports: 16 (2013)
Pipelines: gas 4,456 km; oil 174 km; oil/gas/water 104 km (2013)
Railways: *total:* 27,311 km
standard gauge: 4,800 km 1.435-m gauge (4,800 km electrified)

dual gauge: 132 km 1.435–1.067-m gauge (132 km electrified)

narrow gauge: 124 km 1.372-m gauge (124 km electrified); 22,207 km 1.067-m gauge (15,430 km electrified); 48 km 0.762-m gauge (48 km electrified) (2015)

country comparison to the world: 12

Roadways: total: 1,218,772 km

paved: 992,835 km (includes 8,428 km of expressways)

unpaved: 225,937 km (2015)

country comparison to the world: 6

Waterways: 1,770 km (seagoing vessels use inland seas) (2010)

country comparison to the world: 44

Merchant marine: total: 684

by type: bulk carrier 168, cargo 34, carrier 3, chemical tanker 29, container 2, liquefied gas 58, passenger 11, passenger/cargo 117, petroleum tanker 152, refrigerated cargo 4, roll on/roll off 52, vehicle carrier 54

registered in other countries: 3,122 (Bahamas 88, Bermuda 2, Burma 1, Cambodia 1, Cayman Islands 23, China 2, Cyprus 16, Honduras 4, Hong Kong 79, Indonesia 8, Isle of Man 19, Liberia 110, Luxembourg 3, Malaysia 2, Malta 5, Marshall Islands 59, Mongolia 2, Netherlands 1, Panama 2372, Philippines 77, Portugal 9, Saint Kitts and Nevis 2, Saint Vincent and the Grenadines 3, Sierra Leone 4, Singapore 164, South Korea 14, Tanzania 1, UK 5, Vanuatu 39, unknown 7) (2010)

country comparison to the world: 16

Ports and terminals: major seaport(s): Chiba, Kawasaki, Kobe, Mizushima, Moji, Nagoya, Osaka, Tokyo, Tomakomai, Yokohama

container port(s) (TEUs): Kobe (2,725,304), Nagoya (2,471,821), Osaka (2,172,797), Tokyo (4,416,119), Yokohama (2,992,517)

LNG terminal(s) (import): Chita, Fukwoke, Futtsu, Hachinone, Hakodate, Hatsukaichi, Higashi Ohgishima, Higashi Niigata, Himeiji, Joetsu, Kagoshima, Kawagoe, Kita Kyushu, Mizushima, Nagasaki, Naoetsu, Negishi, Ohgishima, Oita, Sakai, Sakaide, Senboku, Shimizu, Shin Minato, Sodegaura, Tobata, Yanai, Yokkaichi, Okinawa—Nakagusuku

MILITARY AND SECURITY

Military branches: Japanese Ministry of Defense (MOD): Ground Self-Defense Force (Rikujou Jieitai, GSDF), Maritime Self-Defense Force (Kaijou Jieitai, MSDF), Air Self-Defense Force (Koukuu Jieitai, ASDF) (2011)

Military service age and obligation: 18 years of age for voluntary military service; no conscription; mandatory retirement at age 53 for senior enlisted personnel and at 62 years for senior service officers (2012)

Military expenditures: 0.97% of GDP (2012)

1.01% of GDP (2011)

0.99% of GDP (2010)

country comparison to the world: 102

TRANSNATIONAL ISSUES

Disputes—international: the sovereignty dispute over the islands of Etorofu, Kunashiri, and Shikotan, and the Habomai group, known in Japan as the "Northern Territories" and in Russia as the "Southern Kuril Islands," occupied by the Soviet Union in 1945, now administered by Russia and claimed by Japan, remains the primary sticking point to signing a peace treaty formally ending World War II hostilities; Japan and South Korea claim Liancourt Rocks (Take-shima/Tok-do) occupied by South Korea since 1954; the Japanese-administered Senkaku Islands are also claimed by China and Taiwan

Refugees and internally displaced persons: stateless persons: 603 (2015)

JERSEY

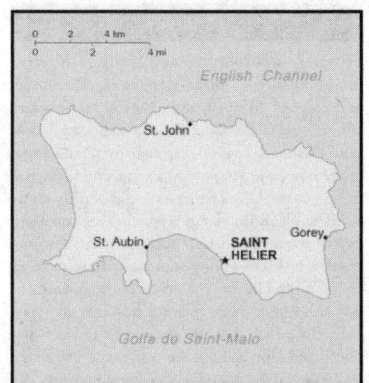

INTRODUCTION

Background: Jersey and the other Channel Islands represent the last remnants of the medieval Dukedom of Normandy that held sway in both France and England. These islands were the only British soil occupied by German troops in World War II. Jersey is a British crown dependency but is not part of the UK or of the EU. However, the UK Government is constitutionally responsible for its defense and international representation.

GEOGRAPHY

Location: Western Europe, island in the English Channel, northwest of France

Geographic coordinates: 49 15 N, 2 10 W

Map references: Europe

Area: total: 116 sq km

land: 116 sq km

water: 0 sq km

country comparison to the world: 225

Area—comparative: about two-thirds the size of Washington, DC

Land boundaries: 0 km

Coastline: 70 km

Maritime claims: territorial sea: 3 nm

exclusive fishing zone: 12 nm

Climate: temperate; mild winters and cool summers

Terrain: gently rolling plain with low, rugged hills along north coast

Elevation: mean elevation: NA

elevation extremes: lowest point: Atlantic Ocean 0 m

highest point: unnamed elevation 143 m

Natural resources:

arable land:

Land use: agricultural land: 66%

arable land: 66%

permanent crops: 0%

permanent pasture: 0%

forest: 0%

other: 34% (2011 est.)

Irrigated land: NA

Natural hazards: NA

Environment—current issues: NA

Geography—note: largest and southernmost of Channel Islands; about 30% of population concentrated in Saint Helier

PEOPLE AND SOCIETY

Nationality: noun: Channel Islander(s)

adjective: Channel Islander

Ethnic groups: Jersey 46.4%, British 32.7%, Portuguese/Madeiran 8.2%, Polish 3.3%, Irish, French, and other white 7.1%, other 2.4% (2011 est.)

Languages: English 94.5% (official), Portuguese 4.6%, other 0.9% (2001 census)

Religions: Protestant (Anglican, Baptist, Congregational New Church, Methodist, Presbyterian), Roman Catholic

Population: 97,294 (July 2015 est.)

country comparison to the world: 197

Age structure: 0–14 years: 16.02% (male 8,066/female 7,517)

15–24 years: 14.52% (male 7,241/female 6,883)

25–54 years: 41.31% (male 20,130/female 20,063)

55–64 years: 12.24% (male 5,797/female 6,109)

65 years and over: 15.92% (male 6,597/female 8,891) (2015 est.)

Dependency ratios: total dependency ratio: 47%

youth dependency ratio: 21.6%

elderly dependency ratio: 25.4%

potential support ratio: 3.9%

note: data represents the Channel Islands (2015 est.)

Median Age: total: 39 years

male: 36.6 years

female: 41.4 years (2015 est.)

country comparison to the world: 57

Population growth rate: 0.8% (2015 est.)

country comparison to the world: 140

Birth rate: 11.91 births/1,000 population (2015 est.)

country comparison to the world: 167

Death rate: 7.68 deaths/1,000 population (2015 est.)

country comparison to the world: 107

Net migration rate: 3.76 migrant(s)/1,000 population (2015 est.)

country comparison to the world: 36

Urbanization: *urban population:* 31.4% of total population (2014)

rate of urbanization: 0.76% annual rate of change (2010–15 est.)

note: data is for the Channel Islands

Sex ratio: *at birth:* 1.06 male(s)/female

0–14 years: 1.07 male(s)/female

15–24 years: 1.05 male(s)/female

25–54 years: 1 male(s)/female

55–64 years: 0.95 male(s)/female

65 years and over: 0.74 male(s)/female

total population: 0.97 male(s)/female (2015 est.)

Infant mortality rate: *total:* 3.82 deaths/1,000 live births

male: 4.03 deaths/1,000 live births

female: 3.59 deaths/1,000 live births (2015 est.)

country comparison to the world: 197

Life expectancy at birth: *total population:* 81.76 years

male: 79.3 years

female: 84.37 years (2015 est.)

country comparison to the world: 17

Total fertility rate: 1.66 children born/woman (2015 est.)

country comparison to the world: 175

HIV/AIDS—adult prevalence rate: NA

HIV/AIDS—people living with HIV/AIDS: NA

HIV/AIDS—deaths: NA

GOVERNMENT

Country name: *conventional long form:* Bailiwick of Jersey

conventional short form: Jersey

etymology: the name is of Old Norse origin, but the meaning of the root "Jer(s)" is uncertain; the "-ey" ending means "island"

Dependency status: British crown dependency

Government type: parliamentary democracy (Assembly of the States of Jersey); a Crown dependency of the UK

Capital: *name:* Saint Helier

Geographic coordinates: 49 11 N, 2 06 W

time difference: UTC 0 (5 hours ahead of Washington, DC, during Standard Time)

daylight saving time: +1hr, begins last Sunday in March; ends last Sunday in October

Administrative divisions: none (British crown dependency); there are no first-order administrative divisions as defined by the US Government, but there are 12 parishes; Grouville, Saint Brelade, Saint Clement, Saint Helier, Saint John, Saint Lawrence, Saint Martin, Saint Mary, Saint Ouen, Saint Peter, Saint Saviour, and Trinity

Independence: none (British crown dependency)

National holiday: Liberation Day, 9 May (1945)

Constitution: unwritten; partly statutes, partly common law and practice

Legal system: the laws of the UK, where applicable, apply; local statutes

Citizenship: see United Kingdom

Suffrage: 16 years of age; universal

Executive branch: *chief of state:* Queen ELIZABETH II (since 6 February 1952); represented by Lieutenant Governor Sir John MCCOLL (since 26 September 2011)

head of government: Chief Minister Ian GORST (18 December 2011); Bailiff Michael BIRT (since 9 July 2009)

cabinet: Council of Ministers appointed individually by the states

elections/appointments: the monarchy is hereditary; Council of Ministers including the chief minister indirectly elected by the Assembly of States; lieutenant governor and bailiff appointed by the monarch

Legislative branch: *description:* unicameral Assembly of the States of Jersey (54 seats; 49 voting members directly elected by simple majority vote include 8 senators to serve 6-year terms, and 29 deputies and 12 constables or heads of parishes to serve 3-year terms; 5 non-voting members appointed by the monarch include the bailiff, lieutenant governor, dean of Jersey, attorney general, and the solicitor general)

elections: last held on 15 October 2014 (next to be held in 2017)

election results: percent of vote—NA; seats—independents 49

Judicial branch: highest court(s): Jersey Court of Appeal (consists of the bailiff, deputy bailiff, and 12 judges and organized into Heritage, Family, Probate, and Civil and Criminal Divisions); Royal Court (consists of the bailiff, deputy bailiff, 6 commissioners (part-time judges), and NA lay people referred to as jurats)

judge selection and term of office: Jersey Court of Appeal bailiffs and judges appointed by the Crown upon the advice of the Secretary of State for Justice; bailiffs and judges appointed for extent of good behavior; Royal Court bailiffs appointed by the Crown upon the advice of the Secretary of State for Justice; commissioners appointed by the bailiff; jurats appointed by the Electoral College; bailiffs and commissioners appointed for extent of good behavior; jurats appointed until retirement at age 72

subordinate courts: Magistrate's Court; Youth Court; Petty Debts Court; Parish Hall Enquires (a process of preliminary investigation into youth and minor adult offenses to determine need for presentation before a court)

Political parties and leaders: *one registered party:* Reform Jersey [Sam MEZEC]

note: most senators and deputies sit as independents

Political pressure groups and leaders: Institute of Directors, Jersey branch (provides business support)

Jersey Hospitality Association [Ian BARNES] (trade association)

Jersey Rights Association [David ROTHERHAM] (human rights)

La Societe Jersiaise (education And conservation group)

Progress Jersey [Daren O'TOOLE, Gino RISOLI] (human rights)

Royal Jersey Agriculture and Horticultural Society or RJA&HS (development and management of the Jersey breed of cattle)

Save Jersey's Heritage (protects heritage through building preservation)

Diplomatic representation in the US: none (British crown dependency)

Diplomatic representation from the US: none (British crown dependency)

Flag description: white with a diagonal red cross extending to the corners of the flag; in the upper quadrant, surmounted by a yellow crown, a red shield with three lions in yellow; according to tradition, the ships of Jersey—in an attempt to differentiate themselves from English ships flying the horizontal cross of St. George—rotated the cross to the "X" (saltire) configuration; because this arrangement still resembled the Irish cross of St. Patrick, the yellow Plantagenet crown and Jersey coat of arms were added

National symbol(s): Jersey cow; national colors: red, white

National anthem: *name:* "Isle de Siez Nous" (Island Home)

lyrics/music: Gerard LEFEUVRE

note: adopted 2008; serves as a local anthem; as a British crown dependency, "God Save the Queen" is official (see United Kingdom)

ECONOMY

Economy—overview: Jersey's economy is based on international financial services, agriculture, and tourism. In 2010, the financial services sector accounted for about 50% of the island's output. Potatoes, cauliflower, tomatoes, and especially flowers are important export crops, shipped mostly to the UK. The Jersey breed of dairy cattle is known worldwide and represents an important export income earner. Tourism accounts for one-quarter of GDP. Living standards come close to those of the UK. In recent years, the government has encouraged light industry to locate in Jersey with the result that an electronics industry has developed, displacing more traditional industries. All raw material and energy requirements are imported as well as a large share of Jersey's food needs. Light taxes and death duties make the island a popular tax haven. In october 2014, Jersey signed an OECD agreement to automatically exchange some financial account information to limit tax avoidance and evasion.

GDP (purchasing power parity): $5.771 billion (FY12/13 est.)

$5.786 billion (FY11/12)

note: data are in 2013 US dollars

country comparison to the world: 170

GDP (official exchange rate): $5.771 billion (FY 2012/13 est.)

GDP—real growth rate: -0.3% (FY12/13 est.)

country comparison to the world: 201

GDP—per capita (PPP): $57,000 (2005 est.)

country comparison to the world: 17

GDP—composition, by sector of origin: *agriculture:* 2%

industry: 2%

services: 96% (2010)

Agriculture—products: potatoes, cauliflower, tomatoes; beef, dairy products

Industries: tourism, banking and finance, dairy, electronics

Industrial production growth rate: NA%

Labor force: 53,380 (June 2012)

country comparison to the world: 190

Unemployment rate: 1.7% (2012 est.)

2.2% (2006 est.)

country comparison to the world: 8

Population below poverty line: NA%

Household income or consumption by percentage share: *lowest:* 10%: NA%

highest: 10%: NA%

Budget: revenues: $829 million

expenditures: $851 million (2005)

Taxes and other revenues: 14.4% of GDP (2005)

country comparison to the world: 197

Budget surplus (+) or deficit (-): -0.4% of GDP (2005)

country comparison to the world: 41

Fiscal year: 1 April—31 March

Inflation rate (consumer prices): 3.7% (2006)

country comparison to the world: 151

Market value of publicly traded shares: $NA

Exports: $NA

Exports—commodities: light industrial and electrical goods, dairy cattle, foodstuffs, textiles, flowers

Imports: $NA

Imports—commodities: machinery and transport equipment, manufactured goods, foodstuffs, mineral fuels, chemicals

Debt—external: $NA

Exchange rates: Jersey pounds (JEP) per US dollar—

0.6528 (2012)

0.607 (2014)

0.607 (2013)

0.6391 (2011 est.)

ENERGY

Electricity—consumption: 630.1 million kWh (2004 est.)

country comparison to the world: 167

COMMUNICATIONS

Telephones—fixed lines: *total subscriptions:* 83,900

subscriptions per 100 inhabitants: 95 (2014 est.)

country comparison to the world: 148

Telephones—mobile cellular: *total:* 83,900

subscriptions per 100 inhabitants: 105 (2004)

country comparison to the world: 194

Telephone system: *general assessment:* increasingly modern system, with broadband access

domestic: digital telephone system launch announced in 2006 now implemented; fixed-line and mobile-cellular services widely available; combined fixed-line and mobile-cellular density exceeds 100 per 100 persons

international: country code—44; submarine cable connectivity to Guernsey, the UK, and France (2010)

Broadcast media: multiple UK terrestrial television broadcasts are received via a transmitter in Jersey; satellite packages available; BBC Radio Jersey and 1 other radio station operating (2009)

Radio broadcast stations: AM NA, FM 1, shortwave 0 (UK radio broadcasts carried via local relays) (2008)

Television broadcast stations: 2 (UK television carried by local relays with a switch to digital broadcasts scheduled for 2010) (2008)

Internet country code: .je

Internet hosts: 264 (2012)

country comparison to the world: 193

Internet users: *total:* 29,500

percent of Population: 31.9% (2009)

country comparison to the world: 197

TRANSPORTATION

Airports: 1 (2013)

country comparison to the world: 223

Airports—with paved runways: *total:* 1

1,524 to 2,437 m: 1 (2013)

Roadways: *total:* 576 km (2010)

country comparison to the world: 192

Merchant marine: *registered in other countries:* 14 (Gibraltar 1, India 2, Marshall Islands 11) (2010)

country comparison to the world: 102

Ports and terminals: *major seaport(s):* Gorey, Saint Aubin, Saint Helier

MILITARY AND SECURITY

Military—note: defense is the responsibility of the UK

TRANSNATIONAL ISSUES

Disputes—international: none

JORDAN

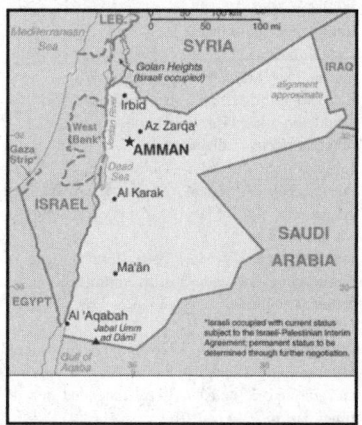

INTRODUCTION

Background: Following World War I and the dissolution of the Ottoman Empire, the League of Nations awarded Britain the mandate to govern much of the Middle East. Britain demarcated a semi-autonomous region of Transjordan from Palestine in the early 1920s. The area gained its independence in 1946 and thereafter became The Hashemite Kingdom of Jordan. The country's long-time ruler, King HUSSEIN (1953–99), successfully navigated competing pressures from the major powers (US, USSR, and UK), various Arab states, Israel, and a large internal Palestinian population. Jordan lost the West Bank to Israel in the 1967 Six-Day War. King HUSSEIN in 1988 permanently relinquished Jordanian claims to the West Bank; in 1994 he signed a peace treaty with Israel. King ABDALLAH II, King HUSSEIN's eldest son, assumed the throne following his father's death in 1999. He implemented modest political and economic reforms, but in the wake of the 2011 "Arab Revolution" across the Middle East, Jordanians continue to press for further political liberalization, government reforms, and economic improvements. Jordan held a nonpermanent seat on the UN Security Council for the 2014–15 term.

GEOGRAPHY

Location: Middle East, northwest of Saudi Arabia, between Israel (to the west) and Iraq

Geographic coordinates: 31 00 N, 36 00 E

Map references: Middle East

Area: *total:* 89,342 sq km

land: 88,802 sq km

water: 540 sq km

country comparison to the world: 112

Area—comparative: about three-quarters the size of Pennsylvania; slightly smaller than Indiana

Land boundaries: *total:* 1,744 km

border countries (5): Iraq 179 km, Israel 307 km, Saudi Arabia 731 km, Syria 379 km, West Bank 148 km

Coastline: 26 km

Maritime claims: *territorial sea:* 3 nm

Climate: mostly arid desert; rainy season in west (November to April)

Terrain: mostly desert plateau in east, highland area in west; Great Rift Valley separates eastern and western banks of the Jordan River

Elevation: *mean elevation:* 812 m

elevation extremes: *lowest point:* Dead Sea -408 m
highest point: Jabal Umm ad Dami 1,854 m
Natural resources: phosphates, potash, shale oil
Land use: *agricultural land:* 11.4%
arable land: 2%
permanent crops: 1%
permanent pasture: 8.4%
forest: 1.1%
other: 87.5% (2011 est.)
Irrigated land: 964 sq km (2012)
Total renewable water resources: 0.94 cu km (2011)
Freshwater withdrawal (domestic/industrial/agricultural): *total:* 0.94 cu km/yr (31%/4%/65%)
per capita: 166 cu m/yr (2005)
Natural hazards: droughts; periodic earthquakes
Environment—current issues: limited natural freshwater resources; deforestation; overgrazing; soil erosion; desertification
Environment—international agreements: *party to:* Biodiversity, Climate Change, Climate Change-Kyoto Protocol, Desertification, Endangered Species, Hazardous Wastes, Law of the Sea, Marine Dumping, Ozone Layer Protection, Wetlands
signed, but not ratified: none of the selected agreements
Geography—note: strategic location at the head of the Gulf of Aqaba and as the Arab country that shares the longest border with Israel and the occupied West Bank

PEOPLE AND SOCIETY

Nationality: *noun:* Jordanian(s)
adjective: Jordanian
Ethnic groups: Arab 98%, Circassian 1%, Armenian 1%
Languages: Arabic (official), English (widely understood am ong upper and m iddle classes)
Religions: Muslim 97.2% (official; predominantly Sunni), Christian 2.2% (majority Greek Orthodox, but some Greek and Roman Catholics, Syrian Orthodox, Coptic Orthodox, Armenian Orthodox, and Protestant denominations), Buddhist 0.4%, Hindu 0.1%, Jewish <0.1, folk religionist <0.1, unaffiliated <0.1, other <0.1 (2010 est.)
Population: 8,117,564
note: increased estim ate reflects revised assumptions about the net migration rate due to the increased flow of Syrian refugees (July 2015 est.)
country comparison to the world: 98
Age structure: *0–14 years:* 35.42% (male 1,474,464/female 1,400,926)
15–24 years: 20.25% (male 840,714/female 803,237)
25–54 years: 36.12% (male 1,468,388/female 1,463,452)
55–64 years: 4.3% (male 169,857/female 179,275)
65 years and over: 3.91% (male 149,207/female 168,044) (2015 est.)
Dependency ratios: *total dependency ratio:* 64.8%
youth dependency ratio: 58.5%
elderly dependency ratio: 6.2%
potential support ratio: 16% (2015 est.)

Median Age: *total:* 22 years
male: 21.7 years
female: 22.4 years (2015 est.)
country comparison to the world: 179
Population growth rate: 0.83% (2015 est.)
country comparison to the world: 132
Birth rate: 25.37 births/1,000 population (2015 est.)
country comparison to the world: 50
Death rate: 3.79 deaths/1,000 population (2015 est.)
country comparison to the world: 211
Net migration rate: -13.24 migrant(s)/1,000 population (2015 est.)
country comparison to the world: 217
Urbanization: *urban population:* 83.7% of total population (2015)
rate of urbanization: 3.79% annual rate of change (2010–15 est.)
Major urban areas—population: AMMAN (capital) 1.155 million (2015)
Sex ratio: *at birth:* 1.06 male(s)/female
0–14 years: 1.05 male(s)/female
15–24 years: 1.05 male(s)/female
25–54 years: 1 male(s)/female
55–64 years: 0.95 male(s)/female
65 years and over: 0.89 male(s)/female
total population: 1.02 male(s)/female (2015 est.)
Mother's mean Age at first birth: 24.7
note: median Age at first birth among women 25–29 (2012 est.)
Maternal mortality rate: 58 deaths/100,000 live births (2015 est.)
country comparison to the world: 97
Infant mortality rate: *total:* 15.18 deaths/1,000 live births
male: 16.05 deaths/1,000 live births
female: 14.25 deaths/1,000 live births (2015 est.)
country comparison to the world: 104
Life expectancy at birth: *total population:* 74.35 years
male: 73 years
female: 75.78 years (2015 est.)
country comparison to the world: 122
Total fertility rate: 3.17 children born/woman (2015 est.)
country comparison to the world: 50
Contraceptive prevalence rate: 61.2% (2012)
Health expenditures: 7.2% of GDP (2013)
country comparison to the world: 25
Physicians density: 2.56 physicians/1,000 population (2010)
Hospital bed density: 1.8 beds/1,000 population (2012)
Drinking water source:
improved:
urban: 97.8% of population
rural: 92.3% of population
total: 96.9% of population
unimproved:
urban: 2.2% of population
rural: 7.7% of population
total: 3.1% of population (2015 est.)
Sanitation facility access:
improved:
urban: 98.6% of population

rural: 98.9% of population
total: 98.6% of population
unimproved:
urban: 1.4% of population
rural: 1.1% of population
total: 1.4% of population (2015 est.)
HIV/AIDS—adult prevalence rate: NA
HIV/AIDS—people living with HIV/AIDS: NA
HIV/AIDS—deaths: NA
Obesity—adult prevalence rate: 28.1% (2014)
country comparison to the world: 28
Children under the age of 5 years underweight: 3% (2012)
country comparison to the world: 114
Education expenditures: NA
Literacy: *definition:* age 15 and over can read and write
total populati on: 95.4%
male: 97.7%
female: 92.9% (2015 est.)
School life expectancy (primary to tertiary education): *total:* 13 years
male: 12 years
female: 13 years (2012)
Unemployment, youth ages 15–24: *total:* 29.3%
male: 25.2%
female: 48.8% (2012 est.)
country comparison to the world: 27

GOVERNMENT

Country name: *conventional long form:* Hashemite Kingdom of Jordan
conventional short form: Jordan
local long form: Al Mamlakah al Urduniyah al Hashimiyah
local short form: Al Urdun
former: Transjordan
etymology: named for the Jordan River, which makes up part of Jordan's northwest border
Government type: parliamentary constitutional monarchy
Capital: *name:* Amman
Geographic coordinates: 31 57 N, 35 56 E
time difference: UTC+2 (7 hours ahead of Washington, DC, during Standard Time)
daylight saving time: +1hr, begins last Friday in March; ends last Friday in October
Administrative divisions: 12 governorates (muhafazat, singular—muhafazah); 'Ajlun, Al 'Aqabah, Al Balqa', Al Karak, Al Mafraq, Al'Asimah, At Tafilah, Az Zarqa', Irbid, Jarash, Ma'an, Madaba
Independence: 25 May 1946 (from League of Nations mandate under British administration)
National holiday: Independence Day, 25 May (1946)
Constitution: previous 1928 (preindependence); latest initially adopted 28 November 1947, revised and ratified 1 January 1952; amended several times, last in 2014 (2016)
Legal system: mixed system developed from codes instituted by the Ottoman Empire (based on French law), British common law, and Islamic law

International law organization participation: has not submitted an ICJ jurisdiction declaration; accepts ICCt jurisdiction

Citizenship: *citizenship by birth:* no

citizenship by descent only: the father must be a citizen of Jordan

dual citizenship recognized: yes

residency requirement for naturalization: 15 years

Citizenship

Suffrage: 18 years of age; universal

Executive branch: *chief of state:* King ABDALLAH II (since 7 February 1999); Crown Prince HUSSEIN (born 28 June 1994), eldest son of King ABDALLAH II

head of government: Prime Minister Hani MULKI (since 1 June 2016)

cabinet: Cabinet appointed by the prime minister in consultation with the monarch

elections/appointments: the monarchy is hereditary; prime minister appointed by the monarch

Legislative branch: *description:* bicameral National Assembly or Majlis al-'Umma consists of the Senate, or the House of notables or Majlis al-Ayan (60 seats; members appointed by the monarch to serve 4-year terms) and the Chamber of Deputies or House of Representatives or Majlis al-Nuwaab (150 seats; 108 members directly elected in single- and multi-seat constituencies by simple majority vote, 27 directly elected in a single national constituency by proportional representation vote, and 15 seats reserved for women; members serve 4-year terms); note—the electoral law enacted in July 2012 allocated an additional 10 seats—6 for women, 2 for Amman, and 1 seat each for the cities of Az Zarqa' and Irbid; unchanged are 9 seats reserved for Christian candidates, 9 for Bedouin candidates, and 3 for Jordanians of Chechen or Circassian descent

elections: Chamber of Deputies—last held on 23 January 2013 (next on 20 September 2016); note—the King dissolved the previous Chamber of Deputies in november 2012, midway through the parliamentary term

election results: Chamber of Deputies—percent of vote by party—NA; seats by party—27 elected on closed national list including: Islamic Centrist Party 3, Nation 2, National Union 2, Stronger Jordan 2, Ahl al-Himma 1, Al-Bayyan 1, Citizenship 1, Construction 1, Cooperation 1, Dawn 1, Dignity 1, Free Voice 1, Labor and Trade 1, National Accord Youth Block 1, National Action 1, National Current 1 (member resigned in February 2013), National Unity 1, nobel Jerusalem 1, Salvation 1, The People 1, Unified Front 1, Voice of Nation 1; other 123; note—the IAF boycotted the election

Judicial branch: *highest court(s):* Court of Cassation or Supreme Court (consists of 15 judges including the chief justice; 7-judge panels for important cases and 5-judge panels for most appeals cases)

judge selection and term of office: chief justice appointed by the king; other judges nominated by the Higher Judicial Council and approved by the king; judge tenure NA

subordinate courts: Courts of Appeal; Major Felonies Court; Courts of First Instance; Magistrate's Courts; State Security Court; religious courts; military courts

Political parties and leaders: Ahl al-Himma

Al-Bayy an

Al-Hayah Jordanian Party [Zahier AMR]

Arab Ba'ath Socialist Party [Akram al-HIMSI]

Ba'ath Arab Progressive Party [Fuad DABBOUR]

Citizenship

Construction

Cooperation

Dawn

Democratic People's Party [Ablah ABUULBAH]

Democratic Popular Unity Party [Sa'id DIAB]

Dignity

Du'a Party [Muhammed ABUBAKR]

Free Voice

Islamic Action Front or IAF [Hamzah MANSOUR]

Islamic Centrist Party [Muhammad al-HAJ]

Jordanian Communist Party [Munir HAMARNAH]

Jordanian National Party [Muna ABUBAKR]

Jordanian United Front [Amjad al-MAJALI]

Labor and Trade

Muslim Center Party [Haitham ALAMAERAH]

Nation

National Accord Youth Block

National Action

National Constitution Party [Ahmad al-SHUNAQ]

National Current Party [Abd al-Hadi al-MAJALI]

National Movement for Direct Democracy [Muhammad al-QAQ]

National Union

National Unity

Nobel Jerusalem

Risalah Party [Hazem QASHOU]

Salvation

Stronger Jordan

The Direct Democratic Nationalists Movement Party [Nash'at KHALIFAH]

The Homeland (Hizb Al-Watan)

The People

Unified Front

United Front

Voice of the Nation; qtgan

Political pressure groups and leaders: 15 April Movement [Mohammad SUNEID, chairman]

24 March Movement [Mu'az al-KHAWALIDAH, Abdel Rahman HASANEIN, spokespersons]

1952 Constitution Movement

Anti-Normalization Committee [Hamzah MANSOUR, chairman]

Economic and Social Association of Retired Servicemen And Veterans or ESARSV [Abdulsalam al-HASSANAT, chairman]

Group of 36

Higher Coordination Committee of Opposition Parties [Said DIAB]

Higher National Committee for Military Retirees or HNCMR [Ali al-HABASHNEH, chairman]

Hirak

Jordan Bar Association [Saleh al-ARMUTI, chairman]

Jordanian Campaign for Change or Jayin

Jordanian Muslim Brotherhood [Dr. Hamam SAID, controller general]

Jordanian Press Association [Sayf al-SHARIF, president]

National Front for Reform or NFR [Ahmad OBEIDAT, chairman]

Popular Gathering for Reform

Professional Associations Council [Abd al-Hadial-FALAHAT, chairman]

Sons of Jordan

International organization participation: ABEDA, AFESD, AMF, CAEU, CD, CICA, EBRD, FAO, G-11, G-77, IAEA, IBRD, ICAO, ICC (national committees), ICCt, ICRM, IDA, IDB, IFAD, IFC, IFRCS, ILO, IMF, IMO, IMSO, Interpol, IOC, IOM, IPU, ISO, ITSO, ITU, ITUC (NGOs), LAS, MIGA, MINUSTAH, MINUSMA, MONUSCO, NAM, OIC, OPCW, OSCE (partner), PCA, UN, UN Security Council (temporary), UNAMID, UNCTAD, UNESCO, UNHCR, UNIDO, UNMIL, UNMISS, UNOCI, UNRWA, UNWTO, UPU, WCO, WFTU (NGOs), WHO, WIPO, WMO, WTO

Diplomatic representation in the US: *chief of mission:* Ambassador Dina Khalil Tawiq KAWAR (since 27 June 2016)

chancery: 3504 International Drive NW, Washington, DC 20008

telephone: [1] (202) 966-2664

FAX: [1] (202) 966-3110

Diplomatic representation from the US: *chief of mission:* Ambassador Alice G. WELLS (since 31 August 2014)

embassy: Abdoun, Al-Umawyeen St., Amman

mailing address: P. O. Box 354, Amman 11118 Jordan; Unit 70200, Box 5, DPO AE 09892–0200

telephone: [962] (6) 590-6000

FAX: [962] (6) 592-0163

Flag description: three equal horizontal bands of black (top), representing the Abbassid Caliphate, white, representing the Ummayyad Caliphate, and green, representing the Fatimid Caliphate; a red isosceles triangle on the hoist side, representing the Great Arab Revolt of 1916, and bearing a small white seven-pointed star symbolizing the seven verses of the opening Sura (Al-Fatiha) of the Holy Koran; the seven points on the star represent faith in One God, humanity, national spirit, humility, social justice, virtue, and aspirations; design is based on the Arab Revolt flag of World War I

National symbol(s): eagle; national colors: black, white, green, red

National anthem: *name:* "As-salam al-malaki al-urdoni" (Long Live the King of Jordan)

lyrics/music: Abdul-Mone'm al-RIFAI'/Abdul-Qader al-TANEER

note: adopted 1946; the shortened version of the anthem is used most commonly, while the full version is reserved for special occasions

ECONOMY

Economy—overview: Jordan's economy is among the smallest in the Middle East, with insufficient supplies of water, oil, and other natural resources, underlying the government's heavy reliance on foreign Assistance. Other economic challenges for the government include chronic high rates of poverty, unemployment and underemployment, and chronic budget and current account deficits, and government debt. King ABDALLAH, during the first decade of the 2000s, implemented significant economic reforms, such as expanding foreign trade and privatizing state-owned companies that attracted foreign investment and contributed to average annual economic growth of 8% for 2004 through 2008. The global economic slowdown and regional turmoil contributed to slower growth from 2010 to 2014—with growth averaging 2.8% per year—and hurt export-oriented sectors, construction, and tourism. Through 2014, Jordan's finances were strained by a series of natural gas pipeline attacks in Egypt, disrupting natural gas exports to Jordan, and led Jordan to rely on more expensive diesel imports, primarily from Saudi Arabia, to generate electricity.

To diversify its energy mix, Jordan has secured several contracts for liquefied natural gas, and is currently exploring nuclear power generation, exploitation of abundant oil shale reserves and renewable technologies, as well as the import of Israeli offshore gas. in August 2015, Jordan completed a $2.1 billion, three year IMF Stand-By Arrangement, which the government had entered to help correct budgetary and balance of payments imbalances. Jordan plans to expand on its fiscal reform measures enacted over the previous few years with a follow-on IMF agreement in 2016 to boost government revenues, reduce the budget deficit, and manage its burgeoning debt, brought on in part by an influx of over 630,000 Syrian refugees since 2011, which put additional pressure on expenditures.

GDP (purchasing power parity): $82.73 billion (2015 est.)
$80.71 billion (2014 est.)
$78.28 billion (2013 est.)
note: data are in 2015 US dollars
country comparison to the world: 89
GDP (official exchange rate): $37.62 billion (2015 est.)
GDP—real growth rate: 2.5% (2015 est.)
3.1% (2014 est.)
2.8% (2013 est.)
country comparison to the world: 121
GDP—per capita (PPP): $12,100 (2015 est.)
$12,100 (2014 est.)
$12,000 (2013 est.)
note: data are in 2015 US dollars
country comparison to the world: 125
Gross national saving: 11.4% of GDP (2015 est.)
14.7% of GDP (2014 est.)
10.5% of GDP (2013 est.)
country comparison to the world: 144
GDP—composition, by end use:
household consumption: 78.9%
government consumption: 23.1%
investment in fixed capital: 28%
investment in inventories: 0.2%
exports of goods and services: 36.8%
imports of goods and services: —67% (2015 est.)

GDP—composition, by sector of origin:
agriculture: 3.8%
industry: 29.9%
services: 66.3% (2015 est.)
Agriculture—products: citrus, tomatoes, cucumbers, olives, strawberries, stone fruits; sheep, poultry, dairy
Industries: tourism, information technology, clothing, fertilizers, potash, phosphate mining, pharmaceuticals, petroleum refining, cement, inorganic chemicals, light manufacturing
Industrial production growth rate: 3.6% (2015 est.)
country comparison to the world: 66
Labor force: 2.02 million (2015 est.)
country comparison to the world: 122

Labor force—by occupation: *agriculture:* 2%
industry: 20%
services: 78% (2013 est.)
Unemployment rate: 13% (2015 est.)
11.9% (2014 est.)
note: official rate; unofficial rate is approximately 30%
country comparison to the world: 142
Population below poverty line: 14.2% (2002 est.)
Household income or consumption by percentage share: *lowest:* 10%: 3.4%
highest: 10%: 28.7% (2010 est.)
Distribution of family income—Gini index: 39.7 (2007)
36.4 (1997)
country comparison to the world: 65

Budget: *revenues:* $8.707 billion
expenditures: $11.01 billion (2015 est.)
Taxes and other revenues: 22.8% of GDP (2015 est.)
country comparison to the world: 137
Budget surplus (+) or deficit (-): -6% of GDP (2015 est.)
country comparison to the world: 180
Public debt: 79.2% of GDP (2015 est.)
80.8% of GDP (2014 est.)
note: data cover central government debt, and include debt instruments issued (or owned) by government entities other than the treasury; the data include treasury debt held by foreign entities; the data exclude debt issued by subnational entities, as well as intra-governmental debt; intra-governmental debt consists of treasury borrowings from surpluses in the social funds, such as for retirement, medical care, and unemployment; debt instruments for the social funds are not sold at public auctions
country comparison to the world: 33
Fiscal year: calendar year
Inflation rate (consumer prices): -0.9% (2015 est.)
2.9% (2014 est.)
country comparison to the world: 16
Central bank discount rate: 0.3% (31 December 2010)
4.75% (31 December 2009)
country comparison to the world: 133
Commercial bank prime lending rate: 8.4% (31 December 2015 est.)
8.84% (31 December 2014 est.)
country comparison to the world: 105

Stock of narrow money: $13.91 billion (31 December 2015 est.)
$13 billion (31 December 2014 est.)
country comparison to the world: 69
Stock of broad money: $43.64 billion (31 December 2015 est.)
$41.18 billion (31 December 2014 est.)
country comparison to the world: 71
Stock of domestic credit: $40.83 billion (31 December 2015 est.)
$38.71 billion (31 December 2014 est.)
country comparison to the world: 66
Market value of publicly traded shares: $27 billion (31 December 2012 est.)
$27.18 billion (31 December 2011)
$30.86 billion (31 December 2010 est.)
country comparison to the world: 60
Current account balance: -$3.299 billion (2015 est.)
-$2.362 billion (2014 est.)
country comparison to the world: 161
Exports: $7.882 billion (2015 est.)
$8.385 billion (2014 est.)
country comparison to the world: 97
Exports—commodities: textiles, fertilizers, potash, phosphates, vegetables, pharmaceuticals
Exports—partners: US 21%, Saudi Arabia 16.5%, Iraq 10.3%, India 8.7%, UAE 4.8%, Kuwait 4.4% (2015)
Imports: $17.76 billion (2015 est.)
$20.18 billion (2014 est.)
country comparison to the world: 77
Imports—commodities: crude oil, refined petroleum products, machinery, transport equipment, iron, cereals
Imports—partners: Saudi Arabia 15.4%, China 12.8%, US 6.2%, Germany 4.7%, UAE 4.2% (2015)
Reserves of foreign exchange and gold: $17.22 billion (31 December 2015 est.)
$16.04 billion (31 December 2014 est.)
country comparison to the world: 64
Debt—external: $25.02 billion (31 December 2014 est.)
$23.85 billion (31 December 2013 est.)
country comparison to the world: 80
Stock of direct foreign investment—at home: $30.02 billion (31 December 2015 est.)
$28.73 billion (31 December 2014 est.)
country comparison to the world: 71
Stock of direct foreign investment—abroad: $623 million (31 December 2015 est.)
$608 million (31 December 2014 est.)
country comparison to the world: 86
Exchange rates: Jordanian dinars (JOD) per US dollar—
0.71 (2015 est.)
0.71 (2014 est.)
0.71 (2013 est.)
0.709 (2012 est.)
0.709 (2011 est.)

ENERGY

Electricity—production: 15.6 billion kWh (2012 est.)
country comparison to the world: 83

Electricity—consumption: 14.56 billion kWh (2013 est.)
country comparison to the world: 79
Electricity—exports: 59 million kWh (2013 est.)
country comparison to the world: 83
Electricity—imports: 381 million kWh (2013 est.)
country comparison to the world: 81
Electricity—installed generating capacity: 3.193 million kW (2013 est.)
country comparison to the world: 92
Electricity—from fossil fuels: 99.6% of total installed capacity (2013 est.)
country comparison to the world: 45
Electricity—from nuclear fuels: 0% of total installed capacity (2013 est.)
country comparison to the world: 117
Electricity—from hydroelectric plants: 0.3% of total installed capacity (2013 est.)
country comparison to the world: 148
Electricity—from other renewable sources: 0.1% of total installed capacity (2013 est.)
country comparison to the world: 122
Crude oil—production: 22 bbl/day (2014 est.)
country comparison to the world: 100
Crude oil—exports: 0 bbl/day (2013 est.)
country comparison to the world: 143
Crude oil—imports: 59,440 bbl/day (2013 est.)
country comparison to the world: 53
Crude oil—proved reserves: 1 million bbl (1 January 2015 est.)
country comparison to the world: 98
Refined petroleum products—production: 57,790 bbl/day (2013 est.)
country comparison to the world: 79
Refined petroleum products—consumption: 134,000 bbl/day (2013 est.)
country comparison to the world: 70
Refined petroleum products—exports: 0 bbl/day (2013 est.)
country comparison to the world: 191
Refined petroleum products—imports: 68,040 bbl/day (2013 est.)
country comparison to the world: 64
Natural gas—production: 150 million cu m (2013 est.)
country comparison to the world: 81
Natural gas—consumption: 1.016 billion cu m (2013 est.)
country comparison to the world: 90
Natural gas—exports: 0 cu m (2013 est.)
country comparison to the world: 124
Natural gas—imports: 865 million cu m (2013 est.)
country comparison to the world: 60
Natural gas—proved reserves: 6.031 billion cu m (1 January 2014 est.)
country comparison to the world: 88

Carbon dioxide emissions from consumption of energy: 16.86 million Mt (2012 est.)
country comparison to the world: 85

COMMUNICATIONS

Telephones—fixed lines: *total subscriptions:* 380,000
subscriptions per 100 inhabitants: 5 (2014 est.)
country comparison to the world: 107
Telephones—mobile cellular: *total:* 11.1 million
subscriptions per 100 inhabitants: 140 (2014 est.)
country comparison to the world: 81
Telephone system: *general assessment:* service has improved recently with increased use of digital switching equipment; microwave radio relay transmission and coaxial and fiber-optic cable are employed on trunk lines; growing mobile-cellular usage in both urban and rural areas is reducing use of fixed-line services
domestic: 1995 telecommunications law opened all non-fixed-line services to private competition; in 2005, monopoly over fixed-line services terminated and the entire telecommunications sector was opened to competition; currently multiple mobile-cellular providers with subscribership reaching 115 per 100 persons in 2011
international: country code—962; landing point for the Fiber-Optic Link Around the Globe (FLAG) FEA and FLAG Falcon submarine cable networks; satellite earth stations—33 (3 Intelsat, 1 Arabsat, and 29 land and maritime Inmarsat terminals); fiber-optic cable to Saudi Arabia and microwave radio relay link with Egypt and Syria; participant in Medarabtel (2011)
Broadcast media: radio and TV dominated by the government-owned Jordan Radio and Television Corporation (JRTV) that operates a main network, a sports network, a film network, and a satellite channel; first independent TV broadcaster aired in 2007; international satellite TV and Israeli and Syrian TV broadcasts are available; roughly 30 radio stations with JRTV operating the main government-owned station; transmissions of multiple international radio broadcasters are available (2007)
Radio broadcast station: AM 1, FM 28 (2010)
Television broadcast stations: 4 (2009)
Internet country code: .jo
Internet hosts: 69,473 (2012)
country comparison to the world: 89
Internet users: *total:* 3.6 million
percent of Population: 45.0% (2014 est.)
country comparison to the world: 82

TRANSPORTATION

Airports: 18 (2013)
country comparison to the world: 140

Airports—with paved runways: *total:* 16
over 3,047 m: 8
2,438 to 3,047 m: 5
1,524 to 2,437 m: 2
914 to 1,523 m: 1 (2013)
Airports—with unpaved runways: *total:* 2
under 914 m: 2 (2013)
Heliports: 1 (2012)
Pipelines: gas 473 km; oil 49 km (2013)
Railways: *total:* 507 km
narrow gauge: 507 km 1.050-m gauge (2008)
country comparison to the world: 114
Roadways: total: 7,203 km
paved: 7,203 km (2011)
country comparison to the world: 144
Merchant marine: *total:* 12
by type: cargo 4, passenger/cargo 6, petroleum tanker 1, roll on/roll off 1
foreign-owned: 2 (UAE 2)
registered in other countries: 16 (Bahamas 2, Egypt 2, Indonesia 1, Panama 11) (2010)
country comparison to the world: 106
Ports and terminals: *major seaport(s):* Al 'Aqabah

MILITARY AND SECURITY

Military branches: Jordanian Armed Forces (JAF): Royal Jordanian Land Force (RJLF), Royal Jordanian Navy, Royal Jordanian Air Force (Al-Quwwat al-Jawwiya al-Malakiya al-Urduniya, RJAF), Special Operations Command (Socom); Public Security Directorate (normally falls under Ministry of Interior, but comes under JAF in wartime or crisis) (2013)
Military service age and obligation: years of age for voluntary male military service; initial service term 2 years, with option to reenlist for years; conscription at age 18 suspended in 1999; women not subject to conscription, but can volunteer to serve in noncombat military positions in the Royal Jordanian Arab Army Women's Corps and RJAF (2013)
Military expenditures:
4.65% of GDP (2012)
4.64% of GDP (2011)
4.65% of GDP (2010)
country comparison to the world: 7

TRANSNATIONAL ISSUES

Disputes—international: 2004 Agreement settles border dispute with Syria pending demarcation

Refugees and internally displaced persons: *refugees (country of origin):* 2,097,338 (Palestinian refugees) (2014); 52,643 (Iraq) (2015); 657,433 (Syria) (2016)

KAZAKHSTAN

INTRODUCTION

Background: Ethnic Kazakhs, a mix of Turkic and Mongol nomadic tribes who migrated to the region by the 13th century, were rarely united as a single nation. The area was conquered by Russia in the 18th century, and Kazakhstan became a Soviet Republic in 1936. During the 1950s and 1960s agricultural "Virgin Lands" program, Soviet citizens were encouraged to help cultivate Kazakhstan's northern pastures. This influx of immigrants (mostly Russians, but also some other deported nationalities) skewed the ethnic mixture and enabled non-ethnic Kazakhs to outnumber natives. Non-Muslim ethnic minorities departed Kazakhstan in large numbers from the mid-1990s through the mid-2000s and a national program has repatriated about a million ethnic Kazakhs back to Kazakhstan. These trends have allowed Kazakhs to become the titular majority again. This dramatic demographic shift has also undermined the previous religious diversity and made the country more than 70 percent Muslim. Kazakhstan's economy is larger than those of all the other Central Asian states largely due to the country's vast natural resources. Current issues include: developing a cohesive national identity; managing Islamic revivalism; expanding the development of the country's vast energy resources and exporting them to world markets; diversifying the economy outside the oil, gas, and mining sectors; enhancing Kazakhstan's economic competitiveness; developing a multiparty parliament and advancing political and social reform; and strengthening relations with neighboring states and other foreign powers.

GEOGRAPHY\

Location: Central Asia, northwest of China; a small portion west of the Ural (Zhayyq) River in easternmost Europe

Geographic coordinates: 48 00 N, 68 00 E

Map references: Asia

Area: *total:* 2,724,900 sq km
land: 2,699,700 sq km
water: 25,200 sq km
country comparison to the world: 9

Area—comparative: slightly less than four times the size of Texas

Land boundaries: *total:* 13,364 km
border countries (5): China 1,765 km, Kyrgyzstan 1,212 km, Russia 7,644 km, Turkmenistan 413 km, Uzbekistan 2,330 km

Coastline: 0 km (landlocked); note—Kazakhstan borders the Aral Sea, now split into two bodies of water (1,070 km), and the Caspian Sea (1,894 km)

Maritime claims: none (landlocked)

Climate: continental, cold winters and hot summers, arid and semiarid

Terrain: vast flat steppe extending from the Volga in the west to the Altai Mountains in the east and from the plains of western Siberia in the north to oases and deserts of Central Asia in the south

Elevation: *mean elevation:* 387 m

elevation extremes: *lowest point:* Vpadina Kaundy -132 m
highest point: Khan Tangiri Shyngy (Pik Khan-Tengri) 6,995 m

Natural resources: major deposits of petroleum, natural gas, coal, ironore, manganese, chromeore, nickel, cobalt, copper, molybdenum, lead, zinc, bauxite, gold, uranium

Land use: *agricultural land:* 77.4%
arable land: 8.9%
permanent crops: 0%
permanent pasture: 68.5%
forest: 1.2%
other: 21.4% (2011 est.)

Irrigated land: 20,660 sq km (2012)

Total renewable water resources: 107.5 cu km (2011)

Freshwater withdrawal (domestic/industrial/agricultural): *total:* 21.14 cu km/yr (4%/30%/66%)
per capita: 1,304 cu m/yr (2010)

Natural hazards: earthquakes in the south; mudslides around Alm aty

Environment—current issues: radioactive or toxic chemical sites associated with former defense industries and test ranges scattered throughout the country pose health risks for humans and animals; industrial pollution is severe in some cities; because the two main rivers that flowed into the Aral Sea have been diverted for irrigation, it is drying up and leaving behind a harmful layer of chemical pesticides and natural salts; these substances are then picked up by the wind and blown into noxious dust storms; pollution in the Caspian Sea; soil pollution from overuse of agricultural chemicals and salination from poor infrastructure and wasteful irrigation practices

Environment—international agreements: *party to:* Air Pollution, Biodiversity, Climate Change, Desertification, Endangered Species, Environmental Modification, Hazardous Wastes, Ozone Layer Protection, Ship Pollution, Wetlands
signed, but not ratified: Climate Change-Kyoto Protocol

Geography—note: world's largest landlocked country; Russia leases approximately 6,000 sq km of territory enclosing the Baykonur Cosmodrome; in January 2004, Kazakhstan and Russia extended the lease to 2050

PEOPLE AND SOCIETY

Nationality: *noun:* Kazakhstani(s)
adjective: Kazakhstani

Ethnic groups: Kazakh (Qazaq) 63.1%, Russian 23.7%, Uzbek 2.9%, Uighur 1.4%, Tatar 1.3%, German 1.1%, other 4.4% (2009 est.)

Languages: Kazakh (official, Q azaq) 74% (understand spoken language), Russian (official, used in everyday business, designated the "language of interethnic communication") 94.4% (understand spoken language) (2009 est.)

Religions: Muslim 70.2%, Christian 26.2% (mainly Russian Orthodox), other 0.2%, atheist 2.8%, unspecified 0.5% (2009 est.)

Population: 18,157,122 (July 2015 est.)
country comparison to the world: 61

Age structure: *0–14 years:* 25.41% (male 2,294,513/female 2,319,233)
15–24 years: 15.33% (male 1,417,344/female 1,366,655)
25–54 years: 42.59% (male 3,768,418/female 3,965,188)
55–64 years: 9.49% (male 753,011/female 970,569)
65 years and over: 7.17% (male 448,857/female 853,334) (2015 est.)

Dependency ratios: *total dependency ratio:* 50.3%
youth dependency ratio: 40.1%
elderly dependency ratio: 10.1%
potential support ratio: 9.9% (2015 est.)

Median age: *total:* 30 years
male: 28.7 years
female: 31.3 years (2015 est.)
country comparison to the world: 113

Population growth rate: 1.14% (2015 est.)
country comparison to the world: 107

Birth rate: 19.15 births/1,000 population (2015 est.)
country comparison to the world: 91

Death rate: 8.21 deaths/1,000 population (2015 est.)
country comparison to the world: 86

Net migration rate: 0.41 migrant(s)/1,000 population (2015 est.)
country comparison to the world: 73

Urbanization: *urban population:* 53.2% of total population (2015)
rate of urban ization: 0.86% annual rate of change (2010–15 est.)

Major urban areas—population: Almaty 1.523 million; ASTANA (capital) 759,000 (2015)

Sex ratio: *at birth:* 0.94 male(s)/female
0–14 years: 0.99 male(s)/female
15–24 years: 1.04 male(s)/female
25–54 years: 0.95 male(s)/female
55–64 years: 0.78 male(s)/female
65 years and over: 0.53 male(s)/female
total population: 0.92 male(s)/female (2015 est.)

Mother's mean age at first birth: 25 (2011 est.)

Maternal mortality rate: 12 deaths/100,000 live births (2015 est.)
country comparison to the world: 107

Infant mortality rate: *total:* 20.92 deaths/1,000 live births
male: 23.63 deaths/1,000 live births

female: 18.39 deaths/1,000 live births (2015 est.)
country comparison to the world: 84
Life expectancy at birth: *total population:* 70.55 years
male: 65.3 years
female: 75.46 years (2015 est.)
country comparison to the world: 152
Total fertility rate: 2.31 children born/woman (2015 est.)
country comparison to the world: 92
Contraceptive prevalence rate: 51% (2010/11)
Health expenditures: 4.3% of GDP (2013)
country comparison to the world: 157
Physicians density: 3.62 physicians/1,000 population (2013)
Hospital bed density: 7.2 beds/1,000 population (2012)
Drinking water source:
improved:
urban: 99.4% of population
rural: 85.6% of population
total: 92.9% of population
unimproved:
urban: 0.6% of population
rural: 14.4% of population
total: 7.1% of population (2015 est.)
Sanitation facility access:
improved:
urban: 97% of population
rural: 98.1% of population
total: 97.5% of population
unimproved:
urban: 3% of population
rural: 1.9% of population
total: 2.5% of population (2015 est.)
HIV/AIDS—adult prevalence rate: 0.19% (2014 est.)
country comparison to the world: 98
HIV/AIDS—people living with HIV/AIDS: 20,300 (2014 est.)
country comparison to the world: 78
HIV/AIDS—deaths: 500 (2014 est.)
country comparison to the world: 87
Obesity—adult prevalence rate: 23.5% (2014)
country comparison to the world: 74
Children under the age of 5 years underweight: 3.7% (2011)
country comparison to the world: 100
Education expenditures: 3.1% of GDP (2009)
country comparison to the world: 138
Literacy: *definition:* age 15 and over can read and write
total population: 99.8%
male: 99.8%
female: 99.8% (2015 est.)
School life expectancy (primary to tertiary education): *total:* 15 years
male: 15 years
female: 15 years (2015)
Child labor—children ages 5–14: *total number:* 59,254
percentage: 2% (2006 est.)
Unemployment, youth ages 15–24: *total:* 3.9%
male: 2.9%
female: 5.1% (2012 est.)
country comparison to the world: 128

GOVERNMENT

Country name: *conventional long form:* Republic of Kazakhstan

conventional short form: Kazakhstan
local long form: Qazaqstan Respublikasy
local short form: Qazaqstan
former: Kazakh Soviet Socialist Republic
etymology: the name "Kazakh" derives from the Turkic word "kaz" meaning "to wander, " recalling the Kazakh's nomadic lifestyle; the Persian suffix "-stan" means "place of" or "country," so the word Kazakhstan literally means "Land of the wanderers"
Government type: presiden tial republic
Capital: *name:* Astana
Geographic coordinates: 51 10 N, 71 25 E
time difference: UTC+6 (11 hours ahead of Washington, DC, during Standard Time)
note: Kazakhstan has two time zon es
Administrative divisions: 14 provinces (oblystar, singular—oblys) and 3 cities* (qalalar, singular—qala); Almaty (Taldy qorghan), Almaty*, Aqmola (Kokshetau), Aqtobe, Astana*, Atyrau, Batys Qazaqstan [West Kazakhstan] (Oral), Bayqongyr [Baykonur]*, Mangghystau (Aqtau), Ongtustik Qazaqstan [South Kazakhstan] (Shymkent), Pavlodar, Qaraghan dy, Qostan ay, Qyzylorda, Shyghys Qazaqstan [East Kazakhstan] (O skemen), Soltustik Qazaqstan [North Kazakhstan] (Petropavl), Zhambyl (Taraz)
note: admin istrative divisions have the same names as their administrative centers (exceptions have the administrative center name following in parentheses); in 1995, the Governments of Kazakhstan and Russia entered into an agreement whereby Russia would lease for a period of 20 years an area of 6,000 sq km enclosing the Baykonur space launch facilities and the city of Bayqongyr (Baykonur, formerly Leninsk); in 2004, a new agreement extended the lease to 2050
Independence: 16 December 1991 (from the Soviet Union)
National holiday: Independence Day, 16 December (1991)
Constitution: previous 1937, 1978 (preindependence); latest adopted 28 January 1993, approved by referendum 30 August 1995, effective 5 September 1995; amended several times, last in 2011 (2016)
Legal system: civil law system in fluenced by Roman-Germanic law and by the theory and practice of the Russian Federation
International law organization participation: has not submitted an ICJ jurisdiction declaration; non-party state to the ICCt
Citizenship: *citizenship by birth:* no
citizenship by descent only: at least one parent must be a citizen of Kazakhstan
dual citizenship recognized: no
residency requirement for naturalization: 5 years
Suffrage: 18 years of age; universal
Executive branch: *chief of state:* President Nursultan Abishuly NAZARBAYEV (chairman of the Supreme Soviet from 22 February 1990, elected president 1 December 1991)

head of government: Prime Minister Karim MASIMOV (since 2 April 2014); First Deputy Prime Minister Bakytzhan SAGINTAYEV (since

16 January 2013); Deputy Prime Minister Dariga NAZARBAYEVA (since September 2015)
cabinet: Council of Ministers appointed by the president
elections/appointments: president directly elected by simple majority popular vote for a 5-year term (eligible for a second term); election last held on 26 April 2015 (next to be held in 2020); prime minister and deputy prime minister appointed by the president, approved by the Mazhilis; note—constitutional amendments in May 2007 shortened the presidential term from 7 to 5 years and established a 2-consecutive-term limit; NAZARBAYEV has official status as the "First President of Kazakhstan" and is allowed unlimited terms
election results: Nursultan Abishuly NAZARBAYEV reelected president; percent of vote—Nursultan Abishuly NAZARBAYEV (Nur Otan) 97.8%, other 2.2%
Legislative branch: *description:* bicameral Parliament consists of the Senate (47 seats; 32 members indirectly elected by majority two-round vote by the oblast-level assemblies and 15 members appointed by the president; members serve 6-year terms, with one-half of the membership renewed every 3 years) and the Mazhilis (107 seats; 98 members directly elected in a single national constituency by proportional representation vote to serve 5-year terms and 9 indirectly elected by the Assembly of People of Kazakhstan, a 350-member, presidentially appointed advisory body designed to represent the country's ethnic minorities)
elections: Senate—last held on 1 October 2014 (next to be held in 2017); Mazhilis—last held on 20 March 2016 (next to be held by 2021)
election results: Senate—percent of vote by party—NA; seats by party—Nur Otan 16; Mazhilis -percent of vote by party—Nur Otan 82.2%, Ak Zhol 7.2%, Communist People's Party 7.1%, other 3.5%; seats by party—Nur Otan 84, Ak Zhol 7, Communist People's Party 7
Judicial branch: *highest court(s):* Supreme Court of the Republic (consists of 44 members); Constitutional Council (consists of 7 members)
judge selection and term of office: Supreme Court judges proposed by the president of the republic on recommendation of the Supreme Judicial Council, and confirmed by the Senate; judge tenure NA; Constitutional Council—the president of the republic, the Senate chairperson, the Majilis chairperson each appoints 1 member for a 3-year term and each appoints 1 member for a 6-year term; chairperson of the Constitutional Council appointed by the president of the republic for a 6-year term
subordinate courts: regional and local courts
Political parties and leaders: Ak Zhol (Bright Path) Party or Democratic Party of Kazakhstan Ak Zhol [Azat PERUASHEV]
Auyl National Patriotic Party [Ali BEKTAYEV] (Auyl is a September 2015 merger of the Patriots' Party and the Auyl Social Democratic Party)
Birlik (Unity) [Seril SULTANGALI] (Birlik is an April 2013 merger of Adilet (Justice; formerly Democratic

Party of Kazakhstan) and Rukhaniyat (Spirituality))

Communist People's Party of Kazakhstan [Vladislav KOSAREV]

National Social Democratic Party or NSDP [Zharmakhan TUYAKBAY]

Nur Otan (Radiant Fatherland) Democratic People's Party [Nursultan NAZAR BAYEV] (the Agrarian, Asar, and Civic parties merged with Otan)

Political pressure groups and leaders: Adil-Soz [Tamara KALEYEVA]

Confederation of Free Trade Unions [Larissa KHARKOVA]

Foundation for Support of Civil Initiatives [Nurul RAKHIMBEK]

International Legal Initiative [Aina SHORMAN BAYEVA]

Kazakhstan International Bureau on Human Rights [Yevgeniy ZHOVTIS, Chairman of Bureau's Council, Roza AKYLBEKOVA, director]

Legal Media Centre (sometimes known as the north Kazakhstan Legal Media Centre) [Diana OKREMOVA]

Public Foundation for Parliamentary Development [Zauresh BATTALOVA]

Republican Network of International Monitors [Daniyar LIVAZOV]

Transparency International [Sergey ZLOTNIKOV]

International organization participation: ADB, CICA, CIS, CSTO, EAEC, EAEU, EAPC, EBRD, ECO, EITI (compliant country), FAO, GCTU, IAEA, IBRD, ICAO, ICC (NGOs), ICRM, IDA, IDB, IFAD, IF C, IF RCS, ILO, IMF, IMO, Interpol, IOC, IOM, IPU, ISO, ITSO, ITU, MIGA, MINURSO, NAM (observer), NSG, OAS (observer), OIC, OPCW, OSCE, PFP, SCO, UN, UNCTAD, UNESCO, UNIDO, UNWTO, UPU, WCO, WFTU (NGOs), WHO, WIPO, WMO, WTO (observer), ZC

Diplomatic representation in the US: *chief of mission:* Ambassador Kayrat UMAROV (since 14 January 2013)

chancery: 1401 16th Street NW, Washington, DC 20036

telephone: [1] (202) 232-5488

FAX: [1] (202) 232-5845

consulate(s) general: New York

Diplomatic representation from the US: *chief of mission:* Ambassador George KROL (since 18 March 2015)

embassy: Rakhymzhan Koshkarbayev Ave. no 3, Astana 010010

mailing address: use embassy street address

telephone: [7] (7172) 70-21-00

FAX: [7] (7172) 54-09-14

Consulate(s) General: Almaty

Flag description: a gold sun with 32 rays above a soaring golden steppe eagle, both centered on a sky blue background; the hoist side displays a national ornamental pattern "koshkar-muiz" (the horns of the ram) in gold; the blue color is of religious significance to the Turkic peoples of the country, and so symbolizes cultural and ethnic unity; it also represents the endless sky as well as water; the sun, a source of life and energy, exemplifies wealth

and plenitude; the sun's rays are shaped like grain, which is the basis of abundance and prosperity; the eagle has appeared on the flags of Kazakh tribes for centuries and represents freedom, power, and the flight to the future; blue and yellow are the national colors

National symbol(s): golden eagle; national colors: blue, yellow

National anthem: *name:* "Menin Qazaqstanim" (My Kazakhstan)

lyrics/music: Zhumeken NAZHIMEDENOV and Nursultan NAZARBAYEV/Shamshi KALDAYAKOV

note: adopted 2006; President Nursultan NAZARBAYEV played a role in revising the lyrics

ECONOMY

Economy—overview: Kazakhstan, geographically the largest of the former Soviet republics, excluding Russia, possesses substantial fossil fuel reserves and other minerals and metals, such as uranium, copper, and zinc. It also has a large agricultural sector featuring livestock and grain. The government realizes that its economy suffers from an overreliance on oil and extractive industries and has embarked on an ambitious diversification program, aimed at developing targeted sectors like transport, pharmaceuticals, telecommunications, petrochemicals and food processing. Kazakhstan's vast hydrocarbon and mineral reserves form the backbone of its economy. Kazakhstan is landlocked and depends on Russia to export its oil to Europe. In 2010, Kazakhstan joined Russia and Belarus to establish a Customs Union in an effort to boost foreign investment and improve trade. The Customs Union evolved into a Single Economic Space in 2012 and the Eurasian Economic Union (EEU) in January 2015. The economic downturn of its EEU partner, Russia, and the decline in global commodity prices have contributed to an economic slowdown in Kazakhstan, which is experiencing its slowest economic growth since the financial crises of 2008–09. Kazakhstan devalued its currency, the tenge, by 19% in February 2014, and in november 2014, the government announced a stimulus package to cope with its economic challenges. In spring 2015, Kazakhstan embarked on an ambitious reform agenda to modernize its economy and improve its institutions. In the face of further decline in the ruble, oil prices, and the regional economic slowdown, Kazakhstan announced in August 2015 that it would cancel its currency band in favor of a floating exchange rate that sparked further devaluation of the tenge. In 2015, Kazakhstan's president signed into law a new Entrepreneurial Code and a new Labor Code, both aimed at improving the business environment. Despite some positive institutional and legislative changes, investors remain concerned about corruption, bureaucracy, and arbitrary law enforcement, especially at the regional and municipal levels.

GDP (purchasing power parity): $429.1 billion (2015 est.)

$424.2 billion (2014 est.)

$406.7 billion (2013 est.)

note: data are in 2015 US dollars

country comparison to the world: 43

GDP (official exchange rate): $173.2 billion (2015 est.)

GDP—real growth rate: 1.2% (2015 est.)

4.3% (2014 est.)

6% (2013 est.)

country comparison to the world: 165

GDP—per capita (PPP): $24,300 (2015 est.)

$24,300 (2014 est.)

$23,700 (2013 est.)

note: data are in 2015 US dollars

country comparison to the world: 78

Gross national saving: 24.2% of GDP (2015 est.)

27% of GDP (2014 est.)

24.3% of GDP (2013 est.)

country comparison to the world: 52

GDP—composition, by end use:

household consumption: 56.1%

government consumption: 13.7%

investment in fixed capital: 24%

investment in inventories: 1.2%

exports of goods and services: 30.9%

imports of goods and services: -25.9% (2015 est.)

GDP—composition, by sector of origin:

agriculture: 4.8%

industry: 35.3%

services: 59.9% (2015 est.)

Agriculture—products: grain (mostly spring wheat and barley), potatoes, vegetables, melons; livestock

Industries: oil, coal, iron ore, manganese, chromite, lead, zinc, copper, titanium, bauxite, gold, silver, phosphates, sulfur, uranium, iron and steel; tractors and other agricultural machinery, electric motors, construction materials

Industrial production growth rate: 0.8% (2015 est.)

country comparison to the world: 153

Labor force: 8.965 million (2015 est.)

country comparison to the world: 55

Labor force—by occupation: *agriculture:* 25.8%

industry: 11.9%

services: 62.3% (2012)

Unemployment rate: 5% (2015 est.)

5% (2014 est.)

country comparison to the world: 51

Population below poverty line: 5.3% (2011 est.)

Household income or consumption by percentage share: *lowest:* 10%: 3.9%

highest: 10%: 23.7% (2011 est.)

Distribution of family income—Gini index: 28.9 (2011)

31.5 (2003)

country comparison to the world: 127

Budget: *revenues:* $34.1 billion

expenditures: $38.08 billion (2015 est.)

Taxes and other revenues: 17.5% of GDP (2015 est.)

country comparison to the world: 174

Budget surplus (+) or deficit (–): -2% of GDP (2015 est.)

country comparison to the world: 74

Public debt: 17.6% of GDP (2015 est.)

15.5% of GDP (2014 est.)

country comparison to the world: 157

Fiscal year: calendar year

Inflation rate (consumer prices): 6.5% (2015 est.)
6.7% (2014 est.)
country comparison to the world: 190
Central bank discount rate: 16% (31 December 2015)
5.5% (31 December 2014)
country comparison to the world: 9
Commercial bank prime lending rate: 10.9% (31 December 2015 est.)
7.24% (31 December 2014 est.)
country comparison to the world: 75
Stock of narrow money: $9.802 billion (31 December 2015 est.)
$16.35 billion (31 December 2014 est.)
country comparison to the world: 79
Stock of broad money: $52.89 billion (31 December 2014 est.)
$56.49 billion (31 December 2013 est.)
country comparison to the world: 67
Stock of domestic credit: $50.51 billion (31 December 2015 est.)
$78.46 billion (31 December 2014 est.)
country comparison to the world: 60
Market value of publicly traded shares: $23.5 billion (31 December 2012 est.)
$43.3 billion (31 December 2011)
$60.74 billion (31 December 2010 est.)
country comparison to the world: 63
Current account balance: -$4.5 billion (2015 est.)
$5.994 billion (2014 est.)
country comparison to the world: 165
Exports: $45.37 billion (2015 est.)
$80.28 billion (2014 est.)
country comparison to the world: 55
Exports—commodities: oil and oil products, natural gas, ferrous metals, chemicals, machinery, grain, wool, meat, coal
Exports—partners: China 15.1%, Russia 12.3%, France 9.2%, Germany 7.9%, Italy 6.7%, Greece 4.1% (2015)
Imports: $31.64 billion (2015 est.)
$43.58 billion (2014 est.)
country comparison to the world: 64
Imports—commodities: machinery and equipment, metal products, foodstuffs
Imports—partners: Russia 32.9%, China 25.9%, Germany 4.2% (2015)
Reserves of foreign exchange and gold: $29.31 billion (31 December 2015 est.)
$28.92 billion (31 December 2014 est.)
country comparison to the world: 50
Debt—external: $157.1 billion (31 December 2014 est.)
$149.9 billion (31 December 2013 est.)
country comparison to the world: 39
Stock of direct foreign investment—at home: $142.4 billion (31 December 2015 est.)
$136.6 billion (31 December 2014 est.)
country comparison to the world: 39
Stock of direct foreign investment—abroad: $33.46 billion (31 December 2015 est.)
$31.46 billion (31 December 2014 est.)
country comparison to the world: 51
Exchange rates: tenge (KZT) per US dollar—
214.1 (2015 est.)
179.19 (2014 est.)

179.19 (2013 est.)
149.11 (2012 est.)
146.62 (2011 est.)

ENERGY

Electricity—production: 90.53 billion kWh (2012 est.)
country comparison to the world: 36
Electricity—consumption: 80.29 billion kWh (2012 est.)
country comparison to the world: 37
Electricity—exports: 2.933 billion kWh (2012 est.)
country comparison to the world: 36
Electricity—imports: 4.252 billion kWh (2012 est.)
country comparison to the world: 44
Electricity—installed generating capacity: 17.84 million kW (2012 est.)
country comparison to the world: 43
Electricity—from fossil fuels: 87.3% of total installed capacity (2012 est.)
country comparison to the world: 83
Electricity—from nuclear fuels: 0% of total installed capacity (2012 est.)
country comparison to the world: 124
Electricity—from hydroelectric plants: 12.7% of total installed capacity (2012 est.)
country comparison to the world: 107
Electricity—from other renewable sources: 0% of total installed capacity (2012 est.)
country comparison to the world: 191
Crude oil—production: 1.632 million bbl/day (2014 est.)
country comparison to the world: 15
Crude oil—exports: 1.365 million bbl/day (2012 est.)
country comparison to the world: 9
Crude oil—imports: 118,400 bbl/day (2012 est.)
country comparison to the world: 41
Crude oil—proved reserves: 30 billion bbl (1 January 2015 est.)
country comparison to the world: 12
Refined petroleum products—production: 294,800 bbl/day (2012 est.)
country comparison to the world: 44
Refined petroleum products—consumption: 248,000 bbl/day (2013 est.)
country comparison to the world: 49
Refined petroleum products—exports: 142,800 bbl/day (2012 est.)
country comparison to the world: 40
Refined petroleum products—imports: 51,600 bbl/day (2012 est.)
country comparison to the world: 80
Natural gas—production: 20.4 billion cu m (2013 est.)
country comparison to the world: 32
Natural gas—consumption: 15.7 billion cu m (2013 est.)
country comparison to the world: 42
Natural gas—exports: 11.2 billion cu m (2013 est.)
country comparison to the world: 19
Natural gas—imports: 6.5 billion cu m (2013 est.)
country comparison to the world: 32

Natural gas—proved reserves: 2.407 trillion cu m (1 January 2014 est.)
country comparison to the world: 15
Carbon dioxide emissions from consumption of energy: 224.2 million Mt (2012 est.)
country comparison to the world: 27

COMMUNICATIONS

Telephones—fixed lines: *total subscriptions:* 4.34 million
subscriptions per 100 inhabitants: 24 (2014 est.)
country comparison to the world: 39
Telephones—mobile cellular: *total:* 28 million
subscriptions per 100 inhabitants: 156 (2014 est.)
country comparison to the world: 45
Telephone system: *general assessment:* inherited an outdated telecommunications network from the Soviet era requiring modernization
domestic: intercity by landline and microwave radio relay; number of fixed-line connections is gradually increasing and fixed-line teledensity now roughly 25 per 100 persons; mobile-cellular usage has increased rapidly and the subscriber base now exceeds 140 per 100 persons
international: country code—7; international traffic with other former Soviet republics and China carried by landline and microwave radio relay and with other countries by satellite and by the Trans-Asia-Europe (TAE) fiber-optic cable; satellite earth stations—2 Intelsat (2008)
Broadcast media: state owns nearly all radio and TV transmission facilities and operates national TV and radio networks; nearly all nationwide TV networks are wholly or partly owned by the government; some former state-owned media outlets have been privatized; households with satellite dishes have access to foreign media; a small number of commercial radio stations operate along with state-run radio stations; recent legislation requires all media outlets to register with the government and all TV providers to broadcast in digital format by 2018 (2015)
Radio broadcast stations: AM 60, FM 18, shortwave 9 (2008)
Television broadcast stations: 12 (plus 9 repeaters) (1998)
Internet country code: .kz
Internet hosts: 67,464 (2012)
country comparison to the world: 90
Internet users: *total:* 10.6 million
percent of population: 59.3% (2014 est.)
country comparison to the world: 45

TRANSPORTATION

Airports: 96 (2013)
country comparison to the world: 59
Airports—with paved runways: *total:* 63
over 3,047 m: 10
2,438 to 3,047 m: 25
1,524 to 2,437 m: 15
914 to 1,523 m: 5
under 914 m: 8 (2013)
Airports—with unpaved runways: *total:* 33
over 3,047 m: 5
2,438 to 3,047 m: 7

1,524 to 2,437 m: 3
914 to 1,523 m: 5
under 914 m: 13 (2013)
Heliports: 3 (2013)
Pipelines: condensate 658 km; gas 12,432 km; oil 11,313 km; refined products 1,095 km; water 1,465 km (2013)
Railways: *total:* 14,184 km
broad gauge: 14,184 km 1.520-m gauge (4,056 km electrified) (2014)
country comparison to the world: 19
Roadways: *total:* 97,418 km
paved: 87,140 km
unpaved: 10,278 km (2012)
country comparison to the world: 46
Waterways: 4,000 km (on the Ertis (Irtysh) River (80%) and Syr Darya (Syrdariya) River) (2010)
country comparison to the world: 25
Merchant marine: *total:* 11
by type: cargo 1, petroleum tanker 8, refrigerated cargo 1, specialized tanker 1
foreign-owned: 3 (Austria 1, Ireland 1, Turkey 1) (2010)

country comparison to the world: 109
Ports and terminals: *major seaport(s):* Caspian Sea—Aqtau (Shevchenko), Atyrau (Gur'yev)
river port(s): Oskemen (Ust-Kamenogorsk), Pavlodar, Semey (Semipalatinsk) (Irtysh River)

MILITARY AND SECURITY

Military branches: Kazakhstan Armed Forces: Ground Forces, Navy, Air Mobile Forces, Air Defense Forces (2013)
Military service age and obligation: 18 is the legal minimum age for compulsory military service; conscript service obligation is 2 years, but Kazakhstan may be transitioning to a contract force; 19 is the legal minimum age for voluntary service; military cadets in intermediate (ages 15–17) and higher (ages 17–21) education institutes are classified as military service personnel (2012)
Military expenditures:
1.21% of GDP (2012)
0.97% of GDP (2011)
1.21% of GDP (2010)
country comparison to the world: 81

TRANSNATIONAL ISSUES

Disputes—international: Kyrgyzstan has yet to ratify the 2001 boundary delimitation with Kazakhstan; field demarcation of the boundaries commenced with Uzbekistan in 2004 and with Turkmenistan in 2005; ongoing demarcation with Russia began in 2007; demarcation with China was completed in 2002; creation of a seabed boundary with Turkmenistan in the Caspian Sea remains under discussion; Azerbaijan, Kazakhstan, and Russia ratified Caspian seabed delimitation treaties based on equidistance, while Iran continues to insist on a one-fifth slice of the sea
Refugees and internally displaced persons: *stateless persons:* 7,909 (2015)
Illicit drugs: significant illicit cultivation of cannabis for CIS markets, as well as limited cultivation of opium poppy and ephedra (for the drug ephedrine); limited government eradication of illicit crops; transit point for Southwest Asian narcotics bound for Russia and the rest of Europe; significant consumer of opiates

KENYA

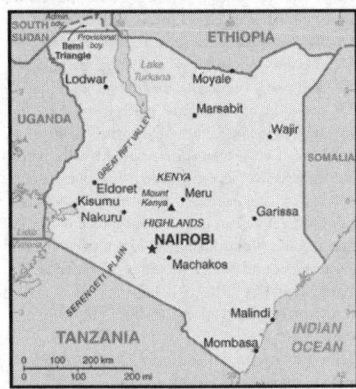

GEOGRAPHY

Location: Eastern Africa, bordering the Indian Ocean, between Somalia and Tanzania
Geographic coordinates: 1 00 N, 38 00 E
Map references: Africa
Area: *total:* 580,367 sq km
land: 569,140 sq km
water: 11,227 sq km
country comparison to the world: 49
Area—comparative: five times the size of Ohio; slightly more than twice the size of Nevada
Land boundaries: *total:* 3,457 km
border countries (5): Ethiopia 867 km, Somalia 684 km, South Sudan 317 km, Tanzania 775 km, Uganda 814 km
Coastline: 536 km
Maritime claims: *territorial sea:* 12 nm

exclusive economic zone: 200 nm
continental shelf: 200-m depth or to the depth of exploitation
Climate: varies from tropical along coast to arid in interior
Terrain: low plains rise to central highlands bisected by Great Rift Valley; fertile plateau in west
Elevation: *mean elevation:* 762 m
elevation extremes: *lowest point:* Indian Ocean 0 m
highest point: Mount Kenya 5,199 m
Natural resources: limestone, soda ash, salt, gemstones, fluorspar, zinc, diatomite, gypsum, wildlife, hydropower
Land use: *agricultural land:* 48.1%
arable land: 9.8%
permanent crops: 0.9%
permanent pasture: 37.4%
forest: 6.1%
other: 45.8% (2011 est.)
Irrigated land: 1,030 sq km (2012)
Total renewable water resources: 30.7 cu km (2011)
Freshwater withdrawal (domestic/industrial/agricultural): *total:* 2.74 cu km/yr (17%/4%/79%)
per capita: 72.96 cu m/yr (2003)
Natural hazards: recurring drought; flooding during rainy seasons
volcanism: limited volcanic activity; the Barrier (elev. 1,032 m) last erupted in 1921; South Island is the only other historically active volcano
Environment—current issues: water pollution from urban and industrial wastes; degradation of water quality from increased use of pesticides and fertilizers; water hyacinth infestation in Lake

Victoria; deforestation; soil erosion; desertification; poaching
Environment—international agreements: *party to:* Biodiversity, Climate Change, Climate Change-Kyoto Protocol, Desertification, Endangered Species, Hazardous Wastes, Law of the Sea, Marine Dumping, Marine Life Conservation, Ozone Layer Protection, Ship Pollution, Wetlands, Whaling
signed, but not ratified: none of the selected agreements
Geography—note: the Kenyan Highlands comprise one of the most successful agricultural production regions in Africa; glaciers are found on Mount Kenya, Africa's second highest peak; unique physiography supports abundant and varied wildlife of scientific and economic value

PEOPLE AND SOCIETY

Nationality: *noun:* Kenyan(s)
adjective: Kenyan
Ethnic groups: Kikuyu 22%, Luhya 14%, Luo 13%, Kalenjin 12%, Kamba 11%, Kisii 6%, Meru 6%, other African 15%, non-African (Asian, European, and Arab) 1%
Languages: English (official), Kiswahili (official), numerous indigenous languages
Religions: Christian 83% (Protestant 47.7%, Catholic 23.4%, other Christian 11.9%), Muslim 11.2%, Traditionalists 1.7%, other 1.6%, none 2.4%, unspecified 0.2% (2009 est.)
Population: 45,925,301
note: estimates for this country explicitly take into account the effects of excess mortality due to AIDS; this can result in lower life expectancy, higher infant mortality, higher death rates, lower population growth rates, and changes in the

distribution of population by age and sex than would otherwise be expected (July 2015 est.)
country comparison to the world: 31

Age structure: *0–14 years:* 41.56% (male 9,572,641/female 9,512,607)

15–24 years: 18.66% (male 4,280,499/female 4,289,960)

25–54 years: 33.17% (male 7,700,801/female 7,530,526)

55–64 years: 3.76% (male 784,775/female 944,041)

65 years and over: 2.85% (male 568,784/female 740,667) (2015 est.)

Dependency ratios: *total dependency ratio:* 80.9%

youth dependency ratio: 75.8%
elderly dependency ratio: 5.1%
potential support ratio: 19.7% (2015 est.)

Median age: *total:* 19.3 years
male: 19.1 years
female: 19.4 years (2015 est.)
country comparison to the world: 200

Population growth rate: 1.93% (2015 est.)
country comparison to the world: 54

Birth rate: 26.4 births/1,000 population (2015 est.)
country comparison to the world: 46

Death rate: 6.89 deaths/1,000 population (2015 est.)
country comparison to the world: 136

Net migration rate: -0.22 migrant(s)/1,000 population (2015 est.)
country comparison to the world: 120

Urbanization: *urban population:* 25.6% of total population (2015)
rate of urbanization: 4.34% annual rate of change (2010–15 est.)

Major urban areas—population: NAIROBI (capital) 3.915 million; Mombassa 1.104 million (2015)

Sex ratio: *at birth:* 1.02 male(s)/female
0–14 years: 1.01 male(s)/female
15–24 years: 1 male(s)/female
25–54 years: 1.02 male(s)/female
55–64 years: 0.83 male(s)/female
65 years and over: 0.77 male(s)/female
total population: 1 male(s)/female (2015 est.)

Mother's mean age at first birth: 20.3
note: median age at first birth among women 25–29 (2014 est.)

Maternal mortality rate: 510 deaths/100,000 live births (2015 est.)
country comparison to the world: 30

Infant mortality rate: *total:* 39.38 deaths/1,000 live births
male: 43.92 deaths/1,000 live births
female: 34.75 deaths/1,000 live births (2015 est.)
country comparison to the world: 51

Life expectancy at birth: *total population:* 63.77 years
male: 62.3 years
female: 65.26 years (2015 est.)
country comparison to the world: 185

Total fertility rate: 3.31 children born/woman (2015 est.)
country comparison to the world: 46

Contraceptive prevalence rate: 45.5% (2008/09)

Health expenditures: 4.5% of GDP (2013)

country comparison to the world: 148

Physicians density: 0.2 physicians/1,000 population (2013)

Hospital bed density: 1.4 beds/1,000 population (2010)

Drinking water source:
improved:
urban: 81.6% of population
rural: 56.8% of population
total: 63.2% of population
unimproved:
urban: 18.4% of population
rural: 43.2% of population
total: 36.8% of population (2015 est.)

Sanitation facility access:
improved:
urban: 31.2% of population
rural: 29.7% of population
total: 30.1% of population
unimproved:
urban: 68.8% of population
rural: 70.3% of population
total: 69.9% of population (2015 est.)

HIV/AIDS—adult prevalence rate: 5.3% (2014 est.)
country comparison to the world: 13

HIV/AIDS—people living with HIV/AIDS: 1,366,900 (2014 est.)
country comparison to the world: 8

HIV/AIDS—deaths: 33,000 (2014 est.)
country comparison to the world: 9

Major infectious diseases: *degree of risk:* very high
food or waterborne diseases: bacterial and protozoal diarrhea, hepatitis A, and typhoid fever
vectorborne disease: malaria, dengue fever, and Rift Valley fever
water contact disease: schistosomiasis
animal contact disease: rabies (2013)

Obesity—adult prevalence rate: 5.9% (2014)
country comparison to the world: 171

Children under the age of 5 years underweight: 11% (2014)
country comparison to the world: 42

Education expenditures: 5.5% of GDP (2010)
country comparison to the world: 28

Literacy: *definition:* age 15 and over can read and write
total population: 78%
male: 81.1%
female: 74.9% (2015 est.)

School life expectancy (primary to tertiary education): *total:* 11 years
male: 11 years
female: 11 years (2009)

GOVERNMENT

Country name: *conventional long form:* Republic of Kenya
conventional short form: Kenya
local long form: Republic of Kenya/Jamh uri ya Kenya
local short form: Kenya
former: British East Africa
etymolgy: named for Mount Kenya; the meaning of the name is unclear but may derive from the Kikuyu, Embu, and Kamba words "kirinyaga,"

"kirenyaa," and "kiinyaa"—all of which mean "God's resting place"

Government type: presidential republic

Capital: *name:* Nairobi

Geographic coordinates: 1 17 S, 36 49 E
time difference: UTC+3 (8 hours ahead of Washington, DC, during Standard Time)

Administrative divisions: 47 counties; Baringo, Bomet, Bungoma, Busia, Elgeyo/Marakwet, Embu, Garissa, Homa Bay, Isiolo, Kajiado, Kakamega, Kericho, Kiambu, Kilifi, Kirinyaga, Kisii, Kisumu, Kitui, Kwale, Laikipia, Lamu, Machakos, Makueni, Mandera, Marsabit, Meru, Migori, Mombasa, Murang'a, Nairobi City, Nakuru, Nandi, Narok, Nyamira, Nyandarua, Nyeri, Samburu, Siaya, Taita/Taveta, Tana River, Tharaka-Nithi, Trans Nzoia, Turkana, Uasin Gishu, Vihiga, Wajir, West Pokot

Independence: 12 December 1963 (from the UK)

National holiday: Independence Day, 12 December (1963); Madaraka Day, 1 June (1963); Mashujaa Day (or Heroes' Day), 20 October (2010)

Constitution: previous 1963, 1969; latest drafted 6 May 2010, passed by referendum 4 August 2010, promulgated 27 August 2010 (2016)

Legal system: mixed legal system of English common law, Islamic law, and customary law; judicial review in a new Supreme Court established pursuant to the new constitution

International law organization participation: accepts compulsory ICJ jurisdiction with reservations; accepts ICCt jurisdiction

Citizenship: *citizenship by birth:* no
citizenship by descent only: at least one parent must be a citizen of Kenya
dual citizenship recognized: no
residency requirement for naturalization: 4 out of the previous 7 years

Suffrage: 18 years of age; universal

Executive branch: *chief of state:* President Uhuru KENYATTA (since 9 April 2013); Deputy President William RUTO (since 9 April 2013); note—the president is both chief of state and head of government

head of government: President Uhuru KENYATTA (since 9 April 2013); Deputy President William RUTO (since 9 April 2013); note—position of the prime minister abolished after the March 2013 elections

cabinet: Cabinet appointed by the president, subject to confirmation by the Natioal Assembly

elections/appointments: president and deputy president directly elected on the same ballot by qualified majority popular vote for a 5-year term (eligible for a second term); in addition to receiving an absolute majority popular vote, the presidential candidate must also win at least 25% of the votes cast in each of more than half of the 47 counties to avoid a runoff; election last held on 4 March 2013 (next to be held in 2017)

election results: U huru KEN YATTA elected president in first round; percent of vote—U huru KEN YATTA (TNA) 50.1%, Raila ODINGA (ODM) 43.7%, Musalia MUDAVADI (UDF) 4.0%, other 2.2%

Legislative branch: *description:* bicameral parliament consists of the Senate (67 seats; 47 members directly elected in single-seat constituencies by simple majority vote and 20 directly elected by proportional representation vote—16 women, 2 representing youth, and 2 representing the disabled; members serve 5-year terms) and the National Assembly (349 seats; 290 members directly elected in single-seat constituencies by simple majority vote, 47 women in single-seat constituencies elected by simple majority vote, and 12 members nominated by the National Assembly—6 representing youth and 6 representing the disabled; members serve 5-year terms)

elections: last held on 4 March 2013 (next to be held in 2017)

election results: Senate—percent of vote by party/coalition—NA; seats by party/coalition—Jubilee Alliance 30 (TNA 17, URP 12, NARC 1); CORD Coalition 28 (ODM 17, FORD-K 5, WDM-K 5, other 1); Amani Coalition 6 (KANU 3, UDF 3), APK 3; National Assembly—percent of vote by party/coalition—NA; seats by party/coalition—Jubilee Alliance 167 (TNA 89, URP 75, NARC 3), CORD Coalition 141 (ODM 96, WDM-K 26, FORD-K 10, other 9), Amani Coalition 24 (UDF 12, KANU 6, NFK 6), Eagle Coalition 2 (KNC 2), APK 5, FORD-P 4, independent 4, other 2

Judicial branch: *highest court(s):* Supreme Court (consists of chief and deputy chief justices and 5 judges)

judge selection and term of office: the president nominates chief and deputy chief justices from among three candidates proposed by Judicial Service Commission (JSC) and appointed by president with approval of the National Assembly; other judges nominated by the JSC and appointed by president; chief justice serves nonrenewable 10-year terms or until age 70 whichever comes first; other judges serve until age 70

subordinate courts: High Court; Court of Appeal; courts martial; magistrates' courts; religious courts

Political parties and leaders: Alliance Party of Kenya or APK [Kiraitu MURUNGI]
Amani National Congress [Musalia MUDAVADI]
Coalition for Reforms and Democracy or CORD (includes ODM, WDM-K, FORD-K) [Raila ODINGA]
Federal Party of Kenya or FPK [Cyrus JIRONGA]
Forum for the Restoration of Democracy-Kenya or FORD-K [Moses WETANGULA]
Forum for the Restoration of Democracy-People or FORD-P [Henry OBWOCHA]
Jubilee Alliance (includes TNA, URP, NARC) [Uhuru KENYATTA]
Kenya African National Union or KANU [Gideon MOI]
National Rainbow Coalition or NARC [Charity NGILU]
New Ford Kenya or NFK [Ken LUSAKA]
Orange Democratic Movement Party of Kenya or ODM [Raila ODINGA]
The National Alliance or TNA [Uhuru KENYATTA]
United Republican Party or URP [William RUTO]

Wiper Democratic Movement-K or WD M-K (formerly Orange Democratic Movement-Kenya or ODM-K) [Kalonzo MUSYOKA]

Political pressure groups and leaders: African Center for Open Governance [Gladwell OTIENO]
Anglican Church of Kenya [Archbishop Eliud WABUKALA]
Council of Imams and Preachers of Kenya or CIPK [Sheikh Mohammed KHALIFA]
Federation of Women Lawyers in Kenya
Kenya Association of Manufacturers
Kenya Human Rights Commission or KHRC [George KEGORO]
Kenya Private Sector Alliance
Kenyans for Peace with Truth and Justice (umbrella group of more than 30 NGOs)
Muslim Human Rights Forum [Ali-Amin KIMATHI]
National Muslim Leaders Forum or NAMLEF [Abdullahi ABDI]
Protestant National Council of Churches of Kenya or NCCK [Canon Peter Karanja MWANGI]
Roman Catholic Church [Cardinal John NJUE]
Supreme Council of Kenya Muslims or SUPKEM [Adan WACHU, secretary general]
other: labor Unions, other Christian churches

International organization participation: ACP, AFDB, AU, C, CD, COMESA, EAC, EADB, FAO, G-15, G-77, IAEA, IBRD, ICAO, ICCt, ICRM, IDA, IFAD, IFC, IFRCS, IGAD, ILO, IMF, IMO, IMSO, Interpol, IOC, IOM, IPU, ISO, ITSO, ITU, ITUC (NGOs), MIGA, MIN USMA, MON USCO, NAM, OPCW, PCA, UN, UNAMID, UNCTAD, UNESCO, UNHCR, UNIDO, UNIFIL, UNMIL, UNMISS, UNWTO, UPU, WCO, WHO, WMO, WTO

Diplomatic representation in the US: *chief of mission:* Ambassador Robinson GITHAE (since 18 November 2014)

chancery: 2249 R Street NW, Washington, DC 20008

telephone: [1] (202) 387-6101

FAX: [1] (202) 462-3829

consulate(s) general: Los Angeles

consulate(s): New York

Diplomatic representation from the US: *chief of mission:* Ambassador Robert F. GODEC (since 16 January 2013)

embassy: United Nations Avenue, Nairobi; P. O. Box 606 Village Market, Nairobi 00621

mailing address: American Embassy Nairobi, U.S. Department of State, Washington, DC 20521–8900

telephone: [254] (20) 363-6000

FAX: [254] (20) 363-6157

Flag description: three equal horizontal bands of black (top), red, and green; the red band is edged in white; a large Maasai warrior's shield covering crossed spears is superimposed at the center; black symbolizes the majority population, red the blood shed in the struggle for freedom, green stands for natural wealth, and white for peace; the shield and crossed spears symbolize the defense of freedom

National symbol(s): lion; national colors: black, red, green, white

National anthem: *name:* "Ee Mungu nguvu Yetu" (Oh God of All Creation)

lyrics/music: Graham HYSLOP, Thomas KALUME, Peter KIBUKOSYA, Washington OMONDI, and George W. SENOGA-ZAKE/traditional, adapted by Graham HYSLOP, Thomas KALUME, Peter KIBUKOSYA, Washington OMONDI, and George W. SENOGA-ZAKE

note: adopted 1963; based on a traditional Kenyan folk song

ECONOMY

Economy—overview: Kenya is the economic and transport hub of East Africa. Kenya's real GDP growth has averaged over 5% for the last seven years. Since 2014 Kenya has been ranked as a lower middle income country because its per capita GDP crossed a World Bank threshold. While Kenya has a growing entrepreneurial middle class and faster growth, its economic and development trajectory is threatened by weak governance and corruption. Unemployment and under-employment are high, but reliable numbers are hard to find. Agriculture remains the backbone of the Kenyan economy, contributing 25% of GD P. About 80% of Kenya's population of roughly 42 million work at least part-time in the agricultural sector, including livestock and pastoral activities. Over 75% of agricultural output is from small-scale, rain-fed farming or livestock production.

Inadequate infrastructure continue to hamper Kenya's efforts to improve its economic growth to the 8–10% range so that it can meaningfully address poverty and unemployment. The KENYATTA administration sought external investment in infrastructure development. International financial institutions and donors remain important to Kenya's economic growth and development, but Kenya has also successfully raised capital in the global bond market. Kenya issued its first sovereign bond offering in mid-2014. Nairobi has contracted with a Chinese company to construct a new standard gauge railway connecting Mombasa and Nairobi, with completion expected in 2017. The country is in the process of devolving some state revenues and responsibilities to the counties. Inflationary pressures and sharp currency depreciation peaked in early 2012 but have since abated following low global food and fuel prices and monetary interventions by the Central Bank. Chronic budget deficits, including a shortage of funds in mid-2015, hampered the government's ability to implement proposed development programs, but the economy is back in balance with many indicators, including foreign exchange reserves, interest rates, inflation, and FDI moving in the right direction.

Tourism holds a significant place in Kenya's economy. Multiple terror attacks by the Somalia-based group al-Shabaab in the time since the 2013 attack on Nairobi's Westgate mall, which killed at least 67, had a negative effect on international tourism earnings, but the sector is starting to recover. Kenya's success in hosting a series of incident-free high-profile events in the second half of 2015, including the visit of President Obama, has helped improve the outlook for tourism.

GDP (purchasing power parity): $141.6 billion (2015 est.)
$134.3 billion (2014 est.)
$127.6 billion (2013 est.)
note: data are in 2015 US dollars
country comparison to the world: 75
GDP (official exchange rate): $61.41 billion (2015 est.)
GDP—real growth rate: 5.4% (2015 est.)
5.3% (2014 est.)
5.7% (2013 est.)
country comparison to the world: 34
GDP—per capita (PPP): $3,200 (2015 est.)
$3,100 (2014 est.)
$3,100 (2013 est.)
note: data are in 2015 US dollars
country comparison to the world: 186
Gross national saving: 14.4% of GDP (2015 est.)
11% of GDP (2014 est.)
11.2% of GDP (2013 est.)
country comparison to the world: 124

GDP—composition, by end use: *household consumption:* 78.7%
government consumption: 13.7%
investment in fixed capital: 23.6%
investment in inventories: -1%
exports of goods and services: 16.1%
imports of goods and services: -31.1% (2015 est.)
GDP—composition, by sector of origin:
agriculture: 29.9%
industry: 19.5%
services: 50.6% (2015 est.)
Agriculture—products: tea, coffee, corn, wheat, sugarcane, fruit, vegetables; dairy products, beef, fish, pork, poultry, eggs
Industries: small-scale consumer goods (plastic, furniture, batteries, textiles, clothing, soap, cigarettes, flour), agricultural products, horticulture, oil refining; aluminum, steel, lead; cement, commercial ship repair, tourism
Industrial production growth rate: 6.1% (2015 est.)
country comparison to the world: 20
Labor force: 18.21 million (2015 est.)
country comparison to the world: 34
Labor force—by occupation:
agriculture: 75%
industry and services: 25% (2011 est.)
Unemployment rate: 40% (2013 est.)
40% (2001 est.)
country comparison to the world: 195
Population below poverty line: 43.4% (2012 est.)
Household income or consumption by percentage share: *lowest:* 10%: 1.8%
highest: 10%: 37.8% (2005)
Distribution of family income—Gini index: 42.5 (2008 est.)
44.9 (1997)
country comparison to the world: 52
Budget: *revenues:* $10.6 billion
expenditures: $14.55 billion (2015 est.)
Taxes and other revenues: 16.8% of GDP (2015 est.)
country comparison to the world: 180

Budget surplus (+) or deficit (–): -6.3% of GDP (2015 est.)
country comparison to the world: 184
Public debt: 48.6% of GDP (2015 est.)
58.9% of GDP (2014 est.)
country comparison to the world: 86
Fiscal year: 1 July—30 June
Inflation rate (consumer prices): 6.6% (2015 est.)
6.9% (2014 est.)
country comparison to the world: 191
Central bank discount rate: 11.5% (20 January 2016)
7% (31 December 2010)
country comparison to the world: 47
Commercial bank prime lending rate: 16% (31 December 2015 est.)
16.5% (31 December 2014 est.)
country comparison to the world: 31
Stock of narrow money: $10.01 billion (31 December 2015 est.)
$10.34 billion (31 December 2014 est.)
country comparison to the world: 78
Stock of broad money: $24.02 billion (31 December 2014 est.)
$18.92 billion (31 December 2013 est.)
country comparison to the world: 83
Stock of domestic credit: $26.61 billion (31 December 2015 est.)
$26.37 billion (31 December 2014 est.)
country comparison to the world: 78
Market value of publicly traded shares: $26.16 billion (31 December 2014 est.)
$22.09 billion (31 December 2013)
$14.79 billion (31 December 2012 est.)
country comparison to the world: 69
Current account balance: -$5.011 billion (2015 est.)
-$6.339 billion (2014 est.)
country comparison to the world: 169
Exports: $5.679 billion (2015 est.)
$6.174 billion (2014 est.)
country comparison to the world: 105
Exports—commodities: tea, horticultural products, coffee, petroleum products, fish, cement
Exports—partners: Uganda 11.3%, US 8.3%, Tanzania 8.1%, Netherlands 7.4%, UK 6%, Pakistan 4.2% (2015)
Imports: $16.2 billion (2015 est.)
$17.61 billion (2014 est.)
country comparison to the world: 82
Imports—commodities: machinery and transportation equipment, petroleum products, motor vehicles, iron and steel, resins and plastics
Imports—partners: China 30.1%, India 15.5%, UAE 5.7%, US 4.8%, Japan 4.7% (2015)
Reserves of foreign exchange and gold: $7.356 billion (31 December 2015 est.)
$7.911 billion (31 December 2014 est.)
country comparison to the world: 84
Debt—external: $17.16 billion (31 December 2014 est.)
$13.47 billion (31 December 2013 est.)
country comparison to the world: 94
Stock of direct foreign investment—at home: $4.762 billion (31 December 2015 est.)
$3.902 billion (31 December 2014 est.)

country comparison to the world: 99
Stock of direct foreign investment—abroad: $NA (31 December 2015 est.)
$NA (31 December 2014 est.)
Exchange rates: Kenyan shillings (KES) per US dollar—
99.73 (2015 est.)
87.921 (2014 est.)
87.921 (2013 est.)
84.53 (2012 est.)
88.811 (2011 est.)

ENERGY

Electricity—production: 8.123 billion kWh (2012 est.)
country comparison to the world: 102
Electricity—consumption: 6.627 billion kWh (2012 est.)
country comparison to the world: 107
Electricity—exports: 31 million kWh (2012 est.)
country comparison to the world: 86
Electricity—imports: 42 million kWh (2012 est.)
country comparison to the world: 104
Electricity—installed generating capacity: 2.281 million kW (2015 est.)
country comparison to the world: 111
Electricity—from fossil fuels: 42.4% of total installed capacity (2012 est.)
country comparison to the world: 163
Electricity—from nuclear fuels: 0% of total installed capacity (2012 est.)
country comparison to the world: 118
Electricity—from hydroelectric plants: 43.9% of total installed capacity (2012 est.)
country comparison to the world: 54
Electricity—from other renewable sources: 13.8% of total installed capacity (2012 est.)
country comparison to the world: 23
Crude oil—production: 0 bbl/day (2014 est.)
country comparison to the world: 151
Crude oil—Exports: 0 bbl/day (2012 est.)
country comparison to the world: 144
Crude oil—imports: 19,830 bbl/day (2012 est.)
country comparison to the world: 70
Crude oil—proved reserves: 0 bbl (1 January 2015 est.)
country comparison to the world: 150
Refined petroleum products—production: 20,510 bbl/day (2012 est.)
country comparison to the world: 93
Refined petroleum products—consumption: 84,000 bbl/day (2013 est.)
country comparison to the world: 82
Refined petroleum products—exports: 843.8 bbl/day (2012 est.)
country comparison to the world: 111
Refined petroleum products—imports: 65,450 bbl/day (2012 est.)
country comparison to the world: 68
Natural gas—production: 0 cu m (2013 est.)
country comparison to the world: 205
Natural gas—consumption: 0 cu m (2013 est.)
country comparison to the world: 158
Natural gas—exports: 0 cu m (2013 est.)
country comparison to the world: 125
Natural gas—imports: 0 cu m (2013 est.)

country comparison to the world: 87
Natural gas—proved reserves: 0 cu m (1 January 2014 est.)
country comparison to the world: 154
Carbon dioxide emissions from consumption of energy: 13.45 million Mt (2012 est.)
country comparison to the world: 92

COMMUNICATIONS

Telephones—fixed lines: *total subscriptions:* 180,000
subscriptions per 100 inhabitants: less than 1 (2014 est.)
country comparison to the world: 129
Telephones—mobile cellular: *total:* 33.6 million
subscriptions per 100 inhabitants: 75 (2014 est.)
country comparison to the world: 35
Telephone system: *general assessment:* the mobile-cellular system is generally good, especially is urban areas; fixed-line telephone system is small and inefficient; trunks are primarily microwave radio relay; business data commonly transferred by a very small aperture terminal (VSAT) system
domestic: sole fixed-line provider, Telkom Kenya, privatized and as of 2013 is 70% owned by France Telecom; multiple providers in the mobile-cellular segment of the market fostering a boom in mobile-cellular telephone usage with teledensity reaching 78 per 100 persons in 2015
international: country code—254; landing point for the EASSy, TEAMS and SEACOM fiber-optic submarine cable systems; satellite earth stations—4 Intelsat (2015)
Broadcast media: about a half-dozen large-scale privately owned media companies with TV and radio stations, as well as a state-owned TV broadcaster, provide service nationwide; satellite and cable TV subscription services available; state-owned radio broadcaster operates 2 national radio channels and provides regional and local radio services in multiple languages; many private radio stations broadcast on a national level along with over 100 private and non-profit provincial stations broadcasting in local languages; transmissions of several international broadcasters available (2014)
Radio broadcast stations: AM 24, FM 82, shortwave 6 (2008)
Television broadcast stations: 8 (2008)
Internet country code: .ke
Internet hosts: 71,018 (2012)
country comparison to the world: 88
Internet users: *total:* 16.5 million
percent of population: 36.7% (2014 est.)
country comparison to the world: 33

TRANSPORTATION

Airports: 197 (2013)
country comparison to the world: 28
Airports—with paved runways: *total:* 16
over 3,047 m: 5
2,438 to 3,047 m: 2
1,524 to 2,437 m: 2
914 to 1,523 m: 6
under 914 m: 1 (2013)
Airports—with unpaved runways: *total:* 181
1,524 to 2,437 m: 14
914 to 1,523 m: 107
under 914 m: 60 (2013)
Pipelines: oil 4 km; refined products 928 km (2013)
Railways: *total:* 3,334 km
narrow gauge: 3,334 km 1.000-m gauge (2014)
country comparison to the world: 54
Roadways: *total:* 160,878 km
paved: 11,189 km
unpaved: 149,689 km
note: includes 99 km of urban and other roads (2013)
country comparison to the world: 30
Waterways: none specifically; the only significant inland waterway is the part of Lake Victoria within the boundaries of Kenya; Kisumu is the main port and has ferry connections to Uganda and Tanzania (2011)
Merchant marine: *registered in other countries:* 5 (Comoros 2, Saint Vincent and the Grenadines 2, unknown 1) (2010)
country comparison to the world: 125
Ports and terminals: *major seaport(s):* Kisumu, Mombasa
LNG terminal(s) (import): Mombasa

MILITARY AND SECURITY

Military branches: Kenya Defence Forces: Kenya Army, Kenya Navy, Kenya Air Force (2012)
Military service age and obligation: 18–26 years of age for male and female voluntary service (under 18 with parental consent), with a 9-year obligation (7 years for Kenyan Navy); applicants must be Kenyan citizens and provide a national identity card (obtained at age 18) and a school-leaving certificate; women serve under the same terms and conditions as men; mandatory retirement at age 55 (2012)
Military expenditures:
1.96% of GDP (2012)
1.88% of GDP (2011)
1.96% of GDP (2010)

country comparison to the world: 41

TRANSNATIONAL ISSUES

Disputes—international: Kenya served as an important mediator in brokering Sudan's north-south separation in February 2005; Kenya provides shelter to an estimated 580,000 refugees, including Ugandans who flee across the border periodically to seek protection from Lord's Resistance Army rebels; Kenya works hard to prevent the clan and militia fighting in Somalia from spreading across the border, which has long been open to nomadic pastoralists; the boundary that separates Kenya's and Sudan's sovereignty is unclear in the "Ilemi Triangle," which Kenya has administered since colonial times
Refugees and internally displaced persons: *refugees (country of origin):* 413,170 (Somalia); 86,874 (South Sudan) (refugees and asylum seekers); 21,537 (Ethiopia); 12,972 (Democratic Republic of the Congo) (2016)
IDPs: 309,000 (represents people displaced since the 1990s by ethnic and political violence and land disputes and who sought refuge mostly in camps; persons who took refuge in host communities or were evicted in urban areas are not included in the data; data is not available on pastoralists displaced by cattle rustling, violence, natural disasters, and development projects; the largest displacement resulted from 200708 post-election violence (2014)
stateless persons: 20,000 (2015); note—the stateless population consists of Nubians, Kenyan Somalis, and coastal Arabs; the Nubians are descendants of Sudanese soldiers recruited by the British to fight for them in East Africa more than a century ago; Nubians did not receive Kenyan citizenship when the country became independent in 1963; only recently have Nubians become a formally recognized tribe and had less trouble obtaining national IDs; Galjeel and other Somalis who have lived in Kenya for decades are included with more recent Somali refugees and denied ID cards
Illicit drugs: widespread harvesting of small plots of marijuana; transit country for South Asian heroin destined for Europe and North America; Indian methaqualone also transits on way to South Africa; significant potential for money-laundering activity given the country's status as a regional financial center; massive corruption, and relatively high levels of narcotics-associated activities

KIRIBATI

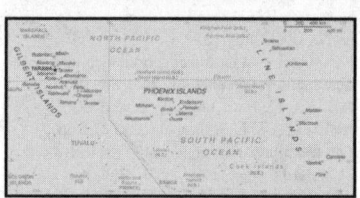

INTRODUCTION

Background: The Gilbert Islands became a British protectorate in 1892 and a colony in 1915; they were captured by the Japanese in the Pacific War in 1941. The islands of Makin and Tarawa were the sites of major US amphibious victories over entrenched Japanese garrisons in 1943. The Gilbert Islands were granted self-rule by the UK in 1971 and complete independence in 1979 under the new name of Kiribati. The US relinquished all claims to the sparsely inhabited Phoenix and Line Island groups in a 1979 treaty of friendship with Kiribati.

GEOGRAPHY

Location: Oceania, group of 33 coral atolls in the Pacific Ocean, straddling the Equator; the capital Tarawa is about halfway between Hawaii and Australia

Geographic coordinates: 1 25 N, 173 00 E

Map references: Oceania

Area: *total:* 811 sq km
land: 811 sq km
water: 0 sq km
note: includes three island groups—Gilbert Islands, Line Islands, and Phoenix Islands—dispersed over about 3.5 million sq km (1.35 million sq mi)
country comparison to the world: 187

Area—comparative: four times the size of Washington, DC

Land boundaries: 0 km

Coastline: 1,143 km

Maritime claims: *territorial sea:* 12 nm
exclusive economic zone: 200 nm

Climate: tropical; marine, hot and humid, moderated by trade winds

Terrain: mostly low-lying coral atolls surrounded by extensive reefs

Elevation: *mean elevation:* NA

elevation extremes: *lowest point:* Pacific Ocean 0 m
highest point: unnamed elevation on Banaba 81 m

Natural resources: phosphate (production discontinued in 1979), coconuts (copra), fish

Land use: *agricultural land:* 42%
arable land: 2.5%
permanent crops: 39.5%
permanent pasture: 0%
forest: 15%
other: 43% (2011 est.)

Irrigated land: 0 sq km (2012)

Natural hazards: typhoons can occur any time, but usually November to March; occasional tornadoes; low level of some of the islands make them sensitive to changes in sea level

Environment—current issues: heavy pollution in lagoon of south Tarawa atoll due to heavy migration mixed with traditional practices such as lagoon latrines and open-pit dumping; ground water at risk

Environment—international agreements: *party to:* Biodiversity, Climate Change, Climate Change-Kyoto Protocol, Desertification, Hazardous Wastes, Law of the Sea, Marine Dumping, Ozone Layer Protection, Whaling
signed, but not ratified: none of the selected agreements

Geography—note: 21 of the 33 islands are inhabited; Banaba (Ocean Island) in Kiribati is one of the three great phosphate rock islands in the Pacific Ocean—the others are Makatea in French Polynesia, and Nauru; Kiribati is the only country in the world to fall into all four hemispheres (northern, southern, eastern, and western)

PEOPLE AND SOCIETY

Nationality: *noun:* I-Kiribati (singular and plural)
adjective: I-Kiribati

Ethnic groups: I—Kiribati 89.5%, I-Kiribati/mixed 9.7%, Tuvaluan 0.1%, other 0.8% (2010 est.)

Languages: I-Kiribati, English (official)

Religions: Roman Catholic 55.8%, Kempsville Presbyterian Church 33.5%, Mormon 4.7%, Baha'i 2.3%, Seventh Day Adventist 2%, other 1.5%, none 0.2%, unspecified 0.05% (2010 est.)

Population: 105,711 (July 2015 est.)
country comparison to the world: 193

Age structure: *0–14 years:* 30.77% (male 16,582/female 15,950)
15–24 years: 21.28% (male 11,202/female 11,296)
25–54 years: 38.23% (male 19,446/female 20,965)
55–64 years: 5.66% (male 2,706/female 3,281)
65 years and over: 4.05% (male 1,689/female 2,594) (2015 est.)

Dependency ratios: *total dependency ratio:* 63%
youth dependency ratio: 57%
elderly dependency ratio: 6%
potential support ratio: 16.6% (2015 est.)

Median age: *total:* 23.9 years
male: 23.1 years
female: 24.8 years (2015 est.)
country comparison to the world: 160

Population growth rate: 1.15% (2015 est.)
country comparison to the world: 105

Birth rate: 21.46 births/1,000 population (2015 est.)
country comparison to the world: 75

Death rate: 7.12 deaths/1,000 population (2015 est.)
country comparison to the world: 127

Net migration rate: -2.87 migrant(s)/1,000 population (2015 est.)

country comparison to the world: 179

Urbanization: *urban population:* 44.3% of total population (2015)
rate of urbanization: 1.78% annual rate of change (2010–15 est.)

Major urban areas—population: TARAWA (capital) 46,000 (2014)

Sex ratio: *at birth:* 1.05 male(s)/female
0–14 years: 1.04 male(s)/female
15–24 years: 0.99 male(s)/female
25–54 years: 0.93 male(s)/female
55–64 years: 0.83 male(s)/female
65 years and over: 0.65 male(s)/female
total population: 0.95 male(s)/female (2015 est.)

Mother's mean age at first birth: 23.1
note: median age at first birth among women 25–29 (2009 est.)

Maternal mortality rate: 90 deaths/100,000 live births (2015 est.)
country comparison to the world: 155

Infant mortality rate: *total:* 34.26 deaths/1,000 live births
male: 35.48 deaths/1,000 live births
female: 32.99 deaths/1,000 live births (2015 est.)
country comparison to the world: 62

Life expectancy at birth: *total population:* 65.81 years
male: 63.36 years
female: 68.39 years (2015 est.)
country comparison to the world: 174

Total fertility rate: 2.48 children born/woman (2015 est.)
country comparison to the world: 79

Contraceptive prevalence rate: 22.3% (2009)
Health expenditures: 10.1% of GDP (2013)
country comparison to the world: 17

Physicians density: 0.38 physicians/1,000 population (2010)

Hospital bed density: 1.3 beds/1,000 population (2011)

Drinking water source:
improved:
urban: 87.3% of population
rural: 50.6% of population
total: 66.9% of population
unimproved:
urban: 12.7% of population
rural: 49.4% of population
total: 33.1% of population (2015 est.)

Sanitation facility access:
improved:
urban: 51.2% of population
rural: 30.6% of population
total: 39.7% of population
unimproved:
urban: 48.8% of population
rural: 69.4% of population
total: 60.3% of population (2015 est.)

HIV/AIDS—adult prevalence rate: NA

HIV/AIDS—people living with HIV/AIDS: NA

HIV/AIDS—deaths: NA

Obesity—adult prevalence rate: 40.1% (2014)

country comparison to the world: 8
Children under the age of 5 years underweight: 14.9% (2009)
country comparison to the world: 48
School life expectancy (primary to tertiary education): *total:* 12 years
male: 11 years
female: 12 years (2008)
Unemployment, youth ages 15–24: *total:* 54%
male: 47.6%
female: 61.8% (2010 est.)

GOVERNMENT

Country name: *conventional long form:* Republic of Kiribati
conventional short form: Kiribati
local long form: Republic of Kiribati
local short form: Kiribati
note: pron oun ced keer-ree-bahss
former: Gilbert Islands
etymology: the name is the local pronunciation of "Gilberts," the former designation of the islands; originally named after explorer Thomas GILBERT, who mapped many of the islands in 1788
Government type: presidential republic
Capital: *name:* Tarawa
Geographic coordinates: 1 21 N, 173 02 E
time difference: UTC + 12 (17 hours ahead of Washington, DC, during Standard Time)
note: on 1 January 1995, Kiribati proclaimed that all of its territory was in the same time zone as its Gilbert Islands group (UTC +12) even though the Phoenix Islands and the Line Islands under its jurisdiction were on the other side of the International Date Line
Administrative divisions: 3 geographical units: Gilbert Islands, Line Islands, Phoenix Islands; *note*—there are no first-order admin istrative divisions but there are 6 districts (Banaba, Central Gilberts, Line Islands, northern Gilberts, Southern Gilberts, Tarawa) and 21 island councils—one for each of the in habited islands (Abaiang, Abemama, Aranuka, Arorae, Banaba, Beru, Butaritari, Kanton, Kiritimati, Kuria, Maiana, Makin, Marakei, Nikunau, Nonouti, Onotoa, Tabiteuea, Tabuaeran, Tamana, Tarawa, Teraina)
Independence: 12 July 1979 (from the UK)
National holiday: Independence Day, 12 July (1979)
Constitution: The Gilbert and Ellice Islands Order in Council 1915, The Gilbert Islands Order in Council 1975 (preindependence); latest promulgated 12 July 1979 (at independence); amended 1995, 2013 (2016)
Legal system: English common law supplemented by customary law
International law organization participation: has not submitted an ICJ jurisdiction declaration; non-party state to the ICCt
Citizenship: *citizenship by birth:* no
citizenship by descent only: at least one parent must be a native-born citizen of Kiribati
dual citizenship recognized: no
residency requirement for naturalization: 7 years
Suffrage: 18 years of age; universal

Executive branch: *chief of state:* President Taneti MAAMAU (since 11 March 2016); Vice President Kourabi NENEM (since 17 March 2016); *note*—the president is both chief of state and head of government
head of government: President Taneti MAAMAU (since 11 March 2016); Vice President Kourabi NENEM (since 17 March 2016)
cabinet: Cabinet appointed by the president from among House of Assembly members
elections/appointments: president directly elected by simple majority popular vote following nomination of candidates from among House of Assembly members; term is 4 years (eligible for 2 additional terms); election last held on 13 January 2012 (next to be held in 2015); vice president appointed by the president
election results: Taneti MAAMAU elected president; percent of vote—Taneti MAAMAU 60%, Rimeta BENIAMINA (BTK) 38.5%, Taneti IOANE (BTK) 1.5%
Legislative branch: *description:* unicameral House of Assembly or Maneaba Ni Maungatabu (46 seats; 44 members directly elected in single- and multi-seat constituencies by absolute majority vote in two-rounds, 1 member appointed by the Rabi Council of Leaders—representing Banaba Island, and 1 ex officio member—the attorney general; members serve 4-year terms)
elections: legislative elections were held in two rounds—the first on 21 October 2011 and the second on 28 October 2011 (next to be held in 2015)
election results: percent of vote by party—NA; seats by party—NA, other 2 (includes attorney general)
Judicial branch: *highest court(s):* High Court (consists of a chief justice and other judges as prescribed by the president); *note*—the High Court has jurisdiction on constitutional issues
judge selection and term of office: chief justice appointed by the president on the advice of the cabinet in consultation with the Public Service Commission (PSC); other judges appointed by the president on the advice of the chief justice along with the PSC
subordinate courts: Court of Appeal; magistrates' courts
Political parties and leaders: Boutokaan Te Koaua Party or BTK [Anote TONG]
Kamaeuraoan Te I-Kiribati Party or KTK [Tetaua TAITAI]
Maurin Kiribati Pati or MKP [Rimeta BENIAMINA]
note: there is no tradition of formally organized political parties in Kiribati; they more closely resemble factions or interest groups because they have no party headquarters, formal platforms, or party structures
International organization participation: ABEDA, ACP, ADB, AOSIS, C, FAO, IBRD, ICAO, ICRM, IDA, IFAD, IFC, IFRCS, ILO, IMF, IMO, IOC, ITU, ITUC (NGOs), OPCW, PIF, Sparteca, SPC, UN, UNCTAD, UNESCO, UPU, WHO, WIPO, WMO
Diplomatic representation in the US: none; the Kiribati Permanent Mission to the UN serves as

the Embassy; it is headed by Makurita BAARO (since 21 May 2014); address: 800 Second Avenue, Suite 400A, New York, NY 10017
telephone: [1] (212)867-3310
FAX: [1](212)867-3320
note: there is an honorary consulate in Honolulu
Diplomatic representation from the US: the US does not have an embassy in Kiribati; the US Ambassador to Fiji is accredited to Kiribati
Flag description: the upper half is red with a yellow frigatebird flying over a yellow rising sun, and the lower half is blue with three horizontal wavy white stripes to represent the Pacific ocean; the white stripes represent the three island groups—the Gilbert, Line, and Phoenix Islands; the 17 rays of the sun represent the 16 Gilbert Islands and Banaba (formerly Ocean Island); the frigatebird symbolizes authority and freedom
National symbol(s): frigatebird; national colors: red, white, blue, yellow
National anthem: *name:* "Teirake kaini Kiribati" (Stand Up, Kiribati)
lyrics/music: Urium Tamuera IOTEBA
note: adopted 1979

ECONOMY

Economy—overview: A remote country of 33 scattered coral atolls, Kiribati has few natural resources and is one of the least developed Pacific Island countries. Commercially viable phosphate deposits were exhausted by the time of independence from the United Kingdom in 1979. Earnings from fishing licenses and seafarer remittances are important sources of income, however, remittances and the number of seafarers employed have declined since the global crisis. In 2013, fishing license revenues contributed close to half of government's total revenue and total remittances from seafarers were equivalent to 6% of GDP. Economic development is constrained by a shortage of skilled workers, weak infrastructure, and remoteness from international markets. The public sector dominates economic activity, with on going capital projects in infrastructure including the road rehabilitation, water and sanitation projects, and renovations to the international airport, spurring some growth. Kiribati is dependent on foreign aid, which was estimated to have contributed over 43% in 2013 to the government's finances. The country's sovereign fund, the Revenue Equalization Reserve Fund (RERF), which is held offshore, had an estimated balance of $668 million in 2013, equivalent to 381% of GDP. The RERF seeks to avoid exchange rate risk by holding investments in more than 20 currencies, including the Australian dollar, United States dollar, the Japanese yen, and the Euro. Drawdowns from the RERF helped finance the government's annual budget
GDP (purchasing power parity): $203 million (2015 est.)
$194.8 million (2014 est.)
$190.3 million (2013 est.)
note: data are in 2015 US dollars
country comparison to the world: 220
GDP (official exchange rate): $162 million (2015 est.)

GDP—real growth rate: 4.2% (2015 est.)
2.4% (2014 est.)
5.8% (2013 est.)
country comparison to the world: 59
GDP—per capita (PPP): $1,800 (2015 est.)
$1,700 (2014 est.)
$1,700 (2013 est.)
note: data are in 2015 US dollars
country comparison to the world: 209
GDP—composition, by sector of origin:
agriculture: 26.3%
industry: 9.2%
services: 64.5% (2012 est.)
Agriculture—products: copr , bread fruit, fish
Industries: fishing, handicrafts
Industrial production growth rate: 1.1% (2012 est.)
country comparison to the world: 142
Labor force: 39,000
note: economically active, not including subsistence farmers (2010 est.)
country comparison to the world: 198

Labor force—by occupation: *agriculture:* 15%
industry: 10%
services: 75% (2010)
Unemployment rate: 30.6% (2010 est.)
6.1% (2005)
country comparison to the world: 188
Population below poverty line: NA%

Household income or consumption by percentage share: *lowest:* 10%: NA%
highest: 10%: NA%
Budget: *revenues:* $197.9 million
expenditures: $179.9 million (2013 est.)
Taxes and other revenues: 120.7% of GDP (2013 est.)
country comparison to the world: 3
Budget surplus (+) or deficit (–): 11% of GDP (2013 est.)
country comparison to the world: 3
Public debt: 8.6% of GDP (2013 est.)
8% of GDP (2012 est.)
country comparison to the world: 170
Fiscal year: NA
Inflation rate (consumer prices): 1.4% (2015 est.)
2.1% (2014 est.)
country comparison to the world: 92
Market value of publicly traded shares: $NA
Current account balance: $74 million (2015 est.)
$45 million (2014 est.)
country comparison to the world: 49
Exports: $84.75 million (2013 est.)
$62.31 million (2012 est.)
country comparison to the world: 197
Exports—commodities: fish, coconut products
Imports: $182.2 million (2013 est.)
$172.5 million (2012 est.)
country comparison to the world: 208
Imports—commodities: food, machinery and equipment, miscellaneous manufactured goods, fuel
Reserves of foreign exchange and gold: $8.37 million (31 December 2010 est.)
Debt—external: $13.6 million (2013 est.)
$14.1 million (2012 est.)
country comparison to the world: 199
Stock of direct foreign investment—at home: $NA
Exchange rates: Australian dollars (AUD) per US dollar—
1.33 (2015 est.)
1.1094 (2014 est.)

0.9695 (2013 est.)
0.9695 (2012 est.)
0.9695 (2011 est.)
note: the Australian dollar circulates as legal tender

ENERGY

Electricity—production: 26 million kWh (2012 est.)
country comparison to the world: 212
Electricity—consumption: 24.18 million kWh (2012 est.)
country comparison to the world: 211
Electricity—exports: 0 kWh (2013 est.)
country comparison to the world: 157
Electricity—imports: 0 kWh (2013 est.)
country comparison to the world: 167
Electricity—installed generating capacity: 5,000 kW (2012 est.)
country comparison to the world: 212
Electricity—from fossil fuels: 100% of total installed capacity (2012 est.)
country comparison to the world: 15
Electricity—from nuclear fuels: 0% of total installed capacity (2012 est.)
country comparison to the world: 121
Electricity—from hydroelectric plants: 0% of total installed capacity (2012 est.)
country comparison to the world: 180
Electricity—from other renewable sources: 0% of total installed capacity (2012 est.)
country comparison to the world: 188
Crude oil—production: 0 bbl/day (2014 est.)
country comparison to the world: 153
Crude oil—exports: 0 bbl/day (2012 est.)
country comparison to the world: 147
Crude oil—imports: 0 bbl/day (2012 est.)
country comparison to the world: 209
Crude oil—proved reserves: 0 bbl (1 January 2015 est.)
country comparison to the world: 152
Refined petroleum products—production: 0 bbl/day (2012 est.)
country comparison to the world: 197
Refined petroleum products—consumption: 400 bbl/day (2013 est.)
country comparison to the world: 209
Refined petroleum products—exports: 0 bbl/day (2012 est.)
country comparison to the world: 193
Refined petroleum products—imports: 420.4 bbl/day (2012 est.)
country comparison to the world: 206
Natural gas—production: 0 cu m (2013 est.)
country comparison to the world: 207
Natural gas—consumption: 0 cu m (2013 est.)
country comparison to the world: 160
Natural gas—exports: 0 cu m (2013 est.)
country comparison to the world: 128
Natural gas—imports: 0 cu m (2013 est.)
country comparison to the world: 89
Natural gas—proved reserves: 0 cu m (1 January 2014 est.)
country comparison to the world: 156
Carbon dioxide emissions from consumption of energy: 58,450 Mt (2012 est.)
country comparison to the world: 208

COMMUNICATIONS

Telephones—fixed lines: *total subscriptions:* 9,200

subscriptions per 100 inhabitants: 9 (2014 est.)
country comparison to the world: 200
Telephones—mobile cellular: *total:* 18,100
subscriptions per 100 inhabitants: 17 (2014 est.)
country comparison to the world: 211
Telephone system: *general assessment:* generally good quality national and international service
domestic: wireline service available on Tarawa and Kiritimati (Christmas Island); connections to outer islands by HF/VHF radiotelephone; wireless service available in Tarawa since 1999
international: country code—686; Kiribati is being linked to the Pacific Ocean Cooperative Telecommunications Network, which should improve telephone service; satellite earth station—1 Intelsat (Pacific Ocean) (2010)
Broadcast media: 1 TV broadcast station that provides about 1 hour of local programming Monday-Friday; multi-channel TV packages provide access to Australian and US stations; 1 government-operated radio station broadcasts on AM, FM, and shortwave (2009)
Radio broadcast station: AM 1, FM 2, shortwave 1 (may be inactive) (2002)
Television broadcast stations: 1 (possibly inactive) (2002)
Internet country code: .ki
Internet hosts: 327 (2012)
country comparison to the world: 188
Internet users: *total:* 12,200
percent of population: 11.7% (2014 est.)
country comparison to the world: 204

TRANSPORTATION

Airports: 19 (2013)
country comparison to the world: 138
Airports—with paved runways: *total:* 4
1,524 to 2,437 m: 4 (2013)
Airports—with unpaved runways: *total:* 15
914 to 1,523 m: 10
under 914 m: 5 (2013)
Roadways: *total:* 670 km (2011)
country comparison to the world: 191
Waterways: 5 km (small network of canals in Line Islands) (2012)
country comparison to the world: 107
Merchant marine: *total:* 77
by type: bulk carrier 7, cargo 35, chemical tanker 6, passenger 1, passenger/cargo 1, petroleum tanker 12, refrigerated cargo 15
foreign-owned: 43 (China 26, Hong Kong 2, Russia 1, Singapore 9, South Korea 1, Taiwan 2, Vietnam 2) (2010)
country comparison to the world: 59
Ports and terminals: *major seaport(s):* Betio (Tarawa Atoll), Canton Island, English Harbor

MILITARY AND SECURITY

Military branches: no regular military forces (establishment prevented by the constitution); Police Force (2011)

Military—note: Kiribati does not have military forces; defense assistance is provided by Australia and NZ

TRANSNATIONAL ISSUES

Disputes—international: none

KOREA, NORTH

INTRODUCTION

Background: An independent kingdom for much of its long history, Korea was occupied by Japan beginning in 1905 following the Russo-Japanese War. Five years later, Japan formally annexed the entire peninsula. Following World War II, Korea was split with the northern half coming under Soviet-sponsored communist control. After failing in the Korean War (1950–53) to conquer the US-backed Republic of Korea (ROK) in the southern portion by force, North Korea (DPR K), under its founder President KIM Il Sung, adopted a policy of ostensible diplomatic and economic "self-reliance" as a check against outside influence. The DPRK demonized the US as the ultimate threat to its social system through state-funded propaganda, and molded political, economic, and military policies around the core ideological objective of eventual unification of Korea under Pyongyang's control. KIM Il Sung's son, KIM Jong Il, was officially designated as his father's successor in 1980, assuming a growing political and managerial role until the elder KIM's death in 1994. KIM Jong Un was publicly unveiled as his father's successor in 2010. Following KIM Jong Il's death in 2011, KIM Jong UN quickly assumed power and has now taken on most of his father's former titles and duties. After decades of economic mismanagement and resource misallocation, the DPRK since the mid-1990s has relied heavily on international aid to feed its population. The DPRK began to ease restrictions to allow semi-private markets, starting in 2002, but then sought to roll back the scale of economic reforms in 2005 and 2009. North Korea's history of regional military provocations; proliferation of military-related items; long-range missile development; WMD programs including tests of nuclear devices in 2006, 2009, 2013, and 2016; and massive conventional armed forces are of major concern to the international community. The regime in 2013 announced a new policy calling for the simultaneous development of its nuclear weapons program and its economy.

GEOGRAPHY

Location: Eastern Asia, northern half of the Korean Peninsula bordering the Korea Bay and the Sea of Japan, between China and South Korea

Geographic coordinates: 40 00 N, 127 00 E

Map references: Asia

Area: total: 120,538 sq km

land: 120,408 sq km

water: 130 sq km

country comparison to the world: 99

Area—comparative: slightly larger than Virginia; slightly smaller than Mississippi

Land boundaries: total: 1,607 km

border countries (3): China 1,352 km, South Korea 237 km, Russia 18 km

Coastline: 2,495 km

Maritime claims: territorial sea: 12 nm

exclusive economic zone: 200 nm

note: military boundary line 50 nm in the Sea of Japan and the exclusive economic zone limit in the Yellow Sea where all foreign vessels and aircraft without permission are banned

Climate: temperate, with rainfall concentrated in summer; long, bitter winters

Terrain: mostly hills and mountains separated by deep, narrow valleys; wide coastal plains in west, discontinuous in east

Elevation: mean elevation: 600 m

elevation extremes: lowest point: Sea of Japan 0 m

highest point: Paektu-san 2,744 m

Natural resources: coal, lead, tungsten, zinc, graphite, magnesite, iron ore, copper, gold, pyrites, salt, fluorspar, hydropower

Land use: agricultural land: 21.8%

arable land: 19.5%

permanent crops: 1.9%

permanent pasture: 0.4%

forest: 46%

other: 32.2% (2011 est.)

Irrigated land: 14,600 sq km (2012)

Total renewable water resources: 77.15 cu km (2011)

Freshwater withdrawal (domestic/industrial/agricultural): total: 8.66 cu km/yr (10%/13%/76%)

per capita: 360.6 cu m/yr (2005)

Natural hazards: late spring droughts often followed by severe flooding; occasional typhoons during the early fall

volcanism: Changbaishan (elev. 2,744 m) (also known as Baitoushan, Baegdu or P'aektu-san), on the Chinese border, is considered historically active

Environment—current issues: water pollution; inadequate supplies of potable water; waterborne disease; deforestation; soil erosion and degradation

Environment—international agreements: party to: Antarctic Treaty, Biodiversity, Climate Change, Climate Change-Kyoto Protocol, Desertification, Environmental Modification, Hazardous Wastes, Ozone Layer Protection, Ship Pollution

signed, but not ratified: Law of the Sea

Geography—note: strategic location bordering China, South Korea, and Russia; mountainous interior is isolated and sparsely populated

PEOPLE AND SOCIETY

Nationality: noun: Korean(s)

adjective: Korean

Ethnic groups: racially homogeneous; there is a small Chinese community and a few ethnic Japanese

Languages: Korean

Religions: traditionally Buddhist and Confucianist, some Christian and syncretic Chondogyo (Religion of the Heavenly Way)

note: autonomous religious activities now almost nonexistent; government-sponsored religious groups exist to provide illusion of religious freedom

Population: 24,983,205 (July 2015 est.)

country comparison to the world: 51

Age structure: 0–14 years: 21.21% (male 2,692,482/female 2,606,842)

15–24 years: 16.08% (male 2,027,480/female 1,989,839)

25–54 years: 44.04% (male 5,511,569/female 5,491,236)

55–64 years: 8.76% (male 1,034,064/female 1,154,141)

65 years and over: 9.91% (male 852,962/female 1,622,590) (2015 est.)

Dependency ratios: total dependency ratio: 44.3%

youth dependency ratio: 30.5%

elderly dependency ratio: 13.8%

potential support ratio: 7.3% (2015 est.)

Median age: total: 33.6 years

male: 32 years

female: 35.2 years (2015 est.)

country comparison to the world: 86

Population growth rate: 0.53% (2015 est.)

country comparison to the world: 157

Birth rate: 14.52 births/1,000 population (2015 est.)

country comparison to the world: 134

Death rate: 9.21 deaths/1,000 population (2015 est.)

country comparison to the world: 64

Net migration rate: -0.04 migrant(s)/1,000 population (2015 est.)

country comparison to the world: 113

Urbanization: urban population: 60.9% of total population (2015)

rate of urbanization: 0.75% annual rate of change (2010–15 est.)

Major urban areas—population: PYONGYANG (capital) 2.863 million (2015)

Sex ratio: at birth: 1.05 male(s)/female

0–14 years: 1.03 male(s)/female

15–24 years: 1.02 male(s)/female

25–54 years: 1 male(s)/female

55–64 years: 0.9 male(s)/female

65 years and over: 0.53 male(s)/female

total population: 0.94 male(s)/female (2015 est.)

Maternal mortality rate: 82 deaths/100,000 live births (2015 est.)
country comparison to the world: 82
Infant mortality rate: *total:* 23.68 deaths/1,000 live births
male: 26.29 deaths/1,000 live births
female: 20.94 deaths/1,000 live births (2015 est.)
country comparison to the world: 74
Life expectancy at birth: *total population:* 70.11 years
male: 66.26 years
female: 74.16 years (2015 est.)
country comparison to the world: 156
Total fertility rate: 1.97 children born/woman (2015 est.)
country comparison to the world: 127
Contraceptive prevalence rate: 70.6%
note: percent of women aged 20–49 (2010)
Hospital bed density: 13.2 beds/1,000 population (2012)
Drinking water source:
improved:
urban: 99.9% of population
rural: 99.4% of population
total: 99.7% of population
unimproved:
urban: 0.1% of population
rural: 0.6% of population
total: 0.3% of population (2015 est.)
Sanitation facility access:
improved:
urban: 87.9% of population
rural: 72.5% of population
total: 81.9% of population
unimproved:
urban: 12.1% of population
rural: 27.5% of population
total: 18.1% of population (2015 est.)
HIV/AIDS—adult prevalence rate: NA
HIV/AIDS—deaths: NA
Obesity—adult prevalence rate: 2.5% (2014)
country comparison to the world: 173
Children under the age of 5 years underweight: 15.2% (2012)
country comparison to the world: 46
Education expenditures: NA
Literacy: *definition:* age 15 and over can read and write
total population: 100%
male: 100%
female: 100% (2015 est.)
School life expectancy (primary to tertiary education): *total:* 12 years
male: 12 years
female: 12 years (2009)

GOVERNMENT

Country name: *conventional long form:* Democratic People's Republic of Korea
conventional short form: north Korea
local long form: Choson-minjujuui-inmin-konghwaguk
local short form: Choson
abbreviation: DPRK
etymology: derived from the Chinese name for Goryeo, which was the Korean dynasty that united

the peninsula in the 10th century A.D.; the North Korean name "Choson" means "[land of the] morning calm"
Government type: communist state
Capital: *name:* Pyongyang
Geographic coordinates: 39 01 N, 125 45 E
time difference: UTC+8.5 (13.5 hours ahead of Washington, DC, during Standard Time)
note: on 15 August 2015, north Korea reverted to U TC+8.5, a time zone that had been observed during pre-colonial times
Administrative divisions: 9 provinces (do, singular and plural) and 2 municipalities (si, singular and plural)
provinces: Chagang-do (Chagang), Hamgyong-bukto (North Hamgyong), Hamgyong-namdo (South Hamgyong), Hwanghae-bukto (North Hwanghae), Hwanghae-namdo (South Hwanghae), Kangwon-do (Kangwon), P'yongan-bukto (North Pyongan), P'yongan-namdo (South Pyongan), Yanggang-do (Yanggang)
cities: Nason-si, P'yongyang-si (Pyongyang)
note: Nason-si is sometimes designated as a special city and P'yongyang-si as a capital city
Independence: 15 August 1945 (from Japan)
National holiday: Founding of the Democratic People's Republic of Korea (DPRK), 9 September (1948)
Constitution: previous 1948, 1972; latest adopted 1998 (during KIM Jong II era); revised 2009, 2012, 2013 (2016)
Legal system: civil law system based on the Prussian model; system influenced by Japanese traditions and Communist legal theory
International law organization participation: has not submitted an ICJ jurisdiction declaration; non-party state to the ICCt
Citizenship: *citizenship by birth:* no
citizenship by descent only: at least one parent must be a citizen of North Korea
dual citizenship recognized: no
residency requirement for naturalization: unknown
Suffrage: 17 years of age; universal
Executive branch: *chief of state:* KIM Jong Un (since 17 December 2011)
head of government: Premier PAK Pong Ju (since 2 April 2013); Vice Premiers IM Chol Ung (since 29 May 2014), KIM Tok Hun (since 19 June 2013), KIM Yong Jin (since 6 January 2012), RI Chol Man (since 13 April 2012), RI Mu Yong (since 31 May 2011), RO Tu Chol (since 3 September 2003)
cabinet: Cabinet or Naegak members appointed by the Supreme People's Assembly except the Minister of People's Armed Forces
elections/appointments: chief of state and premier indirectly elected by the Supreme People's Assembly; election last held on 9 March 2014 (next election NA)
election results: KIM Jong Unelected unopposed
note: the Korean Workers' Party continues to list deceased leaders KIM II Sung and KIM Jong II as Eternal President and Eternal General Secretary respectively

Legislative branch: *description:* unicameral Supreme People's Assembly or Ch'oego Inmin Hoeui (687 seats; members directly elected by absolute majority vote to serve 5-year terms); *note*—the Korean Workers' Party selects all candidates
elections: last held on 9 March 2014 (next to be held in March 2019)
election results: percent of vote by party—NA; seats by party—NA; ruling party approves a list of candidates who are elected without opposition; a token number of seats are reserved for minor parties
Judicial branch: *highest court(s):* Supreme Court or Central Court (consists of the chief justice and 2 "People's Assessors" and for some cases, 3 judges)
judge selection and term of office: judges elected by the Supreme People's Assembly for 5-year terms
subordinate courts: provincial, municipal, military, special courts; people' courts (lowest level)
Political parties and leaders: *major party:* Korean Workers' Party or KWP [KIM Jong Un]
minor parties: Chondoist Chongu Party [RYU MiYong] (under KWP control)
Social Democratic Party [KIM Yong Dae] (under KWP control)
Political pressure groups and leaders: none
International organization participation: ARF, FAO, G-77, ICAO, ICRM, IFAD, IFRCS, IHO, IMO, IMSO, IOC, IPU, ISO, ITSO, ITU, NAM, UN, UNCTAD, UNESCO, UNIDO, UNWTO, UPU, WFTU (NGOs), WHO, WIPO, WMO
Diplomatic representation in the US: none; north Korea has a Permanent Mission to the UN in New York
Diplomatic representation from the US: none; *note*—Swedish Embassy in Pyongyang represents the US as consular protecting power
Flag description: three horizontal bands of blue (top), red (triple width), and blue; the red band is edged in white; on the hoist side of the red band is a white disk with a red five-pointed star; the broad red band symbolizes revolutionary traditions; the narrow white bands stand for purity, strength, and dignity; the blue bands signify sovereignty, peace, and friendship; the red star represents socialism
National symbol(s): red star, chollima (winged horse); national colors: red, white, blue
National anthem: *name:* "Aegukka" (Patriotic Song)
lyrics/music: PAK Se Yong/KIM Won Gyun
note: adopted 1947; both North Korea's and South Korea's anthems share the same name and have a vaguely similar melody but have different lyrics; the north Korean anthem is also known as "Ach'imun pinnara" (Let Morning Shine)

ECONOMY

Economy—overview: north Korea, one of the world's most centrally directed and least open economies, faces chronic economic problems. Industrial capital stock is nearly beyond repair as a result of years of underinvestment, shortages of spare parts, and poor maintenance. Large-scale military spending draws off resources needed for investment and civilian consumption. Industrial and power outputs have stagnated for years at a fraction of pre-1990 levels. Frequent weather-related crop failures aggravated chronic food shortages caused by on-going systemic problems, including a lack of arable land, collective farming practices, poor soil quality, insufficient fertilization, and persistent shortages of tractors and fuel. The mid 1990s were marked by severe famine and widespread starvation. Significant food aid was provided by the international community through 2009. Since that time, food assistance has declined significantly. In the last few years, domestic corn and rice production has been somewhat better, although domestic production does not fully satisfy demand. A large portion of the population continues to suffer from prolonged malnutrition and poor living conditions. Since 2002, the government has allowed informal markets to begin selling a wider range of goods. It also implemented changes in the management process of communal farms in an effort to boost agricultural output.

In December 2009, north Korea carried out a redenomination of its currency, capping the amount of north Korean won that could be exchanged for the new notes, and limiting the exchange to a one-week window. A concurrent crackdown on markets and foreign currency use yielded severe shortages and inflation, forcing Pyongyang to ease the restrictions by February 2010. In response to the sinking of the South Korean warship Cheonan and the shelling of Yeonpyeong Island in 2010, South Korea's government cut off most aid, trade, and bilateral cooperation activities, with the exception of operations at the Kaesong Industrial Complex. north Korea continued efforts to develop special economic zones and expressed willingness to permit construction of a trilateral gas pipeline that would carry Russian natural gas to South Korea. north Korea is also working with Russia to refurbish north Korea's dilapidated rail network and jointly rebuilt a link between a North Korean port in the Rason Special Economic Zone and the Russian rail network.

The North Korean government continues to stress its goal of improving the overall standard of living, but has taken few steps to make that goal a reality for its populace. In 2013–14, the regime rolled out 20 new economic development zones—now totaling 25—set up for foreign investors, although the initiative remains in its infancy. Firm political control remains the government's overriding concern, which likely will inhibit changes to North Korea's current economic system.

GDP (purchasing power parity): $40 billion (2014 est.) $40 billion (2013 est.) $40 billion (2012 est.)
note: data are in 2014 US dollars;
North Korea does not publish reliable National Income Accounts data; the data shown are derived from purchasing power parity (PPP) GDP estimates for North Korea that were made by Angus MADDISON in a study conducted for the OECD; his figure for 1999 was extrapolated to 2011 using estimated real growth rates for North Korea's GDP and an inflation factor based on the US GDP

deflator; the results were rounded to the nearest $10 billion.
country comparison to the world: 114
GDP (official exchange rate): $28 billion (2013 est.)
GDP—real growth rate: 1% (2014 est.) 1.1% (2013 est.) 1.3% (2012 est.)
country comparison to the world: 171
GDP—per capita (PPP): $1,800 (2014 est.) $1,800 (2013 est.) $1,800 (2012 est.)
note: data are in 2014 US dollars
country comparison to the world: 210
Gross national saving: NA%
GDP—composition, by end use:
house holdconsumption: NA%
government consumption: NA%
investment in fixed capital: NA%
investment in inventories: NA%
exports of goods and services: 5.9%
imports of goods and services: -11.1% (2013 est.)
GDP—composition, by sector of origin:
agriculture: 22%
industry: 47%
services: 31% (2014 est.)
Agriculture—products: rice, corn, potatoes, soybeans, pulses, beef, pork, eggs
Industries: military products; machine building, electric power, chemicals; mining (coal, iron ore, limestone, magnesite, graphite, copper, zinc, lead, and precious metals), metallurgy; textiles, food processing; tourism
Industrial production growth rate: 1% (2014 est.)
country comparison to the world: 148
Labor force: 14 million
note: estimates vary widely (2014 est.)
country comparison to the world: 42
Labor force—by occupation: *agriculture:* 37% *industry and services:* 63% (2008 est.)
Unemployment rate: 25.6% (2013 est.) 25.5% (2012 est.)
country comparison to the world: 178
Population below poverty line: NA%
Household income or consumption by percentage share: *lowest:* 10%: NA% *highest:* 10%: NA%
Budget: *revenues:* $3.2 billion *expenditures:* $3.3 billion (2007 est.)
Taxes and other revenues: 11.4% of GDP
note: excludes earnings from state-operated enterprises (2007 est.)
country comparison to the world: 208
Budget surplus (+) or deficit (–): -0.4% of GDP (2007 est.)
country comparison to the world: 43
Fiscal year: calen dar year
Inflation rate (consumer prices): NA%
Exports: $4.4 billion (2014 est.) $4 billion (2013 est.)
country comparison to the world: 114
Exports—commodities: minerals, metallurgical products, manufactures (including armaments), textiles, agricultural and fishery products
Exports—partners: China 75.7% (2015)

Imports: $5.2 billion (2014 est.) $4.8 billion (2013 est.)
country comparison to the world: 124
Imports—commodities: petroleum, coking coal, machinery and equipment, textiles, grain
Imports—partners: China 76.4%, Republic of the Congo 5.5% (2015)
Debt—external: $5 billion (2013 est.)
country comparison to the world: 129
Exchange rates: north Korean won (KPW) per US dollar (average market rate)
8,200 (2015 est.)
7,900 (2014 est.)
98.5 (2013 est.)
155.5 (2012 est.)
140 (2011 est.)

ENERGY

Electricity—production: 18.76 billion kWh (2012 est.)
country comparison to the world: 77
Electricity—consumption: 16 billion kWh (2012 est.)
country comparison to the world: 77
Electricity—exports: 0 kWh (2013 est.)
country comparison to the world: 156
Electricity—imports: 0 kWh (2013 est.)
country comparison to the world: 166
Electricity—installed generating capacity: 7.243 million kW (2013 est.)
country comparison to the world: 66
Electricity—from fossil fuels: 47.4% of total installed capacity (2012 est.)
country comparison to the world: 152
Electricity—from nuclear fuels: 0% of total installed capacity (2012 est.)
country comparison to the world: 120
Electricity—from hydroelectric plants: 52.6% of total installed capacity (2012 est.)
country comparison to the world: 46
Electricity—from other renewable sources: 0% of total installed capacity (2012 est.)
country comparison to the world: 187
Crude oil—production: 0 bbl/day (2014 est.)
country comparison to the world: 152
Crude oil—exports: 0 bbl/day (2012 est.)
country comparison to the world: 146
Crude oil—imports: 70,000 bbl/day (2013 est.)
country comparison to the world: 51
Crude oil—proved reserves: 0 bbl (1 January 2015 est.)
country comparison to the world: 151
Refined petroleum products—production: 11,120 bbl/day (2012 est.)
country comparison to the world: 103
Refined petroleum products—consumption: 17,000 bbl/day (2013 est.)
country comparison to the world: 136
Refined petroleum products—exports: 0 bbl/day (2013 est.)
country comparison to the world: 192
Refined petroleum products—imports: 4,000 bbl/day (2012 est.)
country comparison to the world: 167
Natural gas—production: 0 cu m (2013 est.)
country comparison to the world: 206

Natural gas—consumption: 0 cu m (2013 est.)
country comparison to the world: 159
Natural gas—exports: 0 cu m (2013 est.)
country comparison to the world: 127
Natural gas—imports: 0 cu m (2013 est.)
country comparison to the world: 88
Natural gas—proved reserves: 0 cu m (1 January 2014 est.)
country comparison to the world: 155
Carbon dioxide emissions from consumption of energy: 45.4 million Mt (2012 est.)
country comparison to the world: 63

COMMUNICATIONS

Telephones—fixed lines: *total subscriptions:* 1.18 million
subscriptions per 100 inhabitants: 5 (2014 est.)
country comparison to the world: 70
Telephones—mobile cellular: *total:* 2.8 million
subscriptions per 100 inhabitants: 11 (2014 est.)
country comparison to the world: 142
Telephone system: *general assessment:* adequate system; nationwide fiber-optic network; mobile-cellular service expanding beyond Pyongyang
domestic: fiber-optic links installed down to the county level; telephone directories unavailable; GSM mobile-cellular service initiated in 2002 but suspended in 2004; Orascom Telecom Holding, an Egyptian company, launched W-CDMA mobile service on 15 December 2008 for the Pyongyang area, has expanded service to several large cities and now has a 1-million-person subscriber base
international: country code—850; satellite earth stations—2 (1 Intelsat—Indian Ocean, 1 Russian-Indian Ocean region); other international connections through Moscow and Beijing (2011)
Broadcast media: no independent media; radios and TVs are pre-tuned to government stations; 4 government-owned TV stations; the Korean Workers' Party owns and operates the Korean Central Broadcasting Station, and the state-run Voice of Korea operates an external broadcast service; the government prohibits listening to and jams foreign broadcasts (2008)
Radio broadcast station: AM 17 (including 11 stations of Korean Central Broadcasting Station; North Korea has a "national intercom" cable radio station wired throughout the country that is a significant source of information for the average North Korean citizen; it is wired into most residences and workplaces and carries news and commentary), FM 14, shortwave 14 (2006)
Television broadcast stations: 4 (includes Korean Central Television, Mansudae Television, Korean Educational and Cultural Network, and Kaesong Television targeting South Korea) (2003)
Internet country code: .kp
Internet hosts: 8 (2012)
country comparison to the world: 226

TRANSPORTATION

Airports: 82 (2013)
country comparison to the world: 67
Airports—with paved runways: *total:* 39
over 3,047 m: 3
2,438 to 3,047 m: 22
1,524 to 2,437 m: 8
914 to 1,523 m: 2
under 914 m: 4 (2013)
Airports—with unpaved runways: *total:* 43
2,438 to 3,047 m: 3
1,524 to 2,437 m: 17
914 to 1,523 m: 15
under 914 m: 8 (2013)
Heliports: 23 (2013)
Pipelines: oil 6 km (2013)
Railways: *total:* 7,435 km
standard gauge: 7,435 km 1.435-m gauge (5,400 km electrified)
note: figures are approximate; some narrow-gauge railway also exists (2014)
country comparison to the world: 29

Roadways: *total:* 25,554 km
paved: 724 km
unpaved: 24,830 km (2006)
country comparison to the world: 100
Waterways: 2,250 km (most navigable only by small craft) (2011)
country comparison to the world: 38
Merchant marine: *total:* 158
by type: bulk carrier 6, cargo 131, carrier 1, chemical tanker 1, container 4, passenger/cargo 1, petroleum tanker 12, refrigerated cargo 2
foreign-owned: 13 (Belgium 1, China 3, Nigeria 1, Singapore 1, South Korea 1, Syria 4, UAE 2)
registered in other countries: 6 (Mongolia 1, Sierra Leone 2, unknown 3) (2010)
country comparison to the world: 37

Ports and terminals: *major seaport(s):* Ch'ongjin, Haeju, Hungnam (Hamhung), Namp'o, Senbong, Songnim, Sonbong (formerly Unggi), Wonsan

MILITARY AND SECURITY

Military branches: North Korean People's Army: Ground Forces, Navy, Air Force; civil security forces (2005)
Military service age and obligation: 18 is presumed to be the legal minimum age for compulsory military service; 16–17 is the presumed legal minimum age for voluntary service (2012)

TRANSNATIONAL ISSUES

Disputes—international: risking arrest, imprisonment, and deportation, tens of thousands of North Koreans cross into China to escape famine, economic privation, and political oppression; North Korea and China dispute the sovereignty of certain islands in Yalu and Tumen rivers; Military Demarcation Line within the 4-km-wide Demilitarized Zone has separated North from South Korea since 1953; periodic incidents in the Yellow Sea with South Korea which claims the Northern Limiting Line as a maritime boundary; North Korea supports South Korea in rejecting Japan's claim to Liancourt Rocks (Tok-do/Take-shima)

Refugees and internally displaced persons: *IDPs:* undetermined (periodic flooding and famine during mid-1990s) (2007)
Trafficking in persons: *current situation:* north Korea is a source country for men, women, and children who are subjected to forced labor and sex trafficking; many north Korean workers recruited to work abroad under bilateral contracts with foreign governments, most often Russia and China, are subjected to forced labor and do not have a choice in the work the government assigns them, are not free to change jobs, and face government reprisals if they try to escape or complain to outsiders; tens of thousands of North Koreans, including children, held in prison camps are subjected to forced labor, including logging, mining, and farming; many North Korean women and girls, lured by promises of food, jobs, and freedom, have migrated to China illegally to escape poor social and economic conditions only to be forced into prostitution, domestic service, or agricultural work through forced marriages

tier rating: Tier 3—North Korea does not fully comply with minimum standards for the elimination of trafficking and is not making significant efforts to do so; the government continued to participate in human trafficking through its use of domestic forced labor camps and the provision of forced labor to foreign governments through bilateral contracts; officials did not demonstrate any efforts to address human trafficking through prosecution, protection, or prevention measures; no known investigations, prosecutions, or convictions of trafficking offenders or officials complicit in trafficking-related offenses were conducted; the government also made no efforts to identify or protect trafficking victims and did not permit NGOs to assist victims (2015)

Illicit drugs: for years, from the 1970s into the 2000s, citizens of the Democratic People's Republic of (North) Korea (DPRK), many of them diplomatic employees of the government, were apprehended abroad while trafficking in narcotics, including two in Turkey in December 2004; police investigations in Taiwan and Japan in recent years have linked North Korea to large illicit shipments of heroin and methamphetamine, including an attempt by the North Korean merchant ship Pong Su to deliver 150 kg of heroin to Australia in April 2003

KOREA, SOUTH

INTRODUCTION

Background: An independent kingdom for much of its long history, Korea was occupied by Japan beginning in 1905 following the Russo-Japanese War. In 1910, Tokyo formally annexed the entire Peninsula. Korea regained its independence following Japan's surrender to the US in 1945. After World War II, a democratic-based government (Republic of Korea, ROK) was set up in the southern half of the Korean Penin sula while a communist-style government was installed in the north (Democratic People's Republic of Korea, DPR K). During the Korean War (1950–53), US troops and UN forces fought alongside ROK soldiers to defend South Korea from a DPRK invasion supported by China and the Soviet Union. A 1953 armistice split the Peninsula along a demilitarized zone at about the 38th parallel. PARK Chung-hee took over leadership of the country in a 1961 coup. During his regime, from 1961 to 1979, South Korea achieved rapid economic growth, with per capita income rising to roughly 17 times the level of north Korea. South Korea held its first free presidential election under a revised democratic constitution in 1987, with former ROK Army general ROH Tae-woo winning a close race. In 1993, KIM Young-sam (1993–98) became the first civilian president of South Korea's new democratic era. President KIM Dae-jung (1998–2003) won the Nobel Peace Prize in 2000 for his contributions to South Korean democracy and his "Sunshine" policy of engagement with north Korea. President PARK Geun-hye, daughter of former ROK President PARK Chung-hee, took office in February 2013 and is South Korea's first female leader. South Korea held a non-permanent seat (2013–14) on the UN Security Council and will host the 2018 Winter Olympic Games. Discord with North Korea has permeated inter-Korean relations for much of the past decade, highlighted by the north's attacks on a South Korean ship and island in 2010, multiple nuclear and missile tests, and the exchange of artillery fire across the DMZ.

GEOGRAPHY

Location: Eastern Asia, southern half of the Korean Peninsula bordering the Sea of Japan and the Yellow Sea

Geographic coordinates: 37 00 N, 127 30 E
Map references: Asia
Area: *total:* 99,720 sq km
land: 96,920 sq km
water: 2,800 sq km
country comparison to the world: 109
Area—comparative: slightly smaller than Pennsylvania; slightly larger than Indiana
Land boundaries: *total:* 237 km
border countries (1): North Korea 237 km
Coastline: 2,413 km
Maritime claims: *territorial sea:* 12 nm; between 3 nm and 12 nm in the Korea Strait
contiguous zone: 24 nm
exclusive economic zone: 200 nm
continental shelf: not specified
Climate: temperate, with rainfall heavier in summer than winter; cold winters
Terrain: mostly hills and mountains; wide coastal plains in west and south
Elevation: *mean elevation:* 282 m
elevation extremes: lowest point: Sea of Japan 0 m
highest point: Halla-san 1,950 m
Natural resources: coal, tungsten, graphite, molybdenum, lead, hydropower potential
Land use: *agricultural land:* 18.1%
arable land: 15.3%
permanent crops: 2.2%
permanent pasture: 0.6%
forest: 63.9%
other: 18% (2011 est.)
Irrigated land: 7,780 sq km (2012)
Total renewable water resources: 69.7 cu km (2011)
Freshwater withdrawal (domestic/industrial/agricultural): *total:* 25.47 cu km/yr (26%/12%/62%)
per capita: 548.7 cu m/yr (2003)
Natural hazards: occasional typhoons bring high winds and floods; low-level seismic activity common in southwest
volcanism: Halla (elev. 1,950 m) is considered historically active although it has not erupted in many centuries
Environment—current issues: air pollution in large cities; acid rain; water pollution from the discharge of sewage and industrial effluents; drift net fishing
Environment—international agreements: *party to:* Antarctic-Environmental Protocol, Antarctic-Marine Living Resources, Antarctic Treaty, Biodiversity, Climate Change, Climate Change-Kyoto Protocol, Desertification, Endangered Species, Environmental Modification, Hazardous Wastes, Law of the Sea, Marine Dumping, Ozone Layer Protection, Ship Pollution, Tropical Timber 83, Tropical Timber 94, Wetlands, Whaling

signed, but not ratified: none of the selected agreements
Geography—note: strategic location on Korea Strait

PEOPLE AND SOCIETY

Nationality: *noun:* Korean(s)
adjective: Korean
Ethnic groups: homogeneous (except for about 20,000 Chinese)
Languages: Korean, English (widely taught in junior high and high school)
Religions: Christian 31.6% (Protestant 24.0%, Catholic 7.6%), Buddhist 24.2%, other or unknown 0.9%, none 43.3% (2010 est.)
Population: 49,115,196 (July 2015 est.)
country comparison to the world: 28
Age structure: *0–14 years:* 13.69% (male 3,489,464/female 3,232,372)
15–24 years: 13.52% (male 3,518,488/female 3,122,997)
25–54 years: 46.63% (male 11,687,846/female 11,214,687)
55–64 years: 13.14% (male 3,190,093/female 3,264,411)
65 years and over: 13.02% (male 2,662,353/female 3,732,485) (2015 est.)
Dependency ratios: *total dependency ratio:* 37.2%
youth dependency ratio: 19.2%
elderly dependency ratio: 18%
potential support ratio: 5.6% (2015 est.)
Median age: *total:* 40.8 years
male: 39.2 years
female: 42.2 years (2015 est.)
country comparison to the world: 40
Population growth rate: 0.14% (2015 est.)
country comparison to the world: 186
Birth rate: 8.19 births/1,000 population (2015 est.)
country comparison to the world: 220
Death rate: 6.75 deaths/1,000 population (2015 est.)
country comparison to the world: 139
Net migration rate: 0 migrant(s)/1,000 population (2015 est.)
country comparison to the world: 92
Urbanization: *urban population:* 82.5% of total population (2015)
rate of urbanization: 0.66% annual rate of change (2010–15 est.)
Major urban areas—population: SEOUL (capital) 9.774 million; Busan (Pusan) 3.216 million; Incheon (Inch'on) 2.685 million; Daegu (Taegu) 2.244 million; Daejon (Taejon) 1.564 million; Gwangju (Kwangju) 1.536 million (2015)
Sex ratio: *at birth:* 1.07 male(s)/female
0–14 years: 1.08 male(s)/female
15–24 years: 1.13 male(s)/female
25–54 years: 1.04 male(s)/female
55–64 years: 0.98 male(s)/female
65 years and over: 0.71 male(s)/female
total population: 1 male(s)/female (2015 est.)

Mother's mean age at first birth: 30.3 (2011 est.)

Maternal mortality rate: 11 deaths/100,000 live births (2015 est.)

country comparison to the world: 143

Infant mortality rate: *total:* 3.86 deaths/1,000 live births

male: 4.05 deaths/1,000 live births

female: 3.66 deaths/1,000 live births (2015 est.)

country comparison to the world: 194

Life expectancy at birth: *total population:* 80.04 years

male: 76.95 years

female: 83.34 years (2015 est.)

country comparison to the world: 39

Total fertility rate: 1.25 children born/woman (2015 est.)

country comparison to the world: 220

Contraceptive prevalence rate: 80%

note: percent of women aged 15–44 (2009)

Health expenditures: 7.2% of GDP (2013)

country comparison to the world: 69

Physicians density: 2.14 physicians/1,000 population (2012)

Hospital bed density: 10.3 beds/1,000 population (2009)

Drinking water source:

improved:

urban: 99.7% of population

rural: 87.9% of population

total: 97.8% of population

unimproved:

urban: 0.3% of population

rural: 12.1% of population

total: 2.2% of population (2012 est.)

Sanitation facility access:

improved:

urban: 100% of population

rural: 100% of population

total: 100% of population

unimproved:

urban: 0% of population

rural: 0% of population

total: 0% of population (2015 est.)

HIV/AIDS—adult prevalence rate: NA

HIV/AIDS—people living with HIV/AIDS: NA

HIV/AIDS—deaths: NA

Obesity—adult prevalence rate: 6.3% (2014)

country comparison to the world: 139

Children under the age of 5 years underweight: 0.6% (2011)

country comparison to the world: 135

Education expenditures: 4.6% of GDP (2012)

country comparison to the world: 75

School life expectancy (primary to tertiary education): *total:* 17 years

male: 17 years

female: 16 years (2013)

Unemployment, youth ages 15–24: *total:* 9.3%

male: 9.8%

female: 9% (2013 est.)

country comparison to the world: 107

GOVERNMENT

Country name: *conventional long form:* Republic of Korea

conventional short form: South Korea

local long form: Taehan-min'guk

local short form: Han'guk

abbreviation: ROK

etymology: derived from the Chinese name for Goryeo, which was the Korean dynasty that united the peninsula in the 10th century A.D.; the South Korean name "Han'guk" means "land of the Han," where "han" refers to a "great [leader]" (similar to the title "khan")

Government type: presidential republic

Capital: *name:* Seoul

Geographic coordinates: 37 33 N, 126 59 E

time difference: UTC+9 (14 hours ahead of Washington, DC, during Standard Time)

Administrative divisions: 9 provinces (do, singular and plural), 6 metropolitan cities (gwangyeoksi, singular and plural), 1 special city (teugbyeolsi), and 1 special self-governing city (teukbyeoljachisi)

provinces: Chungbuk (North Chungcheong), Chungnam (South Chungcheong), Gangwon, Gyeongbuk (North Gyeongsang), Gyeonggi, Gyeongnam (South Gyeongsang), Jeju, Jeonbuk (North Jeolla), Jeonnam (South Jeolla)

metropolitan cities: Busan (Pusan), Daegu (Taegu), Daejeon (Taejon), Gwangju (Kwangju), Incheon (Inch'on), Ulsan

special city: Seoul

special self-governing city: Sejong

Independence: 15 August 1945 (from Japan)

National holiday: Liberation Day, 15 August (1945)

Constitution: effective 17 July 1948; amended several times, last in 1987 (2016)

Legal system: mixed legal system combining European civil law, Anglo-American law, and Chinese classical thought

International law organization participation: has not submitted an ICJ jurisdiction declaration; accepts ICCt jurisdiction

Citizenship: *citizenship by birth:* no

citizenship by descent only: at least one parent must be a citizen of South Korea

dual citizenship recognized: no

residency requirement for naturalization: 5 years

Suffrage: 19 years of age; universal

Executive branch: *chief of state:* President PARK Geun-hye (since 25 February 2013)

head of government: Prime Minister HWANG Kyo-ahn (since 18 June 2015); Deputy Prime Ministers

YOO Il-ho (since 13 January 2016), LEE Joon-sik (since 13 January 2016)

cabinet: State Council appointed by the president on the prime minister's recommendation

elections/appointments: president directly elected by simple majority popular vote for a single 5-year term; election last held on 19 December 2012 (next to be held in December 2017); prime minister appointed by president, approved by National Assembly

election results: PARK Geun-Hye elected president; percent of vote—PARK Geun-Hye (NFP) 51.6%, MOON Jae-In (DUP) 48%, other 0.4%

Legislative branch: *description:* unicameral National Assembly or Kuk Hoe (300 seats; 246 members directly elected in single-seat constituencies by simple majority vote and 54 directly elected in a single national constituency by proportional representation vote; members serve 4-year terms)

elections: last held on 13 April 2016 (next to be held in 2020)

election results: percent of vote by party—Saenuri 33.5%, PP 26.7%, MPK 25.5%, JP 7.2%, other 7.1%; seats by party—MPK 123, Saenuri 122, PP 38, Justice Party 6, independent 11

Judicial branch: *highest court(s):* Supreme Court of South Korea (consists of a chief justice and 13 justices); Constitutional Court (consists of a court head and 8 justices)

judge selection and term of office: Supreme Court chief justice appointed by the president with the consent of the National Assembly; other justices appointed by the president upon the recommendation of the chief justice and consent of the National Assembly; position of the chief justice is a 6-year non-renewable term; other justices serve 6-year renewable terms; Constitutional Court justices appointed—3 by the president, 3 by the National Assembly, and 3 by the Supreme Court chief justice; court head serves until retirement at age 70, while other justices serve 6-year renewable terms with mandatory retirement at age 65

subordinate courts: High Courts; District Courts; Branch Courts (organized under the District Courts); specialized courts for family and administrative issues

Political parties and leaders: Justice Party [SIM Sang-jeong]

Minjoo Party of Korea or MPK (formerly New Politics Alliance for Democracy or NPAD) [KIM Jong-in] (NPAD was a merger of the Democratic Party or DP (formerly DUP) [KIM Han-gil] and the New Political Vision Party or NPVP [AHN Cheol-soo] in March 2014)

New Frontier Party (NFP) or Saenuri (formerly Grand National Party) [Interim Chairman WON Yoo-chul] People's Party or PP [AHN Cheol-soo and CHUN Jung-bae]

Political pressure groups and leaders: Catholic Priests' Association for Justice

Christian Council of Korea

Citizen's Coalition for Economic Justice

Federation of Korean Industries

Federation of Korean Trade Unions

Korean Confederation of Trade Unions

Korean Veterans' Association

Lawyers for a Democratic Society

National Council of Churches in Korea

People's Solidarity for Participatory Democracy

International organization participation: ADB, AfDB (nonregional member), APEC, Arctic Council (observer), ARF, ASEAN (dialogue partner), Australia Group, BIS, CD, CICA, CP, EAS, EBRD, FAO, FATF, G-20, IADB, IAEA, IBRD, ICAO, ICC (national committees), ICCt, ICRM, IDA, IEA, IFAD, IFC, IFRCS, IHO, ILO, IMF, IMO, IMSO, Interpol, IOC, IOM, IPU, ISO, ITSO, ITU, ITUC (NGOs), LAIA (observer), MIGA, MINURSO, MINUSTAH, NEA, NSG, OAS (observer), OECD, OPCW, OSCE (partner), Pacific Alliance (observer), Paris Club (associate),

PCA, PIF (partner), SAARC (observer), SICA (observer), UN, UNAMID, UNCTAD, UNESCO, UNHCR, UNIDO, UNIFIL, UNMIL, UNMISS, UNMOGIP, UNOCI, UNWTO, UPU, WCO, WHO, WIPO, WMO, WTO, ZC

Diplomatic representation in the US: *chief of mission:* Ambassador AHN Ho-young (since 7 June 2013)

chancery: 2450 Massachusetts Avenue NW, Washington, DC 20008

telephone: [1] (202) 939-5600

FAX: [1] (202) 797-0595

consulate(s) general: Agana (G uam), Anchorage (AK), Atlanta, Boston, Chicago, Honolulu, Houston, Los Angeles, New York, San Francisco, Seattle

Diplomatic representation from the US: *chief of mission:* Ambassador Mark William LIPPERT (since 21 November 2014)

embassy: 188 Sejong-daero, Jongno-gu, Seoul 110–710

mailing address: US Embassy Seoul, UNit

telephone: [82] (2) 397-4114

FAX: [82] (2) 725-0152

Flag description: white with a red (top) and blue yin-yang symbol in the center; there is a different black trigram from the ancient I Ching (Book of Changes) in each corner of the white field; the South Korean national flag is called Taegukki; white is a traditional Korean color and represents peace and purity; the blue section represents the negative cosmic forces of the yin, while the red symbolizes the opposite positive forces of the yang; each trigram (kwae) denotes one of the four universal elements, which together express the principle of movement and harmony

National symbol(s): taegeuk (yin yang symbol), Hibiscus syriacus (Rose of Sharon); national colors: red, white, blue, black

National anthem: *name:* "Aegukga" (Patriotic Song)

lyrics/music: YUN Ch'i-Ho or AN Ch'ang-Ho/ AHN Eaktay

note: adopted 1948, well-known by 1910; both North Korea's and South Korea's anthems share the same name and have a vaguely similar melody but have different lyrics

ECONOMY

Economy—overview: South Korea over the past four decades has demonstrated incredible economic growth and global integration to become a high-tech industrialized economy. In the 1960s, GDP per capita was comparable with levels in the poorer countries of Africa and Asia. In 2004, South Korea joined the trillion-dollar club of world economies.

A system of close government and business ties, including directed credit and import restrictions, initially made this success possible. The government promoted the import of raw materials and technology at the expense of consumer goods and encouraged savings and investment over consumption. The Asian financial crisis of 1997–98 exposed longstanding weaknesses in South Korea's development model, including high debt/equity ratios and massive short-term foreign borrowing. GDP plunged by 7% in 1998, and then recovered by 9% in 1999–2000. South Korea adopted numerous economic reforms following the crisis, including greater openness to foreign investment and imports. Growth moderated to about 4% annually between 2003 and 2007.

South Korea's export focused economy was hit hard by the 2008 global economic downturn, but quickly rebounded in subsequent years, reaching over 6% growth in 2010. The US-Korea Free Trade Agreement was ratified by both governments in 2011 and went into effect in March 2012. Between 2012 and 2015, the economy experienced slow growth—2%-3% per year—due to sluggish domestic consumption and investment. The administration in 2015 faced the challenge of balancing heavy reliance on exports with developing domestic-oriented sectors, such as services. The South Korean economy's long-term challenges include a rapidly aging population, inflexible labor market, dominance of large conglomerates (chaebols), and the heavy reliance on exports, which comprise about half of GDP. In an effort to address the long term challenges and sustain economic growth, the current government has prioritized structural reforms, deregulation, promotion of entrepreneurship and creative industries, and the competitiveness of small- and medium-sized enterprises.

GDP (purchasing power parity): $1.849 trillion (2015 est.)

$1.802 trillion (2014 est.)

$1.744 trillion (2013 est.)

note: data are in 2015 US dollars

country comparison to the world: 14

GDP (official exchange rate): $1.377 trillion (2015 est.)

GDP—real growth rate: 2.6% (2015 est.)

3.3% (2014 est.)

2.9% (2013 est.)

country comparison to the world: 117

GDP—per capita (PPP): $36,500 (2015 est.)

$35,700 (2014 est.)

$34,700 (2013 est.)

note: data are in 2015 US dollars

country comparison to the world: 48

Gross national saving: 35.7% of GDP (2015 est.)

35.1% of GDP (2014 est.)

35.3% of GDP (2013 est.)

country comparison to the world: 8

GDP—composition, by end use:

household consumption: 49%

government consumption: 14.8%

investment in fixed capital: 27.5%

investment in inventories: 0.3%

exports of goods and services: 44.2%

imports of goods and services: -35.8% (2015 est.)

GDP—composition, by sector of origin:

agriculture: 2.3%

industry: 38%

services: 59.7% (2015 est.)

Agriculture—products: rice, root crops, barley, vegetables, fruit; cattle, pigs, chickens, milk, eggs; fish

Industries: electronics, telecommunications, automobile production, chemicals, shipbuilding, steel

Industrial production growth rate: -1.5% (2015 est.)

country comparison to the world: 177

Labor force: 26.89 million (2015 est.)

country comparison to the world: 25

Labor force—by occupation: *agriculture:* 5.7%

industry: 24.2%

services: 70.2% (2015 est.)

Unemployment rate: 3.5% (2015 est.)

3.5% (2014 est.)

country comparison to the world: 30

Population below poverty line: 14.6% (2013 est.)

Household income or consumption by percentage share: *lowest:* 10%: 6.8%

highest: 10%: 37.8% (Q4 2014)

Distribution of family income—Gini index: 30.2 (2014 est.)

35.8 (2000)

country comparison to the world: 121

Budget: *revenues:* $291.3 billion

expenditures: $294.1 billion (2015 est.)

Taxes and other revenues: 20.9% of GDP (2015 est.)

country comparison to the world: 149

Budget surplus (+) or deficit (−): -0.2% of GDP (2015 est.)

country comparison to the world: 35

Public debt: 34.9% of GDP (2015 est.)

34.5% of GDP (2014 est.)

country comparison to the world: 128

Fiscal year: calendar year

Inflation rate (consumer prices): 0.7% (2015 est.)

1.3% (2014 est.)

country comparison to the world: 68

Central bank discount rate: 1.5% (31 December 2015)

2% (31 December 2014)

country comparison to the world: 120

Commercial bank prime lending rate: 3.7% (31 December 2015 est.)

4.27% (31 December 2014 est.)

country comparison to the world: 161

Stock of narrow money: $541.3 billion (31 December 2015 est.)

$532.9 billion (31 December 2014 est.)

country comparison to the world: 10

Stock of broad money: $1.973 trillion (31 December 2014 est.)

$1.754 trillion (31 December 2013 est.)

country comparison to the world: 9

Stock of domestic credit: $2.397 trillion (31 December 2015 est.)

$2.406 trillion (31 December 2014 est.)

country comparison to the world: 11

Market value of publicly traded shares: $1.263 trillion (31 December 2015 est.)

$1.269 trillion (31 December 2014)

$1.193 trillion (31 December 2013 est.)

country comparison to the world: 12

Current account balance: $105.9 billion (2015 est.)

$84.37 billion (2014 est.)

country comparison to the world: 5

Exports: $535.5 billion (2015 est.)

$621.3 billion (2014 est.)

country comparison to the world: 6

Exports—commodities: semiconductors, petro-chemicals, automobile/auto parts, ships, wireless communication equipment, flat display displays, steel, electronics, plastics, computers

Exports—partners: China 26%, US 13.3%, Hong Kong 5.8%, Vietnam 5.3%, Japan 4.9% (2015)

Imports: $430.8 billion (2015 est.)
$528.6 billion (2014 est.)
country comparison to the world: 12

Imports—commodities: crude oil/petroleum products, semiconductors, natural gas, coal, steel, computers, wireless communication equipment, automobiles, fine chemical, textiles

Imports—partners: China 20.7%, Japan 10.5%, US 10.1%, Germany 4.8%, Saudi Arabia 4.5% (2015)

Reserves of foreign exchange and gold: $368.5 billion (31 December 2015 est.)
$363.6 billion (31 December 2014 est.)
country comparison to the world: 9

Debt—external: $409.1 billion (31 December 2014 est.)
$424.4 billion (31 December 2013 est.)
country comparison to the world: 30

Stock of direct foreign investment—at home: $191.3 billion (31 December 2015 est.)
$182 billion (31 December 2014 est.)
country comparison to the world: 30

Stock of direct foreign investment—abroad: $293.2 billion (31 December 2015 est.)
$261.8 billion (31 December 2014 est.)
country comparison to the world: 22

Exchange rates: South Korean won (KRW) per US dollar—
1,129.7 (2015 est.)
1,052.96 (2014 est.)
1,052.96 (2013 est.)
1,126.47 (2012 est.)
1,108.29 (2011 est.)

ENERGY

Electricity—production: 522 billion kWh (2014 est.)
country comparison to the world: 11

Electricity—consumption: 482.4 billion kWh (2012 est.)
country comparison to the world: 10

Electricity—exports: 0 kWh (2014 est.)
country comparison to the world: 158

Electricity—imports: 0 kWh (2014 est.)
country comparison to the world: 168

Electricity—installed generating capacity: 94.35 million kW (2012 est.)
country comparison to the world: 13

Electricity—from fossil fuels: 69.6% of total installed capacity (2013 est.)
country comparison to the world: 108

Electricity—from nuclear fuels: 26.8% of total installed capacity (2013 est.)
country comparison to the world: 6

Electricity—from hydroelectric plants: 1.7% of total installed capacity (2013 est.)
country comparison to the world: 140

Electricity—from other renewable sources: 1.9% of total installed capacity (2013 est.)
country comparison to the world: 82

Crude oil—production: 0 bbl/day (2014 est.)
country comparison to the world: 154

Crude oil—exports: 5,578 bbl/day (2013 est.)
country comparison to the world: 70

Crude oil—imports: 2.949 million bbl/day (2014 est.)
country comparison to the world: 5

Crude oil—proved reserves: 0 bbl
country comparison to the world: 153

Refined petroleum products—production: 2.697 million bbl/day (2013 est.)
country comparison to the world: 7

Refined petroleum products—consumption: 2.35 million bbl/day (2014 est.)
country comparison to the world: 11

Refined petroleum products—exports: 1.175 million bbl/day (2013 est.)
country comparison to the world: 8

Refined petroleum products—imports: 920,000 bbl/day (2013 est.)
country comparison to the world: 6

Natural gas—production: 322 million cu m (2014 est.)
country comparison to the world: 75

Natural gas—consumption: 47.76 billion cu m (2014 est.)
country comparison to the world: 19

Natural gas—exports: 0 cu m (2014 est.)
country comparison to the world: 129

Natural gas—imports: 49.08 billion cu m (2014 est.)
country comparison to the world: 7

Natural gas—proved reserves: 5.748 billion cu m (1 January 2014 est.)
country comparison to the world: 90

Carbon dioxide emissions from consumption of energy: 688.3 million Mt (2012 est.)
country comparison to the world: 8

COMMUNICATIONS

Telephones—fixed lines: *total subscriptions:* 29.48 million
subscriptions per 100 inhabitants: 60 (2014 est.)
country comparison to the world: 12

Telephones—mobile cellular: *total:* 57.2 million
subscriptions per 100 inhabitants: 117 (2014 est.)
country comparison to the world: 27

Telephone system: *general assessment:* excellent domestic and international services featuring rapid incorporation of new technologies
domestic: fixed-line and mobile-cellular services widely available with a combined telephone subscribership of roughly 170 per 100 persons; rapid assimilation of a full range of telecommunications technologies leading to a boom in e-commerce
international: country code—82; numerous submarine cables provide links throughout Asia, Australia, the Middle East, Europe, and US; satellite earth stations—66 (2011)

Broadcast media: multiple national TV networks with 2 of the 3 largest networks publicly operated; the largest privately owned network, Seoul Broadcasting Service (SBS), has ties with other commercial TV networks; cable and satellite TV subscription services available; publicly operated radio broadcast networks and many privately owned radio broadcasting networks, each with multiple affiliates, and independent local stations (2010)
Radio broadcast station: AM 96, FM 322, shortwave 1 (2008)
Television broadcast stations: 57 (plus 103 cable operators and 119 relay cable operators) (2008)

Internet country code: .kr

Internet hosts: 315,697 (2012)
country comparison to the world: 62

Internet users: *total:* 44.9 million
percent of population: 91.5% (2014 est.)
country comparison to the world: 13

TRANSPORTATION

Airports: 111 (2013)
country comparison to the world: 53

Airports—with paved runways: *total:* 71
over 3,047 m: 4
2,438 to 3,047 m: 19
1,524 to 2,437 m: 12
914 to 1,523 m: 13
under 914 m: 23 (2013)

Airports—with unpaved runways: *total:* 40
914 to 1,523 m: 2
under 914 m: 38 (2013)

Heliports: 466 (2013)

Pipelines: gas 2,216 km; oil 16 km; refined products 889 km (2013)

Railways: *total:* 3,460 km
standard gauge: 3,460 km 1.435-m gauge (1,422 km electrified) (2014)
country comparison to the world: 52

Roadways: total: 104,983 km
paved: 83,199 km (includes 3,779 km of expressways)
unpaved: 21,784 km (2009)
country comparison to the world: 44

Waterways: 1,600 km (most navigable only by small craft) (2011)
country comparison to the world: 50

Merchant marine: *total:* 786
by type: bulk carrier 191, cargo 235, carrier 8, chemical tanker 130, container 72, liquefied gas 44, passenger 5, passenger/cargo 15, petroleum tanker 55, refrigerated cargo 15, roll on/roll off 10, vehicle carrier 6
foreign-owned: 31 (China 6, France 2, Japan 14, Taiwan 1, US 8)
registered in other countries: 457 (Bahamas 1, Cambodia 10, Ghana 1, Honduras 6, Hong Kong 3, Indonesia 2, Kiribati 1, Liberia 2, Malta 2, Marshall Islands 41, North Korea 1, Panama 373, Philippines 1, Russia 1, Singapore 3, Tuvalu 1, unknown 8) (2010)
country comparison to the world: 14

Ports and terminals: *major seaport(s):* Busan, Incheon, Gunsan, Kwangyang, Mokpo, Pohang, Ulsan, Yeosu
container port(s) (TEUs): Busan (16,163,842), Kwangyang (2,061,958), Incheon (1,924,644)
LNG terminal(s) (import): Incheon, Kwangyang, Pyeongtaek, Samcheok, Tongyeong, Yeosu

MILITARY AND SECURITY

Military branches: Republic of Korea Army, Navy (includes Marine Corps), Air Force (2011)

Military service age and obligation: 20–30 years of age for compulsory military service, with middle school education required; minimum conscript service obligation—21 months (Army, Marines), 23 months (Navy), 24 months (Air Force); 18–26 years of age for voluntary military service; women, in service since 1950, admitted to 7 service branches, including infantry, but excluded from artillery, armor, anti-air, and chaplaincy corps; HIV-positive individuals are exempt from military service (2012)

Military expenditures:

2.8% of GDP (2012)
2.77% of GDP (2011)
2.8% of GDP (2010)
country comparison to the world: 25

TRANSNATIONAL ISSUES

Disputes—international: Military Demarcation Line within the 4-km-wide Demilitarized Zone has separated North from South Korea since 1953; periodic incidents with North Korea in the Yellow Sea over the Northern Limit Line, which South Korea claims as a maritime boundary; South Korea and Japan claim Liancourt Rocks (Tok-do/Take-shima), occupied by South Korea since 1954

Refugees and internally displaced persons: *stateless persons:* 197 (2015)

KOSOVO

INTRODUCTION

Background: The central Balkans were part of the Roman and Byzantine Empires before ethnic Serbs migrated to the territories of modern Kosovo in the 7th century. During the medieval period, Kosovo became the center of a Serbian Empire and saw the construction of many important Serb religious sites, including many architecturally significant SerbiaNorthodox monasteries. The defeat of Serbian forces at the Battle of Kosovo in 1389 led to five centuries of Ottoman rule during which large numbers of Turks and Albanians moved to Kosovo. By the end of the 19th century, Albanians replaced Serbs as the dominant ethnic group in Kosovo. Serbia reacquired control over the region from the Ottoman Empire during the First Balkan War of 1912. After World War II, Kosovo's present-day boundaries were established when Kosovo became an autonomous province of Serbia in the Socialist Federal Republic of Yugoslavia (S.F.R.Y.). Despite legislative concessions, Albanian nationalism increased in the 1980s, which led to riots and calls for Kosovo's independence. The Serbs—many of whom viewed Kosovo as their cultural heartland—instituted a new constitution in 1989 revoking Kosovo's autonomous status. Kosovo's Alban ian leaders responded in 1991 by organizing a referendum declaring Kosovo independent. Serbia undertook repressive measures against the Kosovar Albanians in the 1990s, provoking a Kosovar Albanian insurgency.

Beginning in 1998, Serbia conducted a brutal counterinsurgency campaign that resulted in massacres and massive expulsions of ethnic Albanians (some 800,000 ethnic Albanians were forced from their homes in Kosovo). After international attempts to mediate the conflict failed, a three-month NATO military operation against Serbia beginning in March 1999 forced the Serbs to agree to withdraw their military and police forces from Kosovo. UN Security Council Resolution 1244 (1999) placed Kosovo under a transitional administration, the UN Interim Administration Mission in Kosovo (UNMIK), pending a determination of Kosovo's future status. A UN-led process began in late 2005 to determine Kosovo's final status. The 200607 negotiations ended without agreement between Belgrade and Pristina, though the UN issued a comprehensive report on Kosovo's final status that endorsed independence. On 17 February 2008, the Kosovo Assembly declared Kosovo independent. Since then, over 100 countries have recognized Kosovo, and it has joined numerous international organizations. In october 2008, Serbia sought an advisory opinion from the International Court of Justice (ICJ) on the legality under international law of Kosovo's declaration of independence. The ICJ released the advisory opinion in July 2010 affirming that Kosovo's declaration of independence did not violate general principles of international law, UN Security Council Resolution 1244, or the Constitutive Framework. The opinion was closely tailored to Kosovo's unique history and circumstances.

Serbia continues to reject Kosovo's independence, but the two countries reached an agreement to normalize their relations in April 2013 through EU -facilitated talks and are currently engaged in the implementation process. Kosovo seeks full integration into the international community, and has pursued bilateral recognitions and eventual membership in international organizations, such as the UN, EU, and NATO.

GEOGRAPHY

Location: Southeast Europe, between Serbia and Macedonia

Geographic coordinates: 42 35 N, 21 00 E

Map references: Europe

Area: *total:* 10,887 sq km

land: 10,887 sq km

water: 0 sq km

country comparison to the world: 169

Area—comparative: slightly larger than Delaware

Land boundaries: *total:* 714 km

border countries (4): Albania 112 km, Macedonia 160 km, Montenegro 76 km, Serbia 366 km

Coastline: 0 km (landlocked)

Maritime claims: none (landlocked)

Climate: influenced by continental air masses resulting in relatively cold winters with heavy snowfall and hot, dry summers and autumns; Mediterranean and alpine influences create regional variation; maximum rainfall between October and December

Terrain: flat fluvial basin at an elevation of 400–700 m above sea level surrounded by several high mountain ranges with elevations of 2,000 to 2,500 m

Elevation: *mean elevation:* NA

elevation extremes: *lowest point:* Drini i Bardhe/ Beli Drim 297 m (located on the border with Albania)

highest point: Gjeravica/Deravica 2,656 m

Natural resources: nickel, lead, zinc, magnesium, lignite, kaolin, chrome, bauxite

Land use: *agricultural land:* 52.8%

arable land: 27.4%

permanent crops: 1.9%

permanent pasture: 23.5%

forest: 41.7%

other: 5.5% (2001 est.)

Irrigated land: NA

Geography—note: the 41-km long Nerodimka River represents the only instance in Europe where a river divides into two branches each of which flows into a different sea: the northern branch flows into the Sitnica River, which via the Ibar, Morava, and Danube Rivers ultimately flows into the Black Sea; the southern branch flows via the Lepenac and Vardar Rivers into the Aegean Sea

PEOPLE AND SOCIETY

Nationality: *noun:* Kosovar (Albanian), Kosovac (Serbian)

adjective: Kosovar (Albanian), Kosovski (Serbian)

note: Kosovan, a neutral term, is sometimes also used as a noun or adjective

Ethnic groups: Albanians 92.9%, Bosniaks 1.6%, Serbs 1.5%, Turk 1.1%, Ashkali 0.9%, Egyptian 0.7%, Gorani 0.6%, Roma 0.5%, other/unspecified 0.2%

note: these estimates may under-represent Serb, Roma, and some other ethnic minorities because they are based on the 2011 Kosovo national census, which excluded northern Kosovo (a largely Serb-inhabited region) and was partially boycotted by Serb and Roma communities in southern Kosovo (2011 est.)

Languages: Albanian (official) 94.5%, Bosnian 1.7%, Serbian (official) 1.6%, Turkish 1.1%, other 0.9% (includes Romani), unspecified 0.1%

note: in municipalities where a community's mother tongue is not one of Kosovo's official languages, the language of that community may be given official status according to the 2006 Law on the Use of Languages (2011 est.)

Religions: Muslim 95.6%, Roman Catholic 2.2%, Orthodox 1.5%, other 0.07%, none 0.07%, unspecified 0.6% (2011 est.)

Population: 1,870,981 (July 2015 est.)

country comparison to the world: 151

Age structure: *0–14 years:* 25.82% (male 250,907/female 232,112)

15–24 years: 17.74% (male 174,208/female 157,791)

25–54 years: 42.01% (male 414,684/female 371,339)

55–64 years: 7.4% (male 69,030/female 69,338)

65 years and over: 7.03% (male 55,107/female 76,465) (2015 est.)

Median age: *total:* 28.2 years

male: 27.9 years

female: 28.6 years (2015 est.)

country comparison to the world: 128

Major urban areas—population: PRISTINA (capital) 207,062 (2014)

Sex ratio: *at birth:* 1.08 male(s)/female

0–14 years: 1.08 male(s)/female

15–24 years: 1.1 male(s)/female

25–54 years: 1.12 male(s)/female

55–64 years: 1 male(s)/female

65 years and over: 0.72 male(s)/female

total population: 1.06 male(s)/female (2015 est.)

Literacy: *definition:* age 15 and over can read and write

total population: 91.9%

male: 96.6%

female: 87.5% (2003 est.)

Unemployment, youth ages 15–24: *total:* 55.3%

male: 52%

female: 63.8% (2012 est.)

country comparison to the world: 2

GOVERNMENT

Country name: *conventional long form:* Republic of Kosovo

conventional short form: Kosovo

local long form: Republikae Kosoves (Republika Kosovo)

local short form: Kosova (Kosovo)

etymology: name derives from the Serbian "kos" meaning "blackbird, " an ellipsis (linguistic omission) for "kosove polje" or "field of the blackbirds"

Government type: parliamentary republic

Capital: *name:* Pristina (Prishtine, Prishtina)

Geographic coordinates: 42 40 N, 21 10 E

time difference: UTC + 1 (6 hours ahead of Washington, DC during Standard Time)

daylight saving time: +1hr, begins last Sunday in March; ends last Sunday in October

Administrative divisions: 38 municipalities (komunat, singular—komuna (Albanian); opstine, singular—opstina (Serbian)); Decan (Decani), Dragash (Dragas), Ferizaj (Urosevac), Fushe Kosove (Kosovo Polje), Gjakove (Dakovica), Gjilan (Gnjilane), Gllogovc (Glogovac), Gracanice (Gracanica), Hani i Elezit (Deneral Jankovic), Istog (Istok), Junik, Kacanik, Kamenice (Kamenica), Kline (Klina), Kllokot (Klokot), Leposaviq (Leposavic), Lipjan (Lipljan), Malisheve (Malisevo), Mamushe (Mamusa), Mitrovicee Jug (Juzna Mitrovica) [South Mitrovica], Mitrovicee Veriut (Severna Mitrovica) [North Mitrovica], Novoberde (Novo Brdo), Obiliq (Obilic), Partesh (Partes), Peje (Pec), Podujeve (Podujevo), Prishtine (Pristina), Prizren, Rahovec (Orahovac), Ranillug (Ranilug), Shterpce (Strpce), Shtime (Stimlje), Skenderaj (Srbica), Suhareke (Suva Reka), Viti (Vitina), Vushtrri (Vucitrn), Zubin Potok, Zvecan

Independence: 17 February 2008 (from Serbia)

National holiday: Independence Day, 17 February (2008)

Constitution: previous 1974, 1990; latest (postindependence) draft finalized 2 April 2008, signed 7 April 2008, ratified 9 April 2008, entered into force 15 June 2008; amended several times, last in 2016 (2016); note—amendment 24, passed by the Assembly in March 2016, established the Kosovo Relocated Specialist Institution, a court established to try war crimes allegedly committed by the Kosovo Liberation Army in the late 1990s (2016)

Legal system: civil law system; note- the European Union Rule of Law Mission (EULEX) retains limited executive powers related to the investigation of such issues as war crimes

International law organization participation: has not submitted an ICJ jurisdiction declaration; non-party state to the ICCt

Citizenship: *citizenship by birth:* no

citizenship by descent only: at least one parent must be a citizen of Kosovo

dual citizenship recognized: yes

residency requirement for naturalization: 5 years

Suffrage: 18 years of age; universal

Executive branch: *chief of state:* President Hashim THACI (since 7 April 2016)

head of government: Prime Minister Isa MUSTAFA (since 9 December 2014)

cabinet: Cabinet elected by the Assembly

elections/appointments: president indirectly elected by two-thirds majority vote of the Assembly for a 5-year term; if a candidate does not receive a two-third majority in the first two ballots, the candidate receiving a simple majority of votes in the third ballot is elected (eligible for a second term); election last held on 26 February

2016 (next to be held in 2021); prime minister indirectly elected by the Assembly

election results: Hashim THACI elected president; Assembly vote—Hashim THACI (PDK) 71, Rafet RAMA (PDK) 0 in the third round (10 votes invalid); Isa MUSTAFA (LDK) selected prime minister by the President in consultation with the LDK/PDK/PD/LB/PSHDK/PK coalition

Legislative branch: *description:* unicameral Assembly or Kuvendi i Kosoves/Skupstina Kosova (120 seats; 100 members directly elected by proportional represen tation vote with 20 seats reserved for ethnic minorities—10 for Serbs and 10 for other ethnic minorities; members serve 4-year terms)

elections: last held on 8 June 2014 (next expected to be held in June 2018)

election results: percent of vote by party/coalition—PDK/PD/LB/PSHDK/PK 30.4%, LDK 25.2%, VV 13.6%, AAK 9.5%, Serb List 5.2%, NISMA 5.2%, KDTP 1.0%, other 9.9%; seats by party/coalition -PDK/PD/LB/PSHDK/PK 37, LDK 30, VV 16, AAK 11, Serb List 9, NISMA 6, KDTP 2, VAKAT 2, other 7

Judicial branch: *highest court(s):* Supreme Court (consists of the court president and at least 15 percent of judges to reflect Kosovo's territorial ethnic composition); Constitutional Court (consists of the court president, vice president, and 7 judges)

judge selection and term of office: Supreme Court judges nominated by the Kosovo Judicial Council, an independent body staffed by judges and lay members, and also responsible for overall administration of Kosovo's judicial system; judges appointed by the president of the Republic of Kosovo; judges appointed until mandatory retirement age; Constitutional Court judges nominated by the Kosovo Assembly and appointed by the president of the republic to serve single, 9-year terms

subordinate courts: Court of Appeals (organized into 4 departments: General, Serious Crime, Commercial Matters, and Administrative Matters; Basic Court (located in 7 municipalities, each with several branches)

note: in March 2016, the Kosovo Assembly approved a constitutional amendment that establishes the Kosovo Relocated Specialist Judicial Institution; the court—to be located at the Hague in the Netherlands and expected to be in operation by the end of 2016—will try alleged crimes by members of the Kosovo Liberation Army during the late 1990s; the court will be attached to each level of the Kosovo court system and consist of 4 Specialist Chambers with international judges and the Prosecutor's Office

Political parties and leaders: Albanian Christian Democratic Party of Kosovo or PSHDK [Uke BERISHA]

Alliance for the Future of Kosovo or AAK [Ramush HARADINAJ]

Conservative Party of Kosovo or PK [Munir BASHA]

Democratic League of Kosovo or LDK [Isa MUSTAFA]

Democratic Party of Kosovo or PDK [Kadri VESELI, acting chairman]

Initiative for Kosovo or NISMA [Fatmir LIMAJ]

Justice Party of Kosovo or PD [Ferid AGANI]

Movement for Self-Determination (Vetevendosje) or VV [Visar YMERI]

Movement for UNification or LB [Valon MURATI]

Serb List [Slavko SIMIC]

Turkish Democratic Party of Kosovo or KDTP [Mahir YAGCILAR]

Vakat Coalition or VAKAT [Rasim DEMIRI]

Political pressure groups and leaders: CiviKos Platform [Valdete IDRIZI]

Council for the Defense of Human Rights and Freedom (human rights) [Behxhet SHALA]

Group for Political and Legal Studies [Fisnik KORENICA]

KLA War Veterans Organization [Muharrem XHEMAJLI]

Kosova Women's Network [Igballe ROGOVA]

Kosovar Civil Society Foundation [Venera HAJRULLAHU]

Kosovo Democratic Institute [Ismet KRYEZIU]

Organization for Democracy, Anti-Corruption and Dignity Rise! [Arton DEMHASAJ, acting chairman]

Serb National Council (SNV)

Speak Up [Petrit ZOGAJ, executive director]

International organization participation: IBRD, IDA, IFC, IMF, ITUC (NGOs), MIGA, OIF (observer)

Diplomatic representation in the US: *chief of mission:* Ambassador Vlora CITAKU (since 17 September 2015)

chancery: 2175 K Street, NW, Suite 300, Washington, DC 20037

telephone: 202-450-2130

FAX: 202-735-0609

consulate(s) general: New York

consulate(s): Des Moines (IA)

Diplomatic representation from the US: *chief of mission:* Ambassador Gregory T. DELAWIE (since 21 August 2015)

embassy: Arberia/Dragodan, Nazim Hikmet 30, Pristina, Kosovo

mailing address: use embassy street address

telephone: [381] 38 59 59 3000

FAX: [381] 38 549 890

Flag description: centered on a dark blue field is the geographical shape of Kosovo in a gold color surmounted by six white, five-pointed stars arrayed in a slight arc; each star represents one of the major ethnic groups of Kosovo: Albanians, Serbs, Turks, Gorani, Roma, and Bosniaks

National symbol(s): six, five-pointed, white stars; national colors: blue, gold, white

National anthem: *name:* "Europe"

lyrics/music: no lyrics/Mendi MENGJIQI

note: adopted 2008; Kosovo chose to exclude lyrics in its anthem so as not to offend the country's minority ethnic groups

ECONOMY

Economy—overview: Kosovo's economy has shown progress in transitioning to a market-based system and maintaining macroeconomic stability, but it is still highly dependent on the international community and the diaspora for financial and technical assistance. Remittances from the diaspora—located mainly in Germany, Switzerland, and the Nordic countries—are estimated to account for about 15% of GDP and international donor assistance accounts for approximately 10% of GDP. With international assistance, Kosovo has been able to privatize a majority of its state-owned enterprises.

Kosovo's citizens are the poorest in Europe with a per capita GDP (PPP) of $8,000 in 2014. An unemployment rate of 31%, and a youth unemployment rate near 60%, in a country where the average age is 26, encourages emigration and fuels a significant informal, unreported economy. Most of Kosovo's population lives in rural towns outside of the capital, Pristina. Inefficient, near-subsistence farming is common—the result of small plots, limited mechanization, and a lack of technical expertise. Kosovo enjoys lower labor costs than the rest of the region. However, high levels of corruption, little contract enforcement, and unreliable electricity supply have discouraged potential investors. Minerals and metals production—including lignite, lead, zinc, nickel, chrome, aluminum, magnesium, and a wide variety of construction materials—once the backbone of industry, has declined because of ageing equipment and insufficient investment. A limited and unreliable electricity supply is a major impediment to economic development, but Kosovo has received technical assistance to help improve the sector's performance. In 2012, Kosovo privatized its electricity supply and distribution network. The US Government is cooperating with the Ministry of Economic Development (MED) and the World Bank to conclude a commercial tender for the construction of a new power plant, Kosovo C. MED also has plans for the rehabilitation of an older coal power plant, Kosovo B, and the development of a coal mine that could supply both plants.

In June 2009, Kosovo joined the World Bank and International Monetary Fund, and began servicing its share of the former Yugoslavia's debt. In order to help integrate Kosovo into regional economic structures, UNMIK signed (on behalf of Kosovo) its accession to the Central Europe Free Trade Area (CEF TA) in 2006. Serbia and Bosnia previously had refused to recognize Kosovo's customs stamp or extend reduced tariff privileges for Kosovo products under CEFTA, but both countries resumed trade with Kosovo in 2011. Kosovo joined the European Bank for Reconstruction and Development in 2012 and the Council of Europe Development Bank in 2013. In 2014, Kosovo concluded the Stabilization and Association Agreement negotiations (SAA) with the EU, focused on trade liberalization, and signed it into law in 2015. In 2015, Kosovo negotiated a $185 million Stand-by Arrangement (SBA) with the IMF following the conclusion of its previous SBA in 2014. The official currency of Kosovo is the euro, but the Serbian dinar is also used illegally in Serb majority communities. Kosovo's tie to the euro has helped keep core inflation low. Kosovo experienced its first federal budget deficit in 2012, when government expenditures climbed sharply. In May 2014, the government introduced a 25% salary increase for public sector employees and an equal increase in certain social benefits. Central revenues could not sustain these increases, and the government was forced to reduce its planned capital investments. The government, led by Prime Minister MUSTAFA—a trained economist—recently made several changes to its fiscal policy, expanding the list of duty-free imports, decreasing the Value Added Tax (VAT) for basic food items and public utilities, and increasing the VAT for all other goods. In August 2015, as part of its EU-facilitated normalization process with Serbia, Kosovo signed agreements on telecommunications and energy distribution, but disagreements over who owns economic assets within Kosovo continue.

GDP (purchasing power parity): $17.39 billion (2015 est.)

$16.84 billion (2014 est.)

$16.63 billion (2013 est.)

note: data are in 2015 US dollars

country comparison to the world: 150

GDP (official exchange rate): $6.355 billion (2015 est.)

GDP—real growth rate: 3.3% (2015 est.)

1.2% (2014 est.)

3.4% (2013 est.)

country comparison to the world: 91

GDP—per capita (PPP): NA (2015 est.)

NA (2014 est.)

NA (2013 est.)

note: data are in 2015 US dollars

Gross national saving: 12.5% of GDP (2015 est.)

12.7% of GDP (2014 est.)

12.5% of GDP (2013 est.)

country comparison to the world: 135

GDP—composition, by end use:

household consumption: 90.5%

government consumption: 16%

investment in fixed capital: 28.2%

investment in inventories: 3%

exports of goods and services: 5.8%

imports of goods and services: -43.5% (2012 est.)

GDP—composition, by sector of origin:

agriculture: 12.9%

industry: 22.6%

services: 64.5% (2009 est.)

Agriculture—products: wheat, corn, berries, potatoes, peppers, fruit; dairy, livestock; fish

Industries: mineral mining, construction materials, base metals, leather, machinery, appliances, foodstuffs and beverages, textiles

Labor force: 483,200

note: includes th ose estimated to be employed in the grey economy (2013 est.)

country comparison to the world: 156

Labor force—by occupation: *agriculture:* 5.9%

industry: 16.8%

services: 77.3% (2013)

Unemployment rate: 35.3% (2014 est.)

30.9% (2013 est.)

note: Kosovo has a large informal sector that may not be reflected in these data

country comparison to the world: 192

Population below poverty line: 30% (2013 est.)

Distribution of family income—Gini index: 30 (FY05/06)
country comparison to the world: 123

Budget: *revenues:* $1.396 billion
expenditures: $1.61 billion (2014 est.)
Taxes and other revenues: 22.1% of GDP (2014 est.)
country comparison to the world: 140

Budget surplus (+) or deficit (−): -3.4% of GDP (2014 est.)
country comparison to the world: 127

Public debt: 10.6% of GDP (2014 est.)
9.1% of GDP (2013)
country comparison to the world: 166

Inflation rate (consumer prices): -0.5% (2015 est.)
0.4% (2014 est.)
country comparison to the world: 29

Commercial bank prime lending rate: 12.8% (30 June 2013 est.)
13.7% (31 December 2012 est.)
country comparison to the world: 58

Stock of broad money: $2.511 billion (2014 est.)
$2.773 billion (2012 est.)
country comparison to the world: 147

Stock of domestic credit: $2.02 billion (2014 est.)
$2.505 billion (2013 est.)
country comparison to the world: 139

Current account balance: -$512 million (2015 est.)
-$582 million (2014 est.)
country comparison to the world: 97

Exports: $349 million (2014 est.)
$408 million (2013 est.)
country comparison to the world: 181

Exports—commodities: mining and processed metal products, scrap metals, leather products, machinery, appliances, prepared foodstuffs, beverages and tobacco, vegetable products, textiles and apparel

Exports—partners: Italy 25.8%, Albania 14.6%, Macedonia 9.6%, China 5.5%, Germany 5.4%, Switzerland 5.4%, Turkey 4.1% (2012 est.)

Imports: $2.687 billion (2014 est.)
$3.398 billion (2013 est.)
country comparison to the world: 150

Imports—commodities: foodstuffs, livestock, wood, petroleum, chemicals, machinery, minerals, textiles, stone, ceramic and glass products, electrical equipment

Imports—partners: Germany 11.9%, Macedonia 11.5%, Serbia 11.1%, Italy 8.5%, Turkey 9%, China 6.4%, Albania 4.4% (2012 est.)

Reserves of foreign exchange and gold: $NA
Debt—external: $411.6 million (2014 est.)
$448.2 million (2013 est.)
country comparison to the world: 183

Stock of direct foreign investment—at home: $21.2 billion (31 December 2015 est.)
$29.41 billion (31 December 2014 est.)
country comparison to the world: 76

Exchange rates: euros (EUR) per US dollar—
0.885 (2015 est.)
0.7525 (2014 est.)
0.7634 (2013 est.)
0.78 (2012 est.)
0.7185 (2011 est.)

ENERGY

Electricity—production: 5.324 billion kWh (2014 est.)
country comparison to the world: 118

Electricity—consumption: 2.887 billion kWh (2014 est.)
country comparison to the world: 135

Electricity—exports: 474.8 million kWh (2014 est.)
country comparison to the world: 68

Electricity—imports: 875 million kWh (2014 est.)
country comparison to the world: 67

Electricity—installed generating capacity: 1.589 million kW (2012 est.)
country comparison to the world: 115

Electricity—from fossil fuels: 97.1% of total installed capacity (2012 est.)
country comparison to the world: 59

Electricity—from nuclear fuels: 0% of total installed capacity (2012 est.)
country comparison to the world: 123

Electricity—from hydroelectric plants: 2.9% of total installed capacity (2012 est.)
country comparison to the world: 132

Electricity—from other renewable sources: 0% of total installed capacity (2012 est.)
country comparison to the world: 190

Crude oil—production: NA bbl/day (2014 est.)
Crude oil—exports: 0 bbl/day (2012 est.)
country comparison to the world: 148

Crude oil—imports: 0 bbl/day (2012 est.)
country comparison to the world: 211

Crude oil—proved reserves: NA bbl (1 January 2015 est.)

Refined petroleum products—production: 0 bbl/day (2012 est.)
country comparison to the world: 198

Refined petroleum products—consumption: NA bbl/day (2011 est.)

Natural gas—production: 0 cu m (2007)
country comparison to the world: 208

Natural gas—consumption: 0 cu m (2007)
country comparison to the world: 161

Natural gas—proved reserves: NA cu m
Carbon dioxide emissions from consumption of energy: 7.576 million Mt (2012 est.)
country comparison to the world: 113

COMMUNICATIONS

Telephones—fixed lines: *total:* 110,000
subscriptions per 100 inhabitants: 6 (2006)

country comparison to the world: 143
Telephones—mobile cellular: *total:* 562,000
subscriptions per 100 inhabitants: 31 (2007)
country comparison to the world: 168

TRANSPORTATION

Airports: 6 (2013)
country comparison to the world: 172
Airports—with paved runways: *total:* 3
2,438 to 3,047 m: 1
1,524 to 2,437 m: 1
under 914 m: 1 (2013)
Airports—with unpaved runways: *total:* 3
under 914 m: 3 (2013)
Heliports: 2 (2013)
Railways: *total:* 333 km
standard gauge: 333 km 1.435-m gauge (2014)
country comparison to the world: 121

Roadways: *total:* 2,003 km
paved: 1,883 km (includes 38 km of expressways)
unpaved: 120 km (2014)
country comparison to the world: 147

MILITARY AND SECURITY

Military branches: Kosovo does not have a military force; the Kosovo Security Force was established in 2009 and maintains a non-military mandate in four core competencies: search-and-rescue, firefighting, demining, and hazardous material response (2015)

TRANSNATIONAL ISSUES

Disputes—international: Serbia with several other states protest the US and other states' recognition of Kosovo's declaration of its status as a sovereign and independent state in February 2008; ethnic Serbian municipalities along Kosovo's northern border challenge final status of Kosovo-Serbia boundary; several thousand NATO-led Kosovo Force peacekeepers under UN Interim Administration Mission in Kosovo authority continue to keep the peace within Kosovo between the ethnic Albanian majority and the Serb minority in Kosovo; Kosovo and Macedonia completed demarcation of their boundary in September 2008

Refugees and internally displaced persons: *IDPs:* 17,000 (primarily ethnic Serbs displaced during the 1998–1999 war fearing reprisals from the majority ethnic-Albanian population; a smaller number of ethnic Serbs, Roma, Ashkali, and Egyptians fled their homes in 2004 as a result of violence) (2015)

KUWAIT

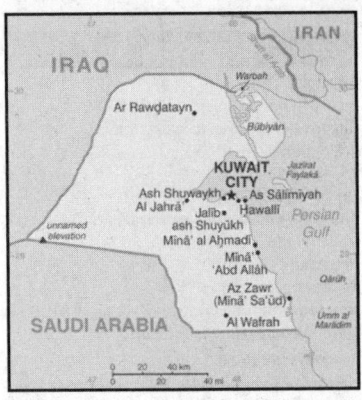

INTRODUCTION

Background: Kuwait has been ruled by the AL-SABAH dynasty since the 18th century. The threat of Ottoman invasion in 1899 prompted Amir Mubarak AL-SABAH to seek protection from Britain, ceding foreign and defense responsibility to Britain until 1961, when the country attained its independence. Kuwait was attacked and overrun by Iraq on 2 August 1990. Following several weeks of aerial bombardment, a US-led UN coalition began a ground assault on 23 February 1991 that liberated Kuwait in four days. Kuwait spent more than $5 billion to repair oil infrastructure damaged during 1990–91. The AL-SABAH family returned to power in 1991 and established one of the most independent legislatures in the Arab World. The country witnessed the historic election in 2009 of four women to its National Assembly. Amid the 2010–11 uprisings and protests across the Arab world, stateless Arabs, known as bidoon, staged small protests in February and March 2011 demanding citizenship, jobs, and other benefits available to Kuwaiti nationals. Youth activist groups -supported by opposition legislators—rallied repeatedly in 2011 for the prime minister's dismissal amid allegations of widespread government corruption, ultimately prompting the prime minister to resign in late 2011. Demonstrations, following a short lull, renewed in late 2012 in response to an Amiri decree amending the electoral law to reduce the number of votes per person from four to one. The opposition, led by a coalition of Sunni Islamists, tribalists, some liberals, and myriad youth groups, largely boycotted legislative elections in 2012 and 2013, which ushered in a legislature more amenable to the government's agenda. Since coming to power in 2006, the Amir has dissolved the National Assembly on five occasions (the Constitutional Court annulled the Assembly in June 2012 and again in June 2013) and shuffled the cabinet over a dozen times, usually citing political stagnation and gridlock between the legislature and the government.

GEOGRAPHY

Location: Middle East, bordering the Persian Gulf, between Iraq and Saudi Arabia

Geographic coordinates: 29 30 N, 45 45 E

Map references: Middle East

Area: *total:* 17,818 sq km

land: 17,818 sq km

water: 0 sq km

country comparison to the world: 158

Area—comparative: slightly smaller than New Jersey

Land boundaries: *total:* 475 km

border countries (2): Iraq 254 km, Saudi Arabia 221 km

Coastline: 499 km

Maritime claims: *territorial sea:* 12 nm

Climate: dry desert; intensely hot summers; short, cool winters

Terrain: flat to slightly undulating desert plain

Elevation: *mean elevation:* 108 m

elevation extremes: *lowest point:* Persian Gulf 0 m

highest point: unnamed elevation 306 m

Natural resources: petroleum, fish, shrimp, natural gas

Land use: *agricultural land:* 8.5%

arable land: 0.6%

permanent crops: 0.3%

permanent pasture: 7.6%

forest: 0.4%

other: 91.1% (2011 est.)

Irrigated land: 105 sq km (2012)

Total renewable water resources: 0.02 cu km (2011)

Freshwater withdrawal (domestic/industrial/agricultural): *total:* 0.91 cu km/yr (47%/2%/51%)

per capita: 441.2 cu m/yr (2005)

Natural hazards: sudden cloudbursts are common from October to April and bring heavy rain, which can damage roads and houses; sandstorms and dust storms occur throughout the year but are most common between March and August

Environment—current issues: limited natural freshwater resources; some of world's largest and most sophisticated desalination facilities provide much of the water; air and water pollution; desertification

Environment—international agreements: *party to:* Biodiversity, Climate Change, Climate Change-Kyoto Protocol, Desertification, Endangered Species, Environmental Modification, Hazardous Wastes, Law of the Sea, Ozone Layer Protection

signed, but not ratified: Marine Dumping

Geography—note: strategic location at head of Persian Gulf

PEOPLE AND SOCIETY

Nationality: *noun:* Kuwaiti(s)

adjective: Kuwaiti

Ethnic groups: Kuwaiti 31.3%, other Arab 27.9%, Asian 37.8%, African 1.9%, other 1.1% (includes

European, north American, South American, and Australian) (2013 est.)

Languages: Arabic (official), English widely spoken

Religions: Muslim (official) 76.7%, Christian 17.3%, other and unspecified 5.9%

note: represents the total population; about 69% of the population consists of immigrants (2013 est.)

Population: 2,788,534 (July 2015 est.)

note: Kuwait's Public Authority for Civil Information estimates the country's total population to be 4,183,658 for 2015, with immigrants accounting more than 69%

country comparison to the world: 141

Age structure: *0–14 years:* 25.32% (male 367,176/ female 338,883)

15–24 years: 15.21% (male 233,306/female 190,903)

25–54 years: 52.32% (male 924,103/female 534,769)

55–64 years: 4.82% (male 76,707/female 57,663)

65 years and over: 2.33% (male 30,681/female 34,343) (2015 est.)

Dependency ratios: *total dependency ratio:* 32.1%

youth dependency ratio: 29.5%

elderly dependency ratio: 2.6%

potential support ratio: 38.4% (2015 est.)

Median age: *total:* 29 years

male: 30.2 years

female: 27 years (2015 est.)

country comparison to the world: 121

Population growth rate: 1.615% (2015 est.)

country comparison to the world: 73

Birth rate: 19.91 births/1,000 population (2015 est.)

country comparison to the world: 84

Death rate: 2.18 deaths/1,000 population (2015 est.)

country comparison to the world: 223

Net migration rate: -1.58 migrant(s)/1,000 population (2015 est.)

country comparison to the world: 158

Urbanization: *urban population:* 98.3% of total population (2015)

rate of urbanization: 3.63% annual rate of change (2010–15 est.)

Major urban areas—population: KUWAIT (capital) 2.779 million (2015)

Sex ratio: *at birth:* 1.05 male(s)/female

0–14 years: 1.08 male(s)/female

15–24 years: 1.22 male(s)/female

25–54 years: 1.73 male(s)/female

55–64 years: 1.33 male(s)/female

65 years and over: 0.89 male(s)/female

total population: 1.41 male(s)/female (2015 est.)

Maternal mortality rate: 4 deaths/100,000 live births (2015 est.)

country comparison to the world: 145

Infant mortality rate: *total:* 7.31 deaths/1,000 live births

male: 7.09 deaths/1,000 live births
female: 7.54 deaths/1,000 live births (2015 est.)
country comparison to the world: 158
Life expectancy at birth: *total population:* 77.82 years
male: 76.51 years
female: 79.19 years (2015 est.)
country comparison to the world: 64
Total fertility rate: 2.48 children born/woman (2015 est.)
country comparison to the world: 80
Health expenditures: 2.9% of GDP (2013)
country comparison to the world: 187
Physicians density: 1.79 physicians/1,000 population (2009)
Hospital bed density: 2.2 beds/1,000 population (2012)
Drinking water source:
improved:
urban: 99% of population
rural: 99% of population
total: 99% of population
unimproved:
urban: 1% of population
rural: 1% of population
total: 1% of population (2015 est.)
Sanitation facility access:
improved:
urban: 100% of population
rural: 100% of population
total: 100% of population
unimproved:
urban: 0% of population
rural: 0% of population
total: 0% of population (2015 est.)
HIV/AIDS—people living with HIV/AIDS: NA
HIV/AIDS—deaths: NA
Obesity—adult prevalence rate: 38.3% (2014)
country comparison to the world: 10
Children under the age of 5 years underweight: 3% (2014)
country comparison to the world: 120
Education expenditures: 3.8% of GDP (2006)
country comparison to the world: 116
Literacy: *definition:* age 15 and over can read and write
total population: 96.3%
male: 96.5%
female: 95.8% (2015 est.)
School life expectancy (primary to tertiary education): *total:* 13 years
male: 12 years
female: 14 years (2013)
Unemployment, youth ages 15–24: *total:* 14.55%
male: N/A
female: N/A (2011 est.)
country comparison to the world: 94

GOVERNMENT

Country name: *conventional long form:* State of Kuwait
conventional short form: Kuwait
local long form: Dawlat al Kuwayt
local short form: Al Kuwayt

etymology: the name derives from the capital city, which is from Arabic "al-Kuwayt" a diminutive of "kut" meaning "fortress encircled by water"
Government type: constitutional monarchy
Capital: *name:* Ku wait City
Geographic coordinates: 29 22 N, 47 58 E
time difference: UTC+3 (8 hours ahead of Washington, DC, during Standard Time)
Administrative divisions: 6 governorates (muhafazat, singular—muhafazah); Al Ahmadi, Al 'Asimah, Al Farwaniyah, Al Jahra', Hawalli, Mubarak al Kabir
Independence: 19 June 1961 (from the UK)
National holiday: National Day, 25 February (1950)
Constitution: approved and promulgated 11 November 1962 (2016)
Legal system: mixed legal system consisting of English common law, French civil law, and Islamic religious law
International law organization participation: has not submitted an ICJ jurisdiction declaration; non-party state to the ICCt
Citizenship: *citizenship by birth:* no
citizenship by descent only: at least one parent must be a citizen of Kuwait
dual citizenship recognized: no
residency requirement for naturalization: not specified
Suffrage: 21 years of age; universal; note—members of the military or police by law cannot vote; all voters must have been citizens for 20 years
Executive branch: *chief of state:* Amir SABAH al-Ahmad al-Jabir al-Sabah (since 29 January 2006); Crown Prince NAWAF al-Ahmad al-J abir al-Sabah (born 25 June 1937)

head of government: Prime Minister JABIR AL-MUBARAK al-Hamad al-Sabah (since 30 November 2011); First Deputy Prime Minister SABAH Khaled al-Hamad al-Sabah; Deputy Prime Ministers al-KHALD al- Jarrah al-Sabah, MUHAMMAD AL-KHALID al-Hamad al-Sabah, Abdulmohsen MUDEJ
cabinet: Council of Ministers appointed by the prime minister, approved by the amir
elections/appointments: amir chosen from within the ruling family, confirmed by the National Assembly; prime minister and deputy prime ministers appointed by the amir
Legislative branch: *description:* unicameral National Assembly or Majlis al-U mma (65 seats; 50 members directly elected in multi-seat constituencies by simple majority vote and 15 ex-officio members—cabinet ministers—appointed by the prime minister; members serve 4-year terms)
elections: last held 27 July 2013 (next to be held in July 2017)
election results: seats won—pro-government 30, liberal 9, Shiite 8, Sunni 3
Judicial branch: *highest court(s):* Constitutional Court (consists of 5 judges); Supreme Court or Court of Cassation (organized into several circuits, each with 5 judges)
judge selection and term of office: all Kuwaiti judges appointed by the Amir upon recommendation of the Supreme Judicial Council, a

consultative body comprised of Kuwaiti judges and Ministry of Justice officials
subordinate courts: High Court of Appeal; Court of First Instance; Summary Court
Political parties and leaders: none; while the formation of political parties is not permitted, they are not forbidden by law
Political pressure groups and leaders: *other:* Islamists; merchants; political groups; secular liberals and pro-governmental deputies; Shia activists; tribal groups
International organization participation: ABEDA, AfDB (nonregional member), AFESD, AMF, BDEAC, CAEU, CD, FAO, G-77, GCC, IAEA, IBRD, ICAO, ICC (national committees), ICRM, IDA, IDB, IFAD, IFC, IFRCS, IHO, ILO, IMF, IMO, IMSO, Interpol, IOC, IPU, ISO, ITSO, ITU, ITUC (NGOs), LAS, MIGA, NAM, OAPEC, OIC, OPCW, OPEC, Paris Club (associate), PCA, UN, UNCTAD, UNESCO, UNIDO, UNRWA, UNWTO, UPU, WCO, WFTU (NGOs), WHO, WIPO, WMO, WTO
Diplomatic representation in the US: *chief of mission:* Ambassador SALIM al-Abdallah al-Jabir al-Sabah (since 10 October 2001)
chancery: 2940 Tilden Street NW, Washington, DC 20008
telephone: [1] (202) 966-0702
FAX: [1] (202) 966-8468
consulate(s) general: Los Angeles
Diplomatic representation from the US: *chief of mission:* Ambassador Douglas A. SILLIMAN (since 31 August 2014)
embassy: Bayan 36302, Block 13, Al-Masjed Al-Aqsa Street (near the Bayan palace), Kuwait City
mailing address: P. O. Box 77 Safat 13001 Kuwait; or PSC 1280 APO AE 09880–9000
telephone: [965] 2259-1001
FAX: [965] 2538-6562
Flag description: three equal horizontal bands of green (top), white, and red with a black trapezoid based on the hoist side; colors and design are based on the Arab Revolt flag of World War I; green represents fertile fields, white stands for purity, red denotes blood on Kuwaiti swords, black signifies the defeat of the enemy
National symbol(s): golden falcon; national colors: green, white, red, black
National anthem: *name:* "Al-Nasheed Al-Watani" (National Anthem)
lyrics/music: Ahmad MUSHARI al-Adwani/Ibrahim Nasir al-SOULA
note: adopted 1978; the anthem is only used on formal occasions

ECONOMY

Economy—overview: Kuwait has a geographically small, but wealthy, relatively open economy with crude oil reserves of about 102 billion barrels—more than 6% of world reserves. Kuwaiti officials plan to increase oil production to 4 million barrels per day by 2020. Petroleum accounts for over half of GDP, 94% of export revenues, and 90% of government income.
In 2015, Kuwait, for the first time in 15 years, realized a budget deficit after decades of high oil

prices. Kuwaiti authorities have tried to reduce the deficit by decreasing spending on subsidies for the local population, but with limited success. Despite Kuwait's dependence on oil, the government has cushioned itself against the impact of lower oil prices, by saving annually at least 10% of government revenue in the Fund for Future Generations. Kuwait has failed to diversify its economy or bolster the private sector, because of a poor business climate, a large public sector that crowds out private employment of Kuwaiti nationals, and an acrimonious relationship between the National Assembly and the executive branch that has stymied most economic reforms. The Kuwaiti government has made little progress on its long-term economic development plan first passed in 2010. While the government planned to spend up to $104 billion over four years to diversify the economy, attract more investment, and boost private sector participation in the economy, many of the projects did not materialize because of an uncertain political situation.

GDP (purchasing power parity): $288.4 billion (2015 est.)
$285.8 billion (2014 est.)
$285.7 billion (2013 est.)
note: data are in 2015 US dollars
country comparison to the world: 54

GDP (official exchange rate): $120.7 billion (2015 est.)

GDP—real growth rate: 0.9% (2015 est.)
0% (2014 est.)
1% (2013 est.)
country comparison to the world: 177

GDP—per capita (PPP): $70,200 (2015 est.)
$71,500 (2014 est.)
$73,500 (2013 est.)
note: data are in 2015 US dollars
country comparison to the world: 10

Gross national saving: 31.4% of GDP (2015 est.)
46.9% of GDP (2014 est.)
56.6% of GDP (2013 est.)
country comparison to the world: 20

GDP—composition, by end use:
household consumption: 36.1%
government consumption: 25.4%
investment in fixed capital: 20.2%
investment in inventories: 0%
exports of goods and services: 55.5%
imports of goods and services: -37.2% (2015 est.)

GDP—composition, by sector of origin:
agriculture: 0.4%
industry: 59.4%
services: 40.2% (2015 est.)

Agriculture—products: fish

Industries: petroleum, petrochemicals, cement, shipbuilding and repair, water desalination, food processing, construction materials

Industrial production growth rate: -4% (2015 est.)
country comparison to the world: 187

Labor force: 2.473 million
note: non-Kuwaitis represent about 60% of the labor force (2015 est.)
country comparison to the world: 116

Labor force—by occupation: *agriculture:* NA%
industry: NA%

services: NA%
Unemployment rate: 3% (2015 est.)
3% (2014 est.)
country comparison to the world: 22
Population below poverty line: NA%
Household income or consumption by percentage share: *lowest:* 10%: NA%
highest: 10%: NA%
Budget: *revenues:* $61.08 billion
expenditures: $66.5 billion (2015 est.)
Taxes and other revenues: 49.6% of GDP (2015 est.)
country comparison to the world: 15
Budget surplus (+) or deficit (–): -4.4% of GDP (2015 est.)
country comparison to the world: 158
Public debt: 9.5% of GDP (2015 est.)
6.5% of GDP (2014 est.)
country comparison to the world: 168
Fiscal year: 1 April–31 March
Inflation rate (consumer prices): 3.4% (2015 est.)
2.9% (2014 est.)
country comparison to the world: 147
Central bank discount rate: 1.25% (31 December 2010)
3% (31 December 2009)
country comparison to the world: 122
Commercial bank prime lending rate: 4.3% (31 December 2015 est.)
4.3% (31 December 2014 est.)
country comparison to the world: 157
Stock of narrow money: $31.83 billion (31 December 2015 est.)
$32.8 billion (31 December 2014 est.)
country comparison to the world: 60
Stock of broad money: $114.8 billion (31 December 2015 est.)
$116 billion (31 December 2014 est.)
country comparison to the world: 52
Stock of domestic credit: $96.93 billion (31 December 2015 est.)
$96.65 billion (31 December 2014 est.)
country comparison to the world: 53
Market value of publicly traded shares: $99.77 billion (31 December 2014 est.)
$100.9 billion (31 December 2011)
$119.6 billion (31 December 2010 est.)
country comparison to the world: 44
Current account balance: $13.89 billion (2015 est.)
$53.8 billion (2014 est.)
country comparison to the world: 17
Exports: $57.13 billion (2015 est.)
$103.4 billion (2014 est.)
country comparison to the world: 47
Exports—commodities: oil and refined products, fertilizers
Exports—partners: South Korea 14.6%, China 12.1%, India 12.1%, Japan 10.4%, US 7.6%, Pakistan 5.9%, Singapore 4.3% (2015)
Imports: $25.67 billion (2015 est.)
$27.38 billion (2014 est.)
country comparison to the world: 68
Imports—commodities: food, construction materials, vehicles and parts, clothing

Imports—partners: China 13%, US 9.5%, Saudi Arabia 7.6%, Japan 6.4%, Germany 5%, France 4.3%, India 4.2% (2015)
Reserves of foreign exchange and gold: $31.43 billion (31 December 2015 est.)
$32.23 billion (31 December 2014 est.)
country comparison to the world: 49
Debt—external: $35.22 billion (31 December 2014 est.)
$36.04 billion (31 December 2013 est.)
country comparison to the world: 72
Stock of direct foreign investment—at home: $4.031 billion (31 December 2015 est.)
$3.882 billion (31 December 2014 est.)
country comparison to the world: 101
Stock of direct foreign investment—abroad: $39.46 billion (31 December 2015 est.)
$36.85 billion (31 December 2014 est.)
country comparison to the world: 47
Exchange rates: Kuwaiti dinars (KD) per US dollar—
0.301 (2015 est.)
0.2845 (2014 est.)
0.2845 (2013 est.)
0.28 (2012 est.)
0.276 (2011 est.)

ENERGY

Electricity—production: 58.9 billion kWh (2012 est.)
country comparison to the world: 48
Electricity—consumption: 50 billion kWh (2012 est.)
country comparison to the world: 48
Electricity—exports: 0 kWh (2013 est.)
country comparison to the world: 159
Electricity—imports: 0 kWh (2013 est.)
country comparison to the world: 169
Electricity—installed generating capacity: 14.7 million kW (2012 est.)
country comparison to the world: 48
Electricity—from fossil fuels: 100% of total installed capacity (2012 est.)
country comparison to the world: 16
Electricity—from nuclear fuels: 0% of total installed capacity (2012 est.)
country comparison to the world: 122
Electricity—from hydroelectric plants: 0% of total installed capacity (2012 est.)
country comparison to the world: 181
Electricity—from other renewable sources: 0% of total installed capacity (2012 est.)
country comparison to the world: 189
Crude oil—production: 2.619 million bbl/day (2014 est.)
country comparison to the world: 9
Crude oil—exports: 1.824 million bbl/day (2012 est.)
country comparison to the world: 7
Crude oil—imports: 0 bbl/day (2012 est.)
country comparison to the world: 210
Crude oil—proved reserves: 104 billion bbl (1 January 2015 est.)
country comparison to the world: 6
Refined petroleum products—production: 772,300 bbl/day (2012 est.)

country comparison to the world: 25
Refined petroleum products—consumption: 467,000 bbl/day (2013 est.)
country comparison to the world: 35
Refined petroleum products—exports: 533,100 bbl/day (2012 est.)
country comparison to the world: 12
Refined petroleum products—imports: 0 bbl/day (2012 est.)
country comparison to the world: 210
Natural gas—production: 16.31 billion cu m (2013 est.)
country comparison to the world: 35
Natural gas—consumption: 16.88 billion cu m (2013 est.)
country comparison to the world: 40
Natural gas—exports: 0 cu m (2013 est.)
country comparison to the world: 130
Natural gas—imports: 571 million cu m (2013 est.)
country comparison to the world: 63
Natural gas—proved reserves: 1.798 trillion cu m (1 January 2014 est.)
country comparison to the world: 21
Carbon dioxide emissions from consumption of energy: 105.7 million Mt (2012 est.)
country comparison to the world: 39

COMMUNICATIONS

Telephones—fixed lines: *total subscriptions:* 490,000
subscriptions per 100 inhabitants: 18 (2014 est.)
country comparison to the world: 97
Telephones—mobile cellular: *total:* 7.6 million
subscriptions per 100 inhabitants: 277 (2014 est.)
country comparison to the world: 100
Telephone system: *general assessment:* the quality of service is excellent
domestic: new telephone exchanges provide a large capacity for new subscribers; trunk traffic is carried by microwave radio relay, coaxial cable, and open-wire and fiber-optic cable; a mobile-cellular telephone system operates throughout Kuwait, and the country is well-supplied with pay telephones
international: country code—965; linked to international submarine cable Fiber-Optic Link Around the Globe (FLAG); linked to Bahrain, Qatar, UAE via the Fiber-Optic Gulf (FOG) cable; coaxial cable and microwave radio relay to Saudi Arabia; satellite earth stations—6 (3 Intelsat—1 Atlantic Ocean and 2 Indian Ocean, 1 Inmarsat—Atlantic Ocean, and 2 Arabsat) (2011)
Broadcast media: state-owned TV broadcaster operates 4 networks and a satellite channel; several private TV broadcasters have emerged since 2003; satellite TV available with pan-Arab TV stations especially popular; state-owned Radio Kuwait broadcasts on a number of channels in Arabic and English; first private radio station

emerged in 2005; transmissions of at least 2 international radio broadcasters are available (2007)
Radio broadcast station: AM 6, FM 11, shortwave 1 (1998)
Television broadcast stations: 13 (plus several satellite channels) (1997)
Internet country code: .kw
Internet hosts: 2,771 (2012)
country comparison to the world: 156
Internet users: *total:* 2.4 million
percent of population: 86.9% (2014 est.)
country comparison to the world: 93

TRANSPORTATION

Airports: 7 (2013)
country comparison to the world: 168
Airports—with paved runways: *total:* 4
over 3,047 m: 1
2,438 to 3,047 m: 2
914 to 1,523 m: 1 (2013)
Airports—with unpaved runways: *total:* 3
1,524 to 2,437 m: 1
under 914 m: 2 (2013)
Heliports: 4 (2013)
Pipelines: gas 261 km; oil 540 km; refined products 57 km (2013)
Roadways: total: 6,608 km (2010)
country comparison to the world: 149
Merchant marine: *total:* 34
by type: bulk carrier 2, carrier 3, container 6, liquefied gas 4, petroleum tanker 19
registered in other countries: 45 (Bahamas 1, Bahrain 5, Comoros 1, Libya 1, Malta 3, Marshall Islands 2, Panama 12, Qatar 6, Saudi Arabia 4, UAE 10) (2010)
country comparison to the world: 82
Ports and terminals: *major seaport(s):* Ash Shu'aybah, Ash Shuwaykh, Az Zawr (Mina' Sa'ud), Mina' 'Abd Allah, Mina' al Ahmadi

MILITARY AND SECURITY

Military branches: Kuwaiti Land Forces (KLF), Kuwaiti Navy, Kuwaiti Air Force (Al-Quwwat al-Jawwiya al-Kuwaitiya; includes Kuwaiti Air Defense Force, KADF), Kuwaiti National Guard (KNG) (2013)
Military service age and obligation: 17–21 years of age for voluntary military service; conscription suspended (2012)
Military expenditures:
0% of GDP (2012)
3.35% of GDP (2011)
0% of GDP (2010)
country comparison to the world: 132

TRANSNATIONAL ISSUES

Disputes—international: Kuwait and Saudi Arabia continue negotiating a joint maritime boundary

with Iran; no maritime boundary exists with Iraq in the Persian Gulf
Refugees and internally displaced persons: *stateless persons:* 93,000 (2015); note—Kuwait's 1959 Nationality Law defined citizens as persons who settled in the country before 1920 and who had maintained normal residence since then; one-third of the population, descendants of Bedouin tribes, missed the window of opportunity to register for nationality rights after Kuwait became independent in 1961 and were classified as bidun (meaning without); since the 1980s Kuwait's bidun have progressively lost their rights, including opportunities for employment and education, amid official claims that they are nationals of other countries who have destroyed their identification documents in hopes of gaining Kuwaiti citizenship; Kuwaiti authorities have delayed processing citizenship applications and labeled biduns as "illegal residents," denying them access to civil documentation, such as birth and marriage certificates
Trafficking in persons: *current situation:* Kuwait is a destination country for men and women subjected to forced labor and, to a lesser degree, forced prostitution; men and women migrate from South and Southeast Asia, Egypt, the Middle East, and increasingly Africa to work in Kuwait, most of them in the domestic service, construction, and sanitation sectors; although most of these migrants enter Kuwait voluntarily, upon arrival some are subjected to conditions of forced labor by their sponsors and labor agents, including debt bondage; Kuwait's sponsorship law restricts workers' movements and penalizes them for running away from abusive workplaces, making domestic workers particularly vulnerable to forced labor in private homes

tier rating: Tier 3—Kuwait does not fully comply with the minimum standards for the elimination of trafficking and is not making sufficient efforts to do so; although investigations into visa fraud rings lead to the referral of hundreds of people for prosecution, including complicit officials, the government has not prosecuted or convicted any suspected traffickers; authorities made no effort to enforce the prohibition against withholding workers' passports, as mandated under Kuwaiti law; punishment of forced labor cases was limited to shutting down labor recruitment firms, assessing fines, and ordering the return of withheld passports and the paying of back-wages; the government made progress in victims' protection by opening a high-capacity shelter for runaway domestic workers but still lacks formal procedures to identify and refer victims to care services (2015)

KYRGYZSTAN

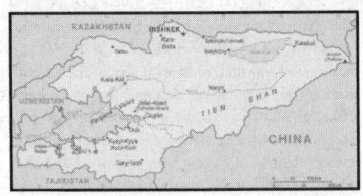

INTRODUCTION

Background: A Central Asian country of incredible natural beauty and proud nomadic traditions, most of the territory of present-day Kyrgyzstan was formally annexed to the Russian Empire in 1876. The Kyrgyz staged a major revolt against the Tsarist Empire in 1916 in which almost one-sixth of the Kyrgyz population was killed. Kyrgyzstan became a Soviet republic in 1936 and achieved independence in 1991 when the USSR dissolved. Nationwide demonstrations in the spring of 2005 resulted in the ouster of President Askar AKAEV, who had run the country since 1990. Former prime minister Kurmanbek BAKIEV overwhelmingly won the presidential election in the summer of 2005. Over the next few years, he manipulated the parliament to accrue new powers for the presidency. In July 2009, after months of harassment against his opponents and media critics, BAKIEV won reelection in a presidential campaign that the international community deemed flawed. In April 2010, violent protests in Bishkek led to the collapse of the BAKIEV regime and his eventual flight to Minsk, Belarus. His successor, Roza OTUN BAEVA, served as transitional president until Almazbek ATAMBAEV was inaugurated in December 2011, marking the first peaceful transfer of presidential power in independent Kyrgyzstan's history. Continuing concerns include: the trajectory of democratization, endemic corruption, poor interethnic relations, border security vulnerabilities, and potential terrorist threats.

GEOGRAPHY

Location: Central Asia, west of China, south of Kazakhstan
Geographic coordinates: 41 00 N, 75 00 E
Map references: Asia
Area: *total:* 199,951 sq km
land: 191,801 sq km
water: 8,150 sq km
country comparison to the world: 87
Area—comparative: slightly smaller than South Dakota
Land boundaries: *total:* 4,573 km
border countries (4): China 1,063 km, Kazakhstan 1,212 km, Tajikistan 984 km, Uzbekistan 1,314 km
Coastline: 0 km (landlocked)
Maritime claims: none (landlocked)
Climate: dry continental to polar in high Tien Shan Mountains; subtropical in southwest

(Fergana Valley); temperate in northern foothill zone
Terrain: peaks of the Tien Shan mountain range and associated valleys and basins encompass the entire country
Elevation: *mean elevation:* 2,988 m
elevation extremes: *lowest point:* Kara-Daryya (Karadar'ya) 132 m
highest point: Jengish Chokusu (Pik Pobedy) 7,439 m
Natural resources: abundant hydropower; gold, rare earth metals; locally exploitable coal, oil, and natural gas; other deposits of nepheline, mercury, bismuth, lead, and zinc
Land use: *agricultural land:* 55.4%
arable land: 6.7%
permanent crops: 0.4%
permanent pasture: 48.3%
forest: 5.1%
other: 39.5% (2011 est.)
Irrigated land: 10,233 sq km (2012)
Total renewable water resources: 23.62 cu km (2011)
Freshwater withdrawal (domestic/industrial/agricultural): *total:* 8.01 cu km/yr (3%/4%/93%)
per capita: 1,558 cu m/yr (2006)
Natural hazards: NA
Environment—current issues: water pollution; many people get their water directly from contaminated streams and wells; as a result, water-borne diseases are prevalent; increasing soil salinity from faulty irrigation practices
Environment—international agreements: *party to:* Air Pollution, Biodiversity, Climate Change, Climate Change-Kyoto Protocol, Desertification, Hazardous Wastes, Ozone Layer Protection, Wetlands
signed, but not ratified: none of the selected agreements
Geography—note: landlocked; entirely mountainous, dominated by the Tien Shan range; 94% of the country is 1,000 m above sea level with an average elevation of 2,750 m; many tall peaks, glaciers, and high-altitude lakes

PEOPLE AND SOCIETY

Nationality: *noun:* Kyrgyzstani(s)
adjective: Kyrgyzstani
Ethnic groups: Kyrgyz 70.9%, Uzbek 14.3%, Russian 7.7%, Dungan 1.1%, other 5.9% (includes Uyghur, Tajik, Turk, Kazakh, Tatar, Ukrainian, Korean, German) (2009 est.)
Languages: Kyrgyz (official) 71.4%, Uzbek 14.4%, Russian (official) 9%, other 5.2% (2009 est.)
Religions: Muslim 75%, Russian orthodox 20%, other 5%
Population: 5,664,939 (July 2015 est.)
country comparison to the world: 115
Age structure: *0–14 years:* 29.92% (male 867,668/female 827,235)
15–24 years: 18.18% (male 523,347/female 506,453)

25–54 years: 39.55% (male 1,096,430/female 1,144,265)
55–64 years: 7.34% (male 180,874/female 234,733)
65 years and over: 5.01% (male 108,776/female 175,158) (2015 est.)
Dependency ratios: *total dependency ratio:* 55.3%
youth dependency ratio: 48.8%
elderly dependency ratio: 6.6%
potential support ratio: 15.2% (2015 est.)
Median age: *total:* 26 years
male: 25 years
female: 27 years (2015 est.)
country comparison to the world: 147
Population growth rate: 1.11% (2015 est.)
country comparison to the world: 109
Birth rate: 22.98 births/1,000 population (2015 est.)
country comparison to the world: 68
Death rate: 6.65 deaths/1,000 population (2015 est.)
country comparison to the world: 142
Net migration rate: -5.22 migrant(s)/1,000 population (2015 est.)
country comparison to the world: 194
Urbanization: *urban population:* 35.7% of total population (2015)
rate of urbanization: 1.58% annual rate of change (2010–15 est.)
Major urban areas—population: BISHKEK (capital) 865,000 (2015)
Sex ratio: *at birth:* 1.07 male(s)/female
0–14 years: 1.05 male(s)/female
15–24 years: 1.03 male(s)/female
25–54 years: 0.96 male(s)/female
55–64 years: 0.77 male(s)/female
65 years and over: 0.62 male(s)/female
total population: 0.96 male(s)/female (2015 est.)
Mother's mean age at first birth: 22.6
note: median age at first birth among women 25–29 (2012 est.)
Maternal mortality rate: 76 deaths/100,000 live births (2015 est.)
country comparison to the world: 86
Infant mortality rate: *total:* 27.73 deaths/1,000 live births
male: 31.94 deaths/1,000 live births
female: 23.24 deaths/1,000 live births (2015 est.)
country comparison to the world: 67
Life expectancy at birth: *total population:* 70.36 years
male: 66.19 years
female: 74.8 years (2015 est.)
country comparison to the world: 155
Total fertility rate: 2.66 children born/woman (2015 est.)
country comparison to the world: 73
Contraceptive prevalence rate: 36.3% (2012)
Health expenditures: 6.7% of GDP (2013)
country comparison to the world: 77

Physicians density: 1.97 physicians/1,000 population (2013)
Hospital bed density: 4.8 beds/1,000 population (2012)
Drinking water source:
improved:
urban: 96.7% of population
rural: 86.2% of population
total: 90% of population
unimproved:
urban: 3.3% of population
rural: 13.8% of population
total: 10% of population (2015 est.)
Sanitation facility access:
improved:
urban: 89.1% of population
rural: 95.6% of population
total: 93.3% of population
unimproved:
urban: 10.9% of population
rural: 4.4% of population
total: 6.7% of population (2015 est.)
HIV/AIDS—adult prevalence rate: 0.26% (2014 est.)
country comparison to the world: 92
HIV/AIDS—people living with HIV/AIDS: 9,300 (2014 est.)
country comparison to the world: 95
HIV/AIDS—deaths: 400 (2014 est.)
country comparison to the world: 95
Obesity—adult prevalence rate: 13.3% (2014)
country comparison to the world: 118
Children under the age of 5 years underweight: 2.8% (2014)
country comparison to the world: 101
Education expenditures: 6.8% of GDP (2013)
country comparison to the world: 25
Literacy: *definition:* age 15 and over can read and write
total population: 99.5%
male: 99.6%
female: 99.4% (2015 est.)
School life expectancy (primary to tertiary education): *total:* 13 years
male: 13 years
female: 13 years (2014)
Child labor—children ages 5–14: *total number:* 563,920
percentage: 40.3%
note: data represent children ages 5–17 (2007 est.)
Unemployment, youth ages 15–24:
total: 13.4%
male: 12%
female: 15.8% (2013 est.)
country comparison to the world: 80

GOVERNMENT

Country name: *conventional long form:* Kyrgyz Republic
conventional short form: Kyrgyzstan
local long form: Kyrgyz Respublikasy
local short form: Kyrgyzstan
former: Kirghiz Soviet Socialist Republic
etymology: a combination of the Turkic words "kyrg" (forty) and "-yz" (tribes) with the Persian suffix "stan" (country) creating the meaning

"Land of the forty tribes"; the name refers to the forty clans united by the legendary Kyrgyz hero, MANAS
Government type: parliamentary republic
Capital: *name:* Bishkek
Geographic coordinates: 42 52 N, 74 36 E
time difference: UTC+6 (11 hours ahead of Washington, DC, during Standard Time)
Administrative divisions: 7 provinces (oblustar, singular—oblus) and 2 cities* (shaarlar, singular—shaar); Batken Oblusu, Bishkek Shaary*, Chuy Oblusu (Bishkek), Jalal-Abad Oblusu, Naryn Oblusu, Osh Oblusu, Osh Shaary*, Talas Oblusu, Ysyk-Kol Oblusu (Karakol)
note: administrative divisions have the same names as their administrative centers (exceptions have the administrative center name following in parentheses)
Independence: 31 August 1991 (from the Soviet Union)
National holiday: Independence Day, 31 August(1991)
Constitution: previous 1993; latest adopted 27 June 2010, effective 2 July 2010; note—the current constitution prohibits any change until 2020 (2016)
Legal system: civil law system which includes features of French civil law and Russian Federation laws
International law organization participation: has not submitted an ICJ jurisdiction declaration; non-party state to the ICCt
Citizenship: *citizenship by birth:* no
citizenship by descent only: at least one parent must be a citizen of Kyrgyzstan
dual citizenship recognized: yes, but only if a mutual treaty on dual citizenship is in force
residency requirement for naturalization: 5 years
Suffrage: 18 years of age; universal
Executive branch: *chief of state:* President Almazbek ATAMBAEV (since 1 December 2011)
head of government: Prime Minister Sooronbay JEENBEKOV (since 13 April 2016)
cabinet: Cabinet of Ministers proposed by the prime minister, appointed by the president; defense and security committee chairs appointed by the president
elections/appointments: president directly elected by absolute majority popular vote in 2 rounds if needed for a single 6-year term; election last held on 30 October 2011 (next to be held in 2017); prime minister nominated by the majority party or majority coalition in the Supreme Council, appointed by the president
election results: Almazbek ATAMBAEV elected president; percent of vote—Almazbek ATAMBAEV (SDPK) 63.2%, Adakhan MADUMAROV (All Kyrgyzstan) 14.7%, Kamchybek TASHIEV (Homeland) 14.3%, other 7.8%; Sooronbay JEENBEKOV elected prime minister; Supreme Council vote—115 to 0
Legislative branch: *description:* unicameral Supreme Council or Jogorku Kengesh (120 seats; members directly elected in a single nationwide

constituency by proportional representation vote to serve 5-year terms)
elections: last held on 4 October 2015 (next to be held in 2020)
election results: Supreme Council—percent of vote by party—SDPK 27.4%, Respublika-Ata-Jurt 20.1%, Kyrgyzstan Party 12.9%, Onuguu-Progress 9.3%, Bir Bol 8.5%, Ata-Meken 7.8%, other 14%; seats by party—SDPK 38, Respublika-Ata-Jurt 28, Kyrgyzstan Party 18, Onuguu-Progress 13, Bir Bol 12, Ata-Meken 11
Judicial branch: *highest court(s):* Supreme Court (consists of 25 judges); Constitutional Court (consists of 9 judges)
judge selection and term of office: Supreme Court and Constitutional Court judges appointed by the Supreme Council on the recommendation of the president; Supreme Court judges serve for 10 years, Constitutional Court judges serve for 15 years; mandatory retirement at age 70 for judges of both courts
subordinate courts: Higher Court of Arbitration; oblast (provincial) and city courts
Political parties and leaders: Ata-Jurt-Respublika (Homeland-Republic) [Omurbek BABANOV, Kamchybek TASHIEV]
Ata-Meken (Fatherland) [Omurbek TEKEBAEV]
Bir Bol (Stay United) [Altynbek SULAIMANOV]
Kyrgyzstan Party [Kanatbek ISAEV, Kanybek IMANALIEV]
Onuguu-Progress [Bakyt TOROBAEV]
Social-Democratic Party of Kyrgyzstan or SDPK [Almazbek ATAMBAEV]
Political pressure groups and leaders: Adilet (Justice) Legal Clinic [Cholpon JAKUPOVA]
Citizens Against Corruption [Tolekan ISMAILOVA]
Coalition for Democracy and Civil Society [Dinara OSHURAKHUNOVA]
Kylym Shamy (Torch of the Century) [Aziza ABDIRASU LOVA]
Precedent Partnership Group [Nurbek TOKTAKUNOV]
Societal Analysis Public Association [Rita KARASARTOVA]
Union of True Muslims [Nurlan MOTUEV]
International organization participation: ADB, CICA, CIS, CSTO, EAEC, EAEU, EAPC, EBRD, ECO, EITI (compliant country), FAO, GCTU, IAEA, IBRD, ICAO, ICC (NGOs), ICRM, IDA, IDB, IFAD, IFC, IFRCS, ILO, IMF, Interpol, IOC, IOM, IPU, ISO (correspondent), ITSO, ITU, MIGA, NAM (observer), OIC, OPCW, OSCE, PCA, PFP, SCO, UN, UNAMID, UNCTAD, UNESCO, UNIDO, UNISFA, UNMIL, UNMISS, UNWTO, UPU, WCO, WFTU (NGOs), WHO, WIPO, WMO, WTO
Diplomatic representation in the US: *chief of mission:* Ambassador Kadyr TOKTOGULOV (since 23 February 2015)
chancery: 2360 Massachusetts Ave. NW, Washington, DC 20008
telephone: [1] (202) 449-9822-23
FAX: [1] (202) 386-7550
consulate(s): New York

Diplomatic representation from the US: *chief of mission:* Ambassador Sheila GWALTNEY (14 October 2015)
embassy: 171 Prospect Mira, Bishkek 720016
mailing address: use embassy street address
telephone: [996] (312) 551-241, (517) 777-217
FAX: [996] (312) 551-264

Flag description: red field with a yellow sun in the center having 40 rays representing the 40 Kyrgyz tribes; on the obverse side the rays run counterclockwise, on the reverse, clockwise; in the center of the sun is a red ring crossed by two sets of three lines, a stylized representation of a "tunduk"—the crown of a traditional Kyrgyz yurt; red symbolizes bravery and valor, the sun evinces peace and wealth

National symbol(s): gyrfalcon; national colors: red, yellow

National anthem: *name:* "Kyrgyz Respublikasynyn Mamlekettik Gimni" (National Anthem of the Kyrgyz Republic)
lyrics/music: Djamil SADYKOV and Eshmambet KULUEV/Nasyr DAVLESOV and Kalyi MOLDOBASANOV
note: adopted 1992

ECONOMY

Economy—overview: Kyrgyzstan is a poor, mountainous country with an economy dominated by minerals extraction, agriculture, and reliance on remittances from citizens working abroad. Cotton, wool, and meat are the main agricultural products, although only cotton is exported in any quantity. Other exports include gold, mercury, uranium, natural gas, and—in some years—electricity. The country has sought to attract foreign investment to expand its export base, including construction of hydroelectric dams, but a difficult investment climate and an ongoing legal battle with Canadian investors in the nation's largest gold mine deter potential investors. Remittances from Kyrgyz migrant workers in Russia and Kazakhstan are equivalent to about a quarter of Kyrgyzstan's GDP. Following independence, Kyrgyzstan rapidly carried out market reforms, such as improving the regulatory system and instituting land reform. Kyrgyzstan was the first Commonwealth of Independent States (CIS) country to be accepted into the World Trade Organization. The government has privatized much of its ownership shares in public enterprises. Despite these reforms, the country suffered a severe drop in production in the early 1990s and has again faced slow growth in recent years as the global financial crisis and declining oil prices have damaged economies across Central Asia.

Kyrgyz leaders hope the country's August 2015 accession to the Eurasian Economic Union will bolster trade and investment, but slowing economies in Russia and China, low commodity prices, and currency fluctuations continue to hamper economic growth. The keys to future growth include progress in fighting corruption, improving administrative transparency, restructuring domestic industry, and attracting foreign aid and investment.

GDP (purchasing power parity): $20.1 billion (2015 est.)
$19.42 billion (2014 est.)
$18.75 billion (2013 est.)
note: data are in 2015 US dollars
country comparison to the world: 146

GDP (official exchange rate): $6.65 billion (2015 est.)

GDP—real growth rate: 3.5% (2015 est.)
3.6% (2014 est.)
10.5% (2013 est.)
country comparison to the world: 83

GDP—per capita (PPP): $3,400 (2015 est.)
$3,300 (2014 est.)
$3,200 (2013 est.)
note: data are in 2015 US dollars
country comparison to the world: 181

Gross national saving: 14.2% of GDP (2015 est.)
10% of GDP (2014 est.)
11% of GDP (2013 est.)
country comparison to the world: 125

GDP—composition, by end use:
household consumption: 96.2%
government consumption: 16.2%
investment in fixed capital: 31.1%
investment in inventories: 2.6%
exports of goods and services: 32.9%
imports of goods and services: -79% (2015 est.)

GDP—composition, by sector of origin:
agriculture: 18%
industry: 25.5%
services: 56.4% (2015 est.)

Agriculture—products: cotton, potatoes, vegetables, grapes, fruits and berries; sheep, goats, cattle, wool

Industries: small machinery, textiles, food processing, cement, shoes, sawn logs, refrigerators, furniture, electric motors, gold, rare earth metals

Industrial production growth rate: -3% (2015 est.)
country comparison to the world: 183

Labor force: 2.65 million (2015 est.)
country comparison to the world: 111

Labor force—by occupation: *agriculture:* 48%
industry: 12.5%
services: 39.5% (2005 est.)

Unemployment rate: 8% (2013 est.)
8% (2013 est.)
country comparison to the world: 93

Population below poverty line: 33.7% (2011 est.)

Household income or consumption by percentage share: *lowest:* 10%: 2.8%
highest: 10%: 27.8% (2009 est.)

Distribution of family income—Gini index: 33.4 (2007)
29 (2001)
country comparison to the world: 104

Budget: *revenues:* $2.113 billion
expenditures: $2.202 billion (2015 est.)
Taxes and other revenues: 29.5% of GDP (2015 est.)
country comparison to the world: 84

Budget surplus (+) or deficit (−): -1.2% of GDP (2015 est.)
country comparison to the world: 59

Fiscal year: calendar year

Inflation rate (consumer prices): 6.5% (2015 est.)
7.5% (2014 est.)
country comparison to the world: 189

Central bank discount rate: 13.73% (22 December 2011)
2.5% (31 December 2010)
country comparison to the world: 15

Commercial bank prime lending rate: 20.5% (31 December 2015 est.)
16.87% (31 December 2014 est.)
country comparison to the world: 12

Stock of narrow money: $1.052 billion (31 December 2015 est.)
$1.061 billion (31 December 2014 est.)
country comparison to the world: 151

Stock of broad money: $1.333 billion (31 December 2015 est.)
$1.399 billion (31 December 2014 est.)
country comparison to the world: 166

Stock of domestic credit: $1.023 billion (31 December 2015 est.)
$1.074 billion (31 December 2014 est.)
country comparison to the world: 158

Market value of publicly traded shares: $165 million (31 December 2012 est.)
$165 million (31 December 2011)
$79 million (31 December 2010 est.)
country comparison to the world: 118

Current account balance: -$979 million (2015 est.)
-$1.245 billion (2014 est.)
country comparison to the world: 119

Exports: $1.933 billion (2015 est.)
$1.892 billion (2014 est.)
country comparison to the world: 140

Exports—commodities: gold, cotton, wool, garments, meat; mercury, uranium, electricity; machinery; shoes

Exports—partners: Switzerland 26%, Uzbekistan 22.5%, Kazakhstan 20.8%, UAE 4.9%, Turkey 4.5%, Afghanistan 4.5%, Russia 4.2% (2015)

Imports: $4.268 billion (2015 est.)
$5.29 billion (2014 est.)
country comparison to the world: 131

Imports—commodities: oil and gas, machinery and equipment, chemicals, foodstuffs

Imports—partners: China 56.4%, Russia 17.1%, Kazakhstan 9.9% (2015)

Reserves of foreign exchange and gold: $1.916 billion (31 December 2015 est.)
$1.957 billion (31 December 2014 est.)
country comparison to the world: 119

Debt—external: $7.101 billion (31 December 2014 est.)
$6.804 billion (31 December 2013 est.)
country comparison to the world: 117

Stock of direct foreign investment—at home: $3.857 billion (31 December 2015 est.)
$3.537 billion (31 December 2014 est.)
country comparison to the world: 102

Stock of direct foreign investment—abroad: $444 million (31 December 2015 est.)
$444 million (31 December 2014 est.)
country comparison to the world: 88

Exchange rates: soms (KGS) per US dollar—
60.58 (2015 est.)
53.654 (2014 est.)
53.654 (2013 est.)
47.01 (2012 est.)
46.144 (2011 est.)

ENERGY

Electricity—production: 14.97 billion kWh (2012 est.)
country comparison to the world: 85
Electricity—consumption: 9.943 billion kWh (2012 est.)
country comparison to the world: 90
Electricity—exports: 1.84 billion kWh (2012 est.)
country comparison to the world: 46
Electricity—imports: 177 million kWh (2012 est.)
country comparison to the world: 88
Electricity—installed generating capacity: 3.766 million kW (2012 est.)
country comparison to the world: 84
Electricity—from fossil fuels: 21.1% of total installed capacity (2012 est.)
country comparison to the world: 193
Electricity—from nuclear fuels: 0% of total installed capacity (2012 est.)
country comparison to the world: 119
Electricity—from hydroelectric plants: 78.9% of total installed capacity (2012 est.)
country comparison to the world: 16
Electricity—from other renewable sources: 0% of total installed capacity (2012 est.)
country comparison to the world: 186
Crude oil—production: 1,000 bbl/day (2014 est.)
country comparison to the world: 92
Crude oil—exports: 0 bbl/day (2012 est.)
country comparison to the world: 145
Crude oil—imports: 0 bbl/day (2012 est.)
country comparison to the world: 208
Crude oil—proved reserves: 40 million bbl (1 January 2015 est.)
country comparison to the world: 81
Refined petroleum products—production: 1,666 bbl/day (2012 est.)
country comparison to the world: 108
Refined petroleum products—consumption: 33,000 bbl/day (2013 est.)
country comparison to the world: 113
Refined petroleum products—exports: 1,732 bbl/day (2012 est.)
country comparison to the world: 108
Refined petroleum products—imports: 38,070 bbl/day (2012 est.)
country comparison to the world: 87
Natural gas—production: 32 million cu m (2013 est.)
country comparison to the world: 85
Natural gas—consumption: 406 million cu m (2013 est.)
country comparison to the world: 100
Natural gas—exports: 0 cu m (2013 est.)
country comparison to the world: 126
Natural gas—imports: 374 million cu m (2013 est.)
country comparison to the world: 66
Natural gas—proved reserves: 5.663 billion cu m (1 January 2014 est.)
country comparison to the world: 93
Carbon dioxide emissions from consumption of energy: 9.278 million Mt (2012 est.)
country comparison to the world: 104

COMMUNICATIONS

Telephones—fixed lines: *total subscriptions:* 440,000
subscriptions per 100 inhabitants: 8 (2014 est.)
country comparison to the world: 100
Telephones—mobile cellular: *total:* 7.6 million
subscriptions per 100 inhabitants: 135 (2014 est.)
country comparison to the world: 101
Telephone system: *general assessment:* telecommunications infrastructure is being upgraded; loans from the European Bank for Reconstruction and Development (EBRD) are being used to install a digital network, digital radio-relay stations, and fiber-optic links
domestic: fixed-line penetration remains low and concentrated in urban areas; multiple mobile-cellular service providers with growing coverage; mobile-cellular subscribership was about 115 per 100 persons in 2011
international: country code—996; connections with other CIS countries by landline or microwave radio relay and with other countries by leased connections with Moscow international gateway switch and by satellite; satellite earth stations—2 (1 Intersputnik, 1 Intelsat); connected internationally by the Trans-Asia-Europe (TAE) fiber-optic line (2011)
Broadcast media: state-run TV broadcaster operates 2 nationwide networks and 6 regional stations; roughly 20 private TV stations operating with most rebroadcasting other channels; state-run radio broadcaster operates 2 networks; about 20 private radio stations (2007)
Radio broadcast stations: AM 3 (plus 10 repeater stations), FM 23, shortwave 2 (2009)
Television broadcast stations: 8 (2 countrywide and 6 regional stations; state-owned); note—there are about 20 private TV stations, most of which rebroadcast other channels (2007)
Internet country code: .kg
Internet hosts: 115,573 (2012)
country comparison to the world: 81
Internet users: *total:* 1.4 million
percent of population: 24.2% (2014 est.)
country comparison to the world: 113

TRANSPORTATION

Airports: 28 (2013)
country comparison to the world: 122
Airports—with paved runways: *total:* 18

over 3,047 m: 1
2,438 to 3,047 m: 3
1,524 to 2,437 m: 11
under 914 m: 3 (2013)
Airports—with unpaved runways: *total:* 10
1,524 to 2,437 m: 1
914 to 1,523 m: 1
under 914 m: 8 (2013)
Pipelines: gas 480 km; oil 16 km (2013)
Railways: *total:* 470 km
broad gauge: 470 km 1.520-m gauge (2014)
country comparison to the world: 116
Roadways: *total:* 34,000 km (2007)
country comparison to the world: 94
Waterways: 600 km (2010)
country comparison to the world: 78
Ports and terminals: lake port(s): Balykchy (Ysyk-Kolor Rybach'ye)(Lake Ysyk-Kol)

MILITARY AND SECURITY

Military branches: State Committee on Defense Affairs (GKDO): Ground Forces, Air Force (includes Air Defense Forces) (2015)
Military service age and obligation: 18–27 years of age for compulsory or voluntary male military service in the Armed Forces or Interior Ministry; 1-year service obligation, with optional fee-based 3-year service in the callup mobilization reserve; women may volunteer at age 19; 16–17 years of age for military cadets, who cannot take part in military operations (2013)
Military expenditures: NA% (2012)
3.74% of GDP (2011)

TRANSNATIONAL ISSUES

Disputes—international: Kyrgyzstan has yet to ratify the 2001 boundary delimitation with Kazakhstan; disputes in Isfara Valley delay completion of delimitation with Tajikistan; delimitation of 130 km of border with Uzbekistan is hampered by serious disputes over enclaves and other areas
Refugees and internally displaced persons: *stateless persons:* 9,118 (2015); note—most stateless people were born in Kyrgyzstan, have lived there many years, or married Kyrgyz citizens; in 2009, Kyrg yzstan adopted a national action plan to speed up the exchange of old Soviet passports for Kyrgyz ones; stateless people are unable to register marriages and births, to travel within the country or abroad, to own property, or to receive social benefits

Illicit drugs: limited illicit cultivation of cannabis and opium poppy for CIS markets; limited government eradication of illicit crops; transit point for Southwest Asian narcotics bound for Russia and the rest of Europe; major consumer of opiates

Background: Modern-day Laos has its roots in the ancient Lao kingdom of Lan Xang, established in the 14th century under King FANGUM. For 300 years Lan Xang had influence reaching into present-day Cambodia and Thailand, as well as over all of what is now Laos. After centuries of gradual decline, Laos came under the domination of Siam (Thailand) from the late 18th century until the late 19th century when it became part of French Indochina. The Franco-Siamese Treaty of 1907 defined the current Lao border with Thailand. In 1975, the communist Pathet Lao took control of the government ending a six-century-old monarchy and instituting a strict socialist regime closely aligned to Vietnam. Agradual, limited return to private enterprise and the liberalization of foreign investment laws began in 1988. Laos became a member of ASEAN in 1997 and the WTO in 2013.

GEOGRAPHY

Location: Southeastern Asia, northeast of Thailand, west of Vietnam
Geographic coordinates: 18 00 N, 105 00 E
Map references: Southeast Asia
Area: *total:* 236,800 sq km
land: 230,800 sq km
water: 6,000 sq km
country comparison to the world: 84
Area—comparative: slightly larger than Utah

Land boundaries: *total:* 5,274 km
border countries (5): Burma 238 km, Cambodia 555 km, China 475 km, Thailand 1,845 km, Vietnam 2,161 km
Coastline: 0 km (landlocked)
Maritime claims: none (landlocked)
Climate: tropical monsoon; rainy season (May to November); dry season (December to April)
Terrain: mostly rugged mountains; some plains and plateaus

Elevation: *mean elevation:* 710 m

elevation extremes: *lowest point:* Mekong River 70 m

highest point: Phu Bia 2,817 m
Natural resources: timber, hydropower, gypsum, tin, gold, gemstones
Land use: *agricultural land:* 10.6%
arable land: 6.2%
permanent crops: 0.7%
permanent pasture: 3.7%
forest: 67.9%
other: 21.5% (2011 est.)
Irrigated land: 3,100 sq km (2012)
Total renewable water resources: 333.5 cu km (2011)
Freshwater withdrawal (domestic/industrial/agricultural): *total:* 3.49 cu km/yr (4%/5%/91%)
per capita: 588.9 cu m/yr (2005)
Natural hazards: floods, droughts
Environment—current issues: unexploded ordnance; deforestation; soil erosion; most of the population does not have access to potable water
Environment—international agreements: *party to:* Biodiversity, Climate Change, Climate Change-Kyoto Protocol, Desertification, Endangered Species, Environmental Modification, Law of the Sea, Ozone Layer Protection
signed, but not ratified: none of the selected agreements
Geography—note: landlocked; most of the country is mountainous and thickly forested; the Mekong River forms a large part of the western boundary with Thailand

PEOPLE AND SOCIETY

Nationality: *noun:* Lao(s) or Laotian(s)
adjective: Lao or Laotian
Ethnic groups: Lao 54.6%, Khmou 10.9%, Hmong 8%, Tai 3.8%, Phuthai 3.3%, Lue 2.2%, Katang 2.1%, Makong 2.1%, Akha 1.6%, other 10.4%, unspecified 1% (2005 est.)
Languages: Lao (official), French, English, various ethnic languages
Religions: Buddhist 66.8%, Christian 1.5%, other 31%, unspecified 0.7% (2005 est.)
Population: 6,911,544 (July 2015 est.)
country comparison to the world: 104
Age structure: *0–14 years:* 34.1% (male 1,190,119/female 1,166,774)
15–24 years: 21.31% (male 731,531/female 741,107)
25–54 years: 35.54% (male 1,211,600/female 1,245,010)
55–64 years: 5.23% (male 177,142/female 184,409)
65 years and over: 3.82% (male 119,392/female 144,460) (2015 est.)
Dependency ratios: *total dependency ratio:* 62.8%
youth dependency ratio: 56.6%
elderly dependency ratio: 6.2%
potential support ratio: 16.1% (2015 est.)
Median age: *total:* 22.3 years
male: 22 years
female: 22.6 years (2015 est.)
country comparison to the world: 176

Population growth rate: 1.55% (2015 est.)
country comparison to the world: 79
Birth rate: 24.25 births/1,000 population (2015 est.)
country comparison to the world: 60
Death rate: 7.63 deaths/1,000 population (2015 est.)
country comparison to the world: 110
Net migration rate: -1.09 migrant(s)/1,000 population (2015 est.)
country comparison to the world: 149
Urbanization: *urban Population:* 38.6% of total population (2015)
rate of urbanization: 4.93% annual rate of change (2010–15 est.)
Major urban areas—Population: VIENTIANE (capital) 997,000 (2015)
Sex ratio: *at birth:* 1.04 male(s)/female
0–14 years: 1.02 male(s)/female
15–24 years: 0.99 male(s)/female
25–54 years: 0.97 male(s)/female
55–64 years: 0.96 male(s)/female
65 years and over: 0.83 male(s)/female
total population: 0.99 male(s)/female (2015 est.)
Maternal mortality rate: 197 deaths/100,000 live births (2015 est.)
country comparison to the world: 21
Infant mortality rate: *total:* 52.97 deaths/1,000 live births
male: 58.52 deaths/1,000 live births
female: 47.21 deaths/1,000 live births (2015 est.)
country comparison to the world: 32
Life expectancy at birth: *total population:* 63.88 years
male: 61.88 years
female: 65.95 years (2015 est.)
country comparison to the world: 181
Total fertility rate: 2.82 children born/woman (2015 est.)
country comparison to the world: 62
Contraceptive prevalence rate: 49.8% (2011/12)
Health expenditures: 2% of GDP (2013)
country comparison to the world: 181
Physicians density: 0.18 physicians/1,000 population (2012)
Hospital bed density: 1.5 beds/1,000 population (2012)
Drinking water source:
improved:
urban: 85.6% of population
rural: 69.4% of population
total: 75.7% of population
unimproved:
urban: 14.4% of population
rural: 30.6% of population
total: 24.3% of population (2015 est.)
Sanitation facility access:
improved:
urban: 94.5% of population
rural: 56% of population
total: 70.9% of population
unimproved:
urban: 5.5% of population
rural: 44% of population

total: 29.1% of population (2015 est.)

HIV/AIDS—adult prevalence rate: 0.26% (2014 est.)

country comparison to the world: 91

HIV/AIDS—people living with HIV/AIDS: 11,100 (2014 est.)

country comparison to the world: 91

HIV/AIDS—deaths: 500 (2014 est.)

country comparison to the world: 86

Major infectious diseases: *degree of risk:* very high

food or waterborne diseases: bacterial and protozoal diarrhea, hepatitis A, and typhoid fever

vectorborne diseases: dengue fever and malaria

note: highly pathogenic H5N1 avian influenza has been identified in this country; it poses a negligible risk with extremely rare cases possible among US citizens who have close contact with birds (2013)

Obesity—adult prevalence rate: 3% (2014)

country comparison to the world: 179

Children under the age of 5 years underweight: 26.5% (2012)

country comparison to the world: 22

Education expenditures: 4.2% of GDP (2014)

country comparison to the world: 147

Literacy: *definition:* age 15 and over can read and write

total population: 79.9%

male: 87.1%

female: 72.8% (2015 est.)

School life expectancy (primary to tertiary education): *total:* 11 years

male: 11 years

female: 10 years (2014)

Child labor—children ages 5–14: *total number:* 175,138

percentage: 11% (2006 est.)

GOVERNMENT

Country name: *conventional long form:* Lao People's Democratic Republic

conventional short form: Laos

local long form: Sathalanalat Paxathipatai Paxaxon Lao

local short form: Pathet Lao (unofficial)

etymology: name means "Land of the Lao [people]"

Government type: communist state

Capital: *name:* Vientiane (Viangchan)

Geographic coordinates: 17 58 N, 102 36 E

time difference: UTC+7 (12 hours ahead of Washington, DC, during Standard Time)

Administrative divisions: 17 provinces (khoueng, singular and plural) and 1 capital city* (nakhon luang, singular and plural); Attapu, Bokeo, Bolikhamxai, Champasak, Houaphan, Khammouan, Louangnamtha, Louangphabang, Oudomxai, Phongsali, Salavan, Savannakhet, Viangchan (Vientiane)*, Viangchan, Xaignabouli, Xaimsomboun, Xekong, Xiangkhouang

Independence: 19 July 1949 (from France)

National holiday: Republic Day, 2 December (1975)

Constitution: previous 1947 (preindependence); latest promulgated 13–15 August 1991; amended 2003,2015 (2016)

Legal system: civil law system similar in form to the French system

International law organization participation: has not submitted an ICJ jurisdiction declaration; non-party state to the ICCt

Citizenship: *citizenship by birth:* no

citizenship by descent only: at least one parent must be a citizen of Laos

dual citizenship recognized: no

residency requirement for naturalization: 10 years

Suffrage: 18 years of age; universal

Executive branch: *chief of state:* President BOUNNYANG Vorachit (since 20 April 2016); Vice President PHANKHAM Viphavan (since 20 April 2016)

head of government: Prime Minister THONGLOUN Sisoulit (since 20 April 2016); Deputy Prime Ministers BOUNTHONG Chitmani, SONXAI Siphandon, SOMDI Douangdi (since 20 April 2016)

cabinet: Council of Ministers appointed by the president, approved by the National Assembly

elections/appointments: president and vice president indirectly elected by the National Assembly for a 5-year term (no term limits); election last held on 20 April 2016 (next to be held in 2021); prime minister nominated by the president, elected by the National Assembly for 5-year term

election results: BOUNNYANG Vorachit (LPRP) elected president; PHAN KHAM Viphavan (LPRP) elected vice president; percent of National Assembly vote—NA; THONGLOUN Sisoulit (LPRP) elected prime minister; percent of National Assembly vote—NA

Legislative branch: *description:* unicameral National Assembly or Sapha Heng Xat (132 seats; members directly elected in multi-seat constituencies by simple majority vote from candidate lists provided by the Lao People's Revolutionary Party; members serve 5-year terms)

elections: last held on 20 April 2016 (next to be held in 2021)

election results: percent of vote by party—NA; seats by party—LPRP 128, independent 4

Judicial branch: *highest court(s):* People's Supreme Court (consists of NA judges)

judge selection and term of office: president of People's Supreme Court elected by National Assembly on recommendation of National Assembly Standing Committee; vice president of People's Supreme Court and judges appointed by National Assembly Standing Committee; judge tenure NA

subordinate courts: provincial, municipal, district, and military courts

Political parties and leaders: Lao People's Revolutionary Party or LPRP [BOUNNYANG Vorachit]

note: other parties proscribed

Political pressure groups and leaders: NA

International organization participation: ADB, ARF, ASEAN, CP, EAS, FAO, G-77, IAEA, IBRD, ICAO, ICRM, IDA, IFAD, IFC, IFRCS, ILO, IMF, Interpol, IOC, IPU, ISO (subscriber), ITU, MIGA, NAM, OIF, OPCW, PCA, UN, UNCTAD, UNESCO, UNIDO, UNWTO, UPU,

WCO, WFTU (NGOs), WHO, WIPO, WMO, WTO

Diplomatic representation in the US: *chief of mission:* Ambassador MAI Xaignavong (since 3 August 2015)

chancery: 2222 S Street NW, Washington, DC 20008

telephone: [1] (202) 332-6416

FAX: [1] (202) 332-4923

consulate(s): New York

Diplomatic representation from the US: *chief of mission:* Ambassador David A. CLUNE (since 16 September 2013)

embassy: Thadeua Road, Kilometer 9, Ban Somvang Tai, Hatsayfong District, Vientiane

mailing address: American Embassy Vientiane, Unit 8165, APO AP 96546

telephone: [856] 21-48-7000

FAX: [856] 21-48-7190

Flag description: three horizontal bands of red (top), blue (double width), and red with a large white disk centered in the blue band; the red bands recall the blood shed for liberation; the blue band represents the Mekong River and prosperity; the white disk symbolizes the full moon against the Mekong River, but also signifies the unity of the people under the Lao People's Revolutionary Party, as well as the country's bright future

National symbol(s): elephant; national colors: red, white, blue

National anthem: *name:* "Pheng Xat Lao" (Hymn of the Lao People)

lyrics/music: SISANA Sisane/THONGDY Southonevichit

note: music adopted 1945, lyrics adopted 1975; the anthem's lyrics were changed following the 1975 Communist revolution that overthrew the monarchy

ECONOMY

Economy—overview: The government of Laos, one of the few remaining one-party communist states, began decentralizing control and encouraging private enterprise in 1986. Economic growth averaged 6% per year from 19882008 except during the short-lived drop caused by the Asian financial crisis that began in 1997. Laos' growth has more recently been amongst the fastest in Asia and averaged nearly 8% per year for the last decade.

Nevertheless, Laos remains a country with an underdeveloped infrastructure, particularly in rural areas. It has a basic, but improving, road system, and limited external and internal land-line telecommunications. Electricity is available to 83% of the population. Agriculture, dominated by rice cultivation in lowland areas, accounts for about 25% of GDP and 73% of total employment. Laos' economy is heavily dependent on capital-intensive natural resource exports. The economy has benefited from high-profile foreign direct investment in hydropower dams along the Mekong river, copper and gold mining, logging, and construction, although some projects in these industries have drawn criticism for their environmental impacts.

Laos gained Normal Trade Relations status with the US in 2004 and applied for Generalized

System of Preferences trade benefits in 2013 after being admitted to the World Trade Organization earlier in the year. Laos began a one-year chairmanship of ASEAN in January 2016. Laos is in the process of implementing a value-added tax system. The government appears committed to raising the country's profile among foreign investors and has developed special economic zones replete with generous tax incentives, but a small labor pool remains an impediment to investment. Laos also has ongoing problems with the business environment, including onerous registration requirements, a gap between legislation and implementation, and unclear or conflicting regulations.

GDP (purchasing power parity): $37.32 billion (2015 est.)

$34.88 billion (2014 est.)

$32.47 billion (2013 est.)

note: data are in 2015 US dollars

country comparison to the world: 116

GDP (official exchange rate): $12.5 billion (2015 est.)

GDP—real growth rate: 7% (2015 est.)

7.4% (2014 est.)

8% (2013 est.)

country comparison to the world: 13

GDP—per capita (PPP): $5,300 (2015 est.)

$5,100 (2014 est.)

$4,800 (2013 est.)

note: data are in 2015 US dollars

country comparison to the world: 165

Gross national saving: 26.5% of GDP (2015 est.)

25.3% of GDP (2014 est.)

25.8% of GDP (2013 est.)

country comparison to the world: 41

GDP—composition, by end use:

household consumption: 58.2%

government consumption: 14.4%

investment in fixed capital: 36.6%

investment in inventories: 1.6%

exports of goods and services: 42.9%

imports of goods and services: -53.7% (2015 est.)

GDP—composition, by sector of origin:

agriculture: 23.1%

industry: 33.4%

services: 43.5% (2015 est.)

Agriculture—products: sweet potatoes, vegetables, corn, coffee, sugarcane, tobacco, cotton, tea, peanuts, rice; cassava (manioc, tapioca), water buffalo, pigs, cattle, poultry

Industries: mining (copper, tin, gold, gypsum); timber, electric power, agricultural processing, rubber, construction, garments, cement, tourism

Industrial production growth rate: 10% (2015 est.)

country comparison to the world: 5

Labor force: 3.532 million (2015 est.)

country comparison to the world: 99

Labor force—by occupation: *agriculture:* 73.1%

industry: 6.1%

services: 20.6% (2012 est.)

Unemployment rate: 1.3% (2012 est.)

1.4% (2013 est.)

country comparison to the world: 7

Population below poverty line: 22% (2013 est.)

Household income or consumption by percentage share: *lowest:* 10%: 3.3%

highest: 10%: 30.3% (2008)

Distribution of family income—Gini index: 36.7 (2008)

34.6 (2002)

country comparison to the world: 83

Budget: *revenues:* $3.095 billion

expenditures: $3.723 billion (2015 est.)

Taxes and other revenues: 24.7% of GDP (2015 est.)

country comparison to the world: 124

Budget surplus (+) or deficit (–): -5% of GDP (2015 est.)

country comparison to the world: 169

Public debt: 48.6% of GDP (2015 est.)

47.6% of GDP (2014 est.)

country comparison to the world: 85

Fiscal year: 1 October—30 September

Inflation rate (consumer prices): 5.3% (2015 est.)

5.5% (2014 est.)

country comparison to the world: 178

Central bank discount rate: 4.3% (31 December 2010)

4% (31 December 2009)

country comparison to the world: 85

Commercial bank prime lending rate: 19% (31 December 2015 est.)

19.2% (31 December 2014 est.)

country comparison to the world: 15

Stock of narrow money: $1.166 billion (31 December 2015 est.)

$1.154 billion (31 December 2014 est.)

country comparison to the world: 147

Stock of broad money: $6.509 billion (31 December 2015 est.)

$6.461 billion (31 December 2014 est.)

country comparison to the world: 120

Stock of domestic credit: $6.529 billion (31 December 2015 est.)

$6.241 billion (31 December 2014 est.)

country comparison to the world: 114

Market value of publicly traded shares: $1.012 billion (2012 est.)

$576.8 million (2011)

country comparison to the world: 106

Current account balance: -$2.905 billion (2015 est.)

-$2.71 billion (2014 est.)

country comparison to the world: 157

Exports: $3.115 billion (2015 est.)

$2.662 billion (2014 est.)

country comparison to the world: 128

Exports—commodities: wood products, coffee, electricity, tin, copper, gold, cassava

Exports—partners: Thailand 30.4%, China 27%, Vietnam 17.6% (2015)

Imports: $4.912 billion (2015 est.)

$4.271 billion (2014 est.)

country comparison to the world: 125

Imports—commodities: machinery and equipment, vehicles, fuel, consumer goods

Imports—partners: Thailand 60.9%, China 18.6%, Vietnam 7.3% (2015)

Reserves of foreign exchange and gold: $976.3 million (31 December 2015 est.)

$889.7 million (31 December 2014 est.)

country comparison to the world: 132

Debt—external: $9.552 billion (31 December 2014 est.)

$8.615 billion (31 December 2013 est.)

country comparison to the world: 108

Stock of direct foreign investment—at home: $15.14 billion (31 December 2012 est.)

$12.44 billion (31 December 2011 est.)

country comparison to the world: 86

Exchange rates: kips (LAK) per US dollar—8,151.6 (2015 est.)

8,049 (2014 est.)

8,049 (2013 est.)

8,007.3 (2012 est.)

8,035.1 (2011 est.)

ENERGY

Electricity—production: 12.1 billion kWh (2012 est.)

country comparison to the world: 92

Electricity—consumption: 2.874 billion kWh (2012 est.)

country comparison to the world: 136

Electricity—exports: 2.537 billion kWh (2013 est.)

country comparison to the world: 42

Electricity—imports: 1.127 billion kWh (2012 est.)

country comparison to the world: 61

Electricity—installed generating capacity: 3.217 million kW (2013 est.)

country comparison to the world: 91

Electricity—from fossil fuels: 1.7% of total installed capacity (2012 est.)

country comparison to the world: 208

Electricity—from nuclear fuels: 0% of total installed capacity (2012 est.)

country comparison to the world: 125

Electricity—from hydroelectric plants: 98.3% of total installed capacity (2012 est.)

country comparison to the world: 7

Electricity—from other renewable sources: 0% of total installed capacity (2012 est.)

country comparison to the world: 192

Crude oil—production: 0 bbl/day (2014 est.)

country comparison to the world: 155

Crude oil—exports: 0 bbl/day (2012 est.)

country comparison to the world: 149

Crude oil—imports: 0 bbl/day (2012 est.)

country comparison to the world: 212

Crude oil—proved reserves: 0 bbl (1 January 2015 est.)

country comparison to the world: 154

Refined petroleum products—production: 0 bbl/day (2012 est.)

country comparison to the world: 199

Refined petroleum products—consumption: 3,200 bbl/day (2013 est.)

country comparison to the world: 180

Refined petroleum products—exports: 0 bbl/day (2012 est.)

country comparison to the world: 194

Refined petroleum products—imports: 3,160 bbl/day (2012 est.)

country comparison to the world: 173

Natural gas—production: 0 cu m (2013 est.)

country comparison to the world: 209

Natural gas—consumption: 0 cu m (2013 est.)
country comparison to the world: 162
Natural gas—exports: 0 cu m (2013 est.)
country comparison to the world: 131
Natural gas—imports: 0 cu m (2013 est.)
country comparison to the world: 90
Natural gas—proved reserves: 0 cu m (1 January 2014 est.)
country comparison to the world: 157
Carbon dioxide emissions from consumption of energy: 1.623 million Mt (2012 est.)
country comparison to the world: 156

COMMUNICATIONS

Telephones—fixed lines: *total subscriptions:* 920,000
subscriptions per 100 inhabitants: 14 (2014 est.)
country comparison to the world: 81

Telephones—mobile cellular: *total:* 4.6 million
subscriptions per 100 inhabitants: 68 (2014 est.)
country comparison to the world: 122

Telephone system: *general assessment:* service to general public is improving; the government relies on a radiotelephone network to communicate with remote areas
domestic: 4 service providers with mobile cellular usage growing very rapidly
international: country code—856; satellite earth station—1 Intersputnik (Indian Ocean region) and a second to be developed by China (2012)

Broadcast media: 6 TV stations operating out of Vientiane—3 government-operated and the others commercial; 17 provincial stations operating with nearly all programming relayed via satellite from the government-operated stations in Vientiane; Chinese and Vietnamese programming relayed via satellite from Lao National TV; broadcasts available from stations in Thailand and Vietnam in border areas; multi-channel satellite and cable TV systems provide access to a wide range of foreign stations; state-controlled radio with state-operated Lao National Radio (LNR) broadcasting on 5 frequencies—1 AM, 1 SW, and 3 FM; LNR's AM and FM programs are relayed via satellite constituting a large part of the programming schedules of the provincial radio stations; Thai radio broadcasts available in border areas and transmissions of multiple international broadcasters are also accessible (2012)
Radio broadcast stations: AM 3, FM 34, shortwave 3 (2010)
Television broadcast stations: 28 (2010)
Internet country code: .la
Internet hosts: 1,532 (2012)
country comparison to the world: 166
Internet users: *total:* 300,000

percent of population: 5.8% (2009)
country comparison to the world: 142

TRANSPORTATION

Airports: 41 (2013)
country comparison to the world: 103
Airports—with paved runways: *total:* 8
2,438 to 3,047 m: 3
1,524 to 2,437 m: 4
914 to 1,523 m: 1 (2013)
Airports—with unpaved runways: *total:* 33
1,524 to 2,437 m: 2
914 to 1,523 m: 9
under 914 m: 22 (2013)
Pipelines: refined products 540 km (2013)

Roadways: *total:* 39,586 km
paved: 5,415 km
unpaved: 34,171 km (2009)
country comparison to the world: 89
Waterways: 4,600 km (primarily on the Mekong River and its tributaries; 2,900 additional km are intermittently navigable by craft drawing less than 0.5 m) (2012)
country comparison to the world: 23

MILITARY AND SECURITY

Military branches: Lao People's Armed Forces (LPAF): Lao People's Army (LPA; includes Riverine Force), Air Force (2011)
Military service age and obligation: 18 years of age for compulsory or voluntary military service; conscript service obligation—minimum 18-months (2012)
Military expenditures: NA% (2012) 0.23% of GDP (2011)
Military—note: serving one of the world's least developed countries, the Lao People's Armed Forces (LPAF) is small, poorly funded, and ineffectively resourced; its mission focus is border and internal security, primarily in countering ethnic Hmong insurgent groups; together with the Lao People's Revolutionary Party and the government, the Lao People's Army (LPA) is the third pillar of state machinery, and as such is expected to suppress political and civil unrest and similar national emergencies; there is no perceived external threat to the state and the LPA maintains strong ties with the neighboring Vietnamese military (2012)

TRANSNATIONAL ISSUES

Disputes—international: southeast Asian states have enhanced border surveillance to check the spread of avian flu; talks continue on completion of demarcation with Thailand but disputes remain over islands in the Mekong River; concern among

Mekong River Commission members that China's construction of dams on the Mekong River and its tributaries will affect water levels; Cambodia and Vietnam are concerned about Laos' extensive upstream dam construction

Trafficking in persons: *current situation:* Laos is a source and, to a lesser extent, transit and destination country for men, women, and children subjected to forced labor and sex trafficking; Lao economic migrants may encounter conditions of forced labor or sexual exploitation in destination countries, most often Thailand; Lao women and girls are exploited in Thailand's commercial sex trade, domestic service, factories, and agriculture; a small, possibly growing, number of Lao women and girls are sold as brides in China and South Korea and subsequently sex trafficked; Lao men and boys are victims of forced labor in the Thai fishing, construction, and agriculture industries; some Lao children, as well as Vietnamese and Chinese women and girls are subjected to sex trafficking in Laos; other Vietnamese and Chinese, and possibly Burmese, adults and girls transit Laos for sexual and labor exploitation in neighboring countries, particularly Thailand

tier rating: Tier 2 Watch List—Laos does not fully comply with the minimum standards for the elimination of trafficking; however, it is making significant efforts to do so; authorities sustained moderate efforts to investigate, prosecute, and convict trafficking offenders; the government failed to make progress in proactively identifying victims exploited within the country or among those deported from abroad; the government continues to rely almost entirely on local and international organizations to provide and fund services to trafficking victims; although Lao men and boys are trafficked, most protective services are only available to women and girls, and long-term support is lacking; modest prevention efforts include the promotion of anti-trafficking awareness on state-controlled media (2015)

Illicit drugs: estimated opium poppy cultivation in 2008 was 1900 hectares, about a 73% increase from 2007; estimated potential opium production in 2008 more than tripled to 17 metric tons; unsubstantiated reports of domestic methamphetamine production; growing domestic methamphetamine problem (2009)

LATVIA

INTRODUCTION

Background: Several eastern Baltic tribes merged in medieval times to form the ethnic core of the Latvian people (ca.8th-12th centuries A.D.). The region subsequently came under the control of Germans, Poles, Swedes, and finally, Russians. A Latvian republic emerged following World War I, but it was annexed by the USSR in 1940—an action never recognized by the US and many other countries. Latvia reestablished its independence in 1991 following the breakup of the Soviet Union. Although the last Russian troops left in 1994, the status of the Russian minority (some 26% of the population) remains of concern to Moscow. Latvia acceded to both NATO and the EU in the spring of 2004; it joined the euro zone in 2014.

GEOGRAPHY

Location: Eastern Europe, bordering the Baltic Sea, between Estonia and Lithuania
Geographic coordinates: 57 00 N, 25 00 E
Map references: Europe
Area: *total:* 64,589 sq km
land: 62,249 sq km
water: 2,340 sq km
country comparison to the world: 124
Area—comparative: slightly larger than West Virginia
Land boundaries: *total:* 1,370 km
border countries (4): Belarus 161 km, Estonia 333 km, Lithuania 544 km, Russia 332 km
Coastline: 498 km
Maritime claims: *territorial sea:* 12 nm
exclusive economic zone: limits as agreed to by Estonia, Finland, Latvia, Sweden, and Russia
continental shelf: 200 m depth or to the depth of exploitation
Climate: maritime; wet, moderate winters
Terrain: low plain
Elevation: *mean elevation:* 87 m
elevation extremes: *lowest point:* Baltic Sea 0 m
highest point: Gaizina Kalns 312 m

Natural resources: peat, limestone, dolomite, amber, hydropower, timber, arable land
Land use: *agricultural land:* 29.2%
arable land: 18.6%
permanent crops: 0.1%
permanent pasture: 10.5%
forest: 54.1%
other: 16.7% (2011 est.)
Irrigated land: 12 sq km
note: land in Latvia is often too wet and in need of drainage not irrigation; approximately 16,000 sq km or 85% of agricultural land has been improved by drainage (2012)
Total renewable water resources: 35.45 cu km (2011)
Freshwater withdrawal (domestic/industrial/agricultural): *total:* 0.42 cu km/yr (42%/45%/13%)
per capita: 177.9 cu m/yr (2007)
Natural hazards: NA
Environment—current issues: Latvia's environment has benefited from a shift to service industries after the country regained independence; improvements have occurred in drinking water quality, sewage treatm ent, household and hazardous waste management, as well as reduction of air pollution
Environment—international agreements: *party to:* Air Pollution, Air Pollution-Persistent Organic Pollutants, Biodiversity, Climate Change, Climate Change-Kyoto Protocol, Desertification, Endangered Species, Hazardous Wastes, Law of the Sea, Ozone Layer Protection, Ship Pollution, Wetlands *signed, but not ratified:* none of the selected agreements
Geography—note: most of the coun try is composed of fertile low-lying plains with some hills in the east

PEOPLE AND SOCIETY

Nationality: *noun:* Latvian(s)
adjective: Latvian
Ethnic groups: Latvian 61.1%, Russian 26.2%, Belarusian 3.5%, Ukrainian 2.3%, Polish 2.2%, Lithuanian 1.3%, other 3.4% (2013 est.)
Languages: Latvian (official) 56.3%, Russian 33.8%, other 0.6% (in cludes Polish, Ukrainian, and Belarusian), un specified 9.4%
note: represents lanuage usually spoken at home (2011 est.)
Religions: Lutheran 19.6%, Orthodox 15.3%, other Christian 1%, other 0.4%, unspecified 63.7% (2006)
Population: 1986,705 (July 2015 est.)
country comparison to the world: 147
Age structure: *0–14 years:* 14.86% (male 151,296/female 143,968)
15–24 years: 10.47% (male 107,301/female 100,779)
25–54 years: 42.25% (male 414,648/female 424,745)
55–64 years: 13.44% (male 117,851/female 149,063)

65 years and over: 18.98% (male 122,507/female 254,547) (2015 est.)
Dependency ratios: *total dependency ratio:* 52.2%
youth dependency ratio: 22.7%
elderly dependency ratio: 29.5%
potential support ratio: 3.4% (2015 est.)
Median age: *total:* 42.9 years
male: 39.2 years
female: 46.3 years (2015 est.)
country comparison to the world: 18
Population growth rate: -1.06% (2015 est.)
country comparison to the world: 231
Birth rate: 10 births/1,000 population (2015 est.)
country comparison to the world: 194
Death rate: 14.31 deaths/1,000 population (2015 est.)
country comparison to the world: 5
Net migration rate: -6.26 migrant(s)/1,000 population (2015 est.)
country comparison to the world: 200
Urbanization: *urban Population:* 67.4% of total population (2015)
rate of urbanization: -0.67% annual rate of change (2010–15 est.)
Major urban areas—Population: RIGA (capital) 621,000 (2015)
Sex ratio: *at birth:* 1.05 male(s)/female
0–14 years: 1.05 male(s)/female
15–24 years: 1.07 male(s)/female
25–54 years: 0.98 male(s)/female
55–64 years: 0.79 male(s)/female
65 years and over: 0.48 male(s)/female
total population: 0.85 male(s)/female (2015 est.)
Mother's mean age at first birth: 26.4 (2011 est.)
Maternal mortality rate: 18 deaths/100,000 live births (2015 est.)
country comparison to the world: 120
Infant mortality rate: *total:* 5.36 deaths/1,000 live births
male: 5.76 deaths/1,000 live births
female: 4.95 deaths/1,000 live births (2015 est.)
country comparison to the world: 174
Life expectancy at birth: *total population:* 74.23 years
male: 69.62 years
female: 79.07 years (2015 est.)
country comparison to the world: 123
Total fertility rate: 1.5 children born/woman (2015 est.)
country comparison to the world: 195
Health expenditures: 5.7% of GDP (2013)
country comparison to the world: 110
Physicians density: 3.58 physicians/1,000 population (2012)
Hospital bed density: 5.9 beds/1,000 population (2011)
Drinking water source:
improved:
urban: 99.8% of population
rural: 98.3% of population
total: 99.3% of population

unimproved:
urban: 0.2% of population
rural: 1.7% of population
total: 0.7% of population (2015 est.)
Sanitation facility access:
improved:
urban: 90.8% of population
rural: 81.5% of population
total: 87.8% of population
unimproved:
urban: 9.2% of population
rural: 18.5% of population
total: 12.2% of population (2015 est.)
HIV/AIDS—adult prevalence rate: NA
HIV/AIDS—people living with HIV/AIDS: NA
HIV/AIDS—deaths: NA
Major infectious diseases: *degree of risk:* intermediate
vectorborne diseases: tickborne encephalitis (2013)
Obesity—adult prevalence rate: 25.6% (2014)
country comparison to the world: 62
Education expenditures: 4.9% of GDP (2013)
country comparison to the world: 77
Literacy: *definition:* age 15 and over can read and write
total population: 99.9%
male: 99.9%
female: 99.9% (2015 est.)
School life expectancy (primary to tertiary education): *total:* 16 years
male: 16 years
female: 17 years (2014)
Unemployment, youth ages 15–24: *total:* 23.2%
male: 21.8%
female: 24.9% (2013 est.)
country comparison to the world: 28

GOVERNMENT

Country name: *conventional long form:* Republic of Latvia
conventional short form: Latvia
local long form: Latvijas Republika
local short form: Latvija
former: Latvian Soviet Socialist Republic
etymology: the name "Latvia" originates from the ancient Latgalians, one of four eastern Baltic tribes that formed the ethnic core of the Latvian people (ca.8th-12th centuries A.D.)
Government type: parliamentary republic
Capital: *name:* Riga
Geographic coordinates: 56 57 N, 24 06 E
time difference: UTC+2 (7 hours ahead of Washington, DC, during Standard Time)
daylight saving time: +1hr, begins last Sunday in March; ends last Sunday in October
Administrative divisions: 110 municipalities (novadi, singular—novads) and 9 cities
municipalities: Adazu Novads, Aglonas Novads, Aizkraukles Novads, Aizputes Novads, Aknistes Novads, Alojas Novads, Alsungas Novads, Aluksnes Novads, Amatas Novads, Apes Novads, Auces Novads, Babites Novads, Baldones Novads, Baltinavas Novads, Balvu Novads, Bauskas Novads, Beverinas Novads, Brocenu Novads, Burtnieku Novads, Carnikavas Novads, Cesu

Novads, Cesvaines Novads, Ciblas Novads, Dagdas Novads, Daugavpils Novads, Dobeles Novads, Dundagas Novads, Durbes Novads, Engures Novads, Erglu Novads, Garkalnes Novads, Grobinas Novads, Gulbenes Novads, Iecavas Novads, Ikskiles Novads, Ilukstes Novads, Incukalna Novads, Jaunjelgavas Novads, Jaunpiebalgas Novads, Jaunpils Novads, Jekabpils Novads, Jelgavas Novads, Kandavas Novads, Karsavas Novads, Keguma Novads, Kekavas Novads, Kocenu Novads, Kokneses Novads, Kraslavas Novads, Krimuldas Novads, Krustpils Novads, Kuldigas Novads, Lielvardes Novads, Ligatnes Novads, Limbazu Novads, Livanu Novads, Lubanas Novads, Ludzas Novads, Madonas Novads, Malpils Novads, Marupes Novads, Mazsalacas Novads, Mersraga Novads, Nauksenu Novads, Neretas Novads, Nicas Novads, Ogres Novads, Olaines Novads, Ozolnieku Novads, Pargaujas Novads, Pavilostas Novads, Plavinu Novads, Preilu Novads, Priekules Novads, Priekulu Novads, Raunas Novads, Rezeknes Novads, Riebinu Novads, Rojas Novads, Ropazu Novads, Rucavas Novads, Rugaju Novads, Rujienas Novads, Rundales Novads, Salacgrivas Novads, Salas Novads, Salaspils Novads, Saldus Novads, Saulkrastu Novads, Sejas Novads, Siguldas Novads, Skriveru Novads, Skrundas Novads, Smiltenes Novads, Stopinu Novads, Str encu Novads, Talsu Novads, Tervetes Novads, Tukuma Novads, Vainodes Novads, Valkas Novads, Varaklanu Novads, Varkavas Novads, Vecpiebalgas Novads, Vecumnieku Novads, Ventspils Novads, Viesites Novads, Vilakas Novads, Vilanu Novads, Zilupes Novads
cities: Daugavpils, Jekabpils, Jelgava, Jurmala, Liepaja, Rezekne, Riga, Valmiera, Ventspils
Independence: 4 May 1990 (declared); 6 September 1991 (recognized by the Soviet Union)
National holiday: Independence Day, 18 November (1918); note—18 November 1918 was the date Latvia established its statehood and its concomitant independence from Soviet Russia; 4 May 1990 was the date it declared the restoration of Latvian statehood and its concomitant independence from the Soviet Union
Constitution: several previous (pre-1991 independence); note—following the restoration of independence in 1991, parts of the 1922 constitution were reinforced and fully reinforced 6 July 1993; amended several times, last in 2014 (2016)
Legal system: civil law system with traces of socialist legal traditions and practices
International law organization participation: has not submitted an ICJ jurisdiction declaration; accepts ICCt jurisdiction
Citizenship: *citizenship by birth:* no
citizenship by descent only: at least one parent must be a citizen of Latvia
dual citizenship recognized: no
residency requirement for naturalization: 5 years
Suffrage: 18 years of age; universal
Executive branch: *chief of state:* President Raimonds VEJONIS (since 8 July 2015)
head of government: Prime Minister Maris KUCINSKIS (since 11 February 2016); Deputy

Prime Minister Arvils ASERADENS (since 11 February 2016)
cabinet: Cabinet of Ministers nominated by the prime minister, appointed by Parliament
elections/appointments: president indirectly elected by Parliament for a 4-year term (eligible for a second term); election last held on 3 June 2015 (next to be held in 2019); prime minister appointed by the president, confirmed by Parliament
election results: Raimonds VEJONIS elected president; Parliament vote—Raimonds VEJONIS 55 of 100
Legislative branch: *description:* unicameral Parliament or Saeima (100 seats; members directly elected in multi-seat constituencies by proportional representation vote; members serve 4-year terms)
elections: last held on 4 October 2014 (next to be held in October 2018)
election results: percent of vote by party—SC 23%, Unity 21.9%, ZZS 19.5%, NA 16.6%, NSL 6.9%, LRA 6.7%, other 5.4%; seats by party—SC 24, Unity 23, ZZS 21, NA 17, LRA 8, NSL 7
Judicial branch: *highest court(s):* Supreme Court (consists of the Senate with 27 judges and Supreme Court of Chambers with 22 judges); Constitutional Court (consists of 7 judges)
judge selection and term of office: Supreme Court judges nominated by chief justice and confirmed by the Saeima; judges serve until age 70, but term can be extended 2 years; Constitutional Court judges—3 nominated by Saeima members, 2 by Cabinet ministers, and 2 by plenum of Supreme Court; all judges confirmed by Saeima majority vote; Constitutional Court president and vice president serve in their positions for 3 years; all judges serve 10-year terms; mandatory retirement at age 70
subordinate courts: district (city) and regional courts
Political parties and leaders: Alliance of Regions or LRA [Martins BONDARS]
For Latvia from the Heart or NSL [Inguna SUDRABA]
Social Democratic Party "Harmony" or SC [Nils USAKOVS]
National Alliance "All For Latvia!"-"For Fatherland and Freedom/LNNK" or NA [Gaidis BERZINS, Raivis DZINTARS]
Union of Greens and Farmers or ZZS [Augusts BRIGMANIS]
Unity [Solvita ABOLTINA]
Political pressure groups and leaders: Employers' Confederation of Latvia [Vitalijs GAVRILOVS]
Farmers' Parliament [Juris LAZDINS]
Free Trade Union Confederation of Latvia [Peteris KRIGERS]
International organization participation: Australia Group, BA, BIS, CBSS, CD, CE, EAPC, EBRD, ECB, EIB, EMU, ESA (cooperating state), EU, FAO, IAEA, IBRD, ICAO, ICC (NGOs), ICCt, ICRM, IDA, IFC, IFRCS, IHO, ILO, IMF, IMO, IMSO, Interpol, IOC, IOM, IPU, ISO (correspondent), ITU, ITUC (NGOs), MIGA, NATO, NIB, NSG, OAS (observer), OIF (observer),

OPCW, OSCE, PCA, Schengen Convention, UN, UNCTAD, UNESCO, UNHCR, UNWTO, UPU, WCO, WHO, WIPO, WMO, WTO

Diplomatic representation in the US: *chief of mission:* Ambassador Andris RAZANS (since 27 July 2012)

chancery: 2306 Massachusetts Ave. NW, Washington, DC 20008

telephone: [1] (202) 328-2840

FAX: [1] (202) 328-2860

Diplomatic representation from the US: *chief of mission:* Ambassador Nancy Bikoff PETTIT (since 8 September 2015)

embassy: 1 Samnera Velsa St, Riga LV-1510

mailing address: Embassy of the United States of America, 1 Samnera Velsa St, Riga, LV-1510, Latvia

telephone: [371] 6710-7000

FAX: [371] 6710-7050

Flag description: three horizontal bands of maroon (top), white (half-width), and maroon; the flag is one of the older banners in the world; a medieval chronicle mentions a red standard with a white stripe being used by Latvian tribes in about 1280

National symbol(s): white wagtail (bird); national colors: maroon, white

National anthem: *name:* "Dievs, sveti Latviju! " (God Bless Latvia)

lyrics/music: Karlis BAUMANIS

note: adopted 1920, restored 1990; first performed in 1873 while Latvia was a part of Russia; banned during the Soviet occupation from 1940 to 1990

ECONOMY

Economy—overview: Latvia is a small, open economy with exports contributing nearly a third of GDP. Due to its geographical location, transit services are highly-developed, along with timber and wood-processing, agriculture and food products, and manufacturing of machinery and electronics industries. Corruption continues to be an impediment to attracting foreign direct investment and Latvia's low birth rate and decreasing population are major challenges to its long-term economic vitality. Latvia's economy experienced GDP growth of more than 10% per year during 2006–07, but entered a severe recession in 2008 as a result of an unsustainable current account deficit and large debt exposure amid the softening world economy. Triggered by the collapse of the second largest bank, GDP plunged 18% in 2009. The economy has not returned to pre-crisis levels despite strong growth, especially in the export sector in 2011–14. The IMF, EU, and other international donors provided substantial financial assistance to Latvia as part of an agreement to defend the currency's peg to the euro in exchange for the government's commitment to stringent austerity measures. The IMF/EU program successfully concluded in December 2011. The majority of companies, banks, and real estate have been privatized, although the state still holds sizable stakes in a few large enterprises, including 99.8% ownership of the Latvian national airline. Latvia officially joined the World Trade Organization in February 1999 and the EU in May 2004. Latvia joined the euro zone in 2014.

GDP (purchasing power parity): $49.08 billion (2015 est.)

$47.77 billion (2014 est.)

$46.67 billion (2013 est.)

note: data are in 2015 US dollars

country comparison to the world: 110

GDP (official exchange rate): $27.05 billion (2015 est.)

GDP—real growth rate: 2.7% (2015 est.)

2.4% (2014 est.)

3% (2013 est.)

country comparison to the world: 111

GDP—per capita (PPP): $24,700 (2015 est.)

$23,900 (2014 est.)

$23,100 (2013 est.)

note: data are in 2015 US dollars

country comparison to the world: 76

Gross national saving: 20.6% of GDP (2015 est.)

21.5% of GDP (2014 est.)

21.7% of GDP (2013 est.)

country comparison to the world: 78

GDP—composition, by end use:

household consumption: 62%

government consumption: 17.4%

investment in fixed capital: 23.3%

investment in inventories: 0.8%

exports of goods and services: 68%

imports of goods and services: -71.5% (2015 est.)

GDP—composition, by sector of origin:

agriculture: 3.4%

industry: 23.2%

services: 73.4% (2015 est.)

Agriculture—products: grain, rapeseed, potatoes, vegetables; pork, poultry, milk, eggs; fish

Industries: processed foods, processed wood products, textiles, processed metals, pharmaceuticals, railroad cars, synth etic fibers, electronics

Industrial production growth rate: 3% (2015 est.)

country comparison to the world: 83

Labor force: 993,500 (2015 est.)

country comparison to the world: 143

Labor force—by occupation: *agriculture:* 8.8%

industry: 24%

services: 67.2% (2010 est.)

Unemployment rate: 8.7% (2015 est.)

8.9% (2014 est.)

country comparison to the world: 101

Population below poverty line: NA%

Household income or consumption by percentage share: *lowest:* 10%: 2.7%

highest: 10%: 27.6% (2008)

Distribution of family income—Gini index: 35.2 (2010)

32 (1999)

country comparison to the world: 94

Budget: *revenues:* $9.394 billion

expenditures: $9.707 billion (2015 est.)

Taxes and other revenues: 33.8% of GDP (2015 est.)

country comparison to the world: 67

Budget surplus (+) or deficit (–): -1.1% of GDP (2015 est.)

country comparison to the world: 58

Public debt: 38.5% of GDP (2015 est.)

40% of GDP (2014 est.)

note: data cover general government debt, and includes debt instruments issued (or owned) by government entities, including sub-sectors of central government, state government, local government, and social secu rity funds

country comparison to the world: 122

Fiscal year: calendar year

Inflation rate (consumer prices): 0.2% (2015 est.)

0.7% (2014 est.)

country comparison to the world: 56

Central bank discount rate: 0.05% (31 December 2013)

0.3% (31 December 2012)

country comparison to the world: 139

Commercial bank prime lending rate: 4.5% (31 December 2015 est.)

4.6% (31 December 2014 est.)

country comparison to the world: 153

Stock of narrow money: $7.543 billion (31 December 2015 est.)

$8.969 billion (31 December 2014 est.)

country comparison to the world: 88

Stock of broad money: $12.88 billion (31 December 2014 est.)

$13.41 billion (31 December 2013 est.)

country comparison to the world: 99

Stock of domestic credit: $12.54 billion (31 December 2015 est.)

$15.46 billion (31 December 2014 est.)

country comparison to the world: 97

Market value of publicly traded shares: $1.115 billion (31 December 2012 est.)

$1.076 billion (31 December 2011)

$1.252 billion (31 December 2010 est.)

country comparison to the world: 105

Current account balance: -$433 million (2015 est.)

-$620 million (2014 est.)

country comparison to the world: 94

Exports: $13.33 billion (2015 est.)

$13.41 billion (2014 est.)

country comparison to the world: 80

Exports—commodities: foodstuffs, wood and wood products, metals, machinery and equipment, textiles

Exports—partners: Lithuania 17.8%, Russia 11.5%, Estonia 11.1%, Germany 6.3%, Poland 5.6%, Sweden 5.2%, UK 5%, Denmark 4% (2015)

Imports: $16.4 billion (2015 est.)

$16.65 billion (2014 est.)

country comparison to the world: 80

Imports—commodities: machinery and equipment, consumer goods, chemicals, fuels, vehicles

Imports—partners: Lithuania 16.9%, Germany 11.2%, Poland 10.5%, Russia 8.1%, Estonia 7.7%, Finland 5.2%, Netherlands 4% (2015)

Reserves of foreign exchange and gold: $7.507 billion (31 December 2014 est.)

$7.893 billion (31 December 2013 est.)

country comparison to the world: 82

Debt—external: $40.5 billion (31 December 2014 est.)

$42.06 billion (31 December 2013 est.)

country comparison to the world: 68

Stock of direct foreign investment—at home: $17.45 billion (31 December 2015 est.)

$15.85 billion (31 December 2014 est.)

country comparison to the world: 80

Stock of direct foreign investment—abroad:
$2.714 billion (31 December 2015 est.)
$2.454 billion (31 December 2014 est.)
country comparison to the world: 77
Exchange rates: lati (LVL) per US dollar—
0.932 (2015 est.)
0.7525 (2014 est.)
0.7525 (2013 est.)
0.55 (2012 est.)
0.5012 (2011 est.)

ENERGY

Electricity—production: 6.008 billion kWh (2012 est.)
country comparison to the world: 115
Electricity—consumption: 7.141 billion kWh (2012 est.)
country comparison to the world: 104
Electricity—exports: 3.65 billion kWh (2013 est.)
country comparison to the world: 35
Electricity—imports: 5.005 billion kWh (2013 est.)
country comparison to the world: 40
Electricity—installed generating capacity: 2.245 million kW (2012 est.)
country comparison to the world: 103
Electricity—from fossil fuels: 26.3% of total installed capacity (2012 est.)
country comparison to the world: 186
Electricity—from nuclear fuels: 0% of total installed capacity (2012 est.)
country comparison to the world: 127
Electricity—from hydroelectric plants: 70.2% of total installed capacity (2012 est.)
country comparison to the world: 23
Electricity—from other renewable sources: 3.5% of total installed capacity (2012 est.)
country comparison to the world: 68
Crude oil—production: 0 bbl/day (2014 est.)
country comparison to the world: 157
Crude oil—exports: 117.9 bbl/day (2012 est.)
country comparison to the world: 90
Crude oil—imports: 140 bbl/day (2012 est.)
country comparison to the world: 82
Crude oil—proved reserves: 0 bbl (1 January 2015 est.)
country comparison to the world: 156
Refined petroleum products—production: 0 bbl/day (2012 est.)
country comparison to the world: 201
Refined petroleum products—consumption: 34,000 bbl/day (2013 est.)
country comparison to the world: 111
Refined petroleum products—exports: 11,590 bbl/day (2012 est.)
country comparison to the world: 86
Refined petroleum products—imports: 45,630 bbl/day (2012 est.)
country comparison to the world: 82
Natural gas—production: 0 cu m (2013 est.)
country comparison to the world: 211
Natural gas—consumption: 1.41 billion cu m (2013 est.)
country comparison to the world: 86
Natural gas—exports: 0 cu m (2013 est.)
country comparison to the world: 133

Natural gas—imports: 1.41 billion cu m (2013 est.)
country comparison to the world: 55
Natural gas—proved reserves: 0 cu m (1 January 2014 est.)
country comparison to the world: 159
Carbon dioxide emissions from consumption of energy: 7.897 million Mt (2012 est.)
country comparison to the world: 111

COMMUNICATIONS

Telephones—fixed lines: *total subscriptions:* 390,000
subscriptions per 100 inhabitants: 19 (2014 est.)
country comparison to the world: 106

Telephones—mobile cellular: *total:* 2.5 million
subscriptions per 100 inhabitants: 126 (2014 est.)
country comparison to the world: 145
Telephone system: *general assessment:* recent efforts focused on bringing competition to the telecommunications sector; the number of fixed lines is decreasingas mobile-cellular telephone service expands
domestic: number of telecommunications operators has grown rapidly since the fixed-line market opened to competition in 2003; combined fixed-line and mobile-cellular subscribership roughly 150 per 100 persons
international: country code—371; the Latvian network is now connected via fiber optic cable to Estonia, Finland, and Sweden (2008)
Broadcast media: several national and regional commercial TV stations are foreign-owned, 2 national TV stations are publicly owned; system supplemented by privately owned regional and local TV stations; cable and satellite multichannel TV services with domestic and foreign broadcasts available; publicly owned broadcaster operates 4 radio networks with dozens of stations throughout the country; dozens of private broadcasters also operate radio stations (2007)
Radio broadcast stations: AM 8, FM 62, shortwave 1 (2008)
Television broadcast stations: 37 (plus 31 repeaters) (2008)
Internet country code: .lv
Internet hosts: 359,604 (2012)
country comparison to the world: 58
Internet users: *total:* 1.5 million
percent of population: 76.5% (2014 est.)
country comparison to the world: 110

TRANSPORTATION

Airports: 42 (2013)
country comparison to the world: 101
Airports—with paved runways: *total:* 18
over 3,047 m: 1
2,438 to 3,047 m: 3
1,524 to 2,437 m: 4
914 to 1,523 m: 3
under 914 m: 7 (2013)
Airports—with unpaved runways: *total:* 24
under 914 m: 24 (2013)
Heliports: 1 (2013)
Pipelines: gas 928 km; refined products 415 km (2013)

Railways: *total:* 2,239 km
broad gauge: 2,206 km 1.520-m gauge
narrow gauge: 33 km 0.750-m gauge (2008)
country comparison to the world: 68
Roadways: *total:* 72,440 km
paved: 14,707 km
unpaved: 57,733 km (2013)
country comparison to the world: 64
Waterways: 300 km (navigable year round) (2010)
country comparison to the world: 92
Merchant marine: *total:* 11
by type: cargo 3, chemical tanker 1, passenger/cargo 4, petroleum tanker 2, roll on/roll off 1
foreign-owned: 3 (Estonia 3)
registered in other countries: 79 (Antigua and Barbuda 16, Belize 9, Comoros 2, Dominica 2, Georgia 1, Liberia 5, Malta 8, Marshall Islands 19, Russia 2, Saint Vincent and the Grenadines 15) (2010)
country comparison to the world: 113
Ports and terminals: *major seaport(s):* Riga, Ventspils

MILITARY AND SECURITY

Military branches: National Armed Forces (Nacionalo Brunoto Speku): Land Forces (Latvijas Sauszemes Speki), Navy (Latvijas Juras Speki; includes Coast Guard (Latvijas Kara Flotes)), Latvian Air Force (Latvijas Gaisa Speki), Latvian Home Guard (Latvijas Zemessardze) (2011)
Military service age and obligation: 18 years of age for voluntary male and female military service; no conscription; under current law, every citizen is entitled to serve in the armed forces for life (2012)
Military expenditures:
0.91% of GDP (2014)
0.99% of GDP (2013)
0.92% of GDP (2012)
1.05% of GDP (2011)
0.92% of GDP (2010)
country comparison to the world: 105

TRANSNATIONAL ISSUES

Disputes—international: Russia demands better Latvian treatment of ethnic Russians in Latvia; boundary demarcated with Latvia and Lithuania; the Latvian parliament has not ratified its 1998 maritime boundary treaty with Lithuania, primarily due to concerns over oil exploration rights; as a member state that forms part of the EU's external border, Latvia has implemented the strict Schengen border rules with Russia
Refugees and internally displaced persons: *stateless persons:* 252,195 (2015); note—individuals who were Latvian citizens prior to the 1940 Soviet occupation and their descendants were recognized as Latvian citizens when the country's independence was restored in 1991; citizens of the former Soviet Union residing in Latvia who have neither Latvian nor other citizenship are considered noncitizens (officially the ere is no statelessness in Latvia) and are entitled to non-citizen passports; children born after Latvian independence to stateless parents are entitled to Latvian citizenship upon their parents' request; non-citizens cannot vote or hold certain government jobs and are exempt

from military service but can travel visa-free in the EU under the Schengen accord like Latvian citizens; non-citizens can obtain naturalization if they have been permanent residents of Latvia for at least five years, pass tests in Latvian language and history, and know the words of the Latvian national anthem

Illicit drugs: transshipment and destination point for cocaine, synthetic drugs, opiates, and cannabis from Southwest Asia, Western Europe, Latin America, and neighboring Balkan countries; despite improved legislation, vu lnerable to money laundering due to nascent enforcement capabilities and comparatively weak regulation of offshore

companies and the gaming industry; CIS organized crime (including counterfeiting, corruption, extortion, stolen cars, and prostitution) accounts for most laundered proceeds

LEBANON

INTRODUCTION

Background: Following World War I, France acquired a mandate over the northern portion of the former Ottoman Empire province of Syria. The French demarcated the region of Lebanon in 1920 and granted this area independence in 1943. Since independence the country has been marked by periods of political turmoil interspersed with prosperity built on its position as a regional center for finance and trade. The country's 1975–90 civil war that resulted in an estimated 120,000 fatalities, was followed by years of social and political instability. Sectarianism is a key element of Lebanese political life. Neighboring Syria has historically influenced Lebanon's foreign policy and internal policies, and its military occupied Lebanon from 1976 until 2005. The Lebanon-based Hizballah militia and Israel continued attacks and counterattacks against each other after Syria's withdrawal, and fought a brief war in 2006. Lebanon's borders with Syria and Israel remain unresolved.

GEOGRAPHY

Location: Middle East, bordering the Mediterranean Sea, between Israel and Syria
Geographic coordinates: 33 50 N, 35 50 E
Map references: Middle East
Area: *total:* 10,400 sq km
land: 10,230 sq km
water: 170 sq km
country comparison to the world: 170
Area—comparative: about one-third the size of Maryland

Land boundaries: *total:* 484 km
border countries (2): Israel 81 km, Syria 403 km
Coastline: 225 km
Maritime claims: *territorial sea:* 12 nm
Climate: Mediterranean; mild to cool, wet winters with hot, dry summers; the Lebanon Mountains experience heavy winter snows
Terrain: narrow coastal plain; El Beqaa (Bekaa Valley) separates Lebanon and Anti-Lebanon Mountains
Elevation: *mean elevation:* 1,250 m
elevation extremes: *lowest point:* Mediterranean Sea 0 m
highest point: Qornet es Saouda 3,088 m
Natural resources: limestone, iron ore, salt, water-surplus state in a water-deficit region, arable land
Land use: *agricultural land:* 63.3%
arable land: 11.9%
permanent crops: 12.3%
permanent pasture: 39.1%
forest: 13.4%
other: 23.3% (2011 est.)
Irrigated land: 1,040 sq km (2012)
Total renewable water resources: 4.5 cu km (2011)
Freshwater withdrawal (domestic/industrial/agricultural): *total:* 1.31 cu km/yr (29%/11%/60%)
per capita: 316.8 cu m/yr (2005)
Natural hazards: dust storms, sandstorms
Environment—current issues: deforestation; soil erosion; desertification; air pollution in Beirut from vehicular traffic and the burning of industrial wastes; pollution of coastal waters from raw sewage and oil spills
Environment—international agreements: *party to:* Biodiversity, Climate Change, Climate Change-Kyoto Protocol, Desertification, Hazardous Wastes, Law of the Sea, Ozone Layer Protection, Ship Pollution, Wetlands
signed, but not ratified: Environmental Modification, Marine Life Conservation
Geography—note: smallest country in continental Asia; Nahr el Litani is the only major river in Near East not crossing an international boundary; rugged terrain historically helped isolate, protect, and develop num erous factional groups based on religion, clan, and ethnicity

PEOPLE AND SOCIETY

Nationality: *noun:* Lebanese (singular and plural)
adjective: Lebanese
Ethnic groups: Arab 95%, Armenian 4%, other 1%

note: many Christian Lebanese do not identify them selves as Arab but rather as descendents of the ancient Canaanites and prefer to be called Phoenicians
Languages: Arabic (official), French, English, Armenian
Religions: Muslim 54% (27% Sunni, 27% Shia), Christian 40.5% (includes 21% Maronite Catholic, 8% Greek Orthodox, 5% Greek Catholic, 6.5% other Christian), Druze 5.6%, very small numbers of Jews, Baha'is, Buddhists, Hindus, and Mormons
note: 18 religious sects recognized (2012 est.)
Population: 6,184,701 (July 2015 est.)
country comparison to the world: 109
Age structure: *0–14 years:* 25.08% (male 793,837/female 757,120)
15–24 years: 17.04% (male 539,232/female 514,394)
25–54 years: 44.13% (male 1,378,852/female 1,350,506)
55–64 years: 7.18% (male 205,933/female 237,849)
65 years and over: 6.58% (male 179,983/female 226,995) (2015 est.)
Dependency ratios: *total dependency ratio:* 47.3%
youth dependency ratio: 35.4%
elderly dependency ratio: 12%
potential support ratio: 8.3% (2015 est.)
Median age: *total:* 29.4 years
male: 28.8 years
female: 30 years (2015 est.)
country comparison to the world: 118
Population growth rate: 0.86% (2015 est.)
country comparison to the world: 128
Birth rate: 14.59 births/1,000 population (2015 est.)
country comparison to the world: 133
Death rate: 4.88 deaths/1,000 population (2015 est.)
country comparison to the world: 191
Net migration rate: -1.1 migrant(s)/1,000 population (2015 est.)
country comparison to the world: 150
Urbanization: *urban Population:* 87.8% of total population (2015)
rate of urbanization: 3.18% annual rate of change (2010–15 est.)
Major urban areas—Population: BEIRUT (capital) 2.226 million (2015)
Sex ratio: *at birth:* 1.05 male(s)/female
0–14 years: 1.05 male(s)/female

15–24 years: 1.05 male(s)/female
25–54 years: 1.02 male(s)/female
55–64 years: 0.87 male(s)/female
65 years and over: 0.79 male(s)/female
total population: 1 male(s)/female (2015 est.)
Maternal mortality rate: 15 deaths/100,000 live births (2015 est.)
country comparison to the world: 130
Infant mortality rate: *total:* 7.76 deaths/1,000 live births
male: 8.18 deaths/1,000 live births
female: 7.32 deaths/1,000 live births (2015 est.)
country comparison to the world: 155
Life expectancy at birth: *total population:* 77.4 years
male: 76.18 years
female: 78.69 years (2015 est.)
country comparison to the world: 70
Total fertility rate: 1.73 children born/woman (2015 est.)
country comparison to the world: 169
Health expenditures: 7.2% of GDP (2013)
country comparison to the world: 73
Physicians density: 3.2 physicians/1,000 population (2011)
Hospital bed density: 3.5 beds/1,000 population (2012)
Drinking water source:
improved:
urban: 99% of population
rural: 99% of population
total: 99% of population
unimproved:
urban: 1% of population
rural: 1% of population
total: 1% of population (2015 est.)
Sanitation facility access:
improved:
urban: 80.7% of population
rural: 80.7% of population
total: 80.7% of population
unimproved:
urban: 19.3% of population
rural: 19.3% of population
total: 19.3% of population (2015 est.)
HIV/AIDS—adult prevalence rate: 0.06% (2014 est.)
country comparison to the world: 116
HIV/AIDS—people living with HIV/AIDS: 1,800 (2014 est.)
country comparison to the world: 117
HIV/AIDS—deaths: less than 100 (2014 est.)
country comparison to the world: 117
Obesity—adult prevalence rate: 30.8% (2014)
country comparison to the world: 40
Education expenditures: 2.6% of GDP (2013)
country comparison to the world: 162
Literacy: *definition:* age 15 and over can read and write
total population: 93.9%
male: 96%
female: 91.8% (2015 est.)
School life expectancy (primary to tertiary education): *total:* 12 years
male: 12 years
female: 12 years (2013)

Unemployment, youth ages 15–24: *total:* 22.1%
male: 22.3%
female: 21.5% (2007 est.)
country comparison to the world: 71

GOVERNMENT

Country name: *conventional long form:* Lebanese Republic
conventional short form: Lebanon
local long form: Al Jumhuriyah al Lubnaniyah
local short form: Lubnan
former: Greater Lebanon
etymology: derives from the Semitic root "lbn" meaning "white" and refers to snow-capped Mount Lebanon
Government type: parliamentary republic
Capital: *name:* Beirut
Geographic coordinates: 33 52 N, 35 30 E
time difference: UTC+2 (7 hours ahead of Washington, DC, during Standard Time)
daylight saving time: +1hr, begins last Sunday in March; ends last Sunday in October
Administrative divisions: 8 governorates (mohafazat, singular—mohafazah); Aakkar, Baalbek-Hermel, Beqaa, Beyrouth (Beirut), Liban-Nord (North Lebanon), Liban-Sud (South Lebanon), Mont-Liban (Mount Lebanon), Nabatiye
Independence: 22 November 1943 (from League of Nations mandate under French administration)
National holiday: Independence Day, 22 November (1943)
Constitution: drafted 15 May 1926, adopted 23 May 1926; amended several times, last in 2004 (2016)
Legal system: mixed legal system of civil law based on the French civil code, Ottoman legal tradition, and religious laws covering personal status, marriage, divorce, and other family relations of the Jewish, Islamic, and Christian communities
International law organization participation: has not submitted an ICJ jurisdiction declaration; non-party state to the ICCt
Citizenship: *citizenship by birth:* no
citizenship by descent only: the father must be a citizen of Lebanon
dual citizenship recognized: yes
residency requirement for naturalization: unknown
Suffrage: 21 years of age; compulsory for all males; authorized for women at age 21 with elementary education; excludes military personnel
Executive branch: *chief of state:* President (vacant); note—President Michel SULAYMAN's term expired on 25 May 2014; the prime minister and his cabinet are temporarily assuming the duties of the president; as of June 2016, the National Assembly had failed to elect a president
head of government: Prime Minister Tamam SALAM (since 6 April 2013); Deputy Prime Minister Samir MOQBIL (since 7 July 2011)
cabinet: Cabinet chosen by the prime minister in consultation with the president and National Assembly
elections/appointments: president indirectly elected by the National Assembly for a 6-year term

(eligible for non-consecutive terms); first round of election held on 23 April 2014 (next to be held in 2020); prime minister and deputy prime minister appointed by the president in consultation with the National Assembly
election results: NA; note—the April 2014 parliamentary vote failed to meet the required two-thirds majority vote threshold; subsequent voting from April 2014 through June 2016 also failed to meet a quorum or was postponed
Legislative branch: *description:* unicameral National Assembly or Majlis al-Nuwab in Arabic or Assemblee Nationale in French (128 seats; members directly elected in multi-seat constituencies by majority vote; members serve 4-year terms); note—seats are apportioned among the Christian and Muslim denominations
note: Lebanon's Constitution states the National Assembly cannot conduct regular business until it elects a president when the position is vacant
elections: last held on 7 June 2009 (next delayed due to a failure to elect a new president)
election results: percent of vote by coalition—March 8 Coalition 54.7%, March 14 Coalition 45.3%; seats by coalition—March 14 Coalition 71; March 8 Coalition 57; seats by coalition following 16 July 2012 by election held to fill one seat—March 14 Coalition 72, March 8 Coalition 56
Judicial branch: *highest court(s):* Court of Cassation or Supreme Court (organized into 4 divisions, each with a presiding judge and 2 associate judges); Constitutional Council (consists of 10 members)
judge selection and term of office: Court of Cassation judges appointed by Supreme Judicial Council, headed by the chief justice, and includes other judicial officials; judge tenure NA; Constitutional Council members appointed—5 by the Council of Ministers and 5 by parliament; members serve 5-year terms
subordinate courts: Courts of Appeal; Courts of First Instance; specialized tribunals, religious courts; military courts
Political parties and leaders: *14 March Coalition:* Democratic Left Movement or DLM [Elias ATALLAH]
Future Movement Bloc [Sa'ad al-HARIRI]
Kata'ib Party [Sami GEMAYEL]
Lebanese Forces [Samir JA'JA]
Marada Movement [Sulayman FRANJIEH]
Social Democratic Hunchakian Party [Hagop DIKRANIAN]
8 March Coalition: Amal Movement [Nabih BERRI]
Free Patriotic Movement [Gibran BASSIL]
Lebanese Democratic Party [Emir Talal ARSLAN]
Loyalty to the Resistance Bloc [Mohammad RA'AD] (includes Hizballah [Hassan NASRALLAH])
Marada Movement [Sulayman FRANJIEH]
Syrian Ba'th Party [Abdel Mouin GHAZI]
Syrian Social Nationalist Party [Ali QANSO]
Independent: Metn Bloc [Michel MURR]
Progressive Socialist Party or PSP [Walid JUNBLATT]
Tashnag or ARF [Hagop DHATCHERIAN]

Political pressure groups and leaders: Maronite Church [Patriarch Bishara al-Ra'i]

note: most sects retain militias and a number of militant groups operate in Palestinian refugee camps

International organization participation: ABEDA, AFESD, AMF, CAEU, FAO, G-24, G-77, IAEA, IBRD, ICAO, ICC (national committees), ICRM, IDA, IDB, IFAD, IFC, IFRCS, ILO, IMF, IMO, IMSO, Interpol, IOC, IPU, ISO, ITSO, ITU, LAS, MIGA, NAM, OAS (observer), OIC, OIF, OPCW, PCA, UN, UNCTAD, UNESCO, UNHCR, UNIDO, UNRWA, UNWTO, UPU, WCO, WFTU (NGOs), WHO, WIPO, WMO, WTO (observer)

Diplomatic representation in the US: *chief of mission:* Ambassador (vacant); Charge d'Affaries Carla JAZZAR (since 28 January 2016)

chancery: 2560 28th Street NW, Washington, DC 20008

telephone: [1] (202) 939-6300

FAX: [1] (202) 939-6324

consulate(s) general: Detroit, New York, Los Angeles

Diplomatic representation from the US: *chief of mission:* Ambassador Elizabeth H. RICHARD (since May 2016)

embassy: Awkar, Lebanon (Awkar facing the Municipality)

mailing address: P.O. Box 70–840, Antelias, Lebanon; from US: US Embassy Beirut, 6070 Beirut Place, Washington, DC 20521–6070

telephone: [961] (4) 542600,543600

FAX: [961] (4) 544136

Flag description: three horizontal bands consisting of red (top), white (middle, double width), and red (bottom) with a green cedar tree centered in the white band; the red bands symbolize blood shed for liberation, the white band denotes peace, the snow of the mountains, and purity; the green cedar tree is the symbol of Lebanon and represents eternity, steadiness, happiness, and prosperity

National symbol(s): cedar tree; national colors: red, white, green

National anthem: *name:* "Kulluna lil-watan" (All Of Us, For Our Country!)

lyrics/music: Rachid NAKHLE/Wadih SABRA

note: adopted 1927; chosen following a nation-wide competition

ECONOMY

Economy—overview: Lebanon has a free-market economy and a strong laissez-faire commercial tradition. The government does not restrict foreign investment; however, the investment climate suffers from red tape, corruption, arbitrary licensing decisions, complex customs procedures, high taxes, tariffs, and fees, archaic legislation, and weak intellectual property rights. The Lebanese economy is service-oriented; main growth sectors include banking and tourism.

The 1975–90 civil war seriously damaged Lebanon's economic infrastructure, cut national output by half, and derailed Lebanon's position as a Middle Eastern entrepot and banking hub. Following the civil war, Lebanon rebuilt much of its war-torn

physical and financial infrastructure by borrowing heavily, mostly from domestic banks, which saddled the government with a huge debt burden. Pledges of economic and financial reforms made at separate international donor conferences during the 2000s have mostly gone unfulfilled, including those made during the Paris III Donor Conference in 2007, following the July 2006 war.

Spillover from the Syrian conflict, including the influx of more than 1.1 million registered Syrian refugees, has increased internal tension and slowed economic growth to the 1–2% range in 2011–15, after four years of averaging 8% growth. Syrian refugees have increased the labor supply, but pushed more Lebanese into unemployment. Chronic fiscal deficits have increased Lebanon's debt-to-GDP ratio, the fourth highest in the world; most of the debt is held internally by Lebanese banks. Weak economic growth limits tax revenues, while the largest government expenditures remain debt servicing, salaries for government workers, and transfers to the electricity sector. These limitations constrain other government spending and limit the government's ability to invest in necessary infrastructure improvements, such as water, electricity, and transportation.

GDP (purchasing power parity): $83.06 billion (2015 est.)

$82.23 billion (2014 est.)

$80.62 billion (2013 est.)

note: data are in 2015 US dollars

country comparison to the world: 88

GDP (official exchange rate): $51.17 billion (2015 est.)

GDP—real growth rate: 1% (2015 est.)

2% (2014 est.)

2.5% (2013 est.)

country comparison to the world: 175

GDP—per capita (PPP): $18,200 (2015 est.)

$18,200 (2014 est.)

$18,000 (2013 est.)

note: data are in 2015 US dollars

country comparison to the world: 91

Gross national saving: -3.7% of GDP (2015 est.)

-3% of GDP (2014 est.)

-2.6% of GDP (2013 est.)

country comparison to the world: 172

GDP—composition, by end use:

household consumption: 88%

government consumption: 12.4%

investment in fixed capital: 26.1%

investment in inventories: 0.5%

exports of goods and services: 20.4%

imports of goods and services: -47.4% (2015 est.)

GDP—composition, by sector of origin:

agriculture: 5.6%

industry: 24.7%

services: 69.7% (2015 est.)

Agriculture—products: citrus, grapes, tomatoes, apples, vegetables, potatoes, olives, tobacco; sheep, goats

Industries: banking, tourism, food processing, wine, jewelry, cement, textiles, mineral and chemical products, wood and furniture products, oil refining, metal fabricating

Industrial production growth rate: 1.7% (2015 est.)

country comparison to the world: 126

Labor force: 1.628 million

note: does not include as many as 1 million foreign workers, nor refugees (2013 est.)

country comparison to the world: 128

Labor force—by occupation: *agriculture:* NA%

industry: NA%

services: NA%

Unemployment rate: NA%

Population below poverty line: 28.6% (2004 est.)

Household income or consumption by percentage share: *lowest:* 10%: NA%

highest: 10%: NA%

Budget: *revenues:* $10.28 billion

expenditures: $14.28 billion (2015 est.)

Taxes and other revenues: 20.1% of GDP (2015 est.)

country comparison to the world: 154

Budget surplus (+) or deficit (–): -7.8% of GDP (2015 est.)

country comparison to the world: 197

Public debt: 138.8% of GDP (2015 est.)

135.4% of GDP (2014 est.)

note: data cover central government debt, and exclude debt instruments issued (or owned) by government entities other than the treasury; the data include treasury debt held by foreign entities; the data include debt issued by subnational entities, as well as intra-governmental debt; intra-governmental debt consists of treasury borrowings from surpluses in the social funds, such as for retirement, medical care, and unemployment

country comparison to the world: 4

Fiscal year: calendar year

Inflation rate (consumer prices): -3.7% (2015 est.)

1.9% (2014 est.)

country comparison to the world: 2

Central bank discount rate: 3.5% (31 December 2010)

10% (31 December 2009)

country comparison to the world: 100

Commercial bank prime lending rate: 7.1% (31 December 2015 est.)

7.27% (31 December 2014 est.)

country comparison to the world: 120

Stock of narrow money: $6.085 billion (31 December 2015 est.)

$5.506 billion (31 December 2014 est.)

country comparison to the world: 93

Stock of broad money: $52.94 billion (31 December 2015 est.)

$48.69 billion (31 December 2014 est.)

country comparison to the world: 66

Stock of domestic credit: $96.44 billion (31 December 2015 est.)

$89.13 billion (31 December 2014 est.)

country comparison to the world: 54

Market value of publicly traded shares: $11.22 billion (30 December 2014 est.)

$10.54 billion (30 December 2013)

$10.42 billion (28 December 2012 est.)

country comparison to the world: 72

Current account balance: -$12.78 billion (2015 est.)

-$13.42 billion (2014 est.)

country comparison to the world: 181

Exports: $3.475 billion (2015 est.)
$3.787 billion (2014 est.)
country comparison to the world: 126
Exports—commodities: jewelry, base metals, chemicals, consumer goods, fruit and vegetables, tobacco, construction minerals, electric power machinery and switchgear, textile fibers, paper
Exports—partners: Saudi Arabia 12.4%, UAE 10.5%, Iraq 7.8%, Syria 7.3%, South Africa 4.8% (2015)
Imports: $16.27 billion (2015 est.)
$18.99 billion (2014 est.)
country comparison to the world: 81
Imports—commodities: petroleum products, cars, medicinal products, clothing, meat and live animals, consumer goods, paper, textile fabrics, tobacco, electrical machinery and equipment, chemicals
Imports—partners: China 12.7%, Italy 7.4%, US 6.2%, France 6.1%, Germany 5.6%, Greece 4.5% (2015)
Reserves of foreign exchange and gold: $49.61 billion (31 December 2015 est.)
$50.5 billion (31 December 2014 est.)
country comparison to the world: 40
Debt—external: $31.59 billion (31 December 2014 est.)
$32.2 billion (31 December 2013 est.)
country comparison to the world: 73
Stock of direct foreign investment—at home: $NA
Stock of direct foreign investment—abroad: $NA
Exchange rates: Lebanese pounds (LBP) per US dollar—
1,507.5 (2015 est.)
1,507.5 (2014 est.)
1,507.5 (2013 est.)
1,507.5 (2012 est.)
1,507.5 (2011 est.)

ENERGY

Electricity—production: 13.99 billion kWh (2012 est.)
country comparison to the world: 87
Electricity—consumption: 12.94 billion kWh (2012 est.)
country comparison to the world: 83
Electricity—exports: 0 kWh (2013 est.)
country comparison to the world: 160
Electricity—imports: 323 million kWh (2012 est.)
country comparison to the world: 84
Electricity—installed generating capacity: 2.26 million kW (2012 est.)
country comparison to the world: 102
Electricity—from fossil fuels: 90.2% of total installed capacity (2012 est.)
country comparison to the world: 76
Electricity—from nuclear fuels: 0% of total installed capacity (2012 est.)
country comparison to the world: 126
Electricity—from hydroelectric plants: 9.8% of total installed capacity (2012 est.)
country comparison to the world: 117
Electricity—from other renewable sources: 0% of total installed capacity (2012 est.)
country comparison to the world: 193
Crude oil—production: 0 bbl/day (2014 est.)

country comparison to the world: 156
Crude oil—exports: 0 bbl/day (2012 est.)
country comparison to the world: 150
Crude oil—imports: 0 bbl/day (2012 est.)
country comparison to the world: 213
Crude oil—proved reserves: 0 bbl (1 January 2015 est.)
country comparison to the world: 155
Refined petroleum products—production: 0 bbl/day (2012 est.)
country comparison to the world: 200
Refined petroleum products—consumption: 125,000 bbl/day (2013 est.)
country comparison to the world: 73
Refined petroleum products—exports: 0 bbl/day (2012 est.)
country comparison to the world: 195
Refined petroleum products—imports: 126,600 bbl/day (2012 est.)
country comparison to the world: 45
Natural gas—production: 0 cu m (2013 est.)
country comparison to the world: 210
Natural gas—consumption: 0 cu m (2013 est.)
country comparison to the world: 163
Natural gas—exports: 0 cu m (2013 est.)
country comparison to the world: 132
Natural gas—imports: 0 cu m (2013 est.)
country comparison to the world: 91
Natural gas—proved reserves: 0 cu m (1 January 2014 est.)
country comparison to the world: 158
Carbon dioxide emissions from consumption of energy: 16.44 million Mt (2012 est.)
country comparison to the world: 88

COMMUNICATIONS

Telephones—fixed lines: *total subscriptions:* 970,000
subscriptions per 100 inhabitants: 16 (2014 est.)
country comparison to the world: 77
Telephones—mobile cellular: *total:* 4.4 million
subscriptions per 100 inhabitants: 75 (2014 est.)
country comparison to the world: 125
Telephone system: *general assessment:* repair of the telecommunications system, severely damaged during the civil war, now complete
domestic: two mobile-cellular networks provide good service; combined fixed-line and mobile-cellular subscribership roughly 100 per 100 persons
international: country code—961; submarine cable links to Cyprus, Egypt, and Syria; satellite earth stations—2 Intelsat (1 Indian Ocean and 1 Atlantic Ocean); coaxial cable to Syria (2011)
Broadcast media: 7 TV stations, 1 of which is state owned; more than 30 radio stations, 1 of which is state owned; satellite and cable TV services available; transmissions of at least 2 international broadcasters are accessible through partner stations (2007)
Radio broadcast stations: AM 20, FM 30 (plus about a dozen unlicensed stations operating), shortwave 4 (2009)
Television broadcast stations: 12 (2009)
Internet country code: .lb
Internet hosts: 64,926 (2012)

country comparison to the world: 91
Internet users: *total:* 4 million
percent of population: 67.2% (2014 est.)
country comparison to the world: 76

TRANSPORTATION

Airports: 8 (2013)
country comparison to the world: 161
Airports—with paved runways: *total:* 5
over 3,047 m: 1
2,438 to 3,047 m: 2
1,524 to 2,437 m: 1
under 914 m: 1 (2013)
Airports—with unpaved runways: *total:* 3
914 to 1,523 m: 2
under 914 m: 1 (2013)
Heliports: 1 (2013)
Pipelines: gas 88 km (2013)
Railways: *total:* 401 km
standard gauge: 319 km 1.435-m gauge
narrow gauge: 82 km 1.050-m gauge
note: rail system unusable due to damage sustained from fighting in the 1980s and in 2006 (2008)
country comparison to the world: 120
Roadways: *total:* 6,970 km (includes 170 km of expressways) (2005)
country comparison to the world: 146
Merchant marine: *total:* 29
by type: bulk carrier 4, cargo 7, carrier 17, vehicle carrier 1
foreign-owned: 2 (Syria 2)
registered in other countries: 34 (Barbados 2, Cambodia 5, Comoros 2, Egypt 1, Georgia 1, Honduras 2, Liberia 1, Malta 6, Moldova 1, Panama 2, Saint Vincent and the Grenadines 2, Sierra Leone 2, Togo 6, unknown 1) (2010)
country comparison to the world: 85
Ports and terminals: *major seaport(s):* Beirut, Tripoli
container port(s) (TEUs): Beirut (1,034,249)

MILITARY AND SECURITY

Military branches: Lebanese Armed Forces (LAF): Lebanese Army ((Al Jaysh al Lubnani) includes Lebanese Navy (Al Quwwat al Bahiriyya al Lubnaniya), Lebanese Air Force (Al Quwwat al Jawwiya al Lubnaniya)) (2013)
Military service age and obligation: 17–30 years of age for voluntary military service; 18–24 years of age for officer candidates; no conscription (2013)
Military expenditures: 4.04% of GDP (2012)
4.06% of GDP (2011) 4.04% of GDP (2010)
country comparison to the world: 11

TRANSNATIONAL ISSUES

Disputes—international: lacking a treaty or other documentation describing the boundary, portions of the Lebanon-Syria boundary are unclear with several sections in dispute; since 2000, Lebanon has claimed Shab'a Farms area in the Israeli-occupied Golan Heights; the roughly 2,000-strong UN Interim Force in Lebanon has been in place since 1978

Refugees and internally displaced persons: *refugees (country of origin):* 449,957 (Palestinian refugees); 5,986 (Iraq) (2014); 1,033,513 (Syria) (2016)

IDPs: 12,000 (2007 Lebanese security forces' destruction of Palestinian refugee camp) (2015)

stateless persons: undetermined (2014); note— tens of thousands of persons are stateless in Lebanon, including many Palestinian refugees and their descendants, Syrian Kurds denaturalized in Syria in 1962, children born to Lebanese women married to foreign or stateless men; most babies born to Syrian refugees, and Lebanese children whose births are unregistered

Trafficking in persons: *current situation:* Lebanon is a source and destination country for women and children subjected to forced labor and sex trafficking and a transit point for Eastern European women and children subjected to sex trafficking in other Middle Eastern countries; women and girls from South and Southeast Asia and an increasing

number from East and West Africa are recruited by agencies to work in domestic service but are subject to conditions of forced labor; under Lebanon's artiste visa program, women from Eastern Europe, North Africa, and the Dominican Republic enter Lebanon to work in the adult entertainment industry but are often forced into the sex trade; Lebanese children are reportedly forced into street begging and commercial sexual exploitation, with small numbers of Lebanese girls sex trafficked in other Arab countries; Syrian refugees are vulnerable to forced labor and prostitution

tier rating: Tier 2 Watch List—Lebanon does not fully comply with the minimum standards for the elimination of trafficking; however, it is making significant efforts to do so; in 2014, Lebanon was granted a waiver from an otherwise required downgrade to Tier 3 because its government has a written plan that, if implemented would constitute making significant efforts to bring itself into

compliance with the minimum standards for the elimination of trafficking; law enforcement efforts in 2014 were uneven; the number of convicted traffickers increased, but judges lack of familiarity with anti-trafficking law meant that many offenders were not brought to justice; the government relied heavily on an NGO to identify and provide service to trafficking victims; and its lack of thoroughly implemented victim identification procedures resulted in victims continuing to be arrested, detained, and deported for crimes committed as a direct result of being trafficked (2015)

Illicit drugs: cannabis cultivation dramatically reduced to 2,500 hectares in 2002 despite continued significant cannabis consum ption; opium poppy cultivation minimal; small amounts of Latin American cocaine and Southwest Asian heroin transit country on way to European markets and for Middle Eastern consumption; money laundering of drug proceeds fuels concern that extremists are benefiting from drug trafficking

LESOTHO

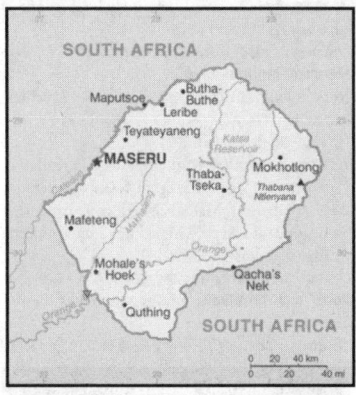

INTRODUCTION

Background: Basutoland was renamed the Kingdom of Lesotho upon independence from the UK in 1966. The Basuto National Party ruled the country during its first two decades. King MOSHOESHOE was exiled in 1990, but returned to Lesotho in 1992 and was reinstated in 1995 and subsequently succeeded by his son, King LETSIE III, in 1996. Constitutional government was restored in 1993 after seven years of military rule. In 1998, violent protests and a military mutiny following a contentious election prompted a brief but bloody intervention by South African and Batswana military forces under the aegis of the Southern African Development Community. Subsequent constitutional reforms restored relative political stability. Peaceful parliamentary elections were held in 2002, but the National Assembly elections of February 2007 were hotly contested and aggrieved parties disputed how the electoral law was applied to award proportional seats in the Assembly. In May 2012, competitive

elections involving 18 parties saw Prime Minister Motsoahae Thomas THABANE form a coalition government—the first in the country's history— that ousted the 14-year incumbent, Pakalitha MOSISILI, who peacefully transferred power the following month. MOSISILI returned to power in snap elections in February 2015 after the collapse of THABANE's coalition government and an alleged attempted military coup.

GEOGRAPHY

Location: Southern Africa, an enclave of South Africa

Geographic coordinates: 29 30 S, 28 30 E

Map references: Africa

Area: *total:* 30,355 sq km
land: 30,355 sq km
water: 0 sq km
country comparison to the world: 142

Area—comparative: slightly smaller than Maryland

Land boundaries: *total:* 1,106 km
border countries (1): South Africa 1,106 km

Coastline: 0 km (landlocked)

Maritime claims: none (landlocked)

Climate: temperate; cool to cold, dry winters; hot, wet summers

Terrain: mostly highland with plateaus, hills, and mountains

Elevation: *mean elevation:* 2,161 m

elevation extremes: *lowest point:* junction of the Orange and Makhaleng Rivers 1,400 m
highest point: Thabana Ntlenyana 3,482 m

Natural resources: water, agricultural and grazing land, diamonds, sand, clay, building stone

Land use: *agricultural land:* 76.1%
arable land: 10.1%
permanent crops: 0.1%
permanent pasture: 65.9%

forest: 1.5%
other: 22.4% (2011 est.)

Irrigated land: 30 sq km (2012)

Total renewable water resources: 3.02 cu km (2011)

Freshwater withdrawal (domestic/industrial/agricultural): *total:* 0.04 cu km/yr (46%/46%/9%)
per capita: 21.79 cu m/yr (2000)

Natural hazards: periodic droughts

Environment—current issues: population pressure forcing settlement in marginal areas results in overgrazing, severe soil erosion, and soil exhaustion; desertification; Highlands Water Project controls, stores, and redirects water to South Africa

Environment—international agreements: *party to:* Biodiversity, Climate Change, Climate Change-Kyoto Protocol, Desertification, Endangered Species, Hazardous Wastes, Law of the Sea, Marine Life Conservation, Ozone Layer Protection, Wetlands
signed, but not ratified: none of the selected agreements

Geography—note: landlocked, completely surrounded by South Africa; mountainous, more than 80% of the country is 1,800 m above sea level

PEOPLE AND SOCIETY

Nationality: *noun:* Mosotho (singular), Basòtho (plural)
adjective: Basotho

Ethnic groups: Sotho 99.7%, Europeans, Asians, and other 0.3%

Languages: Sesotho (official) (southern Sotho), English (official), Zulu, Xhosa

Religions: Christian 80%, indigenous beliefs 20%

Population: 1947,701

note: estimates for this country explicitly take into account the effects of excess mortality due to AIDS; this can result in lower life expectancy, higher infant mortality, higher death rates, lower population growth rates, and changes in the distribution of population by age and sex than would otherwise be expected (July 2015 est.)

country comparison to the world: 150

Age structure: *0–14 years:* 32.67% (male 319,592/female 316,672)

15–24 years: 19.73% (male 182,697/female 201,510)

25–54 years: 37.2% (male 354,193/female 370,287)

55–64 years: 4.98% (male 51,693/female 45,234)

65 years and over: 5.43% (male 53,706/female 52,117) (2015 est.)

Dependency ratios: *total dependency ratio:* 67.3%

youth dependency ratio: 60.3%

elderly dependency ratio: 6.9%

potential support ratio: 14.4% (2015 est.)

Median age: *total:* 23.8 years

male: 23.8 years

female: 23.8 years (2015 est.)

country comparison to the world: 162

Population growth rate: 0.32% (2015 est.)

country comparison to the world: 172

Birth rate: 25.47 births/1,000 population (2015 est.)

country comparison to the world: 49

Death rate: 14.89 deaths/1,000 population (2015 est.)

country comparison to the world: 1

Net migration rate: -7.36 migrant(s)/1,000 population (2015 est.)

country comparison to the world: 205

Urbanization: *urban Population:* 27.3% of total population (2015)

rate of urbanization: 3.05% annual rate of change (2010–15 est.)

Major urban areas—Population: MASERU (capital) 267,000 (2014)

Sex ratio: *at birth:* 1.03 male(s)/female

0–14 years: 1.01 male(s)/female

15–24 years: 0.91 male(s)/female

25–54 years: 0.96 male(s)/female

55–64 years: 1.14 male(s)/female

65 years and over: 1.03 male(s)/female

total population: 0.98 male(s)/female (2015 est.)

Mother's mean age at first birth: 21.2

note: median age at first birth among women 25–29 (2009 est.)

Maternal mortality rate: 487 deaths/100,000 live births (2015 est.)

country comparison to the world: 12

Infant mortality rate: *total:* 49.03 deaths/1,000 live births

male: 52.82 deaths/1,000 live births

female: 45.13 deaths/1,000 live births (2015 est.)

country comparison to the world: 37

Life expectancy at birth: *total population:* 52.86 years

male: 52.76 years

female: 52.97 years (2015 est.)

country comparison to the world: 215

Total fertility rate: 2.72 children born/woman (2015 est.)

country comparison to the world: 69

Contraceptive prevalence rate: 47% (2009/10)

Health expenditures: 11.5% of GDP (2013)

country comparison to the world: 10

Hospital bed density: 1.3 beds/1,000 population (2006)

Drinking water source:

improved:

urban: 94.6% of population

rural: 77% of population

total: 81.8% of population

unimproved:

urban: 5.4% of population

rural: 23% of population

total: 18.2% of population (2015 est.)

Sanitation facility access:

improved:

urban: 37.3% of population

rural: 27.6% of population

total: 30.3% of population

unimproved:

urban: 62.7% of population

rural: 72.4% of population

total: 69.7% of population (2015 est.)

HIV/AIDS—adult prevalence rate: 23.39% (2014 est.)

country comparison to the world: 3

HIV/AIDS—people living with HIV/AIDS: 314,600 (2014 est.)

country comparison to the world: 20

HIV/AIDS—deaths: 9,300 (2014 est.)

country comparison to the world: 25

Obesity—adult prevalence rate: 11.9% (2014)

country comparison to the world: 120

Children under the age of 5 years underweight: 10.3% (2014)

country comparison to the world: 54

Education expenditures: 13% of GDP (2008)

country comparison to the world: 1

Literacy: *definition:* age 15 and over can read and write

total population: 79.4%

male: 70.1%

female: 88.3% (2015 est.)

School life expectancy (primary to tertiary education): *total:* 11 years

male: 10 years

female: 11 years (2014)

Unemployment, youth ages 15–24: *total:* 34.4%

male: 29%

female: 41.9% (2013 est.)

country comparison to the world: 18

GOVERNMENT

Country name: *conventional long form:* Kingdom of Lesotho

conventional short form: Lesotho

local long form: Kingdom of Lesotho

local short form: Lesotho

former: Basutoland

etymology: the name translates as "Land of the Sesotho speakers"

Government type: parliamentary constitutional monarchy

Capital: *name:* Maseru

Geographic coordinates: 29 19 S, 27 29 E

time difference: UTC+2 (7 hours ahead of Washington, DC, during Standard Time)

Administrative divisions: 10 districts; Berea, Butha-Buthe, Leribe, Mafeteng, Maseru, Mohale's Hoek, Mokhotlong, Qacha's Nek, Quthing, Thaba-Tseka

Independence: 4 October 1966 (from the UK)

National holiday: Independence Day, 4 October (1966)

Constitution: previous 1959,1967; latest adopted 2 April 1993 (effectively restoring the 1967 version); amended several times, last in 2011 (2016)

Legal system: mixed legal system of English common law and Roman-Dutch law; judicial review of legislative acts in High Court and Court of Appeal

International law organization participation: accepts compulsory ICJ jurisdiction with reservations; accepts ICCt jurisdiction

Citizenship: *citizenship by birth:* yes

citizenship by descent: yes

dual citizenship recognized: no

residency requirement for naturalization: 5 years

Suffrage: 18 years of age; universal

Executive branch: *chief of state:* King LETSIE III (since 7 February 1996); note—King LETSIE III formerly occupied the throne from November 1990 to February 1995 while his father was in exile

head of government: *Prime Minister Pakalitha MOSISILI (since 18 March 2015)*

cabinet: Cabinet

elections/appointments: the monarchy is hereditary but under the terms of the constitution that came into effect after the March 1993 election, the monarch is a "living symbol of national unity" with no executive or legislative powers; under traditional law, the college of chiefs has the power to depose the monarch, to determine next in line of succession, or to serve as regent in the event that a successor is not of mature age; following legislative elections, the leader of the majority party or majority coalition in the Assembly automatically becomes prime minister

Legislative branch: *description:* bicameral Parliament consists of the Senate (33 seats; 22 principal chiefs and 11 other senators nominated by the king with the advice of the Council of State, a 13-member body of key government and nongovernment officials; members serve 5-year terms) and the National Assembly (120 seats; 80 members directly elected in single-seat constituencies by simple majority vote and 40 directly elected in single-seat constituencies by proportional representation vote; members serve 5-year terms)

elections: last held on 28 February 2015 (next to be held in 2020)

election results: National Assembly—percent of vote by party—DC 38.4%, ABC 37.8%, LCD 9.9%, BNP 5.5%, PFD 1.7%, RCL 1.2%, NIP 1.0%, MFP 0.6%, BCP 0.5%, LPC 0.3%, other 3.1%; seats by party—DC 47, ABC 46, LCD 12, BNP 7, PFD 2, RCL 2, NIP 1, MFP 1, BCP 1, LPC 1

Judicial branch: *highest court(s):* Court of Appeal (consists of the court president, such number of justices of appeal as set by Parliament, and the Chief Justice and the puisne judges of the High Court ex officio); High Court (consists of the chief justice and such number of puisne judges as set by Parliament); note—both the Court of Appeal and the High Court have jurisdiction in constitutional issues

495

judge selection and term of office: Court of Appeal president and High Court chief justice appointed by the monarch on the advice of the prime minister; puisne judges appointed by the monarch on advice of the Judicial Service Commission, an independent body of judicial officers and officials designated by the monarch; judges of both courts can serve until age 75

subordinate courts: Magistrate Courts; customary or traditional courts; Courts Martial

Political parties and leaders: All Basotho Convention or ABC [Motsoahae Thomas THABANE] Basotho Congress Party or BCP [Thulo MAHLAKENG]
Basotho National Party or BNP [Thesele MASERIBANE]
Democratic Congress or DC [Pakalitha MOSISILI]
Lesotho Congress for Democracy or LCD [Mothetjoa METSING]
Lesotho Peoples Congress or LPC [Molahlehi LETLOTLO]
Marematlou Freedom Party or MFP [Vincent MALEBO]
National Independent Party or NIP [Kimetso MATHABA]
Popular Front for Democracy of PFD [Lekhetho RAKUOANE]
Reformed Congress of Lesotho or RCL [Keketso RANTSO]

Political pressure groups and leaders: Media Institute of Southern Africa, Lesotho chapter [Tsebo MATASA] (pushes for media freedom)

International organization participation: ACP, AfDB, AU, C, CD, FAO, G-77, IAEA, IBRD, ICAO, ICCt, ICRM, IDA, IFAD, IFC, IFRCS, ILO, IMF, Interpol, IOC, IOM, IPU, ISO (correspondent), ITU, MIGA, NAM, OPCW, SACU, SADC, UN, UNAMID, UNCTAD, UNESCO, UNHCR, UNIDO, UNWTO, UPU, WCO, WFTU (NGOs), WHO, WIPO, WMO, WTO

Diplomatic representation in the US: *chief of mission:* Ambassador Eliachim Molapi SEBATANE (since 2 November 2011)
chancery: 2511 Massachusetts Avenue NW, Washington, DC 20008
telephone: [1] (202) 797-5533
FAX: [1] (202) 234-6815

Diplomatic representation from the US: *chief of mission:* Ambassador Matthew T. HARRINGTON (since October 2014)
embassy: 254 Kingsway Road, Maseru West (Consular Section)
mailing address: P.O. Box 333, Maseru 100, Lesotho
telephone: [266] 22312666
FAX: [266] 22310116

Flag description: three horizontal stripes of blue (top), white, and green in the proportions of 3: 4: 3; the colors represent rain, peace, and prosperity respectively; centered in the white stripe is a black Basotho hat representing the indigenous people; the flag was unfurled in October 2006 to celebrate 40 years of independence

National symbol(s): mokorotio (Basotho hat); national colors: blue, white, green, black

National anthem: *name:* "Lesotho fatse la bo ntat'a rona" (Lesotho, Land of Our Fathers)
lyrics/music: Francois COILLARD/Ferdinand-Samuel LAUR

note: adopted 1967; music derives from an 1823 Swiss songbook

ECONOMY

Economy—overview: Small, mountainous, and completely landlocked by South Africa, Lesotho depends on a narrow economic base of textile manufacturing, agriculture, remittances, and regional customs revenue. About three-fourths of the people live in rural areas and engage in animal herding and subsistence agriculture, although Lesotho produces less than 20% of the nation's demand for food. Agriculture is vulnerable to weather and climate variability.

Lesotho relies on South Africa for much of its economic activity; Lesotho imports 90% of the goods it consumes from South Africa, including most agricultural inputs. Households depend heavily on remittances from family members working in South Africa, in mines, on farms, and as domestic workers, though mining employment has declined substantially since the 1990s. Lesotho is a member of the Southern Africa Customs Union (SACU), and revenues from SACU accounted for roughly 44% of total government revenue in 2014. The South African Government also pays royalties for water transferred to South Africa from a dam and reservoir system in Lesotho. However, the government continues to strengthen its tax system to reduce dependency on customs duties and other transfers.

The government maintains a large presence in the economy—government consumption accounted for 37% of GDP in 2014 and the government remains Lesotho's largest employer. Access to credit remains a problem for the private sector. Lesotho's large st private employer is the textile and garment industry -approximately 36,000 Basotho, mainly women, work in factories producing garments for export to South Africa and the US. Diamond mining in Lesotho has grown in recent years and may contribute 8.5% to GDP by 2015, according to current forecasts.

GDP (purchasing power parity): $5.77 billion (2015 est.)
$5.631 billion (2014 est.)
$5.443 billion (2013 est.)
note: data are in 2015 US dollars
country comparison to the world: 171

GDP (official exchange rate): $2.032 billion (2015 est.)

GDP—real growth rate: 2.5% (2015 est.) 3.4% (2014 est.)
3.6% (2013 est.)
country comparison to the world: 120

GDP—per capita (PPP): $3,000 (2015 est.)
$2,900 (2014 est.)
$2,800 (2013 est.)
note: data are in 2015 US dollars
country comparison to the world: 189

Gross national saving: 27% of GDP (2015 est.)
24.8% of GDP (2014 est.)
24.4% of GDP (2013 est.)
country comparison to the world: 38

GDP—composition, by end use:
household consumption: 79.7%

government consumption: 32%
investment in fixed capital: 29.6%
investment in inventories: -3.9%
exports of goods and services: 39%
imports of goods and services: -76.4% (2015 est.)

GDP—composition, by sector of origin: *agriculture:* 5.6%
industry: 29.8%
services: 64.6% (2013 est.)

Agriculture—products: corn, wheat, pulses, sorghum, barley; livestock

Industries: food, beverages, textiles, apparel assembly, handicrafts, construction, tourism

Industrial production growth rate: 0.8% (2015 est.)
country comparison to the world: 151

Labor force: 899,100 (2015 est.)
country comparison to the world: 147

Labor force—by occupation: *agriculture:* 86%
industry and services: 14%
note: most of the resident population is engaged in subsistence agriculture; roughly 35% of the active male wage earners work in South Africa (2002 est.)

Unemployment rate: 28.1% (2014 est.)
25% (2008 est.)
country comparison to the world: 183

Population below poverty line: 57.1% (2010 est.)

Household income or consumption by percentage share: *lowest:* 10%: 1%
highest: 10%: 39.4% (2003)

Distribution of family income—Gini index: 63.2 (1995)
56 (1986–87)
country comparison to the world: 1

Budget: *revenues:* $1.161 billion
expenditures: $1.256 billion (2015 est.)
Taxes and other revenues: 57% of GDP (2015 est.)
country comparison to the world: 7

Budget surplus (+) or deficit (–): -4.7% of GDP (2015 est.)
country comparison to the world: 162

Public debt: 53.4% of GDP (2015 est.)
47.8% of GDP (2014)

Fiscal year: 1 April—31 March

Inflation rate (consumer prices): 4.9% (2015 est.)
5.9% (2014)
country comparison to the world: 170

Central bank discount rate: 6.75% (2 February 2016)
6.25% (31 December 2015)
country comparison to the world: 29

Commercial bank prime lending rate: 10.5% (31 December 2015 est.)
10.34% (31 December 2014 est.)
country comparison to the world: 80

Stock of narrow money: $270.1 million (31 December 2015 est.)
$209.8 million (31 December 2014 est.)
country comparison to the world: 172

Stock of broad money: $535.4 million (31 December 2015 est.)
$569.1 million (31 December 2014 est.)
country comparison to the world: 172

Stock of domestic credit: $14.06 million (31 December 2015 est.)
$14.77 million (31 December 2014 est.)

country comparison to the world: 187
Current account balance: -$54 million (2015 est.)
-$176 million (2014 est.)
country comparison to the world: 64
Exports: $786.7 million (2015 est.) $815 million (2014 est.)
country comparison to the world: 167
Exports—commodities: manufactures (clothing, footwear), wool and mohair, food and live animals, electricity, water, diamonds
Imports: $1.671 billion (2015 est.) $1.837 billion (2014 est.)
country comparison to the world: 169
Imports—commodities: food; building materials, vehicles, machinery, medicines, petroleum products
Reserves of foreign exchange and gold: $980.8 million (31 December 2015 est.)
$1.071 billion (31 December 2014 est.)
country comparison to the world: 131
Debt—external: $900.4 million (31 December 2014 est.)
$885.2 million (31 December 2013 est.)
country comparison to the world: 167
Stock of direct foreign investment—at home: $427.4 million (31 December 2015 est.)
$370.6 million (31 December 2014 est.)
country comparison to the world: 115
Exchange rates: maloti (LSL) per US dollar—
12.58 (2015 est.)
10.85 (2014 est.)
10.85 (2013 est.)
8.2 (2012 est.)
7.26 (2011 est.)

ENERGY

Electricity—production: 486 million kWh (2012 est.)
country comparison to the world: 162
Electricity—consumption: 707 million kWh (2012 est.)
country comparison to the world: 163
Electricity—exports: 0 kWh (2013 est.)
country comparison to the world: 162
Electricity—imports: 255 million kWh (2012 est.)
country comparison to the world: 85
Electricity—installed generating capacity: 80,000 kW (2012 est.)
country comparison to the world: 180
Electricity—from fossil fuels: 0% of total installed capacity (2012 est.)
country comparison to the world: 214
Electricity—from nuclear fuels: 0% of total installed capacity (2012 est.)
country comparison to the world: 130
Electricity—from hydroelectric plants: 100% of total installed capacity (2012 est.)
country comparison to the world: 1
Electricity—from other renewable sources: 0% of total installed capacity (2012 est.)
country comparison to the world: 195
Crude oil—production: 0 bbl/day (2014 est.)
country comparison to the world: 159
Crude oil—exports: 0 bbl/day (2012 est.)
country comparison to the world: 152
Crude oil—imports: 0 bbl/day (2012 est.)
country comparison to the world: 87

Crude oil—proved reserves: 0 bbl (1 January 2015 est.)
country comparison to the world: 158
Refined petroleum products—production: 0 bbl/day (2012 est.)
country comparison to the world: 203
Refined petroleum products—consumption: 1,600 bbl/day (2013 est.)
country comparison to the world: 192
Refined petroleum products—exports: 0 bbl/day (2012 est.)
country comparison to the world: 197
Refined petroleum products—imports: 1,553 bbl/day (2012 est.)
country comparison to the world: 187
Natural gas—production: 0 cu m (2013 est.)
country comparison to the world: 214
Natural gas—consumption: 0 cu m (2013 est.)
country comparison to the world: 165
Natural gas—exports: 0 cu m (2013 est.)
country comparison to the world: 136
Natural gas—imports: 0 cu m (2013 est.)
country comparison to the world: 93
Natural gas—proved reserves: 0 cu m (1 January 2014 est.)
country comparison to the world: 162
Carbon dioxide emissions from consumption of energy: 270,100 Mt (2012 est.)
country comparison to the world: 191

COMMUNICATIONS

Telephones—fixed lines: *total subscriptions:* 51,200
subscriptions per 100 inhabitants: 3 (2014 est.)
161
country comparison to the world: 161
Telephones—mobile cellular: *total:* 2.1 million
subscriptions per 100 inhabitants: 110 (2014 est.)
country comparison to the world: 151
Telephone system: *general assessment:* rudimentary system consisting of a modest number of landlines, a small microwave radio relay system, and a small radiotelephone communication system; mobile-cellular telephone system is expanding
domestic: privatized in 2001, Telecom Lesotho was tasked with providing an additional 50,000 fixed-line connections within five years, a target not met; mobile-cellular service dominates the market and is expanding with a subscribership roughly 65 per 100 persons in 2011; rural services are scant
international: country code—266; satellite earth station—1 Intelsat (Atlantic Ocean) (2011)
Broadcast media: 1 state-owned TV station and 2 state-owned radio stations; government controls most private broadcast media; satellite TV subscription service available; transmissions of multiple international broadcasters obtainable (2008)
Radio broadcast stations: AM 1, FM 3, shortwave 1 (2007)
Television broadcast stations: 1 (2007)
Internet country code: .ls
Internet hosts: 11,030 (2012)
country comparison to the world: 131
Internet users: *total:* 102,000
percent of population: 5.3% (2014 est.)
country comparison to the world: 169

TRANSPORTATION

Airports: 24 (2013)
country comparison to the world: 132
Airports—with paved runways: *total:* 3
over 3,047 m: 1
914 to 1,523 m: 1
under 914 m: 1 (2013)
Airports—with unpaved runways: *total:* 21
914 to 1,523 m: 5
under 914 m: 16 (2013)
Road ways: *total:* 5,940 km
paved: 1,069 km
unpaved: 4,871 km (2011)
country comparison to the world: 151

MILITARY AND SECURITY

Military branches: Lesotho Defense Force (LDF): Army (includes Air Wing) (2012)
Military service age and obligation: 18–24 years of age for voluntary military service; no conscription; women serve as commissioned officers (2012)
Military expenditures:
1.94% of GDP (2012)
2.3% of GDP (2011)
1.94% of GDP (2010)
country comparison to the world: 43
Military—note: Lesotho's declared policy for its military is the maintenance of the country's sovereignty and the preservation of internal security; in practice, external security is guaranteed by South Africa

TRANSNATIONAL ISSUES

Disputes—international: South Africa has placed military units to assist police operations along the border of Lesotho, Zimbabwe, and Mozambique to control smuggling, poaching, and illegal migration
Trafficking in persons: *current situation:* Lesotho is a source, transit, and destination country for women and children subjected to forced labor and sex trafficking and for men subjected to forced labor; in Lesotho and South Africa, Basotho women and children are subjected to domestic servitude, and Basotho children increasingly endure commercial sexual exploitation; some Basotho men who voluntarily migrate to South Africa for work become victims of forced labor in agriculture and mining or are coerced into committing crimes; foreign nationals continue to traffic fellow citizens in Lesotho

tier rating: Tier 2 Watch List—Lesotho does not fully comply with the minimum standards for the elimination of trafficking; however, it is making significant efforts to do so; in 2014, Lesotho was granted a waiver from an otherwise required downgrade to Tier 3 because its government has a written plan that, if implemented would constitute making significant efforts to bring itself into compliance with the minimum standards for the elimination of trafficking; the government failed to initiate any prosecutions against alleged traffickers and has not convicted any offenders under the 2011 anti-trafficking act, which remains unimplemented for a fifth year; authorities did not develop formal victim identification and referral procedures, did not establish victim care centers, as required under the 2011 anti-trafficking act, and did not support NGOs offering victims protective services (2015)

LIBERIA

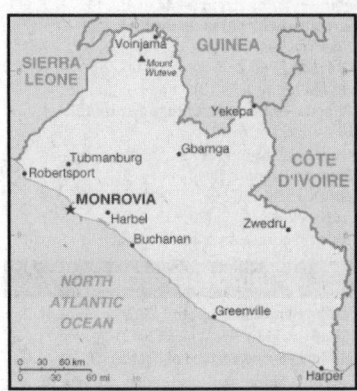

INTRODUCTION

Background: Settlement of freed slaves from the US in what is today Liberia began in 1822; by 1847, the Americo-Liberians were able to establish a republic. William TUBMAN, president from 1944–71, did much to promote foreign investment and to bridge the economic, social, and political gaps between the descendants of the original settlers and the inhabitants of the interior. In 1980, a military coup led by Samuel DOE ushered in a decade of authoritarian rule. In December 1989, Charles TAYLOR launched a rebellion against DOE's regime that led to a prolonged civil war in which DOE was killed. A period of relative peace in 1997 allowed for an election that brought TAYLOR to power, but major fighting resumed in 2000. An August 2003 peace agreement ended the war and prompted the resignation of former president Charles TAYLOR, who was convicted by the UN -backed Special Court for Sierra Leone in The Hague for his involvement in Sierra Leone's civil war. After two years of rule by a transitional government, democratic elections in late 2005 brought President Ellen JOHNSON SIRLEAF to power. She subsequently won reelection in 2011 and remains challenged to rebuild Liberia's economy, particularly following the 2014–15 Ebola epidemic, and to reconcile a nation still recovering from 14 years of fighting. The UN Security Council in September 2015 passed Resolution 2239, which renewed the mandate for the UN Mission in Liberia for another year. in July 2016, the UN handed over peacekeeping responsibility to Liberia and reduced the UN troop presence, which now serves a support role.

GEOGRAPHY

Location: Western Africa, bordering the North Atlantic Ocean, between Cote d'I voire and Sierra Leone

Geographic coordinates: 6 30 N, 9 30 W

Map references: Africa

Area: total: 111,369 sq km

land: 96,320 sq km

water: 15,049 sq km

country comparison to the world: 104

Area—comparative: slightly larger than Tennessee

Land boundaries: total: 1,667 km

border countries (3): Guinea 590 km, Cote d'Ivoire 778 km, Sierra Leone 299 km

Coastline: 579 km

Maritime claims: territorial sea: 200 nm

Climate: tropical; hot, humid; dry winters with hot days and cool to cold nights; wet, cloudy summers with frequent heavy showers

Terrain: mostly flat to rolling coastal plains rising to rolling plateau and low mountains in northeast

Elevation: mean elevation: 243 m

elevation extremes: lowest point: Atlantic Ocean 0 m

highest point: Mount Wuteve 1,380 m

Natural resources: iron ore, timber, diamonds, gold, hydropower

Land use: agricultural land: 28.1%

arable land: 5.2%

permanent crops: 2.1%

permanent pasture: 20.8%

forest: 44.6%

other: 27.3% (2011 est.)

Irrigated land: 30 sq km (2012)

Total renewable water resources: 232 cu km (2011)

Freshwater withdrawal (domestic/industrial/agricultural): total: 0.13 cu km/yr (55%/37%/8%)

per capita: 43.66 cu m/yr (2005)

Natural hazards: dust-laden harmattan winds blow from the Sahara (December to March)

Environment—current issues: tropical rain forest deforestation; soil erosion; loss of biodiversity; pollution of coastal waters from oil residue and raw sewage

Environment—international agreements: party to: Biodiversity, Climate Change, Climate Change-Kyoto Protocol, Desertification, Endangered Species, Hazardous Wastes, Law of the Sea, Ozone Layer Protection, Ship Pollution, Tropical Timber 83, Tropical Timber 94, Wetlands

signed, but not ratified: Environm ental Modification, Marine Life Conservation

Geography—note: facing the Atlantic Ocean, the coastline is characterized by lagoons, m angrove swam ps, and river-deposited sandbars; the inland grassy plateau supports lim ited agriculture

PEOPLE AND SOCIETY

Nationality: noun: Liberian(s)

adjective: Liberian

Ethnic groups: Kpelle 20.3%, Bassa 13.4%, Grebo 10%, Gio 8%, Mano 7.9%, Kru 6%, Lorma 5.1%, Kissi 4.8%, Gola 4.4%, other 20.1% (2008 Census)

Languages: English 20% (official), some 20 ethnic group languages few of which can be written or used in correspondence

Religions: Christian 85.6%, Muslim 12.2%, Traditional 0.6%, other 0.2%, none 1.4% (2008 Census)

Population: 4,195,666 (July 2015 est.)

country comparison to the world: 128

Age structure: 0–14 years: 42.75% (male 904,495/female 889,198)

15–24 years: 18.3% (male 376,224/female 391,568)

25–54 years: 31.51% (male 658,291/female 663,954)

55–64 years: 4.3% (male 87,606/female 92,831)

65 years and over: 3.13% (male 64,697/female 66,802) (2015 est.)

Dependency ratios: total dependency ratio: 82.9%

youth dependency ratio: 77.4%

elderly dependency ratio: 5.5%

potential support ratio: 18.2% (2015 est.)

Median age: total: 18.1 years

male: 17.9 years

female: 18.3 years (2015 est.)

country comparison to the world: 212

Population growth rate: 2.47% (2015 est.)

country comparison to the world: 24

Birth rate: 34.41 births/1,000 population (2015 est.)

country comparison to the world: 26

Death rate: 9.69 deaths/1,000 population (2015 est.)

country comparison to the world: 51

Net migration rate: 0 migrant(s)/1,000 population (2015 est.)

country comparison to the world: 91

Urbanization: urban Population: 49.7% of total population (2015)

rate of urbanization: 3.36% annual rate of change (2010–15 est.)

Major urban areas—Population: MONROVIA (capital) 1.264 million (2015)

Sex ratio: at birth: 1.03 male(s)/female

0–14 years: 1.02 male(s)/female

15–24 years: 0.96 male(s)/female

25–54 years: 0.99 male(s)/female

55–64 years: 0.94 male(s)/female

65 years and over: 0.97 male(s)/female

total population: 0.99 male(s)/female (2015 est.)

Mother's mean age at first birth: 19

note: median age at first birth among women 20–24 (2013 est.)

Maternal mortality rate: 725 deaths/100,000 live births (2015 est.)

country comparison to the world: 8

Infant mortality rate: total: 67.5 deaths/1,000 live births

male: 71.71 deaths/1,000 live births

female: 63.16 deaths/1,000 live births (2015 est.)

country comparison to the world: 15

Life expectancy at birth: total population: 58.6 years

male: 56.94 years

female: 60.32 years (2015 est.)

country comparison to the world: 201
Total fertility rate: 4.7 children born/woman (2015 est.)
country comparison to the world: 21
Contraceptive prevalence rate: 20.2% (2013)
Health expenditures: 10% of GDP (2013)
country comparison to the world: 3
Physicians density: 0.01 physicians/1,000 population (2008)
Hospital bed density: 0.8 beds/1,000 population (2010)
Drinking water source:
improved:
urban: 88.6% of population
rural: 62.6% of population
total: 75.6% of population
unimproved:
urban: 11.4% of population
rural: 37.4% of population
total: 24.4% of population (2015 est.)
Sanitation facility access:
improved:
urban: 28% of population
rural: 5.9% of population
total: 16.9% of population
unimproved:
urban: 72% of population
rural: 94.1% of population
total: 83.1% of population (2015 est.)
HIV/AIDS—adult prevalence rate: 1.17% (2014 est.)
country comparison to the world: 39
HIV/AIDS—people living with HIV/AIDS: 33,100 (2014 est.)
country comparison to the world: 66
HIV/AIDS—deaths: 2,000 (2014 est.)
country comparison to the world: 56
Major infectious diseases: *degree of risk:* very high
food or waterborne diseases: bacterial and protozoal diarrhea, hepatitis A, and typhoid fever
vectorborne diseases: malaria, dengue fever, and yellow fever
water contact disease: schistosomiasis
aerosolized dust or soil contact disease: Lassa fever
animal contact disease: rabies (2013)
Obesity—adult prevalence rate: 5.8% (2014)
country comparison to the world: 161
Children under the age of 5 years underweight: 15.3% (2013)
country comparison to the world: 28
Education expenditures: 2.8% of GDP (2012)
country comparison to the world: 144
Literacy: *definition:* age 15 and over can read and write
total population: 47.6%
male: 62.4%
female: 32.8% (2015 est.)
Child labor—children ages 5–14: *total number:* 177,160
percentage: 21% (2007 est.)
Unemployment, youth ages 15–24: *total:* 5.1%
male: 3.4%
female: 6.6% (2010 est.)
country comparison to the world: 126

GOVERNMENT

Country name: *conventional long form:* Republic of Liberia
conventional short form: Liberia
etymology: name derives from the Latin word "liber" meaning "free"; so named because the nation was created as a homeland for liberated African-American slaves
Government type: presidential republic
Capital: *name:* Monrovia
Geographic coordinates: 6 18 N, 10 48 W
time difference: UTC 0 (5 hours ahead of Washington, DC, during Standard Time)
Administrative divisions: 15 counties; Bomi, Bong, Gbarpolu, Grand Bassa, Grand Cape Mount, Grand Gedeh, Grand Kru, Lofa, Margibi, Maryland, Montserrado, Nimba, River Cess, River Gee, Sinoe
Independence: 26 July 1847
National holiday: Independence Day, 26 July (1847)
Constitution: previous 1847 (at independence); latest drafted 19 October 1983, revised version adopted by referendum 3 July 1984, effective 6 January 1986; amended 2011; note—a series of amendment proposals approved by the Constitution Review Conference in early 2015 are pending government review (2016)
Legal system: mixed legal system of common law (based on Anglo-American law) and customary law
International law organization participation: accepts compulsory ICJ jurisdiction with reservations; accepts ICCt jurisdiction
Citizenship: *citizenship by birth:* no
citizenship by descent only: at least one parent must be a citizen of Liberia
dual citizenship recognized: no
residency requirement for naturalization: 2 years
Suffrage: 18 years of age; universal
Executive branch: *chief of state:* President Ellen JOHNSON SIRLEAF (since 16 January 2006); Vice President Joseph BOAKAI (since 16 January 2006); note—the president is both chief of state and head of government
head of government: President Ellen JOHNSON SIRLEAF (since 16 January 2006); Vice President Joseph BOAKAI (since 16 January 2006)
cabinet: Cabinet appointed by the president, confirmed by the Senate
elections/appointments: president directly elected by absolute majority popular vote in 2 rounds if needed for a 6-year term (eligible for a second term); election last held on 11 October and 8 November 2011 (next to be held in 2017)
election results: Ellen JOHNSON SIRLEAF reelected president; percent of vote in second round—Ellen JOHNSON SIRLEAF (UP) 90.7%, Winston TUBMAN (NDPL) 9.3%
Legislative branch: *description:* bicameral National Assembly consists of the Senate (30 seats; members directly elected in 15 two-seat constituencies by simple majority vote to serve 9-year staggered terms with half the membership renewed at 3- and 6-year intervals; eligible for a second term; and the House of Representatives (73 seats; members directly elected in single-seat constituencies by simple majority vote to serve 6-year terms; eligible for a second term)
elections: Senate—last held on 20 December 2014 (originally scheduled for 14 October 2014, but postponed due to Ebola-virus epidemic; next to be held in fall 2020); House of Representatives—last held on 11 October 2011 (next to be held in 2017)
election results: Senate—percent of vote by party—CDC 29.8%, LP 11.5%, NPP 6.1%, PUP 4.9%, NDC 1.3%, other parties 11.8%, independent 24.3%; seats by party—UP 4, CDC 2, LP 2, ANC 1, NDC 1, NPP 1, PUP 1, independent 3; House of Representatives—percent of vote by party—UP 17.8%, CDC 12.8%, LP 9.2%, NDC 5.7%, LTP 4.5%, PUP 3.9%, NPP 3.3%, MPC 2.4%, LDP 1.0%, NRP 0.8%, other parties 16.8% independent 19.7%; seats by party—UP 24, CDC 11, LP 7, PUP 6, NDC 5, APD 3, NPP 3, MPC 2, LDP 1, LTP 1, NRP 1, independent 9
Judicial branch: *highest court(s):* Supreme Court (consists of a chief justice and 4 associate justices); note—the Supreme Court has jurisdiction for all constitutional cases
judge selection and term of office: chief justice and associate justices appointed by the president of Liberia with consent of the Senate; judges can serve until age 70
subordinate courts: judicial circuit courts; special courts including criminal, civil, labor, traffic; magistrate and traditional or customary courts
Political parties and leaders: Alliance for Peace and Democracy or APD [Marcus S. G. DAHN]
Alternative National Congress or ANC [Orishil GOULD]
Congress for Democratic Change or CDC [George WEAH]
Liberia Destiny Party or LDP [Nathaniel BARNES]
Liberia Transformation Party or LTP [Julius SUKU]
Liberty Party or LP [J. Fonati KOFFA]
Movement for Progressive Change or MPC [Simeon FREEMAN]
National Democratic Coalition or NDC [Dew MAYSON]
National Democratic Party of Liberia or NDPL [D. Nyandeh SIEH]
National Patriotic Party or NPP
National Reformist Party or NRP [Maximillian T. W. DIABE]
National Union for Democratic Progress or NUDP [Victor BARNEY]
People's Unification Party [Isobe GBORKORKOLLIE]
Unity Party or UP [Varney SHERMAN]
Political pressure groups and leaders: *other:* demobilized former military officers
International organization participation: ACP, AfDB, AU, ECO WAS, EITI (compliant country), FAO, G-77, IAEA, IBRD, ICAO, ICC (NGOs), ICCt, ICRM, IDA, IFAD, IFC, IFRCS, ILO, IMF, IMO, IMSO, Interpol, IOC, IOM, ISO

499

(correspondent), ITU, ITUC (NGOs), MIGA, MINUSMA, NAM, OPCW, UN, UNCTAD, UNESCO, UNIDO, UNWTO, UPU, WCO, WFTU (NGOs), WHO, WIPO, WMO, WTO (observer)

Diplomatic representation in the US: *chief of mission:* Ambassador Jeremiah Congbeh SULUNTEH (since 25 April 2012)
chancery: 520116th Street NW, Washington, DC 20011
telephone: [1] (202) 723-0437
FAX: [1] (202) 723-0436
consulate(s) general: New York

Diplomatic representation from the US: *chief of mission:* Ambassador Christine A. ELDER (since 23 June 2016)
embassy: U.S. Embassy, P.O. Box 98,502 Benson Street, Monrovia
mailing address: P.O. Box 98, Monrovia
telephone: [231] 77-677-7000
FAX: [231] 77-677-7370

Flag description: 11 equal horizontal stripes of red (top and bottom) alternating with white; a white five-pointed star appears on a blue square in the upper hoist-side corner; the stripes symbolize the signatories of the Liberian Declaration of Independence; the blue square represents the African mainland, and the star represents the freedom granted to the ex-slaves; according to the constitution, the blue color signifies liberty, justice, and fidelity, the white color purity, cleanliness, and guilelessness, and the red color steadfastness, valor, and fervor
note: the design is based on the US flag

National symbol(s): white star; national colors: red, white, blue

National anthem: *name:* "All Hail, Liberia Hail!"
lyrics/music: Daniel Bashiel WARNER/Olmstead LUCA
note: lyrics adopted 1847, music adopted 1860; the anthem's author later became the third president of Liberia

ECONOMY

Economy—overview: Liberia is a low income country that relies heavily on foreign assistance. It is richly endowed with water, mineral resources, forests, and a climate favorable to agriculture. Its principal exports are iron ore, rubber, gold and timber. The government has attempted to revive raw timber extraction and is encouraging oil exploration. In the 1990s and early 2000s, civil war and government mismanagement destroyed much of Liberia's economy, especially infrastructure in and around the capital. With the conclusion of fighting and the installation of a democratically elected government in 2006, businesses that had fled the country began to return. The country achieved high growth due to 2010–13 due to favorable world prices for its commodities. However, in 2014 as the Ebolavirus began to spread, the economy declined and many businesses departed, taking capital and expertise with them. The epidemic forced the government to divert scarce resources to combat the spread of the virus, reducing funds available for

needed public investment. The cost of addressing the Ebola epidemic will weigh heavily on public finances at the same time decreased economic activity reduces government revenue, although higher donor support will partly offset this loss. Revitalizing the economy in the future will depend on increasing investment and trade, higher global commodity prices, sustained foreign aid and remittances, development of infrastructure and institutions, and maintaining political stability and security.

GDP (purchasing power parity): $3.749 billion (2015 est.)
$3.748 billion (2014 est.)
$3.723 billion (2013 est.)
note: data are in 2015 US dollars
country comparison to the world: 179

GDP (official exchange rate): $2.035 billion (2015 est.)

GDP—real growth rate: 0% (2015 est.)
0.7% (2014 est.)
8.7% (2013 est.)
country comparison to the world: 195

GDP—per capita (PPP): $900 (2015 est.)
$900 (2014 est.)
$900 (2013 est.)
note: data are in 2015 US dollars
country comparison to the world: 225

Gross national saving: NA% (2014 est.)
-35% of GDP (2013 est.)
-2.3% of GDP (2012 est.)

GDP—composition, by end use:
household consumption: 116.3%
government consumption: 20.7%
investment in fixed capital: 25.4%
investment in inventories: -5.2%
exports of goods and services: 32.4%
imports of goods and services: -89.5% (2015 est.)

GDP—composition, by sector of origin:
agriculture: 36%
industry: 16%
services: 48% (2012 est.)

Agriculture—products: rubber, coffee, cocoa, rice, cassava (manioc, tapioca), palm oil, sugarcane, bananas; sheep, goats; timber

Industries: mining (iron ore), rubber processing, palm oil processing, timber, diamonds

Industrial production growth rate: -0.5% (2015 est.)
country comparison to the world: 168

Labor force: 1.6 million (2015 est.)
country comparison to the world: 129

Labor force—by occupation: *agriculture:* 70%
industry: 8%
services: 22% (2000 est.)

Unemployment rate: 85% (2003 est.)
country comparison to the world: 206

Population below poverty line: 63.8% (2007 est.)

Household income or consumption by percentage share: *lowest:* 10%: 2.4%
highest: 10%: 30.1% (2007)

Budget: *revenues:* $681.5 million
expenditures: $809.2 million (2015 est.)
Taxes and other revenues: 33.8% of GDP (2015 est.)

country comparison to the world: 68

Budget surplus (+) or deficit (–): -6.3% of GDP (2015 est.)
country comparison to the world: 186

Public debt: 6.7% of GDP (2015 est.)
0.5% of GDP (2014 est.)
country comparison to the world: 175

Fiscal year: calendar year

Inflation rate (consumer prices): 7.7% (2015 est.)
9.9% (2014 est.)
country comparison to the world: 198

Commercial bank prime lending rate: 14.2% (31 December 2015 est.)
13.5% (31 December 2014 est.)
country comparison to the world: 47

Stock of narrow money: $444.1 million (31 December 2015 est.)
$449.7 million (31 December 2014 est.)
country comparison to the world: 167

Stock of broad money: $738.7 million (31 December 2014 est.)
$656 million (31 December 2013 est.)
country comparison to the world: 175

Stock of domestic credit: $558.3 million (31 December 2015 est.)
$678.8 million (31 December 2014 est.)
country comparison to the world: 168

Market value of publicly traded shares: $NA

Current account balance: -$801 million (2015 est.)
-$635 million (2014 est.)
country comparison to the world: 113

Exports: $440.1 million (2015 est.)
$468.2 million (2014 est.)
country comparison to the world: 177

Exports—commodities: rubber, timber, iron, diamonds, cocoa, coffee

Exports—partners: Poland 32.9%, China 20.8%, India 9.3%, US 5.1%, Greece 4.7%, France 4.3% (2015)

Imports: $1.21 billion (2015 est.)
$1.052 billion (2014 est.)
country comparison to the world: 175

Imports—commodities: fuels, chemicals, machinery, transportation equipment, manufactured goods; foodstuffs

Imports—partners: Singapore 28.7%, China 16%, South Korea 15.3%, Japan 10.3%, Philippines 6.6% (2015)

Debt—external: $652.2 million (31 December 2014 est.)
$541.5 million (31 December 2013 est.)
country comparison to the world: 174

Stock of direct foreign investment—at home: $17.01 billion (31 December 2014 est.)
$16.56 billion (31 December 2013 est.)
country comparison to the world: 83

Stock of direct foreign investment—abroad: $201 million (31 December 2013 est.)
$201 million (31 December 2012 est.)
country comparison to the world: 91

Exchange rates: Liberian dollars (LRD) per US dollar—
86.13 (2015 est.)
83.893 (2014 est.)
83.893 (2013 est.)
73.52 (2012 est.)

72.227 (2011 est.)

ENERGY

Electricity—production: 300 million kWh (2012 est.)
country comparison to the world: 179
Electricity—consumption: 276.9 million kWh (2012 est.)
country comparison to the world: 183
Electricity—exports: 0 kWh (2013 est.)
country comparison to the world: 161
Electricity—imports: 0 kWh (2013 est.)
country comparison to the world: 170
Electricity—installed generating capacity: 23,000 kW (2012 est.)
country comparison to the world: 202
Electricity—from fossil fuels: 100% of total installed capacity (2012 est.)
country comparison to the world: 17
Electricity—from nuclear fuels: 0% of total installed capacity (2012 est.)
country comparison to the world: 129
Electricity—from hydroelectric plants: 0% of total installed capacity (2012 est.)
country comparison to the world: 182
Electricity—from other renewable sources: 0% of total installed capacity (2012 est.)
country comparison to the world: 194
Crude oil—production: 0 bbl/day (2014 est.)
country comparison to the world: 158
Crude oil—exports: 0 bbl/day (2012 est.)
country comparison to the world: 151
Crude oil—imports: 0 bbl/day (2012 est.)
country comparison to the world: 214
Crude oil—proved reserves: 0 bbl (1 January 2015 est.)
country comparison to the world: 157
Refined petroleum products—production: 0 bbl/day (2012 est.)
country comparison to the world: 202
Refined petroleum products—consumption: 3,750 bbl/day (2013 est.)
country comparison to the world: 176
Refined petroleum products—exports: 0 bbl/day (2012 est.)
country comparison to the world: 196
Refined petroleum products—imports: 3,750 bbl/day (2012 est.)
country comparison to the world: 168
Natural gas—production: 0 cu m (2013 est.)
country comparison to the world: 213
Natural gas—consumption: 0 cu m (2013 est.)
country comparison to the world: 164
Natural gas—exports: 0 cu m (2013 est.)
country comparison to the world: 135
Natural gas—imports: 0 cu m (2013 est.)
country comparison to the world: 92
Natural gas—proved reserves: 0 cu m (1 January 2014 est.)
country comparison to the world: 161
Carbon dioxide emissions from consumption of energy: 541,600 Mt (2012 est.)
country comparison to the world: 179

COMMUNICATIONS

Telephones—fixed lines: *total subscriptions:* 10,000
subscriptions per 100 inhabitants: less than 1 (2014 est.)
country comparison to the world: 198
Telephones—mobile cellular: *total:* 3.2 million
subscriptions per 100 inhabitants: 79 (2014 est.)
country comparison to the world: 136
Telephone system: *general assessment:* the limited services available are found almost exclusively in the capital, Monrovia; fixed-line service stagnant and extremely limited; telephone coverage extended to a number of other towns and rural areas by four mobile-cellular network operators
domestic: mobile-cellular subscription base growing and teledensity reached 50 per 100 persons in 2011
international: country code—231; satellite earth station—1 Intelsat (Atlantic Ocean) (2010)
Broadcast media: 3 private TV stations; satellite TV service available; 1 state-owned radio station; about 15 independent radio stations broadcasting in Monrovia, with another 25 local stations operating in other areas; transmissions of 2 international broadcasters are available (2007)
Radio broadcast stations: AM 0, FM 10, shortwave 2 (2007)
Television broadcast stations: 5 (plus 4 repeaters) (2007)
Internet country code: .lr
Internet hosts: 7 (2012)
country comparison to the world: 228
Internet users: *total:* 177,600
percent of population: 4.3% (2014 est.)
country comparison to the world: 158

TRANSPORTATION

Airports: 29 (2013)
country comparison to the world: 117
Airports—with paved runways: *total:* 2
over 3,047 m: 1
1,524 to 2,437 m: 1 (2013)
Airports—with unpaved runways: *total:* 27
1,524 to 2,437 m: 5
914 to 1,523 m: 8
under 914 m: 14 (2013)
Pipelines: oil 4 km (2013)
Railways: *total:* 429 km
standard gauge: 345 km 1.435-m gauge
narrow gauge: 84 km 1.067-m gauge
note: most sections of the railways inoperable due to damage sustained during the civil wars from 1980 to 2003, but many are being rebuilt (2008)
country comparison to the world: 119
Roadways: *total:* 10,600 km
paved: 657 km
unpaved: 9,943 km (2000)
country comparison to the world: 134
Merchant marine: *total:* 2,771
by type: barge carrier 5, bulk carrier 662, cargo 143, carrier 2, chemical tanker 248, combination ore/

oil 8, container 937, liquefied gas 92, passenger 2, passenger/cargo 2, petroleum tanker 526, refrigerated cargo 102, roll on/roll off 5, specialized tanker 10, vehicle carrier 27
foreign-owned: 2,559 (Angola 1, Argentina 1, Australia 1, Belgium 1, Bermuda 4, Brazil 20, Canada 2, Chile 9, China 4, Croatia 1, Cyprus 9, Denmark 8, Egypt 3, Germany 1185, Gibraltar 5, Greece 505, Hong Kong 48, India 8, Indonesia 4, Israel 34, Italy 47, Japan 110, Latvia 5, Lebanon 1, Monaco 8, Netherlands 31, Nigeria 4, Norway 38, Poland 13, Qatar 5, Romania 3, Russia 109, Saudi Arabia 20, Singapore 22, Slovenia 7, South Korea 2, Sweden 12, Switzerland 25, Syria 1, Taiwan 94, Turkey 16, UAE 37, UK 32, Ukraine 10, Uruguay 1, US 53) (2010)
country comparison to the world: 2
Ports and terminals: *major seaport(s):* Buchanan, Monrovia

MILITARY AND SECURITY

Military branches: Armed Forces of Liberia (AFL): Army, Navy, Air Force
Military service age and obligation: 18 years of age for voluntary military service; no conscription (2012)
Military expenditures:
0.82% of GDP (2012)
0.86% of GDP (2011)
0.82% of GDP (2010)
country comparison to the world: 114

TRANSNATIONAL ISSUES

Disputes—international: although civil unrest continues to abate with the assistance of 6,500 UN Mission in Liberia peacekeepers, as of January 2013, Liberian refugees still remain in Guinea, Cote d'Ivoire, Sierra Leone, and Ghana; Liberia, in turn, shelters refugees fleeing turmoil in Cote d'Ivoire; despite the presence of over 9,000 UN forces in Cote d'I voire since 2004, ethnic conflict continues to spread into neighboring states who can no longer send their migrant workers to Ivorian cocoa plantations; UN sanctions ban Liberia from exporting diamonds and timber
Refugees and internally displaced persons: *refugees (country of origin):* 38,090 (Cote d'Ivoire) (2015)
IDPs: up to 23,000 (civil war from 1990–2004; post-election violence in March and April 2011; many dwell in slums in Monrovia) (2014)
stateless persons: 1 (2015)
Illicit drugs: transshipment point for Southeast and Southwest Asian heroin and South American cocaine for the European and US markets; corruption, criminal activity, arms-dealing, and diamond trade provide significant potential for money laundering, but the lack of well-developed financial system limits the country's utility as a major money-laundering center

LIBYA

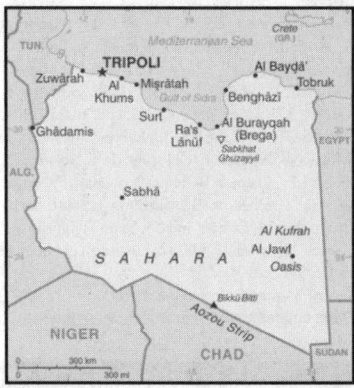

INTRODUCTION

Background: The Italians supplanted the Ottoman Turks in the area around Tripoli in 1911 and did not relinquish their hold until 1943 when defeated in World War II. Libya then passed to UN administration and achieved independence in 1951. Following a 1969 military coup, Col. Muammar al-QADHAFI assumed leadership and began to espouse his political system at home, which was a combination of socialism and Islam. During the 1970s, QADHAFI used oil revenues to promote his ideology outside Libya, supporting subversive and terrorist activities that included the downing of two airliners—one over Scotland, another in Northern Africa—and a discotheque bombing in Berlin. UN sanctions in 1992 isolated QADHAFI politically and economically following the attacks; sanctions were lifted in 2003 following Libyan acceptance of responsibility for the bombings and agreement to claimant compensation. QADHAFI also agreed to end Libya's program to develop weapons of mass destruction, and he made significant strides in normalizing relations with Western nations.

Unrest that began in several Middle Eastern and North African countries in late 2010 erupted in Libyan cities in early 2011. QADHAFI's brutal crackdown on protesters spawned a civil war that triggered UN authorization of air and naval intervention by the international community. After months of seesaw fighting between government and opposition forces, the QADHAFI regime was toppled in mid-2011 and replaced by a transitional government. Libya in 2012 formed a new parliament and elected a new prime minister. The country subsequently elected the House of Representatives in 2014, but remnants of the outgoing legislature refused to leave office and created a rival, Islamist-led government, the General National Congress. in October 2015, UN envoy to Libya, Bernardino LEON, proposed a power-sharing arrangement—known as the Libyan Political Agreement, which was signed by the rival governments two months later and subsequently endorsed by the UN . The agreement called for the formation of an interim Government of National Accord or GNA and the holding of general elections within two years.

GEOGRAPHY

Location: Northern Africa, bordering the Mediterranean Sea, between Egypt, Tunisia, and Algeria
Geographic coordinates: 25 00 N, 17 00 E
Map references: Africa
Area: *total:* 1,759,540 sq km
land: 1,759,540 sq km
water: 0 sq km
country comparison to the world: 17
Area—comparative: about 2.5 times the size of Texas; slightly larger than Alaska
Land boundaries: *total:* 4,339 km
border countries (6): Algeria 989 km, Chad 1,050 km, Egypt 1,115 km, Niger 342 km, Sudan 382 km, Tunisia 461 km
Coastline: 1,770 km
Maritime claims: *territorial sea:* 12 nm
note: Gulf of Sidra closing line—32 degrees, 30 minutes north
exclusive fishing zone: 62 nm
Climate: Mediterranean along coast; dry, extreme desert interior
Terrain: mostly barren, flat to undulating plains, plateaus, depressions
Elevation: *mean elevation:* 423 m
elevation extremes: *lowest point:* Sabkhat Ghuzayyil -47 m
highest point: Bikku Bitti 2,267 m
Natural resources: petroleum, natural gas, gypsum
Land use: *agricultural land:* 8.8%
arable land: 1%
permanent crops: 0.2%
permanent pasture: 7.6%
forest: 0.1%
other: 91.1% (2011 est.)
Irrigated land: 4,700 sq km (2012)
Total renewable water resources: 0.7 cu km (2011)
Freshwater withdrawal (domestic/industrial/agricultural): *total:* 4.33 cu km/yr (14%/3%/83%)
per capita: 796.1 cu m/yr (2000)
Natural hazards: hot, dry, dust-laden ghibli is a southern wind lasting one to four days in spring and fall; dust storms, sandstorms
Environment—current issues: desertification; limited natural freshwater resources; the Great Manmade River Project, the largest water development scheme in the world, brings water from large aquifers under the Sahara to coastal cities
Environment—international agreements: *party to:* Biodiversity, Climate Change, Climate Change-Kyoto Protocol, Desertification, Endangered Species, Hazardous Wastes, Marine Dumping, Ozone Layer Protection, Ship Pollution, Wetlands
signed, but not ratified: Law of the Sea
Geography—note: more than 90% of the country is desert or semidesert

PEOPLE AND SOCIETY

Nationality: *noun:* Libyan(s)
adjective: Libyan
Ethnic groups: Berber and Arab 97%, other 3% (includes Greeks, Maltese, Italians, Egyptians, Pakistanis, Turks, Indians, and Tunisians)
Languages: Arabic (official), Italian, English (all widely understood in the major cities); Berber (Nafusi, Ghadamis, Suknah, Awjilah, Tamasheq)
Religions: Muslim (official; virtually all Sunni) 96.6%, Christian 2.7%, Buddhist 0.3%, Hindu <0.1, Jewish <0.1, folk religion <0.1, unafilliated 0.2%, other <0.1
note: non-Sunni Muslims include native Ibadhi Muslims (<1% of the population) and foreign Muslims (2010 est.)
Population: 6,411,776 (July 2015 est.)
note: immigrants make up just over 12% of the total population, according to UN data (2015) (July 2015 est.)
country comparison to the world: 108
Age structure: 0–14 years: 26.52% (male 869,583/female 830,751)
15–24 years: 17.77% (male 588,243/female 551,139)
25–54 years: 46.62% (male 1,567,608/female 1,421,246)
55–64 years: 4.97% (male 163,133/female 155,703)
65 years and over: 4.12% (male 132,740/female 131,630) (2015 est.)
Dependency ratios: *total dependency ratio:* 52.4%
youth dependency ratio: 45.5%
elderly dependency ratio: 6.9%
potential support ratio: 14.5% (2015 est.)
Median age: *total:* 28 years
male: 28.2 years
female: 27.8 years (2015 est.)
country comparison to the world: 129
Population growth rate: 2.23% (2015 est.)
country comparison to the world: 38
Birth rate: 18.03 births/1,000 population (2015 est.)
country comparison to the world: 104
Death rate: 3.58 deaths/1,000 population (2015 est.)
country comparison to the world: 214
Net migration rate: 7.8 migrant(s)/1,000 population (2015 est.)
country comparison to the world: 15
Urbanization: *urban Population:* 78.6% of total population (2015)
rate of urbanization: 1.13% annual rate of change (2010–15 est.)
Major urban areas—Population: TRIPOLI (capital) 1.126 million (2015)
Sex ratio: *at birth:* 1.05 male(s)/female
0–14 years: 1.05 male(s)/female
15–24 years: 1.07 male(s)/female
25–54 years: 1.1 male(s)/female
55–64 years: 1.05 male(s)/female

65 years and over: 1.01 male(s)/female

total population: 1.08 male(s)/female (2015 est.)

Maternal mortality rate: 9 deaths/100,000 live births (2015 est.)

country comparison to the world: 102

Infant mortality rate: *total:* 11.48 deaths/1,000 live births

male: 12.42 deaths/1,000 live births

female: 10.5 deaths/1,000 live births (2015 est.)

country comparison to the world: 125

Life expectancy at birth: *total population:* 76.26 years

male: 74.54 years

female: 78.06 years (2015 est.)

country comparison to the world: 88

Total fertility rate: 2.05 children born/woman (2015 est.)

country comparison to the world: 113

Contraceptive prevalence rate: 41.9% (2007)

Health expenditures: 4.3% of GDP (2013)

country comparison to the world: 162

Physicians density: 1.9 physicians/1,000 population (2009)

Hospital bed density: 3.7 beds/1,000 population (2012)

Drinking water source:

improved:

urban: 54.2% of population

rural: 54.9% of population

total: 54.4% of population

unimproved:

urban: 45.8% of population

rural: 45.1% of population

total: 45.6% of population (2001 est.)

Sanitation facility access:

improved:

urban: 96.8% of population

rural: 95.7% of population

total: 96.6% of population

unimproved:

urban: 3.2% of population

rural: 4.3% of population

total: 3.4% of population (2015 est.)

HIV/AIDS—people living with HIV/AIDS: NA

HIV/AIDS—deaths: NA

Obesity—adult prevalence rate: 31.9% (2014)

country comparison to the world: 35

Children under the age of 5 years underweight: 5.6% (2007)

country comparison to the world: 86

Education expenditures: NA

Literacy: *definition:* age 15 and over can read and write

total population: 91%

male: 96.7%

female: 85.6% (2015 est.)

Unemployment, youth ages 15–24: *total:* 48.7%

male: 40.8%

female: 67.8% (2012 est.)

GOVERNMENT

Country name: *conventional long form:* none

conventional short form: Libya

local long form: none

local short form: Libiya

note: name derives from the Libu, an ancient Libyan tribe first mentioned in texts from the 13th century B.C.

Government type: in transition

Capital: *name:* Tripoli (Tarabulus)

Geographic coordinates: 32 53 N, 13 10 E

time difference: UTC+2 (7 hours ahead of Washington, DC, during Standard Time)

Administrative divisions: 22 districts (shabiyat, singular—shabiyat); Al Butnan, Al Jabal al Akhdar, Al Jabal al Gharbi, Al Jafarah, Al Jufrah, Al Kufrah, Al Marj, Al Marqab, Al Wahat, An Nuqat al Khams, Az Zawiyah, Banghazi, Darnah, Ghat, Misratah, Murzuq, Nalut, Sabha, Surt, Tarabulus, Wadi al Hayat, Wadi ash Shati

Independence: 24 December 1951 (from UN trusteeship)

National holiday: Liberation Day, 23 October (2011)

Constitution: previous 1951, 1977; latest 2011 (interim); note—the Constitution Draftingassembly continued drafting a new constitution as of early 2016 (2016)

Legal system: Libya's post-revolution legal system is in flux and driven by state and non-state entities

International law organization participation: has not submitted an ICJ jurisdiction declaration; non-party state to the ICCt

Citizenship: *citizenship by birth:* no

citizenship by descent only: at least one parent or grandparent must be a citizen of Libya

dual citizenship recognized: no

residency requirement for naturalization: varies from 3 to 5 years

Suffrage: 18 years of age, universal

Executive branch: *chief of state:* Speaker of the House of Representatives Aqilah Salah ISSA (since 5 August 2014)

head of government: Prime Minister Abdullah al-THINI (since 11 March 2014); Deputy Prime Ministers Abd al-Salam al-BADRI (since 4 August 2014), Al-Mahdi Hasan Muftah al-LABAD (since 4 August 2014), Abd al-Rahman al-Tahir al-UHAYRISH (since 4 August 2014)

cabinet: new cabinet approved by the House of Representatives in September 2014

elections/appointments: prime minister and speaker of the house elected by the House of Representatives

election results: NA

Legislative branch: *description:* unicameral Council of Deputies or Majlis Al Nuwab (200 seats including 32 reserved for women; members elected by direct popular vote; member term NA)

elections: election last held in June 2014; note—the Libyan Supreme Court in November 2014 declared the House election unconstitutional, but the Council rejected the ruling; no country has officially recognized the rival government

election results: percent of vote by party—NA; seats by party—independent 200; note—not all 200 seats were filled in the June election because of boycotts and lack of security at some polling stations; some elected members of the Council also boycotted the election

Judicial branch: *highest court(s):* NA; note—government in transition

Political parties and leaders: Al-Watan (Homeland) Party

Justice and Construction Party or JCP [Mohamed SOWAN]

National Forces Alliance or NFA [Mahmoud JIBRIL] (includes many political organizations, NGOs, and independents)

National Front (initially the National Front for the Salvation of Libya, formed in 1981 as a diaspora opposition group)

Union for the Homeland [Abd al-Rahman al-SUWAYHILI]

note: partial list of the larger political parties and leaders

Political pressure groups and leaders: NA

International organization participation: ABEDA, AFDB, AFESD, AMF, AMU, AU, BDEAC, CAEU, COMESA, FAO, G-77, IAEA, IBRD, ICAO, ICC (NGOs), ICRM, IDA, IDB, IFAD, IFC, IFRCS, ILO, IMF, IMO, IMSO, Interpol, IOC, IOM, IPU, ISO, ITSO, ITU, LAS, MIGA, NAM, OAPEC, OIC, OPCW, OPEC, PCA, UN, UNCTAD, UNESCO, UNIDO, UNWTO, UPU, WCO, WFTU (NGOs), WHO, WIPO, WMO, WTO (observer)

Diplomatic representation in the US: *chief of mission:* Ambassador (vacant); Charge d'Affaires Wafa M.T. BUGHAIGHIS (since 5 December 2014)

chancery: 2600 Virginia Avenue NW, Suite 705, Washington, DC 20037

telephone: [1] (202) 944-9601

FAX: [1] (202) 944-9606

Diplomatic representation from the US: *chief of mission:* Ambassador Peter William BODDE (since 21 December 2015)

note: on 11 September 2012, US Ambassador Christopher STEVENS and three other American diplomats were killed in an attack by heavily armed militants ONAUS diplomatic post in the eastern city of Benghazi; the US Government evacuated its Embassy in Tripoli in July 2014

embassy: Sidi Slim Area/Walie Al-Ahed Road, Tripoli

mailing address: US Embassy, 8850 Tripoli Place, Washington, DC 20521-8850

telephone: [218] (0) 91-220-3239

Flag description: three horizontal bands of red (top), black (double width), and green with a white crescent and star centered on the black stripe; the National Transitional Council reintroduced this flag design of the former Kingdom of Libya (1951–1969) on 27 February 2011; it replaced the former all-green banner promulgated by the QADHAFI regime in 1977; the colors represent the three major regions of the country: red stands for Fezzan, black symbolizes Cyrenaica, and green denotes Tripolitania; the crescent and star represent Islam, the main religion of the country

National symbol(s): star and crescent, hawk; national colors: red, black, green

National anthem: *name:* "Libya, Libya, Libya"

lyrics/music: Al Bashir ALAREBI/Mohamad Abdel WAHAB

503

note: also known as "Ya Beladi" or "Oh, My Country!"; adopted 1951; readopted 2011 with some modification to the lyrics; during the QADHAFI years between 1969 and 2011, the anthem was "Allahu Akbar, " (God is Great) a marching song of the Egyptian Army in the 1956 Suez War

ECONOMY

Economy—overview: Libya's economy, almost entirely dependent on oil and gas exports, struggled during 2015 as the country plunged into civil war and world oil prices dropped to seven-year lows. In early 2015, armed conflict between rival forces for control of the country's largest oil terminals caused a decline in Libyan crude oil production, which never recovered to more than one-third of the average pre-Revolution highs of 1.6 million barrels per day. The Central Bank of Libya continued to pay government salaries to a majority of the Libyan workforce and to fund subsidies for fuel and food, resulting in an estimated budget deficit about 49% of GDP.

Libya's economic transition away from QADAFI's notionally socialist model has completely stalled as political chaos persists and security continues to deteriorate. Libya's leaders have hindered economic development by failing to use its financial resources to invest in national infrastructure. The country suffers from widespread power outages in its largest cities, caused by shortages of fuel for power generation. Living conditions, including access to clean drinking water, medical services, and safe housing, have all declined as the civil war has caused more people to become internally displaced, further straining local resources.

Extremists affiliated with the Islamic State of Iraq and the Levant (ISIL) attacked Libyan oilfields in the first half of 2015; ISIL has a presence in many cities across Libya including near oil infrastructure, threatening future government revenues from oil and gas.

GDP (purchasing power parity): $92.61 billion (2015 est.)
$98.92 billion (2014 est.)
$130.2 billion (2013 est.)
note: data are in 2015 US dollars
country comparison to the world: 84

GDP (official exchange rate): $38.3 billion (2015 est.)

GDP—real growth rate: -6.4% (2015 est.)
-24% (2014 est.)
-13.6% (2013 est.)
country comparison to the world: 217

GDP—per capita (PPP): $14,600 (2015 est.)
$15,800 (2014 est.)
$20,800 (2013 est.)
note: data are in 2015 US dollars
country comparison to the world: 111

Gross national saving: -24.6% of GDP (2015 est.)
1.4% of GDP (2014 est.)
37.3% of GDP (2013 est.)
country comparison to the world: 179

GDP—composition, by end use: *household consumption:* 80%
government consumption: 21.8%

investment in fixed capital: 4.1%
investment in inventories: 0.8%
exports of goods and services: 27.3%
imports of goods and services: -34% (2015 est.)

GDP—composition, by sector of origin:
agriculture: 1.8%
industry: 40.2%
services: 58% (2015 est.)

Agriculture—products: wheat, barley, olives, dates, citrus, vegetables, peanuts, soybeans; cattle

Industries: petroleum, petrochemicals, aluminum, iron and steel, food processing, textiles, handicrafts, cement

Industrial production growth rate: -13% (2015 est.)
country comparison to the world: 198

Labor force: 1.195 million (2015 est.)
country comparison to the world: 137

Labor force—by occupation: *agriculture:* 17%
industry: 23%
services: 59% (2004 est.)

Unemployment rate: 30% (2004 est.)
country comparison to the world: 186

Population below poverty line: NA%
note: about one-third of Libyans live at or below the national poverty line

Household income or consumption by percentage share: *lowest:* 10%: NA%
highest: 10%: NA%

Budget: *revenues:* $10.19 billion
expenditures: $24.85 billion (2015 est.)
Taxes and other revenues: 34.3% of GDP (2015 est.)
country comparison to the world: 64

Budget surplus (+) or deficit (–): -49.3% of GDP (2015 est.)
country comparison to the world: 219

Public debt: 6.6% of GDP (2015 est.)
6.5% of GDP (2014 est.)
country comparison to the world: 176

Fiscal year: calendar year

Inflation rate (consumer prices): 8% (2015 est.)
2.8% (2014 est.)
country comparison to the world: 201

Central bank discount rate: 9.52% (31 December 2010)
3% (31 December 2009)
country comparison to the world: 26

Commercial bank prime lending rate: 7% (31 December 2015 est.)
6% (31 December 2014 est.)
country comparison to the world: 121

Stock of narrow money: $45.42 billion (31 December 2015 est.)
$48.02 billion (31 December 2014 est.)
country comparison to the world: 53

Stock of broad money: $54.66 billion (31 December 2014 est.)
$53.34 billion (31 December 2013 est.)
country comparison to the world: 64

Stock of domestic credit: -$13.84 billion (31 December 2015 est.)
-$16.48 billion (31 December 2014 est.)
country comparison to the world: 191

Market value of publicly traded shares: $NA

Current account balance: -$16.7 billion (2015 est.)
-$12.36 billion (2014 est.)
country comparison to the world: 184

Exports: $10.51 billion (2015 est.)
$16.46 billion (2014 est.)
country comparison to the world: 88

Exports—commodities: crude oil, refined petroleum products, natural gas, chemicals

Exports—partners: Italy 32%, Germany 11.3%, China 8%, France 8%, Spain 5.6%, Netherlands 5.4%, Syria 5.3% (2015)

Imports: $11.24 billion (2015 est.)
$20.43 billion (2014 est.)
country comparison to the world: 93

Imports—commodities: machinery, semi-finished goods, food, transport equipment, consumer products

Imports—partners: China 14.8%, Italy 12.9%, Turkey 11.1%, Tunisia 6.5%, France 6.1%, Spain 4.6%, Syria 4.5%, Egypt 4.4%, South Korea 4.2% (2015)

Reserves of foreign exchange and gold: $61.63 billion (31 December 2015 est.)
$89.25 billion (31 December 2014 est.)
country comparison to the world: 35

Debt—external: $5.244 billion (31 December 2014 est.)
$6.028 billion (31 December 2013 est.)
country comparison to the world: 128

Stock of direct foreign investment—at home: $16.04 billion (31 December 2015 est.)
$16.04 billion (31 December 2014 est.)
country comparison to the world: 84

Stock of direct foreign investment—abroad: $21.59 billion (31 December 2015 est.)
$20.91 billion (31 December 2014 est.)
country comparison to the world: 54

Exchange rates: Libyan dinars (LYD) per US dollar—
1.378 (2015 est.)
1.2724 (2014 est.)
1.2724 (2013 est.)
1.26 (2012 est.)
1.224 (2011 est.)

ENERGY

Electricity—production: 31.94 billion kWh
note: persistent electricity shortages have contributed to the ongoing instability throughout the country (2012 est.)
country comparison to the world: 62

Electricity—consumption: 27.54 billion kWh (2012 est.)
country comparison to the world: 63

Electricity—exports: 14 million kWh (2012 est.)
country comparison to the world: 88

Electricity—imports: 61 million kWh (2012 est.)
country comparison to the world: 99

Electricity—installed generating capacity: 7.121 million kW (2012 est.)
country comparison to the world: 67

Electricity—from fossil fuels: 99.2% of total installed capacity (2012 est.)
country comparison to the world: 49

Electricity—from nuclear fuels: 0% of total installed capacity (2012 est.)
country comparison to the world: 132

Electricity—from hydroelectric plants: 0% of total installed capacity (2012 est.)

country comparison to the world: 183
Electricity—from other renewable sources: 0.8% of total installed capacity (2012 est.)
country comparison to the world: 98
Crude oil—production: 470,000 bbl/day (2014 est.)
country comparison to the world: 30
Crude oil—Exports: 735,000 bbl/day
note: Libyan crude oil export values are highly volatile because of continuing protests and other disruptions across the country (2013 est.)
country comparison to the world: 18
Crude oil—imports: 0 bbl/day (2012 est.)
country comparison to the world: 89
Crude oil—proved reserves: 48.36 billion bbl (1 January 2015 est.)
country comparison to the world: 9
Refined petroleum products—production: 171,600 bbl/day (2012 est.)
country comparison to the world: 58
Refined petroleum products—consumption: 242,000 bbl/day (2013 est.)
country comparison to the world: 51
Refined petroleum products—Exports: 35,630 bbl/day (2012 est.)
country comparison to the world: 65
Refined petroleum products—Imports: 108,500 bbl/day (2012 est.)
country comparison to the world: 49
Natural gas—production: 12 billion cu m (2013 est.)
country comparison to the world: 40
Natural gas—consumption: 6.487 billion cu m (2013 est.)
country comparison to the world: 54
Natural gas—exports: 5.513 billion cu m (2013 est.)
country comparison to the world: 29
Natural gas—imports: 0 cu m (2013 est.)
country comparison to the world: 94
Natural gas—proved reserves: 1.549 trillion cu m (1 January 2014 est.)
country comparison to the world: 22
Carbon dioxide emissions from consumption of energy: 54.6 million Mt (2012 est.)
country comparison to the world: 55

COMMUNICATIONS

Telephones—fixed lines: *total subscriptions:* 710,000
subscriptions per 100 inhabitants: 11 (2014 est.)
country comparison to the world: 89

Telephones—mobile cellular: *total:* 10.1 million
subscriptions per 100 inhabitants: 161 (2014 est.)
country comparison to the world: 85
Telephone system: *general assessment:* telecommunications system is state-owned and service is poor, but investment is being made to upgrade; state retains monopoly in fixed-line services;

mobile-cellular telephone system became operational in 1996
domestic: multiple providers for a mobile telephone system that is growing rapidly; combined fixed-line and mobile-cellular teledensity has soared
international: country code—218; satellite earth stations—4 Intelsat, NA Arabsat, and NA Intersputnik; submarine cable to France and Italy; microwave radio relay to Tunisia and Egypt; tropospheric scatter to Greece; participant in Medarabtel (2010)
Broadcast media: state-funded and private TV stations; some provinces operate local TV stations; pan-Arab satellite TV stations are available; state-funded radio (2012)
Radio broadcast stations: AM 16, FM 3, shortwave 3 (2001)
Television broadcast stations: 12 (plus 1 repeater) (1999)
Internet country code: .ly
Internet hosts: 17,926 (2012)
country comparison to the world: 121
Internet users: *total:* 1.4 million
percent of population: 21.8% (2014 est.)
country comparison to the world: 114

TRANSPORTATION

Airports: 146 (2013)
country comparison to the world: 41
Airports—with paved runways: *total:* 68
over 3,047 m: 23
2,438 to 3,047 m: 7
1,524 to 2,437 m: 30
914 to 1,523 m: 7
under 914 m: 1 (2013)
Airports—with unpaved runways: *total:* 78
over 3,047 m: 2
2,438 to 3,047 m: 5
1,524 to 2,437 m: 14
914 to 1,523 m: 37
under 914 m: 20 (2013)
Heliports: 2 (2013)
Pipelines: condensate 882 km; gas 3,743 km; oil 7,005 km (2013)

Roadways: *total:* 100,024 km
paved: 57,214 km
unpaved: 42,810 km (2003)
country comparison to the world: 45
Merchant marine: *total:* 23
by type: cargo 2, chemical tanker 4, liquefied gas 3, petroleum tanker 13, roll on/roll off 1
foreign-owned: 2 (Kuwait 1, Norway 1)
registered in other countries: 6 (Hong Kong 1, Malta 5) (2010)
country comparison to the world: 91
Ports and terminals: *major seaport(s):* Marsa al Burayqah (Marsa el Brega), Tripoli
oil terminal(s): Az Zawiyah, Ra's Lanuf
LNG terminal (export): Marsa el Brega

Military branches: note—in transition; government has affiliated Army, Air Force, and Navy forces (2015)
Military service age and obligation: 18 years of age for mandatory or voluntary service (2012)

TRANSNATIONAL ISSUES

Disputes—international: dormant disputes include Libyan claims of about 32,000 sq km still reflected on its maps of southeastern Algeria and the FLN's assertions of a claim to Chirac Pastures in southeastern Morocco; various Chadian rebels from the Aozou region reside in southern Libya
Refugees and internally displaced persons: *refugees (country of origin):* 18,653 (Syria); 5,391 (West Bank and Gaza Strip) (2014)
IDPs: 425,250 (conflict between pro-Qadhafi and anti-Qadhafi forces in 2011; post-Qadhafi tribal clashes 2014) (2016)
Trafficking in persons: *current situation:* Libya is a destination and transit country for men and women from sub-Saharan Africa and Asia subjected to forced labor and forced prostitution; migrants who seek employment in Libya as laborers and domestic workers or who transit Libya en route to Europe are vulnerable to forced labor; private employers also exploit migrants from detention centers as forced laborers on farms and construction sites, returning them to detention when they are no longer needed; some sub-Saharan women are reportedly forced to work in Libyan brothels, particularly in the country's south; since 2013, militia groups and other informal armed groups, including some affiliated with the government, are reported to conscript Libyan children under the age of 18; large-scale violence driven by militias, civil unrest, and increased lawlessness increased in 2014, making it more difficult to obtain information on human trafficking
tier rating: Tier 3—the Libyan Government does not fully comply with the minimum standards for the elimination of trafficking and is not making significant efforts to do so; in 2014, the government's capacity to address human trafficking was hampered by the ongoing power struggle and violence; the judicial system was not functioning, preventing any efforts to investigate, prosecute, or convict traffickers, complicit detention camp guards or government officials, or militias or armed groups that used child soldiers; the government failed to identify or provide protection to trafficking victims, including child conscripts, and continued to punish victims for unlawful acts committed as a direct result of being trafficked; no public anti-trafficking awareness campaigns were conducted (2015)

LIECHTENSTEIN

INTRODUCTION

Background: The Principality of Liechtenstein was established within the Holy Roman Empire in 1719. Occupied by both French and Russian troops during the Napoleonic Wars, it became a sovereign state in 1806 and joined the Germanic Confederation in 1815. Liechtenstein became fully independent in 1866 when the Confederation dissolved. Until the end of World War I, it was closely tied to Austria, but the economic devastation caused by that conflict forced Liechtenstein to enter into a customs and monetary union with Switzerland. Since World War II (in which Liechtenstein remained neutral), the country's low taxes have spurred outstanding economic growth. In 2000, shortcomings in banking regulatory oversight resulted in concerns about the use of financial institutions for money laundering. However, Liechtenstein implemented anti-money laundering legislation and a Mutual Legal Assistance Treaty with the US that went into effect in 2003.

GEOGRAPHY

Location: Central Europe, between Austria and Switzerland
Geographic coordinates: 47 16 N, 9 32 E
Map references: Europe
Area: *total:* 160 sq km
land: 160 sq km
water: 0 sq km
country comparison to the world: 219
Area—comparative: about 0.9 times the size of Washington, DC

Land boundaries: *total:* 75 km
border countries (2): Austria 34 km, Switzerland 41 km
Coastline: 0 km (doubly landlocked)
Maritime claims: none (landlocked)
Climate: continental; cold, cloudy winters with frequent snow or rain; cool to moderately warm, cloudy, humid summers
Terrain: mostly mountainous (Alps) with Rhine Valley in western third

Elevation: *mean elevation:* NA
elevation extremes: *lowest point:* Ruggeller Riet 430 m
highest point: Vorder-Grauspitz 2,599 m
Natural resources: hydroelectric potential, arable land
Land use: *agricultural land:* 37.6%
arable land: 18.8%
permanent crops: 0%
permanent pasture: 18.8%
forest: 43.1%
other: 19.3% (2011 est.)
Irrigated land: 0 sq km (2012)
Natural hazards: NA
Environment—current issues: NA
Environment—international agreements: *party to:* Air Pollution, Air Pollution-Nitrogen Oxides, Air Pollution-Persistent Organic Pollutants, Air Pollution-Sulfur 85, Air Pollution-Sulfur 94, Air Pollution-Volatile Organic Compounds, Biodiversity, Climate Change, Climate Change-Kyoto Protocol, Desertification, Endangered Species, Hazardous Wastes, Ozone Layer Protection, Wetlands
signed, but not ratified: Law of the Sea
Geography—note: along with Uzbekistan, one of only two doubly landlocked countries in the world; variety of microclimatic variations based on elevation

PEOPLE AND SOCIETY:: LIECHTENSTEIN

Nationality: *noun:* Liechtensteiner(s)
adjective: Liechtenstein
Ethnic groups: Liechtensteiner 66.3%, other 33.7% (2013 est.)
Languages: German 94.5% (official) (Alemannic is the main dialect), Italian 1.1%, other 4.3% (2010 est.)
Religions: Roman Catholic (official) 75.9%, Protestant Reformed 6.5%, Muslim 5.4%, Lutheran 1.3%, other 2.9%, none 5.4%, unspecified 2.6% (2010 est.)
Population: 37,624 (July 2015 est.)
country comparison to the world: 214
Age structure: *0–14 years:* 15.54% (male 3,142/female 2,706)
15–24 years: 11.73% (male 2,182/female 2,230)
25–54 years: 42.65% (male 8,013/female 8,035)
55–64 years: 13.58% (male 2,504/female 2,606)
65 years and over: 16.49% (male 2,837/female 3,369) (2015 est.)
Median age: *total:* 42.7 years
male: 41.5 years
female: 43.8 years (2015 est.)
country comparison to the world: 19
Population growth rate: 0.84% (2015 est.)
country comparison to the world: 130
Birth rate: 10.45 births/1,000 population (2015 est.)
country comparison to the world: 187
Death rate: 7.12 deaths/1,000 population (2015 est.)
country comparison to the world: 128

Net migration rate: 5.08 migrant(s)/1,000 population (2015 est.)
country comparison to the world: 26
Urbanization: *urban Population:* 14.3% of total population (2015)
rate of urbanization: 0.48% annual rate of change (2010–15 est.)
Major urban areas—Population: VADUZ (capital) 5,000 (2014)
Sex ratio: *at birth:* 1.26 male(s)/female
0–14 years: 1.16 male(s)/female
15–24 years: 0.98 male(s)/female
25–54 years: 1 male(s)/female
55–64 years: 0.96 male(s)/female
65 years and over: 0.84 male(s)/female
total population: 0.99 male(s)/female (2015 est.)
Infant mortality rate: *total:* 4.29 deaths/1,000 live births
male: 4.59 deaths/1,000 live births
female: 3.92 deaths/1,000 live births (2015 est.)
country comparison to the world: 189
Life expectancy at birth: *total population:* 81.77 years
male: 79.6 years
female: 84.5 years (2015 est.)
country comparison to the world: 16
Total fertility rate: 1.69 children born/woman (2015 est.)
country comparison to the world: 173
HIV/AIDS—adult prevalence rate: NA
HIV/AIDS—people living with HIV/AIDS: NA
HIV/AIDS—deaths: NA
Education expenditures: 2.6% of GDP (2011)
country comparison to the world: 166
School life expectancy (primary to tertiary education): *total:* 15 years
male: 16 years
female: 13 years (2014)

GOVERNMENT

Country name: *conventional long form:* Principality of Liechtenstein
conventional short form: Liechtenstein
local long form: Fuerstentum Liechtenstein
local short form: Liechtenstein
etymology: named after the Liechtenstein dynasty that purchased and united the counties of Schellenburg and Vaduz and that were allowed by the Holy Roman Emperor in 1719 to rename the new property after their family; the name in German means "light (bright) stone"
Government type: constitutional monarchy
Capital: *name:* Vaduz
Geographic coordinates: 47 08 N, 9 31 E
time difference: UTC + 1 (6 hours ahead of Washington, DC, during Standard Time)
daylight saving time: +1hr, begins last Sunday in March; ends last Sunday in October
Administrative divisions: 11 communes (Gemeinden, singular—Gemeinde); Balzers, Eschen, Gamprin, Mauren, Planken, Ruggell, Schaan, Schellenberg, Triesen, Triesenberg, Vaduz

Independence: 23 January 1719 (Principality of Liechtenstein established); 12 July 1806 (independence from the Holy Roman Empire); 24 August 1866 (independence from the German Confederation)

National holiday: Assumption Day, 15 August, and National Day, 15 August (1940)

Constitution: previous 1862; latest adopted 5 October 1921; amended many times, last in 2011 (2016)

Legal system: civil law system influenced by Swiss, Austrian, and German law

International law organization participation: accepts compulsory ICJ jurisdiction with reservations; accepts ICCt jurisdiction

Citizenship: *citizenship by birth:* no

citizenship by descent only: the father must be a citizen of Liechtenstein; in the case of a child born out of wedlock, the mother must be a citizen

dual citizenship recognized: no

residency requirement for naturalization: 5 years

Suffrage: 18 years of age; universal

Executive branch: *chief of state:* Prince HANS ADAM II (since 13 November 1989, assumed executive powers on 26 August 1984); Heir Apparent Prince ALOIS, son of the monarch (born 11 June 1968); note—on 15 August 2004, HANSADAMII tran sferred the official duties of the ruling prince to ALOIS, but HANS ADAM II retains powers of chief of state

head of government: *Prime Minister Adrian HASLER (since 27 March 2013)*

cabinet: Cabinet elected by the Parliament, confirmed by the monarch

elections/appointments: the monarchy is hereditary; following legislative elections, the leader of the majority party in the Landtag usually appointed the head of government by the monarch, and the leader of the largest minority party in the Landtag usually appointed the deputy head of government by the monarch if there is a coalition government

Legislative branch: *description:* unicameral Parliament or Landtag (25 seats; members directly elected in multi-seat constituencies by proportional representation vote to serve 4-year terms)

elections: last held on 3 February 2013 (next to be held in February 2017)

election results: percent of vote by party—FBP 40.0%, VU 33.5%, DU 15.3% FL 11.1%; seats by party -FBP 10, VU 8, DU 4, FL 3

Judicial branch: *highest court(s):* Supreme Court or Oberster Gerichtshof (consists of 5 judges); Constitutional Court or Verfassungsgericht (consists of 5 judges and 5 alternates)

judge selection and term of office: judges of both courts elected by the Landtag and appointed by the monarch; Supreme Court judges serve 4-year renewable terms; Constitutional Court judge tenure NA

subordinate courts: Court of Appeal or Obergericht (second instance), Court of Justice (first instance), Administrative Court, county courts

Political parties and leaders: Fatherland Union (Vaterlaendische Union) or VU [Jakob BUECHEL]

Progressive Citizens' Party (Fortschrittliche Buergerpartei) or FBP [Elfried HASLER]

The Free List (Die Freie Liste) or FL [Wolfgang MARXER]

the independents (Die Unabhaengigen) or DU [Harry QUADERER]

International organization participation: CD, CE, EBRD, EFTA, IAEA, ICCt, ICRM, IFRCS, Interpol, IOC, IPU, ITSO, ITU, ITUC (NGOs), OAS (observer), OPCW, OSCE, PCA, Schengen Convention, UN, UNCTAD, UPU, WIPO, WTO

Diplomatic representation in the US: *chief of mission:* Ambassador Claudia FRITSCHE (since 7 December 2000)

chancery: 2900 K Street, NW, Suite 602B, Washington, DC 20007

telephone: [1] (202) 331-0590

FAX: [1] (202) 331-3221

Diplomatic representation from the US: the US does not have an embassy in Liechtenstein; the US Ambassador to Switzerland is accredited to Liechtenstein

Flag description: two equal horizontal bands of blue (top) and red with a gold crown on the hoist side of the blue band; the colors may derive from the blue and red livery design used in the principality's household in the 18th century; the prince's crown was introduced in 1937 to distinguish the flag from that of Haiti

National symbol(s): princely hat (crown); national colors: blue, red

National anthem: *name:* "Oben am jungen Rhein" (High Above the Young Rhine)

lyrics/music: Jakob Joseph JAUCH/Josef FROMMELT

note: adopted 1850, revised 1963; uses the tune of "God Save the Queen"

ECONOMY

Economy—overview: Despite its small size and lack of natural resources, Liechtenstein has developed into a prosperous, highly industrialized, free-enterprise economy with a vital financial service sector and the third highest per capita income in the world, after Qatar and Luxembourg. The Liechtenstein economy is widely diversified with a large number of small businesses. Low business taxes—the maximum tax rate is 20%—and easy incorporation rules have induced many holding companies to establish nominal offices in Liechtenstein, providing 30% of state revenues. The country participates in a customs union with Switzerland and uses the Swiss franc as its national currency. It imports more than 90% of its energy requirements. Liechtenstein has beeNA member of the European Economic Area (an organ ization servingas a bridge between the European Free Trade Association and the EU) since May 1995. The government is working to harmonize its economic policies with those of an integrated Europe. Since 2008, Liechtenstein has faced renewed international pressure—particularly from Germany and the US—to improve transparency in

its banking and tax systems. in December 2008, Liechtenstein signed a Tax Information Exchange Agreement with the US. Upon Liechtenstein's conclusion of 12 bilateral information-sharing agreements, the OECD in October 2009 removed the principality from its "grey list" of countries that had yet to implement the organization's Model Tax Convention. By the end of 2010, Liechtenstein had signed 25 Tax Information Exchange Agreements or Double Tax Agreements. In 2011, Liechtenstein joined the Schengen area, which allows passport-free travel across 26 European countries.

GDP (purchasing power parity): $3.2 billion (2009 est.) $3.216 billion (2008 est.)

$3.159 billion (2007 est.)

country comparison to the world: 183

GDP (official exchange rate): $5.113 billion (2010 est.)

GDP—real growth rate: 1.8% (2012 est.)

-0.5% (2009 est.)

3.1% (2007 est.)

country comparison to the world: 141

GDP—per capita (PPP): $89,400 (2009 est.) $90,600 (2008 est.)

$89,700 (2007 est.)

country comparison to the world: 4

GDP—composition, by sector of origin:

agriculture: 8%

industry: 37%

services: 55% (2009)

Agriculture—products: wheat, barley, corn, potatoes; livestock, dairy products

Industries: electronics, metal manufacturing, dental products, ceramics, pharmaceuticals, food products, precision instruments, tourism, optical instruments

Industrial production growth rate: NA%

Labor force: 35,830 (2012)

note: 51% of the labor force in Liechtenstein commute daily from Austria, Switzerland, and Germany (2012 est.)

country comparison to the world: 201

Labor force—by occupation: *agriculture:* 0.8%

industry: 39.4%

services: 59.9% (2012)

Unemployment rate: 3.4% (2014)

2.3% (2012)

country comparison to the world: 29

Population below poverty line: NA%

Household income or consumption by percentage share: *lowest:* 10%: NA%

highest: 10%: NA%

Budget: *revenues:* $995.3 million

expenditures: $890.4 million (2012 est.)

Taxes and other revenues: 19.5% of GDP (2012 est.)

country comparison to the world: 162

Budget surplus (+) or deficit (–): 2.1% of GDP (2012 est.)

country comparison to the world: 14

Fiscal year: calendar year

Inflation rate (consumer prices): -0.2% (2013) -0.7% (2012)

country comparison to the world: 37

Market value of publicly traded shares: $NA

Exports: $3.801 billion (2012 est.)

$3.757 billion (2011 est.)

note: trade data exclude trade with Switzerland
country comparison to the world: 122

Exports—commodities: small specialty machinery, connectors for audio and video, parts for motor vehicles, dental products, hardware, prepared foodstuffs, electronic equipment, optical products

Imports: $2.09 billion (2012 est.)

$2.218 billion (2011 est.)

note: trade data exclude trade with Switzerland
country comparison to the world: 161

Imports—commodities: agricultural products, raw materials, energy products, machinery, metal goods, textiles, foodstuffs, motor vehicles

Debt—external: $0 (2001)

note: public external debt only; private external debt unavailable

country comparison to the world: 206

Exchange rates: Swiss francs (CHF) per US dollar—

0.9381 (2015)

0.9377 (2012)

0.9377 (2012)

0.94 (2012 est.)

0.8876 (2011 est.)

ENERGY

Electricity—production: 145.3 million kWh (2012)

country comparison to the world: 193

Electricity—consumption: 1.36 billion kWh (2012)

country comparison to the world: 148

Electricity—imports: 1.214 billion kWh (2012)

country comparison to the world: 59

COMMUNICATIONS

Telephones—fixed lines: *total subscriptions:* 18,000

subscriptions per 100 inhabitants: 48 (2014 est.)

country comparison to the world: 187

Telephones—mobile cellular: *total:* 38,800

subscriptions per 100 inhabitants: 104 (2014 est.)

country comparison to the world: 204

Telephone system: *general assessment:* automatic telephone system

domestic: fixed-line and mobile-cellular services widely available; combined telephone service subscribership exceeds 150 per 100 persons

international: country code—423; linked to Swiss networks by cable and microwave radio relay (2011)

Broadcast media: relies on foreign terrestrial and satellite broadcasters for most broadcast media services; first Liechtenstein-based TV station established August 2008; Radio Liechtenstein operates multiple radio stations; a Swiss-based broadcaster operates several radio stations in Liechtenstein (2008)

Radio broadcast stations: AM 0, FM 4, shortwave 0 (1998)

Television broadcast stations: NA (linked to Swiss networks) (1997)

Internet country code: .li

Internet hosts: 14,278 (2012)

country comparison to the world: 128

Internet users: *total:* 34,500

percent of population: 92.4% (2014 est.)

country comparison to the world: 193

TRANSPORTATION

Pipelines: gas 20 km (2013)

Railways: *total:* 9 km

standard gauge: 9 km 1.435-m gauge (electrified)

note: belongs to the Austrian Railway System connecting Austria and Switzerland (2008)

country comparison to the world: 136

Roadways: *total:* 380 km

paved: 380 km (2012)

country comparison to the world: 202

Waterways: 28 km (2010)

country comparison to the world: 105

MILITARY AND SECURITY

Military branches: no regular military forces; National Police maintains close relations with neighboring forces (2013)

Military—note: Liechtenstein has no military forces, but the modern National Police maintains close relations with neighboring forces (2013)

TRANSNATIONAL ISSUES

Disputes—international: none

Illicit drugs: has strength ened money laundering controls, but money laundering remains a concern due to Liechtenstein's sophisticated offshore financial services sector

LITHUANIA

INTRODUCTION

Background: Lithuanian lands were united under MINDAUGAS in 1236; over the next century, through alliances and conquest, Lithuania extended its territory to include most of present-day Belarus and Ukraine. By the end of the 14th century Lithuania was the largest state in Europe. An alliance with Poland in 1386 led the two countries into a union through the person of a common ruler. In 1569, Lithuania and Poland formally united into a single dual state, the Polish-Lithuanian Commonwealth. This entity survived until 1795 when its remnants were partitioned by surrounding countries. Lithuania regained its independence following World War I but was annexed by the USSR in 1940—an action never recognized by the US and many other countries. On 11 March 1990, Lithuania became the first of the Soviet republics to declare its independence, but Moscow did not recognize this proclamation until September of 1991 (following the abortive coup in Moscow) . The last Russian troops withdrew in 1993. Lithuania subsequently restructured its economy for integration into Western European institutions; it joined both NATO and the EU in the spring of 2004. In January 2014, Lithuania assumed a nonpermanent seat on the UN Security Council for the 2014–15 term; in January 2015, Lithuania joined the euro zone.

GEOGRAPHY

Location: Eastern Europe, bordering the Baltic Sea, between Latvia and Russia, west of Belarus

Geographic coordinates: 56 00 N, 24 00 E

Map references: Europe

Area: *total:* 65,300 sq km

land: 62,680 sq km

water: 2,620 sq km

country comparison to the world: 123

Area—comparative: slightly larger than West Virginia

Land boundaries: *total:* 1,549 km

border countries (4): Belarus 640 km, Latvia 544 km, Poland 104 km, Russia (Kaliningrad) 261 km

Coastline: 90 km

Maritime claims: *territorial sea:* 12 nm

Climate: transitional, between maritime and continental; wet, moderate winters and summers

Terrain: lowland, many scattered small lakes, fertile soil

Elevation: *mean elevation:* 110 m

elevation extremes: *lowest point:* Baltic Sea 0 m

highest point: Aukstojas 294 m

Natural resources: peat, arable land, amber

Land use: *agricultural land:* 44.8%

arable land: 34.9%

permanent crops: 0.5%

permanent pasture: 9.4%

forest: 34.6%

other: 20.6% (2011 est.)

Irrigated land: 44 sq km (2012)

Total renewable water resources: 24.9 cu km (2011)

Freshwater withdrawal (domestic/industrial/agricultural): *total:* 2.38 cu km/yr (7%/90%/3%)
per capita: 703.8 cu m/yr (2009)
Natural hazards: NA
Environment—current issues: contam ination of soil and groundwater with petroleum products and chem icals at military bases
Environment—international agreements: *party to:* Air Pollution, Air Pollution-Nitrogen Oxides, Air Pollution-Persistent Organic Pollutants, Air Pollution-Sulphur 85, Air Pollution-Sulphur 94, Air Pollution-Volatile Organic Compounds, Biodiversity, Climate Change, Climate Change-Kyoto Protocol, Desertification, Endangered Species, Environmental Modification, Hazardous Wastes, Law of the Sea, Ozone Layer Protection, Ship Pollution, Wetlands
signed, but not ratified: none of the selected agreem ents
Geography—note: fertile central plains are separated by hilly uplands that are ancient glacial deposits

PEOPLE AND SOCIETY

Nationality: *noun:* Lithuanian(s)
adjective: Lithuanian
Ethnic groups: Lithuanian 84.1%, Polish 6.6%, Russian 5.8%, Belarusian 1.2%, other 1.1%, unspecified 1.2% (2011 est.)
Languages: Lithuanian (official) 82%, Russian 8%, Polish 5.6%, other 0.9%, unspecified 3.5% (2011 est.)
Religions: Roman Catholic 77.2%, RussiaNorthodox 4.1%, Old Believer 0.8%, Evangelical Lutheran 0.6%, Evangelical Reformist 0.2%, other (including Sunni Muslim, Jewish, Greek Catholic, and Karaite) 0.8%, none 6.1%, unspecified 10.1% (2011 est.)
Population: 2,884,433 (July 2015 est.)
country comparison to the world: 140
Age structure: *0–14 years:* 14.91% (male 220,460/female 209,501)
15–24 years: 11.97% (male 178,332/female 166,985)
25–54 years: 40.71% (male 575,323/female 598,912)
55–64 years: 13.26% (male 168,354/female 214,201)
65 years and over: 19.15% (male 186,458/female 365,907) (2015 est.)
Dependency ratios: *total dependency ratio:* 50.1%
youth dependency ratio: 21.8%
elderly dependency ratio: 28.3%
potential support ratio: 3.5% (2015 est.)
Median age: *total:* 43.1 years
male: 39.3 years
female: 46.3 years (2015 est.)
country comparison to the world: 14
Population growth rate: -1.04% (2015 est.)
country comparison to the world: 230
Birth rate: 10.1 births/1,000 population (2015 est.)
country comparison to the world: 193
Death rate: 14.27 deaths/1,000 population (2015 est.)
country comparison to the world: 7

Net migration rate: -6.27 migrant(s)/1,000 population (2015 est.)
country comparison to the world: 201
Urbanization: *urban Population:* 66.5% of total population (2015)
rate of urbanization: -0.53% annual rate of change (2010–15 est.)
Major urban areas—Population: VILNIUS (capital) 517,000 (2015)
Sex ratio: *at birth:* 1.06 male(s)/female
0–14 years: 1.05 male(s)/female
15–24 years: 1.07 male(s)/female
25–54 years: 0.96 male(s)/female
55–64 years: 0.79 male(s)/female
65 years and over: 0.51 male(s)/female
total population: 0.85 male(s)/female (2015 est.)
Mother's mean age at first birth: 26.7 (2011 est.)
Maternal mortality rate: 10 deaths/100,000 live births (2015 est.)
country comparison to the world: 163
Infant mortality rate: *total:* 3.84 deaths/1,000 live births
male: 4.3 deaths/1,000 live births
female: 3.36 deaths/1,000 live births (2015 est.)
country comparison to the world: 196
Life expectancy at birth: *total population:* 74.69 years
male: 69.24 years
female: 80.46 years (2015 est.)
country comparison to the world: 113
Total fertility rate: 1.59 children born/woman (2015 est.)
country comparison to the world: 182
Contraceptive prevalence rate: 62.9%
note: percent of women aged 18–49 (2006)
Health expenditures: 6.2% of GDP (2013)
country comparison to the world: 90
Physicians density: 4.12 physicians/1,000 population (2012)
Hospital bed density: 7 beds/1,000 population (2011)
Drinking water source:
improved:
urban: 99.7% of population
rural: 90.4% of population
total: 96.6% of population
unimproved:
urban: 0.3% of population
rural: 9.6% of population
total: 3.4% of population (2015 est.)
Sanitation facility access:
improved:
urban: 97.2% of population
rural: 82.8% of population
total: 92.4% of population
unimproved:
urban: 2.8% of population
rural: 17.2% of population
total: 7.6% of population (2015 est.)
HIV/AIDS—adult prevalence rate: NA
HIV/AIDS—people living with HIV/AIDS: NA
HIV/AIDS—deaths: NA
Major infectious diseases: *degree of risk:* intermediate
vectorborne diseases: tickborne encephalitis (2013)

Obesity—adult prevalence rate: 27.5% (2014)
country comparison to the world: 38
Education expenditures: 4.8% of GDP (2012)
country comparison to the world: 61
Literacy: *definition:* age 15 and over can read and write
total population: 99.8%
male: 99.8%
female: 99.8% (2015 est.)
School life expectancy (primary to tertiary education): *total:* 17 years
male: 16 years
female: 17 years (2014)
Unemployment, youth ages 15–24: *total:* 19.3%
male: 19.6%
female: 18.7% (2014 est.)
country comparison to the world: 35

GOVERNMENT

Country name: *conventional long form:* Republic of Lithuania
conventional short form: Lithuania
local long form: Lietuvos Respublika
local short form: Lietuva
former: Lithuanian Soviet Socialist Republic
etymology: meaning of the name "Lietuva" remains unclear; it may derive from the Lietava, a stream in east central Lithuania
Government type: semi-presidential republic
Capital: *name:* Vilnius
Geographic coordinates: 54 41 N, 25 19 E
time difference: UTC+2 (7 hours ahead of Washington, DC, during Standard Time)
daylight saving time: +1hr, begins last Sunday in March; ends last Sunday in October
Administrative divisions: 60 municipalities (savivaldybe, singular—savivaldybe); Akmene, Alytaus Miestas, Alytus, Anksciai, Birstono, Birzai, Druskininkai, Elektrenai, Ignalina, Jonava, Joniskis, Jurbarkas, Kaisiadorys, Kalvarijos, Kauno Miestas, Kaunas, Kazlu Rudos, Kedainiai, Kelme, Klaipedos Miestas, Klaipeda, Kretinga, Kupiskis, Lazdijai, Marijampole, Mazeikiai, Moletai, Neringa, Pagegiai, Pakruojis, Palangos Miestas, Panevezio Miestas, Panevezys, Pasvalys, Plunge, Prienai, Radviliskis, Raseiniai, Rietavo, Rokiskis, Sakiai, Salcininkai, Siauliu Miestas, Siauliai, Silale, Silute, Sirvintos, Skuodas, Svencionys, Taurage, Telsiai, Trakai, Ukmerge, Utena, Varena, Vilkaviskis, Vilniaus Miestas, Vilnius, Visaginas, Zarasai
Independence: 11 March 1990 (declared); 6 September 1991 (recognized by the Soviet Union); notable earlier dates: 6 July 1253 (coronation of MINDAUGAS, traditional founding date),1 July 1569 (Polish-Lithuanian Commonwealth created), 16 February 1918 (independence from Soviet Russia)
National holiday: Independence Day, 16 February (1918); note—16 February 1918 was the date Lithuania established its statehood and its comitant independence from Soviet Russia and Germany; 11 March 1990 was the date it declared the restoration of Lithuanian statehood and its concomitant independence from the Soviet Union
Constitution: several previous; latest adopted by referendum 25 October 1992, entered into force

509

2 November 1992; amended 1996, 2003, 2006 (2016)

Legal system: civil law system; legislative acts can be appealed to the constitutional court

International law organization participation: accepts compulsory ICJ jurisdiction with reservations; accepts ICCt jurisdiction

Citizenship: *citizenship by birth:* no

citizenship by descent only: at least one parent must be a citizen of Lithuania

dual citizenship recognized: no

residency requirement for naturalization: 10 years

Suffrage: 18 years of age; universal

Executive branch: *chief of state:* President Dalia GRYBAUSKAITE (since 12 July 2009)

head of government: *Prime Minister Algirdas BUTKEVICIUS (since 22 November 2012)*

cabinet: Council of Ministers nominated by the prime minister, appointed by the president, and approved by Parliament

elections/appointments: president directly elected by absolute majority popular vote in 2 rounds if needed for a 5-year term (eligible for a second term); election last held on 11 and 25 May 2014 (next to be held in May 2019); prime minister appointed by the president, approved by Parliament

election results: Dalia GRYBAUSKAITE reelected president; percent of vote—Dalia GRYBAUSKAITE (independent) 59%, Zigmantas BALCYTIS (LSDP) 41%; Algirdas BUTKEVICIUS (LSDP) approved as prime minister by Parliament vote—90 of 130

Legislative branch: *description:* unicameral Parliament or Seimas (141 seats; 71 members directly elected in single-seat constituencies by absolute majority vote and 70 directly elected in a single nationwide constituency by proportional representation vote; members serve 4-year terms)

elections: last held on 14 and 28 October 2012 (next to be held in October 2016)

election results: percent of vote by party—DP 19.8%, LSDP 18.4%, TS-LKD 15.1%, LS 8.6%, DK 8%, TT 7.3%, LLRA 5.8%, LVZS 3.9%, other 13.1%; seats by party—LSDP 38, TS-LKD 33, DP 29, TT 11, LS 11, LLRA 8, DK 7, LVZS 1, independent 3

Judicial branch: *highest court(s):* Supreme Court (consists of 37 judges); Constitutional Court (consists of 9 judges)

judge selection and term of office: Supreme Court judges nominated by the president and appointed by the Seimas; judges serve 5-year renewable terms; Constitutional Court judges selected by the Seimas from among nominations by the president, by the Seimas chairperson, and Supreme Court chairperson; judges serve 9-year, nonrenewable terms; note—one-third of court judges reconstituted every 3 years

subordinate courts: Court of Appeals; district and local courts

Political parties and leaders: Electoral Action of Lithuanian Poles or LLRA [Valdemar TOMASEVSKI]

Homeland Union-Lithuanian Christian Democrats or TS-LKD [Gabrielius LANDSBERGIS]

Labor Party or DP [Valentinas MAZURONIS]

Liberal Movement or LS or LRLS [Eligijus MASIULIS]

Lithuanian Green Party or LZP [Linas BALSYS]

Lithuanian Social Democratic Party or LSDP [Algirdas BUTKEVICIUS]

Order and Justice Party or TT [Rolandas PAKSAS]

Peasant and Greens Union or LVZS [Ramunas KARBAUSKIS]

Way of Courage or DK [Jonas VARKALA]

International organization participation: Australia Group, BA, BIS, CBSS, CD, CE, EAPC, EBRD, ECB, EIB, EU, FAO, IAEA, IBRD, ICAO, ICC (national committees), ICCt, ICRM, IDA, IFC, IFRCS, ILO, IMF, IMO, Interpol, IOC, IOM, IPU, ISO, ITU, ITUC (NGOs), MIGA, NATO, NIB, NSG, OAS (observer), OIF (observer), OPCW, OSCE, PCA, Schengen Convention, UN, UN Security Council (non-permanent), UNCTAD, UNESCO, UNIDO, UNWTO, UPU, WCO, WHO, WIPO, WMO, WTO

Diplomatic representation in the US: *chief of mission:* Ambassador Rolandas KRISCIUNAS (since 17 September 2015)

chancery: 2622 16th Street NW, Washington, DC 20009

telephone: [1] (202) 234-5860

FAX: [1] (202) 328-0466

consulate(s) general: Chicago, Los Angeles, New York

Diplomatic representation from the US: *chief of mission:* Ambassador Deborah A. MCCARTHY (since 5 February 2013)

embassy: Akmenu gatve 6, Vilnius, LT-03106

mailing address: American Embassy, Akmenu Gatve 6, Vilnius LT-03106

telephone: [370] (5) 266-5500

FAX: [370] (5) 266-5510

Flag description: three equal horizontal bands of yellow (top), green, and red; yellow symbolizes golden fields, as well as the sun, light, and goodness; green represents the forests of the countryside, in addition to nature, freedom, and hope; red stands for courage and the blood spilled in defense of the homeland

National symbol(s): mounted knight known as Vytis (the Chaser), white stork; national colors: yellow, green, red

National anthem: *name:* "Tautiska giesme" (The National Song)

lyrics/music: Vincas KUDIRKA

note: adopted 1918, restored 1990; written in 1898 while Lithuania was a part of Russia; banned during the Soviet occupation from 1940 to 1990

ECONOMY

Economy—overview: Lithuania gained membership in the WTO in May 2001 and joined the EU in May 2004. Lithuania's trade with the EU and CIS countries accounts for approximately 87.3% of total trade. Foreign investment and EU funding have aided in the transition from the former planned economy to a market economy. The three former Soviet Baltic republics were severely hit

by the 2008–09 financial crisis, but Lithuania has rebounded and become one of the fastest growing economies in the EU. Lithuania's ongoing recovery hinges on export growth, which is being hampered by economic slowdowns in the EU and Russia. Lithuania joined the euro zone on 1 January 2015 and is under review for membership in the OECD.

GDP (purchasing power parity): $82.36 billion (2015 est.)

$81.06 billion (2014 est.)

$78.68 billion (2013 est.)

note: data are in 2015 US dollars

country comparison to the world: 90

GDP (official exchange rate): $41.27 billion (2015 est.)

GDP—real growth rate: 1.6% (2015 est.)

3% (2014 est.) 3.5% (2013 est.)

country comparison to the world: 147

GDP—per capita (PPP): $28,400 (2015 est.)

$27,600 (2014 est.)

$26,600 (2013 est.)

note: data are in 2015 US dollars

country comparison to the world: 65

Gross national saving: 16.4% of GDP (2015 est.)

21.9% of GDP (2014 est.)

20.7% of GDP (2013 est.)

country comparison to the world: 101

GDP—composition, by end use:

household consumption: 64.5%

government consumption: 16.5%

investment in fixed capital: 20.3%

investment in inventories: 3.7%

exports of goods and services: 83.2%

imports of goods and services: -88.2% (2015 est.)

GDP—composition, by sector of origin:

agriculture: 3.5%

industry: 30.7%

services: 65.8% (2015 est.)

Agriculture—products: grain, potatoes, sugar beets, flax, vegetables; beef, milk, eggs, pork, cheese; fish

Industries: metal-cutting machine tools, electric motors, television sets, refrigerators and freezers, petroleum refining, shipbuilding (small ships), furniture, textiles, food processing, fertilizers, agricultural machinery, optical equipment, lasers, electronic components, computers, amber jewelry, information technology, video game development, biotechnology

Industrial production growth rate: 3.6% (2015 est.)

country comparison to the world: 65

Labor force: 1.464 million (2015 est.)

country comparison to the world: 133

Labor force—by occupation: *agriculture:* 7.9%

industry: 19.6%

services: 72.5% (2012 est.)

Unemployment rate: 8.2% (2015 est.)

10.7% (2014 est.)

country comparison to the world: 95

Population below poverty line: 4% (2008 est.)

Household income or consumption by percentage share: *lowest:* 10%: 2.6%

highest: 10%: 29.1% (2008)

Distribution of family income— Gini index: 35.5 (2009)

34 (1999)

country comparison to the world: 91

Budget: *revenues:* $13.31 billion
expenditures: $13.97 billion (2015 est.)
Taxes and other revenues: 31.9% of GDP (2015 est.)
country comparison to the world: 78
Budget surplus (+) or deficit (–): -1.6% of GDP (2015 est.)
country comparison to the world: 64
Public debt: 38.8% of GDP (2015 est.)
39.3% of GDP (2014 est.)
note: official data; data cover general government debt, and includes debt instruments issued (or owned) by government entities other than the treasury; the data include treasury debt held by foreign entities, debt issued by subnational entities, as well as intra-governmental debt; intragovernmental debt consists of treasury borrowings from surpluses in the social funds, such as for retirement, medical care, and unemployment; debt instruments for the social funds are sold at public auctions
country comparison to the world: 120
Fiscal year: calen dar year
Inflation rate (consumer prices): -0.7% (2015 est.)
0.2% (2014 est.)
country comparison to the world: 19
Central bank discount rate: 0.05% (31 December 2013)
0.3% (31 December 2012)
country comparison to the world: 140
Commercial bank prime lending rate: 3.2% (31 December 2015 est.)
3.5% (31 December 2014 est.)
country comparison to the world: 168
Stock of narrow money: $17.4 billion (31 December 2015 est.)
$14.67 billion (31 December 2014 est.)
country comparison to the world: 67
Stock of broad money: $22.25 billion (31 December 2015 est.)
$22.41 billion (31 December 2013 est.)
country comparison to the world: 86
Stock of domestic credit: $21.08 billion (31 December 2015 est.)
$22.34 billion (31 December 2014 est.)
country comparison to the world: 84
Market value of publicly traded shares: $3.964 billion (31 December 2012 est.)
$4.075 billion (31 December 2011)
$5.661 billion (31 December 2010 est.)
country comparison to the world: 92
Current account balance: -$932 million (2015 est.)
$1.734 billion (2014 est.)
country comparison to the world: 117
Exports: $30.92 billion (2015 est.)
$31.55 billion (2014 est.)
country comparison to the world: 62
Exports—commodities: refined fuel, machinery and equipment, chemicals, textiles, foodstuffs, plastics
Exports—partners: Russia 13.7%, Latvia 9.8%, Poland 9.7%, Germany 7.8%, Estonia 5.3%, Belarus 4.6%, UK 4.5%, US 4.4%, Netherlands 4% (2015)
Imports: $33.97 billion (2015 est.)
$33.54 billion (2014 est.)
country comparison to the world: 62

Imports—commodities: oil, natural gas, machinery and equipment, transport equipment, chemicals, textiles and clothing, metals
Imports—partners: Russia 16.9%, Germany 11.5%, Poland 10.3%, Latvia 7.6%, Netherlands 5.1%, Italy 4.5% (2015)
Reserves of foreign exchange and gold: $8.728 billion (31 December 2014 est.)
$8.072 billion (31 December 2013 est.)
country comparison to the world: 78
Debt—external: $30.81 billion (31 December 2014 est.)
$33.64 billion (31 December 2013 est.)
country comparison to the world: 74
Stock of direct foreign investment—at home: $17.1 billion (31 December 2015 est.)
$15.8 billion (31 December 2014 est.)
country comparison to the world: 82
Stock of direct foreign investment—abroad: $4.164 billion (31 December 2015 est.)
$3.814 billion (31 December 2014 est.)
country comparison to the world: 70
Exchange rates: litai (LTL) per US dollar—
0.9091 (2015 est.)
0.7525 (2014 est.)
0.7525 (2013 est.)
2.69 (2012 est.)
2.481 (2011 est.)

ENERGY

Electricity—production: 3.927 billion kWh (2012 est.)
country comparison to the world: 126
Electricity—consumption: 9.664 billion kWh (2012 est.)
country comparison to the world: 91
Electricity—exports: 1.127 billion kWh (2013 est.)
country comparison to the world: 53
Electricity—imports: 8.073 billion kWh (2013 est.)
country comparison to the world: 29
Electricity—installed generating capacity: 3.714 million kW (2012 est.)
country comparison to the world: 86
Electricity—from fossil fuels: 68.8% of total installed capacity (2012 est.)
country comparison to the world: 112
Electricity—from nuclear fuels: 0% of total installed capacity (2012 est.)
country comparison to the world: 128
Electricity—from hydroelectric plants: 3.1% of total installed capacity (2012 est.)
country comparison to the world: 131
Electricity—from other renewable sources: 7.6% of total installed capacity (2012 est.)
country comparison to the world: 50
Crude oil—production: 2,000 bbl/day (2014 est.)
country comparison to the world: 88
Crude oil—exports: 1,552 bbl/day (2012 est.)
country comparison to the world: 80
Crude oil—imports: 181900 bbl/day (2012 est.)
country comparison to the world: 35
Crude oil—proved reserves: 12 million bbl (1 January 2015 est.)
country comparison to the world: 90

Refined petroleum products—production: 192,000 bbl/day (2012 est.)
country comparison to the world: 56
Refined petroleum products—consumption: 55,000 bbl/day (2013 est.)
country comparison to the world: 94
Refined petroleum products—exports: 160,300 bbl/day (2012 est.)
country comparison to the world: 39
Refined petroleum products—imports: 22,620 bbl/day (2012 est.)
country comparison to the world: 105
Natural gas—production: 0 cu m (2013 est.)
country comparison to the world: 212
Natural gas—consumption:
3.24 billion cu m (2013 est.)
country comparison to the world: 69
Natural gas—exports: 0 cu m (2013 est.)
country comparison to the world: 134
Natural gas—imports: 3.24 billion cu m (2013 est.)
country comparison to the world: 40
Natural gas—proved reserves: 0 cu m (1 January 2014 est.)
country comparison to the world: 160
Carbon dioxide emissions from consumption of energy: 16.69 million Mt (2012 est.)
country comparison to the world: 86

COMMUNICATIONS

Telephones—fixed lines: *total subscriptions:* 590,000
subscriptions per 100 inhabitants: 20 (2014 est.)
country comparison to the world: 93
Telephones—mobile cellular: *total:* 4.4 million
subscriptions per 100 inhabitants: 152 (2014 est.)
country comparison to the world: 124
Telephone system: *general assessment:* adequate; being modernized to provide improved international capability and better residential access
domestic: rapid expansion of mobile-cellular services has resulted in a steady decline in the number of fixed-line connections; mobile-cellular teledensity stands at about 140 per 100 persons
international: country code—370; major international connections to Denmark, Sweden, and Norway by submarine cable for further transmission by satellite; landline connections to Latvia and Poland (2010)
Broadcast media: public broadcaster operates 3 channels with the third channel—a satellite channel—introduced in 2007; various privately owned commercial TV broadcasters operate national and multiple regional channels; many privately owned local TV stations; multi-channel cable and satellite TV services available; publicly owned broadcaster operates 3 radio networks; many privately owned commercial broadcasters, with repeater stations in various regions throughout the country (2007)
Radio broadcast stations: AM 29, FM 142, shortwave 1 (2001)
Television broadcast stations: 44 (may have as many as 100 transmitters, including repeater stations) (2008)
Internet country code: .lt

511

Internet hosts: 1.205 million (2012)
country comparison to the world: 43
Internet users: *total:* 2 million
percent of population: 70.3% (2014 est.)
country comparison to the world: 97

TRANSPORTATION

Airports: 61 (2013)
country comparison to the world: 79
Airports—with paved runways: *total:* 22
over 3,047 m: 3
2,438 to 3,047 m: 1
1,524 to 2,437 m: 7
914 to 1,523 m: 2
under 914 m: 9 (2013)
Airports—with unpaved runways: *total:* 39
over 3,047 m: 1
914 to 1,523 m: 2
under 914 m: 36 (2013)
Pipelines: gas 1921 km; refined products 121 km (2013)
Railways: *total:* 1,768 km
broad gauge: 1,746 km 1.520-m gauge (122 km electrified)
standard gauge: 22 km 1.435-m gauge (2014)
country comparison to the world: 76
Roadways: *total:* 84,166 km
paved: 72,297 km (includes 312 km of expressways)
unpaved: 11,869 km (2012)
country comparison to the world: 56
Waterways: 441 km (navigable year round) (2007)

country comparison to the world: 86
Merchant marine: *total:* 38
by type: cargo 20, container 1, passenger/cargo 6, refrigerated cargo 9, roll on/roll off 2
foreign-owned: 8 (Denmark 8)
registered in other countries: 22 (Antigua and Barbuda 3, Belize 1, Comoros 1, Cook Islands 1, Norway 1, Panama 3, Saint Vincent and the Grenadines 9, unknown 3) (2010)
country comparison to the world: 77
Ports and terminals: *major seaport(s):* Klaipeda
oil terminals: Butinge oil terminal
LNG terminal(s) (import): Klaipeda

MILITARY AND SECURITY

Military branches: Lithuanian Armed Forces (Lietuvos Ginkluotosios Pajegos): Land Forces (Sausumos Pajegos), Naval Forces (Karines Juru Pajegos), Air Forces (Karines Oro Pajegos), Special Forces (Specialiuju Operaciju Pajegos); Volunteer Forces (Savanoriu Pajegos) (2015)
Military service age and obligation: 18 years of age for military service; 9-month service obligation; Lithuania converted to a professional military in the fall of 2008, although the decision continues under judicial review; a new law passed in March 2015 restored conscription on a limited, 5-year basis; in March 2016, Lithuania's National Security and Defense Council recommended permanently restoring conscription service (2016)
Military expenditures: 1.48% of GDP (2016)

1.11% of GDP (2015)
0.9% of GDP (2014)
0.8% of GDP (2013)
0.97% of GDP (2012)
country comparison to the world: 103

TRANSNATIONAL ISSUES

Disputes—international: Lithuania and Russia committed to demarcating their boundary in 2006 in accordance with the land and maritime treaty ratified by Russia in May 2003 and by Lithuania in 1999; Lithuania operates a simplified transit regime for Russian nationals traveling from the Kaliningrad coastal exclave into Russia, while still conforming, as a EU member state having an external border with a non-EU member, to strict Schengen border rules; boundary demarcated with Latvia and Lithuania; as of January 2007, ground demarcation of the boundary with Belarus was complete and mapped with final ratification documents in preparation
Refugees and internally displaced persons: *stateless persons:* 3,466 (2015)
Illicit drugs: transshipment and destination point for cannabis, cocaine, ecstasy, and opiates from Southwest Asia, Latin America, Western Europe, and neighboring Baltic countries; growing production of high-quality amphetamines, but limited production of cannabis, methamphetamines; susceptible to money laundering despite changes to banking legislation

LUXEMBOURG

INTRODUCTION

Background: Founded in 963, Luxembourg became a grand duchy in 1815 and an independent state under the Netherlands. It lost more than half of its territory to Belgium in 1839 but gained a larger measure of autonomy. Full independence was attained in 1867. Overrun by Germany in both world wars, it ended its neutrality in 1948 when

it entered into the Benelux Customs Union and when it joined NATO the following year. in 1957, Luxembourg became one of the six founding countries of the European Economic Community (later the EU), and in 1999 it joined the euro currency area.

GEOGRAPHY

Location: Western Europe, between France and Germany
Geographic coordinates: 49 45 N, 6 10 E
Map references: Europe
Area: *total:* 2,586 sq km
land: 2,586 sq km
water: 0 sq km
country comparison to the world: 179
Area—comparative: slightly smaller than Rhode Island
Land boundaries: *total:* 327 km
border countries (3): Belgium 130 km, France 69 km, Germany 128 km
Coastline: 0 km (landlocked)
Maritime claims: none (landlocked)
Climate: modified continental with mild winters, cool summers
Terrain: mostly gently rolling uplands with broad, shallow valleys; uplands to slightly mountainous in

the north; steep slope down to Moselle flood plain in the southeast
Elevation: *mean elevation:* 325 m
elevation extremes: *lowest point:* Moselle River 133 m
highest point: Buurgplaatz 559 m
Natural resources: iron ore (no longer exploited), arable land
Land use: *agricultural land:* 50.7%
arable land: 24%
permanent crops: 0.6%
permanent pasture: 26.1%
forest: 33.5%
other: 15.8% (2011 est.)
Irrigated land: 0 sq km (2012)
Total renewable water resources: 3.1 cu km (2011)
Freshwater withdrawal (domestic/industrial/agricultural): *total:* 0.06 cu km/yr (65%/33%/1%)
per capita: 135.9 cu m/yr (2010)
Natural hazards: NA
Environment—current issues: air and water pollution in urban areas, soil pollution of farmland
Environment—international agreements: *party to:* Air Pollution, Air Pollution-Nitrogen Oxides, Air Pollution-Persistent Organic Pollutants, Air Pollution-Sulfur 85, Air Pollution-Sulfur 94, Air Pollution-Volatile Organic Compounds, Biodiversity, Climate Change, Climate Change-Kyoto

Protocol, Desertification, Endangered Species, Hazardous Wastes, Law of the Sea, Marine Dumping, Ozone Layer Protection, Ship Pollution, Tropical Timber 83, Tropical Timber 94, Wetlands
signed, but not ratified: Environmental Modification
Geography—note: landlocked; the only Grand Duchy in the world

PEOPLE AND SOCIETY

Nationality: *noun:* Luxembourger(s)
adjective: Luxembourg
Ethnic groups: Luxembourger 54.1%, Portuguese 16.4%, French 7%, Italian 3.5%, Belgian 3.3%, German 2.3%, British 1.1%, other 12.3%
note: represents population by nationality (2015 est.)
Languages: Luxembourgish (official administrative and judicial language and national language (spoken vernacular)) 88.8%, French (official administrative, judicial, and legislative language) 4.2%, Portuguese 2.3%, German (official administrative and judicial language) 1.1%, other 3.5% (2011 est.)
Religions: Roman Catholic 87%, other (includes Protestant, Jewish, and Muslim) 13% (2000)
Population: 570,252 (July 2015 est.)
country comparison to the world: 173
Age structure: *0–14 years:* 16.93% (male 49,677/female 46,886)
15–24 years: 12.28% (male 35,983/female 34,062)
25–54 years: 44.37% (male 129,660/female 123,355)
55–64 years: 11.51% (male 33,280/female 32,351)
65 years and over: 14.91% (male 37,460/female 47,538) (2015 est.)
Dependency ratios: *total dependency ratio:* 43.7%
youth dependency ratio: 23.6%
elderly dependency ratio: 20.1%
potential support ratio: 5% (2015 est.)
Median age: *total:* 39.2 years
male: 38.6 years
female: 39.9 years (2015 est.)
country comparison to the world: 52
Population growth rate: 2.13% (2015 est.)
country comparison to the world: 44
Birth rate: 11.37 births/1,000 population (2015 est.)
country comparison to the world: 173
Death rate: 7.24 deaths/1,000 population (2015 est.)
country comparison to the world: 122
Net migration rate: 17.16 migrant(s)/1,000 population (2015 est.)
country comparison to the world: 3
Urbanization: *urban Population:* 90.2% of total population (2015)
rate of urbanization: 1.71% annual rate of change (2010–15 est.)
Major urban areas—Population: LUXEMBOURG (capital) 107,000 (2014)
Sex ratio: *at birth:* 1.06 male(s)/female
0–14 years: 1.06 male(s)/female
15–24 years: 1.06 male(s)/female

25–54 years: 1.05 male(s)/female
55–64 years: 1.03 male(s)/female
65 years and over: 0.79 male(s)/female
total population: 1.01 male(s)/female (2015 est.)
Mother's mean age at first birth: 30.2 (2012 est.)
Maternal mortality rate: 10 deaths/100,000 live births (2015 est.)
country comparison to the world: 141
Infant mortality rate: *total:* 3.46 deaths/1,000 live births
male: 3.84 deaths/1,000 live births
female: 3.05 deaths/1,000 live births (2015 est.)
country comparison to the world: 205
Life expectancy at birth: *total population:* 82.17 years
male: 79.73 years
female: 84.76 years (2015 est.)
country comparison to the world: 12
Total fertility rate: 1.61 children born/woman (2015 est.)
country comparison to the world: 178
Health expenditures: 7.1% of GDP (2013)
country comparison to the world: 82
Physicians density: 2.9 physicians/1,000 population (2013)
Hospital bed density: 5.4 beds/1,000 population (2010)
Drinking water source:
improved:
urban: 100% of population
rural: 100% of population
total: 100% of population
unimproved:
urban: 0% of population
rural: 0% of population
total: 0% of population (2015 est.)
Sanitation facility access:
improved:
urban: 97.5% of population
rural: 98.5% of population
total: 97.6% of population
unimproved:
urban: 2.5% of population
rural: 1.5% of population
total: 2.4% of population (2015 est.)
HIV/AIDS—adult prevalence rate: NA
HIV/AIDS—people living with HIV/AIDS: NA
HIV/AIDS—deaths: NA
Obesity—adult prevalence rate: 24.8% (2014)
country comparison to the world: 50
School life expectancy (primary to tertiary education): *total:* 14 years
male: 14 years
female: 14 years (2012)
Unemployment, youth ages 15–24: *total:* 15.5%
male: 18.7%
female: 10.9% (2013 est.)
country comparison to the world: 59

GOVERNMENT

Country name: *conventional long form:* Grand Duchy of Luxembourg
conventional short form: Luxembourg
local long form: Grand Duchee de Luxembourg
local short form: Luxembourg

etymology: from the Celtic "lucilem" (little) and the German "burg" (castle or fortress) to produce the meaning of the "little castle"
Government type: constitutional monarchy
Capital: *name:* Luxembourg
Geographic coordinates: 49 36 N, 6 07 E
time difference: UTC+1 (6 hours ahead of Washington, DC, during Standard Time)
daylight saving time: +1hr, begins last Sunday in March; ends last Sunday in October
Administrative divisions: 12 cantons (cantons, singular—canton); Capellen, Clervaux, Diekirch, Echternach, Esch-sur-Alzette, Grevenmacher, Luxembourg, Mersch, Redange, Remich, Vianden, Wiltz
Independence: 1839 (from the Netherlands)
National holiday: National Day (birthday of Grand Duke Henri) 23 June; note—this date of birth is not the true date of birth for any of the Royals, but the festivities were shifted to allow observance during a more favorable time of year
Constitution: previous 1842 (heavily amended 1848,1856); latest effective 17 October 1868; amended many times, last in 2009 (2016)
Legal system: civil law system
International law organization participation: accepts compulsory ICJ jurisdiction; accepts ICCt jurisdiction
Citizenship: *citizenship by birth:* no
citizenship by descent only: at least one parent must be a citizen of Luxembourg
dual citizenship recognized: no
residency requirement for naturalization: 10 years
Suffrage: 18 years of age; universal and compulsory
Executive branch: *chief of state:* Grand Duke HENRI (since 7 October 2000); Heir Apparent Prince GUILLAUME (son of the monarch, born 11 November 1981)

head of government: Prime Minister Xavier BETTEL (since 4 December 2013); Deputy Prime Minister Etienne SCHNEIDER (since 4 December 2013)

cabinet: Council of Ministers recommended by the prime minister, appointed by the monarch
elections/appointments: the monarchy is hereditary; following elections to the Chamber of Deputies, the leader of the majority party or majority coalition usually appointed prime minister by the monarch; deputy prime minister appointed by the monarch; prime minister and deputy prime minister are responsible to the Chamber of Deputies
Legislative branch: *description:* unicameral Chamber of Deputies or Chambre des Deputes (60 seats; members directly elected in multi-seat constituencies by proportional representation vote; members serve 5-year terms); note—a 21-member Council of State appointed by the Grand Duke on the advice of the prime minister serves as an advisory body to the Chamber of Deputies
elections: last held on 20 October 2013 (next to be held by June 2018)
election results: percent of vote by party—CSV 33.7%, LSAP 20.3%, DP 18.3%, Green Party 10.1%, ADR 6.6%, The Left 4.9%, other 6.1%;

seats by party—CSV 23, LSAP 13, DP 13, Green Party 6, ADR 3, The Left 2

Judicial branch: *highest court(s):* Superior Court of Justice includes Court of Appeal and Court of Cassation (consists of 27 judges on 9 benches); Constitutional Court (consists of 9 members)
judge selection and term of office: judges of both courts appointed by the monarch for life
subordinate courts: district and local tribunals and courts

Political parties and leaders: Alternative Democratic Reform Party or ADR [Jean SCHOOS]
Christian Social People's Party or CSV [Claude WISELER]
Democratic Party or DP [Corinne CAHEN]
Green Party [Francoise FOLMER and Christian KMIOTEK]
Luxembourg Socialist Workers' Party or LSAP [Claude HAAGEN]
The Left (dei Lenk/la Gauche) [Central Committee]
other minor parties

Political pressure groups and leaders: Business Federation Luxembourg or FEDIL [Nicolas BUCK, chairman]
Centrale Paysanne [Marc FISCH] (federation of agricultural producers)
Chamber of Artisans (Chambre des Metiers) [Roland KUHN]
Chamber of Commerce (Chambre de Commerce) [Carlo THELEN]
Chambre des Salaires or CSL [Jean-Claude REDING]
General Association of Officials (Confederation Generale de la Fonction Publique or CGFP [Romain WOLFF] (trade union representing civil service) Greenpeace [Kumi NAIDOO]
LCGP [Patrick DURY] (center-right trade union)
Luxembourgassociation of Bankers and Insurance Employees or ALEBA [Roberto SCOLATI]
Luxembourg Bankers Association or ABBL [Yves MAAS]
Mouvement Ecologique [Blanche WEBER] (environment protection)
OGB-L [Andre ROELTGEN] (center-left trade union)

International organization participation: ADB (nonregional member), Australia Group, Benelux, BIS, CD, CE, EAPC, EBRD, ECB, EIB, EMU, ESA, EU, FAO, FATF, IAEA, IBRD, ICAO, ICC (national committees), ICCt, ICRM, IDA, IEA, IFAD, IFC, IFRCS, ILO, IMF, IMO, Interpol, IOC, IOM, IPU, ISO, ITSO, ITU, ITUC (NGOs), MIGA, NATO, NEA, NSG, OAS (observer), OECD, OIF, OPCW, OSCE, PCA, Schengen Convention, UN, UNCTAD, UNESCO, UNHCR, UNIDO, UNRWA, UPU, WCO, WHO, WIPO, WMO, WTO, ZC

Diplomatic representation in the US: *chief of mission:* Ambassador Jean-Louis WOLZFELD (since 11 September 2012)
chancery: 2200 Massachusetts Avenue NW, Washington, DC 20008
telephone: [1] (202) 265-4171 through 72
FAX: [1] (202) 328-8270
consulate(s) general: New York, San Francisco

Diplomatic representation from the US: *chief of mission:* Ambassador David MCKEAN (since 14 April 2016)
embassy: 22 Boulevard Emmanuel Servais, L-2535 Luxembourg City
mailing address: American Embassy Luxembourg, Unit 1410, APOAE 09126–1410 (official mail); American Embassy Luxembourg, PSC 9, Box 9500, APOAE 09123 (personal mail)
telephone: [352] 46-01-23
FAX: [352] 46-14-01

Flag description: three equal horizontal bands of red (top), white, and light blue; similar to the flag of the Netherlands, which uses a darker blue and is shorter; the coloring is derived from the Grand Duke's coat of arms (a red lion on a white and blue striped field)

National symbol(s): lion; national colors: red, white, light blue

National anthem: *name:* "Ons Heemecht" (Our Motherland); "De Wilhelmus" (The William)
lyrics/music: Michel LENTZ/Jean-Antoine ZINNEN; Nikolaus WELTER/unknown
note: "Ons Heemecht, " adopted 1864, is the national anthem, while "De Wilhelmus, " adopted 1919, serves as a royal anthem for use when members of the grand ducal family enter or exit a ceremony in Luxembourg

ECONOMY

Economy—overview: This small, stable, high-income economy has historically featured solid growth, low inflation, and low unemployment. The industrial sector, initially dominated by steel, has become increasingly diversified to include chemicals, machinery and equipment, rubber, automotive components, and other products. The financial sector, which accounts for about 36% of GDP, is the leading sector in the economy. The economy depends on foreign and cross-border workers for about 39% of its labor force.
Luxembourg experienced uneven economic growth in the aftermath of the global economic crisis that began in late 2008. Luxembourg's GDP contracted 3.6% in 2009, rebounded in 2010–12, fell again in 2013, but recovered in 2014. Unemployment has remained below the EU average despite having increased from a historically low rate of 4% in the 2000s to 7% in 2014.
The country continues to enjoy an extraordinarily high standard of living—GDP per capita ranks among the highest in the world and is the highest in the euro zone. Luxembourg has one of the highest current account surpluses as a share of GDP in the euro zone, and it maintains a healthy budgetary position and the lowest public debt level in the region.
Luxembourg has lost some of its advantage as a favorable tax location because of OECD and EU pressure. In 2015, the government's compliance with EU requirements to implement automatic exchange of tax information on savings accounts—thus ending banking secrecy—has depressed banking activity and dampened GDP growth. Likewise, changes to the way EU members collect taxes from e-Commerce has cut Luxembourg's tax revenues,

requiring the government to raise additional levies and to reduce some direct social benefits.

GDP (purchasing power parity): $55.73 billion (2015 est.)
$53.32 billion (2014 est.)
$51.23 billion (2013 est.)
note: data are in 2015 US dollars
country comparison to the world: 107

GDP (official exchange rate): $57.42 billion (2015 est.)

GDP—real growth rate: 4.5% (2015 est.)
4.1% (2014 est.)
4.3% (2013 est.)
country comparison to the world: 48

GDP—per capita (PPP): $99,000 (2015 est.)
$96,900 (2014 est.)
$95,400 (2013 est.)
note: data are in 2015 US dollars
country comparison to the world: 2

Gross national saving: 23.4% of GDP (2015 est.)
24.8% of GDP (2014 est.)
24% of GDP (2013 est.)
country comparison to the world: 61

GDP—composition, by end use:
household consumption: 28.9%
government consumption: 16.1%
investment in fixed capital: 17.6%
investment in inventories: 0.6%
exports of goods and services: 200.5%
imports of goods and services: -163.7% (2015 est.)

GDP—composition, by sector of origin:
agriculture: 0.3%
industry: 11.3%
services: 88.3% (2015 est.)

Agriculture—products: grapes, barley, oats, potatoes, wheat, fruits; dairy and livestock products

Industries: banking and financial services, construction, real estate services, iron, metals, and steel, information technology, telecommunications, cargo transportation and logistics, chemicals, engineering, tires, glass, aluminum, tourism, biotechnology

Industrial production growth rate: 1% (2015 est.)
country comparison to the world: 146

Labor force: 265,800
note: data exclude foreign workers; in addition to the figure for domestic labor force, about 150,000 workers commute daily from France, Belgium, and Germany (2015 est.)
country comparison to the world: 165

Labor force—by occupation: *agriculture:* 1.1%
industry: 20%
services: 78.9% (2013 est.)

Unemployment rate: 6.9% (2015 est.)
7.1% (2014 est.)
country comparison to the world: 83

Population below poverty line: NA%

Household income or consumption by percentage share: *lowest:* 10%: 3.5%
highest: 10%: 23.8% (2000)

Distribution of family income— Gini index: 30.4 (2013 est.)
26 (2005 est.)
country comparison to the world: 118

Budget: *revenues:* $23.65 billion

expenditures: $23.65 billion (2015 est.)

Taxes and other revenues: 40.8% of GDP (2015 est.)

country comparison to the world: 36

Budget surplus (+) or deficit (–): 0% of GDP (2015 est.)

country comparison to the world: 30

Public debt: 21.7% of GDP (2015 est.)

22.5% of GDP (2014 est.)

note: data cover general government debt, and includes debt instruments issued (or owned) by government entities other than the treasury; the data include treasury debt held by foreign entities; the data include debt issued by subnational entities, as well as intra-governmental debt; intra-governmental debt consists of treasury borrowings from surpluses in the social funds, such as for retirement, medical care, and unemployment; debt instruments for the social funds are not sold at public auctions

country comparison to the world: 153

Fiscal year: calendar year

Inflation rate (consumer prices): 0.1% (2015 est.) 0.7% (2014 est.)

country comparison to the world: 45

Central bank discount rate: 0.05% (31 December 2013) 0.3% (31 December 2010)

note: this is the European Central Bank's rate on the marginal lending facility, which offers overnight credit to banks in the euro area

country comparison to the world: 142

Stock of narrow money: $215.7 billion (31 December 2015 est.)

$211.9 billion (31 December 2014 est.)

note: see entry for the European Union for money supply for the entire euro area; the European Central Bank (ECB) controls monetary policy for the 18 members of the Economic and Monetary Union (EMU); individual members of the EMU do not control the quantity of money circulating within their own borders

country comparison to the world: 20

Stock of broad money: $268.6 billion (31 December 2015 est.)

$275 billion (31 December 2014 est.)

country comparison to the world: 36

Stock of domestic credit: $114.2 billion (31 December 2015 est.)

$116.9 billion (31 December 2014 est.)

country comparison to the world: 49

Market value of publicly traded shares: $70.34 billion (31 December 2012 est.)

$67.63 billion (31 December 2011)

$101.1 billion (31 December 2010 est.)

country comparison to the world: 48

Current account balance: $3 billion (2015 est.)

$3.581 billion (2014 est.)

country comparison to the world: 29

Exports: $20.9 billion (2015 est.)

$24.22 billion (2014 est.)

country comparison to the world: 71

Exports—commodities: machinery and equipment, steel products, chemicals, rubber products, glass

Exports—partners: Germany 22.1%, Belgium 16.7%, France 16.6%, UK 4.7%, Italy 4.6%, Netherlands 4% (2015)

Imports: $21.9 billion (2015 est.)

$24.79 billion (2014 est.)

country comparison to the world: 72

Imports—commodities: commercial aircraft, minerals, chemicals, metals, foodstuffs, luxury consumer goods

Imports—partners: Belgium 27.6%, Germany 22.9%, China 11.7%, France 9.5%, US 8.4%, Netherlands 4.2%, Mexico 4.1% (2015)

Reserves of foreign exchange and gold: $1 billion (31 December 2015 est.)

$863 million (31 December 2014 est.)

country comparison to the world: 130

Debt—external: $3.331 trillion (31 December 2014 est.)

$3.525 trillion (31 December 2013 est.)

country comparison to the world: 8

Stock of direct foreign investment—at home: $NA

$11.21 billion (31 December 2008 est.)

Stock of direct foreign investment—abroad: $NA

Exchange rates: euros (EUR) per US dollar—

0.885 (2015 est.)

0.7525 (2014 est.)

0.7634 (2013 est.)

0.78 (2012 est.)

0.7185 (2011 est.)

ENERGY

Electricity—production: 2.119 billion kWh (2012 est.)

country comparison to the world: 137

Electricity—consumption: 6.108 billion kWh (2012 est.)

country comparison to the world: 109

Electricity—exports: 1.907 billion kWh (2013 est.)

country comparison to the world: 44

Electricity—imports: 6.889 billion kWh (2013 est.)

country comparison to the world: 33

Electricity—installed generating capacity: 1.79 million kW (2012 est.)

country comparison to the world: 112

Electricity—from fossil fuels: 27.5% of total installed capacity (2012 est.)

country comparison to the world: 185

Electricity—from nuclear fuels: 0% of total installed capacity (2012 est.)

country comparison to the world: 131

Electricity—from hydroelectric plants: 1.9% of total installed capacity (2012 est.)

country comparison to the world: 137

Electricity—from other renewable sources: 9.1% of total installed capacity (2012 est.)

country comparison to the world: 40

Crude oil—production: 0 bbl/day (2014 est.)

country comparison to the world: 160

Crude oil—exports: 0 bbl/day (2013 est.)

country comparison to the world: 153

Crude oil—imports: 0 bbl/day (2013 est.)

country comparison to the world: 88

Crude oil—proved reserves: 0 bbl (1 January 2015 est.)

country comparison to the world: 159

Refined petroleum products—production: 0 bbl/day (2013 est.)

country comparison to the world: 204

Refined petroleum products—consumption: 56,610 bbl/day (2014 est.)

country comparison to the world: 93

Refined petroleum products—exports: 42.36 bbl/day (2013 est.)

country comparison to the world: 121

Refined petroleum products—imports: 58,890 bbl/day (2013 est.)

country comparison to the world: 73

Natural gas—production: 5 million cu m (2014 est.)

country comparison to the world: 93

Natural gas—consumption: 983 million cu m (2014 est.)

country comparison to the world: 92

Natural gas—exports: 0 cu m (2014 est.)

country comparison to the world: 137

Natural gas—imports: 979 million cu m (2014 est.)

country comparison to the world: 58

Natural gas—proved reserves: 0 cu m (1 January 2014 est.)

country comparison to the world: 163

Carbon dioxide emissions from consumption of energy: 11.69 million Mt (2012 est.)

country comparison to the world: 98

COMMUNICATIONS

Telephones—fixed lines: *total subscriptions:* 270,000

subscriptions per 100 inhabitants: 48 (2014 est.)

country comparison to the world: 119

Telephones—mobile cellular: *total:* 796,400

subscriptions per 100 inhabitants: 143 (2014 est.)

country comparison to the world: 162

Telephone system: *general assessment:* highly developed, completely automated and efficient system, mainly buried cables

domestic: fixed-line teledensity over 50 per 100 persons; nationwide mobile-cellular telephone system with market for mobile-cellular phones virtually saturated

international: country code—352 (2010)

Broadcast media: Luxembourg has a long tradition of operating radio and TV services for pan-European audiences and is home to Europe's largest privately owned broadcast media group, the RTL group, which operates 46 TV stations and 29 radio stations in Europe; also home to Europe's largest satellite operator, Societe Europeenne des Satellites (SES); domestically, the RTL group operates TV and radio networks; other domestic private radio and TV operators and French and German stations available; satellite and cable TV services available (2008)

Radio broadcast stations: AM 2, FM 9, shortwave 2 (1999)

Television broadcast stations: 5 (1999)

Internet country code: .lu

Internet hosts: 250,900 (2012)

country comparison to the world: 68

515

Internet users: *total:* 530,400
percent of population: 95.0% (2014 est.)
country comparison to the world: 130

TRANSPORTATION

Airports: 2 (2013)
country comparison to the world: 202
Airports—with paved runways: *total:* 1
over 3,047 m: 1 (2013)
Airports—with unpaved runways: *total:* 1
under 914 m: 1 (2013)
Heliports: 1 (2013)
Pipelines: gas 142 km; refined products 27 km
(2013)
Railways: *total:* 275 km
standard gauge: 275 km 1.435-m gauge (275 km
electrified) (2014)
country comparison to the world: 125

Roadways: *total:* 2,899 km

paved: 2,899 km (includes 152 km of expressways)
(2011)
country comparison to the world: 168
Waterways: 37 km (on Moselle River) (2010)
country comparison to the world: 104
Merchant marine: *total:* 49
by type: bulk carrier 2, cargo 3, chemical tanker
20, container 10, petroleum tanker 2, roll on/roll
off 12
foreign-owned: 48 (Belgium 11, Denmark 1,
France 15, Germany 9, Japan 3, Netherlands 3,
Switzerland 1, UK 5)
registered in other countries: 18 (Italy 14, Malta
3, Panama 1) (2010)
country comparison to the world: 71
Ports and terminals: *river port(s):* Mertert
(Moselle)

MILITARY AND SECURITY

Military branches: Luxembourg Army (Armee
Luxembourgeoise) (2015)

Military service age and obligation: 18–24 years of
age for male and female voluntary military service;
no conscription; Luxembourg citizen or EU citizen
with 3-year residence in Luxembourg (2012)
Military expenditures: 0.5% of GDP (2015)
0.39% of GDP (2014)
0.38% of GDP (2013)
0.38% of GDP (2012)
0.39% of GDP (2011)
country comparison to the world: 123

TRANSNATIONAL ISSUES

Disputes—international: none
Refugees and internally displaced persons: *stateless persons:* 82 (2015)

INTRODUCTION

Background: Colonized by the Portuguese in the 16th century, Macau was the first European settlement in the Far East. Pursuant to an agreement signed by China and Portugal on 13 April 1987, Macau became the Macau Special Administrative Region of the People's Republic of China on 20 December 1999. In this agreement, China promised that, under its "one country, two systems" formula, China's political and economic system would not be imposed on Macau, and that Macau would enjoy a "high degree of autonomy" in all matters except foreign affairs and defense for the subsequent 50 years.

GEOGRAPHY

Location: Eastern Asia, bordering the South China Sea and China

Geographic coordinates: 22 10 N, 113 33 E

Map references: Southeast Asia

Area: *total:* 28.2 sq km
land: 28.2 sq km
water: 0 sq km
country comparison to the world: 237

Area—comparative: less than one-sixth the size of Washington, DC

Land boundaries: *total:* 3 km

regional border (1): China 3 km

Coastline: 41 km

Maritime claims: not specified

Climate: subtropical; marine with cool winters, warm summers

Terrain: generally flat

Elevation: *mean elevation:* NA

elevation extremes: *lowest point:* South China Sea 0 m
highest point: Coloane Alto 172 m

Natural resources: NEGL

Land use: *agricultural land:* 0%
arable land: 0%;

permanent crops: 0%;
permanent pasture: 0%
forest: 0%
other: 100% (urban area) (2011 est.)

Irrigated land: 0 sq km (2012)

Natural hazards: typhoons

Environment—current issues: NA

Environment—international agreements: *party to:* Marine Dumping (associate member), Ship Pollution (associate member)

Geography—note: essentially urban; an area of land reclaimed from the sea measuring 5.2 sq km and known as Cotai now connects the islands of Coloane and Taipa; the island area is connected to the mainland peninsula by th ree bridges

PEOPLE AND SOCIETY

Nationality: *noun:* Chinese
adjective: Chinese

Ethnic groups: Chinese 92.4%, Portuguese 0.6%, mixed 1.1%, other 5.9% (includes Macanese—mixed Portuguese and Asian ancestry) (2011 est.)

Languages: Cantonese 83.3%, Mandarin 5%, Hokkien 3.7%, English 2.3%, other Chinese dialects 2%, Tagalog 1.7%, Portuguese 0.7%, other 1.3%
note: Chinese and Portuguese are official languages (2011 est.)

Religions: Buddhist 50%, Roman Catholic 15%, none or other 35% (1997 est.)

Population: 592,731
note: Macau's statistical agency estimated the total population to be approximately 646,800 as of 31 December 2015 (July 2015 est.)
country comparison to the world: 170

Age structure: *0–14 years:* 14.31% (male 44,335/female 40,481)
15–24 years: 13.02% (male 40,337/female 36,862)
25–54 years: 50.67% (male 133,897/female 166,418)
55–64 years: 12.42% (male 37,118/female 36,527)
65 years and over: 9.58% (male 26,555/female 30,201) (2015 est.)

Dependency ratios: *total dependency ratio:* 28.2%
youth dependency ratio: 16.7%
elderly dependency ratio: 11.5%
potential support ratio: 8.7% (2015 est.)

Median age: *total:* 38.2 years
male: 38.7 years
female: 37.9 years (2015 est.)
country comparison to the world: 59

Population growth rate: 0.8% (2015 est.)
country comparison to the world: 138

Birth rate: 8.88 births/1,000 population (2015 est.)
country comparison to the world: 211

Death rate: 4.22 deaths/1,000 population (2015 est.)
country comparison to the world: 205

Net migration rate: 3.37 migrant(s)/1,000 population (2015 est.)
country comparison to the world: 37

Urbanization: *urban Population:* 100% of total population (2015)
rate of urbanization: 1.78% annual rate of change (2010–15 est.)

Sex ratio: *at birth:* 1.05 male(s)/female
0–14 years: 1.1 male(s)/female
15–24 years: 1.09 male(s)/female
25–54 years: 0.81 male(s)/female
55–64 years: 1.02 male(s)/female
65 years and over: 0.88 male(s)/female
total population: 0.91 male(s)/female (2015 est.)

Infant mortality rate: *total:* 3.12 deaths/1,000 live births
male: 3.27 deaths/1,000 live births
female: 2.95 deaths/1,000 live births (2015 est.)
country comparison to the world: 214

Life expectancy at birth: *total population:* 84.51 years
male: 81.55 years
female: 87.61 years (2015 est.)
country comparison to the world: 4

Total fertility rate: 0.94 children born/woman (2015 est.)
country comparison to the world: 223

HIV/AIDS—adult prevalence rate: NA

HIV/AIDS—people living with HIV/AIDS: NA

HIV/AIDS—deaths: NA

Education expenditures: 2.1% of GDP (2013)
country comparison to the world: 148

Literacy: *definition:* age 15 and over can read and write
total population: 96.2%
male: 98%
female: 94.6% (2015 est.)

Unemployment, youth ages 15–24: *total:* 4.2%
male: 5.5%
female: 3.2% (2013 est.)
country comparison to the world: 123

GOVERNMENT

Country name: *conventional long form:* Macau Special Administrative Region
conventional short form: Macau
official long form: Aomen Tebie Xingzhengqu (Chinese); Regiao Administrativa Especial de Macau (Portuguese)
official short form: Aomen (Chinese); Macau (Portuguese)
etymology: name is thought to derive from the A-Ma Temple—built in 1488 and dedicated to Mazu, the goddess of seafarers and fishermen—which is referred to locally as "Maa Gok" and which in Portuguese became "Macau"; the Chinese name Aomen means "inlet gates"

Dependency status: special administrative region of the People's Republic of China

Government type: presidential limited democracy; a special administrative region of the PRC

Administrative divisions: none (special administrative region of the People's Republic of China)

Independence: none (special administrative region of China)

National holiday: National Day (anniversary of the Founding of the People's Republic of China), 1 October (1949); note—20 December 1999 is celebrated as Macau Special Administrative Region Establishment Day

Constitution: previous 1976 (Organic Statute of Macau, under Portuguese authority); latest adopted 31 March 1993, effective 20 December 1999 (Basic Law of the Macau Special Administrative Region of the People's Republic of China serves as Macau's constitution); amended 2005,2012 (2016)

Legal system: civil law system based on the Portuguese model

Citizenship: see China

Suffrage: 18 years of age in direct elections for some legislative positions, universal for permanent residents living in Macau for the past seven years; note—indirect elections are limited to organizations registered as "corporate voters" (973 were registered in the 2009 legislative elections) and a 400-member Election Committee for the Chief Executive drawn from broad regional groupings, municipal organizations, central government bodies, and elected Macau officials

Executive branch: *chief of state:* President of China XI Jinping (since 14 March 2013)

head of government: Chief Executive Fernando CHUI Sai On (since 20 December 2009)

cabinet: Executive Council appointed by the chief executive

elections/appointments: president indirectly elected by National People's Congress for a 5-year term (eligible for a second term); chief executive chosen by a 400-member Election Committee for a 5-year term (eligible for a second term); election last held on 29 August 2014 (next to be held in 2019); note—the Legislative Assembly in August 2012 voted to expand the Election Committee to 400 from 300 seats for the 2014 election

election results: Fernando CHUI Sai On re-elected chief executive; Election Committee vote count—380 of 396

Legislative branch: *description:* unicameral Legislative Council or Regiao Administrativa Especial de Macau (33 seats; 14 members directly elected by proportional representation vote, 12 indirectly elected by an electoral college of professional and commercial interest groups, and 7 appointed by the chief executive; members serve 4-year terms)

elections: last held on 15 September 2013 (next to be held in September 2017)

election results: percent of vote—ACUM 18.0%, UMG 11.1%, UPP 10.8%, NE 9.0%, NUDM 8.9%, UPD 8.2%, APMD 7.5%, ANMD 6.0%, APM 6.0%, other 14.5%; seats by political group—ACUM 3, UMG 2, UPP 2, NE 2, NUDM 1, UPD 1, APMD 1, ANMD 1, APM 1; 12 seats

filled by professional and business groups; 7 members appointed by the chief executive

Judicial branch: *highest court(s):* Court of Final Appeal of Macau Special Administrative Region (consists of the court president and 2 associate justices)

judge selection and term of office: justices appointed by the Macau chief executive upon the recommendation of an independent commission of judges, lawyers, and "eminent" persons; judge tenure NA

subordinate courts: Court of Second Instance; Court of First instance; Lower Court; Administrative Court

Political parties and leaders: Alliance for Change or APM [Melinda CHAN Mei-yi]
Macau-Guangdong Union or UMG [MAK Soi-kun]
New Democratic Macau Association or ANMD (an electoral list of the New Macau Association)
New Hope or NE [Jose Maria Pereira COUTINHO]
New Macau Association or ANM [Sulu SOUKa-hou]
New Union for Macau's Development or NUDM [Angela LEONGOn-kei]
Prosperous Democratic Macau Association or APMD (an electoral list of the New Macau Association)
Union for Development or UPD [KWAN Tsui-hang]
Union for Promoting Progress or UPP [HOIon-sang]
United Citizens Association of Macau or ACUM [CHANM eng-kam]
note: there is no political party ordinance, so there are no registered political parties; politically active groups register as societies or companies

Political pressure groups and leaders: Bar-Bending Workers' Association [WONG Wai-Man]
Civic Power [Agnes LAM lok-fong]
Democratic Action [LEE Kin-yun]
Macau New Chinese Youth Association [LEONG Sin-man]
Macau Worker's Union [HO Heng-kuok]
New Macau Association [Antonio NG Kuok-cheong]
Workers' Self-Help Union [CHEONG Weng-fat]

International organization participation: ICC (national committees), IHO, IMF, IMO (associate), Interpol (subbureau), ISO (correspondent), UNESCO (associate), UNWTO (associate), UPU, WCO, WMO, WTO

Diplomatic representation in the US: none (Special Administrative Region of China)

Diplomatic representation from the US: the US has no offices in Macau; US Consulate General in Hong Kong is accredited to Macau

Flag description: green with a lotus flower above a stylized bridge and water in white, beneath an arc of five gold, five-pointed stars: one large in the center of the arc and two smaller on either side; the lotus is the floral emblem of Macau, the three petals represent the peninsula and two islands that

make up Macau; the five stars echo those on the flag of China

National symbol(s): lotus blossom; national colors: green, white, yellow

National anthem: *note:* as a Special Administrative Region of China, "Yiyongjun Jinxingqu" is the official anthem (see China)

ECONOMY

Economy—overview: Since opening up its locally-controlled casino industry to foreign competition in 2001, Macau has attracted tens of billions of dollars in foreign investment, transforming the territory into one of the world's largest gaming centers. Macau's gaming and tourism businesses were fueled by China's decision to relax travel restrictions on Chinese citizens wishing to visit Macau. In 2015, Macau's gaming-related taxes accounted for more than 76% of total government revenue. Macau's economy slowed dramatically in 2009 as a result of the global economic slowdown, but strong growth resumed in 2010–13, largely on the back of tourism from mainland China and the gaming sectors. In 2015, this city of 646,800 hosted nearly 30.7 million visitors. Almost 67% came from mainland China. Macau's traditional manufacturing industry has slowed greatly since the termination of the Multi-Fiber Agreement in 2005. Services export—primarily gaming—increasingly has driven Macau's economic performance. Mainland China's ongoing anti-corruption campaign has brought Macau's gambling boom to a halt, with spending in casinos contracting 34.3% in 2015. As a result, Macau's inflation-adjusted GDP contracted 20.3% from 2014, down from double-digit expansion rates in 2010–13. Non-inflation adjusted exports of goods and services dropped 1.8% from 2014, reflecting the slowdown in gaming exports. Macau continues to face the challenges of managing its growing casino industry, risks from money-laundering activities, and the need to diversify the economy away from heavy dependence on gaming revenues. Macau's currency, the pataca, is closely tied to the Hong Kong dollar, which is also freely accepted in the territory.

GDP (purchasing power parity):
$65.38 billion (2015 est.)
$82.09 billion (2014 est.)
$82.79 billion (2013 est.)
note: data are in 2013 US dollars
country comparison to the world: 99

GDP (official exchange rate): $46.18 billion (2015 est.)

GDP—real growth rate: -20.3% (2015 est.)
-0.9% (2014 est.)
11.2% (2013 est.)
country comparison to the world: 223

GDP—per capita (PPP): $98,200 (2015 est.)
$129,100 (2014 est.)
$136,200 (2013 est.)
country comparison to the world: 3

GDP—composition, by end use:
household consumption: 26.2%
government consumption: 9.7%

investment in fixed capital: 21.4%
investment in inventories: -0.1%
exports of goods and services: 84.2%
imports of goods and services: -41.4% (2015 est.)

GDP—composition, by sector of origin:
agriculture: 0%
industry: 8.4%
services: 91.6% (2013 est.)

Agriculture—products: only 2% of land area is cultivated, mainly by vegetable growers; fishing, mostly for crustaceans, is important; some of the catch is exported to Hong Kong

Industries: tourism, gambling, clothing, textiles, electronics, footwear, toys

Industrial production growth rate: 4% (2015 est.)
country comparison to the world: 55

Labor force: 394,800 (2014 est.)
country comparison to the world: 159

Labor force—by occupation: *manufacturing:* 2.5%
construction: 9.8%
transport and communications: 4.4%
Wholesale and retail trade: 12.4%
restaurants and hotels: 15%
gambling: 25.9%
public sector: 7.1%
financial services: 2.6%
other services: 20.3% (2013)

Unemployment rate: *1.9% (2013 est.)*
1.7% (2014 est.)
country comparison to the world: 10

Population below poverty line: NA%

Household income or consumption by percentage share: *lowest:* 10%: NA%
highest: 10%: NA%

Distribution of family income—Gini index: 35 (2013)
38 (2008)
country comparison to the world: 95

Budget: *revenues:* $14.16 billion
expenditures: $6.433 billion (2015 est.)
Taxes and other revenues: 27.4% of GDP (2015 est.)
country comparison to the world: 99

Budget surplus (+) or deficit (−): 14.9% of GDP (2015 est.)
country comparison to the world: 2

Fiscal year: calendar year

Inflation rate (consumer prices): 4.6% (2015 est.)
6% (2014 est.)
country comparison to the world: 166

Commercial bank prime lending rate: 5.3% (31 December 2015 est.)
5.25% (31 December 2014 est.)
country comparison to the world: 142

Stock of narrow money: $6.632 billion (31 December 2015 est.)
$7.678 billion (31 December 2014 est.)
country comparison to the world: 92

Stock of broad money: $64.67 billion (31 December 2014 est.)
$55.29 billion (31 December 2013 est.)

country comparison to the world: 63

Stock of domestic credit:
$475.6 million (31 December 2015 est.)
-$147.8 million (31 December 2014 est.)
country comparison to the world: 172

Market value of publicly traded shares:
$85.5 billion (2 March 2012 est.)
$46.1 billion (31 February 2011)
$2.3 billion (31 December 2008 est.)
country comparison to the world: 45

Current account balance: $12.11 billion (2015 est.)
$21.08 billion (2014 est.)
country comparison to the world: 21

Exports: $1.137 billion (2013 est.)
$1.384 billion (2012 est.)
note: in cludes reexports
country comparison to the world: 156

Exports—commodities: clothing, textiles, footwear, toys, electron ics, machinery and parts

Exports—partners: Hong Kong 63.4%, China 18.2% (2015)

Imports: $10.13 billion (2013 est.)
$8.866 billion (2012 est.)
country comparison to the world: 99

Imports—commodities: raw materials and semi-manufactured goods, consumer goods (foodstuffs, beverages, tobacco, garments and footwear, motor vehicles), capital goods, mineral fuels and oils

Imports—partners: China 33.8%, Hong Kong 8.8%, Japan 8.5%, Switzerland 8%, France 6.9%, Italy 6.7%, US 6.7% (2015)

Reserves of foreign exchange and gold:
$16.44 billion (31 December 2014 est.)
$16.15 billion (31 December 2013 est.)
note: the Fiscal Reserves Act that came into force on 1 January 2012 requires the fiscal reserves to be separated from the foreign exchange reserves and to be managed separately; the transfer of assets took place in February 2012
country comparison to the world: 66

Debt—external: $0 (31 December 2013)
$0 (31 December 2012)
country comparison to the world: 205

Stock of direct foreign investment—at home:
$18.91 billion (31 December 2011 est.)
$14.91 billion (31 December 2011 est.)
country comparison to the world: 79

Stock of direct foreign investment—abroad:
$1.166 billion (2012 est.)
$667.8 million (2011 est.)
country comparison to the world: 83

Exchange rates: patacas (MOP) per US dollar—
7.99 (2015 est.)
7.9871 (2014 est.)
7.9871 (2013 est.)
7.99 (2012 est.)
8.0182 (2011 est.)

ENERGY

Electricity—production: 413.7 million kWh (2013 est.)
country comparison to the world: 166

Electricity—consumption: 4.291 billion kWh (2013 est.)
country comparison to the world: 123

Electricity—exports: 0 kWh (2013 est.)
country comparison to the world: 164

Electricity—imports: 3.855 billion kWh (2012 est.)
country comparison to the world: 47

Electricity—installed generating capacity: 472,000 kW (2013 est.)
country comparison to the world: 142

Electricity—from fossil fuels: 100% of total installed capacity (2013 est.)
country comparison to the world: 18

Electricity—from nuclear fuels: 0% of total installed capacity (2013 est.)
country comparison to the world: 134

Electricity—from hydroelectric plants: 0% of total installed capacity (2013 est.)
country comparison to the world: 184

Electricity—from other renewable sources: 0% of total installed capacity (2013 est.)
country comparison to the world: 196

Crude oil—production: 0 bbl/day (2014 est.)
country comparison to the world: 162

Crude oil—exports: 0 bbl/day (2013 est.)
country comparison to the world: 155

Crude oil—imports: 0 bbl/day (2013 est.)
country comparison to the world: 91

Crude oil—proved reserves: 0bbl (1January 2015 est.)
country comparison to the world: 161

Refined petroleum products—production: *0 bbl/day (2013 est.)*
country comparison to the world: 206

Refined petroleum products—consumption: 10,680 bbl/day (2013 est.)
country comparison to the world: 153

Refined petroleum products—exports: 0 bbl/day (2013 est.)
country comparison to the world: 199

Refined petroleum products—imports: 5,780 bbl/day (2013 est.)
country comparison to the world: 155

Natural gas—production: 0 cu m (2013 est.)
country comparison to the world: 216

Natural gas—consumption: 355,000 cu m (2013 est.)
country comparison to the world: 113

Natural gas—exports: 0 cu m (2013 est.)
country comparison to the world: 139

Natural gas—imports: 371,000 cu m (2013 est.)
country comparison to the world: 74

Natural gas—proved reserves: 0 cu m (1 January 2014 est.)
country comparison to the world: 164

Carbon dioxide emissions from consumption of energy:
1.694 million Mt (2012 est.)
country comparison to the world: 153

COMMUNICATIONS

Telephones—fixed lines: *total:* 160,000
subscriptions per 100 inhabitants: 28 (2012)
country comparison to the world: 133

Telephones—mobile cellular: *total:* 1.6 million
subscriptions per 100 inhabitants: 279 (2012)
country comparison to the world: 154

Telephone system: *general assessment:* fairly modern communication facilities maintained for domestic and international services
domestic: termination of monopoly over mobile-cellular telephone services in 2001 spurred sharp increase in subscriptions with mobile-cellular teledensity exceeding 290 per 100 persons; fixed-line subscribership appears to have peaked and is now in decline
international: country code—853; landing point for the SEA-ME-WE-3 submarine cable network that provides links to Asia, the Middle East, and Europe; HF radiotelephone communication facility; satellite earth station—1 Intelsat (Indian Ocean) (2011)

Broadcast media: local government dominates broadcast media; 2 television stations operated by the government with one broadcasting in Portuguese and the other in Cantonese and Mandarin; 1 cable TV and 4 satellite TV services available; 3 radio stations broadcasting, of which 2 are government-operated (2015)
Radio broadcast stations: AM 1, FM 2, shortwave 0 (2009)
Television broadcast stations: 1 (2009)

Internet country code: .mo

Internet hosts: 327 (2012)
country comparison to the world: 189

Internet users: *total:* 270,200
percent of population: 48.3% (2009)
country comparison to the world: 150

TRANSPORTATION

Airports: 1 (2013)
country comparison to the world: 224

Airports—with paved runways: *total:* 1
over 3,047 m: 1 (2013)

Heliports: 2 (2013)

Road ways: *total:* 424 km
paved: 424 km (2014)
country comparison to the world: 200

Ports and terminals: *major seaport(s):* Macau

MILITARY AND SECURITY

Military branches: no regular indigenous military forces

Military—note: defense is the responsibility of China

TRANSNATIONAL ISSUES

Disputes—international: none

Illicit drugs: transshipment point for drugs going into mainland China; consumer of opiates and amphetamines

MACEDONIA

INTRODUCTION

Background: Macedonia gained its independence peacefully from Yugoslavia in 1991. Greek objection to Macedonia's name, insisting it implies territorial pretensions to the northern Greek province of the same name, have stalled the country's movement toward Euro-Atlantic integration. Immediately after Macedonia declared independence, Greece sought to block Macedonian efforts to gain UN membership if the name "Macedonia" was used. Macedonia was eventually admitted to the UN in 1993 as "The Former Yugoslav Republic of Macedonia, " and at the same time it agreed to UN-sponsored negotiations on the name dispute. In 1995, Greece lifted a 20-month trade embargo and the two countries agreed to normalize relations, but the issue of the name remained unresolved and negotiations for a solution are ongoing.

Since 2004, the US and over 130 other nations have recognized Macedonia by its constitutional name, Republic of Macedonia. Ethnic Albanian grievances over perceived political and economic inequities escalated into an insurgency in 2001 that eventually led to the internationally brokered Ohrid Framework Agreement, which ended the fighting and established guidelines for constitutional amendments and the creation of new laws that enhanced the rights of minorities. Relations between Macedonians and ethnic Albanians remain fragile, however. Although Macedonia became an EU candidate in 2005, the country still faces challenges, including overcoming the ongoing political crisis that began in 2015 when opposition party SDSM began releasing wiretap content that it alleged showed widespread government corruption, the ongoing migration crisis, fully implementing the Framework Agreement, resolving the outstanding name dispute with Greece, improving relations with Bulgaria, halting democratic backsliding, and stimulating economic growth and development. Macedonia's membership in NATO was blocked by Greece at the Alliance's Summit of Bucharest in 2008.

GEOGRAPHY

Location: Southeastern Europe, north of Greece

Geographic coordinates: 41 50 N, 22 00 E

Map references: Europe

Area: *total:* 25,713 sq km
land: 25,433 sq km
water: 280 sq km
country comparison to the world: 150

Area—comparative: slightly larger than Vermont

Land boundaries: *total:* 838 km

border countries (5): Albania 181 km, Bulgaria 162 km, Greece 234 km, Kosovo 160 km, Serbia 101 km

Coastline: 0 km (landlocked)

Maritime claims: none (landlocked)

Climate: warm, dry summers and autumns; relatively cold winters with heavy snowfall

Terrain: mountainous with deep basins and valleys; three large lakes, each divided by a frontier line; country bisected by the Vardar River

Elevation: *mean elevation:* 741 m

elevation extremes: *lowest point:* Vardar River 50 m
highest point: Golem Korab (Majae Korabit) 2,764 m

Natural resources: low-grade iron ore, copper, lead, zinc, chromite, manganese, nickel, tungsten, gold, silver, asbestos, gypsum, timber, arable land

Land use: *agricultural land:* 44.3%
arable land: 16.4%;
permanent crops: 1.4%;
permanent pasture: 26.5%
forest: 39.8%
other: 15.9% (2011 est.)

Irrigated land: 1,280 sq km (2012)

Total renewable water resources: 6.4 cu km (2011)

Freshwater withdrawal (domestic/industrial/agricultural): *total:* 1.03 cu km/yr (21%/67%/12%)
per capita: 502 cu m/yr (2007)

Natural hazards: high seismic risks

Environment—current issues: air pollution from metallurgical plants

Environment—international agreements: *party to:* Air Pollution, Biodiversity, Climate Change, Climate Change-Kyoto Protocol, Desertification,

Endangered Species, Hazardous Wastes, Law of the Sea, Ozone Layer Protection, Wetlands

signed, but not ratified: none of the selected agreements

Geography—note: landlocked; major transportation corridor from Western and Central Europe to Aegean Sea and Southern Europe to Western Europe

PEOPLE AND SOCIETY

Nationality: *noun:* Macedonian(s)
adjective: Macedonian

Ethnic groups: Macedonian 64.2%, Albanian 25.2%, Turkish 3.9%, Roma (Gypsy) 2.7%, Serb 1.8%, other 2.2% (2002 est.)

Languages: Macedonian (official) 66.5%, Albanian (official) 25.1%, Turkish 3.5%, Roma 1.9%, Serbian 1.2%, other 1.8% (2002 est.)

Religions: MacedoniaNorthodox 64.8%, Muslim 33.3%, other Christian 0.4%, other and unspecified 1.5% (2002 est.)

Population: 2,096,015 (July 2015 est.)
country comparison to the world: 146

Age structure: *0–14 years:* 17.48% (male 189,719/female 176,751)
15–24 years: 13.88% (male 150,048/female 140,834)
25–54 years: 43.69% (male 464,811/female 450,914)
55–64 years: 12.21% (male 125,327/female 130,617)
65 years and over: 12.74% (male 114,357/female 152,637) (2015 est.)

Dependency ratios: *total dependency ratio:* 41.4%
youth dependency ratio: 24%
elderly dependency ratio: 17.4%
potential support ratio: 5.7% (2015 est.)

Median age: *total:* 37.2 years
male: 36.1 years
female: 38.3 years (2015 est.)
country comparison to the world: 65

Population growth rate: 0.2% (2015 est.)
country comparison to the world: 184

Birth rate: 11.55 births/1,000 population (2015 est.)
country comparison to the world: 170

Death rate: 9.08 deaths/1,000 population (2015 est.)
country comparison to the world: 67

Net migration rate: -0.48 migrant(s)/1,000 population (2015 est.)
country comparison to the world: 135

Urbanization: *urban Population:* 57.1% of total population (2015)
rate of urbanization: 0.11% annual rate of change (2010–15 est.)

Major urban areas—Population: SKOPJE (capital) 503,000 (2015)

Sex ratio: *at birth:* 1.08 male(s)/female
0–14 years: 1.07 male(s)/female
15–24 years: 1.07 male(s)/female

25–54 years: 1.03 male(s)/female
55–64 years: 0.96 male(s)/female
65 years and over: 0.75 male(s)/female
total population: 0.99 male(s)/female (2015 est.)

Mother's mean age at first birth: 26.2 (2011 est.)

Maternal mortality rate: 8 deaths/100,000 live births (2015 est.)
country comparison to the world: 153

Infant mortality rate: *total:* 7.7 deaths/1,000 live births
male: 7.96 deaths/1,000 live births
female: 7.42 deaths/1,000 live births (2015 est.)
country comparison to the world: 156

Life expectancy at birth: *total population:* 76.02 years
male: 73.44 years
female: 78.79 years (2015 est.)
country comparison to the world: 90

Total fertility rate: 1.6 children born/woman (2015 est.)
country comparison to the world: 180

Contraceptive prevalence rate: 40.2% (2011)

Health expenditures: 6.4% of GDP (2013)
country comparison to the world: 79

Physicians density: 2.62 physicians/1,000 population (2009)

Hospital bed density: 4.5 beds/1,000 population (2011)

Drinking water source:
improved:
urban: 99.8% of population
rural: 98.9% of population
total: 99.4% of population
unimproved:
urban: 0.2% of population
rural: 1.1% of population
total: 0.6% of population (2015 est.)

Sanitation facility access:
improved:
urban: 97.2% of population
rural: 82.6% of population
total: 90.9% of population
unimproved:
urban: 2.8% of population
rural: 17.4% of population
total: 9.1% of population (2015 est.)

HIV/AIDS—adult prevalence rate: 0.01% (2013 est.)
country comparison to the world: 131

HIV/AIDS—people living with HIV/AIDS: 200 (2013 est.)
country comparison to the world: 126

HIV/AIDS—deaths: fewer than 100 (2013 est.)
country comparison to the world: 106

Obesity—adult prevalence rate: 20.8% (2014)
country comparison to the world: 92

Children under the age of 5 years underweight: 1.3% (2011)
country comparison to the world: 128

Literacy: *definition:* age 15 and over can read and write
total population: 97.8%

male: 98.8%
female: 96.8% (2015 est.)

School life expectancy (primary to tertiary education): *total:* 13 years
male: 13 years
female: 13 years (2012)

Child labor—children ages 5–14: *total number:* 16,782
percentage: 6% (2005 est.)

Unemployment, youth ages 15–24: *total:* 51.9%
male: 52.5%
female: 51% (2013 est.)
country comparison to the world: 4

GOVERNMENT

Country name: *conventional long form:* Republic of Macedonia
conventional short form: Macedonia
local long form: Republika Makedonija
local short form: Makedonija
note: the provisional designation used by the UN, EU, and NATO is the "former Yugoslav Republic of Macedonia" (FYROM)
former: People's Republic of Macedonia, Socialist Republic of Macedonia
etymology: the country name derives from the ancient kingdom of Macedon (7th to 2nd centuries B.C.)

Government type: parliamentary republic

Capital: *name:* Skopje

Geographic coordinates: 42 00 N, 21 26 E
time difference: UTC+1 (6 hours ahead of Washington, DC, during Standard Time)
daylight saving time: +1hr, begins last Sunday in March; ends last Sunday in October

Administrative divisions: 70 municipalities (opstini, singular—opstina) and 1 city* (grad); Aracinovo, Berovo, Bitola, Bogdanci, Bogovinje, Bosilovo, Brvenica, Caska, Centar Zupa, Cesinovo-Oblesevo, Cucer Sandevo, Debar, Debarca, Delcevo, Demir Hisar, Demir Kapija, Dojran, Dolneni, Gevgelija, Gostivar, Gradsko, Ilinden, Jegunovce, Karbinci, Kavadarci, Kicevo, Kocani, Konce, Kratovo, Kriva Palanka, Krivogastani, Krusevo, Kumanovo, Lipkovo, Lozovo, Makedonska Kamenica, Makedonski Brod, Mavrovo i Rostusa, Mogila, Negotino, Novaci, Novo Selo, Ohrid, Pehcevo, Petrovec, Plasnica, Prilep, Probistip, Radovis, Rankovce, Resen, Rosoman, Skopje*, Sopiste, Staro Nagoricane, Stip, Struga, Strumica, Studenicani, Sveti Nikole, Tearce, Tetovo, Valandovo, Vasilevo, Veles, Vevcani, Vinica, Vrapciste, Zelenikovo, Zelino, Zrnovci

Independence: 8 September 1991 (referendum by registered voters endorsed independence from Yugoslavia)

National holiday: Independence Day, 8 September (1991); also known as National Day

Constitution: several previous; latest adopted 17 November 1991, effective 20 November 1991; amended several times, last in 2015 (2016)

Legal system: civil law system; judicial review of legislative acts

International law organization participation: has not submitted an ICJ jurisdiction declaration; accepts ICCt jurisdiction

Citizenship: *citizenship by birth:* no
citizenship by descent only: at least one parent must be a citizen of Macedonia
dual citizenship recognized: no
residency requirement for naturalization: 8 years

Suffrage: 18 years of age; universal

Executive branch: *chief of state:* President Gjorge IVANOV (since 12 May 2009)

head of government: Interim Prime Minister Emil DIMITRIEV (since 18 January 2016); Prime Minister Nikola GRUEVSKI (since 26 August 2006) resigned on 15 January 2016
cabinet: Council of Ministers elected by the Assembly by simple majority vote; note—the 2014 cabinet formed by the government coalition parties VMRO-DPMNE, DUI, and several small parties; as a result of an agreement reached in July 2015 between the largest parties to resolve a 16-month opposition boycott of parliament, several minister and deputy minister positions were also given to the opposition SDSM
elections/appointments: president directly elected by absolute majority popular vote in 2 rounds if needed for a 5-year term (eligible for a second term); election last held on 13 and 27 April 2014 (next to be held in 2019); following legislative elections, the leader of the majority party or majority coalition usually elected prime minister by the Assembly
election results: Gjorge IVANOV reelected president in second round; percent of vote—Gjorge IVANOV (independent) 55.3%, Stevo PENDAROVSKI (SDSM) 41.1%, other 3.6%

Legislative branch: *description:* unicameral Assembly or Sobranie (123 seats; 120 members directly elected in multi-seat constituencies by proportional representation vote and 3 directly elected in diaspora constituencies worldwide by simple majority vote; members serve 4-year terms)
elections: last held on 27 April 2014 (the election-scheduled for 5 June 2016 has been postponed)
election results: percent of vote by party—VMRO-DPMNE 43.0%, SDSM 25.3%, BDI 13.7%, PDSh 5.9%, GROM 2.8%, RDK 1.6%, other 4.3%, invalid 3.4%; seats by party—VMRO-DPMNE 61, SDSM 34, BDI 19, PDSh 7, GROM 1, RDK 1

Judicial branch: *highest court(s):* Supreme Court (consist of NA judges); Constitutional Court (consists of 9 judges)
judge selection and term of office: Supreme Court judges nominated by the Judicial Council, a 7-member body of legal professionals, and appointed by the Assembly; judge tenure NA; Constitutional Court judges appointed by the legislature for nonrenewable, 9-year terms
subordinate courts: Courts of Appeal; Basic Courts

Political parties and leaders: Citizens Option for Macedonia or GROM [Stevco JAKIMOVSKI]

Democratic Party of Albanians or PDSh [Menduh THACI]
Democratic Union for Integration or BDI [Ali AHMETI]
Internal Macedonian Revolutionary Organization—Democratic Party for Macedonian National Unity or VMRO-DPMNE [Nikola GRUEVSKI]
National Democratic Revival or RDK [Vesel MEMEDI]
Social Democratic Union of Macedonia or SDSM [Zoran ZAEV]
note: during the 2014 parliamentary elections VMRO-DPMNE, SDSM, and GROM each led coalitions

Political pressure groups and leaders: Federation of Free Trade Unions [Mirjana ANDREVSKA]
Federation of Trade Unions [Zivko MITREVSKI]
Trade Union of Education, Science and Culture or SONK [Jakim NEDELKOV]
Student Plenum
Eco Guerilla [Arianit XHAFERI]

International organization participation: BIS, CD, CE, CEI, EAPC, EBRD, EU (candidate country), FAO, IAEA, IBRD, ICAO, ICC (NGOs), ICCt, ICRM, IDA, IFAD, IFC, IFRCS, ILO, IMF, IMO, Interpol, IOC, IOM, IPU, ISO, ITU, ITUC (NGOs), MIGA, OAS (observer), OIF, OPCW, OSCE, PCA, PFP, SELEC, UN, UNCTAD, UNESCO, UNHCR, UNIDO, UNIFIL, UNWTO, UPU, WCO, WHO, WIPO, WMO, WTO

Diplomatic representation in the US: *chief of mission:* Ambassador Vasko NAUMOVSKI (since 18 November 2014)
chancery: 2129 Wyoming Avenue NW, Washington, DC 20008
telephone: [1] (202) 667-0501
FAX: [1] (202) 667-2131
consulate(s) general: Chicago, Detroit, New York

Diplomatic representation from the US: *chief of mission:* Ambassador Jess L. BAILY (since 12 February 2015)
embassy: Str. Samolilova, Nr.21, 1000 Skopje
mailing address: American Embassy Skopje, US Department of State, 7120 Skopje Place, Washington, DC 20521-7120 (pouch)
telephone: [389] (2) 310-2000
FAX: [389] (2) 310-2499

Flag description: a yellow sun (the Sun of Liberty) with eight broadening rays extending to the edges of the red field; the red and yellow colors have long been associated with Macedonia

National symbol(s): eight-rayed sun; national colors: red, yellow

National anthem: *name:* "Denes nad Makedonija" (Today Over Macedonia)
lyrics/music: Vlado MALESKI/Todor SKALOVSKI
note: adopted 1991; written in 1943, the song previously served as the anthem of the Socialist Republic of Macedonia while part of Yugoslavia

ECONOMY

Economy—overview: Since its independence in 1991, Macedonia has made progress in liberalizing its economy and improving its business environment, but has lagged the Balkan region in attracting foreign investment. Corruption and weak rule of law remain significant problems. Some businesses complain of opaque regulations and unequal enforcement of the law.

Macedonia's economy is closely linked to Europe as a customer for exports and source of investment, and has suffered as a result of prolonged weakness in the euro zone. Unemployment has remained consistently high at more than 30% since 2008, but may be overstated based on the existence of an extensive gray market, estimated to be between 20% and 45% of GDP, which is not captured by official statistics.

Macedonia maintained macroeconomic stability through the global financial crisis by conducting prudent monetary policy, which keeps the domestic currency pegged against the euro, and by limiting fiscal deficits. The government has been loosening fiscal policy, however, and the budget deficit was 4.2% of GDP in both 2013 and 2014, gradually falling to 3.7% in 2015. By yearend 2015, public debt was 40.3%, which although low by regional comparison, is significant for a small economy.

GDP (purchasing power parity):
$29.04 billion (2015 est.)
$28.01 billion (2014 est.)
$27.05 billion (2013 est.)
note: data are in 2015 US dollars; Macedonia has a large informal sector that may not be reflected in th ese data
country comparison to the world: 131

GDP (official exchange rate): $9.922 billion (2015 est.)

GDP—real growth rate: 3.7% (2015 est.)
3.5% (2014 est.)
2.9% (2013 est.)
country comparison to the world: 74

GDP—per capita (PPP):
$14,000 (2015 est.)
$13,500 (2014 est.)
$13,100 (2013 est.)
note: data are in 2015 US dollars
country comparison to the world: 114

Gross national saving: 30% of GDP (2015 est.)
29.7% of GDP (2014 est.)
27.2% of GDP (2013 est.)
country comparison to the world: 26

GDP—composition, by end use:
household consumpti on: 69.1%
government consumption: 16.6%
investment in fixed capital: 24%
investment in inventories: 6.8%
exports of goods and servi ces: 52%
imports of goods and services: -68.5% (2015 est.)

GDP—composition, by sector of origin:
agriculture: 10.2%
industry: 24.9%
services: 64.9% (2015 est.)

Agriculture—products: grapes, tobacco, vegetables, fruits; milk, eggs

Industries: food processing, beverages, textiles, chemicals, iron, steel, cement, energy, pharmaceuticals, automotive parts

Industrial production growth rate: 3% (2015 est.)
country comparison to the world: 88

Labor force: 961900 (2015 est.)
country comparison to the world: 145

Labor force—by occupation: *agriculture:* 18.3%
industry: 29.1%
services: 52.6% (2014 est.)

Unemployment rate: 26.9% (2015 est.)
28% (2014 est.)
country comparison to the world: 180

Population below poverty line: 30.4% (2011 est.)

Household income or consumption by percentage share: *lowest:* 10%: 2.2%
highest: 10%: 34.5% (2009 est.)

Distribution of family income—Gini index: 43.6 (2013)
39.2 (2011)
country comparison to the world: 49

Budget: *revenues:* $2.709 billion
expenditures: $3.084 billion (2015 est.)
Taxes and other revenues: 26.8% of GDP (2015 est.)
country comparison to the world: 107

Budget surplus (+) or deficit (−): -3.7% of GDP (2015 est.)
country comparison to the world: 136

Public debt: 40.3% of GDP (2015 est.)
31.4% of GDP (2014 est.)
note: official data from Ministry of Finance; data cover central government debt; this data excludes debt instruments issued (or owned) by government entities other than the treasury; includes treasury debt held by foreign entitites; excludes debt issued by sub-national entities, as well as intra-governmental debt; there are no debt instruments sold for social funds
country comparison to the world: 112

Fiscal year: calendar year

Inflation rate (consumer prices): -0.2% (2015 est.)
-0.1% (2014 est.)
country comparison to the world: 36

Central bank discount rate: 3.25% (31 December 2014)
3.25% (31 December 2013)
note: series discontinued in January 2010; the discount rate has been replaced by a referent rate for calculating the penalty rate
country comparison to the world: 101

Commercial bank prime lending rate: 8.5% (31 December 2015 est.)
8.16% (31 December 2014 est.)
country comparison to the world: 104

Stock of narrow money:
$1.424 billion (31 December 2015 est.)
$1.686 billion (31 December 2014 est.)
country comparison to the world: 142

Stock of broad money:
$6.129 billion (31 December 2014 est.)
$6.282 billion (31 December 2013 est.)
country comparison to the world: 123

Stock of domestic credit:
$4.436 billion (31 December 2015 est.)
$5.093 billion (31 December 2014 est.)
country comparison to the world: 125

Market value of publicly traded shares:
$2.084 billion (31 December 2014)
$2.302 billion (31 December 2013)
$2.423 billion (31 December 2012)
country comparison to the world: 98

Current account balance: -$141 million (2015 est.)
-$91 million (2014 est.)
country comparison to the world: 73

Exports: $3.945 billion (2015 est.)
$3.681 billion (2014 est.)
country comparison to the world: 118

Exports—commodities: foodstuffs, beverages, tobacco; textiles, miscellaneous manufactures, iron, steel; automotive parts

Exports—partners: Germany 33.2%, Kosovo 11.5%, Bulgaria 5.1%, Greece 4.5% (2015)

Imports: $6.212 billion (2015 est.)
$6.15 billion (2014 est.)
country comparison to the world: 118

Imports—commodities: machinery and equipment, automobiles, chemicals, fuels, food products

Imports—partners: Germany 15.9%, UK 13.6%, Greece 10.9%, Serbia 8.7%, Bulgaria 6.7%, Turkey 5.5%, Italy 4.7% (2015)

Reserves of foreign exchange and gold: $2.615 billion (31 December 2015 est.)
$2.963 billion (31 December 2014 est.)
country comparison to the world: 112

Debt—external: $7.241 billion (31 December 2014 est.)
$7.194 billion (31 December 2013 est.)
country comparison to the world: 115

Stock of direct foreign investment—at home:
$6.277 billion (31 December 2015 est.)
$6.007 billion (31 December 2014 est.)
country comparison to the world: 95

Stock of direct foreign investment—abroad:
$543.5 million (31 December 2015 est.)
$500.5 million (31 December 2014 est.)
country comparison to the world: 87

Exchange rates: Macedonian denars (MKD) per US dollar—
57.38 (2015 est.)
46.437 (2014 est.)
46.437 (31 December 2013 est.)
47.89 (2012 est.)
44.231 (2011 est.)

ENERGY

Electricity—production: 4.569 billion kWh (2014 est.)
country comparison to the world: 120

Electricity—consumption: 6.96 billion kWh (2014 est.)
country comparison to the world: 105

Electricity—exports: 112.9 million kWh (2014 est.)
country comparison to the world: 78

Electricity—imports: 3.073 billion kWh (2014 est.)
country comparison to the world: 52

Electricity—installed generating capacity: 2.011 million kW (2014 est.)
country comparison to the world: 107

Electricity—from fossil fuels: 64.5% of total installed capacity (2014 est.)
country comparison to the world: 121

Electricity—from nuclear fuels: 0% of total installed capacity (2014 est.)
country comparison to the world: 140

Electricity—from hydroelectric plants: 33% of total installed capacity (2014 est.)
country comparison to the world: 70

Electricity—from other renewable sources: 2.6% of total installed capacity (2014 est.)
country comparison to the world: 76

Crude oil—production: 0 bbl/day (2014 est.)
country comparison to the world: 167

Crude oil—exports: 0 bbl/day (2014)
country comparison to the world: 160

Crude oil—imports: 146 bbl/day (2014 est.)
country comparison to the world: 81

Crude oil—proved reserves: 0 bbl (1 January 2015 est.)
country comparison to the world: 167

Refined petroleum products—production: 5,246 bbl/day (2012 est.)
country comparison to the world: 106

Refined petroleum products—consumption: 15,070 bbl/day (2014 est.)
country comparison to the world: 141

Refined petroleum products—exports: 2,616 bbl/day (2014 est.)
country comparison to the world: 101

Refined petroleum products—imports: 17,950 bbl/day (2014 est.)
country comparison to the world: 117

Natural gas—production: 0 cu m (2014)
country comparison to the world: 102

Natural gas—consumption: 134.7 million cu m (2014 est.)
country comparison to the world: 107

Natural gas—exports: 0 cu m (2014)
country comparison to the world: 145

Natural gas—imports: 134.7 million cu m (2014 est.)
country comparison to the world: 71

Natural gas—proved reserves: 0 cu m (31 December 2014 est.)
country comparison to the world: 170

Carbon dioxide emissions from consumption of energy: 8.084 million Mt (2012 est.)
country comparison to the world: 110

COMMUNICATIONS

Telephones—fixed lines: *total subscriptions:* 390,000
subscriptions per 100 inhabitants: 19 (2014 est.)
country comparison to the world: 105
Telephones—mobile cellular: *total:* 2.3 million
subscriptions per 100 inhabitants: 110 (2014 est.)
country comparison to the world: 147

Telephone system: *general assessment:* competition from the mobile-cellular segment of the telecommunications market has led to a drop in fixed-line telephone subscriptions
domestic: combined fixed-line and mobile-cellular telephone subscribership about 130 per 100 persons
international: country code—389 (2012)

Broadcast media: public TV broadcaster operates 3 national channels and a satellite network; 5 privately owned TV channels broadcast nationally using terrestrial transmitters and about 15 broadcast on national level via satellite; roughly 75 local commercial TV stations; large number of cable operators offering domestic and international programming; public radio broadcaster operates over multiple stations; 3 privately owned radio stations broadcast nationally; about 70 local commercial radio stations (2012)
Radio broadcast stations: AM 1, FM 68, shortwave 0 (2009)
Television broadcast stations: 76 (2009)

Internet country code: .mk

Internet hosts: 62,826 (2012)
country comparison to the world: 92

Internet users: 1.1 million
51.1% (2009)
country comparison to the world: 121

TRANSPORTATION

Airports: 10 (2013)
country comparison to the world: 155
Airports—with paved runways: *total:* 8
2,438 to 3,047 m: 2
under 914 m: 6 (2013)
Airports—with unpaved runways: *total:* 2
914 to 1,523 m: 1
under 914 m: 1 (2013)
Pipelines: gas 268 km; oil 120 km (2013)
Railways: *total:* 699 km
standard gauge: 699 km 1.435-m gauge (223 km electrified) (2014)
country comparison to the world: 101
Roadways: *total:* 14,182 km (includes 242 km of expressways)
paved: 9,633 km
unpaved: 4,549 km (2014)
country comparison to the world: 124

MILITARY AND SECURITY

Military branches: Army of the Republic of Macedonia (ARM; includes General Staff and subordinate Joint Operational Command, Training and Doctrine Command, Special Operations Regiment) (2012)

Military service age and obligation: 18 years of age for voluntary military service; conscription abolished in 2008 (2013)

Military expenditures: 1.08% of GDP (2015)
1.17% of GDP (2014)
1.14% of GDP (2013)
1.2% of GDP (2012)
1.3% of GDP (2011)
country comparison to the world: 92

TRANSNATIONAL ISSUES

Disputes—international: Kosovo and Macedonia completed demarcation of their boundary in September 2008; Greece continues to reject the use of the name Macedonia or Republic of Macedonia

Refugees and internally displaced persons: *stateless persons:* 667 (2015)
note: 472,903 estimated refugee and migrant arrivals (2015—June 2016)

Illicit drugs: major transshipment point for Southwest Asian heroin and hashish; minor transit point for South American cocaine destined for Europe; although not a financial center and most criminal activity is thought to be domestic, money laundering is a problem due to a mostly cash-based economy and weak enforcement

MADAGASCAR

INTRODUCTION

Background: Madagascar was one of the last major landmasses on earth to be colonized by humans. The earliest settlers from present-day Indonesia arrived between A.D.350 and 550. The island attracted Arab and Persian traders as early as the 7th century, and migrants from Africa arrived around A.D.1000. Madagascar was a pirate stronghold during the late 17th and early 18th centuries, and served as a slave trading center into the 19th century. From the 16th to the late 19th century, a native Merina Kingdom dominated much of Madagascar. The island was conquered by the French in 1896 who made it a colony; independence was regained in 1960. During 1992–93, free presidential and National Assembly elections were held ending 17 years of single-party rule. in 1997, in the second presidential race, Didier RATSIRAKA, the leader during the 1970s and 1980s, was returned to the presidency. The 2001 presidential election was contested between the followers of Didier RATSIRAKA and Marc RAVALOMANANA, nearly causing secession of half of the country. In April 2002, the High Constitutional Court announced RAVALOMANANA the winner. RAVALOMANANA won a second term in 2006 but, following protests in 2009, handed over power to the military, which then conferred the presidency on the mayor of Antananarivo, Andry RAJOELINA, in what amounted to a coup d'etat.

Following a lengthy mediation process led by the Southern African Development Community, Madagascar held UN-supported presidential and parliamentary elections in 2013. Former de facto finance minister Hery RAJAONARIMAMPIANINA won a runoff election in December 2013 and was inaugurated in January 2014.

GEOGRAPHY

Location: Southern Africa, island in the Indian Ocean, east of Mozambique

Geographic coordinates: 20 00 S, 47 00 E

Map references: Africa

Area: *total:* 587,041 sq km
land: 581,540 sq km
water: 5,501 sq km
country comparison to the world: 47

Area—comparative: slightly less than twice the size of Arizona

Land boundaries: 0 km

Coastline: 4,828 km

Maritime claims: *territorial sea:* 12 nm
contiguous zone: 24 nm
exclusive economic zone: 200 nm
continental shelf: 200 nm or 100 nm from the 2,500-m isobath

Climate: tropical along coast, temperate inland, arid in south

Terrain: narrow coastal plain, high plateau and mountains in center

Elevation: *mean elevation:* 615 m

elevation extremes: *lowest point:* Indian Ocean 0 m
highest point: Maromokotro 2,876 m

Natural resources: graphite, ch romite, coal, bauxite, rare earth elements, salt, quartz, tar sands, semiprecious stones, mica, fish, hydropower

Land use: *agricultural land:* 71.1%
arable land: 6%;
permanent crops: 1%;
permanent pasture: 64.1%
forest: 21.5%
other: 7.4% (2011 est.)

Irrigated land: 10,860 sq km (2012)

Total renewable water resources: 337 cu km (2011)

Freshwater withdrawal (domestic/industrial/agricultural): *total:* 16.5 cu km/yr (2%/1%/97%)
per capita: 1,010 cu m/yr (2005)

Natural hazards: periodic cyclones; drough t; and locust infestation
volcanism: Madagascar's volcanoes have not erupted in historical times

Environment—current issues: soil erosion results from deforestation and overgrazing; desertification; surface water contaminated with raw sewage

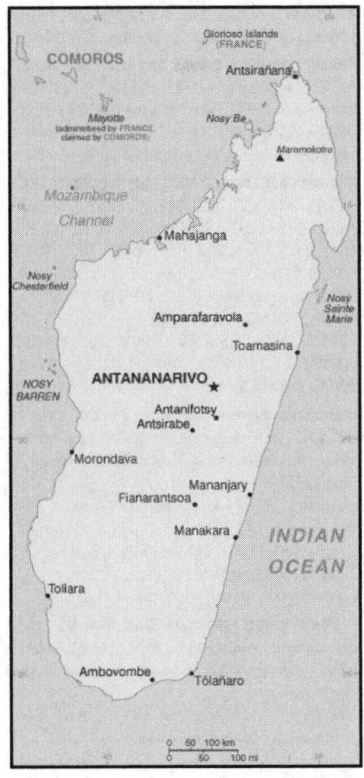

and other organic wastes; several endangered species of flora and fauna unique to the island

Environment—international agreements: *party to:* Biodiversity, Climate Change, Climate Change-Kyoto Protocol, Desertification, Endangered Species, Hazardous Wastes, Law of the Sea, Marine Life Conservation, Ozone Layer Protection, Ship Pollution, Wetlands
signed, but not ratified: none of the selected agreements

Geography—note: world's fourth -largest island; strategic location along Mozambique Channel

PEOPLE AND SOCIETY

Nationality: *noun:* Malagasy (singular and plural) *adjective:* Malagasy

Ethnic groups: Malayo-Indonesian (Merina and related Betsileo), Cotiers (mixed African, Malayo-Indonesian, and Arab ancestry—Betsimisaraka, Tsimihety, Antaisaka, Sakalava), French, Indian, Creole, Comoran

Languages: French (official), Malagasy (official), English

Religions: Christian, indigenous believer, Muslim *note:* population largely practices Christianity or an indigenous religion; small sh are of population is Muslim

Population: 23,812,681 (July 2015 est.)
country comparison to the world: 52

Age structure: *0–14 years:* 40.45% (male 4,856,231/female 4,775,025)
15–24 years: 20.53% (male 2,450,164/female 2,439,035)
25–54 years: 31.56% (male 3,760,230/female 3,755,775)
55–64 years: 4.24% (male 488,315/female 521,690)
65 years and over: 3.22% (male 347,151/female 419,065) (2015 est.)

Dependency ratios: *total dependency ratio:* 80.3%
youth dependency ratio: 75.2%
elderly dependency ratio: 5.1%
potential support ratio: 19.5% (2015 est.)

Median age: *total:* 19.4 years
male: 19.2 years
female: 19.5 years (2015 est.)
country comparison to the world: 196

Population growth rate: 2.58% (2015 est.)
country comparison to the world: 21

Birth rate: 32.61 births/1,000 population (2015 est.)
country comparison to the world: 33

Death rate: 6.81 deaths/1,000 population (2015 est.)
country comparison to the world: 138

Net migration rate: 0 migrant(s)/1,000 population (2015 est.)
country comparison to the world: 90

Urbanization: *urban Population:* 35.1% of total population (2015)
rate of urbanization: 4.69% annual rate of change (2010–15 est.)

Major urban areas—Population: ANTANANARIVO (capital) 2.61 million (2015)

Sex ratio: *at birth:* 1.03 male(s)/female
0–14 years: 1.02 male(s)/female
15–24 years: 1.01 male(s)/female
25–54 years: 1 male(s)/female
55–64 years: 0.94 male(s)/female
65 years and over: 0.83 male(s)/female
total population: 1 male(s)/female (2015 est.)

Mother's mean age at first birth: 19.4
note: median age at first birth among women 20–24 (2008/09 est.)

Maternal mortality rate: 353 deaths/100,000 live births (2015 est.)
country comparison to the world: 48

Infant mortality rate: *total:* 43.67 deaths/1,000 live births
male: 47.59 deaths/1,000 live births
female: 39.63 deaths/1,000 live births (2015 est.)
country comparison to the world: 47

Life expectancy at birth: *total population:* 65.55 years
male: 64.09 years
female: 67.05 years (2015 est.)
country comparison to the world: 175

Total fertility rate: 4.2 children born/woman (2015 est.)
country comparison to the world: 33

Contraceptive prevalence rate: 39.9% (2008/09)

Health expenditures: 4.2% of GDP (2013)
country comparison to the world: 158

Physicians density: 0.16 physicians/1,000 population (2007)

Hospital bed density: 0.2 beds/1,000 population (2010)

Drinking water source:
improved:
urban: 81.6% of population
rural: 35.3% of population
total: 51.5% of population
unimproved:
urban: 18.4% of population
rural: 64.7% of population
total: 48.5% of population (2015 est.)

Sanitation facility access:
improved:
urban: 18% of population
rural: 8.7% of population
total: 12% of population
unimproved:
urban: 82% of popu lation
rural: 91.3% of population
total: 88% of population (2015 est.)

HIV/AIDS—adult prevalence rate: 0.29% (2014 est.)
country comparison to the world: 82

HIV/AIDS—people living with HIV/AIDS: 39,100 (2014 est.)
country comparison to the world: 62

HIV/AIDS—deaths: 3,200 (2014 est.)
country comparison to the world: 43

Major infectious diseases: *degree of risk:* very high
food or waterborne diseases: bacterial diarrhea, hepatitis A, and typhoid fever
vectorborne diseases: malaria and dengue fever
water contact disease: schistosomiasis
animal contact disease: rabies (2013)

Obesity—adult prevalence rate: 4.6% (2014)
country comparison to the world: 187

Education expenditures: 2.1% of GDP (2013)
country comparison to the world: 150

Literacy: *definition:* age 15 and over can read and write
total population: 64.7%
male: 66.7%
female: 62.6% (2015 est.)

School life expectancy (primary to tertiary education): *total:* 10 years
male: 11 years
female: 10 years (2012)

Child labor—children ages 5–14: *total number:* 1,827,423
percentage: 28%
note: data represent children ages 5–17 (2007 est.)

Unemployment, youth ages 15–24: *total:* 2.6%
male: 2.2%
female: 3% (2012 est.)
country comparison to the world: 133

GOVERNMENT

Country name: *conventional long form:* Republic of Madagascar conventional short form: Madagascar

local long form: Republique de Madagascar/ Repoblikan'i Madagasikara

local short form: Madagascar/Madagasikara

former: Malagasy Republic

note: the name "Madageiscar" was first used by the 13th-century Venetian explorer Marco POLO, as a corrupted transliteration of Mogadishu, the Somali port with which POLO con fused the island

Government type: semi-presidential republic

Capital: name: Antananarivo

Geographic coordinates: 18 55 S, 47 31 E

time difference: UTC+3 (8 hours ahead of Washington, DC, during Standard Time)

Administrative divisions: 6 provinces (faritany); Antananarivo, Antsiranana, Fianarantsoa, Mahajanga, Toamasina, Toliara

Independence: 26 June 1960 (from France)

National holiday: Independence Day, 26 June (1960)

Constitution: previous 1992; latest passed by referendum 17 November 2010, promulgated 11 December 2010 (2016)

Legal system: civil law system based on the old French civil code and customary law in matters of marriage, family, and obligation

International law organization participation: accepts compulsory ICJ jurisdiction with reservations; accepts ICCt jurisdiction

Citizenship: citizenship by birth: no

citizenship by descent only: the father must be a citizen of Madagascar; in the case of a child born out of wedlock, the mother must be a citizen

dual citizenship recognized: no

residency requirement for naturalization: unknown

Suffrage: 18 years of age; universal

Executive branch: chief of state: President Hery Martial RAJAONARIMAMPIANINA Rakotoarimana (since 25 January 2014)

head of government: Prime Minister Olivier Mahafaly SOLONANDRASANA (since 13 April 2016); Prime Minister Jean RAVELONARIVO (since 17 January 2015) resigned 8 April 2016

cabinet: Council of Ministers appointed by the prime minister

elections/appointments: president directly elected by absolute majority popular vote in 2 rounds if needed for a 5-year term (eligible for a second term); election last held on 20 December 2013 (next to be held in 2018); prime minister nominated by the National Assembly, appointed by the president

election results: Hery Martial RAJ AO NARI-MAMPIANINA elected president; percent of vote in second round—Hery Martial RAJ AO NARIMAMPIANINA (FIDO) 53.5%, Jean Louis ROBINSON (AVANA) 46.5%

note: on 17 March 2009, democratically elected President Marc RAVALOMANANA stepped down, handing the government over to the military, which in turn conferred the presidency on opposition leader and Antananarivo mayor Andry

RAJOELINA; a power-sharing agreement established a 15-month transition period to conclude with a general election in 2010, which failed to occur; a subsequent agreement aimed for an early 2013 election—the first round was held on 25 October 2013 and the second on 20 December 2013

Legislative branch: description: unicameral National Assembly or Antenimierampirenena (151 seats; 87 members directly elected in single-seat constituencies by simple majority vote and 64 directly elected in two-seat constituencies by proportional representation vote; members serve 4-year terms)

elections: National Assembly—last held on 20 December 2013 (next to be held in 2017); note—a power-sharing agreement in the summer of 2009 established a 15-month transition, concluding in general elections held in 2013 after repeated delays

election results: National Assembly—percent of vote by party—MPAR 17.3%, MR 10.8%, VPM MMM 8.2%, PHI 3.8%, AMHM 3.5%, LF 2.8%, FFF 1.6%, AIM 1.0%, SFN 0.3%, independent and other 50.6%; seats by party—MPAR 49, MR 20, VPMMMM 13, PHI 5, AMHM 2, LF 5, FFF 2, AIM 2, SFN 2, other 22, independent 25, seats with delayed elections 4

Judicial branch: highest court(s): Supreme Court or Cour Supreme (consists of 11 members; addresses judicial administration issues only); High Constitutional Court or Haute Cour Constitutionnelle (consists of 9 members; note—the judiciary includes a high Court of Justice responsible for adjudicating crimes and misdemeanors by government officials including the president

judge selection and term of office: Supreme Court heads elected by the president and judiciary officials to serve single-renewable, 3-year terms; High Constitutional Court members appointed—3 each by the president, by both legislative bodies, and by the Council of Magistrates; members serve single, 6-year terms

subordinate courts: Courts of Appeal; provincial and city tribunals

Political parties and leaders: AVANA Party [Jean-Louis ROBINSON]

Economic Liberalism and Democratic Action for National Recovery/LEADER Fanilo or LF [Manasse ESOAVELOMANDROSO]

Green Party/Parti Vert or AMHM [Sarah Georget RABEHARISOA]

National Unity, Freedom, and Development or FFF [Benjamin RADAVIDSON Andriamparany]

New Force for Madagascar or FIDIO [Hery RAJAONARIMAMPIANINA]

Parti Hiaraka Isika or PHI [Albert Camille VITAL] Party of Andry Rajoelina or MPAR [Andry RAJOELINA]

Pillar of Madagascar or AIM [Andry RAKOTOVAO]

Ravlomanana Movement or MR [Marc RAVALOMANANA]

Sambo Fiaran'i Noe or SFN

Union Party or Tambatra [Pety RAKOTONIAINA]

Vondrona Politika Miara dia Malagasy Miara Miainga or VPM MMM [Milavonjy ANDRIASY]

Political pressure groups and leaders: Committee for the Defense of Truth and Justice or KMMR Committee for National Reconciliation or CRN [Albert ZAFY]

National Council of Christian Churches or FFKM

International organization participation: ACP, AFDB, AU, CD, CO MESA, EITI (candidate country), FAO, G-77, IAEA, IBR D, ICAO, ICC (NGOs), ICCt, ICRM, ID A, IFAD, IFC, IFRCS, ILO, IMF, IMO, InOC, Interpol, IOC, IOM, IPU, ISO (correspondent), ITSO, ITU, ITUC (NGOs), MIGA, NAM, OIF, OPCW, PCA, SADC, UN, UNCTAD, UNESCO, UNHCR, UNIDO, UNWTO, UPU, WCO, WFTU (NGOs), WHO, WIPO, WMO, WTO

Diplomatic representation in the US: chief of mission: Ambassador (vacant); Charge d'Affaires Velotiana Rakotoanosy RAOBELINA (since 20 June 2011)

chancery: 2374 Massachusetts Avenue NW, Washington, DC 20008

telephone: [1] (202) 265–5525 through 5526

FAX: [1] (202) 265–3034

consulate(s) general: New York

Diplomatic representation from the US: chief of mission: Ambassador Robert T. YAMATE (since 13 January 2015); note—also accredited to Comoros

embassy: Lot 207A, Point Liberty, Andranoro, Antehiroka, 105 Antananarivo

mailing address: B.P. 620, Antsahavola, Antananarivo

telephone: [261] (23) 480 00/01

FAX: [261] (23) 480 35

Flag description: two equal horizontal bands of red (top) and green with a vertical white band of the same width on hoist side; by tradition, red stands for sovereignty, green for hope, white for purity

National symbol(s): traveller's palm, zebu; national colors: red, green, white

National anthem: name: "Ry Tanindraza nay malala o" (Oh, Our Beloved Fatherland)

lyrics/music: Pasteur RAHAJASON/Norbert RAHARISOA

note: adopted 1959

ECONOMY

Economy—overview: Agriculture, including fishing and forestry, is a mainstay of the economy, accounting for more than one-fourth of GDP and employing roughly 80% of the population. Deforestation and erosion, aggravated by the use of firewood as the primary source of fuel, are serious concerns.

After discarding socialist economic policies in the mid-1990s, Madagascar followed a World Bank-and IMF-led policy of privatization and liberalization until the onset of a political crisis, which lasted from 2009 to 2013. The free market strategy had placed the country on a slow and steady growth path from an extremely low starting point. Exports of apparel boomed after gaining duty-free access to the US in 2000; however, Madagascar's failure to comply with the requirements of the African Growth and Opportunity Act (AGOA) led to the termination of the country's duty-free access in January 2010, a sharp fall in textile production, and a loss of more than 100,000 jobs. Madagascar regained AGOA access in January 2015 following the democratic election of a new President the previous year. in November 2015, the International Monetary Fund (IMF) approved a Rapid Credit Facility to Madagascar worth about $42.1 million to help the government meet its balance of payments needs. The IMF also approved a staff monitoring program to guide policy implementation and indicated that Madagascar must demonstrate the capability to sustain reforms to qualify for future requests for a credit facility.

GDP (purchasing power parity):
$35.44 billion (2015 est.)
$34.39 billion (2014 est.)
$33.29 billion (2013 est.)
note: data are in 2015 US dollars
country comparison to the world: 121

GDP (official exchange rate): $9.737 billion (2015 est.)

GDP—real growth rate: 3% (2015 est.)
3.3% (2014 est.)
2.3% (2013 est.)
country comparison to the world: 100

GDP—per capita (PPP):
$1,500 (2015 est.)
$1,500 (2014 est.)
$1,500 (2013 est.)
note: data are in 2015 US dollars
country comparison to the world: 217

Gross national saving: 14.9% of GDP (2015 est.)
15.3% of GDP (2014 est.)
10% of GDP (2013 est.)
country comparison to the world: 118

GDP—composition, by end use:
household consumption: 77.6%
government consumption: 15.3%
investment in fixed capital: 15.8%
investment in inventories: -0.1%
exports of goods and services: 22.7%
imports of goods and services: -31.3% (2015 est.)

GDP—composition, by sector of origin:
agriculture: 26.5%
industry: 16.9%
services: 56.6% (2015 est.)

Agriculture—products: coffee, vanilla, sugarcane, cloves, cocoa, rice, cassava (manioc, tapioca), beans, bananas, peanuts; livestock products

Industries: meat processing, seafood, soap, beer, leather, sugar, textiles, glassware, cement, automobile assembly plant, paper, petroleum, tourism, mining

Industrial production growth rate: 3.8% (2015 est.)
country comparison to the world: 63

Labor force: 12.57 million (2015 est.)
country comparison to the world: 44

Unemployment rate: NA% (2015 est.)
3.6% (2014 est.)

Population below poverty line: 75.3% (2010 est.)

Household income or consumption by percentage share: *lowest:* 10%: 2.2%
highest: 10%: 34.7% (2010 est.)

Distribution of family income—Gini index: 47.5 (2001)
38.1 (1999)
country comparison to the world: 27

Budget: *revenues:* $2.533 billion
expenditures: $2.854 billion (2015 est.)
Taxes and other revenues: 26.6% of GDP (2015 est.)
country comparison to the world: 110

Budget surplus (+) or deficit (−): -3.3% of GDP (2015 est.)
country comparison to the world: 126

Fiscal year: calendar year

Inflation rate (consumer prices): 7.4% (2015 est.)
6.1% (2014 est.)
country comparison to the world: 196

Central bank discount rate: 5% (31 December 2010)
country comparison to the world: 79

Commercial bank prime lending rate: 62% (31 December 2015 est.)
60% (31 December 2014 est.)
country comparison to the world: 1

Stock of narrow money: $1.535 billion (31 December 2015 est.)
$1.506 billion (31 December 2014 est.)
country comparison to the world: 140

Stock of broad money: $2.745 billion (31 December 2015 est.)
$2.399 billion (31 December 2014 est.)
country comparison to the world: 146

Stock of domestic credit: $1.89 billion (31 December 2015 est.) $1.658 billion (31 December 2014 est.)
country comparison to the world: 141

Market value of publicly traded shares: $NA

Current account balance: -$211 million (2015 est.)
-$34 million (2014 est.)
country comparison to the world: 83

Exports: $2.447 billion (2015 est.) $2.187 billion (2014 est.)
country comparison to the world: 133

Exports—commodities: coffee, vanilla, shellfish, sugar, cotton cloth, clothing, chromite, petroleum products

Exports—partners: France 15.2%, US 12.7%, China 7.1%, South Africa 5.9%, Japan 5.5%, Netherlands 5.4%, Germany 5.1%, Belgium 5%, India 4.4% (2015)

Imports: $3.041 billion (2015 est.) $2.927 billion (2014 est.)
country comparison to the world: 145

Imports—commodities: capital goods, petroleum, consumer goods, food

Imports—partners: China 24.8%, France 10.3%, Bahrain 5.6%, India 5.5%, Kuwait 4.5%, Mauritius 4.5%, South Africa 4.3% (2015)

Reserves of foreign exchange and gold: $962.9 million (31 December 2015 est.)
$773.8 million (31 December 2014 est.)
country comparison to the world: 134

Debt—external: $3.444 billion (31 December 2014 est.)
$2.849 billion (31 December 2013 est.)
country comparison to the world: 141

Stock of direct foreign investment—at home: $NA

Stock of direct foreign investment—abroad: $NA

Exchange rates: Malagasy ariary (MGA) per US dollar—
2,872.7 (2015 est.)
2,414.8 (2014 est.)
2,414.8 2,414.8 (2013 est.)
2,195 (2012 est.)
2,025.1 (2011 est.)

ENERGY

Electricity—production: 2.025 billion kWh (2012 est.)
country comparison to the world: 139

Electricity—consumption: 1.883 billion kWh (2012 est.)
country comparison to the world: 143

Electricity—exports: 0 kWh (2013 est.)
country comparison to the world: 163

Electricity—imports: 0 kWh (2013 est.)
country comparison to the world: 171

Electricity—installed generating capacity: m 544,200 kW (2012 est.)
country comparison to the world: 138

Electricity—from fossil fuels: 69.6% of total installed capacity (2012 est.)
country comparison to the world: 107

Electricity—from nuclear fuels: 0% of total installed capacity (2012 est.)
country comparison to the world: 133

Electricity—from hydroelectric plants: 30.1% of total installed capacity (2012 est.)
country comparison to the world: 75

Electricity—from other renewable sources: 0.2% of total installed capacity (2012 est.)
country comparison to the world: 109

Crude oil—production: 0 bbl/day (2014 est.)
country comparison to the world: 161

Crude oil—exports: 0 bbl/day (2012 est.)
country comparison to the world: 154

Crude oil—imports: 0 bbl/day (2012 est.)
country comparison to the world: 90

Crude oil—proved reserves: 0 bbl (1 January 2015 est.)
country comparison to the world: 160

Refined petroleum products—production: 0 bbl/day (2012 est.)
country comparison to the world: 205

Refined petroleum products—consumption: 12,000 bbl/day (2013 est.)
country comparison to the world: 149

Refined petroleum products—exports: 0 bbl/day (2012 est.)

country comparison to the world: 198

Refined petroleum products—imports: 12,120 bbl/day (2012 est.)
country comparison to the world: 132

Natural gas—production: 0 cu m (2013 est.)
country comparison to the world: 215

Natural gas—consumption: 0 cu m (2013 est.)
country comparison to the world: 166

Natural gas—exports: 0 cu m (2013 est.)
country comparison to the world: 138

Natural gas—imports: 0 cu m (2013 est.)
country comparison to the world: 95

Natural gas—proved reserves: 2.01 billion cu m (1 January 2012 est.)
country comparison to the world: 99

Carbon dioxide emissions from consumption of energy: 2.886 million Mt (2012 est.)
country comparison to the world: 142

COMMUNICATIONS

Telephones—fixed lines: *total subscriptions:* 250,000
subscriptions per 100 inhabitants: 1 (2014 est.)
country comparison to the world: 121

Telephones—mobile cellular: *total:* 9 million
subscriptions per 100 inhabitants: 39 (2014 est.)
country comparison to the world: 91

Telephone system: *general assessment:* system is above average for the region; Antananarivo's main telephone exchange modernized in the late 1990s, but the rest of the analogue-based telephone system is poorly developed
domestic: combined fixed-line and mobile-cellular teledensity about 40 per 100 persons
international: country code—261; landing point for the EASSy, SEACOM, and LION fiber-optic submarine cable systems; satellite earth stations—2 (1 Intelsat—Indian Ocean, 1 Intersputnik—Atlantic Ocean region) (2010)

Broadcast media: state-owned Radio Nationale Malagasy (RNM) and Television Malagasy (TVM) have an extensive national network reach; privately owned radio and TV broadcasters in cities and major towns; state-run radio dominates in rural areas; relays of 2 international broadcasters are available in Antananarivo (2007)
Radio broadcast stations: AM 2, FM 9, shortwave 6 (2001)
Television broadcast stations: 1 (plus 36 repeaters) (2001)

Internet country code: .mg

Internet hosts: 38,392 (2012)
country comparison to the world: 102

Internet users: *total:* 17 million
percent of population: 73.5% (2014 est.)
country comparison to the world: 31

TRANSPORTATION

Airports: 83 (2013)
country comparison to the world: 65

Airports—with paved runways: *total:* 26
over 3,047 m: 1
2,438 to 3,047 m: 2
1,524 to 2,437 m: 6
914 to 1,523 m: 16
under 914 m: 1 (2013)

Airports—with unpaved runways: *total:* 57
1,524 to 2,437 m: 1
914 to 1,523 m: 38
under 914 m: 18 (2013)

Railways: *total:* 836 km
narrow gauge: 836 km 1.000-m gauge (2014)
country comparison to the world: 95

Roadways: *total:* 37,476 km
paved: 6,103 km
unpaved: 31,373 km (2010)
country comparison to the world: 92

Waterways: 600 km (432 km navigable) (2011)

country comparison to the world: 79

Merchant marine: *total:* 1
by type: cargo 1
registered in other countries: 1 (unknown 1) (2010)
country comparison to the world: 152

Ports and terminals: *major seaport(s):* Antsiranana (Diego Suarez), Mahajanga, Toamasina, Toliara (Tulear)

MILITARY AND SECURITY

Military branches: People's Armed Forces: Intervention Force, Development Force, and Aeronaval Force (navy and air); National Gendarmerie

Military service age and obligation: 18–25 years of age for male-only voluntary military service; no conscription; service obligation is 18 months for military or equivalent civil service; 20–30 years of age for National Gendarmerie recruits and 35 years of age for those with military experience (2012)

Military expenditures: 0.69% of GDP (2012)
0.73% of GDP (2011)
0.69% of GDP (2010)
country comparison to the world: 119

TRANSNATIONAL ISSUES

Disputes—international: claims Bassas da India, Europa Island, Glorioso Islands, and Juan de Nova Island (all administered by France); the vegetated drying cays of Banc du Geyser, which were claimed by Madagascar in 1976, also fall within the EEZ claims of the Comoros and France (Glorioso Islands, part of the French Southern and Antarctic Lands)

Refugees and internally displaced persons: *IDPs:* 21,475 (floods in 2015) (2015)

Illicit drugs: illicit producer of cannabis (cultivated and wild varieties) used mostly for domestic consumption; transshipment point for heroin

MALAWI

INTRODUCTION

Background: Established in 1891, the British protectorate of Nyasaland became the independent nation of Malawi in 1964. After three decades of one-party rule under President Hastings Kamuzu BANDA, the country held multiparty presidential and parliamentary elections in 1994, under a provisional constitution that came into full effect the following year. President Bingu wa MUTHARIKA, elected in May 2004 after a failed attempt by the previous president to amend the constitution to permit another term, struggled to assert his authority against his predecessor and subsequently started his own party, the Democratic Progressive Party in 2005. MUTHARIKA was reelected to a second term in May 2009. He oversaw some economic improvement in his first term, but was accused of economic mismanagement and poor

governance in his second term. He died abruptly in April 2012 and was succeeded by vice president, Joyce BANDA, who had earlier started her own party, the People's Party. MUTHARIKA's brother, Peter MUTHARIKA, defeated BANDA in the May 2014 election. Population growth, increasing pressure on agricultural lands, corruption, and the scourge of HIV/AIDS pose major problems for Malawi.

GEOGRAPHY

Location: Southern Africa, east of Zambia, west and north of Mozambique

Geographic coordinates: 13 30 S, 34 00 E

Map references: Africa

Area: *total:* 118,484 sq km
land: 94,080 sq km

water: 24,404 sq km
country comparison to the world: 100

Area—comparative: slightly smaller than Pennsylvania

Land boundaries: *total:* 2,857 km
border countries (3): Mozambique 1,498 km, Tanzania 512 km, Zambia 847 km

Coastline: 0 km (landlocked)

Maritime claims: none (landlocked)

Climate: sub-tropical; rainy season (November to May); dry season (May to November)

Terrain: narrow elongated plateau with rolling plains, rounded hills, some mountains

Elevation: *mean elevation:* 779 m

elevation extremes: *lowest point:* junction of the Shire River and international boundary with Mozambique 37 m

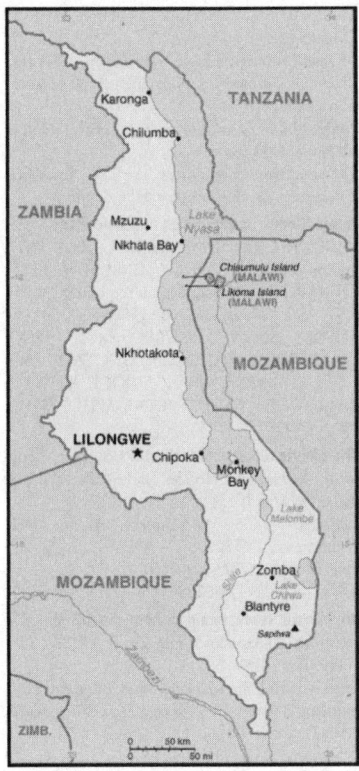

highest point: Sapitwa (Mount Mlanje) 3,002 m

Natural resources: limestone, arable land, hydropower, unexploited deposits of uranium, coal, and bauxite

Land use: *agricultural land:* 59.2%
arable land: 38.2%;
permanent crops: 1.4%;
permanent pasture: 19.6%
forest: 34%
other: 6.8% (2011 est.)

Irrigated land: 740 sq km (2012)

Total renewable water resources: 17.28 cu km (2011)

Freshwater withdrawal (domestic/industrial/agricultural): *total:* 1.36 cu km/yr (11%/4%/86%)
per capita: 99.86 cu m/yr (2005)

Natural hazards: NA

Environment—current issues: deforestation; land degradation; water pollution from agricultural runoff, sewage, industrial wastes; siltation of spawning grounds endangers fish populations

Environment—international agreements: *party to:* Biodiversity, Climate Change, Climate Change-Kyoto Protocol, Desertification, Endangered Species, Environmental Modification, Hazardous Wastes, Marine Life Conservation, Ozone Layer Protection, Ship Pollution, Wetlands
signed, but not ratified: Law of the Sea

Geography—note: landlocked; Lake Nyasa, some 580 km long, is the country's most prominent physical feature; it contains more fish species than any other lake on earth

PEOPLE AND SOCIETY

Nationality: *noun:* Malawian(s)
adjective: Malawian

Ethnic groups: Chewa 32.6%, Lomwe 17.6%, Yao 13.5%, Ngoni 11.5%, Tumbuka 8.8%, Nyanja 5.8%, Sena 3.6%, Tonga 2.1%, Ngonde 1%, other 3.5%

Languages: English (official), Chichewa (common), Chinyanja, Chiyao, Chitumbuka, Chilomwe, Chinkhonde, Chingoni, Chisena, Chitonga, Chinyakyusa, Chilambya

Religions: Christian 82.6%, Muslim 13%, other 1.9%, none 2.5% (2008 est.)

Population: 17,964,697
note: estimates for this country explicitly take into account the effects of excess mortality due to AIDS; this can result in lower life expectancy, higher infant mortality, higher death rates, lower population growth rates, and changes in the distribution of population by age and sex than would otherwise be expected (July 2015 est.)
country comparison to the world: 63

Age structure: *0–14 years:* 46.73% (male 4,175,706/female 4,218,955)
15–24 years: 20.38% (male 1,820,047/female 1,841,331)
25–54 years: 27.14% (male 2,418,126/female 2,457,419)
55–64 years: 3.06% (male 262,067/female 287,637)
65 years and over: 2.69% (male 213,735/female 269,674) (2015 est.)

Dependency ratios: *total dependency ratio:* 94.5%
youth dependency ratio: 87.9%
elderly dependency ratio: 6.7%
potential support ratio: 14.9% (2015 est.)

Median age: *total:* 16.4 years
male: 16.3 years
female: 16.5 years (2015 est.)
country comparison to the world: 226

Population growth rate: 3.32% (2015 est.)
country comparison to the world: 2

Birth rate: 41.56 births/1,000 population (2015 est.)
country comparison to the world: 7

Death rate: 8.41 deaths/1,000 population (2015 est.)
country comparison to the world: 82

Net migration rate: 0 migrant(s)/1,000 population (2015 est.)
country comparison to the world: 89

Urbanization: *urban Population:* 16.3% of total population (2015)
rate of urbanization: 3.77% annual rate of change (2010–15 est.)

Major urban areas—Population: LILONGWE (capital) 905,000; Blantyre-Limbe 808,000 (2015)

Sex ratio: *at birth:* 1.02 male(s)/female
0–14 years: 0.99 male(s)/female
15–24 years: 0.99 male(s)/female
25–54 years: 0.98 male(s)/female
55–64 years: 0.91 male(s)/female
65 years and over: 0.79 male(s)/female
total population: 0.98 male(s)/female (2015 est.)

Mother's mean age at first birth: 18.9
note: median age at first birth among women 20–24 (2010 est.)

Maternal mortality rate: 634 deaths/100,000 live births (2015 est.)
country comparison to the world: 24

Infant mortality rate: *total:* 46.26 deaths/1,000 live births
male: 53.07 deaths/1,000 live births
female: 39.35 deaths/1,000 live births (2015 est.)
country comparison to the world: 42

Life expectancy at birth: *total population:* 60.66 years
male: 58.67 years
female: 62.69 years (2015 est.)
country comparison to the world: 196

Total fertility rate: 5.6 children born/woman (2015 est.)
country comparison to the world: 8

Contraceptive prevalence rate: 46.1% (2010)

Health expenditures: 8.3% of GDP (2013)
country comparison to the world: 35

Physicians density: 0.02 physicians/1,000 population (2009)

Hospital bed density: 1.3 beds/1,000 population (2011)

Drinking water source:
improved:
urban: 95.7% of population
rural: 89.1% of population
total: 90.2% of population
unimproved:
urban: 4.3% of population
rural: 10.9% of population
total: 9.8% of population (2015 est.)

Sanitation facility access:
improved:
urban: 47.3% of population
rural: 39.8% of population
total: 41% of population
unimproved:
urban: 52.7% of population
rural: 60.2% of population
total: 59% of population (2015 est.)

HIV/AIDS—adult prevalence rate: 10.04% (2014 est.)
country comparison to the world: 9

HIV/AIDS—people living with HIV/AIDS: 1,063,900 (2014 est.)
country comparison to the world: 10

HIV/AIDS—deaths: 32,600 (2014 est.)
country comparison to the world: 11

Major infectious diseases: *degree of risk:* very high
food or waterborne diseases: bacterial and protozoal diarrhea, hepatitis A, and typhoid fever

vectorborne diseases: malaria and dengue fever
water contact disease: schistosomiasis
animal contact disease: rabies (2013)

Obesity—adult prevalence rate: 4.3% (2014)
country comparison to the world: 168

Children under the age of 5 years underweight: 16.7% (2014)
country comparison to the world: 52

Education expenditures: 6.9% of GDP (2014)
country comparison to the world: 60

Literacy: *definition:* age 15 and over can read and write
total population: 65.8%
male: 73%
female: 58.6% (2015 est.)

School life expectancy (primary to tertiary education): *total:* 11 years
male: 11 years
female: 11 years (2011)

Child labor—children ages 5–14: *total number:* 993,318
percentage: 26% (2006 est.)

Unemployment, youth ages 15–24: *total:* 8.6%
male: 9.1%
female: 8.2% (2013 est.)

GOVERNMENT

Country name: *conventional long form:* Republic of Malawi
conventional short form: Malawi
local long form: Dziko la Malawi
local short form: Malawi
former: British Central African Protectorate, Nyasaland Protectorate, Nyasaland
etymology: named for the East African Maravi kingdom of the 16th century; the word "maravi" means "fire flames"

Government type: presidential republic

Capital: *name:* Lilongwe

Geographic coordinates: 13 58 S, 33 47 E
time difference: UTC+2 (7 hours ahead of Washington, DC, during Standard Time)

Administrative divisions: 28 districts; Balaka, Blantyre, Chikwawa, Chiradzulu, Chitipa, Dedza, Dowa, Karonga, Kasungu, Likoma, Lilongwe, Machinga, Mangochi, Mchinji, Mulanje, Mwanza, Mzimba, Neno, Ntcheu, Nkhata Bay, Nkhotakota, Nsanje, Ntchisi, Phalombe, Rumphi, Salima, Thyolo, Zomba

Independence: 6 July 1964 (from the UK)

National holiday: Independence Day (Republic Day),6 July (1964)

Constitution: previous 1953 (preindependence),1966; latest drafted January to May 1994, approved 16 May 1994, entered into force 18 May 1995; amended several times, last in 2013 (2016)

Legal system: mixed legal system of English common law and customary law; judicial review of legislative acts in the Supreme Co urt of Appeal

International law organization participation: accepts compulsory ICJ jurisdiction with reservations; accepts ICCt jurisdiction

Citizenship: *citizenship by birth:* no
citizenship by descent only: at least one parent must be a citizen of Malawi
dual citizenship recognized: no
residency requirement for naturalization: 7 years

Suffrage: 18 years of age; universal

Executive branch: *chief of state:* President Arthur Peter MUTHARIKA (since 31 May 2014); Vice President Saulos CHILIMA (since 31 May 2014); note—the president is both chief of state and head of government

head of government: President Arthur Peter MUTHARIKA (since 31 May 2014); Vice President Saulos CHILIMA (since 31 May 2014)
cabinet: Cabinet named by the president
elections/appointments: president directly elected by simple majority popular vote for a 5-year term (eligible for a second term); election last held on 20 May 2014 (next to be held in May 2019)
election results: Peter MUTHARIKA elected president; percent of vote—Peter MUTHARIKA (DPP) 36.4%, Lazarus CHAKWERA (MCP) 27.8%, Joyce BANDA (PP) 20.2%, Atupele MULUZI (UDF) 13.7%, other 1.9%

Legislative branch: *description:* unicameral National Assembly (193 seats; members directly elected in single-seat constituencies by simple majority vote to serve 5-year terms)
elections: last held on 20–22 May 2014 (next to be held in May 2019)
election results: percent of vote by party—DPP 22.0%, MCP 17.4%, PP 18.5%, UDF 9.6%, other 2.8%, independent 29.7%; seats by party—DPP 51, MCP 48, PP 26, UDF 14, other 2, independent 52

Judicial branch: *highest court(s):* Supreme Court of Appeal (consists of the chief justice and at least 3 judges)
judge selection and term of office: Supreme Court chief justice appointed by the president and confirmed by the National Assembly; other judges appointed by the president upon recommendation of the Judicial Service Commission, which regulates judicial officers; judges serve until age 65
subordinate courts: High Court; magistrate courts; Industrial Relations Court; district and city traditional or local courts

Political parties and leaders: Alliance for Democracy or AFORD [Godfrey SHAWA]
Chipani Cha Fuko or CCP [Davis KATSONGA PHIRI]; note—party disbanded in fall of 2015
Democratic Progressive Party or DPP [Peter MUTHARIKA]
Malawi Congress Party or MCP [Lazarus CHAKWERA]
People's Party or PP [Joyce BANDA]
United Democratic Front or UDF [Atupele MULUZI]

Political pressure groups and leaders: Council for NGOs in Malawi or CONGOMA (human rights, democracy, and development)

Human Rights Consultative Committee or HRCC (human rights)
Malawi Economic Justice Network or MEJN (pro economic growth, development, government accountability)
Malawi Law Society (an umbrella organization of all lawyers in Malawi)
Public Affairs Committee or PAC (promotes democracy, development, peace and unity)

International organization participation: ACP, AfDB, AU, C, CD, CO MESA, FAO, G-77, IAEA, IBRD, ICAO, ICCt, ICRM, ID A, IFAD, IFC, IFRCS, ILO, IMF, IMO, Interpol, IOC, IOM, IPU, ISO (correspondent), ITSO, ITU, ITUC (NGOs), MIGA, MINURSO, MONU SCO, NAM, OPCW, SADC, UN, UNCTAD, UNESCO, UNIDO, UNISFA, UNOCI, UNWTO, UPU, WCO, WFTU (NGOs), WHO, WIPO, WMO, WTO

Diplomatic representation in the US: *chief of mission:* Ambassador Necton Darlington MHURA (since 18 May 2015)
chancery: 2408 Massachusetts Avenue NW, Washington, DC 20008
telephone: [1] (202) 721-0270
FAX: [1] (202) 721-0288

Diplomatic representation from the US: *chief of mission:* Ambassador Virginia E. PALMER (since 5 February 2015)
embassy: 16 Jomo Kenyatta Road, Lilongwe 3
mailing address: P.O. Box 30016, Lilongwe 3, Malawi
telephone: [265] (1) 773-166
FAX: [265] (1) 770-471

Flag description: three equal horizontal bands of black (top), red, and green with a radiant, rising, red sun centered on the black band; black represents the native peoples, red the blood shed in their struggle for freedom, and green the color of nature; the rising sun represents the hope of freedom for the continent of Africa

National symbol(s): lion; national colors: black, red, green

National anthem: *name:* "Mulungu dalitsa Malawi" (Oh God Bless Our Land of Malawi)
lyrics/music: Michael-F redrick Paul SAU KA
note: adopted 1964

ECONOMY

Economy—overview: Landlocked Malawi ranks among the world's most densely populated and least developed countries. The country's economic performance has historically been constrained by policy inconsistency, macroeconomic instability, limited connectivity to the region and the world, and poor health and education outcomes that limit labor productivity. The economy is predominately agricultural with about 80% of the population living in rural areas. Agriculture accounts for about one-third of GDP and 90% of export revenues. The performance of the tobacco sector is key to short-term growth as tobacco accounts for more than half of exports.

The economy depends on substantial inflows of economic assistance from the IMF, the World Bank, and individual donor nations. In 2006, Malawi was approved for relief under the Heavily Indebted Poor Countries program. Between 2005 and 2009 Malawi's government exhibited improved financial discipline under the guidance of Finance Minister Goodall GONDWE and signed a three-year IMF Poverty Reduction and Growth Facility worth $56 million. The government announced infrastructure projects that could yield improvements, such as a new oil pipeline for better fuel access, and the potential for a waterway link through Mozambican rivers to the ocean for better transportation options.

Since 2009, however, Malawi has experienced some setbacks, including a general shortage of foreign exchange, which has damaged its ability to pay for imports, and fuel shortages that hinder transportation and productivity. In October 2013, the African Development Bank, the IMF, several European countries, and the US indefinitely froze $150 million in direct budgetary support in response to a high level corruption scandal, called "Cashgate, " citing a lack of trust in the government's financial management system and civil service. Most of the frozen donor funds—which accounted for 40% of the budget—have been channeled through non-governmental organizations in the country. The government has failed to address barriers to investment such as unreliable power, water shortages, poor telecommunications infrastructure, and the high costs of services. Investment had fallen continuously for several years, but rose 4 percentage points in 2014 to 17% of GDP.

The government faces many challenges, including developing a market economy, improving educational facilities, addressing environmental problems, dealing with HIV/AIDS, and satisfying foreign donors on anti-corruption efforts.

GDP (purchasing power parity):
$20.36 billion (2015 est.)
$19.78 billion (2014 est.)
$18.71 billion (2013 est.)
note: data are in 2015 US dollars
country comparison to the world: 145

GDP (official exchange rate): $6.416 billion (2015 est.)

GDP—real growth rate: 3% (2015 est.)
5.7% (2014 est.)
5.2% (2013 est.)
country comparison to the world: 101

GDP—per capita (PPP): $1,100 (2015 est.)
$1,100 (2014 est.)
$1,100 (2013 est.)
note: data are in 2015 US dollars
country comparison to the world: 223

Gross national saving: 4.1% of GDP (2015 est.)
4% of GDP (2014 est.)
4% of GDP (2013 est.)
country comparison to the world: 165

GDP—composition, by end use:
household consumption: 77.5%
government consumption: 17.4%
investment in fixed capital: 12.4%

investment in inventories: 2.7%
exports of goods and services: 43.5%
imports of goods and services: -53.5% (2015 est.)

GDP—composition, by sector of origin:
agriculture: 32.9%
industry: 17.1%
services: 50.1% (2015 est.)

Agriculture—products: tobacco, sugarcane, cotton, tea, corn, potatoes, cassava (manioc, tapioca), sorghum, pulses, groundnuts, Macadamia nuts; cattle, goats

Industries: tobacco, tea, sugar, sawmill products, cement, consumer goods

Industrial production growth rate: 4.1% (2015 est.)
country comparison to the world: 53

Labor force: 5.747 million (2007 est.)
country comparison to the world: 72

Labor force—by occupation: *agriculture:* 90%
industry and services: 10% (2003 est.)

Unemployment rate: NA%

Population below poverty line: 52.4% (2004 est.)

Household income or consumption by percentage share: *lowest:* 10%: 3%
highest: 10%: 31.9% (2004)

Distribution of family income—Gini index: 39 (2004)
country comparison to the world: 70

Budget: *revenues:* $1.188 billion
expenditures: $1.388 billion (2015 est.)
Taxes and other revenues: 18.6% of GDP (2015 est.)
country comparison to the world: 168

Budget surplus (+) or deficit (–): -3.1% of GDP (2015 est.)
country comparison to the world: 115

Public debt: 61.1% of GDP (2015 est.)
60.9% of GDP (2014 est.)
country comparison to the world: 60

Fiscal year: 1 July—30 June

Inflation rate (consumer prices): 21.9% (2015 est.)
23.8% (2014 est.)
country comparison to the world: 220

Central bank discount rate: 15% (31 December 2009)
15% (31 December 2008)
country comparison to the world: 12

Commercial bank prime lending rate: 41% (31 December 2015 est.)
44.29% (31 December 2014 est.)
country comparison to the world: 3

Stock of narrow money: $456.9 million (31 December 2015 est.)
$549.8 million (31 December 2014 est.)
country comparison to the world: 166

Stock of broad money: $1.481 billion (31 December 2014 est.)
$1.2 billion (31 December 2013 est.)
country comparison to the world: 164

Stock of domestic credit: $647 million (31 December 2015 est.)
$800.2 million (31 December 2014 est.)

country comparison to the world: 163

Market value of publicly traded shares:
$753.6 million (31 December 2012 est.)
$1.384 billion (31 December 2011)
$1.363 billion (31 December 2010 est.)
country comparison to the world: 109

Current account balance: -$568 million (2015 est.)
-$494 million (2014 est.)
country comparison to the world: 103

Exports: $1.185 billion (2015 est.)
$1.366 billion (2014 est.)
country comparison to the world: 155

Exports—commodities: tobacco 53%, tea, sugar, cotton, coffee, peanuts, wood products, apparel (2010 est.)

Exports—partners: Belgium 15.8%, Zimbabwe 12%, India 6.9%, South Africa 6.2%, US 6%, Russia 5.6%, Germany 4.6% (2015)

Imports: $2.664 billion (2015 est.)
$2.808 billion (2014 est.)
country comparison to the world: 151

Imports—commodities: food, petroleum products, semi-manufactures, consumer goods, transportation equipment

Imports—partners: South Africa 26.4%, China 16.7%, India 12%, Zambia 10.3%, Tanzania 6% (2015)

Reserves of foreign exchange and gold: $743.4 million (31 December 2015 est.)
$625.2 million (31 December 2014 est.)
country comparison to the world: 140

Debt—external: $1.884 billion (31 December 2014 est.)
$1.558 billion (31 December 2013 est.)
country comparison to the world: 151

Stock of direct foreign investment—at home: $NA

Stock of direct foreign investment—abroad: $NA

Exchange rates: Malawian kwachas (MWK) per US dollar—
520.5 (2015 est.
424.9 (2014 est.)
424.9 (2013 est.)
249.11 (2012 est.)
156.93 (2011 est.)

ELECTRICITY

Energy: 2.18 billion kWh (2012 est.)
country comparison to the world: 135

Electricity—consumption: 2.027 billion kWh (2012 est.)
country comparison to the world: 142

Electricity—exports: 0 kWh (2013 est.)
country comparison to the world: 167

Electricity—imports: 0 kWh (2013 est.)
country comparison to the world: 173

Electricity—installed generating capacity: 302,000 kW (2012 est.)
country comparison to the world: 151

Electricity—from fossil fuels: 0.7% of total installed capacity (2012 est.)
country comparison to the world: 211

Electricity—from nuclear fuels: 0% of total installed capacity (2012 est.)
country comparison to the world: 138

Electricity—from hydroelectric plants: 99.3% of total installed capacity (2012 est.)
country comparison to the world: 5

Electricity—from other renewable sources: 0% of total installed capacity (2012 est.)
country comparison to the world: 199

Crude oil—production: 0 bbl/day (2014 est.)
country comparison to the world: 165

Crude oil—exports: 0 bbl/day (2012 est.)
country comparison to the world: 158

Crude oil—imports: 0 bbl/day (2012 est.)
country comparison to the world: 95

Crude oil—proved reserves: 0 bbl (1 January 2015 est.)
country comparison to the world: 165

Refined petroleum products—production: 0 bbl/day (2012 est.)
country comparison to the world: 209

Refined petroleum products—consumption: 6,000 bbl/day (2013 est.)
country comparison to the world: 165

Refined petroleum products—exports: 0 bbl/day (2012 est.)
country comparison to the world: 202

Refined petroleum products—imports: 6,059 bbl/day (2012 est.)
country comparison to the world: 153

Natural gas—production: 0 cu m (2013 est.)
country comparison to the world: 100

Natural gas—consumption: 0 cu m (2013 est.)
country comparison to the world: 169

Natural gas—exports: 0 cu m (2013 est.)
country comparison to the world: 143

Natural gas—imports: 0 cu m (2013 est.)
country comparison to the world: 98

Natural gas—proved reserves: 0 cu m (1 January 2014 est.)
country comparison to the world: 168

Carbon dioxide emissions from consumption of energy: 1.91 million Mt (2012 est.)
country comparison to the world: 150

COMMUNICATIONS

Telephones—fixed lines: *total subscriptions:* 64,200

subscriptions per 100 inhabitants: less than 1 (2014 est.)
country comparison to the world: 153

Telephones—mobile cellular: *total:* 5.1 million
subscriptions per 100 inhabitants: 30 (2014 est.)
country comparison to the world: 117

Telephone system: *general assessment:* rudimentary; privatization of Malawi Telecommunications (MTL), a necessary step in bringing improvement to telecommunications services, completed in 2006
domestic: limited fixed-line subscribership of about 1 per 100 persons; mobile-cellular services are expanding but network coverage is limited and is based around the main urban areas; mobile-cellular subscribership about 25 per 100 persons
international: country code—265; satellite earth stations—2 Intelsat (1 Indian Ocean, 1 Atlantic Ocean) (2010)

Broadcast media: radio is the main broadcast medium; privately owned Zodiac radio has the widest national broadcasting reach, followed by state-run radio; about a dozen private and community radio stations broadcast in cities and towns around the country; the largest TV network is government-owned, but two private TV networks now broadcast in urban areas and more plan to begin broadcasting in 2014; relays of multiple international broadcasters are available (2014)
Radio broadcast stations: AM 9, FM 5 (plus 15 repeater stations), shortwave 2 (plus one shortwave station on standby) (2001)
Television broadcast stations: 1 (2001)

Internet country code: .mw

Internet hosts: 1,099 (2012)
country comparison to the world: 171

Internet users: *total:* 387,500
percent of population: 2.2% (2014 est.)
country comparison to the world: 135

TRANSPORTATION

Airports: 32 (2013)
country comparison to the world: 113

Airports—with paved runways: *total:* 7
over 3,047 m: 1
1,524 to 2,437 m: 2
914 to 1,523 m: 4 (2013)

Airports—with unpaved runways: *total:* 25
1,524 to 2,437 m: 1
914 to 1,523 m: 11

under 914 m: 13 (2013)

Railways: *total:* 767 km
narrow gauge: 767 km 1.067-m gauge (2014)
country comparison to the world: 98

Roadways: *total:* 15,450 km
paved: 6,951 km
unpaved: 8,499 km (2011)
country comparison to the world: 120

Waterways: 700 km (on Lake Nyasa [Lake Malawi] and Shire River) (2010)
country comparison to the world: 75

Ports and terminals: *lake port(s):* Chipoka, Monkey Bay, Nkhata Bay, Nkhotakota, Chilumba (Lake Nyasa)

MILITARY AND SECURITY

Military branches: Malawi Defense Forces (MDF): Army (includes Air Wing, Marine Unit) (2012)

Military service age and obligation: 18 years of age for voluntary military service; high school equivalent required for enlisted recruits and college equivalent for officer recruits; initial engagement is 7 years for enlisted personnel and 10 years for officers (2014)

Military expenditures: 0.93% of GDP (2012)
0.79% of GDP (2011)
0.93% of GDP (2010)
country comparison to the world: 104

TRANSNATIONAL ISSUES

Disputes—international: dispute with Tanzania over the boundary in Lake Nyasa (Lake Malawi) and the meandering Songwe River; Malawi contends that the entire lake up to the Tanzanian shoreline is its territory, while Tanzania claims the border is in the center of the lake; the conflict was reignited in 2012 when Malawi awarded a license to a British company for oil exploration in the lake

Refugees and internally displaced persons: *refugees (country of origin):* 11,315 (Congo, Democratic Republic of the); 5,260 (Rwanda) (2015); nearly 11,500 (Mozambique) (2016)
IDPs: 107,000 (floods in 2015) (2015)

MALAYSIA

INTRODUCTION

Background: During the late 18th and 19th centuries, Great Britain established colonies and protectorates in the area of current Malaysia; these were occupied by Japan from 1942 to 1945. In 1948, the British-ruled territories on the Malay Peninsula except Singapore formed the Federation of Malaya, which became independent in 1957. Malaysia was formed in 1963 when the former British colonies of Singapore, as well as Sabah and Sarawak on the northern coast of Borneo, joined the Federation. The first several years of the country's independence were marred by a communist insurgency, Indonesian confrontation with Malaysia, Philippine claims to Sabah, and Singapore's withdrawal in 1965. During the 22-year term of Prime Minister MAHATHIR bin Mohamad (1981–2003), Malaysia was successful in diversifying its economy from dependence on exports of raw materials to the development of manufacturing, services, and tourism. Prime Minister Mohamed NAJIB bin Abdul Razak (in office since April 2009) has continued these pro-business policies. Malaysia assum ed a nonpermanent seat on the UN Security Council for the 2015–16 term.

GEOGRAPHY

Location: Southeastern Asia, peninsula bordering Thailand and northern one-third of the island of Borneo, bordering Indonesia, Brunei, and the South China Sea, south of Vietnam

Geographic coordinates: 2 30 N, 112 30 E

Map references: Southeast Asia

Area: *total:* 329,847 sq km
land: 328,657 sq km
water: 1,190 sq km
country comparison to the world: 67

Area—comparative: slightly larger than New Mexico

Land boundaries: *total:* 2,742 km
border countries (3): Brunei 266 km, Indonesia 1,881 km, Thailand 595 km

Coastline: 4,675 km (Peninsular Malaysia 2,068 km, East Malaysia 2,607 km)

Maritime claims: *territorial sea:* 12 nm
exclusive economic zone: 200 nm
continental shelf: 200-m depth or to the depth of exploitation; specified boundary in the South China Sea

Climate: tropical; annual southwest (April to October) and northeast (October to February) monsoons

Terrain: coastal plains rising to hills and mountains

Elevation: *mean elevation:* 419 m

elevation extremes: *lowest point:* Indian Ocean 0 m
highest point: Gunung Kinabalu 4,100 m

Natural resources: tin, petroleum, timber, copper, iron ore, natural gas, bauxite

Land use: *agricultural land:* 23.2%
arable land: 2.9%;
permanent crops: 19.4%;
permanent pasture: 0.9%
forest: 62%
other: 14.8% (2011 est.)

Irrigated land: 3,800 sq km (2012)

Total renewable water resources: 580 cu km (2011)

Freshwater withdrawal (domestic/industrial/agricultural): *total:* 11.2 cu km/yr (35%/43%/22%)
per capita: 414 cu m/yr (2005)

Natural hazards: flooding; landslides; forest fires

Environment—current issues: air pollution from industrial and vehicular emissions; water pollution from raw sewage; deforestation; smoke/haze from Indonesian forest fires

Environment—international agreements: *party to:* Biodiversity, Climate Change, Climate Change-Kyoto Protocol, Desertification, Endangered Species, Hazardous Wastes, Law of the Sea, Marine Life Conservation, Ozone Layer Protection, Ship Pollution, Tropical Timber 83, Tropical Timber 94, Wetlands
signed, but not ratified: none of the selected agreements

Geography—note: strategic location along Strait of Malacca and southern South China Sea

PEOPLE AND SOCIETY

Nationality: *noun:* Malaysian(s)
adjective: Malaysian

Ethnic groups: Malay 50.1%, Chinese 22.6%, indigenous 11.8%, Indian 6.7%, other 0.7%, non-citizens 8.2% (2010 est.)

Languages: Bahasa Malaysia (official), English, Chinese (Cantonese, Mandarin, Hokkien, Hakka, Hainan, Foochow), Tamil, Telugu, Malayalam, Panjabi, Thai
note: in East Malaysia there are several indigenous languages; most widely spoken are Iban and Kadazan

Religions: Muslim (official) 61.3%, Buddhist 19.8%, Christian 9.2%, Hindu 6.3%, Confucianism, Taoism, other traditional Chinese religions 1.3%, other 0.4%, none 0.8%, unspecified 1% (2010 est.)

Population: 30,513,848 (July 2015 est.)

country comparison to the world: 43

Age structure: *0–14 years:* 28.49% (male 4,472,457/female 4,221,384)
15–24 years: 16.91% (male 2,615,356/female 2,543,039)
25–54 years: 41.12% (male 6,352,742/female 6,194,303)
55–64 years: 7.84% (male 1,215,315/female 1,175,868)
65 years and over: 5.65% (male 817,766/female 905,618) (2015 est.)

Dependency ratios: *total dependency ratio:* 43.6%
youth dependency ratio: 35.2%
elderly dependency ratio: 8.4%
potential support ratio: 11.9% (2015 est.)

Median age: *total:* 27.9 years
male: 27.7 years
female: 28.2 years (2015 est.)
country comparison to the world: 130

Population growth rate: 1.44% (2015 est.)
country comparison to the world: 83

Birth rate: 19.71 births/1,000 population (2015 est.)
country comparison to the world: 86

Death rate: 5.03 deaths/1,000 population (2015 est.)
country comparison to the world: 188

Net migration rate: -0.33 migrant(s)/1,000 population (2015 est.)
country comparison to the world: 130

Urbanization: *urban Population:* 74.7% of total population (2015)
rate of urbanization: 2.66% annual rate of change (2010–15 est.)

Major urban areas—Population: KUALA LUMPUR (capital) 6.837 million; Johor Bahru 912,000 (2015)

Sex ratio: *at birth:* 1.07 male(s)/female
0–14 years: 1.06 male(s)/female
15–24 years: 1.03 male(s)/female
25–54 years: 1.03 male(s)/female
55–64 years: 1.03 male(s)/female
65 years and over: 0.9 male(s)/female
total population: 1.03 male(s)/female (2015 est.)

Maternal mortality rate: 40 deaths/100,000 live births (2015 est.)
country comparison to the world: 125

Infant mortality rate: *total:* 13.27 deaths/1,000 live births
male: 15.33 deaths/1,000 live births
female: 11.07 deaths/1,000 live births (2015 est.)
country comparison to the world: 113

Life expectancy at birth: *total population:* 74.75 years
male: 71.97 years
female: 77.73 years (2015 est.)
country comparison to the world: 112

Total fertility rate: 2.55 children born/woman (2015 est.)
country comparison to the world: 76

Health expenditures: 4% of GDP (2013)
country comparison to the world: 161

Physicians density: 1.2 physicians/1,000 population (2010)

Hospital bed density: 1.9 beds/1,000 population (2012)

Drinking water source:
improved:
urban: 100% of population
rural: 93% of population
total: 98.2% of population
unimproved:
urban: 0% of population
rural: 7% of population
total: 1.8% of population (2015 est.)

Sanitation facility access:
improved:
urban: 96.1% of population
rural: 95.9% of population
total: 96% of population
unimproved:
urban: 3.9% of population
rural: 4.1% of population
total: 4% of population (2015 est.)

HIV/AIDS—adult prevalence rate: 0.45% (2014 est.)
country comparison to the world: 72

HIV/AIDS—people living with HIV/AIDS: 100,800 (2014 est.)
country comparison to the world: 44

HIV/AIDS—deaths: 9,000 (2014 est.)
country comparison to the world: 27

Major infectious diseases: *degree of risk:* intermediate
food or waterborne diseases: bacterial diarrhea
vectorborne diseases: dengue fever
water contact disease: leptospirosis
note: highly pathogenic H5N1 avian influenza has been identified in this country; it poses a negligible risk with extremely rare cases possible among US citizens who have close contact with birds (2013)

Obesity—adult prevalence rate: 12.9% (2014)
country comparison to the world: 123

Children under the age of 5 years underweight: 12.9% (2006)
country comparison to the world: 58

Education expenditures: 6.1% of GDP (2013)
country comparison to the world: 46

Literacy: *definition:* age 15 and over can read and write
total population: 94.6%
male: 96.2%
female: 93.2% (2015 est.)

School life expectancy (primary to tertiary education): *total:* 14 years
male: NA
female: NA (2014)

Unemployment, youth ages 15–24: *total:* 10.4%
male: 9.3%
female: 12% (2013 est.)

country comparison to the world: 100

GOVERNMENT

Country name: *conventional long form:* none
conventional short form: Malaysia
local long form: none
local short form: Malaysia
former: Federation of Malaya
etymology: the name means "Land of the Malays"

Government type: federal constitutional monarchy
note: nominally headed by paramount ruler (commonly referred to as the king) and a bicameral Parliament consisting of a nonelected upper house and an elected lower house; all Peninsular Malaysian states have hereditary rulers (commonly referred to as sultans) except Melaka (Malacca) and Pulau Pinang (Penang); those two states along with Sabah and Sarawak in East Malaysia have governors appointed by government; powers of state governments are limited by federal constitution; under terms of federation, Sabah and Sarawak retain certain constitutional prerogatives (e.g., right to maintain their own immigration controls)

Capital: *name:* Kuala Lumpur; note—Putrajaya is referred to as an administrative center not the capital; Parliament meets in Kuala Lumpur

Geographic coordinates: 3 10 N, 101 42 E
time difference: UTC+8 (13 hours ahead of Washington, DC, during Standard Time)

Administrative divisions: 13 states (negeri-negeri, singular—negeri); Johor, Kedah, Kelantan, Melaka, Negeri Sembilan, Pahang, Perak, Perlis, Pulau Pinang, Sabah, Sarawak, Selangor, Terengganu; and 1 federal territory (Wilayah Persekutuan) with 3 components, Kuala Lumpur, Labuan, and Putrajaya

Independence: 31 August 1957 (from the UK)

National holiday: Independence Day 31 August (1957) (independence of Malaya); Malaysia Day 16 September (1963) (formation of Malaysia)

Constitution: previous 1948; latest drafted 21 February 1957, effective 27 August 1957; amended many times, last in 2010 (2016)

Legal system: mixed legal system of English common law, Islamic law, and customary law; judicial review of legislative acts in the Federal Court at request of supreme head of the federation

International law organization participation: has not submitted an ICJ jurisdiction declaration; non-party state to the ICCt

Citizenship: *citizenship by birth:* no
citizenship by descent only: at least one parent must be a citizen of Malaysia
dual citizenship recognized: no
residency requirement for naturalization: 10 out 12 years preceding application

Suffrage: 21 years of age; universal

Executive branch: *chief of state:* King Tuanku ABDUL HALIM Mu'adzam Shah (selected on 13 December 2011; installed on 11 April 2012); the position of the king is primarily ceremonial but he

is the final arbiter on the appointment of the prime minister

head of government: Prime Minister Mohamed NAJIB bin Abdul Najib Razak (since 3 April 2009); Deputy Prime Minister Ahmad ZAHID Hamidi (since 29 July 2015)
cabinet: Cabinet appointed by the prime minister from among members of Parliament with the consent of the king
elections/appointments: king elected by and from the hereditary rulers of 9 states for a 5-year term; election is on a rotational basis among rulers of the 9 states; election last held on 14 October 2011 (next to be held in 2016); prime minister designated from among members of the House of Representatives; following legislative elections, the leader who commands support of the majority of members in the House becomes prime minister
election results: Tuanku ABDUL HALIM Mu'adzam Shah elected king; Mohamed NAJIB bin Abdul Najib Razak (UMNO) sworn in as prime minister for second term on 3 April 2009

Legislative branch: *description:* bicameral Parliament or Parlimen consists of the Senate or Dewan Negara (70 seats; 44 members appointed by the king and 26 indirectly elected by 13 state legislatures; members serve 3-year terms) and the House of Representatives or Dewan Rakyat (222 seats; members directly elected in single-seat constituencies by simple majority vote to serve 5-year terms)
elections: House of Representatives—last held on 5 May 2013 (next to be held by May 2018)
election results: House of Representatives—percent of vote by party/coalition—BN 47.4%, People's Alliance (DAP, PAS, PKR) 50.9%, other 1.7%; seats by party/coalition—BN 133, People's Alliance (DAP, PAS, PKR) 89
note: seats by party/coalition as of October 2015—BN 132, PH 72, PAS 14, PSM 1, TERAS 1, independent 2

Judicial branch: *highest court(s):* Federal Court (consists of the chief justice, president of the Court of Appeal, chief justice of the High Court of Malaya, chief judge of the High Court of Sabah and Sarawak and 7 judges); note—Malaysia has a dual judicial hierarchy of civil and religious (sharia) courts
judge selection and term of office: Federal Court justices appointed by the monarch on advice of the prime minister; judges serve until mandatory retirement at age 65
subordinate courts: Court of Appeal; High Court; Sessions Court; Magistrates' Court

Political parties and leaders: National Front (Barisan Nasional) or BN: Gerakan Rakyat Malaysia Party or GERAKAN [MAH Siew Keong]
Liberal Democratic Party (Parti Liberal Demokratik—Sabah) or LDP [TEO Chee Kang]
Malaysian Chinese Association (Persatuan China Malaysia) or MCA [LIOW Tiong Lai]
Malaysian Indian Congress (Kongres India Malaysia) or MIC [S. SUBRAMANIAM]
Parti Bersatu Rakyat Sabah or PBRS [Joseph KURUP]

Parti Bersatu Sabah or PBS [Joseph PAIRIN Kitingan]

Parti Pesaka Bumiputera Bersatu or PBB [Adenan SATEM]

Parti Rakyat Sarawak or PRS [James MASING]

Sarawak Progressive Democratic Party or SPDP [TIONG King Sing]

Sarawak United People's Party (Parti Bersatu Rakyat Sarawak) or SUPP [Dr. SIM Kui Hian]

United Malays National Organization or UMNO [NAJIB bin Abdul Razak]

United Pasokmomogun Kadazandusun Murut Organization (Pertubuhan Pasko Momogun Kadazan Dusun Bersatu) or UPKO [Wilfred Madius TANGAU]

People's Progressive Party (Parti Progresif Pendu duk Malaysia) or PPP [M. Kayveas]

Coalition of Hope (Pakatan Harapan) or PH: Democratic Action Party (Parti Tindakan Demokratik) or DAP [TAN Kok Wai, Acting National Chairman]

National Trust Party (Parti Amanah Negara) or Amanah [Mohamad SABU]

People's Justice Party (Parti Keadilan Rakyat) or PKR [WAN AZIZAH Wan Ismail]

other: Islamic Party of Malaysia (Parti Islam se Malaysia) or PAS [Abdul HADI Awang]

Sarawak People's Energy Party or TERAS [William Mawan IKOM]

Socialist Party of Malaysia (Parti Sosialis Malaysia) or PSM [Mohd Nasir HASHIM]

Political pressure groups and leaders: Bar Council BERSIH (electoral reform coalition)
ISMA (Muslim NGO)
PERKASA (defense of Malay rights)
other: religious groups; women's groups; youth groups

International organization participation: ADB, APEC, ARF, ASEAN, BIS, C, CICA (observer), CP, D-8, EAS, FAO, G-15, G-77, IAEA, IBRD, ICAO, ICC (national committees), ICRM, IDA, IDB, IFAD, IFC, IFRCS, IHO, ILO, IMF, IMO, IMSO, Interpol, IOC, IPU, ISO, ITSO, ITU, ITUC (NGOs), MIGA, MINURSO, MONUSCO, NAM, OIC, OPCW, PCA, PIF (partner), UN, UN Security Council (temporary), UNAMID, UNCTAD, UNESCO, UNIDO, UNIFIL, UNISFA, UNMIL, UNWTO, UPU, WCO, WFTU (NGOs), WHO, WIPO, WMO, WTO

Diplomatic representation in the US: chief of mission: Ambassador AWANG ADEK Bin Hussin (since 21 May 2015)
chancery: 3516 International Court NW, Washington, DC 20008
telephone: [1] (202) 572-9700
FAX: [1] (202) 572-9882
consulate(s) general: Los Angeles, New York

Diplomatic representation from the US: chief of mission: Ambassador Joseph Y. YUN (since 2 October 2013)
embassy: 376 Jalan Tun Razak, 50400 Kuala Lumpur
mailing address: US Embassy Kuala Lumpur, APO AP 96535–8152

telephone: [60] (3) 2168-5000
FAX: [60] (3) 2142-2207

Flag description: 14 equal horizontal stripes of red (top) alternating with white (bottom); there is a blue rectangle in the upper hoist-side corner bearing a yellow crescent and a yellow 14-pointed star; the flag is often referred to as Jalur Gemilang (Stripes of Glory); the 14 stripes stand for the equal status in the federation of the 13 member states and the federal government; the 14 points on the star represent the unity between these entities; the crescent is a traditional symbol of Islam; blue symbolizes the unity of the Malay people and yellow is the royal color of Malay rulers
note: the design is based on the flag of the US

National symbol(s): tiger, hibiscus; national colors: red, white, blue, yellow

National anthem: name: "Negaraku" (My Country)
lyrics/music: collective, led by Tunku ABDUL RAHMAN/Pierre Jean DE BERANGER
note: adopted 1957; full version only performed in the presence of the king; the tune, which was adopted from a popular French melody titled "La Rosalie, " was originally the anthem of Perak, one of Malaysia's 13 states

ECONOMY

Economy—overview: Malaysia, a middle-income country, has transformed itself since the 1970s from a producer of raw materials into an emerging multi-sector economy. Under current Prime Minister NAJIB, Malaysia is attempting to achieve high-income status by 2020 and to move farther up the value-added production chain by attracting investments in Islamic finance, high technology industries, biotechnology, and services. NAJIB's Economic Transformation Program is a series of projects and policy measures intended to accelerate the country's economic growth. The government has also taken steps to liberalize some services sub-sectors. Malaysia is vulnerable to a fall in world commodity prices or a general slowdown in global economic activity.

The NAJIB administration is continuing efforts to boost domestic demand and reduce the economy's dependence on exports. Nevertheless, exports—particularly of electronics, oil and gas, palm oil, and rubber—remaiNA significant driver of the economy. Gross exports of goods and services constitute more than 80% of GDP. The oil and gas sector supplied about 29% of government revenue in 2014. As an oil and gas exporter, Malaysia has previously profited from higher world energy prices, although the rising cost of domestic gasoline and diesel fuel, combined with sustained budget deficits, has forced Kuala Lumpur to begin to address fiscal shortfalls, through initial reductions in energy and sugar subsidies and the announcement of the 2015 implementation of a 6% goods and services tax. Falling global oil prices in the second half of 2014 have strained government finances, shrunk Malaysia's current account surplus and put downward pressure on the ringgit.

The government is trying to lessen its dependence on state oil producer Petronas.

Bank Negara Malaysia (the central bank) maintains healthy foreign exchange reserves; a well-developed regulatory regime has limited Malaysia's exposure to riskier financial instruments and the global financial crisis. in order to attract increased investment, NAJIB raised possible revisions to the special economic and social preferences accorded to ethnic Malays under the New Economic Policy of 1970, but retreated in 2013 after he encountered significant opposition from Malay nationalists and other vested interests. In September 2013 NAJIB launched the new Bumiputra Economic Empowerment Program, policies that favor and advance the economic condition of ethnic Malays.

Malaysia is a member of the 12-nation Trans-Pacific Partnership free trade agreement negotiations and, with the nine other ASEAN members, will form the ASEAN Economic Community in 2015.

GDP (purchasing power parity):
$815.6 billion (2015 est.)
$777.2 billion (2014 est.)
$733.2 billion (2013 est.)
note: data are in 2015 US dollars
country comparison to the world: 29

GDP (official exchange rate): $296.2 billion (2015 est.)

GDP—real growth rate: 5% (2015 est.)
6% (2014 est.) 4.7% (2013 est.)
country comparison to the world: 40

GDP—per capita (PPP): $26,300 (2015 est.)
$25,400 (2014 est.)
$24,500 (2013 est.)
note: data are in 2015 US dollars
country comparison to the world: 69

Gross national saving: 28% of GDP (2015 est.)
29.3% of GDP (2014 est.)
29.4% of GDP (2013 est.)
country comparison to the world: 31

GDP—composition, by end use:
household consumption: 54%
government consumption: 13.6%
investment in fixed capital: 26.9%
investment in inventories: 0%
exports of goods and services: 74.6%
imports of goods and services: -69.1% (2015 est.)

GDP—composition, by sector of origin:
agriculture: 8.9%
industry: 35%
services: 56.1% (2015 est.)

Agriculture—products: Peninsular Malaysia—palm oil, rubber, cocoa, rice; Sabah—palm oil, subsistence crops; rubber, timber; Sarawak—palm oil, rubber, timber; pepper

Industries: Peninsular Malaysia—rubber and oil palm processing and manufacturing, petroleum and natural gas, light manufacturing, pharmaceuticals, medical technology, electronics and semiconductors, timber processing; Sabah—logging, petroleum and natural gas production; Sarawak—agriculture processing, petroleum and natural gas production, logging

Industrial production growth rate: 5.5% (2015 est.)
country comparison to the world: 26

Labor force: 14.3 million (2015 est.)
country comparison to the world: 41

Labor force—by occupation: *agriculture:* 11%
industry: 36%
services: 53% (2012 est.)

Unemployment rate: 2.7% (2015 est.)
2.9% (2014 est.)
country comparison to the world: 18

Population below poverty line: 3.8% (2009 est.)

Household income or consumption by percentage share: *lowest:* 10%: 1.8%
highest: 10%: 34.7% (2009 est.)

Distribution of family income—Gini index: 46.2 (2009)
49.2 (1997)
country comparison to the world: 34

Budget: *revenues:* $52.97 billion
expenditures: $64.25 billion (2015 est.)
Taxes and other revenues: 16.9% of GDP (2015 est.)
country comparison to the world: 179

Budget surplus (+) or deficit (–): -3.6% of GDP (2015 est.)
country comparison to the world: 134

Public debt: 53.5% of GDP (2015 est.)
52.7% of GDP (2014 est.)
note: this figure is based on the amount of federal government debt; this includes Malaysian Treasury bills and other government securities, as well as loans raised externally and bonds and notes issued overseas; this figure excludes debt issued by non-financial public enterprises and guaranteed by the federal government
country comparison to the world: 71

Fiscal year: calendar year

Inflation rate (consumer prices): 2.1% (2015 est.)
3.1% (2014 est.)
note: approximately 30% of goods are price-controlled
country comparison to the world: 116

Central bank discount rate: 3% (31 December 2011)
2.83% (31 December 2010)
country comparison to the world: 105

Commercial bank prime lending rate: 4.8% (31 December 2015 est.)
4.67% (31 December 2014 est.)
country comparison to the world: 148

Stock of narrow money: $84.18 billion (31 December 2015 est.)
$99.12 billion (31 December 2014 est.)
country comparison to the world: 40

Stock of broad money: $478.7 billion (31 December 2014 est.)
$440.3 billion (31 December 2013 est.)
country comparison to the world: 24

Stock of domestic credit: $381.2 billion (31 December 2015 est.)
$444.8 billion (31 December 2014 est.)
country comparison to the world: 31

Market value of publicly traded shares: $476.3 billion (31 December 2012 est.)

$395.1 billion (31 December 2011)
$410.5 billion (31 December 2010 est.)
country comparison to the world: 24

Current account balance: $8.712 billion (2015 est.)
$14.46 billion (2014 est.)
country comparison to the world: 25

Exports: $203.8 billion (2015 est.)
$224.9 billion (2014 est.)
country comparison to the world: 24

Exports—commodities: semiconductors and electronic equipment, palm oil, petroleum and liquefied natural gas, wood and wood products, palm oil, rubber, textiles, chemicals, solar panels

Exports—partners: Singapore 13.9%, China 13%, Japan 9.5%, US 9.4%, Thailand 5.7%, Hong Kong 4.7%, India 4.1% (2015)

Imports: $174.7 billion (2015 est.)
$189.8 billion (2014 est.)
country comparison to the world: 26

Imports—commodities: electronics, machinery, petroleum products, plastics, vehicles, iron and steel products, chemicals

Imports—partners: China 18.8%, Singapore 12%, US 8.1%, Japan 7.8%, Thailand 6.1%, South Korea 4.5%, Indonesia 4.5% (2015)

Reserves of foreign exchange and gold: $89.86 billion (31 December 2015 est.)
$115.9 billion (31 December 2014 est.)
country comparison to the world: 27

Debt—external: $213.9 billion (31 December 2014 est.)
$212.3 billion (31 December 2013 est.)
country comparison to the world: 34

Stock of direct foreign investment—at home: $166.8 billion (31 December 2015 est.)
$155.8 billion (31 December 2014 est.)
country comparison to the world: 33

Stock of direct foreign investment—abroad: $161.5 billion (31 December 2015 est.)
$149.5 billion (31 December 2014 est.)
country comparison to the world: 27

Exchange rates: ringgits (MYR) per US dollar—
3.902 (2015 est.)
3.27 (2014 est.)
3.27 (2013 est.)
3.09 (2012 est.)
3.06 (2011 est.)

ENERGY

Electricity—production: 126.8 billion kWh (2012 est.)
country comparison to the world: 30

Electricity—consumption: 118.5 billion kWh (2012 est.)
country comparison to the world: 29

Electricity—exports: 12 million kWh (2012 est.)
country comparison to the world: 89

Electricity—imports: 372 million kWh (2013 est.)
country comparison to the world: 82

Electricity—installed generating capacity: 28.53 million kW (2012 est.)

country comparison to the world: 30

Electricity—from fossil fuels: 87.6% of total installed capacity (2012 est.)
country comparison to the world: 82

Electricity—from nuclear fuels: 0% of total installed capacity (2012 est.)
country comparison to the world: 148

Electricity—from hydroelectric plants: 11.6% of total installed capacity (2012 est.)
country comparison to the world: 110

Electricity—from other renewable sources: 0.8% of total installed capacity (2012 est.)
country comparison to the world: 96

Crude oil—production: 597,500 bbl/day (2014 est.)
country comparison to the world: 26

Crude oil—exports: 244,600 bbl/day (2012 est.)
country comparison to the world: 28

Crude oil—imports: 200,200 bbl/day (2012 est.)
country comparison to the world: 33

Crude oil—proved reserves: 4 billion bbl (1 January 2015 est.)
country comparison to the world: 27

Refined petroleum products—production: 560,700 bbl/day (2012 est.)
country comparison to the world: 30

Refined petroleum products—consumption: 680,000 bbl/day (2013 est.)
country comparison to the world: 30

Refined petroleum products—exports: 235,600 bbl/day (2012 est.)
country comparison to the world: 29

Refined petroleum products—imports: 302,700 bbl/day (2012 est.)
country comparison to the world: 23

Natural gas—production: 64 billion cu m (2013 est.)
country comparison to the world: 14

Natural gas—consumption: 31.86 billion cu m (2013 est.)
country comparison to the world: 30

Natural gas—exports: 35.4 billion cu m (2013 est.)
country comparison to the world: 10

Natural gas—imports: 2.34 billion cu m (2012 est.)
country comparison to the world: 46

Natural gas—proved reserves: 2.35 trillion cu m (1 January 2014 est.)
country comparison to the world: 16

Carbon dioxide emissions from consumption of energy: 198.8 million Mt (2012 est.)
country comparison to the world: 30

COMMUNICATIONS

Telephones—fixed lines: *total subscriptions:* 4.41 million
subscriptions per 100 inhabitants: 15 (2014 est.)
country comparison to the world: 37

Telephones—mobile cellular: *total:* 44.9 million
subscriptions per 100 inhabitants: 149 (2014 est.)

country comparison to the world: 31

Telephone system: *general assessment:* modern system featuring good intercity service on Peninsular Malaysia provided mainly by microwave radio relay and an adequate intercity microwave radio relay network between Sabah and Sarawak via Brunei; international service excellent

domestic: domestic satellite system with 2 earth stations; combined fixed-line and mobile-cellular teledensity roughly 140 per 100 persons

international: country code—60; landing point for several major international submarine cable networks that provide connectivity to Asia, Middle East, and Europe; satellite earth stations—2 Intelsat (1 Indian Ocean, 1 Pacific Ocean) (2011)

Broadcast media: state-owned TV broadcaster operates 2 TV networks with relays throughout the country, and the leading private commercial media group operates 4 TV stations with numerous relays throughout the country; satellite TV subscription service is available; state-owned radio broadcaster operates multiple national networks, as well as regional and local stations; many private commercial radio broadcasters and some subscription satellite radio services are available; about 55 radio stations overall (2012)

Radio broadcast stations: AM 35, FM 391, shortwave 15 (2001)

Television broadcast stations: 88 (mainland Malaysia 51, Sabah 16, and Sarawak 21) (2006)

Internet country code: .my

Internet hosts: 422,470 (2012)
country comparison to the world: 53

Internet users: *total:* 12.1 million
percent of population: 40.3% (2014 est.)
country comparison to the world: 40

TRANSPORTATION

Airports: 114 (2013)
country comparison to the world: 51

Airports—with paved runways: *total:* 39
over 3,047 m: 8
2,438 to 3,047 m: 8
1,524 to 2,437 m: 7
914 to 1,523 m: 8
under 914 m: 8 (2013)

Airports—with unpaved runways: *total:* 75
914 to 1,523 m: 6
under 914 m: 69 (2013)

Heliports: 4 (2013)

Pipelines: condensate 354 km; gas 6,439 km; liquid petroleum gas 155 km; oil 1937 km; oil/gas/water 43 km; refined products 114 km; water 26 km (2013)

Railways: *total:* 1,849 km
standard gauge: 59 km 1.435-m gauge (59 km electrified)
narrow gauge: 1,792 km 1.000-m gauge (339 km electrified) (2014)
country comparison to the world: 74

Roadways: *total:* 144,403 km (excludes local roads)

paved: 116,169 km (includes 1,821 km of expressways)
unpaved: 28,234 km (2010)
country comparison to the world: 33

Waterways: 7,200 km (Peninsular Malaysia 3,200 km; Sabah 1,500 km; Sarawak 2,500 km) (2011)
country comparison to the world: 19

Merchant marine: *total:* 315
by type: bulk carrier 11, cargo 83, carrier 2, chemical tanker 47, container 41, liquefied gas 34, passenger/cargo 4, petroleum tanker 86, roll on/roll off 2, vehicle carrier 5
foreign-owned: 26 (Denmark 1, Hong Kong 8, Japan 2, Russia 2, Singapore 13)
registered in other countries: 82 (Bahamas 13, India 1, Indonesia 1, Isle of Man 6, Malta 1, Marshall Islands 11, Panama 12, Papua New Guinea 1, Philippines 1, Saint Kitts and Nevis 1, Singapore 27, Thailand 3, US 2, unknown 2) (2010)
country comparison to the world: 31

Ports and terminals: *major seaport(s):* Bintulu, Johor Bahru, George Town (Penang), Port Kelang (Port Klang), Tanjung Pelepas
container port(s) (TEUs): George Town (Penang) (1,202,180), Port Kelang (Port Klang) (9,435,403), Tanjung Pelepas (7,302,461)
LNG terminal(s) (export): Bintulu (Sarawak)
LNG terminal(s) (import): Sungei Udang

Transportation—note: the International Maritime Bureau reports that the territorial and offshore waters in the Strait of Malacca and South China Sea remain high risk for piracy and armed robbery against ships; in the past, commercial vessels have been attacked and hijacked both at anchor and while underway; hijacked vessels are often disguised and cargo diverted to ports in East Asia; crews have been murdered or cast adrift; 24 attacks were reported in 2014

MILITARY AND SECURITY

Military branches: Malaysian Armed Forces (Angkatan Tentera Malaysia, ATM): Malaysian Army (Tentera Darat Malaysia), Royal Malaysian Navy (Tentera Laut Diraja Malaysia, TLDM), Royal Malaysian Air Force (Tentera Udara Diraja Malaysia, TUDM) (2013)

Military service age and obligation: 17 years 6 months of age for voluntary military service (younger with parental consent and proof of age); mandatory retirement age 60; women serve in the Malaysian Armed Forces; no conscription (2013)

Military expenditures: 1.5% of GDP (2014)
1.5% of GDP (2013)
1.55% of GDP (2012)
1.67% of GDP (2011)
1.55% of GDP (2010)
country comparison to the world: 58

TRANSNATIONAL ISSUES

Disputes—international: while the 2002 "Declaration on the Conduct of Parties in the South China Sea" has eased tensions over the Spratly Islands, it is not the legally binding "code of conduct" sought by some parties; Malaysia was not party to the

March 2005 joint accord among the national oil companies of China, the Philippines, and Vietnam on conducting marine seismic activities in the Spratly Islands; disputes continue over deliveries of fresh water to Singapore, Singapore's land reclamation, bridge construction, and maritime boundaries in the Johor and Singapore Straits; in 2008, ICJ awarded sovereignty of Pedra Branca (Pulau Batu Puteh/Horsburgh Island) to Singapore, and Middle Rocks to Malaysia, but did not rule on maritime regimes, boundaries, or disposition of South Ledge; land and maritime negotiations with Indonesia are ongoing, and disputed areas include the controversial Tanjung Datu and Camar Wulan border area in Borneo and the maritime boundary in the Ambalat oil block in the Celebes Sea; separatist violence in Thailand's predominantly Muslim southern provinces prompts measures to close and monitor border with Malaysia to stem terrorist activities; Philippines retains a dormant claim to Malaysia's Sabah State in northern Borneo; per Letters of Exchange signed in 2009, Malaysia in 2010 ceded two hydrocarbon concession blocks to Brunei in exchange for Brunei's sultan dropping claims to the Limbang corridor, which divides Brunei; piracy remains a problem in the Malacca Strait

Refugees and internally displaced persons: *refugees (country of origin):* 93,866 (Burma) (2014)
stateless persons: 11,689 (2015); note—Malaysia's stateless population consists of Rohingya refugees from Burma, ethnic Indians, and the children of Filipino and Indonesian illegal migrants; Burma stripped the Rohingya of their nationality in 1982; Filipino and Indonesian children who have not have been registered for birth certificates by their parents or who received birth certificates stamped "foreigner" are not eligible to attend government schools; these children are vulnerable to statelessness should they not be able to apply to their parents' country of origin for passports

Trafficking in persons: *current situation:* Malaysia is a destination and, to a lesser extent, a source and transit country for men, women, and children subjected to forced labor and women and children subjected to sex trafficking; Malaysia is mainly a destination country for foreign workers who migrate willingly from countries, including Indonesia, Bangladesh, the Philippines, Nepal, Burma, and other Southeast Asian countries, but subsequently encounter forced labor or debt bondage in agriculture, construction, factories, and domestic service at the hands of employers, employment agents, and labor recruiters; women from Southeast Asia and, to a much lesser extent, Africa, are recruited for legal work in restaurants, hotels, and salons but are forced into prostitution; refugees, including Rohingya adults and children, are not legally permitted to work and are vulnerable to trafficking; a small number of Malaysians are trafficked internally and subjected to sex trafficking abroad

tier rating: Tier 2 Watch list—Malaysia does not fully comply with the minimum standards for the elimination of trafficking; however, it is making significant efforts to do so; in 2014, amendments to strengthen existing anti-trafficking laws, including enabling victims to move freely and to work and for NGOs to run protective facilities, were drafted by the government and are pending approval from Parliament; authorities more than doubled investigations and prosecutions but convicted only three

traffickers for forced labor and none for sex trafficking, a decline from 2013 and a disproportionately small number compared to the scale of the country's trafficking problem; NGOs provided the majority of victim rehabilitation and counseling services with no financial support from the government (2015)

Illicit drugs: drug trafficking prosecuted vigorously, including enforcement of the death penalty; heroin still primary drug of abuse, but synthetic drug demand remains strong; continued ecstasy and methamphetamine producer for domestic users and, to a lesser extent, the regional drug market

MALDIVES

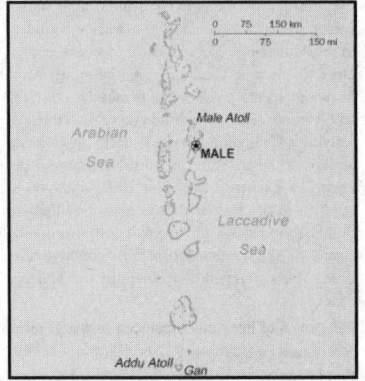

INTRODUCTION

Background: A sultanate since the 12th century, the Maldives became a British protectorate in 1887. It became a republic in 1968, three years after independence. President Maumoon Abdul GAYOOM dominated the islands' political scene for 30 years, elected to six successive terms by single-party referendums. Following political demonstrations in the capital Male in August 2003, the president and his government pledged to embark upon a process of liberalization and democratic reforms, including a more representative political system and expanded political freedoms. Progress was sluggish, however, and many promised reforms were slow to be realized. Nonetheless, political parties were legalized in 2005. In June 2008, a constituent assembly—termed the "Special Majlis"—finalized a new constitution, wh ich was ratified by the president in August. The first-ever presidential elections under a multi-candidate, multiparty system were held in October 2008. GAYOOM was defeated in a runoff poll by Mohamed NASHEED, a political activist who had been jailed several years earlier by the former regime. President NASHEED faced a number of challenges including strengthening democracy and combating poverty and drug abuse. in early February 2012, after several weeks of street protests following his sacking of a top judge, NASHEED resigned the presidency and handed over power to Vice President Mohammed WAHEED Hassan Maniku. in mid-2012, a Commission of National Inquiry was set by the government to probe events leading up to NASHEED's resignation. Though the commission found no

evidence of a coup, the report recommended the need to strengthen the country's democratic institutions to avert similar events in the future, and to further investigate alleged police misconduct during the crisis. Maldivian officials have played a prominent role in international climate change discussions (due to the islands' low elevation and the threat from sea-level rise) on the UN Human Rights Council and in other international forums, as well as in encouraging regional cooperation, especially between India and Pakistan.

GEOGRAPHY

Location: Southern Asia, group of atolls in the Indian Ocean, south-southwest of India

Geographic coordinates: 3 15 N, 73 00 E

Map references: Asia

Area: *total:* 298 sq km
land: 298 sq km
water: 0 sq km
country comparison to the world: 210

Area—comparative: about 1.7 times the size of Washington, DC

Land boundaries: 0 km

Coastline: 644 km

Maritime claims: measured from claimed archipelagic straight baselines
territorial sea: 12 nm
contiguous zone: 24 nm
exclusive economic zone: 200 nm

Climate: tropical; hot, humid; dry, northeast monsoon (November to March); rainy, southwest monsoon (June to August)

Terrain: flat, with white sandy beaches

Elevation: *mean elevation:* 1.8 m

elevation extremes: *lowest point:* Indian Ocean 0 m
highest point: unnamed location on Viligili in the Addu Atholhu 2.4 m

Natural resources: fish

Land use: *agricultural land:* 23.3%
arable land: 10%;
permanent crops: 10%;
permanent pasture: 3.3%
forest: 3%
other: 73.7% (2011 est.)

Irrigated land: 0 sq km (2012)

Total renewable water resources: 0.03 cu km (2011)

Freshwater withdrawal (domestic/industrial/agricultural): *total:* 0.01 cu km/yr (95%/5%/0%)
per capita: 18.44 cu m/yr (2008)

Natural hazards: tsunamis; low elevation of islands makes them sensitive to sea level rise

Environment—current issues: depletion of freshwater aquifers threatens water supplies; coral reef bleaching

Environment—international agreements: *party to:* Biodiversity, Climate Change, Climate Change-Kyoto Protocol, Desertification, Hazardous Wastes, Law of the Sea, Ozone Layer Protection, Ship Pollution
signed, but not ratified: none of the selected agreements

Geography—note: smallest Asian country; archipelago of 1,190 coral islands grouped into 26 atolls (200 inhabited islands, plus 80 islands with tourist resorts); strategic location astride and along major sea lanes in Indian Ocean

PEOPLE AND SOCIETY

Nationality: *noun:* Maldivian(s)
adjective: Maldivian

Ethnic groups: South Indians, Sinhalese, Arabs

Languages: Dhivehi (official, dialect of Sinhala, script derived from Arabic), English (spoken by most government officials)

Religions: Sunni Muslim (official)

Population: 393,253 (July 2015 est.)
country comparison to the world: 177

Age structure: *0–14 years:* 21.05% (male 42,230/female 40,555)
15–24 years: 22.41% (male 51,141/female 36,970)
25–54 years: 47.08% (male 107,436/female 77,713)
55–64 years: 5.14% (male 10,243/female 9,968)
65 years and over: 4.32% (male 7,994/female 9,003) (2015 est.)

Dependency ratios: *total dependency ratio:* 47.4%
youth dependency ratio: 40.5%
elderly dependency ratio: 6.9%
potential support ratio: 14.4% (2015 est.)

Median age: *total:* 27.4 years
male: 27.5 years
female: 27.3 years (2015 est.)
country comparison to the world: 135

Population growth rate: -0.08% (2015 est.)
country comparison to the world: 205

Birth rate: 15.75 births/1,000 population (2015 est.)
country comparison to the world: 125

Death rate: 3.89 deaths/1,000 population (2015 est.)
country comparison to the world: 209

Net migration rate: -12.68 migrant(s)/1,000 population (2015 est.)
country comparison to the world: 216

Urbanization: *urban population:* 45.5% of total population (2015)
rate of urbanization: 4.49% annual rate of change (2010–15 est.)

Major urban areas—Population: MALE (capital) 156,000 (2014)

Sex ratio: *at birth:* 1.05 male(s)/female
0–14 years: 1.04 male(s)/female
15–24 years: 1.38 male(s)/female
25–54 years: 1.38 male(s)/female
55–64 years: 1.03 male(s)/female
65 years and over: 0.89 male(s)/female
total population: 1.26 male(s)/female (2015 est.)

Mother's mean age at first birth: 23.9
note: median age at first birth among women 25–29 (2009 est.)

Maternal mortality rate: 68 deaths/100,000 live births (2015 est.)
country comparison to the world: 100

Infant mortality rate: *total:* 23.7 deaths/1,000 live births
male: 26.11 deaths/1,000 live births
female: 21.17 deaths/1,000 live births (2015 est.)
country comparison to the world: 73

Life expectancy at birth: *total population:* 75.37 years
male: 73.06 years
female: 77.8 years (2015 est.)
country comparison to the world: 101

Total fertility rate: 1.74 children born/woman (2015 est.)
country comparison to the world: 166

Contraceptive prevalence rate: 34.7% (2009)

Health expenditures: 10.8% of GDP (2013)
country comparison to the world: 50

Physicians density: 1.42 physicians/1,000 population (2010)

Hospital bed density: 4.3 beds/1,000 population (2009)

Drinking water source:
improved:
urban: 99.5% of population
rural: 97.9% of population
total: 98.6% of population
unimproved:
urban: 0.5% of population
rural: 2.1% of population
total: 1.4% of population (2015 est.)

Sanitation facility access:
improved:
urban: 97.5% of population
rural: 98.3% of population
total: 97.9% of population

unimproved:
urban: 2.5% of population
rural: 1.7% of population
total: 2.1% of population (2015 est.)

HIV/AIDS—adult prevalence rate: 0.01% (2013 est.)
country comparison to the world: 133

HIV/AIDS—people living with HIV/AIDS: fewer than 100 (2013 est.)
country comparison to the world: 127

HIV/AIDS—deaths: fewer than 100 (2013 est.)
country comparison to the world: 113

Obesity—adult prevalence rate: 7% (2014)
country comparison to the world: 126

Children under the age of 5 years underweight: 17.8% (2009)
country comparison to the world: 36

Education expenditures: 5.2% of GDP (2012)
country comparison to the world: 26

Literacy: *definition:* age 15 and over can read and write
total population: 99.3%
male: 99.8%
female: 98.8% (2015 est.)

Unemployment, youth ages 15–24: *total:* 25.4%
male: 29.1%
female: 21.4% (2010 est.)
country comparison to the world: 48

GOVERNMENT

Country name: *conventional long form:* Republic of Maldives
conventional short form: Maldives
local long form: Dhivehi Raajjeyge Jumhooriyyaa
local short form: Dhivehi Raajje
etymology: archipelago apparently named after the main island (and capital) of Male; the word "Maldives" means "the islands (dives) of Male"; alternatively, the name may derive from the Sanskrit word "maladvipa" meaning "garland of islands"; Dhivehi Raajje in Maldivian means "Kingdom of the Dhivehi people"

Government type: presidential republic

Capital: *name:* Male

Geographic coordinates: 4 10 N, 73 30 E
time difference: UTC+5 (10 hours ahead of Washington, DC, during Standard Time)

Administrative divisions: 7 provinces and 1 municipality*; Dhekunu (South), Maale*, Mathi Dhekunu (Upper South), Mathi Uthuru (Upper North), Medhu (Central), Medhu Dhekunu (South Central), Medhu Uthuru (North Central), Uthuru (North)

Independence: 26 July 1965 (from the UK)

National holiday: Independence Day, 26 July (1965)

Constitution: many previous; latest ratified 7 August 2008; amended 2015 (2016)

Legal system: Islamic religious legal system with English common law influences, primarily in commercial matters

International law organization participation: has not submitted an ICJ jurisdiction declaration; accepts ICCt jurisdiction

Citizenship: *citizenship by birth:* no
citizenship by descent only: at least one parent must be a citizen of the Maldives
dual citizenship recognized: yes
residency requirement for naturalization: unknown

Suffrage: 18 years of age; universal

Executive branch: *chief of state:* President Abdulla YAMEEN Abdul Gayoom (since 17 November 2013); Vice President Abdulla JIHAD (since 21 June 2016); note—the president is both chief of state and head of government; Vice President Ahmed ADHEEB Abdul Ghafoor (since 22 July 2015) was removed from office 5 November 2015

head of government: President Abdulla YAME EN Abdul Gayoom (since 17 November 2013); Vice President Abdulla JI HAD (since 22 June 2016); note—Vice President Ahmed ADHEEB Abdul Ghafoor (since 22 July 2015) was removed from office 5 November 2015
cabinet: Cabinet of Ministers appointed by the president
elections/appointments: president directly elected by absolute majority popular vote in 2 rounds if needed for a 5-year term (eligible for a second term); the election held on 7 September 2013 was annulled by the Supreme Court; rerun of first round held on 9 November 2013 and a ru noff held on 16 November (next election to be held in 2018)
election results: first round—percent of vote—Mohamed NASH EED (MDP) 46.9%, Abdulla YAM EEN Abdul Gayoom (PPM) 29.7%, Qasim IBRAHIM (JP) 23.3%; runoff second round—percent of vote—Abdulla YAMEEN Abdul Gayoom elected president 51.4%, Mohamed NASHEED 48.6%

Legislative branch: *description:* unicameral Parliament or People's Majlis (85 seats; members directly elected in multi-seat constituencies by simple majority vote to serve 5-year terms)
elections: last held on 22 March 2014 (next to be held in 2019)
election results: percent of vote—MDP 40.8%, MDP 27.7%, JP 13.6%, MDA 4.0%, AP 2.7% other 0.3%, independent 10.9%; seats by party—PPM 33, MDP 26, JP 15, MDA 5, AP 1, independent 5

Judicial branch: *highest court(s):* Supreme Court (consists of the chief justice and 6 judges)
judge selection and term of office: Supreme Court judges appointed by the president in consultation with the Judicial Service Commission—a separate 10-member body of selected high government officials and the public—and upon confirmation by voting members of the People's Majlis; judges serve until mandatory retirement at age 70
subordinate courts: High Court; Criminal, Civil, Family, Juvenile, and Drug Courts; Magistrate Courts (on each of the inhabited islands)

Political parties and leaders: Adhaalath (Justice) Party or AP [Sheikh Imran ABDULLA]

Maldives Development Alliance or MDA [Ahmed Shiyam Mohamed]

Maldavian Democratic Party or MDP [Ali WAHEED]

Progressive Party of Maldives or PPM [Maumoon Abdul GAYOOM]

Republican (Jumhooree) Party or JP [Qasim IBRAHIM]

Political pressure groups and leaders: *other*: various unregistered political parties

International organization participation: ADB, AOSIS, C, CP, FAO, G-77, IBRD, ICAO, ICC (NGOs), ICCt, IDA, IDB, IFAD, IFC, IFRCS, ILO, IMF, IMO, Interpol, IOC, IOM, IPU, ITU, MIGA, NAM, OIC, OPCW, SAARC, SACEP, UN, UNCTAD, UNESCO, UNIDO, UNWTO, UPU, WCO, WHO, WIPO, WMO, WTO

Diplomatic representation in the US: *chief of mission:* Ambassador Ahmed SAREER (since 11 January 2013)

chancery: 800 2nd Avenue, Suite 400E, New York, NY 10017

telephone: [1] (212) 599-6195

FAX: [1] (212) 661-6405

Diplomatic representation from the US: the US does not have an embassy in Maldives; the US Ambassador to Sri Lanka is accredited to Maldives and makes periodic visits

Flag description: red with a large green rectangle in the center bearing a vertical white crescent moon; the closed side of the crescent is on the hoist side of the flag; red recalls those who have sacrificed their lives in defense of their country, the green rectangle represents peace and prosperity, and the white crescent signifies Islam

National symbol(s): coconut palm, yellowfin tuna; national colors: red, green, white

National anthem: *name:* "Gaumee Salaam" (National Salute)

lyrics/music: Mohamed Jameel DIDI/Wannaku-wattawaduge DON AMARADEVA

note: lyrics adopted 1948, music adopted 1972; between 1948 and 1972, the lyrics were sung to the tune of "Auld Lang Syne"

ECONOMY

Economy—overview: Maldives has rapidly grown into a middle-income country, driven by tourism development. in 2015, the economy's growth slowed to 4.8%, mainly due to lower tourism sector growth as tourist arrivals from China declined. However, the slowdown is expected to reverse in 2016. Tourism, construction, transport, and the communications sector accounted for 50% of the output on average. Tourism-related tax receipts increased by 13% in 2015 due to higher tax rates. This increase in dollar tax receipts directly led to higher usable reserves in 2015. The current account deficit widened to $400 million in 2015 due to increases in construction related imports. A large and growing fiscal deficit remains an ongoing

economic challenge. In July 2015, Maldives' Parliament passed a constitutional amendment legalizing foreign ownership of land; foreign land-buyers must reclaim at least 70% of the desired land from the ocean and invest at least $1 billion in a construction project approved by Parliament. Diversifying the economy beyond tourism and fishing, reforming public finance, increasing employment opportunities, and combating corruption, cronyism, and a growing drug problem are near-term challenges facing the government. Over the longer term Maldivian authorities worry about the impact of erosion and possible global warming on their low-lying country; 80% of the area is 1 meter or less above sea level.

GDP (purchasing power parity):
$5.191 billion (2015 est.)
$5.094 billion (2014 est.)
$4.784 billion (2013 est.)
note: data are in 2015 US dollars
country comparison to the world: 174

GDP (official exchange rate): $3.13 billion (2015 est.)

GDP—real growth rate: 1.9% (2015 est.)
6.5% (2014 est.) 4.7% (2013 est.)
country comparison to the world: 138

GDP—per capita (PPP): $14,900 (2015 est.)
$14,900 (2014 est.)
$14,200 (2013 est.)
note: data are in 2015 US dollars
country comparison to the world: 109

Gross national saving: 12% of GDP (2015 est.)
15.9% of GDP (2014 est.)
15.7% of GDP (2013 est.)
country comparison to the world: 139

GDP—composition, by end use:
household consumption: NA%
government consumption: NA%
investment in fixed capital: NA%
investment in inventories: NA%
exports of goods and services: 108.2%
imports of goods and services: 89.3% (2014 est.)

GDP—composition, by sector of origin:
agriculture: 3.5%
industry: 19.3%
services: 77.2% (2014 est.)

Agriculture—products: coconuts, corn, sweet potatoes; fish

Industries: tourism, fish processing, shipping, boat building, coconut processing, woven mats, rope, handicrafts, coral and sand mining

Industrial production growth rate: 14% (2012 est.)
country comparison to the world: 2

Labor force: 195,100 (2014)
country comparison to the world: 174

Labor force—by occupation: *agriculture:* 15%
industry: 15%
services: 70% (2010 est.)

Unemployment rate: 11.6% (2013 est.)
11% (2012 est.)
country comparison to the world: 130

Population below poverty line: 16% (2008 est.)

Household income or consumption by percentage share: *lowest:* 10%: 1.2%
highest: 10%: 33.3% (FY09/10)

Distribution of family income—Gini index: 37.4 (2004 est.)
country comparison to the world: 79

Budget: *revenues:* $960 million
expenditures: $1.148 billion (2014 est.)
Taxes and other revenues: 31.7% of GDP (2014 est.)
country comparison to the world: 80

Budget surplus (+) or deficit (–): -6% of GDP (2016 est.)
country comparison to the world: 181

Public debt: 72.8% of GDP (2014)
66.7% of GDP (2013)
country comparison to the world: 42

Fiscal year: calendar year

Inflation rate (consumer prices): 1.4% (2015 est.)
2.5% (2014 est.)
country comparison to the world: 97

Central bank discount rate: 7% (31 December 2013)
6.96% (31 December 2011)
country comparison to the world: 48

Commercial bank prime lending rate: 10.5% (31 December 2012 est.)
10.2% (31 December 2011 est.)
country comparison to the world: 81

Stock of narrow money: $623 million (31 December 2013 est.)
$547.1 million (31 December 2012 est.)
country comparison to the world: 162

Stock of broad money: $1.538 billion (31 December 2013 est.)
$1.298 billion (31 December 2012 est.)
country comparison to the world: 163

Stock of domestic credit: $1.559 billion (31 December 2012 est.)
$1.601 billion (31 December 2011 est.)
country comparison to the world: 149

Market value of publicly traded shares: $555 million (31 December 2011 est.)
country comparison to the world: 113

Current account balance: -$251 million (2015 est.)
-$125 million (2014 est.)
country comparison to the world: 85

Exports: $300.9 million (2014 est.)
$331 million (2013 est.)
country comparison to the world: 182

Exports—commodities: fish

Exports—partners: Thailand 17.9%, France 12.1%, Germany 10.7%, US 9.6%, Italy 6.8%, UK 6.4%, Sri Lanka 5.8%, Japan 4.6% (2015)

Imports: $1.993 billion (2014 est.) $1.733 billion (2013 est.)
country comparison to the world: 163

Imports—commodities: petroleum products, clothing, intermediate and capital goods

Imports—partners: UAE 18.3%, Singapore 13.8%, China 10.6%, India 10.4%, Malaysia 6.9%, Sri Lanka 5.5%, Thailand 4.9% (2015)

Reserves of foreign exchange and gold: $627.4 million (31 December 2014 est.)
$381.9 million (31 December 2013 est.)
country comparison to the world: 143

Debt—external: $741.6 million (2014 est.)
$792.2 million (2013 est.)
country comparison to the world: 170

Exchange rates: rufiyaa (MVR) per US dollar—
15.25 (2015)
15.365 (2014)

ENERGY

Electricity—production: 287.2 million kWh (2012 est.)
country comparison to the world: 180

Electricity—consumption: 267.1 million kWh (2012 est.)
country comparison to the world: 184

Electricity—exports: 0 kWh (2013 est.)
country comparison to the world: 173

Electricity—imports: 0 kWh (2013 est.)
country comparison to the world: 179

Electricity—installed generating capacity: 77,000 kW (2012 est.)
country comparison to the world: 181

Electricity—from fossil fuels: 100% of total installed capacity (2012 est.)
country comparison to the world: 21

Electricity—from nuclear fuels: 0% of total installed capacity (2012 est.)
country comparison to the world: 147

Electricity—from hydroelectric plants: 0% of total installed capacity (2012 est.)
country comparison to the world: 189

Electricity—from other renewable sources: 0% of total installed capacity (2012 est.)
country comparison to the world: 204

Crude oil—production: 0 bbl/day (2014 est.)
country comparison to the world: 171

Crude oil—Exports: 0 bbl/day (2012 est.)
country comparison to the world: 165

Crude oil—imports: 0 bbl/day (2012 est.)
country comparison to the world: 102

Crude oil—proved reserves: 0 bbl (1 January 2015 est.)
country comparison to the world: 171

Refined petroleum products—production: 0 bbl/day (2012 est.)
country comparison to the world: 113

Refined petroleum products—consumption: 6,900 bbl/day (2013 est.)
country comparison to the world: 161

Refined petroleum products—exports: 0 bbl/day (2012 est.)
country comparison to the world: 206

Refined petroleum products—imports: 6,941 bbl/day (2012 est.)
country comparison to the world: 147

Natural gas—production: 0 cu m (2013 est.)
country comparison to the world: 107

Natural gas—consumption: 0 cu m (2013 est.)
country comparison to the world: 175

Natural gas—exports: 0 cu m (2013 est.)
country comparison to the world: 151

Natural gas—imports: 0 cu m (2013 est.)
country comparison to the world: 104

Natural gas—proved reserves: 0 cu m (1 January 2014 est.)
country comparison to the world: 174

Carbon dioxide emissions from consumption of energy: 1.123 million Mt (2012 est.)
country comparison to the world: 165

COMMUNICATIONS

Telephones—fixed lines: *total subscriptions:* 21,500
subscriptions per 100 inhabitants: 5 (2014 est.)
country comparison to the world: 183

Telephones—mobile cellular: *total:* 665,800
subscriptions per 100 inhabitants: 169 (2014 est.)
country comparison to the world: 164

Telephone system: *general assessment:* telephone services have improved; inter-atoll communication through microwave links; all inhabited islands and resorts are connected with telephone and fax service
domestic: each island now has at least 1 public telephone, and there are mobile-cellular networks with a rapidly expanding subscribership that has reached 135 per 100 persons
international: country code—960; linked to international submarine cable Fiber-Optic Link Around the Globe (FLAG); satellite earth station—3 Intelsat (Indian Ocean) (2011)

Broadcast media: state-owned radio and TV monopoly until recently; state-owned TV operates 2 channels; 3 privately owned TV stations; state owns Voice of Maldives and operates both an entertainment and a music-based station; 5 privately owned radio stations (2012)
Radio broadcast stations: AM 1, FM 6, shortwave 1 (2009)
Television broadcast stations: 2 (2009)

Internet country code: .mv

Internet hosts: 3,296 (2012)
country comparison to the world: 153

Internet users: *total:* 18,600
percent of population: 4.7% (2014 est.)
country comparison to the world: 201

TRANSPORTATION

Airports: 9 (2013)
country comparison to the world: 159

Airports—with paved runways: *total:* 7
over 3,047 m: 1
2,438 to 3,047 m: 1
1,524 to 2,437 m: 1
914 to 1,523 m: 4 (2013)

Airports—with unpaved runways: *total:* 2
914 to 1,523 m: 2 (2013)

Roadways: *total:* 88 km
paved roads: 88 km—60 km in Male; 14 km on Addu Atolis; 14 km on Laamu
note: island roads are mainly compacted coral (2013)
country comparison to the world: 216

Merchant marine: *total:* 18
by type: bulk carrier 1, cargo 14, petroleum tanker 1, refrigerated cargo 2
foreign-owned: 4 (Singapore 4)
registered in other countries: 4 (Panama 2, Tuvalu 1, unknown 1) (2010)
country comparison to the world: 97

Ports and terminals: *major seaport(s):* Male

MILITARY AND SECURITY

Military branches: Maldives National Defense Force (MNDF): Marine Corps, Security Protection Group, Coast Guard (2010)

Military service age and obligation: 18–28 years of age for voluntary service; no conscription; 10th grade or equivalent education required; must not be a member of a political party (2012)

Military—note: the Maldives National Defense Force (MNDF), with its small size and with little serviceable equipment, is inadequate to prevent external aggression and is primarily tasked to reinforce the Maldives Police Service (MPS) and ensure security in the exclusive economic zone (2008)

TRANSNATIONAL ISSUES

Disputes—international: none

Trafficking in persons: *current situation:* Maldives is a destination country for men, women, and children subjected to forced labor and sex trafficking and a source country for women and children subjected to labor and sex trafficking; primarily Bangladeshi and Indian migrants working both legally and illegally in the construction and service sectors face conditions of forced labor, including fraudulent recruitment, confiscation of identity and travel documents, nonpayment and withholding of wages, and debt bondage; a small number of women from Asia, Eastern Europe, and former Soviet states are trafficked to Maldives for sexual exploitation; Maldivian women may be subjected to sex trafficking domestically or in Sri Lanka; some Maldivian children are transported to the capital for domestic service, where they may also be victims of sexual abuse and forced labor

tier rating: Tier 2 Watch List—Maldives does not fully comply with the minimum standards for the elimination of trafficking; however, it is making significant efforts to do so; the government adopted a national action plan for 2015–2019 and is continuing to develop victim identification, protection, and referral procedures, but overall its anti-trafficking efforts did not increase; only five trafficking investigations were conducted, no new prosecutions were initiated for the second consecutive year, and no convictions were made, down from one in 2013; some officials warned businesses in advanced of planned raids for suspected trafficking offenses; victim protection deteriorated when the state-run shelter for female victims barred access to victims shortly after opening

in January 2014, in part because of bureaucratic disputes, which dissuaded victims from pursuing charges against perpetrators; the government did

not prosecute or hold accountable any employers or government officials for withholding passports (2015)

MALI

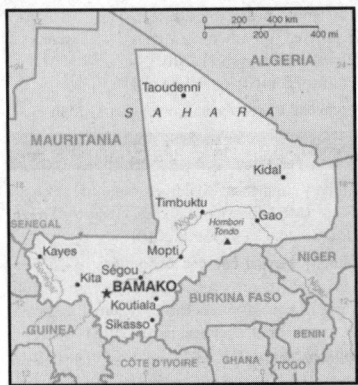

INTRODUCTION

Background: The Sudanese Republic and Senegal became independent of France in 1960 as the Mali Federation. When Senegal withdrew after only a few months, what formerly made up the Sudanese Republic was renamed Mali. Rule by dictatorship was brought to a close in 1991 by a military coup that ushered in a period of democratic rule. President Alpha KONARE won Mali's first two democratic presidential elections in 1992 and 1997. In keeping with Mali's two-term constitutional limit, he stepped down in 2002 and was succeeded by Amadou Toumani TOURE, who was elected to a second term in a 2007 election that was widely judged to be free and fair. Malian returnees from Libya in 2011 exacerbated tensions in northern Mali, and Tuareg ethnic militias rebelled in January 2012. Low- and mid-level soldiers, frustrated with the poor handling of the rebellion, overthrew TOURE on 22 March. Intensive mediation efforts led by the Economic Community of West African States (ECOWAS) returned power to a civilian administration in April with the appointment of Interim President Dioncounda TRAORE. The post-coup chaos led to rebels expelling the Malian military from the country's three northern regions and allowed Islamic militants to set up strongholds. Hundreds of thousands of northern Malians fled the violence to southern Mali and neighboring countries, exacerbating regional food shortages in host communities. An international military intervention to retake the three northern regions began in January 2013 and within a month most of the north had been retaken. in a democratic presidential election conducted in July and August of 2013, Ibrahim Boubacar KEITA was elected president. The Malian Government and northern

armed groups signed an internationally-mediated peace accord in June 2015.

GEOGRAPHY

Location: interior Western Africa, southwest of Algeria, north of Guinea, Cote d'Ivoire, and Burkina Faso, west of Niger

Geographic coordinates: 17 00 N, 4 00 W

Map references: Africa

Area: *total:* 1,240,192 sq km
land: 1,220,190 sq km
water: 20,002 sq km
country comparison to the world: 24

Area—comparative: slightly less than twice the size of Texas

Land boundaries: *total:* 7,908 km
border countries (7): Algeria 1,359 km, Burkina Faso 1,325 km, Cote d'Ivoire 599 km, Guinea 1,062 km, Mauritania 2,236 km, Niger 838 km, Senegal 489 km

Coastline: 0 km (landlocked)

Maritime claims: none (landlocked)

Climate: subtropical to arid; hot and dry (February to June); rainy, humid, and mild (June to November); cool and dry (November to February)

Terrain: mostly flat to rolling northern plains covered by sand; savanna in south, rugged hills in northeast

Elevation: *mean elevation:* 343 m

elevation extremes: *lowest point:* Senegal River 23 m
highest point: Hombori Tondo 1,155 m

Natural resources: gold, phosphates, kaolin, salt, lim estone, uranium, gypsum, granite, hydropower
note: bauxite, iron ore, manganese, tin, and copper deposits are known but not exploited

Land use: *agricultural land:* 34.1%
arable land: 5.6%;
permanent crops: 0.1%;
permanent pasture: 28.4%
forest: 10.2%
other: 55.7% (2011 est.)

Irrigated land: 3,780 sq km (2012)

Total renewable water resources: 100 cu km (2011)

Freshwater withdrawal (domestic/industrial/agricultural): *total:* 6.55 cu km/yr (9%/1%/90%)
per capita: 545.4 cu m/yr (2000)

Natural hazards: hot, dust-laden harmattan haze common during dry seasons; recurring droughts; occasional Niger River flooding

Environment—current issues: deforestation; soil erosion; desertification; inadequate supplies of potable water; poaching

Environment—international agreements: *party to:* Biodiversity, Climate Change, Climate Change-Kyoto Protocol, Desertification, Endangered Species, Hazardous Wastes, Law of the Sea, Ozone Layer Protection, Wetlands, Whaling
signed, but not ratified: none of the selected agreem ents

Geography—note: landlocked; divided into three natural zones: the southern, cultivated Sudanese; the central, semiarid Sahelian; and the northern, arid Saharan

PEOPLE AND SOCIETY

Nationality: *noun:* Malian(s)
adjective: Malian

Ethnic groups: Bambara 34.1%, Fulani (Peul) 14.7%, Sarakole 10.8%, Senufo 10.5%, Dogon 8.9%, Malinke 8.7%, Bobo 2.9%, Songhai 1.6%, Tuareg 0.9%, other Malian 6.1%, from member of Economic Community of West African States 0.3%, other 0.4% (2012–13 est.)

Languages: French (official), Bambara 46.3%, Peul/Foulfoulbe 9.4%, Dogon 7.2%, Maraka/Soninke 6.4%, Malinke 5.6%, Sonrhai/Djerma 5.6%, Minianka 4.3%, Tamacheq 3.5%, Senoufo 2.6%, Bobo 2.1%, unspecified 0.7%, other 6.3%
note: Mali has 13 national languages in addition to its official language (2009 est.)

Religions: Muslim 94.8%, Christian 2.4%, Animist 2%, none 0.5%, unspecified 0.3% (2009 est.)

Population: 16,955,536 (July 2015 est.)
country comparison to the world: 66

Age structure: *0–14 years:* 47.44% (male 4,038,801/female 4,005,256)
15–24 years: 19.09% (male 1,543,751/female 1,693,410)
25–54 years: 26.75% (male 2,106,889/female 2,428,643)
55–64 years: 3.75% (male 317,513/female 317,957)
65 years and over: 2.97% (male 251,693/female 251,623) (2015 est.)

Dependency ratios: *total dependency ratio:* 100.2%
youth dependency ratio: 95.1%
elderly dependency ratio: 5%
potential support ratio: 19.8% (2015 est.)

Median age: *total:* 16.1 years
male: 15.5 years
female: 16.8 years (2015 est.)
country comparison to the world: 227

Population growth rate: 2.98% (2015 est.)
country comparison to the world: 8

Birth rate: 44.99 births/1,000 population (2015 est.)
country comparison to the world: 2

Death rate: 12.89 deaths/1,000 population (2015 est.)
country comparison to the world: 19

Net migration rate: -2.26 migrant(s)/1,000 population (2015 est.)
country comparison to the world: 172

Urbanization: *urban Population:* 39.9% of total population (2015)
rate of urbanization: 5.08% annual rate of change (2010–15 est.)

Major urban areas—Population: BAMAKO (capital) 2.515 million (2015)

Sex ratio: *at birth:* 1.03 male(s)/female
0–14 years: 1.01 male(s)/female
15–24 years: 0.91 male(s)/female
25–54 years: 0.87 male(s)/female
55–64 years: 1 male(s)/female
65 years and over: 1 male(s)/female
total population: 0.95 male(s)/female (2015 est.)

Mother's mean age at first birth: 18.3
note: median age at first birth among women 20–24 (2012/13 est.)

Maternal mortality rate: 587 deaths/100,000 live births (2015 est.)
country comparison to the world: 18

Infant mortality rate: *total:* 102.23 deaths/1,000 live births
male: 108.88 deaths/1,000 live births
female: 95.37 deaths/1,000 live births (2015 est.)
country comparison to the world: 2

Life expectancy at birth: *total population:* 55.34 years
male: 53.48 years
female: 57.25 years (2015 est.)
country comparison to the world: 208

Total fertility rate: 6.06 children born/woman (2015 est.)
country comparison to the world: 3

Contraceptive prevalence rate: 10.3% (2012/13)

Health expenditures: 7.1% of GDP (2013)
country comparison to the world: 119

Physicians density: 0.08 physicians/1,000 population (2010)

Hospital bed density: 0.1 beds/1,000 population (2010)

Drinking water source:
improved:
urban: 96.5% of population
rural: 64.1% of population
total: 77% of population
unimproved:
urban: 3.5% of population
rural: 35.9% of population
total: 23% of population (2015 est.)

Sanitation facility access:
improved:
urban: 37.5% of population

rural: 16.1% of population
total: 24.7% of population
unimproved:
urban: 62.5% of population
rural: 83.9% of population
total: 75.3% of population (2015 est.)

HIV/AIDS—adult prevalence rate: 1.42% (2014 est.)
country comparison to the world: 35

HIV/AIDS—people living with HIV/AIDS: 133,400 (2014 est.)
country comparison to the world: 35

HIV/AIDS—deaths: 5,300 (2014 est.)
country comparison to the world: 29

Major infectious diseases: *degree of risk:* very high
food or waterborne diseases: bacterial and protozoal diarrhea, hepatitis A, and typhoid fever
vectorborne diseases: malaria and dengue fever
water contact disease: schistosomiasis
respiratory disease: meningococcal meningitis
animal contact disease: rabies (2013)

Obesity—adult prevalence rate: 5.7% (2014)
country comparison to the world: 166

Children under the age of 5 years underweight: 27.9% (2006)
country comparison to the world: 20

Education expenditures: 4.3% of GDP (2014)
country comparison to the world: 83

Literacy: *definition:* age 15 and over can read and write
total population: 38.7%
male: 48.2%
female: 29.2% (2015 est.)

School life expectancy (primary to tertiary education): *total:* 8 years
male: 9 years
female: 7 years (2011)

Child labor—children ages 5–14: *total number:* 1,485,027
percentage: 36% (2010 est.)

Unemployment, youth ages 15–24: *total:* 10.7%
male: 7.9%
female: 14.1% (2010 est.)

GOVERNMENT

Country name: *conventional long form:* Republic of Mali
conventional short form: Mali
local long form: Republique de Mali
local short form: Mali
former: French Sudan and Sudanese Republic
note: name derives from the West African Mali Empire of the 13th to 16th centuries A.D.

Government type: semi-presidential republic

Capital: *name:* Bamako

Geographic coordinates: 12 39 N, 8 00 W
time difference: UTC 0 (5 hours ahead of Washington, DC, during Standard Time)

Administrative divisions: 8 regions (regions, singular—region),1 district*; District de Bamako*,

Gao, Kayes, Kidal, Koulikoro, Mopti, Segou, Sikasso, Tombouctou (Timbuktu)

Independence: 22 September 1960 (from France)

National holiday: Independence Day, 22 September (1960)

Constitution: several previous; latest drafted August 1991, approved by referendum 12 January 1992, effective 25 February 1992; amended 1999, suspended briefly in 2012 (2016)

Legal system: civil law system based on the French civil law model and influenced by customary law; judicial review of legislative acts in Constitutional Court

International law organization participation: has not submitted an ICJ jurisdiction declaration; accepts ICCt jurisdiction

Citizenship: *citizenship by birth:* no
citizenship by descent only: at least one parent must be a citizen of Mali
dual citizenship recognized: yes
residency requirement for naturalization: 5 years

Suffrage: 18 years of age; universal

Executive branch: *chief of state:* President Ibrahim Boubacar KEITA (since 4 September 2013)

head of government: Prime Minister Modibo KEITA (since 8 January 2015)
cabinet: Council of Ministers appointed by the prime minister
elections/appointments: president directly elected by absolute majority popular vote in 2 rounds if needed for a 5-year term (eligible for a second term); election last held on 28 July 2013 with a runoff on 11 August 2013 (election delayed from April 2012 due to a coup in March 2012); prime minister appointed by the president
election results: Ibrahim Boubacar KEITA elected president in runoff; percent of vote—Ibrahim Boubacar KEITA (RPM) 77.6%, Soumaila CISSE (URD) 22.4%

Legislative branch: *description:* unicameral National Assembly or Assemblee Nationale (147 seats; members directly elected in single-seat constituencies by absolute majority vote in two rounds if needed; members serve 5-year terms)
elections: last held in two rounds on 24 November and 15 December 2013 (next to be held in 2018); note—the scheduled July 2012 election was canceled due to a coup d'etat and the Tuareg Rebellion
election results: percent of vote by party—NA; seats by party—FDR coalition 69 (RPM 66, PARENA 3), ADP coalition 37 (ADEMA-PASG 16, URD 17, CNID 4), FARE 6, CODEM 5, SADI 5, ASMA-CFP 3, PDES 3, MPR 3, independent 4, other 12; note—13 seats were from voters abroad

Judicial branch: *highest court(s):* Supreme Court or Cour Supreme (consists of 19 members organized into 3 civil chambers and a criminal chamber); Constitutional Court (consists of 9 members)
judge selection and term of office: Supreme Court members appointed by the Ministry of Justice to serve 5-year terms; Constitutional Court

543

members selected—3 each by the president, the National Assembly, and the Supreme Council of the Magistracy; members serve single renewable 7-year terms

subordinate courts: High Court of Justice (jurisdiction limited to cases of high treason or criminal offenses by the president or ministers while in office)

Political parties and leaders: African Solidarity for Democracy and Independence or SADI [Oumar MARIKO]

Alliance for Democracy in Mali-Pan-African Party for Liberty, Solidarity, and Justice or ADEMA-PASJ [Dioncounda TRAORE]

Alliance for Democracy and Progress or ADP (coalition including ADEMA and URD formed in December 2006 to support the presidential candidacy of Amadou TOURE)

Alliance for the Solidarity of Mali-Convergence of Patriotic Forces or ASM A-CFP [Soumeylou Boubeye MAIGA]

Alternative Forces for Renewal and Emergence or FARE [Modibo SIDIBE]

Convergence for the Development of Mali or CODEM [Housseyni Amion GUINDO]

Economic and Social Development Party or PDES [Jamille BITTAR]

Front for Democracy and the Republic or FDR (coalition including RPM and PARENA formed to oppose the presidential candidacy of Amadou TOURE)

National Congress for Democratic Initiative or CNID [Mountaga TALL]

Party for National Renewal or PARENA [Tiebile DRAME]

Patriotic Movement for Renewal or MPR [Choguel Kokalla MAIGA]

Rally for Mali or RPM [Ibrahim Boubacar KEITA] (ruling party)

Union for Republic and Democracy or URD [Younoussi TOURE]

Political pressure groups and leaders: *other:* the army; Islamic authorities; state-run cotton company CMDT

International organization participation: ACP, AfDB, AU, CD, ECOWAS, EITI (compliant country), FAO, FZ, G-77, IAEA, IBRD, ICAO, ICCt, ICRM, IDA, IDB, IFAD, IFC, IFRCS, ILO, IMF, Interpol, IOC, IOM, IPU, ISO, ITSO, ITU, ITUC (NGOs), MIGA, MONUSCO, NAM, OIC, OIF, OPCW, UN, UNAMID, UNCTAD, UNESCO, UNIDO, UNISFA, UNMISS, UNWTO, UPU, WADB (regional), WAEMU, WCO, WFTU (NGOs), WHO, WIPO, WMO, WTO

Diplomatic representation in the US: *chief of mission:* Ambassador Tiena COULIBALY (since 18 November 2014)

chancery: 2130 R Street NW, Washington, DC 20008

Telephone: [1] (202) 332-2249,939-8950

FAX: [1] (202) 332-6603

Diplomatic representation from the US: *chief of mission:* Ambassador Paul A. FOLMSBEE (since 2015)

embassy: located just off the RoiBin Fahad Aziz Bridge just west of the Bamako central district

mailing address: ACI 2000, Rue 243, Porte 297, Bamako

telephone: [223] 2070–2300

FAX: [223] 2070–2479

Flag description: three equal vertical bands of green (hoist side), yellow, and red

note: uses the popular Pan-African colors of Ethiopia; the colors from left to right are the same as those of neighboring Senegal (which has an additional green central star) and the reverse of those on the flag of neighboring Guinea

National symbol(s): Great Mosque of Djenne; national colors: green, yellow, red

National anthem: *name:* "Le Mali" (Mali)

lyrics/music: Seydou Badian KOUYATE/Banzoumana SISSOKO

note: adopted 1962; also known as "Pour L'Afrique et pour toi, Mali" (For Africa and for You, Mali) and "A ton appel Mali" (At Your Call, Mali)

ECONOMY

Economy—overview: Among the 25 poorest countries in the world, Mali is a landlocked country that depends on gold mining and agricultural exports for revenue. The country's fiscal status fluctuates with gold and agricultural commodity prices and the harvest; cotton and gold exports make up around 80% of export earnings. Mali remains dependent on foreign aid.

Economic activity is largely confined to the riverine area irrigated by the Niger River and about 65% of its land area is desert or semidesert. About 10% of the population is nomadic and about 80% of the labor force is engaged in farming and fishing. Industrial activity is concentrated on processing farm commodities. The government subsidizes the production of cereals to decrease the country's dependence on imported foodstuffs and to reduce its vulnerability to food price shocks.

Mali is developing its iron ore extraction industry to diversify foreign exchange earnings away from gold, but the pace will largely depend on global price trends. Mali's economic performance has improved since 2013 although physical insecurity, high population growth, corruption, weak infrastructure, and low levels of human capital remain hindrances to sustained growth.

GDP (purchasing power parity): $35.83 billion (2015 est.)

$33.76 billion (2014 est.)

$31.41 billion (2013 est.)

note: data are in 2015 US dollars

country comparison to the world: 119

GDP (official exchange rate): $13.07 billion (2015 est.)

GDP—real growth rate: 6.1% (2015 est.) 7.5% (2014 est.)

2.3% (2013 est.)

country comparison to the world: 28

GDP—per capita (PPP): $2,200 (2015 est.)

$2,100 (2014 est.)

$2,100 (2013 est.)

note: data are in 2015 US dollars

country comparison to the world: 200

Gross national saving: 21.2% of GDP (2015 est.)

23.2% of GDP (2014 est.)

22.6% of GDP (2013 est.)

country comparison to the world: 76

GDP—composition, by end use:

household consumption: 83.3%

government consumption: 18.1%

investment in fixed capital: 16.7%

investment in inventories: -0.1%

exports of goods and services: 30.1%

imports of goods and services: -48.1% (2015 est.)

GDP—composition, by sector of origin:

agriculture: 38.5%

industry: 23.3%

services: 38.2% (2015 est.)

Agriculture—products: cotton, millet, rice, corn, vegetables, peanuts; cattle, sheep, goats

Industries: food processing; construction; phosphate and gold mining

Industrial production growth rate: 5.2% (2015 est.)

country comparison to the world: 28

Labor force: 5.644 million (2015 est.)

country comparison to the world: 73

Labor force—by occupation: *agriculture:* 80%

industry and services: 20% (2005 est.)

Unemployment rate: 30% (2015 est.)

8.2% (2014 est.)

country comparison to the world: 185

Population below poverty line: 36.1% (2005 est.)

Household income or consumption by percentage share: *lowest:* 10%: 3.5%

highest: 10%: 25.8% (2010 est.)

Distribution of family income—Gini index: 40.1 (2001)

50.5 (1994)

country comparison to the world: 63

Budget: *revenues:* $2.409 billion

expenditures: $2.756 billion (2015 est.)

Taxes and other revenues: 22% of GDP (2015 est.)

country comparison to the world: 142

Budget surplus (+) or deficit (–): -3.2% of GDP (2015 est.)

country comparison to the world: 119

Public debt: 39% of GDP (2015 est.)

33.8% of GDP (2014 est.)

country comparison to the world: 118

Fiscal year: calendar year

Inflation rate (consumer prices): 1.4% (2015 est.)

0.9% (2014 est.)

country comparison to the world: 93

Central bank discount rate: 16% (31 December 2010)

4.25% (31 December 2009)

country comparison to the world: 11

Commercial bank prime lending rate: 9.3% (31 December 2015 est.)

9.3% (31 December 2014 est.)

country comparison to the world: 89

Stock of narrow money: $2.213 billion (31 December 2015 est.)
$2.612 billion (31 December 2014 est.)
country comparison to the world: 123

Stock of broad money: $3.984 billion (31 December 2014 est.)
$3.817 billion (31 December 2013 est.)
country comparison to the world: 140

Stock of domestic credit: $2.16 billion (31 December 2015 est.)
$2.541 billion (31 December 2014 est.)
country comparison to the world: 136

Market value of publicly traded shares: $NA

Current account balance: -$371 million (2015 est.)
-$664 million (2014 est.)
country comparison to the world: 91

Exports: $2.191 billion (2015 est.)
$2.253 billion (2014 est.)
country comparison to the world: 136

Exports—commodities: cotton, gold, livestock

Exports—partners: Switzerland 48.7%, China 9.4%, India 9.1%, Bangladesh 8%, Thailand 4.5%, Indonesia 4.4% (2015)

Imports: $2.919 billion (2015 est.)
$3.14 billion (2014 est.)
country comparison to the world: 148

Imports—commodities: petroleum, machinery and equipment, construction materials, foodstuffs, textiles

Imports—partners: Cote dIvoire 9.9%, France 9.5%, Senegal 7.7%, China 7% (2015)

Debt—external: $3.633 billion (31 December 2014 est.) $3.423 billion (31 December 2013 est.)
country comparison to the world: 138

Stock of direct foreign investment—at home: $3.159 billion (31 December 2015 est.)
$2.624 billion (31 December 2014 est.)
country comparison to the world: 104

Stock of direct foreign investment—abroad: $27.26 million (31 December 2015 est.)
$7.28 million (31 December 2014 est.)
country comparison to the world: 100

Exchange rates: Communaute Financiere Africaine francs (XOF) per US dollar—
580.5 (2015 est.)
494.42 (2014 est.)
494.42 (2013 est.)
510.53 (2012 est.)
471.87 (2011 est.)

ENERGY

Electricity—production: 949 million kWh (2012 est.)
country comparison to the world: 152

Electricity—consumption: 882.6 million kWh (2012 est.)
country comparison to the world: 159

Electricity—exports: 0 kWh (2013 est.)
country comparison to the world: 168

Electricity—imports: 0 kWh (2013 est.)
country comparison to the world: 174

Electricity—installed generating capacity: 304,000 kW (2012 est.)
country comparison to the world: 150

Electricity—from fossil fuels: 48.4% of total installed capacity (2012 est.)
country comparison to the world: 151

Electricity—from nuclear fuels: 0% of total installed capacity (2012 est.)
country comparison to the world: 141

Electricity—from hydroelectric plants: 51.6% of total installed capacity (2012 est.)
country comparison to the world: 47

Electricity—from other renewable sources: 0% of total installed capacity (2012 est.)
country comparison to the world: 201

Crude oil—production: 0 bbl/day (2014 est.)
country comparison to the world: 168

Crude oil—exports: 0 bbl/day (2012 est.)
country comparison to the world: 161

Crude oil—imports: 0 bbl/day (2012 est.)
country comparison to the world: 97

Crude oil—proved reserves: 0 bbl (1 January 2015 est.)
country comparison to the world: 168

Refined petroleum products—production: 0 bbl/day (2012 est.)
country comparison to the world: 211

Refined petroleum products—consumption: 4,700 bbl/day (2013 est.)
country comparison to the world: 173

Refined petroleum products—exports: 0 bbl/day (2012 est.)
country comparison to the world: 203

Refined petroleum products—imports: 4,698 bbl/day (2012 est.)
country comparison to the world: 165

Natural gas—production: 0 cu m (2013 est.)
country comparison to the world: 103

Natural gas—consumption: 0 cu m (2013 est.)
country comparison to the world: 171

Natural gas—exports: 0 cu m (2013 est.)
country comparison to the world: 146

Natural gas—imports: 0 cu m (2013 est.)
country comparison to the world: 100

Natural gas—proved reserves: 0 cu m (1 January 2014 est.)
country comparison to the world: 171

Carbon dioxide emissions from consumption of energy: 773,900 Mt (2012 est.)
country comparison to the world: 170

COMMUNICATIONS

Telephones—fixed lines: *total subscriptions:* 160,000
subscriptions per 100 inhabitants: 1 (2014 est.)
country comparison to the world: 136

Telephones—mobile cellular: *total:* 23.5 million
subscriptions per 100 inhabitants: 143 (2014 est.)
country comparison to the world: 50

Telephone system: *general assessment:* domestic system unreliable but improving; increasing use of local radio loops to extend network coverage to remote areas
domestic: fixed-line subscribership remains less than 1 per 100 persons; mobile-cellular subscribership has increased sharply to about 70 per 100 persons
international: country code—223; satellite communications center and fiber-optic links to neighboring countries; satellite earth stations—2 Intelsat (1 Atlantic Ocean, 1 Indian Ocean) (2010)

Broadcast media: national public TV broadcaster; 2 privately owned companies provide subscription services to foreign multi-channel TV packages; national public radio broadcaster supplemented by a large number of privately owned and community broadcast stations; transmissions of multiple international broadcasters are available (2007)
Radio broadcast stations: AM 1, FM 230 (27 regional and government stations, and 203 private stations), shortwave 1 (2001)
Television broadcast stations: 2 (plus repeaters) (2007)

Internet country code: .ml

Internet hosts: 437 (2012)
country comparison to the world: 186

Internet users: *total:* 12.4 million
percent of population: 75.2% (2014 est.)
country comparison to the world: 38

TRANSPORTATION

Airports: 25 (2013)
country comparison to the world: 129

Airports—with paved runways: *total:* 8
over 3,047 m: 1
2,438 to 3,047 m: 4
1,524 to 2,437 m: 2
914 to 1,523 m: 1 (2013)

Airports—with unpaved runways: *total:* 17
1,524 to 2,437 m: 3
914 to 1,523 m: 9
under 914 m: 5 (2013)

Heliports: 2 (2013)

Railways: *total:* 593 km
narrow gauge: 593 km 1.000-m gauge (2014)
country comparison to the world: 111

Roadways: *total:* 22,474 km
paved: 5,522 km
unpaved: 16,952 km (2009)
country comparison to the world: 103

Waterways: 1,800 km (downstreAmof Koulikoro; low water levels on the River Niger cause problems in dry years; in the months before the rainy season the river is not navigable by commercial vessels) (2011)
country comparison to the world: 43

Ports and terminals: *river port(s):* Koulikoro (Niger)

MILITARY AND SECURITY

Military branches: Malian Armed Forces: Army (Armee de Terre), Republic of Mali Air Force (Force Aerienne de la Republique du Mali,

545

FARM), National Guard (Garde National du Mali) (2013)

Military service age and obligation: 18 years of age for selective compulsory and voluntary military service; 2-year conscript service obligation (2012)

Military expenditures: 1.44% of GDP (2012)
1.51% of GDP (2011)
1.44% of GDP (2010)
country comparison to the world: 68

TRANSNATIONAL ISSUES

Disputes—international: demarcation is underway with Burkina Faso

Refugees and internally displaced persons: *refugees (country of origin):* 12,898 (Mauritania) (2014)
IDPs: 37,561 (Tuareg rebellion since 2012) (2016)

Trafficking in persons: *current situation:* Mali is a source, transit, and destination country for men, women, and children subjected to forced labor and sex trafficking; internal trafficking is more prevalent than transnational trafficking, but foreign women and girls are forced into domestic servitude, agricultural labor, and support roles in gold mines, as well as subjected to sex trafficking; Malian boys are forced to work in agricultural settings, gold mines, the informal commercial sector and to beg within Mali and neighboring countries; Malians and other Africans who travel through Mali to Mauritania, Algeria, or Libya in hopes of reaching Europe are particularly at risk of becoming victims of human trafficking; men and boys, primarily of Songhai ethnicity, are subjected to debt bondage in the salt mines of Taoudenni in northern Mali; some members of Mali's Tamachek community are subjected to hereditary slavery-related practices; Malian women and girls are victims of sex trafficking in Gabon, Libya, Lebanon, and Tunisia; the recruitment of child soldiers by armed groups in northern Mali decreased

tier rating: Tier 2 Watch List—Mali does not fully comply with the minimum standards for the elimination of trafficking; however, it is making significant efforts to do so; in 2014, Mali was granted a waiver from an otherwise required downgrade to Tier 3 because its government has a written plan that, if implemented would constitute making significant efforts to bring itself into compliance with the minimum standards for the elimination of trafficking; officials failed to distribute the 2012 anti-trafficking law to judicial and law enforcement personnel, perpetuating a lack of understanding and awareness of the legislation; anti-trafficking law enforcement efforts decreased in 2014, with only one case investigated and no prosecutions or convictions; fewer victims were identified, and the government did not support the privately funded NGOs and international organizations it relied upon to provide victims with services; the government did not conduct any awareness-raising campaigns, workshops, or training sessions (2015)

MALTA

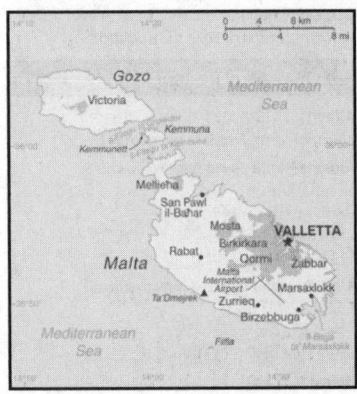

INTRODUCTION

Background: Great Britain formally acquired possession of Malta in 1814. The island staunchly supported the UK through both world wars and remained in the Commonwealth when it became independent in 1964; a decade later it declared itself a republic. Since about the mid-1980s, the island has transformed itself into a freight transshipment point, a financial center, and a tourist destination while its key industries moved toward more service-oriented activities. Malta became an EU member in May 2004 and began using the euro as currency in 2008.

GEOGRAPHY

Location: Southern Europe, islands in the Mediterranean Sea, south of Sicily (Italy)

Geographic coordinates: 35 50 N, 14 35 E

Map references: Europe

Area: *total:* 316 sq km
land: 316 sq km
water: 0 sq km
country comparison to the world: 208

Area—comparative: slightly less than twice the size of Washington, DC

Land boundaries: 0 km

Coastline: 196.8 km (excludes 56 km for the island of Gozo)

Maritime claims: *territorial sea:* 12 nm
contiguous zone: 24 nm
continental shelf: 200-m depth or to the depth of exploitation
exclusive fishing zone: 25 nm

Climate: Mediterranean; mild, rainy winters; hot, dry summers

Terrain: mostly low, rocky, flat to dissected plains; many coastal cliffs

Elevation: *mean elevation:* NA

elevation extremes: *lowest point:* Mediterranean Sea 0 m
highest point: Ta'Dmejrek 253 m (near Dingli)

Natural resources: limestone, salt, arable land

Land use: *agricultural land:* 32.3%
arable land: 28.4%;
permanent crops: 3.9%;
permanent pasture: 0%
forest: 0.9%
other: 66.8% (2011 est.)

Irrigated land: 35 sq km (2012)

Total renewable water resources: 0.05 cu km (2011)

Freshwater withdrawal (domestic/industrial/agricultural): *total:* 0.05 cu km/yr (64%/1%/35%)
per capita: 134.1 cu m/yr (2009)

Natural hazards: NA

Environment—current issues: limited natural freshwater resources; increasing reliance on desalination

Environment—international agreements: *party to:* Air Pollution, Biodiversity, Climate Change, Climate Change-Kyoto Protocol, Desertification, Endangered Species, Hazardous Wastes, Law of the Sea, Marine Dumping, Ozone Layer Protection, Ship Pollution, Wetlands
signed, but not ratified: none of the selected agreements

Geography—note: the country comprises an archipelago, with only the three largest islands (Malta, Ghawdex or Gozo, and Kemmuna or Comino) being inhabited; numerous bays provide good harbors; Malta and Tunisia are discussing the commercial exploitation of the continental shelf between their countries, particularly for oil exploration

PEOPLE AND SOCIETY

Nationality: *noun:* Maltese (singular and plural)
adjective: Maltese

Ethnic groups: Maltese (descendants of ancient Carthaginians and Phoenicians with strong elements of Italian and other Mediterranean stock)

Languages: Maltese (official) 90.1%, English (official) 6%, multilingual 3%, other 0.9% (2005 est.)

Religions: Roman Catholic (official) more than 90% (2011 est.)

Population: 413,965 (July 2015 est.)
country comparison to the world: 176

Age structure: *0–14 years:* 15.05% (male 31943/female 30,341)
15–24 years: 12.22% (male 26,028/female 24,570)
25–54 years: 40.24% (male 85,145/female 81,447)
55–64 years: 13.98% (male 28,702/female 29,185)

65 years and over: 18.5% (male 34,345/female 42,259) (2015 est.)

Dependency ratios: *total dependency ratio:* 50.8%
youth dependency ratio: 21.8%
elderly dependency ratio: 29%
potential support ratio: 3.4% (2015 est.)

Median age: *total:* 41.2 years
male: 40 years
female: 42.4 years (2015 est.)
country comparison to the world: 36

Population growth rate: 0.31% (2015 est.)
country comparison to the world: 174

Birth rate: 10.18 births/1,000 population (2015 est.)
country comparison to the world: 192

Death rate: 9.09 deaths/1,000 population (2015 est.)
country comparison to the world: 66

Net migration rate: 1.98 migrant(s)/1,000 population (2015 est.)
country comparison to the world: 51

Urbanization: *urban Population:* 95.4% of total population (2015)
rate of urbanization: 0.46% annual rate of change (2010–15 est.)

Major urban areas—Population: VALLETTA (capital) 197,000 (2014)

Sex ratio: *at birth:* 1.06 male(s)/female
0–14 years: 1.05 male(s)/female
15–24 years: 1.06 male(s)/female
25–54 years: 1.05 male(s)/female
55–64 years: 0.98 male(s)/female
65 years and over: 0.81 male(s)/female
total population: 0.99 male(s)/female (2015 est.)

Mother's mean age at first birth: 26.9
note: data refer to the average of the different childbearing ages of first-order births (2010 est.)

Maternal mortality rate: 9 deaths/100,000 live births (2015 est.)
country comparison to the world: 161

Infant mortality rate: *total:* 3.56 deaths/1,000 live births
male: 3.97 deaths/1,000 live births
female: 3.14 deaths/1,000 live births (2015 est.)
country comparison to the world: 203

Life expectancy at birth: *total population:* 80.25 years
male: 77.92 years
female: 82.71 years (2015 est.)
country comparison to the world: 36

Total fertility rate: 1.54 children born/woman (2015 est.)
country comparison to the world: 190

Health expenditures: 8.7% of GDP (2013)
country comparison to the world: 36

Physicians density: 3.49 physicians/1,000 population (2013)

Hospital bed density: 4.8 beds/1,000 population (2012)

Drinking water source:
improved:

urban: 100% of population
rural: 100% of population
total: 100% of population
unimproved:
urban: 0% of population
rural: 0% of population
total: 0% of population (2015 est.)

Sanitation facility access:
improved:
urban: 100% of population
rural: 100% of population
total: 100% of population
unimproved:
urban: 0% of population
rural: 0% of population
total: 0% of population (2015 est.)

HIV/AIDS—adult prevalence rate: NA

HIV/AIDS—people living with HIV/AIDS: NA

HIV/AIDS—deaths: NA

Obesity—adult prevalence rate: 28.7% (2014)
country comparison to the world: 32

Education expenditures: 6.8% of GDP (2012)
country comparison to the world: 23

Literacy: *definition:* age 15 and over can read and write
total population: 94.4%
male: 93.1%
female: 95.8% (2015 est.)

School life expectancy (primary to tertiary education): *total:* 15 years
male: 15 years
female: 14 years (2014)

Unemployment, youth ages 15–24: *total:* 13%
male: 15.2%
female: 10.4% (2013 est.)
country comparison to the world: 82

GOVERNMENT

Country name: *conventional long form:* Republic of Malta
conventional short form: Malta
local long form: Repubblika ta' Malta
local short form: Malta
etymology: the ancient Greeks called the island "Melite" meaning "honey-sweet" from the Greek word "meli" meaning "honey" and referring to the island's honey production

Government type: parliamentary republic

Capital: *name:* Valletta

Geographic coordinates: 35 53 N, 1 4 30 E
time difference: UTC + 1 (6 hours ahead of Washington, DC, during Standard Time)
daylight saving time: +1hr, begins last Sunday in March; ends last Sunday in October

Administrative divisions: 68 localities (Il-lokalita); Attard, Balzan, Birgu, Birkirkara, Birzebbuga, Bormla, Dingli, Fgura, Floriana, Fontana, Ghajnsielem, Gharb, Gharghur, Ghasri, Ghaxaq, Gudja, Gzira, Hamrun, Iklin, Imdina, Imgarr, Imqabba, Imsida, Imtarfa, Isla, Kalkara, Kercem, Kirkop, Lija, Luqa, Marsa, Marsaskala, Marsaxlokk, Mellieha, Mosta, Munxar, Nadur, Naxxar, Paola,

Pembroke, Pieta, Qala, Qormi, Qrendi, Rabat, Rabat (Ghawdex), Safi, San Giljan/Saint Julian, San Gwann/Saint John, San Lawrenz/Saint Lawrence, Sannat, San Pawl il-Bahar/Saint Paul's Bay, Santa Lucija/Saint Lucia, Santa Venera/Saint Venera, Siggiewi, Sliema, Swieqi, Tarxien, Ta' Xbiex, Valletta, Xaghra, Xewkija, Xghajra, Zabbar, Zebbug, Zebbug (Ghawdex), Zejtun, Zurrieq

Independence: 21 September 1964 (from the UK)

National holiday: Independence Day, 21 September (1964); Republic Day, 13 December (1974)

Constitution: many previous; latest adopted 21 September 1964; amended many times, last in 2015 (2016)

Legal system: mixed legal system of English common law and civil law (based on the Roman and Napoleonic civil codes)

International law organization participation: accepts compulsory ICJ jurisdiction with reservations; accepts ICCt jurisdiction

Citizenship: *citizenship by birth:* no
citizenship by descent only: at least one parent must be a citizen of Malta
dual citizenship recognized: no
residency requirement for naturalization: 5 years

Suffrage: 18 years of age (16 in Local Council elections); universal

Executive branch: *chief of state:* President Marie-Louise Coleiro PR ECA (since 4 April 2014)

head of government: Prime Minister Joseph MUSCAT (since 11 March 2013)
cabinet: Cabinet appointed by the president on the advice of the prime minister
elections/appointments: president indirectly elected by the House of Representatives for a 5-year term (1-term limit); election last held on 4 April 2014 (next to be held by April 2019); following legislative elections, the leader of the majority party or majority coalition usually appointed prime minister by the president for a 5-year term; deputy prime minister appointed by the president on the advice of the prime minister
election results: Marie-Louise Coleiro PRECA (PL) elected president; House of Representatives vote -unanimous; Joseph MUSCAT (PL) appointed prime minister

Legislative branch: *description:* unicameral House of Representatives or Il-Kamra Tad-Deputati, a component of the Parliament of Malta (normally 65 seats, but can include at-large members; members directly elected in 5 multi-seat constituencies by proportional representation vote; members serve 5-year terms); note—the parliament elected in 2013 has 69 seats
elections: last held on 9 March 2013 (next to be held by mid-summer 2018)
election results: percent of vote by party—PL 54.8%, PN 43.3%, other 1.9%; seats by party—PL 39, PN 30

Judicial branch: *highest court(s):* Court of Appeal (consists of either 1 or 3 judges); Constitutional

Court (consists of 3 judges); Court of Criminal Appeal (consists of either 1 or 3 judges)

judge selection and term of office: Court of Appeal and Constitutional Court judges appointed by the president, usually upon the advice of the prime minister; judges of both courts serve until age 65

subordinate courts: Civil Court (divided into the General Jurisdiction Section, Family Section, and Voluntary Section); Criminal Court; Court of Magistrates; Gozo Courts (for the islands of Gozo and Comino)

Political parties and leaders: Alternativa Demokratika or AD (Green Party) [Arnold CASSOLA]
Labor Party or PL [Joseph MUSCAT]
Nationalist Party or PN [Simon BUSUTTIL]

Political pressure groups and leaders: Alliance of Liberal Democrats Malta (Alleanza Liberali-Demokratika Malta) or ALDM (for divorce, abortion, gay marriage, women's rights)
Alliance for Change (Alleanza Bidla) (Euros-septic)
Together for a Better Environment (Flimkien Ghal-Ambjent Ahjar) or FAA (pro-environment)
other: environmentalists

International organization participation: Australia Group, C, CD, CE, EAPC, EBRD, ECB, EIB, EMU, EU, FAO, IAEA, IBRD, ICAO, ICC (NGOs), ICCt, ICRM, IDA, IFAD, IFC, IFRCS, ILO, IMF, IMO, IMSO, Interpol, IOC, IOM, IPU, ISO, ITSO, ITU, ITUC (NGOs), MIGA, NSG, OAS (observer), OPCW, OSCE, PCA, PFP, Schengen Convention, UN, UNCTAD, UNESCO, UNIDO, Union Latina (observer), UNWTO, UPU, WCO, WHO, WIPO, WMO, WTO

Diplomatic representation in the US: *chief of mission:* Ambassador Pierre Clive AGIUS (since 2 March 2016)
chancery: 2017 Connecticut Avenue NW, Washington, DC 20008
telephone: [1] (202) 462-3611 through 3612
FAX: [1] (202) 387-5470

Diplomatic representation from the US: *chief of mission:* Ambassador G. Kathleen HILL (since 25 February 2016)
embassy: Ta' Qali National Park, Attard, ATD 4000
mailing address: 5800 Valletta Place, Dulles, VA 20189
telephone: [356] 2561 4000
FAX: [356] 2124 3229

Flag description: two equal vertical bands of white (hoist side) and red; in the upper hoist-side corner is a representation of the George Cross, edged in red; according to legend, the colors are taken from the red and white checkered banner of Count Roger of Sicily who removed a bi-colored corner and granted it to Malta in 1091; an uncontested explanation is that the colors are those of the Knights of Saint John who ruled Malta from 1530 to 1798; in 1942, King George VI of the United Kingdom awarded the George Cross to the islanders for their exceptional bravery and gallantry in World War II; since independence in 1964, the George Cross bordered in red has appeared directly on the white field

National symbol(s): Maltese eight-pointed cross; national colors: red, white

National anthem: *name:* "L-Innu Malti" (The Maltese Anthem)
lyrics/music: Dun Karm PSAILA/Robert SAMMUT
note: adopted 1945; written in the form of a prayer

ECONOMY

Economy—overview: Malta—the smallest economy in the eurozone—produces only about 20% of its food needs, has limited fresh water supplies, and has few domestic energy sources. Malta's economy is dependent on foreign trade, manufacturing, and tourism. Malta joined the EU in 2004 and adopted the euro on 1 January 2008. Malta has weathered the eurozone crisis better than most EU member states due to a low debt-to-GDP ratio and financially sound banking sector. It has low unemployment relative to other European countries, and growth has recovered since the 2009 recession. in 2014 and 2015, Malta led the eurozone in growth, expanding by nearly 3.5% each year.

Malta's services sector continued to grow in 2015, with noted increases in the financial services and online gaming sectors. Malta continues to enhance its regulation of the financial services sector, and passed additional legislation in 2014 and 2015 to improve anti-money laundering oversight for financial and gaming activities. Expanding EU discussions of anti-tax avoidance measures, including the "Anti-Tax Avoidance Package" submitted in early 2016, have raised concerns among Malta's financial services and insurance providers about passage of laws governing EU tax practices, which could have a significant impact on those sectors.

Malta's 2015 GDP growth was bolstered by energy infrastructure investments, and revenue growth is expected to continue, supported by a strong labor market and proceeds from a citizenship by investment program equal to roughly 0.9% of GDP. Malta's geographic position between Europe and North Africa makes it a route for irregular migration. Historically, Malta's fertility rate has been below the EU average, and population growth in recent years has been largely from immigration, increasing pressure on the pension system. The government has implemented new programs, including free child care, to encourage increased labor participation. The high cost of borrowing and small labor market remain potential constraints to future economic growth.

GDP (purchasing power parity):
$15.38 billion (2015 est.)
$14.6 billion (2014 est.)
$14.03 billion (2013 est.)
note: data are in 2015 US dollars
country comparison to the world: 152

GDP (official exchange rate): $9.801 billion (2015 est.)

GDP—real growth rate: 5.4% (2015 est.)
4.1% (2014 est.)
4% (2013 est.)
country comparison to the world: 35

GDP—per capita (PPP): $35,900 (2015 est.)
$34,300 (2014 est.)
$33,300 (2013 est.)
note: data are in 2012 US dollars
country comparison to the world: 51

Gross national saving: 25.1% of GDP (2015 est.)
22.1% of GDP (2014 est.)
21.5% of GDP (2013 est.)
country comparison to the world: 48

GDP—composition, by end use:
household consumption: 52.7%
government consumption: 19.4%
investment in fixed capital: 21.1%
investment in inventories: -0.1%
exports of goods and services: 141.5%
imports of goods and services: -134.6% (2015 est.)

GDP—composition, by sector of origin:
agriculture: 1.4%
industry: 15.5%
services: 83.1% (2015 est.)

Agriculture—products: potatoes, cauliflower, grapes, wheat, barley, tomatoes, citrus, cut flowers, green peppers; pork, milk, poultry, eggs

Industries: tourism, electronics, ship building and repair, construction, food and beverages, pharmaceuticals, footwear, clothing, tobacco, aviation services, financial services, information technology services

Industrial production growth rate: 5.9% (2015)
country comparison to the world: 23

Labor force: 186,900 (2015 est.)
country comparison to the world: 176

Labor force—by occupation: *agriculture:* 1.7%
industry: 18.3%
services: 80% (2015)

Unemployment rate: 5.2% (2015 est.)
5.7% (2014 est.)
country comparison to the world: 55

Population below poverty line: 15.9% (2014 est.)

Household income or consumption by percentage share: *lowest:* 10%: NA%
highest: 10%: NA%

Distribution of family income—Gini index: 27.7 (2014) 27.9 (2013)
country comparison to the world: 131

Budget: *revenues:* $4.031 billion
expenditures: $3.39 billion (2015 est.)
Taxes and other revenues: 41.3% of GDP (2015 est.)
country comparison to the world: 32

Budget surplus (+) or deficit (–): 6.6% of GDP (2015 est.)
country comparison to the world: 6

Public debt: 60.6% of GDP (2015 est.)
58.3% of GDP (2014 est.)
note: Malta reports public debt at nominal value outstanding at the end of the year, according to guidelines set out in the Maastricht Treaty for

general government gross debt; the data include the following categories of government liabilities (as defined in ESA95): currency and deposits (AF.2), securities other than shares excluding financial derivatives (AF.3, excluding AF.34), and loans (AF.4); general government comprises the cen tral government, state govern men t, local government and social security funds
country comparison to the world: 61

Fiscal year: calendar year

Inflation rate (consumer prices): 1.2% (2015 est.) 0.8% (2014 est.)
country comparison to the world: 89

Central bank discount rate: -0.21% (31 December 2015)
-0.09% (31 December 2013)
note: this is the European Central Bank's rate on the marginal lending facility, which offers overnight credit to banks in the euro area
country comparison to the world: 156

Commercial bank prime lending rate: 4.18% (31 December 2015 est.)
5.15% (31 December 2014 est.)
country comparison to the world: 159

Stock of narrow money: $11.82 billion (31 December 2015 est.)
$10.55 billion (31 December 2014 est.)
note: see entry for the European Union for money supply for the entire euro area; the European Central Bank (ECB) controls monetary policy for the 18 members of the Economic and Monetary Union (EMU); individual members of the EMU do not control the quantity of money circulating within their own borders
country comparison to the world: 73

Stock of broad money: $17.65 billion (31 December 2015 est.)
$15.97 billion (31 December 2014 est.)
country comparison to the world: 94

Stock of domestic credit: $12.42 billion (31 December 2015 est.)
$14.55 billion (31 December 2014 est.)
country comparison to the world: 98

Market value of publicly traded shares: $4.468 billion (31 December 2015 est.)
$3.353 billion (31 December 2015)
$3.636 billion (31 December 2015 est.)
country comparison to the world: 89

Current account balance: $403 million (2015 est.)
$417 million (2014 est.)
country comparison to the world: 45

Exports: $3.896 billion (2015 est.)
$4.145 billion (2014 est.)
country comparison to the world: 120

Exports—commodities: machinery and mechanical appliances; mineral fuels, oils and petroleum products; pharmaceutical products; books and newspapers; aircraft/spacecraft and parts; toys, games, and sports equipment

Exports—partners: Germany 13.3%, France 10.2%, Hong Kong 7.4%, Singapore 7.3%, UK 6.4%, US 5.8%, Italy 5.6%, Japan 4.7% (2015)

Imports: $6.669 billion (2015 est.)

$7.097 billion (2014 est.)
country comparison to the world: 116

Imports—commodities: mineral fuels, oils and products; electrical machinery; aircraft/spacecraft and parts thereof; machinery and mechanical appliances; plastic and other semi-manufactured goods; vehicles and parts

Imports—partners: Italy 23%, Netherlands 8.4%, UK 7.5%, Germany 6.8%, Canada 6.1%, China 4.1%, France 4% (2015)

Reserves of foreign exchange and gold: $415.5 million (31 December 2015 est.)
$448 million (31 December 2014 est.)
country comparison to the world: 154

Debt—external: $99.02 billion (31 December 2015 est.)
$103.8 billion (30 December 2014 est.)
country comparison to the world: 50

Stock of direct foreign investment—at home: $164.4 billion (30 June 2015 est.)
$158.7 billion (December 31,2014 est.)
country comparison to the world: 34

Stock of direct foreign investment—abroad: $69.09 billion (31 June 2015 est.)
$67.32 billion (30 December 2014 est.)
country comparison to the world: 37

Exchange rates: euros (EUR) per US dollar—
0.885 (2015 est.)
0.7525 (2014 est.)
0.7634 (2013 est.)
0.78 (2012 est.)
0.7185 (2011 est.)

ENERGY

Electricity—production: 2.17 billion kWh (2014 est.)
country comparison to the world: 136

Electricity—consumption: 174,700 kWh (2014 est.)
country comparison to the world: 218

Electricity—exports: 0 kWh (2013 est.)
country comparison to the world: 171

Electricity—imports: 0 kWh (2013 est.)
country comparison to the world: 177

Electricity—installed generating capacity: 620,000 kW (2014 est.)
country comparison to the world: 136

Electricity—from fossil fuels: 91.7% of total installed capacity (2014 est.)
country comparison to the world: 71

Electricity—from nuclear fuels: 0% of total installed capacity (2013 est.)
country comparison to the world: 145

Electricity—from hydroelectric plants: 0% of total installed capacity (2013 est.)
country comparison to the world: 187

Electricity—from other renewable sources: 8.3% of total installed capacity (2014 est.)
country comparison to the world: 46

Crude oil—production: 0 bbl/day (2014 est.)
country comparison to the world: 170

Crude oil—exports: 0 bbl/day (2014 est.)

country comparison to the world: 164

Crude oil—imports: 0 bbl/day (2014 est.)
country comparison to the world: 100

Crude oil—proved reserves: 0 bbl (July 6,1905 est.)
country comparison to the world: 170

Refined petroleum products—production: 0 bbl/day (2014 est.)
country comparison to the world: 214

Refined petroleum products—consumption: 42,000 bbl/day (2013 est.)
country comparison to the world: 105

Refined petroleum products—exports: 14,410 bbl/day (2013 est.)
country comparison to the world: 79

Refined petroleum products—imports: 36,480 bbl/day (2013 est.)
country comparison to the world: 91

Natural gas—production: 0 cu m (2014 est.)
country comparison to the world: 106

Natural gas—consumption: 0 cu m (2014 est.)
country comparison to the world: 174

Natural gas—exports: 0 cu m (2014 est.)
country comparison to the world: 150

Natural gas—imports: 0 cu m (2013 est.)
country comparison to the world: 103

Natural gas—proved reserves: 0 cu m (1 January 2014 est.)
country comparison to the world: 173

Carbon dioxide emissions from consumption of energy: 1.457 million Mt (2014 est.)
country comparison to the world: 158

COMMUNICATIONS

Telephones—fixed lines: *total subscriptions:* 230,000
subscriptions per 100 inhabitants: 56 (2014 est.)
country comparison to the world: 126

Telephones—mobile cellular: *total:* 546,200
subscriptions per 100 inhabitants: 132 (2014 est.)
country comparison to the world: 169

Telephone system: *general assessment:* automatic system featuring submarine cable and microwave radio relay between islands
domestic: combined fixed-line and mobile-cellular subscribership exceeds 180 per 100 persons
international: country code—356; submarine cable connects to Italy; satellite earth station—1 Intelsat (Atlantic Ocean) (2011)

Broadcast media: 2 publicly owned TV stations, Television Malta (TVM) broadcasting nationally plus an educational channel; several privately owned national television stations, two of which are owned by political parties; Italian and British broadcast programs are available; multi-channel cable and satellite TV services are available; publicly owned radio broadcaster operates 3 stations; roughly 20 commercial radio stations (2016)
Radio broadcast stations: AM 1, FM 18, shortwave 6 (1999)
Television broadcast stations: 6 (2009)

Internet country code: .mt

Internet hosts: 14,754 (2012)
country comparison to the world: 125

Internet users: total: 166,000
percent of population: 40.2% (2014 est.)
country comparison to the world: 160

TRANSPORTATION

Airports: 1 (2013)
country comparison to the world: 225

Airports—with paved runways: *total:* 1
over 3,047 m: 1 (2013)

Heliports: 2 (2013)

Roadways: *total:* 3,096 km
paved: 2,704 km
unpaved: 392 km (2008)
country comparison to the world: 165

Merchant marine: *total:* 1,650
by type: bulk carrier 544, cargo 351, carrier 1,
chemical tanker 324, container 117, liquefied gas

36, passenger 50, passenger/cargo 18, petroleum
tanker 160, refrigerated cargo 7, roll on/roll off 22,
specialized tanker 2, vehicle carrier 18
foreign-owned: 1,437 (Angola 7, Azerbaijan 1,
Belgium 7, Bermuda 15, Bulgaria 8, Canada 5,
China 6, Croatia 6, Cyprus 32, Denmark 34, Egypt
1, Estonia 16, Finland 3, France 8, Germany 135,
Greece 469, Hong Kong 4, India 3, Iran 48, Ireland 4, Israel 3, Italy 45, Japan 5, Kuwait 3, Latvia
8, Lebanon 6, Libya 5, Luxembourg 3, Malaysia
1, Monaco 3, Netherlands 3, Norway 96, Oman
5, Poland 21, Portugal 3, Romania 7, Russia 45,
Saudi Arabia 2, Singapore 4, Slovenia 4, South
Korea 2, Spain 8, Sweden 1, Switzerland 20, Syria
4, Turkey 233, UAE 1, UK 21, Ukraine 29, US 34)
registered in other countries: 2 (Panama 2)
(2010)
country comparison to the world: 4

Ports and terminals: *major seaport(s):* Marsaxlokk
(Malta Freeport), Valletta

container port(s) (TEUs): Marsaxlokk
(2,360,000)

MILITARY AND SECURITY

Military branches: Armed Forces of Malta (AFM;
includes land, maritime, and air elements) (2013)

Military service age and obligation: 18 years of
age for voluntary military service; no conscription
(2014)

Military expenditures: 0.61% of GDP (2013)
0.61% of GDP (2012)
0.61% of GDP (2011)
0.61% of GDP (2010)
country comparison to the world: 122

TRANSNATIONAL ISSUES

Disputes—international: none

Illicit drugs: minor transshipment point for hashish from North Africa to Western Europe

MARSHALL ISLANDS

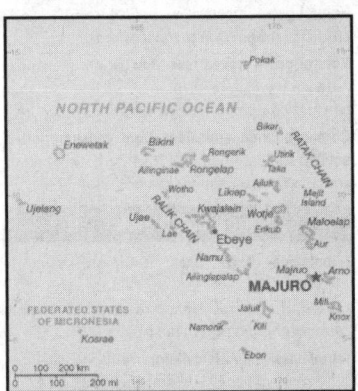

INTRODUCTION

Background: After almost four decades under US
administration as the easternmost part of the UN
Trust Territory of the Pacific Islands, the Marshall
Islands attained independence in 1986 under a
Compact of Free Association. Compensation
claims continue as a result of US nuclear testing
on some of the atolls between 1947 and 1962. The
Marshall Islands hosts the US Army Kwajalein
Atoll Reagan Missile Test Site, a key installation
in the US missile defense network. Kwajalein also
hosts one of four dedicated ground antennas (the
others are on Ascension (Saint Helena, Ascen-
sion, and Tristan da Cunha), Diego Garcia (British
Indian Ocean Territory), and at Cape Canaveral,
Florida (US)) that assist in the operation of the
Global Positioning System (GPS) navigation
system.

GEOGRAPHY

Location: Oceania, two archipelagic island chains
of 29 atolls, each made up of many small islets,
and five single islands in the North Pacific Ocean,
about halfway between Hawaii and Australia

Geographic coordinates: 9 00 N, 168 00 E

Map references: Oceania

Area: *total:* 181 sq km
land: 181 sq km
water: 0 sq km
note: the archipelago includes 11,673 sq km
of lagoon waters and encompasses the atolls of
Bikini, Enewetak, Kwajalein, Majuro, Rongelap,
and Utirik
country comparison to the world: 217

Area—comparative: about the size of Washington,
DC

Land boundaries: 0 km

Coastline: 370.4 km

Maritime claims: *territorial sea:* 12 nm
contiguous zone: 24 nm
exclusive economic zone: 200 nm

Climate: tropical; hot and humid; wet season May
to November; islands border typhoon belt

Terrain: low coral limestone and sand islands

Elevation: *mean elevation:* NA

elevation extremes: *lowest point:* Pacific Ocean
0 m
highest point: unnamed location on Likiep 10 m

Natural resources: coconut products, marine products, deep seabed minerals

Land use: *agricultural land:* 50.7%
arable land: 7.8%;
permanent crops: 31.2%;
permanent pasture: 11.7%

forest: 49.3%
other: 0% (2011 est.)

Irrigated land: 0 sq km (2012)

Natural hazards: infrequent typhoons

Environment—current issues: inadequate supplies of potable water; pollution of Majuro lagoon
from household waste and discharges from fishing
vessels

Environment—international agreements: *party to:*
Biodiversity, Climate Change, Climate Change-
Kyoto Protocol, Desertification, Hazardous
Wastes, Law of the Sea, Ozone Layer Protection,
Ship Pollution, Wetlands, Whaling
signed, but not ratified: none of the selected
agreements

Geography—note: the islands of Bikini and
Enewetak are former US nuclear test sites; Kwajalein atoll, famous as a World War II battleground,
surrounds the world's largest lagoon and is used as a
US missile test range; the island city of Ebeye is the
second largest settlement in the Marshall Islands,
after the capital of Majuro, and one of the most
densely populated locations in the Pacific

PEOPLE AND SOCIETY

Nationality: *noun:* Marshallese (singular and
plural)
adjective: Marshallese

Ethnic groups: Marshallese 92.1%, mixed Marshallese 5.9%, other 2% (2006)

Languages: Marshallese (official) 98.2%, other
languages 1.8% (1999 census)
note: English (official), widely spoken as a second
language

Religions: Protestant 54.8%, Assembly of God
25.8%, Roman Catholic 8.4%, Bukot nan Jesus

2.8%, Mormon 2.1%, other Christian 3.6%, other 1%, none 1.5% (1999 census)

Population: 72,191 (July 2015 est.)
country comparison to the world: 203

Age structure: *0–14 years:* 36.02% (male 13,256/female 12,749)
15–24 years: 17.4% (male 6,391/female 6,171)
25–54 years: 37.25% (male 13,681/female 13,210)
55–64 years: 5.73% (male 2,120/female 2,017)
65 years and over: 3.6% (male 1,276/female 1,320) (2015 est.)

Median age: *total:* 22.6 years
male: 22.5 years
female: 22.7 years (2015 est.)
country comparison to the world: 172

Population growth rate: 1.66% (2015 est.)
country comparison to the world: 71

Birth rate: 25.6 births/1,000 population (2015 est.)
country comparison to the world: 48

Death rate: 4.21 deaths/1,000 population (2015 est.)
country comparison to the world: 206

Net migration rate: -4.83 migrant(s)/1,000 population (2015 est.)
country comparison to the world: 192

Urbanization: *urban Population:* 72.7% of total population (2015)
rate of urbanization: 0.59% annual rate of change (2010–15 est.)

Major urban areas—Population: MAJURO (capital) 31,000 (2014)

Sex ratio: *at birth:* 1.05 male(s)/female
0–14 years: 1.04 male(s)/female
15–24 years: 1.04 male(s)/female
25–54 years: 1.04 male(s)/female
55–64 years: 1.05 male(s)/female
65 years and over: 0.97 male(s)/female
total population: 1.04 male(s)/female (2015 est.)

Mother's mean age at first birth: 20.7
note: median age at first birth among women 25–29 (2007 est.)

Infant mortality rate: *total:* 20.66 deaths/1,000 live births
male: 23.29 deaths/1,000 live births
female: 17.9 deaths/1,000 live births (2015 est.)
country comparison to the world: 85

Life expectancy at birth: *total population:* 72.84 years
male: 70.67 years
female: 75.13 years (2015 est.)
country comparison to the world: 136

Total fertility rate: 3.15 children born/woman (2015 est.)
country comparison to the world: 52

Contraceptive prevalence rate: 44.6% (2007)

Health expenditures: 16.5% of GDP (2013)
country comparison to the world: 2

Physicians density: 0.44 physicians/1,000 population (2010)

Hospital bed density: 2.7 beds/1,000 population (2010)

Drinking water source: improved:

urban: 93.5% of population
rural: 97.6% of population
total: 94.6% of population
unimproved:
urban: 6.5% of population
rural: 2.4% of population
total: 5.4% of population (2015 est.)

Sanitation facility access:
improved:
urban: 84.5% of population
rural: 56.2% of population
total: 76.9% of population
unimproved:
urban: 15.5% of population
rural: 43.8% of population
total: 23.1% of population (2015 est.)

HIV/AIDS—adult prevalence rate: NA

HIV/AIDS—people living with HIV/AIDS: NA

HIV/AIDS—d eaths: NA

Obesity—adult prevalence rate: 42.3% (2014)
country comparison to the world: 9

GOVERNMENT

Country Name: *conventional long form:* Republic of the Marshall Islands
conventional short form: Marshall Islands
local long form: Republic of the Marshall Islands
local short form: Marshall Islands
abbreviation: RMI
former: Trust Territory of the Pacific Islands, Marshall Islands District
etymology: named after British Captain John MARSHALL, who charted many of the islands in 1788

Government type: presidential republic in free association with the US

Capital: *name:* Majuro

Geographic coordinates: 7 06 N, 1 71 23 E
time difference: UTC+12 (17 hours ahead of Washin gton, DC, during Standard Time)

Administrative divisions: 24 municipalities; Ailinglaplap, Ailuk, Arno, Aur, Bikini & Kili, Ebon, Enewetak & Ujelang, Jabat, Jaluit, Kwajalein, Lae, Lib, Likiep, Majuro, Maloelap, Mejit, Mili, Namdrik, Namu, Rongelap, Ujae, Utrik, Wotho, Wotje

Independence: 21 October 1986 (from the US-administered UN trusteeship)

National holiday: Constitution Day, 1 May (1979)

Constitution: effective 1 May 1979; amended several times, last in 1995 (2016)

Legal system: mixed legal system of US and English common law, customary law, and local statutes

International law organization participation: accepts compulsory ICJ jurisdiction with reservation s; accepts ICCt jurisdiction

Citizenship: *citizenship by birth:* no
citizenship by descent only: at least one parent must be a citizen of the Marshall Islands
dual citizenship recognized: no
residency requirement for naturalization: 5 years

Suffrage: 18 years of age; universal

Executive branch: *chief of state:* President Hilda C. HEINE (since 28 January 2016); note—the president is both chief of state and head of government

head of government: President Hilda C. HEINE (since 28 January 2016)
cabinet: Cabinet nominated by the president from among members of the Nitijela, appointed by Nitijela speaker
elections/appointments: president indirectly elected by the Nitijela from among its members for a 4-year term (no term limits); election last held on 27 January 2016 (next to be held in 2020)
election results: Hilda C. HEINE elected president on 27 January 2016; Parliament vote—Hilda C. HEINE 24, she was the only candidate

Legislative branch: *description:* bicameral legislature consists of the Council of Iroij (12 seats; consists of tribal chiefs chosen by holders of the chieftainship among the constituent islands) and the National Parliament or Nitijela (33 seats); members directly elected by simple majority vote to serve 4-year terms); note—the Council of Iroij advises the Presidential Cabinet and reviews legislation affecting customary law or any traditional practice)
elections: last held on 21 November 2011 (next to be held by November 2015)
election results: percent of vote by party—NA; seats by party—independents 33

Judicial branch: *highest court (s):* Supreme Court (consists of the chief justice and other judges as prescribed by law)
judge selection and term of office: judges appointed by the Cabinet on the recommendation of the Judicial Service Commission and upon the approval of the Nitijela; judges appointed until retirement, normally at age 72
subordinate courts: High Court; District Courts; Traditional Rights Court; Community Courts

Political parties and leaders: traditionally there have been no formally organized political parties; what has existed more closely resembles factions or interest groups because they do not have party headquarters, formal platforms, or party structures; the following two "groupings" have competed in legislative balloting in recent years -Aelon Kein Ad Party [Michael KABUA] and United Democratic Party or UDP [Litokwa TOMEING]

Political pressure groups and leaders: NA

International organization participation: ACP, ADB, AOSIS, FAO, G-77, IAEA, IBRD, ICAO, ICCt, IDA, IFAD, IFC, ILO, IMF, IMO, IMSO, Interpol, IOC, IOM, ITU, OPCW, PIF, Sparteca, SPC, UN, UNCTAD, UNESCO, WHO

Diplomatic representation in the US: *chief of mission:* Ambassador (vacant); Charge d'Affaires Junior AINI (since 25 April 2015)
chancery: 2433 Massachusetts Avenue NW, 1st Floor, Washington, DC 20008
telephone: [1] (202) 234-5414
FAX: [1] (202) 232-3236
consulate(s) general: Honolulu, Springdale (AR)
consulate(s): Agana (Guam)

Diplomatic representation from the US: *chief of mission:* Ambassador Thomas H. ARM-BRUSTER (since 16 August 2012)
embassy: Oceanside, Mejen Weto, Long Island, Majuro
mailing address: P.O. Box 1379, Majuro, Republic of the Marshall Islands 96960-1379
telephone: [692] 247-4011
FAX: [692] 247-4012

Flag description: blue with two stripes radiating from the lower hoist-side corner—orange (top) and white; a white star with four large rays and 20 small rays appears on the hoist side above the two stripes; blue represents the Pacific Ocean, the orange stripe signifies the Ralik Chain or sunset and courage, while the white stripe signifies the Ratak Chain or sunrise and peace; the star symbolizes the cross of Christianity, each of the 24 rays designates one of the electoral districts in the country and the four larger rays highlight the principal cultural centers of Majuro, Jaluit, Wotje, and Ebeye; the rising diagonal band can also be interpreted as representing the equator, with the star showing the archipelago's position just to the north

National symbol(s): a 24-rayed star; national colors: blue, white, orange

National anthem: *name:* "Forever Marshall Islands"
lyrics/music: Amata KABUA
note: adopted 1981

ECONOMY

Economy—overview: US assistance and lease payments for the use of Kwajalein Atoll as a US military base are the mainstay of this small island country. Agricultural production, primarily subsistence, is concentrated on small farms; the most important commercial crops are coconuts and breadfruit. Industry is limited to handicrafts, tuna processing, and copra. Tourism holds some potential. The islands and atolls have few natural resources, and imports exceed exports.
The Marshall Islands received roughly $1 billion in aid from the US during 1986–2001 under the original Compact of Free Association (Compact). In 2002 and 2003, the US and the Marshall Islands renegotiated the Compact's financial package for a 20-year period, from 2004 to 2024. Under the amended Compact, the Marshall Islands will receive roughly $1.5 billion in direct US assistance. Under the amended Compact, the US and Marshall Islands are also jointly funding a Trust Fund for the people of the Marshall Islands that will provide an income stream beyond 2024, when direct Compact aid ends.

GDP (purchasing power parity): $175 million (2015 est.)
$172.3 million (2014 est.
$170.6 million (2013 est.)
note: data are in 2015 US dollars
country comparison to the world: 222

GDP (official exchange rate): $183 million (2015 est.)

GDP—real growth rate: 1.6% (2015 est.)
1% (2014 est.)
-1.1% (2013 est.)
country comparison to the world: 148

GDP—per capita (PPP): $3,200 (2015 est.)
$3,200 (2014 est.)
$3,200 (2013 est.)
note: data are in 2015 US dollars
country comparison to the world: 185

GDP—composition, by sector of origin:
agriculture: 4.4%
industry: 9.9%
services: 85.7% (2013 est.)

Agriculture—products: coconuts, tomatoes, melons, taro, breadfruit, fruits; pigs, chickens

Industries: copra, tuna processing, tourism, craft items (from seashells, wood, and pearls)

Industrial production growth rate: NA%

Labor force: 10,670 (2013 est.)
country comparison to the world: 217

Labor force—by occupation: *agriculture:* 11%
industry: 16.3%
services: 72.7% (2011 est.)

Unemployment rate: 36% (2006 est.)
30.9% (2000 est.)
country comparison to the world: 193

Population below poverty line: NA%

Household income or consumption by percentage share: *lowest:* 10%: NA%
highest: 10%: NA%

Budget: *revenues:* $116.7 million
expenditures: $113.9 million (2013 est.)
Taxes and other revenues: 59.8% of GDP (2013 est.)
country comparison to the world: 6

Budget surplus (+) or deficit (–): 1.4% of GDP (2013 est.)
country comparison to the world: 17

Public debt: 51.3% of GDP (2013)
country comparison to the world: 79

Fiscal year: 1 October—30 September

Inflation rate (consumer prices): -4% (2015 est.)
1.1% (2014 est.)
country comparison to the world: 1

Current account balance: -$1 million (2015 est.)
-$14 million (2014 est.)
country comparison to the world: 53

Exports: $53.7 million (2013 est.)
$58.1 million (2012)
country comparison to the world: 201

Exports—commodities: copra cake, coconut oil, handicrafts, fish

Imports: $133.7 million (2013 est.)
$120.9 million (2012)
country comparison to the world: 214

Imports—commodities: foodstuffs, machinery and equipment, fuels, beverages, tobacco

Debt—external: $97.96 million (2013 est.)
$87 million (2008 est.)
country comparison to the world: 194

Exchange rates: the US dollar is used

COMMUNICATIONS

Telephones—fixed lines: *total subscriptions:* 2,400
subscriptions per 100 inhabitants: 3 (2014 est.)
country comparison to the world: 213

Telephones—mobile cellular: *total:* 15,500
subscriptions per 100 inhabitants: 22 (2014 est.)
country comparison to the world: 212

Telephone system: *general assessment:* digital switching equipment; modern services include telex, cellular, Internet, international calling, caller ID, and leased data circuits
domestic: Majuro Atoll and Ebeye and Kwajalein islands have regular, seven-digit, direct-dial telephones; other islands interconnected by high frequency radiotelephone (used mostly for government purposes) and mini-satellite telephones
international: country code—692; satellite earth stations—2 Intelsat (Pacific Ocean); US Government satellite communications system on Kwajalein (2005)

Broadcast media: no TV broadcast station; a cable network is available on Majuro with programming via videotape replay and satellite relays; 4 radio broadcast stations; American Armed Forces Radio and Television Service (AFRTS) provides satellite radio and television service to Kwajalein Atoll (2009)
Radio broadcast stations: AM 1, FM 3, shortwave 0 (additionally, the American Armed Forces Radio and Television Service (Central Pacific Network) operates one FM and one AM station on Kwajalein Island) (2005)
Television broadcast stations: 2 (both are US military stations; Marshalls Broadcasting Service, a cable company, operates on Majuro) (2005)

Internet country code: .mh

Internet hosts: 3 (2012)
country comparison to the world: 232

Internet users: *total:* 1,700
percent of population: 2.4% (2014 est.)
country comparison to the world: 210

TRANSPORTATION

Airports: 15 (2013)
country comparison to the world: 146

Airports—with paved runways: *total:* 4
1,524 to 2,437 m: 3
914 to 1,523 m: 1 (2013)

Airports—with unpaved runways: *total:* 11
914 to 1,523 m: 10
under 914 m: 1 (2013)

Roadways: total: 2,028 km
paved: 75 km
note: roads are mostly unimproved (2007)
country comparison to the world: 176

Merchant marine: *total:* 1,593
by type: barge carrier 1, bulk carrier 524, cargo 65, carrier 1, chemical tanker 351, container 226, liquefied gas 88, passenger 7, passenger/cargo 1, petroleum tanker 297, refrigerated cargo 13, roll on/roll off 9, vehiclecarrier 10

foreign-owned: 1,465 (Belgium 1, Bermuda 35, Brazil 1, Canada 8, China 14, Croatia 12, Cyprus 40, Denmark 7, Egypt 1, France 7, Germany 248, Greece 408, Hong Kong 3, India 10, Indonesia 1, Iraq 2, Ireland 6, Italy 1, Japan 59, Jersey 11, Kuwait 2, Latvia 19, Malaysia 11, Mexico 2, Monaco 30, Netherlands 21, Norway 75, Pakistan 1, Qatar 29, Romania 2, Russia 5, Singapore 30, Slovenia 6, South Korea 41, Sweden 1, Switzerland 12, Taiwan 8, Turkey 70, UAE 12, UK 12, Ukraine 1, US 200) (2010)
country comparison to the world: 7

Ports and terminals: *major seaport(s):* Enitwetak Island, Kwajalein, Majuro

MILITARY AND SECURITY

Military branches: no regular military forces; Marshall Islands Police (2012)

Military—note: defense is the responsibility of the US

TRANSNATIONAL ISSUES

Disputes—international: claims US territory of Wake Island

Trafficking in persons: *currentsituation:* The Marshall Islands is a source and destination country for Marshallese women and girls and women from East Asia subjected to sex trafficking; Marshallese and foreign women are forced into prostitution in businesses frequented by crew members of fishing and transshipping vessels that dock in Majuro; some Chinese women are recruited to the Marshall Islands with promises of legitimate work and are subsequently forced into prostitution

tier rating: Tier 3—The Marshall Islands do not fully comply with the minimum standards for the elimination of trafficking and is not making significant efforts to do so; the government made no anti-trafficking law enforcement efforts, including developing a written plan to combat trafficking; no new trafficking investigations were opened in 2014, and no prosecutions or convictions were made for the fourth consecutive year; no efforts were made to identify trafficking victims, especially among women in prostitution or men working on foreign fishing vessels in Marshallese waters, and no attempt was made to ensure their access to protective services; limited awareness-raising events were conducted by an international organization (2015)

MAURITANIA

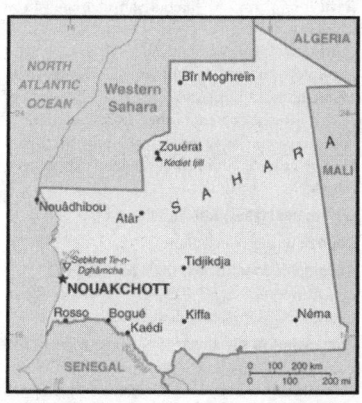

INTRODUCTION

Background: Independent from France in 1960, Mauritania annexed the southern third of the former Spanish Sahara (now Western Sahara) in 1976 but relinquished it after three years of raids by the Polisario guerrilla front seeking independence for the territory. Maaouya Ould Sid Ahmed TAYA seized power in a coup in 1984 and ruled Mauritania with a heavy hand for more than two decades. A series of presidential elections that he held were widely seen as flawed. A bloodless coup in August 2005 deposed President TAYA and ushered in a military council that oversaw a transition to democratic rule. Independent candidate Sidi Ould Cheikh ABDALLAHI was inaugurated in April 2007 as Mauritania's first freely and fairly elected president. His term ended prematurely in August 2008 when a military junta led by General Mohamed Ould Abdel AZIZ deposed him and installed a military council government. AZIZ was subsequently elected president in July 2009 and sworn in the following month. AZIZ sustained injuries from

an accidental shooting by his own troops in October 2012 but has continued to maintain his authority. He was reelected in 2014 to a second and final term as president (according to the present constitu tion) . The country continues to experience ethnic tensions among three major groups: Arabic-speaking descendants of slaves (Haratines), Arabic-speaking "White Moors" (Bidhan), and members of Sub-Saharan ethnic groups mostly originating in the Senegal River valley (Halpulaar, Soninke, and Wolof). Mauritania confronts a terrorism threat by al-Qa'ida in the Islamic Maghreb, which launched successful attacks between 2005 and 2010.

GEOGRAPHY

Location: Western Africa, bordering the North Atlantic Ocean, between Senegal and Western Sahara

Geographic coordinates: 20 00 N, 12 00 W

Map references: Africa

Area: *total:* 1,030,700 sq km
land: 1,030,700 sq km
water: 0 sq km
country comparison to the world: 29

Area—comparative: slightly larger than three times the size of New Mexico

Land boundaries: *total:* 5,002 km
border countries (4): Algeria 460 km, Mali 2,236 km, Senegal 742 km, Western Sahara 1,564 km

Coastline: 754 km

Maritime claims: *territorial sea:* 12 nm
contiguous zone: 24 nm
exclusive economic zone: 200 nm
continental shelf: 200 nm or to the edge of the continental margin

Climate: desert; constantly hot, dry, dusty

Terrain: mostly barren, flat plains of the Sahara; some central hills

Elevation: *mean elevation:* 276 m

elevation extremes: *lowest point:* Sebkhet Te-n-Dghamcha -5 m
highest point: Kediet Ijill 915 m

Natural resources: iron ore, gypsum, copper, phosphate, diamonds, gold, oil, fish

Land use: *agricultural land:* 38.5%
arable land: 0.4%;
permanent crops: 0%;
permanent pasture: 38.1%
forest: 0.2%
other: 61.3% (2011 est.)

Irrigated land: 450 sq km (2012)

Total renewable water resources: 11.4 cu km (2011)

Freshwater withdrawal (domestic/industrial/agricultural): *total:* 1.35 cu km/yr (7%/2%/91%)
per capita: 420.2 cu m/yr (2005)

Natural hazards: hot, dry, dust/sand-laden sirocco wind primarily in March and April; periodic droughts

Environment—current issues: overgrazing, deforestation, and soil erosion aggravated by drought are contributing to desertification; limited natural freshwater resources away from the Senegal, which is the only perennial river; locust infestation

Environment—international agreements: *party to:* Biodiversity, Climate Change, Climate Change-Kyoto Protocol, Desertification, Endangered Species, Hazardous Wastes, Law of the Sea, Ozone Layer Protection, Ship Pollution, Wetlands, Whaling
signed, but not ratified: none of the selected agreements

Geography—note: Mauritania is considered both a part of North Africa's Maghreb region and West Africa's Sahel region; most of the population is concentrated in the cities of Nouakchott and

Nouadhibou and along the Senegal River in the southern part of the country

PEOPLE AND SOCIETY

Nationality: *noun:* Mauritanian(s)
adjective: Mauritanian

Ethnic groups: black Moors (Haratines—Arab-speaking slaves, former slaves, and their descendants of African origin, enslaved by white Moors) 40%, white Moors (of Arab-Berber descent, known as Bidhan) 30%, black Africans (non-Arabic speaking, Halpulaar, Soninke, Wolof, and Bamara ethnic groups) 30%

Languages: Arabic (official and national), Pulaar, Soninke, Wolof (all national languages), French
note: the spoken Arabic in Mauritania differs considerably from the modern standard Arabic used for official written purposes or in the media; the Mauritanian dialect, which incorporates many Berber words, is referred to as Hassaniya

Religions: Muslim (official) 100%

Population: 3,596,702 (July 2015 est.)
country comparison to the world: 132

Age structure: *0–14 years:* 39.18% (male 707,528/female 701,681)
15–24 years: 19.9% (male 350,283/female 365,578)
25–54 years: 32.71% (male 544,670/female 631,891)
55–64 years: 4.55% (male 73,737/female 90,000)
65 years and over: 3.65% (male 55,736/female 75,598) (2015 est.)

Dependency ratios: *total dependency ratio:* 76.1%
youth dependency ratio: 70.5%
elderly dependency ratio: 5.7%
potential support ratio: 17.7% (2015 est.)

Median age: *total:* 20.1 years
male: 19.2 years
female: 21 years (2015 est.)
country comparison to the world: 189

Population growth rate: 2.23% (2015 est.)
country comparison to the world: 37

Birth rate: 31.34 births/1,000 population (2015 est.)
country comparison to the world: 36

Death rate: 8.2 deaths/1,000 population (2015 est.)
country comparison to the world: 88

Net migration rate: -0.83 migrant(s)/1,000 population (2015 est.)
country comparison to the world: 144

Urbanization: *urban Population:* 59.9% of total population (2015)
rate of urbanization: 3.54% annual rate of change (2010–15 est.)

Major urban areas—Population: NOUAKCHOTT (capital) 968,000 (2015)

Sex ratio: *at birth:* 1.03 male(s)/female
0–14 years: 1.01 male(s)/female
15–24 years: 0.96 male(s)/female
25–54 years: 0.86 male(s)/female

55–64 years: 0.82 male(s)/female
65 years and over: 0.74 male(s)/female
total population: 0.93 male(s)/female (2015 est.)

Maternal mortality rate: 602 deaths/100,000 live births (2015 est.)
country comparison to the world: 19

Infant mortality rate: *total:* 54.68 deaths/1,000 live births
male: 59.61 deaths/1,000 live births
female: 49.6 deaths/1,000 live births (2015 est.)
country comparison to the world: 28

Life expectancy at birth: *total population:* 62.65 years
male: 60.35 years
female: 65.02 years (2015 est.)
country comparison to the world: 189

Total fertility rate: 4 children born/woman (2015 est.)
country comparison to the world: 39

Contraceptive prevalence rate: 9.3% (2007)

Health expenditures: 3.8% of GDP (2013)
country comparison to the world: 100

Physicians density: 0.13 physicians/1,000 population (2009)

Hospital bed density: 0.4 beds/1,000 population (2006)

Drinking water source:
improved:
urban: 58.4% of population
rural: 57.1% of population
total: 57.9% of population
unimproved:
urban: 41.6% of population
rural: 42.9% of population
total: 42.1% of population (2015 est.)

Sanitation facility access:
improved:
urban: 57.5% of population
rural: 13.8% of population
total: 40% of population
unimproved:
urban: 42.5% of population
rural: 86.2% of population
total: 60% of population (2015 est.)

HIV/AIDS—adult prevalence rate: 0.66% (2014 est.)
country comparison to the world: 57

HIV/AIDS—people living with HIV/AIDS: 15,900 (2014 est.)
country comparison to the world: 87

HIV/AIDS—deaths: 1,100 (2014 est.)
country comparison to the world: 66

Major infectious diseases: *degree of risk:* very high
food or waterborne diseases: bacterial and protozoal diarrhea, hepatitis A, and typhoid fever
vectorborne diseases: malaria and dengue fever
respiratory disease: meningococcal meningitis
animal contact disease: rabies (2013)

Obesity—adult prevalence rate: 8.6% (2014)
country comparison to the world: 127

Children under the age of 5 years underweight: 19.5% (2012)
country comparison to the world: 32

Education expenditures: 3.3% of GDP (2013)
country comparison to the world: 120

Literacy: *definition:* age 15 and over can read and write
total population: 52.1%
male: 62.6%
female: 41.6% (2015 est.)

School life expectancy (primary to tertiary education): *total:* 8 years
male: 9 years
female: 8 years (2013)

Child labor—children ages 5–14: *total number:* 127,251
percentage: 16% (2007 est.)

GOVERNMENT

Country name: *conventional long form:* Islamic Republic of Mauritania
conventional short form: Mauritania
local long form: Al Jumhuriyah al Islamiyah al Muritaniyah
local short form: Muritaniyah
etymology: named for the ancient Kingdom of Mauretania (3rd century B.C. to 1st century A.D.), which existed further north in present-day Morocco; the name derives from the Mauri (Moors), the Berber-speaking peoples of northwest Africa

Government type: presidential republic

Capital: *name:* Nouakchott

Geographic coordinates: 18 04 N, 15 58 W
time difference: UTC 0 (5 hours ahead of Washington, DC, during Standard Time)

Administrative divisions: 15 regions (wilayas, singular—wilaya); Adrar, Assaba, Brakna, Dakhlet Nouadhibou, Gorgol, Guidimaka, Hodh ech Chargui, Hodh ElGharbi, Inchiri, Nouakchott Nord, Nouakchott Ouest, Nouakchott Sud, Tagant, Tiris Zemmour, Trarza

Independence: 28 November 1960 (from France)

National holiday: Independence Day, 28 November (1960)

Constitution: previous 1964; latest adopted 12 July 1991; amended 2004,2006,2012 (2016)

Legal system: mixed legal system of Islamic and French civil law

International law organization participation: has not submitted an ICJ jurisdiction declaration; non-party state to the ICCt

Citizenship: *citizenship by birth:* no
citizenship by descent only: at least one parent must be a citizen of Mauritania
dual citizenship recognized: no
residency requirement for naturalization: 5 years

Suffrage: 18 years of age; universal

Executive branch: *chief of state:* President Mohamed Ould Abdel AZIZ (since 5 August 2009); note—AZIZ deposed President Sidi Ould

Cheikh ABDELLAHI in a coup and installed himself as president in August 2008; he subsequently retired from the military, stepped down from the appropriated presidency in April 2009 to run for the legitimate presidency, and was elected president on 18 July 2009

head of government: Prime Minister Yahya Ould HADEMINE (since 21 August 2014)
cabinet: Council of Ministers appointed by the president
elections/appointments: president directly elected by absolute majority popular vote in 2 rounds if needed for a 5-year term (eligible for a second term); election last held on 21 June 2014 (next to be held by 2019); prime minister appointed by the president
election results: Mohamed Ould Abdel AZIZ elected president; percent of vote—Mohamed Ould Abdel AZIZ (UPR) 81.9%, Biram Dah ABEID (independent) 8.7%, Boidiel Ould HOUMEIT (El Wiam) 4.5%, Ibrahima Moctar SARR (SJD/MR) 4.4%, other 0.5%

Legislative branch: *description:* bicameral Parliament or Barlamane consists of the Senate or Majlis al-Shuyukh (56 seats; 53 members indirectly elected by municipal leaders by simple majority vote and 3 directly elected by Mauritanians abroad; members serve a 6-year term with one-third of membership renewed every 2 years) and the National Assembly or A IJamiya Al Wataniya (146 seats; 106 members directly elected in single- and two-seat constituencies by absolute majority vote in two rounds if needed and 40 directly elected in constituencies with three or more seats by proportional representation vote; members serve a 5-year term)
elections: Senate—last held on 23 November 2013 (next electionscheduled for 2015 but delayed because of opposition party threats to boycott election); National Assembly—first round last held on 23 November and second round on 21 December 2013 (next to be held in 2018)
election results: Senate—percent of vote by party—NA; seats by party—NA; National Assembly -percent of vote by party—NA; seats by party—UPR 75, RNRD-TAWASSOUL 16, El Wiam 10, APP 7, El Karama Party 6, UDP 6, AJD/MR 4, Burst of Youth for the Nation 4, El Vadila Party 3, PRDR 3, PUD 3, Ravah Party 3, other 6; note—parties winning fewer than 3 seats sit as independents unless they joiNA coalition

Judicial branch: *highest court(s):* Supreme Court or Cour Supreme (subdivided into 1 criminal and 2 civil chambers, each with a president and 5 counselors); Constitutional Council (consists of 6 members)
judge selection and term of office: Supreme Court president appointed by the president of the republic to serve a 5-year renewable term; Constitutional Council members appointed—3 by the president of the republic, 2 by the president of the National Assembly, and 1 by the president of the Senate; members serve single, 9-year terms with one-third of membership renewed every 3 years

subordinate courts: High Court of Justice (cases involving treason and criminal acts of high government officials); courts of appeal; wilaya (regional) courts (located at the headquarters of each of the 13 regions); commercial and labor courts; criminal courts; moughataa (district) courts; informal/customary courts

Political parties and leaders: Alliance for Justice and Democracy/Movement for Renewal or AJD/MR [Ibrahima Moctar SARR]
Burst of Youth for the Nation [Lalla CHERIVA]
Coalition for Pacific Alternation or CAP (coalition of opposition parties, including APP, El Wiam)
Coalition of Majority Parties or CPM (including UPR, UDP)
Coordination of Democratic Opposition or COD [Ahmed Ould DADDAH] (coalition including RNRD—TAWASSOUL)
El Karama Party [Cheikhna Ould Mohamed Ould HAJBOU]
El Vadila Party [Ethmane Ould Ahmed ABOULMAALY]
El Wiam [Boidiel Ould HOUMEIT]
National Rally for Reform and Development or RNRD-TAWASSO UL [Mohamed Jamil Ould MANSOUR]
Party of Unity and Development or PUD [Mohamed BARO]
Popular Progressive Alliance or APP [Messaoud Ould BOULKHEIR]
Ravah Party
Republican Party for Democracy and Renewal or PRDR [Sidi Mohamed Ould Mohamed VALL]
Union for Democracy and Progress or UDP [Naha Mint MOUKNASS]
Union for the Republic or UPR [Sidi Mohamed Ould MAHAM]

Political pressure groups and leaders: General Confederation of Mauritanian Workers or CGTM [Abdallahi Ould MOHAMED, secretary general]
Independent Confederation of Mauritanian Workers or CLTM and El Hor [Samory Ould BEYE] (civil society organization)
Mauritanian Workers Union or UTM [Mohamed Ely Ould BRAHIM, secretary general] SO S-Esclaves [Boubacar MESSAOUD] (anti-slavery group)
other: Arab nationalists; Ba'athists; Islamists; Nasserists

International organization participation: ABEDA, ACP, AfDB, AFESD, AMF, AMU, AU, CAEU (candidate), EITI (compliant country), FAO, G-77, IAEA, IBRD, ICAO, ICC (NGOs), ICRM, IDA, IDB, IFAD, IFC, IFRCS, IHO (pending member), ILO, IMF, IMO, Interpol, IOC, IOM, IPU, ISO (correspondent), ITSO, ITU, ITUC (NGOs), LAS, MIGA, MIUSMA, NAM, OIC, OIF, OPCW, UN, UNCTAD, UNESCO, UNIDO, UNWTO, UPU, WCO, WHO, WIPO, WMO, WTO

Diplomatic representation in the US: *chief of mission:* Ambassador Mohamedoun DADDAH (since 27 June 2016)

chancery: 2129 Leroy Place NW, Washington, DC 20008
telephone: [1] (202) 232-5700 through 5701
FAX: [1] (202) 319-2623

Diplomatic representation from the US: *chief of mission:* Ambassador Larry Edward ANDRE, Jr. (since 25 September 2014)
embassy: 288 Rue Abdallaye, Rue 42–100 (between Presidency building and Spanish Embassy), Nouakchott
mailing address: BP 222, Nouakchott
telephone: [222] 4525-2660, -2663
FAX: [222] 4525-1592

Flag description: green with a yellow five-pointed star above a yellow, horizontal crescent; the closed side of the crescent is down; the crescent, star, and color green are traditional symbols of Islam; green also represents hope for a bright future; the yellow color stands for the sands of the Sahara

National symbol(s): star and crescent; national colors: green, yellow

National anthem: *name:* "Hymne National de la Republique Islamique de Mauritanie" (National Anthem of the Islamic Republic of Mauritania)
lyrics/music: Baba Ould CHEIKH/traditional, arranged by Tolia NIKIPROWETZKY
note: adopted 1960; the unique rhythm of the Mauritanian anthem makes it particularly challenging to sing

ECONOMY

Economy—overview: Mauritania's economy is dominated by natural resources and agriculture. Half the population still depends on agriculture and livestock for a livelihood, even though many nomads and subsistence farmers were forced into the cities by recurrent droughts in the 1970s and 1980s. Recently, GDP growth has been driven by foreign investment in the mining and oil sectors. Mauritania's extensive mineral resources include iron ore, gold, copper, gypsum, and phosphate rock, and exploration is ongoing for uranium, crude oil, and natural gas. Extractive commodities make up about three-quarters of Mauritania's total exports, subjecting the economy to price swings in world commodity markets. Mining is also a growing source of government revenue, rising from 13% to 29% of total revenue between 2006 and 2013. The nation's coastal waters are among the richest fishing areas in the world, and fishing accounts for about 25% of budget revenues, but overexploitation by foreigners threatens this key source of revenue.
Risks to Mauritania's economy include its recurring droughts, dependence on foreign aid and investment, and insecurity in neighboring Mali, as well as significant shortages of infrastructure, institutional capacity, and human capital. Mauritania has sought additional IMF support by focusing efforts on poverty reduction. Investment in agriculture and infrastructure are the largest components of the country's public expenditures.

GDP (purchasing power parity): $16.29 billion (2015 est.)

$15.98 billion (2014 est.)
$15 billion (2013 est.)
note: data are in 2015 US dollars
country comparison to the world: 151

GDP (official exchange rate): $4.752 billion (2015 est.)

GDP—real growth rate: 1.9% (2015 est.)
6.6% (2014 est.)
6.4% (2013 est.)
country comparison to the world: 136

GDP—per capita (PPP): $4,400 (2015 est.)
$4,400 (2014 est.)
$4,200 (2013 est.)
note: data are in 2015 US dollars
country comparison to the world: 173

Gross national saving: 16.3% of GDP (2015 est.)
21.9% of GDP (2014 est.)
29.8% of GDP (2013 est.)
country comparison to the world: 105

GDP—composition, by end use:
household consumption: 50.6%
government consumption: 30.7%
investment in fixed capital: 41%
investment in inventories: 6.6%
exports of goods and services: 24.3%
imports of goods and services: -53.2% (2015 est.)

GDP—composition, by sector of origin:
agriculture: 23.2%
industry: 37.4%
services: 39.4% (2015 est.)

Agriculture—products: dates, millet, sorghum, rice, corn; cattle, sheep

Industries: fish processing, oil production, mining (iron ore, gold, copper)
note: gypsum deposits have never been exploited

Industrial production growth rate: 9.6% (2015 est.)
country comparison to the world: 8

Labor force: 1.318 million (2015 est.)
country comparison to the world: 134

Labor force—by occupation: *agriculture:* 50%
industry: 2%
services: 48% (2001 est.)

Unemployment rate: 31% (2013 est.)
country comparison to the world: 189

Population below poverty line: 40% (2004 est.)

Household income or consumption by percentage share: *lowest:* 10%: 2.5%
highest: 10%: 29.5% (2000)

Distribution of family income—Gini index: 39 (2000)
37.3 (1995)
country comparison to the world: 71

Budget: *revenues:* $2.076 billion
expenditures: $2.22 billion (2015 est.)
Taxes and other revenues: 44.4% of GDP (2015 est.)
country comparison to the world: 26

Budget surplus (+) or deficit (–): -3.1% of GDP (2015 est.)
country comparison to the world: 116

Fiscal year: calendar year

Inflation rate (consumer prices): 0.5% (2015 est.)
3.8% (2014 est.)
country comparison to the world: 64

Central bank discount rate: 9% (31 December 2009)
12% (31 December 2007)
country comparison to the world: 33

Commercial bank prime lending rate: 18% (31 December 2015 est.)
18% (31 December 2014 est.)
country comparison to the world: 21

Stock of domestic credit: $2.157 billion (31 December 2015 est.)
$1.969 billion (31 December 2014 est.)
country comparison to the world: 137

Market value of publicly traded shares: $NA

Current account balance: -$917 million (2015 est.)
-$1.471 billion (2014 est.)
country comparison to the world: 116

Exports: $1.705 billion (2015 est.)
$2.265 billion (2014 est.)
country comparison to the world: 145

Exports—commodities: iron ore, fish and fish products, gold, copper, petroleum

Exports—partners: China 32.7%, Switzerland 11.1%, Spain 8.6%, Italy 6.7%, Cote dIvoire 6.6%, Japan 5.7% (2015)

Imports: $2.142 billion (2015 est.)
$2.74 billion (2014 est.)
country comparison to the world: 160

Imports—commodities: machinery and equipment, petroleum products, capital goods, foodstuffs, consumer goods

Imports—partners: China 25.5%, Algeria 8.4%, France 6.3%, Morocco 5.1%, Spain 4.8%, Brazil 4.5%, US 4% (2015)

Debt—external: $3.807 billion (31 December 2014 est.)
$3.571 billion (31 December 2013 est.)
country comparison to the world: 135

Exchange rates: ouguiyas (MRO) per US dollar—
301.5 (2015 est.)
299.5 (2014 est.)
299.5 (2013 est.)
296.6 (2012 est.)
281.12 (2011 est.)

ENERGY

Electricity—production: 1.035 billion kWh (2012 est.)
country comparison to the world: 148

Electricity—consumption: 962.6 million kWh (2012 est.)
country comparison to the world: 153

Electricity—exports: 0 kWh (2013 est.)
country comparison to the world: 170

Electricity—imports: 0 kWh (2013 est.)
country comparison to the world: 176

Electricity—installed generating capacity: 293,000 kW (2012 est.)
country comparison to the world: 152

Electricity—from fossil fuels: 66.9% of total installed capacity (2012 est.)
country comparison to the world: 119

Electricity—from nuclear fuels: 0% of total installed capacity (2012 est.)
country comparison to the world: 144

Electricity—from hydroelectric plants: 33.1% of total installed capacity (2012 est.)
country comparison to the world: 68

Electricity—from other renewable sources: 0% of total installed capacity (2012 est.)
country comparison to the world: 202

Crude oil—production: 6,003 bbl/day (2014 est.)
country comparison to the world: 83

Crude oil—exports: 11,250 bbl/day (2012 est.)
country comparison to the world: 65

Crude oil—imports: 0 bbl/day (2012 est.)
country comparison to the world: 99

Crude oil—proved reserves: 20 million bbl (1 January 2015 est.)
country comparison to the world: 85

Refined petroleum products—production: 0 bbl/day (2012 est.)
country comparison to the world: 213

Refined petroleum products—consumption: 12,800 bbl/day (2013 est.)
country comparison to the world: 147

Refined petroleum products—exports: 0 bbl/day (2012 est.)
country comparison to the world: 205

Refined petroleum products—imports: 12,810 bbl/day (2012 est.)
country comparison to the world: 130

Natural gas—production: 0 cu m (2013 est.)
country comparison to the world: 105

Natural gas—consumption: 0 cu m (2013 est.)
country comparison to the world: 173

Natural gas—exports: 0 cu m (2013 est.)
country comparison to the world: 149

Natural gas—imports: 0 cu m (2013 est.)
country comparison to the world: 102

Natural gas—proved reserves: 28.32 billion cu m (1 January 2014 est.)
country comparison to the world: 70

Carbon dioxide emissions from consumption of energy: 2.408 million Mt (2012 est.)
country comparison to the world: 146

COMMUNICATIONS

Telephones—fixed lines: *total subscriptions:* 51,400
subscriptions per 100 inhabitants: 1 (2014 est.)
country comparison to the world: 160

Telephones—mobile cellular: *total:* 3.8 million
subscriptions per 100 inhabitants: 107 (2014 est.)
country comparison to the world: 126

Telephone system: *general assessment:* limited system of cable and open-wire lines, minor microwave radio relay links, and radiotelephone communications stations; mobile-cellular services expanding rapidly *domestic:* Mauritel, the national telecommunications company, was privatized in 2001 but remains the monopoly provider of fixed-line services; fixed-line teledensity 2 per 100 persons; mobile-cellular network coverage extends mainly to urban areas with a teledensity of roughly 106 per 100 persons; mostly cable and open-wire lines; a domestic satellite telecommunications system links Nouakchott with regional capitals

international: country code—222; satellite earth stations—3 (1 Intelsat—Atlantic Ocean, 2 Arabsat); fiber-optic and asymmetric digital subscriber line cables for Internet access (2009)

Broadcast media: one state-run TV (Television de Mauritanie) and one state-run radio network (Radio de Mauritanie); Television de Mauritanie has three channels, AlMahadra station (for Islamic content) and Channels 1 and 2, which cover news, sports, and other programming; Radio de Mauritanie runs 12 regional stations, as well as a radio station for youth and the Holy Quran station; five private TV channels and five private radio stations also broadcast from Mauritania; six private international radio stations broadcast in Mauritania on the FM band; with satellite connections, Mauritanians also have access to hundreds of foreign TV channels (2013)

Radio broadcast stations: AM 1, FM 14, shortwave 1 (2001)

Television broadcast stations: 1 (2002)

Internet country code: .mr

Internet hosts: 22 (2012)
country comparison to the world: 220

Internet users: *total:* 402,000
percent of population: 11.4% (2014 est.)
country comparison to the world: 134

TRANSPORTATION

Airports: 30 (2013)
country comparison to the world: 116
Airports—with paved runways: *total:* 9
2,438 to 3,047 m: 5
1,524 to 2,437 m: 4 (2013)
Airports—with unpaved runways: *total:* 21
2,438 to 3,047 m: 1
1,524 to 2,437 m: 10
914 to 1,523 m: 8
under 914 m: 2 (2013)
Railways: *total:* 728 km
standard gauge: 728 km 1.435-m gauge (2014)
country comparison to the world: 99
Roadways: *total:* 10,628 km
paved: 3,158 km
unpaved: 7,470 km (2010)
country comparison to the world: 133
Waterways: (some navigation possible on the Senegal River) (2011)
Ports and terminals: *major seaport(s):* Nouadhibou, Nouakchott

MILITARY AND SECURITY

Military branches: Mauritanian Armed Forces: Army, Mauritanian Navy (Marine Mauritanienne; includes naval infantry), Islamic Republic of Mauritania Air Group (Groupement Aerienne Islamique de Mauritanie, GAIM) (2013)

Military service age and obligation: 18 is the legal minimum age for voluntary military service; no conscription (2012)

TRANSNATIONAL ISSUES

Disputes—international: Mauritanian claims to Western Sahara remain dormant

Refugees and internally displaced persons: *refugees (country of origin):* 26,001 (Western Saharan—Sahrawis) (2014); 41,255 (Mali) (2016)

Trafficking in persons: *current situation:* Mauritania is a source and destination country for men, women, and children subjected to forced labor and sex trafficking; adults and children from traditional slave castes are subjected to slavery-related practices rooted in ancestral master-slave relationships; Mauritanian boy students called talibes are trafficked within the country by religious teachers for forced begging; Mauritanian girls, as well as girls from Mali, Senegal, The Gambia, and other West African countries, are forced into domestic servitude; Mauritanian women and girls are forced into prostitution domestically or transported to countries in the Middle East for the same purpose, sometimes through forced marriages

tier rating: Tier 3—Mauritania does not fully comply with the minimum standards for the elimination of trafficking and is not making significant efforts to do so; anti-trafficking law enforcement efforts were negligible; one slavery case identified by an NGO was investigated, but no prosecutions or convictions were made, including among the 4,000 child labor cases NGOs referred to the police; the 2007 anti-slavery law remains ineffective because it requires slaves, most of whom are illiterate, to file their own legal complaint, and the government agency that can submit claims on them did not file any in 2014; authorities arrested, prosecuted, and convicted several anti-slavery activists; NGOs continued to provide the majority of protective services to trafficking victims without support from the government; some steps were taken to raise public awareness about human trafficking (2015)

MAURITIUS

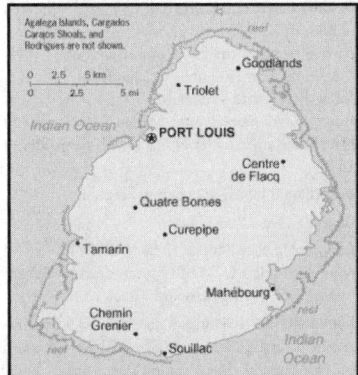

first explored by the Portuguese in the 16th century and subsequently settled by the Dutch—who named it in honor of Prince Maurits van NASSAU—in the 17th century. The French assumed control in 1715, developing the island into an important naval base overseeing Indian Ocean trade, and establishing a plantation economy of sugar cane. The British captured the island in 1810, during the Napoleonic Wars. Mauritius remained a strategically important British naval base, and later an air station, playing an important role during World War II for anti-submarine and convoy operations, as well as the collection of signals intelligence. Independence from the UK was attained in 1968. A stable democracy with regular free elections and a positive human rights record, the country has attracted considerable foreign investment and has one of Africa's highest per capita incomes.

INTRODUCTION

Background: Although known to Arab and Malay sailors as early as the 10th century, Mauritius was

GEOGRAPHY

Location: Southern Africa, island in the Indian Ocean, about 800 km (500 mi) east of Madagascar

Geographic coordinates: 20 17 S, 57 33 E

Map references: Africa

Area: *total:* 2,040 sq km
land: 2,030 sq km
water: 10 sq km
note: includes Agalega Islands, Cargados Carajos Shoals (Saint Brandon), and Rodrigues
country comparison to the world: 181

Area—comparative: almost 11 times the size of Washington, DC

Land boundaries: 0 km

Coastline: 177 km

Maritime claims: measured from claimed archipelagic straight baselines
territorial sea: 12 nm
exclusive economic zone: 200 nm
continental shelf: 200 nm or to the edge of the continental margin

Climate: tropical, modified by southeast trade winds; warm, dry winter (May to November); hot, wet, humid summer (November to May)

Terrain: small coastal plain rising to discontinuous mountains encircling central plateau

Elevation: *mean elevation:* NA

elevation extremes: *lowest point:* Indian Ocean 0 m
highest point: Mont Piton 828 m

Natural resources: arable land, fish

Land use: *agricultural land:* 43.8%
arable land: 38.4%;
permanent crops: 2%;
permanent pasture: 3.4%
forest: 17.3%
other: 38.9% (2011 est.)

Irrigated land: 190 sq km (2012)

Total renewable water resources: 2.75 cu km (2011)

Freshwater withdrawal (domestic/industrial/agricultural): *total:* 0.73 cu km/yr (30%/3%/68%)
per capita: 568.2 cu m/yr (2003)

Natural hazards: cyclones (November to April); almost completely surrounded by reefs that may pose maritime hazards

Environment—current issues: water pollution, degradation of coral reefs

Environment—international agreements: *party to:* Antarctic-Marine Living Resources, Biodiversity, Climate Change, Climate Change-Kyoto Protocol, Desertification, Endangered Species, Environmental Modification, Hazardous Wastes, Law of the Sea, Marine Life Conservation, Ozone Layer Protection, Ship Pollution, Wetlands
signed, but not ratified: none of the selected agreements

Geography—note: the main island, from which the country derives its name, is of volcanic origin and is almost entirely surrounded by coral reefs; former home of the dodo, a large flightless bird related to pigeons, driven to extinction by the end of the 17th century through a combination of hunting and the introduction of predatory species

PEOPLE AND SOCIETY

Nationality: *noun:* Mauritian(s)

adjective: Mauritian

Ethnic groups: Indo-Mauritian 68%, Creole 27%, Sino-Mauritian 3%, Franco-Mauritian 2%

Languages: Creole 86.5%, Bhojpuri 5.3%, French 4.1%, two languages 1.4%, other 2.6% (includes English, the official language, which is spoken by less than 1% of the population), unspecified 0.1% (2011 est.)

Religions: Hindu 48.5%, Roman Catholic 26.3%, Muslim 17.3%, other Christian 6.4%, other 0.6%, none 0.7%, unspecified 0.1% (2011 est.)

Population: 1,339,827 (July 2015 est.)
country comparison to the world: 157

Age structure: *0–14 years:* 20.74% (male 141928/ female 135,918)
15–24 years: 15.3% (male 103,549/female 101,469)
25–54 years: 44% (male 294,700/female 294,863)

55–64 years: 11.15% (male 70,810/female 78,599)
65 years and over: 8.81% (male 47,900/female 70,091) (2015 est.)

Dependency ratios: *total dependency ratio:* 40.6%
youth dependency ratio: 27.2%
elderly dependency ratio: 13.4%
potential support ratio: 7.4% (2015 est.)

Median age: *total:* 34.4 years
male: 33.5 years
female: 35.3 years (2015 est.)
country comparison to the world: 77

Population growth rate: 0.64% (2015 est.)
country comparison to the world: 150

Birth rate: 13.29 births/1,000 population (2015 est.)
country comparison to the world: 151

Death rate: 6.91 deaths/1,000 population (2015 est.)
country comparison to the world: 135

Net migration rate: 0 migrant(s)/1,000 population (2015 est.)
country comparison to the world: 88

Urbanization: *urban Population:* 39.7% of total population (2015)
rate of urbanization: -0.08% annual rate of change (2010–15 est.)

Major urban areas—Population: PORT LOUIS (capital) 135,000 (2014)

Sex ratio: *at birth:* 1.05 male(s)/female
0–14 years: 1.04 male(s)/female
15–24 years: 1.02 male(s)/female
25–54 years: 1 male(s)/female
55–64 years: 0.9 male(s)/female
65 years and over: 0.68 male(s)/female
total population: 0.97 male(s)/female (2015 est.)

Maternal mortality rate: 53 deaths/100,000 live births (2015 est.)
country comparison to the world: 99

Infant mortality rate: *total:* 10.3 deaths/1,000 live births
male: 12.24 deaths/1,000 live births
female: 8.26 deaths/1,000 live births (2015 est.)
country comparison to the world: 135

Life expectancy at birth: *total population:* 75.4 years
male: 71.94 years
female: 79.03 years (2015 est.)
country comparison to the world: 100

Total fertility rate: 1.76 children born/woman (2015 est.)
country comparison to the world: 160

Health expenditures: 4.8% of GDP (2013)
country comparison to the world: 145

Physicians density: 1.62 physicians/1,000 population (2013)

Hospital bed density: 3.4 beds/1,000 population (2011)

Drinking water source:
improved:
urban: 99.9% of population
rural: 99.8% of population

total: 99.9% of population
unimproved:
urban: 0.1% of population
rural: 0.2% of population
total: 0.1% of population (2015 est.)

Sanitation facility access:
improved:
urban: 93.9% of population
rural: 92.6% of population
total: 93.1% of population
unimproved:
urban: 6.1% of population
rural: 7.4% of population
total: 6.9% of population (2015 est.)

HIV/AIDS—adult prevalence rate: 0.92% (2014 est.)
country comparison to the world: 49

HIV/AIDS—people living with HIV/AIDS: 8,300 (2014 est.)
country comparison to the world: 101

HIV/AIDS—deaths: 500 (2014 est.)
country comparison to the world: 88

Obesity—adult prevalence rate: 18.8% (2014)
country comparison to the world: 105

Education expenditures: 5% of GDP (2014)
country comparison to the world: 123

Literacy: *definition:* age 15 and over can read and write
total population: 90.6%
male: 92.9%
female: 88.5% (2015 est.)

School life expectancy (primary to tertiary education): *total:* 15 years
male: 15 years
female: 16 years (2014)

Unemployment, youth ages 15–24: *total:* 23.2%
male: 17.3%
female: 32% (2013 est.)
country comparison to the world: 41

GOVERNMENT

Country name: *conventional long form:* Republic of Mauritius
conventional short form: Mauritius
local long form: Republic of Mauritius
local short form: Mauritius
note: island named after Prince Maurice VAN NASSAU, stadtholder of the Dutch Republic, in 1598

Government type: parliamentary republic

Capital: *name:* Port Louis

Geographic coordinates: 20 09 S, 57 29 E
time difference: UTC+4 (9 hours ahead of Washington, DC, during Standard Time)

Administrative divisions: 9 districts and 3 dependencies*; Agalega Islands*, Black River, Cargados Carajos Shoals*, Flacq, Grand Port, Moka, Pamplemousses, Plaines Wilhems, Port Louis, Riviere du Rempart, Rodrigues*, Savanne

Independence: 12 March 1968 (from the UK)

National holiday: Independence Day, 12 March (1968); Republic Day, 12 March (1992)

Constitution: several previous; latest adopted 12 March 1968; amended many times, last in 2015 (2016)

Legal system: civil legal system based on French civil law with some elements of English common law

International law organization participation: accepts compulsory ICJ jurisdiction with reservations; accepts ICCt jurisdiction

Citizenship: *citizenship by birth:* yes
citizenship by descent: yes
dual citizenship recognized: yes
residency requirement for naturalization: 5 out of the previous 7 years including the last 12 months

Suffrage: 18 years of age; universal

Executive branch: *chief of state:* President Ameenah GURIB-FAKIM (since 5 June 2015); Vice President Paramaslyum (aka Barlen) Pillay VYAPOORY (since 4 April 2016)

head of government: Prime Minister Sir Anerood JUGNAUTH (since 17 December 2014)
cabinet: Cabinet of Ministers (Council of Ministers) appointed by the president on the recommendation of the prime minister
elections/appointments: president and vice president indirectly elected by the National Assembly for a 5-year term (eligible for a second term); election last held on 4 June 2015 (next to be held in 2020); prime minister and deputy prime minister appointed by the president, responsible to the National Assembly
election results: Ameenah GURIB-FAKIM (independent) elected president by the National Assembly-unanimo US vote

Legislative branch: *description:* unicameral National Assembly or Assemblee Nationale (70 seats maximum; 62 members directly elected in single- and multi-seat constituencies by simple majority vote and up to 8 seats allocated to non-elected party candidates by the Electoral Commissioner's Office to ensure fair and adequate representation of each community and party in the Assembly, as outlined in the Constitution; members serve 5-year terms)
elections: last held on 10 December 2014 (next to be held by 2019); note—the National Assembly was dissolved on 6 October 2014, resulting in early elections
election results: percent of vote by party—Alliance Lepep 49.8%, PTR-MMM 38.5%, FSM 2.1%, OPR 1.1%, other 8.5%; elected seats by party—Alliance Lepep 47, PTR-MMM 13, OPR 2; appointed seats Alliance Lepep 4, PTR-MMM 3, non-elected candidate 1

Judicial branch: *highest court(s):* Supreme Court of Mauritius (consists of the chief justice, a senior puisne judge, and 17 puisne judges); note—the Judicial Committee of the Privy Council (in London) serves as the final court of appeal
judge selection and term of office: chief justice appointed by the president after consultation with the prime minister; senior puisne judge appointed by the president with the advice of the chief justice; other puisne judges appointed by the president with the advice of the Judicial and Legal Commission, a 4-member body of judicial officials including the chief justice; all judges serve until retirement at age 67
subordinate courts: Court of Civil Appeal; Court of Criminal Appeal; Public Bodies Appeal Tribunal (formed by a 2008 constitutional amendment)

Political parties and leaders: Alliance Lepep (Alliance of the People) [Sir Anerood JUGNAUTH] (coalition including MSM, PMSD, and ML)
Labor Party (Parti Travailliste) or PTR or MLP [Navinchandra RAMGOOLAM]
Mauritian Militant Movement (Mouvement Militant Mauricien) or MMM [Paul BERENGER]
Mauritian Social Democratic Party (Parti Mauricien Social Democrate) or PMSD [Xavier Luc DUVAL]
Mauritian Solidarity Front (Front Solidarite Mauricienne) or FSM [Ceh FAKEERM EEAH, known as Cehl MEEAH]
Militant Socialist Movement (Mouvement Socialist Mauricien) or MSM [Pravind JUGNAUTH]
Muvman Liberator or ML [Ivan COLLENDAVELLOO]
Rodrigues Peoples Organization (Organisation du Peuple Rodriguais) or OPR [Serge CLAIR]

Political pressure groups and leaders: Lalit Political Party
Rezizans ek Alternativ (Resistance and Alternative) Say No to Coal!
other: various labor unions

International organization participation: ACP, AfDB, AOSIS, AU, C, CD, COMESA, CPLP (associate), FAO, G-77, IAEA, IBRD, ICAO, ICC (NGOs), ICCt, ICRM, IDA, IFAD, IFC, IFRCS, IHO, ILO, IMF, IMO, IMSO, InO C, Interpol, IOC, IOM, IPU, ISO, ITSO, ITU, ITUC (NGOs), MIGA, NAM, OIF, OPCW, PCA, SAARC (observer), SADC, UN, UNCTAD, UNESCO, UNIDO, UNWTO, UPU, WCO, WFTU (NGOs), WHO, WIPO, WMO, WTO

Diplomatic representation in the US: *chief of mission:* Ambassador Sooroojdev PHOKEER (since 3 August 2015)
chancery: 1709 N Street NW, Washington, DC 20036; administrative offices at 3201 Connecticut Avenue NW, Suite 441, Washington, DC 20036
telephone: [1] (202) 244-1491 through 1492
FAX: [1] (202) 966-0983

Diplomatic representation from the US: *chief of mission:* Ambassador (vacant); Charge d'Affaires Susan FALATKO (since 26 February 2016); note—also accredited to Seychelles
embassy: 4th Floor, Rogers House, John Kennedy Street, Port Louis
mailing address: international mail: P.O. Box 544, Port Louis; US mail: American Embassy, Port Louis, US Department of State, Washington, DC 20521-2450
telephone: [230] 202-4400
FAX: [230] 208-9534

Flag description: four equal horizontal bands of red (top), blue, yellow, and green; red represents self-determination and independence, blue the Indian Ocean surrounding the island, yellow has been interpreted as the new light of independence, golden sunshine, or the bright future, and green can symbolize either agriculture or the lush vegetation of the island

National symbol(s): dodo bird; national flower: Trochetia Boutoniana; nation al colors: red, blue, yellow, green

National anthem: *name:* "Motherland"
lyrics/music: Jean Georges PROSPER/Philippe GENTIL
note: adopted 1968

ECONOMY

Economy—overview: Since independence in 1968, Mauritius has undergone a remarkable economic transformation from a low-income, agriculturally based economy to a diversified, upper middle-income economy with growing industrial, financial, and tourist sectors. Mauritius has achieved steady growth over the last several decades, resulting in more equitable income distribution, increased life expectancy, lowered infant mortality, and a much-improved infrastructure.

The economy currently rests on sugar, tourism, textiles and apparel, and financial services, but is expanding into fish processing, information and communications technology, and hospitality and property development. Sugarcane is grown on about 90% of the cultivated land area and accounts for 15% of export earnings. The government's development strategy centers on creating vertical and horizontal clusters of development in these sectors. Mauritius has attracted more than 32,000 offshore entities, many aimed at commerce in India, South Africa, and China. Investment in the banking sector alone has reached over $1 billion. Mauritius' textile sector has taken advantage of the Africa Growth and Opportunity Act, a preferential trade program that allows duty free access to the US market, with Mauritian exports to the US growing by 40% from 2000 to 2014.

Mauritius' sound economic policies and prudent banking practices helped to mitigate negative effects of the global financial crisis in 2008–09. GDP grew in the 3–4% per year range in 2010–14, and the country continues to expand its trade and investment outreach around the globe. Growth in the US and Europe fostered goods and services exports, including tourism, while lower oil prices kept inflation low in 2015.

GDP (purchasing power parity): $24.57 billion (2015 est.)
$23.76 billion (2014 est.)
$22.93 billion (2013 est.)
note: data are in 2015 US dollars
country comparison to the world: 138

GDP (official exchange rate): $11.61 billion (2015 est.)

GDP—real growth rate: 3.4% (2015 est.)
3.6% (2014 est.)
3.2% (2013 est.)
country comparison to the world: 86

GDP—per capita (PPP): $19,500 (2015 est.)
$18,900 (2014 est.)
$18,200 (2013 est.)
note: data are in 2015 US dollars
country comparison to the world: 87

Gross national saving: 20.4% of GDP (2015 est.)
18.4% of GDP (2014 est.)
19.8% of GDP (2013 est.)
country comparison to the world: 80

GDP—composition, by end use:
household consumption: 73.1%
government consumption: 14.8%
investment in fixed capital: 20.7%
investment in inventories: 2.7%
exports of goods and servi ces: 57.9%
imports of goods and services: -69.2% (2015 est.)

GDP—composition, by sector of origin:
agriculture: 4.5%
industry: 21.7%
services: 73.8% (2015 est.)

Agriculture—products: sugarcane, tea, corn, potatoes, bananas, pulses; cattle, goats; fish

Industries: food processing (largely sugar milling), textiles, clothing, mining, chemicals, metal products, transport equipment, nonelectrical machinery, tourism

Industrial production growth rate: 0.9% (2015 est.)
country comparison to the world: 149

Labor force: 610,400 (2015 est.)
country comparison to the world: 155

Labor force—by occupation: *agriculture and fish ing:* 9%
construction and industry: 30%
transportation and communication: 7%
trade, restaurants, hotels: 22%
finance: 6%
other services: 25% (2007)

Unemployment rate: 7.7% (2015 est.)
7.8% (2014 est.)
country comparison to the world: 90

Population below poverty line: 8% (2006 est.)

Household income or consumption by percentage share: *lowest:* 10%: NA%
highest: 10%: NA%

Distribution of family income—Gini index: 35.9 (2012 est.)
39 (2006 est.)
country comparison to the world: 89

Budget: *revenues:* $2.212 billion
expenditures: $2.602 billion (2015 est.)
Taxes and other revenues: 19.1% of GDP (2015 est.)
country comparison to the world: 165

Budget surplus (+) or deficit (–): -3.4% of GDP (2015 est.)
country comparison to the world: 128

Public debt: 61.1% of GDP (2015 est.)
61% of GDP (2014 est.)
country comparison to the world: 59

Fiscal year: 1 July—30 June

Inflation rate (consumer prices): 1.3% (2015 est.)
3.2% (2014 est.)
country comparison to the world: 90

Central bank discount rate: 9% (31 December 2010)
country comparison to the world: 36

Commercial bank prime lending rate: 8.5% (31 December 2015 est.)
8.5% (31 December 2014 est.)
country comparison to the world: 103

Stock of narrow money: $2.324 billion (31 December 2015 est.)
$2.634 billion (31 December 2014 est.)
country comparison to the world: 122

Stock of broad money: $12.6 billion (31 December 2014 est.)
$12.15 billion (31 December 2013 est.)
country comparison to the world: 100

Stock of domestic credit: $12.39 billion (31 December 2015 est.)
$14.08 billion (31 December 2014 est.)
country comparison to the world: 99

Market value of publicly traded shares:
$7.093 billion (31 December 2012 est.)
$7.667 billion (31 December 2011)
$7.442 billion (31 December 2010 est.)
country comparison to the world: 81

Current account balance: -$590 million (2015 est.)
-$713 million (2014 est.)
country comparison to the world: 105

Exports: $2.826 billion (2015 est.)
$3.109 billion (2014 est.)
country comparison to the world: 129

Exports—commodities: clothing and textiles, sugar, cut flowers, molasses, fish, primates (for research)

Exports—partners: UK 13.2%, UAE 12.4%, France 11.9%, US 10.7%, South Africa 8.6%, Madagascar 6.5%, Italy 5.4%, Spain 4.4% (2015)

Imports: $4.573 billion (2015 est.)
$5.361 billion (2014 est.)
country comparison to the world: 130

Imports—commodities: manufactured goods, capital equipment, foodstuffs, petroleum products, chemicals

Imports—partners: India 18.7%, China 17.8%, France 7.1%, South Africa 6.5%, Vietnam 4.4% (2015)

Reserves of foreign exchange and gold: $3.732 billion (31 December 2015 est.)
$3.919 billion (31 December 2014 est.)
country comparison to the world: 101

Debt—external: $11.83 billion (31 December 2014 est.)
$10.92 billion (31 December 2013 est.)
country comparison to the world: 102

Stock of direct foreign investment—at home: NA

Stock of direct foreign investment—abroad: $NA

Exchange rates: Mauritian rupees (MUR) per US dollar—
36.81 (2015 est.)
30.622 (2014 est.)
30.622 (2013 est.)
30.05 (2012 est.)
28.706 (2011 est.)

ENERGY

Electricity—production: 2.885 billion kWh (2013 est.)
country comparison to the world: 134

Electricity—consumption: 2.658 billion kWh (2013 est.)
country comparison to the world: 139

Electricity—exports: 0 kWh (2013 est.)
country comparison to the world: 169

Electricity—imports: 0 kWh (2013 est.)
country comparison to the world: 175

Electricity—installed generating capacity: 778,200 kW (2013 est.)
country comparison to the world: 129

Electricity—from fossil fuels: 96.5% of total installed capacity (2013 est.)
country comparison to the world: 60

Electricity—from nuclear fuels: 0% of total installed capacity (2013 est.)
country comparison to the world: 143

Electricity—from hydroelectric plants: 3.3% of total installed capacity (2013 est.)
country comparison to the world: 130

Electricity—from other renewable sources: 0.2% of total installed capacity (2013 est.)
country comparison to the world: 107

Crude oil—production: 0 bbl/day (2014 est.)
country comparison to the world: 169

Crude oil—exports: 0 bbl/day (2012 est.)
country comparison to the world: 163

Crude oil—imports: 0 bbl/day (2012 est.)
country comparison to the world: 98

Crude oil—proved reserves: 0 bbl (1 January 2015 est.)
country comparison to the world: 169

Refined petroleum products—production: 0 bbl/day (2012 est.)
country comparison to the world: 212

Refined petroleum products—consumption: 24,000 bbl/day (2013 est.)
country comparison to the world: 123

Refined petroleum products—exports: 0 bbl/day (2012 est.)
country comparison to the world: 204

Refined petroleum products—imports: 23,980 bbl/day (2012 est.)
country comparison to the world: 103

Natural gas—production: 0 cu m (2013 est.)
country comparison to the world: 104

Natural gas—consumption: 0 cu m (2013 est.)
country comparison to the world: 172

Natural gas—exports: 0 cu m (2013 est.)
country comparison to the world: 148

Natural gas—imports: 0 cu m (2013 est.)
country comparison to the world: 101

Natural gas—proved reserves: 0 cu m (1 January 2014 est.)
country comparison to the world: 172

Carbon dioxide emissions from consumption of energy: 5.317 million Mt (2012 est.)
country comparison to the world: 126

COMMUNICATIONS

Telephones—fixed lines: *total subscriptions:* 370,000
subscriptions per 100 inhabitants: 28 (2014 est.)
country comparison to the world: 110

Telephones—mobile cellular: *total:* 1.7 million
subscriptions per 100 inhabitants: 124 (2014 est.)
country comparison to the world: 153

Telephone system: *general assessment:* small system with good service
domestic: monopoly over fixed-line services terminated in 2005; fixed-line teledensity roughly 30 per 100 persons; mobile-cellular services launched in 1989 with current teledensity roughly 100 per 100 persons
international: country code—230; landing point for the SAFE submarine cable that provides links to Asia and South Africa where it connects to the SAT-3/WASC submarine cable that provides further links to parts of East Africa, and Europe; satellite earth station—1 Intelsat (Indian Ocean); new microwave link to Reunion; HF radiotelephone links to several countries (2011)

Broadcast media: the government maintains control over TV broadcasting through the Mauritius Broadcasting Corporation (MBC), which operates 3 analog and 10 digital TV stations; MBC is a shareholder in a local company that operates 2 pay-TV station s; the state retains the largest radio broadcast network with multiple station s; several private radio broadcasters have entered the market sin ce 2001; tran smissions of at least 2 in tern ation al broadcasters are available (2007)
Radio broadcast stations: AM 4, FM 9, shortwave 0 (2001)
Television broadcast stations: 2 (plus several repeaters) (1997)

Internet country code: .mu

Internet hosts: 51,139 (2012)
country comparison to the world: 95

Internet users: *total:* 81,700
percent of population: 6.1% (2014 est.)
country comparison to the world: 175

TRANSPORTATION

Airports: 5 (2013)
country comparison to the world: 182

Airports—with paved runways: *total:* 2
over 3,047 m: 1
914 to 1,523 m: 1 (2013)

Airports—with unpaved runways: *total:* 3
914 to 1,523 m: 2
under 914 m: 1 (2013)

Roadways: *total:* 2,149 km
paved: 2,149 km (includes 75 km of expressways) (2012)
country comparison to the world: 174

Merchant marine: *total:* 4
by type: passen ger/cargo 2, petroleum tan ker 1, refrigerated cargo 1 (2010)
country comparison to the world: 132

Ports and terminals: *major seaport(s):* Port Louis

MILITARY AND SECURITY

Military branches: no regular military forces; Mauritius Police Force, Special Mobile Force, National Coast Guard (2011)

Military expenditures: 0.19% of GDP (2012)
0.16% of GDP (2011)
0.19% of GDP (2010)
country comparison to the world: 130

TRANSNATIONAL ISSUES

Disputes—international: Mauritius and Seychelles claim the Chagos Islands; claims French-administered Tromelin Island

Trafficking in persons: *current situation:* Mauritius is a source, transit, and destination country for men, women, and children subjected to forced labor and sex trafficking; Mauritian girls are induced or sold into prostitution, often by peers, family members, or businessmen offering other forms of employment; Mauritian adults have been identified as labor trafficking victims in the UK, Belgium, and Canada, while Mauritian women from Rodrigues Island are also subject to domestic servitude in Mauritius; Malagasy women transit Mauritius en route to the Middle East for jobs as domestic servants and subsequently are subjected to forced labor; Cambodian men are victims of forced labor on foreign fishing vessels in Mauritius' territorial waters; other migrant workers from East and South Asia and Madagascar are also subject to forced labor in Mauritius' manufacturing and construction sectors

tier rating: Tier 2 Watch List—Mauritius does not fully comply with the minimum standards for the elimination of trafficking; however, it is making significant efforts to do so; in 2014, the government made modest efforts to address child sex trafficking but none related to adult forced labor; law enforcement lacks an understanding of trafficking crimes outside of child sex trafficking, despite increasing evidence of other forms of human trafficking; authorities made no trafficking prosecutions or convictions and made modest efforts to assist a couple of child sex trafficking victims; officials sustained an extensive public awareness campaign to prevent child sex trafficking, but no efforts were made to raise awareness or reduce demand for forced adult or child labor (2015)

Illicit drugs: consumer and transshipment point for heroin from South Asia; small amounts of cannabis produced and consumed locally; significant offshore financial industry creates potential for money laundering, but corruption levels are relatively low and the government appears generally to be committed to regulating its banking industry

MEXICO

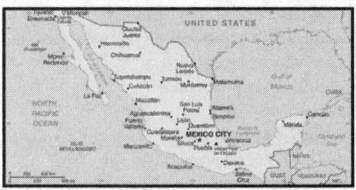

INTRODUCTION

Background: The site of several advanced Amerindian civilizations—including the Olmec, Toltec, Teotihuacan, Zapotec, Maya, and Aztec—Mexico was conquered and colonized by Spain in the early 16th century. Administered as the Viceroyalty of New Spain for three centuries, it achieved independence early in the 19th century. Elections held in 2000 marked the first time since the 1910 Mexican Revolution that an opposition candidate—Vicente FOX of the National Action Party (PAN)—defeated the party in government, the Institutional Revolutionary Party (PRI) . He was succeeded in 2006 by another PAN candidate Felipe CALDERON, but Enrique PENA NIETO regained the presidency for the PRI in 2012. The global financial crisis in late 2008 caused a massive economic downturn in Mexico the following year, although growth returned quickly in 2010. Ongoing economic and social concerns include low real wages, high underemployment, inequitable income distribution, and few advancement opportunities for the largely indigenous population in the impoverished southern states. Since 2007, Mexico's powerful drug-trafficking organizations have engaged in bloody feuding, resulting in tens of thousands of drug-related homicides.

GEOGRAPHY

Location: North America, bordering the Caribbean Sea and the Gulf of Mexico, between Belize and the United States and bordering the North Pacific Ocean, between Guatemala and the United States

Geographic coordinates: 23 00 N, 102 00 W

Map references: North America

Area: *total:* 1964,375 sq km
land: 1943,945 sq km
water: 20,430 sq km
country comparison to the world: 14

Area—comparative: slightly less than three times the size of Texas

Land boundaries: *total:* 4,389 km
border countries (3): Belize 276 km, Guatemala 958 km, US 3,155 km

Coastline: 9,330 km

Maritime claims: *territorial sea:* 12 nm
contiguous zone: 24 nm
exclusive economic zone: 200 nm
continental shelf: 200 nm or to the edge of the continental margin

Climate: varies from tropical to desert

Terrain: high, rugged mountains; low coastal plains; high plateaus; desert

Elevation: mean elevation: 1,111 m

elevation extremes: *lowest point:* Laguna Salada -10 m
highest point: Volcan Pico de Orizaba 5,675 m

Natural resources: petroleum, silver, copper, gold, lead, zinc, natural gas, timber

Land use: *agricultural land:* 54.9%;
arable land: 11.8%;
permanent crops: 1.4%;
permanent pasture: 41.7%;
forest: 33.3%
other: 11.8% (2011 est.)

Irrigated land: 65,000 sq km (2012)

Total renewable water resources: 457.2 cu km (2011)

Freshwater withdrawal (domestic/industrial/agricultural): *total:* 80.4 cu km/yr (14%/9%/77%)
per capita: 700.4 cu m/yr (2009)

Natural hazards: tsunam is along the Pacific coast, volcanoes and destructive earthquakes in the center and south, and hurricanes on the Pacific, Gulf of Mexico, and Caribbean coasts
volcanism: volcanic activity in the central-southern part of the country; the volcanoes in Baja California are mostly dormant; Colima (elev. 3,850 m), which erupted in 2010, is Mexico's most active volcano and is responsible for causing periodic evacuations of nearby villagers; it has been deemed a Decade Volcano by the International Association of Volcanology and Chemistry of the Earth's Interior, worthy of study due to its explosive history and close proxim ity to hum an populations; Popocatepetl (elev. 5, 426 m) poses a threat to Mexico City; other historically active volcanoes include Barcena, Ceboruco, El Chichon, Michoacan-Guanajuato, Pico de Orizaba, San Martin, Socorro, and Tacana

Environment—current issues: scarcity of hazardous waste disposal facilities; rural to urban migration; natural freshwater resources scarce and polluted in north, inaccessible and poor quality in center and extreme southeast; raw sewage and industrial effluents polluting rivers in urban areas; deforestation; widespread erosion; desertification; deteriorating agricultural lands; serious air and water pollution

in the national capital and urban centers along US-Mexico border; land subsidence in Valley of Mexico caused by groundwater depletion
note: the government considers the lack of clean water and deforestation national security issues

Environment—international agreements: *party to:* Biodiversity, Climate Change, Climate Change-Kyoto Protocol, Desertification, Endangered Species, Hazardous Wastes, Law of the Sea, Marine Dumping, Marine Life Conservation, Ozone Layer Protection, Ship Pollution, Wetlands, Whaling
signed, but not ratified: none of the selected agreements

Geography—note: strategic location on southern border of US; corn (maize), one of the world's major grain crops, is thought to have originated in Mexico

PEOPLE AND SOCIETY

Nationality: *noun:* Mexican(s)
adjective: Mexican

Ethnic groups: mestizo (Amerindian-Spanish) 62%, predominantly Amerindian 21%, Amerindian 7%, other 10% (mostly European)
note: Mexico does not collect census data on ethnicity (2012 est.)

Languages: Spanish only 92.7%, Spanish and indigenous languages 5.7%, indigenous only 0.8%, unspecified 0.8%
note: indigenous languages include various Mayan, Nahuatl, and other regional languages (2005)

Religions: Roman Catholic 82.7%, Pentecostal 1.6%, Jehovah's Witnesses 1.4%, other Evangelical Churches 5%, other 1.9%, none 4.7%, unspecified 2.7% (2010 est.)

Population: 121,736,809 (July 2015 est.)
country comparison to the world: 12

Age structure: *0–14 years:* 27.59% (male 17,178,327/female 16,412,337)
15–24 years: 17.9% (male 11,027,564/female 10,759,446)
25–54 years: 40.55% (male 23,785,345/female 25,576,645)
55–64 years: 7.19% (male 4,017,721/female 4,734,391)
65 years and over: 6.77% (male 3,709,873/female 4,535,160) (2015 est.)

Dependency ratios: *total dependency ratio:* 51.7%
youth dependency ratio: 41.9%
elderly dependency ratio: 9.8%
potential support ratio: 10.2% (2015 est.)

Median age: *total:* 27.6 years
male: 26.6 years
female: 28.7 years (2015 est.)
country comparison to the world: 131

Population growth rate: 1.18% (2015 est.)
country comparison to the world: 102

Birth rate: 18.78 births/1,000 population (2015 est.)
country comparison to the world: 92

Death rate: 5.26 deaths/1,000 population (2015 est.)

country comparison to the world: 181

Net migration rate: -1.68 migrant(s)/1,000 population (2015 est.)
country comparison to the world: 160

Urbanization: *urban Population:* 79.2% of total population (2015)
rate of urbanization: 1.57% annual rate of change (2010–15 est.)

Major urban areas—Population: MEXICO CITY (capital) 20.999 million; Guadalajara 4.843 million; Monterrey 4.513 million; Puebla 2.984 million; Toluca de Lerdo 2.164 million; Tijuana 1.987 million (2015)

Sex ratio: *at birth:* 1.05 male(s)/female
0–14 years: 1.05 male(s)/female
15–24 years: 1.03 male(s)/female
25–54 years: 0.93 male(s)/female
55–64 years: 0.85 male(s)/female
65 years and over: 0.82 male(s)/female
total population: 0.96 male(s)/female (2015 est.)

Mother's mean age at first birth: 21.3 (2008 est.)

Maternal mortality rate: 38 deaths/100,000 live births (2015 est.)
country comparison to the world: 108

Infant mortality rate: *total:* 12.23 deaths/1,000 live births
male: 13.64 deaths/1,000 live births
female: 10.74 deaths/1,000 live births (2015 est.)
country comparison to the world: 122

Life expectancy at birth: *total population:* 75.65 years
male: 72.88 years
female: 78.55 years (2015 est.)
country comparison to the world: 95

Total fertility rate: 2.27 children born/woman (2015 est.)
country comparison to the world: 94

Contraceptive prevalence rate: 72.5% (2009)

Health expenditures: 6.2% of GDP (2013)
country comparison to the world: 108

Physicians density: 2.1 physicians/1,000 population (2011)

Hospital bed density: 1.5 beds/1,000 population (2011)

Drinking water source:
improved:
urban: 97.2% of population
rural: 92.1% of population
total: 96.1% of population
unimproved:
urban: 2.8% of population
rural: 7.9% of popu lation
total: 3.9% of population (2015 est.)

Sanitation facility access:
improved:
urban: 88% of population
rural: 74.5% of population
total: 85.2% of population
unimproved:
urban: 12% of population
rural: 25.5% of population

total: 14.8% of population (2015 est.)

HIV/AIDS—adult prevalence rate: 0.23% (2014 est.)
country comparison to the world: 95

HIV/AIDS—people living with HIV/AIDS: 194,100 (2014 est.)
country comparison to the world: 30

HIV/AIDS—deaths: 6,000 (2014 est.)
country comparison to the world: 28

Major infectious diseases: *degree of risk:* intermediate
food or waterborne diseases: bacterial diarrhea and hepatitis A
vectorborne disease: dengue fever (2013)
Obesity—adult prevalence rate: 27.6% (2014)
country comparison to the world: 23

Children under the age of 5 years underweight: 2.8% (2012)
country comparison to the world: 117

Education expenditures: 5.2% of GDP (2011)
country comparison to the world: 72

Literacy: *definition:* age 15 and over can read and write
total population: 95.1%
male: 96.2%
female: 94.2% (2012 est.)

School life expectancy (primary to tertiary education): *total:* 13 years
male: 13 years
female: 13 years (2014)

Child labor—children ages 5–14: *total number:* 1,105,617
percentage: 5% (2009 est.)

Unemployment, youth ages 15–24: *total:* 9.2%
male: 8.5%
female: 10.5% (2013 est.)
country comparison to the world: 104

GOVERNMENT

Country name: *conventional long form:* United Mexican States
conventional short form: Mexico
local long form: Estados Unidos Mexicanos
local short form: Mexico
etymology: named after the Mexica, the largest and most powerful branch of the Aztecs; the meaning of the name is uncertain

Government type: federal presidential republic

Capital: *name:* Mexico City (Distrito Federal)

Geographic coordinates: 19 26 N, 99 08 W
time difference: UTC-6 (1 hour behind Washington, DC, during Standard Time)
daylight saving time: +1hr, begins first Sunday in April; ends last Sunday in October
note: Mexico has four time zones

Administrative divisions: 31 states (estados, singular—estado) and 1 federal district* (distrito federal); Aguascalientes, Baja California, Baja California Sur, Campeche, Chiapas, Chihuahua, Coahuila de Zaragoza, Colima, Distrito Federal*, Durango, Guanajuato, Guerrero, Hidalgo, Jalisco, Mexico, Michoacan de Ocampo, Morelos, Nayarit, Nuevo Leon, Oaxaca, Puebla, Queretaro, Quintana Roo, San Luis Potosi, Sinaloa, Sonora, Tabasco, Tamaulipas, Tlaxcala, Veracruz de Ignacio de la Llave (Veracruz), Yucatan, Zacatecas

Independence: 16 September 1810 (declared); 27 September 1821 (recognized by Spain)

National holiday: Independence Day, 16 September (1810)

Constitution: several previous; latest approved 5 February 1917; amended many times, last in 2015 (2016)

Legal system: civil law system with US constitutional law influence; judicial review of legislative acts

International law organization participation: accepts compulsory ICJ jurisdiction with reservations; accepts ICCt jurisdiction

Citizenship: *citizenship by birth:* yes
citizenship by descent: yes
dual citizenship recognized: not specified
residency requirement for naturalization: 5 years

Suffrage: 18 years of age; universal and compulsory

Executive branch: *chief of state:* President Enrique PENA NIETO (since 1 December 2012); note—the president is both chief of state and head of government

head of government: President Enrique PENA NIETO (since 1 December 2012)
cabinet: Cabinet appointed by the president; note—appointment of attorney general, the head of the Bank of Mexico, and senior treasury officials require consent of the Senate
elections/appointments: president directly elected by simple majority popular vote for a single 6-year term; election last held on 1 July 2012 (next to be held in July 2018)
election results: Enrique PENA NIETO elected president; percent of vote—Enrique PENA NIETO (PRI) 38.2%, Andres Manuel LOPEZ OBRADOR (PRD) 31.6%, Josefina Eugenia VAZQUEZ Mota (PAN) 25.4%, other 4.8%

Legislative branch: *description:* bicameral National Congress or Congreso de la Union consists of the Senate or Camara de Senadores (128 seats; 96 members directly elected in multi-seat constituencies by simple majority vote and 32 directly elected in a single, nationwide constituency by proportional representation vote; members serve 6-year terms) and the Chamber of Deputies or Camara de Diputados (500 seats; 300 members directly elected in single-seat constituencies by simple majority vote and 200 directly elected in a single, nationwide constituency by proportional representation vote; members serve 3-year terms)
elections: Senate—last held on 1 July 2012 for all of the seats (next to be held 1 July 2018); Chamber of Deputies—last held on 7 June 2015 (next to be held on 1 July 2018)
election results: Senate—percent of vote by party—NA; seats by party—PRI 52, PAN 38, PRD 22, PVEM 9, PT 4, Movimiento Ciudadano 2, PANAL 1; Chamber of Deputies—percent of vote by party—NA; seats by party—PRI 203, PAN 108, PRD 56, PVEM 47, MORENA 35, MC 26, PNA/PANAL 10, PES 8, PT 6, independent 1

Judicial branch: *highest court(s):* Supreme Court of Justice or Suprema Corte de Justicia de la Nacion (consists of the chief justice and 11 justices and organized into civil, criminal, administrative, and labor panels) and the Electoral Tribunal of the Federal Judiciary (organized into the superior court, with 7 judges including the court president and 5 regional courts, each with 3 judges)
judge selection and term of office: Supreme Court justices nominated by the president of the republic and approved by two-th irds vote of the members present in the Senate; justices serve for life; Electoral Tribunal superior and regional court judges nominated by the Supreme Court and elected by two-thirds vote of members present in the Senate; superior court president elected from among its members to hold office for a single-renewable 4-year term; other judges of the superior and regional courts serve staggered, single-renewable 9-year terms
subordinate courts: federal level includes circuit, collegiate, and unitary courts; state and district level courts

Political parties and leaders: Citizen's Movement (Movimiento Ciudadano) or MC [Dante DELGADO Rannaoro]
Institutional Revolutionary Party (Partido Revolucionario Institucional) or PRI [Cesar CAMACHO Quiroz]
Labor Party (Partido del Trabajo) or PT [Alberto ANAYA Gutierrez]
Mexican Green Ecological Party (Partido Verde Ecologista de Mexico) or PVEM [Jorge Emilio GONZALEZ Torres]
Movement for National Regeneration (Movimiento Regeneracion Nacional) or MORENA [Marti BATRES]
National Action Party (Partido Accion Nacional) or PAN [Gustavo MADERO Munoz]
New Alliance Party (Partido Nueva Alianza) or PNA/PANAL [Luis CASTRO Obregon]
Party of the Democratic Revolution (Partido de la Revolucion Democratica) or PRD [Jesus ZAMBRANO Grijalva]
Social Encounter Party (Partido Encuentro Social) or PES [Hugo Eric FLORES Cervantes]

Political pressure groups and leaders: Businessmen's Coordinating Council or CCE
Confederation of Employers of the Mexican Republic or COPARMEX
Confederation of Industrial Chambers or CONCAMIN
Confederation of Mexican Workers or CTM
Confederation of National Chambers of Commerce or CONCANACO
Coordinator for Foreign Trade Business Organizations or COECE
Federation of Unions Providing Goods and Services or FESEBES
National Chamber of Transformation Industries or CANACINTRA
National Confederation of Popular Organizations or CNOP

National Coordinator for Education Workers or CNTE

National Peasant Confederation or CNC

National Small Business Chamber or CANACOPE

National Syndicate of Education Workers or SNTE

National Union of Workers or UNT

Popular Assembly of the People of Oaxaca or APPO

Roman Catholic Church

International organization participation: APEC, Australia Group, BCIE, BIS, CAN (observer), Caricom (observer), CD, CDB, CE (observer), CELAC, CSN (observer), EBRD, FAO, FATF, G-3, G-15, G-20, G-24, G-5, IADB, IAEA, IBRD, ICAO, ICC (national committees), ICCt, ICRM, IDA, IFAD, IFC, IFRCS, IHO, ILO, IMF, IMO, IMSO, Interpol, IOC, IOM, IPU, ISO, ITSO, ITU, ITUC (NGOs), LAES, LAIA, MIGA, NAFTA, NAM (observer), NEA, NSG, OAS, OECD, OPANAL, OPCW, Pacific Alliance, Paris Club (associate), PCA, SICA (observer), UN, UNASUR (observer), UNCTAD, UNESCO, UNHCR, UNIDO, Union Latina (observer), UNWTO, UPU, WCO, WFTU (NGOs), WHO, WIPO, WMO, WTO

Diplomatic representation in the US: *chief of mission:* Ambassador Miguel BASANEZ Ebergenyi (since 17 September 2015)

chancery: 1911 Pennsylvania Avenue NW, Washington, DC 20006

telephone: [1] (202) 728-1600

FAX: [1] (202) 728-1698

consulate(s) general: Atlanta, Austin, Boston, Chicago, Dallas, Denver, El Paso (TX), Houston, Laredo (TX), Los Angeles, Miami, New York, Ngales (AZ), Phoenix, Sacramento (CA), San Antonio (TX), San Diego, San Francisco, San Jose (CA), San Juan (Puerto Rico), Saint Paul (MN)

consulate(s): Albuquerque (NM), Anchorage (AK), Boise (ID), Brownsville (TX), Calexico (CA), Del Rio (TX), Detroit, Douglas (AZ), Eagle Pass (TX), Fresno (CA), Indianapolis (IN), Kansas City (MO), Las Vegas (N V), Little Rock (AR), McAllen (TX), Minneapolis (MN), New Orleans, Omaha (NE), Orlando (FL), Oxnard (CA), Philadelphia, Portland (OR), Presidio (TX), Raleigh (NC), Salt Lake City, San Bernardino (CA), Santa Ana (CA), Seattle, Tucson (AZ), Yuma (AZ); note—Washington DC Consular Section is located in a separate building from the Mexican Embassy and has jurisdiction over DC, parts of Virginia, Maryland, and West Virginia

Diplomatic representation from the US: *chief of mission:* Ambassador Roberta JACOBSON (since 20 June 2016)

embassy: Paseo de la Reforma 305, Colonia Cuauhtemoc, 06500 Mexico, Distrito Federal

mailing address: P.O. Box 9000, Brownsville, TX 78520–9000

telephone: [52] (55) 5080-2000

FAX: [52] (55) 5080-2834

consulate(s) general: Ciudad Juarez, Guadalajara, Hermosillo, Matamoros, Merida, Monterrey, Nogales, Nuevo Laredo, Tijuana

Flag description: three equal vertical bands of green (hoist side), white, and red; Mexico's coat of arms (an eagle with a snake in its beak perched on a cactus) is centered in the white band; green signifies hope, joy, and love; white represents peace and honesty; red stands for hardiness, bravery, strength, and valor; the coat of arms is derived from a legend that the wandering Aztec people were to settle at a location where they would see an eagle on a cactus eating a snake; the city they founded, Tenochtitlan, is now Mexico City

note: similar to the flag of Italy, which is shorter, uses lighter shades of red and green, and does not display anything in its white band

National symbol(s): golden eagle; national colors: green, white, red

National anthem: *name:* "Himno Nacional Mexicano" (National Anthem of Mexico)

lyrics/music: Francisco Gonzalez BOCANEGRA/ Jaime Nuno ROCA

note: adopted 1943, in use since 1854; also known as "Mexicanos, algrito de Guerra" (Mexicans, to the War Cry); according to tradition, Francisco Gonzalez BOCANEGRA, an accomplished poet, was uninterested in submitting lyrics to a national anthem contest; his fiancee locked him in a room and refused to release him until the lyrics were completed

ECONOMY

Economy—overview: Mexico's $2.2 trillion economy has become increasingly oriented toward manufacturing in the 22 years since the North American Free Trade Agreement (NAFTA) entered into force. Per capita income is roughly one-third that of the US; income distribution remains highly unequal.

Mexico has become the US' second-largest export market and third-largest source of imports. In 2014, two-way trade in goods and services exceeded $590 billion. Mexico has free trade agreements with 46 countries, putting more than 90% of trade under free trade agreements. In 2012, Mexico formally joined the Trans-Pacific Partnership negotiations and formed the Pacific Alliance with Peru, Colombia, and Chile. Mexico's current government, led by President Enrique PENA NIETO, emphasized economic reforms during its first two years in office, passing and implementing sweeping education, energy, financial, fiscal, and telecommunications reform legislation, among others, with the long-term aim to improve competitiveness and economic growth across the Mexican economy. Mexico began holding public auctions of exploration and development rights to select oil and gas resources in 2015 as a part of reforms that allow for private investment in the oil, gas, and electricity sectors. The second and third auctions demonstrated the capacity for the Mexican Government to adapt and improve the terms of the contracts to garner sufficient interest from investors amid low oil prices.

Although the economy experienced stronger growth in 2014–15 as a result of increased investment and stronger demand for Mexican exports, growth is predicted to remain below potential

given falling oil production, weak oil prices, structural issues such as low productivity, high inequality, a large informal sector employing over half of the workforce, weak rule of law, and corruption. Over the medium-term, the economy is vulnerable to global economic pressures, such as lower external demand, rising interest rates, and low oil prices—approximately 20% of government revenue comes from the state-owned oil company, PEMEX. The increasing integration of supply chains, development of energy sectors, and government-to-government focus on trade facilitation will continue to make the North American region increasingly competitive and contribute to Mexican economic development and strength.

GDP (purchasing power parity):
$2.227 trillion (2015 est.)
$2.172 trillion (2014 est.)
$2.124 trillion (2013 est.)
note: data are in 2015 US dollars
country comparison to the world: 12

GDP (official exchange rate): $1.144 trillion (2015 est.)

GDP—real growth rate: 2.5% (2015 est.)
2.3% (2014 est.)
1.3% (2013 est.)
country comparison to the world: 119

GDP—per capita (PPP):
$17,500 (2015 est.)
$17,300 (2014 est.)
$17,200 (2013 est.)
note: data are in 2015 US dollars
country comparison to the world: 94

Gross national saving: 19.9% of GDP (2015 est.)
19.6% of GDP (2014 est.)
19.3% of GDP (2013 est.)
country comparison to the world: 83

GDP—composition, by end use:
household consumption: 67.3%
government consumption: 12.1%
investment in fixed capital: 21.2%
investment in inventories: -0.7%
exports of goods and services: 38.4%
imports of goods and services: -38.3% (2015 est.)

GDP—composition, by sector of origin:
agriculture: 3.5%
industry: 34.1%
services: 62.4% (2015 est.)

Agriculture—products: corn, wheat, soybeans, rice, beans, cotton, coffee, fruit, tomatoes; beef, poultry, dairy products; wood products

Industries: food and beverages, tobacco, chemicals, iron and steel, petroleum, mining, textiles, clothing, motor vehicles, consumer durables, tourism

Industrial production growth rate: 3.3% (2015 est.)
country comparison to the world: 75

Labor force: 52.81 million (2015 est.)
country comparison to the world: 13

Labor force—by occupation: *agriculture:* 13.4%
industry: 24.1%
services: 61.9% (2011)

Unemployment rate: 4.5% (2015 est.)
4.8% (2014 est.)
note: underemployment may be as high as 25%

country comparison to the world: 44

Population below poverty line: 52.3%
note: based on food-based definition of poverty; asset-based poverty amounted to more than 47% (2012 est.)

Household income or consumption by percentage share: *lowest:* 10%: 2%
highest: 10%: 37.5% (2010)

Distribution of family income—Gini index: 48.3 (2008)
53.1 (1998)
country comparison to the world: 26

Budget: *revenues:* $259.6 billion
expenditures: $300.5 billion (2015 est.)
Taxes and other revenues: 22.3% of GDP (2015 est.)
country comparison to the world: 139

Budget surplus (+) or deficit (–): -3.5% of GDP (2015 est.)
country comparison to the world: 131

Public debt: 45.2% of GDP (2015 est.)
42.1% of GDP (2014 est.)
country comparison to the world: 98

Fiscal year: calendar year

Inflation rate (consumer prices): 2.7% (2015 est.)
4% (2014 est.)
country comparison to the world: 132

Central bank discount rate: 4.5% (31 December 2012)
4.5% (31 December 2011)
country comparison to the world: 83

Commercial bank prime lending rate: 3.7% (31 December 2015 est.)
3.55% (31 December 2014 est.)
country comparison to the world: 163

Stock of narrow money: $180.8 billion (31 December 2015 est.)
$195.6 billion (31 December 2014 est.)
country comparison to the world: 23

Stock of broad money: $826.7 billion (31 December 2014 est.)
$727 billion (31 December 2013 est.)
country comparison to the world: 20

Stock of domestic credit: $389 billion (31 December 2015 est.)
$412.5 billion (31 December 2014 est.)
country comparison to the world: 30

Market value of publicly traded shares:
$525.1 billion (31 December 2012 est.)
$408.7 billion (31 December 2011)
$454.3 billion (31 December 2010 est.)
country comparison to the world: 22

Current account balance: -$32.38 billion (2015 est.)
-$24.85 billion (2014 est.)
country comparison to the world: 191

Exports: $430.9 billion (2015 est.)
$398.3 billion (2014 est.)
country comparison to the world: 12

Exports—commodities: manufactured goods, oil and oil products, silver, fruits, vegetables, coffee, cotton

Exports—partners: US 81.1% (2015)

Imports: $434.8 billion (2015 est.)
$400.4 billion (2014 est.)
country comparison to the world: 10

Imports—commodities: metalworking machines, steel mill products, agricultural machinery, electrical equipment, automobile parts for assem bly and repair, aircraft, aircraft parts

Imports—partners: US 47.3%, China 17.7%, Japan 4.4% (2015)

Reserves of foreign exchange and gold: $204.1 billion (31 December 2015 est.)
$195.9 billion (31 December 2014 est.)
country comparison to the world: 13

Debt—external: $424.1 billion (31 December 2014 est.)
$397.3 billion (31 December 2013 est.)
country comparison to the world: 29

Stock of direct foreign investment—at home: $361 billion (31 December 2015 est.)
$338 billion (31 December 2014 est.)
country comparison to the world: 19

Stock of direct foreign investment—abroad: $142.8 billion (31 December 2015 est.)
$131.2 billion (31 December 2014 est.)
country comparison to the world: 29

Exchange rates: Mexican pesos (MXN) per US dollar—
15.88 (2015 est.)
13.292 (2014 est.)
13.292 (2013 est.)
13.17 (2012 est.)
12.423 (2011 est.)

ENERGY

Electricity—production: 278.7 billion kWh (2012 est.)
country comparison to the world: 15

Electricity—consumption: 234 billion kWh (2012 est.)
country comparison to the world: 16

Electricity—exports: 1.288 billion kWh (2013 est.)
country comparison to the world: 51

Electricity—imports: 607 million kWh (2013 est.)
country comparison to the world: 73

Electricity—installed generating capacity: 62.29 million kW (2012 est.)
country comparison to the world: 17

Electricity—from fossil fuels: 74.2% of total installed capacity (2012 est.)
country comparison to the world: 101

Electricity—from nuclear fuels: 2.5% of total installed capacity (2012 est.)
country comparison to the world: 28

Electricity—from hydroelectric plants: 18.7% of total installed capacity (2012 est.)
country comparison to the world: 96

Electricity—from other renewable sources: 4.7% of total installed capacity (2012 est.)
country comparison to the world: 60

Crude oil—production: 2.459 million bbl/day (2014 est.)

country comparison to the world: 11

Crude oil—exports: 1.22 million bbl/day (2013 est.)
country comparison to the world: 13

Crude oil—imports: 9,884 bbl/day (2013 est.)
country comparison to the world: 76

Crude oil—proved reserves: 9.812 billion bbl (1 January 2015 est.)
country comparison to the world: 17

Refined petroleum products—production: 1.438 million bbl/day (2013 est.)
country comparison to the world: 14

Refined petroleum products—consumption: 1.966 million bbl/day (2014 est.)
country comparison to the world: 12

Refined petroleum products—exports: 171,200 bbl/day (2013 est.)
country comparison to the world: 37

Refined petroleum products—imports: 563,300 bbl/day (2013 est.)
country comparison to the world: 13

Natural gas—production: 45.4 billion cu m (2014 est.)
country comparison to the world: 19

Natural gas—consumption: 73.26 billion cu m (2014 est.)
country comparison to the world: 10

Natural gas—exports: 172 million cu m (2014 est.)
country comparison to the world: 43

Natural gas—imports: 27.39 billion cu m (2014 est.)
country comparison to the world: 13

Natural gas—proved res erves: 483.5 billion cu m (1 January 2014 est.)
country comparison to the world: 31

Carbon dioxide emissions from consumption of energy: 453.8 million Mt (2012 est.)
country comparison to the world: 16

COMMUNICATIONS

Telephones—fixed lines: *total subscriptions:* 21.1 million
subscriptions per 100 inhabitants: 18 (2014 est.)
country comparison to the world: 14

Telephones—mobile cellular: *total:* 102.2 million
subscriptions per 100 inhabitants: 85 (2014 est.)
country comparison to the world: 14

Telephone system: *general assessment:* adequate telephone service for business and government; improving quality and increasing mobile cellular availability, with mobile subscribers far outnumbering fixed-line subscribers; domestic satellite system with 120 earth stations; extensive microwave radio relay network; considerable use of fiber-optic cable and coaxial cable
domestic: despite the opening to competition in January 1997, Telmex remains dominant; fixed-line teledensity is less than 20 per 100 persons; mobile-cellular teledensity is about 80 per 100 persons
international: country code—52; Columbus-2 fiber-optic submarine cable with access to the

US, Virgin Islands, Canary Islands, Spain, and Italy; the Americas Region Caribbean Ring System (ARCOS-1) and the MAYA-1 submarine cable system together provide access to Central America, parts of South America and the Caribbean, and the US; satellite earth stations—120 (32 Intelsat, 2 Solidaridad (giving Mexico improved access to South America, Central America, and much of the US as well as enhancing domestic communications),1 Panamsat, numerous Inmarsat mobile earth stations); linked to Central American Microwave System of trunk connections (2011)

Broadcast media: many TV stations and more than 1,400 radio stations with most privately owned; the Televisa group once had a virtual monopoly in TV broadcasting, but new broadcasting groups and foreign satellite and cable operators are now available (2012)
Radio broadcast stations: AM 851, FM 726, shortwave 15 (2009)
Television broadcast stations: 729 (2009)

Internet country code: . mx
Internet hosts: 16.233 million (2012)
country comparison to the world: 9
Internet users: total: 49.5 million
percent of population: 41.1% (2014 est.)
country comparison to the world: 12

TRANSPORTATION

Airports: 1,714 (2013)
country comparison to the world: 3

Airports—with paved runways: total: 243
over 3,047 m: 12
2,438 to 3,047 m: 32
1,524 to 2,437 m: 80
914 to 1,523 m: 86
under 914 m: 33 (2013)

Airports—with unpaved runways: total: 1,471
over 3,047 m: 1
2,438 to 3,047 m: 1
1,524 to 2,437 m: 42
914 to 1,523 m: 281
under 914 m: 1,146 (2013)

Heliports: 1 (2013)

Pipelines: gas 18,074 km; liquid petroleum 2,102 km; oil 8,775 km; oil/gas/water 369 km; refined products 7,565 km; water 123 km (2013)

Railways: total: 15,389 km
standard gauge: 15,389 km 1.435-m gauge (27 km electrified) (2014)
country comparison to the world: 18

Roadways: total: 377,660 km
paved: 137,544 km (includes 7,176 km of expressways)
unpaved: 240,116 km (2012)
country comparison to the world: 19

Waterways: 2,900 km (navigable rivers and coastal canals mostly connected with ports on the country's east coast) (2012)
country comparison to the world: 33

Merchant marine: total: 52
by type: bulk carrier 5, cargo 3, chemical tanker 11, liquefied gas 3, passenger/cargo 10, petroleum tanker 17, roll on/roll off 3
foreign-owned: 5 (France 1, Greece 2, South Africa 1, UAE 1)
registered in other countries: 12 (Antigua and Barbuda 1, Marshall Islands 2, Panama 5, Portugal 1, Spain 1, Venezuela 1, unknown 1) (2010)
country comparison to the world: 70

Ports and terminals: *major seaport(s):* Altamira, Coatzacoalcos, Lazaro Cardenas, Manzanillo, Veracruz
container port(s) (TEUs): Manzanillo (1992,176), Lazaro Cardenas (1,242,777) (2012)
oil terminals: Cayo Arcas terminal, Dos Bocas terminal
LNG terminal(s) (import): Altamira, Ensenada
cruise port(s): Cancun, Cozumel, Ensenada

MILITARY AND SECURITY

Military branches: Secretariat of National Defense (Secretaria de Defensa Nacional, Sedena): Army (Ejercito), Mexican Air Force (Fuerza Aerea Mexicana, FAM); Secretariat of the Navy (Secretaria de Marina, Semar): Mexican Navy (Armada de Mexico (ARM); includes Naval Air Force (FAN), Mexican Naval Infantry Corps (Cuerpo de Infanteria de Marina, Mexmar or CIM)) (2013)

Military service age and obligation: 18 years of age for compulsory military service, conscript service obligation is 12 months; 16 years of age with consent for voluntary enlistment; conscripts serve only in the Army; Navy and Air Force service is all voluntary; women are eligible for voluntary military service; cadets enrolled in military schools from the age of 15 are considered members of the armed forces (2012)

Military expenditures: 0.59% of GDP (2012)
0.56% of GDP (2011)
0.59% of GDP (2010)
country comparison to the world: 124

TRANSNATIONAL ISSUES

Disputes—international: abundant rainfall in recent years along much of the Mexico-US border region has ameliorated periodically strained water-sharing arrangements; the US has intensified security measures to monitor and control legal and illegal personnel, transport, and commodities across its border with Mexico; Mexico must deal with thousands of impoverished Guatemalans and other Central Americans who cross the porous border looking for work in Mexico and the US; Belize and Mexico are working to solve minor border demarcation discrepancies arising from inaccuracies in the 1898 border treaty

Refugees and internally displaced persons: *IDPs:* 287,000 (government's quashing of Zapatista uprising in 1994 in eastern Chiapas Region; drug cartel violence and government's military response since 2007; violence between and within indigenous groups) (2015)
stateless persons: 13 (2015)

Illicit drugs: major drug-producing and transit nation; world's second largest opium poppy cultivator; opium poppy cultivation in 2009 rose 31% over 2008 to 19,500 hectares yielding a potential production of 50 metric tons of pure heroin, or 125 metric tons of "black tar" heroin, the dominant form of Mexican heroin in the western United States; marijuana cultivation increased 45% to 17,500 hectares in 2009; government conducts the largest independent illicit-crop eradication program in the world; continues as the primary transshipment country for US-bound cocaine from South America, with an estimated 95% of annual cocaine movements toward the US stopping in Mexico; major drug syndicates control the majority of drug trafficking throughout the country; producer and distributor of ecstasy; significant money-laundering center; major supplier of heroin and largest foreign supplier of marijuana and methamphetamine to the US market (2007)

MICRONESIA, FEDERATED STATES OF

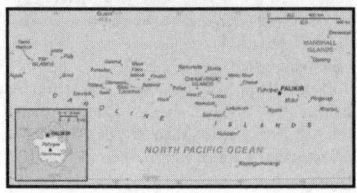

INTRODUCTION

Background: The Caroline Islands are a widely scattered archipelago in the western Pacific Ocean; they became part of a UN Trust Territory under US administration following World War II. The eastern four island groups adopted a constitution in 1979 and chose to become the Federated States of Micronesia. (The westernmost island group became Palau.) Independence came in 1986 under a Compact of Free Association with the US, which was amended and renewed in 2004. Present concerns include large-scale unemployment, overfishing, overdependence on US foreign aid, and state perception of inequitable allocation of US aid.

GEOGRAPHY

Location: Oceania, island group in the North Pacific Ocean, about three-quarters of the way from Hawaii to Indonesia

Geographic coordinates: 6 55 N, 158 15 E

Map references: Oceania

Area: *total:* 702 sq km
land: 702 sq km
water: 0 sq km (fresh water only)
note: includes Pohnpei (Ponape), Chuuk (Truk) Islands, Yap Islands, and Kosrae (Kosaie)
country comparison to the world: 191

Area—comparative: four times the size of Washington, DC (land area only)

Land boundaries: 0 km

Coastline: 6,112 km

Maritime claims: *territorial sea:* 12 nm
exclusive economic zone: 200 nm

Climate: tropical; heavy year-round rainfall, especially in the eastern islands; located on southern edge of the typhoon belt with occasionally severe damage

Terrain: islands vary geologically from high mountainous islands to low, coral atolls; volcanic outcroppings on Pohnpei, Kosrae, and Chuuk

Elevation: *mean elevation:* NA

elevation extremes: *lowest point:* Pacific Ocean 0 m
highest point: Dolohmwar (Totolom) 791 m

Natural resources: timber, marine products, deepseabed minerals, phosphate

Land use: *agricultural land:* 25.5%
arable land: 2.3%;
permanent crops: 19.7%;
permanent pasture: 3.5%
forest: 74.5%
other: 0% (2011 est.)

Irrigated land: 0 sq km NA (2012)

Natural hazards: typhoons (June to December)

Environment—current issues: overfishing, climate change, pollution

Environment—international agreements: *party to:* Biodiversity, Climate Change, Climate Change-Kyoto Protocol, Desertification, Hazardous Wastes, Law of the Sea, Ozone Layer Protection
signed, but not ratified: none of the selected agreements

Geography—note: composed of four major island groups totaling 607 islands

PEOPLE AND SOCIETY

Nationality: *noun:* Micronesian(s)
adjective: Micronesian; Chuukese, Kosraen(s), Pohnpeian(s), Yapese

Ethnic groups: Chuukese/Mortlockese 49.3%, Pohnpeian 29.8%, Kosraean 6.3%, Yapese 5.7%, Yap outer islanders 5.1%, Polynesian 1.6%, Asian 1.4%, other 0.8% (2010 est.)

Languages: English (official and common language), Chuukese, Kosrean, Pohnpeian, Yapese, Ulithian, Woleaian, Nukuoro, Kapingamarangi

Religions: Roman Catholic 54.7%, Protestant 41.1% (includes Congregational 38.5%, Baptist 1.1%, Seventh Day Adventist 0.8%, Assembly

of God 0.7%), Mormon 1.5%, other 1.9%, none 0.7%, unspecified 0.1% (2010 est.)

Population: 105,216 (July 2015 est.)
country comparison to the world: 194

Age structure: *0–14 years:* 31.34% (male 16,761/female 16,215)
15–24 years: 20% (male 10,576/female 10,469)
25–54 years: 38.41% (male 19,583/female 20,827)
55–64 years: 6.72% (male 3,494/female 3,580)
65 years and over: 3.53% (male 1,660/female 2,051) (2015 est.)

Dependency ratios: *total dependency ratio:* 62.4%
youth dependency ratio: 55.3%
elderly dependency ratio: 7.1%
potential support ratio: 14.1% (2015 est.)

Median age: *total:* 24.2 years
male: 23.6 years
female: 24.9 years (2015 est.)
country comparison to the world: 158

Population growth rate: -0.46% (2015 est.)
country comparison to the world: 223

Birth rate: 20.54 births/1,000 population (2015 est.)
country comparison to the world: 81

Death rate: 4.23 deaths/1,000 population (2015 est.)
country comparison to the world: 204

Net migration rate: -20.93 migrant(s)/1,000 population (2015 est.)
country comparison to the world: 221

Urbanization: *urban Population:* 22.4% of total population (2015)
rate of urbanization: 0.27% annual rate of change (2010–15 est.)

Major urban areas—Population: PALIKIR (capital) 7,000 (2014)

Sex ratio: *at birth:* 1.05 male(s)/female
0–14 years: 1.03 male(s)/female
15–24 years: 1.01 male(s)/female
25–54 years: 0.94 male(s)/female
55–64 years: 0.98 male(s)/female
65 years and over: 0.81 male(s)/female
total population: 0.98 male(s)/female (2015 est.)

Maternal mortality rate: 100 deaths/100,000 live births (2015 est.)
country comparison to the world: 71

Infant mortality rate: *total:* 21.18 deaths/1,000 live births
male: 23.46 deaths/1,000 live births
female: 18.79 deaths/1,000 live births (2015 est.)
country comparison to the world: 82

Life expectancy at birth: *total population:* 72.62 years
male: 70.59 years
female: 74.75 years (2015 est.)
country comparison to the world: 137

Total fertility rate: 2.49 children born/woman (2015 est.)
country comparison to the world: 77

Health expenditures: 12.6% of GDP (2013)
country comparison to the world: 6

Physicians density: 0.18 physicians/1,000 population (2009)

Hospital bed density: 3.2 beds/1,000 population (2009)

Drinking water source:
improved:
urban: 94.8% of population
rural: 87.4% of population
total: 89% of population
unimproved:
urban: 5.2% of population
rural: 12.6% of population
total: 11% of population (2015 est.)

Sanitation facility access:
improved:
urban: 85.1% of population
rural: 49% of population
total: 57.1% of population
unimproved:
urban: 14.9% of population
rural: 51% of population
total: 42.9% of population (2015 est.)

HIV/AIDS—adult prevalence rate: NA

HIV/AIDS—people living with HIV/AIDS: NA

HIV/AIDS—deaths: NA

Obesity—adult prevalence rate: 33.2% (2014)
country comparison to the world: 12

Education expenditures: NA

GOVERNMENT

Country name: *conventional long form:* Federated States of Micronesia
conventional short form: none
local long form: Federated States of Micronesia
local short form: none
former: Trust Territory of the Pacific Islands, Ponape, Truk, and Yap Districts
abbreviation: FSM
etymology: the term "Micronesia" is a 19th-century construct of two Greek words, "micro" (small) and "nesoi" (islands), and refers to thousands of small islands in the western Pacific Ocean

Government type: federal republic in free association with the US

Capital: *name:* Palikir

Geographic coordinates: 6 55 N, 158 09 E
time difference: UTC + 11 (16 hours ahead of Washington, DC, during Standard Time)

Administrative divisions: 4 states; Chuuk (Truk), Kosrae (Kosaie), Pohnpei (Ponape), Yap

Independence: 3 November 1986 (from the US-administered UN trusteeship)

National holiday: Constitution Day, 10 May (1979)

Constitution: drafted June 1975, ratified 1 October 1978, entered into force 10 May 1979; amended 1990; note—in 2001, all 26 amendments proposed by the FSM constitutional convention were defeated in a national referendum (2016)

Legal system: mixed legal system of common and customary law

International law organization participation: has not submitted an ICJ jurisdiction declaration; non-party state to the ICCt

Citizenship: *citizenship by birth:* no
citizenship by descent only: at least one parent must be a citizen of FSM
dual citizenship recognized: no
residency requirement for naturalization: 5 years

Suffrage: 18 years of age; universal

Executive branch: *chief of state:* President Peter M. CHRISTIAN (since 12 May 2015); Vice President Yosiwo P. GEORGE (since 12 May 2015); note—the president is both chief of state and head of government

head of government: President Peter M. CHRISTIAN (since 12 May 2015); Vice President Yosiwo P. GEORGE (since 12 May 2015)
cabinet: Cabinet includes the vice president and the heads of the 8 executive departments
elections/appointments: president and vice president indirectly elected by Congress from among the 4 'at large' senators for a 4-year term (eligible for a second term); election last held on 11 May 2011 (next to be held in May 2015)
election results: Peter M. CHRISTIAN elected president by Congress; Yosiwo P. GEORGE elected vice president

Legislative branch: *description:* unicameral Congress (14 seats; 10 members directly elected in single-seat constituencies by simple majority vote to serve 2-year terms and 4 directly elected from each of the 4 states by proportional representation vote to serve 4-year terms)
elections: last held on 5 March 2013 (next to be held in March 2015)
election results: percent of vote—NA; seats—independent 14

Judicial branch: *highest court(s):* Federated States of Micronesia (FSM) Supreme Court (consists of the chief justice and not more than 5 associate justices and organized into appellate and criminal divisions)
judge selection and term of office: justices appointed by the president of the Federated States of Micronesia with the approval of two-thirds of Congress; justices appointed for life
subordinate courts: the highest state-level courts are: Chuuk Supreme Court; Korsae State Court; Pohnpei State Court; Yap State Court

Political parties and leaders: no formal parties

Political pressure groups and leaders: NA

International organization participation: ACP, ADB, AOSIS, FAO, G-77, IBRD, ICAO, ICRM, IDA, IFC, IFRCS, IMF, IOC, IOM, IPU, ITSO, ITU, MIGA, OPCW, PIF, Sparteca, SPC, UN, UNCTAD, UNESCO, WHO, WMO

Diplomatic representation in the US: *chief of mission:* Ambassador Asterio R. TAKESY (since 13 January 2012)
chancery: 1725 N Street NW, Washington, DC 20036
telephone: [1] (202) 223-4383
FAX: [1] (202) 223-4391

consulate(s) general: Honolulu, Tamuning (Guam)

Diplomatic representation from the US: *chief of mission:* Ambassador Dorothea-Maria (Doria) ROSEN (since9 August 2012)
embassy: 101 Upper Pics Road, Kolonia
mailing address: P.O. Box 1286, Kolonia, Pohnpei, 96941; U.S. Embassy in Micronesia, 4120 Kolonia Place, Washington, D.C.20521-4120
telephone: [691] 320-2187
FAX: [691] 320-2186

Flag description: light blue with four white five-pointed stars centered; the stars are arranged in a diamond pattern; blue symbolizes the Pacific Ocean, the stars represent the four island groups of Chuuk, Kosrae, Pohnpei, and Yap

National symbol(s): four, five-pointed, white stars on a light blue field; national colors: light blue, white

National anthem: *name:* "Patriots of Micronesia"
lyrics/music: unknown
note: adopted 1991; also known as "Across All Micronesia"; the music is based on the 1820 German patriotic song "Ich hab mich ergeben", which was the West German national anthem from 1949–1950; variants of this tune are used in Johannes Brahms' "Festival Overture" and Gustav Mahler's "Third Symphony"

ECONOMY

Economy—overview: Economic activity consists largely of subsistence farming and fishing, and government, which employs two-thirds of the adult working population and receives funding largely—58% in 2013—from Compact of Free Association assistance provided by the US. The islands have few commercially valuable mineral deposits. The potential for tourism is limited by isolation, lack of adequate facilities, and limited internal air and water transportation.
Under the terms of the original Compact, the US provided $1.3 billion in grants and aid from 1986 to 2001. The US and the Federated States of Micronesia (FSM) negotiated a second (amended) Compact agreement in 2002–03 that took effect in 2004. The amended Compact runs for a 20-year period to 2023; during which the US will provide roughly $2.1 billion to the FSM. The amended Compact also develops a Trust Fund for the FSM that will provide a comparable income stream beyond 2024 when Compact grants end.
The country's medium-term economic outlook appears fragile because of dependence on US assistance and lackluster performance of its small and stagnant private sector.

GDP (purchasing power parity): $306 million (2015 est.)
$306.5 million (2014 e+st.)
$317.3 million (2013 est.)
note: data are in 2013 US dollars; GDP supplemented by grant aid, averaging about $100 million annually
country comparison to the world: 216

GDP (official exchange rate): $318 million (2015 est.)

GDP—real growth rate: -0.2% (2015 est.)
-3.4% (2014 est.)
-3.6% (2013 est.)
country comparison to the world: 199

GDP—per capita (PPP): $3,000 (2015 est.)
$2,900 (2014 est.)
$3,100 (2013 est.)
note: data are in 2015 US dollars
country comparison to the world: 190

GDP—composition, by end use:
household consumption: 83.5%
government consumption: 41.8%
investment in fixed assets: 24.3%
investment in inventories: 0%
exports of goods and services: 26.6%
imports of goods and services: -76.2% (2013 est.)

GDP—composition, by sector of origin:
agriculture: 26.3%
industry: 18.9%
services: 54.8% (2013 est.)

Agriculture—products: taro, yams, coconuts, bananas, cassava (manioc, tapioca), sakau (kava), Kosraen citrus, betel nuts, black pepper, fish, pigs, chickens

Industries: tourism, construction; specialized aquaculture, craft items (shell and wood)

Industrial production growth rate: NA%

Labor force: 37,920 (2010 est.)
country comparison to the world: 199

Labor force—by occupation: *agriculture:* 0.9%
industry: 5.2%
services: 93.9%
note: two-thirds of the labor force are government employees (2013 est.)

Unemployment rate: 16.2% (2010 est.)
country comparison to the world: 156

Population below poverty line: 26.7% (2000 est.)

Household income or consumption by percentage share: *lowest:* 10%: NA%
highest: 10%: NA%

Distribution of family income—Gini index: 61.1 (2013 est.)
country comparison to the world: 6

Budget: *revenues:* $213.8 million
expenditures: $192.1 million (FY12/13 est.)
Taxes and other revenues: 69.6% of GDP (FY12/13 est.)
country comparison to the world: 5

Budget surplus (+) or deficit (–): 7.1% of GDP (FY12/13 est.)
country comparison to the world: 5

Public debt: 28% of GDP (2013)
27% of GDP (2012)
country comparison to the world: 145

Fiscal year: 1 October—30 September

Inflation rate (consumer prices): -1% (2015 est.)
0.6% (2014 est.)
country comparison to the world: 13

Commercial bank prime lending rate: 7.1% (2013 est.)

6.4% (2012 est.)
country comparison to the world: 119

Stock of narrow money: $196 million (31 December 2013 est.)
country comparison to the world: 182

Stock of broad money: $225.2 million (31 December 2013 est.)
country comparison to the world: 189

Stock of domestic credit: $56.98 million (2013 est.)
$56.77 million (31 December 2011 est.)
country comparison to the world: 185

Market value of publicly traded shares: $NA

Current account balance: $3 million (2015 est.)
$22 million (2014 est.)
country comparison to the world: 52

Exports: $88.3 million (2013 est.)
$95.7 million (2012 est.)
country comparison to the world: 196

Exports—commodities: fish, sakau (kava), betel nuts, black pepper

Imports: $258.5 million (2013 est.)
$263.4 million (2012 est.)
country comparison to the world: 203

Imports—commodities: food, beverages, clothing, computers, household electronics, appliances, manufactured goods, automobiles, machinery and equipment, furniture, tools

Reserves of foreign exchange and gold: $75.06 million (31 December 2011 est.)
country comparison to the world: 167

Debt—external: $93.6 million (2013 est.)
$93.5 million (2012 est.)
country comparison to the world: 195

Stock of direct foreign investment—at home: $15.8 million (2013 est.)
$34.4 million (2012 est.)
country comparison to the world: 119

Exchange rates: the US dollar is used

ENERGY

Electricity—production: 192 million kWh (2002)
country comparison to the world: 187

Electricity—consumption: 178.6 million kWh (2002)
country comparison to the world: 188

Electricity—exports: 0 kWh (2013 est.)
country comparison to the world: 138

Electricity—imports: 0 kWh (2013 est.)

country comparison to the world: 149

Electricity—installed generating capacity: 18,000 kW (2015 est.)
country comparison to the world: 204

Electricity—from fossil fuels: 96% of total installed capacity (2015 est.)
country comparison to the world: 64

Electricity—from nuclear fuels: 0% of total installed capacity (2015 est.)
country comparison to the world: 92

Electricity—from hydroelectric plants: 1% of total installed capacity (2013 est.)
country comparison to the world: 143

Electricity—from other renewable sources: 3% of total installed capacity (2013 est.)
country comparison to the world: 72

Crude oil—production: 0 bbl/day (2014)
country comparison to the world: 136

Crude oil—Exports: 0 bbl/day (2014)
country comparison to the world: 125

Crude oil—imports: 0 bbl/day (2014)
country comparison to the world: 190

Crude oil—proved reserves: 0 bbl (1 January 2014)
country comparison to the world: 134

Refined petroleum products—production: 0 bbl/day (2014)
country comparison to the world: 182

Refined petroleum products—exports: 0 bbl/day
country comparison to the world: 181

Natural gas—production: 0 cu m (2014)
country comparison to the world: 187

Natural gas—exports: 2,014 cu m
country comparison to the world: 51

Natural gas—proved reserves: 0 cu m
country comparison to the world: 139

Carbon dioxide emissions from consumption of energy: 105 Mt (2010 est.)
country comparison to the world: 212

COMMUNICATIONS

Telephones—fixed lines: *total subscriptions:* 7,000
subscriptions per 100 inhabitants: 7 (2014 est.)
country comparison to the world: 204

Telephones—mobile cellular: *total:* 31,400
subscriptions per 100 inhabitants: 30 (2013)
country comparison to the world: 208

Telephone system: *general assessment:* adequate system
domestic: islands interconnected by shortwave radiotelephone (used mostly for government purposes), satellite (Intelsat) ground stations, and some coaxial and fiber-optic cable; mobile-cellular service available on Kosrae, Pohnpei, and Yap
international: country code—691; satellite earth stations—5 Intelsat (Pacific Ocean) (2002)

Broadcast media: no TV broadcast stations; each state has a multi-channel cable service with TV transmissions carrying roughly 95% imported programming and 5% local programming; about a half dozen radio stations (2009)
Radio broadcast stations: AM 5, FM 1, shortwave 0 (2004)
Television broadcast stations: 3 (cable TV also available) (2004)

Internet country code: .fm

Internet hosts: 4,668 (2012)
country comparison to the world: 147

Internet users: *total:* 29,900
percent of population: 28.3% (2014 est.)
country comparison to the world: 196

TRANSPORTATION

Airports: 6 (2013)
country comparison to the world: 173

Airports—with paved runways: *total:* 6
1,524 to 2,437 m: 4
914 to 1,523 m: 2 (2013)

Roadways: *total:* 388 km
paved: 184 km
unpaved: 204 km (2015)
country comparison to the world: 208

Merchant marine: *total:* 3
by type: cargo 1, passenger/cargo 2 (2010)
country comparison to the world: 139

Ports and terminals: *major seaport(s):* Colonia (Tomil Harbor), Lele Harbor, Pohnepi Harbor

MILITARY AND SECURITY

Military branches: no regular military forces (2012)

Military—note: defense is the responsibility of the US

TRANSNATIONAL ISSUES

Disputes—international: none

Illicit drugs: major consum er of cannabis

MOLDOVA

INTRODUCTION

Background: Part of Romania during the interwar period, Moldova was incorporated into the Soviet Union at the close of World War II. Although the country has been independent from the USSR since 1991, Russian forces have remained on Moldovan territory east of the Nistru River supporting the breakaway region of Transnistria, composed of a Slavic majority population (mostly Ukrainians and Russians), but with a sizable ethnic Moldovan minority. Europe's poorest economy, Moldova became the first former Soviet state to elect a communist, Vladimir VORONIN, as its president in 2001. VORONIN served as Moldova's president until he resigned in September 2009. Four Moldovan opposition parties then formed a new coalition, the Alliance for European Integration (AEI),

GEOGRAPHY

Location: Eastern Europe, northeast of Romania

Geographic coordinates: 47 00 N, 29 00 E

Map references: Europe

Area: *total:* 33,851 sq km
land: 32,891 sq km
water: 960 sq km
country comparison to the world: 140

iterations of which acted as Moldova's governing coalitions over the next several years. In May 2013, two of the original AEI parties and a splinter group from a third re-formed a ruling coalition called the Pro-European Coalition. The Moldovan Government in summer 2014 signed and ratified an Association Agreement with the EU, advancing the Coalition's policy priority of EU integration. Following the country's most recent legislative election in November 2014, the three pro-European parties that entered Parliament won a total of 55 of the body's 101 seats. Infighting among coalition members led to prolonged legislative gridlock and political instability, as well as the collapse of two governments, all ruled by pro-European coalitions centered around the Liberal Democratic Party (PLDM) and the Democratic Party (PDM). A political impasse ended in January 2016 when a new parliamentary majority led by PDM, joined by defectors from the Communists and PLDM, supported Pavel FILIP as prime minister.

Area—comparative: slightly larger than Maryland

Land boundaries: *total:* 1,885 km
border countries (2): Romania 683 km, Ukraine 1,202 km

Coastline: 0 km (landlocked)

Maritime claims: none (landlocked)

Climate: moderate winters, warm summers

Terrain: rolling steppe, gradual slope south to Black Sea

Elevation: *mean elevation:* 139 m

elevation extremes: *lowest point:* Dniester (Nistru) 2 m
highest point: Dealul Balanesti 430 m

Natural resources: lignite, phosphorites, gypsum, limestone, arable land

Land use: *agricultural land:* 74.9%
arable land: 55.1%;
permanent crops: 9.1%;
permanent pasture: 10.7%;
forest: 11.9%
other: 13.2% (2011 est.)

Irrigated land: 2,283 sq km (2012)

Total renewable water resources: 11.65 cu km (2011)

Freshwater withdrawal (domestic/industrial/agricultural): *total:* 1.07 cu km/yr (14%/83%/4%)
per capita: 290 cu m/yr (2010)

Natural hazards: landslides

Environment—current issues: heavy use of agricultural chemicals, including banned pesticides such as DDT, has contaminated soil and groundwater; extensive soil erosion from poor farming methods

Environment—international agreements: *party to:* Air Pollution, Air Pollution-Persistent Organic Pollutants, Biodiversity, Climate Change, Climate Change-Kyoto Protocol, Desertification, Endangered Species, Hazardous Wastes, Ozone Layer Protection, Ship Pollution, Wetlands
signed, but not ratified: none of the selected agreements

Geography—note: landlocked; well endowed with various sedimentary rocks and minerals including sand, gravel, gypsum, and limestone

PEOPLE AND SOCIETY

Nationality: *noun:* Moldovan(s)
adjective: Moldovan

Ethnic groups: Moldovan 75.8%, Ukrainian 8.4%, Russian 5.9%, Gagauz 4.4%, Romanian 2.2%, Bulgarian 1.9%, other 1%, unspecified 0.4%
note: internal disputes with ethnic Slavs in the Transnistrian region (2004 est.)

Languages: Moldovan 58.8% (official; virtually the same as the Romanian language), Romanian 16.4%, Russian 16%, Ukrainian 3.8%, Gagauz 3.1% (a Turkish language), Bulgarian 1.1%, other 0.3%, unspecified 0.4%
note: represents lanugage usually spoken (2004 est.)

Religions: Orthodox 93.3%, Baptist 1%, other Christian 1.2%, other 0.9%, atheist 0.4%, none 1%, unspecified 2.2% (2004 est.)

Population: 3,546,847 (July 2015 est.)
country comparison to the world: 133

Age structure: *0–14 years:* 17.86% (male 326,681/female 306,763)
15–24 years: 13.49% (male 247,183/female 231,389)
25–54 years: 43.73% (male 777,648/female 773,401)
55–64 years: 13.24% (male 214,846/female 254,818)
65 years and over: 11.68% (male 159,145/female 254,973) (2015 est.)

Dependency ratios: *total dependency ratio:* 34.6%
youth dependency ratio: 21.2%
elderly depen dency ratio: 13.4%
potential support ratio: 7.5% (2015 est.)

Median age: *total:* 36 years
male: 34.2 years
female: 38 years (2015 est.)
country comparison to the world: 71

Population growth rate: -1.03% (2015 est.)
country comparison to the world: 229

Birth rate: 12 births/1,000 population (2015 est.)
country comparison to the world: 165

Death rate: 12.59 deaths/1,000 population (2015 est.)
country comparison to the world: 22

Net migration rate: -9.67 migrant(s)/1,000 population (2015 est.)
country comparison to the world: 214

Urbanization: *urban population:* 45% of total population (2015)
rate of urbanization: -0.73% annual rate of change (2010–15 est.)

Major urban areas—Population: CHISINAU (capital) 725,000 (2015)

Sex ratio: *at birth:* 1.06 male(s)/female
0–14 years: 1.07 male(s)/female
15–24 years: 1.07 male(s)/female
25–54 years: 1.01 male(s)/female
55–64 years: 0.84 male(s)/female
65 years and over: 0.62 male(s)/female
total population: 0.95 male(s)/female (2015 est.)

Mother's mean age at first birth: 23.7 (2011 est.)

Maternal mortality rate: 23 deaths/100,000 live births (2015 est.)
country comparison to the world: 114

Infant mortality rate: *total:* 12.59 deaths/1,000 live births
male: 14.44 deaths/1,000 live births
female: 10.62 deaths/1,000 live births (2015 est.)
country comparison to the world: 120

Life expectancy at birth: *total population:* 70.42 years
male: 66.55 years
female: 74.54 years (2015 est.)
country comparison to the world: 154

Total fertility rate: 1.56 children born/woman (2015 est.)
country comparison to the world: 187

Contraceptive prevalence rate: 67.8% (2005)

Health expenditures: 11.8% of GDP (2013)
country comparison to the world: 8

Physicians density: 2.98 physicians/1,000 population (2013)

Hospital bed density: 6.2 beds/1,000 population (2012)

Drinking water source:
improved:
urban: 96.9% of population
rural: 81.4% of population
total: 88.4% of population
unimproved:
urban: 3.1% of population
rural: 18.6% of population
total: 11.6% of population (2015 est.)

Sanitation facility access:
improved:
urban: 87.8% of population
rural: 67.1% of population
total: 76.4% of population
unimproved:
urban: 12.2% of population
rural: 32.9% of population
total: 23.6% of population (2015 est.)

HIV/AIDS—adult prevalence rate: 0.63% (2014 est.)
country comparison to the world: 60

HIV/AIDS—people living with HIV/AIDS: 17,600 (2014 est.)
country comparison to the world: 81

HIV/AIDS—deaths: 800 (2014 est.)
country comparison to the world: 72

Obesity—adult prevalence rate: 15.7% (2014)
country comparison to the world: 91

Children under the age of 5 years underweight: 2.2% (2012)
country comparison to the world: 111

Education expenditures: 7.5% of GDP (2014)
country comparison to the world: 10

Literacy: *definition:* age 15 and over can read and write
total population: 99.4%
male: 99.7%
female: 99.1% (2015 est.)

School life expectancy (primary to tertiary education): *total:* 12 years
male: 12 years
female: 12 years (2013)

Child labor—children ages 5–14: *total number:* 72,364
percentage: 16% (2009 est.)

Unemployment, youth ages 15–24: *total:* 12.2%
male: 11.9%
female: 12.7% (2013 est.)
country comparison to the world: 87

GOVERNMENT

Country name: *conventional long form:* Republic of Moldova

conventional short form: Moldova
local long form: Republica Moldova
local short form: Moldova
former: Moldavian Soviet Socialist Republic, Moldovan Soviet Socialist Republic
etymology: named for the Moldova River in neighboring eastern Romania

Government type: parliamentary republic

Capital: *name:* Chisinau in Romanian (Kishinev in Russian)
note: pronounced KEE-shee-now (KIH-shi-nyov)

Geographic coordinates: 47 00 N, 28 51 E
time difference: UTC+2 (7 hours ahead of Washington, DC, during Standard Time)
daylight saving time: +1hr, begins last Sunday in March; ends last Sunday in October

Administrative divisions: 32 raions (raioane, singular—raion), 3 municipalities (municipii, singular—municipiul), 1 autonomous territorial unit (unitatea teritoriala autonoma), and 1 territorial unit (unitatea teritoriala)
raions: Anenii Noi, Basarabeasca, Briceni, Cahul, Cantemir, Calarasi, Causeni, Cimislia, Criuleni, Donduseni, Drochia, Dubasari, Edinet, Falesti, Floresti, Glodeni, Hincesti, Ialoveni, Leova, Nisporeni, Ocnita, Orhei, Rezina, Riscani, Singerei, Soldanesti, Soroca, Stefan-Voda, Straseni, Taraclia, Telenesti, Ungheni
municipalities: Balti, Bender, Chisinau
autonomous territorial unit: Gagauzia
territorial unit: Stinga Nistrului (Transnistria)

Independence: 27 August 1991 (from the Soviet Union)

National holiday: Independence Day, 27 August (1991)

Constitution: previous 1978; latest adopted 29 July 1994, effective 27 August 1994; amended several times, last in 2010; note—in early 2016, a Moldovan Constitutional Court decision allows for direct presidential elections, reversing a constitutional amendment allowing Parliament to select the president (2016)

Legal system: civil law system with Germanic law influences; Constitutional Court review of legislative acts

International law organization participation: has not submitted an ICJ jurisdiction declaration; accepts ICCt jurisdiction

Citizenship: *citizenship by birth:* no
citizenship by descent only: at least one parent must be a citizen of Moldova
dual citizenship recognized: no
residency requirement for naturalization: 10 years

Suffrage: 18 years of age; universal

Executive branch: *chief of state:* President Nicolae TIMOFTI (since 23 March 2012)

head of government: Prime Minister Pavel FILIP (since 20 January 2016)
cabinet: Cabinet proposed by the prime minister-designate, nominated by the president, approved through a vote of confidence in Parliament

elections/appointments: president directly elected for a 4-year term (eligible for a second term); election last held on 16 March 2012 (under the previous system of indirect election by the Parliament; next to be held in fall 2016); prime minister designated by the president upon consultation with Parliament; within 15 days from designation, the prime minister-designate must request a vote of confidence for his/her proposed work program from the Parliament
election results: Nicolae TIMOFTI (independent) elected president; Parliament vote—62 of 101; Pavel FILIP (Democratic Party) designated prime minister; Parliament vote—57 of 101

Legislative branch: *description:* unicameral Parliament (101 seats; members directly elected in a single, nationwide constituency by proportional representation vote to serve 4-year terms)
elections: last held on 30 November 2014 (next to be held in November 2018)
election results: percent of vote by party—PSRM 20.5%, PLDM 20.2%, PCRM 17.5%, PDM 15.8%, PL 9.7%, other 16.3%; seats by party—PSRM 25, PLDM 23, PCRM 21, PDM 19, PL 13

Judicial branch: *highest court(s):* Supreme Court of Justice (consists of a chief judges, 3 deputy-chief judges, 45 judges, and 7 assistant judges); Constitutional Court (consists of the court president and 6 judges); note—the Constitutional Court is autonomous to the other branches of government; the Court interprets the Constitution and reviews the constitutionality of parliamentary laws and decisions, decrees of the president, and acts of the government
judge selection and term of office: Supreme Court of Justice judges appointed by Parliament upon the recommendation of the Supreme Council of the Magistracy; all judges serve 4-year renewable terms; Constitutional Court judges appointed 2 each by Parliament, the Moldovan president, and the Higher Council of Magistracy; court president elected by other court judges for a 3-year term; other judges appointed for 6-year terms
subordinate courts: Courts of Appeal; Court of Business Audit; municipal courts

Political parties and leaders: *represented in Parliament:* Communist Party of the Republic of Moldova or PCRM [Vladimir VORONIN]
Democratic Party of Moldova or PDM [Marian LUPU]
Liberal Democratic Party of Moldova or PLDM [Valeriu STRELET, acting]
Liberal Party or PL [Mihai GHIMPU]
Socialist Party of the Republic of Moldova or PSRM [Igor DODON]
not represented in Parliament: Anti-Mafia Movement [Sergiu MOCANU]
Christian Democratic People's Party or PPCD [Victor CIOBANU]
Conservative Party or PC [Natalia NIRCA]
Dignity and Truth Party [Andrei NASTASE]
Ecological Party of Moldova "Green Alliance" or PEMAVE [Vladimir BRAGA]
European People's Party of Moldova (EPPM) [Iurie LEANCA]

Humanist Party of Moldova or PUM [Valeriu PASAT]

Labor Party or PM [Gheorghe SIMA]

Liberal Reformers Party or PLR [Ion HADARCA]

National Liberal Party or PNL [Vitalia PAVLICENKO]

Our Home Moldova [Grigore PETRENCO]

Our Party [Renato USATII]

Patriots of Moldova Party or PPM [Mihail GARBUZ]

Republican Party of Moldova or PRM [Andrei STRATAN]

Revival Party [Vadim MISIN]

Roma Social Political Movement of the Republic of Moldova or MRRM [Ion BUCUR]

Social Democratic Party or PSD [Victor SELIN]

Social Political Movement "Equality" or MR [Valeriy KLIMENCO]

United Moldova Party or PMU EM [Vladimir TURCAN]

Political pressure groups and leaders: NA

International organization participation: BSEC, CD, CE, CEI, CIS, EAEC (observer), EAPC, EBRD, FAO, GCTU, GUAM, IAEA, IBRD, ICAO, ICC (NGOs), ICCt, ICR M, IDA, IFAD, IFC, IFRCS, ILO, IMF, IMO, Interpol, IOC, IOM, IPU, ISO (correspondent), ITU, ITUC (NGOs), MIGA, OIF, OPCW, OSCE, PFP, SELEC, UN, UNCTAD, UNESCO, UNHCR, UNIDO, Union Latina, UNMIL, UNMISS, UNOCI, UNWTO, UPU, WCO, WHO, WIPO, WMO, WTO

Diplomatic representation in the US: *chief of mission:* Ambassador (vacant); Charge d'Affaires Veaceslav PITUSCAN (since 26 August 2015)

chancery: 2101 S Street NW, Washington, DC 20008

telephone: [1] (202) 667-1130

FAX: [1] (202) 667-1204

Diplomatic representation from the US: *chief of mission:* Ambassador James D. PETTIT (since 29 January 2015)

embassy: 103 Mateevici Street, Chisinau MD-2009

mailing address: use embassy street address

telephone: [373] (22) 40-8300

FAX: [373] (22) 23-3044

Flag description: three equal vertical bands of blue (hoist side), yellow, and red; emblem in center of flag is of a Roman eagle of gold outlined in black with a red beak and talons carrying a yellow cross in its beak and a green olive branch in its right talons and a yellow scepter in its left talons; on its breast is a shield divided horizontally red over blue with a stylized aurochs head, star, rose, and crescent all in black-outlined yellow; based on the color scheme of the flag of Romania—with which Moldova shares a history and culture—but Moldova's blue band is lighter; the reverse of the flag does not display any coat of arms

note: one of only three national flags that differ on their obverse and reverse sides—the others are Paraguay and Saudi Arabia

National symbol(s): aurochs (a type of wild cattle); national colors: blue, yellow, red

National anthem: *name:* "Limba noastra" (Our Language)

lyrics/music: Alexei MATEEVICI/Alexandru CRISTEA

note: adopted 1994

ECONOMY

Economy—overview: Despite recent progress, Moldova remains one of the poorest countries in Europe. With a moderate climate and productive farmland, Moldova's economy relies heavily on its agriculture sector, featuring fruits, vegetables, wine, and tobacco. Moldova also depends on annual remittances of about $1.12 billion from the roughly one million Moldovans working in Europe, Russia, and other former Soviet Bloc countries. With few natural energy resources, Moldova imports almost all of its energy supplies from Russia and Ukraine. Moldova's depen dence on Russian energy is underscored by a more than $5 billion debt to Russian natural gas supplier Gazprom, largely the result of unreimbursed natural gas consumption in the breakaway region of Transnistria. Moldova and Romania inaugurated the Ungheni-I asi natural gas interconnector project in August 2014. The 43-kilometer pipeline between Moldova and Romania, allows for both the import and export of natural gas. Several technical and regulatory delays kept gas from flowing into Moldova until March 2015. Romanian gas exports to Moldova are largely symbolic. Moldova hopes to build a pipeline connecting Ungheni to Chisinau, bringing the gas to Moldovan population centers. The government's stated goal of EU integration has resulted in some market-oriented progress. Moldova experienced better than expected economic growth in 2014 due to increased agriculture production, to economic policies adopted by the Moldovan government since 2009, and to the receipt of EU trade preferences. Moldova signed an Association Agreement and a Deep and Comprehensive Free Trade Agreement with the EU during fall 2014, connecting Moldovan products to the world's largest market. Still, a $1 billion asset-stripping heist of Moldovan banks in late 2014 delivered a significant shock to the economy in 2015; a subsequent bank bailout increased inflationary pressures and contributed to the depreciation of the leu. Moldova's growth has also been hampered by endemic corru ption and a Russian import ban on Moldova's agricultural products.

Over the longer term, Moldova's economy remains vulnerable to corruption, political uncertainty, weak administrative capacity, vested bureaucratic interests, higher fuel prices, Russian political and economic pressure, and unresolved separatism in Moldova's Transnistria region.

GDP (purchasing power parity):
$17.79 billion (2015 est.)
$17.99 billion (2014 est.)
$17.17 billion (2013 est.)
note: data are in 2015 US dollars
country comparison to the world: 149

GDP (official exchange rate): $6.414 billion (2015 est.)

GDP—real growth rate: -1.1% (2015 est.)
4.8% (2014 est.)
9.4% (2013 est.)
country comparison to the world: 204

GDP—per capita (PPP): $5,000 (2015 est.)
$5,100 (2014 est.)
$4,800 (2013 est.)
note: data are in 2015 US dollars
country comparison to the world: 169

Gross national saving: 12.9% of GDP (2015 est.)
20.7% of GDP (2014 est.)
19.6% of GDP (2013 est.)
country comparison to the world: 132

GDP—composition, by end use:
household consumption: 87.4%
government consumption: 19.8%
investment in fixed capital: 24.3%
investment in inventories: -0.4%
exports of goods and services: 42.8%
imports of goods and services: -73.9% (2015 est.)

GDP—composition, by sector of origin:
agriculture: 16.2%
industry: 20.7%
services: 63.2% (2015 est.)

Agriculture—products: vegetables, fruits, grapes, grain, sugar beets, sunflower seeds, tobacco; beef, milk; wine

Industries: sugar, vegetable oil, food processing, agricultural machinery; foundry equipment, refrigerators and freezers, washing machines; hosiery, shoes, textiles

Industrial production growth rate: 0.6% (2015 est.)
country comparison to the world: 158

Labor force: 1.222 million (2015 est.)
country comparison to the world: 136

Labor force—by occupation: *agriculture:* 30.5%
industry: 12.2%
services: 57.3% (2014 est.)

Unemployment rate: 6% (2015 est.)
3.9% (2014 est.)
country comparison to the world: 65

Population below poverty line: 20.8% (2013 est.)

Household income or consumption by percentage share: *lowest:* 10%: 3.3%
highest: 10%: 26% (2010 est.)

Distribution of family income—Gini index: 28.5 (2013)
33.2 (2003)
country comparison to the world: 129

Budget: *revenues:* $2.32 billion
expenditures: $2.466 billion
note: National Public Budget (2015 est.)
Taxes and other revenues: 36.8% of GDP (2015 est.)
country comparison to the world: 51

Budget surplus (+) or deficit (–): -2.3% of GDP (2015 est.)
country comparison to the world: 81

Public debt: 51.9% of GDP (2015 est.)
country comparison to the world: 77

Fiscal year: calendar year

Inflation rate (consumer prices): 9.6% (2015 est.)
5.1% (2014 est.)
country comparison to the world: 209

Central bank discount rate: 19.5% (31 December 2015)
6.5% (31 December 2014)
note: this is the basic rate on short-term operations
country comparison to the world: 7

Commercial bank prime lending rate: 15.46% (31 December 2015 est.)
10.95% (31 December 2014 est.)
country comparison to the world: 37

Stock of narrow money: $1.578 billion (31 December 2015 est.)
$1.718 billion (31 December 2014 est.)
country comparison to the world: 137

Stock of broad money:
$3.402 billion (31 December 2015 est.)
$4.685 billion (31 December 2014 est.)
country comparison to the world: 144

Stock of domestic credit:
$2.03 billion (31 December 2015 est.)
$2.674 billion (31 December 2014 est.)
country comparison to the world: 138

Market value of publicly traded shares:
$9.723 million (31 December 2014 est.)
$50.47 million (31 December 2014)
$51.46 million (31 December 2012 est.)
country comparison to the world: 120

Current account balance: -$426 million (2015 est.)
-$294 million (2014 est.)
country comparison to the world: 93

Exports: $1.967 billion (2015 est.)
$2.34 billion (2014 est.)
country comparison to the world: 138

Exports—commodities: foodstuffs, textiles, machinery

Exports—partners: Romania 23.1%, Italy 10.2%, Turkey 9.4%, Russia 8.1%, Germany 6.6%, Belarus 6.5% (2015)

Imports: $3.987 billion (2015 est.)
$5.317 billion (2014 est.)
country comparison to the world: 134

Imports—commodities: mineral products and fuel, machinery and equipment, chemicals, textiles

Imports—partners: Russia 22.7%, Romania 18.1%, Ukraine 11.5%, Germany 7%, Italy 4.8%, Turkey 4.4% (2015)

Reserves of foreign exchange and gold: $1.757 billion (31 December 2015 est.)
$2.157 billion (31 December 2013 est.)
country comparison to the world: 123

Debt—external: $6.57 billion (31 December 2014 est.)
$6.674 billion (31 December 2013 est.)
country comparison to the world: 122

Stock of direct foreign investment—at home:
$3.647 billion (31 December 2014 est.)
$3.615 billion (31 December 2013 est.)
country comparison to the world: 103

Stock of direct foreign investment—abroad:
$108.2 million (31 December 2012)

$88.42 million (31 December 2011)
country comparison to the world: 95

Exchange rates: Moldovan lei (MDL) per US dollar—
18.816 (2015 est.)
14.036 (2014 est.)
14.036 (2013 est.)
12.11 (2012 est.)
11.738 (2011 est.)

ENERGY

Electricity—production: 3.574 billion kWh (2014 est.)
country comparison to the world: 128

Electricity—consumption: 4.305 billion kWh (2014 est.)
country comparison to the world: 121

Electricity—exports: 0 kWh (2014 est.)
country comparison to the world: 165

Electricity—imports: 731 million kWh (2014 est.)
country comparison to the world: 70

Electricity—installed generating capacity: 439,900 kW
note: excludes Transnistria (2013 est.)
country comparison to the world: 143

Electricity—from fossil fuels: 96.4% of total installed capacity (2013 est.)
country comparison to the world: 62

Electricity—from nuclear fuels: 0% of total installed capacity (2013 est.)
country comparison to the world: 135

Electricity—from hydroelectric plants: 3.6% of total installed capacity (2013 est.)
country comparison to the world: 129

Electricity—from other renewable sources: 0% of total installed capacity (2013 est.)
country comparison to the world: 197

Crude oil—production: 0 bbl/day (2014 est.)
country comparison to the world: 163

Crude oil—exports: 0 bbl/day (2012 est.)
country comparison to the world: 156

Crude oil—imports: 0 bbl/day (2012 est.)
country comparison to the world: 92

Crude oil—proved reserves: 0 bbl (1 January 2015 est.)
country comparison to the world: 162

Refined petroleum products—production: 354 bbl/day (2012 est.)
country comparison to the world: 112

Refined petroleum products—consumption: 16,000 bbl/day (2013 est.)
country comparison to the world: 140

Refined petroleum products—exports: 579.3 bbl/day (2012 est.)
country comparison to the world: 114

Refined petroleum products—imports: 16,320 bbl/day (2012 est.)
country comparison to the world: 121

Natural gas—production: 0 cu m (2015 est.)
country comparison to the world: 97

Natural gas—consumption: 3.28 billion cu m

note: includes Transnistria; excluding Transnistria, consumption amounted to 2.92 billion cu m in 2015 (2013 est.)
country comparison to the world: 68

Natural gas—exports: 0 cu m (2013 est.)
country comparison to the world: 140

Natural gas—imports: 3.28 billion cu m
note: includes Transnistria; excluding Transnistria, imports amounted to 2.92 billion cu m in 2015 (2013 est.)
country comparison to the world: 38

Natural gas—proved reserves: 0 cu m (1 January 2014 est.)
country comparison to the world: 165

Carbon dioxide emissions from consumption of energy: 9.415 million Mt (2012 est.)
country comparison to the world: 102

COMMUNICATIONS

Telephones—fixed lines: *total subscriptions:* 1.22 million
subscriptions per 100 inhabitants: 34 (2014 est.)
country comparison to the world: 69

Telephones—mobile cellular: *total:* 3.7 million
subscriptions per 100 inhabitants: 104 (2014 est.)
country comparison to the world: 127

Telephone system: *general assessment:* poor service outside Chisinau; some modernization is under way
domestic: multiple private operators of GSM mobile-cellular telephone service are operating; GPRS system is being introduced; a CDMA mobile telephone network began operations in 2007; combined fixed-line and mobile-cellular teledensity 100 per 100 persons
international: country code—373; service through Romania and Russia via landline; satellite earth stations—at least 3 (Intelsat, Eutelsat, and Intersputnik) (2011)

Broadcast media: state-owned national radio-TV broadcaster operates 1 TV and 1 radio stations; a total of nearly 70 terrestrial TV channels and some 50 radio stations are in operation; Russian and Romanian channels also are available (2016)
Radio broadcast stations: AM 2, FM 29, shortwave NA (2006)
Television broadcast stations: 40 (2006)

Internet country code: .md

Internet hosts: 711,564 (2012)
country comparison to the world: 51

Internet users: *total:* 1.6 million
percent of population: 44.8% (2014 est.)
country comparison to the world: 106

TRANSPORTATION

Airports: 7 (2013)
country comparison to the world: 169

Airports—with paved runways: *total:* 5
over 3,047 m: 1
2,438 to 3,047 m: 2
1,524 to 2,437 m: 2 (2013)

Airports—with unpaved runways: *total:* 2

1,524 to 2,437 m: 1
under 914 m: 1 (2013)

Pipelines: gas 1906 km (2013)

Railways: *total:* 1,171 km
broad gauge: 1,157 km 1.520-m gauge
standard gauge: 14 km 1.435-m gauge (2014)
country comparison to the world: 86

Roadways: *total:* 9,352 km
paved: 8,835 km
unpaved: 517 km (2012)
country comparison to the world: 137

Waterways: 558 km (in public use on Danube, Dniester and Prut rivers) (2011)
country comparison to the world: 82

Merchant marine: *total:* 121
by type: bulk carrier 7, cargo 88, carrier 1, chemical tanker 3, passenger/cargo 7, petroleum tanker 2, refrigerated cargo 1, roll on/roll off 11, specialized tanker 1
foreign-owned: 63 (Bulgaria 1, Denmark 1, Egypt 5, Greece 1, Israel 2, Lebanon 1, Pakistan

1, Romania 2, Russia 5, Syria 5, Turkey 18, UK 3, Ukraine 14, Yemen 4) (2010)
country comparison to the world: 45

MILITARY AND SECURITY

Military branches: National Army: Land Forces Command, Air Forces Command (includes air defense unit); Carabinieri Troops: a component of the Ministry of Internal Affairs that also has official status as a service of the Armed Forces (2016)

Military service age and obligation: 18 years of age for compulsory or voluntary military service; male registration required at age 16; 1-year service obligation (2016)

Military expenditures: 0.3% of GDP (2015 projected)
0.3% of GDP (2014)
0.3% of GDP (2012)
0.3% of GDP (2011)
0.3% of GDP (2010)
country comparison to the world: 128

TRANSNATIONAL ISSUES

Disputes—international: Moldova and Ukraine operate joint customs posts to monitor the transit of people and commodities through Moldova's break-away Transnistria region, which remains under the auspices of an Organization for Security and Cooperation in Europe-mandated peacekeeping mission comprised of Moldovan, Transnistrian, Russian, and Ukrainian troops

Refugees and internally displaced persons: *refugees (country of origin):* 6,779 applicants for forms of legal stay other than asylum (Ukraine) (2015)
stateless persons: 5,014 (2015)

Illicit drugs: limited cultivation of opium poppy and cannabis, mostly for CIS consumption; transshipment point for illicit drugs from Southwest Asia via Central Asia to Russia, Western Europe, and possibly the US; widespread crime and underground economic activity

MONACO

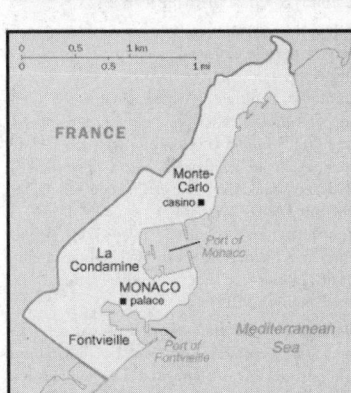

INTRODUCTION

Background: The Genoese built a fortress on the site of present day Monaco in 1215. The current ruling GRIMALDI family first seized temporary control in 1297, and again in 1331, but was not able to permanently secure its holding until 1419. Economic development was spurred in the late 19th century with a railroad linkup to France and the opening of a casino. Since then, the principality's mild climate, splendid scenery, and gambling facilities have made Monaco world famous as a tourist and recreation center.

GEOGRAPHY

Location: Western Europe, bordering the Mediterranean Sea on the southern coast of France, near the border with Italy

Geographic coordinates: 43 44 N, 7 24 E

Map references: Europe

Area: *total:* 2 sq km
land: 2 sq km
water: 0 sq km
country comparison to the world: 254

Area—comparative: about three times the size of the National Mall in Washington, DC

Land boundaries: *total:* 6 km
border countries (1): France 6 km

Coastline: 4.1 km

Maritime claims: *territorial sea:* 12 nm
exclusive economic zone: 12 nm

Climate: Mediterranean with mild, wet winters and hot, dry summers

Terrain: hilly, rugged, rocky

Elevation: *mean elevation:* NA

elevation extremes: *lowest point:* Mediterranean Sea 0 m
highest point: Mont Agel 140 m

Natural resources: none

Land use: *agricultural land:* 1%
arable land: 0%;
permanent crops: 1%;
permanent pasture: 0%
forest: 0%
other: 99% (2011 est.)

Irrigated land: 0 sq km (2012)

Natural hazards: NA

Environment—current issues: NA

Environment—international agreements: *party to:* Air Pollution, Air Pollution-Sulfur 94, Air Pollution-Volatile Organic Compounds, Biodiversity, Climate Change, Climate Change-Kyoto Protocol, Desertification, Endangered Species,

Hazardous Wastes, Law of the Sea, Marine Dumping, Ozone Layer Protection, Ship Pollution, Wetlands, Whaling
signed, but not ratified: none of the selected agreements

Geography—note: second-smallest independent state in the world (after the Holy See); smallest country with a coastline; almost entirely urban

PEOPLE AND SOCIETY

Nationality: *noun:* Monegasque(s) or Monacan(s)
adjective: Monegasque or Monacan

Ethnic groups: French (official) 47%, Monegasque 16%, Italian 16%, other 21%

Languages: French (official), English, Italian, Monegasque

Religions: Roman Catholic 90% (official), other 10%

Population: 37,731 (July 2015 est.)
note: immigrants make up more than 55% of the total population, according to UN data (2015)
country comparison to the world: 218

Age structure: *0–14 years:* 11.41% (male 1,793/female 1,692)
15–24 years: 9.03% (male 1,420/female 1,337)
25–54 years: 34.47% (male 5,239/female 5,286)
55–64 years: 14.71% (male 2,255/female 2,238)
65 years and over: 30.37% (male 4,146/female 5,129) (2015 est.)

Median age: *total:* 51.7 years
male: 50.6 years
female: 53 years (2015 est.)
country comparison to the world: 1

Population growth rate: 0.12% (2015 est.)
country comparison to the world: 187

Birth rate: 6.65 births/1,000 population (2015 est.)
country comparison to the world: 224

Death rate: 9.24 deaths/1,000 population (2015 est.)
country comparison to the world: 63

Net migration rate: 3.83 migrant(s)/1,000 population (2015 est.)
country comparison to the world: 35

Urbanization: *urban Population:* 100% of total population (2015)
rate of urbanization: 0.79% annual rate of change (2010–15 est.)

Major urban areas—Population: MONACO (capital) 38,000 (2014)

Sex ratio: *at birth:* 1.04 male(s)/female
0–14 years: 1.06 male(s)/female
15–24 years: 1.06 male(s)/female
25–54 years: 0.99 male(s)/female
55–64 years: 1.01 male(s)/female
65 years and over: 0.81 male(s)/female
total population: 0.95 male(s)/female (2015 est.)

Infant mortality rate: *total:* 1.82 deaths/1,000 live births
male: 2.06 deaths/1,000 live births
female: 1.57 deaths/1,000 live births (2015 est.)
country comparison to the world: 224

Life expectancy at birth: *total population:* 89.52 years
male: 85.63 years
female: 93.58 years (2015 est.)
country comparison to the world: 1

Total fertility rate: 1.52 children born/woman (2015 est.)
country comparison to the world: 193

Health expenditures: 4% of GDP (2013)
country comparison to the world: 155

Physicians density: 7.17 physicians/1,000 population (2012)

Hospital bed density: 13.8 beds/1,000 population (2012)

Drinking water source:
improved:
urban: 100% of population
total: 100% of population
unimproved:
urban: 0% of population
total: 0% of population (2015 est.)

Sanitation facility access:
improved:
urban: 100% of population
rural: NA
total: 100% of population
unimproved:
urban: 0% of population
rural: NA
total: 0% of population (2015 est.)

HIV/AIDS—adult prevalence rate: NA

HIV/AIDS—people living with HIV/AIDS: NA

HIV/AIDS—deaths: NA

Education expenditures: 1% of GDP (2014)
country comparison to the world: 169

GOVERNMENT

Country name: *conventional long form:* Principality of Monaco
conventional short form: Monaco
local long form: Principaute de Monaco
local short form: Monaco
etymology: founded as a Greek colony in the 6th century B.C., the name derives from two Greek words "monos" (single, alone) and "oikos" (house) to convey the sense of a people "living apart" or in a "single habitation"

Government type: constitutional monarchy

Capital: *name:* Monaco

Geographic coordinates: 43 44 N, 7 25 E
time difference: UTC+1 (6 hours ahead of Washington, DC, during Standard Time)
daylight saving time: +1hr, begins last Sunday in March; ends last Sunday in October

Administrative divisions: none; there are no first-order administrative divisions as defined by the US Government, but there are 4 quarters (quartiers, singular—quartier); Fontvieille, La Condamine, Monaco-Ville, Monte-Carlo; note—Moneghetti, a part of La Condamine, is sometimes called the 5th quarter of Monaco

Independence: 1419 (beginning of permanent rule by the House of GRIMALDI)

National holiday: National Day (Saint Rainier's Day),19 November (1857)

Constitution: previous 1911 (suspended 1959); latest adopted 17 December 1962; amended 2002 (2016)

Legal system: civil law system influenced by French legal tradition

International law organization participation: has not submitted an ICJ jurisdiction declaration; non-party state to the ICCt

Citizenship: *citizenship by birth:* no
citizenship by descent only: the father must be a citizen of Monaco; in the case of a child born out of wedlock, the mother must be a citizen and father unknown
dual citizenship recognized: no
residency requirement for naturalization: 10 years

Suffrage: 18 years of age; universal

Executive branch: *chief of state:* Prince ALBERT II (since 6 April 2005)

head of government: Minister of State Serge TELLE (since 1 February 2016)
cabinet: Council of Government under the authority of the monarch
elections/appointments: the monarchy is hereditary; minister of state appointed by the monarch from a list of three French national candidates presented by the French Government

Legislative branch: *description:* unicameral National Council or Conseil National (24 seats; 16 members directly elected in multi-seat constituencies by simple majority vote and 8 directly elected by proportional representation vote; members serve 5-year terms)
elections: last held on 10 February 2013 (next to be held in February 2018)
election results: percent of vote by party—Horizon Monaco 50.3%, Union Monegasque 39%, Renaissance 10.7%; seats by party—Horizon Monaco 20, Union Monegasque 3, Renaissance 1

Judicial branch: *highest court(s):* Supreme Court (consists of 5 permanent members and 2 substitutes)
judge selection and term of office: Supreme Court members appointed by the monarch upon the proposals of the National Council, State Council, Crown Council, Court of Appeal, and Trial Court
subordinate courts: Court of Appeal; Civil Court of First Instance

Political parties and leaders: Horizon Monaco [Laurent NOUVION]
Renaissance [SBM (public corporation)]
Union Monegasque [Jean-Francois ROBILLON]

Political pressure groups and leaders: NA

International organization participation: CD, CE, FAO, IAEA, ICAO, ICC (national committees), ICRM, IFRCS, IHO, IMO, IMSO, Interpol, IOC, IPU, ITSO, ITU, OAS (observer), OIF, OPCW, OSCE, Schengen Convention (de facto member), UN, UNCTAD, UNESCO, UNIDO, Union Latina, UNWTO, UPU, WHO, WIPO, WMO

Diplomatic representation in the US: *chief of mission:* Ambassador Maguy MACCARIO-DOYLE (since 3 December 2013)
chancery: 3400 International Drive NW, Suite 2K-100, Washington, DC 20008
telephone: (202) 234-1530
FAX: (202) 244-7656
consulate(s) general: New York

Diplomatic representation from the US: the US does not have an embassy in Monaco; the US Ambassador to France is accredited to Monaco; the US Consul General in Marseille (France), under the authority of the US ambassador to France, handles diplomatic and consular matters concerning Monaco

Flag description: two equal horizontal bands of red (top) and white; the colors are those of the ruling House of Grimaldi and have been in use since 1339, making the flag one of the world's oldest national banners
note: similar to the flag of Indonesia which is longer and the flag of Poland which is white (top) and red

National symbol(s): red and white lozenges (diamond shapes); national colors: red, white

National anthem: *name:* "A Marcia de Muneghu" (The March of Monaco)
lyrics/music: Louis NOTARI/Charles ALBRECHT
note: music adopted 1867, lyrics adopted 1931; although French is commonly spoken, only the Monegasque lyrics are official; the French version is known as "Hymne Monegasque" (Monegasque

Anthem); the words are generally only sung on official occasions

ECONOMY

Economy—overview: Monaco, bordering France on the Mediterranean coast, is a popular resort, attracting tourists to its casino and pleasant climate. The principality also is a banking center and has successfully sought to diversify into services and small, high-value-added, nonpolluting industries. The state retains monopolies in a number of sectors, including tobacco, the telephone network, and the postal service. Living standards are high, roughly comparable to those in prosperous French metropolitan areas.

The state has no income tax and low business taxes and thrives as a tax haven both for individuals who have established residence and for foreign companies that have set up businesses and offices. Monaco, however, is not a tax-free shelter; it charges nearly 20% value-added tax, collects stamp duties, and companies face a 33% tax on profits unless they can show that three-quarters of profits are generated within the principality. Monaco was formally removed from the OECD's "grey list" of uncooperative tax jurisdictions in late 2009, but continues to face international pressure to abandon its banking secrecy laws and help combat tax evasion. In October 2014, Monaco officially became the 84th jurisdiction participating in the OECD's Multilateral Convention on Mutual Administrative Assistance in Tax Matters, an effort to combat offshore tax avoidance and evasion.

Monaco's reliance on tourism and banking for its economic growth has left it vulnerable to a downturn in France and other European economies which are the principality's main trade partners. in 2009, Monaco's GDP fell by 11.5% as the euro-zone crisis precipitated a sharp drop in tourism and retail activity and home sales. A modest recovery ensued in 2010 and intensified in 2013, with GDP growth of more than 9%, but Monaco's economic prospects remain uncertain, and tied to future euro-zone growth.

GDP (purchasing power parity):
$6.79 billion (2013 est.)
$6.213 billion (2012 est.)
$5.748 billion (2011 est.)
note: data are in 2012 US dollars
country comparison to the world: 166

GDP (official exchange rate): $6.063 billion (2013 est.)

GDP—real growth rate: 9.3% (2013 est.)
1.2% (2012 est.)
7% (2011 est.)
country comparison to the world: 4

GDP—per capita (PPP): $78,700 (2013 est.)
$73,200 (2012 est.)
$72,600 (2011 est.)
country comparison to the world: 9

GDP—composition, by sector of origin: agriculture: 0%
industry: 14%

services: 86% (2013)

Agriculture—products: none

Industries: banking, insurance, tourism, construction, small-scale industrial and consumer products

Industrial production growth rate: 20% (2013)
country comparison to the world: 1

Labor force: 52,000
note: includes all foreign workers (2014 est.)
country comparison to the world: 191

Labor force—by occupation: agriculture: 0%
industry: 16.1%
services: 83.9% (2012 est.)

Unemployment rate: 2% (2012)
country comparison to the world: 13

Population below poverty line: NA%

Household income or consumption by percentage share: lowest: 10%: NA%
highest: 10%: NA%

Budget: revenues: $1.075 billion
expenditures: $1.144 billion (2011 est.)
Taxes and other revenues: 17.7% of GDP (2011 est.)
country comparison to the world: 173

Budget surplus (+) or deficit (–): -1.1% of GDP (2011 est.)
country comparison to the world: 57

Fiscal year: calendar year

Inflation rate (consumer prices): 1.5% (2010)
country comparison to the world: 100

Market value of publicly traded shares: $NA

Exports: $1.115 billion (2011)
$684.9 million (2010)
note: full customs integration with France, which collects and rebates Monegasque trade duties; also participates in EU market system through customs union with France
country comparison to the world: 157

Exports—partners: Europe 73.2%, Africa 14.6%, America 5.2%, Asia 4.9% (2013 est.)

Imports: $1.162 billion (2011)
$850.2 million (2010)
note: full customs integration with France, which collects and rebates Monegasque trade duties; also participates in EU market system through customs union with France
country comparison to the world: 176

Imports—partners: Europe 70.4%, Asia 20.8%, America 4.4%, Africa 4.1% (2013 est.)

Debt—external: $NA

Exchange rates: euros (EUR) per US dollar—
0.885 (2015 est.)
0.7525 (2014 est.)
0.7634 (2013 est.)
0.78 (2012 est.)
0.7185 (2011 est.)

COMMUNICATIONS

Telephones—fixed lines: total subscriptions: 50,600
subscriptions per 100 inhabitants: 166 (2014 est.)
country comparison to the world: 162

Telephones—mobile cellular: total: 33,700
subscriptions per 100 inhabitants: 110 (2014 est.)
country comparison to the world: 207

Telephone system: general assessment: modern automatic telephone system; the country's sole fixed-line operator offers a full range of services to residential and business customers
domestic: combined fixed-line and mobile-cellular teledensity exceeds 200 per 100 persons
international: country code—377; no satellite earth stations; connected by cable into the French communications system (2011)

Broadcast media: TV Monte-Carlo (TMC) operates a TV network; cable TV available; Radio Monte-Carlo has extensive radio networks in France and Italy with French-language broadcasts to France beginning in the 1960s and Italian-language broadcasts to Italy beginning in the 1970s; other radio stations include Riviera Radio and Radio Monaco (2012)
Radio broadcast stations: AM 1, FM 11, short-wave 1 (2008)
Television broadcast stations: 5 (1998)

Internet country code: .mc

Internet hosts: 26,009 (2012)
country comparison to the world: 111

Internet users: total: 27,400
percent of population: 89.9% (2014 est.)
country comparison to the world: 199

TRANSPORTATION

Heliports: 1 (2012)

Roadways: total: 77 km
paved: 77 km (2010)
country comparison to the world: 218

Merchant marine: registered in other countries: 64 (Bahamas 8, Bermuda 2, Liberia 8, Malta 3, Marshall Islands 30, Panama 11, Saint Vincent and the Grenadines 2) (2010)
country comparison to the world: 63

Ports and terminals: major seaport(s): Monaco

MILITARY AND SECURITY

Military branches: no regular military forces; Directorate of Public Security (2012)

Military—note: defense is the responsibility of France

TRANSNATIONAL ISSUES

Disputes—international: none

MONGOLIA

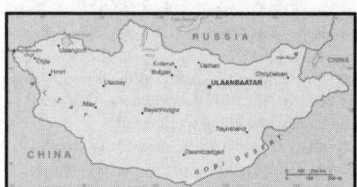

INTRODUCTION

Background: The Mongols gained fame in the 13th century when under Chinggis KHAAN they established a huge Eurasian empire through conquest. After his death the empire was divided into several powerful Mongol states, but these broke apart in the 14th century. The Mongols eventually retired to their original steppe homelands and in the late 17th century came under Chinese rule. Mongolia won its independence in 1921 with Soviet backing and a communist regime was installed in 1924. The modern country of Mongolia, however, represents only part of the Mongols' historical homeland; today, more ethnic Mongolians live in the Inner Mongolia Autonomous Region in the People's Republic of China than in Mongolia. Following a peaceful democratic revolution in 1990, the ex-communist Mongolian People's Revolutionary Party (MPRP) won most parliamentary elections and stayed in power either governing alone or in coalition. In 2009, current President ELBEGDORJ of the Democratic Party (DP) was elected to office and was re-elected for a second and final term in June 2013. In 2010, the MPRP voted to retake the name of the Mongolian People's Party (MPP), a name it used in the early 1920s. Shortly thereafter, a new party was formed by former President ENKHBAYAR, which confusingly adopted for itself the MPRP name. Following the 2012 parliamentary elections, a coalition of four political parties was formed but then dissolved in November 2014 when Prime Minister ALTANKHUYAG was voted out of office. A new five-party grand coalition was formed in December 2014 under the leadership of Prime Minister SAIKHANBILEG. The coalition had been expected to last until the next parliamentary elections in the summer of 2016. However, in August 2015, the grand coalition also dissolved, and Prime Minister SAI KHANBILEG took charge of a new governing coalition comprising three parties. Parliamentary elections are scheduled for 29 June 2016.

GEOGRAPHY

Location: Northern Asia, between China and Russia

Geographic coordinates: 46 00 N, 105 00 E

Map references: Asia

Area: *total:* 1,564,116 sq km
land: 1,553,556 sq km
water: 10,560 sq km

country comparison to the world: 19

Area—comparative: slightly smaller than Alaska; more than twice the size of Texas

Land boundaries: *total:* 8,082 km
border countries (2): China 4,630 km, Russia 3,452 km

Coastline: 0 km (landlocked)

Maritime claims: none (landlocked)

Climate: desert; continental (large daily and seasonal temperature ranges)

Terrain: vast semidesert and desert plains, grassy steppe, mountains in west and southwest; Gobi Desert in south-central

Elevation: *mean elevation:* 1,528 m

elevation extremes: *lowest point:* Hoh Nuur 560 m
highest point: Nayramadlin Orgil (Huyten Orgil) 4,374 m

Natural resources: oil, coal, copper, molybdenum, tungsten, phosphates, tin, nickel, zinc, fluorspar, gold, silver, iron

Land use: *agricultural land:* 73%
arable land: 0.4%;
permanent crops: 0%;
permanent pasture: 72.6%
forest: 7%
other: 20% (2011 est.)

Irrigated land: 840 sq km (2012)

Total renewable water resources: 34.8 cu km (2011)

Freshwater withdrawal (domestic/industrial/agricultural): *total:* 0.55 cu km/yr (13%/43%/44%)
per capita: 196.8 cu m/yr (2009)

Natural hazards: dust storms; grassland and forest fires; drought; "zud, " which is harsh winter conditions

Environment—current issues: limited natural freshwater resources in some areas; the policies of former Communist regimes promoted rapid urbanization and industrial growth that had negative effects on the environment; the burning of soft coal in power plants and the lack of enforcement of environmental laws severely polluted the air in Ulaanbaatar; deforestation, overgrazing, and the converting of virgin land to agricultural production increased soil erosion from wind and rain; desertification and mining activities had a deleterious effect on the environment

Environment—international agreements: *party to:* Biodiversity, Climate Change, Climate Change-Kyoto Protocol, Desertification, Endangered Species, Environmental Modification, Hazardous Wastes, Law of the Sea, Ozone Layer Protection, Ship Pollution, Wetlands, Whaling
signed, but not ratified: none of the selected agreements

Geography—note: landlocked; strategic location between China and Russia

PEOPLE AND SOCIETY

Nationality: *noun:* Mongolian(s)
adjective: Mongolian

Ethnic groups: Khalkh 81.9%, Kazak 3.8%, Dorvod 2.7%, Bayad 2.1%, Buryat-Bouriates 1.7%, Zakhchin 1.2%, Dariganga 1%, Uriankhai 1%, other 4.6% (2010 est.)

Languages: Khalkha Mongol 90% (official), Turkic, Russian (1999)

Religions: Buddhist 53%, Muslim 3%, Christian 2.2%, Shamanist 2.9%, other 0.4%, none 38.6% (2010 est.)

Population: 2,992,908 (July 2015 est.)
country comparison to the world: 138

Age structure: *0–14 years:* 26.87% (male 409,994/female 394,195)
15–24 years: 17.69% (male 267,507/female 261,869)
25–54 years: 45.04% (male 653,195/female 694,688)
55–64 years: 6.29% (male 86,401/female 101,714)
65 years and over: 4.12% (male 50,372/female 72,973) (2015 est.)

Dependency ratios: *total dependency ratio:* 47.6%
youth dependency ratio: 41.7%
elderly dependency ratio: 6%
potential support ratio: 16.7% (2015 est.)

Median age: *total:* 27.5 years
male: 26.7 years
female: 28.3 years (2015 est.)
country comparison to the world: 134

Population growth rate: 1.31% (2015 est.)
country comparison to the world: 92

Birth rate: 20.25 births/1,000 population (2015 est.)
country comparison to the world: 83

Death rate: 6.35 deaths/1,000 population (2015 est.)
country comparison to the world: 152

Net migration rate: -0.84 migrant(s)/1,000 population (2015 est.)
country comparison to the world: 146

Urbanization: *urban population:* 72% of total population (2015)
rate of urbanization: 2.78% annual rate of change (2010–15 est.)

Major urban areas—Population: ULAANBAATAR (capital) 1.377 million (2015)

Sex ratio: *at birth:* 1.05 male(s)/female
0–14 years: 1.04 male(s)/female
15–24 years: 1.02 male(s)/female
25–54 years: 0.94 male(s)/female
55–64 years: 0.85 male(s)/female
65 years and over: 0.69 male(s)/female
total population: 0.96 male(s)/female (2015 est.)

Mother's mean age at first birth: 20.5

note: median age at first birth among women 20–24 (2008 est.)

Maternal mortality rate: 44 deaths/100,000 live births (2015 est.)
country comparison to the world: 96

Infant mortality rate: *total:* 22.44 deaths/1,000 live births
male: 25.64 deaths/1,000 live births
female: 19.09 deaths/1,000 live births (2015 est.)
country comparison to the world: 78

Life expectancy at birth: *total population:* 69.29 years
male: 65.04 years
female: 73.76 years (2015 est.)
country comparison to the world: 159

Total fertility rate: 2.17 children born/woman (2015 est.)
country comparison to the world: 100

Contraceptive prevalence rate: 54.9% (2010)

Health expenditures: 6% of GDP (2013)
country comparison to the world: 105

Physicians density: 2.84 physicians/1,000 population (2011)

Hospital bed density: 6.8 beds/1,000 population (2012)

Drinking water source:
improved:
urban: 66.4% of population
rural: 59.2% of population
total: 64.4% of population
unimproved:
urban: 33.6% of population
rural: 40.8% of population
total: 35.6% of population (2015 est.)

Sanitation facility access:
improved:
urban: 66.4% of population
rural: 42.6% of population
total: 59.7% of population
unimproved:
urban: 33.6% of population
rural: 57.4% of population
total: 40.3% of population (2015 est.)

HIV/AIDS—adult prevalence rate: 0.04% (2013 est.)
country comparison to the world: 124

HIV/AIDS—people living with HIV/AIDS: 600 (2013 est.)
country comparison to the world: 124

HIV/AIDS—deaths: fewer than 100 (2013 est.)
country comparison to the world: 115

Obesity—adult prevalence rate: 15.7% (2014)
country comparison to the world: 122

Children under the age of 5 years underweight: 1.6% (2013)
country comparison to the world: 92

Education expenditures: 4.6% of GDP (2011)
country comparison to the world: 58

Literacy: *definition:* age 15 and over can read and write
total population: 98.4%
male: 98.2%

female: 98.6% (2015 est.)

School life expectancy (primary to tertiary education): *total:* 15 years
male: 14 years
female: 15 years (2014)

Child labor—children ages 5–14: *total number:* 106,203
percentage: 18% (2005 est.)

Unemployment, youth ages 15–24: *total:* 16.6%
male: 14.7%
female: 19.1% (2013 est.)
country comparison to the world: 92

GOVERNMENT

Country name: *conventional long form:* none
conventional short form: Mongolia
local long form: none
local short form: Mongol Uls
former: Outer Mongolia
etymology: the name means "Land of the Mongols" in Latin; the Mongolian name Mongol Uls translates as "Mongol State"

Government type: semi-presidential republic

Capital: *name:* Ulaanbaatar

Geographic coordinates: 47 55 N, 106 55 E
time difference: UTC+8 (13 hours ahead of Washington, DC, during Standard Time)
daylight saving time: +1hr, begins last Saturday in March; ends last Saturday in September
note: Mongolia has two time zones—Ulaanbaatar Time (8 hours in advance of UTC) and Hovd Time (7 hours in advance of UTC)

Administrative divisions: 21 provinces (aymguud, singular—aymag) and 1 municipality* (singular—hot); Arhangay, Bayanhongor, Bayan-Olgiy, Bulgan, Darhan-Uul, Dornod, Dornogovi, Dundgovi, Dzavhan (Zavkhan), Govi-Altay, Govisumber, Hentiy, Hovd, Hovsgol, Omnogovi, Orhon, Ovorhangay, Selenge, Suhbaatar, Tov, Ulaanbaatar*, Uvs

Independence: 11 July 1921 (from China)

National holiday: Independence Day/Revolution Day, 11 July (1921)

Constitution: several previous; latest adopted 13 January 1992, effective 12 February 1992; amended 1999, 2001; legislation on amendments proposed in 2015 continued into 2016 (2016)

Legal system: civil law system influenced by Soviet and Romano-Germanic legal systems; constitution ambiguous on judicial review of legislative acts

International law organization participation: has not submitted an ICJ jurisdiction declaration; accepts ICCt jurisdiction

Citizenship: *citizenship by birth:* no
citizenship by descent only: both parents must be citizens of Mongolia; one parent if born within Mongolia
dual citizenship recognized: no
residency requirement for naturalization: 5 years

Suffrage: 18 years of age; universal

Executive branch: *chief of state:* President Tsakhia ELBEGDORJ (since 18 June 2009)

head of government: Prime Minister Jargaltulga ERDENEBAT (since 7 July 2016); Deputy Prime Minister Tserendash OYUNBAATAR (since 8 September 2015)
cabinet: Cabinet nominated by the prime minister in consultation with the president, confirmed by the State Great Hural (parliament)
elections/appointments: presidential candidates nominated by political parties represented in the State Great Hural and directly elected by simple majority popular vote for a 4-year term (eligible for a second term); election last held on 26 June 2013 (next to be held in June 2017); following legislative elections, the leader of the majority party or majority coalition usually elected prime minister by the State Great Hural
election results: Tsakhia ELBEGDORJ reelected president; percent of vote—Tsakhia ELBEGDORJ (DP) 50.2%, Badmaanyambuu BAT-ERDENE (MPP) 42%, Natsag UDVAL (MPRP) 6.5%, other 1.3%

Legislative branch: *description:* unicameral State Great Hural or Ulsyn Ikh Khural (76 seats; 48 members directly elected in multi-seat constituencies by simple majority vote and 28 members directly elected in multi-seat constituencies by proportional representation vote; members serve 4-year terms)
elections: last held on 29 June 2016 (next to be held in June 2020)
election results: MPRP 1, independent 1

Judicial branch: *highest court(s):* Supreme Court (consists of the chief justice and 24 judges organized into civil, criminal, and administrative chambers); Constitutional Court or Tsets (consists of a chairman and 8 members)
judge selection and term of office: Supreme Court chief justice and judges appointed by the president upon recommendation to the State Great Hural by the General Council of Courts, a 14-member body of judges and judicial officials; term of appointment is for life; chairman of the Constitutional Court elected from among its members; members appointed by the State Great Hural upon nominations—3 each by the president, the State Great Hural, and the Supreme Court; term of appointment is 6 years; chairmanship limited to a single renewable 3-year term
subordinate courts: aimag (provincial) and capital city appellate courts; soum, inter-soum, and district courts; Administrative Cases Courts (established in 2004)

Political parties and leaders: Civil Will-Green Party or CWGP [Sanjaasuren OYUN, Sambuu DEMBEREL, Tserendorj GANKHUYAG]
Democratic Party or DP [Zandaakhuu ENKHBOLD]
Mongolian National Democratic Party or MNDP [Mendsaikhan ENKHSAIKHAN]
Mongolian People's Party or MPP [Miyegombo ENKHBOLD]
Mongolian People's Revolutionary Party or MPRP [Nambar ENKHBAYAR]

New Labor Party or XYH [S. GANBAATAR]

Political pressure groups and leaders: *other:* human rights groups; women's rights groups; disability rights groups

International organization participation: ADB, ARF, CD, CICA, CP, EBRD, EITI (compliant country), FAO, G-77, IAEA, IBRD, ICAO, ICC (NGOs), ICCt, ICRM, IDA, IFAD, IFC, IFRCS, ILO, IMF, IMO, IMSO, Interpol, IOC, IOM, IPU, ISO, ITSO, ITU, ITUC, MIGA, MIN URSO, MON USCO, NAM, OPCW, OSCE, SCO (observer), UN, UN AMID, UNCTAD, UNESCO, UNIDO, UNISFA, UNMISS, UNWTO, UPU, WCO, WHO, WIPO, WMO, WTO

Diplomatic representation in the US: *chief of mission:* Ambassador Bulgaa ALTANGEREL (since 8 January 2013)
chancery: 2833 M Street NW, Washington, DC 20007
telephone: [1] (202) 333-7117
FAX: [1] (202) 298-9227
consulate(s) general: New York, San Francisco

Diplomatic representation from the US: *chief of mission:* Ambassador Jennifer Zimdahl GALT (since 5 October 2015)
embassy: Denver Street
mailing address: PSC 461, Box 300, FPO AP 96521–0002; P.O. Box 341, Ulaanbaatar-14192
telephone: [976] 7007-6001
FAX: [976] 7007-6016

Flag description: three, equal vertical bands of red (hoist side), blue, and red; centered on the hoist-side red band in yellow is the national emblem ("soyombo"—a columnar arrangement of abstract and geometric representation for fire, sun, moon, earth, water, and the yin-yang symbol); blue represents the sky, red symbolizes progress and prosperity

National symbol(s): soyombo emblem; national colors: red, blue, yellow

National anthem: *name:* "Mongol ulsyn toriin duulal" (National Anthem of Mongolia)
lyrics/music: Tsendiin DAMDINSUREN/Bilegiin DAMDINSUREN and Luvsanjamts MURJORJ
note: music adopted 1950, lyrics adopted 2006; lyrics altered on numerous occasions

ECONOMY

Economy—overview: Foreign direct investment in Mongolia's extractive industries—which are based on extensive deposits of copper, gold, coal, molybdenum, fluorspar, uranium, tin, and tungsten—has transformed Mongolia's landlocked economy from its traditional dependence on herding and agriculture. Exports now account for more than half of GDP. Mongolia depends on China for more than 60% of its external trade—China receives some 90% of Mongolia's exports and supplies Mongolia with more than one-third of its imports. Mongolia also relies on Russia for 90% of its energy supplies, leaving it vulnerable to price increases. Remittances from Mongolians working abroad, particularly in South Korea, are significant. Soviet assistance, at its height one-third of GDP, disappeared

almost overnight in 1990 and 1991 at the time of the dismantlement of the USSR. The following decade saw Mongolia endure both deep recession, because of political inaction, and natural disasters, as well as strong economic growth, because of market reforms and extensive privatization of the formerly state-run economy. The country opened a fledgling stock exchange in 1991. Mongolia joined the WTO in 1997 and seeks to expand its participation in regional economic and trade regimes. Growth averaged nearly 9% per year in 2004–08 largely because of high copper prices globally and new gold production. By late 2008, Mongolia was hit by the global financial crisis and Mongolia's real economy contracted 1.3% in 2009. In early 2009, the IMF reached a $236 million Stand-by Arrangement with Mongolia and it emerged from the crisis with a stronger banking sector and better fiscal management. in October 2009, Mongolia passed long-awaited legislation on an investment agreement to develop the Oyu Tolgoi (OT) mine, among the world's largest untapped copper-gold deposits. However, a dispute with foreign investors developing OT called into question the attractiveness of Mongolia as a destination for foreign investment. This caused a severe drop in FDI, and a slowing economy, leading to the dismissal of Prime Minister ALTANKHUYAG in November 2014. The economy had grown more than 10% per year between 2011 and 2013—largely on the strength of commodity exports and high government spending -before slowing to 7.8% in 2014 and 2.3% in 2015.

The current government has made restoring investor trust and reviving the economy its top priority, but has failed to invigorate the economy in the face of the large drop off in foreign direct investment. Mongolia's economy faces near-term economic risks from the government's loose fiscal and monetary policies, from uncertainties in foreign demand for Mongolian exports, and on Mongolia's ability to access financing. The May 2015 agreement with Rio Tinto to restart the OT mine and the subsequent $4.4 billion finance package signing in December 2015 have served to increase investor confidence but are unlikely to overcome the downward economic pressures in the shortterm.

GDP (purchasing power parity):
$36.07 billion (2015 est.)
$35.26 billion (2014 est.)
$32.68 billion (2013 est.)
note: data are in 2015 US dollars
country comparison to the world: 118

GDP (official exchange rate): $11.74 billion (2015 est.)

GDP—real growth rate: 2.3% (2015 est.)
7.9% (2014 est.)
11.6% (2013 est.)
country comparison to the world: 130

GDP—per capita (PPP): $12,100 (2015 est.)
$12,100 (2014 est.)
$11,300 (2013 est.)
note: data are in 2015 US dollars
country comparison to the world: 124

Gross national saving: 21.7% of GDP (2015 est.)
23.4% of GDP (2014 est.)
26.3% of GDP (2013 est.)
country comparison to the world: 70

GDP—composition, by end use:
household consumption: 58.5%
government consumption: 12.8%
investment in fixed capital: 18.1%
investment in inventories: 7.1%
exports of goods and services: 60.7%
imports of goods and services: -57.4% (2015 est.)

GDP—composition, by sector of origin:
agriculture: 16.6%
industry: 33.1%
services: 50.3% (2015 est.)

Agriculture—products: wheat, barley, vegetables, forage crops; sheep, goats, cattle, camels, horses

Industries: construction and construction materials; mining (coal, copper, molybdenum, fluorspar, tin, tungsten, gold); oil; food and beverages; processing of animal products, cashmere and natural fiber manufacturing

Industrial production growth rate: 2.9% (2015 est.)
country comparison to the world: 91

Labor force: 1.164 million (2015 est.)
country comparison to the world: 139

Labor force—by occupation: *agriculture:* 28.6%
industry: 21%
services: 50.4% (2014)

Unemployment rate: 8.3% (2015 est.)
7.7% (2014 est.)
country comparison to the world: 96

Population below poverty line: 21.6% (2014 est.)

Household income or consumption by percentage share: *lowest:* 10%: 3%
highest: 10%: 28.4% (2008)

Distribution of family income—Gini index: 36.5 (2008) 32.8 (2002)
country comparison to the world: 84

Budget: *revenues:* $2.994 billion
expenditures: $3.354 billion (2015 est.)
Taxes and other revenues: 32.4% of GDP (2015 est.)
country comparison to the world: 76

Budget surplus (+) or deficit (–): -7.3% of GDP (2015 est.)
country comparison to the world: 194

Public debt: 72% of GDP (31 September 2015 est.)
country comparison to the world: 44

Fiscal year: calendar year

Inflation rate (consumer prices): 5.9% (2015 est.)
12.9% (2014 est.)
country comparison to the world: 185

Central bank discount rate: 12% (14 January 2016)
13% (15 January 2015)
country comparison to the world: 16

Commercial bank prime lending rate: 19.1% (31 December 2015 est.)
19.54% (31 December 2014 est.)
country comparison to the world: 14

Stock of narrow money: $844 million (31 December 2015 est.)

$963.5 million (31 December 2014 est.)
country comparison to the world: 157

Stock of broad money: $5.036 billion (31 December 2015 est.)
$5.648 billion (31 December 2014 est.)
country comparison to the world: 130

Stock of domestic credit: $5.86 billion (31 December 2015 est.)
$6.64 billion (31 December 2014 est.)
country comparison to the world: 118

Market value of publicly traded shares:
$632.6 million (31 December 2015 est.)
$766.1 million (31 December 2014)
$1.095 billion (31 December 2013 est.)
country comparison to the world: 110

Current account balance: -$567 million (2015 est.)
-$1.405 billion (2014 est.)
country comparison to the world: 102

Exports: $5.272 billion (2015 est.)
$5.825 billion (2014 est.)
country comparison to the world: 109

Exports—commodities: copper, apparel, livestock, animal products, cashmere, wool, hides, fluorspar, other nonferrous metals, coal, crude oil

Exports—partners: China 84%, Switzerland 9% (2015)

Imports: $3.923 billion (2015 est.)
$4.738 billion (2014 est.)
country comparison to the world: 135

Imports—commodities: machinery and equipment, fuel, cars, food products, industrial consumer goods, chemicals, building materials, cigarettes and tobacco, appliances, soap and detergent

Imports—partners: China 39.9%, Russia 28.4%, Japan 6.4%, South Korea 6.2% (2015)

Debt—external: $20.94 billion (31 December 2014 est.)
$19.02 billion (31 December 2013 est.)
country comparison to the world: 85

Stock of direct foreign investment—at home:
$17.3 billion (31 December 2015 est.)
$16.25 billion (31 December 2014 est.)
country comparison to the world: 81

Stock of direct foreign investment—abroad:
$1.241 billion (31 December 2013 est.)
$1.191 billion (31 December 2012 est.)
country comparison to the world: 82

Exchange rates: togrog/tugriks (MNT) per US dollar—
2,042 (2016 est.)
1,883 (2015 est.)
1,817.9 (2013 est.)
1,357.6 (2012 est.)
1,265.5 (2011 est.)

ENERGY

Electricity—production: 4.534 billion kWh (2012 est.)
country comparison to the world: 121

Electricity—consumption: 4.204 billion kWh (2012 est.)
country comparison to the world: 125

Electricity—exports: 21 million kWh (2012 est.)
country comparison to the world: 87

Electricity—imports: 366 million kWh (2012 est.)
country comparison to the world: 83

Electricity—installed generating capacity: 833,300 kW (2012 est.)
country comparison to the world: 128

Electricity—from fossil fuels: 99.8% of total installed capacity (2012 est.)
country comparison to the world: 42

Electricity—from nuclear fuels: 0% of total installed capacity (2012 est.)
country comparison to the world: 136

Electricity—from hydroelectric plants: 0% of total installed capacity (2012 est.)
country comparison to the world: 185

Electricity—from other renewable sources: 0.2% of total installed capacity (2012 est.)
country comparison to the world: 108

Crude oil—production: 20,850 bbl/day (2014 est.)
country comparison to the world: 69

Crude oil—exports: 9,780 bbl/day (2012 est.)
country comparison to the world: 66

Crude oil—imports: 0 bbl/day (2012 est.)
country comparison to the world: 93

Crude oil—proved reserves: NA bbl 0 bbl
country comparison to the world: 163

Refined petroleum products—production: 0 bbl/day (2012 est.)
country comparison to the world: 207

Refined petroleum products—consumption: 24,000 bbl/day (2013 est.)
country comparison to the world: 122

Refined petroleum products—exports: 0 bbl/day (2012 est.)
country comparison to the world: 200

Refined petroleum products—imports: 24,600 bbl/day (2012 est.)
country comparison to the world: 102

Natural gas—production: 0 cu m (2013 est.)
country comparison to the world: 98

Natural gas—consumption: 0 cu m (2013 est.)
country comparison to the world: 167

Natural gas—exports: 0 cu m (2013 est.)
country comparison to the world: 141

Natural gas—imports: 0 cu m (2013 est.)
country comparison to the world: 96

Natural gas—proved reserves: 0 cu m (1 January 2014 est.)
country comparison to the world: 166

Carbon dioxide emissions from consumption of energy: 11.36 million Mt (2012 est.)
country comparison to the world: 99

COMMUNICATIONS

Telephones—fixed lines: *total subscriptions:* 230,000
subscriptions per 100 inhabitants: 8 (2014 est.)
country comparison to the world: 125

Telephones—mobile cellular: *total:* 3 million
subscriptions per 100 inhabitants: 103 (2014 est.)

country comparison to the world: 139

Telephone system: *general assessment:* network is improving with international direct dialing available in many areas; a fiber-optic network has been installed that is improving broadband and communication services between major urban centers with multiple companies providing inter-city fiber-optic cable services
domestic: very low fixed-line teledensity; there are multiple mobile-cellular providers and subscribership is increasing
international: country code—976; satellite earth stations—7 (2011)

Broadcast media: following a law passed in 2005, Mongolia's state-run radio and TV provider converted to a public service provider; also available are private radio and TV broadcasters, as well as multi-channel satellite and cable TV providers; more than 100 radio stations, including some 20 via repeaters for the public broadcaster; transmissions of multiple international broadcasters are available (2008)
Radio broadcast stations: AM 7, FM 108 (includes 20 national radio broadcaster repeaters), shortwave 4 (2009)
Television broadcast stations: 99 (2009)

Internet country code: .mn

Internet hosts: 20,084 (2012)
country comparison to the world: 118

Internet users: total: 527,100
percent of population: 17.9% (2014 est.)
country comparison to the world: 131

TRANSPORTATION

Airports: 44 (2013)
country comparison to the world: 98

Airports—with paved runways: *total:* 15
over 3,047 m: 2
2,438 to 3,047 m: 10
1,524 to 2,437 m: 3 (2013)

Airports—with unpaved runways: *total:* 29
over 3,047 m: 2
2,438 to 3,047 m: 2
1,524 to 2,437 m: 24
under 914 m: 1 (2013)

Heliports: 1 (2013)

Railways: *total:* 1,815 km
broad gauge: 1,815 km 1.520-m gauge
note: national operator Ulannbaator Railway is jointly owned by the Mongolian Government and by the Russian State Railway (2016)
country comparison to the world: 75

Roadways: *total:* 49,249 km
paved: 4,800 km
unpaved: 44,449 km (2013)
country comparison to the world: 77

Waterways: 580 km (the only waterway in operation is Lake Hovsgol) (135 km); Selenge River (270 km) and Orhon River (175 km) are navigable but carry little traffic; lakes and rivers ice free from May to September) (2010)
country comparison to the world: 81

Merchant marine: *total:* 57
by type: bulk carrier 21, cargo 25, chemical tanker 1, container 2, liquefied gas 2, passenger/cargo 2, roll on/roll off 3, vehicle carrier 1

foreign-owned: 44 (Indonesia 2, Japan 2, North Korea 1, Russia 2, Singapore 3, Ukraine 1, Vietnam 33) (2010)
country comparison to the world: 68

MILITARY AND SECURITY

Military branches: Mongolian Armed Forces (Mongol ulsyn zevsegt huchin): Mongolian Army, Mongolian Air Force (2016)

Military service age and obligation: 18–27 years of age for compulsory and voluntary military service; 1 -year conscript service obligation in land or air forces or police for males only; after conscription, soldiers can contract into military service for 2 or 4 years; citizens can also voluntarily join the armed forces (2015)

Military expenditures: 0.98% of GDP (2015)
1.12% of GDP (2012)

0.99% of GDP (2011)
1.12% of GDP (2010)
country comparison to the world: 90

MONGOLIA

Disputes—international: none

MONTENEGRO

INTRODUCTION

Background: The use of the name Crna Gora or Black Mountain (Montenegro) began in the 13th century in reference to a highland region in the Serbian province of Zeta. The later medieval state of Zeta maintained its existence until 1496 when Montenegro finally fell under Ottoman rule. Over subsequent centuries, Montenegro managed to maintain a level of autonomy within the Ottoman Empire. From the 16th to 19th centuries, Montenegro was a theocracy ruled by a series of bishop princes; in 1852, it transformed into a secular principality. Montenegro was recognized as an independent sovereign principality at the Congress of Berlin in 1878. After World War I, during which Montenegro fought on the side of the Allies, Montenegro was absorbed by the Kingdom of Serbs, Croats, and Slovenes, which became the Kingdom of Yugoslavia in 1929; at the conclusion of World War II, it became a constituent republic of the Socialist Federal Republic of Yugoslavia. When the latter dissolved in 1992, Montenegro federated with Serbia, creating the Federal Republic of Yugoslavia and, after 2003, shifting to a looser State Union of Serbia and Montenegro. In May 2006, Montenegro invoked its right under the Constitutional Charter of Serbia and Montenegro to hold a referendum on independence from the state union. The vote for severing ties with Serbia barely exceeded 55%—the threshold set by the

EU—allowing Montenegro to formally restore its independence on 3 June 2006.

GEOGRAPHY

Location: Southeastern Europe, between the Adriatic Sea and Serbia

Geographic coordinates: 42 30 N, 19 18 E

Map references: Europe

Area: total: 13,812 sq km
land: 13,452 sq km
water: 360 sq km
country comparison to the world: 162

Area—comparative: slightly smaller than Connecticut

Land boundaries: total: 680 km
border countries (5): Albania 186 km, Bosnia and Herzegovina 242 km, Croatia 19 km, Kosovo 76 km, Serbia 157 km

Coastline: 293.5 km

Maritime claims: territorial sea: 12 nm
continental shelf: defined by treaty

Climate: Mediterranean climate, hot dry summers and autumns and relatively cold winters with heavy snowfalls inland

Terrain: highly indented coastline with narrow coastal plain backed by rugged high limestone mountains and plateaus

Elevation: mean elevation: 1,086 m

elevation extremes: lowest point: Adriatic Sea 0 m
highest point: Bobotov Kuk 2,522 m

Natural resources: bauxite, hydroelectricity

Land use: agricultural land: 38.2%
arable land: 12.9%;
permanent crops: 1.2%;
permanent pasture: 24.1%
forest: 40.4%
other: 21.4% (2011 est.)

Irrigated land: 24 sq km (2012)

Natural hazards: destructive earthquakes

Environment—current issues: pollution of coastal waters from sewage outlets, especially in tourist-related areas such as Kotor

Environment—international agreements: party to: Air Pollution, Biodiversity, Climate Change,

Climate Change-Kyoto Protocol, Desertification, Hazardous Wastes, Law of the Sea, Marine Dumping, Marine Life Conservation, Ozone Layer Protection, Ship Pollution
signed, but not ratified: none of the selected agreements

Geography—note: strategic location along the Adriatic coast

PEOPLE AND SOCIETY

Nationality: noun: Montenegrin(s)
adjective: Montenegrin

Ethnic groups: Montenegrin 45%, Serbian 28.7%, Bosniak 8.7%, Albanian 4.9%, Muslim 3.3%, Roma 1%, Croat 1%, other 2.6%, unspecified 4.9% (2011 est.)

Languages: Serbian 42.9%, Montenegrin (official) 37%, Bosnian 5.3%, Albanian 5.3%, Serbo-Croat 2%, other 3.5%, unspecified 4% (2011 est.)

Religions: Orthodox 72.1%, Muslim 19.1%, Catholic 3.4%, atheist 1.2%, other 1.5%, unspecified 2.6% (2011 est.)

Population: 647,073 (July 2015 est.)
country comparison to the world: 168

Age structure: 0–14 years: 15.18% (male 48,138/female 50,095)
15–24 years: 10.27% (male 30,681/female 35,776)
25–54 years: 47.02% (male 164,104/female 140,142)
55–64 years: 13.12% (male 42,354/female 42,542)
65 years and over: 14.41% (male 37,040/female 56,201) (2015 est.)

Dependency ratios: total dependency ratio: 47.7%
youth dependency ratio: 27.6%
elderly dependency ratio: 20.2%
potential support ratio: 5% (2015 est.)

Median age: total: 39.7 years
male: 38.7 years
female: 40.9 years (2015 est.)
country comparison to the world: 48

Population growth rate: -0.42% (2015 est.)
country comparison to the world: 221

Birth rate: 10.42 births/1,000 population (2015 est.)
country comparison to the world: 188

Death rate: 9.43 deaths/1,000 population (2015 est.)
country comparison to the world: 57

Urbanization: *urban Population:* 64% of total population (2015)
rate of urbanization: 0.34% annual rate of change (2010–15 est.)

Major urban areas—Population: PODGORICA (capital) 165,000 (2014)

Sex ratio: *at birth:* 1.06 male(s)/female
0–14 years: 0.96 male(s)/female
15–24 years: 0.86 male(s)/female
25–54 years: 1.17 male(s)/female
55–64 years: 1 male(s)/female
65 years and over: 0.66 male(s)/female
total population: 0.99 male(s)/female (2015 est.)

Mother's mean age at first birth: 26.3 (2010 est.)

Maternal mortality rate: 7 deaths/100,000 live births (2015 est.)
country comparison to the world: 160

Contraceptive prevalence rate: 39.4% (2005/06)

Health expenditures: 6.5% of GDP (2013)
country comparison to the world: 65

Physicians density: 2.11 physicians/1,000 population (2013)

Hospital bed density: 4 beds/1,000 population (2011)

Drinking water source:
improved:
urban: 100% of population
rural: 99.2% of population
total: 99.7% of population
unimproved:
urban: 0% of population
rural: 0.8% of population
total: 0.3% of population (2015 est.)

Sanitation facility access:
improved:
urban: 98% of population
rural: 92.2% of population
total: 95.9% of population
unimproved:
urban: 2% of population
rural: 7.8% of population
total: 4.1% of population (2015 est.)

HIV/AIDS—adult prevalence rate: NA

HIV/AIDS—people living with HIV/AIDS: NA

HIV/AIDS—deaths: NA

Major infectious diseases: *degree of risk:* intermediate
food or waterborne diseases: bacterial diarrhea

vectorborne disease: Crimean-Congo hemorrhagic fever (2013)

Obesity—adult prevalence rate: 21.4% (2014)
country comparison to the world: 79

Children under the age of 5 years underweight: 1% (2013)
country comparison to the world: 133

Education expenditures: NA

Literacy: *definition:* age 15 and over can read and write

total population: 98.7%
male: 99.5%
female: 98% (2015 est.)

School life expectancy (primary to tertiary education): *total:* 15 years
male: 15 years
female: 15 years (2010)

Child labor—children ages 5–14: *total number:* 8,520
percentage: 10% (2005 est.)

Unemployment, youth ages 15–24: *total:* 41.1%
male: 42.3%
female: 39.7% (2012 est.)
country comparison to the world: 11

GOVERNMENT

Country name: *conventional long form:* none
conventional short form: Montenegro
local long form: none
local short form: CrNA Gora
former: People's Republic of Monten egro, Socialist Republic of Mon ten egro, Republic of Montenegro
etymology: the country's name locally as well as in most Western European languages means "black moun tain " and refers to the dark coniferous forests on Mount Lovcen and the surrounding area

Government type: parliamentary republic

Capital: *name:* Podgorica; *note*—Cetinje retains the status of "Old Royal Capital"

Geographic coordinates: 42 26 N, 19 16 E
time difference: UTC + 1 (6 hours ahead of Washington, DC, during Standard Time)
daylight saving time: +1 hr, begins last Sunday in March; ends last Sunday in October

Administrative divisions: 23 municipalities (opstine, singular—opstina); Andrijevica, Bar, Berane, Bijelo Polje, Budva, Cetinje, Danilovgrad, Gusinje, Herceg Novi, Kolasin, Kotor, Mojkovac, Niksic, Petnijica, Plav, Pljevlja, Pluzine, Podgorica, Rozaje, Savnik, Tivat, Ulcinj, Zabljak

Independence: 3 June 2006 (from the State Union of Serbia and Montenegro)

National holiday: National Day, 13 July (1878, the day the Berlin Congress recognized Montenegro as the 27th independent state in the world, and 1941, the day the Montenegrins staged an uprising against Nazi occupiers and sided with the partisan Communist movement)

Constitution: several previous; latest adopted 22 October 2007; amended 2013,2014 (2016)

Legal system: civil law

International law organization participation: has not submitted an ICJ jurisdiction declaration; accepts ICC jurisdiction

Citizenship: *citizenship by birth:* no
citizenship by descent only: at least one parent must be a citizen of Montenegro
dual citizenship recognized: no
residency requirement for naturalization: 10 years

Suffrage: 18 years of age; universal

Executive branch: *chief of state:* President Filip VUJANOVIC (since 6 April 2008)

head of government: Prime Minister Milo DJUKANOVIC (since 4 December 2012)
cabinet: Ministers act as cabinet

elections/appointments: president directly elected by absolute majority popular vote in 2 rounds if needed for a 5-year term (eligible for a second term); election last held on 7 April 2013 (next to be held in 2018); prime minister nominated by the president, approved by the Assembly
election results: Filip VUJANOVIC reelected president; Filip VUJANOVIC (DPS) 51.2%, Miodrag LEKIC (independent) 48.8%%

Legislative branch: *description:* unicameral Assembly or Skupstina (81 seats; members directly elected in a single nationwide constituency by proportional representation vote; members serve 4-year terms)
elections: last held on 14 October 2012 (next to be held by October 2016)
election results: percent of vote by party/coalition—Coalition for European Montenegro (including DPS, LP, SDP) 45.6%, Democratic Front 22.8%, SNP 11.1%, Positive Montenegro 8.2%, Bosniak Party 4.2%, other (including Albanian and Croatian minority parties) 8.1%; seats by party/coalition—Coalition for European Montenegro (includinGDPS, LP, SDP) 39, Democratic Front 20, SNP 9, Positive Montenegro 7, Bosniak Party 3, Albanian and Croatian minority parties 3
note: seats by party/coalition as of February 2016—DPS 30, DF 15, SDP 6, SNP 6, Positive Montenegro 3, DEMOS 4, DCG 3, Bosniak Party 3, Albanian and Croatian minority parties 3, SD 2, URA 2, LP 1, independent 3

Judicial branch: *highest court(s):* Supreme Court or Vrhovni Sud (consists of the court president, deputy president and 15 judges); Constitutional Court or Ustavni Sud (consists of the court president and 7 judges)
judge selection and term of office: Supreme Court president proposed by general session of the Supreme Court and elected by the Judicial Council, a 9-member body consisting of judges, lawyers designated by the Assembly, and the minister of judicial affairs; Supreme Court president elected for a single renewable, 5-year term; other judges elected by the Judicial Council for life; Constitutional Court judges—2 proposed by the president of Montenegro and 5 by the Assembly, and elected by the Assembly; court president elected from among the court members; court president elected for 3 years, other judges 9 years

subordinate courts: Administrative Courts; Appellate Court; Commercial Courts; high Courts; basic courts

Politicalparties and leaders: Albanian parties (include New Democratic Power or FORCA [Nazif CUNGU] and Democratic Party [Fatmir GJEKA])
Bosniak Party or BS [Rafet HUSOVIC]
Croatian Civic Initiative or HGI [Marija VUCINOVIC]
Democratic Alliance or DEMOS [Miodrag LEKIC]

Democratic Front or DF (includes New Serb Democracy or NOVA [Andrija MANDIC] and Movement for Change or PZP [Nebojsa MEDOJEVIC])

Democratic Montenegro or DCG [Aleksa BECIC]

Democratic Party of Socialists or DPS [Milo DJUKANOVIC]

Liberal Party of Montenegro or LP [Andrija POPOVIC]

Positive Montenegro [Darko PAJOVIC]

Social Democratic Party or SDP [Ranko KRIVOKAPIC]

Social Democrats or SD [Ivan BRAJOVIC]

Socialist People's Party or SNP [Srdjan MILIC]

United Reform Action or URA [Zarko RAKCEVIC]

Political pressure groups and leaders: NA

International organization participation: CE, CEI, EAPC, EBRD, FAO, IAEA, IBRD, ICAO, ICC (NGOs), ICCt, ICRM, IDA, IFC, IFRCS, IHO, ILO, IMF, IMO, IMSO, Interpol, IOC, IOM, IPU, ISO (correspondent), ITSO, ITU, ITUC (NGOs), MIGA, OAS (observer), OIF (observer), OPCW, OSCE, PCA, PFP, SELEC, UN, UNCTAD, UNESCO, UNHCR, UNIDO, UNWTO, UPU, WCO, WHO, WIPO, WMO, WTO

Diplomatic representation in the US: *chief of mission:* Ambassador Srdjan DARMANOVIC (since 30 November 2010)

chancery: 1610 New Hampshire Avenue NW, Washington, DC, 20009

telephone: [1] (202) 234-6108

FAX: [1] (202) 234-6109

consulate(s) general: New York

Diplomatic representation from the US: *chief of mission:* Ambassador Margaret UYEHARA (since 19 February 2015)

embassy: Dzona Dzeksona 2,81000 Podgorica, Montenegro

mailing address: use embassy street address

telephone: [382] (0) 20 410 500

FAX: [382] (0) 20 241 358

Flag description: a red field bordered by a narrow golden-yellow stripe with the Montenegrin coat of arms centered; the arms consist of a double-headed golden eagle—symbolizing the unity of church and state—surmounted by a crown; the eagle holds a golden scepter in its right claw and a blue orb in its left; the breast shield over the eagle shows a golden lion passant on a green field in front of a blue sky; the lion is symbol of episcopal authority and harkens back to the three and a half centuries that Montenegro was ruled as a theocracy

National symbol(s): double-headed eagle; national colors: red, gold

National anthem: *name:* "Oj, svijetla majska zoro" (Oh, Bright Dawn of May)

lyrics/music: Sekula DRLJEVIC/unknown, arranged by Zarko MIKOVIC

note: adopted 2004; music based on a Montenegrin folk song

ECONOMY

Economy—overview: Montenegro's economy is transitioning to a market system. From the beginning of the privatization process in 1999 through 2015, around 85% of Montenegrin state-owned companies have been privatized, including 100% of banking, telecommunications, and oil distribution. Tourism brings in twice as many visitors as Montenegro's total population every year. Several new luxury tourism complexes are in various stages of development along the coast, and a number are being offered in connection with nearby boating and yachting facilities.

Montenegro uses the euro as its domestic currency, though it is not an official member of the eurozone. In January 2007, Montenegro joined the World Bank and IMF, and in December 2011, the WTO. Montenegro began negotiations to join the EC in June, 2012, having met the conditions set down by the European Council, which called on Montenegro to take steps to fight corruption and organized crime. The government recognizes the need to remove impediments in order to remain competitive and open the economy to foreign investors. The biggest foreign investors in Montenegro are Italy, Norway, Austria, Russia, Hungary and the UK. Net foreign direct investment in 2014 reached $483 million and investment per capita is one of the highest in Europe.

Montenegro is currently planning major overhauls of its road and rail networks, and possible expansions of its air transportation system. In 2014, the Government of Montenegro selected two Chinese companies to construct a 41 km-long section of the country's highway system. Construction will cost around $1.1 billion. Montenegro first instituted a value added tax (VAT) in April 2003, and introduced differentiated VAT rates of 17% and 7% (for tourism) in January 2006. In May 2013, the Montenegrin Government raised the higher level VAT rate to 19%.

GDP (purchasing power parity): $10.04 billion (2015 est.)

$9.642 billion (2014 est.)

$9.473 billion (2013 est.)

note: data are in 2015 US dollars

country comparison to the world: 158

GDP (official exchange rate): $4.039 billion (2015 est.)

GDP—real growth rate: 4.1% (2015 est.)

1.8% (2014 est.)

3.5% (2013 est.)

country comparison to the world: 61

GDP—per capita (PPP): $16,100 (2015 est.)

$15,500 (2014 est.)

$15,300 (2013 est.)

note: data are in 2015 US dollars

country comparison to the world: 102

Gross national saving: 14.7% of GDP (2015 est.)

4.6% of GDP (2014 est.)

5.1% of GDP (2013 est.)

country comparison to the world: 121

GDP—composition, by end use:

household consumption: 81.8%

government consumption: 21.2%

investment in fixed capital: 19.5%

investment in inventories: -0.1%

exports of goods and services: 42.1%

imports of goods and services: -64.5% (2013 est.)

GDP—composition, by sector of origin:

agriculture: 8.3%

industry: 21.2%

services: 70.5% (2013 est.)

Agriculture—products: tobacco, potatoes, citrus fruits, olives, grapes; sheep

Industries: steelmaking, aluminum, agricultural processing, consumer goods, tourism

Industrial production growth rate: 4.5% (2013 est.)

country comparison to the world: 39

Labor force: 263,200 (2014 est.)

country comparison to the world: 166

Labor force—by occupation: *agriculture:* 5.3%

industry: 17.9%

services: 76.8% (2014 est.)

Unemployment rate: 18.5% (2014 est.)

19.1% (2013 est.)

country comparison to the world: 165

Population below poverty line: 8.6% (2013 est.)

Distribution of family income—Gini index: 26.2 (2013 est.)

24.3 (2010)

country comparison to the world: 137

Budget: *revenues:* $1.56 billion

expenditures: $1.63 billion (2014 est.)

Taxes and other revenues: 39.1% of GDP (2014 est.)

country comparison to the world: 42

Budget surplus (+) or deficit (–): -1.8% of GDP (2014 est.)

country comparison to the world: 68

Public debt: 59.5% of GDP (31 December 2014 est.)

57.9% of GDP (2013 est.)

note: data cover general government debt, and includes debt instruments issued (or owned) by government entities other than the treasury; the data include treasury debt held by foreign entities; the data include debt issued by subnational entities, as well as intra-governmental debt; intra-governmental debt consists of treasury borrowings from surpluses in the social funds, such as for retirement, medical care, and unemployment; debt instruments for the social funds are not sold at public auctions

country comparison to the world: 64

Fiscal year: calendar year

Inflation rate (consumer prices): 1.6% (2015 est.)

-0.7% (2014 est.)

country comparison to the world: 103

Commercial bank prime lending rate: 9.22% (31 December 2014 est.)

9.36% (31 December 2013 est.)

country comparison to the world: 91

Stock of narrow money: $749 million (31 December 2011 est.)

$783.3 million (31 December 2010 est.)

country comparison to the world: 158

Stock of broad money: $1.982 billion (31 December 2011 est.)

$2.01 billion (31 December 2010 est.)

country comparison to the world: 156

Stock of domestic credit: $2.63 billion (31 December 2014 est.)

$2.682 billion (31 December 2013 est.)

country comparison to the world: 133

Market value of publicly traded shares: $7.532 billion (31 December 2014 est.)

$3.827 billion (31 December 2012)

$3.322 billion (31 December 2011 est.)
country comparison to the world: 79

Current account balance: -$535 million (2015 est.)
-$699 million (2014 est.)
country comparison to the world: 100

Exports: $370.2 million (2014 est.)
$489.2 million (2012 est.)
country comparison to the world: 180

Exports—partners: Croatia 22.7%, Serbia 22.7%, Slovenia 7.8% (2012 est.)

Imports: $1.982 billion (2014 est.)
$2.4 billion (2012 est.)
country comparison to the world: 164

Imports—partners: Serbia 29.3%, Greece 8.7%, China 7.1% (2012 est.)

Reserves of foreign exchange and gold: $599.6 million (31 December 2014 est.)
country comparison to the world: 46

Debt—external: $1.576 billion (31 December 2014 est.)
$1.433 billion (31 December 2013 est.)
country comparison to the world: 155

Stock of direct foreign investment—at home: $483 million (31 December 2014 est.)
$446.5 million (31 December 2013 est.)
country comparison to the world: 114

Stock of direct foreign investment—abroad: $133 million (31 December 2014 est.)
country comparison to the world: 94

Exchange rates: euros (EUR) per US dollar—
0.885 (2015 est.)
0.7525 (2014 est.)
0.7634 (2013 est.)
0.78 (2012 est.)
0.7185 (2011 est.)

ENERGY

Electricity—production: 3.809 billion kWh (2013 est.)
country comparison to the world: 127

Electricity—consumption: 3.465 billion kWh (2013 est.)
country comparison to the world: 130

Electricity—exports: 696 million kWh (2013 est.)
country comparison to the world: 61

Electricity—imports: 410 million kWh (2013 est.)
country comparison to the world: 78

Electricity—installed generating capacity: 885,500 kW (2013 est.)
country comparison to the world: 126

Electricity—from fossil fuels: 24.6% of total installed capacity (20113 est.)
country comparison to the world: 189

Electricity—from nuclear fuels: 0% of total installed capacity (2013 est.)
country comparison to the world: 139

Electricity—from hydroelectric plants: 75.3% of total installed capacity (2013 est.)
country comparison to the world: 19

Electricity—from other renewable sources: 0% of total installed capacity (2013 est.)
country comparison to the world: 200

Crude oil—production: 0 bbl/day (2014 est.)

country comparison to the world: 166

Crude oil—exports: 0 bbl/day (2013)
country comparison to the world: 159

Crude oil—imports: 0 bbl/day (2013 est.)
country comparison to the world: 96

Crude oil—proved reserves: 0 bbl (1 January 2012 est.)
country comparison to the world: 166

Refined petroleum products—production: 0 bbl/day (2013 est.)
country comparison to the world: 210

Refined petroleum products—consumption: 6,000 bbl/day (2013 est.)
country comparison to the world: 164

Refined petroleum products—exports: 622 bbl/day (2013 est.)
country comparison to the world: 113

Refined petroleum products—imports: 12,270 bbl/day (2013 est.)
country comparison to the world: 131

Natural gas—production: 0 cu m (2013 est.)
country comparison to the world: 101

Natural gas—consumption: 0 cu m (2013 est.)
country comparison to the world: 170

Natural gas—exports: 0 cu m (2013 est.)
country comparison to the world: 144

Natural gas—imports: 0 cu m (2013 est.)
country comparison to the world: 99

Natural gas—proved reserves: 0 cu m (1 January 2014)
country comparison to the world: 169

Carbon dioxide emissions from consumption of energy: 19.72 million Mt (2012 est.)
country comparison to the world: 83

COMMUNICATION

Telephones—fixed lines: *total subscriptions:* 160,000
subscriptions per 100 inhabitants: 25 (2014 est.)
country comparison to the world: 135

Telephones—mobile cellular: *total:* 1 million
subscriptions per 100 inhabitants: 156 (2014 est.)
country comparison to the world: 158

Telephone system: *general assessment:* modern telecommunications system with access to European satellites
domestic: GSM mobile-cellular service, available through multiple providers with national coverage, is growing
international: country code—382; 2 international switches connect the national system (2011)

Broadcast media: state-funded national radio-TV broadcaster operates 2 terrestrial TV networks, 1 satellite TV channel, and 2 radio networks; 4 public TV stations and some 20 private TV stations; 14 local public radio stations and more than 40 private radio stations (2007)
Radio broadcast stations: 31 (station frequency types NA) (2004)
Television broadcast stations: 13 (2004)

Internet country code: .me

Internet hosts: 10,088 (2012)

country comparison to the world: 135

Internet users: *total:* 381,700
percent of population: 58.7% (2014 est.)
country comparison to the world: 136

TRANSPORTATION

Airports: 5 (2013)
country comparison to the world: 181

Airports—with paved runways: *total:* 5
2,438 to 3,047 m: 2
1,524 to 2,437 m: 1
914 to 1,523 m: 1
under 914 m: 1 (2013)

Heliports: 1 (2012)

Railways: *total:* 250 km
standard gauge: 250 km 1.435-m gauge (169 km electrified) (2014)
country comparison to the world: 126

Roadways: *total:* 7,762 km
paved: 7,141 km
unpaved: 621 km (2010)
country comparison to the world: 142

Merchant marine: *total:* 2
by type: cargo 1, passenger/cargo 1
registered in other countries: 4 (Bahamas 2, Honduras 1, Slovakia 1) (2010)
country comparison to the world: 146

Ports and terminals: *major seaport(s):* Bar

MILITARY AND SECURITY

Military branches: Armed Forces of the Republic of Montenegro: Army of Montenegro (includes Montenegrin Navy (Mornarica Crne Gore, MCG)), Air Force (2011)

Military service age and obligation: 18 is the legal minimum age for voluntary military service; no conscription (2012)

Military expenditures: 1.65% of GDP (2015)
1.74% of GDP (2014)
1.59% of GDP (2013)
1.69% of GDP (2012)
1.75% of GDP (2011)
country comparison to the world: 46

TRANSNATIONAL ISSUES

Disputes—international: none

Refugees and internally displaced persons: *refugees (country of origin):* 5,633 (Serbia and Kosovo) (2014)
stateless persons: 3,262 (2015)

MONTSERRAT

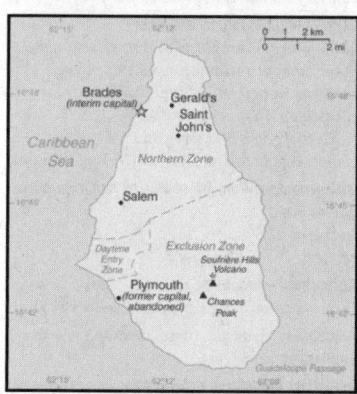

INTRODUCTION

Background: English and Irish colonists from St. Kitts first settled on Montserrat in 1632; the first African slaves arrived three decades later. The British and French fought for possession of the island for most of the 18th century, but it finally was confirmed as a British possession in 1783. The island's sugar plantation economy was converted to small farm landholdings in the mid-19th century. Much of this island was devastated and two-thirds of the population fled abroad because of the eruption of the Soufriere Hills Volcano that began on 18 July 1995. Montserrat has endured volcanic activity since, with the last eruption occurring in July 2003.

GEOGRAPHY

Location: Caribbean, island in the Caribbean Sea, southeast of Puerto Rico

Geographic coordinates: 16 45 N, 62 12 W

Map references: Central America and the Caribbean

Area: *total:* 102 sq km
land: 102 sq km
water: 0 sq km
country comparison to the world: 226

Area—comparative: about 0.6 times the size of Washington, DC

Land boundaries: 0 km

Coastline: 40 km

Maritime claims: *territorial sea:* 3 nm
exclusive fishing zone: 200 nm

Climate: tropical; little daily or seasonal temperature variation

Terrain: volcanic island, mostly mountainous, with small coastal lowland

Elevation: *mean elevation:* NA
elevation extremes: *lowest point:* Caribbean Sea 0 m

highest point: Soufriere Hills volcano pre-eruption height was 915 m; current lava dome is subject to periodic build up and collapse; estimated dome height was 1050 m in 2015

Natural resources: NEGL

Land use: agricultural *land:* 30%
arable land: 20%;
permanent crops: 0%;
permanent pasture: 10%
forest: 25%
other: 45% (2011 est.)

Irrigated land: 0 sq km (2012)

Natural hazards: volcanic eruptions; severe hurricanes (June to November)
volcanism: Soufriere Hills volcano (elev. 915 m), has erupted continuously since 1995; a massive eruption in 1997 destroyed most of the capital, Plymouth, and resulted in approximately half of the island becoming uninhabitable

Environment—current issues: land erosion occurs on slopes that have been cleared for cultivation

Geography—note: the island is entirely volcanic in origin and comprised of three major volcanic centers of differing ages

PEOPLE AND SOCIETY

Nationality: *noun:* Montserratian(s)
adjective: Montserratian

Ethnic groups: African/black 88.4%, mixed 3.7%, hispanic/Spanish 3%, caucasian/white 2.7%, East Indian/Indian 1.5%, other 0.7% (2011 est.)

Languages: English

Religions: Protestant 67.1% (includes Anglican 21.8%, Methodist 17%, Pentecostal 14.1%, Seventh Day Adventist 10.5%, and Church of God 3.7%), Roman Catholic 11.6%, Rastafarian 1.4%, other 6.5%, none 2.6%, unspecified 10.8% (2001 est.)

Population: 5,241
note: an estimated 8,000 refugees left the island following the resumption of volcanic activity in July 1995; some have returned (July 2015 est.)
country comparison to the world: 229

Age structure: *0–14 years:* 17.99% (male 485/female 458)
15–24 years: 20.89% (male 567/female 528)
25–54 years: 47.89% (male 1,202/female 1,308)
55–64 years: 6.98% (male 163/female 203)
65 years and over: 6.24% (male 201/female 126) (2015 est.)

Median age: *total:* 31.9 years
male: 31.5 years
female: 32.5 years (2015 est.)
country comparison to the world: 98

Population growth rate: 0.5% (2015 est.)
country comparison to the world: 160

Birth rate: 11.26 births/1,000 population (2015 est.)
country comparison to the world: 175

Death rate: 6.3 deaths/1,000 population (2015 est.)
country comparison to the world: 153

Net migration rate: 0 migrant(s)/1,000 population (2015 est.)
country comparison to the world: 87

Urbanization: *urban Population:* 9% of total population (2015)
rate of urbanization: 0.65% annual rate of change (2010–15 est.)

Sex ratio: *at birth:* 1.03 male(s)/female
0–14 years: 1.06 male(s)/female
15–24 years: 1.07 male(s)/female
25–54 years: 0.92 male(s)/female
55–64 years: 0.8 male(s)/female
65 years and over: 1.6 male(s)/female
total population: 1 male(s)/female (2015 est.)

Infant mortality rate: *total:* 13.17 deaths/1,000 live births
male: 10.22 deaths/1,000 live births
female: 16.25 deaths/1,000 live births (2015 est.)
country comparison to the world: 114

Life expectancy at birth: *total population:* 74.14 years
male: 75.64 years
female: 72.57 years (2015 est.)
country comparison to the world: 124

Total fertility rate: 1.3 children born/woman (2015 est.)
country comparison to the world: 217

Drinking water source:
improved:
urban: 99% of population
rural: 99% of population
total: 99% of population
unimproved:
urban: 1% of population
rural: 1% of population
total: 1% of population (2015 est.)

Sanitation facility access:
improved:
urban: 82.9% of population
rural: 82.9% of population
total: 82.9% of population
unimproved:
urban: 17.1% of population
rural: 17.1% of population
total: 17.1% of population (2007 est.)

HIV/AIDS—adult prevalence rate: NA

HIV/AIDS—people living with HIV/AIDS: NA

HIV/AIDS—deaths: NA

Education expenditures: 5.1% of GDP (2009)

School life expectancy (primary to tertiary education): *total:* 15 years
male: 14 years
female: 17 years (2007)

GOVERNMENT

Country name: *conventional long form:* none
conventional short form: Montserrat

585

etymology: island named by explorer Christopher COLUMBUS in 1493 after the Benedictine abbey Santa Maria de Montserrat, near Barcelona, Spain

Dependency status: overseas territory of the UK

Government type: parliamentary democracy (Legislative Council); self-governing overseas territory of the UK

Capital: *name:* Plymouth; note—Plymouth was abandoned in 1997 because of volcanic activity; interim government buildings have been built at Brades Estate in the Carr's Bay/Little Bay vicinity at the northwest end of Montserrat

Geographic coordinates: 16 42 N, 62 13 W
time difference: UTC-4 (1 hour ahead of Washington, DC, during Standard Time)

Administrative divisions: 3 parishes; Saint Anthony, Saint Georges, Saint Peter

Independence: none (overseas territory of the UK)

National holiday: birthday of Queen ELIZABETH II, second Saturday in June (1926)

Constitution: previous 1960; latest effective 1 September 2010; amended 2011 (2016)

Legal system: English common law

Citizenship: see United Kingdom

Suffrage: 18 years of age; universal

Executive branch: *chief of state:* Queen ELIZABETH II (since 6 February 1952); represented by Governor Elizabeth CARRIERE (since 5 August 2015)

head of government: Premier Donaldson ROMERO (since 12 September 2014); note—effective with the new Constitution Order of October 2010, the office of premier replaced the office of chief minister

cabinet: Executive Council consists of the governor, the premier, 3 other ministers, the attorney general, and the finance secretary

elections/appointments: the monarchy is hereditary; governor appointed by the monarch; following legislative elections, the leader of the majority party usually becomes premier

Legislative branch: *description:* unicameral Legislative Council (11 seats;9 members directly elected in a single constituency by absolute majority vote in two rounds to serve 5-year terms and 2 ex-officio members—the attorney general and financial secretary)
elections: last held on 11 September 2014 (next to be held by 2019)
election results: percent of vote by party—PDM 50%, MCAP 35.4%, other 14.6%; seats by party—PDM 7, MCAP 2

Judicial branch: *highest court(s):* the Eastern Caribbean Supreme Court (ECSC) is the itinerant superior court of record for the 9-member Organization of Eastern Caribbean States to include Montserrat; the ECSC—with its headquarters on St. Lucia—is headed by the chief justice and is comprised of the Court of Appeal with 3 justices and the High Court with 16 judges; sittings of the Court of Appeal and High Court rotate among the 9 member states; 1 judge of the Supreme Court is a resident of Montserrat and presides over the High Court; note—Montserrat is also a member of the Caribbean Court of Justice

judge selection and term of office: Eastern Caribbean Supreme Court chief justice appointed by Her Majesty, Queen ELIZABETH II; other justices and judges appointed by the Judicial and Legal Services Commission; Court of Appeal justices appointed for life with mandatory retirement at age 65; High Court judges appointed for life with mandatory retirement at age 62

subordinate courts: magistrate's court

Political parties and leaders: Movement for Change and Prosperity or MCAP [Reuben MEADE]
People's Democratic Movement or PDM [Shirley OSBORNE]

Political pressure groups and leaders: NA

International organization participation: Caricom, CDB, Interpol (subbureau), OECS, UPU

Diplomatic representation in the US: none (overseas territory of the UK)

Diplomatic representation from the US: none (overseas territory of the UK)

Flag description: blue with the flag of the UK in the upper hoist-side quadrant and the Montserratian coat of arms centered in the outer half of the flag; the arms feature a woman in green dress, Erin, the female personification of Ireland, standing beside a yellow harp and embracing a large dark cross with her right arm; Erin and the harp are symbols of Ireland reflecting the territory's Irish ancestry; blue represents awareness, trustworthiness, determination, and righteousness

National anthem: *note:* as a territory of the UK, "God Save the Queen" is official (see United Kingdom)

ECONOMY

Economy—overview: Severe volcanic activity, which began in July 1995, has put a damper on this small, open economy. A catastrophic eruption in June 1997 closed the airport and seaports, causing further economic and social dislocation. Two-thirds of the 12,000 inhabitants fled the island. Some began to return in 1998 but lack of housing limited the number. The agriculture sector continued to be affected by the lack of suitable land for farming and the destruction of crops.

Prospects for the economy depend largely on developments in relation to the volcanic activity and on public sector construction activity. Half of the island remains uninhabitable. In January 2013, the EU announced the disbursement of a $55.2 million aid package to Montserrat in order to boost the country's economic recovery, with a specific focus on public finance management, public sector reform, and prudent economic management.

GDP (purchasing power parity): $43.78 million (2006 est.)
country comparison to the world: 226

GDP (official exchange rate): $NA

GDP—real growth rate: 3.5% (2008 est.)

country comparison to the world: 82

GDP—per capita (PPP): $8,500 (2006 est.)
country comparison to the world: 142

GDP—composition, by end use:
household consumption: 87.3%
government consumption: 48.1%
investment in fixed capital: 22.7%
investment in inventories: 0.1%
exports of goods and services: 18.1%
imports of goods and services: -76.3% (2015 est.)

GDP—composition, by sector of origin: *agriculture:* 1.6%
industry: 22.5%
services: 75.9% (2015 est.)

Agriculture—products: cabbages, carrots, cucumbers, tomatoes, onions, peppers; livestock products

Industries: tourism, rum, textiles, electronic appliances

Industrial production growth rate: 2% (2015 est.)
country comparison to the world: 117

Labor force: 4,521 (2012)
country comparison to the world: 222

Unemployment rate: 6% (1998 est.)
country comparison to the world: 66

Population below poverty line: NA%

Household income or consumption by percentage share: *lowest:* 10%: NA%
highest: 10%: NA%

Budget: *revenues:* $0
expenditures: $37.04 million (2015 est.)

Fiscal year: 1 April—31 March

Inflation rate (consumer prices): 2.2% (2015 est.)
1.5% (2014 est.)
country comparison to the world: 120

Central bank discount rate: 10.99% (31 December 2010)
6.5% (31 December 2009)
country comparison to the world: 20

Commercial bank prime lending rate: 8.1% (31 December 2015 est.)
8.02% (31 December 2014 est.)
country comparison to the world: 108

Stock of narrow money: $18.51 million (31 December 2015 est.)
$16.69 million (31 December 2014 est.)
country comparison to the world: 192

Stock of broad money: $97.44 million (31 December 2015 est.)
$88.59 million (31 December 2014 est.)
country comparison to the world: 193

Stock of domestic credit: $5.185 million (31 December 2014 est.)
$5.185 million (31 December 2014 est.)
country comparison to the world: 188

Exports: $3.6 million (2015 est.)
$3.6 million (2014 est.)
country comparison to the world: 219

Exports—commodities: electronic components, plastic bags, apparel; hot peppers, limes, live plants; cattle

Imports: $30 million (2015 est.)

$30 million (2014 est.)
country comparison to the world: 220

Imports—commodities: machinery and transportation equipment, foodstuffs, manufactured goods, fuels, lubricants

Reserves of foreign exchange and gold: $32.08 million (31 December 2012 est.)
$40.51 million (31 December 2013 est.)
country comparison to the world: 169

Debt—external: $8.9 million (1997)
country comparison to the world: 200

Exchange rates: East Caribbean dollars (XCD) per US dollar—
2.7 (2015 est.)
2.7 (2014 est.)
2.7 (2013 est.)
2.7 (2012 est.)
2.7 (2011 est.)

ENERGY

Electricity—production: 25 million kWh (2012 est.)
country comparison to the world: 213

Electricity—consumption: 23.25 million kWh (2012 est.)
country comparison to the world: 212

Electricity—exports: 0 kWh (2013 est.)
country comparison to the world: 166

Electricity—imports: 0 kWh (2013 est.)
country comparison to the world: 172

Electricity—installed generating capacity: 10,000 kW (2012 est.)
country comparison to the world: 207

Electricity—from fossil fuels: 100% of total installed capacity (2012 est.)
country comparison to the world: 19

Electricity—from nuclear fuels: 0% of total installed capacity (2012 est.)
country comparison to the world: 137

Electricity—from hydroelectric plants: 0% of total installed capacity (2012 est.)
country comparison to the world: 186

Electricity—from other renewable sources: 0% of total installed capacity (2012 est.)
country comparison to the world: 198

Crude oil—production: 0 bbl/day (2014 est.)
country comparison to the world: 164

Crude oil—Exports: 0 bbl/day (2012 est.)
country comparison to the world: 157

Crude oil—imports: 0 bbl/day (2012 est.)
country comparison to the world: 94

Crude oil—proved reserves: 0 bbl (1 January 2015 est.)
country comparison to the world: 164

Refined petroleum products—production: 0 bbl/day (2012 est.)
country comparison to the world: 208

Refined petroleum products—consumption: 570 bbl/day (2013 est.)
country comparison to the world: 207

Refined petroleum products—exports: 0 bbl/day (2012 est.)
country comparison to the world: 201

Refined petroleum products—imports: 568.5 bbl/day (2012 est.)
country comparison to the world: 204

Natural gas—production: 0 cu m (2013 est.)
country comparison to the world: 99

Natural gas—consumption: 0 cu m (2013 est.)
country comparison to the world: 168

Natural gas—exports: 0 cu m (2013 est.)
country comparison to the world: 142

Natural gas—imports: 0 cu m (2013 est.)
country comparison to the world: 97

Natural gas—proved reserves: 0 cu m (1 January 2014 est.)
country comparison to the world: 167

Carbon dioxide emissions from consumption of energy: 88,010 Mt (2012 est.)
country comparison to the world: 207

COMMUNICATIONS

Telephones—fixed lines: *total subscriptions:* 3,100
subscriptions per 100 inhabitants: 59 (2014 est.)
country comparison to the world: 210

Telephones—mobile cellular: *total:* 4,500
subscriptions per 100 inhabitants: 86 (2014 est.)
country comparison to the world: 215

Telephone system: *general assessment:* modern and fully digitalized

country comparison to the world: 164

domestic: combined fixed-line and mobile-cellular teledensity exceeds 100 per 100 persons
international: country code—1–664; landing point for the East Caribbean Fiber System (ECFS) optic submarine cable with links to 13 other islands in the eastern Caribbean extending from the British Virgin Islands to Trinidad (2011)

Broadcast media: Radio Montserrat, a public radio broadcaster, transmits on 1 station and has a repeater transmission to second station; repeater transmissions from the GEM Radio Network of Trinidad and Tobago provide another 2 radio stations; cable and satellite TV available (2007)
Radio broadcast stations: AM 1, FM 2, shortwave 0 (2008)
Television broadcast stations: 1 (1997)

Internet country code: .ms

Internet hosts: 2,431 (2012)
country comparison to the world: 160

Internet users: *total:* 1,200
percent of population: 23.5% (2009)
country comparison to the world: 212

TRANSPORTATION

Airports: 1 (2013)
country comparison to the world: 226

Airports—with paved runways: *total:* 1
under 914 m: 1 (2013)

Roadways: *note:* volcanic eruptions that began in 1995 destroyed most of the 227 km road system; a new road infrastructure has been built on the north end of the island (2008)

Ports and terminals: *major seaport(s):* Little Bay, Plymouth

MILITARY AND SECURITY

Military branches: no regular military forces; Royal Montserrat Police Force (2011)

Military—note: defense is the responsibility of the UK

TRANSNATIONAL ISSUES

Disputes—international: none

Illicit drugs: transshipment point for South American narcotics destined for the US and Europe

---

MOROCCO

INTRODUCTION

Background: In 788, about a century after the Arab conquest of North Africa, a series of Moroccan Muslim dynasties began to rule in Morocco. In the 16th century, the Sa'adi monarchy, particularly under Ahmad al-MANSUR (1578-1603), repelled foreign invaders and inaugurated a golden age. The Alaouite Dynasty, to which the current Moroccan royal family belongs, dates from the 17th century. In 1860, Spain occupied northern Morocco and ushered in a half century of trade rivalry among European powers that saw Morocco's sovereignty steadily erode; in 1912, the French imposed a protectorate over the country. A protracted independence struggle with France ended successfully in 1956. The internationalized city of Tangier and most Spanish possessions were turned over to the new country that same year. Sultan MOHAMMEDV, the current monarch's grandfather, organized the new state as a constitutional monarchy and in 1957 assumed the title of king.

Since Spain's 1976 withdrawal from what is today called Western Sahara, Morocco has extended its de facto administrative control to roughly 80% of this territory; however, the UN does not recognize Morocco as the administering power for Western Sahara. The UN since 1991 has monitored a cease-fire between Morocco and the Polisario Front—Western Sahara's liberation movement -and leads ongoing negotiations over the status of the territory.

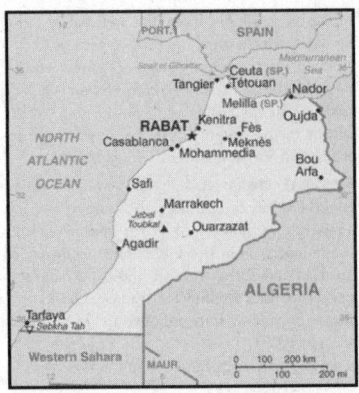

King MOHAMMED VI in early 2011 responded to the spread of pro-democracy protests in the region by implementing a reform program that included a new constitution, passed by popular referendum in July 2011, under which some new powers were extended to parliament and the prime minister but ultimate authority remains in the hands of the monarch. In November 2011, the Justice and Development Party—a moderate Islamist party—won the largest number of seats in parliamentary elections, becoming the first Islamist party to lead the Moroccan Government. In September 2015, Morocco held its first ever direct elections for regional councils, one of the reforms included in the 2011 constitution. Nationwide parliamentary elections are scheduled for October 2016.

GEOGRAPHY

Location: Northern Africa, bordering the North Atlantic Ocean and the Mediterranean Sea, between Algeria and Western Sahara

Geographic coordinates: 32 00 N, 5 00 W

Map references: Africa

Area: *total:* 446,550 sq km
land: 446,300 sq km
water: 250 sq km
country comparison to the world: 58

Area—comparative: slightly more than three times the size of New York; slightly larger than California

Land boundaries: *total:* 2,362.5 km
border countries (3): Algeria 1900 km, Western Sahara 444 km, Spain (Ceuta) 8 km, Spain (Melilla) 10.5 km
note: an additional 75-meter border segment exists between Morocco and the Spanish exclave of Penon de Velez de la Gomera

Coastline: 1,835 km

Maritime claims: *territorial sea:* 12 nm
contiguous zone: 24 nm
exclusive economic zone: 200 nm
continental shelf: 200-m depth or to the depth of exploitation

Climate: Mediterranean, becoming more extreme in the interior

Terrain: mountainous northern coast (Rif Mountains) and interior (Atlas Mountains) bordered by large plateaus with interMontane valleys, and fertile coastal plains

Elevation: *mean elevation:* 909 m

elevation extremes: lowest point: Sebkha Tah -55 m
highest point: Jebel Toubkal 4,165 m

Natural resources: phosphates, iron ore, m anganese, lead, zinc, fish, salt

Land use: *agricultural land:* 67.5%
arable land: 17.5%;
permanent crops: 2.9%;
permanent pasture: 47.1%
forest: 11.5%
other: 21% (2011 est.)

Irrigated land: 14,850 sq km (2012)

Total renewable water resources: 29 cu km (2011)

Freshwater withdrawal (domestic/industrial/agricultural): *total:* 12.61 cu km/yr (12%/4%/84%)
per capita: 428.1 cu m/yr (2005)

Natural hazards: northern mountains geologically unstable and subject to earthquakes; periodic droughts

Environment—current issues: land degradation/desertification (soil erosion resulting from farming of m arginal areas, overgrazing, destruction of vegetation); water supplies contam inated by raw sewage; siltation of reservoirs; oil pollution of coastal waters

Environment—international agreements: party to: Biodiversity, Climate Change, Climate Change-Kyoto Protocol, Desertification, Endangered Species, Hazardous Wastes, Law of the Sea, Marine Dumping, Ozone Layer Protection, Ship Pollution, Wetlands, Whaling
signed, but not ratified: Environmental Modification

Geography—note: strategic location along Strait of Gibraltar; the only African nation to have both Atlantic and Mediterranean coastlines

PEOPLE AND SOCIETY

Nationality: *noun:* Moroccan(s)
adjective: Moroccan

Ethnic groups: Arab-Berber 99%, other 1%

Languages: Arabic (official), Berber languages (Tamazight (official), Tachelhit, Tarifit), French (often the language of business, government, and diplomacy)

Religions: Muslim 99% (official; virtually all Sunni, <0.1% Shia), other 1% (includes Christian, Jewish, and Baha'i);
note—Jewish about 6,000 (2010 est.)

Population: 33,322,699 (July 2015 est.)
country comparison to the world: 40

Age structure: *0–14 years:* 26.41% (male 4,469,461/female 4,330,904)
15–24 years: 17.42% (male 2,886,637/female 2,919,324)
25–54 years: 42.13% (male 6,788,601/female 7,249,887)
55–64 years: 7.6% (male 1,262,634/female 1,271,492)
65 years and over: 6.43% (male 964,900/female 1,178,859) (2015 est.)

Dependency ratios: *total dependency ratio:* 50.1%
youth dependency ratio: 40.9%
elderly dependency ratio: 9.3%
potential support ratio: 10.8% (2015 est.)

Median age: *total:* 28.5 years
male: 27.9 years
female: 29.1 years (2015 est.)
country comparison to the world: 125

Population growth rate: 1% (2015 est.)
country comparison to the world: 117

Birth rate: 18.2 births/1,000 population (2015 est.)
country comparison to the world: 101

Death rate: 4.81 deaths/1,000 population (2015 est.)
country comparison to the world: 194

Net migration rate: -3.36 migrant(s)/1,000 population (2015 est.)
country comparison to the world: 185

Urbanization: *urban Population:* 60.2% of total population (2015)
rate of urbanization: 2.26% annual rate of change (2010–15 est.)

Major urban areas—Population: Casablanca 3.515 million; RABAT (capital) 1.967 million; Fes 1.172 million; Marrakech 1.134 million; Tangier 982,000 (2015)

Sex ratio: *at birth:* 1.05 male(s)/female
0–14 years: 1.03 male(s)/female
15–24 years: 0.99 male(s)/female
25–54 years: 0.94 male(s)/female
55–64 years: 0.99 male(s)/female
65 years and over: 0.82 male(s)/female
total population: 0.97 male(s)/female (2015 est.)

Maternal mortality rate: 121 deaths/100,000 live births (2015 est.)
country comparison to the world: 70

Infant mortality rate: *total:* 23.6 deaths/1,000 live births
male: 27.92 deaths/1,000 live births
female: 19.05 deaths/1,000 live births (2015 est.)
country comparison to the world: 75

Life expectancy at birth: *total population:* 76.71 years
male: 73.64 years
female: 79.94 years (2015 est.)
country comparison to the world: 79

Total fertility rate: 2.13 children born/woman (2015 est.)
country comparison to the world: 104

Contraceptive prevalence rate: 67.4% (2010/11)

Health expenditures: 6% of GDP (2013)
country comparison to the world: 101

Physicians density: 0.62 physicians/1,000 population (2009)

Hospital bed density: 0.9 beds/1,000 population (2012)

Drinking water source:
improved:
urban: 98.7% of population

rural: 65.3% of population
total: 85.4% of population
unimproved:
urban: 1.3% of population
rural: 34.7% of population
total: 14.6% of population (2015 est.)

Sanitation facility access:
improved:
urban: 84.1% of population
rural: 65.5% of population
total: 76.7% of population
unimproved:
urban: 15.9% of population
rural: 34.5% of population
total: 23.3% of population (2015 est.)

HIV/AIDS—adult prevalence rate: 0.14% (2014 est.)
country comparison to the world: 107

HIV/AIDS—people living with HIV/AIDS: 28,700 (2014 est.)
country comparison to the world: 73

HIV/AIDS—deaths: 1,100 (2014 est.)
country comparison to the world: 65

Obesity—adult prevalence rate: 21.7% (2014)
country comparison to the world: 114

Children under the age of 5 years underweight: 3.1% (2011)
country comparison to the world: 113

Education expenditures: 5.3% of GDP (2009)
country comparison to the world: 59

Literacy: *definition:* age 15 and over can read and write
total population: 68.5%
male: 78.6%
female: 58.8% (2015 est.)

School life expectancy (primary to tertiary education): *total:* 12 years
male: 13 years
female: 12 years (2012)

Child labor—children ages 5–14: *total number:* 500,960
percentage: 8% (2007 est.)

Unemployment, youth ages 15–24: *total:* 19.1%
male: 19.4%
female: 18.2% (2013 est.)
country comparison to the world: 60

GOVERNMENT

Country name: *conventional long form:* Kingdom of Morocco
conventional short form: Morocco
local long form: Al Mamlakah al Maghribiyah
local short form: Al Maghrib
note: the English name "Morocco" derives from, respectively, the Spanish and Portuguese names "Marruecos" and "Marrocos, " wh ich stem from "Marrakesh " the Latin name for the former capital of ancient Morocco; the Arabic name "AlMaghrib" translates as "The West"

Government type: parliamentary constitutional monarchy

Capital: *name:* Rabat

Geographic coordinates: 34 01 N, 6 49 W
time difference: UTC 0 (5 hours ahead of Washington, DC, during Standard Time)
daylight saving time: +1 hr, begins last Sunday in April; ends last Sunday in September

Administrative divisions: 11 regions (recognized); Beni Mellal-Khenifra, Casablanca-Settat, Draa-Tafilalet, Fes-Meknes, Guelmim-Oued Noun, Laay oune-Sakia al Hamra, Oriental, Marrakech-Safi, Rabat-Sale-Kenitra, Souss-Massa, Tanger-Tetouan-Al Hoceima
note: Morocco claims the territory of Western Sah ara, the political status of which is considered undetermined by the USG overnment; portions of the regions Guelmim-Oued Noun and Laayoune-Sakia al Hamra as claimed by Morocco lie with in Western Sahara; Morocco also claims a 12th region, Dakh la-Oued ed Dahab, that falls entirely with in Western Sahara

Independence: 2 March 1956 (from France)

National holiday: Throne Day (accession of King MOHAMMED VI to the throne),30 July (1999)

Constitution: several previous; latest drafted 17 June 2011, approved by referendum 1 July 2011; *note*—sources disagree on whether the 2011 referendum was for a new constitution or for reforms to the previous constitution (2016)

Legal system: mixed legal system of civil law based on French law and Islamic law; judicial review of legislative acts by Constitutional Court

International law organization participation: has not submitted an ICJ jurisdiction declaration; non-party state to the ICCt

Citizenship: *citizenship by birth:* no
citizenship by descent only: the father must be a citizen of Morocco; if the father is unknown or stateless, the mother must be a citizen
dual citizenship recognized: yes
residency requirement for naturalization: 5 years

Suffrage: 18 years of age; universal

Executive branch: *chief of state:* King MOHAMMED VI (since 30 July 1999)

head of government: Prime Minister Abdelillah BENKIRANE (since 29 November 2011)
cabinet: Council of Ministers chosen by the prime minister in consultation with Parliament and appointed by the monarch
elections/appointments: the monarchy is hereditary; prime minister appointed by the monarch from the majority party following legislative elections

Legislative branch: *description:* bicameral Parliament consists of the Chamber of Advisors (120 seats; members indirectly elected by an electoral college of local councils, professional organizations, and labor unions; members serve 6-year terms) and the Chamber of Representatives (395 seats; 305 members directly elected in multi-seat constituencies by proportional representation vote and 90 directly elected in a single nationwide constituency by proportional representation vote; members serve 5-year terms); *note*—in the national constituency, 60 seats are reserved for women and 30 reserved for those under age 40
elections: Chamber of Advisors- last held on 2 October 2015 (next to be held in fall 2021); Chamber of Representatives—last held on 25 November 2011 (next to be held on 7 October 2016)
election results: Chamber of Advisors- percent of vote by party—NA; seats by party—NA; Chamber of Representatives—percent of vote by party—NA; seats by party—PJD 107, PI 60, RNI 52, PAM 47, USFP 39, MP 32, UC 23, PPS 18, other 17

Judicial branch: *highest court(s):* Supreme Court or Court of Cassation (consists of 5-judge panels organized into civil, family matters, commercial, administrative, social, and criminal sections); Constitutional Court (consists of 12 members)
judge selection and term of office: Supreme Court judges appointed by the Superior Council of Judicial Power, a 20-member body presided by the monarch and including the Supreme Court president, the prosecutor general, representatives of the appeals and first instance courts—among them 1 woman magistrate, the president of the National Council of the Rights of Man, and 5 "notable persons" appointed by the monarch; judges appointed for life; Constitutional Court members—6 designated by the monarch and 6 elected by Parliament; court president appointed by the monarch from among the court members; members serve 9-year non-renewable terms
subordinate courts: courts of appeal; High Court of Justice; administrative and commercial courts; regional and sadad courts (for religious, civil and administrative, and penal adjudication); first instance courts

Political parties and leaders: Action Party or PA [Mohammed EL IDRISSI]
Amal (hope) Party [Mohamed BANI]
An-Nahj Ad-Dimocrati or An-Nahj [Mustapha BRAHMA]
Authenticity and Modernity Party or PAM [Ilyas EL OMARI]
Choura et Istiqlal (Consultation and Independence) Party or PCI [Abdelwahed MAACH]
Constitutional Union Party or UC [Mohamed SAJID]
Democratic and Social Movement or MDS [Abdessamad ARCHANE]
Democratic Forces Front or FFD [Mustapha BENALI]
Democratic Oath Party or SD [Najib EL OUAZZANI]
Democratic Socialist Vanguard Party or PADS [Abderrahman BENAMROU]
Democratic Society Party [Zhour CHAKKAFI]
Environment and Development Party or PED [Karim HRITAN]
Green Left Party [Mohamed FARES]
Istiqlal (Independence) Party or PI [Hamid CHABAT]
Ittihadi National Congress or CNI [Abdesalam EL AZIZ]
Labor Party or PT [Abdelkrim BENATIK]
Moroccan Liberal Party or PML [Mohammed ZIANE]

Moroccan Union for Democracy or UMD [Jamal MANDRI]

National Rally of Independents or RNI [Salaheddine MEZOUAR]

Neo-Democrats Party [Mohamed DARIF]

Party of Citizen Forces or PFC [Abderrahim LAHJOUJI]

Party of Development Reform or PRD [Abderrahmane EL KOHEN]

Party of Justice and Development or PJD [Abdelillah BENKIRANE]

Party of Liberty and Social Justice [Miloud MOUSSAOUI]

Popular Movement or MP [Mohand LAENSER]

Progress and Socialism Party or PPS [Nabil BENABDELLAH]

Renaissance and Virtue Party [Mohamed KHALIDI]

Renaissance Party [Said EL GHENNIOUI]

Renewal and Equity Party or PRE [Chakir ACHEHABAR]

Shoura (consultation) and Istiqlal Party [Ahmed BELGHAZI]

Social Center Party or PCS [Lahcen MADIH]

Socialist Party [Abdelmajid BOUZOUBAA]

Socialist Union of Popular Forces or USFP [Driss LACHGAR]

Unified Socialist Party or GSU [Nabila MOUNIB]

Unity and Democracy Party [Ahmed FITRI]

Political pressure groups and leaders: Democratic Confederation of Labor or CDT [Noubir ELAMAOUI]

General Union of Moroccan Workers or UGTM [Mohamed KAFI CHERRAT]

Justice and Charity Organization or JCO [Mohammed ben Abdesslam ABBADI]

Moroccan Employers Association or CGEM [Miriem BENSALAH-CHAQROUN]

National Labor Union of Morocco or UNMT [Mohamed YATIM]

Union of Moroccan Workers or UMT [Miloudi EL MOUKHARIK]

International organization participation: ABEDA, AfDB, AFESD, AMF, AMU, CAEU, CD, EBRD, FAO, G-11, G-77, IAEA, IBRD, ICAO, ICC (national committees), ICRM, IDA, IDB, IFAD, IFC, IFRCS, IHO, ILO, IMF, IMO, IMSO, Interpol, IOC, IOM, IPU, ISO, ITSO, ITU, ITUC (NGOs), LAS, MIGA, MONUSCO, NAM, OAS (observer), OIC, OIF, OPCW, OSCE (partner), Pacific Alliance (observer), Paris Club (associate), PCA, SICA (observer), UN, UNCTAD, UNESCO, UNHCR, UNIDO, UNOCI, UNSC (temporary), UNWTO, UPU, WCO, WHO, WIPO, WMO, WTO

Diplomatic representation in the US: *chief of mission:* Ambassador Mohammed Rachad BOUHLAL (since 22 December 2011)
chancery: 1601 21st Street NW, Washington, DC 20009
telephone: [1] (202) 462-7980
FAX: [1] (202) 462-7643
consulate(s) general: New York

Diplomatic representation from the US: *chief of mission:* Ambassador Dwight L. BUSH, Sr. (since 8 April 2014)
embassy: Km 5.7 Avenue Mohammed VI, Souissi, Rabat
mailing address: Unit 9400, Box Front Office, DPO, AE 09718
telephone: [212] 537 63 7777
FAX: [212] 537 63 7201
consulate(s) general: Casablanca

Flag description: red with a green pentacle (five-pointed, linear star) known as Sulayman's (Solomon's) seal in the center of the flag; red and green are traditional colors in Arab flags, although the use of red is more commonly associated with the Arab states of the Persian Gulf; the pentacle represents the five pillars of Islam and signifies the association between God and the nation; design dates to 1912

National symbol(s): pentacle symbol, lion; national colors: red, green

National anthem: *name:* "Hymne Cherifien" (Hymn of the Sharif)
lyrics/music: Ali Squalli HOUSSAINI/Leo MORGAN
note: music adopted 1956, lyrics adopted 1970

ECONOMY

Economy—overview: Morocco has capitalized on its proximity to Europe and relatively low labor costs to work towards building a diverse, open, market-oriented economy. Key sectors of the economy include agriculture, tourism, aerospace, automotive, phosphates, textiles, apparel, and subcomponents. Morocco has increased investment in its port, transportation, and industrial infrastructure to position itself as a center and broker for business throughout Africa. Industrial development strategies and infrastructure improvements—most visibly illustrated by a new port and free trade zone near Tangier—are improving Morocco's competitiveness.

In the 1980s, Morocco was a heavily indebted country before pursuing austerity measures and pro-market reforms, overseen by the IMF. Since taking the throne in 1999, King MOHAMMED VI has presided over a stable economy marked by steady growth, low inflation, and gradually falling unemployment, although poor harvests and economic difficulties in Europe contributed to an economic slowdown. To boost exports, Morocco entered into a bilateral Free Trade Agreement with the US in 2006 and an Advanced Status agreement with the EU in 2008. In late 2014, Morocco eliminated subsidies for gasoline, diesel, and fuel oil, dramatically reducing outlays that weighted on the country's budget and current account. Subsidies on butane gas and certain food products remain in place. Morocco also seeks to expand its renewable energy capacity with a goal of making renewable more than 50% of installed electricity generation capacity by 2030.

Despite Morocco's economic progress, the country suffers from high unemployment, poverty, and illiteracy, particularly in rural areas. Key economic challenges for Morocco include reforming the education system and the judiciary.

GDP (purchasing power parity):
$273.5 billion (2015 est.)
$261.8 billion (2014 est.)
$255.7 billion (2013 est.)
note: data are in 2015 US dollars
country comparison to the world: 58

GDP (official exchange rate): $103.1 billion (2015 est.)

GDP—real growth rate: 4.5% (2015 est.)
2.4% (2014 est.)
4.7% (2013 est.)
country comparison to the world: 49

GDP—per capita (PPP):
$8,200 (2015 est.)
$7,900 (2014 est.)
$7,800 (2013 est.)
note: data are in 2015 US dollars
country comparison to the world: 147

Gross national saving: 32% of GDP (2015 est.)
28% of GDP (2014 est.)
26.8% of GDP (2013 est.)
country comparison to the world: 18

GDP—composition, by end use:
household consumption: 60.2%
government consumption: 19.1%
investment in fixed capital: 28.5%
investment in inventories: 2.6%
exports of goods and services: 34.4%
imports of goods and services: -44.8% (2015 est.)

GDP—composition, by sector of origin:
agriculture: 13.8%
industry: 29%
services: 57.2% (2015 est.)

Agriculture—products: barley, wheat, citrus fruits, grapes, vegetables, olives; livestock; wine

Industries: automotive parts, phosphate mining and processing, aerospace, food processing, leather goods, textiles, construction, energy, tourism

Industrial production growth rate: 4.3% (2015 est.)
country comparison to the world: 49

Labor force: 12.27 million (2015 est.)
country comparison to the world: 46

Labor force—by occupation: *agriculture:* 39.1%
industry: 20.3%
services: 40.5% (2014 est.)

Unemployment rate: 9.7% (2015 est.)
9.9% (2014 est.)
country comparison to the world: 113

Population below poverty line: 15% (2007 est.)

Household income or consumption by percentage share: *lowest:* 10%: 2.7%
highest: 10%: 33.2% (2007)

Distribution of family income—Gini index: 40.9 (2007 est.)
39.5 (1999 est.)
country comparison to the world: 58

Budget: *revenues:* $24.49 billion
expenditures: $29.04 billion (2015 est.)
Taxes and other revenues: 23.8% of GDP (2015 est.)
country comparison to the world: 132

Budget surplus (+) or deficit (–): -4.4% of GDP (2015 est.)
country comparison to the world: 157

Public debt: 73.4% of GDP (2015 est.)
73.8% of GDP (2014 est.)
country comparison to the world: 40

Fiscal year: calendar year

Inflation rate (consumer prices): 1.6% (2015 est.)
0.4% (2014 est.)
country comparison to the world: 104

Central bank discount rate: 6.5% (31 December 2010)
3.31% (31 December 2009)
country comparison to the world: 59

Commercial bank prime lending rate: 5.9% (31 December 2015 est.)
6% (31 December 2014 est.)
country comparison to the world: 132

Stock of narrow money: $70.65 billion (31 December 2015 est.)
$73.27 billion (31 December 2014 est.)
country comparison to the world: 42

Stock of broad money: $92.72 billion (31 December 2014 est.)
$92.2 billion (31 December 2013 est.)
country comparison to the world: 56

Stock of domestic credit: $108.6 billion (31 December 2015 est.)
$115.4 billion (31 December 2014 est.)
country comparison to the world: 52

Market value of publicly traded shares:
$52.63 billion (31 December 2012 est.)
$60.09 billion (31 December 2011)
$69.15 billion (31 December 2010 est.)
country comparison to the world: 52

Current account balance: -$1.413 billion (2015 est.)
-$6.226 billion (2014 est.)
country comparison to the world: 137

Exports: $21.15 billion (2015 est.)
$23.72 billion (2014 est.)
country comparison to the world: 69

Exports—commodities: clothing and textiles, automobiles, electric components, inorganic chemicals, transistors, crude minerals, fertilizers (including phosphates), petroleum products, citrus fruits, vegetables, fish

Exports—partners: Spain 22.1%, France 19.7%, India 4.9%, US 4.3%, Italy 4.3% (2015)

Imports: $37.32 billion (2015 est.)
$46.16 billion (2014 est.)
country comparison to the world: 58

Imports—commodities: crude petroleum, textile fabric, telecommunications equipment, wheat, gas and electricity, transistors, plastics

Imports—partners: Spain 13.9%, France 12.4%, China 8.5%, US 6.5%, Germany 5.8%, Italy 5.5%, Russia 4.4%, Turkey 4.3% (2015)

Reserves of foreign exchange and gold: $21.35 billion (31 December 2015 est.)
$20.41 billion (31 December 2014 est.)
country comparison to the world: 58

Debt—external: $43.99 billion (31 December 2014 est.)
$39.85 billion (31 December 2013 est.)
country comparison to the world: 66

Stock of direct foreign investment—at home:
$59.11 billion (31 December 2015 est.)
$55.4 billion (31 December 2014 est.)
country comparison to the world: 57

Stock of direct foreign investment—abroad:
$1.518 billion (31 December 2015 est.)
$2.083 billion (31 December 2014 est.)
country comparison to the world: 81

Exchange rates: Moroccan dirhams (MAD) per US dollar—
9.592 (2015 est.)
8.3798 (2014 est.)
8.3798 (2013 est.)
8.6 (2012 est.)
8.0899 (2011 est.)

ENERGY

Electricity—production: 25.35 billion kWh (2012 est.)
country comparison to the world: 69

Electricity—consumption: 26.7 billion kWh (2012 est.)
country comparison to the world: 65

Electricity—exports: 818 million kWh (2012 est.)
country comparison to the world: 58

Electricity—imports: 5.66 billion kWh (2012 est.)
country comparison to the world: 39

Electricity—installed generating capacity: 6.763 million kW (2012 est.)
country comparison to the world: 69

Electricity—from fossil fuels: 69% of total installed capacity (2012 est.)
country comparison to the world: 109

Electricity—from nuclear fuels: 0% of total installed capacity (2012 est.)
country comparison to the world: 142

Electricity—from hydroelectric plants: 19.3% of total installed capacity (2012 est.)
country comparison to the world: 94

Electricity—from other renewable sources: 4.8% of total installed capacity (2012 est.)
country comparison to the world: 58

Crude oil—production: 500 bbl/day (2014 est.)
country comparison to the world: 95

Crude oil—exports: 0 bbl/day (2012 est.)
country comparison to the world: 162

Crude oil—imports: 148,500 bbl/day (2012 est.)
country comparison to the world: 38

Crude oil—proved reserves: 680,000 bbl (1 January 2015 est.)
country comparison to the world: 99

Refined petroleum products—production: 155,200 bbl/day (2012 est.)
country comparison to the world: 62

Refined petroleum products—consumption: 293,000 bbl/day (2013 est.)
country comparison to the world: 43

Refined petroleum products—exports: 13,380 bbl/day (2012 est.)
country comparison to the world: 80

Refined petroleum products—imports: 161,000 bbl/day (2012 est.)
country comparison to the world: 34

Natural gas—production: 79 million cu m (2013 est.)
country comparison to the world: 83

Natural gas—consumption: 1.181 billion cu m
country comparison to the world: 87

Natural gas—exports: 0 cu m (2013 est.)
country comparison to the world: 147

Natural gas—imports: 1.102 billion cu m (2013 est.)
country comparison to the world: 56

Natural gas—proved reserves: 1.444 billion cu m (1 January 2014 est.)
country comparison to the world: 101

Carbon dioxide emissions from consumption of energy: 39.35 million Mt (2012 est.)
country comparison to the world: 68

COMMUNICATIONS

Telephones—fixed lines: *total subscriptions:* 2.49 million
subscriptions per 100 inhabitants: 8 (2014 est.)
country comparison to the world: 54

Telephones—mobile cellular: *total:* 44.1 million
subscriptions per 100 inhabitants: 134 (2014 est.)
country comparison to the world: 32

Telephone system: *general assessment:* good system composed of open-wire lines, cables, and microwave radio relay links; principal switching centers are Casablanca and Rabat; national network nearly 100% digital using fiber-optic links; improved rural service employs microwave radio relay; Internet available but expensive
domestic: fixed-line teledensity is roughly 10 per 100 persons; mobile-cellular subscribership exceeds 100 per 100 persons
international: country code—212; landing point for the Atlas Offshore, Estepona-Tetouan, Euroafrica, Spain-Morocco, and SEA-ME-WE-3 fiber-optic telecommunications undersea cables that provide connectivity to Asia, the Middle East, and Europe; satellite earth stations—2 Intelsat (Atlantic Ocean) and 1 Arabsat; microwave radio relay to Gibraltar, Spain, and Western Sahara; coaxial cable and microwave radio relay to Algeria; participant in Medarabtel; fiber-optic cable link from Agadir to Algeria and Tunisia (2011)

Broadcast media: 2 TV broadcast networks with state-run Radio-Television Marocaine (RTM) operating one network and the state partially owning the other; foreign TV broadcasts are available via satellite dish; 3 radio broadcast networks with RTM operating one; the government-owned network includes 10 regional radio channels in addition to its national service (2007)
Radio broadcast stations: AM NA, FM 15, shortwave NA (2009)
Television broadcast stations: 8 (2009)

Internet country code: .ma

Internet hosts: 277,338 (2012)
country comparison to the world: 66

Internet users: total: 19.9 million
percent of population: 60.3% (2014 est.)
country comparison to the world: 29

TRANSPORTATION

Airports: 55 (2013)
country comparison to the world: 86

Airports—with paved runways: total: 31
over 3,047 m: 11
2,438 to 3,047 m: 9
1,524 to 2,437 m: 7
914 to 1,523 m: 4 (2013)

Airports—with unpaved runways: total: 24
2,438 to 3,047 m: 1
1,524 to 2,437 m: 7
914 to 1,523 m: 11
under 914 m: 5 (2013)

Heliports: 1 (2013)

Pipelines: gas 944 km; oil 270 km; refined products 175 km (2013)

Railways: total: 2,067 km
standard gauge: 2,067 km 1.435-m gauge (1,022 km electrified) (2014)
country comparison to the world: 71

Roadways: total: 58,395 km

paved: 41,116 km (includes 1,080 km of expressways)
unpaved: 17,279 km (2010)
country comparison to the world: 73

Merchant marine: total: 26
by type: cargo 1, chemical tanker 3, container 6, passenger/cargo 14, roll on/roll off 2
foreign-owned: 14 (France 3, Germany 1, Italy 1, Spain 9)
registered in other countries: 4 (Gibraltar 4) (2010)
country comparison to the world: 88

Ports and terminals: major seaport(s): Casablanca, Jorf Lasfar, Mohammedia, Safi, Tangier
container port(s) (TEUs): Tangier (2,093,408)
LNG terminal(s) (import): Jorf Lasfar

MILITARY AND SECURITY

Military branches: Royal Armed Forces (Forces Armees Royales, FAR): Royal Moroccan Army (includes Air Defense), Royal Moroccan Navy (includes Coast Guard, Marines), Royal Moroccan Air Force (Al Quwwat al Jawyiya al Malakiya Marakishiy a; Force Aerienne Royale Marocaine) (2010)

Military service age and obligation: 20 years of age for voluntary military service; no conscription; service obligation—18 months (2012)

Military expenditures: 3.7% of GDP (2014)
3.91% of GDP (2013)

3.55% of GDP (2012)
3.37% of GDP (2011)
3.55% of GDP (2010)
country comparison to the world: 14

TRANSNATIONAL ISSUES

Disputes—international: claims and administers Western Sahara whose sovereignty remains unresolved; Morocco protests Spain's control over the coastal enclaves of Ceuta, Melilla, and Penon de Velez de la Gomera, the islands of Penon de Alhucemas and Islas Chafarinas, and surrounding waters; both countries claim Isla Perejil (Leila Island); discussions have not progressed on a comprehensive maritime delimitation, setting limits on resource exploration and refugee interdiction, since Morocco's 2002 rejection of Spain's unilateral designation of a median line from the Canary Islands; Morocco serves as one of the primary launching areas of illegal migration into Spain from North Africa; Algeria's border with Morocco remains an irritant to bilateral relations, each nation accusing the other of harboring militants and arms smuggling; the National Liberation Front's assertions of a claim to Chirac Pastures in southeastern Morocco is a dormant dispute

Illicit drugs: one of the world's largest producers of illicit hashish; shipments of hashish mostly directed to Western Europe; transit point for cocaine from South America destined for Western Europe; significant consumer of cannabis

MOZAMBIQUE

INTRODUCTION

Background: Almost five centuries as a Portuguese colony came to a close with independence in 1975. Large-scale emigration, economic dependence on South Africa, a severe drought, and a prolonged civil war hindered the country's development until the mid-1990s. The ruling Front for the Liberation of Mozambique (FRELIMO) party formally abandoned Marxism in 1989, and a new constitution the following year provided for multiparty elections and a free market economy. A UN-negotiated peace agreement between FRELIMO and rebel Mozambique National Resistance (RENAMO) forces ended the fighting in 1992. In December 2004, Mozambique underwent a delicate transition as Joaquim CHISSANO stepped down after 18 years in office. His elected successor, Armando GUEBUZA, served two terms and then passed executive power to Philipe NYUSI in October 2014. RENAMO's residual armed forces engaged in a low-level insurgency from 2012 to 2014.

GEOGRAPHY

Location: Southeastern Africa, bordering the Mozambique Channel, between South Africa and Tanzania

Geographic coordinates: 18 15 S, 35 00 E

Map references: Africa

Area: total: 799,380 sq km
land: 786,380 sq km
water: 13,000 sq km
country comparison to the world: 35

Area—comparative: slightly less than twice the size of California

Land boundaries: total: 4,783 km
border countries (6): Malawi 1,498 km, South Africa 496 km, Swaziland 108 km, Tanzania 840 km, Zambia 439 km, Zimbabwe 1,402 km

Coastline: 2,470 km

Maritime claims: territorial sea: 12 nm
exclusive economic zone: 200 nm

Climate: tropical to subtropical

Terrain: mostly coastal lowlands, uplands in center, high plateaus in northwest, mountains in west

Elevation: mean elevation: 345 m

elevation extremes: lowest point: Indian Ocean 0 m
highest point: Monte Binga 2,436 m

Natural resources: coal, titanium, natural gas, hydropower, tantalum, graphite

Land use: agricultural land: 56.3%
arable land: 6.4%;
permanent crops: 0.3%;

permanent pasture: 49.6%
forest: 43.7%
other: 0% (2011 est.)

Irrigated land: 1,180 sq km (2012)

Total renewable water resources: 217.1 cu km (2011)

Freshwater withdrawal (domestic/industrial/agricultural): total: 0.88 cu km/yr (26%/4%/70%)
per capita: 46.05 cu m/yr (2005)

Natural hazards: severe droughts; devastating cyclones and floods in central and southern provinces

Environment—current issues: increased migration of the population to urban and coastal areas with adverse environmental consequences; desertification; pollution of surface and coastal waters; elephant poaching for ivory is a problem

Environment—international agreements: party to: Biodiversity, Climate Change, Climate Change-Kyoto Protocol, Desertification, Endangered Species, Hazardous Wastes, Law of the Sea, Ozone Layer Protection, Ship Pollution, Wetlands
signed, but not ratified: none of the selected agreements

Geography—note: the Zambezi River flows through the north-central and most fertile part of the country

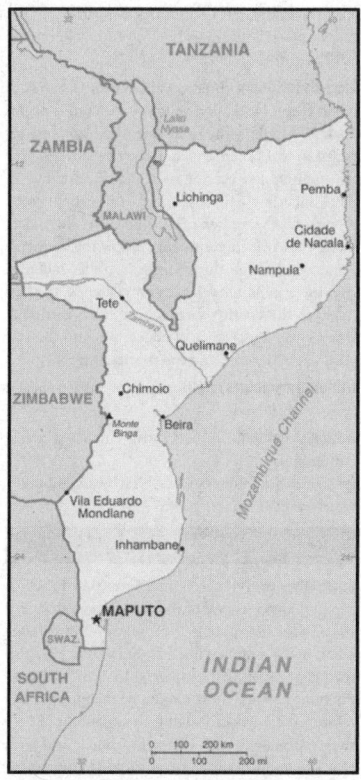

Nationality: *noun:* Mozambican(s)
adjective: Mozambican

Ethnic groups: African 99.66% (Makhuwa, Tsonga, Lomwe, Sena, and others), Europeans 0.06%, Euro-Africans 0.2%, Indians 0.08%

Languages: Emakhuwa 25.3%, Portuguese (official) 10.7%, Xichangana 10.3%, Cisena 7.5%, Elomwe 7%, Echuwabo 5.1%, other Mozambican languages 30.1%, other 4% (1997 census)

Religions: Roman Catholic 28.4%, Muslim 17.9%, Zionist Christian 15.5%, Protestant 12.2% (includes Pentecostal 10.9% and Anglican 1.3%), other 6.7%, none 18.7%, unspecified 0.7% (2007 est.)

Population: 25,303,113
note: estimates for this country explicitly take into account the effects of excess mortality due to AIDS; this can result in lower life expectancy, higher infant mortality, higher death rates, lower population growth rates, and changes in the distribution of population by age and sex than would otherwise be expected (July 2015 est.)
country comparison to the world: 50

Age structure: *0–14 years:* 45.13% (male 5,740,743/female 5,677,563)
15–24 years: 21.43% (male 2,657,099/female 2,764,109)

25–54 years: 27.09% (male 3,201,321/female 3,654,012)
55–64 years: 3.44% (male 415,357/female 455,450)
65 years and over: 2.91% (male 338,552/female 398,907) (2015 est.)

Dependency ratios: *total dependency ratio:* 94.8%
youth dependency ratio: 88.2%
elderly dependency ratio: 6.5%
potential support ratio: 15.3% (2015 est.)

Median age: *total:* 17 years
male: 16.4 years
female: 17.6 years (2015 est.)
country comparison to the world: 224

Population growth rate: 2.45% (2015 est.)
country comparison to the world: 28

Birth rate: 38.58 births/1,000 population (2015 est.)
country comparison to the world: 10

Death rate: 12.1 deaths/1,000 population (2015 est.)
country comparison to the world: 26

Net migration rate: -1.98 migrant(s)/1,000 population (2015 est.)
country comparison to the world: 166

Urbanization: *urban Population:* 32.2% of total population (2015)
rate of urbanization: 3.27% annual rate of change (2010–15 est.)

Major urban areas—Population: MAPUTO (capital) 1.187 million; Matola 937,000 (2015)

Sex ratio: *at birth:* 1.02 male(s)/female
0–14 years: 1.01 male(s)/female
15–24 years: 0.96 male(s)/female
25–54 years: 0.88 male(s)/female
55–64 years: 0.91 male(s)/female
65 years and over: 0.85 male(s)/female
total population: 0.95 male(s)/female (2015 est.)

Mother's mean age at first birth: 18.7
median age at first birth among women 20–24 (2011 est.)

Maternal mortality rate: 489 deaths/100,000 live births (2015 est.)
country comparison to the world: 20

Infant mortality rate: *total:* 70.21 deaths/1,000 live births
male: 72.29 deaths/1,000 live births
female: 68.09 deaths/1,000 live births (2015 est.)
country comparison to the world: 13

Life expectancy at birth: *total population:* 52.94 years
male: 52.18 years
female: 53.72 years (2015 est.)
country comparison to the world: 214

Total fertility rate: 5.21 children born/woman (2015 est.)
country comparison to the world: 12

Contraceptive prevalence rate: 11.6% (2011)

Health expenditures: 6.8% of GDP (2013)
country comparison to the world: 99

Physicians density: 0.04 physicians/1,000 population (2012)

Hospital bed density: 0.7 beds/1,000 population (2011)

Drinking water source:
improved:
urban: 80.6% of population
rural: 37% of population
total: 51.1% of population
unimproved:
urban: 19.4% of population
rural: 63% of population
total: 48.9% of population (2015 est.)

Sanitation facility access:
improved:
urban: 42.4% of population
rural: 10.1% of population
total: 20.5% of population
unimproved:
urban: 57.6% of population
rural: 89.9% of population
total: 79.5% of population (2015 est.)

HIV/AIDS—adult prevalence rate: 10.58% (2014 est.)
country comparison to the world: 8

HIV/AIDS—people living with HIV/AIDS: 1.543 million (2014 est.)
country comparison to the world: 5

HIV/AIDS—deaths: 44,900 (2014 est.)
country comparison to the world: 5

Major infectious diseases: *degree of risk:* very high
food or waterborne diseases: bacterial and protozoal diarrhea, hepatitis A, and typhoid fever
vectorb orne diseases: malaria and dengue fever
water contact di sease: schistosomiasis
animal contact disease: rabies (2013)
Obesity—adult prevalence rate: 4.5% (2014)
country comparison to the world: 158

Children under the age of 5 years underweight: 15.6% (2011)
country comparison to the world: 44

Education expenditures: 6.5% of GDP (2013)
country comparison to the world: 78

Literacy: *definition:* age 15 and over can read and write
total population: 58.8%
male: 73.3%
female: 45.4% (2015 est.)

School life expectancy (primary to tertiary education): *total:* 9 years
male: 10 years
female: 9 years (2014)

Child labor—children ages 5–14: *total number:* 1,369,080
percentage: 22% (2008 est.)

Unemployment, youth ages 15–24: *total:* 39.4%
male: 40.2%
female: 38.7% (2012 est.)

Country name: *conventional long form:* Republic of Mozambique conventional short form: Mozambique

local long form: Republica de Mocambique

local short form: Mocambique

former: Portuguese East Africa

etymology: named for the offshore island of Mozambique; the island was apparently named after Mussa al-BIK, an influential Arab slave trader who set himself up as sultan on the island in the 15th century

Government type: presidential republic

Capital: name: Maputo

Geographic coordinates: 25 57 S, 32 35 E

time difference: UTC+2 (7 hours ahead of Washington, DC, during Standard Time)

Administrative divisions: 10 provinces (provincias, singular—provincia),1 city (cidade) *; Cabo Delgado, Gaza, Inhambane, Manica, Maputo, Cidade de Maputo*, Nampula, Niassa, Sofala, Tete, Zambezia

Independence: 25 June 1975 (from Portugal)

National holiday: Independence Day, 25 June (1975)

Constitution: previous 1975, 1990; latest adopted 16 November 2004, effective 21 December 2004; amended 2007; note—amendments drafted in late 2013 were rejected by parliament in late 2015 (2016)

Legal system: mixed legal system of Portuguese civil law, and customary law; note—in rural, predominately Muslim villages with no formal legal system, Islamic law may be applied

International law organization participation: has not submitted an ICJ jurisdiction declaration; non-party state to the ICCt

Citizenship: citizenship by birth: no

citizenship by descent only: at least one parent must be a citizen of Mozambique

dual citizenship recognized: no

residency requirement for naturalization: 5 years

Suffrage: 18 years of age; universal

Executive branch: chief of state: President Filipe Jacinto NYUSI (since 15 January 2015)

head of government: Prime Minister Carlos Agostinho DO ROSARIO (since 17 January 2015); Alberto Clementino Antonio VAQUINA removed from office 9 January 2015

cabinet: Cabinet appointed by the president

elections/appointments: president elected directly elected by absolute majority popular vote in 2 rounds if needed for a 5-year term (eligible for 2 consecutive terms); election last held on 15 October 2014 (next to be held in October 2019); prime minister appointed by the president

election results: Filipe NYUSI elected president; percent of vote—Filipe NYUSI (FRELIMO) 57.0%, Afonso DHLAKAMA (RENAMO) 36.6%, Daviz SIMANGO (MDM) 6.4%

Legislative branch: description: unicameral Assembly of the Republic or Assembleia da Republica (250 seats; members -including 2 representing Mozambicans abroad—directly elected in single- and multi-seat constituencies by proportional representation vote; members serve 5-year terms)

elections: last held on 15 October 2014 (next to be held in October 2019)

election results: percent of vote by party—FRELIMO 55.9%, RENAMO 32.5%, MDM 8.4%, other 3.3%; seats by party—FRELIMO 144, RENAMO 89, MDM 17

Judicial branch: highest court(s): Supreme Court (consists of the court president, vice president, and 5 judges); Constitutional Council (consists of 7 judges); note—the Higher Council of the Judiciary is responsible for judiciary management and discipline

judge selection and term of office: Supreme Court president and vice president appointed by Mozambique president in consultation with the Higher Council of the Judiciary (CSMJ) and with ratification by the legislature; other judges elected by the legislature; judges serve 5-year renewable terms; Constitutional Council judges appointed—1 by the president, 5 by the legislature, and 1 by the CSMJ; judges serve 5-year nonrenewable terms

subordinate courts: Administrative Court (capital city only); provincial courts or Tribunais Judicias de Provincia; District Courts or Tribunais Judicias de Districto; customs courts; maritime courts; courts marshal; labor courts; community courts

Political parties and leaders: Democratic Movement of Mozambique (Movimento Democratico de Mocambique) or MDM [Daviz SIMANGO] Front for the Liberation of Mozambique (Frente de Liberatacao de Mocambique) or FRELIMO [Filipe NYOSOI]

Mozambique National Resistance (Resistencia Nacional Mocambicana) or RENAMO [Afonso DHLAKAMA]

Political pressure groups and leaders: Mozambican League of Human Rights (Liga Mocambicana dos Direitos Humanos) or LDH [Alice MABOTE, president]

International organization participation: ACP, AfDB, AU, C, CD, CPLP, EITI (compliant country), FAO, G-77, IAEA, IBRD, ICAO, ICC (NGOs), ICRM, IDA, IDB, IFAD, IFC, IFRCS, IHO, ILO, IMF, IMO, IMSO, Interpol, IOC, IOM, IPU, ISO (correspondent), ITSO, ITU, ITUC (NGOs), MIGA, NAM, OIC, OIF (observer), OPCW, SADC, UN, UNCTAD, UNESCO, UNHCR, UNIDO, Union Latina, UNISFA, UNWTO, UPU, WCO, WFTU (NGOs), WHO, WIPO, WMO, WTO

Diplomatic representation in the US: chief of mission: Ambassador Carlos dos SANTOS (since 28 January 2016)

chancery: 1525 New Hampshire Avenue NW, Washington, DC 20036

telephone: [1] (202) 293-7146

FAX: [1] (202) 835-0245

Diplomatic representation from the US: chief of mission: Ambassador Douglas M. GRIFFITHS (since 6 July 2012)

embassy: Avenida Kenneth Kuanda 193, Maputo

mailing address: P. O. Box 783, Maputo

telephone: [258] (21) 492797

FAX: [258] (21) 490114

Flag description: three equal horizontal bands of green (top), black, and yellow with a red isosceles triangle based on the hoist side; the black band is edged in white; centered in the triangle is a yellow five-pointed star bearing a crossed rifle and hoe in black superimposed on an open white book; green represents the riches of the land, white peace, black the African continent, yellow the country's minerals, and red the struggle for independence; the rifle symbolizes defense and vigilance, the hoe refers to the country's agriculture, the open book stresses the importance of education, and the star represents Marxism and internationalism

National symbol(s): national colors: green, black, yellow, white, red

National anthem: name: "Patria Amada" (Lovely Fatherland)

lyrics/music: Salomao J. MANHICA/unknown

note: adopted 2002

ECONOMY

Economy—overview: At independence in 1975, Mozambique was one of the world's poorest countries. Socialist policies, economic mismanagement, and a brutal civil war from 1977 to 1992 further impoverished the country. In 1987, the government embarked on a series of macroeconomic reforms designed to stabilize the economy. These steps, combined with donor assistance and with political stability since the multi-party elections in 1994, propelled the country's GDP from $4 billion in 1993, following the war, to about $34 billion in 2015. Fiscal reforms, including the introduction of a value-added tax and reform of the customs service, have improved the government's revenue collection abilities.

In spite of these gains, more than half the population remains below the poverty line. Subsistence agriculture continues to employ the vast majority of the country's work force. Citizens rioted in September 2010 after fuel, water, electricity, and bread price increases were announced. in an attempt to lessen the negative impact on the population, the government implemented subsidies, decreased taxes and tariffs, and instituted other fiscal measures.

A substantial trade imbalance persists, although aluminum production from the Mozal Aluminum Smelter has significantly boosted export earnings in recent years. In 2012, The Mozambican Government took over Portugal's last remaining share in the Cahora Bassa Hydroelectricity Company, a significant contributor to the Southern African Power Pool. The government has plans to expand the Cahora Bassa Dam and build additional dams to increase its electricity exports and fulfill the needs of its burgeoning domestic industries.

Mozambique's once substantial foreign debt was reduced through forgiveness and rescheduling under the IMF's Heavily Indebted Poor Countries (HIPC) and Enhanced HIPC initiatives. However, in 2013, the Mozambique Tuna Company

(EMATUM) issued an $850 million bond fully guaranteed by the Mozambican government primarily for the purpose of purchasing tuna boats. The government is attempting to reschedule this debt, in the expectation that a pending deal with a consortium led by a US company will provide enough revenue to pay off this debt. The pending deal has the potential to transform Mozambique's economy and dramatically increase GDP.

Mozambique grew at an average annual rate of 6%-8% in the decade up to 2015, one of Africa's strongest performances. Mozambique's ability to attract large investment projects in natural resources is expected to sustain high growth rates in coming years although weaker global demand for commodities is likely to weaken expected revenues from these vast resources, including natural gas, coal, titanium, and hydroelectric capacity.

GDP (purchasing power parity):
$33.19 billion (2015 est.)
$31.22 billion (2014 est.)
$29.06 billion (2013 est.)
note: data are in 2015 US dollars
country comparison to the world: 125

GDP (official exchange rate): $14.97 billion (2015 est.)

GDP—real growth rate: 6.3% (2015 est.)
7.4% (2014 est.)
7.1% (2013 est.)
country comparison to the world: 26

GDP—per capita (PPP): $1,200 (2015 est.)
$1,100 (2014 est.)
$1,100 (2013 est.)
note: data are in 2015 US dollars
country comparison to the world: 220

Gross national saving: -13.1% of GDP (2015 est.)
11.8% of GDP (2014 est.)
15.4% of GDP (2013 est.)
country comparison to the world: 178

GDP—composition, by end use:
household consumption: 67.5%
government consumption: 19.3%
investment in fixed capital: 14.7%
investment in inventories: 2%
exports of goods and services: 20.7%
imports of goods and services: -24.2% (2015 est.)

GDP—composition, by sector of origin:
agriculture: 28.1%
industry: 21.6%
services: 50.2% (2015 est.)

Agriculture—products: cotton, cashew nuts, sugarcane, tea, cassava (manioc, tapioca), corn, coconuts, sisal, citrus and tropical fruits, potatoes, sunflowers; beef, poultry

Industries: aluminum, petroleum products, chemicals (fertilizer, soap, paints), textiles, cement, glass, asbestos, tobacco, food, beverages

Industrial production growth rate: 9.1% (2015 est.)
country comparison to the world: 11

Labor force: 12.92 million (2015 est.)
country comparison to the world: 43

Labor force—by occupation: *agriculture:* 81%
industry: 6%

services: 13% (1997 est.)

Unemployment rate: 17% (2007 est.)
21% (1997 est.)
country comparison to the world: 158

Population below poverty line: 52% (2009 est.)

Household income or consumption by percentage share: *lowest:* 10%: 1.9%
highest: 10%: 36.7% (2008)

Distribution of family income—Gini index: 45.6 (2008)
47.3 (2002)
country comparison to the world: 40

Budget: *revenues:* $4.587 billion
expenditures: $5.775 billion (2015 est.)
Taxes and other revenues: 27% of GDP (2015 est.)
country comparison to the world: 102

Budget surplus (+) or deficit (–): -7% of GDP (2015 est.)
country comparison to the world: 190

Public debt: 58.3% of GDP (2015 est.)
59.8% of GDP (2014 est.)
country comparison to the world: 65

Fiscal year: calendar year

Inflation rate (consumer prices): 2.4% (2015 est.)
2.3% (2014 est.)
country comparison to the world: 127

Central bank discount rate: 9.5% (17 January 2013)
3.25% (31 December 2010)
country comparison to the world: 28

Commercial bank prime lending rate: 14.7% (31 December 2015 est.)
14.8% (31 December 2014 est.)
country comparison to the world: 45

Stock of narrow money: $5.333 billion (31 December 2015 est.)
$5.405 billion (31 December 2014 est.)
country comparison to the world: 96

Stock of broad money: $7.48 billion (31 December 2015 est.)
$7.871 billion (31 December 2014 est.)
country comparison to the world: 118

Stock of domestic credit: $5.164 billion (31 December 2015 est.)
$5.529 billion (31 December 2014 est.)
country comparison to the world: 123

Market value of publicly traded shares: $NA

Current account balance: -$6.185 billion (2015 est.)
-$5.797 billion (2014 est.)
country comparison to the world: 172

Exports: $3.605 billion (2015 est.)
$3.92 billion (2014 est.)
country comparison to the world: 124

Exports—commodities: aluminum, prawns, cashews, cotton, sugar, citrus, timber; bulk electricity

Exports—partners: South Africa 24.9%, China 10.2%, Italy 8.9%, India 8.9%, Belgium 7.9%, Spain 4.4% (2015)

Imports: $7.068 billion (2015 est.)
$7.958 billion (2014 est.)

country comparison to the world: 113

Imports—commodities: machinery and equipment, vehicles, fuel, chemicals, metal products, foodstuffs, textiles

Imports—partners: South Africa 26.8%, China 19.3%, India 13.9% (2015)

Reserves of foreign exchange and gold: $2.528 billion (31 December 2015 est.)
$3.22 billion (31 December 2014 est.)
country comparison to the world: 113

Debt—external: $8.049 billion (31 December 2014 est.)
$6.89 billion (31 December 2013 est.)
country comparison to the world: 113

Exchange rates: meticais (MZM) per US dollar—
37.79 (2015 est.)
31.367 (2014 est.)
31.367 (2013 est.)
28.38 (2012 est.)
29.075 (2011 est.)

ENERGY

Electricity—production: 15.01 billion kWh (2012 est.)
country comparison to the world: 84

Electricity—consumption: 11.28 billion kWh (2012 est.)
country comparison to the world: 87

Electricity—exports: 9.791 billion kWh (2012 est.)
country comparison to the world: 22

Electricity—imports: 8.304 billion kWh (2012 est.)
country comparison to the world: 25

Electricity—installed generating capacity: 2.436 million kW (2012 est.)
country comparison to the world: 100

Electricity—from fossil fuels: 10.2% of total installed capacity (2012 est.)
country comparison to the world: 198

Electricity—from nuclear fuels: 0% of total installed capacity (2012 est.)
country comparison to the world: 149

Electricity—from hydroelectric plants: 89.8% of total installed capacity (2012 est.)
country comparison to the world: 13

Electricity—from other renewable sources: 0% of total installed capacity (2012 est.)
country comparison to the world: 205

Crude oil—production: 0 bbl/day (2014 est.)
country comparison to the world: 172

Crude oil—exports: 0 bbl/day (2012 est.)
country comparison to the world: 166

Crude oil—imports: 0 bbl/day (2012 est.)
country comparison to the world: 103

Crude oil—proved reserves: 0 bbl (1 January 2015 est.)
country comparison to the world: 172

Refined petroleum products—production: 0 bbl/day (2012 est.)
country comparison to the world: 114

Refined petroleum products—consumption: 17,000 bbl/day (2013 est.)
country comparison to the world: 135

Refined petroleum products—exports: 0 bbl/day (2012 est.)
country comparison to the world: 207

Refined petroleum products—imports: 17,560 bbl/day (2012 est.)
country comparison to the world: 118

Natural gas—production: 4.309 billion cu m (2013 est.)
country comparison to the world: 54

Natural gas—consumption: 191 million cu m (2013 est.)
country comparison to the world: 105

Natural gas—exports: 4.118 billion cu m (2013 est.)
country comparison to the world: 31

Natural gas—imports: 0 cu m (2013 est.)
country comparison to the world: 105

Natural gas—proved reserves: 2.832 trillion cu m (1 January 2014 est.)
country comparison to the world: 14

Carbon dioxide emissions from consumption of energy: 4.789 million Mt (2012 est.)
country comparison to the world: 128

COMMUNICATIONS

Telephones—fixed lines: *total subscriptions:* 68,800
subscriptions per 100 inhabitants: less than 1 (2014 est.)
country comparison to the world: 151

Telephones—mobile cellular: *total:* 18.4 million
subscriptions per 100 inhabitants: 75 (2014 est.)
country comparison to the world: 59

Telephone system: *general assessment:* a fair telecommunications system that is shackled with a heavy state presence, lack of competition, and high operating costs and charges
domestic: stagnation in the fixed-line network contrasts with rapid growth in the mobile-cellular network; mobile-cellular coverage now includes all the main cities and key roads, including those from Maputo to the South African and Swaziland borders, the national highway through Gaza and Inhambane provinces, the Beira corridor, and from Nampula to Nacala; extremely low fixed-line teledensity; despite significant growth in mobile-cellular services, teledensity remains low at about 35 per 100 persons
international: country code—258; landing point for the EASSy and SEACOM fiber-optic submarine cable systems; satellite earth stations—5 Intelsat (2 Atlantic Ocean and 3 Indian Ocean) (2011)

Broadcast media: 1 state-run TV station supplemented by private TV station; Portuguese state TV's African service, RTP Africa, and Brazilian-owned TV Miramar are available; state-run radio provides nearly 100% territorial coverage and broadcasts in multiple languages; a number of privately owned and community-operated stations; transmissions of multiple international broadcasters are available (2007)
Radio broadcast stations: AM 13, FM 17, shortwave 11 (2001)
Television broadcast stations: 4 (2008)

Internet country code: .mz

Internet hosts: 89,737 (2012)
country comparison to the world: 82

Internet users: *total:* 1.4 million
percent of population: 5.5% (2014 est.)
country comparison to the world: 111

TRANSPORTATION

Airports: 98 (2013)
country comparison to the world: 57

Airports—with paved runways: *total:* 21
over 3,047 m: 1
2,438 to 3,047 m: 2
1,524 to 2,437 m: 9
914 to 1,523 m: 5
under 914 m: 4 (2013)

Airports—with unpaved runways: *total:* 77
2,438 to 3,047 m: 1
1,524 to 2,437 m: 9
914 to 1,523 m: 29
under 914 m: 38 (2013)

Pipelines: gas 972 km; refined products 278 km (2013)

Railways: *total:* 4,787 km
narrow gauge: 4,787 km 1.067-m gauge (2014)
country comparison to the world: 39

Roadways: *total:* 30,331 km
paved: 6,303 km
unpaved: 24,028 km (2009)
country comparison to the world: 96

Waterways: 460 km (Zambezi River navigable to Tete and along Cahora Bassa Lake) (2010)
country comparison to the world: 85

Merchant marine: *total:* 2
by type: cargo 2
foreign-owned: 2 (Belgium 2) (2010)
country comparison to the world: 144

Ports and terminals: *major seaport(s):* Beira, Maputo, Nacala

MILITARY AND SECURITY

Military branches: Mozambique Armed Defense Forces (Forcas Armadas de Defesa de Mocambique, FADM): Mozambique Army, Mozambique Navy (Marinha de Guerra de Mocambique, MGM), Mozambique Air Force (Forca Aerea de Mocambique, FAM) (2012)

Military service age and obligation: registration for military service is mandatory for all males and females at 18 years of age; 18–35 years of age for selective compulsory military service; 18 years of age for voluntary service; 2-year service obligation; women may serve as officers or enlisted (2012)

TRANSNATIONAL ISSUES

Disputes—international: South Africa has placed military units to assist police operations along the border of Lesotho, Zimbabwe, and Mozambique to control smuggling, poaching, and illegal migration

Refugees and internally displaced persons: *refugees (country of origin):* 9,082 (Congo, Democratic Republic of the) (2015)
IDPs: 61,102 (2015 floods) (2015)

Illicit drugs: southern African transit point for South Asian hashish and heroin, and South American cocaine probably destined for the European and South African markets; producer of cannabis (for local consumption) and methaqualone (for export to South Africa); corruption and poor regulatory capability make the banking system vulnerable to money laundering, but the lack of a well-developed financial infrastructure limits the country's utility as a money-laundering center

Background: South Africa occupied the German colony of South-West Africa during World War I and administered it as a mandate until after World War II, when it annexed the territory. In 1966, the Marxist South-West Africa People's Organization (SWAPO) guerrilla group launched a war of independence for the area that became Namibia, but it was not until 1988 that South Africa agreed to end its administration in accordance with a UN peace plan for the entire region. Namibia has been governed by SWAPO since the country won independence in 1990, though the party has dropped much of its Marxist ideology. Prime Minister Hage GEINGOB was elected president in November 2014 in a landslide victory, replacing Hifikepunye POHAMBA who stepped down after serving two terms. SWAPO retained its parliamentary super majority in the November 2014 elections and established a system of gender parity in parliamentary positions.

GEOGRAPHY

Location: Southern Africa, bordering the South Atlantic Ocean, between Angola and South Africa

Geographic coordinates: 22 00 S, 17 00 E
Map references: Africa
Area: *total:* 824,292 sq km
land: 823,290 sq km
water: 1,002 sq km
country comparison to the world: 34
Area—comparative: slightly more than half the size of Alaska

Land boundaries: *total:* 4,220 km
border countries (4): Angola 1,427 km, Botswana 1,544 km, South Africa 1,005 km, Zambia 244 km
Coastline: 1,572 km
Maritime claims: *territorial sea:* 12 nm
contiguous zone: 24 nm
exclusive economic zone: 200 nm
Climate: desert; hot, dry; rainfall sparse and erratic
Terrain: mostly high plateau; Namib Desert along coast; Kalahari Desert in east

Elevation: *mean elevation:* 1,141 m
elevation extremes: *lowest point:* Atlantic Ocean 0 m
highest point: Konigstein 2,606 m
Natural resources: diamonds, copper, uranium, gold, silver, lead, tin, lithium, cadmium, tungsten, zinc, salt, hydropower, fish
note: suspected deposits of oil, coal, and iron ore

Land use: *agricultural land:* 47.2%
arable land: 1%
permanent crops: 0%
permanent pasture: 46.2%
forest: 8.8%
other: 44% (2011 est.)
Irrigated land: 80 sq km (2012)
Total renewable water resources: 17.72 cu km (2011)
Freshwater withdrawal (domestic/industrial/agricultural): *total:* 0.29 cu km/yr (25%/5%/70%)
per capita: 146 cu m/yr (2002)
Natural hazards: prolonged periods of drought
Environment—current issues: limited natural freshwater resources; desertification; wildlife poaching; land degradation has led to few conservation areas
Environment—international agreements: *party to:* Antarctic-Marine Living Resources, Biodiversity, Climate Change, Climate Change-Kyoto Protocol, Desertification, Endangered Species, Hazardous Wastes, Law of the Sea, Ozone Layer Protection, Wetlands
signed, but not ratified: none of the selected agreements
Geography—note: first country in the world to incorporate the protection of the environment into its constitution; some 14% of the land is protected, including virtually the entire Namib Desert coastal strip

PEOPLE AND SOCIETY

Nationality: *noun:* Namibian(s)
adjective: Namibian
Ethnic groups: black 87.5%, white 6%, mixed 6.5%
note: about 50% of the population belong to the Ovambo tribe and 9% to the Kavangos tribe; other ethnic groups include Herero 7%, Damara 7%, Nama 5%, Caprivian 4%, Bushmen 3%, Baster 2%, Tswana 0.5%
Languages: Oshiwambo languages 48.9%, Nama/Damara 11.3%, Afrikaans 10.4% (common language of most of the population and about 60% of the white population), Otjiherero languages 8.6%, Kavango languages 8.5%, Caprivi languages 4.8%, English (official) 3.4%, other African languages 2.3%, other 1.7%
note: Namibia has 13 recognized national languages, including 10 indigenous African languages and 3 Indo-European languages (2011 est.)
Religions: Christian 80% to 90% (at least 50% Lutheran), indigenous beliefs 10% to 20%
Population: 2,212,307
note: estimates for this country explicitly take into account the effects of excess mortality due

to AIDS; this can result in lower life expectancy, higher infant mortality, higher death rates, lower population growth rates, and changes in the distribution of population by age and sex than would otherwise be expected (July 2015 est.)
country comparison to the world: 143
Age structure: *0–14 years:* 30.95% (male 345,767/female 339,026)
15–24 years: 23.11% (male 258,586/female 252,773)
25–54 years: 36.57% (male 422,026/female 386,948)
55–64 years: 4.88% (male 48,406/female 59,545)
65 years and over: 4.49% (male 42,635/female 56,595) (2015 est.)
Dependency ratios: *total dependency ratio:* 67.3%
youth dependency ratio: 61.4%
elderly dependency ratio: 5.9%
potential support ratio: 17% (2015 est.)
Median age: *total:* 23.1 years
male: 23.1 years
female: 23.1 years (2015 est.)
country comparison to the world: 169
Population growth rate: 0.59% (2015 est.)
country comparison to the world: 151
Birth rate: 19.8 births/1,000 population (2015 est.)
country comparison to the world: 85
Death rate: 13.91 deaths/1,000 population (2015 est.)
country comparison to the world: 8
Net migration rate: 0 migrant(s)/1,000 population (2015 est.)
country comparison to the world: 86
Urbanization: *urban population:* 46.7% of total population (2015)
rate of urbanization: 4.16% annual rate of change (2010–15 est.)
Major urban areas—population: WINDHOEK (capital) 368,000 (2015)
Sex ratio: *at birth:* 1.03 male(s)/female
0–14 years: 1.02 male(s)/female
15–24 years: 1.02 male(s)/female
25–54 years: 1.09 male(s)/female
55–64 years: 0.81 male(s)/female
65 years and over: 0.75 male(s)/female
total population: 1.02 male(s)/female (2015 est.)
Mother's mean age at first birth: 21.5
note: median age at first birth among women 25–29 (2013 est.)
Maternal mortality rate: 265 deaths/100,000 live births (2015 est.)
country comparison to the world: 53
Infant mortality rate: *total:* 45.62 deaths/1,000 live births
male: 48.48 deaths/1,000 live births
female: 42.67 deaths/1,000 live births (2015 est.)
country comparison to the world: 44
Life expectancy at birth: *total population:* 51.62 years
male: 52.05 years
female: 51.18 years (2015 est.)
country comparison to the world: 220

Total fertility rate: 2.17 children born/woman (2015 est.)
country comparison to the world: 101
Contraceptive prevalence rate: 55.1% (2006/07)
Health expenditures: 7.7% of GDP (2013)
country comparison to the world: 54
Physicians density: 0.37 physicians/1,000 population (2007)
Hospital bed density: 2.7 beds/1,000 population (2009)
Drinking water source:
improved:
urban: 98.2% of population
rural: 84.6% of population
total: 91% of population
unimproved:
urban: 1.8% of population
rural: 15.4% of population
total: 9% of population (2015 est.)
Sanitation facility access:
improved:
urban: 54.5% of population
rural: 16.8% of population
total: 34.4% of population
unimproved:
urban: 45.5% of population
rural: 83.2% of population
total: 65.6% of population (2015 est.)
HIV/AIDS—adult prevalence rate: 15.97% (2014 est.)
country comparison to the world: 6
HIV/AIDS—people living with HIV/AIDS: 245,400 (2013 est.)
country comparison to the world: 24
HIV/AIDS—deaths: 5,100 (2014 est.)
country comparison to the world: 31
Major infectious diseases: *degree of risk:* high
food or waterborne diseases: bacterial diarrhea, hepatitis A, and typhoid fever
vectorborne disease: malaria
water contact disease: schistosomiasis (2013)
Obesity—adult prevalence rate: 16.8% (2014)
country comparison to the world: 133
Children under the age of 5 years underweight: 13.2% (2013)
country comparison to the world: 37
Education expenditures: 8.3% of GDP (2010)
country comparison to the world: 9
Literacy: *definition:* age 15 and over can read and write
total population: 81.9%
male: 79.2%
female: 84.5% (2015 est.)
School life expectancy (primary to tertiary education): *total:* 11 years
male: 11 years
female: 11 years (2006)
Unemployment, youth ages 15–24: *total:* 56.2%
male: 49.4%
female: 62.2% (2013 est.)
country comparison to the world: 19

GOVERNMENT

Country name: *conventional long form:* Republic of Namibia
conventional short form: Namibia

local long form: Republic of Namibia
local short form: Namibia
former: German South-West Africa (Deutsch Suedwest Afrika), South-West Africa
etymology: named for the coastal Namib Desert; the name "namib" means "vast place" in the Nama/Damara language
Government type: presidential republic
Capital: *name:* Windhoek
Geographic coordinates: 22 34 S, 17 05 E
time difference: UTC + 1 (6 hours ahead of Washington, DC, during Standard Time)
daylight saving time: +1hr, begins first Sunday in September; ends first Sunday in April
Administrative divisions: 14 regions; Erongo, Hardap,//Karas, Kavango East, Kavango West, Khomas, Kunene, Ohangwena, Omaheke, Omusati, Oshana, Oshikoto, Otjozondjupa, Zambezi; note—the Karas Region was renamed//Karas in September 2013 to include the alveolar lateral click of the Khoekhoegowab language
Independence: 21 March 1990 (from South African mandate)
National holiday: Independence Day, 21 March (1990)
Constitution: drafted 9 February 1990, signed 16 March 1990, entered into force 21 March 1990; amended 1998, 2010, 2014 (2016)
Legal system: mixed legal system of uncodified civil law based on Roman-Dutch law and customary law
International law organization participation: has not submitted an ICJ jurisdiction declaration; accepts ICCt jurisdiction
Citizenship: *citizenship by birth:* no
citizenship by descent only: at least one parent must be a citizen of Namibia
dual citizenship recognized: no
residency requirement for naturalization: 5 years
Suffrage: 18 years of age; universal
Executive branch: *chief of state:* President Hage GEINGOB (since 21 March 2015); note—the president is both chief of state and head of government
head of government: President Hage GEINGOB (since 21 March 2015); Prime Minister Saara KUUGONGELWA-AMADHILA (since 21 March 2015)
cabinet: Cabinet appointed by the president from among members of the National Assembly
elections/appointments: president elected by absolute majority popular vote in 2 rounds if needed for a 5-year term (eligible for a second term); election last held on 27–28 November 2009 (next to be held on 28 November 2014)
election results: Hage GEINGOB elected president; percent of vote—Hage GEINGOB (SWAPO) 86.7%, McHenry VENAANI (DTA) 5.0%, Hidipo HAMUTENYA (RDP) 3.4%, Asser MBAI (NUDO) 1.9%, Henk MUDGE (RP) 1.0%, other 2.0%
Legislative branch: *description:* bicameral Parliament consists of the National Assembly (104 seats; 96 members directly elected in multi-seat constituencies by proportional representation vote to serve

5-year terms and 8 nonvoting members appointed by the president) and the National Council, which primarily reviews legislation passed and referred by the National Assembly (26 seats (to be expanded to 42 in 2016); members indirectly elected 2 each by the 13 regional councils to serve 5-year terms)
elections: National Council—elections for regional councils to determine members of the National Council held on 27 November 2015 (next to be held in November 2020); National Assembly—last held on 28 November 2014 (next to be held in November 2019)
election results: National Council—percent of vote by party—NA; seats by party—SWAPO 24, UDF 1, DTA 1; National Assembly—percent of vote by party—SWAPO 80.0%, DTA 4.8%, RDP 3.5%, APP 2.3%, UDF 2.1%, NUDO 2.0%, CPN 1.5%, other 3.8%; seats by party—SWAPO 77, DTA 5, RDP 3, APP 2, UDF 2, NUDO 2, CPN 2, SWANU 1, UPM 1, RP 1
Judicial branch: *highest court (s):* Supreme Court (consists of the chief justice and at least 3 judges in quorum sessions)
judge selection and term of office: judges appointed by the president of Namibia upon the recommendation of the Judicial Service Commission; judges serve until age 65 but can be extended by the president until age 70
subordinate courts: High Court; Labor Court; regional and district magistrates' courts; community courts
Political parties and leaders: All People's Party or APP [Ignatius SHIXWAMENI]
Communist Party of Namibia or CPN (formerly known as Workers' Revolutionary Party or WRP) [Attie BEUKES and Harry BOESAK]
Democratic Turnhalle Alliance of Namibia or DTA [McHenry VENAANI]
National Unity Democratic Organization or NUDO [Asser MBAI]
Rally for Democracy and Progress or RDP [Jeremiah NAMBINGA]
Republican Party or RP [Henk MUDGE]
South West Africa National Union or SWANU [Usutuaije MAAMBERUA]
South West Africa People's Organization or SWAPO [Hage GEINGOB, acting president]
United Democratic Front or UDF [Justus IIGAROEB]
United People's Movement or UPM [Jan J. VAN WYK]
Political pressure groups and leaders: National Society for Human Rights or NAM RIGHTS
The Affirmative Repositioning Movement or AR [Job AMUPANDA, Dimbulukweni NAUYOM A, George KAMBALA]
other: various labor unions
International organization participation: ACP, AfDB, AU, C, CD, CPLP (associate observer), FAO, G-77, IAEA, IBRD, ICAO, ICCt, ICRM, IDA, IFAD, IFC, IFRCS, ILO, IMF, IMO, Interpol, IOC, IOM, IPU, ISO, ITSO, ITU, ITUC (NGOs), MIGA, NAM, OPCW, SACU, SADC, UN, UNAMID, UNCTAD, UNESCO, UNHCR, UNIDO, UNISFA, UNMIL, UNMISS, UNOCI,

UNWTO, UPU, WCO, WHO, WIPO, WMO, WTO

Diplomatic representation in the US: *chief of mission:* Ambassador Martin ANDJABA (since 3 September 2010)

chancery: 1605 New Hampshire Avenue NW, Washington, DC 20009

telephone: [1] (202) 986-0540

FAX: [1] (202) 986-0443

Diplomatic representation from the US: *chief of mission:* Ambassador Thomas Frederick DAUGHTON (since 6 October 2014)

embassy: 14 Lossen Street, Windhoek

mailing address: Private Bag 12029 Ausspannplatz, Windhoek

telephone: [264] (61) 295-8500

FAX: [264] (61) 295-8603

Flag description: a wide red stripe edged by narrow white stripes divides the flag diagonally from lower hoist corner to upper fly corner; the upper hoist-side triangle is blue and charged with a yellow, 12-rayed sunburst; the lower fly-side triangle is green; red signifies the heroism of the people and their determination to build a future of equal opportunity for all; white stands for peace, unity, tranquility, and harmony; blue represents the Namibian sky and the Atlantic Ocean, the country's precious water resources and rain; the yellow sun denotes power and existence; green symbolizes vegetation and agricultural resources

National symbol(s): oryx (antelope); national colors: blue, red, green, white, yellow

National anthem: *name:* "Namibia, Land of the Brave"

lyrics/music: Axali DOESEB

note: adopted 1991

ECONOMY

Economy—overview: The economy is heavily dependent on the extraction and processing of minerals for export. Mining accounts for 11.5% of GDP, but provides more than 50% of foreign exchange earnings. Rich alluvial diamond deposits make Namibia a primary source for gem-quality diamonds. Marine diamond mining is increasingly important as the terrestrial diamond supply has dwindled. The rising cost of m ining diamonds, increasingly from the sea, combined with increased diamond production in Russia and China, has reduced profit margins. Namibian authorities have emphasized the need to add value to raw materials, do more in-country manufacturing, and exploit the services market, especially in the logistics and transportation sectors.

Namibia is the world's fifth-largest producer of uranium. The Chinese owned Husab uranium mine in expected to start producing uranium ore in 2017. Once the Husab mine reaches full production, Namibia is expected to become the world's second-largest producer of uranium. Namibia also produces large quantities of zinc and is a smaller producer of gold and copper. The mining and quarrying sectors employ 2% of the population. Namibia's economy remains vulnerable to world commodity price fluctuations, and drought.

Namibia normally imports about 50% of its cereal requirements; in drought years food shortages can be a problem in rural areas. A high per capita GDP, relative to the region, hides one of the world's most unequal income distributions. A priority of the current government is poverty eradication.

A five-year, Millennium Challenge Corporation compact ended in September 2014. As an upper middle income country, Namibia is ineligible for a second compact. The Namibian economy is closely linked to South Africa with the Namibian dollar pegged one-to-one to the South African rand. Namibia receives 30%–40% of its revenues from the Southern African Customs Union (SACU). Volatility in the size of Namibia's annual SACU allotment complicates budget planning.

GDP (purchasing power parity): $25.34 billion (2015 est.)

$24.25 billion (2014 est.)

$22.8 billion (2013 est.)

note: data are in 2015 US dollars

country comparison to the world: 135

GDP (official exchange rate): $12.83 billion (2015 est.)

GDP—real growth rate: 4.5% (2015 est.)

6.4% (2014 est.)

5.7% (2013 est.)

country comparison to the world: 51

GDP—per capita (PPP): $11,400 (2015 est.)

$11,000 (2014 est.)

$10,500 (2013 est.)

note: data are in 2015 US dollars

country comparison to the world: 130

Gross national saving: 19.6% of GDP (2015 est.)

25.3% of GDP (2014 est.)

21.1% of GDP (2013 est.)

country comparison to the world: 84

GDP—composition, by end use:

household consumption: 69.2%

government consumption: 27.3%

investment in fixed capital: 29.9%

investment in inventories: -1.2%

exports of goods and services: 39.6%

imports of goods and services: -64.8% (2015 est.)

GDP—composition, by sector of origin:

agriculture: 6.2%

industry: 30%

services: 63.8% (2015 est.)

Agriculture—products: millet, sorghum, peanuts, grapes; livestock; fish

Industries: meatpacking, fish processing, dairy products, pasta, beverages; mining (diamonds, lead, zinc, tin, silver, tungsten, uranium, copper)

Industrial production growth rate: 4.3% (2015 est.)

country comparison to the world: 48

Labor force: 1.188 million (2015 est.)

country comparison to the world: 138

Labor force—by occupation: *agriculture:* 31%

industry: 14%

services: 54%

note: about half of Namibia's people are unemployed while about two-thirds live in rural areas; roughly two-thirds of rural dwellers rely on subsistence agriculture (2013 est.)

Unemployment rate: 28.1% (2014 est.)

29.6% (2013 est.)

country comparison to the world: 182

Population below poverty line: 28.7% (2010 est.)

Household income or consumption by percentage share: *lowest:* 10%: 2.4%

highest: 10%: 42% (2010)

Distribution of family income—Gini index: 59.7 (2010)

70.7 (2003)

country comparison to the world: 8

Budget: *revenues:* $4.617 billion

expenditures: $5.333 billion (2015 est.)

Taxes and other revenues: 35.9% of GDP (2015 est.)

country comparison to the world: 53

Budget surplus (+) or deficit (−): -5.6% of GDP (2015 est.)

country comparison to the world: 176

Public debt: 28.2% of GDP (2015 est.)

24% of GDP (2014 est.)

country comparison to the world: 144

Fiscal year: 1 April–31 March

Inflation rate (consumer prices): 3.4% (2015 est.)

5.3% (2014 est.)

country comparison to the world: 146

Central bank discount rate: 6.25% (17 February 2016)

6.5% (31 December 2015)

country comparison to the world: 64

Commercial bank prime lending rate: 10.5% (17 February 2016 est.)

10.25% (31 December 2015 est.)

country comparison to the world: 90

Stock of narrow money: $2.786 billion (31 December 2015 est.)

$3.17 billion (31 December 2014 est.)

country comparison to the world: 118

Stock of broad money: $7.496 billion (31 December 2014 est.)

$6.574 billion (31 December 2013 est.)

country comparison to the world: 117

Stock of domestic credit: $5.863 billion (31 December 2015 est.)

$6.655 billion (31 December 2014 est.)

country comparison to the world: 117

Market value of publicly traded shares: $1.305 billion (31 December 2012 est.)

$1.152 billion (31 December 2011)

$1.176 billion (31 December 2010 est.)

country comparison to the world: 104

Current account balance: -$1.253 billion (2015 est.)

-$1.12 billion (2014 est.)

country comparison to the world: 129

Exports: $5.042 billion (2015 est.)

$4.626 billion (2014 est.)

country comparison to the world: 110

Exports—commodities: diamonds, copper, gold, zinc, lead, uranium; cattle, white fish and mollusks

Imports: $7.205 billion (2015 est.)

$7.36 billion (2014 est.)

country comparison to the world: 112

Imports—commodities: foodstuffs; petroleum products and fuel, machinery and equipment, chemicals

Reserves of foreign exchange and gold: $1.135 billion (31 December 2015 est.)

$1.209 billion (31 December 2014 est.)

country comparison to the world: 127
Debt—external: $5.993 billion (31 December 2014 est.)
$5.306 billion (31 December 2013 est.)
country comparison to the world: 125
Stock of direct foreign investment—at home: $NA
Stock of direct foreign investment—abroad: $NA
Exchange rates: Namibian dollars (NAD) per US dollar—
12.58 (2015 est.)
10.8526 (2014 est.)
10.8526 (2013 est.)
8.2 (2012 est.)
7.2597 (2011 est.)

ENERGY

Electricity—production: 1.796 billion kWh (2012 est.)
country comparison to the world: 141
Electricity—consumption: 4.238 billion kWh (2013 est.)
country comparison to the world: 124
Electricity—exports: 89 million kWh (2013 est.)
country comparison to the world: 79
Electricity—imports: 2.907 billion kWh (2013 est.)
country comparison to the world: 54
Electricity—installed generating capacity: 1.087 million kW (2013 est.)
country comparison to the world: 122
Electricity—from fossil fuels: 31.8% of total installed capacity (2013 est.)
country comparison to the world: 179
Electricity—from nuclear fuels: 0% of total installed capacity (2013 est.)
country comparison to the world: 207
Electricity—from hydroelectric plants: 68.2% of total installed capacity (2013 est.)
country comparison to the world: 25
Electricity—from other renewable sources: 0% of total installed capacity (2013 est.)
country comparison to the world: 142
Crude oil—production: 0 bbl/day (2014 est.)
country comparison to the world: 208
Crude oil—exports: 0 bbl/day (2014 est.)
country comparison to the world: 208
Crude oil—imports: 0 bbl/day (2012 est.)
country comparison to the world: 147
Crude oil—proved reserves: 0 bbl (1 January 2015 est.)
country comparison to the world: 209
Refined petroleum products—production: 0 bbl/day (2012 est.)
country comparison to the world: 145
Refined petroleum products—consumption: 22,000 bbl/day (2013 est.)
country comparison to the world: 126
Refined petroleum products—exports: 0 bbl/day (2012 est.)
country comparison to the world: 147
Refined petroleum products—imports: 21990 bbl/day (2012 est.)
country comparison to the world: 107
Natural gas—production: 0 cu m (2013 est.)
country comparison to the world: 146
Natural gas—consumption: 0 cu m (2013 est.)
country comparison to the world: 209
Natural gas—exports: 0 cu m (2013 est.)
country comparison to the world: 210

Natural gas—imports: 0 cu m (2013 est.)
country comparison to the world: 79
Natural gas—proved reserves: 62.29 billion cu m (1 January 2014 est.)
country comparison to the world: 61
Carbon dioxide emissions from consumption of energy: 3.716 million Mt (2012 est.)
country comparison to the world: 135

COMMUNICATIONS

Telephones—fixed lines: total subscriptions: 180,000
subscriptions per 100 inhabitants: 8 (2014 est.)
country comparison to the world: 128
Telephones—mobile cellular: total: 2.7 million
subscriptions per 100 inhabitants: 121 (2014 est.)
country comparison to the world: 143
Telephone system: general assessment: good system; core fiber-optic network links most centers with digital connections
domestic: multiple mobile-cellular providers with a combined subscribership of more than 100 telephones per 100 persons
international: country code—264; fiber-optic cable to South Africa, microwave radio relay link to Botswana, direct links to other neighboring countries; connected to the South African Far East (SAFE) submarine cable through South Africa; connected to the West Africa Cable System (WACS), an ultra-high capacity fiber optic submarine cable linking southern and western African countries to Europe; satellite earth stations—4 Intelsat (2012)
Broadcast media: 1 private and 1 state-run TV station; satellite and cable TV service available; state-run radio service broadcasts in multiple languages; about a dozen private radio stations; transmissions of multiple international broadcasters available (2007)
Radio broadcast stations: AM 2, FM 39, shortwave 4 (2001)
Television broadcast stations: 2 (2007)
Internet country code: .na
Internet hosts: 78,280 (2012)
country comparison to the world: 84
Internet users: total: 325,400
percent of population: 14.8% (2014 est.)
country comparison to the world: 140

TRANSPORTATION

Airports: 112 (2013)
country comparison to the world: 52
Airports—with paved runways: total: 19
over 3,047 m: 4
2,438 to 3,047 m: 2
1,524 to 2,437 m: 12
914 to 1,523 m: 1 (2013)
Airports—with unpaved runways: total: 93
1,524 to 2,437 m: 25
914 to 1,523 m: 52
under 914 m: 16 (2013)
Railways: total: 2,628 km
narrow gauge: 2,628 km 1.067-m gauge (2014)
country comparison to the world: 62
Roadways: total: 44,138 km
paved: 6,387 km
unpaved: 37,751 km (2010)
country comparison to the world: 81
Merchant marine: total: 1

by type: cargo 1 (2010)
country comparison to the world: 153
Ports and terminals: major seaport(s): Luderitz, Walvis Bay

MILITARY AND SECURITY

Military branches: Namibian Defense Force (NDF): Army, Navy, Air Force (2013)
Military service age and obligation: 18 years of age for voluntary military service; no conscription (2012)
Military expenditures:
4.2% of GDP (2015)
3.11% of GDP (2012)
3.38% of GDP (2011)
3.11% of GDP (2010)
country comparison to the world: 20

TRANSNATIONAL ISSUES

Disputes—international: concerns from international experts and local populations over the Okavango Delta ecology in Botswana and human displacement scuttled Namibian plans to construct a hydroelectric dam on Popa Falls along the Angola-Namibia border; the governments of South Africa and Namibia have not signed or ratified the text of the 1994 Surveyor's General agreement placing the boundary in the middle of the Orange River; Namibia has supported, and in 2004 Zimbabwe dropped objections to, plans between Botswana and Zambia to build a bridge over the Zambezi River, thereby de facto recognizing a short, but not clearly delimited, Botswana-Zambia boundary in the river
Trafficking in persons: current situation: Namibia is a country of origin and destination for children and, to a lesser extent, women subjected to forced labor and sex trafficking; victims, lured by promises of legitimate jobs, are forced to work in urban centers and on commercial farms; traffickers exploit Namibian children, as well as children from Angola, Zambia, and Zimbabwe, for forced labor in agriculture, cattle herding, domestic service, fishing, and street vending; children are also forced into prostitution, often catering to tourists from southern Africa and Europe; San and Zemba children are particularly vulnerable; foreign adults and Namibian adults and children are reportedly subjected to forced labor in Chinese-owned retail, construction, and fishing operations
tier rating: Tier 2 Watch List—Namibia does not fully comply with the minimum standards for the elimination of trafficking; however, it is making significant efforts to do so; Namibia was granted a waiver from an otherwise required downgrade to Tier 3 because its government has a written plan that, if implemented would constitute making significant efforts to bring itself into compliance with the minimum standards for the elimination of trafficking; in 2015, the Child Care and Protection Bill passed, criminalizing child trafficking; the government's first sex trafficking prosecution remained pending; no new prosecutions were initiated and no trafficking offenders have ever been convicted; accusations of forced labor at Chinese construction and mining companies continue to go uninvestigated; authorities failed to fully implement victim identification and referral processes, which led to the deportation of possible victims (2015)

NAURU

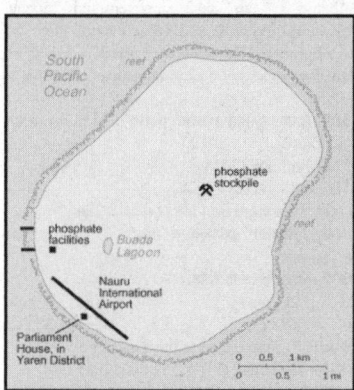

INTRODUCTION

Background: The exact origins of the Nauruans are unclear since their language does not resemble any other in the Pacific region. Germany annexed the island in 1888. A German-British consortium began mining the island's phosphate deposits early in the 20th century. Australian forces occupied Nauru in World War I; it subsequently became a League of Nations mandate. After the Second World War—and a brutal occupation by Japan—Nauru became a UN trust territory. It achieved independence in 1968 and joined the UN in 1999 as the world's smallest independent republic.

GEOGRAPHY

Location: Oceania, island in the South Pacific Ocean, south of the Marshall Islands

Geographic coordinates: 0 32 S, 166 55 E

Map references: Oceania

Area: *total:* 21 sq km

land: 21 sq km

water: 0 sq km

country comparison to the world: 240

Area—comparative: about 0.1 times the size of Washington, DC

Land boundaries: 0 km

Coastline: 30 km

Maritime claims: *territorial sea:* 12 nm

contiguous zone: 24 nm

exclusive economic zone: 200 nm

Climate: tropical with a monsoonal pattern; rainy season (November to February)

Terrain: sandy beach rises to fertile ring around raised coral reefs with phosphate plateau in center

Elevation: *mean elevation:* NA

elevation extremes: *lowest point:* Pacific Ocean 0 m

highest point: unnamed elevation along plateau rim 61 m

Natural resources: phosphates, fish

Land use: *agricultural land:* 20%

arable land: 0%

permanent crops: 20%

permanent pasture: 0%

forest: 0%

other: 80% (2011 est.)

Irrigated land: 0 sq km (2012)

Natural hazards: periodic droughts

Environment—current issues: limited natural freshwater resources, roof storage tanks collect rainwater but mostly dependent on a single, aging desalination plant; a century of intensive phosphate mining beginning in 1906—mainly by a UK, Australia, and NZ consortium—left the central 90% of Nauru a wasteland and threatens limited remaining land resources

Environment—international agreements: *party to:* Biodiversity, Climate Change, Climate Change-Kyoto Protocol, Desertification, Hazardous Wastes, Law of the Sea, Marine Dumping, Ozone Layer Protection, Whaling

signed, but not ratified: none of the selected agreements

Geography—note: world's smallest island country; situated just 53 km south of the Equator; Nauru is one of the three great phosphate rock islands in the Pacific Ocean—the others are Banaba (Ocean Island) in Kiribati and Makatea in French Polynesia

PEOPLE AND SOCIETY

Nationality: *noun:* Nauruan(s)

adjective: Nauruan

Ethnic groups: Nauruan 58%, other Pacific Islander 26%, Chinese 8%, European 8%

Languages: Nauruan 93% (official, a distinct Pacific Island language), English 2% (widely understood, spoken, and used for most government and com mercial purposes), other 5% (includes I-Kiribati 2% and Chinese 2%)

note: percentages represent main language spoken at home; Nauruan is spoken by 95% of the population, English by 66%, and other languages by 12% (2011 est.)

Religions: Protestant 60.4% (includes Nauru Congregational 35.7%, Assembly of God 13%, Nauru Independent Church 9.5%, Baptist 1.5%, and Seventh Day Adventist 0.7%), Roman Catholic 33%, other 3.7%, none 1.8%, unspecified 1.1% (2011 est.)

Population: 9,540 (July 2015 est.)

country comparison to the world: 225

Age structure: *0–14 years:* 32.45% (male 1,360/female 1,736)

15–24 years: 16.13% (male 785/female 754)

25–54 years: 43.19% (male 2,059/female 2,061)

55–64 years: 6.11% (male 231/female 352)

65 years and over: 2.12% (male 78/female 124) (2015 est.)

Median age: *total:* 25.7 years

male: 26.1 years

female: 25.3 years (2015 est.)

country comparison to the world: 148

Population growth rate: 0.55% (2015 est.)

country comparison to the world: 154

Birth rate: 24.95 births/1,000 population (2015 est.)

country comparison to the world: 52

Death rate: 5.87 deaths/1,000 population (2015 est.)

country comparison to the world: 171

Net migration rate: -13.63 migrant(s)/1,000 population (2015 est.)

country comparison to the world: 218

Urbanization: *urban population:* 100% of total population (2015)

rate of urbanization: 0.19% annual rate of change (2010–15 est.)

Sex ratio: *at birth:* 0.83 male(s)/female

0–14 years: 0.78 male(s)/female

15–24 years: 1.04 male(s)/female

25–54 years: 1 male(s)/female

55–64 years: 0.66 male(s)/female

65 years and over: 0.63 male(s)/female

total population: 0.9 male(s)/female (2015 est.)

Mother's mean age at first birth: 22.1

note: median age at first birth among women 25–29 (2007 est.)

Infant mortality rate: *total:* 8.07 deaths/1,000 live births

male: 10.34 deaths/1,000 live births

female: 6.17 deaths/1,000 live births (2015 est.)

country comparison to the world: 154

Life expectancy at birth: *total population:* 66.75 years

male: 62.64 years

female: 70.19 years (2015 est.)

country comparison to the world: 170

Total fertility rate: 2.88 children born/woman (2015 est.)

country comparison to the world: 58

Contraceptive prevalence rate: 35.6% (2007)

Health expenditures: 6.3% of GDP (2013)

country comparison to the world: 67

Physicians density: 0.71 physicians/1,000 population (2010)

Hospital bed density: 5 beds/1,000 population (2010)

Drinking water source:

improved:

urban: 96.5% of population

total: 96.5% of population

unimproved:

urban: 3.5% of population

total: 3.5% of population (2015 est.)

Sanitation facility access:

improved:

urban: 65.6% of population

total: 65.6% of population

unimproved:

urban: 34.4% of population

total: 34.4% of population (2015 est.)

HIV/AIDS—adult prevalence rate: NA

HIV/AIDS—people living with HIV/AIDS: NA

HIV/AIDS—deaths: NA

Obesity—adult prevalence rate: 45.1% (2014)

country comparison to the world: 2

Children under the age of 5 years underweight:
4.8% (2007)

country comparison to the world: 91

Education expenditures: NA

School life expectancy (primary to tertiary education): *total:* 9 years
male: 9 years
female: 10 years (2008)

GOVERNMENT

Country name: *conventional long form:* Republic of Nauru

conventional short form: Nauru

local long form: Republic of Nauru

local short form: Nauru

former: Pleasant Island

etymology: the island name may derive from the Nauruan word "anaoero" meaning "I go to the beach"

Government type: parliamen tary republic

Capital: no official capital; government offices in Yaren District

time difference: UTC + 12 (17 hours ahead of Washington, DC, during Standard Time)

Administrative divisions: 14 districts; Aiwo, Anabar, Anetan, Anibare, Baiti, Boe, Buada, Denigomodu, Ewa, Ijuw, Meneng, Nibok, Uaboe, Yaren

Independence: 31 January 1968 (from the Australia-, NZ-, and UK-administered UN trusteeship)

National holiday: independence Day, 31 January (1968)

Constitution: effective 29 January 1968; amended 1968, 2009, 2014 (2016)

Legal system: mixed legal system of common law based on the English model and customary law

International law organization participation: has not submitted an ICJ jurisdiction declaration; accepts ICCt jurisdiction

Suffrage: 20 years of age; universal and compulsory

Executive branch: *chief of state:* President Baron WAQA (since 11 June 2013); note—the president is both chief of state and head of government

head of government: President Baron WAQA (since 11 June 2013)

cabinet: Cabinet appointed by the president from among members of Parliament

elections/appointments: president indirectly elected by Parliament for a 3-year renewable term; election last held on 11 June 2013 (next to be held in 2016)

election results: Baron WAQA reelected president on 11 June 2013; Parliament vote—Baron WAQA (independent) 13, Roland KUN (Nauru First) 5

Legislative branch: *description:* unicameral parliament (19 seats; members directly elected in multi-seat constituencies by majority vote; members serve 3-year terms)

elections: last held on 9 July 2016 (next to be held in 2019)

election results: percent of vote—NA; seats—independent 19

Judicial branch: *highest court(s):* Supreme Court (consists of a chief justice and 1 judge)

judge selection and term of office: judges appointed by the president to serve until age 65

subordinate courts: District Court, Family Court

Political parties and leaders: Democratic Party [Kennan ADEANG]

Nauru First (Naoero Amo) Party

Nauru Party (informal)

note: loose multiparty system

Political pressure groups and leaders: Woman Information and News Agency (women's issues)

International organization participation: ACP, ADB, AOSIS, C, FAO, G-77, ICAO, ICCt, IFAD, Interpol, IOC, IOM, ITU, OPCW, PIF, Sparteca, SPC, UN, UNCTAD, UNESCO, UPU, WHO

Diplomatic representation in the US: *chief of mission:* Ambassador Marlene Inemwin MOSES (since 10 February 2006)

chancery: 800 2nd Avenue, Suite 400 D, New York, NY 10017

telephone: [1] (212) 937-0074

FAX: [1] (212) 937-0079

Diplomatic representation from the US: the US does not have an embassy in Nauru; the US Ambassador to FijiIs accredited to Nauru

Flag description: blue with a narrow, horizontal, yellow stripe across the center and a large white 12-pointed star below the stripe on the hoist side; blue stands for the Pacific Ocean, the star indicates the country's location in relation to the Equator (the yellow stripe) and the 12 points symbolize the 12 original tribes of Nauru

National symbol(s): frigatebird, calophyllum flower; national colors: blue, yellow, white

National anthem: *name:* "Nauru Bwiema" (Song of Nauru)

lyrics/music: Margaret HENDRIE/Laurence Henry HICKS

note: adopted 1968

ECONOMY

Economy—overview: Revenues of this tiny island—a coral atoll with a land area of 21 square kilometers—traditionally have come from exports of phosphates. Few other resources exist, with most necessities being imported, mainly from Australia, its former occupier and later major source of support. Primary reserves of phosphates were exhausted and mining ceased in 2006, but mining of a deeper layer of "secondary phosphate" in the interior of the island began the following year. The secondary phosphate deposits may last another 30 years. Earnings from Nauru's export of phosphate remains an important source of income. Few comprehensive statistics on the Nauru economy exist; estimates of Nauru's GDP vary widely. The rehabilitation of mined land and the replacement of income from phosphates are serious long-term problems. in anticipation of the exhaustion of Nauru's phosphate deposits, substantial amounts of phosphate income were invested in trust funds to help cushion the transition and provide for Nauru's economic future.

Although revenue sources for government are limited, the opening of the Australian Regional Processing Center for asylum seekers since 2012 has sparked growth in the economy. Revenue derived from fishing licenses under the "vessel day scheme" has also boosted government income. Housing, hospitals, and other capital plant are deteriorating. The cost to Australia of keeping the government and economy afloat continues to climb.

GDP (purchasing power parity): $150.8 million (2015 est.)

$139.7 million (2014 est.)

$127 million (2013 est.)

country comparison to the world: 224

GDP (official exchange rate): $150.8 million (2015 est.)

GDP—real growth rate: 8% (2015 est.)

10% (2014 est.)

4.5% (2013 est.)

country comparison to the world: 8

GDP—per capita (PPP): $14,800 (2015 est.)

$13,700 (2014 est.)

$12,500 (2013 est.)

note: data are in 2015 US dollars

country comparison to the world: 110

GDP—composition, by sector of origin:

agriculture: 6.1%

industry: 33%

services: 60.8% (2009 est.)

Agriculture—products: coconuts

Industries: phosphate mining, offshore banking, coconut products

Industrial production growth rate: NA%

Labor force: NA

Labor force—by occupation: *note:* most of the labor force is employed in phosphate mining, public administration, education, and transportation

Unemployment rate: 23% (2011 est.)

90% (2004 est.)

country comparison to the world: 175

Population below poverty line: NA%

Household income or consumption by percentage share: *lowest:* 10%: NA%

highest: 10%: NA%

Budget: *revenues:* $57.8 million

expenditures: $51.8 million (2010 est.)

Fiscal year: 1 July–30 June

Inflation rate (consumer prices): 8% (2015 est.)

5% (2014 est.)

country comparison to the world: 200

Exports: $125 million (2013 est.)

$110.3 million (2012 est.)

country comparison to the world: 192

Exports—commodities: phosphates

Imports: $143.1 million (2013 est.)

$41.2 million (2012 est.)

country comparison to the world: 211

Imports—commodities: food, fuel, manufactures, building materials, machinery

Debt—external: $33.3 million (2004 est.)

country comparison to the world: 198

Exchange rates: Australian dollars (AUD) per US dollar—

1.33 (2015 est.)

1.1094 (2014 est.)

1.0358 (2013 est.)

0.97 (2012 est.)

0.9695 (2011 est.)

ENERGY

Electricity—production: 25 million kWh (2012 est.)
country comparison to the world: 214
Electricity—consumption: 23.25 million kWh (2012 est.)
country comparison to the world: 213
Electricity—exports: 0 kWh (2013 est.)
country comparison to the world: 179
Electricity—imports: 0 kWh (2013 est.)
country comparison to the world: 184
Electricity—installed generating capacity: 6,000 kW (2012 est.)
country comparison to the world: 210
Electricity—from fossil fuels: 100% of total installed capacity (2012 est.)
country comparison to the world: 24
Electricity—from nuclear fuels: 0% of total installed capacity (2012 est.)
country comparison to the world: 157
Electricity—from hydroelectric plants: 0% of total installed capacity (2012 est.)
country comparison to the world: 193
Electricity—from other renewable sources: 0% of total installed capacity (2012 est.)
country comparison to the world: 209
Crude oil—production: 0 bbl/day (2014 est.)
country comparison to the world: 177
Crude oil—Exports: 0 bbl/day (2012 est.)
country comparison to the world: 171
Crude oil—imports: 0 bbl/day (2012 est.)
country comparison to the world: 110
Crude oil—proved reserves: 0 bbl (1 January 2015 est.)
country comparison to the world: 177

Refined petroleum products—production: 0 bbl/day (2012 est.)
country comparison to the world: 120
Refined petroleum products—consumption: 1,000 bbl/day (2013 est.)
country comparison to the world: 200
Refined petroleum products—exports: 0 bbl/day (2012 est.)
country comparison to the world: 212
Refined petroleum products—imports: 1,075 bbl/day (2012 est.)
country comparison to the world: 195
Natural gas—production: 0 cu m (2013 est.)
country comparison to the world: 113
Natural gas—consumption: 0 cu m (2013 est.)
country comparison to the world: 181
Natural gas—exports: 0 cu m (2013 est.)
country comparison to the world: 157
Natural gas—imports: 0 cu m (2013 est.)
country comparison to the world: 113
Natural gas—proved reserves: 0 cu m (1 January 2014 est.)
country comparison to the world: 180
Carbon dioxide emissions from consumption of energy: 168,700 Mt (2012 est.)
country comparison to the world: 197

COMMUNICATIONS

Telephones—fixed lines: *total subscriptions:* 0 *subscriptions per 100 inhabitants:* less than 1 (2014 est.)
country comparison to the world: 218
Telephones—mobile cellular: *total:* 6,800 *subscriptions per 100 inhabitants:* 73 (2012)
country comparison to the world: 214

Telephone system: *general assessment:* adequate local and international radiotelephone communication provided via Au stralian facilities
international: country code—674; satellite earth station—1 Intelsat (Pacific Ocean)
Broadcast media: 1 government-owned TV station broadcasting programs from New Zealand sent via satellite or on videotape; 1 government-owned radio station, broadcasting on AM and FM, utilizes Australian and British programs (2009)
Radio broadcast stations: AM 1, FM 0, shortwave 0 (1998)
Television broadcast stations: 1 (1997)
Internet country code: .nr
Internet hosts: 8,162 (2012)
country comparison to the world: 138

TRANSPORTATION

Airports: 1 (2013)
country comparison to the world: 227
Airports—with paved runways: *total:* 1
1,524 to 2,437 m: 1 (2013)
Roadways: *total:* 30 km
paved: 24 km
unpaved: 6 km (2002)
country comparison to the world: 220
Ports and terminals: *major seaport(s):* Nauru

MILITARY AND SECURITY

Military branches: no regular military forces (2012)
Military—note: Nauru maintains no defense forces; under an informal agreement, defense is the responsibility of Australia

TRANSNATIONAL ISSUES

Disputes—international: none

NAVASSA ISLAND

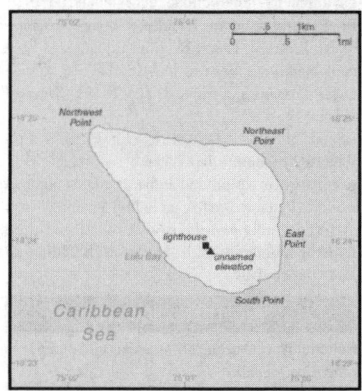

INTRODUCTION

Background: This uninhabited island was claimed by the US in 1857 for its guano. Mining took place between 1865 and 1898. The lighthouse, built in 1917, was shut down in 1996 and administration of Navassa Island transferred from the US Coast Guard to the Department of the Interior, Office of Insular Affairs. A 1998 scientific expedition to the island described it as a "unique preserve of Caribbean biodiversity. "The following year it became a National Wildlife Refuge and annual scientific expeditions have continued.

GEOGRAPHY

Location: Caribbean, island in the Caribbean Sea, 30 nm west of Tiburon Peninsula of Haiti
Geographic coordinates: 18 25 N, 75 02 W
Map references: Central America and the Caribbean
Area: *total:* 5.4 sq km
land: 5.4 sq km
water: 0 sq km
country comparison to the world: 248
Area—comparative: about nine times the size of the National Mall in Washington, DC
Land boundaries: 0 km
Coastline: 8 km

Maritime claims: *territorial sea:* 12 nm
exclusive economic zone: 200 nm
Climate: marine, tropical
Terrain: raised flat to undulating coral and limestone plateau; ringed by vertical white cliffs (9 to 15 m high)
Elevation: *mean elevation:* NA
elevation extremes: *lowest point:* Caribbean Sea 0 m
highest point: unnamed elevation on southwest side 77 m
Natural resources: guano
Land use: *agricultural land:* 0%
arable land: 0%
permanent crops: 0%
permanent pasture: 0%
forest: 0%
other: 100% (2011 est.)
Natural hazards: hurricanes
Environment—current issues: NA
Geography—note: strategic location 160 km south of the US Naval Base at Guantanamo Bay, Cuba; mostly exposed rock with numerous solution holes

(limestone sinkholes) but with enough grassland to support goat herds; dense stands of fig trees, scattered cactus

PEOPLE AND SOCIETY

Population: uninhabited
note: transient Haitian fishermen and others camp on the island

GOVERNMENT

Country name: *conventional long form:* none
conventional short form: Navassa Island
etymology: the flat island was named "Navaza" by some of Christopher COLUMBUS' sailers in 1504; the name derives from the Spanish term "nava" meaning "flat land, plain, or field"
Dependency status: unorganized, unincorporated territory of the US; administered by the Fish and

Wildlife Service, US Department of the Interior from the Caribbean Islands National Wildlife Refuge in Boqueron, Puerto Rico; in September 1996, the Coast Guard ceased operations and maintenance of Navassa Island Light, a 46-meter-tall lighthouse on the southern side of the island; there has also been a private claim advanced against the island
Legal system: the laws of the US, where applicable, apply
Diplomatic representation from the US: none (territory of the US)
Flag description: the flag of the US is used

ECONOMY

Economy—overview: Subsistence fishing and commercial trawling occur within refuge waters.

TRANSPORTATION

Ports and terminals: none; offshore anchorage only

MILITARY AND SECURITY

Military—note: defense is the responsibility of the US
Disputes—international:

TRANSNATIONAL ISSUES

claimed by Haiti, source of subsistence fishing

NEPAL

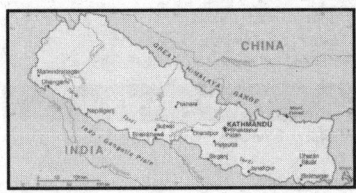

INTRODUCTION

Background: In 1951, the Nepali monarch ended the century-old system of rule by hereditary premiers and instituted a cabinet system that brought political parties into the government. That arrangement lasted until 1960, when political parties were again banned, but was reinstated in 1990 with the establishment of a multiparty democracy within the framework of a constitutional monarchy. An insurgency led by Maoists broke out in 1996. The ensuing 10-year civil war between Maoist and government forces witnessed the dissolution of the cabinet and parliament and the reassumption of absolute power by the king in 2002. Several weeks of mass protests in April 2006 were followed by several months of peace negotiations between the Maoists and government officials, and culminated in a late 2006 peace accord and the 2007 promulgation of an interim constitution. Following a nationwide Constituent Assembly (CA) election in 2008, the newly formed CA declared Nepal a federal democratic republic, abolished the monarchy, and elected the country's first president. After the CA failed to draft a constitution by a May 2012 deadline set by the Supreme Court, then-Prime Minister Baburam BHATTARAI dissolved the CA. Months of negotiations ensued until March 2013 when the major political parties agreed to create an interim government headed by then-Chief Justice Khil Raj REGMI with a mandate to hold elections for a new CA. Elections

were held in November 2013, in which the Nepali Congress won the largest share of seats in the CA and in February 2014 formed a coalition government with the second place Communist Party of Nepal-Unified Marxist-Leninist and with Nepali Congress President Sushil KOIRALA as prime minister. Nepal's new constitution came into effect in September 2015.

GEOGRAPHY

Location: Southern Asia, between China and India
Geographic coordinates: 28 00 N, 84 00 E
Map references: Asia
Area: *total:* 147,181 sq km
land: 143,351 sq km
water: 3,830 sq km
country comparison to the world: 94
Area—comparative: slightly larger than Arkansas
Land boundaries: *total:* 3,159 km
border countries (2): China 1,389 km, India 1,770 km
Coastline: 0 km (landlocked)
Maritime claims: none (landlocked)
Climate: varies from cool summers and severe winters in north to subtropical summers and mild winters in south
Terrain: Tarai or flat river plain of the Ganges in south; central hill region with rugged Himalayas in north
Elevation: *mean elevation:* 2,565 m
elevation extremes: *lowest point:* Kanchan Kalan 70 m
highest point: Mount Everest 8,850 m (highest peak in Asia and highest point on earth above sea level)
Natural resources: quartz, water, timber, hydropower, scenic beauty, small deposits of lignite, copper, cobalt, iron ore
Land use: *agricultural land:* 28.8%
arable land: 15.1%
permanent crops: 1.2%

permanent pasture: 12.5%
forest: 25.4%
other: 45.8% (2011 est.)
Irrigated land: 13,320 sq km (2012)
Total renewable water resources: 210.2 cu km (2011)
Freshwater withdrawal (domestic/industrial/agricultural): *total:* 9.5 cu km/yr (2%/0%/98%)
per capita: 334.7 cu m/yr (2006)
Natural hazards: severe thunderstorm s; flooding; landslides; drought and famine depending on the timing, intensity, and duration of the summer monsoons
Environment—current issues: deforestation (overuse of wood for fuel and lack of alternatives); contam inated water (with human and anim al wastes, agricultural runoff, and industrial effluents); wildlife conservation; vehicular emissions
Environment—international agreements: *party to:* Biodiversity, Climate Change, Climate Change-Kyoto Protocol, Desertification, Endangered Species, Hazardous Wastes, Law of the Sea, Ozone Layer Protection, Tropical Timber 83, Tropical Timber 94, Wetlands
signed, but not ratified: M arine Life Conservation
Geography—note: landlocked; strategic location between China and India; contains eight of world's 10 highest peaks, including Mount Everest and Kanchenjunga—the world's tallest and third tallest mountains—on the borders with China and India respectively

PEOPLE AND SOCIETY

Nationality: *noun:* Nepali (singular and plural)
adjective: Nepali
Ethnic groups: Chhettri 16.6%, Brahman-Hill 12.2%, Magar 7.1%, Tharu 6.6%, Tamang 5.8%, Newar 5%, Kami 4.8%, Muslim 4.4%, Yadav 4%, Rai 2.3%, Gurung 2%, Damai/Dholii 1.8%, Thakuri 1.6%, Limbu 1.5%, Sarki 1.4%, Teli 1.4%, Chamar/Harijan/Ram 1.3%, Koiri/Kushwaha 1.2%, other 19%

note: 125 caste/ethnic groups were reported in the 2011 national census (2011 est.)

Languages: Nepali (official) 44.6%, Maithali 11.7%, Bhojpuri 6%, Tharu 5.8%, Tamang 5.1%, Newar 3.2%, Magar 3%, Bajjika 3%, Urdu 2.6%, Avadhi 1.9%, Limbu 1.3%, Gurung 1.2%, other 10.4%, unspecified 0.2%

note: 123 languages reported as mother tongue in 2011 national census; many in government and business also speak English (2011 est.)

Religions: Hindu 81.3%, Buddhist 9%, Muslim 4.4%, Kirant 3.1%, Christian 1.4%, other 0.5%, unspecified 0.2% (2011 est.)

Population: 31,551,305 (July 2015 est.)
country comparison to the world: 42

Age structure: *0–14 years:* 30.72% (male 4,937,627/female 4,755,972)

15–24 years: 22.51% (male 3,580,083/female 3,522,047)

25–54 years: 36.5% (male 5,552,621/female 5,964,599)

55–64 years: 5.67% (male 874,350/female 913,683)

65 years and over: 4.6% (male 668,760/female 781,563) (2015 est.)

Dependency ratios: *total dependency ratio:* 61.8%

youth dependency ratio: 52.9%
elderly dependency ratio: 9%
potential support ratio: 11.1% (2015 est.)

Median age: *total:* 23.4 years
male: 22.8 years
female: 24 years (2015 est.)
country comparison to the world: 165

Population growth rate: 1.79% (2015 est.)
country comparison to the world: 64

Birth rate: 20.64 births/1,000 population (2015 est.)
country comparison to the world: 80

Death rate: 6.56 deaths/1,000 population (2015 est.)
country comparison to the world: 146

Net migration rate: 3.86 migrant(s)/1,000 population (2015 est.)
country comparison to the world: 33

Urbanization: *urban population:* 18.6% of total population (2015)
rate of urbanization: 3.18% annual rate of change (2010–15 est.)

Major urban areas—population: KATHMANDU (capital) 1.183 million (2015)

Sex ratio: *at birth:* 1.04 male(s)/female
0–14 years: 1.04 male(s)/female
15–24 years: 1.02 male(s)/female
25–54 years: 0.93 male(s)/female
55–64 years: 0.96 male(s)/female
65 years and over: 0.86 male(s)/female
total population: 0.98 male(s)/female (2015 est.)

Mother's mean age at first birth: 20.1
note: median age at first birth among women 25–29 (2011 est.)

Maternal mortality rate: 258 deaths/100,000 live births (2015 est.)
country comparison to the world: 60

Infant mortality rate: *total:* 39.14 deaths/1,000 live births

male: 39.24 deaths/1,000 live births
female: 39.04 deaths/1,000 live births (2015 est.)
country comparison to the world: 52

Life expectancy at birth: *total population:* 67.52 years
male: 66.18 years
female: 68.92 years (2015 est.)
country comparison to the world: 166

Total fertility rate: 2.24 children born/woman (2015 est.)
country comparison to the world: 96

Contraceptive prevalence rate: 49.7% (2011)

Health expenditures: 6% of GDP (2013)
country comparison to the world: 125

Hospital bed density: 5 beds/1,000 population (2006)

Drinking water source:
improved:
urban: 90.9% of population
rural: 91.8% of population
total: 91.6% of population
unimproved:
urban: 9.1% of population
rural: 8.2% of population
total: 8.4% of population (2015 est.)

Sanitation facility access:
improved:
urban: 56% of population
rural: 43.5% of population
total: 45.8% of population
unimproved:
urban: 44% of population
rural: 56.5% of population
total: 54.2% of population (2015 est.)

HIV/AIDS—adult prevalence rate: 0.2% (2014 est.)
country comparison to the world: 97

HIV/AIDS—people living with HIV/AIDS: 39,200 (2014 est.)
country comparison to the world: 63

HIV/AIDS—deaths: 2,600 (2014 est.)
country comparison to the world: 50

Major infectious diseases: *degree of risk:* high
food or waterborne diseases: bacterial diarrhea, hepatitis A and E, and typhoid fever
vectorborne disease: Japanese encephalitis, malaria, and dengue fever (2013)

Obesity—adult prevalence rate: 2.9% (2014)
country comparison to the world: 189

Children under the age of 5 years underweight: 30.1% (2014)
country comparison to the world: 17

Education expenditures: 4.7% of GDP (2014)
country comparison to the world: 87

Literacy: *definition:* age 15 and over can read and write
total population: 63.9%
male: 76.4%
female: 53.1% (2015 est.)

School life expectancy (primary to tertiary education): *total:* 12 years
male: 12 years
female: 13 years (2013)

Child labor—children ages 5–14: *total number:* 2,467,549
percentage: 34% (2008 est.)

Unemployment, youth ages 15–24: *total:* 3.5%

male: 4.2%
female: 2.9% (2008 est.)

Country name: *conventional long form:* Federal Democratic Republic of Nepal
conventional short form: Nepal
local long form: Sanghiya Loktantrik Ganatantra Nepal
local short form: Nepal
etymology: the Newar people of the Kathmandu Valley and surrounding areas apparently gave their name to the country; the terms "Nepal," "Newar," "Nepar," and "Newal" are phonetically different forms of the same word

Government type: federal parliamentary republic

Capital: *name:* Kathmandu

Geographic coordinates: 27 43 N, 85 19 E
time difference: UTC+5.75 (10.75 hours ahead of Washington, DC, during Standard Time)

Administrative divisions: 14 zones (anchal, singular and plural); Bagmati, Bheri, Dhawalagiri, Gandaki, Janakpur, Karnali, Kosi, Lumbini, Mahakali, Mechi, Narayani, Rapti, Sagarmatha, Seti

Independence: 1768 (unified by Prithvi Narayan SHAH)

National holiday: Republic Day, 28 May (2008), the abdication of Gyanendra SHAH, last Nepalese monarch, and the establishment of a federal republic

Constitution: several previous; latest adopted 20 September 2015; amended January 2016

Legal system: English common law and Hindu legal concepts

International law organization participation: has not submitted an ICJ jurisdiction declaration; non-party state to the ICCt

Citizenship: *citizenship by birth:* yes
citizenship by descent: yes
dual citizenship recognized: no
residency requirement for naturalization: 15 years

Suffrage: 18 years of age; universal

Executive branch: *chief of state:* President Bidhya Devi BHANDARI (since 29 October 2015); Vice President Nanda Bahadar PUN (since 31 October 2015)

head of government: Prime Minister Khadga Prasad OLI (since 12 October 2015)
cabinet: Council of Ministers appointed by the prime minister; cabinet dominated by the Nepali Congress and the Communist Party of Nepal-United Marxist-Leninist
elections/appointments: president indirectly elected by the Constituency Assembly; term extends until the new constitution is promulgated; president elected on 29 October 2015 (next election NA); prime minister indirectly elected by the Constituent Assembly
election results: Bidhya Devi BHANDARI elected president; Constituent Assembly vote count—Bidhya Devi BHANDARI (CPN-UML) 327, Kul Bahadur GURUNG (NC) 214; BHANDARIIs Nepal's first woman president

Legislative branch: *description:* unicameral Constituent Assembly or Sambidhan Sabha (601 seats; 240 members directly elected in single-seat constituencies by simple majority vote, 335 directly elected in a single nationwide constituency by proportional representation (PR) vote and 26 appointed by the cabinet (Council of Ministers); note—political parties allocated more than 30 percent of the PR seats are obliged to follow specified quotas for ethnic groups and within them equal percentages of men and women

elections: last held on 19 November 2013 (next to be held NA)

election results: percent of vote by party—NC 26%, CPN-UML 24%, Unified Communist Party of Nepal (Maoist) 15%, Rastriya Prajatantra Party Nepal 7%; other 28%; seats by party—NC 196, CPN-UML 175, UCPN(M) 80, Rastriya Prajantantra Party Nepal 24, other smaller parties 100; note—26 seats filled by the new Cabinet have not yet been appointed

Judicial branch: *highest court(s):* Supreme Court (consists of the chief justice and up to 14 judges)

judge selection and term of office: the Supreme Court chief justice appointed by the prime minister on the recommendation of the Constitutional Council; other judges appointed by the prime minister on the recommendation of the Judicial Council; judges serve until age 65

subordinate courts: appellate and district courts

note: Nepal's judiciary was restructured under its 2007 Interim Constitution

Political parties and leaders: *note:* 122 political parties participated in the 19 November 2013 election and the 30 parties listed below were elected to serve in the Constituent Assembly

Akhanda Nepal Party [Kumar KHADKA]

Communist Party of Nepal-Marxist Leninist or CPN-ML [C.P. MAINALI]

Communist Party of Nepal-Unified Marxist-Leninist or CPN -UML [Jhala Nath KHANAL]

Communist Party of Nepal (United) or CPN (United) [Jaydev JOSHI]

Dalit Janajati Party [Bishwendra PASHWAN]

Federal Socialist Party [Ashok RAI]

Jana Jagaran Party Nepal (Awareness Party Nepal) [Lok Mani DHAKAL]

Khambuwan Rastriya Morcha-Nepal [Ram Kumar RAI]

Madhesi People's Rights Forum-Democratic [Bijay Kumar GACHCHADAR]

Madhesi People's Rights Forum-Nepal [Upendra YADAV]

Madhesi People's Rights Forum-Republican

Madhesh Samata Party Nepal [Meghraj SAHANI]

National Madhes Socialist Party [Sharat Singh BHANDARI]

Nepal Rastriya Party [Keshav Man SHAKYA]

Nepal Pariwar Dal [Ek Nath DHAKAL]

Nepal Workers and Peasants Party [Narayan Man BIJUKCHHE]

Nepali Congress or NC [Sushil KOIRALA]

Nepali Janata Dal [Hari Charan SHAH]

Rastriya Janamorcha Nepal [Chitra Bahadur K. C.]

Rastriya Janamukti Party [Malwar Singh THAPA]

Rastriya Prajatantra Party

Rastriya Prajatantra Party-Nepal [Kamal THAPA]

Sadbhavana Party [Rajendra MAHATO]

Samajbadi Prajatanytrik Janata Party Nepal [Prem Bahadur SINGH]

Sanghiya Sadbhavana Party [Anil Kumar JHA]

Sanghiye Loktantrik Rastriya Manch [Rukmini CHAUDHARY]

Terai Madhesh Democratic Party [Mahantha THAKUR]

Terai-Madhesh Sadbhavana Party-Nepal [Mahendra YADAV]

Tharuhat Terai Party Nepal [Bhanuram CHAUDARY]

Unified Communist Party of Nepal (Maoist) or UCPN (M) [Pushpa Kamal DAHAL, also known as Comrade PRACHANDA]

Political pressure groups and leaders: *other:* various groups advocating regional autonomy such as the Federal State Limbuwan Council in far eastern Nepal

International organization participation: ADB, BIMSTEC, CD, CP, FAO, G-77, IAEA, IBRD, ICAO, ICC (NGOs), ICRM, IDA, IFAD, IFC, IFRCS, ILO, IMF, IMO, Interpol, IOC, IOM, IPU, ISO, ITSO, ITU, ITUC (NGOs), MIGA, MINURSO, MINUSMA, MINUSTAH, MONUSCO, NAM, OPCW, SAARC, SACEP, UN, UNAMID, UNCTAD, UND OF, UNESCO, UNIDO, UNIFIL, UNML, UNMISS, UNOCI, UNTSO, UNWTO, UPU, WCO, WFTU (NGOs), WHO, WIPO, WMO, WTO

Diplomatic representation in the US: *chief of mission:* Ambassador Arjun Kumar KARKI (since 18 May 2015)

chancery: 2131 Leroy Place NW, Washington, DC 20008

telephone: [1] (202) 667-4550

FAX: [1] (202) 667-5534

consulate(s) general: Cleveland (OH), New York

Diplomatic representation from the US: *chief of mission:* Ambassador Alaina B. TEPLITZ (since 7 October 2015)

embassy: Maharajgunj, Kathmandu

mailing address: use embassy street address

telephone: [977] (1) 423-4000

FAX: [977] (1) 400-7272

Flag description: red with a blue border around the unique shape of two overlapping right triangles; the smaller, upper triangle bears a white stylized half moon and the larger, lower triangle displays a white 12-pointed sun; the color red represents the rhododendron (Nepal's national flower) and is a sign of victory and bravery, the blue border signifies peace and harmony; the two right triangles are a combination of two single pennons (pennants) that originally symbolized the Himalaya Mountains while their charges represented the families of the king (upper) and the prime minister, but today they are understood to denote Hinduism and Buddhism, the country's two main religions; the moon represents the serenity of the Nepalese people and the shade and cool weather in the Himalaya, while the sun depicts the heat and higher temperatures of the lower parts of Nepal; the moon and the sun are also said to express the hope that the nation will endure as long as these heavenly bodies

note: Nepal is the only country in the world whose flag is not rectangular or square

National symbol(s): rhododendron blossom; national color: red

National anthem: *name:* "Sayaun Thunga Phool Ka" (Hundreds of Flowers)

lyrics/music: Pradeep Kumar RAI/Ambar GURUNG

note: adopted 2007; after the abolition of the monarchy in 2006, a new anthem was required because of the previous anthem's praise for the king

ECONOMY

Economy—overview: Nepal is among the poorest and least developed countries in the world, with about one-quarter of its population living below the poverty line. Nepal is heavily dependent on remittances, which amount to as much as 29% of GDP. Agriculture is the mainstay of the economy, providing a livelihood for almost 70% of the population and accounting for about one-third of GDP. Industrial activity mainly involves the processing of agricultural products, including pulses, jute, sugarcane, tobacco, and grain. Nepal has considerable scope for exploiting its potential in hydropower, with an estimated 42,000 MW of commercially feasible capacity. Nepal and India signed trade and investment agreements in 2014 that increase Nepal's hydropower potential, but political uncertainty and a difficult business climate have hampered foreign investment.

Nepal was hit by massive earthquakes in early 2015, which damaged or destroyed infrastructure and homes and set back economic development. Political gridlock in the past several years and recent public protests, predominantly in the southern Tarai region, have hindered post-earthquake recovery and prevented much-needed economic reform. Additional challenges to Nepal's growth include its landlocked geographic location, persistent power shortages, and underdeveloped transportation infrastructure.

GDP (purchasing power parity): $70.09 billion (2015 est.)

$67.81 billion (2014 est.)

$64.35 billion (2013 est.)

note: data are in 2015 US dollars

country comparison to the world: 98

GDP (official exchange rate): $21.36 billion (2015 est.)

GDP—real growth rate: 3.4% (2015 est.)

5.4% (2014 est.)

4.1% (2013 est.)

country comparison to the world: 89

GDP—per capita (PPP): $2,500 (2015 est.)

$2,400 (2014 est.)

$2,300 (2013 est.)

note: data are in 2015 US dollars

country comparison to the world: 197

Gross national saving: 33.9% of GDP (2015 est.)

33.3% of GDP (2014 est.)

33.1% of GDP (2013 est.)

country comparison to the world: 12

GDP—composition, by end use: *household consumption:* 77.2%
government consumption: 12.4%
investment in fixed capital: 24.4%
investment in inventories: 12.3%
exports of goods and services: 9.9%
imports of goods and services: -36.2% (2015 est.)
GDP—composition, by sector of origin:
agriculture: 31.7%
industry: 15.1%
services: 53.2% (FY2014/15 est.)
Agriculture—products: pulses, rice, corn, wheat, sugarcane, jute, root crops; milk, water buffalo meat
Industries: tourism, carpets, textiles; small rice, jute, sugar, and oilseed mills; cigarettes, cement and brick production
Industrial production growth rate: 2.6% (2015 est.)
country comparison to the world: 98
Labor force: 15.2 million
note: severe lack of skilled labor (2013 est.)
country comparison to the world: 39
Labor force—by occupation:
agriculture: 69%
industry: 12%
services: 19% (2014 est.)
Unemployment rate: 46% (2008 est.)
42% (2004 est.)
country comparison to the world: 199
Population below poverty line: 25.2% (2011 est.)
Household income or consumption by percent Age share: *lowest:* 10%: 3.2%
highest: 10%: 29.5% (2011)
Distribution of family income—Gini index : 32.8 (2010)
47.2 (2008 est.)
country comparison to the world: 106
Budget: *revenues:* $4.257 billion
expenditures: $4.203 billion (2015 est.)
Taxes and other revenues: 19.9% of GDP (2015 est.)
country comparison to the world: 159
Budget surplus (+) or deficit (–): 0.2% of GDP (2015 est.)
country comparison to the world: 26
Public debt: 30% of GDP (FY 2012/13 est.)
32% of GDP (2013 est.) (FY11/12)
country comparison to the world: 143
Fiscal year: 16 July—15 July
Inflation rate (consumer prices): 7.2% (2015 est.)
9% (2014 est.)
country comparison to the world: 194
Central bank discount rate: 8% (31 July 2015)
8% (31 July 2014)
country comparison to the world: 40
Commercial bank prime lending rate: 9.8% (31 December 2015 est.)
10.6% (31 December 2014 est.)
country comparison to the world: 84
Stock of narrow money: $4.002 billion (31 December 2015 est.)
$3.567 billion (31 December 2014 est.)
country comparison to the world: 107
Stock of broad money: $17.83 billion (31 December 2015 est.)
$16.36 billion (31 December 2014 est.)
country comparison to the world: 93

Stock of domestic credit: $14.33 billion (31 December 2015 est.)
$13.97 billion (31 December 2014 est.)
country comparison to the world: 93
Market value of publicly traded shares: $11.81 billion (31 October 2015 est.)
$9.574 billion (31 October 2014)
$5.235 billion (31 December 2010 est.)
country comparison to the world: 71
Current account balance: $1.067 billion (2015 est.)
$908 million (2014 est.)
country comparison to the world: 36
Exports: $924.2 million (2015 est.)
$1.078 billion (2014 est.)
country comparison to the world: 163
Exports—commodities: clothing, pulses, carpets, textiles, juice, jute goods
Exports—partners: India 61.2%, US 9.4% (2015)
Imports: $8.56 billion (2015 est.)
$7.72 billion (2014 est.)
country comparison to the world: 106
Imports—commodities: petroleum products, machinery and equipment, gold, electrical goods, medicine
Imports—partners: India 61.4%, China 15.4% (2015)
Reserves of foreign exchange and gold: $71.83 billion (30 July 2015 est.)
$6.191 billion (30 July 2014 est.)
country comparison to the world: 32
Debt—external: $3.727 billion (31 December 2014 est.)
$3.833 billion (31 December 2013 est.)
country comparison to the world: 137
Stock of direct foreign investment—at home: $103 million (31 July 2013 est.)
country comparison to the world: 117
Stock of direct foreign investment—abroad: $NA
Exchange rates: Nepalese rupees (NPR) per US dollar—
102.4 (2015 est.)
97.6 (2014 est.)
99.53 (2013 est.)
85.2 (2012 est.)
74.02 (2011 est.)

ENERGY

Electricity—production: 3.516 billion kWh (2012 est.)
country comparison to the world: 129
Electricity—consumption: 3.239 billion kWh (2012 est.)
country comparison to the world: 131
Electricity—exports: 4 million kWh (2012 est.)
country comparison to the world: 92
Electricity—imports: 793 million kWh (2012 est.)
country comparison to the world: 68
Electricity—installed generating capacity: 763,000 kW (2012 est.)
country comparison to the world: 131
Electricity—from fossil fuels: 7.5% of total installed capacity (2012 est.)
country comparison to the world: 202
Electricity—from nuclear fuels: 0% of total installed capacity (2012 est.)

country comparison to the world: 156
Electricity—from hydroelectric plants: 92.5% of total installed capacity (2012 est.)
country comparison to the world: 11
Electricity—from other renewable sources: 0% of total installed capacity (2012 est.)
country comparison to the world: 208
Crude oil—production: 0 bbl/day (2014 est.)
country comparison to the world: 176
Crude oil—exports: 0 bbl/day (2012 est.)
country comparison to the world: 170
Crude oil—imports: 0 bbl/day (2012 est.)
country comparison to the world: 109
Crude oil—proved reserves: 0 bbl (1 January 2015 est.)
country comparison to the world: 176
Refined petroleum products—production: 0 bbl/day (2012 est.)
country comparison to the world: 119
Refined petroleum products—consumption: 20,000 bbl/day (2013 est.)
country comparison to the world: 128
Refined petroleum products—exports: 0 bbl/day (2012 est.)
country comparison to the world: 211
Refined petroleum products—imports: 19,990 bbl/day (2012 est.)
country comparison to the world: 113
Natural gas—production: 0 cu m (2013 est.)
country comparison to the world: 112
Natural gas—consumption: 0 cu m (2013 est.)
country comparison to the world: 180
Natural gas—exports: 0 cu m (2013 est.)
country comparison to the world: 156
Natural gas—imports: 0 cu m (2013 est.)
country comparison to the world: 112
Natural gas—proved reserves: 0 cu m (1 January 2014 est.)
country comparison to the world: 179
Carbon dioxide emissions from consumption of energy: 3.638 million Mt (2012 est.)
country comparison to the world: 136

COMMUNICATIONS

Telephones—fixed lines: *total subscriptions:* 840,000
subscriptions per 100 inhabitants: 3 (2014 est.)
country comparison to the world: 85
Telephones—mobile cellular: *total:* 23.2 million
subscriptions per 100 inhabitants: 75 (2014 est.)
country comparison to the world: 52
Telephone system: *general assessment:* poor telephone and telegraph service; fair radiotelephone communication service and mobile-cellular telephone network
domestic: mobile-cellular telephone subscribership base is increasing with roughly 90% of the population living in areas covered by mobile carriers
international: country code—977; radiotelephone communications; microwave and fiber landlines to India; satellite earth station—1 Intelsat (Indian Ocean) (2011)
Broadcast media: state operates 2 TV stations, as well as national and regional radio stations; roughly 30 independent TV channels are registered with

only about half in regular operation; nearly 400 FM radio stations are licensed with roughly 300 operational (2007)

Radio broadcast stations: AM 6, FM 80, shortwave 4 (2008)

Television broadcast stations: 9 (plus9 repeaters) (2008)

Internet country code: .np

Internet hosts: 41,256 (2012)

country comparison to the world: 100

Internet users: *total:* 3.8 million

percent of population: 12.1% (2014 est.)

country comparison to the world: 80

TRANSPORTATION

Airports: 47 (2013)

country comparison to the world: 95

Airports—with paved runways: *total:* 11

over 3,047 m: 1

1,524 to 2,437 m: 3

914 to 1,523 m: 6

under 914 m: 1 (2013)

Airports—with unpaved runways: *total:* 36

1,524 to 2,437 m: 1

914 to 1,523 m: 6

under 914 m: 29 (2013)

Railways: *total:* 53 km

narrow gauge: 53 km 0.762-m gauge (2014)

country comparison to the world: 131

Roadways: *total:* 10,844 km

paved: 4,952 km

unpaved: 5,892 km (2010)

country comparison to the world: 132

MILITARY AND SECURITY

Military branches: Nepal Army (2012)

Military service age and obligation: 18 years of age for voluntary military service; no conscription (2014)

Military expenditures: NA% (2012)

1.41% of GDP (2011)

TRANSNATIONAL ISSUES

Disputes—international: joint border commission continues to work on contested sections of boundary with India, including the 400 sq km dispute over the source of the Kalapani River; India has instituted a stricter border regime to restrict transit of Maoist insurgents and illegal cross-border activities

Refugees and internally displaced persons: *refugees (country of origin):* 15,000 (Tibet/China) (2014); fewer than 18,000 (Bhutan) (2015)

IDPs: 40,700 (remaining from ten-year Maoist insurgency that officially ended in 2006; figure does not include people displaced since 2007 by inter-communal violence and insecurity in the Terai region; 2015 earthquakes) (2015)

stateless persons: undetermined (2015); note— the UNHCR is working with the Nepali Government to address the large number of individuals lacking citizenship certificates in Nepal; smaller numbers of Bhutanese Hindu refugees of Nepali origin (the Lhotsampa) who were stripped of Bhutanese nationality and forced to flee their country in the late 1980s and early 1990s—and undocumented Tibetan refugees who arrived in Nepal prior to the 1990s—are considered stateless

Illicit drugs: illicit producer of cannabis and hashish for the domestic and international drug markets; transit point for opiates from Southeast Asia to the West

NETHERLANDS

INTRODUCTION

Background: The Dutch United Provinces declared their independence from Spain in 1579; during the 17th century, they became a leading seafaring and commercial power, with settlements and colonies around the world. After a 20-year French occupation, a Kingdom of the Netherlands was formed in 1815. In 1830, Belgium seceded and formed a separate kingdom. The Netherlands remained neutral in World War I, but suffered German invasion and occupation in World War II. A modern, industrialized nation, the Netherlands is also a large exporter of agricultural products. The country was a founding member of NATO and the EEC (now the EU) and participated in the introduction of the euro in 1999. In October 2010, the former Netherlands Antilles was dissolved and the three smallest islands—Bonaire, Sint Eustatius, and Saba—became special municipalities in the Netherlands administrative structure. The larger islands of Sint Maarten and Curacao joined the Netherlands and Aruba as constituent countries forming the Kingdom of the Netherlands.

GEOGRAPHY

Location: Western Europe, bordering the North Sea, between Belgium and Germany

Geographic coordinates: 52 30 N, 5 45 E

Map references: Europe

Area: *total:* 41,543 sq km

land: 33,893 sq km

water: 7,650 sq km

country comparison to the world: 135

Area—comparative: slightly less than twice the size of New Jersey

Land boundaries: *total:* 1,053 km

border countries (2): Belgium 478 km, Germany 575 km

Coastline: 451 km

Maritime claims: *territorial sea:* 12 nm

contiguous zone: 24 nm

exclusive fishing zone: 200 nm

Climate: temperate; marine; cool summers and mild winters

Terrain: mostly coastal lowland and reclaimed land (polders); some hills in southeast

Elevation: *mean elevation:* 30 m

elevation extremes: *lowest point:* Zuidplaspolder -7 m

highest point: Mount Scenery 862 m (on the island of Saba in the Caribbean, now considered an integral part of the Netherlands following the dissolution of the Netherlands Antilles)

note: the highest point on continental Netherlands is Vaalserberg at 322 m

Natural resources: natural gas, petroleum, peat, limestone, salt, sand and gravel, arable land

Land use: *agricultural land:* 55.1%

arable land: 29.8%

permanent crops: 1.1%

permanent pasture: 24.2%

forest: 10.8%

other: 34.1% (2011 est.)

Irrigated land: 4,860 sq km (2012)

Total renewable water resources: 91 cu km (2011)

Freshwater withdrawal (domestic/industrial/agricultural): *total:* 10.61 cu km/yr (12%/88%/1%)

per capita: 636.7 cu m/yr (2008)

Natural hazards: flooding

Environment—current issues: water pollution in the form of heavy metals, organic compounds, and nutrients such as nitrates and phosphates; air pollution from vehicles and refining activities; acid rain

Environment—international agreements: *party to:* Air Pollution, Air Pollution-Nitrogen Oxides, Air Pollution-Persistent Organic Pollutants, Air Pollution-Sulfur 85, Air Pollution-Sulfur 94, Air Pollution-Volatile Organic Compounds, Antarctic-Environmental Protocol, Antarctic-Marine Living Resources, Antarctic Treaty, Biodiversity, Climate Change, Climate Change-Kyoto Protocol, Desertification, Endangered Species, Environmental Modification, Hazardous Wastes, Law of the Sea, Marine Dumping, Marine Life Conservation, Ozone Layer Protection, Ship Pollution,

Tropical Timber 83, Tropical Timber 94, Wetlands, Whaling

signed, but not ratified: none of the selected agreements

Geography—note: located at mouths of three major European rivers (Rhine, Maas or Meuse, and Schelde)

PEOPLE AND SOCIETY

Nationality: *noun:* Dutchman(men), Dutchwoman (women)
adjective: Dutch

Ethnic groups: Dutch 78.6%, EU 5.8%, Turkish 2.4%, Indonesian 2.2%, Moroccan 2.2%, Surinamese 2.1%, Bonairian, Saba Islander, Sint Eustatian 0.8%, other 5.9% (2014 est.)

Languages: Dutch (official)
note: Frisian is an official language in Fryslan province; Frisian, Low Saxon, Limburgish, Romani, and Yiddish have protected status under the European Charter for Regional or Minority Languages; Dutch is the official language of the three special municipalities of the Caribbean Netherlands, while English is a recognized regional language on Sint Eustatius and Saba and Papiamento is a recognized regional language on Bonaire

Religions: Roman Catholic 28%, Protestant 19% (includes Dutch Reformed 9%, Protestant Church of The Netherlands, 7%, Calvinist 3%), other 11% (includes about 5% Muslim and lesser numbers of Hindu, Buddhist, Jehovah's Witness, and Orthodox), none 42% (2009 est.)

Population: 16,947,904 (July 2015 est.)
country comparison to the world: 67

Age structure: *0–14 years:* 16.73% (male 1,450,957/female 1,384,576)
15–24 years: 12.15% (male 1,049,802/female 1,009,250)
25–54 years: 40.12% (male 3,412,016/female 3,388,119)
55–64 years: 13.02% (male 1,099,594/female 1,107,401)
65 years and over: 17.97% (male 1,373,111/female 1,673,078) (2015 est.)

Dependency ratios: *total dependency ratio:* 53.3%
youth dependency ratio: 25.3%
elderly dependency ratio: 27.9%
potential support ratio: 3.6% (2015 est.)

Median age: *total:* 42.3 years
male: 41.3 years
female: 43.2 years (2015 est.)
country comparison to the world: 23

Population growth rate: 0.41% (2015 est.)
country comparison to the world: 164

Birth rate: 10.83 births/1,000 population (2015 est.)
country comparison to the world: 181

Death rate: 8.66 deaths/1,000 population (2015 est.)
country comparison to the world: 74

Net migration rate: 1.95 migrant(s)/1,000 population (2015 est.)
country comparison to the world: 52

Urbanization: *urban population:* 90.5% of total population (2015)

rate of urbanization: 1.05% annual rate of change (2010–15 est.)

Major urban areas—population: AMSTERDAM (capital) 1.091 million; Rotterdam 993,000; The Hague (seat of government) 650,000 (2015)

Sex ratio: *at birth:* 1.05 male(s)/female
0–14 years: 1.05 male(s)/female
15–24 years: 1.04 male(s)/female
25–54 years: 1.01 male(s)/female
55–64 years: 0.99 male(s)/female
65 years and over: 0.82 male(s)/female
total population: 0.98 male(s)/female (2015 est.)

Mother's mean age at first birth: 29.4 (2011 est.)

Maternal mortality rate: 7 deaths/100,000 live births (2015 est.)
country comparison to the world: 171

Infant mortality rate: *total:* 3.62 deaths/1,000 live births
male: 3.91 deaths/1,000 live births
female: 3.32 deaths/1,000 live births (2015 est.)
country comparison to the world: 201

Life expectancy at birth: *total population:* 81.23 years
male: 79.11 years
female: 83.47 years (2015 est.)
country comparison to the world: 24

Total fertility rate: 1.78 children born/woman (2015 est.)
country comparison to the world: 155

Contraceptive prevalence rate: 69%
note: percent of women aged 18–45 (2008)

Health expenditures: 12.9% of GDP (2013)
country comparison to the world: 7

Hospital bed density: 4.7 beds/1,000 population (2009)

Drinking water source:
improved:
urban: 100% of population
rural: 100% of population
total: 100% of population
unimproved:
urban: 0% of population
rural: 0% of population
total: 0% of population (2015 est.)

Sanitation facility access:
improved:
urban: 97.5% of population
rural: 99.9% of population
total: 97.7% of population
unimproved:
urban: 2.5% of population
rural: 0.1% of population
total: 2.3% of population (2015 est.)

HIV/AIDS—adult prevalence rate: NA

HIV/AIDS—people living with HIV/AIDS: NA

HIV/AIDS—deaths: NA

Obesity—adult prevalence rate: 21.9% (2014)
country comparison to the world: 103

Education expenditures: 5.6% of GDP (2013)
country comparison to the world: 45

School life expectancy (primary to tertiary education): *total:* 18 years
male: 18 years
female: 18 years (2012)

Unemployment, youth ages 15–24: *total:* 11%
male: 10.8%

female: 11.2% (2013 est.)
country comparison to the world: 102

GOVERNMENT

Country name: *conventional long form:* Kingdom of the Netherlands
conventional short form: Netherlands
local long form: Koninkrijk der Nederlanden
local short form: Nederland
etymology: the country name literally means "the lowlands" and refers to the geographic features of the land being both flat and down river from higher areas (i.e., at the estuaries of the Scheldt, Meuse, and Rhine Rivers; only about half of the Netherlands is more than 1 meter above sea level)

Government type: parliamentary constitutional monarchy; part of the Kingdom of the Netherlands

Capital: *name:* Amsterdam; note—The Hague is the seat of government

Geographic coordinates: 52 21 N, 4 55 E
time difference: UTC + 1 (6 hours ahead of Washington, DC, during Standard Time)
daylight saving time: +1hr, begins last Sunday in March; ends last Sunday in October
note: time descriptions apply to the continental Netherlands only, not to the Caribbean components

Administrative divisions: 12 provinces (provincies, singular—provincie); Drenthe, Flevoland, Fryslan (Friesland), Gelderland, Groningen, Limburg, Noord-Brabant (North Brabant), Noord-Holland (North Holland), Overijssel, Utrecht, Zeeland (Zealand), Zuid-Holland (South Holland)
note 1: the Netherlands is one of four constituent parts (countries) of the Kingdom of the Netherlands; the other three parts, Aruba, Curacao, and Sint Maarten, are all islands in the Caribbean; while all four parts are considered equal partners, in practice, most of the Kingdom's affairs are administered by the Netherlands, which makes up about 98% of the Kingdom's total land area and population
note 2: three other Caribbean islands, Bonaire, Saint Eustatius, and Saba, are considered to be special municipalities of the Netherlands proper

Dependent areas: Aruba, Curacao, Sint Maarten

Independence: 23 January 1579 (the northern provinces of the Low Countries conclude the Union of Utrecht breaking with Spain; on 26 July 1581 they formally declared their independence with an Act of Abjuration; however, it was not until 30 January 1648 and the Peace of Westphalia that Spain recognized this independence)

National holiday: King's Day (the King's birthday of 27 April (1967); celebrated on 26 April if 27 April is a Sunday)

Constitution: previous 1597, 1798; latest adopted 24 August 1815 (substantially revised in 1848); amended many times, last in 2010 (2016)

Legal system: civil law system based on the French system; constitution does not permit judicial review of acts of the States General

International law organization participation: accepts compulsory ICJ jurisdiction with reservations; accepts ICCt jurisdiction

Citizenship: *citizenship by birth:* no

citizenship by descent only: at least one parent must be a citizen of the Netherlands

dual citizenship recognized: no

residency requirement for naturalization: 5 years

Suffrage: 18 years of age; universal

Executive branch: *chief of state:* King WILLEM-ALEXANDER (since 30 April 2013); Heir Apparent Princess Catharina-Amalia (since 30 April 2013)

head of government: Prime Minister Mark RUTTE (since 14 October 2010); Deputy Prime Minister Lodewijk ASSCHER (since 5 November 2012); note—Mark RUTTE heads his second cabinet since 5 November 2012

cabinet: Council of Ministers appointed by the monarch; note—there is also a Council of State composed of the monarch, heir apparent, and councilors that provides advice to the cabinet on legislative and administrative policy

elections/appointments: the monarchy is hereditary; following Second Chamber elections, the leader of the majority party or majority coalition usually appointed prime minister by the monarch; deputy prime ministers appointed by the monarch

Legislative branch: *description:* bicameral States General or Staten Generaal consists of the First Chamber or Eerste Kamer (75 seats; members indirectly elected by the country's 12 provincial council members by proportional representation vote; members serve 4-year terms) and the Second Chamber or Tweede Kamer (150 seats; members directly elected in multi-seat constituencies by proportional representation vote to serve up to 4-year terms)

elections: First Chamber—last held on 26 May 2015 (next to be held in May 2019); Second Chamber -last held on 12 September 2012 (next to be held no later than 15 March 2017)

election results: First Chamber—percent of vote by party—NA; seats by party—VVD 13, CDA 12, D66 10, PVV 9, SP 9, PvdA 8, GL 4, CU 3, other 7; Second Chamber—percent of vote by party—VVD 26.6%, PvdA 24.8%, PVV, 10.1%, SP 9.7%, CDA 8.5%, D66 8.0%, CU 3.1%, GL 2.3%, other 6.9%; seats by party—VVD 41, PvdA 38, PVV 15, SP 15, CDA 13, D66 12, CU 5, GL 4, other 7

Judicial branch: *highest court(s):* Supreme Court or Hoge Raad (consists of 41 judges: the president, 6 vice-presidents, 31 justices or raadsheren, and 3 justices in exceptional service, referred to as buitengewone dienst); the court is divided into criminal, civil, tax, and ombuds chambers

judge selection and term of office: justices appointed by the monarch from a list provided by the Second Chamber of the States General; justices appointed for life or until mandatory retirement at age 70

subordinate courts: courts of appeal; district courts, each with up to 5 subdistrict courts

Political parties and leaders: Christian Democratic Appeal or CDA [Sybrand VAN HAERSMA BUMA]

Christian Union or CU [Gert-Jan SEGERS]

Democrats 66 or D66 [Alexander PECHTOLD]

50 Plus [Jan NAGEL]

Green Left or GL [Jesse KLAVER]

Labor Party or PvdA [Diederik SAMSOM]

Party for Freedom or PVV [Geert WILDERS]

Party for the Animals or PvdD [Marianne THIEME]

People's Party for Freedom and Democracy or VVD [Mark RUTTE]

Reformed Political Party or SGP [Kees VANDERSTAAIJ]

Socialist Party or SP [Emile ROEMER]

plus a few minor parties

Political pressure groups and leaders: Christian Trade Union Federation or CNV [Maurice LIMMEN]

Confederation of Netherlands Industry and Employers or VNO-NCW [Hans DE BOER]

Federation for Small and Medium-sized Businesses or MKB [Michael VAN STRAALEN]

Netherlands Trade Union Federation or FNV [Ton HEERTS]

Social Economic Council or SER [Mariette HAMER]

Trade Union Federation of Middle and High Personnel or MHP [Reginald VISSER]

International organization participation: ADB (nonregional member), AfDB (nonregional member), Arctic Council (observer), Australia Group, Benelux, BIS, CBSS (observer), CD, CE, CERN, EAPC, EBRD, ECB, EIB, EITI (implementing country), EMU, ESA, EU, FAO, FATF, G-10, IADB, IAEA, IBRD, ICAO, ICC (national committees), ICCt, ICRM, IDA, IEA, IFAD, IFC, IFRCS, IGAD (partners), IHO, ILO, IMF, IMO, IMSO, Interpol, IOC, IOM, IPU, ISO, ITSO, ITU, ITUC (NGOs), MIGA, MINU SMA, NATO, NEA, NSG, OAS (observer), OECD, OPCW, OSCE, Pacific Alliance (observer), Paris Club, PCA, Schengen Convention, SELEC (observer), UN, UNCTAD, UNDOF, UNESCO, UNHCR, UNIDO, UNMISS, UNRWA, UNTSO, UNWTO, UPU, WCO, WHO, WIPO, WMO, WTO, ZC

Diplomatic representation in the US: *chief of mission:* Ambassador Henne SCHUWER (since 17 September 2015)

chancery: 4200 Linnean Avenue NW, Washington, DC 20008

telephone: [1] (202) 244-5300, [1] 877–388–2443

FAX: [1] (202) 362-3430

consulate(s) general: Chicago, Miami, New York, San Francisco

Diplomatic representation from the US: *chief of mission:* Ambassador (vacant); Charge d'Affaires Adam H. STERLING (since 12 February 2016)

embassy: Lange Voorhout 102,2514 EJ, The Hague

mailing address: PSC 71, Box 1000, APO AE 09715

telephone: [31] (70) 310-2209

FAX: [31] (70) 310-2207

consulate(s) general: Amsterdam

Flag description: three equal horizontal bands of red (top), white, and blue; similar to the flag of Luxembourg, which uses a lighter blue and is longer; the colors were those of WILLIAM I, Prince of Orange, who led the Dutch Revolt against Spanish sovereignty in the latter half of the 16th century; originally the upper band was orange, but because it tended to fade to red over time, the red shade was eventually made the permanent color; the banner is perhaps the oldest tricolor in continuous use

National symbol(s): lion, tulip; national color: orange

National anthem: *name:* "Het Wilhelmus" (The William)

lyrics/music: Philips VAN MARNIX van Sint Aldegonde (presumed)/unknown

note: adopted 1932, in use since the 17th century, making it the oldest national anthem in the world; also known as "Wilhelmus van Nassouwe" (William of Nassau), it is in the form of an acrostic, where the first letter of each stanza spells the name of the leader of the Dutch Revolt

ECONOMY

Economy—overview: The Netherlands, the sixth-largest economy in the European Union, plays an important role as a European transportation hub, with a persistently high trade surplus, stable industrial relations, and moderate unemployment. Industry focuses on food processing, chemicals, petroleum refining, and electrical machinery. A highly mechanized agricultural sector employs only 2% of the labor force but provides large surpluses for food-processing and underpins the country's status as the world's second largest agricultural exporter.

The Netherlands is part of the eurozone, and as such, its monetary policy is controlled by the European Central Bank. The Dutch financial sector is highly concentrated, with four commercial banks possessing over 90% of bankingassets. The sector suffered as a result of the global financial crisis and required billions of dollars of government support, but the European Banking Authority completed stringent reviews in 2014 and deemed Dutch banks to be well-capitalized. To address the 2009 and 2010 economic downturns, the government sought to stimulate the domestic economy by accelerating infrastructure programs, offering corporate tax breaks for employers to retain workers, and expanding export credits. The stimulus programs and bank bailouts, however, resulted in a government budget deficit of 5.3% of GDP in 2010 that contrasted sharply with a surplus of 0.7% in 2008.

The government of Prime Minister Mark RUTTE has since implemented significant austerity measures to improve public finances and has instituted broad structural reforms in key policy areas, including the labor market, the housing sector, the energy market, and the pension system. As a result, the government budget deficit at the end of 2015 dropped to 2% of GDP. Following a protracted recession during which unemployment doubled to 7.4% and household consumption contracted for nearly three consecutive years, 2014 saw fragile GDP growth of 1% and a rise in most economic indicators. Growth picked up in 2015 as households boosted purchases through reduced saving. Drivers of growth included increased exports and business investments, as well as newly invigorated household consumption.

GDP (purchasing power parity): $832.6 billion (2015 est.)
$816.9 billion (2014 est.)
$808.7 billion (2013 est.)
note: data are in 2015 US dollars
country comparison to the world: 28

GDP (official exchange rate): $738.4 billion (2015 est.)

GDP—real growth rate: 1.9% (2015 est.)
1% (2014 est.)
-0.5% (2013 est.)
country comparison to the world: 139

GDP—per capita (PPP): $49,200 (2015 est.)
$48,400 (2014 est.)
$48,100 (2013 est.)
note: data are in 2012 US dollars
country comparison to the world: 25

Gross national saving: 28.3% of GDP (2015 est.)
28.7% of GDP (2014 est.)
29% of GDP (2013 est.)
country comparison to the world: 30

GDP—composition, by end use:
household consumption: 45%
government consumption: 25.3%
investment in fixed capital: 19%
investment in inventories: -0.1%
exports of goods and services: 83.6%
imports of goods and services: -72.8% (2015 est.)

GDP—composition, by sector of origin:
agriculture: 1.6%
industry: 18.8%
services: 79.6% (2015 est.)

Agriculture—products: grains, potatoes, sugar beets, fruits, vegetables; livestock

Industries: agroindustries, metal and engineering products, electrical machinery and equipment, chemicals, petroleum, construction, microelectronics, fishing

Industrial production growth rate: 1% (2015 est.)
country comparison to the world: 145

Labor force: 7.884 million (2015 est.)
country comparison to the world: 62

Labor force—by occupation: *agriculture:* 1.8%
industry: 17%
services: 81.2% (2013 est.)

Unemployment rate: 6.9% (2015 est.)
7.4% (2014 est.)
country comparison to the world: 82

Population below poverty line: 9.1% (2013 est.)

Household income or consumption by percentage share: *lowest:* 10%: 2.1%
highest: 10%: 24.5% (2012 est.)

Distribution of family income—Gini index: 25.1 (2013 est.)
32.6 (1994 est.)
country comparison to the world: 140

Budget: *revenues:* $336.5 billion
expenditures: $351.8 billion (2015 est.)
Taxes and other revenues: 44.8% of GDP (2015 est.)
country comparison to the world: 25

Budget surplus (+) or deficit (–): -2% of GDP (2015 est.)
country comparison to the world: 73

Public debt: 68.9% of GDP (2015 est.)
68.8% of GDP (2014 est.)
note: data cover general government debt, and includes debt instruments issued (or owned) by government entities other than the treasury; the data include treasury debt held by foreign entities; the data include debt issued by subnational entities, as well as intra-governmental debt; intra-governmental debt consists of treasury borrowings from surpluses in the social funds, such as for retirement, medical care, and unemployment, debt instruments for the social funds are not sold at public auctions
country comparison to the world: 47

Fiscal year: calendar year

Inflation rate (consumer prices): 0.2% (2015 est.)
0.3% (2014 est.)
country comparison to the world: 54

Central bank discount rate: 0.05% (31 December 2013)
0.3% (31 December 2010)
note: this is the European Central Bank's rate on the marginal lending facility, which offers overnight credit to banks in the euro area
country comparison to the world: 149

Commercial bank prime lending rate: 2% (31 December 2015 est.)
2.27% (31 December 2014 est.)
country comparison to the world: 179

Stock of narrow money: $357.8 billion (31 December 2015 est.)
$388.6 billion (31 December 2014 est.)
note: see entry for the European Union for money supply for the entire euro area; the European Central Bank (ECB) controls monetary policy for the 18 members of the Economic and Monetary Union (EMU); individual members of the EMU do not control the quantity of money circulating within their own borders
country comparison to the world: 15

Stock of broad money: $1.119 trillion (31 December 2014 est.)
$1.158 trillion (31 December 2013 est.)
country comparison to the world: 17

Stock of domestic credit: $1.712 trillion (31 December 2015 est.)
$1.853 trillion (31 December 2014 est.)
country comparison to the world: 13

Market value of publicly traded shares: $671.7 billion (31 December 2014 est.)
$698.6 billion (31 December 2013)
$578.9 billion (31 December 2012 est.)
country comparison to the world: 20

Current account balance: $80.99 billion (2015 est.)
$93.4 billion (2014 est.)
country comparison to the world: 6

Exports: $488.3 billion (2015 est.)
$571.8 billion (2014 est.)
country comparison to the world: 9

Exports—commodities: machinery and equipment, chemicals, fuels; foodstuffs

Exports—partners: Germany 24.5%, Belgium 11.1%, UK 9.3%, France 8.4%, Italy 4.2% (2015)

Imports: $404.6 billion (2015 est.) $469 billion (2014 est.)
country comparison to the world: 13

Imports—commodities: machinery and transport equipment, chemicals, fuels, foodstuffs, clothing

Imports—partners: Germany 14.7%, China 14.5%, Belgium 8.2%, US 8.1%, UK 5.1% (2015)

Reserves of foreign exchange and gold: $42.92 billion (31 December 2014 est.)
$46.25 billion (31 December 2013 est.)
country comparison to the world: 43

Debt—external: $4.154 trillion (31 December 2014 est.)
$4.524 trillion (31 December 2013 est.)
country comparison to the world: 7

Stock of direct foreign investment—at home: $561.4 billion (31 December 2015 est.)
$540.9 billion (31 December 2014 est.)
country comparison to the world: 16

Stock of direct foreign investment—abroad: $1.029 trillion (31 December 2015 est.)
$930.1 billion (31 December 2014 est.)
country comparison to the world: 12

Exchange rates: euros (EU R) per US dollar—
0.885 (2015 est.)
0.7525 (2014 est.)
0.7634 (2013 est.)
0.78 (2012 est.)
0.7185 (2011 est.)

ENERGY

Electricity—production: 98.57 billion kWh (2013 est.)
country comparison to the world: 34

Electricity—consumption: 116.8 billion kWh (2013 est.)
country comparison to the world: 31

Electricity—exports: 15.02 billion kWh (2013 est.)
country comparison to the world: 13

Electricity—imports: 33.25 billion kWh (2013 est.)
country comparison to the world: 6

Electricity—installed generating capacity: 29.85 million kW (2012 est.)
country comparison to the world: 29

Electricity—from fossil fuels: 83.7% of total installed capacity (2012 est.)
country comparison to the world: 91

Electricity—from nuclear fuels: 1.6% of total installed capacity (2012 est.)
country comparison to the world: 30

Electricity—from hydroelectric plants: 0.1% of total installed capacity (2012 est.)
country comparison to the world: 152

Electricity—from other renewable sources: 14.5% of total installed capacity (2012 est.)
country comparison to the world: 22

Crude oil—production: 28,120 bbl/day (2014 est.)
country comparison to the world: 65

Crude oil—exports: 48,820 bbl/day (2013 est.)
country comparison to the world: 46

Crude oil—imports: 1.204 million bbl/day (2013 est.)
country comparison to the world: 11
Crude oil—proved reserves: 144.7 million bbl (1 January 2015 est.)
country comparison to the world: 67
Refined petroleum products—production: 1.186 million bbl/day (2013 est.)
country comparison to the world: 21
Refined petroleum products—consumption: 960,600 bbl/day (2014 est.)
country comparison to the world: 22
Refined petroleum products—exports: *2.089 million bbl/day (2013 est.)*
country comparison to the world: 4
Refined petroleum products—imports: *1.838 million bbl/day (2013 est.)*
country comparison to the world: 3
Natural gas—production: 70.25 billion cu m
note: the Netherlands has curbed gas production due to seismic activity in the province of Groningen, largest source of gas reserves (2014 est.)
country comparison to the world: 13
Natural gas—consumption: 39.98 billion cu m (2014 est.)
country comparison to the world: 22
Natural gas—exports: 59.3 billion cu m (2014 est.)
country comparison to the world: 7
Natural gas—imports: 29.1 billion cu m (2014 est.)
country comparison to the world: 12
Natural gas—proved reserves: 1.044 trillion cu m (1 January 2014 est.)
country comparison to the world: 26
Carbon dioxide emissions from consumption of energy: 239.6 million Mt (2012 est.)
country comparison to the world: 25

COMMUNICATIONS

Telephones—fixed lines: *total subscriptions:* 7.13 million
subscriptions per 100 inhabitants: 42 (2014 est.)
country comparison to the world: 25
Telephones—mobile cellular: *total:* 19.6 million
subscriptions per 100 inhabitants: 116 (2014 est.)
country comparison to the world: 58
Telephone system: *general assessment:* highly developed and well maintained
domestic: extensive fixed-line fiber-optic network; large cellular telephone system with 5 major operators utilizing the third generation of the Global System for Mobile Communications (GSM) technology; one in five households now use Voice over the Internet Protocol (VoIP) services

international: country code—31; submarine cables provide links to the US and Europe; satellite earth stations—5 (3 Intelsat—1 Indian Ocean and 2 Atlantic Ocean, 1 Eutelsat, and 1 Inmarsat (2011)
Broadcast media: more than 90% of households are connected to cable or satellite TV systems that provide a wide range of domestic and foreign channels; public service broadcast system includes multiple broadcasters, 3 with a national reach and the remainder operating in regional and local markets; 2 major nationwide commercial television companies, each with 3 or more stations, and many commercial TV stations in regional and local markets; nearly 600 radio stations with a mix of public and private stations providing national or regional coverage (2008)
Radio broadcast stations: AM 4, FM 567, shortwave 1 (2009)
Television broadcast stations: 342 (2009)
Internet country code: .nl
Internet hosts: 13.699 million (2012)
country comparison to the world: 11
Internet users: *total:* 16.2 million
percent of population: 96.1% (2014 est.)
country comparison to the world: 34

TRANSPORTATION

Airports: 29 (2013)
country comparison to the world: 120
Airports—with paved runways: *total:* 23
over 3,047 m: 3
2,438 to 3,047 m: 11
1,524 to 2,437 m: 1
914 to 1,523 m: 6
under 914 m: 2 (2013)
Airports—with unpaved runways: *total:* 6
914 to 1,523 m: 4
under 914 m: 2 (2013)
Heliports: 1 (2013)
Pipelines: condensate 81 km; gas 8,531 km; oil 578 km; refined products 716 km (2013)
Railways: *total:* 3,223 km
standard gauge: 3,223 km 1.435-m gauge (2,321 km electrified) (2014)
country comparison to the world: 56
Roadways: *total:* 138,641 km (includes 3,530 km of expressways) (2014)
country comparison to the world: 36
Waterways: 6,237 km (navigable by ships up to 50 tons) (2012)
country comparison to the world: 21
Merchant marine: *total:* 744
by type: bulk carrier 4, cargo 514, carrier 15, chemical tanker 56, container 67, liquefied gas

21, passenger 17, passenger/cargo 14, petroleum tanker 4, refrigerated cargo 10, roll on/roll off 19, specialized tanker 3
foreign-owned: 196 (Australia 1, Bermuda 1, Denmark 27, Finland 13, France 2, Germany 86, Ireland 8, Italy 6, Japan 1, Norway 19, Sweden 12, UAE 4, US 16)
registered in other countries: 233 (Antigua and Barbuda 17, Bahamas 23, Belize 1, Canada 1, Curacao 43, Cyprus 23, Germany 1, Gibraltar 34, Italy 2, Liberia 31, Luxembourg 3, Malta 3, Marshall Islands 21, Panama 6, Paraguay 1, Philippines 17, Russia 2, Saint Vincent and the Grenadines 1, Singapore 1, UK 1, unknown 1) (2010)
country comparison to the world: 15
Ports and terminals: *major seaport(s):* I Jmuiden, Vlissingen
river port(s): Amsterdam (Nordsee Kanaal); Moerdijk (Hollands Diep River); Rotterdam (Rhine River); Terneuzen (Western Scheldt River)
container port(s) (TEUs): Rotterdam (11,876,920)
LNG terminal(s) (import): Rotterdam

MILITARY AND SECURITY

Military branches: Royal Netherlands Army, Royal Netherlands Navy (includes Naval Air Service and Marine Corps), Royal Netherlands Air Force (Koninklijke Luchtmacht, KLu), Royal Marechaussee (Military Police) (2015)
Military service age and obligation: 17 years of age for an all-volunteer force (2014)
Military expenditures:
1.15% of GDP (2014)
1.16% of GDP (2013)
1.23% of GDP (2012)
1.26% of GDP (2011)
1.34% of GDP (2010)
country comparison to the world: 79

TRANSNATIONAL ISSUES

Disputes—international: none
Refugees and internally displaced persons:
refugees (country of origin): 18,687 (Somalia); 14,396 (Iraq); 8,692 (Syria); 6,294 (Eritrea); 6,244 (Afghanistan) (2014)
stateless persons: 1951 (2015)
Illicit drugs: major European producer of synthetic drugs, including ecstasy, and cannabis cultivator; important gateway for cocaine, heroin, and hashish entering Europe; major source of US-bound ecstasy; large financial sector vulnerable to money laundering; significant consumer of ecstasy

NEW CALEDONIA

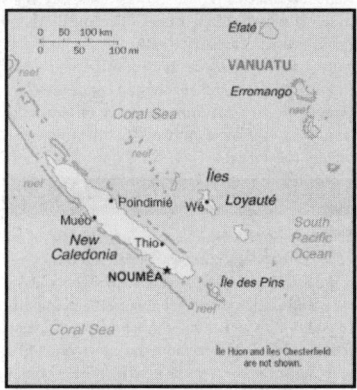

INTRODUCTION

Background: Settled by both Britain and France during the first half of the 19th century, the island became a French possession in 1853. It served as a penal colony for four decades after 1864. Agitation for independence during the 1980s and early 1990s ended in the 1998 Noumea Accord, which over a period of 15 to 20 years will transfer an increasing amount of governing responsibility from France to New Caledonia. The agreement also commits France to conduct a referendum between 2014 and 2018 to decide whether New Caledonia should assume full sovereignty and independence.

GEOGRAPHY

Location: Oceania, islands in the South Pacific Ocean, east of Australia
Geographic coordinates: 21 30 S, 165 30 E
Map references: Oceania
Area: total: 18,575 sq km
land: 18,275 sq km
water: 300 sq km
country comparison to the world: 156
Area—comparative: slightly smaller than New Jersey
Land boundaries: 0 km
Coastline: 2,254 km
Maritime claims: territorial sea: 12 nm
exclusive economic zone: 200 nm
Climate: tropical; modified by southeast trade winds; hot, humid
Terrain: coastal plains with interior mountains
Elevation: mean elevation: NA
elevation extremes: lowest point: Pacific Ocean 0 m
highest point: Mont Panie 1,628 m
Natural resources: nickel, chrome, iron, cobalt, manganese, silver, gold, lead, copper
Land use: agricultural land: 10.4%
arable land: 0.4%
permanent crops: 0.2%
permanent pasture: 9.8%

forest: 45.9%
other: 43.7% (2011 est.)
Irrigated land: 100 sq km (2012)
Natural hazards: cyclones, most frequent from November to March
volcanism: Matthew and Hunter Islands are historically active
Environment—current issues: erosion caused by mining exploitation and forest fires
Geography—note: consists of the main island of New Caledonia (one of the largest in the Pacific Ocean), the archipelago of Iles Loyaute, and numerous small, sparsely populated islands and atolls

PEOPLE AND SOCIETY

Nationality: noun: New Caledonian(s)
adjective: New Caledonian
Ethnic groups: Kanak 40.3%, European 29.2%, Wallisian, Futunian 8.7%, Tahitian 2%, Indonesian 1.6%, Vietnamese 1%, Ni-Vanuatu 0.9%, other 16.2% (2009 est.)
Languages: French (official), 33 Melanesian-Polynesian dialects
Religions: Roman Catholic 60%, Protestant 30%, other 10%
Population: 271,615 (July 2015 est.)
country comparison to the world: 184
Age structure: 0–14 years: 23.19% (male 32,178/female 30,804)
15–24 years: 16.89% (male 23,435/female 22,448)
25–54 years: 42.99% (male 58,769/female 57,994)
55–64 years: 8.21% (male 10,874/female 11,417)
65 years and over: 8.72% (male 10,558/female 13,138) (2015 est.)
Dependency ratios: total dependency ratio: 47.9%
youth dependency ratio: 32.9%
elderly dependency ratio: 15%
potential support ratio: 6.6% (2015 est.)
Median age: total: 31.4 years
male: 30.7 years
female: 32 years (2015 est.)
country comparison to the world: 103
Population growth rate: 1.38% (2015 est.)
country comparison to the world: 86
Birth rate: 15.33 births/1,000 population (2015 est.)
country comparison to the world: 130
Death rate: 5.52 deaths/1,000 population (2015 est.)
country comparison to the world: 176
Net migration rate: 4.01 migrant(s)/1,000 population
note: there has been steady emigration from Wallis and Futuna to New Caledonia (2015 est.)
country comparison to the world: 32
Urbanization: urban population: 70.2% of total population (2015)
rate of urbanization: 2.17% annual rate of change (2010–15 est.)

Major urban areas—population: NOUMEA (capital) 181,000 (2014)
Sex ratio: at birth: 1.05 male(s)/female
0–14 years: 1.05 male(s)/female
15–24 years: 1.04 male(s)/female
25–54 years: 1.01 male(s)/female
55–64 years: 0.95 male(s)/female
65 years and over: 0.8 male(s)/female
total population: 1 male(s)/female (2015 est.)
Infant mortality rate: total: 5.37 deaths/1,000 live births
male: 6.33 deaths/1,000 live births
female: 4.37 deaths/1,000 live births (2015 est.)
country comparison to the world: 173
Life expectancy at birth: total population: 77.5 years
male: 73.49 years
female: 81.71 years (2015 est.)
country comparison to the world: 69
Total fertility rate: 1.97 children born/woman (2015 est.)
country comparison to the world: 125
Drinking water source:
improved:
urban: 98.5% of population
rural: 98.5% of population
total: 98.5% of population
unimproved:
urban: 1.5% of population
rural: 1.5% of population
total: 1.5% of population (2015 est.)
Sanitation facility access:
improved:
urban: 100% of population
rural: 100% of population
total: 100% of population
unimproved:
urban: 0% of population
rural: 0% of population
total: 0% of population (2015 est.)
HIV/AIDS—adult prevalence rate: NA
HIV/AIDS—people living with HIV/AIDS: NA
HIV/AIDS—deaths: NA
Literacy: definition: age 15 and over can read and write
total population: 96.9%
male: 97.3%
female: 96.5% (2015 est.)

GOVERNMENT

Country name: conventional long form: Territory of New Caledonia and Dependencies
conventional short form: New Caledonia
local long form: Territoire des Nouvelle-Caledonieet Dependances
local short form: Nouvelle-Caledonie
etymology: British explorer Captain James COOK discovered and named New Caledonia in 1774; he used the appellation because the northeast of the island reminded him of Scotland (Caledonia is the Latin designation for Scotland)

613

Dependency status: territorial collectivity (or a sui generis collectivity) of France since 1998

Government type: parliamentary democracy (Territorial Congress); an overseas collectivity of France

Capital: *name:* Noumea

Geographic coordinates: 22 16 S, 166 27 E

time difference: UTC + 11 (16 hours ahead of Washington, DC during Standard Time)

Administrative divisions: 3 provinces; Province Iles (Islands Province), Province Nord (North Province), and Province Sud (South Province)

Independence: none (overseas territory of France); note—a referendum on independence was held in 1998 but was rejected; a new referendum must be held before 2019

National holiday: Fete de la Federation, 14 July (1789); note—the local holiday is New Caledonia Day, 24 September (1853)

Constitution: 4 October 1958 (French Constitution with changes as reflected in Noumea Accord of 5 May 1998) (2016)

Legal system: civil law system based on French law; the 1988 Matignon Accords (signed in the Matignon Hotel) set up a 10-year period of development during which the Kanak community received substantial autonomy but agreed not to raise the independence issue

Citizenship: see France

Suffrage: 18 years of age; universal

Executive branch: *chief of state:* President Francois HOLLANDE (since 15 May 2012); represented by High Commissioner Jean-Jacques BROT (since 2 February 2013)

head of government: President of the Government Philippe GERMAINE (since 1 April 2015); Vice President Jean-Louis D'ANGLEBERME (since 1 April 2015)

cabinet: Cabinet elected from and by the Territorial Congress

elections/appointments: French president directly elected by absolute majority popular vote in 2 rounds if needed for a 5-year term (eligible for a second term); high commissioner appointed by the French president on the advice of the French Ministry of Interior; president of New Caledonia elected by Territorial Congress for a 5-year term (no term limits); election last held on 10 June 2011 (next to be held in June 2016)

election results: Philippe GERMAINE (Caledonia Together) elected president by Territorial Congress; vote NA

Legislative branch: unicameral Territorial Congress or Congres du Territoire (54 seats; members indirectly selected proportionally by the partisan makeup of the 3 Provincial Assemblies or Assemblees Provinciales; members of the 3 Provincial Assemblies directly elected by proportional representation vote; members serve 5-year terms)

note: the Customary Senate is the assembly of the various traditional councils of the Kanaks, the indigenous population, which rules on laws affecting the indigenous population; New Caledonia holds two seats in the French Senate; elections last held on 28 September 2014 (next to be held not later than September 2017); results—percent of vote by party—NA; seats by party—UMP 2; New Caledonia also elects two seats to the French National Assembly; elections last held on 17 June 2012 (next to be held by June 2017); results—percent of vote by party—NA; seats by party—UMP 2

elections: last held on 11 May 2014 (next to be held on May 2019); note—the government that was elected on 11 May 2014 collapsed within 6 months leading to a new election on 31 December 2015 which re-elected the same government

election results: percent of vote by party—NA; seats by party—Caledonia Together 13, FLNKS 9, UMP 7, Union for Caledonia in France 6, Build Our Rainbow Nation 6, National Union for Independence 6, other 7

Judicial branch: *highest resident court(s):* Court of Appeal in Noumea or Cour d'Appel; organized into civil, commercial, social, and pre-trial investigation chambers; number of judges NA); Administrative Court; number of judges NA);

judge selection and term of office: NA

subordinate courts: Courts of First Instance include: civil, juvenile, commercial, labor, police, criminal, Assizes, and also a pre-trial investigation chamber; Joint Commerce Tribunal; administrative courts

Political parties and leaders: Build Our Rainbow Nation

Caledonia Together [Philippe GOMES]

Caledonian Union or UC [Daniel GOA]

Future Together (l'Avenir Ensemble) [Harold MARTIN]

Kanak Socialist Front for National Liberation or FLNKS (alliance includes PALIKA, UNI, UC, and UPM) [Roch WAMYTAN]

Labor Party (Parti Travailliste) or PT [Louis Kotra UREGEI]

National Union for Independence (Union Nationale pour l'Independance) or UNI

Party of Kanak Liberation (Parti de Liberation Kanak) or PALIKA [Paul NEAOUTYINE]

Socialist Kanak Liberation or LKS [Nidoish NAISSELINE]

The Republicans (formerly The Rally or UMP) [Pierre FROGIER]

Union for Caledonia in France; note—dissolved in July 2014

Political pressure groups and leaders: NA

International organization participation: ITUC (NGOs), PIF (associate member), SPC, UPU, WFTU (NGOs), WMO

Diplomatic representation in the US: none (overseas territory of France)

Diplomatic representation from the US: none (overseas territory of France)

Flag description: New Caledonia has two official flags; alongside the flag of France, the Kanak (indigenous Melanesian) flag has equal status; the latter consists of three equal horizontal bands of blue (top), red, and green; a large yellow disk—diameter two-thirds the height of the flag—shifted slightly to the hoist side is edged in black and displays a black fleche faitiere symbol, a native rooftop adornment

National symbol(s): fleche faitiere (native rooftop adornment), kagu bird; national colors: blue, red, green, yellow, black

National anthem: *name:* "Soyons unis, devenons freres" (Let Us Be United, Let Us Become Brothers) *lyrics/music:* Chorale Melodia (a local choir) *note:* adopted 2008; contains a mixture of lyrics in both French and Nengone (an indigenous language); as a self-governing territory of France, in addition to the local anthem, "La Marseillaise" is official (see France)

ECONOMY

Economy—overview: New Caledonia has about 25% of the world's known nickel reserves. Only a small amount of the land is suitable for cultivation, and food accounts for about 20% of imports. In addition to nickel, substantial financial support from France—equal to more than 15% of GDP—and tourism are keys to the health of the economy. During 2009–10, France sent more development assistance to New Caledonia than to any of its other overseas territories. In October 2014, French Prime Minster Manuel VALLS confirmed financial support to New Caledonia totaling $500 million for the period 2016–20. The new government, which inherited a $112 million deficit in 2013, is expected to focus on bringing the territory's budget back into balance. Substantial new investment in the nickel industry—including two major new plants—combined with the recovery of global nickel prices, has brightened the economic outlook for the next several years. in 2015, New Caledonia helped fill China's shortfall in nickel supplies left by an Indonesian ban on nickel ore exports.

GDP (purchasing power parity): $11.1 billion (2014 est.)

$10.8 billion (2013 est.)

$10.57 billion (2012)

country comparison to the world: 155

GDP (official exchange rate): $11.1 billion (2014 est.)

GDP—real growth rate: 2.8% (2014 est.)

2.2% (2013)

2.9% (2012)

country comparison to the world: 108

GDP—per capita (PPP): $38,800 (2012 est.)

$36,500 (2010 est.)

$27,300 (2005)

country comparison to the world: 41

GDP—composition, by end use:

household consumption: 62.8%

government consumption: 25%

investment in fixed capital: 43.1%

investment in inventories: 0%

exports of goods and services: 21.9%

imports of goods and services: -52.8% (2015 est.)

GDP—composition, by sector of origin:

agriculture: 1.4%

industry: 26.4%

services: 72.2% (2015 est.)

Agriculture—products: vegetables; beef, venison, other livestock products; fish

Industries: nickel mining and smelting

Industrial production growth rate: 5% (2015 est.)

country comparison to the world: 31
Labor force: 106,400 (2010 est.)
country comparison to the world: 183

Labor force—by occupation: *agriculture:* 2.7%
industry: 22.4%
services: 74.9% (2010)
Unemployment rate: 17.1% (2004)
country comparison to the world: 159
Population below poverty line: NA%

Household income or consumption by percentage share: *lowest:* 10%: NA%
highest: 10%: NA%
Budget: *revenues:* $996 million
expenditures: $1.072 billion (2001 est.)
Budget surplus (+) or deficit (–): NA% of GDP
Fiscal year: calendar year
Inflation rate (consumer prices): 0.7% (2015 est.)
0.2% (2014 est.)
country comparison to the world: 69
Market value of publicly traded shares: $NA
Exports: $1.565 billion (2014 est.)
$1.565 billion (2014 est.)
country comparison to the world: 149
Exports—commodities: ferron ickels, nickel ore, fish
Exports—partners: China 31.8%, Japan 15.2%, South Korea 10.7%, Australia 8.1%, France 7.4%, Belgium 5.1% (2015)
Imports: $3.323 billion (2014 est.)
$3.323 billion (2014 est.)
country comparison to the world: 141
Imports—commodities: machin ery and equipmen t, fuels, chemicals, foodstuffs
Imports—partners: France 35.3%, Australia 11.4%, South Korea 8.6%, Singapore 5.4%, Malaysia 5.3%, China 4.5%, NZ 4.1% (2015)
Debt—external: $112 million (31 December 2013 est.)
$79 million (31 December 1998 est.)
country comparison to the world: 193
Exchange rates: Comptoirs Francais du Pacifique fran cs (XPF) per US dollar—
89.8 (2015 est.)
89.8 (2014 est.)
85.74 (2011 est.)

ENERGY

Electricity—production: 2.92 billion kWh (2012 est.)
country comparison to the world: 133
Electricity—consumption: 2.716 billion kWh (2012 est.)
country comparison to the world: 138
Electricity—exports: 0 kWh (2013 est.)
country comparison to the world: 174
Electricity—imports: 0 kWh (2013 est.)
country comparison to the world: 180
Electricity—installed generating capacity: 499,200 kW (2012 est.)
country comparison to the world: 140
Electricity—from fossil fuels: 76.7% of total installed capacity (2012 est.)
country comparison to the world: 97
Electricity—from nuclear fuels: 0% of total installed capacity (2012 est.)

country comparison to the world: 150
Electricity—from hydroelectric plants: 15.6% of total installed capacity (2012 est.)
country comparison to the world: 100
Electricity—from other renewable sources: 7.7% of total installed capacity (2012 est.)
country comparison to the world: 48
Crude oil—production: 0 bbl/day (2014 est.)
country comparison to the world: 173
Crude oil—exports: 0 bbl/day (2012 est.)
country comparison to the world: 167
Crude oil—imports: 0 bbl/day (2012 est.)
country comparison to the world: 104
Crude oil—proved reserves: 0 bbl (1 January 2015 est.)
country comparison to the world: 173
Refined petroleum products—production: 0 bbl/day (2012 est.)
country comparison to the world: 115
Refined petroleum products—consumption: 14,500 bbl/day (2013 est.)
country comparison to the world: 144
Refined petroleum products—exports: 116.9 bbl/day (2012 est.)
country comparison to the world: 120
Refined petroleum products—imports: 14,670 bbl/day (2012 est.)
country comparison to the world: 128
Natural gas—production: 0 cu m (2013 est.)
country comparison to the world: 108
Natural gas—consumption: 0 cu m (2013 est.)
country comparison to the world: 176
Natural gas—exports: 0 cu m (2013 est.)
country comparison to the world: 152
Natural gas—imports: 0 cu m (2013 est.)
country comparison to the world: 106
Natural gas—proved reserves: 0 cu m (1 January 2014 est.)
country comparison to the world: 175
Carbon dioxide emissions from consumption of energy: 3.071 million Mt (2012 est.)
country comparison to the world: 139

COMMUNICATIONS

Telephones—fixed lines: *total subscriptions:* 88,500
subscriptions per 100 inhabitants: 33 (2014 est.)
country comparison to the world: 146
Telephones—mobile cellular: *total:* 243,100
subscriptions per 100 inhabitants: 91 (2014 est.)
country comparison to the world: 179
Telephone system: *general assessment:* a submarine cable network connection between New Caledonia and Australia, completed in 2007, increased network capacity and improved high-speed connectivity and access to international networks
domestic: combined fixed-line and mobile-cellular telephone subscribership exceeds 100 per 100 persons
international: country code—687; satellite earth station—1 Intelsat (Pacific Ocean) (2010)
Broadcast media: the publicly owned French Overseas Network (RFO), which operates in France's overseas departments and territories,

broadcasts over the RFO Nouvelle Caledonie TV and radio stations; a small number of privately owned radio stations also broadcast (2008)
Radio broadcast stations: AM 1, FM 5, shortwave 0 (1998)
Television broadcast stations: 6 (plus 25 repeaters) (1997)
Internet country code: .nc
Internet hosts: 34,231 (2012)
country comparison to the world: 104
Internet users: *total:* 169,100
percent of population: 63.1% (2014 est.)
country comparison to the world: 159

TRANSPORTATION

Airports: 25 (2013)
country comparison to the world: 128
Airports—with paved runways: *total:* 12
over 3,047 m: 1
914 to 1,523 m: 10
under 914 m: 1 (2013)
Airports—with unpaved runways: *total:* 13
914 to 1,523 m: 5
under 914 m: 8 (2013)
Heliports: 8 (2013)
Roadways: *total:* 5,622 km (2006)
country comparison to the world: 152
Merchant marine: *registered in other countries:* 3 (France 3) (2010)
country comparison to the world: 137
Ports and terminals: *major seaport(s):* Noumea

MILITARY AND SECURITY

Military branches: no regular military forces; French military, police, and gendarmerie (2012)
Military—note: defense is the responsibility of France

TRANSNATIONAL ISSUES

Disputes—international: Matthew and Hunter Islands east of New Caledonia claimed by France and Vanuatu

NEW ZEALAND

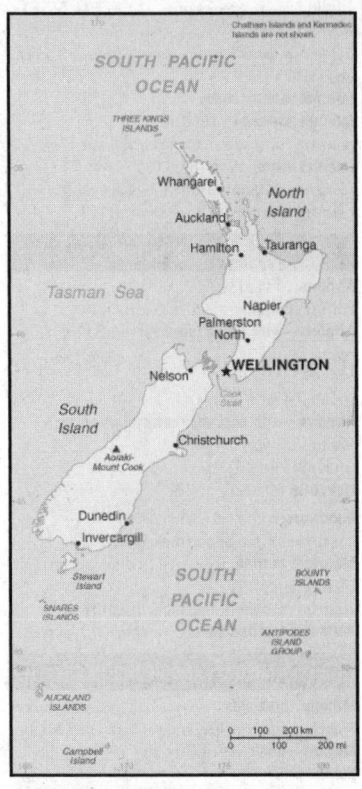

INTRODUCTION

Background: The Polynesian Maori reached New Zealand in about A.D.800. In 1840, their chieftains entered into a compact with Britain, the Treaty of Waitangi, in which they ceded sovereignty to Queen Victoria while retaining territorial rights. That same year, the British began the first organized colonial settlement. A series of land wars between 1843 and 1872 ended with the defeat of the native peoples. The British colony of New Zealand became an independent dominion in 1907 and supported the UK militarily in both world wars. New Zealand's full participation in a number of defense alliances lapsed by the 1980s. in recent years, the government has sought to address longstanding Maori grievances. New Zealand assumed a nonpermanent seat on the UN Security Council for the 2015–16 term.

GEOGRAPHY

Location: Oceania, islands in the South Pacific Ocean, southeast of Australia
Geographic coordinates: 4100 S, 174 00 E
Map references: Oceania
Area: *total:* 268,838 sq km
land: 264,537 sq km

water: 4,301 sq km
note: includes Antipodes Islands, Auckland Islands, Bounty Islands, Campbell Island, Chatham Islands, and Kermadec Islands
country comparison to the world: 76
Area—comparative: almost twice the size of North Carolina; about the size of Colorado
Land boundaries: 0 km
Coastline: 15,134 km
Maritime claims: *territorial sea:* 12 nm
contiguous zone: 24 nm
exclusive economic zone: 200 nm
continental shelf: 200 nm or to the edge of the continental margin
Climate: temperate with sharp regional contrasts
Terrain: predominately mountainous with large coastal plains
Elevation: *mean elevation:* 388 m

elevation extremes: *lowest point:* Pacific Ocean 0 m
highest point: Aoraki-Mount Cook 3,754 m
Natural resources: natural gas, iron ore, sand, coal, timber, hydropower, gold, limestone
Land use: *agricultural land:* 43.2%
arable land: 1.8%
permanent crops: 0.3%
permanent pasture: 41.1%
forest: 31.4%
other: 25.4% (2011 est.)
Irrigated land: 7,210 sq km (2012)
Total renewable water resources: 327 cu km (2011)
Freshwater withdrawal (domestic/industrial/agricultural): *total:* 4.75 cu km/yr (23%/5%/72%)
per capita: 1,200 cu m/yr (2010)
Natural hazards: earthquakes are common, though usually not severe; volcanic activity
volcanism: significant volcanism on North Island; Ruapehu (elev. 2,797 m), which last erupted in 2007, has a history of large eruptions in the past century; Taranaki has the potential to produce dangerous avalanches and lahars; other historically active volcanoes include Okataina, Raoul Island, Tongariro, and White Island
Environment—current issues: deforestation; soil erosion; native flora and fauna hard-hit by invasive species
Environment—international agreements: *party to:* Antarctic-Environmental Protocol, Antarctic-Marine Living Resources, Antarctic Treaty, Biodiversity, Climate Change, Climate Change-Kyoto Protocol, Desertification, Endangered Species, Environmental Modification, Hazardous Wastes, Law of the Sea, Marine Dumping, Ozone Layer Protection, Ship Pollution, Tropical Timber 83, Tropical Timber 94, Wetlands, Whaling
signed, but not ratified: Antarctic Seals, Marine Life Conservation
Geography—note: almost 90% of the population lives in cities; Wellington is the southernmost national capital in the world

PEOPLE AND SOCIETY

Nationality: *noun:* New Zealander(s)
adjective: New Zealand
Ethnic groups: European 71.2%, Maori 14.1%, Asian 11.3%, Pacific peoples 7.6%, Middle Eastern, Latin American, African 1.1%, other 1.6%, not stated or unidentified 5.4%
note: based on the 2013 census of the usually resident population; percentages add up to more than 100% because respondents were able to identify more than one ethnic group (2013 est.)
Languages: English (de facto official) 89.8%, Maori (de jure official) 3.5%, Samoan 2%, Hindi 1.6%, French 1.2%, Northern Chinese 1.2%, Yue 1%, other or not stated 20.5%, New Zealand Sign Language (de jure official)
note: shares sum to 120.8% due to multiple responses on census (2013 est.)
Religions: Christian 44.3% (Catholic 11.6%, Anglican 10.8%, Presbyterian and Congregational 7.8%, Methodist, 2.4%, Pentecostal 1.8%, other 9.9%), Hindu 2.1%, Buddhist 1.4%, Maori Christian 1.3%, Islam 1.1%, other religion 1.4% (includes Judaism, Spiritualism and New Age religions, Baha'i, Asian religions other than Buddhism), no religion 38.5%, not stated or unidentified 8.2%, objected to answering 4.1%
note: based on the 2013 census of the usually resident population; percentages add up to more than 100% because people were able to identify more than one religion (2013 est.)
Population: 4,438,393 (July 2015 est.)
country comparison to the world: 127
Age structure: *0–14 years:* 19.87% (male 451,684/female 430,084)
15–24 years: 13.74% (male 313,140/female 296,654)
25–54 years: 40.25% (male 894,475/female 891973)
55–64 years: 11.52% (male 249,765/female 261,670)
65 years and over: 14.62% (male 299,862/female 349,086) (2015 est.)
Dependency ratios: *total dependency ratio:* 54%
youth dependency ratio: 31.1%
elderly dependency ratio: 22.9%
potential support ratio: 4.4% (2015 est.)
Median age: *total:* 37.7 years
male: 36.8 years
female: 38.5 years (2015 est.)
country comparison to the world: 64
Population growth rate: 0.82% (2015 est.)
country comparison to the world: 136
Birth rate: 13.33 births/1,000 population (2015 est.)
country comparison to the world: 150
Death rate: 7.36 deaths/1,000 population (2015 est.)
country comparison to the world: 116
Net migration rate: 2.21 migrant(s)/1,000 population (2015 est.)
country comparison to the world: 48

Urbanization: *urban population:* 86.3% of total population (2015)
rate of urbanization: 1.05% annual rate of change (2010–15 est.)
Major urban areas—population: Auckland 1.344 million; WELLINGTON (capital) 383,000 (2015)
Sex ratio: *at birth:* 1.05 male(s)/female
0–14 years: 1.05 male(s)/female
15–24 years: 1.06 male(s)/female
25–54 years: 1 male(s)/female
55–64 years: 0.96 male(s)/female
65 years and over: 0.86 male(s)/female
total population: 0.99 male(s)/female (2015 est.)
Mother's mean age at first birth: 27.8
note: median age at first birth (2009 est.)
Maternal mortality rate: II deaths/100,000 live births (2015 est.)
country comparison to the world: 144
Infant mortality rate: *total:* 4.52 deaths/1,000 live births
male: 5.07 deaths/1,000 live births
female: 3.96 deaths/1,000 live births (2015 est.)
country comparison to the world: 181
Life expectancy at birth: *total population:* 81.05 years
male: 78.97 years
female: 83.22 years (2015 est.)
country comparison to the world: 28
Total fertility rate: 2.04 children born/woman (2015 est.)
country comparison to the world: 115
Health expenditures: 9.7% of GDP (2013)
country comparison to the world: 20
Physicians density: 2.74 physicians/1,000 population (2010)
Hospital bed density: 2.3 beds/1,000 population (2011)
Drinking water source:
improved:
urban: 100% of population
rural: 100% of population
total: 100% of population
unimproved:
urban: 0% of population
rural: 0% of population
total: 0% of population (2015 est.)
HIV/AIDS—adult prevalence rate: NA
HIV/AIDS—people living with HIV/AIDS: NA
HIV/AIDS—deaths: NA
Obesity—adult prevalence rate: 30.6% (2014)
country comparison to the world: 34
Education expenditures: 6.4% of GDP (2014)
country comparison to the world: 16
School life expectancy (primary to tertiary education): *total:* 19 years
male: 18 years
female: 20 years (2014)
Unemployment, youth ages 15–24: *total:* 15.8%
male: 15.3%
female: 16.3% (2013 est.)
country comparison to the world: 64

GOVERNMENT

Country name: *conventional long form:* none
conventional short form: New Zealand
abbreviation: NZ

etymology: Dutch explorer Abel TASMAN was the first European to reach New Zealand in 1642; he named it Staten Landt, but Dutch cartographers renamed it Nova Zeelandia in 1645 after the Dutch province of Zeeland; British explorer Captain James COOK subsequently anglicized the name to New Zealand when he mapped the islands in 1769
Government type: parliamentary democracy (New Zealand Parliament) under a constitutional monarchy; a Commonwealth realm
Capital: *name:* Wellington
Geographic coordinates: 41 18 S, 174 47 E
time difference: UTC + 12 (17 hours ahead of Washington, DC, during Standard Time)
daylight saving time: +1hr, begins last Sunday in September; ends first Sunday in April
note: New Zealand has two time zones—New Zealand standard time (12 hours in advance of UTC), and Chatham Islands time (45 minutes in advance of New Zealand standard time)
Administrative divisions: 16 regions and 1 territory*; Auckland, Bay of Plenty, Canterbury, Chatham Islands*, Gisborne, Hawke's Bay, Manawatu-Wanganui, Marlborough, Nelson, Northland, Otago, Southland, Taranaki, Tasman, Waikato, Wellington, West Coast
Dependent areas: Cook Islands, Niue, Tokelau
Independence: 26 September 1907 (from the UK)
National holiday: Waitangi Day (Treaty of Waitangi established British sovereignty over New Zealand), 6 February (1840); ANZAC Day (commemorated as the anniversary of the landing of troops of the Australian and New Zealand Army Corps during World War I at Gallipoli, Turkey), 25 April (1915)
Constitution: Constitution Act 1986 (the principal formal charter) adopted and effective 1 January 1987; amended 1999, 2005, 2014 (2016)
Legal system: common law system, based on English model, with special legislation and land courts for the Maori
International law organization participation: accepts compulsory ICJ jurisdiction with reservations; accepts ICCt jurisdiction
Citizenship: *citizenship by birth:* no
citizenship by descent only: at least one parent must be a citizen of New Zealand
dual citizenship recognized: yes
residency requirement for naturalization: 3 years
Suffrage: 18 years of age; universal
Executive branch: *chief of state:* Queen ELIZABETH II (since 6 February 1952); represented by Governor General Lt. Gen. Sir Jerry MATEPARAE (since 31 August 2011)
head of government: Prime Minister John KEY (since 19 November 2008); Deputy Prime Minister Simon William ENGLISH (since 19 November 2008)
cabinet: Executive Council appointed by the governor general on the recommendation of the prime minister
elections/appointments: the monarchy is hereditary; governor general appointed by the monarch; following legislative elections, the leader of

the majority party or majority coalition usually appointed prime minister by the governor general; deputy prime minister appointed by the governor general
Legislative branch: *description:* unicameral House of Representatives—commonly called Parliament (usually 120 seats; 70 members directly elected in single-seat constituencies, including 7 Maori constituencies, by simple majority vote and 50 directly elected by proportional representation vote; members serve 3-year terms)
elections: last held on 20 September 2014 (next to be held by September 2017)
election results: percent of vote by party—National Party 47%, Labor Party 25.1%, Green Party 10.7%, NZ First 8.7%, Maori 1.3%, ACT Party .7%, United Future .2%, other 6.3%; seats by party—National Party 60, Labor Party 32, Green Party 14, NZ First 11, Maori 2, ACT Party 1, United Future 1
Judicial branch: *highest court(s):* Supreme Court (consists of 5 justices including the chief justice); note—the Supreme Court in 2004 replaced the Judicial Committee of the Privy Council in London as the final appeals court
judge selection and term of office: justices appointed by the governor-general on the recommendation of the attorney-general; justices appointed for life
subordinate courts: Court of Appeal; High Court; tribunals and authorities; district courts; specialized courts for issues related to employment, environment, Maori lands, and military
Political parties and leaders: ACT New Zealand [Rodney HIDE]
Green Party [Russel NORMAN and Metiria TUREI]
Jim Anderton's Progressive Party [James (Jim) ANDERTON]
Mana Party [Hone HARAWIRA]
Maori Party [Tariana TURIA and Dr. Pita SHARPLES]
New Zealand First Party or NZ First [Winston PETERS]
New Zealand Labor Party [Phil GOFF]
New Zealand National Party [John KEY]
United Future New Zealand [Peter DUNNE]
Political pressure groups and leaders: Wom en 's Electoral Lobby or WEL
other: apartheid groups; civil rights groups; farmers groups; Maori; nuclear weapons groups; women's rights groups
International organization participation: ADB, ANZUS (US suspended security obligations to NZ on 11 August 1986), APEC, ARF, ASEAN (dialogue partner), Australia Group, BIS, C, CD, CP, EAS, EBRD, FAO, FATF, IAEA, IBRD, ICAO, ICC (national committees), ICCt, ICRM, IDA, IEA, IFAD, IFC, IFRCS, IHO, ILO, IMF, IMO, IMSO, Interpol, IOC, IOM, IPU, ISO, ITSO, ITU, ITUC (NGOs), MIGA, NSG, OECD, OPCW, Pacific Alliance (observer), Paris Club (associate), PCA, PIF, SICA (observer), Sparteca, SPC, UN, UN Security Council (temporary), UNCTAD, UNESCO, UNHCR, UNIDO, UNMISS, UNT

SO, UPU, WCO, WFTU (NGOs), WHO, WIPO, WMO, WTO

Diplomatic representation in the US: *chief of mission:* Ambassador Timothy John GROSER (since 28 January 2016)

chancery: 37 Observatory Circle NW, Washington, DC 20008

telephone: [1] (202) 328-4800

FAX: [1] (202) 667-5227[1] (202) 667-5227

consulate(s) general: Honolulu (HI), Los Angeles, New York

Diplomatic representation from the US: *chief of mission:* Ambassador Mark GILBERT (since9 February 2015) note—also accredited to Samoa

embassy: 29 Fitzherbert Terrace, Thorndon, Wellington

mailing address: P.O. Box 1190, Wellington; PSC 467, Box 1, APO AP 96531–1034

telephon e: [64] (4) 462–6000

FAX: [64] (4) 499–0490

consulate(s) general: Auckland

Flag description: blue with the flag of the UK in the upper hoist-side quadrant with four red five-pointed stars edged in white centered in the outer half of the flag; the stars represent the Southern Cross constellation

National symbol(s): Southern Cross constellation (four, five-pointed stars), kiwi (bird), silver fern; national colors: black, white, red (ochre)

National anthem: *name:* "God Defend New Zealand"

lyrics/music: Thomas BRACKEN [English], Thomas Henry SMITH [Maori]/John Joseph WOODS

note: adopted 1940 as national song, adopted 1977 as co-national anthem; New Zealand has two national anthems with equal status; as a commonwealth realm, in addition to "God Defend New Zealand, ""God Save the Queen" serves as a national anthem (see United Kingdom); "God Save the Queen" normally played only when a member of the royal family or the governor-general is present; in all other cases, "God Defend New Zealand" is played

ECONOMY

Economy—overview: Over the past 30 years, the government has transformed New Zealand from an agrarian economy, dependent on concessionary British market access, to a more industrialized, free market economy that can compete globally. This dynamic growth has boosted real incomes—but left behind some at the bottom of the ladder—and broadened and deepened the technological capabilities of the industrial sector. Per capita income rose for ten consecutive years until 2007 in purchasing power parity terms, but fell in 2008–09. Debt-driven consumer spending drove robust growth in the first half of the decade, fueling a large balance of payments deficit that posed a challenge for policymakers. Inflationary pressures caused the central bank to raise its key rate steadily from January 2004 until it was among the highest in the OECD in 2007–08. The higher rate attracted international capital inflows, which

strengthened the currency and housing market while aggravating the current account deficit.

The economy fell into recession before the start of the global financial crisis and contracted for five consecutive quarters in 2008–09. In line with global peers, the central bank cut interest rates aggressively and the government developed fiscal stimulus measures. The economy pulled out of recession in 2009, and achieved 2%-3% growth from 2011 to 2015. Nevertheless, key trade sectors remain vulnerable to weak external demand and lower commodity prices. in the aftermath of the 2010 Canterbury earthquakes, the government has continued programs to expand export markets, develop capital markets, invest in innovation, raise productivity growth, and develop infrastructure, while easing its fiscal austerity.

GDP (purchasing power parity): $168.2 billion (2015 est.)

$162.7 billion (2014 est.)

$158 billion (2013 est.)

note: data are in 2015 US dollars

country comparison to the world: 69

GDP (official exchange rate): $172.2 billion (2015 est.)

GDP—real growth rate: 3.4% (2015 est.)

3% (2014 est.)

1.7% (2013 est.)

country comparison to the world: 88

GDP—per capita (PPP): $36,200 (2015 est.)

$35,700 (2014 est.)

$35,300 (2013 est.)

note: data are in 2015 US dollars

country comparison to the world: 49

Gross national saving: 19.2% of GDP (2015 est.)

19.4% of GDP (2014 est.)

19.3% of GDP (2013 est.)

country comparison to the world: 86

GDP—composition, by end use:

household consumption: 56.1%

government consumption: 18.7%

investment in fixed capital: 22.8%

investment in inventories: 0.3%

exports of goods and services: 27.9%

imports of goods and services: -25.8% (2015 est.)

GDP—composition, by sector of origin:

agriculture: 4.1%

industry: 26.8%

services: 69% (2015 est.)

Agriculture—products: dairy products, sheep, beef, poultry, fruit, vegetables, wine, seafood, wheat and barley

Industries: agriculture, forestry, fishing, logs and wood articles, manufacturing, mining, construction, financial services, real estate services, tourism

Industrial production growth rate: 2.5% (2015 est.)

country comparison to the world: 101

Labor force: 2.522 million (2015 est.)

country comparison to the world: 115

Labor force—by occupation: *agriculture:* 7%

industry: 19%

services: 74% (2006 est.)

Unemployment rate: 5.8% (2015 est.)

5.7% (2014 est.)

country comparison to the world: 63

Population below poverty line: NA%

Household income or consumption by percentage share: *lowest:* 10%: NA%

highest: 10%: NA%

Distribution of family income—Gini index: 36.2 (1997)

country comparison to the world: 86

Budget: *revenues:* $73.52 billion

expenditures: $73.34 billion (2015 est.)

Taxes and other revenues: 43.1% of GDP (2015 est.)

country comparison to the world: 30

Budget surplus (+) or deficit (–): 0.1% of GDP (2015 est.)

country comparison to the world: 27

Public debt: 33.5% of GDP (2015 est.)

34.6% of GDP (2014 est.)

country comparison to the world: 133

Fiscal year: 1 April–31 March

note: this is the fiscal year for tax purposes

Inflation rate (consumer prices): 0.3% (2015 est.)

1.2% (2014 est.)

country comparison to the world: 58

Central bank discount rate: 2.5% (31 December 2009)

5% (31 December 2008)

country comparison to the world: 107

Commercial bank prime lending rate: 5.5% (31 December 2015 est.)

5.8% (31 December 2014 est.)

country comparison to the world: 139

Stock of narrow money: $28.33 billion (31 December 2015 est.)

$33.16 billion (31 December 2014 est.)

country comparison to the world: 62

Stock of broad money: $105.1 billion (31 December 2014 est.)

$97.74 billion (31 December 2013 est.)

country comparison to the world: 55

Stock of domestic credit: $240.2 billion (31 December 2015 est.)

$271.8 billion (31 December 2014 est.)

country comparison to the world: 39

Market value of publicly traded shares: $79.8 billion (31 December 2012 est.)

$71.66 billion (31 December 2011)

$71.83 billion (31 December 2010 est.)

country comparison to the world: 46

Current account balance: -$5.249 billion (2015 est.)

-$6.185 billion (2014 est.)

country comparison to the world: 170

Exports: $34.33 billion (2015 est.)

$41.96 billion (2014 est.)

country comparison to the world: 61

Exports—commodities: dairy products, meat and edible offal, logs and wood articles, fruit, crude oil, wine

Exports—partners: China 17.5%, Australia 16.9%, US 11.8%, Japan 6% (2015)

Imports: $35.34 billion (2015 est.)

$41 billion (2014 est.)

country comparison to the world: 61

Imports—commodities: petroleum and products, mechanical machinery, vehicles and parts, electrical machinery, textiles

Imports—partners: China 19.4%, Australia 11.8%, US 11.7%, Japan 6.6%, Germany 4.7%, Thailand 4.2% (2015)

Reserves of foreign exchange and gold: $17.84 billion (31 December 2015 est.)
$15.86 billion (31 December 2014 est.)
country comparison to the world: 62

Debt—external: $189.8 billion (31 December 2014 est.)
$192.1 billion (31 December 2013 est.)
country comparison to the world: 35

Stock of direct foreign investment—at home: $87.6 billion (31 December 2015 est.)
$85.44 billion (31 December 2014 est.)
country comparison to the world: 49

Stock of direct foreign investment—abroad: $59.08 billion (31 December 2009)
country comparison to the world: 38

Exchange rates: New Zealand dollars (NZD) per US dollar—
1.452 (2015 est.)
1.2039 (2014 est.)
1.2039 (2013 est.)
1.23 (2012 est.)
1.263 (2011 est.)

ENERGY

Electricity—production: 43.28 billion kWh (2012 est.)
country comparison to the world: 57

Electricity—consumption: 40.3 billion kWh (2012 est.)
country comparison to the world: 56

Electricity—exports: 0 kWh (2013 est.)
country comparison to the world: 181

Electricity—imports: 0 kWh (2013 est.)
country comparison to the world: 186

Electricity—installed generating capacity: 9.521 million kW (2012 est.)
country comparison to the world: 57

Electricity—from fossil fuels: 29% of total installed capacity (2012 est.)
country comparison to the world: 183

Electricity—from nuclear fuels: 0% of total installed capacity (2012 est.)
country comparison to the world: 160

Electricity—from hydroelectric plants: 55.2% of total installed capacity (2012 est.)
country comparison to the world: 43

Electricity—from other renewable sources: 15.8% of total installed capacity (2012 est.)
country comparison to the world: 18

Crude oil—production: 39,860 bbl/day (2014 est.)
country comparison to the world: 61

Crude oil—exports: 29,620 bbl/day (2013 est.)
country comparison to the world: 53

Crude oil—imports: 101,200 bbl/day (2013 est.)
country comparison to the world: 47

Crude oil—proved reserves: 67.2 million bbl (1 January 2015 est.)
country comparison to the world: 78

Refined petroleum products—production: 113,300 bbl/day (2013 est.)
country comparison to the world: 70

Refined petroleum products—consumption: 156,600 bbl/day (2014 est.)
country comparison to the world: 64

Refined petroleum products—exports: 5,218 bbl/day (2013 est.)
country comparison to the world: 94

Refined petroleum products—imports: 44,520 bbl/day (2013 est.)
country comparison to the world: 84

Natural gas—production: 5.295 billion cu m (2014 est.)
country comparison to the world: 51

Natural gas—consumption: 5.38 billion cu m (2014 est.)
country comparison to the world: 58

Natural gas—exports: 0 cu m (2014 est.)
country comparison to the world: 160

Natural gas—imports: 0 cu m (2014 est.)
country comparison to the world: 116

Natural gas—proved reserves: 29.42 billion cu m (1 January 2014 est.)
country comparison to the world: 68

Carbon dioxide emissions from consumption of energy: 37.89 million Mt (2012 est.)
country comparison to the world: 69

COMMUNICATIONS

Telephones—fixed lines: *total subscriptions:* 1.85 million
subscriptions per 100 inhabitants: 42 (2014 est.)
country comparison to the world: 62

Telephones—mobile cellular: *total:* 5.1 million
subscriptions per 100 inhabitants: 116 (2014 est.)
country comparison to the world: 116

Telephone system: *general assessment:* excellent domestic and international systems
domestic: combined fixed-line and mobile-cellular telephone subscribership exceeds 150 per 100 persons
international: country code—64; the Southern Cross submarine cable system provides links to Australia, Fiji, and the US; satellite earth stations—8 (1 Inmarsat—Pacific Ocean, 7 other) (2011)

Broadcast media: state-owned Television New Zealand operates multiple TV networks and state-owned Radio New Zealand operates 3 radio networks and an external shortwave radio service to the South Pacific region; a small number of national commercial TV and radio stations and many regional commercial television and radio stations are available; cable and satellite TV systems are available (2008)
Radio broadcast stations: AM 124, FM 290, shortwave 4 (1998)
Television broadcast stations: 41 (plus about 700 repeaters) (1997)

Internet country code: .nz

Internet hosts: 3.026 million (2012)
country comparison to the world: 34

Internet users: *total:* 4 million
percent of population: 91.5% (2014 est.)
country comparison to the world: 77

TRANSPORTATION

Airports: 123 (2013)
country comparison to the world: 48

Airports—with paved runways: *total:* 39
over 3,047 m: 2
2,438 to 3,047 m: 1
1,524 to 2,437 m: 12
914 to 1,523 m: 23
under 914 m: 1 (2013)

Airports—with unpaved runways: *total:* 84
1,524 to 2,437 m: 3
914 to 1,523 m: 33
under 914 m: 48 (2013)

Pipelines: condensate 331 km; gas 1936 km; liquid petroleum gas 172 km; oil 288 km; refined products 198 km (2013)

Railways: *total:* 4,128 km
narrow gauge: 4,128 km 1.067-m gauge (503 km electrified) (2014)
country comparison to the world: 42

Roadways: *total:* 94,902 km
paved: 62,759 km (includes 199 km of expressways)
unpaved: 32,143 km (2012)
country comparison to the world: 50

Merchant marine: *total:* 15
by type: bulk carrier 3, cargo 3, chemical tanker 1, container 1, passenger/cargo 5, petroleum tanker 2
foreign-owned: 7 (Germany 2, Hong Kong 1, South Africa 1, Switzerland 2, UK 1)
registered in other countries: 5 (Antigua and Barbuda 2, Cook Islands 2, Samoa 1) (2010)
country comparison to the world: 101

Ports and terminals: *major seaport(s):* Auckland, Lyttelton, Manukau Harbor, Marsden Point, Tauranga, Wellington

MILITARY AND SECURITY

Military branches: New Zealand Defense Force (NZDF): New Zealand Army, Royal New Zealand Navy, Royal New Zealand Air Force (Te Hokowhitu o Kahurangi, RNZAF) (2013)

Military service age and obligation: 17 years of age for voluntary military service; soldiers cannot be deployed until the age of 18; no conscription; 3 years of secondary education required; must be a citizen of NZ, the UK, Australia, Canada, or the US, and resident of NZ for the previous 5 years (2013)

Military expenditures:
1.13% of GDP (2012)
1.12% of GDP (2011)
1.13% of GDP (2010)
country comparison to the world: 87

TRANSNATIONAL ISSUES

Disputes—international: asserts a territorial claim in Antarctica (Ross Dependency)

Illicit drugs: significant consumer of amphetamines

NICARAGUA

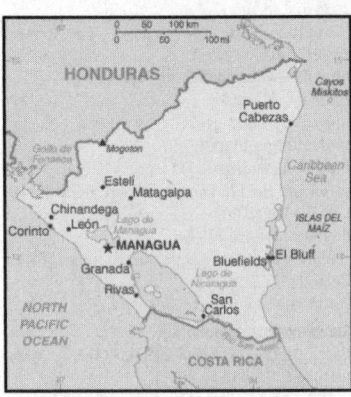

INTRODUCTION

Background: The Pacific coast of Nicaragua was settled as a Spanish colony from Panama in the early 16th century. Independence from Spain was declared in 1821 and the country became an independent republic in 1838. Britain occupied the Caribbean Coast in the first half of the 19th century, but gradually ceded control of the region in subsequent decades. Violent opposition to governmental manipulation and corruption spread to all classes by 1978 and resulted in a short-lived civil war that brought the Marxist Sandinista guerrillas to power in 1979. Nicaraguan aid to leftist rebels in El Salvador prompted the US to sponsor anti-Sandinista contra guerrillas through much of the 1980s. After losing free and fair elections in 1990,1996, and 2001, former Sandinista President Daniel ORTEGA Saavedra was elected president in 2006 and reelected in 2011. The 2008 municipal elections, 2010 regional elections, 2011 presidential election, 2012 municipal elections, and 2013 regional elections were marred by widespread irregularities. Nicaragua's infrastructure and economy—hard hit by the earlier civil war and by Hurricane Mitch in 1998—are slowly being rebuilt, but democratic institutions have been weakened under the ORTEGA administration.

GEOGRAPHY

Location: Central America, bordering both the Caribbean Sea and the North Pacific Ocean, between Costa Rica and Honduras

Geographic coordinates: 13 00 N, 85 00 W

Map references: Central America and the Caribbean

Area: *total:* 130,370 sq km
land: 119,990 sq km
water: 10,380 sq km
country comparison to the world: 98

Area—comparative: slightly larger than Pennsylvania; slightly smaller than New York state

Land boundaries: *total:* 1,253 km

border countries (2): Costa Rica 313 km, Honduras 940 km

Coastline: 910 km

Maritime claims: *territorial sea:* 12 nm
contiguous zone: 24 nm
continental shelf: natural prolongation

Climate: tropical in lowlands, cooler in highlands

Terrain: extensive Atlantic coastal plains rising to central interior mountains; narrow Pacific coastal plain interrupted by volcanoes

Elevation: *mean elevation:* 298 m

elevation extremes: *lowest point:* Pacific Ocean 0 m
highest point: Mogoton 2,438 m

Natural resources: gold, silver, copper, tungsten, lead, zinc, tim ber, fish

Land use: *agricultural land:* 42.2%
arable land: 12.5%
permanent crops: 2.5%
permanent pasture: 27.2%
forest: 25.3%
other: 32.5% (2011 est.)

Irrigated land: 1990 sq km (2012)

Total renewable water resources: 196.6 cu km (2011)

Freshwater withdrawal (domestic/industrial/agricultural): *total:* 1.39 cu km/yr (23%/4%/73%)
per capita: 265.9 cu m/yr (2008)

Natural hazards: destructive earth quakes; volcanoes; landslides; extremely susceptible to hurricanes
volcanism: significant volcanic activity; Cerro Negro (elev. 728 m), which last erupted in 1999, is one of Nicaragua's most active volcanoes; its lava flows and ash have been known to cause significant damage to farmland and buildings; other historically active volcanoes include Concepcion, Cosiguina, Las Pilas, Masaya, Momotombo, San Cristobal, and Telica

Environment—current issues: deforestation; soil erosion; water pollution

Environment—international agreements: *party to:* Biodiversity, Climate Change, Climate Change-Kyoto Protocol, Desertification, Endangered Species, Environmental Modification, Hazardous Wastes, Law of the Sea, Ozone Layer Protection, Ship Pollution, Wetlands, Whaling
signed, but not ratified: none of the selected agreements

Geography—note: largest country in Central America; contains the largest freshwater body in Central America, Lago de Nicaragua

PEOPLE AND SOCIETY

Nationality: *noun:* Nicaraguan(s)
adjective: Nicaraguan

Ethnic groups: mestizo (mixed Amerindian and white) 69%, white 17%, black 9%, Amerindian 5%

Languages: Spanish (official) 95.3%, Miskito 2.2%, Mestizo of the Caribbean coast 2%, other 0.5%

note: English and indigenous languages found on the Caribbean coast (2005 est.)

Religions: Roman Catholic 58.5%, Protestant 23.2% (Evangelical 21.6%, Moravian 1.6%), Jehovah's Witnesses 0.9%, other 1.6%, none 15.7% (2005 est.)

Demographic profile: Despite being one of the poorest countries in Latin America, Nicaragua has improved its access to potable water and sanitation and has ameliorated its life expectancy, infant and child mortality, and immunization rates. However, income distribution is very uneven, and the poor, agriculturalists, and indigenous people continue to have less access to healthcare services. Nicaragua's total fertility rate has fallen from around 6 children per woman in 1980 to just above replacement level today, but the high birth rate among adolescents perpetuates a cycle of poverty and low educational attainment.

Nicaraguans emig rate primarily to Costa Rica and to a lesser extent the United States. Nicaraguan men have been migrating seasonally to Costa Rica to harvest bananas and coffee since the early 20th century. Political turmoil, civil war, and natural disasters from the 1970s through the 1990s dramatically increased the flow of refugees and permanent migrants seeking jobs, higher wages, and better social and healthcare benefits. Since 2000, Nicaraguan emigration to Costa Rica has slowed and stabilized. Today roughly 300,000 Nicaraguans are permanent residents of Costa Rica—about 75% of the foreign population—and thousands more migrate seasonally for work, many illegally.

Population: 5,907,881 (July 2015 est.)
country comparison to the world: 111

Age structure: *0–14 years:* 28.57% (male 860,721/female 827,136)
15–24 years: 22.16% (male 657,339/female 651,744)
25–54 years: 38.69% (male 1,081,081/female 1,204,669)
55–64 years: 5.6% (male 153,711/female 177,334)
65 years and over: 4.98% (male 131965/female 162,181) (2015 est.)

Dependency ratios: *total dependency ratio:* 54.1%
youth dependency ratio: 46.3%
elderly dependency ratio: 7.8%
potential support ratio: 12.8% (2015 est.)

Median age: *total:* 24.7 years
male: 23.8 years
female: 25.5 years (2015 est.)
country comparison to the world: 154

Population growth rate: 1% (2015 est.)
country comparison to the world: 118

Birth rate: 18.03 births/1,000 population (2015 est.)
country comparison to the world: 103

Death rate: 5.08 deaths/1,000 population (2015 est.)
country comparison to the world: 185

Net migration rate: -3 migrant(s)/1,000 population (2015 est.)

country comparison to the world: 181

Urbanization: *urban population:* 58.8% of total population (2015)

rate of urbanization: 1.96% annual rate of change (2010–15 est.)

Major urban areas—population: MANAGUA (capital) 956,000 (2015)

Sex ratio: *at bi rth:* 1.05 male(s)/female

0–14 years: 1.04 male(s)/female

15–24 years: 1.01 male(s)/female

25–54 years: 0.9 male(s)/female

55–64 years: 0.87 male(s)/female

65 years and over: 0.81 male(s)/female

total population: 0.95 male(s)/female (2015 est.)

Mother's mean age at first birth: 19.7

note: median age at first birth among women 20–24 (2006/07 est.)

Maternal mortality rate: 150 deaths/100,000 live births (2015 est.)

country comparison to the world: 76

Infant mortality rate: *total:* 19.65 deaths/1,000 live births

male: 22.56 deaths/1,000 live births

female: 16.59 deaths/1,000 live births (2015 est.)

country comparison to the world: 88

Life expectancy at birth: *total population:* 72.98 years

male: 70.81 years

female: 75.26 years (2015 est.)

country comparison to the world: 134

Total fertility rate: 1.94 children born/woman (2015 est.)

country comparison to the world: 132

Contraceptive prevalence rate: 80.4% (2011/12)

Health expenditures: 8.4% of GDP (2013)

country comparison to the world: 55

Physicians density: 0.9 physicians/1,000 population (2014)

Hospital bed density: 0.9 beds/1,000 population (2012)

Drinking water source:

improved:

urban: 99.3% of population

rural: 69.4% of population

total: 87% of population

unimproved:

urban: 0.7% of population

rural: 30.6% of population

total: 13% of population (2015 est.)

Sanitation facility access:

improved:

urban: 76.5% of population

rural: 55.7% of population

total: 67.9% of population

unimproved:

urban: 23.5% of population

rural: 44.3% of population

total: 32.1% of population (2015 est.)

HIV/AIDS—adult prevalence rate: 0.27% (2014 est.)

country comparison to the world: 88

HIV/AIDS—people living with HIV/AIDS: 10,000 (2014 est.)

country comparison to the world: 107

HIV/AIDS—deaths: 400 (2014 est.)

country comparison to the world: 91

Major infectious diseases: *degree of risk:* high

food or waterborne diseases: bacterial diarrhea, hepatitis A, and typhoid fever

vectorborne disease: dengue fever and malaria (2013)

Obesity—adultprevalence rate: 15.5% (2014)

country comparison to the world: 81

Children under the age of 5 years underweight: 5.7% (2007)

country comparison to the world: 85

Education expenditures: 4.5% of GDP (2010)

country comparison to the world: 88

Literacy: *definition:* age 15 and over can read and write

total population: 82.8%

male: 82.4%

female: 83.2% (2015 est.)

Child labor—children ages 5–14: *total number:* 223,992

percentage: 14%

note: data represent children ages 5–17 (2005 est.)

Unemployment, youth ages 15–24: *total:* 11.9%

male: 9.8%

female: 15.6% (2010 est.)

country comparison to the world: 110

GOVERNMENT

Country name: *conventional long form:* Republic of Nicaragua

conventional short form: Nicaragua

local long form: Republica de Nicaragua

local short form: Nicaragua

etymology: Nicarao was the name of the largest indigenous settlement at the time of Spanish arrival; conquistador Gil GONZALEZ Davila, who explored the area (1622–23), combined the name of the community with the Spanish word "agua" (water), referring to the two large lakes in the west of the country (Lake Managua and Lake Nicaragua)

Government type: presidential republic

Capital: *name:* Managua

Geographic coordinates: 12 08 N, 86 15 W

time difference: UTC-6 (1 hour behind Washington, DC, during Standard Time)

Administrative divisions: 15 departments (departamentos, singular—departamento) and 2 autonomous regions* (regiones autonomistas, singular—region autonoma); Atlantico Norte*, Atlantico Sur*, Boaco, Carazo, Chinandega, Chontales, Esteli, Granada, Jinotega, Leon, Madriz, Managua, Masaya, Matagalpa, Nueva Segovia, Rio San Juan, Rivas

Independence: 15 September 1821 (from Spain)

National holiday: Independence Day, 15 September (1821)

Constitution: several previous; latest adopted 19 November 1986, effective 9 January 1987; amended several tim es, last in 2014 (2016)

Legal system: civil law system; Supreme Court may review administrative acts

International law organization participation: accepts compulsory ICJ jurisdiction with reservations; non-party state to the ICCt

Citizenship: *citizenship by birth:* yes

citizenship by descent: yes

dual citizenship recognized: no, except in cases where bilateral agreements exist

residency requirement for naturalization: 4 years

Suffrage: 16 years of age; universal

Executive branch: *chief of state:* President Jose Daniel ORTEGA Saavedra (since 10 January 2007); Vice President Moises Omar HALLESLEV-ENS Acevedo (since 10 January 2012); note—the president is both chief of state and head of government

head of government: President Jose Daniel ORTEGA Saavedra (since 10 January 2007); Vice President Moises Omar HALLESLEVENS Acevedo (since 10 January 2012)

cabinet: Council of Ministers appointed by the president

elections/appointments: president and vice president directly elected on the same ballot by simple majority popular vote for a 5-year term (no term limits); election last held on 6 November 2011 (next to be held by November 2016)

election results: Jose Daniel ORTEG A Saavedra reelected president; percent of vote—Jose Daniel ORTEGA Saavedra (FSLN) 62.5%, Fabio GADEA Mantilla (PLI) 31%, Arnoldo ALEMAN (PLC) 5.9%, other 0.6%

Legislative branch: *description:* unicameral National Assembly or Asamblea Nacional (92 seats; 70 members in multi-seat constituencies and 20 members in a single nationwide constituency directly elected by proportional representation vote; 2 seats reserved for the previous president and the runner-up candidate in the previous presidential election; members serve 5-year terms;)

elections: last held on 6 November 2011 (next to be held by November 2016)

election results: percent of vote by party—NA; seats by party—FSLN 62, PLI/MRS 26, PLC 2

Judicial branch: *highest court(s):* Supreme Court or Corte Suprema de Justicia (consists of 16 judges organized into administrative, civil, criminal, and constitutional chambers)

judge selection and term of office: Supreme Court judges elected by the National Assembly to serve 5-year staggered terms

subordinate courts: Appeals Court; first instance civil, criminal, and military courts

Political parties and leaders: Alliance for the Republic or APRE [Carlos CANALES]

Conservative Party or PC [Alejandro BOLANOS Davis]

Independent Liberal Party or PLI [Indalecio RODRIGUEZ]

Liberal Constitutionalist Party or PLC [Maria Haydee OSUNA]

Nicaraguan Liberal Alliance or ALN [Alejandro MEJIA Ferreti]

Sandinista National Liberation Front or FSLN [Jose Daniel ORTEG A Saavedra]

Sandinista Renovation Movement or MRS [Ana Margarita VIJIL]

Political pressure groups and leaders: National Workers Front or FNT (a Sandinista umbrella group

of eight labor unions including: Farm Workers Association or ATC, Health Workers Federation or FETASALUD, Heroes and Martyrs Confederation of Professional Associations or CO NAPRO, National Association of Educators of Nicaragua or ANDEN, National Union of Employees or UNE, National Union of Farmers and Ranchers or UNAG, Sandinista Workers Central or CST, and Union of Journalists of Nicaragua or UPN)
Nicaraguan Workers' Central or CTN (an independent labor union)
Permanent Congress of Workers or CPT (an umbrella group of four non-Sandinista labor unions including: Autonomous Nicaraguan Workers Central or CTN-A, Confederation of Labor Unification or CUS, Independent General Confederation of Labor or CGT-I, and Labor Action and Unity Central or CAUS) Superior Council of Private Enterprise or COSEP (a confederation of business groups)
International organization participation: BCIE, CACM, CD, CELAC, FAO, G-77, IADB, IAEA, IBRD, ICAO, ICRM, IDA, IFAD, IFC, IFRCS, ILO, IMF, IMO, Interpol, IOC, IOM, IPU, ISO (correspondent), ITSO, ITU, ITUC (NGOs), LAES, LAIA (observer), MIGA, NAM, OAS, OPANAL, OPCW, PCA, Petrocaribe, SICA, UN, UNCTAD, UNESCO, UNHCR, UNIDO, Union Latina, UNWTO, UPU, WCO, WHO, WIPO, WMO, WTO
Diplomatic representation in the US: hief of mission: Ambassador Francisco Obadiah CAMPBELL Hooker (since 23 June 2010)
chancery: 1627 New Hampshire Avenue NW, Washington, DC 20009
telephone: [1] (202) 939-6570,6573
FAX: [1] (202) 939-6545
consulate(s) general: Houston, Los Angeles, Miami, New York, San Francisco
Diplomatic representation from the US: chief of mission: Ambassador Phyllis M. POWERS (since 24 April 2012)
embassy: Kilometer 5.5 Carretera Sur, Managua
mailing address: American Embassy Managua, APO AA 34021
telephone: [505] 2252-7100,2252–7888; 2252-7634 (after hours)
FAX: [505] 2252-7250
Flag description: three equal horizontal bands of blue (top), white, and blue with the national coat of arms centered in the white band; the coat of arms features a triangle encircled by the words REPUBLICA DE NICARAGUA on the top and AMERICA CENTRAL on the bottom; the banner is based on the former blue-white-blue flag of the Federal Republic of Central America; the blue bands symbolize the Pacific Ocean and the Caribbean Sea, while the white band represents the land between the two bodies of water
note: similar to the flag of El Salvador, which features a round emblem encircled by the words REPUBLICA DE EL SALVADOR EN LA AMERICA CENTRAL centered in the white band; also similar to the flag of Honduras, which has five blue stars arranged in an X pattern centered in the white band

National symbol(s): turquoise-browed motmot (bird); national colors: blue, white
National anthem: name: "Salve a ti, Nicaragua" (Hail to Thee, Nicaragua)
lyrics/music: Salomon Ibarra MAYORGA/traditional, arranged by Luis Abraham DELGADILLO
note: although only officially adopted in 1971, the music was approved in 1918 and the lyrics in 1939; the tune, originally from Spain, was used as an anthem for Nicaragua from the 1830s until 1876

ECONOMY

Economy—overview: Nicaragua, the poorest country in Central America and the second poorest in the Western Hemisphere, has widespread underemployment and poverty. Textiles and agriculture combined account for nearly 50% of Nicaragua's exports.
The Dominican Republic-Central America-United States Free Trade Agreement (CAFTA-DR) has been in effect since April 2006 and has expanded export opportunities for many Nicaraguan agricultural and manufactured goods.
In 2013, the government granted a 50-year concession to a newly formed Chinese-run company to finance and build an inter-oceanic canal and related projects, at an estimated cost of $50 billion. The canal construction has not started.
GDP (purchasing power parity): $31.33 billion (2015 est.)
$29.98 billion (2014 est.)
$28.64 billion (2013 est.)
note: data are in 2015 US dollars
country comparison to the world: 127
GDP (official exchange rate): $12.22 billion (2015 est.)
GDP—real growth rate: 4.5% (2015 est.)
4.7% (2014 est.)
4.5% (2013 est.)
country comparison to the world: 50
GDP—per capita (PPP): $5,000 (2015 est.)
$4,800 (2014 est.)
$4,700 (2013 est.)
note: data are in 2015 US dollars
country comparison to the world: 171
Gross national saving: 19.3% of GDP (2015 est.)
19.6% of GDP (2014 est.)
17.6% of GDP (2013 est.)
country comparison to the world: 85
GDP—composition, by end use:
household consumption: 82.7%
government consumption: 6.5%
investment in fixed capital: 28.8%
investment in inventories: 0%
exports of goods and services: 40.7%
imports of goods and services: -58.7% (2015 est.)
GDP—composition, by sector of origin:
agriculture: 18.1%
industry: 22.9%
services: 58.9% (2015 est.)
Agriculture—products: coffee, bananas, sugarcane, rice, corn, tobacco, cotton, sesame, soya, beans; beef, veal, pork, poultry, dairy products; shrimp, lobsters
Industries: food processing, chemicals, machinery and metal products, knit and woven apparel, petroleum refining and distribution, beverages,

footwear, wood, electric wire harness manufacturing, mining
Industrial production growth rate: 4% (2015 est.)
country comparison to the world: 56
Labor force: 2.98 million (2015 est.)
country comparison to the world: 104
Labor force—by occupation: agriculture: 31%
industry: 18%
services: 50% (2011 est.)
Unemployment rate: 6.1% (2015 est.)
6% (2014 est.)
note: underemployment was 46.5% in 2008
country comparison to the world: 68
Population below poverty line: 29.6% (2015 est.)
Household income or consumption by percentage share: lowest: 10%: 1.4%
highest: 10%: 41.8% (2005)
Distribution of family income—Gini index: 40.5 (2010)
60.3 (1998)
country comparison to the world: 60
Budget: revenues: $1.975 billion
expenditures: $2.443 billion (2015 est.)
Taxes and other revenues: 16% of GDP (2015 est.)
country comparison to the world: 185
Budget surplus (+) or deficit (–): -3.8% of GDP (2015 est.)
country comparison to the world: 139
Public debt: 42.6% of GDP (2015 est.)
40.8% of GDP (2014 est.)
note: official data; data cover general Government Debt, and includes debt instruments issued (or owned) by Government entities other than the treasury; the data include treasury debt held by foreign entities, as well as intra-governmental debt; intra-governmental debt consists of treasury borrowings from surpluses in the social funds, such as retirement, medical care, and unemployment, debt instruments for the social funds are not sold at public auctions; Nicaragua rebased its GDP figures in 2012, which reduced the figures for debt as a percentage of GDP
country comparison to the world: 107
Fiscal year: calendar year
Inflation rate (consumer prices): 4% (2015 est.)
6% (2014 est.)
country comparison to the world: 153
Central bank discount rate: 3% (31 December 2010)
country comparison to the world: 104
Commercial bank prime lending rate: 13.5% (31 December 2015 est.)
13.54% (31 December 2014 est.)
country comparison to the world: 52
Stock of narrow money: $1.033 billion (31 December 2015 est.)
$943.8 million (31 December 2014 est.)
country comparison to the world: 152
Stock of broad money: $4.453 billion (31 December 2013 est.)
$4.136 billion (31 December 2012 est.)
country comparison to the world: 136
Stock of domestic credit: $5.265 billion (31 December 2015 est.)
$5.146 billion (31 December 2014 est.)
country comparison to the world: 122
Market value of publicly traded shares: $NA
Current account balance: -$1.079 billion (2015 est.)
-$838 million (2014 est.)

country comparison to the world: 127
Exports: $4.492 billion (2015 est.)
$4.974 billion (2014 est.)
country comparison to the world: 111
Exports—commodities: coffee, beef, gold, sugar, peanuts, shrimp and lobster, tobacco, cigars, automobile wiring harnesses, textiles, apparel, cotton
Exports—partners: US 56.5%, Mexico 10.7%, Venezuela 5.4%, El Salvador 4.3% (2015)
Imports: $5.902 billion (2015 est.)
$5.746 billion (2014 est.)
country comparison to the world: 120
Imports—commodities: consumer goods, machinery and equipment, raw materials, petroleum products
Imports—partners: US 19.9%, Mexico 14.9%, China 10.6%, Venezuela 7%, Costa Rica 7%, El Salvador 5.7%, Guatemala 5.6%, Netherlands Antilles 5.5% (2015)
Reserves of foreign exchange and gold: $2.32 billion (31 December 2015 est.)
$2.276 billion (31 December 2014 est.)
country comparison to the world: 116
Debt—external: $10.19 billion (31 December 2014 est.)
$9.631 billion (31 December 2013 est.)
country comparison to the world: 105
Exchange rates: cordobas (NIO) per US dollar—
27.31 (2015 est.)
26.01 (2014 est.)
26.01 (2013 est.)
23.55 (2012 est.)
22.424 (2011 est.)

ENERGY

Electricity—production: 4.438 billion kWh (2014 est.)
country comparison to the world: 122
Electricity—consumption: 4.412 billion kWh (2014 est.)
country comparison to the world: 120
Electricity—exports: 48.98 million kWh (2014 est.)
country comparison to the world: 85
Electricity—imports: 22.32 million kWh (2014 est.)
country comparison to the world: 107
Electricity—installed generating capacity: 1.331 million kW (2015 est.)
country comparison to the world: 121
Electricity—from fossil fuels: 54.4% of total installed capacity (2015 est.)
country comparison to the world: 143
Electricity—from nuclear fuels: 0% of total installed capacity (2015 est.)
country comparison to the world: 159
Electricity—from hydroelectric plants: 10.2% of total installed capacity (2015 est.)
country comparison to the world: 115
Electricity—from other renewable sources: 35.4% of total installed capacity (2015 est.)
country comparison to the world: 3
Crude oil—production: 0 bbl/day (2015 est.)
country comparison to the world: 178
Crude oil—exports: 0 bbl/day (2015 est.)
country comparison to the world: 173
Crude oil—imports: 13,580 bbl/day (2014 est.)
country comparison to the world: 74
Crude oil—proved reserves: 0 bbl (1 January 2015 est.)

country comparison to the world: 178
Refined petroleum products—production: 10,810 bbl/day (2012 est.)
country comparison to the world: 104
Refined petroleum products—consumption: 28,700 bbl/day (2014 est.)
country comparison to the world: 116
Refined petroleum products—exports: 396 bbl/day (2014 est.)
country comparison to the world: 116
Refined petroleum products—imports: 16,500 bbl/day (2014 est.)
country comparison to the world: 119
Natural gas—production: 0 cu m (2016 est.)
country comparison to the world: 115
Natural gas—consumption: 0 cu m (2016 est.)
country comparison to the world: 183
Natural gas—exports: 0 cu m (2016 est.)
country comparison to the world: 159
Natural gas—imports: 0 cu m (2016 est.)
country comparison to the world: 115
Natural gas—proved reserves: 0 cu m (1 January 2015 est.)
country comparison to the world: 182
Carbon dioxide emissions from consumption of energy: 5.285 million Mt (2012 est.)
country comparison to the world: 127

COMMUNICATIONS

Telephones—fixed lines: *total subscriptions:* 340,000
subscriptions per 100 inhabitants: 6 (2014 est.)
country comparison to the world: 111
Telephones—mobile cellular: *total:* 7.1 million
subscriptions per 100 inhabitants: 121 (2014 est.)
country comparison to the world: 105
Telephone system: *general assessment:* system being upgraded by foreign investment; nearly all installed telecommunications capacity now uses digital technology, owing to investments since privatization of the formerly state-owned telecommunications company
domestic: since privatization, access to fixed-line and mobile-cellular services has improved; fixed-line teledensity roughly 6 per 100 persons; mobile-cellular telephone subscribership has increased to roughly 114 per 100 persons
international: country code—505; the Americas Region Caribbean Ring System (ARCOS-1) fiber optic submarine cable provides connectivity to South and Central America, parts of the Caribbean, and the US; satellite earth stations—1 Intersputnik (Atlantic Ocean region) and 1 Intelsat (Atlantic Ocean) (2011)
Broadcast media: multiple terrestrial TV stations, supplemented by cable TV in most urban areas; nearly all are government-owned or affiliated; more than 300 radio stations, both government-affiliated and privately owned (2016)
Radio broadcast stations: AM 63, FM 32, shortwave 1 (1998)
Television broadcast stations: 16 (2009)
Internet country code: .ni
Internet hosts: 296,068 (2012)
country comparison to the world: 63
Internet users: *total:* 845,100
percent of population: 14.5% (2014 est.)
country comparison to the world: 123

TRANSPORTATION

Airports: 147 (2013)
country comparison to the world: 40

Airports—with paved runways: *total:* 12
2,438 to 3,047 m: 3
1,524 to 2,437 m: 2
914 to 1,523 m: 3
under 914 m: 4 (2013)
Airports—with unpaved runways: *total:* 135
1,524 to 2,437 m: 1
914 to 1,523 m: 15
under 914 m: 119 (2013)
Pipelines: oil 54 km (2013)
Roadways: *total:* 23,897 km
paved: 3,346 km
unpaved: 20,551 km (2014)
country comparison to the world: 101
Waterways: 2,220 km (navigable waterways as well as the use of the large Lake Managua and Lake Nicaragua; rivers serve only the sparsely populated eastern part of the country) (2011)
country comparison to the world: 39
Ports and terminals: *major seaport(s):* Bluefields, Corinto

MILITARY AND SECURITY

Military branches: National Army of Nicaragua (Ejercito Nacional de Nicaragua, ENN; includes Navy, Air Force) (2013)
Military service age and obligation: 18–30 years of age for voluntary military service; no conscription; tour of duty 18–36 months; requires Nicaraguan nationality and 6th-grade education (2012)
Military expenditures:
0.63% of GDP (2012)
0.53% of GDP (2011)
0.63% of GDP (2010)
country comparison to the world: 120

TRANSNATIONAL ISSUES

Disputes—international: the 1992 ICJ ruling for El Salvador and Honduras advised a tripartite resolution to establish a maritime boundary in the Gulf of Fonseca, which considers Honduran access to the Pacific; Nicaragua and Costa Rica regularly file border dispute cases over the delimitations of the San Juan River and the northern tip of Calero Island to the ICJ; in 2009, the ICJ ruled that Costa Rican vessels carrying out police activities could not use the river, but official Costa Rican vessels providing essential services to riverside inhabitants and Costa Rican tourists could travel freely on the river; in 2011, the ICJ provisionally ruled that both countries must remove personnel from the disputed area; in 2013, the ICJ rejected Nicaragua's 2012 suit to halt Costa Rica's construction of a highway paralleling the river on the grounds of irreparable environmental damage; in 2013, the ICJ, regarding the disputed territory, ordered that Nicaragua should refrain from dredging or canal construction and refill and repair damage caused by trenches connecting the river to the Caribbean and upheld its 2010 ruling that Nicaragua must remove all personnel; in early 2014, Costa Rica brought Nicaragua to the ICJ over offshore oil concessions in the disputed region
Refugees and internally displaced persons: *stateless persons:* 1 (2015)
Illicit drugs: transshipment point for cocaine destined for the US and transshipment point for arms-for-drugs dealing

NIGER

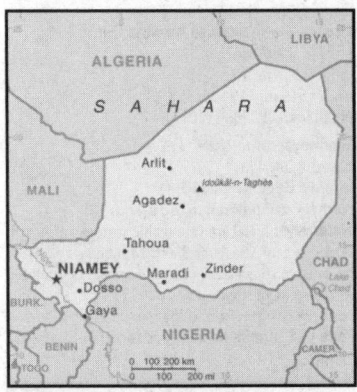

INTRODUCTION

Background: Niger became independent from France in 1960 and experienced single-party and military rule until 1991, when Gen. Ali SAIBOU was forced by public pressure to allow multiparty elections, which resulted in a democratic government in 1993. Political infighting brought the government to a standstill and in 1996 led to a coup by Col. Ibrahim BARE. In 1999, BARE was killed in a counter coup by military officers who restored democratic rule and held elections that brought Mamadou TANDJA to power in December of that year. TANDJA was reelected in 2004 and in 2009 spearheaded a constitutional amendment allowing him to extend his term as president. in February 2010, military officers led a coup that deposed TANDJA and suspended the constitution. ISSO UFOU Mahamadou was elected in April 2011 following the coup and reelected to a second term in early 2016. Niger is one of the poorest countries in the world with minimal government services and insufficient funds to develop its resource base. The largely agrarian and subsistence-based economy is frequently disrupted by extended droughts common to the Sahel region of Africa. A Tuareg rebellion emerged in 2007 and ended in 2009. Niger is facing increased security concerns on its borders from various external threats including insecurity in Libya, spillover from the conflict in Mali, and violent extremism in northeastern Nigeria.

GEOGRAPHY

Location: Western Africa, southeast of Algeria
Geographic coordinates: 16 00 N, 8 00 E
Map references: Africa
Area: *total:* 1.267 million sq km
land: 1,266,700 sq km
water: 300 sq km
country comparison to the world: 22
Area—comparative: slightly less than twice the size of Texas
Land boundaries: *total:* 5,834 km

border countries (7): Algeria 951 km, Benin 277 km, Burkina Faso 622 km, Chad 1,196 km, Libya 342 km, Mali 838 km, Nigeria 1,608 km
Coastline: 0 km (landlocked)
Maritime claims: none (landlocked)
Climate: desert; mostly hot, dry, dusty; tropical in extreme south
Terrain: predominately desert plains and sand dunes; flat to rolling plains in south; hills in north
Elevation: *mean elevation:* 474 m

elevation extremes: *lowest point:* Niger River 200 m
highest point: Idoukal-n-Tagh es 2,022 m
Natural resources: uranium, coal, iron ore, tin, ph osphates, gold, molybdenum, gypsum, salt, petroleum
Land use: *agricultural land:* 35.1%
arable land: 12.3%
permanent crops: 0.1%
permanent pasture: 22.7%
forest: 1%
other: 63.9% (2011 est.)
Irrigated land: 1,000 sq km (2012)
Total renewable water resources: 33.65 cu km (2011)
Freshwater withdrawal (domestic/industrial/agricultural): *total:* 0.98 cu km/yr (30%/3%/67%)
per capita: 70.53 cu m/yr (2005)
Natural hazards: recurring droughts
Environment—current issues: overgrazing; soil erosion; deforestation; desertification; wildlife populations (such as elephant, hippopotamus, giraffe, and lion) threatened because of poaching and habitat destruction
Environment—international agreements: *party to:* Biodiversity, Climate Change, Climate Change-Kyoto Protocol, Desertification, Endangered Species, Environmental Modification, Hazardous Wastes, Ozone Layer Protection, Wetlands
signed, but not ratified: Law of the Sea
Geography—note: landlocked; one of the hottest countries in the world; northern four-fifths is desert, south ern one-fifth is savanna, suitable for livestock and limited agriculture

PEOPLE AND SOCIETY

Nationality: *noun:* Nigerien(s)
adjective: Nigerien
Ethnic groups: Hausa 53.1%, Zarma/Songhai 21.2%, Tuareg 11%, Fulani (Peul) 6.5%, Kanuri 5.9%, Gurma 0.8%, Arab 0.4%, Tubu 0.4%, other/unavailable 0.9% (2006 est.)
Languages: French (official), Hausa, Djerma
Religions: Muslim 80%, other (includes indigenous beliefs and Ch ristian) 20%
Population: 18,045,729 (July 2015 est.)
country comparison to the world: 62
Age structure: *0–14 years:* 49.57% (male 4,512,526/female 4,431944)
15–24 years: 18.61% (male 1,658,537/female 1,699,924)

25–54 years: 25.92% (male 2,336,655/female 2,341,599)
55–64 years: 3.26% (male 305,363/female 283,647)
65 years and over: 2.64% (male 242,025/female 233,509) (2015 est.)
Dependency ratios: *total dependency ratio:* 113%
youth dependency ratio: 107.5%
elderly dependency ratio: 5.5%
potential support ratio: 18.2% (2015 est.)
Median age: *total:* 15.2 years
male: 15.1 years
female: 15.3 years (2015 est.)
country comparison to the world: 229
Population growth rate: 3.25% (2015 est.)
country comparison to the world: 4
Birth rate: 45.45 births/1,000 population (2015 est.)
country comparison to the world: 1
Death rate: 12.42 deaths/1,000 population (2015 est.)
country comparison to the world: 23
Net migration rate: -0.56 migrant(s)/1,000 population (2015 est.)
country comparison to the world: 138

Urbanization: *urban population:* 18.7% of total population (2015)
rate of urbanization: 5.14% annual rate of change (2010–15 est.)
Major urban areas—population: NIAMEY (capital) 1.09 million (2015)
Sex ratio: *at birth:* 1.03 male(s)/female
0–14 years: 1.02 male(s)/female
15–24 years: 0.98 male(s)/female
25–54 years: 1 male(s)/female
55–64 years: 1.08 male(s)/female
65 years and over: 1.04 male(s)/female
total population: 1.01 male(s)/female (2015 est.)
Mother's mean age at first birth: 18.1
note: median age at first birth among women 20–24 (2012 est.)
Maternal mortality rate: 553 deaths/100,000 live births (2015 est.)
country comparison to the world: 14
Infant mortality rate: *total:* 84.59 deaths/1,000 live births
male: 89.12 deaths/1,000 live births
female: 79.92 deaths/1,000 live births (2015 est.)
country comparison to the world: 7
Life expectancy at birth: *total population:* 55.13 years
male: 53.9 years
female: 56.39 years (2015 est.)
country comparison to the world: 209
Total fertility rate: 6.76 children born/woman (2015 est.)
country comparison to the world: 1
Contraceptive prevalence rate: 13.9% (2012)
Health expenditures: 6.5% of GDP (2013)
country comparison to the world: 74
Physicians density: 0.02 physicians/1,000 population (2008)

Drinking water source:
improved:
urban: 100% of popu lation
rural: 48.6% of population
total: 58.2% of population
unimproved:
urban: 0% of population
rural: 51.4% of population
total: 41.8% of population (2015 est.)
Sanitation facility access:
improved:
urban: 37.9% of population
rural: 4.6% of population
total: 10.9% of population
unimproved:
urban: 62.1% of population
rural: 95.4% of population
total: 89.1% of population (2015 est.)
HIV/AIDS—adult prevalence rate: 0.49% (2014 est.)
country comparison to the world: 68
HIV/AIDS—people living with HIV/AIDS: 51,800 (2014 est.)
country comparison to the world: 60
HIV/AIDS—deaths: 3,400 (2014 est.)
country comparison to the world: 42
Major infectious diseases: *degree of risk:* very high
food or waterborne diseases: bacterial and protozoal diarrhea, hepatitis A, and typhoid fever
vectorborne diseases: malaria and dengue fever
water contact disease: schistosomiasis
respiratory disease: meningococcal meningitis
animal contact disease: rabies
note: highly pathogenic H5N1 avian influenza has been identified in this country; it poses a negligible risk with extremely rare cases possible among US citizens who have close contact with birds (2013)
Obesity—adult prevalence rate: 3.7% (2014)
country comparison to the world: 180
Children under the age of 5 years underweight: 37.9% (2012)
country comparison to the world: 4
Education expenditures: 6.8% of GDP (2014)
country comparison to the world: 101
Literacy: *definition:* age 15 and over can read and write
total population: 19.1%
male: 27.3%
female: 11% (2015 est.)
School life expectancy (primary to tertiary education): *total:* 5 years
male: 6 years
female: 5 years (2012)
Child labor—children ages 5–14: *total number:* 1,557,913
percentage: 43% (2006 est.)

GOVERNMENT

Country name: *conventional long form:* Republic of Niger
conventional short form: Niger
local long form: Republique du Niger
local short form: Niger

etymology: named for the Niger River that passes through the southwest of the country; from a native term "Ni Gir" meaning "River Gir"
Government type: semi-presidential republic
Capital: *name:* Niamey

Geographic coordinates: 13 31 N, 2 07 E
time difference: UTC + 1 (6 hours ahead of Washington, DC, during Standard Time)
Administrative divisions: 7 regions (regions, singular—region) and 1 capital district* (communte urbaine); Agadez, Diffa, Dosso, Maradi, Niamey*, Tahoua, Tillaberi, Zinder
Independence: 3 August 1960 (from France)
National holiday: Republic Day, 18 December (1958); note—commemorates the founding of the Republic of Niger which predated independen ce from France in 1960
Constitution: several previous; passed by referendum 31 October 2010, entered into force 25 November 2010 (2016)
Legal system: mixed legal system of civil law (based on French civil law), Islamic law, and customary law
International law organization participation: has not submitted an ICJ jurisdiction declaration; accepts ICCt jurisdiction
Citizenship: *citizenship by birth:* no
citizenship by descent only: at least one parent must be a citizen of Niger
dual citizenship recognized: yes
residency requirement for naturalization: unknown
Suffrage: 18 years of age; universal
Executive branch: *chief of state:* President ISSOUFOU Mahamadou (since 7 April 2011)

head of government: Prime Minister Brigi RAFINI (since 7 April 2011)
cabinet: Cabinet appointed by the president
elections/appointments: president directly elected by absolute majority popular vote in 2 rounds if needed for a 5-year term (eligible for a second term); election last held on 21 February 2016 and 20 March 2016 (next to be held in 2021); prime minister appointed by the president, authorized by the National Assembly
election results: ISSOUFOU Mahamadou reelected president; percent of vote in first round—ISSOUFOU Mahamadou (PNDS-Tarrayya) 48.6%, Hama AMADOU (MODEN/FA Lumana Africa) 17.8%, Seini OUMAROU (MNSD-Nassara) 11.3%, other 22.3%; percent of vote in second round—ISSOUFOU Mahamadou 92%, Hama AMAD OU 8%
Legislative branch: *description:* unicameral National Assembly or Assemblee Nationale (171 seats; 158 members directly elected from 8 multi-member constituencies in 7 regions and Niamey by party-list proportional repr esentation, 8 reserved for minorities elected in special single-seat constituencies by simple majority vote, 5 seats reserved for Nigeriens living abroad—l seat per continent—elected in single-seat constituencies by simple majority vote; members serve 5-year terms); note—the number of National Assembly seats increased from 113 to 171 in the February 2016 legislative election

elections: last held on 21 February 2016 (next to be held in 2021)
election results: percent of vote by party—PNDS-Tarrayya 44.1%, MODEN/FA-Lumana 14.7%, MNSD-Nassara 11.8%, MPR-Jamhuriya 7.1%, MNRD Hankuri-PSDNAlheri 3.5%, MPN-Kishin Kassa 2.9%, ANDP-Zaman Lahiya 2.4%, RSD-Gaskiya 2.4%, CDS-Rahama 1.8%, CPR-Inganci 1.8%, RDP-Jama'a 1.8%, AMENAMIN 3.0%, other 1.4%; seats by party—PNDS-Tarrayya 75, MODEN/FA-Lumana 25, MNSD-Nassara 20, MPR-Jamhuriya 12, MNRD Hankuri-PSD-NAlheri 6, MPN-Kishin Kassa 5, ANDP-Zaman Lahiya 4, RSD-Gaskiya 4, CDS-Rahama 3, CPR-Inganci 3, RDP-Jama'a 3, RDP-Jama'a 3, AM ENAM in 3, other 8
Judicial branch: *highest court(s):* Constitutional Court (consists of 7 judges); High Court of Justice (consists of 7 members)
judge selection and term of office: Constitutional Court judges nominated/elected—1 by the president of the Republic, 1 by the president of the National Assembly, 2 by peer judges, 2 by peer lawyers, 1 law professor by peers, and 1 from within Nigerien society; all appointed by the president; judges serve 6-year nonrenewable terms with one-third of membership renewed every 2 years; High Judicial Court members selected from among the legislature and judiciary; members serve 5-year terms
subordinate courts: Court of Cassation; Council of State; Court of Finances; various specialized tribunals and customary courts
Political parties and leaders: Alliance of Movements for the Emergence of Niger or AMENAMIN [Omar Hamidou TCHIANA]
Congress for the Republic or CPR-Inganci [Kassoum MOCTAR]
Democratic Alliance for Niger or ADN-Fusaha [Habi Mahamadou SALISSOU]
Democratic and Social Convention-Rahama or CDS-Rahama [Abdou LABO]
National Movement for the Development of Society-Nassara or MNSD-Nassara [Seini OUMAROU]
Nigerien Alliance for Democracy and Progress-Zaman Lahiya or ANDP-Zaman Lahiya [Moussa Moumouni DJERMAKOYE]
Nigerien Democratic Movement for an African Federation or MODEN/FA Lumana [Hama AMADOU]
Nigerien Movement for Democratic Renewal or MNRD-Hankuri [Mahamane OUSMANE]
Nigerien Party for Democracy and Socialism or PN DS-Tarrayya [Mahamadou ISSOUFOU]
Nigerien Patriotic Movement or MPN-Kishin Kassa [Ibrahim YACOUBA]
Party for Socialism and Democracy in Niger or PSDN-Alheri
Patriotic Movement for the Republic or MPR-Jamhuriya [Albade ABOUBA]
Rally for Democracy and Progress—Jama'aor RDP-Ja ma'a [Hamid ALGABID]
Social and Democratic Rally or RSD-Gaskiyya [Amadou CHEIFFOU]

Social Democratic Party or PSD-Bassira [Mohamed BEN OMAR]

Union for Democracy and the Republic-Tabbat or UDR-Tabbat [Amadou Boubacar CISSE]

note: the SPLM and SPLM-DC are banned political parties

International organization participation: ACP, AfDB, AU, CD, ECOWAS, EITI (compliant country), Entente, FAO, FZ, G-77, IAEA, IBRD, ICAO, ICCt, ICRM, IDA, IDB, IFAD, IFC, IFRCS, ILO, IMF, Interpol, IOC, IOM, IPU, ISO (correspondent), ITSO, ITU, ITUC (NGOs), MIGA, MINUSMA, MONUSCO, NAM, OIC, OIF, OPCW, UN, UNCTAD, UNESCO, UNIDO, UNMIL, UNOCI, UNWTO, UPU, WADB (regional), WAEMU, WCO, WFTU (NGOs), WHO, WIPO, WMO, WTO

Diplomatic representation in the US: chief of mission: Ambassador Hassana ALIDOU (since 23 February 2015)

chancery: 2204 R Street NW, Washington, DC 20008

telephone: [1] (202) 483-4224 through 4227

FAX: [1] (202) 483-3169

Diplomatic representation from the US: chief of mission: Ambassador Eunice S. REDDICK (since 12 September 2014)

embassy: BP 11201, Rue Des Ambassades, Niamey

mailing address: 2420 Niamey Place, Washington DC 20521-2420

telephone: [227] 20-73-31-69 or [227] 20-72-39-41

FAX: [227] 20-73-55-60

Flag description: three equal horizontal bands of orange (top), white, and green with a small orange disk centered in the white band; the orange band denotes the drier northern regions of the Sahara; white stands for purity and innocence; green symbolizes hope and the fertile and productive southern and western areas, as well as the Niger River; the orange disc represents the sun and the sacrifices made by the people

note: similar to the flag of India, which has a blue spoked wheel centered in the white band

National symbol(s): zebu; national colors: orange, white, green

National anthem: name: "La Nigerienne" (The Nigerien)

lyrics/music: Maurice Albert THIRIET/Robert JACQUET and Nicolas Abel Francois FRIONNET

note: adopted 1961

ECONOMY

Economy—overview: Niger is a landlocked, sub-Saharan nation, whose economy centers on subsistence crops, livestock, and some of the world's largest uranium deposits. Agriculture contributes nearly 40% of GDP and provides livelihood for most of the population. The UN ranked Niger as the least developed country in the world in 2015 due to multiple factors such as food insecurity, lack of industry, high population growth, a weak educational sector, and few prospects for work outside of subsistence farming and herding.

Since 2011 public debt has increased due to efforts to scale-up public investment, particularly that related to infrastructure. The government relies on foreign donor resources for a large portion of its fiscal budget. The economy in recent years has been hurt by terrorist activity and kidnappings near its uranium mines and by instability in Mali and in the Diffa region of the country; concerns about security have resulted in increased support from regional and international partners on defense. Low uranium prices, demographics, and security expenditures may continue to put pressure on the government's finances.

Future growth may be sustained by exploitation of oil, gold, coal, and other mineral resources. Although Niger has sizable reserves of oil, the profitability of these commodities has been called in to question due to the prolonged drop in oil prices. Food insecurity and drought remain perennial problems for Niger, and the government plans to invest a little more in the agriculture sector, most notably irrigation. Niger's three-year $131 million IMF Extended Credit Facility agreement for years 2012–15 was extended until the end of 2016, although formal private sector investment needed for economic diversification and growth remains a challenge, given the country's limited domestic markets, access to credit, and competitiveness.

GDP (purchasing power parity): $19.05 billion (2015 est.)

$18.32 billion (2014 est.)

$17.11 billion (2013 est.)

note: data are in 2015 US dollars

country comparison to the world: 147

GDP (official exchange rate): $7.151 billion (2015 est.)

GDP—real growth rate: 4% (2015 est.)

7.1% (2014 est.)

5.3% (2013 est.)

country comparison to the world: 65

GDP—per capita (PPP): $1,100 (2015 est.)

$1,100 (2014 est.)

$1,000 (2013 est.)

note: data are in 2015 US dollars

country comparison to the world: 222

Gross national saving: 24.1% of GDP (2015 est.)

24.3% of GDP (2014 est.)

25.2% of GDP (2013 est.)

country comparison to the world: 54

GDP—composition, by end use:

household consumption: 72.1%

government consumption: 7.7%

investment in fixed capital: 38.1%

investment in inventories: 2%

exports of goods and services: 24.2%

imports of goods and services: -44.1% (2015 est.)

GDP—composition, by sector of origin:

agriculture: 37.3%

industry: 18.9%

services: 43.8% (2015 est.)

Agriculture—products: cowpeas, cotton, peanuts, millet, sorghum, cassava (manioc, tapioca), rice; cattle, sheep, goats, camels, donkeys, horses, poultry

Industries: uranium mining, petroleum, cement, brick, soap, textiles, food processing, chemicals, slaughterhouses

Industrial production growth rate: 6.8% (2015 est.)

country comparison to the world: 18

Labor force: 6.3 million (2015 est.)

country comparison to the world: 69

Labor force—by occupation: agriculture: 90%

industry: 6%

services: 4% (1995)

Unemployment rate: 5.1% (2015 est.)

5.1% (2013 est.)

country comparison to the world: 53

Population below poverty line: 63% (1993 est.)

Household income or consumption by percentage share: lowest: 10%: 3.7%

highest: 10%: 28.5% (2007)

Distribution of family income—Gini index: 34 (2007) 50.5 (1995)

country comparison to the world: 99

Budget: revenues: $1.975 billion

expenditures: $2.181 billion (2015 est.)

Taxes and other revenues: 27.7% of GDP (2015 est.)

country comparison to the world: 97

Budget surplus (+) or deficit (–): -2.9% of GDP (2015 est.)

country comparison to the world: 105

Fiscal year: calendar year

Inflation rate (consumer prices): 1% (2015 est.)

-0.9% (2014 est.)

country comparison to the world: 78

Central bank discount rate: 4.25% (31 December 2009)

4.75% (31 December 2008)

country comparison to the world: 93

Commercial bank prime lending rate: 3.5% (31 December 2015 est.)

3.5% (31 December 2014 est.)

country comparison to the world: 165

Stock of narrow money: $1.518 billion (31 December 2015 est.)

$1.657 billion (31 December 2014 est.)

country comparison to the world: 141

Stock of broad money: $2.027 billion (31 December 2015 est.)

$2.047 billion (31 December 2014 est.)

country comparison to the world: 154

Stock of domestic credit: $917.2 million (31 December 2015 est.)

$922.7 million (31 December 2014 est.)

country comparison to the world: 161

Market value of publicly traded shares: $NA

Current account balance: -$1.289 billion (2015 est.)

-$1.318 billion (2014 est.)

country comparison to the world: 131

Exports: $1.378 billion (2015 est.)

$1.469 billion (2014 est.)

country comparison to the world: 152

Exports—commodities: uranium ore, livestock, cowpeas, onions

Exports—partners: France 53.1%, Nigeria 20.3%, China 13.8% (2015)

Imports: $2.168 billion (2015 est.)

$2.158 billion (2014 est.)

country comparison to the world: 159

Imports—commodities: foodstuffs, machinery, vehicles and parts, petroleum, cereals

Imports—partners: France 12%, China 10.4%, Nigeria 9.5%, French Polynesia 9%, Togo 6.1%, Belgium 5.3%, Cote dIvoire 5.3%, US 4.3% (2015)
Debt—external: $2.983 billion (31 December 2014 est.)
$2.656 billion (31 December 2013 est.)
country comparison to the world: 143
Exchange rates: Communaute Financiere Africaine francs (XOF) per US dollar—
580.5 (2015 est.)
494.42 (2014 est.)
494.42 (2013 est.)
510.53 (2012 est.)
471.87 (2011 est.)

ENERGY

Electricity—production: 355 million kWh (2012 est.)
country comparison to the world: 168
Electricity—consumption: 930.2 million kWh (2012 est.)
country comparison to the world: 155
Electricity—exports: 0 kWh (2013 est.)
country comparison to the world: 176
Electricity—imports: 600 million kWh (2012 est.)
country comparison to the world: 74
Electricity—installed generating capacity: 134,000 kW (2012 est.)
country comparison to the world: 168
Electricity—from fossil fuels: 100% of total installed capacity (2012 est.)
country comparison to the world: 23
Electricity—from nuclear fuels: 0% of total installed capacity (2012 est.)
country comparison to the world: 152
Electricity—from hydroelectric plants: 0% of total installed capacity (2012 est.)
country comparison to the world: 191
Electricity—from other renewable sources: 0% of total installed capacity (2012 est.)
country comparison to the world: 207
Crude oil—production: 20,000 bbl/day (2014 est.)
country comparison to the world: 73
Crude oil—exports: 20,000 bbl/day (2012 est.)
country comparison to the world: 58
Crude oil—imports: 0 bbl/day (2012 est.)
country comparison to the world: 106
Crude oil—proved reserves: 150 million bbl (July 7,1905 est.)
country comparison to the world: 64
Refined petroleum products—production: 0 bbl/day (2012 est.)
country comparison to the world: 117
Refined petroleum products—consumption: 5,000 bbl/day (2013 est.)
country comparison to the world: 168
Refined petroleum products—exports: 0 bbl/day (2012 est.)
country comparison to the world: 209
Refined petroleum products—imports: 5,136 bbl/day (2012 est.)
country comparison to the world: 159
Natural gas—production: 0 cu m (2013 est.)
country comparison to the world: 110
Natural gas—consumption: 0 cu m (2013 est.)

country comparison to the world: 178
Natural gas—exports: 0 cu m (2013 est.)
country comparison to the world: 154
Natural gas—imports: 0 cu m (2013 est.)
country comparison to the world: 108
Natural gas—proved reserves: 0 cu m (1 January 2014 est.)
country comparison to the world: 177
Carbon dioxide emissions from consumption of energy: 1.411 million Mt (2012 est.)
country comparison to the world: 159

COMMUNICATIONS

Telephones—fixed lines: *total subscriptions:* 110,000
subscriptions per 100 inhabitants: 1 (2014 est.)
country comparison to the world: 142
Telephones—mobile cellular: *total:* 8.2 million
subscriptions per 100 inhabitants: 47 (2014 est.)
country comparison to the world: 95
Telephone system: *general assessment:* inadequate; small system of wire, radio telephone communications, and microwave radio relay links concentrated in southwestern Niger
domestic: combined fixed-line and mobile-cellular teledensity remains only about 39 per 100 persons despite a rapidly increasing cellular subscribership base; domestic satellite system with 3 earth stations and 1 planned
international: country code—227; satellite earth stations—2 Intelsat (1 Atlantic Ocean and 1 Indian Ocean) (2015)
Broadcast media: state-run TV station; 3 private TV stations provide a mix of local and foreign programming; state-run radio has only radio station with national coverage; about 30 private radio stations operate locally; as many as 100 community radio stations broadcast; transmissions of multiple international broadcasters are available (2007)
Radio broadcast stations: AM 5, FM 6, shortwave 4 (2001)
Television broadcast stations: 5 (2007)
Internet country code: .ne
Internet hosts: 454 (2012)
country comparison to the world: 185
Internet users: *total:* 281,200
percent of population: 1.6% (2014 est.)
country comparison to the world: 145

TRANSPORTATION

Airports: 30 (2013)
country comparison to the world: 115
Airports—with paved runways: *total:* 10
2,438 to 3,047 m: 3
1,524 to 2, 437 m: 6
914 to 1,523 m: 1 (2013)
Airports—with unpaved runways: *total:* 20
1,524 to 2,437 m: 3
914 to 1,523 m: 15
under 914 m: 2 (2013)
Heliports: 1 (2013)
Road ways: *total:* 18,949 km
paved: 3,912 km
unpaved: 15,037 km (2010)
country comparison to the world: 114

Waterways: 300 km (the Niger, the only major river, is navigable to Gaya between September and March) (2012)
country comparison to the world: 93

MILITARY AND SECURITY

Military branches: Nigerien Armed Forces (Forces Armees Nigeriennes, FAN): Army, Nigerien Air Force (Force Aerienne du Niger) (2012)
Military service age and obligation: 18 is the presumed legal minimum age for compulsory or voluntary military service; enlistees must be Nigerien citizens and unmarried; 2-year service term; women may serve in health care (2012)
Military expenditures: 1.06% of GDP (2012)
NA% (2011)
1.06% of GDP (2010)
country comparison to the world: 95

TRANSNATIONAL ISSUES

Disputes—international: Libya claims about 25,000 sq km in a currently dormant dispute in the Tommo region; location of Benin-Niger-Nigeria tripoint is unresolved; only Nigeria and Cameroon have heeded the Lake Chad Commission's admonition to ratify the delimitation treaty that also includes the Chad-Niger and Niger-Nigeria boundaries; the dispute with Burkina Faso was referred to the ICJ in 2010
Refugees and internally displaced persons: *refugees (country of origin):* 97,744 (Nigeria) (2015); 60,574 (Mali) (2016)
IDPs: 137,337 (unknown how many of the 11,000 people displaced by clashes between government forces and the Tuareg militant group, Niger Movem ent for Justice, in 2007 are still displaced; inter-communal violence; Boko Haram attacks in southern Niger, 2015) (2015)

NIGERIA

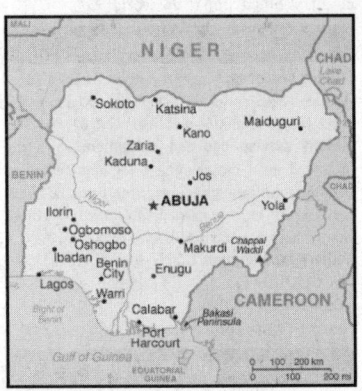

INTRODUCTION

Background: British influence and control over what would become Nigeria and Africa's most populous country grew through the 19th century. A series of constitutions after World War II granted Nigeria greater autonomy. After independence in 1960, politics were marked by coups and mostly military rule, until the death of a military head of state in 1998 allowed for a political transition. In 1999, a new constitution was adopted and a peaceful transition to civilian government was completed. The government continues to face the daunting task of institutionalizing democracy and reforming a petroleum-based economy, whose revenues have been squandered through corruption and mismanagement. in addition, Nigeria continues to experience longstanding ethnic and religious tensions. Although both the 2003 and 2007 presidential elections were marred by significant irregularities and violence, Nigeria is currently experiencing its longest period of civilian rule since independence. The general elections of April 2007 marked the first civilian-to-civilian transfer of power in the country's history and the elections of 2011 were generally regarded as credible. The 2015 election is considered the most well run in Nigeria since the return to civilian rule, with the umbrella opposition party, the All Progressives Congress, defeating the long-ruling Peoples Democratic Party that had governed since 1999.

GEOGRAPHY

Location: Western Africa, bordering the Gulf of Guinea, between Benin and Cameroon
Geographic coordinates: 10 00 N, 8 00 E
Map references: Africa
Area: total: 923,768 sq km
land: 910,768 sq km
water: 13,000 sq km
country comparison to the world: 32

Area—comparative: about six times the size of Georgia; slightly more than twice the size of California
Land boundaries: total: 4,477 km
border countries (4): Benin 809 km, Cameroon 1975 km, Chad 85 km, Niger 1,608 km
Coastline: 853 km
Maritime claims: territorial sea: 12 nm
exclusive economic zone: 200 nm
continental shelf: 200-m depth or to the depth of exploitation
Climate: varies; equatorial in south, tropical in center, arid in north
Terrain: southern lowlands merge into central hills and plateaus; mountains in southeast, plains in north
Elevation: mean elevation: 380 m
elevation extremes: lowest point: Atlantic Ocean 0 m
highest point: Chappal Waddi 2,419 m
Natural resources: natural gas, petroleum, tin, iron ore, coal, limestone, niobium, lead, zinc, arable land
Land use: agricultural land: 78%
arable land: 37.3%
permanent crops: 7.4%
permanent pasture: 33.3%
forest: 9.5%
other: 12.5% (2011 est.)
Irrigated land: 2,930 sq km (2012)
Total renewable water resources: 286.2 cu km (2011)
Freshwater withdrawal (domestic/industrial/agricultural): total: 13.11 cu km/yr (31%/15%/54%)
per capita: 89.21 cu m/yr (2005)
Natural hazards: periodic droughts; flooding
Environment—current issues: soil degradation; rapid deforestation; urban air and water pollution; desertification; oil pollution—water, air, and soil; has suffered serious damage from oil spills; loss of arable land; rapid urbanization
Environment—international agreements: party to: Biodiversity, Climate Change, Climate Change-Kyoto Protocol, Desertification, Endangered Species, Hazardous Wastes, Law of the Sea, Marine Dumping, Marine Life Conservation, Ozone Layer Protection, Ship Pollution, Wetlands
signed, but not ratified: none of the selected agreements
Geography—note: the Niger River enters the country in the northwest and flows southward through tropical rain forests and swamps to its delta in the Gulf of Guinea

PEOPLE AND SOCIETY

Nationality: noun: Nigerian(s)
adjective: Nigerian
Ethnic groups: Nigeria, Africa's most populous country, is composed of more than 250 ethnic groups; the most populous and politically influential are: Hausa and the Fulani 29%, Yoruba 21%, Igbo (Ibo) 18%, Ijaw 10%, Kanuri 4%, Ibibio 3.5%, Tiv 2.5%
Languages: English (official), Hausa, Yoruba, Igbo (Ibo), Fulani, over 500 additional indigenous languages
Religions: Muslim 50%, Christian 40%, indigenous beliefs 10%
Population: 181,562,056
note: estimates for this country explicitly take into account the effects of excess mortality due to AIDS; this can result in lower life expectancy, higher infant mortality, higher death rates, lower population growth rates, and changes in the distribution of population by age and sex than would otherwise be expected (July 2015 est.)
country comparison to the world: 8
Age structure: 0–14 years: 43.01% (male 39,960,275/female 38,123,266)
15–24 years: 19.38% (male 17,978,154/female 17,210,308)
25–54 years: 30.56% (male 28,470,583/female 27,018,101)
55–64 years: 3.94% (male 3,491,784/female 3,669,348)
65 years and over: 3.11% (male 2,687,373/female 2,952,864) (2015 est.)
Dependency ratios: total dependency ratio: 87.7%
youth dependency ratio: 82.6%
elderly dependency ratio: 5.1%
potential support ratio: 19.5% (2015 est.)
Median age: total: 18.2 years
male: 18.2 years
female: 18.3 years (2015 est.)
country comparison to the world: 211
Population growth rate: 2.45% (2015 est.)
country comparison to the world: 27
Birth rate: 37.64 births/1,000 population (2015 est.)
country comparison to the world: 12
Death rate: 12.9 deaths/1,000 population (2015 est.)
country comparison to the world: 18
Net migration rate: -0.22 migrant(s)/1,000 population (2015 est.)
country comparison to the world: 121
Urbanization: urban popu lation: 47.8% of total population (2015)
rate of urbanization: 4.66% annual rate of change (2010–15 est.)
Major urban areas—population: Lagos 13.123 million; Kano 3.587 million; Ibadan 3.16 million; ABUJA (capital) 2.44 million; Port Harcourt 2.343 million; Benin City 1.496 million (2015)
Sex ratio: at birth: 1.06 male(s)/female
0–14 years: 1.05 male(s)/female
15–24 years: 1.05 male(s)/female
25–54 years: 1.05 male(s)/female
55–64 years: 0.95 male(s)/female
65 years and over: 0.91 male(s)/female
total population: 1.04 male(s)/female (2015 est.)
Mother's mean age at first birth: 20.3

note: median age at first birth among women 25–29 (2013 est.)

Maternal mortality rate: 814 deaths/100,000 live births (2015 est.)

country comparison to the world: 11

Infant mortality rate: *total:* 72.7 deaths/1,000 live births

male: 77.55 deaths/1,000 live births

female: 67.55 deaths/1,000 live births (2015 est.)

country comparison to the world: 10

Life expectancy at birth: *total population:* 53.02 years

male: 52 years

female: 54.1 years (2015 est.)

country comparison to the world: 213

Total fertility rate: 5.19 children born/woman (2015 est.)

country comparison to the world: 13

Contraceptive prevalence rate: 15.1% (2013)

Health expenditures: 3.9% of GDP (2013)

country comparison to the world: 109

Physicians density: 0.41 physicians/1,000 population (2009)

Drinking water source:

improved:

urban: 80.8% of population

rural: 57.3% of population

total: 68.5% of population

unimproved:

urban: 19.2% of population

rural: 42.7% of population

total: 31.5% of population (2015 est.)

Sanitation facility access:

improved:

urban: 32.8% of population

rural: 25.4% of population

total: 29% of population

unimproved:

urban: 67.2% of population

rural: 74.6% of population

total: 71% of population (2015 est.)

HIV/AIDS—adult prevalence rate: 3.17% (2014 est.)

country comparison to the world: 20

HIV/AIDS—people living with HIV/AIDS: 3,391,600 (2014 est.)

country comparison to the world: 2

HIV/AIDS—deaths: 174,300 (2014 est.)

country comparison to the world: 1

Major infectious diseases: *degree of risk:* very high

food or waterborne diseases: bacterial and protozoal diarrhea, hepatitis A and E, and typhoid fever

vectorborne diseases: malaria, dengue fever, and yellow fever

water contact diseases: leptospirosis and schistosomiasis

respiratory disease: meningococcal meningitis

aerosolized dust or soil contact disease: one of the most highly endemic areas for Lassa fever

animal contact disease: rabies

note: highly pathogenic H5N1 avian influenza has been identified in this country; it poses a negligible risk with extremely rare cases possible among US citizens who have close contact with birds (2013)

Obesity—adult prevalence rate: 9.7% (2014)

country comparison to the world: 146

Children under the age of 5 years underweight: 19.8% (2014)

country comparison to the world: 12

Education expenditures: NA

Literacy: *definition:* age 15 and over can read and write

total population: 59.6%

male: 69.2%

female: 49.7% (2015 est.)

Child labor—children ages 5–14: *total number:* 11,396,823

percentage: 29% (2007 est.)

GOVERNMENT

Country name: *conventional long form:* Federal Republic of Nigeria

conventional short form: Nigeria

etymology: named for the Niger River that flows through the west of the country to the Atlantic Ocean; from a native term "Ni Gir" meaning "River Gir"

Government type: federal presidential republic

Capital: *name:* Abuja

Geographic coordinates: 9 05 N, 7 32 E

time difference: UTC + 1 (6 hours ahead of Washington, DC, during Standard Time)

Administrative divisions: 36 states and 1 territory*; Abia, Adamawa, Akwa Ibom, Anambra, Bauchi, Bayelsa, Benue, Borno, Cross River, Delta, Ebonyi, Edo, Ekiti, Enugu, Federal Capital Territory*, Gombe, Imo, Jigawa, Kaduna, Kano, Katsina, Kebbi, Kogi, Kwara, Lagos, Nasarawa, Niger, Ogun, Ondo, Osun, Oyo, Plateau, Rivers, Sokoto, Taraba, Yobe, Zamfara

Independence: 1 October 1960 (from the UK)

National holiday: Independence Day (National Day), 1 October (1960)

Constitution: several previous; latest adopted 5 May 1999, effective 29 May 1999; amended several times, last in 2012 (2016)

Legal system: mixed legal system of English common law, Islamic law (in 12 northern states), and traditional law

International law organization participation: accepts compulsory ICJ jurisdiction with reservations; accepts ICCt jurisdiction

Citizenship: *citizenship by birth:* no

citizenship by descent only: at least one parent must be a citizen of Nigeria

dual citizenship recognized: yes

residency requirement for naturalization: 15 years

Suffrage: 18 years of age; universal

Executive branch: *chief of state:* President Maj. Gen. (ret.) Muhammadu BUHARI (since 29 May 2015); Vice President Oluyemi "Yemi" OSINBAJO (since 29 May 2015); note—the president is both chief of state and head of government

head of government: President Maj.Gen. (ret.) Muhammadu BUHARI (since 29 May 2015); Vice President Oluyemi "Yemi" OSINBAJO (since 29 May 2015)

cabinet: Federal Executive Council appointed by the president

elections/appointments: president directly elected by 'qualified' majority popular vote and at least 25% of the votes cast in 24 of Nigeria's 36 states; president elected for a 4-year term (eligible for a second term); election last held on 28–29 March 2015 (next to be held in February 2019)

election results: Muhammadu BUHARI elected president; percent of vote—Muhammadu BUHARI (CPC) 53%, Goodluck JONATHAN (PDP) 46%, other 1%

Legislative branch: *description:* bicameral National Assembly consists of the Senate (109 seats—3 each for the 36 states and 1 for Abuja; members directly elected in single-seat constituencies by simple majority vote to serve 4-year terms) and the House of Representatives (360 seats; members directly elected in single-seat constituencies by simple majority vote to serve 4-year terms)

elections: Senate—last held on 28–29 March 2015 (next to be held in February 2019); House of Representatives—last held on 28–29 March 2015 (next to be held in 2019)

election results: Senate—percent of vote by party—NA; seats by party—APC 60, PDP 49; House of Representatives—percent of vote by party—NA; seats by party—APC 225, PDP 125, other 10

Judicial branch: *highest court(s):* Supreme Court (consists of the chief justice and 15 justices)

judge selection and term of office: judges appointed by the president on the recommendation of the National Judicial Council, a 23-member independent body of federal and state judicial officials; judge appointments confirmed by the Senate; judges serve until age 65

subordinate courts: Court of Appeal; Federal High Court; High Court of the Federal Capital Territory; Sharia Court of Appeal of the Federal Capital Territory; Customary Court of Appeal of the Federal Capital Territory; state court system similar in structure to federal system

Political parties and leaders: Accord Party or ACC [Mohammad Lawal MALADO]

All Progressives Congress or APC [John Odigie OYEGUN]

All Progressives Grand Alliance or APGA [Victor C. UMEH]

Democratic Peoples Party or DPP [Biodun OGUNBIYI]

Labor Party or LP [Alhai Abdulkadir ABDULSALAM]

Peoples Democratic Party or PDP [Uche SECONDUS, acting]

Political pressure groups and leaders: Academic Staff Union for Universities or ASUU

Campaign for Democracy or CD

Civil Liberties Organization or CLO

Committee for the Defense of Human Rights or CDHR

Constitutional Right Project or CRP

Human Right Africa

National Association of Democratic Lawyers or NADL

National Association of Nigerian Students or NANS

Nigerian Bar Association or NBA

Nigerian Labor Congress or NLC
Nigerian Medical Association or NMA
Universal Defenders of Democracy or UDD
other: the press
International organization participation: ACP,
AfDB, AU, C, CD, D-8, ECOWAS, EITI (com-
pliant country), FAO, G-15, G-24, G-77, IAEA,
IBRD, ICAO, ICC (national committees), ICCt,
ICRM, ID A, IDB, IFAD, IFC, IFRCS, IHO, ILO,
IMF, IMO, IMSO, Interpol, IOC, IOM, IPU, ISO,
ITSO, ITU, ITUC (NGOs), MIGA, MINURSO,
MINUSMA, MONUSCO, NAM, OAS
(observer), OIC, OPCW, OPEC, PCA, UN, UN
Security Council (temporary), UNAMID, UNC-
TAD, UNESCO, UNHCR, UNIDO, UNIFIL,
UNISFA, UNITAR, UNMIL, UNMISS, UNOCI,
UNWTO, UPU, WCO, WFTU (NGOs), WHO,
WIPO, WMO, WTO
Diplomatic representation in the US: *chief of
mission:* Ambassador (vacant); Charge d'Affaires
Hakeem Toyin BALOGUN (since 27 August
2015)
chancery: 3519 International Court NW, Wash-
ington, DC 20008
telephone: [1] (202) 986-8400
FAX: [1] (202) 362-6541
consulate(s) general: Atlanta, New York
Diplomatic representation from the US: *chief
of mission:* Ambassador James F. ENTWISTLE
(since 26 November 2013)
embassy: Plot 1075 Diplomatic Drive, Central
District Area, Abuja
mailing address: P.O. Box 5760, Garki, Abuja
telephone: [234] (9) 461-4000
FAX: [234] (9) 461-4171
Flag description: three equal vertical bands of
green (hoist side), white, and green; the color
green represents the forests and abundant natural
wealth of the country, white stands for peace and
unity
National symbol(s): eagle; national colors: green,
white
National anthem: *name:* "Arise Oh Compatriots,
Nigeria's Call Obey"
lyrics/music: John A. ILECHUKWU, Eme Etim
AKPAN, B. A. OGUNNAIKE, Sotu OMOIGUI
and P.O. ADERIBIG BE/Benedict Elide ODIASE
note: adopted 1978; lyrics are a mixture of the five
top entries in a national contest

ECONOMY

Economy—overview: Following an April 2014
statistical "rebasing" exercise, Nigeria has emerged
as Africa's largest economy, with 2015 GDP estimated at $1.1 trillion. Oil has been a dominant
source of income and government revenues since
the 1970s. Following the 2008–9 global financial
crises, the banking sector was effectively recapital-
ized and regulation enhanced. Nigeria's economic
growth over the last five years has been driven
by growth in agriculture, telecommunications,
and services. Economic diversification and strong
growth have not translated into a significant
decline in poverty levels, however—over 62% of
Nigeria's 170 million people still live in extreme
poverty.

Despite its strong fundamentals, oil-rich Nigeria
has been hobbled by inadequate power supply, lack
of infrastructure, delays in the passage of legislative
reforms, an inefficient property registration system,
restrictive trade policies, an inconsistent regulatory environment, a slow and ineffective judicial
system, unreliable dispute resolution mechanisms,
insecurity, and pervasive corruption. Regulatory
constraints and security risks have limited new
investment in oil and natural gas, and Nigeria's oil
production has contracted every year since 2012.
Because of lower oil prices, GDP growth in 2015
fell to around 3%, and government revenues
declined, while the nonoil sector also contracted
due to economic policy uncertainty. President BU
HARI, elected in March 2015, has established a
cabinet of economic ministers that includes several technocrats, and he has announced plans
to increase transparency, diversify the economy
away from oil, and improve fiscal management.
The government is working to develop stronger
public-private partnerships for roads, agriculture,
and power. The medium-term outlook for Nigeria
is positive, assuming oil output stabilizes and oil
prices recover
GDP (purchasing power parity): $1.092 trillion
(2015 est.)
$1.063 trillion (2014 est.)
$1 trillion (2013 est.)
note: data are in 2015 US dollars
country comparison to the world: 23
GDP (official exchange rate): $490.2 billion (2015
est.)
GDP—real growth rate: 2.7% (2015 est.)
6.3% (2014 est.)
5.4% (2013 est.)
country comparison to the world: 112
GDP—per capita (PPP): $6,100 (2015 est.)
$6,100 (2014 est.)
$5,900 (2013 est.)
note: data are in 2015 US dollars
country comparison to the world: 159
Gross national saving: 12% of GDP (2015 est.)
16% of GDP (2014 est.)
18.8% of GDP (2013 est.)
country comparison to the world: 140
GDP—composition, by end use:
household consumption: 74.1%
government consumption: 7.7%
investment in fixed capital: 16.8%
investment in inventories: 0%
exports of goods and services: 13%
imports of goods and services: -11.6% (2015 est.)
GDP—composition, by sector of origin:
agriculture: 20.3%
industry: 23.6%
services: 56.1% (2015 est.)
Agriculture—products: cocoa, peanuts, cotton,
palm oil, corn, rice, sorghum, millet, cassava
(manioc, tapioca), yams, rubber; cattle, sheep,
goats, pigs; timber; fish
Industries: crude oil, coal, tin, columbite; rubber
products, wood; hides and skins, textiles, cement
and other construction materials, food products,
footwear, chemicals, fertilizer, printing, ceramics,
steel

Industrial production growth rate: -2.6% (2015
est.)
country comparison to the world: 182
Labor force: 57.46 million (2015 est.)
country comparison to the world: 11
Labor force—by occupation: *agriculture:* 70%
industry: 10%
services: 20% (1999 est.)
Unemployment rate: 23.9% (2011 est.)
4.9% (2007 est.)
country comparison to the world: 176
Population below poverty line: 70% (2010 est.)
**Household income or consumption by percentage
share:** *lowest:* 10%: 1.8%
highest: 10%: 38.2% (2010 est.)
Distribution of family income—Gini index: 43.7
(2003) 50.6 (1997)
country comparison to the world: 48
Budget: *revenues:* $14.37 billion
expenditures: $21.29 billion (2015 est.)
Taxes and other revenues: 2.9% of GDP (2015
est.)
country comparison to the world: 218
Budget surplus (+) or deficit (–): -1.4% of GDP
(2015 est.)
country comparison to the world: 60
Public debt: 11.7% of GDP (2015 est.)
10.8% of GDP (2014 est.)
country comparison to the world: 165
Fiscal year: calendar year
Inflation rate (consumer prices): 9% (2015 est.)
8% (2014 est.)
country comparison to the world: 205
Central bank discount rate: 4.25% (31 December
2010)
6% (31 December 2009)
country comparison to the world: 94
Commercial bank prime lending rate: 17.3% (31
December 2015 est.)
16.55% (31 December 2014 est.)
country comparison to the world: 24
Stock of narrow money: $29.91 billion (31 Decem-
ber 2015 est.)
$40.69 billion (31 December 2014 est.)
country comparison to the world: 61
Stock of broad money: $89.5 billion (31 December
2015 est.)
$111.5 billion (31 December 2014 est.)
country comparison to the world: 58
Stock of domestic credit: $95.79 billion (31
December 2015 est.)
$115 billion (31 December 2014 est.)
country comparison to the world: 55
Market value of publicly traded shares:
$56.39 billion (31 December 2012 est.)
$39.27 billion (31 December 2011)
$50.88 billion (31 December 2010 est.)
country comparison to the world: 50
Current account balance: -$11.92 billion (2015
est.)
$1.279 billion (2014 est.)
country comparison to the world: 179
Exports: $50.74 billion (2015 est.)
$82.59 billion (2014 est.)
country comparison to the world: 52

Exports—commodities: petroleum and petroleum products 95%, cocoa, rubber (2012 est.)

Exports—partners: India 18.2%, Netherlands 8.5%, Spain 8.2%, Brazil 8.2%, South Africa 7.8%, France 5.2%, Japan 4.5%, Cote dIvoire 4.2%, Ghana 4% (2015)

Imports: $48.41 billion (2015 est.)
$61.59 billion (2014 est.)
country comparison to the world: 51

Imports—commodities: machinery, chemicals, transport equipment, manufactured goods, food and live animals

Imports—partners: China 25.7%, US 6.4%, Netherlands 6.1%, India 4.3% (2015)

Reserves of foreign exchange and gold: $28.76 billion (31 December 2015 est.)
$36.9 billion (31 December 2014 est.)
country comparison to the world: 51

Debt—external: $20.93 billion (31 December 2014 est.)
$18.67 billion (31 December 2013 est.)
country comparison to the world: 86

Stock of direct foreign investment—at home: $95.57 billion (31 December 2015 est.)
$92.75 billion (31 December 2014 est.)
country comparison to the world: 47

Stock of direct foreign investment—abroad: $12.5 billion (31 December 2015 est.)
$10.98 billion (31 December 2014 est.)
country comparison to the world: 57

Exchange rates: nairas (NGN) per US dollar—
196.9 (2015 est.)
158.55 (2014 est.)
158.55 (2013 est.)
156.81 (2012 est.)
154.7 (2011 est.)

ENERGY

Electricity—production: 27.27 billion kWh (2012 est.)
country comparison to the world: 66

Electricity—consumption: 24.78 billion kWh (2012 est.)
country comparison to the world: 67

Electricity—exports: 0 kWh (2013 est.)
country comparison to the world: 178

Electricity—imports: 0 kWh (2013 est.)
country comparison to the world: 183

Electricity—installed generating capacity: 6.09 million kW (2012 est.)
country comparison to the world: 71

Electricity—from fossil fuels: 65% of total installed capacity (2012 est.)
country comparison to the world: 120

Electricity—from nuclear fuels: 0% of total installed capacity (2012 est.)
country comparison to the world: 154

Electricity—from hydroelectric plants: 33.5% of total installed capacity (2012 est.)
country comparison to the world: 67

Electricity—from other renewable sources: 1.5% of total installed capacity (2012 est.)
country comparison to the world: 88

Crude oil—production: 2.423 million bbl/day (2014 est.)
country comparison to the world: 12

Crude oil—exports: 2.411 million bbl/day (2012 est.)
country comparison to the world: 5

Crude oil—imports: 0 bbl/day (2012 est.)
country comparison to the world: 108

Crude oil—proved reserves: 37.07 billion bbl (1 January 2015 est.)
country comparison to the world: 10

Refined petroleum products—production: 101900 bbl/day (2012 est.)
country comparison to the world: 73

Refined petroleum products—consumption: 280,000 bbl/day (2013 est.)
country comparison to the world: 45

Refined petroleum products—exports: 16,120 bbl/day (2012 est.)
country comparison to the world: 76

Refined petroleum products—imports: 180,900 bbl/day (2012 est.)
country comparison to the world: 31

Natural gas—production: 38.41 billion cu m (2013 est.)
country comparison to the world: 24

Natural gas—consumption: 15.69 billion cu m (2013 est.)
country comparison to the world: 44

Natural gas—exports: 22.12 billion cu m (2013 est.)
country comparison to the world: 13

Natural gas—imports: 0 cu m (2013 est.)
country comparison to the world: 110

Natural gas—proved reserves: 5.118 trillion cu m (1 January 2014 est.)
country comparison to the world: 9

Carbon dioxide emissions from consumption of energy: 86.4 million Mt (2012 est.)
country comparison to the world: 43

COMMUNICATIONS

Telephones—fixed lines: *total subscriptions:* 180,000
subscriptions per 100 inhabitants: 10 (2014 est.)
country comparison to the world: 130

Telephones—mobile cellular: *total:* 139 million
su bscriptions per 100 inhabitants: 78 (2014 est.)
country comparison to the world: 9

Telephone system: *general assessment:* further expansion and modernization of the fixed-line telephone network is needed; network quality remains a problem
domestic: the addition of a second fixed-line provider in 2002 resulted in faster growth, but subscribership remains only about 1 per 100 persons; mobile-cellular services growing rapidly, in part responding to the shortcomings of the fixed-line network; multiple cellular providers operate nationally with subscribership base approaching 60 per 100 persons
international: country code—234; landing point for the SAT-3/WASC fiber-optic submarine cable that provides connectivity to Europe and Asia; satellite earth stations—3 Intelsat (2 Atlantic Ocean and 1 Indian Ocean) (2010)

Broadcast media: nearly 70 federal government-controlled national and regional TV stations; all 36 states operate TV stations; several private TV stations operational; cable and satellite TV subscription services are available; network of federal government-controlled national, regional, and state radio stations; roughly 40 state government-owned radio stations typically carry their own programs except for news broadcasts; about 20 private radio stations; transmissions of international broadcasters are available (2007)

Radio broadcast stations: AM 83, FM 36, shortwave 11 (2001)

Television broadcast stations: 3 (the government controls 2 of the broadcasting stations and 15 repeater stations) (2001)

Internet country code: .ng

Internet hosts: 1,234 (2012)
country comparison to the world: 169

Internet users: *total:* 97 million
percent of population: 53.4% (2015 est.)
country comparison to the world: 9

TRANSPORTATION

Airports: 54 (2013)
country comparison to the world: 88

Airports—with paved runways: *total:* 40
over 3,047 m: 10
2,438 to 3,047 m: 12
1,524 to 2,437 m: 9
914 to 1,523 m: 6
under 914 m: 3 (2013)

Airports—with unpaved runways: *total:* 14
1,524 to 2,437 m: 2
914 to 1,523 m: 9
under 914 m: 3 (2013)

Heliports: 5 (2013)

Pipelines: condensate 124 km; gas 4,045 km; liquid petroleum gas 164 km; oil 4,441 km; refined products 3,940 km (2013)

Railways: *total:* 3,798 km
standard gauge: 293 km 1.435-m gauge
narrow gauge: 3,505 km 1.067-m gauge (2014)
country comparison to the world: 47

Roadways: *total:* 193,200 km
paved: 28,980 km
unpaved: 164,220 km (2004)
country comparison to the world: 27

Waterways: 8,600 km (Niger and Benue Rivers and smaller rivers and creeks) (2011)
country comparison to the world: 15

Merchant marine: *total:* 89
by type: cargo 2, chemical tanker 28, liquefied gas 1, passenger/cargo 1, petroleum tanker 56, specialized tanker 1
foreign-owned: 3 (India 1, UK 2)
registered in other countries: 33 (Bahamas 2, Bermuda 11, Comoros 1, Italy 1, Liberia 4, North Korea 1, Panama 6, Seychelles 1, unknown 6) (2010)
country comparison to the world: 54

Ports and terminals: *major seaport(s):* Bonny Inshore Terminal, Calabar, Lagos
LNG terminal(s) (export): Bonn y Island

Transportation—note: the International Maritime Bureau reports the territorial and offshore waters in the Niger Delta and Gulf of Guinea as high risk

631

for piracy and armed robbery of ships; in 2014,18 commercial vessels were boarded or attacked compared with 31 attacks in 2013; crews were robbed and stores or cargoes stolen; Nigerian pirates have extended the range of their attacks to as far away as Cote d'Ivoire

MILITARY AND SECURITY

Military branches: Nigerian Armed Forces: Army, Navy, Air Force (2013)

Military service age and obligation: 18 years of age for voluntary military service; no conscription (2012)

Military expenditures:
0.89% of GDP (2012)
0.98% of GDP (2011)
0.89% of GDP (2010)
country comparison to the world: 108

TRANSNATIONAL ISSUES

Disputes—international: Joint Border Commission with Cameroon reviewed 2002 ICJ ruling on the entire boundary and bilaterally resolved differences, including June 2006 Greentree

Agreement that immediately cedes sovereignty of the Bakassi Peninsula to Cameroon with a phaseout of Nigerian control within two years while resolving patriation issues; the ICJ ruled on an equidistance settlement of Cameroon-Equatorial Guinea-Nigeria maritime boundary in the Gulf of Guinea, but imprecisely defined coordinates in the ICJ decision and a sovereignty dispute between Equatorial Guinea and Cameroon over an island at the mouth of the Ntem River all contribute to the delay in implementation; only Nigeria and Cameroon have heeded the Lake Chad Commission's admonition to ratify the delimitation treaty which also includes the Chad-Niger and Niger-Nigeria boundaries; location of Benin-Niger-Nigeria tripoint is unresolved

Refugees and internally displaced persons: *IDPs:* 2,241,484 (Boko Haram attacks and counterinsurgency efforts in northern Nigeria; communal violence between Christians and Muslims in the middle belt region, political violence; flooding; forced evictions; cattle rustling; competition for resources) (2016)

Illicit drugs: a transit point for heroin and cocaine intended for European, East Asian, and North American markets; consumer of amphetamines; safe haven for Nigerian narcotraffickers operating worldwide; major money-laundering center; massive corruption and criminal activity; Nigeria has improved some anti-money-laundering controls, resulting in its removal from the Financial Action Task Force's (FATF's) Noncooperative Countries and Territories List in June 2006; Nigeria's anti-money-laundering regime continues to be monitored by FATF

NIUE

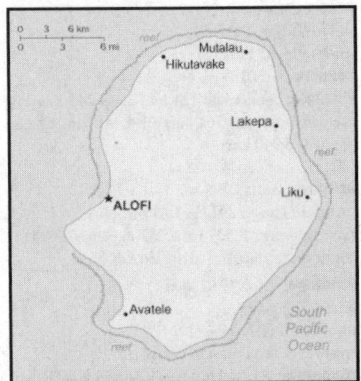

INTRODUCTION

Background: Niue's remoteness, as well as cultural and linguistic differences between its Polynesian inhabitants and those of the adjacent Cook Islands, has caused it to be separately administered by New Zealand. The population of the island continues to drop (from a peak of 5,200 in 1966 to an estimated 1,190 in 2014) with substantial emigration to New Zealand 2,400 km to the southwest.

GEOGRAPHY

Location: Oceania, island in the South Pacific Ocean, east of Tonga

Geographic coordinates: 19 02 S, 169 52 W

Map references: Oceania

Area: *total:* 260 sq km
land: 260 sq km
water: 0 sq km
country comparison to the world: 213

Area—comparative: 1.5 times the size of Washington, DC

Land boundaries: 0 km

Coastline: 64 km

Maritime claims: *territorial sea:* 12 nm
exclusive economic zone: 200 nm

Climate: tropical; modified by southeast trade winds

Terrain: steep limestone cliffs along coast, central plateau

Elevation: *mean elevation:* NA

elevation extremes: *lowest point:* Pacific Ocean 0 m
highest point: unnamed elevation near Mutalau settlement 68 m

Natural resources: fish, arable land

Land use: *agricultural land:* 19.1%
arable land: 3.8%
permanent crops: 11.5%
permanent pasture: 3.8%
forest: 71.2%
other: 9.7% (2011 est.)

Irrigated land: 0 sq km (2012)

Natural hazards: typhoons

Environment—current issues: increasing attention to conservationist practices to counter loss of soil fertility from traditional slash and burn agriculture

Environment—international agreements: *party to:* Biodiversity, Climate Change, Climate Change-Kyoto Protocol, Desertification, Law of the Sea, Ozone Layer Protection

Geography—note: one of world's largest coral islands

PEOPLE AND SOCIETY

Nationality: *noun:* Niuean(s)
adjective: Niuean

Ethnic groups: Niuen 66.5%, part-Niuen 13.4%, non-Niuen 20.1% (includes 12% European and Asian and 8% Pacific Islanders) (2011 est.)

Languages: Niuean (official) 46% (a Polynesian language closely related to Tongan and Samoan), Niuean and English 32%, English (official) 11%, Niuean and others 5%, other 6% (2011 est.)

Religions: Ekalesia Niue (Congregational Christian Church of Niue—a Protestant church founded by missionaries from the London Missionary Society) 67%, other Protestant 3% (includes Seventh Day Adventist 1%, Presbyterian 1%, and Methodist 1%), Mormon 10%, Roman Catholic 10%, Jehovah's Witnesses 2%, other 6%, none 2% (2011 est.)

Population: 1,190 (July 2014 est.)
country comparison to the world: 235

Population growth rate: -0.03% (2014 est.)
country comparison to the world: 202

Urbanization: *urban population:* 42.5% of total population (2015)
rate of urbanization: -0.94% annual rate of change (2010-15 est.)

Major urban areas—population: ALOFI (capital) 1,000 (2014)

Sex ratio: NA

Infant mortality rate: *total:* NA
male: NA
female: NA

Life expectancy at birth: *total population:* NA
male: NA
female: NA
Total fertility rate: NA
Health expenditures: 7.1% of GDP (2013)
country comparison to the world: 87
Physicians density: 3 physicians/1,000 population (2008)
Drinking water source:
improved:
urban: 98.4% of population
rural: 98.6% of population
total: 98.5% of population
unimproved:
urban: 1.6% of population
rural: 1.4% of population
total: 1.5% of population (2015 est.)
Sanitation facility access:
improved:
urban: 100% of population
rural: 100% of population
total: 100% of population
unimproved:
urban: 0% of population
rural: 0% of population
total: 0% of population (2015 est.)
HIV/AIDS—adult prevalence rate: NA
HIV/AIDS—people living with HIV/AIDS: NA
HIV/AIDS—deaths: NA
Obesity—adult prevalence rate: 42.5% (2014)
Education expenditures: NA

GOVERNMENT

Country name: *conventional long form:* none
conventional short form: Niue
note: pronunciation falls between nyu-way and new-way, but not like new-wee
former: Savage Island
etymology: the origin of the name is obscure; in Niuean, the word supposedly translates as "behold the coconut"
Dependency status: self-governing in free association with New Zealand since 1974; Niue fully responsible for internal affairs; New Zealand retains responsibility for external affairs and defense; however, these responsibilities confer no rights of control and are only exercised at the request of the Government of Niue
Government type: self-governing parliamentary democracy (Fouo Ekepule) in free association with New Zealand
Capital: *name:* Alofi
Geographic coordinates: 19 01 S, 169 55 W
time difference: UTC-11 (6 hours behind Washington, DC, during Standard Time)
Administrative divisions: none; note—there are no first-order administrative divisions as defined by the US Government, but there are 14 villages at the second order
Independence: 19 October 1974 (Niue became a self-governing parliamentary government in free association with New Zealand)
National holiday: Waitangi Day (Treaty of Waitangi established British sovereignty over New Zealand), 6 February (1840)

Constitution: several previous (New Zealand colonial statutes); latest 19 October 1974 (Niue Constitution Act 1974); amended 1992, 2007 (2016)
Legal system: English common law
Suffrage: 18 years of age; universal
Executive branch: *chief of state:* Queen ELIZABETH II (since 6 February 1952); represented by Governor General of New Zealand Lt. Gen. Sir Jerry MATEPARAE (since 31 August 2011); the UK and New Zealand are represented by New Zealand High Commissioner Ross ARDEN (since February 2014)
head of government: Premier Toke TALAGI (since 18 June 2008)
cabinet: Cabinet chosen by the premier
elections/appointments: the monarchy is hereditary; premier indirectly elected by the Legislative Assembly for a 3-year term; election last held on 24 April 2014 (next to be held in 2017)
election results: Toke TALAGI reelected premier; Legislative Assembly vote—Toke TALAGI (independent) 12, Stanley KALAUNI 8
Legislative branch: *description:* unicameral Assembly or Fono Ekepule (20 seats; 14 members directly elected in single-seat constituencies by simple majority vote and 6 directly elected from the National Register or "common roll" by majority vote; members serve 3-year terms)
elections: last held on 12 April 2014 (next to be held in 2017)
election results: percent of vote by party—NA; seats by party—20 independents
Judicial branch: *highest resident court(s):* Court of Appeal (consists of the chief justice and up to 3 judges); note—the Judicial Committee of the Privy Council (in London) is the final appeal court beyond the Niue Court of Appeal note—Niue is a participant in the Pacific Judicial Development Program; the program is designed to build governance and the rule of law in 15 Pacific island countries
judge selection and term of office: Niue chief justice appointed by the governor-general on the advice of the Cabinet and tendered by the premier; other judges appointed by the governor-general on the advice of the Cabinet and tendered by the chief justice and the minister of justice; judges serve until age 68
subordinate courts: High Court
Political parties and leaders: Alliance of Independents or AI
Niue People's Action Party or NPP [Young VIVIAN]
Political pressure groups and leaders: NA
International organization participation: ACP, AO SIS, FAO, IFAD, OPCW, PIF, Sparteca, SPC, UNESCO, UPU, WHO, WIPO, WMO
Diplomatic representation in the US: none (self-governing territory in free association with New Zealand)
Diplomatic representation from the US: none (self-governing territory in free association with New Zealand)
Flag description: yellow with the flag of the UK in the upper hoist-side quadrant; the flag of the UK bears five yellow five-pointed stars—a large star on

a blue disk in the center and a smaller star on each arm of the bold red cross; the larger star stands for Niue, the smaller stars recall the Southern Cross constellation on the New Zealand flag and symbolize links with that country; yellow represents the bright sunshine of Niue and the warmth and friendship between Niue and New Zealand
National symbol(s): yellow, five-pointed star; national color: yellow
National anthem: *name:* "Koeiki he Lagi" (The Lord in Heaven)
lyrics/music: unknown/unknown, prepared by Sioeli FUSIKATA
note: adopted 1974

ECONOMY

Economy—overview: The economy suffers from the typical Pacific island problems of geographic isolation, few resources, and a small population. The agricultural sector consists mainly of subsistence gardening, although some cash crops are grown for export. Industry consists primarily of small factories for processing passion fruit, lime oil, honey, and coconut cream. The sale of postage stamps to foreign collectors is an important source of revenue.
Government expenditures regularly exceed revenues, and the shortfall is made up by critically needed grants from New Zealand that are used to pay wages to public employees. Economic aid allocation from New Zealand in FY13/14 was US$10.1 million. Niue has cut government expenditures by reducing the public service by almost half.
The island in recent years has suffered a serious loss of population because of emigration to New Zealand. Efforts to increase GDP include the promotion of tourism and financial services, although the International Banking Repeal Act of 2002 resulted in the termination of all offshore banking licenses.
GDP (purchasing power parity): $10.01 million (2003 est.)
country comparison to the world: 229
GDP (official exchange rate): $10.01 million (2003)
GDP—real growth rate: 6.2% (2003 est.)
country comparison to the world: 27
GDP—per capita (PPP): $5,800 (2003 est.)
country comparison to the world: 162
GDP—composition, by sector of origin:
agriculture: 23.5%
industry: 26.9%
services: 49.5% (2003)
Agriculture—products: coconuts, passion fruit, honey, limes, taro, yams, cassava (manioc, tapioca), sweet potatoes; pigs, poultry, beef cattle
Industries: handicrafts, food processing
Industrial production growth rate: NA%
Labor force: 663 (2001)
country comparison to the world: 231
Labor force—by occupation: *note:* most work on family plantations; paid work exists only in government service, small industry, and the Niue Development Board
Unemployment rate: 12% (2001)
country comparison to the world: 133
Population below poverty line: NA%

Household income or consumption by percentage share: *lowest:* 10%: NA%
highest: 10%: NA%

Budget: *revenues:* $15.07 million
expenditures: $16.33 million (F Y04/05)

Budget surplus (+) or deficit (–): -12.6% of GDP (FY04/05)
country comparison to the world: 209

Fiscal year: 1 April–31 March

Inflation rate (consumer prices): 4% (2005)
country comparison to the world: 159

Exports: $201,400 (2004 est.)
country comparison to the world: 222

Exports—commodities: canned coconut cream, copra, honey, vanilla, passion fruit products, pawpaws, root crops, limes, footballs, stamps, handicrafts

Exports—partners: Germany 25%, Belgium 11%, United Kingdom 8%, France 8%, Italy 4%, United States 4% (2014)

Imports: $9.038 million (2004 est.)
country comparison to the world: 222

Imports—commodities: food, live animals, manufactured goods, mach inery, fuels, lubricants, ch emicals, drugs

Imports—partners: Germany 16%, Belgium 10%, China 9%, United States 7%, United Kingdom 7%, Russia 5%, France 4%, Norway 4% (2014)

Debt—external: $418,000 (2002 est.)
country comparison to the world: 203

Exchange rates: New Zealand dollars (NZD) per US dollar—
1.452 (2015)
1.2187 (2013)
1.2187 (2013)
1.23 (2012)
1.263 (2011)

<!-- -->

ENERGY

Electricity—production: 3 million kWh (2012 est.)
country comparison to the world: 218

Electricity—consumption: 2.79 million kWh (2012 est.)
country comparison to the world: 216

Electricity—exports: 0 kWh (2013 est.)
country comparison to the world: 175

Electricity—imports: 0 kWh (2013 est.)
country comparison to the world: 181

Electricity—installed generating capacity: 1,000 kW (2012 est.)
country comparison to the world: 214

Electricity—from fossil fuels: 100% of total installed capacity (2012 est.)
country comparison to the world: 22

Electricity—from nuclear fuels: 0% of total installed capacity (2012 est.)
country comparison to the world: 151

Electricity—from hydroelectric plants: 0% of total installed capacity (2012 est.)
country comparison to the world: 190

Electricity—from other renewable sources: 0% of total installed capacity (2012 est.)
country comparison to the world: 206

Crude oil—production: 0 bbl/day (2014 est.)
country comparison to the world: 174

Crude oil—Exports: 0 bbl/day (2012 est.)
country comparison to the world: 168

Crude oil—imports: 0 bbl/day (2012 est.)
country comparison to the world: 105

Crude oil—proved reserves: 0 bbl (1 January 2015 est.)
cou ntry comparison to the world: 174

Refined petroleum products—production: 0 bbl/day (2012 est.)
country comparison to the world: 116

Refined petroleum products—consumption: 20 bbl/day (2013 est.)
country comparison to the world: 212

Refined petroleum products—exports: 0 bbl/day (2012 est.)
country comparison to the world: 208

Refined petroleum products—imports: 22.57 bbl/day (2012 est.)
country comparison to the world: 209

Natural gas—production: 0 cu m (2013 est.)
country comparison to the world: 109

Natural gas—consumption: 0 cu m (2013 est.)
country comparison to the world: 177

Natural gas—exports: 0 cu m (2013 est.)
country comparison to the world: 153

Natural gas—imports: 0 cu m (2013 est.)
country comparison to the world: 107

Natural gas—proved reserves: 0 cu m (1 January 2014 est.)
country comparison to the world: 176

Carbon dioxide emissions from consumption of energy: 3,520 Mt (2012 est.)
country comparison to the world: 211

COMMUNICATIONS

Telephone system: *domestic:* single-line telephone system connects all villages on island
international: country code—683 (2001)

Broadcast media: 1 government-owned TV station with many of the programs supplied by Television New Zealand; 1 government-owned radio station broadcasting in AM and FM (2009)

Radio broadcast stations: AM 1, FM 1, shortwave 0 (1998)

Television broad cast stations: 1 (1997)

Internet country code: .nu

Internet hosts: 79,508 (2012)
country comparison to the world: 83

Internet users: *total:* 1,100
percent of population: 92.4% (2014 est.)
country comparison to the world: 213

TRANSPORTATION

Airports: 1 (2013)
country comparison to the world: 228

Airports—with paved runways: *total:* 1
1,524 to 2,437 m: 1 (2012)

Airports—wi th unpaved runways: *total:* 1
1,524 to 2,437 m: 1 (2013)

Roadways: *total:* 120 km
paved: 120 km (2011)
country comparison to the world: 214

Ports and terminals: *major seaport(s):* Alofi

MILITARY AND SECURITY

Military branches: no regular indigenous military forces; Police Force Military—note: defense is the responsibility of New Zealand

TRANSNATIONAL ISSUES

Disputes—international: none

NORFOLK ISLAND

INTRODUCTION

Background: Two British attempts at establishing the island as a penal colony (1788–1814 and 1825–55) were ultimately abandoned. In 1856, the island was resettled by Pitcairn Islanders, descendants of the Bounty mutineers and their Tahitian companions.

GEOGRAPHY

Location: Oceania, island in the South Pacific Ocean, east of Australia

Geographic coordinates: 29 02 S, 167 57 E

Map references: Oceania

Area: *total:* 36 sq km
land: 36 sq km
water: 0 sq km
country comparison to the world: 235

Area—comparative: about 0.2 times the size of Washington, DC

Land boundaries: 0 km

Coastline: 32 km

Maritime claims: *territorial sea:* 12 nm
exclusive fishing zone: 200 nm

Climate: subtropical; mild, little seasonal temperature variation

Terrain: volcanic island with mostly rolling plains

Elevation: *mean elevation:* NA

elevation extremes: *lowest point:* Pacific Ocean 0 m
highest point: Mount Bates 319 m

Natural resources: fish

Land use: *agricultural land:* 25%
arable land: 0%
permanent crops: 0%
permanent pasture: 25%
forest: 11.5%
other: 63.5% (2011 est.)

Irrigated land: 0 sq km (2012)

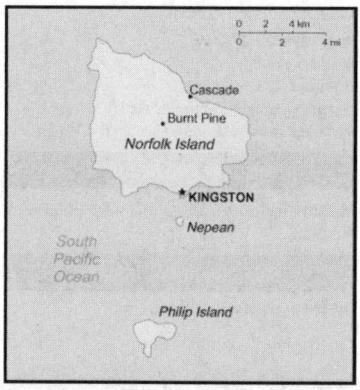

Natural hazards: typhoons (especially May to July)
Environment—current issues: NA
Geography—note: most of the 32 km coastline consists of almost inaccessible cliffs, but the land slopes down to the sea in one small southern area on Sydney Bay, where the capital of Kingston is situated

PEOPLE AND SOCIETY

Nationality: *noun:* Norfolk Islander(s)
adjective: Norfolk Islander(s)
Ethnic groups: Australian 79.5%, New Zealander 13.3%, Fijian 2.5%, Filipino 1.1%, English 1%, other 1.8%, unspecified 0.8% (2011 est.)
Languages: English (official) 67.6%, other 32.4% (includes Norfolk Island 23.7%, which is a mixture of 18th century English and ancient Tahitian) (2011 est.)
Religions: Protestant 49.6% (Anglican 31.8%, Uniting Church in Australia 10.6%, Seventh-Day Adventist 3.2%), Roman Catholic 11.7%, other 8.6%, none 23.5%, unspecified 6.6% (2011 est.)
Population: 2,210 (July 2014 est.)
country comparison to the world: 231
Population growth rate: 0.01% (2014 est.)
country comparison to the world: 194
Sex ratio: NA
Infant mortality rate: *total:* NA
male: NA
female: NA
Life expectancy at birth: *total population:* NA
male: NA
female: NA
Total fertility rate: NA
HIV/AIDS—adult prevalence rate: NA
HIV/AIDS—people living with HIV/AIDS: NA
HIV/AIDS—deaths: NA

GOVERNMENT

Country name: *conventional long form:* Territory of Norfolk Island
conventional short form: Norfolk Island
etymology: named by British explorer Captain James COOK after Mary HOWARD, Duchess of Norfolk, in 1774
Dependency status: self-governing territory of Australia; administered from Canberra by the Department of Regional Australia, Local Government, Arts and Sport
Government type: parliamentary democracy (formerly the Legislative Assembly); overseas territory of Australia; note—in May 2015, the Australian Parliament passed the Norfolk Island Legislation Amendment Bill 2015 which abolished Norfolk Island self-government and replaced it with an interim Advisory Council effective 1 July 2015
Capital: *name:* Kingston
Geographic coordinates: 29 03 S, 167 58 E
time difference: UTC + 11.5 (16.5 hours ahead of Washington, DC, during Standard Time)
Administrative divisions: none (territory of Australia)
Independence: none (territory of Australia)
National holiday: Bounty Day (commemorates the arrival of Pitcairn Islanders), 8 June (1856)
Constitution: previous 1913, 1957; latest effective 7 August 1979; amended many times, last in 2015 (2016)
Legal system: English common law and the laws of Australia
Citizenship: see Australia
Suffrage: 18 years of age; universal
Executive branch: *chief of state:* Queen ELIZABETH II (since 6 February 1952); represented by the Australian governor general
head of government: Administrator Gary HARDGRAVE (since 1 July 2014)
cabinet: Executive Council consists of 4 Legislative Assembly members
elections/appointments: the monarchy is hereditary; governor general appointed by the monarch; administrator appointed by the governor general of Australia for a 2-year term and represents the monarch and Australia
Legislative branch: *description:* unicameral Regional Council (structure to be determined); interim Advisory Council effective 1 July 2015
elections: elections for the new Regional Council will occur in early 2016
election results: interim Advisory Council seats—5 (appointed)
note: following an adminstrative restructuring of local government, the Legislative Assembly was dissolved on 18 June 2015 to be replaced by an interim Norfolk Island Advisory Council effective 1 July 2015; the Advisory Council will consist of 5 members appointed by the Norfolk Island administrator based on nominations from the community; following elections in early 2016, the new Regional Council will commence operations on 1 July 2016
Judicial branch: *highest court(s):* Supreme Court of Norfolk Island (consists of the chief justice and NA justices); note—appeals beyond the Supreme Court of Norfolk Island are heard by the Federal Court of Australia
judge selection and term of office: justices appointed by the governor general of Australia from among justices of the Federal Court of Australia; justices serve until mandatory retirement at age 70
subordinate courts: Petty Court of Sessions; specialized courts including a Coroner's Court and the Employment Tribunal
Political parties and leaders: Norfolk Island Labor Party [Mike KELLY]
Norfolk Liberals [John BROWN]
Political pressure groups and leaders: none
International organization participation: UPU
Diplomatic representation in the US: none (territory of Australia)
Diplomatic representation from the US: none (territory of Australia)
Flag description: three vertical bands of green (hoist side), white, and green with a large green Norfolk Island pine tree centered in the slightly wider white band; green stands for the rich vegetation on the island, and the pine tree—endemic to the island—is a symbol of Norfolk Island
note: somewhat reminiscent of the flag of Canada with its use of only two colors and depiction of a prominent local floral symbol in the central white band; also resembles the green and white triband of Nigeria
National symbol(s): Norfolk Island Pine
National anthem: *name:* "Come Ye Blessed"
lyrics/music: New Testament/John Prindle SCOTT
note: the local anthem, whose lyrics consist of the words from Matthew 25: 34–36, 40, is also known as "The Pitcairn Anthem;" as a territory of Australia, "God Save the Queen" is official (see Australia); however, the island does not recognize "Advance Australia Fair"

ECONOMY

Economy—overview: Norfolk Island is suffering from a severe economic downturn. Tourism, the primary economic activity, is the main driver of economic growth. The agricultural sector has become self-sufficient in the production of beef, poultry, and eggs.
GDP (purchasing power parity): $NA
Agriculture—products: Norfolk Island pine seed, Kentia palm seed, cereals, vegetables, fruit; cattle, poultry
Industries: tourism, light industry, ready mixed concrete
Labor force: 978 (2006)
country comparison to the world: 230
Labor force—by occupation: *agriculture:* 6%
industry: 14%
services: 80% (2006 est.)
Budget: *revenues:* $4.6 million
expenditures: $4.8 million (FY99/00)
Fiscal year: 1 July—30 June
Exports: $NA
Exports—commodities: postage stamps, seeds of the Norfolk Island pine and Kentia palm, small quantities of avocados
Imports: $NA
Imports—commodities: NA
Debt—external: $NA
Exchange rates: Australian dollars (AUD) per US dollar
1.33 (2015)

1.0358 (2013)
1.0358 (2013)
0.97 (2012)
0.9695 (2011)

COMMUNICATIONS

Telephone system: *general assessment:* adequate
domestic: free local calls
international: country code—672; submarine
cable links with Australia and New Zealand; satellite earth station—1
Broadcast media: 1 local radio station; broadcasts
of several Australian radio and TV stations available via satellite (2009)

Radio broadcast stations: AM 1, FM 3, short-wave 0 (2005)
Television broadcast stations: 1 (local programming station plus 2 repeaters that air Australian programs by satellite) (2005)
Internet country code: .nf
Internet hosts: 128 (2012)
country comparison to the world: 204

TRANSPORTATION

Airports: 1 (2013)
country comparison to the world: 229
Airports—with paved runways: *total:* 1

1,524 to 2,437 m: 1 (2013)
Roadways: *total:* 80 km
paved: 53 km
unpaved: 27 km (2008)
country comparison to the world: 217
Ports and terminals: *major seaport(s):* Kingston

MILITARY AND SECURITY

Military—note: defense is the responsibility of
Australia

TRANSNATIONAL ISSUES

Disputes—international: none

NORTHERN MARIANA ISLANDS

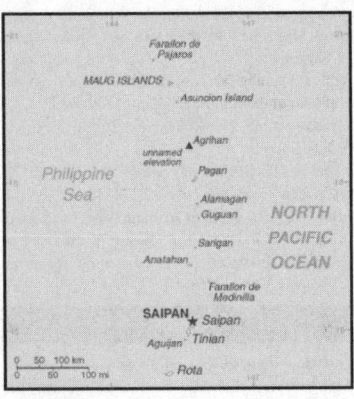

INTRODUCTION

Background: Under US administration as part of
the UN Trust Territory of the Pacific, the people
of the Northern Mariana Islands decided in the
1970s not to seek independence but instead to
forge closer links with the US. Negotiations for
territorial status began in 1972. A covenant to
establish a commonwealth in political union with
the US was approved in 1975, and came into force
on 24 March 1976. A new government and constitution went into effect in 1978.

GEOGRAPHY

Location: Oceania, islands in the North Pacific
Ocean, about three-quarters of the way from
Hawaii to the Philippines
Geographic coordinates: 15 12 N, 145 45 E
Map references: Oceania
Area: *total:* 464 sq km
land: 464 sq km
water: 0 sq km
note: consists of 14 islands including Saipan, Rota,
and Tinian
country comparison to the world: 197
Area—comparative: 2.5 times the size of Washington, DC

Land boundaries: 0 km
Coastline: 1,482 km
Maritime claims: *territorial sea:* 12 nm
exclusive economic zone: 200 nm
Climate: tropical marine; moderated by northeast
trade winds, little seasonal temperature variation;
dry season December to June, rainy season July to
October
Terrain: the southern islands in this north-south
trending archipelago are limestone, with fringing
coral reefs; the northern islands are volcanic, with
active volcanoes on several islands
Elevation: *mean elevation:* NA
elevation extremes: *lowest point:* Pacific Ocean
0 m
highest point: unnamed elevation on Agrihan
965 m
Natural resources: arable land, fish
Land use: *agricultural land:* 6.6%
arable land: 2.2%
permanent crops: 2.2%
permanent pasture: 2.2%
forest: 65.5%
other: 27.9% (2011 est.)
Irrigated land: 1 sq km (2012)
Natural hazards: active volcanoes on Pagan
and Agrihan; typhoons (especially August to
November)
Environment—current issues: contamination of
groundwater on Saipan may contribute to disease;
clean-up of landfill; protection of endangered species conflicts with development
Geography—note: strategic location in the North
Pacific Ocean

PEOPLE AND SOCIETY

Nationality: *noun:* NA (US citizens)
adjective: NA
Ethnic groups: Asian 50% (includes Filipino
35.3%, Chinese 6.8%, Korean 4.2%, and other
Asian 3.7%), Native Hawaiian or other Pacific
Islander 34.9% (includes Chamorro 23.9%, Carolinian 4.6%, and other Native Hawaiian or Pacific
Islander 6.4%), other 2.5%, two or more ethnicities or races 12.7% (2010 est.)

Languages: Philippine languages 32.8%, Chamorro (official) 24.1%, English (official) 17%, other
Pacific island languages 10.1%, Chinese 6.8%,
other Asian languages 7.3%, other 1.9% (2010
est.)
Religions: Christian (Roman Catholic majority,
although traditional beliefs and taboos may still
be found)
Population: 52,344 (July 2015 est.)
country comparison to the world: 209
Age structure: *0–14 years:* 25.6% (male 6,917/
female 6,483)
15–24 years: 14.39% (male 4,216/female 3,317)
25–54 years: 44.3% (male 9,802/female 13,385)
55–64 years: 10.76% (male 3,031/female 2,602)
65 years and over: 4.95% (male 1,240/female
1,351) (2015 est.)
Median age: *total:* 32.1 years
male: 29.6 years
female: 33 years (2015 est.)
country comparison to the world: 93
Population growth rate: 2.18% (2015 est.)
country comparison to the world: 42
Birth rate: 18.32 births/1,000 population (2015
est.)
country comparison to the world: 99
Death rate: 3.71 deaths/1,000 population (2015
est.)
country comparison to the world: 213
Net migration rate: 7.16 migrant(s)/1,000 population (2015 est.)
country comparison to the world: 17
Urbanization: *urban population:* 89.2% of total
population (2015)
rate of urbanization: 0.39% annual rate of
change (2010–15 est.)
Major urban areas—population: SAIPAN (capital) 49,000 (2014)
Sex ratio: *at birth:* 1.06 male(s)/female
0–14 years: 1.07 male(s)/female
15–24 years: 1.27 male(s)/female
25–54 years: 0.73 male(s)/female
55–64 years: 1.17 male(s)/female
65 years and over: 0.92 male(s)/female
total population: 0.93 male(s)/female (2015 est.)

Infant mortality rate: *total:* 5.4 deaths/1,000 live births
male: 5.78 deaths/1,000 live births
*female:*5 deaths/1,000 live births (2015 est.)
country comparison to the world: 172
Life expectancy at birth: *total population:* 77.82 years
male: 75.15 years
*female:*80.65 years (2015 est.)
country comparison to the world: 65
Total fertility rate: 1.98 children born/woman (2015 est.)
country comparison to the world: 124
Drinking water source:
improved:
urban: 97.5% of population
rural: 97.5% of population
total: 97.5% of population
unimproved:
urban: 2.5% of popu lation
rural: 2.5% of population
total: 2.5% of population (2015 est.)
Sanitation facility access:
improved:
urban: 79.7% of population
rural: 79.7% of population
total: 79.7% of population
unimproved:
urban: 20.3% of population
rural: 20.3% of population
total: 20.3% of population (2015 est.)
HIV/AIDS—adult prevalence rate: NA
HIV/AIDS—people living with HIV/AIDS: NA
HIV/AIDS—deaths: NA

GOVERNMENT

Country name: *conventional long form:* Commonwealth of the Northern Mariana Islands
conventional short form: Northern Mariana Islands
abbreviation: CNMI
former: Trust Territory of the Pacific Islands, Mariana Islands District
etymology: formally claimed and named by Spain in 1667 in honor of the Spanish Queen, MARIANA of Austria
Dependency status: commonwealth in political union with the US; federal funds to the Commonwealth administered by the US Department of the Interior, Office of Insular Affairs
Government type: presidential democracy; a commonwealth in political union with the US
Capital: *name:* Saipan
Geographic coordinates: 15 12 N, 145 45 E
time difference: UTC + 10 (15 hours ahead of Washington, DC, during Standard Time)
Administrative divisions: none (commonwealth in political union with the US); there are no first-order administrative divisions as defined by the US Government, but there are 4 municipalities at the second order: Northern Islands, Rota, Saipan, Tinian
Independence: none (commonwealth in political union with the US)

National holiday: Commonwealth Day, 8 January (1978)
Constitution: partially effective 9 January 1978 (Constitution of the Commonwealth of the Northern Mariana Islands); fully effective 4 November 1986 (Covenant Agreement); amended several times, last in 2012 (2016)
Legal system: US system applies, except for customs, wages, immigration laws, and taxation
Citizenship: see United States
Suffrage: 18 years of age; universal; note—indigenous inhabitants are US citizens but do not vote in US presidential elections
Executive branch: *chief of state:* President Barack H. OBAMA (since 20 January 2009); Vice President Joseph R. BIDEN (since 20 January 2009)
head of government: Governor Eloy S. INOS (since 20 February 2013); Lieutenant Governor Ralph TORRES (since 20 February 2013)
cabinet: Cabinet appointed by the governor with the advice and consent of the Senate
elections/appointments: president and vice president indirectly elected on the same ballot by an Electoral College of 'electors' chosen from each state; president and vice president serve a 4-year term (eligible for a second term); under the US Constitution, residents of the Northern Mariana Islands do not vote in elections for US president and vice president; however, they may vote in Democratic and Republican party presidential primary elections; governor directly elected by absolute majority vote in 2 rounds if needed; election last held on 4 November 2014 with a runoff on 21 November 2014 (next to be held in 2018)
election results: Eloy S. INOS reelected governor; percent of vote in runoff—Eloy S. INOS (Republican) 57%, Heinz HOFSCHNEIDER (Republican) 43%; Ralph TORRES reelected lieutenant governor
note: Benigno R. FITIAL was impeached by House of Representatives on 11–12 February 2013 and resigned on 20 February 2013; Eloy INOS (Republican) sworn in as governor the same day
Legislative branch: *description:* bicameral Northern Mariana Commonwealth Legislature consists of the Senate (9 seats; members directly elected in single-seat constituencies by simple majority vote to serve 4-year terms) and the House of Representatives (20 seats; members directly elected in single-seat constituencies by simple majority vote to serve 2-year terms)
elections: Senate—last held on 4 November 2014 (next to be held on 8 November 2016); House of Representatives—last held on 4 November 2014 (next to be held on 8 November 2016)
election results: Senate—percent of vote by party—NA; seats by party—Covenant Party 3, Republican Party 3, Democratic Party 1, independent 2; House of Representatives—percent of vote by party—NA; seats by party—independents 13, Republican Party 7
note: the Northern Mariana Islands directly elects 1 member by simple majority vote to serve a 2-year term as a delegate to the US House of Representatives; the delegate can vote when serving on a committee and when the House meets as

the Committee of the Whole House, but not when legislation is submitted for a "full floor" House vote; election of delegate last held on 4 November 2014 (next to be held on 8 November 2016)
Judicial branch: *highest court(s):* Supreme Court of the Commonwealth of the Northern Marianna Islands or CNMI (consists of the chief justice and 2 associate justices); US Federal District Court (consists of 1 judge); note—US Federal District Court jurisdiction limited to US federal laws; appeals beyond the Northern Mariannas Islands Supreme Court are referred to the US Supreme Court
judge selection and term of office: judges of the Supreme Court of the CNMI appointed by the governor and confirmed by the CNMI Senate; judges appointed for 8-year terms and can serve another term if approved through voter election; US Federal District Court judges appointed by the US president and confirmed by the US Senate; judges appointed for renewable 10-year terms
subordinate courts: Superior Court
Political parties and leaders: Covenant Party [Benigno R. FITIAL]
Democratic Party [Dr. Carlos S. CAMACHO]
Republican Party [Juan S. REYES]
Political pressure groups and leaders: NA
International organization participation: PIF (observer), SPC, UPU
Flag description: blue with a white, five-pointed star superimposed on a gray latte stone (the traditional foundation stone used in building) in the center, surrounded by a wreath; blue symbolizes the Pacific Ocean, the star represents the Commonwealth; the latte stone and the floral head wreath display elements of the native Chamorro culture
National symbol(s): latte stone; national colors: blue, white
National anthem: *name:* "Gi Talo Gi Halom Tasi" (In the Middle of the Sea)
lyrics/music: Jose S. PANGELINAN [Chamoru], David PETER [Carolinian]/Wilhelm GANZHORN
note: adopted 1996; the Carolinian version of the song is known as "Satil Matawal Pacifico;" as a commonwealth of the US, in addition to the local anthem, "The Star-Spangled Banner" is official (see United States)

ECONOMY

Economy—overview: The Northern Mariana Islands' economy benefits substantially from financial assistance from the US. In fiscal year 2013, federal grants accounted for 35.4% of the Commonwealth's total revenues. A small agriculture sector is made up of cattle ranches and small farms producing coconuts, breadfruit, tomatoes, and melons.
The Commonwealth's economy continued to recover in 2013. Real GDP increased 4.4%, following a 2.1% gain in 2012. Economic growth in 2013 reflected increases in consumer spending and exports of services, mainly spending by foreign tourists.

Tourism continued to grow in 2013, after posting double-digit growth in 2012. The tourist industry employs approximately a quarter of the work force and accounts for roughly one-fourth of GDP. The Commonwealth is making a concerted effort to broaden its tourism by extending casino gambling from the small Islands of Tinian and Rota to the main Island of Saipan, its political and commercial center.

GDP (purchasing power parity): $682 million (2013 est.)
$665 million (2012)
$649 million (2011)
note: GDP estimate includes US subsidy
country comparison to the world: 209
GDP (official exchange rate): $1.232 billion (2013 est.)
GDP—real growth rate: 4.5% (2013)
2.1% (2012)
-6.8% (2011)
country comparison to the world: 47
GDP—per capita (PPP): $13,300 (2013 est.)
$12,900 (2012)
$12,400 (2011)
country comparison to the world: 117
GDP—composition, by end use:
household consumption: 91.3%
government consumption: 51.5%
investment in fixed assets: 3.8%
investements in inventories: NA%
exports of goods and services: 42.2%
imports of goods and services: -88.9% (2013)
GDP—composition, by sector of origin:
agriculture: 1.7%
industry: 2.9%
services: 95.4% (2010)
Agriculture—products: vegetables and melons, fruits and nuts; ornamental plants; livestock, poultry, eggs; fish and aquaculture products
Industries: tourism, banking, construction, fishing, handicrafts, other services
Industrial production growth rate: NA%
Labor force: 27,970
note: includes foreign workers (2010 est.)

country comparison to the world: 206
Labor force—by occupation: *agriculture:* 1.9%
industry: 10%
services: 88.1% (2010 est.)
Unemployment rate: 11.2% (2010 est.)
8% (2005 est.)
country comparison to the world: 128
Population below poverty line: NA%
Household income or consumption by percentage share: *lowest:* 10%: NA%
highest: 10%: NA%
Budget: *revenues:* $246.4 million
expenditures: $249.8 million (2013 est.)
Taxes and other revenues: 20% of GDP (2013 est.)
country comparison to the world: 156
Budget surplus (+) or deficit (−): -0.3% of GDP (2013 est.)
country comparison to the world: 40
Fiscal year: 1 October—30 September
Inflation rate (consumer prices): -2.5% (2013 est.)
1.1% (2012)
country comparison to the world: 4
Exports: $288 million (2013)
$268 million (2012)
country comparison to the world: 183
Exports—commodities: garments
Imports: $606 million (2013)
$531 million (2012)
country comparison to the world: 190
Imports—commodities: food, construction equipment and materials, petroleum products
Debt—external: $NA
Exchange rates: the US dollar is used

ENERGY

Electricity—production: 60,600 kWh (January 2009)
country comparison to the world: 219
Electricity—consumption: 48,300 kWh (January 2009)
country comparison to the world: 219
Electricity—exports: 0 kWh (January 2009 est.)
country comparison to the world: 125

Electricity—imports: 0 kWh (January 2009 est.)
country comparison to the world: 135

COMMUNICATIONS

Telephone system: *international:* country code—1–670; satellite earth stations—2 Intelsat (Pacific Ocean)
Broadcast media: 1 TV broadcast station on Saipan; multi-channel cable TV services are available on Saipan; 9 licensed radio broadcast stations (2009)
Radio broadcast stations: AM 1, FM 6, shortwave 1 (2005)
Television broadcast stations: 1 (on Saipan; in addition, 2 cable services on Saipan provide varied programming from satellite networks) (2006)
Internet country code: .mp
Internet hosts: 17 (2012)
country comparison to the world: 222

TRANSPORTATION

Airports: 5 (2013)
country comparison to the world: 180
Airports—with paved runways: *total:* 3
2,438 to 3,047 m: 2
1,524 to 2,437 m: 1 (2013)
Airports—with unpaved runways: *total:* 2
2,438 to 3,047 m: 1
under 914 m: 1 (2013)
Heliports: 1 (2013)
Roadways: *total:* 536 km (2008)
country comparison to the world: 194
Ports and terminals: *major seaport(s):* Saipan, Tinian, Rota

MILITARY AND SECURITY

Military—note: defense is the responsibility of the US

TRANSNATIONAL ISSUES

Disputes—international: none

NORWAY

INTRODUCTION

Background: Two centuries of Viking raids into Europe tapered off following the adoption of Christianity by King Olav TRYGGVASON in 994; conversion of the Norwegian kingdom occurred over the next several decades. In 1397, Norway was absorbed into a union with Denmark that lasted more than four centuries. In 1814, Norwegians resisted the cession of their country to Sweden and adopted a new constitution. Sweden then invaded Norway but agreed to let Norway keep its constitution in return for accepting the union under a Swedish king. Rising nationalism throughout the 19th century led to a 1905 referendum granting Norway independence. Although Norway remained neutral in World War I, it suffered heavy losses to its shipping. Norway

proclaimed its neutrality at the outset of World War II, but was nonetheless occupied for five years by Nazi Germany (1940–45). in 1949, Norway abandoned neutrality and became a member of NATO. Discovery of oil and gas in adjacent waters in the late 1960s boosted Norway's economic fortunes. In referenda held in 1972 and 1994, Norway rejected joining the EU. Key domestic issues include immigration and integration of ethnic minorities, maintaining the country's extensive social safety net with an aging population, and preserving economic competitiveness.

GEOGRAPHY

Location: Northern Europe, bordering the North Sea and the North Atlantic Ocean, west of Sweden

Geographic coordinates: 62 00 N, 10 00 E
Map references: Europe
Area: *total:* 323,802 sq km
land: 304,282 sq km
water: 19,520 sq km
country comparison to the world: 68
Area—comparative: slightly larger than twice the size of Georgia; slightly larger than New Mexico
Land boundaries: *total:* 2,566 km
border countries (3): Finland 709 km, Sweden 1,666 km, Russia 191 km
Coastline: 25,148 km (includes mainland 2,650 km, as well as long fjords, numerous small islands, and minor indentations 22,498 km; length of island coastlines 58,133 km)
Maritime claims: *territorial sea:* 12 nm
contiguous zone: 10 nm
exclusive economic zone: 200 nm

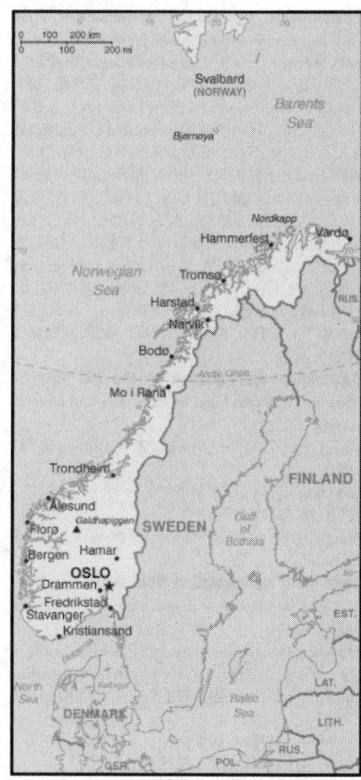

continental shelf: 200 nm

Climate: temperate along coast, modified by North Atlantic Current; colder interior with increased precipitation and colder summers; rainy year-round on west coast

Terrain: glaciated; mostly high plateaus and rugged mountains broken by fertile valleys; small, scattered plains; coastline deeply indented by fjords; arctic tundra in north

Elevation: *mean elevation:* 460 m

elevation extremes: *lowest point:* Norwegian Sea 0 m

highest point: Galdhopiggen 2,469 m

Natural resources: petroleum, natural gas, iron ore, copper, lead, zinc, titanium, pyrites, nickel, fish, timber, hydropower

Land use: *agricultural land:* 2.7%
arable land: 2.2%
permanent crops: 0%
permanent pasture: 0.5%
forest: 27.8%
other: 69.5% (2011 est.)

Irrigated land: 900 sq km (2012)

Total renewable water resources: 382 cu km (2011)

Freshwater withdrawal (domestic/industrial/agricultural): *total:* 2.94 cu km/yr (28%/43%/29%)
per capita: 622.4 cu m/yr (2006)

Natural hazards: rockslides, avalanches

volcanism: Beerenberg (elev. 2,227 m) on Jan Mayen Island in the Norwegian Sea is the country's only active volcano

Environment—current issues: water pollution; acid rain damaging forests and adversely affecting lakes, threatening fish stocks; air pollution from vehicle emissions

Environment—international agreements: *party to:* Air Pollution, Air Pollution-Nitrogen Oxides, Air Pollution-Persistent Organic Pollutants, Air Pollution-Sulfur 85, Air Pollution-Sulfur 94, Air Pollution-Volatile Organic Compounds, Antarctic-Environmental Protocol, Antarctic-Marine Living Resources, Antarctic Seals, Antarctic Treaty, Biodiversity, Climate Change, Climate Change-Kyoto Protocol, Desertification, Endangered Species, Environmental Modification, Hazardous Wastes, Law of the Sea, Marine Dumping, Ozone Layer Protection, Ship Pollution, Tropical Timber 83, Tropical Timber 94, Wetlands, Whaling
signed, but not ratified: none of the selected agreements

Geography—note: about two-thirds mountains; some 50,000 islands off its much-indented coastline; strategic location adjacent to sea lanes and air routes in North Atlantic; one of the most rugged and longest coastlines in the world

PEOPLE AND SOCIETY

Nationality: *noun:* Norwegian(s)
adjective: Norwegian

Ethnic groups: Norwegian 94.4% (includes Sami, about 60,000), other European 3.6%, other 2% (2007 est.)

Languages: Bokmal Norwegian (official), Nynorsk Norwegian (official), small Sami- and Finnish-speaking minorities
note: SamIs an official language in nine municipalities

Religions: Church of Norway (Evangelical Lutheran—official) 82.1%, other Christian 3.9%, Muslim 2.3%, Roman Catholic 1.8%, other 2.4%, unspecified 7.5% (2011 est.)

Population: 5,207,689 (July 2015 est.)
country comparison to the world: 121

Age structure: *0–14 years:* 18.08% (male 482,945/female 458,735)
15–24 years: 12.99% (male 347,535/female 329,113)
25–54 years: 40.91% (male 1,096,539/female 1,033,879)
55–64 years: 11.69% (male 308,142/female 300,895)
65 years and over: 16.32% (male 387,333/female 462,573) (2015 est.)

Dependency ratios: *total dependency ratio:* 52.2%
youth dependency ratio: 27.3%
elderly dependency ratio: 24.9%
potential support ratio: 4% (2015 est.)

Median age: *total:* 39.1 years
male: 38.3 years
female: 39.9 years (2015 est.)
country comparison to the world: 53

Population growth rate: 1.13% (2015 est.)
country comparison to the world: 108

Birth rate: 12.14 births/1,000 population (2015 est.)
country comparison to the world: 163

Death rate: 8.12 deaths/1,000 population (2015 est.)
country comparison to the world: 95

Net migration rate: 7.25 migrant(s)/1,000 population (2015 est.)
country comparison to the world: 16

Urbanization: *urban population:* 80.5% of total population (2015)
rate of urbanization: 1.35% annual rate of change (2010–15 est.)

Major urban areas—population: OSLO (capital) 986,000 (2015)

Sex ratio: *at birth:* 1.06 male(s)/female
0–14 years: 1.05 male(s)/female
15–24 years: 1.06 male(s)/female
25–54 years: 1.06 male(s)/female
55–64 years: 1.02 male(s)/female
65 years and over: 0.84 male(s)/female
total population: 1.01 male(s)/female (2015 est.)

Mother's mean age at first birth: 28.5
note: data is calculated based on actual age at first births (2012 est.)

Maternal mortality rate: 5 deaths/100,000 live births (2015 est.)
country comparison to the world: 167

Infant mortality rate: *total:* 2.48 deaths/1,000 live births
male: 2.79 deaths/1,000 live births
female: 2.16 deaths/1,000 live births (2015 est.)
country comparison to the world: 220

Life expectancy at birth: *total population:* 81.7 years
male: 79.7 years
female: 83.81 years (2015 est.)
country comparison to the world: 20

Total fertility rate: 1.86 children born/woman (2015 est.)
country comparison to the world: 145

Contraceptive prevalence rate: 88.4%
note: percent of women aged 20–44 (2005)

Health expenditures: 9.6% of GDP (2013)
country comparison to the world: 40

Physicians density: 4.28 physicians/1,000 population (2012)

Hospital bed density: 3.3 beds/1,000 population (2011)

Drinking water source:
improved:
urban: 100% of population
rural: 100% of population
total: 100% of population
unimproved:
urban: 0% of population
rural: 0% of population
total: 0% of population (2015 est.)

Sanitation facility access:
improved:
urban: 98% of population
rural: 98.3% of population
total: 98.1% of population
unimproved:
urban: 2% of population
rural: 1.7% of population

total: 1.9% of population (2015 est.)

HIV/AIDS—adult prevalence rate: 0.15% (2014 est.)

country comparison to the world: 105

HIV/AIDS—people living with HIV/AIDS: 5,800 (2014 est.)

HIV/AIDS—deaths: less than 100 (2014 est.)

country comparison to the world: 112

Obesity—adult prevalence rate: 24.8% (2014)

country comparison to the world: 84

Education expenditures: 7.4% of GDP (2014)

cou ntry comparison to the world: 21

School life expectancy (primary to tertiary education): *total:* 18 years

male: 17 years

female: 18 years (2014)

Unemployment, youth ages 15–24: *total:* 9.2%

male: 10.6%

female: 7.7% (2013 est.)

country comparison to the world: 109

GOVERNMENT

Country name: *conventional long form:* Kingdom of Norway

conventional short form: Norway

local long form: Kongeriket Norge

local short form: Norge

etymology: derives from the Old Norse words "nordr" and "vegr" meaning "northern way" and refers to the long coastline of western Norway

Government type: parliamentary constitutional monarchy

Capital: *name:* Oslo

Geographic coordinates: 59 55 N, 10 45 E

time difference: UTC + 1 (6 hours ahead of Washington, DC, during Standard Time)

daylight saving time: +1hr, begins last Sunday in March; ends last Sunday in October

Administrative divisions: 19 counties (fylker, singular—fylke); Akershus, Aust-Agder, Buskerud, Finnmark, Hedmark, Hordaland, More og Romsdal, Nordland, Nord-Trondelag, Oppland, Oslo, Ostfold, Rogaland, Sogn og Fjordane, Sor-Trondelag, Telemark, Troms, Vest-Agder, Vestfold

Dependent areas: Bouvet Island, Jan Mayen, Svalbard

Independence: 7 June 1905 (Norway declared the union with Sweden dissolved); 26 October 1905 (Sweden agreed to the repeal of the union)

National holiday: Constitution Day, 17 May (1814)

Constitution: drafted spring 1814, adopted 16 May 1814, signed by Constituent Assembly 17 May 1814; amended over 400 times, last in 2015 (2016)

Legal system: mixed legal system of civil, common, and customary law; Supreme Court can advise on legislative acts

International law organization participation: accepts compulsory ICJ jurisdiction with reservations; accepts ICCt jurisdiction

Citizenship: *citizenship by birth:* no

citizenship by descent only: at least one parent must be a citizen of Norway

dual citizenship recognized: no

residency requirement for naturalization: 7 years

Suffrage: 18 years of age; universal

Executive branch: *chief of state:* King HARALDV (since 17 January 1991); Heir Apparent Crown Prince HAAKON MAGNUS, son of the monarch (born 20 July 1973)

head of government: Prime Minister Erna SOLBERG (since 16 October 2013)

cabinet: State Council appointed by the monarch, approved by Parliament

elections/appointments: the monarchy is hereditary; following parliamentary elections, the leader of the majority party or majority coalition usually appointed prime minister by the monarch with the approval of the parliament

Legislative branch: *description:* unicameral Parliament or Storting (169 seats; members directly elected in multi-seat constituencies by proportional representation vote; members serve 4-year terms)

elections: last held on 9 September 2013 (next to be held in September 2017)

election results: percent of vote by party—Center-Right Coalition 54.0% (H 26.3%, FrP 16.3%, KrF 5.6%, V 5.2%), Red-Green Coalition 40.6% (Ap 30.8%, SP 5.5%, SV 4.1%), MDG 2.8, other 2.7%; seats by party—Center-Right Coalition 96 (H 48, FrP 29, KrF 10, V 9), Red-Green Coalition 72 (Ap 55, Sp 10, SV 7), MDG 1

Judicial branch: *highest court(s):* Supreme Court or Hoyesterett (consists of the chief justice and 18 associate justices)

judge selection and term of office: justices appointed by the monarch (King in Council) upon the recommendation of the Judicial Appointments Board; justice retirement mandatory at age 70

subordinate courts: Courts of Appeal or Lagmannsrett; regional and district courts; Conciliation Boards; ordinary and special courts; note—in addition to professionally trained judges, elected lay judges sit on the bench with professional judges in the Courts of Appeal and district courts

Political parties and leaders: Center Party or Sp [Trygve Slagsvold VEDUM]

Center-Right Coalition (includes FrP, H, KrF, V)

Christian Democratic Party or KrF [Knut Arild HAREIDE]

Conservative Party or H [Erna SOLBERG]

Green Party or MDG [Rasmus HANSSON and Hilde OPOKU]

Labor Party or Ap [Jonas Gahr STORE]

Liberal Party or V [Trine SKEI GRANDE]

Progress Party or FrP [Siv JENSEN]

Red-G reen Coalition (includes Ap, Sp, SV)

Socialist Left Party or SV [Audun LYSBAKKEN]

Political pressure groups and leaders: Confederation of Norwegian Enterprise (Naeringslivets Hovedorganisasjon) or NHO [President Tore ULSTEIN; CEO Kristin SKOGENLUND]

Norwegian Confederation of Trade Unions (Landsorganisasjonen inorge) or LO [Gerd KRISTIANSEN]

other: environmental groups; media; digital privacy movements

International organization participation: ADB (nonregional member), AfDB (nonregional member), Arctic Council, Australia Group, BIS, CBSS, CD, CE, CERN, EAPC, EBRD, EFTA, EITI (implementing country), ESA, FAO, FATF, IADB, IAEA, IBRD, ICAO, ICC (national committees), ICCt, ICRM, IDA, IEA, IFAD, IFC, IFRCS, IGAD (partners), IHO, ILO, IMF, IMO, IMSO, Interpol, IOC, IOM, IPU, ISO, ITSO, ITU, ITUC (NGOs), MIGA, MINUSMA, NATO, NC, NEA, NIB, NSG, OAS (observer), OECD, OPCW, OSCE, Paris Club, PCA, Schengen Convention, UN, UNCTAD, UNESCO, UNHCR, UNIDO, UNITAR, UNMISS, UNRWA, UNTSO, UNWTO, UPU, WCO, WHO, WIPO, WMO, WTO, ZC

Diplomatic representation in the US: *chief of mission:* Ambassador Kare Reidar AAS (since 22 August 2013)

chancery: 2720 34th Street NW, Washington, DC 20008

telephone: [1] (202) 333-6000

FAX: [1] (202) 459-3990

consulate(s) general: Houston, New York, San Francisco

Diplomatic representation from the US: *chief of mission:* Ambassador Samuel HEINS (since 10 March 2016)

embassy: Henrik Ibsens gate 48,0244 Oslo; note—the embassy will move to Huseby in the near future

mailing address: PSC 69, Box 1000, APO AE 09707

telephone: [47] 21-30-85-40

FAX: [47] 22-44-33-63,22-56-27-51

Flag description: red with a blue cross outlined in white that extends to the edges of the flag; the vertical part of the cross is shifted to the hoist side in the style of the Dannebrog (Danish flag); the colors recall Norway's past political unions with Denmark (red and white) and Sweden (blue)

National symbol(s): lion; national colors: red, white, blue

National anthem: *name:* "Ja, vi elsker dette landet" (Yes, We Love This Country)

lyrics/music: Bjornstjerne BJORNSON/Rikard NORDRAAK

note: adopted 1864; in addition to the national anthem, "Kongesangen" (Song of the King), which uses the tune of "God Save the Queen," serves as the royal anthem

ECONOMY

Economy—overview: Norway's has a stable economy with a vibrant private sector, a large state sector, and an extensive social safety net. Norway opted out of the EU during a referendum in November 1994; nonetheless, as a member of the European Economic Area, it contributes sizably to the EU budget.

The country is richly endowed with natural resources in addition to oil and gas, including hydropower, fish, forests, and minerals. The government manages the country's petroleum resources through extensive regulation. The petroleum sector provides about 9% of jobs, 15% of GDP, and 39% of exports, according to official national estimates. Norway is one of the world's leading petroleum exporters, though oil production in 2015 was close to 50% below its peak in 2000; annual gas production, conversely, more than doubled over the same time period.

In anticipation of eventual declines in oil and gas production, Norway saves state revenue from petroleum sector activities in the world's largest sovereign wealth fund, valued at over $800 billion as of early 2016. The government allows itself to use up to 4% of the fund's value, its annual expected real rate of return, to help balance the federal budget each year. After solid GDP growth in 2004–07, the economy slowed in 2008, and contracted in 2009, before returning to modest, positive growth from 2010 to 2015. Lower oil prices in 2015 caused growth to slow, increased unemployment, and weakened the Norwegian krone. The latter trend has mitigated the negative impact of lower oil and gas prices by making Norwegian exports cheaper for foreign buyers. The government has expressed willingness to increase public spending from the sovereign wealth fund to help prevent a recession.

GDP (purchasing power parity): $356.2 billion (2015 est.)
$350.7 billion (2014 est.)
$343.1 billion (2013 est.)
note: data are in 2015 US dollars
country comparison to the world: 49
GDP (official exchange rate): $389.5 billion (2015 est.)
GDP—real growth rate: 1.6% (2015 est.)
2.2% (2014 est.)
1% (2013 est.)
country comparison to the world: 149
GDP—per capita (PPP): $68,400 (2015 est.)
$68,000 (2014 est.)
$67,300 (2013 est.)
note: data are in 2015 US dollars
country comparison to the world: 11
Gross national saving: 37.6% of GDP (2015 est.)
40.2% of GDP (2014 est.)
38.2% of GDP (2013 est.)
country comparison to the world: 5
GDP—composition, by end use:
household consumption: 42.8%
government consumption: 22.8%
investment in fixed capital: 22.9%
investment in inventories: 5%
exports of goods and services: 36.4%
imports of goods and services: -29.9% (2015 est.)
GDP—composition, by sector of origin:
agriculture: 1.7%
industry: 38.9%
services: 59.4% (2015 est.)
Agriculture—products: barley, wheat, potatoes; pork, beef, veal, milk; fish
Industries: petroleum and gas, shipping, fishing, aquaculture, food processing, shipbuilding, pulp and paper products, metals, chemicals, timber, mining, textiles
Industrial production growth rate: 0% (2015 est.)
country comparison to the world: 166
Labor force: 2.777 million (2015 est.)
country comparison to the world: 106

Labor force—by occupation: *agriculture:* 2.7%
industry: 18.3%
services: 79% (2015 est.)
Unemployment rate: 4.4% (2015 est.)
3.5% (2014 est.)
country comparison to the world: 42
Population below poverty line: NA%
Household income or consumption by percentage share: *lowest:* 10%: 3.8%
highest: 10%: 21.2% (2014)
Distribution of family income—Gini index: 26.8 (2010)
25.8 (1995)
country comparison to the world: 134
Budget: *revenues:* $220.2 billion
expenditures: $193.9 billion (2015 est.)
Taxes and other revenues: 55.4% of GDP (2015 est.)
country comparison to the world: 10
Budget surplus (+) or deficit (–): 6.6% of GDP (2015 est.)
country comparison to the world: 7
Public debt: 39.3% of GDP (2015 est.)
38.6% of GDP (2014 est.)
note: data cover general government debt, and includes debt instruments issued (or owned) by government entities other than the treasury; the data exclude treasury debt held by foreign entities; the data exclude debt issued by subnational entities, as well as intra-governmental debt; intra-governmental debt consists of treasury borrowings from surpluses in the social funds, such as for retirement, medical care, and unemployment; debt instruments for the social funds are not sold at public auctions
country comparison to the world: 117
Fiscal year: calendar year
Inflation rate (consumer prices): 2.2% (2015 est.)
2% (2014 est.)
country comparison to the world: 122
Central bank discount rate: 6.25% (31 December 2010)
1.75% (31 December 2009)
country comparison to the world: 61
Commercial bank prime lending rate: 2.1% (31 December 2015 est.)
2.25% (31 December 2014 est.)
country comparison to the world: 176
Stock of narrow money: $107.9 billion (31 December 2015 est.)
$120.7 billion (31 December 2014 est.)
country comparison to the world: 34
Stock of broad money: $323.9 billion (31 December 2014 est.)
$310 billion (31 December 2013 est.)
country comparison to the world: 32
Stock of domestic credit: $549.8 billion (31 December 2015 est.)
$590.7 billion (31 December 2014 est.)
country comparison to the world: 23
Market value of publicly traded shares:
$252.9 billion (31 December 2012 est.)
$219.2 billion (31 December 2011)
$250.9 billion (31 December 2010 est.)
country comparison to the world: 33

Current account balance: $35.04 billion (2015 est.)
$59.78 billion (2014 est.)
country comparison to the world: 12
Exports: $106.2 billion (2015 est.)
$141.4 billion (2014 est.)
country comparison to the world: 35
Exports—commodities: petroleum and petroleum products, machinery and equipment, metals, chemicals, ships, fish
Exports—partners: UK 22.2%, Germany 17.9%, Netherlands 10.2%, France 6.6%, Sweden 6.1%, Belgium 5%, US 4.5% (2015)
Imports: $71.95 billion (2015 est.)
$91.13 billion (2014 est.)
country comparison to the world: 38
Imports—commodities: machinery and equipment, ch emicals, metals, foodstuffs
Imports—partners: Sweden 12%, Germany 11.8%, China 10.9%, UK 6.7%, US 6.6%, Denmark 6% (2015)
Reserves of foreign exchange and gold: $64.8 billion (31 December 2014 est.)
$58.28 billion (31 December 2013 est.)
country comparison to the world: 33
Debt—external: $661.2 billion (31 December 2014 est.)
$730.1 billion (31 December 2013 est.)
note: Norway is a net external creditor
country comparison to the world: 22
Stock of direct foreign investment—at home:
$290.2 billion (31 December 2015 est.)
$285.1 billion (31 December 2014 est.)
coun try comparison to the world: 23
Stock of direct foreign investment—abroad:
$256.3 billion (31 December 2015 est.)
$256.4 billion (31 December 2014 est.)
country comparison to the world: 24
Exchange rates: Norwegian kroner (NOK) per US dollar—
7.876 (2015 est.)
6.3021 (2014 est.)
6.3021 (2013 est.)
5.82 (2012 est.)
5.6065 (2011 est.)

ENERGY

Electricity—production: 142 billion kWh (2014 est.)
country comparison to the world: 28
Electricity—consumption: 126.4 billion kWh (2014 est.)
country comparison to the world: 28
Electricity—exports: 21.9 billion kWh (2014 est.)
country comparison to the world: 9
Electricity—imports: 6.3 billion kWh (2014 est.)
country comparison to the world: 38
Electricity—installed generating capacity: 33.7 million kW (2014 est.)
country comparison to the world: 28
Electricity—from fossil fuels: 4.7% of total installed capacity (2014 est.)
country comparison to the world: 204
Electricity—from nuclear fuels: 0% of total installed capacity (2014 est.)
country comparison to the world: 155

Electricity—from hydroelectric plants: 92.7% of total installed capacity (2014 est.)
country comparison to the world: 10
Electricity—from other renewable sources: 2.5% of total installed capacity (2014 est.)
country comparison to the world: 78
Crude oil—production: 1.568 million bbl/day (2015 est.)
country comparison to the world: 16
Crude oil—exports: 1.218 million bbl/day (2013 est.)
country comparison to the world: 14
Crude oil—imports: 37,080 bbl/day (2013 est.)
country comparison to the world: 57
Crude oil—proved reserves: 6.435 billion bbl (1 January 2010 est.)
country comparison to the world: 21
Refined petroleum products—production: 349,600 bbl/day (2013 est.)
country comparison to the world: 40
Refined petroleum products—consumption: 225,200 bbl/day (2014 est.)
country comparison to the world: 56
Refined petroleum products—exports: 358,800 bbl/day (2013 est.)
country comparison to the world: 22
Refined petroleum products—imports: 101,600 bbl/day (2013 est.)
country comparison to the world: 51
Natural gas—production: 114.9 billion cu m (2015 est.)
country comparison to the world: 8
Natural gas—consumption: 6.075 billion cu m (2014 est.)
country comparison to the world: 55
Natural gas—exports: 114.4 billion cu m (2015 est.)
country comparison to the world: 3
Natural gas—imports: 0 cu m (2014 est.)
country comparison to the world: 111
Natural gas—proved reserves: 1.856 trillion cu m (1 January 2015 est.)
country comparison to the world: 19
Carbon dioxide emissions from consumption of energy: 41.06 million Mt (2012 est.)
country comparison to the world: 66

COMMUNICATIONS

Telephones—fixed lines: *total subscriptions:* 1.16 million
subscriptions per 100 inhabitants: 22 (2014 est.)
country comparison to the world: 72
Telephones—mobile cellular: *total:* 5.9 million
subscriptions per 100 inhabitants: 115 (2014 est.)
country comparison to the world: 111
Telephone system: *general assessment:* modern in all respects; one of the most advanced telecommunications networks in Europe
domestic: Norway has a domestic satellite system; the prevalence of rural areas encourages the wide use of mobile-cellular systems
international: country code—47; 2 buried coaxial cable systems; submarine cables provide links to other Nordic countries and Europe; satellite earth stations—NA Eutelsat, NA Intelsat (Atlantic Ocean), and 1 Inmarsat (Atlantic and Indian

Ocean regions); note—Norway shares the Inmarsat earth station with the other Nordic countries (Denmark, Finland, Iceland, and Sweden) (2011)
Broadcast media: state-owned public radio-TV broadcaster operates 3 nationwide TV stations, 3 nationwide radio stations, and 16 regional radio stations; roughly a dozen privately owned television stations broadcast nationally and roughly another 25 local TV stations broadcasting; nearly 75% of households have access to multichannel cable or satellite TV; 2 privately owned radio stations broadcast nationwide and another 240 stations operate locally (2008)
Radio broadcast stations: AM 5, FM 160, shortwave 1 (2008)
Television broadcast stations: 69 (2008)
Internet country code: .no
Internet hosts: 3.588 million (2012)
country comparison to the world: 29
Internet users: *total:* 4.9 million
percent of population: 96.2% (2014 est.)
country comparison to the world: 70

TRANSPORTATION

Airports: 95 (2013)
country comparison to the world: 61
Airports—with paved runways: *total:* 67
2,438 to 3,047 m: 14
1,524 to 2,437 m: 10
914 to 1,523 m: 22
under 914 m: 21 (2013)
Airports—with unpaved runways: *total:* 28
914 to 1,523 m: 6
under 914 m: 22 (2013)
Heliports: 1 (2013)
Pipelines: condensate 578 km; condensate/gas 220 km; gas 8,044 km; oil 3,794 km; oil/gas/water 457 km; water 96 km (2013)
Railways: *total:* 4,250 km
standard gauge: 4,250 km 1.435-m gauge (2,518 km electrified) (2014)
country comparison to the world: 41
Roadways: *total:* 93,870 km (includes 393 km of expressways)
paved: 75,754 km
unpaved: 18,116 km (2013)
country comparison to the world: 51
Waterways: 1,577 km (2010)
country comparison to the world: 51
Merchant marine: *total:* 585
by type: bulk carrier 55, cargo 105, carrier 5, chemical tanker 121, combination ore/oil 12, liquefied gas 47, passenger 3, passenger/cargo 121, petroleum tanker 54, refrigerated cargo 9, roll on/roll off 4, vehicle carrier 49
foreign-owned: 81 (Bermuda 24, Canada 1, Cyprus 1, Denmark 7, France 5, Iceland 2, Lithuania 1, Saudi Arabia 3, Sweden 27, US 10)
registered in other countries: 974 (Antigua and Barbuda 9, Bahamas 186, Barbados 38, Belize 2, Bermuda 5, Brazil 3, Canada 4, Chile 1, Comoros 1, Cook Islands 8, Croatia 2, Curacao 2, Cyprus 14, Denmark 2, Dominica 1, Equatorial Guinea 1, Estonia 2, Faroe Islands 13, Gibraltar 46, Hong Kong 48, Indonesia 3, Isle of Man 30, Italy 6, Liberia 38, Libya 1, Malta 96, Marshall Islands

75, Netherlands 19, Panama 81, Portugal 2, Saint Kitts and Nevis 3, Saint Vincent and the Grenadines 13, Singapore 153, Spain 10, Sweden 3, UK 32, US 17, Vanuatu 1, unknown 3) (2010)
country comparison to the world: 19
Ports and terminals: *major seaport(s):* Bergen, Haugesund, Maaloy, Mongstad, Narvik, Sture
LNG terminal(s) (export): Kamoy, Kollsnes, Melkoya Island
LNG terminal(s) (im port): Fredrikstad, Mosjoen

MILITARY AND SECURITY

Military branches: Norwegian Army (Haeren), Royal Norwegian Navy (Kongelige Norske Sjoeforsvaret, RNoN; includes Coastal Rangers and Coast Guard (Kystvakt)), Royal Norwegian Air Force (Kongelige Norske Luftforsvaret, RNoAF), Home Guard (Heimevernet, HV) (2013)
Military service age and obligation: 19–35 years of age for male compulsory military service; 16 years of age in wartime; 17 years of age for male volunteers; 18 years of age for women; 1 -year service obligation followed by 4–5 refresher training periods through ages 35–60, totalling 18 months (2012)
Military expenditures:
1.59% of GDP (2015)
1.58% of GDP (2014)
1.4% of GDP (2013)
1.4% of GDP (2012)
1.47% of GDP (2011)
country comparison to the world: 72

TRANSNATIONAL ISSUES

Disputes—international: Norway asserts a territorial claim in Antarctica (Queen Maud Land and its continental shelf); Denmark (Greenland) and Norway have made submissions to the Commission on the Limits of the Continental Shelf (CLCS) and Russia is collecting additional data to augment its 2001 CLCS submission; Norway and Russia signed a comprehensive maritime boundary agreement in 2010
Refugees and internally displaced persons: *refugees (country of origin):* 8,901 (Somalia); 11,202 (Eritrea); 5,190 (Iraq); 5,454 (Afghanistan) (2014)
stateless persons: 2,561 (2015)

OMAN

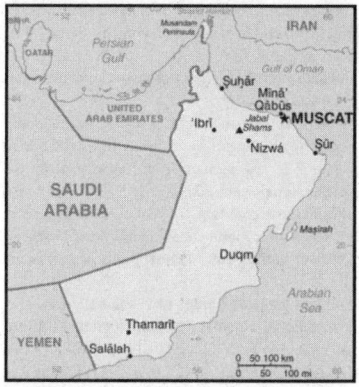

INTRODUCTION

Background: The inhabitants of the area of Oman have long prospered on Indian Ocean trade. In the late 18th century, the nascent sultanate in Muscat signed the first in a series of friendship treaties with Britain. Over time, Oman's dependence on British political and military advisors increased, but it never became a British colony. In 1970, QABOOS bin Said Al-Said overthrew his father, and has since ruled as sultan, but he has never designated a successor. His extensive modernization program has opened the country to the outside world while preserving the longstanding close ties with the UK and US. Oman's moderate, independent foreign policy has sought to maintain good relations with its neighbors and to avoid external entanglements. Inspired by the popular uprisings that swept the Middle East and North Africa beginning in January 2011, some Omanis staged demonstrations, calling for more jobs and economic benefits and an end to corruption. In response to those protester demands, QABOOS in 2011 pledged to implement economic and political reforms, such as granting legislative and regulatory powers to the Majlis al-Shura and increasing unemployment benefits. Additionally, in August 2012, the Sultan announced a royal directive mandating the speedy implementation of a national job creation plan for thousands of public and private sector jobs. As part of the government's efforts to decentralize authority and allow greater citizen participation in local governance, Oman successfully conducted its first municipal council elections in December 2012. Announced by the Sultan in 2011, the municipal councils will have the power to advise the Royal Court on the needs of local districts across Oman's 11 governorates. The Sultan returned to Oman in March 2015 after eight months in Germany, where he received medical treatment and has since appeared publicly on a few occasions.

GEOGRAPHY

Location: Middle East, bordering the Arabian Sea, Gulf of Oman, and Persian Gulf, between Yemen and the UAE

Geographic coordinates: 21 00 N, 57 00 E
Map references: Middle East
Area: *total:* 309,500 sq km
land: 309,500 sq km
water: 0 sq km
country comparison to the world: 71
Area—comparative: twice the size of Georgia; slightly smaller than Kansas

Land boundaries: *total:* 1,561 km
border countries (3): Saudi Arabia 658 km, UAE 609 km, Yemen 294 km
Coastline: 2,092 km
Maritime claims: *territorial sea:* 12 nm
contiguous zone: 24 nm
exclusive economic zone: 200 nm
Climate: dry desert; hot, humid along coast; hot, dry interior; strong southwest summer monsoon (May to September) in far south
Terrain: central desert plain, rugged mountains in north and south
Elevation: *mean elevation:* 310 m
elevation extremes: *lowest point:* Arabian Sea 0 m
highest point: Jabal Shams 2,980 m
Natural resources: petroleum, copper, asbestos, some marble, limestone, chromium, gypsum, natural gas
Land use: *agricultural land:* 4.7%
arable land: 0.1%;
permanent crops: 0.1%;
permanent pasture: 4.5%
forest: 0%
other: 95.3% (2011 est.)
Irrigated land: 590 sq km (2012)
Total renewable water resources: 1.4 cu km (2011)
Freshwater withdrawal (domestic/industrial/agricultural): *total:* 1.32 cu km/yr (10%/1%/88%)
per capita: 515.8 cu m/yr (2003)
Natural hazards: summer winds often raise large sandstorms and dust storms in interior; periodic droughts
Environment—current issues: rising soil salinity; beach pollution from oil spills; limited natural freshwater resources
Environment—international agreements: *party to:* Biodiversity, Climate Change, Climate Change-Kyoto Protocol, Desertification, Hazardous Wastes, Law of the Sea, Marine Dumping, Ozone Layer Protection, Ship Pollution, Whaling
signed, but not ratified: none of the selected agreements
Geography—note: consists of Oman proper and two northern exclaves, Musandam and Al Madhah; the former is a peninsula that occupies a strategic location adjacent to the Strait of Hormuz, a vital transit point for world crude oil

PEOPLE AND SOCIETY

Nationality: *noun:* Omani(s)
adjective: Omani

Ethnic groups: Arab, Baluchi, South Asian (Indian, Pakistani, Sri Lankan, Bangladeshi), African
Languages: Arabic (official), English, Baluchi, Urdu, Indian dialects
Religions: Muslim (official; majority are Ibadhi, lesser numbers of Sunni and Shia) 85.9%, Christian 6.5%, Hindu 5.5%, Buddhist 0.8%, Jewish <0.1, other 1%, unaffiliated 0.2% (2010 est.)
note: approximately 75% of Omani citizens, who compose almost 70% of the country's total population, are Ibadhi Muslims; the Omani government does not keep statistics on religious affiliation (2013)
Population: 3,286,936 (July 2015 est.)
note: immigrants make up over 40% of the total population, according to UN data (2015)
country comparison to the world: 135
Age structure: *0–14 years:* 30.23% (male 509,465/female 484,068)
15–24 years: 19.51% (male 336,286/female 304,994)
25–54 years: 43% (male 822,302/female 590,937)
55–64 years: 3.9% (male 68,460/female 59,756)
65 years and over: 3.37% (male 55,081/female 55,587) (2015 est.)
Dependency ratios: *total dependency ratio:* 30%
youth dependency ratio: 26.7%
elderly dependency ratio: 3.4%
potential support ratio: 29.8% (2015 est.)
Median age: *total:* 25.1 years
male: 26.3 years
female: 23.7 years (2015 est.)
country comparison to the world: 153
Population growth rate: 2.07% (2015 est.)
country comparison to the world: 47
Birth rate: 24.44 births/1,000 population (2015 est.)
country comparison to the world: 56
Death rate: 3.36 deaths/1,000 population (2015 est.)
country comparison to the world: 218
Net migration rate: -0.43 migrant(s)/1,000 population (2015 est.)
country comparison to the world: 132
Urbanization: *urban Population:* 77.6% of total population (2015)
rate of urbanization: 8.54% annual rate of change (2010–15 est.)
Major urban areas—Population: MUSCAT (capital) 838,000 (2015)
Sex ratio: *at birth:* 1.05 male(s)/female
0–14 years: 1.05 male(s)/female
15–24 years: 1.1 male(s)/female
25–54 years: 1.39 male(s)/female
55–64 years: 1.15 male(s)/female
65 years and over: 0.99 male(s)/female
total population: 1.2 male(s)/female (2015 est.)
Maternal mortality rate: 17 deaths/100,000 live births (2015 est.)
country comparison to the world: 122
Infant mortality rate: *total:* 13.55 deaths/1,000 live births

THE CIA WORLD FACTBOOK

male: 13.85 deaths/1,000 live births

female: 13.23 deaths/1,000 live births (2015 est.)

country comparison to the world: 110

Life expectancy at birth: *total population:* 75.21 years

male: 73.29 years

female: 77.23 years (2015 est.)

country comparison to the world: 103

Total fertility rate: 2.86 children born/woman (2015 est.)

country comparison to the world: 59

Contraceptive prevalence rate: 24.4% (2007/08)

Health expenditures: 2.6% of GDP (2013)

country comparison to the world: 185

Physicians density: 2.43 physicians/1,000 population (2012)

Hospital bed density: 1.7 beds/1,000 population (2012)

Drinking water source:

improved:

urban: 95.5% of population

rural: 86.1% of population

total: 93.4% of population

unimproved:

urban: 4.5% of population

rural: 13.9% of population

total: 6.6% of population (2015 est.)

Sanitation facility access:

improved:

urban: 97.3% of population

rural: 94.7% of population

total: 96.7% of population

unimproved:

urban: 2.7% of population

rural: 5.3% of population

total: 3.3% of population (2015 est.)

HIV/AIDS—adult prevalence rate: 0.16% (2014 est.)

country comparison to the world: 101

HIV/AIDS—people living with HIV/AIDS: 2,400 (2014 est.)

HIV/AIDS—deaths: less than 100 (2014 est.)

country comparison to the world: 114

Obesity—adult prevalence rate: 26.5% (2014)

country comparison to the world: 94

Children under the age of 5 years underweight: 9.7% (2014)

country comparison to the world: 73

Education expenditures: 5% of GDP (2013)

country comparison to the world: 100

Literacy: *definition:* age 15 and over can read and write

total population: 91.1%

male: 93.6%

female: 85.6% (2015 est.)

School life expectancy (primary to tertiary education): *total:* 14 years

male: 14 years

female: 14 years (2011)

GOVERNMENT

Country name: *conventional long form:* Sultanate of Oman

conventional short form: Oman

local long form: Saltanat Uman

local short form: Uman

former: Sultanate of Muscat and Oman

etymology: the origin of the name is uncertain, but it apparently dates back at least 2,000 years since an "Omana" is mentioned by Pliny the Elder (1st century A.D.) and an "Omanon" by Ptolemy (2nd century A.D.)

Government type: absolute monarchy

Capital: *name:* Muscat

Geographic coordinates: 23 37 N, 58 35 E

time difference: UTC+4 (9 hours ahead of Washington, DC, during Standard Time)

Administrative divisions: 11 governorates (muhafazat, singular—muhafazat); Ad Dakhiliyah, Al Buraymi, Al Wusta, Az Zahirah, Janub al Batinah (Al Batinah South), Janub ash Sharqiyah (Ash Sharqiyah South), Masqat (Muscat), Musandam, Shamal al Batinah (Al Batinah North), Shamal ash Sharqiyah (Ash Sharqiyah North), Zufar (Dhofar)

Independence: 1650 (expulsion of the Portuguese)

National holiday: Birthday of Sultan QABOOS, 18 November (1940)

Constitution: 1996 (the Basic Law of the Sultanate of Oman serves as the constitution); amended by royal decree in 2011 (2016)

Legal system: mixed legal system of Anglo-Saxon law and Islamic law

International law organization participation: has not submitted an ICJ jurisdiction declaration; non-party state to the ICCt

Citizenship: *citizenship by birth:* no

citizenship by descent only: the father must be a citizen of Oman

dual citizenship recognized: no

residency requirement for naturalization: unknown

Suffrage: 21 years of age; universal; note—members of the military and security forces by law cannot vote

Executive branch: *chief of state:* Sultan and Prime Minister QABOOS bin Said Al-Said (sultan since 23 July 1970 and prime minister since 23 July 1972); note—the monarch is both chief of state and head of government

head of government: Sultan and Prime Minister QABOOS bin Said Al-Said (sultan since 23 July 1970 and prime minister since 23 July 1972)

cabinet: Cabinet appointed by the monarch

elections/appointments: the Ruling Family Council determines a successor from the sultan's extended family; if the Council cannot form a consensus within 3 days of the sultan's death or incapacitation, the Defense Council will relay a predetermined heir as chosen by the sultan

Legislative branch: *description:* bicameral Council of Oman or Majlis Oman consists of the Council of State or Majlis al-Dawla (85 seats including the chairman; members appointed by the sultan from among former government officials and prominent educators, businessmen, and citizens) and the Consultative Council or Majlis al-Shura (85 seats; members directly elected in single- and two-seat constituencies by simple majority popular vote to serve renewable 4-year terms); note—following political reforms in 2011, legislation from the Consultative Council is submitted to the Council of State for review by the Royal Court

elections: Consultative Assembly—last held on 25 October 2015 (next to be held in October 2019)

election results: percent of vote by party—NA; seats by party—NA

Judicial branch: *highest court(s):* Supreme Court (consists of 5 judges)

judge selection and term of office: judges nominated by the 9-member Supreme Judicial Council (chaired by the monarch) and appointed by the monarch; judge tenure NA

subordinate courts: Courts of Appeal; Courts of First Instance; sharia courts; magistrates' courts

Political parties and leaders: political parties are illegal

Political pressure groups and leaders: none

International organization participation: ABEDA, AFESD, AM F, CAEU, FAO, G-77, GCC, IAEA, IBRD, ICAO, ICC (NGOs), IDA, IDB, IFAD, IFC, IHO, ILO, IMF, IMO, IMSO, Interpol, IOC, IPU, ISO, ITSO, ITU, LAS, MIGA, NAM, OIC, OPCW, UN, UNCTAD, UNESCO, UNIDO, UNWTO, UPU, WCO, WFTU (NGOs), WHO, WIPO, WMO, WTO

Diplomatic representation in the US: *chief of mission:* Ambassador Hunaina bint Sultan bin Ahmad al-MUGHAIRI (since9 November 2005)

chancery: 2535 Belmont Road, NW, Washington, DC 20008

telephone: [1] (202) 387-1980

FAX: [1] (202) 745-4933

Diplomatic representation from the US: *chief of mission:* Ambassador Marc J. SIEVERS (since 7 January 2016)

embassy: Jamait Ad Duwal Al Arabiyya Street, Al Khuwair area, Muscat

mailing address: P. O. Box 202, P. C.115, Madinat Al Sultan Qaboos, Muscat

telephone: [968] 24-643-400

FAX: [968] 24-64-37-40

Flag description: three horizontal bands of white, red, and green of equal width with a broad, vertical, red band on the hoist side; the national emblem (a khanjar dagger in its sheath superimposed on two crossed swords in scabbards) in white is centered near the top of the vertical band; white represents peace and prosperity, red recalls battles against foreign invaders, and green symbolizes the Jebel Akhdar (Green Mountains) and fertility

National symbol(s): khanjar dagger superimposed on two crossed swords; national colors: red, white, green

National anthem: *name:* "Nashid as-Salaam as-Sultani" (The Sultan's Anthem)

lyrics/music: Rashid bin Uzayyiz al KHUSAIDI/ James Frederick MILLS, arranged by Bernard EBBINGHAUS

note: adopted 1932; new lyrics written after QABOOS bin Said al Said gained power in 1970; first performed by the band of a British ship as a salute to the Sultan during a 1932 visit to Muscat; the bandmaster of the HMS Hawkins was asked to write a salutation to the Sultan on the occasion of his ship visit

ECONOMY

Economy—overview: Oman is heavily dependent on its dwindling oil resources, which generate 84% of government revenue. In 2015, low global oil prices drove Oman's budget deficit to $6.5 billion, or nearly 11% of GDP. Oman has limited foreign assets and is issuing debt to cover its deficit.

Oman is using enhanced oil recovery techniques to boost production and has actively pursued a development plan that focuses on diversification, industrialization, and privatization, with the objective of reducing the oil sector's contribution to GDP from 46% at present to 9% by 2020. Tourism and gas-based industries are key components of the government's diversification strategy.

Muscat also is focused on creating more jobs to employ the rising number of Omanis entering the workforce. Increases in social welfare benefits, however, particularly since the Arab Spring, have challenged the government's ability to effectively balance its budget, as oil prices decline. Omani officials intend to reduce social entitlements to cut the deficit, but have faced stiff public opposition to spending cuts, hindering their implementation.

GDP (purchasing power parity): $171.4 billion (2015 est.)
$164.6 billion (2014 est.)
$159.9 billion (2013 est.)
note: data are in 2015 US dollars
country comparison to the world: 67
GDP (official exchange rate): $58.49 billion (2015 est.)
GDP—real growth rate: 4.1% (2015 est.)
2.9% (2014 est.) 4.7% (2013 est.)
country comparison to the world: 63
GDP—per capita (PPP): $44,600 (2015 est.)
$44,300 (2014 est.)
$44,500 (2013 est.)
note: data are in 2015 US dollars
country comparison to the world: 33
Gross national saving: 16.9% of GDP (2015 est.)
34.4% of GDP (2014 est.)
34.6% of GDP (2013 est.)
country comparison to the world: 97

GDP—composition, by end use:
household consumption: 35.8%
government consumption: 23.8%
investment in fixed capital: 31.8%
investment in inventories: -0.9%
exports of goods and services: 57.1%
imports of goods and services: -47.6% (2015 est.)
GDP—composition, by sector of origin:
agriculture: 1.4%
industry: 52%
services: 46.6% (2015 est.)
Agriculture—products: dates, limes, bananas, alfalfa, vegetables; camels, cattle; fish
Industries: crude oil production and refining, natural and liquefied natural gas (LNG) production; construction, cement, copper, steel, chemicals, optic fiber
Industrial production growth rate: 1.8% (2015 est.)
country comparison to the world: 123
Labor force: 968,800

note: about 60% of the labor force is non-national (2007 est.)
country comparison to the world: 144
Labor force—by occupation: *agriculture:* NA%
industry: NA%
services: NA%
Unemployment rate: 15% (2004 est.)
country comparison to the world: 150
Population below poverty line: NA%
Household income or consumption by percentage share: *lowest:* 10%: NA%
highest: 10%: NA%
Budget: *revenues:* $30.13 billion
expenditures: $36.62 billion (2015 est.)
Taxes and other revenues: 50.1% of GDP (2015 est.)
country comparison to the world: 14
Budget surplus (+) or deficit (–): -10.8% of GDP (2015 est.)
country comparison to the world: 204
Public debt: 7% of GDP (2015 est.)
4.9% of GDP (2014 est.)
country comparison to the world: 174
Fiscal year: calendar year
Inflation rate (consumer prices): 0.2% (2015 est.)
1% (2014 est.)
country comparison to the world: 55
Central bank discount rate: 2% (31 December 2010)
0.05% (31 December 2009)
country comparison to the world: 114
Commercial bank prime lending rate: 5.3% (31 December 2015 est.)
5.08% (31 December 2014 est.)
country comparison to the world: 143
Stock of narrow money: $13.76 billion (31 December 2015 est.)
$12.5 billion (31 December 2014 est.)
country comparison to the world: 70
Stock of broad money: $39.85 billion (31 December 2015 est.)
$35.8 billion (31 December 2014 est.)
country comparison to the world: 74
Stock of domestic credit: $37.06 billion (31 December 2015 est.)
$33.69 billion (31 December 2014 est.)
country comparison to the world: 68
Market value of publicly traded shares: $20.19 billion (31 December 2014 est.)
$19.07 billion (31 December 2013)
$20.27 billion (31 December 2010 est.)
country comparison to the world: 66
Current account balance: -$7.373 billion (2015 est.)
$4.699 billion (2014 est.)
country comparison to the world: 174
Exports: $39.14 billion (2015 est.)
$53.22 billion (2014 est.)
country comparison to the world: 56
Exports—commodities: petroleum, reexports, fish, metals, textiles
Exports—partners: China 35.4%, UAE 15.2%, South Korea 6.8%, Saudi Arabia 5.8%, Pakistan 4.2% (2015)
Imports: $25.1 billion (2015 est.)
$27.18 billion (2014 est.)

country comparison to the world: 69
Imports—commodities: machinery and transport equipment, manufactured goods, food, livestock, lubricants
Imports—partners: UAE 29.5%, Japan 10.2%, US 7.5%, China 6.7%, India 6.3% (2015)
Reserves of foreign exchange and gold: $15.72 billion (31 December 2015 est.)
$16.32 billion (31 December 2014 est.)
country comparison to the world: 67
Debt—external: $10.18 billion (31 December 2014 est.)
$11.33 billion (31 December 2013 est.)
country comparison to the world: 106
Stock of direct foreign investment—at home: $NA
Stock of direct foreign investment—abroad: $NA
Exchange rates: Omani rials (OMR) per US dollar—
0.3845 (2015 est.)
0.3845 (2014 est.)
0.3845 (2013 est.)
0.3845 (2012 est.)
0.3845 (2011 est.)

ENERGY

Electricity—production: 23.77 billion kWh (2012 est.)
country comparison to the world: 70
Electricity—consumption: 20.36 billion kWh (2012 est.)
country comparison to the world: 70
Electricity—exports: 0 kWh (2013 est.)
country comparison to the world: 172
Electricity—imports: 0 kWh (2013 est.)
country comparison to the world: 178
Electricity—installed generating capacity: 5.809 million kW (2012 est.)
country comparison to the world: 73
Electricity—from fossil fuels: 100% of total installed capacity (2012 est.)
country comparison to the world: 20
Electricity—from nuclear fuels: 0% of total installed capacity (2012 est.)
country comparison to the world: 146
Electricity—from hydroelectric plants: 0% of total installed capacity (2012 est.)
country comparison to the world: 188
Electricity—from other renewable sources: 0% of total installed capacity (2012 est.)
country comparison to the world: 203
Crude oil—production: 943,500 bbl/day (2014 est.)
country comparison to the world: 21
Crude oil—exports: 833,400 bbl/day (2013 est.)
country comparison to the world: 16
Crude oil—imports: 0 bbl/day (2012 est.)
country comparison to the world: 101
Crude oil—proved reserves: 5.151 billion bbl (1 January 2015 est.)
country comparison to the world: 24
Refined petroleum products—production: 216,900 bbl/day (2012 est.)
country comparison to the world: 51
Refined petroleum products—consumption: 172,000 bbl/day (2013 est.)
country comparison to the world: 61

Refined petroleum products—exports: 44,300 bbl/day (2012 est.)
country comparison to the world: 58
Refined petroleum products—imports: 6,529 bbl/day (2012 est.)
country comparison to the world: 149
Natural gas—production: 31.92 billion cu m (2013 est.)
country comparison to the world: 26
Natural gas—consumption: 21.92 billion cu m (2013 est.)
country comparison to the world: 36
Natural gas—exports: 11.5 billion cu m (2013 est.)
country comparison to the world: 18
Natural gas—imports: 1.95 billion cu m (2013 est.)
country comparison to the world: 50
Natural gas—proved reserves: 849.5 billion cu m (1 January 2014 est.)
country comparison to the world: 28
Carbon dioxide emissions from consumption of energy: 62.85 million Mt (2012 est.)
country comparison to the world: 53

COMMUNICATIONS

Telephones—fixed lines: *total subscriptions:* 380,000
subscriptions per 100 inhabitants: 12 (2014 est.)
country comparison to the world: 108

Telephones—mobile cellular: *total:* 6.2 million
subscriptions per 100 inhabitants: 192 (2014 est.)
country comparison to the world: 109

Telephone system: *general assessment:* modern system consisting of open-wire, microwave, and radiotelephone communication stations; limited coaxial cable; domestic satellite system with 8 earth stations
domestic: fixed-line and mobile-cellular subscribership both increasing with fixed-line phone

service gradually being introduced to remote villages using wireless local loop systems
international: country code—968; the Fiber-Optic Link Around the Globe (FLAG) and the SEA-ME-WE-3 submarine cable provide connectivity to Asia, the Middle East, and Europe; satellite earth stations—2 Intelsat (Indian Ocean),1 Arabsat (2008)
Broadcast media: 1 state-run TV broadcaster; TV stations transmitting from Saudi Arabia, the UAE, and Yemen available via satellite TV; state-run radio operates multiple stations; first private radio station began operating in 2007 and 2 additional stations now operating (2007)
Radio broadcast stations: AM 3, FM 9, shortwave 2 (1999)
Television broadcast stations: 13 (plus 25 repeaters) (1999)
Internet country code: .om
Internet hosts: 14,531 (2012)
country comparison to the world: 127
Internet users: *total:* 2.1 million
percent of Population: 65.8% (2014 est.)
country comparison to the world: 96

TRANSPORTATION

Airports: 132 (2013)
country comparison to the world: 44
Airports—with paved runways: *total:* 13
over 3,047 m: 7
2,438 to 3,047 m: 5
914 to 1,523 m: 1 (2013)
Airports—with unpaved runways: *total:* 119
over 3,047 m: 2
2,438 to 3,047 m: 7
1,524 to 2,437 m: 51
914 to 1,523 m: 33
under 914 m: 26 (2013)
Heliports: 3 (2013)
Pipelines: condensate 106 km; gas 4,224 km; oil 3,558 km; oil/gas/water 33 km; refined products 264 km (2013)

Roadways: *total:* 60,230 km
paved: 29,685 km (includes 1943 km of expressways)
unpaved: 30,545 km (2012)
country comparison to the world: 69
Merchant marine: *total:* 5
by type: chemical tanker 1, passenger 1, passenger/cargo 3
registered in other countries: 15 (Malta 5, Panama 10) (2010)
country comparison to the world: 128
Ports and terminals: *major seaport(s):* Mina' Qabus, Salalah, Suhar
container port(s) (TEUs): Salalah (3,200,000)
LNG terminal(s) (export): Qalhat

MILITARY AND SECURITY

Military branches: Sultan's Armed Forces (SAF): Royal Army of Oman, Royal Navy of Oman, Royal Air Force of Oman (al-Quwwat al-Jawwiya al-Sultanat Oman) (2013)
Military service age and obligation: 18–30 years of age for voluntary military service; no conscription (2012)
Military expenditures: 11.8% of GDP (2014)
15% of GDP (2013)
8.61% of GDP (2012)
6.13% of GDP (2011)
8.61% of GDP (2010)
country comparison to the world: 3

TRANSNATIONAL ISSUES

Disputes—international: boundary agreement reportedly signed and ratified with UAE in 2003 for entire border, including Oman's Musandam Peninsula and Al Madhah exclave, but details of the alignment have not been made public
Refugees and internally displaced persons: *refugees (country of origin):* 5,000 (Yemen) (2016)

PACIFIC OCEAN

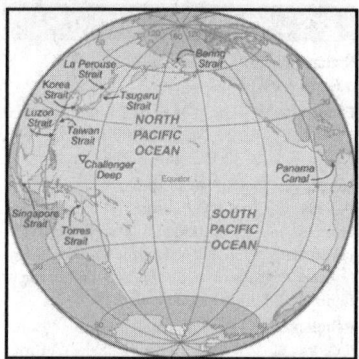

INTRODUCTION

Background: The Pacific Ocean is the largest of the world's five oceans (followed by the Atlantic Ocean, Indian Ocean, Southern Ocean, and Arctic Ocean). Strategically important access waterways include the La Perouse, Tsugaru, Tsushima, Taiwan, Singapore, and Torres Straits. The decision by the International Hydrographic Organization in the spring of 2000 to delimit a fifth ocean, the Southern Ocean, removed the portion of the Pacific Ocean south of 60 degrees south.

GEOGRAPHY

Location: body of water between the Southern Ocean, Asia, Australia, and the Western Hemisphere

Geographic coordinates: 0 00 N, 160 00 W

Map references: Political Map of the World

Area: *total:* 155.557 million sq km
note: includes Bali Sea, Bering Sea, Bering Strait, Coral Sea, East China Sea, Gulf of Alaska, Gulf of Tonkin, Philippine Sea, Sea of Japan, Sea of Okhotsk, South China Sea, Tasman Sea, and other tributary water bodies

Area—comparative: about 15 times the size of the US; covers about 28% of the global surface; almost equal to the total land area of the world

Coastline: 135,663 km

Climate: planetary air pressure systems and resultant wind patterns exhibit remarkable uniformity in the south and east; trade winds and westerly winds are well-developed patterns, modified by seasonal fluctuations; tropical cyclones (hurricanes) may form south of Mexico from June to October and affect Mexico and Central America; continental influences cause climatic uniformity to be much less pronounced in the eastern and western regions at the same latitude in the North Pacific Ocean; the western Pacific is monsoonal—a rainy season occurs during the summer months, when moisture-laden winds blow from the ocean over the land, and a dry season during the winter months, when dry winds blow from the Asian landmass back to the ocean; tropical cyclones (typhoons) may strike southeast and east Asia from May to December

Terrain: surface currents in the northern Pacific are dominated by a clockwise, warm-water gyre (broad circular system of currents) and in the southern Pacific by a counterclockwise, cool-water gyre; in the northern Pacific, sea ice forms in the Bering Sea and Sea of Okhotsk in winter; in the southern Pacific, sea ice from Antarctica reaches its northernmost extent in October; the ocean floor in the eastern Pacific is dominated by the East Pacific Rise, while the western Pacific is dissected by deep trenches, including the Mariana Trench, which is the world's deepest

Elevation: *mean depth:* -3,970 m

elevation extremes: *lowest point:* Challenger Deep in the Mariana Trench -10,924 m
highest point: sea level 0 m

Natural resources: oil and gas fields, polymetallic nodules, sand and gravel aggregates, placer deposits, fish

Natural hazards: surrounded by a zone of violent volcanic and earthquake activity sometimes referred to as the "Pacific Ring of Fire"; subject to tropical cyclones (typhoons) in southeast and east Asia from May to December (most frequent from July to October); tropical cyclones (hurricanes) may form south of Mexico and strike Central America and Mexico from June to October (most common in August and September); cyclical El Nino/La Nina phenomenon occurs in the equatorial Pacific, influencing weather in the Western Hemisphere and the western Pacific; ships subject to superstructure icing in extreme north from October to May; persistent fog in the northern Pacific can be a maritime hazard from June to December

Environment—current issues: endangered marine species include the dugong, sea lion, sea otter, seals, turtles, and whales; oil pollution in Philippine Sea and South China Sea

Geography—note: the major chokepoints are the Bering Strait, Panama Canal, Luzon Strait, and the Singapore Strait; the Equator divides the Pacific Ocean into the North Pacific Ocean and the South Pacific Ocean; dotted with low coral islands and rugged volcanic islands in the southwestern Pacific Ocean

GOVERNMENT

Country name: *etymology:* named by Portuguese explorer Ferdinand MAGELLAN during the Spanish circumnavigation of the world in 1521; encountering favorable winds upon reaching the ocean, he called it "Mar Pacifico, " which means "peaceful sea" in both Portuguese and Spanish

ECONOMY

Economy—overview: The Pacific Ocean is a major contributor to the world economy and particularly to those nations its waters directly touch. It provides low-cost sea transportation between East and West, extensive fishing grounds, offshore oil and gas fields, minerals, and sand and gravel for the construction industry. In 1996, over 60% of the world's fish catch came from the Pacific Ocean. Exploitation of offshore oil and gas reserves is playing an ever-increasing role in the energy supplies of the US, Australia, NZ, China, and Peru. The high cost of recovering offshore oil and gas, combined with the wide swings in world prices for oil since 1985, has led to fluctuations in new drillings.

TRANSPORTATION

Ports and terminals: *major seaport(s):* Bangkok (Thailand), Hong Kong (China), Kao-hsiung (Taiwan), Los Angeles (US), Manila (Philippines), Pusan (South Korea), San Francisco (US), Seattle (US), Shanghai (China), Singapore, Sydney (Australia), Vladivostok (Russia), Wellington (NZ), Yokohama (Japan)

Transportation—note: the Inside Passage offers protected waters from southeast Alaska to Puget Sound (Washington state); the International Maritime Bureau reports the territorial waters of littoral states and offshore waters in the South China Sea as high risk for piracy and armed robbery against ships accounting for 55% of all attacks in 2014; numerous commercial vessels have been attacked and hijacked both at anchor and while underway; hijacked vessels are often disguised and cargoes stolen; crew and passengers are often held for ransom, murdered, or cast adrift

TRANSNATIONAL ISSUES

Disputes—international: some maritime disputes (see littoral states)

PAKISTAN

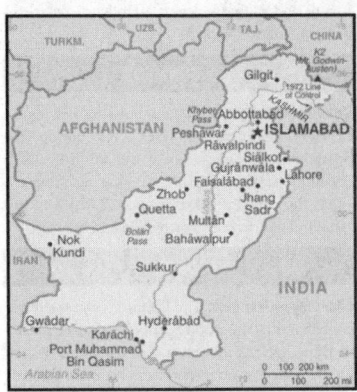

INTRODUCTION

Background: The Indus Valley civilization, one of the oldest in the world and dating back at least 5,000 years, spread over much of what is presently Pakistan. During the second millennium B.C., remnants of this culture fused with the migrating Indo-Aryan peoples. The area underwent successive invasions in subsequent centuries from the Persians, Greeks, Scythians, Arabs (who brought Islam), Afghans, and Turks. The Mughal Empire flourished in the 16th and 17th centuries; the British came to dominate the region in the 18th century. The separation in 1947 of British India into the Muslim state of Pakistan (with West and East sections) and largely Hindu India was never satisfactorily resolved, and India and Pakistan fought two wars—in 1947-48 and 1965—over the disputed Kashmir territory. A third war between these countries in 1971—in which India capitalized on Islamabad's marginalization of Bengalis in Pakistani politics—resulted in East Pakistan becoming the separate nation of Bangladesh. in response to Indian nuclear weapons testing, Pakistan conducted its own tests in 1998. India-Pakistan relations have been rocky since the November 2008 Mumbai attacks, but both countries are taking steps to put relations back on track. Nawaz SHARIF took office as Prime Minister in 2013, marking the first time in Pakistani history that a democratically elected government completed a full term and transitioned to a successive democratically elected government.

GEOGRAPHY

Location: Southern Asia, bordering the Arabian Sea, between India on the east and Iran and Afghanistan on the west and China in the north

Geographic coordinates: 30 00 N, 70 00 E

Map references: Asia

Area: *total:* 796,095 sq km
land: 770,875 sq km

water: 25,220 sq km
country comparison to the world: 36

Area—comparative: slightly more than five times the size of Georgia; slightly less than twice the size of California

Land boundaries: *total:* 7,257 km
border countries (4): Afghanistan 2,670 km, China 438 km, India 3,190 km, Iran 959 km

Coastline: 1,046 km

Maritime claims: *territorial sea:* 12 nm
contiguous zone: 24 nm
exclusive economic zone: 200 nm
continental shelf: 200 nm or to the edge of the continental margin

Climate: mostly hot, dry desert; temperate in northwest; arctic in north

Terrain: divided into three major geographic areas: the northern highlands, the Indus River plain in the center and east, and the Balochistan Plateau in the south and west

Elevation: *mean elevation:* 900 m

elevation extremes: *lowest point:* Indian Ocean 0 m
highest point: K2 (Mt. Godwin-Austen) 8,611 m

Natural resources: arable land, extensive natural gas reserves, limited petroleum, poor quality coal, iron ore, copper, salt, limestone

Land use: *agricultural land:* 35.2%
arable land: 27.6%
permanent crops: 1.1%
permanent pasture: 6.5%
forest: 2.1%
other: 62.7% (2011 est.)

Irrigated land: 202,000 sq km (2012)

Total renewable water resources: 246.8 cu km (2011)

Freshwater withdrawal (domestic/industrial/agricultural): *total:* 183.5 cu km/yr (5%/1%/94%)
per capita: 1,038 cu m/yr (2008)

Natural hazards: frequent earthquakes, occasionally severe especially in north and west; flooding along the Indus after heavy rains (July and August)

Environment—current issues: water pollution from raw sewage, industrial wastes, and agricultural runoff; lim ited natural freshwater resources; most of the population does not have access to potable water; deforestation; soil erosion; desertification

Environment—international agreements: *party to:* Biodiversity, Climate Change, Climate Change-Kyoto Protocol, Desertification, Endangered Species, Environmental Modification, Hazardous Wastes, Law of the Sea, Marine Dumping, Ozone Layer Protection, Ship Pollution, Wetlands
signed, but not ratified: Marine Life Conservation

Geography—note: controls Khyber Pass and Bolan Pass, traditional invasion routes between Central Asia and the Indian Subcontinent

PEOPLE AND SOCIETY

Nationality: *noun:* Pakistani(s)
adjective: Pakistani

Ethnic groups: Punjabi 44.68%, Pashtun (Pathan) 15.42%, Sindhi 14.1%, Sariaki 8.38%, Muhajirs 7.57%, Balochi 3.57%, other 6.28%

Languages: Punjabi 48%, Sindhi 12%, Saraiki (a Punjabi variant) 10%, Pashto (alternate name, Pashtu) 8%, Urdu (official) 8%, Balochi 3%, Hindko 2%, Brahui 1%, English (official; lingua franca of Pakistani elite and most government ministries), Burushaski, and other 8%

Religions: Muslim (official) 96.4% (Sunni 85-90%, Shia 10-15%), other (includes Christian and Hindu) 3.6% (2010 est.)

Population: 199,085,847 (July 2015 est.)
country comparison to the world: 7

Age structure: *0-14 years:* 32.65% (male 33,396,847/female 31,611,641)
15-24 years: 21.44% (male 22,016,207/female 20,673,562)
25-54 years: 36.28% (male 37,526,930/female 34,701,271)
55-64 years: 5.28% (male 5,254,347/female 5,253,526)
65 years and over: 4.35% (male 4,036,727/female 4,614,789) (2015 est.)

Dependency ratios: *total dependency ratio:* 65.3%
youth dependency ratio: 57.9%
elderly dependency ratio: 7.4%
potential support ratio: 13.5% (2015 est.)

Median age: *total:* 23 years
male: 22.9 years
female: 23 years (2015 est.)
country comparison to the world: 170

Population growth rate: 1.46% (2015 est.)
country comparison to the world: 82

Birth rate: 22.58 births/1,000 population (2015 est.)
country comparison to the world: 72

Death rate: 6.49 deaths/1,000 population (2015 est.)
country comparison to the world: 149

Net migration rate: -1.54 migrant(s)/1,000 population (2015 est.)
country comparison to the world: 157

Urbanization: *urban population:* 38.8% of total population (2015)
rate of urbanization: 2.81% annual rate of change (2010-15 est.)

Major urban areas—population: Karachi 16.618 million; Lahore 8.741 million; Faisalabad 3.567 million; Rawalpindi 2.506 million; Multan 1.921 million; ISLAMABAD (capital) 1.365 million (2015)

Sex ratio: *at birth:* 1.05 male(s)/female
0-14 years: 1.06 male(s)/female

15–24 years: 1.07 male(s)/female
25–54 years: 1.08 male(s)/female
55–64 years: 1 male(s)/female
65 years and over: 0.88 male(s)/female
total population: 1.06 male(s)/female (2015 est.)

Mother's mean age at first birth: 23.4
note: median age at first birth among women 25–29 (2012/13 est.)

Maternal mortality rate: 178 deaths/100,000 live births (2015 est.)
country comparison to the world: 44

Infant mortality rate: *total:* 55.67 deaths/1,000 live births
male: 58.84 deaths/1,000 live births
female: 52.35 deaths/1,000 live births (2015 est.)
country comparison to the world: 26

Life expectancy at birth: *total population:* 67.39 years
male: 65.47 years
female: 69.4 years (2015 est.)
country comparison to the world: 167

Total fertility rate: 2.75 children born/woman (2015 est.)
country comparison to the world: 67

Contraceptive prevalence rate: 35.4% (2012/13)

Health expenditures: 2.8% of GDP (2013)
country comparison to the world: 183

Physicians density: 0.83 physicians/1,000 population (2010)

Hospital bed density: 0.6 beds/1,000 population (2012)

Drinking water source:
improved:
urban: 93.9% of population
rural: 89.9% of population
total: 91.4% of population
unimproved:
urban: 6.1% of population
rural: 10.1% of population
total: 8.6% of population (2015 est.)

Sanitation facility access:
improved:
urban: 83.1% of population
rural: 51.1% of population
total: 63.5% of population
unimproved:
urban: 16.9% of population
rural: 48.9% of population
total: 36.5% of population (2015 est.)

HIV/AIDS—adult prevalence rate: 0.09% (2014 est.)
country comparison to the world: 113

HIV/AIDS—people living with HIV/AIDS: 93,900 (2014 est.)
country comparison to the world: 53

HIV/AIDS—deaths: 2,800 (2014 est.)
country comparison to the world: 47

Major infectious diseases: *degree of risk:* high
food or waterborne diseases: bacterial diarrhea, hepatitis A and E, and typhoid fever
vectorborne diseases: dengue fever and malaria
animal contact disease: rabies

note: highly pathogenic H5N1 avian influenza has been identified in this country; it poses a negligible risk with extremely rare cases possible among US citizens who have close contact with birds (2013)

Obesity—adult prevalence rate: 4.8% (2014)
country comparison to the world: 153

Children under the age of 5 years underweight: 31.6% (2013)
country comparison to the world: 11

Education expenditures: 2.5% of GDP (2014)
country comparison to the world: 164

Literacy: *definition:* age 15 and over can read and write
total population: 57.9%
male: 69.5%
female: 45.8% (2015 est.)

School life expectancy (primary to tertiary education): *total:* 8 years
male: 9 years
female: 7 years (2014)

Unemployment, youth ages 15–24: *total:* 7.7%
male: 7%
female: 10.5% (2008 est.)
country comparison to the world: 115

GOVERNMENT

Country name: *conventional long form:* Islamic Republic of Pakistan
conventional short form: Pakistan
local long form: Jamhuryat Islami Pakistan
local short form: Pakistan
former: West Pakistan
etymology: the word "pak" means "pure" in Persian or Pashto, while the Persian suffix "-stan" means "place of" or "country, " so the word Pakistan literally means "Land of the pure"

Government type: federal parliamentary republic

Capital: *name:* Islamabad

Geographic coordinates: 33 41 N, 73 03 E
time difference: UTC+5 (10 hours ahead of Washington, DC, during Standard Time)

Administrative divisions: 4 provinces, 1 territory*, and 1 capital territory**; Balochistan, Federally Administered Tribal Areas*, Islamabad Capital Territory**, Khyber Pakhtunkhwa (formerly North-West Frontier Province), Punjab, Sindh
note: the Pakistani-administered portion of the disputed Jammu and Kashmir region consists of 2 administrative entities: Azad Kashmir and Gilgit-Baltistan

Independence: 14 August 1947 (from British India)

National holiday: Pakistan Day (also referred to as Pakistan Resolution Day or Republic Day), 23 March (1940); note—commemorates both the adoption of the Lahore Resolution by the All-India Muslim League during its 22–24 March 1940 session, which called for the creation of independent Muslim states, and the adoption of the first constitution of Pakistan on 23 March 1956 during the transition to the Islamic Republic of Pakistan

Constitution: several previous; latest endorsed 12 April 1973, passed 19 April 1973, entered into force 14 August 1973 (suspended and restored several times); amended many times, last in 2015 (2016)

Legal system: common law system with Islamic law influence

International law organization participation: accepts compulsory ICJ jurisdiction with reservations; non-party state to the ICCt

Citizenship: *citizenship by birth:* yes
citizenship by descent: at least one parent must be a citizen of Pakistan
dual citizenship recognized: yes, but limited to select countries
residency requirement for naturalization: 4 out of the previous 7 years and including the 12 months preceding application

Suffrage: 18 years of age; universal; note—there are joint electorates and reserved parliamentary seats for women and non-Muslims

Executive branch: *chief of state:* President Mamnoon HUSSAIN (since 9 September 2013)

head of government: Prime Minister Mohammad Nawaz SHARIF (since 5 June 2013)
cabinet: Cabinet appointed by the president upon the advice of the prime minister
elections/appointments: president indirectly elected by the Electoral College consisting of members of the Senate, National Assembly, and provincial assemblies for a 5-year term (eligible for reelection); election last held on 9 September 2013 (next to be held in 2018); prime minister selected by the National Assembly
election results: Mamnoon HUSSAIN elected president; Mamnoon HUSSAIN (PML-N) 432 votes, Wajihuddin AHMED (PTI) 77 votes

Legislative branch: *description:* bicameral Parliament or Majlis-e-Shoora consists of the Senate (104 seats; members indirectly elected by the 4 provincial assemblies and the territories' representatives by proportional representation vote; members serve 6-year terms with one-half of the membership renewed every 3 years) and the National Assembly (342 seats; 272 members directly elected in single-seat constituencies by simple majority vote and 70 members—60 women and 10 non-Muslims—directly elected by proportional representation vote; all members serve 5-year terms)
elections: Senate—last held on 5 March 2015 (next to be held in March 2018); National Assembly—last held on 11 May 2013 (next to be held by 2018)
election results: Senate—percent of vote by party—NA; seats by party—PPPP 27, PML-N 26, MQM 8, ANP 6, PTI 7, JUI-F 5, PML-Q 4, BNP-A 2, NP 1, PML-F 1, other 7, independent 10; National Assembly -percent of vote by party—NA; seats by party as of June 2013—PML-N 126, PPPP 31, PTI 28, MQM 18, JUI-F 10, PML-F 5, other 22, independent 25, unfilled seats 7; 60 seats reserved for women, 10 seats reserved for non-Muslims; seats by party as of August

2015 (includes women and non-Muslim seats)—PML-N 188, PPPP 46, PTI 33, MQM 24, JUI-F 13, PML-F 5, other 24, independent9

Judicial branch: *highest court(s):* Supreme Court of Pakistan (consists of the chief justice and 16 judges)
judge selection and term of office: justices nominated by an 8-member parliamentary committee upon the recommendation of the Judicial Commission (a 9-member body of judges and other judicial professionals), and appointed by the president of Pakistan; justices can serve until age 65
subordinate courts: High Courts; Federal Shariat Court; provincial and district civil and criminal courts; specialized courts for issues such as taxation, banking, customs, etc.

Political parties and leaders: Awami National Party or ANP [Mian Iftikhar HUSSAIN]
Balochistan National Party-Awami or BNP-A [Mir Israr Ullah ZEHRI]
Balochistan National Party-Mengal or BNP-M [Sardar Akhtar Jan MENGAL]
Jamaat-i Islami or JI [Sirajul HAQ]
Jamiat-i Ulema-i Islam Fazl-ur Rehman or JUI-F [Fazlur REHMAN]
Muttahida Qaumi Movement or MQM [Altaf HUSSAIN]
Pakhtun khwa Milli Awami Party or PkMAP [Mahmood Khan ACHAKZAI]
Pakistan Muslim League-Functional or PML-F [Pir PAGARO or Syed Shah Mardan SHAH-II]
Pakistan Muslim League-Nawaz or PML-N [Nawaz SHARIF]
Pakistan Peoples Party Parliamentarians or PPPP [Bilawal Bhutto ZARDARI and Asif Ali ZARDARI]
Pakistan Tehrik-e Insaaf or PTI [Imran KHAN]
Quami Watan Party or QWP [Aftab Ahmed Khan SHERPAO]
note: political alliances in Pakistan shift frequently

Political pressure groups and leaders: *other:* military; ulema (clergy); landowners; industrialists; small merchants

International organization participation: ADB, ARF, ASEAN (dialogue partner), C, CICA, CP, D-8, ECO, FAO, G-11, G-24, G-77, IAEA, IBRD, ICAO, ICC (National committees), ICRM, IDA, IDB, IFAD, IFC, IFRCS, IHO, ILO, IMF, IMO, IMSO, Interpol, IOC, IOM, IPU, ISO, ITSO, ITU, ITUC (NGOs), MIGA, MINURSO, MONUSCO, NAM, OAS (observer), OIC, OPCW, PCA, SAARC, SACEP, SCO (observer), UN, UNAMID, UNCTAD, UNESCO, UNHCR, UNIDO, UNMIL, UNOCI, UNWTO, UPU, WCO, WFTU (NGOs), WHO, WIPO, WMO, WTO

Diplomatic representation in the US: *chief of mission:* Ambassador Jalil Abbas JILANI (since 10 March 2014)
chancery: 3517 International Court, Washington, DC 20008
telephone: [1] (202) 243-6500
FAX: [1] (202) 686-1544
consulate(s) general: Chicago, Houston, Los Angeles, New York

consulate(s): Louisville (KY), San Francisco
Diplomatic representation from the US: *chief of mission:* Ambassador David M. HALE (since 3 December 2015)
embassy: Diplomatic Enclave, Ramna 5, Islamabad
mailing address: 8100 Islamabad Place, Washington, DC 20521-8100
telephone: [92] (51) 208-0000
FAX: [92] (51) 227-6427
consulate(s) general: Karachi
consulate(s): Lahore, Peshawar

Flag description: green with a vertical white band (symbolizing the role of religious minorities) on the hoist side; a large white crescent and star are centered in the green field; the crescent, star, and color green are traditional symbols of Islam

National symbol(s): star and crescent, jasmine; national colors: green, white

National anthem: *name:* "Qaumi Tarana" (National Anthem)
lyrics/music: Abu-Al-Asar Hafeez JULLANDHURI/Ahmed Ghulamali CHAGLA
note: adopted 1954; also known as "Pak sarzamin shad bad" (Blessed Be the Sacred Land)

ECONOMY

Economy—overview: Decades of internal political disputes and low levels of foreign investment have led to slow growth and underdevelopment in Pakistan. Pakistan has a large English-speaking population. Nevertheless, a challenging security environment, electricity shortages, and a burdensome investment climate have deterred investors. Agriculture accounts for more than one-fourth of output and two-fifths of employment. Textiles and apparel account for most of Pakistan's export earnings, and Pakistan's failure to diversify its exports has left the country vulnerable to shifts in world demand. Pakistan's GDP growth has gradually increased since 2012. Official unemployment was 6.5% in 2015, but this fails to capture the true picture, because much of the economy is informal and underemployment remains high. Human development continues to lag behind most of the region. In coordination with the International Monetary Fund (IMF), Pakistan embarked on an economic reform program in 2013. While the reform process has been mixed, and issues like privatization of state-owned enterprises remain unresolved, Pakistan has restored macroeconomic stability, improved its credit rating, and boosted growth. The Pakistani rupee, after heavy depreciation, remained relatively stable against the US dollar in 2014–15. Remittances from overseas workers, averaging more than $1.5 billion a month, are a key revenue source for Pakistan, partly compensating for a lack of foreign investment and a slowdown in portfolio investment. Falling global oil prices in 2015 contributed to a narrowing current account deficit and lower inflation, despite weak export performance. Pakistan's program with the IMF—a three-year, $6.7 billion Extended Fund Facility focusing on reducing energy shortages, stabilizing public finances, expanding revenue,

and improving the external balance—is slated to conclude in September 2016. While passing most quantitative targets, Pakistan has missed targets on structural reforms and performance criteria throughout the program.
Pakistan remains stuck in a low-income, low-growth trap, with growth averaging about 3.5% per year from 2008 to 2013. Pakistan must address long standing issues related to government revenues, with the tax base being narrow at 11% of GDP. Given demographic challenges, Pakistan's leadership wll be pressed to implement economic reforms, promote further development of the energy sector, and attract foreign investment to support sufficient economic growth necessary to employ its growing and rapidly urbanizing population, much of which is under the age of 25. Other long-term challenges include expanding investment in education and healthcare, adapting to the effects of climate change and Natural disasters, improving the country's business climate, and reducing dependence on foreign donors. Pakistan and China are implementing the "China-Pakistan Economic Corridor", a $46 billion investment program targeted towards the energy sector and other infrastructure project that Islamabad and Beijing had agreed on in early 2014.

GDP (purchasing power parity): $931 billion (2015 est.)
$893.1 billion (2014 est.)
$858.5 billion (2013 est.)
note: data are in 2015 US dollars
country comparison to the world: 27

GDP (official exchange rate): $270 billion (2015 est.)

GDP—real growth rate: 4.2% (2015 est.)
4% (2014 est.)
3.7% (2013 est.)
country comparison to the world: 60

GDP—per capita (PPP): $5,000 (2015 est.)
$4,900 (2014 est.)
$4,800 (2013 est.)
note: data are in 2015 US dollars
country comparison to the world: 170

Gross national saving: 14.1% of GDP (2015 est.)
13.7% of GDP (2014 est.)
13.9% of GDP (2013 est.)
country comparison to the world: 126

GDP—composition, by end use:
household consumption: 79.2%
government consumption: 11.8%
investment in fixed capital: 13.5%
investment in inventories: 1.6%
exports of goods and services: 10.9%
imports of goods and services: -17.1% (2015 est.)

GDP—composition, by sector of origin:
agriculture: 25.5%
industry: 19%
services: 55.5% (2015 est.)

Agriculture—products: cotton, wheat, rice, sugarcane, fruits, vegetables; milk, beef, mutton, eggs

Industries: textiles and apparel, food processing, pharmaceuticals, construction materials, paper products, fertilizer, shrimp

Industrial production growth rate: 3.6% (2015 est.)
country comparison to the world: 64

Labor force: 63.34 million
note: extensive export of labor, mostly to the Middle East, and use of child labor (2015 est.)
country comparison to the world: 10

Labor force—by occupation: *agriculture:* 43.7%
industry: 22.4%
services: 33.9% (FY2013 est.)

Unemployment rate: 6.5% (FY2015 est.)
6.7% (FY2014 est.)
note: substantial underemployment exists
country comparison to the world: 76

Population below poverty line: 22.3% (FY2005 est.)

Household income or consumption by percentage share: *lowest:* 10%: 4.2%
highest: 10%: 25.6% (FY2011)

Distribution of family income—Gini index: 29.6 (FY2011)
31.4 (FY2008)
country comparison to the world: 124

Budget: *revenues:* $38.75 billion
expenditures: $53.11 billion (FY2015 est.)
Taxes and other revenues: 15.6% of GDP (FY2015 est.)
country comparison to the world: 188

Budget surplus (+) or deficit (–): -5.8% of GDP (FY2015 est.)
country comparison to the world: 178

Public debt: 64.8% of GDP (FY2015 est.)
65.1% of GDP (FY2014 est.)
country comparison to the world: 55

Fiscal year: 1 July—30 June

Inflation rate (consumer prices): 4.5% (2015 est.)
8.6% (2014 est.)
country comparison to the world: 164

Central bank discount rate: 6% (15 November 2015)
9.5% (18 December 2014)
country comparison to the world: 65

Commercial bank prime lending rate: 6.46% (10 December 2015 est.)
9.74% (10 December 2014 est.)
country comparison to the world: 125

Stock of narrow money: $87.01 billion (31 October 2015 est.)
$77.03 billion (31 December 2014 est.)
country comparison to the world: 39

Stock of broad money: $107 billion (31 October 2015 est.)
$97.95 billion (31 December 2014 est.)
country comparison to the world: 54

Stock of domestic credit: $112 billion (31 October 2015 est.)
$100 billion (31 December 2014 est.)
country comparison to the world: 51

Market value of publicly traded shares: $43.68 billion (31 December 2012 est.)
$32.76 billion (31 December 2011)
$38.17 billion (31 December 2010 est.)
country comparison to the world: 55

Current account balance: -$2.627 billion (2015 est.)
-$3.13 billion (2014 est.)
country comparison to the world: 154

Exports: $23.67 billion (FY2015 est.)
$25.11 billion (FY2014 est.)
country comparison to the world: 68

Exports—commodities: textiles (garments, bed linen, cotton cloth, yarn), rice, leather goods, sporting goods, chemicals, manufactures, carpets and rugs

Exports—partners: US 13.1%, UAE 9.1%, Afghanistan 9.1%, China 8.8%, UK 5.3%, Germany 4.9% (2015)

Imports: $45.83 billion (FY2015 est.)
$45.07 billion (FY2014 est.)
country comparison to the world: 54

Imports—commodities: petroleum, petroleum products, machinery, plastics, transportation equipment, edible oils, paper and paperboard, iron and steel, tea

Imports—partners: China 28.2%, Saudi Arabia 10.9%, UAE 10.8%, Kuwait 5.6% (2015)

Reserves of foreign exchange and gold: $18.68 billion (FY2015 est.)
$14.41 billion (FY2014 est.)
country comparison to the world: 60

Debt—external: $63.58 billion (FY2015 est.)
$61.97 billion (FY2014 est.)
country comparison to the world: 58

Stock of direct foreign investment—at home: $31.17 billion (31 December 2015 est.)
$29.37 billion (31 December 2014 est.)
country comparison to the world: 68

Stock of direct foreign investment—abroad: $1.897 billion (31 December 2015 est.)
$1.847 billion (31 December 2014 est.)
country comparison to the world: 79

Exchange rates: Pakistani rupees (PKR) per US dollar—
101.45 (FY2015 est.)
102.89 (FY2014 est.)
101.1 (FY2013 est.)
93.4 (2012 est.)
86.3434 (2011 est.)

ENERGY

Electricity—production: 97.8 billion kWh (2013 est.)
country comparison to the world: 35

Electricity—consumption: 78.89 billion kWh (2013 est.)
country comparison to the world: 38

Electricity—exports: 0 kWh (2013 est.)
country comparison to the world: 183

Electricity—imports: 392 million kWh (2013 est.)
country comparison to the world: 79

Electricity—installed generating capacity: 24,380 kW (FY2014 est.)
country comparison to the world: 201

Electricity—from fossil fuels: 67.1% of total installed capacity (FY2014 est.)

country comparison to the world: 118

Electricity—from nuclear fuels: 3.2% of total installed capacity (FY2014 est.)
country comparison to the world: 26

Electricity—from hydroelectric plants: 29.2% of total installed capacity (FY2014 est.)
country comparison to the world: 78

Electricity—from other renewable sources: 0.4% of total installed capacity (FY2014 est.)
country comparison to the world: 102

Crude oil—production:
98,000 bbl/day (2014 est.)
country comparison to the world: 46

Crude oil—exports:
0 bbl/day (2012 est.)
country comparison to the world: 175

Crude oil—imports:
372,800 bbl/day (2013 est.)
country comparison to the world: 25

Crude oil—proved reserves: 371 million bbl (1 January 2015 est.)
country comparison to the world: 55

Refined petroleum products—production: 228,000 bbl/day (2012 est.)
country comparison to the world: 49

Refined petroleum products—consumption: 434,000 bbl/day (2013 est.)
country comparison to the world: 36

Refined petroleum products—export: 16,000 bbl/day (2012 est.)
country comparison to the world: 77

Refined petroleum products—imports: 210,000 bbl/day (2012 est.)
country comparison to the world: 30

Natural gas—production:
38.55 billion cu m (2013 est.)
country comparison to the world: 22

Natural gas—consumption:
41.22 billion cu m (2012 est.)
country comparison to the world: 21

Natural gas—exports:
0 cu m (2013 est.)
country comparison to the world: 103

Natural gas—imports:
0 cu m (2013 est.)
country comparison to the world: 120

Natural gas—proved reserves: 754.6 billion cu m (1 January 2014 est.)
country comparison to the world: 29

Carbon dioxide emissions from consumption of energy: 146.9 million Mt (2012 est.)
country comparison to the world: 33

COMMUNICATIONS

Telephones—fixed lines: *total subscriptions:* 4.9 million
subscriptions per 100 inhabitants: 2 (2014 est.)
country comparison to the world: 31

Telephones—mobile cellular: *total:* 135.8 million
subscriptions per 100 inhabitants: 69 (2014 est.)
country comparison to the world: 11

651

Telephone system: *general assessment:* the telecommunications infrastructure is improving, with foreign and domestic investments in fixed-line and mobile-cellular networks; system consists of microwave radio relay, coaxial cable, fiber-optic cable, cellular, and satellite networks; 3G and 4G mobile services introduced
domestic: mobile-cellular subscribership has skyrocketed, exceeding 126 million by the end of 2015, up from only about 300,000 in 2000; more than 90 percent of Pakistanis live within areas that have cell phone coverage, and more than half of all Pakistanis have access to a cell phone; fiber optic networks are being con structed throughout the country to in crease broadband access, though broadband penetration in Pakistan is still relatively low; fixed line availability has risen only margin ally over the same period, and there are still difficulties getting fixed-line service to rural areas
international: country code—92; landing point for the SEA-ME-WE-3 and SEA-ME-WE-4 submarine cable systems that provide links to Asia, the Middle East, and Europe; satellite earth stations—3 Intelsat (1 Atlantic Ocean and 2 Indian Ocean); 3 operational international gateway exchanges (1 at Karachi and 2 at Islamabad); microwave radio relay to neighboring countries (2011)

Broadcast media: media is government regulated; 1 dominant state-owned TV broadcaster, Pakistan Television Corporation (PTV), operates a network consisting of 8 channels; private TV broadcasters are permitted; to date 69 foreign satellite channels are operational; the state-owned radio network operates more than 40 stations; nearly 100 commercially licensed, privately owned radio stations provide programming mostly limited to music and talk shows (2015)
Radio broadcast stations: AM 31, FM 68, shortwave NA (2006)
Television broadcast stations: 20 (5 state-run channels and 15 privately-owned satellite chann els) (2006)

Internet country code: .pk

Internet hosts: 365,813 (2012)
country comparison to the world: 57

Internet users: *total:* 21.3 million
percent of population: 10.8% (2014 est.)
country comparison to the world: 27

TRANSPORTATION

Airports: 151 (2013)
country comparison to the world: 37

Airports—with paved runways: *total:* 108
over 3,047 m: 15
2,438 to 3,047 m: 20
1,524 to 2,437 m: 43
914 to 1,523 m: 20
under 914 m: 10 (2013)

Airports—with unpaved runways: *total:* 43
2,438 to 3,047 m: 1
1,524 to 2,437 m: 9
914 to 1,523 m: 9

under 914 m: 24 (2013)

Heliports: 23 (2013)

Pipelines: gas 12,646 km; oil 2,576 km; refined products 1,087 km (2013)

Railways: *total:* 11,881 km
broad gauge: 11,492 km 1.676-m gauge (293 km electrified)
narrow gauge: 389 km 1.000-m gauge (2015)
country comparison to the world: 28

Roadways: *total:* 263,942 km
paved: 185,063 km (includes 708 km of expressways)
unpaved: 78,879 km (2014)
country comparison to the world: 20

Merchant marine: *total:* 11
by type: bulk carrier 5, cargo 3, petroleum tanker 3
registered in other countries: 11 (Comoros 5, Marshall Islands 1, Moldova 1, Panama 3, Saint Kitts and Nevis 1) (2010)
country comparison to the world: 111

Ports and terminals: *major seaport(s):* Karachi, Port Muhammad Bin Qasim
container port(s) (TEUs): Karachi (1,545,434)
LNG terminal(s) (import): Port Qasim

MILITARY AND SECURITY

Military branches: Pakistan Army (includes National Guard), Pakistan Navy (includes Maritime Security Agency), Pakistan Air Force (Pakistan Fiza'ya) (2015)

Military service age and obligation: 16–23 years of age for voluntary military service; soldiers cannot be deployed for combat until age 18; the Pakistani Air Force and Pakistani Navy have inducted their first female pilots and sailors; the Pakistan Air Force recruits aviation technicians at age 15; service obligation (Navy) 10–18 years; retirement required after 18–30 years service or age 40–52 (2012)

Military expenditures: 3.5% of GDP (2013)
3.5% of GDP (2012)
3.2% of GDP (2011)
country comparison to the world: 21

TRANSNATIONAL ISSUES

Disputes—international: various talks and confidence-building measures cautiously have begun to defuse tensions over Kashmir, particularly since the October 2005 earthquake in the region; Kashmir nevertheless remains the site of the world's largest and most militarized territorial dispute with portions under the de facto administration of China (Aksai Chin), India (Jammu and Kashmir), and Pakistan (Azad Kashmir and Northern Areas); UN Military Observer Group in India and Pakistan has maintained a small group of peacekeepers since 1949; India does not recognize Pakistan's ceding historic Kashmir lands to China in 1964; India and Pakistan have maintained their 2004 cease-fire in Kashmir and initiated discussions on defusing the armed standoff in the Siachen glacier region; Pakistan protests India's fencing the highly militarized Line of Control and construction of the Baglihar

Dam on the Chenab River in Jammu and Kashmir, which is part of the larger dispute on water sharing of the Indus River and its tributaries; to defuse tensions and prepare for discussions on a maritime boundary, India and Pakistan seek technical resolution of the disputed boundary in Sir Creek estuary at the mouth of the Rann of Kutch in the Arabian Sea; Pakistani maps continue to show the Junagadh claim in India's Gujarat State; since 2002, with UN assistance, Pakistan has repatriated 3.8 million Afghan refugees, leaving about 2.6 million; Pakistan has sent troops across and built fences along some remote tribal areas of its treaty-defined Durand Line border with Afghanistan, which serve as bases for foreign terrorists and other illegal activities; Afghan, Coalition, and Pakistan military meet periodically to clarify the alignment of the boundary on the ground and on maps

Refugees and internally displaced persons: *refugees (country of origin):* 2.6 million (1.6 million registered, 1.0 million undocumented) (Afghanistan) (2015)
IDPs: 1.459 million (primarily those who remain displaced by counter-terrorism and counter-insurgency operations and violent conflict between armed non-state groups in the Federally Administered Tribal Areas and Khyber-Paktunkwa Province; more than 1 million displaced in Northern Waziristan in 2014; individuals also have been displaced by repeated monsoon floods) (2015)

Trafficking in persons: *current situation:* Pakistan is a source, transit, and destination country for men, women, and children subjected to forced labor and sex trafficking; the largest human trafficking problem is bonded labor in agriculture, brickmaking and, to a lesser extent, fishing, mining and carpet-making; children are bought, sold, rented, and placed in forced begging rings, domestic service, small shops, brick kilns, or prostitution; militant groups also force children to spy, fight, or die as suicide bombers, kidnapping the children or getting them from poor parents through sale or coercion; women and girls are forced into prostitution or marriages; Pakistani adults migrate to the Gulf States and African and European states for low-skilled jobs and sometimes become victims of forced labor, debt bondage, or prostitution; foreign adults and children, particularly from Afghanistan, Bangladesh, and Sri Lanka, may be subject to forced labor, and foreign women may be sex trafficked in Pakistan, with refugees and ethnic minorities being most vulnerable
tier rating: Tier 2 Watch List—Pakistan does not fully comply with the minimum standards for the elimination of trafficking; however, it is making significant efforts to do so; the government lacks political will and capacity to fully address human trafficking, as evidenced by ineffective law enforcement efforts, official complicity, penalization of victims, and the continued conflation of migrant smuggling and human trafficking by many officials; not all forms of trafficking are prohibited; an anti-trafficking bill drafted in 2013 to address gaps in existing legislation remains pending, and a National action plan drafted in 2014 is not

finalized; feudal landlords and brick kiln owners use their political influence to protect their involvement in bonded labor, while some police personnel have taken bribes to ignore prostitution that may have included sex trafficking; authorities began to use standard procedures for the identification and referral of trafficking victims, but it is not clear how widely these methods were practiced;

in other instances, police were reluctant to assist NGOs with rescues and even punished victims for crimes committed as a direct result of being trafficked (2015)

Illicit drugs: significant transit area for Afghan drugs, including heroin, opium, morphine, and hashish, bound for Iran, Western markets, the Gulf

States, Africa, and Asia; financial crimes related to drug trafficking, terrorism, corruption, and smuggling remain problems; opium poppy cultivation estimated to be 2,300 hectares in 2007 with 600 of those hectares eradicated; federal and provincial authorities continue to conduct anti-poppy campaigns that utilizes forced eradication, fines, and arrests

PALAU

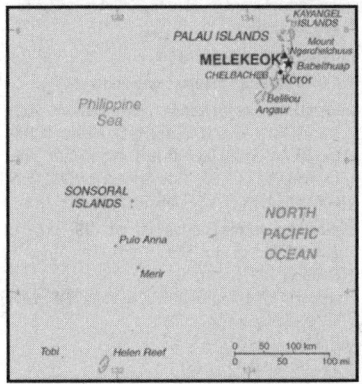

INTRODUCTION

Background: After three decades as part of the UN Trust Territory of the Pacific under US administration, this westernmost cluster of the Caroline Islands opted for independence in 1978 rather than join the Federated States of Micronesia. A Compact of Free Association with the US was approved in 1986 but not ratified until 1993. It entered into force the following year when the islands gained independence.

GEOGRAPHY

Location: Oceania, group of islands in the North Pacific Ocean, southeast of the Philippines

Geographic coordinates: 7 30 N, 134 30 E

Map references: Oceania

Area: *total:* 459 sq km
land: 459 sq km
water: 0 sq km
country comparison to the world: 198

Area—comparative: slightly more than 2.5 times the size of Washington, DC

Land boundaries: 0 km

Coastline: 1,519 km

Maritime claims: *territorial sea:* 3 nm
exclusive fishing zone: 200 nm

Climate: tropical; hot and humid; wet season May to November

Terrain: varying topography from the high, mountainous main island of Babelthuap to low, coral islands usually fringed by large barrier reefs

Elevation: *mean elevation:* NA

elevation extremes: *lowest point:* Pacific Ocean 0 m
highest point: Mount Ngerchelchuus 242 m

Natural resources: forests, minerals (especially gold), marine products, deep-seabed minerals

Land use: *agricultural land:* 10.8%
arable land: 2.2%
permanent crops: 4.3%
permanent pasture: 4.3%
forest: 87.6%
other: 1.6% (2011 est.)

Irrigated land: 0 sq km (2012)

Natural hazards: typhoons (June to December)

Environment—current issues: inadequate facilities for disposal of solid waste; threats to the marine ecosystem from sand and coral dredging, illegal fishing practices, and overfishing

Environment—international agreements: *party to:* Biodiversity, Climate Change, Climate Change-Kyoto Protocol, Desertification, Law of the Sea, Ozone Layer Protection, Wetlands, Whaling
signed, but not ratified: none of the selected agreements

Geography—note: westernmost archipelago in the Caroline chain, consists of six island groups totaling more than 300 islands; includes World War II battleground of Beliliou (Peleliu) and world-famous rock islands

PEOPLE AND SOCIETY

Nationality: *noun:* Palauan(s)
adjective: Palauan

Ethnic groups: Palauan (Micronesian with Malayan and Melanesian admixtures) 72.5%, Carolinian 1%, other Micronesian 2.4%, Filipino 16.3%, Chinese 1.6%, Vietnamese 1.6%, other Asian 3.4%, white 0.9%, other 0.3% (2005 est.)

Languages: Palauan (official on most islands) 66.6%, Carolinian 0.7%, other Micronesian 0.7%, English (official) 15.5%, Filipino 10.8%, Chinese 1.8%, other Asian 2.6%, other 1.3%
note: Sonsoral (Sonsoralese and English are official), Tobi (Tobi and English are official), and Angaur (Angaur, Japanese, and English are official) (2005 est.)

Religions: Roman Catholic 49.4%, Protestant 30.9% (includes Protestant (general) 23.1%, Seventh Day Adventist 5.3%, and other Protestant 2.5%), Modekngei 8.7% (indigenous to Palau), Jehovah's Witnesses 1.1%, other 8.8%, none or unspecified 1.1% (2005 est.)

Population: 21,265 (July 2015 est.)
country comparison to the world: 220

Age structure: *0–14 years:* 20.26% (male 2,225/female 2,084)
15–24 years: 17.18% (male 1,819/female 1,834)
25–54 years: 46.21% (male 5,992/female 3,834)
55–64 years: 9.03% (male 667/female 1,253)
65 years and over: 7.32% (male 418/female 1,139) (2015 est.)

Median age: *total:* 33.2 years
male: 32.6 years
female: 34.4 years (2015 est.)
country comparison to the world: 88

Population growth rate: 0.38% (2015 est.)
country comparison to the world: 167

Birth rate: 11.05 births/1,000 population (2015 est.)
country comparison to the world: 178

Death rate: 7.99 deaths/1,000 population (2015 est.)
country comparison to the world: 100

Net migration rate: 0.71 migrant(s)/1,000 population (2015 est.)
country comparison to the world: 68

Urbanization: *urban population:* 87.1% of total population (2015)
rate of urbanization: 1.66% annual rate of change (2010–15 est.)

Major urban areas—population: MELEKEOK (capital) 299 (2012)

Sex ratio: *at birth:* 1.06 male(s)/female
0–14 years: 1.07 male(s)/female
15–24 years: 0.99 male(s)/female
25–54 years: 1.56 male(s)/female
55–64 years: 0.53 male(s)/female
65 years and over: 0.37 male(s)/female
total population: 1.1 male(s)/female (2015 est.)

Infant mortality rate: *total:* 11.15 deaths/1,000 live births
male: 12.67 deaths/1,000 live births
female: 9.53 deaths/1,000 live births (2015 est.)
country comparison to the world: 129

653

Life expectancy at birth: *total population:* 72.87 years
male: 69.69 years
female: 76.23 years (2015 est.)
country comparison to the world: 135

Total fertility rate: 1.71 children born/woman (2015 est.)
country comparison to the world: 170

Health expenditures: 9.9% of GDP (2013)
country comparison to the world: 28

Physicians density: 1.38 physicians/1,000 population (2010)

Hospital bed density: 4.8 beds/1,000 population (2010)

Drinking water source:
improved:
urban: 97% of popu lation
rural: 86% of population
total: 95.3% of population
unimproved:
urban: 3% of popu lation
rural: 14% of population
total: 4.7% of population (2011 est.)

Sanitation facility access:
improved:
urban: 100% of population
rural: 100% of population
total: 100% of population
unimproved:
urban: 0% of population
rural: 0% of population
total: 0% of population (2015 est.)

HIV/AIDS—adult prevalence rate: NA

HIV/AIDS—people living with HIV/AIDS: NA

HIV/AIDS—deaths: NA

Obesity—adult prevalence rate: 47.1% (2014)
country comparison to the world: 7

Literacy: *definition:* age 15 and over can read and write
total population: 99.5%
male: 99.5%
female: 99.6% (2015 est.)

School life expectancy (primary to tertiary education): *total:* 17 years
male: 16 years
female: 18 years (2013)

GOVERNMENT

Country name: *conventional long form:* Republic of Palau
conventional short form: Palau
local long form: Beluu er a Belau
local short form: Belau
former: Trust Territory of the Pacific Islan ds, Palau District
etymology: from the Palauan name for the islands, Belau, which likely derives from the Palauan word "beluu" meaning "village"

Government type: presidential republic in free association with the US

Capital: *name:* Melekeok

Geographic coordinates: 7 29 N, 134 38 E

time difference: UTC+9 (14 hours ahead of Washington, DC, during Standard Time)

Administrative divisions: 16 states; Aimeliik, Airai, Angaur, Hatohobei, Kayangel, Koror, Melekeok, Ngaraard, Ngarchelong, Ngardmau, Ngatpang, Ngchesar, Ngeremlengui, Ngiwal, Peleliu, Sonsorol

Independence: 1 October 1994 (from the US-administered UN trusteeship)

National holiday: Constitution Day, 9 July (1979), day of a National referendum to pass the new constitution

Constitution: ratified 9 July 1980, effective 1 January 1981; amended 1992, 2004, 2008 (2016)

Legal system: mixed legal system of civil, common, and customary law

International law organization participation: has not submitted an ICJ jurisdiction declaration; non-party state to the ICCt

Citizenship: *citizenship by birth:* no
citizenship by descent only: at least one parent must be a citizen of Palau
dual citizenship recognized: no
residency requirement for naturalization: note—no procedure for naturalization

Suffrage: 18 years of age; universal

Executive branch: *chief of state:* President Tommy REMENGESAU (since 17 January 2013); Vice President Antonio BELLS (since 17 January 2013); note—the president is both chief of state and head of government

head of government: President Tommy REMENGESAU (since 17 January 2013); Vice President Antonio BELLS (since 17 January 2013)
cabinet: Cabinet appointed by the president with the advice and consent of the Senate; also includes the vice president; the Council of Chiefs consists of chiefs from each of the states who advise the president on issues concerning traditional laws, customs, and their relationship to the constitution and laws of Palau
elections/appointments: president and vice president directly elected on separate ballots by absolute majority popular vote in 2 rounds if needed for a 4-year term (eligible for a second term); election last held on 6 November 2012 (next to be held in November 2016)
election results: Tommy REMENGESAU elected president; percent of vote—Tommy REMENGESAU 58%, Johnson TORIBIONG 42%; Antonio BELLS elected vice president

Legislative branch: *description:* bicameral National Congress or Olbiil Era Kelulau consists of the Senate (9 seats; members directly elected in single-seat constituencies by majority vote to serve 4-year terms) and the House of Delegates (16 seats; members directly elected in single-seat constituencies by simple majority vote to serve 4-year terms)
elections: Senate—last held on 6 November 2012 (next to be held in November 2016); House of Delegates—last held on 6 November 2012 (next to be held in November 2016)

election results: Senate—percent of vote—NA; seats—independent 9; House of Delegates—percent of vote—NA; seats—independent 16

Judicial branch: *highest court (s):* Supreme Court (consists of the chief justice and 3 associate justices organized into appellate trial divisions; also within the Supreme Court organization are the Common Pleas and Land Courts)
judge selection and term of office: justices nominated by a 7-member independent body consisting of judges, presidential appointees, and lawyers, and appointed by the president; judges appointed until mandatory retirement at age 65
subordinate courts: National Court and other 'inferior' courts

Political parties and leaders: none

Political pressure groups and leaders: NA

International organization participation: ACP, ADB, AOSIS, FAO, IAEA, IBRD, ICAO, ICRM, IDA, IFC, IFRCS, ILO, IMF, IMO, IMSO, IOC, IPU, MIGA, OPCW, PIF, Sparteca, SPC, UN, UNAMID, UNCTAD, UNESCO, WHO

Diplomatic representation in the US: *chief of mission:* Ambassador Hersey KYOTA (since 12 November 1997)
chancery: 1701 Pennsylvania Avenue NW, Suite 300, Washington, DC 20036
telephone: [1] (202) 452-6814
FAX: [1] (202) 452-6281
consulate(s): Tamuning (Guam)

Diplomatic representation from the US: *chief of mission:* Ambassador Helen P. REED-ROWE (since 27 September 2013)
embassy: Koror (no street address)
mailing address: P. O. Box 6028, Koror, Republic of Palau 96940
telephone: [680] 587-2920
FAX: [680] 587-2911

Flag description: light blue with a large yellow disk shifted slightly to the hoist side; the blue color represents the ocean, the disk represents the moon; Palauans consider the full moon to be the optimum time for human activity; it is also considered a symbol of peace, love, and tranquility

National symbol(s): bai (native meeting house); national colors: blue, yellow

National anthem: *name:* "Belau rekid" (Our Palau)
lyrics/music: multiple/Ymesei O. EZEKIEL
note: adopted 1980

ECONOMY

Economy—overview: The economy consists of tourism and other services such as trade, subsistence agriculture, and fishing. Government is a major employer of the work force relying on financial assistance from the US under the Compact of Free Association (Compact) with the US that took effect after the end of the UN trusteeship on 1 October 1994. The US provided Palau with roughly $700 million in aid for the first 15 years following commencement of the Compact in 1994 in return for unrestricted access to its land and waterways for strategic purposes. The population enjoys a per capita income roughly double that of the Philippines and much of Micronesia.

Business and leisure tourist arrivals numbered over 125,000 in fiscal year 2014, a 13.4% increase over the previous year. Long-run prospects for tourism have been bolstered by the expansion of air travel in the Pacific, the rising prosperity of industrial East Asia, and the willingness of foreigners to finance infrastructure development. Proximity to Guam, the region's major destination for tourists from East Asia, and a regionally competitive tourist infrastructure enhance Palau's advantage as a destination.

GDP (purchasing power parity): $272 million (2015 est.)
$248.7 million (2014 est.)
$238.6 million (2013 est.)
note: GDP estimate includes US subsidy
country comparison to the world: 217

GDP (official exchange rate): $287 million (2015 est.)

GDP—real growth rate: 9.4% (2015 est.)
4.2% (2014 est.)
-2.4% (2013 est.)
country comparison to the world: 3

GDP—per capita (PPP): $15,100 (2015 est.)
$13,800 (2014 est.)
$13,300 (2013 est.)
note: data are in 2015 US dollars
country comparison to the world: 106

GDP—composition, by sector of origin:
agriculture: 3.2%
industry: 20%
services: 76.8% (2012 est.)

Agriculture—products: coconuts, copra, cassava (manioc, tapioca), sweet potatoes; fish

Industries: tourism, craft items (from shell, wood, pearls), construction, garment making

Industrial production growth rate: NA%

Labor force: 10,470 (2014)
country comparison to the world: 218

Labor force—by occupation: *agriculture:* 20%
industry: NA%
services: NA% (1990)

Unemployment rate: 4.2% (2005 est.)
country comparison to the world: 41

Population below poverty line: NA%

Household income or consumption by percentage share: *lowest:* 10%: NA%
highest: 10%: NA%

Budget: *revenues:* $123.6 million
expenditures: $97.53 million (2012 est.)
Taxes and other revenues: 47.4% of GDP (2012 est.)
country comparison to the world: 20

Budget surplus (+) or deficit (–): 10% of GDP (2012 est.)
country comparison to the world: 4

Fiscal year: 1 October—30 September

Inflation rate (consumer prices): 2.2% (2015 est.)
4% (2014 est.)
country comparison to the world: 121

Market value of publicly traded shares: $NA

Current account balance: -$1 million (2015 est.)
-$30 million (2014 est.)
country comparison to the world: 54

Exports: $19.1 million (2014 est.)
$14.4 million (2013 est.)
country comparison to the world: 210

Exports—commodities: shellfish, tuna, copra, garments

Imports: $177.7 million (2014 est.)
$146.5 million (2013 est.)
country comparison to the world: 209

Imports—commodities: machinery and equipment, fuels, metals; foodstuffs

Debt—external: $18.38 billion (31 December 2014 est.)
$16.47 billion (31 December 2013 est.)
country comparison to the world: 89

Exchange rates: the US dollar is used

COMMUNICATIONS

Telephones—fixed lines: *total subscriptions:* 7,100
subscriptions per 100 inhabitants: 34 (2014 est.)

country comparison to the world: 203

Telephones—mobile cellular: *total:* 19,100
subscriptions per 100 inhabitants: 90 (2014 est.)
country comparison to the world: 210

Telephone system: *domestic:* fixed-line and mobile-cellular services available with a combined subscribership of roughly 100 per 100 persons
international: country code—680; satellite earth station—1 Intelsat (Pacific Ocean) (2009)

Broadcast media: no TV stations; a cable TV network covers the major islands and provides access to rebroadcasts, on a delayed basis, of a number of US stations, as well as access to a number of real-time satellite TV channels; about a half dozen radio stations (1 government-owned) (2009)
Radio broadcast stations: AM 1, FM 4, short-wave 1 (2001)
Television broadcast stations: 1 (cable) (2005)

Internet country code: .pw

Internet hosts: 4 (2012)
country comparison to the world: 231

TRANSPORTATION

Airports: 3 (2013)
country comparison to the world: 194

Airports—with paved runways: *total:* 1
1,524 to 2,437 m: 1 (2013)

Airports—with unpaved runways: *total:* 2
1,524 to 2,437 m: 2 (2013)

Ports and terminals: *major seaport(s):* Koror

MILITARY AND SECURITY

Military branches: no regular military forces; Palau National Police (2009)

Military—note: defense is the responsibility of the US; under a Compact of Free Association between Palau and the US, the US military is granted access to the islands for 50 years, but it has not stationed any military forces there (2008)

TRANSNATIONAL ISSUES

Disputes—international: maritime delineation negotiations continue with Philippines, Indonesia

PANAMA

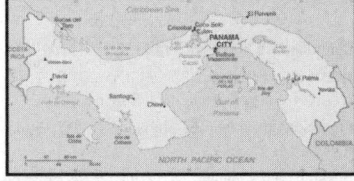

INTRODUCTION

Background: Explored and settled by the Spanish in the 16th century, Panama broke with Spain in 1821 and joined a union of Colombia, Ecuador, and Venezuela—named the Republic of Gran Colombia. When the latter dissolved in 1830, Panama remained part of Colombia. With US backing, Panama seceded from Colombia in 1903 and promptly signed a treaty with the US allowing for the construction of a canal and US sovereignty over a strip of land on either side of the structure (the Panama Canal Zone) . The Panama Canal was built by the US Army Corps of Engineers between 1904 and 1914. In 1977, an agreement was signed for the complete transfer of the Canal from the US to Panama by the end of the century. Certain portions of the Zone and increasing responsibility over the Canal were turned over in the subsequent decades. With US help, dictator Manuel NORIEG

A was deposed in 1989. The entire Panama Canal, the area supporting the Canal, and remaining US military bases were transferred to Panama by the end of 1999. An ambitious expansion project to more than double the Canal's capacity—by allowing for more Canal transits and larger ships—was carried out between 2007 and 2016.

GEOGRAPHY

Location: Central America, bordering both the Caribbean Sea and the North Pacific Ocean, between Colombia and Costa Rica

Geographic coordinates: 9 00 N, 80 00 W

Map references: Central America and the Caribbean

Area: *total:* 75,420 sq km
land: 74,340 sq km
water: 1,080 sq km
country comparison to the world: 118

Area—comparative: slightly smaller than South Carolina

Land boundaries: *total:* 687 km
border countries (2): Colombia 339 km, Costa Rica 348 km

Coastline: 2,490 km

Maritime claims: *territorial sea:* 12 nm
contiguous zone: 24 nm
exclusive economic zone: 200 nm or edge of continental margin

Climate: tropical maritime; hot, humid, cloudy; prolonged rainy season (May to January), short dry season (January to May)

Terrain: interior mostly steep, rugged mountains with dissected, upland plains; coastal plains with rolling hills

Elevation: *mean elevation:* 360 m

elevation extremes: *lowest point:* Pacific Ocean 0 m
highest point: Volcan Baru 3,475 m

Natural resources: copper, mahogany forests, shrimp, hydropower

Land use: *agricultural land:* 30.5%
arable land: 7.3%
permanent crops: 2.5%
permanent pasture: 20.7%
forest: 43.6%
other: 25.9% (2011 est.)

Irrigated land: 321 sq km (2012)

Total renewable water resources: 148 cu km (2011)

Freshwater withdrawal (domestic/industrial/agricultural): *total:* 0.91 cu km/yr (27%/2%/71%)
per capita: 296.1 cu m/yr (2005)

Natural hazards: occasional severe storms and forest fires in the Darien area

Environment—current issues: water pollution from agricultural runoff threatens fish ery resources; deforestation of tropical rain forest; land degradation and soil erosion threatens siltation of Panama Canal; air pollution in urban areas; mining threatens Natural resources

Environment—international agreements: *party to:* Biodiversity, Climate Change, Climate Change-Kyoto Protocol, Desertification, Endangered Species, Environmental Modification, Hazardous Wastes, Law of the Sea, Marine Dumping, Ozone Layer Protection, Ship Pollution, Tropical Timber 83, Tropical Timber 94, Wetlands, Whaling
signed, but not ratified: Marine Life Conservation

Geography—note: strategic location on eastern end of isthmus forming land bridge connecting North and South America; controls Panama Canal that links North Atlantic Ocean via Caribbean Sea with North Pacific Ocean

PEOPLE AND SOCIETY

Nationality: *noun:* Panamanian(s)
adjective: Panamanian

Ethnic groups: mestizo (mixed Amerindian and white) 65%, native American 12.3% (Ngabe 7.6%, Kuna 2.4%, Embera 0.9%, Bugle 0.8%, other 0.4%, unspecified 0.2%), black or African descent 9.2%, mulatto 6.8%, white 6.7% (2010 est.)

Languages: Spanish (official), indigenous languages (including Ngabere (or Guaymi), Buglere, Kuna, Embera, Wounaan, Naso (or Teribe), and Bri Bri), Panamanian English Creole (similar to Jamaican English Creole; a mixture of English and Spanish with elements of Ngabere; also known as Guari Guari and Colon Creole), English, Chinese (Yue and Hakka), Arabic, French Creole, other (Yiddish, Hebrew, Korean, Japanese)
note: many Panamanians are bilingual

Religions: Roman Catholic 85%, Protestant 15%

Demographic profile: Panama is a country of demographic and economic contrasts. It is in the midst of a demographic transition, characterized by steadily declining rates of fertility, mortality, and population growth, but disparities persist based on wealth, geography, and ethnicity. Panama has one of the fastest growing economies in Latin America and dedicates substantial funding to social programs, yet poverty and inequality remain prevalent. The indigenous population accounts for a growing share of Panama's poor and extreme poor, while the non-indigenous rural poor have been more successful at rising out of poverty through rural-to-urban labor migration. The government's large expenditures on untargeted, indirect subsidies for water, electricity, and fuel have been ineffective, but its conditional cash transfer program has shown some promise in helping to decrease extreme poverty among the indigenous population. Panama has expanded access to education and clean water, but the availability of sanitation and, to a lesser extent, electricity remains poor. The increase in secondary schooling—led by female enrollment—is spreading to rural and indigenous areas, which probably will help to alleviate poverty if educational quality and the availability of skilled jobs improve. In adequate access to sanitation contributes to a high incidence of diarrhea in Panama's children, which is one of the main causes of Panama's elevated chronic malnutrition rate, especially among indigenous communities.

Population: 3,657,024 (July 2015 est.)
country comparison to the world: 130

Age structure: *0–14 years:* 27.06% (male 505,079/female 484,471)
15–24 years: 17.2% (male 320,329/female 308,717)
25–54 years: 40.24% (male 745,309/female 726,211)
55–64 years: 7.55% (male 136,506/female 139,513)

65 years and over: 7.95% (male 133,930/female 156,959) (2015 est.)

Dependency ratios: *total dependency ratio:* 53.4%
youth dependency ratio: 41.7%
elderly dependency ratio: 11.7%
potential support ratio: 8.5% (2015 est.)

Median age: *total:* 28.6 years
male: 28.2 years
female: 29 years (2015 est.)
country comparison to the world: 124

Population growth rate: 1.32% (2015 est.)
country comparison to the world: 91

Birth rate: 18.32 births/1,000 population (2015 est.)
country comparison to the world: 98

Death rate: 4.81 deaths/1,000 population (2015 est.)
country comparison to the world: 193

Net migration rate: -0.28 migrant(s)/1,000 population (2015 est.)
country comparison to the world: 125

Urbanization: *urban population:* 66.6% of total population (2015)
rate of urbanization: 2.07% annual rate of change (2010–15 est.)

Major urban areas—population: PANAMA CITY (capital) 1.673 million (2015)

Sex ratio: *at birth:* 1.05 male(s)/female
0–14 years: 1.04 male(s)/female
15–24 years: 1.04 male(s)/female
25–54 years: 1.03 male(s)/female
55–64 years: 0.98 male(s)/female
65 years and over: 0.85 male(s)/female
total population: 1.01 male(s)/female (2015 est.)

Maternal mortality rate: 94 deaths/100,000 live births (2015 est.)
country comparison to the world: 78

Infant mortality rate: *total:* 10.41 deaths/1,000 live births
male: 11.16 deaths/1,000 live births
female: 9.63 deaths/1,000 live births (2015 est.)
country comparison to the world: 134

Life expectancy at birth: *total population:* 78.47 years
male: 75.67 years
female: 81.39 years (2015 est.)
country comparison to the world: 56

Total fertility rate: 2.35 children born/woman (2015 est.)
country comparison to the world: 86

Contraceptive prevalence rate: 52.2% (2009)

Health expenditures: 7.2% of GDP (2013)
country comparison to the world: 64

Physicians density: 1.65 physicians/1,000 population (2013)

Hospital bed density: 2.2 beds/1,000 population (2011)

Drinking water source:
improved:
urban: 97.7% of population
rural: 86.6% of population

total: 94.7% of population
unimproved:
urban: 2.3% of population
rural: 11.4% of population
total: 5.3% of population (2015 est.)

Sanitation facility access:
improved:
urban: 83.5% of population
rural: 58% of population
total: 75% of population
unimproved:
urban: 16.5% of population
rural: 42% of population
total: 25% of population (2015 est.)

HIV/AIDS—adult prevalence rate: 0.65% (2014 est.)
country comparison to the world: 58

HIV/AIDS—people living with HIV/AIDS: 16,600 (2014 est.)
country comparison to the world: 88

HIV/AIDS—deaths: 600 (2014 est.)
country comparison to the world: 81

Major infectious diseases: *degree of risk:* intermediate
food or waterborne diseases: bacterial diarrhea
vectorborne disease: dengue fever (2013)

Obesity—adult prevalence rate: 26.5% (2014)
country comparison to the world: 55

Children under the age of 5 years underweight: 3.9% (2008)
country comparison to the world: 99

Education expenditures: 3.3% of GDP (2011)
country comparison to the world: 122

Literacy: *definition:* age 15 and over can read and write
total population: 95%
male: 95.7%
female: 94.4% (2015 est.)

School life expectancy (primary to tertiary education): *total:* 13 years
male: 12 years
female: 13 years (2013)

Child labor—children ages 5–14: *total number:* 59,294
percentage: 7%
note: data represent children ages 5–17 (2010 est.)

Unemployment, youth ages 15–24: *total:* 10.8%
male: 9%
female: 13.9% (2013 est.)
country comparison to the world: 99

GOVERNMENT

Country name: *conventional long form:* Republic of Panama
conventional short form: Panama
local long form: Republica de Panama
local short form: Panama
etymology: according to tradition, the name derives from a former indigenous fishing village and its nearby beach that were called "Panama" meaning "an abundance of fish"

Government type: presidential republic

Capital: *name:* Panama City

Geographic coordinates: 8 58 N, 79 32 W
time difference: UTC-5 (same time as Washington, DC, during Standard Time)

Administrative divisions: 10 provinces (provincias, singular—provincia) and 3 indigenous territories* (comarcas); Bocas del Toro, Chiriqui, Cocle, Colon, Darien, Embera-Wounaan*, Herrera, Kuna Yala*, Los Santos, Ngobe-Bugle*, Panama, Panama Oeste, Veraguas

Independence: 3 November 1903 (from Colombia; became independent from Spain on 28 November 1821)

National holiday: Independence Day, 3 November (1903)

Constitution: several previous; latest effective 11 October 1972; amended several times, last in 2004 (2016)

Legal system: civil law system; judicial review of legislative acts in the Supreme Court of Justice

International law organization participation: accepts compulsory ICJ jurisdiction with reservations; accepts ICCt jurisdiction

Citizenship: *citizenship by birth:* yes
citizenship by descent: yes
dual citizenship recognized: no
residency requirement for naturalization: 5 years

Suffrage: 18 years of age; universal

Executive branch: *chief of state:* President Juan Carlos VARELA (since 1 July 2014); Vice President Isabel de SAINTMALO de Alvarado (since 1 July 2014); note—the president is both chief of state and head of government

head of government: President Juan Carlos VARELA (since 1 July 2014); Vice President Isabel de SAINTMALO de Alvarado (since 1 July 2014)
cabinet: Cabinet appointed by the president
elections/appointments: president and vice president directly elected on the same ballot by simple majority popular vote for a 5-year term (president eligible for a single non-consecutive term); election last held on 4 May 2014; next to be held in 2019)
election results: Juan Carlos VARELA elected president; percent of vote—Juan Carlos VARELA (PP) 39.1%, Jose Domingo ARIAS (CD) 31.4%, Juan Carlos NAVARRO (PRD) 28.2%, other 1.3%
note: an alliance between the Panamenista Party and Democratic Revolutionary Party (PRD) fractured after the 2014 election, but a loose coalition composed of Panamenista and moderate PRD and CD legislators generally work together to support the president's agenda

Legislative branch: *description:* unicameral National Assembly or Asamblea Nacional (71 seats; 45 members directly elected in multi-seat constituencies—populous towns and cities—by proportional representation vote and 26 directly elected in single-seat constituencies—outlying rural districts—by plurality vote; members serve 5-year terms)

elections: last held on 4 May 2014 (next to be held in May 2019)
election results: percent of vote by party—NA; seats by party—PRD 26, CD 25, Panamenista 16, MOLIR ENA 2, PP 1, independent 1; note—only 57 deputies were officially installed because fourteen runners-up challenged the election

Judicial branch: *highest court(s):* Supreme Court of Justice or Corte Suprema de Justicia (consists of 9 magistrates and 9 alternates and divided into civil, criminal, administrative, and general business chambers)
judge selection and term of office: magistrates appointed by the president for staggered 10-year terms
subordinate courts: appellate courts or Tribunal Superior; Labor Supreme Courts; Court of Audit; circuit courts or Tribunal Circuital (2 each in 9 of the 10 provinces); municipal courts; electoral, family, maritime, and adolescent courts

Political parties and leaders: Democratic Change or CD [Ricardo MARTINELLI Berrocal]
Democratic Revolutionary Party or PRD [Carlos PEREZ Herrera]
Nationalist Republican Liberal Movement or MOLIRENA [Francisco "Pancho" ALEMAN]
Panamenista Party [Juan Carlos VARELA Rodriguez] (formerly the Arnulfista Party)
Popular Party or PP [Milton C. HENRIQUEZ] (formerly Christian Democratic Party or PDC)

Political pressure groups and leaders: Chamber of Commerce
Concertacion Nacional (mechanism for Government of Panama to formally dialogue with representatives of civil society)
National Council of Organized Workers or CONATO
National Council of Private Enterprise or CONEP
National Union of Construction and Similar Workers (SUNTRACS)
Panamanian Association of Business Executives or APEDE
Panamanian Industrialists Society or SIP
Workers Confederation of the Republic of Panama or CTRP

International organization participation: BCIE, CAN (observer), CD, CELAC, FAO, G-77, IADB, IAEA, IBRD, ICAO, ICC (National committees), ICCt, ICRM, IDA, IFAD, IFC, IFRCS, ILO, IMF, IMO, IMSO, Interpol, IOC, IOM, IPU, ISO, ITSO, ITU, ITUC (NGOs), LAES, LAIA, MIGA, NAM, OAS, OPANAL, OPCW, Pacific Alliance (observer), PCA, SICA, UN, UNASUR (observer), UNCTAD, UNESCO, UNIDO, Union Latina, UNWTO, UPU, WCO, WFTU (NGOs), WHO, WIPO, WMO, WTO

Diplomatic representation in the US: *chief of mission:* Ambassador Emanuel Arturo GONZALEZ-REVILLA Lince (since 18 September 2014)
chancery: 2862 McGill Terrace NW, Washington, DC 20007
telephone: [1] (202) 483-1407
FAX: [1] (202) 483-8413

THE CIA WORLD FACTBOOK

consulate(s) general: Atlanta, Houston, Miami, New Orleans, New York, Philadelphia, Tampa, Washington DC

Diplomatic representation from the US: *chief of mission:* Ambassador John D. FEELEY (since 15 February 2015)
embassy: Edificio 783, Avenida Demetrio Basilio Lakas Panama, Apartado Postal 0816–02561, Zona 5, Panama City
mailing address: American Embassy Panama, Unit 0945, APOAA 34002; American Embassy Panama, 9100 Panama City PL, Washington, DC 20521–9100
telephone: [507] 317-5000
FAX: [507] 317-5568

Flag description: divided into four, equal rectangles; the top quadrants are white (hoist side) with a blue five-pointed star in the center and plain red; the bottom quadrants are plain blue (hoist side) and white with a red five-pointed star in the center; the blue and red colors are those of the main political parties (Conservatives and Liberals respectively) and the white denotes peace between them; the blue star stands for the civic virtues of purity and honesty, the red star signifies authority and law

National symbol(s): harpy eagle; national colors: blue, white, red

National anthem: *name:* "Himno Istmeno" (Isthmus Hymn)
lyrics/music: Jeronimo DE LA OSSA/Santos A. JORGE
note: adopted 1925

ECONOMY

Economy—overview: Panama's dollar-based economy rests primarily on a well-developed services sector that accounts for more than three-quarters of GDP. Services include operating the Panama Canal, logistics, banking, the Colon Free Trade Zone, insurance, container ports, flagship registry, and tourism. Panama's transportation and logistics services sectors, along with infrastructure development projects, have boosted economic growth; however, public debt surpassed $32 billion in 2015 because of excessive government spending and public works projects. The US-Panama Trade Promotion Agreement was approved by Congress and signed into law in October 2011, and entered into force in October 2012. Growth will be bolstered by the Panama Canal expansion project that began in 2007 and is estimated to be completed by 2016 at a cost of $5.3 billion—about 10–15% of current GDP. The expansion project will more than double the Canal's capacity, enabling it to accommodate ships that are too large to traverse the existing canal. The US and China are the top users of the Canal. In 2014, Panama completed a metro system in Panama City, valued at $1.2 billion.

Strong economic performance has not translated into broadly shared prosperity, as Panama has the second worst income distribution in Latin America. About one-fourth of the population lives in poverty; however, from 2006 to 2012 poverty was reduced by 10 percentage points.

GDP (purchasing power parity): $87.2 billion (2015 est.)
$82.43 billion (2014 est.)
$77.73 billion (2013 est.)
note: data are in 2015 US dollars
country comparison to the world: 87

GDP (official exchange rate): $52.13 billion (2015 est.)

GDP—real growth rate: 5.8% (2015 est.)
6.1% (2014 est.)
6.6% (2013 est.)
country comparison to the world: 33

GDP—per capita (PPP): $21,800 (2015 est.)
$21,000 (2014 est.)
$20,200 (2013 est.)
note: data are in 2015 US dollars
country comparison to the world: 82

Gross national saving: 41.5% of GDP (2015 est.)
37.3% of GDP (2014 est.)
36% of GDP (2013 est.)
country comparison to the world: 4

GDP—composition, by end use:
household consumption: 51.3%
government consumption: 10.8%
investment in fixed capital: 28.1%
investment in inventories: 8.2%
exports of goods and services: 72.6%
imports of goods and services: -71% (2015 est.)

GDP—composition, by sector of origin:
agriculture: 3%
industry: 20%
services: 77% (2015 est.)

Agriculture—products: bananas, rice, corn, coffee, sugarcane, vegetables; livestock; shrimp

Industries: construction, brewing, cement and other construction materials, sugar milling

Industrial production growth rate: 4.5% (2015 est.)
country comparison to the world: 37

Labor force: 1.587 million
note: shortage of skilled labor, but an oversupply of unskilled labor (2015 est.)
country comparison to the world: 130

Labor force—by occupation: *agriculture:* 17%
industry: 18.6%
services: 64.4% (2009 est.)

Unemployment rate: 4.5% (2015 est.)
4.5% (2014 est.)
country comparison to the world: 45

Population below poverty line: 26% (2012 est.)

Household income or consumption by percentage share: *lowest:* 10%: 1.1%
highest: 10%: 40.1% (2010 est.)

Distribution of family income—Gini index: 51.9 (2010 est.)
56.1 (2003)
country comparison to the world: 16

Budget: *revenues:* $10.18 billion
expenditures: $11.42 billion (2015 est.)
Taxes and other revenues: 21.4% of GDP (2015 est.)
country comparison to the world: 146

Budget surplus (+) or deficit (–): -2.6% of GDP (2015 est.)
country comparison to the world: 96

Public debt: 39.6% of GDP (2015 est.)
37.2% of GDP (2014 est.)
country comparison to the world: 115

Fiscal year: calendar year

Inflation rate (consumer prices): 0.1% (2015 est.)
2.6% (2014 est.)
country comparison to the world: 44

Commercial bank prime lending rate: 6.7% (31 December 2015 est.)
6.83% (31 December 2014 est.)
country comparison to the world: 123

Stock of narrow money: $8.674 billion (31 December 2015 est.)
$8.317 billion (31 December 2014 est.)
country comparison to the world: 85

Stock of broad money: $36.14 billion (31 December 2015 est.)
$34.65 billion (31 December 2014 est.)
country comparison to the world: 75

Stock of domestic credit: $42.53 billion (31 December 2015 est.)
$38.67 billion (31 December 2014 est.)
country comparison to the world: 65

Market value of publicly traded shares:
$12.54 billion (31 December 2012 est.)
$10.68 billion (31 December 2011)
$8.348 billion (31 December 2010 est.)
country comparison to the world: 70

Current account balance: -$3.377 billion (2015 est.)
-$4.794 billion (2014 est.)
country comparison to the world: 162

Exports: $15.85 billion (2015 est.)
$15.34 billion (2014 est.)
note: includes the Colon Free Zone
country comparison to the world: 75

Exports—commodities: fruit and nuts, fish, iron and steel waste, wood

Exports—partners: US 19.7%, Germany 13.2%, Costa Rica 7.7%, China 5.9%, Netherlands 4.1% (2015)

Imports: $23.29 billion (2015 est.)
$23.47 billion (2014 est.)
note: includes the Colon Free Zone
country comparison to the world: 70

Imports—commodities: fuels, machinery, vehicles, iron and steel rods, pharmaceuticals

Imports—partners: US 25.9%, China 9.6%, Mexico 5.1% (2015)

Reserves of foreign exchange and gold: $4.182 billion (31 December 2015 est.)
$4.032 billion (31 December 2014 est.)
country comparison to the world: 99

Debt—external: $15.47 billion (31 December 2014 est.)
$13.88 billion (31 December 2013 est.)
country comparison to the world: 96

Stock of direct foreign investment—at home:
$44.96 billion (31 December 2015 est.)
$41.06 billion (31 December 2014 est.)
country comparison to the world: 61

Stock of direct foreign investment—abroad:
$10.13 billion (31 December 2015 est.)
$9.385 billion (31 December 2014 est.)
country comparison to the world: 60

Exchange rates: balboas (PAB) per US dollar—
1 (2015 est.)
1 (2014 est.)
1 (2013 est.)
1 (2012 est.)
1 (2011 est.)

ENERGY

Electricity—production: 8.361 billion kWh (2012 est.)
country comparison to the world: 101

Electricity—consumption: 7.144 billion kWh (2012 est.)
country comparison to the world: 103

Electricity—exports: 59 million kWh (2012 est.)
country comparison to the world: 84

Electricity—imports: 19 million kWh (2012 est.)
country comparison to the world: 108

Electricity—installed generating capacity: 2.396 million kW (2012 est.)
country comparison to the world: 101

Electricity—from fossil fuels: 38.7% of total installed capacity (2012 est.)
country comparison to the world: 167

Electricity—from nuclear fuels: 0% of total installed capacity (2012 est.)
country comparison to the world: 165

Electricity—from hydroelectric plants: 61.3% of total installed capacity (2012 est.)
country comparison to the world: 34

Electricity—from other renewable sources: 0% of total installed capacity (2012 est.)
country comparison to the world: 212

Crude oil—production: 0 bbl/day (2014 est.)
country comparison to the world: 180

Crude oil—exports: 0 bbl/day (2012 est.)
country comparison to the world: 176

Crude oil—imports: 0 bbl/day (2012 est.)
country comparison to the world: 114

Crude oil—proved reserves: 0 bbl (1 January 2010 est.)
country comparison to the world: 180

Refined petroleum products—production: 0 bbl/day (2012 est.)
country comparison to the world: 122

Refined petroleum products—consumption: 134,000 bbl/day (2013 est.)
country comparison to the world: 69

Refined petroleum products—exports: 22.03 bbl/day (2012 est.)
country comparison to the world: 124

Refined petroleum products—imports: 129,200 bbl/day (2012 est.)
country comparison to the world: 43

Natural gas—production: 0 cu m (2013 est.)
country comparison to the world: 118

Natural gas—consumption: 0 cu m (2013 est.)
country comparison to the world: 186

Natural gas—exports: 0 cu m (2013 est.)
country comparison to the world: 164

Natural gas—imports: 0 cu m (2013 est.)
country comparison to the world: 121

Natural gas—proved reserves: 0 cu m (1 January 2014 est.)
country comparison to the world: 184

Carbon dioxide emissions from consumption of energy: 16.23 million Mt (2012 est.)
country comparison to the world: 89

COMMUNICATIONS

Telephones—fixed lines: *total subscriptions:* 590,000
subscriptions per 100 inhabitants: 16 (2014 est.)
country comparison to the world: 92

Telephones—mobile cellular: *total:* 6.2 million
subscriptions per 100 inhabitants: 172 (2014 est.)
country comparison to the world: 110

Telephone system: *general assessment:* domestic and international facilities well-developed
domestic: mobile-cellular telephone subscriber-ship has increased rapidly
international: country code—507; landing point for the Americas Region Caribbean Ring System (ARCOS-1), the MAYA-1, and PAN-AM submarine cable systems that together provide links to the US and parts of the Caribbean, Central America, and South America; satellite earth stations—2 Intelsat (Atlantic Ocean); connected to the Central American Microwave System (2011)

Broadcast media: multiple privately owned TV networks and a government-owned educational TV station; multi-channel cable and satellite TV subscription services are available; more than 100 commercial radio stations (2007)
Radio broadcast stations: AM 101, FM 134, shortwave 0 (1998)
Television broadcast stations: 38 (including repeaters) (1998)

Internet country code: .pa

Internet hosts: 11,022 (2012)
country comparison to the world: 132

Internet users: *total:* 1.7 million
percent of population: 48.4% (2014 est.)
country comparison to the world: 105

TRANSPORTATION

Airports: 117 (2013)
country comparison to the world: 49

Airports—with paved runways: *total:* 57
over 3,047 m: 1
2,438 to 3,047 m: 3
1,524 to 2,437 m: 3
914 to 1,523 m: 20
under 914 m: 30 (2013)

Airports—with unpaved runways: *total:* 60
1,524 to 2,437 m: 1
914 to 1,523 m: 8
under 914 m: 51 (2013)

Heliports: 3 (2013)

Pipelines: oil 128 km (2013)

Railways: *total:* 77 km
standard gauge: 77 km 1.435-m gauge (2014)
country comparison to the world: 129

Roadways: *total:* 15,137 km
paved: 6,351 km
unpaved: 8,786 km (2010)
country comparison to the world: 122

Waterways: 800 km (includes the 82-km Panama Canal that is being widened) (2011)
country comparison to the world: 72

Merchant marine: *total:* 6,413
by type: barge carrier 1, bulk carrier 2,525, cargo 1,115, carrier 27, chemical tanker 588, combination ore/oil 1, container 742, liquefied gas 205, passenger 42, passenger/cargo 51, petroleum tanker 545, refrigerated cargo 191, roll on/roll off 87, specialized tanker 3, vehicle carrier 290
foreign-owned: 5,157 (Albania 4, Argentina 5, Australia 4, Bahamas 6, Bangladesh 5, Belgium 1, Bermuda 27, Brazil 3, Bulgaria 6, Burma 3, Canada 6, Chile 14, China 534, Colombia 2, Croatia 2, Cuba 2, Cyprus 5, Denmark 41, Ecuador 3, Egypt 11, Finland 2, France 7, Gabon 1, Germany 24, Gibraltar 1, Greece 379, Hong Kong 144, India 24, Indonesia 10, Iran 5, Ireland 1, Israel 1, Italy 25, Japan 2372, Jordan 11, Kuwait 12, Lebanon 2, Lithuania 3, Luxembourg 1, Malaysia 12, Maldives 2, Malta 2, Mexico 5, Monaco 11, Netherlands 6, Nigeria 6, Norway 81, Oman 10, Pakistan 3, Peru 9, Philippines 5, Portugal 10, Qatar 1, Romania 3, Russia 49, Saudi Arabia 11, Singapore 92, South Korea 373, Spain 30, Sweden 2, Switzerland 15, Syria 34, Taiwan 328, Tanzania 2, Thailand 6, Turkey 62, UAE 83, UK 37, Ukraine 8, US 90, Venezuela 13, Vietnam 43, Yemen 4)
registered in other countries: 1 (Honduras 1) (2010)
country comparison to the world: 1

Ports and terminals: *major seaport(s):* Balboa, Colon, Cristobal
container port(s) (TEUs): Balboa (3,232,265), Colon (2,390,976), Manzanillo (2,391,066)

MILITARY AND SECURITY

Military branches: no regular military forces; Panamanian Public Security Forces (subordinate to the Ministry of Public Security), comprising the National Police (PNP), National Air-Naval Service (SENAN), National Border Service (SENAFRONT) (2013)

Military—note: on 10 February 1990, the government of then President ENDARA abolished Panama's military and reformed the security apparatus by creating the Panamanian Public Forces; in October 1994, Panama's Legislative Assembly approved a constitutional amendment prohibiting the creation of a standing military force but allowing the temporary establishment of special police units to counter acts of "external aggression"

TRANSNATIONAL ISSUES

Disputes—international: organized illegal narcotics operations in Colombia operate within the remote border region with Panama

Refugees and internally displaced persons: *refugees (country of origin):* 15,551 (Colombia) (2014)
stateless persons: 2 (2015)

Illicit drugs: major cocaine transshipment point and primary money-laundering center for narcotics revenue; money-laundering activity is especially heavy in the Colon Free Zone; offshore financial center; negligible signs of coca cultivation; monitoring of financial transactions is improving; official corruption remains a major problem

PAPUA NEW GUINEA

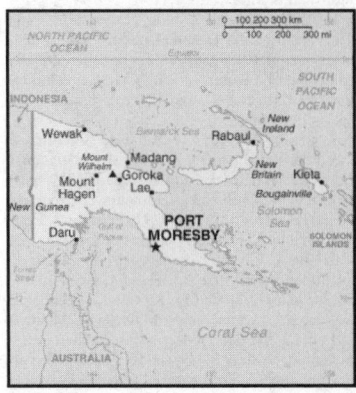

INTRODUCTION

Background: The eastern half of the island of New Guinea—second largest in the world—was divided between Germany (north) and the UK (south) in 1885. The latter area was transferred to Australia in 1902, which occupied the northern portion during World War I and continued to administer the combined areas until independence in 1975. A nine-year secessionist revolt on the island of Bougainville ended in 1997 after claiming some 20,000 lives. Since 2001, Bougainville has experienced autonomy. Under the terms of a peace accord, 2015 is the year that a five-year window opens for a referendum on the question of independence.

GEOGRAPHY

Location: Oceania, group of islands including the eastern half of the island of New Guinea between the Coral Sea and the South Pacific Ocean, east of Indonesia

Geographic coordinates: 6 00 S, 147 00 E

Map references: Oceania

Area: *total:* 462,840 sq km
land: 452,860 sq km
water: 9,980 sq km
country comparison to the world: 55

Area—comparative: slightly larger than California

Land boundaries: *total:* 824 km
border countries (1): Indonesia 824 km

Coastline: 5,152 km

Maritime claims: measured from claimed archipelagic baselines
territorial sea: 12 nm
continental shelf: 200-m depth or to the depth of exploitation
exclusive fishing zone: 200 nm

Climate: tropical; northwest monsoon (December to March), southeast monsoon (May to October); slight seasonal temperature variation

Terrain: mostly mountains with coastal lowlands and rolling foothills

Elevation: *mean elevation:* 667 m

elevation extremes: *lowest point:* Pacific Ocean 0 m
highest point: Mount Wilhelm 4,509 m

Natural resources: gold, copper, silver, Natural gas, timber, oil, fisheries

Land use: *agricultural land:* 2.6%
arable land: 0.7%
permanent crops: 1.5%
permanent pasture: 0.4%
forest: 63.1%
other: 34.3% (2011 est.)

Irrigated land: 0 sq km (2012)

Total renewable water resources: 801 cu km (2011)

Freshwater withdrawal (domestic/industrial/agricultural): *total:* 0.39 cu km/yr (57%/43%/0%)
per capita: 61.3 cu m/yr (2005)

Natural hazards: active volcanism; situated along the Pacific "Ring of Fire"; the country is subject to frequent and sometimes severe earthquakes; mud slides; tsunamis
volcanism: severe volcanic activity; Ulawun (elev. 2,334 m), one of Papua New Guinea's potentially most dangerous volcanoes, has been deemed a Decade Volcano by the International Association of Volcanology and Chemistry of the Earth's Interior, worthy of study due to its explosive history and close proximity to human populations; Rabaul (elev. 688 m) destroyed the city of Rabaul in 1937 and 1994; Lamington erupted in 1951 killing 3,000 people; Manam's 2004 eruption forced the island's abandonment; other historically active volcanoes include Bam, Bagana, Garbuna, Karkar, Langila, Lolobau, Long Island, Pago, St. Andrew Strait, Victory, and Waiowa

Environment—current issues: rain forest subject to deforestation as a result of growing commercial demand for tropical timber; pollution from mining projects; severe drought

Environment—international agreements: *party to:* Antarctic Treaty, Biodiversity, Climate Change, Climate Change-Kyoto Protocol, Desertification, Endangered Species, Environmental Modification, Hazardous Wastes, Law of the Sea, Marine Dumping, Ozone Layer Protection, Ship Pollution, Tropical Timber 83, Tropical Timber 94, Wetlands *signed, but not ratified:* none of the selected agreements

Geography—note: shares island of New Guinea with Indonesia; generally east-west trending highlands break up New Guinea into diverse ecoregions; one of world's largest swamps along southwest coast

PEOPLE AND SOCIETY

Nationality: *noun:* Papua New Guinean(s)

adjective: Papua New Guinean

Ethnic groups: Melanesian, Papuan, Negrito, Micronesian, Polynesian

Languages: Tok Pisin (official), English (official), Hiri Motu (official), some 836 indigenous languages spoken (about 12% of the world's total); most languages have fewer than 1,000 speakers
note: Tok Pisin, a creole language, is widely used and understood; English is spoken by 1%-2%; Hiri Motu is spoken by less than 2%

Religions: Roman Catholic 27%, Protestant 69.4% (Evangelical Lutheran 19.5%, United Church 11.5%, Seventh-Day Adventist 10%, Pentecostal 8.6%, Evangelical Alliance 5.2%, Anglican 3.2%, Baptist 2.5%, other Protestant 8.9%), Baha'i 0.3%, indigenous beliefs and other 3.3% (2000 census)

Population: 6,672,429 (July 2015 est.)
country comparison to the world: 106

Age structure: *0–14 years:* 34.45% (male 1,169,870/female 1,128,631)
15–24 years: 19.77% (male 668,327/female 650,672)
25–54 years: 36.43% (male 1,253,827/female 1,177,004)
55–64 years: 5.3% (male 179,075/female 174,721)
65 years and over: 4.05% (male 139,060/female 131,242) (2015 est.)

Dependency ratios: *total dependency ratio:* 67.1%
youth dependency ratio: 62.1%
elderly dependency ratio: 5%
potential support ratio: 19.9% (2015 est.)

Median age: *total:* 22.6 years
male: 22.8 years
female: 22.5 years (2015 est.)
country comparison to the world: 173

Population growth rate: 1.78% (2015 est.)
country comparison to the world: 66

Birth rate: 24.38 births/1,000 population (2015 est.)
country comparison to the world: 58

Death rate: 6.53 deaths/1,000 population (2015 est.)
country comparison to the world: 147

Net migration rate: 0 migrant(s)/1,000 population (2015 est.)
country comparison to the world: 85

Urbanization: *urban population:* 13% of total population (2015)
rate of urbanization: 2.12% annual rate of change (2010–15 est.)

Major urban areas—population: PORT MORESBY (capital) 345,000 (2015)

Sex ratio: *at birth:* 1.05 male(s)/female
0–14 years: 1.04 male(s)/female
15–24 years: 1.03 male(s)/female
25–54 years: 1.07 male(s)/female
55–64 years: 1.03 male(s)/female

65 years and over: 1.06 male(s)/female
total population: 1.05 male(s)/female (2015 est.)

Maternal mortality rate: 215 deaths/100,000 live births (2015 est.)
country comparison to the world: 51

Infant mortality rate: *total:* 38.55 deaths/1,000 live births
male: 42.12 deaths/1,000 live births
female: 34.81 deaths/1,000 live births (2015 est.)
country comparison to the world: 53

Life expectancy at birth: *total population:* 67.03 years
male: 64.81 years
female: 69.36 years (2015 est.)
country comparison to the world: 169

Total fertility rate: 3.16 children born/woman (2015 est.)
country comparison to the world: 51

Contraceptive prevalence rate: 32.4% (2006/07)

Health expenditures: 4.5% of GDP (2013)
country comparison to the world: 137

Physicians density: 0.06 physicians/1,000 population (2008)

Drinking water source:
improved:
urban: 88% of population
rural: 32.8% of population
total: 40% of population
unimproved:
urban: 12% of population
rural: 67.2% of population
total: 60% of population (2015 est.)

Sanitation facility access:
improved:
urban: 56.4% of population
rural: 13.3% of population
total: 18.9% of population
unimproved:
urban: 43.6% of population
rural: 86.7% of population
total: 81.1% of population (2015 est.)

HIV/AIDS—adult prevalence rate: 0.72% (2014 est.)
country comparison to the world: 53

HIV/AIDS—people living with HIV/AIDS: 37,200 (2014 est.)
country comparison to the world: 69

HIV/AIDS—deaths: 900 (2014 est.)
country comparison to the world: 69

Major infectious diseases: *degree of risk:* very high
food or waterborne diseases: bacterial diarrhea, hepatitis A, and typhoid fever
vectorborne diseases: dengue fever and malaria (2013)

Obesity—adult prevalence rate: 25.5% (2014)
country comparison to the world: 115

Children under the age of 5 years underweight: 27.9% (2011)
country comparison to the world: 19

Education expenditures: NA

Literacy: *definition:* age 15 and over can read and write
total population: 64.2%
male: 65.6%
female: 62.8% (2015 est.)

People—note: the indigenous population of Papua New Guinea (PNG) is one of the most heterogeneous in the world; PNG has several thousand separate communities, most with only a few hundred people; divided by language, customs, and tradition, some of these communities have engaged in low-scale tribal conflict with their neighbors for millennia; the advent of modern weapons and modern migrants into urban areas has greatly magnified the impact of this lawlessness

GOVERNMENT

Country name: *conventional long form:* Independent State of Papua New Guinea
conventional short form: Papua New Guinea
local short form: Papuaniugini
former: Territory of Papua and New Guinea
abbreviation: PNG
etymology: the word "papua" derives from the Malay "papuah" describing the frizzy hair of the Melanesians; Spanish explorer Ynigo ORTIZ de RETEZ applied the term "Nueva Guinea" to the island of New Guinea in 1545 after noting the resemblance of the locals to the peoples of the Guinea coast of Africa

Government type: parliamentary democracy (National Parliament) under a constitutional monarchy; a Commonwealth realm

Capital: *name:* Port Moresby

Geographic coordinates: 9 27 S, 147 11 E
time difference: UTC + 10 (15 hours ahead of Washington, DC, during Standard Time)

Administrative divisions: 20 provinces, 1 autonomous region*, and 1 district**; Bougainville*, Central, Chimbu, Eastern Highlands, East New Britain, East Sepik, Enga, Gulf, Hela, Jiwaka, Madang, Manus, Milne Bay, Morobe, National Capital**, New Ireland, Northern, Southern Highlands, Western, Western Highlands, West New Britain, West Sepik

Independence: 16 September 1975 (from the Australian-administered UN trusteeship)

National holiday: Independence Day, 16 September (1975)

Constitution: adopted 15 August 1975, effective at independence 16 September 1975; amended many times, last in 2013; note—in September 2015, the Supreme Court nullified the 2013 constitutional amendment that increased the grace period on motions of no confidence (2016)

Legal system: mixed legal system of English common law and customary law

International law organization participation: has not submitted an ICJ jurisdiction declaration; non-party state to the ICCt

Citizenship: *citizenship by birth:* no
citizenship by descent only: at least one parent must be a citizen of Papua New Guinea

dual citizenship recognized: no
residency requirement for naturalization: 8 years

Suffrage: 18 years of age; universal

Executive branch: *chief of state:* Queen ELIZABETH II (since 6 February 1952); represented by Governor Michael OGIO (since 25 February 2011)

head of government: Prime Minister Peter Paire O'NEILL (since 2 August 2011); Deputy Prime Minister Leo DION (since 9 August 2012)
cabinet: National Executive Council appointed by the governor general on the recommendation of the prime minister
elections/appointments: the monarchy is hereditary; governor general nominated by the National Parliament and appointed by the chief of state; following legislative elections, the leader of the majority party or majority coalition usually appointed prime minister by the governor general pending the outcome of a National Parliament vote
election results: Peter Paire O'NEILL (PNC) elected prime minister; National Parliament vote—94 to 12

Legislative branch: *description:* unicameral national Parliament (111 seats; members directly elected in single-seat constituencies—91 local and 20 provincial—by majority preferential vote; members serve 5-year terms); note—the constitution allows up to 126 seats
note: 14 other parties won 3 or fewer seats; association with political parties is fluid
elections: last held from 23 June 2012 to 27 July 2012 (next to be held in June 2017)
election results: percent of vote by party—NA; seats by party—People's National Congress Party 27, Triumph Heritage Empowerment Party 12, PNG Party 8, National Alliance Party 7, United Resources Party 7, People's Party 6, People's Progress Party 6, other 22, independent 16

Judicial branch: *highest court(s):* Supreme Court (consists of the chief justice, deputy chief justice, and 28 other judges); National Courts (10 courts located in the province capitals, with a total of 16 resident judges)
judge selection and term of office: chief justice appointed by the governor-general upon advice of the National Executive Council (cabinet) after consultation with the National Justice Administration Minister; deputy chief justice and other justices appointed by the Judicial and Legal Services Commission, a 5-member body to include the Supreme Court chief and deputy chief justices, the chief ombudsman, and a member of the National Parliament; citizen judges appointed for 10-year renewable terms; non-citizen judges appointed for 3-year renewable terms; appointment and tenure of National Court resident judges NA
subordinate courts: district, village, and juvenile courts

Political parties and leaders: National Alliance Party or NA [Patrick PRUAITCHI]
Papua New Guinea Party or PNGP [Beldan NAMAH]

661

People's National Congress Party or PNC [Peter Paire O'NEILL]

People's Party or PP (merged with PNC)

People's Progress Party or PPP [Sir Julius CHAN]

Triumph Heritage Empowerment Party or THE

United Resources Party or URP [William DUMA]

note: as of 13 March 2012, 41 political parties were registered

Political pressure groups and leaders: Centre for Environment Law and Community Rights or Celcor [Damien ASE]

Community Coalition Against Corruption

National Council of Women

Transparency International Papau New Guinea or TIPNG (chapter of Transparency International)

International organization participation: ACP, ADB, AOSIS, APEC, ARF, ASEAN (observer), C, CD, CP, EITI (candidate country), FAO, G-77, IAEA, IBRD, ICAO, ICRM, IDA, IFAD, IFC, IFRCS, IHO, ILO, IMF, IMO, Interpol, IOC, IOM, IPU, ISO (correspondent), ITSO, ITU, MIGA, NAM, OPCW, PIF, Sparteca, SPC, UN, UNCTAD, UNESCO, UNIDO, UNMISS, UNWTO, UPU, WCO, WFTU (NGOs), WHO, WIPO, WMO, WTO

Diplomatic representation in the US: *chief of mission:* Ambassador Rupa Abraham MALINA (since 10 March 2014)

chancery: 1779 Massachusetts Avenue NW, Suite 805, Washington, DC 20036

telephone: [1] (202) 745-3680

FAX: [1] (202) 745-3679

Diplomatic representation from the US: *chief of mission:* Ambassador Catherine EBERT-GRAY (since 23 February 2016); note—also accredited to the Solomon Islands and Vanuatu

embassy: Douglas Street, Port Moresby, N.C.D.

mailing address: 4240 Port Moresby Place, US Department of State, Washington DC 20521–4240

telephone: [675] 321-1455

FAX: [675] 321-3423

Flag description: divided diagonally from upper hoist-side corner; the upper triangle is red with a soaring yellow bird of paradise centered; the lower triangle is black with five, white, five-pointed stars of the Southern Cross constellation centered; red, black, and yellow are traditional colors of Papua New Guinea; the bird of paradise—endemic to the island of New Guinea—is an emblem of regional tribal culture and represents the emergence of Papua New Guinea as a nation; the Southern Cross, visible in the night sky, symbolizes Papua New Guinea's connection with Australia and several other countries in the South Pacific

National symbol(s): bird of paradise; National colors: red, black

National anthem: *name:* "O Arise All You Sons"

lyrics/music: Thomas SHACKLADY

note: adopted 1975

ECONOMY

Economy—overview: Papua New Guinea (PNG) is richly endowed with Natural resources, but exploitation has been hampered by rugged terrain, land tenure issues, and the high cost of developing infrastructure. The economy has a small formal sector, focused mainly on the export of those Natural resources, and an informal sector, employing the majority of the population. Agriculture provides a subsistence livelihood for 85% of the people. The global financial crisis had little impact because of continued foreign demand for PNG's commodities.

Mineral deposits, including copper, gold, and oil, account for nearly two-thirds of export earnings. natural gas reserves amount to an estimated 155 billion cubic meters. A consortium led by a major American oil company is constructing a liquefied natural gas (LNG) production facility that began exporting in April 2014. As the largest investment project in the country's history, it has the potential to double GDP in the near-term and triple Papua New Guinea's export revenue. An American-owned firm also opened PNG's first oil refinery in 2004 and is building a second LNG production facility. The government faces the challenge of ensuring transparency and accountability for revenues flowing from this and other large LNG projects. In 2011 and 2012, the National Parliament passed legislation that created an offshore Sovereign Wealth Fund to manage government surpluses from mineral, oil, and natural gas projects. In recent years, the government has opened up markets in telecommunications and air transport, making both more affordable to the people. Numerous challenges still face the government of Peter O'NEILL, including providing physical security for foreign investors, regaining investor confidence, restoring integrity to state institutions, promoting economic efficiency by privatizing moribund state institutions, and maintaining good relations with Australia, its former colonial ruler. Other socio-cultural challenges could upend the economy including chronic law and order and land tenure issues.

GDP (purchasing power parity): $20.47 billion (2015 est.)

$18.78 billion (2014 est.)

$17.3 billion (2013 est.)

note: data are in 2015 US dollars

country comparison to the world: 143

GDP (official exchange rate): $16.09 billion (2015 est.)

GDP—real growth rate: 9% (2015 est.)

8.5% (2014 est.)

5.5% (2013 est.)

country comparison to the world: 5

GDP—per capita (PPP): $2,700 (2015 est.)

$2,500 (2014 est.)

$2,400 (2013 est.)

note: data are in 2015 US dollars

country comparison to the world: 193

Gross national saving: 24.5% of GDP (2015 est.)

26.4% of GDP (2014 est.)

8.6% of GDP (2013 est.)

country comparison to the world: 50

GDP—composition, by end use:

household consumption: 56.1%

government consumption: 10.5%

investment in fixed capital: 13.4%

investment in inventories: 7.7%

exports of goods and services: 62.6%

imports of goods and services: -50.3% (2015 est.)

GDP—composition, by sector of origin: \

agriculture: 23.3%

industry: 38.3%

services: 38.4% (2015 est.)

Agriculture—products: coffee, cocoa, copra, palm kernels, tea, sugar, rubber, sweet potatoes, fruit, vegetables, vanilla; poultry, pork; shellfish

Industries: copra crushing, palm oil processing, plywood production, wood chip production; mining (gold, silver, copper); crude oil and petroleum products; construction, tourism

Industrial production growth rate: 10.8% (2015 est.)

country comparison to the world: 4

Labor force: 4.267 million (2015 est.)

country comparison to the world: 91

Labor force—by occupation: *agriculture:* 85%

industry: NA%

services: NA% (2005 est.)

Unemployment rate: 1.9% (2008 est.)

1.6% (2004)

country comparison to the world: 11

Population below poverty line: 37% (2002 est.)

Household income or consumption by percentage share: *lowest:* 10%: 1.7%

highest: 10%: 40.5% (1996)

Distribution of family income—Gini index: 50.9 (1996)

country comparison to the world: 18

Budget: *revenues:* $4.142 billion

expenditures: $5.643 billion (2015 est.)

Taxes and other revenues: 23% of GDP (2015 est.)

country comparison to the world: 135

Budget surplus (+) or deficit (–): -8.3% of GDP (2015 est.)

country comparison to the world: 199

Public debt: 48.7% of GDP (2015 est.)

41.3% of GDP (2014 est.)

country comparison to the world: 84

Fiscal year: calendar year

Inflation rate (consumer prices): 6% (2015 est.)

5.3% (2014 est.)

country comparison to the world: 186

Central bank discount rate: 14% (31 December 2010)

6.92% (31 December 2009)

country comparison to the world: 14

Commercial bank prime lending rate: 9.1% (31 December 2015 est.)

9.38% (31 December 2014 est.)

country comparison to the world: 94

Stock of narrow money: $5.113 billion (31 December 2015 est.)

$5.034 billion (31 December 2014 est.)

country comparison to the world: 98

Stock of broad money: $8.085 billion (31 December 2014 est.)

$7.477 billion (31 December 2013 est.)

country comparison to the world: 114

Stock of domestic credit: $6.347 billion (31 December 2015 est.)
$6.125 billion (31 December 2014 est.)
country comparison to the world: 115

Market value of publicly traded shares:
$10.71 billion (31 December 2012 est.)
$8.999 billion (31 December 2011)
$9.742 billion (31 December 2010 est.)
country comparison to the world: 74

Current account balance: $444 million (2015 est.)
-$703 million (2014 est.)
country comparison to the world: 42

Exports: $8.653 billion (2015 est.)
$8.941 billion (2014 est.)
country comparison to the world: 95

Exports—commodities: oil, gold, copper ore, logs, palm oil, coffee, cocoa, crayfish, prawns

Exports—partners: Japan 17.4%, Australia 15.9%, China 12.1% (2015)

Imports: $3.311 billion (2015 est.)
$4.013 billion (2014 est.)
country comparison to the world: 142

Imports—commodities: machinery and transport equipment, manufactured goods, food, fuels, chemicals

Imports—partners: Australia 25.9%, China 20%, Singapore 12.6%, Malaysia 7.2%, US 4.2%, Indonesia 4.1%, South Korea 4% (2015)

Reserves of foreign exchange and gold: $2.966 billion (31 December 2015 est.)
$2.305 billion (31 December 2014 est.)
country comparison to the world: 106

Debt—external: $26.51 billion (31 December 2014 est.)
$21.63 billion (31 December 2013 est.)
country comparison to the world: 77

Stock of direct foreign investment—at home: $NA

Stock of direct foreign investment—abroad: $NA

Exchange rates: kina (PGK) per US dollar—
2.748 (2015 est.)
2.4614 (2014 est.)
2.4614 (2013 est.)
2.08 (2012 est.)
2.371 (2011 est.)

ENERGY

Electricity—production: 3.35 billion kWh (2012 est.)
country comparison to the world: 130

Electricity—consumption: 3.116 billion kWh (2012 est.)
country comparison to the world: 133

Electricity—exports: 0 kWh (2013 est.)
country comparison to the world: 184

Electricity—imports: 0 kWh (2013 est.)
country comparison to the world: 190

Electricity—installed generating capacity: 700,000 kW (2012 est.)
country comparison to the world: 133

Electricity—from fossil fuels: 61.1% of total installed capacity (2012 est.)
country comparison to the world: 129

Electricity—from nuclear fuels: 0% of total installed capacity (2012 est.)
country comparison to the world: 167

Electricity—from hydroelectric plants: 30.9% of total installed capacity (2012 est.)
country comparison to the world: 74

Electricity—from other renewable sources: 8% of total installed capacity (2012 est.)
country comparison to the world: 47

Crude oil—production: 34,210 bbl/day (2014 est.)
country comparison to the world: 63

Crude oil—exports: 25,400 bbl/day (2012 est.)
country comparison to the world: 56

Crude oil—imports: 14,880 bbl/day (2012 est.)
country comparison to the world: 72

Crude oil—proved reserves: 175.2 million bbl (1 January 2015 est.)
country comparison to the world: 62

Refined petroleum products—production: 17,330 bbl/day (2012 est.)
country comparison to the world: 96

Refined petroleum products—consumption: 20,000 bbl/day (2013 est.)
country comparison to the world: 130

Refined petroleum products—exports: 3,536 bbl/day (2012 est.)
country comparison to the world: 99

Refined petroleum products—imports: 5,933 bbl/day (2012 est.)
country comparison to the world: 154

Natural gas—production: 110 million cu m (2013 est.)
country comparison to the world: 82

Natural gas—consumption: 110 million cu m (2013 est.)
country comparison to the world: 108

Natural gas—exports: 0 cu m (2013 est.)
country comparison to the world: 166

Natural gas—imports: 0 cu m (2013 est.)
country comparison to the world: 122

Natural gas—proved reserves: 155.3 billion cu m (1 January 2014 est.)
country comparison to the world: 48

Carbon dioxide emissions from consumption of energy: 3.385 million Mt (2012 est.)
country comparison to the world: 138

COMMUNICATIONS

Telephones—fixed lines: *total subscriptions:* 150,000
subscriptions per 100 inhabitants: 2 (2014 est.)
country comparison to the world: 137

Telephones—mobile cellular: *total:* 3.4 million
subscriptions per 100 inhabitants: 51 (2014 est.)
country comparison to the world: 132

Telephone system: *general assessment:* services are minimal; facilities provide radiotelephone and telegraph, coastal radio, aeronautical radio, and international radio communication services
domestic: access to telephone services is not widely available although combined fixed-line and mobile-cellular teledensity has increased to roughly 40 per 100 persons
international: country code—675; submarine cables to Australia and Guam; satellite earth station—1 Intelsat (Pacific Ocean); international radio communication service (2009)

Broadcast media: TV stations, 1 commercial station operating since the late 1980s, and 1 state-run station launched in 2008; satellite and cable TV services are available; state-run National Broadcasting Corporation operates radio networks with multiple repeaters and about 20 provincial stations; several commercial radio stations with multiple transmission points as well as several community stations; transmissions of several international broadcasters are accessible (2009)

Radio broadcast stations: AM 8, FM 19, shortwave 28 (1998)

Television broadcast stations: 3 (all in the Port Moresby area; stations at Mt. Hagen, Goroka, Lae, and Rabaul are planned) (2004)

Internet country code: .pg

Internet hosts: 5,006 (2012)
country comparison to the world: 145

Internet users: total: 164,500
percent of population: 2.5% (2014 est.)
country comparison to the world: 162

TRANSPORTATION

Airports: 561 (2013)
country comparison to the world: 12

Airports—with paved runways: *total:* 21
over 3,047 m: 1
2,438 to 3,047 m: 2
1,524 to 2,437 m: 12
914 to 1,523 m: 5
under 914 m: 1 (2013)

Airports—with unpaved runways: *total:* 540
1,524 to 2,437 m: 11
914 to 1,523 m: 53
under 914 m: 476 (2013)

Heliports: 2 (2013)

Pipelines: oil 264 km (2013)

Roadways: *total:* 9,349 km
paved: 3,000 km
unpaved: 6,349 km (2011)
country comparison to the world: 138

Waterways: 11,000 km (2011)
country comparison to the world: 11

Merchant marine: *total:* 31
by type: bulk carrier 7, cargo 22, petroleum tanker 2
foreign-owned: 8 (Germany 1, Malaysia 1, UAE 6) (2010)
country comparison to the world: 83

Ports and terminals: *major seaport(s):* Kimbe, Lae, Madang, Rabaul, Wewak
LNG terminal(s) (export): Port Moresby

MILITARY AND SECURITY

Military branches: Papua New Guinea Defense Force (PNGDF; includes Maritime Operations Element, Air Operations Element) (2013)

Military service age and obligation: 16 years of age for voluntary military service (with parental consent); no conscription; graduation from grade 12 required (2013)

Military expenditures: 0.54% of GDP (2012)
0.6% of GDP (2011)
0.54% of GDP (2010)
country comparison to the world: 127

TRANSNATIONAL ISSUES

Disputes—international: relies on assistance from Australia to keep out illegal cross-border activities from primarily Indonesia, including goods smuggling, illegal narcotics trafficking, and squatters and secessionists

Refugees and internally displaced persons: *refugees (country of origin):* 9,368 (Indonesia) (2014) *IDPs:* 6,300 (Natural disasters, tribal conflict, inter-communal violence, development projects) (2015)

Trafficking in persons: *current situation:* Papua New Guinea is a source and destination country for men, women, and children subjected to sex trafficking and forced labor; foreign and Papua New Guinean women and children are subjected to sex trafficking, domestic servitude, forced begging, and street vending; parents may sell girls into forced marriages to settle debts or as peace offerings or trade them to another tribe to forge a political alliance, leaving them vulnerable to forced domestic service, or, in urban areas, they may prostitute their children for income or to pay school fees; Chinese, Malaysian, and local men are forced to labor in logging and mining camps through debt bondage schemes; migrant women from Indonesia, Malaysia, Thailand, China, and the Philippines are subjected to sex trafficking and

domestic servitude at logging and mining camps, fisheries, and entertainment sites

tier rating: Tier 2 Watch List—Papua New Guinea does not fully comply with the minimum standards for the elimination of trafficking; however, it is making significant efforts to do so; the Criminal Code Amendment of 2013, which prohibits all forms of trafficking was brought into force in 2014; the government also formed an anti-trafficking committee, which drafted a National action plan; despite corruption problems, trafficking-related crimes were prosecuted in village courts rather than criminal courts, resulting in restitution to the victim but no prison time for offenders; the government did not investigate, prosecute, or convict any officials or law enforcement personnel complicit in trafficking offenses; the government made no efforts to proactively identify trafficking victims, has no formal victim identification and referral mechanism, and does not provide care facilities to victims or funding to shelters run by NGOs or international organizations (2015)

Illicit drugs: major consumer of cannabis

PARACEL ISLANDS

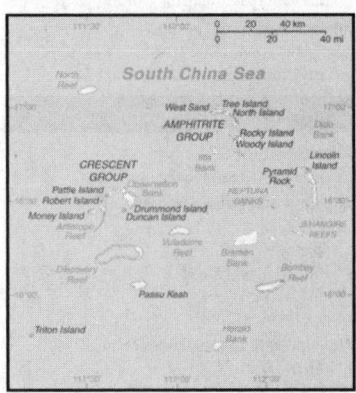

INTRODUCTION

Background: The Paracel Islands are surrounded by productive fishing grounds and by potential oil and gas reserves. In 1932, French Indochina annexed the islands and set up a weather station on Pattle Island; maintenance was continued by its successor, Vietnam. China has occupied all the Paracel Islands since 1974, when its troops seized a South Vietnamese garrison occupying the western islands. China built a military installation on Woody Island with an airfield and artificial harbor. The islands also are claimed by Taiwan and Vietnam.

GEOGRAPHY

Location: Southeastern Asia, group of small islands and reefs in the South China Sea, about one-third

of the way from central Vietnam to the northern Philippines

Geographic coordinates: 16 30 N, 112 00 E

Map references: Southeast Asia

Area: *total:* ca.7.75 sq km
land: ca.7.75 sq km
water: 0 sq km

Area—comparative: land area is about thirteen times the size of the National Mall in Washington, DC

Land boundaries: 0 km

Coastline: 518 km

Maritime claims: NA

Climate: tropical

Terrain: mostly low and flat

Elevation: *mean elevation:* NA

elevation extremes: *lowest point:* South China Sea 0 m
highest point: unnamed location on Rocky Island 14 m

Natural resources: none

Land use: *agricultural land:* 0%
arable land: 0%
permanent crops: 0%
permanent pasture: 0%
forest: 0%
other: 100% (2011 est.)

Irrigated land: 0 sq km (2012)

Natural hazards: typhoons

Environment—current issues: NA

Geography—note: composed of 130 small coral islands and reefs divided into the northeast Amphitrite Group and the western Crescent Group

PEOPLE AND SOCIETY

Population: no indigenous inhabitants
note: there are scattered Chinese garrisons

GOVERNMENT

Country name: *conventional long form:* none
conventional short form: Paracel Islands
etymology: Portuguese navigators began to refer to the "Ilhas do Pracel" in the 16th century as a designation of low lying islets, sandbanks, and reefs scattered over a wide area; over time the name changed to "parcel" and then "paracel"

ECONOMY

Economy—overview: The islands have the potential for oil and gas development. Waters around the islands support commercial fishing, but the islands themselves are not populated on a permanent basis.

TRANSPORTATION

Airports: 1 (2013)
country comparison to the world: 230

Airports—with paved runways: *total:* 1
1,524 to 2,437 m: 1 (2013)

Ports and terminals: small Chinese port facilities on Woody Island and Duncan Island

MILITARY AND SECURITY

Military—note: occupied by China

TRANSNATIONAL ISSUES

Disputes—international: occupied by China, also claimed by Taiwan and Vietnam

PARAGUAY

INTRODUCTION

Background: Paraguay achieved its independence from Spain in 1811. In the disastrous War of the Triple Alliance (1865–70)—between Paraguay and Argentina, Brazil, and Uruguay—Paraguay lost two-thirds of its adult males and much of its territory. The country stagnated economically for the next half century. Following the Chaco War of 1932–35 with Bolivia, Paraguay gained a large part of the Chaco lowland region. The 35-year military dictatorship of Alfredo STROESSNER ended in 1989, and, despite a marked increase in political infighting in recent years, Paraguay has held relatively free and regular presidential elections since the country's return to democracy.

GEOGRAPHY

Location: Central South America, northeast of Argentina, southwest of Brazil

Geographic coordinates: 23 00 S, 58 00 W

Map references: South America

Area: *total:* 406,752 sq km
land: 397,302 sq km
water: 9,450 sq km
country comparison to the world: 60

Area—comparative: slightly smaller than California

Land boundaries: *total:* 4,655 km
border countries (3): Argentina 2,531 km, Bolivia 753 km, Brazil 1,371 km

Coastline: 0 km (landlocked)

Maritime claims: none (landlocked)

Climate: subtropical to temperate; substantial rainfall in the eastern portions, becoming semiarid in the far west

Terrain: grassy plains and wooded hills east of Rio Paraguay; Gran Chaco region west of Rio Paraguay mostly low, marshy plain near the river, and dry forest and thorny scrub elsewhere

Elevation: *mean elevation:* 178 m

elevation extremes: *lowest point:* junction of Rio Paraguay and Rio Parana 46 m
highest point: Cerro Pero 842 m

Natural resources: hydropower, timber, iron ore, manganese, limestone

Land use: *agricultural land:* 53.8%
arable land: 10.8%
permanent crops: 0.2%
permanent pasture: 42.8%
forest: 43.8%
other: 2.4% (2011 est.)

Irrigated land: 1,362 sq km (2012)

Total renewable water resources: 336 cu km (2011)

Freshwater withdrawal (domestic/industrial/agricultural): *total:* 0.49 cu km/yr (20%/8%/71%)
per capita: 88.05 cu m/yr (2000)

Natural hazards: local flooding in southeast (early September to June); poorly drained plains may become boggy (early October to June)

Environment—current issues: deforestation; water pollution; inadequate means for waste disposal pose health risks for many urban residents; loss of wetlands

Environment—international agreements: *party to:* Biodiversity, Climate Change, Climate Change-Kyoto Protocol, Desertification, Endangered Species, Hazardous Wastes, Law of the Sea, Ozone Layer Protection, Wetlands
signed, but not ratified: none of the selected agreements

Geography—note: landlocked; lies between Argentina, Bolivia, and Brazil; population concentrated in southern part of country

PEOPLE AND SOCIETY

Nationality: *noun:* Paraguayan(s)
adjective: Paraguayan

Ethnic groups: mestizo (mixed Spanish and Amerindian) 95%, other 5%

Languages: Spanish (official), Guarani (official)

Religions: Roman Catholic 89.6%, Protestant 6.2%, other Christian 1.1%, other or unspecified 1.9%, none 1.1% (2002 census)

Demographic profile: Paraguay falls below the Latin American average in several socioeconomic categories, including immunization rates, potable water, sanitation, and secondary school enrollment, and has greater rates of income inequality and child and maternal mortality. Paraguay's poverty rate has declined in recent years but remains high, especially in rural areas, with more than a third of the population below the poverty line. However, the well-being of the poor in many regions has improved in terms of housing quality and access to clean water, telephone service, and electricity. The fertility rate continues to drop, declining sharply from an average 4.3 births per woman in the late 1990s to about 2 in 2013, as

a result of the greater educational attainment of women, increased use of contraception, and a desire for smaller families among young women. Paraguay is a country of emigration; it has not attracted large numbers of immigrants because of political instability, civil wars, years of dictatorship, and the greater appeal of neighboring countries. Paraguay first tried to encourage immigration in 1870 in order to rebound from the heavy death toll it suffered during the War of the Triple Alliance, but it received few European and Middle Eastern immigrants. In the 20th century, limited numbers of immigrants arrived from Lebanon, Japan, South Korea, and China, as well as Mennonites from Canada, Russia, and Mexico. Large flows of Brazilian immigrants have been arriving since the 1960s, mainly to work in agriculture. Paraguayans continue to emigrate to Argentina, Brazil, Uruguay, the United States, Italy, Spain, and France.

Population: 6,783,272 (July 2015 est.)
country comparison to the world: 105

Age structure: *0–14 years:* 25.59% (male 882,929/female 852,583)
15–24 years: 20.14% (male 687,025/female 679,420)
25–54 years: 40.04% (male 1,359,281/female 1,356,663)
55–64 years: 7.48% (male 259,086/female 248,636)
65 years and over: 6.75% (male 213,907/female 243,742) (2015 est.)

Dependency ratios: *total dependency ratio:* 56.6%
youth dependency ratio: 47.2%
elderly dependency ratio: 9.4%
potential support ratio: 10.6% (2015 est.)

Median age: *total:* 27.3 years
male: 27 years
female: 27.5 years (2015 est.)
country comparison to the world: 137

Population growth rate: 1.16% (2015 est.)
country comparison to the world: 104

Birth rate: 16.37 births/1,000 population (2015 est.)
country comparison to the world: 116

Death rate: 4.68 deaths/1,000 population (2015 est.)
country comparison to the world: 198

Net migration rate: -0.07 migrant(s)/1,000 population (2015 est.)
country comparison to the world: 115

Urbanization: *urban population:* 59.7% of total population (2015)
rate of urbanization: 2.1% annual rate of change (2010–15 est.)

Major urban areas—population: ASUNCION (capital) 2.356 million (2015)

Sex ratio: *at birth:* 1.05 male(s)/female
0–14 years: 1.04 male(s)/female

15–24 years: 1.01 male(s)/female
25–54 years: 1 male(s)/female
55–64 years: 1.04 male(s)/female
65 years and over: 0.88 male(s)/female
total population: 1.01 male(s)/female (2015 est.)

Mother's mean age at first birth: 22.9
note: median age at first birth among women 25–29 (2008 est.)

Maternal mortality rate: 132 deaths/100,000 live births (2015 est.)
country comparison to the world: 73

Infant mortality rate: total: 20.05 deaths/1,000 live births
male: 23.6 deaths/1,000 live births
female: 16.31 deaths/1,000 live births (2015 est.)
country comparison to the world: 86

Life expectancy at birth: total population: 76.99 years
male: 74.34 years
female: 79.77 years (2015 est.)
country comparison to the world: 74

Total fertility rate: 1.91 children born/woman (2015 est.)
country comparison to the world: 136

Contraceptive prevalence rate: 79.4%
note: percent of women aged 15–44 (2008)

Health expenditures: 9% of GDP (2013)
country comparison to the world: 21

Physicians density: 1.23 physicians/1,000 population (2012)

Hospital bed density: 1.3 beds/1,000 population (2011)

Drinking water source:
improved:
urban: 100% of population
rural: 94.9% of population
total: 98% of population
unimproved:
urban: 0% of population
rural: 5.1% of population
total: 2% of population (2015 est.)

Sanitation facility access:
improved:
urban: 95.5% of population
rural: 78.4% of population
total: 88.6% of population
unimproved:
urban: 4.5% of population
rural: 21.6% of population
total: 11.4% of population (2015 est.)

HIV/AIDS—adult prevalence rate: 0.41% (2014 est.)
country comparison to the world: 75

HIV/AIDS—people living with HIV/AIDS: 16,800 (2014 est.)
country comparison to the world: 83

HIV/AIDS—deaths: 400 (2014 est.)
country comparison to the world: 90

Major infectious diseases: degree of risk: intermediate
food or waterborne diseases: bacterial diarrhea, hepatitis A, and typhoid fever

vectorborne disease: dengue fever (2013)

Obesity—adult prevalence rate: 15.1% (2014)
country comparison to the world: 110

Children under the age of 5 years underweight: 2.6% (2012)
country comparison to the world: 105

Education expenditures: 5% of GDP (2012)
country comparison to the world: 84

Literacy: definition: age 15 and over can read and write
total population: 93.9%
male: 94.8%
female: 92.9% (2010 est.)

School life expectancy (primary to tertiary education): total: 12 years
male: 12 years
female: 13 years (2010)

Child labor—children ages 5–14: total number: 205,297
percentage: 15% (2004 est.)

Unemployment, youth ages 15–24: total: 10.5%
male: 8.9%
female: 13% (2013 est.)
country comparison to the world: 95

GOVERNMENT

Country name: conventional long form: Republic of Paraguay
conventional short form: Paraguay
local long form: Republica del Paraguay
local short form: Paraguay
etymology: the precise meaning of the name Paraguay is unclear, but it seems to derive from the river of the same name; one explanation has the name meaning "water of the Payagua" (an indigenous tribe that lived along the river)

Government type: presidential republic

Capital: name: Asuncion

Geographic coordinates: 25 16 S, 57 40 W
time difference: UTC-4 (1 hour ahead of Washington, DC, during Standard Time)
daylight saving time: +1hr, begins first Sunday in October; ends fourth Sunday in March

Administrative divisions: 17 departments (departamentos, singular—departamento) and 1 capital city*; Alto Paraguay, Alto Parana, Amambay, Asuncion*, Boqueron, Caaguazu, Caazapa, Canindeyu, Central, Concepcion, Cordillera, Guaira, Itapua, Misiones, Neembucu, Paraguari, Presidente Hayes, San Pedro

Independence: 14 May 1811 (from Spain)

National holiday: Independence Day, 14 May 1811 (observed 15 May)

Constitution: several previous; latest approved and promulgated 20 June 1992; amended 2011, 2014 (2016)

Legal system: civil law system with influences from Argentine, Spanish, Roman, and French civil law models; judicial review of legislative acts in Supreme Court of Justice

International law organization participation: accepts compulsory ICJ jurisdiction; accepts ICCt jurisdiction

Citizenship: citizenship by birth: yes
citizenship by descent: at least one parent must be a native-born citizen of Paraguay
dual citizenship recognized: yes
residency requirement for naturalization: 3 years

Suffrage: 18 years of age; universal and compulsory until the age of 75

Executive branch: chief of state: President Horacio CARTES Jara (since 15 August 2013); Vice President Juan AFARA Maciel (since 15 August 2013); note—the president is both chief of state and head of government

head of government: President Horacio CARTES Jara (since 15 August 2013); Vice President Juan AFARA Maciel (since 15 August 2013)
cabinet: Council of Ministers appointed by the president
elections/appointments: president and vice president directly elected on the same ballot by simple majority popular vote for a single 5-year term; election last held on 21 April 2013 (next to be held in April 2018)
election results: Horacio CARTES elected president; percent of vote—Horacio CARTES (ANR) 45.8%, Efrain ALEGRE (PLRA) 36.9%, Mario FERREIRO (AP) 5.9%, Anibal CARRILLO (FG) 3.3%, other 8%

Legislative branch: description: bicameral National Congress or Congreso Nacional consists of the Chamber of Senators or Camara de Senadores (45 seats; members directly elected in a single nationwide constituency by proportional representation vote to serve 5-year terms) and the Chamber of Deputies or Camara de Diputados (80 seats; members directly elected in 18 multi-seat constituencies—corresponding to the country's 17 departments and capital city—by proportional representation vote to serve 5-year terms)
elections: Chamber of Senators—last held on 21 April 2013 (next to be held in April 2018); Chamber of Deputies—last held on 21 April 2013 (next to be held in April 2018)
election results: Chamber of Senators—percent of vote by party—NA; seats by party—ANR 19, PLRA 12, FG 5, PDP 3, Avanza Pais 2, UNACE 2, PEN 1, PPQ 1; Chamber of Deputies—percent of vote by party -NA; seats by party—ANR 44, PLRA 27, Avanza Pais 2, PEN 2, UNACE 2, FG 1, PPQ 1, other 1

Judicial branch: highest court(s): Supreme Court of Justice or Corte Suprema de Justicia (consists of9 justices divided 3 each into the Constitutional Court, Civil and Commercial Chamber, and Criminal Division
judge selection and term of office: justices proposed by the Council of Magistrates or Consejo de la Magistratura, a 6-member independent body, and appointed by the Chamber of Senators with presidential concurrence; judges appointed until mandatory retirement at age 75

subordinate courts: appellate courts; first instance courts; minor courts, including justices of the peace

Political parties and leaders: Asociacion Nacional Republicana—Colorado Party or ANR [Pedro ALLIANA]
Avanza Pais coalition [Adolfo FERREIRO]
Broad Front coalition (Frente Guasu) or FG [Fernando Armindo LUGO Mendez]
Movimiento Union Nacional de Ciudadanos Eticos or UNACE [Jorge OVIEDO MATTO]
Partido del Movimiento al Socialismo or P-MAS [Camilo Ernesto SOARES Machado]
Partido Democratica Progresista or PDP [Desiree MASI]
Partido Encuentro Nacional or PEN [Fernando CAMACHO Paredes]
Partido Liberal Radical Autentico or PLRA [Miguel ABDON SAGUIER]
Partido Pais Solidario or PPS [Carlos Alberto FILIZZOLA Pallares]
Partido Popular Tekojoja [Sixto PEREIRA]
Patria Querida (Beloved Fatherland Party) or PPQ [Sebastian ACHA]

Political pressure groups and leaders: Ahorristas Estafados or AE
National Coordinating Board of Campesino Organizations or MCNOC [Luis AGUAYO]
National Federation of Campesinos or FNC [Odilon ESPINOLA]
National Workers Central or CNT [Secretary General Juan TORRALES]
Paraguayan Workers Confederation or CPT
Rom an Cath olic Church
Unitary Workers Central or CUT [Jorge Guzman ALVARENGA Malgarejo]

International organization participation: CAN (associate), CD, CELAC, FAO, G-11, G-77, IADB, IAEA, IBRD, ICAO, ICC (National committees), ICCt, ICRM, IDA, IFAD, IFC, IFRCS, ILO, IMF, IMO, Interpol, IOC, IOM, IPU, ISO (correspondent), ITSO, ITU, ITUC (NGOs), LAES, LAIA, Mercosur, MIGA, MINURSO, MINUSTAH, MONUSCO, NAM (observer), OAS, OPANAL, OPCW, Pacific Alliance (observer), PCA, UN, UNASUR, UNCTAD, UNESCO, UNFICYP, UNIDO, Union Latina, UNISFA, UNMIL, UNMISS, UNOCI, UNWTO, UPU, WCO, WHO, WIPO, WMO, WTO

Diplomatic representation in the US: *chief of mission:* Ambassador German Hugo ROJAS Irigoyen (since 28 December 2016)
chancery: 2400 Massachusetts Avenue NW, Washington, DC 20008
telephone: [1] (202) 483-6960 through 6962
FAX: [1] (202) 234-4508
consulate(s) general: Los Angeles, Miami, New York

Diplomatic representation from the US: *chief of mission:* Ambassador Leslie A. BASSETT (since 15 January 2015)
embassy: 1776 Avenida Mariscal Lopez, Casilla Postal 402, Asuncion
mailing address: Unit 4711, DPOAA 34036-0001
telephone: [595] (21) 213-715

FAX: [595] (21) 213-728

Flag description: three equal, horizontal bands of red (top), white, and blue with an emblem centered in the white band; unusual flag in that the emblem is different on each side; the obverse (hoist side at the left) bears the National coat of arms (a yellow five-pointed star within a green wreath capped by the words REPUBLICA DEL PARAGUAY, all within two circles); the reverse (hoist side at the right) bears a circular seal of the treasury (a yellow lion below a red Cap of Liberty and the words PAZ Y JUSTICIA (Peace and Justice)); red symbolizes bravery and patriotism, white represents integrity and peace, and blue denotes liberty and generosity
note: the three color bands resemble those on the flag of the Netherlands; one of only three National flags that differ on their obverse and reverse sides—the others are Moldova and Saudi Arabia

National symbol(s): lion; National colors: red, white, blue

National anthem: *name:* "Paraguayos, Republica omuerte!" (Paraguayans, The Republic or Death!)
lyrics/music: Francisco Esteban ACUNA de Figueroa/disputed
note: adopted 1934, in use since 1846; officially adopted following its re-arrangement in 1934

ECONOMY

Economy—overview: Landlocked Paraguay has a market economy distinguished by a large informal sector, featuring re-export of imported consumer goods to neighboring countries, as well as the activities of thousands of microenterprises and urban street vendors. A large percentage of the population, especially in rural areas, derives its living from agricultural activity, often on a subsistence basis. Because of the importance of the informal sector, accurate economic measures are difficult to obtain. On a per capita basis, real income has stagnated at 1980 levels. The economy grew rapidly between 2003 and 2008 as growing world demand for commodities combined with high prices and favorable weather to support Paraguay's commodity-based export expansion. Paraguay is the sixth largest soy producer in the world. Drought hit in 2008, reducing agricultural exports and slowing the economy even before the onset of the global recession. The economy fell 3.8% in 2009, as lower world demand and commodity prices caused exports to contract. The government reacted by introducing fiscal and monetary stimulus packages. Growth resumed in 2010, and has been erratic, although positive, ever since. Severe drought and outbreaks of foot-and-mouth disease led to a drop in beef and other agricultural exports. in addition to the agricultural challenges, political uncertainty, corruption, limited progress on structural reform, and deficient infrastructure are the main obstacles to long-term growth.

GDP (purchasing power parity): $60.98 billion (2015 est.)
$59.19 billion (2014 est.)
$56.52 billion (2013 est.)
note: data are in 2015 US dollars

country comparison to the world: 105

GDP (official exchange rate): $28.08 billion (2015 est.)

GDP—real growth rate: 3% (2015 est.)
4.7% (2014 est.)
14% (2013 est.)
country comparison to the world: 99

GDP—per capita (PPP): $8,700 (2015 est.)
$8,600 (2014 est.)
$8,300 (2013 est.)
note: data are in 2015 US dollars
country comparison to the world: 141

Gross national saving: 14.9% of GDP (2015 est.)
15.8% of GDP (2014 est.)
17.1% of GDP (2013 est.)
country comparison to the world: 119

GDP—composition, by end use:
household consumption: 67.4%
government consumption: 12%
investment in fixed capital: 15.9%
investment in inventories: 0.3%
exports of goods and services: 46.8%
imports of goods and services: -42.4% (2015 est.)

GDP—composition, by sector of origin:
agriculture: 18.9%
industry: 18.5%
services: 62.6% (2015 est.)

Agriculture—products: cotton, sugarcane, soybeans, corn, wheat, tobacco, cassava (manioc, tapioca), fruits, vegetables; beef, pork, eggs, milk; timber

Industries: sugar, cement, textiles, beverages, wood products, steel, base metals, electric power

Industrial production growth rate: 5% (2015 est.)
country comparison to the world: 35

Labor force: 3.243 million (2015 est.)
country comparison to the world: 102

Labor force—by occupation:
agriculture: 26.5%
industry: 18.5%
services: 55% (2008)

Unemployment rate: 5.5% (2015 est.)
5.5% (2014 est.)
country comparison to the world: 60

Population below poverty line: 34.7% (2010 est.)

Household income or consumption by percentage share: *lowest:* 10%: 1%
highest: 10%: 41.1% (2010 est.)

Distribution of family income—Gini index: 53.2 (2009)
57.7 (1998)
country comparison to the world: 13

Budget: *revenues:* $5.294 billion
expenditures: $6.226 billion (2015 est.)
Taxes and other revenues: 18.2% of GDP (2015 est.)
country comparison to the world: 170

Budget surplus (+) or deficit (–): -3.2% of GDP (2015 est.)
country comparison to the world: 120

Public debt: 19.9% of GDP (2015 est.)
17.8% of GDP (2014 est.)
country comparison to the world: 155

Fiscal year: calendar year

Inflation rate (consumer prices): 2.9% (2015 est.)
5% (2014 est.)
country comparison to the world: 136

Central bank discount rate: 5.5% (31 December 2012)
6% (31 December 2011)
country comparison to the world: 72

Commercial bank prime lending rate: 20.6% (31 December 2015 est.)
21.19% (31 December 2014 est.)
country comparison to the world: 11

Stock of narrow money: $4.747 billion (31 December 2015 est.)
$4.806 billion (31 December 2014 est.)
country comparison to the world: 100

Stock of broad money: $9.483 billion (31 December 2014 est.)
$8.546 billion (31 December 2013 est.)
country comparison to the world: 108

Stock of domestic credit: $12.06 billion (31 December 2015 est.)
$12.15 billion (31 December 2014 est.)
country comparison to the world: 101

Market value of publicly traded shares: $962.3 million (31 December 2012 est.)
$958.1 million (31 December 2011)
$42 million (31 December 2010 est.)
country comparison to the world: 107

Current account balance: -$515 million (2015 est.)
-$127 million (2014 est.)
country comparison to the world: 98

Exports: $8.352 billion (2015 est.)
$9.656 billion (2014 est.)
country comparison to the world: 96

Exports—commodities: soybeans, livestock feed, cotton, meat, edible oils, wood, leather

Exports—partners: Brazil 31.7%, Russia 9.1%, Chile 7.1%, Argentina 7% (2015)

Imports: $9.604 billion (2015 est.)
$11.3 billion (2014 est.)
country comparison to the world: 101

Imports—commodities: road vehicles, consumer goods, tobacco, petroleum products, electrical machinery, tractors, chemicals, vehicle parts

Imports—partners: Brazil 25.4%, China 23.7%, Argentina 14.8%, US 7.9% (2015)

Reserves of foreign exchange and gold: $7.028 billion (31 December 2015 est.)
$6.986 billion (31 December 2014 est.)
country comparison to the world: 88

Debt—external: $14.76 billion (31 December 2014 est.)
$13.43 billion (31 December 2013 est.)
country comparison to the world: 98

Stock of direct foreign investment—at home: $6.045 billion (31 December 2015 est.)
$5.479 billion (31 December 2014 est.)
country comparison to the world: 96

Stock of direct foreign investment—abroad: $94.75 million (31 December 2015 est.)

$96.36 million (31 December 2014 est.)
country comparison to the world: 96

Exchange rates: guarani (PYG) per US dollar—
5,087.7 (2015 est.)
4,462.2 (2014 est.)
4,462.2 (2013 est.)
4,424.9 (2012 est.)
4,176.1 (2011 est.)

ENERGY

Electricity—production: 59.63 billion kWh (2012 est.)
country comparison to the world: 47

Electricity—consumption: 8.125 billion kWh (2012 est.)
country comparison to the world: 98

Electricity—exports: 47.37 billion kWh (2013 est.)
country comparison to the world: 5

Electricity—imports: 0 kWh (2013 est.)
country comparison to the world: 188

Electricity—installed generating capacity: 8.816 million kW (2012 est.)
country comparison to the world: 60

Electricity—from fossil fuels: 0.1% of total installed capacity (2012 est.)
country comparison to the world: 213

Electricity—from nuclear fuels: 0% of total installed capacity (2012 est.)
country comparison to the world: 162

Electricity—from hydroelectric plants: 99.9% of total installed capacity (2012 est.)
country comparison to the world: 2

Electricity—from other renewable sources: 0% of total installed capacity (2012 est.)
country comparison to the world: 211

Crude oil—production: 0 bbl/day (2014 est.)
country comparison to the world: 179

Crude oil—exports: 0 bbl/day (2012 est.)
country comparison to the world: 174

Crude oil—imports: 0 bbl/day (2012 est.)
country comparison to the world: 113

Crude oil—proved reserves: 0 bbl (1 January 2015 est.)
country comparison to the world: 179

Refined petroleum products—production: 0 bbl/day (2012 est.)
country comparison to the world: 121

Refined petroleum products—consumption: 35,000 bbl/day (2013 est.)
country comparison to the world: 109

Refined petroleum products—exports: 0 bbl/day (2012 est.)
country comparison to the world: 213

Refined petroleum products—imports: 34,900 bbl/day (2012 est.)
country comparison to the world: 92

Natural gas—production: 0 cu m (2013 est.)
country comparison to the world: 117

Natural gas—consumption: 0 cu m (2013 est.)
country comparison to the world: 185

Natural gas—exports: 0 cu m (2013 est.)

country comparison to the world: 162

Natural gas—imports:
0 cu m (2013 est.)
country comparison to the world: 118

Natural gas—proved reserves: 0 cu m (1 January 2014 est.)
country comparison to the world: 183

Carbon dioxide emissions from consumption of energy: 3.869 million Mt (2012 est.)
country comparison to the world: 133

COMMUNICATIONS

Telephones—fixed lines: *total subscriptions:* 370,000
subscriptions per 100 inhabitants: 6 (2014 est.)
country comparison to the world: 109

Telephones—mobile cellular: *total:* 7.3 million
subscriptions per 100 inhabitants: 109 (2014 est.)
country comparison to the world: 102

Telephone system: *general assessment:* the fixed-line market is a state monopoly and fixed-line telephone service is meager; principal switching center is in Asuncion
domestic: deficiencies in provision of fixed-line service have resulted in a rapid expansion of mobile-cellular services fostered by competition among multiple providers
international: country code—595; satellite earth station—1 Intelsat (Atlantic Ocean) (2010)

Broadcast media: 6 privately owned TV stations; about 75 commercial and community radio stations; 1 state-owned radio network (2010)
Radio broadcast stations: AM 41, FM 121, short-wave 6 (2006)
Television broadcast stations: 6 (2009)

Internet country code: py

Internet hosts: 280,658 (2012)
country comparison to the world: 65

Internet users: *total:* 1.9 million
percent of population: 29.0% (2014 est.)
country comparison to the world: 101

TRANSPORTATION

Airports: 799 (2013)
country comparison to the world: 9

Airports—with paved runways: *total:* 15
over 3,047 m: 3
1,524 to 2,437 m: 7
914 to 1,523 m: 5 (2013)

Airports—with unpaved runways: *total:* 784
1,524 to 2,437 m: 23
914 to 1,523 m: 290
under 914 m: 471 (2013)

Railways: *total:* 30 km
standard gauge: 30 km 1.435-m gauge (2014)
country comparison to the world: 133

Roadways: *total:* 32,059 km
paved: 4,860 km
unpaved: 27,199 km (2010)
country comparison to the world: 95

Waterways: 3,100 km (primarily on the Paraguay and Paran River systems) (2012)

country comparison to the world: 32

Merchant marine: *total:* 19
by type: cargo 13, container 3, passenger 1, petroleum tanker 1, roll on/roll off 1
foreign-owned: 6 (Argentina 5, Netherlands 1) (2010)
country comparison to the world: 96

Ports and terminals: *river port(s):* Asuncion, Villeta, San Antonio, Encarnacion (Parana)

MILITARY AND SECURITY

Military branches: Armed Forces Command (Commando de las Fuerzas Militares): Army, national Navy (Armada nacional, includes Marine Corps, naval Aviation, and Coast Guard), Paraguayan Air Force (Fuerza Aerea Paraguay, FAP), Logistics Command, War Materiel Directorate (2012)

Military service age and obligation: 18 years of age for compulsory and voluntary military service; conscript service obligation is 12 months for Army, 24 months for Navy; volunteers for the Air Force must be younger than 22 years of age with a secondary school diploma (2012)

Military expenditures:
1.66% of GDP (2012)
1.16% of GDP (2011)
1.66% of GDP (2010)
country comparison to the world: 54

TRANSNATIONAL ISSUES

Disputes—international: unruly region at convergence of Argentina-Brazil-Paraguay borders is locus of money laundering, smuggling, arms and illegal narcotics trafficking, and fundraising for violent extremist organizations

Illicit drugs: major illicit producer of cannabis, most or all of which is consumed in Brazil, Argentina, and Chile; transshipment country for Andean cocaine headed for Brazil, other Southern Cone markets, and Europe; weak border controls, extensive corruption and money-laundering activity, especially in the Tri-Border Area; weak anti-money-laundering laws and enforcement

PERU

INTRODUCTION

Background: Ancient Peru was the seat of several prominent Andean civilizations, most notably that of the Incas whose empire was captured by Spanish conquistadors in 1533. Peruvian independence was declared in 1821, and remaining Spanish forces were defeated in 1824. After a dozen years of military rule, Peru returned to democratic leadership in 1980, but experienced economic problems and the growth of a violent insurgency. President Alberto FUJIMORI's election in 1990 ushered in a decade that saw a dramatic turnaround in the economy and significant progress in curtailing guerrilla activity. Nevertheless, the president's increasing reliance on authoritarian measures and an economic slump in the late 1990s generated mounting dissatisfaction with his regime, which led to his resignation in 2000. A caretaker government oversaw a new election in the spring of 2001, which installed Alejandro TOLEDO Manrique as the new head of government—Peru's first democratically elected president of indigenous ethnicity. The presidential election of 2006 saw the return of Alan GARCIA Perez who, after a disappointing presidential term from 1985 to 1990,

oversaw a robust economic rebound. In June 2011, former army officer Ollanta HUMALA Tasso was elected president; he has carried on the sound, market-oriented economic policies of the three preceding administrations.

GEOGRAPHY

Location: Western South America, bordering the South Pacific Ocean, between Chile and Ecuador

Geographic coordinates: 10 00 S, 76 00 W

Map references: South America

Area: *total:* 1,285,216 sq km
land: 1,279,996 sq km
water: 5,220 sq km
country comparison to the world: 20

Area—comparative: almost twice the size of Texas; slightly smaller than Alaska

Land boundaries: *total:* 7,062 km
border countries (5): Bolivia 1,212 km, Brazil 2,659 km, Chile 168 km, Colombia 1,494 km, Ecuador 1,529 km

Coastline: 2,414 km

Maritime claims: *territorial sea:* 200 nm
continental shelf: 200 nm

Climate: varies from tropical in east to dry desert in west; temperate to frigid in Andes

Terrain: western coastal plain (costa), high and rugged Andes in center (sierra), eastern lowland jungle of Amazon Basin (selva)

Elevation: *mean elevation:* 1,555 m

elevation extremes: *lowest point:* Pacific Ocean 0 m
highest point: Nevado Huascaran 6,768 m

Natural resources: copper, silver, gold, petroleum, timber, fish, iron ore, coal, phosphate, potash, hydropower, Natural gas

Land use: *agricultural land:* 18.8%
arable land: 3.1%
permanent crops: 1.1%
permanent pasture: 14.6%
forest: 53%

other: 28.2% (2011 est.)

Irrigated land: 25,800 sq km (2012)

Total renewable water resources: 1913 cu km (2011)

Freshwater withdrawal (domestic/industrial/agricultural): *total:* 19.34 cu km/yr (8%/10%/82%)
per capita: 727.6 cu m/yr (2005)

Natural hazards: earthquakes, tsunamis, flooding, landslides, mild volcanic activity
volcanism: volcanic activity in the Andes Mountains; Ubinas (elev. 5,672 m), which last erupted in 2009, is the country's most active volcano; other historically active volcanoes include El Misti, Huaynaputina, Sabancaya, and Yucamane

Environment—current issues: deforestation (some the result of illegal logging); overgrazing of the slopes of the costa and sierra leading to soil erosion; desertification; air pollution in Lima; pollution of rivers and coastal waters from municipal and mining wastes

Environment—international agreements: *party to:* Antarctic-Environmental Protocol, Antarctic-Marine Living Resources, Antarctic Treaty, Biodiversity, Climate Change, Climate Change-Kyoto Protocol, Desertification, Endangered Species, Hazardous Wastes, Marine Dumping, Ozone Layer Protection, Ship Pollution, Tropical Timber 83, Tropical Timber 94, Wetlands, Whaling
signed, but not ratified: none of the selected agreements

Geography—note: shares control of Lago Titicaca, world's highest navigable lake, with Bolivia; a remote slope of Nevado Mismi, a 5,316 m peak, is the ultimate source of the Amazon River

PEOPLE AND SOCIETY

Nationality: *noun:* Peruvian(s)
adjective: Peruvian

Ethnic groups: Amerindian 45%, mestizo (mixed Amerindian and white) 37%, white 15%, black, Japanese, Chinese, and other 3%

Languages: Spanish (official) 84.1%, Quechua (official) 13%, Aymara (official) 1.7%, Ashaninka 0.3%, other native languages (includes a large number of minor Amazonian languages) 0.7%, other (includes foreign languages and sign language) 0.2% (2007 est.)

Religions: Roman Catholic 81.3%, Evangelical 12.5%, other 3.3%, none 2.9% (2007 est.)

Demographic profile: Peru's urban and coastal communities have benefited much more from recent economic growth than rural, Afro-Peruvian, indigenous, and poor populations of the Amazon and mountain regions. The poverty rate has dropped substantially during the last decade but remains stubbornly high at about 30% (more than 55% in rural areas). After remaining almost static for about a decade, Peru's malnutrition rate began falling in 2005, when the government introduced a coordinated strategy focusing on hygiene, sanitation, and clean water. School enrollment has improved, but achievement scores reflect ongoing problems with educational quality. Many poor children temporarily or permanently drop out of school to help support their families. About a quarter to a third of Peruvian children aged 6 to 14 work, often putting in long hours at hazardous mining or construction sites.

Peru was a country of immigration in the 19th and early 20th centuries, but has become a country of emigration in the last few decades. Beginning in the 19th century, Peru brought in Asian contract laborers mainly to work on coastal plantations. Populations of Chinese and Japanese descent—among the largest in Latin America—are economically and culturally influential in Peru today. Peruvian emigration began rising in the 1980s due to an economic crisis and a violent internal conflict, but outflows have stabilized in the last few years as economic conditions have improved. Nonetheless, more than 2 million Peruvians have emigrated in the last decade, principally to the US, Spain, and Argentina.

Population: 30,444,999 (July 2015 est.)
country comparison to the world: 44

Age structure: *0–14 years:* 26.95% (male 4,174,434/female 4,029,691)
15–24 years: 18.93% (male 2,884,314/female 2,877,403)
25–54 years: 39.65% (male 5,801997/female 6,268,941)
55–64 years: 7.45% (male 1,103,641/female 1,164,821)
65 years and over: 7.03% (male 1,013,806/female 1,125,951) (2015 est.)

Dependency ratios: *total dependency ratio:* 53.2%
youth dependency ratio: 42.7%
elderly dependency ratio: 10.5%
potential support ratio: 9.6% (2015 est.)

Median age: *total:* 27.3 years
male: 26.6 years
female: 28.1 years (2015 est.)
country comparison to the world: 138

Population growth rate: 0.97% (2015 est.)
country comparison to the world: 120

Birth rate: 18.28 births/1,000 population (2015 est.)
country comparison to the world: 100

Death rate: 6.01 deaths/1,000 population (2015 est.)
country comparison to the world: 164

Net migration rate: -2.53 migrant(s)/1,000 population (2015 est.)
country comparison to the world: 174

Urbanization: *urban population:* 78.6% of total population (2015)
rate of urbanization: 1.69% annual rate of change (2010–15 est.)

Major urban areas—population: LIMA (capital) 9.897 million; Arequipa 850,000; Trujillo 798,000 (2015)

Sex ratio: *at birth:* 1.05 male(s)/female
0–14 years: 1.04 male(s)/female
15–24 years: 1 male(s)/female
25–54 years: 0.93 male(s)/female
55–64 years: 0.95 male(s)/female
65 years and over: 0.9 male(s)/female
total population: 0.97 male(s)/female (2015 est.)

Mother's mean age at first birth: 22.2
note: median age at first birth among women 25–29 (2013 est.)

Maternal mortality rate: 68 deaths/100,000 live births (2015 est.)
country comparison to the world: 90

Infant mortality rate: *total:* 19.59 deaths/1,000 live births
male: 21.79 deaths/1,000 live births
female: 17.29 deaths/1,000 live births (2015 est.)
country comparison to the world: 89

Life expectancy at birth: *total population:* 73.48 years
male: 71.45 years
female: 75.6 years (2015 est.)
country comparison to the world: 130

Total fertility rate: 2.18 children born/woman (2015 est.)
country comparison to the world: 99

Contraceptive prevalence rate: 75.5% (2012)

Health expenditures: 5.3% of GDP (2013)
country comparison to the world: 140

Physicians density: 1.13 physicians/1,000 population (2012)

Hospital bed density: 1.5 beds/1,000 population (2012)

Drinking water source:
improved:
urban: 91.4% of population
rural: 69.2% of population
total: 86.7% of population
unimproved:
urban: 8.6% of population
rural: 30.8% of population
total: 13.3% of population (2015 est.)

Sanitation facility access:
improved:
urban: 82.5% of population
rural: 53.2% of population
total: 76.2% of population
unimproved:
urban: 17.5% of population
rural: 46.8% of population
total: 23.8% of population (2015 est.)

HIV/AIDS—adult prevalence rate: 0.36% (2014 est.)

country comparison to the world: 77

HIV/AIDS—people living with HIV/AIDS: 71900 (2014 est.)
country comparison to the world: 51

HIV/AIDS—deaths: 2,500 (2014 est.)
country comparison to the world: 51

Major infectious diseases: *degree of risk:* very high
food or waterborne diseases: bacterial diarrhea, hepatitis A, and typhoid fever
vectorborne disease: dengue fever, malaria, and Bartonellosis (Oroya fever) (2013)

Obesity—adult prevalence rate: 20.4% (2014)
country comparison to the world: 117

Children under the age of 5 years underweight: 3.1% (2014)
country comparison to the world: 103

Education expenditures: 3.7% of GDP (2014)
country comparison to the world: 145

Literacy: *definition:* age 15 and over can read and write
total population: 94.5%
male: 97.3%
female: 91.7% (2015 est.)

School life expectancy (primary to tertiary education): *total:* 13 years
male: 13 years
female: 14 years (2010)

Child labor—children ages 5–14: *total number:* 2,545,855
percen tage: 34%
note: data represents ch ildren ages 5–17 (2007 est.)

Unemployment, youth ages 15–24: *total:* 8.8%
male: 8.3%
female: 9.3% (2013 est.)
country comparison to the world: 101

GOVERNMENT

Country name: *conventional long form:* Republic of Peru
conventional short form: Peru
local long form: Republica del Peru
local short form: Peru
etymology: exact meaning is obscure, but the name may derive from a native word "biru" meaning "river"

Government type: presidential republic

Capital: *name:* Lima

Geographic coordinates: 12 03 S, 77 03 W
time difference: UTC-5 (same time as Wash ington, DC, during Standard Time)

Administrative divisions: 25 regions (regiones, singular—region) and 1 province* (provincia); Amazonas, Ancash, Apurimac, Arequipa, Ayacucho, Cajamarca, Callao, Cusco, Huancavelica, Huanuco, Ica, Junin, La Libertad, Lambayeque, Lima, Lima*, Loreto, Madre de Dios, Moquegua, Pasco, Piura, Puno, San Martin, Tacna, Tumbes, Ucayali
note: Callao, the largest port in Peru, is also referred to as a constitutional province, the only province of the Callao region

Independence: 28 July 1821 (from Spain)

National holiday: Independence Day, 28 July (1821)

Constitution: several previous; latest promulgated 29 December 1993, enacted 31 December 1993; amended several times, last in 2015 (2016)

Legal system: civil law system

International law organization participation: accepts compulsory ICJ jurisdiction with reservations; accepts ICCt jurisdiction

Citizenship: *citizenship by birth:* yes
citizenship by descent: yes
dual citizenship recognized: yes
residency requirement for naturalization: 2 years

Suffrage: 18 years of age; universal and compulsory until the age of 70

Executive branch: *chief of state:* President Ollanta HUMALA Tasso (since 28 July 2011); First Vice President Marisol ESPINOZA Cruz (since 28 July 2011); Second Vice President (vacant); note—the president is both chief of state and head of government

head of government: President Ollanta HUMALA Tasso (since 28 July 2011); First Vice President Marisol ESPINOZA Cruz (since 28 July 2011); Second Vice President (vacant)
cabinet: Council of Ministers appointed by the president
elections/appointments: president directly elected by absolute majority popular vote in 2 rounds if needed for a 5-year term (eligible for nonconsecutive terms); election last held on 10 April 2016 with runoff on 5 June 2016 (next to be held in April 2021)
election results: Pedro Pablo KUCZYNSKI elected president; first round election results from 10 April 2016: percent of vote—Keiko FUJIMORI Higuchi 39.85%, Pedro Pablo KUCZYNSKI 21%, Veronika MENDOZA 18.82%, Alfredo BARNECHEA 6.97%, Alan GARCIA 5.82%; second round election results from 5 June 2016: percent of vote—Pedro Pablo KUCZYNSKI (Peruanos Por el Kambio) 50.1%, Keiko FUJIMORI Higuchi (Fuerza Popular) 49.9%; note—KUCZYNSKI will take office 28 July 2016
note: Prime Minister Pedro CATERIANO Bellido (since 2 April 2015) does not exercise executive power; this power rests with the president; note—Prime Minister ANAJARA was removed from office by Congress in a vote of no confidence on 30 March 2015

Legislative branch: *description:* unicameral Congress of the Republic of Peru or Congreso de la Republica del Peru (130 seats; members directly elected in multi-seat constituencies by closed party list proportional representation vote to serve 5-year terms)
elections: last held on 10 April 2016 with run-off election on 6 June 2016 (next to be held in April 2021)
election results: percent of vote by party—Fuerza Popular 36.34%, PPK 16.47%, Frente Amplio 13.94%, APP 9.23%; APRA 8.31%; AP 7.20%, other 8.51%; seats by party—Fuerza Popular 71, PPK 20, Frente Amplio 20, APP 9; APRA 5; AP 5

Judicial branch: *highest court(s):* Supreme Court (consists of 16 judges and divided into civil, criminal, and constitutional-social sectors)
judge selection and term of office: justices proposed by the National Council of the Judiciary or

National Judicial Council (a 7-member independent body), nominated by the president, and confirmed by the Congress (all appointments reviewed by the Council every 7 years); justices appointed for life or until age 70
subordinate courts: Court of Constitutional Guarantees; Superior Courts or Cortes Superiores; specialized civil, criminal, and mixed courts; 2 types of peace courts in which professional judges and selected members of the local communities preside

Political parties and leaders: Alliance for Progress (Alianza para el Progreso) or APP [Cesar ACUNA Peralta]
Broad Front (Frente Amplio; also known as El Frente Amplio por Justicia, Vida y Libertad), a coalition of left-of-center parties including Tierra y Libertad [Marco ARANA Zegarra], Ciudadanos por el Gran Cambio [Salomon LERNER Ghitis], and Fuerza Social [Susana VILLARAN de la Puente]
Fuerza Popular (formerly Fuerza 2011) [Keiko FUJIMORI Higuchi]
National Solidarity (Solidaridad Nacional) or SN [Luis CASTANEDA Lossio]
Peru Posible or PP (a coalition of Accion Popular and Somos Peru) [Alejandro TOLEDO Manrique]
Peruvian Aprista Party (Partido Aprista Peruano) or PAP [Alan GARCIA Perez] (also referred to by its original name Alianza Popular Revolucion aria Americana or APRA)
Peruvian Nationalist Party [Ollanta HUMALA]
Peruvians for Change (Peruanos Por el Kambio) or PPK [Pedro Pablo KUCZYNSKI]
Popular Action (Accion Popular) or AP [Mesias GUEVARA Amasifuen]
Popular Christian Party (Partido Popular Cristiano) or PPC [Lourdes FLORES nano]

Political pressure groups and leaders: General Workers Confederation of Peru (Confederacion General de Trabajadores del Peru) or CGTP [Mario HUAMAN]
Shining Path (Sendero Luminoso) or SL [Abimael GUZMAN Reynoso (imprisoned), Victor QUISPE Palomino (top leader at-large)] (leftist guerrilla group)

International organization participation: APEC, BIS, CAN, CD, CELAC, EITI (compliant country), FAO, G-24, G-77, IADB, IAEA, IBRD, ICAO, ICC (NGOs), ICCt, ICRM, IDA, IFAD, IFC, IFRCS, IHO, ILO, IMF, IMO, IMSO, Interpol, IOC, IOM, IPU, ISO, ITSO, ITU, ITUC (NGOs), LAES, LAIA, Mercosur (associate), MIGA, MINUSTAH, MONUSCO, NAM, OAS, OPANAL, OPCW, Pacific Alliance, PCA, SICA (observer), UN, UNAMID, UNASUR, UNCTAD, UNESCO, UNHCR, UNIDO, Union Latina, UNISFA, UNMISS, UNOCI, UNWTO, UPU, WCO, WFTU (NGOs), WHO, WIPO, WMO, WTO

Diplomatic representation in the US: *chief of mission:* Ambassador Luis Miguel CASTILLA Rubio (since 4 February 2015)
chancery: 1700 Massachusetts Avenue NW, Washington, DC 20036
telephone: [1] (202) 833-9860 through 9869
FAX: [1] (202) 659-8124
consulate(s) general: Atlanta, Boston, Chicago, Dallas, Denver, Hartford (CT), Houston, Los

Angeles, Miami, New York, Paterson (NJ), San Francisco, Washington DC

Diplomatic representation from the US: *chief of mission:* Ambassador Brian A. NICHOLS (since 30 June 2014)
embassy: Avenida La Encalada, Cuadra 17 s/n, Surco, Lima 33
mailing address: P.O. Box 1995, Lima 1; American Embassy (Lima), APOAA 34031–5000
telephone: [51] (1) 618-2000
FAX: [51] (1) 618-2397

Flag description: three equal, vertical bands of red (hoist side), white, and red with the coat of arms centered in the white band; the coat of arms features a shield bearing a vicuna (representing fauna), a cinchona tree (the source of quinine, signifying flora), and a yellow cornucopia spilling out coins (denoting mineral wealth); red recalls blood shed for independence, white symbolizes peace

National symbol(s): vicuna (a camelid related to the llama); National colors: red, white

National anthem: *name:* "Himno Nacional del Peru" (National Anthem of Peru)
lyrics/music: Jose DELATORRE Ugarte/Jose Bernardo ALZEDO
note: adopted 1822; the song wona National anthem contest

ECONOMY

Economy—overview: Peru's economy reflects its varied topography—an arid lowland coastal region, the central high sierra of the Andes, the dense forest of the Amazon, with tropical lands bordering Colombia and Brazil. A wide range of important mineral resources are found in the mountainous and coastal areas, and Peru's coastal waters provide excellent fishing grounds. Peru is the world's second largest producer of silver and third largest producer of copper.
The Peruvian economy grew by an average of 5.6% from 2009–13 with a stable exchange rate and low inflation, which in 2013 was just below the upper limit of the Central Bank target range of 1% to 3%. This growth was due partly to high international prices for Peru's metals and minerals exports, which account for almost 60% of the country's total exports. Growth slipped in 2014 and 2015, due to weaker world prices for these resources. Despite Peru's strong macroeconomic performance, dependence on minerals and metals exports and imported foodstuffs makes the economy vulnerable to fluctuations in world prices.
Peru's rapid expansion coupled with cash transfers and other programs have helped to reduce the National poverty rate by 28 percentage points since 2002, but inequality persists and continues to pose a challenge for the Ollanta HUMALA administration, which has championed a policy of social inclusion and a more equitable distribution of income. Poor infrastructure hinders the spread of growth to Peru's non-coastal areas. The HUMALA administration passed several economic stimulus packages in 2014 to bolster growth, including reforms to environmental regulations in order to spur investment in Peru's lucrative mining sector, a move that was opposed by some environmental groups. However, in 2015,

mining investment fell as global commodity prices remained low and social conflicts plagued the sector.

Peru's free trade policy has continued under the HUMALA administration; since 2006, Peru has signed trade deals with the US, Canada, Singapore, China, Korea, Mexico, Japan, the EU, the European Free Trade Association, Chile, Thailand, Costa Rica, Panama, Venezuela, concluded negotiations with Guatemala and the Trans-Pacific Partnership, and begun trade talks with Honduras, El Salvador, India, Indonesia, and Turkey. Peru also has signed a trade pact with Chile, Colombia, and Mexico, called the Pacific Allian ce, that seeks integration of services, capital, investment and movement of people. Since the US-Peru Trade Promotion Agreement entered into force in February 2009, total trade between Peru and the US has doubled.

GDP (purchasing power parity): $389.1 billion (2015 est.)
$376.9 billion (2014 est.)
$368.1 billion (2013 est.)
note: data are in 2015 US dollars
country comparison to the world: 48

GDP (official exchange rate): $192.1 billion (2015 est.)

GDP—real growth rate: 3.3% (2015 est.)
2.4% (2014 est.)
5.9% (2013 est.)
country comparison to the world: 93

GDP—per capita (PPP): $12,200 (2015 est.)
$12,000 (2014 est.)
$11900 (2013 est.)
note: data are in 2015 US dollars
country comparison to the world: 122

Gross national saving: 21.6% of GDP (2015 est.)
22.3% of GDP (2014 est.)
23.7% of GDP (2013 est.)
country comparison to the world: 72

GDP—composition, by end use:
household consumption: 63.2%
government consumption: 12.7%
investment in fixed capital: 23.8%
investment in inventories: 1.1%
exports of goods and services: 22.4%
imports of goods and services: -23.2% (2015 est.)

GDP—composition, by sector of origin:
agriculture: 7%
industry: 34.5%
services: 58.5% (2015 est.)

Agriculture—products: artichokes, asparagus, avocados, blueberries, coffee, cocoa, cotton, sugarcane, rice, potatoes, corn, plantains, grapes, oranges, pineapples, guavas, bananas, apples, lemons, pears, coca, tomatoes, mangoes, barley, medicinal plants, quinoa, palm oil, marigold, onion, wheat, dry beans; poultry, beef, pork, dairy products; guinea pigs; fish

Industries: mining and refining of minerals; steel, metal fabrication; petroleum extraction and refining, Natural gas and Natural gas liquefaction; fishing and fish processing, cement, glass, textiles, clothing, food processing, beer, soft drinks, rubber, machinery, electrical machinery, chemicals, furniture

Industrial production growth rate: -0.3% (2015 est.)
country comparison to the world: 167

Labor force: 16.8 million
note: individuals older than 14 years of age (2015 est.)
country comparison to the world: 38

Labor force—by occupation: agriculture: 25.8%
industry: 17.4%
services: 56.8% (2011)

Unemployment rate: 6.1% (2015 est.)
5.5% (2014 est.)
note: data are for metropolitan Lima; widespread underemployment
country comparison to the world: 69

Population below poverty line: 25.8% (2012 est.)

Household income or consumption by percentage share: lowest: 10%: 1.4%
highest: 10%: 36.1% (2010 est.)

Distribution of family income—Gini index: 45.3 (2012)
51 (2005)
country comparison to the world: 43

Budget: revenues: $62.34 billion
expenditures: $63.34 billion (2015 est.)
Taxes and other revenues: 34.6% of GDP (2015 est.)
country comparison to the world: 61

Budget surplus (+) or deficit (–): -0.6% of GDP (2015 est.)
country comparison to the world: 47

Public debt: 19.8% of GDP (2015 est.)
20.1% of GDP (2014 est.)
note: data cover general government debt, and includes debt instruments issued by government entities other than the treasury; the data exclude treasury debt held by foreign entities; the data include debt issued by sub national entities
country comparison to the world: 156

Fiscal year: calendar year

Inflation rate (consumer prices): 3.5% (2015 est.)
3.2% (2014 est.)
note: data are for metropolitan Lima, annual average
country comparison to the world: 148

Central bank discount rate: 5.05% (31 December 2012) 5.05% (31 December 2011)
country comparison to the world: 75

Commercial bank prime lending rate: 15.9% (31 December 2015 est.)
15.74% (31 December 2014 est.)
note: domestic currency lending rate, 90 day maturity
country comparison to the world: 32

Stock of narrow money: $32.08 billion (31 December 2015 est.)
$32.81 billion (31 December 2014 est.)
country comparison to the world: 59

Stock of broad money: $91.26 billion (31 December 2014 est.)
$84.1 billion (31 December 2013 est.)
country comparison to the world: 57

Stock of domestic credit: $48.2 billion (31 December 2015 est.)
$48.24 billion (31 December 2014 est.)
country comparison to the world: 62

Market value of publicly traded shares: $153.4 billion (31 December 2012)
$121.6 billion (31 December 2011)
$160.9 billion (31 December 2010)

country comparison to the world: 39

Current account balance: -$8.431 billion (2015 est.)
-$8.091 billion (2014 est.)
country comparison to the world: 176

Exports: $36.35 billion (2015 est.)
$39.53 billion (2014 est.)
country comparison to the world: 58

Exports—commodities: copper, gold, lead, zinc, tin, iron ore, molybdenum, silver; crude petroleum and petroleum products, Natural gas; coffee, asparagus and other vegetables, fruit, apparel and textiles, fishmeal, fish, chemicals, fabricated metal products and machinery, alloys

Exports—partners: China 22.1%, US 15.2%, Switzerland 8.1%, Canada 7% (2015)

Imports: $38.97 billion (2015 est.)
$40.81 billion (2014 est.)
country comparison to the world: 56

Imports—commodities: petroleum and petroleum products, chemicals, plastics, machinery, vehicles, TV sets, power shovels, front-end loaders, telephones and telecommunication equipment, iron and steel, wheat, corn, soybean products, paper, cotton, vaccines and medicines

Imports—partners: China 22.7%, US 20.7%, Brazil 5.1%, Mexico 4.5% (2015)

Reserves of foreign exchange and gold: $58.99 billion (31 December 2015 est.)
$62.51 billion (31 December 2014 est.)
country comparison to the world: 36

Debt—external: $61.27 billion (31 December 2014 est.)
$56.51 billion (31 December 2013 est.)
country comparison to the world: 60

Stock of direct foreign investment—at home: $87.13 billion (31 December 2015 est.)
$79.65 billion (31 December 2014 est.)
country comparison to the world: 50

Stock of direct foreign investment—abroad: $3.037 billion (31 December 2015 est.)
$3.561 billion (31 December 2014 est.)
country comparison to the world: 75

Exchange rates: nuevo sol (PEN) per US dollar—
3.186 (2015 est.)
2.8383 (2014 est.)
2.8383 (2013 est.)
2.64 (2012 est.)
2.7541 (2011 est.)

ENERGY

Electricity—production: 39.07 billion kWh (2012 est.)
country comparison to the world: 59

Electricity—consumption: 35.69 billion kWh (2012 est.)
country comparison to the world: 59

Electricity—exports: 2 million kWh (2012 est.)
country comparison to the world: 94

Electricity—imports: 0 kWh (2013 est.)
country comparison to the world: 189

Electricity—installed generating capacity: 9.705 million kW (2012 est.)
country comparison to the world: 56

Electricity—from fossil fuels: 63.2% of total installed capacity (2012 est.)
country comparison to the world: 124

Electricity—from nuclear fuels: 0% of total installed capacity (2012 est.)
country comparison to the world: 163

Electricity—from hydroelectric plants: 35.9% of total installed capacity (2012 est.)
country comparison to the world: 64

Electricity—from other renewable sources: 0.9% of total installed capacity (2012 est.)
country comparison to the world: 95

Crude oil—production: 69,300 bbl/day (2014 est.)
country comparison to the world: 51

Crude oil—exports: 27,500 bbl/day (2012 est.)
country comparison to the world: 55

Crude oil—imports: 110,600 bbl/day (2012 est.)
country comparison to the world: 44

Crude oil—proved reserves: 741.2 million bbl (1 January 2015 est.)
country comparison to the world: 43

Refined petroleum products—production: 223,500 bbl/day (2012 est.)
country comparison to the world: 50

Refined petroleum products—consumption: 226,000 bbl/day (2013 est.)
country comparison to the world: 55

Refined petroleum products—exports: 87,600 bbl/day (2012 est.)
country comparison to the world: 46

Refined petroleum products—imports: 57,590 bbl/day (2012 est.)
country comparison to the world: 74

Natural gas—production: 12.2 billion cu m (2013 est.)
country comparison to the world: 39

Natural gas—consumption: 5.9 billion cu m (2013 est.)
country comparison to the world: 56

Natural gas—exports: 5.6 billion cu m (2013 est.)
country comparison to the world: 28

Natural gas—imports: 0 cu m (2013 est.)
country comparison to the world: 119

Natural gas—proved reserves: 435.4 billion cu m (1 January 2014 est.)
country comparison to the world: 33

Carbon dioxide emissions from consumption of energy: 53.58 million Mt (2012 est.)
country comparison to the world: 56

COMMUNICATIONS

Telephones—fixed lines: *total subscriptions:* 3.03 million
subscriptions per 100 inhabitants: 10 (2014 est.)
country comparison to the world: 48

Telephones—mobile cellular: *total:* 31.7 million
subscriptions per 100 inhabitants: 105 (2014 est.)
country comparison to the world: 38

Telephone system: *general assessment:* adequate for most requirements; nationwide microwave radio relay system and a domestic satellite system with 12 earth stations
domestic: fixed-line teledensity is only about 12 per 100 persons; mobile-cellular teledensity, spurred by competition among multiple providers, exceeds 100 telephones per 100 persons
international: country code—51; the South America-1 (SAM-1) and Pan American (PAN-AM) submarine cable systems provide links to parts of Central and South America, the Caribbean, and US; satellite earth stations—2 Intelsat (Atlantic Ocean) (2010)

Broadcast media: 10 major TV networks of which only one, Television Nacional de Peru, is state owned; multi-channel cable TV services are available; in excess of 2,000 radio stations including a substantial number of indigenous language stations (2010)
Radio broadcast stations: AM 472, FM 198, shortwave 189 (1999)
Television broadcast stations: 13 (plus 112 repeaters) (1997)

Internet country code: .pe

Internet hosts: 234,102 (2012)
country comparison to the world: 70

Internet users: *total:* 12.3 million
percent of population: 40.9% (2014 est.)
country comparison to the world: 39

TRANSPORTATION

Airports: 191 (2013)
country comparison to the world: 30

Airports—with paved runways: *total:* 59
over 3,047 m: 5
2,438 to 3,047 m: 21
1,524 to 2,437 m: 16
914 to 1,523 m: 12
under 914 m: 5 (2013)

Airports—with unpaved runways: *total:* 132
2,438 to 3,047 m: 1
1,524 to 2,437 m: 19
914 to 1,523 m: 30
under 914 m: 82 (2013)

Heliports: 5 (2013)

Pipelines: extra heavy crude 786 km; gas 1,526 km; liquid petroleum gas 679 km; oil 1,033 km; refined products 15 km (2013)

Railways: *total:* 1,854.4 km
standard gauge: 1,730.4 km 1.435-m gauge (34 km electrified)
narrow gauge: 124 km 0.914-m gauge (2014)
country comparison to the world: 73

Roadways: *total:* 140,672 km (18,699 km paved)
note: includes 24,593 km of National roads (14,748 km paved), 24,235 km of departmental roads (2,340 km paved), and 91,844 km of local roads (1,611 km paved) (2012)
country comparison to the world: 35

Waterways: 8,808 km (8,600 km of navigable tributaries on the Amazon system and 208 km on Lago Titicaca) (2011)
country comparison to the world: 14

Merchant marine: *total:* 22
by type: cargo 2, chemical tanker 5, liquefied gas 2, petroleum tanker 13
foreign-owned: 8 (Chile 6, Ecuador 1, Spain 1)
registered in other countries: 9 (Panama 9) (2010)
country comparison to the world: 92

Ports and terminals: *major seaport(s):* Callao, Matarani, Paita
river port(s): Iquitos, Pucallpa, Yurimaguas (Amazon)
oil terminals: Conchan oil terminal, La Pampilla oil terminal
container port(s) (TEUs): Callao (1,616,365)

MILITARY AND SECURITY

Military branches: Peruvian Army (Ejercito Peruano), Peruvian Navy (Marina de Guerra del Peru, MGP; includes naval air, naval infantry, and Coast Guard), Air Force of Peru (Fuerza Aerea del Peru, FAP) (2013)

Military service age and obligation: 18–50 years of age for male and 18–45 years of age for female voluntary military service; no conscription (2012)

Military expenditures:
1.28% of GDP (2012)
1.15% of GDP (2011)
1.28% of GDP (2010)
country comparison to the world: 78

TRANSNATIONAL ISSUES

Disputes—international: Chile and Ecuador rejected Peru's November 2005 unilateral legislation to shift the axis of their joint treaty-defined maritime boundaries along the parallels of latitude to equidistance lines which favor Peru; organized illegal narcotics operations in Colombia have penetrated Peru's shared border; Peru rejects Bolivia's claim to restore maritime access through a sovereign corridor through Chile along the Peruvian border

Refugees and internally displaced persons: *IDPs:* 60,000 (civil war from 1980–2000; most IDPs are indigenous peasants in Andean and Amazonian regions; as of 2011, no new information on the situation of these IDPs) (2015)

Illicit drugs: until 1996 the world's largest coca leaf producer, Peru is now the world's second largest producer of coca leaf, though it lags far behind Colombia; cultivation of coca in Peru was estimated at 40,000 hectares in 2009, a slight decrease over 2008; second largest producer of cocaine, estimated at 225 metric tons of potential pure cocaine in 2009; finished cocaine is shipped out from Pacific ports to the international drug market; increasing amounts of base and finished cocaine, however, are being moved to Brazil, Chile, Argentina, and Bolivia for use in the Southern Cone or transshipment to Europe and Africa; increasing domestic drug consumption

PHILIPPINES

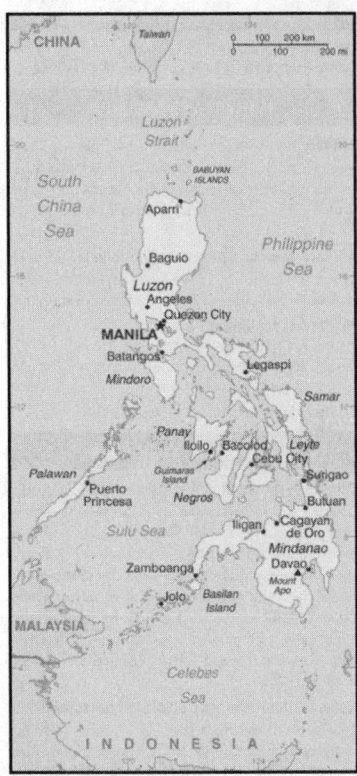

INTRODUCTION

Background: The Philippine Islands became a Spanish colony during the 16th century; they were ceded to the US in 1898 following the Spanish-American War. In 1935 the Philippines became a self-governing commonwealth. Manuel QUEZON was elected president and was tasked with preparing the country for independence after a 10-year transition. In 1942 the islands fell under Japanese occupation during World War II, and US forces and Filipinos fought together during 1944–45 to regain control. On 4 July 1946 the Republic of the Philippines attained its independence. A 20-year rule by Ferdinand MARCOS ended in 1986, whena "people power" movement in Manila ("EDSA 1") forced him into exile and installed Corazon AQUINO as president. Her presidency was hampered by several coup attempts that prevented a return to full political stability and economic development. Fidel RAMOS was elected president in 1992. His administration was marked by increased stability and by progress on economic reforms. in 1992, the US closed its last military bases on the islands. Joseph ESTRADA was elected president in 1998. He was succeeded by his vice-president, Gloria

MACAPAGAL-ARROYO, in January 2001 after ESTRADA's stormy impeachment trial on corruption charges broke down and another "people power" movement ("EDSA 2") demanded his resignation. MACAPAGAL-ARROYO was elected to a six-year term as president in May 2004. Her presidency was marred by several corruption allegations but the Philippine economy was one of the few to avoid contraction following the 2008 global financial crisis, expanding each year of her administration. Benigno AQUINOI II was elected to a six-year term as president in May 2010.

The Philippine Government faces threats from several groups, some of which are on the US Government's Foreign Terrorist Organization list. Manila has waged a decades-long struggle against ethnic Moro insurgencies in the southern Philippines, which has led to a peace accord with the Moro National Liberation Front and ongoing peace talks with the Moro Islamic Liberation Front. The decades-long Maoist-inspired New People's Army insurgency also operates through much of the country. The Philippines faces increased tension with China over disputed territorial and maritime claims in the South China Sea.

GEOGRAPHY

Location: Southeastern Asia, archipelago between the Philippine Sea and the South China Sea, east of Vietnam

Geographic coordinates: 13 00 N, 122 00 E

Map references: Southeast Asia

Area: *total:* 300,000 sq km
land: 298,170 sq km
water: 1,830 sq km
country comparison to the world: 73

Area—comparative: slightly less than twice the size of Georgia; slightly larger than Arizona

Land boundaries: 0 km

Coastline: 36,289 km

Maritime claims: *territorial sea:* irregular polygon extending up to 100 nm from coastline as defined by 1898 treaty; since late 1970s has also claimed polygonal-shaped area in South China Sea as wide as 285 nm
exclusive economic zone: 200 nm
continental shelf: to the depth of exploitation

Climate: tropical marine; northeast monsoon (November to April); southwest monsoon (May to October)

Terrain: mostly mountains with narrow to extensive coastal lowlands

Elevation: *mean elevation:* 442 m

elevation extremes: *lowest point:* Philippine Sea 0 m
highest point: Mount Apo 2,954 m

Natural resources: timber, petroleum, nickel, cobalt, silver, gold, salt, copper

Land use: *agricultural land:* 41%
arable land: 18.2%
permanent crops: 17.8%
permanent pasture: 5%
forest: 25.9%
other: 33.1% (2011 est.)

Irrigated land: 16,270 sq km (2012)

Total renewable water resources: 479 cu km (2011)

Freshwater withdrawal (domestic/industrial/agricultural): *total:* 81.56 cu km/yr (8%/10%/82%)
per capita: 859.9 cu m/yr (2009)

Natural hazards: astride typhoon belt, usually affected by 15 and struck by five to six cyclonic storms each year; landslides; active volcanoes; destructive earthquakes; tsunamis
volcanism: significant volcanic activity; Taal (elev. 311 m), which has shown recent unrest and may erupt in the near future, has been deemed a Decade Volcano by the International Association of Volcanology and Chemistry of the Earth's Interior, worthy of study due to its explosive history and close proximity to human populations; Mayon (elev. 2,462 m), the country's most active volcano, erupted in 2009 forcing over 33,000 to be evacuated; other historically active volcanoes include Biliran, Babuyan Claro, Bulusan, Camiguin, Camiguin de Babuyanes, Didicas, Iraya, Jolo, Kanlaon, Makaturing, Musuan, Parker, Pinatubo and Ragang

Environment—current issues: uncontrolled deforestation especially in watershed areas; soil erosion; air and water pollution in major urban centers; coral reef degradation; increasing pollution of coastal mangrove swamps that are important fish breeding grounds

Environment—international agreements: *party to:* Biodiversity, Clim ate Change, Clim ate Change-Kyoto Protocol, Desertification, Endangered Species, Hazardous Wastes, Law of the Sea, Marine Dumping, Ozone Layer Protection, Ship Pollution, Tropical Timber 83, Tropical Timber 94, Wetlands, Whaling
signed, but not ratified: Air Pollution-Persistent Organic Pollutants

Geography—note: the Philippine archipelago is made up of 7,107 islands; favorably located in relation to m any of Southeast Asia's main water bodies: the South China Sea, Philippine Sea, Sulu Sea, Celebes Sea, and Luzon Strait

PEOPLE AND SOCIETY

Nationality: *noun:* Filipino(s)
adjective: Philippine

Ethnic groups: Tagalog 28.1%, Cebuano 13.1%, Ilocano 9%, Bisay a/Binisay a 7.6%, Hiligaynon Ilonggo 7.5%, Bikol 6%, Waray 3.4%, other 25.3% (2000 census)

Languages: Filipino (official; based on Tagalog) and English (official); eight major dialects—Tagalog, Cebuano, Ilocano, Hili-gaynon or Ilonggo, Bicol, Waray, Pampango, and Pangasinan

Religions: Catholic 82.9% (Roman Catholic 80.9%, Aglipayan 2%), Muslim 5%, Evangelical 2.8%, Iglesia ni Kristo 2.3%, other Christian 4.5%, other 1.8%, unspecified 0.6%, none 0.1% (2000 census)

Population: 100,998,376 (July 2015 est.)
country comparison to the world: 13

Age structure: *0–14 years:* 34.02% (male 17,531,370/female 16,828,067)
15–24 years: 19.18% (male 9,891,032/female 9,484,089)
25–54 years: 36.72% (male 18,810,887/female 18,273,641)
55–64 years: 5.8% (male 2,673,756/female 3,183,809)
65 years and over: 4.28% (male 1,802,632/female 2,519,093) (2015 est.)

Dependency ratios: *total dependency ratio:* 57.6%
youth dependency ratio: 50.3%
elderly dependency ratio: 7.2%
potential support ratio: 13.9% (2015 est.)

Median age: *total:* 23.2 years
male: 22.8 years
female: 23.7 years (2015 est.)
country comparison to the world: 166

Population growth rate: 1.61% (2015 est.)
country comparison to the world: 74

Birth rate: 24.27 births/1,000 population (2015 est.)
country comparison to the world: 59

Death rate: 6.11 deaths/1,000 population (2015 est.)
country comparison to the world: 160

Net migration rate: -2.09 migrant(s)/1,000 population (2015 est.)
country comparison to the world: 169

Urbanization: *urban population:* 44.4% of total population (2015)
rate of urbanization: 1.32% annual rate of change (2010–15 est.)

Major urban areas—population: MANILA (capital) 12.946 million; Davao 1.63 million; Cebu City 951,000; Zamboanga 936,000 (2015)

Sex ratio: *at birth:* 1.05 male(s)/female
0–14 years: 1.04 male(s)/female
15–24 years: 1.04 male(s)/female
25–54 years: 1.03 male(s)/female
55–64 years: 0.84 male(s)/female
65 years and over: 0.72 male(s)/female
total population: 1.01 male(s)/female (2015 est.)

Mother's mean age at first birth: 23
note: median age at first birth among women 25–29 (2013 est.)

Maternal mortality rate: 114 deaths/100,000 live births (2015 est.)
country comparison to the world: 74

Infant mortality rate: *total:* 22.34 deaths/1,000 live births
male: 25.27 deaths/1,000 live births

female: 19.27 deaths/1,000 live births (2015 est.)
country comparison to the world: 80

Life expectancy at birth: *total population:* 68.96 years
male: 65.47 years
female: 72.62 years (2015 est.)
country comparison to the world: 160

Total fertility rate: 3.09 children born/woman (2015 est.)
country comparison to the world: 53

Contraceptive prevalence rate: 48.9% (2011)

Health expenditures: 4.4% of GDP (2013)
country comparison to the world: 150

Hospital bed density: 1 beds/1,000 population (2011)

Drinking water source:
improved:
urban: 93.7% of population
rural: 90.3% of population
total: 91.8% of population
unimproved:
urban: 6.3% of population
rural: 9.7% of population
total: 8.2% of population (2015 est.)

Sanitation facility access:
improved:
urban: 77.9% of population
rural: 70.8% of population
total: 73.9% of population
unimproved:
urban: 22.1% of population
rural: 29.2% of population
total: 26.1% of population (2015 est.)

HIV/AIDS—adult prevalence rate: 0.06% (2014 est.)
country comparison to the world: 118

HIV/AIDS—people living with HIV/AIDS: 35,600 (2014 est.)
country comparison to the world: 64

HIV/AIDS—deaths: 500 (2014 est.)
country comparison to the world: 83

Major infectious diseases: *degree of risk:* high
food or waterborne diseases: bacterial diarrhea, hepatitis A, and typhoid fever
vectorborne diseases: dengue fever and malaria
water contact disease: leptospirosis (2013)

Obesity—adult prevalence rate: 4.7% (2014)
country comparison to the world: 148

Children under the age of 5 years underweight: 19.9% (2014)
country comparison to the world: 29

Education expenditures: 2.7% of GDP (2009)
country comparison to the world: 149

Literacy: *definition:* age 15 and over can read and write
total population: 96.3%
male: 95.8%
female: 96.8% (2015 est.)

School life expectancy (primary to tertiary education): *total:* 13 years
male: 12 years
female: 13 years (2013)

Unemployment, youth ages 15–24: *total:* 16.2%
male: 15.1%
female: 17.8% (2013 est.)
country comparison to the world: 74

Country name: *conventional long form:* Republic of the Philippines
conventional short form: Philippines
local long form: Republika ng Pilipinas
local short form: Pilipinas
etymology: named in honor of King Phillip II of Spain by Spanish explorer Ruy LOPEZ de VILLA-LOBOS, who visited some of the islands in 1543

Government type: presidential republic

Capital: *name:* Manila

Geographic coordinates: 14 36 N, 120 58 E
time difference: UTC+8 (13 hours ahead of Washington, DC, during Standard Time)

Administrative divisions: 80 provinces and 39 chartered cities
provinces: Abra, Agusan del Norte, Agusan del Sur, Aklan, Albay, Antique, Apayao, Aurora, Basilan, Bataan, Batanes, Batangas, Biliran, Benguet, Bohol, Bukidnon, Bulacan, Cagayan, Camarines Norte, Camarines Sur, Camiguin, Capiz, Catanduanes, Cavite, Cebu, Compostela, Cotabato, Davao del Norte, Davao del Sur, Davao Oriental, Dinagat Islands, Eastern Samar, Guimaras, Ifugao, Ilocos Norte, Ilocos Sur, Iloilo, Isabela, Kalinga, Laguna, Lanao del Norte, Lanao del Sur, La Union, Leyte, Maguindanao, Marinduque, Masbate, Mindoro Occidental, Mindoro Oriental, Misamis Occidental, Misamis Oriental, Mountain, Negros Occidental, Negros Oriental, Northern Samar, Nueva Ecija, Nueva Vizcaya, Palawan, Pampanga, Pangasinan, Quezon, Quirino, Rizal, Romblon, Samar, Sarangani, Siquijor, Sorsogon, South Cotabato, Southern Leyte, Sultan Kudarat, Sulu, Surigao del Norte, Surigao del Sur, Tarlac, Tawi-Tawi, Zambales, Zamboanga del Norte, Zamboanga del Sur, Zamboanga Sibugay
chartered cities: Angeles, Antipolo, Bacolod, Baguio, Butuan, Cagayan de Oro, Caloocan, Cebu, Cotabato, Dagupan, Davao, General Santos, Iligan, Iloilo, Lapu-Lapu, Las Pinas, Lucena, Makati, Malabon, Mandaluyong, Mandaue, Manila, Marikina, Muntinlupa, Naga, Navotas, Olongapo, Ormoc, Paranaque, Pasay, Pasig, Puerto Princesa, Quezon, San Juan, Santiago, Tacloban, Taguig, Valenzuela, Zamboanga (2012)

Independence: 4 July 1946 (from the US)

National holiday: Independence Day, 12 June (1898); note—12 June 1898 was date of declaration of independence from Spain; 4 July 1946 was date of independence from the US

Constitution: several previous; latest ratified 2 February 1987, effective 11 February 1987 (2016)

Legal system: mixed legal system of civil, common, Islamic, and customary law

International law organization participation: accepts compulsory ICJ jurisdiction with reservations; accepts ICCt jurisdiction

Citizenship: *citizenship by birth:* no
citizenship by descent only: at least one parent must be a citizen of the Philippines
dual citizenship recognized: no
residency requirement for naturalization: 10 years

Suffrage: 18 years of age; universal

Executive branch: *chief of state:* President Rodrigo DUTERTE (since 30 June 2016); Vice President Leni ROBREDO (since 30 June 2016); note—the president is both chief of state and head of government

head of government: President Rodrigo DUTERTE (since 30 June 2016)
cabinet: Cabinet appointed by the president with the consent of the Commission of Appointments, an independent body of 25 Congressional members including the Senate president (ex officio chairman), appointed by the president
elections/appointments: president and vice president directly elected on separate ballots by sim ple majority popular vote for a single 6-year term; election last held on 9 May 2016 (next to be held on May 2022)
election results: Rodrigo DUTERTE elected president; percent of vote—Rodrigo DUTERTE (PDP-Laban) 39%, Manuel "Mar" ROXAS (LP) 23.4%, Grace POE (independent) 21.4%, Jejomar BINAY (UNA) 12.7%, Miriam Defensor SANTIAGO (PRP) 3%; Leni ROBREDO elected vice president; percent of vote Leni ROBREDO (LP) 35.1%, Bongbong MARCOS (independent) 34.5%

Legislative branch: *description:* bicameral Congress or Kongreso consists of the Senate or Senado (24 seats; members directly elected in m ulti-seat constituencies by majority vote; m embers serve 6-year terms with one-half of the membership renewed every 3 years) and the House of Representatives or Kapulungan Ng Mga Kinatawan (292 seats; 234 members directly elected in single-seat constituencies by simple majority vote and 58 representing minorities directly elected by proportional representation vote; members serve 3-year terms)
elections: Senate—elections last held on 13 May 2013 (next to be held in May 2016); House of Representatives—elections last held on 13 May 2013 (next to be held in May 2016)
election results: Senate—percent of vote by party for 2013 election—UNA 26.94%, NP 15.3%, LP 11.32%, NPC 10.15%, LDP 5.38%, PDP-Laban 4.95%, others 9.72%, independents 16.24%; seats by party after 2013 election—UNA 5, NP 5, LP 4, Lakas 2, NPC 2, LDP 1, PDP-Laban 1, PRP 1, independents 3; House of Representatives—percent of vote by party—LP 38.3%, NPC 17.4%, UNA 11.4%, NUP 8.7%, NP 8.5%, Lakas 5.3%, independents 6.0%, others 4.4%; seats by party—LP 110, NPC 43, NUP 24, NP 17, Lakas 14, UNA 8, independents 6, others 12; party-list 57

Judicial branch: *highest court(s):* Supreme Court (consists of a chief justice and 14 associate justices)
judge selection and term of office: justices are appointed by the president on the recom

mendation of the Judicial and Bar Council, a constitutionally-created, 6-member body that recom mends Supreme Court nom inees; justices serve until age 70
subordinate courts: Court of Appeals; Sandiganbayan (special court for corruption cases of governm ent officials); Court of Tax Appeals; regional, m etropolitan, and municipal trial courts; sharia courts

Political parties and leaders: Laban ng Demokratikong Pilipino (Struggle of Filipino Democrats) or LDP [Edgardo ANGARA]
Lakas ng EDSA-Christian Muslim Democrats or Lakas-CMD [Ferdinand Martin ROMUALDEZ, president]
Liberal Party or LP [Joseph Em ilio ABAYA, president]
Nacionalista Party or NP [Manuel "Manny" VILLAR]
Nationalist People's Coalition or NPC [Eduardo COJUNGCO, Jr.]
PDP-Laban [Aquilino PIMENTEL III]
People's Reform Party or PRP [Miriam Defensor SANTIAGO]
Puwersa ng Masang Pilipino (Force of the Philippine Masses) or PMP [Joseph ESTRADA]
United Nationalist Alliance or UNA [Toby TIANGCO (acting)]—PDP-Laban and PMP coalition for the 2013 election

Political pressure groups and leaders: Black and White Movement [Vicente ROMANO] Kilosbayan [Jovito SALONGA]

International organization participation: ADB, APEC, ARF, ASEAN, BIS, CD, CICA (observer), CP, EAS, FAO, G-24, G-77, IAEA, IBRD, ICAO, ICC (National committees), ICCt, ICRM, IDA, IFAD, IFC, IFRCS, IHO, ILO, IMF, IMO, IMSO, Interpol, IOC, IOM, IPU, ISO, ITSO, ITU, ITUC (NGOs), MIGA, MINUSTAH, NAM, OAS (observer), OPCW, PCA, PIF (partner), UN, UNCTAD, UNESCO, UNHCR, UNIDO, Union Latina, UNMIL, UNMOGIP, UNOCI, UNWTO, UPU, WCO, WFTU (NGOs), WHO, WIPO, WMO, WTO

Diplomatic representation in the US: *chief of mission:* Ambassador Jose L. CUISIAJr. (since 7 April 2011)
chancery: 1600 Massachusetts Avenue NW, Washington, DC 20036
telephone: [1] (202) 467-9300
FAX: [1] (202) 328-7614
consulate(s) general: Chicago, Honolulu, Los Angeles, New Yoek, Saipan (Northern Mariana Islands), San Francisco, Tamuning (Guam)

Diplomatic representation from the US: *chief of mission:* Ambassador Philip S. GOLDBERG (since 2 December 2013)
embassy: 1201 Roxas Boulevard, Manila 1000
mailing address: PSC 500, FPO AP 96515–1000
telephone: [63] (2) 301-2000
FAX: [63] (2) 301-2017

Flag description: two equal horizontal bands of blue (top) and red; a white equilateral triangle is based on the hoist side; the center of the triangle displays a yellow sun with eight primary rays; each

corner of the triangle contains a small, yellow, five-pointed star; blue stands for peace and justice, red symbolizes courage, the white equal-sided triangle represents equality; the rays recall the first eight provinces that sought independence from Spain, while the stars represent the three major geographical divisions of the country: Luzon, Visayas, and Mindanao; the design of the flag dates to 1897
note: in wartime the flag is flown upside down with the red band at the top

National symbol(s): three stars and sun, Philippine eagle; National colors: red, white, blue, yellow

National anthem: *name:* "Lupang Hinirang" (Chosen Land)
lyrics/music: Jose PALMA (revised by Felipe PADILLA de Leon)/Julian FELIPE
note: music adopted 1898, original Spanish lyrics adopted 1899, Filipino (Tagalog) lyrics adopted 1956; although the original lyrics were written in Spanish, later English and Filipino versions were created; today, only the Filipino version is used

ECONOMY

Economy—overview: The economy has been relatively resilient to global economic shocks due to less exposure to troubled international securities, lower dependence on exports, relatively resil ient domestic consumption, large remittances from about 10 million overseas Filipino workers and migrants, and a rapidly expanding outsourcing industry. The current account balance has recorded consecutive surplu ses since 2003, international reserves remain at comfortable levels, and the banking system is stable.

Efforts to improve tax administration and expenditures management have helped ease the Philippines' debt burden and tight financial situation. The Philippines has received investment-grade credit ratings on its sovereign debt under the AQUINO administration and has had little difficulty financing its budget deficits. However, weak absorptive capacity and implementation bottlenecks have prevented the government from maximizing its expenditure plans, which the administration has been working to address. Although it has improved, the low tax-to-GDP ratio remains a constraint to supporting increasingly higher spending levels and sustaining strong growth over the longer term.

Economic growth has accelerated, averaging 6.0% per year from 2011 to 2015, compared with 4.5% under the MACAPAGAL-ARROYO government; and competitiveness rankings have improved. The Philippines has not sustained steady growth in foreign direct investment, which continues to lag regional peers. Although the economy has grown at a faster pace under the AQUINO government, challenges to achieving more inclusive growth remain. The unemployment rate has declined somewhat in recent years but remains high, hovering at around 6.5%; underemployment is also high, ranging from 18% to 19% of the employed. At least 40% of the employed work in the informal sector. Poverty afflicts about a quarter of the population. More than 60% of the poor reside in rural areas, a challenge to raising rural farm and non-farm incomes. The AQUINO administration has been working to boost expenditures for education, health, transfers to the poor, and other social spending programs. Infrastructure remains underfunded and the government is relying on the private sector to help with major projects under its Public-Private Partnership program. Continued efforts are needed to improve governance, the judicial system, the regulatory environment, and the overall ease of doing business.

Notable achievements over the past year include passage of laws that liberalized the entry of foreign banks into the country; partially relaxed the cabotage law by allowing foreign vessels to ply import and export cargo within the archipelago; and passage of anti-trust legislation. Substantial progress has also been made towards passage of a Customs Tariff and Modernization Act to meet international standards and commitments, with strong prospects of enactment into law before President AQUINO steps down from office. However, the Philippine Constitution and other laws restrict foreign ownership in important activities/sectors—such as land ownership and public utilities.

GDP (purchasing power parity): $741 billion (2015 est.)
$700.4 billion (2014 est.)
$659.9 billion (2013 est.)
note: data are in 2015 US dollars
country comparison to the world: 30

GDP (official exchange rate): $292 billion (2015 est.)

GDP—real growth rate: 5.8% (2015 est.)
6.1% (2014 est.)
7.1% (2013 est.)
country comparison to the world: 32

GDP—per capita (PPP): $7,300 (2015 est.)
$7,000 (2014 est.)
$6,700 (2013 est.)
note: data are in 2015 US dollars
country comparison to the world: 153

Gross national saving: 23.7% of GDP (2015 est.)
24.7% of GDP (2014 est.)
24.2% of GDP (2013 est.)
country comparison to the world: 57

GDP—composition, by end use:
household consumption: 73.7%
government consumption: 10.4%
investment in fixed capital: 21.7%
investment in inventories: -0.9%
exports of goods and services: 27.9%
imports of goods and servi ces: -32.9% (2015 est.)

GDP—composition, by sector of origin:
agriculture: 10.3%
industry: 30.9%
services: 58.8% (2015 est.)

Agriculture—products: sugarcane, coconuts, rice, corn, bananas, cassava (manioc, tapioca), pineapples, mangoes; pork, eggs, beef; fish

Industries: electronics assembly, garments, footwear, pharmaceuticals, chemicals, wood products, food processing, petroleum refining, fishing

Industrial production growth rate: 6% (2015 est.)
country comparison to the world: 22

Labor force: 41.37 million (2015 est.)
country comparison to the world: 16

Labor force—by occupation:
agriculture: 29%
industry: 16%
services: 55% (2015 est.)

Unemployment rate: 6.3% (2015 est.)
6.8% (2014 est.)
country comparison to the world: 72

Population below poverty line: 25.2% (2012 est.)

Household income or consumption by percentage share: *lowest:* 10%: 2.9%
highest: 10%: 30.5% (2012 est.)

Distribution of family income—Gini index: 46 (2012)
46.4 (2009)
country comparison to the world: 35

Budget: *revenues:* $46.64 billion
expenditures: $47.76 billion (2015 est.)
Taxes and other revenues: 16% of GDP (2015 est.)
country comparison to the world: 184

Budget surplus (+) or deficit (−): -0.4% of GDP (2015 est.)
country comparison to the world: 42

Public debt: 44.8% of GDP (2015 est.)
45.4% of GDP (2014 est.)
note: data cover debt issued by the National government, and excludes debt instruments issued by government entities other than the treasury; the data include treasury debt held by foreign entities; the data exclude debt issued by social security institutions, government-owned and controlled corporations, the Central Bank, and local government units
country comparison to the world: 101

Fiscal year: calendar year

Inflation rate (consumer prices): 1.4% (2015 est.)
4.2% (2014 est.)
country comparison to the world: 98

Central bank discount rate: 6.13% (31 December 2015)
6.13% (31 December 2014)
country comparison to the world: 63

Commercial bank prime lending rate: 4.4% (31 December 2015 est.)
4.56% (31 December 2014 est.)
country comparison to the world: 155

Stock of narrow money: $56.68 billion (31 December 2015 est.)
$51.8 billion (31 December 2014 est.)
country comparison to the world: 50

Stock of broad money: $179.1 billion (31 December 2015 est.)
$172.3 billion (31 December 2014 est.)
country comparison to the world: 44

Stock of domestic credit: $167 billion (31 December 2015 est.)
$157.7 billion (31 December 2014 est.)
country comparison to the world: 46

Market value of publicly traded shares: $286.1 billion (31 December 2015)
$318.7 billion (31 December 2014)
$268.8 billion (31 December 2013)
country comparison to the world: 31

Current account balance: $8.396 billion (2015 est.)
$10.76 billion (2014 est.)
country comparison to the world: 26

Exports: $58.65 billion (2015 est.)
$62.1 billion (2014 est.)
country comparison to the world: 45

Exports—commodities: semiconductors and electronic products, transport equipment, garments, copper products, petroleum products, coconut oil, fruits

Exports—partners: Japan 21.1%, US 15%, China 10.9%, Hong Kong 10.6%, Singapore 6.2%, Germany 4.5%, South Korea 4.3% (2015)

Imports: $66.69 billion (2015 est.)
$65.4 billion (2014 est.)
country comparison to the world: 40

Imports—commodities: electronic products, mineral fuels, machinery and transport equipment, iron and steel, textile fabrics, grains, chemicals, plastic

Imports—partners: China 16.2%, US 10.8%, Japan 9.6%, Singapore 7%, South Korea 6.5%, Thailand 6.4%, Malaysia 4.8%, Indonesia 4.4% (2015)

Reserves of foreign exchange and gold: $80.67 billion (31 December 2015 est.)
$79.54 billion (31 December 2014 est.)
country comparison to the world: 28

Debt—external: $75.61 billion (30 September 2015 est.)
$77.67 billion (31 December 2014 est.)
country comparison to the world: 55

Stock of direct foreign investment—at home: $58.58 billion (30 September 2015 est.)
$57.09 billion (31 December 2014 est.)
country comparison to the world: 59

Stock of direct foreign investment—abroad: $39.92 billion (31 September 2015 est.)
$36.22 billion (31 December 2014 est.)
country comparison to the world: 46

Exchange rates: Philippine pesos (PHP) per US dollar—
45.503 (2015 est.)
44.395 (2014 est.)
44.395 (2013 est.)
42.23 (2012 est.)
43.313 (2011 est.)

ENERGY

Electricity—production: 75.27 billion kWh (2013 est.)
country comparison to the world: 39

Electricity—consumption: 75.27 billion kWh (2013 est.)
country comparison to the world: 39

Electricity—exports: 0 kWh (2013 est.)
country comparison to the world: 187

Electricity—imports: 0 kWh (2013 est.)
country comparison to the world: 193

Electricity—installed generating capacity: 17.33 million kW (2013 est.)
country comparison to the world: 44

Electricity—from fossil fuels: 68% of total installed capacity (2012 est.)
country comparison to the world: 115

Electricity—from nuclear fuels: 0% of total installed capacity (2012 est.)
country comparison to the world: 171

Electricity—from hydroelectric plants: 20.8% of total installed capacity (2012 est.)
country comparison to the world: 91

Electricity—from other renewable sources: 11.1% of total installed capacity (2012 est.)
country comparison to the world: 31

Crude oil—production: 21,000 bbl/day (2014 est.)
country comparison to the world: 68

Crude oil—exports: 13,990 bbl/day (2012 est.)
country comparison to the world: 61

Crude oil—imports: 1.503 million bbl/day (2014 est.)
country comparison to the world: 7

Crude oil—proved reserves: 138.5 million bbl (1 January 2015 est.)
country comparison to the world: 69

Refined petroleum products—production: 1.373 million bbl/day (2014 est.)
country comparison to the world: 16

Refined petroleum products—consumption: 314,000 bbl/day (2013 est.)
country comparison to the world: 41

Refined petroleum products—exports: 219,800 bbl/day (2014 est.)
country comparison to the world: 32

Refined petroleum products—imports: 1.577 million bbl/day (2014 est.)
country comparison to the world: 4

Natural gas—production: 3.47 billion cu m (2015 est.)
country comparison to the world: 55

Natural gas—consumption: 3.339 billion cu m (2015 est.)
country comparison to the world: 66

Natural gas—exports: 0 cu m (2013 est.)
country comparison to the world: 169

Natural gas—imports: 0 cu m (2013 est.)
country comparison to the world: 125

Natural gas—proved reserves: 98.54 billion cu m (1 January 2014 est.)
country comparison to the world: 53

Carbon dioxide emissions from consumption of energy: 83.95 million Mt (2012 est.)
country comparison to the world: 45

COMMUNICATIONS

Telephones—fixed lines: *total subscriptions:* 3.09 million
subscriptions per 100 inhabitants: 3 (2014 est.)
country comparison to the world: 47

Telephones—mobile cellular: *total:* 111.3 million
subscriptions per 100 inhabitants: 112 (2014 est.)
country comparison to the world: 13

Telephone system: *general assessment:* good international radiotelephone and submarine cable services; domestic and interisland service adequate *domestic:* telecommunications infrastructure includes the following platforms: fixed line, mobile cellular, cable TV, over-the-air TV, radio and Very Small Aperture Terminal (VSAT), fiber-optic cable, and satellite for redundant international connectivity
international: country code—63; a series of submarine cables together provide connectivity to the US, and to countries like Hong Kong, Guam, Singapore, Taiwan, Japan, Brunei, and Malaysia, among others; multiple international gateways (2015)

Broadcast media: multiple National private TV and radio networks; multi-channel satellite and cable TV systems available; more than 350 TV stations—6 major TV networks operating nationwide with 1 being government owned; about 1,300 cable TV providers with more than 2 million subscribers, and some 1,300 radio stations; the Philippines adopted Japan's Integrated Service Digital Broadcast—Terrestrial standard for digital terrestrial television in November 2013 and is scheduled to complete the switch from analog to digital broadcasting by the end of 2015 (2015)
Radio broadcast stations: AM 383, FM 659, shortwave 4 (2008)
Television broadcast stations: 297 (plus 873 CATV networks) (2008)

Internet country code: .ph

Internet hosts: 425,812 (2012)
country comparison to the world: 52

Internet users: *total:* 39.2 million
percent of population: 39.4% (2014 est.)
country comparison to the world: 17

TRANSPORTATION

Airports: 247 (2013)
country comparison to the world: 24

Airports—with paved runways: *total:* 89
over 3,047 m: 4
2,438 to 3,047 m: 8
1,524 to 2,437 m: 33
914 to 1,523 m: 34
under 914 m: 10 (2013)

Airports—with unpaved runways: *total:* 158
1,524 to 2,437 m: 3
914 to 1,523 m: 56
under 914 m: 99 (2013)

Heliports: 2 (2013)

Pipelines: gas 567 km; oil 138 km; refined products 185 km (2013)

Railways: *total:* 995 km
narrow gauge: 995 km 1.067-m gauge (484 km are in operation) (2015)
country comparison to the world: 92

Roadways: *total:* 216,387 km
paved: 61,093 km
unpaved: 155,294 km (2014)
country comparison to the world: 23

Waterways: 3,219 km (limited to vessels with draft less than 1.5 m) (2011)
country comparison to the world: 30

Merchant marine: *total:* 446
by type: bulk carrier 76, cargo 152, carrier 12, chemical tanker 27, container 17, liquefied gas 5, passenger 7, passenger/cargo 65, petroleum tanker 44, refrigerated cargo 20, roll on/roll off 11, vehicle carrier 10
foreign-owned: 159 (Bermuda 47, China 4, Denmark 2, Germany 2, Greece 5, Japan 77, Malaysia 1, Netherlands 17, Singapore 1, South Korea 1, Taiwan 1, UAE 1)
registered in other countries: 7 (Cyprus 1, Panama 5, unknown 1) (2010)
country comparison to the world: 23

Ports and terminals: *major seaport(s):* Batangas, Cagayan de Oro, Cebu, Davao, Liman, Manila
container port(s) (TEUs): Manila (3,342,200)

Transportation—note: the International Maritime Bureau reports the territorial and offshore waters in the South China Sea as high risk for piracy and armed robbery against ships; numerous commercial vessels have been attacked and hijacked both at anchor and while underway; hijacked vessels are often disguised and cargo diverted to ports in East Asia; crews have been murdered or cast adrift

MILITARY AND SECURITY

Military branches: Armed Forces of the Philippines (AFP): Army, Navy (includes Marine Corps), Air Force (2013)

Military service age and obligation: 17–23 years of age (officers 20–24) for voluntary military service; no conscription; applicants must be single male or female Philippine citizens with either 72 college credit hours (enlisted) or a baccalaureate degree (officers) (2013)

Military expenditures:
1.19% of GDP (2012)
1.21% of GDP (2011)
1.19% of GDP (2010)
country comparison to the world: 83

TRANSNATIONAL ISSUES

Disputes—international: Philippines claims sovereignty over Scarborough Reef (also claimed by China together with Taiwan) and over certain of the Spratly Islands, known locally as the Kalayaan (Freedom) Islands, also claimed by China, Malaysia, Taiwan, and Vietnam; the 2002 "Declaration on the Conduct of Parties in the South China Sea, " has eased tensions in the Spratly Islands but falls short of a legally binding "code of conduct" desired by several of the disputants; in March 2005, the National oil companies of China, the Philippines, and Vietnam signed a joint accord to conduct marine seismic activities in the Spratly Islands; Philippines retains a dormant claim to Malaysia's Sabah State in northern Borneo based on the Sultanate of Sulu's granting the Philippines Government power of attorney to pursue a sovereignty claim on his behalf; maritime delimitation negotiations continue with Palau

Refugees and internally displaced persons: *IDPs:* 63,174 (government troops fighting the Moro Islamic Liberation Front, the Abu Sayyaf Group, and the New People's Army; clan feuds; Natural disasters including Typhoon Bopha (December 2012), the Bohol earthquake (October 2013), Typhoon Haiyan (November 2013), and Typhoon Hagupit (December 2014)) (2015)
stateless persons: 7,138 (2015); note—stateless persons are descendants of Indonesian migrants

Illicit drugs: domestic methamphetamine production has beena growing problem in recent years despite government crackdowns; major consumer of amphetamines; longstanding marijuana producer mainly in rural areas where Manila's control is limited

PITCAIRN ISLANDS

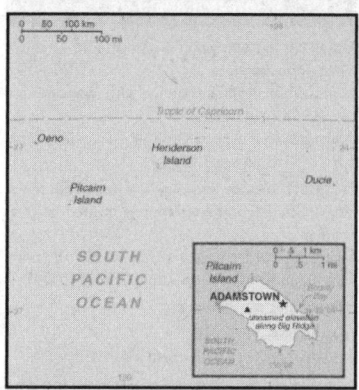

INTRODUCTION

Background: Pitcairn Island was discovered in 1767 by the British and settled in 1790 by the Bounty mutineers and their Tahitian companions. Pitcairn was the first Pacific island to become a British colony (in 1838) and today remains the last vestige of that empire in the South Pacific. Outmigration, primarily to New Zealand, has thinned the population from a peak of 233 in 1937 to less than 50 today.

GEOGRAPHY

Location: Oceania, islands in the South Pacific Ocean, about midway between Peru and New Zealand

Geographic coordinates: 25 04 S, 130 06 W

Map references: Oceania

Area: *total:* 47 sq km
land: 47 sq km
water: 0 sq km
country comparison to the world: 234

Area—comparative: about three-tenths the size of Washington, DC

Land boundaries: 0 km

Coastline: 51 km

Maritime claims: *territorial sea:* 3 nm
exclusive economic zone: 200 nm

Climate: tropical; hot and humid; modified by southeast trade winds; rainy season (November to March)

Terrain: rugged volcanic formation; rocky coastline with cliffs

Elevation: *mean elevation:* NA

elevation extremes: *lowest point:* Pacific Ocean 0 m
highest poin t: Big Ridge 347 m

Natural resources: miro trees (used for handicrafts), fish
note: manganese, iron, copper, gold, silver, and zinc have been discovered offshore

Land use: *agricultural land:* 0%
arable land: 0%
permanent crops: 0%
permanent pasture: 0%
forest: 74.5%
other: 25.5% (2011 est.)

Irrigated land: 0 sq km (2012)

Natural hazards: typhoons (especially November to March)

Environment—current issues: deforestation (only a small portion of the original forest remains because of burning and clearing for settlement)

Geography—note: Britain's most isolated dependency; only the larger island of Pitcairn is inhabited but it has no port or Natural harbor; supplies must be transported by rowed longboat from larger ships stationed offshore

PEOPLE AND SOCIETY

Nationality: *noun:* Pitcairn Islander(s)
adjective: Pitcairn Islander

Ethnic groups: descendants of the Bounty mutineers and their Tahitian wives

Languages: English (official), Pitkern (mixture of an 18th century English dialect and a Tahitian dialect)

Religions: Seventh-Day Adventist 100%

Population: 48 (July 2014 est.)
country comparison to the world: 238

Population growth rate: 0% (2014 est.)
country comparison to the world: 198

Urbanization: *urban population:* 0% of total population (2012)
rate of urbanization: NA

Sex ratio: NA

Infant mortality rate: *total:* NA
male: NA
female: NA

Life expectancy at birth: *total population:* NA
male: NA
*female:*NA

Total fertility rate: NA

HIV/AIDS—adult prevalence rate: NA

HIV/AIDS—people living with HIV/AIDS: NA

HIV/AIDS—deaths: NA

GOVERNMENT

Country name: *conventional long form:* Pitcairn, Henderson, Ducie, and Oeno Islands
conventional short form: Pitcairn Islands
etymology: named after Midshipman Robert PITCAIRN who first sighted the island in 1767

Dependency status: overseas territory of the UK

Government type: parliamentary democracy (Island Council); overseas territory of the UK

Capital: *name:* Adamstown

Geographic coordinates: 25 04 S, 130 05 W
time difference: UTC-9 (4 hours behind Washington, DC, during Standard Time)

Administrative divisions: none (overseas territory of the UK)

Independence: none (overseas territory of the UK)

National holiday: Birthday of Queen ELIZABETH II, second Saturday in June (1926); Discovery Day, 2 July (1767)

Constitution: several previous; latest drafted 10 February 2010, presented 17 February 2010, effective 4 March 2010 (2016)

Legal system: local island by-laws

Citizenship: see United Kingdom

Suffrage: 18 years of age; universal with three years residency

Executive branch: *chief of state:* Queen ELIZABETH II (since 6 February 1952); represented by UK High Commissioner to New Zealand and Governor (nonresident) of the Pitcairn Islands Jonathan SINCLAIR (since August 2014); Commissioner (nonresident) Leslie JAQUES (since September 2003) serves as liaison between the governor and the Island Council

head of government: Mayor and Chairman of the Island Council Shawn CHRISTIAN (since 13 November 2013)
cabinet: none
elections/appointments: the monarchy is hereditary; governor and commissioner appointed by the monarch; island mayor directly elected by majority popular vote for a 3-year term; election last held on 12 November 2013 (next to be held not later than December 2016)
election results: Shawn CHRISTIAN elected mayor and chairman of the Island Council; Island Council vote count in third round—Shawn CHRISTIAN 20, Simon YOUNG 19

Legislative branch: *description:* unicameral Island Council (10 seats; 4 members directly elected by proportional representation vote, 1 nominated by the elected Council members, 2 appointed by the governor, and 3 ex-officio members—the governor, deputy governor, and commissioner; elected members serve 1-year terms)
elections: last held on 13 November 2013 (next to be held not later than December 2015)
election results: percent of vote—NA; seats—5 independent

Judicial branch: *highest resident court(s):* Pitcairn Court of Appeal (consists of the court president, 2 judges, and the Supreme Court chief justice (ex-officio member); Pitcairn Supreme Court (consists of the chief justice and 2 judges); note—appeals beyond the Pitcairn Court of Appeal are heard by the Judicial Committee of the Privy Council (in London); the Court of Appeal was established in 2000 by an Order in Council
judge selection and term of office: all judges of both courts appointed by the governor of the

Pitcairn Islands on the instructions of the Queen of England through the Secretary of State; all judges appointed until retirement, normally at age 75

subordinate courts: Magistrate's Court

Political parties and leaders: none

Political pressure groups and leaders: none

International organization participation: SPC, UPU

Diplomatic representation in the US: none (overseas territory of the UK)

Diplomatic representation from the US: none (overseas territory of the UK)

Flag description: blue with the flag of the UK in the upper hoist-side quadrant and the Pitcairn Islander coat of arms centered on the outer half of the flag; the green, yellow, and blue of the shield represents the island rising from the ocean; the green field features a yellow anchor surmounted by a bible (both the anchor and the bible were items found on the HMS Bounty); sitting on the crest is a Pitcairn Island wheelbarrow from which springs a slip of miro (a local plant)

National anthem: *name:* "We From Pitcairn Island"

lyrics/music: unknown/Frederick M. LEHMAN

note: serves as a local anthem; as a territory of the UK, "God Save the Queen" is official (see United Kingdom)

ECONOMY

Economy—overview: The inhabitants of this tiny isolated economy exist on fishing, subsistence farming, handicrafts, and postage stamps. The fertile soil of the valleys produces a wide variety of fruits and vegetables, including citrus, sugarcane, watermelons, bananas, yams, and beans. Bartering is an important part of the economy. The major sources of revenue are the sale of postage stamps to collectors and the sale of handicrafts to passing ships.

GDP (purchasing power parity): $NA

Agriculture—products: honey; wide variety of fruits and vegetables; goats, chickens; fish

Industries: postage stamps, handicrafts, beekeeping, honey

Labor force: 15 (2004)
country comparison to the world: 233

Labor force—by occupation: *note:* no business community in the usual sense; some public works; subsistence farming and fishing

Budget: *revenues:* $746,000
expenditures: $1.028 million (FY04/05)

Fiscal year: 1 April—31 March

Exports: $NA

Exports—commodities: fruits, vegetables, curios, postage stamps

Imports: $NA

Imports—commodities: fuel oil, machinery, building materials, flour, sugar, other foodstuffs

Exchange rates: New Zealand dollars (NZD) per US dollar—
1.452 (2015)
1.2187 (2013)
1.2187 (2013)
1.23 (2012)
1.263 (2011)

COMMUNICATIONS

Telephone system: *general assessment:* satellite-based phone services
domestic: local phone service with international connections via Internet
international: country code—872; satellite earth station—1 (Inmarsat)

Broadcast media: satellite TV from Fiji-based Sky Pacific offering a wide range of international channels
Radio broadcast stations: AM 1, FM 0, shortwave 0 (15 ham radio operators (VP6)) (2004)

Internet country code: .pn

Internet hosts: 26 (2012)
country comparison to the world: 217

Communications—note: satellite-based local phone service and broadband Internet connections available in all homes

TRANSPORTATION

Ports and terminals: *major seaport(s):* Adamstown (on Bounty Bay)

MILITARY AND SECURITY

Military—note: defense is the responsibility of the UK

TRANSNATIONAL ISSUES

Disputes—international: none

POLAND

INTRODUCTION

Background: Poland's history as a state began near the middle of the 10th century. By the mid-16th century, the Polish-Lithuanian Commonwealth ruled a vast tract of land in central and eastern Europe. During the 18th century, internal disorders weakened the nation, and in a series of agreements between 1772 and 1795, Russia, Prussia, and Austria partitioned Poland among themselves. Poland regained its independence in 1918 only to be overrun by Germany and the Soviet Union in World War II. It became a Soviet satellite state following the war, but its government was comparatively tolerant and progressive. Labor turmoil in 1980 led to the formation of the independent trade union "Solidarity" that over time became a political force with over 10 million members. Free elections in 1989 and 1990 won Solidarity control of the parliament and the presidency, bringing the communist era to a close. A "shock therapy" program during the early 1990s enabled the country to transform its economy into one of the most robust in Central Europe. Poland joined NATO in 1999 and the EU in 2004. With its transformation to a democratic, market-oriented country largely completed and with large investments in defense, energy, and other infrastructure, Poland is an increasingly active member of Euro-Atlantic organizations.

GEOGRAPHY

Location: Central Europe, east of Germany

Geographic coordinates: 52 00 N, 20 00 E

Map references: Europe

Area: *total:* 312,685 sq km
land: 304,255 sq km
water: 8,430 sq km
country comparison to the world: 70

Area—comparative: about twice the size of Georgia; slightly smaller than New Mexico

Land boundaries: *total:* 3,071 km
border countries (7): Belarus 418 km, Czech Republic 796 km, Germany 467 km, Lithuania 104 km, Russia (Kaliningrad Oblast) 210 km, Slovakia 541 km, Ukraine 535 km

Coastline: 440 km

Maritime claims: *territorial sea:* 12 nm
exclusive economic zone: defined by international treaties

Climate: temperate with cold, cloudy, moderately severe winters with frequent precipitation; mild summers with frequent showers and thundershowers

Terrain: mostly flat plain; mountains along southern border

Elevation: *mean elevation:* 173 m

elevation extremes: *lowest point:* near Raczki Elblaskie -2 m
highest point: Rysy 2,499 m

Natural resources: coal, sulfur, copper, Natural gas, silver, lead, salt, amber, arable land

Land use: *agricultural land:* 48.2%
arable land: 36.2%
permanent crops: 1.3%
permanent pasture: 10.7%
forest: 30.6%
other: 21.2% (2011 est.)

Irrigated land: 970 sq km (2012)

Total renewable water resources: 61.6 cu km (2011)

Freshwater withdrawal (domestic/industrial/agricultural): *total:* 11.96 cu km/yr (31%/60%/10%)
per capita: 312.3 cu m/yr (2009)

Natural hazards: flooding

Environment—current issues: decreased emphasis on heavy industry and increased environmental concern by post-communist governments has improved environment; air pollution remains serious because of emissions from coal-fired power plants and the resulting acid rain has caused forest damage; water pollution from industrial and municipal sources is also a problem, as is disposal of hazardous wastes

Environment—international agreements: *party to:* Air Pollution, Antarctic-Environmental Protocol, Antarctic-Marine Living Resources, Antarctic Seals, Antarctic Treaty, Biodiversity, Climate Change, Climate Change-Kyoto Protocol, Desertification, Endangered Species, Environmental Modification, Hazardous Wastes, Law of the Sea, Marine Dumping, Ozone Layer Protection, Ship Pollution, Wetlands
signed, but not ratified: Air Pollution-Nitrogen Oxides, Air Pollution-Persistent Organic Pollutants, Air Pollution-Sulfur 94

Geography—note: historically, an area of conflict because of flat terrain and the lack of Natural barriers on the North European Plain

PEOPLE AND SOCIETY

Nationality: *noun:* Pole(s)
adjective: Polish

Ethnic groups: Polish 96.9%, Silesian 1.1%, German 0.2%, Ukrainian 0.1%, other and unspecified 1.7%
note: represents ethnicity declared first (2011 est.)

Languages: Polish (official) 98.2%, Silesian 1.4%, other 1.1%, unspecified 1.3%
note: data represents the language spoken at home; shares sum to more than 100% because some respondents gave more than one answer on the census; Poland ratified the European Charter for Regional or Minority Languages in 2009 recognizing Kashub as a regional language, Czech, Hebrew, Yiddish, Belarusian, Lithuanian, German, Armenian, Russian, Slovak, and Ukrainian as National minority languages, and Karaim, Lemko, Romani (Polska Roma and Bergitka Roma), and Tatar as ethnic minority languages (2011 est.)

Religions: Catholic 87.2% (includes Roman Catholic 86.9% and Greek Catholic, Armenian Catholic, and Byzantine-Slavic Catholic .3%), Orthodox 1.3% (almost all are Polish Autocephalous Orthodox), Protestant 0.4% (mainly Augsburg Evangelical and Pentacostal), other 0.4% (includes Jehovah's Witness, Buddhist, Hare Krishna, Gaudiya Vaishnavism, Muslim, Jewish, Mormon), unspecified 10.8% (2012 est.)

Population: 38,562,189 (July 2015 est.)
country comparison to the world: 35

Age structure: *0–14 years:* 14.7% (male 2,915,674/female 2,753,218)
15–24 years: 11.52% (male 2,279,404/female 2,163,621)
25–54 years: 43.56% (male 8,471,593/female 8,326,656)
55–64 years: 14.54% (male 2,645,228/female 2,962,305)
65 years and over: 15.67% (male 2,362,421/female 3,682,069) (2015 est.)

Dependency ratios: *total dependency ratio:* 43.8%
youth dependency ratio: 21.5%
elderly dependency ratio: 22.3%
potential support ratio: 4.5% (2015 est.)

Median age: *total:* 39.9 years
male: 38.2 years
female: 41.6 years (2015 est.)
country comparison to the world: 46

Population growth rate: -0.09% (2015 est.)
country comparison to the world: 206

Birth rate: 9.74 births/1,000 population (2015 est.)
country comparison to the world: 200

Death rate: 10.19 deaths/1,000 population (2015 est.)
country comparison to the world: 39

Net migration rate: -0.46 migrant(s)/1,000 population (2015 est.)
country comparison to the world: 134

Urbanization: *urban population:* 60.5% of total population (2015)
rate of urbanization: -0.1% annual rate of change (2010–15 est.)

Major urban areas—population: WARSAW (capital) 1.722 million; Krakow 760,000 (2015)

Sex ratio: *at birth:* 1.06 male(s)/female
0–14 years: 1.06 male(s)/female
15–24 years: 1.05 male(s)/female
25–54 years: 1.02 male(s)/female
55–64 years: 0.89 male(s)/female
65 years and over: 0.64 male(s)/female
total population: 0.94 male(s)/female (2015 est.)

Mother's mean age at first birth: 26.9 (2011 est.)

Maternal mortality rate: 3 deaths/100,000 live births (2015 est.)
country comparison to the world: 175

Infant mortality rate: *total:* 4.5 deaths/1,000 live births
male: 4.89 deaths/1,000 live births
female: 4.09 deaths/1,000 live births (2015 est.)
country comparison to the world: 182

Life expectancy at birth: *total population:* 77.4 years
male: 73.53 years
female: 81.5 years (2015 est.)

country comparison to the world: 71

Total fertility rate: 1.33 children born/woman (2015 est.)
country comparison to the world: 216

Health expenditures: 6.7% of GDP (2013)
country comparison to the world: 89

Physicians density: 2.22 physicians/1,000 population (2012)

Hospital bed density: 6.5 beds/1,000 population (2011)

Drinking water source:
improved:
urban: 99.3% of population
rural: 96.9% of population
total: 98.3% of population
unimproved:
urban: 0.7% of population
rural: 3.1% of population
total: 1.7% of population (2015 est.)

Sanitation facility access:
improved:
urban: 97.5% of population
rural: 96.7% of population
total: 97.2% of population
unimproved:
urban: 2.5% of population
rural: 3.3% of population
total: 2.8% of population (2015 est.)

HIV/AIDS—adult prevalence rate: 0.07% (2014 est.)
country comparison to the world: 115

HIV/AIDS—people living with HIV/AIDS: NA

HIV/AIDS—deaths: NA

Major infectious diseases: *degree of risk:* intermediate
vectorborne disease: tickborne encephalitis
note: highly pathogenic H5N1 avian influenza has been identified in this country; it poses a negligible risk with extremely rare cases possible among US citizens who have close contact with birds (2013)

Obesity—adult prevalence rate: 27% (2014)
country comparison to the world: 56

Education expenditures: 4.8% of GDP (2012)
country comparison to the world: 65

Literacy: *definition:* age 15 and over can read and write
total population: 99.8%
male: 99.9%
female: 99.7% (2015 est.)

School life expectancy (primary to tertiary education): *total:* 16 years
male: 16 years
female: 17 years (2013)

Unemployment, youth ages 15–24: *total:* 27.3%
male: 25.4%
female: 30.1% (2013 est.)
country comparison to the world: 34

GOVERNMENT

Country name: *conventional long form:* Republic of Poland
conventional short form: Poland

local long form: Rzeczpospolita Polska

local short form: Polska

etymology: name derives from the Polanians, a west Slavic tribe that united several surrounding Slavic groups (9th-10th centuries A.D.) and who passed on their name to the country; the name of the tribe likely comes from the Slavic "pole" (field or plain), indicating the flat nature of their country

Government type: parliamentary republic

Capital: *name:* Warsaw

Geographic coordinates: 52 15 N, 21 00 E

time difference: UTC + 1 (6 hours ahead of Washington, DC, during Standard Time)

daylight saving time: +1hr, begins last Sunday in March; ends last Sunday in October

Administrative divisions: 16 provinces (wojewodztwa, singular—wojewodztwo); Dolnoslaskie (Lower Silesia), Kujawsko-Pomorskie (Kuyavia-Pomerania), Lodzkie (Lodz), Lubelskie (Lublin), Lubuskie (Lubusz), Malopolskie (Lesser Poland), Mazowieckie (Masovia), Opolskie (Opole), Podkarpackie (Subcarpathia), Podlaskie, Pomorskie (Pomerania), Slaskie (Silesia), Swietokrzyskie (Holy Cross), Warminsko-Mazurskie (Warmia-Masuria), Wielkopolskie (Greater Poland), Zachodniopomorskie (West Pomerania)

Independence: 11 November 1918 (republic proclaimed); notable earlier dates: 966 (adoption of Christianity, traditional founding date), 1 July 1569 (Polish-Lithuanian Commonwealth created)

National holiday: Constitution Day, 3 May (1791)

Constitution: several previous; latest adopted 2 April 1997, approved by referendum 25 May 1997, effective 17 October 1997; amended 2006, 2009, 2015 (2016)

Legal system: civil law system; judicial review of legislative, administrative, and other governmental acts; constitutional law rulings of the Constitutional Tribunal are final

International law organization participation: accepts compulsory ICJ jurisdiction with reservations; accepts ICCt jurisdiction

Citizenship: *citizenship by birth:* no

citizenship by descent only: both parents must be citizens of Poland

dual citizenship recognized: no

residency requirement for naturalization: 5 years

Suffrage: 18 years of age; universal

Executive branch: *chief of state:* President Andrzej DUDA (since 6 August 2015)

head of government: Prime Minister Beata SZYDLO (since 16 November 2015); Deputy Prime Minister and Minister of Culture and National Heritage Piotr GLINSKI (since 16 November 2015), Deputy Prime Minister and Minister of Science and Higher Education Jaroslaw GOWIN (since 16 November 2015), and Deputy Prime Minister and Minister of Development Mateusz MORAWIECKI (since 16 November 2015)

cabinet: Council of Ministers proposed by the prime minister, appointed by the president, and approved by the Sejm

elections/appointments: president directly elected by absolute majority popular vote in 2 rounds if needed for a 5-year term (eligible for a second term); election last held on 10 and 24 May 2015 (next to be held in 2020); prime minister, deputy prime ministers, and Council of Ministers appointed by the president and confirmed by the Sejm

election results: Andrzej DUDA elected president; percent of vote in runoff—Andrzej DUDA 51.5%, Bronislaw KOMOROWSKI (independent) 48.5%

Legislative branch: *description:* bicameral legislature consists of the Senate or Senat (100 seats; members directly elected in single-seat constituencies by simple majority vote to serve 4-year terms) and the Sejm (460 seats; members directly elected in multi-seat constituencies by proportional representation vote to serve 4-year terms); note—the designation National Assembly or Zgromadzenie narodowe is only used on those rare occasions when the two houses meet jointly

note: the German minority is exempt from the 5% threshold requirement for seats to the Sejm

elections: Senate—last held on 25 October 2015 (next to be held in October 2019); Sejm—last held on 25 October 2015 (next to be held in October 2019)

election results: Senate—percent of vote by party—NA; seats by party—PiS 62, PO 33, PSL 1, independents 4; Sejm—percent of vote by party—PiS 37.6%, PO 24.1%, K158.8%, N 7.6%, PSL 5.1% other 16.8%; seats by party—PiS 234, PO 138, K1540, N29, PSL 16, independent 2, German minority 1

Judicial branch: *highest court(s):* Supreme Court or Sad najwyzszy (consists of the president of the Supreme Court and 116 judges organized in criminal, civil, labor and social insurance, and military chambers); Constitutional Court or Constitutional Tribunal (Trybunal Konstytucyjny) (consits of 15 members)

judge selection and term of office: president of the Supreme Court nominated by the General Assembly of the Supreme Court and selected by the president of Poland; other judges nominated by the 25-member National Judiciary Council, and appointed by the president of Poland; judges appointed until retirement, usually at age 65, but tenure can be extended; Constitutional Court members appointed by the Sjem for 9-year terms

subordinate courts: Constitutional Tribunal; State Tribunal; regional and appellate courts subdivided into military, civil, criminal, labor, and family courts; administrative courts

Political parties and leaders: Civic Platform or PO [Grzegorz SCHETYNA, chairperson; Slawomir NEUMANN, parliamentary caucus leader]
Congress of the New Right or KNP [Michal MARUSIK, chairman]
Democratic Left Alliance or SLD [Wlodzimierz CZARZASTY, chairman]

German Minority of Lower Silesia or MNSO [Ryszard GALLA, representative]
Kukiz 15 [Pawel KUKIZ; chairman, parliamentary caucus leader]
Law and Justice or PiS [Jaroslaw KACZYNSKI, chairman; Ryszard TERLECKI, parliamentary caucus leader]
Nowoczesna ("Modern") or N [Ryszard PETRU; chairman, parliamentary caucus leader]
Polish People's Party or PSL [Wladyslaw KOSINIAK-KAMYSZ; chairman, parliamentary caucus leader]
Razem (Together) [no party chair, led by nine-member management board]

Political pressure groups and leaders: All Poland Trade Union Alliance or OPZZ [Jan GUZ] (trade union)
Independent Self-G overning Trade Union "Solidarity" [Piotr DUDA]
Roman Catholic Church [Archbishop Wojciech POLAK, Archbishop Stanislaw GADECKI]

International organization participation: Arctic Council (observer), Australia Group, BIS, BSEC (observer), CBSS, CD, CE, CEI, CERN, EAPC, EBRD, ECB, EIB, ESA, EU, FAO, IAEA, IBRD, ICAO, ICC (National committees), ICCt, ICRM, IDA, IEA, IFC, IFRCS, IHO, ILO, IMF, IMO, IMSO, Interpol, IOC, IOM, IPU, ISO, ITSO, ITU, ITUC (NGOs), MIGA, MONUSCO, NATO, NEA, NSG, OAS (observer), OECD, OIF (observer), OPCW, OSCE, PCA, Schengen Convention, UN, UNCTAD, UNESCO, UNHCR, UNIDO, UNMIL, UNMISS, UNOCI, UNWTO, UPU, WCO, WFTU (NGOs), WHO, WIPO, WMO, WTO, ZC

Diplomatic representation in the US: *chief of mission:* Ambassador Ryszard SCHNEPF (since 28 September 2012)

chancery: 2640 16th Street NW, Washington, DC 20009

telephone: [1] (202) 234-3800 through 3802

FAX: [1] (202) 328-6271

consulate(s) general: Chicago, Los Angeles, New York

Diplomatic representation from the US: *chief of mission:* Ambassador Paul JONES (since 7 October 2015)

embassy: Aleje Ujazdowskie 29/3100—540 Warsaw

mailing address: American Embassy Warsaw, US Department of State, Washington, DC 20521–5010 (pouch)

telephone: [48] (22) 504-2000

FAX: [48] (22) 504-2688

consulate(s) general: Krakow

Flag description: two equal horizontal bands of white (top) and red; colors derive from the Polish emblem—a white eagle on a red field

note: similar to the flags of Indonesia and Monaco which are red (top) and white

National symbol(s): white eagle; National colors: white, red

National anthem: *name:* "Mazurek Dabrowskiego" (Dabrowski's Mazurka)

lyrics/music: Jozef WYBICKI/traditional

note: adopted 1927; the anthem, commonly known as "Jeszcze Polska nie zginela" (Poland Has Not Yet Perished), was written in 1797; the lyrics resonate strongly with Poles because they reflect the numerous occasions in which the nation's lands have been occupied

ECONOMY

Economy—overview: Poland has pursued a policy of economic liberalization since 1990 and Poland's economy was the only EU country to avoid a recession through the 2008–09 economic downturn. Although EU membership and access to EU structural funds have provided a major boost to the economy since 2004, GDP per capita remains significantly below the EU average and the unemployment rate is now below the EU average. The government of Prime Minister Donald TUSK steered the Polish economy through the economic downturn by skillfully managing public finances and adopting controversial pension and tax reforms to further shore up public finances. While the Polish economy has performed well over the past five years, growth slowed in 2013 and picked back up in 2014–15. Poland's new center-right Law and Justice government plans to introduce expansionary economic policies to spur long-term growth, but social spending programs are expected to lead to increased deficit spending over the medium term. Poland faces several challenges, which include addressing some of the remaining deficiencies in its road and rail infrastructure, business environment, rigid labor code, commercial court system, government red tape, and burdensome tax system, especially for entrepreneurs. Additional long-term challenges include diversifying Poland's energy mix and sources of supply, strengthening investments in innovation, research, and development, and as well as stemming the outflow of educated young Poles to other EU member states, especially in light of a coming demographic contraction due to emigration, persistently low fertility rates, and the aging of the Solidarity-era baby boom generation.

GDP (purchasing power parity): $1.005 trillion (2015 est.)
$970.2 billion (2014 est.)
$938.9 billion (2013 est.)
note: data are in 2015 US dollars
country comparison to the world: 25

GDP (official exchange rate): $474.9 billion (2015 est.)

GDP—real growth rate: 3.6% (2015 est.)
3.3% (2014 est.)
1.3% (2013 est.)
country comparison to the world: 81

GDP—per capita (PPP): $26,500 (2015 est.)
$25,500 (2014 est.)
$24,700 (2013 est.)
note: data are in 2015 US dollars
country comparison to the world: 67

Gross national saving: 19.9% of GDP (2015 est.)
18.2% of GDP (2014 est.)
17.7% of GDP (2013 est.)

country comparison to the world: 82

GDP—composition, by end use:
household consumption: 58.9%
government consumption: 17.8%
investment in fixed capital: 20%
investment in inventories: 0.7%
exports of goods and services: 52.6%
imports of goods and services: -50% (2015 est.)

GDP—composition, by sector of origin:
agriculture: 3.3%
industry: 41.1%
services: 55.6% (2015 est.)

Agriculture—products: potatoes, fruits, vegetables, wheat; poultry, eggs, pork, dairy

Industries: machine building, iron and steel, coal mining, chemicals, shipbuilding, food processing, glass, beverages, textiles

Industrial production growth rate: 4.3% (2015 est.)
country comparison to the world: 51

Labor force: 18.29 million (2015 est.)
country comparison to the world: 33

Labor force—by occupation: *agriculture:* 12.6%
industry: 30.4%
services: 57% (2012)

Unemployment rate: 10.6% (2015 est.)
12.3% (2014 est.)
country comparison to the world: 120

Population below poverty line: 17.3% (2012 est.)

Household income or consumption by percentage share: *lowest:* 10%: 3.3%
highest: 10%: 25.6% (2012 est.)

Distribution of family income—Gini index: 32.4 (2012)
33.7 (2008)
country comparison to the world: 109

Budget: *revenues:* $81.58 billion
expenditures: $90.24 billion (2015 est.)
Taxes and other revenues: 17% of GDP (2015 est.)
country comparison to the world: 178

Budget surplus (+) or deficit (–): -1.8% of GDP (2015 est.)
country comparison to the world: 67

Public debt: 43.4% of GDP (2015 est.)
43.7% of GDP (2014 est.)
note: data cover general government debt, and includes debt instruments issued (or owned) by government entities other than the treasury; the data include treasury debt held by foreign entities, the data include sub national entities, as well as intra-governmental debt; intra-governmental debt consists of treasury borrowings from surpluses in the social funds, such as for retirement, medical care, and unemployment; debt instruments for the social funds are not sold at public auctions
country comparison to the world: 105

Fiscal year: calendar year

Inflation rate (consumer prices): -0.9% (2015 est.)
0% (2014 est.)
country comparison to the world: 14

Central bank discount rate: 2.5% (31 December 2014)

1.5% (31 December 2013)
country comparison to the world: 109

Commercial bank prime lending rate: 5.5% (31 December 2015 est.)
6.18% (31 December 2014 est.)
country comparison to the world: 140

Stock of Narrow money: $167.1 billion (31 December 2015 est.)
$172.9 billion (31 December 2014 est.)
country comparison to the world: 25

Stock of broad money: $306.7 billion (31 December 2014 est.)
$318.8 billion (31 December 2013 est.)
country comparison to the world: 33

Stock of domestic credit: $344 billion (31 December 2015 est.)
$348 billion (31 December 2014 est.)
country comparison to the world: 33

Market value of publicly traded shares: $177.7 billion (31 December 2012 est.)
$138.2 billion (31 December 2011)
$190.2 billion (31 December 2010 est.)
country comparison to the world: 36

Current account balance: -$2.215 billion (2015 est.)
-$11.13 billion (2014 est.)
country comparison to the world: 151

Exports: $190.2 billion (2015 est.)
$210.7 billion (2014 est.)
country comparison to the world: 25

Exports—commodities: machinery and transport equipment 37.8%, intermediate manufactured goods 23.7%, miscellaneous manufactured goods 17.1%, food and live animals 7.6% (2012 est.)

Exports—partners: Germany 27.1%, UK 6.8%, Czech Republic 6.6%, France 5.5%, Italy 4.8%, Netherlands 4.4% (2015)

Imports: $187.5 billion (2015 est.)
$215 billion (2014 est.)
country comparison to the world: 25

Imports—commodities: machinery and transport equipment 38%, intermediate manufactured goods 21%, chemicals 15%, minerals, fuels, lubricants, and related materials 9% (2011 est.)

Imports—partners: Germany 27.6%, China 7.5%, Russia 7.2%, Netherlands 5.9%, Italy 5.2%, France 4.1% (2015)

Reserves of foreign exchange and gold: $94.75 billion (31 December 2015 est.)
$100.4 billion (31 December 2014 est.)
country comparison to the world: 24

Debt—external: $354.2 billion (31 December 2014 est.)
$382.1 billion (31 December 2013 est.)
country comparison to the world: 32

Stock of direct foreign investment—at home: $287.3 billion (31 December 2015 est.)
$280.3 billion (31 December 2014 est.)
country comparison to the world: 24

Stock of direct foreign investment—abroad: $72.19 billion (31 December 2015 est.)
$70.69 billion (31 December 2014 est.)

country comparison to the world: 36

Exchange rates: zlotych (PLN) per US dollar—
3.697 (2015 est.)
3.1538 (2014 est.)
3.1538 (2013 est.)
3.26 (2012 est.)
2.9639 (2011 est.)

ENERGY

Electricity—production: 152.7 billion kWh (2012 est.)
country comparison to the world: 27

Electricity—consumption: 139 billion kWh (2012 est.)
country comparison to the world: 25

Electricity—exports: 12.32 billion kWh (2013)
country comparison to the world: 16

Electricity—imports: 7.8 billion kWh (2013 est.)
country comparison to the world: 30

Electricity—installed generating capacity: 35.22 million kW (2012 est.)
country comparison to the world: 26

Electricity—from fossil fuels: 89.5% of total installed capacity (2013 est.)
country comparison to the world: 79

Electricity—from nuclear fuels: 0% of total installed capacity (2013 est.)
country comparison to the world: 164

Electricity—from hydroelectric plants: 1.5% of total installed capacity (2013 est.)
country comparison to the world: 142

Electricity—from other renewable sources: 8.5% of total installed capacity (2013 est.)
country comparison to the world: 43

Crude oil—production: 19,260 bbl/day (2014 est.)
country comparison to the world: 74

Crude oil—exports: 8,170 bbl/day (2013 est.)
country comparison to the world: 68

Crude oil—imports: 467,400 bbl/day (2013 est.)
country comparison to the world: 19

Crude oil—proved reserves: 142.4 million bbl (1 January 2010 est.)
country comparison to the world: 68

Refined petroleum products—production: 539,200 bbl/day (2013 est.)
country comparison to the world: 31

Refined petroleum products—consumption: 510,400 bbl/day (2014 est.)
country comparison to the world: 33

Refined petroleum products—exports: 127,300 bbl/day (2013 est.)
country comparison to the world: 43

Refined petroleum products—imports: 109,900 bbl/day (2013 est.)
country comparison to the world: 48

Natural gas—production: 6.08 billion cu m (2014 est.)
country comparison to the world: 49

Natural gas—consumption: 17.86 billion cu m (2014 est.)
country comparison to the world: 38

Natural gas—exports: 76 million cu m (2014 est.)
country comparison to the world: 46

Natural gas—imports: 11.82 billion cu m (2014 est.)

country comparison to the world: 23

Natural gas—proved reserves: 92 billion cu m (1 January 2014 est.)
country comparison to the world: 56

Carbon dioxide emissions from consumption of energy: 289.5 million Mt (2012 est.)
country comparison to the world: 24

COMMUNICATIONS

Telephones—fixed lines: *total subscriptions:* 5.04 million
subscriptions per 100 inhabitants: 13 (2014 est.)
country comparison to the world: 30

Telephones—mobile cellular: *total:* 59.8 million
subscriptions per 100 inhabitants: 155 (2014 est.)
country comparison to the world: 26

Telephone system: *general assessment:* modernization of the telecommunications network has accelerated with market-based competition; fixed-line service, dominated by the former state-owned company, is dwarfed by the growth in mobile-cellular services
domestic: mobile-cellular service available since 1993 and provided by four nation-wide networks; coverage is generally good with some gaps in the east; fixed-line service lags in rural areas
international: country code—48; international direct dialing with automated exchanges; satellite earth station—1 with access to Intelsat, Eutelsat, Inmarsat, and Intersputnik (2011)

Broadcast media: state-run public TV operates 2 National channels supplemented by 16 regional channels and several niche channels; privately owned entities operate several National TV networks and a number of special interest channels; many privately owned channels broadcasting locally; roughly half of all households are linked to either satellite or cable TV systems providing access to foreign television networks; state-run public radio operates 5 National networks and 17 regional radio stations; 2 privately owned National radio networks, several commercial stations broadcasting to multiple cities, and many privately owned local radio stations (2007)
Radio broadcast stations: AM 14, FM 63, short-wave 2 (2008)
Television broadcast stations: 75 (2008)

Internet country code: .pl

Internet hosts: 13.265 million (2012)
country comparison to the world: 12

Internet users: *total:* 25.9 million
percent of population: 67.2% (2014 est.)
country comparison to the world: 22

TRANSPORTATION

Airports: 126 (2013)
country comparison to the world: 47

Airports—with paved runways: *total:* 87
over 3,047 m: 5
2,438 to 3,047 m: 30
1,524 to 2,437 m: 36
914 to 1,523 m: 10
under 914 m: 6 (2013)

Airports—with unpaved runways: *total:* 39
1,524 to 2,437 m: 1
914 to 1,523 m: 17

under 914 m: 21 (2013)

Heliports: 6 (2013)

Pipelines: gas 14,198 km; oil 1,374 km; refined products 777 km (2013)

Railways: *total:* 19,837 km
broad gauge: 395 km 1.524-m gauge
standard gauge: 19,442 km 1.435-m gauge (11,899 km electrified) (2014)
country comparison to the world: 16

Roadways: *total:* 412,035 km
paved: 280,719 km (includes 2,418 km of expressways)
unpaved: 131,316 km (2012)
country comparison to the world: 16

Waterways: 3,997 km (navigable rivers and canals) (2009)
country comparison to the world: 27

Merchant marine: *total:* 9
by type: cargo 7, chemical tanker 1, passenger/cargo 1
registered in other countries: 106 (Antigua and Barbuda 2, Bahamas 34, Cyprus 24, Liberia 13, Malta 21, Saint Vincent and the Grenadines 3, Vanuatu 9) (2010)
country comparison to the world: 118

Ports and terminals: *major seaport(s):* Gdansk, Gdynia, Swinoujscie
river port(s): Szczecin (River Oder)
LNG terminal(s) (import): Swinoujscie

MILITARY AND SECURITY

Military branches: Polish Armed Forces: Land Forces, Navy, Air and Air Defense Aviation Forces, Special Forces (2013)

Military service age and obligation: 18–28 years of age for male and female voluntary military service; conscription phased out in 2009–12; service obligation shortened from 12 to 9 months in 2005; women only allowed to serve as officers and non commissioned officers (2013)

Military expenditures:
2% of GDP (2016)
2.27% of GDP (2015)
1.95% of GDP (2014)
1.95% of GDP (2013)
1.91% of GDP (2012)
1.83% of GDP (2011)
country comparison to the world: 44

TRANSNATIONAL ISSUES

Disputes—international: as a member state that forms part of the EU's external border, Poland has implemented the strict Schengen border rules to restrict illegal immigration and trade along its eastern borders with Belarus and Ukraine

Refugees and internally displaced persons: *refugees (country of origin):* 14,277 (Russia) (2014); 71,302 applicants for forms of legal stay other than asylum (Ukraine) (2015)
stateless persons: 10,825 (2015)

Illicit drugs: despite diligent counternarcotics measures and international information sharing on cross-border crimes, a major illicit producer of synthetic drugs for the international market; minor transshipment point for Southwest Asian heroin and Latin American cocaine to Western Europe

PORTUGAL

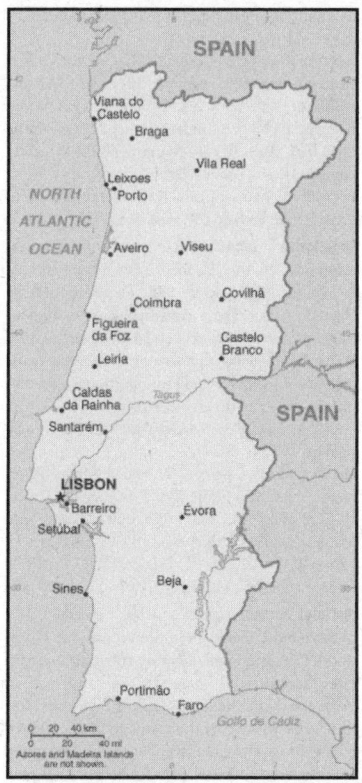

INTRODUCTION

Background: Following its heyday as a global maritime power during the 15th and 16th centuries, Portugal lost much of its wealth and status with the destruction of Lisbon in a 1755 earthquake, occupation during the napoleonic Wars, and the independence of Brazil, its wealthiest colony, in 1822. A 1910 revolution deposed the monarchy; for most of the next six decades, repressive governments ran the country. In 1974, a left-wing military coup installed broad democratic reforms. The following year, Portugal granted independence to all of its African colonies. Portugal is a founding member of NATO and entered the EC (now the EU) in 1986.

GEOGRAPHY

Location: Southwestern Europe, bordering the North Atlantic Ocean, west of Spain

Geographic coordinates: 39 30 N, 8 00 W

Map references: Europe

Area: *total:* 92,090 sq km
land: 91,470 sq km
water: 620 sq km

note: includes Azores and Madeira Islands
country comparison to the world: 111

Area—comparative: slightly smaller than Indiana

Land boundaries: *total:* 1,224 km
border countries (1): Spain 1,224 km

Coastline: 1,793 km

Maritime claims: *territorial sea:* 12 nm
contiguous zone: 24 nm
exclusive economic zone: 200 nm
continental shelf: 200-m depth or to the depth of exploitation

Climate: maritime temperate; cool and rainy in north, warmer and drier in south

Terrain: the west-flowing Tagus River divides the country: the north is mountainous toward the interior, while the south is characterized by rolling plains

Elevation: *mean elevation:* 372 m

elevation extremes: lowest point: Atlantic Ocean 0 m
highest point: Ponta do Pico (Pico or Pico Alto) on Ilha do Pico in the Azores 2,351 m

Natural resources: fish, forests (cork), iron ore, copper, zinc, tin, tungsten, silver, gold, uranium, marble, clay, gypsum, salt, arable land, hydropower

Land use: *agricultural land:* 39.7%
arable land: 11.9%
permanent crops: 7.8%
permanent pasture: 20%
forest: 37.8%
other: 22.5% (2011 est.)

Irrigated land: 5,400 sq km (2012)

Total renewable water resources: 68.7 cu km (2011)

Freshwater withdrawal (domestic/industrial/agricultural): *total:* 8.46 cu km/yr (12%/18%/69%)
per capita: 812 cu m/yr (2005)

Natural hazards: Azores subject to severe earthquakes
volcanism: limited volcanic activity in the Azores Islands; Fayal or Faial (elev. 1,043 m) last erupted in 1958; most volcanoes have not erupted in centuries; historically active volcanoes include Agua de Pau, Furnas, Pico, Picos Volcanic System, San Jorge, Sete Cidades, and Terceira

Environment—current issues: soil erosion; air pollution caused by industrial and vehicle emissions; water pollution, especially in coastal areas

Environment—international agreements: *party to:* Air Pollution, Biodiversity, Climate Change, Climate Change-Kyoto Protocol, Desertification, Endangered Species, Hazardous Wastes, Law of the Sea, Marine Dumping, Marine Life Conservation, Ozone Layer Protection, Ship Pollution, Tropical Timber 83, Tropical Timber 94, Wetlands, Whaling
signed, but not ratified: Air Pollution-Persistent Organic Pollutants, Air Pollution-Volatile Organic Compounds, Environmental Modification

Geography—note: Azores and Madeira Islands occupy strategic locations along western sea approach es to Strait of Gibraltar

PEOPLE AND SOCIETY

Nationality: *noun:* Portuguese (singular and plural)
adjective: Portuguese

Ethnic groups: homogeneous Mediterranean stock; citizens of black African descent WHO immigrated to mainland during decolonization number less than 100,000; since 1990 East Europeans have entered Portugal

Languages: Portuguese (official), Mirandese (official, but locally used)

Religions: Roman Cath olic 81%, other Ch ristian 3.3%, other (includes Jewish, Muslim, oth er) 0.6%, none 6.8%, unspecified 8.3%
note: represents population 15 years of age and older (2011 est.)

Population: 10,825,309 (July 2015 est.)
country comparison to the world: 81

Age structure: *0–14 years:* 15.68% (male 884,389/female 812,685)
15–24 years: 11.41% (male 655,259/female 580,020)
25–54 years: 42.05% (male 2,303,473/female 2,248,914)
55–64 years: 11.97% (male 604,549/female 691,216)
65 years and over: 18.89% (male 836,679/female 1,208,125) (2015 est.)

Dependency ratios: *total dependency ratio:* 53.5%
youth dependency ratio: 21.6%
elderly dependency ratio: 31.9%
potential support ratio: 3.1% (2015 est.)

Median age: *total:* 41.5 years
male: 39.4 years
female: 43.6 years (2015 est.)
country comparison to the world: 31

Population growth rate: 0.09% (2015 est.)
country comparison to the world: 189

Birth rate: 9.27 births/1,000 population (2015 est.)
country comparison to the world: 205

Death rate: 11.02 deaths/1,000 population (2015 est.)
country comparison to the world: 33

Net migration rate: 2.67 migrant(s)/1,000 population (2015 est.)
country comparison to the world: 39

Urbanization: *urban population:* 63.5% of total population (2015)
rate of urbanization: 0.97% annual rate of change (2010–15 est.)

Major urban areas—population: LISBON (capital) 2.884 million; Porto 1.299 million (2015)

Sex ratio: *at birth:* 1.07 male(s)/female
0–14 years: 1.09 male(s)/female

15–24 years: 1.13 male(s)/female
25–54 years: 1.02 male(s)/female
55–64 years: 0.88 male(s)/female
65 years and over: 0.69 male(s)/female
total population: 0.95 male(s)/female (2015 est.)

Mother's mean age at first birth: 29.5 (2012 est.)

Maternal mortality rate: 10 deaths/100,000 live births (2015 est.)
country comparison to the world: 162

Infant mortality rate: *total:* 4.43 deaths/1,000 live births
male: 4.86 deaths/1,000 live births
female: 3.97 deaths/1,000 live births (2015 est.)
country comparison to the world: 185

Life expectancy at birth: *total population:* 79.16 years
male: 75.92 years
female: 82.62 years (2015 est.)
country comparison to the world: 49

Total fertility rate: 1.52 children born/woman (2015 est.)
country comparison to the world: 192

Contraceptive prevalence rate: 86.8% (2005/06)

Health expenditures: 9.7% of GDP (2013)
country comparison to the world: 29

Physicians density: 4.1 physicians/1,000 population (2012)

Hospital bed density: 3.4 beds/1,000 population (2011)

Drinking water source:
improved:
urban: 100% of population
rural: 100% of population
total: 100% of population
unimproved:
urban: 0% of population
rural: 0% of population
total: 0% of population (2015 est.)

Sanitation facility access:
improved:
urban: 99.6% of population
rural: 99.8% of population
total: 99.7% of population
unimproved:
urban: 0.4% of population
rural: 0.2% of population
total: 0.3% of population (2015 est.)

HIV/AIDS—adult prevalence rate: NA

HIV/AIDS—people living with HIV/AIDS: NA

HIV/AIDS—deaths: NA

Obesity—adult prevalence rate: 22.1% (2014)
country comparison to the world: 69

Education expenditures: 5.1% of GDP (2011)
country comparison to the world: 55

Literacy: *definition:* age 15 and over can read and write
total population: 95.7%
male: 97.1%
female: 94.4% (2015 est.)

School life expectancy (primary to tertiary education): *total:* 17 years
male: 17 years

female: 17 years (2014)

Unemployment, youth ages 15–24: *total:* 38.1%
male: 36.7%
female: 39.6% (2013 est.)
country comparison to the world: 16

GOVERNMENT

Country name: *conventional long form:* Portuguese Republic
conventional short form: Portugal
local long form: Republica Portuguesa
local short form: Portugal
etymology: name derives from the Roman designation "Portus Cale" meaning "Port of Cale"; Cale was an ancient Celtic town and port in present-day northern Portugal

Government type: semi-presidential republic

Capital: *name:* Lisbon

Geographic coordinates: 38 43 N, 9 08 W
time difference: UTC 0 (5 hours ahead of Washington, DC, during Standard Time)
daylight saving time: +1hr, begins last Sunday in March; ends last Sunday in October

Administrative divisions: 18 districts (distritos, singular—distrito) and 2 autonomous regions* (regioes autonomas, singular—regiao autonoma); Aveiro, Acores (Azores) *, Beja, Braga, Braganca, Castelo Branco, Coimbra, Evora, Faro, Guarda, Leiria, Lisboa (Lisbon), Madeira*, Portalegre, Porto, Santarem, Setubal, Viana do Castelo, Vila Real, Viseu

Independence: 1143 (Kingdom of Portugal recognized); 5 October 1910 (republic proclaimed)

National holiday: Portugal Day (Dia de Portugal), 10 June (1580); note—also called Camoes Day, the day that revered National poet Luis de Camoes (1524–80) died

Constitution: several previous; latest adopted 2 April 1976, effective 25 April 1976; amended several times, last in 2005 (2016)

Legal system: civil law system; Constitutional Court review of legislative acts

International law organization participation: accepts compulsory ICJ jurisdiction with reservations; accepts ICCt jurisdiction

Citizenship: *citizenship by birth:* no
citizenship by descent only: at least one parent must be a citizen of Portugal
dual citizenship recognized: yes
residency requirement for naturalization: 10 years; 6 years if from a Portuguese speaking country

Suffrage: 18 years of age; universal

Executive branch: *chief of state:* President Marcelo REBELO DE SO USA (since 9 March 2016)

head of government: Prime Minister Antonio Luis Santos da COSTA (since 24 November 2015)
cabinet: Council of Ministers appointed by the president on the recommendation of the prime minister
elections/appointments: president directly elected by absolute majority popular vote in 2 rounds if needed for a 5-year term (eligible for a

second term); election last held on 24 January 2016 (next to be held in January 2021); following legislative elections which must be held by October 2015, the leader of the majority party or majority coalition usually appointed prime minister by the president
election results: Marcelo REBELO DE SOUSA elected president; percent of vote—Marcelo REBELO DE SO USA (PSD) 52%, Antonio Sampaio da NOVA (independent) 22.9%, Marisa MATISA (BE) 10.1%, Maria de BELEM (independent) 4.2%, other 10.8%
note: there is also a Council of State that acts as a consultative body to the president

Legislative branch: *description:* unicameral Assembly of the Republic or Assembleia da Republica (230 seats; 226 members directly elected in multi-seat constituencies by proportional representation vote and 4 members—2 each in 2 constituencies representing Portuguese living abroad—directly elected by proportional representation vote; members serve 4-year terms)
elections: last held on 4 October 2015 (next to be held by October 2019)
election results: percent of vote by party—Portugal Ahead Coalition (PAF) 36.9%, PS 32.3%, B. E.10.2%, CDU 8.2%, PPD/PSD (Azores and Madeira) 1.5%, PAN 1.4%, other 9.5%; seats by party—PAF 102, PS 86, B.E.19, CDU 17, PPD/PSD (Azores and Madeira) 5, PAN 1

Judicial branch: *highest court(s):* Supreme Court or Supremo Tribunal de Justica (consists of 12 justices); Constitutional Court or Tribunal Constitucional (consists of 13 judges)
judge selection and term of office: Supreme Court justices nominated by the president and appointed by the Assembly of the Republic; judges appointed for life; Constitutional Court judges—10 elected by the Assembly and 3 elected by the other Constitutional Court judges; judges elected for 6-year non-renewable terms
subordinate courts: Supreme Administrative Court (Supremo Tribunal Administrativo); Audit Court (Tribunal de Contas); appellate, district, and municipal courts

Political parties and leaders: Democratic and Social Center/Popular Party or CDS/PP [Paulo PORTAS]
Ecologist Party (The Greens) or PEV [Heloisa APOLONIA]
Portuguese Communist Party or PCP [Jeronimo DE SOUSA]
Portugal Ahead Coalition or PAF (includes PSD and CDS/PP)
Social Democratic Party or PPD/PSD [Pedro PASSOS COELHO]
Socialist Party or PS [Antonio COSTA]
The Left Bloc or BE [Catarina Soares MARTINS]
Unitarian Democratic Coalition or CDU [Jeronimo DESOUSA] (includes Portuguese Communist Party or PCP and Ecologist Party ("The Greens") or PEV)

Political pressure groups and leaders: Armed Forces Officers' Association or AOFA [Colonel Pereira CRACEL] the Desperate Generation (youth movement protesting against low wages, precarious labor conditions, and unemployment)

General Workers Union or General Confederation of Portuguese Workers or UGT [Carlos SILVA] Portuguese National Workers' Conference or CGTP [Armenio CARLOS]

TugaLeaks (a website that has become a mouthpiece for publicizing diverse protest action)

other: the media; labor unions

International organization participation: ADB (nonregional member), AfDB (nonregional member), Australia Group, BIS, CD, CE, CERN, CPLP, EAPC, EBRD, ECB, EIB, EMU, ESA, EU, FAO, FATF, IADB, IAEA, IBRD, ICAO, ICC (National committees), ICCt, ICRM, IDA, IEA, IFAD, IFC, IFRCS, IHO, ILO, IMF, IMO, IMSO, Interpol, IOC, IOM, IPU, ISO, ITSO, ITU, ITUC (NGOs), LAIA (observer), MIGA, MINUSMA, NATO, NEA, NSG, OAS (observer), OECD, OPCW, OSCE, Pacific Alliance (observer), Paris Club (associate), PCA, Schengen Convention, SELEC (observer), UN, UNCTAD, UNESCO, UNHCR, UNIDO, Union Latina, UNWTO, UPU, WCO, WFTU (NGOs), WHO, WIPO, WMO, WTO, ZC

Diplomatic representation in the US: *chief of mission:* Ambassador Domingos T?eixeira de Abreu Fezas VITAL (since 28 January 2016)

chancery: 2012 Massachusetts Avenue NW, Washington, DC 20036

telephone: [1] (202) 328-8610

FAX: [1] (202) 462-3726

consulate(s) general: Boston, New York, San Francisco

consulate(s): New Bedford (MA), Newark (NJ), Providence (RI)

Diplomatic representation from the US: *chief of mission:* Ambassador Robert A. SHERMAN (since 30 May 2014)

embassy: Avenida das Forcas Armadas, 1600–081 Lisbon

mailing address: Apartado 43033, 1601–301 Lisboa; PSC 83, APO AE 09726

telephone: [351] (21) 727-3300

FAX: [351] (21) 726-9109

consulate(s): Ponta Delgada (Azores)

Flag description: two vertical bands of green (hoist side, two-fifths) and red (three-fifths) with the National coat of arms (armillary sphere and Portuguese shield) centered on the dividing line; explanations for the color meanings are ambiguous, but a popular interpretation has green symbolizing hope and red the blood of those defending the nation

National symbol(s): armillary sphere (a spherical astrolabe modeling objects in the sky and representing the Republic); national colors: red, green

National anthem: *name:* "A Portugesa" (The Song of the Portuguese)

lyrics/music: Henrique LOPES DE MENDOCA/ Alfredo KEIL

note: adopted 1910; "A Portuguesa" was originally written to protest the Portuguese monarchy's acquiescence to the 1890 British ultimatum forcing Portugal to give up areas of Africa; the lyrics refer to the "insult" that resulted from the event

ECONOMY

Economy—overview: Portugal has become a diversified and increasingly service-based economy since joining the European Community—the EU's predecessor—in 1986. Over the following two decades, successive governments privatized many state-controlled firms and liberalized key areas of the economy, including the financial and telecommunications sectors. The country joined the Economic and Monetary Union in 1999 and began circulating the euro on 1 January 2002 along with 11 other EU members.

The economy grew by more than the EU average for much of the 1990s, but the rate of growth slowed in 2001–08. The economy contracted in 2009, and fell again from 2011 to 2014, as the government implemented spending cuts and tax increases to comply with conditions of an EU-IMF financial rescue package, signed in May 2011. A modest recovery began in 2013 and gathered steam in 2014 due to strong export performance and a rebound in private consumption. Although austerity measures were instituted to reduce the large budget deficit, they contributed to record unemployment and a wave of emigration not seen since the 1960s.

A continued reduction in private- and public-sector debt could weigh on consumption and investment in 2016, holding back a stronger recovery. The prior center-right government passed legislation aimed at reducing labor market rigidity, and, this, along with sustained fiscal discipline, could make Portugal more attractive to foreign direct investment. Under the center-right government, the budget deficit fell from 11.2% of GDP in 2010 to 3.5% in 2015, reaching the EU-IMF target of 4%, but still above its EU fiscal obligations, under the excessive deficit procedure. EU-IMF financing expired in May 2014. The new center-left Socialist government, however, has signaled that it will unwind spending cuts associated with austerity while remaining within EU fiscal targets.

GDP (purchasing power parity): $289.8 billion (2015 est.)

$285.6 billion (2014 est.)

$283 billion (2013 est.)

note: data are in 2015 US dollars

country comparison to the world: 53

GDP (official exchange rate): $199.1 billion (2015 est.)

GDP—real growth rate: 1.5% (2015 est.)

0.9% (2014 est.)

-1.1% (2013 est.)

country comparison to the world: 158

GDP—per capita (PPP): $27,800 (2015 est.)

$27,500 (2014 est.)

$27,100 (2013 est.)

note: data are in 2015 US dollars

country comparison to the world: 66

Gross national saving: 15.6% of GDP (2015 est.)

15.3% of GDP (2014 est.)

15.3% of GDP (2013 est.)

country comparison to the world: 109

GDP—composition, by end use:

household consumption: 66.2%

government consumption: 18.5%

investment in fixed capital: 15.3%

investment in inventories: 0.3%

exports of goods and services: 41.4%

imports of goods and services: -41.7% (2015 est.)

GDP—composition, by sector of origin:

agriculture: 2.3%

industry: 21.6%

services: 76.1% (2015 est.)

Agriculture—products: grain, potatoes, tomatoes, olives, grapes; sheep, cattle, goats, pigs, poultry, dairy products; fish

Industries: textiles, clothing, footwear, wood and cork, paper and pulp, chemicals, lubricants, automobiles and auto parts, base metals, minerals, porcelain and ceramics, glassware, technology, telecommunications; dairy products, wine, other foodstuffs; ship construction and refurbishment; tourism, plastics, financial services, optics

Industrial production growth rate: 2% (2015 est.)

country comparison to the world: 118

Labor force: 5.223 million (2015 est.)

country comparison to the world: 78

Labor force—by occupation: *agriculture:* 8.6%

industry: 23.9%

services: 67.5% (2014 est.)

Unemployment rate: 12.6% (2015 est.)

13.9% (2014 est.)

country comparison to the world: 137

Population below poverty line: 18.7% (2012 est.)

Household income or consumption by percentage share: *lowest:* 10%: 3.1%

highest: 10%: 28.4% (1995 est.)

Distribution of family income—Gini index: 34.2 (2013 est.)

34.2 (2012 est.)

country comparison to the world: 98

Budget: *revenues:* $89.94 billion

expenditures: $96.84 billion (2015 est.)

Taxes and other revenues: 45.5% of GDP (2015 est.)

country comparison to the world: 22

Budget surplus (+) or deficit (–): -3.5% of GDP (2015 est.)

country comparison to the world: 130

Public debt: 129% of GDP (2015 est.)

130.2% of GDP (2014 est.)

note: data cover general government debt, and includes debt instruments issued (or owned) by government entities other than the treasury; the data include treasury debt held by foreign entities; the data include debt issued by sub national entities, as well as intra-governmental debt; intra-governmental debt consists of treasury borrowings from surpluses in the social funds, such as for retirement, medical care, and unemployment; debt instruments for the social funds are not sold at public auctions

country comparison to the world: 6

687

Fiscal year: calendar year

Inflation rate (consumer prices): 0.5% (2015 est.) -0.2% (2014 est.)
country comparison to the world: 63

Central bank discount rate: 0.05% (31 December 2014)
0.25% (31 December 2013)
note: this is the European Central Bank's rate on the marginal lending facility, which offers overnight credit to banks in the euro area
country comparison to the world: 150

Commercial bank prime lending rate: 5.1% (31 December 2015 est.)
5.3% (31 December 2014 est.)
country comparison to the world: 145

Stock of narrow money: $61.64 billion (31 December 2015 est.)
$66.76 billion (31 December 2014 est.)
note: see entry for the European Union for money supply for the entire euro area; the European Central Bank (ECB) controls monetary policy for the 18 members of the Economic and Monetary Union (EMU); individual members of the EMU do not control the quantity of money circulating within their own borders
country comparison to the world: 48

Stock of broad money: $296.1 billion (31 December 2014 est.)
$316.2 billion (31 December 2013 est.)
country comparison to the world: 34

Stock of domestic credit: $335.8 billion (31 December 2015 est.)
$366.2 billion (31 December 2014 est.)
country comparison to the world: 36

Market value of publicly traded shares: $126.8 billion (31 December 2014 est.)
$57.04 billion (31 December 2013)
$65.53 billion (31 December 2012 est.)
country comparison to the world: 40

Current account balance: $901 million (2015 est.)
$280 million (2014 est.)
country comparison to the world: 39

Exports: $57.2 billion (2015 est.)
$62.92 billion (2014 est.)
country comparison to the world: 46

Exports—commodities: agricultural products, foodstuffs, wine, oil products, chemical products, plastics and rubber, hides, leather, wood and cork, wood pulp and paper, textile materials, clothing, footwear, machinery and tools, base metals

Exports—partners: Spain 25%, France 12.1%, Germany 11.8%, UK 6.7%, US 5.2%, Angola 4.2%, Netherlands 4% (2015)

Imports: $66.44 billion (2015 est.)
$74.81 billion (2014 est.)
country comparison to the world: 41

Imports—commodities: agricultural products, chemical products, vehicles and other transport material, optical and precision instruments, computer accessories and parts, semiconductors and related devices, oil products, base metals, food products, textile materials

Imports—partners: Spain 32.9%, Germany 12.9%, France 7.4%, Italy 5.4%, Netherlands 5.1% (2015)

Reserves of foreign exchange and gold: $19.62 billion (31 December 2014 est.)
$17.55 billion (31 December 2013 est.)
country comparison to the world: 59

Debt—external: $493.7 billion (31 December 2014 est.)
$531.6 billion (31 December 2013 est.)
country comparison to the world: 27

Stock of direct foreign investment—at home: $169.1 billion (31 December 2015 est.)
$157.3 billion (31 December 2014 est.)
country comparison to the world: 32

Stock of direct foreign investment—abroad: $99.55 billion (31 December 2015 est.)
$99.55 billion (31 December 2014 est.)
country comparison to the world: 31

Exchange rates: euros (EUR) per US dollar—
0.885 (2015 est.)
0.7525 (2014 est.)
0.7634 (2013 est.)
0.78 (2012 est.)
0.7185 (2011 est.)

ENERGY

Electricity—production: 51.67 billion kWh (2013 est.)
country comparison to the world: 52

Electricity—consumption: 46.25 billion kWh (2013 est.)
country comparison to the world: 51

Electricity—exports: 5.324 billion kWh (2013 est.)
country comparison to the world: 30

Electricity—imports: 8.1 billion kWh (2013 est.)
country comparison to the world: 28

Electricity—installed generating capacity: 19.62 million kW (2013 est.)
country comparison to the world: 41

Electricity—from fossil fuels: 42.4% of total installed capacity (2013 est.)
country comparison to the world: 162

Electricity—from nuclear fuels: 0% of total installed capacity (2013 est.)
country comparison to the world: 166

Electricity—from hydroelectric plants: 28.2% of total installed capacity (2013 est.)
country comparison to the world: 83

Electricity—from other renewable sources: 29.4% of total installed capacity (2013 est.)
country comparison to the world: 6

Crude oil—production: 0 bbl/day (2014 est.)
country comparison to the world: 181

Crude oil—exports: 0 bbl/day (2013 est.)
country comparison to the world: 177

Crude oil—imports: 282,400 bbl/day (2013 est.)
country comparison to the world:

Crude oil—proved reserves: 538,100 bbl (1 January 2015 est.)
country comparison to the world: 100

Refined petroleum products—production: 285,300 bbl/day (2013 est.)
country comparison to the world: 45

Refined petroleum products—consumption: 244,200 bbl/day (2014 est.)
country comparison to the world: 50

Refined petroleum products—exports: 168,000 bbl/day (2013 est.)
country comparison to the world: 38

Refined petroleum products—imports: 86,720 bbl/day (2013 est.)
country comparison to the world: 57

Natural gas—production: 0 cu m (2014 est.)
country comparison to the world: 119

Natural gas—consumption: 4.005 billion cu m (2014 est.)
country comparison to the world: 65

Natural gas—exports: 0 cu m (2014 est.)
country comparison to the world: 165

Natural gas—imports: 4.069 billion cu m (2014 est.)
country comparison to the world: 35

Natural gas—proved reserves: 0 cu m (1 January 2014 est.)
country comparison to the world: 185

Carbon dioxide emissions from consumption of energy: 68.8 million Mt (2012 est.)
country comparison to the world: 49

COMMUNICATIONS

Telephones—fixed lines: *total subscriptions:* 4.59 million
subscriptions per 100 inhabitants: 42 (2014 est.)
country comparison to the world: 34

Telephones—mobile cellular: *total:* 11.9 million
subscriptions per 100 inhabitants: 110 (2014 est.)
country comparison to the world: 76

Telephone system: *general assessment:* Portugal's telephone system has a state-of-the-art network with broadband, highspeed capabilities
domestic: integrated network of coaxial cables, open-wire, microwave radio relay, and domestic satellite earth stations
international: country code—351; a combination of submarine cables provide connectivity to Europe, North and East Africa, South Africa, the Middle East, Asia, and the US; satellite earth stations—3 Intelsat (2 Atlantic Ocean and 1 Indian Ocean), NA Eutelsat; tropospheric scatter to Azores (2010)

Broadcast media: Radio e Televisao de Portugal (RTP), the publicly owned TV broadcaster, operates 2 domestic channels and external service channels to Africa; overall, roughly 40 domestic TV stations; viewers have widespread access to international broadcasters with more than half of all households connected to multi—channel cable or satellite TV systems; publicly owned radio operates 3 National networks and provides regional and external services; several privately owned National radio stations and some 300 regional and local commercial radio stations (2008)
Radio broadcast stations: AM 2, FM 63, shortwave 1 (2008)
Television broadcast stations: 42 (2008)

Internet country code: .pt

Internet hosts: 3.748 million (2012)
country comparison to the world: 28

Internet users: *total:* 7.2 million
percent of population: 66.1% (2014 est.)
country comparison to the world: 52

TRANSPORTATION

Airports: 64 (2013)
country comparison to the world: 77

Airports—with paved runways: *total:* 43
over 3,047 m: 5
2,438 to 3,047 m: 7
1,524 to 2,437 m: 8
914 to 1,523 m: 15
under 914 m: 8 (2013)

Airports—with unpaved runways: *total:* 21
914 to 1,523 m: 1
under 914 m: 20 (2013)

Pipelines: gas 1,344 km; oil 11 km; refined products 188 km (2013)

Railways: *total:* 3,075.1 km
broad gauge: 2,439 km 1.668-m gauge (1,633.4 km electrified)
narrow gauge: 108.1 km 1.000-m gauge
other: 528 km (gauge unspecified) (2014)
country comparison to the world: 58

Roadways: *total:* 82,900 km

paved: 71,294 km (includes 2,613 km of expressways)
unpaved: 11,606 km (2008)
country comparison to the world: 57

Waterways: 210 km (on Douro River from Porto) (2011)
country comparison to the world: 95

Merchant marine: *total:* 109
by type: bulk carrier 8, cargo 35, carrier 1, chemical tanker 21, container 7, liquefied gas 6, passenger 13, passenger/cargo 5, petroleum tanker 3, roll on/roll off 1, vehicle carrier 9
foreign-owned: 81 (Belgium 8, Colombia 1, Denmark 4, Germany 14, Greece 2, Italy 12, Japan 9, Mexico 1, Norway 2, Spain 18, Sweden 3, Switzerland 3, US 4)
registered in other countries: 15 (Cyprus 2, Malta 3, Panama 10) (2010)
country comparison to the world: 48

Ports and terminals: major seaport(s): Leixoes, Lisbon, Setubal, Sines
LNG terminal (import): Sines

MILITARY AND SECURITY

Military branches: Portuguese Army (Exercito Portuguesa), Portuguese Navy (Marinha Portuguesa; includes Marine Corps), Portuguese Air Force (Forca Aerea Portuguesa, FAP) (2013)

Military service age and obligation: 18–30 years of age for voluntary military service; no compulsory military service, but conscription possible if insufficient volunteers available; women serve in the armed forces, on naval ships since 1993, but are prohibited from serving in some combatant specialties; reserve obligation to age 35 (2012)

Military expenditures:
1.29% of GDP (2014)
1.2% of GDP (2013)
1.78% of GDP (2012)
country comparison to the world: 77

TRANSNATIONAL ISSUES

Disputes—international: Portugal does not recognize Spanish sovereignty over the territory of Olivenza based on a difference of interpretation of the 1815 Congress of Vienna and the 1801 Treaty of Badajoz

Refugees and internally displaced persons: *stateless persons:* 14 (2015)

Illicit drugs: seizing record amounts of Latin American cocaine destined for Europe; a European gateway for Southwest Asian heroin; transshipment point for hashish from North Africa to Europe; consumer of Southwest Asian heroin

PUERTO RICO

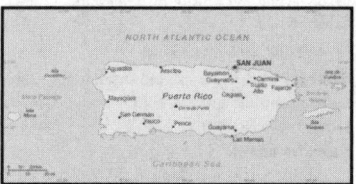

INTRODUCTION

Background: Populated for centuries by aboriginal peoples, the island was claimed by the Spanish Crown in 1493 following Christopher COLUMBUS' second voyage to the Americas. In 1898, after 400 years of colonial rule that saw the indigenous population nearly exterminated and African slave labor introduced, Puerto Rico was ceded to the US as a result of the Spanish-American War. Puerto Ricans were granted US citizenship in 1917. Popularly elected governors have served since 1948. In 1952, a constitution was enacted providing for internal self government. In plebiscites held in 1967, 1993, and 1998, voters chose not to alter the existing political status with the US, but the results of a 2012 vote left open the possibility of American statehood. Economic recession on the island has led to a net population loss since about 2005, as large numbers of residents

moved to the US mainland. The trend has accelerated since 2010; in 2014, Puerto Rico experienced a net population loss to the mainland of 64,000, more than double the net loss of 26,000 in 2010.

GEOGRAPHY

Location: Caribbean, island between the Caribbean Sea and the North Atlantic Ocean, east of the Dominican Republic

Geographic coordinates: 18 15 N, 66 30 W

Map references: Central America and the Caribbean

Area: *total:* 13,791 sq km
land: 8,870 sq km
water: 4,921 sq km
country comparison to the world: 163

Area—comparative: slightly less than three times the size of Rhode Island

Land boundaries: 0 km

Coastline: 501 km

Maritime claims: *territorial sea:* 12 nm
exclusive economic zone: 200 nm

Climate: tropical marine, mild; little seasonal temperature variation

Terrain: mostly mountains with coastal plain in north; precipitous mountains to the sea on west coast; sandy beaches along most coastal areas

Elevation: *mean elevation:* 261 m

elevation extremes: *lowest point:* Caribbean Sea 0 m
highest point: Cerro de Punta 1,338 m

Natural resources: some copper and nickel; potential for onshore and offshore oil

Land use: *agricultural land:* 22%
arable land: 6.6%
permanent crops: 5.6%
permanent pasture: 9.8%
forest: 63.2%
other: 14.8% (2011 est.)

Irrigated land: 220 sq km (2012)

Natural hazards: periodic droughts; hurricanes

Environment—current issues: soil erosion; occasional drought causing water shortages

Geography—note: important location along the Mona Passage—a key shipping lane to the Panama Canal; San Juan is one of the biggest and best Natural harbors in the Caribbean; many small rivers and high central mountains ensure land is well watered; south coast relatively dry; fertile coastal plain belt in north

PEOPLE AND SOCIETY

Nationality: *noun:* Puerto Rican(s) (US citizens)
adjective: Puerto Rican

Ethnic groups: white 75.8%, black/African American 12.4%, other 8.5% (includes American

689

Indian, Alaskan native, native Hawaiian, other Pacific Islander, and others), mixed 3.3%
note: 99% of the population is Latino (2010 est.)

Languages: Spanish, English

Religions: Roman Catholic 85%, Protestant and other 15%

Population: 3,598,357 (July 2015 est.)
country comparison to the world: 131

Age structure: *0–14 years:* 17.72% (male 325,944/female 311,520)
15–24 years: 14.3% (male 263,337/female 251,215)
25–54 years: 38.39% (male 661,124/female 720,160)
55–64 years: 12.1% (male 197,073/female 238,351)
65 years and over: 17.5% (male 271,633/female 358,000) (2015 est.)

Dependency ratios: *total dependency ratio:* 50%
youth dependency ratio: 28.3%
elderly dependency ratio: 21.7%
potential support ratio: 4.6% (2015 est.)

Median age: *total:* 39.1 years
male: 37.1 years
female: 41 years (2015 est.)
country comparison to the world: 54

Population growth rate: -0.6% (2015 est.)
country comparison to the world: 227

Birth rate: 10.86 births/1,000 population (2015 est.)
country comparison to the world: 180

Death rate: 8.67 deaths/1,000 population (2015 est.)
country comparison to the world: 73

Net migration rate: -8.15 migrant(s)/1,000 population (2015 est.)
country comparison to the world: 208

Urbanization: *urban population:* 93.6% of total population (2015)
rate of urbanization: -0.21% annual rate of change (2010–15 est.)

Major urban areas—population: SANJUAN (capital) 2.463 million (2015)

Sex ratio: *at birth:* 1.02 male(s)/female
0–14 years: 1.05 male(s)/female
15–24 years: 1.05 male(s)/female
25–54 years: 0.92 male(s)/female
55–64 years: 0.83 male(s)/female
65 years and over: 0.76 male(s)/female
total population: 0.92 male(s)/female (2015 est.)

Maternal mortality rate: 14 deaths/100,000 live births (2015 est.)
country comparison to the world: 140

Infant mortality rate: *total:* 7.57 deaths/1,000 live births
male: 8.38 deaths/1,000 live births
female: 6.75 deaths/1,000 live births (2015 est.)
country comparison to the world: 157

Life expectancy at birth: *total population:* 79.25 years
male: 75.62 years
female: 82.94 years (2015 est.)

country comparison to the world: 48

Total fertility rate: 1.64 children born/woman (2015 est.)
country comparison to the world: 176

Drinking water source:
improved:
urban: 93.6% of population
rural: 93.6% of population
total: 93.6% of population
unimproved:
urban: 6.4% of population
rural: 6.4% of population
total: 6.4% of population (2001 est.)

Sanitation facility access:
improved:
urban: 99.3% of population
rural: 99.3% of population
total: 99.3% of population
unimproved:
urban: 0.7% of population
rural: 0.7% of population
total: 0.7% of population (2015 est.)

HIV/AIDS—adult prevalence rate: NA

HIV/AIDS—people living with HIV/AIDS: NA

HIV/AIDS—deaths: NA

Education expenditures: 6.4% of GDP (2013)

Literacy: *definition:* age 15 and over can read and write
total population: 93.3%
male: 92.8%
female: 93.8% (2015 est.)

School life expectancy (primary to tertiary education): *total:* 15 years
male: 14 years
female: 15 years (2013)

Unemployment, youth ages 15–24: *total:* 26.6%
male: 28.9%
female: 23.1% (2012 est.)
country comparison to the world: 33

GOVERNMENT

Country name: *conventional long form:* Commonwealth of Puerto Rico
conventional short form: Puerto Rico
etymology: Christopher COLUMBUS named the island San Juan Bautista (Saint John the Baptist) and the capital city and main port Cuidad de Puerto Rico (Rich Port City); over time, however, the names were shortened and transposed and the island came to be called Puerto Rico and its capital San Juan

Dependency status: unincorporated, organized territory of the US with commonwealth status; policy relations between Puerto Rico and the US conducted under the jurisdiction of the Office of the President

Government type: presidential democracy; a self-governing commonwealth in political association with the US

Capital: *name:* San Juan

Geographic coordinates: 18 28 N, 66 07 W

time difference: UTC-4 (1 hour ahead of Washington, DC, during Standard Time)

Administrative divisions: none (territory of the US with commonwealth status); there are no first-order administrative divisions as defined by the US Government, but there are 78 municipalities (municipios, singular—municipio) at the second order; Adjuntas, Aguada, Aguadilla, Aguas Buenas, Aibonito, Anasco, Arecibo, Arroyo, Barceloneta, Barranquitas, Bayamon, Cabo Rojo, Caguas, Camuy, Canovanas, Carolina, Catano, Cayey, Ceiba, Ciales, Cidra, Coamo, Comerio, Corozal, Culebra, Dorado, Fajardo, Florida, Guanica, Guayama, Guayanilla, Guaynabo, Gurabo, Hatillo, Hormigueros, Humacao, Isabela, Jayuya, Juana Diaz, Juncos, Lajas, Lares, Las Marias, Las Piedras, Loiza, Luquillo, Manati, Maricao, Maunabo, Mayaguez, Moca, Morovis, Naguabo, naranjito, Orocovis, Patillas, Penuelas, Ponce, Quebradillas, Rincon, Rio Grande, Sabana Grande, Salinas, San German, San Juan, San Lorenzo, San Sebastian, Santa Isabel, Toa Alta, Toa Baja, Trujillo Alto, Utuado, Vega Alta, Vega Baja, Vieques, Villalba, Yabucoa, Yauco

Independence: none (territory of the US with commonwealth status)

National holiday: US Independence Day, 4 July (1776); Puerto Rico Constitution Day, 25 July (1952)

Constitution: previous 1900 (Organic Act, or Foraker Act); latest ratified 3 March 1952, approved 3 July 1952, effective 25 July 1952 (2016)

Legal system: civil law system based on the Spanish civil code and within the framework of the US federal system

Citizenship: see United States

Suffrage: 18 years of age; universal; note—island residents are US citizens but do not vote in US presidential elections

Executive branch: *chief of state:* President Barack H. OBAMA (since 20 January 2009); Vice President Joseph R. BIDEN (since 20 January 2009)

head of government: Governor Alejandro GARCIA Padilla (since 2 January 2013)
cabinet: Cabinet appointed by governor with the consent of the Legislative Assembly
elections/appointments: president and vice president indirectly elected on the same ballot by an Electoral College of 'electors' chosen from each state; president and vice president serve a 4-year term (eligible for a second term); under the US Constitution, residents of Puerto Rico do not vote in elections for US president and vice president; however, they may vote in Democratic and Republican party presidential primary elections; governor directly elected by simple majority popular vote for a 4-year term (no term limits); election last held on 6 November 2012 (next to be held in November 2016)
election results: Alejandro GARCIA Padilla elected governor; percent of vote—Alejandro GARCIA Padilla (Democratic Party) 48.2%, Luis FORTUNO (PNP) 47.1%, other 4.7%

Legislative branch: *description:* bicameral Legislative Assembly or Asamblea Legislativa consists of the Senate or Senado (27 seats; 16 members directly elected in multi-seat constituencies by simple majority vote and 11 at-large members directly elected by simple majority vote to serve 4-year terms); the House of Representatives or Camara de Representantes (51 seats; members directly elected in single-seat constituencies by simple majority vote to serve 4-year terms)

elections: Senate—last held on 6 November 2012 (next to be held on 8 November 2016); House of Representatives—last held on 6 November 2012 (next to be held on 8 November 2016)

election results: Senate—percent of vote by party—NA; seats by party—PPD 18, PNP 8, PIP 1; House of Representatives—percent of vote by party—NA; seats by party—PPD 28, PNP 23

note: Puerto Rico directly elects 1 member by simple majority vote to serve a 4-year term as a commissioner to the US House of Representatives; the commissioner can vote when serving on a committee and when the House meets as the Committee of the Whole House, but not when legislation is submitted for a "full floor" House vote; election of commissioner last held on 6 November 2012 (next to be held on 8 November 2016)

Judicial branch: *highest court(s):* Supreme Court (consists of the chief justice and 8 associate justices)

judge selection and term of office: justices appointed by the governor and confirmed by majority Senate vote; judges serve until compulsory retirement at age 70

subordinate courts: Court of Appeals; First Instance Court comprised of superior and municipal courts

note: the Commonwealth of Puerto Rico Judiciary Act of 2003 reformed the judicial system

Political parties and leaders: National Democratic Party [Roberto PRATS]

National Republican Party of Puerto Rico [Carlos MENDEZ]

New Progressive Party or PNP [Pedro PIERLUISI] (pro-US statehood)

Popular Democratic Party or PPD [Alejandro Garcia PADILLA] (pro-commonwealth)

Puerto Rican Independence Party or PIP [Ruben BERRIOS Martinez] (pro-independence)

Political pressure groups and leaders: Boricua Popular Army or EPB (a revolutionary group also known as Los Macheteros)

International organization participation: AOSIS (observer), Caricom (observer), Interpol (subbureau), IOC, UNWTO (associate), UPU, WFTU (NGOs)

Diplomatic representation in the US: none (territory of the US)

Diplomatic representation from the US: none (territory of the US with commonwealth status)

Flag description: five equal horizontal bands of red (top, center, and bottom) alternating with white; a blue isosceles triangle based on the hoist side bears a large, white, five-pointed star in the center; the white star symbolizes Puerto Rico; the three sides of the triangle signify the executive, legislative and judicial parts of the government; blue stands for the sky and the coastal waters; red symbolizes the blood shed by warriors, while white represents liberty, victory, and peace

note: design initially influenced by the US flag, but similar to the Cuban flag, with the colors of the bands and triangle reversed

National symbol(s): Puerto Rican spindalis (bird), coqui (frog); National colors: red, white, blue

National anthem: *name:* "La Borinquena" (The Puerto Rican)

lyrics/music: Manuel Fernandez JUNCOS/Felix Astol ARTES

note: music adopted 1952, lyrics adopted 1977; the local anthem's name is a reference to the indigenous name of the island, Borinquen; the music was originally composed as a dance in 1867 and gained popularity in the early 20th century; there is some evidence that the music was written by Francisco RAMIREZ; as a commonwealth of the US, "The Star-Spangled Banner" is official (see United States)

ECONOMY

Economy—overview: Puerto Rico had one of the most dynamic economies in the Caribbean region until 2006; however, growth has been negative for each of the last nine years. The downturn coincided with the phaseout of tax preferences that had led US firms to invest heavily in the Commonwealth since the 1950s, and a steep rise in the price of oil, which generates most of the island's electricity.

Diminished job opportunities prompted a sharp rise in outmigration, as many Puerto Ricans sought jobs on the US mainland. Unemployment reached 16% in 2011, but declined to 13.7% in December 2014. US minimum wage laws apply in Puerto Rico, hampering job expansion. Per capita income is about half that of the US mainland.

The industrial sector greatly exceeds agriculture as the locus of economic activity and in come. Tourism has traditionally been an important source of income with estimated arrivals of more than 3.6 million tourists in 2008. Puerto Rico's merchandise trade surplus is exceptionally strong, with exports nearly 50% greater than imports, and its current account surplus about 10% of GDP.

Closing the budget deficit while restoring economic growth and employment remain the central concerns of the government. The gap between revenues and expenditures narrowed to 0.2% of GDP in 2014, although analysts believe that not all expenditures have been accounted for in the budget and a better accounting of costs would yield an overall deficit of roughly 5% of GDP in 2014. Public debt rose to 105% of GDP in 2015, about $17,000 per person, or nearly three times the per capita debt of the State of Connecticut, the highest in the US. Much of that debt was issued by state-run schools and public corporations, including water and electric utilities. In June 2015, Governor Alejandro GARCIA Padilla announced that the island could not pay back at least $73 billion in debt and that it would seek a deal with its creditors.

GDP (purchasing power parity): $131.9 billion (2015 est.)

$133.6 billion (2014 est.)

$133.7 billion (2013 est.)

note: data are in 2015 US dollars

country comparison to the world: 78

GDP (official exchange rate): $101.6 billion (2015 est.)

GDP—real growth rate: -1.3% (2015 est.)

-0.1% (2014 est.)

0% (2013 est.)

country comparison to the world: 205

GDP—per capita (PPP): $38,000 (2015 est.)

$37,800 (2014 est.)

$37,200 (2013 est.)

note: data are in 2010 US dollars

country comparison to the world: 43

GDP—composition, by end use:

household consumption: 90.7%

government consumption: 15.4%

investment in fixed capital: 12.9%

investment in inventories: 0.2%

exports of goods and services: 110.3%

imports of goods and services: -129.5% (2015 est.)

GDP—composition, by sector of origin:

agriculture: 0.9%

industry: 50.8%

services: 48.4% (2015 est.)

Agriculture—products: sugarcane, coffee, pineapples, plantains, bananas; livestock products, chickens

Industries: pharmaceuticals, electronics, apparel, food products, tourism

Industrial production growth rate: -0.9% (2015 est.)

country comparison to the world: 171

Labor force: 1.139 million (December 2014 est.)

country comparison to the world: 141

Labor force—by occupation: *agriculture:* 2.1%

industry: 19%

services: 79% (2005 est.)

Unemployment rate: 13.7% (December 2014 est.)

15% (December 2013 est.)

country comparison to the world: 146

Population below poverty line: NA%

Household income or consumption by percentage share: *lowest:* 10%: NA%

highest: 10%: NA%

Budget: *revenues:* $8.908 billion

expenditures: $9.402 billion (2015 est.)

Taxes and other revenues: 14.5% of GDP (2015 est.)

country comparison to the world: 196

Budget surplus (+) or deficit (–): -0.8% of GDP (2015 est.)

country comparison to the world: 51

Public debt: 105.4% of GDP (2015 est.)

97.2% of GDP (2014 est.)

country comparison to the world: 14

Fiscal year: 1 July—30 June

691

Inflation rate (consumer prices): -0.8% (2015 est.)
0.6% (2014 est.)
country comparison to the world: 18

Commercial bank prime lending rate: 3.7% (31 December 2015 est.)
3.3% (31 December 2014 est.)
country comparison to the world: 162

Market value of publicly traded shares: $NA

Exports: $68.19 billion (2015 est.)
$68.2 billion (2014 est.)
country comparison to the world: 41

Exports—commodities: chemicals, electronics, apparel, canned tuna, rum, beverage concentrates, medical equipment

Imports: $47.77 billion (2015 est.)
$47.92 billion (2014 est.)
country comparison to the world: 52

Imports—commodities: chemicals, machinery and equipment, clothing, food, fish, petroleum products

Debt—external: $56.82 billion (31 December 2010 est.)
$52.98 billion (31 December 2009 est.)
country comparison to the world: 62

Exchange rates: the US dollar is used

ENERGY

Electricity—production: 20.03 billion kWh (2012 est.)
country comparison to the world: 75

Electricity—consumption: 18.62 billion kWh (2012 est.)
country comparison to the world: 72

Electricity—exports: 0 kWh (2013 est.)
country comparison to the world: 188

Electricity—imports: 0 kWh (2013 est.)
country comparison to the world: 194

Electricity—installed generating capacity: 5.616 million kW (2012 est.)
country comparison to the world: 74

Electricity—from fossil fuels: 96.4% of total installed capacity (2012 est.)
country comparison to the world: 61

Electricity—from nuclear fuels: 0% of total installed capacity (2012 est.)
country comparison to the world: 172

Electricity—from hydroelectric plants: 1.8% of total installed capacity (2012 est.)
country comparison to the world: 138

Electricity—from other renewable sources: 1.8% of total installed capacity (2012 est.)

country comparison to the world: 83

Crude oil—production: 0 bbl/day (2014 est.)
country comparison to the world: 183

Crude oil—exports: 0 bbl/day (2012 est.)
country comparison to the world: 180

Crude oil—imports: 0 bbl/day (2012 est.)
country comparison to the world: 117

Crude oil—proved reserves: 0 bbl (1 January 2014 est.)
country comparison to the world: 182

Refined petroleum products—production: 0 bbl/day (2012 est.)
country comparison to the world: 124

Refined petroleum products—consumption: 133,700 bbl/day (2014 est.)
country comparison to the world: 72

Refined petroleum products—exports: 2,520 bbl/day (2012 est.)
country comparison to the world: 103

Refined petroleum products—imports: 149,700 bbl/day (2012 est.)
country comparison to the world: 37

Natural gas—production: 0 cu m (2014 est.)
country comparison to the world: 121

Natural gas—consumption: 1.663 billion cu m (2014 est.)
country comparison to the world: 82

Natural gas—exports: 0 cu m (2014 est.)
country comparison to the world: 170

Natural gas—imports: 1.663 billion cu m (2014 est.)
country comparison to the world: 52

Natural gas—proved reserves: 0 cu m (1 January 2014 est.)
country comparison to the world: 187

Carbon dioxide emissions from consumption of energy: 26.81 million Mt (2012 est.)
country comparison to the world: 75

COMMUNICATIONS

Telephones—fixed lines: *total subscriptions:* 820,000
subscriptions per 100 inhabitants: 23 (2014 est.)
country comparison to the world: 86

Telephones—mobile cellular: *total:* 3.2 million
subscriptions per 100 inhabitants: 89 (2014 est.)
country comparison to the world: 137

Telephone system: *general assessment:* modern system integrated with that of the US by high-capacity submarine cable and Intelsat with high-speed data capability
domestic: digital telephone system; mobile-cellular services

international: country code—1–787,939; submarine cables provide connectivity to the US, Caribbean, Central and South America; satellite earth station—1 Intelsat (2011)

Broadcast media: more than 30 TV stations operating; cable TV subscription services are available; roughly 125 radio stations (2007)
Radio broadcast stations: AM 74, FM 53, shortwave 0 (2008)
Television broadcast stations: 34 (2008)

Internet country code: .pr

Internet hosts: 469 (2012)
country comparison to the world: 184

Internet users: *total:* 2 million
percent of population: 55.0% (2014 est.)
country comparison to the world: 98

TRANSPORTATION

Airports: 29 (2013)
country comparison to the world: 119

Airports—with paved runways: *total:* 17
over 3,047 m: 2
2,438 to 3,047 m: 1
1,524 to 2,437 m: 2
914 to 1,523 m: 7
under 914 m: 5 (2013)

Airports—with unpaved runways: *total:* 12
1,524 to 2,437 m: 1
914 to 1,523 m: 1
under 914 m: 10 (2013)

Roadways: *total:* 26,862 km (includes 454 km of expressways) (2012)
country comparison to the world: 99

Ports and terminals: *major seaport(s):* En sen ada Honda, Mayaguez, Playa de Guayanilla, Playa de Pon ce, San Juan
container port(s) (TEUs): San Juan (1,484,595)
LNG terminal(s) (imp ort): Guayanilla Bay

MILITARY AND SECURITY

Military branches: no regular indigenous military forces; paramilitary National Guard, Police Force

Military—note: defense is the responsibility of the US

TRANSNATIONAL ISSUES

Disputes—international: increasing numbers of illegal migrants from the Dominican Republic cross the Mona Passage to Puerto Rico each year looking for work

QATAR

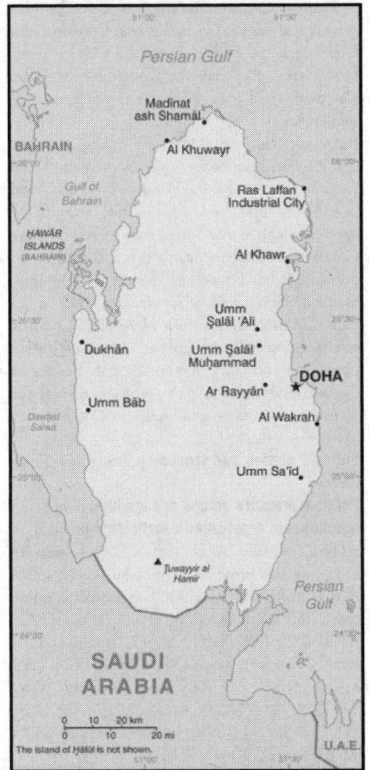

Amir TAMIM bin Hamad—a peaceful abdication rare in the history of Arab Gulf states. TAMIM has prioritized improving the domestic welfare of Qataris, including establishing advanced healthcare and education systems and expanding the country's infrastructure in anticipation of Doha's hosting of the 2022 World Cup.

GEOGRAPHY

Location: Middle East, peninsula bordering the Persian Gulf and Saudi Arabia

Geographic coordinates: 25 30 N, 51 15 E

Map references: Middle East

Area: *total:* 11,586 sq km
land: 11,586 sq km
water: 0 sq km
country comparison to the world: 166

Area—comparative: almost twice the size of Delaware; slightly smaller than Connecticut

Land boundaries: *total:* 87 km
border countries (1): Saudi Arabia 87 km

Coastli ne: 563 km

Maritime claims: *territorial sea:* 12 nm
contiguous zone: 24 nm
exclusive economic zone: as determined by bilateral agreements or the median line

Climate: arid; mild, pleasant winters; very hot, humid summers

Terrain: mostly flat and barren desert

Elevation: *mean elevation:* 28 m

elevation extremes: *lowest point:* Persian Gulf 0 m
highest point: Tuwayyir al Hamir 103 m

Natural resources: petroleum, natural gas, fish

Land use: *agricultural land:* 5.6%
arable land: 1.1%;
permanent crops: 0.2%;
permanent pasture: 4.3%
forest: 0%
other: 94.4% (2011 est.)

Irrigated land: 130 sq km (2012)

Total renewable water resources: 0.06 cu km (2011)

Freshwater withdrawal (domestic/industrial/agricultural): *total:* 0.44 cu km/yr (39%/2%/59%)
per capita: 376.9 cu m/yr (2005)

Natural hazards: haze, dust storms, sandstorms common

Environment—current issues: limited natural freshwater resources are increasing dependence on large-scale desalination facilities

Environment—international agreements: *party to:* Biodiversity, Climate Change, Climate Change-Kyoto Protocol, Desertification, Endangered Species, Hazardous Wastes, Law of the Sea, Ozone Layer Protection, Ship Pollution
signed, but not ratified: none of the selected agreem ents

Geography—note: the peninsula occupies a strategic location in the central Persian Gulf near major petroleum deposits

INTRODUCTION

Background: Ruled by the Al Thani family since the mid-1800s, Qatar transformed itself from a poor British protectorate noted mainly for pearling into an independent state with significant oil and natural gas revenues. During the late 1980s and early 1990s, the Qatari economy was crippled by a continuous siphoning off of petroleum revenues by the amir, who had ruled the country since 1972. His son, HAMAD bin Khalifa Al Thani, overthrew the father in a bloodless coup in 1995. In short order, HAMAD oversaw the creation of the pan-Arab satellite news network Al-Jazeera and Qatar's pursuit of a leadership role in mediating regional conflicts. in the 2000s, Qatar resolved its longstanding border disputes with both Bahrain and Saudi Arabia. As of 2007, oil and natural gas revenues had enabled Qatar to attain the highest per capita income in the world. Qatar has not experienced domestic unrest or violence like that seen in other Near Eastern and North African countries in 2010–11, due in part to its immense wealth. Since the outbreak of regional unrest, however, Doha has prided itself on its support for many of these popular revolutions, particularly in Libya and Syria. In mid-2013, HAMAD transferred power to his 33 year-old son, the current

PEOPLE AND SOCIETY

Nationality: *noun:* Qatari(s)
adjective: Qatari

Ethnic groups: Arab 40%, Indian 18%, Pakistani 18%, Iranian 10%, other 14%

Languages: Arabic (official), English commonly used as a second language

Religions: Muslim 77.5%, Christian 8.5%, other (includes mainly Hindu and other Indian religions) 14% (2004 est.)

Population: 2,194,817 (July 2015 est.)
country comparison to the world: 144

Age structure: *0–14 years:* 12.52% (male 139,353/female 135,514)
15–24 years: 12.96% (male 207,493/female 76,879)
25–54 years: 70.23% (male 1,278,442/female 263,051)
55–64 years: 3.39% (male 57,581/female 16,886)
65 years and over: 0.89% (male 12,365/female 7,253) (2015 est.)

Dependency ratios: *total dependency ratio:* 20.1%
youth dependency ratio: 18.6%
elderly dependency ratio: 1.4%
potential support ratio: 70.4% (2015 est.)

Median age: *total:* 32.8 years
male: 33.9 years
female: 28.1 years (2015 est.)
country comparison to the world: 89

Population growth rate: 3.07% (2015 est.)
country comparison to the world: 6

Birth rate: 9.84 births/1,000 population (2015 est.)
country comparison to the world: 199

Death rate: 1.53 deaths/1,000 population (2015 est.)
country comparison to the world: 225

Net migration rate: 22.39 migrant(s)/1,000 population (2015 est.)
country comparison to the world: 1

Urbanization: *urban Population:* 99.2% of total population (2015)
rate of urbanization: 6.02% annual rate of change (2010–15 est.)

Major urban areas—Population: DOHA (capital) 718,000 (2015)

Sex ratio: *at birth:* 1.02 male(s)/female
0–14 years: 1.03 male(s)/female
15–24 years: 2.7 male(s)/female
25–54 years: 4.86 male(s)/female
55–64 years: 3.41 male(s)/female
65 years and over: 1.71 male(s)/female
total population: 3.39 male(s)/female (2015 est.)

Maternal mortality rate: 13 deaths/100,000 live births (2015 est.)
country comparison to the world: 166

Infant mortality rate: *total:* 6.32 deaths/1,000 live births
male: 6.61 deaths/1,000 live births
female: 6.02 deaths/1,000 live births (2015 est.)
country comparison to the world: 163

Life expectancy at birth: *total population:* 78.59 years
male: 76.58 years
female: 80.65 years (2015 est.)
country comparison to the world: 53
Total fertility rate: 1.91 children born/woman (2015 est.)
country comparison to the world: 137
Contraceptive prevalence rate: 38% (2012)
Health expenditures: 2.2% of GDP (2013)
country comparison to the world: 189
Physicians density: 7.74 physicians/1,000 population (2010)
Hospital bed density: 1.2 beds/1,000 population (2012)
Drinking water source:
improved:
urban: 100% of population
rural: 100% of population
total: 100% of population
unimproved:
urban: 0% of population
rural: 0% of population
total: 0% of population (2015 est.)
Sanitation facility access:
improved:
urban: 98% of population
rural: 98% of population
total: 98% of population
unimproved:
urban: 2% of popu lation
rural: 2% of population
total: 2% of population (2015 est.)
HIV/AIDS—adult prevalence rate: NA
HIV/AIDS—people living with HIV/AIDS: NA
HIV/AIDS—deaths: NA
Obesity—adult prevalence rate: 41% (2014)
country comparison to the world: 16
Education expenditures: 3.5% of GDP (2014)
country comparison to the world: 154
Literacy: *definition:* age 15 and over can read and write
total population: 97.3%
male: 97.4%
female: 96.8% (2015 est.)
School life expectancy (primary to tertiary education): *total:* 13 years
male: 13 years
female: 14 years (2011)
Unemployment, youth ages 15–24: *total:* 1.1%
male: 0.4%
female: 6.2% (2013 est.)
country comparison to the world: 134

GOVERNMENT

Country name: *conventional long form:* State of Qatar
conventional short form: Qatar
local long form: Dawlat Qatar
local short form: Qatar
note: closest approximation of the native pronunciation is cutter
etymology: the origin of the name is uncertain, but it dates back at least 2,000 years since a term "Catharrei" was used to describe the inhabitants of the peninsula by Pliny the Elder (1 st century A.

D.), and a "Catara" peninsula is depicted on a map by Ptolemy (2nd century A. D.)
Government type: absolute monarchy
Capital: *name:* Doha
Geographic coordinates: 25 17 N, 51 32 E
time difference: UTC+3 (8 hours ahead of Washington, DC, during Standard Time)
Administrative divisions: 7 municipalities (baladiyat, singular—baladiyah); Ad Dawhah, Al Khawr wa adh Dhakhirah, Al Wakrah, Ar Rayyan, Ash Shamal, Az Za'ayin, Umm Salal
Independence: 3 September 1971 (from the UK)
National holiday: National Day, 18 December (1878), anniversary of Al Thani family accession to the throne; Independence Day, 3 September (1971)
Constitution: previous 1972 (provisional); latest drafted 2 July 2002, approved by referendum 29 April 2003, endorsed 8 June 2004, effective9 June 2005 (2016)
Legal system: mixed legal system of civil law and Islamic law (in family and personal matters)
International law organization participation: has not submitted an ICJ jurisdiction declaration; non-party state to the ICCt
Citizenship: *citizenship by birth:* no
citizenship by descent only: the father must be a citizen of Qatar
dual citizenship recognized: no
residency requirement for naturalization: 20 years; 15 years if an Arab national
Suffrage: 18 years of age; universal
Executive branch: *chief of state:* Amir TAMIM bin Hamad Al Thani (since 25 June 2013)
head of government: Prime Minister ABDALLAH bin Nasir bin Khalifa Al Thani (since 26 June 2013); Deputy Prime Minister Ahmad bin Abdallah al-MAHMUD (since 20 September 2011)
cabinet: Council of Ministers appointed by the amir
elections/appointments: the monarchy is hereditary; prime minister and deputy prime minister appointed by the amir
Legislative branch: *description:* unicameral Advisory Council or Majlis al-Shura (15 seats; members appointed by the monarch); note—the 2003 constitutional referendum called for the election of 30 members, however; the first electionscheduled for 2013 was postponed and the current term was initially extended until 2016, but in June 2016, the Amir extended it until at least 2019
note: although the Advisory Council has limited legislative authority to draft and approve laws, the Amir has final vote on all legislation; Qatar's first legislative elections were expected to be held in 2013, but HAMAD postponed them in a final legislative act prior to handing over power to TAMIM; in principle, the public would elect 30 members and the Amir would appoint 15; the Advisory Council would have authority to approve the national budget, hold ministers accountable through no-confidence votes, and propose legislation; the 29-member Central Municipal Council—first elected in 1999—has limited consultative authority aimed at improving

municipal services; members elected for a 4-year term; next electionscheduled for May 2019
Judicial branch: *highest court(s):* Supreme Court or Court of Cassation (consists of the court president and several judges); Supreme Constitutional Court (consists of the chief justice and 6 members); note—the Supreme Constitutional Court was established in 1999, but has not been fully implemented
judge selection and term of office: Supreme Court judges nominated by the Supreme Judiciary Council, a 9-member independent body consisting of judiciary heads appointed by the Amir; judges appointed for 3-year renewable terms; Supreme Constitutional Court members nominated by the Supreme Judicial Supreme Council and appointed by the monarch; term of appointment NA
subordinate courts: Courts of Appeal; Courts of First Instance; Sharia Courts; Courts of Justice; Qatar International Court and Dispute Resolution Center, established in 2009, provides dispute services for institutions and bodies in Qatar, as well as internationally
Political parties and leaders: political parties are banned
Political pressure groups and leaders: none
International organization participation: ABEDA, AFESD, AMF, CAEU, CD, CICA (observer), EITI (implementing country), FAO, G-77, GCC, IAEA, IBRD, ICAO, ICC (national committees), ICRM, IDA, IDB, IFAD, IFC, IFRCS, IHO, ILO, IMF, IMO, IMSO, Interpol, IOC, IOM (observer), IPU, ISO, ITSO, ITU, LAS, MIGA, NAM, OAPEC, OAS (observer), OIC, OIF, OPCW, OPEC, PCA, UN, UNCTAD, UNESCO, UNIDO, UNIFIL, UNWTO, UPU, WCO, WHO, WIPO, WMO, WTO
Diplomatic representation in the US: *chief of mission:* Ambassador Muhammad bin Jaham Abd al-Aziz al-KUWARI (since 10 March 2014)
chancery: 2555 M Street NW, Washington, DC 20037
telephone: [1] (202) 274-1600 and 274-1603
FAX: [1] (202) 237-0061
consulate(s) general: Houston, Los Angeles
Diplomatic representation from the US: *chief of mission:* Ambassador Dana Shell SMITH (8 September 2014)
embassy: Al-Luqta District, 22 February Road, Doha
mailing address: P.O. Box 2399, Doha
telephone: [974] 4496-6000
FAX: [974] 4488-4298
Flag description: maroon with a broad white serrated band (nine white points) on the hoist side; maroon represents the blood shed in Qatari wars, white stands for peace; the nine-pointed serrated edge signifies Qatar as the ninth member of the "reconciled emirates" in the wake of the Qatari-British treaty of 1916
note: the other eight emirates are the seven that compose the UAE and Bahrain; according to some sources, the dominant color was formerly red, but this darkened to maroon upon exposure to the sun and the new shade was eventually adopted

National symbol(s): a maroon field surmounted by a white serrated band with nine white points; national colors: maroon, white

National anthem: *name:* "Al-Salam Al-Amiri" (The Peace for the Anthem)

lyrics/music: Sheikh MUBARAK bin Saif al-Thani/Abdul Aziz Nasser OBAIDAN

note: adopted 1996; anthem first performed that year at a meeting of the Gulf Cooperative Council hosted by Qatar

ECONOMY

Economy—overview: Qatar has prospered in the last several years with continued high real GDP growth, but low oil prices have dampened the outlook. Qatar was the only Gulf Cooperation Council member that avoided a budget deficit in 2015, but it projects a $12.8 billion deficit, 6% of GDP in 2016.

GDP is driven largely by the oil and gas sector; however, growth in manufacturing, construction, and financial services have lifted the non-oil sectors to just over half of Qatar's nominal GDP. Economic policy is focused on sustaining Qatar's non-associated natural gas reserves and increasing private and foreign investment in non-energy sectors, but oil and gas still account for roughly 92% of export earnings, and 56% of government revenues. Oil and gas have made Qatar the world's highest per-capita income country and the country with the lowest unemployment. Proved oil reserves in excess of 25 billion barrels should enable continued output at current levels for about 56 years. Qatar's proved reserves of natural gas exceed 25 trillion cubic meters, about 13% of the world total and third largest in the world.

Qatar's successful 2022 World Cup bid is accelerating large-scale infrastructure projects such as it's metro system, light rail system, construction of a new port, roads, stadiums and related sporting infrastructure.

GDP (purchasing power parity): $319.8 billion (2015 est.)
$309.7 billion (2014 est.)
$297.8 billion (2013 est.)
note: data are in 2015 US dollars
country comparison to the world: 52

GDP (official exchange rate): $185.4 billion (2015 est.)

GDP—real growth rate: 3.3% (2015 est.)
4% (2014 est.)
4.6% (2013 est.)
country comparison to the world: 92

GDP—per capita (PPP): $132,100 (2015 est.)
$138,600 (2014 est.)
$145,600 (2013 est.)
note: data are in 2015 US dollars
country comparison to the world: 1

Gross national saving: 54.5% of GDP (2015 est.)
58.3% of GDP (2014 est.)
60.2% of GDP (2013 est.)
country comparison to the world: 1

GDP—composition, by end use:
household consumption: 18.8%
government consumption: 17.8%
investment in fixed capital: 44.6%

investment in inventories: -1.3%
exports of goods and services: 49.9%
imports of goods and services: -29.8% (2015 est.)

GDP—composition, by sector of origin:
agriculture: 0.1%
industry: 58.8%
services: 41.1% (2015 est.)

Agriculture—products: fruits, vegetables; poultry, dairy products, beef; fish

Industries: liquefied natural gas, crude oil production and refining, ammonia, fertilizers, petrochemicals, steel reinforcing bars, cement, commercial ship repair

Industrial production growth rate: 0.7% (2015 est.)
country comparison to the world: 154

Labor force: 1.644 million (2015 est.)
country comparison to the world: 127

Unemployment rate: 0.4% (2015 est.) 0.4% (2014 est.)
country comparison to the world: 2

Population below poverty line: NA%

Household income or consumption by percentage share: *lowest:* 10%: 1.3%
highest 10%: 35.9% (2007)

Budget: *revenues:* $77.22 billion
expenditures: $68.65 billion (2015 est.)
Taxes and other revenues: 40.2% of GDP (2015 est.)
country comparison to the world: 39

Budget surplus (+) or deficit (−): 4.5% of GDP (2015 est.)
country comparison to the world: 9

Public debt: 39.9% of GDP (2015 est.)
31.9% of GDP (2014 est.)
country comparison to the world: 113

Fiscal year: 1 April—31 March

Inflation rate (consumer prices): 1.7% (2015 est.)
3.3% (2014 est.)
country comparison to the world: 107

Central bank discount rate: 4.5% (31 December 2012)
4.93% (31 December 2011)
country comparison to the world: 82

Commercial bank prime lending rate:
4.7% (31 December 2015 est.)
4.5% (31 December 2014 est.)
country comparison to the world: 149

Stock of narrow money: $37.89 billion (31 December 2015 est.)
$34.14 billion (31 December 2014 est.)
country comparison to the world: 56

Stock of broad money: $155.8 billion (31 December 2015 est.)
$138.5 billion (31 December 2014 est.)
country comparison to the world: 48

Stock of domestic credit: $184.1 billion (31 December 2015 est.)
$168.9 billion (31 December 2014 est.)
country comparison to the world: 45

Market value of publicly traded shares:
$126.4 billion (31 December 2012 est.)
$125.4 billion (31 December 2011)
$123.6 billion (31 December 2010 est.)
country comparison to the world: 41

Current account balance: $9.146 billion (2015 est.)

$49.66 billion (2014 est.)
country comparison to the world: 24

Exports: $77.74 billion (2015 est.)
$131.6 billion (2014 est.)
country comparison to the world: 40

Exports—commodities: liquefied natural gas (LNG), petroleum products, fertilizers, steel

Exports—partners: South Korea 18.3%, Japan 18.2%, India 12.4%, UAE 8.8%, China 5.1%, Singapore 4% (2015)

Imports: $37.15 billion (2015 est.)
$38.23 billion (2014 est.)
country comparison to the world: 59

Imports—commodities: machinery and transport equipment, food, ch emicals

Imports—partners: US 13.7%, France 10.1%, UK 9.1%, UAE 7.9%, Germany 7.7%, China 7.4%, Japan 5%, Saudi Arabia 4.4% (2015)

Reserves of foreign exchange and gold: $42.77 billion (31 December 2015 est.)
$43.32 billion (31 December 2014 est.)
country comparison to the world: 44

Debt—external: $156.8 billion (31 December 2014 est.)
$149.2 billion (31 December 2013 est.)
country comparison to the world: 40

Stock of direct foreign investment—at home:
$34.71 billion (31 December 2015 est.)
$33.46 billion (31 December 2014 est.)
country comparison to the world: 65

Stock of direct foreign investment—abroad:
$49.14 billion (31 December 2015 est.)
$45.71 billion (31 December 2014 est.)
country comparison to the world: 40

Exchange rates: Qatari rials (QAR) per US dollar—
3.64 (2015 est.)
3.64 (2014 est.)
3.64 (2013 est.)
3.64 (2012 est.)
3.64 (2011 est.)

ENERGY

Electricity—production: 32.7 billion kWh (2012 est.)
country comparison to the world: 61

Electricity—consumption: 30.53 billion kWh (2012 est.)
country comparison to the world: 61

Electricity—exports: 0 kWh (2013 est.)
country comparison to the world: 186

Electricity—imports: 0 kWh (2013 est.)
country comparison to the world: 192

Electricity—installed generating capacity: 7.947 million kW (2012 est.)
country comparison to the world: 63

Electricity—from fossil fuels: 98.5% of total installed capacity (2012 est.)
country comparison to the world: 53

Electricity—from nuclear fuels: 0% of total installed capacity (2012 est.)
country comparison to the world: 169

Electricity—from hydroelectric plants: 0% of total installed capacity (2012 est.)
country comparison to the world: 195

Electricity—from other renewable sources: 1.5% of total installed capacity (2012 est.)
country comparison to the world: 87
Crude oil—production: 1.54 million bbl/day (2014 est.)
country comparison to the world: 17
Crude oil—exports: 1.232 million bbl/day (2012 est.)
country comparison to the world: 12
Crude oil—imports: 0 bbl/day (2012 est.)
country comparison to the world: 116
Crude oil—proved reserves: 25.24 billion bbl (1 January 2015 est.)
country comparison to the world: 13
Refined petroleum products—production: 310,900 bbl/day (2012 est.)
country comparison to the world: 42
Refined petroleum products—consumption: 230,000 bbl/day (2013 est.)
country comparison to the world: 54
Refined petroleum products—exports: 554,300 bbl/day (2012 est.)
country comparison to the world: 11
Refined petroleum products—imports: 0 bbl/day (2012 est.)
country comparison to the world: 213
Natural gas—production: 158.5 billion cu m (2013 est.)
country comparison to the world: 4
Natural gas—consumption: 32.93 billion cu m (2013 est.)
country comparison to the world: 29
Natural gas—exports: 125.5 billion cu m (2013 est.)
country comparison to the world: 2
Natural gas—imports: 0 cu m (2013 est.)
country comparison to the world: 124
Natural gas—proved reserves: 25.07 trillion cu m (1 January 2014 est.)
country comparison to the world: 3
Carbon dioxide emissions from consumption of energy: 99.17 million Mt (2012 est.)
country comparison to the world: 40

COMMUNICATIONS

Telephones—fixed lines: *total subscriptions:* 420,000
subscriptions per 100 inhabitants: 20 (2014 est.)
country comparison to the world: 101
Telephones—mobile cellular: *total:* 3.3 million
subscriptions per 100 inhabitants: 156 (2014 est.)
country comparison to the world: 134
Telephone system: *general assessment:* modern system centered in Doha
domestic: combined fixed-line and mobile-cellular telephone subscribership exceeds 130 telephones per 100 persons

international: country code—974; landing point for the Fiber-Optic Link Around the Globe (FLAG) submarine cable network that provides links to Asia, Middle East, Europe, and the US; tropospheric scatter to Bahrain; microwave radio relay to Saudi Arabia and the UAE; satellite earth stations—2 Intelsat (1 Atlantic Ocean and 1 Indian Ocean) and 1 Arabsat (2011)
Broadcast media: TV and radio broadcast licensing and access to local media markets are state controlled; home of the satellite TV channel Al-Jazeera, which was originally owned and financed by the Qatari government but has evolved to independent corporate status; Al-Jazeera claims editorial independence in broadcasting; local radio transmissions include state, private, and international broadcasters on FM frequencies in Doha; in August 2013, Qatar's satellite company Es'hailSat launched its first communications satellite Es'hail 1 (manufactured in the US), which entered commercial service in December 2013 to provide improved television broadcasting capability and expand availability of voice and internet; Es'hailSat released a request for proposals in March 2014 for its second satellite to launch in 2016 (2014)
Radio broadcast stations: AM 6, FM 5, shortwave 1 (1998)
Television broadcast stations: 1 (plus 3 repeaters) (2001)
Internet country code: .qa
Internet hosts: 897 (2012)
country comparison to the world: 173
Internet users: *total:* 2.1 million
percent of population: 96.7% (2014 est.)
country comparison to the world: 95

TRANSPORTATION

Airports: 6 (2013)
country comparison to the world: 178
Airports—with paved runways: *total:* 4
over 3,047 m: 3
1,524 to 2,437 m: 1 (2013)
Airports—with unpaved runways: *total:* 2
914 to 1,523 m: 1
under 914 m: 1 (2013)
Heliports: 1 (2013)
Pipelines: condensate 288 km; condensate/gas 221 km; gas 2,383 km; liquid petroleum gas 90 km; oil 745 km; refined products 103 km (2013)
Roadways: *total:* 9,830 km (2010)
country comparison to the world: 136
Merchant marine: *total:* 28
by type: bulk carrier 3, chemical tanker 2, container 13, liquefied gas 6, petroleum tanker 4
foreign-owned: 6 (Kuwait 6)

registered in other countries: 35 (Liberia 5, Marshall Islands 29, Panama 1) (2010)
country comparison to the world: 87
Ports and terminals: *major seaport(s):* Doha, Mesaieed (Umaieed), Ra's Laffan
LNG terminal(s) (export): Ras Laffan

MILITARY AND SECURITY

Military branches: Qatari Emiri Land Force (QELF), Qatari Emiri Navy (QEN), Qatari Emiri Air Force (QEAF) (2013)
Military service age and obligation: conscription for males aged 18–35; 4-month general obligation, 3 months for graduates (2014)

TRANSNATIONAL ISSUES

Disputes—international: none
Refugees and internally displaced persons: *stateless persons:* 1,200 (2015)
Trafficking in persons: *current situation:* Qatar is a destination country for men, women, and children subjected to forced labor, and, to a much lesser extent, forced prostitution; the predominantly foreign workforce migrates to Qatar legally for low- and semi-skilled work but often experiences situations of forced labor, including debt bondage, delayed or nonpayment of salaries, confiscation of passports, abuse, hazardous working conditions, and squalid living arrangements; foreign female domestic workers are particularly vulnerable to trafficking because of their isolation in private homes and lack of protection under Qatari labor laws; some women who migrate for work are also forced into prostitution

tier rating: Tier 2 Watch List—Qatar does not fully comply with the minimum standards for the elimination of trafficking; however, it is making significant efforts to do so; the government investigated 11 trafficking cases but did not prosecute or convict any offenders, including exploitative employers and recruitment agencies; the primary solution for resolving labor violations was to transfer a worker's sponsorship to a new employer with minimal effort to investigate whether a forced labor violation had occurred; authorities increased their efforts to protect some trafficking victims, although many victims of forced labor, particularly domestic workers, remained unidentified and unprotected and were sometimes punished for immigration violations or running away from an employer or sponsor; authorities visited worksites throughout the country to meet and educate workers and employers on trafficking regulations, but the government failed to abolish or reform the sponsorship system, perpetuating Qatar's forced labor problem (2015)

ROMANIA

INTRODUCTION

Background: The principalities of Wallachia and Moldavia—for centuries under the suzerainty of the Turkish Ottoman Empire—secured their autonomy in 1856; they were de facto linked in 1859 and formally united in 1862 under the new name of Romania. The country gained recognition of its independence in 1878. It joined the Allied Powers in World War I and acquired new territories—most notably Transylvania—following the conflict. In 1940, Romania allied with the Axis powers and participated in the 1941 German invasion of the USSR. Three years later, overrun by the Soviets, Romania signed an armistice. The post-war Soviet occupation led to the formation of a communist "people's republic" in 1947 and the abdication of the king. The decades-long rule of dictator Nicolae CEAUSESCU, who took power in 1965, and his Securitate police state became increasingly oppressive and draconian through the 1980s. CEAUSESCU was overthrown and executed in late 1989. Former communists dominated the government until 1996 when they were swept from power. Romania joined NATO in 2004 and the EU in 2007.

GEOGRAPHY

Location: Southeastern Europe, bordering the Black Sea, between Bulgaria and Ukraine

Geographic coordinates: 46 00 N, 25 00 E

Map references: Europe

Area: *total:* 238,391 sq km
land: 229,891 sq km
water: 8,500 sq km
country comparison to the world: 83

Area—comparative: slightly smaller than Oregon

Land boundaries: *total:* 2,844 km
border countries (5): Bulgaria 605 km, Hungary 424 km, Moldova 683 km, Serbia 531 km, Ukraine 601 km

Coastline: 225 km

Maritime claims: *territorial sea:* 12 nm
contiguous zone: 24 nm

exclusive economic zone: 200 nm
continental shelf: 200-m depth or to the depth of exploitation

Climate: temperate; cold, cloudy winters with frequent snow and fog; sunny summers with frequent showers and
thunderstorms

Terrain: central Transy lvanian Basin is separated from the Moldavian Plateau on the east by the Eastern Carpathian Mountains and separated from the Walachian Plain on the south by the Transylvanian Alps

Elevation: *mean elevation:* 414 m
elevation extremes: lowest point: Black Sea 0 m
highest point: Moldoveanu 2,544 m

Natural resources: petroleum (reserves declining), timber, natural gas, coal, iron ore, salt, arable land, hydropower

Land use: *agricultural land:* 60.7%
arable land: 39.1%
permanent crops: 1.9%
permanent pasture: 19.7%
forest: 28.7%
other: 10.6% (2011 est.)

Irrigated land: 31,490 sq km (2012)

Total renewable water resources: 211.9 cu km (2011)

Freshwater withdrawal (domestic/industrial/agricultural): *total:* 6.88 cu km/yr (22%/61%/17%)
per capita: 320.8 cu m/yr (2009)

Natural hazards: earthquakes, most severe in south and southwest; geologic structure and climate promote landslides

Environment—current issues: soil erosion and degradation; water pollution; air pollution in south from industrial effluents; contamination of Danube delta wetlands

Environment—international agreements: *party to:* Air Pollution, Air Pollution-Persistent Organic Pollutants, Antarctic-Environmental Protocol, Antarctic Treaty, Biodiversity, Climate Change, Climate Change-Kyoto Protocol, Desertification, Endangered Species, Environmental Modification, Hazardous Wastes, Law of the Sea, Ozone Layer Protection, Ship Pollution, Wetlands
signed, but not ratified: none of the selected agreements

Geography—note: controls the most easily traversable land route between the Balkans, Moldova, and Ukraine; the Carpathian Mountains dominate the center of the country, while the Danube River forms much of the southern boundary with Serbia and Bulgaria

PEOPLE AND SOCIETY

Nationality: *noun:* Romanian(s)
adjective: Romanian

Ethnic groups: Romanian 83.4%, Hungarian 6.1%, Roma 3.1%, Ukrainian 0.3%, German 0.2%, other 0.7%, unspecified 6.1% (2011 est.)

Languages: Romanian (official) 85.4%, Hungarian 6.3%, Romany (Gypsy) 1.2%, other 1%, unspecified 6.1% (2011 est.)

Religions: Eastern Orthodox (including all sub-denominations) 81.9%, Protestant (various denominations including Reformed and Pentecostal) 6.4%, Roman Catholic 4.3%, other (includes Muslim) 0.9%, none or atheist 0.2%, unspecified 6.3% (2011 est.)

Population: 21,666,350 (July 2015 est.)
country comparison to the world: 58

Age structure: *0–14 years:* 14.49% (male 1,612,090/female 1,526,432)
15–24 years: 10.94% (male 1,215,309/female 1,154,618)
25–54 years: 45.92% (male 5,030,926/female 4,919,140)
55–64 years: 12.92% (male 1,308,475/female 1,491,858)
65 years and over: 15.73% (male 1,376,634/female 2,030,868) (2015 est.)

Dependency ratios: *total dependency ratio:* 48.9%
youth dependency ratio: 23.1%
elderly dependency ratio: 25.8%
potential support ratio: 3.9% (2015 est.)

Median age: *total:* 40.2 years
male: 38.8 years
female: 41.7 years (2015 est.)
country comparison to the world: 44

Population growth rate: -0.3% (2015 est.)
country comparison to the world: 220

Birth rate: 9.14 births/1,000 population (2015 est.)
country comparison to the world: 208

Death rate: 11.9 deaths/1,000 population (2015 est.)
country comparison to the world: 27

Net migration rate: -0.24 migrant(s)/1,000 population (2015 est.)
country comparison to the world: 122

Urbanization: *urban Population:* 54.6% of total population (2015)
rate of urbanization: 0.01% annual rate of change (2010–15 est.)

Major urban areas—population: BUCHAREST (capital) 1.868 million (2015)

Sex ratio: *at birth:* 1.06 male(s)/female
0–14 years: 1.06 male(s)/female
15–24 years: 1.05 male(s)/female
25–54 years: 1.02 male(s)/female
55–64 years: 0.88 male(s)/female
65 years and over: 0.68 male(s)/female
total population: 0.95 male(s)/female (2015 est.)

Mother's mean age at first birth: 26 (2011 est.)

Maternal mortality rate: 31 deaths/100,000 live births (2015 est.)
country comparison to the world: 127

Infant mortality rate: *total:* 9.89 deaths/1,000 live births
male: 11.23 deaths/1,000 live births
female: 8.47 deaths/1,000 live births (2015 est.)
country comparison to the world: 139

Life expectancy at birth: *total population:* 74.92 years

male: 71.46 years

female: 78.59 years (2015 est.)

country comparison to the world: 109

Total fertility rate: 1.33 children born/woman (2015 est.)

country comparison to the world: 215

Contraceptive prevalence rate: 69.8%

note: percent of women aged 18–49 (2005)

Health expenditures: 5.3% of GDP (2013)

country comparison to the world: 138

Physicians density: 2.45 physicians/1,000 population (2012)

Hospital bed density: 6.1 beds/1,000 population (2011)

Drinking water source:

improved:

urban: 100% of population

rural: 100% of population

total: 100% of population

unimproved:

urban: 0% of population

rural: 0% of population

total: 0% of population (2015 est.)

Sanitation facility access:

improved:

urban: 92.2% of population

rural: 63.3% of population

total: 79.1% of population

unimproved:

urban: 7.8% of population

rural: 36.7% of population

total: 20.9% of population (2015 est.)

HIV/AIDS—adult prevalence rate: 0.11% (2013 est.)

country comparison to the world: 111

HIV/AIDS—people living with HIV/AIDS: 16,200 (2013 est.)

country comparison to the world: 85

HIV/AIDS—deaths: 500 (2013 est.)

country comparison to the world: 84

Obesity—adult prevalence rate: 23.4% (2014)

country comparison to the world: 101

Education expenditures: 2.9% of GDP (2012)

country comparison to the world: 104

Literacy: *definition:* age 15 and over can read and write

total population: 98.8%

male: 99.1%

female: 98.5% (2015 est.)

School life expectancy (primary to tertiary education): *total:* 15 years

male: 14 years

*female:*15 years (2012)

Unemployment, youth ages 15–24: *total:* 23.6%

male: 23.5%

female: 23.9% (2013 est.)

country comparison to the world: 45

GOVERNMENT

Country name: *conventional long form:* none

conventional short form: Romania

local long form: none

local short form: Romania

etymology: the name derives from the Latin "Romanus" meaning "citizen of Rome" and was used to stress the common ancient heritage of Romania's three main regions—Moldavia, Transylvania, and Wallachia—during their gradual unification between the mid-19th century and early 20th century

Government type: semi-presidential republic

Capital: *name:* Bucharest

Geographic coordinates: 44 26 N, 26 06 E

time difference: UTC+2 (7 hours ahead of Washington, DC, during Standard Time)

daylight saving time: +1hr, begins last Sunday in March; ends last Sunday in October

Administrative divisions: 41 counties (judete, singular—judet) and 1 municipality* (municipiu); Alba, Arad, Arges, Bacau, Bihor, Bistrita-Nasaud, Botosani, Braila, Brasov, Bucuresti (Bucharest)*, Buzau, Calarasi, Caras-Severin, Cluj, Constanta, Covasna, Dambovita, Dolj, Galati, Gorj, Giurgiu, Harghita, Hunedoara, Ialomita, Iasi, Ilfov, Maramures, Mehedinti, Mures, Neamt, Olt, Prahova, Salaj, Satu Mare, Sibiu, Suceava, Teleorman, Timis, Tulcea, Vaslui, Valcea, Vrancea

Independence: 9 May 1877 (independence proclaimed from the Ottoman Empire; independence recognized on 13 July 1878 by the Treaty of Berlin); 26 March 1881 (kingdom proclaimed); 30 December 1947 (republic proclaimed)

National holiday: Unification Day (of Romania and Transylvania), 1 December (1918)

Constitution: several previous; latest adopted 21 November 1991, approved by referendum and effective 8 December 1991; amended 2003 (2016)

Legal system: civil law system

International law organization participation: accepts compulsory ICJ jurisdiction with reservations; accepts ICCt jurisdiction

Citizenship: *citizenship by birth:* no

citizenship by descent only: at least one parent must be a citizen of Romania

dual citizenship recognized: yes

residency requirement for naturalization: 5 years

Suffrage: 18 years of age; universal

Executive branch: *chief of state:* President Klaus Werner IOHANNIS (since 21 December 2014)

head of government: Prime Minister Dacian CIOLOS (since 17 November 2015); Deputy Prime Ministers Costin Grigore BORC and Vasile DANCU (since 17 November 2015)

cabinet: Council of Ministers appointed by the prime minister

elections/appointments: president directly elected by absolute majority popular vote in 2 rounds if needed for a 5-year term (eligible for a second term); election last held on 2 November 2014 with a runoff on 16 November 2014 (next to be held around 16 November 2019); prime minister appointed by the president with consent of Parliament

election results: Klaus IOHANNIS elected president; percent of vote in runoff—Klaus IOHANNIS (PN L) 54.4%, Victor PONTA (PSD) 45.6%

Legislative branch: *description:* bicameral Parliament or Parlament consists of the Senate or Senat (176 seats; 137 members directly elected in single-seat constituencies by absolute majority vote and 39 directly elected in single-seat constituencies by proportional representation vote; members serve 4-year terms) and the Chamber of Deputies or Camera Deputatilor (412 seats; 315 members directly elected in single-seat con stituencies by absolute majority vote and 97 directly elected in single-seat constituencies by proportional representation vote; members serve 4-year terms)

elections: Senate—last held on 9 December 2012 (next to be held by December 2016); Chamber of Deputies—last held on 9 December 2012 (next to be held by December 2016); note—in the next election the total number of seats will be reduced to 466 (308 members in the Chamber of Deputies [plus 18 reserved seats for non-Hungarian national minorities; ethnic Hungarians compete for regular seats] and 134 in the Senate; the proposed number of members representing the Romanian diaspora has remained unchanged at 6)

election results: Senate—percent of vote by alliance/party—USL 60.1%, ARD 16.7%, PP-DD 14.7%, UDMR 5.2%, other 3.3%; seats by alliance/party—USL 122, ARD 24, PP-DD 21, UDMR 9; Chamber of Deputies—percent of vote by alliance/party—USL 58.6%, ARD 16.5%, PP-DD 14%, UDMR 5.1%, ethnic minorities 2.7%, other 3.1%; seats by alliance/party—USL 273, ARD 56, PP-DD 47, UDMR 18, ethnic minorities 18

Judicial branch: *highest court(s):* High Court of Cassation and Justice (consists of 111 judges organized into civil, penal, commercial, contentious administrative and fiscal business, and joint sections); Supreme Constitutional Court (consists of 9 members)

judge selection and term of office: High Court of Cassation and Justice judges appointed by the president upon nomination by the Superior Council of Magistracy, a 19-member body of judges, prosecutors, and law specialists; judges appointed for 6-year renewable terms; Constitutional Cou rt members—6 elected by Parliament and 3 appointed by the president; members serve 9-year, non-renewable terms

subordinate courts: Courts of Appeal; regional tribunals; first instance courts; military and arbitration courts

Political parties and leaders: Christian-Democratic National Peasants' Party or PNT-CD [Aurelian PAVELESCU] (formerly part of the ARD coalition)

Democratic Union of Hungarians in Romania or UDMR [Hunor KELEMEN]

Green Party [Remus CERNEA]

M10 Party [Monica MACOVEI]

National Liberal Party or PNL [Alina GORGHIU and Vasile BLAGA]—merged with former PDL and FC

National Union for Romania's Progress or UNPR [interim chairman Neculai ONTANU]- merged with former PP-DD

New Republic Party or NR [Alin Ioan BOTA]

Popular Movement Party [Traian BASESCU]

Party of the Alliance of Liberals and Democrats or ALDE [Calin PO PESCU TARI CEANU, Daniel CONSTANTIN]

Romanian Social Party or PSR o [Mircea GEOANA]

Save Bucharest Union Party or Partidul USB [Nicusor DAN]

Social Democratic Party or PSD [Liviu DRAGNEA]

Social Liberal Union or USL (coalition of PSD, PC, and UNPR)

United Romania Party or PRU [Bogdan DIACONU]

Political pressure groups and leaders: *other:* various human rights and professional associations

International organization participation: Australia Group, BIS, BSEC, CBSS (observer), CD, CE, CEI, EAPC, EBRD, ECB, EIB, ESA, EU, FAO, G-9, IAEA, IBRD, ICAO, ICC (national committees), ICCt, ICRM, IDA, IFAD, IFC, IFRCS, IHO, ILO, IMF, IMO, IMSO, Interpol, IOC, IOM, IPU, ISO, ITSO, ITU, ITUC (NGOs), LAIA (observer), MIGA, MO NUSCO, NATO, NSG, OAS (observer), OIF, OPCW, OSCE, PCA, SELEC, UN, UNCTAD, UNESCO, UNHCR, UNIDO, Union Latina, UNMIL, UNMISS, UNOCI, UNWTO, UPU, WCO, WFTU (NGOs), WHO, WIPO, WMO, WTO, ZC

Diplomatic representation in the US: *chief of mission:* Ambassador George Cristian MAIOR (since 17 September 2015)

chancery: 160723rd Street NW, Washington, DC 20008

telephone: [1] (202) 332-4846, 4848, 4851, 4852

FAX: [1] (202) 232-4748

consulate(s) general: Chicago, Los Angeles, New York

Diplomatic representation from the US: *chief of mission:* Ambassador Hans G. KLEMM (since 21 September 2015)

embassy: Bulevardul Dr. Liviu Librescu 4–6, District 1, Bucharest, 015118

mailing address: American Embassy Bucharest, US Department of State, 5260 Bucharest Place, Washington, DC 20521–5260 (pouch)

telephone: [40] (21) 200-3300

FAX: [40] (21) 200-3442

Flag description: three equal vertical bands of blue (hoist side), yellow, and red; modeled after the flag of France, the colors are those of the principalities of Walachia (red and yellow) and Moldavia (red and blue), which united in 1862 to form Romania; the national coat of arms that used to be centered in the yellow band has been removed

note: now similar to the flag of Chad, whose blue band is darker; also resembles the flags of Andorra and Moldova

National symbol(s): golden eagle; national colors: blue, yellow, red

National anthem: *name:* "Desteapta-te romane!" (Wake up, Romanian!)

lyrics/music: Andrei MURESIANU/Anton PANN

note: adopted 1990; the anthem was written during the 1848 Revolution

ECONOMY

Economy—overview: Romania, which joined the EU on 1 January 2007, began the transition from communism in 1989 with a largely obsolete industrial base and a pattern of output unsuited to the country's needs. Romania's macroeconomic gains have only recently started to spur creation of a middle class and to address Romania's widespread poverty. Corruption and red tape continue to permeate the business environment. In the aftermath of the global financial crisis, Romania signed a $26 billion emergency assistance package from the IMF, the EU, and other international lenders, but GDP contracted until 2011. In March 2011, Romania and the IM F/EU/World Bank signed a 24-month precautionary standby agreement, worth $6.6 billion, to promote fiscal discipline, encourage progress on structural reforms, and strengthen financial sector stability; no funds were drawn. in September 2013, Romanian authorities and the IMF/EU agreed to a follow-on standby agreement, worth $5.4 billion, to continue with reforms. This agreement expired in September 2015, and no funds were drawn. Progress on structural reforms has been uneven, and the economy still is vulnerable to external shocks.

Economic growth rebounded in 2013–15, driven by strong industrial exports and excellent agricultural harvests, and the fiscal deficit was reduced substantially. Industry outperformed other sectors of the economy in 2015. Exports remained an engine of economic growth, led by trade with the EU, which accounts for roughly 70% of Romania trade. Domestic demand was a second driver, due to the mid-2015 cut, from 24% to 9%, of the VAT levied upon foodstuffs. In 2015, the government of Romania succeeded in meeting its annual target for the budget deficit, the external deficit remained low, even if it rose due to increasing imports. For the first time since 1989, inflation turned into deflation, allowing for a gradual loosening of monetary policy throughout the period.

An aging population, significant tax evasion, insufficient health care, and an aggressive loosening of the fiscal package jeopardize the low fiscal deficit and public debt and are the economy's top vulnerabilities.

GDP (purchasing power parity):
$413.8 billion (2015 est.)
$398.9 billion (2014 est.)
$387.5 billion (2013 est.)
note: data are in 2015 US dollars
country comparison to the world: 46

GDP (official exchange rate): $177.3 billion (2015 est.)

GDP—real growth rate: 3.7% (2015 est.)
3% (2014 est.)
3.5% (2013 est.)
country comparison to the world: 73

GDP—per capita (PPP): $20,800 (2015 est.)
$20,000 (2014 est.)
$19,400 (2013 est.)
note: data are in 2015 US dollars
country comparison to the world: 85

Gross national saving: 24.4% of GDP (2015 est.)

24.8% of GDP (2014 est.)
24.5% of GDP (2013 est.)
country comparison to the world: 51

GDP—composition, by end use:
household consumption: 68%
government consumption: 7.1%
investment in fixed capital: 24.5%
in vestment in inventories: 1%
exports of goods and services: 40.9%
imports of goods and services: -41.5% (2015 est.)

GDP—composition, by sector of origin:
agriculture: 4.8%
industry: 41.3%
services: 53.9% (2015 est.)

Agriculture—products: wheat, corn, barley, sugar beets, sunflower seed, potatoes, grapes; eggs, sheep

Industries: electric machinery and equipment, auto assembly, textiles and footwear, light machinery, metallurgy, chemicals, food processing, petroleum refining, mining, timber, construction materials

Industrial production growth rate: 4% (2015 est.)
country comparison to the world: 54

Labor force: 9.266 million (2015 est.)
country comparison to the world: 54

Labor force—by occupation: *agriculture:* 28.3%
industry: 28.9%
services: 42.8% (2014)

Unemployment rate: 6.7% (2015 est.)
6.8% (2014 est.)
country comparison to the world: 78

Population below poverty line: 22.4% (2012 est.)

Household income or consumption by percentage share: *lowest:* 10%: 15.3%
highest: 10%: 7.6% (2014 est.)

Distribution of family income—Gini index: 27.3 (2012)
28.2 (2010)
country comparison to the world: 132

Budget: *revenues:* $58.39 billion
expenditures: $60.98 billion (2015 est.)
Taxes and other revenues: 32.9% of GDP (2015 est.)
country comparison to the world: 72

Budget surplus (+) or deficit (–): -1.5% of GDP (2015 est.)
country comparison to the world: 62

Public debt: 39.9% of GDP (2015 est.)
39.8% of GDP (2014 est.)
note: defined by the EU's Maastricht Treaty as consolidated general government gross debt at nominal value, outstanding at the end of the year in the following categories of government liabilities: currency and deposits, securities other than shares excluding financial derivatives, and loans; general government sector comprises the subsectors: central government, state government, local government, and social security funds
country comparison to the world: 114

Fiscal year: calendar year

Inflation rate (consumer prices): -0.6% (2015 est.)
1.1% (2014 est.)
country comparison to the world: 24

Central bank discount rate: 1.75% (31 December 2015)
2.75% (31 December 2014)
country comparison to the world: 118

Commercial bank prime lending rate: 6.21% (31 December 2015 est.)
7.65% (31 December 2014 est.)
country comparison to the world: 126
Stock of narrow money: $37.4 billion (31 December 2015 est.)
$35.5 billion (31 December 2014 est.)
country comparison to the world: 57
Stock of broad money: $71.58 billion (31 December 2015 est.)
$78.18 billion (31 December 2014 est.)
country comparison to the world: 61
Stock of domestic credit: $76.79 billion (31 December 2015 est.)
$88.59 billion (31 December 2014 est.)
country comparison to the world: 56
Market value of publicly traded shares: $36.5 billion (31 December 2015 est.)
$41.04 billion (31 December 2014)
$42.59 billion (31 December 2013 est.)
country comparison to the world: 57
Current account balance: -$1.95 billion (2015 est.)
-$910 million (2014 est.)
country comparison to the world: 143
Exports: $54.51 billion (2015 est.)
$61.79 billion (2014 est.)
country comparison to the world: 51
Exports—commodities: machinery and equipment, other manufactured goods, agricultural products and foodstuffs, metals and metal products, chemicals, minerals and fuels, raw materials
Exports—partners: Germany 19.8%, Italy 12.5%, France 6.8%, Hungary 5.4%, UK 4.4% (2015)
Imports: $63.12 billion (2015 est.)
$70.15 billion (2014 est.)
country comparison to the world: 42
Imports—commodities: machinery and equipment, other manufactured goods, chemicals, agricultural products and foodstuffs, fuels and minerals, metals and metal products, raw materials
Imports—partners: Germany 19.8%, Italy 10.9%, Hungary 8%, France 5.6%, Poland 4.9%, China 4.6%, Netherlands 4% (2015)
Reserves of foreign exchange and gold: $37.33 billion (31 December 2015 est.)
$42.96 billion (31 December 2014 est.)
country comparison to the world: 48
Debt—external: $98.17 billion (31 December 2015 est.)
$114.6 billion (31 December 2014 est.)
country comparison to the world: 51
Stock of direct foreign investment—at home: $76.12 billion (31 December 2015 est.)
$72.84 billion (31 December 2014 est.)
country comparison to the world: 51
Stock of direct foreign investment—abroad: $3.538 billion (31 December 2015 est.)
$3.125 billion (31 December 2014 est.)
country comparison to the world: 73
Exchange rates: lei (RON) per US dollar—
4.0057 (2015 est.)
3.3492 (2014 est.)
3.3492 (2013 est.)
3.47 (2012 est.)
3.0486 (2011 est.)

ENERGY

Electricity—production: 62.04 billion kWh (2014 est.)
country comparison to the world: 46
Electricity—consumption: 50.73 billion kWh (2014 est.)
country comparison to the world: 47
Electricity—exports: 8.2 billion kWh (2014 est.)
country comparison to the world: 24
Electricity—imports: 1.07 billion kWh (2014 est.)
country comparison to the world: 62
Electricity—installed generating capacity: 24 million kW (2014 est.)
country comparison to the world: 36
Electricity—from fossil fuels: 44.3% of total installed capacity (2014 est.)
country comparison to the world: 158
Electricity—from nuclear fuels: 6.1% of total installed capacity (2014 est.)
country comparison to the world: 24
Electricity—from hydroelectric plants: 30% of total installed capacity (2014 est.)
country comparison to the world: 77
Electricity—from other renewable sources: 19.6% of total installed capacity (2014 est.)
country comparison to the world: 16
Crude oil—production: 83,350 bbl/day (2014 est.)
country comparison to the world: 47
Crude oil—exports: 2,077 bbl/day (2012 est.)
country comparison to the world: 78
Crude oil—imports: 104,900 bbl/day (2012 est.)
country comparison to the world: 45
Crude oil—proved reserves: 600 million bbl (1 January 2015 est.)
country comparison to the world: 47
Refined petroleum products—production: 197,300 bbl/day (2012 est.)
country comparison to the world: 54
Refined petroleum products—consumption: 188.000 bbl/day (2013 est.)
country comparison to the world: 60
Refined petroleum products—exports: 72,960 bbl/day (2012 est.)
country comparison to the world: 53
Refined petroleum products—imports: 53,810 bbl/day (2012 est.)
country comparison to the world: 77
Natural gas—production: 11.26 billion cu m (2015 est.)
country comparison to the world: 41
Natural gas—consumption: 11.54 billion cu m (2015 est.)
country comparison to the world: 45
Natural gas—exports: 1.078 million cu m (2015 est.)
country comparison to the world: 49
Natural gas—imports: 277.1 million cu m (2015 est.)
country comparison to the world: 68
Natural gas—proved reserves: 105.5 billion cu m (1 January 2014 est.)
country comparison to the world: 52
Carbon dioxide emissions from consumption of energy: 86.06 million Mt (2012 est.)
country comparison to the world: 44

COMMUNICATIONS

Telephones—fixed lines: *total subscriptions:* 4.6 million
subscriptions per 100 inhabitants: 23 (2014)
country comparison to the world: 33
Telephones—mobile cellular: *total:* 22.9 million
subscriptions per 100 inhabitants: 105 (2014 est.)
country comparison to the world: 53
Telephone system: *general assessment:* the telecommunications sector is being expanded and modernized; domestic and international service improving rapidly, especially mobile-cellular services
domestic: more than 90% of telephone network is automatic; fixed-line teledensity is 23 telephones per 100 persons; mobile-cellular teledensity roughly 114 telephones per 100 persons
international: country code—40; the Black Sea Fiber Optic System provides connectivity to Bulgaria and Turkey; satellite earth stations—10; digital, international, direct-dial exchanges operate in Bucharest (2014)
Broadcast media: a mixture of public and private TV stations; there are 7 public TV stations (2 national, 5 regional) using terrestrial broadcasting and 187 private TV stations (out of which 171 offer local coverage) using terrestrial broadcasting, plus 11 public TV stations using satellite broadcasting and 86 private TV stations using satellite broadcasting; state-owned public radio broadcaster operates 4 national networks and regional and local stations, having in total 20 public radio stations by terrestrial broadcasting plus 4 public radio stations by satellite broadcasting; there are 502 operational private radio stations using terrestrial broadcasting and 26 private radio stations using satellite broadcasting (2014)
Radio broadcast stations: 698 (station frequency type NA) (2006)
Television broadcast stations: 623 (plus 200 repeaters) (2006)
Internet country code: .ro
Internet hosts: 2.667 million (2012)
country comparison to the world: 35
Internet users: *total:* 11.2 million
percent of population: 51.7% (2014 est.)
country comparison to the world: 44

TRANSPORTATION

Airports: 45 (2013)
country comparison to the world: 96
Airports—with paved runways: *total:* 26
over 3,047 m: 4
2, 38 to 3,047 m: 10
1,524 to 2,437 m: 11
under 914 m: 1 (2013)
Airports—with unpaved runways: *total:* 19
914 to 1,523 m: 5
under 914 m: 14 (2013)
Heliports: 2 (2013)
Pipelines: gas 3,726 km; oil 2,451 km (2013)
Railways: *total:* 11,268 km
broad gauge: 60 km 1.524-m gauge
standard gauge: 10,781 km 1.435-m gauge (3,292 km electrified)

narrow gauge: 427 km 0.760-m gauge (2014)
country comparison to the world: 22
Roadways: *total:* 84,185 km
paved: 49,873 km (includes 337 km of expressways)
unpaved: 34,312 km (2012)
country comparison to the world: 55
Waterways: 1,731 km (includes 1,075 km on the Danube River, 524 km on secondary branches, and 132 km on canals) (2010)
country comparison to the world: 45
Merchant marine: *total:* 5
by type: cargo 1, passenger/cargo 2, petroleum tanker 1, roll on/roll off 1
foreign-owned: 1 (Russia 1)
registered in other countries: 31 (Georgia 7, Liberia 3, Malta 7, Marshall Islands 2, Moldova 2, Panama 3, Russia 1, Saint Vincent and the Grenadines 1, Sierra Leone 2, Tanzania 1, Togo 1, unknown 1) (2010)
country comparison to the world: 127
Ports and terminals: *major seaport(s):* Constanta, Midia
river port(s): Braila, Galati (G alatz), M ancanului (Giurgiu), Tulcea (Danube River)

MILITARY AND SECURITY

Military branches: Land Forces, Naval Forces (Fortele Naval, FN), Romanian Air Force (Fortele Aeriene Romane, FAR) (2013)
Military service age and obligation: conscription ended 2006; 18 years of age for male and female voluntary service; all military inductees (including women) contract for an initial 5-year term of service, with subsequent successive 3-year terms until age 36 (2015)
Military expenditures:
1.4% of GDP (2015)
1.42% of GDP (2014 est.)
1.3% of GDP (2013)
1.29% of GDP (2012)
1.3% of GDP (2011)
country comparison to the world: 69

TRANSNATIONAL ISSUES

Disputes—international: the ICJ ruled largely in favor of Romania in its dispute submitted in 2004 over Ukrainian-administered Zmiyinyy/Serpilor (Snake) Island and Black Sea maritime boundary delimitation; Romania opposes Ukraine's reopening of a navigation canal from the Danube border through Ukraine to the Black Sea
Refugees and internally displaced persons: *stateless persons:* 240 (2015)
Illicit drugs: major transshipment point for Southwest Asian heroin transiting the Balkan route and small amounts of Latin American cocaine bound for Western Europe; although not a significant financial center, role as a narcotics conduit leaves it vulnerable to laundering, which occurs via the banking system, currency exchange houses, and casinos

RUSSIA

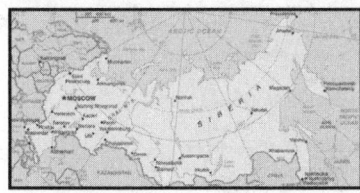

INTRODUCTION

Background: Founded in the 12th century, the Principality of Muscovy was able to emerge from over 200 years of Mongol domination (13th-15th centuries) and to gradually conquer and absorb surrounding principalities. In the early 17th century, a new ROMANOV Dynasty continued this policy of expansion across Siberia to the Pacific. Under PETER I (ruled 1682-1725), hegemony was extended to the Baltic Sea and the country was renamed the Russian Empire. During the 19th century, more territorial acquisitions were made in Europe and Asia. Defeat in the Russo-Japanese War of 1904-05 contributed to the Revolution of 1905, which resulted in the formation of a parliament and other reforms. Repeated devastating defeats of the Russian army in World War I led to widespread rioting in the major cities of the Russian Empire and to the overthrow in 1917 of the imperial household. The communists under Vladimir LEN in seized power soon after and formed the USSR. The brutal rule of Iosif STALIN (1928-53) strengthened communist rule and Russian dominance of the Soviet Union at a cost of tens of millions of lives. After defeating Germany in World War II as part of an alliance with the US (1939-1945), the USSR expanded its territory and influence in Eastern Europe and emerged as a global power. The USSR was the principal adversary of the US during the Cold War (1947-1991). The Soviet economy and society stagnated in the decades following Stalin's rule, until General Secretary Mikhail GORBACHEV (1985-91) introduced glasnost (openness) and perestroika (restructuring) in an attempt to modernize communism, but his initiatives inadvertently released forces that by December 1991 splintered the USSR into Russia and 14 other independent republics. Following economic and political turmoil during President Boris YELTSIN's term (1991-99), Russia shifted toward a centralized authoritarian state under the leadership of President Vladimir PUTIN (2000-2008,2012-present) in which the regime seeks to legitimize its rule through managed elections, populist appeals, a foreign policy focused on enhancing the country's geopolitical influence, and commodity-based economic growth. Russia faces a largely subdued rebel movement in Chechnya and some other surrounding regions, although violence still occurs throughout the North Caucasus.

GEOGRAPHY

Location: North Asia bordering the Arctic Ocean, extending from Europe (the portion west of the Urals) to the North Pacific Ocean
Geographic coordinates: 60 00 N, 100 00 E
Map references: Asia
Area: *total:* 17,098,242 sq km
land: 16,377,742 sq km
water: 720,500 sq km
country comparison to the world: 1
Area—comparative: approximately 1.8 times the size of the US
Land boundaries: *total:* 22,408 km
border countries (14): Azerbaijan 338 km, Belarus 1,312 km, China (southeast) 4,133 km, China (south) 46 km, Estonia 324 km, Finland 1,309 km, Georgia 894 km, Kazakhstan 7,644 km, North Korea 18 km, Latvia 332 km, Lithuania (Kaliningrad Oblast) 261 km, Mongolia 3,452 km, Norway 191 km, Poland (Kaliningrad Oblast) 210 km, Ukraine 1944 km
Coastline: 37,653 km
Maritime claims: *territorial sea:* 12 nm
contiguous zone: 24 nm
exclusive economic zone: 200 nm
continental shelf: 200-m depth or to the depth of exploitation
Climate: ranges from steppes in the south through humid continental in much of European Russia; subarctic in Siberia to tundra climate in the polar north; winters vary from cool along Black Sea coast to frigid in Siberia; summers vary from warm in the steppes to cool along Arctic coast
Terrain: broad plain with low hills west of Urals; vast coniferous forest and tun dra in Siberia; uplan ds and mountains along southern border regions
Elevation: *mean elevation:* 600 m
elevation extremes: *lowest point:* Caspian Sea -28 m
highest point: Gora El'brus 5,633 m (highest point in Europe)
Natural resources: wide natural resource base in cluding major deposits of oil, natural gas, coal, and

many strategic minerals, reserves of rare earthelements, timber

note: formidable obstacles of climate, terrain, and distance hinder exploitation of natural resources

Land use: *agricultural land:* 13.1%
arable land: 7.3%
permanent crops: 0.1%
permanent pasture: 5.7%
forest: 49.4%
other: 37.5% (2011 est.)

Irrigated land: 43,000 sq km (2012)

Total renewable water resources: 4,508 cu km (2011)

Freshwater withdrawal (domestic/industrial/agricultural): *total:* 66.2 cu km/yr (20%/60%/20%)
per capita: 454.9 cu m/yr (2001)

Natural hazards: permafrost over much of Siberia is a major impediment to development; volcanic activity in the Kuril Islands; volcanoes and earthquakes on the Kamchatka Peninsula; spring floods and summer/autumn forest fires throughout Siberia and parts of European Russia

volcanism: significant volcanic activity on the Kamchatka Peninsula and Kuril Islands; the peninsula alone is home to some 29 historically active volcanoes, with dozens more in the Kuril Islands; Kliuchevskoi (elev. 4,835 m), which erupted in 2007 and 2010, is Kamchatka's most active volcano; Avachinsky and Koryaksky volcanoes, which pose a threat to the city of Petropavlovsk-Kamchatskiy, have been deemed Decade Volcanoes by the International Association of Volcanology and Chemistry of the Earth's Interior, worthy of study due to their explosive history and close proximity to human populations; other notable historically active volcanoes include Bezymianny, Chikurachki, Ebeko, Gorely, Grozny, Karymsky, Ketoi, Kronotsky, Ksudach, Medvezhia, Mutnovsky, Sarychev Peak, Shiveluch, Tiatia, Tolbachik, and Zheltovsky

Environment—current issues: air pollution from heavy industry, emissions of coal-fired electric plants, and transportation in major cities; industrial, municipal, and agricultural pollution of inland waterways and seacoasts; deforestation; soil erosion; soil contamination from improper application of agricultural chemicals; scattered areas of sometimes intense radioactive contamination; groundwater contamination from toxic waste; urban solid waste management; abandoned stocks of obsolete pesticides

Environment—international agreements: *party to:* Air Pollution, Air Pollution-Nitrogen Oxides, Air Pollution-Sulfur 85, Antarctic-Environmental Protocol, Antarctic-Marine Living Resources, Antarctic Seals, Antarctic Treaty, Biodiversity, Climate Change, Climate Change-Kyoto Protocol, Desertification, Endangered Species, Environmental Modification, Hazardous Wastes, Law of the Sea, Marine Dumping, Ozone Layer Protection, Ship Pollution, Tropical Timber 83, Wetlands, Whaling
signed, but not ratified: Air Pollution-Sulfur 94

Geography—note: largest country in the world in terms of area but unfavorably located in relation to major sea lanes of the world; despite its size,

much of the country lacks proper soils and climates (either too cold or too dry) for agriculture; Mount El'brus is Europe's tallest peak; Lake Baikal, the deepest lake in the world, is estimated to hold one fifth of the world's fresh water

PEOPLE AND SOCIETY

Nationality: *noun:* Russian(s)
adjective: Russian

Ethnic groups: Russian 77.7%, Tatar 3.7%, Ukrainian 1.4%, Bashkir 1.1%, Chuvash 1%, Chechen 1%, other 10.2%, unspecified 3.9%
note: nearly 200 national and/or ethnic groups are represented in Russia's 2010 census (2010 est.)

Languages: Russian (official) 85.7%, Tatar 3.2%, Chechen 1%, other 10.1%
note: data represent native language spoken (2010 est.)

Religions: RussiaNorthodox 15–20%, Muslim 10–15%, other Christian 2% (2006 est.)
note: estimates are of practicing worshipers; Russia has large populations of non-practicing believers and non-believers, a legacy of over seven decades of Soviet rule; Russia officially recognizes Orthodox Christianity, Islam, Judaism, and Buddhism as traditional religions

Population: 142,423,773 (July 2015 est.)
country comparison to the world: 10

Age structure: *0–14 years:* 16.68% (male 12,204,992/female 11,556,764)
15–24 years: 10.15% (male 7,393,188/female 7,064,060)
25–54 years: 45.54% (male 31,779,688/female 33,086,346)
55–64 years: 14.01% (male 8,545,371/female 11,409,076)
65 years and over: 13.61% (male 5,978,578/female 13,405,710) (2015 est.)

Dependency ratios: *total dependency ratio:* 43.1%
youth dependency ratio: 24%
elderly dependency ratio: 19.1%
potential support ratio: 5.2% (2015 est.)

Median age: *total:* 39.1 years
male: 36.2 years
female: 42.1 years (2015 est.)
country comparison to the world: 55

Population growth rate: -0.04% (2015 est.)
country comparison to the world: 203

Birth rate: 11.6 births/1,000 population (2015 est.)
country comparison to the world: 169

Death rate: 13.69 deaths/1,000 population (2015 est.)
country comparison to the world: 11

Net migration rate: 1.69 migrant(s)/1,000 population (2015 est.)
country comparison to the world: 54

Urbanization: *urban Population:* 74% of total population (2015)
rate of urbanization: -0.13% annual rate of change (2010–15 est.)

Major urban areas—population: MOSCOW (capital) 12.166 million; Saint Petersburg 4.993 million; Novosibirsk 1.497 million; Yekaterinburg 1.379 million; Nizhniy Novgorod 1.212 million; Samara 1.164 million (2015)

Sex ratio: *at birth:* 1.06 male(s)/female
0–14 years: 1.06 male(s)/female
15–24 years: 1.05 male(s)/female
25–54 years: 0.96 male(s)/female
55–64 years: 0.75 male(s)/female
65 years and over: 0.45 male(s)/female
total population: 0.86 male(s)/female (2015 est.)

Mother's mean age at first birth: 24.6 (2009 est.)

Maternal mortality rate: 25 deaths/100,000 live births (2015 est.)
country comparison to the world: 119

Infant mortality rate: *total:* 6.97 deaths/1,000 live births
male: 7.81 deaths/1,000 live births
female: 6.07 deaths/1,000 live births (2015 est.)
country comparison to the world: 159

Life expectancy at birth: *total population:* 70.47 years
male: 64.7 years
female: 76.57 years (2015 est.)
country comparison to the world: 153

Total fertility rate: 1.61 children born/woman (2015 est.)
country comparison to the world: 179

Contraceptive prevalence rate: 68%
note: percent of women aged 15–44 (2011)

Healthexpenditures: 6.5% of GDP (2013)
country comparison to the world: 106

Physicians density: 4.31 physicians/1,000 population (2006)

Hospital bed density: 9.7 beds/1,000 population (2006)

Drinking water source:
improved:
urban: 98.9% of population
rural: 91.2% of population
total: 96.9% of population
unimproved:
urban: 1.1% of population
rural: 8.8% of population
total: 3.1% of population (2015 est.)

Sanitation facility access:
improved:
urban: 77% of population
rural: 58.7% of population
total: 72.2% of population
unimproved:
urban: 23% of population
rural: 41.3% of population
total: 27.8% of population (2015 est.)

HIV/AIDS—adult prevalence rate: NA

HIV/AIDS—people living with HIV/AIDS: NA

HIV/AIDS—deaths: NA

Major infectious diseases: *degree of risk:* intermediate
food or waterborne diseases: bacterial diarrhea
vectorborne disease: tickborne encephalitis
note: highly pathogenic H5N1 avian influenza has been identified in this country; it poses a negligible risk withextremely rare cases possible among US citizens who have close contact with birds (2013)

Obesity—adult prevalence rate: 26.2% (2014)
country comparison to the world: 46

Education expenditures: 4.2% of GDP (2012)
country comparison to the world: 110

Literacy: *definition:* age 15 and over can read and write

total population: 99.7%

male: 99.7%

female: 99.6% (2015 est.)

School life expectancy (primary to tertiary education): *total:* 15 years

male: 15 years

female: 15 years (2014)

Unemployment, youth ages 15–24: *total:* 13.8%

male: 13.3%

female: 14.5% (2013 est.)

country comparison to the world: 78

GOVERNMENT

Country name: *conventional long form:* Russian Federation

conventional short form: Russia

local long form: Rossiyskaya Federatsiya

local short form: Rossiya

former: Russian Empire, Russian Soviet Federative Socialist Republic

etymology: Russian lands were generally referred to as Muscovy until PETER I officially declared the Russian Empire in 1721; the new name sought to invoke the patrimony of the medieval eastern European Rus state centered on Kyiv in present-day Ukraine; the Rus were a Varangian (eastern Viking) elite that imposed their rule and eventually their name on their Slavic subjects

Government type: semi-presidential federation

Capital: *name:* Moscow

Geographic coordinates: 55 45 N, 37 36 E

time difference: UTC+3 (8 hours ahead of Washington, DC, during Standard Time)

note: Russia has 11 time zones, which includes two that were added in 2014

Administrative divisions: 46 provinces (oblastey, singular—oblast), 21 republics (respublik, singular—respublika), 4 autonomous okrugs (avtonomnykh okrugov, singular—avtonomnyy okrug), 9 krays (krayev, singular—kray), 2 federal cities (goroda, singular—gorod), and 1 autonomous oblast (avtonomnaya oblast')

oblasts: Amur (Blagoveshchensk), Arkhangel'sk, Astrakhan', Belgorod, Bryansk, Chelyabinsk, Irkutsk, Ivanovo, Kaliningrad, Kaluga, Kemerovo, Kirov, Kostroma, Kurgan, Kursk, Leningrad, Lipetsk, Magadan, Moscow, Murmansk, Nizhniy Novgorod, Novgorod, Novosibirsk, Omsk, Orenburg, Orel, Penza, Pskov, Rostov, Ryazan', Sakhalin (Yuzhno-Sakhalinsk), Samara, Saratov, Smolensk, Sverdlovsk (Yekaterinburg), Tambov, Tomsk, Tula, Tver', Tyumen', Ul'yanovsk, Vladimir, Volgograd, Vologda, Voronezh, Yaroslavl'

republics: Adygeya (Maykop), Altay (Gorno-Altaysk), Bashkortostan (Ufa), Buryatiya (Ulan-Ude), Chechnya (Groznyy), Chuvashiya (Cheboksary), Dagestan (Makhachkala), Ingushetiya (Magas), Kabardino-Balkariya (Nal'chik), Kalmykiya (Elista), Karachayevo-Cherkesiya (Cherkessk), Kareliya (Petrozavodsk), Khakasiya (Abakan), Komi (Syktyvkar), Mariy-El (Yoshkar-Ola), Mordoviya (Saransk), North Ossetia (Vladikavkaz), Sakha [Yakutiya] (Yakutsk), Tatarstan (Kazan'), Tyva (Kyzyl), Udmurtiya (Izhevsk)

autonomous okrugs: Chukotka (Anadyr'), Khanty-Mansi-Yugra (Khanty-Mansiysk), Nenets (Nar'yan-Mar), Yamalo-Nenets (Salekhard)

krays: Altay (Barnaul), Kamchatka (Petropavlovsk-Kamchatskiy), Khabarovsk, Krasnodar, Krasnoyarsk, Perm', Primorskiy [Maritime] (Vladivostok), Stavropol', Zabaykal'sk (Chita)

federal cities: Moscow [Moskva], Saint Petersburg [Sankt-Peterburg]

autonomous oblast: Yevreyskaya [Jewish] (Birobidzhan)

note 1: administrative divisions have the same names as their administrative centers (exceptions have the administrative center name following in parentheses)

note 2: the United States does not recognize Russia's annexation of Ukraine's Autonomous Republic of Crimea and the municipality of Sevastopol, nor their redesignation as the Republic of Crimea and the Federal City of Sevastopol

Independence: 24 August 1991 (from the Soviet Union); notable earlier dates: 1157 (Principality of Vladimir-Suzdal created); 16 January 1547 (Tsardom of Muscovy established); 22 October 1721 (Russian Empire proclaimed); 30 December 1922 (Soviet Union established)

National holiday: Russia Day, 12 June (1990)

Constitution: several previous (during Russian Empire and Soviet eras); latest drafted 12 July 1993, adopted by referendum 12 December 1993, effective 25 December 1993; amended 2008,2014 (2016)

Legal system: civil law system; judicial review of legislative acts

International law organization participation: has not submitted an ICJ jurisdiction declaration; non-party state to the ICCt

Citizenship: *citizenship by birth:* no

citizenship by descent only: at least one parent must be a citizen of Russia

dual citizenship recognized: yes

residency requirement for naturalization: 3–5 years

Suffrage: 18 years of age; universal

Executive branch: *chief of state:* President Vladimir Vladimirovich PUTIN (since 7 May 2012)

head of government: Premier Dmitriy Anatolyevich MEDVEDEV (since 8 May 2012); First Deputy Premier Igor Ivanovich SHUVALOV (since 12 May 2008); Deputy Premiers Arkadiy Vladimirovich DVORKOVICH (since 21 May 2012), Olga Yuryevna GOLODETS (since 21 May 2012), Aleksandr Gennadiyevich KHLOPONIN (since 19 January 2010), Dmitriy Nikolayevich KOZAK (since 14 October 2008), Dmitriy Olegovich ROGOZIN (since 23 December 2011), Sergey Eduardovich PRIKHODKO (since 22 May 2013), Yuriy Petrovich TRUTNEV (since 31 August 2013)

cabinet: the "Government" is composed of the premier, his deputies, and ministers, all appointed by the president; the premier is also confirmed by the Duma

elections/appointments: president directly elected by absolute majority popular vote in 2

rounds if needed for a 6-year term (eligible for a second term); election last held on 4 March 2012 (next to be held in March 2018); note—term length extended to 6 years from 4 years in late 2008, effective after the 2012 election; there is no vice president; premier appointed by the president with the approval of the Duma

election results: Vladimir PUTIN elected president; percent of vote—Vladimir PUTIN (United Russia) 63.6%, Gennadiy ZYUGANOV (CPRF) 17.2%, Mikhail PROKHOROV(Civic Platform) 8%, Vladimir ZHIRINOVSKIY (LDPR) 6.2%, Sergey MIRONOV (A Just Russia) 3.9%, other 1.1%; Dmitriy MEDVEDEV (United Russia) approved as premier by Duma; vote—299 to 144

note: there is also a Presidential Administration that provides staff and policy support to the president, drafts presidential decrees, and coordinates policy among government agencies; a Security Council also reports directly to the president

Legislative branch: *description:* bicameral Federal Assembly or Federalnoye Sobraniye consists of the Federation Council or Sovet Federatsii (166 seats; 2 members in each of the 83 federal administrative units—oblasts, krays, republics, autonomous okrugs and oblasts, and the federal cities of Moscow and Saint Petersburg-appointed by the top executive and legislative officials; members serve 4-year terms) and the State Duma or Gosudarstvennaya Duma (450 seats; as of February 2014, the electoral system reverted to a mixed electoral system for the 2016 election in which one-half of the members are directly elected by simple majority vote and one-half directly elected by proportional representation vote; members serve 5-year terms)

elections: State Duma—last held on 4 December 2011 (next to be held in September 2016)

election results: State Duma—United Russia 49.3%, CPRF 19.2%, A Just Russia 13.2%, LDPR 11.7%, other 6.6%; seats by party—United Russia 238, CPRF 92, A Just Russia 64, LDPR 56

note: the State Duma now includes 2 representatives each from the Republic of Crimea and Federal City of Sevastopol, two annexed Ukrainian regions that the US does not recognize as part of Russia

Judicial branch: *highest court(s):* Supreme Court of the Russian Federation (consists of 170 members organized into the Judicial Panel for Civil Affairs, the Judicial Panel for Criminal Affairs, and the Military Panel); Constitutional Court (consists of 19 members); note—in February 2014, Russia's Superior Court of Arbitration was abolished and its former authorities transferred to the Supreme Court, which in addition to being the country's highest judicial authority for appeals, civil, criminal, administrative cases, and military cases, and the disciplinary judicial board, now has jurisdiction over economic disputes

judge selection and term of office: all members of Russia's 3 highest courts nominated by the president and appointed by the Federation Council (the upper house of the legislature); members of all 3 courts appointed for life

subordinate courts: Higher Arbitration Court; regional (kray) and provincial (oblast) courts;

Moscow and St. Petersburg city courts; autonomous province and district courts; note—the 14 Russian Republics have court systems specified by their own constitutions

Political parties and leaders: A Just Russia [Sergey MIRONOV]

Communist Party of the Russian Federation or CPRF [Gennadiy ZYUGANOV]

Liberal Democratic Party of Russia or LDPR [Vladimir ZHIRINOVSKIY]

United Russia [D mitriy MEDVEDEV]

note: 78 political parties are registered with Russia's Ministry of Justice (as of October 2015), but only four parties maintain representation in Russia's national legislature

Political pressure groups and leaders: Confederation of Labor of Russia or KTR

Federation of Independent Trade Unions of Russia

Golos Association in Defense of Voters' Rights

Memorial

Movement Against Illegal Migration

Russkiye

Solidarnost

The World Russian People's Congress

Union of the Committees of Soldiers' Mothers

Union of Russian Writers

other: business associations; environmental organizations; religious groups (especially those with Orthodox or Muslim affiliation); veterans groups

International organization participation: APEC, Arctic Council, ARF, ASEAN (dialogue partner), BIS, BRICS, BSEC, CBSS, CD, CE, CERN (observer), CICA, CIS, CSTO, EAEC, EAEU, EAPC, EAS, EBRD, FAO, FATF, G-20, GCTU, IAEA, IBRD, ICAO, ICC (national committees), ICR M, IDA, IFAD, IFC, IFRCS, IHO, ILO, IMF, IMO, IMSO, Interpol, IOC, IOM (observer), IPU, ISO, ITSO, ITU, ITUC (NGOs), LAIA (observer), MIGA, MINURSO, MONUSCO, NEA, NSG, OAS (observer), OIC (observer), OPCW, OSCE, Paris Club, PCA, PFP, SCO, UN, UNCTAD, UNESCO, UNHCR, UNIDO, UNISFA, UNMIL, UNMISS, UNOCI, UNSC (permanent), UNTSO, UNWTO, UPU, WCO, WFTU (NGOs), WHO, WIPO, WMO, WTO, ZC

Diplomatic representation in the US: *chief of mission:* Ambassador Sergey Ivanovich KISLYAK (since 16 September 2008)

chancery: 2650 Wisconsin Avenue NW, Washington, DC 20007

telephone: [1] (202) 298-5700,5701,5704,5708

FAX: [1] (202) 298-5735

consulate(s) general: Houston, New York, San Francisco, Seattle

Diplomatic representation from the US: *chief of mission:* Ambassador John Francis TEFFT (since 19 November 2014)

embassy: Bolshoy Deviatinskiy Pereulok No.8,121099 Moscow

mailing address: PSC -77, APO AE 09721

telephone: [7] (495) 728-5000

FAX: [7] (495) 728-5090

consulate(s) general: Saint Petersburg, Vladivostok, Yekaterinburg

Flag description: three equal horizontal bands of white (top), blue, and red

note: the colors may have been based on th ose of the Dutch flag; despite many popular interpretations, there is no official meaning assigned to the colors of the Russian flag; this flag inspired several other Slav countries to adopt horizontal tricolors of the same colors but in different arrangements, and so red, blue, and wh ite became the Pan-Slav colors

National symbol(s): bear, double-headed eagle; national colors: white, blue, red

National anthem: *name:* "Gimn Rossiyskoy Federatsii" (National Anthem of the Russian Federation)

lyrics/music: Sergey Vladimirovich MIKHALKOV/ Aleksandr Vasilyevich ALEKSANDROV

note: in 2000, Russia adopted the tune of the anthem of the former Soviet Union (composed in 1939); the lyrics, also adopted in 2000, were written by the same person WHO auth ored the Soviet lyrics in 1943

ECONOMY

Economy—overview: Russia has undergone significant ch anges since the collapse of the Soviet Union, moving from a centrally planned economy towards a more market-based system. Botheconomic growth and reform have stalled in recent years, however, and Russia remains a predominantly statist economy with a high concentration of wealth in officials' hands. Economic reforms in the 1990s privatized most industry, with notable exceptions in the energy, transportation, banking, and defense-related sectors. The protection of property righ ts is still weak, and the state continues to interfere in the free operation of the private sector. Russia is one of the world's leading producers of oil and natural gas, and is also a top exporter of metals such as steel and primary aluminum. Russia's reliance on commodity exports makes it vulnerable to boom and bust cycles that follow the volatile swings in global prices.

The economy, which had averaged 7% growth during 1998–2008 as oil prices rose rapidly, has seen diminishing growth rates since then due to the exhaustion of Russia's commodity-based growth model. A combination of falling oil prices, international sanctions, and structural limitations pushed Russia into a deep recession in 2015, with the GDP falling by close to 4%. Most economists expect th is downturn will continue through 2016. Government support for import substitution has increased recently in an effort to diversify the economy away from extractive industries. Alth ough the Russian Ministry of Economic Development is forecasting a modest growth of 0.7% for 2016 as a Whole, the Central Bank of Russia (CBR) is more pessimistic and expects the recovery to begin later in the year and a decline of 0.5% to 1.0% for the full year. Russia is heavily dependent on the movement of world commodity prices and the CBR estimates that if oil prices remain below $40 per barrel beyond 2016, the resulting shock would cause GDP to fall by up to 5%.

GDP (purchasing power parity): $3.718 trillion (2015 est.)

$3.862 trillion (2014 est.)

$3.834 trillion (2013 est.)

note: data are in 2015 US dollars

country comparison to the world: 7

GDP (official exchange rate): $1.325 trillion (2015 est.)

GDP—real growth rate: -3.7% (2015 est.)

0.7% (2014 est.)

1.3% (2013 est.)

country comparison to the world: 210

GDP—per capita (PPP): $25,400 (2015 est.)

$26,400 (2014 est.)

$26,700 (2013 est.)

note: data are in 2015 US dollars

country comparison to the world: 73

Gross national saving: 23.4% of GDP (2015 est.)

24% of GDP (2014 est.)

22.3% of GDP (2013 est.)

country comparison to the world: 62

GDP—composition, by end use:

household consumption: 53.2%

government consumption: 20.2%

investment in fixed capital: 19.1%

investment in inventori es: -3.3%

exports of goods and services: 32.2%

imports of goods and services: -21.4% (2015 est.)

GDP—composition, by sector of origin:

agriculture: 4.4%

industry: 35.8%

services: 59.7% (2015 est.)

Agriculture—products: grain, sugar beets, sunflower seeds, vegetables, fruits; beef, milk

Industries: complete range of mining and extractive industries producing coal, oil, gas, chemicals, and metals; all forms of machine building from rolling mills to high-performance aircraft and space vehicles; defense industries (including radar, missile production, advanced electronic components), shipbuilding; road and rail transportation equipment; communications equipment; agricultural machinery, tractors, and construction equipment; electric power generating and transmitting equipment; medical and scientific instruments; consumer durables, textiles, foodstuffs, handicrafts

Industrial production growth rate: -3.5% (2015 est.)

country comparison to the world: 185

Labor force: 74.89 million (2015 est.)

country comparison to the world: 8

Labor force—by occupation:

agriculture: 9.4%

industry: 27.6%

services: 63% (2014)

Unemployment rate: 5.4% (2015 est.)

5.2% (2014 est.)

country comparison to the world: 58

Population below poverty line: 11.2% (2014 est.)

Household income or consumption by percentage share: *lowest:* 10%: 5.7%

highest: 10%: 42.4% (2011 est.)

Distribution of family income—Gini index: 42 (2014)

41.7 (2011)

country comparison to the world: 55

Budget: *revenues:* $216.3 billion

expenditures: $251.6 billion (2015 est.)

Taxes and other revenues: 17.5% of GDP (2015 est.)

country comparison to the world: 175

Budget surplus (+) or deficit (−): -2.9% of GDP (2015 est.)

country comparison to the world: 107

Public debt: 13.5% of GDP (2015 est.)

10.4% of GDP (2014 est.)

note: data cover general government debt, and includes debt instruments issued (or owned) by government entities other than the treasury; the data include treasury debt held by foreign entities; the data include debt issued by subnational entities, as well as intra-governmental debt; intra-governmental debt consists of treasury borrowings from surpluses in the social funds, such as for retirement, medical care, and unemployment, debt instruments for the social funds are not sold at public auctions

country comparison to the world: 162

Fiscal year: calendar year

Inflation rate (consumer prices): 15.5% (2015 est.)

7.8% (2014 est.)

country comparison to the world: 217

Central bank discount rate: 11% (31 December 2015 est.)

17% (31 December 2014)

note: this is the so-called refinancing rate, but in Russia banks do not get refinancing at this rate; this is a reference rate used primarily for fiscal purposes

country comparison to the world: 19

Commercial bank prime lending rate: 15.9% (31 December 2015 est.)

11.14% (31 December 2014 est.)

country comparison to the world: 33

Stock of narrow money: $171.5 billion (31 December 2015 est.)

$201.4 billion (31 December 2014 est.)

country comparison to the world: 24

Stock of broad money: $926.8 billion (31 October 2014 est.)

$1.087 trillion (31 December 2013 est.)

country comparison to the world: 19

Stock of domestic credit: $676.5 billion (31 December 2015 est.)

$664.8 billion (31 December 2014 est.)

country comparison to the world: 20

Market value of publicly traded shares:

$874.7 billion (31 December 2012 est.)

$796.4 billion (31 December 2011)

$1.005 trillion (31 December 2010 est.)

country comparison to the world: 17

Current account balance: $65.8 billion (2015 est.)

$59.46 billion (2014 est.)

country comparison to the world: 9

Exports: $337.8 billion (2015 est.)

$497.8 billion (2014 est.)

country comparison to the world: 15

Exports—commodities: petroleum and petroleum products, natural gas, metals, wood and wood products, chemicals, and a wide variety of civilian and military manufactures

Exports—partners: Netherlands 11.9%, China 8.3%, Germany 7.4%, Italy 6.5%, Turkey 5.6%, Belarus 4.4%, Japan 4.2% (2015)

Imports: $197.3 billion (2015 est.)

$308 billion (2014 est.)

country comparison to the world: 23

Imports—commodities: machinery, vehicles, pharmaceutical products, plastic, semi-finished metal products, meat, fruits and nuts, optical and medical instruments, iron, steel

Imports—partners: China 19.2%, Germany 11.2%, US 6.4%, Belarus 4.8%, Italy 4.6% (2015)

Reserves of foreign exchange and gold: $377.8 billion (31 December 2015 est.)

$385.5 billion (31 December 2014 est.)

country comparison to the world: 7

Debt—external: $599 billion (31 December 2014 est.)

$728.9 billion (31 December 2013 est.)

country comparison to the world: 23

Stock of direct foreign investment—at home:

$360.9 billion (31 December 2015 est.)

$353.4 billion (31 December 2014 est.)

country comparison to the world: 20

Stock of direct foreign investment—abroad:

$404.4 billion (31 December 2015 est.)

$388.4 billion (31 December 2014 est.)

country comparison to the world: 19

Exchange rates: Russian rubles (RUB) per US dollar—

61.27 (2015 est.)

38.378 (2014 est.)

38.378 (2013 est.)

30.84 (2012 est.)

29.382 (2011 est.)

ENERGY

Electricity—production: 1.064 trillion kWh (2014 est.)

country comparison to the world: 4

Electricity—consumption: 1.065 trillion kWh (2014 est.)

country comparison to the world: 4

Electricity—exports: 8.12 billion kWh (2014 est.)

country comparison to the world: 25

Electricity—imports: 8.87 billion kWh (2014 est.)

country comparison to the world: 24

Electricity—installed generating capacity: 242.2 million kW (2013 est.)

country comparison to the world: 6

Electricity—from fossil fuels: 68.8% of total installed capacity (2012 est.)

country comparison to the world: 110

Electricity—from nuclear fuels: 10.1% of total installed capacity (2012 est.)

country comparison to the world: 18

Electricity—from hydroelectric plants: 20.2% of total installed capacity (2012 est.)

country comparison to the world: 92

Electricity—from other renewable sources: 0.4% of total installed capacity (2012 est.)

country comparison to the world: 103

Crude oil—production: 10.84 million bbl/day (2014 est.)

cou ntry comparison to the world: 1

Crude oil—exports: 4.594 million bbl/day (2014 est.)

country comparison to the world: 2

Crude oil—imports: 29,650 bbl/day (2014 est.)

country comparison to the world: 62

Crude oil—proved reserves: 103.2 billion bbl (1 January 2015 est.)

country comparison to the world: 7

Refined petroleum products—production: 6.053 million bbl/day (2014 est.)

country comparison to the world: 4

Refined petroleum products—consumption: 2.8 million bbl/day (2014 est.)

country comparison to the world: 8

Refined petroleum products—exports: 3.3 million bbl/day (2014 est.)

country comparison to the world: 1

Refined petroleum products—imports: 44,600 bbl/day (2014 est.)

country comparison to the world: 83

Natural gas—production: 578.7 billion cu m (2014 est.)

country comparison to the world: 2

Natural gas—consumption: 409.2 billion cu m (2014 est.)

country comparison to the world: 2

Natural gas—exports: 201.9 billion cu m (2014 est.)

country comparison to the world: 1

Natural gas—imports: 24.2 billion cu m (2014 est.)

country comparison to the world: 14

Natural gas—proved reserves: 32.6 trillion cu m (1 January 2015 est.)

country comparison to the world: 2

Carbon dioxide emissions from consumption of energy: 1.782 billion Mt (2012 est.)

country comparison to the world: 5

COMMUNICATIONS

Telephones—fixed lines: *total subscriptions:* 39.43 million

subscriptions per 100 inhabitants: 28 (2014 est.)

country comparison to the world: 7

Telephones—mobile cellular: *total:* 221 million

subscriptions per 100 inhabitants: 155 (2014 est.)

country comparison to the world: 7

Telephone system: *general assessment:* the telephone system is experiencing significant changes; more than 1,000 companies licensed to offer communication services; access to digital lines has improved, particularly in urban centers; progress made toward building the telecommunications infrastructure necessary for a market economy; the estimated number of mobile subscribers jumped from fewer than 1 million in 1998 to more than 235 million in 2011; fixed-line service has improved but a large demand remains

domestic: cross-country digital trunk lines run from Saint Petersburg to Khabarovsk, and from Moscow to Novorossiysk; the telephone systems in 60 regional capitals have modern digital infrastructures; cellular services, both analog and digital, are available in many areas; in rural areas, telephone services are still outdated, inadequate, and low-density

705

international: country code—7; connected internationally by undersea fiber optic cables; satellite earth stations provide access to Intelsat, Intersputnik, Eutelsat, Inmarsat, and Orbita systems (2011)

Broadcast media: 13 national TV stations with the federal government owning 1 and holding a controlling interest in a second; state-owned Gazprom maintains a controlling interest in 2 of the national channels; government-affiliated Bank Rossiya owns controlling interest in a fourth and fifth, while a sixth national channel is owned by the Moscow city administration; the Russia Northodox Church and the Russian military, respectively, own 2 additional national channels; roughly 3,300 national, regional, and local TV stations with over two-thirds completely or partially controlled by the federal or local governments; satellite TV services are available; 2 state-run national radio networks with a third majority-owned by Gazprom; roughly 2,400 public and commercial radio stations (2016)

Radio broadcast stations: AM 323, FM about 1,500, shortwave 62 (2004)

Television broadcast stations: 7,306 (1998)

Internet country code: .ru; note—Russia also has responsibility for a legacy domain ".su" that was allocated to the Soviet Union and is being phased out

Internet hosts: 14.865 million (2012)
country comparison to the world: 10

Internet users: *total:* 84.4 million
percent of population: 59.3% (2014 est.)
country comparison to the world: 7

TRANSPORTATION

Airports: 1,218 (2013)
country comparison to the world: 5

Airports—with paved runways: *total:* 594
over 3,047 m: 54
2,438 to 3,047 m: 197
1,524 to 2,437 m: 123
914 to 1,523 m: 95
under 914 m: 125 (2013)

Airports—with unpaved runways: *total:* 624
over 3,047 m: 4
2,438 to 3,047 m: 13
1,524 to 2,437 m: 69
914 to 1,523 m: 81
under 914 m: 457 (2013)

Heliports: 49 (2013)

Pipelines: condensate 122 km; gas 163,872 km; liquid petroleum gas 1,378 km; oil 80,820 km; oil/gas/water 40 km; refined products 13,658 km; water 23 km (2013)

Railways: *total:* 87,157 km
broad gauge: 86,200 km 1.520-m gauge (40,300 km electrified)
narrow gauge: 957 km 1.067-m gauge (on Sakhalin Island)
note: an additional 30,000 km of non-common carrier lines serve industries (2014)
country comparison to the world: 3

Roadways: *total:* 1,283,387 km
paved: 927,721 km (includes 39,143 km of expressways)

unpaved: 355,666 km (2012)
country comparison to the world: 5

Waterways: 102,000 km (including 48,000 km with guaranteed depth; the 72,000-km system in European Russia links Baltic Sea, White Sea, Caspian Sea, Sea of Azov, and Black Sea) (2009)
country comparison to the world: 2

Merchant marine: *total:* 1,143
by type: bulk carrier 20, cargo 642, carrier 3, chemical tanker 57, combination ore/oil 42, container 13, passenger 13, passenger/cargo 7, petroleum tanker 244, refrigerated cargo 84, roll on/roll off 13, specialized tanker 3
foreign-owned: 155 (Belgium 4, Cyprus 13, Estonia 1, Ireland 1, Italy 14, Latvia 2, Netherlands 2, Romania 1, South Korea 1, Switzerland 3, Turkey 101, Ukraine 12)
registered in other countries: 439 (Antigua and Barbuda 3, Belgium 1, Belize 30, Bulgaria 2, Cambodia 50, Comoros 12, Cook Islands 1, Cyprus 46, Dominica 3, Georgia 6, Hong Kong 1, Kiribati 1, Liberia 109, Malaysia 2, Malta 45, Marshall Islands 5, Moldova 5, Mongolia 2, Panama 49, Romania 1, Saint Kitts and Nevis 13, Saint Vincent and the Grenadines 11, Sierra Leone 7, Singapore 2, Spain 6, Vanuatu 7, unknown 19) (2010)
country comparison to the world: 11

Ports and terminals: *major seaport(s):* Kaliningrad, Nakhodka, Novorossiysk, Primorsk, Vostochnyy
river port(s): Saint Petersburg (Neva River)
oil terminal(s): Kavkaz oil terminal
container port(s) (TEUs): Saint Petersburg (2,365,174)
LNG terminal(s) (export): Sakhalin Island

MILITARY AND SECURITY

Military branches: Ground Troops (Sukhoputnyye Voyska, SV), Navy (Voyenno-Morskoy Flot, VMF), Air Forces (Voyenno-Vozdushniye Sily, VVS); Airborne Troops (Vozdushno-Desantnyye Voyska, VDV), Missile Troops of Strategic Purpose (Raketnyye Voyska Strategicheskogo Naznacheniya, RVSN) referred to commonly as Strategic Rocket Forces, and Aerospace Defense Troops (Voyska Vozdushno-Kosmicheskoy Oborony or Voyska VKO) are independent "combat arms, " not subordinate to any of the three branches; Russian Ground Troops include the following combat arms: motorized-rifle troops, tank troops, missile and artillery troops, air defense of the Ground Troops (2014)

Military service age and obligation: 18–27 years of age for compulsory or voluntary military service; males are registered for the draft at 17 years of age; 1-year service obligation (conscripts can only be sent to combat zones after 6 months of training); reserve obligation for non-officers to age 50; enrollment in military schools from the age of 16, cadets classified as members of the armed forces
note: the chief of the General Staff Mobilization Directorate announced in March 2015 that for health reasons, only 76% of draftees called up during the spring 2015 draft campaign were fit for military service (2015)

Military expenditures:
3.49% of GDP (2014)
3.18% of GDP (2013)
2.92% of GDP (2012)
2.71% of GDP (2011)
country comparison to the world: 16

TRANSNATIONAL ISSUES

Disputes—international: Russia remains concerned about the smuggling of poppy derivatives from Afghanistan through Central Asian countries; China and Russia have demarcated the once disputed islands at the Amur and Ussuri confluence and in the Argun River in accordance with the 2004 Agreement, ending their centuries-long border disputes; the sovereignty dispute over the islands of Etorofu, Kunashiri, Shikotan, and the Habomai group, known in Japan as the "Northern Territories" and in Russia as the "Southern Kurils, " occupied by the Soviet Union in 1945, now administered by Russia, and claimed by Japan, remains the primary sticking point to signing a peace treaty formally ending World War II hostilities; Russia's military support and subsequent recognition of Abkhazia and South Ossetia independence in 2008 continue to sour relations with Georgia; Azerbaijan, Kazakhstan, and Russia ratified Caspian seabed delimitation treaties based on equidistance, while Iran continues to insist on a one-fifth slice of the sea; Norway and Russia signed a comprehensive maritime boundary agreement in 2010; various groups in Finland advocate restoration of Karelia (Kareliya) and other areas ceded to the Soviet Union following World War II but the Finnish Government asserts no territorial demands; Russia and Estonia signed a technical border agreement in May 2005, but Russia recalled its signature in June 2005 after the Estonian parliament added to its domestic ratification act a historical preamble referencing the Soviet occupation and Estonia's pre-war borders under the 1920 Treaty of Tartu; Russia contends that the preamble allows Estonia to make territorial claims on Russia in the future, while Estonian officials deny that the preamble has any legal impact on the treaty text; Russia demands better treatment of the Russian-speaking population in Estonia and Latvia Lithuania and Russia committed to demarcating their boundary in 2006 in accordance with the land and maritime treaty ratified by Russia in May 2003 and by Lithuania in 1999; Lithuania operates a simplified transit regime for Russian nationals traveling from the Kaliningrad coastal exclave into Russia, while still conforming, as an EU member state with an EU external border, where strict Schengen border rules apply; preparations for the demarcation delimitation of land boundary with Ukraine have commenced; the dispute over the boundary between Russia and Ukraine through the Kerch Strait and Sea of Azov is suspended due to the occupation of Crimea by Russia; Kazakhstan and Russia boundary delimitation was ratified on November 2005 and field demarcation should commence in 2007; Russian Duma has not yet ratified 1990 Bering Sea Maritime Boundary Agreement with the US; Denmark (Greenland)

and Norway have made submissions to the Commission on the Limits of the Continental Shelf (CLCS) and Russia is collecting additional data to augment its 2001 CLCS submission

Refugees and internally displaced persons: *refugees (country of origin):* 383,323 asylum seekers and 911,549 applicants for other forms of legal stay (Ukraine) (2015)

IDPs: 27,000 (armed conflict, human rights violations, generalized violence in North Caucasus, particularly Chechnya and North Ossetia) (2015)

stateless persons: 101,813 (2015); note—Russia's stateless population consists of Roma, Meskhetian Turks, and ex-Soviet citizens from the former republics; between 2003 and 2010 more than 600,000 stateless people were naturalized; most Meskhetian Turks, followers of Islam with origins in Georgia, fled or were evacuated from Uzbekistan after a 1989 pogrom and have lived in Russia for more than the required five-year residency period; they continue to be denied registration for citizenship and basic rights by local Krasnodar Krai authorities on the grounds that they are temporary illegal migrants

Trafficking in persons: *current situation:* Russia is a source, transit, and destination country for men, women, and children who are subjected to forced labor and sex trafficking; with millions of foreign workers, forced labor is Russia's predominant human trafficking problem and sometimes involves organized crime syndicates; workers from Russia, other European countries, Central Asia, and East and Southeast Asia, including North Korea and Vietnam, are subjected to forced labor in the construction, manufacturing, agricultural, textile, grocery store, maritime, and domestic service industries, as well as in forced begging, waste sorting, and street sweeping; women and children from Europe, Southeast Asia, Africa, and Central Asia are subject to sex trafficking in Russia; Russian women and children are victims of sex trafficking domestically and in Northeast Asia, Europe, Central Asia, Africa, the US, and the Middle East

tier rating: Tier 3—Russia does not fully comply with the minimum standards for the elimination of trafficking and is not making a significant effort to do so; prosecutions of trafficking offenders remained low in comparison to the scope of

Russia's trafficking problem; the government did not develop or employ a formal system for identifying trafficking victims or referring them to protective services, although authorities reportedly assisted a limited number of victims on an ad hoc basis; foreign victims, the largest group in Russia, were not entitled to state-provided rehabilitative services and were routinely detained and deported; the government has not reported investigating reports of slave-like conditions among North Korean workers in Russia; authorities have made no effort to reduce the demand for forced labor or to develop public awareness of forced labor or sex trafficking (2015)

Illicit drugs: limited cultivation of illicit cannabis and opium poppy and producer of methamphetamine, mostly for domestic consumption; government has active illicit crop eradication program; used as transshipment point for Asian opiates, cannabis, and Latin American cocaine bound for growing domestic markets, to a lesser extent Western and Central Europe, and occasionally to the US; major source of heroin precursor chemicals; corruption and organized crime are key concerns; major consumer of opiates

RWANDA

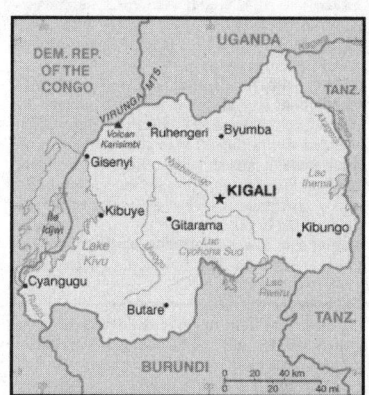

INTRODUCTION

Background: In 1959, three years before independence from Belgium, the majority ethnic group, the Hutus, overthrew the ruling Tutsi king. Over the next several years, thousands of Tutsis were killed, and some 150,000 driven into exile in neighboring countries. The children of these exiles later formed a rebel group, the Rwandan Patriotic Front (RPF), and begaNA civil war in 1990. The war, along with several political and economic upheavals, exacerbated ethnic tensions, culminating in April 1994 in a state-orchestrated genocide, in which Rwandans killed up to a million of their fellow citizens, including approximately three-quarters of the Tutsi population. The genocide ended later that same year when the predominantly Tutsi RPF, operating out of Uganda and northern Rwanda,

defeated the national army and Hutu militias, and established an RPF-led government of national unity. Approximately 2 million Hutu refugees—many fearing Tutsi retribution—fled to neighboring Burundi, Tanzania, Uganda, and former Zaire. Since then, most of the refugees have returned to Rwanda, but several thousand remained in the neighboring Democratic Republic of the Congo (DRC, the former Zaire) and formed an extremist insurgency bent on retaking Rwanda, much as the RPF did in 1990. Rwanda held its first local elections in 1999 and its first post-genocide presidential and legislative elections in 2003. Rwanda in 2009 staged a joint military operation with the Congolese Army in DRC to rout out the Hutu extremist insurgency there, and Kigali and Kinshasa restored diplomatic relations. Rwanda also joined the Commonwealth in late 2009 and assumed a nonpermanent seat on the UN Security Council for the 2013–14 term.

GEOGRAPHY

Location: Central Africa, east of the Democratic Republic of the Congo, north of Burundi

Geographic coordinates: 2 00 S, 30 00 E

Map references: Africa

Area: *total:* 26,338 sq km
land: 24,668 sq km
water: 1,670 sq km
country comparison to the world: 149

Area—comparative: slightly smaller than Maryland

Land boundaries: *total:* 930 km
border countries (4): Burundi 315 km, Democratic Republic of the Congo 221 km, Tanzania 222 km, Uganda 172 km

Coastline: 0 km (landlocked)

Maritime claims: none (landlocked)

Climate: temperate; two rainy seasons (February to April, November to January); mild in mountains with frost and snow possible

Terrain: mostly grassy uplands and hills; relief is mountainous with altitude declining from west to east

Elevation: *mean elevation:* 1,598 m

elevation extremes: *lowest point:* Rusizi River 950 m
highest point: Volcan Karisimbi 4,519 m

Natural resources: gold, cassiterite (tin ore), wolframite (tungsten ore), methane, hydropower, arable land

Land use: *agricultural land:* 74.5%
arable land: 47%
permanent crops: 10.1%
permanent pasture: 17.4%
forest: 18%
other: 7.5% (2011 est.)

Irrigated land: 96 sq km (2012)

Total renewable water resources: 9.5 cu km (2011)

Freshwater withdrawal (domestic/industrial/agricultural): *total:* 0.15 cu km/yr (33%/11%/55%)
per capita: 17.25 cu m/yr (2005)

Natural hazards: periodic droughts; the volcanic Virunga Mountains are in the northwest along the border with Democratic Republic of the Congo

volcanism: Visoke (elev. 3,711 m), located on the border with the Democratic Republic of the Congo, is the country's only historically active volcano

Environment—current issues: deforestation results from uncontrolled cutting of trees for fuel; overgrazing; soil exhaustion; soil erosion; widespread poaching

Environment—international agreements: *party to:* Biodiversity, Climate Change, Climate

Change-Kyoto Protocol, Desertification, Endangered Species, Hazardous Wastes, Ozone Layer Protection, Wetlands

signed, but not ratified: Law of the Sea

Geography—note: landlocked; most of the country is savanna grassland with the population predominantly rural

PEOPLE AND SOCIETY

Nationality: *noun:* Rwandan(s)
adjective: Rwandan

Ethnic groups: Hutu (Bantu) 84%, Tutsi (Hamitic) 15%, Twa (Pygmy) 1%

Languages: Kinyarwanda only (official, universal Bantu vernacular) 93.2%, Kinyarwanda and other language(s) 6.2%, French (official) and other language(s) 0.1%, English (official) and other language(s) 0.1%, Swahili (or Kiswahili, used in commercial centers) 0.02%, other 0.03%, unspecified 0.3% (2002 est.)

Religions: Roman Catholic 49.5%, Protestant 39.4% (includes Adventist 12.2% and other Protestant 27.2%), other Christian 4.5%, Muslim 1.8%, animist 0.1%, other 0.6%, none 3.6% (2001), unspecified 0.5% (2002 est.)

Population: 12,661,733

note: estimates for this country explicitly take into account the effects of excess mortality due to AIDS; this can result in lower life expectancy, higher infant mortality, higher death rates, lower population growth rates, and changes in the distribution of population by age and sex than would otherwise be expected (July 2015 est.)

country comparison to the world: 74

Age structure: *0–14 years:* 41.83% (male 2,670,040/female 2,626,646)

15–24 years: 18.86% (male 1,193,523/female 1,193,953)

25–54 years: 32.72% (male 2,077,406/female 2,065,261)

55–64 years: 4.07% (male 239,924/female 274,829)

65 years and over: 2.53% (male 131,613/female 188,538) (2015 est.)

Dependency ratios: *total dependency ratio:* 78.1%

youth dependency ratio: 73.1%
elderly dependency ratio: 5%
potential support ratio: 20.1% (2015 est.)

Median age: *total:* 18.8 years
male: 18.6 years
female: 19 years (2015 est.)
country comparison to the world: 203

Population growth rate: 2.56% (2015 est.)
country comparison to the world: 22

Birth rate: 33.75 births/1,000 population (2015 est.)
country comparison to the world: 30

Death rate: 8.96 deaths/1,000 population (2015 est.)
country comparison to the world: 69

Net migration rate: 0.85 migrant(s)/1,000 population (2015 est.)
country comparison to the world: 66

Urbanization: *urban Population:* 28.8% of total population (2015)

rate of urbanization: 6.43% annual rate of change (2010–15 est.)

Major urban areas—population: KIGALI (capital) 1.257 million (2015)

Sex ratio: *at birth:* 1.03 male(s)/female

0–14 years: 1.02 male(s)/female
15–24 years: 1 male(s)/female
25–54 years: 1.01 male(s)/female
55–64 years: 0.87 male(s)/female
65 years and over: 0.7 male(s)/female
total population: 0.99 male(s)/female (2015 est.)

Mother's mean age at first birth: 23

note: median age at first birth among women 25–29 (2014/15 est.)

Maternal mortality rate: 290 deaths/100,000 live births (2015 est.)
country comparison to the world: 35

Infant mortality rate: *total:* 58.19 deaths/1,000 live births

male: 61.68 deaths/1,000 live births
female: 54.6 deaths/1,000 live births (2015 est.)
country comparison to the world: 23

Life expectancy at birth: *total population:* 59.67 years

male: 58.11 years
female: 61.27 years (2015 est.)
country comparison to the world: 199

Total fertility rate: 4.53 children born/woman (2015 est.)
country comparison to the world: 27

Contraceptive prevalence rate: 51.6% (2010/11)

Health expenditures: 11.1% of GDP (2013)
country comparison to the world: 18

Physicians density: 0.06 physicians/1,000 population (2010)

Hospital bed density: 1.6 beds/1,000 population (2007)

Drinking water source:
improved:
urban: 86.6% of population
rural: 71.9% of population
total: 76.1% of population
unimproved:
urban: 13.4% of population
rural: 28.1% of population
total: 23.9% of population (2015 est.)

Sanitation facility access:
improved:
urban: 58.5% of population
rural: 62.9% of population
total: 61.6% of population
unimproved:
urban: 41.5% of population
rural: 37.1% of population
total: 38.4% of population (2015 est.)

HIV/AIDS—adult prevalence rate: 2.82% (2014 est.)
country comparison to the world: 21

HIV/AIDS—people living with HIV/AIDS: 210,500 (2014 est.)
country comparison to the world: 29

HIV/AIDS—deaths: 3,000 (2014 est.)
country comparison to the world: 45

Major infectious diseases: *degree of risk:* very high

food or waterborne diseases: bacterial diarrhea, hepatitis A, and typhoid fever
vectorborne diseases: malaria and dengue fever
animal contact disease: rabies (2013)

Obesity—adult prevalence rate: 3.3% (2014)
country comparison to the world: 170

Children under the age of 5 years underweight: 11.7% (2011)
country comparison to the world: 63

Education expenditures: 5% of GDP (2013)
country comparison to the world: 73

Literacy: *definition:* age 15 and over can read and write

total population: 70.5%
male: 73.2%
female: 68% (2015 est.)

School life expectancy (primary to tertiary education): *total:* 11 years

male: 11 years
female: 11 years (2013)

Unemployment, youth ages 15–24: *total:* 4.5%

male: 3.6%
female: 5.2% (2012 est.)

People—note: Rwanda is the most densely populated country in Africa

GOVERNMENT

Country name: *conventional long form:* Republic of Rwanda

conventional short form: Rwanda
local long form: Republikay'u Rwanda
local short form: Rwanda
former: Ruanda, German East Africa
etymology: the name translates as "domain" in the native Kinyarwanda language

Government type: presidential republic

Capital: *name:* Kigali

Geographic coordinates: 1 57 S, 30 03 E

time difference: UTC+2 (7 hours ahead of Washington, DC, during Standard Time)

Administrative divisions: 4 provinces (in French—provinces, singular—province; in Kinyarwanda—intara for singular and plural) and 1 city* (in French—ville; in Kinyarwanda—umujyi); Est (Eastern), Kigali*, Nord (Northern), Ouest (Western), Sud (Southern)

Independence: 1 July 1962 (from Belgium-administered UN trusteeship)

National holiday: Independence Day, 1 July (1962)

Constitution: several previous; latest adopted by referendum 26 May 2003, effective 4 June 2003; amended several times, last in 2015 (2016)

Legal system: mixed legal system of civil law, based on German and Belgian models, and customary law; judicial review of legislative acts in the Supreme Court

International law organization participation: has not submitted an ICJ jurisdiction declaration; non-party state to the ICCt

Citizenship: *citizenship by birth:* no

citizenship by descent only: the father must be a citizen of Rwanda; if the father is stateless or unknown, the mother must be a citizen

dual citizenship recognized: no

residency requirement for naturalization: 10 years

Suffrage: 18 years of age; universal

Executive branch: *chief of state:* President Paul KAGAME (since 22 April 2000)

head of government: Prime Minister Anastase MUREKEZI (since 24 July 2014)

cabinet: Council of Ministers appointed by the president

elections/appointments: president directly elected by simple majority popular vote for a 7-year term (eligible for a second term); election last held on 9 August 2010 (next to be held in 2017); prime minister appointed by the president

election results: Paul KAGAME reelected president; Paul KAGAME (RPF) 93.1%, Jean NTAWUKURIRYAYO (PSD) 5.1%, other 1.8%

Legislative branch: *description:* bicameral Parliament consists of the Senate or Senat (26 seats; 12 members indirectly elected by local councils,

8 appointed by the president, 4 appointed by the Political Organizations Forum—a body of registered political parties, and 2 selected by institutions of higher learning; members serve 8-year terms) and the Chamber of Deputies or Chambre des Deputes (80 seats; 53 members directly elected by proportional representation vote, 24 women elected by special interest groups, and 3 selected by youth and disability organizations; members serve 5-year terms)

elections: Senate—NA; Chamber of Deputies—last held on 16–18 September 2013 (next to be held in 2018)

election results: Chamber of Deputies percent of vote by party—RPF 76.2%, PSD 13%, PL 9.3%, other 1.5%; seats by party—RPF 41, PSD 7, PL 5,27 members indirectly elected

Judicial branch: *highest court(s):* Supreme Court (consists of the court president, vice president, and 12 judges; normally organized into 3—judge benches)

note: the Gacaca Court was established in 2001 by the National Unity Government to try cases of genocide against the Tutsis

judge selection and term of office: judges nominated by the president of the republic after consultation with the Cabinet and the Superior Council of the Judiciary (a 14-member body of judges, other judicial officials, and legal professionals), and approved by the Senate; court president and vice president appointed for 8-year nonrenewable terms; tenure of other judges NA

subordinate courts: High Court of the Republic; commercial courts including the High Commercial Court; intermediate courts; primary courts; Gacaca and military specialized courts

Political parties and leaders: Liberal Party or PL [Protais MITALI]

Party for Progress and Concord or PPC [Christian MARARA]

Rwandan Patriotic Front or RPF [Paul KAGAME]

Social Democratic Party or PSD [Vincent BIRUTA]

Political pressure groups and leaders: IBUKA (association of genocide survivors)

International organization participation: ACP, AFDB, AU, C, CEPGL, COMESA, EAC, EADB, FAO, G-77, IAEA, IBRD, ICAO, ICRM, IDA, IFAD, IFC, IFRCS, ILO, IMF, Interpol, IOC, IOM, IPU, ISO, ITSO, ITU, ITUC (NGOs), MIGA, MINUSMA, NAM, OIF, OPCW, PCA, UN, UNAMID, UNCTAD, UNESCO, UNHCR, UNIDO, UNISFA, UNMISS, UNWTO, UPU, WCO, WHO, WIPO, WMO, WTO

Diplomatic representation in the US: *chief of mission:* Ambassador Mathilde MUKANTABANA (since 5 July 2013)

chancery: 1875 Connecticut Avenue, NW, Suite 418, Washington, DC, 2000

telephone: [1] (202) 232-2882

FAX: [1] (202) 232-4544

Diplomatic representation from the US: *chief of mission:* Ambassador Erica BARKS-RUGGLES (since 26 January 2015)

embassy: 2657 Avenue de la Gendarmerie, Kigali

mailing address: B. P.28, Kigali

telephone: [250] 596-400

FAX: [250] 596-591

Flag description: three horizontal bands of sky blue (top, double width), yellow, and green, with a golden sun with 24 rays near the fly end of the blue band; blue represents happiness and peace, yellow economic development and mineral wealth, green hope of prosperity and natural resources; the sun symbolizes unity, as well as enlightenment and transparency from ignorance

National symbol(s): traditional woven basket with peaked lid; national colors: blue, yellow, green

National anthem: *name:* "Rwanda nziza" (Rwanda, Our Beautiful Country)

lyrics/music: Faustin MURIGO/Jean-Bosco HASHAKAIMANA

note: adopted 2001

ECONOMY

Economy—overview: Rwanda is a rural country with about 90% of the population engaged in subsistence agriculture and some mineral and agro-processing. Tourism, minerals, coffee and tea are Rwanda's main sources of foreign exchange. Despite Rwanda's fertile ecosystem, food production often does not keep pace with demand, requiring food imports. Energy shortages, instability in neighboring states, and lack of adequate transportation linkages to other countries continue to handicap private sector growth. The 1994 genocide decimated Rwanda's fragile economic base, severely impoverished the population, particularly women, and temporarily stalled the country's ability to attract private and external investment. However, Rwanda has made substantial progress in stabilizing and rehabilitating its economy to pre-1994 levels. GDP has rebounded with an average annual growth of 7%-8% since 2003 and inflation has been reduced to single digits. Nonetheless, in 2015, 39% of the population lived below the poverty line, according to government statistics, compared to 57% in 2006.

Africa's most densely populated country is trying to overcome the limitations of its small, landlocked economy by leveraging regional trade; Rwanda joined the East African Community and is aligning its budget, trade, and immigration policies with its regional partners. The government has embraced an expansionary fiscal policy to reduce poverty by improving education, infrastructure, and foreign and domestic investment, and pursuing market-oriented reforms. in recognition of Rwanda's successful management of its macro economy, in 2010, the IMF graduated Rwanda to a Policy Support Instrument. The Rwandan Government is seeking to become a regional leader in information and communication technologies. In 2012, Rwanda completed the first modern Special Economic Zone (SEZ) in Kigali. The SEZ seeks to attract investment in all sectors, but specifically in agribusiness, information and communications, trade and logistics, mining, and construction.

GDP (purchasing power parity): $20.42 billion (2015 est.)

$19.1 billion (2014 est.)

$17.85 billion (2013 est.)

note: data are in 2015 US dollars

country comparison to the world: 144

GDP (official exchange rate): $8.267 billion (2015 est.)

GDP—real growth rate: 6.9% (2015 est.)

7% (2014 est.)

4.7% (2013 est.)

country comparison to the world: 19

GDP—per capita (PPP): $1,800 (2015 est.)

$1,700 (2014 est.)

$1,700 (2013 est.)

note: data are in 2015 US dollars

country comparison to the world: 207

Gross national saving: 11.2% of GDP (2015 est.)

14.6% of GDP (2014 est.)

19.1% of GDP (2013 est.)

country comparison to the world: 146

GDP—composition, by end use:

household consumption: 73.7%

government consumption: 14.7%

investment in fixed capital: 25.6%

investment in inventories: 0.8%

exports of goods and services: 13.6%

imports of goods and services: -28.4% (2015 est.)

GDP—composition, by sector of origin:

agriculture: 32.6%

industry: 14.1%

services: 53.3% (2015 est.)

Agriculture—products: coffee, tea, pyrethrum (insecticide made from chrysanthemums), bananas, beans, sorghum, potatoes; livestock

Industries: cement, agricultural products, small-scale beverages, soap, furniture, shoes, plastic goods, textiles, cigarettes

Industrial production growth rate: 4.4% (2015 est.)

country comparison to the world: 45

Labor force: 6.247 million (2015 est.)

country comparison to the world: 70

Labor force—by occupation:

agriculture: 90%

industry and services: 10% (2000)

Unemployment rate: NA%

Population below poverty line: 39.1% (2015 est.)

Household income or consumption by percentage share: *lowest:* 10%: 2.1%

highest: 10%: 43.2% (2011 est.)

Distribution of family income—Gini index: 46.8 (2000)

28.9 (1985)

country comparison to the world: 31

Budget: *revenues:* $1.857 billion

expenditures: $2.255 billion (2015 est.)

Taxes and other revenues: 21.9% of GDP (2015 est.)

country comparison to the world: 143

Budget surplus (+) or deficit (–): -4.7% of GDP (2015 est.)

country comparison to the world: 163

Public debt: 33.7% of GDP (2015 est.)

30.7% of GDP (2014 est.)

country comparison to the world: 132

Fiscal year: calendar year

Inflation rate (consumer prices): 2.5% (2015 est.)

1.8% (2014 est.)

country comparison to the world: 129

Central bank discount rate: 7.75% (31 December 2010)

11.25% (31 December 2008)

country comparison to the world: 42

Commercial bank prime lending rate: 17.2% (31 December 2015 est.)

17.25% (31 December 2014 est.)

country comparison to the world: 27

Stock of narrow money: $845.1 million (31 December 2015 est.)

$820.3 million (31 December 2014 est.)

country comparison to the world: 156

Stock of broad money: $1.576 billion (31 December 2015 est.)

$1.407 billion (31 December 2014 est.)

country comparison to the world: 161

Stock of domestic credit: $1.577 billion (31 December 2015 est.)

$1.261 billion (31 December 2014 est.)

country comparison to the world: 148

Market value of publicly traded shares: $NA

Current account balance: -$1.139 billion (2015 est.)

-$909 million (2014 est.)

country comparison to the world: 128

Exports: $726.1 million (2015 est.)
$719.9 million (2014 est.)
country comparison to the world: 168
Exports—commodities: coffee, tea, hides, tin ore
Exports—partners: Democratic Republic of the Congo 19.8%, US 10.8%, China 10.3%, Swaziland 7.9%, Malaysia 7%, Pakistan 6.2%, Germany 5.9%, Thailand 5.5% (2015)
Imports: $1.913 billion (2015 est.)
$1.984 billion (2014 est.)
country comparison to the world: 166
Imports—commodities: foodstuffs, machinery and equipment, steel, petroleum products, cement and construction material
Imports—partners: Uganda 15.7%, Kenya 11.8%, India 8.7%, China 8.7%, UAE 8.6%, Russia 6.6%, Tanzania 5.1% (2015)
Reserves of foreign exchange and gold: $1.028 billion (31 December 2015 est.)
$1.005 billion (31 December 2014 est.)
country comparison to the world: 129
Debt—external: $1.778 billion (31 December 2014 est.)
$1.691 billion (31 December 2013 est.)
country comparison to the world: 153
Stock of direct foreign investment—at home: $1.198 billion (31 December 2015 est.)
$1.016 billion (31 December 2014 est.)
country comparison to the world: 110
Stock of direct foreign investment—abroad: $12.9 million (31 December 2015 est.)
$12.9 million (31 December 2014 est.)
country comparison to the world: 102
Exchange rates: Rwandan francs (RWF) per US dollar—
726.9 (2015 est.)
680.95 (2014 est.)
680.95 (2013 est.)
616.6 (2012 est.)
601.83 (2011 est.)

ENERGY

Electricity—production: 310.2 million kWh (2012 est.)
country comparison to the world: 176
Electricity—consumption: 365.5 million kWh (2012 est.)
country comparison to the world: 173
Electricity—exports: 3 million kWh (2012 est.)
country comparison to the world: 93
Electricity—imports: 80 million kWh (2012 est.)
country comparison to the world: 96
Electricity—installed generating capacity: 99,000 kW (2012 est.)
country comparison to the world: 174
Electricity—from fossil fuels: 34.3% of total installed capacity (2012 est.)
country comparison to the world: 170
Electricity—from nuclear fuels: 0% of total installed capacity (2012 est.)
country comparison to the world: 173
Electricity—from hydroelectric plants: 65.7% of total installed capacity (2012 est.)
country comparison to the world: 32
Electricity—from other renewable sources: 0% of total installed capacity (2012 est.)
country comparison to the world: 124
Crude oil—production: 0 bbl/day (2014 est.)
country comparison to the world: 184
Crude oil—exports: 0 bbl/day (2012 est.)
country comparison to the world: 181
Crude oil—imports: 0 bbl/day (2012 est.)
country comparison to the world: 118
Crude oil—proved reserves: 0 bbl (1 January 2015 est.)

country comparison to the world: 183
Refined petroleum products—production:
0 bbl/day (2012 est.)
country comparison to the world: 125
Refined petroleum products—consumption:
5,300 bbl/day (2013 est.)
country comparison to the world: 167
Refined petroleum products—exports:
0 bbl/day (2012 est.)
country comparison to the world: 128
Refined petroleum products—imports:
5,302 bbl/day (2012 est.)
country comparison to the world: 158
Natural gas—production: 0 cu m (2013 est.)
country comparison to the world: 122
Natural gas—consumption: 0 cu m (2013 est.)
country comparison to the world: 188
Natural gas—exports: 0 cu m (2013 est.)
country comparison to the world: 171
Natural gas—imports: 0 cu m (2013 est.)
country comparison to the world: 126
Natural gas—proved reserves: 56.63 billion cu m (1 January 2014 est.)
country comparison to the world: 63
Carbon dioxide emissions from consumption of energy: 769,300 Mt (2012 est.)
country comparison to the world: 171

COMMUNICATIONS

Telephones—fixed lines: *total subscriptions:* 49,600
subscriptions per 100 inhabitants: less than 1 (2014 est.)
country comparison to the world: 163
Telephones—mobile cellular: *total:* 7.7 million
subscriptions per 100 inhabitants: 63 (2014 est.)
country comparison to the world: 98
Telephone system: *general assessment:* small, inadequate telephone system primarily serves business, education, and government
domestic: the capital, Kigali, is connected to provincial centers by microwave radio relay and, recently, by cellular telephone service; much of the network depends on wire and HF radiotelephone; combined fixed-line and mobile-cellular telephone density has increased and now exceeds 40 telephones per 100 persons
international: country code—250; international connections employ microwave radio relay to neighboring countries and satellite communications to more distant countries; satellite earth stations—1 Intelsat (Indian Ocean) in Kigali (includes telex and telefax service) (2010)
Broadcast media: government owns and operates the only TV station; government-owned and operated Radio Rwanda has a national reach;9 private radio stations; transmissions of multiple international broadcasters are available (2007)
Radio broadcast stations: AM 0, FM 10 (two main FM programs are broadcast through a system of repeaters; international FM programming includes the BBC, VOA, and Deutchewelle) (2007)
Television broadcast stations: 2 (2004)
Internet country code: .rw
Internet hosts: 1,447 (2012)
country comparison to the world: 168
Internet users: *total:* 1.1 million
percent of population: 9.2% (2014 est.)
country comparison to the world: 120

TRANSPORTATION

Airports: 7 (2013)
country comparison to the world: 167
Airports—with paved runways: *total:* 4
over 3,047 m: 1
914 to 1,523 m: 2
under 914 m: 1 (2013)
Airports—with unpaved runways: *total:* 3
914 to 1,523 m: 2
under 914 m: 1 (2013)
Roadways: total: 4,700 km
paved: 1,207 km
unpaved: 3,493 km (2012)
country comparison to the world: 153
Waterways: (Lac Kivu navigable by shallow-draft barges and native craft) (2011)

Ports and terminals: *lake port(s):* Cyangugu, Gisenyi, Kibuye (Lake Kivu)

MILITARY AND SECURITY

Military branches: Rwanda Defense Force (RDF): Rwanda Army (Rwanda Land Force), Rwanda Air Force (Force Aerienne Rwandaise, FAR) (2013)
Military service age and obligation: 18 years of age for voluntary military service; no conscription; Rwandan citizenship is required, as is a 9th-grade education for enlisted recruits and an A-level certificate for officer candidates; enlistment is either as contract (5-years, renewable twice) or career; retirement (for officers and senior NCOs) after 20 years of service or at 40–60 years of age (2012)
Military expenditures:
1.12% of GDP (2012)
1.19% of GDP (2011)
1.12% of GDP (2010)
country comparison to the world: 91

TRANSNATIONAL ISSUES

Disputes—international: Burundi and Rwanda dispute two sq km (0.8 sq mi) of Sabanerwa, a farmed area in the Rukurazi Valley where the Akany aru/Kany aru River shifted its course southward after heavy rains in 1965; fighting among ethnic groups—loosely associated political rebels, armed gangs, and various government forces in Great Lakes region transcending the boundaries of Burundi, Democratic Republic of the Congo (DROC), Rwanda, and Uganda—abated substantially from a decade ago due largely to UN peacekeeping, international mediation, and efforts by local governments to create civil societies; nonetheless, 57,000 Rwandan refugees still reside in 21 African states, including Zambia, Gabon, and 20,000 who fled to Burundi in 2005 and 2006 to escape drought and recriminations from traditional cou rts investigating the 1994 massacres; the 2005 DROC and Rwanda border verification mechanism to stem rebel actions on both sides of the border remains in place
Refugees and internally displaced persons: *refugees (country of origin):* 79,057 (Burundi); 73,264 (Democratic Republic of the Congo) (2016)
IDPs: undetermined (fighting between governm ent and insurgency in 1998–99; returning refugees) (2012)

SAINT BARTHELEMY

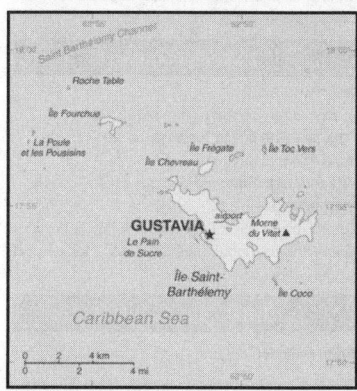

INTRODUCTION

Background: Discovered in 1493 by Christopher COLUMBUS who named it for his brother Bartolomeo, Saint Barthelemy was first settled by the French in 1648. In 1784, the French sold the island to Sweden, which renamed the largest town Gustavia, after the Swedish King GUSTAV III, and made it a free port; the island prospered as a trade and supply center during the colonial wars of the 18th century. France repurchased the island in 1877 and took control the following year. It was placed under the administration of Guadeloupe. Saint Barthelemy retained its free port status along with various Swedish appellations such as Swedish street and town names, and the three-crown symbol on the coat of arms. In 2003 the islanders voted to secede from Guadeloupe, and in 2007 the island became a French overseas collectivity. In 2012, it became an overseas territory of the EU, allowing it to exert local control over the permanent and temporary immigration of foreign workers including non-French European citizens.

GEOGRAPHY

Location: Caribbean, island between the Caribbean Sea and the North Atlantic Ocean; located in the Leeward Islands (northern) group; Saint Barthelemy lies east of the US Virgin Islands

Geographic coordinates: 17 90 N, 62 85 W

Map references: Central America and the Caribbean

Area: *total:* 25 sq km
land: 25 sq km
water: NEGL

Area—comparative: less than one-eighth the size of Washington, DC

Land boundaries: 0 km

Climate: tropical, with practically no variation in temperature; has two seasons (dry and humid)

Terrain: hilly, almost completely surrounded by shallow-water reefs, with plentiful beaches

Elevation: *mean elevation:* NA

elevation extremes: *lowest point:* Caribbean Ocean 0 m
highest point: Morne du Vitet 286 m

Natural resources: few Natural resources; beaches foster tourism

Environment—current issues: with no Natural rivers or streams, fresh water is in short supply, especially in summer, and provided by desalination of sea water, collection of rain water, or imported via water tanker

Geography—note: a 1,200-hectare marine nature reserve, the Reserve Naturelle, is made up of five zones around the island that form a network to protect the island's coral reefs, seagrass, and endangered marine species

PEOPLE AND SOCIETY

Ethnic groups: white, Creole (mulatto), black, Guadeloupe Mestizo (French-East Asia)

Languages: French (primary), English

Religions: Roman Catholic, Protestant, Jehovah's Witnesses

Population: 7,237 (July 2015 est.)
country comparison to the world: 227

Age structure: *0–14 years:* 17.36% (male 645/female 611)
15–24 years: 7.03% (male 269/female 240)
25–54 years: 45.32% (male 1,783/female 1,497)
55–64 years: 15.3% (male 602/female 505)
65 years and over: 14.99% (male 542/female 543) (2015 est.)

Median age: *total:* 43 years
male: 43 years
female: 43 years (2015 est.)
country comparison to the world: 17

Sex ratio: *at birth:* 1.06 male(s)/female
0–14 years: 1.06 male(s)/female
15–24 years: 1.12 male(s)/female
25–54 years: 1.19 male(s)/female
55–64 years: 1.19 male(s)/female
65 years and over: 1 male(s)/female
total population: 1.13 male(s)/female (2015 est.)

GOVERNMENT

Country name: *conventional long form:* Overseas Collectivity of Saint Barthelemy
conventional short form: Saint Barthelemy
local long form: Collectivite d'outre mer de Saint-Barthelemy
local short form: Saint-Barthelemy
abbreviation: Saint-Barth (French); St. Barts or St. Barths (English)
etymology: explorer Christopher COLUMBUS named the island in honor of his brother Bartolomeo's namesake saint in 1493

Dependency status: overseas collectivity of France

Capital: *name:* Gustavia

Geographic coordinates: 17 53 N, 62 51 W
time difference: UTC-4 (1 hour ahead of Washington, DC, during Standard Time)

Independence: none (overseas collectivity of France)

National holiday: Fete de la Federation, 14 July (1789); note—local holiday is St. Barthelemy Day, 24 August (1572)

Constitution: a 4 October 1958 (French Constitution)

Legal system: French civil law

Citizenship: see France

Suffrage: 18 years of age, universal

Executive branch: *chief of state:* President Francois HOLLANDE (since 15 May 2012), represented by Prefect Philippe CHOPIN (since 16 November 2011)

head of government: President of Territorial Council Bruno MAGRAS (since 16 July 2007)
cabinet: Executive Council elected by the Territorial Council; note—there is also an advisory, economic, social, and cultural council
elections/appointments: French president directly elected by absolute majority popular vote in 2 rounds if needed for a 5-year term (eligible for a second term); prefect appointed by the French president on the advice of French Ministry of Interior; president of Territorial Council indirectly elected by its members for a 5-year term; election last held in July 2012 (next to be held in 2017)
election results: Bruno MAGRAS (SBA) reelected president; Territorial Council vote NA

Legislative branch: *description:* unicameral Territorial Council (19 seats; members elected by absolute majority vote in the first round vote and proportional representation vote in the second round; members serve 5-year terms)
note: Saint Barthelemy holds 1 seat in the French Senate; elections last held on 28 September 2014 (next to be held not later than September 2017); results—percent of vote by party NA; seats by party UMP 1; Saint Barthelemy elects 1 seat to the French National Assembly; elections last held on 17 June 2012 (next to be held by June 2017); results—percent of vote by party NA; seats by party UMP 1
elections: last held on 18 March 2012 (next to be held in July 2017)
election results: percent of vote by party—SBA 73.8%, Ensemble pour Saint-Barthelemy 15.9%, Tous Unis pour Saint-Barthelemy 10.3%; seats by party—SBA 16, Ensemble pour Saint-Barthelemy 2, Tous Unis pour Saint-Barthelemy 1

Political parties and leaders: All for Saint-Barth (Tous pour Saint-Barth) [Benoit CHAUVIN]
Saint-Barth First! (Saint-Barth d'Abord!) or SBA [Bruno MAGRAS]; affiliated with UMP Saint-Barth in Motion (Saint-Barth en Mouvement) [Maxime DESOUCHES]

International organization participation: UPU

Diplomatic representation in the US: none (overseas collectivity of France)

Diplomatic representation from the US: none (overseas collectivity of France)

Flag description: the flag of France is used

National symbol(s): pelican

National anthem: *name:* "L'Hymne a St. Barthelemy" (Hymn to St. Barthelemy) *lyrics/music:* Isabelle Massart DERAVIN/Michael VALENTI

note: local anthem in use since 1999; as a collectivity of France, "La Marseillaise" is official (see France)

ECONOMY

Economy—overview: The economy of Saint Barthelemy is based upon high-end tourism and duty-free luxury commerce, serving visitors primarily from North America. The luxury hotels and villas host 70,000 visitors each year with another 130,000 arriving by boat. The relative isolation and high cost of living inhibits mass tourism. The construction and public sectors also enjoy significant investment in support of tourism. With limited fresh water resources, all food must be imported, as must all energy resources and most manufactured goods.

Employment is strong and attracts labor from Brazil and Portugal.

Exchange rates: euros (EUR) per US dollar—
0.885 (2015 est.)
0.7525 (2014 est.)
0.7634 2013 est.)
0.7752 (2012 est.)
0.7185 (2011 est.)

COMMUNICATIONS

Telephone system: *general assessment:* fully integrated access
domestic: direct dial capability with both fixed and wireless systems
international: country code—590; undersea fiber-optic cable provides voice and data connectivity to Puerto Rico and Guadeloupe (2008)

Broadcast media: no local TV broadcasters; 3 FM radio channels (2 via repeater)

Internet country code: .bl;
note—.gp, the internet country code for Guadeloupe, and .fr, the internet country code for France, might also be encountered

TRANSPORTATION

Airports: 1 (2013)
country comparison to the world: 231
Airports—with paved runways: *total:* 1
under 914 m: 1 (2013)
Ports and terminals: *major seaport(s):* Gustavia
Transportation—note:
nearest airport for International flights is Princess Juliana International Airport (SXM) located on Sint Maarten

MILITARY AND SECURITY

Military—note: defense is the responsibility of France

SAINT HELENA, ASCENSION, AND TRISTAN DA CUNHA

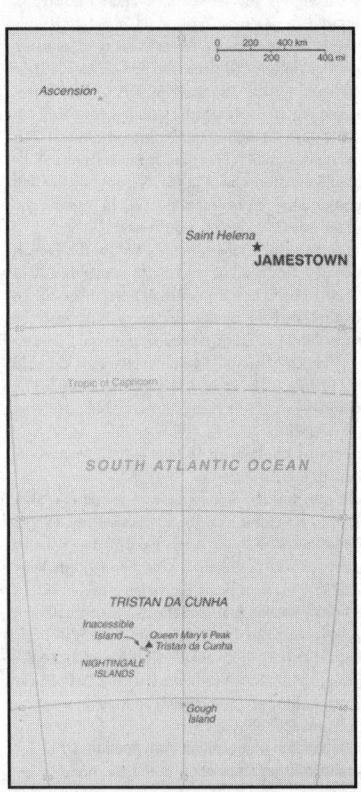

INTRODUCTION

Background: Saint Helena is a British Overseas Territory consisting of Saint Helena and Ascension Islands, and the island group of Tristan da Cunha.

Saint Helena: Uninhabited when first discovered by the Portuguese in 1502, Saint Helena was garrisoned by the British during the 17th century. It acquired fame as the place of Napoleon BONAPARTE's exile from 1815 until his death in 1821, but its importance as a port of call declined after the opening of the Suez Canal in 1869. During the Anglo-Boer War in South Africa, several thousand Boer prisoners were confined on the island between 1900 and 1903.

Ascension Island: This barren and uninhabited island was discovered and named by the Portuguese in 1503. The British garrisoned the island in 1815 to prevent a rescue of Napoleon from Saint Helena. It served as a provisioning station for the Royal Navy's West Africa Squadron on anti-slavery patrol. The island remained under Admiralty control until 1922, when it became a dependency of Saint Helena. During World War II, the UK permitted the US to construct an airfield on Ascension in support of transatlantic flights to Africa and anti-submarine operations in the South Atlantic. in the 1960s the island became an important space tracking station for the US. In 1982, Ascension was an essential staging area for British forces during the Falklands War. It remains a critical refueling point in the air-bridge from the UK to the South Atlantic. The island hosts one of four dedicated ground antennas (the others are on Diego Garcia (British Indian Ocean Territory), Kwajalein (Marshall Islands), and at Cape Canaveral, Florida (US)) that assist in the operation of the Global Positioning System (GPS) navigation system. NASA and the US Air Force also operate a Meter-Class Autonomous Telescope (MCAT) on Ascension as part of the deep space surveillance system for tracking orbital debris, which can be a hazard to spacecraft and astronauts.

Tristan da Cunha: The island group consists of Tristan da Cunha, Nightingale, Inaccessible, and Gough Islands. Tristan da Cunha is named after

its Portuguese discoverer (1506); it was garrisoned by the British in 1816 to prevent any attempt to rescue Napoleon from Saint Helena. Gough and Inaccessible Islands have been designated World Heritage Sites. South Africa leases a site for a meteorological station on Gough Island.

GEOGRAPHY

Location: islands in the South Atlantic Ocean, about midway between South America and Africa; Ascension Island lies 1,300 km (800 mi) northwest of Saint Helena; Tristan da Cunha lies 4,300 km (2,700 mi) southwest of Saint Helena

Geographic coordinates:
Saint Helena: 15 57 S, 5 42 W
Ascension Island: 7 57 S, 14 22 W
Tristan da Cunha island group: 37 15 S, 12 30 W
Map references: Africa
Area: *total:* 308 sq km
land: Saint Helena Island 122 sq km; Ascension Island 88 sq km; Tristan da Cunha island group 98 sq km
water: 0 sq km
country comparison to the world: 209
Area—comparative: slightly more than twice the size of Washington, DC
Land boundaries: 0 km
Coastline: *Saint Helena:* 60 km
Ascension Island: NA Tristan da Cunha: 40 km
Maritime claims: *territorial sea:* 12 nm
exclusive fishing zone: 200 nm
Climate: *Saint Helena:* tropical marine; mild, tempered by trade winds Ascension Is
land: tropical marine; mild, semi-arid
Tristan da Cunha: temperate marine; mild, tempered by trade winds (tends to be cooler than Saint Helena)
Terrain: the islands of this group are of volcanic origin associated with the Atlantic Mid-Ocean Ridge

Saint Helena: rugged, volcanic; small scattered plateaus and plains

Ascension: surface covered by lava flows and cinder cones of 44 dormant volcanoes; terrain rises to the east

Tristan da Cunha: sheer cliffs line the coastline of the nearly circular island; the flanks of the central volcanic peak are deeply dissected; narrow coastal plain lies between The Peak and the coastal cliffs

Elevation: *mean elevation:* NA

elevation extremes: *lowest point:* Atlantic Ocean 0 m

highest point: Queen Mary's Peak on Tristan da Cunha 2,060 m; Green Mountain on Ascension Island 859 m; Mount Actaeon on Saint Helena Island 818 m

Natural resources: fish, lobster

Land use: *agricultural land:* 30.8%

arable land: 10.3%

permanent crops: 0%

permanent pasture: 20.5%

forest: 5.1%

other: 64.1% (2011 est.)

Irrigated land: 0 sq km (2012)

Natural hazards: active volcanism on Tristan da Cunha

volcanism: the island volcanoes of Tristan da Cunha (elev. 2,060 m) and Nightingale Island (elev. 365 m) experience volcanic activity; Tristan da Cunha erupted in 1962 and Nightingale in 2004

Environment—current issues: NA

Geography—note: Saint Helena harbors at least 40 species of plants unknown elsewhere in the world; Ascension is a breeding ground for sea turtles and sooty terns; Queen Mary's Peak on Tristan da Cunha is the highest island mountain in the South Atlantic and a prominent landmark on the sea lanes around southern Africa

PEOPLE AND SOCIETY

Nationality: *noun:* Saint Helenian(s)

adjective: Saint Helenian

note: referred to locally as "Saints"

Ethnic groups: African descent 50%, white 25%, Chinese 25%

Languages: English

Religions: Protestant (Anglican (majority), Baptist, Seventh-Day Adventist), Roman Catholic

Population: 7,795

note: only Saint Helena, Ascension, and Tristan da Cunha islands are inhabited, none of the other nearby islands/islets (July 2015 est.)

country comparison to the world: 226

Age structure: *0–14 years:* 16.55% (male 658/female 632)

15–24 years: 12.06% (male 479/female 461)

25–54 years: 44.67% (male 1,719/female 1,763)

55–64 years: 12.6% (male 519/female 463)

65 years and over: 14.12% (male 560/female 541) (2015 est.)

Median age: *total:* 41 years

male: 41 years

female: 41 years (2015 est.)

country comparison to the world: 39

Population growth rate: 0.24% (2015 est.)

country comparison to the world: 179

Birth rate: 9.88 births/1,000 population (2015 est.)

country comparison to the world: 197

Death rate: 7.44 deaths/1,000 population (2015 est.)

country comparison to the world: 114

Net migration rate: 0 migrant(s)/1,000 population (2015 est.)

country comparison to the world: 84

Urbanization: *urban population:* 39.4% of total population (2015)

rate of urbanization: -0.59% annual rate of change (2010–15 est.)

Major urban areas—population: JAMESTOWN (capital) 1,000 (2014)

Sex ratio: *at birth:* 1.05 male(s)/female

0–14 years: 1.04 male(s)/female

15–24 years: 1.04 male(s)/female

25–54 years: 0.98 male(s)/female

55–64 years: 1.12 male(s)/female

65 years and over: 1.04 male(s)/female

total population: 1.02 male(s)/female (2015 est.)

Infant mortality rate: *total:* 14.19 deaths/1,000 live births

male: 16.75 deaths/1,000 live births

female: 11.5 deaths/1,000 live births (2015 est.)

country comparison to the world: 107

Life expectancy at birth: *total population:* 79.36 years

male: 76.42 years

female: 82.44 years (2015 est.)

country comparison to the world: 45

Total fertility rate: 1.58 children born/woman (2015 est.)

country comparison to the world: 185

HIV/AIDS—adult prevalence rate: NA

HIV/AIDS—people living with HIV/AIDS: NA

HIV/AIDS—deaths: NA

GOVERNMENT

Country name: *conventional long form:* Saint Helena, Ascension, and Tristan da Cunha

conventional short form: none

etymology: Saint Helena was discovered in 1502 by Galician navigator Joao da NOVA, sailing in the service of the Kingdom of Portugal, who named it "Santa Helena"; Ascension was named in 1503 by Portuguese navigator Afonso de ALBUQUERQUE who sighted the island on the Feast Day of the Ascension; Tristan da Cunha was discovered in 1506 by Portuguese explorer Tristao da CUNHA who christened the main island after himself (the name was subsequently anglicized)

Dependency status: overseas territory of the UK

Government type: parliamentary democracy (Legislative Council); limited self-governing overseas territory of the UK

Capital: *name:* Jamestown

Geographic coordinates: 15 56 S, 5 43 W

time difference: UTC 0 (5 hours ahead of Washington, DC, during Standard Time)

Administrative divisions: 3 administrative areas; Ascension, Saint Helena, Tristan da Cunha

Independence: none (overseas territory of the UK)

National holiday: Birthday of Queen ELIZABETH II, third Monday in April (1926)

Constitution: several previous; latest effective 1 September 2009 (The St. Helena, Ascension and Tristan da Cunha Constitution Order 2009) (2016)

Legal system: English common law and local statutes

Citizenship: see United Kingdom

Suffrage: 18 years of age

Executive branch: *chief of state:* Queen ELIZABETH II (since 6 February 1952)

head of government: Governor Lisa PHILLIPS (since 25 April 2016)

cabinet: Executive Council consists of the governor, 3 ex-officio officers, and 5 elected members of the Legislative Council

elections/appointments: none; the monarchy is hereditary; governor appointed by the monarch

note: the constitution order provides for an Administrator for Ascension and Tristan da Cunha appointed by the governor

Legislative branch: *description:* unicameral Legislative Council (17 seats including the speaker and deputy speaker; 12 members directly elected in a single countrywide constituency by simple majority vote and 3 ex-officio members—the chief secretary, financial secretary, and attorney general; members serve 4-year terms)

note: each voter can vote for up to 12 candidates; the Constitution Order provides for separate Island Councils for both Ascension and Tristan da Cunha

elections: last held on 17 July 2013 (next to be held in 2017)

election results: percent of vote—NA; seats—independents 12

Judicial branch: *highest resident court(s):* Court of Appeal (consists of the court president and 2 justices); Supreme Court (consists of the chief justice—a non-resident—and NA judges); note—appeals beyond the Court of Appeal are heard by the Judicial Com mittee of the Privy Council (in London)

judge selection and term of office: court judges' appointments and tenures NA

subordinate courts: Magistrate's Court; Small Claims Court; Juvenile Court

Political parties and leaders: none

Political pressure groups and leaders:

other: private sector; unions

International organization participation: UPU

Diplomatic representation in the US: none (overseas territory of the UK)

Diplomatic representation from the US: none (overseas territory of the UK)

Flag description: blue with the flag of the UK in the upper hoist-side quadrant and the Saint Helenian shield centered on the outer half of the flag; the upper third of the shield depicts a white plover (wire bird) on a yellow field; the remainder of the shield depicts a rocky coastline on the left, offshore is a three-masted sailing ship with sails furled but flying an English flag

National symbol(s): Saint Helena plover (bird)

National anthem: *note:* as a territory of the UK, "God Save the Queen" is official (see United Kingdom)

713

ECONOMY

Economy—overview: The economy depends largely on financial assistance from the UK, which amounted to about $27 million in FY06/07 or more than twice the level of annual budgetary revenues. The local population earns income from fishing, raising livestock, and sales of handicrafts. Because there are few jobs, 25% of the work force has left to seek employment on Ascension Island, on the Falklands, and in the UK.

GDP (purchasing power parity): $31.1 million (FY09/10 est.)
country comparison to the world: 228
GDP (official exchange rate): $NA
GDP—real growth rate: NA%
GDP—per capita (PPP): $7,800 (FY09/10 est.)
country comparison to the world: 149
GDP—composition, by sector of origin:
agriculture: NA%
industry: NA%
services: NA%
Agriculture—products: coffee, corn, potatoes, vegetables; fish, lobster; livestock; timber
Industries: construction, crafts (furniture, lacework, fancy woodwork), fishing, collectible postage stamps
Industrial production growth rate: NA%
Labor force: 2,486 (1998 est.)
country comparison to the world: 227
Labor force—by occupation: *agriculture:* 6%
industry: 48%
services: 46% (1987 est.)
Unemployment rate: 14% (1998 est.)
country comparison to the world: 147
Population below poverty line: NA%

Household income or consumption by percentage share: *lowest:* 10%: NA%
highest: 10%: NA%

Budget: *revenues:* $10.01 million
expenditures: $24.6 million
note: revenue data reflect locally raised revenues only; the budget deficit is resolved by grant aid from the UK (FY06/07 est.)
Fiscal year: 1 April—31 March
Inflation rate (consumer prices): 4% (2012 est.)
country comparison to the world: 155
Exports: $19 million (2004 est.)
country comparison to the world: 211
Exports—commodities: fish (frozen, canned, and salt-dried skipjack, tuna), coffee, handicrafts
Imports: $20.53 million (2010 est.)
country comparison to the world: 221
Imports—commodities: food, beverages, tobacco, fuel oils, animal feed, building materials, motor vehicles and parts, machinery and parts
Debt—external: $NA
Exchange rates: Saint Helenian pounds (SHP) per US dollar—
0.6528 (2015)
0.6391 (2013)
0.6391 (2013)
0.63 (2012)
0.624 (2011)

ENERGY

Electricity—production: 8 million kWh (2012 est.)
country comparison to the world: 217

Electricity—consumption: 7.44 million kWh (2012 est.)
country comparison to the world: 215
Electricity—exports: 0 kWh (2013 est.)
country comparison to the world: 194
Electricity—imports: 0 kWh (2013 est.)
country comparison to the world: 200
Electricity—installed generating capacity: 5,000 kW (2012 est.)
country comparison to the world: 213
Electricity—from fossil fuels: 100% of total installed capacity (2012 est.)
country comparison to the world: 27
Electricity—from nuclear fuels: 0% of total installed capacity (2012 est.)
country comparison to the world: 179
Electricity—from hydroelectric plants: 0% of total installed capacity (2012 est.)
country comparison to the world: 201
Electricity—from other renewable sources: 0% of total installed capacity (2012 est.)
country comparison to the world: 126
Crude oil—production: 0 bbl/day (2014 est.)
country comparison to the world: 189
Crude oil—exports: 0 bbl/day (2012 est.)
country comparison to the world: 187
Crude oil—imports: 0 bbl/day (2012 est.)
country comparison to the world: 123
Crude oil—proved reserves: 0 bbl (1 January 2015 est.)
country comparison to the world: 188
Refined petroleum products—production: 0 bbl/day (2012 est.)
country comparison to the world: 129
Refined petroleum products—consumption: 60 bbl/day (2013 est.)
country comparison to the world: 211
Refined petroleum products—exports: 0 bbl/day (2012 est.)
country comparison to the world: 131
Refined petroleum products—imports: 63.12 bbl/day (2012 est.)
country comparison to the world: 208
Natural gas—production: 0 cum (2013 est.)
country comparison to the world: 126
Natural gas—consumption: 0 cum (2013 est.)
country comparison to the world: 192
Natural gas—exports: 0 cum (2013 est.)
country comparison to the world: 178
Natural gas—imports: 0 cum (2013 est.)
country comparison to the world: 132
Natural gas—proved reserves: 0 cum (1 January 2014 est.)
country comparison to the world: 192
Carbon dioxide emissions from consumption of energy: 12,080 Mt (2012 est.)
country comparison to the world: 210

COMMUNICATIONS

Telephone—fixed lines: *total:* 3,000
subscriptions per 100 inhabitants: 39 (2012)
country comparison to the world: 211
Telephone system: *general assessment:* can communicate worldwide
domestic: automatic digital network
international: country code (Saint Helena)—290, (Ascension Island)—247; International direct dialing; satellite voice and data communications;

satellite earth stations—5 (Ascension Island—4, Saint Helena—1) (2010)
Broadcast media: Saint Helena has no local TV station; 2 local radio stations, one of which is relayed to Ascension Island; satellite TV stations rebroadcast terrestrially; Ascension Island has no local TV station but has 1 local radio station and receives relays of broadcasts from 1 radio station on Saint Helena; broadcasts from the British Forces Broadcasting Service (BFBS) are available, as well as TV services for the US Military; Tristan da Cunha has 1 local radio station and receives BFBS TV and radio broadcasts (2007)
Radio broadcast stations: Saint Helena: AM 1, FM 1, shortwave 0 Ascension: AM 1, FM 1, shortwave 1 (2005)
Television broadcast stations: 0 (3 television channels are received via satellite and distributed by UHF) (2005)
Internet country code: .sh; note—Ascension Island assigned . ac
Internet hosts: 6,729 (2012)
country comparison to the world: 141
Internet users: *total:* 900
percent of population: 11.8% (2009)
country comparison to the world: 214

Communications—note: South Africa maintains A meteorological station on gough Island

TRANSPORTATION

Airports: 2 (2015)
country comparison to the world: 232
Airports—with paved runways: *total:* 2
over 3,047 m: 1 Ascension Island (Wideawake Field)
1,524 to 2,437 m: 1 Saint Helena; note—opening to commercial flights in February 2016 (2015)
Roadways: *total:* 198 km (Saint Helena 138 km, Ascension 40 km, Tristan da Cunha 20 km)
paved: 168 km (Saint Helena 118 km, Ascension 40 km, Tristan da Cunha 10 km)
unpaved: 30 km (Saint Helena 20 km, Tristan da Cunha 10 km) (2002)
country comparison to the world: 210
Ports and terminals: *major seaport(s):*
Saint Helena: Jamestown Ascension Is
land: Georgetown Tristan da Cunha: Calshot Harbor (Edinburgh)
Transportation—note:
there is no air connection to Saint Helena or Tristan da Cunha; construction on the new International airport for Saint Helena began in 2012 with an estimated completion date of late 2015 or early 2016; the new airport will have a runway of 1,550 m capable of handling B737/A319 size aircraft

MILITARY AND SECURITY

Military—note: defense is the responsibility of the UK

TRANSNATIONAL ISSUES

Disputes—International: none

SAINT KITTS AND NEVIS

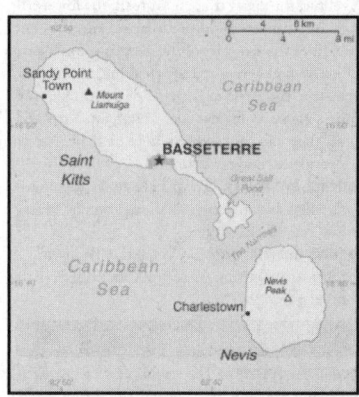

INTRODUCTION

Background: Carib Indians occupied the islands of the West Indies for hundreds of years before the British began settlement in 1623. In 1967, the island territory of Saint Christopher-Nevis-Anguilla became an associated state of the UK with full internal autonomy. The island of Anguilla rebelled and was allowed to secede in 1971. The remaining islands achieved independence in 1983 as Saint Kitts and Nevis. In 1998, a referendum on Nevis to separate from Saint Kitts fell short of the two-thirds majority vote needed. Nevis continues in its efforts to separate from Saint Kitts.

GEOGRAPHY

Location: Caribbean, islands in the Caribbean Sea, about one-third of the way from Puerto Rico to Trinidad and Tobago

Geographic coordinates: 17 20 N, 62 45 W

Map references: Central America and the Caribbean

Area: *total:* 261 sq km (Saint Kitts 168 sq km; Nevis 93 sq km)
land: 261 sq km
water: 0 sq km
country comparison to the world: 212

Area—comparative: 1.5 times the size of Washington, DC

Land boundaries: 0 km

Coastline: 135 km

Maritime claims: *territorial sea:* 12 nm
contiguous zone: 24 nm
exclusive economic zone: 200 nm
continental shelf: 200 nm or to the edge of the continental margin

Climate: tropical, tempered by constant sea breezes; little seasonal temperature variation; rainy season (May to November)

Terrain: volcanic with mountainous interiors

Elevation: *mean elevation:* NA

elevation extremes: *lowest point:* Caribbean Sea 0 m
highest point: Mount Liamuiga 1,156 m

Natural resources: arable land

Land use: *agricultural land:* 23.1%
arable land: 19.2%
permanent crops: 0.4%
permanent pasture: 3.5%
forest: 42.3%
other: 34.6% (2011 est.)

Irrigated land: 8 sq km (2012)

Total renewable water resources: 0.02 cu km (2011)

Natural hazards: hurricanes (July to October)

Environment—current issues: NA

Environment—international agreements: *party to:* Biodiversity, Climate Change, Climate Change-Kyoto Protocol, Desertification, Endangered Species, Hazardous Wastes, Law of the Sea, Marine Dumping, Ozone Layer Protection, Ship Pollution, Whaling
signed, but not ratified: none of the selected agreements

Geography—note: smallest country in the Americas and Western Hemisphere; with coastlines in the shape of a baseball bat and ball, the two volcanic islands are separated by a 3-km-wide channel called The Narrows; on the southern tip of long, baseball bat-shaped Saint Kitts lies the Great Salt Pond; Nevis Peak sits in the center of its almost circular namesake island and its ball shape complements that of its sister island

PEOPLE AND SOCIETY

Nationality: *noun:* Kittitian(s), Nevisian(s)
adjective: Kittitian, Nevisian

Ethnic groups: predominantly black; some British, Portuguese, and Lebanese

Languages: English (official)

Religions: Anglican, other Protestant, Roman Catholic

Population: 51,936 (July 2015 est.)
country comparison to the world: 210

Age structure: *0–14 years:* 20.99% (male 5,457/female 5,445)
15–24 years: 15.1% (male 3,845/female 3,999)
25–54 years: 45.01% (male 11,951/female 11,427)
55–64 years: 10.79% (male 2,806/female 2,800)
65 years and over: 8.1% (male 1,912/female 2,294) (2015 est.)

Median age: *total:* 34 years
male: 34.2 years
female: 33.9 years (2015 est.)
country comparison to the world: 82

Population growth rate: 0.76% (2015 est.)
country comparison to the world: 144

Birth rate: 13.5 births/1,000 population (2015 est.)
country comparison to the world: 147

Death rate: 7.09 deaths/1,000 population (2015 est.)
country comparison to the world: 130

Net migration rate: 1.21 migrant(s)/1,000 population (2015 est.)
country comparison to the world: 61

Urbanization: *urban population:* 32% of total population (2015)
rate of urbanization: 1.27% annual rate of change (2010–15 est.)

Major urban areas—population: BASSETERRE (capital) 14,000 (2014)

Sex ratio: *at birth:* 1.02 male(s)/female
0–14 years: 1 male(s)/female
15–24 years: 0.96 male(s)/female
25–54 years: 1.05 male(s)/female
55–64 years: 1 male(s)/female
65 years and over: 0.83 male(s)/female
total population: 1 male(s)/female (2015 est.)

Infant mortality rate: *total:* 8.77 deaths/1,000 live births
male: 6.03 deaths/1,000 live births
female: 11.56 deaths/1,000 live births (2015 est.)
country comparison to the world: 147

Life expectancy at birth: *total population:* 75.52 years
male: 73.09 years
female: 77.99 years (2015 est.)
country comparison to the world: 97

Total fertility rate: 1.78 children born/woman (2015 est.)
country comparison to the world: 154

Health expenditures: 6.4% of GDP (2013)
country comparison to the world: 117

Hospital bed density: 2.3 beds/1,000 population (2012)

Drinking water source:
improved:
urban: 98.3% of population
rural: 98.3% of population
total: 98.3% of population
unimproved:
urban: 1.7% of population
rural: 1.7% of population
total: 1.7% of population (2015 est.)

Sanitation facility access:
improved:
urban: 87.3% of population
rural: 87.3% of population
total: 87.3% of population
unimproved:
urban: 12.7% of population
rural: 12.7% of population
total: 12.7% of population (2007 est.)

HIV/AIDS—adult prevalence rate: NA

HIV/AIDS—people living with HIV/AIDS: NA

HIV/AIDS—deaths: NA

Obesity—adult prevalence rate: 28.4% (2014)
country comparison to the world: 11

Education expenditures: 4.2% of GDP (2007)
country comparison to the world: 105

School life expectancy (primary to tertiary education): *total:* 14 years
male: 14 years

female: 15 years (2014)

GOVERNMENT

Country name: *conventional long form:* Federation of Saint Kitts and Nevis
conventional short form: Saint Kitts and Nevis
former: Federation of Saint Christopher and Nevis
etymology: Saint Kitts was, and still is, referred to as Saint Christopher and this name was well established by the 17th century (although who first applied the name is unclear); in the 17th century a common nickname for Christopher was Kit or Kitt, so the island began to be referred to as "Saint Kitt's Island" or just "Saint Kitts"; Nevis is derived from the original Spanish name "Nuestra Senora de las Nieves" (Our Lady of the Snows) and refers to the white halo of clouds that generally wreathes Nevis Peak

Government type: federal parliamen tary democracy (National Assembly) un der a con stitution al monarchy; a Common wealth realm

Capital: *name:* Basseterre

Geographic coordinates: 17 18 N, 62 43 W
time difference: UTC-4 (1 hour ahead of Washington, DC, during Standard Time)

Administrative divisions: 14 parishes; Christ Church Nichola Town, Saint Anne Sandy Point, Saint George Basseterre, Saint George Gingerland, Saint James Windward, Saint John Capesterre, Saint John Figtree, Saint Mary Cayon, Saint Paul Capesterre, Saint Paul Charlestown, Saint Peter Basseterre, Saint Thomas Lowland, Saint Thomas Middle Island, Trinity Palmetto Point

Independence: 19 September 1983 (from the UK)

National holiday: independence Day, 19 September (1983)

Constitution: several previous (preindependence); latest presented 22 June 1983, effective 23 June 1983 (2016)

Legal system: English common law

International law organization participation: has not submitted an ICJ jurisdiction declaration; accepts ICCt jurisdiction

Citizenship: *citizenship by birth:* yes citizenship by descent: yes
dual citizenship recognized: yes
residency requirement for naturalization: 14 years

Suffrage: 18 years of age; universal

Executive branch: *chief of state:* Queen ELIZABETH II (since 6 February 1952); represented by Governor General Samuel W. T. SEATON (since 2 September 2015); note—SEATON was acting Governor General from 20 May to 2 September 2015

head of government: Prime Minister Timothy HARRIS (since 18 February 2015); Deputy Prime Minister Shawn RICHARDS (since 22 February 2015)
cabinet: Cabinet appointed by governor general in consultation with prime minister
elections/appointments: the monarchy is hereditary; governor general appointed by the monarch; following legislative elections, the leader of the majority party or majority coalition usually

appointed prime minister by governor general; deputy prime minister appointed by governor general

Legislative branch: *description:* unicameral National Assembly (14 seats; 11 members directly elected in single-seat constituencies by simple majority vote and 3 appointed by the governor general; members serve 5-year terms)
elections: last held on 16 February 2015 (next to be held by 2020)
election results: percent of vote by party—NA; seats by party—PAM 4, SKNLP 3, CCM 2, PLP 1, NRP 1

Judicial branch: *highest court(s):* the Eastern Caribbean Supreme Court (ECSC) is the itinerant superior court of record for the 9-member Organization of Eastern Caribbean States, which includes Saint Kitts and Nevis; the ECSC—with its headquarters on St. Lucia—is headed by the chief justice and comprised of the Court of Appeal with 3 justices and the High Court with 16 judges; sittings of the Court of Appeal and High Court rotate among the member states; 2 High Court judges reside on Saint Kitts and Nevis; note—the Eastern Caribbean Supreme Court in 2003 replaced the Judicial Committee of the Privy Council (in London) as the final court of appeal on Saint Kitts and Nevis; Saint Kitts and Nevis is also a member of the Caribbean Court of Justice
judge selection and term of office: Eastern Caribbean Supreme Court chief justice appointed by Her Majesty, Queen ELIZABETH II; other justices and judges appointed by the Judicial and Legal Services Commission; Court of Appeal justices appointed for life with mandatory retirement at age 65; High Court judges appointed for life with mandatory retirement at age 62
subordinate courts: magistrates' courts

Political parties and leaders: Concerned Citizens Movement or CCM [Vance AMORY]
Nevis Reformation Party or NRP [Joseph PARRY]
People's Action Movement or PAM [Shawn RICHARDS]
People's Labour Party or PLP [Timothy HARRIS]
Saint Kitts and Nevis Labor Party or SKNLP [Dr. Denzil DOUGLAS]

Political pressure groups and leaders: NA

International organization participation: ACP, AOSIS, C, Caricom, CDB, CELAC, FAO, G-77, IBRD, ICAO, ICCt, ICRM, IDA, IFAD, IFC, IFRCS, ILO, IMF, IMO, Interpol, IOC, ITU, MIGA, OAS, OECS, OPANAL, OPCW, Petrocaribe, UN, UNCTAD, UNESCO, UNIDO, UPU, WHO, WIPO, WTO

Diplomatic representation in the US: *chief of mission:* Ambassador Thelma Patricia Phillip BROWNE (since 28 January 2016)
chancery: 3216 New Mexico Avenue NW, Washington, DC 20016
telephone: [1] (202) 686-2636
FAX: [1] (202) 686-5740
consulate(s) general: Los Angeles, New York

Diplomatic representation from the US: the US does not have an embassy in Saint Kitts and Nevis; the US Ambassador to Barbados is accredited to Saint Kitts and Nevis

Flag description: divided diagonally from the lower hoist side by a broad black band bearing two white, five-pointed stars; the black band is edged in yellow; the upper triangle is green, the lower triangle is red; green signifies the island's fertility, red symbolizes the struggles of the people from slavery, yellow denotes year-round sunshine, and black represents the African heritage of the people; the white stars stand for the islands of Saint Kitts and Nevis, but can also express hope and liberty, or independence and optimism

National symbol(s): brown pelican, Royal Poinciana (Flamboyant) tree; National colors: green, yellow, red, black, white

National anthem: *name:* "Oh Land of Beauty!"
lyrics/music: Kenrick Anderson GEORGES
note: adopted 1983

ECONOMY

Economy—overview: The economy of Saint Kitts and Nevis depends on tourism; since the 1970s, tourism has replaced sugar as the economy's traditional mainstay. Roughly 200,000 tourists visited the islands in 2009, but reduced tourism arrivals and foreign investment led to an economic con traction in 2009–2013, and the economy return ed to growth only in 2014. Like other tourist destinations in the Caribbean, St. Kitts and Nevis is vulnerable to damage from Natural disasters and shifts in tourism demand.

Following the 2005 harvest, the government closed the sugar industry after several decades of losses. To compensate for lost jobs, the government has embarked on a program to diversify the agricultural sector and to stimulate other sectors of the economy, such as export-oriented manufacturing and offshore ban king. The government has made notable progress in reducing its public debt, from 154% of GDP in 2011 to 83% in 2013, although it still faces one of the highest levels in the world, largely attributable to public enterprise losses.

GDP (purchasing power parity): $1.379 billion (2015 est.)
$1.294 billion (2014 est.)
$1.22 billion (2013 est.)
note: data are in 2015 US dollars
country comparison to the world: 200

GDP (official exchange rate): $896 million (2015 est.)

GDP—real growth rate: 6.6% (2015 est.)
6.1% (2014 est.)
6.2% (2013 est.)
country comparison to the world: 21

GDP—per capita (PPP): $24,600 (2015 est.)
$23,500 (2014 est.)
$22,600 (2013 est.)
note: data are in 2015 US dollars
country comparison to the world: 77

Gross National saving: 16.9% of GDP (2015 est.)
21.4% of GDP (2014 est.)
21.1% of GDP (2013 est.)
country comparison to the world: 98

GDP—composition, by end use:
household consumption: 73.6%
government consumption: 10.7%

investment in fixed capital: 29.3%
investment in inventories: 0%
exports of goods and services: 25.3%
imports of goods and services: -38.9% (2015 est.)
GDP—composition, by sector of origin:
agriculture: 1.7%
industry: 24.1%
services: 74.2% (2015 est.)
Agriculture—products: sugarcane, rice, yams, vegetables, bananas; fish
Industries: tourism, cotton, salt, copra, clothing, footwear, beverages
Industrial production growth rate: 0.5% (2015 est.)
country comparison to the world: 162
Labor force: 18,170 (June 1995 est.)
country comparison to the world: 213
Unemployment rate: 4.5% (1997)
country comparison to the world: 43
Population below poverty line: NA%
Household income or consumption by percentage share: *lowest:* 10%: NA%
highest: 10%: NA%

Budget: *revenues:* $296.3 million
expenditures: $259.3 million (2015 est.)
Taxes and other revenues: 33.3% of GDP (2015 est.)
country comparison to the world: 70
Budget surplus (+) or deficit (–): 4.2% of GDP (2015 est.)
country comparison to the world: 10
Public debt: 83% of GDP (2013 est.) 144% of GDP (2012 est.)
country comparison to the world: 30
Fiscal year: calendar year
Inflation rate (consumer prices): -2.8% (2015 est.) 0.7% (2014 est.)
country comparison to the world: 3
Central bank discount rate: 6.5% (31 December 2009)
6.5% (31 December 2008)
country comparison to the world: 56
Commercial bank prime lending rate: 9.4% (31 December 2015 est.)
9.28% (31 December 2014 est.)
country comparison to the world: 88
Stock of narrow money: $220.1 million (31 December 2015 est.)
$215.6 million (31 December 2014 est.)
country comparison to the world: 181
Stock of broad money: $964.8 million (31 December 2015 est.)
$1.094 billion (31 December 2014 est.)
country comparison to the world: 170
Stock of domestic credit: $333.3 million (31 December 2015 est.)
$396.7 million (31 December 2014 est.)
country comparison to the world: 179
Market value of publicly traded shares: $598.4 million (31 December 2011)
$598.4 million (31 December 2011)
$623.9 million (31 December 2010)
country comparison to the world: 112
Current account balance: -$117 million (2015 est.)
-$65 million (2014 est.)
country comparison to the world: 70
Exports: $61.3 million (2015 est.)

$62.9 million (2014 est.)
country comparison to the world: 199
Exports—commodities: machinery, food, electronics, beverages, tobacco
Exports—partners: US 44.4%, Poland 14.6%, Bangladesh 10.1%, Azerbaijan 4.3% (2015)
Imports: $240.3 million (2015 est.) $241.8 million (2014 est.)
country comparison to the world: 204
Imports—commodities: machinery, manufactures, food, fuels
Imports—partners: US 37.7%, Trinidad and Tobago 22.7%, Barbados 4.4% (2015)
Debt—external: $156.1 million (31 December 2014 est.)
$158.8 million (31 December 2013 est.)
country comparison to the world: 190
Exchange rates: East Caribbean dollars (XCD) per US dollar—
2.7 (2015 est.)
2.7 (2014 est.)
2.7 (2013 est.)
2.7 (2012 est.)
2.7 (2011 est.)

ENERGY

Electricity—production: 140 million kWh (2012 est.)
country comparison to the world: 195
Electricity—consumption: 130.2 million kWh (2012 est.)
country comparison to the world: 195
Electricity—exports: 0 kWh (2013 est.)
country comparison to the world: 191
Electricity—imports: 0 kWh (2013 est.)
country comparison to the world: 197
Electricity—installed generating capacity: 46,200 kW (2012 est.)
country comparison to the world: 189
Electricity—from fossil fuels: 95.2% of total installed capacity (2012 est.)
country comparison to the world: 69
Electricity—from nuclear fuels: 0% of total installed capacity (2012 est.)
country comparison to the world: 176
Electricity—from hydroelectric plants: 0% of total installed capacity (2012 est.)
country comparison to the world: 198
Electricity—from other renewable sources: 4.8% of total installed capacity (2012 est.)
country comparison to the world: 59
Crude oil—production: 0 bbl/day (2014 est.)
country comparison to the world: 186
Crude oil—exports: 0 bbl/day (2012 est.)
country comparison to the world: 183
Crude oil—imports: 0 bbl/day (2012 est.)
country comparison to the world: 121
Crude oil—proved reserves: 0 bbl (1 January 2015 est.)
country comparison to the world: 185
Refined petroleum products—production: 0 bbl/day (2012 est.)
country comparison to the world: 127
Refined petroleum products—consumption: 1,700 bbl/day (2013 est.)
country comparison to the world: 190

Refined petroleum products—exports: 0 bbl/day (2012 est.)
country comparison to the world: 129
Refined petroleum products—imports: 1,690 bbl/day (2012 est.)
country comparison to the world: 186
Natural gas—production: 0 cum (2013 est.)
country comparison to the world: 124
Natural gas—consumption: 0 cum (2013 est.)
country comparison to the world: 190
Natural gas—exports: 0 cum (2013 est.)
country comparison to the world: 174
Natural gas—imports: 0 cum (2013 est.)
country comparison to the world: 129
Natural gas—proved reserves: 0 cum (1 January 2014 est.)
country comparison to the world: 189
Carbon dioxide emissions from consumption 250,700 Mt (2012 est.)
country comparison to the world: 195

COMMUNICATIONS

Telephones—fixed lines: *total subscriptions:* 19,100
subscriptions per 100 inhabitants: 37 (2014 est.)
country comparison to the world: 198
Telephone—mobile cellular: *total:* 76,600
subscriptions per 100 inhabitants: 149 (2014 est.)
country comparison to the world: 196
Telephone system: *general assessment:* good interisland and International connections
domestic: interisland links via Eastern Caribbean Fiber Optic cable; construction of enhanced wireless infrastructure launched in November 2004; fixed-line teledensity about 40 per 100 persons; mobile-cellular teledensity is roughly 170 per 100 persons
international: country code—1-869; connected Internationally by the East Caribbean Fiber Optic System (ECFS) and Southern Caribbean fiber optic system (SCF) submarine cables (2010)
Broadcast media: the government operates a National TV network that broadcasts on 2 channels; cable subscription services provide access to local and International channels; the government operates a National radio network; a mix of government-owned and privately owned broadcasters operate roughly 15 radio stations (2007)
Radio broadcast stations: AM 3, FM 8, short-wave 0 (2008)
Television broadcast stations: 1 (plus 3 repeaters) (2003)
Internet country code: .kn
Internet hosts: 54 (2012)
country comparison to the world: 213
Internet users: *total:* 17,000
percent of population: 34.4% (2009)
country comparison to the world: 203

TRANSPORTATION

Airports: 2 (2013)
country comparison to the world: 209
Airports—with paved runways: *total:* 2
1,524 to 2,437 m: 1
914 to 1,523 m: 1 (2013)

Railways: *total:* 50 km
Narrow gauge: 50 km 0.762-m gauge on Saint Kitts for tourists (2008)
country comparison to the world: 132
Roadways: *total:* 383 km
paved: 163 km
unpaved: 220 km (2002)
country comparison to the world: 201
Merchant marine: *total:* 152
by type: bulk carrier 16, cargo 81, chemical tanker 4, combination ore/oil 1, container 2, liquefied gas 3, passenger 2, passenger/cargo 7, petroleum tanker 27, refrigerated cargo 4, roll on/roll off 4, specialized tanker 1

foreign-owned: 73 (Belgium 1, China 1, Egypt 1, Greece 2, India 2, Japan 2, Malaysia 1, Norway 3, Pakistan 1, Russia 13, Singapore 10, Turkey 18, UAE 8, UK 1, Ukraine 8, US 1) (2010)
country comparison to the world: 38
Ports and terminals: *major seaport(s):* Basseterre, Charlestown

MILITARY AND SECURITY

Military branches: Ministry of Foreign Affairs, National Security, Labour, Immigration, and Social Security: Royal Saint Kitts and Nevis Defense Force (includes Coast Guard), Royal Saint Kitts and Nevis Police Force (2013)

Military service age and obligation: 18 years of age for voluntary military service; no conscription (2012)

TRANSNATIONAL ISSUES

Disputes—International: joins other Caribbean states to counter Venezuela's claim that Aves Island sustains human habitation, a criterion under UN Convention on the Law of the Sea, which permits Venezuela to extend its EEZ/continental shelf over a large portion of the eastern Caribbean Sea
Illicit drugs: transshipment point for South American drugs destined for the US and Europe; some money-laundering activity

SAINT LUCIA

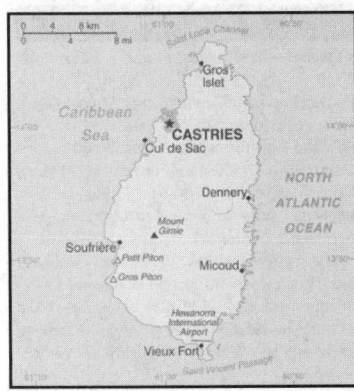

INTRODUCTION

Background: The island, with its fine Natural harbor at Castries, was contested between England and France throughout the 17th and early 18th centuries (changing possession 14 times); it was finally ceded to the UK in 1814. Even After the abolition of slavery on its plantations in 1834, Saint Lucia remained an agricultural island, dedicated to producing tropical commodity crops. Self-government was granted in 1967 and independence in 1979.

GEOGRAPHY

Location: Caribbean, island between the Caribbean Sea and North Atlantic Ocean, north of Trinidad and Tobago
Geographic coordinates: 13 53 N, 60 58 W
Map references: Central America and the Caribbean
Area: *total:* 616 sq km
land: 606 sq km
water: 10 sq km
country comparison to the world: 193
Area—comparative: three and a half times the size of Washington, DC

Land boundaries: 0 km
Coastline: 158 km
Maritime claims: *territorial sea:* 12 nm
contiguous zone: 24 nm
exclusive economic zone: 200 nm
continental shelf: 200 nm or to the edge of the continental margin
Climate: tropical, moderated by northeast trade winds; dry season January to April, rainy season May to August
Terrain: volcanic and mountainous with broad, fertile valleys
Elevation: *mean elevation:* NA
elevation extremes: *lowest point:* Caribbean Sea 0 m
highest point: Mount Gimie 950 m
Natural resources: forests, sandy beaches, minerals (pumice), mineral springs, geothermal potential
Land use: *agricultural land:* 17.4%
arable land: 4.9%
permanent crops: 11.5%
permanent pasture: 1%
forest: 77%
other: 5.6% (2011 est.)
Irrigated land: 30 sq km (2012)
Freshwater withdrawal (domestic/industrial/agricultural): *total:* 0.02 cu km/yr
per capita: 98.22 cu m/yr (2005)
Natural hazards: hurricanes; volcanic activity
Environment—current issues: deforestation; soil erosion, particularly in the northern region
Environment—International agreements: *party to:* Biodiversity, Climate Change, Climate Change-Kyoto Protocol, Desertification, Endangered Species, Environmental Modification, Hazardous Wastes, Law of the Sea, Marine Dumping, Ozone Layer Protection, Ship Pollution, Wetlands, Whaling
signed, but not ratified: none of the selected agreements
Geography—note: the twin Pitons (Gros Piton and Petit Piton), striking cone-shaped peaks south of Soufriere, are one of the scenic Natural highlights of the Caribbean

PEOPLE AND SOCIETY

Nationality: *noun:* Saint Lucian(s)
adjective: Saint Lucian
Ethnic groups: black/African descent 85.3%, mixed 10.9%, East Indian 2.2%, other 1.6%, unspecified 0.1% (2010 est.)
Languages: English (official), French patois
Religions: Roman Catholic 61.5%, Protestant 25.5% (includes Seventh Day Adventist 10.4%, Pentecostal 8.9%, Baptist 2.2%, Anglican 1.6%, Church of God 1.5%, other Protestant 0.9%), other Christian 3.4% (includes Evangelical 2.3% and Jehovah's Witness 1.1%), Rastafarian 1.9%, other 0.4%, none 5.9%, unspecified 1.4% (2010 est.)
Population: 163,922 (July 2015 est.)
country comparison to the world: 187
Age structure: *0–14 years:* 20.75% (male 17,508/female 16,503)
15–24 years: 16.3% (male 13,541/female 13,177)
25–54 years: 42.93% (male 33,812/female 36,565)
55–64 years: 9.18% (male 6,964/female 8,084)
65 years and over: 10.84% (male 8,036/female 9,732) (2015 est.)
Dependency ratios: *total dependency ratio:* 47.3%
youth dependency ratio: 34.1%
elderly dependency ratio: 13.3%
potential support ratio: 7.5% (2015 est.)
Median age: *total:* 33.5 years
male: 32.4 years
female: 34.6 years (2015 est.)
country comparison to the world: 87
Population growth rate: 0.34% (2015 est.)
country comparison to the world: 170
Birth rate: 13.7 births/1,000 population (2015 est.)
country comparison to the world: 143
Death rate: 7.42 deaths/1,000 population (2015 est.)
country comparison to the world: 115
Net migration rate: -2.93 migrant(s)/1,000 population (2015 est.)
country comparison to the world: 180

Urbanization: *urban population:* 18.5% of total population (2015)
rate of urbanization: 0.89% annual rate of change (2010–15 est.)
Major urban areas—population: CASTRIES (capital) 22,000 (2014)
Sex ratio: *at birth:* 1.06 male(s)/female
0–14 years: 1.06 male(s)/female
15–24 years: 1.03 male(s)/female
25–54 years: 0.93 male(s)/female
55–64 years: 0.86 male(s)/female
65 years and over: 0.83 male(s)/female
total population: 0.95 male(s)/female (2015 est.)
Maternal mortality rate: 48 deaths/100,000 live births (2015 est.)
country comparison to the world: 117
Infant mortality rate: *total:* 11.45 deaths/1,000 live births
male: 10.9 deaths/1,000 live births
female: 12.02 deaths/1,000 live births (2015 est.)
country comparison to the world: 126
Life expectancy at birth: *total population:* 77.6 years
male: 74.87 years
female: 80.47 years (2015 est.)
country comparison to the world: 68
Total fertility rate: 1.76 children born/woman (2015 est.)
country comparison to the world: 162
Health expenditures: 8.5% of GDP (2013)
country comparison to the world: 51
Physicians density: 0.11 physicians/1,000 population (2009)
Hospital bed density: 1.6 beds/1,000 population (2011)
Drinking water source:
improved:
urban: 99.5% of population
rural: 95.6% of population
total: 96.3% of population
unimproved:
urban: 0.5% of population
rural: 4.4% of population
total: 3.7% of population (2015 est.)
Sanitation facility access:
improved:
urban: 84.7% of population
rural: 91.9% of population
total: 90.5% of population
unimproved:
urban: 15.3% of population
rural: 8.1% of population
total: 9.5% of population (2015 est.)
HIV/AIDS—adult prevalence rate: NA
HIV/AIDS—people living with HIV/AIDS: NA
HIV/AIDS—deaths: NA
Obesity—adult prevalence rate: 27% (2014)
country comparison to the world: 87
Children under the age of 5 years underweight: 2.8% (2012)
country comparison to the world: 116
Education expenditures: 4.8% of GDP (2014)
country comparison to the world: 107
School life expectancy (primary to tertiary education): *total:* 13 years
male: 12 years

female: 13 years (2007)
Unemployment, youth ages 15–24: *total:* 27.5%
male: 21.5%
female: 35.2% (2007 est.)
country comparison to the world: 12

GOVERNMENT

Country name: *conventional long form:* none
conventional short form: Saint Lucia
etymology: named after Saint LUCY of Syracuse by French sailors who were shipwrecked on the island on 13 December 1502, the saint's feast day
Government type: parliamentary democracy (Parliament) under a constitutional monarchy; a Commonwealth realm
Capital: *name:* Castries

Geographic coordinates: 14 00 N, 61 00 W
time difference: UTC-4 (1 hour ahead of Washington, DC, during Standard Time)
Administrative divisions: 10 districts; Anse-la-Raye, Canaries, Castries, Choiseul, Dennery, Gros-Islet, Laborie, Micoud, Soufriere, Vieux-Fort
Independence: 22 February 1979 (from the UK)
National holiday: Independence Day, 22 February (1979)
Constitution: previous 1958, 1960 (preindependence); latest presented 20 December 1978, effective 22 February 1979;
note—in mid-2015, an amendment was proposed to replace the London-based Privy Council with the Caribbean Court of Justice as the country's highest appellate court (2016)
Legal system: English common law
International law organization participation: has not submitted an ICJ jurisdiction declaration; accepts ICCt jurisdiction
Citizenship: *citizenship by birth:* yes
citizenship by descent: at least one parent must be a citizen of Saint Lucia
dual citizenship recognized: yes
residency requirement for naturalization: 8 years
Suffrage: 18 years of age; universal
Executive branch: *chief of state:* Queen ELIZABETH II (since 6 February 1952); represented by Governor General Dame Pearlette LOUISY (since September 1997)

head of government: Prime Minister Allen CHASTANET (since 7 June 2016)
cabinet: Cabinet appointed by the governor general on the advice of the prime minister
elections/appointments: the monarchy is hereditary; governor general appointed by the monarch; following legislative elections, the leader of the majority party or majority coalition usually appointed prime minister by governor general; deputy prime minister appointed by governor general
Legislative branch: *description:* bicameral Parliament consists of the Senate (11 seats; 6 members appointed on the advice of the prime minister, 3 on the advice of the leader of the opposition, and 2 upon consultation with religious, economic, and social groups; members serve 5-year terms) and the House of Assembly (17 seats; members directly

elected in single-seat constituencies by simple majority vote to serve 5-year terms)
elections: House of Assembly—last held on 6 June 2016 (next to be held in 2021)
election results: House of Assembly—percent of vote by party—UWP 54.8%, SLP 44.1%; seats by party—UWP 11, SLP 6
Judicial branch: *highest court(s):* the Eastern Caribbean Supreme Court (ECSC) is the itinerant superior court of record for the 9-member Organization of Eastern Caribbean States; the ECSC—with its headquarters on St. Lucia-is headed by the chief justice and is comprised of the Court of Appeal with 3 justices and the High Court with 16 judges; sittings of the Court of Appeal and High Court rotate among the member states; 3 High Court judges reside on Saint Lucia; note—Saint Lucia is a member of the Caribbean Court of Justice
judge selection and term of office: Eastern Caribbean Supreme Court chief justice appointed by Her Majesty, Queen ELIZABETH II; other justices and judges appointed by the Judicial and Legal Services Commission; Court of Appeal justices appointed for life with mandatory retirement at age 65; High Court judges appointed for life with mandatory retirement at age 62
subordinate courts: magistrate's court
Political parties and leaders: Lucian People's Movement or LPM [Therold PRUDENT]
Saint Lucia Labor Party or SLP [Kenny ANTHONY]
United Workers Party or UWP [Allen CHASTANET]
Political pressure groups and leaders: NA
International organization participation: ACP, AOSIS, C, Caricom, CD, CDB, CELAC, FAO, G-77, IBRD, ICAO, ICCt, ICRM, IDA, IFAD, IFC, IFRCS, ILO, IMF, IMO, Interpol, IOC, ISO, ITU, ITUC (NGOs), MIGA, NAM, OAS, OECS, OIF, OPANAL, OPCW, Petrocaribe, UN, UNCTAD, UNESCO, UNIDO, UPU, WCO, WFTU (NGOs), WHO, WIPO, WMO, WTO
Diplomatic representation in the US: *chief of mission:* Ambassador Elizabeth Darius CLARKE (since 3 August 2015)
chancery: 3216 New Mexico Avenue NW, Washington, DC 20016
telephone: [1] (202) 364-6792 through 6795
FAX: [1] (202) 364-6723
consulate(s) general: New York
Diplomatic representation from the US: the US does not have an embassy in Saint Lucia; the US Ambassador to Barbados is accredited to Saint Lucia
Flag description: cerulean blue with a gold isosceles triangle below a black arrowhead; the upper edges of the arrowhead have a white border; the blue color represents the sky and sea, gold stands for sunshine and prosperity, and white and black the racial composition of the island (with the latter being dominant); the two major triangles invoke the twin Pitons (Gros Piton and Petit Piton), cone-shaped volcanic plugs that are a symbol of the island

National symbol(s): twin pitons (volcanic peaks), Saint Lucia parrot; National colors: cerulean blue, gold, black, white

National anthem: *name:* "Sons and Daughters of St. Lucia"

lyrics/music: Charles JESSE/Leton Felix THOMAS
note: adopted 1967

ECONOMY

Economy—overview: The island nation has been able to attract foreign business and investment, especially in its offshore banking and tourism industries. Tourism is Saint Lucia's main source of jobs and income—accounting for 65% of GDP—and the island's main source of foreign exchange earnings. The manufacturing sector is the most diverse in the Eastern Caribbean Area. Crops such as bananas, mangos, and avocados continue to be grown for export, but St. Lucia's once solid banana industry has been devastated by strong competition.

Saint Lucia is vulnerable to a variety of external shocks, including volatile tourism receipts, Natural disasters, and dependence on foreign oil. Furthermore, high public debt—77% of GDP in 2012—and high debt servicing obligations constrain the ANTHONY administration's ability to respond to adverse external shocks.

St. Lucia has experienced anemic growth since the onset of the global financial crisis in 2008, largely because of a slowdown in tourism—airlines cut back on their routes to St. Lucia in 2012. Also, St. Lucia introduced a value added tax in 2012 of 15%, becoming the last country in the Eastern Caribbean to do so. in 2013, the government introduced a National Competitiveness and Productivity Council to address St. Lucia's high public wages and lack of productivity.

GDP (purchasing power parity): $2.03 billion (2015 est.)
$1.998 billion (2014 est.)
$1.989 billion (2013 est.)
note: data are in 2015 US dollars
country comparison to the world: 195

GDP (official exchange rate): $1.416 billion (2015 est.)

GDP—real growth rate: 1.6% (2015 est.)
0.5% (2014 est.) 0.1% (2013 est.)
country comparison to the world: 146

GDP—per capita (PPP): $11,700 (2015 est.)
$11,600 (2014 est.)
$11,600 (2013 est.)
note: data are in 2015 US dollars
country comparison to the world: 128

Gross National saving: 16.1% of GDP (2015 est.)
12% of GDP (2014 est.)
11.5% of GDP (2013 est.)
country comparison to the world: 106

GDP—composition, by end use:
household consumption: 52.4%
government consumption: 19.3%
investment in fixed capital: 32.1%
investment in inventories: 0.1%
exports of goods and services: 51.7%
imports of goods and services: -55.6% (2015 est.)

GDP—composition, by sector of origin:

agriculture: 2.7%
industry: 15.3%
services: 82.1% (2015 est.)

Agriculture—products: bananas, coconuts, vegetables, citrus, root crops, cocoa

Industries: tourism; clothing, assembly of electronic components, beverages, corrugated cardboard boxes, lime processing, coconut processing

Industrial production growth rate: 3.5% (2015 est.)
country comparison to the world: 70

Labor force: 79,700 (2012 est.)
country comparison to the world: 184

Labor force—by occupation: *agriculture:* 21.7%
industry: 24.7%
services: 53.6% (2002 est.)

Unemployment rate: 20% (2003 est.)
country comparison to the world: 169

Population below poverty line: NA%

Household income or consumption by percentage share: *lowest:* 10%: NA%
highest: 10%: NA%

Budget: *revenues:* $185.2 million
expenditures: $222.2 million (2011 est.)
Taxes and other revenues: 12.9% of GDP (2011 est.)
country comparison to the world: 204

Budget surplus (+) or deficit (–): -2.6% of GDP (2011 est.)
country comparison to the world: 95

Public debt: 77% of GDP (2012 est.)
77% of GDP (2010 est.)
country comparison to the world: 34

Fiscal year: 1 April–31 March

Inflation rate (consumer prices): -0.7% (2015 est.)
3.5% (2014 est.)
country comparison to the world: 21

Central bank discount rate: 6.5% (31 December 2010)
6.5% (31 December 2009)
country comparison to the world: 52

Commercial bank prime lending rate: 9% (31 December 2015 est.)
9% (31 December 2014 est.)
country comparison to the world: 97

Stock of narrow money: $282.7 million (31 December 2015 est.)
$277.3 million (31 December 2014 est.)
country comparison to the world: 175

Stock of broad money: $1.104 billion (31 December 2014 est.)
$1.057 billion (31 December 2013 est.)
country comparison to the world: 169

Stock of domestic credit: $1.546 billion (31 December 2015 est.)
$1.519 billion (31 December 2014 est.)
country comparison to the world: 150

Current account balance: -$106 million (2015 est.)
-$94 million (2014 est.)
country comparison to the world: 69

Exports: $207 million (2015 est.)
$203.3 million (2014 est.)
country comparison to the world: 186

Exports—commodities: bananas 41%, clothing, cocoa, avocados, mangoes, coconut oil (2010 est.)

Exports—partners: Dominican Republic 25.1%, US 15.9%, Suriname 9.1%, Antigua and Barbuda

7%, Dominica 6.8%, Trinidad and Tobago 6.3%, Barbados 6.1%, UK 4.8%, Grenada 4.6% (2015)

Imports: $540.6 million (2015 est.)
$558.8 million (2014 est.)
country comparison to the world: 193

Imports—commodities: food, manufactured goods, machinery and transportation equipment, chemicals, fuels

Imports—partners: Brazil 34.9%, US 25.7%, Trinidad and Tobago 14.4%, Colombia 10.9% (2015)

Debt—external: $497.5 million (31 December 2014 est.)
$485.9 million (31 December 2013 est.)
country comparison to the world: 179

Exchange rates: East Caribbean dollars (XCD) per US dollar—
2.7 (2015 est.)
2.7 (2014 est.)
2.7 (2013 est.)
2.7 (2012)
2.7 (2011)

ENERGY

Electricity—production: 361.7 million kWh (2012 est.)
country comparison to the world: 167

Electricity—consumption: 336.4 million kWh (2012 est.)
country comparison to the world: 174

Electricity—exports: 0 kWh (2013 est.)
country comparison to the world: 198

Electricity—imports: 0 kWh (2013 est.)
country comparison to the world: 204

Electricity—installed generating capacity: 89,000 kW (2012 est.)
country comparison to the world: 175

Electricity—from fossil fuels: 100% of total installed capacity (2012 est.)
country comparison to the world: 29

Electricity—from nuclear fuels: 0% of total installed capacity (2012 est.)
country comparison to the world: 183

Electricity—from hydroelectric plants: 0% of total installed capacity (2012 est.)
country comparison to the world: 204

Electricity—from other renewable sources: 0% of total installed capacity (2012 est.)
country comparison to the world: 129

Crude oil—production: 0 bbl/day (2014 est.)
country comparison to the world: 193

Crude oil—exports: 0 bbl/day (2012 est.)
country comparison to the world: 191

Crude oil—imports: 0 bbl/day (2012 est.)
country comparison to the world: 127

Crude oil—proved reserves: 0 bbl (1 January 2015 est.)
country comparison to the world: 193

Refined petroleum products—production: 0 bbl/day (2012 est.)
country comparison to the world: 133

Refined petroleum products—consumption: 3,000 bbl/day (2013 est.)
country comparison to the world: 182

Refined petroleum products—exports: 0 bbl/day (2012 est.)
country comparison to the world: 134

Refined petroleum products—imports: 3,041 bbl/day (2012 est.)
country comparison to the world: 175
Natural gas—production: 0 cu m (2013 est.)
country comparison to the world: 130
Natural gas—consumption: 0 cu m (2013 est.)
country comparison to the world: 195
Natural gas—exports: 0 cu m (2013 est.)
country comparison to the world: 183
Natural gas—imports: 0 cu m (2013 est.)
country comparison to the world: 135
Natural gas—proved reserves: 0 cu m (1 January 2014 est.)
country comparison to the world: 196
Carbon dioxide emissions from consumption of energy: 415,700 Mt (2012 est.)
country comparison to the world: 186

COMMUNICATIONS

Telephones—fixed lines: *total subscriptions:* 32,800
subscriptions per 100 inhabitants: 20 (2014 est.)
country comparison to the world: 171
Telephones—mobile cellular: *total:* 188,400
subscriptions per 100 inhabitants: 115 (2014 est.)
country comparison to the world: 181
Telephone system: *general assessment:* an adequate system that is automatically switched
domestic: fixed-line teledensity is 25 per 100 persons and mobile-cellular teledensity is roughly 130 per 100 persons

international: country code—1-758; the East Caribbean Fiber Optic System (ECFS) and Southern Caribbean fiber optic system (SCF) submarine cables, along with intelsat from Martinique, carry calls Internationally; direct microwave radio relay link with Martinique and Saint Vincent and the Grenadines; tropospheric scatter to Barbados (2010)
Broadcast media: 3 privately owned TV stations; 1 public TV station operating on a cable network; multi-channel cable TV service available; a mix of state-owned and privately owned broadcasters operate nearly 25 radio stations including repeater transmission stations (2007)
Radio broadcast stations: AM 2, FM 11, short-wave 0 (2008)
Television broadcast stations: 2 (1 commercial broadcast station and 1 community antenna television or CATV channel) (2003)
Internet country code: .lc
Internet hosts: 100 (2012)
country comparison to the world: 209
Internet users: *total:* 142,900
percent of population: 89.2% (2009)
country comparison to the world: 166

TRANSPORTATION

Airports: 2 (2013)
country comparison to the world: 204
Airports—with paved runways: *total:* 2
2,438 to 3,047 m: 1
1,524 to 2,437 m: 1 (2013)

Roadways: *total:* 1,210 km
paved: 847 km
unpaved: 363 km (2011)
country comparison to the world: 182
Ports and terminals: *major seaport(s):* Castries, Cul-de-Sac, Vieux-Fort

MILITARY AND SECURITY

Military branches: no regular military forces; Royal Saint Lucia Police Force (includes Special Service Unit, Marine Unit) (2012)
Military service age and obligation: 18 years of age for voluntary security service; no National army (2012)

TRANSNATIONAL ISSUES

Disputes—International: joins other Caribbean states to counter Venezuela's claim that Aves Island sustains human habitation, a criterion under UN Convention on the Law of the Sea, which permits Venezuela to extend its EEZ/continental shelf over a large portion of the eastern Caribbean Sea
Illicit drugs: transit point for South American drugs destined for the US and Europe

SAINT MARTIN

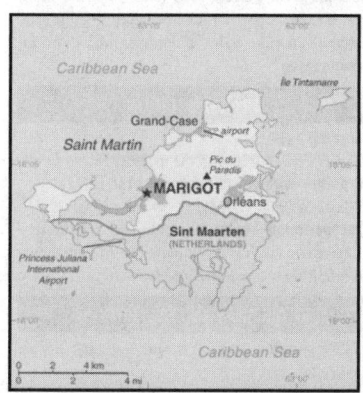

INTRODUCTION

Background: Although sighted by Christopher COLUMBUS in 1493 and claimed for Spain, it was the Dutch who occupied the island in 1631 and set about exploiting its salt deposits. The Spanish retook the island in 1633, but continued to be harassed by the Dutch. The Spanish finally relinquished Saint Martin to the French and Dutch, who divided it between themselves in 1648. Friction between the two sides caused the border to frequently fluctuate over the next two centuries, with the French eventually holding the greater portion of the island (about 57%). The cultivation of sugar cane introduced African slavery to the island in the late 18th century; the practice was not abolished until 1848. The island became a free port in 1939; the tourism industry was dramatically expanded during the 1970s and 1980s. In 2003, the populace of Saint Martin voted to secede from Guadeloupe and in 2007, the northern portion of the island became a French overseas collectivity. in 2010, the southern Dutch portion of the island became the independent nation of Sint Maarten within the Kingdom of the Netherlands.

GEOGRAPHY

Location: Caribbean, located in the Leeward Islands (northern) group; French part of the island of Saint Martin in the Caribbean Sea; Saint Martin lies east of the US Virgin Islands
Geographic coordinates: 18 05 N, 63 57 W
Map references: Central America and the Caribbean
Area: *total:* 54.4 sq km
land: 54.4 sq km
water: NEGL

country comparison to the world: 231
Area—comparative: more than one-third the size of Washington, DC
Land boundaries: *total:* 16 km
border countries (1): Sint Maarten 16 km
Coastline: 58.9 km (for entire island)
Climate: temperature averages 27–29 degrees Celsius all year long; low humidity, gentle trade winds, brief, intense rain showers; hurricane season stretches from July to November
Elevation: *mean elevation:* NA
elevation extremes: lowest point: Caribbean Ocean 0 m
highest point: Pic du Paradis 424 m
Natural resources: salt
Natural hazards: subject to hurricanes from July to November
Environment—current issues: freshwater supply is dependent on desalination of sea water
Geography—note: the island of Saint Martin is the smallest landmass in the world shared by two independent states, the French territory of Saint Martin and the Dutch territory of Sint Maarten

PEOPLE AND SOCIETY

Ethnic groups: Creole (mulatto), black, Guadeloupe Mestizo (French-East Asia), white, East Indian

Languages: French (official), English, Dutch, French Patois, Spanish, Papiamento (dialect of Netherlands Antilles)

Religions: Roman Catholic, Jehovah's Witnesses, Protestant, Hindu

Population: 31,754 (July 2015 est.)
country comparison to the world: 217

Age structure: *0–14 years:* 26.51% (male 4,192/female 4,225)

15–24 years: 10.58% (male 1,682/female 1,677)

25–54 years: 47.05% (male 7,101/female 7,838)

55–64 years: 8.57% (male 1,267/female 1,455)

65 years and over: 7.3% (male 1,033/female 1,284) (2015 est.)

Median age: *total:* 32 years

male: 31 years

female: 32.9 years (2015 est.)

country comparison to the world: 96

Sex ratio: *at birth:* 1.04 male(s)/female

0–14 years: 0.99 male(s)/female

15–24 years: 1 male(s)/female

25–54 years: 0.91 male(s)/female

55–64 years: 0.87 male(s)/female

65 years and over: 0.81 male(s)/female

total population: 0.93 male(s)/female (2015 est.)

GOVERNMENT

Country name: *conventional long form:* Overseas Collectivity of Saint Martin

conventional short form: Saint Martin

local long form: Collectivite d'outre mer de Saint-Martin

local short form: Saint-Martin

etymology: explorer Christopher COLUMBUS named the island after Saint MARTIN of Tours because the 11 November 1493 day of discovery was the saint's feast day

Dependency status: overseas collectivity of France

Capital: *name:* Marigot

Geographical coordinates: 18 04 N, 63 05 W

time difference: UTC-4 (1 hour ahead of Washington, DC, during Standard Time)

Independence: none (overseas collectivity of France)

National holiday: Fete de la Federation, 14 July (1789); note—local holiday is Schoalcher Day (Slavery Abolition Day) 12 July (1848)

Constitution: 4 October 1958 (French Constitution)

Legal system: French civil law

Citizenship: see France

Suffrage: 18 years of age, universal

Executive branch: *chief of state:* President Francois HOLLANDE (since 15 May 2012); represented by Deputy Prefect Philippe CHOPIN (since 16 November 2011)

head of government: President of Territorial Council Aline HANSON (since 17 April 2013)

cabinet: Executive Council; note—there is also an advisory economic, social, and cultural council

elections/appointments: French president directly elected by absolute majority popular vote in 2 rounds if needed for a 5-year term (eligible for a second term); prefect appointed by French president on the advice of French Ministry of Interior; president of Territorial Council elected by its members for a 5-year term; election last held on 17 April 2013 (next to be held in 2018)

election results: Aline HANSON elected president by the Territorial Council

Legislative branch: *description:* unicameral Territorial Council (23 seats; members directly elected by absolute majority vote to serve 5-year terms)

note: Saint Martin elects 1 member to the French Senate; election last held on 28 September 2014 (next to be held not later than September 2017); results—percent of vote by party—NA; seats by party—UMP 1; one seat (shared with Saint Barthelemy) was elected to the French National Assembly on 17 June 2012 (next to be held by June 2017); results—percent of vote by party—NA; seats by party—UMP 1

elections: last held on 18 and 25 March 2012 (next to be held in July 2017)

election results: percent of seats by party—RRR 34.1%, Team Daniel Gibbs 2012 32%, UPP 13.3%, Saint-Martin pour tous 9.4%, other 11.2%; seats by party—NA; second round, percent of seats by party -RRR 56.9%, Team Daniel Gibbs 43.1%; seats by party—RRR 17, Team Daniel Gibbs 6

Political parties and leaders: Rally Responsibility Success (Rassemblement Responsabilite Reussite or RRR [Alain RICHARDSON]

Team Daniel Gibbs [Daniel GIBBS])

Union for Progress (Union Pour le Progres or UPP) [Louis-Constant FLEMING]; affiliated with UMP

Political pressure groups and leaders: NA

International organization participation: UPU

Diplomatic representation in the US: none (overseas collectivity of France)

Diplomatic representation from the US: none (overseas collectivity of France)

Flag description: the flag of France is used

National symbol(s): brown pelican

National anthem: *name:* "O Sweet Saint Martin's Land"

lyrics/music: Gerard KEMPS

note: the song, written in 1958, is used as an unofficial anthem for the entire island (both French and Dutch sides); as a collectivity of France, in addition to the local anthem, "La Marseillaise" remains official on the French side (see France); as a constituent part of the Kingdom of the Netherlands, in addition to the local anthem, "Het Wilhelmus" remains official on the Dutch side (see Netherlands)

ECONOMY

Economy—overview: The economy of Saint Martin centers on tourism with 85% of the labor force engaged in this sector. Over one million visitors come to the island each year with most arriving through the Princess Juliana International Airport in Sint Maarten. No significant agriculture and limited local fishing means that almost all food must be imported. Energy resources and manufactured goods are also imported, primarily from Mexico and the US. Saint Martin is reported to have the highest per capita income in the Caribbean.

GDP (purchasing power parity): $561.5 million (2005 est.)

country comparison to the world: 212

GDP (official exchange rate): $561.5 million (2005 est.)

GDP—per capita (PPP): $19,300 (2005 est.)

country comparison to the world: 88

GDP—composition, by sector of origin:

agriculture: 1%

industry: 15%

services: 84% (2000)

Industries: tourism, light industry and manufacturing, heavy industry

Labor force: 17,300 (2008 est.)

country comparison to the world: 214

Labor force—by occupation: 85% directly or indirectly employed in tourist industry

Imports—commodities: crude petroleum, food, manufactured items

Exchange rates: euros (EUR) per US dollar—

0.885 (2015 est.)

0.7489 (2014 est.)

0.7634 (2013 est.)

0.7752 (2012 est.)

0.7185 (2011 est.)

COMMUNICATIONS

Telephone system: *general assessment:* fully integrated access

domestic: direct dial capability with both fixed and wireless systems

international: country code—590; undersea fiber-optic cable provides voice and data connectivity to Puerto Rico and Guadeloupe (2009)

Broadcast media: 1 local TV station; access to about 20 radio stations, including RFO Guadeloupe radio broadcasts via repeater (2008)

Radio broadcast stations: AM 0, FM 3, shortwave 0 (2007)

Internet country code: . mf; note—.gp, the internet country code for Guadeloupe, and .fr, the internet country code for France, might also be encountered

TRANSPORTATION

Airports: 1 (2013)

country comparison to the world: 233

Airports—with paved runways: *total:* 1

914 to 1,523 m: 1 (2013)

Transportation—note: nearest airport for International flights is Princess Juliana International Airport (SXM) located on Sint Maarten

MILITARY AND SECURITY

Military—note: defense is the responsibility of France

SAINT PIERRE AND MIQUELON

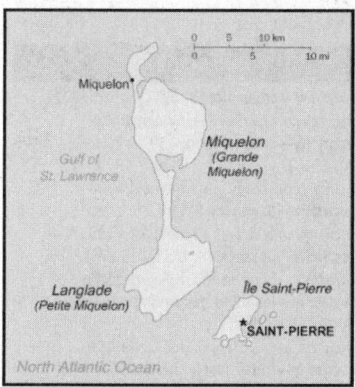

INTRODUCTION

Background: First settled by the French in the early 17th century, the islands represent the sole remaining vestige of France's once vast North American possessions.

GEOGRAPHY

Location: Northern North America, islands in the North Atlantic Ocean, south of Newfoundland (Canada)

Geographic coordinates: 46 50 N, 56 20 W
Map references: North America
Area: *total:* 242 sq km
land: 242 sq km
water: 0 sq km
note: includes eight small islands in the Saint Pierre and the Miquelon groups
country comparison to the world: 214
Area—comparative: one and half times the size of Washington, DC
Land boundaries: 0 km
Coastline: 120 km
Maritime claims: *territorial sea:* 12 nm
exclusive economic zone: 200 nm
Climate: cold and wet, with considerable mist and fog; spring and autumn are often windy
Terrain: mostly barren rock
Elevation: *mean elevation:* NA

elevation extremes: *lowest point:* Atlantic Ocean 0 m
highest point: Morne de la Grande Montagne 240 m
Natural resources: fish, deepwater ports
Land use: *agricultural land:* 8.7%
arable land: 8.7%
permanent crops: 0%
permanent pasture: 0%
forest: 12.5%
other: 78.8% (2011 est.)
Irrigated land: 0 sq km (2012)
Natural hazards: persistent fog throughout the year can be a maritime hazard

Environment—current issues: recent test drilling for oil in waters around Saint Pierre and Miquelon may bring future development that would impact the environment
Geography—note: vegetation scanty; the islands are actually part of the northern appalachians along with Newfoundland

PEOPLE AND SOCIETY

Nationality: *noun:* French man(men), French woman (women)
adjective: French
Ethnic groups: Basques and Bretons (French fishermen)
Languages: French (official)
Religions: Roman Catholic 99%, other 1%
Population: 5,657 (July 2015 est.)
country comparison to the world: 228
Age structure: *0–14 years:* 15.96% (male 465/female 438)
15–24 years: 8.75% (male 256/female 239)
25–54 years: 42.87% (male 1,199/female 1,226)
55–64 years: 13.68% (male 404/female 370)
65 years and over: 18.74% (male 443/female 617) (2015 est.)
Median age: *total:* 45.2 years
male: 44.8 years
female: 45.6 years (2015 est.)
country comparison to the world: 4
Population growth rate: -1.08% (2015 est.)
country comparison to the world: 232
Birth rate: 7.42 births/1,000 population (2015 est.)
country comparison to the world: 223
Death rate: 9.72 deaths/1,000 population (2015 est.)
country comparison to the world: 50
Net migration rate: -8.49 migrant(s)/1,000 population (2015 est.)
country comparison to the world: 210
Urbanization: *urban population:* 90.4% of total population (2015)
rate of urbanization: 0.1% annual rate of change (2010–15 est.)
Major urban areas—population: SAINT-PIERRE (capital) 5,000 (2014)
Sex ratio: *at birth:* 1.05 male(s)/female
0–14 years: 1.06 male(s)/female
15–24 years: 1.07 male(s)/female
25–54 years: 0.98 male(s)/female
55–64 years: 1.09 male(s)/female
65 years and over: 0.72 male(s)/female
total population: 0.96 male(s)/female (2015 est.)
Infant mortality rate: *total:* 6.78 deaths/1,000 live births
male: 7.87 deaths/1,000 live births
female: 5.63 deaths/1,000 live births (2015 est.)
country comparison to the world: 161
Life expectancy at birth: *total population:* 80.39 years
male: 78.06 years
female: 82.85 years (2015 est.)
country comparison to the world: 35

Total fertility rate: 1.56 children born/woman (2015 est.)
country comparison to the world: 186
HIV/AIDS—adult prevalence rate: NA
HIV/AIDS—people living with HIV/AIDS: NA
HIV/AIDS—deaths: NA

GOVERNMENT

Country name: *conventional long form:* Territorial Collectivity of Saint Pierre and Miquelon
conventional short form: Saint Pierre and Miquelon
local long form: Departement de Saint-Pierre et Miquelon
local short form: Saint-Pierre et Miquelon
etymology: Saint-Pierre is named after Saint PETER, the patron saint of fishermen; Miquelon may be a corruption of the Basque name Mikelon
Dependency status: self-governing territorial overseas collectivity of France
Government type: parliamentary democracy (Territorial Council); overseas collectivity of France
Capital: *name:* Saint-Pierre

Geographic coordinates: 46 46 N, 56 11 W
time difference: UTC-3 (2 hours ahead of Washington, DC, during Standard Time)
daylight saving time: +1 hr, begins second Sunday in March; ends first Sunday in November
Administrative divisions: none (territorial overseas collectivity of France); note—there are no first-order administrative divisions as defined by the US Government, but there are 2 communes at the second order—Saint Pierre, Miquelon
Independence: none (territorial collectivity of France; has been under French control since 1763)
National holiday: Fete de la Federation, 14 July (1789)
Constitution: 4 October 1958 (French Constitution)
Legal system: French civil law
Citizenship: see France
Suffrage: 18 years of age; universal
Executive branch: *chief of state:* President Francois HOLLANDE (since 15 May 2012); represented by Prefect Jean-Christophe BOUVIER (since September 2014)

head of government: President of Territorial Council Stephane ARTANO (since 21 February 2007)
cabinet: Le Cabinet du Prefet
elections/appointments: French president directly elected by absolute majority popular vote in 2 rounds if needed for a 5-year term (eligible for a second term); election last held on 6 May 2012 (next to be held in 2017); prefect appointed by French president on the advice of French Ministry of Interior
Legislative branch: *description:* unicameral Territorial Council or Conseil Territorial (19 seats—15 from Saint Pierre and 4 from Miquelon; members directly elected in single-seat constituencies by absolute majority vote to serve 6-year terms)

note: Saint Pierre and Miquelon elect 1 member to the French Senate; elections last held on 28 September 2014 (next to be held not later than September 2017); results—percent of vote by party—NA; seats by party—AD 1 (affiliated with UMP); Saint Pierre and Miquelon also elects 1 member to the French National Assembly; elections last held on 17 June 2012 (next to be held by June 2017); results—percent of vote by party—NA; seats by party—Ensemble pour l'Avenir 1 (affiliated with PRG)

elections: elections last held on 18 March 2012 (next to be held in March 2018)

election results: percent of vote by party—AD 52.5%, Ensemble pour l'Avenir 47.5%; seats by party -AD 14, Ensemble pour l'Avenir 5

Judicial branch: *highest court(s):* Superior Tribunal of Appeals or Tribunal Superieur d'Appel (composition NA)

judge selection and term of office: judge selection and tenure NA

subordinate courts: NA

Political parties and leaders: Archipelago Tomorrow or AD [Stephane ARTANO] (affiliated with UMP)

Togerther for the Future (Ensemble pour l'Avenir) [Annick GIRARDIN] (affiliated with PRG)

Political pressure groups and leaders: NA

International organization participation: UPU, WFTU (NGOs)

Diplomatic representation in the US: none (territorial overseas collectivity of France)

Diplomatic representation from the US: none (territorial overseas collectivity of France)

Flag description: a yellow three-masted sailing ship facing the hoist side rides on a blue background with scattered, white, wavy lines under the ship; a continuous black-over-white wavy line divides the ship from the white wavy lines; on the hoist side, a vertical band is divided into three parts: the top part (called ikkurina) is red with a green diagon al cross extending to the corners overlaid by a white cross dividing the rectangle into four sections; the middle part has a white background with an ermine pattern; the third part has a red background with two stylized yellow lions outlined in black, one above the other; these three heraldic arms represent settlement by colonists from the Basque Country (top), Brittany, and Normandy; the blue on the main portion of the flag symbolizes the Atlantic Ocean and the stylized ship represents the Grande Hermine in which Jacques Cartier "discovered" the islands in 1536

note: the flag of France used for official occasions

National symbol(s): 16th-century sailing ship

National anthem: *note:* as a collectivity of France, "La Marseillaise" is official (see France)

ECONOMY

Economy—overview: The inhabitants have traditionally earned their livelihood by fishing and by servicing fishing fleets operating off the coast of Newfoundland. The economy has been declining, however, because of disputes with Canada over fishing quotas and a steady decline in the number of ships stopping at Saint Pierre. in 1992, an arbitration panel awarded the islands an exclusive economic zone of 12,348 sq km to settle a long-standing territorial dispute with Canada, although it represents only 25% of what France had sought. France heavily subsidizes the islands to the great betterment of living standards.

The government hopes an expansion of tourism will boost economic prospects. Fish farming, crab fishing, and agriculture are being developed to diversify the local economy. Recent test drilling for oil may pave the way for development of the energy sector.

GDP (purchasing power parity): $215.3 million (2006 est.)

note: supplemented by annual payments from France of about $60 million

country comparison to the world: 219

GDP (official exchange rate): $215.3 million (2006 est.)

GDP—real growth rate: NA%

GDP—per capita (PPP): $34,900 (2006 est.)

country comparison to the world: 53

GDP—composition, by sector of origin:

agriculture: 2%

industry: 15%

services: 83% (2006 est.)

Agriculture—products: vegetables; poultry, cattle, sheep, pigs; fish

Industries: fish processing and supply base for fishing fleets; tourism

Industrial production growth rate: NA%

Labor force: 3,194 (2006)

country comparison to the world: 224

Labor force—by occupation: *agriculture:* 18%

industry: 41%

services: 41% (1996 est.)

Unemployment rate: 9.9% (2008 est.)

country comparison to the world: 115

Population below poverty line: NA%

Household income or consumption by percentage share: *lowest:* 10%: NA%

highest: 10%: NA%

Budget: *revenues:* $70 million

expenditures: $60 million (1996 est.)

Taxes and other revenues: 32.5% of GDP (1996 est.)

country comparison to the world: 75

Budget surplus (+) or deficit (–): 4.6% of GDP (1996 est.)

country comparison to the world: 8

Fiscal year: calendar year

Inflation rate (consumer prices): 4.5% (2010) 8.1% (2005)

country comparison to the world: 165

Exports: $6.641 million (2010 est.) $5.5 million (2005 est.)

country comparison to the world: 217

Exports—commodities: fish and fish products, soybeans, animal feed, mollusks and crustaceans, fox and mink pelts

Imports: $95.35 million (2010 est.) $68.2 million (2005 est.)

country comparison to the world: 217

Imports—commodities: meat, clothing, fuel, electrical equipment, machinery, building materials

Debt—external: $NA

Exchange rates: euros (EUR) per US dollar—

0.885 (2015 est.)

0.7525 (2014 est.)

0.7634 (2013 est.)

0.7752 (2012 est.)

0.7185 (2011 est.)

ENERGY

Electricity—production: 43 million kWh (2012 est.)

country comparison to the world: 209

Electricity—consumption: 39.99 million kWh (2012 est.)

country comparison to the world: 208

Electricity—exports: 0 kWh (2013 est.)

country comparison to the world: 190

Electricity—imports: 0 kWh (2013 est.)

country comparison to the world: 196

Electricity—installed generating capacity: 26,600 kW (2012 est.)

country comparison to the world: 199

Electricity—from fossil fuels: 97.7% of total installed capacity (2012 est.)

country comparison to the world: 57

Electricity—from nuclear fuels: 0% of total installed capacity (2012 est.)

country comparison to the world: 175

Electricity—from hydroelectric plants: 0% of total installed capacity (2012 est.)

country comparison to the world: 197

Electricity—from other renewable sources: 2.3% of total installed capacity (2012 est.)

country comparison to the world: 79

Crude oil—production: 0 bbl/day (2014 est.)

country comparison to the world: 185

Crude oil—exports: 0 bbl/day (2012 est.)

country comparison to the world: 182

Crude oil—Imports: 0 bbl/day (2012 est.)

country comparison to the world: 120

Crude oil—proved reserves: 0 bbl (1 January 2015 est.)

country comparison to the world: 184

Refined petroleum products—production: 0 bbl/day (2012 est.)

country comparison to the world: 126

Refined petroleum products—consumption: 600 bbl/day (2013 est.)

country comparison to the world: 206

Refined petroleum products—exports: 1.24 bbl/day (2012 est.)

country comparison to the world: 127

Refined petroleum products—imports: 604.4 bbl/day (2012 est.)

country comparison to the world: 203

Natural gas—production: 0 cu m (2013 est.)

country comparison to the world: 123

Natural gas—consumption: 0 cu m (2013 est.)

country comparison to the world: 189

Natural gas—exports: 0 cu m (2013 est.)

country comparison to the world: 173

Natural gas—imports: 0 cu m (2013 est.)

country comparison to the world: 128

Natural gas—proved reserves: 0 cu m (1 January 2014 est.)

country comparison to the world: 188

Carbon dioxide emissions from consumption 151,100 Mt (2012 est.)

country comparison to the world: 203

COMMUNICATIONS

Telephones—fixed lines: *total subscriptions:* 4,800
subscriptions per 100 inhabitants: 81 (2014 est.)
country comparison to the world: 209
Telephone system: *general assessment:* adequate
international: country code—508; radiotelephone communication with most countries in the world; satellite earth station—1 in French domestic satellite system
Broadcast media: 2 TV stations with a third repeater station, all part of the French Overseas Network; radio stations on St. Pierre and on

Miquelon are part of the French Overseas Network (2007)
Radio broadcast stations: AM 1, FM 4, shortwave 0 (1998)
Television broadcast stations: 0 (2 repeaters rebroadcast programs from France, Canada, and the US) (1997)
Internet country code: .pm
Internet hosts: 15 (2012)
country comparison to the world: 224

TRANSPORTATION

Airports: 2 (2013)
country comparison to the world: 205
Airports—with paved runways: *total:* 2

1,524 to 2,437 m: 1
914 to 1,523 m: 1 (2013)
Roadways: *total:* 117 km
paved: 80 km
unpaved: 37 km (2009)
country comparison to the world: 215
Ports and terminals: *major seaport(s):* Saint-Pierre

MILITARY AND SECURITY

Military—note: defense is the responsibility of France

TRANSNATIONAL ISSUES

Disputes—International: none

SAINT VINCENT AND THE GRENADINES

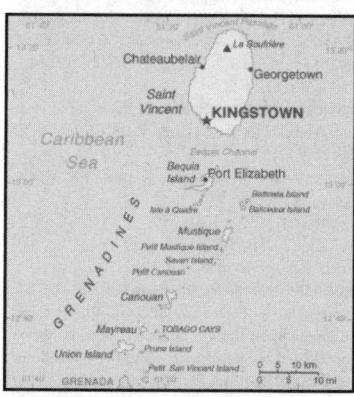

INTRODUCTION

Background: Resistance by native Caribs prevented colonization on Saint Vincent until 1719. Disputed between France and the UK for most of the 18th century, the island was ceded to the latter in 1783. Between 1960 and 1962, Saint Vincent and the Grenadines was a separate administrative unit of the Federation of the West Indies. Autonomy was granted in 1969 and independence in 1979.

GEOGRAPHY

Location: Caribbean, islands between the Caribbean Sea and North Atlantic Ocean, north of Trinidad and Tobago
Geographic coordinates: 13 15 N, 6112 W
Map references: Central America and the Caribbean
Area: *total:* 389 sq km (Saint Vincent 344 sq km)
land: 389 sq km
water: 0 sq km
country comparison to the world: 204
Area—comparative: twice the size of Washington, DC
Land boundaries: 0 km
Coastline: 84 km
Maritime claims: *territorial sea:* 12 nm

contiguous zone: 24 nm
exclusive economic zone: 200 nm
continental shelf: 200 nm
Climate: tropical; little seasonal temperature variation; rainy season (May to November)
Terrain: volcanic, mountainous
Elevation: *mean elevation:* NA

elevation extremes: *lowest point:* Caribbean Sea 0 m
highest point: La Soufriere 1,234 m
Natural resources: hydropower, arable land

Land use: *agricultural land:* 25.6%
arable land: 12.8%
permanent crops: 7.7%
permanent pasture: 5.1%
forest: 68.7%
other: 5.7% (2011 est.)
Irrigated land: 10 sq km (2012)
Freshwater withdrawal (domestic/industrial/agricultural): *total:* 0.01 cu km/yr
per capita: 92.59 cu m/yr (1995)
Natural hazards: hurricanes; Soufriere volcano on the island of Saint Vincent is a constant threat
Environment—current issues: pollution of coastal waters and shorelines from discharges by pleasure yachts and other effluents; in some areas, pollution is severe enough to make swimming prohibitive
Environment—International agreements: *party to:* Biodiversity, Climate Change, Climate Change-Kyoto Protocol, Desertification, Endangered Species, Environmental Modification, Hazardous Wastes, Law of the Sea, Marine Dumping, Ozone Layer Protection, Ship Pollution, Whaling
signed, but not ratified: none of the selected agreements
Geography—note: the administration of the islands of the Grenadines group is divided between Saint Vincent and the Grenadines and Grenada; Saint Vincent and the Grenadines is comprised of 32 islands and cays

PEOPLE AND SOCIETY

Nationality: *noun:* Saint Vincentian(s) or Vincentian(s)
adjective: Saint Vincentian or Vincentian

Ethnic groups: black 66%, mixed 19%, East Indian 6%, European 4%, Carib Amerindian 2%, other 3%
Languages: English, French patois
Religions: Protestant 75% (Anglican 47%, Methodist 28%), Roman Catholic 13%, other (includes Hindu, Seventh-Day Adventist, other Protestant) 12%
Population: 102,627 (July 2015 est.)
country comparison to the world: 196
Age structure: *0–14 years:* 22.31% (male 11,548/ female 11,351)
15–24 years: 16.49% (male 8,537/female 8,384)
25–54 years: 42.66% (male 22,742/female 21,034)
55–64 years: 9.73% (male 5,124/female 4,864)
65 years and over: 8.81% (male 4,203/female 4,840) (2015 est.)
Dependency ratios: *total dependency ratio:* 46.8%
youth dependency ratio: 36%
elderly dependency ratio: 10.8%
potential support ratio: 9.3% (2015 est.)
Median age: *total:* 32.5 years
male: 32.6 years
female: 32.3 years (2015 est.)
country comparison to the world: 91
Population growth rate: -0.28% (2015 est.)
country comparison to the world: 218
Birth rate: 13.57 births/1,000 population (2015 est.)
country comparison to the world: 146
Death rate: 7.18 deaths/1,000 population (2015 est.)
country comparison to the world: 124
Net migration rate: -9.17 migrant(s)/1,000 population (2015 est.)
country comparison to the world: 213
Urbanization: *urban population:* 50.6% of total population (2015)
rate of urbanization: 0.72% annual rate of change (2010–15 est.)
Major urban areas—population: KINGSTOWN (capital) 27,000 (2014)
Sex ratio: *at birth:* 1.03 male(s)/female
0–14 years: 1.02 male(s)/female
15–24 years: 1.02 male(s)/female

25–54 years: 1.08 male(s)/female

55–64 years: 1.05 male(s)/female

65 years and over: 0.87 male(s)/female

total population: 1.03 male(s)/female (2015 est.)

Maternal mortality rate: 45 deaths/100,000 live births (2015 est.)

country comparison to the world: 109

Infant mortality rate: *total:* 12.69 deaths/1,000 live births

male: 13.83 deaths/1,000 live births

female: 11.52 deaths/1,000 live births (2015 est.)

country comparison to the world: 119

Life expectancy at birth: *total population:* 75.09 years

male: 73.11 years

female: 77.13 years (2015 est.)

country comparison to the world: 107

Total fertility rate: 1.82 children born/woman (2015 est.)

country comparison to the world: 150

Health expenditures: 5.2% of GDP (2013)

country comparison to the world: 136

Hospital bed density: 5.2 beds/1,000 population (2012)

Drinking water source:

improved:

urban: 95.1% of population

rural: 95.1% of population

total: 95.1% of population

unimproved:

urban: 4.9% of population

rural: 4.9% of population

total: 4.9% of population (2015 est.)

Sanitation facility access:

improved:

urban: 76.1% of population

rural: 76.1% of population

total: 76.1% of population

unimproved:

urban: 23.9% of population

rural: 23.9% of population

total: 23.9% of population (2007 est.)

HIV/AIDS—adult prevalence rate: NA

HIV/AIDS—people living with HIV/AIDS: NA

HIV/AIDS—deaths: NA

Obesity—adult prevalence rate: 24.1% (2014)

country comparison to the world: 75

Education expenditures: 5.1% of GDP (2010)

country comparison to the world: 69

Unemployment, youth ages 15–24: *total:* 33.8%

male: 27.8%

female: 41.4% (2008 est.)

GOVERNMENT

Country name: *conventional long form:* none

conventional short form: Saint Vincent and the Grenadines

etymology: Saint Vincent was named by explorer Christopher COLUMBUS after Saint VINCENT of Saragossa because the 22 January 1498 day of discovery was the saint's feast day

Government type: parliamentary democracy (House of Assembly) under a constitutional monarchy; a Commonwealth realm

Capital: *name:* Kings town

Geographic coordinates: 13 08 N, 61 13 W

time difference: UTC-4 (1 hour ahead of Washington, DC, during Standard Time)

Administrative divisions: 6 parishes; Charlotte, Grenadines, Saint Andrew, Saint David, Saint George, Saint Patrick

Independence: 27 October 1979 (from the UK)

National holiday: Independence Day, 27 October (1979)

Constitution: several previous; latest passed by the House of Assembly 3 September 2009 (The Saint Vincent and The Grenadines Constitution act, 2009) (2016)

Legal system: English common law

International law organization participation: has not submitted an ICJ jurisdiction declaration; accepts ICCt jurisdiction

Citizenship: *citizenship by birth:* yes

citizenship by descent: at least one parent must be a citizen of Saint Vincent and the Grenadines

dual citizenship recognized: yes

residency requirement for naturalization: 7 years

Suffrage: 18 years of age; universal

Executive branch: *chief of state:* Queen ELIZABETH II (since 6 February 1952); represented by Governor General Sir Fredrick Nathaniel BALLANTYNE (since 2 September 2002)

head of government: Prime Minister Ralph E. GONSALVES (since 29 March 2001)

cabinet: Cabinet appointed by the governor general on the advice of the prime minister

elections/appointments: the monarchy is hereditary; governor general appointed by the monarch; following legislative elections, the leader of the majority party usually appointed prime minister by the governor general; deputy prime minister appointed by the governor general on the advice of the prime minister

Legislative branch: *description:* unicameral House of Assembly (21 seats; 15 members directly elected in single-seat constituencies by simple majority vote and 6 appointed by the governor general; members serve 5-year terms)

elections: last held on 9 December 2015 (next to be held in 2020)

election results: percent of vote by party—ULP 52.3%, NDP 47.4%, other 0.3%; seats by party—ULP 8, NDP 7

Judicial branch: *highest court(s):* the Eastern Caribbean Supreme Court (ECSC) is the itinerant superior court of record for the 9-member Organization of Eastern Caribbean States to include Saint Vincent and the Grenadines; the ECSC—with its headquarters on Saint Lucia—is headed by the chief justice and is comprised of the Court of Appeal with 3 justices and the High Court with 16 judges; sittings of the Court of Appeal and High Court rotate among the member states; 2 High Court judges reside on Saint Vincent and the Grenadines;

note—Saint Vincent and the Grenadines is a member of the Caribbean Court of Justice

judge selection and term of office: Eastern Caribbean Supreme Court chief justice appointed by Her Majesty, Queen ELIZABETH II; other justices

and judges appointed by the Judicial and Legal Services Commission; Court of Appeal justices appointed for life with mandatory retirement at age 65; High Court judges appointed for life with mandatory retirement at age 62

subordinate courts: magistrates' courts

Political parties and leaders: Democratic Republican Party or DRP [Anesia BAPTISTE]

New Democratic Party or NDP [Arnhim EUSTACE]

Unity Labor Party or ULP [Ralph GONSALVES] (formed by the coalition of Saint Vincent Labor Party or SVLP and the Movement for National Unity or MNU)

SVG Green Party or SVGP [Ivan O'N EAL]

Political pressure groups and leaders: NA

International organization participation: ACP, AOSIS, C, Caricom, CDB, CELAC, FAO, G-77, IBRD, ICAO, ICCt, ICRM, IDA, IFAD, IFRCS, ILO, IMF, IMO, Interpol, IOC, IOM, ISO (subscriber), ITU, MIGA, NAM, OAS, OECS, OPANAL, OPCW, Petrocaribe, UN, UNCTAD, UNESCO, UNIDO, UPU, WFTU (NGOs), WHO, WIPO, WTO

Diplomatic representation in the US: *chief of mission:* Ambassador La Celia A. PRINCE (since 30 May 2008)

chancery: 3216 New Mexico Avenue NW, Washington, DC 20016

telephone: [1] (202) 364-6730

FAX: [1] (202) 364-6736

consulate(s) general: New York

Diplomatic representation from the US: the US does not have an embassy in Saint Vincent and the Grenadines; the US Ambassador to Barbados is accredited to Saint Vincent and the Grenadines

Flag description: three vertical bands of blue (hoist side), gold (double width), and green; the gold band bears three green diamonds arranged in a V pattern, which stands for Vincent; the diamonds recall the islands as the "Gems of the Antilles"; blue conveys the colors of a tropical sky and crystal waters, yellow signifies the golden Grenadine sands, and green represents lush vegetation

National symbol(s): Saint Vincent parrot; National colors: blue, gold, green

National anthem: *name:* "St. Vincent! Land So Beautiful!"

lyrics/music: Phyllis Joyce MCCLEAN PUNNETT/Joel Bertram MIGUEL

note: adopted 1967

ECONOMY

Economy—overview: Success of the economy hinges upon seasonal variations in Agriculture, tourism, and construction activity as well as remittances. Much of the workforce is employed in banana production and tourism, but persistent high unemployment has prompted many to leave the islands. Saint Vincent is home to a small offshore banking sector and has moved to adopt International regulatory standards.

This lower-middle-income country is vulnerable to Natural disasters—tropical storms wiped out substantial portions of crops in 1994, 1995, and 2002. Floods and mudslides caused by unseason able rainfall in 2013, caused substantial damage to infrastructure, homes, and crops, which the World Bank estimated at US$112 million. The government's ability to invest in social programs and respond to external shocks is constrained by its high public debt burden, which was 67% of GDP—one of the lowest levels in the Eastern Caribbean—at the end of 2013.

In 2013, the islands had more than 200,000 tourist arrivals, mostly to the Grenadines. Arrivals represented a marginal increase from 2012 but remain 26% below St. Vincent's 2009 peak. Weak recovery in the tourism and construction sectors limited growth in 2015.

GDP (purchasing power parity): $1.205 billion (2015 est.)
$1.186 billion (2014 est.)
$1.189 billion (2013 est.)
note: data are in 2015 US dollars
country comparison to the world: 202
GDP (official exchange rate): $757 million (2015 est.)
GDP—real growth rate: 1.6% (2015 est.)
-0.2% (2014 est.)
2.3% (2013 est.)
country comparison to the world: 152
GDP—per capita (PPP): $11,000 (2015 est.)
$10,800 (2014 est.)
$10,800 (2013 est.)
note: data are in 2015 US dollars
country comparison to the world: 133
Gross National saving: -4.1% of GDP (2015 est.)
-7.3% of GDP (2014 est.)
-6.2% of GDP (2013 est.)
country comparison to the world: 174
GDP—composition, by end use:
household consumption: 97.8%
government consumption: 17.3%
investment in fixed capital: 24.2%
investment in inventories: -0.2%
exports of goods and services: 15.2%
imports of goods and services: -54.3% (2015 est.)
GDP—composition, by sector of origin:
agriculture: 7.1%
industry: 17.9%
services: 75% (2015 est.)
Agriculture—products: bananas, coconuts, sweet potatoes, spices; small numbers of cattle, sheep, pigs, goats; fish
Industries: tourism; food processing, cement, furniture, clothing, starch
Industrial production growth rate: 2.2% (2015 est.)
country comparison to the world: 111
Labor force: 57,520 (2007 est.)
country comparison to the world: 189
Labor force—by occupation: *agriculture:* 26%
industry: 17%
services: 57% (1980 est.)
Unemployment rate: 18.8% (2008 est.)
country comparison to the world: 166
Population below poverty line: NA%
Household income or consumption by percentage share: *lowest:* 10%: NA%
highest: 10%: NA%
Budget: *revenues:* $185.2 million
expenditures: $222.2 million (2015 est.)

Taxes and other revenues: 24.2% of GDP (2015 est.)
country comparison to the world: 128
Budget surplus (+) or deficit (–): -4.8% of GDP (2015 est.)
country comparison to the world: 165
Public debt: 67% of GDP (2013 est.)
68% of GDP (2011 est.)
country comparison to the world: 51
Fiscal year: calendar year
Inflation rate (consumer prices): -1.7% (2015 est.)
0.2% (2014 est.)
country comparison to the world: 5
Central bank discount rate: 6.5% (31 December 2010)
6.5% (31 December 2009)
country comparison to the world: 51
Commercial bank prime lending rate: 9.5% (31 December 2015 est.)
9% (31 December 2014 est.)
country comparison to the world: 85
Stock of narrow money: $172.3 million (31 December 2015 est.)
$157.9 million (31 December 2014 est.)
country comparison to the world: 184
Stock of broad money: $547.8 million (31 December 2015 est.)
$521.7 million (31 December 2014 est.)
country comparison to the world: 179
Stock of domestic credit: $433.9 million (31 December 2015 est.)
$422 million (31 December 2014 est.)
country comparison to the world: 174
Current account balance: -$188 million (2015 est.)
-$216 million (2014 est.)
country comparison to the world: 79
Exports: $49.8 million (2015 est.)
$48.2 million (2014 est.)
country comparison to the world: 202
Exports—commodities: bananas, eddoes and dasheen (taro), arrowroot starch; tennis racquets
Exports—partners: Trinidad and Tobago 18.9%, St. Lucia 14.8%, Barbados 12.3%, Dominica 9.7%, Grenada 9.3%, Antigua and Barbuda 8.4%, Poland 7.1%, St. Kitts and Nevis 4.1% (2015)
Imports: $320.7 million (2015 est.)
$313.6 million (2014 est.)
country comparison to the world: 197
Imports—commodities: foodstuffs, machinery and equipment, chemicals and fertilizers, minerals and fuels
Imports—partners: Trinidad and Tobago 29.3%, US 17.2%, Singapore 8.7%, China 8%, Barbados 6%, Poland 5.5%, Turkey 4.4% (2015)
Reserves of foreign exchange and gold: $135 million (31 December 2015 est.)
$157.4 million (31 December 2014 est.)
country comparison to the world: 164
Debt—external: $282.7 million (31 December 2014 est.)
$292.7 million (31 December 2013 est.)
country comparison to the world: 187
Exchange rates: East Caribbean dollars (XCD) per US dollar—
2.7 (2015 est.)
2.7 (2014 est.)
2.7 (2013 est.)
2.7 (2012 est.)
2.7 (2011 est.)

ENERGY

Electricity—production: 137 million kWh (2012 est.)
country comparison to the world: 196
Electricity—consumption: 127.4 million kWh (2012 est.)
country comparison to the world: 196
Electricity—exports: 0 kWh (2013 est.)
country comparison to the world: 211
Electricity—imports: 0 kWh (2013 est.)
country comparison to the world: 214
Electricity—installed generating capacity: 47,000 kW (2012 est.)
country comparison to the world: 188
Electricity—from fossil fuels: 85.1% of total installed capacity (2012 est.)
country comparison to the world: 89
Electricity—from nuclear fuels: 0% of total installed capacity (2012 est.)
country comparison to the world: 202
Electricity—from hydroelectric plants: 14.9% of total installed capacity (2012 est.)
country comparison to the world: 101
Electricity—from other renewable sources: 0% of total installed capacity (2012 est.)
country comparison to the world: 139
Crude oil—production: 0 bbl/day (2014 est.)
country comparison to the world: 205
Crude oil—exports: 0 bbl/day (2012 est.)
country comparison to the world: 205
Crude oil—imports: 0 bbl/day (2012 est.)
country comparison to the world: 142
Crude oil—proved reserves: 0 bbl (1 January 2015 est.)
country comparison to the world: 206
Refined petroleum products—production: 0 bbl/day (2012 est.)
country comparison to the world: 143
Refined petroleum products—consumption: 1,500 bbl/day (2013 est.)
country comparison to the world: 193
Refined petroleum products—exports: 0 bbl/day (2012 est.)
country comparison to the world: 144
Refined petroleum products—imports: 1,514 bbl/day (2012 est.)
country comparison to the world: 188
Natural gas—production: 0 cu m (2013 est.)
country comparison to the world: 143
Natural gas—consumption: 0 cu m (2013 est.)
country comparison to the world: 206
Natural gas—exports: 0 cu m (2013 est.)
country comparison to the world: 204
Natural gas—imports: 0 cu m (2013 est.)
country comparison to the world: 150
Natural gas—proved reserves: 0 cu m (1 January 2014 est.)
country comparison to the world: 204
Carbon dioxide emissions from consumption 268,900 Mt (2012 est.)
country comparison to the world: 192

COMMUNICATIONS

Telephones—fixed lines: *total subscriptions:* 23,900

727

subscriptions per 100 inhabitants: 23 (2014 est.)
country comparison to the world: 175
Telephones—mobile cellular: total: 115,000
subscriptions per 100 inhabitants: 112 (2014 est.)
country comparison to the world: 188
Telephone system: general assessment: adequate islandwide, fully automatic telephone system
domestic: fixed-line teledensity exceeds 20 per 100 persons and mobile-cellular teledensity exceeds 125 per 100 persons
international: country code—1-784; the East Caribbean Fiber Optic System (ECFS) and Southern Caribbean fiber optic system (SCF) submarine cables carry International calls; connectivity also provided by VHF/UHF radiotelephone from Saint Vincent to Barbados; SHF radiotelephone to Grenada and Saint Lucia; access to intelsat earth station in Martinique through Saint Lucia (2011)
Broadcast media: St. Vincent and the Grenadines Broadcasting Corporation operates 1 TV station and 5 repeater stations that provide near total coverage to the multi-island state; multi-channel cable TV service available; a partially government-funded National radio service broadcasts on 1 station and has 2 repeater stations; about a dozen privately owned radio stations and repeater stations (2007)
Radio broadcast stations: AM 1, FM 8, shortwave 0 (2008)
Television broadcast stations: 1 (plus 3 repeaters) (2004)
Internet country code: .vc
Internet hosts: 305 (2012)
country comparison to the world: 190
Internet users: total: 76,000
percent of population: 72.7% (2009)
country comparison to the world: 177

TRANSPORTATION

Airports: 6 (2013)

country comparison to the world: 175
Airports—with paved runways: total: 5
1,524 to 2,437 m: 1
914 to 1,523 m: 3
under 914 m: 1 (2013)
Airports—with unpaved runways: total: 1
under 914 m: 1 (2013)
Roadways: total: 829 km
paved: 580 km
unpaved: 249 km (2003)
country comparison to the world: 188
Merchant marine: total: 412
by type: bulk carrier 64, cargo 263, carrier 14, chemical tanker 4, container 18, liquefied gas 3, passenger 2, passenger/cargo 7, petroleum tanker 9, refrigerated cargo 12, roll on/roll off 15, specialized tanker 1
foreign-owned: 325 (Austria 1, Azerbaijan 1, Bangladesh 1, Belgium 7, Bermuda 1, Bulgaria 9, China 65, Croatia 8, Cyprus 3, Czech Republic 1, Denmark 9, Dominica 1, Egypt 2, Estonia 8, France 2, Germany 3, Greece 42, Guyana 2, Hong Kong 5, Israel 3, Italy 4, Japan 3, Kenya 2, Latvia 15, Lebanon 2, Lithuania 9, Monaco 2, Netherlands 1, Norway 13, Poland 3, Romania 1, Russia 11, Singapore 5, Slovenia 1, Sweden 10, Switzerland 7, Syria 9, Turkey 13, UAE 3, UK 6, Ukraine 12, US 18, Venezuela 1) (2010)
country comparison to the world: 25
Ports and terminals: major seaport(s): Kingstown

MILITARY AND SECURITY

Military branches: no regular military forces; Royal Saint Vincent and the Grenadines Police Force (RSVPF) (2013)

TRANSNATIONAL ISSUES

Disputes—International: joins other Caribbean states to counter Venezuela's claim that Aves Island sustains human habitation, a criterion under UN Convention on the Law of the Sea, which permits Venezuela to extend its EEZ/continental shelf over a large portion of the eastern Caribbean Sea

Trafficking in persons: current situation: Saint Vincent and the Grenadines is a source, transit, and destination country for men, women, and children subjected to forced labor and sex trafficking; some children under 18 are pressured to engage in sex acts in exchange for money or gifts; foreign workers may experience forced labor and are particularly vulnerable when employed by small, foreign-owned companies; adults and children are vulnerable to forced labor domestically, especially in the agriculture sector

tier rating: Tier 2 Watch List—Saint Vincent and the Grenadines does not fully comply with the minimum standards for the elimination of trafficking; however, it is making significant efforts to do so; the government for the first time acknowledged a trafficking problem, launched an anti-trafficking public awareness campaign, and conducted anti-trafficking training for law enforcement, immigration, and labor officials; in 2014, authorities initiated three trafficking investigations, two of which were ultimately determined not to be trafficking cases, and did not prosecute or convict any trafficking offenders; the government did not identify or refer any potential trafficking victims to care (2015)

Illicit drugs: transshipment point for South American drugs destined for the US and Europe; small-scale cannabis cultivation

SAMOA

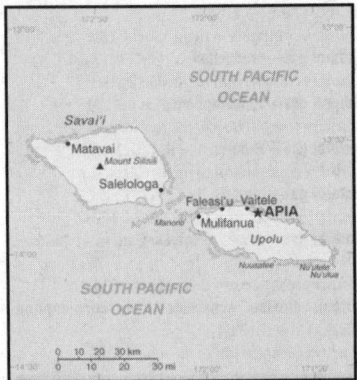

INTRODUCTION

Background: New Zealand occupied the German protectorate of Western Samoa at the outbreak of World War I In 1914. It continued to administer the islands as a mandate and then as a trust territory until 1962, when the islands became the first Polynesian nation to reestablish independence in the 20th century. The country dropped the "Western" from its name in 1997.

GEOGRAPHY

Location: Oceania, group of islands in the South Pacific Ocean, about halfway between Hawaii and New Zealand
Geographic coordinates: 13 35 S, 172 20 W
Map references: Oceania
Area: total: 2,831 sq km
land: 2,821 sq km
water: 10 sq km

country comparison to the world: 178
Area—comparative: slightly smaller than Rhode Island
Land boundaries: 0 km
Coastline: 403 km
Maritime claims: territorial sea: 12 nm
contiguous zone: 24 nm
exclusive economic zone: 200 nm
Climate: tropical; rainy season (November to April), dry season (May to October)
Terrain: two main islands (Savaii, Upolu) and several smaller islands and uninhabited islets; narrow coastal plain with volcanic, rugged mountains in interior
Elevation: mean elevation: NA
elevation extremes: lowest point: Pacific Ocean 0 m
highest point: Mount Silisili 1,857 m
Natural resources: hardwood forests, fish, hydropower

Land use: *agricultural land:* 12.4%
arable land: 2.8%
permanent crops: 7.8%
permanent pasture: 1.8%
forest: 60.4%
other: 27.2% (2011 est.)
Irrigated land: 0 sq km (2012)
Natural hazards: occasional typhoons; active volcanism
volcanism: Savai'I Island (elev. 1,858 m), which last erupted in 1911, is historically active
Environment—current issues: soil erosion, deforestation, invasive species, overfishing
Environment—International agreements: *party to:* Biodiversity, Climate Change, Climate Change-Kyoto Protocol, Desertification, Hazardous Wastes, Law of the Sea, Ozone Layer Protection, Ship Pollution, Wetlands
signed, but not ratified: none of the selected agreements
Geography—note: occupies an almost central position within Polynesia

PEOPLE AND SOCIETY

Nationality: *noun:* Samoan(s)
adjective: Samoan
Ethnic groups: Samoan 92.6%, Euronesians (persons of European and Polynesian blood) 7%, Europeans 0.4% (2001 census)
Languages: Samoan (Polynesian) (official), English
Religions: Protestant 57.4% (Congregation alist 31.8%, Methodist 13.7%, Assembly of God 8%, Seventh-Day Adventist 3.9%), Roman Catholic 19.4%, Mormon 15.2%, Worship Centre 1.7%, other Christian 5.5%, other 0.7%, none 0.1%, unspecified 0.1% (2011 est.)
Population: 197,773
note: prior estimates used official net migration data by sex, but a highly unusual pattern for 1993 lead to a significant imbalance in the sex ratios (more men and fewer women) and a seeming reduction in the female population; the revised total was calculated using a 1993 number that was an Average of the 1992 and 1994 migration figures (July 2015 est.)
country comparison to the world: 185
Age structure: *0–14 years:* 32.72% (male 33,393/female 31,324)
15–24 years: 19.96% (male 20,253/female 19,217)
25–54 years: 35.58% (male 36,374/female 33,993)
55–64 years: 6.24% (male 6,283/female 6,057)
65 years and over: 5.5% (male 4,730/female 6,149) (2015 est.)
Dependency ratios: *total dependency ratio:* 74%
youth dependency ratio: 64.9%
elderly dependency ratio: 9.1%
potential support ratio: 11% (2015 est.)
Median age: *total:* 23.5 years
male: 23.3 years
female: 23.8 years (2015 est.)
country comparison to the world: 164
Population growth rate: 0.58% (2015 est.)
country comparison to the world: 152
Birth rate: 20.87 births/1,000 population (2015 est.)

country comparison to the world: 78
Death rate: 5.32 deaths/1,000 population (2015 est.)
country comparison to the world: 178
Net migration rate: -9.78 migrant(s)/1,000 population (2015 est.)
country comparison to the world: 215
Urbanization: *urban population:* 19.1% of total population (2015)
rate of urbanization: -0.24% annual rate of change (2010–15 est.)
Major urban areas—population: APIA (capital) 37,000 (2014)
Sex ratio: *at birth:* 1.05 male(s)/female
0–14 years: 1.07 male(s)/female
15–24 years: 1.05 male(s)/female
25–54 years: 1.07 male(s)/female
55–64 years: 1.04 male(s)/female
65 years and over: 0.77 male(s)/female
total population: 1.04 male(s)/female (2015 est.)
Mother's mean age at first birth: 23.6
note: Median Age at first birth among women 25–29 (2009 est.)
Maternal mortality rate: 51 deaths/100,000 live births (2015 est.)
country comparison to the world: 72
Infant mortality rate: *total:* 19.57 deaths/1,000 live births
male: 23.1 deaths/1,000 live births
female: 15.87 deaths/1,000 live births (2015 est.)
country comparison to the world: 90
Life expectancy at birth: *total population:* 73.46 years
male: 70.58 years
female: 76.48 years (2015 est.)
country comparison to the world: 131
Total fertility rate: 2.84 children born/woman (2015 est.)
country comparison to the world: 60
Contraceptive prevalence rate: 28.7% (2009)
Health expenditures: 7.5% of GDP (2013)
country comparison to the world: 83
Physicians density: 0.45 physicians/1,000 population (2008)
Drinking water source:
improved:
urban: 97.5% of population
rural: 99.3% of population
total: 99% of population
unimproved:
urban: 2.5% of population
rural: 0.7% of population
total: 1% of population (2015 est.)
Sanitation facility access:
improved:
urban: 93.3% of population
rural: 91.1% of population
total: 91.5% of population
unimproved:
urban: 6.7% of population
rural: 8.9% of population
total: 8.5% of population (2015 est.)
HIV/AIDS—adult prevalence rate: NA
HIV/AIDS—people living with HIV/AIDS: NA
HIV/AIDS—deaths: NA
Obesity—adult prevalence rate: 41.6% (2014)

country comparison to the world: 6
Education expenditures: 5.1% of GDP (2008)
country comparison to the world: 48
Literacy: *definition:* age 15 and over can read and write
total population: 99%
male: 99.1%
female: 98.8% (2015 est.)
Unemployment, youth ages 15–24: *total:* 19.1%
male: 15.6%
female: 25.3% (2012 est.)
country comparison to the world: 75

GOVERNMENT

Country name: *conventional long form:* Independent State of Samoa
conventional short form: Samoa
local long form: Malo Sa'oloto Tuto'atasio Samoa
local short form: Samoa
former: Western Samoa
note: the name "Samoa" is composed of two parts, "sa" meaning sacred and "moa" meaning center, so the name can mean Holy Center; alternatively, it can mean "place of the sacred moa bird" of Polynesian mythology
Government type: parliamentary republic
Capital: *name:* Apia
Geographic coordinates: 13 49 S, 171 46 W
time difference: UTC + 13 (18 hours ahead of Washington, DC, during Standard Time) + 1 hr, begins last Sunday in September; ends first Sunday in April
Administrative divisions: 11 districts; A'ana, Aiga-i-le-Tai, Atua, Fa'asaleleaga, Gaga'emauga, Gagaifomauga, Palauli, Satupa'itea, Tuamasaga, Va'a-o-Fonoti, Vaisigano
Independence: 1 January 1962 (from New Zealand-administered UN trusteeship)
National holiday: Independence Day Celebration, 1 June (1962); note—1 January 1962 is the date of independence from the New Zealand-administered UN trusteeship; it is observed in June
Constitution: several previous (preindependence); latest 1 January 1962; amended several times, last in 2015 (2016)
Legal system: mixed legal system of English common law and customary law; judicial review of legislative acts with respect to fundamental rights of the citizen
International law organization participation: has not submitted an ICJ jurisdiction declaration; accepts ICCt jurisdiction
Citizenship: *citizenship by birth:* no
citizenship by descent only: at least one parent must be a citizen of Samoa
dual citizenship recognized: no
residency requirement for naturalization: 5 years
Suffrage: 21 years of age; universal
Executive branch: *chief of state:* TUI ATUA Tupua Tamasese Efi (since 20 June 2007)
head of government: Prime Minister TUILA'EPA Lupesoliai Sailele Malielegaoi (since 1998); Deputy Prime Minister FONOTOE Pierre Lauofo (since 2011)

cabinet: Cabinet appointed by the chief of state on the prime minister's advice

elections/appointments: chief of state indirectly elected by the Legislative Assembly to serve a 5-year term (no term limits); election last held on 20 July 2012 (next to be held in 2017); following legislative elections, the leader of the majority party usually appointed prime minister by the chief of state, approved by the Legislative Assembly

election results: TUI ATUA Tupua Tamasese Efi unanimously elected by the Legislative Assembly

Legislative branch: *description:* unicameral Legislative Assembly or Fono (49 seats; 47 members—traditional family chiefs or matai and 2 members—part-Samoan or non-Samoan—directly elected by simple majority vote; members serve 5-year terms)

elections: election last held on 4 March 2016 (next election to be held no later than March 2021)

election results: percent of vote by party—NA; seats by party—HRPP 44, Tautua Samoa 3, independents 2

Judicial branch: *highest court(s):* Court of Appeal (consists of the chief justice and 2 Supreme Court judges and meets once or twice a year); Supreme Court (consists of the chief justice and several judges)

judge selection and term of office: chief justice appointed by the head of state upon the advice of the prime minister; other Supreme Court judges appointed by the Judicial Service Commission, a 3-member body chaired by the chief justice and includes the attorney general and an appointee of the Minister of Justice; judges normally appointed until retirement at age 68

subordinate courts: District Court; Magistrates' Courts; Land and Titles Courts; village fono or village chief councils

Political parties and leaders: Human Rights Protection Party or HRPP [Sailele Malielegaoi TUILA'EPA]

Samoa Christian Party or TCP [Tuala Tiresa MALI ETOA]

Samoa Progressive Political Party or SPPP [Toalepaiali'i Toesulusulu S'ieva POSE II]

Tautua Samoa [Leatinu'u Salole LESA]

Political pressure groups and leaders: NA

International organization participation: ACP, ADB, AOSIS, C, FAO, G-77, IBRD, ICAO, ICCt, ICRM, IDA, IFAD, IFC, IFRCS, ILO, IMF, IMO, Interpol, IOC, IPU, ITU, ITUC (NGOs), MIGA, OPCW, PIF, Sparteca, SPC, UN, UNCTAD, UNESCO, UNIDO, UPU, WCO, WHO, WIPO, WMO, WTO

Diplomatic representation in the US: *chief of mission:* Ambassador Aliioaiga Feturi ELISAIA (since 4 December 2003)

chancery: 800 Second Avenue, Suite 400J, New York, NY 10017

telephone: [1] (212) 599-6196 through 6197

FAX: [1] (212) 599-0797

consulate(s) general: Pago Pago (American Samoa)

Diplomatic representation from the US: *chief of mission:* the US does not have an embassy in Samoa; the US Ambassador to New Zealand is accredited to Samoa

embassy: Accident Corporation Building, 5th Floor, Matafele, Apia

mailing address: P.O. Box 3430, Matafele, Apia

telephone: [685] 21436/21631/21452/22696

FAX: [685] 22030

Flag description: red with a blue rectangle in the upper hoist-side quadrant bearing five white five-pointed stars representing the Southern Cross constellation; red stands for courage, blue represents freedom, and white signifies purity

National symbol(s): Southern Cross constellation (five, five-pointed stars); National colors: red, white, blue

National anthem: *name:* "OleFu'aole Sa'olotogao Samoa" (The Banner of Freedom)

lyrics/music: Sauni Liga KURESA

note: adopted 1962; also known as "Samoa Tula'i" (Samoa Arise)

ECONOMY

Economy—overview: The economy of Samoa has traditionally been dependent on development aid, family remittances from overseas, tourism, agriculture, and fishing. It has a nominal GDP of $780 million. Agriculture, including fishing, employs roughly two-thirds of the labor force and furnishes 90% of exports, featuring fish, coconut oil, nonu products, and taro. The manufacturing sector mainly processes agricultural products. One factory in the Foreign Trade Zone employs 1,000 people to make automobile electrical harnesses for an assembly plant in Australia, and accounts for 65% of total exports. Industry accounts for nearly 15% of GDP while employing less than 6% of the work force. The service sector accounts for nearly three-quarters of GDP and employs approximately 50% of the labor force. Tourism is an expanding sector accounting for 25% of GDP; 132,000 tourists visited the islands in 2013.

The country is vulnerable to devastating storms. in September 2009, an earthquake and the resulting tsunami severely damaged Samoa and nearby American Samoa, disrupting transportation and power generation, and resulting in about 200 deaths. in December 2012, extensive flooding and wind damage from Tropical Cyclone Evan killed four people, displaced over 6,000, and damaged or destroyed an estimated 1,500 homes on Samoa's Upolu Island.

The Samoan Government has called for deregulation of the country's financial sector, encouragement of investment, and continued fiscal discipline, while at the same time protecting the environment. Foreign reserves are relatively healthy and inflation is low, but external debt is approximately 55% of GDP. Samoa became the 155th member of the WTO in May 2012, and graduated from least developed country (LDC) status in January 2014.

GDP (purchasing power parity): $1 billion (2015 est.)

$983.5 million (2014 est.)

$971.8 million (2013 est.)

note: data are in 2015 US dollars

country comparison to the world: 204

GDP (official exchange rate): $838 million (2015 est.)

GDP—real growth rate: 1.7% (2015 est.)

1.2% (2014 est.)

-1.9% (2013 est.)

country comparison to the world: 143

GDP—per capita (PPP): $5,200 (2015 est.)

$5,100 (2014 est.)

$5,100 (2013 est.)

note: data are in 2015 US dollars

country comparison to the world: 166

GDP—composition, by sector of origin:

agriculture: 10.9%

industry: 28.3%

services: 60.8% (2012 est.)

Agriculture—products: coconuts, nonu, bananas, taro, yams, coffee, cocoa

Industries: food processing, building materials, auto parts

Industrial production growth rate: -5% (2015 est.)

country comparison to the world: 191

Labor force: 49,180 (2013 est.)

country comparison to the world: 194

Labor force—by occupation: *agriculture:* 65%

industry: NA%

services: NA%

Unemployment rate: NA%

Population below poverty line: NA%

Household income or consumption by percentage share: *lowest:* 10%: NA%

highest: 10%: NA%

Budget: *revenues:* $234.8 million

expenditures: $234.8 million (2015 est.)

Taxes and other revenues: 27.1% of GDP (2015 est.)

country comparison to the world: 101

Budget surplus (+) or deficit (–): 0% of GDP (2015 est.)

country comparison to the world: 31

Fiscal year: June 1—May 31

Inflation rate (consumer prices): 0.9% (2015 est.)

-0.4% (2014 est.)

country comparison to the world: 77

Commercial bank prime lending rate: 9.5% (31 December 2015 est.)

10% (31 December 2014 est.)

country comparison to the world: 86

Stock of narrow money: $114.8 million (31 December 2015 est.)

$113.8 million (31 December 2014 est.)

country comparison to the world: 185

Stock of broad money: $366 million (31 December 2014 est.)

$318.7 million (31 December 2013 est.)

country comparison to the world: 187

Stock of domestic credit: $414.3 million (31 December 2015 est.)

$371.4 million (31 December 2014 est.)

country comparison to the world: 176

Market value of publicly traded shares: $NA

Current account balance: -$33 million (2015 est.)

-$62 million (2014 est.)

country comparison to the world: 61

Exports: $24 million (2013 est.)

$24 million (2013 est.)

country comparison to the world: 209

Exports—commodities: fish, coconut oil and cream, nonu, copra, taro, automotive parts, garments, beer

Exports—partners: American Samoa 57.1%, Australia 17.2% (2015)

Imports: $325.3 million (2013 est.)

$325.3 million (2013 est.)

country comparison to the world: 196

Imports—commodities: machinery and equipment, industrial supplies, foodstuffs

Imports—partners: Fiji 22.6%, NZ 18.8%, China 15.8%, South Korea 7.9%, Australia 6%, US 5.6%, Singapore 5.2% (2015)

Reserves of foreign exchange and gold: $140.7 million (31 December 2014 est.)

$170.7 million (31 December 2013 est.)

country comparison to the world: 163

Debt—external: $447.2 million (31 December 2013 est.)

$422.9 million (31 December 2012 est.)

country comparison to the world: 181

Exchange rates: tala (SAT) per US dollar—
2.555 (2015 est.)
2.3318 (2014 est.)
2.3318 (2013 est.)
2.29 (2012 est.)
2.3175 (2011 est.)

ENERGY

Electricity—production: 97.2 million kWh (2012 est.)

country comparison to the world: 199

Electricity—consumption: 90.4 million kWh (2012 est.)

country comparison to the world: 199

Electricity—exports: 0 kWh (2013 est.)

country comparison to the world: 216

Electricity—imports: 0 kWh (2013 est.)

country comparison to the world: 218

Electricity—installed generating capacity: 42,000 kW (2012 est.)

country comparison to the world: 194

Electricity—from fossil fuels: 71.4% of total installed capacity (2012 est.)

country comparison to the world: 103

Electricity—from nuclear fuels: 0% of total installed capacity (2012 est.)

country comparison to the world: 210

Electricity—from hydroelectric plants: 28.6% of total installed capacity (2012 est.)

country comparison to the world: 82

Electricity—from other renewable sources: 0% of total installed capacity (2012 est.)

country comparison to the world: 145

Crude oil—production: 0 bbl/day (2014 est.)

country comparison to the world: 211

Crude oil—exports: 0 bbl/day (2012 est.)

country comparison to the world: 211

Crude oil—imports: 0 bbl/day (2012 est.)

country comparison to the world: 146

Crude oil—proved reserves: 0 bbl (1 January 2015 est.)

country comparison to the world: 212

Refined petroleum products—production: 0 bbl/day (2012 est.)

country comparison to the world: 148

Refined petroleum products—consumption: 1,100 bbl/day (2013 est.)

country comparison to the world: 199

Refined petroleum products—exports: 0 bbl/day (2012 est.)

country comparison to the world: 146

Refined petroleum products—imports: 1,150 bbl/day (2012 est.)

country comparison to the world: 194

Natural gas—production: 0 cu m (2013 est.)

country comparison to the world: 149

Natural gas—consumption: 0 cu m (2013 est.)

country comparison to the world: 212

Natural gas—exports: 0 cu m (2013 est.)

country comparison to the world: 209

Natural gas—imports: 0 cu m (2013 est.)

country comparison to the world: 82

Natural gas—proved reserves: 0 cu m (1 January 2014 est.)

country comparison to the world: 209

Carbon dioxide emissions from consumption of energy: 161,000 Mt (2012 est.)

country comparison to the world: 199

COMMUNICATIONS

Telephones—fixed lines: *total subscriptions:* 11,800

subscriptions per 100 inhabitants: 6 (2014 est.)

country comparison to the world: 196

Telephones—mobile cellular: *total:* 106,500

subscriptions per 100 inhabitants: 54 (2014 est.)

country comparison to the world: 190

Telephone system: *general assessment:* adequate

domestic: combined fixed-line and mobile-cellular teledensity roughly 100 telephones per 100 persons

International: country code—685; satellite earth station—1 intelsat (Pacific Ocean) (2007)

Broadcast media: state-owned TV station privatized in 2008; 4 privately owned television broadcast stations; about a half dozen privately owned radio stations and one state-owned radio station; TV and radio broadcasts of several stations from American Samoa are available (2009)

Radio broadcast stations: AM 2, FM 5, short-wave 0 (2004)

Television broadcast stations: 2 (2002)

Internet country code: .ws

Internet hosts: 18,013 (2012)

country comparison to the world: 120

Internet users: *total:* 27,600

percent of population: 14.1% (2014 est.)

country comparison to the world: 198

TRANSPORTATION

Airports: 4 (2013)

country comparison to the world: 188

Airports—with paved runways: *total:* 1

2,438 to 3,047 m: 1 (2013)

Airports—with unpaved runways: *total:* 3

under 914 m: 3 (2013)

Roadways: *total:* 2,337 km

paved: 332 km

unpaved: 2,005 km (2001)

country comparison to the world: 173

Merchant marine: *total:* 2

by type: cargo 1, passenger/cargo 1

foreign-owned: 1 (NZ 1) (2010)

country comparison to the world: 145

Ports and terminals: *major seaport(s):* Apia

MILITARY AND SECURITY

Military branches: no regular military forces; Samoa Police Force

Military—note: Samoa has no formal defense structure or regular armed forces; informal defense ties exist with NZ, which is required to consider any Samoan request for assistance under the 1962 Treaty of Friendship

TRANSNATIONAL ISSUES

Disputes—International: none

SAN MARINO

INTRODUCTION

Background: Geographically the third smallest state in Europe (after the Holy See and Monaco), San Marino also claims to be the world's oldest republic. According to tradition, it was founded by a Christian stonemason named MARINUS in A.D. 301. San Marino's foreign policy is aligned with that of the EU, although it is not a member; social and political trends in the republic track closely with those of its larger neighbor, Italy.

GEOGRAPHY

Location: Southern Europe, an enclave in central Italy
Geographic coordinates: 43 46 N, 12 25 E
Map references: Europe
Area: *total:* 61 sq km
land: 61 sq km
water: 0 sq km
country comparison to the world: 229
Area—comparative: about one-third the size of Washington, DC
Land boundaries: *total:* 37 km
border countries (1): Italy 37 km
Coastline: 0 km (landlocked)
Maritime claims: none (landlocked)
Climate: Mediterranean; mild to cool winters; warm, sunny summers
Terrain: rugged mountains
Elevation: *mean elevation:* NA
elevation extremes: *lowest point:* Torrente Ausa 55 m
highest point: Monte Titano 755 m
Natural resources: building stone
Land use: *agricultural land:* 16.7%
arable land: 16.7%
permanent crops: 0%
permanent pasture: 0%
forest: 0%
other: 83.3% (2011 est.)
Irrigated land: 0 sq km (2012)
Natural hazards: NA

Environment—current issues: air pollution; urbanization decreasing rural farmlands
Environment—international agreements: *party to:* Biodiversity, Climate Change, Desertification, Whaling
signed, but not ratified: Air Pollution
Geography—note: landlocked; smallest independent state in Europe after the Holy See and Monaco; dominated by the Apennine Mountains

PEOPLE AND SOCIETY

Nationality: *noun:* Sammarinese (singular and plural)
adjective: Sammarinese
Ethnic groups: Sammarinese, Italian
Languages: Italian
Religions: Roman Catholic
Population: 33,020 (July 2015 est.)
country comparison to the world: 216
Age structure: *0–14 years:* 15.69% (male 2,756/female 2,424)
15–24 years: 11.15% (male 1,890/female 1,792)
25–54 years: 41.88% (male 6,518/female 7,310)
55–64 years: 12.19% (male 2,009/female 2,015)
65 years and over: 19.1% (male 2,822/female 3,484) (2015 est.)
Median age: *total:* 43.9 years
male: 42.9 years
female: 44.7 years (2015 est.)
country comparison to the world: 7
Population growth rate: 0.82% (2015 est.)
country comparison to the world: 134
Birth rate: 8.63 births/1,000 population (2015 est.)
country comparison to the world: 215
Death rate: 8.45 deaths/1,000 population (2015 est.)
country comparison to the world: 79
Net migration rate: 8.03 migrant(s)/1,000 population (2015 est.)
country comparison to the world: 14
Urbanization: *urban population:* 94.2% of total population (2015)
rate of urbanization: 0.62% annual rate of change (2010–15 est.)
Major urban areas—population: SAN MARINO 4,000 (2014)
Sex ratio: *at birth:* 1.1 male(s)/female
0–14 years: 1.14 male(s)/female
15–24 years: 1.06 male(s)/female
25–54 years: 0.89 male(s)/female
55–64 years: 1 male(s)/female
65 years and over: 0.81 male(s)/female
total population: 0.94 male(s)/female (2015 est.)
Infant mortality rate: *total:* 4.45 deaths/1,000 live births
male: 4.65 deaths/1,000 live births
female: 4.24 deaths/1,000 live births (2015 est.)
country comparison to the world: 183
Life expectancy at birth: *total population:* 83.24 years
male: 80.69 years
female: 86.01 years (2015 est.)

country comparison to the world: 5
Total fertility rate: 1.49 children born/woman (2015 est.)
country comparison to the world: 198
Health expenditures: 6.5% of GDP (2013)
country comparison to the world: 94
Physicians density: 5.1 physicians/1,000 population (2013)
Hospital bed density: 3.8 beds/1,000 population (2012)
HIV/AIDS—adult prevalence rate: NA
HIV/AIDS—people living with HIV/AIDS: NA
HIV/AIDS—deaths: NA
Education expenditures: 2.4% of GDP (2011)
School life expectancy (primary to tertiary education): *total:* 15 years
male: 15 years
female: 16 years (2012)

GOVERNMENT

Country name: *conventional long form:* Republic of San Marino
conventional short form: San Marino
local long form: Repubblica di San Marino
local short form: San Marino
etymology: named after Saint MARINUS, the traditional founder of the country
Government type: parliamentary republic
Capital: *name:* San Marino (city)
Geographic coordinates: 43 56 N, 12 25 E
time difference: UTC + 1 (6 hours ahead of Washington, DC, during Standard Time)
daylight saving time: +1 hr, begins last Sunday in March; ends last Sunday in October
Administrative divisions: 9 municipalities (castelli, singular—castello); Acquaviva, Borgo Maggiore, Chiesanuova, Domagnano, Faetano, Fiorentino, Montegiardino, San Marino Citta, Serravalle
Independence: 3 September 301 (traditional founding date)
National holiday: Founding of the Republic, 3 September (A.D. 301)
Constitution: consists of several legislative instruments, chief among them the Statutes (Leges Statuti) of 1600 and the Declaration of Citizen Rights of 1974; latter document amended several times, last in 2012 (2016)
Legal system: civil law system with Italian civil law influences
International law organization participation: has not submitted an ICJ jurisdiction declaration; accepts ICCt jurisdiction
Citizenship: *citizenship by birth:* no
citizenship by descent only: at least one parent must be a citizen of San Marino
dual citizenship recognized: no
residency requirement for naturalization: 30 years
Suffrage: 18 years of age; universal
Executive branch: *chief of state:* co-chiefs of state Captain Regent Gian Nicola BERTI and

Captain Regent Massimo Andrea UGOLINI (for the period 1 April 2016—1 October 2016)

head of government: Secretary of State for Foreign and Political Affairs Pasquale VALENTINI (since 5 December 2012)

cabinet: Congress of State elected by the Grand and General Council

elections/appointments: co-chiefs of state (captains regent) indirectly elected by the Grand and General Council for a single 6-month term; election last held in March 2016 (next to be held in September 2016); secretary of state for Foreign and political affairs indirectly elected by the Grand and General Council for a single 5-year term; election last held on 11 November 2012 (next to be held by November 2017)

election results: Gian Nicola BERTI(NS) and Massimo Andrea UGOLINI (PDCS) elected captains regent; percent of Grand and General Council vote—NA; Pasquale VALENTINI (PDCS) elected secretary of state for Foreign and political affairs; percent of Grand and General Council vote—NA

note: the directly elected parliament (Grand and General Council) selects 2 of its members to serve as the captains regent (co-chiefs of state) for a 6-month period; they preside over meetings of the Grand and General Council and its cabinet (Congress of State), which has 9 other members, all are selected by the Grand and General Council; assisting the captains regent are 9 secretaries of state; the secretary of state for Foreign Affairs has some prime ministerial roles

Legislative branch: *description:* unicameral Grand and General Council or Consiglio Grandee Generale (60 seats; members directly elected by proportional representation vote; members serve 5-year terms)

elections: last held on 11 November 2012 (next to be held by November 2017)

election results: percent of vote by party—San Marino Common good coalition (San Marino Bene Comune) 50.7% (including PDCS 29.5%, PSD 14.3%, AP 6.7%), Entente for the Country coalition (Intesa per Il Paese) 22.3% (including PS 12.1%, UPR 8.4%, USDM 1.7%), Active Citizenry coalition (Cittadinanza Attiva) 16.1% (including SU 9.1%, Civic 10 6.7%), Civic Movement R.E.T.E. 6.3%, For San Marino 2.8%, San Marino 3.0 1.8%; seats by party—San Marino CommoNGOod coalition 35 (PDCS 21, PSD 10, AP 4), Entente for the Country coalition 12 (PS 7, UPR 5), Active Citizenry 9 (SU 5, Civic 10 4), Civic Movement R. E. T. E. 4

Judicial branch: *highest court(s):* Council of Twelve or Consiglio dei XII (consists of 12 members); note—the College of Guarantors for the Constitutionality and General Norms functions as San Marino's constitutional court

judge selection and term of office: judges elected by the Grand and General Council from among its own to serve 5-year terms

subordinate courts: first instance and first appeal criminal, administrative, and civil courts; justices of the peace or conciliatory judges

Political parties and leaders: San Marino Common good (includes Sammarinese Christian Democratic Party or PDCS [Marco GATTI], We Sammarinese or NS [Marco ARZILLI], Party of Socialists and Democrats or PSD [Paride ANDREOLI], Popular Alliance or AP [Gabriele GATTI])

Entente for the Country (Intesa per il Paese; includes Sammarinese Union of Moderates or USDM; dissolved after 2012 election, Socialist Party or PS [Alessandro BEVITORI], Union for the Republic or UPR [Marco PODESCHI)

Active Citizenship (includes Civic 10 [Mateo CIACCI], United Left or SU [Gastone PASOLINI])

Political pressure groups and leaders: NA

International organization participation: CE, FAO, IAEA, IBRD, ICAO, ICC (NGOs), ICCt, ICRM, IDA, IFRCS, ILO, IMF, IMO, Interpol, IOC, IOM (observer), IPU, ITU, ITUC (NGOs), LAIA (observer), OPCW, OSCE, Schengen Convention (de facto member), UN, UNCTAD, UNESCO, Union Latina, UNWTO, UPU, WHO, WIPO

Diplomatic representation in the US: *chief of mission:* Ambassador Paolo RONDELLI (since 16 July 2007)

chancery: 1711 N Street NW, 2nd floor, Washington, DC 20036

telephone: 202-250-1535

FAX: 202-223-2748

Diplomatic representation from the US: the US does not have an embassy in San Marino; the US Ambassador to Italy is accredited to San Marino

Flag description: two equal horizontal bands of white (top) and light blue with the National coat of arms superimposed in the center; the main colors derive from the shield of the coat of arms, which features three white towers on three peaks on a blue field; the towers represent three castles built on San Marino's highest feature, Mount Titano: Guaita, Cesta, and Montale; the coat of arms is flanked by a wreath, below a crown and above a scroll bearing the word LIBERTAS (Liberty); the white and blue colors are also said to stand for peace and liberty respectively

National symbol(s): three peaks each displaying a tower; National colors: white, blue

National anthem: *name:* "Inno Nazion ale della Repubblica" (National Anthem of the Republic)

lyrics/music: no lyrics/Federico CONSOLO

note: adopted 1894; the music for the lyric-less anthem is based on a 10th century chorale piece

ECONOMY

Economy—overview: San Marino's economy relies heavily on tourism, banking, and the manufacture and export of ceramics, clothing, fabrics, furniture, paints, spirits, tiles, and wine. The manufacturing and financial sectors account for more than half of San Marino's GDP. The per capita level of output and standard of living are comparable to those of the most prosperous regions of Italy.

San Marino's economy has been contracting since 2008, largely due to weakened demand from Italy-which accounts for nearly 90% of its export market—and financial sector consolidation. Difficulties in the banking sector, the recent global economic downturn, and the sizable decline in tax revenues have contributed to negative real GDP growth. The government has adopted measures to counter the downturn, including subsidized credit to businesses and is seeking to shift its growth model away from a reliance on bank and tax secrecy. San Marino does not issue public debt securities; when necessary, it finances deficits by drawing down central bank deposits.

The economy benefits from foreign investment due to its relatively low corporate taxes and low taxes on interest earnings. The income tax rate is also very low, about one-third the average EU level. San Marino continues to work towards harmonizing its fiscal laws with EU and International standards. in September 2009, the OECD removed San Marino from its list of tax havens that have yet to fully adopt global tax standards, and in 2010 San Marino signed Tax Information Exchange Agreements with most major countries. in 2013, the San Marino Government signed a Double Taxation agreement with Italy, but a referendum on EU membership failed to reach the quorum needed to bring it to a vote.

GDP (purchasing power parity): $1.982 billion (2015 est.)

$1.963 billion (2014 est.)

$1.982 billion (2013 est.)

note: data are in 2015 US dollars

country comparison to the world: 196

GDP (official exchange rate): $1.566 billion (2015 est.)

GDP—real growth rate: 1% (2015 est.) -1% (2014 est.)

-3% (2013 est.)

country comparison to the world: 174

GDP—per capita (PPP): $63,900 (2015 est.)

$63,300 (2014 est.)

$63,900 (2013 est.)

note: data are in 2015 US dollars

country comparison to the world: 15

GDP—composition, by end use:

household consumption: NA%

government consumption: NA%

investment in fixed capital: NA%

investments in inventories: NA%

exports of goods and services: 176.6%

imports of goods and services: -153.3% (2011)

GDP—composition, by sector of origin:

agriculture: 0.1%

industry: 39.2%

services: 60.7% (2009)

Agriculture—products: wheat, grapes, corn, olives; cattle, pigs, horses, beef, cheese, hides

Industries: tourism, banking, textiles, electronics, ceramics, cement, wine

Industrial production growth rate: -1.1% (2012 est.)

country comparison to the world: 174

Labor force: 21,960 (September 2013 est.)

country comparison to the world: 212

Labor force—by occupation: *agriculture:* 0.2%

industry: 33.5%

services: 66.3% (September 2013 est.)

Unemployment rate: 8.7% (2014 est.) 8.1% (2013 est.)

country comparison to the world: 103

Population below poverty line: NA%

Household income or consumption by percentage share: *lowest:* 10%: NA%

highest: 10%: NA%

Budget: *revenues:* $667.7 million

expenditures: $713.1 million (2011 est.)

Taxes and other revenues: 43.3% of GDP (2011 est.)

country comparison to the world: 29

Budget surplus (+) or deficit (–): -2.9% of GDP (2011 est.)

country comparison to the world: 108

Public debt: 25.8% of GDP (2013 est.)

20.3% of GDP (2012 est.)

country comparison to the world: 149

Fiscal year: calendar year

Inflation rate (consumer prices): 0.4% (2015 est.)

1.1% (2014 est.)

country comparison to the world: 60

Commercial bank prime lending rate: 5.92% (31 December 2011 est.)

5.38% (31 December 2010 est.)

country comparison to the world: 131

Stock of narrow money: $NA

$1.326 billion (31 December 2007)

Stock of broad money: $NA

$4.584 billion (31 December 2007)

Stock of domestic credit: $8.822 billion (30 September 2010)

$8.008 billion (31 December 2009)

country comparison to the world: 106

Market value of publicly traded shares: $NA

Exports: $3.827 billion (2011 est.)

$2.576 billion (2010 est.)

country comparison to the world: 121

Exports—commodities: building stone, lime, wood, chestnuts, wheat, wine, baked goods, hides, ceramics

Exports—partners: Italy 82.3% (2012 est.)

Imports: $2.551 billion (2011 est.)

$2.132 billion (2010 est.)

country comparison to the world: 154

Imports—commodities: wide variety of consumer manufactures, food, energy

Imports—partners: Italy 81.8% (2012 est.)

Reserves of foreign exchange and gold:

$392 million (2014 est.)

$539.3 million (2013 est.)

country comparison to the world: 155

Debt—external: $NA

Exchange rates: euros (EUR) per US dollar—

0.885 (2015 est.)

0.7525 (2014 est.)

0.7634 (2013 est.)

0.7752 2012 est.)

0.7185 (2011 est.)

COMMUNICATIONS

Telephones—fixed lines: *total subscriptions:* 18,600

subscriptions per 100 inhabitants: 57 (2014 est.)

country comparison to the world: 186

Telephones—mobile cellular: *total:* 37,600

subscriptions per 100 inhabitants: 115 (2014 est.)

country comparison to the world: 206

Telephone system: *general assessment:* automatic telephone system completely integrated into Italian system

domestic: combined fixed-line and mobile-cellular teledensity 170 telephones per 100 persons

International: country code—378; connected to Italian International network (2011)

Broadcast media: state-owned public broadcaster operates 1 TV station and 3 radio stations; receives radio and TV broadcasts from Italy (2012)

Radio broadcast stations: AM 0, FM 2, shortwave 0 (2008)

Television broadcast stations: 1 (San Marino residents also receive broadcasts from Italy) (1997)

Internet country code: .sm

Internet hosts: 11,015 (2012)

country comparison to the world: 133

Internet users: *total:* 17,200

percent of population: 52.6% (2014 est.)

country comparison to the world: 202

TRANSPORTATION

Roadways: *total:* 292 km

paved: 292 km (2006)

country comparison to the world: 206

MILITARY AND SECURITY

Military branches: no regular military forces; voluntary Military Corps (Corpi Militari) performs ceremonial duties and limited police support functions (2010)

Military service age and obligation: 18 is the legal minimum age for voluntary military service; no conscription; government has the authority to call up all San Marino citizens from 16–60 years of age to service in the military (2012)

Military—note: defense is the responsibility of Italy

TRANSNATIONAL ISSUES

Disputes—International: none

SAO TOME AND PRINCIPE

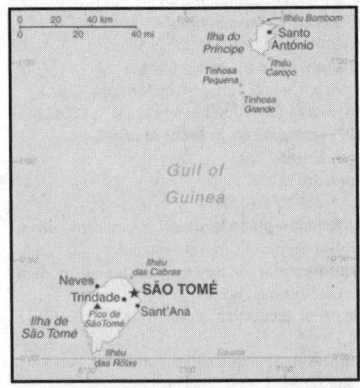

INTRODUCTION

Background: Discovered and claimed by Portugal in the late 15th century, the islands' sugar-based economy gave way to coffee and cocoa in the 19th century—all grown with African plantation slave labor, a form of which lingered into the 20th century. While independence was achieved in 1975, democratic reforms were not instituted until the late 1980s. The country held its first free elections in 1991, but frequent internal wrangling between the various political parties precipitated repeated changes in leadership and four failed, non-violent coup attempts in 1995, 1998, 2003, and 2009. In 2012, three opposition parties combined in a no confidence vote to bring down the majority government of former Prime Minister Patrice TROVOADA, but in 2014, legislative elections returned him to the office. New oil discoveries in the Gulf of Guinea may attract increased attention to the small island nation.

GEOGRAPHY

Location: Central Africa, islands in the Gulf of Guinea, just north of the Equator, west of Gabon

Geographic coordinates: 1 00 N, 7 00 E

Map references: Africa

Area: *total:* 964 sq km

land: 964 sq km

water: 0 sq km

country comparison to the world: 185

Area—comparative: more than five times the size of Washington, DC

Land boundaries: 0 km

Coastline: 209 km

Maritime claims: measured from claimed Archipelagic baselines territorial sea: 12 nm

exclusive economic zone: 200 nm

Climate: tropical; hot, humid; one rainy season (October to May)

Terrain: volcanic, mountainous

Elevation: *mean elevation:* NA

elevation extremes: *lowest point:* Atlantic Ocean 0 m

highest point: Pico de Sao Tome 2,024 m

Natural resources: fish, hydropower

Land use: *agricultural land:* 50.7%

arable land: 9.1%

permanent crops: 40.6%

permanent pasture: 1%

forest: 28.1%

other: 21.2% (2011 est.)

Irrigated land: 100 sq km (2012)

Natural hazards: NA

Environment—current issues: deforestation; soil erosion and exhaustion

Environment—International agreements: *party to:* Biodiversity, Climate Change, Climate Change-Kyoto Protocol, Desertification, Endangered Species, Environmental Modification, Law of the Sea, Ozone Layer Protection, Ship Pollution, Wetlands *signed, but not ratified:* none of the selected agreements

Geography—note: the smallest country in Africa; the two main islands form part of a chain of extinct volcanoes and both are mountainous

PEOPLE AND SOCIETY

Nationality: *noun:* Sao Tomean(s)
adjective: Sao Tomean

Ethnic groups: mestico, angolares (descendants of Angolan slaves), forros (descendants of freed slaves), servicais (contract laborers from Angola, Mozambique, and Cabo Verde), tongas (children of servicais born on the islands), Europeans (primarily Portuguese), Asians (mostly Chinese)

Languages: Portuguese 98.4% (official), Forro 36.2%, Cabo Verdian 8.5%, French 6.8%, Angolar 6.6%, English 4.9%, Lunguie 1%, other (including sign language) 2.4%

note: shares sum to more than 100% because some respondents gave more than one answer on the census (2012 est.)

Religions: Catholic 55.7%, Adventist 4.1%, Assembly of God 3.4%, New Apostolic 2.9%, Mana 2.3%, Universal Kingdom of God 2%, Jehovah's Witness 1.2%, other 6.2%, none 21.2%, unspecified 1% (2012 est.)

Population: 194,006 (July 2015 est.)
country comparison to the world: 186

Age structure: *0–14 years:* 43.04% (male 42,460/female 41,036)

15–24 years: 20.03% (male 19,692/female 19,159)
25–54 years: 30.47% (male 28,985/female 30,125)
55–64 years: 3.59% (male 3,173/female 3,787)
65 years and over: 2.88% (male 2,508/female 3,081) (2015 est.)

Dependency ratios: *total dependency ratio:* 84.2%

youth dependency ratio: 78.5%
elderly dependency ratio: 5.7%
potential support ratio: 17.6% (2015 est.)

Median age: *total:* 17.9 years
male: 17.5 years
female: 18.4 years (2015 est.)
country comparison to the world: 215

Population growth rate: 1.84% (2015 est.)
country comparison to the world: 61

Birth rate: 34.23 births/1,000 population (2015 est.)
country comparison to the world: 27

Death rate: 7.24 deaths/1,000 population (2015 est.)
country comparison to the world: 121

Net migration rate: -8.63 migrant(s)/1,000 population (2015 est.)
country comparison to the world: 212

Urbanization: *urban population:* 65.1% of total population (2015)

rate of urbanization: 3.58% annual rate of change (2010–15 est.)

Major urban areas—population: SAO TOME (capital) 71,000 (2014)

Sex ratio: *at birth:* 1.03 male(s)/female
0–14 years: 1.04 male(s)/female
15–24 years: 1.03 male(s)/female
25–54 years: 0.96 male(s)/female
55–64 years: 0.84 male(s)/female
65 years and over: 0.81 male(s)/female
total population: 1 male(s)/female (2015 est.)

Mother's mean age at first birth: 19.4
note: Median Age at first birth among women 25–29 (2008/09 est.)

Maternal mortality rate: 156 deaths/100,000 live births (2015 est.)
country comparison to the world: 88

Infant mortality rate: *total:* 47.88 deaths/1,000 live births
male: 49.85 deaths/1,000 live births
female: 45.85 deaths/1,000 live births (2015 est.)
country comparison to the world: 41

Life expectancy at birth: *total population:* 64.58 years
male: 63.27 years
female: 65.92 years (2015 est.)
country comparison to the world: 178

Total fertility rate: 4.54 children born/woman (2015 est.)
country comparison to the world: 26

Contraceptive prevalence rate: 38.4% (2008/09)

Health expenditures: 6.9% of GDP (2013)
country comparison to the world: 60

Hospital bed density: 2.9 beds/1,000 population (2011)

Drinking water source:
improved:
urban: 98.9% of population
rural: 93.6% of population
total: 97.1% of population
unimproved:
urban: 1.1% of population
rural: 6.4% of population
total: 2.9% of population (2015 est.)

Sanitation facility access:
improved:
urban: 40.8% of population
rural: 23.3% of population
total: 34.7% of population
unimproved:
urban: 59.2% of population
rural: 76.7% of population
total: 65.3% of population (2015 est.)

HIV/AIDS—adult prevalence rate: 0.78% (2014 est.)
country comparison to the world: 52

HIV/AIDS—people living with HIV/AIDS: 1,000 (2014 est.)
country comparison to the world: 119

HIV/AIDS—deaths: 100 (2014 est.)
country comparison to the world: 129

Major infectious diseases: *degree of risk:* high *food or waterborne diseases:* bacterial diarrhea, hepatitis A, and typhoid fever
vectorborne diseases: malaria and dengue fever
water contact disease: schistosomiasis (2013)

Obesity—adult prevalence rate: 10.6% (2014)
country comparison to the world: 132

Children under the age of 5 years underweight: 8.8% (2014)
country comparison to the world: 50

Education expenditures: 3.9% of GDP (2014)
country comparison to the world: 6

Literacy: *definition:* age 15 and over can read and write
total population: 74.9%
male: 81.8%
female: 68.4% (2015 est.)

School life expectancy (primary to tertiary education): *total:* 13 years
male: 13 years
female: 13 years (2015)

Child labor—children ages 5–14: *total number:* 3,235
percentage: 8% (2006 est.)

GOVERNMENT

Country name: *conventional long form:* Democratic Republic of Sao Tome and Principe
conventional short form: Sao Tome and Principe
local long form: Republica Democratica de Sao Tomee Principe
local short form: Sao Tomee Principe
etymology: Sao Tome was named after Saint THOMAS the Apostle by the Portuguese who discovered the island on 21 December 1470 (or 1471), the saint's feast day; Principe is a shortening of the original Portuguese name of "Ilha do Principe" (Isle of the Prince) referring to the Prince of Portugal to whom duties on the island's sugar crop were paid

Government type: semi-presidential republic

Capital: *name:* Sao Tome

Geographic coordinates: 0 20 N, 6 44 E
time difference: UTC 0 (5 hours ahead of Washington, DC, during Standard Time)

Administrative divisions: 2 provinces; Principe, Sao Tome

Independence: 12 July 1975 (from Portugal)

National holiday: Independence Day, 12 July (1975)

Constitution: approved 5 November 1975; revised several times, last in 2006 (2016)

Legal system: mixed legal system of civil law base on the Portuguese model and customary law

International law organization participation: has not submitted an ICJ jurisdiction declaration; non-party state to the ICCt

Citizenship: *citizenship by birth:* no
citizenship by descent only: at least one parent must be a citizen of Sao Tome and Principe
dual citizenship recognized: no
residency requirement for naturalization: 5 years

Suffrage: 18 years of age; universal

Executive branch: *chief of state:* President Manuel Pinto DA COSTA (since 3 September 2011)

head of government: Prime Minister Patrice Emery TROVOADA (since 29 November 2014)
cabinet: Council of Ministers proposed by the prime minister, appointed by the president

elections/appointments: president directly elected by absolute majority popular vote in 2 rounds if needed for a 5-year term (eligible for a second term); election last held on 17 July and 7 August 2011 (next to be held on 17 July 2016); prime minister chosen by the National Assembly and approved by the president

election results: Manuel Pinto DA COSTA elected president in runoff; percent of vote—Manuel Pinto DA COSTA (independent) 52.9%, Evaristo CARVALHO (ADI) 47.1%

Legislative branch: *description:* unicameral National Assembly or Assembleia Nacional (55 seats; members directly elected in multi-seat constituencies by proportional representation vote to serve 4-year terms)

elections: last held on 12 October 2014 (next expected in October 2018)

election results: percent of vote by party—NA; seats by party—ADI 33, MLSTP-PSD 16, PCD-GR 5, other 1

Judicial branch: *highest court(s):* Supreme Court (consists of 5 judges); Constitutional Court (consists of 5 judges, 3 of which are from the Supreme Court)

judge selection and term of office: Supreme Court judges appointed by the National Assembly; judge tenure NA; Constitutional Court judges nominated by the president of the republic and elected by the National Assembly for 5-year terms

subordinate courts: Court of First Instance; Audit Court

Political parties and leaders: Democratic Movement of Forces for Change or MDFM [Fradique Bandeira Melo DE MENEZES]

Independent Democratic Action or ADI [Patrice TROVOADA]

Movement for the Liberation of Sao Tome and Principe-Social Democratic Party or MLSTP-PSD [Aurelio MARTINS]

Party for Democratic Convergence or PCD [Leonel Mario D'ALVA] other small parties

Political pressure groups and leaders: Association of Sao Tome and Principe NGOs or FONG

other: the media

International organization participation: ACP, AfDB, AOSIS, AU, CD, CEMAC, CPLP, EITI (candidate country), FAO, G-77, IBRD, ICAO, ICRM, IDA, IFAD, IFC, IFRCS, ILO, IMF, IMO, Interpol, IOC, IOM (observer), IPU, ITU, ITUC (NGOs), MIGA, NAM, OIF, OPCW, PCA, UN, UNCTAD, UNESCO, UNIDO, Union Latina, UNWTO, UPU, WCO, WHO, WIPO, WMO, WTO (observer)

Diplomatic representation in the US: *chief of mission:* Ambassador Carlos Filomeno Azevedo Agostinho das NEVES (since 3 December 2013)

chancery: 675 Third Avenue, Suite 1807, New York, NY 10017

telephone: [1] (212) 651-8116

FAX: [1] (212) 651-8117

Diplomatic representation from the US: the US does not have an embassy in Sao Tome and Principe; the US Ambassador to Gabon is accredited to Sao Tome and Principe on a nonresident basis and makes periodic visits to the islands

Flag description: three horizontal bands of green (top), yellow (double width), and green with two black five-pointed stars placed side by side in the center of the yellow band and a red isosceles triangle based on the hoist side; green stands for the country's rich vegetation, red recalls the struggle for independence, and yellow represents cocoa, one of the country's main agricultural products; the two stars symbolize the two main islands

note: uses the popular Pan-African colors of Ethiopia

National symbol(s): palm tree; National colors: green, yellow, red, black

National anthem: *name:* "Independencia total" (Total Independence)

lyrics/music: Alda Neves DA GRACA do Espirito Santo/Manuel dos Santos Barreto de Sousae ALMEIDA

note: adopted 1975

ECONOMY

Economy—overview: This small, poor island economy has become increasingly dependent on cocoa since independence in 1975. Cocoa production has substantially declined in recent years because of drought and mismanagement. Sao Tome and Principe has to import fuels, most manufactured goods, consumer goods, and food, making it vulnerable to fluctuations in global commodity prices. Maintaining control of inflation, fiscal discipline, and increasing flows of foreign direct investment into the oil sector are major economic problems facing the country. The government also has attempted to reduce price controls and subsidies. Over the years, Sao Tome and Principe has had difficulty servicing its external debt and has relied heavily on concessional aid and debt rescheduling. It benefited from $200 million in debt relief in December 2000 under the Highly Indebted Poor Countries program, which helped bring down the country's $300 million debt burden. in August 2005, the government signed on to a new 3-year IMF Poverty Reduction and Growth Facility program worth $4.3 million. In April 2011, the country completed a Threshold Country Program with The Millennium Challenge Corporation to help increase tax revenues, reform customs, and improve the business environment.

Considerable potential exists for development of a tourist industry, and the government has taken steps to expand facilities in recent years. Potential also exists for the development of petroleum resources in Sao Tome and Principe's territorial waters in the oil-rich Gulf of Guinea, which are being jointly developed in a 60–40 split with Nigeria, but any actual production is at least several years off. The first production licenses were sold in 2004, though a dispute over licensing with Nigeria delayed the country's receipt of more than $20 million in signing bonuses for almost a year.

GDP (purchasing power parity): $658 million (2015 est.)

$632.7 million (2014 est.)

$605.4 million (2013 est.)

note: data are in 2015 US dollars

country comparison to the world: 210

GDP (official exchange rate): $318 million (2015 est.)

GDP—real growth rate: 4% (2015 est.)

4.5% (2014 est.)

4% (2013 est.)

country comparison to the world: 66

GDP—per capita (PPP): $3,200 (2015 est.)

$3,200 (2014 est.)

$3,100 (2013 est.)

note: data are in 2015 US dollars

country comparison to the world: 184

Gross National saving: 15% of GDP (2015 est.)

-1.8% of GDP (2014 est.)

8.1% of GDP (2013 est.)

country comparison to the world: 116

GDP—composition, by end use:

household consumption: 85%

government consumption: 13.2%

investment in fixed capital: 48.4%

investment in inventories: -0.1%

exports of goods and services: 12.3%

imports of goods and services: -58.8% (2015 est.)

GDP—composition, by sector of origin:

agriculture: 18.4%

industry: 16%

services: 65.6% (2012 est.)

Agriculture—products: cocoa, coconuts, palm kernels, copra, cinnamon, pepper, coffee, bananas, papayas, beans; poultry; fish

Industries: light construction, textiles, soap, beer, fish processing, timber

Industrial production growth rate: 4.3% (2015 est.)

country comparison to the world: 47

Labor force: 68,640 (2015 est.)

country comparison to the world: 187

Labor force—by occupation: *note:* population mainly engaged in subsistence agriculture and fishing; shortages of skilled workers

Unemployment rate: 13.5% (2014 est.)

13.7% (2013 est.)

country comparison to the world: 144

Population below poverty line: 66.2% (2009 est.)

Household income or consumption by percentage share: *lowest:* 10%: NA%

highest: 10%: NA%

Budget: *revenues:* $84.33 million

expenditures: $101.3 million (2015 est.)

Taxes and other revenues: 25.9% of GDP (2015 est.)

country comparison to the world: 113

Budget surplus (+) or deficit (–): -5.2% of GDP (2015 est.)

country comparison to the world: 173

Public debt: 93.9% of GDP (2015 est.)

69.6% of GDP (2014 est.)

country comparison to the world: 22

Fiscal year: calendar year

Inflation rate (consumer prices): 5.3% (2015 est.)

7% (2014 est.)

country comparison to the world: 177

Central bank discount rate: 16% (31 December 2009)

28% (31 December 2008)

country comparison to the world: 10

Commercial bank prime lending rate: 15% (31 December 2015 est.)

16% (31 December 2014 est.)
country comparison to the world: 40
Stock of narrow money: $62.19 million (31 December 2015 est.)
$54.91 million (31 December 2014 est.)
country comparison to the world: 189
Stock of broad money: $133.1 million (31 December 2014 est.)
$120.8 million (31 December 2013 est.)
country comparison to the world: 192
Stock of domestic credit: $74.86 million (31 December 2015 est.)
$80.91 million (31 December 2014 est.)
country comparison to the world: 184
Market value of publicly traded shares: $NA
Current account balance: -$36 million (2015 est.)
-$93 million (2014 est.)
country comparison to the world: 62
Exports: $18.1 million (2015 est.)
$17.4 million (2014 est.)
country comparison to the world: 213
Exports—commodities: cocoa 80%, copra, coffee, palm oil (2010 est.)
Exports—partners: Netherlands 29.2%, Belgium 22.4%, Spain 15.5%, US 6.6%, Nigeria 5.1% (2015)
Imports: $138.7 million (2015 est.)
$145.6 million (2014 est.)
country comparison to the world: 212
Imports—commodities: machinery and electrical equipment, food products, petroleum Products
Imports—partners: Portugal 65.1%, China 8%, Gabon 7.3% (2015)
Reserves of foreign exchange and gold: $64.1 million (31 December 2015 est.) $63.52 million (31 December 2014 est.)
country comparison to the world: 168
Debt—external: $234.1 million (31 December 2014 est.) $214.4 million (31 December 2013 est.)
country comparison to the world: 188
Exchange rates: dobras (STD) per US dollar—
21,681 (2015 est.)
18,466 (2014 est.)
18,466 (2013 est.)
19,068 (2012 est.)
17,623 (2011 est.)

ENERGY

Electricity—production: 65 million kWh (2012 est.)
country comparison to the world: 204
Electricity—consumption: 60.45 million kWh (2012 est.)
country comparison to the world: 203
Electricity—exports: 0 kWh (2013)
country comparison to the world: 205
Electricity—imports: 0 kWh (2013 est.)
country comparison to the world: 209
Electricity—installed generating capacity: 16,000 kW (2012 est.)
country comparison to the world: 205
Electricity—from fossil fuels: 75% of total installed capacity (2012 est.)
country comparison to the world: 100
Electricity—from nuclear fuels: 0% of total installed capacity (2012 est.)

country comparison to the world: 192
Electricity—from hydroelectric plants: 25% of total installed capacity (2012 est.)
country comparison to the world: 86
Electricity—from other renewable sources: 0% of total installed capacity (2012 est.)
country comparison to the world: 134
Crude oil—production: 0 bbl/day (2014 est.)
country comparison to the world: 199
Crude oil—exports: 0 bbl/day (2012 est.)
country comparison to the world: 198
Crude oil—imports: 0 bbl/day (2012 est.)
country comparison to the world: 135
Crude oil—proved reserves: 0 bbl (1 January 2010 est.)
country comparison to the world: 200
Refined petroleum products—production: 0 bbl/day (2012 est.)
country comparison to the world: 137
Refined petroleum products—consumption: 900 bbl/day (2013 est.)
country comparison to the world: 203
Refined petroleum products—exports: 0 bbl/day (2012 est.)
country comparison to the world: 138
Refined petroleum products—imports: 905.6 bbl/day (2012 est.)
country comparison to the world: 199
Natural gas—production: 0 cu m (2013 est.)
country comparison to the world: 137
Natural gas—consumption: 0 cu m (2013 est.)
country comparison to the world: 201
Natural gas—exports: 0 cu m (2013 est.)
country comparison to the world: 194
Natural gas—imports: 0 cu m (2013 est.)
country comparison to the world: 142
Natural gas—proved reserves: 0 cu m (1 January 2014 est.)
country comparison to the world: 201
Carbon dioxide emissions from consumption of energy: 137,800 Mt (2012 est.)
country comparison to the world: 205

COMMUNICATIONS

Telephone—fixed lines: *total subscriptions:* 6,800
subscriptions per 100 inhabitants: 4 (2014 est.)
country comparison to the world: 205
Telephones—mobile cellular: *total:* 128,500
subscriptions per 100 inhabitants: 67 (2014 est.)
country comparison to the world: 187
Telephone system: *general assessment:* local telephone network of adequate quality with most lines connected to digital switches
domestic: combined fixed-line and mobile-cellular teledensity roughly 65 telephones per 100 persons
international: country code—239; satellite earth station—1 intelsat (Atlantic Ocean) (2010)
Broadcast media: 1 government-owned TV station; 1 government-owned radio station; 3 independent local radio stations authorized in 2005 with 2 operating at the end of 2006; transmissions of multiple International broadcasters are available (2007)
Radio broadcast stations: AM 1, FM 5, shortwave 1 (2001)
Television broadcast stations: 2 (2001)

Internet country code: .st
Internet hosts: 1,678 (2012)
country comparison to the world: 165
Internet users: *total:* 47,000
percent of population: 24.7% (2014 est.)
country comparison to the world: 186

TRANSPORTATION

Airports: 2 (2013)
country comparison to the world: 206
Airports—with paved runways: *total:* 2
1,524 to 2,437 m: 1
914 to 1,523 m: 1 (2013)
Roadways: *total:* 320 km
paved: 218 km
unpaved: 102 km (2000)
country comparison to the world: 204
Merchant marine: *total:* 3
by type: bulk carrier 1, cargo 2
foreign-owned: 2 (China 1, Greece 1) (2010)
country comparison to the world: 138
Ports and terminals: *major seaport(s):* Sao Tome

MILITARY AND SECURITY

Military branches: Armed Forces of Sao Tome and Principe (Forcas Armadas de Sao Tome e Principe, FASTP): Army, Coast Guard of Sao Tome e Principe (Guarda Costeira de Sao Tome e Principe, GCSTP; also called "Navy"), Presidential Guard, National Guard (2015)
Military service age and obligation: 18 is the legal minimum age for compulsory military service; 17 is the legal minimum age for voluntary service (2012)
Military—note: Sao Tome and Principe's army is a tiny force with almost no resources at its disposal and would be wholly ineffective operating unilaterally; infantry equipment is considered simple to operate and maintain but may require refurbishment or replacement after 25 years in tropical climates; poor pay, working conditions, and alleged nepotism in the promotion of officers have been problems in the past, as reflected in the 1995 and 2003 coups; these issues are being addressed with foreig assistance aimed at improving the army and its focus on realistic security concerns; command is exercised from the president, through the Minister of Defense, to the Chief of the Armed Forces (infantry, technical issues) and the Chief of the General Staff (logistics, administration, finances) (2012)

TRANSNATIONAL ISSUES

Disputes—International: none

SAUDI ARABIA

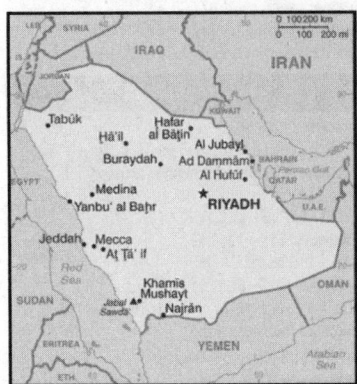

INTRODUCTION

Background: Saudi Arabia is the birthplace of Islam and home to Islam's two holiest shrines in Mecca and Medina. The king's official title is the Custodian of the Two Holy Mosques. The modern Saudi state was founded in 1932 by ABDAL-AZIZ BIN Abdal-Rahman AL SAUD (Ibn Saud) after a 30-year campaign to unify most of the Arabian Peninsula. One of his male descendants rules the country today, as required by the country's 1992 Basic Law. Following Iraq's invasion of Kuwait in 1990, Saudi Arabia accepted the Kuwaiti royal family and 400,000 refugees while allowing Western and Arab troops to deploy on its soil for the liberation of Kuwait the following year. The continuing presence of foreign troops on Saudi soil after the liberation of Kuwait became a source of tension between the royal family and the public until all operation al US troops left the country in 2003. Major terrorist attacks in May and November 2003 spurred a strong ongoing campaign against domestic terrorism and extremism.

From 2005 to 2015, King ABDALLAH incrementally modernized the Kingdom. Driven by person al ideology and political pragmatism, he introduced a series of social and economic initiatives, including expanding employment and social opportunities for women, attracting foreign investment, increasing the role of the private sector in the economy, and discouraging businesses from hiring foreign workers. Saudi Arabia saw protests during the 2011 Arab Spring among Shia Muslims in the Eastern Province, who protested primarily against the detention of political prisoners, endemic discrimination, and Bahraini and Saudi Government actions in Bahrain. Riyadh took a cautious but firm approach by arresting some protesters but releasing most of them quickly and by using its state-sponsored clerics to counter political and Islamist activism. in addition, protests were met by a strong police presence, with some arrests, but not the level of bloodshed seen in protests elsewhere in the region.

The government held its first-ever elections in 2005 and 2011, when Saudis went to the polls to elect municipal councilors. in December 2015, women were allowed to vote and stand as candidates for the first time in municipal council elections, with 21 women winning seats. King SALMAN BIN Abd al-Aziz Al Saud ascended to the throne in 2015 and placed the first next-generation prince, MUHAMMAD BIN NAIF BIN Abd al-Aziz Al Saud, in the line of succession as Crown Prince. He designated his son, MUHAMMAD BIN SALMAN BIN Abd al-Aziz Al Saud, as the Deputy Crown Prince. In March 2015, Saudi Arabia led a coalition of 10 countries in a military campaign to restore the government of Yemen, which had been ousted by Huthi forces allied with former president ALI ABDULLAH al-Salih. The war in Yemen has led to civilian casualties and shortages of basic supplies, which has drawn considerable International criticism. in December 2015, Deputy Crown Prince MUHAMMAD BIN SALMAN announced Saudi Arabia would lead a 34-nation Islamic Coalition to fight terrorism. In January 2016, Saudi Arabia executed 47 people on charges of terrorism, including Shia Muslim cleric NIMR al-Nimr. Iranian protesters overran Saudi diplomatic facilities in Iran to protest al-NIMR's execution and the Saudi government responded by cutting off diplomatic ties with Iran.

GEOGRAPHY

Location: Middle East, bordering the Persian Gulf and the Red Sea, north of Yemen

Geographic coordinates: 25 00 N, 45 00 E

Map references: Middle East

Area: *total:* 2,149,690 sq km
land: 2,149,690 sq km
water: 0 sq km
country comparison to the world: 13

Area—comparative: slightly more than one-fifth the size of the US

Land boundaries: *total:* 4,272 km
border countries (7): Iraq 811 km, Jordan 731 km, Kuwait 221 km, Oman 658 km, Qatar 87 km, UAE 457 km, Yemen 1,307 km

Coastline: 2,640 km

Maritime claims: *territorial sea:* 12 nm
contiguous zone: 18 nm
continental shelf: not specified

Climate: harsh, dry desert with great temperature extremes

Terrain: mostly sandy desert

Elevation: *mean elevation:* 665 m

elevation extremes: *lowest point:* Persian Gulf 0 m
highest point: Jabal Sawda' 3,133 m

Natural resources: petroleum, Natural gas, iron ore, gold, copper

Land use: *agricultural land:* 80.7%
arable land: 1.5%
permanent crops: 0.1%

permanent pasture: 79.1%
forest: 0.5%
other: 18.8% (2011 est.)

Irrigated land: 16,200 sq km (2012)

Total renewable water resources: 2.4 cu km (2011)

Freshwater withdrawal (domestic/industrial/agricultural): *total:* 23.67 cu km/yr (9%/3%/88%)
per capita: 928.1 cu m/yr (2006)

Natural hazards: frequent sand and dust storms
volcanism: despite many volcanic formations, there has been little activity in the past few centuries; volcanoes include Harrat Rahat, Harrat Khaybar, Harrat Lunayyir, and Jabal Yar

Environment—current issues: desertification; depletion of underground water resources; the lack of perennial rivers or permanent water bodies has prompted the development of extensive seawater desalination facilities; coastal pollution from oil spills

Environment—International agreements: *party to:* Biodiversity, Climate Change, Climate Change-Kyoto Protocol, Desertification, Endangered Species, Hazardous Wastes, Law of the Sea, Marine Dumping, Ozone Layer Protection, Ship Pollution
signed, but not ratified: none of the selected agreements

Geography—note: Saudi Arabia is the largest country in the world without a river; extensive coastlines on the Persian Gulf and Red Sea provide great leverage on shipping (especially crude oil) through the Persian Gulf and Suez Canal

PEOPLE AND SOCIETY

Nationality: *noun:* Saudi(s)
adjective: Saudi or Saudi Arabian

Ethnic groups: Arab 90%, Afro-Asian 10%

Languages: Arabic (official)

Religions: Muslim (official; citizens are 85–90% Sunni and 10–15% Shia), other (includes Eastern Orthodox, Protestant, Roman Catholic, Jewish, Hindu, Buddhist, and Sikh) (2012 est.)
note: despite having a large expatriate community of various faiths (more than 30% of the population), most forms of public religious expression inconsistent with the government-sanctioned interpretation of Sunni Islam are restricted; non-Muslims are not allowed to have Saudi citizenship and non-Muslim places of worship are not permitted (2013)

Population: 27,752,316 (July 2015 est.)
note: immigrants make up more than 30% of the total population, according to UN data (2015)
country comparison to the world: 47

Age structure: *0–14 years:* 27.07% (male 3,850,992/female 3,661,194)
15–24 years: 19.11% (male 2,839,161/female 2,463,216)
25–54 years: 45.9% (male 7,244,386/female 5,495,284)
55–64 years: 4.68% (male 710,827/female 587,281)

65 years and over: 3.24% (male 460,209/female 439,766) (2015 est.)

Dependency ratios: *total dependency ratio:* 45.9%

youth dependency ratio: 41.7%
elderly dependency ratio: 4.2%
potential support ratio: 24% (2015 est.)

Median age: *total:* 26.8 years
male: 27.6 years
female: 25.8 years (2015 est.)
country comparison to the world: 143

Population growth rate: 1.46% (2015 est.)
country comparison to the world: 81

Birth rate: 18.51 births/1,000 population (2015 est.)
country comparison to the world: 94

Death rate: 3.33 deaths/1,000 population (2015 est.)
country comparison to the world: 219

Net migration rate: -0.55 migrant(s)/1,000 population (2015 est.)
country comparison to the world: 137

Urbanization: *urban population:* 83.1% of total population (2015)
rate of urbanization: 2.1% annual rate of change (2010–15 est.)

Major urban areas—population: RIYADH (capital) 6.195 million; Jeddah 4.076 million; 1.064 million (2015)

Sex ratio: *at birth:* 1.05 male(s)/female
0–14 years: 1.05 male(s)/female
15–24 years: 1.15 male(s)/female
25–54 years: 1.32 male(s)/female
55–64 years: 1.21 male(s)/female
65 years and over: 1.05 male(s)/female
total population: 1.19 male(s)/female (2015 est.)

Maternal mortality rate: 12 deaths/100,000 live births (2015 est.)
country comparison to the world: 133

Infant mortality rate: *total:* 14.09 deaths/1,000 live births
male: 16.16 deaths/1,000 live births
female: 11.9 deaths/1,000 live births (2015 est.)
country comparison to the world: 108

Life expectancy at birth: *total population:* 75.05 years
male: 73 years
female: 77.2 years (2015 est.)
country comparison to the world: 108

Total fertility rate: 2.12 children born/woman (2015 est.)
country comparison to the world: 105

Contraceptive prevalence rate: 23.8% (2007)
Health expenditures: 3.2% of GDP (2013)
country comparison to the world: 178

Physicians density: 2.49 physicians/1,000 population (2012)

Hospital bed density: 2.1 beds/1,000 population (2012)

Drinking water source:
improved:
urban: 97% of population
rural: 97% of population
total: 97% of population
unimproved:
urban: 3% of population

rural: 3% of population
total: 3% of population (2015 est.)

Sanitation facility access:
improved:
urban: 100% of population
rural: 100% of population
total: 100% of population
unimproved:
urban: 0% of population
rural: 0% of population
total: 0% of population (2015 est.)

HIV/AIDS—adult prevalence rate: NA
HIV/AIDS—people living with HIV/AIDS: NA
HIV/AIDS—deaths: NA
Mecca 1.771 million; Medina 1.28 million; Ad Dammam

Obesity—adult prevalence rate: 33.7% (2014)
country comparison to the world: 19

Children under the age of 5 years underweight: 5.3% (2005)
country comparison to the world: 88

Education expenditures: 5.1% of GDP (2008)
country comparison to the world: 68

Literacy: *definition:* age 15 and over can read and write
total population: 94.7%
male: 97%
female: 91.1% (2015 est.)

School life expectancy (primary to tertiary education): *total:* 16 years
male: 17 years
female: 15 years (2014)

Unemployment, youth ages 15–24: *total:* 29.5%
male: 21.1%
female: 55.3% (2013 est.)
country comparison to the world: 29

GOVERNMENT

Country name: *conventional long form:* Kingdom of Saudi Arabia
conventional short form: Saudi Arabia
local long form: Al Mamlakah al Arabiyah as Suudiyah
local short form: Al Arabiyah as Suudiyah
etymology: named after the ruling dynasty of the country, the House of Saud; the name "Arabia" can be traced back many centuries B.C., the ancient Egyptians referred to the region as "Ar Rabi"

Government type: absolute monarchy
Capital: *name:* Riyadh

Geographic coordinates: 24 39 N, 46 42 E
time difference: UTC+3 (8 hours ahead of Washington, DC, during Standard Time)

Administrative divisions: 13 provinces (mintaqat, singular—mintaqah); Al Bahah, Al Hududash Shamaliyah (Northern Border), Al Jawf, Al Madinah (Medina), Al Qasim, Ar Riyad (Riyadh), Ash Sharqiyah (Eastern),'Asir, Ha'il, Jazan, Makkah (Mecca), Najran, Tabuk

Independence: 23 September 1932 (unification of the kingdom)

National holiday: Unification of the Kingdom, 23 September (1932)

Constitution: 1 March 1992—Basic Law of Government, issued by royal decree, serves as the constitutional framework and is based on the Qur'an and the life and tradition of the Prophet Muhammad

Legal system: Islamic (sharia) legal system with some elements of Egyptian, French, and customary law; note—several secular codes have been introduced; commercial disputes handled by special committees

International law organization participation: has not submitted an ICJ jurisdiction declaration; non-party state to the ICCt

Citizenship: *citizenship by birth:* no
citizenship by descent only: the father must be a citizen of Saudi Arabia; a child born out of wedlock in Saudi Arabia to a Saudi mother and unknown father
dual citizenship recognized: no
residency requirement for naturalization: 5 years

Suffrage: 21 years of age; male; male and female for municipal elections

Executive branch: *chief of state:* King and Prime Minister SALMAN BIN Abd al-Aziz Al Saud (since 23 January 2015); Crown Prince and Deputy Prime Minister MUHAMMAD BIN NAYIF BIN Abd al-Aziz Al Saud (born 30 August 1959); Deputy Crown Prince and Second Deputy Prime Minister MUHAMMAD BIN SALMAN BIN Abdal-Aziz Al Saud (born 31 August 1985); note—the monarch is both chief of state and head of government

head of government: King and Prime Minister SALMAN BIN Abd al-Aziz Al Saud (since 23 January 2015); Crown Prince and Deputy Prime Minister MUHAMMAD BIN NAYIF BIN Abd al-Aziz Al Saud (born 30 August 1959); Crown Prince and Second Deputy Prime Minister MUHAMMAD BIN SALMAN BIN Abd al-Aziz Al Saud (born 31 August 1985)

cabinet: Council of Ministers appointed by the monarch every 4 years and includes many royal family members
elections/appointments: none; the monarchy is hereditary; note—an Allegiance Council created by royal decree in October 2006 established a committee of Saudi princes to a role in selecting future Saudi kings

Legislative branch: *description:* unicameral Consultative Council or Majlisal-Shura (150 seats; members appointed by the monarch to serve 4-year terms); note—in early 2013, the monarch granted women 30 seats on the Council

Judicial branch: *highest court(s):* High Court (consists of the court chief and organized into circuits with 3-judge panels except the criminal circuit which has a 5-judge panel for cases involving major punishments)
judge selection and term of office: the High Court chief and chiefs of the High Court Circuits appointed by royal decree following the recommendation of the Supreme Judiciary Council, a 10-member body of high level judges and other judicial heads; new judges and assistant judges

serve 1—and 2-year probations, respectively, before permanent assignment

subordinate courts: Court of Appeals; Specialized Criminal Court, first-degree courts composed of general, criminal, person al status, and commercial courts, and the Labor Court; hierarchy of administrative courts

Political parties and leaders: none

Political pressure groups and leaders:
other: gas companies; religious groups

International organization participation: ABEDA, AfDB (nonRegional member), AFESD, AMF, BIS, CAEU, CP, FAO, G-20, G-77, GCC, IAEA, IBRD, ICAO, ICC (National committees), ICRM, IDA, IDB, IFAD, IFC, IFRCS, IHO, ILO, IMF, IMO, IMSO, Interpol, IOC, IOM (observer), IPU, ISO, ITSO, ITU, LAS, MIGA, NAM, OAPEC, OAS (observer), OIC, OPCW, OPEC, PCA, UN, UNCTAD, UNESCO, UNIDO, UNRWA, UNWTO, UPU, WCO, WFTU (NGOs), WHO, WIPO, WMO, WTO

Diplomatic representation in the US: *chief of mission:* Ambassador ABDALLAH BIN Faysal BIN Turki BIN Abdallah Al Saud (since 28 January 2016)

chancery: 601 New Hampshire Avenue NW, Washington, DC 20037

telephone: [1] (202) 342-3800

FAX: [1] (202) 944-3113

consulate(s) general: Houston, Los Angeles, New York

Diplomatic representation from the US: *chief of mission:* Ambassador Joseph William WEST-PHAL (since 26 March 2014)

embassy: Collector Road M, Diplomatic Quarter, Riyadh

mailing address: American Embassy, Unit 61307, APO AE 09803-1307; International Mail: P.O. Box 94309, Riyadh 11693

telephone: [966] (1) 488-3800

FAX: [966] (1) 488-7360

consulate(s) general: Dhahran, Jiddah (Jeddah)

Flag description: green, a traditional color in Islamic flags, with the Shahada or Muslim creed in large white Arabic script (translated as "There is no god but God; Muhammad is the Messenger of God") above a white horizontal saber (the tip points to the hoist side); design dates to the early twentieth century and is closely associated with the Al Saud family which established the kingdom in 1932; the flag is manufactured with differing obverse and reverse sides so that the Shahada reads—and the sword points—correctly from right to left on both sides

note: the only National flag to display an inscription as its principal design; one of only three National flags that differ on their obverse and reverse sides—the others are Moldova and Paraguay

National symbol(s): palm tree surmounting two crossed swords; National colors: green, white

National anthem: *name:* "Aash Al Maleek" (Long Live Our Beloved King)

lyrics/music: Ibrahim KHAFAJI/Abdul Rahma-NAI-KH ATEEB

note: music adopted 1947, lyrics adopted 1984

ECONOMY

Economy—overview: Saudi Arabia has an oil-based economy with strong government controls over major economic activities. It possesses about 16% of the world's proven petroleum reserves, ranks as the largest exporter of petroleum, and plays a leading role in OPEC. The petroleum sector accounts for roughly 87% of budget revenues, 42% of GDP, and 90% of export earnings.

Saudi Arabia is encouraging the growth of the private sector in order to diversify its economy and to employ more Saudi Nationals. Over 6 million foreign workers play an important role in the Saudi economy, particularly in the oil and service sectors; at the same time, however, Riyadh is struggling to reduce unemployment among its own Nationals. Saudi officials are particularly focused on employing its large youth population, which generally lacks the education and technical skills the private sector needs. In 2015, the Kingdom incurred a budget deficit estimated at 13% of GDP, and it faces a deficit of $87 billion in 2016, which will be financed by bond sales and drawing down reserves. Although the Kingdom can finance high deficits for several years by drawing down its considerable foreign assets or by borrowing, it has announced plans to cut capital spending in 2016. Some of these plans to cut deficits include introducing a value-added tax and reducing subsidies on electricity, water, and petroleum Products. In January 2016, Crown Prince and Deputy Prime Minister MUHAMMAD BIN SALMAN announced that Saudi Arabia intends to list shares of its state-owned petroleum company, ARAMCO—another move to increase revenue and outside investment. The government has also looked at privatization and diversification of the economy more closely in the wake of a diminished oil market. Historically, Saudi Arabia has focused diversification efforts on power generation, telecommunications, Natural gas exploration, and petrochemical sectors. More recently, the government has approached investors about expanding the role of the private sector in the healthcare, education and tourism industries. While Saudi Arabia has emphasized their goals of diversification for some time, current low oil prices may force the government to make more drastic changes ahead of their long-run timeline.

GDP (purchasing power parity): $1.683 trillion (2015 est.)

$1.628 trillion (2014 est.)

$1.571 trillion (2013 est.)

note: data are in 2015 US dollars

country comparison to the world: 15

GDP (official exchange rate): $653.2 billion (2015 est.)

GDP—real growth rate: 3.4% (2015 est.)

3.6% (2014 est.)

2.7% (2013 est.)

country comparison to the world: 87

GDP—per capita (PPP): $53,600 (2015 est.)

$52,900 (2014 est.)

$52,400 (2013 est.)

note: data are in 2015 US dollars

country comparison to the world: 22

Gross National saving: 21.2% of GDP (2015 est.)

38.3% of GDP (2014 est.)

44.4% of GDP (2013 est.)

country comparison to the world: 75

GDP—composition, by end use:
household consumption: 38.3%
government consumption: 31%
investment in fixed capital: 29.3%
investment in inventories: 4%
exports of goods and services: 35%
imports of goods and services: -37.6% (2015 est.)

GDP—composition, by sector of origin:
agriculture: 2.3%
industry: 46.9%
services: 50.8% (2015 est.)

Agriculture—products: wheat, barley, tomatoes, melons, dates, citrus; mutton, chickens, eggs, milk

Industries: crude oil production, petroleum refining, basic petrochemicals, ammonia, industrial gases, sodium hydroxide (caustic soda), cement, fertilizer, plastics, metals, commercial ship repair, commercial aircraft repair, construction

Industrial production growth rate: 2.8% (2015 est.)

country comparison to the world: 93

Labor force: 11.67 million

note: about 80% of the labor force is non-national (2015 est.)

country comparison to the world: 49

Labor force—by occupation: *agriculture:* 6.7%

industry: 21.4%

services: 71.9% (2005 est.)

Unemployment rate: 11.4% (2015 est.)

11.6% (2014 est.)

note: data are for Saudi males only (local bank estimates; some estimates are as high as 25%)

country comparison to the world: 129

Population below poverty line: NA%

Household income or consumption by percentage share: *lowest:* 10%: NA%

highest: 10%: NA%

Distribution of family income—Gini index: 45.9 (2013 est.)

country comparison to the world: 38

Budget: *revenues:* $193 billion

expenditures: $318 billion (2015 est.)

Taxes and other revenues: 28.3% of GDP (2015 est.)

country comparison to the world: 91

Budget surplus (+) or deficit (–): -18.3% of GDP (2015 est.)

country comparison to the world: 216

Public debt: 7.8% of GDP (2015 est.)

9.3% of GDP (2014 est.)

country comparison to the world: 172

Fiscal year: calendar year

Inflation rate (consumer prices): 2.2% (2015 est.)

2.7% (2014 est.)

country comparison to the world: 119

Central bank discount rate: 2.5% (31 December 2008)

country comparison to the world: 108

Commercial bank prime lending rate: 6.7% (31 December 2015 est.)

6.8% (31 December 2014 est.)

country comparison to the world: 122

Stock of narrow money: $341.3 billion (31 December 2015 est.)

$304.8 billion (31 December 2014 est.)

country comparison to the world: 16

Stock of broad money: $513.3 billion (31 December 2015 est.)

$461.2 billion (31 December 2014 est.)

country comparison to the world: 23

Stock of domestic credit: $24 billion (31 December 2015 est.)

-$38.16 billion (31 December 2014 est.)

country comparison to the world: 82

Market value of publicly traded shares:

$373.4 billion (31 December 2012 est.)

$338.9 billion (31 December 2011)

$353.4 billion (31 December 2010 est.)

country comparison to the world: 26

Current account balance: -$41.48 billion (2015 est.)

$73.76 billion (2014 est.)

country comparison to the world: 192

Exports: $224.6 billion (2015 est.)

$342.3 billion (2014 est.)

country comparison to the world: 22

Exports—commodities: petroleum and petroleum Products 90% (2012 est.)

Exports—partners: China 13.1%, Japan 10.9%, US 9.6%, India 9.6%, South Korea 8.5% (2015)

Imports: $156.9 billion (2015 est.)

$158.5 billion (2014 est.)

country comparison to the world: 28

Imports—commodities: machinery and equipment, foodstuffs, chemicals, motor vehicles, textiles

Imports—partners: China 13.9%, US 12.6%, Germany 7.1%, South Korea 6.1%, India 4.5%, Japan 4.4%, UK 4.3% (2015)

Reserves of foreign exchange and gold: $660.1 billion (31 December 2015 est.)

$732.4 billion (31 December 2014 est.)

country comparison to the world: 4

Debt—external: $166.1 billion (31 December 2014 est.)

$155.7 billion (31 December 2013 est.)

country comparison to the world: 38

Stock of direct foreign investment—at home:

$250.3 billion (31 December 2015 est.)

$242.6 billion (31 December 2014 est.)

country comparison to the world: 26

Stock of direct foreign investment—abroad:

$37.32 billion (31 December 2015 est.)

$32.46 billion (31 December 2014 est.)

country comparison to the world: 49

Exchange rates: Saudi riyals (SAR) per US dollar—

3.75 (2015 est.)

3.75 (2014 est.)

3.75 (2013 est.)

3.75 (2012 est.)

3.75 (2011 est.)

ENERGY

Electricity—production: 255.4 billion kWh (2012 est.)

country comparison to the world: 17

Electricity—consumption: 231.6 billion kWh (2012 est.)

country comparison to the world: 17

Electricity—exports: 0 kWh (2013 est.)

country comparison to the world: 189

Electricity—imports: 0 kWh (2013 est.)

country comparison to the world: 195

Electricity—installed generating capacity: 53.62 million kW (2012 est.)

country comparison to the world: 21

Electricity—from fossil fuels: 99.9% of total installed capacity (2012 est.)

country comparison to the world: 37

Electricity—from nuclear fuels: 0% of total installed capacity (2012 est.)

country comparison to the world: 174

Electricity—from hydroelectric plants: 0% of total installed capacity (2012 est.)

country comparison to the world: 196

Electricity—from other renewable sources: 0.1% of total installed capacity (2012 est.)

country comparison to the world: 119

Crude oil—production: 9.735 million bbl/day (2014 est.)

country comparison to the world: 2

Crude oil—exports: 7.658 million bbl/day (2012 est.)

country comparison to the world: 1

Crude oil—imports: 0 bbl/day (2012 est.)

country comparison to the world: 119

Crude oil—proved reserves: 268.3 billion bbl (1 January 2015 est.)

country comparison to the world: 2

Refined petroleum products—production: 1.971 million bbl/day (2012 est.)

country comparison to the world: 10

Refined petroleum products—consumption: 2.961 million bbl/day (2013 est.)

country comparison to the world: 7

Refined petroleum products—exports: 1.524 million bbl/day (2012 est.)

country comparison to the world: 6

Refined petroleum products—imports: 338,800 bbl/day (2012 est.)

country comparison to the world: 21

Natural gas—production: 102.4 billion cu m (2014 est.)

country comparison to the world: 9

Natural gas—consumption: 102.4 billion cu m (2014 est.)

country comparison to the world: 8

Natural gas—exports: 0 cu m (2014 est.)

country comparison to the world: 172

Natural gas—imports: 0 cu m (2014 est.)

country comparison to the world: 127

Natural gas—proved reserves: 8.235 trillion cu m (1 January 2014 est.)

country comparison to the world: 6

Carbon dioxide emissions from consumption of energy: 582.7 million Mt (2012 est.)

country comparison to the world: 10

COMMUNICATIONS

Telephone—fixed lines: *total subscriptions:* 3.92 million

subscriptions per 100 inhabitants: 14 (2014 est.)

country comparison to the world: 42

Telephones—mobile cellular: *total:* 52.7 million

subscriptions per 100 inhabitants: 193 (2014 est.)

country comparison to the world: 29

Telephone system: *general assessment:* modern system including a comBination of extensive microwave radio relays, coaxial cables, and fiber-optic cables

domestic: mobile-cellular subscribership has been increasing rapidly

international: country code—966; landing point for the International submarine cable Fiber-Optic Link Around the Globe (FLAG) and for both the SEA-M E-WE-3 and SEA-M E-WE-4 submarine cable networks providing connectivity to Asia, Middle East, Europe, and US; microwave radio relay to Bahrain, Jordan, Kuwait, Qatar, UAE, Yemen, and Sudan; coaxial cable to Kuwait and Jordan; satellite earth stations—5 intelsat (3 Atlantic Ocean and 2 Indian Ocean), 1 Arabsat, and 1 Inmarsat (Indian Ocean region) (2011)

Broadcast media: broadcast media are state-controlled; state-run TV operates 4 networks; Saudi Arabia is a major market for pan-Arab satellite TV broadcasters; state-run radio operates several networks; multiple International broadcasters are available (2007)

Radio broadcast stations: AM 43, FM 31, shortwave 2 (1998)

Television broadcast stations: 117 (1997)

Internet country code: .sa

Internet hosts: 145,941 (2012)

country comparison to the world: 79

Internet users: *total:* 16.2 million

percent of population: 59.2% (2014 est.)

country comparison to the world: 35

TRANSPORTATION

Airports: 214 (2013)

country comparison to the world: 26

Airports—with paved runways: *total:* 82

over 3,047 m: 33

2,438 to 3,047 m: 16

1,524 to 2,437 m: 27

914 to 1,523 m: 2

under 914 m: 4 (2013)

Airports—with unpaved runways: *total:* 132

2,438 to 3,047 m: 7

1,524 to 2,437 m: 7

2 914 to 1,523 m: 37

under 914 m: 16 (2013)

Heliports: 10 (2013)

Pipelines: condensate 209 km; gas 2,940 km; liquid petroleum gas 1,183 km; oil 5,117 km; refined products 1,151 km (2013)

Railways: *total:* 1,378 km

standard gauge: 1,378 km 1.435-m gauge (with branch lines and sidings) (2014)

country comparison to the world: 80

Roadways: *total:* 221,372 km

paved: 47,529 km (includes 3,891 km of expressways)

unpaved: 173,843 km (2006)

country comparison to the world: 22

Merchant marine: *total:* 72

by type: cargo 1, chemical tanker 25, container 4, liquefied gas 2, passenger/cargo 10, petroleum tanker 20, refrigerated cargo 3, roll on/roll off 7

foreign-owned: 15 (Egypt 1, Greece 4, Kuwait 4, UAE 6)

registered in other countries: 55 (Bahamas 16, Dominica 2, Liberia 20, Malta 4, Norway 3, Panama 11, Tanzania 1) (2010)

country comparison to the world: 61

Ports and terminals: *major seaport(s):* Ad Dammam, Al Jubayl, Jeddah, Yanbu al Bahr
container port(s) (TEUs): Ad Dammam (1,492,315), Jeddah (4,010,448)

MILITARY AND SECURITY

Military branches: Ministry of Defense: Royal Saudi Land Forces, Royal Saudi Naval Forces (includes Marine Forces and Special Forces), Royal Saudi Air Force (Al-Quwwat al-Jawwiya al-Malakiya as-Sa'udiy a), Royal Saudi Air Defense Forces, Royal Saudi Strategic Rocket Forces, Ministry of the National Guard (SANG) (2015)

Military service age and obligation: 17 is the legal minimum age for voluntary military service; no conscription (2012)

Military expenditures: 12.6% of GDP (2015 planned)
10.7% of GDP (2014 planned)
9.4% of GDP (2013)
7.98% of GDP (2012)
7.25% of GDP (2011)
7.98% of GDP (2010)
country comparison to the world: 4

TRANSNATIONAL ISSUES

Disputes—International: Saudi Arabia has reinforced its concrete-filled security barrier along sections of the now fully demarcated border with Yemen to stem illegal cross-border activities; Kuwait and Saudi Arabia continue discussions on a maritime boundary with Iran; Saudi Arabia

claims Egyptian-administered islands of Tiran and Sanafir

Refugees and internally displaced persons: *refugees (country of origin):* 30,000 (Yemen) (2016)
stateless persons: 70,000 (2015); note—thousands of biduns (stateless Arabs) are descendants of nomadic tribes who were not officially registered when National borders were established, while others migrated to Saudi Arabia in search of jobs; some have temporary identification cards that must be renewed every five years, but their rights remain restricted; most Palestinians have only legal resident status; some Naturalized Yemenis were made stateless after being stripped of their passports when Yemen backed Iraq in its invasion of Kuwait in 1990; Saudi women cannot pass their citizenship on to their children, so if they marry a non-national, their children risk statelessness

Trafficking in persons: *current situation:* Saudi Arabia is a destination country for men and women subjected to forced labor and, to a lesser extent, forced prostitution; men and women from South and East Asia, the Middle East, and Africa who voluntarily travel to Saudi Arabia as domestic servants or low-skilled laborers subsequently face conditions of involuntary servitude, including nonpayment and withholding of passports; some migrant workers are forced to work indefinitely beyond the term of their contract because their employers will not grant them a required exit visa; female domestic workers are particularly vulnerable because of their isolation in private homes; women, primarily from Asian and African countries, are believed to be forced into prostitution

in Saudi Arabia, while other foreign women were reportedly kidnapped and forced into prostitution after running away from abusive employers; children from South Asia, East Africa, and Yemen are subjected to forced labor as beggars and street vendors in Saudi Arabia, facilitated by criminal gangs

tier rating: Tier 2 Watch List—Saudi Arabia does not fully comply with the minimum standards for the elimination of trafficking; however, it is making significant efforts to do so; government officials and high-level religious leaders demonstrated greater political will to combat trafficking and publically acknowledged the problem—specifically forced labor; the government reported increased numbers of prosecutions and convictions of trafficking offenders; however, it did not proactively investigate and prosecute employers for potential labor trafficking crimes following their withholding of workers' wages and passports, which are illegal; authorities did not systematically use formal criteria to proactively identify victims, resulting in some unidentified victims being arrested, detained, deported, and sometimes prosecuted; more victims were identified and referred to protective services in 2014 than the previous year, but victims of sex trafficking and male trafficking victims were not provided with shelter and remained vulnerable to punishment (2015)

Illicit drugs: regularly enforces the death penalty for drug traffickers, with foreigners being convicted and executed disproportion ately; improving anti-money-laundering legislation and enforcement

SENEGAL

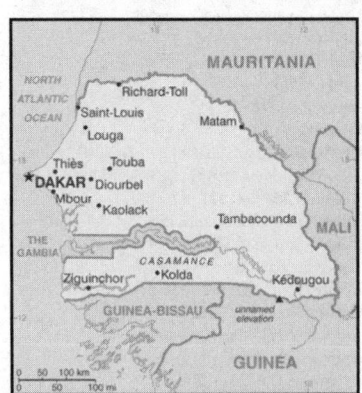

INTRODUCTION

Background: The French colonies of Senegal and French Sudan were merged in 1959 and granted independence in 1960 as the Mali Federation. The union broke up after only a few months. Senegal joined with The Gambia to form the nominal confederation of Senegambia in 1982. The envisaged

integration of the two countries was never implemented, and the union was dissolved in 1989. The Movement of Democratic Forces in the Casamance has led a low-level separatist insurgency in southern Senegal since the 1980s, and several peace deals have failed to resolve the conflict. Nevertheless, Senegal remains one of the most stable democracies in Africa and has a long history of participating in International peacekeeping and Regional mediation. Senegal was ruled by a Socialist Party for 40 years until Abdoulaye WADE was elected president in 2000. He was reelected in 2007 and during his two terms amended Senegal's constitution over a dozen times to increase executive power and weaken the opposition. His decision to run for a third presidential termsparked a large public backlash that led to his defeat in a March 2012 runoff with Macky SALL, whose term runs until 2019. A 2016 constitutional referendum reduced the term to five years with a maximum of two consecutive terms for future presidents.

GEOGRAPHY

Location: Western Africa, bordering the North Atlantic Ocean, between Guinea-Bissau and Mauritania

Geographic coordinates: 14 00 N, 14 00 W

Map references: Africa

Area: *total:* 196,722 sq km
land: 192,530 sq km
water: 4,192 sq km
country comparison to the world: 88

Area—comparative: slightly smaller than South Dakota

Land boundaries: *total:* 2,684 km
border countries (5): The Gambia 749 km, Guinea 363 km, Guinea-Bissau 341 km, Mali 489 km, Mauritania 742 km

Coastline: 531 km

Maritime claims: *territorial sea:* 12 nm
contiguous zone: 24 nm
exclusive economic zone: 200 nm
continental shelf: 200 nm or to the edge of the continental margin

Climate: tropical; hot, humid; rainy season (May to November) has strong southeast winds; dry season (December to April) dominated by hot, dry, harmattan wind

Terrain: generally low, rolling, plains rising to foothills in southeast

Elevation: *mean elevation:* 69 m

elevation extremes: *lowest point:* Atlantic Ocean 0 m

highest point: unnamed elevation southwest of Kedougou 581 m

Natural resources: fish, phosphates, iron ore

Land use: *agricultural land:* 46.8%

arable land: 17.4%

permanent crops: 0.3%

permanent pasture: 29.1%

forest: 43.8%

other: 9.4% (2011 est.)

Irrigated land: 1,200 sq km (2012)

Total renewable water resources: 38.8 cu km (2011)

Freshwater withdrawal (domestic/industrial/agricultural): *total:* 2.22 cu km/yr (4%/3%/93%)

per capita: 221.6 cu m/yr (2002)

Natural hazards: lowlands season ally flooded; periodic droughts

Environment—current issues: wildlife populations threatened by poaching; deforestation; overgrazing; soil erosion; desertification; over fishing

Environment—international agreements: *party to:* Biodiversity, Climate Change, Climate Change-Kyoto Protocol, Desertification, Endangered Species, Hazardous Wastes, Law of the Sea, Marine Life Conservation, Ozone Layer Protection, Ship Pollution, Wetlands, Whaling

signed, but not ratified: none of the selected agreements

Geography—note: westernmost country on the African continent; The Gambia is almost an enclave within Senegal

PEOPLE AND SOCIETY

Nationality: *noun:* Senegalese (singular and plural)

adjective: Senegalese

Ethnic groups: Wolof 38.7%, Pular 26.5%, Serer 15%, Mandinka 4.2%, Jola 4%, Soninke 2.3%, other 9.3% (includes Europeans and persons of Lebanese descent) (2010–11 est.)

Languages: French (official), Wolof, Pulaar, Jola, Mandinka

Religions: Muslim 95.4% (most adhere to one of the four main Sufi brotherhoods), Christian 4.2% (mostly Roman Catholic), animist 0.4% (2010–11 est.)

Population: 13,975,834 (July 2015 est.)

country comparison to the world: 73

Age structure: *0–14 years:* 42.16% (male 2,960,395/female 2,931,298)

15–24 years: 20.4% (male 1,420,180/female 1,431,571)

25–54 years: 30.67% (male 1,960,745/female 2,325,620)

55–64 years: 3.84% (male 233,892/female 303,394)

65 years and over: 2.92% (male 184,196/female 224,543) (2015 est.)

Dependency ratios: *total dependency ratio:* 87.6%

youth dependency ratio: 82.1%

elderly dependency ratio: 5.5%

potential support ratio: 18.2% (2015 est.)

Median age: *total:* 18.5 years

male: 17.7 years

female: 19.4 years (2015 est.)

country comparison to the world: 207

Population growth rate: 2.45% (2015 est.)

country comparison to the world: 29

Birth rate: 34.52 births/1,000 population (2015 est.)

country comparison to the world: 24

Death rate: 8.46 deaths/1,000 population (2015 est.)

country comparison to the world: 78

Net migration rate: -1.59 migrant(s)/1,000 population (2015 est.)

country comparison to the world: 159

Urbanization: *urban population:* 43.7% of total population (2015)

rate of urbanization: 3.59% annual rate of change (2010–15 est.)

Major urban areas—population: DAKAR (capital) 3.52 million (2015)

Sex ratio: *at birth:* 1.03 male(s)/female

0–14 years: 1.01 male(s)/female

15–24 years: 0.99 male(s)/female

25–54 years: 0.84 male(s)/female

55–64 years: 0.77 male(s)/female

65 years and over: 0.82 male(s)/female

total population: 0.94 male(s)/female (2015 est.)

Mother's mean age at first birth: 21.4

note: Median Age at first birth among women 25–29 (2010/11 est.)

Maternal mortality rate: 315 deaths/100,000 live births (2015 est.)

country comparison to the world: 28

Infant mortality rate: *total:* 51.54 deaths/1,000 live births

male: 57.62 deaths/1,000 live births

female: 45.29 deaths/1,000 live births (2015 est.)

country comparison to the world: 34

Life expectancy at birth: *total population:* 61.32 years

male: 59.29 years

female: 63.42 years (2015 est.)

country comparison to the world: 195

Total fertility rate: 4.44 children born/woman (2015 est.)

country comparison to the world: 30

Contraceptive prevalence rate: 17.8% (2012/13)

Health expenditures: 4.2% of GDP (2013)

country comparison to the world: 141

Physicians density: 0.06 physicians/1,000 population (2008)

Hospital bed density: 0.3 beds/1,000 population (2008)

Drinking water source:

improved:

urban: 92.9% of population

rural: 67.3% of population

total: 78.5% of population

unimproved:

urban: 7.1% of population

rural: 32.7% of population

total: 21.5% of population (2015 est.)

Sanitation facility access:

improved:

urban: 65.4% of population

rural: 33.8% of population

total: 47.6% of population

unimproved:

urban: 34.6% of population

rural: 66.2% of population

total: 52.4% of population (2015 est.)

HIV/AIDS—adult prevalence rate: 0.53% (2014 est.)

country comparison to the world: 66

HIV/AIDS—people living with HIV/AIDS: 44,000 (2014 est.)

country comparison to the world: 58

HIV/AIDS—deaths: 2,400 (2014 est.)

country comparison to the world: 52

Major infectious diseases: *degree of risk:* very high

food or waterborne diseases: bacterial and protozoal diarrhea, hepatitis A, and typhoid fever

vectorborne diseases: dengue fever, malaria, and yellow fever

water contact disease: schistosomiasis

respiratory disease: meningococcal meningitis

animal contact disease: rabies (2013)

Obesity—adult prevalence rate: 8.3% (2014)

country comparison to the world: 145

Children under the age of 5 years underweight: 12.8% (2014)

country comparison to the world: 40

Education expenditures: 5.6% of GDP (2010)

country comparison to the world: 53

Literacy: *definition:* age 15 and over can read and write

total population: 57.7%

male: 69.7%

female: 46.6% (2015 est.)

School life expectancy (primary to tertiary education): *total:* 8 years

male: 8 years

female: 8 years (2010)

Child labor—children ages 5–14: *total number:* 657,216

percentage: 22% (2005 est.)

Unemployment, youth ages 15–24: *total:* 12.7%

male: 8.3%

female: 19% (2011 est.)

country comparison to the world: 77

GOVERNMENT

Country name: *conventional long form:* Republic of Senegal

conventional short form: Senegal

local long form: Republique du Senegal

local short form: Senegal

former: Senegambia (along with The Gambia), Mali Federation

etymology: named for the Senegal River that forms the northern border of the country; many theories exist for the origin of the river name; perhaps the most widely cited derives the name from "Azenegue," the Portuguese appellation for the Berber Zenaga people who lived north of the river

Government type: presidential republic

Capital: *name:* Dakar

Geographic coordinates: 14 44 N, 17 38 W

time difference: UTC 0 (5 hours ahead of Washington, DC, during Standard Time)

Administrative divisions: 14 regions (regions, singular—region); Dakar, Diourbel, Fatick, Kaffrine, Kaolack, Kedougou, Kolda, Louga, Matam, Saint-Louis, Sedhiou, Tambacounda, Thies, Ziguinchor

Independence: 4 April 1960 (from France); note—complete independence achieved upon dissolution of federation with Mali on 20 August 1960

National holiday: Independence Day, 4 April (1960)

Constitution: previous 1959 (preindependence), 1963; latest adopted by referendum 7 January 2001, promulgated 22 January 2001; amended many times, last in 2016 (2016)

Legal system: civil law system based on French law; judicial review of legislative acts in Constitutional Court

International law organization participation: accepts compulsory ICJ jurisdiction with reservations; accepts ICCt jurisdiction

Citizenship: *citizenship by birth:* no
citizenship by descent only: at least one parent must be a citizen of Senegal
dual citizenship recognized: no, but Senegalese citizens do not automatically lose their citizenship if they acquire citizenship in another state
residency requirement for naturalization: 5 years

Suffrage: 18 years of age; universal

Executive branch: *chief of state:* President Macky SALL (since 2 April 2012)

head of government: Prime Minister Mohammed Abdallah Boun DIONNE (since 4 July 2014)

cabinet: Council of Ministers appointed by the prime minister in consultation with the president

elections/appointments: president directly elected by absolute majority popular vote in 2 rounds if needed for a 5-year term (eligible for a second consecutive term); election last held on 26 February 2012 with a runoff on 25 March 2012 (next to be held in 2019); prime minister appointed by the president

election results: Macky SALL elected president; percent of vote in runoff—Macky SALL (Alliance for the Republic-Yakaar) 65.8%, Abdoulaye WADE (PDS) 34.2%

Legislative branch: *description:* unicameral National Assembly or Assemblee Nationale (150 seats; 90 members directly elected in single- and multi-seat constituencies by simple majority vote and 60 directly elected in single- and multi-seat constituencies by proportional representation vote; members serve 5-year terms)

elections: National Assembly—last held on 1 July 2012 (next to be held in 2017)

election results: National Assembly results—percent of vote by party—NA; seats by party—Benno Bokk Yakaar coalition 119, PDS 12, Bokk Gis Gis coalition 4, MCRN-Bes Du Nakk 4, PVD 2, MRSD 2, URD 1, AJ/PADS 1, other 5

Judicial branch: *highest court(s):* Court of Final Appeals or Cour de Cassation (consists of NA judges); Constitutional Council (consists of 7 members to include the court president, vice-president, and 5 judges)

judge selection and term of office: Court of Final Appeals judges appointed by the president

upon recommendation of the Higher Council of the Judiciary, a body chaired by the president of the republic; judge tenure NA; Constitutional Council members—5 appointed by the president of the republic and 2 chosen by the president of the National Assembly to serve 6-year terms with renewal of 3 members every 2 years

subordinate courts: High Court of Justice (for crime of high treason by president); Supreme Court (for abuses by government executives and local officials); Court of Auditors; Courts of Appeal; Assize Courts (4); Regional and District Courts, Labor Court

Political parties and leaders: Alliance for the Republic-Yakaar or APR-Yakaar [Macky SALL]
Alliance of Forces of Progress or AFP [Moustapha NIASSE]
And-Jef/African Party for Democracy and Socialism or AJ/PADS [Mamadou DIOP]
And-Jef/African Party for Democracy and Socialism or AJ/PAD S-A [Landing SAVAN E]
Bokk G is G is coalition [Pape DIOP]
Citizen Movement for National Reform or MCRN-Bes Du NAkk
Democratic League-Labor Party Movement or LD-MPT [Mamadou NDOYE]
Front for Socialism and Democracy/Benno Jubel or FSD/BJ [Cheikh Abdoulaye Bamba DIEYE]
Gainde Centrist Bloc or BGC [J ean-Paul DIAS]
Grand Party or GP [Malick GACKOU]
Independence and Labor Party or PIT [Magatte THIAM]
Jef-Jel [Talla SYLLA]
National Democratic Rally or RND [Madior DIOUF]
Party for Truth and Development or PVD [Cheikh Ahmadou Kara MBAKE]
People's Labor Party or PTP [El Hadji DIOUF]
Reform Party or PR [Abdourahim AGNE]
Republican Movement for Socialism and Democracy or MRSD
Rewmi Party [I drissa SECK]
Senegalese Democratic Party or PDS [Abdoulaye WADE]
Socialist Party or PS [Ousmane Tanor DIENG]
Union for Democratic Renewal or URD [Djibo Leyti KA]

Political pressure groups and leaders: *other:* Catholic clergy; labor; religious groups; students; Sufi brotherhoods, including the Mourides and Tidjanes; teachers

International organization participation: ACP, AfDB, AU, CD, CPLP (associate), ECOWAS, EITI (candidate country), FAO, FZ, G-15, G-77, IAEA, IBRD, ICAO, ICC (National committees), ICCt, ICRM, IDA, IDB, IFAD, IFC, IFRCS, ILO, IMF, IMO, IMSO, Interpol, IOC, IOM, IPU, ISO, ITSO, ITU, ITUC (NGOs), MIGA, MINUSMA, MONUSCO, NAM, OIC, OIF, OPCW, PCA, UN, UNAMID, UNCTAD, UNESCO, UNHCR, UNIDO, UNMIL, UNMISS, UNOCI, UNWTO, UPU, WADB (regional), WAEMU, WCO, WFTU (NGOs), WHO, WIPO, WMO, WTO

Diplomatic representation in the US: *chief of mission:* Ambassador Babacar DIAGNE (since 18 November 2014)

embassy: 2215 M Street, NW, Washington, DC 20007
telephone: [1] (202) 234-0540
FAX: [1] (202) 629-2961
consulate(s) general: Houston, New York

Diplomatic representation from the US: *chief of mission:* Ambassador James P. ZUMWALT (since 9 January 2015); note—also accredited to Guinea-Bissau
embassy: Route des Almadies, Dakar
mailing address: B. P. 49, Dakar
telephone: [221] 33-879-4000
FAX: [221] 33-822-2991

Flag description: three equal vertical bands of green (hoist side), yellow, and red with a small green five-pointed star centered in the yellow band; green represents Islam, progress, and hope; yellow signifies Natural wealth and progress; red symbolizes sacrifice and determination; the star denotes unity and hope
note: uses the popular Pan-African colors of Ethiopia; the colors from left to right are the same as those of neighboring Mali and the reverse of those on the flag of neighboring Guinea

National symbol(s): lion; National colors: green, yellow, red

National anthem: *name:* "Pincez Tous vos Koras, Frappez les Balafons" (Pluck Your Koras, Strike the Balafons)
lyrics/music: Leopold Sedar SENGHOR/Herbert PEPPER
note: adopted 1960; lyrics written by Leopold Sedar SEN GH OR, Senegal's first president; the anthem sometimes played incorporating the Koras (harp-like stringed instruments) and Balafons (types of xylophones) mentioned in the title

ECONOMY

Economy—overview: Senegal's economy is driven by mining, construction, tourism, fisheries and agriculture, which is the primary source of employment in rural areas. The country's key export industries include phosphate mining, fertilizer production, agricultural products and commercial fishing and it is also working on oil exploration projects. Senegal relies heavily on donor assistance, remittances and foreign direct investment. For the first time in the past twelve years, Senegal reached a growth rate of 6.5% in 2015 due in part to a buoyant performance in agriculture because of higher rainfall and productivity in the sector. President Macky SALL, who was elected in March 2012 under a reformist policy agenda, inherited an economy with high energy costs, a challenging business environment, and a culture of overspending. President SALL unveiled an ambitious economic plan, the Emerging Senegal Plan (ESP), which aims to implement priority economic reforms and investment projects to increase economic growth while preserving macroeconomic stability and debt sustainability. Bureaucratic bottlenecks and a challenging business climate are among the perennial challenges that may slow the implementation of this plan. Senegal is receiving technical support from the IMF from 2015–2017 under a Policy Support Instrument (PSI) to assist with implementation of the ESP. The PSI implementation continues to be satisfactory as concluded by the IMF's second review mission in March 2016. Investors have signaled confidence in the country through Senegal's successful Eurobond issuances in recent years, including in 2014. The government will focus on 19 projects under the ESP for the 2016 budget to continue the structural transformation of the economy. These 19 projects include the Thies-Touba Highway, including the new airport- Mbour-Thies Highway. Senegal will increase the National family allowances program and the community development emergency program in 2016. Electricity supply is a chief constraint for Senegal's development. Electricity prices in Senegal are among the highest in the world. Power Africa, a program led by USAID and OPIC, plans to increase the current 500 mW of generating capacity to over 1,000 mW in the next three to five years. Recent gas discoveries on the Senegal-Mauritanian border, as well as just south of Dakar, will help alleviate some of the energy shortages.

GDP (purchasing power parity): $36.69 billion (2015 est.)
$34.45 billion (2014 est.)
$33.02 billion (2013 est.)
note: data are in 2015 US dollars
country comparison to the world: 117
GDP (official exchange rate): $13.67 billion (2015 est.)
GDP—real growth rate: 6.5% (2015 est.)
4.3% (2014 est.)
3.6% (2013 est.)
country comparison to the world: 22
GDP—per capita (PPP): $2,500 (2015 est.)
$2,400 (2014 est.)
$2,300 (2013 est.)
note: data are in 2015 US dollars
country comparison to the world: 196
Gross National saving: 17.7% of GDP (2015 est.)
16.1% of GDP (2014 est.)
17.3% of GDP (2013 est.)
country comparison to the world: 93
GDP—composition, by end use:
household consumption: 76.5%
government consumption: 15.2%
investment in fixed capital: 25.7%
investment in inventories: 0.9%
exports of goods and services: 27%
imports of goods and services: -45.3% (2015 est.)
GDP—composition, by sector of origin:
agriculture: 17.1%
industry: 24.3%
services: 58.6% (2015 est.)
Agriculture—products: peanuts, millet, corn, sorghum, rice, cotton, tomatoes, green vegetables; cattle, poultry, pigs; fish
Industries: agricultural and fish processing, phosphate mining, fertilizer production, petroleum refining, zircon, and gold mining, construction materials, ship construction and repair
Industrial production growth rate: 5.8% (2015 est.)
country comparison to the world: 24
Labor force: 6.515 million (2015 est.)
country comparison to the world: 67

Labor force—by occupation: *agriculture:* 77.5%
industry and services: 22.5% (2007 est.)
Unemployment rate: 48% (2007 est.)
country comparison to the world: 200
Population below poverty line: 46.7% (2011 est.)
Household income or consumption by percentage share: *lowest:* 10%: 2.5%
highest: 10%: 31.1% (2011)
Distribution of family income—Gini index: 40.3 (2011)
country comparison to the world: 61
Budget: *revenues:* $3.394 billion
expenditures: $4.031 billion (2015 est.)
Taxes and other revenues: 24.3% of GDP (2015 est.)
country comparison to the world: 126
Budget surplus (+) or deficit (–): -4.6% of GDP (2015 est.)
country comparison to the world: 161
Public debt: 55.7% of GDP (2015 est.) 53.4% of GDP (2014 est.)
country comparison to the world: 69
Fiscal year: calendar year
Inflation rate (consumer prices): 0.1% (2015 est.)
-1.1% (2014 est.)
country comparison to the world: 43
Central bank discount rate: 0.25% (31 December 2010)
4.25% (31 December 2009)
country comparison to the world: 135
Commercial bank prime lending rate: 14.3% (31 December 2015 est.)
14.5% (31 December 2014 est.)
country comparison to the world: 46
Stock of narrow money: $4.067 billion (31 December 2015 est.)
$3.931 billion (31 December 2014 est.)
country comparison to the world: 105
Stock of broad money: $6.351 billion (31 December 2015 est.)
$6.446 billion (31 December 2014 est.)
country comparison to the world: 122
Stock of domestic credit: $5.315 billion (31 December 2015 est.)
$4.882 billion (31 December 2014 est.)
country comparison to the world: 121
Market value of publicly traded shares: $NA
Current account balance: -$1.033 billion (2015 est.)
-$1.373 billion (2014 est.)
country comparison to the world: 124
Exports: $2.307 billion (2015 est.)
$2.678 billion (2014 est.)
country comparison to the world: 134
Exports—commodities: fish, groundnuts (peanuts), petroleum Products, phosphates, cotton
Exports—partners: Mali 12.8%, Switzerland 9.7%, India 5.9%, Cote dIvoire 5.3%, China 5.1%, UAE 4.1%, France 4.1% (2015)
Imports: $4.668 billion (2015 est.) $5.696 billion (2014 est.)
country comparison to the world: 127
Imports—commodities: food and beverages, capital goods, fuels

Imports—partners: France 17.9%, China 10%, Nigeria 8.7%, India 5.6%, Spain 4.9%, Netherlands 4.5% (2015)
Reserves of foreign exchange and gold: $2.099 billion (31 December 2015 est.)
$2.038 billion (31 December 2014 est.)
country comparison to the world: 118
Debt—external: $6.536 billion (31 December 2014 est.)
$5.223 billion (31 December 2013 est.)
country comparison to the world: 124
Exchange rates: Communaute Financiere Africaine francs (XOF) per US dollar—
580.5 (2015 est.)
494.42 (2014 est.)
494.42 (2013 est.)
510.53 (2012 est.)
471.87 (2011 est.)

ENERGY

Electricity—production: 3.148 billion kWh (2012 est.)
country comparison to the world: 131
Electricity—consumption: 2.586 billion kWh (2012 est.)
country comparison to the world: 140
Electricity—exports: 0 kWh (2013 est.)
country comparison to the world: 193
Electricity—imports: 0 kWh (2013 est.)
country comparison to the world: 199
Electricity—installed generating capacity: 623,000 kW (2012 est.)
country comparison to the world: 134
Electricity—from fossil fuels: 99.7% of total installed capacity (2012 est.)
country comparison to the world: 44
Electricity—from nuclear fuels: 0% of total installed capacity (2012 est.)
country comparison to the world: 178
Electricity—from hydroelectric plants: 0% of total installed capacity (2012 est.)
country comparison to the world: 200
Electricity—from other renewable sources: 0.3% of total installed capacity (2012 est.)
country comparison to the world: 105
Crude oil—production: 0 bbl/day (2014 est.)
country comparison to the world: 188
Crude oil—exports: 0 bbl/day (2012 est.)
country comparison to the world: 186
Crude oil—imports: 15,560 bbl/day (2012 est.)
country comparison to the world: 71
Crude oil—proved reserves: 0 bbl (1 January 2015 est.)
country comparison to the world: 187
Refined petroleum products—production: 16,190 bbl/day (2012 est.)
country comparison to the world: 97
Refined petroleum products consumption: 38,000 bbl/day (2013 est.)
country comparison to the world: 108
Refined petroleum products—exports: 2,070 bbl/day (2012 est.)
country comparison to the world: 106
Refined petroleum products—imports: 23,820 bbl/day (2012 est.)
country comparison to the world: 104

Natural gas—production: 46 million cu m (2013 est.)
country comparison to the world: 84
Natural gas—consumption: 46 million cu m (2013 est.)
country comparison to the world: 110
Natural gas—exports: 0 cu m (2013 est.)
country comparison to the world: 177
Natural gas—imports: 0 cu m (2013 est.)
country comparison to the world: 131
Natural gas—proved reserves: 0 cu m (1 January 2014 est.)
country comparison to the world: 191
Carbon dioxide emissions from consumption of energy: 7.139 million Mt (2012 est.)
country comparison to the world: 115

COMMUNICATIONS

Telephones—fixed lines: *total subscriptions:* 310,000
subscriptions per 100 inhabitants: 2 (2014 est.)
country comparison to the world: 105 (2014 est.)
Telephones—mobile cellular: *total:* 14.4 million
subscriptions per 100 inhabitants: 105 (2014 est.)
country comparison to the world: 67
Telephone system: *general assessment:* good system with microwave radio relay, coaxial cable and fiber-optic cable in trunk system
domestic: above-average urban system with a fiber-optic network; nearly two-thirds of all fixed-line connections are in Dakar where a call-center industry is emerging; expansion of fixed-line services in rural areas needed; mobile-cellular service is expanding rapidly
international: country code—221; the SAT-3/WASC fiber-optic cable provides connectivity to Europe and Asia while Atlantis-2 provides

connectivity to South America; satellite earth station—1 intelsat (Atlantic Ocean) (2010)
Broadcast media: state-run Radiodiffusion Television Senegalaise (RTS) operates 2 TV stations; a few private TV subscription channels rebroadcast foreign channels without providing any local news or programs; RTS operates a National radio network and a number of Regional FM stations; many community and private-broadcast radio stations are available; transmissions of at least 2 International broadcasters are accessible on FM in Dakar (2007)
Radio broadcast stations: AM 8, FM 20, short-wave 1 (2001)
Television broadcast stations: 7 (2008)
Internet country code: .sn
Internet hosts: 237 (2012)
country comparison to the world: 197
Internet users: *total:* 3 million
percent of population: 22.0% (2014 est.)
country comparison to the world: 84

TRANSPORTATION

Airports: 20 (2013)
country comparison to the world: 136
Airports—with paved runways: *total:* 9
over 3,047 m: 2
1,524 to 2,437 m: 6
914 to 1,523 m: 1 (2013)
Airports—with unpaved runways: *total:* 11
1,524 to 2,437 m: 7
914 to 1,523 m: 3
under 914 m: 1 (2013)
Pipelines: gas 43 km; refined products 8 km (2013)
Railways: *total:* 906 km
narrow gauge: 906 km 1.000-m gauge (2014)
country comparison to the world: 91
Roadways: *total:* 15,000 km
paved: 5,300 km (includes 7 km of expressways)

unpaved: 9,700 km (2015)
country comparison to the world: 125
Waterways: 1,000 km (primarily on the Senegal, Saloum, and Casamance Rivers) (2012)
country comparison to the world: 64
Merchant marine: *total:* 1
by type: passenger/cargo 1 (2010)
country comparison to the world: 154
Ports and terminals: *major seaport(s):* Dakar

MILITARY AND SECURITY

Military branches: Senegalese Armed Forces: Army, Senegalese National Navy (Marine Senegalaise, MNS), Senegalese Air Force (Armee de l'Air du Senegal) (2013)
Military service age and obligation: 18 years of age for voluntary military service; 20 years of age for selective conscript service; 2-year service obligation; women have been accepted into military service since 2008 (2013)

TRANSNATIONAL ISSUES

Disputes—International: The Gambia and Guinea-Bissau attempt to stem separatist violence, cross border raids, and arms smuggling into their countries from southern Senegal's Casamance region

Refugees and internally displaced persons: *refugees (country of origin):* 13,699 (Mauritania) (2014)
IDPs: 24,000 (clashes between government troops and separatists in Casamance region) (2015)
Illicit drugs: transshipment point for Southwest and Southeast Asian hero in and South American cocaine moving to Europe and North America; illicit cultivator of cannabis

SERBIA

INTRODUCTION

Background: The Kingdom of Serbs, Croats, and Slovenes was formed in 1918; its name was changed to Yugoslavia in 1929. Communist

Partisans resisted the Axis occupation and division of Yugoslavia from 1941 to 1945 and fought Nationalist opponents and collaborators as well. The military and political movement headed by Josip Broz "TITO" (Partisans) took full control of Yugoslavia when their domestic rivals and the occupiers were defeated in 1945. Although communists, TITO and his successors (Tito died in 1980) managed to steer their own path between the Warsaw Pact nations and the West for the next four and a half decades. In 1989, Slobodan MILOSEVIC became president of the Republic of Serbia and his ultraNationalist calls for Serbian domination led to the violent breakup of Yugoslavia along ethnic lines. In 1991, Croatia, Slovenia, and Macedonia declared independence, followed by Bosnia in 1992. The remaining republics of Serbia and Montenegro declared a new Federal Republic of Yugoslavia (FRY) in April 1992 and under MILOSEVIC's leadership, Serbia led various military campaigns to unite ethnic Serbs in neighboring republics into a "Greater Serbia." These actions ultimately failed and, after International

intervention, led to the signing of the Dayton Peace Accords in 1995.
MILOSEVIC retained control over Serbia and eventually became president of the FRY in 1997. In 1998, an ethnic Albanian insurgency in the formerly autonomous Serbian province of Kosovo provoked a Serbian counterinsurgency campaign that resulted in massacres and massive expulsions of ethnic Albanians living in Kosovo. The MILOSEVIC government's rejection of a proposed International settlement led to NATO's bomBing of Serbia in the spring of 1999. Serbian military and police forces withdrew from Kosovo in June 1999, and the UN Security Council authorized an interim UN Administration and a NATO-led security force in Kosovo. FRY elections in late 2000 led to the ouster of MILOSEVIC and the installation of democratic government. In 2003, the FRY became the State Union of Serbia and Montenegro, a loose federation of the two republics. Widespread violence predominantly targeting ethnic Serbs in Kosovo in March 2004 led to more intense calls to address Kosovo's status, and the UN began facilitating status talks in 2006. In June

2006, Montenegro seceded from the federation and declared itself an independent nation. Serbia subsequently gave notice that it was the successor state to the union of Serbia and Montenegro. in February 2008, after nearly two years of inconclusive negotiations, Kosovo declared itself independent of Serbia—an action Serbia refuses to recognize. At Serbia's request, the UN General Assembly (UNGA) in October 2008 sought an advisory opinion from the International Court of Justice (ICJ) on whether Kosovo's unilateral declaration of independence was in accordance with International law. in a ruling considered unfavorable to Serbia, the ICJ issued an advisory opinion in July 2010 stating that International law did not prohibit declarations of independence. in late 2010, Serbia agreed to an EU-drafted UNGA Resolution acknowledging the ICJ's decision and calling for a new round of talks between Serbia and Kosovo, this time on practical issues rather than Kosovo's status. Serbia and Kosovo signed the first agreement of principles governing the normalization of relations between the two countries in April 2013 and are in the process of implementing its provisions. Prime Minister Aleksandar VUCIC, has promoted an ambitious goal of Serbia joining the EU by 2020. Under his leadership, in January 2014 Serbia opened formal negotiations for accession.

GEOGRAPHY

Location: Southeastern Europe, between Macedonia and Hungary

Geographic coordinates: 44 00 N, 2100 E

Map references: Europe

Area: *total:* 77,474 sq km
land: 77,474 sq km
water: 0 sq km
country comparison to the world: 117

Area—comparative: slightly smaller than South Carolina

Land boundaries: *total:* 2,322 km
border countries (8): Bosnia and Herzegovina 345 km, Bulgaria 344 km, Croatia 314 km, Hungary 164 km, Kosovo 366 km, Macedonia 101 km, Montenegro 157 km, Romania 531 km

Coastline: 0 km (landlocked)

Maritime claims: none (landlocked)

Climate: in the north, continental climate (cold winters and hot, humid summers with well-distributed rainfall); in other parts, continental and Mediterranean climate (relatively cold winters with heavy snowfall and hot, dry summers and autumns)

Terrain: extremely varied; to the north, rich fertile plains; to the east, limestone ranges and basins; to the southeast, ancient mountains and hills

Elevation: *mean elevation:* 442 m

elevation extremes: *lowest point:* Danube and Timok Rivers 35 m
highest point: Midzor 2,169 m

Natural resources: oil, gas, coal, iron ore, copper, zinc, antimony, chromite, gold, silver, magnesium, pyrite, limestone, marble, salt, arable land

Land use: *agricultural land:* 57.9%
arable land: 37.7%

permanent crops: 3.4%
permanent pasture: 16.8%
forest: 31.6%
other: 10.5% (2011 est.)

Irrigated land: 950 sq km (2012)

Total renewable water resources: 162.2 cu km (note—includes Kosovo) (2011)

Natural hazards: destructive earthquakes

Environment—current issues: air pollution around Belgrade and other industrial cities; water pollution from industrial wastes dumped into the Sava which flows into the Danube

Environment—International agreements: *party to:* Air Pollution, Biodiversity, Climate Change, Climate Change-Kyoto Protocol, Desertification, Endangered Species, Hazardous Wastes, Law of the Sea, Marine Dumping, Marine Life Conservation, Ozone Layer Protection, Ship Pollution, Wetlands
Gulf none of the selected agreements

Geography—note: controls one of the major land routes from Western Europe to Turkey and the Near East

PEOPLE AND SOCIETY

Nationality: *noun:* Serb(s)
adjective: Serbian

Ethnic groups: Serb 83.3%, Hungarian 3.5%, Romany 2.1%, Bosniak 2%, other 5.7%, undeclared or unknown 3.4% (2011 est.)

Languages: Serbian (official) 88.1%, Hungarian 3.4%, Bosnian 1.9%, Romany 1.4%, other 3.4%, undeclared or unknown 1.8%
note: Serbian, Hungarian, Slovak, Romanian, Croatian, and Rusyn Are official in Vojvodina (2011 est.)

Religions: Serbian Orthodox 84.6%, Catholic 5%, Muslim 3.1%, Protestant 1%, atheist 1.1%, other 0.8%, undeclared or unknown 4.5% (2011 est.)

Population: 7,176,794
note: does not include the population of Kosovo (July 2015 est.)
country comparison to the world: 102

Age structure: *0–14 years:* 14.74% (male 545,685/female 512,443)
15–24 years: 11.46% (male 423,785/female 398,878)
25–54 years: 41.52% (male 1,503,100/female 1,476,843)
55–64 years: 14.66% (male 506,796/female 545,165)
65 years and over: 17.61% (male 519,501/female 744,598) (2015 est.)

Dependency ratios: *total dependency ratio:* 50.1%
youth dependency ratio: 24.5%
elderly dependency ratio: 25.6%
potential support ratio: 3.9% (2015 est.)

Median age: *total:* 42.1 years
male: 40.4 years
female: 43.8 years (2015 est.)
country comparison to the world: 24

Population growth rate: -0.46% (2015 est.)
country comparison to the world: 222

Birth rate: 9.08 births/1,000 population (2015 est.)
country comparison to the world: 209

Death rate: 13.66 deaths/1,000 population (2015 est.)
country comparison to the world: 12

Net migration rate: 0 migrant(s)/1,000 population (2015 est.)
country comparison to the world: 83

Urbanization: *urban population:* 55.6% of total population (2015)
rate of urbanization: -0.34% annual rate of change (2010–15 est.)

Major urban areas—population: BELGRADE (capital) 1.182 million (2015)

Sex ratio: *at birth:* 1.07 male(s)/female
0–14 years: 1.07 male(s)/female
15–24 years: 1.06 male(s)/female
25–54 years: 1.02 male(s)/female
55–64 years: 0.93 male(s)/female
65 years and over: 0.7 male(s)/female
total population: 0.95 male(s)/female (2015 est.)

Mother's mean age at first birth: 27.5 (2011 est.)

Maternal mortality rate: 17 deaths/100,000 live births (2015 est.)
country comparison to the world: 149

Infant mortality rate: *total:* 6.05 deaths/1,000 live births
male: 6.96 deaths/1,000 live births
female: 5.07 deaths/1,000 live births (2015 est.)
country comparison to the world: 166

Life expectancy at birth: *total population:* 75.26 years
male: 72.39 years
female: 78.31 years (2015 est.)
country comparison to the world: 102

Total fertility rate: 1.43 children born/woman (2015 est.)
country comparison to the world: 209

Contraceptive prevalence rate: 60.8% (2010)

Health expenditures: 10.6% of GDP (2013)
country comparison to the world: 19

Physicians density: 2.11 physicians/1,000 population (2009)

Hospital bed density: 5.4 beds/1,000 population (2009)

Drinking water source:
improved:
urban: 99.4% of population
rural: 98.9% of population
total: 99.2% of population
unimproved:
urban: 0.6% of population
rural: 1.1% of population
total: 0.8% of population (2015 est.)

Sanitation facility access:
improved:
urban: 98.2% of population
rural: 94.2% of population
total: 96.4% of population
unimproved:
urban: 1.8% of population
rural: 5.8% of population
total: 3.6% of population (2015 est.)

HIV/AIDS—adult prevalence rate: 0.05% (2013 est.)
country comparison to the world: 121

HIV/AIDS—people living with HIV/AIDS: 3,000 (2013 est.)

country comparison to the world: 115
HIV/AIDS—deaths: 100 (2013 est.)
country comparison to the world: 111

Major infectious diseases: *degree of risk:* intermediate
food or waterborne diseases: bacterial diarrhea
note: highly pathogenic H5N1 avian influenza has been identified in this country; it poses a negligible risk with extremely rare cases possible among US citizens who have close contact with birds (2013)
Obesity—adult prevalence rate: 21.1% (2014)
country comparison to the world: 63
Children under the age of 5 years underweight: 1.8% (2014)
country comparison to the world: 125
Education expenditures: 4.4% of GDP (2012)
country comparison to the world: 82
Literacy: *definition:* age 15 and over can read and write
total population: 98.1%
male: 99.1%
female: 97.2% (2015 est.)
School life expectancy (primary to tertiary education): *total:* 14 years
male: 14 years
female: 15 years (2014)

Child labor—children ages 5–14: *total number:* 36,141
percentage: 4% (2005 est.)
Unemployment, youth ages 15–24: *total:* 49.4%
male: N/A
female: N/A (2013 est.)
country comparison to the world: 7

GOVERNMENT

Country name: *conventional long form:* Republic of Serbia
conventional short form: Serbia
local long form: Republika Srbija
local short form: Srbija
former: People's Republic of Serbia, Socialist Republic of Serbia
etymology: the origin of the name in uncertain, but seems to be related to the name of the West Slavic Sorbs who reside in the Lusatian region in present-day eastern Germany; by tradition, the Serbs migrated from that region to the Balkans in about the 6th century A. D.
Government type: parliamentary republic
Capital: *name:* Belgrade (Beograd)
Geographic coordinates: 44 50 N, 20 30 E
time difference: UTC + 1 (6 hours ahead of Washington, DC, during Standard Time)
daylight saving time: +1 hr, begins last Sunday in March; ends last Sunday in October
Administrative divisions: 119 municipalities (opstine, singular—opstina) and 26 cities (gradovi, singular—grad)
municipalities: Ada*, Aleksandrovac, Aleksinac, Alibunar*, Apatin*, Arandelovac, Arilje, Babusnica, Bac*, Backa Palanka*, Backa Topola*, Backi Petrovac*, Bajina Basta, Batocina, Becej*, Bela Crkva*, Bela Palanka, Beocin*, Blace, Bogatic, Bojnik, Boljevac, Bor, Bosilegrad, Brus, Bujanovac, Cajetina, Cicevac, Coka*, Crna Trava,

Cuprija, Despotovac, Dimitrov, Doljevac, Gadzin Han, Golubac, Gornji Milanovac, Indija*, Irig*, Ivanjica, Kanjiza*, Kladovo, Knic, Knjazevac, Koceljeva, Kosjeric, Kovacica*, Kovin*, Krupanj, Kucevo, Kula*, Kursumlija, Lajkovac, Lapovo, Lebane, Ljig, Ljubovija, Lucani, Majdanpek, Mali Idos*, Mali Zvornik, Malo Crnice, Medveda, Merosina, Mionica, Negotin, Nova Crnja*, Nova Varos, Novi Becej*, Novi Knezevac*, Odzaci*, Opovo*, Osecina, Paracin, Pecinci*, Petrovacna Mlavi, Plandiste*, Pozega, Presevo, Priboj, Prijepolje, Prokuplje, Raca, Raska, Razanj, Rekovac, Ruma*, Secanj*, Senta*, Sid*, Sjenica, Smederevska Palanka, Sokobanja, Srbobran*, Sremski Karlovci*, Stara Pazova*, Surdulica, Svilajnac, Svrljig, Temerin*, Titel*, Topola, Trgoviste, Trstenik, Tutin, Ub, Varvarin, Velika Plana, Veliko Gradiste, Vladicin Han, Vladimirci, Vlasotince, Vrbas*, Vrnjacka Banja, Zabalj*, Zabari, Zagubica, Zitiste*, Zitorada cities: Beograd, Cacak, Jagodina, Kikinda*, Kragujevac, Kraljevo, Krusevac, Leskovac, Loznica, Nis, Novi Pazar, Novi Sad*, Pancevo*, Pirot, Pozarevac, Sabac, Smederevo, Sombor*, Sremska Mitrovica*, Subotica*, Uzice, Valjevo, Vranje, Vrsac, Zajecar, Zrenjanin*
note: the northern 39 municipalities and 6 cities—about 28% of Serbia's area—compose the autonomous province of Vojvodina and are indicated with *

Independence: 5 June 2006 (from the State Union of Serbia and Montenegro)
National holiday: National Day, 15 February (1835), the day the first constitution of the country was adopted
Constitution: many previous; latest approved by referendum 28–29 October 2006, adopted 30 September 2006, effective 8 November 2006;
note—proposed amendments to establish a special court for war crimes were defeated in June 2015 by the National Assembly (2016)
Legal system: civil law system
International law organization participation: has not submitted an ICJ jurisdiction declaration; accepts ICCt jurisdiction
Citizenship: *citizenship by birth:* no
citizenship by descent only: at least one parent must be a citizen of Serbia
dual citizenship recognized: yes
residency requirement for naturalization: 3 years
Suffrage: 18 years of age, 16 if employed; universal
Executive branch: *chief of state:* President Tomislav NIKOLIC (since 11 June 2012)

head of government: Prime Minister Aleksandar VUCIC (since 27 April 2014)
cabinet: Cabinet elected by the National Assembly
elections/appointments: president directly elected by absolute majority popular vote in 2 rounds if needed for a 5-year term (eligible for a second term); election last held on 20 May 2012 (next to be held in 2017); prime minister elected by the National Assembly
election results: Tomislav NIKOLIC elected president; percent of vote in second round—Tomislav

NIKOLIC (SNS) 51.2%, Boris TADIC (NDS-Z) 48.8%
Legislative branch: *description:* unicameral National Assembly or Narodna Skupstina (250 seats; members directly elected in a single nationwide constituency by party list proportional representation vote to serve 4-year terms)
elections: last held on 24 April 2016 (next to be held by April 2020)
election results: percent of vote by party/coalition—Serbia is Winning 48.2%, SPS-JS-ZS-KP 11.0%, SRS 8.1%, For a Just Serbia 6.0%, Enough is Enough 6.0%, Alliance for a Better Serbia 5.0%, Dveri-DSS 5.0%, SVM 1.5%, other 9.2%; seats by party/coalition Serbia is Winning 131, SPS-JS-ZS-KP 29, SRS 22, For a Just Serbia 16, Enough is Enough 16, Alliance for a Better Serbia 13, Dveri-DSS 13, SVM 4, other 6

Judicial branch: *highest court(s):* Supreme Court of Cassation (consists of more than 60 judges organized into 3- and 5-member panels for criminal, civil, and administrative cases); Constitutional Court (consists of 15 judges)
judge selection and term of office: Supreme Court justices proposed by the High Judicial Council (HJC), an 11-member body of which 7 are judges, and elected by the National Assembly; Constitutional Court judges appointed—5 each by the National Assembly, the president, and the Supreme Court of Cassation; judges of both courts appointed to permanent tenure by the JC
subordinate courts: appellate courts, higher courts, and municipal and district courts; courts of special jurisdiction include the Administrative Court, Appellate Commercial Court, and 2 levels of misdemeanor courts
note: in 2003, specialized panels on war crimes were established within the Serbian court system; the panels have jurisdiction over alleged violations of the Basic Criminal Code and crimes against humanity, International law, and criminal acts as defined by the Statute of the International Criminal Tribunal for the former Yugoslavia
Political parties and leaders: Alliance for a Better Serbia—coalition includes LDP, LSV, SDS
Alliance of Vojvodina Hungarians or SVM [Istvan PASZTOR]
Communist Party or KP [Josip Joska BROZ]
Democratic Alliance of Croats in Vojvodina [Petar KUNTIC]
Democratic Party or DS [Bojan PAJTIC]
Democratic Party of Serbia or DSS [Sanda RASKOVIC-I VIC]
Dveri [Bosko OBRADOVIC]
Enough of Enough [Sasa RADU LOVIC]
For a Just Serbia—coalition includes DS, NS, RS, DSVH, VVS, Together for Sumadija Greens of Serbia or ZS [Ivan KARIC]
League of Social Democrats of Vojvodina or LSV [Nenad CANAK]
Liberal Democratic Party or LDP [Cedomir JOVANOVIC]
Movement of Socialists or PS [Aleksandar VULIN]
New Serbia or NS [Velimir ILIC]

Party for Democratic Action or PDD [Riza HALIMI]

Party of Democratic Action of the Sandzak or SDA [Sulejman UGLJANIN]

Party of United Pensioners of Serbia or PUPS [Milan KRKOBABIC]

Reformist Party or RS [Aleksandar VI SNJIC]

Serbia is Winning—coalition includes SNS, SDPS, PUPS, NS, SPO, PS, PSS, NDSS, SNP

Serbian People's Party or SNP [Nenad POPOVIC]

Serbian Progressive Party or SNS [Aleksandar VUCIC]

Serbian Radical Party or SRS [Vojislav SESELJ]

Serbian Renewal Movement or SPO [Vuk DRASKOVIC]

Social Democratic Party or SDS [Boris TADIC]

Social Democratic Party of Serbia or SDPS [Rasim LJAJIC]

Socialist Party of Serbia or SPS [Ivica DACIC]

Strength of Serbia or PSS [Bogoljub KARIC]

Together for Serbia or ZZS [Dusan PETROVIC]

Together for Sumadija [Veroljub STEVAN OVIC]

note: as of April 2016, Serbia had 111 registered political parties and citizens' associations

Political pressure groups and leaders: Independent Association of Journalists of Serbia or NUNS

Journalists Association of Serbia (Udruzenje novinara Srbije) or UNS

Obraz (Orthodox clero-fascist organization)

SNP 1389 (Serbian Nationalist movement)

SNP NASI 1389 (Serbian National Movement NASI) Eastern alternative (pro-Russian association)

International organization participation: BIS, BSEC, CD, CE, CEI, EAPC, EBRD, EU (candidate country), FAO, G-9, IAEA, IBRD, ICAO, ICC (National committees), ICCt, ICRM, IDA, IFC, IFRCS, IHO, ILO, IMF, IMO, IMSO, Interpol, IOC, IOM, IPU, ISO, ITSO, ITU, ITUC (NGOs), MI GA, MONUSCO, NAM (observer), NSG, OAS (observer), OIF (observer), OPCW, OSCE, PCA, PFP, SELEC, UN, UNCTAD, UNESCO, UNFICYP, UNHCR, UNIDO, UNIFIL, UNMIL, UNOCI, UNTSO, UNWTO, UPU, WCO, WHO, WIPO, WMO, WTO (observer)

Diplomatic representation in the US: *chief of mission:* Ambassador Djerdj MATKOVIC (since 23 February 2015)

chancery: 2233 Wisconsin Ave NW

telephone: [1] (202) 332-0333

FAX: [1] (202) 332-3933

consulate(s) general: Chicago, New York

Diplomatic representation from the US: *chief of mission:* Ambassador Kyle SCOTT (since 4 February 2016)

embassy: 92 Bulevar kneza Aleksandra Karadjordjevica, 11040 Belgrade, Serbia

mailing address: 5070 Belgrade Place, Washington, DC 20521-5070

telephone: [381] (11) 706-4000

FAX: [381] (11) 706-4005

Flag description: three equal horizontal stripes of red (top), blue, and white—the Pan-Slav colors representing freedom and revolution ary ideals; charged with the coat of arms of Serbia shifted slightly to the hoist side; the principal field of the coat of arms represents the Serbian state and displays a white two-headed eagle on a red shield; a smaller red shield on the eagle represents the Serbian nation, and is divided into four quarters by a white cross; interpretations vary as to the meaning and origin of the white, curved symbols resembling firesteels or Cyrillic "C's" in each quarter; a royal crown surmounts the coat of arms

note: the Pan-Slav colors were inspired by the 19th-century flag of Russia

National symbol(s): double-headed eagle; National colors: red, blue, white

National anthem: *name:* "Boze pravde" (God of Justice)

lyrics/music: Jovan DORDEVIC/Davorin JENKO

note: adopted 1904; song originally written as part of a play in 1872 and has been used as an anthem by the Serbian people throughout the 20th and 21 st centuries

ECONOMY

Economy—overview: Serbia has a transitional economy largely dominated by market forces, but the state sector remains significant in certain Areas and many institution al reforms are needed. The economy relies on manufacturing and exports, driven largely by foreign investment. MILOSEVIC-era mismanagement of the economy, an extended period of International economic sanctions, civil war, and the damage to Yugoslavia's infrastructure and industry during the NATO airstrikes in 1999 left the economy only half the size it was in 1990.

After former Federal Yugoslav President MILOSEVIC was ousted in September 2000, the Democratic Opposition of Serbia (DOS) coalition Government implemented stabilization measures and embarked on a market reform program. Serbia renewed its membership in the IMF in December 2000 and rejoined the World Bank and the European Bank for Reconstruction and Development. Serbia has made progress in trade liberalization and enterprise restructuring and privatization, but many large enterprises—including the power utilities, telecommunications company, Natural gas company, and others—remain state-owned. Serbia has made some progress towards EU membership, signing a Stabilization and Association agreement with Brussels in May 2008, and with full implementation of the Interim Trade Agreement with the EU in February 2010, gained candidate status in March 2012. in January 2014, Serbia's EU accession talks officially opened. Serbia's negotiations with the WTO are advanced, with the country's complete ban on the trade and cultivation of agricultural biotechnology products representing the primary remaining obstacle to accession. Serbia's program with the IMF was frozen in early 2012 because the 2012 budget approved by parliament deviated from the program parameters; the arrangement is now void. in late 2014, Serbia and the IMF announced a tentative plan for a precautionary loan worth approximately $1 billion, but the government will be challenged to implement IMF-mandated reforms that will target social spending and the large public sector.

High unemployment and stagnant household incomes are ongoing political and economic problems. Structural economic reforms needed to ensure the country's long-term prosperity have largely stalled since the onset of the global financial crisis. Growing budget deficits constrain the use of stimulus efforts to revive the economy and contribute to growing concern of a public debt crisis, given that Serbia's total public debt as a share of GDP more than doubled between 2008 and 2014. Serbia's concerns about inflation and exchange-rate stability preclude the use of expansion ary monetary policy. During 2014 the SNS party addressed issues with the fiscal deficit, state-owned enterprises, the labor market, construction permits, bankruptcy and privatization, and other areas.

Major challenges ahead include: high unemployment rates and the need for job creation; high government expenditures for salaries, pensions, healthcare, and unemployment benefits; a growing need for new government borrowing; rising public and private foreign debt; attracting new foreign direct investment; and getting the IMF program back on track. Other serious longer-term challenges include an inefficient judicial system, high levels of corruption, and an Aging population. Factors favorable to Serbia's economic growth include its strategic location, a relatively inexpensive and skilled labor force, and free trade agreements with the EU, Russia, Turkey, and countries that are members of the Central European Free Trade Agreement.

GDP (purchasing power parity): $97.5 billion (2015 est.)

$96.78 billion (2014 est.)

$98.59 billion (2013 est.)

note: data are in 2015 US dollars

country comparison to the world: 83

GDP (official exchange rate): $36.51 billion (2015 est.)

GDP—real growth rate: 0.7% (2015 est.)

-1.8% (2014 est.)

2.6% (2013 est.)

country comparison to the world: 184

GDP—per capita (PPP): $13,700 (2015 est.)

$13,600 (2014 est.)

$13,800 (2013 est.)

note: data are in 2015 US dollars

country comparison to the world: 116

Gross National saving: 12.9% of GDP (2015 est.)

11.5% of GDP (2014 est.)

11.5% of GDP (2013 est.)

country comparison to the world: 131

GDP—composition, by end use:

household consumption: 81%

government consumption: 17.9%

investment in fixed capital: 17.8%

investment in inventories: -10.1%

exports of goods and services: 46%

imports of goods and services: -52.6% (2015 est.)

GDP—composition, by sector of origin:

agriculture: 10.4%

industry: 38.5%

services: 51.1% (2015 est.)

Agriculture—products: wheat, maize, sunflower, sugar beets, grapes/wine, fruits (raspberries, apples, sour cherries), vegetables (tomatoes, peppers, potatoes), beef, pork, and meat products, milk and dairy products

Industries: automobiles, base metals, furniture, food processing, machinery, chemicals, sugar, tires, clothes, pharmaceuticals

Industrial production growth rate: -2% (2015 est.)
country comparison to the world: 180

Labor force: 2.9 million (2015 est.)
country comparison to the world: 105

Labor force—by occupation: *agriculture:* 21.9%
industry: 15.6%
services: 62.5% (2014 est.)

Unemployment rate: 19.3% (2015 est.)
19.7% (2014 est.)
country comparison to the world: 167

Population below poverty line: 9.2% (2013 est.)

Distribution of family income—Gini index: 38.7 (2014 est.)
28.2 (2008 est.)
country comparison to the world: 72

Budget: *revenues:* $14.91 billion
expenditures: $16.4 billion
note: this is the consolidated budget, including both central government and local government budgets (2015 est.)
Taxes and other revenues: 40.8% of GDP (2015 est.)
country comparison to the world: 35

Budget surplus (+) or deficit (–): -4.1% of GDP (2015 est.)
country comparison to the world: 146

Public debt: 75% of GDP (2015 est.)
70% of GDP (2014 est.)
note: data cover general government debt, and includes debt instruments issued or owned by government entities other than the treasury (for which the Government of Singapore issued guarantees); the data include treasury debt held by foreign entities; the data include debt issued by sub-National entities (for which the GOS also issued guarantees), as well as intra-governmental debt; intra-governmental debt consists of treasury borrowings from surpluses in the social funds, such as for retirement, medical care, and unemployment, debt instruments for the social funds are not sold at public auctions
country comparison to the world: 37

Inflation rate (consumer prices): 1.4% (2015 est.)
2.1% (2014 est.)
country comparison to the world: 96

Central bank discount rate: 9.5% (18 March 2014)
11.75% (6 February 2013)
country comparison to the world: 27

Commercial bank prime lending rate: 12% (31 December 2015 est.)
14.8% (31 December 2014 est.)
country comparison to the world: 68

Stock of narrow money: $4.282 billion (31 December 2015 est.)
$4.332 billion (31 December 2014 est.)
country comparison to the world: 103

Stock of broad money: $18.37 billion (31 December 2015 est.)

$18.75 billion (31 December 2014 est.)
country comparison to the world: 91

Stock of domestic credit: $19.79 billion (31 December 2015 est.)
$20.59 billion (31 December 2014 est.)
country comparison to the world: 85

Market value of publicly traded shares: $7.696 billion (31 December 2014 est.)
$8.1 billion (31 December 2013)
$7.451 billion (31 December 2012 est.)
country comparison to the world: 78

Current account balance: -$1.765 billion (2015 est.)
-$2.632 billion (2014 est.)
country comparison to the world: 142

Exports: $12.8 billion (2015 est.)
$14.22 billion (2014 est.)
country comparison to the world: 81

Exports—commodities: iron and steel, rubber, clothes, wheat, fruit and vegetables, nonferrous metals, electric appliances, metal products, weapons and ammunition, automobiles

Exports—partners: Italy 16.2%, Germany 12.6%, Bosnia and Herzegovina 8.7%, Romania 5.6%, Russia 5.4% (2015)

Imports: $17.21 billion (2015 est.)
$19.56 billion (2014 est.)
country comparison to the world: 79

Imports—partners: Germany 12.4%, Italy 10.6%, Russia 9.6%, China 8.5%, Hungary 4.8%, Poland 4.2% (2015)

Reserves of foreign exchange and gold: $11.68 billion (31 December 2015 est.)
$12.05 billion (31 December 2014 est.)
country comparison to the world: 74

Debt—external: $36.09 billion (31 December 2014 est.)
$36.4 billion (31 December 2013 est.)
country comparison to the world: 71

Stock of direct foreign investment—at home: $31.21 billion (31 December 2009 est.)
$11.95 billion (2006 est.)
country comparison to the world: 67

Stock of direct foreign investment—abroad: $NA

Exchange rates: Serbian dinars (RSD) per US dollar—
106.6 (2015 est.)
88.405 (2014 est.)
88.405 (2013 est.)
87.99 (2012 est.)
72.455 (2011 est.)

ENERGY

Electricity—production: 34.4 billion kWh (2014 est.)
country comparison to the world: 60

Electricity—consumption: 26.91 billion kWh (2014 est.)
country comparison to the world: 64

Electricity—exports: 4.806 billion kWh (2014 est.)
country comparison to the world: 34

Electricity—imports: 6.864 billion kWh (2014 est.)
country comparison to the world: 34

Electricity—installed generating capacity: 7.368 million kW (2014 est.)
country comparison to the world: 65

Electricity—from fossil fuels: 59.2% of total installed capacity (2014 est.)
country comparison to the world: 136

Electricity—from nuclear fuels: 0% of total installed capacity (2013 est.)
country comparison to the world: 170

Electricity—from hydroelectric plants: 40.6% of total installed capacity (2014 est.)
country comparison to the world: 59

Electricity—from other renewable sources: 0.2% of total installed capacity (2014 est.)
country comparison to the world: 115

Crude oil—production: 16,840 bbl/day (2014 est.)
country comparison to the world: 75

Crude oil—exports: 0 bbl/day (2014 est.)
country comparison to the world: 179

Crude oil—imports: 31,730 bbl/day (2014 est.)
country comparison to the world: 61

Crude oil—proved reserves: 77.5 million bbl (1 January 2015 est.)
country comparison to the world: 76

Refined petroleum products—production: 61,590 bbl/day (2014 est.)
country comparison to the world: 77

Refined petroleum products—consumption: 67,980 bbl/day (2014 est.)
country comparison to the world: 91

Refined petroleum products—exports: 12,050 bbl/day (2014 est.)
country comparison to the world: 83

Refined petroleum products—imports: 20,080 bbl/day (2014 est.)
country comparison to the world: 112

Natural gas—production: 562.2 million cu m (2014 est.)
country comparison to the world: 70

Natural gas—consumption: 2.43 billion cu m (2014 est.)
country comparison to the world: 78

Natural gas—exports: 0 cu m (2013 est.)
country comparison to the world: 168

Natural gas—imports: 1.629 billion cu m (2014 est.)
country comparison to the world: 53

Natural gas—proved reserves: 48.14 billion cu m (1 January 2014 est.)
country comparison to the world: 65

Carbon dioxide emissions from consumption of energy: 46 million Mt (2014 est.)
country comparison to the world: 62

COMMUNICATIONS

Telephone—fixed lines: *total subscriptions:* 2.86 million
subscriptions per 100 inhabitants: 40 (2014 est.)
country comparison to the world: 51

Telephones—mobile cellular: *total:* 9.3 million
subscriptions per 100 inhabitants: 130 (2014 est.)
country comparison to the world: 89

Telephone system: *general assessment:* replacements of, and upgrades to, telecommunications equipment damaged during the 1999 war resulted in a modern digitalized telecommunications system

domestic: wireless service, available through multiple providers with National coverage, is growing very rapidly; best telecommunications services are centered in urban centers; 3G mobile network launched in 2007

international: country code—381 (2011)

Radio broadcast stations: 308 (station frequency types NA) (2009)

Television broadcast stations: 138 (2009)

Internet country code: .rs

Internet hosts: 1.102 million (2012)

country comparison to the world: 44

Internet users: *total:* 3.6 million

percent of population: 49.7% (2014 est.)

country comparison to the world: 83

TRANSPORTATION

Airports: 26 (2013)

country comparison to the world: 127

Airports—with paved runways: *total:* 10

over 3,047 m: 2 *2,438 to 3,047 m:* 3

1,524 to 2,437 m: 3

914 to 1,523 m: 2 (2013)

Airports—with unpaved runways: *total:* 16

1,524 to 2,437 m: 1

914 to 1,523 m: 10

under 914 m: 5 (2013)

Heliports: 2 (2012)

Railways: *total:* 3,808 km

standard gauge: 3,808 km 1.435-m gauge (1,196 km electrified) (2014)

country comparison to the world: 46

Roadways: *total:* 44,248 km

paved: 28,000 km

unpaved: 16,248 km (2010)

country comparison to the world: 80

Waterways: 587 km (primarily on the Danube and Sava rivers) (2009)

country comparison to the world: 80

Ports and terminals: river port(s): Belgrade (Danube)

MILITARY AND SECURITY

Military branches: Serbian Armed Forces (Vojska Srbije, VS): Land Forces (includes Riverine Component, consisting of a river flotilla on the Danube), Air and Air Defense Forces (2016)

Military service age and obligation: 18 years of age for voluntary military service; conscription abolished December 2010; reserve obligation to age 60 for men and age 50 for women (2013)

Military expenditures: 1.37% of GDP (2016 est.)

1.41% of GDP (2015)

1.49% of GDP (2014)

1.48% of GDP (2013)

1.77% of GDP (2012)

country comparison to the world: 36

TRANSNATIONAL ISSUES

Disputes—International: Serbia with several other states protest the US and other states' recognition of Kosovo's declaration of its status as a sovereign and independent state in February 2008; ethnic Serbian municipalities along Kosovo's northern border challenge final status of Kosovo-Serbia boundary; several thousand NATO-led Kosovo Force peacekeepers under UN Interim Administration Mission in Kosovo authority continue to keep the peace within Kosovo between the ethnic Albanian majority and the Serb minority in Kosovo; Serbia delimited about half of the boundary with Bosnia and Herzegovina, but sections along the Drina River remain in dispute

Refugees and internally displaced persons: *refugees (country of origin):* 32,408 (Croatia); 11,325 (Bosnia and Herzegovina) (2014)

IDPs: 220,002 (most are Kosovar Serbs, some are Roma, Ashkalis, and Egyptian (RAE); some RAE IDPs are unregistered) (2015)

stateless persons: 2,700 (includes stateless persons in Kosovo) (2015)

note: 668,402 estimated refugee and migrant arrivals (2015—June 2016)

Illicit drugs: transshipment point for Southwest Asian heroin moving to Western Europe on the Balkan route; economy vulnerable to money laundering

SEYCHELLES

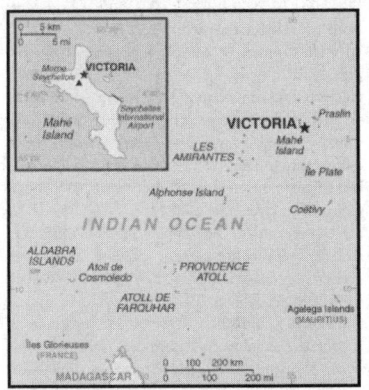

INTRODUCTION

Background: A lengthy struggle between France and Great Britain for the islands ended in 1814, when they were ceded to the latter. Independence came in 1976. Single-party rule was brought to a close with a new constitution and free elections in 1993. President France-Albert RENE, who had served since 1977, was reelected in 2001, but stepped down in 2004. Vice President James Alix MICHEL took over the presidency and in July 2006 was elected to a new five-year term; he

was reelected in May 2011 and again in December 2015.

GEOGRAPHY

Location: archipelago in the Indian Ocean, northeast of Madagascar

Geographic coordinates: 4 35 S, 55 40 E

Map references: Africa

Area: *total:* 455 sq km

land: 455 sq km

water: 0 sq km

country comparison to the world: 199

Area—comparative: 2.5 times the size of Washington, DC

Land boundaries: 0 km

Coastline: 491 km

Maritime claims: *territorial sea:* 12 nm

contiguous zone: 24 nm

exclusive economic zone: 200 nm

continental shelf: 200 nm or to the edge of the continental margin

Climate: tropical marine; humid; cooler season during southeast monsoon (late May to September); warmer season during northwest monsoon (March to May)

Terrain: Mahe Group is volcanic with a narrow coastal strip and rocky, hilly interior; others are coral, flat, elevated reefs

Elevation: *mean elevation:* NA

elevation extremes: *lowest point:* Indian Ocean 0 m

highest point: Morne Seychellois 905 m

Natural resources: fish, coconuts (copra), cinnamon trees

Land use: *agricultural land:* 6.5%

arable land: 2.2%

permanent crops: 4.3%

permanent pasture: 0%

forest: 88.5%

other: 5% (2011 est.)

Irrigated land: 3 sq km (2012)

Natural hazards: lies outside the cyclone belt, so severe storms are rare; occasional short droughts

Environment—current issues: water supply depends on catchments to collect rainwater

Environment—International agreements: *party to:* Biodiversity, Climate Change, Climate Change-Kyoto Protocol, Desertification, Endangered Species, Hazardous Wastes, Law of the Sea, Marine Dumping, Ozone Layer Protection, Ship Pollution, Wetlands

signed, but not ratified: none of the selected agreements

Geography—note: smallest African country; the constitution of the Republic of Seychelles lists 155 islands: 42 granitic and 113 coralline; by far the largest island is Mahe, which is home to about 90% of the population and the site of the capital city of Victoria

PEOPLE AND SOCIETY

Nationality: *noun:* Seychellois (singular and plural)
adjective: Seychellois

Ethnic groups: mixed French, African, Indian, Chinese, and Arab

Languages: Seychellois Creole (official) 89.1%, English (official) 5.1%, French (official) 0.7%, other 3.8%, unspecified 1.4% (2010 est.)

Religions: Roman Catholic 76.2%, Protestant 10.6% (Anglican 6.1%, Pentecoastal Assembly 1.5%, Seventh-Day Adventist 1.2%, other Protestant 1.6), other Christian 2.4%, Hindu 2.4%, Muslim 1.6%, other non-Christian 1.1%, unspecified 4.8%, none 0.9% (2010 est.)

Population: 92,430 (July 2015 est.)
country comparison to the world: 199

Age structure: *0–14 years:* 20.53% (male 9,731/female 9,243)
15–24 years: 13.92% (male 6,740/female 6,125)
25–54 years: 49.4% (male 24,076/female 21,586)
55–64 years: 8.74% (male 4,190/female 3,888)
65 years and over: 7.41% (male 2,670/female 4,181) (2015 est.)

Dependency ratios: *total dependency ratio:* 43.5%
youth dependency ratio: 33.6%
elderly dependency ratio: 9.9%
potential support ratio: 10.1% (2015 est.)

Median age: *total:* 34.4 years
male: 33.9 years
female: 35 years (2015 est.)
country comparison to the world: 78

Population growth rate: 0.83% (2015 est.)
country comparison to the world: 133

Birth rate: 14.19 births/1,000 population (2015 est.)
country comparison to the world: 138

Death rate: 6.89 deaths/1,000 population (2015 est.)
country comparison to the world: 137

Net migration rate: 1 migrant(s)/1,000 population (2015 est.)
country comparison to the world: 64

Urbanization: *urban population:* 53.9% of total population (2015)
rate of urbanization: 1.14% annual rate of change (2010–15 est.)

Major urban areas—population: VICTORIA (capital) 26,000 (2014)

Sex ratio: *at birth:* 1.03 male(s)/female
0–14 years: 1.05 male(s)/female
15–24 years: 1.1 male(s)/female
25–54 years: 1.12 male(s)/female
55–64 years: 1.08 male(s)/female
65 years and over: 0.64 male(s)/female
total population: 1.05 male(s)/female (2015 est.)

Infant mortality rate: *total:* 10.49 deaths/1,000 live births
male: 13.12 deaths/1,000 live births
female: 7.78 deaths/1,000 live births (2015 est.)
country comparison to the world: 132

Life expectancy at birth: *total population:* 74.49 years
male: 69.92 years

female: 79.2 years (2015 est.)
country comparison to the world: 117

Total fertility rate: 1.87 children born/woman (2015 est.)
country comparison to the world: 143

Health expenditures: 4% of GDP (2013)
country comparison to the world: 147

Physicians density: 1.07 physicians/1,000 population (2012)

Hospital bed density: 3.6 beds/1,000 population (2011)

Drinking water source:
improved:
urban: 95.7% of population
rural: 95.7% of population
total: 95.7% of population
unimproved:
urban: 4.3% of population
rural: 4.3% of population
total: 4.3% of population (2015 est.)

Sanitation facility access:
improved:
urban: 98.4% of population
rural: 98.4% of population
total: 98.4% of population
unimproved:
urban: 1.6% of population
rural: 1.6% of population
total: 1.6% of population (2015 est.)

HIV/AIDS—adult prevalence rate: NA

HIV/AIDS—people living with HIV/AIDS: NA

HIV/AIDS—deaths: NA

Obesity—adult prevalence rate: 26.9% (2014)
country comparison to the world: 70

Children under the age of 5 years underweight: 3.6% (2012)

Education expenditures: 3.6% of GDP (2011)
country comparison to the world: 121

Literacy: *definition:* age 15 and over can read and write
total population: 91.8%
male: 91.4%
female: 92.3% (2012 est.)

School life expectancy (primary to tertiary education): *total:* 14 years
male: 13 years
female: 15 years (2014)

Unemployment, youth ages 15–24: *total:* 11%
male: 8.4%
female: 14.2% (2011 est.)

GOVERNMENT

Country name: *conventional long form:* Republic of Seychelles
conventional short form: Seychelles
local long form: Republic of Seychelles
local short form: Seychelles
etymology: named by French Captain Corneille Nicholas MORPHEY after Jean Moreau de SECHELLES, the finance minister of France, in 1756

Government type: presidential republic

Capital: *name:* Victoria

Geographic coordinates: 4 37 S, 55 27 E
time difference: UTC+4 (9 hours ahead of Washington, DC, during Standard Time)

Administrative divisions: 25 administrative districts; Anse aux Pins, Anse Boileau, Anse Etoile, Anse Royale, Au Cap, Baie Lazare, Baie Sainte Anne, Beau Vallon, Bel Air, Bel Ombre, Cascade, Glacis, Grand Anse Mahe, Grand Anse Praslin, Inner Islands, La Riviere Anglaise, Les Mamalles, Mont Buxton, Mont Fleuri, Plaisance, Pointe Larue, Port Glaud, Roche Caiman, Saint Louis, Takamaka

Independence: 29 June 1976 (from the UK)

National holiday: Constitution Day (National Day), 18 June (1993); Independence Day, 29 June (1976)

Constitution: previous 1970, 1979; latest drafted May 1993, approved by referendum 18 June 1993, effective 23 June 1993; amended several times, last in 2011 (2016)

Legal system: mixed legal system of English common law, French civil law, and customary law

International law organization participation: has not submitted an ICJ jurisdiction declaration; accepts ICCt jurisdiction

Citizenship: *citizenship by birth:* no
citizenship by descent only: at least one parent must be a citizen of the Seychelles
dual citizenship recognized: no
residency requirement for naturalization: 5 years

Suffrage: 18 years of age; universal

Executive branch: *chief of state:* President James Alix MICHEL (since 14 April 2004); Vice President Danny FAURE (since 1 July 2010); note—the president is both chief of state and head of government
head of government: President James Alix MICHEL (since 14 April 2004); Vice President Danny FAURE (since 1 July 2010)
cabinet: Council of Ministers appointed by the president
elections/appointments: president directly elected by absolute majority popular vote in two rounds if needed for a 5-year term (eligible for 2 more terms); election last held on 3–5 December with runoff on 16–18 December 2015 (next expected in December 2020)
election results: President James MICHEL reelected president; percent of vote in second round—James MICHEL (PP) 50.2%, Wavel RAMKALAWAN (SNP) 49.8%

Legislative branch: *description:* unicameral National Assembly or Assemblee Nationale (34 seats; 25 members directly elected in single-seat constituencies by simple majority vote and 9 members directly elected in single-seat constituencies by proportional representation vote; members serve 5-year terms)
elections: last held on 29 September—1 October 2011 (next to be held in October 2016); note—the National Assembly was dissolved in July 2011 resulting in early elections
election results: percent of vote by party—PL 88.6%, PDM 10.9%, independent 0.6%; seats by party -PL 33, PDM 1; note—the SNP and NDP boycotted the 2011 elections

Judicial branch: *highest court(s):* Seychelles Court of Appeal (consists of the court president and 4

justices; Supreme Court of Seychelles (consists of the chief justice and 9 puisine judges); Constitutional Court (consists of 3 Supreme Court judges) *judge selection and term of office:* all judges appointed by the president of the republic upon the recommendation of the Constitutional Appointments Committee, a 3-member body, with 1 member appointed by the president of the republic, 1 by the opposition leader in the National Assembly, and 1 by the other 2 appointees; judges appointed until retirement at age 70

subordinate courts: Magistrates' Courts of Seychelles; Family Tribunal for issues such as domestic violence, and child custody and maintenance; Employment Tribunal for labor related disputes

Political parties and leaders: People's Party (Parti Lepep) or PL [James Alix MICHEL] (formerly SPPF) Popular Democratic Movement or PDM [David PIERRE]

Seychelles National Party or SNP [Wavel RAM KALAWAN] (formerly the United Opposition or UO) Seselwa (Seychelles) United Party or SUP [Robert ERN ESTA] (formerly the New Democratic Party or NDP)

International organization participation: ACP, AfDB, AOSIS, AU, C, CD, COMESA, EITI (candidate country), FAO, G-77, IAEA, IBRD, ICAO, ICC (NGOs), ICCt, ICRM, IDA, IFAD, IFC, IFRCS, ILO, IMF, IMO, InOC, Interpol, IOC, IOM, IPU, ISO (correspondent), ITU, MIGA, NAM, OIF, OPCW, SADC, UN, UNCTAD, UNESCO, UNIDO, UNWTO, UPU, WCO, WHO, WIPO, WMO, WTO (observer)

Diplomatic representation in the US: *chief of mission:* Ambassador Marie-Louise Cecile POTTER (since 6 September 2012)

chancery: 800 Second Avenue, Suite 400C, New York, NY 10017

telephone: [1] (212) 972-1785

FAX: [1] (212) 972-1786

consulate(s) general: New York

Diplomatic representation from the US: the US does not have an embassy in Seychelles; the US Ambassador to Mauritius is accredited to Seychelles

Flag description: five oblique bands of blue (hoist side), yellow, red, white, and green (bottom) radiating from the bottom of the hoist side; the oblique bands are meant to symbolize a dynamic new country moving into the future; blue represents sky and sea, yellow the sun giving light and life, red the peoples' determination to work for the future in unity and love, white social justice and harmony, green the land and Natural environment

National symbol(s): coco de mer (sea coconut); National colors: blue, yellow, red, white, green

National anthem: *name:* "Koste Seselwa" (Seychellois Unite)

lyrics/music: David Francois Marc ANDRE and George Charles Robert PAYET

note: adopted 1996

ECONOMY

Economy—overview: Since independence in 1976, per capita output in this Indian Ocean Archipelago has expanded to roughly seven times the pre-independence, near-subsistence level, moving the island into the upper-middle-income group of countries. Growth has been led by the tourist sector, which employs about 30% of the labor force and provides more than 70% of hard currency earnings, and by tuna fishing. in recent years, the government has encouraged foreign investment to upgrade hotels and other services. At the same time, the government has moved to reduce the dependence on tourism by promoting the development of farming, fishing, and small-scale manufacturing.

In 2008, having depleted its foreign exchange reserves, Seychelles defaulted on interest payments due on a $230 million Eurobond, requested assistance from the IMF, and immediately enacted a number of significant structural reforms, including liberalization of the exchange rate, reform of the public sector to include layoffs, and the sale of some state assets. In December 2013, the IMF declared that Seychelles had successfully transitioned to a market-based economy with full employment and a fiscal surplus. Seychelles grew at 4.3% in 2015 because of a strong tourist sector and expanding private sector credits; its fiscal surplus reached 4% of GDP.

GDP (purchasing power parity): $2.417 billion (2015 est.)

$2.316 billion (2014 est.)

$2.181 billion (2013 est.)

note: data are in 2015 US dollars

country comparison to the world: 192

GDP (official exchange rate): $1.375 billion (2015 est.)

GDP—real growth rate: 4.4% (2015 est.)

6.2% (2014 est.)

5% (2013 est.)

country comparison to the world: 52

GDP—per capita (PPP): $26,300 (2015 est.)

$25,400 (2014 est.)

$24,200 (2013 est.)

note: data are in 2015 US dollars

country comparison to the world: 70

Gross National saving: 17.6% of GDP (2015 est.)

15.4% of GDP (2014 est.)

26.3% of GDP (2013 est.)

country comparison to the world: 95

GDP—composition, by end use:

household consumption: 53.4%

government consumption: 21.7%

investment in fixed capital: 38.8%

investment in inventories: 0.2%

exports of goods and services: 70.8%

imports of goods and services: -84.9% (2015 est.)

GDP—composition, by sector of origin:

agriculture: 3%

industry: 14.6%

services: 82.4% (2015 est.)

Agriculture—products: coconuts, cinnamon, vanilla, sweet potatoes, cassava (manioc, tapioca), copra, bananas; tuna

Industries: fishing, tourism, beverages

Industrial production growth rate: 3.5% (2015 est.)

country comparison to the world: 71

Labor force: 39,560 (2006 est.)

country comparison to the world: 196

Labor force—by occupation: *agriculture:* 3%

industry: 23%

services: 74% (2006)

Unemployment rate: 3% (2014 est.)

3.3% (2013 est.)

country comparison to the world: 25

Population below poverty line: NA%

Household income or consumption by percentage share: *lowest:* 10%: 4.7%

highest: 10%: 15.4% (2007)

Budget: *revenues:* $478.7 million

expenditures: $423.7 million (2015 est.)

Taxes and other revenues: 34.8% of GDP (2015 est.)

country comparison to the world: 59

Budget surplus (+) or deficit (–): 4% of GDP (2015 est.)

country comparison to the world: 11

Public debt: 54.8% of GDP (2015 est.)

65.3% of GDP (2014 est.)

country comparison to the world: 70

Fiscal year: calendar year

Inflation rate (consumer prices): 4% (2015 est.)

1.4% (2014 est.)

country comparison to the world: 154

Central bank discount rate: 11.17% (31 December 2010)

country comparison to the world: 18

Commercial bank prime lending rate: 12.2% (31 December 2015 est.)

11.65% (31 December 2014 est.)

country comparison to the world: 65

Stock of narrow money: $467.8 million (31 December 2015 est.)

$407.2 million (31 December 2014 est.)

country comparison to the world: 165

Stock of broad money: $567.8 million (31 December 2014 est.)

$529.3 million (31 December 2013 est.)

country comparison to the world: 178

Stock of domestic credit: $476.2 million (31 December 2015 est.)

$427.3 million (31 December 2014 est.)

country comparison to the world: 171

Market value of publicly traded shares: $NA

Current account balance: -$195 million (2015 est.)

-$300 million (2014 est.)

country comparison to the world: 80

Exports: $450.6 million (2015 est.)

$538.9 million (2014 est.)

country comparison to the world: 176

Exports—commodities: canned tuna, frozen fish, petroleum Products (reexports)

Exports—partners: France 18.2%, UK 17.8%, Mauritius 10%, Japan 9.2%, Italy 7.7%, Spain 4.5% (2015)

Imports: $1.05 billion (2015 est.)

$1.081 billion (2014 est.)

country comparison to the world: 178

Imports—commodities: machinery and equipment, foodstuffs, petroleum Products, chemicals, other manufactured goods

Imports—partners: Saudi Arabia 22.5%, Spain 11.1%, Singapore 7.4%, China 4.5%, South Africa 4.1%, France 4% (2015)

Reserves of foreign exchange and gold: $549.8 million (31 December 2015 est.)
$465 million (31 December 2014 est.)
country comparison to the world: 148
Debt—external: $2.823 billion (31 December 2014 est.)
$2.714 billion (31 December 2013 est.)
country comparison to the world: 145
Exchange rates: Seychelles rupees (SCR) per US dollar—
13.37 (2015 est.)
12.747 (2014 est.)
12.747 (2013 est.)
13.7 (2012 est.)
12.381 (2011 est.)

ENERGY

Electricity—production: 316 million kWh (2012 est.)
country comparison to the world: 172
Electricity—consumption: 293.9 million kWh (2012 est.)
country comparison to the world: 176
Electricity—exports: 0 kWh (2013 est.)
country comparison to the world: 192
Electricity—imports: 0 kWh (2013 est.)
country comparison to the world: 198
Electricity—installed generating capacity: 89,000 kW (2012 est.)
country comparison to the world: 176
Electricity—from fossil fuels: 100% of total installed capacity (2012 est.)
country comparison to the world: 26
Electricity—from nuclear fuels: 0% of total installed capacity (2012 est.)
country comparison to the world: 177
Electricity—from hydroelectric plants: 0% of total installed capacity (2012 est.)
country comparison to the world: 199
Electricity—from other renewable sources: 0% of total installed capacity (2012 est.)
country comparison to the world: 125
Crude oil—production: 0 bbl/day (2014 est.)
country comparison to the world: 187
Crude oil—exports: 0 bbl/day (2012 est.)
country comparison to the world: 184
Crude oil—imports: 0 bbl/day (2012 est.)
country comparison to the world: 122
Crude oil—proved reserves: 0 bbl (1 January 2010 est.)
country comparison to the world: 186

Refined petroleum products—production: 0 bbl/day (2012 est.)
country comparison to the world: 128
Refined petroleum products—consumption: 6,800 bbl/day (2013 est.)
country comparison to the world: 162
Refined petroleum products—exports: 0 bbl/day (2012 est.)
country comparison to the world: 130
Refined petroleum products—imports: 6,805 bbl/day (2012 est.)
country comparison to the world: 148
Natural gas—production: 0 cu m (2013 est.)
country comparison to the world: 125
Natural gas—consumption: 0 cu m (2013 est.)
country comparison to the world: 191
Natural gas—exports: 0 cu m (2013 est.)
country comparison to the world: 175
Natural gas—imports: 0 cu m (2013 est.)
country comparison to the world: 130
Natural gas—proved reserves: 0 cu m (1 January 2014 est.)
country comparison to the world: 190
Carbon dioxide emissions from consumption of energy: 1.304 million Mt (2012 est.)
country comparison to the world: 164

COMMUNICATIONS

Telephone—fixed lines: *total subscriptions:* 21,200
subscriptions per 100 inhabitants: 23 (2014 est.)
country comparison to the world: 184
Telephones—mobile cellular: *total:* 151,300
subscriptions per 100 inhabitants: 165 (2014 est.)
country comparison to the world: 184
Telephone system: *general assessment:* effective system
domestic: combined fixed-line and mobile-cellular teledensity exceeds 170 telephones per 100 persons; radiotelephone communications between islands in the archipelago
international: country code—248; direct radiotelephone communications with adjacent island countries and African coastal countries; satellite earth station—1 intelsat (Indian Ocean) (2011)
Broadcast media: the government operates the only terrestrial TV station, which provides local programming and airs broadcasts from International services; multi-channel cable and satellite TV are available; the government operates 1 AM and 1 FM radio station; transmissions of 2

International broadcasters are accessible in Victoria (2007)
Radio broadcast stations: AM 1, FM 1, shortwave 2 (2001)
Television broadcast stations: 2 (plus 9 repeaters) (1997)
Internet country code: .sc
Internet hosts: 247 (2012)
country comparison to the world: 195
Internet users: *total:* 49,300
percent of population: 53.8% (2014 est.)
country comparison to the world: 184

TRANSPORTATION

Airports: 14 (2013)
country comparison to the world: 150
Airports—with paved runways: *total:* 7
2,438 to 3,047 m: 1
914 to 1,523 m: 5
under 914 m: 1 (2013)
Airports—with unpaved runways: *total:* 7
914 to 1,523 m: 2
under 914 m: 5 (2013)
Heliports: 1 (2013)
Roadways: *total:* 508 km
paved: 490 km
unpaved: 18 km (2010)
country comparison to the world: 195
Merchant marine: *total:* 9
by type: cargo 1, carrier 1, chemical tanker 6, petroleum tanker 1
foreign-owned: 3 (Hong Kong 1, Nigeria 1, South Africa 1) (2010)
country comparison to the world: 117
Ports and terminals: *major seaport(s):* Victoria

MILITARY AND SECURITY

Military branches: Seychelles People's Defense Forces (SPDF): Army, Coast Guard (includes Naval Wing, Air Wing), National Guard (2015)
Military service age and obligation: 18 years of age for voluntary military service (younger with parental consent); no conscription (2012)
Military expenditures: 0.89% of GDP (2012)
0.82% of GDP (2011)
0.89% of GDP (2010)
country comparison to the world: 109

TRANSNATIONAL ISSUES

Disputes—International: Mauritius and Seychelles claim the Chagos Islands (UK-administered British Indian Ocean Territory)

SIERRA LEONE

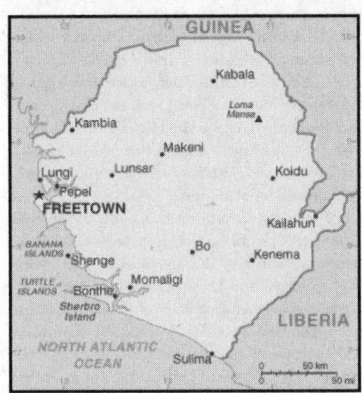

INTRODUCTION

Background: The British set up a trading post near present-day Freetown in the 17th century. Originally the trade involved timber and ivory, but later it expanded into slaves. Following the American Revolution, a colony was established in 1787 and Sierra Leone became a destination for resettling black loyalists who had originally been resettled in Nova Scotia. After the abolition of the slave trade in 1807, British crews delivered thousands of Africans liberated from illegal slave ships to Sierra Leone, particularly Freetown. The colony gradually expanded inland during the course of the 19th century; independence was attained in 1961. Democracy is slowly being reestablished after the civil war (1991–2002) that resulted in tens of thousands of deaths and the displacement of more than 2 million people (about one third of the population). The military, which took over full responsibility for security following the departure of UN peacekeepers at the end of 2005, has developed as a guarantor of the country's stability; the armed forces remained on the sideline during the 2007 and 2012 National elections. In March 2014, the closure of the UN Integrated Peacebuilding Office in Sierra Leone marked the end of more than 15 years of peacekeeping and political operations in Sierra Leone. The government's stated priorities include furthering development—including recovering from the Ebola epidemic—creating jobs, and stamping out endemic corruption.

GEOGRAPHY

Location: Western Africa, bordering the North Atlantic Ocean, between Guinea and Liberia
Geographic coordinates: 8 30 N, 1130 W
Map references: Africa
Area: *total:* 71,740 sq km
land: 71,620 sq km
water: 120 sq km
country comparison to the world: 119
Area—comparative: slightly smaller than South Carolina

Land boundaries: *total:* 1,093 km
border countries (2): Guinea 794 km, Liberia 299 km
Coastline: 402 km
Maritime claims: *territorial sea:* 12 nm
contiguous zone: 24 nm
exclusive economic zone: 200 nm
continental shelf: 200 nm
Climate: tropical; hot, humid; summer rainy season (May to December); winter dry season (December to April)
Terrain: coastal belt of mangrove swamps, wooded hill country, upland plateau, mountains in east
Elevation: *mean elevation:* 279 m

elevation extremes: *lowest point:* Atlantic Ocean 0 m
highest point: Loma Mansa (Bintimani) 1,948 m
Natural resources: diamonds, titanium ore, bauxite, iron ore, gold, chromite

Land use: *agricultural land:* 56.2%
arable land: 23.4%
permanent crops: 2.3
permanent pasture: 30.5%
forest: 37.5%
other: 6.3% (2011 est.)
Irrigated land: 300 sq km (2012)
Total renewable water resources: 160 cu km (2011)
Freshwater withdrawal (domestic/industrial/agricultural): *total:* 0.21 cu km/yr (52%/26%/22%)
per capita: 38.74 cu m/yr (2005)
Natural hazards: dry, sand-laden harmattan winds blow from the Sahara (December to February); sandstorms, dust storms
Environment—current issues: rapid population growth pressuring the environment; overharvesting of timber, expansion of cattle grazing, and slash-and-burn Agriculture have resulted in deforestation and soil exhaustion; civil war depleted Natural resources; overfishing
Environment—International agreements: *party to:* Biodiversity, Climate Change, Climate Change-Kyoto Protocol, Desertification, Endangered Species, Law of the Sea, Marine Life Conservation, Ozone Layer Protection, Ship Pollution, Wetlands
signed, but not ratified: Environmental Modification
Geography—note: rainfall along the coast can reach 495 cm (195 inches) a year, making it one of the wettest places along coastal, western Africa

PEOPLE AND SOCIETY

Nationality: *noun:* Sierra Leonean(s)
adjective: Sierra Leonean
Ethnic groups: Temne 35%, Mende 31%, Limba 8%, Kono 5%, Kriole 2% (descendants of freed Jamaican slaves who were settled in the Freetown area in the late-18th century; also known as Krio), Mandingo 2%, Loko 2%, other 15% (includes refugees from Liberia's recent civil war, and small numbers of Europeans, Lebanese, Pakistanis, and Indians) (2008 census)

Languages: English (official, regular use limited to literate minority), Mende (principal vernacular in the south), Temne (principal vernacular in the north), Krio (English-based Creole, spoken by the descendants of freed Jamaican slaves who were settled in the Freetown Area, a lingua franca and a first language for 10% of the population but understood by 95%)
Religions: Muslim 60%, Christian 10%, indigenous beliefs 30%
Population: 5,879,098 (July 2015 est.)
country comparison to the world: 112
Age structure: *0–14 years:* 41.93% (male 1,228,380/female 1,236,475)
15–24 years: 18.67% (male 532,738/female 564,828)
25–54 years: 31.85% (male 898,538/female 973,908)
55–64 years: 3.82% (male 102,915/female 121,864)
65 years and over: 3.73% (male 92,777/female 126,675) (2015 est.)
Dependency ratios: *total dependency ratio:* 81.9%
youth dependency ratio: 77.1%
elderly dependency ratio: 4.9%
potential support ratio: 20.6% (2015 est.)
Median age: *total:* 19 years
male: 18.4 years
female: 19.6 years (2015 est.)
country comparison to the world: 201
Population growth rate: 2.35% (2015 est.)
country comparison to the world: 32
Birth rate: 37.03 births/1,000 population (2015 est.)
country comparison to the world: 14
Death rate: 10.81 deaths/1,000 population (2015 est.)
country comparison to the world: 35
Net migration rate: -2.77 migrant(s)/1,000 population (2015 est.)
country comparison to the world: 178
Urbanization: *urban population:* 39.9% of total population (2015)
rate of urbanization: 2.75% annual rate of change (2010–15 est.)
Major urban areas—population: FREETOWN (capital) 1.007 million (2015)
Sex ratio: *at birth:* 1.03 male(s)/female
0–14 years: 0.99 male(s)/female
15–24 years: 0.94 male(s)/female
25–54 years: 0.92 male(s)/female
55–64 years: 0.85 male(s)/female
65 years and over: 0.73 male(s)/female
total population: 0.94 male(s)/female (2015 est.)
Mother's mean age at first birth: 19.2
note: Median Age at first birth among women 25–29 (2013 est.)
Maternal mortality rate: 1,360 deaths/100,000 live births (2015 est.)
country comparison to the world: 5

Infant mortality rate: *total:* 71.68 deaths/1,000 live births

male: 80.14 deaths/1,000 live births

female: 62.96 deaths/1,000 live births (2015 est.)

country comparison to the world: 11

Life expectancy at birth: *total population:* 57.79 years

male: 55.23 years

female: 60.42 years (2015 est.)

country comparison to the world: 204

Total fertility rate: 4.8 children born/woman (2015 est.)

country comparison to the world: 19

Contraceptive prevalence rate: 16.6% (2013)

Health expenditures: 11.8% of GDP (2013)

country comparison to the world: 5

Physicians density: 0.02 physicians/1,000 population (2010)

Hospital bed density: 0.4 beds/1,000 population (2006)

Drinking water source:

improved:

urban: 84.9% of population

rural: 47.8% of population

total: 62.6% of population

unimproved:

urban: 15.1% of population

rural: 52.2% of population

total: 37.4% of population (2015 est.)

Sanitation facility access:

improved:

urban: 22.8% of population

rural: 6.9% of population

total: 13.3% of population

unimproved:

urban: 77.2% of population

rural: 93.1% of population

total: 86.7% of population (2015 est.)

HIV/AIDS—adult prevalence rate: 1.4% (2014 est.)

country comparison to the world: 36

HIV/AIDS—people living with HIV/AIDS: 54,000 (2014 est.)

country comparison to the world: 54

HIV/AIDS—deaths: 2,700 (2014 est.)

country comparison to the world: 48

Major infectious diseases: *degree of risk:* very high

food or waterborne diseases: bacterial and protozoal diarrhea, hepatitis A, and typhoid fever

vectorborne diseases: malaria, dengue fever, and yellow fever

water contact disease: schistosomiasis

animal contact disease: rabies

aerosolized dust or soil contact disease: Lassa fever (2013)

Obesity—adult prevalence rate: 6.6% (2014)

country comparison to the world: 144

Children under the age of 5 years underweight: 18.1% (2013)

country comparison to the world: 34

Education expenditures: 2.8% of GDP (2014)

country comparison to the world: 141

Literacy: *definition:* age 15 and over can read and write English, Mende, Temne, or Arabic

total population: 48.1%

male: 58.7%

female: 37.7% (2015 est.)

Child labor—children ages 5–14: *total number:* 573,287

percentage: 48% (2005 est.)

GOVERNMENT

Country name: *conventional long form:* Republic of Sierra Leone

conventional short form: Sierra Leone

local long form: Republic of Sierra Leone

local short form: Sierra Leone

etymology: the Portuguese explorer Pedro de SINTRA named the country "Serra Leoa" (Lion Mountains) for the impressive Mountains he saw while sailing the West African coast in 1462

Government type: presidential republic

Capital: *name:* Freetown

Geographic coordinates: 8 29 N, 13 14 W

time difference: UTC 0 (5 hours ahead of Washington, DC, during Standard Time)

Administrative divisions: 3 provinces and 1 area*; Eastern, Northern, Southern, Western*

Independence: 27 April 1961 (from the UK)

National holiday: Independence Day, 27 April (1961)

Constitution: several previous; latest in effect 1 October 1991; amended several times, last in 2013 (2016)

Legal system: mixed legal system of English common law and customary law

International law organization participation: has not submitted an ICJ jurisdiction declaration; accepts ICCt jurisdiction

Citizenship: *citizenship by birth:* no

citizenship by descent only: at least one parent or grandparent must be a citizen of Sierra Leone

dual citizenship recognized: yes

residency requirement for naturalization: 5 years

Suffrage: 18 years of age; universal

Executive branch: *chief of state:* President Ernest Bai KOROMA (since 17 September 2007); note—the president is both chief of state and head of government

head of government: President Ernest Bai KOROMA (since 17 September 2007)

cabinet: Ministers of State appointed by the president, approved by Parliament; the cabinet is responsible to the president

elections/appointments: president directly elected by absolute majority popular vote in 2 rounds if needed for a 5-year term (eligible for a second term); election last held on 17 November 2012 (next to be held in 2017)

election results: Ernest Bai KOROMA reelected president; percent of vote—Ernest Bai KOROMA (APC) 58.7%, Julius Maada BIO (SLPP) 37.4%, other 3.9%

Legislative branch: *description:* unicameral Parliament (124 seats; 112 members directly elected in single-seat constituencies by simple majority vote and 12 seats filled in separate elections by non-partisan members of Parliament called "paramount chiefs; " members serve 5-year terms)

elections: last held on 17 November 2012 (next to be held in 2017)

election results: percent of vote by party—NA; seats by party—APC 69, SLPP 43

Judicial branch: *highest court(s):* Superior Court of Judicature (consists of the Supreme Court—at the apex—with the chief justice and 4 other judges, the Court of Appeal with the chief justice and 7 other judges, and the High Court of Justice with the chief justice and 9 other judges; note—the Judicature has jurisdiction in all civil, criminal, and constitutional matters

judge selection and term of office: Supreme Court chief justice and other judges of the Judicature appointed by the president on the advice of the Judicial and Legal Service Commission (a 7-member independent body of judges, presidential appointees, and the Commission chairman) and subject to the approval of Parliament; all Judicature judges appointed until retirement at age 65

subordinate courts: Magistrates' courts; District Appeals Court; local courts

Political parties and leaders: All People's Congress or APC [Ernest Bai KOROMA]

Sierra Leone People's Party or SLPP [Somano KAPEN] numerous other parties

Political pressure groups and leaders:

other: student unions; trade unions

International organization participation: ACP, AfDB, AU, C, ECOWAS, EITI (compliant country), FAO, G-77, IAEA, IBRD, ICAO, ICCt, ICRM, IDA, IDB, IFAD, IFC, IFRCS, IHO (pending member), ILO, IMF, IMO, Interpol, IOC, IOM, IPU, ISO (correspondent), ITU, ITUC (NGOs), MIGA, MINUSMA, NAM, OIC, OPCW, UN, UNAMID, UNCTAD, UNESCO, UNIDO, UNIFIL, UNISFA, UNWTO, UPU, WCO, WFTU (NGOs), WHO, WIPO, WMO, WTO

Diplomatic representation in the US: *chief of mission:* Ambassador Bockari Kortu STEVENS (since 28 March 2008)

chancery: 170119th Street NW, Washington, DC 20009

telephone: [1] (202) 939-9261 through 9263

FAX: [1] (202) 483-1793

Diplomatic representation from the US: *chief of mission:* Ambassador John HOOVER (since 4 November 4 December 2014)

embassy: Southridge-Hill Station, Freetown

mailing address: use embassy street address

telephone: [232] (76) 515 000 or (76) 515 000

FAX: [232] (76) 515 355

Flag description: three equal horizontal bands of green (top), white, and blue; green symbolizes agriculture, mountains, and Natural resources, white represents unity and justice, and blue the sea and the Natural harbor in Freetown

National symbol(s): lion; National colors: green, white, blue

National anthem: *name:* "High We Exalt Thee, Realm of the Free"

lyrics/music: Clifford Nelson FYLE/John Joseph AKA

note: adopted 1961

ECONOMY

Economy—overview: Sierra Leone is extremely poor and nearly half of the working-age population engages in subsistence agriculture. The country possesses substantial mineral, agricultural, and fishery resources, but it is still recovering from a civil war that destroyed most institutions before ending in the early 2000s. In recent years economic growth has been driven by mining—particularly iron ore. The country's principal exports are iron ore, diamonds, and rutile, and the economy is vulnerable to fluctuations in International prices. Until 2014, the government had relied on external assistance to support its budget, but it was gradually becoming more independent. The Ebola outbreak of 2014 and 2015, combined with falling global commodities prices, caused a significant contraction of economic activity in all areas. While the World Health Organization declared an end to the Ebola outbreak in Sierra Leone in November 2015, economic recovery will depend on rising commodities prices and increased efforts to diversify the sources of growth. Pervasive corruption and undeveloped human capital will continue to deter foreign investors. Sustained International donor support in the near future will partially offset these fiscal constraints.

GDP (purchasing power parity): $9.966 billion (2015 est.)
$12.69 billion (2014 est.)
$12.13 billion (2013 est.)
note: data are in 2015 US dollars
country comparison to the world: 159

GDP (official exchange rate): $4.167 billion (2015 est.)

GDP—real growth rate: -21.5% (2015 est.)
4.6% (2014 est.)
20.7% (2013 est.)
country comparison to the world: 224

GDP—per capita (PPP): $1,600 (2015 est.)
$2,000 (2014 est.)
$2,000 (2013 est.)
note: data are in 2015 US dollars
country comparison to the world: 214

Gross National saving: 3.9% of GDP (2015 est.)
-7.9% of GDP (2014 est.)
-4.8% of GDP (2013 est.)
country comparison to the world: 166

GDP—composition, by end use:
household consumption: 87.5%
government consumption: 10.6%
investment in fixed capital: 15.6%
investment in inventories: 0.5%
exports of goods and services: 7.6%
imports of goods and services: -21.8% (2015 est.)

GDP—composition, by sector of origin:
agriculture: 66.8%
industry: 3.4%
services: 29.8% (2015 est.)

Agriculture—products: rice, coffee, cocoa, palm kernels, palm oil, peanuts, cashews; poultry, cattle, sheep, pigs; fish

Industries: diamond mining; iron ore, rutile and bauxite mining; small-scale manufacturing (beverages, textiles, footwear)

Industrial production growth rate: -51% (2015 est.)
country comparison to the world: 201

Labor force: 2.53 million (2015 est.)
country comparison to the world: 114

Labor force—by occupation: *agriculture:* 61.1%
industry: NA%
services: 33.4% (2014 est.)

Unemployment rate: 9.1% (2014 est.)

Population below poverty line: 70.2% (2004 est.)

Household income or consumption by percentage share: *lowest:* 10%: 2.6%
highest: 10%: 33.6% (2003)

Distribution of family income—Gini Index: 34 (2011)
62.9 (1989)
country comparison to the world: 3

Budget: *revenues:* $544.1 million
expenditures: $737.3 million (2015 est.)

Taxes and other revenues: 12.8% of GDP (2015 est.)
country comparison to the world: 205

Budget surplus (+) or deficit (–): -4.5% of GDP (2015 est.)
country comparison to the world: 159

Public debt: 48.5% of GDP (2015 est.)
39.3% of GDP (2014 est.)
country comparison to the world: 87

Fiscal year: calendar year

Inflation rate (consumer prices): 9% (2015 est.)
8.3% (2014 est.)
country comparison to the world: 206

Central bank discount rate: NA%

Commercial bank prime lending rate: 19% (31 December 2015 est.)
19.41% (31 December 2014 est.)
country comparison to the world: 17

Stock of narrow money: $509.6 million (31 December 2015 est.)
$431.9 million (31 December 2014 est.)
country comparison to the world: 164

Stock of broad money: $960.1 million (31 December 2014 est.)
$857.3 million (31 December 2013 est.)
country comparison to the world: 171

Stock of domestic credit: $574 million (31 December 2015 est.)
$516 million (31 December 2014 est.)
country comparison to the world: 165

Market value of publicly traded shares: $NA

Current account balance: -$574 million (2015 est.)
-$911 million (2014 est.)
country comparison to the world: 104

Exports: $533.3 million (2015 est.)
$2.086 billion (2014 est.)
country comparison to the world: 171

Exports—commodities: Iron ore, diamonds, rutile, cocoa, coffee, fish

Exports—partners: China 31.1%, Belgium 27.6%, Romania 11.3%, US 7.2% (2015)

Imports: $929.3 million (2015 est.)
$1.829 billion (2014 est.)
country comparison to the world: 183

Imports—commodities: foodstuffs, machinery and equipment, fuels and lubricants, chemicals

Imports—partners: China 23%, India 7.9%, US 6.4%, Netherlands 5.1% (2015)

Debt—external: $1.368 billion (31 December 2014 est.)
$1.395 billion (31 December 2013 est.)
country comparison to the world: 157

Stock of direct foreign investment—at home: $1.064 billion (31 December 2015 est.)
$1.012 billion (31 December 2014 est.)
country comparison to the world: 111

Stock of direct foreign investment—abroad: $9.7 million (31 December 2015 est.)
$6.7 million (31 December 2014 est.)
country comparison to the world: 103

Exchange rates: leones (SLL) per US dollar—
4,923.8 (2015 est.)
4,524.2 (2014 est.)
4,524.2 (2013 est.)
4,344 (2012 est.)
4,336.1 (2011 est.)

ENERGY

Electricity—production: 145 million kWh (2012 est.)
country comparison to the world: 194

Electricity—consumption: 134.9 million kWh (2012 est.)
country comparison to the world: 194

Electricity—exports: 0 kWh (2013 est.)
country comparison to the world: 195

Electricity—imports: 0 kWh (2013 est.)
country comparison to the world: 201

Electricity—installed generating capacity: 100,000 kW (2015 est.)
country comparison to the world: 178

Electricity—from fossil fuels: 33.3% of total installed capacity (2012 est.)
country comparison to the world: 173

Electricity—from nuclear fuels: 0% of total installed capacity (2012 est.)
country comparison to the world: 180

Electricity—from hydroelectric plants: 66.7% of total installed capacity (2012 est.)
country comparison to the world: 28

Electricity—from other renewable sources: 0% of total installed capacity (2012 est.)
country comparison to the world: 127

Crude oil—production: 0 bbl/day (2014 est.)
country comparison to the world: 190

Crude oil—exports: 0 bbl/day (2012 est.)
country comparison to the world: 189

Crude oil—imports: 0 bbl/day (2012 est.)
country comparison to the world: 125

Crude oil—proved reserves: 0 bbl (1 January 2015 est.)
country comparison to the world: 190

Refined petroleum products—production: 0 bbl/day (2012 est.)
country comparison to the world: 131

Refined petroleum products—consumption: 4,400 bbl/day (2013 est.)
country comparison to the world: 175

Refined petroleum products—production: 0 bbl/day (2012 est.)
country comparison to the world: 132

Refined petroleum products—consumption: 4,428 bbl/day (2012 est.)
country comparison to the world: 166

Natural gas—production: 0 cu m (2013 est.)
country comparison to the world: 127
Natural gas—consumption: 0 cu m (2013 est.)
country comparison to the world: 193
Natural gas—exports: 0 cu m (2013 est.)
country comparison to the world: 180
Natural gas—imports: 0 cu m (2013 est.)
country comparison to the world: 133
Natural gas—proved reserves: 0 cu m (1 January 2014 est.)
country comparison to the world: 194
Carbon dioxide emissions from consumption of energy: 1.311 million Mt (2012 est.)
country comparison to the world: 163

COMMUNICATIONS

Telephone—fixed lines: *total subscriptions:* 16,500
subscriptions per 100 inhabitants: less than 1 (2014 est.)
country comparison to the world: 192
Telephone—mobile cellular: *total:* 4.8 m illion
subscriptions per 100 inhabitants: 83 (2014 est.)
country comparison to the world: 120
Telephone system: *general assessment:* marginal telephone service with poor infrastructure
domestic: the National microwave radio relay trunk system connects Freetown to Bo and Kenem a; while mobile—cellular service is growing rapidly from a small base, service are a coverage remains limited
international: country code—232; satellite earth station—1 intelsat (Atlantic Ocean) (2009)
Broadcast media: 1 government-owned TV station; 3 private TV stations; a pay-TV service began operations in late 2007; 1 government-owned

National radio station; about two dozen private radio stations primarily clustered in major cities; transmissions of several International broadcasters are available (2016)
Radio broadcast stations: AM 1, FM 9, short-wave 1 (2001)
Television broadcast stations: 2 (1999)
Internet country code: .sl
Internet hosts: 282 (2012)
country comparison to the world: 191
Internet users: *total:* 85,600
percent of population: 1.5% (2014 est.)
country comparison to the world: 173

TRANSPORTATION

Airports: 8 (2013)
country comparison to the world: 164
Airports—with paved runways: *total:* 1
over 3,047 m: 1 (2013)
Airports—with unpaved runways: *total:* 7
914 to 1,523 m: 7 (2013)
Heliports: 2 (2013)
Roadways: *total:* 11,300 km
paved: 904 km
unpaved: 10,396 km (2002)
country comparison to the world: 131
Waterways: 800 km (600 km navigable year round) (2011)
country comparison to the world: 71
Merchant marine: *total:* 215
by type: bulk carrier 22, cargo 120, carrier 2, chemical tanker 19, container 6, liquefied gas 3, passenger/cargo 2, petroleum tanker 28, refrigerated cargo 7, roll on/roll off 4, specialized tanker 1, vehicle carrier 1

foreign-owned: 98 (Bangladesh 1, China 19, Cyprus 2, Egypt 3, Estonia 2, Hong Kong 7, Japan 4, Lebanon 2, North Korea 2, Romania 2, Russia 7, Singapore 9, Syria 13, Taiwan 7, Turkey 9, UAE 1, UK 1, Ukraine 5, Yemen 2) (2010)
country comparison to the world: 34
Ports and terminals: *major seaport(s):* Freetown, Pepel, Sherbro Islands

MILITARY AND SECURITY

Military branches: Republic of Sierra Leone Armed Forces (RSLAF): Army (includes Maritime Wing and Air Wing) (2013)
Military service age and obligation: 18 is the legal minimum age for voluntary military service (younger with parental consent); women are eligible to serve; no conscription; candidates must be HIV negative (2012)
Military expenditures: 0.72% of GDP (2012)
0.8% of GDP (2011)
0.72% of GDP (2010)
country comparison to the world: 118

TRANSNATIONAL ISSUES

Disputes—International: Sierra Leone opposes Guinean troops' continued occupation of Yenga, a small village on the Makon a River that serves as a border with Guinea; Guinea's forces came to Yenga in the mid-1990s to help the Sierra Leonean military to suppress rebels and to secure their common border but have remained there even after both countries signed a 2005 agreement acknowledging that Yenga belonged to Sierra Leone; in 2012, the two sides signed a declaration to demilitarize the area

SINGAPORE

INTRODUCTION

Background: Singapore was founded as a British trading colony in 1819. It joined the Malaysian Federation in 1963 but was ousted two years later

and became independent. Singapore subsequently became one of the world's most prosperous countries with strong International trading links (its port is one of the world's busiest in terms of tonnage handled) and with per capita GDP equal to that of the leading nations of Western Europe.

GEOGRAPHY

Location: Southeastern Asia, islands between Malaysia and Indonesia
Geographic coordinates: 122 N, 103 48 E
Map references: Southeast Asia
Area: *total:* 697 sq km
land: 687 sq km
water: 10 sq km
country comparison to the world: 192
Area—comparative: slightly more than 3.5 times the size of Washington, DC
Land boundaries: 0 km
Coastline: 193 km
Maritime claims: *territorial sea:* 3 nm
exclusive fishing zone: within and beyond territorial sea, as defined in treaties and practice

Climate: tropical; hot, humid, rainy; two distinct monsoon seasons—northeastern monsoon (December to March) and southwestern monsoon (June to September); inter-monsoon—frequent afternoon and early evening thunderstorms
Terrain: lowlying, gently undulating central plateau
Elevation: *mean elevation:* NA
elevation extremes: *lowest point:* Singapore Strait 0 m
highest point: Bukit Timah 166 m
Natural resources: fish, deepwater ports
Land use: *agricultural land:* 1%
arable land: 0.9%
permanent crops: 0.1%
permanent pasture: 0%
forest: 3.3%
other: 95.7% (2011 est.)
Irrigated land: 0 sq km (2012)
Total renewable water resources: 0.6 cu km (2011)
Freshwater withdrawal (domestic/industrial/agricultural): *total:* 0.19 cu km/yr (47%/53%/0%)
per capita: 81.97 cu m/yr (2005)
Natural hazards: NA

Environment—current issues: industrial pollution; limited Natural freshwater resources; limited land availability presents waste disposal problems; seasonal smoke/haze resulting from forest fires in Indonesia

Environment—international agreements: *party to:* Biodiversity, Climate Change, Climate Change-Kyoto Protocol, Desertification, Endangered Species, Hazardous Wastes, Law of the Sea, Ozone Layer Protection, Ship Pollution
signed, but not ratified: none of the selected agreements

Geography—note: focal point for Southeast Asian sea routes

PEOPLE AND SOCIETY

Nationality: *noun:* Singaporean(s)
adjective: Singapore

Ethnic groups: Chinese 74.2%, Malay 13.3%, Indian 9.2%, other 3.3% (2013 est.)

Languages: Mandarin (official) 36.3%, English (official) 29.8%, Malay (official) 11.9%, Hokkien 8.1%, Cantonese 4.1%, Tamil (official) 3.2%, Teochew 3.2%, other Indian languages 1.2%, other Chinese dialects 1.1%, other 1.1% (2010 est.)

Religions: Buddhist 33.9%, Muslim 14.3%, Taoist 11.3%, Catholic 7.1%, Hindu 5.2%, other Christian 11%, other 0.7%, none 16.4% (2010 est.)

Population: 5,674,472 (July 2015 est.)
country comparison to the world: 114

Age structure: *0–14 years:* 13.14% (male 381,404/female 364,424)
15–24 years: 17.43% (male 486,979/female 502,159)
25–54 years: 50.39% (male 1,393,686/female 1,465,601)
55–64 years: 10.16% (male 288,489/female 287,992)
65 years and over: 8.88% (male 229,117/female 274,621) (2015 est.)

Dependency ratios: *total dependency ratio:* 37.4%
youth dependency ratio: 21.4%
elderly dependency ratio: 16.1%
potential support ratio: 6.2% (2015 est.)

Median age: *total:* 34 years
male: 33.9 years
female: 34.1 years (2015 est.)
country comparison to the world: 83

Population growth rate: 1.89% (2015 est.)
country comparison to the world: 57

Birth rate: 8.27 births/1,000 population (2015 est.)
country comparison to the world: 219

Death rate: 3.43 deaths/1,000 population (2015 est.)
country comparison to the world: 217

Net migration rate: 14.05 migrant(s)/1,000 population (2015 est.)
country comparison to the world: 5

Urbanization: *urban population:* 100% of total population (2015)
rate of urbanization: 2.02% annual rate of change (2010–15 est.)

Major urban areas—population: SINGAPORE (capital) 5.619 million (2015)

Sex ratio: *at birth:* 1.07 male(s)/female

0–14 years: 1.05 male(s)/female
15–24 years: 0.97 male(s)/female
25–54 years: 0.95 male(s)/female
55–64 years: 1 male(s)/female
65 years and over: 0.83 male(s)/female
total population: 0.96 male(s)/female (2015 est.)

Mother's mean age at first birth: 29.8 (2010 est.)

Maternal mortality rate: 10 deaths/100,000 live births (2015 est.)
country comparison to the world: 182

Infant mortality rate: *total:* 2.48 deaths/1,000 live births
male: 2.65 deaths/1,000 live births
female: 2.28 deaths/1,000 live births (2015 est.)
country comparison to the world: 221

Life expectancy at birth: *total population:* 84.68 years
male: 82.06 years
female: 87.5 years (2015 est.)
country comparison to the world: 3

Total fertility rate: 0.81 children born/woman (2015 est.)
country comparison to the world: 224

Health expenditures: 4.6% of GDP (2013)
country comparison to the world: 146

Physicians density: 1.95 physicians/1,000 population (2013)

Hospital bed density: 2 beds/1,000 population (2011)

Drinking water source:
improved:
urban: 100% of population
total: 100% of population
unimproved:
urban: 0% of population
total: 0% of population (2015 est.)

Sanitation facility access:
improved:
urban: 100% of population
total: 100% of population
unimproved:
urban: 0% of population
total: 0% of population (2015 est.)

HIV/AIDS—adult prevalence rate: NA

HIV/AIDS—people living with HIV/AIDS: NA

HIV/AIDS—deaths: NA

Obesity—adult prevalence rate: 6.8% (2014)
country comparison to the world: 142

Education expenditures: 2.9% of GDP (2013)
country comparison to the world: 140

Literacy: *definition:* age 15 and over can read and write
total population: 96.8%
male: 98.6%
female: 95% (2015 est.)

Unemployment, youth ages 15–24: *total:* 7%
male: 5.4%
female: 9% (2013)
country comparison to the world: 121

GOVERNMENT

Country name: *conventional long form:* Republic of Singapore
conventional short form: Singapore
local long form: Republic of Singapore
local short form: Singapore

etymology: name derives from the Sanskrit words "singa" (lion) and "pura" (city) to describe the city-state's leonine symbol

Government type: parliamentary republic

Capital: *name:* Singapore

Geographic coordinates: 117 N, 103 51 E

time difference: UTC+8 (13 hours ahead of Washington, DC, during Standard Time)

Administrative divisions: none

Independence: 9 August 1965 (from Malaysian Federation)

National holiday: National Day, 9 August (1965)

Constitution: several previous; latest adopted 22 December 1965; amended many times, last in 2015 (2016)

Legal system: English common law

International law organization participation: has not submitted an ICJ jurisdiction declaration; non-party state to the ICCt

Citizenship: *citizenship by birth:* no
citizenship by descent only: at least one parent must be a citizen of Singapore
dual citizenship recognized: no
residency requirement for naturalization: 10 years

Suffrage: 21 years of age; universal and compulsory

Executive branch: *chief of state:* President Tony TAN Keng Yam (since 1 September 2011)

head of government: Prime Minister LEE Hsien Loong (since 12 August 2004); Deputy Prime Ministers TEO Chee Hean (since 1 April 2009) and Tharman SHANMUGARATNAM (since 21 May 2011)

cabinet: Cabinet appointed by the president on the advice of the prime minister; Cabinet responsible to Parliament

elections/appointments: president directly elected by simple majority popular vote for a single 6-year term; election last held on 27 August 2011 (next to be held by August 2017); following legislative elections, leader of majority party or majority coalition usually appointed prime minister by president; deputy prime ministers appointed by the president

election results: Tony TAN Keng Yam elected president; percent of vote—Tony TAN Keng Yam (independent) 35.2%, TAN Cheng Bock (independent) 34.9%, TAN Jee Say (independent) 25%, TAN Kin Lian (PP) 4.9%

Legislative branch: *description:* unicameral Parliament (101 seats; 89 members directly elected by popular vote, 9 nominated by the president, and up to 9—but currently 3—non-constituency members from opposition parties to ensure political diversity; members serve 5-year terms)

elections: last held on 11 September 2015 (next to be held in 2020)

election results: percent of vote by party—PAP 69.9%, WP 12.5%, other 17.6%; seats by party—PAP 83, WP 6

Judicial branch: *highest court(s):* Supreme Court (consists of the president or chief justice and 16 justices and organized into an upper tier Appeal Court and a lower tier High Court)

judge selection and term of office: all judges appointed by the president from candidates recommended by the prime minister after consultation with the chief justice; justices appointed for life

subordinate courts: district, magistrates', juvenile, family, community, and coroners' courts; small claims tribunals

Political parties and leaders: National Solidarity Party or NSP [LIM Tean]

People's Action Party or PAP [LEE Hsien Loong]

Singapore Democratic Party or SDP [CHEE Soon Juan]

Workers' Party or WP [LOW Thia Khiang]

Political pressure groups and leaders: none

International organization participation: ADB, AOSIS, APEC, Arctic Council (observer), ARF, ASEAN, BIS, C, CP, EAS, FAO, FATF, G-77, IAEA, IBRD, ICAO, ICC (National committees), ICCt, ICRM, IDA, IFC, IFRCS, IHO, ILO, IMF, IMO, IMSO, Interpol, IOC, IPU, ISO, ITSO, ITU, ITUC (NGOs), MIGA, NAM, OPCW, Pacific Alliance (observer), PCA, UN, UNCTAD, UNESCO, UNHCR, UPU, WCO, WHO, WIPO, WMO, WTO

Diplomatic representation in the US: *chief of mission:* Ambassador Ashok Kumar MIRPURI (since 24 July 2012)

chancery: 3501 International Place NW, Washington, DC 20008

telephone: [1] (202) 537-3100

FAX: [1] (202) 537-0876

consulate(s) general: San Francisco

consulate(s): New York

Diplomatic representation from the US: *chief of mission:* Ambassador Kirk W. WAGAR (since 25 September 2013)

embassy: 27 Napier Road, Singapore 258508

mailing address: FPO AP 96507–0001

telephone: [65] 6476-9100

FAX: [65] 6476-9340

Flag description: two equal horizontal bands of red (top) and white; near the hoist side of the red band, there is a vertical, white crescent (closed portion is toward the hoist side) partially enclosing five white five-pointed stars arranged in a circle; red denotes brotherhood and equality; white signifies purity and virtue; the waxing crescent moon symbolizes a young nation on the ascendancy; the five stars represent the nation's ideals of democracy, peace, progress, justice, and equality

National symbol(s): lion, merlion (mythical half lion-half fish creature), orchid; National colors: red, white

National anthem: *name:* "Majulah Singapura" (Onward Singapore)

lyrics/music: ZUBIR Said

note: adopted 1965; first performed in 1958 at the Victoria Theatre, the anthem is sung only in Malay

ECONOMY

Economy—overview: Singapore has a highly developed and successful free-market economy. It enjoys a remarkably open and corruption-free environment, stable prices, and a per capita GDP higher than that of most developed countries. Unemployment is very low. The economy depends heavily on exports, particularly of consumer electronics, information technology products, medical and optical devices, pharmaceuticals, and on its vibrant transportation, business, and financial services sectors.

The economy contracted 0.6% in 2009 as a result of the global financial crisis, but has continued to grow since 2010 on the strength of renewed exports. Growth in 2014–15 was slower at under 3%, largely a result of soft demand for exports amid a sluggish global economy and weak growth in Singapore's manufacturing sector.

The government is attempting to restructure Singapore's economy by weaning its dependence on foreign labor, addressing weak productivity, and increasing Singaporean wages. Singapore has attracted major investments in pharmaceuticals and medical technology production and will continue efforts to strengthen its position as Southeast Asia's leading financial and high-tech hub. Singapore is a member of the 12-nation Trans-Pacific Partnership free trade negotiations, as well as the Regional Comprehensive Economic Partnership negotiations with the nine other ASEAN members plus Australia, China, India, Japan, South Korea, and New Zealand. in 2015, Singapore formed, with the other ASEAN members, the ASEAN Economic Community.

GDP (purchasing power parity): $471.9 billion (2015 est.)

$462.6 billion (2014 est.)

$448 billion (2013 est.)

note: data are in 2015 US dollars

country comparison to the world: 42

GDP (official exchange rate): $292.7 billion (2015 est.)

GDP—real growth rate: 2% (2015 est.)

3.3% (2014 est.)

4.7% (2013 est.)

country comparison to the world: 135

GDP—per capita (PPP): $85,300 (2015 est.)

$84,600 (2014 est.)

$83,000 (2013 est.)

note: data are in 2015 US dollars

country comparison to the world: 6

Gross National saving: 46% of GDP (2015 est.)

46.3% of GDP (2014 est.)

48% of GDP (2013 est.)

country comparison to the world: 2

GDP—composition, by end use:

household consumption: 38.8%

government consumption: 10.1%

investment in fixed capital: 26.2%

investment in inventories: -0.5%

exports of goods and services: 184.3%

imports of goods and services: -158.9% (2015 est.)

GDP—composition, by sector of origin:

agriculture: 0%

industry: 23.8%

services: 76.2% (2014 est.)

Agriculture—products: orchids, vegetables; poultry, eggs; fish, ornamental fish

Industries: electronics, chemicals, financial services, oil drilling equipment, petroleum refining, rubber processing and rubber products, processed food and beverages, ship repair, offshore platform construction, life sciences, entrepot trade

Industrial production growth rate: -3.5% (2015 est.)

country comparison to the world: 184

Labor force: 3.588 million

note: excludes non-residents (2015 est.)

country comparison to the world: 98

Labor force—by occupation: *agriculture:* 1.3%

industry: 14.8%

services: 83.9%

note: excludes non-residents (2014)

Unemployment rate: 2% (2015 est.)

2% (2014 est.)

country comparison to the world: 12

Population below poverty line: NA%

Household income or consumption by percentage share: *lowest:* 10%: 2.3%

highest: 10%: 11% (2014)

Distribution of family income—Gini index: 46.4 (2014) 46.3 (2013)

country comparison to the world: 33

Budget: *revenues:* $44.06 billion

expenditures: $45.48 billion

note: expenditures include both operational and development expenditures (2015 est.)

Taxes and other revenues: 15% of GDP (2015 est.)

country comparison to the world: 191

Budget surplus (+) or deficit (–): -0.5% of GDP (2015 est.)

country comparison to the world: 46

Public debt: 105.6% of GDP (2015 est.)

99.3% of GDP (2014 est.)

note: Singapore's public debt consists largely of Singapore Government Securities (SGS) issued to assist the Central Provident Fund (CPF), which administers Singapore's defined contribution pension fund; special issues of SGS are held by the CPF, and are non-tradable; the government has not borrowed to finance deficit expenditures since the 1980s; Singapore has no external public debt

country comparison to the world: 13

Fiscal year: 1 April—31 March

Inflation rate (consumer prices): -0.5% (2015 est.)

1% (2014 est.)

country comparison to the world: 28

Central bank discount rate: 0.2484% (2014)

0.0698% (2013)

Commercial bank prime lending rate: 5.4% (31 December 2015 est.)

5.35% (31 December 2014 est.)

country comparison to the world: 141

Stock of narrow money: $114.3 billion (31 December 2015 est.)

$121.3 billion (31 December 2014 est.)

country comparison to the world: 32

Stock of broad money: $413.7 billion (31 December 2014 est.)

$405.1 billion (31 December 2013 est.)

country comparison to the world: 27

Stock of domestic credit: $479.8 billion (31 December 2014 est.)

$458.9 billion (31 December 2013 est.)

country comparison to the world: 26

Market value of publicly traded shares: $787.3 billion (31 December 2014 est.)

$751.1 billion (31 December 2013)
$747.8 billion (31 December 2012 est.)
country comparison to the world: 18
Current account balance: $57.56 billion (2015 est.)
$53.18 billion (2014 est.)
country comparison to the world: 10
Exports: $384.6 billion (2015 est.)
$437.3 billion (2014 est.)
country comparison to the world: 14
Exports—commodities: machinery and equipment (including electronics and telecommunications), pharmaceuticals and other chemicals, Refined petroleum products, foodstuffs and beverages
Exports—partners: China 13.7%, Hong Kong 11.5%, Malaysia 10.8%, Indonesia 8.2%, US 6.9%, Japan 4.4%, South Korea 4.1% (2015)
Imports: $294.2 billion (2015 est.) $360.9 billion (2014 est.)
country comparison to the world: 16
Imports—commodities: machinery and equipment, mineral fuels, chemicals, foodstuffs, consumer goods
Imports—partners: China 14.2%, US 11.2%, Malaysia 11.2%, Japan 6.3%, South Korea 6.1%, Indonesia 4.8% (2015)
Reserves of foreign exchange and gold: $262 billion (31 December 2015 est.)
$256.9 billion (31 December 2014 est.)
country comparison to the world: 12
Debt—external: $1.33 trillion (31 December 2014 est.)
$1.323 trillion (31 December 2013 est.)
country comparison to the world: 15
Stock of direct foreign investment—at home:
$981.1 billion (31 December 2015 est.)
$912.4 billion (31 December 2014 est.)
country comparison to the world: 11
Stock of direct foreign investment—at abroad:
$614 billion (31 December 2015 est.)
$576.4 billion (31 December 2014 est.)
country comparison to the world: 16
Exchange rates: Singapore dollars (SGD) per US dollar—
1.38 (2015 est.)
1.2671 (2014 est.)
1.2671 (2013 est.)
1.25 (2012 est.)
1.258 (2011 est.)

ENERGY

Electricity—production: 49.31 billion kWh (2014 est.)
country comparison to the world: 54
Electricity—consumption: 47.18 billion kWh (2014 est.)
country comparison to the world: 50
Electricity—exports: 0 kWh (2014 est.)
country comparison to the world: 196
Electricity—imports: 0 kWh (2014 est.)
country comparison to the world: 202
Electricity—installed generating capacity: 10.75 million kW (2012 est.)
country comparison to the world: 54
Electricity—from fossil fuels: 95.3% of total installed capacity (2014 est.)

country comparison to the world: 68
Electricity—from nuclear fuels: 0% of total installed capacity (2014 est.)
country comparison to the world: 181
Electricity—from hydroelectric plants: 0% of total installed capacity (2014 est.)
country comparison to the world: 202
Electricity—from other renewable sources: 3.9% of total installed capacity (2014 est.)
country comparison to the world: 63
Crude oil—production: 0 bbl/day (2014 est.)
country comparison to the world: 191
Crude oil—exports: 5,900 bbl/day (2012 est.)
country comparison to the world: 69
Crude oil—imports: 976,100 bbl/day (2012 est.)
country comparison to the world: 13
Crude oil—proved reserves: 0 bbl (1 January 2015 est.)
country comparison to the world: 191
Refined petroleum products—production: 1.099 million bbl/day (2012 est.)
country comparison to the world: 22
Refined petroleum products—consumption: 1.24 million bbl/day (2013 est.)
country comparison to the world: 17
Refined petroleum products—exports: 1.685 million bbl/day (2012 est.)
country comparison to the world: 5
Refined petroleum products—imports: 1.914 million bbl/day (2012 est.)
country comparison to the world: 2
Natural gas—production: 0 cu m (2013 est.)
country comparison to the world: 128
Natural gas—consumption: 9.62 billion cu m (2013 est.)
country comparison to the world: 47
Natural gas—exports: 0 cu m (2013 est.)
country comparison to the world: 181
Natural gas—imports: 9.62 billion cu m (2013 est.)
country comparison to the world: 27
Natural gas—proved reserves: 0 cu m (1 January 2014 est.)
country comparison to the world: 195
Carbon dioxide emissions from consumption of energy: 208 million Mt (2012 est.)
country comparison to the world: 28

COMMUNICATIONS

Telephones—fixed lines: *total subscriptions:* 1.96 million
subscriptions per 100 inhabitants: 35 (2014 est.)
country comparison to the world: 58
Telephones—mobile cellular: *total:* 8.7 million
subscriptions per 100 inhabitants: 157 (2014 est.)
country comparison to the world: 92
Telephone system: *general assessment:* excellent service
domestic: excellent domestic facilities; launched 3G wireless service in February 2005; combined fixed-line and mobile-cellular teledensity more than 180 telephones per 100 persons; multiple providers of highspeed internet connectivity and the government is close to completing an island-wide roll out of a highspeed fiber-optic broadband network

international: country code—65; numerous submarine cables provide links throughout Asia, Australia, the Middle East, Europe, and US; satellite earth stations—4; supplemented by VSAT coverage (2011)
Broadcast media: state controls broadcast media; 8 domestic TV stations operated by MediaCorp which is wholly owned by a state investment company; broadcasts from Malaysian and Indonesian stations available; satellite dishes banned; multichannel cable TV service available; a total of 18 domestic radio stations broadcasting with Media Corp operating more than a dozen and another 4 stations are closely linked to the ruling party or controlled by the Singapore Armed Forces Reservists Association; many Malaysian and Indonesian radio stations are available
Radio broadcast stations: AM 0, FM 19, shortwave 1 (2008)
Television broadcast stations: 1 (broadcasting on 8 channels); addition al reception of numerous UHF and VHF signals originating in Malaysia and Indonesia (2008)
Internet country code: .sg
Internet hosts: 1.96 million (2012)
country comparison to the world: 39
Internet users: *total:* 4.5 million
percent of population: 80.7% (2014 est.)
country comparison to the world: 73

TRANSPORTATION

Airports: 9 (2013)
country comparison to the world: 158
Airports—with paved runways: *total:* 9
over 3,047 m: 2
2,438 to 3,047 m: 2
1,524 to 2,437 m: 3
914 to 1,523 m: 1
under 914 m: 1 (2013)
Pipelines: gas 122 km; refined products 8 km (2013)
Roadways: *total:* 3,425 km
paved: 3,425 km (includes 161 km of expressways) (2012)
country comparison to the world: 164
Merchant marine: *total:* 1,599
by type: bulk carrier 247, cargo 109, carrier 6, chemical tanker 256, container 339, liquefied gas 131, petroleum tanker 436, refrigerated cargo 13, roll on/roll off 5, vehicle carrier 57
foreign-owned: 966 (Australia 12, Bangladesh 1, Belgium 1, Bermuda 25, Brazil 9, Chile 6, China 29, Cyprus 6, Denmark 149, France 3, Germany 32, Greece 22, Hong Kong 46, India 21, Indonesia 60, Italy 5, Japan 164, Malaysia 27, Netherlands 1, Norway 153, Russia 2, South Africa 13, South Korea 3, Sweden 11, Switzerland 3, Taiwan 77, Thailand 33, UAE 10, UK 6, US 36)
registered in other coun tries: 344 (Australia 2, Bahamas 7, Bangladesh 7, Belize 4, Cambodia 3, Cyprus 1, France 3, Honduras 11, Hong Kong 13, Indonesia 46, Italy 1, Kiribati 9, Liberia 22, Malaysia 13, Maldives 4, Malta 4, Marshall Islands 30, Mongolia 3, North Korea 1, Panama 92, Philippines 1, Saint Kitts and Nevis 10, Saint Vincent and the Grenadines 5, Sierra Leone 9, Thailand 1, Tuvalu 19, US 16, Vanuatu 2, unknown 5) (2010)
country comparison to the world: 6

Ports and terminals: *major seaport(s):* Singapore *container port(s)(TEUs):* Singapore (31,649,400) *LNG terminal(s) (import):* Singapore

Transportation—note: the International Maritime Bureau reports the territorial and offshore waters in the South China Sea as high risk for piracy and armed robbery against ships; numerous commercial vessels have been attacked and hijacked both at anchor and while underway; hijacked vessels are often disguised and cargo diverted to ports in East Asia; crews have been murdered or cast adrift; in 2014, 8 commercial vessels were attacked in the Singapore Straits

MILITARY AND SECURITY

Military branches: Singapore Armed Forces: Army, Navy, Air Force (includes Air Defense) (2013)

Military service age and obligation: 18–21 years of age for male compulsory military service; 16 1/2 years of age for volunteers; 2-year conscript service obligation, with a reserve obligation to age 40 (enlisted) or age 50 (officers) (2012)

Military expenditures: 3.52% of GDP (2012) 3.47% of GDP (2011) 3.52% of GDP (2010) *country comparison to the world:* 15

TRANSNATIONAL ISSUES

Disputes—International: disputes persist with Malaysia over deliveries of fresh water to Singapore, Singapore's extensive land reclamation works, bridge construction, and maritime boundaries in the Johor and Singapore Straits; in 2008, ICJ awarded sovereignty of Pedra Branca (Pulau Batu Puteh/Horsburgh Island) to Singapore, and Middle Rocks to Malaysia, but did not rule on maritime regimes, boundaries, or disposition of South Ledge; Indonesia and Singapore continue to work on finalization of their 1973 maritime boundary agreement by defining unresolved areas north of Indonesia's Batam Island; piracy remains a problem in the Malacca Strait

Illicit drugs: drug abuse limited because of aggressive law enforcement efforts, including carrying out death sentences; as a transportation and financial services hub, Singapore is vulnerable, despite strict laws and enforcement, as a venue for money laundering

SINT MAARTEN

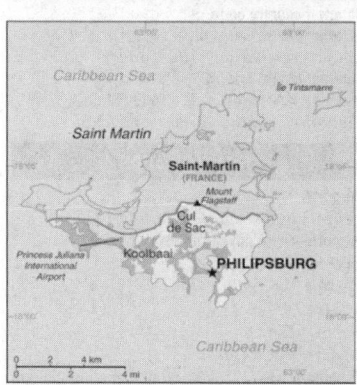

INTRODUCTION

Background: Although sighted by Christopher COLUMBUS in 1493 and claimed for Spain, it was the Dutch who occupied the island in 1631 and began exploiting its salt deposits. The Spanish retook the island in 1633, but continued to be harassed by the Dutch. The Spanish finally relinquished the island of Saint Martin to the French and Dutch, who divided it amongst themselves in 1648. The establishment of cotton, tobacco, and sugar plantations dramatically expanded African slavery on the island in the 18th and 19th centuries; the practice was not abolished in the Dutch half until 1863. The island's economy declined until 1939 when it became a free port; the tourism industry was dramatically expanded beginning in the 1950s. In 1954, Sint Maarten And several other Dutch Caribbean possessions became part of the Kingdom of the Netherlands as the Netherlands Antilles. in a 2000 referendum, the citizens of Sint Maarten voted to become a self-governing country within the Kingdom of the Netherlands. The change in status became effective in October of 2010 with the dissolution of the Netherlands Antilles.

GEOGRAPHY

Location: Caribbean, located in the Leeward Islands (northern) group; Dutch part of the island of Saint Martin in the Caribbean Sea; Sint Maarten lies east of the US Virgin Islands

Geographic coordinates: 18 4 N, 63 4 W

Map references: Central America and the Caribbean

Area: *total:* 34 sq km

land: 34 sq km

water: 0 sq km

note: Dutch part of the island of Saint Martin *country comparison to the world:* 236

Area—comparative: one-fifth the size of Washington, DC

Land boundaries: *total:* 16 km

border countries (1): Saint Martin (France) 16 km

Coastline: 58.9 km (for entire island)

Maritime claims: *territorial sea:* 12 nm

exclusive fishing zone: 12 nm

Climate: tropical marine climate, ameliorated by northeast trade winds, results in moderate temperatures; average rainfall of 150 cm/year; hurricane season stretches from July to November

Terrain: low, hilly terrain, volcanic origin

Elevation: *mean elevation:* NA

elevation extremes: *lowest point:* Caribbean Sea 0 m

highest point: Mount Flagstaff 386 m

Natural resources: fish, salt

Natural hazards: subject to hurricanes from July to November

Environment—current issues: NA

Geography—note: the northern border is shared with the French overseas collectivity of Saint Martin; together, these two entities make up the smallest landmass in the world shared by two self-governing states

PEOPLE AND SOCIETY

Languages: English (official) 67.5%, Spanish 12.9%, Creole 8.2%, Dutch (official) 4.2%, Papiamento (a Spanish-Portuguese-Dutch-English dialect) 2.2%, French 1.5%, other 3.5% (2001 census)

Religions: Protestant 41.9% (Pentecostal 14.7%, Methodist 10.0%, Seventh Day Adventist 6.6%, Baptist 4.7%, Anglican 3.1%, other Protestant 2.8%), Roman Catholic 33.1%, Hindu 5.2%, Christian 4.1%, Jehovah's Witness 1.7%, Evangelical 1.4%, Muslim/Jewish 1.1%, other 1.3% (includes Buddhist, Sikh, Rastafarian), none 7.9%, no response 2.4% (2011 est.)

Population: 37,132 (2014 est.)

country comparison to the world: 213

Age structure: *0–14 years:* 19.7% (male 3,986/female 3,704)

15–24 years: 16.3% (male 3,130/female 3,253)

25–54 years: 45.3% (male 8,626/female 9,077)

55–64 years: 12.9% (male 2,448/female 2,596)

65 years and over: 5.8% (male 1,087/female 1,181) (2013 est.)

Median age: *total:* 40.4 years

male: 39.6 years

female: 41.3 years (2015 est.)

country comparison to the world: 43

Population growth rate: 1.51% (2013 est.)

country comparison to the world: 80

Birth rate: 13 births/1,000 population (2013 est.)

country comparison to the world: 153

Death rate: 4.51 deaths/1,000 population (2013 est.)

country comparison to the world: 202

Net migration rate: 6.63 migrant(s)/1,000 population (2013 est.)

country comparison to the world: 18

Urbanization: *urban population:* 100% of total population (2015)

rate of urbanization: 1.97% annual rate of change (2010–15 est.)

Major urban areas—population: PHILIPSBURG (capital) 1,327 (2011)

Sex ratio: *at birth:* 1.05 male(s)/female

0–14 years: 1.08 male(s)/female

15–24 years: 0.96 male(s)/female

25–54 years: 0.95 male(s)/female
55–64 years: 0.94 male(s)/female
65 years and over: 0.92 male(s)/female
total population: 0.97 male(s)/female (2013 est.)
Infant mortality rate: *total:* 9.05 deaths/1,000 live births
male: 9.84 deaths/1,000 live births
female: 8.22 deaths/1,000 live births (2013 est.)
country comparison to the world: 144
Life expectancy at birth: *total population:* 77.61 years
male: 75.34 years
female: 79.99 years (2013 est.)
country comparison to the world: 67
Total fertility rate: 2.09 children born/woman (2013 est.)
country comparison to the world: 108
HIV/AIDS—adult prevalence rate: NA
HIV/AIDS—people living with HIV/AIDS: NA
HIV/AIDS—deaths: NA

GOVERNMENT

Country name: *Dutch long form:* Land Sint Maarten
Dutch short form: Sint Maarten
English long form: Country of Sint Maarten
English short form: Sint Maarten
former: Netherlands Antilles; Curacao and Dependencies
etymology: explorer Christopher COLUMBUS named the island after Saint MARTIN of Tours because the 11 November 1493 day of discovery was the saint's feast day
Dependency status: constituent country within the Kingdom of the Netherlands; full autonomy in internal affairs granted in 2010; Dutch Government responsible for defense and Foreign Affairs
Government type: Capital: *name:* Philipsburg
Geographic coordinates: 18 1 N, 63 2 W
time difference: UTC-4 (1 hour ahead of Washington, DC, during Standard Time)
Administrative divisions: none (part of the Kingdom of the Netherlands)
note: Sint Maarten is one of four constituent parts (countries) of the Kingdom of the Netherlands; the other three parts are the Netherlands, Aruba, and Curacao
Independence: none (part of the Kingdom of the Netherlands)
National holiday: King's Day (birthday of King WILLEM-ALEXANDER), 27 April (1967)
Constitution: Staatsregeling, 10 October 2010; revised Kingdom Charter pending previous 1947, 1955; latest adopted 21 July 2010, entered into force 10 October 2010 (regulates governance of Sint Maarten but is subordinate to the Charter for the Kingdom of the Netherlands); note—in October 2010, with the dissolution of the Netherlands Antilles, Sint Maarten became a constituent country within the Kingdom of the Netherlands
Legal system: based on Dutch civil law system with some English common law influence
Citizenship: see the Netherlands
Suffrage: 18 years of age; universal

Executive branch: *chief of state:* Queen BEATRIX of the Netherlands (since 30 April 1980); represented by Governor General Eugene HOLIDAY (since 10 October 2010)
head of government: Prime Minister William MARLIN (since 19 November 2015)
cabinet: Cabinet nominated by the prime minister and appointed by the governor-general
elections/appointments: the monarch is hereditary; governor general appointed by the monarch for a 6-year term; following legislative elections, the leader of the majority party is usually elected prime minister by the legislature
Legislative branch: *description:* unicameral Estates of Sint Maarten or Staten (15 seats; members directly elected by proportional representation vote to serve 4-year terms)
elections: last held 17 September 2010 (next to be held in 2014)
election results: percent of vote by party—National Alliance 45.9%, UPP 36.1%, Democratic Party 17.1%, other .9%; seats by party—National Alliance 7, UPP 6, Democratic Party 2
Judicial branch: *highest court(s):* Joint Court of Justice of Aruba, Curacao, Sint Maarten, and of Bonaire, Sint Eustatius, and Saba or "Joint Court of Justice" (consists of the presiding judge, other members, and their substitutes); final appeals heard by the Supreme Court, in The Hague, Netherlands; note—prior to 2010, the Joint Court of Justice was the Common Court of Justice of the Netherlands Antilles and Aruba
judge selection and term of office: Joint Court judges appointed by the monarch for life
subordinate courts: Courts in First Instance
Political parties and leaders: Concordia Political Alliance or CPA [Jeffery RICHARDSON]
Democratic Party or DP [Sarah WESCOTT-WILLIAMS]
National Alliance or NA [William MARLIN]
United People's Party or UPP [Theodore HEYLIGER]
Diplomatic representation in the US: none (represented by the Kingdom of the Netherlands)
Diplomatic representation from the US: the US does not have an embassy in Sint Maarten; the Consul General to Curacao is accredited to Sint Maarten
Flag description: two equal horizontal bands of red (top) and blue with a white isosceles triangle based on the hoist side; the center of the triangle displays the Sint Maarten coat of arms; the arms consist of an orange-bordered blue shield prominently displaying the white court house in Philipsburg, as well as a bouquet of yellow sage (the National flower) in the upper left, and the silhouette of a Dutch-French friendship monument in the upper right; the shield is surmounted by a yellow rising sun in front of which is a brown pelican in flight; a yellow scroll below the shield bears the motto: SEMPER PROGREDIENS (Always Progressing); the three main colors are identical to those on the Dutch flag
note: the flag somewhat resembles that of the Philippines, but with the main red and blue bands reversed; the banner more closely evokes the wartime Philippine flag
National symbol(s): brown pelican, yellow sage (flower); National colors: red, white, blue
National anthem: *name:* "O Sweet Saint Martin's Land"
lyrics/music: Gerard KEMPS
note: the song, written in 1958, is used as an unofficial anthem for the entire island (both French and Dutch sides); as a collectivity of France, in addition to the local anthem, "La Marseillaise" is official on the French side (see France); as a constituent part of the Kingdom of the Netherlands, in addition to the local anthem, "Het Wilhelmus" is official on the Dutch side (see Netherlands)

ECONOMY

Economy—overview: The economy of Sint Maarten centers around tourism with nearly four-fifths of the labor force engaged in this sector. Nearly 1.8 million visitors came to the island by cruise ship and roughly 500,000 visitors arrived through Princess Juliana International Airport in 2013. Cruise ships and yachts also call on Sint Maarten's numerous ports and harbors. Limited agriculture and local fishing means that almost all food must be imported. Energy resources and manufactured goods are also imported. Sint Maarten had the highest per capita income among the five islands that formerly comprised the Netherlands Antilles.
GDP (purchasing power parity): $365.8 million (2014 est.)
$353.5 million (2013 est.)
$339.6 million (2012 est.)
note: data rare in 2014 US dollars
country comparison to the world: 215
GDP (official exchange rate): $304.1 billion (2014 est.)
GDP—real growth rate: 3.6% (2014 est.)
4.1% (2013 est.)
1.9% (2012 est.)
country comparison to the world: 79
GDP—per capita (PPP): $66,800 (2014 est.)
$65,500 (2013 est.)
$63,900 (2012 est.)
note: data are in 2015 US dollars
country comparison to the world: 13
GDP—composition, by sector of origin:
agriculture: 0.4%
industry: 18.3%
services: 81.3% (2008 est.)
Agriculture—products: sugar
Industries: tourism, light industry
Labor force: 23,200 (2008 est.)
country comparison to the world: 210
Labor force—by occupation: *agriculture:* 1.1%
industry: 15.2%
services: 83.7% (2008 est.)
Unemployment rate: 12% (2012 est.)
10.6% (2008 est.)
country comparison to the world: 132
Inflation rate (consumer prices): 4% (2012 est.)
0.7% (2009 est.)
country comparison to the world: 156
Exports—commodities: sugar

Exchange rates: Netherlands Antillean guilders (AN G) per US dollar—
1.79 (2014)
1.79 (2013)
1.79 (2013)
1.79 (2012)
1.79 (2011)

ENERGY

Electricity—production: 304.3 million kWh (2008 est.)
country comparison to the world: 178

COMMUNICATIONS

Telephone system: *general assessment:* generally adequate facilities

domestic: extensive interisland microwave radio relay links
international: country code—1-721; the Americas Region Caribbean Ring System (ARCOS-1) and the Americas-2 submarine cable systems provide connectivity to Central America, parts of South America and the Caribbean, and the US; satellite earth stations—2 intelsat (Atlantic Ocean) (2010)
Internet country code: . sx;
note—IANA has designated .sx for Sint Maarten, but has not yet assigned it to a sponsoring organization
Internet hosts: NA
Internet users: NA

TRANSPORTATION

Airports: 1 (2013)
country comparison to the world: 234
Airports—with paved runways: *total:* 1
1,524 to 2,437 m: 1 (2012)
Roadways: *total:* 53 km
country comparison to the world: 219
Ports and terminals: *major seaport(s):* Philipsburg
oil terminals: Coles Bay oil terminal

MILITARY AND SECURITY

Military branches: no regular military forces (2012)
Military—note: defense is the responsibility of the Kingdom of the Netherlands

SLOVAKIA

INTRODUCTION

Background: Slovakia's roots can be traced to the 9th century state of Great Moravia. Subsequently, the Slovaks became part of the Hungarian Kingdom, where they remained for the next 1,000 years. Following the formation of the dual Austro-Hungarian monarchy in 1867, language and education policies favoring the use of Hungarian (Magyarization) resulted in a strengthening of Slovak Nationalism and a cultivation of cultural ties with the closely related Czechs, who were under Austrian rule. After the dissolution of the Austro-Hungarian Empire at the close of World War I, the Slovaks joined the Czechs to form Czechoslovakia. During the interwar period, Slovak Nationalist leaders pushed for autonomy within Czechoslovakia, and in 1939 Slovakia became an independent state allied with Nazi Germany. Following World War II, Czechoslovakia was reconstituted and came under communist rule within Soviet-dominated Eastern Europe. In 1968, an invasion by Warsaw Pact troops ended the efforts of the country's leaders to liberalize communist rule and create "socialism with a human face," ushering in a period of repression known As "normalization." The peaceful "Velvet Revolution" swept the Communist Party from power at the end of 1989 and inaugurated a return to democratic rule and a market economy. On 1 January 1993, the country underwent a nonviolent "velvet divorce" into its two National components, Slovakia and the Czech Republic. Slovakia joined both NATO and

the EU in the spring of 2004 and the euro zone on 1 January 2009.

GEOGRAPHY

Location: Central Europe, south of Poland
Geographic coordinates: 48 40 N, 19 30 E
Map references: Europe
Area: *total:* 49,035 sq km
land: 48,105 sq km
water: 930 sq km
country comparison to the world: 131
Area—comparative: about twice the size of New Hampshire
Land boundaries: *total:* 1,611 km
border countries (5): Austria 105 km, Czech Republic 241 km, Hungary 627 km, Poland 541 km, Ukraine 97 km
Coastline: 0 km (landlocked)
Maritime claims: none (landlocked)
Climate: temperate; cool summers; cold, cloudy, humid winters
Terrain: rugged mountains in the central and northern part and lowlands in the south
Elevation: *mean elevation:* 458 m
elevation extremes: *lowest point:* Bodrok River 94 m
highest point: Gerlachovsky Stit 2,655 m
Natural resources: lignite, small amounts of iron ore, copper and manganese ore; salt; arable land
Land use: *agricultural land:* 40.1%
arable land: 28.9%
permanent crops: 0.4%
permanent pasture: 10.8%
forest: 40.2%
other: 19.7% (2011 est.)
Irrigated land: 869 sq km (2012)
Total renewable water resources: 50.1 cu km (2011)
Freshwater withdrawal (domestic/industrial/agricultural): *total:* 0.69 cu km/yr (47%/51%/3%)
per capita: 126.7 cu m/yr (2010)
Natural hazards: NA

Environment—current issues: air pollution from metallurgical plants presents human health risks; acid rain damaging forests
Environment—International agreements: *party to:* Air Pollution, Air Pollution-Nitrogen Oxides, Air Pollution-Persistent Organic Pollutants, Air Pollution-Sulfur 85, Air Pollution-Sulfur 94, Air Pollution-Volatile Organic Compounds, Antarctic Treaty, Biodiversity, Climate Change, Climate Change-Kyoto Protocol, Desertification, Endangered Species, Environmental Modification, Hazardous Wastes, Law of the Sea, Ozone Layer Protection, Ship Pollution, Wetlands, Whaling
signed, but not ratified: none of the selected agreements
Geography—note: landlocked; most of the country is rugged and mountainous; the Tatra Mountains in the north are interspersed with many scenic lakes and valleys

PEOPLE AND SOCIETY

Nationality: *noun:* Slovak(s)
adjective: Slovak
Ethnic groups: Slovak 80.7%, Hungarian 8.5%, Roma 2%, other and unspecified 8.8% (2011 est.)
Languages: Slovak (official) 78.6%, Hungarian 9.4%, Roma 2.3%, Ruthenian 1%, other or unspecified 8.8% (2011 est.)
Religions: Roman Catholic 62%, Protestant 8.2%, Greek Catholic 3.8%, other or unspecified 12.5%, none 13.4% (2011 est.)
Population: 5,445,027 (July 2015 est.)
country comparison to the world: 118
Age structure: *0–14 years:* 15.14% (male 422,297/female 402,154)
15–24 years: 11.78% (male 330,116/female 311,144)
25–54 years: 45.17% (male 1,241,594/female 1,217,885)
55–64 years: 13.56% (male 349,304/female 388,904)
65 years and over: 14.35% (male 299,097/female 482,532) (2015 est.)

Dependency ratios: *total dependency ratio:* 40.8%

youth dependency ratio: 21.3%
elderly dependency ratio: 19.5%
potential support ratio: 5.1% (2015 est.)
Median age: *total:* 39.6 years
male: 37.9 years
female: 41.4 years (2015 est.)
country comparison to the world: 51
Population growth rate: 0.02% (2015 est.)
country comparison to the world: 191
Birth rate: 9.91 births/1,000 population (2015 est.)
country comparison to the world: 195
Death rate: 9.74 deaths/1,000 population (2015 est.)
country comparison to the world: 49
Net migration rate: 0.04 migrant(s)/1,000 population (2015 est.)
country comparison to the world: 76
Urbanization: *urban population:* 53.6% of total population (2015)
rate of urbanization: -0.31% annual rate of change (2010–15 est.)
Major urban areas—population: BRATISLAVA (capital) 401,000 (2015)
Sex ratio: *at birth:* 1.07 male(s)/female
0–14 years: 1.05 male(s)/female
15–24 years: 1.06 male(s)/female
25–54 years: 1.02 male(s)/female
55–64 years: 0.9 male(s)/female
65 years and over: 0.62 male(s)/female
total population: 0.94 male(s)/female (2015 est.)
Mother's mean age at first birth: 27.8 (2010 est.)
Maternal mortality rate: 6 deaths/100,000 live births (2015 est.)
country comparison to the world: 172
Infant mortality rate: *total:* 5.27 deaths/1,000 live births
male: 5.91 deaths/1,000 live births
female: 4.58 deaths/1,000 live births (2015 est.)
country comparison to the world: 175
Life expectancy at birth: *total population:* 76.88 years
male: 73.3 years
female: 80.71 years (2015 est.)
country comparison to the world: 77
Total fertility rate: 1.39 children born/woman (2015 est.)
country comparison to the world: 212
Health expenditures: 8.2% of GDP (2013)
country comparison to the world: 62
Physicians density: 3.32 physicians/1,000 population (2012)
Hospital bed density: 6 beds/1,000 population (2011)
Drinking water source:
improved:
urban: 100% of population
rural: 100% of population
total: 100% of population
unimproved:
urban: 0% of population
rural: 0% of population
total: 0% of population (2015 est.)
Sanitation facility access:
improved:

urban: 99.4% of population
rural: 98.2% of population
total: 98.8% of population
unimproved:
urban: 0.6% of population
rural: 1.8% of population
total: 1.2% of population (2015 est.)
HIV/AIDS—adult prevalence rate: 0.02% (2014 est.)
country comparison to the world: 129
HIV/AIDS—people living with HIV/AIDS: NA
HIV/AIDS—deaths: less than 100 (2014 est.)
country comparison to the world: 116
Obesity—adult prevalence rate: 27.4% (2014)
country comparison to the world: 54
Education expenditures: 4.1% of GDP (2013)
country comparison to the world: 103
School life expectancy (primary to tertiary education): *total:* 15 years
male: 14 years
female: 16 years (2014)
Unemployment, youth ages 15–24: *total:* 33.6%
male: 34.9%
female: 31.6% (2013 est.)
country comparison to the world: 21

GOVERNMENT

Country name: *conventional long form:* Slovak Republic
conventional short form: Slovakia
local long form: Slovenska republika
local short form: Slovensko
etymology: related to the Slavic autonym (self-designation) "Slovenin, " a derivation from "slovo" (word), denoting "people who speak (the same language)" (i. e., people who understand each other)
Government type: parliamentary republic
Capital: *name:* Bratislava
Geographic coordinates: 48 09 N, 17 07 E
time difference: UTC + 1 (6 hours ahead of Washington, DC,. during Standard Time)
daylight saving time: +1 hr, begins last Sunday in March; ends last Sunday in October
Administrative divisions: 8 regions (kraje, singular—kraj); Banskobystricky, Bratislavsky, Kosicky, Nitriansky, Presovsky, Trenciansky, Trnavsky, Zilinsky
Independence: 1 January 1993 (Czechoslovakia split into the Czech Republic and Slovakia)
National holiday: Constitution Day, 1 September (1992)
Constitution: several previous (preindependence); latest passed by legislature 1 September 1992, signed 3 September 1992, effective 1 October 1992; amended many times, last in 2015 (2016)
Legal system: civil law system based on austro-Hungarian codes; note—legal code modified to comply with the obligations of Organization on Security and Cooperation in Europe
International law organization participation: accepts compulsory ICJ jurisdiction with reservations; accepts ICCt jurisdiction
Citizenship: *citizenship by birth:* no

citizenship by descent only: at least one parent must be a citizen of Slovakia
dual citizenship recognized: no
residency requirement for naturalization: 5 years
Suffrage: 18 years of age; universal
Executive branch: *chief of state:* President Andrej KISKA (since 15 June 2014)
head of government: Prime Minister Robert FICO (since 4 April 2012); Deputy Prime Ministers Robert KALINAK, Peter KAZIMIR, Miroslav LAJCAK (since 4 April 2012), Lubomir VAZNY (since 26 November 2012)
cabinet: Cabinet appointed by the president on the recommendation of the prime minister
elections/appointments: president directly elected by absolute majority popular vote in 2 rounds if needed for a 5-year term (eligible for a second term); election last held in 2 rounds on 15 and 29 March 2014 (next to be held in March 2019); following National Council elections, the leader of the majority party or majority coalition usually appointed prime minister by the president
election results: Andrej KISKA elected president; percent of vote in second round—Andrej KISKA (independent) 59.4%, Robert FICO (Smer-SD) 40.6%
Legislative branch: *description:* unicameral National Council or Narodna Rada (150 seats; members directly elected in a single National constituency by proportional representation vote; members serve 4-year terms)
elections: last held on 5 March 2016 (next to be held in March 2020)
election results: percent of vote by party—Smer-SD 28.3%, SaS 12.1%, OLaNO-NOVA 11%, SNS 8.6%, LSNS 8%, SME-Rodina 6.6%, Most-Hid 6.5%, Siet 5.6%, other 13.3%; seats by party—Smer-SD 49, SaS 21, OLaNO-NOVA 19, SNS 15, LSNS 14, SME-Rodina 11, Most-Hid 11, Siet 10
Judicial branch: *highest court(s):* Supreme Court of the Slovak Republic (consists of 85 judges—as of 2015—organized into criminal, civil, commercial, and administrative divisions with 3- and 5-judge panels; Constitutional Court (consists of 13 judges)
judge selection and term of office: Supreme Court judge candidates proposed by the Judicial Council of the Slovak Republic, a 17-member independent body to include the Supreme Court chief justice and presidential and governmental appointees; judges appointed by the president for life with mandatory retirement at age 65; Constitutional Court judges nominated by the National Council of the Republic and appointed by the president; judges appointed for 12-year terms
subordinate courts: regional and district civil courts; Higher Military Court; military district courts; Court of Audit

Political parties and leaders: *parties in the Parliament:* Direction-Social Democracy or Smer-SD [Robert FICO]
Bridge or Most-Hid [Bela BUGAR]
Freedom and Solidarity or SaS [Richard SULI K]
Network or Siet [Radoslav PROCHAZKA]

765

Ordinary People and Independent Person ali-ties—New Majority or OLaN O-NOVA [Igor MATOVIC]

People's Party—Our Slovakia or LSNS [Marian KOTLEBA]

Slovak National Party or SNS [Andrej DAN KO]

We Are Family or SM E-Rodina [Boris KOLLAR]

selected parties outside the Parliament: Chris-tian Democratic Movement or KDH [Jan FIGEL]

JUMP! or SKOK! [Juraj MISKOV]

Party of the Hungarian Coalition or SMK [Jozsef BERENYI]

Slovak Democratic and Christian Union-Demo-cratic Party or SDKU-DS [Pavol FRESO]

Political pressure groups and leaders: Alliance of Companies Employing 500 or More Employees or Klub500 Association of Towns and Villages or ZM OS Confederation of Trade Unions or KOZ Entrepreneurs Association of Slovakia or ZPS Fed-eration of Employers' Associations of the Slovak Republic or AZZZ Medical Trade Association or LOZ National Union of Employers or RUZ Slovak Chamber of Commerce and Industry or SOPK The Business Alliance of Slovakia or PAS

International organization participation: Australia Group, BIS, BSEC (observer), CBSS (observer), CD, CE, CEI, CERN, EAPC, EBRD, ECB, EIB, EMU, EU, FAO, IAEA, IBRD, ICAO, ICC (National committees), ICRM, IDA, IEA, IFC, IFRCS, ILO, IMF, IMO, IMSO, Interpol, IOC, IOM, IPU, ISO, ITU, ITUC (NGOs), MIGA, NATO, NEA, NSG, OAS (observer), OECD, OIF (observer), OPCW, OSCE, PCA, Schengen Convention, SELEC (observer), UN, UNC-TAD, UNESCO, UNFICYP, UNIDO, UNTSO, UNWTO, UPU, WCO, WFTU (NGOs), WHO, WIPO, WMO, WTO, ZC

Diplomatic representation in the US: *chief of mis-sion:* Ambassador Peter KMEC (since 17 Septem-ber 2012)

chancery: 3523 International Court NW, Wash-ington, DC 20008

telephone: [1] (202) 237-1054

FAX: [1] (202) 237-6438

consulate(s) general: Los Angeles, New York

Diplomatic representation from the US: *chief of mission:* Charge d'Affaires J. Liam WASLEY (since September 2015)

embassy: Hviezdoslavovo Namestie 4,81102 Bratislava

mailing address: P.O . Box 309, 814 99 Bratislava

telephone: [421] (2) 5443-3338

FAX: [421] (2) 5441-8861

Flag description: three equal horizontal bands of white (top), blue, and red derive from the Pan-Slav colors; the Slovakian coat of arms (consisting of a red shield bordered in white and bearing a white double-barred cross of St. Cyril and St. Methodius surmounting three blue hills) is centered over the bands but offset slightly to the hoist side

note: the Pan-Slav colors were inspired by the 19th-century flag of Russia

National symbol(s): double-barred cross (Cross of St. Cyril and St. Methodius) surmounting three peaks; National colors: white, blue, red

National anthem: *name:* "Nad Tatrou sa blyska" (Lightning Over the Tatras)

lyrics/music: Janko MATUSKA/traditional

note: adopted 1993, in use since 1844; music based on the Slovak folk song "Kopala studienku"

ECONOMY

Economy—overview: Slovakia has made signifi-cant economic reforms since its separation from the Czech Republic in 1993. With a population of 5.4 million, the Slovak Republic has a small, open economy, with exports, at about 93% of GDP, serv-ingas the main driver of GDP growth. Slovakia joined the EU in 2004 and the eurozone in 2009. The country's banking sector is sound.

Slovakia has led the region garnering FDI, because of its relatively low-cost, highly-skilled labor force, reason able tax rates, and favorable geographic location in the heart of Central Europe. How-ever, recent increases in corporate taxes, as well as changes to the Labor Code, slow dispute resolu-tion, and ongoing corruption potentially threaten the attractiveness of the Slovak market. Moreover, the energy sector is characterized by high costs, unpredictable regulatory oversight, and growing government interference.

GDP (purchasing power parity): $161 billion (2015 est.)

$155.4 billion (2014 est.)

$151.6 billion (2013 est.)

note: data are in 2015 US dollars

country comparison to the world: 73

GDP (official exchange rate): $86.63 billion (2015 est.)

GDP—real growth rate: 3.6% (2015 est.)

2.5% (2014 est.)

1.4% (2013 est.)

country comparison to the world: 80

GDP—per capita (PPP): $29,700 (2015 est.)

$28,700 (2014 est.)

$28,000 (2013 est.)

note: data are in 2015 US dollars

country comparison to the world: 62

Gross National saving: 21.8% of GDP (2015 est.)

21.1% of GDP (2014 est.)

22.9% of GDP (2013 est.)

country comparison to the world: 68

GDP—composition, by end use:

household consumption: 56.8%

government consumption: 18.2%

investment in fixed capital: 22.2%

investment in inventories: -0.5%

exports of goods and services: 101.2%

imports of goods and services: -97.9% (2015 est.)

GDP—composition, by sector of origin:

agriculture: 3.4%

industry: 30.4%

services: 66.2% (2015 est.)

Agriculture—products: grains, potatoes, sugar beets, hops, fruit; pigs, cattle, poultry; forest products

Industries: automobiles; metal and metal products; electricity, gas, coke, oil, nuclear fuel; chemi-cals, synthetic fibers, wood and paper products; machinery; earthenware and ceramics; textiles;

electrical and optical apparatus; rubber products; food and beverages; pharmaceutical

Industrial production growth rate: 4.5% (2015 est.)

country comparison to the world: 40

Labor force: 2.745 million (2015 est.)

country comparison to the world: 109

Labor force—by occupation: *agriculture:* 4.2%

industry: 22.6%

services: 73.2% (2015)

Unemployment rate: 10.6% (2015 est.) 12.3% (2014 est.)

country comparison to the world: 121

Population below poverty line: 12.6% (2014 est.)

Household income or consumption by percentage share: *lowest:* 10%: 4.4%

highest: 10%: 26% (2013 est.)

Distribution of family income—Gini index: 26 (2013)

25.7 (2011)

country comparison to the world: 138

Budget: *revenues:* $16.23 billion

expenditures: $18.17 billion (2015 est.)

Taxes and other revenues: 40.2% of GDP (2015 est.)

country comparison to the world: 38

Budget surplus (+) or deficit (–): -2.5% of GDP (2015 est.)

country comparison to the world: 92

Public debt: 52.5% of GDP (2015 est.)

53.5% of GDP (2014 est.)

note: data cover general Government Gross Debt, and includes debt instruments issued (or owned) by Government entities, including sub-sectors of central government, state government, local gov-ernment, and social security funds

country comparison to the world: 74

Fiscal year: calendar year

Inflation rate (consumer prices): -0.3% (2015 est.)

-0.1% (2014 est.)

country comparison to the world: 34

Central bank discount rate: 0.05% (9 December 2015)

0.05% (10 September 2014)

note: this is the European Central Bank's rate on the marginal lending facility, which offers over-night credit to banks from the euro area; Slovakia became a member of the Economic and Monetary Union (EMU) on 1 January 2009

country comparison to the world: 141

Commercial bank prime lending rate: 3.9% (31 December 2015 est.)

3.6% (31 December 2014 est.)

country comparison to the world: 160

Stock of narrow money: $18.24 billion (31 Decem-ber 2015 est.)

$18.17 billion (31 December 2014 est.)

note: see entry for the European Union for money supply for the entire euro area; the European Cen-tral Bank (ECB) controls monetary policy for the 18 members of the Economic and Monetary Union (EMU); individual members of the EMU do not control the quantity of money circulating within their own borders

country comparison to the world: 66

Stock of broad money: $53.7 billion (31 December 2015 est.)

$48.34 billion (31 December 2014 est.)
country comparison to the world: 65
Stock of domestic credit: $45.23 billion (31 December 2015 est.)
$40.41 billion (31 December 2014 est.)
country comparison to the world: 64
Market value of publicly traded shares:
$4.634 billion (31 December 2015 est.)
$4.732 billion (31 December 2014)
$4.805 billion (31 December 2013 est.)
country comparison to the world: 86
Current account balance: -$996 million (2015 est.)
$133 million (2014 est.)
country comparison to the world: 122
Exports: $56.39 billion (2015 est.)
$64.8 billion (2014 est.)
country comparison to the world: 49
Exports—commodities: vehicles and related parts 27%, machinery and electrical equipment 20%, nuclear reactors and furnaces 12%, iron and steel 4%, mineral oils and fuels 5% (2015 est.)
Exports—partners: Germany 22.7%, Czech Republic 12.5%, Poland 8.5%, Austria 5.7%, Hungary 5.7%, France 5.6%, UK 5.5%, Italy 4.5% (2015)
Imports: $53.3 billion (42278 est.)
$60.15 billion (2014 est.)
country comparison to the world: 49
Imports—commodities: machinery and electrical equipment 20%, vehicles and related parts 14%, nuclear reactors and furnaces 12%, fuel and mineral oils 9% (2015 est.)
Imports—partners: Germany 19.4%, Czech Republic 17.4%, Austria 9.1%, Hungary 6.3%, Poland 6.3%, South Korea 5.5%, Russia 5.2%, China 4.1% (2015)
Reserves of foreign exchange and gold:
$2.64 billion (31 December 2015 est.)
$2.17 billion (31 December 2014 est.)
country comparison to the world: 111
Debt—external: $67.66 billion (30 September 2015 est.)
$67.78 billion (31 December 2014 est.)
country comparison to the world: 57
Stock of direct foreign investment—at home:
$63.27 billion (31 December 2015 est.)
$43.23 billion (31 December 2014 est.)
country comparison to the world: 54
Stock of direct foreign investment—abroad:
$10.63 billion (31 December 2015 est.)
$2.47 billion (31 December 2014 est.)
country comparison to the world: 59
Exchange rates: euros (EUR) per US dollar—
0.885 (2015 est.)
0.7525 (2014 est.)
0.7634 (2013 est.)
0.7752 (2012 est.)
0.7185 (2011 est.)

ENERGY

Electricity—production: 27.25 billion kWh (2014 est.)
country comparison to the world: 67
Electricity—consumption: 28.36 billion kWh (2014 est.)
country comparison to the world: 62

Electricity—exports: 11.86 billion kWh (2014 est.)
country comparison to the world: 18
Electricity—imports: 12.96 billion kWh (2014 est.)
country comparison to the world: 13
Electricity—installed generating capacity: 8.076 million kW (2014 est.)
country comparison to the world: 62
Electricity—from fossil fuels: 33.2% of total installed capacity (2014 est.)
country comparison to the world: 174
Electricity—from nuclear fuels: 24% of total installed capacity (2014 est.)
country comparison to the world: 8
Electricity—from hydroelectric plants: 31.4% of total installed capacity (2014 est.)
country comparison to the world: 72
Electricity—from other renewable sources: 11.2% of total installed capacity (2014 est.)
country comparison to the world: 30
Crude oil—production: 200 bbl/day (2014 est.)
country comparison to the world: 98
Crude oil—exports: 185.8 bbl/day (2013 est.)
country comparison to the world: 89
Crude oil—imports: 117,600 bbl/day (2013 est.)
country comparison to the world: 42
Crude oil—proved reserves: 9 million bbl (1 January 2015 est.)
country comparison to the world: 94
Refined petroleum products—production: 137,100 bbl/day (2013 est.)
country comparison to the world: 66
Refined petroleum products—consumption: 73,320 bbl/day (2014 est.)
country comparison to the world: 87
Refined petroleum products—exports: 84,830 bbl/day (2013 est.)
country comparison to the world: 48
Refined petroleum products—imports: 24,940 bbl/day (2013 est.)
country comparison to the world: 100
Natural gas—production: 910.7 million cu m (2014 est.)
country comparison to the world: 68
Natural gas—consumption: 4.3 billion cu m (2014 est.)
country comparison to the world: 63
Natural gas—exports: 3 million cu m (2014 est.)
country comparison to the world: 48
Natural gas—imports: 4.21 billion cu m (2014 est.)
country comparison to the world: 34
Natural gas—proved reserves: 14.16 billion cu m (1 January 2014 est.)
country comparison to the world: 78
Carbon dioxide emissions from consumption of energy: 23.04 million Mt (2012 est.)
country comparison to the world: 79

COMMUNICATIONS

Telephone—fixed lines: *total subscriptions:* 920,000
subscriptions per 100 inhabitants: 17 (2014 est.)
country comparison to the world: 80
Telephones—mobile cellular: *total:* 6.4 million
subscriptions per 100 inhabitants: 117 (2014 est.)
country comparison to the world: 108

Telephone system: *general assessment:* a modern telecommunications system that has expanded dramatically in recent years with the growth of cellular services
domestic: analog system is now receiving digital equipment and is being enlarged with fiber-optic cable, especially in the larger cities; 3 companies provide nationwide cellular services
international: country code—421; 3 International exchanges (1 in Bratislava and 2 in Banska Bystrica) are available; Slovakia is participating in several International telecommunications projects that will increase the availability of external services (2011)
Broadcast media: state-owned public broadcaster, Radio and Television of Slovakia (RTVS), operates 2 National TV stations and multiple National and Regional radio networks; roughly 50 privately owned TV stations operating Nationally, region ally, and locally; about 40% of households are connected to multi-channel cable or satellite TV; 32 privately owned radio stations (2016)
Radio broadcast stations: AM 1, FM 22, short-wave 1 (2008)
Television broadcast stations: 37 (2008)
Internet country code: .sk
Internet hosts: 1.384 million (2012)
country comparison to the world: 41
Internet users: *total:* 4.5 million
percent of population: 82.7% (2014 est.)
country comparison to the world: 72

TRANSPORTATION

Airports: 35 (2013)
country comparison to the world:
Airports—with paved runways: *total:* 21
over 3,047 m: 2
2,438 to 3,047 m: 2
1,524 to 2,437 m: 3
914 to 1,523 m: 3
under 914 m: 11 (2013)
Airports—with unpaved runways: *total:* 14
914 to 1,523 m: 9
under 914 m: 5 (2013)
Heliports: 1 (2013)
Pipelines: gas 6,774 km; oil 419 km (2013)
Railways: *total:* 3,624 km
broad gauge: 99 km 1.520-m gauge
standard gauge: 3,475 km 1.435-m gauge (1,616 km electrified) *narrow gauge:* 50 km 1.000-m or 0.750-m gauge (2014)
country comparison to the world: 49
Roadways: *total:* 54,869 km (includes local roads, National roads, and 420 km of highways) (2012)
country comparison to the world: 82
Waterways: 172 km (on Danube River) (2012)
country comparison to the world: 99
Merchant marine: *total:* 11
by type: cargo 9, refrigerated cargo 2
foreign-owned: 11 (Germany 3, Ireland 1, Italy 2, Montenegro 1, Slovenia 1, Turkey 1, Ukraine 2) (2010)
country comparison to the world: 112
Ports and terminals: *river port(s):* Bratislava, Komarno (Danube)

MILITARY AND SECURITY

Military branches: Armed Forces of the Slovak Republic (Ozbrojene Sily Slovenskej Republiky): Land Forces (Pozemne Sily), Air Forces (Vzdusne Sily) (2010)

Military service age and obligation: 18–30 years of age for voluntary military service; conscription in peacetime suspended in 2006; women are eligible to serve (2012)

Military expenditures: 1.03% of GDP (2015)

1.01% of GDP (2014)
1% of GDP (2013)
1.12% of GDP (2012)
1.1% of GDP (2011)
country comparison to the world: 89

TRANSNATIONAL ISSUES

Disputes—International: bilateral government, legal, technical and economic working group negotiations continued in 2006 between Slovakia and Hungary over Hungary's completion of its portion of the Gabcikovo-Nagymaros hydroelectric dam project along the Danube; as a member state that forms part of the EU's external border, Slovakia has implemented the strict Schengen border rules

Refugees and internally displaced persons: *stateless persons:* 1,523 (2015)

Illicit drugs: transshipment point for Southwest Asian heroin bound for Western Europe; producer of synthetic drugs for Regional market; consumer of ecstasy

SLOVENIA

INTRODUCTION

Background: The Slovene lands were part of the Austro-Hungarian Empire until the latter's dissolution at the end of World War I. In 1918, the Slovenes joined the Serbs and Croats in forming a new multi national state, which was named Yugoslavia in 1929. After World War II, Slovenia became a republic of the renewed Yugoslavia, which though communist, distanced itself from Moscow's rule. Dissatisfied with the exercise of power by the majority Serbs, the Slovenes succeeded in establishing their independence in 1991 after a short 10-day war. Historical ties to Western Europe, a strong economy, and a stable democracy have assisted in Slovenia's transformation to a modern state. Slovenia acceded to both NATO and the EU in the spring of 2004; it joined the euro zone and the Schengen zone in 2007.

GEOGRAPHY

Location: south Central Europe, Julian Alps between Austria and Croatia

Geographic coordinates: 46 07 N, 14 49 E

Map references: Europe

Area: *total:* 20,273 sq km
land: 20,151 sq km
water: 122 sq km
country comparison to the world: 155

Area—comparative: slightly smaller than New Jersey

Land boundaries: *total:* 1,211 km
border countries (4): Austria 299 km, Croatia 600 km, Hungary 94 km, Italy 218 km

Coastline: 46.6 km

Maritime claims: *territorial sea:* 12 nm

Climate: Mediterranean climate on the coast, continental climate with mild to hot summers and cold winters in the plateaus and valleys to the east

Terrain: a short southwestern coastal strip of Karst topography on the Adriatic; an alpine mountain region lies adjacent to Italy and Austria in the north; mixed mountains and valleys with numerous rivers to the east

Elevation: *mean elevation:* 492 m

elevation extremes: *lowest point:* Adriatic Sea 0 m
highest point: Triglav 2,864 m

Natural resources: lignite, lead, zinc, building stone, hydropower, forests

Land use: *agricultural land:* 22.8%
arable land: 8.4%
permanent crops: 1.3%
permanent pasture: 13.1%
forest: 62.3%
other: 14.9% (2011 est.)

Irrigated land: 60 sq km (2012)

Total renewable water resources: 31.87 cu km (2011)

Freshwater withdrawal (domestic/industrial/agricultural): *total:* 0.94 cu km/yr (18%/82%/0%)
per capita: 462.9 cu m/yr (2009)

Natural hazards: flooding; earth quakes

Environment—current issues: Sava River polluted with domestic and industrial waste; pollution of coastal waters with heavy metals and toxic chemicals; forest damage from urban Air pollution and resulting acid rain

Environment—International agreements: *party to:* Air Pollution, Air Pollution-Nitrogen Oxides, Air Pollution-Persistent Organic Pollutants, Air Pollution-Sulfur 94, Biodiversity, Climate Change, Climate Change-Kyoto Protocol, Desertification, Endangered Species, Environmental Modification, Hazardous Wastes, Law of the Sea, Marine Dumping, Ozone Layer Protection, Ship Pollution, Wetlands, Whaling
signed, but not ratified: none of the selected agreements

Geography—note: despite its small size, this eastern alpine country controls some of Europe's major transit routes

PEOPLE AND SOCIETY

Nationality: *noun:* Slovene(s)
adjective: Slovenian

Ethnic groups: Slovene 83.1%, Serb 2%, Croat 1.8%, Bosniak 1.1%, other or unspecified 12% (2002 census)

Languages: Slovenian (official) 91.1%, Serbo-Croatian 4.5%, other or unspecified 4.4%, Italian (official, only in municipalities where Italian National communities reside), Hungarian (official, only in municipalities where Hungarian National communities reside) (2002 census)

Religions: Catholic 57.8%, Muslim 2.4%, Orthodox 2.3%, other Christian 0.9%, unaffiliated 3.5%, other or unspecified 23%, none 10.1% (2002 census)

Population: 1,983,412 (July 2015 est.)
country comparison to the world: 148

Age structure: *0–14 years:* 13.38% (male 136,839/female 128,560)
15–24 years: 9.76% (male 99,207/female 94,471)
25–54 years: 43.65% (male 437,238/female 428,439)
55–64 years: 14.81% (male 144,737/female 148,929)
65 years and over: 18.4% (male 147,745/female 217,247) (2015 est.)

Dependency ratios: *total dependency ratio:* 48.7%
youth dependency ratio: 22%
elderly dependency ratio: 26.7%
potential support ratio: 3.7% (2015 est.)

Median age: *total:* 43.8 years
male: 42.1 years
female: 45.6 years (2015 est.)
country comparison to the world: 9

Population growth rate: -0.26% (2015 est.)
country comparison to the world: 217

Birth rate: 8.42 births/1,000 population (2015 est.)
country comparison to the world: 218

Death rate: 11.37 deaths/1,000 population (2015 est.)
country comparison to the world: 31

Net migration rate: 0.37 migrant(s)/1,000 population (2015 est.)
country comparison to the world: 74

Urbanization: *urban population:* 49.6% of total population (2015)
rate of urbanization: 0.08% annual rate of change (2010–15 est.)
Major urban areas—population: LJUBLJANA (capital) 279,000 (2014)
Sex ratio: *at birth:* 1.07 male(s)/female
0–14 years: 1.06 male(s)/female
15–24 years: 1.05 male(s)/female
25–54 years: 1.02 male(s)/female
55–64 years: 0.97 male(s)/female
65 years and over: 0.68 male(s)/female
total population: 0.95 male(s)/female (2015 est.)
Mother's mean age at first birth: 28.8 (2011 est.)
Maternal mortality rate: 9 deaths/100,000 live births (2015 est.)
country comparison to the world: 150
Infant mortality rate: *total:* 4 deaths/1,000 live births
male: 4.51 deaths/1,000 live births
female: 3.46 deaths/1,000 live births (2015 est.)
country comparison to the world: 192
Life expectancy at birth: *total population:* 78.01 years
male: 74.4 years
female: 81.86 years (2015 est.)
country comparison to the world: 61
Total fertility rate: 1.34 children born/woman (2015 est.)
country comparison to the world: 214
Health expenditures: 9.2% of GDP (2013)
country comparison to the world: 43
Physicians density: 2.54 physicians/1,000 population (2010)
Hospital bed density: 4.6 beds/1,000 population (2013)
Drinking water source:
improved:
urban: 99.7% of population
rural: 99.4% of population
total: 99.5% of population
unimproved:
urban: 0.3% of population
rural: 0.6% of population
total: 0.5% of population (2015 est.)
Sanitation facility access:
improved:
urban: 99.1% of population
rural: 99.1% of population
total: 99.1% of population
unimproved:
urban: 0.9% of population
rural: 0.9% of population
total: 0.9% of population (2015 est.)
HIV/AIDS—adult prevalence rate: 0.08% (2014 est.)
country comparison to the world: 114
HIV/AIDS—people living with HIV/AIDS: 900 (2014 est.)
country comparison to the world: 120
HIV/AIDS—deaths: less than 100 (2014 est.)
country comparison to the world: 109
Obesity—adult prevalence rate: 27.4% (2014)
country comparison to the world: 33
Education expenditures: 5.7% of GDP (2012)
country comparison to the world: 51

Literacy: *definition:* NA
total population: 99.7%
male: 99.7%
female: 99.7% (2015 est.)
School life expectancy (primary to tertiary education): *total:* 17 years
male: 17 years
female: 18 years (2014)
Unemployment, youth ages 15–24: *total:* 21.6%
male: 20.1%
female: 23.7% (2013 est.)
country comparison to the world: 54

GOVERNMENT

Country name: *conventional long form:* Republic of Slovenia
conventional short form: Slovenia
local long form: Republika Slovenija
local short form: Slovenija
former: People's Republic of Slovenia, Socialist Republic of Slovenia
etymology: related to the Slavic autonym (self-designation) "Slovenin," a derivation from "slovo" (word), denoting "people who speak (the same language) " (i. e., people who understand each other)
Government type: parliamentary republic
Capital: *name:* Ljubljana
Geographic coordinates: 46 03 N, 14 31 E
time difference: UTC + 1 (6 hours ahead of Washington, DC, during Standard Time)
daylight saving time: +1 hr, begins last Sunday in March; ends last Sunday in October
Administrative divisions: 201 municipalities (obcine, singular—obcina) and 11 urban municipalities (mestne obcine, singular-mest naobcina)
municipalities: Ajdovscina, Ankaran, Apace, Beltinci, Benedikt, Bistrica ob Sotli, Bled, Bloke, Bohinj, Borovnica, Bovec, Braslovce, Brda, Brezice, Brezovica, Cankova, Cerklje na Gorenjskem, Cerknica, Cerkno, Cerkvenjak, Cirkulane, Crensovci, Crna na Koroskem, Crnomelj, Destrnik, Divaca, Dobje, Dobrepolje, Dobrna, Dobrova-Polhov Gradec, Dobrovnik/D obron ak, Dolenjske Toplice, Dol pri Ljubljani, Domzale, Dornava, Dravograd, Duplek, Gorenja Vas-Poljane, Gorisnica, Gorje, Gornja Radgon a, Gornji Grad, Gornji Petrovci, Grad, Grosuplje, Hajdina, Hoce-Slivnica, Hodos, Horjul, Hrastnik, Hrpelje-Kozina, Idrija, Ig, Ilirska Bistrica, Ivancna Gorica, Izola/Isola, Jesenice, Jezersko, Jursinci, Kamnik, Kanal, Kidricevo, Kobarid, Kobilje, Kocevje, Komen, Komenda, Kosanjevica na Krki, Kostel, Kozje, Kranjska Gora, Krizevci, Krsko, Kungota, Kuzma, Lasko, Lenart, Lendava/Lendva, Litija, Ljubno, Ljutomer, Log-Dragomer, Logatec, Loska Dolina, Loski Potok, Lovrenc na Pohorju, Luce, Lukovica, Majsperk, Makole, Markovci, Medvode, Menges, Metlika, Mezica, Miklavzna Dravskem Polju, Miren-Kostanjevica, Mirna, Mirna Pec, Mislinja, Mokronog-Trebelno, Moravce, Moravske Toplice, Mozirje, Muta, Naklo, NAzarje, Odranci, Oplotnica, Ormoz, Osilnica, Pesnica, Piran/Pirano, Pivka, Podcetrtek, Podlehnik, Podvelka, Poljcane, Polzela, Postojna, Prebold, Preddvor, Prevalje, Puconci, Race-Fram, Radece,

Radenci, Radlje ob Dravi, Radovljica, Ravne na Koroskem, Razkrizje, Recica ob Savinji, Rence-Vogrsko, Ribnica, Ribnica na Pohorju, Rogaska Slatina, Rogasovci, Rogatec, Ruse, Selnica ob Dravi, Semic, Sevnica, Sezana, Slovenska Bistrica, Slovenske Konjice, Sodrazica, Solcava, Sredisce ob Dravi, Starse, Straza, Sveta Ana, Sveta Trojica v Slovenskih Goricah, Sveti Andraz v Slovenskih Goricah, Sveti Jurijob Scavnici, Sveti Jurij v Slovenskih Goricah, Sveti Tomaz, Salovci, Sempeter-Vrtojba, Sencur, Sentilj, Sentjernej, Sentjur, Sentrupert, Skocjan, Skofja Loka, Skofljica, Smarjepri Jelsah, Smarjeske Toplice, Smartno ob Paki, Smartno pri Litiji, Sostanj, Store, Tabor, Tisina, Tolmin, Trbovlje, Trebnje, Trnovska Vas, Trzic, Trzin, Turnisce, Velika Polana, Velike Lasce, Verzej, Videm, Vipava, Vitanje, Vodice, Vojnik, Vransko, Vrhnika, Vuzenica, Zagorje ob Savi, Zalec, Zavrc, Zelezniki, Zetale, Ziri, Zirovnica, Zrece, Zuzemberk
urban municipalities: Celje, Koper-Capodistria, Kranj, Ljubljana, Maribor, Murska Sobota, Nova Gorica, Novo Mesto, Ptuj, Slovenj Gradec, Velenje
Independence: 25 June 1991 (from Yugoslavia)
National holiday: Independence Day/Statehood Day, 25 June (1991)
Constitution: previous 1974 (preindependence); latest passed by legislature 23 December 1991; amended several times, last in 2015 (2016)
Legal system: civil law system
International law organization participation: has not submitted an ICJ jurisdiction declaration; accepts ICCt jurisdiction
Citizenship: *citizenship by birth:* no
citizenship by descent only: at least one parent must be a citizen of Slovenia; both parents if the child is born outside of Slovenia dual
citizenship recognized: yes, for select cases
residency requirement for naturalization: 10 years, the last 5 of which have been continuous
Suffrage: 18 years of age, 16 if employed; universal
Executive branch: *chief of state:* President Borut PAHOR (since 22 December 2012)
head of government: Prime Minister Miro CERAR (since 18 September 2014)
cabinet: Council of Ministers nominated by the prime minister, elected by the National Assembly
elections/appointments: president directly elected by absolute majority popular vote in 2 rounds if needed for a 5-year term (eligible for a second term); election last held on 11 November 2012 with a runoff on 2 December 2012 (next to be held in 2017); following National Assembly elections, the leader of the majority party or majority coalition usually nominated prime minister by the president and elected by the National Assembly
election results: Borut PAHOR elected president; percent of vote in second round—Borut PAHOR (SD) 67.4%, Danilo TURK (independent) 32.6%; note—a snap election was held in July 2014 following the resignation of Prime Minister Alenka BRATUSEK in May 2014, Miro CERAR (SMC) elected prime minister; National Assembly vote—57 to 11

Legislative branch: *description:* bicameral Parliament consists of the National Council or Drzavni Svet (40 seats; members indirectly elected by an electoral college to serve 5-year terms) and the National Assembly or Drzavni Zbor (90 seats; 88 members directly elected in single-seat constituencies by proportional representation vote and 2 directly elected in special constituencies for Italian and hungarian minorities by simple majority vote; members serve 4-year terms); note—the National Council is primarily an advisory body with limited legislative powers

elections: National Assembly—last held on 13 July 2014 (next to be held in 2018)

election results: percent of vote by party—SMC 34.6%, SDS 20.7%, DeSUS 10.2%, ZL 6%, SD 6%, NSi 5.6%, ZaAB 4.3%, other 12.6%; seats by party—SMC 36, SDS 21, DeSUS 10, ZL 6, SD 6, NSi, 5, ZaAB 4, Hungarian minority 1, Italian minority 1

Judicial branch: *highest court(s):* Supreme Court (consists of the court president and 37 judges organized into 7 departments—civil, criminal, commercial, labor and social security, administrative, registry, and International cooperation); Constitutional Court (consists of the court president, vice president, and 7 judges)

judge selection and term of office: Supreme Court president and vice president appointed by the National Assembly upon the proposal of the Minister of Justice based on the opinions of the Judicial Council, an 11-member independent body elected by the National Assembly from proposals submitted by the president, attorneys, law universities, and sitting judges; other Supreme Court judges elected by the National Assembly from candidates proposed by the Judicial Council; Supreme Court judge term NA; Constitutional Court judges appointed by the National Assembly from nominations by the president of the republic; Constitutional Court president selected from among their own for a 3-year term; other judges elected for single 9-year terms

subordinate courts: county, district, region al, and high courts; specialized labor-related and social courts; Court of Audit; Administrative Court

Political parties and leaders: Alliance of Alenka Bratusek or ZaAB [Alenka BRATUSEK]
Democratic Party of Pensioners of Slovenia or DeSUS [Karl ERJAVEC]
Modern Center Party or SMC [Miro CERAR]
New Slovenia or NSI [Ljudmila NoVAK]
Slovenian Democratic Party or SDS [Janez JANSA]
Social Democrats or SD [Dejan ZIDAN]
United Left or ZL (collective leadership)

Political pressure groups and leaders: Catholic Church

other: various trade and public sector employee unions

International organization participation: Australia Group, BIS, CD, CE, CEI, EAPC, EBRD, ECB, EIB, EMU, ESA (cooperating state), EU, FAO, IADB, IAEA, IBRD, ICAO, ICC (National committees), ICCt, ICRM, IDA, IFC, IFRCS, IHO, ILO, IMF, IMO, Interpol, IOC, IOM, IPU, ISO, ITU, MIGA, NATO, NEA, NSG, OAS (observer), OECD, OIF (observer), OPCW, OSCE, PCA, Schengen Convention, SELEC, UN, UNCTAD, UNESCO, UNHCR, UNIDO, UNIFIL, UNTSO, UNWTO, UPU, WCO, WHO, WIPO, WMO, WTO, ZC

Diplomatic representation in the US: *chief of mission:* Ambassador Bozo CERAR (since 6 September 2013)

chancery: 2410 California Street N.W., Washington, DC 20008

telephone: [1] (202) 386-6601

FAX: [1] (202) 386-6633

consulate(s) general: Cleveland (OH)

Diplomatic representation from the US: *chief of mission:* Ambassador Brent Robert HARTLEY (since 12 February 2015)

embassy: Presernova 31,1000 Ljubljana

mailing address: American Embassy Ljubljana, US Department of State, 7140 Ljubljana Place, Washington, DC 20521-7140

telephone: [386] (1) 200-5500

FAX: [386] (1) 200-5555

Flag description: three equal horizontal bands of white (top), blue, and red, derive from the medieval coat of arms of the Duchy of Carniola; the Slovenian seal (a shield with the image of Triglav, Slovenia's highest peak, in white against a blue background at the center; beneath it are two wavy blue lines depicting seas and rivers, and above it are three six-pointed stars arranged in an inverted triangle, which are taken from the coat of arms of the Counts of Celje, the great Slovene dynastic house of the late 14th and early 15th centuries) appears in the upper hoist side of the flag centered on the white and blue bands

National symbol(s): Mount Triglav; National colors: white, blue, red

National anthem: *name:* "Zdravljica" (A Toast)
lyrics/music: France PRESEREN/Stanko PREMRL
note: adopted 1989; originally written in 1848; the full poem, whose seventh verse is used as the anthem, speaks of pan-Slavic Nationalism

ECONOMY

Economy—overview: With excellent infrastructure, a well-educated work force, and a strategic location between the Balkans and Western Europe, Slovenia has one of the highest per capita GDPs in Central Europe, despite having suffered a protracted recession in 2008–2009 in the wake of the global financial crisis. Slovenia became the first 2004 EU entrant to adopt the euro (on 1 January 2007) and has experienced one of the most stable political transitions in Central and Southeastern Europe.

In March 2004, Slovenia became the first transition country to graduate from borrower status to donor partner at the World Bank. in 2007, Slovenia was invited to begin the process for joining the OECD; it became a member in 2012. However, long-delayed privatizations, particularly within Slovenia's largely state-owned and increasingly indebted banking sector, have fueled investor concerns since 2012 that the country would need EU-IMF financial assistance. in 2013, the European Commission granted Slovenia permission to begin recapitalizing ailing lenders and transferring their nonperformingassets into a "bad bank" established to restore bank balance sheets. Export-led growth fueled by demand in larger European markets pushed GDP growth to 3.0% in 2014, while stubbornly-high unemployment fell slightly to 12%. Prime Minister CERAR's government took office in September 2014, pledging to press ahead with commitments to privatize a select group of state-run companies, ration alize public spending, and further stabilize the banking sector.

GDP (purchasing power parity):
$63.96 billion (2015 est.)
$62.17 billion (2014 est.)
$60.33 billion (2013 est.)
note: data are in 2015 US dollars
country comparison to the world: 101

GDP (official exchange rate):
$42.77 billion (2015 est.)

GDP—real growth rate: 2.9% (2015 est.)
3% (2014 est.)
-1.1% (2013 est.)
country comparison to the world: 105

GDP—per capita (PPP): $31,000 (2015 est.)
$30,200 (2014 est.)
$29,300 (2013 est.)
note: data are in 2015 US dollars
country comparison to the world: 60

Gross National saving: 27.5% of GDP (2015 est.)
26.8% of GDP (2014 est.)
25% of GDP (2013 est.)
country comparison to the world: 35

GDP—composition, by end use:
household consumption: 53.6%
government consumption: 18.8%
investment in fixed capital: 20.2%
investment in inventories: 0.5%
exports of goods and services: 82.6%
imports of goods and services: -75.7% (2015 est.)

GDP—composition, by sector of origin:
agriculture: 2.2%
industry: 33.4%
services: 64.4% (2015 est.)

Agriculture—products: hops, wheat, coffee, corn, apples, pears; cattle, sheep, poultry

Industries: ferrous metallurgy and aluminium Products, lead and zinc smelting; electronics (including military electronics), trucks, automobiles, electric power equipment, wood products, textiles, chemicals, machine tools

Industrial production growth rate: 4.9% (2015 est.)
country comparison to the world: 36

Labor force: 916,000 (2015 est.)
country comparison to the world: 146

Labor force—by occupation: *agriculture:* 8.3%
industry: 30.8%
services: 60.9% (2012 est.)

Unemployment rate: 12% (2015 est.)
13.1% (2014 est.)
country comparison to the world: 131

Population below poverty line: 13.5% (2012 est.)

Household income or consumption by percentage share: *lowest:* 10%: 3.7%
highest: 10%: 21.1% (2012)

Distribution of family income—Gini index: (2012) (2005)
country comparison to the world: 145
Budget: *revenues:* $17.38 billion
expenditures: $18.59 billion (2015 est.)
Taxes and other revenues: 40.7% of GDP (2015 est.)
country comparison to the world: 37
Budget surplus (+) or deficit (–): -1% of GDP (2015 est.)
country comparison to the world: 53
Public debt: 62.7% of GDP (2015 est.) 60.9% of GDP (2014 est.)
note: defined by the EU's Maastricht Treaty as consolidated general government gross debt at nominal value, outstanding at the end of the year in the following categories of government liabilities: currency and deposits, securities other than shares excluding financial derivatives, and loans; *general government sector comprises the subsectors:* central government, state government, local government, and social security funds
country comparison to the world: 57
Fiscal year: calendar year
Inflation rate (consumer prices): -0.5% (2015 est.) 0.2% (2014 est.)
country comparison to the world: 27
Central bank discount rate: 0.3% (10 September 2014)
0.75% (31 December 2013)
note: this is the European Central Bank's rate on the marginal lending facility, which offers overnight credit to banks in the euro area
country comparison to the world: 132
Commercial bank prime lending rate: 5.5% (31 December 2015 est.)
5.02% (31 December 2014 est.)
country comparison to the world: 136
Stock of narrow money: $11.82 billion (31 December 2015 est.)
$12.85 billion (31 December 2014 est.)
note: see entry for the European Union for money supply for the entire euro area; the European Central Bank (ECB) controls monetary policy for the 18 members of the Economic and Monetary Union (EMU); individual members of the EMU do not control the quantity of money circulating within their own borders
country comparison to the world: 74
Stock of broad money: $26.11 billion (31 December 2014 est.)
$25.92 billion (31 December 2013 est.)
country comparison to the world: 80
Stock of domestic credit: $25.2 billion (31 December 2015 est.)
$31.08 billion (31 December 2014 est.)
country comparison to the world: 79
Market value of publicly traded shares:
$6.87 billion (31 December 2013 est.)
$6.31 billion (31 December 2012)
$6.783 billion (31 December 2011 est.)
country comparison to the world: 82
Current account balance:
$3.118 billion (2015 est.)
$3.464 billion (2014 est.)
country comparison to the world: 28

Exports: $28.09 billion (2015 est.)
$30.55 billion (2014 est.)
country comparison to the world: 65
Exports—commodities: manufactured goods, machinery and transport equipment, chemicals, food
Exports—partners: Germany 19.1%, Italy 10.6%, Austria 8%, Croatia 6.8%, Slovakia 4.7%, Hungary 4.4%, France 4.2% (2015)
Imports: $27.1 billion (2015 est.)
$28.94 billion (2014 est.)
country comparison to the world: 67
Imports—commodities: machinery and transport equipment, manufactured goods, chemicals, fuels and lubricants, food
Imports—partners: Germany 16.5%, Italy 13.6%, Austria 10.2%, China 5.5%, Croatia 5.1%, Turkey 4% (2015)
Reserves of foreign exchange and gold: $961.8 million (31 December 2015 est.)
$1.016 billion (31 December 2014 est.)
country comparison to the world: 135
Debt—external: $56.11 billion (31 December 2014 est.)
$55.45 billion (31 December 2013 est.)
country comparison to the world: 63
Stock of direct foreign investment—at home:
$15.83 billion (31 December 2015 est.)
$14.73 billion (31 December 2014 est.)
country comparison to the world: 85
Stock of direct foreign investment—abroad:
$7.958 billion (31 December 2015 est.)
$8.178 billion (31 December 2014 est.)
country comparison to the world: 62
Exchange rates: euros (EUR) per US dollar—
0.885 (2015 est.)
0.7525 (2014 est.)
0.7634 (2013 est.)
0.7752 (2012 est.)
0.7185 (2011 est.)

ENERGY

Electricity—production: 14.81 billion kWh (2012 est.)
country comparison to the world: 86
Electricity—consumption: 13.02 billion kWh (2012 est.)
country comparison to the world: 82
Electricity—exports: 8.684 billion kWh (2013 est.)
country comparison to the world: 23
Electricity—imports: 7.522 billion kWh (2013 est.)
country comparison to the world: 31
Electricity—installed generating capacity: 3.353 million kW (2012 est.)
country comparison to the world: 90
Electricity—from fossil fuels: 34.1% of total installed capacity (2013 est.)
country comparison to the world: 171
Electricity—from nuclear fuels: 33.6% of total installed capacity (2013 est.)
country comparison to the world: 4
Electricity—from hydroelectric plants: 29.2% of total installed capacity (2013 est.)
country comparison to the world: 79

Electricity—from other renewable sources: 3% of total installed capacity (2013 est.)
country comparison to the world: 71
Crude oil—production: 5 bbl/day (2014 est.)
country comparison to the world: 101
Crude oil—exports: 0 bbl/day (2013 est.)
country comparison to the world: 188
Crude oil—imports: 0 bbl/day (2013 est.)
country comparison to the world: 124
Crude oil—proved reserves: 0 bbl (1 January 2015 est.)
country comparison to the world: 189
Refined petroleum products—production: 0 bbl/day (2013 est.)
country comparison to the world: 130
Refined petroleum products—consumption: 49,100 bbl/day (2014 est.)
country comparison to the world: 101
Refined petroleum products—exports: 13,200 bbl/day (2013 est.)
country comparison to the world: 81
Refined petroleum products—imports: 65,660 bbl/day (2013 est.)
country comparison to the world: 66
Natural gas—production: 3 million cu m (2014 est.)
country comparison to the world: 95
Natural gas—consumption: 770 million cu m (2014 est.)
country comparison to the world: 94
Natural gas—exports: 0 cu m (2014 est.)
country comparison to the world: 179
Natural gas—imports: 767 million cu m (2014 est.)
country comparison to the world: 61
Natural gas—proved reserves: 0 cu m (1 January 2014 est.)
country comparison to the world: 193
Carbon dioxide emissions from consumption of energy: 15.87 million Mt (2012 est.)
country comparison to the world: 90

COMMUNICATIONS

Telephones—fixed lines: *total subscriptions:* 770,000
subscriptions per 100 inhabitants: 39 (2014 est.)
country comparison to the world: 88
Telephone—mobile cellular: *total:* 2.3 million
subscriptions per 100 inhabitants: 117 (2014 est.)
country comparison to the world: 149
Telephone system: *general assessment:* well-developed telecommunications infrastructure
domestic: combined fixed-line and mobile-cellular teledensity roughly 150 telephones per 100 persons
international: country code—386 (2011)
Broadcast media: public TV broadcaster, Radio-televizija Slovenija (RTV), operates a system of National and Regional TV stations; 35 domestic commercial TV stations operating Nationally, region ally, and locally; about 60% of households are connected to multi-channel cable TV; public radio broadcaster operates 3 National and 4 Regional stations; more than 75 Regional and local commercial and non-commercial radio stations (2007)

Radio broadcast stations: AM 10, FM 230, short-wave 0 (2006)

Television broadcast stations: 31 (2006)

Internet country code: .si

Internet hosts: 415,581 (2012)

country comparison to the world: 54

Internet users: *total:* 1.4 million

percent of population: 72.3% (2014 est.)

country comparison to the world: 115

TRANSPORTATION

Airports: 16 (2013)

country comparison to the world: 143

Airports—with paved runways: *total:* 7

over 3,047 m: 1

2,438 to 3,047 m: 1

1,524 to 2,437 m: 1

914 to 1,523 m: 3 under 914 m: 1 (2013)

Airports—with unpaved runways: *total:* 9

1,524 to 2,437 m: 1

914 to 1,523 m: 3

under 914 m: 5 (2013)

Pipelines: gas 844 km; oil 5 km (2013)

Railways: *total:* 1,229 km

standard gauge: 1,229 km 1.435-m gauge (503 km electrified) (2014)

country comparison to the world: 84

Roadways: *total:* 38,985 km

paved: 38,985 km (includes 769 km of expressways) (2012)

country comparison to the world: 91

Waterways: (some transport on the Drava River) (2012)

Merchant marine: *registered in other countries:* 24 (Cyprus 5, Liberia 7, Malta 4, Marshall Islands 6, Saint Vincent and the Grenadines 1, Slovakia 1) (2010)

country comparison to the world: 90

Ports and terminals: *major seaport(s):* Koper

MILITARY AND SECURITY

Military branches: Slovenian Armed Forces (Slovenska Vojska, SV): Forces Command (with ground units, Naval element, air and air defense brigade); Administration for Civil Protection and Disaster Relief (ACPDR) (2013)

Military service age and obligation: 18–25 years of age for voluntary military service; conscription abolished in 2003 (2012)

Military expenditures: 0.97% of GDP (2015)

1% of GDP (2014)

1.05% of GDP (2013)

1.18% of GDP (2012)

1.32% of GDP (2011)

country comparison to the world: 85

TRANSNATIONAL ISSUES

Disputes—International: since the breakup of Yugoslavia in the early 1990s, Croatia and Slovenia have each claimed sovereignty over Pirin Bay and four villages, and Slovenia has objected to Croatia's claim of an exclusive economic zone in the Adriatic Sea; in 2009, however Croatia and Slovenia signed a Binding International arbitration agreement to define their disputed land and maritime borders, which led to Slovenia lifting its objections to Croatia joining the EU; as a member state that forms part of the EU's external border, Slovenia has implemented the strict Schengen border rules to curb illegal migration and commerce through Southeastern Europe while encouraging close cross-border ties with Croatia; Slovenia continues to impose a hard border Schengen regime with Croatia, which joined the EU in 2013 but has not yet fulfilled Schengen requirements

Refugees and internally displaced persons: *stateless persons:* 4 (2015)

note: 477,791 estimated refugee and migrant arrivals (2015—March 2016)

Illicit drugs: minor transit point for cocaine and Southwest Asian heroin bound for Western Europe, and for precursor chemicals

SOLOMON ISLANDS

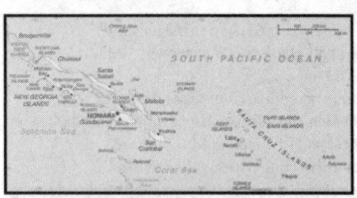

INTRODUCTION

Background: The UK established a protectorate over the Solomon Islands in the 1890s. Some of the bitterest fighting of World War II occurred on this archipelago. Self-government was achieved in 1976 and independence two years later. Ethnic violence, government malfeasance, endemic crime, and a narrow economic base have undermined stability and civil society. In June 2003, then Prime Minister Sir Allan KEMAKEZA sought the assistance of Australia in reestablishing law and order; the following month, an australian led multinational force arrived to restore peace and disarm ethnic militias. The Regional Assistance Mission to the Solomon Islands (RAMSI) has generally been effective in restoring law and order and rebuilding government institutions.

GEOGRAPHY

Location: Oceania, group of islands in the South Pacific Ocean, east of Papua New Guinea

Geographic coordinates: 8 00 S, 159 00 E

Map references: Oceania

Area: *total:* 28,896 sq km

land: 27,986 sq km

water: 910 sq km

country comparison to the world: 144

Area—comparative: slightly smaller than Maryland

Land boundaries: 0 km

Coastline: 5,313 km

Maritime claims: measured from claimed Archipelagic baselines

territorial sea: 12 nm

exclusive economic zone: 200 nm

continental shelf: 200 nm

Climate: tropical monsoon; few temperature and weather extremes

Terrain: mostly rugged mountains with some low coral atolls

Elevation: *mean elevation:* NA

elevation extremes: *lowest point:* Pacific Ocean 0 m

highest point: Mount Popomanaseu 2,310 m

Natural resources: fish, forests, gold, bauxite, phosphates, lead, zinc, nickel

Land use: *agricultural land:* 3.9%

arable land: 0.7%

permanent crops: 2.9%

permanent pasture: 0.3%

forest: 78.9%

other: 17.2% (2011 est.)

Irrigated land: 0 sq km NA (2012)

Total renewable water resources: 44.7 cu km (2011)

Natural hazards: typhoons, but rarely destructive; geologically active region with frequent earthquakes, tremors, and volcanic activity; tsunamis

volcanism: Tinakula (elev. 851 m) has frequent eruption activity, while an eruption of Savo (elev. 485 m) could affect the capital Honiara on nearby Guadalcanal

Environment—current issues: deforestation; soil erosion; many of the surrounding coral reefs are dead or dying

Environment—International agreements: *party to:* Biodiversity, Climate Change, Climate Change-Kyoto Protocol, Desertification, Environmental Modification, Law of the Sea, Marine Dumping, Marine Life Conservation, Ozone Layer Protection, Whaling

signed, but not ratified: none of the selected agreements

Geography—note: strategic location on sea routes between the South Pacific Ocean, the Solomon Sea, and the Coral Sea; on 2 April 2007 an undersea earthquake measuring 8.1 on the Richter scale occurred 345 km WNW of the capital Honiara; the resulting tsunami devastated coastal areas of Western and Choiseul provinces with dozens of deaths and thousands dislocated; the provincial capital of Gizo was especially hard hit

PEOPLE AND SOCIETY

Nationality: *noun:* Solomon Islander(s)

adjective: Solomon Islander

Ethnic groups: Melanesian 95.3%, Polynesian 3.1%, Micronesian 1.2%, other 0.3% (2009 est.)

Languages: Melanesian pidgin (in much of the country is lingua franca), English (official but spoken by only 1% -2% of the population), 120 indigenous languages

Religions: Protestant 73.4% (Church of Melanesia 31.9%, South Sea Evangelical 17.1%, Seventh Day Adventist 11.7%, United Church 10.1%, Christian Fellowship Church 2.5%), Roman Catholic 19.6%, other Christian 2.9%, other 4%, none 0.03%, unspecified 0.1% (2009 est.)

Population: 622,469 (July 2015 est.)
country comparison to the world: 169

Age structure: *0–14 years:* 35.68% (male 114,349/female 107,750)
15–24 years: 20.01% (male 64,036/female 60,512)
25–54 years: 35.73% (male 113,306/female 109,133)
55–64 years: 4.45% (male 13,863/female 13,820)
65 years and over: 4.13% (male 12,315/female 13,385) (2015 est.)

Dependency ratios: *total dependency ratio:* 75.1%
youth dependency ratio: 69.1%
elderly dependency ratio: 5.9%
potential support ratio: 16.8% (2015 est.)

Median age: *total:* 21.9 years
male: 21.7 years
female: 22.1 years (2015 est.)
country comparison to the world: 180

Population growth rate: 2.02% (2015 est.)
country comparison to the world: 49

Birth rate: 25.77 births/1,000 population (2015 est.)
country comparison to the world: 47

Death rate: 3.85 deaths/1,000 population (2015 est.)
country comparison to the world: 210

Net migration rate: -1.75 migrant(s)/1,000 population (2015 est.)
country comparison to the world: 162

Urbanization: *urban population:* 22.3% of total population (2015)
rate of urbanization: 4.25% annual rate of change (2010–15 est.)

Major urban areas—population: HONIARA (capital) 73,000 (2014)

Sex ratio: *at birth:* 1.05 male(s)/female
0–14 years: 1.06 male(s)/female
15–24 years: 1.06 male(s)/female
25–54 years: 1.04 male(s)/female
55–64 years: 1 male(s)/female
65 years and over: 0.92 male(s)/female
total population: 1.04 male(s)/female (2015 est.)

Mother's mean age at first birth: 21.6
note: Median Age at first birth among women 25–29 (2006/07 est.)

Maternal mortality rate: 114 deaths/100,000 live births (2015 est.)
country comparison to the world: 77

Infant mortality rate: *total:* 15.65 deaths/1,000 live births
male: 17.84 deaths/1,000 live births
female: 13.35 deaths/1,000 live births (2015 est.)
country comparison to the world: 102

Life expectancy at birth: *total population:* 75.12 years
male: 72.49 years
female: 77.88 years (2015 est.)
country comparison to the world: 106

Total fertility rate: 3.28 children born/woman (2015 est.)
country comparison to the world: 47

Contraceptive prevalence rate: 34.6% (2006/07)

Health expenditures: 5.1% of GDP (2013)
country comparison to the world: 59

Physicians density: 0.22 physicians/1,000 population (2009)

Hospital bed density: 1.3 beds/1,000 population (2012)

Drinking water source:
improved:
urban: 93.2% of population
rural: 77.2% of population
total: 80.8% of population
unimproved:
urban: 6.8% of population
rural: 22.8% of population
total: 19.2% of population (2015 est.)

Sanitation facility access:
improved:
urban: 81.4% of population
rural: 15% of population
total: 29.8% of population
unimproved:
urban: 18.6% of population
rural: 85% of population
total: 70.2% of population (2015 est.)

HIV/AIDS—adult prevalence rate: NA

HIV/AIDS—people living with HIV/AIDS: NA

HIV/AIDS—deaths: NA

Obesity—adult prevalence rate: 25% (2014)
country comparison to the world: 27

Children under the age of 5 years underweight: 11.5% (2007)
country comparison to the world: 65

Education expenditures: 10% of GDP (2010)
country comparison to the world: 18

Literacy: *definition:* age 15 and over can read and write
total population: 84.1%
male: 88.9%
female: 79.2% (2009 est.)

School life expectancy (primary to tertiary education): *total:* 9 years
male: 10 years
female: 9 years (2007)

GOVERNMENT

Country name: *conventional long form:* none
conventional short form: Solomon Islands
local long form: none
local short form: Solomon Islands
former: British Solomon Islands
etymology: Spanish explorer Alvaro de MENDANA named the isles in 1568 after the wealthy biblical King SOLOMON in the mistaken belief that the islands contained great riches

Government type: parliamentary democracy (National Parliament) under a constitutional monarchy; a Commonwealth realm

Capital: *name:* Honiara

Geographic coordinates: 9 26 S, 159 57 E
time difference: UTC + 11 (16 hours ahead of Washington, DC, during Standard Time)

Administrative divisions: 9 provinces and 1 city*; Central, Choiseul, Guadalcanal, Honiara*, Isabel, Makira and Ulawa, Malaita, Rennell and Bellona, Temotu, Western

Independence: 7 July 1978 (from the UK)

National holiday: Independence Day, 7 July (1978)

Constitution: adopted 31 May 1978, effective 7 July 1978; new constitution drafted in 2014 (2016)

Legal system: mixed legal system of English common law and customary law

International law organization participation: has not submitted an ICJ jurisdiction declaration; non-party state to the ICCt

Citizenship: *citizenship by birth:* no
citizenship by descent only: at least one parent must be a citizen of the Solomon Islands
dual citizenship recognized: no
residency requirement for naturalization: 7 years

Suffrage: 21 years of age; universal

Executive branch: *chief of state:* Queen ELIZABETH II (since 6 February 1952); represented by Governor General Frank KABUI (since 7 July 2009)

head of government: Prime Minister Manasseh SOGAVARE (since 9 December 2014)
cabinet: Cabinet appointed by the governor general on the advice of the prime minister
elections/appointments: the monarchy is hereditary; governor general appointed by the monarch on the advice of the National Parliament for up to 5 years (eligible for a second term); following legislative elections, the leader of the majority party or majority coalition usually elected prime minister by the National Parliament; deputy prime minister appointed by the governor general on the advice of the prime minister from among members of the National Parliament
election results: Manasseh SOGAVARE (independent) elected prime minister; National Parliament vote—31 to 19

Legislative branch: *description:* unicameral National Parliament (50 seats; members directly elected in single-seat constituencies by simple majority vote to serve 4-year terms)
elections: last held on 19 November 2014 (next to be held in 2018)
election results: percent of vote by party—NA; seats by party—independents 32, DAP 7, UDP 5, PAP 3, KPSI 1, SIPFP 1, SIPRA 1

Judicial branch: *highest court(s):* Court of Appeal (consists of the court president, and ex officio members to include the High Court chief justice and its puisne judges); High Court (consists of the chief justice and puisne judges as prescribed by the National Parliament)
judge selection and term of office: Court of Appeal and High Court president, chief justices, and puisne judges appointed by the governor-general upon recommendation of the Judicial and Legal Service Commission, chaired by the chief justice to include 5 members, mostly

773

judicial officials and legal profession als; all judges appointed until retirement at age 60

subordinate courts: Magistrates' Courts; local courts; Customary Land Appeal Court

Political parties and leaders: Democratic Alliance Party or DAP [Steve ABANA]

Kadere Party of Solomon Islands or KPSI [Alfred LEGUA]

People's Alliance Party or PAP [Nathaniel WAENA]

Solomon Islands People First Party or SIPFP [Jimmie RODGERS]

Solomon Islands Party for Rural Advancement or SIPRA [Manasseh MAELANGA]

United Democratic Party [Thomas Ko CHAN]

note: in general, Solomon Islands politics is characterized by fluid coalitions

Political pressure groups and leaders: Isatabu Freedom Movement or IFM Malaita Eagle Force or MEF

note: these rival armed ethnic factions crippled the Solomon Islands in a wave of violence from 1999 to 2003

International organization participation: ACP, ADB, AOSIS, C, EITI (candidate country), ESCAP, FAO, G-77, IBRD, ICAO, ICRM, IDA, IFAD, IFC, IFRCS, ILO, IMF, IMO, IOC, ITU, MIGA, OPCW, PIF, Sparteca, SPC, UN, UNCTAD, UNESCO, UPU, WFTU, WHO, WMO, WTO

Diplomatic representation in the US: *chief of mission:* Ambassador Collin David BECK (since 31 March 2004)

chancery: 800 Second Avenue, Suite 400L, New York, NY 10017

telephone: [1] (212) 599-6192, 6193

FAX: [1] (212) 661-8925

Diplomatic representation from the US: the US does not have an embassy in the Solomon Islands; the US Ambassador to Papua New Guinea is accredited to the Solomon Islands

Flag description: divided diagon ally by a thin yellow stripe from the lower hoist-side corner; the upper triangle (hoist side) is blue with five white five-pointed stars arranged in an X pattern; the lower triangle is green; blue represents the ocean; green the land; and yellow sunshine; the five stars stand for the five main island groups of the Solomon Islands

National symbol(s): National colors: blue, yellow, green, white

National anthem: *name:* "God Save Our Solomon Islands"

lyrics/music: Panapasa BALEKANA and Matila BALEKANA/Panapasa BALEKANA

note: adopted 1978

ECONOMY

Economy—overview: The bulk of the population depends on agriculture, fishing, and forestry for at least part of its livelihood. Most manufactured goods and petroleum Products must be imported. The islands are rich in undeveloped mineral resources such as lead, zinc, nickel, and gold. Prior to the arrival of The Regional Assistance Mission to the Solomon Islands (RAMSI), severe ethnic

violence, the closure of key businesses, and an empty government treasury culminated in economic collapse. RAMSI's efforts to restore law and order and economic stability have led to modest growth as the economy rebuilds.

GDP (purchasing power parity): $1.146 billion (2015 est.)

$1.11 billion (2014 est.)

$1.088 billion (2013 est.)

note: data are in 2015 US dollars

country comparison to the world: 203

GDP (official exchange rate): $1.147 billion (2015 est.)

GDP—real growth rate: 3.3% (2015 est.)

2% (2014 est.)

3% (2013 est.)

country comparison to the world: 90

GDP—per capita (PPP): $1,900 (2015 est.)

$1,900 (2014 est.)

$1,900 (2013 est.)

note: data are in 2015 US dollars

country comparison to the world: 205

Gross National saving: 17.1% of GDP (2015 est.)

14.9% of GDP (2014 est.)

21.6% of GDP (2013 est.)

country comparison to the world: 96

GDP—composition, by sector of origin:

agriculture: 51.2%

industry: 10.2%

services: 38.7% (2015 est.)

Agriculture—products: cocoa, coconuts, palm kernels, rice, fruit; cattle, pigs; fish; timber

Industries: fish (tuna), mining, timber

Industrial production growth rate: 4.3% (2015 est.)

country comparison to the world: 46

Labor force: 202,500 (2007 est.)

country comparison to the world: 170

Labor force—by occupation: *agriculture:* 75%

industry: 5%

services: 20% (2000 est.)

Unemployment rate: NA%

Population below poverty line: NA%

Household income or consumption by percentage share: *lowest:* 10%: NA%

highest: 10%: NA%

Budget: *revenues:* $415.5 million

expenditures: $440.7 million (2015 est.)

Taxes and other revenues: 34.5% of GDP (2015 est.)

country comparison to the world: 63

Budget surplus (+) or deficit (–): -2.1% of GDP (2015 est.)

country comparison to the world: 78

Fiscal year: calendar year

Inflation rate (consumer prices): -0.4% (2015 est.)

5.2% (2014 est.)

country comparison to the world: 30

Commercial bank prime lending rate: 10.9% (31 December 2015 est.)

10.91% (31 December 2014 est.)

country comparison to the world: 76

Stock of narrow money: $348.4 million (31 December 2015 est.)

$360.5 million (31 December 2014 est.)

country comparison to the world: 170

Stock of broad money: $452.1 million (31 December 2014 est.)

$467.9 million (31 December 2013 est.)

country comparison to the world: 184

Stock of domestic credit: $48.89 million (31 December 2015 est.)

$45.12 million (31 December 2014 est.)

country comparison to the world: 186

Current account balance: -$30 million (2015 est.)

-$50 million (2014 est.)

country comparison to the world: 59

Exports: $493.1 million (2012 est.)

$448.1 million (2013 est.)

country comparison to the world: 173

Exports—commodities: timber, fish, copra, palm oil, cocoa

Exports—partners: China 61.7%, India 5.9%, Italy 5.9% (2015)

Imports: $446 million (2012 est.)

$464.5 million (2013 est.)

country comparison to the world: 195

Imports—commodities: food, plant and equipment, manufactured goods, fuels, chemicals

Imports—partners: Australia 24.7%, China 18.4%, Malaysia 6.3%, Singapore 5.8%, Fiji 4.7%, NZ 4.6%, Papua New Guinea 4.6% (2015)

Debt—external: $491.5 million (31 December 2013 est.)

$228.1 million (31 December 2012 est.)

country comparison to the world: 180

Stock of direct foreign investment—at home: $850.1 million (31 December 2015 est.)

$799 million (31 December 2014 est.)

country comparison to the world: 112

Stock of direct foreign investment—abroad: $47.3 million (31 December 2015 est.)

$47.3 million (31 December 2014 est.)

country comparison to the world: 99

Exchange rates: Solomon Islands dollars (SBD) per US dollar—

7.942 (2015 est.)

7.3754 (2014 est.)

7.3754 (2013 est.)

7.36 (2012 est.)

7.6413 (2011 est.)

ENERGY

Electricity—production: 85 million kWh (2012 est.)

country comparison to the world: 203

Electricity—consumption: 79.05 million kWh (2012 est.)

country comparison to the world: 202

Electricity—exports: 0 kWh (2013 est.)

country comparison to the world: 112

Electricity—imports: 0 kWh (2013 est.)

country comparison to the world: 125

Electricity—installed generating capacity: 36,000 kW (2012 est.)

country comparison to the world: 195

Electricity—from fossil fuels: 100% of total installed capacity (2012 est.)

country comparison to the world: 6

Electricity—from nuclear fuels: 0% of total installed capacity (2012 est.)

country comparison to the world: 58

Electricity—from hydroelectric plants: 0% of total installed capacity (2012 est.)
country comparison to the world: 163
Electricity—from other renewable sources: 0% of total installed capacity (2012 est.)
country comparison to the world: 161
Crude oil—production: 0 bbl/day (2014 est.)
country comparison to the world: 113
Crude oil—exports: 0 bbl/day (2012 est.)
country comparison to the world: 103
Crude oil—imports: 0 bbl/day (2012 est.)
country comparison to the world: 165
Crude oil—proved reserves: 0 bbl (1 January 2015 est.)
country comparison to the world: 111
Refined petroleum products—production: 0 bbl/day (2012 est.)
country comparison to the world: 161
Refined petroleum products—consumption: 1,500 bbl/day (2013 est.)
country comparison to the world: 194
Refined petroleum products—exports: 0 bbl/day (2012 est.)
country comparison to the world: 161
Refined petroleum products—imports: 1,491 bbl/day (2012 est.)
country comparison to the world: 189
Natural gas—production: 0 cu m (2013 est.)
country comparison to the world: 163
Natural gas—consumption: 0 cu m (2013 est.)
country comparison to the world: 122
Natural gas—exports: 0 cu m (2013 est.)
country comparison to the world: 69
Natural gas—imports: 0 cu m (2013 est.)
country comparison to the world: 168
Natural gas—proved reserves: 0 cu m (1 January 2014 est.)
country comparison to the world: 117
Carbon dioxide emissions from consumption of energy: 266,000 Mt (2012 est.)
country comparison to the world: 193

COMMUNICATIONS

Telephones—fixed lines: *total subscriptions:* 7,500
subscriptions per 100 inhabitants: 1 (2014 est.)
country comparison to the world: 201
Telephones—mobile cellular: *total:* 376,700

subscriptions per 100 inhabitants: 62 (2014 est.)
country comparison to the world: 174
Telephone system: *domestic:* mobile-cellular telephone density is about 50 per 100 persons
international: country code—677; satellite earth station—1 intelsat (Pacific Ocean) (2011)
Broadcast media: Solomon Islands Broadcasting Corporation (SI BC) is the sole TV broadcaster with 1 station; multi-channel pay-TV is available; SIBC operates 2 National radio stations and 2 provincial stations; 2 local commercial radio stations; Radio Australia is available via satellite feed (2009)
Radio broadcast stations: AM 1, FM 1, shortwave 1 (2004)
Internet country code: .sb
Internet hosts: 4,370 (2012)
country comparison to the world: 148
Internet users: *total:* 46,400
percent of population: 7.6% (2014 est.)
country comparison to the world: 187

TRANSPORTATION

Airports: 36 (2013)
country comparison to the world: 109
Airports—with paved runways: *total:* 1
1,524 to 2,437 m: 1 (2013)
Airports—with unpaved runways: *total:* 35
1,524 to 2,437 m: 1
914 to 1,523 m: 10
under 914 m: 24 (2013)
Heliports: 3 (2013)
Roadways: *total:* 1,390 km
paved: 34 km
unpaved: 1,356 km
note: includes 920 km of private plantation roads (2011)
country comparison to the world: 179
Ports and terminals: *major seaport(s):* Honiara, Malloco Bay, Viru Harbor, Tulaghi

MILITARY AND SECURITY

Military branches: no regular military forces; Royal Solomon Islands Police Force (2013)

TRANSNATIONAL ISSUES

Disputes—International: since 2003, the Regional Assistance Mission to Solomon Islands, consisting of police, military, and civilian advisors drawn from 15 countries, has assisted in reestablishing and maintaining civil and political order while reinforcing regional stability and security

Trafficking in persons: *current situation:* the Solomon Islands is a source and destination country for local adults and children and Southeast Asian men and women subjected to forced labor and forced prostitution; women from China, Indonesia, Malaysia, and the Philippines are recruited for legitimate work and upon arrival are forced into prostitution; men from Indonesia and Malaysia recruited to work in the Solomon Islands' mining and logging industries may be subjected to forced labor; local children are forced into prostitution near foreign logging camps, on fishing vessels, at hotels, and entertainment venues; some local children are also sold by their parents for marriage to foreign workers or put up for "informal adoption" to pay off debts and then find themselves forced into domestic servitude or forced prostitution

tier rating: Tier 2 Watch List—the Solomon Islands does not fully comply with the minimum standards for the elimination of trafficking; however, it is making significant efforts to do so; in 2014, the Solomon Islands was granted a waiver from an otherwise required downgrade to Tier 3 because its government has a written plan that, if implemented, would constitute making significant efforts to bring itself into compliance with the minimum standards for the elimination of trafficking; the government gazetted implementing regulations for the 2012 immigration act prohibiting Transnational trafficking, but the penalties are not sufficiently stringent because they allow the option of paying a fine; a new draft law to address these weaknesses awaits parliamentary review; no new trafficking investigations were conducted, even after labor inspections at logging and fishing companies, no existing cases led to prosecutions or convictions, and no funding was allocated for National anti-trafficking efforts; authorities did not identify or protect any victims and lack any procedures or shelters to do so; civil society and religious organizations provide most of the limited services available; a lack of understanding of the crime of trafficking remains a serious challenge (2015)

SOMALIA

INTRODUCTION

Background: Britain withdrew from British Somaliland in 1960 to allow its protectorate to join with Italian Somaliland and form the new nation of Somalia. In 1969, a coup headed by Mohamed SIAD Barre ushered in an authoritarian socialist rule characterized by the persecution, jailing, and torture of political opponents and dissidents. After the regime's collapse early in 1991, Somalia descended into turmoil, factional fighting, and anarchy. In May 1991, northern clans declared an independent Republic of Somaliland that now includes the administrative regions of Awdal, Woqooyi Galbeed, Togdheer, Sanaag, and Sool. Although not recognized by any government, this entity has maintained a stable existence and continues efforts to establish a constitutional democracy, including holding municipal, parliamentary, and presidential elections. The regions of Bari, Nugaal, and northern Mudug comprise a neighboring semi-autonomous state of Puntland, which has been self-governing since 1998 but does not aim at independence; it has also made strides toward reconstructing a legitimate, representative government but has suffered some civil strife. Puntland disputes its border with Somaliland as it also claims the regions of Sool and Sanaag, and portions of Togdheer. Beginning in 1993, a two-year UN humanitarian effort (primarily in south-central Somalia) was able to alleviate famine conditions, but when the UN withdrew in 1995, having suffered significant casualties, order still had not been restored. In 2000, the Somalia National Peace Conference (SNPC) held in Djibouti resulted in the formation of an interim government, known as the Transitional National Government (TNG). When the TNG failed to establish adequate security or governing institutions, the Government of Kenya, under the auspices of the Intergovernmental Authority on Development (IGAD), led a subsequent peace process that concluded in October 2004 with the election of Abdullahi YUSUF Ahmed

as President of a second interim government, known as the Transitional Federal Government (TFG) of the Somali Republic. The TFG included a 275-member parliamentary body, known as the Transitional Federal Parliament (TFP). President YUSUF resigned late in 2008 while United Nations-sponsored talks between the TFG and the opposition alliance for the Re-Liberation of Somalia (ARS) were underway in Djibouti. In January 2009, following the creation of a TFG-ARS unity government, Ethiopian military forces, which had entered Somalia in December 2006 to support the TFG in the face of advances by the opposition Islamic Courts Union (ICU), withdrew from the country. The TFP was doubled in size to 550 seats with the addition of 200 ARS and 75 civil society members of parliament. The expanded parliament elected Sheikh SHARIF Sheikh Ahmed, the former ICU and ARS chairman as president in January 2009. The creation of the TFG was based on the Transitional Federal Charter (TFC), which outlined a five-year mandate leading to the establishment of a new Somali constitution and a transition to a representative government following National elections. In 2009, the TFP amended the TFC to extend TFG's mandate until 2011 and in 2011 Somali principals agreed to institute political transition by August 2012. The transition process ended in September 2012 when clan elders replaced the TFP by appointing 275 members to a new parliament who subsequently elected a new president.

GEOGRAPHY

Location: Eastern africa, bordering the Gulf of Aden and the Indian Ocean, east of Ethiopia

Geographic coordinates: 10 00 N, 49 00 E

Map references: Africa

Area: *total:* 637,657 sq km
land: 627,337 sq km
water: 10,320 sq km
country comparison to the world: 44

Area—comparative: almost five times the size of Alabama; slightly smaller than Texas

Land boundaries: *total:* 2,385 km
border countries (3): Djibouti 61 km, Ethiopia 1,640 km, Kenya 684 km

Coastline: 3,025 km

Maritime claims: *territorial sea:* 200 nm

Climate: principally desert; northeast monsoon (December to February), moderate temperatures in north and hot in south; southwest monsoon (May to October), torrid in the north and hot in the south, irregular rainfall, hot and humid periods (tangambili) between monsoons

Terrain: mostly flat to undulating plateau rising to hills in north

Elevation: *mean elevation:* 410 m

elevation extremes: *lowest point:* Indian Ocean 0 m
highest point: Shimbiris 2,416 m

Natural resources: uranium and largely unexploited reserves of iron ore, tin, gypsum, bauxite, copper, salt, Natural gas, likely 0I1 reserves

Land use: *agricultural land:* 70.3%
arable land: 1.8%
permanent crops: 0%
permanent pasture: 68.5%
forest: 10.6%
other: 19.1% (2011 est.)

Irrigated land: 2,000 sq km (2012)

Total renewable water resources: 14.7 cu km (2011)

Freshwater withdrawal (domestic/industrial/agricultural): *total:* 3.3 cu km/yr (0%/0%/100%)
per capita: 377.6 cu m/yr (2003)

Natural hazards: recurring droughts; frequent dust storms over eastern plains in summer; floods during rainy season

Environment—current issues: famine; use of contaminated water contributes to human health problems; deforestation; overgrazing; soil erosion; desertification

Environment—International agreements: *party to:* Biodiversity, Desertification, Endangered Species, Law of the Sea, Ozone Layer Protection
signed, but not ratified: none of the selected agreements

Geography—note: strategic location on Horn of Africa along southern approaches to Babel Mandeb and route through Red Sea and Suez Canal

PEOPLE AND SOCIETY

Nationality: *noun:* Somali(s)
adjective: Somali

Ethnic groups: Somali 85%, Bantu and other non-Somali 15% (including 30,000 Arabs)

Languages: Somali (official), Arabic (official, according to the Transition al Federal Charter), Italian, English

Religions: Sunni Muslim (Islam) (official, according to the Transition al Federal Charter)

Population: 10,616,380
note: this estimate was derived from an official census taken in 1975 by the Somali Government; population counting in Somalia is complicated by the large number of nomads and by refugee movements in response to famine and clan warfare (July 2015 est.)
country comparison to the world: 86

Age structure: *0–14 years:* 43.72% (male 2,317,935/female 2,323,681)
15–24 years: 18.85% (male 1,012,447/female 988,251)
25–54 years: 31.36% (male 1,722,230/female 1,607,117)
55–64 years: 3.83% (male 196,664/female 209,983)
65 years and over: 2.24% (male 92,658/female 145,414) (2015 est.)

Dependency ratios: *total dependency ratio:* 98.1%
youth dependency ratio: 92.5%
elderly dependency ratio: 5.6%

potential support ratio: 17.9% (2015 est.)
Median age: *total:* 17.8 years
male: 18 years
female: 17.7 years (2015 est.)
country comparison to the world: 217
Population growth rate: 1.83% (2015 est.)
country comparison to the world: 62
Birth rate: 40.45 births/1,000 population (2015 est.)
country comparison to the world: 8
Death rate: 13.62 deaths/1,000 population (2015 est.)
country comparison to the world: 13
Net migration rate: -8.49 migrant(s)/1,000 population (2015 est.)
country comparison to the world: 211
Urbanization: *urban population:* 39.6% of total population (2015)
rate of urbanization: 4.06% annual rate of change (2010–15 est.)
Major urban areas—population: MOGADISHU (capital) 2.138 million; Hargeysa 760,000 (2015)
Sex ratio: *at birth:* 1.03 male(s)/female
0–14 years: 1 male(s)/female
15–24 years: 1.02 male(s)/female
25–54 years: 1.07 male(s)/female
55–64 years: 0.94 male(s)/female
65 years and over: 0.64 male(s)/female
total population: 1.01 male(s)/female (2015 est.)
Maternal mortality rate: 732 deaths/100,000 live births (2015 est.)
country comparison to the world: 3
Infant mortality rate: *total:* 98.39 deaths/1,000 live births
male: 107.07 deaths/1,000 live births
female: 89.45 deaths/1,000 live births (2015 est.)
country comparison to the world: 3
Life expectancy at birth: *total population:* 51.96 years
male: 49.93 years
female: 54.06 years (2015 est.)
country comparison to the world: 218
Total fertility rate: 5.99 children born/woman (2015 est.)
country comparison to the world: 4
Contraceptive prevalence rate: 14.6% (2006)
Physicians density: 0.04 physicians/1,000 population (2006)
Drinking water source:
improved:
urban: 69.6% of population
rural: 8.8% of population
total: 31.7% of population
unimproved:
urban: 30.4% of population
rural: 91.2% of population
total: 68.3% of population (2011 est.)
Sanitation facility access:
improved:
urban: 52% of population
rural: 6.3% of population
total: 23.6% of population
unimproved:
urban: 48% of population
rural: 93.7% of population
total: 76.4% of population (2011 est.)

HIV/AIDS—adult prevalence rate: 0.55% (2014 est.)
country comparison to the world: 63
HIV/AIDS—people living with HIV/AIDS: 34,900 (2014 est.)
country comparison to the world: 65
HIV/AIDS—deaths: 2,400 (2014 est.)
country comparison to the world: 54
Major infectious diseases: *degree of risk:* very high
food or waterborne diseases: bacterial and protozoal diarrhea, hepatitis A and E, and typhoid fever
vectorborne diseases: dengue fever, malaria, and Rift Valley fever
water contact disease: schistosomiasis animal contact disease: rabies (2013)
Obesity—adult prevalence rate: 3.9% (2014)
country comparison to the world: 162
Children under the age of 5 years underweight: 23% (2009)
country comparison to the world: 9
Education expenditures: NA
Child labor—children ages 5–14: *total number:* 1,148,265
percentage: 49% (2006 est.)

GOVERNMENT

Country name: *conventional long form:* Federal Republic of Somalia
conventional short form: Somalia
local long form: Jamhuuriyadda Federaalkaa Soomaaliya
local short form: Soomaaliya
former: Somali Republic, Somali Democratic Republic etymology: "Land of the Somali" (ethnic group)
Government type: federal parliamentary republic
Capital: *name:* Mogadishu
Geographic coordinates: 2 04 N, 45 20 E
time difference: UTC+3 (8 hours ahead of Washington, DC, during Standard Time)
Administrative divisions: 18 regions (plural—NA, singular—gobolka); Awdal, Bakool, Banaadir, Bari, Bay, Galguduud, Gedo, Hiiraan, Jubbada Dhexe (Middle Jubba), Jubbada Hoose (Lower Jubba), Mudug, Nugaal, Sanaag, Shabeellaha Dhexe (Middle Shabeelle), Shabeellaha Hoose (Lower Shabeelle), Sool, Togdheer, Woqooyi Galbeed
Independence: 1 July 1960 (from a merger of British Somaliland that became independent from the UK on 26 June 1960 and Italian Somaliland that became independent from the Italian-administered UN trusteeship on 1 July 1960 to form the Somali Republic)
National holiday: Foundation of the Somali Republic, 1 July (1960); note—26 June (1960) in Somaliland
Constitution: previous 1961, 1979; latest drafted 12 June 2012, approved 1 August 2012 (provisional) (2016)
Legal system: mixed legal system of civil law, Islamic law, and customary law (referred to as Xeer)

International law organization participation: accepts compulsory ICJ jurisdiction with reservations; non-party state to the ICCt
Citizenship: *citizenship by birth:* no
citizenship by descent only: the father must be a citizen of Somalia
dual citizenship recognized: no
residency requirement for naturalization: 7 years
Suffrage: 18 years of age; universal
Executive branch: *chief of state:* President HASSAN SHEIKH Mohamud (since 10 September 2012)
head of government: Prime Minister Omar Abdirashid Ali SHARMARKE (since 24 December 2014); Deputy Prime Minister Mohamad Omar ARTEH (since 6 February 2015)
cabinet: Cabinet appointed by the prime minister, approved by the National Parliament
elections/appointments: president indirectly elected by the Federal Parliament by two-thirds majority vote in 2 rounds if needed for a single 4-year term; election last held on 10 September 2012 (next to be held in 2016); prime minister appointed by the president, approved by the Federal Parliament
election results: HASSAN SHEIKH Mohamud elected president; Federal Parliament second round vote -HASSAN SHEIKH Mohamud (PDP) 190, Sheikh SHARIF Sheikh Ahmed (ARS) 79; Omar Abdirashid Ali SHARMARKE approved as prime minister; Federal Parliament vote—218 for approval, none against (6 members not present for vote)
Legislative branch: *description:* unicameral National Parliament or Golaha Shacabka Soomaaliya consists of the House of the People (275 seats; members directly elected to serve 4-year terms)
note: the inaugural House of the People was appointed in September 2012 by clan elders; slated for 2016, the National Parliament will become bicameral with the formation of an upper house that will consist of 54 seats with members indirectly elected by regional governing councils to serve 4-year terms
Judicial branch: *highest court(s):* the provisional constitution stipulates the establishment of the Constitutional Court (consists of 5 judges including the chief judge and deputy chief judge); note—under the terms of the 2004 Transitional National Charter, a Supreme Court based in Mogadishu and an appeal Court were established; yet most regions have reverted to local forms of conflict resolution, either secular, traditional Somali customary law, or sharia Islamic law
judge selection and term of office: judges appointed by the president upon proposal of the Judicial Service Commission, a 9-member judicial and administrative body; judge tenure NA
subordinate courts: federal-level and federal member state-level courts; military courts; sharia (Islamic) courts
Political parties and leaders: CADHI [Abdirahman IBRAHIM]

Cosmopolitan Democratic Party [Yarow Sharef ADEN]

Democratic Green Party of Somalia or DGPS [Abdullahi Y. MAHAMOUD]

Democratic Party of Somalia or DPS [Maslah Mohamed SIAD]

Green Leaf for Democracy or GLED Hiil Qaran Justice and Communist Party [Mohamed NUR]

Liberal Party of Somalia National Unity Party (Xisbiga MIdnimo-Quaran) [Abdurahman BAADIYOW]

Peace and Development Party or PDP Somali National Party or SNP [Mohammed Ameen Saeed AHMED]

Somali People's Party [Mahamud Hassan RAG E]

Somali Green Party (local chapter of Federation of Green Parties of Africa) Tayo or TPP [M ohamed Abdullahi MOHAMED]

Tiir Party [Fadhil Sheik MOHAMUD]

United and Democratic Party [Salad Ali JELLE]

United Somali Parliamentarians

Political pressure groups and leaders:

other: numerous political associations and clan and sub-clan factions exist both in support and in opposition to the incumbent president

International organization participation: ACP, AfDB, AFESD, AMF, AU, CAEU (candidate), FAO, G-77, IBRD, ICAO, ICRM, IDA, IDB, IFAD, IFC, IFRCS, IGAD, ILO, IMF, IMO, Interpol, IOC, IOM, IPU, ITSO, ITU, LAS, NAM, OIC, OPCW, OPCW (signatory), UN, UNCTAD, UNESCO, UNHCR, UNIDO, UPU, WFTU (NGOs), WHO, WIPO, WMO

Diplomatic representation in the US: *chief of mission:* Ambassador Ahmed Issa AWAD (since 17 September 2015)

chancery: 425 East 61 st Street, Suite 702, New York City, NY 10021

telephone: [1] (212) 688-9410, 688-5046

FAX: [1] (212) 759-0651

Diplomatic representation from the US: the US Mission in Somalia, operating out of the US Embassy in Nairobi, Kenya, is headed by Charge d'Affaires Ambassador (Retired) David H. KAEU-PER (since 1 October 2015)

Flag description: light blue with a large white five-pointed star in the center; the blue field was origi-nally influenced by the flag of the UN, but today is said to denote the sky and the neighboring Indian Ocean; the five points of the star represent the five regions in the horn of Africa that are inhabited by Somali people: the former British Somaliland and Italian Somaliland (which together make up Somalia), Djibouti, Ogaden (Ethiopia), and the North East Province (Kenya)

National symbol(s): leopard; National colors: blue, white

National anthem: *name:* "Qolobaa Calankeed" (Every Nation Has its own Flag)

lyrics/music: Abdullahi QARSHE

note: adopted 2012; written in 1959

Government—note: regional and local governing bodies continue to exist and control various areas of the country, including the self-declared Repub-lic of Somaliland in northwestern Somalia and the semi-autonomous state of Puntland in northeast-ern Somalia

ECONOMY

Economy—overview: Despite the lack of effec-tive National governance, Somalia maintains an informal economy largely based on livestock, remittance/money transfer companies, and tel-ecommunications. Somalia's government lacks the ability to collect domestic revenue and external debt—mostly in arrears—was estimated at 93% of GDP in 2014.

Agriculture is the most important sector, with livestock normally accounting for about 40% of GDP and more than 50% of export earnings. Nomads and semi-pastoralists, who are depend-ent upon livestock for their livelihood, make up a large portion of the population. Economic activ-ity is estimated to have increased by 3.7% in 2014 because of growth in the agriculture, construction and telecommunications sector. Somalia's small industrial sector, based on the processing of agri-cultural products, has largely been looted and the machinery sold as scrap metal.

In recent years, Somalia's capital city, Mogadishu, has witnessed the development of the city's first gas stations, supermarkets, and airline flights to Tur-key since the collapse of central authority in 1991. Mogadishu's main market offers a variety of goods from food to electronic gadgets. Hotels continue to operate and are supported with private-security militias. Economic growth has yet to expand out-side of Mogadishu, and within the city, security concerns dominate business. Telecommunication firms provide wireless services in most major cit-ies and offer the lowest International call rates on the continent in the absence of a formal banking sector, money transfer/remittance services have sprouted throughout the country, handling up to $1.6 billion in remittances annually, although International concerns over the money transfers into Somalia continues to threaten these services.

GDP (purchasing power parity): $4.431 billion (2014 est.)

$4.186 billion (2013 est.)

$5.607 billion (2008 est.)

note: data are in 2010 US dollars

country comparison to the world: 177

GDP (official exchange rate): $5.8 billion (2014 est.)

GDP—real growth rate: 2.6% (2010 est.)

2.6% (2009 est.)

2.6% (2008 est.)

country comparison to the world: 113

GDP—per capita (PPP): $400 (2014 est.)

$400 (2013 est.)

$600 (2008 est.)

country comparison to the world: 229

GDP—composition, by end use:

household consumption: 72.7%

government consumption: 8.7%

investment in fixed capital: 19.9%

investment in inventories: 0.4%

exports of goods and services: 0.3%

imports of goods and services: -2% (2011 est.)

GDP—composition, by sector of origin:

agriculture: 60.2%

industry: 7.4%

services: 32.5% (2013 est.)

Agriculture—products: bananas, sorghum, corn, coconuts, rice, sugarcane, mangoes, sesame seeds, beans; cattle, sheep, goats; fish

Industries: light industries, including sugar refin-ing, textiles, wireless communication

Industrial production growth rate: 2.5% (2013 est.)

country comparison to the world: 103

Labor force: 3.109 million (2013 est.)

country comparison to the world: 103

Labor force—by occupation: *agriculture:* 71%

industry and services: 29% (1975)

Unemployment rate: NA%

Population below poverty line: NA%

Household income or consumption by percentage share: *lowest:* 10%: NA%

highest: 10%: NA%

Budget: *revenues:* $145.3 million

expenditures: $151.1 million (2014 est.)

Taxes and other revenues: 2.5% of GDP (2014 est.)

country comparison to the world: 219

Budget surplus (+) or deficit (–): -0.1% of GDP (2014 est.)

country comparison to the world: 34

Fiscal year: NA

Inflation rate (consumer prices): NA%

note: businesses print their own money, so infla-tion rates cannot be easily determined

Central bank discount rate: NA%

Commercial bank prime lending rate: NA%

Current account balance: -$644 million (2014 est.)

country comparison to the world: 110

Exports: $819 million (2014 est.)

$779 million (2013 est.)

country comparison to the world: 166

Exports—commodities: livestock, bananas, hides, fish, charcoal, scrap metal

Exports—partners: UAE 45.7%, Yemen 19.7%, Oman 15.9% (2015)

Imports: $3.482 billion (2014 est.)

$3.322 billion (2013 est.)

country comparison to the world: 138

Imports—commodities: manufactures, petroleum Products, foodstuffs, construction materials, qat

Imports—partners: Djibouti 18.7%, India 16.5%, China 11.8%, Oman 8.7%, Kenya 6.1%, Pakistan 4.4% (2015)

Reserves of foreign exchange and gold: $30.45 million (2014 est.)

country comparison to the world: 170

Debt—external: $3.054 billion (31 December 2013 est.)

$3.055 billion (31 December 2012 est.)

country comparison to the world: 142

Stock of direct foreign investment—at home: $NA

Exchange rates: Somali shillings (SOS) per US dollar—

20,227 (2014 est.)

19,276 (2013 est.)

ENERGY

Electricity—production: 315 million kWh (2012 est.)

country comparison to the world: 174
Electricity—consumption: 293 million kWh (2012 est.)
country comparison to the world: 177
Electricity—exports: 0 kWh (2013 est.)
country comparison to the world: 197
Electricity—imports: 0 kWh (2013 est.)
country comparison to the world: 203
Electricity—installed generating capacity: 80,000 kW (2012 est.)
country comparison to the world: 179
Electricity—from fossil fuels: 100% of total installed capacity (2012 est.)
country comparison to the world: 28
Electricity—from nuclear fuels: 0% of total installed capacity (2012 est.)
country comparison to the world: 182
Electricity—from hydroelectric plants: 0% of total installed capacity (2012 est.)
country comparison to the world: 203
Electricity—from other renewable sources: 0% of total installed capacity (2012 est.)
country comparison to the world: 128
Crude oil—production: 0 bbl/day (2014 est.)
country comparison to the world: 192
Crude oil—exports: 0 bbl/day (2012 est.)
country comparison to the world: 190
Crude oil—imports: 0 bbl/day (2012 est.)
country comparison to the world: 126
Crude oil—proved reserves: 0 bbl (1 January 2015 est.)
country comparison to the world: 192
Refined petroleum products—production: 0 bbl/day (2012 est.)
country comparison to the world: 132
Refined petroleum products—consumption: 5,600 bbl/day (2013 est.)
country comparison to the world: 166
Refined petroleum products—exports: 0 bbl/day (2012 est.)
country comparison to the world: 133
Refined petroleum products—imports: 5,556 bbl/day (2012 est.)
country comparison to the world: 157
Natural gas—production: 0 cu m (2013 est.)
country comparison to the world: 129
Natural gas—consumption: 0 cu m (2013 est.)
country comparison to the world: 194
Natural gas—exports: 0 cu m (2013 est.)
country comparison to the world: 182
Natural gas—imports: 0 cu m (2013 est.)
country comparison to the world: 134
Natural gas—proved reserves: 5.663 billion cu m (1 January 2014 est.)
country comparison to the world: 91
Carbon dioxide emissions from consumption of energy: 855,800 Mt (2012 est.)
country comparison to the world: 169

COMMUNICATIONS

Telephone—fixed lines: *total subscriptions:* 57,200

subscriptions per 100 inhabitants: 1 (2014 est.)
country comparison to the world: 157
Telephone—mobile cellular: *total:* 5.5 million
subscriptions per 100 inhabitants: 53 (2014 est.)
country comparison to the world: 113
Telephone system: *general assessment:* the public telecommunications system was almost completely destroyed or dismantled during the civil war; private companies offer limited local fixed-line service, and private wireless companies offer service in most major cities, while charging the lowest International rates on the continent
domestic: local cellular telephone systems have been established in Mogadishu and in several other population centers with one company beginning to provide 3G services in late 2012
international: country code—252; Mogadishu is a landing point for the Eassy fiber-optic submarine cable system linking East Africa with Europe and North America (2010)
Broadcast media: 2 private TV stations rebroadcast Al-Jazeera and CNN; Somaliland has 1 government-operated TV station and Puntland has 1 private TV station; the transitional government operates Radio Mogadishu; 1 SW and roughly 10 private FM radio stations broadcast in Mogadishu; several radio stations operate in central and southern regions; Somaliland has 1 government-operated radio station; Puntland has roughly a half dozen private radio stations; transmissions of at least 2 International broadcasters are available (2007)
Radio broadcast stations: AM 0, FM 11 (also 1 station each in Puntland and Somaliland), shortwave 1 (in Mogadishu) (2001)
Television broadcast stations: 4 (2 in Mogadishu and 2 in Hargeisa) (2001)
Internet country code: .so
Internet hosts: 186 (2012)
country comparison to the world: 202
Internet users: *total:* 157,500
percent of population: 1.5% (2014 est.)
country comparison to the world: 164

TRANSPORTATION

Airports: 61 (2013)
country comparison to the world: 81
Airports—with paved runways: *total:* 6
over 3,047 m: 4
2,438 to 3,047 m: 1
1,524 to 2,437 m: 1 (2013)
Airports—with unpaved runways: *total:* 55
over 3,047 m: 1
2,438 to 3,047 m: 5
1,524 to 2,437 m: 20
914 to 1,523 m: 23
under 914 m: 6 (2013)
Roadways: *total:* 22,100 km
paved: 2,608 km
unpaved: 19,492 km (2000)
country comparison to the world: 105
Merchant marine: *total:* 1

by type: cargo 1 (2008)
country comparison to the world: 155
Ports and terminals: *major seaport(s):* Berbera, Kismaayo
Transportation—note:
despite a dramatic drop in the number of attacks in 2014, the International Maritime Bureau continues to report the territorial and offshore waters in the Gulf of Aden and Indian Ocean as a region of significant risk for piracy and armed robbery again st ships accounting for 4% of all attacks in 2014; 11 vessels were attacked or hijacked in 2014 compared with 237 in 2011; the presence of several Naval task forces in the Gulf of Aden and additional anti-piracy measures on the part of ship operators, including the use of on board armed security teams, have reduced piracy incidents in that body of water; in response Somali-based pirates, using hijacked fishing trawlers as "mother ships" to extend their range, shifted operations as far south as the Mozambique Channel, eastward to the vicinity of the Maldives, and northeastward to the Strait of Hormuz

MILITARY AND SECURITY

Military branches: National Security Force (NSF): Somali Army (2011)
Military service age and obligation: 18 is the legal minimum age for compulsory and voluntary military service (2012)

TRANSNATIONAL ISSUES

Disputes—International: Ethiopian forces invaded southern Somalia and routed Islamist Courts from Mogadishu in January 2007; "Somaliland" secessionists provide port facilities in Berbera to land-locked Ethiopia and have established commercial ties with other regional states; "Puntland" and "Somaliland" "governments" seek International support in their secessionist aspirations and overlapping border claims; the undemarcated former British administrative line has little meaningas a political separation to rival clans within Ethiopia's Ogaden and southern Somalia's Oromo region; Kenya works hard to prevent the clan and militia fighting in Somalia from spreading south across the border, which has long been open to nomadic pastoralists

Refugees and internally displaced persons:
refugees (country of origin): 3,268 (Yemen) (2015)
IDPs: 1.133 million (civil war since 1988, clan-based competition for resources; 2011 famine; insecurity because of fighting between Al-Shabaab and the Transitional Federal Government's allied forces) (2015)

SOUTH AFRICA

INTRODUCTION

Background: Dutch traders landed at the southern tip of modern day South Africa in 1652 and established a stopover point on the spice route between the Netherlands and the Far East, founding the city of Cape Town. After the British seized the Cape of Good Hope area in 1806, many of the Dutch settlers (Afrikaners, called "Boers" (farmers) by the British) trekked north to found their own republics in lands taken from the indigenous black inhabitants. The discovery of diamonds (1867) and gold (1886) spurred wealth and immigration and intensified the subjugation of the native inhabitants. The Afrikaners resisted British encroachments but were defeated in the Second South African War (1899–1902); however, the British and the Afrikaners, ruled together beginning in 1910 under the Union of South Africa, which became a republic in 1961 after a whites-only referendum. in 1948, the Afrikaner-dominated National Party was voted into power and instituted a policy of apartheid—the separate development of the races—which favored the white minority at the expense of the black majority. The African National Congress (ANC) led the opposition to apartheid and many top ANC leaders, such as Nelson MANDELA, spent decades in South Africa's prisons. Internal protests and insurgency, as well as boycotts by some Western nations and institutions, led to the regime's eventual willingness to negotiate a peaceful transition to majority rule. The first multi-racial elections in 1994 following the end of apartheid ushered in majority rule under an ANC-led government. South Africa has since struggled to address apartheid-era imbalances in decent housing, education, and health care. ANC infighting came to a head in 2008 when President Thabo MBEKI was recalled by Parliament, and Deputy President Kgalema MOTLANTHE, succeeded him as interim president. Jacob ZUMA became president after the ANC won general elections in 2009; he was reelected in 2014.

GEOGRAPHY

Location: Southern Africa, at the southern tip of the continent of Africa

Geographic coordinates: 29 00 S, 24 00 E

Map references: Africa

Area: *total:* 1,219,090 sq km

land: 1,214,470 sq km

water: 4,620 sq km

note: includes Prince Edward Islands (Marion Island and Prince Edward Island)

country comparison to the world: 25

Area—comparative: slightly less than twice the size of Texas

Land boundaries: *total:* 5,244 km

border countries (6): Botswana 1,969 km, Lesotho 1,106 km, Mozambique 496 km, Namibia 1,005 km, Swaziland 438 km, Zimbabwe 230 km

Coastline: 2,798 km

Maritime claims: *territorial sea:* 12 nm

contiguous zone: 24 nm

exclusive economic zone: 200 nm

continental shelf: 200 nm or to edge of the continental margin

Climate: mostly semiarid; subtropical along east coast; sunny days, cool nights

Terrain: vast interior plateau rimmed by rugged hills and narrow coastal plain

Elevation: *mean elevation:* 1,034 m

elevation extremes: *lowest point:* Atlantic Ocean 0 m

highest point: Njesuthi 3,408 m

Natural resources: gold, chromium, antimony, coal, iron ore, manganese, nickel, phosphates, tin, rare earth elements, uranium, gem diamonds, platinum, copper, vanadium, salt, Natural gas

Land use: *agricultural land:* 79.4%

arable land: 9.9%

permanent crops: 0.3%

permanent pasture: 69.2%

forest: 7.6%

other: 13% (2011 est.)

Irrigated land: 16,700 sq km (2012)

Total renewable water resources: 51.4 cu km (2011)

Freshwater withdrawal (domestic/industrial/agricultural): *total:* 12.5 cu km/yr (36%/7%/57%)

per capita: 271.7 cu m/yr (2005)

Natural hazards: prolonged droughts

volcanism: the volcano forming Marion Island in the Prince Edward Islands, which last erupted in 2004, is South Africa's only active volcano

Environment—current issues: lack of important arterial rivers or lakes requires extensive water conservation and control measures; growth in water usage outpacing supply; pollution of rivers from agricultural runoff and urban discharge; air pollution resulting in acid rain; soil erosion; desertification

Environment—International agreements: *party to:* Antarctic-Environmental Protocol, Antarctic-Marine Living Resources, Antarctic Seals,

Antarctic Treaty, Biodiversity, Climate Change, Climate Change-Kyoto Protocol, Desertification, Endangered Species, Hazardous Wastes, Law of the Sea, Marine Dumping, Marine Life Conservation, Ozone Layer Protection, Ship Pollution, Wetlands, Whaling

signed, but not ratified: none of the selected agreements

Geography—note: South Africa completely surrounds Lesotho and almost completely surrounds Swaziland

PEOPLE AND SOCIETY

Nationality: *noun:* South African(s)

adjective: South African

Ethnic groups: black African 80.2%, white 8.4%, colored 8.8%, Indian/Asian 2.5%

note: colored is a term used in South Africa, including on the National census, for persons of mixed race ancestry (2014 est.)

Languages: IsiZulu (official) 22.7%, IsiXhosa (official) 16%, Afrikaans (official) 13.5%, English (official) 9.6%, Sepedi (official) 9.1%, Setswana (official) 8%, Sesotho (official) 7.6%, Xitsonga (official) 4.5%, siSwati (official) 2.5%, Tshivenda (official) 2.4%, isiNdebele (official) 2.1%, sign language 0.5%, other 1.6% (2011 est.)

Religions: Protestant 36.6% (Zionist Christian 11.1%, Pentecostal/Charismatic 8.2%, Methodist 6.8%, Dutch Reformed 6.7%, Anglican 3.8%), Catholic 7.1%, Muslim 1.5%, other Christian 36%, other 2.3%, unspecified 1.4%, none 15.1% (2001 census)

Population: 53,675,563

note: estimates for this country explicitly take into account the effects of excess mortality due to AIDS; this can result in lower life expectancy, higher infant mortality, higher death rates, lower population growth rates, and changes in the distribution of population by age and sex than would otherwise be expected (July 2015 est.)

country comparison to the world: 26

Age structure: *0–14 years:* 28.43% (male 7,660,173/female 7,598,013)

15–24 years: 18.52% (male 4,937,169/female 5,002,201)

25–54 years: 41.07% (male 11,120,423/female 10,923,422)

55–64 years: 6.53% (male 1,628,183/female 1,874,946)

65 years and over: 5.46% (male 1,231,627/female 1,699,406) (2015 est.)

Dependency ratios: *total dependency ratio:* 52.1%

youth dependency ratio: 44.5%

elderly dependency ratio: 7.7%

potential support ratio: 13.1% (2015 est.)

Median age: *total:* 26.5 years

male: 26.2 years

female: 26.7 years (2015 est.)

country comparison to the world: 145

Population growth rate: 1.33% (2015 est.)

country comparison to the world: 90

Birth rate: 20.75 births/1,000 population (2015 est.)

country comparison to the world: 79

Death rate: 9.91 deaths/1,000 population (2015 est.)

country comparison to the world: 46

Net migration rate: 2.42 migrant(s)/1,000 population (2015 est.)

country comparison to the world: 42

Urbanization: *urban population:* 64.8% of total population (2015)

rate of urbanization: 1.59% annual rate of change (2010–15 est.)

Major urban areas—population: Johannesburg (includes Ekurhuleni) 9.399 million; Cape Town (legislative capital) 3.66 million; Durban 2.901 million; PRETORIA (capital) 2.059 million; Port Elizabeth 1.179 million; Vereeniging 1.155 million (2015)

Sex ratio: *at birth:* 1.02 male(s)/female

0–14 years: 1.01 male(s)/female

15–24 years: 0.99 male(s)/female

25–54 years: 1.02 male(s)/female

55–64 years: 0.87 male(s)/female

65 years and over: 0.73 male(s)/female

total population: 0.98 male(s)/female (2015 est.)

Maternal mortality rate: 138 deaths/100,000 live births (2015 est.)

country comparison to the world: 38

Infant mortality rate: *total:* 32.99 deaths/1,000 live births

male: 36.62 deaths/1,000 live births

female: 29.27 deaths/1,000 live births (2015 est.)

country comparison to the world: 64

Life expectancy at birth: *total population:* 62.34 years

male: 60.83 years

female: 63.87 years (2015 est.)

country comparison to the world: 191

Total fertility rate: 2.33 children born/woman (2015 est.)

country comparison to the world: 88

Health expenditures: 8.9% of GDP (2013)

country comparison to the world: 42

Physicians density: 0.78 physicians/1,000 population (2013)

Drinking water source:

improved:

urban: 99.6% of population

rural: 81.4% of population

total: 93.2% of population

unimproved:

urban: 0.4% of population

rural: 18.6% of population

total: 6.8% of population (2015 est.)

Sanitation facility access:

improved:

urban: 69.6% of population

rural: 60.5% of population

total: 66.4% of population

unimproved:

urban: 30.4% of population

rural: 39.5% of population

total: 33.6% of population (2015 est.)

HIV/AIDS—adult prevalence rate: 18.92% (2014 est.)

country comparison to the world: 4

HIV/AIDS—people living with HIV/AIDS: 6,836,500 (2014 est.)

country comparison to the world: 1

HIV/AIDS—deaths: 138,400 (2014 est.)

country comparison to the world: 2

Major infectious diseases: *degree of risk:* intermediate

food or waterborne diseases: bacterial diarrhea, hepatitis A, and typhoid fever

water contact disease: schistosomiasis (2013)

Obesity—adult prevalence rate: 25.6% (2014)

country comparison to the world: 24

Children under the age of 5 years underweight: 8.7% (2008)

country comparison to the world: 72

Education expenditures: 6.1% of GDP (2014)

country comparison to the world: 42

Literacy: *definition:* age 15 and over can read and write

total population: 94.3%

male: 95.5%

female: 93.1% (2015 est.)

School life expectancy (primary to tertiary education): *total:* 13 years

male: 12 years

female: 14 years (2013)

Unemployment, youth ages 15–24: *total:* 51.4%

male: 48%

female: 55.5% (2013 est.)

country comparison to the world: 6

GOVERNMENT

Country name: *conventional long form:* Republic of South Africa

conventional short form: South Africa

former: Union of South Africa

abbreviation: RSA

etymology: self-descriptive name from the country's location on the continent; "Africa" is derived from the Roman designation of the area corresponding to present-day Tunisia "Africa terra," which meant "Land of the Afri" (the tribe resident in that area), but which eventually came to mean the entire continent

Government type: parliamentary republic

Capital: *name:* Pretoria (administrative capital); Cape Town (legislative capital); Bloemfontein (judicial capital)

Geographic coordinates: 25 42 S, 28 13 E

time difference: UTC+2 (7 hours ahead of Washington, DC, during Standard Time)

Administrative divisions: 9 provinces; Eastern Cape, Free State, Gauteng, KwaZulu-Natal, Limpopo, Mpumalanga, Northern Cape, North West, Western Cape

Independence: 31 May 1910 (Union of South Africa formed from four British colonies: Cape Colony, Natal, Transvaal, and Orange Free State); 31 May 1961 (republic declared); 27 April 1994 (majority rule)

National holiday: Freedom Day, 27 April (1994)

Constitution: several previous; latest drafted 8 May 1996, approved 4 December 1996, effective 4 February 1997; amended many times, last in 2013 (2016)

Legal system: mixed legal system of Roman-Dutch civil law, English common law, and customary law

International law organization participation: has not submitted an ICJ jurisdiction declaration; accepts ICCt jurisdiction

Citizenship: *citizenship by birth:* no

citizenship by descent only: at least one parent must be a citizen of South Africa

dual citizenship recognized: yes, but requires prior permission of the government

residency requirement for naturalization: 1 year

Suffrage: 18 years of age; universal

Executive branch: *chief of state:* President Jacob ZUMA (since 9 May 2009); Deputy President Matamela Cyril RAMAPHOSA (since 26 May 2014) note—the president is both chief of state and head of government

head of government: President Jacob ZUMA (since 9 May 2009); Deputy President Matamela Cyril RAMAPHOSA (since 26 May 2014)

cabinet: Cabinet appointed by the president

elections/appointments: president indirectly elected by the National Assembly for a 5-year term (eligible for a second term); election last held on 21 May 2014 (next to be held in May 2019)

election results: Jacob ZUMA (ANC) reelected president by the National Assembly unopposed

Legislative branch: *description:* bicameral Parliament consists of the National Council of Provinces (90 seats; 10-member delegations appointed by each of the 9 provincial legislatures to serve 5-year terms; note—this council has special powers to protect regional interests, including safeguarding cultural and linguistic traditions among ethnic minorities) and the National Assembly (400 seats; members directly elected in multi-seat constituencies by proportional representation vote to serve 5-year terms)

elections: National Assembly and National Council of Provinces—last held on 7 May 2014 (next to be held in 2019)

election results: National Council of Provinces—percent of vote by party—NA; seats by party—ANC 60, DA 20, EFF 7, NFP 1, IFP 1, UDM 1; National Assembly—percent of vote by party—ANC 62.2%, DA 22.2%, EFF 6.4%, IFP 2.4%, NFP 1.6%, UDM 1.0%, other 4.2%; seats by party—ANC 249, DA 89, EFF 25, IFP 10, NFP 6, UDM 4, other 17

Judicial branch: *highest court(s):* Supreme Court of Appeals (consists of the court president, deputy president, and 21 judges); Constitutional Court (consists of the chief and deputy chief justices and 9 judges)

judge selection and term of office: Supreme Court of Appeals president and vice-president appointed by the National president after consultation with the Judicial Services Commission (JSC), a 23-member body chaired by the chief justice and includes other judges and judicial executives, members of parliament, practicing lawyers and advocates, a teacher of law, and several members designated by the National president; other

781

Supreme Court judges appointed by the National president on the advice of the JSC and hold office until discharged from active service by terms of an Act of Parliament; Constitutional Court chief and deputy chief justices appointed by the National president after consultation with the JSC and with heads of the National Assembly; other Constitutional Court judges appointed by the National president after consultation with the chief justice and leaders of the National Assembly; Constitutional Court judges appointed for 12-year non-renewable terms or until age 70

subordinate courts: High Courts; Magistrates' Courts; labor courts; land claims courts

Political parties and leaders: African Christian Democratic Party or ACDP [Kenneth MESHOE] African Independent Congress or AIC [Mandla GALD] African National Congress or ANC [Jacob ZUMA] African People's Convention or APC [Themba God I] Agamg SA [Andries TLOUAMMA] Congress of the People or COPE [Mosiuoa LEKO TA] Democratic Alliance or DA [Mmusi MAIMAN E] Economic Freedom Fighters or EFF [Julius MALEMA] Freedom Front Plus or FF+ [Pieter MULDER] I nkatha Freedom Party or IFP [Mangosuthu BU THELEZI] National Freedom Party or NFP [Zanele kaMAGWAZA-MSIBI] Pan-Africanist Congress of Azania or PAC [Alton MPH ETHI] United Christian Democratic Party or UCDP [Isaac Sipho MFUNDISI] United Democratic Movement or UDM [Bantu HOLOMISA]

Political pressure groups and leaders: Congress of South African Trade Unions or COSATU [Zwel-inzima VAVI, general secretary] South African Communist Party or SACP [Blade NZIMANDE, general secretary] South African National Civic Organization or SAN CO [Richard MDAKANE, National president]
note: COSATU and SACP are in a formal alliance with the African National Congress

International organization participation: ACP, AfDB, AU, BIS, BRICS, C, CD, FAO, FATF, G-20, G-24, G-5, G-77, IAEA, IBRD, ICAO, ICC (National committees), ICCt, ICRM, IDA, IFAD, IFC, IFRCS, IHO, ILO, IMF, IMO, IMSO, Interpol, IOC, IOM, IPU,ISO, ITSO, ITU, ITUC (NGOs), MIGA, MONUSCO, NAM, NSG, OECD (Enhanced Engagement, OPCW, Paris Club (associate), PCA, SACU, SADC, UN, UNAMID, UNCTAD, UNESCO, UNHCR, UNIDO, UNITAR, UNWTO, UPU, WCO, WFTU (NGOs), WHO, WIPO, WMO, WTO, ZC

Diplomatic representation in the US: *chief of mission:* Ambassador Mninwa Johnnes MAHL-ANGU (since 23 February 2015)
chancery: 3051 Massachusetts Avenue NW, Washington, DC 20008

telephone: [1] (202) 232-4400
FAX: [1] (202) 265-1607
consulate(s) general: Chicago, Los Angeles, New York

Diplomatic representation from the US: *chief of mission:* Ambassador Patrick Hubert GASPARD (since 16 October 2013)
embassy: 877 Pretorius Street, Arcadia, Pretoria
mailing address: P.O . Box 9536, Pretoria 0001
telephone: [27] (12) 431-4000
FAX: [27] (12) 342-2299
consulate(s) general: Cape Town, Durban, Johannesburg

Flag description: two equal width horizontal bands of red (top) and blue separated by a central green band that splits into a horizontal Y, the arms of which end at the corners of the hoist side; the Y embraces a black isosceles triangle from which the arms are separated by narrow yellow bands; the red and blue bands are separated from the green band and its arms by narrow white stripes; the flag colors do not have any official symbolism, but the Y stands for the "convergence of diverse elements within South African society, taking the road ahead in unity"; black, yellow, and green are found on the flag of the African National Congress, while red, white, and blue are the colors in the flags of the Netherlands and the UK, whose settlers ruled South Africa during the colonial era
note: the South African flag is one of only two National flags to display six colors as part of its primary design, the other is South Sudan's

National symbol(s): springbok (antelope); king protea flower; National colors: red, green, blue, yellow, black, white

National anthem: *name:* "National Anthem of South Africa"
lyrics/music: Enoch SONTONGA and Cornelius Jacob LANGENHOVEN/Enoch SONTONGA and Marthinus LOU RENS de Villiers
note: adopted 1994; a combination of "N'kosi Sikelel' iAfrica" (God Bless Africa) and "Die Stem van Suid Afrika" (The Call of South Africa), which were respectively the anthems of the non-white and white communities under apartheid; official lyrics contain a mixture of Xhosa, Zulu, Sesotho, Afrikaans, and English (i. e., the five most widely spoken of South Africa's 11 official languages); music incorporates the melody used in the Tanzanian and zambian Anthems

ECONOMY

Economy—overview: South Africa is a middle-income emerging market with an abundant supply of Natural resources; well-developed financial, legal, communications, energy, and transport sectors; and a stock exchange that is Africa's largest and among the top 20 in the world.
Economic growth has decelerated in recent years, slowing to just 1.5% in 2014. Unemployment, poverty, and inequality—among the highest in the world—remain a challenge. Official unemployment is roughly 25% of the workforce, and runs significantly higher among black youth. Even though the country's modern infrastructure supports a relatively efficient distribution of goods

to major urban centers throughout the region, unstable electricity supplies retard growth. Eskom, the state-run power company, is building three new power stations and is installing new power demand management programs to improve power grid reliability. Load shedding and resulting rolling blackouts gripped many parts of South Africa in late 2014 and early 2015 because of electricity supply constraints due to technical problems at some generation units, unavoidable planned maintenance, and an Accident at a power station in Mpumalanga province. The rolling blackouts were the worst the country faced since 2008. Construction delays at two additional plants, however, mean South Africa will continue to operate on a razor thin margin; economists judge that growth cannot exceed 3% until electrical supply problems are resolved.
South Africa's economic policy has focused on controlling inflation; however, the country faces structural constraints that also limit economic growth, such as skills shortages, declining global competitiveness, and frequent work stoppages due to strike action. The current government faces growing pressure from urban constituencies to improve the delivery of basic services to low-income areas and to increase job growth.

GDP (purchasing power parity): $723.5 billion (2015 est.)
$714.4 billion (2014 est.)
$703.5 billion (2013 est.)
note: data are in 2015 US dollars
country comparison to the world: 31

GDP (official exchange rate): $313 billion (2015 est.)

GDP—real growth rate: 1.3% (2015 est.)
1.5% (2014 est.)
2.2% (2013 est.)
country comparison to the world: 162

GDP—per capita (PPP): $13,200 (2015 est.)
$13,200 (2014 est.)
$13,200 (2013 est.)
note: data are in 2015 US dollars
country comparison to the world: 118

Gross National saving: 15.1% of GDP (2015 est.)
14.9% of GDP (2014 est.)
14.4% of GDP (2013 est.)
country comparison to the world: 112

GDP—composition, by end use:
household consumption: 59.6%
government consumption: 20%
investment in fixed capital: 22.2%
investment in inventories: -0.6%
exports of goods and services: 31.5%
imports of goods and services: -32.7% (2015 est.)

GDP—composition, by sector of origin:
agriculture: 2.4%
industry: 30.3%
services: 67.4% (2015 est.)

Agriculture—products: corn, wheat, sugarcane, fruits, vegetables; beef, poultry, mutton, wool, dairy products

Industries: mining (world's largest producer of platinum, gold, chromium), automobile assembly, metalworking, machinery, textiles, iron and steel, chemicals, fertilizer, foodstuffs, commercial ship repair

Industrial production growth rate: 1.7% (2015 est.)
country comparison to the world: 125
Labor force: 20.86 million (2015 est.)
country comparison to the world: 30
Labor force—by occupation: *agriculture:* 4%
industry: 18%
services: 66% (2014 est.)
Unemployment rate: 25.9% (2015 est.)
25.1% (2014 est.)
country comparison to the world: 179
Population below poverty line: 35.9% (2012 est.)
Household income or consumption by percentage share: *lowest:* 10%: 1.2%
highest: 10%: 51.7% (2009 est.)
Distribution of family income—Gini index: 62.5 (2013 est.)
59.3 (1994)
country comparison to the world: 4
Budget: *revenues:* $84.15 billion
expenditures: $98.26 billion (2015 est.)
Taxes and other revenues: 26.5% of GDP (2015 est.)
country comparison to the world: 111
Budget surplus (+) or deficit (–): -4.4% of GDP (2015 est.)
country comparison to the world: 156
Public debt: 45.4% of GDP (2015 est.)
44.8% of GDP (2014 est.)
country comparison to the world: 97
Fiscal year: 1 April—31 March
Inflation rate (consumer prices): 4.6% (2015 est.)
6.1% (2014 est.)
country comparison to the world: 167
Central bank discount rate: 5.75% (31 December 2014)
7% (31 December 2009)
country comparison to the world: 69
Commercial bank prime lending rate: 9.5% (31 December 2015 est.)
9.13% (31 December 2014 est.)
country comparison to the world: 87
Stock of narrow money: $97.33 billion (31 December 2015 est.)
$107.5 billion (31 December 2014 est.)
country comparison to the world: 36
Stock of broad money: $172.7 billion (31 December 2015 est.)
$192.9 billion (31 December 2014 est.)
country comparison to the world: 46
Stock of domestic credit: $218.5 billion (31 December 2015 est.)
$245.5 billion (31 December 2014 est.)
country comparison to the world: 41
Market value of publicly traded shares: $1.007 trillion (31 December 2013)
$1.038 trillion (31 December 2012)
$855.7 billion (31 December 2011)
country comparison to the world: 15
Current account balance: -$13.67 billion (2015 est.)
-$19.06 billion (2014 est.)
country comparison to the world: 182
Exports: $85.14 billion (2015 est.)
$92.54 billion (2014 est.)

country comparison to the world: 38
Exports—commodities: gold, diamonds, platinum, other metals and minerals, machinery and equipment
Exports—partners: China 11.3%, US 7.3%, Germany 6%, Namibia 5.2%, Botswana 5.2%, Japan 4.7%, UK 4.3%, India 4.2% (2015)
Imports: $86.81 billion (2015 est.)
$98.87 billion (2014 est.)
country comparison to the world: 35
Imports—commodities: machinery and equipment, chemicals, petroleum Products, scientific instruments, foodstuffs
Imports—partners: China 17.6%, Germany 11.2%, US 6.7%, Nigeria 5%, India 4.7%, Saudi Arabia 4.1% (2015)
Reserves of foreign exchange and gold: $44.28 billion (31 December 2015 est.)
$49.09 billion (31 December 2014 est.)
country comparison to the world: 42
Debt—external: $145.1 billion (31 December 2014 est.)
$137.1 billion (31 December 2013 est.)
country comparison to the world: 43
Stock of direct foreign investment—at home: $164 billion (31 December 2015 est.)
$157.9 billion (31 December 2014 est.)
country comparison to the world: 35
Stock of direct foreign investment—abroad: $143 billion (31 December 2015 est.)
$135.7 billion (31 December 2014 est.)
country comparison to the world: 28
Exchange rates: rand (ZAR) per US dollar—
12.63 (2015 est.)
10.8469 (2014 est.)
10.8469 (2013 est.)
8.2 (2012 est.)
7.2597 (2011 est.)

ENERGY

Electricity—production: 239 billion kWh (2012 est.)
country comparison to the world: 19
Electricity—consumption: 211.6 billion kWh (2012 est.)
country comparison to the world: 19
Electricity—exports: 13.93 billion kWh (2013 est.)
country comparison to the world: 15
Electricity—imports: 9.428 billion kWh (2013 est.)
country comparison to the world: 23
Electricity—installed generating capacity: 44.15 million kW (2013 est.)
country comparison to the world: 24
Electricity—from fossil fuels: 90.4% of total installed capacity (2013 est.)
country comparison to the world: 74
Electricity—from nuclear fuels: 4.4% of total installed capacity (2013 est.)
country comparison to the world: 25
Electricity—from hydroelectric plants: 4.5% of total installed capacity (2013 est.)
country comparison to the world: 128
Electricity—from other renewable sources: 0.7% of total installed capacity (2013 est.)

country comparison to the world: 99
Crude oil—production: 3,000 bbl/day (2014 est.)
country comparison to the world: 87
Crude oil—exports: 0 bbl/day (2012 est.)
country comparison to the world: 185
Crude oil—imports: 414,000 bbl/day (2013 est.)
country comparison to the world: 22
Crude oil—proved reserves: 15 million bbl (1 January 2015 est.)
country comparison to the world: 87
Refined petroleum products—production: 456,500 bbl/day (2012 est.)
country comparison to the world: 36
Refined petroleum products—consumption: 612,000 bbl/day (2013 est.)
country comparison to the world: 32
Refined petroleum products—exports: 81,660 bbl/day (2012 est.)
country comparison to the world: 50
Refined petroleum products—imports: 137,900 bbl/day (2012 est.)
country comparison to the world: 40
Natural gas—production: 1.17 billion cu m (2013 est.)
country comparison to the world: 64
Natural gas—consumption: 4.889 billion cu m (2013 est.)
country comparison to the world: 59
Natural gas—exports: 0 cu m (2013 est.)
country comparison to the world: 176
Natural gas—imports: 3.771 billion cu m (2013 est.)
country comparison to the world: 36
Natural gas—proved reserves: 15.01 billion cu m (1 January 2012 est.)
country comparison to the world: 77
Carbon dioxide emissions from consumption of energy: 473.2 million Mt (2012 est.)
country comparison to the world: 14

COMMUNICATIONS

Telephones—fixed lines: *total subscriptions:* 4.3 million
subscriptions per 100 inhabitants: 8 (2014 est.)
country comparison to the world: 40
Telephones—mobile cellular: *total:* 79.5 million
subscriptions per 100 inhabitants: 150 (2014 est.)
country comparison to the world: 19
Telephone system: *general assessment:* the system is the best-developed and most modern in Africa
domestic: combined fixed-line and mobile-cellular teledensity is roughly 140 telephones per 100 persons; consists of carrier-equipped open-wire lines, coaxial cables, microwave radio relay links, fiber-optic cable, radiotelephone communication stations, and wireless local loops; key centers are Bloemfontein, Cape Town, Durban, Johannesburg, Port Elizabeth, and Pretoria
international: country code—27; the SAT-3/WASC and SAFE fiber-optic submarine cable systems connect South Africa to Europe and Asia; the EASSy fiber-optic cable system connects with Europe and North America; satellite earth stations—3 intelsat (1 Indian Ocean and 2 Atlantic Ocean) (2011)

Broadcast media: the South African Broadcasting Corporation (SABC) operates 4 TV stations, 3 are free-to-air and 1 is pay TV; e. tv, a private station, is accessible to more than half the population; multiple subscription TV services provide a mix of local and International channels; well-developed mix of public and private radio stations at the National, regional, and local levels; the SABC radio network, state-owned and controlled but nominally independent, operates 18 stations, one for each of the 11 official languages, 4 community stations, and 3 commercial stations; more than 100 community-based stations extend coverage to rural areas (2007)

Radio broadcast stations: AM 14, FM 347 (plus 243 repeaters), shortwave 1 (1998)

Television broadcast stations: 556 (plus 144 network repeaters) (1997)

Internet country code: .za

Internet hosts: 4.761 million (2012)
country comparison to the world: 23

Internet users: *total:* 24.8 million
percent of population: 46.9% (2014 est.)
country comparison to the world: 24

TRANSPORTATION

Airports: 566 (2013)
country comparison to the world: 11
Airports—with paved runways: *total:* 144
over 3,047 m: 11
2,438 to 3,047 m: 7
1,524 to 2,437 m: 52
914 to 1,523 m: 65
under 914 m: 9 (2013)
Airports—with unpaved runways: *total:* 422
2,438 to 3,047 m: 1
1,524 to 2,437 m: 3

1914 to 1,523 m: 258
under 914 m: 132 (2013)
Heliports: 1 (2013)
Pipelines: condensate 94 km; gas 1,293 km; oil 992 km; refined products 1,460 km (2013)
Railways: *total:* 20,986 km
standard gauge: 80 km 1.435-m gauge (80 km electrified)
narrow gauge: 19,756 km 1.065-m gauge (8,271 km electrified)
other: 1,150 km (passenger rail, gauge unspecified, 1,115.5 km electrified) (2014)
country comparison to the world: 14
Roadways: *total:* 747,014 km
paved: 158,952 km
unpaved: 588,062 km (2014)
country comparison to the world: 10
Merchant marine: *total:* 3
by type: petroleum tanker 3
registered in other countries: 19 (Australia 1, Isle of Man 2, Mexico 1, NZ 1, Seychelles 1, Singapore 13) (2010)
country comparison to the world: 136
Ports and terminals: *major seaport(s):* Cape Town, Durban, Port Elizabeth, Richards Bay, Saldanha Bay
container port(s) (TEUs): Durban (2,712,975)
LNG terminal(s) (import): Mossel Bay

MILITARY AND SECURITY

Military branches: South African National Defense Force (SANDF): South Africam Army, South African Navy (SAN), South African Air Force (SAAF), South African Military Health Services (2013)
Military service age and obligation: 18 years of age for voluntary military service; women are eligible to serve in noncombat roles; 2-year service obligation (2012)

Military expenditures: 1.2% of GDP (2014)
1% of GDP (2013)
1.16% of GDP (2012)
1.14% of GDP (2011)
1.16% of GDP (2010)
country comparison to the world: 100
Military—note: with the end of apartheid and the establishment of majority rule, former military, black homelands forces, and ex-opposition forces were integrated into the South African National Defense Force (SANDF)

TRANSNATIONAL ISSUES

Disputes—International: South Africa has placed military units to assist police operations along the border of Lesotho, Zimbabwe, and Mozambique to control smuggling, poaching, and illegal migration; the governments of South Africa and Namibia have not signed or ratified the text of the 1994 Surveyor's General agreement placing the boundary in the middle of the Orange River

Refugees and internally displaced persons: *refugees (country of origin):* 40,133 (Somalia); 30,125 (Democratic Republic of the Congo); 18,830 (Ethiopia); 6,217 (Zimbabwe); 6,035 (Republic of the Congo) (2014)

Illicit drugs: transshipment center for heroin, hashish, and cocaine, as well as a major cultivator of marijuana in its own right; cocaine and heroin consumption on the rise; world's largest market for illicit methaqualone, usually imported illegally from India through various east African countries, but increasingly producing its own synthetic drugs for domestic consumption; attractive venue for money launderers given the increasing level of organized criminal and narcotics activity in the region and the size of the South African economy

SOUTH GEORGIA AND SOUTH SANDWICH ISLANDS

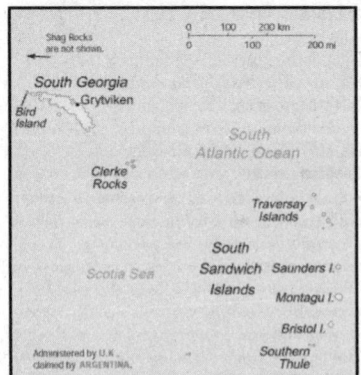

INTRODUCTION

Background: The islands, with large bird and seal populations, lie approximately 1,000 km east of the Falkland Islands and have been under British administration since 1908—except for a brief

period in 1982 when Argentina occupied them. Grytviken, on South Georgia, was a 19th and early 20th century whaling station. Famed explorer Ernest SHACKLETON stopped there in 1914 en route to his ill-fated attempt to cross Antarctica on foot. He returned some 20 months later with a few companions in a small boat and arranged a successful rescue for the rest of his crew, stranded off the Antarctic Peninsula. He died in 1922 on a subsequent expedition and is buried in Grytviken. Today, the station houses scientists from the British Antarctic Survey. Recognizing the importance of preserving the marine stocks in adjacent waters, the UK, in 1993, extended the exclusive fishing zone from 12 nm to 200 nm around each island.

GEOGRAPHY

Location: Southern South America, islands in the South Atlantic Ocean, east of the tip of South America

Geographic coordinates: 54 30 S, 37 00 W
Map references: Antarctic Region
Area: *total:* 3,903 sq km
land: 3,903 sq km

water: 0 sq km
note: includes Shag Rocks, Black Rock, Clerke Rocks, South Georgia Island, Bird Island, and the South Sandwich Islands, which consist of 11 islands
country comparison to the world: 177
Area—comparative: slightly larger than Rhode Island
Land boundaries: 0 km
Coastline: NA
Maritime claims: *territorial sea:* 12 nm
exclusive fishing zone: 200 nm
Climate: variable, with mostly westerly winds throughout the year interspersed with periods of calm; nearly all precipitation falls ass Now
Terrain: most of the islands are rugged and mountainous rising steeply from the sea; South Georgia is largely barren with steep, glacier-covered mountains; the South Sandwich Islands are of volcanic origin with some still active volcanoes
Elevation: *mean elevation:* NA
elevation extremes: *lowest point:* Atlantic Ocean 0 m

highest point: Mount Paget (South Georgia) 2,934 m

Natural resources: fish

Land use: *agricultural land:* 0%
arable land: 0%
permanent crops: 0%
permanent pasture: 0%
forest: 0%
other: 100% (2011 est.)

Irrigated land: 0 sq km (2011)

Natural hazards: the South Sandwich Islands have prevailing weather conditions that generally make them difficult to approach by ship; they are also subject to active volcanism

Environment—current issues: reindeer—introduced to the islands on several occasions in the 20th century—devastated the native flora and bird species; some reindeer were translocated to the Falkland Islands in 2001, the rest were exterminated (2013–14)

Geography—note: the north coast of South Georgia has several large bays, which provide good anchorage

PEOPLE AND SOCIETY

Population: no indigenous inhabitants

note: the small military garrison on South Georgia withdrew in March 2001, replaced by a permanent group of scientists of the British Antarctic Survey, which also has a biological station on Bird Island; the South Sandwich Islands are uninhabited

GOVERNMENT

Country name: *conventional long form:* South Georgia and the South Sandwich Islands

conventional short form: South Georgia and South Sandwich Islands

abbreviation: SGSSI

etymology: South Georgia was named "the Isle of Georgia" in 1775 by Captain James COOK in honor of British King GEORGE III; the explorer also discovered the Sandwich Islands Group that year, which he named "Sandwich Land" after John MONTAGU, the Earl of Sandwich and First Lord of the Admiralty; the word "South" was later added to distinguish these islands from the other Sandwich Islands, now known as the Hawaiian Islands

Dependency status: overseas territory of the UK, also claimed by Argentina; administered from the Falkland Islands by a commissioner, who is concurrently governor of the Falkland Islands, representing Queen ELIZABETH II

Legal system: the laws of the UK, where applicable, apply

Diplomatic representation in the US: none (overseas territory of the UK, also claimed by Argentina)

Diplomatic representation from the US: none (overseas territory of the UK, also claimed by Argentina)

Flag description: blue with the flag of the UK in the upper hoist-side quadrant and the South Georgia and South Sandwich Islands coat of arms centered on the outer half of the flag; the coat of arms features a shield with a golden lion rampant, holding a torch; the shield is supported by a fur seal on the left and a Macaroni penguin on the right; a reindeer appears above the crest, and below the shield on a scroll is the motto LEO TERRAM PROPRIAM PROTEGAT (Let the Lion

Protect its Own Land)); the lion with the torch represents the UK and discovery; the background of the shield, blue and white estoiles, are found in the coat of arms of James Cook, discoverer of the islands; all the outer supporting animals represented are native to the islands

ECONOMY

Economy—overview: Some fishing takes place in adjacent waters. Harvesting finfish and krill are potential sources of income. The islands receive income from postage stamps produced in the UK, the sale of fishing licenses, and harbor and landing fees from tourist vessels. Tourism from specialized cruise ships is increasing rapidly.

COMMUNICATIONS

Radio broadcast stations: AM 0, FM 0, shortwave 0 (2003)

Television broadcast stations: 0 (2003)

TRANSPORTATION

Ports and terminals: *major seaport(s):* Grytviken

MILITARY AND SECURITY

Military—note: defense is the responsibility of the UK

TRANSNATIONAL ISSUES

Disputes—International: Argentina, which claims the islands in its constitution and briefly occupied them by force in 1982, agreed in 1995 to no longer seek settlement by force

---

SOUTH SUDAN

INTRODUCTION

Background: Egypt attempted to colonize the region of southern Sudan by establishing the province of Equatoria in the 1870s. Islamic Mahdist revolution aries overran the region in 1885, but in 1898 a British force was able to overthrow the Mahdist regime. An Anglo-Egyptian Sudan was established the following year with Equatoria being the southernmost of its eight provinces. The isolated region was largely left to itself over the following decades, but Christian missionaries converted much of the population and facilitated the spread of English. When Sudan gained its independence in 1956, it was with the understanding that the southerners would be able to participate fully in the political system. When the Arab Khartoum government reneged on its promises, a mutiny began that led to two prolonged periods of conflict (1955–1972 and 1983–2005) in which perhaps 2.5 million people died—mostly civilians—due to starvation and drought. Ongoing peace talks finally resulted in a Comprehensive Peace Agreement, signed in January 2005. As part of this agreement, the south was granted a six-year period of autonomy to be followed by a referendum on final status. The result of this referendum, held in January 2011, was a vote of 98% in favor of secession. Since independence on 9 July 2011, South Sudan has struggled with good governance and nation building and has attempted to control

rebel militia groups operating in its territory. Economic conditions have deteriorated since January 2012 when the government decided to shut down oil production following bilateral disagreements with Sudan. In December 2013, conflict between government and opposition forces led to a humanitarian crisis with millions of South Sudanese displaced and food insecure. The warring parties signed a peace agreement in August 2015, which calls for a transitional government of National unity, but its formation has been delayed as of early 2016.

GEOGRAPHY

Location: East-Central Africa; south of Sudan, north of Uganda and Kenya, west of Ethiopia

Geographic coordinates: 8 00 N, 30 00 E

Map references: Africa

Area: *total:* 644,329 sq km
land: NA
water: NA
country comparison to the world: 42

Area—comparative: more than four times the size of Georgia; slightly smaller than Texas

Land boundaries: *total:* 6,018 km
border countries (6): Central African Republic 1,055 km, Democratic Republic of the Congo 714 km, Ethiopia 1,299 km, Kenya 317 km, Sudan 2,158 km, Uganda 475 km
note: South Sudan-Sudan boundary represents 1 January 1956 alignment; final alignment pending negotiations and demarcation; final sovereignty status of Abyei Area pending negotiations between South Sudan and Sudan
Coastline: 0 km (landlocked)
Maritime claims: none (landlocked)
Climate: hot with seasonal rainfall influenced by the annual shift of the Inter-Tropical Convergence Zone; rainfall heaviest in upland areas of the south and diminishes to the north
Terrain: plains in the north and center rise to southern highlands along the border with Uganda and Kenya; the White Nile, flowing north out of the uplands of Central Africa, is the major geographic feature of the country; The Sudd (a name derived from floating vegetation that hinders navigation) is a large swampy area of more than 100,000 sq km fed by the waters of the White Nile that dominates the center of the country
Elevation: *mean elevation:* NA

elevation extremes: *lowest point:* NA
highest point: Kinyeti 3,187 m
Natural resources: hydropower, fertile agricultural land, gold, diamonds, petroleum, hardwoods, limestone, iron ore, copper, chromium ore, zinc, tungsten, mica, silver
Irrigated land: 1,000 sq km (2012)
Geography—note: The Sudd is a vast swamp in South Sudan, formed by the White Nile, comprising more than 15% of the country's total area; it is one of the world's largest wetlands

PEOPLE AND SOCIETY

Nationality: *noun:* South Sudanese (singular and plural)
adjective: South Sudanese
Ethnic groups: Dinka 35.8%, Nuer 15.6%, Shilluk, Azande, Bari, Kakwa, Kuku, Murle, Mandari, Didinga, Ndogo, Bviri, Lndi, Anuak, Bongo, Lango, Dungotona, Acholi (2011 est.)
Languages: English (official), Arabic (includes Juba and Sudanese variants), regional languages include Dinka, Nuer, Bari, Zande, Shilluk
Religions: animist, Christian
Population: 12,042,910 (July 2015 est.)
country comparison to the world: 75
Age structure: *0–14 years:* 45.34% (male 2,783,904/female 2,676,370)
15–24 years: 20.08% (male 1,274,328/female 1,144,181)
25–54 years: 29.25% (male 1,701,044/female 1,821,277)
55–64 years: 3.23% (male 210,231/female 179,076)
65 years and over: 2.1% (male 140,993/female 111,506) (2015 est.)
Dependency ratios: *total dependency ratio:* 83.7%
youth dependency ratio: 77.3%

elderly dependency ratio: 6.4%
potential support ratio: 15.7% (2015 est.)
Median age: *total:* 17 years
male: 16.8 years
female: 17.1 years (2015 est.)
country comparison to the world: 222
Population growth rate: 4.02% (2015 est.)
country comparison to the world: 1
Birth rate: 36.91 births/1,000 population (2015 est.)
country comparison to the world: 15
Death rate: 8.18 deaths/1,000 population (2015 est.)
country comparison to the world: 91
Net migration rate: 11.47 migrant(s)/1,000 population (2015 est.)
country comparison to the world: 9
Urbanization: *urban population:* 18.8% of total population (2015)
rate of urbanization: 5.05% annual rate of change (2010–15 est.)
Major urban areas—population: JUBA (capital) 321,000 (2015)
Maternal mortality rate: 789 deaths/100,000 live births (2015 est.)
country comparison to the world: 1
Infant mortality rate: *total:* 66.39 deaths/1,000 live births
male: 71.05 deaths/1,000 live births
female: 61.49 deaths/1,000 live births (2015 est.)
country comparison to the world: 16
Total fertility rate: 5.31 children born/woman (2015 est.)
country comparison to the world: 11
Contraceptive prevalence rate: 4% (2010)
Health expenditures: 2.2% of GDP (2013)
country comparison to the world: 186
Drinking water source:
improved:
urban: 66.7% of population
rural: 56.9% of population
total: 58.7% of population
unimproved:
urban: 33.3% of population
rural: 43.1% of population
total: 41.3% of population (2015 est.)
Sanitation facility access:
improved:
urban: 16.4% of population
rural: 4.5% of population
total: 6.7% of population
unimproved:
urban: 83.6% of population
rural: 95.5% of population
total: 93.3% of population (2015 est.)
HIV/AIDS—adult prevalence rate: 2.71% (2014 est.)
country comparison to the world: 23
HIV/AIDS—people living with HIV/AIDS: 193,400 (2014 est.)
country comparison to the world: 31
HIV/AIDS—deaths: 12,700 (2014 est.)
country comparison to the world: 19
Major infectious diseases: *degree of risk:* very high

food or waterborne disease: bacterial and protozoal diarrhea, hepatitis A and E, and typhoid fever
vectorborne disease: malaria, dengue fever, trypanosomiasis-Gambiense (African sleeping sickness)
water contact disease: schistosomiasis
respiratory disease: meningococcal meningitis
animal contact disease: rabies (2013)
Obesity—adult prevalence rate: 6.6% (2014)
Children under the age of 5 years underweight: 27.6% (2010)
country comparison to the world: 10
Education expenditures: 0.8% of GDP (2011)
Literacy: *definition:* age 15 and over can read and write
total population: 27%
male: 40%
female: 16% (2009 est.)
Unemployment, youth ages 15–24: *total:* 18.5%
male: 20%
female: 17% (2008 est.)

GOVERNMENT

Country name: *conventional long form:* Republic of South Sudan
conventional short form: South Sudan
etymology: self-descriptive name from the country's former position within Sudan prior to independence; the name "Sudan" derives from the Arabic "bilad-as-sudan" meaning "Land of the black [peoples]"
Government type: presidential republic
Capital: *name:* Juba

Geographic coordinates: 04 51 N, 3137 E
time difference: UTC+3 (8 hours ahead of Washington, DC, during Standard Time)
Administrative divisions: 10 states; Central Equatoria, Eastern Equatoria, Jonglei, Lakes, Northern Bahr el Ghazal, Unity, Upper Nile, Warrap, Western Bahr el Ghazal, Western Equatoria
Independence: 9 July 2011 (from Sudan)
National holiday: Independence Day, 9 July (2011)
Constitution: previous 2005 (preindependence); latest signed 7 July 2011, effective 9 July 2011 (Transitional Constitution of the Republic of South Sudan, 2011); amended 2013, 2015 (2016)
Citizenship: *citizenship by birth:* no
citizenship by descent only: at least one parent must be a citizen of South Sudan
dual citizenship recognized: yes
residency requirement for naturalization: 10 years
Suffrage: 18 years of age; universal
Executive branch: *chief of state:* President Salva KIIR Mayardit (since 9 July 2011); First Vice President Riek MACHAR Teny Dhurgon (since 11 February 2016); Vice President James Wani IGGA (since 12 February 2016);
note—the president is both chief of state and head of government
head of government: President Salva KIIR Mayardit (since 9 July 2011); First Vice President Riek MACHAR Teny Dhurgon (since 11 February 2016); Vice President James Wani IGGA (since 12 February 2016)

cabinet: National Council of Ministers appointed by the president, approved by National Legislative Assembly

elections/appointments: president directly elected by simple majority popular vote for a 4-year term (eligible for a second term); election last held on 11–15 April 2010 (the next election has been postponed from 2015 to 2018 due to instability and violence)

election results: Salva KIIR Mayardit elected president; percent of vote—Salva KIIR Mayardit (SPLM) 93%, Lam AKOL (SPLM-DC) 7%

Legislative branch: description: bicameral National Legislature consists of the Council of States (50 seats; the Council of States, established by presidential decree in August 2011, includes 50 members—20 former members of the Council of States and 30 appointed representatives) and the National Legislative Assembly (400 seats; the National Assembly, also established by presidential decree in August 2011, includes 170 members elected in April 2010, 96 members of the former National Assembly, 66 members appointed after independence, and 68 members added as a result of the Agreement on the Resolution of the Conflict in the Republic of South Sudan)

elections: National Legislative Assembly—last held 11–15 April 2010 but did not take office until July 2011; because of political instability, current parliamentary term extended until next election on 9 July 2018); Council of States—established and members appointed 1 August 2011

election results: Council of States—percent of vote by party—NA; seats by party—SPLM 20, unknown 30; National Legislative Assembly—percent of vote by party—NA; seats by party—SPLM 251, SPLM-DC 6, DCP 4, independent 6, unknown 65

Judicial branch: highest court(s): Supreme Court of South Sudan (consists of 7 justices including the court president and deputy president and organized into panels of 3 justices except when sitting as a Constitutional panel of all 7 justices)

judge selection and term of office: judges appointed by the president upon proposal of the Judicial Service Council, a 9-member judicial and administrative body; judge tenure NA

subordinate courts: National level—Courts of Appeal; High Courts; County Courts; state level—High Courts; County Courts; customary courts; other specialized courts and tribunals

Political parties and leaders: Sudan People's Liberation Movement or SPLM [Salva KIIR Mayardit] Democratic Change Party or DCP [Lam AKOL]

International organization participation: AU, FAO, G-77, IBRD, ICAO, ICRM, IDA, IFAD, IFC, IFRCS, ILO, IMF, Interpol, IOM, IPU, ITU, MIGA, UN, UNCTAD, UNESCO, UPU, WCO, WHO, WMO

Diplomatic representation in the US: chief of mission: Ambassador Garang Diing AKUONG (since 23 February 2015)

chancery: 1015 31 st St., NW, Third Floor, Washington, DC, 20007

telephone: [1] (202) 293-7940

FAX: [1] (202) 293-7941

Diplomatic representation from the US: chief of mission: Ambassador Mary Catherine PHEE (since July 2015)

embassy: Kololo Road adjacent to the EU's compound, Juba

telephone: [211] (0) 912-105-188

Flag description: three equal horizontal bands of black (top), red, and green; the red band is edged in white; a blue isosceles triangle based on the hoist side contains a gold, five-pointed star; black represents the people of South Sudan, red the blood shed in the struggle for freedom, green the verdant land, and blue the waters of the Nile; the gold star represents the unity of the states making up South Sudan

note: resembles the flag of Kenya; one of only two National flags to display six colors as part of its primary design, the other is South Africa's

National symbol(s): African fish eagle; National colors: red, green, blue, yellow, black, white

National anthem: name: South Sudan Oyee! (Hooray!)

lyrics/music: collective of 49 poets/Juba University students and teachers

note: adopted 2011; anthem selected in a National contest

ECONOMY

Economy—overview: Following several decades of civil war with Sudan, industry and infrastructure in landlocked South Sudan are severely underdeveloped and poverty is widespread. Subsistence agriculture provides a living for the vast majority of the population. Property rights are insecure and price signals are weak, because markets are not well organized. After independence, South Sudan's central bank issued a new currency, the South Sudanese Pound, allowing a short grace period for turning in the old currency. South Sudan has little infrastructure—approximately 200 kilometers of paved roads. Electricity is produced mostly by costly diesel generators, and indoor plumbing and potable water are scarce. South Sudan depends largely on imports of goods, services, and capital—mainly from Uganda, Kenya and Sudan.

Nevertheless, South Sudan does have abundant Natural resources. At independence in 2011, South Sudan produced nearly three-fourths of former Sudan's total oil output of nearly a half million barrels per day. The government of South Sudan derives the vast majority of its budget revenues from oil. Oil is exported through two pipelines that run to refineries and shipping facilities at Port Sudan on the Red Sea. The economy of South Sudan will remain linked to Sudan for some time, given the long lead time and great expense required to build another pipeline, should the government decide to do so in January 2012, South Sudan suspended production of oil because of its dispute with Sudan over transshipment fees. This suspension lasted 15 months and had a devastating impact on GDP, which declined by 48% in 2012. With the resumption of oil flows the economy rebounded strongly during the second half of calendar year 2013. This occurred in spite of the fact that oil production, at an average level of 222,000

barrels per day, was 40% lower compared with 2011, prior to the shutdown. GDP grew by nearly 30% in 2013. However, the outbreak of conflict on 15 December 2013 combined with a further reduction of oil production and exports, meant that GDP growth fell significantly in 2014 and poverty and food insecurity rose. South Sudan holds one of the richest agricultural areas in Africa with fertile soils and abundant water supplies. Currently the region supports 10–20 million head of cattle.

South Sudan is currently burdened by considerable debt because of increased military spending and revenue shortfalls due to low oil prices and decreased production. South Sudan has received more than $4 billion in foreign aid since 2005, largely from the UK, the US, Norway, and the Netherlands. Annual inflation peaked at 79.5% in May 2012 but declined rapidly thereafter, to 1.7% in 2014, before jumping back to 52.8% in 2015, following the December 2013 outbreak of violence. The decision in December 2015 by the central bank to abandon a fixed exchange rate and allow the South Sudanese Pound to float has not reduced inflation in the short term. Long-term challenges include diversifying the formal economy, alleviating poverty, maintaining macroeconomic stability, improving tax collection and financial management and improving the business environment.

GDP (purchasing power parity): $23.69 billion (2015 est.)
$23.73 billion (2014 est.)
$23.06 billion (2013 est.)
note: data are in 2015 US dollars
country comparison to the world: 139

GDP (official exchange rate): $2.627 billion (2015 est.)

GDP—real growth rate: -0.2% (2015 est.)
2.9% (2014 est.)
29.3% (2013 est.)
country comparison to the world: 198

GDP—per capita (PPP): $2,000 (2015 est.)
$2,100 (2014 est.)
$2,100 (2013 est.)
note: data are in 2015 US dollars
country comparison to the world: 203

Gross National saving: 7.1% of GDP (2015 est.)
13.6% of GDP (2014 est.)
11.3% of GDP (2013 est.)
country comparison to the world: 161

GDP—composition, by end use:
household consumption: 34.9%
government consumption: 17.1%
investment in fixed capital: 10.4%
exports of goods and services: 64.9%
imports of goods and services: -27.2% (2011 est.)

Agriculture—products: sorghum, maize, rice, millet, wheat, gum arabic, sugarcane, mangoes, papayas, bananas, sweet potatoes, sunflower seeds, cotton, sesame seeds, cassava (manioc, tapioca), beans, peanuts; cattle, sheep

Population below poverty line: 50.6% (2009 est.)

Distribution of family income—Gini index: 46 (2010 est.)
country comparison to the world: 37

Budget: revenues: $437 million

expenditures: $2.259 billion (FY 2013 est.)
Taxes and other revenues: 3.4% of GDP (FY 2013 est.)
country comparison to the world: 217
Budget surplus (+) or deficit (−): -14.1% of GDP (FY 2013 est.)
country comparison to the world: 214
Inflation rate (consumer prices): 52.8% (2015 est.)
1.7% (2014 est.)
country comparison to the world: 225
Stock of narrow money: $1.873 billion (31 December 2013)
$2.032 billion (31 December 2012)
country comparison to the world: 129
Stock of broad money: $2.194 billion (31 December 2013 est.)
$2.23 billion (31 December 2012 est.)
country comparison to the world: 150
Current account balance: -$332 million (2015 est.)
$290 million (2014 est.)
country comparison to the world: 89
Exchange rates: South Sudanese pounds (SSP) per US dollar—
0.885 (2015 est.)
0.7525 (2014 est.)
0.7634 (2013 est.)
0.78 (2012 est.)
0.7185 (2011 est.)

ENERGY

Electricity—production: 881.3 million kWh (2012 est.)
country comparison to the world: 154
Electricity—consumption: 694.1 million kWh (2012 est.)
country comparison to the world: 164
Electricity—exports: 0 kWh (2013 est.)
country comparison to the world: 182
Electricity—imports: 0 kWh (2013 est.)
country comparison to the world: 187
Electricity—installed generating capacity: 255,200 kW (2012 est.)
country comparison to the world: 155
Electricity—from fossil fuels: 30.7% of total installed capacity (2010 est.)
country comparison to the world: 180
Electricity—from nuclear fuels: 0% of total installed capacity (2010 est.)
country comparison to the world: 161
Electricity—from hydroelectric plants: 66.3% of total installed capacity (2010 est.)
country comparison to the world: 31
Electricity—from other renewable sources: 3% of total installed capacity (2010 est.)
country comparison to the world: 70
Crude oil—production: 220,000 bbl/day (Second half, 2013 est.)
country comparison to the world: 38
Crude oil—exports: 291,800 bbl/day (2010 est.)
country comparison to the world: 26
Crude oil—imports: 0 bbl/day (2012 est.)
country comparison to the world: 112
Crude oil—proved reserves: 3.75 billion bbl (1 January 2015 est.)
country comparison to the world: 28
Refined petroleum products—Imports: 13,050 bbl/day
country comparison to the world: 129
Natural gas—production: 0 cu m (2013 est.)
country comparison to the world: 116

Natural gas—consumption: 0 cu m (2013 est.)
country comparison to the world: 184
Natural gas—exports: 0 cu m (2013 est.)
country comparison to the world: 161
Natural gas—Imports: 0 cu m (2013 est.)
country comparison to the world: 117
Natural gas—proved reserves: 63.71 billion cu m (1 January 2013 est.)
country comparison to the world: 60
Carbon dioxide emissions from consumption of energy: 2.016 million Mt (2011 est.)
country comparison to the world: 149

COMMUNICATIONS

Telephone—mobile cellular: *total:* 2.9 million
subscriptions per 100 inhabitants: 25 (2014 est.)
country comparison to the world: 141
Telephone system: *international:* country code—211
Broadcast media: TV is controlled by the government; several private FM stations are operation al in South Sudan; some foreign radio broadcasts are available
Internet country code: .ss

TRANSPORTATION

Airports: 85 (2013)
country comparison to the world: 64
Airports—with paved runways: *total:* 3
2,438 to 3,047 m: 1
1,524 to 2,437 m: 2 (2013)
Airports—with unpaved runways: *total:* 82
2,438 to 3,047 m: 1
1,524 to 2,437 m: 12
914 to 1,523 m: 35
under 914 m: 34 (2013)
Heliports: 1 (2013)
Railways: *total:* 248 km
note: a narrow guage, single-track railroad between Babonosa (Sudan) and Wau, the only existing rail system, was repaired in 2010 with $250 million in UN funds (2014)
country comparison to the world: 127
Roadways: *total:* 7,000 km
note: most of the road network is unpaved and much of it is in disrepair; a 192-km paved road between the capital, Juba, and Nimule on the Ugandan border was constructed with USAID funds in 2012 (2012)
country comparison to the world: 145
Waterways: see entry for Sudan

MILITARY AND SECURITY

Military branches: Sudan People's Liberation army (SPLA)
Military service age and obligation: 18 is the legal minimum age for compulsory and voluntary military service; the Government of South Sudan signed a revised action plan with the UN in March 2012 to demobilize all child soldiers within the SPLA, but recruitment of child soldiers by the SPLA and the opposition increased in 2014; as of the end of 2015, UNICEF estimates that 15,000 to 16,000 child soldiers had been used by the SPLA and rebel forces in the country's civil war since it began in December 2013 (2015)
Military expenditures: 10.32% of GDP (2012)
5.8% of GDP (2011) 10.32% of GDP (2010)

country comparison to the world: 1

TRANSNATIONAL ISSUES

Disputes—International: South Sudan-Sudan boundary represents 1 January 1956 alignment, final alignment pending negotiations and demarcation; final sovereignty status of Abyei Area pending negotiations between South Sudan and Sudan; periodic violent skirmishes with South Sudanese residents over water and grazing rights persist among related pastoral populations along the border with the Central African Republic; the boundary that separates Kenya and South Sudan's sovereignty is unclear in the "Ilemi Triangle," which Kenya has administered since colonial times

Refugees and internally displaced persons:
refugees (country of origin): 251,216 (Sudan); 14,799 (Democratic Republic of the Congo) (2016)
IDPs: 1,790,427 (alleged coup attempt and ethnic conflict beginning in December 2013; information is lacking on those displaced in earlier years by: fighting in Abyei between the Sudanese Armed Forces and the Sudan People's Liberation army (SPLA) in May 2011; clashes between the SPLA and dissident militia groups in South Sudan; inter-ethnic conflicts over resources and cattle; attacks from the Lord's Resistance Army; floods and drought) (2015)

Trafficking in persons: *current situation:* South Sudan is a source and destination country for men, women, and children subjected to forced labor and sex trafficking; South Sudanese women and girls, particularly those who are internally displaced, orphaned, refugees, or from rural areas, are vulnerable to forced labor and sexual exploitation, often in urban centers; children may be victims of forced labor in construction, market vending, shoe shining, car washing, rock breaking, brick making, delivery cart pulling, and begging; girls are also forced into marriages and subsequently subjected to sexual slavery or domestic servitude; women and girls migrate willingly from Uganda, Kenya, Ethiopia, Eritrea, and the Democratic Republic of the Congo to South Sudan with the promise of legitimate jobs and are forced into the sex trade; inter-ethnic abductions and abductions by criminal groups continue, with abductees subsequently forced into domestic servitude, herding, or sex trafficking; in 2014, the recruitment and use of child soldiers increased significantly within government security forces and was also prevalent among opposition forces

tier rating: Tier 3—South Sudan does not fully comply with the minimum standards for the elimination of trafficking and is not making significant efforts to do so; despite the government's formal recommitment to an action plan to eliminate the recruitment and use of child soldiers by 2016, the practice expanded during 2014, and the government did not hold any officers criminally responsible; government officials reportedly are complicit in trafficking offenses but these activities continue to go uninvestigated; authorities reportedly identified five trafficking victims but did not transfer them to care facilities; law enforcement continued to arrest and imprison individuals for prostitution, including trafficking victims; no known steps were taken to address the exploitation of South Sudanese Nationals working abroad or foreign workers in South Sudan (2015)

SOUTHERN OCEAN

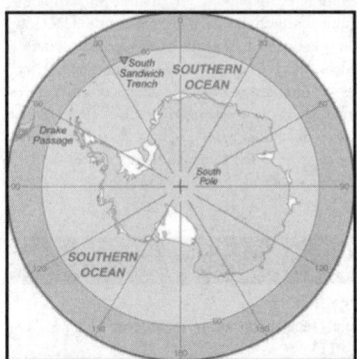

INTRODUCTION

Background: A large body of recent oceanographic research has shown that the Antarctic Circumpolar Current (ACC), an ocean current that flows from west to east around Antarctica, plays a crucial role in global ocean circulation. The region where the cold waters of the ACC meet and mingle with the warmer waters of the north defines a distinct border—the Antarctic Convergence—which fluctuates with the seasons, but which encompasses a discrete body of water and a unique ecologic region. The Convergence concentrates nutrients, which promotes marine plant life, and which, in turn, allows for a greater abundance of animal life. In 2000, the International Hydrographic Organization delimited the waters within the Convergence as a fifth world ocean—the Southern Ocean—by combining the southern portions of the Atlantic Ocean, Indian Ocean, and Pacific Ocean. The Southern Ocean extends from the coast of Antarctica north to 60 degrees south latitude, which coincides with the Antarctic Treaty region and which approximates the extent of the Antarctic Convergence. As such, the Southern Ocean is now the fourth largest of the world's five oceans (after the Pacific Ocean, Atlantic Ocean, and Indian Ocean, but larger than the Arctic Ocean). It should be noted that inclusion of the Southern Ocean does not imply recognition of this feature as one of the world's primary oceans by the US Government.

GEOGRAPHY

Location: body of water between 60 degrees south latitude and Antarctica

Geographic coordinates: 60 00 S, 90 00 E (nominally), but the Southern Ocean has the unique distinction of being a large circumpolar body of water totally encircling the continent of Antarctica; this ring of water lies between 60 degrees south latitude and the coast of Antarctica and encompasses 360 degrees of longitude

Map references: Antarctic Region

Area: *total:* 20.327 million sq km

note: includes Amundsen Sea, Bellingshausen Sea, part of the Drake Passage, Ross Sea, a small part of the Scotia Sea, Weddell Sea, and other tributary water bodies

Area—comparative: slightly more than twice the size of the US

Coastline: 17,968 km

Climate: sea temperatures vary from about 10 degrees Celsius to -2 degrees Celsius; cyclonic storms travel eastward around the continent and frequently are intense because of the temperature contrast between ice and open ocean; the ocean area from about latitude 40 south to the Antarctic Circle has the strongest average winds found anywhere on Earth; in winter the ocean freezes outward to 65 degrees south latitude in the Pacific sector and 55 degrees south latitude in the Atlantic sector, lowering surface temperatures well below 0 degrees Celsius; at some coastal points intense persistent drainage winds from the interior keep the shoreline ice-free throughout the winter

Terrain: the Southern Ocean is 4,000 to 5,000-m deep over most of its extent with only limited areas of shallow water; the Antarctic continental shelf is generally narrow and unusually deep, its edge lying at depths of 400 to 800 m (the global mean is 133 m); the Antarctic icepack grows from an average minimum of 2.6 million sq km in March to about 18.8 million sq km in September, better than a sixfold increase in area; the Antarctic Circumpolar Current (21,000 km long) moves perpetually eastward, the world's largest ocean current, it transports 130 million cubic meters of water per second—100 times the flow of all the world's rivers

Elevation: mean depth: -3,270 m

elevation extremes: *lowest point:* southern end of the South Sandwich Trench -7,235 m

highest point: sea level 0 m

Natural resources: probable large oil and gas fields on the continental margin; manganese nodules, possible placer deposits, sand and gravel, fresh water as icebergs; squid, whales, and seals—none exploited; krill, fish

Natural hazards: huge icebergs with drafts up to several hundred meters; smaller bergs and iceberg fragments; sea ice (generally 0.5 to 1 m thick) with sometimes dynamic short-term variations and with large annual and interannual variations; deep continental shelf floored by glacial deposits varying widely over short distances; high winds and large waves much of the year; ship icing, especially May-October; most of region is remote from sources of search and rescue

Environment—current issues: increased solar ultraviolet radiation resulting from the Antarctic ozone hole in recent years, reducing marine primary productivity (phytoplankton), damaging the DNA of some fish, and causing sun damage to some mammals; large amount of mortality of seabirds resulting from long-line fishing for toothfish; ocean Acidification

note: the now-protected fur seal population is making a strong comeback after severe overexploitation in the 18th and 19th centuries

Environment—International agreements: the Southern Ocean is subject to all International agreements regarding the world's oceans; in addition, it is subject to these agreements specific to the Antarctic region: International Whaling Commission (prohibits commercial whaling south of 40 degrees south [south of 60 degrees south between 50 degrees and 130 degrees west]); Convention on the Conservation of Antarctic Seals (limits sealing); Convention on the Conservation of Antarctic Marine Living Resources (regulates fishing)

note: many nations (including the US) prohibit mineral resource exploration and exploitation south of the fluctuating Polar Front (Antarctic Convergence), which is in the middle of the Antarctic Circumpolar Current and serves as the dividing line between the cold polar surface waters to the south and the warmer waters to the north

Geography—note: the major chokepoint is the Drake Passage between South America and Antarctica; the Polar Front (Antarctic Convergence) is the best Natural definition of the northern extent of the Southern Ocean; it is a distinct region at the middle of the Antarctic Circumpolar Current that separates the cold polar surface waters to the south from the warmer waters to the north; the Front and the Current extend entirely around Antarctica, reaching south of 60 degrees south near New Zealand and near 48 degrees south in the far South Atlantic coinciding with the path of the maximum westerly winds

GOVERNMENT

Country name: etymology: the International Hydrographic Organization (IHO) included the Ocean and its definition as the waters south of 60 degrees south in its year 2000 revision, but this has not formally been adopted; the 2000 IHO definition, however, was circulated in a draft edition in 2002 and has acquired de facto usage by many nations and organizations, including the CIA

ECONOMY

Economy—overview: Fisheries in 2013–14 landed 302,960 metric tons, of which 96% (291,370 tons-the highest reported catch since 1991) was krill and 4% (11,590 tons) Patagonian toothfish (also known as Chilean sea bass), compared to 15,330 tons in 2012–13 (estimated fishing from the area covered by the Convention of the Conservation of Antarctic Marine Living Resources, which extends slightly beyond the Southern OceanArea). International agreements were adopted in late 1999 to reduce illegal, unreported, and unregulated fishing, which in the 2000–01 season landed, by one estimate, 8,376 metric tons of Patagonian and Antarctic toothfish. In the 2014–15 Antarctic summer, 36,702 tourists visited the Southern Ocean, slightly lower than the 37,405 visitors in 2013–14 (estimates provided to the Antarctic Treaty by the International Association of Antarctica Tour Operators, and does not include passengers on overflights and those flying directly in and out of Antarctica).

TRANSPORTATION

Ports and terminals: *major seaport(s):* McMurdo, Palmer, and offshore anchorages in Antarctica
note: few ports or harbors exist on the southern side of the Southern Ocean; ice conditions limit use of most to short periods in midsummer; even then some cannot be entered without icebreaker escort; most Antarctic ports are operated by government research stations and, except in an emergency, are not open to commercial or private vessels

Transportation—note: Drake Passage offers alternative to transit through the Panama Canal

TRANSNATIONAL ISSUES

Disputes—International: Antarctic Treaty defers claims (see Antarctica entry), but Argentina, Australia, Chile, France, NZ, Norway, and UK assert claims (some overlapping), including the continental shelf in the Southern Ocean; several states have expressed an interest in extending those continental shelf claims under the UN Convention on the Law of the Sea to include undersea ridges; the US and most other states do not recognize the land or maritime claims of other states and have made no claims themselves (the US and Russia have reserved the right to do so); no formal claims exist in the waters in the sector between 90 degrees west and 150 degrees west

SPAIN

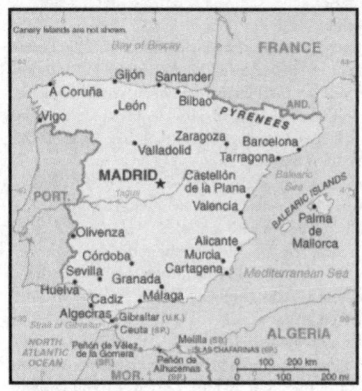

INTRODUCTION

Background: Spain's powerful world empire of the 16th and 17th centuries ultimately yielded command of the seas to England. Subsequent failure to embrace the mercantile and industrial revolutions caused the country to fall behind Britain, France, and Germany in economic and political power. Spain remained neutral in World War I and II but suffered through a devastating civil war (1936–39). A peaceful transition to democracy following the death of dictator Francisco FRANCO in 1975, and rapid economic modernization (Spain joined the EU in 1986) gave Spain A dynamic and rapidly growing economy and made it a global champion of freedom and human rights. More recently the government has focused on measures to reverse a severe economic recession that began in mid-2008. Austerity measures implemented to reduce a large budget deficit and reassure foreign investors have led to one of the highest unemployment rates in Europe. Spain Assumed a nonpermanent seat on the UN Security Council for the 2015–16 term.

GEOGRAPHY

Location: Southwestern Europe, bordering the Mediterranean Sea, North Atlantic Ocean, Bay of Biscay, and Pyrenees Mountains; southwest of France

Geographic coordinates: 40 00 N, 4 00 W

Map references: Europe
Area: *total:* 505,370 sq km
land: 498,980 sq km
water: 6,390 sq km
note: there are two autonomous cities—Ceuta and Melilla—and 17 autonomous communities including Balearic Islands and Canary Islands, and three small Spanish possessions off the coast of Morocco—Islas Chafarinas, Penon de Alhucemas, and Penon de Velez de la Gomera
country comparison to the world: 52
Area—comparative: almost five times the size of Kentucky; slightly more than twice the size of Oregon
Land boundaries: *total:* 1,952.7 km
border countries (5): Andorra 63 km, France 646 km, Gibraltar 1.2 km, Portugal 1,224 km, Morocco (Ceuta) 8 km, Morocco (Melilla) 10.5 km
note: an Additional 75-meter border segment exists between Morocco and the Spanish exclave of Penon de Velez de la Gomera
Coastline: 4,964 km
Maritime claims: *territorial sea:* 12 nm
contiguous zone: 24 nm
exclusive economic zone: 200 nm (applies only to the Atlantic Ocean)
Climate: temperate; clear, hot summers in interior, more moderate and cloudy along coast; cloudy, cold winters in interior, partly cloudy and cool along coast
Terrain: large, flat to dissected plateau surrounded by rugged hills; Pyrenees Mountains in north
Elevation: *mean elevation:* 660 m
elevation extremes: *lowest point:* Atlantic Ocean 0 m
highest point: Pico de Teide (Tenerife) on Canary Islands 3,718 m
Natural resources: coal, lignite, iron ore, copper, lead, zinc, uranium, tungsten, mercury, pyrites, magnesite, fluorspar, gypsum, sepiolite, kaolin, potash, hydropower, arable land
Land use: *agricultural land:* 54.1%
arable land: 24.9%
permanent crops: 9.1%
permanent pasture: 20.1%
forest: 36.8%
other: 9.1% (2011 est.)
Irrigated land: 38,000 sq km (2012)

Total renewable water resources: 111.5 cu km (2011)
Freshwater withdrawal (domestic/industrial/agricultural): *total:* 32.46 cu km/yr (18%/22%/61%)
per capita: 698.7 cu m/yr (2008)
Natural hazards: periodic droughts, occasional flooding
volcanism: volcanic activity in the Canary Islands, located off Africa's northwest coast; Teide (elev. 3,715 m) has been deemed a Decade Volcano by the International Association of Volcanology and Chemistry of the Earth's Interior, worthy of study due to its explosive history and close proximity to human populations; La Palma (elev. 2,426 m), which last erupted in 1971, is the most active of the Canary Islands volcanoes; Lanzarote is the only other historically active volcano
Environment—current issues: pollution of the Mediterranean Sea from raw sewage and effluents from the offshore production of oil and gas; water quality and quantity nationwide; air pollution; deforestation; desertification
Environment—International agreements: *party to:* Air Pollution, Air Pollution-Nitrogen Oxides, Air Pollution-Sulfur 94, Air Pollution-Volatile Organic Compounds, Antarctic-Environmental Protocol, Antarctic-Marine Living Resources, Antarctic Treaty, Biodiversity, Climate Change, Climate Change-Kyoto Protocol, Desertification, Endangered Species, Environmental Modification, Hazardous Wastes, Law of the Sea, Marine Dumping, Marine Life Conservation, Ozone Layer Protection, Ship Pollution, Tropical Timber 83, Tropical Timber 94, Wetlands, Whaling
signed, but not ratified: Air Pollution-Persistent Organic Pollutants
Geography—note: strategic location along approaches to Strait of Gibraltar; Spain controls a number of territories in northern Morocco including the enclaves of Ceuta and Melilla, and the islands of Penon de Velez de la Gomera, Penon de Alhucemas, and Islas Chafarinas

PEOPLE AND SOCIETY

Nationality: *noun:* Spaniard(s)
adjective: Spanish
Ethnic groups: composite of Mediterranean And Nordic types

Languages: Castilian Spanish (official nationwide) 74%, Catalan (official in Catalonia, the Balearic Islands, and the Valencian Community (where it is known as Valencian)) 17%, Galician (official in Galicia) 7%, Basque (official in the Basque Country and in the Basque-speaking area of Navarre) 2%, Aranese (official in the northwest corner of Catalonia (Vall d'Aran) along with Catalan; <5,000 speakers)

note: Aragonese, Aranese Asturian, Basque, Calo, Catalan, Galician, and Valencian are recognized as regional languages under the European Charter for Regional or Minority Languages

Religions: Roman Catholic 94%, other 6%

Population: 48,146,134 (July 2015 est.)
country comparison to the world: 29

Age structure: *0–14 years:* 15.45% (male 3,827,552/female 3,610,910)

15–24 years: 9.56% (male 2,379,676/female 2,223,159)

25–54 years: 45.57% (male 11,180,532/female 10,762,002)

55–64 years: 11.67% (male 2,738,802/female 2,877,648)

65 years and over: 17.75% (male 3,642,559/female 4,903,294) (2015 est.)

Dependency ratios: *total dependency ratio:* 50.8%

youth dependency ratio: 22.4%
elderly dependency ratio: 28.3%
potential support ratio: 3.5% (2015 est.)

Median age: *total:* 42 years
male: 40.8 years
female: 43.2 years (2015 est.)
country comparison to the world: 28

Population growth rate: 0.89% (2015 est.)
country comparison to the world: 127

Birth rate: 9.64 births/1,000 population (2015 est.)
country comparison to the world: 201

Death rate: 9.04 deaths/1,000 population (2015 est.)
country comparison to the world: 68

Net migration rate: 8.31 migrant(s)/1,000 population (2015 est.)
country comparison to the world: 13

Urbanization: *urban population:* 79.6% of total population (2015)

rate of urbanization: 0.52% annual rate of change (2010–15 est.)

Major urban areas—population: MADRID (capital) 6.199 million; Barcelona 5.258 million; Valencia 810,000 (2015)

Sex ratio: *at birth:* 1.07 male(s)/female
0–14 years: 1.06 male(s)/female
15–24 years: 1.07 male(s)/female
25–54 years: 1.04 male(s)/female
55–64 years: 0.95 male(s)/female
65 years and over: 0.74 male(s)/female
total population: 0.98 male(s)/female (2015 est.)

Mother's mean age at first birth: 29.8 (2010 est.)

Maternal mortality rate: 5 deaths/100,000 live births (2015 est.)
country comparison to the world: 170

Infant mortality rate: *total:* 3.3 deaths/1,000 live births
male: 3.63 deaths/1,000 live births

female: 2.96 deaths/1,000 live births (2015 est.)
country comparison to the world: 211

Life expectancy at birth: *total population:* 81.57 years
male: 78.57 years
female: 84.77 years (2015 est.)
country comparison to the world: 21

Total fertility rate: 1.49 children born/woman (2015 est.)
country comparison to the world: 197

Contraceptive prevalence rate: 65.7% (2006)

Health expenditures: 8.9% of GDP (2013)
country comparison to the world: 26

Physicians density: 4.95 physicians/1,000 population (2013)

Hospital bed density: 3.1 beds/1,000 population (2011)

Drinking water source:
improved:
urban: 100% of population
rural: 100% of population
total: 100% of population
unimproved:
urban: 0% of population
rural: 0% of population
total: 0% of population (2015 est.)

Sanitation facility access:
improved:
urban: 99.8% of population
rural: 100% of population
total: 99.9% of population
unimproved:
urban: 0.2% of population
rural: 0% of population
total: 0.1% of population (2015 est.)

HIV/AIDS—adult prevalence rate: 0.42% (2013 est.)
country comparison to the world: 73

HIV/AIDS—people living with HIV/AIDS: 150,400 (2013 est.)
country comparison to the world: 32

HIV/AIDS—deaths: 800 (2013 est.)
country comparison to the world: 70

Obesity—adult prevalence rate: 26.5% (2014)
country comparison to the world: 45

Education expenditures: 4.3% of GDP (2013)
country comparison to the world: 80

Literacy: *definition:* age 15 and over can read and write
total population: 98.1%
male: 98.7%
female: 97.5% (2015 est.)

School life expectancy (primary to tertiary education): *total:* 18 years
male: 17 years
female: 18 years (2014)

Unemployment, youth ages 15–24: *total:* 55.5%
male: 56.2%
female: 54.6% (2013 est.)
country comparison to the world: 5

GOVERNMENT

Country name: *conventional long form:* Kingdom of Spain
conventional short form: Spain
local long form: Reino de Espana

local short form: Espana

etymology: derivation of the name "Espana" is uncertain, but may come from the Phoenician term "span," related to the word "spy," meaning "to forge metals," so, "i-spn-ya" would mean "place where metals are forged"; the ancient Phoenicians long exploited the Iberian Peninsula for its mineral wealth

Government type: parliamentary constitutional monarchy

Capital: *name:* Madrid

Geographic coordinates: 40 24 N, 3 41 W

time difference: UTC + 1 (6 hours ahead of Washington, DC, during Standard Time)

daylight saving time: +1 hr, begins last Sunday in March; ends last Sunday in October

note: Spain has two time zones including the Canary Islands

Administrative divisions: 17 semi-autonomous communities (comunidades autonomas, singular—comunidad autonoma) and 2 autonomous cities* (ciudades autonomas, singular—ciudad autonoma); Andalucia; Aragon; Asturias; Canarias (Canary Islands); Cantabria; Castilla-La Mancha; Castilla-Leon; Cataluna (Castilian), Catalunya (Catalan), Catalonha (Aranese) [Catalonia]; Ceuta*; Comunidad Valenciana (Castilian), Comunitat Valenciana (Valencian) [Valencian Community]; Extremadura; Galicia; Illes Baleares (Balearic Islands); La Rioja; Madrid; Melilla*; Murcia; Navarra (Castilian), Nafarroa (Basque) [Navarre]; Pais Vasco (Castilian), EUS kadi (Basque) [Basque Country]

note: the autonomous cities of Ceuta and Melilla plus three small islands of Islas Chafarinas, Penon de Alhucemas, and Penon de Velez de la Gomera, administered directly by the Spanish central government, are all along the coast of Morocco and are collectively referred to as Places of Sovereignty (Plazas de Soberania)

Independence: 1492; the Iberian peninsula was characterized by a variety of independent kingdoms prior to the Muslim occupation that began in the early 8th century A.D. and lasted nearly seven centuries; the small Christian redoubts of the north began the reconquest almost immediately, culminating in the seizure of Granada in 1492; this event completed the unification of several kingdoms and is traditionally considered the forging of present-day Spain

National holiday: National Day, 12 October (1492); year when Columbus first set foot in the Americas

Constitution: previous 1812; latest approved by the General Courts 31 October 1978, passed by referendum 6 December 1978, signed by the king 27 December 1978, effective 29 December 1978; amended 1992, 2007, 2011 (2016)

Legal system: civil law system with Regional variations

International law organization participation: accepts compulsory ICJ jurisdiction with reservations; accepts ICCt jurisdiction

Citizenship: *citizenship by birth:* no
citizenship by descent only: at least one parent must be a citizen of Spain

dual citizenship recognized: only with select Latin American countries

residency requirement for naturalization: 10 years for persons with no ties to Spain

Suffrage: 18 years of age; universal

Executive branch: *chief of state:* King FELIPE VI (since 19 June 2014); Heir Apparent Princess LEONOR, Princess of Asturias, daughter of the monarch, born 31 October 2005

head of government: Acting President of the Government or Acting Prime Minister Mariano RAJOY (since 20 December 2011); Vice President (and Minister of the President's Office) Soraya SAENZ DE SANTAMARIA (since 22 December 2011)

cabinet: Council of Ministers designated by the president

elections/appointments: the monarchy is hereditary; following legislative elections, the monarch usually proposes the leader of the party or coalition with the largest majority of seats as president, who is then indirectly elected by the Congress of Deputies; election last held on 20 December 2015; vice president and Council of Ministers appointed by the president;

note—because no party received a majority of the votes in both houses, and because the leaders of the parties with the most votes were unable to form a coalition to form a majority, new elections will be most likely held on 26 June 2016

election results: percent of National Assembly vote—NA

note: there is also a Council of State that is the supreme consultative organ of the government, but its recommendations are non-Binding

Legislative branch: *description:* bicameral General Courts or Las Cortes Generales consists of the Senate or Senado (266 seats as of 2013; 208 members directly elected in multi-seat constituencies by simple majority vote and 58 appointed by the regional legislatures; members serve 4-year terms) and the Congress of Deputies or Congreso de los Diputados (350 seats; 348 members directly elected in 50 multi-seat constituencies by proportional representation vote and 2 directly elected from the North African Ceuta and Melilla enclaves by simple majority vote; members serve 4-year terms or until the government is dissolved)

elections: Senate—last held on 20 December 2015 (next to be held 26 June 2016); Congress of Deputies—last held on 20 December 2015 (next to be held on 26 June 2016); note—the four main parties were unable to form a government so a second election is being held six months later

election results: Senate—percent of vote by party—PP 54.5%, PSOE 24.8%, Podemos 8.6%, DiL 4.9%, ERC 2.6%, EAJ-PNV 2.6%, C's 0.8%, CC-PNC 0.8%, independent 0.4%, other 1.5%; seats by party—PP 145, PSOE 66, Podemos 23, DiL 9, ERC 7, EAJ/PNV 7, CC/PNC 2, C's 2, other 4, independent 1; Congress of Deputies—percent of vote by party—PP 28.7%, PSOE 22.0%, Podemos 20.7%, C's 13.9%, IU/UP 3.7%, ERC 2.4%, DiL 2.3%, EAJ/PNV 1.2%, other 5.1%; seats by party—PP 123, PSOE 90, Podemos 69, C's 40, ERC 9, DiL 8, EAJ/PN V 6, IU/UP 2, other 3

Judicial branch: *highest court(s):* Supreme Court or Tribunal Supremo (consists of the court president and organized into the Civil Room with a president and 9 magistrates, the Penal Room with a president and 14 magistrates, the Administrative Room with a president and 32 magistrates, the Social Room with a president and 12 magistrates, and the Military Room with a president and 7 magistrates); Constitutional Court or Tribunal Constitucion al de Espana (consists of 12 judges)

judge selection and term of office: Supreme Court judges appointed by the monarch from candidates proposed by the General Council of the Judiciary Power, a 20-member governing board chaired by the monarch that includes presidential appointees, and lawyers and jurists confirmed by the National Assembly; judge tenure NA; Constitutional Court judges nominated by the National Assembly, executive branch, and the General Council of the Judiciary, and appointed by the monarch for 9-year terms

subordinate courts: National Court; High Courts of Justice (in each of the autonomous communities); provincial courts; courts of first instance

Political parties and leaders: Amaiur [Xabier ERREKONDO] (a separatist political coalition that advocates Basque independence from Spain)

Asturias Forum or FAC [Cristina COTO]

Basque Country Unite (Euskal Herria Bildu) or EH Bildu [Pello URIZAR] (coalition of 4 Basque pro-independence parties)

Basque Nationalist Party or PNV or EAJ [Andoni ORTUZAR]

Canarian Coalition or CC [Claudina MORALES Rodriguez] (coalition of five parties)

Canarian Nationalist Party or PNC [Juan Manuel GARCIA Ramos]

Catalan Agreement of Progress (Entesa Catalonia de Progress) or ECP [Carles BONET i Reves] (Senate coalition of Catalan parties—PSC, ERC, ICV, EUA)

Change or Cambio-Aldaketa

Ciudadamos Party or C's [Albert RIVERA]

Democracy and Freedom or DiL [Francesc HOMS Molist] (2015 merger of Cemocratic Convergence of Catalonia or CDC, Democrats of Catalonia, Reagrupament)

Democratic Union of Catalonia or UDC [Josep Antoni DURAN i LLEIDA]

Galician Nationalist Bloc or BNG [Xavier VENCE]

Gomera Socialist Group or ASG

Initiative for Catalonia Greens or ICV [Joan HERRERA i Torres and Dolors CAMATS]

Podemos [Pablo I GLESI AS Turrion]

Popular Party or PP [Mariano RAJOY Brey]

Republican Left of Catalonia or ERC [Oriol JUNQUERAS i Vies]

Spanish Socialist Workers Party or PSOE [Pedro SANCHEZ]

Union of People of Navarra or UPN [Yolanda BARCINA Angulo]

Union, Progress and Democracy or UPyD [Rosa DIEZ Gonzalez]

United Left or IU [Alberto GARZON] (a coalition of parties including the Communist Party of

Spain or PCE and other small parties; ran as Popular Unity or UP in 2015 election) Yes to the Future or Geroa Bai [Uxue BARKOS] (a coalition of four Navarran parties)

Political pressure groups and leaders: Association for Victims of Terrorism or AVT (grassroots organization devoted primarily to supporting victims of the Basque Fatherland and Liberty (ETA) terrorist organization) Catholic Church Socialist General Union of Workers or UGT (includes the smaller independent Workers Syndical Union or USO) Trade Union Confederation of Workers' Commissions or CC. OO. Spanish Confederation of Employers' Organizations or CEOE

other: business and landowning interests; free labor unions (authorized in April 1977); university students

International organization participation: ADB (nonregional member), AfDB (nonRegional member), Arctic Council (observer), Australia Group, BCIE, BIS, CAN (observer), CBSS (observer), CD, CE, CERN, EAPC, EBRD, ECB, EIB, EITI (implementing country), EMU, ESA, EU, FAO, FATF, IADB, IAEA, IBRD, ICAO, ICC (National committees), ICCt, ICRM, IDA, IEA, IFAD, IFC, IFRCS, IHO, ILO, IMF, IMO, IMSO, Interpol, IOC, IOM, IPU, ISO, ITSO, ITU, ITUC (NGOs), LAIA (observer), MIGA, NATO, NEA, NSG, OAS (observer), OECD, OPCW, OSCE, Pacific Alliance (observer), Paris Club, PCA, PIF (partner), Schengen Convention, SELEC (observer), SICA (observer), UN, UN Security Council (temporary), UNCTAD, UNESCO, UNHCR, UNIDO, UNIFIL, Union Latina, UNOCI, UNRWA, UNWTO, UPU, WCO, WHO, WIPO, WMO, WTO, ZC

Diplomatic representation in the US: *chief of mission:* Ambassador Ramon GIL-CASARES Satrustegui (since 5 June 2012)

chancery: 2375 Pennsylvania Avenue NW, Washington, DC 20037

telephone: [1] (202) 452-0100, 728-2340

FAX: [1] (202) 833-5670

consulate(s) general: Boston, Chicago, Houston, Los Angeles, Miami, New York, San Francisco, San Juan (Puerto Rico) consulate(s): Kansas City (MO)

Diplomatic representation from the US: *chief of mission:* Ambassador James COSTOS (since 24 September 2013); note—also accredited to An dorra

embassy: Serrano 75,28006 Madrid

mailing address: PSC 61, APO AE 09642

telephone: [34] (91) 587-2200

FAX: [34] (91) 587-2303

consulate(s) general: Barcelona

Flag description: three horizontal bands of red (top), yellow (double width), and red with the National coat of arms on the hoist side of the yellow band; the coat of arms is quartered to display the emblems of the traditional kingdoms of Spain (clockwise from upper left, Castile, Leon, Navarre, and Aragon) while Granada is represented by the stylized pomegranate at the bottom of the shield; the arms are framed by two columns representing the Pillars of Hercules, which are the two promontories (Gibraltar and Ceuta) on either side of the eastern end of the Strait of Gibraltar; the red scroll across the two columns bears the imperial motto of "Plus Ultra" (further beyond) referring to Spanish lands beyond Europe; the triband arrangement with the center stripe twice the width of the outer dates to the 18th century

note: the red and yellow colors are related to those of the oldest Spanish kingdoms: Aragon, Castile, Leon, and Navarre

National symbol(s): Pillars of Hercules; National colors: red, yellow

National anthem: *name:* "Himno Nacion al Espanol" (National Anthem of Spain)

lyrics/music: no lyrics/unknown

note: officially in use between 1770 and 1931, restored in 1939; the Spanish anthem is the first anthem to be officially adopted, but it has no lyrics; in the years prior to 1931 it became known as "Marcha Real" (The Royal March); it first appeared in a 1761 military bugle call book and was replaced by "Himno de Riego" in the years between 1931 and 1939; the long version of the anthem is used for the king, while the short version is used for the prince, prime minister, and occasions such as sporting events

ECONOMY

Economy—overview: After experiencing a prolonged recession in the wake of the global financial crisis that began in 2008, in 2014 Spain marked the first full year of positive economic growth in seven years, largely due to increased private consumption. At the onset of the financial crisis, Spain's GDP contracted by 3.7% in 2009, ending a 16-year growth trend, and continued contracting through most of 2013. In 2013, the government successfully shored up struggling banks—exposed to the collapse of Spain's depressed real estate and construction sectors—and in January 2014 completed an EU -funded restructuring and recapitalization program.

Until 2014, credit contraction in the private sector, fiscal austerity, and high unemployment weighed on domestic consumption and investment. The unemployment rate rose from a low of about 8% in 2007 to more than 26% in 2013, but labor reforms prompted a modest reduction to 22% in 2015. High unemployment strained Spain's public finances, as spending on social benefits increased while tax revenues fell. Spain's budget deficit peaked at 11.4% of GDP in 2010, but Spain gradually reduced the deficit to just under 7% of GDP in 2013–14, and 4.7% of GDP in 2015. Public debt has increased substantially—from 60.1% of GDP in 2010 to nearly 101% in 2015.

Exports were resilient throughout the economic downturn and helped to bring Spain's current account into surplus in 2013 for the first time since 1986, where it remained in 2014–15. Rising labor productivity and an internal devaluation resulting from moderating labor costs and lower inflation have helped to improve foreign investor interest in the economy and positive FDI flows have been restored.

The government's efforts to implement labor, pension, healthcare, tax, and education reforms—aimed at supporting investor sentiment—have become overshadowed by political activity in 2015 in anticipation of the National parliamentary elections in December. The European Commission criticized Spain's 2016 budget for its easing of austerity measures and its alleged overly optimistic growth and deficit projections. Spain's borrowing costs are dramatically lower since their peak in mid-2012, and despite the recent uptick in economic activity, inflation has dropped sharply, from 1.5% in 2013 to a negative 0.6% in 2015.

GDP (purchasing power parity): $1.615 trillion (2015 est.)

$1.565 trillion (2014 est.)

$1.544 trillion (2013 est.)

note: data are in 2015 US dollars

country comparison to the world: 17

GDP (official exchange rate): $1.2 trillion (2015 est.)

GDP—real growth rate: 3.2% (2015 est.)

1.4% (2014 est.)

-1.7% (2013 est.)

country comparison to the world: 94

GDP—per capita (PPP): $34,800 (2015 est.)

$33,700 (2014 est.)

$33,100 (2013 est.)

note: data are in 2015 US dollars

country comparison to the world: 54

Gross National saving: 22% of GDP (2015 est.)

20.8% of GDP (2014 est.)

20.7% of GDP (2013 est.)

country comparison to the world: 67

GDP—composition, by end use:

household consumption: 58.8%

government consumption: 18.7%

investment in fixed capital: 19.3%

investment in inventories: 0.3%

exports of goods and services: 32.2%

imports of goods and services: -29.3% (2015 est.)

GDP—composition, by sector of origin:

agriculture: 2.5%

industry: 22.7%

services: 74.8% (2015 est.)

Agriculture—products: grain, vegetables, olives, wine grapes, sugar beets, citrus; beef, pork, poultry, dairy products; fish

Industries: textiles and apparel (including footwear), food and beverages, metals and metal manufactures, chemicals, shipbuilding, automobiles, machine tools, tourism, clay and refractory products, footwear, pharmaceuticals, medical equipment

Industrial production growth rate: 1.5% (2015 est.)

country comparison to the world: 131

Labor force: 22.98 million (2015 est.)

country comparison to the world: 29

Labor force—by occupation: *agriculture:* 2.9%

industry: 15%

services: 58.4% (2014 est.)

Unemployment rate: 22.5% (2015 est.)

24.5% (2014 est.)

country comparison to the world: 173

Population below poverty line: 21.1% (2012 est.)

Household income or consumption by percentage share: *lowest:* 10%: 2.5%

highest: 10%: 24% (2011)

Distribution of family income—Gini index: 35.9 (2012)

32 (2005)

country comparison to the world: 88

Budget: *revenues:* $473.6 billion

expenditures: $527.9 billion (2015 est.)

Taxes and other revenues: 38.8% of GDP (2015 est.)

country comparison to the world: 43

Budget surplus (+) or deficit (–): -4.4% of GDP (2015 est.)

country comparison to the world: 155

Public debt: 101% of GDP (2015 est.)

97.7% of GDP (2014 est.)

country comparison to the world: 17

Fiscal year: calendar year

Inflation rate (consumer prices): -0.5% (2015 est.)

-0.1% (2014 est.)

country comparison to the world: 26

Central bank discount rate: 0.05% (10 September 2014)

0.25% (13 November 2013)

note: this is the European Central Bank's rate on the marginal lending facility, which offers overnight credit to banks in the euro area

country comparison to the world: 152

Commercial bank prime lending rate: 9.1% (31 December 2015 est.)

9.44% (31 December 2014 est.)

country comparison to the world: 93

Stock of narrow money: $778.9 billion (31 December 2015 est.)

$858.2 billion (31 December 2014 est.)

note: see entry for the European Union for money supply for the entire euro area; the European Central Bank (ECB) controls monetary policy for the 18 members of the Economic and Monetary Union (EMU); individual members of the EMU do not control the quantity of money circulating within their own borders

country comparison to the world: 8

Stock of broad money: $1.257 trillion (31 December 2015 est.)

$1.369 trillion (31 December 2014 est.)

country comparison to the world: 15

Stock of domestic credit: $2.428 trillion (31 December 2015 est.)

$2.662 trillion (31 December 2014 est.)

country comparison to the world: 10

Market value of publicly traded shares:

$995.1 billion (31 December 2012 est.)

$1.031 trillion (31 December 2011)

$1.172 trillion (31 December 2010 est.)

country comparison to the world: 16

Current account balance: $16.48 billion (2015 est.)

$13.6 billion (2014 est.)

country comparison to the world: 16

Exports: $277.3 billion (2015 est.) $317.1 billion (2014 est.)

country comparison to the world: 20

Exports—commodities: machinery, motor vehicles; foodstuffs, pharmaceuticals, medicines, other consumer goods

Exports—partners: France 15.7%, Germany 11%, Italy 7.4%, UK 7.4%, Portugal 7.1%, US 4.5% (2015)

Imports: $298.3 billion (2015 est.) $345.6 billion (2014 est.)

country comparison to the world: 15

Imports—commodities: machinery and equipment, fuels, chemicals, semi-finished goods, foodstuffs, consumer goods, measuring and medical control instruments

Imports—partners: Germany 14.4%, France 11.7%, China 7.1%, Italy 6.5%, Netherlands 5%, UK 4.9% (2015)

Reserves of foreign exchange and gold: $50.35 billion (31 December 2014 est.) $46.31 billion (31 December 2013 est.)

country comparison to the world: 39

Debt—external: $2.064 trillion (31 December 2014 est.) $2.238 trillion (31 December 2013 est.)

country comparison to the world: 10

Stock of direct foreign investment—at home: $746.8 billion (31 December 2015 est.) $721.9 billion (31 December 2014 est.)

country comparison to the world: 14

Stock of direct foreign investment—abroad: $707 billion (31 December 2015 est.) $674 billion (31 December 2014 est.)

country comparison to the world: 14

Exchange rates: euros (EU R) per US dollar— 0.885 (2015 est.) 0.7525 (2014 est.) 0.7634 (2013 est.) 0.7752 (2012 est.) 0.7185 (2011 est.)

ENERGY

Electricity—production: 280 billion kWh (2012 est.)

country comparison to the world: 14

Electricity—consumption: 243.1 billion kWh (2012 est.)

country comparison to the world: 15

Electricity—exports: 16.94 billion kWh (2013 est.)

country comparison to the world: 12

Electricity—imports: 10.2 billion kWh (2013 est.)

country comparison to the world: 22

Electricity—installed generating capacity: 102.3 million kW (2014 est.)

country comparison to the world: 12

Electricity—from fossil fuels: 43% of total installed capacity (2014 est.)

country comparison to the world: 161

Electricity—from nuclear fuels: 7.7% of total installed capacity (2014 est.)

country comparison to the world: 22

Electricity—from hydroelectric plants: 19.6% of total installed capacity (2014 est.)

country comparison to the world: 93

Electricity—from other renewable sources: 30% of total installed capacity (2014 est.)

country comparison to the world: 5

Crude oil—production: 6,419 bbl/day (2014 est.)

country comparison to the world: 82

Crude oil—exports: 75,640 bbl/day (2013 est.)

country comparison to the world: 39

Crude oil—imports: 1.224 million bbl/day (2013 est.)

country comparison to the world: 9

Crude oil—proved reserves: 150 million bbl (1 January 2015 est.)

country comparison to the world: 65

Refined petroleum products—production: 1.25 million bbl/day (2013 est.)

country comparison to the world: 19

Refined petroleum products—consumption: 1.209 million bbl/day (2014 est.)

country comparison to the world: 19

Refined petroleum products—exports: 372,200 bbl/day (2013 est.)

country comparison to the world: 20

Refined petroleum products—imports: 285,000 bbl/day (2013 est.)

country comparison to the world: 26

Natural gas—production: 24 million cu m (2014 est.)

country comparison to the world: 86

Natural gas—consumption: 27.16 billion cu m (2014 est.)

country comparison to the world: 31

Natural gas—exports: 8.219 billion cu m (2014 est.)

country comparison to the world: 25

Natural gas—imports: 36.39 billion cu m (2014 est.)

country comparison to the world: 11

Natural gas—proved reserves: 2.548 billion cu m (1 January 2014 est.)

country comparison to the world: 98

Carbon dioxide emissions from consumption of energy: 312.4 million Mt (2012 est.)

country comparison to the world: 20

COMMUNICATIONS

Telephones—fixed lines: *total subscriptions:* 19.09 million

subscriptions per 100 inhabitants: 40 (2014 est.)

country comparison to the world: 16

Telephone—mobile cellular: *total:* 50.8 million subscriptions per 100 inhabitants: 106 (2014 est.)

country comparison to the world: 30

Telephone system: *general assessment:* well-developed, modern facilities; fixed-line teledensity exceeds 40 per 100 persons

domestic: combined fixed-line and mobile-cellular teledensity exceeds 150 telephones per 100 persons

international: country code—34; submarine cables provide connectivity to Europe, Middle East, Asia, and US; satellite earth stations—2 intelsat (1 Atlantic Ocean and 1 Indian Ocean), NA Eutelsat; tropospheric scatter to adjacent countries (2011)

Broadcast media: a mixture of both publicly operated and privately owned TV and radio stations; overall, hundreds of TV channels are available including National, regional, local, public, and International channels; satellite and cable TV systems available; multiple National radio networks, a large number of Regional radio networks, and a larger number of local radio stations; overall, hundreds of radio stations (2008)

Radio broadcast stations: AM 18, FM 250, shortwave 2 (2008)

Television broadcast stations: 379 (2008)

Internet country code: .es

Internet hosts: 4.228 million (2012)

country comparison to the world: 26

Internet users: *total:* 35.5 million

percent of population: 74.4% (2014 est.)

country comparison to the world: 20

TRANSPORTATION

Airports: 150 (2013)

country comparison to the world: 38

Airports—with paved runways: *total:* 99

over 3,047 m: 18

2,438 to 3,047 m: 14

1,524 to 2,437 m: 19

914 to 1,523 m: 24

under 914 m: 24 (2013)

Airports—with unpaved runways: *total:* 51

1,524 to 2,437 m: 2

914 to 1,523 m: 13

under 914 m: 36 (2013)

Heliports: 10 (2013)

Pipelines: gas 10,481 km; oil 616 km; refined products 3,461 km (2013)

Railways: *total:* 16,101.5 km

broad gauge: 11,873 km 1.668-m gauge (6,488 km electrified) standard gauge: 2,312 km 1.435-m gauge (2,312 km electrified)

narrow gauge: 1,884.9 km 1.000-m gauge (807 km electrified); 28 km 0.914-m gauge (28 km electrified); 3.6 km 0.600-m gauge (2014)

country comparison to the world: 17

Roadways: *total:* 683,175 km

paved: 683,175 km (includes 16,205 km of expressways) (2011)

country comparison to the world: 11

Waterways: 1,000 km (2012)

country comparison to the world: 63

Merchant marine: *total:* 132

by type: bulk carrier 7, cargo 19, chemical tanker 8, container 5, liquefied gas 12, passenger/cargo 43, petroleum tanker 18, refrigerated cargo 4, roll on/roll off 9, vehicle carrier 7

foreign-owned: 27 (Canada 4, Germany 4, Italy 1, Mexico 1, Norway 10, Russia 6, Switzerland 1)

registered in other countries: 103 (Angola 1, Argentina 3, Bahamas 6, Brazil 12, Cabo Verde 1, Cyprus 6, Ireland 1, Malta 8, Morocco 9, Panama 30, Peru 1, Portugal 18, Uruguay 5, Venezuela 1, unknown 1) (2010)

country comparison to the world: 44

Ports and terminals: *major seaport(s):* Algeciras, Barcelon a, Bilbao, Cartagena, Huelva, Tarragon a, Valencia (all in Spain); Las Palmas, Santa Cruz de Tenerife (in the Canary Islands)

container port(s) (TEUs): Algeciras (3,608,301), Barcelon a (2,033,747), Valencia (4,327,371); Las Palmas (1,287,389)

LNG terminal(s) (import): Barcelon a, Bilbao, Cartagena, Huelva, Mugardos, Sagunto

MILITARY AND SECURITY

Military branches: Spanish Armed Forces: Army (Ejercito de Tierra), Spanish Navy (Armada

Espanola, AE; includes Marine Corps), Spanish Air Force (Ejercito del Aire Espanola, EdA) (2013)

Military service age and obligation: 18–26 years of age for voluntary military service by a Spanish citizen or legal immigrant, 2–3 year obligation; women allowed to serve in all SAF branches, including combat units; no conscription, but Spanish Government retains right to mobilize citizens 19–25 years of age in a National emergency; mandatory retirement of non-NCO enlisted personnel at age 45 or 58, depending on service length (2013)

Military expenditures: 0.86% of GDP (2012)
0.95% of GDP (2011)
0.86% of GDP (2010)
country comparison to the world: 110

TRANSNATIONAL ISSUES

Disputes—International: in 2002, Gibraltar residents voted overwhelmingly by referendum to reject any "shared sovereignty" arrangement; the Government of Gibraltar insists on equal participation in talks between the UK and Spain; Spain disapproves of UK plans to grant Gibraltar greater autonomy; Morocco protests Spain's control over the coastal enclaves of Ceuta, Melilla, and the islands of Penon de Velez de la Gomera, Penon de Alhucemas, and Islas Chafarinas, and surrounding waters; both countries claim Isla Perejil (Leila Island); Morocco serves as the primary launching site of illegal migration into Spain from North Africa; Portugal does not recognize Spanish sovereignty over the territory of Olivenza based on a difference of interpretation of the 1815 Congress of Vienna and the 1801 Treaty of Badajoz

Refugees and internally displaced persons: *stateless persons:* 440 (2015)

Illicit drugs: despite rigorous law enforcement efforts, North African, Latin American, Galician, and other European traffickers take advantage of Spain's long coastline to land large shipments of cocaine and hashish for distribution to the European market; consumer for Latin american cocaine and North African hashish; destination and minor transshipment point for Southwest Asian heroin; money-laundering site for Colombian narcotics trafficking organizations and organized crime

SPRATLY ISLANDS

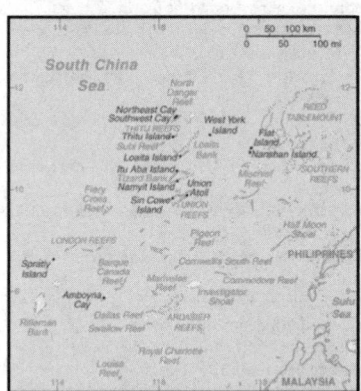

INTRODUCTION

Background: The Spratly Islands consist of more than 100 small islands or reefs surrounded by rich fishing grounds -and potentially by gas and oil deposits. They are claimed in their entirety by China, Taiwan, and Vietnam, while portions are claimed by Malaysia and the Philippines. About 45 islands are occupied by relatively small numbers of military forces from China, Malaysia, the Philippines, Taiwan, and Vietnam. Since 1985 Brunei has claimed a continental shelf that overlaps a southern reef but has not made any formal claim to the reef. Brunei claims an exclusive economic zone over this area.

GEOGRAPHY

Location: Southeastern Asia, group of reefs and islands in the South China Sea, about two-thirds of the way from southern Vietnam to the southern Philippines

Geographic coordinates: 8 38 N, 11155 E

Map references: Southeast Asia

Area: *total:* less than 5 sq km
land: less than 5 sq km
water: 0 sq km
note: includes 100 or so islets, coral reefs, and sea mounts scattered over an Area of nearly 410,000 sq km (158,000 sq mi) of the central South China Sea

country comparison to the world: 249

Area—comparative: land area is about seven times the size of the National Mall in Washington, DC

Land boundaries: 0 km

Coastline: 926 km

Maritime claims: NA

Climate: tropical

Terrain: flat

Elevation: *mean elevation:* NA

elevation extremes: *lowest point:* South China Sea 0 m

highest point: unnamed location on Southwest Cay 4 m

Natural resources: fish, guano, undetermined oil and Natural gas potential

Land use: *agricultural land:* 0%
arable land: 0%
permanent crops: 0%
permanent pasture: 0%
forest: 0%
other: 100% (2011 est.)

Natural hazards: typhoons; numerous reefs and shoals pose a serious maritime hazard

Environment—current issues: NA

Geography—note: strategically located near several primary shipping lanes in the central South China Sea; includes numerous small islands, atolls, shoals, and coral reefs

PEOPLE AND SOCIETY

Population: no indigenous inhabitants
note: there are scattered garrisons occupied by military personnel of several claimant states

GOVERNMENT

Country name: *conventional long form:* none
conventional short form: Spratly Islands
etymology: named after a British whaling captain Richard SPRATLY, who sighted Spratly Island in 1843; the name of the island eventually passed to the entire archipelago

ECONOMY

Economy—overview: Economic activity is limited to commercial fishing. The proximity to nearby oil- and gas-producing sedimentary basins indicate potential oil and gas deposits, but the region is largely unexplored. No reliable estimates of potential reserves are available. Commercial exploitation has yet to be developed.

TRANSPORTATION

Airports: 4 (2013)
country comparison to the world: 189

Airports—with paved runways: *total:* 3
914 to 1,523 m: 2
under 914 m: 1 (2013)

Airports—with unpaved runways: *total:* 1
914 to 1,523 m: 1 (2013)

Heliports: 3 (2013)

Ports and terminals: None; offshore anchor age only

MILITARY AND SECURITY

Military—note: Spratly Islands consist of more than 100 small islands or reefs of which about 45 are claimed and occupied by China, Malaysia, the Philippines, Taiwan, and Vietnam

TRANSNATIONAL ISSUES

Disputes—International: all of the Spratly Islands are claimed by China (including Taiwan) and Vietnam; parts of them are claimed by Brunei, Malaysia and the Philippines; despite no public territorial claim to Louisa Reef, Brunei implicitly lays claim by including it within the Natural prolongation of its continental shelf and basis for a seabed median with Vietnam; claimants in November 2002 signed the "Declaration on the Conduct of Parties in the South China Sea," which has eased tensions but falls short of a legally Binding "code of conduct"; in March 2005, the National oil companies of China, the Philippines, and Vietnam signed a joint accord to conduct marine seismic activities in the Spratly Islands

795

SRI LANKA

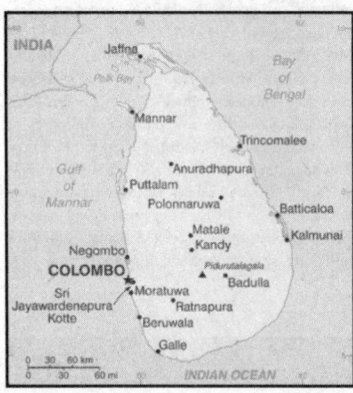

INTRODUCTION

Background: The first Sinhalese arrived in Sri Lanka late in the 6th century B.C., probably from northern India. Buddhism was introduced circa 250 B.C., and a great civilization developed at the cities of Anuradhapura (kingdom from circa 200 B.C. to circa A.D. 1000) and Polonnaruwa (from about 1070 to 1200). In the 14th century, a south Indian dynasty established a Tamil kingdom in northern Sri Lanka. The Portuguese controlled the coastal areas of the island in the 16th century and the Dutch in the 17th century. The island was ceded to the British in 1796, became a crown colony in 1802, and was formally united under British rule by 1815. As Ceylon, it became independent in 1948; its name was changed to Sri Lanka in 1972. Tensions between the Sinhalese majority and Tamil separatists erupted into war in 1983. After two decades of fighting, the government and Liberation Tigers of Tamil Eelam (LTTE) formalized a cease-fire in February 2002 with Norway brokering peace negotiations. Violence between the LTTE and government forces intensified in 2006, but the government regained control of the Eastern Province in 2007 and by May 2009, the remnants of the LTTE had been defeated. Since the end of the conflict, the government has enacted an Ambitious program of economic development projects, many of which are financed by loans from the Government of China. In addition to efforts at reconstructing its economy, the government has resettled more than 95% of those civilians displaced during the final phase of the conflict and released the vast majority of former LTTE combatants captured by Government Security Forces. At the same time, there has been little progress on more contentious and politically difficult issues such as reaching a political settlement with Tamil elected representatives and holding accountable those alleged to have been involved in human rights violations and other abuses during the conflict.

GEOGRAPHY

Location: Southern Asia, island in the Indian Ocean, south of India

Geographic coordinates: 700 N, 8100 E

Map references: Asia

Area: *total:* 65,610 sq km
land: 64,630 sq km
water: 980 sq km
country comparison to the world: 122

Area—comparative: slightly larger than West Virginia

Land boundaries: 0 km

Coastline: 1,340 km

Maritime claims: *territorial sea:* 12 nm
contiguous zone: 24 nm
exclusive economic zone: 200 nm
continental shelf: 200 nm or to the edge of the continental margin

Climate: tropical monsoon; northeast monsoon (December to March); southwest monsoon (June to October)

Terrain: mostly low, flat to rolling plain; mountains in south-central interior

Elevation: *mean elevation:* 228 m

elevation extremes: *lowest point:* Indian Ocean 0 m
highest point: Pidurutalagala 2,524 m

Natural resources: limestone, graphite, mineral sands, gem s, phosphates, clay, hydropower, arable land

Land use: *agricultural land:* 43.5%
arable land: 20.7%
permanent crops: 15.8%
permanent pasture: 7%
forest: 29.4%
other: 27.1% (2011 est.)

Irrigated land: 5,700 sq km (2012)

Total renewable water resources: 52.8 cu km (2011)

Freshwater withdrawal (domestic/industrial/agricultural): *total:* 12.95 cu km/yr (6%/6%/87%)
per capita: 638.8 cu m/yr (2005)

Natural hazards: occasional cyclones and tornadoes

Environment—current issues: deforestation; soil erosion; wildlife populations threatened by poaching and urbanization; coastal degradation from mining activities and increased pollution; freshwater resources being polluted by industrial wastes and sewage runoff; waste disposal; air pollution in Colombo

Environment—International agreements: *party to:* Biodiversity, Climate Change, Climate Change-Kyoto Protocol, Desertification, Endangered Species, Environmental Modification, Hazardous Wastes, Law of the Sea, Ozone Layer Protection, Ship Pollution, Wetlands
signed, but not ratified: Marine Life Conservation

Geography—note: strategic location near major Indian Ocean sea lanes

PEOPLE AND SOCIETY

Nationality: *noun:* Sri Lankan(s)
adjective: Sri Lankan

Ethnic groups: Sinhalese 74.9%, Sri Lankan Tamil 11.2%, Sri Lankan Moors 9.2%, Indian Tamil 4.2%, other 0.5% (2012 est.)

Languages: Sinhala (official and National language) 74%, Tamil (National language) 18%, other 8%
note: English, spoken competently by about 10% of the population, is commonly used in government and is referred to as the link language in the constitution

Religions: Buddhist (official) 70.2%, Hindu 12.6%, Muslim 9.7%, Roman Catholic 6.1%, other Christian 1.3%, other 0.05% (2012 est.)

Population: 22,053,488 (July 2015 est.)
country comparison to the world: 57

Age structure: *0–14 years:* 24.58% (male 2,764,848/female 2,655,218)
15–24 years: 14.77% (male 1,652,884/female 1,604,089)
25–54 years: 41.9% (male 4,523,146/female 4,718,156)
55–64 years: 9.72% (male 992,750/female 1,149,828)
65 years and over: 9.04% (male 847,805/female 1,144,764) (2015 est.)

Dependency ratios: *total dependency ratio:* 51.2%
youth dependency ratio: 37.2%
elderly dependency ratio: 14.1%
potential support ratio: 7.1% (2015 est.)

Median age: *total:* 32.1 years
male: 30.9 years
female: 33.3 years (2015 est.)
country comparison to the world: 94

Population growth rate: 0.84% (2015 est.)
country comparison to the world: 131

Birth rate: 15.85 births/1,000 population (2015 est.)
country comparison to the world: 124

Death rate: 6.11 deaths/1,000 population (2015 est.)
country comparison to the world: 159

Net migration rate: -1.35 migrant(s)/1,000 population (2015 est.)
country comparison to the world: 154

Urbanization: *urban population:* 18.4% of total population (2015)
rate of urbanization: 0.72% annual rate of change (2010–15 est.)

Major urban areas—population: Sri Jayewardenepura Kotte (legislative capital) 128,000 (2014); COLOMBO (capital) 707,000 (2015)

Sex ratio: *at birth:* 1.04 male(s)/female
0–14 years: 1.04 male(s)/female
15–24 years: 1.03 male(s)/female
25–54 years: 0.96 male(s)/female
55–64 years: 0.86 male(s)/female
65 years and over: 0.74 male(s)/female

total population: 0.96 male(s)/female (2015 est.)
Mother's mean age at first birth: 25.4
note: Median Age at first birth among women 30–34 (2006/07 est.)
Maternal mortality rate: 30 deaths/100,000 live births (2015 est.)
country comparison to the world: 118
Infant mortality rate: *total:* 8.8 deaths/1,000 live births
male: 9.75 deaths/1,000 live births
female: 7.82 deaths/1,000 live births (2015 est.)
country comparison to the world: 146
Life expectancy at birth: *total population:* 76.56 years
male: 73.06 years
female: 80.19 years (2015 est.)
country comparison to the world: 84
Total fertility rate: 2.1 children born/woman (2015 est.)
country comparison to the world: 106
Contraceptive prevalence rate: 68.4% (2006/07)
Health expenditures: 3.2% of GDP (2013)
country comparison to the world: 177
Physicians density: 0.68 physicians/1,000 population (2010)
Hospital bed density: 3.6 beds/1,000 population (2012)
Drinking water source:
improved:
urban: 98.5% of population
rural: 95% of population
total: 95.6% of population
unimproved:
urban: 1.5% of population
rural: 5% of population
total: 4.4% of population (2015 est.)
Sanitation facility access:
improved:
urban: 88.1% of population
rural: 96.7% of population
total: 95.1% of population
unimproved:
urban: 11.9% of population
rural: 3.3% of population
total: 4.9% of population (2015 est.)
HIV/AIDS—adult prevalence rate: 0.03% (2014 est.)
country comparison to the world: 127
HIV/AIDS—people living with HIV/AIDS: 3,300 (2014 est.)
country comparison to the world: 113
HIV/AIDS—deaths: 100 (2014 est.)
country comparison to the world: 127
Major infectious diseases: *degree of risk:* high
food or waterborne diseases: bacterial diarrhea and hepatitis A
vectorborne disease: dengue fever
water contact disease: leptospirosis animal contact disease: rabies (2013)
Obesity—adult prevalence rate: 6.8% (2014)
country comparison to the world: 155
Children under the age of 5 years underweight: 26.3% (2012)
country comparison to the world: 23
Education expenditures: 1.6% of GDP (2013)
country comparison to the world: 168

Literacy: *definition:* age 15 and over can read and write
total population: 92.6%
male: 93.6%
female: 91.7% (2015 est.)
School life expectancy (primary to tertiary education): *total:* 14 years
male: 14 years
female: 14 years (2013)
Unemployment, youth ages 15–24: *total:* 20.1%
male: 15%
female: 27.8% (2013 est.)
country comparison to the world: 69

GOVERNMENT

Country name: *conventional long form:* Democratic Socialist Republic of Sri Lanka
conventional short form: Sri Lanka
local long form: Shri Lanka Prajatantrika Samajavadi Janarajaya/Ilankai Jananayaka Choshalichak Kutiyarachu
local short form: Shri Lanka/Ilankai
former: Serendib, Ceylon
note: the name means "resplendent island" in Sanskrit
Government type: presidential republic
Capital: *name:* Colombo; note—Sri Jayewardenepura Kotte is the legislative capital
Geographic coordinates: 6 55 N, 79 50 E
time difference: UTC+5.5 (10.5 hours ahead of Washington, DC, during Standard Time)
Administrative divisions: 9 provinces; Central, Eastern, North Central, Northern, North Western, Sabaragamuwa, Southern, Uva, Western
Independence: 4 February 1948 (from the UK)
National holiday: Independence Day, 4 February (1948)
Constitution: several previous; latest adopted 16 August 1978, certified 31 August 1978; amended many times, last in 2015 (2016)
Legal system: mixed legal system of Roman-Dutch civil law, English common law, and Jaffna Tamil customary law
International law organization participation: has not submitted an ICJ jurisdiction declaration; non-party state to the ICCt
Citizenship: *citizenship by birth:* no
citizenship by descent only: at least one parent must be a citizen of Sri Lanka
dual citizenship recognized: no, except in cases where the government rules it is to the benefit of Sri Lanka
residency requirement for naturalization: 7 years
Suffrage: 18 years of age; universal
Executive branch: *chief of state:* President Maithripala SIRISENA (since 9 January 2015); note—the president is both chief of state and head of government; Ranil WICKREMESINGHE (since 9 January 2015) holds the title of prime minister
head of government: President Maithripala SIRISENA (since 9 January 2015)
cabinet: Cabinet appointed by the president in consultation with the prime minister
elections/appointments: president directly elected by preferential majority popular vote for a

6-year term (eligible for a second term); election last held on 8 January 2015 (next to be held by January 2021); note—the January 2015 election was held nearly 2 years ahead of schedule
election results: Maithripala SIRISENA elected president; percent of vote—Maithripala SIRISENA (Sri Lanka Freedom Party) 51.3%, Mahinda Percy RAJAPAKSA (Sri Lanka Freedom Party) 47.6%, other 1.1%
Legislative branch: *description:* unicameral Parliament (225 seats; 196 members directly elected in multi-seat constituencies by proportional representation vote using a preferential method in which voters select 3 candidates in order of preference; remaining 29 seats allocated to other political parties and groups in proportion to share of National vote; members serve 6-year terms)
elections: last held on 17 August 2015 following President SIRISENA's dissolution of Parliament in late June in an effort to consolidate power and pass reforms (next to be held in 2021)
election results: percent of vote by alliance/party—EYJP 45.7%, UPFA 42.4%, JVP 4.9%, TNA 4.6%, SLMC 0.4%, EPDP 0.3% other 1.7%; seats by alliance/party EYJP 106, UPFA 95, TNA 16, JVP 6, SLMC 1, EPDP 1
Judicial branch: *highest court(s):* Supreme Court of the Republic (consists of the chief justice and 10 justices);
note—the court has exclusive jurisdiction to review legislation
judge selection and term of office: the chief justice appointed by the president; the other justices appointed by the president with the advice of the chief justice; all justices hold office until age 65
subordinate courts: Court of Appeals; High Courts; Magistrate's Courts; municipal and primary courts
Political parties and leaders: Eelam People's Democratic Party or EPDP
Janatha Vimukthi Peramuna or JVP [Anura Kumara DISSANAYAKE]
Jathika Hela Urumaya or JHU [Patali Champika RANAWAKA]
Sri Lanka Freedom Party or SLFP [Maithripala SIRISENA]
Sri Lanka Muslim Congress or SLMC [Rauff HAKEEM]
Tamil National Alliance or TNA [R. SAMPANTHAN]
United National Front for Good Governance or EYJP (coalition includes UNP)
United National Party or UNP [Ranil WICKREMESIN GH E]
United People's Freedom Alliance or UPFA (coalition includes SLFP)
Political pressure groups and leaders: Buddhist clergy Sinhalese Buddhist lay groups
other: labor unions; hard-line Nationalist Sinhalese groups such as the National Movement Against Terrorism
International organization participation: ABEDA, ADB, ARF, BIMSTEC, C, CD, CICA (observer), CP, FAO, G-11, G-15, G-24, G-77, IAEA, IBRD, ICAO, ICC (National committees), ICRM, IDA, IFAD, IFC, IFRCS, IHO, ILO, IMF, IMO, IMSO,

Interpol, IOC, IOM, IPU, ISO, ITSO, ITU, ITUC (NGOs), MIGA, MINURSO, MINUSTAH, MONUSCO, NAM, OAS (observer), OPCW, PCA, SAARC, SACEP, SCO (dialogue member), UN, UNCTAD, UNESCO, UNIDO, UNIFIL, UNISFA, UNMISS, UNWTO, UPU, WCO, WFTU (NGOs), WHO, WIPO, WMO, WTO

Diplomatic representation in the US: *chief of mission:* Ambassador Prasad KARIYAWASAM (since 14 July 2014)

chancery: 2148 Wyoming Avenue NW, Washington, DC 20008

telephone: [1] (202) 483-4025 through 4028

FAX: [1] (202) 232-7181

consulate(s) general: Los Angeles, New York

Diplomatic representation from the US: *chief of mission:* Ambassador Atul KESHAP (since 21 August 2015); note—also accredited to Maldives

embassy: 210 Galle Road, Colombo 3

mailing address: P.O. Box 106, Colombo

telephone: [94] (11) 249-8500

FAX: [94] (11) 243-7345

Flag description: yellow with two panels; the smaller hoist-side panel has two equal vertical bands of green (hoist side) and orange; the other larger panel depicts a yellow lion holding a sword on a maroon rectangular field that also displays a yellow bo leaf in each corner; the yellow field appears as a border around the entire flag and extends between the two panels; the lion represents Sinhalese ethnicity, the strength of the nation, and bravery; the sword demonstrates the sovereignty of the nation; the four boleaves—symbolizing Buddhism and its influence on the country—stand for the four virtues of kindness, friendliness, happiness, and equanimity; orange signifies Sri Lankan Tamils, green Sri Lankan Moors, and maroon the Sinhalese majority; yellow denotes other Ethnic groups; also referred to as the Lion Flag

National symbol(s): lion, water lily; National colors: maroon, yellow

National anthem: *name:* "Sri Lanka Matha" (Mother Sri Lanka)

lyrics/music: Ananda SAMARKONE

note: adopted 1951

ECONOMY

Economy—overview: Sri Lanka continues to experience strong economic growth following the end of the government's 26-year conflict with the Liberation Tigers of Tamil Eelam. The government has been pursuing large-scale reconstruction and development projects in its efforts to spur growth in war-torn and disadvantaged areas, develop small and medium enterprises, and increase agricultural productivity.

The government's high debt payments and bloated civil service have contributed to historically high budget deficits and low tax revenues remain a concern. Government debt of about 72% of GDP remains among the highest in emerging markets. The new government in 2015 drastically increased wages for public sector employees, which boosted demand for consumer goods but hurt the overall balance of payments and reduced foreign exchange reserves.

GDP (purchasing power parity): $223 billion (2015 est.)

$212 billion (2014 est.)

$203 billion (2013 est.)

note: data are in 2015 US dollars

country comparison to the world: 63

GDP (official exchange rate): $82.1 billion (2015 est.)

GDP—real growth rate: 5.2% (2015 est.)

4.5% (2014 est.)

3.4% (2013 est.)

country comparison to the world: 38

GDP—per capita (PPP): $10,600 (2015 est.)

$10,100 (2014 est.)

$9,700 (2013 est.)

note: data are in 2015 US dollars

country comparison to the world: 135

Gross National saving: 25.8% of GDP (2015 est.)

24.7% of GDP (2014 est.)

26.1% of GDP (2013 est.)

country comparison to the world: 45

GDP—composition, by end use:

household consumption: 67.6%

government consumption: 13.5%

investment in fixed capital: 28.4%

investment in inventories: -0.9%

exports of goods and services: 21.2%

imports of goods and services: -29.8% (2015 est.)

GDP—composition, by sector of origin:

agriculture: 8.1%

industry: 29.1%

services: 62.8% (2015 est.)

Agriculture—products: rice, sugarcane, grains, pulses, oilseed, spices, vegetables, fruit, tea, rubber, coconuts; milk, eggs, hides, beef; fish

Industries: processing of rubber, tea, coconuts, tobacco and other agricultural commodities; telecommunications, insurance, banking; tourism, shipping; clothing, textiles; cement, petroleum refining, information technology services, construction

Industrial production growth rate: 2.7% (2015 est.)

country comparison to the world: 96

Labor force: 8.928 million (2015 est.)

country comparison to the world: 56

Labor force—by occupation: *agriculture:* 28.4%

industry: 25.7%

services: 45.9% (30 Jun 2015)

Unemployment rate: 4.2% (2015 est.)

4.3% (2014 est.)

country comparison to the world: 39

Population below poverty line: 8.9% (2010 est.)

Household income or consumption by percentage share: *lowest:* 10%: 1.6%

highest: 10%: 39.5% (2009)

Distribution of family income—Gini index: 49 (2010) 46 (1995)

country comparison to the world: 23

Budget: *revenues:* $9.785 billion

expenditures: $15.38 billion (2015 est.)

Taxes and other revenues: 12.3% of GDP (2015 est.)

country comparison to the world: 206

Budget surplus (+) or deficit (–): -7% of GDP (2015 est.)

country comparison to the world: 191

Public debt: 74.7% of GDP (2015 est.)

71.8% of GDP (2014 est.)

note: covers central government debt, and excludes debt instruments directly owned by government entities other than the treasury (e.g. commercial bank borrowings of a government corporation); the data includes treasury debt held by foreign entities as well as intra-governmental debt; intra-governmental debt consists of treasury borrowings from surpluses in the social funds, such as for retirement; sub-national entities are usually not permitted to sell debt instruments

country comparison to the world: 38

Fiscal year: calendar year

Inflation rate (consumer prices): 0.9% (2015 est.)

3.3% (2014 est.)

country comparison to the world: 75

Central bank discount rate: 6% (31 December 2015) 6.5% (31 December 2013)

country comparison to the world: 66

Commercial bank prime lending rate: 7.4% (31 December 2015 est.)

7.84% (31 December 2014 est.)

country comparison to the world: 117

Stock of narrow money: $5.007 billion (31 December 2015 est.)

$4.591 billion (31 December 2014 est.)

country comparison to the world: 99

Stock of broad money: $26.79 billion (31 December 2015 est.)

$25.95 billion (31 December 2014 est.)

country comparison to the world: 79

Stock of domestic credit: $35.91 billion (31 December 2015 est.)

$33.21 billion (31 December 2014 est.)

country comparison to the world: 69

Market value of publicly traded shares: $18.48 billion (31 November 2013 est.)

$17.05 billion (31 December 2012)

$19.44 billion (31 Decem ber 2011 est.)

country comparison to the world: 67

Current account balance: -$1.681 billion (2015 est.)

-$2.018 billion (2014 est.)

country comparison to the world: 141

Exports: $11.28 billion (2015 est.)

$11.13 billion (2014 est.)

country comparison to the world: 85

Exports—commodities: textiles and apparel, tea and spices; rubber manufactures; precious stones; coconut products, fish

Exports—partners: US 26.1%, UK 9%, India 7.2%, Germany 4.3% (2015)

Imports: $20.14 billion (2015 est.)

$19.42 billion (2014 est.)

country comparison to the world: 74

Imports—commodities: petroleum, textiles, machinery and transportation equipment, building materials, mineral products, food stuffs

Imports—partners: India 24.6%, China 20.6%, UAE 7.1%, Singapore 5.9%, Japan 5.7% (2015)

Reserves of foreign exchange and gold: $7.065 billion (31 December 2015 est.)

$8.209 billion (31 December 2014 est.)

country comparison to the world: 87

Debt—external: $45 billion (31 December 2015 est.)

$42 billion (31 December 2014 est.)

country comparison to the world: 65

Stock of direct foreign investment—at home: $NA

Stock of direct foreign investment—abroad: $NA

Exchange rates: Sri Lankan rupees (LKR) per US dollar—

140 (2015 est.)

130.57 (2014 est.)
130.57 (2013 est.)
127.6 (2012 est.)
110.57 (2011 est.)

ENERGY

Electricity—production: 11.36 billion kWh (2012 est.)
country comparison to the world: 94
Electricity—consumption: 10.17 billion kWh (2012 est.)
country comparison to the world: 89
Electricity—exports: 0 kWh (2013 est.)
country comparison to the world: 118
Electricity—imports: 0 kWh (2013 est.)
country comparison to the world: 129
Electricity—installed generating capacity: 3.373 million kW (2012 est.)
country comparison to the world: 89
Electricity—from fossil fuels: 51.1% of total installed capacity (2012 est.)
country comparison to the world: 147
Electricity—from nuclear fuels: 0% of total installed capacity (2012 est.)
country comparison to the world: 64
Electricity—from hydroelectric plants: 47% of total installed capacity (2012 est.)
country comparison to the world: 52
Electricity—from other renewable sources: 1.9% of total installed capacity (2012 est.)
country comparison to the world: 81
Crude oil—production: 0 bbl/day (2014 est.)
country comparison to the world: 117
Crude oil—exports: 0 bbl/day (2012 est.)
country comparison to the world: 108
Crude oil—imports: 32,520 bbl/day (2012 est.)
country comparison to the world: 59
Crude oil—proved reserves: 0 bbl (1 January 2015 est.)
country comparison to the world: 116
Refined petroleum products—production: 31,150 bbl/day (2012 est.)
country comparison to the world: 86
Refined petroleum products—consumption: 108,000 bbl/day (2013 est.)
country comparison to the world: 77
Refined petroleum products—exports: 0 bbl/day (2012 est.)
country comparison to the world: 166
Refined petroleum products—imports: 72,790 bbl/day (2012 est.)
country comparison to the world: 62
Natural gas—production: 0 cu m (2013 est.)
country comparison to the world: 169
Natural gas—consumption: 0 cu m (2013 est.)
country comparison to the world: 128
Natural gas—exports: 0 cu m (2013 est.)
country comparison to the world: 76
Natural gas—imports: 0 cu m (2013 est.)
country comparison to the world: 175
Natural gas—proved reserves: 0 cu m (1 January 2014 est.)
country comparison to the world: 123
Carbon dioxide emissions from consumption of energy: 15.23 million Mt (2012 est.)
country comparison to the world: 91

COMMUNICATIONS

Telephone—fixed lines: *total subscriptions:* 2.7 million
subscriptions per 100 inhabitants: 12 (2014 est.)
country comparison to the world: 52
Telephones—mobile cellular: *total:* 22.1 million
subscriptions per 100 inhabitants: 101 (2014 est.)
country comparison to the world: 55
Telephone system: *general assessment:* telephone services have improved significantly and are available in most parts of the country
domestic: national trunk network consists mostly of digital microwave radio relay; fiber-optic links now in use in Colombo area and fixed wireless local loops have been installed; competition is strong in mobile cellular systems and mobile cellular subscribership is increasing
international: country code—94; the SEA-ME-WE-3 and SEA-ME-WE-4 submarine cables provide connectivity to Asia, Australia, Middle East, Europe, US; satellite earth stations—2 intelsat (Indian Ocean) (2011)
Broadcast media: government operates 8 TV channels and a radio network; multi-channel satellite and cable TV subscription services available; 35 private TV stations and about 50 radio stations (2012)
Radio broadcast stations: AM 15, FM 52, shortwave 4 (2007)
Television broadcast stations: 12 (2009)
Internet country code: .lk
Internet hosts: 9,552 (2012)
country comparison to the world: 136
Internet users: *total:* 4.4 million
percent of population: 19.9% (2014 est.)
country comparison to the world: 74

TRANSPORTATION

19 (2013)
country comparison to the world: 137
Airports—with paved runways: *total:* 15
over 3,047 m: 2
1,524 to 2,437 m: 6
914 to 1,523 m: 7 (2013)
Airports—with unpaved runways: *total:* 4
914 to 1,523 m: 1
under 914 m: 3 (2013)
Heliports: 1 (2013)
Railways: *total:* 1,447 km
broad gauge: 1,447 km 1.676-m gauge (2014)
country comparison to the world: 79
Roadways: *total:* 114,093 km
paved: 16,977 km
unpaved: 97,116 km (2010)
country comparison to the world: 41
Waterways: 160 km (primarily on rivers in southwest) (2012)
country comparison to the world: 100
Merchant marine: *total:* 21
by type: bulk carrier 4, cargo 13, chemical tanker 1, container 1, petroleum tanker 2
foreign-owned: 8 (Germany 8) (2010)
country comparison to the world: 94
Ports and terminals: *major seaport(s):* Colombo

container port(s) (TEUs): Colombo (3,651,963)

MILITARY AND SECURITY

Military branches: Sri Lanka Army, Sri Lanka Navy, Sri Lanka Air Force, Sri Lanka Coast Guard (2015)
Military service age and obligation: 18–22 years of age for voluntary military service; no conscription; 5-year service obligation (Air Force) (2012)
Military expenditures: 2.43% of GDP (2012)
2.89% of GDP (2011)
2.43% of GDP (2010)
country comparison to the world: 29

TRANSNATIONAL ISSUES

Disputes—International: none
Refugees and internally displaced persons: *IDPs:* 44,934 (civil war; more than half displaced prior to 2008; many of the more than 480,000 IDPs registered as returnees have not reached durable solutions) (2015)
Trafficking in persons: *current situation:* Sri Lanka is primarily a source and, to a lesser extent, a destination country for men, women, and children subjected to forced labor and sex trafficking; some Sri Lankan adults and children who migrate willingly to the Middle East, Southeast Asia, and Afghanistan to work in the construction, garment, and domestic service sectors are subsequently subjected to forced labor or debt bondage (incurred through high recruitment fees or money advances); some Sri Lankan women are forced into prostitution in Jordan, Maldives, Malaysia, Singapore, and other countries; within Sri Lanka, women and children are subjected to sex trafficking, and children are also forced to beg and work in the agriculture, fireworks, and fish-drying industries; a small number of women from Asia, Central Asia, Europe, and the Middle East have been forced into prostitution in Sri Lanka in recent years
tier rating: Tier 2 Watch List—Sri Lanka does not fully comply with the minimum standards for the elimination of trafficking; however, it is making significant efforts to do so; in 2014, Sri Lanka was granted a waiver from an otherwise required downgrade to Tier 3 because its government has a written plan that, if implemented, would constitute making significant efforts to bring itself into compliance with the minimum standards for the elimination of trafficking; law enforcement continues to demonstrate a lack of understanding of trafficking crimes and inadequate investigations, relying on trafficking cases to be prosecuted under the procurement statute rather than the trafficking statute, which carries more stringent penalties; authorities convicted only one offender under the procurement statue, a decrease from 2013; the government approved guidelines for the identification of victims and their referral to protective services but failed to ensure that victims were not jailed and charged for crimes committed as a direct result of being trafficked; no government employees were investigated or prosecuted, despite allegations of complicity (2015)

799

SUDAN

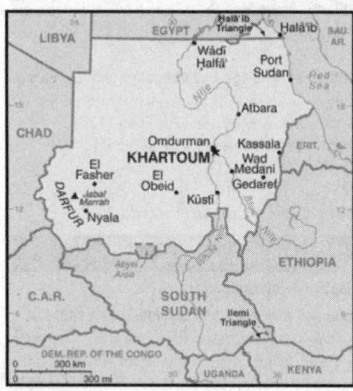

INTRODUCTION

Background: Military regimes favoring Islamic-oriented governments have dominated National politics since independence from Anglo-Egyptian co-rule in 1956. Sudan was embroiled in two prolonged civil wars during most of the remainder of the 20th century. These conflicts were rooted in northern economic, political, and social domination of largely non-Muslim, non-Arab southern Sudanese. The first civil war ended in 1972 but another broke out in 1983. Peace talks gained momentum in 2002–04 with the signing of several accords. The final North/South Comprehensive Peace Agreement (CPA), signed in January 2005, granted the southern rebels autonomy for six years followed by a referendum on independence for Southern Sudan. The referendum was held in January 2011 and indicated overwhelming support for independence. South Sudan became independent on 9 July 2011. Sudan and South Sudan have yet to fully implement security and economic agreements signed in September 2012 relating to the normalization of relations between the two countries. The final disposition of the contested Abyei region has also to be decided.

Since South Sudan's independence, conflict has broken out between the government and the Sudan People's Liberation Movement-North in Southern Kordofan and Blue Nile states, which has resulted in 1.2 million internally displaced persons or severely affected persons needing humanitarian Assistance. A separate conflict, which broke out in the western region of Darfur in 2003, displaced nearly two million people and caused an estimated 200,000 to 400,000 deaths. Violence in Darfur in 2013 resulted in an Additional estimated 6,000 civilians killed and 500,000 displaced. The UN and the African Union have jointly commanded a Darfur peacekeeping operation known as the African Union-United Nations Hybrid Mission in Darfur (UNAMID) since 2007. Peacekeeping troops have struggled to stabilize the situation and have increasingly become targets

for attacks by armed groups. Sudan also has faced refugee influxes from neighboring countries, primarily Ethiopia, Eritrea, Chad, Central African Republic, and South Sudan. Armed conflict, poor transport infrastructure, and government denial of access have impeded the provision of humanitarian Assistance to affected populations.

GEOGRAPHY

Location: north-eastern Africa, bordering the Red Sea, between Egypt and Eritrea

Geographic coordinates: 15 00 N, 30 00 E

Map references: Africa

Area: *total:* 1,861,484 sq km

land: NA

water: NA

country comparison to the world: 16

Area—comparative: slightly less than one-fifth the size of the US

Land boundaries: *total:* 6,819 km

border countries (7): Central African Republic 174 km, Chad 1,403 km, Egypt 1,276 km, Eritrea 682 km, Ethiopia 744 km, Libya 382 km, South Sudan 2,158 km

note: Sudan-South Sudan boundary represents 1 January 1956 alignment; final alignment pending negotiations and demarcation; final sovereignty status of Abyei region pending negotiations between Sudan and South Sudan

Coastline: 853 km

Maritime claims: *territorial sea:* 12 nm

contiguous zone: 18 nm

continental shelf: 200-m depth or to the depth of exploitation

Climate: hot and dry; arid desert; rainy season varies by region (April to November)

Terrain: generally flat, featureless plain; desert dominates the north

Elevation: *mean elevation:* 568 m

elevation extremes: *lowest point:* Red Sea 0 m

highest point: Jabal Marrah 3,071 m

Natural resources: petroleum; small reserves of iron ore, copper, chromium ore, zinc, tungsten, mica, silver, gold; hydropower

Land use: *agricultural land:* 100%

arable land: 15.7%

permanent crops: 0.2%

permanent pasture: 84.2%

forest: 0%

other: 0% (2011 est.)

Irrigated land: 18,900 sq km (2012)

Total renewable water resources: 64.5 cu km (2011)

Freshwater withdrawal (domestic/industrial/agricultural): *total:* 27.59 cu km/yr (4%/1%/95%)

per capita: 683.4 cu m/yr (2005)

Natural hazards: dust storms and periodic persistent droughts

Environment—current issues: inadequate supplies of potable water; wildlife populations threatened

by excessive hunting; soil erosion; desertification; periodic drought

Environment—International agreements: *party to:* Biodiversity, Climate Change, Climate Change-Kyoto Protocol, Desertification, Endangered Species, Hazardous Wastes, Law of the Sea, Ozone Layer Protection, Wetlands

signed, but not ratified: none of the selected agreements

Geography—note: dominated by the Nile and its tributaries

PEOPLE AND SOCIETY

Nationality: *noun:* Sudanese (singular and plural)

adjective: Sudanese

Ethnic groups: Sudanese Arab (approximately 70%), Fur, Beja, Nuba, Fallata

Languages: Arabic (official), English (official), Nubian, Ta Bedawie, Fur

note: program of "Arabization" in process

Religions: Sunni Muslim, small Christian minority

Population: 36,108,853 (July 2015 est.)

country comparison to the world: 38

Age structure: *0–14 years:* 40.15% (male 7,359,547/female 7,138,348)

15–24 years: 20.5% (male 3,815,524/female 3,587,177)

25–54 years: 32.08% (male 5,620,201/female 5,964,277)

55–64 years: 4.02% (male 765,137/female 685,577)

65 years and over: 3.25% (male 638,495/female 534,570) (2015 est.)

Dependency ratios: *total dependency ratio:* 78%

youth dependency ratio: 72.1%

elderly dependency ratio: 5.9%

potential support ratio: 16.9% (2015 est.)

Median age: *total:* 19.3 years

male: 19.1 years

female: 19.6 years (2015 est.)

country comparison to the world: 198

Population growth rate: 1.72% (2015 est.)

country comparison to the world: 68

Birth rate: 29.19 births/1,000 population (2015 est.)

country comparison to the world: 43

Death rate: 7.66 deaths/1,000 population (2015 est.)

country comparison to the world: 109

Net migration rate: -4.29 migrant(s)/1,000 population (2015 est.)

country comparison to the world: 190

Urbanization: *urban population:* 33.8% of total population (2015)

rate of urbanization: 2.54% annual rate of change (2010–15 est.)

Major urban areas—population: KHARTOUM (capital) 5.129 million (2015)

Sex ratio: *at birth:* 1.05 male(s)/female

0–14 years: 1.03 male(s)/female

15–24 years: 1.06 male(s)/female

25–54 years: 0.94 male(s)/female

55–64 years: 1.12 male(s)/female
65 years and over: 1.19 male(s)/female
total population: 1.02 male(s)/female (2015 est.)
Maternal mortality rate: 311 deaths/100,000 live births (2015 est.)
country comparison to the world: 9
Infant mortality rate: *total:* 51.52 deaths/1,000 live births
male: 56.87 deaths/1,000 live births
female: 45.9 deaths/1,000 live births (2015 est.)
country comparison to the world: 35
Life expectancy at birth: *total population:* 63.68 years
male: 61.61 years
female: 65.85 years (2015 est.)
country comparison to the world: 186
Total fertility rate: 3.79 children born/woman (2015 est.)
country comparison to the world: 41
Contraceptive prevalence rate: 9% (2010)
Health expenditures: 6.5% of GDP (2013)
country comparison to the world: 75
Physicians density: 0.28 physicians/1,000 population (2008)
Hospital bed density: 0.8 beds/1,000 population (2012)
Drinking water source:
improved:
urban: 66% of population
rural: 50.2% of population
total: 55.5% of population
unimproved:
urban: 34% of population
rural: 49.8% of population
total: 44.5% of population (2012 est.)
Sanitation facility access:
improved:
urban: 43.9% of population
rural: 13.4% of population
total: 23.6% of population
unimproved:
urban: 56.1% of population
rural: 86.6% of population
total: 76.4% of population (2012 est.)
HIV/AIDS—adult prevalence rate: 0.25% (2014 est.)
country comparison to the world: 93
HIV/AIDS—people living with HIV/AIDS: 53,200 (2014 est.)
country comparison to the world: 55
HIV/AIDS—deaths: 2,900 (2014 est.)
country comparison to the world: 46
Major infectious diseases: *degree of risk:* very high
food or waterborne diseases: bacterial and protozoal diarrhea, hepatitis A and E, and typhoid fever
vectorborne diseases: malaria, dengue fever, and Rift Valley fever
water contact disease: schistosomiasis
respiratory disease: meningococcal meningitis
animal contact disease: rabies
note: highly pathogenic H5N1 avian influenza has been identified in this country; it poses a negligible risk with extremely rare cases possible among US citizens who have close contact with birds (2013)
Obesity—adult prevalence rate: 6.6% (2014)

country comparison to the world: 150
Children under the age of 5 years underweight: 33% (2014)
country comparison to the world: 21
Education expenditures: 2.2% of GDP (2009)
Literacy: *definition:* age 15 and over can read and write
total population: 75.9%
male: 83.3%
female: 68.6% (2015 est.)
School life expectancy (primary to tertiary education): *total:* 7 years
male: 7 years
female: 7 years (2013)
Unemployment, youth ages 15–24: *total:* 22.9%
male: 21.2%
fem ale: 25.7% (2008 est.)

GOVERNMENT

Country name: *conventional long form:* Republic of the Sudan
conventional short form: Sudan
local long form: Jumhuriyat as-Sudan
local short form: As-Sudan
former: Anglo-Egyptian Sudan
etymology: the name "Sudan" derives from the Arabic "bilad-as-sudan" meaning "Land of the black [peoples]"
Government type: presidential republic
Capital: *name:* Khartoum
Geographic coordinates: 15 36 N, 32 32 E
time difference: UTC+3 (8 hours ahead of Washington, DC, during Standard Time)
Administrative divisions: 18 states (wilayat, singular—wilayah); Al Gazira, Al Gedaref, Blue Nile, Central Darfur, East Darfur, Kassala, Khartoum, North Darfur, North Kordofan, Northern, Red Sea, River Nile, Sennar, South Darfur, South Kordofan, West Darfur, Western Kordofan, White Nile
Independence: 1 January 1956 (from Egypt and the UK)
National holiday: Independence Day, 1 January (1956)
Constitution: previous 1998; latest adopted 6 July 2005, effective 9 July 2005 (interim constitution); amended 2015; note—in 2011, the Government of Sudan initiated a process for drafting a new constitution (2016)
Legal system: mixed legal system of Islamic law and English common law
International law organization participation: accepts compulsory ICJ jurisdiction with reservations; withdrew acceptance of ICCt jurisdiction in 2008
Citizenship: *citizenship by birth:* no
citizenship by descent only: the father must be a citizen of Sudan
dual citizenship recognized: no
residency requirement for naturalization: 10 years
Suffrage: 17 years of age; universal
Executive branch: *chief of state:* President Umar Hassan Ahmad al-BASHIR (since 16 October 1993); First Vice President BAKRI Hassan Salih,

Second Vice President Hasabu Mohamed ABDEL RAHM in (both since 3 December 2013); note—the president is both chief of state and head of government
head of government: President Umar Hassan Ahmad al-BASHIR (since 16 October 1993); First Vice President BAKRI Hassan Salih, Second Vice President Hasabu Mohamed ABDEL RAHMAN (both since 9 December 2013)
cabinet: Council of Ministers appointed by the president; note—the NCP, formerly the National Islamic Front or NIF, dominates al-BASHIR's cabinet
elections/appointments: president directly elected by absolute majority popular vote in 2 rounds if needed; last held on 13–16 April 2015 (next to be held in 2020)
election results: Umar Hassan Ahmadal-BASHIR reelected president; percent of vote—Umar Hassan Ahmad al-BASHIR (NCP) 94.1%, other (15 candidates) 5.9%
Legislative branch: *description:* bicameral National Legislature consists of the Council of States or Majlis Weleyat (50 seats; members indirectly elected—2 each by the 25 state legislatures to serve 6-year terms) and the National Assembly or Majlis Watani (426 seats; 213 members directly elected in single-seat constituencies by simple majority vote, 128 for women only directly elected by proportional representation vote, and 85 directly elected by proportional representation vote; members serve 6-year terms)
elections: last held on 13–15 April 2015 (next to be held in 2021)
election results: National Assembly—percent of vote by party—NA; seats by party—NCP 323, DUP 25, Democratic Unionist Party 15, other 44, independent 19
note: the mandate of the members from the south was terminated upon independence by the Republic of South Sudan effective 9 July 2011 and membership in Sudan's National Assembly was reduced to 354; it is unclear whether this total will be retained for the next election or whether the previous total of 450 will be reconstituted
Judicial branch: *highest court(s):* National Supreme Court (consists of 70 judges organized into panels of 3 judges; court includes 4 circuits that operate outside the capital); Constitutional Court (consists of 9 justices including the court president); note—the Constitutional Court resides outside the National judiciary
judge selection and term of office: National Supreme Court and Constitutional Court judges appointed by the president of the republic upon the recommendation of the National Judicial Service Commission, an independent body chaired by the chief justice of the republic and members including other judges and judicial and legal officials; Supreme Court judge tenure NA; Constitutional Court judges appointed for 7 years
subordinate courts: National Court of Appeals; other National courts (not specified in the 2005 Interim National Constitution as to National or local authority); township and rural (peoples') courts

Political parties and leaders: Democratic Unionist Party or DUP [Jalal al-DIGAIR]

Democratic Unionist Party [Muhammad Uthman Al-MIRGHANI]

M uslim Brotherhood or MB

National Congress Party or NCP [Umar Hassan Al-BASHIR]

National Umma Party or UP [Siddiq al-MAH DI]

Popular Congress Party or PCP [Hassan Al-TURABI]

Reform Now Party or RNP [Dr. Ghazi Salah al-DEEN]

Sudanese Communist Party or SCP [Mohammed Moktar Al-KH ATEEB]

Sudanese Congress Party [I brahim Al-SHEI KH]

Unionist Movement Party or UMP [Nagla AL-AZHARI]

Political pressure groups and leaders: Darfur rebel groups including the Justice and Equality Movement or JEM [Gibril Fidaill BRAHIM],

Sudan Liberation Movement or SLM-AW [Abdel Wahid NU R, various faction al leaders]

Sudan Liberation Movement or SLM-MM [Minni Arkou MINAWI]

National Consensus Front or NCF [Farouq ABUISSA]

Sudan People's Liberation Movement-North or SPLM-N [Malik AGAR]

Sudan Revolution ary Front or SRF [Malik AGAR]

International organization participation: ABEDA, ACP, AfDB, AFESD, AMF, AU, CAEU, COMESA, FAO, G-77, IAEA, IBRD, ICAO, ICC (NGOs), ICRM, IDA, IDB, IFAD, IFC, IFRCS, IGAD, ILO, IMF, IMO, Interpol, IOC, IOM, IPU, ISO, ITSO, ITU, LAS, MIGA, NAM, OIC, OPCW, PCA, UN, UNCTAD, UNESCO, UNHCR, UNIDO, UNWTO, UPU, WCO, WFTU (NGOs), WHO, WIPO, WMO, WTO (observer)

Diplomatic representation in the US: *chief of mission:* Ambassador (vacant); Charge d'Affaires Maowia Osman KHALID (since 31 January 2014)

chancery: 2210 Massachusetts Avenue NW, Washington, DC 20008

telephone: [1] (202) 338-8565

FAX: [1] (202) 667-2406

Diplomatic representation from the US: *chief of mission:* Ambassador (vacant); Charge d'Affaires Benjamin MOELING (since February 2016)

embassy: Sharia Ali Abdul Latif Street, Khartoum

mailing address: P.O. Box 699, Kilo 10, Soba, Khartoum; APO AE 09829

telephone: [249] (187)-0-(22000)

FAX: [249] (183) 774-137

Flag description: three equal horizontal bands of red (top), white, and black with a green isosceles triangle based on the hoist side; colors and design based on the Arab Revolt flag of World War I, but the meanings of the colors are expressed as follows: red signifies the struggle for freedom, white is the color of peace, light, and love, black represents the people of Sudan (in Arabic 'Sudan' means black), green is the color of Islam, agriculture, and prosperity

National symbol(s): secretary bird; National colors: red, white, black, green

National anthem: *name:* "Nahnu Djundulla Djundulwatan" (We Are the Army of God and of Our Land)

lyrics/music: Sayed Ahmad Muhammad SALIH/ Ahmad MURJAN

note: adopted 1956; originally served as the anthem of the Sudanese military

ECONOMY

Economy—overview: Sudan has experienced protracted social conflict, civil war, and, in July 2011, the loss of three-quarters of its oil production due to the secession of South Sudan. The oil sector had driven much of Sudan's GDP growth since 1999. For nearly a decade, the economy boomed on the back of rising oil production, high oil prices, and significant inflows of foreign direct investment. Since the economic shock of South Sudan's secession, Sudan has struggled to stabilize its economy and make up for the loss of foreign exchange earnings. The interruption of oil production in South Sudan in 2012 for over a year and the consequent loss of oil transit fees further exacerbated the fragile state of Sudan's economy. Ongoing conflicts in Southern Kordofan, Darfur, and the Blue Nile states, lack of basic infrastructure in large areas, and reliance by much of the population on subsistence agriculture keep close to half of the population at or below the poverty line.

Sudan is also subject to comprehensive US sanctions. Sudan is attempting to develop non-oil sources of revenues, such as gold mining, while carrying out an Austerity program to reduce expenditures. The world's largest exporter of gum Arabic, Sudan produces 75–80% of the world's total output. Agriculture continues to employ 80% of the workforce.

Sudan introduced a new currency, still called the Sudanese pound, following South Sudan's secession, but the value of the currency has fallen since its introduction. Khartoum formally devalued the currency in June 2012, when it passed austerity measures that included gradually repealing fuelsubsidies. Sudan also faces high inflation, which reached 47% on an annual basis in November 2012 but subsided to just under 18% in 2015.

GDP (purchasing power parity): $167 billion (2015 est.)

$161.3 billion (2014 est.)

$156.2 billion (2013 est.)

note: data are in 2015 US dollars

country comparison to the world: 71

GDP (official exchange rate): $83.61 billion (2015 est.)

GDP—real growth rate: 3.5% (2015 est.)

3.3% (2014 est.)

3.9% (2013 est.)

country comparison to the world: 84

GDP—per capita (PPP): $4,300 (2015 est.)

$4,300 (2014 est.)

$4,300 (2013 est.)

note: data are in 2015 US dollars

country comparison to the world: 174

Gross National saving: 9.5% of GDP (2015 est.)

10.5% of GDP (2014 est.)

11.5% of GDP (2013 est.)

country comparison to the world: 154

GDP—composition, by end use:

household consumption: 78.7%

government consumption: 6.7%

investment in fixed capital: 19%

investment in inventories: 1%

exports of goods and services: 7.6%

imports of goods and services: -13% (2015 est.)

GDP—composition, by sector of origin:

agriculture: 28.9%

industry: 20.4%

services: 50.7% (2015 est.)

Agriculture—products: cotton, groundnuts (peanuts), sorghum, millet, wheat, gum arabic, sugarcane, cassava (manioc, tapioca), mangoes, papaya, bananas, sweet potatoes, sesame seeds; sheep and other livestock

Industries: oil, cotton ginning, textiles, cement, edible oils, sugar, soap distilling, shoes, petroleum refining, pharmaceuticals, armaments, automobile/light truck assembly

Industrial production growth rate: 2.7% (2015 est.)

country comparison to the world: 97

Labor force: 11.92 million (2007 est.)

country comparison to the world: 47

Labor force—by occupation: *agriculture:* 80%

industry: 7%

services: 13% (1998 est.)

Unemployment rate: 13.6% (2014 est.)

14.8% (2013 est.)

country comparison to the world: 145

Population below poverty line: 46.5% (2009 est.)

Household income or consumption by percentage share: *lowest:* 10%: 2.7%

highest: 10%: 26.7% (2009 est.)

Budget: *revenues:* $6.518 billion

expenditures: $9.754 billion (2015 est.)

Taxes and other revenues: 7.7% of GDP (2015 est.)

country comparison to the world: 213

Budget surplus (+) or deficit (–): -3.8% of GDP (2015 est.)

country comparison to the world: 138

Public Debt: 72.1% of GDP (2015 est.) 73.4% of GDP (2014 est.)

country comparison to the world: 43

Fiscal year: calendar year

Inflation rate (consumer prices): 16.9% (2015 est.) 36.9% (2014 est.)

country comparison to the world: 218

Stock of narrow money: $8.345 billion (31 December 2015 est.)

$8.024 billion (31 December 2014 est.)

country comparison to the world: 87

Stock of broad money: $13.47 billion (31 December 2015 est.)

$13 billion (31 December 2014 est.)

country comparison to the world: 98

Stock of domestic credit: $15.16 billion (31 December 2015 est.)

$14.83 billion (31 December 2014 est.)

country comparison to the world: 92

Market value of publicly traded shares: $NA

Current account balance: -$6.457 billion (2015 est.)

-$4.999 billion (2014 est.)

country comparison to the world: 173

Exports: $4.392 billion (2015 est.)

$4.35 billion (2014 est.)

country comparison to the world: 116

Exports—commodities: gold; oil and petroleum Products; cotton, sesame, livestock, peanuts, gum arabic, sugar

Exports—partners: UAE 32%, China 16.2%, Saudi Arabia 15.5%, Australia 4.7%, India 4.2% (2015)

Imports: $8.287 billion (2015 est.)

$8.106 billion (2014 est.)

country comparison to the world: 108

Imports—commodities: foodstuffs, manufactured goods, refinery and transport equipment, medicines, chemicals, textiles, wheat

Imports—partners: China 26.3%, UAE 10%, India 9%, Egypt 5.6%, Turkey 4.7%, Saudi Arabia 4.4% (2015)

Reserves of foreign exchange and gold: $172.4 million (31 December 2015 est.)

$181.5 million (31 December 2014 est.)

country comparison to the world: 161

Debt—external: $48.17 billion (31 December 2014 est.)

$45.56 billion (31 December 2013 est.)

country comparison to the world: 64

Stock of direct foreign investment—at home: $0 (31 December 2015 est.)

$22.69 billion (31 December 2014 est.)

country comparison to the world: 120

Exchange rates: Sudanese pounds (SDG) per US dollar—

6.47 (2015 est.)

5.74 (2014 est.)

5.74 (2013 est.)

3.57 (2012 est.)

2.68 (2011 est.)

ENERGY

Electricity—production: 7.193 billion kWh (2012 est.)

country comparison to the world: 108

Electricity—consumption: 5.665 billion kWh (2010 est.)

country comparison to the world: 110

Electricity—exports: 0 kWh (2013 est.)

country comparison to the world: 199

Electricity—imports: 0 kWh (2013 est.)

country comparison to the world: 205

Electricity—installed generating capacity: 2.083 million kW (2012 est.)

country comparison to the world: 105

Electricity—from fossil fuels: 30.7% of total installed capacity (2012 est.)

country comparison to the world: 181

Electricity—from nuclear fuels: 0% of total installed capacity (2012 est.)

country comparison to the world: 184

Electricity—from hydroelectric plants: 66.3% of total installed capacity (2012 est.)

country comparison to the world: 30

Electricity—from other renewable sources: 3% of total installed capacity (2012 est.)

country comparison to the world: 73

Crude oil—production: 64,770 bbl/day (2014 est.)

country comparison to the world: 53

Crude oil—exports: 5,355 bbl/day (2012 est.)

country comparison to the world: 71

Crude oil—imports: 0 bbl/day (2012 est.)

country comparison to the world: 128

Crude oil—proved reserves: 1.25 billion bbl (1 January 2015 est.)

country comparison to the world: 39

Refined petroleum products—production: 124,900 bbl/day (2010 est.)

country comparison to the world: 68

Refined petroleum products—consumption: 26,750 bbl/day (2013 est.)

country comparison to the world: 118

Refined petroleum products—exports: 1,496 bbl/day (2012 est.)

country comparison to the world: 109

Refined petroleum products—imports: 6,199 bbl/day (2012 est.)

country comparison to the world: 151

Imports: Natural gas—production: 0 cu m (2013 est.)

country comparison to the world: 131

Natural gas—consumption: 0 cu m (2013 est.)

country comparison to the world: 196

Natural gas—exports: 0 cu m (2013 est.)

country comparison to the world: 184

Natural gas—imports: 0 cu m (2013 est.)

country comparison to the world: 136

Natural gas—proved reserves: 21.24 billion cu m (1 January 2013 est.)

country comparison to the world: 75

Carbon dioxide emissions from consumption of energy: 16.45 million Mt (2011 est.)

country comparison to the world: 87

COMMUNICATIONS

Telephones—fixed lines: *total subscriptions:* 420,000

subscriptions per 100 inhabitants: 1 (2014 est.)

country comparison to the world: 102

Telephones—mobile cellular: *total:* 27.8 million

subscriptions per 100 inhabitants: 78 (2014 est.)

country comparison to the world: 46

Telephone system: *general assessment:* well-equipped system by Regional standards and being upgraded; cellular communications started in 1996 and have expanded substantially with wide coverage of most major cities

domestic: consists of microwave radio relay, cable, fiber optic, radiotelephone communications, tropospheric scatter, and a domestic satellite system with 14 earth stations

international: country code—249; linked to the EASSy and FLAG fiber-optic submarine cable systems; satellite earth stations—1 intelsat (Atlantic Ocean), 1 Arabsat (2010)

Broadcast media: the Sudanese Government directly controls TV and radio, requiring that both media reflect government policies; TV has a permanent military censor; a private radio station is in operation (2007)

Radio broadcast stations: AM 12, FM 1, shortwave 1 (1998)

Television broadcast stations: 3 (1997)

Internet country code: .sd

Internet hosts: 99 (2012)

country comparison to the world: 210

Internet users: *total:* 8.5 million

percent of population: 24.0% (2014 est.)

country comparison to the world: 48

TRANSPORTATION

Airports: 74 (2013)

country comparison to the world: 71

Airports—with paved runways: *total:* 16

over 3,047 m: 2 2,438 to 3,047 m: 1 01,524 to 2,437 m: 2 under 914 m: 2 (2013)

Airports—with unpaved runways: *total:* 58

2,438 to 3,047 m: 1

1,524 to 2,437 m: 17

914 to 1,523 m: 28

under 914 m: 12 (2013)

Heliports: 6 (2013)

Pipelines: gas 156 km; oil 4,070 km; refined products 1,613 km (2013)

Railways: *total:* 7,251 km

narrow gauge: 5,851 km 1.067-m gauge; 1,400 km 0.600-m gauge for cotton plantations (20014)

country comparison to the world: 31

Roadways: *total:* 11,900 km

paved: 4,320 km

unpaved: 7,580 km (2000)

country comparison to the world: 128

Waterways: 4,068 km (1,723 km open year round on White and Blue Nile Rivers) (2011)

country comparison to the world: 24

Merchant marine: *total:* 2

by type: cargo 2 (2010)

country comparison to the world: 143

Ports and terminals: *major seaport(s):* Port Sudan

MILITARY AND SECURITY

Military branches: Sudanese Armed Forces (SAF): Land Forces, Navy (includes Marines), Sudanese Air Force (Sikakh al-Jawwiya as-Sudaniya), Popular Defense Forces (2011)

Military service age and obligation: 18–33 years of age for male and female compulsory or voluntary military service; 1-2 year service obligation; a requirement that completion of National service was mandatory before entering public or private sector employment has been cancelled (2012)

TRANSNATIONAL ISSUES

Disputes—International: the effects of Sudan's almost constant ethnic and rebel militia fighting since the mid-20th century have penetrated all of the neighboring states; Chad wishes to be a helpful mediator in resolving the Darfur conflict, and in 2010 established a joint border monitoring force with Sudan, which has helped to reduce cross-border banditry and violence; as of mid-2013, Chad, Egypt, Ethiopia, Israel, the Central African Republic, and South Sudan provided shelter for more than 600,000 Sudanese refugees; during the same period, Sudan, in turn, hosted about 115,000

Eritreans, 32,000 Chadians, and smaller numbers of Ethiopians and Central Africans; Sudan accuses Eritrea of supporting Sudanese rebel groups; efforts to demarcate the porous boundary with Ethiopia proceed slowly due to civil and ethnic fighting in eastern Sudan; Sudan claims but Egypt de facto administers security and economic development of the Halaib region north of the 22nd parallel boundary; periodic violent skirmishes with Sudanese residents over water and grazing rights persist among related pastoral populations along the border with the Central African Republic; South Sudan-Sudan boundary represents 1 January 1956 alignment, final alignment pending negotiations and demarcation; final sovereignty status of Abyei Area pending negotiations between South Sudan and Sudan

Refugees and internally displaced persons: *refugees (country of origin):* 109,196 (Eritrea); 42,334 (Chad); 5,495 (Ethiopia) (2014); 5,540 (Yemen) (2015); 231,581 (South Sudan) (2016)

IDPs: 3,218,234 (civil war 1983–2005; ongoing conflict in Darfur region; government and rebel fighting along South Sudan border; inter-tribal clashes) (2015)

Trafficking in persons: *current situation:* Sudan is a source, transit, and destination country for men, women, and children who are subjected to forced labor and sex trafficking; Sudanese women and girls, particularly those from rural areas or who are internally displaced, or refugees are vulnerable to domestic servitude in country, as well as domestic servitude and sex trafficking abroad; migrants from East and West Africa, South Sudan, Syria, and Nigeria smuggled into or through Sudan are vulnerable to exploitation; Ethiopian, Eritrean, and Filipina women are subjected to domestic servitude in Sudanese homes, and East African And possibly Thai women are forced into prostitution in Sudan; Sudanese children continue to be recruited and used as combatants by government forces and armed groups

tier rating: Tier 2 Watch List—Sudan does not fully comply with the minimum standards for the elimination of trafficking; however, it is making significant efforts to do so; the government increased its efforts to publically address and prevent trafficking, established a National anti-trafficking council, and began drafting a National action plan against trafficking; the government acknowledges cross-border trafficking but still denies the existence of forced labor, sex trafficking, and the recruitment of child soldiers domestically; law enforcement and judicial officials struggled to apply the National anti-trafficking law, often relying on other statutes with lesser penalties; authorities did not use systematic procedure to identify victims or refer them to care and relied on International organizations and domestic groups to provide protective services; some foreign victims were penalized for unlawful acts committed as a direct result of being trafficked, such as immigration or prostitution violations (2015)

SURIANAME

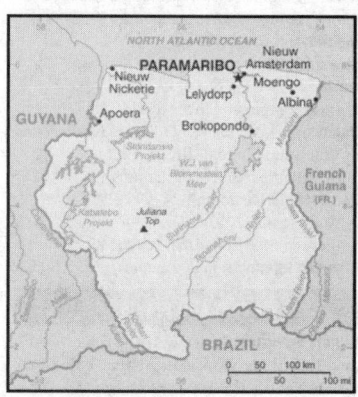

INTRODUCTION

Background: First explored by the Spaniards in the 16th century and then settled by the English in the mid-17th century, Suriname became a Dutch colony in 1667. With the abolition of African slavery in 1863, workers were brought in from India and Java. The Netherlands granted the colony independence in 1975. Five years later the civilian Government was replaced by a military regime that soon declared a socialist republic. It continued to exert control through a succession of nominally civilian administrations until 1987, when International pressure finally forced a democratic election. In 1990, the military overthrew the civilian leadership, but a democratically elected government—a four-party coalition—returned to power in 1991. The coalition expanded to eight parties in 2005 and ruled until August 2010, when voters returned former military leader Desire

BOUTERSE and his opposition coalition to power. President BOUTERSE was reelected unopposed in 2015.

GEOGRAPHY

Location: Northern South America, bordering the North Atlantic Ocean, between French Guiana and Guyana

Geographic coordinates: 4 00 N, 56 00 W

Map references: South America

Area: *total:* 163,820 sq km

land: 156,000 sq km

water: 7,820 sq km

country comparison to the world: 92

Area—comparative: slightly larger than Georgia

Land boundaries: *total:* 1,907 km

border countries (3): Brazil 515 km, French Guiana 556 km, Guyana 836 km

Coastline: 386 km

Maritime claims: *territorial sea:* 12 nm

exclusive economic zone: 200 nm

Climate: tropical; moderated by trade winds

Terrain: mostly rolling hills; narrow coastal plain with swamps

Elevation: *mean elevation:* 246 m

elevation extremes: *lowest point:* unnamed location in the coastal plain -2 m

highest point: Juliana Top 1,230 m

Natural resources: timber, hydropower, fish, kaolin, shrimp, bauxite, gold, and small amounts of nickel, copper, platinum, iron ore

Land use: agricultural *land:* 0.5%

arable land: 0.4%

permanent crops: 0%

permanent pasture: 0.1%

forest: 94.6%

other: 4.9% (2011 est.)

Irrigated land: 570 sq km (2012)

Total renewable water resources: 122 cu km (2011)

Freshwater withdrawal (domestic/industrial/agricultural): *total:* 0.67 cu km/yr (6%/4%/90%)

per capita: 1,396 cu m/yr (2006)

Natural hazards: NA

Environment—current issues: deforestation as timber is cut for export; pollution of inland waterways by small-scale mining activities

Environment—International agreements: *party to:* Biodiversity, Climate Change, Climate Change-Kyoto Protocol, Desertification, Endangered Species, Law of the Sea, Marine Dumping, Ozone Layer Protection, Ship Pollution, Tropical Timber 94, Wetlands, Whaling

signed, but not ratified: none of the selected agreements

Geography—note: smallest independent country on South American continent; mostly tropical rain forest; great diversity of flora and fauna that, for the most part, is increasingly threatened by new development; relatively small population, mostly along the coast

PEOPLE AND SOCIETY

Nationality: *noun:* Surinamer(s)

adjective: Surinamese

Ethnic groups: Hindustani (also known locally as "East Indians"; their ancestors emigrated from northern India in the latter part of the 19th century) 37%, Creole (mixed white and black) 31%, Javanese 15%, "Maroons" (their African Ancestors were brought to the country in the 17th and 18th centuries as slaves and escaped to the interior) 10%, Amerindian 2%, Chinese 2%, white 1%, other 2%

Languages: Dutch (official), English (widely spoken), Sranang Tongo (Surinamese, sometimes called Taki-Taki, is native language of Creoles and much of the younger population and is lingua franca among others), Caribbean Hindustani (adialect of Hindi), Javanese

Religions: Hindu 27.4%, Protestant 25.2% (predominantly Moravian), Roman Catholic 22.8%, Muslim 19.6%, indigenous beliefs 5%

Demographic profile: Suriname is a pluralistic society consisting primarily of Creoles (persons of mixed African and European heritage), the descendants of escaped African slaves known as Maroons, and the descendants of Indian and Javanese contract workers. The country overall is in full, post-industrial demographic transition, with a low fertility rate, a moderate mortality rate, and a rising life expectancy. However, the Maroon population of the rural interior lags behind because of lower educational attainment and contraceptive use, higher malnutrition, and significantly less access to electricity, potable water, sanitation, infrastructure, and health care.

Some 350,000 people of Surinamese descent live in the Netherlands, Suriname's former colonial ruler. In the 19th century, better-educated, largely Dutch-speaking Surinamese began emigrating to the Netherlands. World War II interrupted the outflow, but it resumed after the war when Dutch labor demands grew—emigrants included all segments of the Creole population. Suriname still is strongly influenced by the Netherlands because most Surinamese have relatives living there and it is the largest supplier of development aid. Other emigration destinations include French Guiana and the United States. Suriname's immigration rules are flexible, and the country is easy to enter illegally because rainforests obscure its borders. Since the mid-1980s, Brazilians have settled in Suriname's capital, Paramaribo, or eastern Suriname, where they mine gold. This immigration is likely to slowly re-orient Suriname toward its Latin american roots.

Population: 579,633 (July 2015 est.)
country comparison to the world: 171

Age structure: *0–14 years:* 25.66% (male 75,791/female 72,934)
15–24 years: 17.48% (male 51,657/female 49,662)
25–54 years: 44.3% (male 130,726/female 126,048)
55–64 years: 6.81% (male 19,291/female 20,198)
65 years and over: 5.75% (male 14,395/female 18,931) (2015 est.)

Dependency ratios: *total dependency ratio:* 50.8%
youth 40.4%
elderly dependency ratio: 10.4%
potential support ratio: 9.6% (2015 est.)

Median age: *total:* 29.1 years
male: 28.7 years
female: 29.4 years (2015 est.)
country comparison to the world: 120

Population growth rate: 1.08% (2015 est.)
country comparison to the world: 113

Birth rate: 16.34 births/1,000 population (2015 est.)
country comparison to the world: 117

Death rate: 6.13 deaths/1,000 population (2015 est.)
country comparison to the world: 157

Net migration rate: 0.56 migrant(s)/1,000 population (2015 est.)
country comparison to the world: 70

Urbanization: *urban population:* 66% of total population (2015)
rate of urbanization: 0.78% annual rate of change (2010–15 est.)

Major urban areas—population: PARAMARIBO (capital) 234,000 (2014)

Sex ratio: *at birth:* 1.05 male(s)/female
0–14 years: 1.04 male(s)/female
15–24 years: 1.04 male(s)/female
25–54 years: 1.04 male(s)/female
55–64 years: 0.96 male(s)/female
65 years and over: 0.76 male(s)/female
total population: 1.01 male(s)/female (2015 est.)

Maternal mortality rate: 155 deaths/100,000 live births (2015 est.)
country comparison to the world: 63

Infant mortality rate: *total:* 26.17 deaths/1,000 live births
male: 30.48 deaths/1,000 live births
female: 21.65 deaths/1,000 live births (2015 est.)
country comparison to the world: 68

Life expectancy at birth: *total population:* 71.97 years
male: 69.57 years
female: 74.48 years (2015 est.)
country comparison to the world: 146

Total fertility rate: 1.97 children born/woman (2015 est.)
country comparison to the world: 126

Contraceptive prevalence rate: 47.6% (2010)

Hospital bed density: 3.1 beds/1,000 population (2010)

Drinking water source:
improved:
urban: 98.1% of population
rural: 88.4% of population
total: 94.8% of population
unimproved:
urban: 1.9% of population
rural: 11.6% of population
total: 5.2% of population (2015 est.)

Sanitation facility access:
improved:
urban: 88.4% of population
rural: 61.4% of population
total: 79.2% of population
unimproved:
urban: 11.6% of population
rural: 38.6% of population
total: 20.8% of population (2015 est.)

HIV/AIDS—adult prevalence rate: 1.02% (2014 est.)
country comparison to the world: 47

HIV/AIDS—people living with HIV/AIDS: 3,800 (2014 est.)
country comparison to the world: 110

HIV/AIDS—deaths: 200 (2014 est.)
country comparison to the world: 100

Major infectious diseases: *degree of risk:* very high

food or waterborne diseases: bacterial and protozoal diarrhea, hepatitis A, and typhoid fever
vectorborne disease: dengue fever and malaria (2013)

Obesity—adult prevalence rate: 26.1% (2014)
country comparison to the world: 60

Children under the age of 5 years underweight: 5.8% (2010)
country comparison to the world: 83

Education expenditures: NA

Literacy: *definition:* age 15 and over can read and write
total population: 95.6%
male: 96.1%
female: 95% (2015 est.)

Child labor—children ages 5–14: *total number:* 6,094
percentage: 6% (2006 est.)

Unemployment, youth ages 15–24: *total:* 15.3%
male: 11.6%
female: 21.7% (2013 est.)
country comparison to the world: 51

GOVERNMENT

Country name: *conventional long form:* Republic of Suriname
conventional short form: Suriname
local long form: Republiek Suriname
local short form: Suriname *former:* Netherlands Guiana, Dutch Guiana
etymology: name may derive from the indigenous "Surinen" people who inhabited the area at the time of European contact

Government type: presidential republic

Capital: *name:* Paramaribo

Geographic coordinates: 5 50 N, 55 10 W
time difference: UTC-3 (2 hours ahead of Washington, DC, during Standard Time)

Administrative divisions: 10 districts (distrikten, singular—distrikt); Brokopondo, Commewijne, Coronie, Marowijne, Nickerie, Para, Para maribo, Saramacca, Sipaliwini, Wanica

Independence: 25 November 1975 (from the Netherlands)

National holiday: Independence Day, 25 November (1975)

Constitution: previous 1975; latest ratified 30 September 1987, effective 30 October 1987; amended 1992 (2016)

Legal system: civil law system influenced by Dutch civil law; note—the Commissie Nieuw Surinaamse Burgerlijk Wetboek completed drafting a new civil code in February 2009

International law organization participation: accepts compulsory ICJ jurisdiction with reservations; accepts ICCt jurisdiction

Citizenship: *citizenship by birth:* no
citizenship by descent only: at least one parent must be a citizen of Suriname
dual citizenship recognized: no
residency requirement for naturalization: 5 years

Suffrage: 18 years of age; universal

Executive branch: *chief of state:* President Desire Delano BOUTERSE (since 12 August 2010);

Vice President Ashwin ADHIN (since 12 August 2015); note—the president is both chief of state and head of government

head of government: President Desire Delano BOUTERSE (since 12 August 2010); Vice President Ashwin ADHIN (since 12 August 2015)

cabinet: Cabinet of Ministers appointed by the president

elections/appointments: president and vice president indirectly elected by the National Assembly; president and vice president serve a 5-year term (no term limits); election last held on 25 May 2015 (next to be held on 25 May 2020)

election results: Desire Delano BOUTERSE reelected president; National Assembly vote—NA

Legislative branch: *description:* unicameral National Assembly or Nationale Assemblee (51 seats; members directly elected in multi-seat constituencies by proportional representation vote to serve 5-year terms)

elections: last held on 25 May 2015 (next to be held in May 2020)

election results: percent of vote by party—NDP 45.5%, V7 37.2%, A-Com 10.5%, DOE 4.3%, PALU .7%, other 1.7%; seats by party—NDP 26, V7 18, A-Com 5, DOE 1, PALU 1

Judicial branch: *highest resident court(s):* High Court of Justice of Suriname (consists of the court president, vice president, and 4 judges); note—Suriname can appeal beyond its High Court to the Caribbean Court of Justice, with final appeal to the Judicial Committee of the Privy Council (in London)

judge selection and term of office: court judges appointed by the National president after consultation with the High Court; judges appointed for life

subordinate courts: cantonal courts

Political parties and leaders: Alternative ComBination or A-Com (a coalition that includes ABOP, KTPI, PDO)

Brotherhood and Unity in Politics or BEP [Celsius WATERBERG]

Democratic Alternative'91 or DA91[Winston JESSURUN]

General Liberation and Development Party or ABOP [Ronnie BRUNSWIJK]

National Democratic Party or NDP [Desire Delano BOUTERSE]

National Party of Suriname or NPS [Gregory RUSLAN D]

Party for Democracy and Development or PDO [Waldy NAIN]

Party for Democracy and Development in Unity or DOE [Carl BREEVELD]

Party for National Unity and Solidarity or KTPI [Willy SOEMITA]

People's Alliance, Pertjaja Luhur or PL [Paul SOMOHARDJO]

Progressive Worker and Farmer's Union or PALU [Jim HOK]

Surinamese Labor Party or SPA [Guno CASTELEN]

United Reform Party or VHP [Chandrikapersad SANTOKHI] Victory 7 or V7 (formerly the New Front for Democracy and Development or NF) (a coalition including NPS, VH P, DA91, PL, SPA) [Chandrikapresad SAN TOKHI]

Political pressure groups and leaders: Association of Indigenous Village Chiefs [Ricardo PANE] Association of Saramaccan authorities or Maroon

[Head Captain WASE] Women's Parliament Forum or PVF [Iris GILLIAD]

International organization participation: ACP, AOSIS, Caricom, CD, CDB, CELAC, FAO, G-77, IADB, IBRD, ICAO, ICCt, ICRM, IDA, IDB, IFAD, IFC, IFRCS, IHO, ILO, IMF, IMO, Interpol, IOC, IOM, IPU, ISO (correspondent), ITU, ITUC (NGOs), LAES, MIGA, NAM, OAS, OIC, OPANAL, OPCW, PCA, Petrocaribe, UN, UNASUR, UNCTAD, UNESCO, UNIDO, UPU, WHO, WIPO, WMO, WTO

Diplomatic representation in the US: *chief of mission:* Ambassador (vacant); Charge d'Affaires Sylvana Elvira SIMSON (since 1 September 2015)

chancery: Suite 460,4301 Connecticut Avenue NW, Washington, DC 20008

telephone: [1] (202) 244-7488

FAX: [1] (202) 244-5878

consulate(s) general: Miami

Diplomatic representation from the US: *chief of mission:* Ambassador Jay N. ANANIA (since 1 October 2012)

embassy: Dr. Sophie Redmondstraat 129, Paramaribo

mailing address: US Department of State, PO Box 1821, Paramaribo

telephone: [597] 472-900

FAX: [597] 410-972

Flag description: five horizontal bands of green (top, double width), white, red (quadruple width), white, and green (double width); a large, yellow, five-pointed star is centered in the red band; red stands for progress and love; green symbolizes hope and fertility; white signifies peace, justice, and freedom; the star represents the unity of all Ethnic groups; from its yellow light the nation draws strength to bear sacrifices patiently while working toward a golden future

National symbol(s): royal palm, faya lobi (flower); National colors: green, white, red

National anthem: *name:* "Godzij metons Suriname!" (God Be With Our Suriname)

lyrics/music: Cornelis Atses HOEKSTRA and Henry DE ZIEL/Johannes Corstianus DEPUY

note: adopted 1959; originally adapted from a Sunday school song written in 1893 and contains lyrics in both Dutch and Sranang Tongo

ECONOMY

Economy—overview: The economy is dominated by the mining industry, with exports of oil, gold, and alumina accounting for about 85% of exports and 27% of government revenues, making the economy highly vulnerable to mineral price volatility.

Economic growth has declined annually from just under 5% in 2012 to 1.5% in 2015. In January 2011, the government devalued the currency by 20% and raised taxes to reduce the budget deficit. As a result of these measures, inflation receded to less than 4% in 2015.

Suriname's economic prospects for the medium term will depend on continued commitment to responsible monetary and fiscal policies and to the introduction of structural reforms to liberalize markets and promote competition. The government's reliance on revenue from extractive industries will temper Suriname's economic outlook, especially if gold prices continue their downward trend.

GDP (purchasing power parity): $9.09 billion (2015 est.) $9.077 billion (2014 est.) $8.913 billion (2013 est.)

note: data are in 2015 US dollars

country comparison to the world: 161

GDP (official exchange rate): $5.192 billion (2015 est.)

GDP—real growth rate: 0.1% (2015 est.) 1.8% (2014 est.) 2.8% (2013 est.)

country comparison to the world: 193

GDP—per capita (PPP): $16,300 (2015 est.) $16,200 (2014 est.) $16,200 (2013 est.)

note: data are in 2015 US dollars

country comparison to the world: 100

Gross National saving: 24.2% of GDP (2015 est.) 24.5% of GDP (2014 est.) 25.7% of GDP (2013 est.)

country comparison to the world: 53

GDP—composition, by end use:

household consumption: 52%

government consumption: 11.2%

investment in fixed capital: 11.9%

investment in inventories: 26.5%

exports of goods and services: 24.2%

imports of goods and services: -25.8% (2015 est.)

GDP—composition, by sector of origin:

agriculture: 6.2%

industry: 48.7%

services: 45.1% (2015 est.)

Agriculture—products: rice, bananas, palm kernels, coconuts, plantains, peanuts; beef, chickens; shrimp; forest products

Industries: bauxite and gold mining, alumina production; oil, lumbering, food processing, fishing

Industrial production growth rate: 2% (2015 est.)

country comparison to the world: 114

Labor force: 165,600 (2007 est.)

country comparison to the world: 177

Labor force—by occupation: *agriculture:* 11.2%

industry: 19.5%

services: 69.3% (2010)

Unemployment rate: 8.9% (2014 est.) 8.5% (2013 est.)

country comparison to the world: 106

Population below poverty line: 70% (2002 est.)

Household income or consumption by percentage share: *lowest:* 10%: NA%

highest: 10%: NA%

Budget: *revenues:* $1.061 billion

expenditures: $1.455 billion (2015 est.)

Taxes and other revenues: 21% of GDP (2015 est.)

country comparison to the world: 148

Budget surplus (+) or deficit (−): -7.8% of GDP (2015 est.)

country comparison to the world: 198

Fiscal year: calendar year

Inflation rate (consumer prices): 6.9% (2015 est.) 3.4% (2014 est.)

country comparison to the world: 193

Central bank discount rate: 10% (2013) 9% (2012)

country comparison to the world: 22

Commercial bank prime lending rate: 12.5% (31 December 2015 est.) 12.28% (31 December 2014 est.)

country comparison to the world: 62

Stock of narrow money: $1.55 billion (31 December 2015 est.) $1.409 billion (31 December 2014 est.)

country comparison to the world: 139
Stock of broad money: $3.461 billion (31 December 2015 est.)
$2.885 billion (31 December 2014 est.)
country comparison to the world: 143
Stock of domestic credit: $2.424 billion (31 December 2015 est.)
$2.029 billion (31 December 2014 est.)
country comparison to the world: 134
Market value of publicly traded shares: $NA
Current account balance: -$808 million (2015 est.)
-$415 million (2014 est.)
country comparison to the world: 114
Exports: $1.829 billion (2015 est.) $2.149 billion (2014 est.)
country comparison to the world: 142
Exports—commodities: alumina, gold, crude oil, lumber, shrimp and fish, rice, bananas
Exports—partners: Switzerland 21.8%, UAE 14.5%, India 13.9%, Belgium 9.7%, US 8.9%, France 8.1%, Canada 6.6% (2015)
Imports: $2.06 billion (2015 est.)
$1.966 billion (2014 est.)
country comparison to the world: 162
Imports—commodities: capital equipment, petroleum, foodstuffs, cotton, consumer goods
Imports—partners: US 26.8%, Netherlands 14.3%, China 12.2%, Trinidad and Tobago 7.4%, Japan 4.8% (2015)
Reserves of foreign exchange and gold: $625.2 million (31 December 2014 est.) $778.8 million (31 December 2013 est.)
country comparison to the world: 144
Debt—external: $1.067 billion (31 December 2014 est.) $983 million (31 December 2013 est.)
country comparison to the world: 163
Exchange rates: Surinamese dollars (SRD) per US dollar—
-3.3 (2015 est.)
3.3 (2014 est.)
3.3 (2013 est.)
3.3 (2012 est.)
3.2683 (2011 est.)

ENERGY

Electricity—production: 1.75 billion kWh (2012 est.)
country comparison to the world: 144
Electricity—consumption: 1.572 billion kWh (2012 est.)
country comparison to the world: 146
Electricity—exports: 0 kWh (2013 est.)
country comparison to the world: 180
Electricity—imports: 0 kWh (2013 est.)
country comparison to the world: 185
Electricity—Installed generating capacity: 412,000 kW (2012 est.)
country comparison to the world: 145
Electricity—from fossil fuels: 54.1% of total installed capacity (2012 est.)
country comparison to the world: 144
Electricity—from nuclear fuels: 0% of total installed capacity (2012 est.)
country comparison to the world: 158
Electricity—from hydroelectric plants: 45.9% of total installed capacity (2012 est.)
country comparison to the world: 53
Electricity—from other renewable sources: 0% of total installed capacity (2012 est.)
country comparison to the world: 210

Crude oil—production: 15,000 bbl/day (2014 est.)
country comparison to the world: 77
Crude oil—exports: 0 bbl/day (2012 est.)
country comparison to the world: 172
Crude oil—imports: 0 bbl/day (2012 est.)
country comparison to the world: 111
Crude oil—proved reserves: 88.97 million bbl (1 January 2015 est.)
country comparison to the world: 73
Refined petroleum products—production: 15,980 bbl/day (2012 est.)
country comparison to the world: 98
Refined petroleum products—consumption: 17,000 bbl/day (2013 est.)
country comparison to the world: 137
Refined petroleum products—exports: 8,884 bbl/day (2012 est.)
country comparison to the world: 89
Refined petroleum products—imports: 10,070 bbl/day (2012 est.)
country comparison to the world: 137
Natural gas—production: 0 cu m (2013 est.)
country comparison to the world: 114
Natural gas—consumption: 0 cu m (2013 est.)
country comparison to the world: 182
Natural gas—exports: 0 cu m (2013 est.)
country comparison to the world: 158
Natural gas—imports: 0 cu m (2013 est.)
country comparison to the world: 114
Natural gas—proved reserves: 0 cu m (1 January 2011 est.)
country comparison to the world: 181
Carbon dioxide emissions from consumption of energy: 2.268 million Mt (2012 est.)
country comparison to the world: 147

COMMUNICATIONS

Telephones—fixed lines: *total subscriptions:* 84,900
subscriptions per 100 inhabitants: 15 (2014 est.)
country comparison to the world: 147
Telephones—mobile cellular: *total:* 927,800
subscriptions per 100 inhabitants: 162 (2014 est.)
country comparison to the world: 159
Telephone system: *general assessment:* International facilities are good
domestic: combined fixed-line and mobile-cellular teledensity 185 telephones per 100 persons; microwave radio relay network
international: country code—597; satellite earth stations—2 intelsat (Atlantic Ocean) (2010)
Broadcast media: 2 state-owned TV stations; 1 state-owned radio station; multiple private radio and TV stations (2007)
Radio broadcast stations: AM 4, FM 23, shortwave 3 (2008)
Television broadcast stations: 3 (plus 7 repeaters) (2000)
Internet country code: .sr
Internet hosts: 188 (2012)
country comparison to the world: 201
Internet users: *total:* 212,900
percent of population: 37.1% (2014 est.)
country comparison to the world: 154

TRANSPORTATION

Airports: 55 (2013)
country comparison to the world: 85
Airports—with paved runways: *total:* 6
over 3,047 m: 1
under 914 m: 5 (2013)

Airports—with unpaved runways: *total:* 49
914 to 1,523 m: 4
under 914 m: 45 (2013)
Pipelines: oil 50 km (2013)
Roadways: *total:* 4,304 km
paved: 1,130 km
unpaved: 3,174 km (2003)
country comparison to the world: 155
Waterways: 1,200 km (most navigable by ships with drafts up to 7 m) (2011)
country comparison to the world: 58
Ports and terminals: major seaport(s): Paramaribo, Wageningen

MILITARY AND SECURITY

Military branches: Suriname Armed Forces: Ground Forces, Naval Forces, Air Forces (2010)
Military service age and obligation: 18 is the legal minimum age for voluntary military service; no conscription; personnel drawn almost exclusively from the Creole community (2012)

TRANSNATIONAL ISSUES

Disputes—International: area claimed by French Guiana between Riviere Litani and Riviere Marouini (both headwaters of the Lawa); Suriname claims a triangle of land between the New and Kutari/Koetari rivers in a historic dispute over the headwaters of the Courantyne; Guyana seeks UN Convention on the Law of the Sea arbitration to resolve the longstanding dispute with Suriname over the axis of the territorial sea boundary in potentially oil-rich waters

Trafficking in persons: *current situation:* Suriname is a source, transit, and destination country for women and children subjected to sex trafficking and men, women, and children subjected to forced labor; women and girls from Suriname, Guyana, Brazil, and the Dominican Republic are subjected to sex trafficking in the country, sometimes in interior mining camps; migrant workers in Agriculture and on fishing boats and children working in informal urban sectors and gold mines are vulnerable to forced labor; traffickers from Suriname exploit victims in the Netherlands

tier rating: Tier 2 Watch List—Suriname does not fully comply with the minimum standards for the elimination of trafficking; however, it is making significant efforts to do so; in 2014, Suriname was granted a waiver from an otherwise required downgrade to Tier 3 because its government has a written plan that, if implemented, would constitute making significant efforts to bring itself into compliance with the minimum standards for the elimination of trafficking; authorities increased the number of trafficking investigations, prosecutions, and convictions as compared to 2013, but resources were insufficient to conduct investigations in the country's interior; more trafficking victims were identified in 2014 than in 2013, but protective services for adults and children were inadequate, with a proposed government shelter for women and child trafficking victims remaining unopened (2015)

Illicit drugs: growing transshipment point for South American drugs destined for Europe via the Netherlands and Brazil; transshipment point for arms-for-drugs dealing

SVALBARD

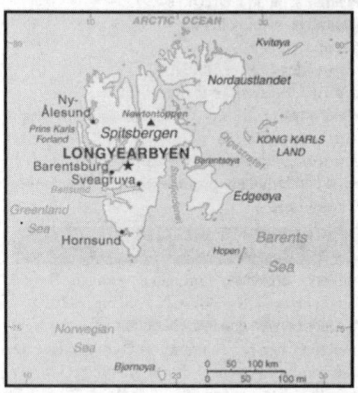

INTRODUCTION

Background: The archipelago may have been first discovered by Norse explorers in the 12th century; the islands served as an International whaling base during the 17th and 18th centuries. Norway's sovereignty was Internationally recognized by treaty in 1920, and five years later it officially took over the territory. In the 20th century coal mining started and today a Norwegian and a Russian company are still functioning. Travel between the settlements is accomplished with snowmobiles, aircraft, and boats.

GEOGRAPHY

Location: Northern Europe, islands between the Arctic Ocean, Barents Sea, Greenland Sea, and Norwegian Sea, north of Norway

Geographic coordinates: 78 00 N, 20 00 E

Map references: Arctic Region

Area: *total:* 62,045 sq km

land: 62,045 sq km

water: 0 sq km

note: includes Spitsbergen and Bjornoya (Bear Island)

country comparison to the world: 125

Area—comparative: slightly smaller than West Virginia

Land boundaries: 0 km

Coastline: 3,587 km

Maritime claims: *territorial sea:* 4 nm

exclusive fishing zone: 200 nm unilaterally claimed by Norway but not recognized by Russia

Climate: arctic, tempered by warm North Atlantic Current; cool summers, cold winters; North Atlantic Current flows along west and north coasts of Spitsbergen, keeping water open and navigable most of the year

Terrain: rugged mountains; much of the upland areas are ice covered; west coast clear of ice about half the year; fjords along west and north coasts

Elevation: *mean elevation:* NA

elevation extremes: *lowest point:* Arctic Ocean 0 m

highest point: Newtontoppen 1,717 m

Natural resources: coal, iron ore, copper, zinc, phosphate, wildlife, fish

Land use: *agricultural land:* 0%

arable land: 0%

permanent crops: 0%

permanent pasture: 0%

forest: 0%

other: 100% (2011 est.)

Natural hazards: ice floes often block the entrance to Bellsund (a transit point for coal export) on the west coast and occasionally make parts of the northeastern coast inaccessible to maritime traffic

Environment—current issues: NA

Geography—note: northernmost part of the Kingdom of Norway; consists of nine main islands; glaciers and snowfields cover 60% of the total area; Spitsbergen Island is the site of the Svalbard Global Seed Vault, a seed repository established by the Global Crop Diversity Trust and the Norwegian government

PEOPLE AND SOCIETY

Ethnic groups: Norwegian 55.4%, Russian and Ukrainian 44.3%, other 0.3% (1998)

Languages: Norwegian, Russian

Population: 1,872 (July 2014 est.)

country comparison to the world: 232

Population growth rate: -0.03% (2014 est.)

country comparison to the world: 201

Sex ratio: NA

Infant mortality rate: *total:* NA

male: NA

female: NA

Life expectancy at birth: *total population:* NA

male: NA

female: NA

Total fertility rate: NA

GOVERNMENT

Country name: *conventional long form:* none

conventional short form: Svalbard (sometimes referred to as Spitsbergen, the largest island in the archipelago)

etymology: 12th century Norse accounts speak of the discovery of a "Svalbard"—literally "cold shores"—but they may have referred to Jan Mayen island or eastern Greenland; the archipelago was traditionally known as Spitsbergen, but Norway renamed it Svalbard in the 1920s when it assumed sovereignty of the islands

Dependency status: territory of Norway; administered by the Polar Department of the Ministry of Justice, through a governor (sysselmann) residing in Longy earby en, Spitsbergen; by treaty (9 February 1920) sovereignty was awarded to Norway

Government type: **Capital:** *name:* Longyearbyen

Geographic coordinates: 78 13 N, 15 38 E

time difference: UTC + 1 (6 hours ahead of Washington, DC, during Standard Time)

daylight saving time: +1 hr, begins last Sunday in March; ends last Sunday in October

Independence: none (territory of Norway)

Legal system: the laws of Norway where applicable apply; only the laws of Norway made explicitly applicable to Svalbard have effect there; the Svalbard Act and the Svalbard Environmental Protection act, and certain regulations, apply only to Svalbard; the Spitsbergen Treaty and the Svalbard Treaty grants certain rights to citizens and corporations of signatory nations

Citizenship: see Norway

Executive branch: *chief of state:* King HARALDV of Norway (since 17 January 1991)

head of government: Governor Kjersti NASKHOLT (since 1 October 2015); Assistant Governor Lars Erik ALHEIM

elections/appointments: none; the monarchy is hereditary; governor and assistant governor responsible to the Polar Department of the Ministry of Justice

Legislative branch: *description:* unicameral Longyear by en Community Council (15 seats; members elected by direct vote to serve four-year-terms)

elections: last held on 6 October 2015 (next to be held October 2019)

election resulta: seats by party—Conservatives 5, Green Party 2, Labor Party 5, Liberals 3

note: the Council's main reponsibilities are infrastructures and utilities, including power, land-use and community planning, education, and child welfare; however, healthcare services are provided by the state

Judicial branch: *highest court(s):* none; note—Svalbard is subordinate to Norway's Nord-Troms District Court and Halogal and Court of Appeal, both located in Tromso

Political parties and leaders: Svalbard Conservative Party; Svalbard Green Party [Espen Klungseth ROTEVATN]; Svalbard Labor Party [Chjristin KRISTOFFERSEN]; Svalbard Liberal Party

Political pressure groups and leaders: NA

International organization participation: none

Flag description: the flag of Norway is used

National anthem: *note:* as a territory of Norway, "Javielsker dette landet" is official (see Norway)

ECONOMY

Economy—overview: Tourism and International research are Svalbard's major revenue sources. Coal mining has historically been the dominant economic activity, and a treaty of 9 February 1920 gave the 41 signatories equal rights to exploit mineral deposits, subject to Norwegian regulation. Although US, UK, Dutch, and Swedish coal companies have mined in the past, the only companies still engaging in this are Norwegian and Russian. Low coal prices have forced the Norwegian coal company, Store Norske Spitsbergen Kulkompani, to close one of its two mines and to considerably reduce the activity of the other. Since the 1990s, the tourism and hospitality industry has grown rapidly, and Svalbard now receives 60,000 visitors annually.

The settlements on Svalbard were established as company towns, and at their height in the 1950s, the Norwegian state-owned coal company supported around 1,000 jobs. Today, around 300 people work in the mining industry. Goods such as alcohol, tobacco, and vehicles, normally highly taxed on mainland Norway, are considerably cheaper in Svalbard in an effort by the Norwegian Government to entice more people to live on the Arctic archipelago. By law, Norway collects only enough taxes to pay for the needs of the local government; none of tax proceeds go to the central government.

GDP—real growth rate: NA%
Labor force: 1,590 (2013)
country comparison to the world: 229
Budget: *revenues:* $NA
expenditures: $NA
Taxes and other revenues: NA% of GDP
Budget surplus (+) or deficit (–): NA% of GDP
Exports: $NA
Imports: $NA
Exchange rates: Norwegian kroner (NOK) per US dollar—
7.876 (2015)
5.876 (2013)
5.876 (2013)
5.82 (2012)
5.6065 (2011)

ENERGY

Crude oil—production: 194,300 bbl/day (2014 est.)
country comparison to the world: 39

Crude oil—exports: 16,070 bbl/day (2012 est.)
country comparison to the world: 60
Crude oil—imports: 0 bbl/day (2012 est.)
country comparison to the world: 129
Refined petroleum products—consumption: 80,250 bbl/day (2013 est.)
country comparison to the world: 84
Refined petroleum products—exports: 4,488 bbl/day (2012 est.)
country comparison to the world: 96
Refined petroleum products—imports: 18,600 bbl/day (2012 est.)
country comparison to the world: 114
Natural gas—production: 0 cu m (2013 est.)
country comparison to the world: 132
Natural gas—consumption: 0 cu m (2013 est.)
country comparison to the world: 197
Natural gas—exports: 0 cu m (2013 est.)
country comparison to the world: 185
Natural gas—imports: 0 cu m (2013 est.)
country comparison to the world: 137

COMMUNICATIONS

Telephone system: *general assessment:* adequate
domestic: local telephone service
international: country code—47-790; satellite earth station—1 of unknown type (for communication with Norwegian mainland only) (2005)
Broadcast media: the Norwegian Broadcasting Corporation (NRK) began direct TV transmission to Svalbard via satellite in 1984; Longyearbyen

households have access to 3 NRK radio and 2 TV stations (2008)
Radio broadcast stations: AM 1, FM 1 (plus 2 repeaters), shortwave 0 (1998)
Television broadcast stations: NA
Internet country code: .sj

TRANSPORTATION

Airports: 4 (2013)
country comparison to the world: 190
Airports—with paved runways: *total:* 1
2,438 to 3,047 m: 1 (2013)
Airports—with unpaved runways: *total:* 3
under 914 m: 3 (2013)
Heliports: 1 (2013)
Ports and terminals: *major seaport(s):* Barentsburg, Longyearbyen, Ny-Alesund, Pyramiden

MILITARY AND SECURITY

Military branches: No regular Military forces
Military—note: Svalbard is a territory of Norway, demilitarized by treaty on 9 February 1920; Norwegian military activity is limited to fisheries surveillance by the Norwegian Coast Guard

TRANSNATIONAL ISSUES

Disputes—International: despite recent discussions, Russia and Norway dispute their maritime limits in the Barents Sea and Russia's fishing rights beyond Svalbard's territorial limits within the Svalbard Treaty zone

SWAZILAND

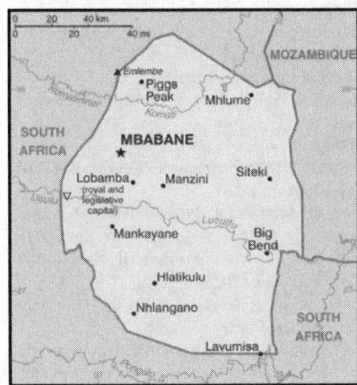

INTRODUCTION

Background: Autonomy for the Swazis of southern Africa was guaranteed by the British in the late 19th century; independence was granted in 1968. Student and labor unrest during the 1990s pressured King MSWATI III, Africa's last absolute monarch, to grudgingly allow political reform and greater democracy, although he has backslid on these promises in recent years. A constitution

came into effect in 2006, but the legal status of political parties was not defined and their status remains unclear. Swaziland has surpassed Botswana as the country with the world's highest known HIV/AIDS prevalence rate.

GEOGRAPHY

Location: Southern Africa, between Mozambique and South Africa
Geographic coordinates: 26 30 S, 3130 E
Map references: Africa
Area: *total:* 17,364 sq km
land: 17,204 sq km
water: 160 sq km
country comparison to the world: 159
Area—comparative: slightly smaller than New Jersey
Land boundaries: *total:* 546 km
border countries (2): Mozambique 108 km, South Africa 438 km
Coastline: 0 km (landlocked)
Maritime claims: none (landlocked)
Climate: varies from tropical to near temperate
Terrain: mostly mountains and hills; some moderately sloping plains
Elevation: *mean elevation:* 305 m

elevation extremes: *lowest point:* Great Usutu River 21 m
highest point: Emlembe 1,862 m
Natural resources: asbestos, coal, clay, cassiterite, hydropower, forests, small gold and diamond deposits, quarry stone, and talc
Land use: *agricultural land:* 68.3%
arable land: 9.8%
permanent crops: 0.8%
permanent pasture: 57.7%
forest: 31.7%
other: 0% (2011 est.)
Irrigated land: 500 sq km (2012)
Total renewable water resources: 4.51 cu km (2011)
Freshwater withdrawal (domestic/industrial/agricultural): *total:* 1.04 cu km/yr (4%/2%/94%)
per capita: 962.1 cu m/yr (2005)
Natural hazards: drought
Environment—current issues: limited supplies of potable water; wildlife populations being depleted because of excessive hunting; overgrazing; soil degradation; soil erosion
Environment—International agreements: *party to:* Biodiversity, Climate Change, Climate Change-Kyoto Protocol, Desertification, Endangered Species, Hazardous Wastes, Ozone Layer Protection
signed, but not ratified: Law of the Sea

Geography—note: landlocked; almost completely surrounded by South Africa

PEOPLE AND SOCIETY

Nationality: *noun:* Swazi(s)
adjective: Swazi

Ethnic groups: African 97%, European 3%

Languages: English (official, used for government business), siswati (official)

Religions: Zionist 40% (a blend of Christianity and indigenous ancestral worship), Roman Catholic 20%, Muslim 10%, other 30% (includes Anglican, Baha'i, Methodist, Mormon, Jewish)

Population: 1,435,613

note: estimates for this country explicitly take into account the effects of excess mortality due to AIDS; this can result in lower life expectancy, higher infant mortality, higher death rates, lower population growth rates, and changes in the distribution of population by age and sex than would otherwise be expected (July 2015 est.)
country comparison to the world: 155

Age structure: 0–14 years: 35.99% (male 261,213/female 255,489)

15–24 years: 22.26% (male 161,626/female 157,990)

25–54 years: 33.64% (male 249,233/female 233,703)

55–64 years: 4.26% (male 24,229/female 36,968)

65 years and over: 3.84% (male 21,582/female 33,580) (2015 est.)

Dependency ratios: *total dependency ratio:* 69.3%
youth dependency ratio: 63.2%
elderly dependency ratio: 6.1%
potential support ratio: 16.5% (2015 est.)

Median age: *total:* 21.2 years
male: 21 years
female: 21.5 years (2015 est.)
country comparison to the world: 183

Population growth rate: 1.11% (2015 est.)
country comparison to the world: 111

Birth rate: 24.67 births/1,000 population (2015 est.)
country comparison to the world: 55

Death rate: 13.56 deaths/1,000 population (2015 est.)
country comparison to the world: 14

Net migration rate: 0 migrant(s)/1,000 population (2015 est.)
country comparison to the world: 82

Urbanization: *urban population:* 21.3% of total population (2015)
rate of urbanization: 1.32% annual rate of change (2010–15 est.)

Major urban areas—population: MBABANE (capital) 66,000 (2014)

Sex ratio: *at birth:* 1.03 male(s)/female
0–14 years: 1.02 male(s)/female
15–24 years: 1.02 male(s)/female
25–54 years: 1.07 male(s)/female
55–64 years: 0.66 male(s)/female
65 years and over: 0.64 male(s)/female
total population: 1 male(s)/female (2015 est.)

Mother's mean age at first birth: 19.8

note: Median Age at first birth among women 20–24 (2006/07 est.)

Maternal mortality rate: 389 deaths/100,000 live births (2015 est.)
country comparison to the world: 36

Infant mortality rate: *total:* 52.57 deaths/1,000 live births
male: 56.49 deaths/1,000 live births
female: 48.53 deaths/1,000 live births (2015 est.)
country comparison to the world: 33

Life expectancy at birth: *total population:* 51.05 years
male: 51.6 years
female: 50.5 years (2015 est.)
country comparison to the world: 221

Total fertility rate: 2.8 children born/woman (2015 est.)
country comparison to the world: 63

Contraceptive prevalence rate: 65.2% (2010)

Health expenditures: 8.4% of GDP (2013)
country comparison to the world: 49

Physicians density: 0.17 physicians/1,000 population (2009)

Hospital bed density: 2.1 beds/1,000 population (2011)

Drinking water source:
improved:
urban: 93.6% of population
rural: 68.9% of population
total: 74.1% of population
unimproved:
urban: 6.4% of population
rural: 31.1% of population
total: 25.9% of population (2015 est.)

Sanitation facility access:
improved:
urban: 63.1% of population
rural: 56% of population
total: 57.5% of population
unimproved:
urban: 36.9% of population
rural: 44% of population
total: 42.5% of population (2015 est.)

HIV/AIDS—adult prevalence rate: 27.73% (2014 est.)
country comparison to the world: 1

HIV/AIDS—people living with HIV/AIDS: 214,300 (2014 est.)
country comparison to the world: 26

HIV/AIDS—deaths: 3,500 (2014 est.)
country comparison to the world: 41

Major infectious diseases: *degree of risk:* intermediate
food or waterborne diseases: bacterial diarrhea, hepatitis A, and typhoid fever
vectorborne disease: malaria water contact disease: schistosomiasis (2013)

Obesity—adult prevalence rate: 14.8% (2014)
country comparison to the world: 98

Children under the age of 5 years underweight: 5.8% (2014)
country comparison to the world: 84

Education expenditures: 8.6% of GDP (2011)
country comparison to the world: 12

Literacy: *definition:* age 15 and over can read and write

total population: 87.5%
male: 87.4%
female: 87.5% (2015 est.)

School life expectancy (primary to tertiary education): *total:* 11 years
male: 12 years
female: 11 years (2013)

GOVERNMENT

Country name: *conventional long form:* Kingdom of Swaziland
conventional short form: Swaziland
local long form: Umbuso weSwatini
local short form: eSwatini
etymology: "Land of the Swazi" people; the name "Swazi" derives from 19th century King MSWATI II, under whose rule Swazi territory was expanded and unified

Government type: absolute monarchy

Capital: *name:* Mbabane; note—Lobamba is the royal and legislative capital

Geographic coordinates: 26 19 S, 3108 E
time difference: UTC+2 (7 hours ahead of Washington, DC, during Standard Time)

Administrative divisions: 4 districts; Hhohho, Lubombo, Manzini, Shiselweni

Independence: 6 September 1968 (from the UK)

National holiday: Independence Day, 6 September (1968)

Constitution: previous 1968, 1978; latest signed by the king 26 July 2005, effective 8 February 2006 (2016)

Legal system: mixed legal system of civil, common, and customary law

International law organization participation: accepts compulsory ICJ jurisdiction with reservations; non-party state to the ICCt

Citizenship: *citizenship by birth:* no
citizenship by descent only: both parents must be citizens of Swaziland
dual citizenship recognized: no
residency requirement for naturalization: 5 years

Suffrage: 18 years of age

Executive branch: *chief of state:* King MSWATI III (since 25 April 1986)

head of government: Prime Minister Barnabas Sibusiso DLAMINI (since 23 October 2008); Deputy Prime Minister Themba Nhlanganiso MASUKU (since 2008)

cabinet: Cabinet recommended by the prime minister, confirmed by the monarch

elections/appointments: the monarchy is hereditary; prime minister appointed by the monarch from among elected members of the House of Assembly

Legislative branch: *description:* bicameral Parliament or Libandla consists of the Senate (30 seats; 20 members appointed by the monarch and 10 indirectly elected by simple majority vote by the House of Assembly; members serve 5-year terms) and the House of Assembly (65 seats; 55 members directly elected in single-seat constituencies by simple majority vote and 10 members appointed by the monarch; members serve 5-year terms) *elections:* House of Assembly—last held on 20 September 2013 (next scheduled for September 2018)

election results: House of Assembly—no results of the election were released; note—balloting is done on a nonparty basis; for each constituency the three candidates with the most votes in the first round of voting are narrowed to a single winner by a second round

Judicial branch: *highest court(s):* the Supreme Court of the Judicature comprising the Supreme Court (consists of the chief justice and at least 5 justices) and the High Court (consists of the chief justice—ex officio—and at least 4 justices); note—the Supreme Court has jurisdiction in all constitutional matters

judge selection and term of office: justices of the Supreme Court of the Judicature are appointed by the monarch on the advice of the Judicial Service Commission or JCS, a judicial advisory body consisting of the Supreme Court Chief Justice, 4 members appointed by the monarch, and the JCS head; justices of both courts eligible for retirement at age 65 with mandatory retirement at age 75 for Supreme Court justices and at age 70 for High Court justices

subordinate courts: magistrates' courts; National Swazi Courts for administering customary/traditional laws (jurisdiction restricted to customary law for Swazi citizens)

note: the National constitution as amended in 2006 shifted judicial power from the monarch and vested it exclusively in the judiciary

Political parties and leaders: the status of political parties, previously banned, is unclear under the 2006 Constitution; the following are considered *political associations:* African United Democratic Party or AUDP [Stanley MAUNDZISA] Ngwane National Liberatory Congress or NNLC [Alvit DLAMINI] People's United Democratic Movement or PUDEMO [Mario MASUKU] Swaziland Democratic Party roswadepa [Jan SITHOLE]

Political pressure groups and leaders: Swaziland Democracy Campaign Swaziland Federation of Trade Unions Swaziland Solidarity Network or SSN

International organization participation: ACP, AfDB, AU, C, COMESA, FAO, G-77, IAEA, IBRD, ICAO, ICRM, IDA, IFAD, IFC, IFRCS, ILO, IMF, IMO, Interpol, IOC, IOM, ISO (correspondent), ITSO, ITU, ITUC (NGOs), MIGA, NAM, OPCW, PCA, SACU, SADC, UN, UN CTAD, UNESCO, UNIDO, UNWTO, UPU, WCO, WHO, WIPO, WMO, WTO

Diplomatic representation in the US: *chief of mission:* Ambassador Abednigo Mandlan TSH AN Gase (since 19 July 2010)

chancery: 1712 New Hampshire Avenue, NW, Washington, DC 20009

telephone: [1] (202) 234-5002

FAX: [1] (202) 234-8254

Diplomatic representation from the US: *chief of mission:* Ambassador Lisa PETERSON (since January 2016)

embassy: 7th Floor, Central Bank Building, Mahlokohla St., Mbabane

mailing address: P.O . Box 199, Mbabane

telephone: [268] 404-6441

FAX: [268] 404-5959

Flag description: three horizontal bands of blue (top), red (triple width), and blue; the red band is edged in yellow; centered in the red band is a large black and white shield covering two spears and a staff decorated with feather tassels, all placed horizontally; blue stands for peace and stability, red represents past struggles, and yellow the mineral resources of the country; the shield, spears, and staff symbolize protection from the country's enemies, while the black and white of the shield are meant to portray black and white people living in peaceful coexistence

National symbol(s): lion, elephant; National colors: blue, yellow, red

National anthem: *name:* "Nkulunkulu Mnikati wetibusiso temaSwati" (Oh God, Bestower of the Blessings of the Swazi)

lyrics/music: Andrease Enoke Fanyana SIMELANE/David Kenneth RYCROFT

note: adopted 1968; uses elements of both ethnic Swazi and Western music styles

ECONOMY

Economy—overview: Surrounded by South Africa, except for a short border with Mozambique, Swaziland depends on South Africa for 60% of its exports and for more than 90% of its imports. Swaziland's currency is pegged to the South African rand, effectively relinquishing Swaziland's monetary policy to South Africa. The government is heavily dependent on customs duties from the Southern African Customs Union (SACU), and worker remittances from South Africa supplement domestically earned income. Swaziland's GDP per capita makes it a lower middle income country, but its income distribution is highly skewed, with an estimated 20% of the population controlling 80% of the nation's wealth. As of 2013, more than one-quarter of the adult population was infected by HIV/AIDS; Swaziland has the world's highest HIV prevalence rate.

Subsistence agriculture employs approximately 70% of the population. The manufacturing sector diversified in the 1980s and 1990s, but manufacturing has grown little in the last decade. Sugar and wood pulp had been major foreign exchange earners until the wood pulp producer closed in January 2010, and sugar is now the main export earner. Mining has declined in importance in recent years. Coal, gold, diamond, and quarry stone mines are smallscale, and the only iron ore mine closed in 2014. With an estimated 40% unemployment rate, Swaziland's need to increase the number and size of small and medium enterprises and to attract foreign direct investment is acute. Overgrazing, soil depletion, drought, and floods are persistent problems. On 1 January 2015, Swaziland lost its eligibility for benefits under the US African Growth and Opportunity Act, resulting in the loss of thousands of jobs.

The IMF forecasted that Swaziland's economy will grow at a slower pace in 2016/2017 because of a region-wide drought, which is likely to hurt Swaziland's revenue from sugar exports and other agricultural products, and a decline in the tourism and transport sectors. Swaziland's revenue from SACU receipts and remittances from Swazi citizens abroad will also decline in 2016/2017, making it harder to maintain fiscal balance.

GDP (purchasing power parity): $10.85 billion (2015 est.)

$10.67 billion (2014 est.)

$10.41 billion (2013 est.)

note: data are in 2015 US dollars

country comparison to the world: 156

GDP (official exchange rate): $4.028 billion (2015 est.)

GDP—real growth rate: 1.7% (2015 est.)

2.5% (2014 est.)

2.9% (2013 est.)

country comparison to the world: 145

GDP—per capita (PPP): $8,500 (2015 est.)

$8,400 (2014 est.)

$8,300 (2013 est.)

note: data are in 2015 US dollars

country comparison to the world: 143

Gross National saving: 11.4% of GDP (2015 est.)

12.5% of GDP (2014 est.)

12.7% of GDP (2013 est.)

country comparison to the world: 143

GDP—composition, by end use:

household consumption: 78.7%

government consumption: 24%

investment in fixed capital: 11.6%

investment in inventories: -0.1%

exports of goods and services: 50.7%

imports of goods and services: -64.9% (2015 est.)

GDP—composition, by sector of origin:

agriculture: 11.9%

industry: 46.6%

services: 41.5% (2015 est.)

Agriculture—products: sugarcane, cotton, corn, tobacco, rice, citrus, pineapples, sorghum, peanuts; cattle, goats, sheep

Industries: coal, forestry, sugar, soft drink concentrates, textiles and apparel

Industrial production growth rate: 1.1% (2015 est.)

country comparison to the world: 141

Labor force: 446,100 (2013 est.)

country comparison to the world: 158

Labor force—by occupation: *agriculture:* 70%

industry: NA%

services: NA%

Unemployment rate: 40% (2006 est.)

country comparison to the world: 194

Population below poverty line: 69% (2006 est.)

Household income or consumption by percentage share: *lowest:* 10%: 1.7%

highest: 10%: 40.1% (2010 est.)

Distribution of family income—Gini index: 50.4 (2001)

country comparison to the world: 19

Budget: *revenues:* $1.153 billion

expenditures: $1.264 billion (2015 est.)

Taxes and other revenues: 26.8% of GDP (2015 est.)

811

country comparison to the world: 106
Budget surplus (+) or deficit (–): -2.6% of GDP (2015 est.)
country comparison to the world: 97
Fiscal year: 1 April—31 March
Inflation rate (consumer prices): 5% (2015 est.)
5.7% (2014 est.)
country comparison to the world: 174
Central bank discount rate: 6.5% (31 December 2010)
6.5% (31 December 2009)
country comparison to the world: 58
Commercial bank prime lending rate: 8.7% (31 December 2015 est.)
8.63% (31 December 2014 est.)
country comparison to the world: 100
Stock of narrow money: $317.1 million (31 December 2015 est.)
$367.8 million (31 December 2014 est.)
country comparison to the world: 174
Stock of broad money: $825.6 million (31 December 2015 est.)
$1.008 billion (31 December 2014 est.)
country comparison to the world: 173
Stock of domestic credit: $562.6 million (31 December 2015 est.)
$685 million (31 December 2014 est.)
country comparison to the world: 166
Market value of publicly traded shares: $NA
$203.1 million (31 December 2007)
$199.9 million (31 December 2006)
Current account balance: $20 million (2015 est.)
$145 million (2014 est.)
country comparison to the world: 51
Exports: $1.575 billion (2015 est.)
$1.803 billion (2014 est.)
country comparison to the world: 148
Exports—commodities: soft drink concentrates, sugar, timber, cotton yarn, refrigerators, citrus and canned fruit
Imports: $1.581 billion (2015 est.)
$1.687 billion (2014 est.)
country comparison to the world: 171
Imports—commodities: motor vehicles, machinery, transport equipment, foodstuffs, petroleum Products, chemicals
Reserves of foreign exchange and gold: $572.3 million (31 December 2015 est.)
$690.8 million (31 December 2014 est.)
country comparison to the world: 147
Debt—external: $561.3 million (31 December 2014 est.)
$463.6 million (31 December 2013 est.)
country comparison to the world: 176
Stock of direct foreign investment—at home: $NA
Stock of direct foreign investment—abroad: $NA
Exchange rates: emalangeni per US dollar—
12.58 (2015 est.)
10.8469 (2014 est.)
10.8469 (2013 est.)
8.2 (2012 est.)
7.2597 (2011 est.)

ENERGY

Electricity—production: 425 million kWh (2012 est.)

country comparison to the world: 164
Electricity—consumption: 1.295 billion kWh (2012 est.)
country comparison to the world: 149
Electricity—exports: 0 kWh (2013)
country comparison to the world: 217
Electricity—imports: 900 million kWh (2012 est.)
country comparison to the world: 66
Electricity—installed generating capacity: 149,000 kW (2012 est.)
country comparison to the world: 165
Electricity—from fossil fuels: 59.7% of total installed capacity (2012 est.)
country comparison to the world: 135
Electricity—from nuclear fuels: 0% of total installed capacity (2012 est.)
country comparison to the world: 211
Electricity—from hydroelectric plants: 40.3% of total installed capacity (2012 est.)
country comparison to the world: 60
Electricity—from other renewable sources: 0% of total installed capacity (2012 est.)
country comparison to the world: 146
Crude oil—production: 0 bbl/day (2014 est.)
country comparison to the world: 212
Crude oil—exports: 0 bbl/day (2012 est.)
country comparison to the world: 212
Crude oil—imports: 0 bbl/day (2012 est.)
country comparison to the world: 150
Crude oil—proved reserves: 0 bbl (1 January 2010 est.)
country comparison to the world: 213
Refined petroleum products—production: 0 bbl/day (2012 est.)
country comparison to the world: 149
Refined petroleum products—consumption: 4,800 bbl/day (2013 est.)
country comparison to the world: 172
Refined petroleum products—exports: 0 bbl/day (2012 est.)
country comparison to the world: 149
Refined petroleum products—imports: 4,785 bbl/day (2012 est.)
country comparison to the world: 164
Natural gas—production: 0 cu m (2013 est.)
country comparison to the world: 150
Natural gas—consumption: 0 cu m (2013 est.)
country comparison to the world: 213
Natural gas—exports: 0 cu m (2013 est.)
country comparison to the world: 213
Natural gas—imports: 0 cu m (2013 est.)
country comparison to the world: 83
Natural gas—proved reserves: 0 cu m (1 January 2014 est.)
country comparison to the world: 210
Carbon dioxide emissions from consumption of energy: 936,900 Mt (2012 est.)
country comparison to the world: 167

COMMUNICATIONS

Telephone—fixed lines: *total subscriptions:* 44,400
subscriptions per 100 inhabitants: 3 (2014 est.)
country comparison to the world: 160
Telephone—mobile cellular: *total:* 916,800
subscriptions per 100 inhabitants: 65 (2014 est.)

country comparison to the world:
Telephone system: *general assessment:* a somewhat modern but not an advanced system
domestic: single source for mobile-cellular service with a geographic coverage of about 90% and a rising subscribership base; combined fixed-line and mobile cellular teledensity roughly 60 telephones per 100 persons in 2011; telephone system consists of carrier-equipped, open-wire lines and low-capacity, microwave radio relay
international: country code—268; satellite earth station—1 intelsat (Atlantic Ocean) (2009)
Broadcast media: state-owned TV station; satellite dishes are able to access South African providers; state-owned radio network with 3 channels; 1 private radio station (2007)
Radio broadcast stations: AM 3, FM 2 (plus 4 repeaters), shortwave 3 (2004)
Television broadcast stations: 12 (includes 7 relay stations) (2004)
Internet country code: .sz
Internet hosts: 2,744 (2012)
country comparison to the world: 158
Internet users: *total:* 337,300
percent of population: 23.8% (2014 est.)
country comparison to the world: 137

TRANSPORTATION

Airports: 14 (2013)
country comparison to the world: 149
Airports—with paved runways: *total:* 2
over 3,047 m: 1
2,438 to 3,047 m: 1 (2013)
Airports—with unpaved runways: *total:* 12
914 to 1,523 m: 5
under 914 m: 7 (2013)
Railways: *total:* 301 km
narrow gauge: 301 km 1.067-m gauge (2014)
country comparison to the world: 123
Roadways: *total:* 3,594 km
paved: 1,078 km
unpaved: 2,516 km (2002)
country comparison to the world: 161

MILITARY AND SECURITY

Military branches: Umbutfo Swaziland Defense Force (USDF): Ground Force (includes Air Wing (no operation al aircraft)) (2013)
Military service age and obligation: 18–30 years of age for male and female voluntary military service; no conscription; compulsory HIV testing required, only HIV-negative applicants accepted (2012)
Military expenditures: 3.17% of GDP (2012)
3.11% of GDP (2011)
3.17% of GDP (2010)
country comparison to the world: 18

TRANSNATIONAL ISSUES

Disputes—International: in 2006, Swazi king advocated resorting to ICJ to claim parts of Mpumalanga and KwaZulu-Natal from South Africa

SWEDEN

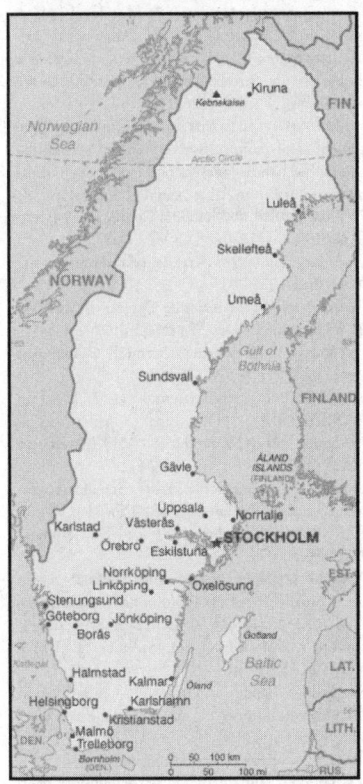

INTRODUCTION

Background: A military power during the 17th century, Sweden has not participated in any war for two centuries. An armed neutrality was preserved in both world wars. Sweden's long-successful economic formula of a capitalist system intermixed with substantial welfare elements was challenged in the 1990s by high unemployment and in 2000–02 and 2009 by the global economic downturns, but fiscal discipline over the past several years has allowed the country to weather economic vagaries. Sweden joined the EU in 1995, but the public rejected the introduction of the euro in a 2003 referendum.

GEOGRAPHY

Location: Northern Europe, bordering the Baltic Sea, Gulf of Bothnia, Kattegat, and Skagerrak, between Finland and Norway

Geographic coordinates: 62 00 N, 15 00 E

Map references: Europe

Area: *total:* 450,295 sq km
land: 410,335 sq km
water: 39,960 sq km
country comparison to the world: 56

Area—comparative: slightly larger than California

Land boundaries: *total:* 2,211 km
border countries (2): Finland 545 km, Norway 1,666 km

Coastline: 3,218 km

Maritime claims: *territorial sea:* 12 nm (adjustments made to return a portion of straits to high seas)
exclusive economic zone: agreed boundaries or midlines
continental shelf: 200-m depth or to the depth of exploitation

Climate: temperate in south with cold, cloudy winters and cool, partly cloudy summers; subarctic in north

Terrain: mostly flat or gently rolling lowlands; mountains in west

Elevation: *mean elevation:* 320 m

elevation extremes: *lowest point:* reclaimed bay of Lake Hammarsjon, near Kristianstad -2.4 m
highest point: Kebnekaise 2,111 m

Natural resources: iron ore, copper, lead, zinc, gold, silver, tungsten, uranium, arsenic, feldspar, timber, hydropower

Land use: *agricultural land:* 7.5%
arable land: 6.4%
permanent crops: 0%
permanent pasture: 1.1%
forest: 68.7%
other: 23.8% (2011 est.)

Irrigated land: 1,640 sq km (2012)

Total renewable water resources: 174 cu km (2011)

Freshwater withdrawal (domestic/industrial/agricultural): *total:* 2.62 cu km/yr (37%/59%/4%)
per capita: 285.6 cu m/yr (2007)

Natural hazards: ice floes in the surrounding waters, especially in the Gulf of Bothnia, can interfere with maritime traffic

Environment—current issues: acid rain damage to soils and lakes; pollution of the North Sea and the Baltic Sea

Environment—international agreements: *party to:* Air Pollution, Air Pollution-Nitrogen Oxides, Air Pollution-Persistent Organic Pollutants, Air Pollution-Sulfur 85, Air Pollution-Sulfur 94, Air Pollution-Volatile Organic Compounds, Antarctic-Environmental Protocol, Antarctic-Marine Living Resources, Antarctic Treaty, Biodiversity, Climate Change, Climate Change-Kyoto Protocol, Desertification, Endangered Species, Environmental Modification, Hazardous Wastes, Law of the Sea, Marine Dumping, Ozone Layer Protection, Ship Pollution, Tropical Timber 83, Tropical Timber 94, Wetlands, Whaling
signed, but not ratified: none of the selected agreements

Geography—note: strategic location along Danish Straits linking Baltic and North Seas

PEOPLE AND SOCIETY

Nationality: *noun:* Swede(s)

adjective: Swedish

Ethnic groups: *indigenous Population:* Swedes with Finnish and Sami minorities; foreign-born or first-generation immigrants: Finns, Yugoslavs, Danes, Norwegians, Greeks, Turks

Languages: Swedish (official), small Sami- and Finnish-speaking minorities

Religions: Lutheran 87%, other (includes Roman Catholic, Orthodox, Baptist, Muslim, Jewish, and Buddhist) 13%

Population: 9,801,616 (July 2015 est.)
country comparison to the world: 91

Age structure: *0–14 years:* 17.12% (male 863,125/female 814,803)
15–24 years: 11.97% (male 603,615/female 569,289)
25–54 years: 39.3% (male 1,957,869/female 1,894,064)
55–64 years: 11.63% (male 571,318/female 568,293)
65 years and over: 19.99% (male 900,070/female 1,059,170) (2015 est.)

Dependency ratios: *total dependency ratio:* 59.3%
youth dependency ratio: 27.5%
elderly dependency ratio: 31.8%
potential support ratio: 3.1% (2015 est.)

Median age: *total:* 41.2 years
male: 40.2 years
female: 42.2 years (2015 est.)
country comparison to the world: 37

Population growth rate: 0.8% (2015 est.)
country comparison to the world: 139

Birth rate: 11.99 births/1,000 population (2015 est.)
country comparison to the world: 166

Death rate: 9.4 deaths/1,000 population (2015 est.)
country comparison to the world: 59

Net migration rate: 5.42 migrant(s)/1,000 population (2015 est.)
country comparison to the world: 25

Urbanization: *urban population:* 85.8% of total population (2015)
rate of urbanization: 0.83% annual rate of change (2010–15 est.)

Major urban areas—population: STOCKHOLM (capital) 1.486 million (2015)

Sex ratio: *at birth:* 1.06 male(s)/female
0–14 years: 1.06 male(s)/female
15–24 years: 1.06 male(s)/female
25–54 years: 1.03 male(s)/female
55–64 years: 1.01 male(s)/female
65 years and over: 0.85 male(s)/female
total population: 1 male(s)/female (2015 est.)

Mother's mean age at first birth: 28.9 (2010 est.)

Maternal mortality rate: 4 deaths/100,000 live births (2015 est.)
country comparison to the world: 179

Infant mortality rate: *total:* 2.6 deaths/1,000 live births
male: 2.87 deaths/1,000 live births
female: 2.31 deaths/1,000 live births (2015 est.)

813

country comparison to the world: 217
Life expectancy at birth: *total population:* 81.98 years
male: 80.09 years
female: 83.99 years (2015 est.)
country comparison to the world: 15
Total fertility rate: 1.88 children born/woman (2015 est.)
country comparison to the world: 141
Health expenditures: 9.7% of GDP (2013)
country comparison to the world: 27
Physicians density: 3.93 physicians/1,000 population (2011)
Hospital bed density: 2.7 beds/1,000 population (2011)
Drinking water source:
improved:
urban: 100% of population
rural: 100% of population
total: 100% of population
unimproved:
urban: 0% of population
rural: 0% of population
total: 0% of population (2015 est.)
Sanitation facility access:
improved:
urban: 99.3% of population
rural: 99.6% of population
total: 99.3% of population
unimproved:
urban: 0.7% of population
rural: 0.4% of population
total: 0.7% of population (2015 est.)
HIV/AIDS—adult prevalence rate: 0.18% (2014 est.)
country comparison to the world: 99
HIV/AIDS—people living with HIV/AIDS: NA
HIV/AIDS—deaths: 100 (2014 est.)
country comparison to the world: 108
Obesity—adult prevalence rate: 22% (2014)
country comparison to the world: 104
Education expenditures: 7.7% of GDP (2013)
country comparison to the world: 20
School life expectancy (primary to tertiary education): *total:* 18 years
male: 17 years
female: 20 years (2014)
Unemployment, youth ages 15–24: *total:* 23.6%
male: 24.8%
female: 22.3% (2013 est.)
country comparison to the world: 40

GOVERNMENT

Country name: *conventional long form:* Kingdom of Sweden
conventional short form: Sweden
local long form: Konungariket Sverige
local short form: Sverige
etymology: name ultimately derives from the North Germanic Svear tribe, which inhabited central Sweden and is first mentioned in the first centuries A.D.
Government type: parliamentary constitutional monarchy
Capital: *name:* Stockholm

Geographic coordinates: 59 20 N, 18 03 E
time difference: UTC + 1 (6 hours ahead of Washington, DC, during Standard Time)
daylight saving time: +1 hr, begins last Sunday in March; ends last Sunday in October
Administrative divisions: 21 counties (lan, singular and plural); Blekinge, Dalarna, Gavleborg, Gotland, Halland, Jamtland, Jonkoping, Kalmar, Kronoberg, Norrbotten, Orebro, Ostergotland, Skane, Sodermanland, Stockholm, Uppsala, Varmland, Vasterbotten, Vasternorrland, Vastmanland, Vastra Gotaland
Independence: 6 June 1523 (Gustav VASA elected king)
National holiday: National Day, 6 June (1983); note—from 1916 to 1982 this date was celebrated as Swedish Flag Day
Constitution: several previous; latest adopted 1 January 1975; amended several times, last in 2014 (Riksdag Act) (2016)
Legal system: civil law system influenced by Roman-Germanic law and customary law
International law organization participation: accepts compulsory ICJ jurisdiction with reservations; accepts ICCt jurisdiction
Citizenship: *citizenship by birth:* no
citizenship by descent only: the father must be a citizen of Sweden; in the case of a child born out of wedlock, the mother must be a citizen of Sweden and the father unknown
dual citizenship recognized: no, unless the other citizenship was acquired involuntarily
residency requirement for naturalization: 5 years
Suffrage: 18 years of age; universal
Executive branch: *chief of state:* King CARL XVI GUSTAF (since 19 September 1973); Heir Apparent Princess VICTORIA Ingrid Alice Desiree, daughter of the monarch (born 14 July 1977)
head of government: Prime Minister Stefan LOFVEN (since 3 October 2014); Deputy Prime Minister Isabella LOVIN (since 25 May 2016)
cabinet: Cabinet appointed by the prime minister
elections/appointments: the monarchy is hereditary; following legislative elections, the leader of the majority party or majority coalition usually becomes the prime minister
Legislative branch: *description:* unicameral Parliament or Riksdag (349 seats; 310 members directly elected in multi-seat constituencies by proportional representation vote and 39 members in "at-large" seats directly elected by proportional representation vote; members serve 4-year terms)
elections: last held on 14 September 2014 (next to be held in September 2018)
election results: percent of vote by party—SAP 31.0%, M 23.3%, SD 12.9%, MP 6.9%, C 6.1%, V 5.7%, FP 5.4%, KD 4.6%, others 4.1%; seats by party—SAP 113, M 84, SD 49, MP 25, C 22, V 21, FP 19, KD 16
Judicial branch: *highest court(s):* Supreme Court of Sweden (consists of 16 justices including the court chairman; Supreme Administrative Court (consists of 18 justices including the court president)

judge selection and term of office: Supreme Court and Supreme Administrative Court justices nominated by the Board of Judges, a 9-member nominating body consisting of high-level judges, prosecutors, and members of Parliament; justices appointed by the Government; following a probation ary period, justices' appointments are permanent
subordinate courts: first instance and appellate general and administrative courts; specialized courts that handle cases such as land and environment, immigration, labor, markets, and patents
Political parties and leaders: Center Party (Centerpartiet) or C [Annie LOOF]
Christian Democrats (Kristdemokraterna) or KD [Ebba Busch THOR]
Green Party (Miljopartiet de Grona) or MP [Asa ROMSOn and Gustav FRI DOLIn]
Left Party (Vansterpartiet) (formerly Communist Party) or V [Jon as SJOSTEDT]
Liberal Party (Liberalerna) or L [Jan BJORKLUND]
Moderate Party (Moderaterna) or M [Anna KIn BERG BATRA]
Swedish Social Democratic Party (Socialdemokraterna) or SAP [Stefan LOFVEN] Sweden Democrats (Sverigedemokraterna) or SD [Jimmie AKESSON]
Political pressure groups and leaders: Swedish Confederation of Professional Associations or SACO [GoraNARRI US] Swedish Confederation of Profession al Employees or TCO [Eva NORDMARK]
Swedish Trade Union Confederation (Landsorganisationen) or LO [Karl-Petter THORWALDSSON]
other: environmental groups; media
International organization participation: ADB (nonregional member), AfDB (nonRegional member), Arctic Council, Australia Group, BIS, CBSS, CD, CE, CERN, EAPC, EBRD, ECB, EIB, EITI (implementing country), EMU, ESA, EU, FAO, FATF, G-9, G-10, IADB, IAEA, IBRD, ICAO, ICC (National committees), ICCt, ICRM, IDA, IEA, IFAD, IFC, IFRCS, IGAD (partners), IHO, ILO, IMF, IMO, IMSO, Interpol, IOC, IOM, IPU, ISO, ITSO, ITU, ITUC (NGOs), MIGA, MINUSMA, MONUSCO, NC, NEA, NIB, NSG, OAS (observer), OECD, OPCW, OSCE, Paris Club, PCA, PFP, Schengen Convention, UN, UNCTAD, UNESCO, UNHCR, UNIDO, UNMISS, UNMOGIP, UNRWA, UNTSO, UPU, WCO, WFTU (NGOs), WHO, WIPO, WMO, WTO, ZC
Diplomatic representation in the US: *chief of mission:* Ambassador Bjorn O. LYRVALL (since 12 September 2013)
chancery: The House of Sweden, 2900 K Street NW, Washington, DC 20007
telephone: [1] (202) 467-2600
FAX: [1] (202) 467-2699
consulate(s) general: New York
Diplomatic representation from the US: *chief of mission:* Ambassador Azita RAJI (since 15 March 2016)

embassy: Dag Hammarskjolds Vag 31, SE-11589 Stockholm

mailing address: American Embassy Stockholm, US Department of State, 5750 Stockholm Place, Washington, DC 20521–5750

telephone: [46] (08) 783 53 00

FAX: [46] (08) 66119 64

Flag description: blue with a golden yellow cross extending to the edges of the flag; the vertical part of the cross is shifted to the hoist side in the style of the Dannebrog (Danish flag); the colors reflect those of the Swedish coat of arms—three gold crowns on a blue field

National symbol(s): three crowns, lion; National colors: blue, yellow

National anthem: *name:* "Du Gamla, Du Fria" (Thou Ancient, Thou Free)

lyrics/music: Richard DYBECK/traditional

note: in use since 1844; also known as "Sang till Norden" (Song of the North), is based on a Swedish folk tune; it has never been officially adopted by the government; "Kungssangen" (The King's Song) serves as the royal anthem and is played in the presence of the royal family and during certain state ceremonies

ECONOMY

Economy—overview: Sweden has achieved an enviable standard of living with its combination of free-market capitalism and extensive welfare benefits. Sweden remains outside the euro zone largely out of concern that joining the European Economic and Monetary Union would diminish the country's sovereignty over its welfare system. Timber, hydropower, and iron ore constitute the resource base of an economy heavily oriented toward foreign trade.

Economic growth slowed in 2013, as a result of continued economic weakness in Sweden's European trading partners; Sweden's economy experienced modest growth in 2014–15, with real GDP growth above 2%, but continues to struggle with deflationary pressure.

GDP (purchasing power parity): $473.4 billion (2015 est.)

$454.8 billion (2014 est.)

$444.7 billion (2013 est.)

note: data are in 2015 US dollars

country comparison to the world: 41

GDP (official exchange rate): $492.6 billion (2015 est.)

GDP—real growth rate: 4.1% (2015 est.)

2.3% (2014 est.)

1.2% (2013 est.)

country comparison to the world: 62

GDP—per capita (PPP): $47,900 (2015 est.)

$46,700 (2014 est.)

$46,100 (2013 est.)

note: data are in 2015 US dollars

country comparison to the world: 26

Gross National saving: 30.4% of GDP (2015 est.)

29.1% of GDP (2014 est.)

28.5% of GDP (2013 est.)

country comparison to the world: 24

GDP—composition, by end use:

household consumption: 45.4%

government consumption: 25.6%

investment in fixed capital: 24.1%

investment in inventories: 0%

exports of goods and services: 45.3%

imports of goods and services: -40.4% (2015 est.)

GDP—composition, by sector of origin:

agriculture: 1.8%

industry: 33.5%

services: 64.7% (2015 est.)

Agriculture—products: barley, wheat, sugar beets; meat, milk

Industries: iron and steel, precision equipment (bearings, radio and telephone parts, armaments), wood pulp and paper products, processed foods, motor vehicles

Industrial production growth rate: 3.5% (2015 est.)

country comparison to the world: 69

Labor force: 5.184 million (2015 est.)

country comparison to the world: 79

Labor force—by occupation: *agriculture:* 2%

industry: 12%

services: 86% (2014 est.)

Unemployment rate: 7.4% (2015 est.)

7.9% (2014 est.)

country comparison to the world: 88

Population below poverty line: 14% (2011 est.)

Household income or consumption by percentage share: *lowest:* 10%: 3.4%

highest: 10%: 24% (2012)

Distribution of family income—Gini index: 24.9 (2013)

25 (1992)

country comparison to the world: 142

Budget: *revenues:* $250.8 billion

expenditures: $256.1 billion (2015 est.)

Taxes and other revenues: 51.8% of GDP (2015 est.)

country comparison to the world: 11

Budget surplus (+) or deficit (–): -1.1% of GDP (2015 est.)

country comparison to the world: 56

Public debt: 44% of GDP (2015 est.)

43.8% of GDP (2014 est.)

note: data cover general government debt, and includes debt instruments issued (or owned) by government entities other than the treasury; the data include treasury debt held by foreign entities; the data include debt issued by subnational entities, as well as intra-governmental debt; intra-governmental debt consists of treasury borrowings from surpluses in the social funds, such as for retirement, medical care, and unemployment; debt instruments for the social funds are not sold at public auctions

country comparison to the world: 104

Fiscal year: calendar year

Inflation rate (consumer prices): 0.7% (2015 est.)

0.2% (2014 est.)

country comparison to the world: 70

Central bank discount rate: 0% (31 December 2014) 1% (31 December 2013)

note: the Discount rate was abolished in 2002, and replaced by a "Reference rate" with no bearing on monetary policy; the rate quoted here is the Reference rate

country comparison to the world: 155

Commercial bank prime lending rate: 2% (31 December 2015 est.)

2.53% (31 December 2014 est.)

country comparison to the world: 178

Stock of narrow money: $272.7 billion (31 December 2015 est.)

$258.7 billion (31 December 2014 est.)

country comparison to the world: 17

Stock of broad money: $326.9 billion (31 December 2015 est.)

$322.1 billion (31 December 2014 est.)

country comparison to the world: 31

Stock of domestic credit: $785.8 billion (31 December 2015 est.)

$788.4 billion (31 December 2014 est.)

country comparison to the world: 17

Market value of publicly traded shares:

$560.5 billion (31 December 2012 est.)

$470.1 billion (31 December 2011)

$581.2 billion (31 December 2010 est.)

country comparison to the world: 21

Current account balance: $29.19 billion (2015 est.)

$30.58 billion (2014 est.)

country comparison to the world: 14

Exports: $151.1 billion (2015 est.) $178.8 billion (2014 est.)

country comparison to the world: 31

Exports—commodities: machinery 35%, motor vehicles, paper products, pulp and wood, iron and steel products, chemicals (2012 est.)

Exports—partners: Norway 10.3%, Germany 10.3%, US 7.7%, UK 7.2%, Denmark 6.8%, Finland 6.7%, Netherlands 5.2%, Belgium 4.4%, France 4.2% (2015)

Imports: $133.2 billion (2015 est.) $161.4 billion (2014 est.)

country comparison to the world: 32

Imports—commodities: machinery, petroleum and petroleum Products, chemicals, motor vehicles, iron and steel; foodstuffs, clothing

Imports—partners: Germany 17.9%, Netherlands 8.1%, Norway 7.8%, Denmark 7.7%, China 6%, UK 5.5%, Finland 4.6%, France 4.3%, Belgium 4.3% (2015)

Reserves of foreign exchange and gold: $62.5 billion (31 December 2014 est.)

$65.38 billion (31 December 2013 est.)

country comparison to the world: 34

Debt—external: $1.01 trillion (31 December 2014 est.)

$1.107 trillion (31 December 2013 est.)

country comparison to the world: 18

Stock of direct foreign investment—at home:

$432.2 billion (31 December 2015 est.)

$429 billion (31 December 2014 est.)

country comparison to the world: 18

Stock of direct foreign investment—abroad:

$504.8 billion (31 December 2015 est.)

$487.4 billion (31 December 2014 est.)

country comparison to the world: 17

Exchange rates: Swedish kronor (SEK) per US dollar—

8.23 (2015 est.)

6.8612 (2014 est.)

6.8612 (2013 est.)

6.77 (2012 est.)
6.4918 (2011 est.)

ENERGY

Electricity—production: 161 billion kWh (2012 est.)
country comparison to the world: 24
Electricity—consumption: 130.5 billion kWh (2012 est.)
country comparison to the world: 27
Electricity—exports: 22.68 billion kWh (2013 est.)
country comparison to the world: 8
Electricity—imports: 12.67 billion kWh (2013 est.)
country comparison to the world: 15
Electricity—installed generating capacity: 37.94 million kW (2012 est.)
country comparison to the world: 25
Electricity—from fossil fuels: 9.5% of total installed capacity (2012 est.)
country comparison to the world: 199
Electricity—from nuclear fuels: 24.8% of total installed capacity (2012 est.)
country comparison to the world: 7
Electricity—from hydroelectric plants: 43% of total installed capacity (2012 est.)
country comparison to the world: 56
Electricity—from other renewable sources: 22.7% of total installed capacity (2012 est.)
country comparison to the world: 14
Crude oil—production: 0 bbl/day (2014 est.)
country comparison to the world: 194
Crude oil—exports: 12,590 bbl/day (2013 est.)
country comparison to the world: 62
Crude oil—imports: 352,300 bbl/day (2013 est.)
country comparison to the world: 26
Crude oil—proved reserves: 0 bbl (1 January 2015 est.)
country comparison to the world: 194
Refined petroleum products—production: 355,700 bbl/day (2013 est.)
country comparison to the world: 39
Refined petroleum products—consumption: 295,200 bbl/day (2014 est.)
country comparison to the world: 42
Refined petroleum products—exports: 192,900 bbl/day (2013 est.)
country comparison to the world: 34
Refined petroleum products—imports: 152,700 bbl/day (2013 est.)
country comparison to the world: 36
Natural gas—production: 0 cu m (2014 est.)
country comparison to the world: 133
Natural gas—consumption: 892 million cu m (2014 est.)
country comparison to the world: 93
Natural gas—exports: 0 cu m (2014 est.)
country comparison to the world: 186
Natural gas—imports: 892 million cu m (2014 est.)
country comparison to the world: 59
Natural gas—proved reserves: 0 cu m (1 January 2014 est.)
country comparison to the world: 197
Carbon dioxide emissions from consumption of energy: 51.08 million Mt (2012 est.)

country comparison to the world: 58

COMMUNICATIONS

Telephones—fixed lines: *total subscriptions:* 3.82 million
subscriptions per 100 inhabitants: 39 (2014 est.)
country comparison to the world: 43
Telephone—mobile cellular: *total:* 12.3 million
subscriptions per 100 inhabitants: 127 (2014 est.)
country comparison to the world: 75
Telephone system: *general assessment:* highly developed telecommunications infrastructure; ranked among leading countries for fixed-line, mobile-cellular, internet and broadband penetration
domestic: coaxial and multiconductor cables carry most of the voice traffic; parallel microwave radio relay systems carry some additional telephone channels
international: country code—46; submarine cables provide links to other Nordic countries and Europe; satellite earth stations—1 Intelsat (Atlantic Ocean), 1 Eutelsat, and 1 Inmarsat (Atlantic and Indian Ocean regions); note—Sweden shares the Inmarsat earth station with the other Nordic countries (Denmark, Finland, Iceland, and Norway) (2011)
Broadcast media: publicly owned TV broadcaster operates 2 terrestrial networks plus Regional stations; multiple privately owned TV broadcasters operating Nationally, region ally, and locally; about 50 local TV stations; widespread access to pan-Nordic and International broadcasters through multi-channel cable and satellite TV; publicly owned radio broadcaster operates 3 National stations and a network of 25 Regional channels; roughly 100 privately owned local radio stations with some consolidating into near National networks; an estimated 900 community and neighborhood radio stations broadcast intermittently (2008)
Radio broadcast stations: AM 1, FM 124, shortwave 0 (2008)
Television broadcast stations: 252 (2008)
Internet country code: .se
Internet hosts: 5.978 million (2010)
country comparison to the world: 19
Internet users: *total:* 8.7 million
percent of population: 89.1% (2014 est.)
country comparison to the world: 47

TRANSPORTATION

Airports: 231 (2013)
country comparison to the world: 25
Airports—with paved runways: *total:* 149
over 3,047 m: 3
2,438 to 3,047 m: 12
1,524 to 2,437 m: 75
914 to 1,523 m: 22
under 914 m: 37 (2013)
Airports—with unpaved runways: *total:* 82
914 to 1,523 m: 5
under 914 m: 77 (2013)
Heliports: 2 (2013)
Pipelines: gas 1,626 km (2013)
Railways: *total:* 11,915 km

standard gauge: 11,850 km 1.435-m gauge (7,567 km electrified)
narrow gauge: 65 km 0.891-m gauge (65 km electrified) (2014)
country comparison to the world: 21
Roadways: *total:* 579,564 km (includes 1,913 km of expressways)
paved: 135,444 km
unpaved: 444,412 km
note: includes 104,705 km of state roads, 433,034 km of private roads, and 41,825 km of municipal roads (2010)
country comparison to the world: 13
Waterways: 2,052 km (2010)
country comparison to the world: 40
Merchant marine: *total:* 135
by type: bulk carrier 4, cargo 16, carrier 1, chemical tanker 15, passenger 5, passenger/cargo 36, petroleum tanker 11, roll on/roll off 30, vehicle carrier 17
foreign-owned: 35 (Denmark 4, Estonia 3, Finland 16, Germany 3, Ireland 1, Italy 5, Norway 3)
registered in other countries: 189 (Bahamas 11, Barbados 4, Bermuda 14, Canada 2, Cook Islands 3, Cyprus 5, Denmark 15, Faroe Islands 11, Finland 1, France 4, Gibraltar 11, Italy 1, Liberia 12, Malta 1, Marshall Islands 1, Netherlands 12, Norway 27, Panama 2, Portugal 3, Saint Vincent and the Grenadines 10, Singapore 11, UK 28) (2010)
country comparison to the world: 42
Ports and terminals: *major seaport(s):* Brofjorden, Goteborg, Helsingborg, Karlshamn, Lulea, Malmo, Stockholm, Trelleborg, Visby
LNG terminal(s) (import): Brunnsviksholme, Lysekil

MILITARY AND SECURITY

Military branches: Swedish Armed Forces (Forsvarsmakten): Army (Armen), Royal Swedish Navy (Marinen), Swedish Air Force (Svenska Flygvapn et) (2010)
Military service age and obligation: 18–47 years of age for male and female voluntary military service; Swedish citizenship required; service obligation: 7.5 months (Army), 7–15 months (NAvy), 8–12 months (Air Force); the Swedish Parliament has abolished compulsory military service, with exclusively voluntary recruitment as of July 2010; conscription remains an option in emergencies; after completing initial service, soldiers have a reserve commitment until age 47 (2013)
Military expenditures: 1.1% of GDP (2015)
1.1% of GDP (2014)
1.1% of GDP (2013)
1.18% of GDP (2012)
1.17% of GDP (2011)
country comparison to the world: 84

TRANSNATIONAL ISSUES

Disputes—International: none
Refugees and internally displaced persons: *refugees (country of origin):* 34,285 (Syria); 24,184 (Iraq); 21,189 (Somalia); 14,107 (Eritrea); 12,090 (Afghanistan) (2014)
stateless persons: 31,062 (2015); note—the majority of stateless people are from the Middle East and Somalia

SWITZERLAND

INTRODUCTION

Background: The Swiss Confederation was founded in 1291 as a defensive alliance among three cantons. In succeeding years, other localities joined the original three. The Swiss Confederation secured its independence from the Holy Roman Empire in 1499. A constitution of 1848, subsequently modified in 1874, replaced the confederation with a centralized federal government. Switzerland's sovereignty and neutrality have long been honored by the major European powers, and the country was not involved in either of the two world wars. The political and economic integration of Europe over the past half century, as well as Switzerland's role in many UN and International organizations, has strengthened Switzerland's ties with its neighbors. However, the country did not officially become a UN member until 2002. Switzerland remains active in many UN And International organizations but retains a strong commitment to neutrality.

GEOGRAPHY

Location: Central Europe, east of France, north of Italy

Geographic coordinates: 47 00 N, 8 00 E

Map references: Europe

Area: *total:* 41,277 sq km
land: 39,997 sq km
water: 1,280 sq km
country comparison to the world: 136

Area—comparative: slightly less than twice the size of New Jersey

Land boundaries: *total:* 1,770 km
border countries (5): Austria 158 km, France 525 km, Italy 698 km, Liechtenstein 41 km, Germany 348 km

Coastline: 0 km (landlocked)

Maritime claims: none (landlocked)

Climate: temperate, but varies with altitude; cold, cloudy, rainy/snowy winters; cool to warm, cloudy, humid summers with occasional showers

Terrain: mostly mountains (Alps in south, Jura in northwest) with a central plateau of rolling hills, plains, and large lakes

Elevation: *mean elevation:* 1,350 m

elevation extremes: *lowest point:* Lake Maggiore 195 m
highest point: Dufourspitze 4,634 m

Natural resources: hydropower potential, timber, salt

Land use: *agricultural land:* 38.7%
arable land: 10.2%
permanent crops: 0.6%
permanent pasture: 27.9%
forest: 31.5%
other: 29.8% (2011 est.)

Irrigated land: 630 sq km (2012)

Total renewable water resources: 53.5 cu km (2011)

Freshwater withdrawal (domestic/industrial/agricultural): *total:* 2.61 cu km/yr (39%/58%/3%)
per capita: 360.3 cu m/yr (2010)

Natural hazards: avalanches, landslides; flash floods

Environment—current issues: air pollution from vehicle emissions and open-air burning; acid rain; water pollution from increased use of agricultural fertilizers; loss of biodiversity

Environment—International agreements: *party to:* Air Pollution, Air Pollution-Nitrogen Oxides, Air Pollution-Persistent Organic Pollutants, Air Pollution-Sulfur 85, Air Pollution-Sulfur 94, Air Pollution-Volatile Organic Compounds, Antarctic Treaty, Biodiversity, Climate Change, Climate Change-Kyoto Protocol, Desertification, Endangered Species, Environmental Modification, Hazardous Wastes, Marine Dumping, Marine Life Conservation, Ozone Layer Protection, Ship Pollution, Tropical Timber 83, Tropical Timber 94, Wetlands, Whaling
signed, but not ratified: Law of the Sea

Geography—note: landlocked; crossroads of northern and southern Europe; along with Southeastern France, northern Italy, and southwestern Austria has the highest elevations in the Alps

PEOPLE AND SOCIETY

Nationality: *noun:* Swiss (singular and plural)
adjective: Swiss

Ethnic groups: German 65%, French 18%, Italian 10%, Romansch 1%, other 6%

Languages: German (official) 63.5%, French (official) 22.5%, Italian (official) 8.1%, English 4.4%, Portuguese 3.4%, Albanian 3.1%, Serbo-Croatian 2.5%, Spanish 2.2%, Romansch (official) 0.5%, other 6.6%
note: German, French, Italian, and Romansch are all National and official languages; totals more than 100% because some respondents indicated more than one main language (2013 est.)

Religions: Roman Catholic 38.2%, Protestant 26.9%, other Christian 5.6%, Muslim 5%, other 1.6%, none 21.4%, unspecified 1.3% (2013 est.)

Population: 8,121,830 (July 2015 est.)
country comparison to the world: 97

Age structure: *0–14 years:* 15.09% (male 630,944/female 594,465)
15–24 years: 11.29% (male 468,036/female 449,309)
25–54 years: 43.67% (male 1,780,039/female 1,766,820)

55–64 years: 12.18% (male 494,285/female 495,107)
65 years and over: 17.76% (male 631,204/female 811,621) (2015 est.)

Dependency ratios: *total dependency ratio:* 48.8%
youth dependency ratio: 22%
elderly dependency ratio: 26.9%
potential support ratio: 3.7% (2015 est.)

Median age: *total:* 42.1 years
male: 41.1 years
female: 43.1 years (2015 est.)
country comparison to the world: 27

Population growth rate: 0.71% (2015 est.)
country comparison to the world: 147

Birth rate: 10.5 births/1,000 population (2015 est.)
country comparison to the world: 186

Death rate: 8.13 deaths/1,000 population (2015 est.)
country comparison to the world: 94

Net migration rate: 4.74 migrant(s)/1,000 population (2015 est.)
country comparison to the world: 27

Urbanization: *urban population:* 73.9% of total population (2015)
rate of urbanization: 1.08% annual rate of change (2010–15 est.)

Major urban areas—population: Zurich 1.246 million; BERN (capital) 358,000 (2015)

Sex ratio: *at birth:* 1.06 male(s)/female
0–14 years: 1.06 male(s)/female
15–24 years: 1.04 male(s)/female
25–54 years: 1.01 male(s)/female
55–64 years: 1 male(s)/female
65 years and over: 0.78 male(s)/female
total population: 0.97 male(s)/female (2015 est.)

Mother's mean age at first birth: 30.4 (2012 est.)

Maternal mortality rate: 5 deaths/100,000 live births (2015 est.)
country comparison to the world: 159

Infant mortality rate: *total:* 3.67 deaths/1,000 live births
male: 4.03 deaths/1,000 live births
female: 3.29 deaths/1,000 live births (2015 est.)
country comparison to the world: 199

Life expectancy at birth: *total population:* 82.5 years
male: 80.22 years
female: 84.92 years (2015 est.)
country comparison to the world: 9

Total fertility rate: 1.55 children born/woman (2015 est.)
country comparison to the world: 188

Health expenditures: 11.5% of GDP (2013)
country comparison to the world: 12

Physicians density: 4.05 physicians/1,000 population (2012)

Hospital bed density: 5 beds/1,000 population (2011)

Drinking water source:
improved:
urban: 100% of population

rural: 100% of population
total: 100% of population
unimproved:
urban: 0% of population
rural: 0% of population
total: 0% of population (2015 est.)
Sanitation facility access:
improved:
urban: 99.9% of population
rural: 99.8% of population
total: 99.9% of population
unimproved:
urban: 0.1% of population
rural: 0.2% of population
total: 0.1% of population (2015 est.)
HIV/AIDS—adult prevalence rate: 0.35% (2013 est.)
country comparison to the world: 78
HIV/AIDS—people living with HIV/AIDS: 20,200 (2013 est.)
country comparison to the world: 79
HIV/AIDS—deaths: 300 (2013 est.)
country comparison to the world: 99
Obesity—adult prevalence rate: 21% (2014)
country comparison to the world: 111
Education expenditures: 5.1% of GDP (2012)
country comparison to the world: 66
School life expectancy (primary to tertiary education): *total:* 16 years
male: 16 years
female: 16 years (2014)
Unemployment, youth ages 15–24: *total:* 8.5%
male: 8.8%
female: 8.3% (2013 est.)
country comparison to the world: 111

GOVERNMENT

Country name: *conventional long form:* Swiss Confederation
conventional short form: Switzerland
local long form: Schweizerische Eidgenossenschaft (German); Confederation Suisse (French); Confederazione Svizzera (Italian); Confederaziun Svizra (Romansh)
local short form: Schweiz (German); Suisse (French); Svizzera (Italian); Svizra (Romansh)
etymology: name derives from the canton of Schwyz, one of the founding cantons of the Old Swiss Confederacy that formed in the 14th century
Government type: federal republic (formally a confederation)
Capital: *name:* Bern
Geographic coordinates: 46 55 N, 7 28 E
time difference: UTC + 1 (6 hours ahead of Washington, DC, during Standard Time)
daylight saving time: +1 hr, begins last Sunday in March; ends last Sunday in October
Administrative divisions: 26 cantons (cantons, singular—canton in French; cantoni, singular—cantone in Italian; Kantone, singular-Kanton in German); Aargau, Appenzell Ausserrhoden, Appenzell Innerrhoden, Basel-Landschaft, Basel-Stadt, Berne/Bern, Fribourg/Freiburg, Geneve, Glarus, Graubuenden/Grigioni/Grischun, Jura, Luzern, Neuchatel, Nidwalden, Obwalden, Sankt

Gallen, Schaffhausen, Schwyz, Solothurn, Thurgau, Ticino, Uri, Valais/Wallis, Vaud, Zug, Zuerich
note: 6 of the cantons—Appenzell Ausserrhoden, Appenzell Innerrhoden, Basel-Landschaft, Basel-Stadt, Nidwalden, Obwalden—are referred to as half cantons because they elect only one member to the Council of States and, in popular referendums where a majority of popular votes and a majority of cantonal votes are required, these six cantons only have a half vote
Independence: 1 August 1291 (founding of the Swiss Confederation)
National holiday: Founding of the Swiss Confederation in 1291; note—since 1 August 1891 celebrated as Swiss National Day
Constitution: previous 1848, 1874; latest adopted by referendum 18 April 1999, effective 1 January 2000; amended many times, last in 2016 (2016)
Legal system: civil law system; judicial review of legislative acts, except for federal decrees of a general obligatory character
International law organization participation: accepts compulsory ICJ jurisdiction with reservations; accepts ICCt jurisdiction
Citizenship: *citizenship by birth:* no
citizenship by descent only: at least one parent must be a citizen of Switzerland
dual citizenship recognized: yes
residency requirement for naturalization: 12 years including at least 3 of the last 5 years prior to application
Suffrage: 18 years of age; universal
Executive branch: *chief of state:* President of the Swiss Confederation Johann N. SCHNEIDER-AMMANN (since 1 January 2016); Vice President Doris LEUTARD (since 1 January 2016; note—the Federal Council, which is comprised of 7 federal councillors, constitutes the federal government of Switzerland; council members rotate in a 1-year term as federal president (chief of state and head of government)
head of government: President of the Swiss Confederation Johann N. SCHNEIDER-AMMANN (since 1 January 2016); Vice President Doris LEUTARD (since 1 January 2016)
cabinet: Federal Council or Bundesrat (in German), Conseil Federal (in French), Consiglio Federale (in Italian) indirectly elected usually from among its members by the Federal Assembly for a 4-year term
elections/appointments: president and vice president indirectly elected by the Federal Assembly from among members of the Federal Council for a 1-year, non-consecutive term; election last held on 9 December 2015 (next to be held in early December 2016)
election results: Johann N. SCHNEIDER-AMMANN elected president; Federal Assembly vote—196 of 208; Doris LEUTHARD elected vice president
Legislative branch: *description:* bicameral Federal Assembly or Bundesversammlung—in German, Assemblee Federale—in French, Assemblea Federale—in Italian consists of the Council of States or Staenderat—in German, Conseil des Etats—in French, Consiglio degli Stati—in Italian (46 seats;

members in multi-seat constituencies representing cantons and single-seat constituencies representing half cantons directly elected by simple majority vote; members serve 4-year terms) and the National Council or Nationalrat—in German, Conseil National—in French, Consiglio nazionale—in Italian (200 seats; 195 members in cantons directly elected by proportional representation vote and 5 in half cantons directly elected by simple majority vote; members serve 4-year terms)
elections: Council of States—last held in most cantons on 18 October 2015 (each canton determines when the next election will be held); National Council—last held on 18 October 2015 (next to be held in October 2019)
election results: Council of States—percent of vote by party—NA; seats by party (as of 18 October 2015)—Christian Democratic People's Party 13, FDP.The Liberals 13, SDP 12, Swiss People's Party 6, other 2; National Council—percent of vote by party—SVP 29.4%, SPS 18.8%, FDP 16.4%, CVP 11.6%, Green Party 7.1%, GLP 4.6%, BDP 4.1%, other 8.0%; seats by party—SVP 65, SPS 43, FDP 33, CVP 27, Green Party 11, GLP 7, BDP 7, other 7
Judicial branch: *highest court(s):* Federal Supreme Court (consists of 38 judges and 31 substitutes and organized into 5 sections)
judge selection and term of office: judges elected by the Federal Assembly for 6-year terms;
note—judges are affiliated with political parties and are elected according to linguistic and Regional criteria in approximate proportion to the level of party representation in the Federal Assembly
subordinate courts: Federal Criminal Court (began in 2004); Federal Administrative Court (began in 2007); note—each of Switzerland's 26 cantons has its own courts
Political parties and leaders: Christian Democratic People's Party (Christlichdemokratische Volkspartei der Schweiz or CVP, Parti Democrate-Chretien Suisse or PDC, Partito Popolare Democratico Svizzero or PPD, Partida Cristiandemocratica dalla Svizra or PCD) [Christophe DARBELLAY]
Conservative Democratic Party (Buergerlich-Demokratische Partei Schweiz or BDP, Parti Bourgeois Democratique Suisse or PBD, Partito Borghese Democratico Svizzero or PBD, Partido burgais democratica Svizera or PBD) [Martin LANDOLT]
Free Democratic Party or FDP. The Liberals (FDP. Die Liberalen, PLR. Les Liberaux-Radicaux, PLR.I Liberali, IIs Liberals) [Philipp MUELLER]
Green Liberal Party (Grunliberale or GLP, Parti vert liberale or PVL, Partito Verde-Liberale or PVL, Partida Verde Liberale or PVL) [Martin BAEUMLE]
Green Party (Gruene Partei der Schweiz or Gruene, Parti Ecologiste Suisse or Les Verts, Partito Ecologista Svizzero or IVerdi, Partida Ecologica Svizra or La Verda) [Adele THORENS GOUMAZ and Regula RYTZ]
Social Democratic Party (Sozialdemokratische Partei der Schweiz or SPS, Parti Socialiste Suisse

or PSS, Partito Socialista Svizzero or PSS, Partida Socialdemocratica de la Svizra or PSS) [Christian LEVRAT]

Swiss People's Party (Schweizerische Volkspartei or SVP, Union Democratique du Centre or UDC, Unione Democratica di Centro or UDC, Uniun Democratica dal Center or UDC) [Toni BRUNNER] other minor parties

Political pressure groups and leaders: NA
International organization participation: ADB (nonregional member), AfDB (nonregional member), Australia Group, BIS, CD, CE, CERN, EAPC, EBRD, EFTA, EITI (implementing country), ESA, FAO, FATF, G-10, IADB, IAEA, IBRD, ICAO, ICC (National committees), ICCt, ICRM, IDA, IEA, IFAD, IFC, IFRCS, IGAD (partners), ILO, IMF, IMO, IMSO, Interpol, IOC, IOM, IPU, ISO, ITSO, ITU, ITUC (NGOs), LAIA (observer), MIGA, MINUSMA, MONUSCO, NEA, NSG, OAS (observer), OECD, OIF, OPCW, OSCE, Pacific Alliance (observer), Paris Club, PCA, PFP, Schengen Convention, UN, UNCTAD, UNESCO, UNHCR, UNIDO, UNITAR, UNMISS, UNMOGIP, UNRWA, UNTSO, UNWTO, UPU, WCO, WHO, WIPO, WMO, WTO, ZC
Diplomatic representation in the US: *chief of mission:* Ambassador Martin DAHINDEN (since 18 November 2014)
chancery: 2900 Cathedral Avenue NW, Washington, DC 20008
telephone: [1] (202) 745-7900
FAX: [1] (202) 387-2564
consulate(s) general: Atlanta, Chicago, Los Angeles, New York, San Francisco
Diplomatic representation from the US: *chief of mission:* Ambassador Suzan G. LEVINE (since 2 June 2014); note—also accredited to Liechtenstein
embassy: Sulgeneckstrasse 19, CH-3007 Bern
mailing address: use embassy street address
telephone: [41] (031) 357-70-11
FAX: [41] (031) 357-73-44
Flag description: red square with a bold, equilateral white cross in the center that does not extend to the edges of the flag; various medieval legends purport to describe the origin of the flag; a white cross used as identification for troops of the Swiss Confederation is first attested at the Battle of Laupen (1339)
National symbol(s): Swiss cross (white cross on red field, arms equal length);
National colors: red, white
National anthem: the Swiss anthem has four names: "Schweizerpsalm" [German]
"Cantique Suisse" [French]
"Salmo svizzero," [Italian]
"Psalm svizzer" [Romansch] (Swiss Psalm)
lyrics/music: Leonhard WIDMER [German], Charles CHATELANAT [French], Camillo VALSANGIACOMO [Italian], and Flurin CAMATHIAS [Romansch]/Alberik ZWYSSIG
note: unofficially adopted 1961, officially 1981; the anthem has been popular in a number of Swiss cantons since its composition (in German) in 1841; translated into the other three official

languages of the country (French, Italian, and Romansch), it is official in each of those languages

ECONOMY

Economy—overview: Switzerland, a country that espouses neutrality, is a prosperous and modern market economy with low unemployment, a highly skilled labor force, and a per capita GDP among the highest in the world. Switzerland's economy benefits from a highly developed service sector, led by financial services, and a manufacturing industry that specializes in high-technology, knowledge-based production. Its economic and political stability, transparent legal system, exceptional infrastructure, efficient capital markets, and low corporate tax rates also make Switzerland one of the world's most competitive economies. The Swiss have brought their economic practices largely into conformity with the EU's to enhance their International competitiveness, but some trade protectionism remains, particularly for its small agricultural sector. The fate of the Swiss economy is tightly linked to that of its neighbors in the euro zone, which purchases half of Swiss exports. The global financial crisis of 2008 and resulting economic downturn in 2009 stalled demand for Swiss exports and put Switzerland into a recession. During this period, the Swiss National Bank (SNB) implemented a zero-interest rate policy to boost the economy, as well as to prevent appreciation of the franc, and Switzerland's economy began to recover in 2010.

The sovereign debt crises unfolding in neighboring eurozone countries, however, coupled with ongoing economic instability in Russia and other eastern European economies continue to pose a significant risk to the Swiss economy, driving up demand for the Swiss franc by investors seeking a safe-haven currency. In January 2015, the SNB abandoned the Swiss franc's peg to the euro, roiling global currency markets and making active SNB intervention a necessary hallmark of present-day Swiss monetary policy. The independent SNB has upheld its zero interest rate policy and conducted major market interventions to prevent further appreciation of the Swiss franc, but parliamentarians have urged it to do more to weaken the currency. The franc's strength has made Swiss exports less competitive and weakened the country's growth outlook; GDP growth fell below 2% per year from 2011–15.

In recent years, Switzerland has responded to increasing pressure from neighboring countries and trading partners to reform its banking secrecy laws, by agreeing to conform to OECD regulations on administrative assistance in tax matters, including tax evasion. The Swiss government has also renegotiated its double taxation agreements with numerous countries, including the US, to incorporate OECD standards, and is openly considering the possibility of imposing taxes on bank deposits held by foreigners .
GDP (purchasing power parity): $482.3 billion (2015 est.)
$478.3 billion (2014 est.)
$469.4 billion (2013 est.)

note: data are in 2015 US dollars
country comparison to the world: 40
GDP (official exchange rate): $664.6 billion (2015 est.)
GDP—real growth rate: 0.9% (2015 est.)
1.9% (2014 est.)
1.8% (2013 est.)
country comparison to the world: 178
GDP—per capita (PPP): $58,600 (2015 est.)
$58,800 (2014 est.)
$58,400 (2013 est.)
note: data are in 2015 US dollars
country comparison to the world: 16
Gross National saving: 33.3% of GDP (2015 est.)
32.2% of GDP (2014 est.)
33.7% of GDP (2013 est.)
country comparison to the world: 13
GDP—composition, by end use:
household consumption: 54.4%
government consumption: 11.1%
investment in fixed capital: 24%
investment in inventories: -1.1%
exports of goods and services: 56.2%
imports of goods and services: -44.6% (2015 est.)
GDP—composition, by sector of origin:
agriculture: 0.8%
industry: 26.7%
services: 72.6% (2015 est.)
Agriculture—products: grains, fruits, vegetables; meat, eggs
Industries: machinery, chemicals, watches, textiles, precision instruments, tourism, banking, insurance
Industrial production growth rate: 2.2% (2015 est.)
country comparison to the world: 108
Labor force: 5.097 million (2015 est.)
country comparison to the world: 82
Labor force—by occupation: *agriculture:* 3.4%
industry: 23.4%
services: 73.2% (2010)
Unemployment rate: 3.3% (2015 est.)
3.2% (2014 est.)
country comparison to the world: 28
Population below poverty line: 7.6% (2011 est.)
Household income or consumption by percentage share: *lowest:* 10%: 7.5%
highest: 10%: 19% (2007)
Distribution of family income—Gini index: 28.7 (2012 est.) 33.1 (1992)
country comparison to the world: 128
Budget: *revenues:* $221.9 billion
expenditures: $220.8 billion
note: includes federal, cantonal, and municipal budgets (2015 est.)
Taxes and other revenues: 32.8% of GDP (2015 est.)
country comparison to the world: 73
Budget surplus (+) or deficit (–): 0.2% of GDP (2015 est.)
country comparison to the world: 24
Public debt: 34% of GDP (2015 est.)
34.7% of GDP (2014 est.)
note: general government gross debt; gross debt consists of all liabilities that require payment or payments of interest and/or principal by the debtor to the creditor at a date or dates in the

future; includes debt liabilities in the form of Special Drawing Rights (SDRs), currency and deposits, debt securities, loans, insurance, pensions and standardized guarantee schemes, and other accounts payable; all liabilities in the GFSM 2001 system are debt, except for equity and investment fund shares and financial derivatives and employee stock options
country comparison to the world: 130

Fiscal year: calendar year

Inflation rate (consumer prices): -1.1% (2015 est.) 0% (2014 est.)
country comparison to the world: 10

Central bank discount rate: 0.5% (31 December 2010)
0.75% (31 December 2009)
country comparison to the world: 128

Commercial bank prime lending rate: 2.6% (31 December 2015 est.)
2.69% (31 December 2014 est.)
country comparison to the world: 173

Stock of narrow money: $519.8 billion (31 December 2015 est.)
$514.1 billion (31 December 2014 est.)
country comparison to the world: 11

Stock of broad money: $1.347 trillion (31 December 2014 est.)
$1.301 trillion (31 December 2013 est.)
country comparison to the world: 14

Stock of domestic credit: $1.197 trillion (31 December 2015 est.)
$1.138 trillion (31 December 2014 est.)
country comparison to the world: 16

Market value of publicly traded shares: $1.079 trillion (31 December 2012 est.)
$932.2 billion (31 December 2011)
$1.229 trillion (31 December 2010 est.)
country comparison to the world: 14

Current account balance: $75.82 billion (2015 est.)
$61.9 billion (2014 est.)
country comparison to the world: 8

Exports: $270.6 billion (2015 est.)
$327.6 billion (2014 est.)
note: trade data exclude trade with Switzerland
country comparison to the world: 21

Exports—commodities: machinery, chemicals, metals, watches, agricultural products

Exports—partners: Germany 14.2%, US 10.6%, Hong Kong 8.7%, India 7.3%, China 6.9%, France 6.1%, Italy 5.4%, UK 4.8% (2015)

Imports: $214.8 billion (2015 est.)
$272.6 billion (2014 est.)
country comparison to the world: 20

Imports—commodities: machinery, chemicals, vehicles, metals; agricultural products, textiles

Imports—partners: Germany 20.7%, UK 12.8%, US 8.1%, Italy 7.8%, France 6.7%, China 5.1% (2015)

Reserves of foreign exchange and gold: $545.5 billion (31 December 2014 est.)
$535.9 billion (31 December 2013 est.)
country comparison to the world: 5

Debt—external: $1.533 trillion (31 December 2014 est.)
$1.601 trillion (31 December 2013 est.)

country comparison to the world: 12

Stock of direct foreign investment—at home: $1.136 trillion (31 December 2015 est.)
$1.107 trillion (31 December 2014 est.)
country comparison to the world: 8

Stock of direct foreign investment—abroad: $1.487 trillion (31 December 2015 est.)
$1.464 trillion (31 December 2014 est.)
country comparison to the world: 7

Exchange rates: Swiss francs (CHF) per US dollar—
0.9381 (2015 est.)
0.9152 (2014 est.)
0.9152 (2013 est.)
0.94 (2012 est.)
0.8876 (2011 est.)

ENERGY

Electricity—production: 64.81 billion kWh (2012 est.)
country comparison to the world: 42

Electricity—consumption: 58.01 billion kWh (2012 est.)
country comparison to the world: 44

Electricity—exports: 32.27 billion kWh (2013 est.)
country comparison to the world: 6

Electricity—imports: 29.87 billion kWh (2013 est.)
country comparison to the world: 7

Electricity—installed generating capacity: 20.31 million kW (2012 est.)
country comparison to the world: 39

Electricity—from fossil fuels: 2.5% of total installed capacity (2012 est.)
country comparison to the world: 206

Electricity—from nuclear fuels: 16.1% of total installed capacity (2012 est.)
country comparison to the world: 13

Electricity—from hydroelectric plants: 67.8% of total installed capacity (2012 est.)
country comparison to the world: 26

Electricity—from other renewable sources: 4.6% of total installed capacity (2012 est.)
country comparison to the world: 61

Crude oil—production: 0 bbl/day (2014 est.)
country comparison to the world: 195

Crude oil—exports: 0 bbl/day (2013 est.)
country comparison to the world: 193

Crude oil—imports: 101,400 bbl/day (2013 est.)
country comparison to the world: 46

Crude oil—proved reserves: 0 bbl (1 January 2015 est.)
country comparison to the world: 195

Refined petroleum products—production: 105,400 bbl/day (2013 est.)
country comparison to the world: 72

Refined petroleum products—consumption: 238,500 bbl/day (2014 est.)
country comparison to the world: 52

Refined petroleum products—exports: 10,450 bbl/day (2013 est.)
country comparison to the world: 87

Refined petroleum products—imports: 157,900 bbl/day (2013 est.)
country comparison to the world: 35

Natural gas—production: 20 million cu m (2014 est.)
country comparison to the world: 88

Natural gas—consumption: 3.281 billion cu m (2014 est.)
country comparison to the world: 67

Natural gas—exports: 0 cu m (2014 est.)
country comparison to the world: 188

Natural gas—imports: 3.261 billion cu m (2014 est.)
country comparison to the world: 39

Natural gas—proved reserves: NA cu m (1 January 2011 est.)

Carbon dioxide emissions from consumption of energy: 42.97 million Mt (2012 est.)
country comparison to the world: 65

COMMUNICATIONS

Telephones—fixed lines: *total subscriptions:* 4.37 million
subscriptions per 100 inhabitants: 54 (2014 est.)
country comparison to the world: 38

Telephones—mobile cellular: *total:* 11.5 million
subscriptions per 100 inhabitants: 142 (2014 est.)
country comparison to the world: 79

Telephone system: *general assessment:* highly developed telecommunications infrastructure with excellent domestic and International services
domestic: ranked among leading countries for fixed-line teledensity and infrastructure; mobile-cellular subscribership roughly 125 per 100 persons; extensive cable and microwave radio relay networks
international: country code—41; satellite earth stations—2 intelsat (Atlantic Ocean and Indian Ocean) (2011)

Broadcast media: the publicly owned radio and TV broadcaster, Swiss Broadcasting Corporation (SRG/SSR), operates 7 National TV networks, 3 broadcasting in German, 2 in Italian, and 2 in French; private commercial TV stations broadcast region ally and locally; TV broadcasts from stations in Germany, Italy, and France are widely available via multi-channel cable and satellite TV services; SR G/SSR operates 18 radio stations that, along with private broadcasters, provide National to local coverage (2009)

Radio broadcast stations: AM 3, FM 106 (plus many low-power stations), shortwave 3 (2008)
Television broadcast stations: 106 (2007)

Internet country code: .ch

Internet hosts: 5.301 million (2012)
country comparison to the world: 20

Internet users: *total:* 7.1 million
percent of population: 88.0% (2014 est.)
country comparison to the world: 54

TRANSPORTATION

Airports: 63 (2013)
country comparison to the world: 78
Airports—with paved runways: *total:* 40
over 3,047 m: 3
2,438 to 3,047 m: 2
1,524 to 2,437 m: 12
914 to 1,523 m: 6
under 914 m: 17 (2013)

Airports—with unpaved runways: *total:* 23
under 914 m: 23 (2013)
Heliports: 2 (2013)
Pipelines: gas 1,800 km; oil 94 km; refined products 7 km (2013)
Railways: *total:* 5,651.5 km
standard gauge: 4,424.8 km 1.435-m gauge (3,634.1 km electrified)
narrow gauge: 2 km 1.200-m gauge (2 km electrified); 1,188.3 km 1.000-m gauge (1,167.3 km electrified); 36.4 km 0.800-m gauge (36.4 km electrified) (2014)
country comparison to the world: 33
Roadways: *total:* 71,464 km
paved: 71,464 km (includes 1,415 of expressways) (2011)
country comparison to the world: 65
Waterways: 1,292 km (there are 1,227 km of waterways on lakes and rivers for public transport and 65 km on the Rhine River between Basel-Rheinfelden and Schaffhausen-Bodensee for commercial goods transport) (2010)
country comparison to the world: 57
Merchant marine: *total:* 38

by type: bulk carrier 19, cargo 9, chemical tanker 5, container 4, petroleum tanker 1
registered in other countries: 127 (Antigua and Barbuda 7, Bahamas 1, Belize 1, Cayman Islands 1, France 5, Germany 2, Hong Kong 5, Italy 13, Liberia 25, Luxembourg 1, Malta 20, Marshall Islands 12, NZ 2, Panama 15, Portugal 3, Russia 3, Saint Vincent and the Grenadines 7, Singapore 3, Spain 1) (2010)
country comparison to the world: 76
Ports and terminals: river port(s): Basel (Rhine)

Military branches: Swiss Armed Forces: Land Forces, Swiss Air Force (Schweizer Luftwaffe) (2013)
Military service age and obligation: 19–26 years of age for male compulsory military service; 18 years of age for voluntary male and female military service; every Swiss male has to serve at least 260 days in the armed forces; conscripts receive 18 weeks of mandatory training, followed by seven 3-week intermittent recalls for training during the next

10 years (2012)
Military expenditures: 0.64% of GDP (2014)
0.69% of GDP (2013)
0.76% of GDP (2012)
0.75% of GDP (2011)
0.76% of GDP (2010)
country comparison to the world: 117

Disputes—International: none
Refugees and internally displaced persons: *refugees (country of origin):* 16,091 (Eritrea); 5,161 (Syria) (2014) stateless persons: 69 (2015)
Illicit drugs: a major International financial center vulnerable to the layering and integration stages of money laundering; despite significant legislation and reporting requirements, secrecy rules persist and nonresidents are permitted to conduct business through offshore entities and various intermediaries; transit country for and consumer of South American cocaine, Southwest Asian heroin, and Western European synthetics; domestic cannabis cultivation and limited ecstasy production

SYRIA

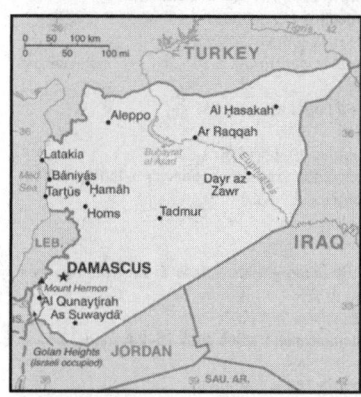

Background: Following World War I, France acquired a mandate over the northern portion of the former Ottoman Empire province of Syria. The French administered the area as Syria until granting it independence in 1946. The new country lacked political stability and experienced a series of military coups. Syria united with Egypt in February 1958 to form the United Arab Republic. In September 1961, the two entities separated, and the Syrian Arab Republic was reestablished. In the 1967 Arab-Israeli War, Syria lost the Golan Heights region to Israel. During the 1990s, Syria and Israel held occasional, albeit unsuccessful, peace talks over its return. In November 1970, Hafizal-ASAD, a member of the socialist Ba'th Party and the minority Alawi sect, seized power

in a bloodless coup and brought political stability to the country. Following the death of President Hafizal-ASAD, his son, Bashar al-ASAD, was approved as president by popular referendum in July 2000. Syrian troops—stationed in Lebanon since 1976 in an ostensible peacekeeping role—were withdrawn in April 2005. During the July-August 2006 conflict between Israel and Hizballah, Syria placed its military forces on alert but did not intervene directly on behalf of its ally Hizballah. In May 2007, Basharal-ASAD's second term as president was approved by popular referendum. Influenced by major uprisings that began elsewhere in the region, and compounded by additional social and economic factors, antigovernment protests broke out first in the southern province of Dar'a in March 2011 with protesters calling for the repeal of the restrictive Emergency Law allowing arrests without charge, the legalization of political parties, and the removal of corrupt local officials. Demonstrations and violent unrest spread across Syria with the size and intensity of protests fluctuating. The government responded to unrest with a mix of concessions—including the repeal of the Emergency Law, new laws permitting new political parties, and liberalizing local and National elections—and military force. However, the government's response has failed to meet opposition demands for ASAD's resignation, and the government's ongoing violence to quell unrest and widespread armed opposition activity has led to extended clashes between government forces and oppositionists. International pressure on the ASAD regime has intensified since late 2011, as the Arab League, EU, Turkey, and the US expanded economic sanctions against the regime. In December 2012, the Syrian National Coalition,

was recognized by more than 130 countries as the sole legitimate representative of the Syrian people. Peace talks between the Coalition and Syrian regime at the UN-sponsored Geneva II conference in 2014 failed to produce a resolution of the conflict. Unrest continues in Syria, and according to a January 2015 UN estimate, the death toll among Syrian Government forces, opposition forces, and civilians had reached 220,000. As of January 2016, approximately 13.5 million people were in need of humanitarian Assistance in Syria, with 6.5 million people displaced internally, and an Additional 4.4 million Syrian refugees, making the Syrian situation the largest humanitarian crisis worldwide.

Location: Middle East, bordering the Mediterranean Sea, between Lebanon and Turkey
Geographic coordinates: 35 00 N, 38 00 E
Map references: Middle East
Area: *total:* 185,180 sq km
land: 183,630 sq km
water: 1,550 sq km
note: includes 1,295 sq km of Israeli-occupied territory
country comparison to the world: 89
Area—comparative: slightly more than 1.5 times the size of Pennsylvania
Land boundaries: *total:* 2,363 km
border countries (5): Iraq 599 km, Israel 83 km, Jordan 379 km, Lebanon 403 km, Turkey 899 km
Coastline: 193 km
Maritime claims: *territorial sea:* 12 nm
contiguous zone: 24 nm
Climate: mostly desert; hot, dry, sunny summers (June to August) and mild, rainy winters

(December to February) along coast; cold weather with snow or sleet periodically in Damascus

Terrain: primarily semiarid and desert plateau; narrow coastal plain; mountains in west

Elevation: *mean elevation:* 514 m

elevation extremes: *lowest point:* unnamed location near Lake Tiberias -200 m

highest point: Mount Hermon 2,814 m

Natural resources: petroleum, phosphates, chrome and manganese ores, asphalt, iron ore, rock salt, marble, gypsum, hydropower

Land use: *agricultural land:* 75.8%

arable land: 25.4%

permanent crops: 5.8%

permanent pasture: 44.6%

forest: 2.7%

oth er: 21.5% (2011 est.)

Irrigated land: 14,280 sq km (2012)

Total renewable water resources: 16.8 cu km (2011)

Freshwater withdrawal (domestic/industrial/agricultural): *total:* 16.76 cu km/yr (9%/4%/88%)

per capita: 867.4 cu m/yr (2005)

Natural hazards: dust storms, sandstorms

volcanism: Syria's two historically active volcanoes, Es Safa and an unnamed volcano near the Turkish border have not erupted in centuries

Environment—current issues: deforestation; overgrazing; soil erosion; desertification; water pollution from raw sewage and petroleum refining wastes; inadequate potable water

Environment—international agreements: *party to:* Biodiversity, Climate Change, Climate Change-Kyoto Protocol, Desertification, Endangered Species, Hazardous Wastes, Ozone Layer Protection, Ship Pollution, Wetlands

signed, but not ratified: Environmental Modification

Geography—note: the capital of Damascus—located at an oasis fed by the Barada River—is thought to be one of the world's oldest continuously inhabited cities; there are 42 Israeli settlements and civilian land use sites in the Israeli-occupied Golan Heights (2014 est.)

PEOPLE AND SOCIETY

Nationality: *noun:* Syrian(s)

adjective: Syrian

Ethnic groups: Arab 90.3%, Kurds, Armenians, and other 9.7%

Languages: Arabic (official), Kurdish, Armenian, Aramaic, Circassian (widely understood); French, English (somewhat understood)

Religions: Muslim 87% (official; includes Sunni 74% and Alawi, Ismaili, and Shia 13%), Christian 10% (includes Orthodox, Uniate, and Nestorian), Druze 3%, Jewish (few remaining in Damascus and Aleppo)

Population: 17,064,854 (July 2014 est.)

note: approximately 20,500 Israeli settlers live in the Golan Heights (2014) (July 2015 est.)

country comparison to the world: 65

Age structure: *0–14 years:* 32.49% (male 2,841,760/female 2,701,998)

15–24 years: 19.85% (male 1,713,286/female 1,673,560)

25–54 years: 38.57% (male 3,283,267/female 3,298,387)

55–64 years: 5.07% (male 427,655/female 438,105)

65 years and over: 4.02% (male 309,947/female 376,889) (2015 est.)

Dependency ratios: *total dependency ratio:* 70%

youth dependency ratio: 63.1%

elderly dependency ratio: 6.9%

potential support ratio: 14.5% (2015 est.)

Median age: *total:* 23.8 years

male: 23.3 years

female: 24.1 years (2015 est.)

country comparison to the world: 161

Population growth rate: -0.16% (2015 est.)

country comparison to the world: 213

Birth rate: 22.17 births/1,000 population (2015 est.)

country comparison to the world: 74

Death rate: 4 deaths/1,000 population (2015 est.)

country comparison to the world: 208

Net migration rate: -19.79 migrant(s)/1,000 population (2015 est.)

country comparison to the world: 220

Urbanization: *urban population:* 57.7% of total population (2015)

rate of urbanization: 1.37% annual rate of change (2010–15 est.)

Major urban areas—population: Aleppo 3.562 million; DAMASCUS (capital) 2.566 million; Hims (Homs) 1.641 million; Hamah 1.237 million; Lattakia 781,000 (2015)

Sex ratio: *at birth:* 1.06 male(s)/female

0–14 years: 1.05 male(s)/female

15–24 years: 1.02 male(s)/female

25–54 years: 1 male(s)/female

55–64 years: 0.98 male(s)/female

65 years and over: 0.82 male(s)/female

total population: 1.01 male(s)/female (2015 est.)

Maternal mortality rate: 68 deaths/100,000 live births (2015 est.)

country comparison to the world: 87

Infant mortality rate: *total:* 15.61 deaths/1,000 live births

male: 17.95 deaths/1,000 live births

female: 13.13 deaths/1,000 live births (2015 est.)

country comparison to the world: 103

Life expectancy at birth: *total population:* 74.69 years

male: 72.31 years

female: 77.21 years (2015 est.)

country comparison to the world: 114

Total fertility rate: 2.6 children born/woman (2015 est.)

country comparison to the world: 74

Contraceptive prevalence rate: 53.9% (2009/10)

Health expenditures: 3.3% of GDP (2013)

country comparison to the world: 176

Physicians density: 1.46 physicians/1,000 population (2010)

Hospital bed density: 1.5 beds/1,000 population (2012)

Drinking water source:

improved:

urban: 92.3% of population

rural: 87.2% of population

total: 90.1% of population

unimproved:

urban: 7.7% of population

rural: 12.8% of population

total: 9.9% of population (2015 est.)

Sanitation facility access:

improved:

urban: 96.2% of population

rural: 95.1% of population

total: 95.7% of population

unimproved:

urban: 3.8% of population

rural: 4.9% of population

total: 4.3% of population (2015 est.)

HIV/AIDS—adult prevalence rate: 0.01% (2014 est.)

country comparison to the world: 132

HIV/AIDS—people living with HIV/AIDS: 900 (2014 est.)

country comparison to the world: 121

HIV/AIDS—deaths: less than 100 (2014 est.)

country comparison to the world: 110

Obesity—adult prevalence rate: 21.6% (2014)

country comparison to the world: 41

Children under the age of 5 years underweight: 10.1% (2009)

country comparison to the world: 70

Education expenditures: 5.1% of GDP (2009)

country comparison to the world: 70

Literacy: *definition:* age 15 and over can read and write

total population: 86.4%

male: 91.7%

female: 81% (2015 est.)

School life expectancy (primary to tertiary education): *total:* 9 years

male: 9 years

female: 9 years (2013)

Child labor—children ages 5–14: *total number:* 192,915

percentage: 4% (2006 est.)

Unemployment, youth ages 15–24: *total:* 35.8%

male: 26.6%

female: 71.1% (2011 est.)

country comparison to the world: 58

GOVERNMENT

Country name: *conventional long form:* Syrian Arab Republic

conventional short form: Syria

local long form: Al Jumhuriyahal Arabiyah as Suriyah

local short form: Suriyah

former: United Arab Republic (with Egypt)

etymology: name ultimately derived from the ancient Assyrians who dominated northern Mesopotamia, but whose reach also extended westward to the Levant; over time, the name came to be associated more with the western area

Government type: presidential republic; highly authoritarian regime

Capital: *name:* Damascus

Geographic coordinates: 33 30 N, 36 18 E

time difference: UTC+2 (7 hours ahead of Washington, DC, during Standard Time)

daylight saving time: +1 hr, begins midnight on the last Friday in March; ends at midnight on the first Friday in November

Administrative divisions: 14 provinces (muhafazat, singular—muhafazah); Al Hasakah, Al Ladhiqiyah (Latakia), Al Qunaytirah, Ar Raqqah, As Suwayda', Dar'a, Dayraz Zawr, Dimashq (Damascus), Halab, Hamah, Hims (Homs), Idlib, Rif Dimashq (Damascus Countryside), Tartus

Independence: 17 April 1946 (from League of Nations mandate under French administration)

National holiday: Independence Day, 17 April (1946)

Constitution: several previous; latest issued 15 February 2012, passed by referendum 26 February 2012 (2016)

Legal system: mixed legal system of civil and Islamic law (for family courts)

International law organization participation: has not submitted an ICJ jurisdiction declaration; non-party state to the ICCt

Citizenship: *citizenship by birth:* no

citizenship by descent only: the father must be a citizen of Syria; if the father is unknown or stateless, the mother must be a citizen of Syria

dual citizenship recognized: yes

residency requirement for naturalization: 10 years

Suffrage: 18 years of age; universal

Executive branch: *chief of state:* President Bashar al-ASAD (since 17 July 2000); Vice President Najah al-ATTAR (since 23 March 2006)

head of government: Prime Minister Imad Muhammad Dib KHAMIS (since 3 July 2016); Deputy Prime Ministers Fahd Jasim al-FURAYJ, Lt. Gen. Walid al-MUALEM

cabinet: Council of Ministers appointed by the president

elections/appointments: president directly elected by simple majority popular vote for a 7-year term (eligible for a second term); election last held on 3 June 2014 (next to be held in June 2021); the president appoints the vice presidents, prime minister, and deputy prime ministers

election results: Bashar al-ASAD approved as president; percent of vote—Bashar al-ASAD (Ba'th Party) 88.7%, Hassan Al-NOURI (independent) 4.3%, Maher HAJJER (independent) 3.2%, other/invalid 3.8%

Legislative branch: *description:* unicameral People's Assembly or Majlis al-Shaab (250 seats; members directly elected in multi-seat constituencies by proportional representation vote to serve 4-year terms)

elections: last held on 13 April 2016 (next to be held in 2020)

election results: percent of vote by party—NPF 80%, other 20%; seats by party—NPF 200, other 50

Judicial branch: *highest court(s):* Court of Cassation (organized into civil, criminal, religious, and military divisions, each with 3 judges); Supreme Constitutional Court (consists of 4 members)

judge selection and term of office: Court of Cassation judges appointed by the Supreme Judicial

Council or SJC, a judicial management body headed by the minister of justice with 7 members including the National president; judge tenure NA; Supreme Constitutional Court judges nominated by the president and appointed by the SJC; judges appointed for 4-year renewable terms

subordinate courts: courts of first instance; magistrates' courts; religious and military courts; Economic Security Court

Political parties and leaders: legal parties/alliances: Arab Socialist Union of Syria or ASU [Safwan Al-QUDSI]

National Progressive Front or NPF [Bashar al-ASAD, Suleiman QADDAH] (alliance includes Arab Socialist Renaissance (Ba'th) Party [President Bashar al-ASAD], Socialist Unionist Democratic Party [Fadlallah Nasr al-DIN]

Syrian Communist Party (two branches) [Wissal Farha BAKD ASH, Yusuf Rashid FAYSAL]

Syrian Social Nationalist Party or SSNP [As'ad HARDAN]

Unionist Socialist Party [Fayez ISMAIL]) Kurdish parties (considered illegal): Kurdish Azadi Party

Kurdish Democratic Accord Party (al Wifaq)

Kurdish Democratic Party (al Parti-I brahim wing)

Kurdish Democratic Party (al Parti-Mustafa wing)

Kurdish Democratic Party in Syria or KDP-S

Kurdish Democratic Patriotic/National Party

Kurdish Democratic Progressive Party or KDPP-Darwish

Kurdish Democratic Progressive Party or KDPP-Muhammad

Kurdish Democratic Union Party or PYD [Salih Muslim MOHAMMAD]

Kurdish Democratic Unity Party

Kurdish Democratic Yekiti Party

Kurdish Future Party [Rezan HASSAN]

Kurdish Left Party

Kurdish Yekiti (Union) Party

Syrian Kurdish Democratic Party

other: Syrian Democratic Party [Mustafa QALAAJI]

Political pressure groups and leaders: Free Syrian Army Syrian Muslim Brotherhood or SMB [Muhammad Riyad al-SHAQFAH] (operates in exile in London) Syrian Opposition Coalition or National Coalition of Syrian Revolution ary and Opposition Forces [Anasal-ABDAH]

note: there are also hundreds of local and provincial political and armed opposition groups that organize protests, provide civilian services, and stage armed attacks

International organization participation: ABEDA, AFESD, AMF, CAEU, FAO, G-24, G-77, IAEA, IBRD, ICAO, ICC (National committees), ICRM, IDA, IDB, IFAD, IFC, IFRCS, IHO, ILO, IMF, IMO, Interpol, IOC, IPU, ISO, ITSO, ITU, LAS, MIGA, NAM, OAPEC, OIC, OPCW, UN, UNCTAD, UNESCO, UNIDO, UNRWA, UNWTO, UPU, WCO, WFTU (NGOs), WHO, WIPO, WMO, WTO (observer)

Diplomatic representation in the US: *note:* Embassy ceased operation and closed on 18 March 2014

chief of mission: Ambassador (vacant); Charge d'Affaires Mounir KOUDMANI (since 1 June 2012)

chancery: 2215 Wyoming Avenue NW, Washington, DC 20008

telephone: [1] (202) 232-6313

FAX: [1] (202) 234-9548

Diplomatic representation from the US: *chief of mission:* ambassador (vacant); Special Envoy to Syria Michael RATNEY (since July 2015); note—on 6 February 2012, the US closed its embassy in Damascus

embassy: Abou Roumaneh, Al-M ansour Street, No.2, Damascus

mailing address: P.O. Box 29, Damascus

telephone: [963] (11) 3391-4444

FAX: [963] (11) 3391-3999

Flag description: three equal horizontal bands of red (top), white, and black; two small, green, five-pointed stars in a horizontal line centered in the white band; the band colors derive from the Arab Liberation flag and represent oppression (black), overcome through bloody struggle (red), to be replaced by a bright future (white); identical to the former flag of the United Arab Republic (1958–1961) where the two stars represented the constituent states of Syria and Egypt; the current design dates to 1980

note: similar to the flag of Yemen, which has a plain white band, Iraq, which has an Arabic inscription centered in the white band, and that of Egypt, which has a gold Eagle of Saladin centered in the white band

National symbol(s): hawk; National colors: red, white, black, green

National anthem: *name:* "Humatad-Diyar" (Guardians of the Homeland)

lyrics/music: Khalil Mardam BEY/Mohammad Salim FLAYFEL and Ahmad Salim FLAYFEL

note: adopted 1936, restored 1961; between 1958 and 1961, while Syria was a member of the United Arab Republic with Egypt, the country had a different anthem

ECONOMY

Economy—overview: Syria's economy continues to deteriorate amid the ongoing conflict that began in 2011, declining by 62% from 2010 to 2014. The government has struggled to address the effects of International sanctions, widespread infrastructure damage, diminished domestic consumption and production, reduced subsidies, and high inflation, which have caused dwindling foreign exchange reserves, rising budget and trade deficits, a decreasing value of the Syrian pound, and falling household purchasing power. During 2014, the ongoing conflict and continued unrest and economic decline worsened the humanitarian crisis and elicited a greater need for International assistance, as the number of people in need inside Syria increased from 9.3 million to 12.2 million, and the number of Syrian refugees increased from 2.2 million to more than 3.3 million.

Prior to the turmoil, Damascus had begun liberalizing economic policies, including cutting lending interest rates, opening private banks, consolidating multiple exchange rates, raising prices on some subsidized items, and establishing the Damascus Stock Exchange, but the economy remains highly regulated. Long-run economic constraints include foreign trade barriers, declining oil production, high unemployment, rising budget deficits, increasing pressure on water supplies caused by heavy use in Agriculture, rapid population growth, industrial expansion, water pollution, and widespread infrastructure damage.

GDP (purchasing power parity): $55.8 billion (2014 est.)

$61.9 billion (2013 est.)

$97.5 billion (2012 est.)

note: data are in 2014 US dollars the war-driven deterioration of the economy resulted in a disappearance of quality National level statistics in the 2012–13 period

country comparison to the world: 106

GDP (official exchange rate): $24.6 billion (2014 est.)

GDP—real growth rate: -9.9% (2015 est.)

-36.5% (2014 est.)

-30.9% (2013 est.)

country comparison to the world: 219

GDP—per capita (PPP): $5,100 (2011 est.)

$5,100 (2010 est.)

$5,200 (2010 est.)

note: data are in 2011 US dollars

country comparison to the world: 168

Gross National saving: NA% (2015 est.)

-16.7% of GDP (2014 est.)

NA% (2013 est.)

GDP—composition, by end use:

household consumption: 100.9%

government consumption: 28.1%

investment in fixed capital: 10.9%

investment in inventories: 2.8%

exports of goods and services: 18.1%

imports of goods and services: -60.8% (2014 est.)

GDP—composition, by sector of origin:

agriculture: 19.5%

industry: 18.9%

services: 61.6% (2015 est.)

Agriculture—products: wheat, barley, cotton, lentils, chickpeas, olives, sugar beets; beef, mutton, eggs, poultry, milk

Industries: petroleum, textiles, food processing, beverages, tobacco, phosphate rock mining, cement, oil seeds crushing, automobile assembly

Industrial production growth rate: -4.8% (2015 est.)

country comparison to the world: 188

Labor force: 3.798 million (2015 est.)

country comparison to the world: 95

Labor force—by occupation: *agriculture:* 17%

industry: 16%

services: 67% (2008 est.)

Unemployment rate: 57.7% (2014 est.)

49.7% (2013 est.)

country comparison to the world: 202

Population below poverty line: 82.5% (2014 est.)

House holding come or consumption by percentage share: *lowest 10%:* NA%

highest 10%: NA%

Budget: *revenues:* $3.9 billion

expenditures: $5.7 billion

note: government projections for FY2016

Taxes and other revenues: 15.9% of GDP (2016 est.)

country comparison to the world: 186

Budget surplus (+) or deficit (–): -7.3% of GDP (2016 est.)

country comparison to the world: 195

Public debt: 57.2% of GDP (2015 est.)

51.1% of GDP (2014 est.)

country comparison to the world: 67

Fiscal year: calendar year

Inflation rate (consumer prices): 33.6% (2015 est.) 29.2% (2014 est.)

country comparison to the world: 223

Central bank discount rate: 0.75% (31 December 2015)

5% (31 December 2014)

country comparison to the world: 125

Commercial bank prime lending rate: 17.5% (31 December 2015 est.)

17% (31 December 2014 est.)

country comparison to the world: 23

Stock of narrow money: $4.009 billion (31 December 2015 est.)

$5.536 billion (31 December 2014 est.)

country comparison to the world: 106

Stock of broad money: $11.05 billion (31 December 2014 est.)

$12.71 billion (31 December 2013 est.)

country comparison to the world: 106

Stock of domestic credit: $4.009 billion (31 December 2015 est.)

$6.119 billion (31 December 2014 est.)

country comparison to the world: 126

Market value of publicly traded shares: $NA

Current account balance: -$3.148 billion (2015 est.)

-$3.667 billion (2014 est.)

country comparison to the world: 160

Exports: $1.849 billion (2015 est.)

$3.015 billion (2014 est.)

country comparison to the world: 141

Exports—commodities: crude oil, minerals, petroleum Products, fruits and vegetables, cotton fiber, textiles, clothing, meat and live animals, wheat

Exports—partners: Iraq 64.7%, Saudi Arabia 11.2%, Kuwait 7.1%, UAE 6.1%, Libya 4.6% (2015)

Imports: $6.557 billion (2015 est.) $8.028 billion (2014 est.)

country comparison to the world: 117

Imports—commodities: machinery and transport equipment, electric power machinery, food and livestock, metal and metal products, chemicals and chemical products, plastics, yarn, paper

Imports—partners: Saudi Arabia 27.9%, UAE 13.7%, Iran 10.1%, Turkey 9%, Iraq 8.3%, China 6.1% (2015)

Reserves of foreign exchange and gold: $967.6 million (31 December 2015 est.) $1.428 billion (31 December 2014 est.)

country comparison to the world: 133

Debt—external: $5.812 billion (31 December 2014 est.)

$4.753 billion (31 December 2013 est.)

country comparison to the world: 126

Exchange rates: Syrian pounds (SYP) per US dollar—

234.5 (2015 est.)

153.695 (2014 est.)

153.695 (2013 est.)

64.39 (2012 est.)

48.371 (2011 est.)

ENERGY

Electricity—production: 29.48 billion kWh (2012 est.)

country comparison to the world: 64

Electricity—consumption: 25.7 billion kWh (2012 est.)

country comparison to the world: 66

Electricity—exports: 0 kWh (2012 est.)

country comparison to the world: 200

Electricity—imports: 1.234 billion kWh (2012 est.)

country comparison to the world: 58

Electricity—installed generating capacity: 8.958 million kW (2012 est.)

country comparison to the world: 59

Electricity—from fossil fuels: 82.9% of total installed capacity (2012 est.)

country comparison to the world: 93

Electricity—from nuclear fuels: 0% of total installed capacity (2012 est.)

country comparison to the world: 185

Electricity—from hydroelectric plants: 16.8% of total installed capacity (2012 est.)

country comparison to the world: 99

Electricity—from other renewable sources: 0.3% of total installed capacity (2012 est.)

country comparison to the world: 106

Crude oil—production: 22,660 bbl/day (2014 est.)

country comparison to the world: 66

Crude oil—exports: 0 bbl/day (2012 est.)

country comparison to the world: 192

Crude oil—imports: 0 bbl/day (2012 est.)

country comparison to the world: 130

Crude oil—proved reserves: 2.5 billion bbl (1 January 2015 est.)

country comparison to the world: 32

Refined petroleum products—production: 168,800 bbl/day (2012 est.)

country comparison to the world: 60

Refined petroleum products—consumption: 224,000 bbl/day (2013 est.)

country comparison to the world: 57

Refined petroleum products—exports: 18,940 bbl/day (2012 est.)

country comparison to the world: 73

Refined petroleum products—imports: 63,820 bbl/day (2012 est.)

country comparison to the world: 71

Natural gas—production: 5.3 billion cu m (2013 est.)

country comparison to the world: 50

Natural gas—consumption: 5.65 billion cu m (2013 est.)

country comparison to the world: 57

Natural gas—exports: 0 cu m (2013 est.)

country comparison to the world: 187

Natural gas—imports: 350 million cu m (2013 est.)
country comparison to the world: 67
Natural gas—proved reserves: 240.7 billion cu m (1 January 2014 est.)
country comparison to the world: 45
Carbon dioxide emissions from consumption of energy: 50.92 million Mt (2012 est.)
country comparison to the world: 59

COMMUNICATIONS

Telephones—fixed lines: *total subscriptions:* 3.99 million
subscriptions per 100 inhabitants: 22 (2014 est.)
country comparison to the world:
Telephone—mobile cellular: *total:* 15.6 million 41
subscriptions per 100 inhabitants: 87 (2014 est.)
country comparison to the world: 66
Telephone system: *general assessment:* fair system currently undergoing significant improvement and digital upgrades, including fiber-optic technology and expansion of the network to rural areas; the armed insurgency that began in 2011 has led to major disruptions to the network and has caused telephone and internet outages throughout the country
domestic: the number of fixed-line connections has increased markedly since 2000; mobile-cellular service growing with telephone subscribership nearly 60 per 100 persons in 2011
international: country code—963; submarine cable connection to Egypt, Lebanon, and Cyprus; satellite earth stations—1 intelsat (Indian Ocean) and 1 Intersputnik (Atlantic Ocean region); coaxial cable and microwave radio relay to Iraq, Jordan, Lebanon, and Turkey; participant in Medarabtel (2011)
Broadcast media: state-run TV and radio broadcast networks; state operates 2 TV networks and a satellite channel; roughly two-thirds of Syrian homes have a satellite dish providing access to foreign TV broadcasts; 3 state-run radio channels; first private radio station launched in 2005; private radio broadcasters prohibited from transmitting news or political content (2007)
Radio broadcast stations: AM 14, FM 15, short-wave 26 (2010)
Television broadcast stations: 44 (plus 17 repeaters) (1995)
Internet country code: .sy
Internet hosts: 416 (2012)
country comparison to the world: 187
Internet users: *total:* 4.8 million
percent of population: 26.7% (2014 est.)
country comparison to the world: 71

TRANSPORTATION

Airports: 90 (2013)
country comparison to the world: 62
Airports—with paved runways: *total:* 29
over 3,047 m: 5
2,438 to 3,047 m: 16
914 to 1,523 m: 3
under 914 m: 5 (2013)
Airports—with unpaved runways: *total:* 61

1,524 to 2,437 m: 1914 to 1,523 m: 12
under 914 m: 48 (2013)
Heliports: 6 (2013)
Pipelines: gas 3,170 km; oil 2,029 km (2013)
Railways: *total:* 2,052 km
standard gauge: 1,801 km 1.435-m gauge
narrow gauge: 251 km 1.050-m gauge (2014)
country comparison to the world: 72
Roadways: *total:* 69,873 km
paved: 63,060 km
unpaved: 6,813 km (2010)
country comparison to the world: 67
Waterways: 900 km (navigable but not economically significant) (2011)
country comparison to the world: 68
Merchant marine: *total:* 19
by type: bulk carrier 4, cargo 14, carrier 1
registered in other countries: 166 (Barbados 1, Belize 4, Bolivia 4, Cambodia 22, Comoros 5, Dominica 4, Georgia 24, Lebanon 2, Liberia 1, Malta 4, Moldova 5, North Korea 4, Panama 34, Saint Vincent and the Grenadines 9, Sierra Leone 13, Tanzania 23, Togo 6, unknown 1) (2010)
country comparison to the world: 95
Ports and terminals: *major seaport(s):* Baniyas, Latakia, Tartus

MILITARY AND SECURITY

Military branches: Syrian Armed Forces: Land Forces, Naval Forces, Air Forces (includes Air Defense Forces) (2013)
Military service age and obligation: 18 years of age for compulsory and voluntary military service; conscript service obligation is 18 months; women are not conscripted but may volunteer to serve; re-enlistment obligation 5 years, with retirement after 15 years or age 40 (enlisted) or 20 years or age 45 (NCOs) (2012)

TRANSNATIONAL ISSUES

Disputes—International: Golan Heights is Israeli-occupied with the almost 1,000-strong UN Disengagement Observer Force patrolling a buffer zone since 1964; lacking a treaty or other documentation describing the boundary, portions of the Lebanon-Syria boundary are unclear with several sections in dispute; since 2000, Lebanon has claimed Shab'a Farms in the Golan Heights; 2004 Agreement and pending demarcation would settle border dispute with Jordan
Refugees and internally displaced persons: *refugees (country of origin):* 526,744 (Palestinian Refugees) (2014); undetermined (Iraq) (2015)
note: the ongoing civil war has created more than 4.8 million Syrian refugees—dispersed in Egypt, Iraq, Jordan, Lebanon, and Turkey—as of July 2016
IDPs: 6,563,462 (ongoing civil war since 2011) (2015)
stateless persons: 160,000 (2015); note—Syria's stateless population consists of Kurds and Palestinians; stateless persons are prevented from voting, owning land, holding certain jobs, receiving food subsidies or public healthcare, enrolling in public schools, or being legally married to Syrian citizens;

in 1962, some 120,000 Syrian Kurds were stripped of their Syrian citizenship, rendering them and their descendants stateless; in 2011, the Syrian government granted citizenship to thousands of Syrian Kurds as a means of appeasement; however, resolving the question of statelessness is not a priority given Syria's ongoing civil war
Trafficking in persons: *current situation:* as conditions continue to deteriorate due to Syria's civil war, human trafficking has increased; Syrians remaining in the country and those that are refugees abroad are vulnerable to trafficking; Syria is a source and destination country for men, women and children subjected to forced labor and sex trafficking; Syrian children continue to be forcibly recruited by government forces, pro-regime militias, armed opposition groups, and terrorist organizations to serve as soldiers, human shields, and executioners; ISIL forces Syrian women and girls and Yazidi women and girls taken from Iraq to marry its fighters, where they experience domestic servitude and sexual violence; Syrian refugee women and girls are forced into exploitive marriages or prostitution in neighboring countries, while displaced children are forced into street begging domestically and abroad
tier rating: Tier 3—the government does not fully comply with the minimum standards for the elimination of trafficking and is not making significant efforts to do so; in 2014, Syria's violent conditions enabled human trafficking to flourish; the government made no effort to investigate, prosecute, or convict trafficking offenders or complicit government officials, including those who forcibly recruited child soldiers; authorities did not identify victims and failed to ensure victims, including child soldiers, were protected from arrest, detention, and severe abuse as a result of being trafficked (2015)
Illicit drugs: a transit point for opiates, hashish, and cocaine bound for regional and Western markets; weak anti-money-laundering controls and bank privatization may leave it vulnerable to money laundering

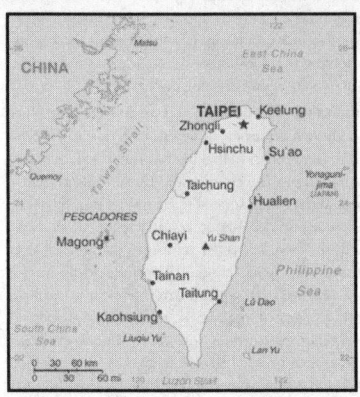

INTRODUCTION

Background: First inhabited by Austronesian people, Taiwan became home to Han immigrants beginning in the late Ming Dynasty (17th century). In 1895, military defeat forced China's Qing Dynasty to cede Taiwan to Japan, which governed Taiwan for 50 years. Taiwan came under Chinese Nationalist control after World War II. In the four years leading to the communist victory on the mainland in 1949, 2 million Nationalists fled to Taiwan and established a government under the 1947 constitution drawn up for all of China. The Nationalist government established authoritarian rule under martial law in 1948. Beginning in the late 1970s, the ruling authorities gradually democratized and incorporated the local population within the governing structure. This process expanded rapidly in the 1980s, with the founding of the first opposition party (the Democratic Progressive Party or DPP) in 1986 and the lifting of martial law in 1987. Taiwan held its first direct presidential election in 1996. In 2000, Taiwan underwent its first peaceful transfer of power from the Nationalist Party (Kuomintang or KMT) to the DPP. Throughout this period, the island prospered and became one of East Asia's economic "Tigers." The dominant political issues continue to be management of sensitive relations between Taiwan and China—specifically the question of Taiwan's eventual status—as well as domestic priorities for economic reform and growth.

GEOGRAPHY

Location: Eastern asia, islands bordering the East China Sea, Philippine Sea, South China Sea, and Taiwan Strait, north of the Philippines, off the southeastern coast of China

Geographic coordinates: 23 30 N, 121 00 E

Map references: Southeast Asia

Area: *total:* 35,980 sq km
land: 32,260 sq km
water: 3,720 sq km

note: includes the Pescadores, Matsu, and Quemoy islands
country comparison to the world: 139

Area—comparative: slightly smaller than Maryland and Delaware combined

Land boundaries: 0 km

Coastline: 1,566.3 km

Maritime claims: *territorial sea:* 12 nm
exclusive economic zone: 200 nm

Climate: tropical; marine; rainy season during southwest monsoon (June to August); persistent and extensive cloudiness all year

Terrain: eastern two-thirds mostly rugged mountains; flat to gently rolling plains in west

Elevation: *mean elevation:* 1,150 m

elevation extremes: *lowest point:* South China Sea 0 m
highest point: Yu Shan 3,952 m

Natural resources: small deposits of coal, Natural gas, limestone, marble, asbestos, arable land

Land use: *agricultural land:* 22.7%
arable land: 16.9%
permanent crops: 5.8%
permanent pasture: NA
forest: NA
other: 77.3% (2011 est.)

Irrigated land: 3,820 sq km (2012)

Total renewable water resources: 67 cu km (2011)

Natural hazards: earthquakes; typhoons
volcanism: Kueishantao Island (elev. 401 m), east of Taiwan, is its only historically active volcano, although it has not erupted in centuries

Environment—current issues: air pollution; water pollution from industrial emissions, raw sewage; contamination of drinking water supplies; trade in endangered species; low-level radioactive waste disposal

Environment—international agreements: *party to:* none of the selected agreements because of Taiwan's international status

Geography—note: strategic location adjacent to both the Taiwan Strait and the Luzon Strait

PEOPLE AND SOCIETY

Nationality: *noun:* Taiwan (singular and plural)
note: example—he or she is from Taiwan; they are from Taiwan
adjective: Taiwan (or Taiwanese)

Ethnic groups: Taiwanese (including Hakka) 84%, mainland Chinese 14%, indigenous 2%

Languages: Mandarin Chinese (official), Taiwanese (Min), Hakka dialects

Religions: mixture of Buddhist and Taoist 93%, Christian 4.5%, other 2.5%

Population: 23,415,126 (July 2015 est.)
country comparison to the world: 54

Age structure: *0–14 years:* 13.52% (male 1,632,763/female 1,531,895)
15–24 years: 13.36% (male 1,606,940/female 1,521,617)
25–54 years: 47.06% (male 5,505,063/female 5,513,395)
55–64 years: 13.59% (male 1,556,205/female 1,625,436)
65 years and over: 12.48% (male 1,348,686/female 1,573,126) (2015 est.)

Median age: *total:* 39.7 years
male: 39 years
female: 40.4 years (2015 est.)
country comparison to the world: 49

Population growth rate: 0.23% (2015 est.)
country comparison to the world: 181

Birth rate: 8.47 births/1,000 population (2015 est.)
country comparison to the world: 216

Death rate: 7.11 deaths/1,000 population (2015 est.)
country comparison to the world: 129

Net migration rate: 0.89 migrant(s)/1,000 population (2015 est.)
country comparison to the world: 65

Major urban areas—population: TAIPEI (capital) 2.666 million; Kaohsiung 1.523 million; Taichung 1.225 million; Tainan 815,000 (2015)

Sex ratio: *at birth:* 1.07 male(s)/female
0–14 years: 1.07 male(s)/female
15–24 years: 1.06 male(s)/female
25–54 years: 1 male(s)/female
55–64 years: 0.96 male(s)/female
65 years and over: 0.86 male(s)/female
total population: 0.99 male(s)/female (2015 est.)

Infant mortality rate: *total:* 4.44 deaths/1,000 live births
male: 4.84 deaths/1,000 live births
female: 4.01 deaths/1,000 live births (2015 est.)
country comparison to the world: 184

Life expectancy at birth: *total population:* 79.98 years
male: 76.85 years
female: 83.33 years (2015 est.)
country comparison to the world: 40

Total fertility rate: 1.12 children born/woman (2015 est.)
country comparison to the world: 222

HIV/AIDS—adult prevalence rate: NA

HIV/AIDS—people living with HIV/AIDS: NA

HIV/AIDS—deaths: NA

Literacy: *definition:* age 15 and over can read and write
total population: 98.5%
male: 99.7%
female: 97.3% (2014 est.)

GOVERNMENT

Country name: *conventional long form:* none
conventional short form: Taiwan

local long form: none
local short form: Taiwan
former: Formosa
etymology: "Tayowan" was the name of the coastal sandbank where the Dutch erected their colonial headquarters on the island in the 17th century; the former name "Formosa" means "beautiful" in Portuguese

Government type: semi-presidential republic

Capital: *name:* Taipei

Geographic coordinates: 25 02 N, 121 31 E
time difference: UTC+8 (13 hours ahead of Washington, DC, during Standard Time)

Administrative divisions: includes main island of Taiwan plus smaller islands nearby and off coast of China's Fujian Province; Taiwan is divided into 13 counties (xian, singular and plural), 3 cities (shi, singular and plural), and 6 special municipalities directly under the jurisdiction of the Executive Yuan
counties: Changhua, Chiayi, Hsinchu, Hualien, Kinmen, Lienchiang, Miaoli, Nantou, Penghu, Pingtung, Taitung, Yilan, Yunlin
cities: Chiayi, Hsinchu, Keelung
special municipalities: Kaohsiung (city), New Taipei (city), Taichung (city), Tainan (city), Taipei (city), Taoyuan (city)
note: Taiwan uses a variety of romanization systems; while a modified Wade-Giles system still dominates, the city of Taipei has adopted a Pinyin romanization for street and place names within its boundaries; other local authorities use different romanization systems

National holiday: Republic Day (Anniversary of the Chinese Revolution), 10 October (1911)

Constitution: previous 1912, 1931; latest adopted 25 December 1946, promulgated 1 January 1947, effective 25 December 1947; revised several times, last in 2005 (2016)

Legal system: civil law system

International law organization participation: has not submitted an ICJ jurisdiction declaration; non-party state to the ICCt

Citizenship: *citizenship by birth:* no
citizenship by descent only: at least one parent must be a citizen of Taiwan
dual citizenship recognized: yes, except that citizens of TaiwaNAre not recognized as dual citizens of the People's Republic of China
residency requirement for naturalization: 5 years

Suffrage: 20 years of age; universal

Executive branch: *chief of state:* President TSAI Ing-wen (since 20 May 2016); Vice President CHEN Chien-jen (since 20 May 2016)

head of government: Premier LIN Chuan (President of the Executive Yuan) (since 20 May 2016); Vice Premier LIN Hsi-yao, Vice President of the Executive Yuan (since 20 May 2016)
cabinet: Executive Yuan—ministers appointed by president on recommendation of premier
elections/appointments: president and vice president directly elected on the same ballot by simple

majority popular vote for a 4-year term (eligible for a second term); election last held on 16 January 2016 (next to be held in 2020); premier appointed by the president; vice premiers appointed by the president on the recommendation of the premier
election results: TSAI Ing-wen elected president; percent of vote—TSAI Ing-wen (DPP) 56.1%, Eric CHU Li-lun (KMT) 31.0%, James SOONG Chu-yu (PFP) 12.8%; note—TSAI is the first woman elected president of Taiwan

Legislative branch: *description:* unicameral Legislative Yuan (113 seats; 73 members directly elected in single-seat constituencies by simple majority vote, 34 directly elected in a single island-wide constituency by proportional representation vote, and 6 directly elected in multi-seat aboriginal constituencies by proportional representation vote; members serve 4-year terms)
elections: Legislative Yuan—last held on 16 January 2016 (next to be held in January 2020)
election results: Legislative Yuan—percent of vote by party—DPP 44.1%, KMT 26.9%, PFP 6.5%, NPP 6.1%, other 16.4%; seats by party—DPP 68, KMT 35, NPP 5, PFP 3, NPSU 1, independent 1

Judicial branch: *highest court(s):* Supreme Court (consists of the court president, vice president, and approximately 100 judges organized into 8 civil and 12 criminal divisions, each with a division chief justice and 4 associate justices); Constitutional Court (consists of the court president, vice president, and 13 justices)
judge selection and term of office: Supreme Court justices appointed by the president; Constitutional Court justices appointed by the president with approval of the Legislative Yuan; Supreme Court justices appointed for life; Constitutional Court justices appointed for 8-year terms with half the membership renewed every 4 years
subordinate courts: high courts; district courts; hierarchy of administrative courts

Political parties and leaders: Democratic Progressive Party or DPP [TSAI Ing-wen]
Kuomintang or KMT (Nationalist Party) [Eric Chu Li-lun]
New Power Party or NPP [HUANG Kuo-chang]
Non-Partisan Solidarity Union or NPSU [LIn Pin-kuan]
People First Party or PFP [James SOONG Chu-yu]
Taiwan Solidarity Union or TSU [HUANG Kun-huei]

Political pressure groups and leaders: *other:* environmental groups; independence movement; various business groups
note: public opinion polls consistently show most Taiwanese support maintaining Taiwan's status quo; advocates of Taiwan independence oppose unification with mainland China; most advocates of eventual unification predicate their goal on the democratic transformation of the mainland

International organization participation: ADB (Taipei, China), APEC (Chinese Taipei), BCIE, ICC (National committees), IOC, ITUC (NGOs), SICA (observer), WTO (Taipei, China)

Diplomatic representation in the US: none; commercial and cultural relations with the people

in the United States are maintained through an unofficial instrumentality, the Taipei Economic and Cultural Representative Office in the United States (TECRO), a private nonprofit corporation that performs citizen and consular services similar to those at diplomatic posts
representative: KAO Shuo-tai (a.k.a. Stanley KAO) (since 5 June 2016) office: 4201 Wisconsin Avenue NW, Washington, DC 20016
telephone: [1] 202895-1800
Taipei Economic and Cultural Offices (branch offices): Atlanta, Boston, Chicago, Denver (CO), Hagatna (Guam), Houston, Honolulu, Los Angeles, Miami, New York, San Francisco, Seattle

Diplomatic representation from the US: none; commercial and cultural relations with the people on Taiwan are maintained through an unofficial instrumentality, the American Institute in Taiwan (AIT), a private nonprofit corporation that performs citizen and consular services similar to those at diplomatic posts office:
telephone: [1] [886] (02) 2162-2000
FAX: [1] [886] (02) 2162-2251
other offices: Kaohsiung (Branch Office)

Flag description: red field with a dark blue rectangle in the upper hoist-side corner bearing a white sun with 12 triangular rays; the blue and white design of the canton (symbolizing the sun of progress) dates to 1895; it was later adopted as the flag of the Kuomintang Party; blue signifies liberty, justice, and democracy; red stands for fraternity, sacrifice, and Nationalism, white represents equality, frankness, and the people's livelihood; the 12 rays of the sun are those of the months and the twelve traditional Chinese hours (each ray equals two hours)

National symbol(s): white, 12-rayed sun on blue field; National colors: blue, white, red

National anthem: *name:* "Zhonghua Minguo guoge" (National Anthem of the Republic of China)
lyrics/music: HU Han-min, TAI Chi-t'ao, and LIAO Chung-k'ai/CHENG Mao-Yun
note: adopted 1930; also the song of the Kuomintang Party; it is informally known as "San Min Chu I "or "San Min Zhu Yi" (Three Principles of the People); because of political pressure from China, "Guo Qi Ge" (National Banner Song) is used at international events rather than the official anthem of Taiwan; the "National Banner Song" has gained popularity in Taiwaa and is commonly used during flag raisings

ECONOMY

Economy—overview: Taiwan has a dynamic capitalist economy with gradually decreasing government guidance on investment and foreign trade. Exports, led by electronics, machinery, and petrochemicals have provided the primary impetus for economic development. This heavy dependence on exports exposes the economy to fluctuations in world demand. Taiwan's diplomatic isolation, low birth rate, and rapidly aging population are other major long-term challenges.

Free trade agreements have proliferated in East Asia over the past several years. Following the landmark

Economic Cooperation Framework Agreement (ECFA) signed with China in June 2010, Taiwan in July 2013 signed a free trade deal with New Zealand—Taipei's first-ever with a country with which it does not maintain diplomatic relations—and, in November, inked a trade pact with Singapore. However, follow-on components of the ECFA, including a signed agreement on trade in services and negotiations on trade in goods and dispute resolution, have stalled. In early 2014, the government bowed to public demand and proposed a new law governing the oversight of cross-Strait agreements, before any addition al deals with China are implemented; the legislature has yet to vote on such legislation, leaving the future of ECFA up in the air as of the conclusion of President MA's second and final term in May 2016. MA portrayed ECFA as Taiwan's key to greater participation in East Asia's free trade networks, and has also expressed interest in Taiwan joining the Trans-Pacific Partnership.

Taiwan's total fertility rate of just over one child per woman is among the lowest in the world, raising the prospect of future labor shortages, falling domestic demand, and declining tax revenues. Taiwan's population is aging quickly, with the number of people over 65 expected to account for nearly 20% of the island's total population by 2025.

The island runs a trade surplus, largely because of its surplus with China, and its foreign reserves are the world's fifth largest, behind those of China, Japan, Saudi Arabia, and Switzerland. In 2006 China overtook the US to become Taiwan's second-largest source of imports after Japan. China is also the island's number one destination for foreign direct investment. Taiwan since 2009 has gradually loosened rules governing Chinese investment on the island and has also secured greater market access for its investors in the mainland. In August 2012, the Taiwan Central Bank signed a memorandum of understanding (MOU) on cross-Strait currency settlement with its Chinese counterpart. The MOU allows for the direct settlement of Chinese Renminbi (RMB) and the New Taiwan Dollar across the Strait, which has helped Taiwan develop into a local RMB hub.

Closer economic links with the mainland bring opportunities for Taiwan's economy but also pose challenges as political differences remain unsolved and China's economic growth is slowing. Domestic economic issues loomed large in public debate ahead of the 16 January 2016 presidential and legislative elections, including concerns about stagnant wages, high housing prices, youth unemployment, job security, and financial security in retirement.

GDP (purchasing power parity): $1.099 trillion (2015 est.)
$1.091 trillion (2014 est.)
$1.05 trillion (2013 est.)
note: data are in 2015 US dollars
country comparison to the world: 22

GDP (official exchange rate): $523.6 billion (2015 est.)

GDP—real growth rate: 0.7% (2015 est.)
3.9% (2014 est.)

2.2% (2013 est.)
country comparison to the world: 185

GDP—per capita (PPP): $46,800 (2015 est.)
$46,600 (2014 est.)
$44,900 (2013 est.)
note: data are in 2015 US dollars
country comparison to the world: 29

Gross National saving: 36.3% of GDP (2015 est.)
34.5% of GDP (2014 est.)
33.3% of GDP (2013 est.)
country comparison to the world: 7

GDP—composition, by end use:
household consumption: 52.2%
government consumption: 13.9%
investment in fixed capital: 20.8%
investment in inventories: 0.1%
exports of goods and services: 64.5%
imports of goods and services: -51.5% (2015 est.)

GDP—composition, by sector of origin:
agriculture: 1.8%
industry: 35.4%
services: 62.8% (2015 est.)

Agriculture—products: rice, vegetables, fruit, tea, flowers; pigs, poultry; fish

Industries: electronics, communications and information technology products, petroleum refining, chemicals, textiles, iron and steel, machinery, cement, food processing, vehicles, consumer products, pharmaceuticals

Industrial production growth rate: 1.2% (2015 est.)
country comparison to the world: 139

Labor force: 11.64 million (2015 est.)
country comparison to the world: 50

Labor force—by occupation: agriculture: 5%
industry: 36%
services: 59% (2015 est.)

Unemployment rate: 3.8% (2015 est.)
4% (2014 est.)
country comparison to the world: 33

Population below poverty line: 1.5% (2012 est.)

Household income or consumption by percentage share: lowest: 10%: 6.4%
highest: 10%: 40.3% (2010)

Distribution of family income—Gini index: 33.6 (2014)
32.6 (2000)
country comparison to the world: 102

Budget: revenues: $78.36 billion
expenditures: $83.46 billion (2015 est.)
Taxes and other revenues: 15.1% of GDP (2015 est.)
country comparison to the world: 190

Budget surplus (+) or deficit (–): -1% of GDP (2015 est.)
country comparison to the world: 55

Public debt: 32.8% of GDP (2015 est.)
33.4% of GDP (2014 est.)
note: data for central government
country comparison to the world: 136

Fiscal year: calendar year

Inflation rate (consumer prices): -0.3% (2015 est.)
1.2% (2014 est.)

country comparison to the world: 32

Central bank discount rate: 1.63% (31 December 2015)
1.88% (31 December 2014)
country comparison to the world: 119

Commercial bank prime lending rate: 2.83% (31 December 2015 est.)
2.88% (31 December 2014 est.)
country comparison to the world: 171

Stock of narrow money: $467.6 billion (31 December 2015 est.)
$451.2 billion (31 December 2014 est.)
country comparison to the world: 12

Stock of broad money: $1.249 trillion (31 December 2014 est.)
$1.186 trillion (31 December 2013 est.)
country comparison to the world: 16

Stock of domestic credit: $762.4 billion (31 December 2015 est.)
$739.8 billion (31 December 2014 est.)
country comparison to the world: 18

Market value of publicly traded shares: $741.1 billion (31 December 2015)
$847.8 billion (31 December 2014)
$818.7 billion (31 December 2013)
country comparison to the world: 19

Current account balance: $76.17 billion (2015 est.)
$65.42 billion (2014 est.)
country comparison to the world: 7

Exports: $284.9 billion (2015 est.)
$317.8 billion (2014 est.)
country comparison to the world: 18

Exports—commodities: semiconductors, petrochemicals, automobile/auto parts, ships, wireless communication equipment, flat display displays, steel, electronics, plastics, computers

Exports—partners: China 27.1%, Hong Kong 13.2%, US 10.3%, Japan 6.4%, Singapore 4.4% (2012 est.)

Imports: $228.6 billion (2015 est.)
$274 billion (2014 est.)
country comparison to the world: 19

Imports—commodities: oil/petroleum, semiconductors, Natural gas, coal, steel, computers, wireless communication equipment, automobiles, fine chemicals, textiles

Imports—partners: Japan 17.6%, China 16.1%, US 9.5% (2012 est.)

Reserves of foreign exchange and gold: $426 billion (31 December 2015 est.)
$419 billion (31 December 2014 est.)
country comparison to the world: 6

Debt—external: $173.5 billion (31 December 2015 est.)
$177.9 billion (31 December 2014 est.)
country comparison to the world: 36

Stock of direct foreign investment—at home: $69.09 billion (31 December 2015 est.)
$66.29 billion (31 December 2014 est.)
country comparison to the world: 52

Stock of direct foreign investment—abroad: $271.9 billion (31 December 2015 est.) $258.6 billion (31 December 2014 est.) *country comparison to the world:* 23

Exchange rates: New Taiwan dollars (TWD) per US dollar—
33.066 (2015 est.)
31.72 (2014 est.)
30.363 (2013 est.)
29.62 (2012 est.)
29.47 (2011 est.)

ENERGY

Electricity—production: 258 billion kWh (2015 est.)
country comparison to the world: 16

Electricity—consumption: 249.5 billion kWh (2015 est.)
country comparison to the world: 14

Electricity—exports: 0 kWh (2015 est.)
country comparison to the world: 208

Electricity—imports: 0 kWh (2015 est.)
country comparison to the world: 212

Electricity—installed generating capacity: 48.48 million kW (2014 est.)
country comparison to the world: 22

Electricity—from fossil fuels: 75.6% of total installed capacity (2014 est.)
country comparison to the world: 99

Electricity—from nuclear fuels: 10.6% of total installed capacity (2014 est.)
country comparison to the world: 17

Electricity—from hydro electric plants: 5.4% of total installed capacity (2014 est.)
country comparison to the world: 124

Electricity—from other renewable sources: 8.4% of total installed capacity (2014 est.)
country comparison to the world: 44

Crude oil—production: 159 bbl/day (2015 est.)
country comparison to the world: 99

Crude oil—exports: 0 bbl/day (2015 est.)
country comparison to the world: 200

Crude oil—imports: 841,300 bbl/day (2015 est.)
country comparison to the world: 15

Crude oil—proved reserves: 10.06 million bbl (1 January 2015 est.)
country comparison to the world: 92

Refined petroleum products—production: 1.299 million bbl/day (2015 est.)
country comparison to the world: 17

Refined petroleum products—consumption: 818,700 bbl/day (2015 est.)
country comparison to the world: 23

Refined petroleum products—exports: 315,000 bbl/day (2015 est.)
country comparison to the world: 25

Refined petroleum products—imports: 363,100 bbl/day (2015 est.)
country comparison to the world: 18

Natural gas—production: 1.294 billion cu m (2015 est.)
country comparison to the world: 61

Natural gas—consumption: 17.79 billion cu m (2015 est.)
country comparison to the world: 39

Natural gas—exports: 0 cu m (2015 est.)
country comparison to the world: 198

Natural gas—imports: 18.95 billion cu m (2015 est.)
country comparison to the world: 19

Natural gas—proved reserves: 6.229 billion cu m (31 December 2015 est.)
country comparison to the world: 87

Carbon dioxide emissions from consumption of energy: 26.69 million Mt (2014 est.)
country comparison to the world: 76

COMMUNICATIONS

Telephones—fixed lines: *total subscriptions:* 14.04 million
subscriptions per 100 inhabitants: 60 (2014 est.)
country comparison to the world: 18

Telephones—mobile cellular: *total:* 30.4 million
subscriptions per 100 inhabitants: 130 (2014 est.)
country comparison to the world: 43

Telephone system: *general assessment:* provides telecommunications service for every business and private need
domestic: thoroughly modern; completely digitalized
international: country code—886; roughly 15 submarine fiber cables provide links throughout Asia, Australia, the Middle East, Europe, and the US; satellite earth stations—2 (2011)

Broadcast media: 5 nationwide television networks operating roughly 75 TV stations; about 85% of households utilize multi–channel cable TV; National and region al radio networks with about 170 radio stations (2008)
Radio broadcast stations: AM 21, FM 143, short-wave 1 (2008)
Television broadcast stations: 76 (5 television networks with 46 digital and 30 analog stations) (2007)

Internet country code: .tw

Internet hosts: 6.272 million (2012)
country comparison to the world: 18

Internet users: *total:* 16.1 million
percent of population: 70.0% (2009)
country comparison to the world: 36

TRANSPORTATION

Airports: 37 (2013)
country comparison to the world: 107

Airports—with paved runways: *total:* 35
over 3,047 m: 8
2,438 to 3,047 m: 7
1,524 to 2,437 m: 10
914 to 1,523 m: 8
under 914 m: 2 (2013)

Airports—with unpaved runways: *total:* 2
1,524 to 2,437 m: 1
under 914 m: 1 (2013)

Heliports: 31 (2013)

Pipelines: condensate 25 km; gas 802 km; oil 241 km (2013)

Railways: *total:* 1,597 km
standard gauge: 345 km 1.435-m gauge (345 km electrified)
narrow gauge: 1,102 km 1.067-m gauge (692 km electrified); 150 km 0.762-m gauge

note: the 0.762-gauge track belongs to three entities: the Forestry Bureau, Taiwan Cement, and TaiPower (2014)
country comparison to the world: 78

Roadways: *total:* 42,520 km
paved: 42,078 km (includes 1,348 km of highways and 737 km of expressways)
unpaved: 442 km (2013)
country comparison to the world: 85

Merchant marine: *total:* 112
by type: bulk carrier 35, cargo 20, chemical tanker 1, container 31, passenger/cargo 4, petroleum tanker 12, refrigerated cargo 7, roll on/roll off 2
foreign-owned: 3 (France 2, Vietnam 1)
registered in other countries: 579 (Argentina 2, Cambodia 1, Honduras 1, Hong Kong 25, Indonesia 1, Italy 10, Kiribati 2, Liberia 94, Marshall Islands 8, Panama 328, Philippines 1, Sierra Leone 7, Singapore 77, South Korea 1, Thailand 1, UK 11, Vanuatu 1, unknown 8) (2010)
country comparison to the world: 47

Ports and terminals: *major seaport(s):* Chilung (Keelung), Kaohsiung, Hualian, Taichung
container port(s) (TEUs): Chilung (Keelung) (1,749,388), Kaohsiung (9,363,289), Taichung (1,383,578)
LNG terminal (import): Yung An (Kaohsiung), Taichung

MILITARY AND SECURITY

Military branches: Army, Navy (includes Marine Corps), Air Force, Military Police Command, Armed Forces Reserve Command, Coast Guard Administration (2016)

Military service age and obligation: starting with those born in 1994, males 18–36 years of age may volunteer for military service or must complete 4 months of compulsory military training (or substitute civil service in some cases); women may enlist; women in Air Force service are restricted to noncombat roles; for men born before December 1993, compulsory service (military or civil) is 1 year; for 8 years after discharge, men are subject to training recall four times for periods not to exceed 20 days (2016)

TRANSNATIONAL ISSUES

Disputes—international: involved in complex dispute with Brunei, China, Malaysia, the Philippines, and Vietnam over the Spratly Islands, and with China and the Philippines over Scarborough Reef; the 2002 "D eclaration on the Conduct of Parties in the South China Sea" has eased tensions but falls short of a legally Binding "code of conduct" desired by several of the disputants; Paracel Islands are occupied by China, but claimed by Taiwaa and Vietnam; in 2003, China and Taiwan became more vocal in rejecting both Japan's claims to the uninhabited islands of the Senkaku-shoto (Diaoyu Tai) and Japan's unilaterally declared exclusive economic zone in the East China Sea where all parties engage in hydrocarbon prospecting

Illicit drugs: region al transit point for heroin, methamphetamine, and precursor chemicals; transshipment point for drugs to Japan; major problem with domestic consumption of methamphetamine and heroin; rising problems with use of ketamine and club drugs

TAJIKISTAN

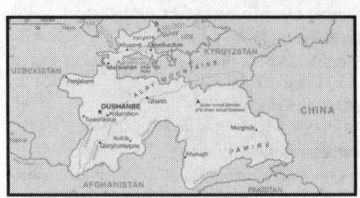

INTRODUCTION

Background: The Tajik people came under Russian rule in the 1860s and 1870s, but Russia's hold on Central Asia weakened following the Revolution of 1917. Bands of indigenous guerrillas (called "basmachi") fiercely contested Bolshevik control of the area, which was not fully reestablished until 1925. Tajikistan was first created as an autonomous republic within Uzbekistan in 1924, but the USSR designated Tajikistan a separate republic in 1929 and transferred to it much of present-day Sughd province. Ethnic Uzbeks form a substantial minority in Tajikistan, and ethnic Tajiks an even larger minority in Uzbekistan. Tajikistan became independent in 1991 following the breakup of the Soviet Union, and experienced a civil war between region al factions from 1992 to 1997. Tajikistan has endured several domestic security incidents since 2010, including armed conflict between government forces and local strongmen in the Rasht Valley and between government forces and criminal groups in gorno-Badakhshan autonomous Oblast. The most recent incidents were a series of attacks on security personnel in September 2015 led by a former high-ranking official in the Ministry of Defense. The country remains the poorest in the former Soviet sphere. Tajikistan became a member of the World Trade Organization in March 2013. However, its economy continues to face major challenges, including dependence on remittances from Tajikistanis working in Russia, pervasive corruption, and the major role narco-trafficking plays in the country's informal economy.

GEOGRAPHY

Location: Central Asia, west of China, south of Kyrgyzstan

Geographic coordinates: 39 00 N, 71 00 E

Map references: Asia

Area: *total:* 144,100 sq km
land: 141,510 sq km
water: 2,590 sq km
country comparison to the world: 96

Area—comparative: slightly smaller than Wisconsin

Land boundaries: *total:* 4,130 km
border countries (4): Afghanistan 1,357 km, China 477 km, Kyrgyzstan 984 km, Uzbekistan 1,312 km

Coastline: 0 km (landlocked)

Maritime claims: none (landlocked)

Climate: mid-latitude continental, hot summers, mild winters; semiarid to polar in Pamir Mountains

Terrain: mountainous region dominated by the Trans-Alay Range in the north and the Pamirs in the southeast; western Fergana Valley in north, Kofarnihon and Vakhsh Valleys in southwest

Elevation: *mean elevation:* 3,186 m

elevation extremes: *lowest point:* Syr Darya (Sirdaryo) 300 m
highest point: Qullai Ismoili Somoni 7,495 m

Natural resources: hydropower, some petroleum, uranium, mercury, brown coal, lead, zinc, antimony, tungsten, silver, gold

Land use: *agricultural land:* 34.7%
arable land: 6.1%
permanent crops: 0.9%
permanent pasture: 27.7%
forest: 2.9%
other: 62.4% (2011 est.)

Irrigated land: 7,420 sq km (2012)

Total renewable water resources: 21.91 cu km (2011)

Freshwater withdrawal (domestic/industrial/agricultural): *total:* 11.49 cu km/yr (6%/4%/91%)
per capita: 1,740 cu m/yr (2006)

Natural hazards: earthquakes; floods

Environment—current issues: inadequate sanitation facilities; increasing levels of soil salinity; industrial pollution; excessive pesticides

Environment—international agreements: *party to:* Biodiversity, Climate Change, Climate Change-Kyoto Protocol, Desertification, Environmental Modification, Ozone Layer Protection, Wetlands
signed, but not ratified: none of the selected agreements

Geography—note: landlocked; highest point, Qullai Ismoili Somoni (formerly Communism Peak), was the tallest mountain in the former USSR

PEOPLE AND SOCIETY

Nationality: *noun:* Tajikistani(s)
adjective: Tajikistani

Ethnic groups: Tajik 84.3%, Uzbek 13.8% (includes Lakai, Kongrat, Katagan, Barlos, Yuz), other 2% (includes Kyrgyz, Russian, Turkmen, Tatar, Arab) (2010 est.)

Languages: Tajik (official), Russian widely used in Government and business
note: different ethnic groups speak Uzbek, Kyrgyz, and Pashto

Religions: Sunni Muslim 85%, Shia Muslim 5%, other 10% (2003 est.)

Population: 8,191,958 (July 2015 est.)
country comparison to the world: 96

Age structure: *0–14 years:* 32.75% (male 1,365,565/female 1,317,285)
15–24 years: 19.7% (male 818,661/female 795,125)

25–54 years: 39.26% (male 1,590,051/female 1,626,091)
55–64 years: 5.1% (male 191,688/female 226,134)
65 years and over: 3.19% (male 109,084/female 152,274) (2015 est.)

Dependency ratios: *total dependency ratio:* 60.9%
youth dependency ratio: 56%
elderly dependency ratio: 4.8%
potential support ratio: 20.7% (2015 est.)

Median age: *total:* 23.9 years
male: 23.4 years
female: 24.4 years (2015 est.)
country comparison to the world: 159

Population growth rate: 1.71% (2015 est.)
country comparison to the world: 69

Birth rate: 24.38 births/1,000 population (2015 est.)
country comparison to the world: 57

Death rate: 6.18 deaths/1,000 population (2015 est.)
country comparison to the world: 156

Net migration rate: -1.15 migrant(s)/1,000 population (2015 est.)
country comparison to the world: 151

Urbanization: *urban population:* 26.8% of total population (2015)
rate of urbanization: 2.62% annual rate of change (2010–15 est.)

Major urban areas—population: DUSHANBE (capital) 822,000 (2015)

Sex ratio: *at birth:* 1.05 male(s)/female
0–14 years: 1.04 male(s)/female
15–24 years: 1.03 male(s)/female
25–54 years: 0.98 male(s)/female
55–64 years: 0.85 male(s)/female
65 years and over: 0.72 male(s)/female
total population: 0.99 male(s)/female (2015 est.)

Mother's mean age at first birth: 22.8
note: Median age at first birth among women 25–29 (2012 est.)

Maternal mortality rate: 32 deaths/100,000 live births (2015 est.)
country comparison to the world: 93

Infant mortality rate: *total:* 33.93 deaths/1,000 live births
male: 38.23 deaths/1,000 live births
female: 29.42 deaths/1,000 live births (2015 est.)
country comparison to the world: 63

Life expectancy at birth: *total population:* 67.39 years
male: 64.28 years
female: 70.66 years (2015 est.)
country comparison to the world: 168

Total fertility rate: 2.71 children born/woman (2015 est.)
country comparison to the world: 70

Contraceptive prevalence rate: 27.9% (2012)

Health expenditures: 6.8% of GDP (2013)

country comparison to the world: 120

Physicians density: 1.92 physicians/1,000 population (2013)

Hospital bed density: 5.5 beds/1,000 population (2011)

Drinking water source:
improved:
urban: 93.1% of population
rural: 66.7% of population
total: 73.8% of population
unimproved:
urban: 6.9% of population
rural: 33.3% of population
total: 26.2% of population (2015 est.)

Sanitation facility access:
improved:
urban: 93.8% of population
rural: 95.5% of population
total: 95% of population
unimproved:
urban: 6.2% of population
rural: 4.5% of population
total: 5% of population (2015 est.)

HIV/AIDS—adult prevalence rate: 0.35% (2014 est.)
country comparison to the world: 79

HIV/AIDS—people living with HIV/AIDS: 16,400 (2014 est.)
country comparison to the world: 84

HIV/AIDS—deaths: 700 (2014 est.)
country comparison to the world: 73

Major infectious diseases: *degree of risk:* high
food or waterborne diseases: bacterial diarrhea, hepatitis A, and typhoid fever
vectorborne disease: malaria (2013)

Obesity—adult prevalence rate: 12% (2014)
country comparison to the world: 136

Children under the age of 5 years underweight: 13.3% (2012)
country comparison to the world: 56

Education expenditures: 4% of GDP (2012)
country comparison to the world: 114

Literacy: *definition:* age 15 and over can read and write
total population: 99.8%
male: 99.8%
female: 99.7% (2015 est.)

School life expectancy (primary to tertiary education): *total:* 11 years
male: 12 years
female: 11 years (2013)

Child labor—children ages 5–14: *total number:* 164,432
percentage: 10% (2005 est.)

Unemployment, youth ages 15–24: *total:* 16.7%
male: 19.2%
female: 13.7% (2009 est.)
country comparison to the world: 72

GOVERNMENT

Country name: *conventional long form:* Republic of Tajikistan

conventional short form: Tajikistan
local long form: Jumhurii Tojikiston
local short form: Tojikiston
former: Tajik Soviet Socialist Republic
etymology: the Persian suffix "-stan" means "place of" or "country," so the word Tajikistan literally means "Land of the Tajik [People]"

Government type: presidential republic

Capital: *name:* Dushanbe

Geographic coordinates: 38 33 N, 68 46 E
time difference: UTC+5 (10 hours ahead of Washington, DC, during Standard Time)

Administrative divisions: 2 provinces (viloyatho, singular—viloyat), 1 autonomous province* (viloyati mukhtor), 1 capital region** (viloyati poytakht), and 1 area referred to as Districts Under Republic Administration***; Dushanbe**, Khatlon (Qurghonteppa), Kuhistoni Badakhshon [Gorno-Badakhshan]* (Khorugh), Nohiyahoi Tobei Jumhuri***, Sughd (Khujand)
note: the administrative center name follows in parentheses

Independence: 9 September 1991 (from the Soviet Union)

National holiday: Independence Day (or National Day), 9 September (1991)

Constitution: several previous; latest adopted 6 November 1994; amended 1999, 2003, 2014 (2016)

Legal system: civil law system

International law organization participation: has not submitted an ICJ jurisdiction declaration; accepts ICCt jurisdiction

Citizenship: *citizenship by birth:* no
citizenship by descent only: at least one parent must be a citizen of Tajikistan
dual citizenship recognized: no
residency requirement for naturalization: 5 years or 3 years of continuous residence prior to application

Suffrage: 18 years of age; universal

Executive branch: *chief of state:* President Emomali RAHMON (since 6 November 1994; head of state and Supreme Assembly chairman since 19 November 1992)

head of government: Prime Minister Qohir RASULZODA (since 23 November 2013)
cabinet: Council of Ministers appointed by the president, approved by the Supreme Assembly
elections/appointments: president directly elected by simple majority popular vote for a 7-year term (eligible for 2 terms); election last held on 6 November 2013 (next to be held in November 2020); prime minister appointed by the president
election results: Emomali RAHMON reelected president; percent of vote—Emomali RAHMON (PDPT) 83.9%, Ismoil TALBAKOV (CPT) 5%, other 11.1%

Legislative branch: *description:* bicameral Supreme Assembly or Majlisi Oli consists of the National Assembly or Majlisi Milli (34 seats; 25 members indirectly elected by local representative assemblies or majlisi, 8 appointed by the president,

and 1 reserved for the former president; members serve 5-year terms) and the Assembly of Representatives or Majlisi Namoyandagon (63 seats; 41 members directly elected in single-seat constituencies by two-round absolute majority vote and 22 directly elected in a single nationwide constituency by proportional representation vote; members serve 5-year terms)
elections: National Assembly—last held on 1 March 2015 (next to be held in 2020); Assembly of Representatives—last held on 1 March 2015 (next to be held in 2020)
election results: National Assembly—percent of vote by party—NA; seats by party—NA; Assembly of Representatives—percent of vote by party—PDPT 65.4%, APT 11.7%, PERT 7.5%, SPT 5.5%, CPT 2.2%, DPT 1.7%, other 6%; seats by party—PDPT 51, APT 5, PERT 3, SPT 1, CPT 2, DPT 1

Judicial branch: *highest court(s):* Supreme Court (consists of the chairman, deputy chairmen, and 34 judges organized into civil, criminal, and military chambers); Constitutional Court (consists of the court chairman, vice-president, and 5 judges); High Economic Court (consists 16 judicial positions)
judge selection and term of office: Supreme Court, Constitutional Court, and High Economic Court judges nominated by the president of the republic and approved by the National Assembly; judges of all 3 courts appointed for 10-year renewable terms with no limit on terms, but last appointment must occur before the age of 65
subordinate courts: region al and district courts; Dushanbe City Court; viloyat (province level) courts; Court of Gorno-Badakhshan Autonomous Region

Political parties and leaders: Agrarian Party of Tajikistan or APT [Rustam LATIFZODA]
Communist Party of Tajikistan or CPT [Shodi SHABDOLOV]
Democratic Party of Tajikistan or DPT [Saidjafar ISMONOV]
Party of Economic Reform of Tajikistan or PERT [Olimjon BOBOEV]
People's Democratic Party of Tajikistan or PDPT [Emomali RAHMON]
Social Democratic Party of Tajikistan or SDPT [Rahmatullo ZOIROV]
Socialist Party of Tajikistan or SPT [Abduhalim GHAFOROV]

Political pressure groups and leaders: New Tajikistan Party [Zayd SAIDOV] (unregistered)
Presidential Candidate of Union of Reformist Forces of Tajikistan Oynihol BOBONAZAROVA (unregistered) Vatandor (Patriot) Movement [Dodojon aTOVULLOEV]
Youth for the Revival of Tajikistan [Maqsud IBROHIMOV]
Youth Party of Tajikistan [Izzat AMON] (unregistered)
Islamic Renaissance Party of Tajikistan or IRPT [Muhiddin KABIRI] (banned)

International organization participation: ADB, CICA, CIS, CSTO, EAEC, EAPC, EBRD, ECO,

EITI (candidate country), FAO, G-77, GCTU, IAEA, IBRD, ICAO, ICC (NGOs), ICCt, ICRM, IDA, IDB, IFAD, IFC, IFRCS, ILO, IMF, Interpol, IOC, IOM, IPU, ISO (correspondent), ITSO, ITU, MIGA, NAM (observer), OIC, OPCW, OSCE, PFP, SCO, UN, UNCTAD, UNESCO, UNIDO, UNWTO, UPU, WCO, WFTU (NGOs), WHO, WIPO, WMO, WTO

Diplomatic representation in the US: *chief of mission:* Ambassador Farhod SALIM (since 21 May 2014)
chancery: 1005 New Hampshire Avenue NW, Washington, DC 20037
telephone: [1] (202) 223-6090
FAX: [1] (202) 223-6091

Diplomatic representation from the US: *chief of mission:* Ambassador Elisabeth MILLARD (since 11 March 2016)
embassy: 109-A Ismoili Somoni Avenue, Dushanbe 734019
mailing address: 7090 DUShanbe Place, Dulles, VA20189
telephone: [992] (37) 229-20-00
FAX: [992] (37) 229-20-50

Flag description: three horizontal stripes of red (top), a wider stripe of white, and green; a gold crown surmounted by seven gold, five-pointed stars is located in the center of the white stripe; red represents the sun, victory, and the unity of the nation, white stands for purity, cotton, and mountain snows, while green is the color of Islam and the bounty of nature; the crown symbolizes the Tajik people; the seven stars signify the Tajik magic number "seven"—a symbol of perfection and the embodiment of happiness

National symbol(s): crown surmounted by seven, five-pointed stars; National colors: red, white, green

National anthem: *name:* "Surudi milli" (National Anthem)
lyrics/music: Gulnazar KELDI/Sulaimon YUDAKOV
note: adopted 1991; after the fall of the Soviet Union, Tajikistan kept the music of the anthem from its time as a Soviet republic but adopted new lyrics

ECONOMY

Economy—overview: Tajikistan is a poor, mountainous country with an economy dominated by minerals extraction, metals processing, agriculture, and reliance on remittances from citizens working abroad. The 1992–97 civil war severely damaged an already weak economic infrastructure and caused a sharp decline in industrial and agricultural production, and today, Tajikistan has one of the lowest per capita GDPs among the 15 former Soviet republics. Less than 7% of the land area is arable and cotton is the most important crop. Tajikistan imports approximately 60% of its food. Mineral resources include silver, gold, uranium, antimony, and tungsten. Industry consists mainly of small obsolete factories in food processing and light industry, substantial hydropower

facilities, and a large aluminum plant—currently operating well below its capacity. Because of a lack of employment opportunities in Tajikistan, more than one million Tajik citizens work abroad—roughly 90% in Russia—supporting families back home through remittances that have been equivalent to nearly 50% of GDP. Some experts estimate the value of narcotics transiting Tajikistan is equivalent to 30–50% of GDP.

Since the end of the devastating, five-year civil war, the country has pursued half-hearted reforms and privatizations, but the poor business climate remains a hurdle to attracting investment. Tajikistan has sought to develop its substantial hydroelectricity potential through partnership with Russian and Iranian investors, and is pursuing completion of the Roghun dam—which, if built according to plan, would be the tallest dam in the world. However, the project will take at least 8 to 11 years to construct and faces financing shortfalls and opposition from downstream Uzbekistan.

Recent slowdowns in the Russian and Chinese economies, low commodity prices, and currency fluctuations are hampering economic growth in Tajikistan. By some estimates, the dollar value of remittances from Russia to Tajikistan dropped by more than 65% in 2015. The government faces challenges financing the public debt, which is equivalent to 35% of GDP, and the National Bank of Tajikistan has aggressively spent down reserves to bolster the weakening somoni, leaving little space for fiscal or monetary measures to counter any additional economic shocks.

GDP (purchasing power parity): $23.31 billion (2015 est.)
$22.63 billion (2014 est.)
$21.21 billion (2013 est.)
note: data are in 2015 US dollars
country comparison to the world: 140

GDP (official exchange rate): $7.816 billion (2015 est.)

GDP—real growth rate: 3% (2015 est.)
6.7% (2014 est.)
7.4% (2013 est.)
country comparison to the world: 103

GDP—per capita (PPP): $2,700 (2015 est.)
$2,700 (2014 est.)
$2,600 (2013 est.)
note: data are in 2015 US dollars
country comparison to the world: 192

Gross National saving: 8.5% of GDP (2015 est.)
6.1% of GDP (2014 est.)
12.2% of GDP (2013 est.)
country comparison to the world: 156

GDP—composition, by end use:
household consumption: 116.9%
government consumption: 12.6%
investment in fixed capital: 13.9%
investment in inventories: 3.4%
exports of goods and services: 17.2%
imports of goods and services: -64% (2015 est.)

GDP—composition, by sector of origin:
agriculture: 25.7%
industry: 17.3%
services: 57% (2015 est.)

Agriculture—products: cotton, grain, fruits, grapes, vegetables; cattle, sheep, goats

Industries: aluminum, cement, vegetable oil

Industrial production growth rate: 2% (2015 est.)
country comparison to the world: 115

Labor force: 2.209 million (2013 est.)
country comparison to the world: 120

Labor force—by occupation: *agriculture:* 46.5%
industry: 10.7%
services: 42.8% (2013 est.)

Unemployment rate: 2.5% (2013 est.)
2.5% (2012 est.)
note: official rates; actual unemployment is much higher
country comparison to the world: 16

Population below poverty line: 35.6% (2013 est.)

Household income or consumption by percentage share: *lowest:* 10%: NA%
highest: 10%: NA% (2009 est.)

Distribution of family income—Gini index: *32.6* (2006)
34.7 (1998)
country comparison to the world: 107

Budget: *revenues:* $2.432 billion
expenditures: $2.481 billion (2015 est.)
Taxes and other revenues: 30.2% of GDP (2015 est.)
country comparison to the world: 81

Budget surplus (+) or deficit (–): -0.6% of GDP (2015 est.)
country comparison to the world: 49

Public debt: 6.5% of GDP (2013 est.)
NA%
country comparison to the world: 177

Fiscal year: calendar year

Inflation rate (consumer prices): 5.8% (2015 est.)
6.1% (2014 est.)
country comparison to the world: 184

Central bank discount rate: 4.8% (31 December 2013)
6.5% (31 December 2012)
country comparison to the world: 80

Commercial bank prime lending rate: 22% (31 December 2015 est.)
21.62% (31 December 2014 est.)
country comparison to the world: 10

Stock of narrow money: $1.28 billion (31 December 2015 est.)
$1.42 billion (31 December 2014 est.)
country comparison to the world: 146

Stock of broad money: $2.085 billion (31 December 2014 est.)
$1.778 billion (31 December 2013 est.)
country comparison to the world: 152

Stock of domestic credit: $1.135 billion (31 December 2015 est.)
$1.338 billion (31 December 2014 est.)
country comparison to the world: 156

Market value of publicly traded shares: $NA
$NA
$NA

Current account balance: -$795 million (2015 est.)

-$892 million (2014 est.)
country comparison to the world: 112

Exports: $555.6 million (2015 est.)
$526.8 million (2014 est.)
country comparison to the world: 170

Exports—commodities: aluminum, electricity, cotton, fruits, vegetable oil, textiles

Exports—partners: Turkey 19.7%, Kazakhstan 17.6%, Switzerland 13.7%, Iran 8.7%, Afghanistan 7.5%, Russia 5.1%, China 4.9%, Italy 4.8% (2015)

Imports: $3.162 billion (2015 est.)
$4.509 billion (2014 est.)
country comparison to the world: 143

Imports—commodities: petroleum Products, aluminum oxide, machinery and equipment, foodstuffs

Imports—partners: China 42.3%, Russia 17.9%, Kazakhstan 13.1%, Iran 4.7% (2015)

Reserves of foreign exchange and gold: $430.3 million (31 December 2015 est.)
$502.8 million (31 December 2014 est.)
country comparison to the world: 153

Debt—external: $3.612 billion (31 December 2014 est.)
$3.538 billion (31 December 2013 est.)
country comparison to the world: 139

Stock of direct foreign investment—at home: $2.272 billion (31 December 2013 est.)
country comparison to the world: 107

Stock of direct foreign investment—abroad: $NA
$16.3 billion (31 December 2009 est.)

Exchange rates: Tajikistani somoni (TJS) per US dollar—
6.208 (2015 est.)
4.9348 (2014 est.)
4.9348 (2013 est.)
4.76 (2012 est.)
4.6103 (2011 est.)

ENERGY

Electricity—production: 17.09 billion kWh (2013 est.)
country comparison to the world: 80

Electricity—consumption: 14.42 billion kWh (2012 est.)
country comparison to the world: 80

Electricity—exports: 1 billion kWh (2013 est.)
country comparison to the world: 56

Electricity—imports: 114 million kWh (2012 est.)
country comparison to the world: 92

Electricity—installed generating capacity: 4.476 million kW (2013 est.)
country comparison to the world: 76

Electricity—from fossil fuels: 9% of total installed capacity (2013 est.)
country comparison to the world: 200

Electricity—from nuclear fuels: 0% of total installed capacity (2013 est.)
country comparison to the world: 188

Electricity—from hydro electric plants: 91% of total installed capacity (2013 est.)

country comparison to the world: 12

Electricity—from other renewable sources: 0% of total installed capacity (2013 est.)
country comparison to the world: 130

Crude oil—production: 206 bbl/day (2014 est.)
country comparison to the world: 97

Crude oil—exports: 0 bbl/day (2013 est.)
country comparison to the world: 194

Crude oil—imports: 0 bbl/day (2013 est.)
country comparison to the world: 131

Crude oil—proved reserves: 12 million bbl (29 February 2016 est.)
country comparison to the world: 91

Refined petroleum products—production: 400 bbl/ day (2013 est.)
country comparison to the world: 111

Refined petroleum products—consumption: 12,000 bbl/day (2013 est.)
country comparison to the world: 151

Refined petroleum products—exports: 500 bbl/day (2013 est.)
country comparison to the world: 115

Refined petroleum products—imports: 20,090 bbl/ day (2013 est.)
country comparison to the world: 111

Natural gas—production: 13 million cu m (2013 est.)
country comparison to the world: 91

Natural gas—consumption: 211 million cu m (2013 est.)
country comparison to the world: 109

Natural gas—exports: 0 cu m (2013 est.)
country comparison to the world: 190

Natural gas—imports: 198 million cu m (2013 est.)
country comparison to the world: 70

Natural gas—proved reserves: 5.663 billion cu m (1 January 2014 est.)
country comparison to the world: 94

Carbon dioxide emissions from consumption of energy: 2.618 million Mt (2013 est.)
country comparison to the world: 143

COMMUNICATIONS

Telephones—fixed lines: *total subscriptions:* 440,000
subscriptions per 100 inhabitants: 5 (2014 est.)
country comparison to the world: 98

Telephones—mobile cellular: *total:* 8 million
subscriptions per 100 inhabitants: 99 (2014 est.)
country comparison to the world: 96

Telephone system: *general assessment:* foreign investment in the telephone system has resulted in major improvements; conversion of the existing fixed network from analogue to digital was completed in 2012
domestic: fixed line availability has not changed significantly since 1998, while mobile cellular subscribership, aided by competition among multiple operators, has expanded rapidly; coverage now extends to all major cities and towns

international: country code—992; linked by cable and microwave radio relay to other CIS republics and by leased connections to the Moscow international gateway switch; Dushanbe linked by Intelsat to international gateway switch in ankara (Turkey); satellite earth stations—3 (2 Intelsat and 1 Orbita); established a single gateway for Internet traffic in December 2015, which is expected to limit the connectivity of nonstate-owned telecom, Internet, and mobile companies (2016)

Broadcast media: state-run TV broadcasters transmit Nationally on 9 TV and 10 radio stations, and region ally on 4 stations; 31 independent TV and 20 radio stations broadcast locally and regionally; many households are able to receive Russian and other foreign stations via cable and satellite (2016)
Radio broadcast stations: 16 (number of licensed stations with only about 10 broadcasting) (2009)
Television broadcast stations: 24 (number of licensed stations with only about 15 active) (2009)

Internet country code: .tj

Internet hosts: 6,258 (2012)
country comparison to the world: 142

Internet users: *total:* 1.3 million
percent of population: 16.1% (2014 est.)
country comparison to the world: 118

TRANSPORTATION

Airports: 24 (2013)
country comparison to the world: 131

Airports—with paved runways: *total:* 17
over 3,047 m: 2
2,438 to 3,047 m: 4
1,524 to 2,437 m: 5
914 to 1,523 m: 3
under 914 m: 3 (2013)

Airports—with unpaved runways: *total:* 7
1,524 to 2,437 m: 1
914 to 1,523 m: 1
under 914 m: 5 (2013)

Pipelines: gas 549 km; oil 38 km (2013)

Railways: *total:* 680 km
broad gauge: 680 km 1.520-m gauge (2014)
country comparison to the world: 103

Roadways: *total:* 27,767 km (2000)
country comparison to the world: 98

Waterways: 200 km (along Vakhsh River) (2011)
country comparison to the world: 98

MILITARY AND SECURITY

Military branches: Ground Forces, Air and Air Defense Forces, Mobile Forces (2013)

Military service age and obligation: 18–27 years of age for compulsory or voluntary military service; 2-year conscript service obligation; males required to undergo compulsory military training between Ages 16 and 55; males can enroll in military schools from at least age 15 (2012)

Military expenditures: 1.1% of GDP (2014)
1% of GDP (2008)

833

Disputes—international: in 2006, China and Tajikistan pledged to commence demarcation of the revised boundary agreed to in the delimitation of 2002; talks continue with Uzbekistan to delimit border and remove minefields; disputes in Isfara Valley delay delim itation with Kyrgyzstan

Refugees and internally displaced persons: *stateless persons:* 19,469 (2015)

Illicit drugs: major transit country for Afghan narcotics bound for Russian and, to a lesser extent, Western European markets; limited illicit cultivation of opium poppy for domestic consumption; Tajikistan seizes roughly 80% of all drugs captured in Central Asia and stands third worldwide in seizures of opiates (heroin and raw opium); significant consumer of opiates

TANZANIA

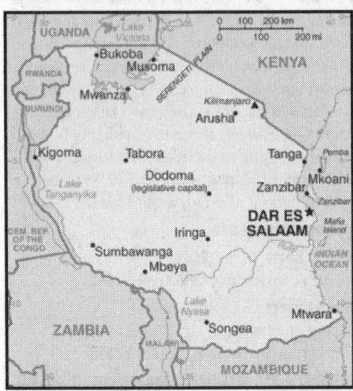

INTRODUCTION

Background: Shortly after achieving independence from Britain in the early 1960s, Tanganyika and Zanzibar merged to form the United Republic of Tanzania in 1964. One-party rule ended in 1995 with the first democratic elections held in the country since the 1970s. Zanzibar's semi-autonomous status and popular opposition led to two contentious elections since 1995, which the ruling party won despite international observers' claims of voting irregularities. The formation of a government of National unity between Zanzibar's two leading parties succeeded in minimizing electoral tension in 2010.

GEOGRAPHY

Location: Easter Africa, bordering the Indian Ocean, between Kenya and Mozambique

Geographic coordinates: 6 00 S, 35 00 E

Map references: Africa

Area: *total:* 947,300 sq km
land: 885,800 sq km
water: 61,500 sq km
note: includes the islands of Mafia, Pemba, and Zanzibar
country comparison to the world: 31

Area—comparative: more than six times the size of Georgia; slightly larger than twice the size of California

Land boundaries: *total:* 4,161 km
border countries (8): Burundi 589 km, Democratic Republic of the Congo 479 km, Kenya 775 km, Malawi 512 km, Mozambique 840 km, Rwanda 222 km, Uganda 391 km, Zambia 353 km

Coastline: 1,424 km

Maritime claims: *territorial sea:* 12 nm
exclusive economic zone: 200 nm

Climate: varies from tropical along coast to temperate in highlands

Terrain: plains along coast; central plateau; highlands in north, south

Elevation: *mean elevation:* 1,018 m

elevation extremes: *lowest point:* Indian Ocean 0 m
highest point: Kilimanjaro 5,895 m (highest point in Africa)

Natural resources: hydropower, tin, phosphates, iron ore, coal, diamonds, gemstones, gold, Natural gas, nickel

Land use: *agricultural land:* 43.7%
arable land: 14.3%
permanent crops: 2.3%
permanent pasture: 27.1%
forest: 37.3%
other: 19% (2011 est.)

Irrigated land: 1,840 sq km (2012)

Total renewable water resources: 96.27 cu km (2011)

Freshwater withdrawal (domestic/industrial/agricultural): *total:* 5.18 cu km/yr (10%/0%/89%)
per capita: 144.7 cu m/yr (2002)

Natural hazards: flooding on the central plateau during the rainy season; drought
volcanism: limited volcanic activity; Ol Doinyo Lengai (elev. 2,962 m) has emitted lava in recent years; other historically active volcanoes include Kieyo and Meru

Environment—current issues: soil degradation; deforestation; desertification; destruction of coral reefs threatens marine habitats; recent droughts affected marginal agriculture; wildlife threatened by illegal hunting and trade, especially for ivory

Environment—international agreements: *party to:* Biodiversity, Climate Change, Climate Change-Kyoto Protocol, Desertification, Endangered Species, Hazardous Wastes, Law of the Sea, Ozone Layer Protection, Wetlands
signed, but not ratified: none of the selected agreements

Geography—note: Kilimanjaro is the highest point in Africa and one of only two mountains on the continent that has glaciers (the other is Mount Kenya); bordered by three of the largest lakes on the continent: Lake Victoria (the world's second-largest freshwater lake) in the north, Lake Tanganyika (the world's second deepest) in the west, and Lake Nyasa (Lake Malawi) in the southwest

PEOPLE AND SOCIETY

Nationality: *noun:* Tanzanian(s)
adjective: Tanzanian

Ethnic groups: mainland—African 99% (of which 95% are Bantu consisting of more than 130 tribes), other 1% (consisting of Asian, European, and Arab); Zanzibar—Arab, African, mixed Arab and African

Languages: Kiswahili or Swahili (official), Kiunguja (name for Swahili in Zanzibar), English (official, primary language of commerce, administration, and higher education), Arabic (widely spoken in Zanzibar), many local languages
note: Kiswahili (Swahili) is the mother tongue of the Bantu people living in Zanzibar and nearby coastal Tanzania; although Kiswahili is Bantu in structure and origin, its vocabulary draws on a variety of sources including Arabic and English; it has become the lingua franca of central and Easter Africa; the first language of most people is one of the local languages

Religions: Christian 61.4%, Muslim 35.2%, folk religion 1.8%, other 0.2%, unaffiliated 1.4%
note: Zanzibar is almost entirely Muslim (2010 est.)

Population: 51,045,882
note: estimates for this country explicitly take into account the effects of excess mortality due to AIDS; this can result in lower life expectancy, higher infant mortality, higher death rates, lower population growth rates, and changes in the distribution of population by age and sex than would otherwise be expected (July 2015 est.)
country comparison to the world: 27

Age structure: *0–14 years:* 44.34% (male 11,428,872/female 11,205,695)
15–24 years: 19.59% (male 4,999,410/female 4,999,503)
25–54 years: 29.61% (male 7,588,196/female 7,524,554)
55–64 years: 3.49% (male 772,258/female 1,010,744)
65 years and over: 2.97% (male 648,851/female 867,799) (2015 est.)

Dependency ratios: *total dependency ratio:* 93.8%

youth dependency ratio: 87.6%
elderly dependency ratio: 6.2%
potential support ratio: 16.1% (2015 est.)

Median age: *total:* 17.5 years
male: 17.2 years
female: 17.8 years (2015 est.)
country comparison to the world: 219

Population growth rate: 2.79% (2015 est.)
country comparison to the world: 14

Birth rate: 36.39 births/1,000 population (2015 est.)
country comparison to the world: 17

Death rate: 8 deaths/1,000 population (2015 est.)
country comparison to the world: 99

Net migration rate: -0.54 migrant(s)/1,000 population (2015 est.)
country comparison to the world: 136

Urbanization: *urban population:* 31.6% of total population (2015)
rate of urbanization: 5.36% annual rate of change (2010–15 est.)

Major urban areas—population: DAR ES SALAAM (capital) 5.116 million; Mwanza 838,000 (2015)

Sex ratio: *at birth:* 1.03 male(s)/female
0–14 years: 1.02 male(s)/female
15–24 years: 1 male(s)/female
25–54 years: 1.01 male(s)/female
55–64 years: 0.76 male(s)/female
65 years and over: 0.75 male(s)/female
total population: 0.99 male(s)/female (2015 est.)

Mother's mean age at first birth: 19.5
note: Median age at first birth among women 20–24 (2010 est.)

Maternal mortality rate: 398 deaths/100,000 live births (2015 est.)
country comparison to the world: 23

Infant mortality rate: *total:* 42.43 deaths/1,000 live births
male: 44.47 deaths/1,000 live births
female: 40.33 deaths/1,000 live births (2015 est.)
country comparison to the world: 49

Life expectancy at birth: *total population:* 61.71 years
male: 60.34 years
female: 63.13 years (2015 est.)
country comparison to the world: 192

Total fertility rate: 4.89 children born/woman (2015 est.)
country comparison to the world: 17

Contraceptive prevalence rate: 34.4% (2009/10)

Health expenditures: 7.3% of GDP (2013)
country comparison to the world: 81

Physicians density: 0.03 physicians/1,000 population (2012)

Hospital bed density: 0.7 beds/1,000 population (2010)

Drinking water source:
improved:
urban: 77.2% of population
rural: 45.5% of population
total: 55.6% of population

unimproved:
urban: 22.1% of population
rural: 56% of population
total: 46.8% of population (2015 est.)

Sanitation facility access:
improved:
urban: 31.3% of population
rural: 8.3% of population
total: 15.6% of population
unimproved:
urban: 68.7% of population
rural: 91.7% of population
total: 84.4% of population (2015 est.)

HIV/AIDS—adult prevalence rate: 5.34% (2014 est.)
country comparison to the world: 12

HIV/AIDS—people living with HIV/AIDS: 1,499,400 (2014 est.)
country comparison to the world: 6

HIV/AIDS—deaths: 46,100 (2014 est.)
country comparison to the world: 4

Major infectious diseases: *degree of risk:* very high
food or waterborne diseases: bacterial diarrhea, hepatitis A, and typhoid fever
vectorborne diseases: malaria, dengue fever, and Rift Valley fever
water contact diseases: schistosomiasis and leptospirosis
animal contact disease: rabies (2013)

Obesity—adult prevalence rate: 5.9% (2014)
country comparison to the world: 156

Children under the age of 5 years underweight: 13.6% (2011)
country comparison to the world: 53

Education expenditures: 3.5% of GDP (2014)
country comparison to the world: 37

Literacy: *definition:* age 15 and over can read and write Kiswahili (Swahili), English, or Arabic
total population: 70.6%
male: 75.9%
female: 65.4% (2015 est.)

School life expectancy (primary to tertiary education): *total:* 8 years
male: 8 years
female: 8 years (2013)

Child labor—children ages 5–14: *total number:* 2,815,085
percentage: 21%
note: data represent children ages 5–17 and does not include Zanzibar (2006 est.)

Unemployment, youth ages 15–24: *total:* 5.8%
male: 4.5%
female: 7.2% (2013 est.)
country comparison to the world: 120

GOVERNMENT

Country name: *conventional long form:* United Republic of Tanzania
conventional short form: Tanzania
local long form: Jamhuri ya Muungano wa Tanzania
local short form: Tanzania

former: United Republic of Tanganyika and Zanzibar
note: the country's name is a comBination of the first letters of Tanganyika and Zanzibar, the two states that merged to form Tanzania in 1964

Government type: presidential republic

Capital: *name:* Dodoma; note—officially changed in 1996; serves as the meeting place for the National Assembly; the executive branch offices and diplomatic representation remain in Dar es Salaam, the largest city and commercial capital

Geographic coordinates: 6 8 S, 39 17 E
time difference: UTC+3 (8 hours ahead of Washington, DC, during Standard Time)

Administrative divisions: 30 regions; Arusha, Dar es Salaam, Dodoma, Geita, Iringa, Kagera, Kaskazini Pemba (Pemba North), Kaskazini Unguja (Zanzibar North), Katavi, Kigoma, Kilimanjaro, Kusini Pemba (Pemba South), Kusini Unguja (Zanzibar Central/South), Lindi, Manyara, Mara, Mbeya, Mjini Magharibi (Zanzibar Urban/West), Morogoro, Mtwara, Mwanza, Njombe, Pwani (Coast), Rukwa, Ruvuma, Shinyanga, Simiyu, Singida, Tabora, Tanga

Independence: 26 April 1964; Tanganyika became independent on 9 December 1961 (from UK-administered UN trusteeship); Zanzibar became independent on 10 December 1963 (from UK); Tanganyika united with Zanzibar on 26 April 1964 to form the United Republic of Tanganyika and Zanzibar; renamed United Republic of Tanzania on 29 October 1964

National holiday: Union Day (Tanganyika and Zanzibar), 26 April (1964)

Constitution: several previous; latest adopted 25 April 1977; amended many times, last in 2012; note—in 2012, the Tanzania Constitutional Review Commission was formed, and in June 2013, completed the first draft of a new constitution and a second version in December; a 640-member Constituent Assembly, formed in February 2014, passed a new constitution draft in October; a National referendum planned for April 2015 has been postponed (2016)

Legal system: English common law; judicial review of legislative acts limited to matters of interpretation

International law organization participation: has not submitted an ICJ jurisdiction declaration; accepts ICCt jurisdiction

Citizenship: *citizenship by birth:* no
citizenship by descent only: at least one parent must be a citizen of Tanzania; if a child is borNAbroad, the father must be a citizen of Tanzania
dual citizenship recognized: no
residency requirement for naturalization: 5 years

Suffrage: 18 years of age; universal

Executive branch: *chief of state:* President John MAGUFULI (since 5 November 2015); Vice President Samia SULUHU (since 5 November 2015); note—the president is both chief of state and head of government

head of government: President John MAGU-FULI, Dr. (since 5 November 2015); Vice President Samia SULUHU (since 5 November 2015); note—Prime Minister Kassim Majaliwa MAJAL-IWA (since 20 November 2015) has authority over the day-to-day functions of the government, is the leader of government busines in the National Assembly, and is head of the Cabinet

cabinet: Cabinet appointed by the president from among members of the National Assembly

elections/appointments: president and vice president directly elected on the same ballot by simple majority popular vote for a 5-year term (eligible for a second term); election last held on 25 October 2015 (next to be held in October 2020); prime minister appointed by the president

election results: John MAGU FULI elected president; percent of vote—John MAGU FULI (CCM) 58.5%, Edward LOWASSA (CHADEMA) 40%, other 1.5%

note: Zanzibar elects a president as head of government for matters internal to Zanzibar; election held on 25 October 2015 was annulled by the Zanzibar Electoral Commission and rerun on 20 March 2016; President Ali Mohamed SHEIN reelected; percent of vote—Ali Mohamed SHEIN 91.4%, Hamad Rashid MOHAMED 3%, other 5.6%

Legislative branch: *description:* unicameral National Assembly or Parliament (Bunge) (357 seats; 239 members directly elected in single-seat constituencies by simple majority vote, 102 women directly elected by proportional representation vote, 5 indirectly elected by simple majority vote by the Zanzibar House of Representatives, 10 appointed by the president, and 1 seat reserved for the attorney general; members serve a 5-year term); note—in addition to enacting laws that apply to the entire United Republic of Tanzania, the National Assembly enacts laws that apply only to the mainland; Zanzibar has its own House of Representatives or Baraza La Wawakilishi (81 seats; 50 members directly elected in single-seat constituencies by simple majority vote, 15 women directly elected by proportional representation vote, 10 appointed by the Zanzibar president, 5 seats reserved for government appointed region al commissioners, and 1 seat for the attorney general; elected members serve a 5-year term)

elections: Tanzania National Assembly and Zanzibar House of Representatives elections last held on 25 October 2015 (next National Assembly election to be held in October 2020; next Zanzibar election NA; note the Zanzibar Electoral Commission annulled the 2015 election; no date for repoll announced as of early November)

election results: National Assembly—percent of vote by party—NA; seats by party—NA Zanzibar House of Representatives—election annulled

Judicial branch: *highest court(s):* Court of Appeal of the United Republic of Tanzania (consists of the chief justice and 14 justices); High Court of the United Republic for Mainland Tanzania (consists of the principal judge and 30 judges organized into commercial, land, and labor courts); High Court of Zanzibar (consists of the chief justice and NA judges)

judge selection and term of office: Court of Appeal and High Court justices appointed by the National president after consultation with the Judicial Service Commission for Tanzania, a judicial body of high level judges and 2 members appointed by the National president; Court of Appeal and High Court judges appointed until mandatory retirement at age 60 but can be extended; High Court of Zanzibar judges appointed by the National president after consultation with the Judicial Commission of Zanzibar; judge tenure NA

subordinate courts: Resident Magistrates Courts; Kadhi courts (for Islamic family matters); district and primary courts

Political parties and leaders: Civic United Front or CUF (Chama Cha Wananchi [Seif Shariff HAMAD, Secretary General]

National Convention for Construction and Reform—Mageuzi or NCCR-M [James Francis MBATCA]

Party of Democracy and Development or CHADEMA (Chama Cha Demokrasia na Maendeleo) [Freeman MBOWE]

Revolution ary Party or CCM (Chama Cha Mapinduzi) [John MAGUFULI]

Tanzania Labor Party or TLP [Augustine MREMA]

United Democratic Party or UDP [John Momose CHEYO]

note: in March 2014, four opposition parties (CUF, CHADEMA, NCCR-Mageuzi, and the National League for Democracy) united to form Umoja wa Katiba ya Wananchi (Coalition for the People's Constituion) or UKAWA; during local elections held in October, 2014, UKAWA entered one candidate representing the three parties united in the coalition

Political pressure groups and leaders: Economic and Social Research Foundation or ESRF Free Zanzibar Tanzania Media Women's Association or TAMWA

Tanzania Private Sector Foundation or TPSF Twaweza

International organization participation: ACP, AfDB, AU, C, CD, EAC, EADB, EITI, FAO, G-77, IAEA, IBRD, ICAO, ICC (NGOs), ICCt, ICRM, IDA, IFAD, IFC, IFRCS, ILO, IMF, IMO, IMSO, Interpol, IOC, IOM, IPU, ISO, ITSO, ITU, ITUC (NGOs), MIGA, MONUSCO, NAM, OPCW, SADC, UN, UNAMID, UNC-TAD, UNESCO, UNHCR, UNIDO, UNIFIL, UNISFA, UNMISS, UNWTO, UPU, WCO, WFTU (NGOs), WHO, WIPO, WMO, WTO

Diplomatic representation in the US: *chief of mission:* Ambassador Wilson MASILINGI (since 17 September 2015)

chancery: 1232 22nd Street NW, Washington, DC 20037

telephone: [1] (202) 939-6125

FAX: [1] (202) 797-7408

Diplomatic representation from the US: *chief of mission:* Ambassador Mark Bradley CHILDRESS (since 22 May 2014)

embassy: 686 Old Bagamoyo Road, Msasani, Dares Salaam

mailing address: P. O. Box 9123, Dares Salaam P. O. Box 9123, Dar es Salaam

telephone: [255] (22) 229-4000

FAX: [255] (22) 229-4970 or 4971

Flag description: divided diagon ally by a yellow-edged black band from the lower hoist-side corner; the upper triangle (hoist side) is greeNAnd the lower triangle is blue; the banner comBines colors found on the flags of Tanganyika and Zanzibar; green represents the Natural vegetation of the country, gold its rich mineral deposits, black the native Swahili people, and blue the country's many lakes and rivers, as well as the Indian Ocean

National symbol(s): Uhuru (Freedom) torch, giraffe; National colors: green, yellow, blue, black

National anthem: *name:* "Mungu ibariki Afrika" (God Bless Africa)

lyrics/music: collective/Enoch Mankayi SONTONGA

note: adopted 1961; the anthem, which is also a popular song in Africa, shares the same melody with that of Zambia, but has different lyrics; the melody is also incorporated into South Africa's anthem

ECONOMY

Economy—overview: Tanzania is one of the world's poorest economies in terms of per capita income, but has achieved high growth rates based on its vast Natural resource wealth and tourism. GDP growth in 2009–15 was an impressive 6–7% per year. Dar es Salaam used fiscal stimulus measures and easier monetary policies to lessen the impact of the global recession. Tanzania has largely completed its transition to a market economy, though the government retains a presence in sectors such as telecommunications, banking, energy, and mining.

The economy depends on agriculture, which accounts for more than one-quarter of GDP, provides 85% of exports, and employs about 80% of the work force; agriculture accounts for 7% of government expenditures. All land in Tanzania is owned by the government, which can lease land for up to 99 years. Proposed reforms to allow for land ownership, particularly foreign land ownership, remain unpopular. The financial sector in Tanzania has expanded in recent years and foreign-owned banks account for about 48% of the banking industry's total assets. Competition among foreign commercial banks has resulted in significant improvements in the efficiency and quality of financial services, though interest rates are still relatively high, reflecting high fraud risk. Recent banking reforms have helped increase private-sector growth and investment.

The World Bank, the IMF, and bilateral donors have provided funds to rehabilitate Tanzania's aging infrastructure, including rail and port, that provide important trade links for inland countries. In 2013, Tanzania completed the world's largest Millennium Challenge Compact grant, worth $698 million, and, in December 2014, the Millennium Challenge Corporation selected Tanzania for a second Compact. in late 2014, a highly publicized scandal in the energy sector involving senior Tanzanian officials resulted in international donors freezing nearly $500 million in direct budget support to the government. The Tanzanian shilling weakened in 2015 because of lower gold prices, election-related political risk, and outflows from emerging market currencies generally.

GDP (purchasing power parity): $138.5 billion (2015 est.)
$129.4 billion (2014 est.)
$121 billion (2013 est.)
note: data are in 2015 US dollars
country comparison to the world: 76

GDP (official exchange rate): $44.9 billion (2015 est.)

GDP—real growth rate: 7% (2015 est.)
7% (2014 est.)
7.3% (2013 est.)
country comparison to the world: 14

GDP—per capita (PPP): $2,900 (2015 est.)
$2,800 (2014 est.)
$2,600 (2013 est.)
note: data are in 2015 US dollars
country comparison to the world: 191

Gross National saving: 22.6% of GDP (2015 est.)
21.7% of GDP (2014 est.)
14.9% of GDP (2013 est.)
country comparison to the world: 65

GDP—composition, by end use:
household consumption: 68%
government consumption: 16.1%
investment in fixed capital: 29.3%
investment in inventories: -0.3%
exports of goods and services: 18.7%
imports of goods and services: -31.8% (2015 est.)

GDP—composition, by sector of origin:
agriculture: 26.5%
industry: 25.6%
services: 47.9% (2014 est.)

Agriculture—products: coffee, sisal, tea, cotton, pyrethrum (insecticide made from chrysanthemums), cashew nuts, tobacco, cloves, corn, wheat, cassava (manioc, tapioca), bananas, fruits, vegetables; cattle, sheep, goats

Industries: agricultural processing (sugar, beer, cigarettes, sisal twine); mining (diamonds, gold, and iron), salt, soda ash; cement, oil refining, shoes, apparel, wood products, fertilizer

Industrial production growth rate: 5.3% (2015 est.)
country comparison to the world: 27

Labor force: 26.11 million (2015 est.)
country comparison to the world: 26

Labor force—by occupation: *agriculture:* 80%
industry and services: 20% (2002 est.)

Unemployment rate: NA%

Population below poverty line: 67.9% (2011 est.)

Household income or consumption by percentage share: *lowest:* 10%: 2.8%
highest: 10%: 29.6% (2007)

Distribution of family income—Gini index: 37.6 (2007)

34.6 (2000)
country comparison to the world: 77

Budget: *revenues:* $6.819 billion
expenditures: $8.431 billion (2015 est.)
Taxes and other revenues: 14.8% of GDP (2015 est.)
country comparison to the world: 194

Budget surplus (+) or deficit (–): -3.5% of GDP (2015 est.)
country comparison to the world: 129

Public debt: 36.9% of GDP (2015 est.)
31.7% of GDP (2014 est.)
country comparison to the world: 125

Fiscal year: 1 July—30 June

Inflation rate (consumer prices): 5.6% (2015 est.)
6.1% (2014 est.)
country comparison to the world: 181

Central bank discount rate: 8.25% (31 December 2010)
3.7% (31 December 2009)
country comparison to the world: 38

Commercial bank prime lending rate: 15.2% (31 December 2015 est.)
15.75% (31 December 2014 est.)
country comparison to the world: 39

Stock of narrow money: $3.957 billion (31 December 2015 est.)
$4.805 billion (31 December 2014 est.)
country comparison to the world: 108

Stock of broad money: $8.072 billion (31 December 2014 est.)
$7.533 billion (31 December 2013 est.)
country comparison to the world: 115

Stock of domestic credit: $7.726 billion (31 December 2015 est.)
$9.318 billion (31 December 2014 est.)
country comparison to the world: 110

Market value of publicly traded shares: $1.803 billion (31 December 2012 est.)
$1.539 billion (31 December 2011)
$1.264 billion (31 December 2010 est.)
country comparison to the world: 102

Current account balance: -$3.886 billion (2015 est.)
-$4.583 billion (2014 est.)
country comparison to the world: 164

Exports: $5.365 billion (2015 est.)
$5.319 billion (2014 est.)
country comparison to the world: 107

Exports—commodities: gold, coffee, cashew nuts, manufactures, cotton

Exports—partners: India 21.4%, China 8.1%, Japan 5.1%, Kenya 4.6%, Belgium 4.3% (2015)

Imports: $10.49 billion (2015 est.)
$10.92 billion (2014 est.)
country comparison to the world: 97

Imports—commodities: consumer goods, machinery and transportation equipment, industrial raw materials, crude oil

Imports—partners: China 34.7%, India 13.5%, South Africa 4.7%, UAE 4.4%, Kenya 4.1% (2015)

Reserves of foreign exchange and gold: $4.021 billion (31 December 2015 est.)
$4.39 billion (31 December 2014 est.)
note: excludes gold
country comparison to the world: 100

Debt—external: $14.12 billion (31 December 2014 est.)
$13.02 billion (31 December 2013 est.)
country comparison to the world: 99

Stock of direct foreign investment—at home: $NA

Stock of direct foreign investment—abroad: $NA

Exchange rates: Tanzanian shillings (TZS) per US dollar—
2,039.4 (2015 est.)
1,654 (2014 est.)
1,654 (2013 est.)
1,583 (2012 est.)
1,572.1 (2011 est.)

ENERGY

Electricity—production: 5.532 billion kWh (2012 est.)
country comparison to the world: 116

Electricity—consumption: 4.545 billion kWh (2012 est.)
country comparison to the world: 119

Electricity—exports: 0 kWh (2013 est.)
country comparison to the world: 209

Electricity—imports: 61 million kWh (2012 est.)
country comparison to the world: 100

Electricity—installed generating capacity: 845,000 kW (2012 est.)
country comparison to the world: 127

Electricity—from fossil fuels: 33.5% of total installed capacity (2012 est.)
country comparison to the world: 172

Electricity—from nuclear fuels: 0% of total installed capacity (2012 est.)
country comparison to the world: 197

Electricity—from hydro electric plants: 66.5% of total installed capacity (2012 est.)
country comparison to the world: 29

Electricity—from other renewable sources: 0% of total installed capacity (2012 est.)
country comparison to the world: 136

Crude oil—production: 0 bbl/day (2014 est.)
country comparison to the world: 201

Crude oil—exports: 0 bbl/day (2012 est.)
country comparison to the world: 201

Crude oil—imports: 0 bbl/day (2012 est.)
country comparison to the world: 139

Crude oil—proved reserves: 0 bbl (1 January 2015 est.)
country comparison to the world: 203

Refined petroleum products—production: 0 bbl/day (2012 est.)
country comparison to the world: 140

Refined petroleum products—consumption: 35,000 bbl/day (2013 est.)
country comparison to the world: 110

Refined petroleum products—exports: 0 bbl/day (2012 est.)

country comparison to the world: 141

Refined petroleum products—imports: 34,850 bbl/day (2012 est.)
country comparison to the world: 93

Natural gas—production: 995 million cu m (2013 est.)
country comparison to the world: 66

Natural gas—consumption: 995 million cu m (2013 est.)
country comparison to the world: 91

Natural gas—exports: 0 cu m (2013 est.)
country comparison to the world: 199

Natural gas—imports: 0 cu m (2013 est.)
country comparison to the world: 146

Natural gas—proved reserves: 6.513 billion cu m (1 January 2014 est.)
country comparison to the world: 86

Carbon dioxide emissions from consumption of energy: 9.295 million Mt (2012 est.)
country comparison to the world: 103

COMMUNICATIONS

Telephone—fixed lines: *total subscriptions:* 150,000
subscriptions per 100 inhabitants: less than 1 (2014 est.)
country comparison to the world: 139

Telephones—mobile cellular: *total:* 31.9 million
subscriptions per 100 inhabitants: 64 (2014 est.)
country comparison to the world: 37

Telephone system: *general assessment:* telecommunications services are marginal; system operating below capacity and being modernized for better service; small aperture terminal (VSAT) system under construction
domestic: fixed-line telephone network inadequate with less than 1 connection per 100 persons; mobile-cellular service, aided by multiple providers, is increasing rapidly and in 2011 exceeded a subscriber base of 50 telephones per 100 persons; trunk service provided by open-wire, microwave radio relay, tropospheric scatter, and fiber-optic cable; some links being made digital
international: country code—255; landing point for the EASSy fiber-optic submarine cable system linking East Africa with Europe and North America; satellite earth stations—2 Intelsat (1 Indian Ocean, 1 Atlantic Ocean) (2010)

Broadcast media: a state-owned TV station and multiple privately owned TV stations; state-owned National radio station supplemented by more than 40 privately owned radio stations; transmissions of several international broadcasters are available (2007)
Radio broadcast stations: AM 12, FM 11, shortwave 2 (1998)
Television broadcast stations: 3 (1999)

Internet country code: .tz

Internet hosts: 26,074 (2012)
country comparison to the world: 110

Internet users: *total:* 7.4 million
percent of population: 15.0% (2014 est.)

country comparison to the world: 51

TRANSPORTATION

Airports: 166 (2013)
country comparison to the world: 34

Airports—with paved runways: *total:* 10
over 3,047 m: 2
2,438 to 3,047 m: 2
1,524 to 2,437 m: 4
914 to 1,523 m: 2 (2013)

Airports—with unpaved runways: *total:* 156
over 3,047 m: 1
1,524 to 2,437 m: 24
914 to 1,523 m: 98
under 914 m: 33 (2013)

Pipelines: gas 311 km; oil 891 km; refined products 8 km (2013)

Railways: *total:* 4,567 km
narrow gauge: 1,860 km 1.067-m gauge; 2,707 km 1.000-m gauge (2014)
country comparison to the world: 40

Roadways: *total:* 86,472 km
paved: 7,092 km
unpaved: 79,380 km (2010)
country comparison to the world: 53

Waterways: (Lake Tanganyika, Lake Victoria, and Lake Nyasa (Lake Malawi) are the principal avenues of commerce with neighboring countries; the rivers are not navigable) (2011)

Merchant marine: *total:* 94
by type: bulk carrier 6, cargo 66, carrier 4, chemical tanker 1, container 1, passenger/cargo 2, petroleum tanker 10, refrigerated cargo 1, roll on/roll off 3
foreign-owned: 42 (Japan 1, Romania 1, Saudi Arabia 1, Syria 23, Turkey 13, UAE 3)
registered in other countries: 3 (Panama 2, UK 1) (2010)
country comparison to the world: 52

Ports and terminals: *major seaport(s):* Dares Salaam, Zanzibar

Transportation—note: the International Maritime Bureau reports that shipping in territorial and offshore waters in the Indian Ocean remain at risk for piracy and armed robbery against ships, especially as Somali-based pirates extend their activities south; numerous commercial vessels have been attacked and hijacked both at anchor and while underway; crews have been robbed and stores or cargoes stolen

MILITARY AND SECURITY

Military branches: Tanzania People's Defense Force (Jeshi la Wananchi la Tanzania, JWTZ): Army, Naval Wing (includes Coast Guard), Air Defense Command (includes Air Wing), National Service (2007)

Military service age and obligation: 18 years of age for voluntary military service; no conscription (2012)

Military expenditures: 1.13% of GDP (2012)
1.12% of GDP (2011)
1.13% of GDP (2010)
country comparison to the world: 88

TRANSNATIONAL ISSUES

Disputes—international: dispute with Tanzania over the boundary in Lake Nyasa (Lake M alawi) and the meandering Songwe River; Malawi contends that the entire lake up to the Tanzanian shoreline is its territory, while Tanzania claims the border is in the center of the lake; the conflict was reignited in 2012 when M alawi awarded a license to a British company for oil exploration in the lake

Refugees and internally displaced persons: *refugees (country of origin):* 143,138 (Burundi); 61,090 (Democratic Republic of the Congo) (2016)

Trafficking in persons: *current situation:* Tanzania is a source, transit, and destination country for men, women, and children subjected to forced labor and sex trafficking; the exploitation of young girls in domestic servitude continues to be Tanzania's largest human trafficking problem; Tanzanian boys are subject to forced labor mainly on farms but also in mines and quarries, in the informal commercial sector, in factories, in the sex trade, and possibly on small fishing boats; Tanzanian children and adults are subjected to domestic servitude, other forms of forced labor, and sex trafficking in other African countries, the Middle East, Europe, and the US; internal trafficking is more prevalent than Transnational trafficking and is usually facilitated by friends, family members, or intermediaries with false offers of education or legitimate jobs; trafficking victims from Burundi, Kenya, South Asia, and Yemen are forced to work in Tanzania's agricultural, mining, and domestic service sectors or may be sex trafficked

tier rating: Tier 2 Watch List—Tanzania does not fully comply with the minimum standards for the elimination of trafficking; however, it is making significant efforts to do so; in 2014, Tanzania was granted a waiver from an otherwise required downgrade to Tier 3 because its government has a written plan that, if implemented, would constitute making significant efforts to bring itself into compliance with the minimum standards for the elimination of trafficking; the government adopted a three-year National action plan and implementing regulations for the 2008 anti-trafficking law; authorities somewhat increased their number of trafficking investigations and prosecutions and convicted one offender, but the penalty was a fine in lieu of prison, which was inadequate given the severity of the crime; the government did not operate any shelters for victims and relied on NGOs to provide protective services (2015)

Illicit drugs: targeted by traffickers moving hashish, Afghan heroin, and South American cocaine transported down the East African coastline, through airports, or overland through Central Africa; Zanzibar likely used by traffickers for drug smuggling; traffickers in the past have recruited Tanzanian couriers to move drugs through Iran into East Asia

THAILAND

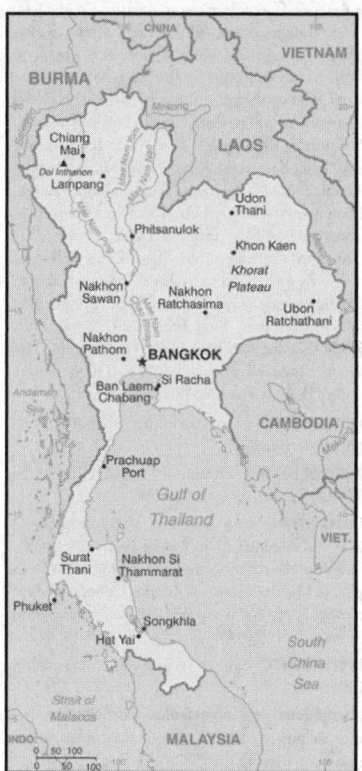

INTRODUCTION

Background: A unified Thai kingdom was established in the mid-14th century. Known as Siam until 1939, Thailand is the only Southeast Asian country never to have been colonized by a European power. A bloodless revolution in 1932 led to the establishment of a constitutional monarchy. In alliance with Japan during World War II, Thailand became a US treaty ally in 1954 after sending troops to Korea and later fighting alongside the US in Vietnam. Thailand since 2005 has experienced several rounds of political turmoil including a military coup in 2006 that ousted then Prime Minister THAKSIN Chinnawat, followed by large-scale street protests by competing political factions in 2008, 2009, and 2010. THAKSIN's youngest sister, YINGLAK Chinnawat, in 2011 led the Puea Thai Party to an electoral win and assumed control of the government. A blanket amnesty bill for individuals involved in street protests, altered at the last minute to include all political crimes—including all convictions against THAKSIN—triggered months of large-scale anti-government protests in Bangkok beginning in November 2013. In early May 2014 YINGLAK was removed from office by the Constitutional Court and in late

May 2014 the Royal Thai Army staged a coup against the caretaker government. The head of the Royal Thai Army, Gen. PRAYUT Chan-ocha, was appointed prime minister in August 2014. The interim military government created several interim institutions to promote reform and draft a new constitution. Elections are tentatively set for mid-2017. Thailand has also experienced violence associated with the ethno-Nationalist insurgency in its southern Malay-Muslim majority provinces. Since January 2004, thousands have been killed and wounded in the insurgency.

GEOGRAPHY

Location: SouthEastern asia, bordering the Andaman Sea and the Gulf of Thailand, southeast of Burma

Geographic coordinates: 15 00 N, 100 00 E

Map references: Southeast Asia

Area: *total:* 513,120 sq km
land: 510,890 sq km
water: 2,230 sq km
country comparison to the world: 51

Area—comparative: about three times the size of Florida; slightly more than twice the size of Wyoming

Land boundaries: *total:* 5,673 km
border countries (4): Burma 2,416 km, Cambodia 817 km, Laos 1,845 km, Malaysia 595 km

Coastline: 3,219 km

Maritime claims: *territorial sea:* 12 nm
exclusive economic zone: 200 nm
continental shelf: 200-m depth or to the depth of exploitation

Climate: tropical; rainy, warm, cloudy southwest monsoon (mid-May to September); dry, cool northeast monsoon (November to mid-March); southern isthmus always hot and humid

Terrain: central plain; Khorat Plateau in the east; mountains elsewhere

Elevation: *mean elevation:* 287 m

elevation extremes: *lowest point:* Gulf of Thailand 0 m
highest point: Doi Inthanon 2,576 m

Natural resources: tin, rubber, Natural gas, tungsten, tantalum, timber, lead, fish, gypsum, lignite, fluorite, arable land

Land use: *agricultural land:* 41.2%
arable land: 30.8%
permanent crops: 8.8%
permanent pasture: 1.6%
forest: 37.2%
other: 21.6% (2011 est.)

Irrigated land: 64,150 sq km (2012)

Total renewable water resources: 438.6 cu km (2011)

Freshwater withdrawal (domestic/industrial/agricultural): *total:* 57.31 cu km/yr (5%/5%/90%)

per capita: 845.3 cu m/yr (2007)

Natural hazards: land subsidence in Bangkok area resulting from the depletion of the water table; droughts

Environment—current issues: air pollution from vehicle emissions; water pollution from organic and factory wastes; deforestation; soil erosion; wildlife populations threatened by illegal hunting

Environment—international agreements: *party to:* Biodiversity, Climate Change, Climate Change-Kyoto Protocol, Desertification, Endangered Species, Hazardous Wastes, Marine Life Conservation, Ozone Layer Protection, Tropical Timber 83, Tropical Timber 94, Wetlands
signed, but not ratified: Law of the Sea

Geography—note: controls only land route from Asia to Malaysia and Singapore

PEOPLE AND SOCIETY

Nationality: *noun:* Thai (singular and plural)
adjective: Thai

Ethnic groups: Thai 95.9%, Burmese 2%, other 1.3%, unspecified 0.9% (2010 est.)

Languages: Thai (official) 90.7%, Burmese 1.3%, other 8%
note: English is a secondary language of the elite (2010 est.)

Religions: Buddhist (official) 93.6%, Muslim 4.9%, Christian 1.2%, other 0.2%, none 0.1% (2010 est.)

Population: 67,976,405
note: estimates for this country explicitly take into account the effects of excess mortality due to AIDS; this can result in lower life expectancy, higher infant mortality, higher death rates, lower population growth rates, and changes in the distribution of population by age and sex than would otherwise be expected (July 2015 est.)
country comparison to the world: 21

Age structure: *0–14 years:* 17.41% (male 6,062,868/female 5,774,631)
15–24 years: 14.78% (male 5,119,387/female 4,927,250)
25–54 years: 46.69% (male 15,675,425/female 16,061,864)
55–64 years: 11.26% (male 3,600,695/female 4,053,977)
65 years and over: 9.86% (male 2,935,703/female 3,764,605) (2015 est.)

Dependency ratios: *total dependency ratio:* 39.2%
youth dependency ratio: 24.7%
elderly dependency ratio: 14.6%
potential support ratio: 6.9% (2015 est.)

Median age: *total:* 36.7 years
male: 35.7 years
female: 37.7 years (2015 est.)
country comparison to the world: 67

Population growth rate: 0.34% (2015 est.)

country comparison to the world: 168

Birth rate: 11.19 births/1,000 population (2015 est.)
country comparison to the world: 176

Death rate: 7.8 deaths/1,000 population (2015 est.)
country comparison to the world: 104

Net migration rate: 0 migrant(s)/1,000 population (2015 est.)
country comparison to the world: 81

Urbanization: *urban population:* 50.4% of total population (2015)
rate of urbanization: 2.97% annual rate of change (2010–15 est.)

Major urban areas—population: BANGKOK (capital) 9.27 million; Samut Prakan 1.814 million (2015)

Sex ratio: *at birth:* 1.05 male(s)/female
0–14 years: 1.05 male(s)/female
15–24 years: 1.04 male(s)/female
25–54 years: 0.98 male(s)/female
55–64 years: 0.89 male(s)/female
65 years and over: 0.78 male(s)/female
total population: 0.97 male(s)/female (2015 est.)

Mother's mean age at first birth: 23.3 (2009 est.)

Maternal mortality rate: 20 deaths/100,000 live births (2015 est.)
country comparison to the world: 110

Infant mortality rate: *total:* 9.63 deaths/1,000 live births
male: 10.59 deaths/1,000 live births
female: 8.62 deaths/1,000 live births (2015 est.)
country comparison to the world: 141

Life expectancy at birth: *total population:* 74.43 years
male: 71.24 years
female: 77.78 years (2015 est.)
country comparison to the world: 118

Total fertility rate: 1.51 children born/woman (2015 est.)
country comparison to the world: 194

Contraceptive prevalence rate: 79.3% (2012)

Health expenditures: 4.6% of GDP (2013)
country comparison to the world: 163

Physicians density: 0.39 physicians/1,000 population (2010)

Hospital bed density: 2.1 beds/1,000 population (2010)

Drinking water source:
improved:
urban: 97.6% of population
rural: 98% of population
total: 97.8% of population
unimproved:
urban: 2.4% of population
rural: 2% of population
total: 2.2% of population (2015 est.)

Sanitation facility access:
improved:
urban: 89.9% of population
rural: 96.1% of population
total: 93% of population
unimproved:

urban: 10.1% of population
rural: 3.9% of population
total: 7% of population (2015 est.)

HIV/AIDS—adult prevalence rate: 1.13% (2014 est.)
country comparison to the world: 42

HIV/AIDS—people living with HIV/AIDS: 445,600 (2014 est.)
country comparison to the world: 18

HIV/AIDS—deaths: 19,400 (2014 est.)
country comparison to the world: 15

Major infectious diseases: *degree of risk:* very high
food or waterborne diseases: bacterial diarrhea
vectorborne diseases: dengue fever, Japanese encephalitis, and malaria
note: highly pathogenic H5N1 avian influenza has been identified in this country; it poses a negligible risk with extremely rare cases possible among US citizens who have close contact with birds (2013)

Obesity—adult prevalence rate: 9.2% (2014)
country comparison to the world: 135

Children under the age of 5 years underweight: 9.2% (2012)
country comparison to the world: 71

Education expenditures: 4.1% of GDP (2013)
country comparison to the world: 47

Literacy: *definition:* age 15 and over can read and write
total population: 96.7%
male: 96.6%
female: 96.7% (2015 est.)

School life expectancy (primary to tertiary education): *total:* 14 years
male: 13 years
female: 14 years (2013)

Child labor—children ages 5–14: *total number:* 818,399
percentage: 8% (2006 est.)

Unemployment, youth ages 15–24: *total:* 3.4%
male: 2.8%
female: 4.4% (2013 est.)
country comparison to the world: 132

GOVERNMENT

Country name: *conventional long form:* Kingdom of Thailand
conventional short form: Thailand
local long form: Ratcha Anachak Thai
local short form: Prathet Thai
former: Siam
etymology: "Land of the Tai [People]"; the meaning of "tai" is uncertain, but may originally have meant "human beings" or "people"

Government type: constitutional monarchy; note—interim military-run government since May 2014

Capital: *name:* Bangkok

Geographic coordinates: 13 45 N, 100 31 E
time difference: UTC+7 (12 hours ahead of Washington, DC, during Standard Time)

Administrative divisions: 76 provinces (changwat, singular and plural) and 1 municipality*

(maha nakhon); Amnat Charoen, Ang Thong, Bueng Kan, Buriram, Chachoengsao, Chai Nat, Chaiyaphum, Chanthaburi, Chiang Mai, Chiang Rai, Chon Buri, Chumphon, Kalasin, Kamphaeng Phet, Kanchanaburi, Khon Kaen, Krabi, Krung Thep* (Bangkok), Lampang, Lamphun, Loei, Lop Buri, Mae Hong Son, Maha Sarakham, Mukdahan, Nakhon Nayok, Nakhon Pathom, Nakhon Phanom, Nakhon Ratchasima, Nakhon Sawan, Nakhon Si Thammarat, Nan, Narathiwat, Nong Bua Lamphu, Nong Khai, Nonthaburi, Pathum Thani, Pattani, Phangnga, Phatthalung, Phayao, Phetchabun, Phetchaburi, Phichit, Phitsanulok, Phra Nakhon Si Ayutthaya, Phrae, Phuket, Prachin Buri, Prachuap Khiri Khan, Ranong, Ratchaburi, Rayong, RoiEt, Sa Kaeo, Sakon Nakhon, Samut Prakan, Samut Sakhon, Samut Songkhram, Sara Buri, Satun, Sing Buri, Sisaket, Songkhla, Sukhothai, Suphan Buri, Surat Thani, Surin, Tak, Trang, Trat, Ubon Ratchathani, Udon Thani, Uthai Thani, Uttaradit, Yala, Yasothon

Independence: 1238 (traditional founding date; never colonized)

National holiday: Birthday of King PHUMIPHON (BHUMIBOL), 5 December (1927)

Constitution: many previous; latest enacted 22 May 2014, signed 22 July 2014 (interim); note—a draft constitution completed in April 2015 was rejected by the National Reform Council in September 2015, and a second draft was published in January 2016 (2016)

Legal system: civil law system with common law influences

international law organization participation: has not submitted an ICJ jurisdiction declaration; non-party state to the ICCt

Citizenship: *citizenship by birth:* no
citizenship by descent only: at least one parent must be a citizen of Thailand
dual citizenship recognized: no
residency requirement for naturalization: 5 years

Suffrage: 18 years of age; universal and compulsory

Executive branch: *chief of state:* King PHUMIPHON adunyadet, also spelled BHUMIBOL Adulyadej (since 9 June 1946)

head of government: Interim Prime Minister Gen. PRAYUT Chan-ocha (since 25 August 2014) Deputy Prime Ministers PRAWIT Wongsuwan, Gen. (since 31 August 2014), THANASAK Patimaprakon, Gen. (since 31 August 2014), WISSANU Kruea-ngam (since 31 August 2014), SOMKHIT Chatusiphitak (since 20 August 2015), PRACHIN Chantong (since 20 August 2015), NARONG Phiphatthanasai (since 20 August 2015)
cabinet: Council of Ministers nominated by the prime minister, appointed by the king; a Privy Council advises the king
elections/appointments: the monarchy is hereditary; prime minister appointed by the monarch with a resolution of the National Legislative Assembly (as stated in the 2014 interim constitution)

note: Prime Minister YIn GLAK Chinnawat, also spelled YIn GLUCK Shinawatra, was removed from office on 7 May 2014 after the Constitutional Court ruled she illegally transferred a government official; Thai army declared martial law on 20 May 2014 followed by a coup on 22 May 2014

Legislative branch: *description:* in transition; following the May 2014 military coup, a National Legislative Assembly or Sapha Nitibanyat of no more than 220 members replaced the bicameral National Assembly; elections for a permanent legislative body are currently unscheduled and may not occur until mid-2017

elections: Senate—last held on 30 March 2014; House of Representatives—last held on 2 February 2014, but later declared invalid by the Constitutional Court

election results: Senate—percent of vote by party—NA; seats by party—NA; House of Representatives—percent of vote by party—NA; seats by party—NA

Judicial branch: *highest court(s):* Supreme Court of Justice (consists of court president, 6 vice-presidents, and NA judges, and organized into civil and criminal divisions); Constitutional Court (consists of court president and 8 judges); Supreme Administrative Court (number of judges determined by Judicial Commission of the Administrative Courts)

judge selection and term of office: Supreme Court judges selected by the Judicial Commission of the Courts of Justice and approved by the monarch; judges' terms NA; Constitutional Court justices—3 judges drawn from the Supreme Court, 2 judges drawn from the Administrative Court, and 4 judge candidates selected by the Selective Committee for Judges of the Constitutional Court and confirmed by the Senate; judges appointed by the monarch to serve single 9-year terms; Supreme Administrative Court judges selected by the Judicial Commission of the Administrative Courts and appointed by the monarch; judge tenure NA

subordinate courts: courts of first instance and appeals courts within both the judicial and administrative systems; military courts

Political parties and leaders: Chat Pattana Party or CPN (National Development Party) [WAN-NARAT Channukun]
Chat Thai Phattana Party or CTP (Thai Nation Development Party) [THEERA Wongsamut]
Mahachon party or Mass Party [APHIRAT Sirinawin]
Matubhum party (Motherland Party) [Gen. SON-THI Bunyaratkalin]
Phalang Chon Party (People Chonburi Power Party) [SONTHAYA Khunpluem]
Phumjai (Bhumjai) Thai Party or PJT (Thai Pride) [ANUTH in Chanvirakun]
Prachathipat Party or DP (Democrat Party) [ABHISIT Wechachiwa, also spelled ABHISIT Vejjajiva]
Prachathipathai Mai Party (New Democracy Party) [SURATIN Phichan]
Puea Thai Party (For Thais Party) or PTP [acting leader VIROT Paoin]

Rak Prathet Thai Party (Love Thailand Party) [CHUWIT Kamonwisit]
Rak Santi Party (Peace Conservation Party) [Pol. Lt. Gen. THAW In Surachetphong]

Political pressure groups and leaders: Multicolor Group
People's Alliance for Democracy or PAD
People's Democratic Reform Committee or PDRC
Student and People Network for Thailand's Reform or STR
United Front for Democracy Against Dictatorship or UDD

International organization participation: ADB, APEC, ARF, ASEAN, BIMSTEC, BIS, CD, CICA, CP, EAS, FAO, G-77, IAEA, IBRD, ICAO, ICC (National committees), ICRM, IDA, IFAD, IFC, IFRCS, IHO, ILO, IMF, IMO, IMSO, Interpol, IOC, IOM, IPU, ISO, ITSO, ITU, ITUC (NGOs), MIGA, NAM, OAS (observer), OIC (observer), OIF (observer), OPCW, OSCE (partner), PCA, PIF (partner), UN, UNAMID, UNCTAD, UNESCO, UNHCR, UNIDO, UNMOGIP, UNOCI, UNWTO, UPU, WCO, WFTU (NGOs), WHO, WIPO, WMO, WTO

Diplomatic representation in the US: *chief of mission:* Ambassador PHISAN Manawaphat (since 23 February 2015)
chancery: 1024 WisconsiNAvenue NW, Suite 401, Washington, DC 20007
telephone: [1] (202) 944-3600
FAX: [1] (202) 944-3611
consulate(s) general: Chicago, Los Angeles, New York

Diplomatic representation from the US: *chief of mission:* Ambassador Glyn T. DAVIES (since 27 November 2015)
embassy: 120–122 Wireless Road, Bangkok 10330
mailing address: APO AP 96546
telephone: [66] (2) 205-4000
FAX: [66] (2) 254-2990, 205-4131
consulate(s) general: Chiang Mai

Flag description: five horizontal bands of red (top), white, blue (double width), white, and red; the red color symbolizes the nation and the blood of life; white represents religion and the purity of Buddhism; blue stands for the monarchy
note: similar to the flag of Costa Rica but with the blue and red colors reversed

National symbol(s): garuda (mythical half-man, half-bird figure), elephant; National colors: red, white, blue

National anthem: *name:* "Phleng Chat Thai" (National Anthem of Thailand)
lyrics/music: Luang SARANUPRAPAN/Phra JENDURIYANG
note: music adopted 1932, lyrics adopted 1939; by law, people are required to stand for the National anthem at 0800 and 1800 every day; the anthem is played in schools, offices, theaters, and on television and radio during this time; "Phleng Sansaoen Phra Barami" (A Salute to the Monarch) serves as the royal anthem and is played in the

presence of the royal family and during certain state ceremonies

ECONOMY

Economy—overview: With a well-developed infrastructure, a free-enterprise economy, and generally pro-investment policies, Thailand historically has had a strong economy, but it experienced slow growth in 2013–15 as a result of domestic political turmoil and sluggish global demand, which curbed Thailand's traditionally strong Exports—mostly electronics, agricultural commodities, automobiles and parts, and processed foods. Following the May 2014 coup d'etat, tourism decreased 6–7% but is beginning to recover. The Thaibaht depreciated more than 8% during 2015.

Thailand faces labor shortages, and has attracted an estimated 2–4 million migrant workers from neighboring countries. The Thai Government in 2013 implemented a nationwide 300 baht (roughly \$10) per day minimum wage policy and deployed new tax reforms designed to lower rates on middle-income earners. The household debt to GDP ratio is over 80%.

GDP (purchasing power parity): \$1.108 trillion (2015 est.)
\$1.078 trillion (2014 est.)
\$1.069 trillion (2013 est.)
note: data are in 2015 US dollars
country comparison to the world: 21

GDP (official exchange rate): \$395.3 billion (2015 est.)

GDP—real growth rate: 2.8% (2015 est.)
0.8% (2014 est.)
2.7% (2013 est.)
country comparison to the world: 110

GDP—per capita (PPP): \$16,100 (2015 est.)
\$15,700 (2014 est.)
\$15,700 (2013 est.)
note: data are in 2015 US dollars
country comparison to the world: 101

Gross National saving: 32.9% of GDP (2015 est.)
27.9% of GDP (2014 est.)
26.3% of GDP (2013 est.)
country comparison to the world: 14

GDP—composition, by end use:
household consumption: 52.8%
government consumption: 17.1%
investment in fixed capital: 25.3%
investment in inventories: -0.2%
exports of goods and services: 67.6%
imports of goods and services: -62.6% (2015 est.)

GDP—composition, by sector of origin:
agriculture: 10.4%
industry: 37.7%
services: 51.9% (2015 est.)

Agriculture—products: rice, cassava (manioc, tapioca), rubber, corn, sugarcane, coconuts, palm oil, pineapple, livestock, fish products

Industries: tourism, textiles and garments, agricultural processing, beverages, tobacco, cement, light manufacturing such as jewelry and electric appliances, computers and parts, integrated circuits,

THE CIA WORLD FACTBOOK

furniture, plastics, automobiles and automotive parts, agricultural machinery, air conditioning and refrigeration, ceramics, aluminum, chemical, environmental management, glass, granite and marble, leather, machinery and metal work, petrochemical, petroleum refining, pharmaceuticals, printing, pulp and paper, rubber, sugar, rice, fishing, cassava, world's second-largest tungsten producer and third-largest tin producer

Industrial production growth rate: 4% (2015 est.)
country comparison to the world: 61

Labor force: 39.12 million (2015 est.)
country comparison to the world: 17

Labor force—by occupation: *agriculture:* 32.2%
industry: 16.7%
services: 51.1% (2014 est.)

Unemployment rate: 1% (2015 est.)
0.8% (2014 est.)
country comparison to the world: 5

Population below poverty line: 12.6% (2012 est.)

Household income or consumption by percentage share: *lowest:* 10%: 2.8%
highest: 10%: 31.5% (2009 est.)

Distribution of family income—Gini index: 48.4 (2011) 49 (2009)
country comparison to the world: 25

Budget: *revenues:* $71.48 billion
expenditures: $80.54 billion (2015 est.)
Taxes and other revenues: 19.1% of GDP (2015 est.)
country comparison to the world: 164

Budget surplus (+) or deficit (–): -2.4% of GDP (2015 est.)
country comparison to the world: 88

Public debt: 50.6% of GDP (2015 est.)
46.3% of GDP (2014 est.)
note: data cover general government debt, and includes debt instruments issued (or owned) by government entities other than the treasury; the data include treasury debt held by foreign entities; the data include debt issued by sub national entities, as well as intra-governmental debt; intra-governmental debt consists of treasury borrowings from surpluses in the social funds, such as for retirement, medical care, and unemployment; debt instruments for the social funds are sold at public auctions
country comparison to the world: 81

Fiscal year: 1 October—30 September

Inflation rate (consumer prices): -0.9% (2015 est.)
1.9% (2014 est.)
country comparison to the world: 15

Central bank discount rate: 2% (31 December 2014)
2.25% (31 December 2013)
country comparison to the world: 113

Commercial bank prime lending rate: 6.6% (31 December 2015 est.)
6.77% (31 December 2014 est.)
country comparison to the world: 124

Stock of narrow money: $49.13 billion (31 December 2015 est.)
$51.04 billion (31 December 2014 est.)

country comparison to the world: 51

Stock of broad money: $517.4 billion (31 December 2014 est.)
$524.8 billion (31 December 2013 est.)
country comparison to the world: 22

Stock of domestic credit: $494 billion (31 December 2015 est.)
$509 billion (31 December 2014 est.)
country comparison to the world: 25

Market value of publicly traded shares: $313.8 billion (31 December 2014 est.)
$383.2 billion (31 December 2013)
$245 billion (31 December 2012 est.)
country comparison to the world: 27

Current account balance: $34.82 billion (2015 est.)
$15.42 billion (2014 est.)
country comparison to the world: 13

Exports: $214.8 billion (2015 est.)
$224.8 billion (2014 est.)
country comparison to the world: 23

Exports—commodities: automobiles and parts, computer and parts, jewelry and precious stones, polymers of ethylene in primary forms, refine fuels, electronic integrated circuits, chemical products, rice, fish products, rubber products, sugar, cassava, poultry, machinery and parts, iron and steel and their products

Exports—partners: US 11.2%, China 11.1%, Japan 9.4%, Hong Kong 5.5%, Malaysia 4.8%, Australia 4.6%, Vietnam 4.2%, Singapore 4.1% (2015)

Imports: $196.4 billion (2015 est.)
$200.2 billion (2014 est.)
country comparison to the world: 24

Imports—commodities: machinery and parts, crude oil, electrical machinery and parts, chemicals, iron & steel and product, electronic integrated circuit, automobile's parts, jewelry including silver bars and gold, computers and parts, electrical household appliances, soybean, soybean meal, wheat, cotton, dairy products

Imports—partners: China 20.3%, Japan 15.4%, US 6.9%, Malaysia 5.9%, UAE 4% (2015)

Reserves of foreign exchange and gold: $148.6 billion (31 December 2015 est.)
$157.1 billion (31 December 2014 est.)
country comparison to the world: 16

Debt—external: $140.7 billion (31 December 2014 est.)
$141.9 billion (31 December 2013 est.)
country comparison to the world: 44

Stock of direct foreign investment—at home: $219.4 billion (31 December 2015 est.)
$207.9 billion (31 December 2014 est.)
country comparison to the world: 27

Stock of direct foreign investment—abroad: $81.46 billion (31 December 2015 est.)
$73.46 billion (31 December 2014 est.)
country comparison to the world: 35

Exchange rates: baht per US dollar—34.1 (2015 est.)

32.48 (2014 est.)
32.48 (2013 est.)
31.08 (2012 est.)
30.492 (2011 est.)

ENERGY

Electricity—production: 156.4 billion kWh (2012 est.)
country comparison to the world: 25

Electricity—consumption: 155.9 billion kWh (2012 est.)
country comparison to the world: 24

Electricity—exports: 1.375 billion kWh (2013 est.)
country comparison to the world: 50

Electricity—imports: 12.57 billion kWh (2013 est.)
country comparison to the world: 16

Electricity—installed generating capacity: 53.85 million kW (2012 est.)
country comparison to the world: 20

Electricity—from fossil fuels: 90.2% of total installed capacity (2012 est.)
country comparison to the world: 75

Electricity—from nuclear fuels: 0% of total installed capacity (2012 est.)
country comparison to the world: 187

Electricity—from hydro electric plants: 6.5% of total installed capacity (2012 est.)
country comparison to the world: 123

Electricity—from other renewable sources: 3.3% of total installed capacity (2012 est.)
country comparison to the world: 69

Crude oil—production: 232,900 bbl/day (2014 est.)
country comparison to the world: 37

Crude oil—exports: 43,140 bbl/day (2012 est.)
country comparison to the world: 48

Crude oil—imports: 898,000 bbl/day (2012 est.)
country comparison to the world: 14

Crude oil—proved reserves: 461 million bbl (1 January 2015 est.)
country comparison to the world: 52

Refined petroleum products—production: 1.197 million bbl/day (2012 est.)
country comparison to the world: 20

Refined petroleum products—consumption: 1.171 million bbl/day (2013 est.)
country comparison to the world: 20

Refined petroleum products—exports: 233,800 bbl/day (2012 est.)
country comparison to the world: 31

Refined petroleum products—imports: 67,470 bbl/day (2012 est.)
country comparison to the world: 65

Natural gas—production: 41.8 billion cu m (2013 est.)
country comparison to the world: 21

Natural gas—consumption: 52.27 billion cu m (2013 est.)
country comparison to the world: 15

Natural gas—exports: 0 cu m (2013 est.)

country comparison to the world: 189

Natural gas—imports: 10.47 billion cu m (2013 est.)
country comparison to the world: 25

Natural gas—proved reserves: 255.9 billion cu m (1 January 2014 est.)
country comparison to the world: 43

Carbon dioxide emissions from consumption of energy: 290.7 million Mt (2012 est.)
country comparison to the world: 22

COMMUNICATIONS

Telephones—fixed lines: *total subscriptions:* 5.69 million
subscriptions per 100 inhabitants: 8 (2014 est.)
country comparison to the world: 27

Telephones—mobile cellular: *total:* 97.1 million
subscriptions per 100 inhabitants: 143 (2014 est.)
country comparison to the world: 16

Telephone system: *general assessment:* high quality system, especially in urban Areas like Bangkok
domestic: fixed-line system provided by both a government-owned and commercial provider; wireless service expanding rapidly
international: country code—66; connected to major submarine cable systems providing links throughout Asia, Australia, Middle East, Europe, and US; satellite earth stations—2 Intelsat (1 Indian Ocean, 1 Pacific Ocean) (2011)

Broadcast media: 6 terrestrial TV stations in Bangkok broadcast Nationally via relay stations—2 of the networks are owned by the military, the other 4 are government-owned or controlled, leased to private enterprise, and all are required to broadcast government-produced news programs twice a day; multi-channel satellite and cable TV subscription services are available; radio frequencies have been allotted for more than 500 government and commercial radio stations; many small community radio stations operate with low-power transmitters (2008)
Radio broadcast stations: AM 238, FM 351, shortwave 6 (2007)
Television broadcast stations: 111 (2006)

Internet country code: .th

Internet hosts: 3.399 million (2012)
country comparison to the world: 31

Internet users: *total:* 19.5 million
percent of population: 28.8% (2014 est.)
country comparison to the world: 30

TRANSPORTATION

Airports: 101 (2013)
country comparison to the world: 56

Airports—with paved runways: *total:* 63
over 3,047 m: 8
2,438 to 3,047 m: 12
1,524 to 2,437 m: 23
914 to 1,523 m: 14
under 914 m: 6 (2013)

Airports—with unpaved runways: *total:* 38
2,438 to 3,047 m: 1

1,524 to 2,437 m: 1
914 to 1,523 m: 10
under 914 m: 26 (2013)

Heliports: 7 (2013)

Pipelines: condensate 2 km; gas 5,900 km; liquid petroleum gas 85 km; oil 1 km; refined products 1,097 km (2013)

Railways: *total:* 4,070.8 km
standard gauge: 28.8 km 1.435-m gauge (28.8 km electrified)
narrow gauge: 4,042 km 1.000-m gauge (2014)
country comparison to the world: 43

Roadways: *total:* 180,053 km (includes 450 km of expressways) (2006)
country comparison to the world: 28

Waterways: 4,000 km (3,701 km navigable by boats with drafts up to 0.9 m) (2011)
country comparison to the world: 26

Merchant marine: *total:* 363
by type: bulk carrier 31, cargo 99, chemical tanker 28, container 18, liquefied gas 36, passenger 1, passenger/cargo 10, petroleum tanker 114, refrigerated cargo 24, roll on/roll off 1, vehicle carrier 1
foreign-owned: 13 (China 1, Hong Kong 1, Malaysia 3, Singapore 1, Taiwan 1, UK 6)
registered in other countries: 46 (Bahamas 4, Belize 1, Honduras 2, Panama 6, Singapore 33) (2010)
country comparison to the world: 28

Ports and terminals: *major seaport(s):* Bangkok, Laem Chabang, Map Ta Phut, Prachuap Port, Si Racha
container port(s) TEUs): Bangkok (1,305,229), Laem Chabang (5,731,063)
LNG terminal(s) (import): Map Ta Phut

MILITARY AND SECURITY

Military branches: Royal Thai Army (Kongthap Bok Thai, RTA), Royal Thai Navy (Kongthap Ruea Thai, RTN, includes Royal Thai Marine Corps), Royal Thai Air Force (Kongthap Agard Thai, RTAF) (2013)

Military service age and obligation: 21 years of age for compulsory military service; 18 years of age for voluntary military service; males register at 18 years of age; 2-year conscript service obligation (2012)

Military expenditures: 1.5% of GDP (2013)
1.47% of GDP (2012)
1.6% of GDP (2011)
1.47% of GDP (2010)
country comparison to the world: 63

TRANSNATIONAL ISSUES

Disputes—international: separatist violence in Thailand's predominantly Malay-Muslim southern provinces prompt border closures and controls with Malaysia to stem insurgent activities; Southeast Asian states have enhanced border surveillance to check the spread of avian flu; talks continue on completion of demarcation with Laos but disputes remain over several islands in the Mekong River; despite continuing border committee talks,

Thailand must deal with Karen and other ethnic rebels, refugees, and illegal cross-border activities; Cambodia and Thailand dispute sections of boundary; in 2011 Thailand and Cambodia resorted to arms in the dispute over the location of the boundary on the precipice surmounted by Preah Vihear temple ruins, awarded to Cambodia by ICJ decision in 1962 and part of a planned UN World Heritage site; Thailand is studying the feasibility of jointly constructing the Hatgyi Dam on the Salween river near the border with Burma; in 2004, international environmentalist pressure prompted China to halt construction of 13 dams on the Salween River that flows through China, Burma, and Thailand; 140,000 mostly Karen refugees fleeing civil strife, political upheaval and economic stagnation in Burma live in remote camps in Thailand near the border

Refugees and internally displaced persons: *refugees (country of origin):* 128,863 (Burma) (2014)
IDPs: 35,000 (resurgence in ethno-Nationalist violence in south of country since 2004) (2015)
stateless persons: 443,862 (2015); note—about half of Thailand's northern hill tribe people do not have citizenship and make up the bulk of Thailand's stateless population; most lack documentation showing they or one of their parents were born in Thailand; children born to Burmese refugees are not eligible for Burmese or Thai citizenship and are stateless; most Chao Lay, maritime nomadic peoples, who travel from island to island in the Andaman Sea west of Thailand are also stateless; stateless Rohingya refugees from Burma are considered illegal migrants by Thai authorities and are detained in inhumane conditions or expelled; stateless persons are denied access to voting, property, education, employment, healthcare, and driving
note: Thai Nationality was granted to more than 18,000 stateless persons in the last 3 years (2015)

Trafficking in persons: *current situation:* Thailand is a source, transit, and destination country for men, women, and children subjected to forced labor and sex trafficking; victims from Burma, Cambodia, Laos, China, Vietnam, Uzbekistan, and India, migrate to Thailand in search of jobs but are forced, coerced, or defrauded into labor in commercial fishing, fishing-related industries, factories, domestic work, street begging, or the sex trade; some Thai, Burmese, Cambodian, and Indonesian men forced to work on fishing boats are kept at sea for years; sex trafficking of adults and children from Thailand, Laos, Vietnam, and Burma remains a significant problem; Thailand is a transit country for victims from China, Vietnam, Bangladesh, and Burma subjected to sex trafficking and forced labor in Malaysia, Indonesia, Singapore, Russia, South Korea, the US, and countries in Western Europe; Thai victims are also trafficked in North America, Europe, Africa, Asia, and the Middle East

tier rating: Tier 2 Watch List—Thailand does not fully comply with the minimum standards for the elimination of trafficking, and is not making significant efforts to do so; in 2014, authorities

843

investigated, prosecuted, and convicted fewer traffickers and identified fewer victims; some cases of official complicity were investigated and prosecuted, but trafficking-related corruption continues to hinder progress in combatting trafficking; authorities' efforts to screen for victims among vulnerable populations remained inadequate due to a poor understanding of trafficking indicators, a failure to recognize non-physical forms of coercion, and a shortage of language interpreters; the government passed new labor laws increasing the

minimum age in the fishing industry to 18 years old, guaranteeing the minimum wage, and requiring work contracts, but weak law enforcement and poor coordination among regulatory agencies enabled exploitive labor practices to continue; the government increased efforts to raise public awareness to the dangers of human trafficking and to deny entry to foreign sex tourists (2015)

Illicit drugs: a minor producer of opium, heroin, and marijuana; transit point for illicit heroin en route to the international drug market from Burma and Laos; eradication efforts have reduced the area of cannabis cultivation and shifted some production to neighboring countries; opium poppy cultivation has been reduced by eradication efforts; also a drug money-laundering center; minor role in methamphetamine production for region al consumption; major consumer of methamphetamine since the 1990s despite a series of government crackdowns

TIMOR-LESTE

INTRODUCTION

Background: The Portuguese began to trade with the island of Timor in the early 16th century and colonized it in mid-century. Skirmishing with the Dutch in the region eventually resulted in an 1859 treaty in which Portugal ceded the western portion of the island. Imperial Japan occupied Portuguese Timor from 1942 to 1945, but Portugal resumed colonial authority after the Japanese defeat in World War II. East Timor declared itself independent from Portugal on 28 November 1975 and was invaded and occupied by Indonesian forces nine days later. It was incorporated into Indonesia in July 1976 as the province of Timor Timur (East Timor). An unsuccessful campaign of pacification followed over the next two decades, during which an estimated 100,000 to 250,000 people died. In an August 1999 UN-supervised popular referendum, an overwhelming majority of the people of Timor-Leste voted for independence from Indonesia. However, in the next three weeks, anti-independence Timorese militias—organized and supported by the Indonesian military-commenced a large-scale, scorched-earth campaign of retribution. The militias killed approximately 1,400 Timorese and forced 300,000 people into western Timor as refugees. Most of the country's infrastructure, including homes, irrigation systems, water supply systems, and schools, and nearly all of the country's electrical grid were destroyed. On 20 September 1999, Australian-led peacekeeping troops deployed to

the country and brought the violence to an end. On 20 May 2002, Timor-Leste was Internationally recognized as an independent state.

In 2006, internal tensions threatened the new nation's security when a military strike led to violence and a breakdown of law and order. At Dili's request, aNAustralian-led international Stabilization Force (ISF) deployed to Timor-Leste, and the UN Security Council established the UN Integrated Mission in Timor-Leste (UNMIT), which included aNAuthorized police presence of over 1,600 personnel. The ISF and UNM It restored stability, allowing for presidential and parliamentary elections in 2007 in a largely peaceful atmosphere. In February 2008, a rebel group staged an unsuccessful attack against the president and prime minister. The ringleader was killed in the attack, and most of the rebels surrendered in April 2008. Since the attack, the government has enjoyed one of its longest periods of post-independence stability, including successful 2012 elections for both the parliament and president and a successful transition of power in February 2015. In late 2012, the UN Security Council ended its peacekeeping mission in Timor-Leste and both the ISF and UNMIT departed the country.

GEOGRAPHY

Location: SouthEastern asia, northwest of Australia in the Lesser Sunda Islands at the eastern end of the Indonesian Archipelago; note—Timor-Leste includes the eastern half of the island of Timor, the Oecussi (Ambeno) region on the northwest portion of the island of Timor, and the islands of Pulau Atauro and Pulau Jaco

Geographic coordinates: 8 50 S, 125 55 E

Map references: Southeast Asia

Area: *total:* 14,874 sq km
land: 14,874 sq km
water: 0 sq km
country comparison to the world: 160

Area—comparative: slightly larger than Connecticut

Land boundaries: *total:* 253 km
border countries (1): Indonesia 253 km

Coastline: 706 km

Maritime claims: *territorial sea:* 12 nm

contiguous zone: 24 nm
exclusive fishing zone: 200 nm

Climate: tropical; hot, humid; distinct rainy and dry seasons

Terrain: mountainous

Elevation: *mean elevation:* NA

elevation extremes: *lowest point:* Timor Sea, Savu Sea, and Banda Sea 0 m
highest point: Foho Tatamailau 2,963 m

Natural resources: gold, petroleum, Natural gas, manganese, marble

Land use: *agricultural land:* 25.1%
arable land: 10.1%
permanent crops: 4.9%
permanent pasture: 10.1%
forest: 49.1%
other: 25.8% (2011 est.)

Irrigated land: 350 sq km (2012)

Natural hazards: floods and landslides are common; earthquakes; tsunamis; tropical cyclones

Environment—current issues: widespread use of slash and burn agriculture has led to deforestation and soil erosion

Environment—international agreements: *party to:* Biodiversity, Climate Change, Climate Change-Kyoto Protocol, Desertification
signed, but not ratified: none of the selected agreements

Geography—note: Timor comes from the Malay word for "east"; the island of Timor is part of the Malay Archipelago and is the largest and easternmost of the Lesser Sunda Islands

PEOPLE AND SOCIETY

Nationality: *noun:* Timorese
adjective: Timorese

Ethnic groups: Austronesian (Malayo-Polynesian), Papuan, small Chinese minority

Languages: Tetum (official), Portuguese (official), Indonesian, English
note: there are about 16 indigenous languages; Tetum, Galole, Mambae, and Kemak are spoken by a significant portion of the population

Religions: Roman Catholic 96.9%, Protestant/Evangelical 2.2%, Muslim 0.3%, other 0.6% (2005)

Population: 1,231,116 (July 2015 est.)
country comparison to the world: 159

Age structure: 0–14 years: 41.82% (male 264,636/female 250,184)
15–24 years: 20.02% (male 124,937/female 121,508)
25–54 years: 29.59% (male 175,569/female 188,726)
55–64 years: 4.84% (male 30,584/female 29,010)
65 years and over: 3.73% (male 21,948/female 24,014) (2015 est.)

Dependency ratios: total dependency ratio: 92.3%
youth dependency ratio: 81.5%
elderly dependency ratio: 10.7%
potential support ratio: 9.3% (2015 est.)

Median age: total: 18.6 years
male: 18 years
female: 19.2 years (2015 est.)
country comparison to the world: 205

Population growth rate: 2.42% (2015 est.)
country comparison to the world: 30

Birth rate: 34.16 births/1,000 population (2015 est.)
country comparison to the world: 28

Death rate: 6.1 deaths/1,000 population (2015 est.)
country comparison to the world: 162

Net migration rate: -3.86 migrant(s)/1,000 population (2015 est.)
country comparison to the world: 189

Urbanization: urban population: 32.8% of total population (2015)
rate of urbanization: 3.75% annual rate of change (2010–15 est.)

Major urban areas—population: DILI (capital) 228,000 (2014)

Sex ratio: at birth: 1.07 male(s)/female
0–14 years: 1.06 male(s)/female *15–24 years:* 1.03 male(s)/female
25–54 years: 0.93 male(s)/female
55–64 years: 1.05 male(s)/female
65 years and over: 0.91 male(s)/female
total population: 1.01 male(s)/female (2015 est.)

Mother's mean age at first birth: 22.1
note: Median age at first birth among women 25–29 (2009/10 est.)

Maternal mortality rate: 215 deaths/100,000 live births (2015 est.)
country comparison to the world: 41

Infant mortality rate: total: 37.54 deaths/1,000 live births
male: 40.5 deaths/1,000 live births
female: 34.39 deaths/1,000 live births (2015 est.)
country comparison to the world: 55

Life expectancy at birth: total population: 67.72 years
male: 66.17 years
female: 69.37 years (2015 est.)
country comparison to the world: 165

Total fertility rate: 5.01 children born/woman (2015 est.)
country comparison to the world: 15

Contraceptive prevalence rate: 22.3% (2009/10)

Health expenditures: 1.3% of GDP (2013)
country comparison to the world: 156

Physicians density: 0.07 physicians/1,000 population (2011)

Hospital bed density: 5.9 beds/1,000 population (2010)

Drinking water source:
improved:
urban: 95.2% of population
rural: 60.5% of population
total: 71.9% of population
unimproved:
urban: 4.8% of population
rural: 39.5% of population
total: 28.1% of population (2015 est.)

Sanitation facility access:
improved:
urban: 69% of population
rural: 26.8% of population
total: 40.6% of population
unimproved:
urban: 31% of population
rural: 73.2% of population
total: 59.4% of population (2015 est.)

HIV/AIDS—adult prevalence rate: NA

HIV/AIDS—people living with HIV/AIDS: NA

HIV/AIDS—deaths: NA

Major infectious diseases: degree of risk: very high
food or waterborne diseases: bacterial diarrhea, hepatitis A, and typhoid fever
vectorborne diseases: dengue fever and malaria (2013)

Obesity—adult prevalence rate: 1.8% (2014)
country comparison to the world: 178

Children under the age of 5 years underweight: 37.7% (2013)
country comparison to the world: 1

Education expenditures: 7.7% of GDP (2014)
country comparison to the world: 7

Literacy: definition: age 15 and over can read and write
total population: 67.5%
male: 71.5%
female: 63.4% (2015 est.)

School life expectancy (primary to tertiary education): total: 13 years
male: 14 years
female: 13 years (2010)

Child labor—children ages 5–14: total number: 10,510
percentage: 4% (2002 est.)

Unemployment, youth ages 15–24: total: 14.8%
male: 10.4%
female: 22.7% (2010 est.)
country comparison to the world: 79

GOVERNMENT

Country name: conventional long form: Democratic Republic of Timor-Leste
conventional short form: Timor-Leste
note: pronounced TEE-mor LESS-tay
local long form: Republika Demokratika Timor Lorosa'e [Tetum]; Republica Democratica de Timor-Leste [Portuguese]
local short form: Timor Lorosa'e [Tetum]; Timor-Leste [Portuguese]
former: East Timor, Portuguese Timor
etymology: "timor" derives from the Indonesian and Malay word "timur" meaning "east"; "leste" is the Portuguese word for "east", so "Timor-Leste" literally means "Eastern-East"; the local [Tetum] name "Timor Lorosa'e" translates as "East Rising Sun"

Government type: semi-presidential republic

Capital: *name:* Dili

Geographic coordinates: 8 35 S, 125 36 E
time difference: UTC+9 (14 hours ahead of Washington, DC, during Standard Time)

Administrative divisions: 13 administrative districts; Aileu, Ainaro, Baucau, Bobon aro (Maliana), Cova-Lima (Suai), Dili, Ermera (Gleno), Lautem (Los Palos), Liquica, Manatuto, Manufahi (Same), Oecussi (Ambeno), Viqueque
note: administrative divisions have the same names as their administrative centers (exceptions have the administrative center name following in parentheses)

Independence: 20 May 2002 (from Indonesia); note—28 November 1975 was the date independence was proclaimed from Portugal; 20 May 2002 was the date of international recognition of Timor-Leste's independence from Indonesia

National holiday: Proclamation of Independence Day, 28 November (1975)

Constitution: drafted 2001, approved 22 March 2002, entered into force 20 May 2002 (2016)

Legal system: civil law system based on the Portuguese model; note—penal and civil law codes to replace the Indonesian codes were passed by Parliament and promulgated in 2009 and 2011, respectively

international law organization participation: accepts compulsory ICJ jurisdiction with reservations; accepts ICCt jurisdiction

Citizenship: *citizenship by birth:* no
citizenship by descent only: at least one parent must be a citizen of Timor-Leste
dual citizenship recognized: no
residency requirement for naturalization: 10 years

Suffrage: 17 years of age; universal

Executive branch: *chief of state:* President Taur Matan RUAK, aka Jose Maria de VASCONCELOS (since 20 May 2012); note—the president plays a largely symbolic role but is the commander in chief of the military and is able to veto legislation, dissolve parliament, and call National elections

head of government: Prime Minister Kay Rala Xanana GUSMAO—formerly Jose Alexandre GUSMAO (since 8 August 2007); Vice Prime Minister Fernando "Lasama" de ARAUJO (since 8 August 2012)
cabinet: Council of Ministers proposed by the prime minister and appointed by the president

elections/appointments: president directly elected by absolute majority popular vote in 2 rounds if needed for a 5-year term (eligible for a second term); election last held on 17 March 2012 with a runoff on 16 April 2012; following parliamentary elections, the president appoints the leader of the majority party or majority coalition as the prime minister

election results: Taur Matan RUAK elected president in runoff; percent of vote—Taur Matan RUAK (independent) 61.2%, Francisco GUTTERES (Frenti-Mudanca) 38.8%

Legislative branch: *description:* unicameral National Parliament (65 seats; members directly elected in a single nationwide constituency by proportional representation vote to serve 5-year terms)

elections: elections were held on 7 July 2012 (next to be held in July 2017)

election results: percent of vote by party—CNRT 36%, FRETILIN 30%, PD 10%, Frenti-Mudanca 3%, others 21%; seats by party—CNRT 30, FRETILIN 25, PD 8, Frenti-Mudanca 2

Judicial branch: *highest court(s):* Supreme Court of Justice (operated by the Court of Appeals, consists of the court president and 3 judges)

judge selection and term of office: Supreme Court president appointed by the president of the republic from among the other court judges to serve a 4-year term; other Supreme Court judges appointed—1 by the Parliament, and the others by the Supreme Council for the Judiciary, a body presided by the Supreme Court president and includes mostly presidential and parliamentary appointees; other Supreme Court judges appointed for life

subordinate courts: Court of Appeal; district courts; magistrates' courts

note: the UN Justice System Programme, launched in 2003 and in 2008, is helping strengthen the country's justice system

Political parties and leaders: Democratic Party or PD [Fernando "Lasama" de ARAUJO] Frenti-Mudanca [Jose Luis GUTERRES] National Congress for Timorese Reconstruction or CNRT [Kay Rala Xanana GUSMAO] Revolution ary Front of Independent Timor-Leste or FRETILIN [Mari ALKATIRI] (only parties in Parliament are listed)

Political pressure groups and leaders: NA

International organization participation: ACP, ADB, AOSIS, ARF, ASEAN (observer), CPLP, EITI (compliant country), FAO, G-77, IBRD, ICAO, ICCt, ICRM, IDA, IFAD, IFC, IFRCS, ILO, IMF, IMO, Interpol, IOC, IOM, IPU, ITU, MIGA, NAM, OPCW, PIF (observer), UN, UNCTAD, UNESCO, UNIDO, Union Latina, UNWTO, UPU, WCO, WHO, WMO

Diplomatic representation in the US: *chief of mission:* Ambassador Domingos Sarmento ALVES (since 21 May 2014)

chancery: 4201 Connecticut Avenue NW, Suite 504, Washington, DC 20008

telephone: [1] (202) 966-3202

FAX: [1] (202) 966-3205

Diplomatic representation from the US: *chief of mission:* Ambassador Karen STANTON (since 16 January 2015)

embassy: Avenida de Portugal, Praia dos Coqueiros, Dili

mailing address: US Department of State, 8250 Dili Place, Washington, DC 20521 -8250

telephone: (670) 332-4684

FAX: (670) 331-3206

Flag description: red with a black isosceles triangle (based on the hoist side) superimposed on a slightly longer yellow arrowhead that extends to the center of the flag; a white star—pointing to the upper hoist-side corner of the flag—is in the center of the black triangle; yellow denotes the colonialism in Timor-Leste's past; black represents the obscurantism that needs to be overcome; red stands for the National liberation struggle; the white star symbolizes peace and serves as a guiding light

National symbol(s): Mount Ramelau; National colors: red, yellow, black, white

National anthem: *name:* "Patria" (Fatherland)

lyrics/music: Fransisco Borja DA COSTA/Afonso DE ARAUJO

note: adopted 2002; the song was first used as an anthem when Timor-Leste declared its independence from Portugal in 1975; the lyricist, Fransisco Borja DA COSTA, was killed in the Indonesian invasion just days after independence was declared

ECONOMY

Economy—overview: Since gaining independence in 1999, Timor-Leste has faced great challenges in rebuilding its infrastructure, strengthening the civil administration, and generating jobs for young people entering the work force. The development of offshore oil and gas resources has greatly supplemented government revenues. This technology-intensive industry, however, has done little to create jobs in part because there are no production facilities in Timor-Leste. Gas is currently piped to Australia for processing, but Timor-Leste has expressed interest in developing a domestic processing capacity.

In June 2005, the National Parliament unanimously approved the creation of the Timor-Leste Petroleum Fund to serve as a repository for all petroleum revenues and to preserve the value of Timor-Leste's petroleum wealth for future generations. The Fund held assets of $16.5 billion, as of December 2014. Oil accounts for 90% of government revenues, and the drop in the price of oil in 2014 has led to concerns about the long-term sustainability of government spending. The Ministry of Finance maintains that the Petroleum Fund is sufficient to sustain government operations for the foreseeable future.

Annual government budget expenditures increased markedly between 2009 and 2012 but dropped significantly in 2013–15. Historically, the government failed to spend as much as its budget allowed. The government has focused significant resources on basic infrastructure, including electricity and roads. Limited experience in procurement and infrastructure building has hampered these projects. The underlying economic policy challenge the country faces remains how best to use oil-and-gas wealth to lift the non-oil economy onto a higher growth path and to reduce poverty.

GDP (purchasing power parity): $6.57 billion (2015 est.)

$6.302 billion (2014 est.)

$5.974 billion (2013 est.)

note: data are in 2015 US dollars

country comparison to the world: 167

GDP (official exchange rate): $2.62 billion (2015 est.)

note: non-oil GDP

GDP—real growth rate: 4.3% (2015 est.)

5.5% (2014 est.)

2.8% (2013 est.)

country comparison to the world: 56

GDP—per capita (PPP): $5,600 (2015 est.)

$5,500 (2014 est.)

$5,300 (2013 est.)

note: data are in 2015 US dollars

country comparison to the world: 163

GDP—composition, by end use:

household consumption: 25.8%

government consumption: 29.1%

investment in fixed capital: 16%

investment in inventories: 0%

exports of goods and services: 79.4%

imports of goods and services: -50.3% (2015 est.)

GDP—composition, by sector of origin:

agriculture: 5.9%

industry: 77.4%

services: 16.8% (2015 est.)

Agriculture—products: coffee, rice, corn, cassava (manioc, tapioca), sweet potatoes, soybeans, cabbage, mangoes, bananas, vanilla

Industries: printing, soap manufacturing, handicrafts, woven cloth

Industrial production growth rate: -6% (2015 est.)

country comparison to the world: 192

Labor force: 259,800 (2013 est.)

country comparison to the world: 167

Labor force—by occupation: *agriculture:* 64%

industry: 10%

services: 26% (2010)

Unemployment rate: 11% (2013 est.)

18.4% (2010 est.)

country comparison to the world: 124

Population below poverty line: 37% (2011 est.)

Household income or consumption by percentage share: *lowest:* 10%: 4%

highest: 10%: 27% (2007)

Distribution of family income—Gini index: 31.9 (2007 est.)

38 (2002 est.)

country comparison to the world: 114

Budget: *revenues:* $300 million

expenditures: $2.1 billion (2015 est.)

Taxes and other revenues: 7.1% of GDP (2015 est.)

country comparison to the world: 214

Budget surplus (+) or deficit (–): -42.5% of GDP (2015 est.)

country comparison to the world: 218

Fiscal year: calendar year

Inflation rate (consumer prices): 0.6% (2015 est.)

0.7% (2014 est.)

country comparison to the world: 66

Commercial bank prime lending rate: 13% (31 December 2015 est.)

12.9% (31 December 2014 est.)

country comparison to the world: 54

Stock of narrow money: $282.3 million (31 December 2015 est.)

$342.9 million (31 December 2014 est.)
country comparison to the world: 176

Stock of broad money: $677.8 million (31 December 2015 est.)
$599.8 million (31 December 2014 est.)
country comparison to the world: 176

Stock of domestic credit: $200 million (31 December 2015 est.)
-$469 million (31 December 2013 est.)
country comparison to the world: 180

Market value of publicly traded shares: $NA

Current account balance: $431 million (2015 est.)
$1.096 billion (2014 est.)
country comparison to the world: 44

Exports: $15.5 million (2014 est.)
$15.5 million (2014 est.)
country comparison to the world: 214

Exports—commodities: oil, coffee, sandalwood, marble
note: potential for vanilla exports

Imports: $764.2 million (2014 est.)
$764.2 million (2014 est.)
country comparison to the world: 188

Imports—commodities: food, gasoline, kerosene, machinery

Debt—external: $311.5 million (31 December 2014 est.)
$687 million (31 December 2013 est.)
country comparison to the world: 185

Exchange rates: the US dollar is used

ENERGY

Electricity—production: 349.4 million kWh (2012 est.)
country comparison to the world: 169

Electricity—consumption: 125.3 million kWh (2012 est.)
country comparison to the world: 197

Electricity—exports: 0 kWh (2012 est.)
country comparison to the world: 206

Electricity—imports: 0 kWh (2012 est.)
country comparison to the world: 210

Electricity—installed generating capacity: NA kW (2012 est.)

Crude oil—production: 76,490 bbl/day (2014 est.)
country comparison to the world: 50

Crude oil—exports: 77,280 bbl/day (2013 est.)
country comparison to the world: 38

Crude oil—imports: 0 bbl/day (2012 est.)
country comparison to the world: 136

Crude oil—proved reserves: 0 bbl (1 January 2015 est.)
country comparison to the world: 201

Refined petroleum products—production: 0 bbl/day (2012 est.)
country comparison to the world: 138

Refined petroleum products—consumption: 1,300 bbl/day (2013 est.)
country comparison to the world: 197

Refined petroleum products—exports: 0 bbl/day (2012 est.)
country comparison to the world: 139

Refined petroleum products—imports: 1,264 bbl/day (2012 est.)

country comparison to the world: 191

Natural gas—production: 0 cu m (2012 est.)
country comparison to the world: 138

Natural gas—consumption: 0 cu m (2013 est.)
country comparison to the world: 202

Natural gas—exports: 0 cu m (2012 est.)
country comparison to the world: 196

Natural gas—imports: 0 cu m (2013 est.)
country comparison to the world: 143

Natural gas—proved reserves: 200 billion cu m (1 January 2006 est.)
country comparison to the world: 46

Carbon dioxide emissions from consumption of energy: 496,300 Mt (2012 est.)
country comparison to the world: 180

COMMUNICATIONS

Telephone—fixed lines: *total subscriptions:* 3,000
subscriptions per 100 inhabitants: less than 1 (2014 est.)
country comparison to the world: 212

Telephone—mobile cellular: *total:* 676,900
subscriptions per 100 inhabitants: 56 (2014 est.)
country comparison to the world: 163

Telephone system: *general assessment:* rudimentary service in urban and some rural areas, which is expanding with the entrance of new competitors
domestic: system suffered significant damage during the violence associated with independence; limited fixed-line services; mobile-cellular services have been expanding and are now available in urban and most rural areas
international: country code—670; international service is available (2012)

Broadcast media: 1 public TV broadcast station broadcasting Nationally and 1 public radio broadcaster with stations in each of the 13 administrative districts; 1 commercial TV broadcast station, 3 commercial radio stations, and roughly 20 community radio stations (2012)
Radio broadcast stations: at least 21 (Timor-Leste has one National public broadcaster and 20 community and church radio stations—station frequency types NA) (2007)
Television broadcast stations: 1 (Timor-Leste has one National public broadcaster)

Internet country code: .tl

Internet hosts: 252 (2012)
country comparison to the world: 194

Internet users: *total:* 12,000
percent of population: 1.0% (2014 est.)
country comparison to the world: 205

TRANSPORTATION

Airports: 6 (2013)
country comparison to the world: 176

Airports—with paved runways: *total:* 2
2,438 to 3,047 m: 1
1,524 to 2,437 m: 1 (2013)

Airports—with unpaved runways: *total:* 4
914 to 1,523 m: 2
under 914 m: 2 (2013)

Heliports: 8 (2013)

Roadways: *total:* 6,040 km
paved: 2,600 km
unpaved: 3,440 km (2005)
country comparison to the world: 150

Merchant marine: *total:* 1
by type: passenger/cargo 1 (2010)
country comparison to the world: 151

Ports and terminals: *major seaport(s):* Dili

MILITARY AND SECURITY

Military branches: Timor-Leste Defense Force (Falintil-Forcas de Defesa de Timor-L'este, Falintil (F-FDTL)): Army, Navy (Armada) (2013)

Military service age and obligation: 18 years of age for voluntary military service; 18-month service obligation; no conscription but, as of May 2013, introduction of conscription was under discussion (2013)

Military expenditures: 1.5% of GDP (2014)
1.8% of GDP (2013)
2.92% of GDP (2012)
2.6% of GDP (2011)
2.92% of GDP (2010)
country comparison to the world: 23

TRANSNATIONAL ISSUES

Disputes—international: three stretches of land borders with Timor-Leste have yet to be delimited, two of which are in the Oecussi exclave area, and no maritime or Economic Exclusion Zone boundaries have been established between the countries; maritime boundaries with Indonesia remain unresolved; in 2007, Australia and Timor-Leste signed a 50-year development zone and revenue sharing agreement in lieu of a maritime boundary

Trafficking in persons: *current situation:* Timor Leste is a source and destination country for men, women, and children subjected to forced labor and sex trafficking; Timorese women and girls from rural areas are lured to the capital with promises of legitimate jobs or education prospects and are then forced into prostitution or domestic servitude, and other women and girls may be sent to Indonesia for domestic servitude; Timorese family members force children into bonded domestic or agricultural labor to repay debts; foreign migrant women are vulnerable to sex trafficking in Timor Leste, while men and boys from Burma, Cambodia, and Thailand are forced to work on fishing boats in Timorese waters under inhumane conditions
tier rating: Tier 2 Watch List—Timor Leste does not fully comply with the minimum standards for the elimination of trafficking; however, it is making significant efforts to do so; in 2014, legislation was drafted but not finalized or implemented that outlines procedures for screening potential trafficking victims; law enforcement made modest progress, including one conviction for sex trafficking, but efforts are hindered by prosecutors' and judges' lack of expertise in applying anti-trafficking laws effectively; the government rescued two child victims with support from an NGO but did not provide protective services (2015)

Illicit drugs: NA

TOGO

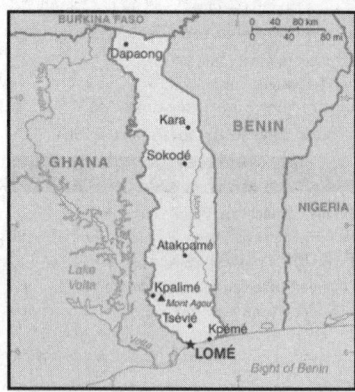

INTRODUCTION

Background: French Togoland became Togo in 1960. Gen. Gnassingbe EYADEMA, installed as military ruler in 1967, ruled Togo with a heavy hand for almost four decades. Despite the facade of multi-party elections instituted in the early 1990s, the government was largely dominated by President EYADEMA, whose Rally of the Togolese People (RPT) party has been in power almost continually since 1967 and its successor, the Union for the Republic, maintains a majority of seats in today's legislature. Upon EYADEMA's death in February 2005, the military installed the president's son, Faure GNASSINGBE, and then engineered his formal election two months later. Democratic gains since then allowed Togo to hold its first relatively free and fair legislative elections in October 2007. After years of political unrest and condemnation from international organizations for human rights abuses, Togo is finally being re-welcomed into the international community.

GEOGRAPHY

Location: Western Africa, bordering the Bight of Benin, between Benin and Ghana

Geographic coordinates: 8 00 N, 1 10 E

Map references: Africa

Area: *total:* 56,785 sq km
land: 54,385 sq km
water: 2,400 sq km
country comparison to the world: 126

Area—comparative: slightly smaller than West Virginia

Land boundaries: *total:* 1,880 km
border countries (3): Benin 651 km, Burkina Faso 131 km, Ghana 1,098 km

Coastline: 56 km

Maritime claims: *territorial sea:* 30 nm
exclusive economic zone: 200 nm

Climate: tropical; hot, humid in south; semiarid in north

Terrain: gently rolling savanna in north; central hills; southern plateau; low coastal plain with extensive lagoons and marshes

Elevation: *mean elevation:* 236 m

elevation extremes: *lowest point:* Atlantic Ocean 0 m
highest point: Mont Agou 986 m

Natural resources: phosphates, limestone, marble, arable land

Land use: *agricultural land:* 67.4%
arable land: 45.2%
permanent crops: 3.8%
permanent pasture: 18.4%
forest: 4.9%
other: 27.7% (2011 est.)

Irrigated land: 70 sq km (2012)

Total renewable water resources: 14.7 cu km (2011)

Freshwater withdrawal (domestic/industrial/agricultural): *total:* 0.17 cu km/yr (63%/3%/34%)
per capita: 33.46 cu m/yr (2005)

Natural hazards: hot, dry harmattan wind can reduce visibility in north during winter; periodic droughts

Environment—current issues: deforestation attributable to slash-and-burn agriculture and the use of wood for fuel; water pollution presents health hazards and hinders the fishing industry; air pollution increasing in urban Areas

Environment—international agreements: *party to:* Biodiversity, Climate Change, Climate Change-Kyoto Protocol, Desertification, Endangered Species, Law of the Sea, Ozone Layer Protection, Ship Pollution, Tropical Timber 83, Tropical Timber 94, Wetlands, Whaling
signed, but not ratified: none of the selected agreements

Geography—note: the country's length allows it to stretch through six distinct geographic regions; climate varies from tropical to savanna

PEOPLE AND SOCIETY

Nationality: *noun:* Togolese (singular and plural)
adjective: Togolese

Ethnic groups: African (37 tribes; largest and most important are Ewe, Mina, and Kabre) 99%, EuropeaNAnd Syrian-Lebanese less than 1%

Languages: French (official, the language of commerce), Ewe and Mina (the two major African languages in the south), Kabye (sometimes spelled Kabiye) and Dagomba (the two major African languages in the north)

Religions: Christian 29%, Muslim 20%, indigenous beliefs 51%

Population: 7,552,318
note: estimates for this country explicitly take into account the effects of excess mortality due to AIDS; this can result in lower life expectancy, higher infant mortality, higher death rates, lower population growth rates, and changes in the distribution of population by age and sex than would otherwise be expected (July 2015 est.)
country comparison to the world: 100

Age structure: *0–14 years:* 40.56% (male 1,536,301/female 1,527,018)
15–24 years: 19.51% (male 735,409/female 738,276)
25–54 years: 32.37% (male 1,214,388/female 1,230,218)
55–64 years: 4.24% (male 150,890/female 169,158)
65 years and over: 3.32% (male 108,474/female 142,186) (2015 est.)

Dependency ratios: *total dependency ratio:* 81.8%
youth dependency ratio: 76.8%
elderly dependency ratio: 5%
potential support ratio: 19.9% (2015 est.)

Median age: *total:* 19.6 years
male: 19.4 years
female: 19.9 years (2015 est.)
country comparison to the world: 193

Population growth rate: 2.69% (2015 est.)
country comparison to the world: 17

Birth rate: 34.13 births/1,000 population (2015 est.)
country comparison to the world: 29

Death rate: 7.26 deaths/1,000 population (2015 est.)
country comparison to the world: 120

Net migration rate: 0 migrant(s)/1,000 population (2015 est.)
country comparison to the world: 80

Urbanization: *urban population:* 40% of total population (2015)
rate of urbanization: 3.83% annual rate of change (2010–15 est.)

Major urban areas—population: LOME (capital) 956,000 (2015)

Sex ratio: *at birth:* 1.03 male(s)/female
0–14 years: 1.01 male(s)/female
15–24 years: 1 male(s)/female
25–54 years: 0.99 male(s)/female
55–64 years: 0.89 male(s)/female
65 years and over: 0.76 male(s)/female
total population: 0.98 male(s)/female (2015 est.)

Mother's mean age at first birth: 21
note: Median age at first birth among women 25–29 (2013/14 est.)

Maternal mortality rate: 368 deaths/100,000 live births (2015 est.)
country comparison to the world: 40

Infant mortality rate: *total:* 45.22 deaths/1,000 live births
male: 51.76 deaths/1,000 live births
female: 38.48 deaths/1,000 live births (2015 est.)
country comparison to the world: 45

Life expectancy at birth: *total population:* 64.51 years
male: 61.91 years
female: 67.17 years (2015 est.)
country comparison to the world: 179

Total fertility rate: 4.48 children born/woman (2015 est.)
country comparison to the world: 28

Contraceptive prevalence rate: 15.2% (2010)

Health expenditures: 8.6% of GDP (2013)
country comparison to the world: 45

Physicians density: 0.05 physicians/1,000 population (2008)

Hospital bed density: 0.7 beds/1,000 population (2011)

Drinking water source:
improved:
urban: 91.4% of population
rural: 44.2% of population
total: 63.1% of population
unimproved:
urban: 8.6% of population
rural: 55.8% of population
total: 36.9% of population (2015 est.)

Sanitation facility access:
improved:
urban: 24.7% of population
rural: 2.9% of population
total: 11.6% of population
unimproved:
urban: 75.3% of population
rural: 97.1% of population
total: 88.4% of population (2015 est.)

HIV/AIDS—adult prevalence rate: 2.4% (2014 est.)
country comparison to the world: 26

HIV/AIDS—people living with HIV/AIDS: 113,700 (2014 est.)
country comparison to the world: 41

HIV/AIDS—deaths: 4,300 (2014 est.)
country comparison to the world: 35

Major infectious diseases: *degree of risk:* very high
food or waterborne diseases: bacterial and protozoal diarrhea, hepatitis A, and typhoid fever
vectorborne diseases: malaria, dengue fever, and yellow fever
respiratory disease: meningococcal meningitis
water contact disease: schistosomiasis
animal contact disease: rabies
note: highly pathogenic H5N1 avian influenza has been identified in this country; it poses a negligible risk with extremely rare cases possible among US citizens who have close contact with birds (2013)

Obesity—adult prevalence rate: 6.4% (2014)
country comparison to the world: 169

Children under the age of 5 years underweight: 16.2% (2014)
country comparison to the world: 41

Education expenditures: 4.8% of GDP (2014)
country comparison to the world: 91

Literacy: *definition:* age 15 and over can read and write

total population: 66.5%
male: 78.3%
female: 55.3% (2015 est.)

School life expectancy (primary to tertiary education): *total:* 12 years
male: NA
female: NA (2011)

Child labor—children ages 5–14: *total number:* 774,801
percentage: 47% (2010 est.)

GOVERNMENT

Country name: *conventional long form:* Togolese Republic
conventional short form: Togo
local long form: Republique Togolaise
local short form: none
former: French Togoland
etymology: derived from the Ewe words "to" (water) and "go" (shore) to give the sense of "by the water"; originally, this designation applied to the town of Togo (now Togoville) on the northern shore of Lake Togo, but the name was eventually extended to the entire nation

Government type: presidential republic

Capital: *name:* Lome

Geographic coordinates: 6 07 N, 1 13 E
time difference: UTC 0 (5 hours ahead of Washington, DC, during Standard Time)

Administrative divisions: 5 regions (regions, singular—region); Centrale, Kara, Maritime, Plateaux, Savanes

Independence: 27 April 1960 (from French-administered UN trusteeship)

National holiday: Independence Day, 27 April (1960)

Constitution: several previous; latest adopted 27 September 1992, effective 14 October 1992; amended 2002, 2007 (2016)

Legal system: customary law system

International law organization participation: accepts compulsory ICJ jurisdiction with reservations; non-party state to the ICCt

Citizenship: *citizenship by birth:* no
citizenship by descent only: at least one parent must be a citizen of Togo
dual citizenship recognized: yes
residency requirement for naturalization: 5 years

Suffrage: 18 years of age; universal

Executive branch: *chief of state:* President Faure GNASSINGBE (since 4 May 2005)

head of government: Prime Minister Komi KLASSOU (since 5 June 2015)
cabinet: Council of Ministers appointed by the president on the advice of the prime minister
elections/appointments: president directly elected by simple majority popular vote for a 5-year term (no term limits); election last held on 25 April 2015 (next to be held in 2020); prime minister appointed by the president
election results: Faure GNASSINGBE reelected president; percent of vote—Faure GNASSINGBE

(UNIR) 58.8%, Jean-Pierre FABRE (ANC) 35.2%, Tchaboure GOGUE 4%, other 2%

Legislative branch: *description:* unicameral National Assembly or Assemblee Nationale (91 seats; members directly elected in multi-seat constituencies by proportional representation vote to serve 5-year terms)
elections: last held on 25 July 2013 (next to be held in 2018)
election results: percent of vote by party—UNIR 46.7%, CST 28.9%, Rainbow Alliance 10.8%, UFC 7.7%, independent 0.8%, other 5.1%; seats by party—UNIR 62, CST 19, Rainbow Alliance 6, UFC 3, independent 1

Judicial branch: *Highest court(s):* Supreme Court or Cour Supreme (organized into the Criminal Chamber and the Administrative Chamber, each with a chamber president and advisors); Constitutional Court (consists of 9 judges including the court president)
judge selection and term of office: Supreme Court president appointed by decree of the president of the republic upon the proposal of the Supreme Council of the Magistracy, a 9-member judicial, advisory, and disciplinary body; other judge appointments and judge tenure NA; Constitutional Court judges appointed by the National Assembly; judge tenure NA
subordinate courts: Court of Assizes (sessions court); appeals courts; tribunals of first instance (divided into civil, commercial, and correctional chambers; Court of State Security; military tribunal

Political parties and leaders: Action Committee for Renewal or CAR [Dodji APEVON]
Democratic Convention of African Peoples or CDPA [Brigitte ADJAMAGBO-JOHNSON]
National Alliance for Change or ANC [Jean-Pierre FABRE]
Pan-African Patriotic Convergence or CPP [Edem KODJO]
Rainbow Alliance (a coalition including CAR and CDPA) [Brigitte ADJAMAGBO-JOHNSON]
Save Togo Collective or CST (a coalition including: ANC and PSR) [Ata Messan Zeus AJAVON]
Socialist Pact for Renewal or PSR [Abi TCHESSA]
Union for Democracy and Social Progress or UDPS [Gagou KOKOU]
Union of Forces for Change or UFC [Gilchrist OLYMPIO]

Political pressure groups and leaders: NA

International organization participation: ACP, AfDB, AU, ECOWAS, EITI (compliant country), Entente, FAO, FZ, G-77, IAEA, IBRD, ICAO, ICRM, IDA, IDB, IFAD, IFC, IFRCS, ILO, IMF, IMO, Interpol, IOC, IOM, IPU, ISO (correspondent), ITSO, ITU, ITUC (NGOs), MIGA, MINURSO, MINUSMA, NAM, OIC, OIF, OPCW, PCA, UN, UNAMID, UNCTAD, UNESCO, UNHCR, UNIDO, UNMIL, UNOCI, UNWTO, UPU, WADB (regional), WAEMU, WCO, WFTU (NGOs), WHO, WIPO, WMO, WTO

849

Diplomatic representation in the US: *chief of mission:* Ambassador (vacant); Charge d'Affaires Yokoudema KADOKALIH (since 26 October 2015)
chancery: 2208 Massachusetts Avenue NW, Washington, DC 20008
telephone: [1] (202) 234-4212
FAX: [1] (202) 232-3190

Diplomatic representation from the US: *chief of mission:* Ambassador Robert E. WHITEHEAD (since 7 May 2012)
embassy: 4332 Blvd. Gnassingbe Eyadema, Cite OUA, Lome
mailing address: B. P.852, Lome; 2300 Lome Place, Washington, DC 20521-2300
telephone: [228] 2261-5470
FAX: [228] 2261-5501

Flag description: five equal horizontal bands of green (top and bottom) alternating with yellow; a white five-pointed star on a red square is in the upper hoist-side corner; the five horizontal stripes stand for the five different regions of the country; the red square is meant to express the loyalty and patriotism of the people; green symbolizes hope, fertility, and agriculture; yellow represents mineral wealth and faith that hard work and strength will bring prosperity; the star symbolizes life, purity, peace, dignity, and Togo's independence
note: uses the popular Pan-African colors of Ethiopia

National symbol(s): lion; National colors: green, yellow, red, white

National anthem: *name:* "Salut a toi, pays de nos aieux" (Hail to Thee, Land of Our Forefathers)
lyrics/music: Alex CASIMIR-DOSSEH
note: adopted 1960, restored 1992; this anthem was replaced by another during one-party rule between 1979 and 1992

ECONOMY

Economy—overview: This small, sub-Saharan economy depends heavily on both commercial and subsistence agriculture, which provides employment for a significant share of the labor force. Some basic foodstuffs must still be imported. Cocoa, coffee, and cotton generate about 40% of export earnings with cotton being the most important cash crop. Togo is among the world's largest producers of phosphate and seeks to develop its carbon ate phosphate reserves.
The government's decade-long effort, supported by the World Bank and the IMF, to implement economic reform measures, encourage foreign investment, and bring revenues in line with expenditures has moved slowly. Togo completed its IMF Extended Credit Facility in 2011 and reached a Heavily Indebted Poor Country debt relief completion point in 2010 at which 95% of the country's debt was forgiven. Togo continues to work with the IMF on structural reforms. Progress depends on follow through on privatization, increased openness in government financial operations, progress toward legislative elections, and continued support from foreign donors.

Togo's 2015 economic growth remained steady at 5.4%, largely driven by infusions of foreign aid, infrastructure investment in the port and mineral sectors, and improvements in the business climate. Foreign direct investment inflows have slowed in recent years.

GDP (purchasing power parity): $10.85 billion (2015 est.)
$10.3 billion (2014 est.)
$9.775 billion (2013 est.)
note: data are in 2015 US dollars
country comparison to the world: 157

GDP (official exchange rate): $4.165 billion (2015 est.)

GDP—real growth rate: 5.3% (2015 est.)
5.4% (2014 est.)
5.4% (2013 est.)
country comparison to the world: 36

GDP—per capita (PPP): $1,500 (2015 est.)
$1,400 (2014 est.)
$1,400 (2013 est.)
note: data are in 2015 US dollars
country comparison to the world: 215

Gross National saving: 11.7% of GDP (2015 est.)
10.7% of GDP (2014 est.)
10.5% of GDP (2013 est.)
country comparison to the world: 142

GDP—composition, by end use:
household consumption: 90.3%
government consumption: 15.6%
investment in fixed capital: 22.5%
investment in inventories: 26.1%
exports of goods and services: 56.8%
imports of goods and services: -111.3% (2015 est.)

GDP—composition, by sector of origin:
agriculture: 29.5%
industry: 21%
services: 49.5% (2015 est.)

Agriculture—products: coffee, cocoa, cotton, yams, cassava (manioc, tapioca), corn, beans, rice, millet, sorghum; livestock; fish

Industries: phosphate mining, agricultural processing, cement, handicrafts, textiles, beverages

Industrial production growth rate: 9.7% (2015 est.)
country comparison to the world: 6

Labor force: 2.595 million (2007 est.)
country comparison to the world: 112

Labor force—by occupation: *agriculture:* 65%
industry: 5%
services: 30% (1998 est.)

Unemployment rate: NA%

Population below poverty line: 32% (1989 est.)

Household income or consumption by percentage share: *lowest:* 10%: 3.3%
highest: 10%: 27.1% (2006)

Budget: *revenues:* $1.025 billion
expenditures: $1.192 billion (2015 est.)
Taxes and other revenues: 24.7% of GDP (2015 est.)
country comparison to the world: 123

Budget surplus (+) or deficit (–): -4% of GDP (2015 est.)
country comparison to the world: 144

Public debt: 48.7% of GDP (2015 est.)
47.4% of GDP (2014 est.)
country comparison to the world: 83

Fiscal year: calendar year

Inflation rate (consumer prices): 1.8% (2015 est.)
0.2% (2014 est.)
country comparison to the world: 108

Central bank discount rate: 2.5% (31 December 2010)
4.25% (31 December 2009)
country comparison to the world: 110

Commercial bank prime lending rate: NA%

Stock of narrow money: $983.4 million (31 December 2015 est.)
$1.036 billion (31 December 2014 est.)
country comparison to the world: 155

Stock of broad money: $2.017 billion (31 December 2015 est.)
$2.025 billion (31 December 2014 est.)
country comparison to the world: 155

Stock of domestic credit: $1.652 billion (31 December 2015 est.)
$1.642 billion (31 December 2014 est.)
country comparison to the world: 145

Market value of publicly traded shares: $NA

Current account balance: -$523 million (2015 est.)
-$592 million (2014 est.)
country comparison to the world: 99

Exports: $1.934 billion (2015 est.)
$1.809 billion (2014 est.)
country comparison to the world: 139

Exports—commodities: reexports, cotton, phosphates, coffee, cocoa

Exports—partners: India 14.3%, Burkina Faso 11.1%, China 11.1%, Lebanon 10%, Benin 9.4%, Ghana 8.8%, Nigeria 6%, Niger 5.8% (2015)

Imports: $2.983 billion (2015 est.) $3.004 billion (2014 est.)
country comparison to the world: 146

Imports—commodities: machinery and equipment, foodstuffs, petroleum Products

Imports—partners: China 22.9%, Belgium 20.3%, Netherlands 11.9%, France 6.6%, India 4.8%, Singapore 4.4% (2015)

Reserves of foreign exchange and gold: $494.3 million (31 December 2015 est.)
$507 million (31 December 2014 est.)
country comparison to the world: 150

Debt—external: $984.4 million (31 December 2014 est.)
$903.3 million (31 December 2013 est.)
country comparison to the world: 164

Exchange rates: Communaute Financiere Africaine francs (XOF) per US dollar—
580.5 (2015 est.)
494.42 (2014 est.)
494.42 (2013 est.)
510.53 (2012 est.)

471.87 (2011 est.)

ENERGY

Electricity—production: 109 million kWh (2012 est.)
country comparison to the world: 197

Electricity—consumption: 976 million kWh (2012 est.)
country comparison to the world: 151

Electricity—exports: 0 kWh (2013 est.)
country comparison to the world: 204

Electricity—imports: 959 million kWh (2012 est.)
country comparison to the world: 64

Electricity—installed generating capacity: 83,000 kW (2012 est.)
country comparison to the world: 177

Electricity—from fossil fuels: 21.7% of total installed capacity (2012 est.)
country comparison to the world: 192

Electricity—from nuclear fuels: 0% of total installed capacity (2012 est.)
country comparison to the world: 191

Electricity—from hydro electric plants: 78.3% of total installed capacity (2012 est.)
country comparison to the world: 17

Electricity—from other renewable sources: 0% of total installed capacity (2012 est.)
country comparison to the world: 133

Crude oil—production: 0 bbl/day (2014 est.)
country comparison to the world: 198

Crude oil—exports: 0 bbl/day (2012 est.)
country comparison to the world: 197

Crude oil—imports: 0 bbl/day (2012 est.)
country comparison to the world: 134

Crude oil—proved reserves: 0 bbl (1 January 2015 est.)
country comparison to the world: 199

Refined petroleum products—production: 0 bbl/day (2012 est.)
country comparison to the world: 136

Refined petroleum products—consumption: 13,000 bbl/day (2013 est.)
country comparison to the world: 146

Refined petroleum products—exports: 0 bbl/day (2012 est.)
country comparison to the world: 137

Refined petroleum products—imports: 11,950 bbl/day (2012 est.)
country comparison to the world: 133

Natural gas—production: 0 cu m (2013 est.)
country comparison to the world: 136

Natural gas—consumption: 0 cu m (2013 est.)
country comparison to the world: 200

Natural gas—exports: 0 cu m (2013 est.)
country comparison to the world: 193

Natural gas—imports: 0 cu m (2013 est.)
country comparison to the world: 141

Natural gas—proved reserves: 0 cu m (1 January 2014 est.)
country comparison to the world: 200

Carbon dioxide emissions from consumption of energy: 1.63 million Mt (2012 est.)
country comparison to the world: 155

COMMUNICATIONS

Telephones—fixed lines: *total subscriptions:* 63,200
subscriptions per 100 inhabitants: 1 (2014 est.)
country comparison to the world: 155

Telephones—mobile cellular: *total:* 4.8 million
subscriptions per 100 inhabitants: 66 (2014 est.)
country comparison to the world: 121

Telephone system: *general assessment:* fair system based on a network of microwave radio relay routes supplemented by open-wire lines and a mobile-cellular system
domestic: microwave radio relay and open-wire lines for conventional system; combined fixed-line and mobile-cellular teledensity roughly 50 telephones per 100 persons with mobile-cellular use predominating
International: country code—228; satellite earth stations—1 Intelsat (Atlantic Ocean), 1 Symphonie (2010)

Broadcast media: 2 state-owned TV stations with multiple transmission sites; 5 private TV stations broadcast locally; cable TV service is available; state-owned radio network with multiple stations; several dozen private radio stations and a few community radio stations; transmissions of multiple international broadcasters available (2007)
Radio broadcast stations: AM 2, FM 9, shortwave 4 (1998)
Television broadcast stations: 3 (plus 2 repeaters) (1997)

Internet country code: .tg

Internet hosts: 1,168 (2012)
country comparison to the world: 170

Internet users: *total:* 336,000
percent of population: 4.6% (2014 est.)
country comparison to the world: 138

TRANSPORTATION

Airports: 8 (2013)
country comparison to the world: 163

Airports—with paved runways: *total:* 2

2,438 to 3,047 m: 2 (2013)

Airports—with unpaved runways: *total:* 6
914 to 1,523 m: 4
under 914 m: 2 (2013)

Railways: *total:* 568 km
narrow gauge: 568 km 1.000-m gauge (2014)
country comparison to the world: 112

Roadways: *total:* 11,652 km
paved: 2,447 km
unpaved: 9,205 km (2007)
country comparison to the world: 129

Waterways: 50 km (season ally navigable by small craft on the Mono River depending on rainfall) (2011)
country comparison to the world: 102

Merchant marine: *total:* 61
by type: bulk carrier 6, cargo 38, carrier 3, chemical tanker 5, container 3, passenger/cargo 1, petroleum tanker 3, refrigerated cargo 1, roll on/roll off 1
foreign-owned: 21 (China 1, Lebanon 6, Romania 1, Syria 6, Turkey 4, UAE 1, US 1, Yemen 1) (2010)
country comparison to the world: 66
Ports and terminals: *major seaport(s):* Kpeme, Lome

MILITARY AND SECURITY

Military branches: Togolese Armed Forces (Forces Armees Togolaise, FAT): Togolese Army (l'Armee de Terre), Togolese Navy (Forces Naval Togolaises), Togolese Air Force (Force Aerienne Togolaise, TAF), National Gendarmerie (2013)

Military service age and obligation: 18 years of age for compulsory and voluntary military service; 2-year service obligation (2012)

Military expenditures: NA% (2012)
1.6% of GDP (2011)

TRANSNATIONAL ISSUES

Disputes—international: in 2001, Benin claimed Togo moved boundary monuments—joint commission continues to resurvey the boundary; talks continue between Benina nd Togo on funding the Adjrala hydro electric dam on the Mon a River

Refugees and internally displaced persons: *refugees (country of origin):* 18,444 (Ghana) (2014)

Illicit drugs: transit hub for Nigerian heroina nd cocaine traffickers; money laundering not a significant problem

TOKELAU

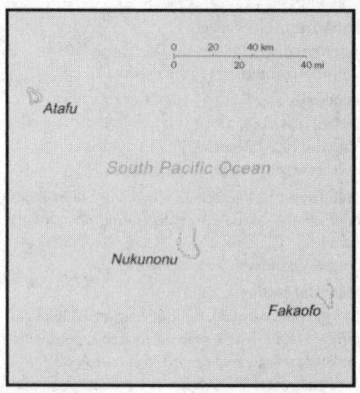

INTRODUCTION

Background: Originally settled by Polynesian emigrants from surrounding island groups, the Tokelau Islands were made a British protectorate in 1889. They were transferred to New Zealand administration in 1925. Referenda held in 2006 and 2007 to change the status of the islands from that of a New Zealand territory to one of free association with New Zealand did not meet the needed threshold for approval.

GEOGRAPHY

Location: Oceania, group of three atolls in the South Pacific Ocean, about one-half of the way from Hawaii to New Zealand

Geographic coordinates: 9 00 S, 172 00 W

Map references: Oceania

Area: *total:* 12 sq km
land: 12 sq km
water: 0 sq km
country comparison to the world: 242

Area—comparative: about 17 times the size of the National Mall in Washington, DC

Land boundaries: 0 km

Coastline: 101 km

Maritime claims: *territorial sea:* 12 nm
exclusive economic zone: 200 nm

Climate: tropical; moderated by trade winds (April to November)

Terrain: low-lying coral atolls enclosing large lagoons

Elevation: *mean elevation:* NA

elevation extremes: *lowest point:* Pacific Ocean 0 m
highest point: unnamed location 5 m

Natural resources: NEGL

Land use: *agricultural land:* 60%
arable land: 0%
permanent crops: 60%

permanent pasture: 0% forest: 0%
other: 40% (2011 est.)

Irrigated land: 0 sq km (2012)

Natural hazards: lies in Pacific typhoon belt

Environment—current issues: limited Natural resources and overcrowding are contributing to emigration to New Zealand

Geography—note: consists of three atolls (Atafu, Fakaofo, Nukunonu), each with a lagoon surrounded by a number of reef-bound islets of varying length and rising to over 3 m above sea level

PEOPLE AND SOCIETY

Nationality: *noun:* Tokelauan(s)
adjective: Tokelauan

Ethnic groups: Tokelauan 65.3%, part Tokelauan/Samoan 8.7%, part Tokelauan/Tuvaluan 6.9%, part Tokelauan/other Pacific islander 1.9%, part Tokelauan/European 1%, Samoan 6.7%, Tuvaluan 2.8%, other Pacific islander 1.1%, other 5.1%, unspecified 0.4% (2011 est.)

Languages: Tokelauan 93.5% (a Polynesian language), English 58.9%, Samoan 45.5%, Tuvaluan 11.6%, Kiribati 2.7%, other 2.5%, none 4.1%, unspecified 0.6%
note: shares sum to more than 100% because some respondents gave more than one answer on the census (2011 ests.)

Religions: Congregation al Christian Church 58.2%, Roman Catholic 36.6%, Presbyterian 1.8%, other Christian 2.8%, Spiritualism and New Age 0.1%, unspecified 0.5% (2011 est.)

Population: 1,337 (July 2014 est.)
country comparison to the world: 234

Population growth rate: -0.01% (2014 est.)
country comparison to the world: 200

Urbanization: *urban population:* 0% of total population (2015)
rate of urbanization: 0% annual rate of change (2010–15 est.)

Sex ratio: NA

Infant mortality rate: *total:* NA
male: NA
female: NA

Life expectancy at birth: *total population:* NA
male: NA
female: NA

Total fertility rate: NA

Drinking water source:
improved:
rural: 100% of population
total: 100% of population
unimproved:
rural: 0% of population
total: 0% of population (2015 est.)

Sanitation facility access:
improved:
rural: 90.5% of population

total: 90.5% of population
unimproved:
rural: 9.5% of population
total: 9.5% of population (2015 est.)

HIV/AIDS—adult prevalence rate: NA

HIV/AIDS—people living with HIV/AIDS: NA

HIV/AIDS—deaths: NA

Education expenditures: NA

GOVERNMENT

Country name: *conventional long form:* none
conventional short form: Tokelau
etymology: "tokelau" is a Polynesian word meaning "north wind"

Dependency status: self-administering territory of New Zealand; note—Tokelau and New Zealand have agreed to a draft constitution as Tokelau moves toward free association with New Zealand; a UN-sponsored referendum on self governance in October 2007 did not produce the two-thirds majority vote necessary for changing the political status

Government type: parliamentary democratic dependency (General Fono); a territory of New Zealand

Capital: none; each atoll has its owNAdmin istrative center
time difference: UTC + 13 (18 hours ahead of Washington, DC during Standard Time)

Administrative divisions: none (territory of New Zealand)

Independence: none (territory of New Zealand)

National holiday: Waitangi Day (Treaty of Waitangi established British sovereignty over New Zealand), 6 February (1840)

Constitution: many previous; latest effective 1 January 1949 (Tokelau Islands Act 1948); amended many times, last in 2007 (2016)

Legal system: common law system of New Zealand

Citizenship: see New Zealand

Suffrage: 21 years of age; un iversal

Executive branch: *chief of state:* Queen ELIZABETH II (since 6 February 1952); represented by Governor General of New Zealand Anand SATYANAND (since 23 August 2006); New Zealand is represented by Administrator Jonathan KINGS (since February 2011)

head of government: Siopili PEREZ (since 23 February 2015); note—position rotates annually among the 3 Faipule (village leaders)
cabinet: the Council for the Ongoing Government of Tokelau functions as a cabinet; consists of 3 Faipule (village leaders) and 3 Pulenuku (village mayors)
elections/appointments: the monarchy is hereditary; governor general appointed by the monarch; administrator appointed by the Minister of Foreign Affairs and Trade in New Zealand; head of

government chosen from the Council of Faipule to serve a 1-year term

Legislative branch: *description:* unicameral General Fono (20 seats apportioned by island—Atafu 7, Fakaofo 7, Nukunonu 6; members directly elected by simple majority vote to serve 3-year terms); note—the Tokelau Amendment Act of 1996 confers limited legislative power to the General Fono

elections: last held on 23 January 2014 (next to be held in 2017)

election results: independent 20

Judicial branch: *highest court(s):* Court of Appeal in New Zealand (consists of the court president and 8 judges sitting in 3- or 5-judge panels depending on the case)

judge selection and term of office: judges nominated by the Judicial Selection Committee and approved by three-quarters majority of the Parliament; judge tenure NA

subordinate courts: High Court, in New Zealand; Council of Elders or Taupulega

Political parties and leaders: none

Political pressure groups and leaders: none

International organization participation: PIF (associate member), SPC, UNESCO (associate), UPU

Diplomatic representation in the US: none (territory of New Zealand)

Diplomatic representation from the US: none (territory of New Zealand)

Flag description: a yellow stylized Tokelauan canoe on a dark blue field sails toward the manu—the Southern Cross constellation of four, white, five-pointed stars at the hoist side; the Southern Cross represents the role of Christianity in Tokelauan culture and, in conjunction with the canoe, symbolizes the country navigating into the future; the color yellow indicates happiness and peace, and the blue field represents the ocean on which the community relies

National symbol(s): tuluma (fishing tackle box); National colors: blue, yellow, white

National anthem: *name:* "Te Atua" (For the Almighty)

lyrics/music: unknown/Falani KALOLO

note: adopted 2008; in preparation for eventual self governance, Tokelau held a National contest to choose an anthem; as a territory of New Zealand, "God Defend New Zealand" and "God Save the Queen" are official (see New Zealand)

ECONOMY

Economy—overview: Tokelau's small size (three villages), isolation, and lack of resources greatly restrain economic development and confine agriculture to the subsistence level. The principal sources of revenue come from sales of copra, postage stamps, souvenir coins, and handicrafts. Money is also remitted to families from relatives in New Zealand. The people rely heavily on aid from New Zealand—about $15 million annually in FY12/13 and FY13/14—to maintain public services. New Zealand's support amounts to 80% of Tokelau's recurrent government budget. An international trust fund, currently worth nearly $32 million, was established in 2004 by New Zealand to provide Tokelau an independent source of revenue.

GDP (purchasing power parity): $1.5 million (1993 est.)

country comparison to the world: 230

GDP (official exchange rate): $NA

GDP—real growth rate: NA%

GDP—per capita (PPP): $1,000 (1993 est.)

country comparison to the world: 224

GDP—composition, by sector of origin:

agriculture: NA%

industry: NA%

services: NA%

Agriculture—products: cocon uts, copra, breadfruit, papayas, bananas; pigs, poultry, goats; fish

Industries: small-scale enterprises for copra production, woodworking, plaited craft goods; stamps, coins; fishing

Labor force: 440 (2001)

country comparison to the world: 232

Unemployment rate: NA%

Population below poverty line: NA%

Budget: *revenues:* $430,800

expenditures: $2.8 million (1987 est.)

Fiscal year: 1 April—31 March

Inflation rate (consumer prices): NA%

Exports: $0 (2002 est.)

country comparison to the world: 224

Exports—commodities: stamps, copra, handicrafts

Imports: $969,200 (2002 est.)

country comparison to the world: 223

Imports—commodities: foodstuffs, building materials, fuel

Exchange rates: New Zealand dollars (NZD) per US dollar—

1.452 (2015)

1.2187 (2013)

1.2187 (2013)

1.23 (2012)

1.263 (2011)

ENERGY

Crude oil—proved reserves: 0 bbl (1 January 2015 est.)

country comparison to the world: 197

COMMUNICATIONS

Telephone system: *general assessment:* modern satellite-based communications system

domestic: radio telephone service between Islands

international: country code—690; radiotelephon eservice to Samoa; government-regulated telephone service (TeleTok); satellite earth stations—3 (2009)

Broadcast media: no TV stations; each atoll operates a radio service that provides shipping news and weather reports (2009)

Radio broadcast stations: AM NA, FM NA, shortwave NA (one radio station provides service to all Islands) (2002)

Internet country code: .tk

Internet hosts: 2,069 (2012)

country comparison to the world: 162

Internet users: *total:* 800

percent of population: 55.4% (2008)

country comparison to the world: 215

TRANSPORTATION

Ports and termimals: none; offs horeanchorage only

MILITARY AND SECURITY

Military—note: defense is the responsibility of New Zealand

TRANSNATIONAL ISSUES

Disputes—international: Tokelau included American Samoa's Swains Island (Olosega) in its 2006 draft independence constitution

TONGA

INTRODUCTION

Background: Tonga—unique among Pacific nations—never completely lost its indigenous governance. The archipelagos of "The Friendly Islands" were united into a Polynesian kingdom in 1845. Tonga became a constitutional monarchy in 1875 and a British protectorate in 1900; it withdrew from the protectorate and joined the Commonwealth of Nations in 1970. Tonga remains the only monarchy in the Pacific.

GEOGRAPHY

Location: Oceania, archipelago in the South Pacific Ocean, about two-thirds of the way from Hawaii to New Zealand

Geographic coordinates: 20 00 S, 175 00 W

Map references: Oceania

Area: *total:* 747 sq km

land: 717 sq km

water: 30 sq km

country comparison to the world: 190

Area—comparative: four times the size of Washington, DC

Land boundaries: 0 km

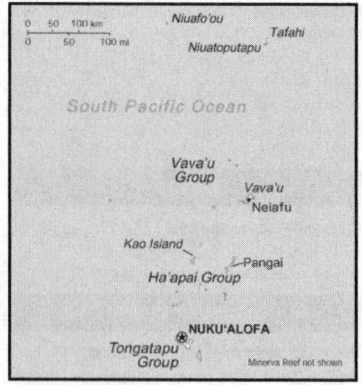

Coastline: 419 km

Maritime claims: *territorial sea:* 12 nm
exclusive economic zone: 200 nm
continental shelf: 200-m depth or to the depth of exploitation

Climate: tropical; modified by trade winds; warm season (December to May), cool season (May to December)

Terrain: mostly flat islands with limestone bedrock formed from uplifted coral formation; others have limestone overlying volcanic rock

Elevation: *mean elevation:* NA

elevation extremes: *lowest point:* Pacific Ocean 0 m
highest point: unnamed elevation on Kao Island 1,033 m

Natural resources: fish, arable land

Land use: *agricultural land:* 43.1%
arable land: 22.2%
permanent crops: 15.3%
permanent pasture: 5.6%
forest: 12.5%
other: 44.4% (2011 est.)

Irrigated land: 0 sq km (2012)

Natural hazards: cyclones (October to April); earthquakes and volcanic activity on Fonuafo'ou *volcanism:* moderate volcanic activity; Fonualei (elev. 180 m) has shown frequent activity in recent years, while Niuafo'ou (elev. 260 m), which last erupted in 1985, has forced evacuations; other historically active volcanoes include Late and Tofua

Environment—current issues: deforestation results as more and more land is being cleared for agriculture and settlement; some damage to coral reefs from starfish and indiscriminate coral and shell collectors; overhunting threatens native sea turtle populations

Environment—international agreements: *party to:* Biodiversity, Climate Change, Climate Change-Kyoto Protocol, Desertification, Law of the Sea, Marine Dumping, Marine Life Conservation, Ozone Layer Protection, Ship Pollution
signed, but not ratified: none of the selected agreements

Geography—note: archipelago of 169 islands (36 inhabited)

PEOPLE AND SOCIETY

Nationality: *noun:* Tongan(s)
adjective: Tongan

Ethnic groups: Tongan 96.6%, part-Tongan 1.7%, other 1.7%, unspecified 0.03% (2006 est.)

Languages: English and Tongan 87%, Tongan (official) 10.7%, English (official) 1.2%, other 1.1%, unspecified 0.03% (2006 est.)

Religions: Protestant 64.9% (includes Free Wesleyan Church 37.3%, Free Church of Tonga 11.4%, Church of Tonga 7.2%, Tokaikolo Christian Church 2.6%, Assembly of God 2.3%, Seventh Day Adventist 2.2%, Constitutional Church of Tonga 0.9%, Anglican 0.8% and Full Gospel Church 0.2%), Mormon 16.8%, Roman Catholic 15.6%, other 1.1%, none 0.03%, unspecified 1.7% (2006 est.)

Population: 106,501 (July 2015 est.)
country comparison to the world: 192

Age structure: *0–14 years:* 35.06% (male 18,971/female 18,370)
15–24 years: 19.44% (male 10,605/female 10,103)
25–54 years: 33.6% (male 17,880/female 17,901)
55–64 years: 5.61% (male 2,924/female 3,047)
65 years and over: 6.29% (male 3,050/female 3,650) (2015 est.)

Dependency ratios: *total dependency ratio:* 74.3%
youth dependency ratio: 64.1%
elderly dependency ratio: 10.2%
potential support ratio: 9.8% (2015 est.)

Median age: *total:* 22.3 years
male: 21.9 years
female: 22.8 years (2015 est.)
country comparison to the world: 177

Population growth rate: 0.03% (2015 est.)
country comparison to the world: 190

Birth rate: 23 births/1,000 population (2015 est.)
country comparison to the world: 66

Death rate: 4.85 deaths/1,000 population (2015 est.)
country comparison to the world: 192

Net migration rate: -17.84 migrant(s)/1,000 population (2015 est.)
country comparison to the world: 219

Urbanization: *urban population:* 23.7% of total population (2015)
rate of urbanization: 0.71% annual rate of change (2010–15 est.)

Major urban areas—population: NUKU'ALOFA 25,000 (2014)

Sex ratio: *at birth:* 1.03 male(s)/female
0–14 years: 1.03 male(s)/female
15–24 years: 1.05 male(s)/female
25–54 years: 1 male(s)/female
55–64 years: 0.96 male(s)/female
65 years and over: 0.84 male(s)/female
total population: 1.01 male(s)/female (2015 est.)

Mother's mean age at first birth: 24.9
note: Median age at first birth among women 25–49 (2012 est.)

Maternal mortality rate: 124 deaths/100,000 live births (2015 est.)
country comparison to the world: 66

Infant mortality rate: *total:* 11.96 deaths/1,000 live births
male: 12.38 deaths/1,000 live births
female: 11.53 deaths/1,000 live births (2015 est.)
country comparison to the world: 123

Life expectancy at birth: *total population:* 76.04 years
male: 74.53 years
female: 77.59 years (2015 est.)
country comparison to the world: 89

Total fertility rate: 3.26 children born/woman (2015 est.)
country comparison to the world: 48

Health expenditures: 4.7% of GDP (2013)
country comparison to the world: 129

Physicians density: 0.56 physicians/1,000 population (2010)

Hospital bed density: 2.6 beds/1,000 population (2010)

Drinking water source:
improved:
urban: 99.7% of population
rural: 99.6% of population
total: 99.6% of population
unimproved:
urban: 0.3% of population
rural: 0.4% of population
total: 0.4% of population (2015 est.)

Sanitation facility access:
improved:
urban: 97.6% of population
rural: 89% of population
total: 91% of population
unimproved:
urban: 2.4% of population
rural: 11% of population
total: 9% of population (2015 est.)

HIV/AIDS—adult prevalence rate: NA

HIV/AIDS—people living with HIV/AIDS: NA

HIV/AIDS—deaths: NA

Obesity—adult prevalence rate: 41.1% (2014)
country comparison to the world: 5

Children under the age of 5 years underweight: 1.9% (2012)

Literacy: *definition:* can read and write Tongan and/or English
total population: 99.4%
male: 99.3%
female: 99.4% (2015 est.)

GOVERNMENT

Country name: *conventional long form:* Kingdom of Tonga
conventional short form: Tonga
local long form: Pule'anga Tonga
local short form: Tonga
former: Friendly Islands
etymology: "tonga" means "south" in the Tongan language and refers to the country's geographic position in relation to central Polynesia

Government type: constitutional monarchy

Capital: *name:* Nuku'alofa

Geographic coordinates: 21 08 S, 175 12 W
time difference: UTC + 13 (18 hours ahead of Washington, DC, during Standard Time)

Administrative divisions: 5 island divisions; 'Eua, Ha'apai, Ongo Niua, Tongatapu, Vava'u

Independence: 4 June 1970 (from UK protectorate)

National holiday: National Day, 4 November (1875)

Constitution: adopted 4 November 1875, revised 1988; amended many times, last in 2014 (2016)

Legal system: English common law

International law organization participation: has not submitted an ICJ jurisdiction declaration; non-party state to the ICCt

Citizenship: *citizenship by birth:* no
citizenship by descent only: the father must be a citizen of Tonga; if a child is born out of wedlock, the mother must be a citizen of Tonga
dual citizenship recognized: yes
residency requirement for naturalization: 5 years

Suffrage: 21 years of age; universal

Executive branch: *chief of state:* King TUPOU VI (since 18 March 2012); note—on 18 March 2012, King George TUPOUV died and his brother, Crown Prince TUPOUTO'A Lavaka, assumed the throne as TUPOU VI

head of government: Prime Minister 'Akilisi POHIVA (since 30 December 2014)
cabinet: Cabinet nominated by the prime minister and appointed by the monarch
elections/appointments: the monarchy is heredi-tary; prime minister and deputy prime minister indirectly elected by the Legislative Assembly and appointed by the monarch; election last held on 21 December 2010 (next to be held in November 2014)
election results: 'Akilisi POHIVA (Democratic Party of the Friendly Islands) elected prime minis-ter by parliament on 29 December 2014; vote—15 of 26 votes
note: a Privy Council advises the monarch

Legislative branch: *description:* unicameral Leg-islative Assembly or Fale Alea (26 seats; 17 peo-ple's representatives directly elected in single-seat constituencies by simple majority vote and 9 indi-rectly elected by hereditary leaders; members serve 3-year terms)
elections: last held on 27 November 2014 (next to be held in 2017)
election results: percent of vote—NA; seats by party—Democratic Party 9, noble's representatives 9, independent 8

Judicial branch: *highest court(s):* Court of Appeal (consists of the court president and a number of judges determined by the monarch); note—appeals beyond the Court of Appeal are brought before the King in Privy Council, the monarch's advisory organ that has both judicial and legisla-tive powers
judge selection and term of office: judge appoint-ments and tenures made by the King in Privy Council, judge appointments subject to consent of the Legislative Assembly
subordinate courts: Supreme Court; Magistrate's Courts; Land Courts

Political parties and leaders: Democratic Party of the Friendly Islands [Samuela 'Akilisi POHIVA] People's Democratic Party or PDP [Tesina FUKO] Sustainable Nation-Building Party [Sione FONUA] Tonga Democratic Labor Party
Tonga Human Rights and Democracy Movement or THRDM

Political pressure groups and leaders: Human Rights and Democracy Movement Tonga or HRDMT [Rev. Simote VEA, chairman]

Public Servant's Association [Finau TUTONE]

International organization participation: ACP, ADB, AOSIS, C, FAO, G-77, IBRD, ICAO, ICRM, IDA, IFAD, IFC, IFRCS, IHO, IMF, IMO, IMSO, Interpol, IOC, IPU, ITU, ITUC (NGOs), OPCW, PIF, Sparteca, SPC, UN, UNCTAD, UNESCO, UNIDO, UPU, WCO, WHO, WIPO, WMO, WTO

Diplomatic representation in the US: *chief of mis-sion:* Ambassador Mahe'uli'uli Sandhurst TUP-OUNIUA (since 10 September 2013)
chancery: 250 E.51st Street, New York, NY, 10022
telephone: [1] (917) 369-1025
FAX: [1] (917) 369-1024 consulate(s) general: San Francisco

Diplomatic representation from the US: the US does not have an embassy in Tonga; the US Ambassador to Fiji is accredited to Tonga

Flag description: red with a bold red cross on a white rectangle in the upper hoist-side corner; the cross reflects the deep-rooted Christianity in Tonga; red represents the blood of Christ and his sacrifice; white signifies purity

National symbol(s): red cross on white field, arms equal length; National colors: red, white

National anthem: *name:* "Koefasi 'oetu"i 'oe 'Otu Tonga" (Song of the King of the Tonga Islands)
lyrics/music: Uelingatoni Ngu TUPOUM-ALOHI/Karl Gustavus SCHMITT
note: in use since 1875; more commonly known as "F asi Fakafonua" (National Song)

ECONOMY

Economy—overview: Tonga has a small, open, island economy and is the last constitutional monarchy among the Pacific Island countries. It has a narrow export base in agricultural goods. Squash, vanilla beans, and yams are the main crops. Agricultural exports, including fish, make up two-thirds of total exports. Tourism is the second-largest source of hard currency earnings following remittances. Tonga had 45,000 visitors in 2013. The country must import a high propor-tion of its food, mainly from New Zealand. The country remains dependent on external aid and remittances from overseas Tongans to offset its trade deficit. The government is emphasizing the development of the private sector, encouraging investment, and is committing increased funds for healthcare and education. Tonga's English-speak-ing and educated workforce offer a viable labor market, and the tropical climate provides fertile soil. Renewable energy and deep sea mining also offer opportunities for investment.
Tonga has a reason ably sound basic infrastructure and well developed social services. The govern-ment faces high unemployment among the young, moderate inflation, pressures for democratic reform, and rising civil service expenditures.

GDP (purchasing power parity): $526 million (2015 est.)
$512.6 million (2014 est.)
$502.4 million (2013 est.)
note: data are in 2015 US dollars
country comparison to the world: 213

GDP (official exchange rate): $414 million (2015 est.)

GDP—real growth rate: 2.6% (2015 est.)
2% (2014 est.)
-0.6% (2013 est.)
country comparison to the world: 118

GDP—per capita (PPP): $5,100 (2015 est.)
$4,900 (2014 est.)
$4,800 (2013 est.)
note: data are in 2015 US dollars
country comparison to the world: 167

GDP—composition, by end use:
household consumption: 79.9%
government consumption: 21.6%
investment in fixed capital: 40.2%
investment in inventories: 0%
exports of goods and services: 18.7%
imports of goods and services: -60.4% (2015 est.)

GDP—composition, by sector of origin:
agriculture: 18.3%
industry: 18.8%
services: 62.9% (2015 est.)

Agriculture—products: squash, coconuts, copra, bananas, vanilla beans, cocoa, coffee, sweet pota-toes, cassava, taro and kava

Industries: tourism, construction, fishing

Industrial production growth rate: 1.2% (2015 est.)
country comparison to the world: 140

Labor force: 33,800 (2011 est.)
country comparison to the world: 202

Labor force—by occupation: *agriculture:* 27.5%
industry: 27.5%
services: 45.1% (2006 est.)

Unemployment rate: 1.1% (2011 est.)
1.1% (2006)
country comparison to the world: 6

Population below poverty line: 24% (FY03/04 est.)

Household income or consumption by percentage share: *lowest:* 10%: NA%
highest: 10%: NA%

Budget: *revenues:* $146.3 million
expenditures: $146.3 million (2015 est.)
Taxes and other revenues: 33% of GDP (2015 est.)
country comparison to the world: 71

Budget surplus (+) or deficit (−): 0% of GDP (2015 est.)
country comparison to the world: 33

Public debt: 45.1% of GDP (2013)
46.5% of GDP (2012)
country comparison to the world: 99

Fiscal year: 1 July—30 June

Inflation rate (consumer prices): -0.1% (2015 est.)
1.2% (2014 est.)
country comparison to the world: 38

Commercial bank prime lending rate: 8.6% (31 December 2015 est.)
8.89% (31 December 2014 est.)
country comparison to the world: 101

Stock of narrow money: $83.91 million (31 December 2015 est.)
$95.17 million (31 December 2014 est.)
country comparison to the world: 188

Stock of broad money: $198.4 million (31 Decem-ber 2014 est.)
$195.1 million (31 December 2013 est.)

country comparison to the world: 190

Stock of domestic credit: $106.6 million (31 December 2015 est.)
$121.2 million (31 December 2014 est.)
country comparison to the world: 183

Market value of publicly traded shares: $NA

Current account balance: -$32 million (2015 est.)
-$37 million (2014 est.)
country comparison to the world: 60

Exports: $29.4 million (2015 est.)
$38.8 million (2014 est.)
country comparison to the world: 206

Exports—commodities: squash, fish, vanilla beans, root crops

Exports—partners: Japan 15.9%, US 15.4%, Fiji 12.7%, NZ 12.5%, South Korea 11%, Samoa 10.7%, Australia 7.5%, American Samoa 6.8% (2015)

Imports: $151.9 million (2015 est.)
$152.7 million (2014 est.)
country comparison to the world: 210

Imports—commodities: foodstuffs, machinery and transport equipment, fuels, chemicals

Imports—partners: Fiji 37.7%, NZ 21.2%, China 14.2%, US 6.4%, Australia 4.5% (2015)

Reserves of foreign exchange and gold: $166.5 million (31 December 2015 est.)
$158.8 million (31 December 2014 est.)
country comparison to the world: 162

Debt—external: $215 million (31 December 2014 est.)
$198.9 million (31 December 2013 est.)
country comparison to the world: 189

Stock of direct foreign investment—at home: $76.97 million (31 December 2015 est.)
$73.97 million (31 December 2014 est.)
country comparison to the world: 118

Exchange rates: pa'anga (TOP) per US dollar—
2.05 (2015 est.)
1.847 (2014 est.)
1.847 (2013 est.)
1.72 (2012 est.)
1.729 (2011 est.)

ENERGY

Electricity—production: 48 million kWh (2012 est.)
country comparison to the world: 208

Electricity—consumption: 44.64 million kWh (2012 est.)
country comparison to the world: 207

Electricity—exports: 0 kWh (2013)
country comparison to the world: 203

Electricity—imports: 0 kWh (2013 est.)
country comparison to the world: 208

Electricity—installed generating capacity: 14,000 kW (2012 est.)
country comparison to the world: 206

Electricity—from fossil fuels: 100% of total installed capacity (2012 est.)
country comparison to the world: 31

Electricity—from nuclear fuels: 0% of total installed capacity (2012 est.)
country comparison to the world: 190

Electricity—from hydro electric plants: 0% of total installed capacity (2012 est.)
country comparison to the world: 207

Electricity—from other renewable sources: 0% of total installed capacity (2012 est.)
country comparison to the world: 132

Crude oil—production: 0 bbl/day (2014 est.)
country comparison to the world: 197

Crude oil—exports: 0 bbl/day (2012 est.)
country comparison to the world: 196

Crude oil—imports: 0 bbl/day (2012 est.)
country comparison to the world: 133

Crude oil—proved reserves: 0 bbl (1 January 2010 est.)
country comparison to the world: 198

Refined petroleum products—production: 0 bbl/day (2012 est.)
country comparison to the world: 135

Refined petroleum products—consumption: 1,200 bbl/day (2013 est.)
country comparison to the world: 198

Refined petroleum products—exports: 0 bbl/day (2012 est.)
country comparison to the world: 136

Refined petroleum products—imports: 1,202 bbl/day (2012 est.)
country comparison to the world: 193

Natural gas—production: 0 cu m (2013 est.)
country comparison to the world: 135

Natural gas—consumption: 0 cu m (2013 est.)
country comparison to the world: 199

Natural gas—exports: 0 cu m (2013 est.)
country comparison to the world: 192

Natural gas—imports: 0 cu m (2013 est.)
country comparison to the world: 140

Natural gas—proved reserves: 0 cu m (1 January 2014 est.)
country comparison to the world: 199

Carbon dioxide emissions from consumption of energy: 188,800 Mt (2012 est.)
country comparison to the world: 196

COMMUNICATIONS

Telephones—fixed lines: *total subscriptions:* 12,000
subscriptions per 100 inhabitants: 11 (2014 est.)
country comparison to the world: 195

Telephone—mobile cellular: *total:* 68,000
subscriptions per 100 inhabitants: 64 (2014 est.)
country comparison to the world: 197

Telephone system: *general assessment:* competition between Tonga Telecommunications Corporation (TCC) and Digicel Tonga Limited is accelerating expansion of telecommunications; both parties provide high speed Internet, mobile telephone networks, and international telecom services; Digicel also holds a telecommunication license after its acquisition of TonFon (a subsidiary of former Shoreline Communications Tonga); submarine cable infrastructure, managed by Tonga Cable Limited, has also been brought to the country by Asian Development Bank and World Bank aid
domestic: combined fixed-line and mobile-cellular teledensity about 80 telephones per 100 persons; fully automatic switched network
international: country code—676; satellite earth station—1 Intelsat (Pacific Ocean) (2015)

Broadcast media: 1 state-owned TV station and 3 privately owned TV stations; satellite and cable TV services are available; 1 state-owned and 3 privately owned radio stations; Radio Australia broadcasts available via satellite (2015)
Radio broadcast stations: AM 1, FM 4, short-wave 1 (2001)
Television broadcast stations: 3 (2004)

Internet country code: .to

Internet hosts: 5,367 (2012)
country comparison to the world: 144

Internet users: *total:* 40,400
percent of population: 37.9% (2014 est.)
country comparison to the world: 191

TRANSPORTATION

Airports: 6 (2013)
country comparison to the world: 177

Airports—with paved runways: *total:* 1
2,438 to 3,047 m: 1 (2013)

Airports—with unpaved runways: *total:* 5
1,524 to 2,437 m: 1
914 to 1,523 m: 3 under 914 m: 1 (2013)

Roadways: *total:* 680 km
paved: 184 km
unpaved: 496 km (2011)
country comparison to the world: 190

Merchant marine: *total:* 7
by type: cargo 4, carrier 1, passenger/cargo 2
foreign-owned: 2 (Australia 1, UK 1) (2010)
country comparison to the world: 122

Ports and terminals: *major seaport(s):* Nuku'alofa, Neiafu, Pangai

MILITARY AND SECURITY

Military branches: Tonga Defense Services (TDS): Land Force (Royal Guard), Maritime Force (includes Royal Marines, Air Wing) (2013)

Military service age and obligation: 16 years of age for voluntary enlistment (with parental consent); no conscription; the king retains the right to call up "all those capable of bearing arms" in wartime (2012)

TRANSNATIONAL ISSUES

Disputes—international: none

TRINIDAD AND TOBAGO

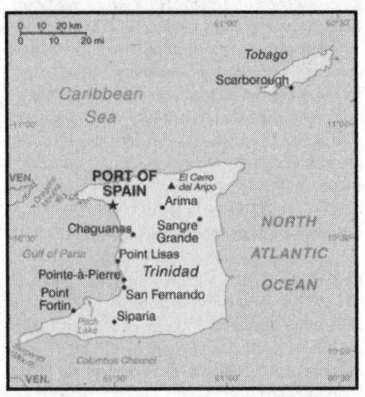

INTRODUCTION

Background: First colonized by the Spanish, the islands came under British control in the early 19th century. The islands' sugar industry was hurt by the emancipation of the slaves in 1834. Manpower was replaced with the importation of contract laborers from India between 1845 and 1917, which boosted sugar production as well as the cocoa industry. The discovery of oil on Trinidad in 1910 added another important export. Independence was attained in 1962. The country is one of the most prosperous in the Caribbean thanks largely to petroleum and Natural gas production and processing. Tourism, mostly in Tobago, is targeted for expansion and is growing. The government is coping with a rise in violent crime.

GEOGRAPHY

Location: Caribbean, islands between the Caribbean Sea and the North Atlantic Ocean, northeast of Venezuela

Geographic coordinates: 11 00 N, 61 00 W

Map references: Central America and the Caribbean

Area: *total:* 5,128 sq km
land: 5,128 sq km
water: 0 sq km
country comparison to the world: 174

Area—comparative: slightly smaller than Delaware

Land boundaries: 0 km

Coastline: 362 km

Maritime claims: measured from claimed Archipelagic baselines
territorial sea: 12 nm
contiguous zone: 24 nm
exclusive economic zone: 200 nm
continental shelf: 200 nm or to the outer edge of the continental margin

Climate: tropical; rainy season (June to December)

Terrain: mostly plains with some hills and low mountains

Elevation: *mean elevation:* 83 m

elevation extremes: *lowest point:* Caribbean Sea 0 m
highest point: El Cerro del Aripo 940 m

Natural resources: petroleum, Natural gas, asphalt

Land use: *agricultural land:* 10.6%
arable land: 4.9%
permanent crops: 4.3%
permanent pasture: 1.4%
forest: 44%
other: 45.4% (2011 est.)

Irrigated land: 70 sq km (2012)

Total renewable water resources: 3.84 cu km (2011)

Freshwater withdrawal (domestic/industrial/agricultural): *total:* 0.23 cu km/yr (67%/25%/8%)
per capita: 177.9 cu m/yr (2005)

Natural hazards: outside usual path of hurricanes and other tropical storms

Environment—current issues: water pollution from agricultural chemicals, industrial wastes, and raw sewage; oil pollution of beaches; deforestation; soil erosion

Environment—international agreements: *party to:* Biodiversity, Climate Change, Climate Change-Kyoto Protocol, Desertification, Endangered Species, Hazardous Wastes, Law of the Sea, Marine Dumping, Marine Life Conservation, Ozone Layer Protection, Ship Pollution, Tropical Timber 83, Tropical Timber 94, Wetlands
signed, but not ratified: none of the selected agreements

Geography—note: Pitch Lake, on Trinidad's southwestern coast, is the world's largest Natural reservoir of asphalt

PEOPLE AND SOCIETY

Nationality: *noun:* Trinidadian(s), Tobagonian(s)
adjective: Trinidadian, Tobagonian

Ethnic groups: East Indian 35.4%, African 34.2%, mixed—other 15.3%, mixed African/East Indian 7.7%, other 1.3%, unspecified 6.2% (2011 est.)

Languages: English (official), Caribbean Hindustani (a dialect of Hindi), French, Spanish, Chinese

Religions: Protestant 32.1% (Pentecostal/Evangelical/Full Gospel 12%, Baptist 6.9%, Anglican 5.7%, Seventh-Day Adventist 4.1%, Presbyterian/Congretation al 2.5%, other Protestant 0.9%), Roman Catholic 21.6%, Hindu 18.2%, Muslim 5%, Jehovah's Witness 1.5%, other 8.4%, none 2.2%, unspecified 11.1% (2011 est.)

Population: 1,222,363 (July 2015 est.)
country comparison to the world: 160

Age structure: *0–14 years:* 19.41% (male 120,876/female 116,336)
15–24 years: 12.59% (male 79,949/female 73,888)

25–54 years: 46.59% (male 295,970/female 273,481)
55–64 years: 11.59% (male 70,466/female 71,196)
65 years and over: 9.83% (male 52,199/female 68,002) (2015 est.)

Dependency ratios: *total dependency ratio:* 43.2%
youth dependency ratio: 29.8%
elderly dependency ratio: 13.5%
potential support ratio: 7.4% (2015 est.)

Median age: *total:* 35 years
male: 34.5 years
female: 35.5 years (2015 est.)
country comparison to the world: 75

Population growth rate: -0.13% (2015 est.)
country comparison to the world: 208

Birth rate: 13.46 births/1,000 population (2015 est.)
country comparison to the world: 148

Death rate: 8.56 deaths/1,000 population (2015 est.)
country comparison to the world: 75

Net migration rate: -6.25 migrant(s)/1,000 population (2015 est.)
country comparison to the world: 199

Urbanization: *urban population:* 8.4% of total population (2015)
rate of urbanization: -1.2% annual rate of change (2010–15 est.)

Major urban areas—population: PORT-OF-SPAIN (capital) 34,000 (2014)

Sex ratio: *at birth:* 1.03 male(s)/female
0–14 years: 1.04 male(s)/female
15–24 years: 1.08 male(s)/female
25–54 years: 1.08 male(s)/female
55–64 years: 0.99 male(s)/female
65 years and over: 0.77 male(s)/female
total population: 1.03 male(s)/female (2015 est.)

Maternal mortality rate: 63 deaths/100,000 live births (2015 est.)
country comparison to the world: 112

Infant mortality rate: *total:* 23.9 deaths/1,000 live births
male: 25.11 deaths/1,000 live births
female: 22.66 deaths/1,000 live births (2015 est.)
country comparison to the world: 72

Life expectancy at birth: *total population:* 72.59 years
male: 69.69 years
female: 75.56 years (2015 est.)
country comparison to the world: 138

Total fertility rate: 1.71 children born/woman (2015 est.)
country comparison to the world: 171

Contraceptive prevalence rate: 42.5% (2006)

Health expenditures: 5.5% of GDP (2013)
country comparison to the world: 131

Physicians density: 1.18 physicians/1,000 population (2007)

Hospital bed density: 2.7 beds/1,000 population (2012)

Drinking water source:
improved:
urban: 95.1% of population
rural: 95.1% of population
total: 95.1% of population
unimproved:
urban: 4.9% of population
rural: 4.9% of population
total: 4.9% of population (2015 est.)

Sanitation facility access:
improved:
urban: 91.5% of population
rural: 91.5% of population
total: 91.5% of population
unimproved:
urban: 8.5% of population
rural: 8.5% of population
total: 8.5% of population (2015 est.)

HIV/AIDS—adult prevalence rate: 1.65% (2013 est.)
country comparison to the world: 30

HIV/AIDS—people living with HIV/AIDS: 14,000 (2013 est.)
country comparison to the world: 90

HIV/AIDS—deaths: 700 (2013 est.)
country comparison to the world: 74

Obesity—adult prevalence rate: 32.3% (2014)
country comparison to the world: 31

Literacy: definition: age 15 and over can read and write
total population: 99%
male: 99.2%
female: 98.7% (2015 est.)

Child labor—children ages 5–14: total number: 1,201
percentage: 1% (2006 est.)

Unemployment, youth ages 15–24: total: 9.2%
male: 7.7%
female: 11.4% (2013 est.)
country comparison to the world: 98

GOVERNMENT

Country name: conventional long form: Republic of Trinidad and Tobago
conventional short form: Trinidad and Tobago
etymology: explorer Christopher COLUMBUS named the larger island "La Isla de la Trinidad" (The Island of the Trinity) on 31 July 1498 on his third voyage; the tobacco grown and smoked by the natives of the smaller island or its elongated cigar shape may account for the "tobago" name, which is spelled "tobaco" in Spanish

Government type: parliamentary republic

Capital: name: Port of Spain

Geographic coordinates: 10 39 N, 61 31 W
time difference: UTC-4 (1 hour ahead of Washington, DC, during Standard Time)

Administrative divisions: 9 regions, 3 boroughs, 2 cities, 1 ward

regions: Couva/Tabaquite/Talparo, Diego Martin, Mayaro/Rio Claro, Penal/Debe, Princes Town, Sangre Grande, San Juan/Laventille, Siparia, Tunapuna/Piarco
borough: Arima, Chaguanas, Point Fortin
cities: Port of Spain, San Fernando ward: Tobago

Independence: 31 August 1962 (from the UK)

National holiday: Independence Day, 31 August (1962)

Constitution: previous 1962; latest 1976; amended many times, last in 2007 (2016)

Legal system: English common law; judicial review of legislative acts in the Supreme Court

International law organization participation: has not submitted an ICJ jurisdiction declaration; accepts ICCt jurisdiction

Citizenship: citizenship by birth: yes
citizenship by descent: yes
dual citizenship recognized: yes
residency requirement for naturalization: 8 years

Suffrage: 18 years of age; universal

Executive branch: chief of state: President Anthony CARMON a (since 18 March 2013)

head of government: Prime Minister Keith ROWLEY (since 9 September 2015)
cabinet: Cabinet appointed from among members of Parliament
elections/appointments: president indirectly elected by an electoral college of selected Senate and House of Representatives members for a 5-year term (eligible for a second term); election last held on 15 February 2013 (next to be held by February 2018); the president usually appoints the leader of the majority party in the House of Representatives as prime minister
election results: Anthony CARMON a (independent) elected president; electoral college vote—100%

Legislative branch: description: bicameral Parliament consists of the Senate (31 seats; 16 members appointed by the ruling party, 9 by the president, and 6 by the opposition party; members serve 5-year terms;) and the House of Representatives (41 seats; members directly elected in single-seat constituencies by simple majority vote to serve 5-year terms)
note: Tobago has a unicameral House of Assembly (16 seats; 12 assemblymen directly elected by simple majority vote and 4 appointed councillors—3 on the advice of the chief secretary and 1 on the advice of the minority leader; members serve 4-year terms)
elections: House of Representatives—last held on 7 September 2015 (next to be held in 2020)
election results: House of Representatives—percent of vote—NA; seats by party—PNM 23, UNC 18

Judicial branch: highest resident court(s): Supreme Court of the Judicature (consists of a chief justice for both the Court of Appeal with 12 judges and the High Court with 24 judges); note—Trinidad and Tobago can file appeals beyond its

Supreme Court to the Caribbean Court of Justice, with final appeal to the Judicial Committee of the Privy Council (in London)
judge selection and term of office: Supreme Court chief justice appointed by the president after consultation with the prime minister and the parliamentary leader of the opposition; other judges appointed by the Judicial Legal Services Commission, headed by the chief justice and 5 members with judicial experience; all judges appointed for life with mandatory retirement normally at age 65
subordinate courts: Courts of Summary Criminal Jurisdiction; Petty Civil Courts; Family Court

Political parties and leaders: Congress of the People or COP [Prakash RAMADHAR]
Democratic Action Congress or DAC [Hochoy CHARLES] (only active in Tobago)
Democratic National Alliance or DNA [Charles CARSON] (coalition of NAR, DDPT, MND)
Movement for National Development or MND [Garvin NICHOLAS]
National Alliance for Reconstruction or NAR [Lennox SANKERSINGH]
People's National Movement or PNM [Keith ROWLEY]
Tobago Organization of the People or TOP [Ashworth JACK]
United National Congress or UNC [Kamla PERSAD-BI SSESSAR]

Political pressure groups and leaders: Jamaat-al Muslimeen [Yasin ABU BAKR]

International organization participation: ACP, AOSIS, C, Caricom, CDB, CELAC, EITI (compliant country), FAO, G-24, G-77, IADB, IAEA, IBRD, ICAO, ICC (NGOs), ICCt, ICRM, IDA, IFAD, IFC, IFRCS, IHO, ILO, IMF, IMO, Interpol, IOC, IOM, IPU, ISO, ITSO, ITU, ITUC (NGOs), LAES, MIGA, NAM, OAS, OPANAL, OPCW, Pacific Alliance (observer), Paris Club (associate), UN, UNCTAD, UNESCO, UNIDO, UPU, WCO, WFTU (NGOs), WHO, WIPO, WMO, WTO

Diplomatic representation in the US: chief of mission: Ambassador (vacant); Charge d'Affaires Colin MIchael CONNELLY (since 15 August 2015
chancery: 1708 Massachusetts Avenue NW, Washington, DC 20036
telephone: [1] (202) 467-6490
FAX: [1] (202) 785-3130
consulate(s) general: Miami, New York

Diplomatic representation from the US: chief of mission: Ambassador John L. ESTRADA (since 19 April 2016)
embassy: 15 Queen's Park West, Port of Spain
mailing address: P. O. Box 752, Port of Spain
telephone: [1] (868) 622-6371 through 6376
FAX: [1] (868) 822-5905

Flag description: red with a white-edged black diagon al band from the upper hoist side to the lower fly side; the colors represent the elements of earth, water, and fire; black stands for the wealth of the land and the dedication of the people; white symbolizes the sea surrounding the islands, the purity of the country's aspirations, and equality;

red symbolizes the warmth and energy of the sun, the vitality of the land, and the courage and friendliness of its people

National symbol(s): scarlet ibis (bird of Trinidad), cocrico (bird of Tobago), Chaconia flower; National colors: red, white, black

National anthem: *name:* "Forged From the Love of Liberty"
lyrics/music: Patrick Stanislaus CASTAGNE
note: adopted 1962; song originally created to serve as an anthem for the West Indies Federation; adopted by Trinidad and Tobago following the Federation's dissolution in 1962

ECONOMY

Economy—overview: Trinidad and Tobago attracts considerable foreign direct investment, particularly in energy, and has one of the highest per capita incomes in Latin America and the Caribbean. Trinidad and Tobago is the leading Caribbean producer of oil and gas, and its economy is heavily dependent upon these resources. It also supplies manufactured goods, notably food products and beverages, as well as cement to the Caribbean region. Oil and gas account for about 40% of GDP and 80% of exports but only 5% of employment. Growth has been fueled by investments in liquefied Natural gas, petrochemicals, and steel with additional upstream and downstream investment planned. Oil production has declined over the last decade as the country focused the majority of its efforts on Natural gas. Economic growth between 2000 and 2007 averaged slightly over 8% per year, significantly above the region al average of about 3.7% for that same period; however, GDP slowed down since then and contracted during 2009–12 due to depressed Natural gas prices and changing markets. The current administration has been working to arrest this decline by opening bid rounds and providing fiscal incentives for investments in onshore and deep water acreage to boost oil reserves and production. The government keeps a close watch on the changing global gas markets and has shown flexibility in diversifying Natural gas export destinations. The economy benefits from a growing trade surplus with the US, Trinidad and Tobago's leading trade partner.

Although Trinidad and Tobago enjoys cheap electricity from Natural gas, the renewable energy sector has recently garnered increased interest. The country is also a region al financial center with a well-regulated and stable financial system. Other sectors the Government of Trinidad and Tobago has targeted for increased investment and projected growth include tourism, agriculture, information and communications technology, and shipping.

The previous MANNING administration benefited from fiscal surpluses fueled by the dynamic exportsector; however, declines in oil and gas prices have reduced government revenues, challenging the current government's commitment to maintaining high levels of public investment. Crime and bureaucratic hurdles continue to be the biggest deterrents for attracting more foreign direct investment and business.

GDP (purchasing power parity): $44.31 billion (2015 est.)
$45.1 billion (2014 est.)
$45.56 billion (2013 est.)
note: data are in 2015 US dollars
country comparison to the world: 111

GDP (official exchange rate): $24.55 billion (2015 est.)

GDP—real growth rate: -1.8% (2015 est.)
-1% (2014 est.)
2.3% (2013 est.)
country comparison to the world: 207

GDP—per capita (PPP): $32,600 (2015 est.)
$33,400 (2014 est.)
$33,900 (2013 est.)
note: data are in 2015 US dollars
country comparison to the world: 57

Gross National saving: 8% of GDP (2015 est.)
18.1% of GDP (2014 est.)
20.7% of GDP (2013 est.)
country comparison to the world: 159

GDP—composition, by end use:
household consumption: 40.1%
government consumption: 12.3%
investment in fixed capital: 8.5%
investment in inventories: 0.5%
exports of goods and services: 66.8%
imports of goods and services: -28.2% (2015 est.)

GDP—composition, by sector of origin:
agriculture: 0.5%
industry: 14.6%
services: 84.9% (2015 est.)

Agriculture—products: cocoa, rice, citrus, coffee; sugar; vegetables; poultry

Industries: petroleum and petroleum Products, liquefied Natural gas (LNG), methanol, ammonia, urea, steel products, beverages, food processing, cement, cotton textiles

Industrial production growth rate: 1% (2015 est.)
country comparison to the world: 147

Labor force: 626,400 (2015 est.)
country comparison to the world: 154

Labor force—by occupation: *agriculture:* 3.8%
manufacturing, mining, and quarrying: 12.8%
constru ction and utilities: 20.4%
services: 62.9% (2007 est.)

Unemployment rate: 3.5% (2015 est.)
3.3% (2014 est.)
country comparison to the world: 31

Population below poverty line: 17% (2007 est.)

Household income or consumption by percentage share: *lowest:* 10%: NA%
highest: 10%: NA%

Budget: *revenues:* $8.802 billion
expenditures: $9.849 billion (2015 est.)
Taxes and other revenues: 31.8% of GDP (2015 est.)
country comparison to the world: 79

Budget surplus (+) or deficit (–): -3.8% of GDP (2015 est.)
country comparison to the world: 141

Public debt: 42.1% of GDP (2015 est.)

39.5% of GDP (2014 est.)
country comparison to the world: 108

Fiscal year: 1 October—30 September

Inflation rate (consumer prices): 4.7% (2015 est.)
5.7% (2014 est.)
country comparison to the world: 168

Central bank discount rate: 4.25% (31 December 2010)
7.25% (31 December 2009)
country comparison to the world: 90

Commercial bank prime lending rate: 8% (31 December 2015 est.)
7.8% (31 December 2014 est.)
country comparison to the world: 109

Stock of narrow money: $7.422 billion (31 December 2015 est.)
$6.907 billion (31 December 2014 est.)
country comparison to the world: 89

Stock of broad money: $17.98 billion (31 December 2015 est.)
$16.92 billion (31 December 2014 est.)
country comparison to the world: 92

Stock of domestic credit: $9.06 billion (31 December 2015 est.)
$8.431 billion (31 December 2014 est.)
country comparison to the world: 105

Market value of publicly traded shares: $15.17 billion (31 December 2012 est.)
$14.73 billion (31 December 2011)
$12.16 billion (31 December 2010 est.)
country comparison to the world: 68

Current account balance: -$1.329 billion (2015 est.) $1.266 billion (2014 est.)
country comparison to the world: 135

Exports: $8.713 billion (2015 est.)
$11.73 billion (2014 est.)
country comparison to the world: 94

Exports—commodities: petroleum and petroleum Products, liquefied Natural gas, methanol, ammonia, urea, steel products, beverages, cereal and cereal products, sugar, cocoa, coffee, citrus fruit, vegetables, flowers

Exports—partners: US 26.3%, Argentina 12%, Brazil 6.6%, Chile 5.3%, Dominican Republic 5.2%, Barbados 5% (2015)

Imports: $7.62 billion (2015 est.)
$8.904 billion (2014 est.)
country comparison to the world: 109

Imports—commodities: mineral fuels, lubricants, machinery, transportation equipment, manufactured goods, food, chemicals, live animals

Imports—partners: US 35.6%, China 6.8%, Gabon 6.6% (2015)

Reserves of foreign exchange and gold: $11.69 billion (31 December 2015 est.)
$11.98 billion (31 December 2014 est.)
country comparison to the world: 73

Debt—external: $4.879 billion (31 December 2014 est.)
$4.676 billion (31 December 2013 est.)
country comparison to the world: 131

Stock of direct foreign investment—at home: $102 billion (31 December 2008 est.)
$12.44 billion (2007)
country comparison to the world: 45

Stock of direct foreign investment—abroad: $3.829 billion (2007)
country comparison to the world: 72

Exchange rates: Trinidad and Tobago dollars (TTD) per US dollar—
6.383 (2015 est.)
6.4041 (2014 est.)
6.4041 (2013 est.)
6.39 (2012 est.)
6.4094 (2011 est.)

ENERGY

Electricity—production: 8.604 billion kWh (2012 est.)
country comparison to the world: 100

Electricity—consumption: 8.365 billion kWh (2012 est.)
country comparison to the world: 96

Electricity—exports: 0 kWh (2013 est.)
country comparison to the world: 201

Electricity—imports: 0 kWh (2013 est.)
country comparison to the world: 206

Electricity—installed generating capacity: 2.104 million kW (2012 est.)
country comparison to the world: 104

Electricity—from fossil fuels: 99.8% of total installed capacity (2012 est.)
country comparison to the world: 40

Electricity—from nuclear fuels: 0% of total installed capacity (2012 est.)
country comparison to the world: 186

Electricity—from hydro electric plants: 0% of total installed capacity (2012 est.)
country comparison to the world: 205

Electricity—from other renewable sources: 0.2% of total installed capacity (2012 est.)
country comparison to the world: 114

Crude oil—production: 81,260 bbl/day (2014 est.)
country comparison to the world: 48

Crude oil—exports: 30,800 bbl/day (2012 est.)
country comparison to the world: 51

Crude oil—imports: 59,180 bbl/day (2012 est.)
country comparison to the world: 54

Crude oil—proved reserves: 728.3 million bbl (1 January 2015 est.)
country comparison to the world: 44

Refined petroleum products—production: 109,000 bbl/day (2012 est.)
country comparison to the world: 71

Refined petroleum products—consumption: 42,000 bbl/day (2013 est.)
country comparison to the world: 106

Refined petroleum products—exports: 111,000 bbl/day (2012 est.)
country comparison to the world: 44

Refined petroleum products—imports: 8,823 bbl/day (2012 est.)
country comparison to the world: 140

Natural gas—production: 42.8 billion cu m (2013 est.)

country comparison to the world: 20

Natural gas—consumption: 20.2 billion cu m (2013 est.)
country comparison to the world: 37

Natural gas—exports: 19.8 billion cu m (2013 est.)
country comparison to the world: 14

Natural gas—imports: 0 cu m (2013 est.)
country comparison to the world: 138

Natural gas—proved reserves: 371.2 billion cu m (1 January 2014 est.)
country comparison to the world: 37

Carbon dioxide emissions from consumption of energy: 51.27 million Mt (2012 est.)
country comparison to the world: 57

COMMUNICATIONS

Telephones—fixed lines: *total subscriptions:* 290,000
subscriptions per 100 inhabitants: 24 (2014 est.)
country comparison to the world: 116

Telephones—mobile cellular: *total:* 2 million
subscriptions per 100 inhabitants: 162 (2014 est.)
country comparison to the world: 152

Telephone system: *general assessment:* excellent international service; good local service
domestic: combined fixed-line and mobile-cellular teledensity roughly 170 telephones per 100 persons
international: country code—1 -868; submarine cable systems provide connectivity to US and parts of the Caribbean and South America; satellite earth station—1 Intelsat (Atlantic Ocean); tropospheric scatter to Barbados and Guyana (2011)

Broadcast media: 5 TV networks, one of which is state-owned, broadcast on multiple stations; multiple cable TV subscription service providers; multiple radio networks, one state-owned, broadcast over about 35 stations (2007)
Radio broadcast stations: AM 2, FM 28, shortwave 0 (2008)
Television broadcast stations: 6 (2005)

Internet country code: .tt

Internet hosts: 241,690 (2012)
country comparison to the world: 69

Internet users: *total:* 779,900
percent of population: 63.7% (2014 est.)
country comparison to the world: 126

TRANSPORTATION

Airports: 4 (2013)
country comparison to the world: 187

Airports—with paved runways: *total:* 2
over 3,047 m: 1
2,438 to 3,047 m: 1 (2013)

Airports—with unpaved runways: *total:* 2
914 to 1,523 m: 1
under 914 m: 1 (2013)

Pipelines: condensate 257 km; condensate/gas 11 km; gas 1,567 km; oil 587 km (2013)

Roadways: *total:* 8,320 km
paved: 4,252 km
unpaved: 4,068 km (2001)
country comparison to the world: 140

Merchant marine: *total:* 4
by type: passenger 1, passenger/cargo 2, petroleum tanker 1

registered in other countries: 2 (unknown 2) (2010)
country comparison to the world: 131

Ports and terminals: *major seaport(s):* Point Fortin, Point Lisas, Port of Spain, Scarborough
oilterminals: Galeota Point terminal
LNG terminal(s) (export): Port Fortin

MILITARY AND SECURITY

Military branches: *Trinidad and Tobago Defense Force (TTDF):* Trinidad and Tobago Army, Coast Guard, Air Guard, Defense Force Reserves (2010)

Military service age and obligation: 18–25 years of age for voluntary military service (16 years of age with parental consent); no conscription; Trinidad and Tobago citizenship and completion of secondary school required (2012)

TRANSNATIONAL ISSUES

Disputes—international: Barbados and Trinidad and Tobago abide by the April 2006 Permanent Court of Arbitration decision delimiting a maritime boundary and limiting catches of flying fish in Trinidad and Tobago's EEZ; in 2005, Barbados and Trinidad and Tobago agreed to compulsory international arbitration under UN Convention on the Law of the Sea challenging whether the northern limit of Trinidad and Tobago's and Venezuela's maritime boundary extends into Barbadian waters; Guyana has expressed its intention to include itself in the arbitration, as the Trinidad and Tobago-Venezuela maritime boundary may also extend into its waters

Trafficking in persons: *current situation:* Trinidad and Tobago is a destination, transit, and possible source country for adults and children subjected to sex trafficking and forced labor; women and girls from Venezuela, the Dominican Republic, Guyana, and Colombia have been subjected to sex trafficking in Trinidad and Tobago's brothels and clubs; some economic migrants from the Caribbean region and Asia are vulnerable to forced labor in domestic service and the retail sector; the steady flow of vessels transiting Trinidad and Tobago's territorial waters may also increase opportunities for forced labor for fishing; international crime organizations are increasingly involved in trafficking, and boys are coerced to sell drugs and guns; corruption among police and immigration officials impedes anti-trafficking efforts

tier rating: Tier 2 Watch List—Trinidad and Tobago does not fully comply with the minimum standards for the elimination of trafficking; however, it is making significant efforts to do so; anti-trafficking law enforcement efforts decreased from the initiation of 12 prosecutions in 2013 to 1 in 2014; the government has yet to convict anyone under its 2011 anti-trafficking law, and all prosecutions from previous years remain pending; the government sustained efforts to identify victims and to refer them for care at NGO facilities, which it provided with funding; the government failed to draft a National action plan as mandated under the 2011 anti-trafficking law and did not launch a sufficiently robust awareness campaign to educate the public and officials (2015)

Illicit drugs: transshipment point for South American drugs destined for the US and Europe; producer of cannabis

TUNISIA

INTRODUCTION

Background: Rivalry between French and Italian interests in Tunisia culminated in a French invasion in 1881 and the creation of a protectorate. Agitation for independence in the decades following World War I was finally successful in convincing the French to recognize Tunisia as an independent state in 1956. The country's first president, Habib BOURGUIBA, established a strict one-party state. He dominated the country for 31 years, repressing Islamic fundamentalism and establishing rights for women unmatched by any other Arab nation. In November 1987, BOURGUIBA was removed from office and replaced by Zine el Abidine BENALI in a bloodless coup. Street protests that began in Tunis in December 2010 over high unemployment, corruption, widespread poverty, and high food prices escalated in January 2011, culminating in rioting that led to hundreds of deaths. On 14 January 2011, the same day BENALI dismissed the government, he fled the country, and by late January 2011, a "National unity government" was formed. Elections for the new Constituent Assembly were held in late October 2011, and in December, it elected

human rights activist Moncef MARZOUKI as interim president. The Assembly began drafting a new constitution in February 2012 and, after several iterations and a months-long political crisis that stalled the transition, ratified the document in January 2014. Parliamentary and presidential elections for a permanent government were held at the end of 2014. Beji CAID ESSEBSI was elected as the first president under the country's new constitution.

GEOGRAPHY

Location: Northern Africa, bordering the Mediterranean Sea, between Algeria and Libya

Geographic coordinates: 34 00 N, 9 00 E

Map references: Africa

Area: *total:* 163,610 sq km
land: 155,360 sq km
water: 8,250 sq km
country comparison to the world: 93

Area—comparative: slightly larger than Georgia

Land boundaries: *total:* 1,495 km
border countries (2): Algeria 1,034 km, Libya 461 km

Coastline: 1,148 km

Maritime claims: *territorial sea:* 12 nm
contiguous zone: 24 nm
exclusive economic zone: 12 nm

Climate: temperate in north with mild, rainy winters and hot, dry summers; desert in south

Terrain: mountains in north; hot, dry central plain; semiarid south merges into the Sahara

Elevation: *mean elevation:* 246 m

elevation extremes: *lowest point:* Shatt al Gharsah -17 m
highest point: Jebelech Chambi 1,544 m

Natural resources: petroleum, phosphates, iron ore, lead, zinc, salt

Land use: *agricultural land:* 64.8%
arable land: 18.3%
permanent crops: 15.4%
permanent pasture: 31.1%
forest: 6.6%
other: 28.6% (2011 est.)

Irrigated land: 4,590 sq km (2012)

Total renewable water resources: 4.6 cu km (2011)

Freshwater withdrawal (domestic/industrial/agricultural): *total:* 2.85 cu km/yr (14%/4%/82%)
per capita: 295.8 cu m/yr (2001)

Natural hazards: NA

Environment—current issues: toxic and hazardous waste disposal is ineffective and poses health risks; water pollution from raw sewage; limited Natural freshwater resources; deforestation; overgrazing; soil erosion; desertification

Environment—international agreements: *party to:* Biodiversity, Climate Change, Climate

Change-Kyoto Protocol, Desertification, Endangered Species, Environmental Modification, Hazardous Wastes, Law of the Sea, Marine Dumping, Ozone Layer Protection, Ship Pollution, Wetlands
signed, but not ratified: Marine Life Conservation

Geography—note: strategic location in central Mediterranean; Malta and Tunisia are discussing the commercial exploitation of the continental shelf between their countries, particularly for oil exploration

PEOPLE AND SOCIETY

Nationality: *noun:* Tunisian(s)
adjective: Tunisian

Ethnic groups: Arab 98%, European 1%, Jewish and other 1%

Languages: Arabic (official, one of the languages of commerce), French (commerce), Berber (Tamazight)
note: despite having no official status, French plays a major role in the country and is spoken by about two-thirds of the population

Religions: Muslim (official; Sunni) 99.1%, other (includes Christian, Jewish, Shia Muslim, and Baha'i) 1%

Population: 11,037,225 (July 2015 est.)
country comparison to the world: 79

Age structure: *0–14 years:* 23.03% (male 1,309,910/female 1,232,149)
15–24 years: 15.53% (male 860,967/female 853,502)
25–54 years: 44.58% (male 2,388,056/female 2,532,035)
55–64 years: 8.82% (male 494,054/female 479,469)
65 years and over: 8.04% (male 435,737/female 451,346) (2015 est.)

Dependency ratios: *total dependency ratio:* 44.8%
youth dependency ratio: 33.8%
elderly dependency ratio: 11%
potential support ratio: 9.1% (2015 est.)

Median age: *total:* 31.9 years
male: 31.5 years
female: 32.3 years (2015 est.)
country comparison to the world: 97

Population growth rate: 0.89% (2015 est.)
country comparison to the world: 126

Birth rate: 16.64 births/1,000 population (2015 est.)
country comparison to the world: 113

Death rate: 5.98 deaths/1,000 population (2015 est.)
country comparison to the world: 166

Net migration rate: -1.73 migrant(s)/1,000 population (2015 est.)
country comparison to the world: 161

Urbanization: *urban population:* 66.8% of total population (2015)

rate of urbanization: 1.38% annual rate of change (2010–15 est.)

Major urban areas—population: TUNIS (capital) 1.993 million (2015)

Sex ratio: *at birth:* 1.07 male(s)/female
0–14 years: 1.06 male(s)/female
15–24 years: 1.01 male(s)/female
25–54 years: 0.94 male(s)/female
55–64 years: 1.03 male(s)/female
65 years and over: 0.97 male(s)/female
total population: 0.99 male(s)/female (2015 est.)

Maternal mortality rate: 62 deaths/100,000 live births (2015 est.)
country comparison to the world: 104

Infant mortality rate: *total:* 22.35 deaths/1,000 live births
male: 25.71 deaths/1,000 live births
female: 18.76 deaths/1,000 live births (2015 est.)
country comparison to the world: 79

Life expectancy at birth: *total population:* 75.89 years
male: 73.79 years
female: 78.14 years (2015 est.)
country comparison to the world: 93

Total fertility rate: 1.99 children born/woman (2015 est.)
country comparison to the world: 122

Contraceptive prevalence rate: 62.5% (2011/12)

Health expenditures: 7.1% of GDP (2013)
country comparison to the world: 80

Physicians density: 1.22 physicians/1,000 population (2010)

Hospital bed density: 2.1 beds/1,000 population (2012)

Drinking water source:
improved:
urban: 100% of population
rural: 93.2% of population
total: 97.7% of population
unimproved:
urban: 0% of population
rural: 6.8% of population
total: 2.3% of population (2015 est.)

Sanitation facility access:
improved:
urban: 97.4% of population
rural: 79.8% of population
total: 91.6% of population
unimproved:
urban: 2.6% of population
rural: 20.2% of population
total: 8.4% of population (2015 est.)

HIV/AIDS—adult prevalence rate: 0.04% (2014 est.)
country comparison to the world: 123

HIV/AIDS—people living with HIV/AIDS: 2,700 (2014 est.)
country comparison to the world: 116

HIV/AIDS—deaths: 100 (2014 est.)
country comparison to the world: 104

Obesity—adult prevalence rate: 27.1% (2014)
country comparison to the world: 80

Children under the age of 5 years underweight: 2.3% (2012)
country comparison to the world: 118

Education expenditures: 6.2% of GDP (2012)
country comparison to the world: 38

Literacy: *definition:* age 15 and over can read and write
total population: 81.8%
male: 89.6%
female: 74.2% (2015 est.)

School life expectancy (primary to tertiary education): *total:* 15 years
male: NA
female: NA (2014)

Unemployment, youth ages 15–24: *total:* 37.6%
male: 35.7%
female: 41.8% (2012 est.)
country comparison to the world: 10

GOVERNMENT

Country name: *conventional long form:* Republic of Tunisia
conventional short form: Tunisia
local long form: Al Jumhuriyah at Tunisiyah
local short form: Tunis
note: the country name derives from the capital city of Tunis

Government type: parliamentary republic

Capital: *name:* Tunis

Geographic coordinates: 36 48 N, 10 11 E
time difference: UTC + 1 (6 hours ahead of Washington, DC, during Standard Time)

Administrative divisions: 24 governorates (wilayat, singular—wilayah); Beja (Bajah), BeNArous (BIN 'Arus), Bizerte (Banzart), Gabes (Qabis), Gafsa (Qafsah), Jendouba (Jundubah), Kairouan (Al Qayrawan), Kasserine (Al Qasrayn), Kebili (Qibili), Kef (Al Kaf), L'Ariana (Aryanah), Mahdia (Al Mahdiyah), Manouba (Manubah), Medenine (Madanin), Mon astir (Al Munastir), Nabeul (Nabul), Sfax (Safaqis), Sidi Bouzid (Sidi Bu Zayd), Siliana (Silyanah), Sousse (Susah), Tataouine (Tatawin), Tozeur (Tawzar), Tunis, Zaghouan (Zaghwan)

Independence: 20 March 1956 (from France)

National holiday: Independence Day, 20 March (1956); Revolution and Youth Day, 14 January (2011)

Constitution: several previous; latest approved by Constituent Assembly 26 January 2014, signed by president on 27 January 2014 (2016)

Legal system: mixed legal system of civil law, based on the French civil code, and Islamic law; some judicial review of legislative acts in the Supreme Court in joint session

International law organization participation: has not submitted an ICJ jurisdiction declaration; accepts ICCt jurisdiction

Citizenship: *citizenship by birth:* no
citizenship by descent only: at least one parent must be a citizen of Tunisia
dual citizenship recognized: yes

residency requirement for naturalization: 5 years

Suffrage: 18 years of age; universal except for active government security forces (including the police and the military), people with mental disabilities, people who have served more than three months in prison (criminal cases only), and people given a suspended sentence of more than six months

Executive branch: *chief of state:* President Beji CAID ESSEBSI (since 31 December 2014)

head of government: Prime Minister Habib ESSID (since 6 February 2015)
cabinet: selected by the prime minister and approved by the Constituent Assembly
elections/appointments: president directly elected by absolute majority popular vote in 2 rounds if needed for a 5-year term (eligible for a second term); election last held on 23 November and 21 December 2014 (next to be held in 2019); following legislative elections, the prime minister is selected by the majority party or majority coalition and appointed by the president
election results: Beji CAID ESSEBSI elected president; percent of vote in runoff—Beji CAID ESSEBSI (Tunisia's Call) 55.7%, Moncef MARZOUKI (CPR) 44.3%

Legislative branch: *description:* unicameral Chamber of the People's Deputies (217 seats); members directly elected in multi-seat constituencies by proportional representation vote; members serve 5-year terms)
elections: initial election held on 26 October 2014 (next to be held in 2019)
election results: percent of vote by party—Tunisia's Call 39.6%, al-Nahda 31.8%, UPL 7.4%, Popular Front 6.9%, Afek Tounes 3.7%, CPR 1.8%, other 8.8%; seats by party—Tunisia's Call 86, al-Nahda 69, UPL 16, Popular Front 15, Afek Tounes 8, CPR 4, other 17, independent 2

Judicial branch: *highest court(s):* Court of Cassation or Cour de Cassation (organized into 1 civil and 3 criminal chambers)
note: the new Tunisian constitution of January 2014 called for the creation of a constitutional court by the end of 2015; the court will consist of 12 members—4 each appointed by the president, Supreme Judicial Council or SJC (an independent 4-part body consisting mainly of elected judges and the remainder specialized persons), and the Chamber of the People's Deputies (parliament); members will serve 9-year terms with one-third of the membership renewed every 3 years; in late 2015, the International Commission of Jurists called on Tunisia's parliament to revise the draft on the constitutional court to ensure compliance with international standards
judge selection and term of office: judges nominated by the SJC; judges appointed by presidential decree; judge tenure NA
subordinate courts: Courts of Appeal; administrative courts; Court of Audit; Housing Court; courts of first instance; lower district courts; military courts

Political parties and leaders: Afek Tounes [Emna MINF]

Congress for the Republic or CPR [Imed DAIMI]

Current of Love [Mohamed HAMDI] (formerly the Popular Petition party)

Democratic Alliance Party [Mohamed HAMDI]

Democratic Current [Mohamed ABBOU]

Ennahda Movement (The Renaissance) [Rachid GHANNOUCHI]

Free Patriotic Union or UPL (Union patriotique libre) [Slim RIAHI]

Movement of Socialist Democrats or MDS [Ahmed KHASKHOUSSI]

National Destourian Initiative or El Moubadra [Kamel MORJANE]

People's Movement [Zouheir MAGHZAOUI]

Popular Front (a coalition of 9 parties including Democractic Patriots' Movement, Workers' Party, Green Tunisia, Tunisian Ba'ath Movement, and Party of the Democractic Arab Vanguard) Popular Petition (Aridha Chaabia) [Hachemi HAMDI]

Republican Party [Maya JRIBI]

The Initiative [Kamel MORJANE] (formerly the Constitutional Democratic Rally or RCD)

Tunisia's Call (Nidaa Tounes) [Mohamed ENNACEUR]

Tunisian Workers' Communist Party or PCOT [Hamma HAMMAMI]

Political pressure groups and leaders: 18 October Group [collective leadership]

Tunisian League for Human Rights or LTDH [Mokhtar TRIFI]

Tunisian General Labor Union or UGTT [Hassine ABASSI]

International organization participation: ABEDA, AfDB, AFESD, AMF, AMU, AU, BSEC (observer), CAEU, CD, EBRD, FAO, G-11, G-77, IAEA, IBRD, ICAO, ICC (National committees), ICCt, ICCt (signatory), ICRM, IDA, IDB, IFAD, IFC, IFRCS, IHO, ILO, IMF, IMO, IMSO, Interpol, IOC, IOM, IPU, ISO, ITSO, ITU, ITUC (NGOs), LAS, MIGA, MONUSCO, NAM, OAS (observer), OIC, OIF, OPCW, OSCE (partner), UN, UNCTAD, UNESCO, UNHCR, UNIDO, UNOCI, UNWTO, UPU, WCO, WFTU (NGOs), WH O, WIPO, WMO, WTO

Diplomatic representation in the US: *chief of mission:* Ambassador Faycal GOUIA (since 18 May 2015)

chancery: 151 5 Massachusetts Avenue NW, Washington, DC 20005

telephone: [1] (202) 862-1850

FAX: [1] (202) 862-1858

Diplomatic representation from the US: *chief of mission:* Ambassador Daniel H. RUBEN STEIn (Since 22 October 2015)

embassy: Zone Nord-Est des Berges du Lac Nordde Tunis 1053

mailing address: Zone Nord-Est des Berges du Lac Nord de Tunis 1053

telephone: [216] 71107-000

FAX: [216] 71963-263

Flag description: red with a white disk in the center bearing a red crescent nearly encircling a red five-pointed star; resembles the Ottoman flag (red banner with white crescent and star) and recalls Tunisia's history as part of the Ottoman Empire; red represents the blood shed by martyrs in the struggle against oppression, white stands for peace; the crescent and star are traditional symbols of Islam

note: the flag is based on that of Turkey, itself a successor state to the Ottoman Empire

National symbol(s): encircled red star and crescent; National colors: red, white

National anthem: *name:* "Humat Al Hima" (Defenders of the Homeland)

lyrics/music: Mustafa Sadik AL-RAFII and Aboul-Qacem ECHEBBI/Mohamad Abdel WAHAB

note: adopted 1957, replaced 1958, restored 1987; Mohamad Abdel WAHAB also composed the music for the anthem of the United Arab Emirates

ECONOMY

Economy—overview: Tunisia's diverse, market-oriented economy has long been cited as a success story in Africa and the Middle East, but it faces an array of challenges following the 2011 Arab Spring revolution. Following an ill-fated experiment with socialist economic policies in the 1960s, Tunisia embarked on a successful strategy focused on bolstering exports, foreign investment, and tourism, all of which have become central to the country's economy. Key exports now include textiles and apparel, food products, petroleum Products, chemicals, and phosphates, with about 80% of exports bound for Tunisia's main economic partner, the EU. Tunisia's liberal strategy, coupled with investments in education and infrastructure, fueled decades of 4–5% annual GDP growth and improving living standards. Former President Zine el Abidine BENALI (1987–2011) continued these policies, but as his reign wore on cronyism and corruption stymied economic performance and unemployment rose among the country's growing ranks of university graduates. These grievances contributed to the January 2011 overthrow of BENALI, sending Tunisia's economy into a tailspin as tourism and investment declined sharply.

Since its establishment in late 2014, Tunisia's new government has faced challenges reassuring businesses and investors, bringing budget and current account deficits under control, shoring up the country's financial system, lowering high unemployment, and reducing economic disparities between the more developed coastal region and the impoverished interior. In 2015, successive terrorist attacks against the tourism sector and worker strikes in the phosphate sector, which combined account for nearly 15% of GDP, slowed growth to less than 1% of GDP.

GDP (purchasing power parity): $127 billion (2015 est.)

$126 billion (2014 est.)

$123.2 billion (2013 est.)

note: data are in 2015 US dollars

country comparison to the world: 80

GDP (official exchange rate): $43.58 billion (2015 est.)

GDP—real growth rate: 0.8% (2015 est.)

2.3% (2014 est.)

2.4% (2013 est.)

country comparison to the world: 183

GDP—per capita (PPP): $11,400 (2015 est.)

$11,500 (2014 est.)

$11,300 (2013 est.)

note: data are in 2015 US dollars

country comparison to the world: 129

Gross National saving: 12.9% of GDP (2015 est.)

14% of GDP (2014 est.)

14.4% of GDP (2013 est.)

country comparison to the world: 130

GDP—composition, by end use:

household consumption: 69.2%

government consumption: 19.3%

investment in fixed capital: 18.7%

investment in inventories: 1.7%

exports of goods and services: 40.9%

imports of goods and services: -49.8% (2015 est.)

GDP—composition, by sector of origin:

agriculture: 9.9%

industry: 29%

services: 61.2% (2015 est.)

Agriculture—products: olives, olive oil, grain, tomatoes, citrus fruit, sugar beets, dates, almonds; beef, dairy products

Industries: petroleum, mining (particularly phosphate, iron ore), tourism, textiles, footwear, agribusiness, beverages

Industrial production growth rate: -0.8% (2015 est.)

country comparison to the world: 170

Labor force: 4.044 million (2015 est.)

country comparison to the world: 92

Labor force—by occupation: *agriculture:* 14.8%

industry: 33.2%

services: 51.7% (2014 est.)

Unemployment rate: 15.4% (2015 est.)

14.9% (2014 est.)

country comparison to the world: 153

Population below poverty line: 15.5% (2010 est.)

Household income or consumption by percentage share: *lowest:* 10%: 2.6%

highest: 10%: 27% (2010 est.)

Distribution of family income—Gini index: 40 (2005 est.)

41.7 (1995 est.)

country comparison to the world: 64

Budget: *revenues:* $10.87 billion

expenditures: $12.78 billion (2015 est.)

Taxes and other revenues: 24.6% of GDP (2015 est.)

country comparison to the world: 125

Budget surplus (+) or deficit (–): -4.3% of GDP (2015 est.)

country comparison to the world: 153

Public debt: 52.6% of GDP (2015 est.)

50.5% of GDP (2014 est.)

country comparison to the world: 73

Fiscal year: calendar year

863

Inflation rate (consumer prices): 4.9% (2015 est.) 4.9% (2014 est.)
country comparison to the world: 172

Central bank discount rate: 5.75% (31 December 2010)
country comparison to the world: 68

Commercial bank prime lending rate: 7.31% (31 December 2014 est.)
6.76% (31 December 2013 est.)
country comparison to the world: 118

Stock of narrow money: $12.32 billion (31 December 2015 est.)
$12.68 billion (31 December 2014 est.)
country comparison to the world: 72

Stock of broad money: $31.32 billion (31 December 2014 est.)
$30.9 billion (31 December 2013 est.)
country comparison to the world: 77

Stock of domestic credit: $34.93 billion (31 December 2015 est.)
$35.82 billion (31 December 2014 est.)
country comparison to the world: 71

Market value of publicly traded shares: $8.887 billion (31 December 2012 est.)
$9.662 billion (31 December 2011)
$10.68 billion (31 December 2010 est.)
country comparison to the world: 76

Current account balance: -$3.875 billion (2015 est.)
-$4.341 billion (2014 est.)
country comparison to the world: 163

Exports: $14.74 billion (2015 est.)
$16.84 billion (2014 est.)
country comparison to the world: 76

Exports—commodities: clothing, semi-finished goods and textiles, agricultural products, mechanical goods, phosphates and chemicals, hydrocarbons, electrical equipment

Exports—partners: France 28.5%, Italy 17.2%, Germany 10.9%, Libya 6.1%, Spain 4.2% (2015)

Imports: $19.42 billion (2015 est.)
$23.4 billion (2014 est.)
country comparison to the world: 75

Imports—commodities: textiles, machinery and equipment, hydrocarbons, chemicals, foodstuffs

Imports—partners: France 19.4%, Italy 16.4%, Algeria 8.2%, Germany 7.4%, China 6% (2015)

Reserves of foreign exchange and gold: $7.225 billion (31 December 2015 est.)
$7.395 billion (31 December 2014 est.)
country comparison to the world: 85

Debt—external: $27.66 billion (31 December 2014 est.)
$26.83 billion (31 December 2013 est.)
country comparison to the world: 76

Stock of direct foreign investment—at home: $36.39 billion (31 December 2015 est.)
$35.46 billion (31 December 2014 est.)
country comparison to the world: 64

Stock of direct foreign investment—abroad: $285 million (31 December 2015 est.)
$285 million (31 December 2014 est.)
country comparison to the world: 90

Exchange rates: Tunisian dinars (TND) per US dollar—
1.954 (2015 est.)
1.6976 (2014 est.)
1.6976 (2013 est.)
1.56 (2012 est.)
1.4078 (2011 est.)

ENERGY

Electricity—production: 16.09 billion kWh (2012 est.)
country comparison to the world: 82

Electricity—consumption: 13.31 billion kWh (2012 est.)
country comparison to the world: 81

Electricity—exports: 426 million kWh (2012 est.)
country comparison to the world: 70

Electricity—imports: 384 million kWh (2012 est.)
country comparison to the world: 80

Electricity—installed generating capacity: 4.203 million kW (2012 est.)
country comparison to the world: 81

Electricity—from fossil fuels: 95.9% of total installed capacity (2012 est.)
country comparison to the world: 66

Electricity—from nuclear fuels: 0% of total installed capacity (2012 est.)
country comparison to the world: 193

Electricity—from hydro electric plants: 1.6% of total installed capacity (2012 est.)
country comparison to the world: 141

Electricity—from other renewable sources: 2.6% of total installed capacity (2012 est.)
country comparison to the world: 77

Crude oil—production: 55,050 bbl/day (2014 est.)
country comparison to the world: 54

Crude oil—exports: 56,060 bbl/day (2012 est.)
country comparison to the world: 43

Crude oil—imports: 22,120 bbl/day (2012 est.)
country comparison to the world: 68

Crude oil—proved reserves: 425 million bbl (1 January 2015 est.)
country comparison to the world: 53

Refined petroleum products—production: 35,860 bbl/day (2012 est.)
country comparison to the world: 85

Refined petroleum products—consumption: 86,000 bbl/day (2013 est.)
country comparison to the world: 81

Refined petroleum products—exports: 18,740 bbl/day (2012 est.)
country comparison to the world: 74

Refined petroleum products—imports: 65,450 bbl/day (2012 est.)
country comparison to the world: 67

Natural gas—production: 1.879 billion cu m (2013 est.)
country comparison to the world: 56

Natural gas—consumption: 4.079 billion cu m (2013 est.)
country comparison to the world: 64

Natural gas—exports: 0 cu m (2013 est.)
country comparison to the world: 195

Natural gas—imports: 2.2 billion cu m (2013 est.)
country comparison to the world: 47

Natural gas—proved reserves: 65.13 billion cu m (1 January 2014 est.)
country comparison to the world: 59

Carbon dioxide emissions from consumption of energy: 20.27 million Mt (2012 est.)
country comparison to the world: 82

COMMUNICATIONS

Telephone—fixed lines: *total subscriptions:* 950,000
subscriptions per 100 inhabitants: 9 (2014 est.)
country comparison to the world: 78

Telephones—mobile cellular: *total:* 14.3 million
subscriptions per 100 inhabitants: 131 (2014 est.)
country comparison to the world: 68

Telephone system: *general assessment:* above the African average and continuing to be upgraded; key centers are Sfax, Sousse, Bizerte, and Tunis; telephone network is completely digitized; Internet access available throughout the country
domestic: in an effort to jumpstart expansion of the fixed-line network, the government has awarded a concession to build and operate a VSAT network with international connectivity; rural areas are served by wireless local loops; competition between the two mobile-cellular service providers has resulted in lower activation and usage charges and a strong surge in subscribership; a third mobile, fixed, and ISP operator was licensed in 2009 and began offering services in 2010; expansion of mobile-cellular services to include multimedia messaging and e-mail and Internet to mobile phone services has also lead to a surge in subscribership; overall fixed-line and mobile-cellular teledensity has reached about 125 telephones per 100 persons
international: country code—216; a landing point for the SEA-ME-WE-4 submarine cable system that provides links to Europe, Middle East, and Asia; satellite earth stations—1 Intelsat (Atlantic Ocean) and 1 Arabsat; coaxial cable and microwave radio relay to Algeria and Libya; participant in Medarabtel; 2 international gateway digital switches (2011)

Broadcast media: broadcast media is mainly government-controlled; the state-run Tunisian Radio and Television Establishment (ERTT) operates 2 National TV networks, several National radio networks, and a number of region al radio stations; 1 TV and 3 radio stations are privately owned and report domestic news stories directly from the official Tunisian news agency; the state retains control of broadcast facilities and transmitters through L'Office National de la Telediffusion; Tunisians also have access to Egyptian, pan-Arab, and European satellite TV channels (2007)
Radio broadcast stations: AM 7, FM 38, shortwave 2 (2007)
Television broadcast stations: 26 (plus 76 repeaters) (1995)

Internet country code: .tn

Internet hosts: 576 (2012)
country comparison to the world: 180

Internet users: *total:* 5 million
percent of population: 45.5% (2014 est.)
country comparison to the world: 65

TRANSPORTATION

Airports: 29 (2013)
country comparison to the world: 118

Airports—with paved runways: *total:* 15
over 3,047 m: 4
2,438 to 3,047 m: 6
1,524 to 2,437 m: 2
914 to 1,523 m: 3 (2013)

Airports—with unpaved runways: *total:* 14
1,524 to 2,437 m: 1
914 to 1,523 m: 5
under 914 m: 8 (2013)

Pipelines: condensate 68 km; gas 3,111 km; oil 1,381 km; refined products 453 km (2013)

Railways: *total:* 2,173 km (1,991 in use)
standard gauge: 471 km 1.435-m gauge
dual gauge: 8 km 1.435–1.000-m gauge
narrow gauge: 1,694 km 1.000-m gauge (65 km electrified) (2014)
country comparison to the world: 69

Roadways: *total:* 19,418 km
paved: 14,756 km (includes 357 km of expressways)
unpaved: 4,662 km (2010)

country comparison to the world: 112

Merchant marine: *total:* 9
by type: bulk carrier 1, cargo 2, passenger/cargo 4, roll on/roll off 2 (2010)
country comparison to the world: 116

Ports and terminals: *major seaport(s):* Bizerte, Gabes, Rades, Sfax, Skhira

MILITARY AND SECURITY

Military branches: Tunisian Armed Forces (Forces Armees Tunisiens, FAT): Tunisian Army (includes Tunisian Air Defense Force), Tunisian Navy, Republic of Tunisia Air Force (Al-Quwwat al-Jawwiya al-Jamahiriyah At'Tunisia) (2012)

Military service age and obligation: 20–23 years of age for compulsory service, 1 -year service obligation; 18–23 years of age for voluntary service; Tunisian Nationality required (2012)

Military expenditures: 1.55% of GDP (2012)
1.34% of GDP (2011)
1.55% of GDP (2010)
country comparison to the world: 57

TRANSNATIONAL ISSUES

Disputes—international: none

Trafficking in persons: *current situation:* Tunisia is a source, destination, and possible transit country for men, women, and children subjected to forced labor and sex trafficking; Tunisia's increased number of street children, rural children working

to support their families, and migrants who have fled unrest in neighboring countries are vulnerable to human trafficking; organized gangs force street children to serve as thieves, beggars, and drug transporters; Tunisian women have been forced into prostitution domestically and elsewhere in the region under false promises of legitimate work; East and West African women may be subjected to forced labor as domestic workers

tier rating: Tier 2 Watch List—Tunisia does not fully comply with the minimum standards for the elimination of trafficking; however, it is making significant efforts to do so; in 2014, Tunisia was granted a waiver from an otherwise required downgrade to Tier 3 because its government has a written plan that, if implemented would constitute making significant efforts to bring itself into compliance with the minimum standards for the elimination of trafficking; in early 2015, the government drafted a National anti-trafficking action plan outlining proposals to raise awareness and enact draft anti-trafficking legislation; authorities did not provide data on the prosecution and conviction of offenders but reportedly identified 24 victims, as opposed to none in 2013, and operated facilities specifically dedicated to trafficking victims, regardless of Nationality and gender; the government did not fully implement its National victim referral mechanism; some unidentified victims were not protected from punishment for unlawful acts directly resulting from being trafficked (2015)

TURKEY

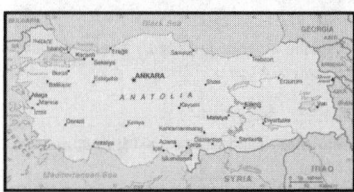

INTRODUCTION

Background: Modern Turkey was founded in 1923 from the Anatolian remnants of the defeated Ottoman Empire by National hero Mustafa KEMAL, who was later honored with the title Ataturk or "Father of the Turks." Under his leadership, the country adopted wide-ranging social, legal, and political reforms. After a period of one-party rule, an experiment with multi-party politics led to the 1950 election victory of the opposition Democratic Party and the peaceful transfer of power. Since then, Turkish political parties have multiplied, but democracy has been fractured by periods of instability and intermittent military coups (1960, 1971, 1980), which in each case eventually resulted in a return of political power to civilians. In 1997, the military again helped engineer the ouster—popularly

dubbed a "post-modern coup"—of the then Islamic-oriented government. Turkey intervened militarily on Cyprus in 1974 to prevent a Greek takeover of the island and has since acted as patron state to the "Turkish Republic of Northern Cyprus," which only Turkey recognizes. A separatist insurgency begun in 1984 by the Kurdistan Workers' Party (PKK)—now knowNAs the Kurdistan People's Congress or Kongra-Gel (KGK)—dominated the Turkish military's attention and claimed more than 30,000 lives. After the capture of the group's leader in 1999, the insurgents largely withdrew from Turkey mainly to northern Iraq. In 2013, the PKK and the Turkish Government agreed to a cease-fire, but fighting resumed in 2015. Turkey joined the UN in 1945 and in 1952 it became a member of NATO. In 1963, Turkey became aNAssociate member of the European Community; it begaNAccession membership talks with the EU in 2005. Over the past decade, economic reforms have contributed to a quickly growing economy.

GEOGRAPHY

Location: Southeastern Europe and Southwestern asia (that portion of Turkey west of the Bosporus is geographically part of Europe), bordering the Black Sea, between Bulgaria and Georgia, and

bordering the Aegean Sea and the Mediterranean Sea, between Greece and Syria

Geographic coordinates: 39 00 N, 35 00 E

Map references: Middle East

Area: *total:* 783,562 sq km
land: 769,632 sq km
water: 13,930 sq km
country comparison to the world: 37

Area—comparative: slightly larger than Texas

Land boundaries: *total:* 2,816 km
border countries (8): Armenia 311 km, Azerbaijan 17 km, Bulgaria 223 km, Georgia 273 km, Greece 192 km, Iran 534 km, Iraq 367 km, Syria 899 km

Coastline: 7,200 km

Maritime claims: *territorial sea:* 6 nm in the Aegean Sea; 12 nm in Black Sea and in Mediterranean Sea
exclusive economic zone: in Black Sea only: to the maritime boundary agreed upon with the former USSR

Climate: temperate; hot, dry summers with mild, wet winters; harsher in interior

Terrain: high central plateau (Anatolia); narrow coastal plain; several mountain ranges

Elevation: *mean elevation:* 1,132 m

elevation extremes: *lowest point:* Mediterranean Sea 0 m

highest point: Mount Ararat 5,166 m

Natural resources: coal, iron ore, copper, chromium, antimony, mercury, gold, barite, borate, celestite (strontium), emery, feldspar, limestone, magnesite, marble, perlite, pumice, pyrites (sulfur), clay, arable land, hydropower

Land use: *agricultural land:* 49.7%
arable land: 26.7%
permanent crops: 4%
permanent pasture: 19%
forest: 14.9%
other: 35.4% (2011 est.)

Irrigated land: 52,150 sq km (2012)

Total renewable water resources: 211.6 cu km (2011)

Freshwater withdrawal (domestic/industrial/agricultural): *total:* 40.1 cu km/yr (14%/10%/76%)
per capita: 572.9 cu m/yr (2008)

Natural hazards: severe earthquakes, especially in northern Turkey, along an arc extending from the Sea of Marm ara to Lake Van

volcanism: limited volcanic activity; its three historically active volcanoes; Ararat, Nemrut Dagi, and Tendurek Dagi have not erupted since the 19th century or earlier

Environment—current issues: water pollution from dumping of chem icals and detergents; air pollution, particularly in urban Areas; deforestation; concern for oil spills from increasing Bosporus ship traffic

Environment—international agreements: *party to:* Air Pollution, Antarctic Treaty, Biodiversity, Climate Change, Desertification, Endangered Species, Hazardous Wastes, Ozone Layer Protection, Ship Pollution, Wetlands
signed, but not ratified: Environmental Modification

Geography—note: strategic location controlling the Turkish Straits (Bosporus, Sea of Marmara, Dardanelles) that link the Black and Aegean Seas; Mount Ararat, the legendary landing place of Noah's ark, is in the far eastern portion of the country

PEOPLE AND SOCIETY

Nationality: *noun:* Turk(s)
adjective: Turkish

Ethnic groups: Turkish 70–75%, Kurdish 18%, other minorities 7–12% (2008 est.)

Languages: Turkish (official), Kurdish, other m inority languages

Religions: Muslim 99.8% (mostly Sunni), other 0.2% (mostly Christians and Jews)

Population: 79,414,269 (July 2015 est.)
country comparison to the world: 19

Age structure: *0–14 years:* 25.45% (male 10,339,731/female 9,868,005)
15–24 years: 16.25% (male 6,587,897/female 6,314,306)

25–54 years: 43.07% (male 17,323,965/female 16,878,498)
55–64 years: 8.15% (male 3,216,877/female 3,253,892)
65 years and over: 7.09% (male 2,498,187/female 3,132,911) (2015 est.)

Dependency ratios: *total dependency ratio:* 49.7%
youth dependency ratio: 38.4%
elderly dependency ratio: 11.3%
potential support ratio: 8.9% (2015 est.)

Median age: *total:* 30.1 years
male: 29.7 years
female: 30.6 years (2015 est.)
country comparison to the world: 112

Population growth rate: 1.26% (2015 est.)
country comparison to the world: 93

Birth rate: 16.33 births/1,000 population (2015 est.)
country comparison to the world: 118

Death rate: 5.88 deaths/1,000 population (2015 est.)
country comparison to the world: 170

Net migration rate: 2.16 migrant(s)/1,000 population (2015 est.)
country comparison to the world: 50

Urbanization: *urban population:* 73.4% of total population (2015)
rate of urbanization: 1.97% annual rate of change (2010–15 est.)

Major urban areas—population: Istanbul 14.164 million; ANKARA (capital) 4.75 million; Izmir 3.04 million; Bursa 1.923 million; Adana 1.83 million; Gaziantep 1.528 million (2015)

Sex ratio: *at birth:* 1.05 male(s)/female
0–14 years: 1.05 male(s)/female
15–24 years: 1.04 male(s)/female
25–54 years: 1.03 male(s)/female
55–64 years: 0.99 male(s)/female
65 years and over: 0.8 male(s)/female
total population: 1.01 male(s)/female (2015 est.)

Mother's mean age at first birth: 22.3 (2010 est.)

Maternal mortality rate: 16 deaths/100,000 live births (2015 est.)
country comparison to the world: 139

Infant mortality rate: *total:* 18.87 deaths/1,000 live births
male: 20.13 deaths/1,000 live births
female: 17.55 deaths/1,000 live births (2015 est.)
country comparison to the world: 93

Life expectancy at birth: *total population:* 74.57 years
male: 72.26 years
female: 77 years (2015 est.)
country comparison to the world: 115

Total fertility rate: 2.05 children born/woman (2015 est.)
country comparison to the world: 114

Contraceptive prevalence rate: 73% (2008)

Health expenditures: 5.6% of GDP (2013)
country comparison to the world: 103

Physicians density: 1.71 physicians/1,000 population (2011)

Hospital bed density: 2.5 beds/1,000 population (2011)

Drinking water source:
improved:
urban: 100% of population
rural: 100% of population
total: 100% of population
unimproved:
urban: 0% of population
rural: 0% of population
total: 0% of population (2015 est.)

Sanitation facility access:
improved:
urban: 98.3% of population
rural: 85.5% of population
total: 94.9% of population
unimproved:
urban: 1.7% of population
rural: 14.5% of population
total: 5.1% of population (2015 est.)

HIV/AIDS—adult prevalence rate: NA

HIV/AIDS—people living with HIV/AIDS: NA

HIV/AIDS—deaths: NA

Obesity—adult prevalence rate: 29.4% (2014)
country comparison to the world: 36

Children under the age of 5 years underweight: 1.9% (2014)
country comparison to the world: 123

Education expenditures: 2.9% of GDP (2006)
country comparison to the world: 142

Literacy: *definition:* age 15 and over can read and write
total population: 95%
male: 98.4%
female: 91.8% (2015 est.)

School life expectancy (primary to tertiary education): *total:* 16 years
male: 17 years
female: 16 years (2013)

Child labor—children ages 5–14: *total number:* 321,866
percentage: 3%
note: data represent children ages 6–14 (2006 est.)

Unemployment, youth ages 15–24: *total:* 18.7%
male: 16.9%
female: 21.9% (2013 est.)
country comparison to the world: 66

GOVERNMENT

Country name: *conventional long form:* Republic of Turkey
conventional short form: Turkey
local long form: Turkiye Cumhuriyeti
local short form: Turkiye
etymology: the name means "Land of the Turks"

Government type: parliamentary republic

Capital: *name:* Ankara

Geographic coordinates: 39 56 N, 32 52 E
time difference: UTC+2 (7 hours ahead of Washington, DC, during Standard Time) daylight

saving time: +1hr, begins last Sunday in March; ends last Sunday in October

Administrative divisions: 81 provinces (iller, singular—ili); Adana, Adiyaman, Afyonkarahisar, Agri, Aksaray, Amasya, Ankara, Antalya, Ardahan, Artvin, Aydin, Balikesir, Bartin, Batman, Bayburt, Bilecik, Bingol, Bitlis, Bolu, Burdur, Bursa, Canakkale, Cankiri, Corum, Denizli, Diyarbakir, Duzce, Edirne, Elazig, Erzincan, Erzurum, Eskisehir, Gaziantep, Giresun, Gumushane, Hakkari, Hatay, Igdir, Isparta, Istanbul, Izmir (Smyrna), Kahramanmaras, Karabuk, Karaman, Kars, Kastamonu, Kayseri, Kilis, Kirikkale, Kirklareli, Kirsehir, Kocaeli, Konya, Kutahya, Malatya, Manisa, Mardin, Mersin, Mugla, Mus, Nevsehir, Nigde, Ordu, Osmaniye, Rize, Sakarya, Samsun, Sanliurfa, Siirt, Sinop, Sirnak, Sivas, Tekirdag, Tokat, Trabzon (Trebizond), Tunceli, Usak, Van, Yalova, Yozgat, Zonguldak

Independence: 29 October 1923 (successor state to the Ottoman Empire)

National holiday: Republic Day, 29 October (1923)

Constitution: several previous; latest ratified 9 November 1982; amended several times, last in 2015 (2016)

Legal system: civil law system based on various European legal systems notably the Swiss civil code

international law organization participation: has not submitted an ICJ jurisdiction declaration; non-party state to the ICCt

Citizenship: *citizenship by birth:* no
citizenship by descent only: at least one parent must be a citizen of Turkey
dual citizenship recognized: yes, but requires prior permission from the government
residency requirement for naturalization: 5 years

Suffrage: 18 years of age; universal

Executive branch: *chief of state:* President Recep Tayyip ERDOGAN (since 10 August 2014)

head of government: Prime Minister Binali YILDIRIM (since 22 May 2016); Deputy Prime Ministers Nurettin CANIKLI (since 24 May 2016), Veysi KAYNAK (since 24 May 2016), Mehmet SIMSEK (since 24 November 2015), Yildirim Tugrul TURKES (since 29 August 2014), Numan KURTULMUS (since 29 August 2014)
cabinet: Council of Ministers nominated by the prime minister, appointed by the president
elections/appointments: president directly elected by absolute majority popular vote in 2 rounds if needed for a 5-year term (eligible for a second term); prime minister appointed by the president from among members of parliament; note—a 2007 constitutional amendment changed the presidential electoral process to direct popular vote; prime minister appointed by the president from among members of the Grand National Assembly of Turkey
election results: Recep Tayyip ERDOGAN elected president; Recep Tayyip ERDOGAN (AKP)

51.8%, Ekmeleddin IHSANOGLU (independent) 38.4%, Selahattin DEMIRTAS (HDP) 9.8%

Legislative branch: *description:* unicameral Grand National Assembly of Turkey or Turkiye Buyuk Millet Meclisi (550 seats; members directly elected in multi-seat constituencies by proportional representation vote to serve 4-year terms)
elections: last held on 1 November 2015 (next to be held on June 2019); note—ERDOGAN was unable to form a coalition government and announced on 24 August 2015 that snap elections would be held; DAVU TOGLU formed the interim government
election results: percent of vote by party—AKP 49.5%, CHP 25.3%, MHP 11.9%, HDP 10.8%, other 2.6%; seats by party—AKP 317, CHP 134, MHP 40, HDP 59; note—only parties surpassing the 10% threshold can win parliamentary seats

Judicial branch: *Highest court:* Constitutional Court or Anayasa Mahkemesi (consists of 17 members); Supreme Court of Appeals (consists of about 390 judges and organized into 15 divisions with 23 civil and 15 criminal chambers); Council of State (organized into 15 divisions—14 judicial and 1 consultative—each with a division head and at least 5 members)
judge selection and term of office: Constitutional Court members—3 appointed by the Grand National Assembly and 14 by the president of the republic from among candidates nominated by the plenary assemblies of the high courts (with the exception of the Court of High Accounts), the Higher Education Council, and from among senior government administrators, lawyers, judges and prosecutors, and Constitutional Court rapporteurs; court president and 2 deputy presidents appointed from among its members for 4-year terms; judges appointed for 12-year, non-renewable terms with mandatory retirement at age 65; Supreme Court of Appeals judges appointed by the Supreme Council of Judges and Public Prosecutors (SCJP), an independent body of judicial officials; judges appointed until retirement at age 65; Council of State members appointed by the SCJP and by the president of the republic; members appointed for renewable, 4-year terms
subordinate courts: basic (first instance) courts, military courts, specialized courts, including administrative and audit

Political parties and leaders: Democratic Party or DP [Gultekin UYSAL]
Felicity Party or SP [Mustafa KAMALAK]
Grand Unity Party or BBP [Mustafa DESTICI]
Justice and Development Party or AKP [Ahmet DAVUTOGLU]
Nationalist Movement Party or MHP [Devlet BAHCELI]
People's Democratic Party or HDP [Selahattin DEMIRTAS and Figen YUKSEKDAG]
Republican People's Party or CHP [Kemal KILICDAROGLU]

Political pressure groups and leaders: Confederation of Businessmen and Industrialists of Turkey or TUSKON [Rizanur MERAL]

Confederation of Public Sector Unions or KESK [Lami OZGEN, Sazyie KOSE, co-chairs]
Confederation of Revolution ary Workers Unions or DISK [Tayfun GORGUN]
Independent Industrialists' and Businessmen's Association or MUSIAD [Nail OLPAK]
Moral Rights Workers Union or Hak-Is [Mahmut ARSLAN]
Turkish Confederation of Employers' Unions or TISK [Tugrul KUDATGOBILIK]
Turkish Confederation of Labor or Turk-Is [Ergu NATALAY]
Turkish Confederation of Tradesmen and Craftsmen or TESK [Bendevi PALANDOKEN]
Turkish Industrialists' and Businessmen's Association or TUSIAD [Muharrem YILMAZ]
Turkish Union of Chambers of Commerce and Commodity Exchanges or TOBB [M. Rifat HISARCIKLIOGLU]

International organization participation: ADB (nonregional member), Australia Group, BIS, BSEC, CBSS (observer), CD, CE, CERN (observer), CICA, CPLP (associate observer), D-8, EAPC, EBRD, ECO, EU (candidate country), FAO, FATF, G-20, IAEA, IBRD, ICAO, ICC (National committees), ICRM, IDA, IDB, IEA, IFAD, IFC, IFRCS, IHO, ILO, IMF, IMO, IMSO, Interpol, IOC, IOM, IPU, ISO, ITSO, ITU, ITUC (NGOs), MIGA, NATO, NEA, NSG, OAS (observer), OECD, OIC, OPCW, OSCE, Pacific Alliance (observer), Paris Club (associate), PCA, PIF (partner), SCO (dialogue member), SELEC, UN, UNCTAD, UNESCO, UNHCR, UNIDO, UNIFIL, UNRWA, UNWTO, UPU, WCO, WFTU (NGOs), WHO, WIPO, WMO, WTO, ZC

Diplomatic representation in the US: *chief of mission:* Ambassador Serdar KILIC (since 21 May 2014)
chancery: 2525 Massachusetts Avenue NW, Washington, DC 20008
telephone: [1] (202) 612-6700
FAX: [1] (202) 612-6744
consulate(s) general: Boston, Chicago, Houston, Los Angeles, New York

Diplomatic representation from the US: *chief of mission:* Ambassador John R. BASS (since 20 October 2014)
embassy: 110 Ataturk Boulevard, Kavaklidere, 06100 Ankara
mailing address: PSC 93, Box 5000, APO AE 09823
telephone: [90] (312) 455-5555
FAX: [90] (312) 467-0019
consulate(s) general: Istanbul
consulate(s): Adana; note—there is a Consular Agent in Izmir

Flag description: red with a vertical white crescent moon (the closed portion is toward the hoist side) and white five-pointed star centered just outside the crescent opening; the flag colors and designs closely resemble those on the banner of the Ottoman Empire, which preceded modern-day Turkey; the crescent moon and star serve as insignia for Turkic peoples (the crescent represents the

867

mythical moon god, Ay Ata, and the star the sun goddess, Gun Ana); according to one legend, the flag represents the reflection of the moon and a star in a pool of blood of Turkish warriors

National symbol(s): star and crescent; National colors: red, white

National anthem: *name:* "Istiklal Marsi" (Independence March)
lyrics/music: Mehmet Akif ERSOY/Zeki UNGOR
note: lyrics adopted 1921, music adopted 1932; the anthem's original music was adopted in 1924; a new composition was agreed upon in 1932

ECONOMY

Economy—overview: Turkey's largely free-market economy is increasingly driven by its industry and service sectors, although its traditional agriculture sector still accounts for about 25% of employment. ANAggressive privatization program has reduced state involvement in basic industry, banking, transport, and communication. An emerging cadre of middle-class entrepreneurs is adding dynamism to the economy and expanding production beyond the traditional textiles and clothing sectors. The automotive, petrochemical, and electronics industries are rising in importance and have surpassed textiles within Turkey's export mix. Oil began to flow through the Baku-Tbilisi-Ceyhan pipeline in May 2006, marking a major milestone that has brought up to 1 million barrels per day from the Caspian region to market. The joint Turkish-Azeri Trans Anatolian Natural Gas Pipeline (TANAP) is moving forward to help transport Caspian gas to Europe through Turkey, helping to address Turkey's dependence on imported gas, which currently meets 98% of its energy needs.

After Turkey experienced a severe financial crisis in 2001, Ankara adopted financial and fiscal reforms as part of an IMF program. The reforms strengthened the country's economic fundamentals and ushered in an era of strong growth averaging more than 6% annually until 2008. Global economic conditions and tighter fiscal policy caused GDP to contract in 2009, but Turkey's well-regulated financial markets and banking system helped the country weather the global financial crisis, and GDP rebounded strongly to around 9% in 2010–11, as exports returned to normal levels following the crisis. Two rating agencies upgraded Turkey's debt to investment grade in 2012 and 2013, and Turkey's public sector debt to GDP ratio fell to 33% in 2014.

The stock value of Foreign Direct Investment reached nearly $195 billion at year end 2014. Despite these positive trends, GDP growth dropped to 4.4% in 2013 and 2.9% in 2014. Growth slowed considerably in the last quarter of 2014, largely due to lackluster consumer demand both domestically and in Europe, Turkey's most important export market. High interest rates have also contributed to the slowdown in growth, as Turkey sharply increased interest rates in January 2014 in order to strengthen the country's currency and reduce inflation. Turkey then cut rates in February 2015 in a bid to spur economic growth.

The Turkish economy retains significant weaknesses. Specifically, Turkey's relatively high current account deficit, uncertain commitment to structural reform, and turmoil within Turkey's neighborhood leave the economy vulnerable to destabilizing shifts in investor confidence. Turkey also remains overly dependent on often volatile, short-term investment to finance its large current account deficit.

GDP (purchasing power parity): $1.589 trillion (2015 est.)
$1.53 trillion (2014 est.)
$1.487 trillion (2013 est.)
note: data are in 2015 US dollars
country comparison to the world: 18

GDP (official exchange rate): $733.6 billion (2015 est.)

GDP—real growth rate: 3.8% (2015 est.)
2.9% (2014 est.)
4.2% (2013 est.)
country comparison to the world: 71

GDP—per capita (PPP): $20,400 (2015 est.)
$19,900 (2014 est.)
$19,500 (2013 est.)
note: data are in 2015 US dollars
country comparison to the world: 86

Gross National saving: 15.6% of GDP (2015 est.)
14.7% of GDP (2014 est.)
12.9% of GDP (2013 est.)
country comparison to the world: 110

GDP—composition, by end use:
household consumption: 68.2%
government consumption: 15.4%
investment in fixed Capital: 19.8%
investment in inventories: 0%
exports of goods and services: 28.7%
imports of goods and services: -32.1% (2015 est.)

GDP—composition, by sector of origin:
agriculture: 8.1%
industry: 27.7%
services: 64.2% (2015 est.)

Agriculture—products: tobacco, cotton, grain, olives, sugar beets, hazelnuts, pulses, citrus; livestock

Industries: textiles, food processing, automobiles, electronics, mining (coal, chromate, copper, boron), steel, petroleum, construction, lumber, paper

Industrial production growth rate: 4.5% (2015 est.)
country comparison to the world: 43

Labor force: 29.4 million
note: about 1.2 million Turks work abroad (2015 est.)
country comparison to the world: 21

Labor force—by occupation: *agriculture:* 25.5%
industry: 26.2%
services: 48.4% (2010)

Unemployment rate: 10.4% (2015 est.)
10% (2014 est.)
country comparison to the world: 118

Population below poverty line: 16.9% (2010 est.)

Household income or consumption by percentage share: *lowest:* 10%: 2.1%

highest: 10%: 30.3% (2008)

Distribution of family income—Gini index: 40.2 (2010)
43.6 (2003)
country comparison to the world: 62

Budget: *revenues:* $175.4 billion
expenditures: $187.4 billion (2015 est.)
Taxes and other revenues: 24.3% of GDP (2015 est.)
country comparison to the world: 127

Budget surplus (+) or deficit (–): -1.7% of GDP (2015 est.)
country comparison to the world: 66

Public debt: 33.1% of GDP (2015 est.)
35% of GDP (2014 est.)
note: data cover central government debt, and excludes debt instruments issued (or owned) by government entities other than the treasury; the data include treasury debt held by foreign entities; the data exclude debt issued by subNational entities, as well as intra-governmental debt; intra-governmental debt consists of treasury borrowings from surpluses in the social funds, such as for retirement, medical care, and unemployment; debt instruments for the social funds are sold at public auctions
country comparison to the world: 135

Fiscal year: calendar year

Inflation rate (consumer prices): 7.7% (2015 est.)
8.9% (2014 est.)
country comparison to the world: 199

Central bank discount rate: 5.25% (31 December 2011) 15%
(22 December 2009)
country comparison to the world: 74

Commercial bank prime lending rate: 13.8% (31 December 2015 est.)
13.38% (31 December 2014 est.)
country comparison to the world: 51

Stock of narrow money: $99.09 billion (31 December 2015 est.)
$111.3 billion (31 December 2014 est.)
country comparison to the world: 35

Stock of broad money: $474.7 billion (31 December 2014 est.)
$425.1 billion (31 December 2013 est.)
country comparison to the world: 25

Stock of domestic credit: $551 billion (31 December 2015 est.)
$618.6 billion (31 December 2014 est.)
country comparison to the world: 22

Market value of publicly traded shares:
$308.8 billion (31 December 2012 est.)
$201.8 billion (31 December 2011)
$306.7 billion (31 December 2010 est.)
country comparison to the world: 29

Current account balance: -$32.19 billion (2015 est.)
-$43.55 billion (2014 est.)
country comparison to the world: 190

Exports: $153.6 billion (2015 est.)
$168.9 billion (2014 est.)
country comparison to the world: 29

Exports—commodities: apparel, foodstuffs, textiles, metal manufactures, transport equipment

Exports—partners: Germany 9.3%, UK 7.3%, Iraq 5.9%, Italy 4.8%, US 4.5%, France 4.1% (2015)

Imports: $204.3 billion (2015 est.)
$232.5 billion (2014 est.)
country comparison to the world: 22

Imports—commodities: machinery, chemicals, semi-finished goods, fuels, transport equipment

Imports—partners: China 12%, Germany 10.3%, Russia 9.9%, US 5.4%, Italy 5.1% (2015)

Reserves of foreign exchange and gold: $118.3 billion (31 December 2015 est.)
$127.3 billion (31 December 2014 est.)
country comparison to the world: 20

Debt—external: $402.4 billion (31 December 2014 est.)
$389.2 billion (31 December 2013 est.)
country comparison to the world: 31

Stock of direct foreign investment—at home: $184.1 billion (31 December 2015 est.)
$169.1 billion (31 December 2014 est.)
country comparison to the world: 31

Stock of direct foreign investment—abroad: $44.98 billion (31 December 2015 est.)
$40.48 billion (31 December 2014 est.)
country comparison to the world: 42

Exchange rates: Turkish liras (TRY) per US dollar—
2.739 (2015 est.)
2.1885 (2014 est.)
2.1885 (2013 est.)
1.8 (2012 est.)
1.675 (2011 est.)

ENERGY

Electricity—production: 228.3 billion kWh (2012 est.)
country comparison to the world: 21

Electricity—consumption: 197 billion kWh (2012 est.)
country comparison to the world: 20

Electricity—exports: 1.236 billion kWh (2013 est.)
country comparison to the world: 52

Electricity—imports: 7.425 billion kWh (2013 est.)
country comparison to the world: 32

Electricity—installed generating capacity: 57.12 million kW (2012 est.)
country comparison to the world: 18

Electricity—from fossil fuels: 61% of total installed capacity (2012 est.)
country comparison to the world: 130

Electricity—from nuclear fuels: 0% of total installed capacity (2012 est.)
country comparison to the world: 194

Electricity—from hydro electric plants: 34.3% of total installed capacity (2012 est.)
country comparison to the world: 65

Electricity—from other renewable sources: 4.6% of total installed capacity (2012 est.)

country comparison to the world: 6

Crude oil—production: 47,670 bbl/day (2014 est.)
country comparison to the world: 59

Crude oil—exports: 4,176 bbl/day (2013 est.)
country comparison to the world: 74

Crude oil—imports: 379,600 bbl/day (2013 est.)
country comparison to the world: 24

Crude oil—proved reserves: 296 million bbl (1 January 2015 est.)
country comparison to the world: 56

Refined petroleum products—production: 483,100 bbl/day (2013 est.)
country comparison to the world: 35

Refined petroleum products—consumption: 718,600 bbl/day (2014 est.)
country comparison to the world: 28

Refined petroleum products—exports: 142,600 bbl/day (2013 est.)
country comparison to the world: 41

Refined petroleum products—imports: 438,600 bbl/day (2013 est.)
country comparison to the world: 16

Natural gas—production: 476 million cu m (2014 est.)
country comparison to the world: 72

Natural gas—consumption: 48.45 billion cu m (2014 est.)
country comparison to the world: 17

Natural gas—exports: 633 million cu m (2014 est.)
country comparison to the world: 39

Natural gas—imports: 48.89 billion cu m (2014 est.)
country comparison to the world: 8

Natural gas—proved reserves: 6.824 billion cu m (1 January 2014 est.)
country comparison to the world: 85

Carbon dioxide emissions from consumption of energy: 296.9 million Mt (2012 est.)
country comparison to the world: 21

COMMUNICATIONS

Telephone—fixed lines: *total subscriptions:* 12.53 million
subscriptions per 100 inhabitants: 16 (2014 est.)
country comparison to the world: 19

Telephones—mobile cellular: *total:* 71.9 million
subscriptions per 100 inhabitants: 92 (2014 est.)
country comparison to the world: 16

Telephone system: *general assessment:* comprehensive telecommunications network undergoing rapid modernization and expansion, especially in mobile-cellular services
domestic: addition al digital exchanges are permitting a rapid increase in subscribers; the construction of a network of technologically advanced intercity trunk lines, using both fiber-optic cable and digital microwave radio relay, is facilitating communication between urban centers; remote areas are reached by a domestic satellite system; combined fixed-line and mobile-cellular teledensity is roughly 100 telephones per 100 persons

international: country code—90; international service is provided by the SEA-ME-WE-3 submarine cable and by submarine fiber-optic cables in the Mediterranean and Black Seas that link Turkey with Italy, Greece, Israel, Bulgaria, Romania, and Russia; satellite earth stations—12 Intelsat; mobile satellite terminals—328 in the Inmarsat and Eutelsat systems (2010)

Broadcast media: Turkish Radio and Television Corporation (TRT) operates multiple TV and radio networks and stations; multiple privately owned National television stations and up to 300 private regional and local television stations; multi-channel cable TV subscriptions available; more than 1,000 private radio broadcast stations (2009)
Radio broadcast stations: 1,090 (station frequency types NA) (2009)
Television broadcast stations: 251 (2009)

Internet country code: .tr

Internet hosts: 7.093 million (2012)
country comparison to the world: 16

Internet users: *total:* 36.6 million
percent of population: 46.6% (2014 est.)
country comparison to the world: 19

TRANSPORTATION

Airports: 98 (2013)
country comparison to the world: 58

Airports—with paved runways: *total:* 91
over 3,047 m: 16
2,438 to 3,047 m: 38
1,524 to 2,437 m: 17
914 to 1,523 m: 16
under 914 m: 4 (2013)

Airports—with unpaved runways: *total:* 7
1,524 to 2,437 m: 1
914 to 1,523 m: 4
under 914 m: 2 (2013)

Heliports: 20 (2013)

Pipelines: gas 12,603 km; oil 3,038 km (2013)

Railways: *total:* 12,008 km
standard gauge: 12,008 km 1.435-m gauge (3,216 km electrified) (2014)
country comparison to the world: 20

Roadways: *total:* 385,754 km
paved: 352,268 km (includes 2,127 km of expressways)
unpaved: 33,486 km (2012)
country comparison to the world: 18

Waterways: 1,200 km (2010)
country comparison to the world: 59

Merchant marine: *total:* 629
by type: bulk carrier 102, cargo 281, chemical tanker 80, container 42, liquefied gas 6, passenger 2, passenger/cargo 60, petroleum tanker 25, refrigerated cargo 1, roll on/roll off 29, specialized tanker 1
foreign-owned: 1 (Italy 1)
registered in other countries: 645 (Albania 1, Antigua and Barbuda 7, Azerbaijan 1, Bahamas 3, Barbados 1, Belize 16, Brazil 1, Cambodia 15, Comoros 8, Cook Islands 4, Curacao 5, Cyprus 1, Dominica 1, Georgia 14, Italy 4, Kazakhstan 1, Liberia 16, Malta 233, Marshall Islands 70,

Moldova 18, Panama 62, Russia 101, Saint Kitts and Nevis 18, Saint Vincent and the Grenadines 13, Sierra Leone 9, Slovakia 1, Tanzania 13, Togo 4, Tuvalu 1, unknown 3) (2010)

country comparison to the world: 18

Ports and terminals: *major seaport(s):* Aliaga, Ambarli, Diliskelesi, Eregli, Izmir, Kocaeli (Izmit), Mersin (Icel), Limani, Yarimca

container port(s) (TEUs): Ambarli (2,121,549), Mersin (Icel) (1,126,866)

LNG terminal (import): Izmir Aliaga, Marmara Ereglisi

MILITARY AND SECURITY

Military branches: Turkish Armed Forces (TSK): Turkish Land Forces (Turk Kara Kuvvetleri), Turkish Naval Forces (Turk Deniz Kuvvetleri; includes Naval air and Naval infantry), Turkish Air Forces (Turk Hava Kuvvetleri) (2013)

Military service age and obligation: 21–41 years of age for male compulsory military service; 18 years of age for voluntary service; 12-month conscript obligation for non-university graduates, 6–12 months for university graduates (graduates of higher education may perform 6 months of military service as short-term privates, or 12 months as reserve officers); conscripts are called to register at age 20, for service at 21; women serve in the Turkish Armed Forces only as officers; reserve obligation to age 41; Turkish citizens with a residence or work permit who have worked abroad for at least 3 years (1095 days) can be exempt from military service in exchange for 6,000 EUR or its equivalent in foreign currencies; a law passed in December 2014 introduced a one-time payment scheme which exempted Turkish citizens 27 and older from conscription in exchange for a payment of $8,150 (2013)

Military expenditures: 2.29% of GDP (2015 est.)
2.36% of GDP (2014)
2.39% of GDP (2013)

2.31% of GDP (2012)
2.28% of GDP (2011)
country comparison to the world: 35

Military—note: the ruling Justice and Development Party (AKP) has actively pursued the goal of asserting civilian control over the military since first taking power in 2002; the Turkish Armed Forces (TSK) role in internal security has been significantly reduced; the TSK leadership continues to be an influential institution within Turkey, but plays a much smaller role in politics; the Turkish military remains focused on the threats emanating from the Syrian civil war, Russia's actions in Ukraine, and the PKK insurgency; primary domestic threats are listed as fundamentalism (with the definition in some dispute with the civilian government), separatism (Kurdish discontent), and the extreme left wing; Ankara strongly opposed establishment of an Autonomous Kurdish region in Iraq; an overhaul of the Turkish Land Forces Command (TLFC) taking place under the "Force 2014" program is to produce 20–30% smaller, more highly trained forces characterized by greater mobility and firepower and capable of joint and combined operations; the TLFC has taken on increasing international peacekeeping responsibilities including in Afghanistan; the Turkish Navy is a region al Naval power that wants to develop the capability to project power beyond Turkey's coastal waters; the Navy is heavily involved in NATO, multinational, and UN operations; its roles include control of territorial waters and security for sea lines of communications; the Turkish Air Force adopted an "Aerospace and Missile Defense Concept" in 2002 and has initiated project work on an integrated missile defense system; Air Force priorities include attaining a modern deployable, survivable, and sustainable force structure, and establishing a sustainable command and control system; Turkey is a NATO ally and hosts

NATO's Land Forces Command in Izmir, as well as the AN/TPY-2 radar as part of NATO Missile Defense (2014)

TRANSNATIONAL ISSUES

Disputes—international: complex maritime, air, and territorial disputes with Greece in the Aegean Sea; status of north Cyprus question remains; Syria and Iraq protest Turkish hydrological projects to control upper Euphrates waters; Turkey has expressed concern over the status of Kurds in Iraq; in 2009, Swiss mediators facilitated an accord reestablishing diplomatic ties between Armenia and Turkey, but neither side has ratified the agreement and the rapprochement effort has faltered; Turkish authorities have complained that blasting from quarries in Armenia might be damaging the medieval ruins of Ani, on the other side of the Arpacay valley

Refugees and internally displaced persons: *refugees (country of origin):* at least 103,000 (Iraq) (2014); 2,733,044 (Syria) (2016)
IDPs: 954,000 (displaced from 1984–2005 because of fighting between the Kurdish PKK and Turkish military; most IDPs are Kurds from eastern and southeastern provinces; no information available on persons displaced by development projects) (2015)
stateless persons: 780 (2015)

Illicit drugs: key transit route for Southwest Asian heroin to Western Europe and, to a lesser extent, the US—via air, land, and sea routes; major Turkish and other international trafficking organizations operate out of Istanbul; laboratories to convert imported morphine base into heroin exist in remote regions of Turkey and near Istanbul; government maintains strict controls over areas of legal opium poppy cultivation and over output of poppy straw concentrate; lax enforcement of money-laundering controls

---

TURKMENISTAN

INTRODUCTION

Background: Present-day Turkmenistan covers territory that has been at the crossroads of civilizations for centuries. The area was ruled in antiquity by various Persian empires, and was conquered by Alexander the Great, Muslim armies, the Mongols, Turkic warriors, and eventually the Russians. In medieval times, Merv (located in present-day Mary province) was one of the great cities of the Islamic world and an important stop on the Silk Road. Annexed by Russia in the late 1800s, Turkmenistan later figured prominently in the anti-Bolshevik movement in Central Asia. In 1924, Turkmenistan became a Soviet republic; it achieved independence upon the dissolution of the USSR in 1991. Extensive hydrocarbon/ Natural gas reserves, which have yet to be fully exploited, have begun to transform the country.

The Government of Turkmenistan is moving to expand its extraction and delivery projects and has attempted to diversify its gas export routes beyond Russia's pipeline network. In 2010, new gas export pipelines that carry Turkmen gas to China and to northern Iran began operating, effectively ending the Russian monopoly on Turkmen gas exports. Subsequently, decreased Russian purchases, as well as limited purchases by Iran, have made China the dominant buyer of Turkmen gas. President for Life Saparmurat NYYAZOW died in December 2006, and Turkmenistan held its first multi-candidate presidential election in February 2007. Gurbanguly BERDIMUHAMEDOW, a deputy cabinet chairman under NYYAZOW, emerged as the country's new president; he was reelected in February 2012 with 97% of the vote, in an election widely regarded as "a democratic sham."

GEOGRAPHY

Location: Central Asia, bordering the Caspian Sea, between Iran and Kazakhstan

Geographic coordinates: 40 00 N, 60 00 E

Map references: Asia

Area: *total:* 488,100 sq km
land: 469,930 sq km
water: 18,170 sq km
country comparison to the world: 53

Area—comparative: slightly larger than California

Land boundaries: *total:* 4,158 km
border countries (4): Afghanistan 804 km, Iran 1,148 km, Kazakhstan 413 km, Uzbekistan 1,793 km

Coastline: 0 km; note—Turkmenistan borders the Caspian Sea (1,768 km)

Maritime claims: none (landlocked)

Climate: subtropical desert

Terrain: flat-to-rolling sandy desert with dunes rising to mountains in the south; low mountains along border with Iran; borders Caspian Sea in west

Elevation: *mean elevation:* 230 m

elevation extremes: *lowest point:* Vpadina Akchanaya -81 m (Sarygamysh Koli is a lake in northern Turkmenistan with a water level that fluctuates above and below the elevation of Vpadina Akchanaya, the lake has dropped as low as -110 m)
highest point: Gora Ayribaba 3,139 m

Natural resources: petroleum, Natural gas, sulfur, salt

Land use: *agricultural land:* 72%
arable land: 4.1%
permanent crops: 0.1%
permanent pasture: 67.8%
forest: 8.8%
other: 19.2% (2011 est.)

Irrigated land: 19,950 sq km (2012)

Total renewable water resources: 24.77 cu km (2011)

Freshwater withdrawal (domestic/industrial/agricultural): *total:* 27.95 cu km/yr (3%/3%/94%)
per capita: 5,752 cu m/yr (2004)

Natural hazards: NA

Environment—current issues: contamination of soil and groundwater with agricultural chemicals, pesticides; salination, water logging of soil due to poor irrigation methods; Caspian Sea pollution; diversion of a large share of the flow of the Amu Darya into irrigation contributes to that river's inability to replenish the Aral Sea; desertification

Environment—international agreements: *party to:* Biodiversity, Climate Change, Climate Change-Kyoto Protocol, Desertification, Hazardous Wastes, Ozone Layer Protection
signed, but not ratified: none of the selected agreements

Geography—note: landlocked; the western and central low-lying desolate portions of the country make up the great Garagum (Kara-Kum) desert, which occupies over 80% of the country; eastern part is plateau

PEOPLE AND SOCIETY

Nationality: *noun:* Turkmen(s)
adjective: Turkmen

Ethnic groups: Turkmen 85%, Uzbek 5%, Russian 4%, other 6% (2003)

Languages: Turkmen (official) 72%, Russian 12%, Uzbek 9%, other 7%

Religions: Muslim 89%, Eastern Orthodox 9%, unknown 2%

Population: 5,231,422 (July 2015 est.)
country comparison to the world: 120

Age structure: *0–14 years:* 26.14% (male 692,800/ female 674,638)
15–24 years: 19.66% (male 517,312/female 510,945)
25–54 years: 42.57% (male 1,104,066/female 1,122,896)
55–64 years: 7.25% (male 178,925/female 200,502)
65 years and over: 4.38% (male 99,878/female 129,460) (2015 est.)

Dependency ratios: *total dependency ratio:* 47.9%
youth dependency ratio: 41.7%
elderly dependency ratio: 6.1%
potential support ratio: 16.3% (2015 est.)

Median age: *total:* 27.1 years
male: 26.6 years
female: 27.5 years (2015 est.)
country comparison to the world: 141

Population growth rate: 1.14% (2015 est.)
country comparison to the world: 106

Birth rate: 19.4 births/1,000 population (2015 est.)
country comparison to the world: 89

Death rate: 6.13 deaths/1,000 population (2015 est.)
country comparison to the world: 158

Net migration rate: -1.84 migrant(s)/1,000 population (2015 est.)
country comparison to the world: 163

Urbanization: *urban population:* 50% of total population (2015)
rate of urbanization: 1.94% annual rate of change (2010–15 est.)

Major urban areas—population: ASHGABAT (capital) 746,000 (2015)

Sex ratio: *at birth:* 1.05 male(s)/female
0–14 years: 1.03 male(s)/female *15–24 years:* 1.01 male(s)/female
25–54 years: 0.98 male(s)/female
55–64 years: 0.89 male(s)/female
65 years and over: 0.77 male(s)/female
total population: 0.98 male(s)/female (2015 est.)

Mother's mean age at first birth: 24.6 (2006 est.)

Maternal mortality rate: 42 deaths/100,000 live births (2015 est.)
country comparison to the world: 89

Infant mortality rate: *total:* 36.82 deaths/1,000 live births
male: 44.13 deaths/1,000 live births
female: 29.14 deaths/1,000 live births (2015 est.)
country comparison to the world: 60

Life expectancy at birth: *total population:* 69.78 years
male: 66.77 years
female: 72.93 years (2015 est.)
country comparison to the world: 157

Total fertility rate: 2.09 children born/woman (2015 est.)
country comparison to the world: 109

Contraceptive prevalence rate: 48% (2006)

Health expenditures: 2% of GDP (2013)
country comparison to the world: 190

Hospital bed density: 4 beds/1,000 population (2012)

Drinking water source:
improved:
urban: 89.1% of population
rural: 53.7% of population
total: 71.1% of population
unimproved:
urban: 10.9% of population
rural: 46.3% of population
total: 28.9% of population (2012 est.)

Sanitation facility access:
improved:
urban: 100% of population
rural: 98.2% of population
total: 99.1% of population
unimproved:
urban: 0% of population
rural: 1.8% of population
total: 0.9% of population (2012 est.)

HIV/AIDS—adult prevalence rate: NA

HIV/AIDS—people living with HIV/AIDS: NA

HIV/AIDS—deaths: NA

Obesity—adult prevalence rate: 18.8% (2014)
country comparison to the world: 125

Children under the age of 5 years underweight: 9.2% (2006)
country comparison to the world: 68

Education expenditures: 3% of GDP (2012)

Literacy: *definition:* age 15 and over can read and write
total population: 99.7%
male: 99.8%
female: 99.6% (2015 est.)

School life expectancy (primary to tertiary education): *total:* 11 years
male: 11 years
female: 11 years (2014)

GOVERNMENT

Country name: *conventional long form:* none
conventional short form: Turkmenistan
local long form: none
local short form: Turkmenistan
former: Turkmen Soviet Socialist Republic

etymology: the suffix "-stan" means "place of" or "country," so Turkmenistan literally means the "Land of the Turkmen [people]"

Government type: presidential republic; highly authoritarian

Capital: *name:* Ashgabat (Ashkhabad)

Geographic coordinates: 37 57 N, 58 23 E

time difference: UTC+5 (10 hours ahead of Washington, DC, during Standard Time)

Administrative divisions: 5 provinces (welayatlar, singular—welayat) and 1 independent city*: Ahal Welayaty (Anew), Ashgabat*, Balkan Welayaty (Balkanabat), Dashoguz Welayaty, Lebap Welayaty (Turkmenabat), Mary Welayaty

note: administrative divisions have the same names as their administrative centers (exceptions have the administrative center name following in parentheses)

Independence: 27 October 1991 (from the Soviet Union)

National holiday: Independence Day, 27 October (1991)

Constitution: adopted 18 May 1992; amended several times, last in 2008; note—in mid-2014, the president established the Constitutional Commission to initiate a process for developing constitutional reforms (2016)

Legal system: civil law system with Islamic law influences

international law organization participation: has not submitted an ICJ jurisdiction declaration; non-party state to the ICCt

Citizenship: *citizenship by birth:* no

citizenship by descent only: at least one parent must be a citizen of Turkmenistan

dual citizenship recognized: yes

residency requirement for naturalization: 7 years

Suffrage: 18 years of age; universal

Executive branch: *chief of state:* President Gurbanguly BERDIMUHAMEDOW (since 14 February 2007); note—the president is both chief of state and head of government

head of government: President Gurbanguly BERDIMUHAMEDOW (since 14 February 2007)

cabinet: Cabinet of Ministers appointed by the president

elections/appointments: president directly elected by absolute majority popular vote in 2 rounds if needed for a 5-year term (eligible for a second term); election last held on 12 February 2012 (next to be held in February 2017); note—while the next presidential election would normally be held in February 2017, that may change as a result of the ongoing constitutional reforms, which are expected to extend the presidential term to 7 years

election results: Gurbanguly BERDIMUHAMEDOW reelected president; percent of vote—Gurbanguly BERDIMUHAMEDOW 97.1%, Annageldi YAZMYRADOW 1.1%, other candidates 1.8%

Legislative branch: *description:* unicameral National Assembly or Mejlis (125 seats; members directly elected in multi-seat constituencies by absolute majority vote in two rounds if needed; members serve 5-year terms); note—in September 2008, a constitutional change abolished a second, 2,507-member People's Council and expanded the membership in the National Assembly to 125 from 65; the powers formerly held by the People's Council were divided between the president and the National Assembly

elections: last held on 15 December 2013 (next to be held in December 2018)

election results: percent of vote by party—NA; seats by party—Democratic Party 47, Organization of Trade and Unions of Turkmenistan 33, Women's Union of Turkmenistan 16, Party of Industrialists and Entrepreneurs 14, Magtymguly Youth Organization 8, independents 7; note—all of these parties support President BERDIMUHAMIDOW

Judicial branch: *highest court(s):* Supreme Court of Turkmenistan (consists of the court president and 21 associate judges)

judge selection and term of office: judges appointed by the president; judge tenure NA

subordinate courts: provincial, district, and city courts; High Commercial Court; military courts

Political parties and leaders: Agrarian Party of Turkmenistan or APT [Rezhep BAZAROV] (government created in September 2014, like the PIE, but not represented in parliament)

Democratic Party of Turkmenistan or DPT [Kasymguly BABAYEW]

Party of Industrialists and Entrepreneurs or PIE [Orazmammet MAMMEDOW]

note: a law authorizing the registration of political parties went into effect in January 2012; unofficial, small opposition movements exist abroad

Political pressure groups and leaders: none

International organization participation: ADB, CIS (associate member, has not ratified the 1993 CIS charter although it participates in meetings and held the chairmanship of the CIS in 2012), EAPC, EBRD, ECO, FAO, G-77, IBRD, ICAO, ICRM, IDA, IDB, IFC, IFRCS, ILO, IMF, IMO, Interpol, IOC, IOM (observer), ISO (correspondent), ITU, MIGA, NAM, OIC, OPCW, OSCE, PFP, UN, UNCTAD, UNESCO, UNHCR, UNIDO, UNWTO, UPU, WCO, WFTU (NGOs), WHO, WIPO, WMO

Diplomatic representation in the US: *chief of mission:* Ambassador Mered Bairamovich ORAZOW (since 14 February 2001)

chancery: 2207 Massachusetts Avenue NW, Washington, DC 20008

telephone: [1] (202) 588-1500

FAX: [1] (202) 588-0697

Diplomatic representation from the US: *chief of mission:* Ambassador Allan MUSTARD (since 20 January 2015)

embassy: No.91984 Street (formerly Pushkin Street), Ashgabat, Turkmenistan 744000

mailing address: 7070 Ashgabat Place, Washington, DC 20521-7070

telephone: [993] (12) 94-00-45

FAX: [993] (12) 94-26-14

Flag description: green field with a vertical red stripe near the hoist side, containing five tribal guls (designs used in producing carpets) stacked above two crossed olive branches; five white stars and a white crescent moon appear in the upper corner of the field just to the fly side of the red stripe; the green color and crescent moon represent Islam; the five stars symbolize the regions or welayats of Turkmenistan; the guls reflect the National identity of Turkmenistan where carpetmaking has long been a part of traditional nomadic life

note: the flag of Turkmenistan is the most intricate of all National flags

National symbol(s): Akhal-Teke horse; National colors: green, white

National anthem: *name:* "Garassyz, Bitarap Turkmenistanyn" (Independent, Neutral, Turkmenistan State Anthem)

lyrics/music: collective/Veli MUKHATOV

note: adopted 1997, lyrics revised 2008; following the death of President Saparmurat NYYAZOW, the lyrics were altered to eliminate references to him

ECONOMY

Economy—overview: Turkmenistan is largely a desert country with intensive agriculture in irrigated oases and significant Natural gas and oil resources. The two largest crops are cotton, most of which is produced for export, and wheat, which is domestically consumed. Although agriculture accounts for roughly 14% of GDP, it continues to employ nearly half of the country's workforce. Hydrocarbon exports (mainly Natural gas) make up 31% of Turkmenistan's GDP, with 60% of gas exports going to China and the remainder to Russia and Iran. Ashgabat has explored two initiatives to bring gas to new markets: a trans-Caspian pipeline that would carry gas to Europe and the Turkmenistan-Afghanistan-Pakistan-India gas pipeline. Both face major financing and security hurdles and are unlikely to be completed soon.

Turkmenistan's autocratic governments under presidents NIYAZOW (1991–2006) and BERDIMUHAMEDOW (since 2007) have made little progress improving the business climate, privatizing state-owned industries, and combatting corruption, limiting economic development outside the energy sector. High energy prices in the mid-2000s allowed the government to undertake extensive development and social spending, including providing heavy utility subsidies.

Low energy prices since mid-2014 are hampering Turkmenistan's economic growth and reducing government revenues. The government has cut subsidies in several areas, and wage arears have increased. in January 2014, the Central Bank of Turkmenistan devalued the manat by 19%, and downward pressure on the currency continues. Turkmenistan continues to report GDP growth of nearly 10% per year and claims substantial foreign currency reserves, but non-transparent data limit international institutions' ability to verify this information.

GDP (purchasing power parity): $88.6 billion (2015 est.)
$83.19 billion (2014 est.)
$75.43 billion (2013 est.)
note: data are in 2015 US dollars
country comparison to the world: 86

GDP (official exchange rate): $35.68 billion (2015 est.)

GDP—real growth rate: 6.5% (2015 est.)
10.3% (2014 est.)
10.2% (2013 est.)
country comparison to the world: 24

GDP—per capita (PPP): $16,400 (2015 est.)
$15,700 (2014 est.)
$14,400 (2013 est.)
note: data are in 2015 US dollars
country comparison to the world: 99

Gross National saving: 32.1% of GDP (2015 est.)
19.3% of GDP (2014 est.)
11.7% of GDP (2013 est.)
country comparison to the world: 16

GDP—composition, by end use:
household consumption: 50%
government consumption: 12.5%
investment in fixed capital: 27.4%
investment in inventories: -0.1%
exports of goods and services: 35.5%
imports of goods and services: -25.3% (2015 est.)

GDP—composition, by sector of origin:
agriculture: 12.7%
industry: 49.3%
services: 37.9% (2015 est.)

Agriculture—products: cotton, grain, melons; livestock

Industries: Natural gas, oil, petroleum Products, textiles, food processing

Industrial production growth rate: 7% (2015 est.)
country comparison to the world: 17

Labor force: 2.305 million (2013 est.)
country comparison to the world: 118

Labor force—by occupation: agriculture: 48.2%
industry: 14%
services: 37.8% (2004 est.)

Unemployment rate: 11% (2014 est.)
10.6% (2013)
country comparison to the world: 125

Population below poverty line: 0.2% (2012 est.)

Household income or consumption by percentage share: lowest: 10%: 2.6%
highest: 10%: 31.7% (1998)

Distribution of family income—Gini index: 40.8 (1998)
country comparison to the world: 59

Budget: revenues: $6.229 billion
expenditures: $6.457 billion (2015 est.)
Taxes and other revenues: 14% of GDP (2015 est.)
country comparison to the world: 201

Budget surplus (+) or deficit (–): -0.5% of GDP (2015 est.)
country comparison to the world: 45

Fiscal year: calendar year

Inflation rate (consumer prices): 5.5% (2015 est.)
6% (2014 est.)
country comparison to the world: 180

Central bank discount rate: 5% (31 December 2014)
5% (31 December 2013)
country comparison to the world: 76

Stock of narrow money: $1.326 billion (31 December 2015 est.) $1.255 billion (31 December 2014 est.)
country comparison to the world: 144

Stock of broad money: $12.23 billion (31 December 2015 est.) $5.632 billion (31 December 2014 est.)
country comparison to the world: 102

Stock of domestic credit: $28.4 billion (31 December 2015 est.)
$13.09 billion (31 December 2014 est.)
country comparison to the world: 75

Market value of publicly traded shares: $NA

Current account balance: -$4.523 billion (2015 est.)
-$3.092 billion (2014 est.)
country comparison to the world: 166

Exports: $21.04 billion (2015 est.)
$20.84 billion (2014 est.)
country comparison to the world: 70

Exports—commodities: gas, crude oil, petrochemicals, textiles, cotton fiber

Exports—partners: China 68.5%, Turkey 4.9% (2015)

Imports: $14.82 billion (2015 est.)
$15.92 billion (2014 est.)
country comparison to the world: 86

Imports—commodities: machinery and equipment, chemicals, foodstuffs

Imports—partners: Turkey 24.9%, Russia 12.3%, China 10.9%, UAE 9.1%, Kazakhstan 5.1%, Germany 4.6%, Iran 4.4% (2015)

Reserves of foreign exchange and gold: $22.64 billion (31 December 2015 est.)
$26.65 billion (31 December 2014 est.)
country comparison to the world: 56

Debt—external: $522.3 million (31 December 2014 est.)
$501.8 million (31 December 2013 est.)
country comparison to the world: 178

Stock of direct foreign investment—at home: $3.061 billion (2013 est.)
$3.117 billion (2012 est.)
country comparison to the world: 105

Exchange rates: Turkmen manat (TMM) per US dollar—
3.5 (2015 est.)
2.85 (2014 est.)
2.85 (2013 est.)
2.85 (2012 est.)
2.85 (2011 est.)

ENERGY

Electricity—production: 22.3 billion kWh (2014 est.)

country comparison to the world: 73

Electricity—consumption: 11.75 billion kWh (2012 est.)
country comparison to the world: 85

Electricity—exports: 2.9 billion kWh (2014 est.)
country comparison to the world: 37

Electricity—imports: 0 kWh (2013 est.)
country comparison to the world: 213

Electricity—installed generating capacity: 4.275 million kW (2014 est.)
country comparison to the world: 79

Electricity—from fossil fuels: 100% of total installed capacity (2014 est.)
country comparison to the world: 32

Electricity—from nuclear fuels: 0% of total installed capacity (2014 est.)
country comparison to the world: 196

Electricity—from hydro electric plants: 0% of total installed capacity (2014 est.)
country comparison to the world: 209

Electricity—from other renewable sources: 0% of total installed capacity (2014 est.)
country comparison to the world: 135

Crude oil—production: 242,900 bbl/day (2014 est.)
country comparison to the world: 35

Crude oil—exports: 60,910 bbl/day (2012 est.)
country comparison to the world: 41

Crude oil—imports: 0 bbl/day (2013 est.)
country comparison to the world: 138

Crude oil—proved reserves: 600 million bbl (1 January 2015 est.)
country comparison to the world: 48

Refined petroleum products—production: 171,000 bbl/day (2012 est.)
country comparison to the world: 59

Refined petroleum products—consumption: 144,000 bbl/day (2013 est.)
country comparison to the world: 66

Refined petroleum products—exports: 44,130 bbl/day (2012 est.)
country comparison to the world: 59

Refined petroleum products—imports: 0 bbl/day (2012 est.)
country comparison to the world: 212

Natural gas—production: 84.8 billion cu m (2013 est.)
country comparison to the world: 10

Natural gas—consumption: 24 billion cu m (2013 est.)
country comparison to the world: 32

Natural gas—exports: 60.8 billion cu m (2013 est.)
country comparison to the world: 6

Natural gas—imports: 0 cu m (2014 est.)
country comparison to the world: 145

Natural gas—proved reserves: 17.5 trillion cu m (1 January 2014 est.)
country comparison to the world: 4

Carbon dioxide emissions from consumption of energy: 64.98 million Mt (2012 est.)

country comparison to the world: 51

COMMUNICATIONS

Telephones—fixed lines: *total subscriptions:* 620,000
subscriptions per 100 inhabitants: 12 (2014 est.)
country comparison to the world: 91

Telephones—mobile cellular: *total:* 7.2 million
subscriptions per 100 inhabitants: 139 (2014 est.)
country comparison to the world: 103

Telephone system: *general assessment:* telecommunications network remains underdeveloped and progress toward improvement is slow; strict government control and censorship inhibits liberalization and modernization
domestic: Turkmentelekom, in cooperation with foreign partners, has installed high-speed fiber-optic lines and has upgraded most of the country's telephone exchanges and switching centers with new digital technology; combined fixed-line and mobile teledensity is about 80 per 100 persons; Russia's Mobile Telesystems, the only foreign mobile-cellular service provider in Turkmenistan, had its operating license suspended in December 2010 but was able to resume operations in September 2012; Turkmenistan's first telecommunication satellite was launched in 2015; it is expected to greatly improve connectivity in the country
international: country code—993; linked by fiber-optic cable and microwave radio relay to other CIS republics and to other countries by leased connections to the Moscow international gateway switch; an exchange in Ashgabat switches international traffic through Turkey via Intelsat; satellite earth stations—1 Orbita and 1 Intelsat (2012)

Broadcast media: broadcast media is government controlled and censored; 7 state-owned TV and 4 state-owned radio networks; satellite dishes and programming provide an alternative to the state-run media; officials sometimes limit access to satellite TV by removing satellite dishes (2007)
Radio broadcast stations: AM 12, FM 9, shortwave 2 (2008)
Television broadcast stations: 4 (government-owned and programmed) (2008)

Internet country code: .tm

Internet hosts: 714 (2012)
country comparison to the world: 176

Internet users: *total:* 414,300

percent of population: 8.0% (2014 est.)
country comparison to the world: 133

TRANSPORTATION

Airports: 26 (2013)
country comparison to the world: 126

Airports—with paved runways: *total:* 21
over 3,047 m: 1
2,438 to 3,047 m: 9
1,524 to 2,437 m: 9
914 to 1,523 m: 2 (2013)

Airports—with unpaved runways: *total:* 5
1,524 to 2,437 m: 1
under 914 m: 4 (2013)

Heliports: 1 (2013)

Pipelines: gas 7,500 km; oil 1,501 km (2013)

Railways: *total:* 2,980 km
broad gauge: 2,980 km 1.520-m gauge (2014)
country comparison to the world: 59

Roadways: *total:* 58,592 km
paved: 47,577 km
unpaved: 11,015 km (2002)
country comparison to the world: 71

Waterways: 1,300 km (Amu Darya and Kara Kum canal are important inland waterways) (2011)
country comparison to the world: 55

Merchant marine: *total:* 11
by type: cargo 4, chemical tanker 1, petroleum tanker 5, refrigerated cargo 1 (2010)
country comparison to the world: 110

Ports and terminals: *major seaport(s):* Caspian Sea—Turkmenbasy

MILITARY AND SECURITY

Military branches: Turkmen Armed Forces: Ground Forces, Navy, Air and Air Defense Forces (2013)

Military service age and obligation: 18–27 years of age for compulsory male military service; 2-year conscript service obligation; 20 years of age for voluntary service; males may enroll in military schools from age 15 (2015)

TRANSNATIONAL ISSUES

Disputes—international: cotton monoculture in Uzbekistan and Turkmenistan creates water-sharing difficulties for Amu Darya river states; field demarcation of the boundaries with Kazakhstan

commenced in 2005, but Caspian seabed delimitation remains stalled with Azerbaijan, Iran, and Kazakhstan due to Turkmenistan's indecision over how to allocate the sea's waters and seabed; bilateral talks continue with Azerbaijan on dividing the seabed and contested oilfields in the middle of the Caspian

Refugees and internally displaced persons: *stateless persons:* 7,125 (2015)

Trafficking in persons: *current situation:* Turkmenistan is a source country for men, women, and children subjected to forced labor and sex trafficking; Turkmen who migrate abroad are forced to work in the textile, agriculture, construction, and domestic service industries, while women and girls may also be sex trafficked; in 2014, men surpassed women as victims; Turkey and Russia are primary trafficking destinations, followed by the Middle East, South and Central Asia, and other parts of Europe; Turkmen also experience forced labor domestically in the informal construction industry; participation in the cotton harvest is still mandatory for some public sector employees

tier rating: Tier 2 Watch List—Turkmenistan does not fully comply with the minimum standards for the elimination of trafficking; however, it is making significant efforts to do so; in 2014, Turkmenistan was granted a waiver from an otherwise required downgrade to Tier 3 because its government has a written plan that, if implemented, would constitute making significant efforts to bring itself into compliance with the minimum standards for the elimination of trafficking; the government made some progress in its law enforcement efforts in 2014, convicting more offenders than in 2013; authorities did not make adequate efforts to identify and protect victims and did not fund international organizations or NGOs that offered protective services; some victims were punished for crimes as a result of being trafficked (2015)

Illicit drugs: transit country for Afghan narcotics bound for Russian and Western European markets; transit point for heroin precursor chemicals bound for Afghanistan

TURKS AND CAICOS ISLANDS

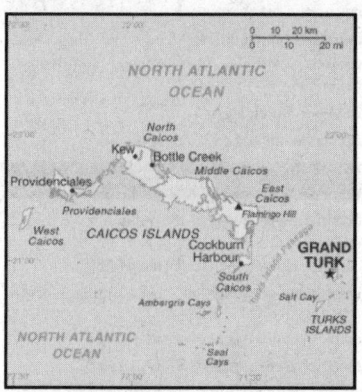

INTRODUCTION

Background: The islands were part of the UK's Jamaican colony until 1962, when they assumed the status of a separate crown colony upon Jamaica's independence. The governor of The Bahamas oversaw affairs from 1965 to 1973. With Bahamian independence, the islands received a separate governor in 1973. Although independence was agreed upon for 1982, the policy was reversed and the islands remaiNA British overseas territory.

GEOGRAPHY

Location: two island groups in the North Atlantic Ocean, southeast of The Bahamas, north of Haiti

Geographic coordinates: 21 45 N, 71 35 W

Map references: Central America and the Caribbean

Area: *total:* 948 sq km
land: 948 sq km
water: 0 sq km
country comparison to the world: 186

Area—comparative: 2.5 times the size of Washington, DC

Land boundaries: 0 km

Coastline: 389 km

Maritime claims: *territorial sea:* 12 nm
exclusive fishing zone: 200 nm

Climate: tropical; marine; moderated by trade winds; sunny and relatively dry

Terrain: low, flat limestone; extensive marshes and mangrove swamps

Elevation: *mean elevation:* NA

elevation extremes: *lowest point:* Caribbean Sea 0 m
highest point: Flamingo Hill 48 m

Natural resources: spiny lobster, conch

Land use: *agricultural land:* 1.1%
arable land: 1.1%
permanent crops: 0%

permanent pasture: 0%
forest: 36.2%
other: 62.7% (2011 est.)

Irrigated land: 0 sq km (2012)

Natural hazards: frequent hurricanes

Environment—current issues: limited Natural freshwater resources, private cisterns collect rainwater

Geography—note: about 40 islands (eight inhabited)

PEOPLE AND SOCIETY

Nationality: *noun:* none
adjective: none

Ethnic groups: black 87.6%, white 7.9%, mixed 2.5%, East Indian 1.3%, other 0.7% (2006)

Languages: English (official)

Religions: Protestant 72.8% (Baptist 35.8%, Church of God 11.7%, Anglican 10%, Methodist 9.3%, Seventh-Day Adventist 6%), Roman Catholic 11.4%, Jehovah's Witnesses 1.8%, other 14%

Population: 50,280 (July 2015 est.)
country comparison to the world: 211

Age structure: *0–14 years:* 22.01% (male 5,637/female 5,429)
15–24 years: 14.64% (male 3,614/female 3,748)
25–54 years: 53.37% (male 13,598/female 13,238)
55–64 years: 5.7% (male 1,558/female 1,309)
65 years and over: 4.27% (male 958/female 1,191) (2015 est.)

Median age: *total:* 32.4 years
male: 32.7 years
female: 32 years (2015 est.)
country comparison to the world: 92

Population growth rate: 2.3% (2015 est.)
country comparison to the world: 35

Birth rate: 16.13 births/1,000 population (2015 est.)
country comparison to the world: 119

Death rate: 3.1 deaths/1,000 population (2015 est.)
country comparison to the world: 220

Net migration rate: 9.94 migrant(s)/1,000 population (2015 est.)
country comparison to the world: 10

Urbanization: *urban population:* 92.2% of total population (2015)
rate of urbanization: 2.48% annual rate of change (2010–15 est.)

Major urban areas—population: GRAND TURK (capital) 5,000 (2014)

Sex ratio: *at birth:* 1.05 male(s)/female
0–14 years: 1.04 male(s)/female
15–24 years: 0.96 male(s)/female
25–54 years: 1.03 male(s)/female
55–64 years: 1.19 male(s)/female
65 years and over: 0.8 male(s)/female
total population: 1.02 male(s)/female (2015 est.)

Infant mortality rate: *total:* 10.65 deaths/1,000 live births

male: 13.29 deaths/1,000 live births
female: 7.88 deaths/1,000 live births (2015 est.)
country comparison to the world: 130

Life expectancy at birth: *total population:* 79.69 years
male: 76.94 years
female: 82.57 years (2015 est.)
country comparison to the world: 42

Total fertility rate: 1.7 children born/woman (2015 est.)
country comparison to the world: 172

Sanitation facility access:
improved:
urban: 81.4% of population
rural: 81.4% of population
total: 81.4% of population
unimproved:
urban: 18.6% of population
rural: 18.6% of population
total: 18.6% of population (2007 est.)

HIV/AIDS—adult prevalence rate: NA

HIV/AIDS—people living with HIV/AIDS: NA

HIV/AIDS—deaths: NA

Education expenditures: 3.3% of GDP (2015)

People—note: destination and transit point for illegal Haitian immigrants bound for the Turks and Caicos Islands, The Bahamas, and the US

GOVERNMENT

Country name: *conventional long form:* none
conventional short form: Turks and Caicos Islands abbreviation: TCI
etymology: the Turks Islands are named after the Turk's cap cactus (native to the islands and appearing on the flag and coat of arms), while the Caicos Islands derive from the native term "caya hico" meaning "string of islands"

Dependency status: overseas territory of the UK

Government type: parliamentary democracy (House of Assembly); self-governing overseas territory of the UK

Capital: *name:* Grand Turk (Cockburn Town)
Geographic coordinates: 21 28 N, 71 08 W
time difference: UTC-5 (same time as Washington, DC, during Standard Time)
daylight saving time: +1hr, begins second Sunday in March; ends first Sunday in November

Administrative divisions: none (overseas territory of the UK)

Independence: none (overseas territory of the UK)

National holiday: Constitution Day, 30 August (1976)

Constitution: several previous; latest signed 7 August 2012, effective 15 October 2012 (Turks and Caicos ConstitutioNorder 2011) (2016)

Legal system: mixed legal system of English common law and civil law

Citizenship: see United Kingdom

Suffrage: 18 years of age; universal

Executive branch: *chief of state:* Queen ELIZA-BETH II (since 6 February 1952); represented by Governor Peter BECKINGHAM (since 9 October 2013)

head of government: Premier Rufus EWING (since 13 November 2012)

cabinet: Cabinet appointed by the governor from among members of the House of Assembly

elections/appointments: the monarch is hereditary; governor appointed by the monarch; following legislative elections, the leader of the majority party is appointed premier by the governor

Legislative branch: *description:* unicameral House of Assembly (19 seats; 15 members in multi-seat constituencies and a single all-islands constituency directly elected by simple majority vote, 1 member nominated by the premier and appointed by the governor, 1 nominated by the opposition party leader and appointed by the governor, and 2 from the Turks and Caicos Islands Civic Society directly appointed by the governor; members serve 4-year terms)

elections: last held on 9 November 2012 (next to be held in 2016)

election results: percent of vote—NA; seats by party—PNP 8, PDM 7

Judicial branch: *highest resident court(s):* Supreme Court (consists of the chief justice and such number of other judges as determined by the governor); Court of Appeal (consists of the court president and 2 justices; note—appeals beyond the Supreme Court are heard by the Judicial Committee of the Privy Council (in London)

judge selection and term of office: Supreme Court and Appeals Court judges appointed by the governor in accordance with the Judicial Service Commission, a 3-member body of high level judicial officials; Supreme Court judges appointed until mandatory retirement at age 65, but can be extended to age 70; Appeals Court judge tenure determined by individual terms of appointment

subordinate courts: magistrates' courts

Political parties and leaders: People's Democratic Movement or PDM [Oswald SKIPPINGS]
People's Progressive Party
Progressive National Party or PNP [Rufus EWING]

Political pressure groups and leaders: NA

International organization participation: Caricom (associate), CDB, Interpol (subbureau), UPU

Diplomatic representation in the US: none (overseas territory of the UK)

Diplomatic representation from the US: none (overseas territory of the UK)

Flag description: blue with the flag of the UK in the upper hoist-side quadrant and the colonial shield centered on the outer half of the flag; the shield is yellow and displays a conch shell, a spiny lobster, and Turk's cap cactus three common elements of the islands' biota

National symbol(s): conch shell, Turk's cap cactus

National anthem: *name:* "This Land of Ours"
lyrics/music: Conrad HOWELL

note: serves as a local anthem; as a territory of the UK, "God Save the Queen" is the official anthem (see United Kingdom)

ECONOMY

Economy—overview: The Turks and Caicos economy is based on tourism, offshore financial services, and fishing. Most capital goods and food for domestic consumption are imported. The US is the leading source of tourists, accounting for more than three-quarters of the more than 1 million visitors that arrived in 2013. Three-quarters of the visitors came by ship. Major sources of government revenue also include fees from offshore financial activities and customs receipts.

GDP (purchasing power parity): $632 million (2007 est.)
$568.3 million (2006 est.)
country comparison to the world: 211

GDP (official exchange rate): $NA

GDP—real growth rate: 11.2% (2007 est.)
country comparison to the world: 1

GDP—per capita (PPP): $29,100 (2007 est.)
country comparison to the world: 63

GDP—composition, by end use:
household consumption: 23.4%
government consumption: 17.2%
investment in fixed capital: 32.2%
investment in inventories: 33.8%
exports of goods and services: 57.4%
imports of goods and services: -64% (2015 est.)

GDP—composition, by sector of origin:
agriculture: 0.5%
industry: 10%
services: 89.5% (2015 est.)

Agriculture—products: corn, beans, cassava (manioc, tapioca), citrus fruits; fish

Industries: tourism, offshore financial services

Industrial production growth rate: 3% (2015 est.)
country comparison to the world: 89

Labor force: 4,848 (1990 est.)
country comparison to the world: 221

Labor force—by occupation: *note:* about 33% in government and 20% in agriculture and fishing; significant numbers in tourism, finan cial, and other services

Unemployment rate: 10% (1997 est.)
country comparison to the world: 116

Population below poverty line: NA%

Household income or consumption by percentage share: *lowest:* 10%: NA%
highest: 10%: NA%

Budget: *revenues:* $218.6 million
expenditures: $183.5 million (2015 est.)

Fiscal year: calendar year

Inflation rate (consumer prices): 2.5% (2015 est.)
3% (2014 est.)
country comparison to the world: 130

Exports: $24.77 million (2008 est.)
country comparison to the world: 208

Exports—commodities: lobster, dried and fresh conch, conch shells

Imports: $591.3 million (2008 est.)
country comparison to the world: 191

Imports—commodities: food and beverages, tobacco, clothing, manufactures, construction materials

Debt—external: $NA

Exchange rates: the US dollar is used

ENERGY

Electricity—production: 180 million kWh (2012 est.)
country comparison to the world: 189

Electricity—consumption: 167.4 million kWh (2012 est.)
country comparison to the world: 191

Electricity—exports: 0 kWh (2013 est.)
country comparison to the world: 202

Electricity—imports: 0 kWh (2013 est.)
country comparison to the world: 207

Electricity—installed generating capacity: 48,000 kW (2012 est.)
country comparison to the world: 187

Electricity—from fossil fuels: 100% of total installed capacity (2012 est.)
country comparison to the world: 30

Electricity—from nuclear fuels: 0% of total installed capacity (2012 est.)
country comparison to the world: 189

Electricity—from hydro electric plants: 0% of total installed capacity (2012 est.)
country comparison to the world: 206

Electricity—from other renewable sources: 0% of total installed capacity (2012 est.)
country comparison to the world: 131

Crude oil—production: 0 bbl/day (2014 est.)
country comparison to the world: 196

Crude oil—exports: 0 bbl/day (2012 est.)
country comparison to the world: 195

Crude oil—imports: 0 bbl/day (2012 est.)
country comparison to the world: 132

Crude oil—proved reserves: 0 bbl (1 January 2015 est.)
country comparison to the world: 196

Refined petroleum products—production: 0 bbl/day (2012 est.)
country comparison to the world: 134

Refined petroleum products—consumption: 1,300 bbl/day (2013 est.)
country comparison to the world: 196

Refined petroleum products—exports: 0 bbl/day (2012 est.)
country comparison to the world: 135

Refined petroleum products—imports: 1,261 bbl/day (2012 est.)
country comparison to the world: 192

Natural gas—production: 0 cu m (2013 est.)
country comparison to the world: 134

Natural gas—consumption: 0 cu m (2013 est.)

country comparison to the world: 198

Natural gas—exports: 0 cu m (2013 est.)
country comparison to the world: 191

Natural gas—imports: 0 cu m (2013 est.)
country comparison to the world: 139

Natural gas—proved reserves: 0 cu m (1 January 2014 est.)
country comparison to the world: 198

Carbon dioxide emissions from consumption of energy: 159,400 Mt (2012 est.)
country comparison to the world: 201

COMMUNICATIONS

Telephone system: *general assessment:* fully digital system with international direct dialing
domestic: full range of services available; GSM wireless service available
international: country code—1–649; the Americas Region Caribbean Ring System (ARCOS-1) fiber optic telecommunications submarine cable provides connectivity to South and Central

America, parts of the Caribbean, and the US; satellite earth station—1 Intelsat (Atlantic Ocean) (2011)

Broadcast media: no local terrestrial TV stations, broadcasts from the Bahamas can be received and multi-channel cable and satellite TV services are available; government-run radio network operates alongside private broadcasters with a total of about 15 stations (2007)
Radio broadcast stations: AM 2, FM 7, shortwave 0 (2003)
Television broadcast stations: 0 (broadcasts received from The Bahamas; 2 cable television networks) (2003)

Internet country code: .tc

Internet hosts: 73,217 (2012)
country comparison to the world: 86

TRANSPORTATION

Airports: 8 (2013)
country comparison to the world: 162

Airports—with paved runways: *total:* 6

2,438 to 3,047 m: 1
1,524 to 2,437 m: 3
914 to 1,523 m: 1
under 914 m: 1 (2013)

Airports—with unpaved runways: *total:* 2
under 914 m: 2 (2013)

Roadways: *total:* 121 km
paved: 24 km
unpaved: 97 km (2003)
country comparison to the world: 213

Ports and terminals: *major seaport(s):* Cockburn Harbour, Grand Turk, Providenciales

MILITARY AND SECURITY

Military—note: defense is the responsibility of the UK

TRANSNATIONAL ISSUES

Disputes—international: have received Haitians fleeing economic and civil disorder

Illicit drugs: transshipment point for South American narcotics destined for the US and Europe

TUVALU

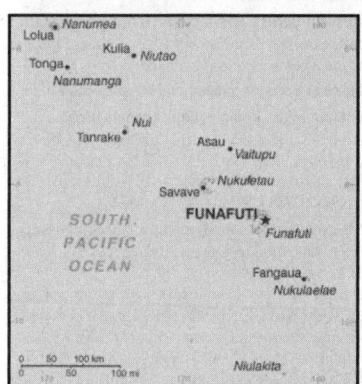

INTRODUCTION

Background: In 1974, ethnic differences within the British colony of the Gilbert and Ellice Islands caused the Polynesians of the Ellice Islands to vote for separation from the Micronesians of the Gilbert Islands. The following year, the Ellice Islands became the separate British colony of Tuvalu. Independence was granted in 1978. In 2000, Tuvalu negotiated a contract leasing its Internet domain name ".tv" for $50 million in royalties over a 12-year period. The agreement was subsequently renegotiated but details were not disclosed.

GEOGRAPHY

Location: Oceania, island group consisting of nine coral atolls in the South Pacific Ocean, about half way from Hawaii to Australia

Geographic coordinates: 8 00 S, 178 00 E

Map references: Oceania

Area: *total:* 26 sq km
land: 26 sq km
water: 0 sq km
country comparison to the world: 238

Area—comparative: 0.1 times the size of Washington, DC

Land boundaries: 0 km

Coastline: 24 km

Maritime claims: *territorial sea:* 12 nm
contiguous zone: 24 nm
exclusive economic zone: 200 nm

Climate: tropical; moderated by easterly trade winds (March to November); westerly gales and heavy rain (November to March)

Terrain: low-lying and narrow coral atolls

Elevation: *mean elevation:* NA

elevation extremes: *lowest point:* Pacific Ocean 0 m
highest point: unnamed location 5 m

Natural resources: fish, coconut (copra)

Land use: *agricultural land:* 60%
arable land: 0%
permanent crops: 60%
permanent pasture: 0%
forest: 33.3%
other: 6.7% (2011 est.)

Irrigated land: 0 sq km (2012)

Natural hazards: severe tropical storms are usually rare, but in 1997 there were three cyclones; low levels of islands make them sensitive to changes in sea level

Environment—current issues: since there are no streams or rivers and groundwater is not potable,

most water needs must be met by catchment systems with storage facilities; beachhead erosion because of the use of sand for building materials; excessive clearance of forest undergrowth for use as fuel; damage to coral reefs from increasing ocean temperatures and acidification; Tuvalu is concerned about global increases in greenhouse gas emissions and their effect on rising sea levels, which threaten the country's underground water table; in 2000, the government appealed to Australia and New Zealand to take in Tuvaluans if rising sea levels should make evacuation necessary

Environment—international agreements: *party to:* Biodiversity, Climate Change, Climate Change-Kyoto Protocol, Desertification, Law of the Sea, Ozone Layer Protection, Ship Pollution, Whaling
signed, but not ratified: none of the selected agreements

Geography—note: one of the smallest and most remote countries on Earth; six of the nine coral atolls—Nanumea, Nui, Vaitupu, Nukufetau, Funafuti, and Nukulaelae—have lagoons open to the ocean; Nanumaya and Niutao have landlocked lagoons; Niulakita does not have a lagoon

PEOPLE AND SOCIETY

Nationality: *noun:* Tuvaluan(s)
adjective: Tuvaluan

Ethnic groups: Polynesian 96%, Micronesian 4%

Languages: Tuvaluan (official), English (official), Samoan, Kiribati (on the island of Nui)

Religions: Protestant 98.4% (Church of Tuvalu (Congregation alist) 97%, Seventh-Day Adventist 1.4%), Baha'i 1%, other 0.6%

Population: 10,869 (July 2015 est.)
country comparison to the world: 223

877

Age structure: *0–14 years:* 29.4% (male 1,639/ female 1,557)
15–24 years: 20.27% (male 1,157/female 1,046)
25–54 years: 36.35% (male 1,946/female 2,005)
55–64 years: 8.41% (male 373/female 541)
65 years and over: 5.57% (male 247/female 358) (2015 est.)

Median age: *total:* 25.2 years
male: 24.1 years
female: 26.6 years (2015 est.)
country comparison to the world: 152

Population growth rate: 0.82% (2015 est.)
country comparison to the world: 135

Birth rate: 23.74 births/1,000 population (2015 est.)
country comparison to the world: 62

Death rate: 8.74 deaths/1,000 population (2015 est.)
country comparison to the world: 71

Net migration rate: -6.81 migrant(s)/1,000 population (2015 est.)
country comparison to the world: 204

Urbanization: *urban population:* 59.7% of total population (2015)
rate of urbanization: 1.9% annual rate of change (2010–15 est.)

Major urban areas—population: FUNAFUTI (capital) 6,000 (2014)

Sex ratio: *at birth:* 1.05 male(s)/female
0–14 years: 1.05 male(s)/female
15–24 years: 1.11 male(s)/female
25–54 years: 0.97 male(s)/female
55–64 years: 0.69 male(s)/female
65 years and over: 0.69 male(s)/female
total population: 0.97 male(s)/female (2015 est.)

Mother's mean age at first birth: 23.5
note: Median age at first birth among women 25–29 (2007 est.)

Infant mortality rate: *total:* 30.8 deaths/1,000 live births
male: 33.46 deaths/1,000 live births
female: 28.01 deaths/1,000 live births (2015 est.)
country comparison to the world: 66

Life expectancy at birth: *total population:* 66.16 years
male: 64.01 years
female: 68.41 years (2015 est.)
country comparison to the world: 173

Total fertility rate: 3 children born/woman (2015 est.)
country comparison to the world: 54

Contraceptive prevalence rate: 30.5% (2007)

Health expenditures: 19.7% of GDP (2013)
country comparison to the world: 4

Physicians density: 1.09 physicians/1,000 population (2009)

Drinking water source:
improved:
urban: 98.3% of population
rural: 97% of population
total: 97.7% of population
unimproved:
urban: 1.7% of population
rural: 3% of population
total: 2.3% of population (2015 est.)

Sanitation facility access:
improved:
urban: 86.3% of population
rural: 80.2% of population
total: 83.3% of population

unimproved:
urban: 13.7% of population
rural: 19.8% of population
total: 16.7% of population (2012 est.)

HIV/AIDS—adult prevalence rate: NA

HIV/AIDS—people living with HIV/AIDS: NA

HIV/AIDS—deaths: NA

Obesity—adult prevalence rate: 39.6% (2014)

Children under the age of 5 years underweight: 1.6% (2007)
country comparison to the world: 126

Education expenditures: NA

GOVERNMENT

Country name: *conventional long form:* none
conventional short form: Tuvalu
local long form: none
local short form: Tuvalu
former: Ellice Islands
note: "tuvalu" means "group of eight" referring to the country's eight traditionally inhabited islands

Government type: parliamentary democracy (House of Assembly) under a constitutional monarchy; a Commonwealth realm

Capital: *name:* Funafuti; *note*—administrative offices are in Vaiaku Village on Fongafale Islet

Geographic coordinates: 8 31 S, 179 13 E
time difference: UTC + 12 (17 hours ahead of Washington, DC, during Standard Time)

Administrative divisions: 7 island councils and 1 town council*; Funafuti*, Nanumaga, Nanumea, Niutao, Nui, Nukufetau, Nukulaelae, Vaitupu

Independence: 1 October 1978 (from the UK)

National holiday: Independence Day, 1 October (1978)

Constitution: previous 1978 (at independence); latest effective 1 October 1986; amended 2007, 2010, 2013 (2016)

Legal system: mixed legal system of English common law and local customary law

international law organization participation: has not submitted an ICJ jurisdiction declaration; non-party state to the ICCt

Citizenship: *citizenship by birth:* yes
citizenship by descent: yes; for a child born abroad, at least one parent must be a citizen of Tuvalu
dual citizenship recognized: yes
residency requirement for naturalization: na

Suffrage: 18 years of age; universal

Executive branch: *chief of state:* Queen ELIZABETH II (since 6 February 1952); represented by Governor General Iakoba TAEIA Italeli (since 16 April 2010)
head of government: Prime Minister Enele SOPOAGA (since 5 August 2013)
cabinet: Cabinet appointed by the governor general on recommendation of the prime minister
elections/appointments: the monarchy is hereditary; governor general appointed by the monarch on recommendation of the prime minister; prime minister and deputy prime minister elected by and from members of House of Assembly following parliamentary elections
election results: Enele SOPOAGA elected prime minister by House of Assembly; House of Assembly vote count on 4 August 2013—8 to 5;

note—Willie TELAVI removed as prime minister by the governor general on 1 August 2013

Legislative branch: *description:* unicameral House of Assembly or Fale I Fono (15 seats; members directly elected in single-and multi-seat constituencies by simple majority vote to serve 4-year terms)
elections: last held on 31 March 2015 (next to be held in 2019)
election results: percent of vote—NA; seats: independent 15; 12 members reelected

Judicial branch: *highest court(s):* Court of Appeal is the Fiji Court of Appeal on Fiji Island (consists of the chief justice who visits twice a year); High Court, located on Fiji, consists of the chief justice of Fiji who presides over its sessions
judge selection and term of office: chief justice appointed by the president of Fiji on the advice of the prime minister following consultation with the parliamentary leader of the opposition; justices of the Court of Appeal, and puisne judges of the High Court are appointed by the president of Fiji, upon the nomination of the Judicial Service Commission, after consulting with the Cabinet Minister and the committee of the House of Representatives responsible for the administration of justice; the chief justice and justices of Appeal generally required to retire at age 70; puisine judges appointed for not less than 4 years nor more than 7 years with mandatory retirement at age 65
subordinate courts: magistrates' courts; island courts; lands courts

Political parties and leaders: there are no political parties but members of parliament usually align themselves in informal groupings

Political pressure groups and leaders: none

International organization participation: ACP, ADB, AOSIS, C, FAO, IBRD, IDA, IFAD, IFRCS (observer), ILO, IMF, IMO, IOC, ITU, OPCW, PIF, Sparteca, SPC, UN, UNCTAD, UNESCO, UNIDO, UPU, WHO, WIPO, WMO

Diplomatic representation in the US: *chief of mission:* Ambassador Aunese Makoi SIMATI (since 11 January 2013)
chancery: note—Tuvalu does not have an embassy in Washington, D. C.; UN office located at 8002nd Avenue, Suite 400D, New York, NY 10017
telephone: [1] (212) 490-0534
FAX: [1] (212) 937-0692

Diplomatic representation from the US: the US does not have an embassy in Tuvalu; the US Ambassador to Fiji is accredited to Tuvalu

Flag description: light blue with the flag of the UK in the upper hoist-side quadrant; the outer half of the flag represents a map of the country with nine yellow, five-pointed stars on a blue field symbolizing the nine atolls in the ocean

National symbol(s): maneapa (native meeting house); National colors: light blue, yellow

National anthem: *name:* "Tuvalu mo te Atua" (Tuvalu for the Almighty)
lyrics/music: Afaese MANOA
note: adopted 1978; the anthem's name is also the nation's motto

ECONOMY

Economy—overview: Tuvalu consists of a densely populated, scattered group of nine coral atolls with poor soil. Only eight of the atolls are inhabited. It is one of the smallest countries in the world, with its highest point at 4.6 meters above sea level.

The country is isolated, almost entirely dependent on imports, particularly of food and fuel, and vulnerable to climate change and rising sea levels, which pose significant challenges to development. The public sector dominates economic activity. Tuvalu has few Natural resources, except for its fisheries. Earnings from fish exports and fishing licenses for Tuvalu's territorial waters are a significant source of government revenue. In 2013, revenue from fishing licenses doubled and totaled more than 45% of GDP. Official aid from foreign development partners has also increased. Tuvalu has substantial assets abroad. The Tuvalu Trust Fund, an international trust fund established in 1987 by development partners, has grown to $141 million in 2013 and is an important cushion for meeting shortfalls in the government's budget. While remittances are another substantial source of income, the value of remittances has declined since the 2008–2009 global financial crisis. Growing income inequality is one of many concerns for the nation.

GDP (purchasing power parity): $37 million (2015 est.)
$36.05 million (2014 est.)
$35.26 million (2013 est.)
note: data are in 2015 US dollars
country comparison to the world: 227

GDP (official exchange rate): $33 million (2015 est.)

GDP—real growth rate: 2.6% (2015 est.)
2.2% (2014 est.)
1.3% (2013 est.)
country comparison to the world: 116

GDP—per capita (PPP): $3,400 (2015 est.)
$3,300 (2014 est.)
$3,200 (2013 est.)
note: data are in 2015 US dollars
country comparison to the world: 182

GDP—composition, by sector of origin:
agriculture: 24.5%
industry: 5.6%
services: 70% (2012 est.)

Agriculture—products: coconuts; fish

Industries: fishing

Industrial production growth rate: -26.1% (2012 est.)
country comparison to the world: 200

Labor force: 3,615 (2004 est.)
country comparison to the world: 223

Labor force—by occupation: *note:* people make a living mainly through exploitation of the sea, reefs, and atolls and through overseas remittances (mostly from workers in the phosphate industry and sailors)

Unemployment rate: NA%

Population below poverty line: 26.3% (2010 est.)

Household income or consumption by percentage share: *lowest:* 10%: NA%
highest: 10%: NA%

Budget: *revenues:* $42.68 million
expenditures: $32.46 million (2013 est.)
Taxes and other revenues: 125.5% of GDP (2013 est.)
country comparison to the world: 2

Budget surplus (+) or deficit (–): 30.1% of GDP (2013 est.)
country comparison to the world: 1

Public debt: 41.1% of GDP (2013 est.)
43.1% of GDP (2012 est.)
country comparison to the world: 110

Fiscal year: calendar year

Inflation rate (consumer prices): 3.3% (2015 est.)
1.1% (2014 est.)
country comparison to the world: 143

Commercial bank prime lending rate: 10.6% (31 December 2013 est.)
10.6% (31 December 2012 est.)
country comparison to the world: 78

Market value of publicly traded shares: $0 (2014)
country comparison to the world: 121

Current account balance: -$9 million (2015 est.)
-$10 million (2014 est.)
country comparison to the world: 57

Exports: $600,000 (2010 est.)
$1 million (2004 est.)
country comparison to the world: 221

Exports—commodities: copra, fish

Imports: $136.5 million (2013 est.) $238.6 million (2012 est.)
country comparison to the world: 213

Imports—commodities: food, animals, mineral fuels, machinery, manufactured goods

Debt—external: $NA

Exchange rates: Tuvaluan dollars or Australian dollars (AUD) per US dollar—
1.33 (2015 est.)
1.67 (2014 est.)
1.1094 (2013 est.)
0.97 (2012 est.)
0.9695 (2011 est.)

ENERGY

Electricity—production: 11.8 million kWh (2011)
country comparison to the world: 216

Electricity—exports: 0 kWh (2014 est.)
country comparison to the world: 207

Electricity—imports: 0 kWh (2014)
country comparison to the world: 211

Electricity—installed generating capacity: 5,100 kW (2011)
country comparison to the world: 211

Electricity—from fossil fuels: 96% of total installed capacity (2015 est.)
country comparison to the world: 65

Electricity—from nuclear fuels: 0% of total installed capacity (2014)
country comparison to the world: 195

Electricity—from hydro electric plants: 0% of total installed capacity (2014)
country comparison to the world: 208

Crude oil—production: 0 bbl/day (2014)
country comparison to the world: 200

Crude oil—exports: 0 bbl/day (2014)
country comparison to the world: 199

Crude oil—imports: 0 bbl/day (2014)
country comparison to the world: 137

Crude oil—proved reserves: 0 bbl (1 January 2015 est.)
country comparison to the world: 202

Refined petroleum products—production: 0 bbl/day (2014 est.)
country comparison to the world: 139

Refined petroleum products—exports: 0 bbl/day
country comparison to the world: 140

Natural gas—production: 0 cu m (2014)
country comparison to the world: 139

Natural gas—consumption: 0 cu m (2014)
country comparison to the world: 203

Natural gas—exports: 0 cu m (2014)
country comparison to the world: 197

Natural gas—imports: 0 cu m (2014)
country comparison to the world: 144

COMMUNICATIONS

Telephone—fixed lines: *total subscriptions:* 1,500
subscriptions per 100 inhabitants: 14 (2014 est.)
country comparison to the world: 215

Telephone—mobile cellular: *total:* 3,800
subscriptions per 100 inhabitants: 35 (2014 est.)
country comparison to the world: 217

Telephone system: *general assessment:* serves particular needs for internal communications
domestic: radio telephone communications between islands
international: country code—688; international calls can be made by satellite (2007)

Broadcast media: no TV stations; many households use satellite dishes to watch foreign TV stations; 1 government-owned radio station, Radio Tuvalu, includes relays of programming from international broadcasters (2009)
Radio broadcast stations: AM 1, FM 1, shortwave 0 (2004)
Television broadcast stations: 0 (2004)

Internet country code: .tv

Internet hosts: 145,158 (2012)
country comparison to the world: 80

Internet users: *total:* 4,100
percent of population: 38.1% (2014 est.)
country comparison to the world: 206

TRANSPORTATION

Airports: 1 (2013)
country comparison to the world: 235

Airports—with unpaved runways: *total:* 1
1,524 to 2,437 m: 1 (2013)

Roadways: *total:* 8 km
paved: 8 km (2011)
country comparison to the world: 223

Merchant marine: *total:* 58
by type: bulk carrier 4, cargo 24, chemical tanker 15, container 1, passenger 2, passenger/cargo 1, petroleum tanker 10, refrigerated cargo 1
foreign-owned: 33 (China 4, Indonesia 1, Maldives 1, Singapore 19, South Korea 1, Turkey 1, Vietnam 6) (2010)
country comparison to the world: 67

Ports and terminals: *major seaport(s):* Funafuti

MILITARY AND SECURITY

Military branches: no regular military forces; Tuvalu Police Force (2012)

TRANSNATIONAL ISSUES

Disputes—international: none

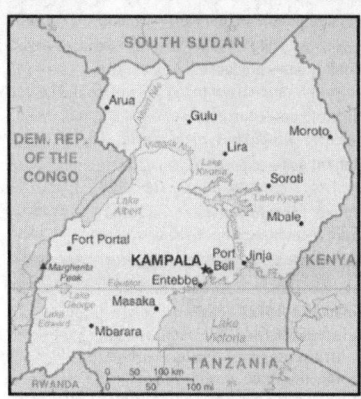

INTRODUCTION

Background: The colonial boundaries created by Britain to delimit Uganda grouped together a wide range of Ethnic groups with different political systems and cultures. These differences complicated the establishment of a working political community after independence was achieved in 1962. The dictatorial regime of Idi AMIN (1971–79) was responsible for the deaths of some 300,000 opponents; guerrilla war and human rights abuses under Milton OBOTE (1980–85) claimed at least another 100,000 lives. The rule of Yoweri MUSEVENI since 1986 has brought relative stability and economic growth to Uganda. A constitutional referendum in 2005 cancelled a 19-year ban on multi-party politics and lifted presidential term limits.

GEOGRAPHY

Location: East-Central Africa, west of Kenya, east of the Democratic Republic of the Congo

Geographic coordinates: 1 00 N, 32 00 E

Map references: Africa

Area: *total:* 241,038 sq km
land: 197,100 sq km
water: 43,938 sq km
country comparison to the world: 81

Area—comparative: slightly smaller than Oregon

Land boundaries: *total:* 2,729 km
border countries (5): Democratic Republic of the Congo 877 km, Kenya 814 km, Rwanda 172 km, South Sudan 475 km, Tanzania 391 km

Coastline: 0 km (landlocked)

Maritime claims: none (landlocked)

Climate: tropical; generally rainy with two dry seasons (December to February, June to August); semiarid in North east

Terrain: mostly plateau with rim of mountains

Elevation: *mean elevation:* NA

elevation extremes: *lowest point:* Lake Albert 621 m
highest point: Margherita Peak on Mount Stanley 5,110 m

Natural resources: copper, cobalt, hydropower, limestone, salt, arable land, gold

Land use: *agricultural land:* 71.2%
arable land: 34.3%
permanent crops: 11.3%
permanent pasture: 25.6%
forest: 14.5%
other: 14.3% (2011 est.)

Irrigated land: 140 sq km (2012)

Total renewable water resources: 66 cu km (2011)

Freshwater withdrawal (domestic/industrial/agricultural): *total:* 0.32 cu km/yr (41%/16%/43%)
per capita: 12.31 cu m/yr (2005)

Natural hazards: NA

Environment—current issues: draining of wetlands for agricultural use; deforestation; overgrazing; soil erosion; water hyacinth infestation in Lake Victoria; widespread poaching

Environment—international agreements: *party to:* Biodiversity, Climate Change, Climate Change-Kyoto Protocol, Desertification, Endangered Species, Hazardous Wastes, Law of the Sea, Marine Life Conservation, Ozone Layer Protection, Wetlands
signed, but not ratified: Environmental Modification

Geography—note: landlocked; fertile, well-watered country with many lakes and rivers

PEOPLE AND SOCIETY

Nationality: *noun:* Ugandan(s)
adjective: Ugandan

Ethnic groups: Baganda 16.9%, Banyankole 9.5%, Basoga 8.4%, Bakiga 6.9%, Iteso 6.4%, Langi 6.1%, Acholi 4.7%, Bagisu 4.6%, Lugbara 4.2%, Bunyoro 2.7%, other 29.6% (2002 census)

Languages: English (official National language, taught in grade schools, used in courts of law and by most newspapers and some radio broadcasts), Ganda or Luganda (most widely used of the Niger-Congo languages, preferred for native language publications in the capital and may be taught in school), other Niger-Congo languages, Nilo-Saharan languages, Swahili, Arabic

Religions: Roman Catholic 41.9%, Protestant 42% (Anglican 35.9%, Pentecostal 4.6%, Seventh-Day Adventist 1.5%), Muslim 12.1%, other 3.1%, none 0.9% (2002 census)

Population: 37,101,745
note: estimates for this country explicitly take into account the effects of excess mortality due to AIDS; this can result in lower life expectancy, higher infant mortality, higher death rates, lower population growth rates, and changes in the distribution of population by age and sex than would otherwise be expected (July 2015 est.)
country comparison to the world: 36

Age structure: *0–14 years:* 48.47% (male 8,966,494/female 9,015,302)
15–24 years: 21.16% (male 3,892,004/female 3,958,998)
25–54 years: 25.91% (male 4,808,534/female 4,803,040)
55–64 years: 2.43% (male 431,112/female 470,359)
65 years and over: 2.04% (male 332,724/female 423,178) (2015 est.)

Dependency ratios: *total dependency ratio:* 102.3%
youth dependency ratio: 97.3%
elderly dependency ratio: 5%
potential support ratio: 19.9% (2015 est.)

Median age: *total:* 15.6 years
male: 15.6 years
female: 15.7 years (2015 est.)
country comparison to the world: 228

Population growth rate: 3.24% (2015 est.)
country comparison to the world: 5

Birth rate: 43.79 births/1,000 population (2015 est.)
country comparison to the world: 3

Death rate: 10.69 deaths/1,000 population (2015 est.)
country comparison to the world: 36

Net migration rate: -0.74 migrant(s)/1,000 population (2015 est.)
country comparison to the world: 143

Urbanization: *urban Population:* 16.1% of total population (2015)
rate of urbanization: 5.43% annual rate of change (2010–15 est.)

Major urban Areas—population: KAMPALA (capital) 1.936 million (2015)

Sex ratio: *at birth:* 1.03 male(s)/female
0–14 years: 1 male(s)/female
15–24 years: 0.98 male(s)/female
25–54 years: 1 male(s)/female
55–64 years: 0.92 male(s)/female
65 years and over: 0.79 male(s)/female
total population: 0.99 male(s)/female (2015 est.)

Mother's mean age at first birth: 19.3
note: Median Age at first birth among women 20–24 (2011 est.)

Maternal mortality rate: 343 deaths/100,000 live births (2015 est.)
country comparison to the world: 37

Infant mortality rate: *total:* 59.21 deaths/1,000 live births
male: 68.39 deaths/1,000 live births
female: 49.75 deaths/1,000 live births (2015 est.)
country comparison to the world: 21

Life expectancy at birth: *total population:* 54.93 years
male: 53.54 years

female: 56.36 years (2015 est.)
country comparison to the world: 211

Total fertility rate: 5.89 children born/woman (2015 est.)
country comparison to the world: 5

Contraceptive prevalence rate: 30% (2011)

Health expenditures: 9.8% of GDP (2013)
country comparison to the world: 58

Physicians density: 0.12 physicians/1,000 population (2005)

Hospital bed density: 0.5 beds/1,000 population (2010)

Drinking water source:
improved:
urban: 95.5% of population
rural: 75.8% of population
total: 79% of population
unimproved:
urban: 4.5% of population
rural: 24.2% of population
total: 21% of population (2015 est.)

Sanitation facility access:
improved:
urban: 28.5% of population
rural: 17.3% of population
total: 19.1% of population
unimproved:
urban: 71.5% of population
rural: 82.7% of population
total: 80.9% of population (2015 est.)

HIV/AIDS—adult prevalence rate: 7.25% (2014 est.)
country comparison to the world: 10

HIV/AIDS—people living with HIV/AIDS: 1,486,600 (2014 est.)
country comparison to the world: 7

HIV/AIDS—deaths: 32,900 (2014 est.)
country comparison to the world: 10

Major infectious diseases: degree of risk: very high
food or waterborne diseases: bacterial diarrhea, hepatitis A and E, and typhoid fever
vectorborne diseases: malaria, dengue fever, and trypanosomiasis-Gambiense (African sleeping sickness)
water contact disease: schistosomiasis
animal contact disease: rabies (2013)

Obesity—adult prevalence rate: 3.9% (2014)
country comparison to the world: 167

Children under the age of 5 years underweight: 14.1% (2011)
country comparison to the world: 51

Education expenditures: 2.2% of GDP (2013)
country comparison to the world: 131

Literacy: definition: age 15 and over can read and write
total population: 78.4%
male: 85.3%
female: 71.5% (2015 est.)

School life expectancy (primary to tertiary education): total: 10 years
male: 10 years
female: 10 years (2011)

Child labor—children ages 5–14: total number: 117,266
percentage: 25%
note: data represent children ages 5–17 (2010 est.)

Unemployment, youth ages 15–24: total: 2.6%
male: 2%
female: 3.2% (2013 est.)
country comparison to the world: 125

GOVERNMENT

Country name: conventional long form: Republic of Uganda
conventional short form: Uganda
etymology: from the Swahili "Buganda," adopted by the British as the name for their East African colony in 1894; Buganda had been a powerful East African state during the 18th and 19th centuries

Government type: presidential republic

Capital: name: Kampala

Geographic coordinates: 0 19 N, 32 33 E
time difference: UTC+3 (8 hours ahead of Washington, DC, during Standard Time)

Administrative divisions: 111 districts and 1 capital city*; Abim, Adjumani, Agago, Alebtong, Amolatar, Amudat, Amuria, Amuru, Apac, Arua, Budaka, Bududa, Bugiri, Buhweju, Buikwe, Bukedea, Bukomansimbi, Bukwa, Bulambuli, Buliisa, Bundibugyo, Bushenyi, Busia, Butaleja, Butambala, Buvuma, Buyende, Dokolo, Gomba, Gulu, Hoima, Ibanda, Iganga, Isingiro, Jinja, Kaabong, Kabale, Kabarole, Kaberamaido, Kalangala, Kaliro, Kalungu, Kampala*, Kamuli, Kamwenge, Kanungu, Kapchorwa, Kasese, Katakwi, Kayunga, Kibaale, Kiboga, Kibuku, Kiruhura, Kiryandongo, Kisoro, Kitgum, Koboko, Kole, Kotido, Kumi, Kween, Kyankwanzi, Kyegegwa, Kyenjojo, Lamwo, Lira, Luuka, Luwero, Lwengo, Lyantonde, Manafwa, Maracha, Masaka, Masindi, Mayuge, Mbale, Mbarara, Mitooma, Mityana, Moroto, Moyo, Mpigi, Mubende, Mukono, Nakapiripirit, Nakaseke, Nakasongola, Namayingo, Namutumba, Napak, Nebbi, Ngora, Ntoroko, Ntungamo, Nwoya, Otuke, Oyam, Pader, Pallisa, Rakai, Rubirizi, Rukungiri, Sembabule, Serere, Sheema, Sironko, Soroti, Tororo, Wakiso, Yumbe, Zombo

Independence: 9 October 1962 (from the UK)

National holiday: Independence Day, 9 October (1962)

Constitution: several previous; latest adopted 27 September 1995, promulgated 8 October 1995; amended many times, last in 2015 (2016)

Legal system: mixed legal system of English common law and customary law

International law organization participation: accepts compulsory ICJ jurisdiction; accepts ICCt jurisdiction

Citizenship: citizenship by birth: no
citizenship by descent only: at least one parent or grandparent must be a native-born citizen of Uganda
dual citizenship recognized: yes

residency requirement for Naturalization: an aggregate of 20 years and continuously for the last 2 years prior to applying for citizenship

Suffrage: 18 years of age; universal

Executive branch: chief of state: President Yoweri Kaguta MUSEVENI (since seizing power on 26 January 1986); Vice President Edward SSEKANDI (since 24 May 2011); note—the president is both chief of state and head of government

head of government: President Yoweri Kaguta MUSEVENI (since seizing power on 26 January 1986); Vice President Edward SSEKANDI (since 24 May 2011); Ruhakana RUGUNDA (since 19 September 2014 note—the prime minister assists the president in supervising the cabinet
cabinet: Cabinet appointed by the president from among elected members of the National Assembly or persons who qualify to be elected as members of the National Assembly
elections/appointments: president directly elected by absolute majority popular vote in 2 rounds if needed for a 5-year term (no term limit); election last held on 18 February 2016 (next to be held in February 2021)
election results: Yoweri Kaguta MUSEVEN I reelected president; percent of vote—Yoweri Kaguta MUSEVENI (NRM) 60.6%, Kizza BESIGYE (FDC) 35.6%, other 3.8%

Legislative branch: description: unicameral National Assembly or Parliament (427 seats; 290 members directly elected in single-seat constituencies by simple majority vote, 112 for women directly elected in single-seat constituencies by simple majority vote, and 25 "representatives" reserved for special interest groups—army 10, disabled 5, youth 5, labor 5; there are 13 ex-officio members appointed by the president; members serve 5-year terms)
elections: last held on 18 February 2016 (next to be held in February 2021)
election results: percent of vote by party—NA; seats by party—NA

Judicial branch: highest court(s): Supreme Court of Uganda (consists of the chief justice and 10 justices)
judge selection and term of office: justices appointed by the president in consultation with the Judicial Service Commission (a 9-member independent advisory body) and with approval of the National Assembly; justices serve until mandatory retirement at age 70
subordinate courts: Court of Appeal (also sits as the Constitutional Court); High Court (includes 12 High Court Circuits and 8 High Court Divisions); Chief Magistrate, Grade One and Grade Two Courts

Political parties and leaders: Conservative Party or CP [Ken LUKYAMUZI]
Democratic Party or DP [Norbert MAO]
Forum for Democratic Change or FDC [Mugisha MUNTU]
Justice Forumor JEEMA [Asuman BASALIRWA]
National Resistance Movement or NRM [Yoweri MUSEVENI]

Ugandan People's Congress or UPC [Olara OTUNNU]

Political pressure groups and leaders: National Association of Women Organizations in Uganda or NAWOU [Florence NEKYON]
Parliamentary Advocacy Forum or PAFO
Ugandan Coalition for Political Accountability to Women or COPAW

International organization participation: ACP, AfDB, AU, C, COMESA, EAC, EADB, FAO, G-77, IAEA, IBRD, ICAO, ICC (National committees), ICCt, IDA, IDB, IFAD, IF C, IFRCS, IGAD, ILO, IMF, IMO, Interpol, IOC, IOM, IPU, ISO (correspondent), ITSO, ITU, ITUC (NGOs), MIGA, NAM, OIC, OPCW, PCA, UN, UNCTAD, UNESCO, UNHCR, UNIDO, UNOCI, UNWTO, UPU, WCO, WFTU (NGOs), WHO, WIPO, WMO, WTO

Diplomatic representation in the US: *chief of mission:* Ambassador Oliver WONEKHA (since 18 July 2013)
chancery: 5911 16th Street NW, Washington, DC 20011
telephone: [1] (202) 726-7100 through 7102, 0416
FAX: [1] (202) 726-1727

Diplomatic representation from the US: *chief of mission:* Ambsssador Deborah R. MALAC (since 27 February 2016)
embassy: 1577 Ggaba Road, Kampala
mailing address: P. O. Box 7007, Kampala
telephone: [256] (414) 259-791 through 93, 95
FAX: [256] (414) 259-794

Flag description: six equal horizontal bands of black (top), yellow, red, black, yellow, and red; a white disk is superimposed at the center and depicts a grey crowned crane (the National symbol) facing the hoist side; black symbolizes the African people, yellow sunshine and vitality, red African brotherhood; the crane was the military badge of Ugandan soldiers under the UK

National symbol(s): grey crowned crane; National colors: black, yellow, red

National anthem: *name:* "Oh Uganda, Land of Beauty!"
lyrics/music: George Wilberforce KAKOMOA
note: adopted 1962

ECONOMY

Economy—overview: Uganda has substantial Natural resources, including fertile soils, regular rainfall, small deposits of copper, gold, and other minerals, and recently discovered oil. Agriculture is the most important sector of the economy, employing one third of the work force. Coffee accounts for the bulk of export revenues. Uganda's economy remains predominantly agricultural with a small industrial sector that is dependent on imported inputs like oil and equipment. Overall productivity is hampered by a number of supply-side constraints, including underinvestment in an agricultural sector that continues to rely on rudimentary technology. Industrial growth is impeded by high-costs due to poor infrastructure, low levels

of private investment, and the depreciation of the Ugandan shilling.

Since 1986, the government—with the support of foreign countries and international agencies—has acted to rehabilitate and stabilize the economy by undertaking currency reform, raising producer prices on export crops, increasing prices of petroleum Products, and improving civil service wages. The policy changes are especially aimed at dampening inflation while encouraging foreign investment to boost production and export earnings. Since 1990 economic reforms ushered in an era of solid economic growth based on continued investment in infrastructure, improved incentives for production and exports, lower inflation, better domestic security, and the return of exiled Indian-Ugandan entrepreneurs. The global economic downturn in 2008 hurt Uganda's exports; however, Uganda's GDP growth has largely recovered due to past reforms and a rapidly growing urban consumer population. Oil revenues and taxes are expected to become a larger source of government fundingas production starts in the next five to 10 years. However, lower oil prices since 2014 and protracted negotiations and legal disputes between the Ugandan government and oil companies may prove a stumbling block to further exploration and development.

Uganda faces many challenges. Instability in South Sudan has led to a sharp increase in Sudanese refugees and is disrupting Uganda's main export market. High energy costs, inadequate transportation and energy infrastructure, insufficient budgetary discipline, and corruption inhibit economic development and investor confidence. During 2015 the Uganda shilling depreciated 22% against the dollar, and inflation rose from 3% to 9%, which led to the Bank of Uganda hiking interest rates from 11% to 17%. As a result, inflation remained below double digits; however, trade and capital-intensive industries were negatively impacted.

The budget for FY2015/16 is dominated by energy and road infrastructure spending, while relying on donor support for long-term economic drivers of growth, including agriculture, health, and education. The largest infrastructure projects are externally financed through low-interest concessional loans. As a result, debt servicing for these loans is expected to rise in 2016/2017 by 22% and consume 15% the domestic budget.

GDP (purchasing power parity): $79.88 billion (2015 est.)
$76.05 billion (2014 est.)
$72.48 billion (2013 est.)
note: data are in 2015 US dollars
country comparison to the world: 91

GDP (official exchange rate): $24.74 billion (2015 est.)

GDP—real growth rate: 5% (2015 est.)
4.9% (2014 est.)
4% (2013 est.)
country comparison to the world: 41

GDP—per capita (PPP): $2,000 (2015 est.)
$2,000 (2014 est.)
$1,900 (2013 est.)

note: data are in 2015 US dollars
country comparison to the world: 204

Gross National saving: 17.7% of GDP (2015 est.)
16.8% of GDP (2014 est.)
20.8% of GDP (2013 est.)
country comparison to the world: 94

GDP—composition, by end use:
household consumption: 72.6%
government consumption: 8.9%
investment in fixed capital: 29.7%
investment in inventories: 0.2%
exports of goods and services: 22.5%
imports of goods and services: -33.9% (2015 est.)

GDP—composition, by sector of origin:
agriculture: 26.3%
industry: 22.3%
services: 51.4% (2015 est.)

Agriculture—products: coffee, tea, cotton, tobacco, cassava (manioc, tapioca), potatoes, corn, millet, pulses, cut flowers; beef, goat meat, milk, poultry, and fish

Industries: sugar, brewing, tobacco, cotton textiles; cement, steel production

Industrial production growth rate: 5.5% (2015 est.)
country comparison to the world: 25

Labor force: 18.58 million (2015 est.)
country comparison to the world: 32

Labor force—by occupation: *agriculture:* 40%
industry: 10%
services: 50% (2015 est.)

Unemployment rate: NA%
9.4% (2013 est.)

Population below poverty line: 19.7% (2013 est.)

Household income or consumption by percentage share: *lowest:* 10%: 2.4%
highest: 10%: 36.1% (2009 est.)

Distribution of family income—Gini index: 39.5 (2013) 45.7 (2002)
country comparison to the world: 67

Budget: *revenues:* $3.29 billion
expenditures: $4.34 billion (2015 est.)
Taxes and other revenues: 13.2% of GDP (2015 est.)
country comparison to the world: 202

Budget surplus (+) or deficit (–): -4.2% of GDP (2015 est.)
country comparison to the world: 150

Public debt: 34.8% of GDP (2015 est.)
30.7% of GDP (2014 est.)
country comparison to the world: 129

Fiscal year: 1 July—30 June

Inflation rate (consumer prices): 5.8% (2015 est.)
4.6% (2014 est.)
country comparison to the world: 183

Central bank discount rate: 17% (30 March 2016)
14% (December 2014)
country comparison to the world: 13

Commercial bank prime lending rate: 24.29% (31 January 2016 est.)
22.2% (31 December 2015 est.)
country comparison to the world: 9

Stock of narrow money: $1.839 billion (31 December 2015 est.)
$2.396 billion (31 December 2014 est.)
country comparison to the world: 132

Stock of broad money: $4.262 billion (31 December 2014 est.)
$3.705 billion (31 December 2013 est.)
country comparison to the world: 137

Stock of domestic credit: $3.327 billion (31 December 2015 est.)
$4.157 billion (31 December 2014 est.)
country comparison to the world: 127

Market value of publicly traded shares: $7.294 billion (31 December 2012 est.)
$7.727 billion (31 December 2011 est.)
$1.788 billion (31 December 2010 est.)
country comparison to the world: 80

Current account balance: -$2.193 billion (2015 est.)
-$2.625 billion (2014 est.)
country comparison to the world: 150

Exports: $2.755 billion (2015 est.)
$2.743 billion (2014 est.)
country comparison to the world: 130

Exports—commodities: coffee, fish and fish products, tea, cotton, flowers, horticultural products; gold

Exports—partners: Rwanda 10.7%, UAE 9.9%, Democratic Republic of the Congo 9.8%, Kenya 9.7%, Italy 5.8%, Netherlands 4.8%, Germany 4.7%, China 4.1% (2015)

Imports: $4.603 billion (2015 est.)
$5.116 billion (2014 est.)
country comparison to the world: 128

Imports—commodities: capital equipment, vehicles, petroleum, medical supplies; cereals

Imports—partners: Kenya 16.4%, UAE 15.5%, India 13.4%, China 13.1% (2015)

Reserves of foreign exchange and gold: $3.681 billion (31 December 2015 est.)
$3.316 billion (31 December 2014 est.)
note: excludes gold
country comparison to the world: 102

Debt—external: $4.97 billion (31 December 2014 est.)
$4.361 billion (31 December 2013 est.)
country comparison to the world: 130

Stock of direct foreign investment—at home: $NA

Stock of direct foreign investment—abroad: $NA

Exchange rates: Ugandan shillings (UGX) per US dollar—
3,339.6 (2015 est.)
2,599.8 (2014 est.)
2,599.8 (2013 est.)
2,505.6 (2012 est.)
2,522.8 (2011 est.)

ENERGY

Electricity—production: 3.045 billion kWh (2012 est.)
country comparison to the world: 132

Electricity—consumption: 2.821 billion kWh (2012 est.)
country comparison to the world: 137

Electricity—exports: 70 million kWh (2012)
country comparison to the world: 82

Electricity—imports: 59 million kWh (2012 est.)
country comparison to the world: 101

Electricity—installed generating capacity: 711,400 kW (2014 est.)
country comparison to the world: 132

Electricity—from fossil fuels: 21% of total installed capacity (2011 est.)
country comparison to the world: 194

Electricity—from nuclear fuels: 0% of total installed capacity (2011 est.)
country comparison to the world: 198

Electricity—from hydroelectric plants: 59.9% of total installed capacity (2014 est.)
country comparison to the world: 36

Electricity—from other renewable sources: 19.2% of total installed capacity (2014 est.)
country comparison to the world: 17

Crude oil—production: 0 bbl/day (2014 est.)
country comparison to the world: 202

Crude oil—exports: 0 bbl/day (2012 est.)
country comparison to the world: 202

Crude oil—imports: 0 bbl/day (2012 est.)
country comparison to the world: 140

Crude oil—proved reserves: 2.5 billion bbl (1 January 2015 est.)
country comparison to the world: 33

Refined petroleum Products—production: 0 bbl/day (2012 est.)
country comparison to the world: 141

Refined petroleum Products—consumption: 22,000 bbl/day (2013 est.)
country comparison to the world: 125

Refined petroleum Products—exports: 0 bbl/day (2012 est.)
country comparison to the world: 142

Refined petroleum Products—Imports: 22,160 bbl/day (2012 est.)
country comparison to the world: 106

Natural gas—production: 0 cu m (2013 est.)
country comparison to the world: 140

Natural gas—consumption: 0 cu m (2013 est.)
country comparison to the world: 204

Natural gas—exports: 0 cu m (2013 est.)
country comparison to the world: 200

Natural gas—imports: 0 cu m (2013 est.)
country comparison to the world: 147

Natural gas—proved reserves: 14.16 billion cu m (1 January 2014 est.)
country comparison to the world: 79

Carbon dioxide emissions from consumption of energy: 2.548 million Mt (2012 est.)
country comparison to the world: 144

COMMUNICATIONS

Telephones—fixed lines: *total subscriptions:* 320,000

subscriptions per 100 inhabitants: 1 (2014 est.)
country comparison to the world: 114

Telephones—mobile cellular: *total:* 20.4 million
subscriptions per 100 inhabitants: 57 (2014 est.)
country comparison to the world: 57

Telephone system: *general assessment:* mobile cellular service is increasing rapidly, but the number of main lines is still deficient; work underway on a National backbone information and communications technology infrastructure; international phone networks and Internet connectivity provided through satellite and and fiber optic cables through Kenya and the Indian Ocean
domestic: intercity traffic by wire, microwave radio relay, and radiotelephone communication stations, fixed-line and mobile-cellular systems for short-range traffic; mobile-cellular teledensity about 50 per 100 persons in 2010
international: country code—256; satellite earth stations—1 Intelsat (Atlantic Ocean) and 1 Inmarsat; analog and digital links to Kenya and Tanzania (2015)

Broadcast media: public broadcaster, Uganda Broadcasting Corporation (UBC), operates radio and TV networks; Uganda first began licensing privately owned stations in the 1990s; by 2007, there were nearly 150 radio and 35 TV stations, mostly based in and around Kampala; transmissions of multiple international broadcasters are available in Kampala (2007)
Radio broadcast stations: AM 7, FM 33, shortwave 2 (2001)
Television broadcast stations: 8 (plus 1 repeater) (2001)

Internet country code: .ug

Internet hosts: 32,683 (2012)
country comparison to the world: 106

Internet users: *total:* 6 million
percent of population: 16.8% (2014 est.)
country comparison to the world: 57

TRANSPORTATION

Airports: 47 (2013)
country comparison to the world: 93

Airports—with paved runways: *total:* 5
over 3,047 m: 3
1,524 to 2,437 m: 1
914 to 1,523 m: 1 (2013)

Airports—with unpaved runways: *total:* 42
over 3,047 m: 1
1,524 to 2,437 m: 8
914 to 1,523 m: 26
under 914 m: 7 (2013)

Railways: *total:* 1,244 km
narrow gauge: 1,244 km 1.000-m gauge (2014)
country comparison to the world: 83

Roadways: *total:* 20,000 km (excludes local roads)
paved: 3,264 km
unpaved: 16,736 km (2011)
country comparison to the world: 109

Waterways: (there are no long navigable stretches of river in Uganda; parts of the Albert Nile that flow out of Lake Albert in the northwestern part of the country are navigable; several lakes including Lake Victoria and Lake Kyoga have substantial traffic; Lake Albert is navigable along a 200-km stretch from its northern tip to its southern shores) (2011)

Ports and terminals: *lake port(s):* Entebbe, Jinja, Port Bell (Lake Victoria)

MILITARY AND SECURITY

Military branches: Uganda People's Defense Force (UPDF): Land Forces (includes Marine Unit), Uganda Air Force (2013)

Military service age and obligation: 18–26 years of age for voluntary military duty; 18–30 years of age for profession als; no conscription; 9-year service obligation; the government has stated that while recruitment under 18 years of age could occur with

proper consent, "no person under the apparent age of 18 years shall be enrolled in the armed forces"; Ugandan citizenship and secondary education required (2012)

Military expenditures: 2.2% of GDP (2013)
1.45% of GDP (2012)
3.73% of GDP (2011)
1.45% of GDP (2010)
country comparison to the world: 67

TRANSNATIONAL ISSUES

Disputes—international: Uganda is subject to armed fighting among hostile Ethnic groups, rebels, armed gangs, militias, and various government forces that extend across its borders; Ugandan refugees as well as members of the Lord's Resistance Army (LRA) seek shelter in southern

SudaNAnd the Democratic Republic of the Congo's Garamba National Park; LRA forces have also attacked Kenyan villages across the border

Refugees and internally displaced persons: *refugees (country of origin):* 229,006 (South Sudan) (refugees and asylum seekers); 193,945 (Democratic Republic of the Congo); 37,410 (Burundi); 36,684 (Somalia) (refugees and asylum seekers); 14,708 (Rwanda) (2016)

IDPs: 30,000 (displaced in northern Uganda because of fighting between government forces and the Lord's Resistance Army; as of 2011, most of the 1.8 million people displaced to IDP camps at the height of the conflict had returned home or resettled, but many had not found durable solutions; intercommunal violence and cattle raids) (2015)

UKRAINE

INTRODUCTION

Background: Ukraine was the center of the first eastern Slavic state, Kyivan Rus, which during the 10th and 11th centuries was the largest and most powerful state in Europe. Weakened by internecine quarrels and Mongol invasions, Kyivan Rus was incorporated into the Grand Duchy of Lithuania and eventually into the Polish-Lithuanian Commonwealth. The cultural and religious legacy of Kyivan Rus laid the foundation for Ukrainian Nationalism through subsequent centuries. A new Ukrainian state, the Cossack Hetmanate, was established during the mid-17th century after an uprising against the Poles. Despite continuous Muscovite pressure, the Hetmanate managed to remain autonomous for well over 100 years. During the latter part of the 18th century, most Ukrainian ethnographic territory was absorbed by the Russian Empire. Following the collapse of czarist Russia in 1917, Ukraine achieved a short-lived period of independence (1917–20), but was reconquered and endured a brutal Soviet rule that engineered two forced famines (1921–22 and 1932–33) in which over 8 million died. In World War II, German and Soviet armies were responsible for 7 to 8 million more deaths. Although Ukraine achieved final independence in 1991 with the dissolution of the USSR, democracy and prosperity remained elusive as the legacy of state control and endemic corruption stalled efforts at economic reform, privatization, and civil liberties.

A peaceful mass protest referred to as the "Orange Revolution" in the closing months of 2004 forced the authorities to overturn a rigged presidential election and to allow a new Internationally monitored vote that swept into power a reformist slate under Viktor YUSHCHENKO. Subsequent internal squabbles in the YUSHCHENKO camp allowed his rival Viktor YANUKOVYCH to stage a comeback in parliamentary (Rada) elections, become prime minister in August 2006, and be elected president in February 2010. In October 2012, Ukraine held Rada elections, widely criticized by Western observers as flawed due to use of government resources to favor ruling party candidates, interference with media access, and harassment of opposition candidates. President YANUKOVYCH's backtracking on a trade and cooperation agreement with the EU in November 2013—in favor of closer economic ties with Russia—and subsequent use of force against civil society activists in favor of the agreement led to a three-month protest occupation of Kyiv's central square. The government's use of violence to break up the protest camp in February 2014 led to all out pitched battles, scores of deaths, international condemnation, and the president's abrupt departure to Russia. New elections in the spring allowed pro-West president Petro POROSHENKO to assume office on 7 June 2014.

Shortly after YANUKOVYCH's departure in late February 2014, Russian President PUTIN ordered the invasion of Ukraine's Crimean Peninsula claiming the action was to protect ethnic Russians living there. Two weeks later, a "referendum" was held regarding the integration of Crimea into the Russian Federation. The "referendum" was condemned as illegitimate by the Ukrainian Government, the EU, the US, and the UN General Assembly (UNGA). Although Russia illegally annexed Crimea after the "referendum," the Ukrainian government, backed by UNGA resolution 68/262, asserts that Crimea remains part of

Ukraine and fully under Ukrainian sovereignty. Russia also continues to supply separatists in two of Ukraine's eastern provinces with manpower, funding, and materiel resulting in an armed conflict with the Ukrainian Government. Representatives from Ukraine, Russia, and the unrecognized separatist republics signed a ceasefire agreement in September 2014. However, this ceasefire failed to stop the fighting. in a renewed attempt to alleviate ongoing clashes, leaders of Ukraine, Russia, France, and Germany negotiated a follow-on peace deal in February 2015 known as the Minsk Agreements. Representatives from Ukraine, Russia, and the Organization for Security and Cooperation in Europe also meet regularly to facilitate implementation of the peace deal. Scattered fighting between Ukrainian and Russian-backed separatist forces is still ongoing in eastern Ukraine.

GEOGRAPHY

Location: Eastern Europe, bordering the Black Sea, between Poland, Romania, and Moldova in the west and Russia in the east

Geographic coordinates: 49 00 N, 32 00 E

Map references: Asia, Europe

Area: *total:* 603,550 sq km
land: 579,330 sq km
water: 24,220 sq km
country comparison to the world: 46

Area—comparative: almost four times the size of Georgia; slightly smaller than Texas

Land boundaries: *total:* 5,618 km
border countries (7): Belarus 1,111 km, Hungary 128 km, Moldova 1,202 km, Poland 535 km, Romania 601 km, Russia 1,944 km, Slovakia 97 km

Coastline: 2,782 km

Maritime claims: *territorial sea:* 12 nm
exclusive economic zone: 200 nm

continental shelf: 200 m or to the depth of exploitation

Climate: temperate continental; Mediterranean only on the southern Crimean coast; precipitation disproportionately distributed, highest in west and north, lesser in east and southeast; winters vary from cool along the Black Sea to cold farther inland; warm summers across the greater part of the country, hot in the south

Terrain: mostly fertile plains (steppes) and plateaus, with mountains found only in the west (the Carpathians) or in the extreme south of the Crimean Peninsula

Elevation: *mean elevation:* 175 m

elevation extremes: *lowest point:* Black Sea 0 m
highest point: Hora Hoverla 2,061 m

Natural resources: iron ore, coal, manganese, Natural gas, oil, salt, sulfur, graphite, titanium, magnesium, kaolin, nickel, mercury, timber, arable land

Land use: *agricultural land:* 71.2%
arable land: 56.1%
permanent crops: 1.5%
permanent pasture: 13.6%
forest: 16.8%
other: 12% (2011 est.)

Irrigated land: 21,670 sq km (2012)

Total renewable water resources: 139.6 cu km (2011)

Freshwater withdrawal (domestic/industrial/agricultural): *total:* 19.24 cu km/yr (24%/69%/7%) per capita: 415.7 cu m/yr (2010)

Natural hazards: NA

Environment—current issues: inadequate supplies of potable water; air and water pollution; deforestation; radiation contamination in the northeast from 1986 accident at Chornobyl' Nuclear Power Plant

Environment—International agreements: *party to:* Air Pollution, Air Pollution-Nitrogen Oxides, Air Pollution-Sulfur 85, Antarctic-Environmental Protocol, Antarctic-Marine Living Resources, Antarctic Treaty, Biodiversity, Climate Change, Climate Change-Kyoto Protocol, Desertification, Endangered Species, Environmental Modification, Hazardous Wastes, Law of the Sea, Marine Dumping, Ozone Layer Protection, Ship Pollution, Wetlands
signed, but not ratified: Air Pollution-Persistent Organic Pollutants, Air Pollution-Sulfur 94, Air Pollution-Volatile Organic Compounds

Geography—note: strategic position at the crossroads between Europe and Asia; second-largest country in Europe after Russia

PEOPLE AND SOCIETY

Nationality: *noun:* Ukrainian(s)
adjective: Ukrainian

Ethnic groups: Ukrainian 77.8%, Russian 17.3%, Belarusian 0.6%, Moldovan 0.5%, Crimean Tatar 0.5%, Bulgarian 0.4%, Hungarian 0.3%, Romanian 0.3%, Polish 0.3%, Jewish 0.2%, other 1.8% (2001 est.)

Languages: Ukrainian (official) 67.5%, Russian (region al language) 29.6%, other (includes small Crimean Tatar-, Moldavian-, and Hungarian-speaking minorities) 2.9% (2001 est.)
note: 2012 legislation enables a language spoken by at least 10% of an oblast's population to be given the status of "region al language," allowing for its use in courts, schools, and other government institutions; Ukrainian remains the country's only official nationwide language

Religions: Orthodox (includes UkrainianAutocephalous Orthodox (UAOC), Ukrainianorthodox—Kyiv Patriarchate (UOC-KP), Ukrainianorthodox—Moscow Patriarchate (UOC-MP), Ukrainian Greek Catholic, Roman Catholic, Protestant, Muslim, Jewish
note: Ukraine's population is overwhelmingly Christian; the vast majority—up to two-thirds—identify themselves as Orthodox, but many do not specify a particular branch; the UOC-KP and the UOC-MP each represent less than a quarter of the country's population, the Ukrainian Greek Catholic Church accounts for 8–10%, and the UAOC accounts for 1–2%; Muslim and Jewish adherents each compose less than 1% of the total population (2013 est.)

Population: 44,429,471 (July 2015 est.)
country comparison to the world: 32

Age structure: *0–14 years:* 15.22% (male 3,480,870/female 3,281,363)
15–24 years: 10.85% (male 2,470,594/female 2,349,313)
25–54 years: 44.63% (male 9,703,407/female 10,126,348)
55–64 years: 13.5% (male 2,563,195/female 3,435,022)
65 years and over: 15.8% (male 2,343,097/female 4,676,262) (2015 est.)

Dependency ratios: *total dependency ratio:* 43.3%
youth dependency ratio: 21.4%
elderly dependency ratio: 21.9%
potential support ratio: 4.6% (2015 est.)

Median age: *total:* 40.1 years
male: 37 years
female: 43.3 years (2015 est.)
country comparison to the world: 45

Population growth rate: -0.6% (2015 est.)
country comparison to the world: 228

Birth rate: 10.72 births/1,000 population (2015 est.)
country comparison to the world: 182

Death rate: 14.46 deaths/1,000 population (2015 est.)
country comparison to the world: 2

Net migration rate: -2.25 migrant(s)/1,000 population (2015 est.)
country comparison to the world: 171

Urbanization: *urban Population:* 69.7% of total population (2015)
rate of urbanization: -0.33% annual rate of change (2010–15 est.)

Major urban Areas—population: KYIV (capital) 2.942 million; Kharkiv 1.441 million; Odesa 1.01 million; Dnipropetrovsk 957,000; Donetsk 934,000; Zaporizhzhya 753,000 (2015)

Sex ratio: *at birth:* 1.06 male(s)/female
0–14 years: 1.06 male(s)/female *15–24 years:* 1.05 male(s)/female
25–54 years: 0.96 male(s)/female
55–64 years: 0.75 male(s)/female
65 years and over: 0.5 male(s)/female
total population: 0.86 male(s)/female (2015 est.)

Mother's mean age at first birth: 25.8 (2010 est.)

Maternal mortality rate: 24 deaths/100,000 live births (2015 est.)
country comparison to the world: 121

Infant mortality rate: *total:* 8.12 deaths/1,000 live births
male: 9.03 deaths/1,000 live births
female: 7.16 deaths/1,000 live births (2015 est.)
country comparison to the world: 153

Life expectancy at birth: *total population:* 71.57 years
male: 66.81 years
female: 76.63 years (2015 est.)
country comparison to the world: 148

Total fertility rate: 1.53 children born/woman (2015 est.)
country comparison to the world: 191

Contraceptive prevalence rate: 65.4% (2012)

Health expenditures: 7.8% of GDP (2013)
country comparison to the world: 66

Physicians density: 3.54 physicians/1,000 population (2013)

Hospital bed density: 9 beds/1,000 population (2012)

Drinking water source:
improved:
urban: 95.5% of population
rural: 97.8% of population
total: 96.2% of population
unimproved:
urban: 4.5% of population
rural: 2.2% of population
total: 3.8% of population (2015 est.)

Sanitation facility access:
improved:
urban: 97.4% of population
rural: 92.6% of population
total: 95.9% of population
unimproved:
urban: 2.6% of population
rural: 7.4% of population
total: 4.1% of population (2015 est.)

HIV/AIDS—adult prevalence rate: 0.83% (2013 est.)
country comparison to the world: 51

HIV/AIDS—people living with HIV/AIDS: 210,700 (2013 est.)
country comparison to the world: 28

HIV/AIDS—deaths: 13,400 (2013 est.)
country comparison to the world: 18

Obesity—adult prevalence rate: 21.7% (2014)

country comparison to the world: 89

Education expenditures: 6.7% of GDP (2013)
country comparison to the world: 35

Literacy: *definition:* age 15 and over can read and write
total population: 99.8%
male: 99.8%
female: 99.7% (2015 est.)

School life expectancy (primary to tertiary education): *total:* 15 years
male: 15 years
female: 16 years (2014)

Child labor—children ages 5–14: total number: 356,213
percentage: 7% (2005 est.)

Unemployment, youth ages 15–24: *total:* 17.4%
male: 18.2%
female: 16.3% (2013 est.)
country comparison to the world: 67

GOVERNMENT

Country name: *conventional long form:* none
conventional short form: Ukraine
local long form: none
local short form: Ukrayina
former: Ukrainian National Republic, Ukrainian State, Ukrainian Soviet Socialist Republic
etymology: name derives from the Old East Slavic word "ukraina" meaning "borderland or march (militarized border region)"

Government type: semi-presidential republic

Capital: *name:* Kyiv (Kiev)
note: pronounced KAY-yiv

Geographic coordinates: 50 26 N, 30 31 E
time difference: UTC+2 (7 hours ahead of Washington, DC, during Standard Time) daylight saving time: +1hr, begins last Sunday in March; ends last Sunday in October

Administrative divisions: 24 provinces (oblasti, singular—oblast'), 1 autonomous republic* (avtonomna respublika), and 2 municipalities (mista, singular—misto) with oblast status**; Cherkasy, Chernihiv, Chernivtsi, Crimea or Avtonomna Respublika Krym* (Simferopol'), Dnipropetrovs'k, Donets'k, Ivano-Frankivs'k, Kharkiv, Kherson, Khmel'nyts'kyy, Kirovohrad, Kyiv**, Kyiv, Luhans'k, L'viv, Mykolayiv, Odesa, Poltava, Rivne, Sevastopol'**, Sumy, Ternopil', Vinnytsya, Volyn' (Luts'k), Zakarpattya (Uzhhorod), Zaporizhzhya, Zhytomyr
note 1: administrative divisions have the same names as their administrative centers (exceptions have the administrative center name following in parentheses)
note 2: the United States does not recognize Russia's annexation of Ukraine's Autonomous Republic of Crimea and the municipality of Sevastopol, nor their redesignation as the Republic of Crimea and the Federal City of Sevastopol

Independence: 24 August 1991 (from the Soviet Union); notable earlier dates: ca. 982 (VOLODYMYRI consolidates Kyivan Rus), 1648 (establishment of the Cossack Hetmanate)

National holiday: Independence Day, 24 August (1991); note—22 January 1918, the day Ukraine first declared its independence (from Soviet Russia) and the day the short-lived Western and Greater (Eastern) Ukrainian republics united (1919), is now celebrated as Unity Day

Constitution: several previous; latest adopted and ratified 28 June 1996; amended 2004,2010,2015 (2016)

Legal system: civil law system; judicial review of legislative acts

International law organization participation: has not submitted an ICJ jurisdiction declaration; non-party state to the ICCt

Citizenship: *citizenship by birth:* no
citizenship by descent only: at least one parent must be a citizen of Ukraine
dual citizenship recognized: no
residency requirement for Naturalization: 5 years

Suffrage: 18 years of age; universal

Executive branch: *chief of state:* President Petro POROSHENKO (since 7 June 2014)

head of government: Prime Minister Volodymyr HROISMAN (since 14 April 2016); Deputy Prime Minister Vyacheslav KYRYLENKO (since 2 December 2014)
cabinet: Cabinet of Ministers nominated by the prime minister, approved by the Verkhovna Rada
elections/appointments: president directly elected by absolute majority popular vote in 2 rounds if needed for a 5-year term (eligible for a second term); election last held on 25 May 2014 (next to be held in 2019); prime minister nominated by the president, confirmed by the Verkhovna Rada
election results: Petro POROSHENKO elected president; percent of vote—Petro POROSHENKO (independent) 54.5%, Yuliya TYMOSHENKO (Fatherland) 12.9%, Oleh LYASHKO (Radical Party) 8.4%, other 24.2%; Volodymyr HROISMAN elected prime minister; Verkhovna Rada vote 257–50
note: there is also a National Security and Defense Council or NSDC originally created in 1992 as the National Security Council; the NSDC staff is tasked with developing National security policy on domestic and international matters and advising the president; a presidential administration helps draft presidential edicts and provides policy support to the president

Legislative branch: *description:* unicameral Supreme Council or Verkhovna Rada (450 seats; 225 members directly elected in single-seat constituencies by simple majority vote and 225 directly elected in a single nationwide constituency by proportional representation vote; members serve 5-year terms); note—because of the Russian annexation of Crimea and the partial occupation of two eastern provinces, 27 of the 450 seats remain unfilled
elections: last held on 26 October 2014 (next to be held fall of 2019)

election results: percent of vote by party—NF 22.1%, BPP 21.8%, Samopomich 11.0%, OB 9.4%, Radical 7.4%, Batkivshchyna 5.7%, Svoboda 4.7%, CPU 3.9%, other 13.9%; seats by party—BPP 132, NF 82, Samopomich 33, OB 29, Radical 22, Batkivshchyna 19, Svoboda 6, other 4, independent 96, vacant 27; note—voting not held in Crimea and parts of two Russian-occupied eastern oblasts leaving 27 seats vacant; seats as of December 2015—BPP 139, NF 81, OB 43, Samopomich 26, Vidrozhennya 23, Radical 21, Batkivshchyna 19, VN 20, independent 50, vacant 28

Judicial branch: *highest court(s):* Supreme Court of Ukraine or SCU (consists of 95 judges organized into civil, criminal, commercial, and administrative chambers, and a military panel); Constitutional Court (consists of 18 justices)
judge selection and term of office: Supreme Court judges proposed by the Supreme Council of Justice or SCJ (a 20-member independent body of judicial officials and other appointees) and appointed by presidential decree; judges initially appointed for 5 years and, if approved by the SCJ, serve until mandatory retirement at age 65; Constitutional Court justices appointed—6 each by the president, by the SCU, and by the Verkhovna Rada; justices appointed for 9-year non-renewable terms
subordinate courts: specialized high courts; Courts of Cassation; Courts of Appeal; region al, district, city, and town courts

Political parties and leaders: Batkivshchyna ("Fatherland") [Yuliya TYMOSHENKO]
Bloc of Petro Poroshenko—Solidarnist or BPP [Vitali KLYCHKO] (formed from the merger of Solidarnist and UDAR)
Narodnyy Front ("People's Front") or NF [Arseniy YATSENIUK]
Opposition Bloc or OB [Yuriy BOYKO]
Radical Party [Oleh LYASHKO]
Samopomich ("Self Reliance") [Andriy SADOVYY]
Svoboda ("Freedom") [Oleh TYAHNYBOK]
UkrainianAssociation of Patriots or UKROP [Hennadiy KORBAN]
Vidrozhennya ("Revival") [Vitaliy KHOMUTYNNIK] (parliamentary group)
Volya Naroda ("People's Will") or VN (parliamentary group)

Political pressure groups and leaders: Centre UA [Oleh RYBACHUK]
Committee of Voters of Ukraine [Oleksandr CHERNENKO]
OPORA [Olha AIVAZOVSKA]

International organization participation: Australia Group, BSEC, CBSS (observer), CD, CE, CEI, CICA (observer), CIS (participating member, has not signed the 1993 CIS charter), EAEC (observer), EAPC, EBRD, FAO, GCTU, GUAM, IAEA, IBRD, ICAO, ICC (National committees), ICRM, IDA, IFC, IFRCS, IHO, ILO, IMF, IMO, IMSO, Interpol, IOC, IOM, IPU, ISO, ITU, ITUC (NGOs), LAIA (observer), MIGA, MONUSCO, NAM (observer), NSG, OAS (observer), OIF (observer), OPCW, OSCE, PCA, PFP, SELEC (observer), UN, UNCTAD,

UNESCO, UNFICYP, UNIDO, UNISFA, UNMIL, UNMISS, UNOCI, UNWTO, UPU, WCO, WFTU (NGOs), WHO, WIPO, WMO, WTO, ZC

Diplomatic representation in the US: *chief of mission:* Ambassador Valeriy CHALYY (since 3 August 2015)
chancery: 3350 M Street NW, Washington, DC 20007
telephone: [1] (202) 349-2920
FAX: [1] (202) 333-0817
consulate(s) general: Chicago, New York, San Francisco

Diplomatic representation from the US: *chief of mission:* Ambassador Geoffrey R. PYATT (since 7 August 2013)
embassy: 4 Igor Sikorsky Street, 04112 Kyiv
mailing address: 5850 Kyiv Place, Washington, DC 20521 -5850
telephone: [380] (44) 521-5000
FAX: [380] (44) 521-5155

Flag description: two equal horizontal bands of azure (top) and golden yellow represent grain fields under a blue sky

National symbol(s): tryzub (trident); National colors: blue, yellow

National anthem: *name:* "Shche ne vmerla UKraina" (Ukraine has not Yet Perished)
lyrics/music: Paul CHUBYNSKYI/Mikhail VERBYTSKYI
note: music adopted 1991, lyrics adopted 2003; song first performed in 1864 at the Ukraine Theatre in Lviv; the lyrics, originally written in 1862, were revised in 2003

ECONOMY

Economy—overview: After Russia, the Ukrainian republic was the most important economic component of the former Soviet Union, producing about four times the output of the next-ranking republic. Its fertile black soil generated more than one-fourth of Soviet agricultural output, and its farms provided substantial quantities of meat, milk, grain, and vegetables to other republics. Likewise, its diversified heavy industry supplied unique equipment, such as, large diameter pipes and vertical drilling apparatus, and raw materials to industrial and mining sites in other regions of the former USSR.

Shortly after independence in August 1991, the Ukrainian Government liberalized most prices and erected a legal framework for privatization, but widespread resistance to reform within the government and the legislature soon stalled reform efforts and led to some backtracking. Output by 1999 had fallen to less than 40% of the 1991 level. Outside institutions—particularly the IMF-encouraged Ukraine to quicken the pace and scope of reforms to foster economic growth. Ukrainian Government officials eliminated most tax and customs privileges in a March 2005 budget law, bringing more economic activity out of Ukraine's large shadow economy. But more improvements are needed, including fighting corruption, developing capital markets, and improving the legislative framework. From 2000 until mid-2008, Ukraine's economy was buoyant despite political turmoil between the prime minister and president.

Ukraine's dependence on Russia for energy supplies and the lack of significant structural reform have made the Ukrainian economy vulnerable to external shocks. Ukraine depends on imports to meet about three-fourths of its annual oil and Natural gas requirements and 100% of its nuclear fuel needs. in January 2009, after a two-week dispute that saw gas supplies cut off to Europe, Ukraine agreed to 10-year gas supply and transit contracts with Russia that brought gas prices to "world" levels. The strict terms of the contracts further hobbled Ukraine's cash-strapped state gas company, Naftohaz. The economy contracted nearly 15% in 2009, among the worst economic performances in the world. in April 2010, Ukraine negotiated a price discount on Russian gas imports in exchange for extending Russia's lease on its Naval base in Crimea.

Ukraine's oligarch-dominated economy grew slowly from 2010 to 2014. After former President YANUKOVYCH fled the country during the Revolution of Dignity, the international community began efforts to stabilize the Ukrainian economy, including a March 2014 IMF assistance package of $14–18 billion. Ukraine has made significant progress on reforms designed to make the country a prosperous, democratic, and transparent country. Russia's occupation of Crimea in March 2014 and on-going aggression in eastern Ukraine have hurt economic growth. With the loss of a major portion of Ukraine's heavy industry in Donbas and ongoing violence, Ukraine's economy contracted by 6.8% in 2014 and by an estimated 10.5% in 2015. Ukraine and Russia have engaged in a trade war with sharply reduced trade between the countries by the end of 2015. The EU-Ukraine Deep and Comprehensive Free Trade Area finally started up on 1 January 2016, and is expected to help Ukraine integrate its economy with Europe by opening up markets and harmonizing regulations.

GDP (purchasing power parity): $339.5 billion (2015 est.)
$376.7 billion (2014 est.)
$403.1 billion (2013 est.)
note: data are in 2015 US dollars
country comparison to the world: 50

GDP (official exchange rate): $90.52 billion (2015 est.)

GDP—real growth rate: -9.9% (2015 est.)
-6.6% (2014 est.)
0% (2013 est.)
country comparison to the world: 220

GDP—per capita (PPP): $7,500 (2015 est.)
$8,300 (2014 est.)
$9,400 (2013 est.)
note: data are in 2015 US dollars
country comparison to the world: 152

Gross National saving: 15% of GDP (2015 est.)
9.4% of GDP (2014 est.)
9.3% of GDP (2013 est.)
country comparison to the world: 114

GDP—composition, by end use:

household consumption: 68.7%
government consumption: 22.3%
investment in fixed capital: 10.2%
investment in inventories: 0.1%
exports of goods and services: 58.5%
imports of goods and services: -59.8% (2015 est.)

GDP—composition, by sector of origin:
agriculture: 13.3%
industry: 24.4%
services: 62.7% (2015 est.)

Agriculture—products: grain, sugar beets, sunflower seeds, vegetables; beef, milk

Industries: coal, electric power, ferrous and nonferrous metals, machinery and transport equipment, chemicals, food processing

Industrial production growth rate: -13.4% (2015 est.)
country comparison to the world: 199

Labor force: 17.4 million (2015 est.)
country comparison to the world: 37

Labor force—by occupation: *agriculture:* 5.8%
industry: 26.5%
services: 67.8% (2014)

Unemployment rate: 9.5% (2015 est.)
9.3% (2014 est.)
note: officially registered workers; large number of unregistered or underemployed workers
country comparison to the world: 111

Population below poverty line: 24.1% (2010 est.)

Household income or consumption by percentage share: *lowest:* 10%: 3.8%
highest: 10%: 22.5% (2011 est.)

Distribution of family income—Gini index: 24.6 (2013)
28.2 (2009)
country comparison to the world: 144

Budget: *revenues:* $25.43 billion
expenditures: $29.36 billion
note: this is the planned, consolidated budget (2015 est.)
Taxes and other revenues: 28.2% of GDP (2015 est.)
country comparison to the world: 92

Budget surplus (+) or deficit (–): -4.4% of GDP (2015 est.)
country comparison to the world: 154

Public debt: 94.9% of GDP (2015 est.)
70.3% of GDP (2014 est.)
note: the total public debt of $64.5 billion consists of: domestic public debt ($23.8 billion); external public debt ($26.1 billion); and sovereign guarantees ($14.6 billion)
country comparison to the world: 21

Fiscal year: calendar year

Inflation rate (consumer prices): 48.7% (2015 est.)
12.1% (2014 est.)
note: Excluding the temporarily occupied territories of the Autonomous Republic of Crimea, the city of Sevastopol and part of the anti-terrorist operation zone
country comparison to the world: 224

Central bank discount rate: 22% (23 December 2015)
7.5% (31 January 2012)
country comparison to the world: 2

Commercial bank prime lending rate:
19% (31 December 2015 est.)
17.72% (31 December 2014 est.)
country comparison to the world: 18

Stock of narrow money:
$17.16 billion (31 December 2015 est.)
$27.62 billion (31 December 2014 est.)
country comparison to the world: 68

Stock of broad money: $78.02 billion (31 December 2014 est.)
$113.4 billion (31 December 2013 est.)
country comparison to the world: 60

Stock of domestic credit: $69.23 billion (31 December 2015 est.)
$95.93 billion (31 December 2014 est.)
country comparison to the world: 58

Market value of publicly traded shares: $20.71 billion (31 December 2012 est.)
$25.56 billion (31 December 2011)
$39.46 billion (31 December 2010 est.)
country comparison to the world: 65

Current account balance: -$260 million (2015 est.)
-$5.332 billion (2014 est.)
country comparison to the world: 87

Exports: $35 billion (2015 est.)
$53.91 billion (2014 est.)
country comparison to the world: 60

Exports—commodities: ferrous and nonferrous metals, fuel and petroleum Products, chemicals, machinery and transport equipment, foodstuffs

Exports—partners: Russia 12.7%, Turkey 7.3%, China 6.3%, Egypt 5.5%, Italy 5.2%, Poland 5.2% (2015)

Imports: $37.15 billion (2015 est.)
$54.38 billion (2014 est.)
country comparison to the world: 60

Imports—commodities: energy, machinery and equipment, chemicals

Imports—partners: Russia 20%, Germany 10.4%, China 10.1%, Belarus 6.5%, Poland 6.2%, Hungary 4.2% (2015)

Reserves of foreign exchange and gold:
$13.15 billion (30 November 2015 est.)
$7.53 billion (31 December 2014 est.)
country comparison to the world: 72

Debt—external: $130.7 billion (31 December 2015 est.)
$142.1 billion (31 December 2013 est.)
country comparison to the world: 45

Stock of direct foreign investment—at home: $62 billion (31 December 2015 est.)
$57.9 billion (31 December 2014 est.)
country comparison to the world: 55

Stock of direct foreign investment—abroad:
$7.945 billion (31 December 2015 est.)
$7.145 billion (31 December 2014 est.)
country comparison to the world: 63

Exchange rates: hryvnia (UAH) per US dollar—

21.85 (2015 est.)
11.8867 (2014 est.)
11.8867 (2013 est.)
7.99 (2012 est.)
7.9676 (2011 est.)

ENERGY

Electricity—production: 187.1 billion kWh (2012 est.)
country comparison to the world: 22

Electricity—consumption: 159.8 billion kWh (2012 est.)
country comparison to the world: 23

Electricity—exports: 6 billion kWh (2012 est.)
country comparison to the world: 28

Electricity—imports: 89 million kWh (2012 est.)
country comparison to the world: 95

Electricity—Installed generating capacity: 55.19 million kW (2012 est.)
country comparison to the world: 19

Electricity—from fossil fuels: 63.7% of total installed capacity (2012 est.)
country comparison to the world: 123

Electricity—from nuclear fuels: 23.7% of total installed capacity (2012 est.)
country comparison to the world: 9

Electricity—from hydroelectricplants: 9.9% of total installed capacity (2012 est.)
country comparison to the world: 116

Electricity—from other renewable sources: 1.1% of total installed capacity (2012 est.)
country comparison to the world: 94

Crude oil—production: 40,490 bbl/day (2014 est.)
country comparison to the world: 60

Crude oil—exports: 1,218 bbl/day (2012 est.)
country comparison to the world: 83

Crude oil—imports: 33,020 bbl/day (2012 est.)
country comparison to the world: 58

Crude oil—proved reserves: 395 million bbl (1 January 2015 est.)
country comparison to the world: 54

Refined petroleum Products—production: 118,700 bbl/day (2012 est.)
country comparison to the world: 69

Refined petroleum Products—consumption: 255,000 bbl/day (2013 est.)
country comparison to the world: 47

Refined petroleum Products—exports: 35,020 bbl/day (2012 est.)
country comparison to the world: 66

Refined petroleum Products—Imports: 175,100 bbl/day (2012 est.)
country comparison to the world: 32

Natural gas—production: 19.9 billion cu m (2015)
country comparison to the world: 33

Natural gas—consumption: 33.8 billion cu m (2015 est.)
country comparison to the world: 28

Natural gas—exports: 0 cu m (2015 est.)
country comparison to the world: 201

Natural gas—imports: 16.4 billion cu m (2015 est.)
country comparison to the world: 22

Natural gas—proved reserves: 1.104 trillion cu m (1 January 2014 est.)
country comparison to the world: 25

Carbon dioxide emissions from consumption of energy: 290.4 million Mt (2012 est.)
country comparison to the world: 23

COMMUNICATIONS

Telephones—fixed lines: *total subscriptions:* 10.46 million
subscriptions per 100 inhabitants: 23 (2014 est.)
country comparison to the world: 20

Telephones—mobile cellular: *total:* 61.2 million
subscriptions per 100 inhabitants: 136 (2014 est.)
country comparison to the world: 25

Telephone system: *general assessment:* Ukraine's telecommunication development plan emphasizes improving domestic trunk lines, international connections, and the mobile-cellular system
domestic: at independence in December 1991, Ukraine inherited a telephone system that was antiquated, inefficient, and in disrepair; more than 3.5 million applications for telephones could not be satisfied; telephone density is rising and the domestic trunk system is being improved; about one-third of Ukraine's networks are digital, and a majority of region al centers now have digital switching stations; improvements in local networks and local exchanges continue to lag; the mobile-cellular telephone system's expansion has slowed, largely due to saturation of the market which has reached 125 mobile phones per 100 people
International: country code—380; 2 new domestic trunk lines are a part of the fiber-optic Trans-Asia-Europe (TAE) system and 3 Ukrainian links have been installed in the fiber-optic Trans-European Lines (TEL) project that connects 18 countries; addition al international service is provided by the Italy-Turkey-Ukraine-Russia (ITUR) fiber-optic submarine cable and by an unknown number of earth stations in the Intelsat, Inmarsat, and Intersputnik satellite systems (2010)

Broadcast media: state-controlled nationwide TV broadcast channel (UT1) and a number of privately owned TV networks provide basic TV coverage; multi-channel cable and satellite TV services are available; Russian television broadcasts have a small audience nationwide, but larger audiences in the eastern and southern regions; the radio broadcast market, a mix of independent and state-owned networks, is comprised of some 300 stations (2007)
Radio broadcast stations: 524 (station frequency types NA) (2006)
Television broadcast stations: 647 (2006)

Internet country code: .ua

Internet hosts: 2.173 million (2012)
country comparison to the world: 37

Internet users: *total:* 16.8 million
percent of population: 37.5% (2014 est.)

country comparison to the world: 32

TRANSPORTATION

Airports: 187 (2013)
country comparison to the world: 31

Airports—with paved runways: *total:* 108
over 3,047 m: 13
2,438 to 3,047 m: 42
1,524 to 2,437 m: 22
914 to 1,523 m: 3
under 914 m: 28 (2013)

Airports—with unpaved runways: *total:* 79
1,524 to 2,437 m: 5
914 to 1,523 m: 5
under 914 m: 69 (2013)

Heliports: 9 (2013)

Pipelines: gas 36,720 km; oil 4,514 km; refined products 4,363 km (2013)

Railways: *total:* 21,733 km
broad gauge: 21,684 km 1.524-m gauge (9,250 km electrified)
standard gauge: 49 km 1.435-m gauge (49 km electrified) (2014)
country comparison to the world: 13

Roadways: *total:* 169,694 km
paved: 166,095 km (includes 17 km of expressways)
unpaved: 3,599 km (2012)
country comparison to the world: 29

Waterways: 1,672 km (most on Dnieper River) (2012)
country comparison to the world: 46

Merchant marine: *total:* 134
by type: bulk carrier 3, cargo 98, chemical tanker 1, passenger 6, passenger/cargo 5, petroleum tanker 8, refrigerated cargo 11, specialized tanker 2
registered in other countries: 172 (Belize 6, Cambodia 35, Comoros 10, Cyprus 3, Dominica 1, Georgia 10, Liberia 10, Malta 29, Marshall Islands 1, Moldova 14, Mongolia 1, Panama 8, Russia 12, Saint Kitts and Nevis 8, Saint Vincent and the Grenadines 12, Sierra Leone 5, Slovakia 2, unknown 5) (2010)
country comparison to the world: 43

Ports and terminals: *major seaport(s):* Feodosiya (Theodosia), Illichivsk, Mariupol', Mykolayiv, Odesa, Yuzhnyy

MILITARY AND SECURITY

Military branches: Ground Forces, Naval Forces, Air Forces (2013)

Military service age and obligation: 20–27 years of age for compulsory military service; conscript service obligation is 18 months (2015)

Military expenditures: 3.8% of GDP (2016)
2.7% of GDP (2015)
1.77% of GDP (2014)
0.97% of GDP (2013)
country comparison to the world: 26

TRANSNATIONAL ISSUES

Disputes—international: 1997 boundary delimitation treaty with Belarus remains unratified due to unresolved financial claims, stalling demarcation and reducing border security; delimitation of land boundary with Russia is complete and demarcation began in 2012; the dispute over the boundary between Russia and Ukraine through the Kerch Strait and Sea of Azov is suspended due to the occupation of Crimea by Russia; Ukraine and Moldova signed an agreement officially delimiting their border in 1999, but the border has not been demarcated due to Moldova's difficulties with the break-away region of Transnistria; Moldova and Ukraine operate joint customs posts to monitor transit of people and commodities through Moldova's Transnistria Region, which remains under the auspices of an Organization for Security and Cooperation in Europe-mandated peacekeeping mission comprised of Moldovan, Transnistrian, Russian, and Ukrainian troops; the ICJ ruled largely in favor of Romania in its dispute submitted in 2004 over Ukrainian-administered Zmiyinyy/Serpilor (Snake) Island and Black Sea maritime boundary delimitation; Romania opposes Ukraine's reopening of a navigation canal from the Danube border through Ukraine to the Black Sea

Refugees and internally displaced persons: *IDPs:* 800,000 (Russian-sponsored separatist violence in Crimea and eastern Ukraine) (2015); note -revised figure reflects updates to UN's IDP verification and registration processes
stateless persons: 35,228 (2015); note—citizens of the former USSR who were permanently resident in Ukraine were granted citizenship upon Ukraine's independence in 1991, but some missed this window of opportunity; people arriving after 1991, Crimean Tatars, ethnic Koreans, people with expired Soviet passports, and people with no documents have difficulty acquiring Ukrainian citizenship; following the fall of the Soviet Union in 1989, thousands of Crimean Tatars and their descendants deported from Ukraine under the STALIN regime returned to their homeland, some being stateless and others holding the citizenship of Uzbekistan or other former Soviet republics; a 1998 bilateral agreement between Ukraine and Uzbekistan simplified the process of renouncing Uzbek citizenship and obtaining Ukrainian citizenship

Trafficking in persons: *current situation:* Ukraine is a source, transit, and destination country for men, women, and children subjected to forced labor and sex trafficking; Ukrainian victims are sex trafficked within Ukraine as well as in Russia, Poland, Iraq, Spain, Turkey, Cyprus, Greece, Seychelles, Portugal, the Czech Republic, Israel, Italy, South Korea, Moldova, China, the United Arab Emirates, Montenegro, UK, Kazakhstan, Tunisia, and other countries; small numbers of foreigners from Moldova, Russia, Vietnam, Uzbekistan, Pakistan, Cameroon, and Azerbaijan were victims of labor trafficking in Ukraine; Ukrainian recruiters most often target Ukrainians from rural areas with limited job prospects using fraud, coercion, and debt bondage

tierrating: Tier 2 Watch List—Ukraine does not fully comply with the minimum standards for the elimination of trafficking; however, it is making significant efforts to do so; the government's focus on its security situation constrained its anti-trafficking capabilities; law enforcement efforts to pursue trafficking cases weakened in 2014, continuing a multi-year decline, and no investigations, prosecutions, or convictions of government officials were made, despite reports of official complicity in the sex and labor trafficking of children living in state-run institutions; fewer victims were identified and referred to NGOs, which continued to provide and to fund the majority of victims' services (2015)

Illicit drugs: limited cultivation of cannabis and opium poppy, mostly for CIS consumption; some synthetic drug production for export to the West; limited government eradication program; used as transshipment point for opiates and other illicit drugs from Africa, Latin America, and Turkey to Europe and Russia; Ukraine has improved anti-money-laundering controls, resulting in its removal from the Financial Action Task Force's (FATF 's) Noncooperative Countries and Territories List in February 2004; Ukraine's anti-money-laundering regime continues to be monitored by FATF

889

UNITED ARAB EMIRATES

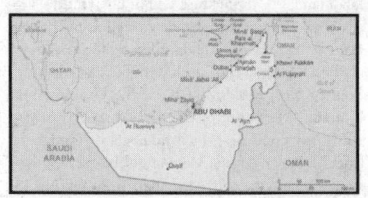

INTRODUCTION

Background: The Trucial States of the Persian Gulf coast granted the UK control of their defense and Foreign Affairs in 19th century treaties. In 1971, six of these states—Abu Dhabi, 'Ajman, Al Fujayrah, Ash Shariqah, Dubayy, and Umm al Qaywayn—merged to form the United Arab Emirates (UAE). They were joined in 1972 by Ra's al Khaymah. The UAE's per capita GDP is on par with those of leading West European nations. Its high oil revenues and its moderate foreign policy stance have allowed the UAE to play a vital role in the affairs of the region. For more than three decades, oil and global finance drove the UAE's economy. However, in 2008–09, the confluence of falling oil prices, collapsing real estate prices, and the international banking crisis hit the UAE especially hard. The UAE has essentially avoided the "Arab Spring" unrest seen elsewhere in the Middle East, though in March 2011, political activists and intellectuals signed a petition calling for greater public participation in governance that was widely circulated on the Internet. in an effort to stem potential further unrest, the government announced a multi-year, $ 1.6-billion infrastructure investment plan for the poorer northern emirates and aggressively pursued advocates of political reform.

GEOGRAPHY

Location: Middle East, bordering the Gulf of Oman and the Persian Gulf, between Oman and Saudi Arabia

Geographic coordinates: 24 00 N, 54 00 E

Map references: Middle East

Area: total: 83,600 sq km
land: 83,600 sq km
water: 0 sq km
country comparison to the world: 115

Area—comparative: slightly larger than South Carolina; slightly smaller than Maine

Land boundaries: total: 1,066 km
border countries (2): Oman 609 km, Saudi Arabia 457 km

Coastline: 1,318 km

Maritime claims: territorial sea: 12 nm
contiguous zone: 24 nm
exclusive economic zone: 200 nm
continental shelf: 200 nm or to the edge of the continental margin

Climate: desert; cooler in eastern mountains

Terrain: flat, barren coastal plain merging into rolling sand dunes of vast desert; mountains in east

Elevation: mean elevation: 149 m

elevation extremes: lowest point: Persian Gulf 0 m
highest point: Jabal Yibir 1,527 m

Natural resources: petroleum, Natural gas

Land use: agricultural land: 4.6%
arable land: 0.5%
permanent crops: 0.5%
permanent pasture: 3.6%
forest: 3.8%
other: 91.6% (2011 est.)

Irrigated land: 923 sq km (2012)

Total renewable water resources: 0.15 cu km (2011)

Freshwater withdrawal (domestic/industrial/agricultural): total: 3.99 cu km/yr (15%/2%/83%)
per capita: 739.5 cu m/yr (2005)

Natural hazards: frequent sand and dust storms

Environment—current issues: lack of Natural freshwater resources compensated by desalination plants; desertification; beach pollution from Oils pills

Environment—International agreements: party to: Biodiversity, Climate Change, Climate Change-Kyoto Protocol, Desertification, Endangered Species, Hazardous Wastes, Marine Dumping, Ozone Layer Protection
signed, but not ratified: Law of the Sea

Geography—note: strategic location along southern approaches to Strait of Hormuz, a vital transit point for world crude oil

PEOPLE AND SOCIETY

Nationality: noun: Emirati(s)
adjective: Emirati

Ethnic groups: Emirati 19%, other Arab and Iranian 23%, South Asian 50%, other expatriates (includes Westerners and East Asians) 8% (1982)
note: less than 20% are UAE citizens (1982)

Languages: Arabic (official), Persian, English, Hindi, Urdu

Religions: Muslim (Islam; official) 76%, Christian 9%, other (primarily Hindu and Buddhist, less than 5% of the population consists of Parsi, Baha'i, Druze, Sikh, Ahmadi, Ismaili, Dawoodi Bohra Muslim, and Jewish) 15%
note: represents the total population; about 85% of the population consists of noncitizens (2005 est.)

Population: 5,779,760 (July 2015 est.)
note: the UN estimates the country's total population to be 9,157,000 as of mid-year 2015; immigrants make up almost 90% of the total population, according to 2015 UN data (2016)
country comparison to the world: 113

Age structure: 0–14 years: 20.85% (male 616,669/female 588,546)
15–24 years: 13.57% (male 466,663/female 317,735)
25–54 years: 61.38% (male 2,704,889/female 842,852)
55–64 years: 3.18% (male 137,753/female 46,214)
65 years and over: 1.01% (male 36,725/female 21,714) (2015 est.)

Dependency ratios: total dependency ratio: 17.8%
youth dependency ratio: 16.4%
elderly dependency ratio: 1.3%
potential support ratio: 74.6% (2015 est.)

Median age: total: 30.3 years
male: 32.1 years
female: 25.1 years (2015 est.)
country comparison to the world: 110

Population growth rate: 2.58% (2015 est.)
country comparison to the world: 20

Birth rate: 15.43 births/1,000 population (2015 est.)
country comparison to the world: 128

Death rate: 1.97 deaths/1,000 population (2015 est.)
country comparison to the world: 224

Net migration rate: 12.36 migrant(s)/1,000 population (2015 est.)
country comparison to the world: 7

Urbanization: urban Population: 85.5% of total population (2015)
rate of urbanization: 2.87% annual rate of change (2010–15 est.)

Major urban Areas—population: Dubai 2.415 million; Sharjah 1.279 million; ABU DHABI (capital) 1.145 million (2015)

Sex ratio: at birth: 1.05 male(s)/female
0–14 years: 1.05 male(s)/female 15–24 years: 1.47 male(s)/female
25–54 years: 3.21 male(s)/female
55–64 years: 2.98 male(s)/female
65 years and over: 1.69 male(s)/female
total population: 2.18 male(s)/female (2015 est.)

Maternal mortality rate: 6 deaths/100,000 live births (2015 est.)
country comparison to the world: 146

Infant mortality rate: total: 10.59 deaths/1,000 live births
male: 12.35 deaths/1,000 live births
female: 8.75 deaths/1,000 live births (2015 est.)
country comparison to the world: 131

Life expectancy at birth: total population: 77.29 years
male: 74.67 years
female: 80.04 years (2015 est.)
country comparison to the world: 72

Total fertility rate: 2.35 children born/woman (2015 est.)
country comparison to the world: 85

Health expenditures: 3.2% of GDP (2013)
country comparison to the world: 182

Physicians density: 2.53 physicians/1,000 population (2010)

Hospital bed density: 1.1 beds/1,000 population (2012)

Drinking water source:
improved:
urban: 99.6% of population
rural: 100% of population
total: 99.6% of population
unimproved:
urban: 0.4% of population
rural: 0% of population
total: 0.4% of population (2015 est.)

Sanitation facility access:
improved:
urban: 98% of population
rural: 95.2% of population
total: 97.6% of population
unimproved:
urban: 2% of popu lation
rural: 4.8% of population
total: 2.4% of population (2015 est.)

HIV/AIDS—adult prevalence rate: NA

HIV/AIDS—people living with HIV/AIDS: NA

HIV/AIDS—deaths: NA

Obesity—adult prevalence rate: 34.5% (2014)
country comparison to the world: 22

Education expenditures: NA

Literacy: *definition:* age 15 and over can read and write
total population: 93.8%
male: 93.1%
female: 95.8% (2015 est.)

Unemployment, youth ages 15–24: *total:* 12.1%
male: 7.9%
female: 21.8% (2008 est.)
country comparison to the world: 91

GOVERNMENT

Country name: *conventional long form:* United Arab Emirates
conventional short form: none
local long form: Al Imarat al Arabiyah al Muttahidah
local short form: none
former: Trucial Oman, Trucial States
abbreviation: UAE
etymology: self-descriptive country name; the name "Arabia" can be traced back many centuries B.C., the ancient Egyptians referred to the region as "Ar Rabi"; "emirates" derives from "amir" the Arabic word for "commander," "lord," or "prince"

Government type: federation of monarchies

Capital: *name:* Abu Dhabi

Geographic coordinates: 24 28 N, 54 22 E
time difference: UTC+4 (9 hours ahead of Washington, DC, during Standard Time)

Administrative divisions: 7 emirates (imarat, singular—imarah); Abu Zaby (Abu Dhabi), 'Ajman,

Al Fujayrah, Ash Shariqah (Sharjah), Dubayy (Dubai), Ra's al Khaymah, Umm al Qaywayn

Independence: 2 December 1971 (from the UK)

National holiday: independence Day, 2 Decembe (1971)

Constitution: previous 1971 (provision al); latest drafted in 1979, became permanent May 1996; amended 2009 (2016)

Legal system: mixed legal system of Islamic law and civil law

international law organization participation: has not submitted an ICJ jurisdiction declaration; non-party state to the ICCt

Citizenship: *citizenship by birth:* no
citizenship by descent only: the father must be a citizen of the United Arab Emirates; if the father is unknown, the mother must be a citizen
dual citizenship recognized: no
residency requirement for Naturalization: 30 years

Suffrage: limited; note—rulers of the seven emirates each select a proportion of voters for the Federal National Council (FNC) that together account for about 12 percent of Emirati citizens

Executive branch: *chief of state:* President KHALIFA BIN Zayid Al-Nuhayyan (since 3 November 2004), ruler of Abu Zaby (Abu Dhabi) (since 4 November 2004); Vice President and Prime Minister MUHAMMAD BIN RASHID Al-Maktum (since 5 January 2006)

head of government: Prime Minister Vice President MUHAMMAD BIN RASHID Al-Maktum (since 5 January 2006); Deputy Prime Ministers SAIF BIN Zayid Al-Nuhayyan, MANSUR BIN Zayid Al-Nuhayyan (both since 11 May 2009)
cabinet: Council of Ministers appointed by the president
elections/appointments: president and vice president indirectly elected by the Federal Supreme Council—composed of the rulers of the 7 emirates—for a 5-year term (no term limits); election last held 3 November 2009 (next election NA); prime minister and deputy prime minister appointed by the president
election results: KHALIFA BIN Zayid Al-Nuhayyan reelected president; FSC vote NA
note: there is also a Federal Supreme Council (FSC) composed of the 7 emirate rulers; the FSC is the highest constitutional authority in the UAE; establishes general policies and sanctions federal legislation; meets 4 times a year; Abu Zaby (Abu Dhabi) and Dubayy (Dubai) rulers have effective veto power

Legislative branch: *description:* unicameral Federal National Council (FNC) or Majlis al-Ittihad al-Watani (40 seats; 20 members appointed by the rulers of the 7 constituent states and 20 indirectly elected by an electoral college whose members are selected by each emirate ruler proportional to its FNC membership; members serve 4-year terms)
elections: last held on 3 October 2015 (next to be held in 2019); note—the electoral college was expanded from 129,274 electors in the December 2011 election to 224,279 in the October 2015

election; elections for candidates rather than political parties; 347 candidates including 78 women ran for 20 contested seats in the 40-member FNC; 80,000 voters, or 35% of eligible voters, turned out to vote and 19 men and one woman were elected
election results: elected FNC seats by emirate— Abu Dhabi 4, Dubai 4, Sharjah 3, Ras al-Khaimah 3, Ajman 2, Fujairah 2, Umm al-Quwain 2; note— only 1 woman (from Ras Al Khaimah) won an FNC seat

Judicial branch: *highest court(s):* Federal Supreme Court (consists of the court president and 4 judges)
judge selection and term of office: judges appointed by the federal president following approval by the Federal Supreme Council, which includes the rulers of the 7 emirates; judge term NA
subordinate courts: Federal Court of Cassation (determines the constitutionality of laws promulgated at the federal and local (emirate) levels; federal level courts of first instance and appeals courts; each emirate has its own court system

Political parties and leaders: none; political parties are banned

Political pressure groups and leaders: NA

International organization participation: ABEDA, AfDB (nonregion al member), AFESD, AMF, BIS, CAEU, CICA, FAO, G-77, GCC, IAEA, IBRD, ICAO, ICC (National committees), ICRM, IDA, IDB, IFAD, IFC, IFRCS, IHO, ILO, IMF, IMO, IMSO, Interpol, IOC, IPU, ISO, ITSO, ITU, LAS, MIGA, NAM, OAPEC, OIC, OIF (observer), OPCW, OPEC, PCA, UN, UNCTAD, UNESCO, UNIDO, UNRWA, UNWTO, UPU, WCO, WHO, WIPO, WMO, WTO

Diplomatic representation in the US: *chief of mission:* Ambassador Yusif BIN Mani BIN Said al-UTAYBA (since 25 July 2008) ch an cery: 3522 Inter National Court NW, Suite 400, Washington, DC 20008
telephone: [1] (202) 243-2400
FAX: [1] (202) 243-2432
consulate(s) general: Los Angeles

Diplomatic representation from the US: *chief of mission:* Ambassador Barbara A. LEAF (since 30 December 2014)
embassy: Embassies District, Plot 38 Sector W59–02, Street No.4, Abu Dhabi mailing address: P. O. Box 4009, Abu Dhabi
telephone: [971] (2) 414-2200
FAX: [971] (2) 414-2603
consulate(s) general: Dubai

Flag description: three equal horizontal bands of green (top), white, and black with a wider vertical red band on the hoist side; the flag incorporates all four Pan-Arab colors, which in this case represent fertility (green), neutrality (white), petroleum resources (black), and unity (red); red was the traditional color incorporated into all flags of the emirates before their unification

National symbol(s): golden falcon; National colors: green, white, black, red

National anthem: *name:* "Nashid al-watani al-imarati" (National Anthem of the UAE)

lyrics/music: AREF Al Sheikh Abdullah Al Hassan/Mohamad Abdel WAHAB

note: music adopted 1971, lyrics adopted 1996; Mohamad Abdel WAH AB also composed the music for the anthem of Tunisia

ECONOMY

Economy—overview: The UAE has an open economy with a high per capita income and a sizable annual trade surplus. Successful efforts at economic diversification have reduced the portion of GDP based on oil and gas output to 25%.

Since the discovery of oil in the UAE more than 30 years ago, the country has undergone a profound transformation from an impoverished region of small desert principalities to a modern state with a high standard of living. The government has increased spending on job creation and infrastructure expansion and is opening up utilities to greater private sector involvement. The country's free trade zones—offering 100% foreign ownership and zero taxes—are helping to attract foreign investors. The global financial crisis of 2008–09, tight international credit, and deflated asset prices constricted the economy in 2009. UAE authorities tried to blunt the crisis by increasing spending and boosting liquidity in the banking sector. The crisis hit Dubai hardest, as it was heavily exposed to depressed real estate prices. Dubai lacked sufficient cash to meet its debt obligations, prompting global concern about its solvency and ultimately a $20 billion bailout from the UAE Central Bank and Abu Dhabi Government that was refinanced in March 2014.

Dependence on oil, a large expatriate workforce, and growing inflation pressures are significant long-term challenges. Low oil prices have prompted the UAE to take steps to reduce its social spending, including eliminating fuelsubsidies in August 2015, but the UAE has sufficient assets to cover its deficits with money from its sovereign investment funds. The UAE's strategic plan for the next few years focuses on economic diversification and creating more job opportunities for Nationals through improved education and increased private sector employment.

GDP (purchasing power parity): $647.8 billion (2015 est.)
$623.3 billion (2014 est.)
$596.1 billion (2013 est.)
note: data are in 2015 US dollars
country comparison to the world: 33

GDP (official exchange rate): $345.5 billion (2015 est.)

GDP—real growth rate: 3.9% (2015 est.)
4.6% (2014 est.)
4.3% (2013 est.)
country comparison to the world: 70

GDP—per capita (PPP): $67,600 (2015 est.)
$67,000 (2014 est.)
$66,000 (2013 est.)
note: data are in 2015 US dollars
country comparison to the world: 12

Gross National saving: 27.8% of GDP (2015 est.)
38.3% of GDP (2014 est.)

41.6% of GDP (2013 est.)
country comparison to the world: 32

GDP—composition, by end use:
household consumption: 55.4%
government consumption: 8.7%
investment in fixed capital: 27.4%
investment in inventories: 0.8%
exports of goods and services: 94.5%
imports of goods and services: -86.8% (2015 est.)

GDP—composition, by sector of origin:
agriculture: 0.7%
industry: 49.4%
services: 49.8% (2015 est.)

Agriculture—products: dates, vegetables, watermelons; poultry, eggs, dairy products; fish

Industries: petroleum and petrochemicals; fishing, aluminum, cement, fertilizers, commercial ship repair, construction materials, handicrafts, textiles

Industrial production growth rate: 2.8% (2015 est.)
country comparison to the world: 94

Labor force: 5.136 million
note: expatriates account for about 85% of the workforce (2015 est.)
country comparison to the world: 80

Labor force—by occupation: *agriculture:* 7%
industry: 15%
services: 78% (2000 est.)

Unemployment rate: 2.4% (2001 est.)
country comparison to the world: 15

Population below poverty line: 19.5% (2003 est.)

Household income or consumption by percentage share: *lowest:* 10%: NA%
highest: 10%: NA%

Budget: *revenues:* $110.1 billion *expenditures:* $119.8 billion
note: the UAE federal budget does not account for emirate-level spending in Abu Dhabi and Dubai (2015 est.)
Taxes and other revenues: 32.5% of GDP (2015 est.)
country comparison to the world: 74

Budget surplus (+) or deficit (–): -2.9% of GDP (2015 est.)
country comparison to the world: 110

Public debt: 52.1% of GDP (2015 est.)
45.4% of GDP (2014 est.)
country comparison to the world: 76

Fiscal year: calendar year

Inflation rate (consumer prices): 4.1% (2015 est.)
2.3% (2014 est.)
country comparison to the world: 161

Central bank discount rate: NA%

Stock of narrow money: $130 billion (31 December 2015 est.)
$118.7 billion (31 December 2014 est.)
country comparison to the world: 28

Stock of broad money: $343.6 billion (31 December 2014 est.)
$287.7 billion (31 December 2013 est.)
country comparison to the world: 30

Stock of domestic credit: $357.6 billion (31 December 2015 est.)

$331.7 billion (31 December 2014 est.)
country comparison to the world: 32

Market value of publicly traded shares: $67.95 billion (31 December 2012 est.)
$71.33 billion (31 December 2011)
$77.08 billion (31 December 2010 est.)
country comparison to the world: 49

Current account balance: $13.55 billion (2015 est.)
$54.63 billion (2014 est.)
country comparison to the world: 18

Exports: $323.8 billion (2015 est.)
$370.6 billion (2014 est.)
country comparison to the world: 16

Exports—commodities: crude oil 45%, Natural gas, reexports, dried fish, dates (2012 est.)

Exports—partners: Iran 14.5%, Japan 9.8%, India 9.2%, China 4.7%, Oman 4.3% (2015)

Imports: $248.2 billion (2015 est.)
$239.8 billion (2014 est.)
country comparison to the world: 18

Imports—commodities: machinery and transport equipment, chemicals, food

Imports—partners: China 15.5%, India 12.7%, US 9.6%, Germany 6.8%, UK 4.3% (2015)

Reserves of foreign exchange and gold: $79.92 billion (31 December 2015 est.)
$78.42 billion (31 December 2014 est.)
country comparison to the world: 29

Debt—external: $171.9 billion (31 December 2014 est.)
$167.1 billion (31 December 2013 est.)
country comparison to the world: 37

Stock of direct foreign investment—at home: $126.4 billion (31 December 2015 est.)
$116.4 billion (31 December 2014 est.)
country comparison to the world: 41

Stock of direct foreign investment—abroad: $86.1 billion (31 December 2015 est.)
$81.6 billion (31 December 2014 est.)
country comparison to the world: 33

Exchange rates: Emirati dirhams (AED) per US dollar—
3.673 (2015 est.)
3.673 (2014 est.)
3.673 (2013 est.)
3.67 (2012 est.)
3.673 (2011 est.)

ENERGY

Electricity—production: 100.5 billion kWh (2012 est.)
country comparison to the world: 33

Electricity—consumption: 93.28 billion kWh (2012 est.)
country comparison to the world: 34

Electricity—exports: 0 kWh (2013 est.)
country comparison to the world: 97

Electricity—imports: 0 kWh (2013 est.)
country comparison to the world: 114

Electricity—installed generating capacity: 27.23 million kW (2012 est.)

country comparison to the world: 31

Electricity—from fossil fuels: 99.8% of total installed capacity (2012 est.)
country comparison to the world: 41

Electricity—from nuclear fuels: 0% of total installed capacity (2012 est.)
country comparison to the world: 36

Electricity—from hydroelectric plants: 0% of total installed capacity (2012 est.)
country comparison to the world: 156

Electricity—from other renewable sources: 0.2% of total installed capacity (2012 est.)
country comparison to the world: 111

Crude oil—production: 2.82 million bbl/day (2014 est.)
country comparison to the world: 8

Crude oil—exports: 2.5 million bbl/day (2013 est.)
country comparison to the world: 4

Crude oil—imports: 0 bbl/day (2012 est.)
country comparison to the world: 152

Crude oil—proved reserves: 97.8 billion bbl (1 January 2015 est.)
country comparison to the world: 8

Refined petroleum Products—consumption: -487,000 bbl/day (2012 est.)
country comparison to the world: 33

Refined petroleum Products—consumption: 694.000 bbl/day (2013 est.)
country comparison to the world: 29

Refined petroleum Products—exports: 364,500 bbl/day (2012 est.)
country comparison to the world: 21

Refined petroleum Products—imports: 341,700 bbl/day (2012 est.)
country comparison to the world: 20

Natural gas—production: 54.6 billion cu m (2013 est.)
country comparison to the world: 18

Natural gas—consumption: 66.69 billion cu m (2013 est.)
country comparison to the world: 12

Natural gas—exports: 7.4 billion cu m (2013 est.)
country comparison to the world: 26

Natural gas—imports: 19.49 billion cu m (2013 est.)
country comparison to the world: 17

Natural gas—proved reserves: 6.089 trillion cu m (1 January 2014 est.)
country comparison to the world: 7

Carbon dioxide emissions from consumption of energy: 234.1 million Mt (2012 est.)
country comparison to the world: 26

COMMUNICATIONS

Telephones—fixed lines: *total subscriptions:* 2.1 million
subscriptions per 100 inhabitants: 37 (2014 est.)
country comparison to the world: 56

Telephones—mobile cellular: *total:* 16.8 million

subscriptions per 100 inhabitants: 299 (2014 est.)
country comparison to the world: 64

Telephone system: *general assessment:* modern fiber-optic integrated services; digital network with rapidly growing use mobile-cellular telephones; key centers are Abu Dhabi and Dubai of *domestic:* microwave radio relay, fiber optic and coaxial cable
International: country code—971; linked to the international submarine cable FLAG (Fiber-Optic Link Around the Globe); landing point for both the SEA-ME-WE-3 and SEA-ME-WE-4 submarine cable networks; satellite earth stations—3 Intelsat (1 Atlantic Ocean and 2 Indian Ocean) and 1 Arabsat; tropospheric scatter to Bahrain; microwave radio relay to Saudi Arabia (2011)

Broadcast media: except for the many organizations now operating in Dubai's Media Free Zone, most TV and radio stations remain government-owned; widespread use of satellite dishes provides access to pan-Arab and other international broadcasts (2007)
Radio broadcast stations: AM 13, FM 8, shortwave 2 (2004)
Television broadcast stations: 15 (2004)

Internet country code: .ae

Internet hosts: 337,804 (2012)
country comparison to the world: 61

Internet users: *total:* 5.2 million
percent of population: 93.2% (2014 est.)
country comparison to the world: 63

TRANSPORTATION

Airports: 43 (2013)
country comparison to the world: 100

Airports—with paved runways: *total:* 25
over 3,047 m: 12
2,438 to 3,047 m: 3
1,524 to 2,437 m: 5
914 to 1,523 m: 3
under 914 m: 2 (2013)

Airports—with unpaved runways: *total:* 18
over 3,047 m: 1
2,438 to 3,047 m: 1
1,524 to 2,437 m: 4
914 to 1,523 m: 6
under 914 m: 6 (2013)

Heliports: 5 (2013)

Pipelines: condensate 533 km; gas 3,277 km; liquid petroleum gas 300 km; oil 3,287 km; oil/gas/water 24 km; refined products 218 km; water 99 km (2013)

Roadways: *total:* 4,080 km
paved: 4,080 km (includes 253 km of expressways) (2008)
country comparison to the world: 158

Merchant marine: *total:* 61
by type: bulk carrier 3, cargo 13, chemical tanker 8, container 7, liquefied gas 1, passenger/cargo 1, petroleum tanker 24, roll on/roll off 4

foreign-owned: 13 (Greece 3, Kuwait 10)
registered in other countries: 253 (Bahamas 23, Barbados 1, Belize 3, Cambodia 2, Comoros 8, Cyprus 3, Georgia 2, Gibraltar 5, Honduras 1, Hong Kong 1, India 4, Iran 2, Jordan 2, Liberia 37, Malta 1, Marshall Islands 12, Mexico 1, Netherlands 4, North Korea 2, Panama 83, Papua New Guinea 6, Philippines 1, Saint Kitts and Nevis 8, Saint Vincent and the Grenadines 3, Saudi Arabia 6, Sierra Leone 1, Singapore 10, Tanzania 3, Togo 1, UK 8, Vanuatu 1, unknown 8) (2010)
country comparison to the world: 65

Ports and terminals: *major seaport(s):* Al Fujayrah, Mina' Jabal 'Ali (Dubai), Khor Fakkan (Khawr Fakkan), Mubarraz Island, Mina' Rashid (Dubai), Mina' Saqr (Ra's al Khaymah)
container port(s) (TEUs): Dubai Port (12,617,595), Khor Fakkan (Khawr Fakkan) (3,234,101)
LNG terminal(s) (export): Das Island

MILITARY AND SECURITY

Military branches: United Arab Emirates Armed Forces: Critical Infrastructure Coastal Patrol Agency (CICPA), Land Forces, Navy, Air Force and Air Defense, Presidential Guard (2015)

Military service age and obligation: 18–30 years of age for compulsory military service for men, optional service for women; 17 years of age for male volunteers with parental approval; 2-year general obligation, 9 months for secondary school graduates; women may train for 9 months regardless of education (2014)

Military expenditures: NA% (2012)
5.5% of GDP (2011)

TRANSNATIONAL ISSUES

Disputes—international: boundary agreement was signed and ratified with Oman in 2003 for entire border, including Oman's Musandam Peninsula and Al Madhah enclaves, but contents of the agreement and detailed maps showing the alignment have not been published; Iran and UAE dispute Tunb Islands and Abu Musa Island, which Iran occupies

Illicit drugs: the UAE is a drug transshipment point for traffickers given its proximity to Southwest Asian drug-producing countries; the UAE's position as a major financial center makes it vulnerable to money laundering; anti-money-laundering controls improving, but informal banking remains unregulated

UNITED KINGDOM

The island of Rockall is not shown.

INTRODUCTION

Background: The United Kingdom has historically played a leading role in developing parliamentary democracy and in advancing literature and science. At its zenith in the 19th century, the British Empire stretched over one-fourth of the earth's surface. The first half of the 20th century saw the UK's strength seriously depleted in two world wars and the Irish Republic's withdrawal from the union. The second half witnessed the dismantling of the Empire and the UK rebuilding itself into a moderNAnd prosperous European nation. As one of five permanent members of the UN Security Council and a founding member of NATO and the Commonwealth, the UK pursues a global approach to foreign policy. The Scottish Parliament, the National Assembly for Wales, and the Northern Ireland Assembly were established in 1999. The latter was suspended until May 2007 due to wrangling over the peace process, but devolution was fully completed in March 2010.

The UK was an active member of the EU from 1973 to 2016, although it chose to remain outside the Economic and Monetary Union. However, frustrated by a remote bureaucracy in Brussels and massive migration into the country, UK citizens on 23 June 2016 narrowly voted to leave the EU. The so-called "Brexit" will take years to carry out but could be the signal for referenda in other EU countries where skepticism of EU membership benefits is strong.

GEOGRAPHY

Location: Western Europe, islands—including the northern one-sixth of the island of Ireland— between the North Atlantic Ocean and the North Sea; northwest of France

Geographic coordinates: 54 00 N, 2 00 W

Map references: Europe

Area: *total:* 243,610 sq km
land: 241,930 sq km
water: 1,680 sq km
note: includes Rockall and Shetland Islands
country comparison to the world: 80

Area—comparative: twice the size of Pennsylvania; slightly smaller than Oregon

Land boundaries: *total:* 443 km
border countries (1): Ireland 443 km

Coastline: 12,429 km

Maritime claims: *territorial sea:* 12 nm
exclusive fishing zone: 200 nm
continental shelf: as defined in continental shelf orders or in accordance with agreed upon boundaries

Climate: temperate; moderated by prevailing southwest winds over the North Atlantic Current; more than one-half of the days are overcast

Terrain: mostly rugged hills and low mountains; level to rolling plains in east and southeast

Elevation: *mean elevation:* 162 m

elevation extremes: *lowest point:* The Fens -4 m
highest point: Ben Nevis 1,343 m

Natural resources: coal, petroleum, Natural gas, iron ore, lead, zinc, gold, tin, limestone, salt, clay, chalk, gypsum, potash, silica sand, slate, arable land

Land use: *agricultural land:* 71%
arable land: 25.1%
permanent crops: 0.2%
permanent pasture: 45.7%
forest: 11.9%
other: 17.1% (2011 est.)

Irrigated land: 950 sq km (2012)

Total renewable water resources: 147 cu km (2011)

Freshwater withdrawal (domestic/industrial/agricultural): *total:* 13.03 cu km/yr (58%/33%/9%)
per capita: 213.2 cu m/yr (2008)

Natural hazards: winter windstorm s; floods

Environment—current issues: continues to reduce greenhouse gas emissions; by 2005 the government reduced the amount of industrial and commercial waste disposed of in landfill sites to 85% of 1998 levels and recycled or composted at least 25% of household waste, increasing to 33% by 2015

Environment—International agreements: *party to:* Air Pollution, Air Pollution-Nitrogen Oxides, Air Pollution-Persistent Organic Pollutants, Air Pollution-Sulfur 94, Air Pollution-Volatile Organic Compounds, Antarctic-Environmental Protocol, Antarctic-Marine Living Resources, Antarctic Seals, Antarctic Treaty, Biodiversity, Climate Change, Climate Change-Kyoto Protocol, Desertification, Endangered Species, Environmental Modification, Hazardous Wastes, Law of the Sea, Marine Dumping, Marine Life Conservation, Ozone Layer Protection, Ship Pollution, Tropical Tim ber 83, Tropical Timber 94, Wetlands, Whaling
signed, but not ratified: none of the selected agreements

Geography—note: lies near vital North Atlantic sea lanes; only 35 km from France and linked by tunnel under the English Channel (the Channel Tunnel or Chunnel); because of heavily indented coastline, no location is more than 125 km from tidal waters

PEOPLE AND SOCIETY

Nationality: *noun:* Briton(s), British (collective plural)
adjective: British

Ethnic groups: white 87.2%, black/African/Caribbean/black British 3%, Asian/Asian British: Indian 2.3%, Asian/Asian British: Pakistani 1.9%, mixed 2%, other 3.7% (2011 est.)

Languages: English
note: the following are recognized regional
Languages: Scots (about 30% of the population of Scotland), Scottish Gaelic (about 60,000 in Scotland), Welsh (about 20% of the population of Wales), Irish (about 10% of the population of Northern Ireland), Cornish (some 2,000 to 3,000 in Cornwall) (2012 est.)

Religions: Christian (includes Anglican, Roman Catholic, Presbyterian, Methodist) 59.5%, Muslim 4.4%, Hindu 1.3%, other 2%, unspecified 7.2%, none 25.7% (2011 est.)

Population: 64,088,222 (July 2015 est.)
country comparison to the world: 23

Age structure: *0–14 years:* 17.37% (male 5,706,871/female 5,424,654)
15–24 years: 12.41% (male 4,060,480/female 3,891,262)
25–54 years: 40.91% (male 13,344,087/female 12,873,234)
55–64 years: 11.58% (male 3,675,565/female 3,746,483)
65 years and over: 17.73% (male 5,086,919/female 6,278,667) (2015 est.)

Dependency ratios: *total dependency ratio:* 55.1%
youth dependency ratio: 27.6%

elderly dependency ratio: 27.6%
potential support ratio: 3.6% (2015 est.)

Median age: *total:* 40.4 years
male: 39.2 years
female: 41.6 years (2015 est.)
country comparison to the world: 42

Population growth rate: 0.54% (2015 est.)
country comparison to the world: 155

Birth rate: 12.17 births/1,000 population (2015 est.)
country comparison to the world: 161

Death rate: 9.35 deaths/1,000 population (2015 est.)
country comparison to the world: 60

Net migration rate: 2.54 migrant(s)/1,000 population (2015 est.)
country comparison to the world: 40

Urbanization: *urban Population:* 82.6% of total population (2015)
rate of urbanization: 0.88% annual rate of change (2010–15 est.)

Major urban Areas—population: LONDON (capital) 10.313 million; Manchester 2.646 million; Birmingham 2.515 million; Glasgow 1.223 million; Southampton/Portsmouth 882,000; Liverpool 870,000 (2015)

Sex ratio: *at birth:* 1.05 male(s)/female
0–14 years: 1.05 male(s)/female *15–24 years:* 1.04 male(s)/female
25–54 years: 1.04 male(s)/female
55–64 years: 0.98 male(s)/female
65 years and over: 0.81 male(s)/female
total population: 0.99 male(s)/female (2015 est.)

Mother's mean age at first birth: 28.1
note: data represents England and Wales only (2012 est.)

Maternal mortality rate: 9 deaths/100,000 live births (2015 est.)
country comparison to the world: 148

Infant mortality rate: *total:* 4.38 deaths/1,000 live births
male: 4.8 deaths/1,000 live births
female: 3.95 deaths/1,000 live births (2015 est.)
country comparison to the world: 187

Life expectancy at birth: *total population:* 80.54 years
male: 78.37 years
female: 82.83 years (2015 est.)
country comparison to the world: 33

Total fertility rate: 1.89 children born/woman (2015 est.)
country comparison to the world: 140

Contraceptive prevalence rate: 84%
note: percent of women aged 16–49 (2008/09)

Health expenditures: 9.1% of GDP (2013)
country comparison to the world: 30

Physicians density: 2.81 physicians/1,000 population (2013)

Hospital bed density: 2.9 beds/1,000 population (2011)

Drinking water source:
improved:

urban: 100% of population
rural: 100% of population
total: 100% of population
unimproved:
urban: 0% of popu lation
rural: 0% of population
total: 0% of population (2015 est.)

Sanitation facility access:
improved:
urban: 99.1% of population
rural: 99.6% of population
total: 99.2% of population
unimproved:
urban: 0.9% of population
rural: 0.4% of population
total: 0.8% of population (2015 est.)

HIV/AIDS—adult prevalence rate: 0.33% (2013 est.)
country comparison to the world: 81

HIV/AIDS—people living with HIV/AIDS: 126,700 (2013 est.)
country comparison to the world: 36

HIV/AIDS—deaths: fewer than 600 (2013 est.)
country comparison to the world: 82

Obesity—adult prevalence rate: 29.8% (2014)
country comparison to the world: 43

Education expenditures: 6.7% of GDP (2013)
country comparison to the world: 36

School life expectancy (primary to tertiary education): *total:* 18 years
male: 17 years
female: 18 years (2014)

Unemployment, youth ages 15–24: *total:* 20.9%
male: 23.3%
female: 18.3% (2013 est.)
country comparison to the world: 52

GOVERNMENT

Country name: *conventional long form:* United Kingdom of Great Britain and Northern Ireland; *note*—the island of Great Britain includes England, Scotland, and Wales
conventional short form: United Kingdom
abbreviation: UK
etymology: self-descriptive country name; the designation "Great Britain," in the sense of "Larger Britain," dates back to medieval times and was used to distinguish the island from "Little Britain," or Brittany in modern France; the name Ireland derives from the Gaelic "Eriu," the matron goddess of Ireland (goddess of the land)

Government type: parliamentary constitutional monarchy; a Commonwealth realm

Capital: *name:* London

Geographic coordinates: 51 30 N, 0 05 W
time difference: UTC 0 (5 hours ahead of Washington, DC, during Standard Time)
daylight saving time: +1hr, begins last Sunday in March; ends last Sunday in October
note: applies to the United Kingdom proper, not to its overseas dependencies or territories

Administrative divisions: *England:* 27 two-tier counties, 32 London boroughs and 1 City of

London or Greater London, 36 metropolitan districts, 56 unitary authorities (including 4 single-tier counties*)
two-tier counties: Buckinghamshire, Cambridgeshire, Cumbria, Derbyshire, Devon, Dorset, East Sussex, Essex, Gloucestershire, Hampshire, Hertfordshire, Kent, Lancashire, Leicestershire, Lincolnshire, Norfolk, North Yorkshire, Northamptonshire, Nottinghamshire, Oxfordshire, Somerset, Staffordshire, Suffolk, Surrey, Warwickshire, West Sussex, Worcestershire
London boroughs and City of London or Greater London: Barking and Dagenham, Barnet, Bexley, Brent, Bromley, Camden, Croydon, Ealing, Enfield, Greenwich, Hackney, Hammersmith and Fulham, Haringey, Harrow, Havering, Hillingdon, Hounslow, Islington, Kensington and Chelsea, Kingston upon Thames, Lambeth, Lewisham, City of London, Merton, Newham, Redbridge, Richmond upon Thames, Southwark, Sutton, Tower Hamlets, Waltham Forest, Wandsworth, Westminster
metropolitan districts: Barnsley, Birmingham, Bolton, Bradford, Bury, Calderdale, Coventry, Doncaster, Dudley, Gateshead, Kirklees, Knowlsey, Leeds, Liverpool, Manchester, Newcastle upon Tyne, North Tyneside, Oldham, Rochdale, Rotherham, Salford, Sandwell, Sefton, Sheffield, Solihull, South Tyneside, St. Helens, Stockport, Sunderland, Tameside, Trafford, Wakefield, Walsall, Wigan, Wirral, Wolverhampton
unitary authorities: Bath and North East Somerset, Blackburn with Darwen, Bedford, Blackpool, Bournemouth, Bracknell Forest, Brighton and Hove, City of Bristol, Central Bedfordshire, Cheshire East, Cheshire West and Chester, Cornwall, Darlington, Derby, Durham County*, East Riding of Yorkshire, Halton, Hartlepool, Herefordshire*, Isle of Wight*, Isles of Scilly, City of Kingston upon Hull, Leicester, Luton, Medway, Middlesbrough, Milton Keynes, North East Lincolnshire, North Lincolnshire, North Somerset, Northumberland*, Nottingham, Peterborough, Plymouth, Poole, Portsmouth, Reading, Redcar and Cleveland, Rutland, Shropshire, Slough, South Gloucestershire, Southampton, Southend-on-Sea, Stockton-on-Tees, Stoke-on-Trent, Swindon, Telford and Wrekin, Thurrock, Torbay, Warrington, West Berkshire, Wiltshire, Windsor and Maidenhead, Wokingham, York
Northern Ireland: 5 borough councils, 4 district councils, 2 city councils
borough councils: Antrim and Newtownabbey; Ards and North Down; Armagh, Banbridge, and Craigavon; Causeway Coast and Glens; Mid and East Antrim
district councils: Derry and Strabane; Fermanagh and Omagh; Mid Ulster; Newry, Murne, and Down
city councils: Belfast; Lisburn and Castlereagh
Scot
land: 32 council areas
council areas: Aberdeen City, Aberdeenshire, Angus, Argyll and Bute, Clackmannanshire, Dumfries and Galloway, Dundee City, East Ayrshire, East Dunbartonshire, East Lothian, East Renfrewshire, City of Edinburgh, Eilean Siar (Western

Isles), Falkirk, Fife, Glasgow City, Highland, Inverclyde, Midlothian, Moray, North Ayrshire, North Lanarkshire, Orkney Islands, Perth and Kinross, Renfrewshire, Shetland Islands, South Ayrshire, South Lanarkshire, Stirling, The Scottish Borders, West Dunbartonshire, West Lothian
Wales: 22 unitary authorities

unitary authorities: Blaenau Gwent, Bridgend, Caerphilly, Cardiff, Carmarthenshire, Ceredigion, Conwy, Denbighshire, Flintshire, Gwynedd, Isle of Anglesey, Merthyr Tydfil, Monmouthshire, Neath Port Talbot, Newport, Pembrokeshire, Powys, Rhondda Cynon Taff, Swansea, The Vale of Glamorgan, Torfaen, Wrexham

Dependent areas: Anguilla, Bermuda, British Indian Ocean Territory, British Virgin Islands, Cayman Islands, Falkland Islands, Gibraltar, Montserrat, Pitcairn Islands, Saint Helena, Ascension, and Tristan da Cunha, South Georgia and the South Sandwich Islands, Turks and Caicos Islands

Independence: 12 April 1927 (Royal and Parliamentary Titles Act establishes current name of the United Kingdom of Great Britain and Northern Ireland); notable earlier dates: 927 (minor English kingdoms united); 3 March 1284 (enactment of the Statute of Rhuddlan uniting England and Wales); 1536 (Act of Union formally incorporates England and Wales); 1 May 1707 (Acts of Union formally unite England and Scotland as Great Britain); 1 January 1801 (Acts of Union formally unite Great Britain and Ireland as the United Kingdom of Great Britain and Ireland); 6 December 1921 (Anglo-Irish Treaty formalizes partition of Ireland; six counties remain part of the United Kingdom and Northern Ireland)

National holiday: the UK does not celebrate one particular National holiday

Constitution: unwritten; partly statutes, partly common law and practice; note—recent additions include the Human Rights Act of 1998, the Constitutional Reform and Governance Act 2010, the Parliamentary Voting System and Constituencies Act 2011, the Fixed-term Parliaments Act 2011, and the House of Lords (Expulsion and Suspension) Act 2015 (2016)

Legal system: common law system; has nonBinding judicial review of Acts of Parliament under the Human Rights Act of 1998

International law organization participation: accepts compulsory ICJ jurisdiction with reservations; accepts ICCt jurisdiction

Citizenship: *citizenship by birth:* no
citizenship by descent only: at least one parent must be a citizen of the United Kingdom
dual citizenship recognized: yes
residency requirement for Naturalization: 5 years

Suffrage: 18 years of age; universal

Executive branch: *chief of state:* Queen ELIZABETH II (since 6 February 1952); Heir Apparent Prince CHARLES (son of the queen, born 14 November 1948)

head of government: Prime Minister Theresa MAY (since 13 July 2016)

cabinet: Cabinet of Ministers appointed by the prime minister
elections/appointments: the monarchy is hereditary; following legislative elections, the leader of the majority party or majority coalition usually becomes the prime minister; Theresea may (Conservative) assumed office 13 July 2016

Legislative branch: *description:* bicameral Parliament consists of the House of Lords (760 seats—membership not fixed (there are 815 lords eligible for taking part in the work of the House of Lords consisting of 701 life peers, 88 hereditary peers, and 26 clergy—as of October 2015; members appointed by the monarch on the advice of the prime minister and non-party political members recommended by the House of Lords Appointments Commission) and the House of Commons (650 seats; members directly elected in single-seat constituencies by first-past-the-post vote to serve 5-year terms unless the House is dissolved earlier)
elections: House of Lords—no elections (note—in 1999, as provided by the House of Lords Act, elections were held in the House of Lords to determine the 92 hereditary peers who would remain there; elections are held only as vacancies in the hereditary peerage arise); House of Commons—last held on 8 May 2015 (next to be held by May 2020)
election results: House of Commons—percent of vote by party—Conservative 36.8%, Labor 30.5%, UKIP 12.7%, Lib Dems 7.9%, SNP 4.7%, Greens 3.8%, DUP 0.6%, Sinn Fein 0.6%, Plaid Cymru 0.6%, SDLP 0.3%, Ulster Unionist Party 0.4%, other 1.1%; seats by party—Conservative 330, Labor 232, SNP 56, Lib Dems 8, DUP 8, Sinn Fein 4, Plaid Cymru 3, SDLP 3, Ulster Unionist Party 2, UKIP 1, Greens 1, other 2

Judicial branch: *highest court(s):* Supreme Court (consists of 12 justices including the court president and deputy president); note—the Supreme Court was established by the Constitutional Reform Act 2005 and implemented in October 2009, replacing the Appellate Committee of the House of Lords as the highest court in the United Kingdom
judge selection and term of office: judge candidates selected by an independent committee of several judicial commissions, followed by their recommendations to the prime minister, and appointed by Her Majesty The Queen; justices appointed during period of good behavior
subordinate courts: England and Wales—Court of Appeal (civil and criminal divisions); High Court; Crown Court; County Courts; Magistrates' Courts; Scotland—Court of Sessions; Sheriff Courts; High Court of Justiciary; tribunals; Northern Ireland—Court of Appeal in Northern Ireland; High Court; county courts; magistrates' courts; specialized tribunals

Political parties and leaders: Alliance Party (Northerm Ireland) [David FORD]
Conservative and Unionist Party [Theresea MAY]
Democratic Unionist Party or DUP (Northern Ireland) [Peter ROBINSON; note—expected to be replaced by Arlene FOSTER around 11 January 2016]

Green Party of England and Wales or Greens [Natalie BENNETT]
Labor Party [J eremy CORBYN]
Liberal Democrats (Lib Dems) [Tim FARRON]
Party of Wales (Plaid Cymru) [Leanne WOOD]
Scottish National Party or SNP [Nicola STURGEON]
Sinn Fein (Northern Ireland) [Gerry ADAMS]
Social Democratic and Labor Party or SDLP (Northern Ireland) [Colum EASTWOOD]
Ulster Unionist Party (Northern Ireland) [Mike NESBITT]
UK Independence Party or UKIP [Nigel FARAGE]

Political pressure groups and leaders: Campaign for Nuclear Disarm Ament Confederation of British Industry National Farmers' Union Trades Union Congress

International organization participation: ADB (nonregional member), AfDB (nonregion al member), Arctic Council (observer), Australia Group, BIS, C, CBSS (observer), CD, CDB, CE, CERN, EAPC, EBR D, ECB, EIB, EITI (implementing country), ESA, EU, FAO, FATF, G-5, G-7, G-8, G-10, G-20, IADB, IAEA, IBRD, ICAO, ICC (National committees), ICCt, ICRM, IDA, IEA, IFAD, IF C, IF RCS, IGAD (partners), IHO, ILO, IMF, IMO, IMSO, Interpol, IOC, IOM, IPU, ISO, ITSO, ITU, ITUC (NGOs), MIGA, MINUSMA, MONUSCO, NATO, NEA, NSG, OAS (observer), OECD, OPCW, OSCE, Pacific Alliance (observer), Paris Club, PCA, PIF (partner), SELEC (observer), SICA (observer), UN, UNCTAD, UNESCO, UNFICYP, UNHCR, UNMISS, UNRWA, UNSC (permanent), UPU, WCO, WHO, WIPO, WMO, WTO, ZC

Diplomatic representation in the US: *chief of mission:* Ambassador Sir Nigel Kim DARROCH (since 28 January 2016)
chancery: 3100 Massachusetts Avenue NW, Washington, DC 20008
telephone: [1] (202) 588-6500
FAX: [1] (202) 588-7870
consulate(s) general: Atlanta, Boston, Chicago, Denver, Houston, Los Angeles, Miami, New York, San Francisco
consulate(s): Orlando (FL), San Juan (PR)

Diplomatic representation from the US: *chief of mission:* Ambassador Matthew Winthrop BARZUN (since 27 November 2013)
embassy: 24 Grosvenor Square, London, W1K 6AH; note—a new embassy is scheduled to open by the end of 2017 in the Nine Elms area of Wandsworth
mailing address: PSC 801, Box 40, FPOAE 09498-4040
telephone: [44] (0) 20 7499-9000
FAX: [44] (0) 20 7629-9124
consulate(s) general: Belfast, Edinburgh

Flag description: blue field with the red cross of Saint George (patron saint of England) edged in white superimposed on the diagonal red cross of Saint Patrick (patron saint of Ireland), which is superimposed on the diagon al white cross of Saint Andrew (patron saint of Scotland); properly known as the Union Flag, but commonly called the Union Jack; the design and colors (especially the Blue Ensign) have been the basis for a number of other flags including other Commonwealth countries and their constituent states or provinces, and British overseas territories

National symbol(s): lion (Britain in general); lion, Tudor rose, oak (England); lion, unicorn, thistle (Scotland); dragon, daffodil, leek (Wales); shamrock, flax (Northern Ireland); National colors: red, white, blue (Britain in general); red, white (England); blue, white (Scotland); red, white, green (Wales)

National anthem: *name:* "God Save the Queen" *lyrics/music:* unknown

note: in use since 1745; by tradition, the song serves as both the National and royal anthem of the UK; it is known as either "God Save the Queen" or "God Save the King," depending on the gender of the reigning monarch; it also serves as the royal anthem of many Commonwealth nations

ECONOMY

Economy—overview: The UK, a leading trading power and financial center, is the third largest economy in Europe after Germany and France. Agriculture is intensive, highly mechanized, and efficient by European standards, producing about 60% of food needs with less than 2% of the labor force. The UK has large coal, Natural gas, and oil resources, but its oil and Natural gas reserves are declining; the UK has been a net importer of energy since 2005. Services, particularly banking, insurance, and business services, are key drivers of British GDP growth. Manufacturing, meanwhile, has declined in importance but still accounts for about 10% of economic output.

In 2008, the global financial crisis hit the economy particularly hard, due to the importance of its financial sector. Falling home prices, high consumer debt, and the global economic slowdown compounded Britain's economic problems, pushing the economy into recession in the latter half of 2008 and prompting the then BROWN (Labour) government to implement a number of measures to stimulate the economy and stabilize the financial markets. Facing burgeoning public deficits and debt levels, in 2010 the CAMERON-led coalition government (between Conservatives and Liberal Democrats) initiated an austerity program, which has continued under the new Conservative majority government. However, the deficit still remains one of the highest in the G-7, standing at 5.1% of GDP as of mid-2015. London intends to eliminate its deficit by 2020, primarily through addition al cuts to public spending and welfare benefits. It has also pledged to lower its corporation tax from 20% to 18% by 2020. In 2012, weak consumer spending and subdued business investment weighed on the economy, however, GDP grew 1.7% in 2013 and 2.8% in 2014, accelerating because of greater consumer spending and a recovering housing market. As of late 2015, the Bank of England is examining when to begin raising interest rates from historically low levels while being cautious not to damage economic growth. While the UK is one of the fastest growing economies in the G-7, economists are concerned about the potential negative impact if the UK votes to leave the EU. The UK has an extensive trade relationship with other EU members through its access to the single market and economic observers have warned an exit could jeopardize its position as the central location for European financial services.

GDP (purchasing power parity): $2.679 trillion (2015 est.)
$2.62 trillion (2014 est.)
$2.548 trillion (2013 est.)
note: data are in 2015 US dollars
country comparison to the world: 10

GDP (official exchange rate): $2.849 trillion (2015 est.)

GDP—real growth rate: 2.2% (2015 est.)
2.9% (2014 est.)
2.2% (2013 est.)
country comparison to the world: 131

GDP—per capita (PPP): $41,200 (2015 est.)
$40,600 (2014 est.)
$39,800 (2013 est.)
note: data are in 2015 US dollars
country comparison to the world: 39

Gross National saving: 12.8% of GDP (2015 est.)
12.3% of GDP (2014 est.)
12.1% of GDP (2013 est.)
country comparison to the world: 134

GDP—composition, by end use:
household consumption: 64.7%
government consumption: 19.1%
investment in fixed capital: 17.2%
investment in inventories: 0.2%
exports of goods and services: 27.6%
imports of goods and services: -28.8% (2015 est.)

GDP—composition, by sector of origin:
agriculture: 0.6%
industry: 19.7%
services: 79.6% (2015 est.)

Agriculture—products: cereals, oilseed, potatoes, vegetables; cattle, sheep, poultry; fish

Industries: machine tools, electric power equipment, automation equipment, railroad equipment, shipbuilding, aircraft, motor vehicles and parts, electronics and communications equipment, metals, chemicals, coal, petroleum, paper and paper products, food processing, textiles, clothing, other consumer goods

Industrial production growth rate: 1.8% (2015 est.)
country comparison to the world: 121

Labor force: 32.94 million (2015 est.)
country comparison to the world: 19

Labor force—by occupation: *agriculture:* 1.3%
industry: 15.2%
services: 83.5% (2014 est.)

Unemployment rate: 5.4% (2015 est.)
6.2% (2014 est.)
country comparison to the world: 59

Population below poverty line: 15% (2013 est.)

Household income or consumption by percentage share: *lowest:* 10%: 1.7%
highest: 10%: 31.1% (2012)

Distribution of family income—Gini index: 32.4 (2012) 33.4 (2010)
country comparison to the world: 108

Budget: *revenues:* $1.101 trillion
expenditures: $1.229 trillion (2015 est.)
Taxes and other revenues: 38.4% of GDP (2015 est.)
country comparison to the world: 45

Budget surplus (+) or deficit (–): -4.5% of GDP (2015 est.)
country comparison to the world: 160

Public debt: 90.6% of GDP (2015 est.)
88.1% of GDP (2014 est.)
note: data cover general government debt, and include debt instruments issued (or owned) by government entities other than the treasury; the data include treasury debt held by foreign entities; the data include debt issued by subNational entities, as well as intra-governmental debt; intra-governmental debt consists of treasury borrowings from surpluses in the social funds, such as for retirement, medical care, and unemployment; debt instruments for the social funds are not sold at public auctions
country comparison to the world: 25

Fiscal year: 6 April—5 April

Inflation rate (consumer prices): 0.1% (2015 est.)
1.5% (2014 est.)
country comparison to the world: 42

Central bank discount rate: 0.5% (31 December 2014)
0.5% (31 December 2013)
country comparison to the world: 127

Commercial bank prime lending rate: 4.5% (31 December 2015 est.)
4.45% (31 December 2014 est.)
country comparison to the world: 152

Stock of narrow money: $109.5 billion (31 December 2015 est.)
$106.4 billion (31 December 2014 est.)
country comparison to the world: 33

Stock of broad money: $3.567 trillion (31 December 2014 est.)
$3.491 trillion (31 December 2013 est.)
country comparison to the world: 6

Stock of domestic credit: $3.276 trillion (31 December 2015 est.)
$3.366 trillion (31 December 2014 est.)
country comparison to the world: 7

Market value of publicly traded shares: $3.019 trillion (31 December 2012 est.)
$2.903 trillion (31 December 2011)
$3.107 trillion (31 December 2010 est.)
country comparison to the world: 6

Current account balance: -$123.5 billion (2015 est.)
-$152.2 billion (2014 est.)
country comparison to the world: 196

Exports: $442 billion (2015 est.)
$480.8 billion (2014 est.)
country comparison to the world: 11

Exports—commodities: manufactured goods, fuels, chemicals; food, beverages, tobacco

Exports—partners: US 14.6%, Germany 10.1%, Switzerland 7%, China 6%, France 5.9%, Netherlands 5.8%, Ireland 5.5% (2015)

Imports: $617.1 billion (2015 est.)
$680.4 billion (2014 est.)
country comparison to the world: 6

Imports—commodities: manufactured goods, machinery, fuels; foodstuffs

Imports—partners: Germany 14.8%, China 9.8%, US 9.2%, Netherlands 7.5%, France 5.8%, Belgium 5% (2015)

Reserves of foreign exchange and gold: $107.7 billion (31 December 2014 est.)
$104.4 billion (31 December 2013 est.)
country comparison to the world: 21

Debt—external: $9.219 trillion (31 December 2014 est.)
$9.411 trillion (31 December 2013 est.)
country comparison to the world: 3

Stock of direct foreign investment—at home: $1.453 trillion (31 December 2015 est.)
$1.411 trillion (31 December 2014 est.)
country comparison to the world: 5

Stock of direct foreign investment—abroad: $1.767 trillion (31 December 2015 est.)
$1.711 trillion (31 December 2014 est.)
country comparison to the world: 4

Exchange rates: British pounds (GBP) per US dollar—
0.6528 (2015 est.)
0.607 (2014 est.)
0.6391 (2013 est.)
0.6324 (2012 est.)
0.624 (2011 est.)

ENERGY

Electricity—production: 335 billion kWh (2014 est.)
country comparison to the world: 12

Electricity—consumption: 319.1 billion kWh (2012 est.)
country comparison to the world: 12

Electricity—exports: 2.72 billion kWh (2014 est.)
country comparison to the world: 40

Electricity—imports: 20.5 billion kWh (2014 est.)
country comparison to the world: 9

Electricity—installed generating capacity: 84.99 million kW (31 December 2014 est.)
country comparison to the world: 14

Electricity—from fossil fuels: 71.1% of total installed capacity (2014 est.)
country comparison to the world: 104

Electricity—from nuclear fuels: 11.7% of total installed capacity (2014 est.)
country comparison to the world: 16

Electricity—from hydroelectric plants: 5.1% of total installed capacity (2014 est.)
country comparison to the world: 126

Electricity—from other renewable sources: 12.2% of total installed capacity (2014 est.)
country comparison to the world: 27

Crude oil—production: 787,200 bbl/day (2014 est.)

country comparison to the world: 24

Crude oil—exports: 703,100 bbl/day (2013 est.)
country comparison to the world: 19

Crude oil—imports: 1.221 million bbl/day (2013 est.)
country comparison to the world: 10

Crude oil—proved reserves: 2.982 billion bbl (1 January 2015 est.)
country comparison to the world: 31

Refined petroleum Products—production: 1.409 million bbl/day (2013 est.)
country comparison to the world: 15

Refined petroleum Products—consumption: 1.505 million bbl/day (2014 est.)
country comparison to the world: 16

Refined petroleum Products—exports: 559,800 bbl/day (2013 est.)
country comparison to the world: 10

Refined petroleum Products—Imports: 603,100 bbl/day (2013 est.)
country comparison to the world: 11

Natural gas—production: 38.52 billion cu m (2014 est.)
country comparison to the world: 23

Natural gas—consumption: 70.24 billion cu m (2014 est.)
country comparison to the world: 11

Natural gas—exports: 10.55 billion cum (2014 est.)
country comparison to the world: 20

Natural gas—imports: 42.83 billion cu m (2014 est.)
country comparison to the world: 9

Natural gas—proved reserves: 241 billion cu m (1 January 2014 est.)
country comparison to the world: 44

Carbon dioxide emissions from consumption of energy: 568.3 million Mt (2013 est.)
country comparison to the world: 11

COMMUNICATIONS

Telephones—fixed lines: *total subscriptions:* 33.24 million
subscriptions per 100 inhabitants: 52 (2014 est.)
country comparison to the world: 9

Telephones—mobile cellular: *total:* 78.5 million
subscriptions per 100 inhabitants: 123 (2014 est.)
country comparison to the world: 20

Telephone system: *general assessment:* technologically advanced domestic and international system domestic: equal mix of buried cables, microwave radio relay, and fiber-optic 'systems International: country code—44; numerous submarine cables provide links throughout Europe, Asia, Australia, the Middle East, and US; satellite earth stations—10 Intelsat (7 Atlantic Ocean and 3 Indian Ocean), 1 Inmarsat (Atlantic Ocean region), and 1 Eutelsat; at least 8 large international switching centers (2011)

Broadcast media: public service broadcaster, British Broadcasting Corporation (BBC), is the largest broadcasting corporation in the world; BBC operates multiple TV networks with region al and local

TV service; a mixed system of public and commercial TV broadcasters along with satellite and cable systems provide access to hundreds of TV stations throughout the world; BBC operates multiple National, region al, and local radio networks with multiple transmission sites; a large number of commercial radio stations, as well as satellite radio services are available (2008)
Radio broadcast stations: AM 206, FM 696, shortwave 3 (2008)
Television broadcast stations: 940 (2008)

Internet country code: .uk

Internet hosts: 8.107 million (2012)
country comparison to the world: 15

Internet users: *total:* 57.3 million
percent of population: 89.9% (2014 est.)
country comparison to the world: 10

TRANSPORTATION

Airports: 460 (2013)
country comparison to the world: 18

Airports—with paved runways: *total:* 271
over 3,047 m: 7
2,438 to 3,047 m: 29
1,524 to 2,437 m: 89
914 to 1,523 m: 80
under 914 m: 66 (2013)

Airports—with unpaved runways: *total:* 189
1,524 to 2,437 m: 3
914 to 1,523 m: 26
under 914 m: 160 (2013)

Heliports: 9 (2013)

Pipelines: condensate 502 km; condensate/gas 9 km; gas 28,603 km; liquid petroleum gas 59 km; oil 5,256 km; oil/gas/water 175 km; refined products 4,919 km; water 255 km (2013)

Railways: *total:* 16,837 km
broad gauge: 303 km 1.600-m gauge (in Northern Ireland)
standard gauge: 16,534 km 1.435-m gauge (5,357 km electrified) (2015)
country comparison to the world: 9

Roadways: *total:* 394,428 km
paved: 394,428 km (includes 3,519 km of expressways) (2009)
country comparison to the world: 17

Waterways: 3,200 km (620 km used for commerce) (2009)
country comparison to the world: 31

Merchant marine: *total:* 504
by type: bulk carrier 33, cargo 76, carrier 4, chemical tanker 58, container 178, lique fied gas 6, passenger 7, passenger/cargo 66, petroleum tanker 18, refrigerated cargo 2, roll on/roll off 31, vehicle carrier 25
foreign-owned: 271 (Australia 1, Bermuda 6, China 7, Denmark 43, France 39, Germany 59, Hong Kong 12, Ireland 1, Italy 3, Japan 5, Netherlands 1, Norway 32, Sweden 28, Taiwan 11, Tanzania 1, UAE 8, US 14)
registered in other countries: 308 (Algeria 15, Antigua and Barbuda 1, Argentina 2, Australia 5, Bahamas 18, Barbados 6, Belgium 2, Belize 4, Bermuda 14, Bolivia 1, Brunei 2, Cabo Verde 1,

Cambodia 1, Cayman Islands 2, Comoros 1, Cook Islands 2, Cyprus 7, Georgia 5, Gibraltar 6, Greece 6, Honduras 1, Hong Kong 33, Indonesia 2, Italy 2, Liberia 22, Liberia 32, Luxembourg 5, Malta 21, Marshall Islands 12, Marshall Islands 3, Moldova 3, Nigeria 2, NZ 1, Panama 37, Panama 5, Saint Kitts and Nevis 1, Saint Vincent and the Grenadines 6, Sierra Leone 1, Singapore 6, Thailand 6, Tonga 1, US 4, unknown 1) (2010)
country comparison to the world: 22

Ports and terminals: *major seaport(s):* Dover, Felixstowe, Immingham, Liverpool, London, Southampton, Teesport (England); Forth Ports (Scotland); Milford Haven (Wales)

oil terminals: Fawley Marine terminal, Liverpool Bay terminal (England); Braefoot Bay terminal, Finnart oil terminal, Hound Point terminal (Scotland)

container port(s) (TEUs): Felixstowe (3,248,592), London (1,932,000), Southampton (1,324,581)

LNG terminal(s) (import): Isle of Grain, Milford Haven, Teesside

MILITARY AND SECURITY

Military branches: Army, Royal Navy (includes Royal Marines), Royal Air Force (2013)

Military service age and obligation: 16–33 years of age (officers 17–28) for voluntary military service

(with parental consent under 18); no conscription; women serve in military services including some ground combat roles; the UK's Defense Ministry is expected to further ease existing women's restrictions by the end of 2016; must be citizen of the UK, Commonwealth, or Republic of Ireland; reservists serve a minimum of 3 years, to age 45 or 55; 17 years 6 months of age for voluntary military service by Nepalese citizens in the Brigade of Gurkhas; 16–34 years of age for voluntary military service by Papua New Guinean citizens (2016)

Military expenditures: 2.07% of GDP (2015)
2.2% of GDP (2014)
2.3% of GDP (2013)
2.49% of GDP (2012)
2.48% of GDP (2011)
country comparison to the world: 28

TRANSNATIONAL ISSUES

Disputes—international: in 2002, Gibraltar residents voted overwhelmingly by referendum to reject any "shared sovereignty" arrangement between the UK and Spain; the Government of Gibraltar insisted on equal participation in talks between the two countries; Spain disapproved of UK plans to grant Gibraltar greater autonomy; Mauritius and Seychelles claim the Chagos Archipelago (British Indian Ocean Territory); in 2001,

the former inhabitants of the archipelago, evicted 1967—1973, were granted UK citizenship and the right of return, followed by Orders in Council in 2004 that banned rehabitation, a High Court ruling reversed the ban, a Court of Appeal refusal to hear the case, and a Law Lords' decision in 2008 denied the right of return; in addition, the UK created the world's largest marine protection area around the Chagos islands prohibiting the extraction of any Natural resources therein; UK rejects sovereignty talks requested by Argentina, which still claims the Falkland Islands (Islas Malvinas) and South Georgia and the South Sandwich Islands; territorial claim iNAntarctica (British Antarctic Territory) overlaps Argentine claim and partially overlaps Chilean claim; Iceland, the UK, and Ireland dispute Denmark's claim that the Faroe Islands' continental shelf extends beyond 200 nm

Refugees and internally displaced persons: *refugees (country of origin):* 11,583 (Eritrea); 11,510 (Iran); 9,467 (Zimbabwe); 9,039 (Afghanistan); 8,509 (Somalia); 5,669 (Pakistan) (2014)
stateless persons: 41 (2015)

Illicit drugs: producer of limited amounts of synthetic drugs and synthetic precursor chemicals; major consumer of Southwest Asian heroin, Latin American cocaine, and synthetic drugs; money-laundering center

UNITED STATES PACIFIC ISLAND WILDLIFE REFUGES

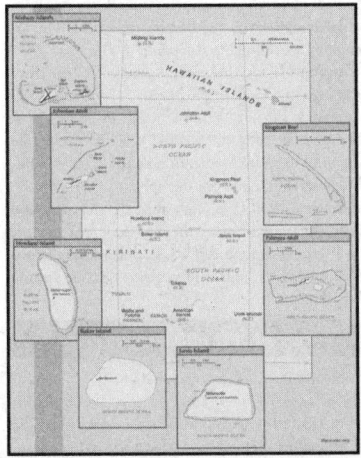

INTRODUCTION

Background: All of the following US Pacific island territories except Midway Atoll constitute the Pacific Remote Islands National Wildlife Refuge (NWR) Complex and as such are managed by the Fish and Wildlife Service of the US Department

of the Interior. Midway Atoll NWR has been included in a Refuge Complex with the Hawaiian Islands NWR and also designated as part of Papahanaumokuakea Marine National Monument. These remote refuges are the most widespread collection of marine- and terrestrial-life protected areas on the planet under a single country's jurisdiction. They sustain many endemic species including corals, fish, shellfish, marine mammals, seabirds, water birds, land birds, insects, and vegetation not found elsewhere.

Baker Island: The US took possession of the island in 1857. Its guano deposits were mined by US and British companies during the second half of the 19th century. In 1935, a short-lived attempt at colonization began on this island but was disrupted by World War II and thereafter abandoned. The island was established as a NWR in 1974.

Howland Island: Discovered by the US early in the 19th century, the uninhabited atoll was officially claimed by the US in 1857. Both US and British companies mined for guano deposits until about 1890. In 1935, a short-lived attempt at colonization began on this island, similar to the effort on nearby Baker Island, but was disrupted by World War II and thereafter abandoned. The famed American aviatrix Amelia EARHART disappeared while seeking out Howland Island as a refueling stop during her 1937 round-the-world flight; Earhart Light, a day beacon near the middle

of the west coast, was named in her memory. The island was established as an WR in 1974.

Jarvis Island: First discovered by the British in 1821, the uninhabited island was annexed by the US in 1858 but abandoned in 1879 after tons of guano had been removed. The UK annexed the island in 1889 but never carried out plans for further exploitation. The US occupied and reclaimed the island in 1935. It was abandoned in 1942 during World War II. The island was established as an WR in 1974.

Johnston atoll: Both the US and the Kingdom of Hawaii annexed Johnston atoll in 1858, but it was the US that mined the guano deposits until the late 1880s. Johnston and Sand Islands were designated wildlife refuges in 1926. The US Navy took over the atoll in 1934. Subsequently, the US Air Force assumed control in 1948. The site was used for high-altitude nuclear tests in the 1950s and 1960s. Until late in 2000 the atoll was maintained as a storage and disposal site for chemical weapons. Munitions destruction, cleanup, and closure of the facility were completed by May 2005. The Fish and Wildlife Service and the US Air Force are currently discussing future management options; in the interim, Johnston atoll and the three-mile Naval Defensive Sea around it remain under the jurisdiction and administrative control of the US Air Force.

Kingman Reef: The US annexed the reef in 1922. Its sheltered lagoon served as a way station for flying boats on Hawaii-to-American Samoa flights during the late 1930s. There are no terrestrial plants on the reef, which is frequently awash, but it does support abundant and diverse marine fauna and flora. in 2001, the waters surrounding the reef out to 12 nm were designated an WR.

Midway Islands: The US took formal possession of the islands in 1867. The laying of the transpacific cable, which passed through the islands, brought the first residents in 1903. Between 1935 and 1947, Midway was used as a refueling stop for transpacific flights. The US Naval victory over a Japanese fleet off Midway in 1942 was one of the turning points of World War II. The islands continued to serve as a Naval station until closed in 1993. Today the islands are an WR and are the site of the world's largest Laysan Albatross colony.

Palmyra Atoll: The Kingdom of Hawaii claimed the atoll in 1862, and the US included it among the Hawaiian Islands when it annexed the archipelago in 1898. The Hawaii Statehood Act of 1959 did not include Palmyra Atoll, which is now partly privately owned by the Nature Conservancy with the rest owned by the Federal government and managed by the US Fish and Wildlife Service. These organizations are managing the atoll as a wildlife refuge. The lagoons and surrounding waters within the 12-nm US territorial seas were transferred to the US Fish and Wildlife Service and designated an WR in January 2001.

GEOGRAPHY

Location: Oceania
Baker Island: atoll in the North Pacific Ocean 1,830 nm southwest of Honolulu, about halfway between Hawaii and Australia
Howland Island: island in the North Pacific Ocean 1,815 nm southwest of Honolulu, about halfway between Hawaii and Australia
Jarvis Island: island in the South Pacific Ocean 1,305 nm south of Honolulu, about halfway between Hawaii and Cook Islands
John stonatoll: atoll in the North Pacific Ocean 717 nm southwest of Honolulu, about one-third of the way from Hawaii to the Marshall Islands
Kingman Reef: reef in the North Pacific Ocean 930 nm south of Honolulu, about halfway between Hawaii and American Samoa
Midway Islands: atoll in the North Pacific Ocean 1,260 nm northwest of Honolulu near the end of the Hawaiian Archipelago, about one-third of the way from Honolulu to Tokyo
Palmyra Atoll: atoll in the North Pacific Ocean 960 nm south of Honolulu, about halfway between Hawaii and American Samoa

Geographic coordinates: *Baker Island:* 0 13 N, 176 28 W
Howland Island: 0 48 N, 176 38 W
Jarvis Island: 0 23 S, 160 01 W
Johnston atoll: 16 45 N, 169 31 W
Kingman Reef: 6 23 N, 162 25 W
Midway Islands: 28 12 N, 177 22 W
Palmyra Atoll: 5 53 N, 162 05 W

Map references: Oceania

Area: total—6,959.41 sq km; emergent land—22.41 sq km; submerged—6,937 sq km
Baker Island: total—129.1 sq km; emergent land—2.1 sq km; submerged—127 sq km
Howland Island: total—138.6 sq km; emergent land—2.6 sq km; submerged—136 sq km
Jarvis Island: total—152 sq km; emergent land—5 sq km; submerged—147 sq km
John stonatoll: total—276.6 sq km; emergent land—2.6 sq km; submerged—274 sq km
Kingman Reef: total—1,958.01 sq km; emergent land—0.01 sq km; submerged—1,958 sq km
Midway Islands: total—2,355.2 sq km; emergent land—6.2 sq km; submerged—2,349 sq km
Palmyra Atoll: total—1,949.9 sq km; emergent land—3.9 sq km; submerged—1,946 sq km
country comparison to the world: 239

Area—comparative: *Baker Island:* about 2.5 times the size of the National Mall in Washington, DC
Howland Island: about three times the size of the National Mall in Washington, DC
Jarvis Island: about eight times the size of the National Mall in Washington, DC
John stonatoll: about 4.5 times the size of the National Mall in Washington, DC
Kingman Reef: a little more than 1.5 times the size of the National Mall in Washington, DC
Midway Islands: about nine times the size of the National Mall in Washington, DC
Palmyra Atoll: about 20 times the size of the National Mall in Washington, DC

Land boundaries: none

Coastline: *Baker Island:* 4.8 km
Howland Island: 6.4 km
Jarvis Island: 8 km
John stonatoll: 34 km
Kingman Reef: 3 km
Midway Islands: 15 km
Palmyra Atoll: 14.5 km

Maritime claims: *territorial sea:* 12 nm
exclusive economic zone: 200 nm

Climate: *Baker, Howland, and Jarvis Islands:* equatorial; scant rainfall, constant wind, burning sun
John stonatoll and Kingman Reef: tropical, but generally dry; consistent northeast trade winds with little season al temperature variation
Midway Islands: subtropical with cool, moist winters (December to February) and warm, dry summers (May to October); moderated by prevailing easterly winds; most of the 107 cm of annual rainfall occurs during the winter
Palmyra Atoll: equatorial, hot; located within the low pressure area of the Intertropical Convergence Zone (ITCZ) where the northeast and southeast trade winds meet, it is extremely wet with between 400–500 cm of rainfall each year

Terrain: low and nearly flat sandy coral islands with narrow fringing reefs that have developed at the top of submerged volcanic mountains, which in most cases rise steeply from the ocean floor

Elevation: *elevation extremes:* lowest point: Pacific Ocean 0 m

highest point: Baker Island, unnamed location—8 m; Howland Island, unnamed location—3 m; Jarvis Island, unnamed location—7 m; Johnston atoll, Sand Island—10 m; Kingman Reef, unnamed location—less than 2 m; Midway Islands, unnamed location—13 m; Palmyra Atoll, unnamed location—3 m

Natural resources: terrestrial and aquatic wildlife

Land use: *agricultural land:* 0%
arable land: 0%
permanent crops: 0%
permanent pasture: 0%
forest: 0%
other: 100% (2011 est.)

Natural hazards: *Baker, Howl and, and Jarvis Islands:* the narrow fringing reef surrounding the island poses a maritime hazard
Kingman Reef: wet or awash most of the time, maximum elevation of less than 2 m makes Kingman Reef a maritime hazard
Midway Islands, Johnston, and Palmyra Atolls: NA

Environment—current issues: Baker, Howl and, and Jarvis Islands, and John stonatoll: no Natural freshwater resources
Kingman Reef: none
Midway Islands and Palmyra Atoll: NA

Geography—note: *Baker, Howl and, and Jarvis Islands:* scattered vegetation consisting of grasses, prostrate vines, and low growing shrubs; primarily a nesting, roosting, and foraging habitat for seabirds, shorebirds, and marine wildlife; closed to the public
John stonatoll: Johnston Island and Sand Island are Natural islands, which have been expanded by coral dredging; North Island (Akau) and East Island (Hikina) are manmade islands formed from coral dredging; the egg-shaped reef is 34 km in circumference; closed to the public
Kingman Reef: barren coral atoll with deep interior lagoon; closed to the public
Midway Islands: a coral atoll managed as a National Wildlife Refuge and open to the public for wildlife-related recreation in the form of wildlife observation and photography
Palmyra Atoll: the high rainfall and resulting lush vegetation make the environment of this atoll unique among the US Pacific Island territories; supports a large undisturbed stand of Pisonia beach forest

PEOPLE AND SOCIETY

Population: no indigenous inhabitants
note: public entry is only by special-use permit from US Fish and Wildlife Service and generally restricted to scientists and educators; visited annually by US Fish and Wildlife Service
Jarvis Island: Millersville settlement on western side of island occasionally used as a weather station from 1935 until World War II, when it was abandoned; reoccupied in 1957 during the international Geophysical Year by scientists who left in 1958; currently unoccupied
Johnston atoll: in previous years, an average of 1,100 US military and civilian contractor

personnel were present; as of May 2005, all US Government personnel had left the island Midway Islands: approximately 40 people make up the staff of US Fish and Wildlife Service and their services contractor living at the atoll
Palmyra Atoll: four to 20 Nature Conservancy, US Fish and Wildlife staff, and researchers

GOVERNMENT

Country name: *conventional long form:* none
conventional short form: Baker Island; Howland Island; Jarvis Island; Johnston atoll; Kingman Reef; Midway Islands; Palmyra Atoll
etymology: self-descriptive name specifying the territories' affiliation and location

Dependency status: unincorporated territories of the US; administered from Washington, DC, by the Fish and Wildlife Service of the US Department of the Interior as part of the National Wildlife Refuge system note on Palmyra Atoll: incorporated Territory of the US; partly privately owned and partly federally owned; administered from Washington, DC, by the Fish and Wildlife Service of the US Department of the Interior; the

Office of Insular Affairs of the US Department of the Interior continues to administer nine excluded areas comprising certain tidal and submerged lands within the 12 nm territorial sea or within the lagoon

Legal system: the laws of the US, where applicable, apply

Diplomatic representation from the US: none (territories of the US)

Flag description: the flag of the US is used

ECONOMY

Economy—overview: No economic activity

TRANSPORTATION

Airports: *Baker Island:* one abandoned World War II runway of 1,665 m covered with vegetation and unusable
Howland Island: airstrip constructed in 1937 for scheduled refueling stop on the round-the-world flight of Amelia EARHART and Fred NOONAN; the aviators left Lae, New Guinea, for Howland

Island but were never seen again; the airstrip is no longer serviceable
Johnston atoll: one closed and not maintained
Kingman Reef: lagoon was used as a halfway station between Hawaii and American Samoa by PaNAmerican airways for flying boats in 1937 and 1938
Midway Islands: 3—one operation al (2,377 m paved); no fuel for sale except emergencies
Palmyra Atoll: 1—1,846 m unpaved runway; privately owned (2013)

Ports and terminals: *major seaport(s):* Baker, Howland, and Jarvis Islands, and Kingman Reef: none; offshore anchorage only
Johnston atoll: Johnston Island
Midway Islands: Sand Island
Palmyra Atoll: West Lagoon

MILITARY AND SECURITY

Military—note: defense is the responsibility of the US

TRANSNATIONAL ISSUES

Disputes—international: none

UNITED STATES

INTRODUCTION

Background: Britain's American colonies broke with the mother country in 1776 and were recognized as the new nation of the United States of America following the Treaty of Paris in 1783. During the 19th and 20th centuries, 37 new states were added to the original 13 as the nation expanded across the North American continent and acquired a number of overseas possessions. The two most traumatic experiences in the nation's history were the Civil War (1861–65), in which a northern Union of states defeated a secessionist Confederacy of 11 southern slave states, and the Great Depression of the 1930s, an economic downturn during which about a quarter of the labor force lost its jobs. Buoyed by victories in World Wars I and II and the end of the Cold War in 1991, the US remains the world's most powerful nation state. Since the end of World War II, the economy has achieved relatively steady growth, low unemployment and inflation, and rapid advances in technology.

GEOGRAPHY

Location: North America, bordering both the North Atlantic Ocean and the North Pacific Ocean, between Canada and Mexico

Geographic coordinates: 38 00 N, 97 00 W

Map references: North America

Area: *total:* 9,833,517 sq km
land: 9,147,593 sq km
water: 685,924 sq km
note: includes only the 50 states and District of Columbia, no overseas territories (2010)
country comparison to the world: 3

Area—comparative: about half the size of Russia; about three-tenths the size of Africa; about half the size of South America (or slightly larger than Brazil); slightly larger than China; more than twice the size of the European Union

Land boundaries: *total:* 12,048 km
border countries (2): Canada 8,893 km (including 2,477 km with Alaska), Mexico 3,155 km
note: US Naval Base at Guantanamo Bay, Cuba is leased by the US and is part of Cuba; the base boundary is 28.5 km

Coastline: 19,924 km

Maritime claims: *territorial sea:* 12 nm
contiguous zone: 24 nm
exclusive economic zone: 200 nm
continental shelf: not specified

Climate: mostly temperate, but tropical in Hawaii and Florida, arctic in Alaska, semiarid in the great plains west of the Mississippi River, and arid in the Great Basin of the southwest; low winter

temperatures in the northwest are ameliorated occasionally in January and February by warm chinook winds from the eastern slopes of the Rocky Mountains

Terrain: vast central plain, mountains in west, hills and low mountains in east; rugged mountains and broad river valleys in Alaska; rugged, volcanic topography in Hawaii

Elevation: *mean elevation:* 760 m

elevation extremes: *lowest point:* Death Valley -86 m (lowest point in North America)
highest point: Denali (Mount McKinley) 6,190 m (highest point in North America)
note: the peak of Mauna Kea (4,205 m above sea level) on the island of Hawaii rises about 10,200 m above the Pacific Ocean floor; by this measurement, it is the world's tallest mountain—higher than Mount Everest (8,850 m), which is recognized as the tallest mountain above sea level

Natural resources: coal, copper, lead, molybdenum, phosphates, rare earth elements, uranium, bauxite, gold, iron, mercury, nickel, potash, silver, tungsten, zinc, petroleum, Natural gas, timber, arable land
note: the US has the world's largest coal reserves with 491 billion short tons accounting for 27% of the world's total

Land use: *agricultural land:* 44.5%
arable land: 16.8%
permanent crops: 0.3%
permanent pasture: 27.4%
forest: 33.3%
other: 22.2% (2011 est.)

901

Irrigated land: 264,000 sq km (2012)

Total renewable water resources: 3,069 cu km (2011)

Freshwater withdrawal (domestic/industrial/agricultural): *total:* 478.4 cu km/yr (14%/46%/40%) *per capita:* 1,583 cu m/yr (2005)

Natural hazards: tsunamis; volcanoes; earthquake activity around Pacific Basin; hurricanes along the Atlantic and Gulf of Mexico coasts; tornadoes in the Midwest and Southeast; mud slides in California; forest fires in the west; flooding; permafrost in northern Alaska, a major impediment to development

volcanism: volcanic activity in the Hawaiian Islands, Western Alaska, the Pacific Northwest, and in the Northern Mariana Islands; both Mauna Loa (elev. 4,170 m) in Hawaii and Mount Rainier (elev. 4,392 m) in Washington have been deemed Decade Volcanoes by the international Association of Volcanology and Chemistry of the Earth's Interior, worthy of study due to their explosive history and close proximity to human populations; Pavlof (elev. 2,519 m) is the most active volcano in Alaska's Aleutian Arc and poses a significant threat to air travel since the area constitutes a major flight path between North America and East Asia; St. Helens (elev. 2,549 m), famous for the devastating 1980 eruption, remains active today; numerous other historically active volcanoes exist, mostly concentrated in the Aleutian Arc and Hawaii; they include: in Alaska: Aniakchak, Augustine, Chiginagak, Fourpeaked, Iliamna, Katmai, Kupreanof, Martin, Novarupta, Redoubt, Spurr, Wrangell; in Hawaii: Trident, Ugashik-Peulik, Ukinrek Maars, Veniaminof; in the Northern Mariana Islands: Anatahan; and in the Pacific Northwest: Mount Baker, Mount Hood

Environment—current issues: large emitter of carbon dioxide from the burning of fossil fuels; air pollution resulting in acid rain in both the US and Canada; water pollution from runoff of pesticides and fertilizers; limited Natural freshwater resources in much of the western part of the country require careful management; desertification

Environment—International agreements: *party to:* Air Pollution, Air Pollution-Nitrogen Oxides, Antarctic-Environmental Protocol, Antarctic-Marine Living Resources, Antarctic Seals, Antarctic Treaty, Climate Change, Desertification, Endangered Species, Environmental Modification, Marine Dumping, Marine Life Conservation, Ozone Layer Protection, Ship Pollution, Tropical Timber 83, Tropical Timber 94, Wetlands, Whaling

signed, but not ratified: Air Pollution-Persistent Organic Pollutants, Air Pollution-Volatile Organic Compounds, Biodiversity, Climate Change-Kyoto Protocol, Hazardous Wastes

Geography—note: world's third-largest country by size (after Russia and Canada) and by population (after China and India); Denali (Mt. McKinley) is the highest point in North America and Death Valley the lowest point on the continent

PEOPLE AND SOCIETY

Nationality: *noun:* American(s) *adjective:* American

Ethnic groups: white 79.96%, black 12.85%, Asian 4.43%, AmerindiaNAnd Alaska native 0.97%, native Hawaiian and other Pacific islander 0.18%, two or more races 1.61% (July 2007 estimate) *note:* a separate listing for Hispanic is not included because the US Census Bureau considers Hispanic to mean persons of Spanish/Hispanic/Latino origin including those of Mexican, Cuban, Puerto Rican, Dominican Republic, Spanish, and Central or South American origin living in the US who may be of any race or ethnic group (white, black, Asian, etc.); about 15.1% of the total US population is Hispanic

Languages: English 79.2%, Spanish 12.9%, other Indo-European 3.8%, Asian and Pacific island 3.3%, other 0.9% (2011 est.) *note:* data represents the language spoken at home; the US has no official National language, but English has acquired official status in 31 of the 50 states; Hawaiian is an official language in the state of Hawaii

Religions: Protestant 51.3%, Roman Catholic 23.9%, Mormon 1.7%, other Christian 1.6%, Jewish 1.7%, Buddhist 0.7%, Muslim 0.6%, other or unspecified 2.5%, unaffiliated 12.1%, none 4% (2007 est.)

Population: 321,368,864 (July 2015 est.) *country comparison to the world:* 4

Age structure: *0–14 years:* 18.99% (male 31,171,623/female 29,845,713) *15–24 years:* 13.64% (male 22,473,687/female 21,358,609) *25–54 years:* 39.76% (male 63,838,086/female 63,947,036) *55–64 years:* 12.73% (male 19,731,664/female 21,172,201) *65 years and over:* 14.88% (male 21,129,978/female 26,700,267) (2015 est.)

Dependency ratios: *total dependency ratio:* 50.9% *youth dependency ratio:* 28.6% *elderly dependency ratio:* 22.3% *potential support ratio:* 4.5% (2015 est.)

Median age: *total:* 37.8 years *male:* 36.5 years *female:* 39.2 years (2015 est.) *country comparison to the world:* 62

Population growth rate: 0.78% (2015 est.) *country comparison to the world:* 141

Birth rate: 12.49 births/1,000 population (2015 est.) *country comparison to the world:* 158

Death rate: 8.15 deaths/1,000 population (2015 est.) *country comparison to the world:* 93

Net migration rate: 3.86 migrant(s)/1,000 population (2015 est.) *country comparison to the world:* 34

Urbanization: *urban Population:* 81.6% of total population (2015) *rate of urbanization:* 1.02% annual rate of change (2010–15 est.)

Major urban Areas—population: New York-Newark 18.593 million; Los Angeles-Long Beach-Santa Ana 12.31 million; Chicago 8.745 million; Miami 5.817 million; Dallas-Fort Worth 5.703 million; WASHINGTON, D.C. (capital) 4.955 million (2015)

Sex ratio: *at birth:* NA *0–14 years:* 1.04 male(s)/female *15–24 years:* 1.05 male(s)/female *25–54 years:* 1 male(s)/female *55–64 years:* 0.93 male(s)/female *65 years and over:* 0.79 male(s)/female *total population:* 0.97 male(s)/female (2015 est.)

Mother's mean age at first birth: 25.6 (2011 est.)

Maternal mortality rate: 14 deaths/100,000 live births (2015 est.) *country comparison to the world:* 136

Infant mortality rate: *total:* 5.87 deaths/1,000 live births *male:* 6.37 deaths/1,000 live births *female:* 5.35 deaths/1,000 live births (2015 est.) *country comparison to the world:* 167

Life expectancy at birth: *total population:* 79.68 years *male:* 77.32 years *female:* 81.97 years (2015 est.) *country comparison to the world:* 43

Total fertility rate: 1.87 children born/woman (2015 est.) *country comparison to the world:* 142

Contraceptive prevalence rate: 76.4% *note:* percent of women aged 15–44 (2006/10)

Health expenditures: 17.1% of GDP (2013) *country comparison to the world:* 1

Physicians density: 2.45 physicians/1,000 population (2011)

Hospital bed density: 2.9 beds/1,000 population (2011)

Drinking water source: improved: *urban:* 99.4% of population *rural:* 98.2% of population *total:* 99.2% of population unimproved: *urban:* 0.6% of population *rural:* 1.8% of population *total:* 0.8% of population (2015 est.)

Sanitation facility access: improved: *urban:* 100% of population *rural:* 100% of population *total:* 100% of population unimproved: *urban:* 0% of popu lation *rural:* 0% of population *total:* 0% of population (2015 est.)

HIV/AIDS—adult prevalence rate: NA

HIV/AIDS—people living with HIV/AIDS: NA

HIV/AIDS—deaths: NA

Obesity—adult prevalence rate: 35% (2014)
country comparison to the world: 18

Children under the age of 5 years underweight: 0.5% (2012)
country comparison to the world: 136

Education expenditures: 5.2% of GDP (2011)
country comparison to the world: 63

School life expectancy (primary to tertiary education): *total:* 17 years
male: 16 years
female: 17 years (2014)

Unemployment, youth ages 15–24: *total:* 13.4%
male: 14.5%
female: 12.2% (2014 est.)
country comparison to the world: 68

GOVERNMENT

Country name: *conventional long form:* United States of America
conventional short form: United States abbreviation: US or USA
etymology: the name America is derived from that of Amerigo VESPUCCI (1454–1512), Italian explorer, navigator, and cartographer

Government type: federal presidential republic

Capital: *name:* Washington, DC

Geographic coordinates: 38 53 N, 77 02 W
time difference: UTC-5 (during Standard Time)
daylight saving time: +1hr, begins second Sunday in March; ends first Sunday in November
note: the 50 United States cover six time zones

Administrative divisions: 50 states and 1 district*; Alabama, Alaska, Arizon a, Arkansas, California, Colorado, Connecticut, Delaware, District of Columbia*, Florida, Georgia, Hawaii, Idaho, Illinois, Indiana, Iowa, Kansas, Kentucky, Louisiana, Maine, Maryland, Massachusetts, Michigan, Minnesota, Mississippi, Missouri, Montana, Nebraska, Nevada, New Hampshire, New Jersey, New Mexico, New York, North Carolina, North Dakota, Ohio, Oklahoma, Oregon, Pennsylvania, Rhode Island, South Carolina, South Dakota, Tennessee, Texas, Utah, Vermont, Virginia, Washington, West Virginia, Wisconsin, Wyoming

Dependent areas: American Samoa, Baker Island, Guam, Howland Island, Jarvis Island, Johnston atoll, Kingman Reef, Midway Islands, Navassa Island, Northern Mariana Islands, Palmyra Atoll, Puerto Rico, Virgin Islands, Wake Island
note: from 18 July 1947 until 1 October 1994, the US administered the Trust Territory of the Pacific Islands; it entered into a political relationship with all four political entities: the Northern Mariana Islands is a commonwealth in political union with the US (effective 3 November 1986); the Republic of the Marshall Islands signed a Compact of Free Association with the US (effective 21 October 1986); the Federated States of Micronesia signed a Compact of Free Association with the US (effective 3 November 1986); Palau concluded a Compact of Free Association with the US (effective 1 October 1994)

Independence: 4 July 1776 (declared); 3 September 1783 (recognized by Great Britain)

National holiday: Independence Day, 4 July (1776)

Constitution: previous 1781 (Articles of Confederation and Perpetual Union); latest drafted July—September 1787, submitted to the Congress of the Confederation 20 September 1787, submitted for states' ratification 28 September 1787, ratification completed by nine states 21 June 1788, effective 4 March 1789; amended many times, last in 1992 (2016)

Legal system: common law system based on English common law at the federal level; state legal systems based on common law except Louisiana, which is based on Napoleonic civil code; judicial review of legislative acts

International law organization participation: withdrew acceptance of compulsory ICJ jurisdiction in 2005; withdrew acceptance of ICCt jurisdiction in 2002

Citizenship: *citizenship by birth:* yes
citizenship by descent: yes
dua citizenship recognized: no, but the US government acknowledges such situtations exist; US citizens are not encouraged to seek dual citizenship since it limits protection by the US
residency requirement for Naturalization: 5 years

Suffrage: 18 years of age; universal

Executive branch: *chief of state:* President Barack H. OBAMA (since 20 January 2009); Vice President Joseph R. BIDEN (since 20 January 2009); note—the president is both chief of state and head of government

head of government: President Barack H. OBAMA (since 20 January 2009); Vice President Joseph R. BI DEN (since 20 January 2009)
cabinet: Cabinet appointed by the president, approved by the Senate
elections/appointments: president and vice president indirectly elected on the same ballot by the Electoral College of 'electors' chosen from each state; president and vice president serve a 4-year term (eligible for a second term); election last held on 6 November 2012 (next to be held on 8 November 2016)
election results: Barack H. OBAMA reelected president; electoral vote count—Barack H. OBAMA (Democratic Party) 332, Mitt ROMNEY 206 (Republican Party); percent of direct popular vote—Barack H. OBAMA 50.6%, Mitt ROMNEY 47.9%, other 1.5%

Legislative branch: *description:* bicameral Congress consists of the Senate (100 seats; 2 members directly elected in each of the 50 state constituencies by simple majority vote except in Georgia and Louisiana which require an absolute majority vote with a second round if needed; members serve 6-year terms with one-third of membership renewed every 2 years) and the House of Representatives (435 seats; members directly elected in single-seat constituencies by simple majority vote except in Georgia which requires an absolute majority vote with a second round if needed; members serve 2-year terms)
elections: Senate—last held on 4 November 2014 (next to be held on 8 November 2016); House of Representatives—last held on 4 November 2014 (next to be held on 8 November 2016)

election results: Senate—percent of vote by party—NA; seats by party—Democratic Party 44, Republican Party 54, independent 2; House of Representatives—percent of vote by party—NA; seats by party—Democratic Party 188, Republican Party 247
note: in addition to the regular members of the House of Representatives there are 6 non-voting delegates elected from the District of Columbia and the US territories of American Samoa, Guam, Puerto Rico, the Northern Mariana Islands, and the Virgin Islands; these are single seat constituencies directly elected by simple majority vote to serve a 2-year term; the delegate can vote when serving on a committee and when the House meets as the Committee of the Whole House, but not when legislation is submitted for a "full floor" House vote; election of delegates last held on 4 November 2014 (next to be held on 1 November 2016)

Judicial branch: *highest court(s):* US Supreme Court (consists of 9 justices—the chief justice and 8 associate justices)
judge selection and term of office: president nominates and, with the advice and consent of the Senate, appoints Supreme Court justices; justices appointed for life
subordinate courts: Courts of Appeal (includes the US Court of Appeal for the Federal District and 12 region al appeals courts); 94 federal district courts in 50 states and territories
note: the US court system consists of the federal court system and the state court systems; although each court system is responsible for hearing certain types of cases, neither is completely independent of the other, and the systems often interact

Political parties and leaders: Democratic Party [Debbie Wasserman SCHULTZ]
Green Party [collective leadership]
Libertarian Party [Nicholas SARWARK]
Republican Party [Reince PRIEBUS]

Political pressure groups and leaders: *other:* environmentalists; business groups; labor unions; churches; Ethnic groups; political action committees or PACs; health groups; education groups; civic groups; youth groups; transportation groups; agricultural groups; veterans groups; women's groups; reform lobbies

International organization participation: ADB (nonregion al member), AfDB (nonregion al member), ANZUS, APEC, Arctic Council, ARF, ASEAN (dialogue partner), Australia Group, BIS, BSEC (observer), CBSS (observer), CD, CE (observer), CERN (observer), CICA (observer), CP, EAPC, EAS, EBRD, EITI (implementing country), FAO, FATF, G-5, G-7, G-8, G-10, G-20, IADB, IAEA, IBRD, ICAO, ICC (National committees), ICRM, IDA, IEA, IFAD, IFC, IFRCS, IGAD (partners), IHO, ILO, IMF, IMO, IMSO, Interpol, IOC, IOM, ISO, ITSO, ITU, ITUC (NGOs), MIGA, MINUSMA, MINUSTAH, MONUSCO, NAFTA, NATO, NEA, NSG, OAS, OECD, OPCW, OSCE, Pacific Alliance (observer), Paris Club, PCA, PIF (partner), SAARC (observer), SELEC (observer), SICA (observer), SPC, UN, UNCTAD, UNESCO, UNHCR, UNITAR, UNMIL, UNMISS, UNRWA, UNSC (permanent), UNTSO, UPU, WCO, WHO, WIPO, WMO, WTO, ZC

Flag description: 13 equal horizontal stripes of red (top and bottom) alternating with white; there is a blue rectangle in the upper hoist-side corner bearing 50 small, white, five-pointed stars arranged in nine offset horizontal rows of six stars (top and bottom) alternating with rows of five stars; the 50 stars represent the 50 states, the 13 stripes represent the 13 original colonies; the blue stands for loyalty, devotion, truth, justice, and friendship; red symbolizes courage, zeal, and fervency, while white denotes purity and rectitude of conduct; commonly referred to by its nickname of Old Glory
note: the design and colors have been the basis for a number of other flags, including Chile, Liberia, Malaysia, and Puer to Rico

National symbol(s): bald eagle; National colors: red, white, blue

National anthem: *name:* "The Star-Spangled Banner"
lyrics/music: Francis Scott KEY/John Stafford SMITH
note: adopted 1931; during the War of 1812, after witnessing the successful American defense of Fort McHenry in Baltimore following British Naval bombardment, Francis Scott KEY wrote the lyrics to what would become the National anthem; the lyrics were set to the tune of "The Anacreontic Song"; only the first verse is sung

ECONOMY

Economy—overview: The US has the most technologically powerful economy in the world, with a per capita GDP of $54,800. US firms are at or near the forefront in technological advances, especially in computers, pharmaceuticals, and medical, aerospace, and military equipment; however, their advantage has narrowed since the end of World War II. Based on a comparison of GDP measured at Purchasing Power Parity conversion rates, the US economy in 2014, having stood as the largest in the world for more than a century, slipped into second place behind China, which has more than tripled the US growth rate for each year of the past four decades.

In the US, private individuals and business firms make most of the decisions, and the federal and state governments buy needed goods and services predominantly in the private marketplace. US business firms enjoy greater flexibility than their counterparts in Western Europe and Japan in decisions to expand capital plant, to lay off surplus workers, and to develop new products. At the same time, businesses face higher barriers to enter their rivals' home markets than foreign firms face entering US markets.

Long-term problems for the US include stagnation of wages for lower-income families, inadequate investment in deteriorating infrastructure, rapidly rising medical and pension costs of an aging population, energy shortages, and sizable current account and budget deficits.

The onrush of technology has been a driving factor in the gradual development of a "two-tier" labor market in which those at the bottom lack the education and the professional/technical skills of those at the top and, more and more, fail to get comparable pay raises, health insurance coverage, and other benefits. But the globalization of trade, and especially the rise of low-wage producers such as China, has put addition al downward pressure on wages and upward pressure on the return to capital. Since 1975, practically all the gains in household income have gone to the top 20% of households. Since 1996, dividends and capital gains have grown faster than wages or any other category of after-tax income.

Imported oil accounts for nearly 55% of US consumption and oil has a major impact on the overall health of the economy. Crude oil prices doubled between 2001 and 2006, the year home prices peaked; higher gasoline prices ate into consumers' budgets and many individuals fell behind in their mortgage payments. Oil prices climbed another 50% between 2006 and 2008, and bank foreclosures more than doubled in the same period. Besides dampening the housing market, soaring oil prices caused a drop in the value of the dollar and a deterioration in the US merchandise trade deficit, which peaked at $840 billion in 2008. Because the US economy is energy-intensive, falling oil prices since 2013 have alleviated many of the problems the earlier increases had created.

The sub-prime mortgage crisis, falling home prices, investment bank failures, tight credit, and the global economic downturn pushed the US into a recession by mid-2008. GDP contracted until the third quarter of 2009, making this the deepest and longest downturn since the Great Depression. To help stabilize financial markets, the US Congress established a $700 billion Troubled Asset Relief Program (TARP) in October 2008. The government used some of these funds to purchase equity in US banks and industrial corporations, much of which had been returned to the government by early 2011. In January 2009, Congress passed and President Barack OBAMA signed a bill providing an additional $787 billion fiscal stimulus to be used over 10 years—two-thirds on additional spending and one-third on tax cuts—to create jobs and to help the economy recover. In 2010 and 2011, the federal budget deficit reached nearly 9% of GDP. In 2012, the Federal Government reduced the growth of spending and the deficit shrank to 7.6% of GDP. US revenues from taxes and other sources are lower, as a percentage of GDP, than those of most other countries.

Wars in Iraq and Afghanistan required major shifts in National resources from civilian to military purposes and contributed to the growth of the budget deficit and public debt. Through 2014, the direct costs of the wars totaled more than $1.5 trillion, according to US Government figures.

In March 2010, President OBAMA signed into law the Patient Protection and Affordable Care Act, a health insurance reform that was designed to extend coverage to an addition al 32 million americans by 2016, through private health insurance

for the general population and Medicaid for the impoverished. Total spending on healthcare—public plus private—rose from 9.0% of GDP in 1980 to 17.9% in 2010. In July 2010, the president signed the DODD-FRANK Wall Street Reform and Consumer Protection act, a law designed to promote financial stability by protecting consumers from financial abuses, ending taxpayer bailouts of financial firms, dealing with troubled banks that are "too big to fail, " and improving accountability and transparency in the financial system—in particular, by requiring certain financial derivatives to be traded in markets that are subject to government regulation and oversight.

In December 2012, the Federal Reserve Board (Fed) announced plans to purchase $85 billion per month of mortgage-backed and Treasury securities in an effort to hold down long-term interest rates, and to keep short term rates near zero until unemployment dropped below 6.5% or inflation rose above 2.5%. in late 2013, the Fed announced that it would begin scaling back long-term bond purchases to $75 billion per month in January 2014 and further reduce them as conditions warranted; the Fed ended the purchases during the summer of 2014. in 2014, the unemployment rate dropped to 6.2%, and continued to fall to 5.5% by mid-2015, the lowest rate of joblessness since before the global recession began; inflation stood at 1.7%, and public debt as a share of GDP continued to decline, following several years of increases.

GDP (purchasing power parity): $17.95 trillion (2015 est.)
$17.52 trillion (2014 est.) $17.11 trillion (2013 est.)
note: data are in 2015 US dollars
country comparison to the world: 3

GDP (official exchange rate): $17.95 trillion (2015 est.)

GDP—real growth rate: 2.4% (2015 est.)
2.4% (2014 est.)
1.5% (2013 est.)
country comparison to the world: 127

GDP—per capita (PPP): $55,800 (2015 est.)
$54,900 (2014 est.)
$54,000 (2013 est.)
note: data are in 2015 US dollars
country comparison to the world: 19

Gross National saving: 18.7% of GDP (2015 est.)
18.8% of GDP (2014 est.)
18.2% of GDP (2013 est.)
country comparison to the world: 91

GDP—composition, by end use:
household consumption: 68.8%
government consumption: 17.6%
investment in fixed capital: 16.3%
investment in inventories: 0.6%
exports of goods and services: 12.7%
imports of goods and services: -16% (2015 est.)

GDP—composition, by sector of origin:
agriculture: 1.6%
industry: 20.8%
services: 77.6% (2015 est.)

Agriculture—products: wheat, corn, other grains, fruits, vegetables, cotton; beef, pork, poultry, dairy products; fish; forest products

Industries: highly diversified, world leading, high-technology innovator, second-largest industrial output in the world; petroleum, steel, motor vehicles, aerospace, telecommunications, chemicals, electronics, food processing, consumer goods, lumber, mining

Industrial production growth rate: 3% (2015 est.)
country comparison to the world: 84

Labor force: 156.4 million
note: includes unemployed (2015 est.)
country comparison to the world: 4

Labor force—by occupation: *farming, forestry, and fishing:* 0.7%
manufacturing, extraction, transportation, and crafts: 20.3%
managerial, professional, and technical: 37.3%
sales and office: 24.2%
other services: 17.6%
note: figures exclude the unemployed (2009)

Unemployment rate: 5.2% (2015 est.)
6.2% (2014 est.)
country comparison to the world: 54

Population below poverty line: 15.1% (2010 est.)

Household income or consumption by percentage share: *lowest:* 10%: 2%
highest: 10%: 30% (2007 est.)

Distribution of family income—Gini index: 45 (2007)
40.8 (1997)
country comparison to the world: 44

Budget: *revenues:* $3.251 trillion
expenditures: $3.677 trillion
note: for the US, revenues exclude social contributions of approximately $1.0 trillion; expenditures exclude social benefits of approximately $2.3 trillion (2015 est.)
Taxes and other revenues: 18.1% of GDP
note: excludes contributions for social security and other programs; if social contributions were added, taxes and other revenues would amount to approximately 22% of GDP (2015 est.)
country comparison to the world: 171

Budget surplus (+) or deficit (–): -2.4% of GDP (2015 est.)
country comparison to the world: 89

Public debt: 73.6% of GDP (2015 est.)
74.4% of GDP (2014 est.)
note: data cover only what the United States Treasury denotes as "Debt Held by the Public," which includes all debt instruments issued by the Treasury that are owned by non-US Government entities; the data include Treasury debt held by foreign entities; the data exclude debt issued by individual US states, as well as intra-governmental debt; intra-governmental debt consists of Treasury borrowings from surpluses in the trusts for Federal Social Security, Federal Employees, Hospital Insurance (Medicare and Medicaid), Disability and Unemployment, and several other smaller trusts; if data for intra-government debt were added, "Gross Debt" would increase by about one-third of GDP

country comparison to the world: 39

Fiscal year: 1 October—30 September

Inflation rate (consumer prices): 0.1% (2015 est.)
1.6% (2014 est.)
country comparison to the world: 41

Central bank discount rate: 0.5% (31 December 2010)
0.5% (31 December 2009)
country comparison to the world: 129

Commercial bank prime lending rate: 3.3% (31 December 2015 est.)
3.25% (31 December 2014 est.)
country comparison to the world: 167

Stock of narrow money: $3.121 trillion (31 December 2015 est.)
$2.807 trillion (31 December 2014 est.)
country comparison to the world: 4

Stock of broad money: $11.79 trillion (31 December 2014 est.)
$10.69 trillion (31 December 2013 est.)
country comparison to the world: 3

Stock of domestic credit: $19.47 trillion (31 December 2014 est.)
$18.56 trillion (31 December 2014 est.)
country comparison to the world: 2

Market value of publicly traded shares: $18.67 trillion (31 December 2012 est.)
$15.64 trillion (31 December 2011)
$17.14 trillion (31 December 2010 est.)
country comparison to the world: 1

Current account balance: -$484.1 billion (2015 est.)
-$389.5 billion (2014 est.)
country comparison to the world: 197

Exports: $1.598 trillion (2015 est.)
$1.633 trillion (2014 est.)
country comparison to the world: 3

Exports—commodities: agricultural products (soybeans, fruit, corn) 9.2%, industrial supplies (organic chemicals) 26.8%, capital goods (transistors, aircraft, motor vehicle parts, computers, telecommunications equipment) 49.0%, consumer goods (automobiles, medicines) 15.0% (2008 est.)

Exports—partners: Canada 18.6%, Mexico 15.7%, China 7.7%, Japan 4.2% (2015)

Imports: $2.347 trillion (2015 est.)
$2.374 trillion (2014 est.)
country comparison to the world: 1

Imports—commodities: agricultural products 4.9%, industrial supplies 32.9% (crude oil 8.2%), capital goods 30.4% (computers, telecommunications equipment, motor vehicle parts, office machines, electric power machinery), consumer goods 31.8% (automobiles, clothing, medicines, furniture, toys) (2008 est.)

Imports—partners: China 21.5%, Canada 13.2%, Mexico 13.2%, Japan 5.9%, Germany 5.5% (2015)

Reserves of foreign exchange and gold: $130.1 billion (31 December 2014 est.)
$144.6 billion (31 December 2013 est.)
country comparison to the world: 19

Debt—external: $17.26 trillion (31 December 2014 est.)

$16.49 trillion (31 December 2013 est.)
note: approximately 4/5ths of US external debt is denominated in US dollars; foreign lenders have been willing to hold US dollar denominated debt instruments because they view the dollar as the world's reserve currency
country comparison to the world: 1

Stock of direct foreign investment—at home: $3.116 trillion (31 December 2015 est.)
$2.901 trillion (31 December 2014 est.)
country comparison to the world: 2

Stock of direct foreign investment—abroad: $5.191 trillion (31 December 2015 est.)
$4.921 trillion (31 December 2014 est.)
country comparison to the world: 2

Exchange rates:
British pounds per US dollar: 0.6528 (2015 est.), 0.607 (2014 est), 0.6391 (2013 est.), 0.6324 (2012 est.), 0.624 (2011 est.)
Canadian dollars per US dollar: 1 (2015 est.), 1.275 (2015 est.), 1.1047 (2014 est.), 1.0298 (2013 est.), 0.9992 (2012 est.), 0.9895 (2011 est)
Chinese yuan per US dollar: 1 (2014 est.), 6.243 (2015 est.), 6.1434 (2014 est.), 6.1958 (2013 est.), 6.3123 (2012 est.), 6.4615 (2011 est.)
euros per US dollar: (2012 est.), 0.885 (2015 est.), 0.7525 (2014 est.), 0.7634 (2013 est.), 0.7752 (2012 est.), 0.7185 (2011 est.)
Japanese yen per US dollar: 122.10 (2015 est.), 105.86 (2014 est.), 97.44 (2013 est.), 79.79 (2012 est.), 79.81 (2011 est.)

ENERGY

Electricity—production: 4.048 trillion kWh (2012 est.)
country comparison to the world: 2

Electricity—consumption: 3.832 trillion kWh (2012 est.)
country comparison to the world: 2

Electricity—exports: 11.28 billion kWh (2013 est.)
country comparison to the world: 19

Electricity—imports: 63.61 billion kWh (2013 est.)
country comparison to the world: 2

Electricity—installed generating capacity: 1.063 billion kW (2012 est.)
country comparison to the world: 2

Electricity—from fossil fuels: 73.5% of total installed capacity (2012 est.)
country comparison to the world: 102

Electricity—from nuclear fuels: 9.6% of total installed capacity (2012 est.)
country comparison to the world: 20

Electricity—from hydroelectric plants: 7.4% of total installed capacity (2012 est.)
country comparison to the world: 122

Electricity—from other renewable sources: 7.4% of total installed capacity (2012 est.)
country comparison to the world: 51

Crude oil—production: 8.653 million bbl/day (2014 est.)
country comparison to the world: 3

Crude oil—exports: 629,400 bbl/day (2013 est.)
country comparison to the world: 20

Crude oil—imports: 9.08 million bbl/day (2013 est.)
country comparison to the world: 1

Crude oil—proved reserves: 36.52 billion bbl (1 January 2015 est.)
country comparison to the world: 11

Refined petroleum Products—production: 19.11 million bbl/day (2013 est.)
country comparison to the world: 1

Refined petroleum Products—consumption: 19.03 million bbl/day (2014 est.)
country comparison to the world: 1

Refined petroleum Products—exports: 2.992 million bbl/day (2013 est.)
country comparison to the world: 2

Refined petroleum Products—imports: 778,800 bbl/day (2013 est.)
country comparison to the world: 8

Natural gas—production: 728.2 billion cu m (2014 est.)
country comparison to the world: 1

Natural gas—consumption: 759.4 billion cu m (2014 est.)
country comparison to the world: 1

Natural gas—exports: 42.73 billion cu m (2014 est.)
country comparison to the world: 9

Natural gas—imports: 76.32 billion cu m (2014 est.)
country comparison to the world: 4

Natural gas—proved reserves: 8.734 trillion cu m (1 January 2013 est.)
country comparison to the world: 5

Carbon dioxide emissions from consumption of energy: 5.27 billion Mt (2012 est.)
country comparison to the world: 2

COMMUNICATIONS

Telephones—fixed lines: *total subscriptions:* 129.4 million
subscriptions per 100 inhabitants: 41 (2014 est.)
country comparison to the world: 3

Telephones—mobile cellular: *total:* 317.4 million
subscriptions per 100 inhabitants: 100 (2014 est.)
country comparison to the world: 5

Telephone system: *general assessment:* a large, technologically advanced, multipurpose communications system domestic: a large system of fiber-optic cable, microwave radio relay, coaxial cable, and domestic satellites carries every form of telephone traffic; a rapidly growing cellular system carries mobile telephone traffic throughout the country
International: country code—1; multiple ocean cable systems provide international connectivity; satellite earth stations—61 Intelsat (45 Atlantic Ocean and 16 Pacific Ocean), 5 Intersputnik (Atlantic Ocean region), and 4 Inmarsat (Pacific and Atlantic Ocean regions) (2011)

Broadcast media: 4 major terrestrial TV networks with affiliate stations throughout the country, plus cable and satellite networks, independent stations, and a limited public broadcasting sector that is largely supported by private grants; overall, thousands of TV stations broadcasting; multiple National radio networks with many affiliate stations; while most stations are commercial, National Public Radio (NPR) has a network of some 600 member stations; satellite radio available; overall, nearly 15,000 radio stations operating (2008)

Radio broadcast stations: AM 4,789, FM 8,961, shortwave 19 (2006)

Television broadcast stations: 2,218 (2006)

Internet country code: .us

Internet hosts: 505 million (2012); note—the US Internet total host count includes the following top-level domain host
addresses: .us, .com, .edu, .gov, .mil, .net, and .org
country comparison to the world: 1

Internet users: *total:* 276.6 million
percent of population: 86.8% (2014 est.)
country comparison to the world: 3

TRANSPORTATION

Airports: 13,513 (2013)
country comparison to the world: 1

Airports—with paved runways: *total:* 5,054
over 3,047 m: 189
2,438 to 3,047 m: 235
1,524 to 2,437 m: 1,478
914 to 1,523 m: 2,249
under 914 m: 903 (2013)

Airports—with unpaved runways: *total:* 8,459 over 3,047 m: 12,438 to 3,047 m: 6
1,524 to 2,437 m: 140
914 to 1,523 m: 1,552
under 914 m: 6,760 (2013)

Heliports: 5,287 (2013)

Pipelines: natural gas 1,984,321 km; petroleum Products 240,711 km (2013)

Railways: *total:* 293,564.2 km
standard gauge: 293,564.2 km 1.435-m gauge (2014)
country comparison to the world: 1

Roadways: *total:* 6,586,610 km
paved: 4,304,715 km (includes 76,334 km of expressways)
unpaved: 2,281,895 km (2012)
country comparison to the world: 1

Waterways: 41,009 km (19,312 km used for commerce; Saint Lawrence Seaway of 3,769 km, including the Saint Lawrence River of 3,058 km, is shared with Canada) (2012)
country comparison to the world: 5

Merchant marine: *total:* 393
by type: barge carrier 6, bulk carrier 55, cargo 51, carrier 2, chemical tanker 30, container 84, passenger 18, passenger/cargo 56, petroleum tanker 35, refrigerated cargo 3, roll on/roll off 27, vehicle carrier 26

foreign-owned: 85 (Australia 1, Bermuda 5, Denmark 31, France 4, Germany 5, Malaysia 2, Norway 17, Singapore 16, UK 4)

registered in other countries: 794 (Antigua and Barbuda 7, Australia 2, Bahamas 109, Belgium 1, Bermuda 26, Canada 10, Cayman Islands 57, Comoros 2, Cyprus 5, Georgia 1, Greece 8, Honduras 1, Hong Kong 44, Indonesia 2, Ireland 2, Isle of Man 1, Italy 23, Liberia 53, Malta 34, Marshall Islands 200, Netherlands 16, Norway 10, Panama 90, Portugal 4, Saint Kitts and Nevis 1, Saint Vincent and the Grenadines 18, Singapore 36, South Korea 8, Togo 1, UK 14, Vanuatu 2, unknown 6) (2010)
country comparison to the world: 26

Ports and terminals: *cargo ports (ton NAge):* Baton Rouge, Corpus Christi, Hampton Roads, Houston, Long Beach, Los Angeles, New Orleans, New York, Plaquemines, Tampa, Texas City
container port(s) (TEUs): Hampton Roads (1,918,029), Houston (1,866,450), Long Beach (6,061,091), Los Angeles (7,940,511), New York/New Jersey (5,503,485), Oakland (2,342,504), Savannah (2,944,678), Seattle (2,033,535)(2011)
cruise departure ports (passengers): Miami (2,032,000), Port Everglades (1,277,000), Port Canaveral (1,189,000), Seattle (430,000), Long Beach (415,000) (2009)
oil terminals: LOOP terminal, Haymark terminal
LNG terminal(s) (import): Cove Point (MD), Elba Island (GA), Everett (MA), Freeport (TX), Golden Pass (TX), Hackberry (LA), Lake Charles (LA), Neptune (offshore), Northeast Gateway (offshore), Pascagoula (MS), SaBine Pass (TX)
LNG terminal(s) (export): Kenai (AK)

MILITARY AND SECURITY

Military branches: United States Armed Forces: US Army, US Navy (includes Marine Corps), US Air Force, US Coast Guard; note—Coast Guard administered in peacetime by the Department of Homeland Security, but in wartime reports to the Department of the Navy (2015)

Military service age and obligation: 18 years of age (17 years of age with parental consent) for male and female voluntary service; no conscription; maximum enlistment age 42 (Army), 27 (Air Force), 34 (Navy), 28 (Marines); 8-year service obligation, including 2–5 years active duty (Army), 2 years active (Navy), 4 years active (Air Force, Marines); DoD is eliminating prohibitions restricting women from assignments in units smaller than brigades or near combat units (2013)

Military expenditures: 4.35% of GDP (2012)
4.75% of GDP (2011)
4.35% of GDP (2010)
country comparison to the world: 9

TRANSNATIONAL ISSUES

Disputes—international: the US has intensified domestic security measures and is collaborating closely with its neighbors, Canada and Mexico, to monitor and control legal and illegal personnel, transport, and commodities across the international borders; abundant rainfall in recent years along much of the Mexico-US border region has ameliorated periodically strained water-sharing arrangements; 1990 Maritime Boundary Agreement in the Bering Sea still awaits Russian Duma ratification; Canada and the United States dispute how to divide the Beaufort Sea and the status of the Northwest Passage but continue to work cooperatively to survey the Arctic continental shelf; The Bahamas and US have not been able to agree on a maritime boundary; US Naval Base at Guantanamo Bay is leased from Cuba

and only mutual agreement or US abandonment of the area can terminate the lease; Haiti claims US-administered Navassa Island; US has made no territorial claim iNAntarctica (but has reserved the right to do so) and does not recognize the claims of any other states; Marshall Islands claims Wake Island; Tokelau included American Samoa's Swains Island among the islands listed in its 2006 draft constitution

Refugees and internally displaced persons: *refugees (country of origin):* 18,386 (Burma); the US admitted 69,933 refugees during FY2015

including: 12,676 (Iraq); 8,858 (Somalia); 7,876 (Democratic Republic of the Congo); 5,775 (Bhutan); 3,109 (Iran); 1,682 (Syria)

Illicit drugs: world's largest consumer of cocaine (shipped from Colombia through Mexico and the Caribbean), Colombian heroin, and Mexican heroin and marijuana; major consumer of ecstasy and Mexican methamphetamine; minor consumer of high-quality Southeast Asian heroin; illicit producer of cannabis, marijuana, depressants, stimulants, hallucinogens, and methamphetamine; money-laundering center

URUGUAY

INTRODUCTION

Background: Montevideo, founded by the Spanish in 1726 as a military stronghold, soon took advantage of its Natural harbor to become an important commercial center. Claimed by Argentina but annexed by Brazil in 1821, Uruguay declared its independence four years later and secured its freedom in 1828 after a three-year struggle. The administrations of President Jose BATLLE in the early 20th century launched widespread political, social, and economic reforms that established a statist tradition. A violent Marxist urban guerrilla movement named the Tupamaros, launched in the late 1960s, led Uruguay's president to cede control of the government to the military in 1973. By yearend, the rebels had been crushed, but the military continued to expand its hold over the government. Civilian rule was not restored until 1985. In 2004, the left-of-center Frente Amplio Coalition won National elections that effectively ended 170 years of political control previously held by the Colorado and Blanco parties. Uruguay's political and labor conditions are among the freest on the continent.

GEOGRAPHY

Location: Southern South America, bordering the South Atlantic Ocean, betweeNArgentina and Brazil

Geographic coordinates: 33 00 S, 56 00 W

Map references: South America

Area: *total:* 176,215 sq km
land: 175,015 sq km
water: 1,200 sq km
country comparison to the world: 91

Area—comparative: slightly smaller than the state of Washington

Land boundaries: *total:* 1,591 km
border countries (2): Argentina 541 km, Brazil 1,050 km

Coastline: 660 km

Maritime claims: *territorial sea:* 12 nm
contiguous zone: 24 nm
exclusive economic zone: 200 nm
continental shelf: 200 nm or the edge of continental margin

Climate: warm temperate; freezing temperatures almost unknown

Terrain: mostly rolling plains and low hills; fertile coastal lowland

Elevation: *mean elevation:* 109 m

elevation extremes: *lowest point:* Atlantic Ocean 0 m
highest point: Cerro Catedral 514 m

Natural resources: arable land, hydropower, minor minerals, fish

Land use: *agricultural land:* 87.2%
arable land: 10.1%
permanent crops: 0.2%
permanent pasture: 76.9%
forest: 10.2%
other: 2.6% (2011 est.)

Irrigated land: 2,380 sq km (2012)

Total renewable water resources: 139 cu km (2011)

Freshwater withdrawal (domestic/industrial/agricultural): *total:* 3.66 cu km/yr (11%/2%/87%) per capita: 1,101 cu m/yr (2000)

Natural hazards: season ally high winds (the pampero is a chilly and occasional violent wind that blows north from the Argentine pampas), droughts, floods; because of the absence of Mountains, which act as weather barriers, all locations

are particularly vulnerable to rapid changes from weather fronts

Environment—current issues: water pollution from m eat packing/tannery industry; inadequate solid/hazardous waste disposal

Environment—International agreements: *party to:* Antarctic-Environmental Protocol, Antarctic-Marine Living Resources, Antarctic Treaty, Biodiversity, Climate Change, Climate Change-Kyoto Protocol, Desertification, Endangered Species, Environmental Modification, Hazardous Wastes, Law of the Sea, Ozone Layer Protection, Ship Pollution, Wetlands
signed, but not ratified: Marine Dumping, Marine Life Conservation

Geography—note: second-smallest South American country (after Suriname); most of the low-lying landscape (three-quarters of the country) is grassland, ideal for cattle and sheep raising

PEOPLE AND SOCIETY

Nationality: *noun:* Uruguayan(s)
adjective: Uruguayan

Ethnic groups: white 88%, mestizo 8%, black 4%, Amerindian (practically nonexistent)

Languages: Spanish (official), Portunol, Bralzero (Portuguese-Spanish mix on the Brazilian frontier)

Religions: Roman Catholic 47.1%, non-Catholic Christians 11.1%, nondenominational 23.2%, Jewish 0.3%, atheist or agnostic 17.2%, other 1.1% (2006)

Demographic profile: Uruguay rates high for most developm ent indicators and is known for its secularism, liberal social laws, and well-developed social security, health, and education al systems. It is one of the few countries in Latin America and the Caribbean where the entire population has access to clean water. Uruguay's provision of free primary through university education has contributed to the country's high levels of literacy and education al attainment. However, the emigration of human capital has diminished the state's return on its investment in education. Remittances from the roughly 18% of Uruguayans abroad am ount to less than 1 percent of National GDP. The

907

emigration of young adults and a low birth rate are causing Uruguay's population to age rapidly.

In the 1960s, Uruguayans for the first time emigrated en masse—primarily to Argentina and Brazil -because of economic decline and the onset of more than a decade of Military dictatorship. Economic crises in the early 1980s and 2002 also triggered waves of emigration, but since 2002 more than 70% of Uruguayan emigrants have selected the US and Spainas destinations because of better job prospects. Uruguay had a tiny population upon its independence in 1828 and welcomed thousands of predominantly ItalianAnd Spanish immigrants, but the country has not experienced large influxes of new arrivals since the afterm ath of World War II. More recent immigrants include Peruvians and Arabs.

Population: 3,341,893 (July 2015 est.)
country comparison to the world: 134

Age structure: 0–14 years: 20.73% (male 352,470/ female 340,275)
15–24 years: 15.89% (male 269,034/female 262,117)
25–54 years: 39.09% (male 644,816/female 661,635)
55–64 years: 10.25% (male 161,190/female 181,478)
65 years and over: 14.03% (male 187,051/female 281,827) (2015 est.)

Dependency ratios: *total dependency ratio:* 55.9%
youth dependency ratio: 33.4%
elderly dependency ratio: 22.5%
potential support ratio: 4.4% (2015 est.)

Median age: *total:* 34.5 years
male: 32.8 years
female: 36.2 years (2015 est.)
country comparison to the world: 76

Population growth rate: 0.27% (2015 est.)
country comparison to the world: 176

Birth rate: 13.07 births/1,000 population (2015 est.)
country comparison to the world: 152

Death rate: 9.45 deaths/1,000 population (2015 est.)
country comparison to the world: 56

Net migration rate: -0.9 migrant(s)/1,000 population (2015 est.)
country comparison to the world: 147

Urbanization: *urban Population:* 95.3% of total population (2015)
rate of urbanization: 0.53% annual rate of change (2010–15 est.)

Major urban Areas—population: MONTEVIDEO (capital) 1.707 million (2015)

Sex ratio: *at birth:* 1.04 male(s)/female
0–14 years: 1.04 male(s)/female *15–24 years:* 1.03 male(s)/female
25–54 years: 0.98 male(s)/female
55–64 years: 0.89 male(s)/female
65 years and over: 0.66 male(s)/female
total population: 0.94 male(s)/female (2015 est.)

Maternal mortality rate: 15 deaths/100,000 live births (2015 est.)
country comparison to the world: 124

Infant mortality rate: *total:* 8.74 deaths/1,000 live births
male: 9.7 deaths/1,000 live births
female: 7.75 deaths/1,000 live births (2015 est.)
country comparison to the world: 148

Life expectancy at birth: *total population:* 77 years
male: 73.86 years
female: 80.26 years (2015 est.)
country comparison to the world: 73

Total fertility rate: 1.82 children born/woman (2015 est.)
country comparison to the world: 151

Health expenditures: 8.8% of GDP (2013)
country comparison to the world: 41

Physicians density: 3.74 physicians/1,000 population (2008)

Hospital bed density: 2.5 beds/1,000 population (2012)

Drinking water source:
improved:
urban: 100% of population
rural: 93.9% of population
total: 99.7% of population
unimproved:
urban: 0% of population
rural: 6.1% of population
total: 0.3% of population (2015 est.)

Sanitation facility access:
improved:
urban: 96.6% of population
rural: 92.6% of population
total: 96.4% of population
unimproved:
urban: 3.4% of population
rural: 7.4% of population
total: 3.6% of population (2015 est.)

HIV/AIDS—adult prevalence rate: 0.7% (2014 est.)
country comparison to the world: 54

HIV/AIDS—people living with HIV/AIDS: 14,400 (2014 est.)
country comparison to the world: 89

HIV/AIDS—deaths: 600 (2014 est.)
country comparison to the world: 79

Obesity—adult prevalence rate: 27.6% (2014)
country comparison to the world: 64

Children under the age of 5 years underweight: 4.5% (2011)
country comparison to the world: 94

Education expenditures: 4.4% of GDP (2011)
country comparison to the world: 92

Literacy: *definition:* age 15 and over can read and write
total population: 98.5%
male: 98.2%
female: 98.8% (2015 est.)

School life expectancy (primary to tertiary education): *total:* 16 years
male: 14 years
female: 17 years (2010)

Child labor—children ages 5–14: *total number:* 51,879
percentage: 7% (2006 est.)

Unemployment, youth ages 15–24: *total:* 19.2%
male: 15.8%
female: 24% (2013 est.)
country comparison to the world: 61

GOVERNMENT

Country name: *conventional long form:* Oriental Republic of Uruguay
conventional short form: Uruguay
local long form: Republica Oriental del Uruguay
local short form: Uruguay former: Banda Oriental, Cisplatine Province
etymology: the Guarani Indians named the Uruguay River, which makes up the western border of the country and whose name later came to be applied to the entire country

Government type: presidential republic

Capital: *name:* Mon tevideo

Geographic coordinates: 34 51 S, 5610 W
time difference: UTC-3 (2 hours ahead of Washington, DC, during Standard Time)

Administrative divisions: 19 departments (departamentos, singular—departamento); Artigas, Canelones, Cerro Largo, Colonia, Durazno, Flores, Florida, Lavalleja, Maldon ado, Montevideo, Paysandu, Rio Negro, Rivera, Rocha, Salto, San Jose, Soriano, Tacuarembo, Treinta y Tres

Independence: 25 August 1825 (from Brazil)

National holiday: Independence Day, 25 August (1825)

Constitution: several previous; latest approved by plebiscite 27 November 1966, effective 15 February 1967; amended several times, last in 2004 (2016)

Legal system: civil law system based on the Spanish civil code

International law organization participation: accepts compulsory ICJ jurisdiction; accepts ICCt jurisdiction

Citizenship: *citizenship by birth:* yes
citizenship by descent: yes
dual citizenship recognized: yes
residency requirement for Naturalization: 3–5 years

Suffrage: 18 years of age; universal and compulsory

Executive branch: *chief of state:* President Tabare VAZQUEZ (since 1 March 2015); Vice President Raul Fernando SENDIC Rodriguez (since 1 March 2015); note—the president is both chief of state and head of government

head of government: President Tabare VAZQUEZ (since 1 March 2015); Vice President Raul Fernando SENDIC Rodriguez (since 1 March 2015)
cabinet: Council of Ministers appointed by the president with approval of the General Assembly
elections/appointments: president and vice president directly elected on the same ballot by absolute majority vote in 2 rounds if needed for a 5-year term (eligible for nonconsecutive terms); election last held on 26 October 2014, with a runoff

election on 30 November 2014 (next to be held on 27 October 2019, and a runoff if needed on 24 November 2019)

election results: Tabare VAZQUEZ elected president in a runoff election; percent of vote—Tabare VAZQUEZ (Socialist Party) 56.5%, Luis Alberto LACALLE Pou (Blanco) 43.4%

Legislative branch: *description:* bicameral General Assembly or Asamblea General consists of the Chamber of Senators or Camara de Senadores (31 seats; members directly elected in a single nationwide constituency by proportional representation vote; the vice-president serves as the presiding ex-officio member; elected members serve 5-year terms) and the Chamber of Representatives or Camara de Representantes (99 seats; members directly elected in multi-seat constituencies by proportional representation vote to serve 5-year terms)

elections: Chamber of Senators—last held on 26 October 2014 (next to be held in October 2019); Chamber of Representatives—last held on 26 October 2014 (next to be held in October 2019)

election results: Chamber of Senators—percent of vote by party—NA; seats by party—Frente Amplio 15, Blanco 10, Colorado Party 4, Independent Party 1; Chamber of Representatives—percent of vote by party—NA; seats by party—Frente Amplio 50, Blanco 32, Colorado Party 13, Independent Party 3, Popular Assembly 1

Judicial branch: *highest court(s):* Supreme Court of Justice (consists of 5 judges)

judge selection and term of office: judges nominated by the president and appointed in joint conference of the General Assembly; judges appointed for 0-year terms, with reelection after a lapse of 5 years following the previous term

subordinate courts: Courts of Appeal; District Courts (Juzgados Letrados); Peace Courts (Juzagados de Paz); Rural Courts (Juzgados Rurales)

Political parties and leaders: Broad Front (Frente Amplio) or EP-FA [Monica XAVIER] (a broad governing coalition that includes
Liber Seregni Front (FLS) [Danilo ASTORI],
Socialist Party [Monica XAVIER],
Vertiente Artiguiste [Enrique RUBIO],
Christian Democratic Party [JuaNAndres ROBALLO],
Popular Participation Movement (MPP) [Jose MUJICA],
Broad Front Commitment [Raul SENDIC],
Action and Thought Current-Freedom (CAP-L) [Eleuterio FERNADEZ HUIDOBRO],
Big House [Constanza MOREIRA],
Communist Party [Marcos CARAMBULA],
The Federal League
Colorado Party (including Vamos Uruguay [Pedro Bordaberry]
and Propuesta Batllista [Jorge AMORIN BAT LLE])
Independent Party [Pablo MIERES]
National Party or Blanco (including All Forward [Luis LACALLE POU] and National Alliance [Jorge LARRANAGA])
Popular Assembly [Gonzalo ABELLA]

Political pressure groups and leaders: B'nai Brith Catholic Church
Chamber of Commerce and Export of Agriproducts
Chamber of Industries (manufacturer's association)
Exporters Union of Uruguay National Chamber of Commerce and Services
PIT/CNT (powerful federation of Uruguayan Unions—umbrella labor organization)
Rural Association of Uruguay (rancher's association) Uruguayan Network of Political Women
other: students

International organization participation: CAN (associate), CD, CELAC, FAO, G-77, IADB, IAEA, IBRD, ICAO, ICC (National committees), ICCt, ICRM, IDA, IFAD, IFC, IFRCS, IHO, ILO, IMF, IMO, Interpol, IOC, IOM, IPU, ISO, ITSO, ITU, LAES, LAIA, Mercosur, MIGA, MINUSTAH, MONUSCO, NAM (observer), OAS, OIF (observer), OPANAL, OPCW, Pacific Alliance (observer), PCA, SICA (observer), UN, UNASUR, UNCTAD, UNESCO, UNIDO, Union Latina, UNMOGIP, UNOCI, UNWTO, UPU, WCO, WFTU (NGOs), WHO, WIPO, WMO, WTO

Diplomatic representation in the US: *chief of mission:* Ambassador Carlos Alberto GIANELLI Derois (since 3 August 2015)

chancery: 1913 I Street NW, Washington, DC 20006

telephone: [1] (202) 331-1313

FAX: [1] (202) 331-8142

consulate(s) general: Chicago, Los Angeles, Miami, New York

Diplomatic representation from the US: *chief of mission:* Ambassador (vacant); Charge d'Affaires Brad FREDEN (since 10 December 2014)

embassy: Lauro Muller 1776, Montevideo 11200

mailing address: APO AA 34035

telephone: [598] (2) 1770-2000

FAX: [598] (2) 1770-2128

Flag description: nine equal horizontal stripes of white (top and bottom) alternating with blue; a white square in the upper hoist-side corner with a yellow sun bearing a human face knowNAs the Sun of May with 16 rays that alternate between triangular and wavy; the stripes represent the nine original departments of Uruguay; the sun symbol evokes the legend of the sun breaking through the clouds on 25 May 1810 as independence was first declared from Spain (Uruguay subsequently won its independence from Brazil); the sun features are said to represent those of Inti, the Inca god of the sun

note: the banner was inspired by the National colors of Argentina and by the design of the US flag

National symbol(s): Sun of May (a sun-with-face symbol); National colors: blue, white, yellow

National anthem: *name:* "Himno Nacion al" (National Anthem of Uruguay)

lyrics/music: Francisco Esteban ACUNA de Figueroa/Francisco Jose DEBALI

note: adopted 1848; the anthem is also known as "Orientales, la Patriaola tumba!" ("Uruguayans, the Fatherland or Death!"); it is the world's

longest National anthem in terms of music (105 bars; almost five minutes); generally only the first verse and chorus are sung

ECONOMY

Economy—overview: Uruguay has a free market economy characterized by an export-oriented agricultural sector, a well-educated workforce, and high levels of social spending. Uruguay has sought to expand trade within the Common Market of the South (Mercosur) and with non-Mercosur members, and President VAZQUEZ has maintained his predecessor's mix of pro-market policies and a strong social safety net. Following financial difficulties in the late 1990s and early 2000s, Uruguay's economic growth averaged 8% annually during the period 2004–08. The 2008–09 global financial crisis put a brake on Uruguay's vigorous growth, which decelerated to 2.6% in 2009. Nevertheless, the country managed to avoid a recession and keep positive growth rates, mainly through higher public expenditure and investment; GDP growth reached 8.9% in 2010 but slowed in 2012–13 as a result of a renewed slowdown in the global economy and in Uruguay's main trade partners and Mercosur counterparts, Argentina and Brazil.

GDP (purchasing power parity): $71.43 billion (2015 est.)
$70.39 billion (2014 est.)
$68.01 billion (2013 est.)
note: data are in 2015 US dollars
country comparison to the world: 97

GDP (official exchange rate): $53.79 billion (2015 est.)

GDP—real growth rate: 1.5% (2015 est.)
3.5% (2014 est.)
5.1% (2013 est.)
country comparison to the world: 157

GDP—per capita (PPP): $21,500 (2015 est.)
$21,300 (2014 est.)
$20,600 (2013 est.)
note: data are in 2015 US dollars
country comparison to the world: 84

Gross National saving: 14.8% of GDP (2015 est.)
17.1% of GDP (2014 est.)
17.8% of GDP (2013 est.)
country comparison to the world: 120

GDP—composition, by end use:
household consumption: 65.9%
government consumption: 13.6%
investment in fixed capital: 22.4%
investment in inventories: 0.5%
exports of goods and services: 23.8%
imports of goods and services: -26.2% (2015 est.)

GDP—composition, by sector of origin:
agriculture: 7.5%
industry: 20.6%
services: 71.9% (2015 est.)

Agriculture—products: soybeans, rice, wheat; beef, dairy products; fish; lumber, cellulose

Industries: food processing, electrical machinery, transportation equipment, petroleum Products, textiles, chemicals, beverages

909

Industrial production growth rate: 3.3% (2015 est.)
country comparison to the world: 78

Labor force: 1.725 million (2015 est.)
country comparison to the world: 125

Labor force—by occupation: *agriculture:* 13%
industry: 14%
services: 73% (2010 est.)

Unemployment rate: 7.1% (2015 est.)
6.6% (2014 est.)
country comparison to the world: 86

Population below poverty line: 18.6% (2010 est.)

Household income or consumption by percentage share: *lowest:* 10%: 1.9%
highest: 10%: 34.4% (2010 est.)

Distribution of family income—Gini index: 45.3
(2010) 44.8 (1999)
country comparison to the world: 42

Budget: *revenues:* $15.94 billion
expenditures: $17.69 billion (2015 est.)
Taxes and other revenues: 29% of GDP (2015 est.)
country comparison to the world: 87

Budget surplus (+) or deficit (–): -3.2% of GDP
(2015 est.)
country comparison to the world: 121

Public debt: 68.6% of GDP (2015 est.)
62.7% of GDP (2014 est.)
note: data cover general government debt, and include debt instruments issued (or owned) by government entities other than the treasury; the data include treasury debt held by foreign entities; the data include debt issued by subNational entities, as well as intra-governmental debt; intra-governmental debt consists of treasury borrowings from surpluses in the social funds, such as for retirement, medical care, and unemployment; debt instruments for the social funds are not sold at public auctions
country comparison to the world: 48

Fiscal year: calendar year

Inflation rate (consumer prices): 8.7% (2015 est.)
8.9% (2014 est.)
country comparison to the world: 204

Central bank discount rate: 9% (31 December 2012)
8.75% (31 December 2011)
note: Uruguay's central bank uses the benchmark interest rate, rather than the discount rate, to conduct monetary policy; the rates shown here are the benchmark rates
country comparison to the world: 32

Commercial bank prime lending rate: 15.5% (31 December 2015 est.)
15.53% (31 December 2014 est.)
country comparison to the world: 35

Stock of narrow money: $4.49 billion (31 December 2015 est.)
$4.89 billion (31 December 2014 est.)
country comparison to the world: 101

Stock of broad money: $8.568 billion (31 December 2014 est.)
$8.919 billion (31 December 2013 est.)
country comparison to the world: 110

Stock of domestic credit: $18.16 billion (31 December 2015 est.)
$19.67 billion (31 December 2014 est.)
country comparison to the world: 89

Market value of publicly traded shares: $175.4 million (31 December 2012 est.)
$174.6 million (31 December 2011)
$156.9 million (31 December 2010 est.)
country comparison to the world: 117

Current account balance: -$2.12 billion (2015 est.)
-$2.494 billion (2014 est.)
country comparison to the world: 146

Exports: $7.672 billion (2015 est.)
$9.134 billion (2014 est.)
country comparison to the world: 100

Exports—commodities: beef, soybeans, cellulose, rice, wheat, wood, dairy products; wool

Exports—partners: China 15%, Brazil 14.4%, US 6.5%, Argentina 4.9% (2015)

Imports: $9.8 billion (2015 est.)
$11.48 billion (2014 est.)
country comparison to the world: 100

Imports—commodities: refined oil, crude oil, passenger and other transportation vehicles, vehicle parts, cellular phones

Imports—partners: Brazil 18.2%, China 17.4%, Argentina 12.6%, US 9.1%, Germany 4.5%, Nigeria 4.1% (2015)

Reserves of foreign exchange and gold: $17.48 billion (31 December 2015 est.)
$17.55 billion (31 December 2014 est.)
country comparison to the world: 63

Debt—external: $24.19 billion (31 December 2014 est.)
$22.86 billion (31 December 2013 est.)
country comparison to the world: 83

Stock of direct foreign investment—at home: $23.97 billion (31 December 2015 est.)
$21.34 billion (31 December 2014 est.)
country comparison to the world: 75

Stock of direct foreign investment—abroad: $180.6 million (31 December 2015 est.)
$156.6 million (31 December 2014 est.)
country comparison to the world: 92

Exchange rates: Uruguayan pesos (UYU) per US dollar—
27 (2015 est.)
23.246 (2014 est.)
23.246 (2013 est.)
20.31 (2012 est.)
19.314 (2011 est.)

ENERGY

Electricity—production: 10.3 billion kWh (2012 est.)
country comparison to the world: 96

Electricity—consumption: 9.559 billion kWh (2012 est.)
country comparison to the world: 92

Electricity—exports: 194 million kWh (2012 est.)
country comparison to the world: 75

Electricity—imports: 742 million kWh (2012 est.)
country comparison to the world: 69

Electricity—installed generating capacity: 2.87 million kW (2012 est.)
country comparison to the world: 95

Electricity—from fossil fuels: 44.5% of total installed capacity (2012 est.)
country comparison to the world: 157

Electricity—fron nuclear fuels: 0% of total installed capacity (2012 est.)
country comparison to the world: 200

Electricity—from hydroelectric plants: 53.6% of total installed capacity (2012 est.)
country comparison to the world: 45

Electricity—from other renewable sources: 2% of total installed capacity (2012 est.)
country comparison to the world: 80

Crude oil—production: 0 bbl/day (2014 est.)
country comparison to the world: 204

Crude oil—exports: 0 bbl/day (2012 est.)
country comparison to the world: 204

Crude oil—imports: 40,880 bbl/day (2012 est.)
country comparison to the world: 55

Crude oil—proved reserves: 0 bbl (1 January 2014 est.)
country comparison to the world: 205

Refined petroleum Products—production: 42,670 bbl/day (2012 est.)
country comparison to the world: 83

Refined petroleum Products—consumption: 64,000 bbl/day (2013 est.)
country comparison to the world: 92

Refined petroleum Products—exports: 2,515 bbl/day (2012 est.)
country comparison to the world: 104

Refined petroleum Products—Imports: 26,910 bbl/day (2012 est.)
country comparison to the world: 99

Natural gas—production: 0 cu m (2013 est.)
country comparison to the world: 142

Natural gas—consumption: 50 million cu m (2013 est.)
country comparison to the world: 109

Natural gas—exports: 0 cu m (2013 est.)
country comparison to the world: 203

Natural gas—imports: 50 million cu m (2013 est.)
country comparison to the world: 73

Natural gas—proved reserves: 0 cu m (1 January 2014 est.)
country comparison to the world: 203

Carbon dioxide emissions from consumption of energy: 7.591 million Mt (2012 est.)
country comparison to the world: 112

COMMUNICATIONS

Telephones—fixed lines: *total subscriptions:* 1.08 million
subscriptions per 100 inhabitants: 32 (2014 est.)
country comparison to the world: 75

Telephones—mobile cellular: *total:* 5.5 million
subscriptions per 100 inhabitants: 165 (2014 est.)
country comparison to the world: 112

Telephone system: *general assessment:* fully digitalized

domestic: most modern facilities concentrated in Montevideo; nationwide microwave radio relay network; overall fixed-line and mobile-cellular teledensity has reached 170 telephones per 100 persons

International: country code—598; the UNISOR submarine cable system provides direct connectivity to Brazil and Argentina; satellite earth stations—2 Intelsat (Atlantic Ocean) (2011)

Broadcast media: mixture of privately owned and state-run broadcast media; more than 100 commercial radio stations and about 20 TV channels; cable TV is available; many community radio and TV stations; adopted the hybrid Japanese/Brazilian HDTV standard (ISDB-T) in December 2010 (2010)

Radio broadcast stations: AM 93, FM 191, shortwave 7 (2005)

Television broadcast stations: 62 (2005)

Internet country code: .uy

Internet hosts: 1.036 million (2012)
country comparison to the world: 45

Internet users: *total:* 2 million
percent of population: 59.0% (2014 est.)
country comparison to the world: 99

TRANSPORTATION

Airports: 133 (2013)
country comparison to the world: 42

Airports—with paved runways: *total:* 11
over 3,047 m: 1

1,524 to 2,437 m: 4
914 to 1,523 m: 4
under 914 m: 2 (2013)

Airports—with unpaved runways: *total:* 122
1,524 to 2,437 m: 3
914 to 1,523 m: 40
under 914 m: 79 (2013)

Pipelines: gas 257 km; oil 160 km (2013)

Railways: *total:* 1,641 km
standard gauge: 1,641 km 1.435-m gauge (2014)
country comparison to the world: 77

Roadways: *total:* 77,732 km
paved: 7,743 km
unpaved: 69,989 km (2010)
country comparison to the world: 62

Waterways: 1,600 km (2011)
country comparison to the world: 48

Merchant marine: *total:* 16
by type: bulk carrier 1, cargo 2, chemical tanker 3, passenger/cargo 6, petroleum tanker 3, roll on/roll off 1
foreign-owned: 8 (Argentina 1, Denmark 1, Greece 1, Spain 5)
registered in other countries: 1 (Liberia 1) (2010)
country comparison to the world: 100

Ports and terminals: *major seaport(s):* Montevideo

MILITARY AND SECURITY

Military branches: Uruguayan Armed Forces: Uruguayan National Army (Ejercito Nacion al Uruguaya, ENU), Uruguayan National Navy (Armada Nacional del Uruguay; includes Naval air arm,

Naval Rifle Corps (Cuerpo de Fusileros Navales, Fusna), Maritime Prefecture in wartime), Uruguayan Air Force (Fuerza Aerea Uruguaya, FAU) (2012)

Military service age and obligation: 18–30 years of age (18–22 years of age for navy) for male or female voluntary military service; up to 40 years of age for specialists; enlistment is voluntary in peacetime, but the government has the authority to conscript in emergencies; minimum 6-year education (2013)

Military expenditures: 1.95% of GDP (2012)
1.94% of GDP (2011)
1.95% of GDP (2010)
country comparison to the world: 42

TRANSNATIONAL ISSUES

Disputes—international: in 2010, the ICJ ruled in favor of Uruguay's operation of two paper mills on the Uruguay River, which forms the border with Argentina; the two countries formed a joint pollution monitoring regime; uncontested boundary dispute between Brazil and Uruguay over Braziliera/Brasiliera Island in the Quarai/Cuareim River leaves the tripoint with Argentina in question; smuggling of firearms and narcotics continues to be an issue along the Uruguay-Brazil border

Illicit drugs: small-scale transit country for drugs mainly bound for Europe, often through sea-borne containers; law enforcement corruption; money laundering because of strict banking secrecy laws; weak border control along Brazilian frontier; increasing consumption of cocaine base and synthetic drugs

UZBEKISTAN

export capacity and increasing its manufacturing base. However, long-serving septuagenarian President Islom KARIMOV, who rose through the ranks of the Soviet-era State Planning Committee (Gosplan), remains wedded to the concepts of a command economy, creating a challenging environment for foreign investment. Current concerns include post-KARIMOV succession, economic stagnation, pervasive corruption, declining quality of social services, persistent inability to adequately meet the country's energy needs outside of Tashkent, the curtailment of human rights, and the lack of democratization.

INTRODUCTION

Background: Russia conquered the territory of present-day Uzbekistan in the late 19th century. Stiff resistance to the Red Army after the Bolshevik Revolution was eventually suppressed and a socialist republic established in 1924. During the Soviet era, intensive production of "white gold" (cotton) and grain led to overuse of agrochemicals and the depletion of water supplies, which have left the land degraded and the Aral Sea and certain rivers half dry. Independent since 1991, the country has gradually lessened its dependence on the cotton monoculture by diversifying agricultural production while developing its mineral and petroleum

GEOGRAPHY

Location: Central Asia, north of Turkmenistan, south of Kazakhstan

Geographic coordinates: 41 00 N, 64 00 E

Map references: Asia

Area: *total:* 447,400 sq km
land: 425,400 sq km
water: 22,000 sq km
country comparison to the world: 57

Area—comparative: about four times the size of Virginia; slightly larger than California

Land boundaries: *total:* 6,893 km
border countries (5): Afghanistan 144 km, Kazakhstan 2,330 km, Kyrgyzstan 1,314 km, Tajikistan 1,312 km, Turkmenistan 1,793 km

Coastline: 0 km (doubly landlocked); note—Uzbekistan includes the southern portion of the Aral Sea with a 420 km shoreline

Maritime claims: none (doubly landlocked)

Climate: mostly mid-latitude desert, long, hot summers, mild winters; semiarid grassland in east

Terrain: mostly flat-to-rolling sandy desert with dunes; broad, flat intensely irrigated river valleys along course of Amu Darya, Syr Darya (Sirdaryo), and Zarafshon; Fergana Valley in east surrounded by mountainous TajikistaNAnd Kyrgyzstan; shrinking Aral Sea in west

Elevation: *mean elevation:* NA

elevation extremes: *lowest point:* Sariqamish Kuli -12 m
highest point: Adelunga Toghi 4,301 m

Natural resources: Natural gas, petroleum, coal, gold, uranium, silver, copper, lead and zinc, tungsten, molybdenum

Land use: *agricultural land:* 62.6%
arable land: 10.1%
permanent crops: 0.8%
permanent pasture: 51.7%
forest: 7.7%
other: 29.7% (2011 est.)

Irrigated land: 42,150 sq km (2012)

Total renewable water resources: 48.87 cu km (2011)

Freshwater withdrawal (domestic/industrial/agricultural): *total:* 56 cu km/yr (7%/3%/90%) per capita: 2,113 cu m/yr (2005)

Natural hazards: NA

Environment—current issues: shrinkage of the Aral Sea has resulted in growing concentrations of chemical pesticides and Natural salts; these substances are then blown from the increasingly exposed lake bed and contribute to desertification and respiratory health problems; water pollution from industrial wastes and the heavy use of fertilizers and pesticides is the cause of many human health disorders; increasing soil salination; soil contamination from buried nuclear processing and agricultural chemicals, including DDT

Environment—International agreements: *party to:* Biodiversity, Climate Change, Climate Change-Kyoto Protocol, Desertification, Endangered Species, Environmental Modification, Hazardous Wastes, Ozone Layer Protection, Wetlands
signed, but not ratified: none of the selected agreements

Geography—note: along with Liechtenstein, one of the only two doubly landlocked countries in the world

PEOPLE AND SOCIETY

Nationality: *noun:* Uzbekistani
adjective: Uzbekistani

Ethnic groups: Uzbek 80%, Russian 5.5%, Tajik 5%, Kazakh 3%, Karakalpak 2.5%, Tatar 1.5%, other 2.5% (1996 est.)

Languages: Uzbek (official) 74.3%, Russian 14.2%, Tajik 4.4%, other 7.1%
note: in the Karakalpakstan Republic, both the Karakalpak language and Uzbek have official status

Religions: Muslim 88% (mostly Sunni), Easter-Northodox 9%, other 3%

Population: 29,199,942 (July 2015 est.)
country comparison to the world: 46

Age structure: *0–14 years:* 24.56% (male 3,676,029/female 3,496,916)
15–24 years: 19.92% (male 2,945,837/female 2,869,483)
25–54 years: 43.46% (male 6,310,206/female 6,379,037)
55–64 years: 7.17% (male 987,930/female 1,104,347)

65 years and over: 4.9% (male 610,272/female 819,885) (2015 est.)

Dependency ratios: *total dependency ratio:* 49.7%
youth dependency ratio: 42.7%
elderly dependency ratio: 7%
potential support ratio: 14.3% (2015 est.)

Median age: *total:* 27.6 years
male: 27.1 years
female: 28.2 years (2015 est.)
country comparison to the world: 132

Population growth rate: 0.93% (2015 est.)
country comparison to the world: 123

Birth rate: 17 births/1,000 population (2015 est.)
country comparison to the world: 108

Death rate: 5.3 deaths/1,000 population (2015 est.)
country comparison to the world: 180

Net migration rate: -2.37 migrant(s)/1,000 population (2015 est.)
country comparison to the world: 173

Urbanization: *urban Population:* 36.4% of total population (2015)
rate of urbanization: 1.45% annual rate of change (2010–15 est.)

Major urban Areas—population: TASHKENT (capital) 2.251 million (2015)

Sex ratio: *at birth:* 1.06 male(s)/female
0–14 years: 1.05 male(s)/female *15–24 years:* 1.03 male(s)/female
25–54 years: 0.99 male(s)/female
55–64 years: 0.9 male(s)/female
65 years and over: 0.74 male(s)/female
total population: 0.99 male(s)/female (2015 est.)

Mother's mean age at first birth: 23.8 (2006 est.)

Maternal mortality rate: 36 deaths/100,000 live births (2015 est.)
country comparison to the world: 126

Infant mortality rate: *total:* 19.2 deaths/1,000 live births
male: 22.78 deaths/1,000 live births
female: 15.4 deaths/1,000 live births (2015 est.)
country comparison to the world: 91

Life expectancy at birth: *total population:* 73.55 years
male: 70.5 years
female: 76.78 years (2015 est.)
country comparison to the world: 128

Total fertility rate: 1.79 children born/woman (2015 est.)
country comparison to the world: 153

Contraceptive prevalence rate: 64.9% (2006)

Health expenditures: 6.1% of GDP (2013)
country comparison to the world: 118

Physicians density: 2.53 physicians/1,000 population (2013)

Hospital bed density: 4.4 beds/1,000 population (2010)

Drinking water source:
improved:
urban: 98.5% of population
rural: 80.9% of population
total: 87.3% of population

unimproved:
urban: 1.5% of population
rural: 19.1% of population
total: 12.7% of population (2012 est.)

Sanitation facility access:
improved:
urban: 100% of population
rural: 100% of population
total: 100% of population
unimproved:
urban: 0% of popu lation
rural: 0% of population
total: 0% of population (2015 est.)

HIV/AIDS—adult prevalence rate: 0.15% (2014 est.)
country comparison to the world: 104

HIV/AIDS—people living with HIV/AIDS: 32,300 (2014 est.)
country comparison to the world: 68

HIV/AIDS—deaths: 2,200 (2014 est.)
country comparison to the world: 55

Obesity—adult prevalence rate: 14.3% (2014)
country comparison to the world: 119

Children under the age of 5 years underweight: 4.4% (2006)
country comparison to the world: 97

Education expenditures: NA

Literacy: *definition:* age 15 and over can read and write
total population: 99.6%
male: 99.7%
female: 99.5% (2015 est.)

School life expectancy (primary to tertiary education): *total:* 12 years
male: 12 years
female: 12 years (2011)

GOVERNMENT

Country name: *conventional long form:* Republic of Uzbekistan
conventional short form: Uzbekistan
local long form: O'zbekiston Respublikasi
local short form: O'zbekiston
former: Uzbek Soviet Socialist Republic
etymology: a comBination of the Turkic words "uz" (self) and "bek" (master) with the Persian suffix "stan" (country) to give the meaning "Land of the free"

Government type: presidential republic; highly authoritarian

Capital: *name:* Tashkent (Toshkent)

Geographic coordinates: 41 19 N, 69 15 E
time difference: UTC+5 (10 hours ahead of Washington, DC, during Standard Time)

Administrative divisions: 12 provinces (viloyatlar, singular—viloyat), 1 autonomous republic* (avtonom respublikasi), and 1 city** (shahar); Andijon Viloyati, Buxoro Viloyati, Farg'on a Viloyati, Jizzax Viloyati, Namangan Viloyati, Navoiy Viloyati, Qashqadaryo Viloyati (Qarshi), Qoraqalpog'iston Respublikasi [Karakalpakstan Republic]* (Nukus), Samarqand Viloyati, Sirdaryo

Viloyati (Guliston), Surxondaryo Viloyati (Termiz), Toshkent Shahri [Tashkent City]**, Toshkent Viloyati [Tashkent province], Xorazm Viloyati (Urganch)

note: administrative divisions have the same names as their administrative centers (exceptions have the administrative center name following in parentheses)

Independence: 1 September 1991 (from the Soviet Union)

National holiday: Independence Day, 1 September (1991)

Constitution: several previous; latest adopted 8 December 1992; amended several times, last in 2014 (2016)

Legal system: civil law system

International law organization participation: has not submitted an ICJ jurisdiction declaration; non-party state to the ICCt

Citizenship: *citizenship by birth:* no
citizenship by descent only: at least one parent must be a citizen of Uzbekistan
dual citizenship recognized: no
residency requirement for Naturalization: 5 years

Suffrage: 18 years of age; universal

Executive branch: *chief of state:* President Islom KARIMOV (since 24 March 1990, when elected president by the former Supreme Soviet; first elected president of independent Uzbekistan in 1991)

head of government: Prime Minister Shavkat MIRZIYOYEV (since 11 December 2003); First Deputy Prime Minister Rustam AZIMOV (since 2 January 2008)
cabinet: Cabinet of Ministers appointed by the president with approval of both chambers of the Supreme Assembly (Oliy Majlis)
elections/appointments: president directly elected by absolute majority popular vote in 2 rounds if needed for a 5-year term (eligible for a second term; previously a 5-year term, extended by a 2002 constitutional amendment to 7 years, and reverted to 5 years in 2011); election last held on 29 March 2015 (next to be held in 2020); prime minister nominated by majority party in legislature since 2011, but appointed along with the ministers and deputy ministers by the president
election results: Islom KARIMOV reelected president; percent of vote—Islom KARIMOV (LDPU) 90.4%, Akmal SAIDOV (Democratic Party of Uzbekistan) 3.1%, Khatamjan KETMANOV (NDP) 2.9%, Nariman UMAROV (Justice Social Democratic Party of Uzbekistan) 2.1%, other 1.5%

Legislative branch: *description:* bicameral Supreme Assembly or Oliy Majlis consists of the Senate (100 seats; 84 members indirectly elected by region al governing councils and 16 appointed by the president; members serve 5-year terms) and the Legislative Chamber or Qonunchilik Palatasi (150 seats; 135 members directly elected in single-seat constituencies by absolute majority vote with a second round if needed and 15 indirectly elected

by the Ecological Movement of Uzbekistan; members serve 5-year terms)
note: all parties in the Supreme Assembly support President Islom KARIMOV
elections: last held on 21 December 2014 and 4 January 2015 (next to be held in December 2019)
election results: Senate—percent of vote by party—NA; seats by party—NA; Legislative Chamber—percent of vote by party—NA; seats by party—LDPU 52, National Rebirth Party 36, NDP 27, Adolat 20, Ecological Movement 15

Judicial branch: *High est cou rt(s):* Supreme Court (consists of 34 judges organized in civil, criminal, and military sections); Constitutional Court (consists of 7 judges); Higher Economic Court (consists of 19 judges)
judge selection and term of office: judges of the 3 highest courts nominated by the president and confirmed by the Oliy Majlis; judges appointed for 5-year terms subject to reappointment
subordinate courts: region al, district, city, and town courts

Political parties and leaders: Ecological Movement of Uzbekistan (O'zbekiston Ekologik Harakati) [Boriy ALI KH ANOV]
Justice (Adolat) Social Democratic Party of Uzbekistan [Narimon UMAROV]
Liberal Democratic Party of Uzbekistan (O 'zbekiston Liberal-Demokratik Partiyasi) or LDPU [I slam KARIMOV]
National Revival Democratic Party of Uzbekistan (O'zbekiston Milliy Tiklanish Demokratik Partiyasi)
[Shavkat MIR ZIYOYEV]
People's Democratic Party of Uzbekistan (Xalq Demokratik Partiyas) or NDP [Hotamjon KET-MONOV] (formerly Communist Party)

Political pressure groups and leaders: no significant opposition political parties or pressure groups in Uzbekistan

International organization participation: ADB, CICA, CIS, CSTO, EAPC, EBRD, ECO, FAO, IAEA, IBRD, ICAO, ICC (National committees), ICCt, ICRM, IDA, IDB, IFAD, IFC, IFRCS, ILO, IMF, Interpol, IOC, ISO, ITSO, ITU, MIGA, NAM, OIC, OPCW, OSCE, PFP, SCO, UN, UN Security Council (temporary), UNCTAD, UNESCO, UNIDO, UNWTO, UPU, WCO, WFTU (NGOs), WHO, WIPO, WMO, WTO (observer)

Diplomatic representation in the US: *chief of mission:* Ambassador Baxtiyor GULOMOV (since 18 July 2013)
chancery: 1746 Massachusetts Avenue NW, Washington, DC 20036
telephone: [1] (202) 887-5300
FAX: [1] (202) 293-6804
consulate(s) general: New York

Diplomatic representation from the US: *chief of mission:* Ambassador Pamela L. SPRATLEN (since 21 January 2015)
embassy: 3 Moyqo'rq'on, 5th Block, Yunusobod District, Tashkent 100093
mailing address: use embassy street address
telephone: [998] (71) 120-5450
FAX: [998] (71) 120-6335

Flag description: three equal horizontal bands of blue (top), white, and green separated by red fimbriations with a white crescent moon (closed side to the hoist) and 12 white stars shifted to the hoist on the top band; blue is the color of the Turkic peoples and of the sky, white signifies peace and the striving for purity in thoughts and deeds, while green represents nature and is the color of Islam; the red stripes are the vital force of all living organisms that links good and pure ideas with the eternal sky and with deeds on earth; the crescent represents Islam and the 12 stars the months and constellations of the Uzbek calendar

National symbol(s): khumo (mythical bird); National colors: blue, white, red, green

National anthem: *name:* "O 'zbekiston Respublikasining Davlat Madhiyasi" (National Anthem of the Republic of Uzbekistan)
lyrics/music: Abdulla ARIPO V/Mutal BURHANOV
note: adopted 1992; after the fall of the Soviet Union, Uzbekistan kept the music of the anthem from its time as a Soviet Republic but adopted new lyrics

ECONOMY

Economy—overview: Uzbekistan is a landlocked country with more than 60% of the population living in densely populated rural communities. Since its independence in September 1991, the government maintained its Soviet-style command economy with subsidies and tight controls on production and prices. Despite ongoing efforts to diversify crops, Uzbekistani agriculture remains largely centered on cotton; Uzbekistan is the world's fifth largest cotton exporter and sixth largest producer. Uzbekistan's growth has been driven primarily by state-led investments, and export of Natural gas, gold, and cotton provides a significant share of foreign exchange earnings. In 2015, Russia's Gazprom announced it would reduce its Natural gas imports from Uzbekistan but Tashkent continues to export Natural gas to China and Chinese investments in the country have substantially increased.

While aware of the need to improve the investment climate, the government continues to intervene in the business sector and has not addressed the impediments to foreign investment in the country. in the past, Uzbekistani authorities have accused US and other foreign companies operating in Uzbekistan of violating Uzbekistani laws and have frozeNAnd seized their assets. At the same time, the Uzbekistani Government has actively courted several major US and international corporations, offering financing and tax advantages. In 2003, the government accepted Article VIII obligations under the IMF, providing for full currency convertibility. However, strict currency controls and tightening of borders have lessened the effects of convertibility and have also led to some shortages that have further stifled economic activity. Recently, lower global commodity prices and economic slowdown in neighboring Russia and China have been hurting Uzbekistan's trade and investment and worsening its problem of currency shortage.

GDP (purchasing power parity): $187.9 billion (2015 est.)
$174 billion (2014 est.)
$161 billion (2013 est.)
note: data are in 2015 US dollars
country comparison to the world: 64

GDP (official exchange rate): $65.68 billion (2015 est.)

GDP—real growth rate: 8% (2015 est.)
8.1% (2014 est.)
8% (2013 est.)
country comparison to the world: 7

GDP—per capita (PPP): $6,100 (2015 est.)
$5,700 (2014 est.)
$5,300 (2013 est.)
note: data are in 2015 US dollars
country comparison to the world: 160

Gross National saving: 30.8% of GDP (2015 est.)
31.6% of GDP (2014 est.)
33.7% of GDP (2013 est.)
country comparison to the world: 23

GDP—composition, by end use:
household consumption: 57.8%
government consumption: 17.3%
investment in fixed capital: 25.4%
investment in inventories: -0.1%
exports of goods and services: 31.5%
imports of goods and services: -31.9% (2015 est.)

GDP—composition, by sector of origin:
agriculture: 18.8%
industry: 33.7%
services: 47.5% (2015 est.)

Agriculture—products: cotton, vegetables, fruits, grain; livestock

Industries: textiles, food processing, machine building, metallurgy, mining, hydrocarbon extraction, chemicals

Industrial production growth rate: 4% (2015 est.)
country comparison to the world: 58

Labor force: 17.54 million (2015 est.)
country comparison to the world: 35

Labor force—by occupation: *agriculture:* 25.9%
industry: 13.2%
services: 60.9% (2012 est.)

Unemployment rate: 4.8% (2015 est.)
4.8% (2014 est.)
note: official data; another 20% are underemployed
country comparison to the world: 47

Population below poverty line: 17% (2011 est.)

Household income or consumption by percentage share: *lowest:* 10%: 2.8%
highest: 10%: 29.6% (2003)

Distribution of family income—Gini index: 36.8 (2003)
44.7 (1998)
country comparison to the world: 81

Budget: *revenues:* $18.74 billion
expenditures: $19.69 billion (2015 est.)
Taxes and other revenues: 28.4% of GDP (2015 est.)

country comparison to the world: 90

Budget surplus (+) or deficit (–): -1.4% of GDP (2015 est.)
country comparison to the world: 61

Public debt: 8.3% of GDP (2015 est.)
7.1% of GDP (2014 est.)
country comparison to the world: 171

Fiscal year: calendar year

Inflation rate (consumer prices): 8.5% (2015 est.)
9.1% (2014 est.)
note: official data; based on independent analysis of consumer prices, inflation reached 22% in 2012
country comparison to the world: 203

Commercial bank prime lending rate: 12.44% (31 December 2013 est.)
11.2% (31 December 2012 est.)
country comparison to the world: 63

Stock of narrow money: $8.504 billion (31 December 2015 est.)
$7.606 billion (31 December 2014 est.)
country comparison to the world: 86

Stock of broad money: $16.56 billion (31 December 2015 est.)
$15.59 billion (31 December 2014 est.)
country comparison to the world: 95

Stock of domestic credit: $13.21 billion (31 December 2015 est.)
$13.09 billion (31 December 2014 est.)
country comparison to the world: 95

Market value of publicly traded shares: $NA (31 December 2012)
$715.3 million (31 December 2006)

Current account balance: -$7 million (2015 est.)
$454 million (2014 est.)
country comparison to the world: 55

Exports: $13.53 billion (2015 est.)
$13.31 billion (2014 est.)
country comparison to the world: 78

Exports—commodities: energy products, cotton, gold, mineral fertilizers, ferrous and nonferrous metals, textiles, foodstuffs, machinery, automobiles

Exports—partners: Switzerland 25.8%, China 17.6%, Kazakhstan 14.2%, Turkey 9.9%, Russia 8.4%, Bangladesh 6.9% (2015)

Imports: $13.5 billion (2015 est.)
$12.92 billion (2014 est.)
country comparison to the world: 88

Imports—commodities: machinery and equipment, foodstuffs, chemicals, ferrous and nonferrous metals

Imports—partners: China 20.8%, Russia 20.8%, South Korea 12%, Kazakhstan 10.8%, Turkey 4.6%, Germany 4.4% (2015)

Reserves of foreign exchange and gold: $15 billion (31 December 2015 est.)
$17.8 billion (31 December 2014 est.)
country comparison to the world: 69

Debt—external: $10.19 billion (31 December 2014 est.)
$10.6 billion (31 December 2013 est.)
country comparison to the world: 104

Stock of direct foreign investment—at home: $NA

Stock of direct foreign investment—abroad: $NA

Exchange rates: Uzbekistani soum (UZS) per US dollar—
2,565.8 (2015 est.)
2,311.4 (2014 est.)
2,311.4 (2013 est.)
1,890.1 (2012 est.)
1,715.8 (2011 est.)

ENERGY

Electricity—production: 49.91 billion kWh (2012 est.)
country comparison to the world: 53

Electricity—consumption: 45.21 billion kWh (2012 est.)
country comparison to the world: 52

Electricity—exports: 12.27 billion kWh (2012 est.)
country comparison to the world: 17

Electricity—imports: 12.18 billion kWh (2012 est.)
country comparison to the world: 17

Electricity—installed generating capacity: 12.57 million kW (2012 est.)
country comparison to the world: 51

Electricity—from fossil fuels: 86.2% of total installed capacity (2012 est.)
country comparison to the world: 86

Electricity—fron nuclear fuels: 0% of total installed capacity (2012 est.)
country comparison to the world: 201

Electricity—from hydroelectric plants: 13.8% of total installed capacity (2012 est.)
country comparison to the world: 107

Electricity—from other renewable sources: 0% of total installed capacity (2012 est.)
country comparison to the world: 138

Crude oil—production: 64,810 bbl/day (2014 est.)
country comparison to the world: 52

Crude oil—exports: 30,000 bbl/day (2012 est.)
country comparison to the world: 52

Crude oil—imports: 340 bbl/day (2012 est.)
country comparison to the world: 80

Crude oil—proved reserves: 594 million bbl (1 January 2015 est.)
country comparison to the world: 49

Refined petroleum Products—production: 71,260 bbl/day (2012 est.)
country comparison to the world: 75

Refined petroleum Products—consumption: 69,000 bbl/day (2013 est.)
country comparison to the world: 90

Refined petroleum Products—exports: 4,331 bbl/day (2012 est.)
country comparison to the world: 97

Refined petroleum Products—Imports: 0 bbl/day (2012 est.)
country comparison to the world: 211

Natural gas—production: 59.63 billion cu m (2013 est.)
country comparison to the world: 16

Natural gas—consumption: 46.13 billion cu m (2013 est.)
country comparison to the world: 20

Natural gas—exports: 13.5 billion cu m (2013 est.)
country comparison to the world: 17

Natural gas—imports: 0 cu m (2013 est.)
country comparison to the world: 149

Natural gas—proved reserves: 1.841 trillion cu m (1 January 2014 est.)
country comparison to the world: 20

Carbon dioxide emissions from consumption of energy: 123.2 million Mt (2012 est.)
country comparison to the world: 38

COMMUNICATIONS

Telephones—fixed lines: *total subscriptions:* 2.51 million
subscriptions per 100 inhabitants: 9 (2014 est.)
country comparison to the world: 53

Telephones—mobile cellular: *total:* 21.6 million
subscriptions per 100 inhabitants: 75 (2014 est.)
country comparison to the world: 56

Telephone system: *general assessment:* digital exchanges in large cities and in rural areas
domestic: the state-owned telecommunications company, Uzbektelecom, owner of the fixed-line telecommunications system, has used loans from the Japanese government and the China Development Bank to upgrade fixed-line services including conversion to digital exchanges; mobile-cellular services are provided by 3 private and 1 state-owned operator with a total subscriber base of 19 million as of January 2014
International: country code—998; linked by fiber-optic cable or microwave radio relay with CIS member states and to other countries by leased connection via the Moscow international gateway switch; the country also has a link to the Trans-Asia-Europe (TAE) fiber-optic cable; Uzbekistan has supported the National fiber optic backbone project of Afghanistan since 2008 (2009)

Broadcast media: government controls media; 14 state-owned broadcasters—10 TV and 4 radio—provide service to virtually the entire country; about 20 privately owned TV stations, overseen by local officials, broadcast to local markets; privately owned TV stations are required to lease transmitters from the government-owned Republic TV and Radio Industry Corporation; in 2013, the government closed TV and radio broadcasters affiliated with the National Association of Electronic Mass Media of Uzbekistan, a government-sponsored NGO for private broadcast media
Radio broadcast stations: AM 20, FM 24, shortwave 3 (2008)
Television broadcast stations: 28 (includes 1 cable rebroadcaster in Tashkent and approximately 20 stations in region al capitals) (2006)

Internet country code: .uz

Internet hosts: 56,075 (2012)
country comparison to the world: 94

Internet users: *total:* 11.8 million

percent of population: 40.6% (2014 est.)
country comparison to the world: 41

TRANSPORTATION

Airports: 53 (2013)
country comparison to the world: 89

Airports—with paved runways: *total:* 33
over 3,047 m: 6
2,438 to 3,047 m: 13
1,524 to 2,437 m: 6
914 to 1,523 m: 4
under 914 m: 4 (2013)

Airports—with unpaved runways: *total:* 20
2,438 to 3,047 m: 2
under 914 m: 18 (2013)

Pipelines: gas 10,401 km; oil 944 km (2013)

Railways: *total:* 3,645 km
broad gauge: 3,645 km 1.520-m gauge (620 km electrified) (2014)
country comparison to the world: 48

Roadways: *total:* 86,496 km
paved: 75,511 km
unpaved: 10,985 km (2000)
country comparison to the world: 52

Waterways: 1,100 km (2012)
country comparison to the world: 62

Ports and terminals: *river port(s):* Termiz (Amu Darya)

MILITARY AND SECURITY

Military branches: Uzbek Armed Forces: Army, Air and Air Defense Forces (2013)

Military service age and obligation: 18 years of age for compulsory military service; 1-month or 1-year conscript service obligation for males; moving toward a professional military, but conscription in some form will continue; the military cannot accommodate everyone who wishes to enlist, and competition for entrance into the military is similar to the competition for admission to universities (2013)

TRANSNATIONAL ISSUES

Disputes—international: prolonged drought and cotton monoculture in Uzbekistan and Turkmenistan created water-sharing difficulties for Amu Darya river states; field demarcation of the boundaries with Kazakhstan commenced in 2004; border delimitation of 130 km of border with Kyrgyzstan is hampered by serious disputes around enclaves and other areas

Refugees and internally displaced persons: *stateless persons:* 86,703 (2015)

Trafficking in persons: *current situation:* Uzbekistan is a source country for men, women, and children subjected to forced labor and women and children subjected to sex trafficking; government-compelled forced labor of adults remained endemic during the 2014 cotton harvest; despite a decree banning the use of persons under 18, children were mobilized to harvest cotton by local officials in some districts; in some regions, local officials

forced teachers, students, private business employees, and others to work in construction, agriculture, and cleaning parks; Uzbekistani women and children are victims of sex trafficking domestically and in the Middle East, Eurasia, and Asia; Uzbekistani men and, to a lesser extent, womeNAre subjected to forced labor in Kazakhstan, Russia, and Ukraine in the construction, oil, agriculture, retail, and food sectors

tier rating: Tier 2 Watch List—Uzbekistan does not fully comply with the minimum standards for the elimination of trafficking; however, it is making significant efforts to do so; law enforcement efforts in 2014 were mixed; the government made efforts to combat sex and Transnational labor trafficking, but government-compelled forced labor of adults in the cotton harvest went unaddressed, and the decree prohibiting forced child labor was not applied universally; official complicity in human trafficking in the cotton harvest remained prevalent; authorities made efforts to identify and protect sex and Transnational labor victims, although a systematic process is still lacking; minimal efforts were made to assist victims of forced labor in the cotton harvest, as the government does not openly acknowledge the existence of this forced labor; the ILO did not have permission or funding to monitor the 2014 harvest, but the government authorized the UN's InterNational Labour Organization to conduct a survey on recruitment practices and working conditions in agriculture, particularly the cotton sector, and to monitor the 2015–17 cotton harvests for child and forced labor in project areas (2015)

Illicit drugs: transit country for Afghan narcotics bound for Russian and, to a lesser extent, Western European markets; limited illicit cultivation of cannabis and small amounts of opium Poppy for domestic consumption; poppy cultivation almost wiped out by government crop eradication program; transit point for heroin precursor chemicals bound for Afghanistan

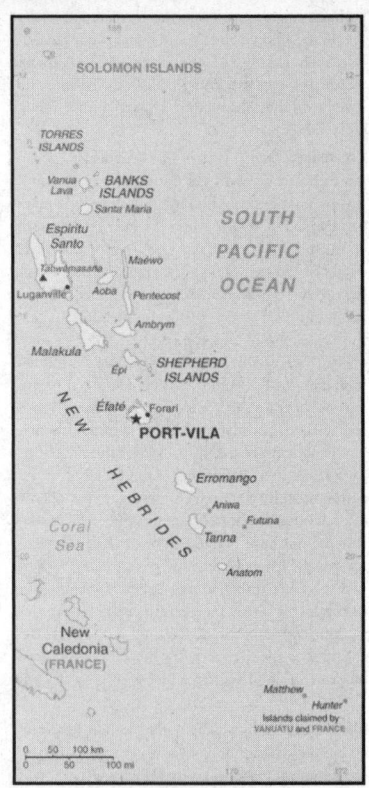

INTRODUCTION

Background: Multiple waves of colonizers, each speaking a distinct language, migrated to the New Hebrides in the millennia preceding European exploration in the 18th century. This settlement pattern accounts for the complex linguistic diversity found on the archipelago to this day. The British and French, who settled the New Hebrides in the 19th century, agreed in 1906 to an Anglo-French Condominium, which administered the islands until independence in 1980, when the new name of Vanuatu was adopted.

GEOGRAPHY

Location: Oceania, group of islands in the South Pacific Ocean, about three-quarters of the way from Hawaii to Australia

Geographic coordinates: 16 00 S, 167 00 E

Map references: Oceania

Area: *total:* 12,189 sq km
land: 12,189 sq km
water: 0 sq km
note: includes more than 80 islands, about 65 of which are inhabited
country comparison to the world: 164

Area—comparative: slightly larger than Connecticut

Land boundaries: 0 km

Coastline: 2,528 km

Maritime claims: measured from claimed Archipelagic baselines
territorial sea: 12 nm
contiguous zone: 24 nm
exclusive economic zone: 200 nm
continental shelf: 200 nm or to the edge of the continental margin

Climate: tropical; moderated by southeast trade winds from May to October; moderate rainfall from November to April; may be affected by cyclones from December to April

Terrain: mostly mountainous islands of volcanic origin; narrow coastal plains

Elevation: *mean elevation:* NA

elevation extremes: *lowest point:* Pacific Ocean 0 m
highest point: Tabwemasana 1,877 m

Natural resources: manganese, hardwood forests, fish

Land use: *agricultural land:* 15.3%
arable land: 1.6%
permanent crops: 10.3%
permanent pasture: 3.4%
forest: 36.1%
other: 48.6% (2011 est.)

Irrigated land: 0 sq km (2012)

Natural hazards: tropical cyclones or typhoons (January to April); volcanic eruption on aoba (Ambae) island began on 27 November 2005, volcanism also causes minor earthquakes; tsunami
volcanism: significant volcanic activity with multiple eruptions in recent years; Yasur (elev. 361 m), one of the world's most active volcanoes, has experienced continuous activity in recent centuries; other historically active volcanoes include, Aoba, Ambrym, Epi, Gaua, Kuwae, Lopevi, Suretamatai, and Traitor's Head

Environment—current issues: most of the population does not have access to a reliable supply of potable water; deforestation

Environment—international agreements: *party to:* Antarctic-Marine Living Resources, Biodiversity, Climate Change, Climate Change-Kyoto Protocol, Desertification, Endangered Species, Law of the Sea, Marine Dumping, Ozone Layer Protection, Ship Pollution, Tropical Timber 94
signed, but not ratified: none of the selected agreements

Geography—note: a Y-shaped chain of four main islands and 80 smaller islands; several of the islands have active volcanoes and there are several underwater volcanoes as well

PEOPLE AND SOCIETY

Nationality: *noun:* Ni-Vanuatu (singular and plural)

adjective: Ni-Vanuatu

Ethnic groups: Ni-Vanuatu 97.6%, part Ni-Vanuatu 1.1%, other 1.3% (2009 est.)

Languages: local languages (more than 100) 63.2%, Bislama (official; creole) 33.7%, English (official) 2%, French (official) 0.6%, other 0.5% (2009 est.)

Religions: Protestant 70% (includes Presbyterian 27.9%, Anglican 15.1%, Seventh Day Adventist 12.5%, Assemblies of God 4.7%, Church of Christ 4.5%, Neil Thomas Ministry 3.1%, and Apostolic 2.2%), Roman Catholic 12.4%, customary beliefs 3.7% (including Jon Frum cargo cult), other 12.6%, none 1.1%, unspecified 0.2% (2009 est.)

Population: 272,264 (July 2015 est.)
country comparison to the world: 183

Age structure: *0–14 years:* 36.71% (male 51,014/female 48,940)
15–24 years: 19.94% (male 26,970/female 27,314)
25–54 years: 34.45% (male 45,935/female 47,864)
55–64 years: 5.13% (male 7,034/female 6,932)
65 years and over: 3.77% (male 5,236/female 5,025) (2015 est.)

Dependency ratios: *total dependency ratio:* 68.7%
youth dependency ratio: 61.6%
elderly dependency ratio: 7.1%
potential support ratio: 14.1% (2015 est.)

Median age: *total:* 21.4 years
male: 21 years
female: 21.7 years (2015 est.)
country comparison to the world: 182

Population growth rate: 1.95% (2015 est.)
country comparison to the world: 52

Birth rate: 25.04 births/1,000 population (2015 est.)
country comparison to the world: 51

Death rate: 4.09 deaths/1,000 population (2015 est.)
country comparison to the world: 207

Net migration rate: -1.47 migrant(s)/1,000 population (2015 est.)
country comparison to the world: 155

Urbanization: *urban population:* 26.1% of total population (2015)
rate of urbanization: 3.42% annual rate of change (2010–15 est.)

Major urban Areas—population: PORT-VILA (capital) 53,000 (2014)

Sex ratio: *at birth:* 1.05 male(s)/female
0–14 years: 1.04 male(s)/female
15–24 years: 0.99 male(s)/female
25–54 years: 0.96 male(s)/female
55–64 years: 1.02 male(s)/female
65 years and over: 1.04 male(s)/female
total population: 1 male(s)/female (2015 est.)

Maternal mortality rate: 78 deaths/100,000 live births (2015 est.)
country comparison to the world: 68

Infant mortality rate: *total:* 15.7 deaths/1,000 live births
male: 16.77 deaths/1,000 live births
female: 14.58 deaths/1,000 live births (2015 est.)
country comparison to the world: 101

Life expectancy at birth: *total population:* 73.06 years
male: 71.47 years
female: 74.72 years (2015 est.)
country comparison to the world: 133

Total fertility rate: 3.25 children born/woman (2015 est.)
country comparison to the world: 49

Contraceptive prevalence rate: 38.4% (2007)

Health expenditures: 3.9% of GDP (2013)
country comparison to the world: 171

Physicians density: 0.12 physicians/1,000 population (2008)

Hospital bed density: 1.8 beds/1,000 population (2008)

Drinking water source:
improved:
urban: 98.9% of population
rural: 92.9% of population
total: 94.5% of population
unimproved:
urban: 1.1% of population
rural: 7.1% of population
total: 5.5% of population (2015 est.)

Sanitation facility access:
improved:
urban: 65.1% of population
rural: 55.4% of population
total: 57.9% of population
unimproved:
urban: 34.9% of population
rural: 44.6% of population
total: 42.1% of population (2015 est.)

HIV/AIDS—adult prevalence rate: NA

HIV/AIDS—people living with HIV/AIDS: NA

HIV/AIDS—deaths: NA

Obesity—adult prevalence rate: 32.9% (2014)
country comparison to the world: 39

Children under the age of 5 years underweight: 10.7% (2013)
country comparison to the world: 62

Education expenditures: 4.9% of GDP (2014)
country comparison to the world: 79

Literacy: *definition:* age 15 and over can read and write
total population: 85.2%
male: 86.6%
female: 83.8% (2015 est.)

Unemployment, youth ages 15–24: *total:* 10.6%
male: 10.2%
female: 11.2% (2009 est.)

GOVERNMENT

Country name: *conventional long form:* Republic of Vanuatu
conventional short form: Vanuatu
local long form: Ripablik blong Vanuatu

local short form: Vanuatu form er: New Hebrides
etymology: derived from the words "vanua" (home or land) and "tu" (stand) that occur in several of the Austonesian languages spoken on the islands and which provide the meaning of "independence" or the sense of "our land"

Government type: parliamentary republic

Capital: *name:* Port-Vila (on Efate)

Geographic coordinates: 17 44 S, 168 19 E
time difference: UTC + 11 (16 hours ahead of Washington, DC, during Standard Time)

Administrative divisions: 6 provinces; Malampa, Penama, Sanma, Shefa, Tafea, Torba

Independence: 30 July 1980 (from France and the UK)

National holiday: Independence Day, 30 July (1980)

Constitution: effective 30 July 1980; amended several times, last in 2013 (2016)

Legal system: mixed legal system of English common law, French law, and customary law

International law organization participation: has not submitted an ICJ jurisdiction declaration; accepts ICCt jurisdiction

Citizenship: *citizenship by birth:* no
citizenship by descent only: both parents must be citizens of Vanuatu; in the case of only one parent, it must be the father who is a citizen
dual citizenship recognized: no
residency requirement for Naturalization: 10 years

Suffrage: 18 years of age; universal

Executive branch: *chief of state:* President Baldwin LONSDALE (since 22 September 2014)

head of government: Prime Minister Charlot SAL-WAI (since 11 February 2016)
cabinet: Council of Ministers appointed by the prime minister, responsible to parliament
elections/appointments: president indirectly elected by an electoral college consisting of Parliament and presidents of the 6 provinces; Vanuatu president serves a 5-year term; election last held on 17 September 2014 (next to be held in 2019); following legislative elections, the leader of the majority party or majority coalition usually elected prime minister by parliament from among its members; election for prime minister last held on 11 February 2016 (next to be held following general elections in 2020)
election results: Baldwin LONSDALE (independent) elected president; Parliament vote—46 out of 52 on the eighth ballot; Charlot SALWAI elected prime minister on 11 February 2016 with 46 votes

Legislative branch: *description:* unicameral Parliament (52 seats; members directly elected in multi-seat constituencies by simple majority vote to serve 4-year terms)
note: the National Council of Chiefs advises on matters of culture and language elections: last held on 22 January 2016 (next to be held in 2020)
election results: percent of vote by party—NA; seats by party—VP 8, PPP 6, UMP 5, GJP 4, NUP 4, IG 3, GC 3, NAG 3, RMC 3, MPP 2, NIPDP

2, PSP 1, VLDP 1, VNP 1, VPDP 1, VRP 1, and independent 4; note -political party associations are fluid

Judicial branch: .*highest court(s):* Supreme Court (consists of a chief justice and 3 judges); note—appeals from the Supreme Court are considered by the Court of Appeal, constituted by 2 or more judges of the Supreme Court sitting together
judge selection and term of office: Supreme Court chief justice appointed by the president after consultation with the prime minister and the leader of the opposition; other judges are appointed by the president on the advice of the Judicial Service Commission, a 4-member advisory body; judges appointed until age of retirement
subordinate courts: magistrates' courts; island courts

Political parties and leaders: Greens Confederation or GC [Moana CARCASSES Kalosil]
Iauko Group or IG [Tony NARI]
Land and Justice Party (Graon mo Jastis Pati) or GJP [Ralph REGENVANU]
Melanesian Progressive Party or MPP [Barak SOPE]
Nagriamel movement or NAG [Frankie STEVENS]
Natatok Indigenous People's Democratic Party or (NATATOK) or NIPDP [Alfred Roland CARLOT]
National United Party or NUP [Ham LINI]
People's Progressive Party or PPP [Sato KILMAN]
People's Service Party or PSP [Don KEN]
Reunification of Movement for Change or RMC [Charlot SALWAI]
Union of Moderate Parties or UMP [Serge VOHOR]
Vanua'aku Pati (Our Land Party) or VP [Edward NATAPEI]
Vanuatu Democratic Party [Maxime Carlot KORMAN]
Vanuatu Liberal Democratic Party or VLDP [Tapangararua WILLIE]
Vanuatu National Party or VNP [Issac HAMARILIU]
Vanuatu National Development Party or VNDP [Robert Bohn SIKOL]
Vanuatu Republican Party or VRP [Marcellino PIPITE]

Political pressure groups and leaders: NA

International organization participation: ACP, ADB, AOSIS, C, FAO, G-77, IBRD, ICAO, ICRM, IDA, IFC, IFRCS, ILO, IMF, IMO, IMSO, IOC, IOM, ITU, ITUC (NGOs), MIGA, NAM, OAS (observer), OIF, OPCW, PIF, Sparteca, SPC, UN, UNCTAD, UNESCO, UNIDO, UNWTO, UPU, WCO, WFTU (NGOs), WHO, WIPO, WMO, WTO

Diplomatic representation in the US: Vanuatu does not have an embassy in the US; it does, however, have a Permanent Mission to the UN

Diplomatic representation from the US: the US does not have an embassy in Vanuatu; the US Ambassador to Papua New Guinea is accredited to Vanuatu

Flag description: two equal horizontal bands of red (top) and green with a black isosceles triangle (based on the hoist side) all separated by a black-edged yellow stripe in the shape of a horizontal Y (the two points of the Y face the hoist side and enclose the triangle); centered in the triangle is a boar's tusk encircling two crossed namele fern fronds, all in yellow; red represents the blood of boars and men, as well as unity, green the richness of the islands, and black the ni-Vanuatu people; the yellow Y-shape—which reflects the pattern of the islands in the Pacific Ocean—symbolizes the light of the Gospel spreading through the islands; the boar's tusk is a symbol of prosperity frequently worn as a pendant on the islands; the fern fronds represent peace

note: one of several flags where a prominent component of the design reflects the shape of the country; other such flags are those of Bosnia and Herzegovina, Brazil, and Eritrea

National symbol(s): boar's tusk with crossed fern fronds; National colors: red, black, green, yellow

National anthem: name: "Yumi, Yumi, Yumi" (We, We, We)

lyrics/music: Francois Vincent AYSSAV

note: adopted 1980; the anthem is written in Bislama, a Creole language that mixes Pidgin English and French

ECONOMY

Economy—overview: This South Pacific island economy is based primarily on small-scale agriculture, which provides a living for about two-thirds of the population. Fishing, offshore financial services, and tourism, with nearly 197,000 visitors in 2008, are other mainstays of the economy. Australia and New Zealand are the main source of tourists and foreign aid. A small light industry sector caters to the local market. Tax revenues come mainly from import duties. Mineral deposits are negligible; the country has no known petroleum deposits. Economic development is hindered by dependence on relatively few commodity exports, vulnerability to Natural disasters, and long distances from main markets and between constituent islands. In response to foreign concerns, the government has promised to tighten regulation of its offshore financial center. Since 2002, the government has stepped up efforts to boost tourism through improved air connections, resort development, and cruise ship facilities. Agriculture, especially livestock farming, is a second target for growth.

GDP (purchasing power parity): $685 million (2015 est.)
$690.5 million (2014 est.)
$674.8 million (2013 est.)
note: data are in 2015 US dollars
country comparison to the world: 208

GDP (official exchange rate): $765 million (2015 est.)

GDP—real growth rate: -0.8% (2015 est.)
2.3% (2014 est.)
2% (2013 est.)

country comparison to the world: 203

GDP—per capita (PPP): $2,500 (2015 est.)
$2,600 (2014 est.)
$2,600 (2013 est.)
note: data are in 2015 US dollars
country comparison to the world: 198

GDP—composition, by end use:
household consumption: 69.8%
government consumption: 18.8%
investment in fixed capital: 25.2%
investment in inventories: 0.1%
exports of goods and services: 45.8%
imports of goods and services: -59.7% (2015 est.)

GDP—composition, by sector of origin:
agriculture: 30.2%
industry: 8.7%
services: 61.1% (2015 est.)

Agriculture—products: copra, coconuts, cocoa, coffee, taro, yams, fruits, vegetables; beef; fish

Industries: food and fish freezing, wood processing, meat canning

Industrial production growth rate: -5% (2015 est.)
country comparison to the world: 189

Labor force: 115,900 (2007 est.)
country comparison to the world: 181

Labor force—by occupation: agriculture: 65%
industry: 5%
services: 30% (2000 est.)

Unemployment rate: 1.7% (1999 est.)
country comparison to the world: 9

Population below poverty line: NA%

Household income or consumption by percentage share: lowest: 10%: NA%
highest: 10%: NA%

Budget: revenues: $141 million
expenditures: $182.7 million (2015 est.)
Taxes and other revenues: 18.3% of GDP (2015 est.)
country comparison to the world: 169

Budget surplus (+) or deficit (–): -5.4% of GDP (2015 est.)
country comparison to the world: 175

Fiscal year: calendar year

Inflation rate (consumer prices): 3.3% (2015 est.)
1% (2014 est.)
country comparison to the world: 144

Central bank discount rate: 20% (31 December 2010)
6% (31 December 2009)
country comparison to the world: 5

Commercial bank prime lending rate: 4.6% (31 December 2015 est.)
4.8% (31 December 2014 est.)
country comparison to the world: 151

Stock of narrow money: $267.5 million (31 December 2015 est.)
$270.3 million (31 December 2014 est.)
country comparison to the world: 178

Stock of broad money: $544.9 million (31 December 2014 est.)
$552.6 million (31 December 2013 est.)
country comparison to the world: 180

Stock of domestic credit: $483.2 million (31 December 2015 est.)
$501.4 million (31 December 2014 est.)
country comparison to the world: 169

Market value of publicly traded shares: $NA

Current account balance: -$77 million (2015 est.)
$4 million (2014 est.)
country comparison to the world: 67

Exports: $38.3 million (2015 est.)
$49.1 million (2014 est.)
country comparison to the world: 205

Exports—commodities: copra, beef, cocoa, timber, kava, coffee

Exports—partners: Japan 35.1%, Turkey 10.5%, Thailand 8.7%, China 8.2%, Venezuela 5.9%, UK 5.6% (2015)

Imports: $314.1 million (2015 est.)
$275.5 million (2014 est.)
country comparison to the world: 198

Imports—commodities: machinery and equipment, foods tuffs, fuels

Imports—partners: China 16.7%, Australia 14.6%, Japan 13.9%, Singapore 10%, Fiji 9.3%, NZ 8.3%, New Caledonia 5.2% (2015)

Reserves of foreign exchange and gold: $213.4 million (31 December 2015 est.) $184 million (31 December 2014 est.)
country comparison to the world: 160

Debt—external: $369.2 million (31 December 2012 est.)
$307.7 million (31 December 2011 est.)
country comparison to the world: 184

Stock of direct foreigninvestment—at home: $749.1 million (31 December 2015 est.)
$694.1 million (31 December 2014 est.)
country comparison to the world: 113

Stock of direct foreign investment—abroad: $26.3 million (31 December 2015 est.)
$26.3 million (31 December 2014 est.)
country comparison to the world: 101

Exchange rates: vatu (VUV) per US dollar—
107.8 (2015 est.)
97.07 (2014 est.)
97.07 (2013 est.)
92.64 (2012 est.)
89.47 (2011 est.)

ENERGY

Electricity—production: 53 million kWh (2012 est.)
country comparison to the world: 206

Electricity—consumption: 49.29 million kWh (2012 est.)
country comparison to the world: 205

Electricity—exports: 0 kWh (2013 est.)
country comparison to the world: 177

Electricity—imports: 0 kWh (2013 est.)
country comparison to the world: 182

Electricity—installed generating capacity: 28,000 kW (2012 est.)
country comparison to the world: 198

Electricity—from fossil fuels: 89.3% of total installed capacity (2012 est.)
country comparison to the world: 80

Electricity—fron nuclear fuels: 0% of total installed capacity (2012 est.)
country comparison to the world: 153

Electricity—from hydroelectric plants: 0% of total installed capacity (2012 est.)
country comparison to the world: 192

Electricity—from other renewable sources: 10.7% of total installed capacity (2012 est.)
country comparison to the world: 33

Crude oil—production: 0 bbl/day (2014 est.)
country comparison to the world: 175

Crude oil—exports: 0 bbl/day (2012 est.)
country comparison to the world: 169

Crude oil—imports: 0 bbl/day (2012 est.)
country comparison to the world: 107

Crude oil—proved reserves: 0 bbl (1 January 2015 est.)
country comparison to the world: 175

Refined petroleum Products—production: 0 bbl/day (2012 est.)
country comparison to the world: 118

Refined petroleum Products—consumption: 1,000 bbl/day (2013 est.)
country comparison to the world: 201

Refined petroleum Products—exports: 0 bbl/day (2012 est.)
country comparison to the world: 210

Refined petroleum Products—imports: 1,015 bbl/day (2012 est.)
country comparison to the world: 196

Natural gas—production: 0 cu m (2013 est.)
country comparison to the world: 111

Natural gas—consumption: 0 cu m (2013 est.)
country comparison to the world: 179

Natural gas—exports: 0 cu m (2013 est.)
country comparison to the world: 155

Natural gas—imports: 0 cu m (2013 est.)
country comparison to the world: 109

Natural gas—proved reserves: 0 cu m (1 January 2014 est.)
country comparison to the world: 178

Carbon dioxide emissions from consumption of energy: 166,100 Mt (2012 est.)
country comparison to the world: 198

COMMUNICATIONS

Telephones—fixed lines:
total subscriptions: 5,700
subscriptions per 100 inhabitants: 2 (2014 est.)
country comparison to the world: 207
Telephones—mobile cellular: *total:* 156,100
subscriptions per 100 inhabitants: 58 (2014 est.)
country comparison to the world: 183

Telephone system: *International:* country code—678; satellite earth station-1 Intelsat (Pacific Ocean)

Broadcast media: 1 state-owned TV station; multi-channel pay TV is available; state-owned Radio Vanuatu operates 2 radio stations; 2 privately owned radio broadcasters; programming from multiple international broadcasters is available (2008)
Radio broadcast stations: AM 2, FM 4, shortwave 1 (2001)
Television broadcast stations: 1 (2004)

Internet country code: .vu

Internet hosts: 5,655 (2012)
country comparison to the world: 143

Internet users: *total:* 30,800
percent of population: 11.5% (2014 est.)
country comparison to the world: 194

TRANSPORTATION

Airports: 31 (2013)
country comparison to the world: 114

Airports—with paved runways: *total:* 3
2,438 to 3,047 m: 1
1,524 to 2,437 m: 1
914 to 1,523 m: 1 (2013)

Airports—with unpaved runways: *total:* 28
914 to 1,523 m: 7
under 914 m: 21 (2013)

Roadways: *total:* 1,070 km
paved: 256 km
unpaved: 814 km (2000)
country comparison to the world: 185

Merchant marine: *total:* 77
by type: bulk carrier 38, cargo 8, chemical tanker 2, container 1, liquefied gas 2, passenger 1, refrigerated cargo 24, vehicle carrier 1
foreign-owned: 72 (Belgium 1, Canada 5, China 1, Greece 3, Japan 39, Norway 1, Poland 9, Russia 7, Singapore 2, Taiwan 1, UAE 1, US 2) (2010)
country comparison to the world: 58

Ports and terminals: *major seaport(s):* Forari Bay, Luganville (Santo, Espiritu Santo), Port-Vila

MILITARY AND SECURITY

Military branches: no regular military forces; Vanuatu Police Force (VPF), Vanuatu Mobile Force (VMF; includes Police Maritime Wing (PMW)) (2013)

TRANSNATIONAL ISSUES

Disputes—international: Matthew and Hunter Islands east of New Caledonia claimed by Vanuatu and France

VENEZUELA

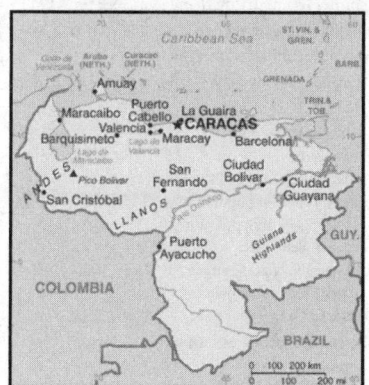

INTRODUCTION

Background: Venezuela was one of three countries that emerged from the collapse of Gran Colombia in 1830 (the others being Ecuador and New Granada, which became Colombia). For most of the first half of the 20th century, Venezuela was ruled by generally benevolent military strongmen, who promoted the oil industry and allowed for some social reforms. Democratically elected governments have held sway since 1959. Under Hugo CHAVEZ, president from 1999 to 2013, and his hand-picked successor, President Nicolas MADURO, the executive branch has exercised increasingly authoritarian control over other branches of government. At the same time, democratic institutions have deteriorated, threats to freedom of expression have increased, and political polarization has grown. The ruling party's economic policies have expanded the state's role in the economy through expropriations of major enterprises, strict currency exchange and price controls that discourage private sector investment and production, and overdependence on the petroleum industry for revenues, among others. Current concerns include: an increasingly politicized military, rampant violent crime, high inflation, and widespread shortages of basic consumer goods, medicine, and medical supplies. Venezuela assumed a nonpermanent seat on the UN Security Council for the 2015–16 term.

GEOGRAPHY

Location: Northern South America, bordering the Caribbean Sea and the North Atlantic Ocean, between Colombia and Guyana

Geographic coordinates: 8 00 N, 66 00 W

Map references: South America

Area: *total:* 912,050 sq km
land: 882,050 sq km
water: 30,000 sq km
country comparison to the world: 33

Area—comparative: almost six times the size of Georgia; slightly more than twice the size of California

Land boundaries: *total:* 5,267 km
border countries (3): Brazil 2,137 km, Colombia 2,341 km, Guyana 789 km

Coastline: 2,800 km

Maritime claims: *territorial sea:* 12 nm
contiguous zone: 15 nm
exclusive economic zone: 200 nm
continental shelf: 200-m depth or to the depth of exploitation

Climate: tropical; hot, humid; more moderate in highlands

Terrain: Andes Mountains and Maracaibo Lowlands in northwest; central plains (llanos); Guiana Highlands in southeast

Elevation: *mean elevation:* 450 m

elevation extremes: *lowest point:* Caribbean Sea 0 m
highest point: Pico Bolivar 5,007 m

Natural resources: petroleum, Natural gas, iron ore, gold, bauxite, other minerals, hydropower, diamonds

Land use: *agricultural land:* 24.5%
arable land: 3.1%
permanent crops: 0.8%
permanent pasture: 20.6%
forest: 52.1%
other: 23.4% (2011 est.)

Irrigated land: 10,550 sq km (2012)

Total renewable water resources: 1,233 cu km (2011)

Freshwater withdrawal (domestic/industrial/agricultural): *total:* 9.06 cu km/yr (23%/4%/74%)
per capita: 358.6 cu m/yr (2008)

Natural hazards: subject to floods, rockslides, mudslides; periodic droughts

Environment—current issues: sewage pollution of Lago de Valencia; oil and urban pollution of Lago de Maracaibo; deforestation; soil degradation; urban and industrial pollution, especially along the Caribbean coast; threat to the rainforest ecosystem from irresponsible mining operations

Environment—International agreements: *party to:* Antarctic Treaty, Biodiversity, Climate Change, Climate Change-Kyoto Protocol, Desertification, Endangered Species, Hazardous Wastes, Marine Life Conservation, Ozone Layer Protection, Ship Pollution, Tropical Timber 83, Tropical Timber 94, Wetlands
signed but not ratified: none of the selected agreements

Geography—note: on major sea and air routes linking North and South America; Angel Falls in the Guiana Highlands is the world's highest waterfall

PEOPLE AND SOCIETY

Nationality: *noun:* Venezuelan(s)
adjective: Venezuelan

Ethnic groups: Spanish, Italian, Portuguese, Arab, German, African, indigenous people

Languages: Spanish (official), numerous indigenous dialects

Religions: nominally Roman Catholic 96%, Protestant 2%, other 2%

Demographic profile: Social investment in Venezuela during the CHAVEZ administration reduced poverty from nearly 50% in 1999 to about 27% in 2011, increased school enrollment, substantially decreased infant and child mortality, and improved access to potable water and sanitation through social investment. "Missions" dedicated to education, nutrition, healthcare, and sanitation were funded through petroleum revenues. The sustainability of this progress remains question able, however, as the continuation of these social programs depends on the prosperity of Venezuela's oil industry. In the long-term, education and health care spending may increase economic growth and reduce income inequality, but rising costs and the staffing of new health care jobs with foreigners are slowing development.

While CHAVEZ was in power, more than one million predominantly middle- and upper-class Venezuelans are estimated to have emigrated. The brain drain is attributed to a repressive political system, lack of economic opportunities, steep inflation, a high crime rate, and corruption. Thousands of oil engineers emigrated to Canada, Colombia, and the United States following CHAVEZ's firing of over 20,000 employees of the state-owned petroleum company during a 2002–03 oil strike. Addition ally, thousands of Venezuelans of European descent have taken up residence in their ancestral homelands. Nevertheless, Venezuela continues to attract immigrants from South America and southern Europe because of its lenient migration policy and the availability of education and health care. Venezuela also has beeNA fairly accommodating host to more than 200,000 Colombian refugees.

Population: 29,275,460 (July 2015 est.)
country comparison to the world: 45

Age structure: *0–14 years:* 27.76% (male 4,143,988/female 3,983,457)
15–24 years: 18.71% (male 2,754,818/female 2,724,039)
25–54 years: 39.7% (male 5,711,044/female 5,911,607)
55–64 years: 7.68% (male 1,067,661/female 1,180,276)
65 years and over: 6.14% (male 791,095/female 1,007,475) (2015 est.)

Dependency ratios: *total dependency ratio:* 52.4% youth 42.8%
elderly dependency ratio: 9.5%
potential support ratio: 10.5% (2015 est.)

Median age: *total:* 27.2 years
male: 26.4 years
female: 27.9 years (2015 est.)

country comparison to the world: 140

Population growth rate: 1.39% (2015 est.)
country comparison to the world: 85

Birth rate: 19.16 births/1,000 population (2015 est.)
country comparison to the world: 90

Death rate: 5.31 deaths/1,000 population (2015 est.)
country comparison to the world: 179

Net migration rate: 0 migrant(s)/1,000 population (2015 est.)
country comparison to the world: 79

Urbanization: *urban population:* 89% of total population (2015)
rate of urbanization: 1.54% annual rate of change (2010–15 est.)

Major urban Areas—population: CARACAS (capital) 2.916 million; Maracaibo 2.196 million; Valencia 1.734 million; Maracay 1.166 million; Barquisimeto 1.039 million (2015)

Sex ratio: *at birth:* 1.05 male(s)/female
0–14 years: 1.04 male(s)/female
15–24 years: 1.01 male(s)/female
25–54 years: 0.97 male(s)/female
55–64 years: 0.91 male(s)/female
65 years and over: 0.79 male(s)/female
total population: 0.98 male(s)/female (2015 est.)

Maternal mortality rate: 95 deaths/100,000 live births (2015 est.)
country comparison to the world: 79

Infant mortality rate: *total:* 18.91 deaths/1,000 live births
male: 22.9 deaths/1,000 live births
female: 15.37 deaths/1,000 live births (2015 est.)
country comparison to the world: 92

Life expectancy at birth: *total population:* 74.54 years
male: 71.4 years
female: 77.83 years (2015 est.)
country comparison to the world: 116

Total fertility rate: 2.32 children born/woman (2015 est.)
country comparison to the world: 91

Health expenditures: 3.6% of GDP (2013)
country comparison to the world: 151

Hospital bed density: 0.9 beds/1,000 population (2011)

Drinking water source:
improved:
urban: 95% of population
rural: 77.9% of population
total: 93.1% of population
unimproved:
urban: 5% of popu lation
rural: 22.1% of population
total: 6.9% of population (2015 est.)

Sanitation facility access:
improved:
urban: 97.5% of population
rural: 69.9% of population
total: 94.4% of population
unimproved:

urban: 2.5% of population
rural: 30.1% of population
total: 5.6% of population (2015 est.)

HIV/AIDS—adult prevalence rate: 0.55% (2014 est.)
country comparison to the world: 61

HIV/AIDS—people living with HIV/AIDS: 106,900 (2014 est.)
country comparison to the world: 43

HIV/AIDS—deaths: 4,400 (2013 est.)
country comparison to the world: 33

Major infectious diseases: *degree of risk:* high
food or waterborne diseases: bacterial diarrhea and hepatitis A
vectorborne diseases: dengue fever and malaria (2013)

Obesity—adult prevalence rate: 24.3% (2014)
country comparison to the world: 26

Children under the age of 5 years underweight: 2.9% (2009)
country comparison to the world: 115

Education expenditures: 6.9% of GDP (2009)
country comparison to the world: 22

Literacy: *definition:* age 15 and over can read and write
total population: 96.3%
male: 96.4%
female: 96.2% (2015 est.)

School life expectancy (primary to tertiary education): *total:* 14 years
male: NA
female: NA (2009)

Unemployment, youth ages 15–24: *total:* 17.1%
male: 14.3%
female: 22.6% (2012 est.)
country comparison to the world: 70

GOVERNMENT

Country name: *conventional long form:* Bolivarian Republic of Venezuela
conventional short form: Venezuela
local long form: Republica Bolivariana de Venezuela
local short form: Venezuela
etymology: native stilt-houses built on Lake Maracaibo reminded early explorers Alonso de OJEDA and Amerigo VESPUCCI in 1499 of buildings in Venice and so they named the region "Venezuola," which in Italian means "Little Venice"

Government type: federal pres iden tial republic

Capital: *name:* Caracas

Geographic coordinates: 10 29 N, 66 52 W
time difference: UTC-4.5 (a half hour ahead of Washington, DC, during Standard Time)

Administrative divisions: 23 states (estados, singular—estado), 1 capital district* (distrito capital), and 1 federal dependency** (dependencia federal); Amazon as, Anzoategui, Apure, Aragua, Barinas, Bolivar, Carabobo, Cojedes, Delta Amacuro, Dependencias Federales (Federal Dependencies)**, Distrito Capital (Capital District) *,

Falcon, Guarico, Lara, Merida, Miranda, Monagas, Nueva Esparta, Portuguesa, Sucre, Tachira, Trujillo, Vargas, Yaracuy, Zulia
note: the federal dependency consists of 11 federally controlled island groups with a total of 72 individual islands

Independence: 5 July 1811 (from Spain)

National holiday: Independence Day, 5 July (1811)

Constitution: many previous; latest adopted 15 December 1999, effective 30 December 1999; amended 2009 (2016)

Legal system: civil law system based on the Spanish civil code

international law organization participation: has not submitted an ICJ jurisdiction declaration; accepts ICCt jurisdiction

Citizenship: *citizenship by birth:* yes citizenship by descen t: yes
dual citizenship recognized: no
residency requirement for Naturalization: 5 years

Suffrage: 18 years of age; universal

Executive branch: *chief of state:* President Nicolas MADURO Moros (since 19 April 2013); Executive Vice President Aristobulo ISTURIZ (since 6 January 2016); note—the president is both chief of state and head of government

head of government: President Nicolas MADURO Moros (since 19 April 2013); Executive Vice President Aristobulo ISTURIZ (since 6 January 2016)
cabinet: Council of Ministers appointed by the president
elections/appointments: president directly elected by simple majority popular vote for a 6-year term (no term limits); election last held on 14 April 2013—a special election held following the death of President Hugo CHAVEZ Frias on 5 March 2013 (next election expected in late 2018 or early 2019 pending official convocation by the country's electoral body)
election results: Nicolas MADURO Moros elected president; percent of vote—Nicolas MADURO Moros (PSUV) 50.6%, Henrique CAPRILES Radonski (PJ) 49.1%, other 0.3%

Legislative branch: *description:* unicameral National Assembly or Asamblea Nacion al (167 seats; 113 members directly elected in single- and multi-seat constituencies by simple majority vote, 51 directly elected in multi-seat constituencies by proportional representation vote, and 3 seats reserved for indigenous peoples of Venezuela; members serve 5-year terms)
elections: last held on 6 December 2015 (next expected to be held in 2020)
election results: percent of vote by party—MUD (opposition coalition) 56.3%, PSUV (pro-government) 40.9%, other 2.8%; seats by party—MUD 112, PSUV 55

Judicial branch: *highest court(s):* Supreme Tribunal of Justice (consists of 32 judges organized into 6 divisions -constitutional, political administrative, electoral, civil appeals, criminal appeals, and social (mainly agrariaNAnd labor issues)

judge selection and term of office: judges proposed by the Committee of Judicial Postulation (an independent body of organizations dealing with legal issues and of the organs of citizen power) and appointed by the National Assembly; judges serve non-renewable 12-year terms
subordinate courts: Superior or Appeals Courts (Tribunales Superiores); District Tribunals (Tribunales de Distrito); Courts of First Instance (Tribunales de Primera Instancia); Parish Courts (Tribunales de Parroquia); Justices of the Peace (Justicia de Paz) Network

Political parties and leaders: A New Time or UNT [Enrique MARQUEZ]
Brave People's Alliance or ABP [Richard BLANCO]
Christian Democrats or COPEI [Roberto ENRIQUEZ]
Coalition of opposition parties—The Democratic Unity Table or MUD [Jesus "Chuo" TORREALBA]
Communist Party of Venezuela or PCV [Oscar FIGUERA]
Democratic Action or AD [Henry RAMOS ALLUP]
Fatherland for All or PPT [Rafael UZCATEGUI]
For Social Democracy or PODEMOS [Didalco Antonio BOLIVAR GRATEROL]
Justice First or PJ [Julio BORGES]
Movement Toward Socialism or MAS [Segundo MELENDEZ]
Popular Will or VP [Leopoldo LOPEZ]
Progressive Wave or AP [Henri FALCON]
The Radical Cause or La Causa R [Americo DE GRAZIA]
United Socialist Party of Venezuela or PSUV [Nicolas MADURO]
Venezuelan Progressive Movement or MPV [Simon CALZADILLA]
Venezuela Projector PV [Henrique Fern and os ALASFEO]

Political pressure groups and leaders: Bolivarian and Socialist Workers' Union (a ruling-party-oriented organized labor union)
Confederacion Venezolana de Industriales or Coindustria (a conservative business group)
Consejos Comunales (pro-government local communal councils)
Federation of Chambers and Associations of Commerce and Production of Venezuela or FEDECAMARAS (a conservative business group)
Union of Oil Workers of Venezuela or FUTPV
Venezuelan Confederation of Workers or CTV (opposition-oriented labor organization)
other: various civil society groups and human rights organizations

International organization participation: Caricom (observer), CD, CDB, CELAC, FAO, G-15, G-24, G-77, IADB, IAEA, IBRD, ICAO, ICC (National committees), ICCt (signatory), ICRM, IDA, IFAD, IFC, IFRCS, IHO, ILO, IMF, IMO, IMSO, Interpol, IOC, IOM, IPU, ITSO, ITU, ITUC (NGOs), LAES, LAIA, LAS (observer), Mercosur, MIGA, NAM, OAS, OPANAL, OPCW, OPEC, PCA, Petrocaribe, UN, UN Security

Council (temporary), UNASUR, UNCTAD, UNESCO, UNHCR, UNIDO, Union Latina, UNWTO, UPU, WCO, WFTU (NGOs), WHO, WIPO, WMO, WTO

Diplomatic representation in the US: *chief of mission:* Ambassador (vacant); Charge d'Affaires Maximilien SANCHEZ Arvelaiz (since July 2014)
chancery: 1099 30th Street NW, Washington, DC 20007
telephone: [1] (202) 342-2214
FAX: [1] (202) 342-6820
consulate(s) general: Boston, Chicago, Houston, Miami, New Orleans, New York, San Francisco, San Juan (Puerto Rico)

Diplomatic representation from the US: *chief of mission:* Ambassador (vacant); Charge d'Affaires Lee MCCLENNY (July 2014)
embassy: Calle Fcon Calle Suapure, Urbanizacion Colinas de Valle Arriba, Caracas 1080
mailing address: P. O. Box 62291, Caracas 1060-A; APO AA 34037
telephone: [58] (212) 975-6411, 907-8400 (after hours)
FAX: [58] (212) 907-8199

Flag description: three equal horizontal bands of yellow (top), blue, and red with the coat of arms on the hoist side of the yellow band and an arc of eight white five-pointed stars centered in the blue band; the flag retains the three equal horizontal bands and three main colors of the banner of Gran Colombia, the South American republic that broke up in 1830; yellow is interpreted as standing for the riches of the land, blue for the courage of its people, and red for the blood shed in attaining independence; the seven stars on the original flag represented the seven provinces in Venezuela that united in the war of independence; in 2006, then President Hugo CHAVEZ ordered an eighth star added to the star arc—a decision that sparked much controversy—to conform with the flag proclaimed by Simon Bolivar in 1827 and to represent the historic province of Guyana

National symbol(s): troupial (bird); National colors: yellow, blue, red

National anthem: *name:* "G loria al bravo pu eblo" (Glory to the Brave People)
lyrics/music: Vicente SALIAS/Juan Jose LANDAETA
note: adopted 1881; lyrics written in 1810, the music some years later; both SALIAS and LANDAETA were executed in 1814 during Venezuela's struggle for independence

ECONOMY

Economy—overview: Venezuela remains highly dependent on oil revenues, which account for almost all export earnings and nearly half of the government's revenue. The country ended 2015 with an estimated 10% contraction in its GDP, 275% inflation, widespread shortages of consumer goods, and declining central bank international reserves. The IMF forecasts that the GDP will shrink another 8% in 2016 and inflation may reach 720%. Falling oil prices since 2014 have aggravated

Venezuela's economic crisis. Insufficient access to dollars, price controls, and rigid labor regulations have led some US and multiNational firms to reduce or shut down their Venezuelan operations. Market uncertainty and state oil company PDVSA's poor cash flow have slowed investment in the petroleum sector, resulting in a decline in oil production. Under President Nicolas MADURO, the Venezuelan Government's response to the economic crisis has been to increase state control over the economy and blame the private sector for the shortages. The Venezuelan Government has maintained strict currency controls since 2003. On 17 February 2016, the Venezuelan Government announced a change from three official currency exchange mechanisms to only two official rates for the sale of dollars to private sector firms and individuals, with rates based on the government's import priorities. The official exchange rate used for food and medicine imports was devalued to 10 bolivars per dollar from 6.3 bolivars per dollar. The second rate moved to a managed float. These currency controls present significant obstacles to trade with Venezuela because importers cannot obtain sufficient dollars to purchase goods needed to maintain their operations. MADURO has used decree powers to enact legislation to deepen the state's role as the primary buyer and distributor of imports, further tighten currency controls, cap business profits, and extend price controls.

GDP (purchasing power parity): $515.7 billion (2015 est.)
$546.9 billion (2014 est.)
$569.1 billion (2013 est.)
note: data are in 2015 US dollars
country comparison to the world: 38

GDP (official exchange rate): $239.6 billion (2015 est.)

GDP—real growth rate: -5.7% (2015 est.)
-3.9% (2014 est.)
1.3% (2013 est.)
country comparison to the world: 216

GDP—per capita (PPP): $16,700 (2015 est.)
$18,000 (2014 est.)
$19,000 (2013 est.)
note: data are in 2015 US dollars
country comparison to the world: 96

Gross National saving: 12.2% of GDP (2015 est.)
15.3% of GDP (2014 est.)
22.2% of GDP (2013 est.)
country comparison to the world: 138

GDP—composition, by end use:
household consumption: 72%
government consumption: 19%
investment in fixed capital: 22.7%
investment in inventories: 8.2%
exports of goods and services: 13.4%
imports of goods and services: -35.2% (2015 est.)

GDP—composition, by sector of origin:
agriculture: 3.9%
industry: 32.9%
services: 63.2% (2015 est.)

Agriculture—products: corn, sorghum, sugarcane, rice, bananas, vegetables, coffee; beef, pork, milk, eggs; fish

Industries: agricultural products, livestock, raw materials, machinery and equipment, transport equipment, construction materials, medical equipment, pharmaceuticals, chemicals, iron and steel products, crude oil and petroleum Products

Industrial production growth rate: -6.8% (2015 est.)
country comparison to the world: 193

Labor force: 14.49 million (2015 est.)
country comparison to the world: 40

Labor force—by occupation: *agriculture:* 7.3%
industry: 21.8%
services: 70.9% (4th quarter, 2011 est.)

Unemployment rate: 8.1% (2015 est.)
7% (2014 est.)
country comparison to the world: 94

Population below poverty line: 32.1% (2013 est.)

Household income or consumption by percentage share: *lowest:* 10%: 1.7%
highest: 10%: 32.7% (2006)

Distribution of family income—Gini index: 39 (2011) 49.5 (1998)
country comparison to the world: 69

Budget: *revenues:* $203.4 billion
expenditures: $348.3 billion (2015 est.)
Taxes and other revenues: 154.3% of GDP (2015 est.)
country comparison to the world: 1

Budget surplus (+) or deficit (–): -109.9% of GDP (2015 est.)
country comparison to the world: 220

Public debt: 51.2% of GDP (2015 est.)
52.4% of GDP (2014 est.)
note: data cover central government debt, as well as the debt of state-owned oil company PDVSA; the data include treasury debt held by foreign entities; the data include some debt issued by sub national entities, as well as intra-governmental debt; intra-governmental debt consists of treasury borrowings from surpluses in the social funds, such as for retirement, medical care, and unemployment; some debt instruments for the social funds are sold at public auctions
country comparison to the world: 80

Fiscal year: calendar year

Inflation rate (consumer prices): 121.7% (2015 est.)
62.2% (2014 est.)
country comparison to the world: 226

Central bank discount rate: 29.5% (2015)
29.5% (2015)
country comparison to the world: 1

Commercial bank prime lending rate: 19.54% (31 December 2015 est.)
17.44% (31 December 2014 est.)
country comparison to the world: 13

Stock of narrow money:
$368.9 billion (31 December 2015 est.)
$314.1 billion (31 December 2014 est.)

country comparison to the world: 13

Stock of broad money: $360 billion (31 December 2014 est.)
$196 billion (31 December 2013 est.)
country comparison to the world: 28

Stock of domestic credit: $399 billion (31 December 2015 est.)
$337 billion (31 December 2014 est.)
country comparison to the world: 29

Market value of publicly traded shares: $25.3 billion (31 December 2012 est.)
$5.143 billion (31 December 2011)
$3.991 billion (31 December 2011)
country comparison to the world: 62

Current account balance: -$18.15 billion (2015 est.) $3.598 billion (2014 est.)
country comparison to the world: 186

Exports: $47.53 billion (2015 est.)
$74.71 billion (2014 est.)
country comparison to the world: 54

Exports—commodities: petroleum and petroleum Products, bauxite and aluminum, minerals, chemicals, agricultural products

Exports—partners: US 26.6%, India 13.7%, China 11.7%, Cuba 6.4% (2015)

Imports: $33.36 billion (2015 est.)
$47.51 billion (2014 est.)
country comparison to the world: 63

Imports—commodities: agricultural products, livestock, raw materials, machinery and equipment, transport equipment, construction materials, medical equipment, petroleum Products, pharmaceuticals, chemicals, iron and steel products

Imports—partners: US 18.4%, China 15.3%, Brazil 9.7%, Colombia 5.9%, Mexico 4.2% (2015)

Reserves of foreign exchange and gold: $15.41 billion (31 December 2015 est.)
$22.09 billion (31 December 2014 est.)
country comparison to the world: 68

Debt—external: $109.5 billion (31 December 2014 est.)
$118.8 billion (31 December 2013 est.)
country comparison to the world: 48

Stock of direct foreign investment—at home: $58.84 billion (31 December 2015 est.)
$58.44 billion (31 December 2014 est.)
country comparison to the world: 58

Stock of direct foreign investment—abroad: $29.17 billion (31 December 2015 est.)
$27.74 billion (31 December 2014 est.)
country comparison to the world: 52

Exchange rates: bolivars (VEB) per US dollar—
6.284 (2015 est.)
6.284 (2014 est.)
6.284 (2013 est.)
4.29 (2012 est.)
4.289 (2011 est.)

ENERGY

Electricity—production: 123 billion kWh (2012 est.)
country comparison to the world: 31

Electricity—consumption: 97.69 billion kWh (2012 est.)
country comparison to the world: 33

Electricity—exports: 705 million kWh (2012 est.)
country comparison to the world: 60

Electricity—imports: 478 million kWh (2013 est.)
country comparison to the world: 76

Electricity—installed generating capacity: 26.31 million kW (2012 est.)
country comparison to the world: 33

Electricity—from fossil fuels: 44.3% of total installed capacity (2012 est.)
country comparison to the world: 159

Electricity—fron nuclear fuels: 0% of total installed capacity (2012 est.)
country comparison to the world: 203

Electricity—from hydroelectric plants: 55.6% of total installed capacity (2012 est.)
country comparison to the world: 42

Electricity—from other renewable sources: 0.1% of total installed capacity (2012 est.)
country comparison to the world: 121

Crude oil—production: 2.5 million bbl/day (2014 est.)
country comparison to the world: 10

Crude oil—exports: 1.358 million bbl/day (2012 est.)
country comparison to the world: 10

Crude oil—imports: 0 bbl/day (2012 est.)
country comparison to the world: 143

Crude oil—proved reserves: 298.4 billion bbl (1 January 2015 est.)
country comparison to the world: 1

Refined petroleum Products—production: 1.036 million bbl/day (2012 est.)
country comparison to the world: 23

Refined petroleum Products—consumption: 746,000 bbl/day (2013 est.)
country comparison to the world: 27

Refined petroleum Products—exports: 463,500 bbl/day (2012 est.)
country comparison to the world: 15

Refined petroleum Products—imports: 36,760 bbl/day (2012 est.)
country comparison to the world: 89

Natural gas—production: 21.88 billion cu m (2014 est.)
country comparison to the world: 29

Natural gas—consumption: 23.72 billion cu m (2014 est.)
country comparison to the world: 33

Natural gas—exports: 0 cu m (2014 est.)
country comparison to the world: 205

Natural gas—imports: 1.839 billion cu m (2014 est.)
country comparison to the world: 51

Natural gas—proved reserves: 5.562 trillion cu m (1 January 2014 est.)
country comparison to the world: 8

Carbondioxideemissions from consumption of energy: 184.8 million Mt (2012 est.)

country comparison to the world: 32

COMMUNICATIONS

Telephones—fixed lines: *total subscriptions:* 7.81 million
subscriptions per 100 inhabitants: 27 (2014 est.)
country comparison to the world: 23

Telephones—mobile cellular: *total:* 30.5 million
subscriptions per 100 inhabitants: 106 (2014 est.)
country comparison to the world: 40

Telephone system: *general assessment:* modern and expanding
domestic: 2 domestic satellite systems with 3 earth stations; recent substantial improvement in telephone service in rural areas; substantial increase in digitalization of exchanges and trunk lines; installation of a National interurban fiber-optic network capable of digital multimedia services; combined fixed-line and mobile-cellular telephone subscribership 130 per 100 persons
International: country code—58; submarine cable systems provide connectivity to Cuba and the Caribbean, Central and South America, and US; satellite earth stations—1 Intelsat (Atlantic Ocean) and 1 PanAmSat; participating with Colombia, Ecuador, Peru, and Bolivia in the construction of an international fiber-optic network (2013)

Broadcast media: government supervises a mixture of state-run and private broadcast media; 13 public service networks, 61 privately owned TV networks, a privately owned news channel with limited National coverage, and a government-backed Pan-American channel; state-run radio network includes roughly 65 news stations and another 30 stations targeted at specific audiences; state-sponsored community broadcasters include 235 radio stations and 44 TV stations; the number of private broadcast radio stations has been declining, but many still remain in operation (2014)
Radio broadcast stations: AM 46, FM 131, shortwave 3 (2008)
Television broadcast stations: 66 (plus 45 repeaters) (1997)

Internet country code: .ve

Internet hosts: 1.016 million (2012)
country comparison to the world: 46

Internet users: *total:* 13.6 million
percent of population: 47.2% (2014 est.)
country comparison to the world: 37

TRANSPORTATION

Airports: 444 (2013)
country comparison to the world: 19

Airports—with paved runways: *total:* 127
over 3,047 m: 6
2,438 to 3,047 m: 9
1,524 to 2,437 m: 33
914 to 1,523 m: 62
under 914 m: 17 (2013)

Airports—with unpaved runways: *total:* 317
2,438 to 3,047 m: 3
1,524 to 2,437 m: 57

914 to 1,523 m: 127
under 914 m: 130 (2013)

Heliports: 3 (2013)

Pipelines: extra heavy crude 981 km; gas 5,941 km; oil 7,588 km; refined products 1,778 km (2013)

Railways: *total:* 447 km
standard gauge: 447 km 1.435-m gauge (41.4 km electrified) (2014)
country comparison to the world: 117

Roadways: *total:* 96,189 km (2014)
country comparison to the world: 48

Waterways: 7,100 km (Orinoco River (400 km) and Lake de Maracaibo navigable by oceangoing vessels) (2011)
country comparison to the world: 20

Merchant marine: *total:* 53
by type: bulk carrier 4, cargo 12, chemical tanker 1, liquefied gas 5, passenger 1, passenger/cargo 14, petroleum tanker 16
foreign-owned: 9 (Denmark 1, Estonia 1, Germany 1, Greece 4, Mexico 1, Spain 1)
registered in other countries: 14 (Panama 13, Saint Vincent and the Grenadines 1) (2010)
country comparison to the world: 69

Ports and terminals: *major seaport(s):* La Guaira, Maracaibo, Puerto Cabello, Punta Cardon
oil terminals: Jose terminal

Transportation—note: the international Maritime Bureau continues to report the territorial and offshore waters in the Caribbean Sea as at risk for piracy and armed robbery against ships; numerous vessels, including commercial shipping and pleasure craft, have been attacked and hijacked both at anchor and while underway; crews have been robbed and stores or cargoes stolen

MILITARY AND SECURITY

Military branches: Bolivarian National Armed Forces (Fuerza Armada Nacion al Bolivariana, FANB): Bolivarian Army (Ejercito Bolivariano, EB), Bolivarian Navy (Armada Bolivariana, AB; includes Naval Infantry, Coast Guard, Naval Aviation), Bolivarian Military Aviation (Aviacion

Militar Bolivariana, AMB; includes Air National Guard), Bolivarian National Guard (Guardia Nacional Bolivaria, GNB) (2015)

Military service age and obligation: all citizens of military service age (18–60 years old) are obligated to register for military service, though mandatory recruitment is forbidden; the minimum conscript service obligation is 12 months (2015)

Military expenditures: 1% of GDP (2015)
1.63% of GDP (2014)
1.4% of GDP (2013)
1.3% of GDP (2012)
country comparison to the world: 98

TRANSNATIONAL ISSUES

Disputes—international: claims all of the area west of the Essequibo River in Guyana, preventing any discussion of a maritime boundary; Guyana has expressed its intention to join Barbados in asserting claims before the UN Convention on the Law of the Sea that Trinidad and Tobago's maritime boundary with Venezuela extends into their waters; dispute with Colombia over maritime boundary and Venezuelan administered Los Monjes islands near the Gulf of Venezuela; Colombian organized illegal narcotics and paramilitary activities penetrate Venezuela's shared border region; US, France, and the Netherlands recognize Venezuela's granting full effect to Aves Island, thereby claiming a Venezuelan Economic Exclusion Zone/continental shelf extending over a large portion of the eastern Caribbean Sea; Dominica, Saint Kitts and Nevis, Saint Lucia, and Saint Vincent and the Grenadines protest Venezuela's full effect claim

Refugees and internally displaced persons: *refugees (country of origin):* 173,519 (Colombia) (2014)

Trafficking in persons: *current situation:* Venezuela is a source and destination country for men, women, and children subjected to sex trafficking and forced labor; Venezuelan women and girls, sometimes lured from poor interior regions to urban and tourist areas, are trafficked for sexual

exploitation within the country, as well as in the Caribbean; Venezuelan children are exploited, frequently by their families, in domestic servitude; people from South America, the Caribbean, Asia, and Africa are sex and labor trafficking victims in Venezuela; thousands of Cuban citizens, particularly doctors, who work in Venezuela on government social programs in exchange for the provision of resources to the Cuban Government experience conditions of forced labor

tier rating: Tier 3—Venezuela does not fully comply with the minimum standards for the elimination of trafficking and is not making significant efforts to do so; in 2014, the government appeared to increase efforts to hold traffickers criminally accountable, but a lack of government data made anti-trafficking law enforcement efforts difficult to assess; publically available information indicated many cases pursued under anti-trafficking law involved illegal adoption rather than sex and labor trafficking; authorities identified a small number of trafficking victims, and victim referrals to limited government services were made on an ad hoc basis; because no specialized facilities are available for trafficking victims, women and child victims accessed centers for victims of domestic violence or at-risk youth, and services for men were virtually nonexistent; NGOs provided some services to sex and labor trafficking victims; Venezuela has no permanent anti-trafficking interagency body, no National anti-trafficking plan, and still has not passed anti-trafficking legislation drafted in 2010 (2015)

Illicit drugs: small-scale illicit producer of opium and coca for the processing of opiates and coca derivatives; however, large quantities of cocaine, heroin, and marijuana transit the country from Colombia bound for US and Europe; significant narcotics-related money-laundering activity, especially along the border with Colombia and on Margarita Island; active eradication program primarily targeting opium; increasing signs of drug-related activities by Colombian insurgents on border

VIETNAM

INTRODUCTION

Background: The conquest of Vietnam by France began in 1858 and was completed by 1884. It became part of French Indochina in 1887. Vietnam declared independence after World War II, but France continued to rule until its 1954 defeat by communist forces under Ho Chi MINH. Under the Geneva Accords of 1954, Vietnam was divided into the communist North and anti-communist South. US economic and military aid to South Vietnam grew through the 1960s in an attempt to bolster the government, but US armed forces were withdrawn following a cease-fire agreement

in 1973. Two years later, North Vietnamese forces overran the South reuniting the country under communist rule. Despite the return of peace, for over a decade the country experienced little economic growth because of conservative leadership policies, the persecution and mass exodus of individuals—many of them successful South Vietnamese merchants—and growing international isolation. However, since the enactment of Vietnam's "doi moi" (renovation) policy in 1986, Vietnamese authorities have committed to increased economic liberalization and enacted structural reforms needed to modernize the economy and to produce more competitive, export-driven industries.

The communist leaders maintain tight control on political expression but have demonstrated some modest steps toward better protection of human rights. The country continues to experience small-scale protests, the vast majority connected to either land-use issues, calls for increased political space, or the lack of equitable mechanisms for resolving disputes. The small-scale protests in the urban Areas are often organized by human rights activists, but many occur in rural areas and involve various ethnic minorities such as the Montagnards of the Central Highlands, H'mong in the Northwest Highlands, and the Khmer Krom in the southern delta region.

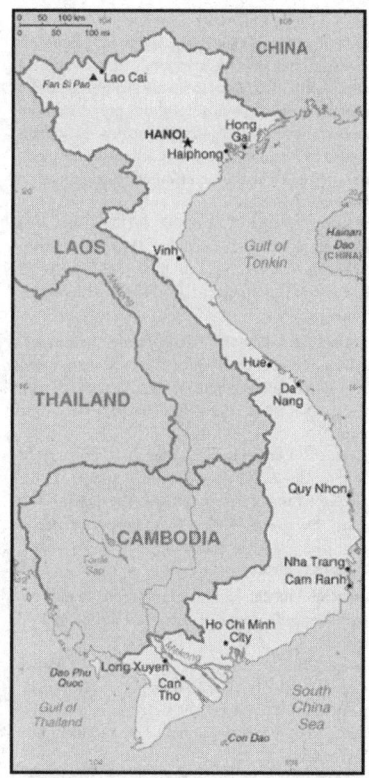

GEOGRAPHY

Location: SouthEastern asia, bordering the Gulf of Thailand, Gulf of Tonkin, and South China Sea, as well as China, Laos, and Cambodia

Geographic coordinates: 16 10 N, 107 50 E

Map references: Southeast Asia

Area: *total:* 331,210 sq km
land: 310,070 sq km
water: 21,140 sq km
country comparison to the world: 66

Area—comparative: about three times the size of Tennesee; slightly larger than New Mexico

Land boundaries: *total:* 4,616 km
border countries (3): Cambodia 1,158 km, China 1,297 km, Laos 2,161 km

Coastline: 3,444 km (excludes islands)

Maritime claims: *territorial sea:* 12 nm
contiguous zone: 24 nm
exclusive economic zone: 200 nm
continental shelf: 200 nm or to the edge of the continental margin

Climate: tropical in south; monsoon al in north with hot, rainy season (May to September) and warm, dry season (October to March)

Terrain: low, flat delta in south and north; central highlands; hilly, mountainous in far north and northwest

Elevation: *mean elevation:* 398 m

elevation extremes: *lowest point:* South China Sea 0 m
highest point: Fan Si Pan 3,144 m

Natural resources: phosphates, coal, manganese, rare earth elements, bauxite, chromate, offshore oil and gas deposits, timber, hydropower, arable land

Land use: *agricultural land:* 34.8%
arable land: 20.6%
permanent crops: 12.1%
permanent pasture: 2.1%
forest: 45%
other: 20.2% (2011 est.)

Irrigated land: 46,000 sq km (2012)

Total renewable water resources: 884.1 cu km (2011)

Freshwater withdrawal (domestic/industrial/agricultural): *total:* 82.03 cu km/yr (1%/4%/95%) per capita: 965 cu m/yr (2005)

Natural hazards: occasional typhoons (May to January) with extensive flooding, especially in the Mekong River delta

Environment—current issues: logging and slash-and-burNAgricultural practices contribute to deforestation and soil degradation; water pollution and overfishing threaten marine life populations; groundwater contamination limits potable water supply; growing urban industrialization and population migration are rapidly degrading environment in Hanoi and Ho Chi Minh City

Environment—International agreements: *party to:* Biodiversity, Climate Change, Climate Change-Kyoto Protocol, Desertification, Endangered Species, Environmental Modification, Hazardous Wastes, Law of the Sea, Ozone Layer Protection, Ship Pollution, Wetlands
signed, but not ratified: none of the selected agreements

Geography—note: extending 1,650 km north to south, the country is only 50 km across at its narrowest point

PEOPLE AND SOCIETY

Nationality: *noun:* Vietnamese (singular and plural)
adjective: Vietnamese

Ethnic groups: Kinh (Viet) 85.7%, Tay 1.9%, Thai 1.8%, Muong 1.5%, Khmer 1.5%, Mong 1.2%, Nung 1.1%, Hoa 1%, other 4.3% (2009 est.)

Languages: Vietnamese (official), English (increasingly favored as a second language), some French, Chinese, and Khmer, mountaiNArea languages (Mon-Khmer and Malayo-Polynesian)

Religions: Buddhist 7.9%, Catholic 6.6%, Hoa Hao 1.7%, Cao Dai 0.9%, Protestant 0.9%, Muslim 0.1%, none 81.8% (2009 est.)

Population: 94,348,835 (July 2015 est.)
country comparison to the world: 15

Age structure: *0–14 years:* 24.1% (male 11,948,130/female 10,786,381)
15–24 years: 17.22% (male 8,411,108/female 7,833,327)

25–54 years: 45.05% (male 21,358,647/female 21,145,416)
55–64 years: 7.81% (male 3,376,706/female 3,995,035)
65 years and over: 5.82% (male 2,115,057/female 3,379,028) (2015 est.)

Dependency ratios: *total dependency ratio:* 42.5%
youth dependency ratio: 32.9%
elderly dependency ratio: 9.6%
potential support ratio: 10.4% (2015 est.)

Median age: *total:* 29.6 years
male: 28.5 years
female: 30.7 years (2015 est.)
country comparison to the world: 116

Population growth rate: 0.97% (2015 est.)
country comparison to the world: 119

Birth rate: 15.96 births/1,000 population (2015 est.)
country comparison to the world: 121

Death rate: 5.93 deaths/1,000 population (2015 est.)
country comparison to the world: 169

Net migration rate: -0.3 migrant(s)/1,000 population (2015 est.)
country comparison to the world: 127

Urbanization: *urban population:* 33.6% of total population (2015)
rate of urbanization: 2.95% annual rate of change (2010–15 est.)

Major urban Areas—population: Ho Chi Minh City 7.298 million; HANOI (capital) 3.629 million; Can Tho 1.175 million; Haiphong 1.075 million; Da Nang 952,000; Bien Hoa 834,000 (2015)

Sex ratio: *at birth:* 1.11 male(s)/female
0–14 years: 1.11 male(s)/female
15–24 years: 1.07 male(s)/female
25–54 years: 1.01 male(s)/female
55–64 years: 0.85 male(s)/female
65 years and over: 0.63 male(s)/female
total population: 1 male(s)/female (2015 est.)

Maternal mortality rate: 54 deaths/100,000 live births (2015 est.)
country comparison to the world: 101

Infant mortality rate: *total:* 18.39 deaths/1,000 live births
male: 18.75 deaths/1,000 live births
female: 17.99 deaths/1,000 live births (2015 est.)
country comparison to the world: 96

Life expectancy at birth: *total population:* 73.16 years
male: 70.69 years
female: 75.9 years (2015 est.)
country comparison to the world: 132

Total fertility rate: 1.83 children born/woman (2015 est.)
country comparison to the world: 147

Contraceptive prevalence rate: 78.1% (2011)

Health expenditures: 6% of GDP (2013)
country comparison to the world: 92

Physicians density: 1.19 physicians/1,000 population (2013)

Hospital bed density: 2 beds/1,000 population (2010)

Drinking water source:
improved:
urban: 99.1% of population
rural: 96.9% of population
total: 97.6% of population
unimproved:
urban: 0.9% of population
rural: 3.1% of population
total: 2.4% of population (2015 est.)

Sanitation facility access:
improved:
urban: 94.4% of population
rural: 69.7% of population
total: 78% of population
unimproved:
urban: 5.6% of population
rural: 30.3% of population
total: 22% of population (2015 est.)

HIV/AIDS—adult prevalence rate: 0.47% (2014 est.)
country comparison to the world: 70

HIV/AIDS—people living with HIV/AIDS: 250,200 (2014 est.)
country comparison to the world: 22

HIV/AIDS—deaths: 10,600 (2014 est.)
country comparison to the world: 22

Major infectious diseases: *degree of risk:* very high
food or waterborne diseases: bacterial diarrhea, hepatitis A, and typhoid fever
vectorborne diseases: dengue fever, malaria, and Japanese encephalitis
note: highly pathogenic H5N1 avian influenza has been identified in this country; it poses a negligible risk with extremely rare cases possible among US citizens who have close contact with birds (2013)

Obesity—adult prevalence rate: 3.5% (2014)
country comparison to the world: 186

Children under the age of 5 years underweight: 12.1% (2013)
country comparison to the world: 60

Education expenditures: 6.3% of GDP (2012)
country comparison to the world: 33

Literacy: *definition:* age 15 and over can read and write
total population: 94.5%
male: 96.3%
female: 92.8% (2015 est.)

Child labor—children ages 5–14: *total number:* 2,545,616
percentage: 16% (2006 est.)

Unemployment, youth ages 15–24: *total:* 6%
male: 5.3%
female: 6.8% (2013 est.)
country comparison to the world: 124

GOVERNMENT

Country name: *conventional long form:* Socialist Republic of Vietnam
conventional short form: Vietnam

local long form: Cong Hoa Xa Hoi Chu Nghia Viet Nam
local short form: Viet Nam
abbreviation: SRV
etymology: "Viet nam" translates as "Viet south" where "Viet" is an ethnic self identification dating to a second century B.C. kingdom and "nam" refers to its location in relation to other Viet kingdoms

Government type: communist state

Capital: *name:* Hanoi (Ha Noi)
Geographic coordinates: 21 02 N, 105 51 E
time difference: UTC+7 (12 hours ahead of Washington, DC, during Standard Time)

Administrative divisions: 58 provinces (tinh, singular and plural) and 5 municipalities (thanh pho, singular and plural)
provinces: An Giang, Bac Giang, Bac Kan, Bac Lieu, Bac Ninh, Ba Ria-Vung Tau, Ben Tre, Binh Dinh, Binh Duong, Binh Phuoc, Binh Thuan, Ca Mau, Cao Bang, Dak Lak, Dak Nong, Dien Bien, Dong Nai, Dong Thap, Gia Lai, Ha Giang, Ha Nam, Ha Tinh, Hai Duong, Hau Giang, Hoa Binh, Hung Yen, Khanh Hoa, Kien Giang, Kon Tum, Lai Chau, Lam Dong, Lang Son, Lao Cai, Long An, Nam Dinh, Nghe An, Ninh Binh, Ninh Thuan, Phu Tho, Phu Yen, Quang Binh, Quang Nam, Quang Ngai, Quang Ninh, Quang Tri, Soc Trang, Son La, Tay Ninh, Thai Binh, Thai Nguyen, Thanh Hoa, Thua Thien-Hue, Tien Giang, Tra Vinh, Tuyen Quang, Vinh Long, Vinh Phuc, Yen Bai
municipalities: Can Tho, Da Nang, Ha Noi, Hai Phong, Ho Chi Minh City (Saigon)

Independence: 2 September 1945 (from France)

National holiday: Independence Day, 2 September (1945)

Constitution: several previous; latest adopted 15 April 1992, effective 1 January 1995; amended 2001,2013 (2016)

Legal system: civil law system; note—the civil code of 2005 reflects a European-style civil law

international law organization participation: has not submitted an ICJ jurisdiction declaration; non-party state to the ICCt

Citizenship: *citizenship by birth:* no
citizenship by descent only: at least one parent must be a citizen of Vietnam
dual citizenship recognized: no
residency requirement for Naturalization: 5 years

Suffrage: 18 years of age; universal

Executive branch: *chief of state:* President Tran Dai QUANG (since 2 April 2016); Vice President Dang Thi Ngoc THINH (since 7 April 2016)

head of government: Prime Minister Nguyen Xuan PHUC (since 7 April 2016); Deputy Prime Ministers Truong Hoa BinH (since 9 April 2016), Vuong Dinh HUE (since 9 April 2016), Vu Duc DAM (since 13 November 2013), Trinh Dinh DUNG (since 9 April 2016), Pham Binh MINH (since 13 November 2013)
cabinet: Cabinet proposed by prime minister, appointed by the president, and confirmed by the National Assembly

elections/appointments: president indirectly elected by National Assembly from among its members for a single 5-year term; election last held on 2 April 2016 (next to be held in spring 2021); prime minister appointed by the president from among members of the National Assembly, confirmed by National Assembly; deputy prime ministers appointed by the prime minister, confirmed by National Assembly
election results: Tran Dai QUANG (CPV) elected president; percent of National Assembly vote—98.9%; Nguyen Xuan PHUC elected prime minister; percent of National Assembly vote—91.0%

Legislative branch: *description:* unicameral National Assembly or Quoc Hoi (500 seats; members directly elected by absolute majority vote with a second round if needed; members serve 5-year terms)
elections: last held on 22 May 2016 (next to be held in May 2021)
election results: percent of vote by party—NA; seats by party—CPV 475, non-party CPV-approved 19, self-nominated 2; note—496 candidates were elected

Judicial branch: *highest court(s):* Supreme People's Court (consists of the chief justice and 13 judges)
judge selection and term of office: chief justice elected by the National Assembly on the recommendation of the president for a 5-year, renewable term; other judges appointed by the president for 5-year terms
subordinate courts: Court of Appeals; administrative, civil, criminal, economic, and labor courts; Central Military Court; People's Special Courts; note—the National Assembly can establish special tribunals

Political parties and leaders: Communist Party of Vietnam or CPV [Nguyen Phu TRONG]
note: other parties proscribed

Political pressure groups and leaders: 8406 Bloc
Democratic Party of Vietnam or DPV
People's Democratic Party Vietnam or PD P-VN
Alliance for Democracy
note: these groups advocate democracy but are not recognized by the government

International organization participation: ADB, APEC, ARF, ASEAN, CICA, CP, EAS, FAO, G-77, IAEA, IBRD, ICAO, ICC (NG Os), ICRM, ID A, IFAD, IFC, IFRCS, ILO, IMF, IMO, IMSO, Interpol, IOC, IOM, IPU, ISO, ITSO, ITU, MIGA, NAM, OIF, OPCW, PCA, UN, UNCTAD, UNESCO, UNIDO, UNWTO, UPU, WCO, WFTU (NGOs), WHO, WIPO, WMO, WTO

Diplomatic representation in the US: *chief of mission:* Ambassador Pham Quang VINH (since 23 February 2015)
chancery: 1233 20th Street NW, Suite 400, Washington, DC 20036
telephone: [1] (202) 861-0737
FAX: [1] (202) 861-0917
consulate(s) general: Houston, San Francisco
consulate: New York

Diplomatic representation from the US: *chief of mission:* Ambassador Ted G. OSIUS III (since 16 December 2014)
embassy: Rose Garden Building, 170 NGOc Khanh St., Hanoi
mailing address: 7 Lang Ha Street, Ba Dinh District, Hanoi; 4550 Hanoi Place, Washington, DC 205214550
telephone: [84] (4) 3850-5000
FAX: [84] (4) 3850-5010
consulate(s) general: Ho Chi Minh City

Flag description: red field with a large yellow five-pointed star in the center; red symbolizes revolution and blood, the fivepointed star represents the five elements of the populace—peasants, workers, intellectuals, traders, and soldiers—that unite to build socialism

National symbol(s): yellow, five-pointed star on red field; lotus blossom; National colors: red, yellow

National anthem: *name:* "Tien quan ca" (The Song of the Marching Troops)
lyrics/music: Nguyen Van CAO
note: adopted as the National anthem of the Democratic Republic of Vietnam in 1945; it became the National anthem of the unified Socialist Republic of Vietnam in 1976; although it consists of two verses, only the first is used as the official anthem

ECONOMY

Economy—overview: Vietnam is a densely populated developing country that has been transitioning from the rigidities of a centrally-planned economy since 1986. Agriculture's share of economic output has shrunk from about 25% in 2000 to 18% in 2014, while industry's share increased from 36% to 38% in the same period. State-owned enterprises now account for only about 40% of GDP. Vietnamese authorities have reaffirmed their commitment to economic modernization and a more open economy. Vietnam joined the WTO in January 2007, which has promoted more competitive, export-driven industries. Vietnam was one of 12-nations that concluded the Trans-Pacific Partnership free trade agreement negotiations in 2015. Hanoi has oscillated between promoting growth and emphasizing macroeconomic stability in recent years. During 2015, Vietnam's managed currency, the dong, depreciated about 5%. Poverty has declined significantly, and Vietnam is working to create jobs to meet the challenge of a labor force that is growing by more than one million people every year.
Vietnam is trying to reform its economy by restructuring public investment, state-owned enterprises, and the banking sector, although Hanoi's progress in meeting its goals is lagging behind the proposed schedule. Vietnam's economy continues to face challenges from an undercapitalized banking sector and Nonper formin gloans .

GDP (purchasing power parity): $552.3 billion (2015 est.)
$517.7 billion (2014 est.)
$488.5 billion (2013 est.)
note: data are in 2015 US dollars

country comparison to the world: 36
GDP (official exchange rate): $191.5 billion (2015 est.)
GDP—real growth rate: 6.7% (2015 est.)
6% (2014 est.) 5.4% (2013 est.)
country comparison to the world: 20
GDP—per capita (PPP): $6,000 (2015 est.)
$5,700 (2014 est.)
$5,400 (2013 est.)
note: data are in 2015 US dollars
country comparison to the world: 161
Gross National saving: 29% of GDP (2015 est.)
31.9% of GDP (2014 est.)
31.1% of GDP (2013 est.)
country comparison to the world: 27
GDP—composition, by end use:
household consumption: 66.5%
government consumption: 6.2%
investment in fixed capital: 24.4%
investment in inventories: 1.7%
exports of goods and services: 86.8%
imports of goods and services: -85.6% (2015 est.)
GDP—composition, by sector of origin:
agriculture: 17.4%
industry: 38.8%
services: 43.7% (2015 est.)
Agriculture—products: rice, coffee, rubber, tea, pepper, soybeans, cashews, sugar cane, peanuts, bananas; poultry; fish, sea food
Industries: food processing, garments, shoes, machine-building; mining, coal, steel; cement, chemical fertilizer, glass, tires, oil, mobile phones
Industrial production growth rate: 7.5% (2015 est.)
country comparison to the world: 15
Labor force: 54.93 million (2015 est.)
country comparison to the world: 12
Labor force—by occupation: *agriculture:* 48%
industry: 21%
services: 31% (2012)
Unemployment rate: 3% (2015 est.)
3.4% (2014 est.)
country comparison to the world: 23
Population below poverty line: 11.3% (2012 est.)
Household income or consumption by percentage share: *lowest:* 10%: 3.2%
highest: 10%: 30.2% (2008)
Distribution of family income—Gini index: 37.6 (2008)
36.1 (1998)
country comparison to the world: 78
Budget: *revenues:* $39.61 billion
expenditures: $47.39 billion (2015 est.)
Taxes and other revenues: 19.9% of GDP (2015 est.)
country comparison to the world: 158
Budget surplus (+) or deficit (–): -3.9% of GDP (2015 est.)
country comparison to the world: 142
Public debt: 52.7% of GDP (2015 est.)
52.9% of GDP (2014 est.)
note: official data; data cover general government debt, and includes debt instruments issued

(or owned) by government entities other than the treasury; the data include treasury debt held by foreign entities; the data include debt issued by sub national entities, as well as intra-governmental debt; intra-governmental debt consists of treasury borrowings from surpluses in the social funds, such as for retirement, medical care, and unemployment; debt instruments for the social funds are not sold at public auctions
country comparison to the world: 72
Fiscal year: calendar year
Inflation rate (consumer prices): 0.6% (2015 est.)
4.1% (2014 est.)
country comparison to the world: 65
Central bank discount rate: 9% (31 December 2012)
15% (31 December 2011)
country comparison to the world: 31
Commercial bank prime lending rate: 8.1% (31 December 2015 est.)
8.67% (31 December 2014 est.)
country comparison to the world: 106
Stock of narrow money: $63.48 billion (31 December 2015 est.)
$56.12 billion (31 December 2014 est.)
country comparison to the world: 46
Stock of broad money: $261.3 billion (31 December 2015 est.)
$235 billion (31 December 2014 est.)
country comparison to the world: 37
Stock of domestic credit: $232.2 billion (31 December 2015 est.) $209.6 billion (31 December 2014 est.)
country comparison to the world: 40
Market value of publicly traded shares: $38.2 billion (31 December 2011 est.)
$26 billion (31 December 2011)
$37 billion (31 December 2010 est.)
country comparison to the world: 56
Current account balance: $2.764 billion (2015 est.)
$9.33 billion (2014 est.)
country comparison to the world: 30
Exports: $158.7 billion (2015 est.)
$150.2 billion (2014 est.)
country comparison to the world: 28
Exports—commodities: clothes, shoes, electronics, seafood, crude oil, rice, coffee, wooden products, machinery
Exports—partners: US 21.2%, China 13.3%, Japan 8.4%, South Korea 5.5%, Germany 4.1% (2015)
Imports: $150.4 billion (2015 est.)
$138.1 billion (2014 est.)
country comparison to the world: 29
Imports—commodities: machinery and equipment, petroleum Products, steel products, raw materials for the clothing and shoe industries, electronics, plastics, automobiles
Imports—partners: China 34.1%, South Korea 14.3%, Singapore 6.5%, Japan 6.4%, Hong Kong 5.1%, Thailand 4.5% (2015)

927

Reserves of foreign exchange and gold: $39.6 billion (31 December 2015 est.)
$34.58 billion (31 December 2014 est.)
country comparison to the world: 45

Debt—external: $69.76 billion (31 December 2014 est.)
$65.46 billion (31 December 2013 est.)
country comparison to the world: 56

Stock of direct foreign investment—at home: $100.5 billion (31 December 2015 est.)
$90.9 billion (31 December 2014 est.)
country comparison to the world: 46

Stock of direct foreign investment—abroad: $7.7 billion (31 December 2009 est.)
$5.3 billion (31 December 2008 est.)
country comparison to the world: 65

Exchange rates: dong (VND) per US dollar—
21,928 (2015 est.)
21,189 (2014 est.)
21,189 (2013 est.)
20,859 (2012 est.)
20,649 (2011 est.)

ENERGY

Electricity—production: 118.2 billion kWh (2012 est.)
country comparison to the world: 32

Electricity—consumption: 108.3 billion kWh (2012 est.)
country comparison to the world: 32

Electricity—exports: 1.078 billion kWh (2012 est.)
country comparison to the world: 54

Electricity—imports: 3.254 billion kWh (2012 est.)
country comparison to the world: 51

Electricity—installed generating capacity: 24.54 million kW (2012 est.)
country comparison to the world: 34

Electricity—from fossil fuels: 48.9% of total installed capacity (2012 est.)
country comparison to the world: 150

Electricity—fron nuclear fuels: 0% of total installed capacity (2012 est.)
country comparison to the world: 205

Electricity—from hydroelectric plants: 50.9% of total installed capacity (2012 est.)
country comparison to the world: 48

Electricity—from other renewable sources: 0.2% of total installed capacity (2012 est.)
country comparison to the world: 113

Crude oil—production: 298,400 bbl/day (2014 est.)
country comparison to the world: 32

Crude oil—exports: 179,500 bbl/day (2012 est.)
country comparison to the world: 32

Crude oil—imports: 0 bbl/day (2012 est.)
country comparison to the world: 145

Crude oil—proved reserves: 4.4 billion bbl (1 January 2015 est.)
country comparison to the world: 25

Refined petroleum Products—production: 150,500 bbl/day (2012 est.)
country comparison to the world: 64

Refined petroleum Products—consumption: 471,000 bbl/day (2013 est.)
country comparison to the world: 34

Refined petroleum Products—exports: 34,670 bbl/day (2012 est.)
country comparison to the world: 67

Refined petroleum Products—imports: 298,400 bbl/day (2012 est.)
country comparison to the world: 24

Natural gas—production: 8.8 billion cu m (2013 est.)
country comparison to the world: 45

Natural gas—consumption: 8.8 billion cu m (2013 est.)
country comparison to the world: 48

Natural gas—exports: 0 cu m (2013 est.)
country comparison to the world: 207

Natural gas—imports: 0 cu m (2013 est.)
country comparison to the world: 77

Natural gas—proved reserves: 699.4 billion cu m (1 January 2014 est.)
country comparison to the world: 30

Carbon dioxide emissions from consumption of energy: 131.7 million Mt (2012 est.)
country comparison to the world: 36

COMMUNICATIONS

Telephones—fixed lines: *total subscriptions:* 5.56 million
subscriptions per 100 inhabitants: 6 (2014 est.)
country comparison to the world: 28

Telephone—mobile cellular: *total:* 136.1 million
subscriptions per 100 inhabitants: 146 (2014 est.)
country comparison to the world: 10

Telephone system: *general assessment:* Vietnam is putting considerable effort into modernization and expansion of its telecommunication system
domestic: all provincial exchanges are digitalized and connected to Hanoi, Da NAng, and Ho Chi Minh City by fiber-optic cable or microwave radio relay networks; main lines have been increased, and the use of mobile telephones is growing rapidly
International: country code—84; a landing point for the SEA-ME-WE-3, the C2C, and Thailand-Vietnam-H ong Kong submarine cable systems; the Asia-America Gateway submarine cable system, completed in 2009, provided new access links to Asia and the US; satellite earth stations—2 Intersputnik (Indian Ocean region) (2011)

Broadcast media: government controls all broadcast media exercising oversight through the Ministry of Information and Communication (MIC); government-controlled National TV provider, Vietnam Television (VTV), operates a network of 9 channels with several region al broadcasting centers; programming is relayed nationwide via a network of provincial and municipal TV stations; law limits access to satellite TV but many households are able to access foreign programming via home satellite equipment; government-controlled

Voice of Vietnam, the National radio broadcaster, broadcasts on 6 channels and is repeated on AM, FM, and shortwave stations throughout Vietnam (2008)
Radio broadcast stations: AM 65, FM 7, shortwave 29 (1999)
Television broadcast stations: 67 (includes 61 relay, provincial, and city TV stations) (2006)

Internet country code: .vn

Internet hosts: 189,553 (2012)
country comparison to the world: 74

Internet users: *total:* 40.1 million
percent of population: 43.0% (2014 est.)
country comparison to the world: 16

TRANSPORTATION

Airports: 45 (2013)
country comparison to the world: 97

Airports—with paved runways: *total:* 38
over 3,047 m: 10
2,438 to 3,047 m: 6
1,524 to 2,437 m: 13
914 to 1,523 m: 9 (2013)

Airports—with unpaved runways: *total:* 7
1,524 to 2,437 m: 1
914 to 1,523 m: 3
under 914 m: 3 (2013)

Heliports: 1 (2013)

Pipelines: condensate 72 km; condensate/gas 398 km; gas 955 km; oil 128 km; oil/gas/water 33 km; refined products 206 km; water 13 km (2013)

Railways: *total:* 2,600 km
standard gauge: 178 km 1.435-m gauge; 253 km mixed gauge
narrow gauge: 2,169 km 1.000-m gauge (2014)
country comparison to the world: 63

Roadways: *total:* 195,468 km
paved: 148,338 km
unpaved: 47,130 km (2013)
country comparison to the world: 24

Waterways: 47,130 km (30,831 km weight under 50 tons) (2011)
country comparison to the world: 4

Merchant marine: *total:* 579
by type: barge carrier 1, bulk carrier 142, cargo 335, chemical tanker 23, container 19, liquefied gas 7, passenger/cargo 1, petroleum tanker 48, refrigerated cargo 1, roll on/roll off 1, specialized tanker 1
registered in other countries: 86 (Cambodia 1, Kiribati 2, Mongolia 33, Panama 43, Taiwan 1, Tuvalu 6) (2010)
country comparison to the world: 20

Ports and terminals: *major seaport(s):* Cam Pha Port, Da Nang, Haiphong, Phu My, Quy Nhon
river port(s): Ho Chi Minh (Mekong)
container port(s) (TEUs): Haiphong (1,018,794), Saigon New Port (3,071,777)

Transportation—note: the InterNational Maritime Bureau reports the territorial and offshore waters in the South China Sea as high risk for piracy and armed robbery against ships; numerous commercial vessels have been attacked and hijacked both at anchor and while underway;

hijacked vessels are often disguised and cargo diverted to ports in East Asia; crews have been murdered or cast adrift

MILITARY AND SECURITY

Military branches: People's Armed Forces: People's Army of Vietnam (PAVN; includes Vietnam People's Navy (with Naval Infantry), Vietnam People's Air and Air Defense Force, Border Defense Command, Coast Guard) (2013)

Military service age and obligation: 18–25 years of age for male compulsory and voluntary military service; females may volunteer for active duty military service; conscription typically takes place twice annually and service obligation is 18 months (Army, Air Defense), 2 years (Navy and Air Force); 18–45 years of age (male) or 18–40 years of age (female) for Militia Force or Self Defense Force service; males may enroll in military schools at age 17 (2013)

Military expenditures: 2.37% of GDP (2012)
2.17% of GDP (2011)
2.37% of GDP (2010)
country comparison to the world: 33

TRANSNATIONAL ISSUES

Disputes—international: southeast Asian states have enhanced border surveillance to check the spread of avian flu; Cambodia and Laos protest Vietnamese squatters and armed encroachments along border; Cambodia accuses Vietnam of a wide variety of illicit cross-border activities; progress on a joint development area with Cambodia is hampered by an unresolved dispute over sovereignty of offshore islands; an estimated 300,000 Vietnamese refugees reside in China; establishment of a maritime boundary with Cambodia is hampered by unresolved dispute over the sovereignty of offshore islands; the decade-long demarcation of the China-Vietnam land boundary was completed in 2009; China occupies the Paracel Islands also claimed by Vietnam and Taiwan; Brunei claims a maritime boundary extending beyond as far as a median with Vietnam, thus asserting an implicit claim to Lousia Reef; the 2002 "D eclaration on the Conduct of Parties in the South China Sea" has eased tensions but falls short of a legally Binding "code of conduct" desired by several of the disputants; Vietnam continues to expand construction of facilities in the Spratly Islands; in March

2005, the National oil companies of China, the Philippines, and Vietnam signed a joint accord to conduct marine seismic activities in the Spratly Islands; Economic Exclusion Zone negotiations with Indonesia are ongoing, and the two countries in Fall 2011 agreed to work together to reduce illegal fishing along their maritime boundary

Refugees and internally displaced persons: *stateless persons:* 11,000 (2015); note—Vietnam's stateless ethnic Chinese Cambodian population dates to the 1970s when thousands of Cambodians fled to Vietnam to escape the Khmer Rouge and were no longer recognized as Cambodian citizens; Vietnamese women who gave up their citizenship to marry foreign men have found themselves stateless after divorcing and returning home to Vietnam; the government addressed this problem in 2009, and Vietnamese womeNAre beginning to reclaim their citizenship

Illicit drugs: minor producer of opiUMPoppy; probable minor transit point for Southeast Asian heroin; government continues to face domestic opium/heroin/methamphetamine addiction problems despite longstanding crackdowns; enforces the death penalty for drug trafficking

VIRGIN ISLANDS

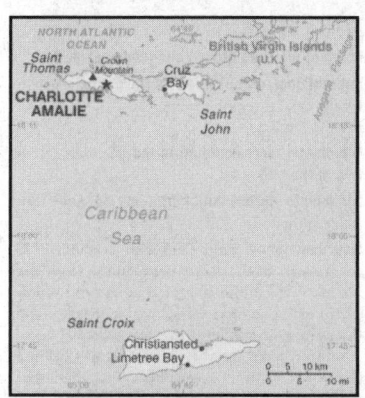

INTRODUCTION

Background: The Danes secured control over the southern Virgin Islands of Saint Thomas, Saint John, and Saint Croix during the 17th and early 18th centuries. Sugarcane, produced by African slave labor, drove the islands' economy during the 18th and early 19th centuries. In 1917, the US purchased the Danish holdings, which had been in economic decline since the abolition of slavery in 1848.

GEOGRAPHY

Location: Caribbean, islands between the Caribbean Sea and the North Atlantic Ocean, east of Puerto Rico

Geographic coordinates: 18 20 N, 64 50 W

Map references: Central America and the Caribbean

Area: *total:* 1,910 sq km
land: 346 sq km
water: 1,564 sq km
country comparison to the world: 182

Area—comparative: twice the size of Washington, DC

Land boundaries: 0 km

Coastline: 188 km

Maritime claims: *territorial sea:* 12 nm exclusive economic zone: 200 nm

Climate: subtropical, tempered by easterly trade winds, relatively low humidity, little season al temperature variation; rainy season September to November

Terrain: mostly hilly to rugged and mountainous with little flat land

Elevation: *mean elevation:* NA

elevation extremes: *lowest point:* Caribbean Sea 0 m
highest point: Crown Mountain 474 m

Natural resources: sun, sand, sea, surf

Land use: *agricultural land:* 11.5%
arable land: 2.9%
permanent crops: 2.9%
permanent pasture: 5.7%
forest: 57.4%
other: 31.1% (2011 est.)

Irrigated land: 1 sq km (2012)

Natural hazards: several hurricanes in recent years; frequent and severe droughts and floods; occasional earthquakes

Environment—current issues: lack of Natural freshwater resources

Geography—note: important location along the Anegada Passage—a key shipping lane for the Panama Canal; Saint Thomas has one of the best Natural deepwater harbors in the Caribbean

PEOPLE AND SOCIETY

Nationality: *noun:* Virgin Islander(s) (US citizens)
adjective: Virgin Islander

Ethnic groups: black 76%, white 15.6%, Asian 1.4%, other 4.9%, mixed 2.1%
note: 17.4% self-identify as latino (2010 est.)

Languages: English 71.6%, Spanish or Spanish Creole 17.2%, French or French Creole 8.6%, other 2.5% (2010 est.)

Religions: Protestant 59% (Baptist 42%, Episcopalian 17%), Roman Catholic 34%, other 7%

Population: 103,574 (July 2015 est.)
country comparison to the world: 195

Age structure: *0–14 years:* 17.47% (male 9,124/female 8,966)
15–24 years: 9.87% (male 4,642/female 5,576)
25–54 years: 38.71% (male 18,103/female 21,994)
55–64 years: 14.49% (male 7,194/female 7,819)
65 years and over: 19.46% (male 9,110/female 11,046) (2015 est.)

Dependency ratios: *total dependency ratio:* 61.2%
youth dependency ratio: 32.8%
elderly dependency ratio: 28.4%
potential support ratio: 3.5% (2015 est.)

Median age: *total:* 44.9 years

male: 45.2 years
female: 44.7 years (2015 est.)
country comparison to the world: 5

Population growth rate: -0.59% (2015 est.)
country comparison to the world: 226

Birth rate: 10.31 births/1,000 population (2015 est.)
country comparison to the world: 189

Death rate: 8.54 deaths/1,000 population (2015 est.)
country comparison to the world: 76

Net migration rate: -7.67 migrant(s)/1,000 population (2015 est.)
country comparison to the world: 206

Urbanization: *urban population:* 95.3% of total population (2015)
rate of urbanization: 0.25% annual rate of change (2010–15 est.)

Major urban Areas—population: CHARLOTTE AMALIE (capital) 52,000 (2014)

Sex ratio: *at birth:* 1.06 male(s)/female
0–14 years: 1.02 male(s)/female
15–24 years: 0.83 male(s)/female
25–54 years: 0.82 male(s)/female
55–64 years: 0.92 male(s)/female
65 years and over: 0.83 male(s)/female
total population: 0.87 male(s)/female (2015 est.)

Infant mortality rate: *total:* 6.64 deaths/1,000 live births
male: 7.35 deaths/1,000 live births
female: 5.89 deaths/1,000 live births (2015 est.)
country comparison to the world: 162

Life expectancy at birth: *total population:* 79.89 years
male: 76.84 years
female: 83.11 years (2015 est.)
country comparison to the world: 41

Total fertility rate: 1.74 children born/woman (2015 est.)
country comparison to the world: 167

Drinking water source: improved:
urban: 100% of population
rural: 100% of population
total: 100% of population
unimproved:
urban: 0% of popu lation
rural: 0% of population
total: 0% of population (2015 est.)

Sanitation facility access: improved:
urban: 96.4% of population
rural: 96.4% of population
total: 96.4% of population
unimproved:
urban: 3.6% of population
rural: 3.6% of population
total: 3.6% of population (2015 est.)

HIV/AIDS—adult prevalence rate: NA

HIV/AIDS—people living with HIV/AIDS: NA

HIV/AIDS—deaths: NA

GOVERNMENT

Country name: *conventional long form:* United States Virgin Islands

conventional short form: Virgin Islands former: Danish West Indies abbreviation: USVI
note: the myriad islets, cays, and rocks surrounding the major islands reminded Christopher COLUMBUS in 1493 of Saint Ursula and her 11,000 virgin followers (Santa Ursula y las Once Mil Virgenes), which over time shortened to the Virgins (las Virgenes)

Dependency status: organized, unincorporated territory of the US with policy relations between the Virgin Islands and the US under the jurisdiction of the Office of Insular Affairs, US Department of the Interior

Government type: presidential democracy; a self-governing territory of the US

Capital: *name:* Ch arlotte Amalie

Geographic coordinates: 18 21 N, 64 56 W
time difference: UTC-4 (1 hour ahead of Washington, DC, during Standard Time)

Administrative divisions: none (territory of the US); there are no first-order administrative divisions as defined by the US Government, but there are 3 islands at the second order; Saint Croix, Saint John, Saint Thomas

Independence: none (territory of the US)

National holiday: Transfer Day (from Denmark to the US), 31 March (1917)

Constitution: 22 July 1954—the Revised Organic Act of the Virgin Islands functions as a constitution for this territory of the US; revised 1962,2000 (2016)

Legal system: US common law

Citizenship: see United States

Suffrage: 18 years of age; universal; note—island residents are US citizens but do not vote in US presidential elections

Executive branch: *chief of state:* President Barack H. OBAMA (since 20 January 2009); Vice President Joseph R. BIDEN (since 20 January 2009)

head of government: Governor Kenneth MAPP (since 5 January 2015), Lieutenant Governor Osbert POTTER (since 5 January 2015)
cabinet: Territorial Cabinet appointed by the governor and confirmed by the Senate
elections/appointments: president and vice president indirectly elected on the same ballot by an Electoral College of 'electors' chosen from each state; president and vice president serve a 4-year term (eligible for a second term); under the US Constitution, residents of the Virgin Islands do not vote in elections for US president and vice president; however, they may vote in the Democratic and Republican presidential primary elections; governor and lieutenant governor directly elected on the same ballot by absolute majority vote in 2 rounds if needed for a 4-year term (eligible for a second term); election last held on 4 November 2014 (next to be held in November 2018)
election results: Kenneth MAPP elected governor; percent of vote in runoff—Kenneth MAPP (independent) 63.9%, Donna CHRISTIAN-CHRISTIANSEN (Democratic Party) 36.1%

Legislative branch: *description:* unicameral Senate (15 seats; members directly elected in single- and multi-seat constituencies by simple majority popular vote to serve 2-year terms)

elections: last held on 4 November 2014 (next to be held on 8 November 2016)
election results: percent of vote by party—NA; seats by party—NA
note: the Virgin Islands directly elects 1 member by simple majority vote to serve a 2-year term as a delegate to the US House of Representatives; the delegate can vote when serving on a committee and when the House meets as the Committee of the Whole House, but not when legislation is submitted for a "full floor" House vote; election of delegate last held on 4 November 2014 (next to be held on 8 November 2016)

Judicial branch: *highest court(s):* Supreme Court of the Virgin Islands (consists of the chief justice and 2 associate justices); note—court established by US Congress in 2004 and assumed appellate jurisdiction in 2007
judge selection and term of office: justices appointed by the governor and confirmed by the Virgin Islands Senate; justices initially serve renewable 10-year terms; chief justice elected to position by peers for a 3 -year term
subordinate courts: Superior Court (Territorial Court renamed in 2004); US Court of Appeals for the Third Circuit (has appellate jurisdiction over the District Court of the Virgin Islands; it is a territorial court and is not associated with a US federal judicial district); District Court of the Virgin Islands

Political parties and leaders: Democratic Party [Arturo WATLINGTON]
Independent Citizens' Movement or ICM [Usie RICHARDS]
Repu blican Party [Gary SPRAUVE]

Political pressure groups and leaders: NA

International organization participation: AOSIS (observer), Interpol (subbureau), IOC, UPU, WFTU (NGOs)

Diplomatic representation in the US: none (territory of the US)

Diplomatic representation from the US: none (territory of the US)

Flag description: white field with a modified US coat of arms in the center between the large blue initials V and I; the coat of arms shows a yellow eagle holding an olive branch in its right talon and three arrows in the left with a superimposed shield of seven red and six white vertical stripes below a blue panel; white is a symbol of purity, the letters stand for the Virgin Islands

National anthem: *name:* "Virgin Islands March"
lyrics/music: multiple/Alton augustus ADAMS, Sr.
note: adopted 1963; serves as a local anthem; as a territory of the US, "The Star-Spangled Banner" is official (see United States)

ECONOMY

Economy—overview: Tourism, trade, and other services are the primary economic activities, accounting for nearly 60% of the Virgin Island's GDP and about half of total civilian employment. The islands host nearly 3 million tourists per year, mostly from visiting cruise ships. The islands are vulnerable to damage from storms. The agriculture sector is small, with most food being imported. Industry and government each account for about one-fifth of GDP. The manufacturing sector consists of rum distilling, electronics, pharmaceuticals, and watch assembly. A refinery on St. Croix, one of the world's largest, processed 350,000 barrels of crude oil a day until it was shut down in February 2012, after operating for 45 years.

Federal programs and grants, totaling $241.4 million in 2013, contributed 19.7% of the territory's total revenues. The economy declined in 2013, due to decreases in exports resulting from the loss of refined oil products. Nevertheless, the economy remains relatively diversified. Along with a vibrant tourism industry, rum exports, trade, and services will be major income sources in future years.

GDP (purchasing power parity): $3.792 billion (2013 est.)
$4.143 billion (2012 est.)
$4.288 billion (2011 est.)
country comparison to the world: 178

GDP (official exchange rate): $5.075 billion (2013)

GDP—real growth rate: -5.4% (2013 est.)
-13.8% (2012 est.)
-7.5% (2011 est.)
country comparison to the world: 215

GDP—per capita (PPP): $36,100 (2013 est.)
$39,300 (2012 est.)
$40,500 (2011 est.)
country comparison to the world: 50

GDP—composition, by end use:
household consumption: 63.6%
government consumption: 28%
investment in fixed assets: 6.1%
investment in inventories: NA%
exports of goods and services: 69.3%
imports of goods and services: -66.9% (2013)

GDP—composition, by sector of origin:
agriculture: 2%
industry: 20%
services: 78% (2012 est.)

Agriculture—products: fruit, vegetables, sorghum; Senepol cattle

Industries: tourism, watch assembly, rum distilling, construction, pharmaceuticals, electronics

Industrial production growth rate: NA%

Labor force: 50,580 (2012 est.)
country comparison to the world: 193

Labor force—by occupation: *agriculture:* 1%
industry: 19%
services: 80% (2003 est.)

Unemployment rate: 13% (2014)
country comparison to the world: 140

Population below poverty line: 28.9% (2002 est.)

Household income or consumption by percentage share: *lowest:* 10%: NA%
highest: 10%: NA%

Budget: *revenues:* $1.223 billion
expenditures: $1.551 billion (2013)
Taxes and other revenues: 24.1% of GDP (2013)
country comparison to the world: 129

Budget surplus (+) or deficit (–): -6.5% of GDP (2013)
country comparison to the world: 189

Public debt: 45.9% of GDP (2014)

country comparison to the world: 94

Fiscal year: 1 October—30 September

Inflation rate (consumer prices): 3.1% (2012)
country comparison to the world: 140

Exports: $2.627 billion (2013)
$3.339 billion (2012)
country comparison to the world: 132

Exports—commodities: rum

Imports: $2.694 billion (2013)
$3.056 billion (2012)
country comparison to the world: 149

Imports—commodities: foodstuffs, consumer goods, building materials

Debt—external: $NA

Exchange rates: the US dollar is used

ENERGY

Electricity—production: 777.9 million kWh (2012 est.)
country comparison to the world: 157

Electricity—consumption: 723.5 million kWh (2012 est.)
country comparison to the world: 162

Electricity—exports: 0 kWh (2013 est.)
country comparison to the world: 213

Electricity—imports: 0 kWh (2013 est.)
country comparison to the world: 216

Electricity—installed generating capacity: 316,000 kW (2012 est.)
country comparison to the world: 149

Electricity—from fossil fuels: 100% of total installed capacity (2012 est.)
country comparison to the world: 34

Electricity—fron nuclear fuels: 0% of total installed capacity (2012 est.)
country comparison to the world: 206

Electricity—from hydroelectric plants: 0% of total installed capacity (2012 est.)
country comparison to the world: 211

Electricity—from other renewable sources: 0% of total installed capacity (2012 est.)
country comparison to the world: 141

Crude oil—production: 0 bbl/day (2014 est.)
country comparison to the world: 207

Crude oil—exports: 0 bbl/day (2012 est.)
country comparison to the world: 207

Crude oil—imports: 4,493 bbl/day (2012 est.)
country comparison to the world: 78

Crude oil—proved reserves: 0 bbl (1 January 2015 est.)
country comparison to the world: 208

Refined petroleum Products—production: 29,350 bbl/day (2012 est.)
country comparison to the world: 87

Refined petroleum Products—consumption: 110,500 bbl/day (2014 est.)
country comparison to the world: 75

Refined petroleum Products—exports: 43,710 bbl/day (2012 est.)
country comparison to the world: 60

Refined petroleum Products—imports: 131,400 bbl/day (2012 est.)
country comparison to the world: 42

Natural gas—production: 0 cu m (2014 est.)
country comparison to the world: 145

Natural gas—consumption: 0 cu m (2014 est.)
country comparison to the world: 208

Natural gas—exports: 0 cu m (2014 est.)
country comparison to the world: 208

Natural gas—imports: 0 cu m (2014 est.)
country comparison to the world: 78

Natural gas—proved reserves: 0 cu m (1 January 2014 est.)
country comparison to the world: 205

Carbon dioxide emissions from consumption of energy: 12.41 million Mt (2012 est.)
country comparison to the world: 96

COMMUNICATIONS

Telephone—fixed lines: *total subscriptions:* 76,100
subscriptions per 100 inhabitants: 73 (2014 est.)
country comparison to the world: 149

Telephones—mobile cellular: *total:* 80,300
subscriptions per 100 inhabitants: 74 (2005)
country comparison to the world: 195

Telephone system: *general assessment:* modern system with total digital switching, uses fiber-optic cable and microwave radio relay
domestic: full range of services available
International: country code—1 -340; submarine cable connections to US, the Caribbean, Central and South America; satellite earth stations—NA (2010)

Broadcast media: about a dozen TV broadcast stations including 1 public TV station; multi-channel cable and satellite TV services are available; 24 radio stations (2009)
Radio broadcast stations: AM 6, FM 16, short-wave 0 (2005)
Television broadcast stations: 5 (2006)

Internet country code: .vi

Internet hosts: 4,790 (2012)
country comparison to the world: 146

Internet users: *total:* 30,000
percent of population: 28.1% (2009)
country comparison to the world: 195

TRANSPORTATION

Airports: 2 (2013)
country comparison to the world: 207

Airports—with paved runways: *total:* 2
over 3,047 m: 1
1,524 to 2,437 m: 1 (2013)

Roadways: *total:* 1,260 km (2008)
country comparison to the world: 181

Ports and terminals: *major seaport(s):* Charlotte Amalie, Christiansted, Cruz Bay, Frederiksted, Limetree Bay

MILITARY AND SECURITY

Military—note: defense is the responsibility of the US

TRANSNATIONAL ISSUES

Disputes—international: none

931

INTRODUCTION

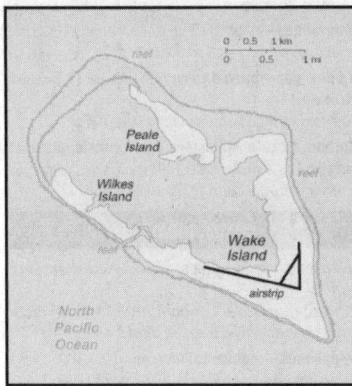

Background: The US annexed Wake Island in 1899 for a cable station. An important air and Naval base was constructed in 1940–41. In December 1941, the island was captured by the Japanese and held until the end of World War II. In subsequent years, Wake became a stopover and refueling site for military and commercial aircraft transiting the Pacific. Since 1974, the island's airstrip has been used by the US military, as well as for emergency landings. Operations on the island were temporarily suspended and all personnel evacuated in 2006 with the approach of super typhoon IOKE (category 5), but resultant damage was comparatively minor. A US Air Force repair team restored full capability to the airfield and facilities, and the island remains a vital strategic link in the Pacific region.

GEOGRAPHY

Location: Oceania, atoll in the North Pacific Ocean, about two-thirds of the way from Hawaii to the Northern Mariana Islands

Geographic coordinates: 19 17 N, 166 39 E

Map references: Oceania

Area: *total:* 6.5 sq km
land: 6.5 sq km
water: 0 sq km
country comparison to the world: 245

Area—comparative: about 11 times the size of the National Mall in Washington, DC

Land boundaries: 0 km

Coastline: 19.3 km

Maritime claims: *territorial sea:* 12 nm
exclusive economic zone: 200 nm

Climate: tropical

Terrain: atoll of three low coral islands, Peale, Wake, and Wilkes, built up on an underwater volcano; central lagoon is former crater, islands are part of the rim

Elevation: *mean elevation:* NA

elevation extremes: *lowest point:* Pacific Ocean 0 m
highest point: unnamed location 6 m

Natural resources: none

Land use: *agricultural land:* 0%
arable land: 0%
permanent crops: 0%
permanent pasture: 0%
forest: 0%
other: 100% (2011 est.)

Irrigated land: 0 sq km (2012)

Natural hazards: occasional typhoons

Environment—current issues: NA

Geography—note: strategic location in the North Pacific Ocean; emergency landing location for transpacific flights

PEOPLE AND SOCIETY

Population: no indigenous inhabitants
note: approximately 150 military personnel and civilian contractors maintain and operate the airfield and communications facilities (2009)

GOVERNMENT

Country name: *conventional long form:* none
conventional short form: Wake Island
etymology: although first discovered by British Captain William WAKE in 1792, the island is named after British Captain Samuel WAKE who rediscovered the island in 1796

Dependency status: unorganized, unincorporated territory of the US; administered from Washington, DC, by the Department of the Interior; activities in the atoll are currently conducted by the US Air Force

Legal system: US common law

Citizenship: see United States

Flag description: the flag of the US is used

ECONOMY

Economy—overview: Economic activity is limited to providing services to military personnel and contractors located on the island. All food and manufactured goods must be imported.

COMMUNICATIONS

Telephone system: *general assessment:* satellite communications; 2 Defense Switched Network circuits off the Overseas Telephone System (OTS); located in the Hawaii area code—808

Broadcast media: AmericaNArmed Forces Radio and Television Service (AFRTS) provides satellite radio/TV broadcasts (2009)
Radio broadcast stations: AM 0, FM 0, shortwave 0 (AmericaNArmed Forces Radio and Television Service (AFRTS)) provides satellite radio service (2005)
Television broadcast stations: 0 (2005)

TRANSPORTATION

Airports: 1 (2013)
country comparison to the world: 211

Airports—with paved runways: *total:* 1
2,438 to 3,047 m: 1 (2013)

Ports and terminals: none; two offshore anchorages for large ships

Transportation—note: there are no commercial or civilian flights to and from Wake Island, except in direct support of island missions; emergency landing is available

MILITARY AND SECURITY

Military—note: defense is the responsibility of the US; the US Air Force is responsible for overall administration and operation of the island facilities; the launch support facility is administered by the US Missile Defense Agency (MDA)

TRANSNATIONAL ISSUES

Disputes—international: claimed by Marshall Islands

WALLIS AND FUTUNA

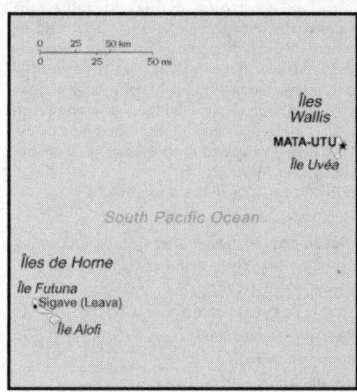

INTRODUCTION

Background: The Futuna island group was discovered by the Dutch in 1616 and Wallis by the British in 1767, but it was the French who declared a protectorate over the islands in 1842, and took official control of them between 1886 and 1888. Notably, Wallis and Futuna was the only French colony to side with the Vichy regime during World War II, a phase that ended in May of 1942 with the arrival of 2,000 American troops. In 1959, the inhabitants of the islands voted to become a French overseas territory and officially assumed this status in July 1961.

GEOGRAPHY

Location: Oceania, islands in the South Pacific Ocean, about two-thirds of the way from Hawaii to New Zealand

Geographic coordinates: 13 18 S, 176 12 W

Map references: Oceania

Area: *total:* 142 sq km
land: 142 sq km
water: 0 sq km
note: includes Ile Uvea (Wallis Island), Ile Futuna (Futuna Island), Ile Alofi, and 20 islets
country comparison to the world: 221

Area—comparative: 1.5 times the size of Washington, DC

Land boundaries: 0 km

Coastline: 129 km

Maritime claims: *territorial sea:* 12 nm
exclusive economic zone: 200 nm

Climate: tropical; hot, rainy season (November to April); cool, dry season (May to October); rains 250–300 cm per year (80% humidity); average temperature 26.6 degrees Celsius

Terrain: volcanic origin; low hills

Elevation: *mean elevation:* NA

elevation extremes: *lowest point:* Pacific Ocean 0 m
highest point: Mont Singavi (on Futuna) 765 m

Natural resources: NEGL

Land use: *agricultural land:* 42.8%
arable land: 7.1%
permanent crops: 35.7%
permanent pasture: 0%
forest: 41.9%
other: 15.3% (2011 est.)

Irrigated land: 0 sq km (2012)

Natural hazards: NA

Environment—current issues: deforestation (only small portions of the original forests remain) largely as a result of the continued use of wood as the main fuelsource; as a consequence of cutting down the forests, the mountainous terrain of Futuna is particularly prone to erosion; there are no permanent settlements on Alofi because of the lack of Natural freshwater resources

Geography—note: both island groups have fringing reefs

PEOPLE AND SOCIETY

Nationality: *noun:* Wallisian(s), Futunan(s), or Wallis and Futuna Islanders
adjective: Wallisian, Futunan, or Wallis and Futuna Islander

Ethnic groups: Polynesian

Languages: Wallisian (indigenous Polynesian language) 58.9%, Futunian 30.1%, French (official) 10.8%, other 0.2% (2003 census)

Religions: Roman Catholic 99%, other 1%

Population: 15,613 (July 2015 est.)
country comparison to the world: 222

Age structure: *0–14 years:* 22.71% (male 1,850/female 1,695)
15–24 years: 17.41% (male 1,426/female 1,292)
25–54 years: 41.11% (male 3,210/female 3,208)
55–64 years: 9.45% (male 731/female 744)
65 years and over: 9.33% (male 697/female 760) (2015 est.)

Median age: *total:* 30.9 years
male: 30 years
female: 32.2 years (2015 est.)
country comparison to the world: 106

Population growth rate: 0.33% (2015 est.)
country comparison to the world: 171

Birth rate: 13.45 births/1,000 population (2015 est.)
country comparison to the world: 149

Death rate: 5.06 deaths/1,000 population (2015 est.)
country comparison to the world: 187

Net migration rate: -5.06 migrant(s)/1,000 population
note: there has been steady emigration from Wallis and Futuna to New Caledonia (2015 est.)
country comparison to the world: ˙93

Urbanization: *urban population:* 0% of total population (2015)
rate of urbanization: 0% annual rate of change (2005–10 est.)

Major urban Areas—population: MATA-UTU (capital) 1,000 (2014)

Sex ratio: *at birth:* 1.05 male(s)/female
0–14 years: 1.09 male(s)/female
15–24 years: 1.1 male(s)/female
25–54 years: 1 male(s)/female
55–64 years: 0.98 male(s)/female
65 years and over: 0.92 male(s)/female
total population: 1.03 male(s)/female (2015 est.)

Infant mortality rate: *total:* 4.43 deaths/1,000 live births
male: 4.66 deaths/1,000 live births
female: 4.18 deaths/1,000 live births (2015 est.)
country comparison to the world: 186

Life expectancy at birth: *total population:* 79.57 years
male: 76.58 years
female: 82.7 years (2015 est.)
country comparison to the world: 44

Total fertility rate: 1.75 children born/woman (2015 est.)
country comparison to the world: 165

Sanitation facility access:
improved:
rural: 96% of population
total: 96% of population
unimproved:
rural: 4% of population
total: 4% of population (2008 est.)

HIV/AIDS—adult prevalence rate: NA

HIV/AIDS—people living with HIV/AIDS: NA

HIV/AIDS—deaths: NA

GOVERNMENT

Country name: *conventional long form:* Territory of the Wallis and Futuna Islands
conventional short form: Wallis and Futuna
local long form: Territoire des Iles Wallis et Futuna
local short form: Wallis et Futuna
etymology: Wallis Island is named after British Captain Samuel WALLIS who discovered it in 1767; Futuna is derived from the native word "futu," which is the name of the fish-poison tree found on the island

Dependency status: overseas territory of France

Government type: parliamentary democracy (Territorial Assembly); overseas collectivity of France

Capital: *name:* Mata-Utu (on Ile Uvea)

Geographic coordinates: 13 57 S, 171 56 W
time difference: UTC + 12 (17 hours ahead of Washington, DC, during Standard Time)

Administrative divisions: 3 administrative precincts (circonscriptions, singular—circonscription) Alo, Sigave, Uvea

Independence: none (overseas territory of France)

National holiday: Bastille Day, 14 July (1789)

Constitution: 4 October 1958 (French Constitution)

Legal system: French civil law

Citizenship: see France

Suffrage: 18 years of age; universal

Executive branch: *chief of state:* President Francois HOLLANDE (since 15 May 2012); represented by High Administrator Marcel RENOUF (since 26 January 2015)

head of government: President of the Territorial Assembly Mikaele KULIMOETOKE (since 26 November 2014)

cabinet: Council of the Territory appointed by the high administrator on the advice of the Territorial Assembly

elections/appointments: French president elected by absolute majority popular vote in 2 rounds if needed for a 5-year term (eligible for a second term); high administrator appointed by the French president on the advice of the French Ministry of the Interior; the presidents of the Territorial Government and the Territorial Assembly elected by assembly members

note: there are 3 traditional kings with limited powers

Legislative branch: *description:* unicameral Territorial Assembly or Assemblee Territoriale (20 seats; members directly elected in multi-seat constituencies by proportional representation to serve 5-year terms)

note: Wallis and Futuna elects 1 senator to the French Senate and 1 deputy to the French National Assembly; French Senate—elections last held on 28 September 2014 (next to be held by September 2017); results—percent of vote by party—NA; seats—UMP 1; French National Assembly—by-election last held on 24 March 2013 (next to be held by 2017); results—percent of vote by party—NA; seats—independent (backed by UMP) 1

elections: last held on 22 March 2012 (next to be held in March 2017)

election results: percent of vote by party—NA; seats by party—PS 4, UMP 4, centrist, 3, other 9

Judicial branch: *highest court(s):* Court of Appeal or Cour d'Appel, located in Noumea, New Caledonia

judge selection and term of office: NA

subordinate courts: note—justice generally administered under French law by the high administrator, but the 3 traditional kings administer customary law, and there is a magistrate in Mata-Utu

Political parties and leaders: Lua Kae Tahi (Giscardians)
Mouvement des Radicaux de Gauche or MRG
Rally for the Republic or RPR (UMP) [Clovis LOGOLOGOFOLAU]
Socialist Party or PS Taumu'a Lelei [Soane Muni UHILA]
Union Populaire Locale or UPL [Falakiko GATA]
Union Pour la Democratie Francaise or UDF

Political pressure groups and leaders: NA

International organization participation: PIF (observer), SPC, UPU

Diplomatic representation in the US: none (overseas territory of France)

Diplomatic representation from the US: none (overseas territory of France)

Flag description: unofficial, local flag has a red field with four white isosceles triangles in the middle, representing the three native kings of the islands and the French administrator; the apexes of the triangles are oriented inward and at right angles to each other; the flag of France, outlined in white on two sides, is in the upper hoist quadrant

note: the design is derived from an original red banner with a white cross pattee that was introduced in the 19th century by French mission aries; the flag of France is used for official occasions

National symbol(s): red saltire (Saint Andrew's Cross) on a white square on a red field; National colors: red, white

National anthem: *note:* as a territory of France, "La Marseillaise" is official (see France)

ECONOMY

Economy—overview: The economy is limited to traditional subsistence agriculture, with 80% of labor force earnings coming from agriculture (coconuts and vegetables), livestock (mostly pigs), and fishing. However, roughly 70% of the labor force is employed in the public sector, although only about 20% of the population is in salaried employment.

Revenues come from French Government subsidies, licensing of fishing rights to Japan and South Korea, import taxes, and remittances from expatriate workers in New Caledonia. France directly finances the public sector and healthcare and education services. It also provides funding for key development projects in a range of areas, including infrastructure, economic development, environmental management, and healthcare facilities. A key concern for Wallis and Futuna is an aging population with consequent economic development issues. Very few people aged 18–30 live on the islands due to the limited formal employment opportunities. Improving job creation is a current priority for the territorial government.

GDP (purchasing power parity): $60 million (2004 est.)

country comparison to the world: 225

GDP (official exchange rate): $NA

GDP—real growth rate: NA%

GDP—per capita (PPP): $3,800 (2004 est.)

country comparison to the world: 178

GDP—composition, by sector of origin:
agriculture: NA%
industry: NA%
services: NA%

Agriculture—products: coconuts, breadfruit, yams, taro, bananas; pigs, goats; fish

Industries: copra, handicrafts, fishing, lumber

Industrial production growth rate: NA%

Labor force: 3,104 (2003)

country comparison to the world: 225

Labor force—by occupation: *agriculture:* 80%
industry: 4%
services: 16% (2001 est.)

Unemployment rate: 12.2% (2008 est.)

country comparison to the world: 136

Population below poverty line: NA%

Household income or consumption by percentage share: *lowest:* 10%: NA%
highest: 10%: NA%

Budget: *revenues:* $29,730
expenditures: $31,330 (2004)
Taxes and other revenues: NA%

Budget surplus (+) or deficit (−): NA%

Public debt: 5.6% of GDP (2004 est.)

note: offical data; data cover general government debt, and includes debt instruments issued (or owned) by government entities other than the treasury; the data include treasury debt held by foreign entities; the data include debt issued by subnational entities, as well as intra-governmental debt; intra-governmental debt consists of treasury borrowings from surpluses in the social funds, such as for retirement, medical care, and unemployment; debt instruments for the social funds are not sold at public auctions

country comparison to the world: 178

Fiscal year: calendar year

Inflation rate (consumer prices): 2.8% (2005)

country comparison to the world: 135

Exports: $47,450 (2004 est.)

country comparison to the world: 223

Exports—commodities: copra, chemicals, construction materials

Imports: $61.17 million (2004)

country comparison to the world: 219

Imports—commodities: chemicals, machinery, consumer goods

Debt—external: $3.67 million (2004)

country comparison to the world: 202

Exchange rates: Comptoirs Francais du Pacifique francs (XPF) per US dollar—
89.85 (2013 est.)
90.56 (2012 est.)
85.74 (2011 est.)

COMMUNICATIONS

Telephone system: *International:* country code—681

Broadcast media: the publicly owned French Overseas Network (RFO), which broadcasts to France's overseas departments and territories, is carried on the RFO Wallis and Fortuna TV and radio stations (2008)

Radio broadcast stations: AM 1, FM 0, shortwave 0 (2000)

Television broadcast stations: 2 (2000)

Internet country code: . wf

Internet hosts: 2,760 (2012)

country comparison to the world: 157

Internet users: *total:* 1,300
percent of population: 8.5% (2009)
country comparison to the world: 211

TRANSPORTATION

Airports: 2 (2013)

country comparison to the world: 208

Airports—with paved runways: *total:* 2
1,524 to 2,437 m: 1
914 to 1,523 m: 1 (2013)

Ports and terminals: *major seaport(s):* Leava, Mata-Utu

MILITARY AND SECURITY

Military—note: defense is the responsibility of France

TRANSNATIONAL ISSUES

Disputes—international: none

WEST BANK

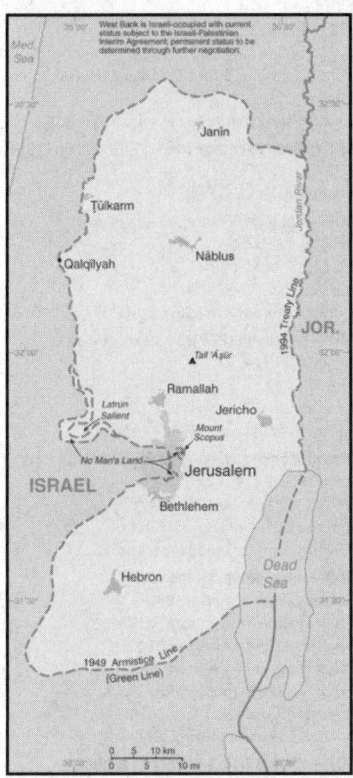

West Bank is Israeli-occupied with current status subject to the Israeli-Palestinian Interim Agreement; permanent status to be determined through further negotiation.

INTRODUCTION

Background: From the early 16th century through 1917, the area now known as the West Bank fell under Ottoman rule. Following World War I, the Allied powers (France, UK, Russia) allocated the area to the British Mandate of Palestine. After World War II, the UN passed a resolution to establish two states within the Mandate, and designated a territory including what is now known as the West Bank as part of the proposed Arab state. Following the 1948 Arab-Israeli War, the area was captured by Transjordan (later renamed Jordan). JordaNAnnexed the West Bank in 1950. In June 1967, Israel captured the West Bank and East Jerusalem during the 1967 Six-Day War. With the exception of East Jerusalem, roughly 60% of the West Bank remains under Israeli military control. Israel transferred security and civilian responsibility for a number of Palestinian-populated areas of the West Bank and Gaza Strip to the PalestiniaNAuthority (PA) under a series of agreements signed between 1994 and 1999, the so-called "Oslo Accords." Negotiations to determine the permanent status of the West Bank and Gaza Strip stalled after the outbreak of an intifada

in mid-2000. In early 2003, the "Quartet" of the US, EU, UN, and Russia, presented a roadmap to a final peace settlement by 2005, calling for two states—Israel and a democratic Palestine. Following Palestinian leader Yassir ARAFAT's death in late 2004 and the subsequent election of Mahmoud ABBAS (head of the Fatah political faction) as PA president, Israel and the Palestinians agreed to move the peace process forward. Israel in late 2005 unilaterally withdrew all of its settlers and soldiers and dismantled its military facilities in the Gaza Strip and redeployed its military from several West Bank settlements but continues to control maritime, airspace, and other access. In early 2006, the Islamic Resistance Movement, HAMAS, won the Palestinian Legislative Council election and took control of the PA government. Attempts to form a unity government failed, and violent clashes between Fatah and HAMAS supporters ensued, culminating in HAMAS's violent seizure of all military and governmental institutions in the Gaza Strip. Fatah and HAMAS have made several attempts at reconciliation, but the factions have been unable to implement details on governance and security. In an attempt to reenergize peace talks between the Israelis and Palestinians, France in June 2016 hosted a ministerial meeting that included participants from 29 countries, although not Israel or the Palestinians, to lay the groundwork for an envisioned "multilateral peace conference" later in the year.

GEOGRAPHY

Location: Middle East, west of Jordan, east of Israel

Geographic coordinates: 32 00 N, 35 15 E

Map references: Middle East

Area: *total:* 5,860 sq km
land: 5,640 sq km
water: 220 sq km
note: includes West Bank, Latrun Salient, and the northwest quarter of the Dead Sea, but excludes Mt. Scopus; East Jerusalem and Jerusalem No Man's Land are also included only as a means of depicting the entire area occupied by Israel in 1967
country comparison to the world: 172

Area—comparative: slightly smaller than Delaware

Land boundaries: *total:* 478 km
border countries (2): Israel 330 km, Jordan 148 km

Coastline: 0 km (landlocked)

Maritime claims: none (landlocked)

Climate: temperate; temperature and precipitation vary with altitude, warm to hot summers, cool to mild winters

Terrain: mostly rugged, dissected upland in west, flat plains descending to Jordan River valley to the east

Elevation: *mean elevation:* NA

elevation extremes: *lowest point:* Dead Sea -408 m
highest point: Tall Asur 1,022 m

Natural resources: arable land

Land use: *agricultural land:* 43.3%
arable land: 7.4%
permanent crops: 11%
permanent pasture: 24.9%
forest: 1.5%
other: 55.2%
note: includes Gaza Strip (2011 est.)

Irrigated land: 240 sq km; note—includes Gaza Strip (2003)

Natural hazards: droughts

Environment—current issues: adequacy of freshwater supply; sewage treatment

Geography—note: landlocked; highlands are main recharge area for Israel's coastal aquifers; there are about 381 Israeli civilian sites, including about 212 settlements and 134 small outpost communities in the West Bank and 35 sites in East Jerusalem (2014 est.)

PEOPLE AND SOCIETY

Nationality: *noun:* NA
adjective: NA

Ethnic groups: PalestiniaNArab and other 83%, Jewish 17%

Languages: Arabic, Hebrew (spoken by Israeli settlers and many Palestinians), English (widely understood)

Religions: Muslim 80–85% (predominantly Sunni), Jewish 12–14%, Christian 1–2.5% (mainly Greek Orthodox), other, unaffiliated, unspecified <1%
note: the proportion of Christians continues to fall mainly as a result of the growth of the Muslim population but also because of migration and the declining birth rate of the Christian population (2012 est.)

Population: 2,785,366 (represents Palestinian population only) (July 2015 est.)
note: approximately 371,000 Israeli settlers live in the West Bank; approximately 211,640 Israeli settlers live in East Jerusalem (2014)
country comparison to the world: 142

Age structure: *0–14 years:* 33.09% (male 473,108/female 448,612)
15–24 years: 21.52% (male 307,020/female 292,465)
25–54 years: 36.96% (male 529,094/female 500,375)
55–64 years: 4.57% (male 64,093/female 63,289)
65 years and over: 3.85% (male 45,303/female 62,007) (2015 est.)

Dependency ratios: *total dependency ratio:* 76%
youth dependency ratio: 70.8%
elderly dependency ratio: 5.2%
potential support ratio: 19.2%

note: data represent Gaza Strip and the West Bank (2015 est.)

Median age: *total:* 22.7 years
male: 22.6 years
female: 22.9 years (2015 est.)
country comparison to the world: 171

Population growth rate: 1.95% (2015 est.)
country comparison to the world: 51

Birth rate: 22.99 births/1,000 population (2015 est.)
country comparison to the world: 67

Death rate: 3.5 deaths/1,000 population (2015 est.)
country comparison to the world: 216

Net migration rate: 0 migrant(s)/1,000 population (2015 est.)
country comparison to the world: 111

Urbanization: *urban population:* 75.3% of total population (2015)
rate of urbanization: 2.81% annual rate of change (2010–15 est.)
note: data represent Gaza Strip and West Bank

Sex ratio: *at birth:* 1.06 male(s)/female
0–14 years: 1.06 male(s)/female *15–24 years:* 1.05 male(s)/female
25–54 years: 1.06 male(s)/female
55–64 years: 1.01 male(s)/female
65 years and over: 0.73 male(s)/female
total population: 1.04 male(s)/female (2015 est.)

Maternal mortality rate: 45 deaths/100,000 live births
note: data represent Gaza Strip and West Bank (2015 est.)
country comparison to the world: 95

Infant mortality rate: *total:* 13.08 deaths/1,000 live births
male: 14.7 deaths/1,000 live births
female: 11.37 deaths/1,000 live births (2015 est.)
country comparison to the world: 115

Life expectancy at birth: *total population:* 75.91 years
male: 73.79 years
female: 78.17 years (2015 est.)
country comparison to the world: 92

Total fertility rate: 2.76 children born/woman (2015 est.)
country comparison to the world: 66

Contraceptive prevalence rate: 52.5% (includes Gaza Strip and West Bank) (2010)

Physicians density: 1.3 physicians/1,000 population (2013)

Hospital bed density: 1.2 beds/1,000 population (2010)

Drinking water source:
improved:
urban: 50.7% of population
rural: 81.5% of population
total: 58.4% of population
unimproved:
urban: 49.3% of population
rural: 18.5% of population
total: 41.6% of population

note: includes Gaza Strip and the West Bank (2015 est.)

Sanitation facility access:
improved:
urban: 93% of population
rural: 90.2% of population
total: 92.3% of population
unimproved:
urban: 7% of population
rural: 9.8% of population
total: 7.7% of population
note: includes Gaza Strip and the West Bank (2015 est.)

HIV/AIDS—adult prevalence rate: NA

HIV/AIDS—people living with HIV/AIDS: NA

HIV/AIDS—deaths: NA

Literacy: *definition:* age 15 and over can read and write
total population: 96.5%
male: 98.4%
female: 94.5%
notes: estimates are for Gaza and West Bank (2015 est.)

School life expectancy (primary to tertiary education): *total:* 13 years
male: 12 years
female: 14 years
note: data represent Gaza and West Bank (2014)

Unemployment, youth ages 15–24: *total:* 41%
male: 37%
female: 64.7%
note: includes Gaza Strip (2013 est.)
country comparison to the world: 15

GOVERNMENT

COUNTRY NAME: *conventional long form:* none
conventional short form: West Bank
etymology: name refers to the location of the region—occupied and administered by Jordan after 1948 that fell on the far side (west bank) of the Jordan River in relation to Jordan proper; the designation was retained following the 1967 Six-Day War and the subsequent changes in government

ECONOMY

Economy—overview: Israeli-Palestinian violence in 2015 exacerbated challenges to economic growth in the West Bank—the larger of the two areas comprising the Palestinian Territories. Increased security restrictions and political instability slowed economic activity, and Israel's four-month withholding of taxes and other fees it collects on the Palestinian authority's (PA) behalf caused the PA to delay salary payments to its employees, which in turn had broader effects on business activity and consumer demand.
Longstanding Israeli closure policies continue to disrupt labor and trade flows and the territory's industrial capacity, limit imports and exports, and constrain private sector development. The PA for the foreseeable future will continue to rely heavily

on donor aid for its budgetary needs and economic activity.

GDP (purchasing power parity): $21.22 billion (2014 est.)
$20.15 billion (2013 est.)
$19.95 billion (2012 est.)
note: data are in 2014 US dollars; includes Gaza Strip
country comparison to the world: 142

GDP (official exchange rate): $9.828 billion (2014 est.)
note: excludes Gaza Strip

GDP—real growth rate: 5.3% (2014 est.)
1% (2013 est.)
6% (2012 est.)
note: excludes Gaza Strip
country comparison to the world: 37

GDP—per capita (PPP): $4,300 (2014 est.)
$4,400 (2013 est.)
$4,600 (2012 est.)
note: includes Gaza Strip
country comparison to the world: 176

Gross National saving: 7.8% of GDP (2014 est.)
9.5% of GDP (2013 est.)
5% of GDP (2012 est.)
note: includes Gaza Strip
country comparison to the world: 160

GDP—composition, by end use:
household consumption: 85.7%
government consumption: 21.9%
investment in fixed capital: 26%
investment in inventories: 2.3%
exports of goods and services: 24.5%
imports of goods and services: -60.4%
note: excludes Gaza Strip (2014 est.)

GDP—composition, by sector of origin:
agriculture: 3.5%
industry: 25.2%
services: 71.4%
note: excludes Gaza Strip (2014 est.)

Agriculture—products: olives, citrus fruit, vegetables; beef, dairy products

Industries: small-scale manufacturing, quarrying, textiles, soap, olive-wood carvings, and mother-of-pearl souvenirs

Industrial production growth rate: -1.7%
note: includes Gaza Strip (2015 est.)
country comparison to the world: 178

Labor force: 828,000
note: excludes Gaza Strip (2015 est.)
country comparison to the world: 148

Labor force—by occupation: *agriculture:* 11.5%
industry: 34.4%
services: 54.1%
note: excludes Gaza Strip (2013 est.)

Unemployment rate: 17.7% (2014 est.)
18.6% (2013 est.)
note: excludes Gaza Strip
country comparison to the world: 162

Population below poverty line: 18% (2011 est.)

Household income or consumption by percentage share: *lowest:* 10%: 3.2%
highest: 10%: 28.2%

note: includes Gaza Strip (2009 est.)

Distribution of family income—Gini index: 34.5 (2009 est.)
38.7 (2007 est.)
note: includes Gaza Strip
country comparison to the world: 97

Budget: *revenues:* $2.75 billion
expenditures: $4.077 billion
note: includes Palestinian authority expenditures in the Gaza Strip (2014 est.)
Taxes and other revenues: 28% of GDP (2014 est.)
country comparison to the world: 95

Budget surplus (+) or deficit (–): -13.5% of GDP (2014 est.)
country comparison to the world: 213

Public debt: 24.4% of GDP (2014 est.)
23.8% of GDP (2013 est.)
country comparison to the world: 150

Fiscal year: calendar year

Inflation rate (consumer prices): 1.2% (2014 est.)
3.1% (2013 est.)
note: excludes Gaza Strip
country comparison to the world: 86

Commercial bank prime lending rate: 7.7% (31 December 2015 est.)
6.41% (31 December 2014 est.)
country comparison to the world: 112

Stock of narrow money: $278.6 million (31 December 2015 est.)
$227.1 million (31 December 2014 est.)
country comparison to the world: 177

Stock of broad money: $2.399 billion (31 December 2014 est.)
$2.16 billion (31 December 2013 est.)
country comparison to the world: 148

Stock of domestic credit: $1.274 billion (31 December 2015 est.)
$1.147 billion (31 December 2014 est.)
country comparison to the world: 152

Market value of publicly traded shares: $2.634 billion (31 December 2012 est.)
$2.532 billion (31 December 2011)
$2.45 billion (31 December 2010 est.)
country comparison to the world: 97

Current account balance: -$2.149 billion (2014 est.) -$2.383 billion (2013 est.)
country comparison to the world: 148

Exports: $937.4 million (2014 est.) $1.692 billion (2013 est.)
note: excludes Gaza Strip
country comparison to the world: 162

Exports—commodities: stone, olives, fruit, vegetables, limestone

Imports: $5.683 billion (2014 est.)
$6.261 billion (2013 est.)
note: data include the Gaza Strip
country comparison to the world: 121

Imports—commodities: food, consumer goods, construction materials, petroleum, chemicals

Debt—external: $1.089 billion (2014 est.)
$1.191 billion (2013 est.)
note: data include the Gaza Strip

country comparison to the world: 162

Exchange rates: new Israeli shekels (ILS) per US dollar—
3.886 (2015 est.)
3.578 (2014 est.)
3.578 (2013 est.)
3.86 (2012 est.)
3.5781 (2011 est.)

ENERGY

Electricity—production: 433 million kWh (2012 est.)
country comparison to the world: 163

Electricity—consumption: 5.312 billion kWh (2012 est.)
country comparison to the world: 113

Electricity—exports: 0 kWh (2013)
country comparison to the world: 214

Electricity—imports: 4.909 billion kWh (2012 est.)
country comparison to the world: 41

Electricity—installed generating capacity: 140,000 kW
note: includes Gaza Strip (2012 est.)
country comparison to the world: 167

Electricity—from fossil fuels: 100% of total installed capacity (2012 est.)
country comparison to the world: 35

Electricity—from nuclear fuels: 0% of total installed capacity (2012 est.)
country comparison to the world: 208

Electricity—from hydroelectric plants: 0% of total installed capacity (2012 est.)
country comparison to the world: 212

Electricity—from other renewable sources: 0% of total installed capacity (2012 est.)
country comparison to the world: 143

Crude oil—production: 0 bbl/day (2014 est.)
country comparison to the world: 209

Crude oil—exports: 0 bbl/day (2012 est.)
country comparison to the world: 209

Crude oil—imports: 0 bbl/day (2012 est.)
country comparison to the world: 148

Crude oil—proved reserves: 0 bbl (1 January 2009 est.)
country comparison to the world: 210

Refined petroleum Products—production: 0 bbl/day (2012 est.)
country comparison to the world: 146

Refined petroleum Products—consumption: 16,000 bbl/day (2013 est.)
country comparison to the world: 139

Refined petroleum Products—exports: 3.84 bbl/day (2012 est.)
country comparison to the world: 126

Refined petroleum Products—Imports: 16,330 bbl/day (2012 est.)
country comparison to the world: 120

Natural gas—production: 0 cu m (2013 est.)
country comparison to the world: 147

Natural gas—consumption: 0 cu m (2013 est.)

country comparison to the world: 210

Natural gas—exports: 0 cu m (2013 est.)
country comparison to the world: 211

Natural gas—imports: 0 cu m (2013 est.)
country comparison to the world: 80

Natural gas—proved reserves: 0 cu m (1 January 2014 est.)
country comparison to the world: 207

Carbon dioxide emissions from consumption of energy: 3.008 million Mt (2012 est.)
country comparison to the world: 141

COMMUNICATIONS

Telephones—fixed lines: *total subscriptions:* 400,000 (includes Gaza Strip)
subscriptions per 100 inhabitants: 15 (2014 est.)
country comparison to the world: 109

Telephones—mobile cellular: *total:* 3.2 million (includes Gaza Strip)
subscriptions per 100 inhabitants: 117 (includes Gaza Strip) (2014 est.)
country comparison to the world: 135

Telephone system: *general assessment:* continuing political and economic instability has impeded significant liberalization of the telecommunications industry
domestic: Israeli company BEZEK and the Palestinian company PALTEL are responsible for fixed-line services; PALTEL plans to establish a fiber-optic connection to Jordan to route domestic mobile calls; the Palestinian JAWWAL company and WATANIYA PALESTINE provide cellular services
International: country code—970; 1 international switch in Ramallah (2009)

Broadcast media: the PalestiniaNAuthority operates 1 TV and 1 radio station; about 20 private TV and 40 radio stations; both Jordanian TV and satellite TV are accessible (2013)
Radio broadcast stations: AM 0, FM 27, shortwave 0 (2010)
Television broadcast stations: 31 (2010)

Internet country code: .ps; note—same as Gaza Strip

Internet users: *total:* 1.4 million (includes Gaza Strip)
percent of population: 34.4% (2009)
country comparison to the world: 112

TRANSPORTATION

Airports: 2 (2013)
country comparison to the world: 203

Airports—with paved runways: *total:* 2
1,524 to 2,437 m: 1
under 914 m: 1 (2013)

Heliports: 1 (2013)

Roadways: *total:* 4,686 km
paved: 4,686 km
note: includes Gaza Strip (2010)
country comparison to the world: 154

TRANSNATIONAL ISSUES

937

Disputes—international: the current status of the West Bank is subject to the Israeli-Palestinian Interim Agreement—permanent status to be determined through further negotiation; Israel continues construction of a "seam line" separation barrier along parts of the Green Line and within the West Bank; Israel withdrew from Gaza and four settlements in the northern West Bank in August 2005; since 1948, about 350 peacekeepers from the UN Truce Supervision Organization (UNTSO), headquartered in Jerusalem, monitor ceasefires, supervise armistice agreements, prevent isolated incidents from escalating, and assist other UN personnel in the region

Refugees and internally displaced persons: *refugees (country of origin):* 762,288 (Palestinian refugees) (2014)

IDPs: 221,000 (includes persons displaced within the Gaza strip due to the intensification of the Israeli-Palestinian conflict since June 2014 and other Palestinian IDPs in the Gaza Strip and West Bank who fled as long ago as 1967, although confirmed cumulative data do not go back beyond 2006) (2015)

WESTERN SAHARA

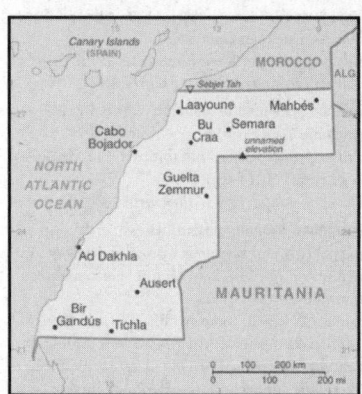

INTRODUCTION

Background: Western Sahara is a disputed territory on the northwest coast of Africa bordered by Morocco, Mauritania, and Algeria. After Spain withdrew from its former colony of Spanish Sahara in 1976, Morocco annexed the northern two-thirds of Western Sahara and claimed the rest of the territory in 1979, following Mauritania's withdrawal. A guerrilla war with the Polisario Front contesting Morocco's sovereignty ended in a 1991 ceasefire and the establishment of a UN peacekeeping operation. As part of this effort, the UN sought to offer a choice to the peoples of the Western Sahara between independence (favored by the Polisario Front) or integration into Morocco. A proposed referendum never took place due to lack of agreement on voter eligibility. The 2,700 km- (1,700 mi-) long defensive sand berm, built by the Moroccans from 1980 to 1987 and running the length of the territory, continues to separate the opposing forces with Morocco controlling the roughly 80 percent of the territory west of the berm. Local demonstrations criticizing the Moroccan Authorities occur regularly, and there are periodic ethnic tensions between the native Sahrawi population and Moroccan immigrants. Morocco maintains a heavy security presence in the territory.

GEOGRAPHY

Location: Northern africa, bordering the North Atlantic Ocean, between Mauritania and Morocco

Geographic coordinates: 24 30 N, 13 00 W

Map references: Africa

Area: *total:* 266,000 sq km
land: 266,000 sq km
water: 0 sq km
country comparison to the world: 78

Area—comparative: about the size of Colorado

Land boundaries: *total:* 2,049 km
border countries (3): Algeria 41 km, Mauritania 1,564 km, Morocco 444 km

Coastline: 1,110 km

Maritime claims: contingent upon resolution of sovereignty issue

Climate: hot, dry desert; rain is rare; cold offshore air currents produce fog and heavy dew

Terrain: mostly low, flat desert with large areas of rocky or sandy surfaces rising to small mountains in south and North east

Elevation: *mean elevation:* 256 m

elevation extremes: *lowest point:* Sebjet Tah -55 m
highest point: unnamed elevation 805 m

Natural resources: phosphates, iron ore

Land use: *agricultural land:* 18.8%
arable land: 0%
permanent crops: 0%
permanent pasture: 18.8%
forest: 2.7%
other: 78.5% (2011 est.)

Irrigated land: 0 sq km (2012)

Natural hazards: hot, dry, dust/sand-laden sirocco wind can occur during winter and spring; widespread harmattan haze exists 60% of time, often severely restricting visibility

Environment—current issues: sparse water and lack of arable land

Geography—note: the waters off the coast are particularly rich fishing areas

PEOPLE AND SOCIETY

Nationality: *noun:* Sahrawi(s), Sahraoui(s)
adjective: Sahrawi, Sahrawian, Sahraouian

Ethnic groups: Arab, Berber

Languages: Standard Arabic (National), Hassaniya Arabic, Moroccan arabic

Religions: Muslim

Population: 570,866 (July 2013 est.)
note: estimate is based on projections by age, sex, fertility, mortality, and migration; fertility and mortality are based on data from neighboring countries (July 2015 est.)
country comparison to the world: 172

Age structure: *0–14 years:* 37.83% (male 109,147/female 106,789)
15–24 years: 19.63% (male 56,412/female 55,624)
25–54 years: 33.93% (male 95,296/female 98,391)
55–64 years: 4.87% (male 12,974/female 14,829)
65 years and over: 3.75% (male 9,406/female 11,998) (2015 est.)

Dependency ratios: *total dependency ratio:* 40.2%
youth dependency ratio: 36.1%
elderly dependency ratio: 4.1%
potential support ratio: 24.4% (2015 est.)

Median age: *total:* 20.9 years
male: 20.5 years
female: 21.4 years (2015 est.)
country comparison to the world: 184

Population growth rate: 2.82% (2015 est.)
country comparison to the world: 12

Birth rate: 30.24 births/1,000 population (2015 est.)
country comparison to the world: 40

Death rate: 8.34 deaths/1,000 population (2015 est.)
country comparison to the world: 84

Urbanization: *urban population:* 80.9% of total population (2015)
rate of urbanization: 3.27% annual rate of change (2010–15 est.)

Major urban Areas—population: Laayoune 262,000 (2014)

Sex ratio: *at birth:* 1.04 male(s)/female
0–14 years: 1.02 male(s)/female
15–24 years: 1.01 male(s)/female
25–54 years: 0.97 male(s)/female
55–64 years: 0.88 male(s)/female
65 years and over: 0.78 male(s)/female
total population: 0.99 male(s)/female (2015 est.)

Infant mortality rate: *total:* 54.7 deaths/1,000 live births
male: 59.61 deaths/1,000 live births
female: 49.6 deaths/1,000 live births (2015 est.)
country comparison to the world: 27

Life expectancy at birth: *total population:* 62.64 years
male: 60.35 years
female: 65.02 years (2015 est.)
country comparison to the world: 190

Total fertility rate: 4 children born/woman (2015 est.)
country comparison to the world: 38

HIV/AIDS—adult prevalence rate: NA

HIV/AIDS—people living with HIV/AIDS: NA

HIV/AIDS—deaths: NA

GOVERNMENT

Country name: *conventional long form:* none
conventional short form: Western Sahara
former: Rio de Oro, Saguia el Hamra, Spanish Sahara
etymology: self-descriptive name specifying the territory's location on the African continent's vast desert

Government type: legal status of territory and issue of sovereignty unresolved-territory contested by Morocco and Polisario Front (Popular Front for the Liberation of the Saguia el Hamra and Rio de Oro), which in February 1976 formally proclaimed a government-in-exile of the Sahrawi Arab Democratic Republic (SADR), near Tindouf, Algeria, led by President Mohamed ABDELAZIZ; territory partitioned between Morocco and Mauritania in April 1976 when Spain withdrew, with Morocco acquiring northern two-thirds; Mauritania, under pressure from Polisario guerrillas, abandoned all claims to its portion in August 1979; Morocco moved to occupy that sector shortly thereafter and has since asserted administrative control; the Polisario's government-inexile was seated as an Organization of African Unity (OAU) member in 1984—Morocco between 1980 and 1987 built a fortified sand berm delineating the roughly 80 percent of Western Sahara west of the barrier that currently is controlled by Morocco; guerrilla activities continued sporadically until a UN-monitored cease-fire was implemented on 6 September 1991 (Security Council Resolution 690) by the United Nations Mission for the Referendum in Western Sahara (MINURSO)

Capital: Laayoune (administrative center)
time difference: UTC 0 (5 hours ahead of Washington, DC, during Standard Time)
daylight saving time: +1hr, begins last Sunday in April; ends last Sunday in September

Administrative divisions: none officially, the territory west of the Moroccan berm falls under de facto Moroccan control; Morocco claims the territory of Western Sahara, the political status of which is considered undetermined by the US Government; portions of the regions Guelmim-Es Smara and Laayoune-Boujdour-Sakia El Hamra as claimed by Morocco lie within Western Sahara; Morocco also claims Oued Eddahab-Lagouira, another region that falls entirely within Western Sahara

Suffrage: none; (residents of Moroccan-controlled Western Sahara participate in Moroccan elections)

Executive branch: none

Political pressure groups and leaders: Polisario Front

International organization participation: AU, CAN (observer), WFTU (NGO s)

Diplomatic representation in the US: none

Diplomatic representation from the US: none

ECONOMY

Economy—overview: Western Sahara has a small market-based economy whose main industries are fishing, phosphate mining, and pastoral nomadism. The territory's arid desert climate makes sedentary agriculture difficult, and Western Sahara imports much of its food. The Moroccan Government administers Western Sahara's economy and is a key source of employment, infrastructure development, and social spending in the territory. Western Sahara's unresolved legal status makes the exploitation of its Natural resources a contentious issue between Morocco and the Polisario. Morocco and the EU in December 2013 finalized a four-year agreement allowing European vessels to fish off the coast of Morocco, including disputed waters off the coast of Western Sahara. Oil has never been found in Western Sahara in commercially significant quantities, but Morocco and the Polisario have quarreled over who has the right to authorize and benefit from oil exploration in the territory. Western Sahara's main long-term economic challenge is the development of a more diverse set of industries capable of providing greater employment and income to the territory. However, following King MOHAMMED VI's November 2015 visit to Western Sahara, the Government of Morocco announced a series of investments aimed at spurring economic activity in the region, while the General Confederation of Moroccan Enterprises announced a $609 million investment initiative in the region in March 2015.

GDP (purchasing power parity): $906.5 million (2007 est.)
country comparison to the world: 205

GDP (official exchange rate): $NA

GDP—real growth rate: NA%

GDP—per capita (PPP): $2,500 (2007 est.)
country comparison to the world: 199

GDP—composition, by sector of origin:
agriculture: NA%
industry: NA%
services: 40% (2007 est.)

Agriculture—products: fruits and vegetables (grown in the few oases); camels, sheep, goats (kept by nomads); fish

Industries: phosphate mining, handicrafts

Industrial production growth rate: NA%

Labor force: 144,000 (2010 est.)
country comparison to the world: 178

Labor force—by occupation: *agriculture:* 50% in du stry and services: 50% (2005 est.)

Unemployment rate: NA%

Population below poverty line: NA%

Household income or consumption by percentage share: *lowest:* 10%: NA%
highest: 10%: NA%

Budget: *revenues:* $NA expenditures: $NA
Taxes and other revenues: NA%

Budget surplus (+) or deficit (–): NA%

Fiscal year: calendar year

Inflation rate (consumer prices): NA%

Exports: $NA

Exports—commodities: phosphates 62% (2012 est.)

Imports: $NA

Imports—commodities: fuel for fishing fleet, foodstuffs

Debt—external: $NA

Exchange rates: Moroccan dirhams (MAD) per US dollar—
9.592 (2015)
8.3803 (2013)
8.3803 (2013)
8.6 (2012)
8.0899 (2011)

ENERGY

Electricity—production: 90 million kWh (2012 est.)
country comparison to the world: 202

Electricity—consumption: 83.7 million kWh (2012 est.)
country comparison to the world: 201

Electricity—exports: 0 kWh (2013 est.)
country comparison to the world: 215

Electricity—imports: 0 kWh (2013 est.)
country comparison to the world: 217

Electricity—installed generating capacity: 58,000 kW (2012 est.)
country comparison to the world: 183

Electricity—from fossil fuels: 100% of total installed capacity (2012 est.)
country comparison to the world: 2

Electricity—fron nuclear fuels: 0% of total installed capacity (2012 est.)
country comparison to the world: 209

Electricity—from hydroelectric plants: 0% of total installed capacity (2012 est.)
country comparison to the world: 213

Electricity—from other renewable sources: 0% of total installed capacity (2012 est.)
country comparison to the world: 144

Crude oil—production: 0 bbl/day (2014 est.)
country comparison to the world: 210

Crude oil—exports: 0 bbl/day (2012 est.)
country comparison to the world: 210

Crude oil—imports: 0 bbl/day (2012 est.)
country comparison to the world: 149

Crude oil—proved reserves: 0 bbl (1 January 2015 est.)
country comparison to the world: 211

Refined petroleum Products—production: 0 bbl/day (2012 est.)
country comparison to the world: 147

939

Refined petroleum Products—consumption: 1,700 bbl/day (2013 est.)
country comparison to the world: 189

Refined petroleum Products—exports: 0 bbl/day (2012 est.)
country comparison to the world: 148

Refined petroleum Products—imports: 1,702 bbl/day (2012 est.)
country comparison to the world: 211

Natural gas—production: 0 cu m (2013 est.)
country comparison to the world: 212

Natural gas—consumption: 0 cu m (2013 est.)
country comparison to the world: 81

Natural gas—exports: 0 cu m (2013 est.)
country comparison to the world: 208

Natural gas—imports: 0 cu m (2013 est.)
country comparison to the world: 189

Natural gas—proved reserves: 0 cu m (1 January 2014 est.)
country comparison to the world: 208

Carbon dioxide emissions from consumption of energy: 316,100 Mt (2012 est.)

country comparison to the world: 189

COMMUNICATIONS

Teleph one system: *general assessment:* sparse and limited system domestic: NA
International: country code—212; tied into Morocco's system by microwave radio relay, tropospheric scatter, and satellite; satellite earth stations—2 Intelsat (Atlantic Ocean) linked to Rabat, Morocco (2008)

Broadcast media: Morocco's state-owned broadcaster, Radio-Television Marocaine (RTM), operates a radio service from Laayoune and relays TV service; a Polisario-backed radio station also broadcasts (2008)
Radio broadcast stations: AM 2, FM 0, shortwave 0 (1998)
Television broadcast stations: NA

Internet country code: .eh

TRANSPORTATION

Airports: 6 (2013)

country comparison to the world: 174

Airports—with paved runways: *total:* 3
2,438 to 3,047 m: 3 (2013)

Airports—with unpaved runways: *total:* 3
1,524 to 2,437 m: 1
914 to 1,523 m: 1
under 914 m: 1 (2013)

Ports and terminals: *major seaport(s):* Ad Dakhla, Laayoune (El Aaiun)

TRANSNATIONAL ISSUES

Disputes—international: many neighboring states reject Moroccan administration of Western Sahara; several states have extended diplomatic relations to the "Sahrawi Arab Democratic Republic" represented by the Polisario Front in exile in algeria, while others recognize Moroccan sovereignty over Western Sahara; approximately 90,000 Sahrawi refugees continue to be sheltered in camps in Tindouf, Algeria, which has hosted Sahrawi refugees sin ce the 1980s

WORLD

INTRODUCTION

Background: Globally, the 20th century was marked by: (a) two devastating world wars; (b) the Great Depression of the 1930s; (c) the end of vast colonial empires; (d) rapid advances in science and technology, from the first airplane flight at Kitty Hawk, North Carolina (US) to the landing on the moon; (e) the Cold War between the Western alliance and the Warsaw Pact nations; (f) a sharp rise in living standards in North America, Europe, and Japan; (g) increased concerns about environmental degradation including deforestation, energy and water shortages, declining biological diversity, and air pollution; (h) the onset of the AIDS epidemic; and (i) the ultimate emergence of the US as the only world superpower. The planet's population continues to explode: from 1 billion in 1820 to 2 billion in 1930, 3 billion in 1960,4 billion in 1974,5 billion in 1987, 6 billion in 1999, and 7 billion in 2012. For the 21st century, the continued exponential growth in science and technology raises both hopes (e. g., advances in medicine and agriculture) and fears (e. g., development of even more lethal weapons of war).

GEOGRAPHY

Geographic overview: The surface of the earth is approximately 70.9% water and 29.1% land. The former portion is divided into large water bodies termed oceans. The World Factbook recognizes and describes five oceans, which are in decreasing order of size: the Pacific Ocean, Atlantic Ocean, Indian Ocean, Southern Ocean, and Arctic

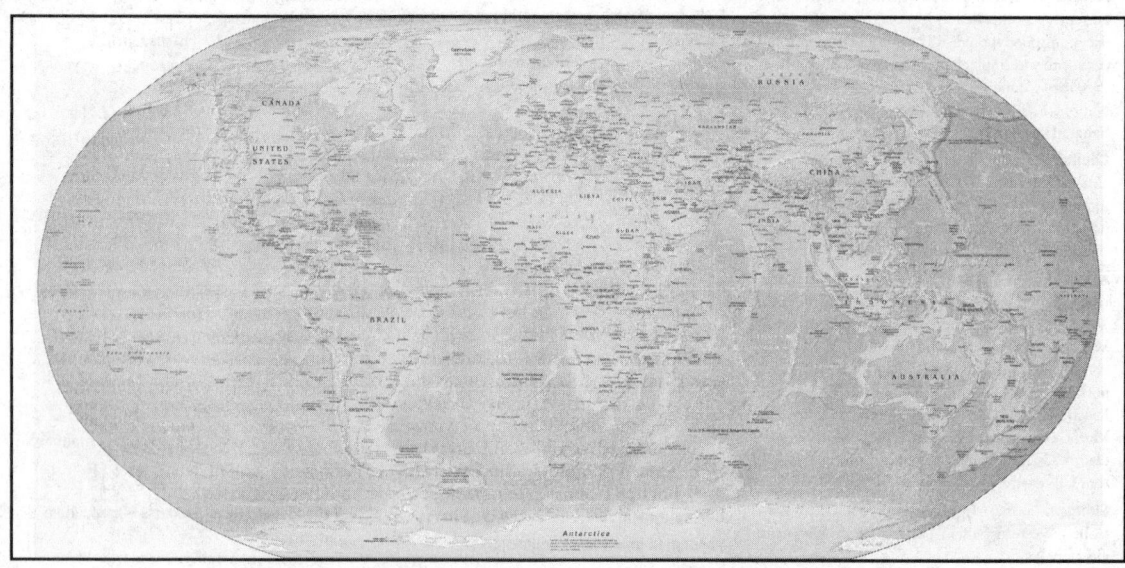

Ocean. The land portion is generally divided into several, large, discrete landmasses termed continents. Depending on the convention used, the number of continents can vary from five to seven. The most common classification recognizes seven, which are (from largest to smallest): Asia, Africa, North America, South America, Antarctica, Europe, and Australia. Asia and Europe are sometimes lumped together into a Eurasian continent resulting in six continents. Alternatively, North and South America are sometimes grouped as simply the Americas, resulting in a continent total of six (or five, if the Eurasia designation is used).

North America is commonly understood to include the island of Greenland, the isles of the Caribbean, and to extend south all the way to the Isthmus of Panama. The easternmost extent of Europe is generally defined as being the Ural Mountains and the Ural River; on the southeast the Caspian Sea; and on the south the Caucasus Mountains, the Black Sea, and the Mediterranean. Portions of Azerbaijan, Georgia, Kazakhstan, Russia, and Turkey fall within both Europe and Asia, but in every instance the larger section is in asia. These countries are considered part of both continents. Armenia and Cyprus, which lie completely in Western asia, are geopolitically European countries.

Asia usually incorporates all the islands of the Philippines, Malaysia, and Indonesia. The islands of the Pacific are often lumped with Australia into a "land mass" termed Oceania or Australasia. Africa's northeast extremity is frequently delimited at the Isthmus of Suez, but for geopolitical purposes, the Egyptian Sinai Peninsula is often included as part of Africa.

Although the above groupings are the most common, different continental dispositions are recognized or taught in certain parts of the world, with some arrangements more heavily based on cultural spheres rather than physical geographic considerations.

Based on the seven-continent model, and grouping islands with adjacent continents, Africa has the most countries with 54. Europe contains 49 countries and Asia 48, but these two continents share five countries: Azerbaijan, Georgia, Kazakhstan, Russia, and Turkey. North America consists of 23 sovereign states, Oceania has 14, and South America 12.

countries by continent: Africa (54): Algeria, Angola, Benin, Botswana, Burkina Faso, Burundi, Cabo Verde, Cameroon, Central African Republic, Chad, Comoros, Democratic Republic of the Congo, Republic of the Congo, Cote d'Ivoire, Djibouti, Egypt, Equatorial Guinea, Eritrea, Ethiopia, Gabon, The Gambia, Ghana, Guinea, Guinea-Bissau, Kenya, Lesotho, Liberia, Libya, Madagascar, Malawi, Mali, Mauritania, Mauritius, Morocco, Mozambique, Namibia, Niger, Nigeria, Rwanda, Sao Tome and Principe, Senegal, Seychelles, Sierra Leone, Somalia, South Africa, South Sudan, Sudan, Swaziland, Tanzania, Togo, Tunisia, Uganda, Zambia, Zimbabwe

Europe (49): Albania, Andorra, Austria, Azerbaijan*, Belarus, Belgium, Bosnia and Herzegovina, Bulgaria, Croatia, Czech Republic, Denmark, Estonia, Finland, France, Georgia*, Germany, Greece, Holy See (Vatican City), Hungary, Iceland, Ireland, Italy, Kazakhstan*, Kosovo, Latvia, Liechtenstein, Lithuania, Luxembourg, Macedonia, Malta, Moldova, Mon aco, Montenegro, Netherlands, Norway, Poland, Portugal, Romania, Russia*, San Marino, Serbia, Slovakia, Slovenia, Spain, Sweden, Switzerland, Turkey*, UKraine, United Kingdom (* indicates part of the country is also in asia)

Asia (48): Afghanistan, Armenia, Azerbaijan*, Bahrain, Bangladesh, Bhutan, Brunei, Burma, Cambodia, China, Cyprus, Georgia*, India, Indonesia, Iran, Iraq, Israel, Japan, Jordan, Kazakhstan*, North Korea, South Korea, Kuwait, Kyrgyzstan, Laos, Lebanon, Malaysia, Maldives, Mongolia, Nepal, Oman, Pakistan, Philippines, Qatar, Russia*, Saudi Arabia, Singapore, Sri Lanka, Syria, Tajikistan, Thailand, Timor-Leste, Turkey*, Turkmenistan, United Arab Emirates, Uzbekistan, Vietnam, Yemen (* indicates part of the country is also in Europe)

North America (23): Antigua and Barbuda, The Bahamas, Barbados, Belize, Canada, Costa Rica, Cuba, Dominica, Dominican Republic, El Salvador, Grenada, Guatemala, Haiti, Honduras, Jamaica, Mexico, Nicaragua, Panama, Saint Kitts and Nevis, Saint Lucia, Saint Vincent and the Grenadines, Trinidad and Tobago, United States

Oceania (14): Australia, Fiji, Kiribati, Marshall Islands, Federated States of Micronesia, Nauru, New Zealand, Palau, Papua New Guinea, Samoa, Solomon Islands, Tonga, Tuvalu, Vanuatu

South America (12): Argentina, Bolivia, Brazil, Chile, Colombia, Ecuador, Guyana, Paraguay, Peru, Suriname, Uruguay, Venezuela

Map references: Physical Map of the World

Area: total: 510.072 million sq km
land: 148.94 million sq km
water: 361.132 million sq km
note: 70.9% of the world's surface is water, 29.1% is land

Area—comparative: land area about 16 times the size of the US

top fifteen World Factbook entities ranked by size: Pacific Ocean 155.557 million sq km; Atlantic Ocean 76.762 million sq km; Indian Ocean 68.556 million sq km; Southern Ocean 20.327 million sq km; Russia 17,098,242 sq km; Arctic Ocean 14.056 million sq km; Antarctica 14 million sq km; Canada 9,984,670 sq km; United States 9,826,675 sq km; China 9,596,960 sq km; Brazil 8,515,770 sq km; Australia 7,741,220 sq km; European Union 4,324,782 sq km; India 3,287,263 sq km; Argentina 2,780,400 sq km

top ten largest water bodies: Pacific Ocean 155.557 million sq km; Atlantic Ocean 76.762 million sq km; Indian Ocean 68.556 million sq km; Southern Ocean 20.327 million sq km; Arctic Ocean 14.056 million sq km; Coral Sea 4,184,100 sq km; South China Sea 3,595,900 sq km; Caribbean Sea 2.834 million sq km; Bering Sea 2.52 million sq km; Mediterranean Sea 2.469 million sq km

top ten largest landmasses: Asia 44,568,500 sq km; Africa 30.065 million sq km; North America 24.473 million sq km; South America 17.819 million sq km; Antarctica 14 million sq km; Europe 9.948 million sq km; Australia 7,741,220 sq km; Greenland 2,166,086 sq km; New Guinea 785,753 sq km; Borneo 751,929 sq km

top ten largest islands: Greenland 2,166,086 sq km; New Guinea (Indonesia, Papua New Guinea) 785,753 sq km; Borneo (Brunei, Indonesia, Malaysia) 751,929 sq km; Madagascar 587,713 sq km; Baffin Island (Canada) 507,451 sq km; Sumatra (Indonesia) 472,784 sq km; Honshu (Japan) 227,963 sq km; Victoria Island (Canada) 217,291 sq km; Great Britain (United Kingdom) 209,331 sq km; Ellesmere Island (Canada) 196,236 sq km

ten smallest independent countries: Holy See (Vatican City) 0.44 sq km; Monaco 2 sq km; Nauru 21 sq km; Tuvalu 26 sq km; San Marino 61 sq km; Liechtenstein 160 sq km; Marshall Islands 181 sq km; Saint Kitts and Nevis 261 sq km; Maldives 298 sq km; Malta 316 sq km

Land boundaries: the land boundaries in the world total 251,060 km (not counting shared boundaries twice); two nations, China and Russia, each border 14 other countries

note: 46 nations and other areas are landlocked, these include: Afghanistan, Andorra, Armenia, Austria, Azerbaijan, Belarus, Bhutan, Bolivia, Botswana, Burkina Faso, Burundi, Central African Republic, Chad, Czech Republic, Ethiopia, Holy See (Vatican City), Hungary, Kazakhstan, Kosovo, Kyrgyzstan, Laos, Lesotho, Liechtenstein, Luxembourg, Macedonia, Malawi, Mali, Moldova, Mongolia, Nepal, Niger, Paraguay, Rwanda, San Marino, Serbia, Slovakia, South Sudan, Swaziland, Switzerland, Tajikistan, Turkmenistan, Uganda, Uzbekistan, West Bank, Zambia, Zimbabwe; two of these, Liechtenstein and Uzbekistan, are doubly landlocked

Coastline: 356,000 km

note: 95 nations and other entities are islands that border no other countries, they include: American Samoa, Anguilla, Antigua and Barbuda, Aruba, Ashmore and Cartier Islands, The Bahamas, Bahrain, Baker Island, Barbados, Bermuda, Bouvet Island, British Indian Ocean Territory, British Virgin Islands, Cabo Verde, Cayman Islands, Christmas Island, Clipperton Island, Cocos (Keeling) Islands, Comoros, Cook Islands, Coral Sea Islands, Cuba, Curacao, Cyprus, Dominica, Falkland Islands (Islas Malvinas), Faroe Islands, Fiji, French Polynesia, French SoutherNAnd Antarctic Lands, Greenland, Grenada, Guam, Guernsey, Heard Island and McDon ald Islands, Howland Island, Iceland, Isle of Man, Jamaica, Jan Mayen, Japan, Jarvis Island, Jersey, Johnston atoll, Kingman Reef, Kiribati, Madagascar, Maldives, Malta, Marshall Islands, Mauritius, Mayotte, Federated States of Micronesia, Midway Islands, Montserrat, Nauru, Navassa Island, New Caledonia, New Zealand, Niue, Norfolk Island, Northern Mariana Islands, Palau, Palmyra Atoll, Paracel Islands, Philippines, Pitcairn Islands, Puerto Rico, Saint Barthelemy, Saint Helena, Saint Kitts and Nevis, Saint Lucia, Saint Pierre and Miquelon, Saint Vincent and the Grenadines, Samoa, Sao Tome and Principe, Seychelles, Singapore, Sint Maarten, Solomon Islands, South Georgia and the South Sandwich Islands, Spratly Islands, Sri Lanka, Svalbard, Taiwan, Tokelau, Tonga, Trinidad and Tobago, Turks and Caicos Islands, Tuvalu, Vanuatu, Virgin Islands, Wake Island, Wallis and Futuna

Maritime claims: a variety of situations exist, but in general, most countries make the following claims measured from the mean low-tide baseline as described in the 1982 UN Convention on the Law of the Sea: territorial sea—12 nm, contiguous zone—24 nm, and exclusive economic zone—200 nm; addition al zones provide for exploitation of continental shelf resources and an exclusive fishing zone; boundary situations with neighboring states prevent many countries from extending their fishing or economic zones to a full 200 nm

Climate: a wide equatorial band of hot and humid tropical climates, bordered north and south by subtropical temperate zones that separate two large areas of cold and dry polar climates

Terrain: the greatest ocean depth is the Mariana Trench at -10,924 m in the Pacific Ocean

Elevation: *mean elevation:* 840 m

elevation extremes: *lowest point:* Bentley Subglacial Trench (Antarctica) -2,555 m (in the oceanic realm, Challenger Deep in the Mariana Trench is the lowest point, lying -10,924 m below the surface of the Pacific Ocean)

highest point: Mount Everest 8,850 m

top ten highest mountains (measured from sea level): Mount Everest (China-Nepal) 8,850 m; K2 (Pakistan) 8,611 m; Kanchenjunga (India-Nepal) 8,598 m; Lhotse (Nepal) 8,516 m; Makalu (China-Nepal) 8,463 m; Cho Oyu (China-Nepal) 8,201 m; Dhaulagiri (Nepal) 8,167 m; Manaslu (Nepal) 8,163 m; Nanga Parbat (Pakistan) 8,125 m; Anapurna (Nepal) 8,091 m

note: Mauna Kea (United States) is the world's tallest mountaiNAs measured from base to summit; the peak of this volcanic colossus lies on the island of Hawaii, but its base begins more than 70 km offshore and at a depth of about 6,000 m; total height estimates range from 9,966 m to 10,203 m

highest point on each continent: Asia—Mount Everest (China-Nepal) 8,850 m; South America—Cerro Aconcagua (Argentina) 6,960 m; North America—Denali (Mount McKinley) (United States) 6,190 m; Africa -Kilimanjaro (Tanzania) 5,895 m; Europe—El'brus (Russia) 5,633 m; Antarctica—Vinson Massif 4,897 m; Australia—Mount Kosciuszko 2,229 m

lowest point on each continent: Antarctica—Bentley Subglacial Trench -2,555 m; Asia—Dead Sea (Israel-Jordan) -408 m; Africa—Lac Assal (Djibouti) -155 m; South America—Laguna del Carbon (Argentina) -105 m; North America—Death Valley (United States) -86 m; Europe—Caspian Sea (Azerbaijan-Kazakhstan-Russia) -28 m; Au stralia—Lake Eyre -15 m

Natural resources: the rapid depletion of nonrenewable mineral resources, the depletion of forest areas and wetlands, the extinction of animal and plant species, and the deterioration in air and water quality (especially in some countries of Eastern Europe, the former USSR, and China) pose serious long-term problems that governments and peoples are only beginning to address

Irrigated land: 3,242,917 sq km (2012 est.)

Total renewable water resources: 53,789.29 cu km (2011)

Natural hazards: large areas subject to severe weather (tropical cyclones); Natural disasters (earthquakes, landslides, tsunamis, volcanic eruptions)

volcanism: volcanism is a fundamental driver and consequence of plate tectonics, the physical process reshaping the Earth's lithosphere; the world is home to more than 1,500 potentially active volcanoes, with over 500 of these having erupted in historical times; an estimated 500 million people live near these volcanoes; associated dangers include lava flows, lahars (mudflows), pyroclastic flows, ash clouds, ash fall, ballistic projectiles, gas emissions, landslides, earthquakes, and tsunamis; in the 1990s, the International Association of Volcanology and Chemistry of the Earth's Interior, created a list of 16 Decade Volcanoes worthy of special study because of their great potential for destruction: Avachinsky-Koryaksky (Russia), Colima (Mexico), Etna (Italy), Galeras (Colombia), Mauna Loa (United States), Merapi (Indonesia), Nyiragongo (Democratic Republic of the Congo), Rainier (United States), Sakurajima (Japan), Santa Maria (Guatemala), Santorini (Greece), Taal (Philippines), Teide (Spain), Ulawun (Papua New Guinea), Unzen (Japan), Vesuvius (Italy)

Environment—current issues: large areas subject to overpopulation, industrial disasters, pollution (air, water, acid rain, toxic substances), loss of vegetation (overgrazing, deforestation, desertification), loss of wildlife, soil degradation, soil depletion, erosion; global warming becoming a greater concern

Geography—note: the world is now thought to be about 4.55 billion years old, just about one-third of the 13.8-billion-year age estimated for the universe

PEOPLE AND SOCIETY

Languages: Mandarin Chinese 11.82%, Spanish 5.77%, English 4.67%, Hindi 3.62%, Arabic 3.3%, Portuguese 2.83%, Bengali 2.69%, Russian 2.33%, Japanese 1.7%, Javanese 1.15%, Standard German 1.09% (2014 est.)

note 1: percents are for "first language" speakers only; the six UN languages—Arabic, Chinese (Mandarin), English, French, Russian, and Spanish (Castilian)—are the mother tongue or second language of about half of the world's population, and are the official languages in more than half the states in the world; some 150 to 200 languages have more thaNA million speakers

note 2: all told, there are an estimated 7,100 languages spoken in the world; approximately 80% of these languages are spoken by less than 100,000 people; about 140 languages are spoken by less than 10 people; communities that are isolated from each other in mountainous regions often develop multiple languages; Papua New Guinea, for example, boasts about 839 separate languages

note 3: approximately 2,300 languages are spoken in asia, 2,140, in Africa, 1,310 in the Pacific, 1,060 in the Americas, and 290 in Europe (2016)

Religions: Christian 31.4%, Muslim 23.2%, Hindu 15%, Buddhist 7.1%, folk religions 5.9%, Jewish 0.2%, other 0.8%, unaffiliated 16.4% (2010 est.)

Population: 7,256,490,011 (July 2015 est.)

top ten most populous countries (in millions): China 1367.49; India 1251.70; United States 321.37; Indonesia 255.99; Brazil 204.26; Pakistan 199.09; Nigeria 181.56; Bangladesh 168.96; Russia 142.42; Japan 126.92

ten least populous countries: Holy See (Vatican City) 1,000; Nauru 9,540; Tuvalu 10,869; Palau 21,265; San Marino 33,020; Liechtenstein 37,624; Monaco 37,731; Saint Kitts and Nevis 51,936; Marshall Islands 72,191; Dominica 73,607

ten most densely populated countries (population per sq km): Monaco 18,866; Singapore 8,260; Holy See (Vatican City) 2,273; Bahrain 1,772; Maldives 1,320; Malta 1,310; Bangladesh 1,298; Barbados 676; Mauritius 660; Lebanon 605

ten least densely populated countries (population per sq km): Mongolia 1.93; Namibia 2.69; Australia 2.96; Iceland 3.31; Mauritania 3.49; Libya 3.64; Suriname 3.72; Guyana 3.73; Botswana 3.85; Canada 3.86

Age structure: *0–14 years:* 25.64% (male 962,504,434/female 897,959,144)

15–24 years: 16.34% (male 610,915,870/female 574,498,881)

25–54 years: 40.98% (male 1,502,925,383/female 1,470,748,023)

55–64 years: 8.56% (male 303,057,587/female 317,738,739)

65 years and over: 8.49% (male 274,517,510/female 341,624,440) (2015 est.)

Dependency ratios: *total dependency ratio:* 52.3%

youth dependency ratio: 39.7%

elderly dependency ratio: 12.6%

potential support ratio: 7.9% (2015 est.)

Median age: *total:* 29.9 years

male: 29.1 years

female: 30.6 years (2015 est.)

Population growth rate: 1.08%

note: this rate results in about 149 net additions to the worldwide population every minute or 2.5 every second (2015 est.)

Birth rate: 18.6 births/1,000 population

note: this rate results in about 256 worldwide births per minute or 4.3 births every second (2015 est.)

Death rate: 7.8 deaths/1,000 population

note: this rate results in about 108 worldwide deaths per minute or 1.8 deaths every second (2015 est.)

Urbanization: *urban population:* 54% of total population (2015)

rate of urbanization: 2.05% annual rate of change (2010–15 est.)

ten *largest urban agglomerations:* Tokyo (Japan)—38,001,000; New Delhi (India)—25,703,000; Shanghai (China)—23,741,000; Sao Paulo (Brazil)—21,066,000; Mumbai (India)—21,043,000; Mexico City (Mexico)—20,999,000; Beijing (China)—20,384,000; Osaka (Japan)—20,238,000; Cairo (Egypt) -18,772,000; New York-Newark (US)—18,593,000 (2015)

Sex ratio: *at birth:* 1.03 male(s)/female
0–14 years: 1.07 male(s)/female
15–24 years: 1.06 male(s)/female
25–54 years: 1.02 male(s)/female
55–64 years: 0.95 male(s)/female
65 years and over: 0.8 male(s)/female
total population: 1.01 male(s)/female (2015 est.)

Maternal mortality rate: 216 deaths/100,000 live births (2015 est.)

Infant mortality rate: *total:* 35.4 deaths/1,000 live births
male: 37.3 deaths/1,000 live births
female: 33.4 deaths/1,000 live births (2015 est.)

Life expectancy at birth: *total population:* 68.7 years
male: 66.7 years
female: 70.8 years (2015 est.)

Total fertility rate: 2.42 children born/woman (2015 est.)

Drinking water source: improved:
urban: 96.5% of population
rural: 84.7% of population
total: 91.1% of population
unimproved:
urban: 3.5% of population
rural: 15.3% of population
total: 8.9% of population (2015 est.)

Sanitation facility access: improved:
urban: 82.3% of population
rural: 50.5% of population
total: 67.7% of population
unimproved:
urban: 17.7% of population
rural: 49.5% of population
total: 32.3% of population (2015 est.)

HIV/AIDS—adult prevalence rate: 0.79% (2014 est.)

HIV/AIDS—people living with HIV/AIDS: 36,872,500 (2014 est.)

HIV/AIDS—deaths: 1,181,700 (2014 est.)

Literacy: *definition:* age 15 and over can read and write
total population: 86.1%
male: 89.9%
female: 82.2% (2015 est.)

note: more than three-quarters of the world's 781 million illiterate adults are found in South and West Asia and sub-Saharan Africa; of all the illiterate adults in the world, almost two-thirds are women (2012)

School life expectancy (primary to tertiary education): *total:* 12 years
male: 12 years
female: 12 years (2014)

GOVERNMENT

Administrative divisions: 195 countries, 72 dependent areas and other entities

Legal system: the legal systems of nearly all countries are generally modeled upon elements of five main types: civil law (including French law, the Napoleonic Code, Roman law, Roman-Dutch law, and Spanish law); common law (including English and US law); customary law; mixed or pluralistic law; and religious law (including Islamic law); an addition al type of legal system—International law—governs the conduct of independent nations in their relationships with one another

international law organization participation: all members of the UN are parties to the statute that established the InterNational Court of Justice (ICJ) or World Court; 61 countries have accepted jurisdiction of the ICJ as compulsory with reservations and 11 countries have accepted ICJ jurisdiction as compulsory without reservations; states parties to the Rome Statute of the Interbational Criminal Court (ICCt) are those countries that have ratified or acceded to the Rome Statute, the treaty that established the Court; a total of 123 (effective 2 January 2015) countries have accepted jurisdiction of the ICCt (see Appendix B for a clarification on the differing mandates of the ICJ and ICCt)

Flag description: *note:* the flags of 11 nations: Austria, Botswana, Jamaica, Japan, Laos, Latvia, Macedonia, Micronesia, Nigeria, Switzerland, and Thailand have no top or bottom and may be flown with either long edge on top without any notice being taken

ECONOMY

Economy—overview: The international financial crisis of 2008–09 led to the first downturn in global output since 1946 and presented the world with a major new challenge: determining what mix of fiscal and monetary policies to follow to restore growth and jobs, while keeping inflation and debt under control. Financial stabilization and stimulus programs that started in 2009–11, comBined with lower tax revenues in 2009–10, required most countries to run large budget deficits. Treasuries issued new public debt—totaling $9.1 trillion since 2008 -to pay for the addition al expenditures. To keep interest rates low, most central banks monetized that debt, injecting large sums of money into their economies—between December 2008 and December 2013 the global money supply increased by more than 35%. Governments are now faced with the difficult task of spurring current growth and employment without saddling their economies with so much debt that they sacrifice long-term growth and financial stability. When economic activity picks up, central

banks will confront the difficult task of containing inflation without raising interest rates so high they snuff out further growth.

Fiscal and monetary data for 2013 are currently available for 180 countries, which together account for 98.5% of world GDP. Of the 180 countries, 82 pursued unequivocally expansion ary policies, boosting government spending while also expanding their money supply relatively rapidly—faster than the world average of 3.1%; 28 followed restrictive fiscal and monetary policies, reducing government spending and holding money growth to less than the 3.1% average; and the remaining 70 followed a mix of counterbalancing fiscal and monetary policies, either reducing government spending while accelerating money growth, or boosting spending while curtailing money growth. (For more information, see attached spreadsheet, Fiscal and Monetary Data, 2008–2012.) in 2013, for many countries the drive for fiscal austerity that began in 2011 abated. While 5 out of 6 countries slowed spending in 2012, only 1 in 2 countries slowed spending in 2013. About 1 in 3 countries actually lowered the level of their expenditures. The global growth rate for government expenditures increased from 1.6% in 2012 to 5.1% in 2013, after falling from a 10.1% growth rate in 2011. On the other hand, nearly 2 out of 3 central banks tightened monetary policy in 2013, decelerating the rate of growth of their money supply, compared with only 1 out of 3 in 2012. Roughly 1 of 4 central banks actually withdrew money from circulation, an increase from 1 out of 7 in 2012. Growth of the global money supply, as measured by the narrowly defined M1, slowed from 8.7% in 2009 and 10.4% in 2010 to 5.2% in 2011,4.6% in 2012, and 3.1% in 2013. Several notable shifts occurred in 2013. By cutting government expenditures and expanding money supplies, the US and Canada moved against the trend in the rest of the world. France reversed course completely. Rather than reducing expenditures and money as it had in 2012, it expanded both. Germany reversed its fiscal policy, sharply expanding federal spending, while continuing to grow the money supply. South Korea shifted monetary policy into high gear, while maintaining a strongly expansion ary fiscal policy. Japan, however, continued to pursue austere fiscal and monetary policies. Austere economic policies have significantly affected economic performance. The global budget deficit narrowed to roughly $2.7 trillion in 2012 and $2.1 trillion in 2013, or 3.8% and 2.5% of World GDP, respectively. But growth of the world economy slipped from 5.1% in 2010 and 3.7% in 2011, to just 3.1% in 2012, and 2.9% in 2013.

Countries with expansion ary fiscal and monetary policies achieved significantly higher rates of growth, higher growth of tax revenues, and greater success reducing the public debt burden than those countries that chose contraction ary policies. in 2013, the 82 countries that followed a pro-growth approach achieved a median GDP growth rate of 4.7%, compared to 1.7% for the 28 countries with restrictive fiscal and monetary policies, a difference of 3 percentage points. Among the 82, China grew 7.7%, Philippines 6.8%, Malaysia 4.7%, Pakistan and Saudi Arabia 3.6%, Argentina 3.5%, South Korea 2.8%, and Russia 1.3%, while among the 28, Brazil grew 2.3%, Japan 2.0%, South Africa 2.0%, Netherlands -0.8%, Croatia -1.0%, Iran -1.5%, Portugal -1.8%, Greece -3.8%, and Cyprus -8.7%.

Faster GDP growth and lower unemployment rates translated into increased tax revenues and a less cumbersome debt burden. Revenues for the 82 expansion ary countries grew at a median rate of 10.7%, whereas tax revenues fell at a median rate of 6.8% for the 28 countries that chose austere economic policies. Budget balances improved for about three-quarters of the 28, but, for most, debt grew faster than GDP, and the median level of their public debt as a share of GDP increased 9.1 percentage points, to 59.2%. On the other hand, budget balances deteriorated for most of the 82 pro-growth countries, but GDP growth outpaced increases in debt, and the median level of public debt as a share of GDP increased just 1.9%, to 39.8%.

The world recession has suppressed inflation rates—world inflation declined 1.0 percentage point in 2012 to about 4.1% and 0.2 percentage point to 3.9% in 2013. In 2013 the median inflation rate for the 82 pro-growth countries was 1.3 percentage points higher than that for the countries that followed more austere fiscal and monetary policies. Overall, the latter countries also improved their current account balances by shedding imports; as a result, current account balances deteriorated for most of the countries that pursued pro-growth policies. Slow growth of world income continued to hold import demand in check and crude oil prices fell. Consequently, the dollar value of world trade grew just 1.3% in 2013.

Beyond the current global slowdown, the world faces several long standing economic challenges. The addition of 80 million people each year to an already overcrowded globe is exacerbating the problems of pollution, waste-disposal, epidemics, water-shortages, famine, over-fishing of oceans, deforestation, desertification, and depletion of non-renewable resources. The nation-state, as a bedrock economic-political institution, is steadily losing control over international flows of people, goods, services, funds, and technology. The introduction of the euro as the common currency of much of Western Europe in January 1999, while paving the way for an integrated economic powerhouse, has created economic risks because the participating nations have varying income levels and growth rates, and hence, require a different mix of monetary and fiscal policies. Governments, especially in Western Europe, face the difficult political problem of channeling resources away from welfare programs in order to increase investment and strengthen incentives to seek employment. Because of their own internal problems and priorities, the industrialized countries are unable to devote sufficient resources to deal effectively with the poorer areas of the world, which, at least from an economic point of view, are becoming further

marginalized. The terrorist attacks on the US on 11 September 2001 accentuated a growing risk to global prosperity—the diversion of resources away from capital investments to counter-terrorism programs.

Despite these vexing problems, the world economy also shows great promise. Technology has made possible further advances in a wide range of fields, from agriculture, to medicine, alternative energy, metallurgy, and transportation. Improved global communications have greatly reduced the costs of international trade, helping the world gain from the international division of labor, raise living standards, and reduce income disparities among nations. Much of the resilience of the world economy in the aftermath of the financial crisis resulted from government and central bank leaders around the globe working in concert to stem the financial onslaught, knowing well the lessons of past economic failures.

GDP (purchasing power parity): $113.7 trillion (2015 est.)
$110.4 trillion (2014 est.)
$106.9 trillion (2013 est.)
note: data are in 2015 US dollars

GDP (official exchange rate): SGWP (gross world product): $74.15 trillion (2015 est.)

GDP—real growth rate: 3% (2015 est.)
3.2% (2014 est.)
3.3% (2013 est.)

GDP—per capita (PPP): $15,800 (2015 est.)
$16,700 (2014 est.)
$16,400 (2013 est.)
note: data are in 2015 US dollars

Gross National saving: 26.7% of GDP (2015 est.)
27.3% of GDP (2014 est.)
27.3% of GDP (2013 est.)

GDP—composition, by end use:
household consumption: 57%
government consumption: 16.4%
investment in fixed capital: 24.9%
investment in inventories: 0.8%
exports of goods and services: 29.6%
imports of goods and services: -28.6% (2015 est.)

GDP—composition, by sector of origin:
agriculture: 6.5%
industry: 31.1%
services: 62.4% (2015 est.)

Industries: dominated by the onrush of technology, especially in computers, robotics, telecommunications, and medicines and medical equipment; most of these advances take place in OECD nations; only a small portion of non-OECD countries have succeeded in rapidly adjusting to these technological forces; the accelerated development of new technologies is complicating already grim environmental problems

Industrial production growth rate: 1.8% (2015 est.)

Labor force: 3.39 billion (2015 est.)

Labor force—by occupation: *agriculture:* 34.6%
industry: 22.2%
services: 43.1% (2011)

Unemployment rate: 8% (2015 est.)

7.3% (2014 est.)
note: 30% combined unemployment and underemployment in many non-industrialized countries; developed countries typically 4%-12% unemployment (2007 est.)

Household income or consumption by percentage share: *lowest:* 10%: 2.6%
highest: 10%: 30.3% (2008 est.)

Distribution of family income—Gini index:
38.1 (2009 est.)
37.3 (2000 est.)

Budget: *revenues:* $20.31 trillion
expenditures: $22.57 trillion (2015 est.)
Taxes and other revenues: 27.4% of GDP (2015 est.)

Budget surplus (+) or deficit (−): -3% of GDP (2015 est.)

Public debt: 58.8% of GDP (2015 est.)
57.9% of GDP (2014 est.)

Inflation rate (consumer prices): *world average:* 3.8% (2015 est.)
0.3% (2015 est.)
developed countries: 5.8% (2015 est.)
0.3% (2014 est.)
developing countries: 5.7% (2015 est.)
4.7% (2014 est.)
note: the above estimates are weighted averages; inflation in developed countries is 0% to 4% typically, in developing countries, 4% to 10% typically; National inflation rates vary widely in individual cases; inflation rates have declined for most countries for the last several years, held in check by increasing international competition from several low wage countries and by soft demand due to the world financial crisis

Stock of narrow money: $27.29 trillion (31 December 2015 est.)
$26.84 trillion (31 December 2014 est.)

Stock of broad money: $81.3 trillion (31 December 2014 est.)
$78.45 trillion (31 December 2013 est.)

Stock of domestic credit: $94.6 trillion (31 December 2015 est.)
$94.55 trillion (31 December 2014 est.)

Market value of publicly traded shares: $59.93 trillion (31 December 2012 est.)
$54.49 trillion (31 December 2011)
$56.6 trillion (31 December 2010 est.)

Exports: $16.64 trillion (2015 est.)
$18.65 trillion (2014 est.)

Exports—commodities: the whole range of industrial and agricultural goods and services
top ten—share of world trade: electrical machinery, including computers 14.8%; mineral fuels, including oil, coal, gas, and refined products 14.4%; nuclear reactors, boilers, and parts 14.2%; cars, trucks, and buses 8.9%; scientific and precision instruments 3.5%; plastics 3.4%; iron and steel 2.7%; organic chemicals 2.6%; pharmaceutical products 2.6%; diamonds, pearls, and precious stones 1.9% (2007 est.)

Imports: $16.12 trillion (2015 est.)
$18.13 trillion (2014 est.)

Imports—commodities: the whole range of industrial and agricultural goods and services

top ten—share of world trade: see listing for exports

Debt—external: $79.12 trillion (31 December 2014 est.)

$78.74 trillion (31 December 2013 est.)

note: this figure is the sum total of all countries' external debt, both public and private

Stock of direct foreign investment—at home: $26.93 trillion (31 December 2015 est.)

$25.14 trillion (31 December 2014 est.)

Stock of direct foreign investment—abroad: $28.04 trillion (31 December 2015 est.)

$26.42 trillion (31 December 2014 est.)

ENERGY

Electricity—production: 22.57 trillion kWh (2012 est.)

Electricity—consumption: 20.99 trillion kWh (2012 est.)

Electricity—exports: 632.9 billion kWh (2013 est.)

Electricity—imports: 678.2 billion kWh (2013 est.)

Electricity—installed generating capacity: 5.847 billion kW (2012 est.)

Electricity—from fossil fuels: 65.3% of total installed capacity (2012 est.)

Electricity—fron nuclear fuels: 6.8% of total installed capacity (2012 est.)

Electricity—from hydroelectric plants: 18.7% of total installed capacity (2012 est.)

Electricity—from other renewable sources: 9.2% of total installed capacity (2012 est.)

Crude oil—production: 79.17 million bbl/day (2014 est.)

Crude oil—exports: 44.07 million bbl/day (2012 est.)

Crude oil—imports: 47.43 million bbl/day (2012 est.)

Crude oil—proved reserves: 1.66 trillion bbl (1 January 2015 est.)

Refined petroleum Products—production: 86.37 million bbl/day (2012 est.)

Refined petroleum Products—consumption: 90.05 million bbl/day (2013 est.)

Refined petroleum Products—exports: 27.09 million bbl/day (2012 est.)

Refined petroleum Products—Imports: 24.5 million bbl/day (2012 est.)

Natural gas—production: 3.43 trillion cu m (2013 est.)

Natural gas—consumption: 3.42 trillion cu m (2013 est.)

Natural gas—exports: 1.136 trillion cu m (2013 est.)

Natural gas—Imports: 1.449 trillion cu m (2013 est.)

Natural gas—proved reserves: 191.4 trillion cu m (1 January 2014 est.)

Carbon dioxide emissions from consumption of energy: 34.18 billion Mt (2012 est.)

COMMUNICATIONS

Telephones—fixed lines: 1.1 billion (2014 est.)

Telephones—mobile cellular: total 7 billion (2014 est.)

Radio broadcast stations: AMNA, FMNA, shortwave NA

Television broadcast stations: NA

Internet users: 2.8 billion

top ten countries by Internet usage (in millions): China 626.6; United States 276.6; India 237.3; Japan 109.4; Brazil 108.2; Russia 84.4; Germany 70.3; Nigeria 66.6; United Kingdom 57.3; France 56.8 (2014 est.)

TRANSPORTATION

Airports: total Airports—41,821 (2013)

top ten by passengers: Atlanta (ATL)—94,431,224; Beijing (PEK)—83,712,355; London (LHR) -72,368,061; Tokyo (HND)—68,906,509; Chicago (ORD)—66,777,161; Los Angeles (LAX)—66,667,619; Dubai (DXB)—66,431,533; Paris (CDG)—62,052,917; Dallas/Fort Worth (DFW)—60,470,507; Jakarta (CGK)—60,137,347 (2013)

top ten by cargo (metric tons): Hong Kong (HKG)—4,166,303; Memphis, TN (MEM)—4,137,801; Shanghai (PVG)—2,928,527; Incheon (ICN)—2,464,384; Dubai (D XB)—2,435,567; Anchorage, AK (ANC)— 2,421,145; Louisville, KY (SDF)—2,216,079; Frankfurt (FRA)—2,094,453; Paris (CDG)—2,069,200; Tokyo (NRT)—2,019,844 (2013)

Heliports: 6,524 (2013)

Railways: *total:* 1,148,186 km (2013)

Roadways: *total:* 64,285,009 km (2013)

Waterways: 2,293,412 km

top ten longest rivers: Nile (Africa) 6,693 km; Amazon (South America) 6,436 km; Mississippi-Missouri (North America) 6,238 km; Yenisey-Angara (Asia) 5,981 km; Ob-Irtysh (Asia) 5,569 km; Yangtze (Asia) 5,525 km; Yellow (Asia) 4,671 km; Amur (Asia) 4,352 km; Lena (Asia) 4,345 km; Congo (Africa) 4,344 km

note: rivers are not necessarily navigable along the entire length; if measured by volume, the Amazon is the largest river in the world

top ten largest Natural lakes (by surface area): Caspian Sea (Azerbaijan, Iran, Kazakhstan, Russia, Turkmenistan) 372,960 sq km; Lake Superior (Canada, United States) 82,414 sq km; Lake Victoria (Kenya, Tanzania, Uganda) 69,490 sq km; Lake Huron (Canada, United States) 59,596 sq km; Lake Michigan (United States) 57,441 sq km; Lake Tanganyika (Burundi, Democratic Republic of the Congo, Tanzania, Zambia) 32,890 sq km; Great Bear Lake (Canada) 31,800 sq km; Lake Baikal (Russia) 31,494 sq km; Lake Nyasa (Malawi, Mozambique, Tanzania) 30,044 sq km; Great Slave Lake (Canada) 28,400 sq km

note: the areas of the lakes are subject to season al variation; only the Caspian Sea is saline, the rest are fresh water (2013)

Ports and terminals: *top ten container ports as measured by Twenty-Foot Equivalent Units (TEUs) throughput:* Shanghai (China)—33,617,000; Singapore (Singapore)—32,578,000; Shenzhen (China)—23,278,000; Hong Kong (China)—22,352,000; Busan (South Korea)—17,611,882; Ningbo (China)—17,326,800; Qingdao (China)—15,520,000; Guangzhou (China)—15,309,200; Dubai (UAE)—13,600,000;—Tianjin (China) -12,996,510 (2013)

Transportation—note: the international Maritime Bureau (IMB) reports that 2014 saw a continued decrease in global pirate activities declining 7% over 2013; in 2014, pirates attacked a total of 245 ships world-wide including hijacking 21 ships, capturing 442 seafarers, and killing 4; the Horn of Africa continued to see a drop in pirate activities with only 11 incidents in 2014 compared with 15 in 2013 and 236 in 2011; the decrease in successful pirate attacks off the Horn of Africa is due, in part, to more aggressive anti-piracy operations by international Naval forces, the hardening of vessels, and the increased use of armed security teams aboard merchant ships; despite these preventative measures, the assessed risk remains high; attacks in the Straits of Malacca and South China Sea accounted for 55% of ships attacked in 2014; West African piracy is a growing threat accounting for 16% of all attacks in 2014; Nigerian pirates are very aggressive, operatingas far as 200 nm offshore and linked with at least four hijackings that occurred in this area; attacks in South Asian waters remaiNAt low levels although incidents have increased each year since 2010 reaching 34 in 2014; as of October 2015, there were 190 attacks worldwide with 15 hijackings in the Straits of Malacca/South China Sea region and West African waters

MILITARY AND SECURITY

Military expenditures: 2.42% of GDP (2012)

2.51% of GDP (2011)

2.42% of GDP (2010)

TRANSNATIONAL ISSUES

Disputes—international: stretching over 250,000 km, the world's 325 international land boundaries separate 195 independent states and 71 dependencies, areas of special sovereignty, and other miscellaneous entities; ethnicity, culture, race, religion, and language have divided states into separate political entities as much as history, physical terrain, political fiat, or conquest, resulting in sometimes arbitrary and imposed boundaries; most maritime states have claimed limits that include territorial seas and exclusive economic zones; overlapping limits due to adjacent or opposite coasts create the potential for 430 bilateral maritime boundaries of which 209 have agreements that include contiguous and non-contiguous segments; boundary, borderland/resource, and territorial disputes vary

945

in intensity from managed or dormant to violent or militarized; undemarcated, indefinite, porous, and unmanaged boundaries tend to encourage illegal cross-border activities, uncontrolled migration, and confrontation; territorial disputes may evolve from historical and/or cultural claims, or they may be brought on by resource competition; ethnic and cultural clashes continue to be responsible for much of the territorial fragmentation and internal displacement of the estimated 20.8 million people and cross-border displacements of approximately 12.1 million refugees and asylum seekers around the world as of mid-2013; over half a million refugees were repatriated during 2012; other sources of contention include access to water and mineral (especially hydrocarbon) resources, fisheries, and arable land; armed conflict prevails not so much between the uniformed armed forces of independent states as between stateless armed entities that detract from the sustenance and welfare of local populations, leaving the community of nations to cope with resultant refugees, hunger, disease, impoverishment, and environmental degradation

Refugees and internally displaced persons: the UN High Commissioner for Refugees (UNHCR) estimated that as of the end of 2015 there were 65.3 million people forcibly displaced worldwide, the highest level ever recorded; this includes 21.3 million refugees, 3.2 million asylum seekers, and 40.8 million conflict

IDPs: the UNHCR estimates there are currently at least 10 million stateless persons (2016)

Trafficking in persons: *current situation:* the Inter National Labour Organization conservatively estimated that 20.9 million people in 2012 were victims of forced labor, representing the full range of human trafficking (also referred to as "modern-day slavery") for labor and sexual exploitation; about one-third of reported cases involved crossing international borders, which is often associated with sexual exploitation; trafficking in persons is most prevalent in southeastern Europe, Eurasia, and Africa and least frequent in EU member states, Canada, the US, and other developed countries (2012)

Tier 2 Watch List: countries that do not fully comply with the minimum standards for the elimination of trafficking but are making significant efforts to do so; (44 countries) Antigua and Barbuda, Bolivia, Botswana, Bulgaria, Burkina Faso, Burma, Cambodia, China, Democratic Republic of the Congo, Republic of the Congo, Costa Rica, Cuba, Djibouti, Egypt, Gabon, Ghana, Guinea, Guyana, Haiti, Jamaica, Laos, Lebanon, Lesotho, Malaysia, Maldives, Mali, Mauritius, Namibia, Pakistan, Papua New Guinea, Qatar, Saudi Arabia, Saint Vincent and the Grenadines, Solomon Islands, Sri Lanka, Sudan, Suriname, Tanzania, Timor-Leste, Trinidad and Tobago, Tunisia, Turkmenistan, UKraine, Uzbekistan

Tier 3: countries that neither satisfy the minimum standards for the elimination of trafficking nor demonstrate a significant effort to do so; (23 countries) Algeria, Belarus, Belize, Burundi, Central African Republic, Comoros, Equatorial Guinea, Eritrea, The Gambia, Guinea-Bissau, Iran, North Korea, Kuwait, Libya, Marshall Islands, Mauritania, Russia, South Sudan, Syria, Thailand, Venezuela, Yemen, Zimbabwe (2015)

Illicit drugs: cocaine: worldwide coca leaf cultivation in 2013 likely amounted to 165,000 hectares, assuming a stable crop in Bolivia; Colombia produced slightly less than half of the worldwide crop, followed by Peru and Bolivia; potential pure cocaine production increased 7% to 640 metric tons in 2013; Colombia conducts an aggressive coca eradication campaign, Peru has increased its eradication efforts, but remains hesitant to eradicate coca in key growing areas

opiates: worldwide illicit opium poppy cultivation increased in 2013, with potential opium Production reaching 6,800 metric tons; Afghanistan is world's primary opium Producer, accounting for 82% of the global supply; Southeast Asia was responsible for 12% of global opium; Pakistan produced 3% of global opium; Latin america produced 4% of global opium, and most was refined into heroin destined for the US market (2015)

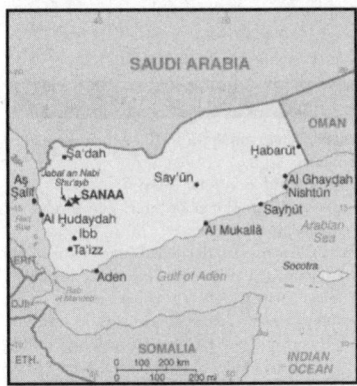

INTRODUCTION

Background: North Yemen became independent from the Ottoman Empire in 1918. The British, who had set up a protectorate area around the southern port of Aden in the 19th century, withdrew in 1967 from what became South Yemen. Three years later, the southern Government adopted a Marxist orientation. The massive exodus of hundreds of thousands of Yemenis from the south to the north contributed to two decades of hostility between the states. The two countries were formally unified as the Republic of Yemen in 1990. A southern secessionist movement and brief civil war in 1994 was quickly subdued. In 2000, Saudi Arabia and Yemen agreed to delineate their border. Fighting in the northwest between the government and the Huthis, a Zaydi Shia Muslim minority, began in 2004 and has since resulted in six rounds of fighting that ended in early 2010 with a cease-fire. The southern secessionist movement was revitalized in 2008. Public rallies in Sana'a against then President SALIH—inspired by similar demonstrations in Tunisia and Egypt—slowly built momentum starting in late January 2011 fueled by complaints over high unemployment, poor economic conditions, and corruption. By the following month, some protests had resulted in violence, and the demonstrations had spread to other major cities. By March the opposition had hardened its demands and was unifying behind calls for SALIH's immediate ouster. In April 2011, the Gulf Cooperation Council (GCC), in an attempt to mediate the crisis in Yemen, proposed the GGC Initiative, an agreement in which the president would step down in exchange for immunity from prosecution. SALIH's refusal to sign an agreement led to further violence. The UN Security Council passed Resolution 2014 in October 2011 calling for an end to the violence and completing a power transfer deal. In November 2011, SALIH signed the GCC Initiative to step down and to transfer some of his powers to Vice President Abd Rabuh Mansur HADI. Following HADI's election

victory in February 2012, SALIH formally transferred his powers. In accordance with the GCC initiative, Yemen launched a National Dialogue Conference (NDC) in March 2013 to discuss key constitutional, political, and social issues. HADI concluded the NDC in January 2014. Subsequent steps in the transition process include constitutional drafting, a constitutional referendum, and National elections. Since the Arab Awakening in 2011, the Huthis have expanded their influence, culminating in a major offensive against military units and tribes affiliated with their Yemeni rivals and enabling their forces to overrun the capital, Sana'a, in September 2014. In January 2015, the Huthis attacked the presidential palace and President HADI's residence and surrounded key government facilities, prompting HADI and the cabinet to submit their resignations. HADI fled to Aden, and in February 2015 rescinded his resignation. He subsequently escaped to Saudi Arabia and asked the GCC to intervene militarily in Yemen to protect the legitimate government from the Huthis. In March, the Kingdom of Saudi Arabia launched Operation Decisive Storm, a series of airstrikes against Huthi and Huthi-affiliated forces. In April 2015, the Saudi Government announced completion of the operation and initiated Operation Restoring Hope, which focuses on humanitarian aid and a return to political dialogue. However, fighting continued through the remainder of 2015 and into early 2016. In April, the UN brokered a "cessation of hostilities" among the warring parties and initiated peace talks in Kuwait, but by early June the talks had stalled.

GEOGRAPHY

Location: Middle East, bordering the Arabian Sea, Gulf of Aden, and Red Sea, between Oman and Saudi Arabia

Geographic coordinates: 15 00N, 48 00E

Map references: Middle East

Area: *total:* 527,968 sq km
land: 527,968 sq km
water: 0 sq km
note: includes Perim, Socotra, the former Yemen Arab Republic (YAR or North Yemen), and the former People's Democratic Republic of Yemen (PDRY or South Yemen)
country comparison to the world: 50

Area—comparative: almost four times the size of Alabama; slightly larger than twice the size of Wyoming

Land boundaries: *total:* 1,601 km
border countries (2): Oman 294 km, Saudi Arabia 1,307 km

Coastline: 1,906 km

Maritime claims: *territorial sea:* 12 nm
contiguous zone: 24 nm
exclusive economic zone: 200 nm
continental shelf: 200 nm or to the edge of the continental margin

Climate: mostly desert; hot and humid along west coast; temperate in western mountains affected by seasonal monsoon; extraordinarily hot, dry, harsh desert in east

Terrain: narrow coastal plain backed by flat-topped hills and rugged mountains; dissected upland desert plains in center slope into the desert interior of the Arabian Peninsula

Elevation: *mean elevation:* 999 m

elevation extremes: *lowest point:* Arabian Sea 0 m
highest point: Jabal an Nabi Shu'ayb 3,760 m

Natural resources: petroleum, fish, rock salt, marble; small deposits of coal, gold, lead, nickel, and copper; fertile soil in west

Land use: *agricultural land:* 44.5%
arable land: 2.2%
permanent crops: 0.6%
permanent pasture: 41.7%
forest: 1%
other: 54.5% (2011 est.)

Irrigated land: 6,800 sq km (2012)

Total renewable water resources: 2.1 cu km (2011)

Freshwater withdrawal (domestic/industrial/agricultural): *total:* 3.57 cu km/yr (7%/2%/91%)
per capita: 162.4 cu m/yr (2005)

Natural hazards: sandstorms and dust storms in summer
volcanism: limited volcanic activity; Jebel at Tair (Jabal al-Tair, Jebel Teir, Jabal al-Tayr, Jazirat at-Tair) (elev. 244 m), which forms an island in the Red Sea, erupted in 2007 after awakening from dormancy; other historically active volcanoes include Harra of Arhab, Harras of Dhamar, Harra es-Sawad, and Jebel Zubair, although many of these have not erupted in over a century

Environment—current issues: limited Natural freshwater resources; inadequate supplies of potable water; overgrazing; soil erosion; desertification

Environment—International agreements: *party to:* Biodiversity, Climate Change, Climate Change-Kyoto Protocol, Desertification, Endangered Species, Environmental Modification, Hazardous Wastes, Law of the Sea, Ozone Layer Protection
signed, but not ratified: none of the selected agreements

Geography—note: strategic location on Bab el Mandeb, the strait linking the Red Sea and the Gulf of Aden, one of world's most active shipping lanes

PEOPLE AND SOCIETY

Nationality: *noun:* Yemeni(s)
adjective: Yemeni

Ethnic groups: predominantly Arab; but also Afro-Arab, South Asians, Europeans

Languages: Arabic (official)

note: a distinct Socotri language is widely used on Socotra Island and Archipelago; Mahri is still fairly widely spoken in eastern Yemen

Religions: Muslim 99.1% (official; virtually all are citizens, an estimated 65% are Sunni and 35% are Shia), other 0.9% (includes Jewish, Baha'i, Hindu, and Christian; many are refugees or temporary foreign residents) (2010 est.)

Population: 26,737,317 (July 2015 est.)
country comparison to the world: 48

Age structure: *0–14 years:* 41.09% (male 5,588,316/female 5,399,365)
15–24 years: 21.12% (male 2,865,453/female 2,782,109)
25–54 years: 31.33% (male 4,280,258/female 4,096,280)
55–64 years: 3.79% (male 468,869/female 543,336)
65 years and over: 2.67% (male 330,966/female 382,365) (2015 est.)

Dependency ratios: *total dependency ratio:* 75.6%
youth dependency ratio: 70.7%
elderly dependency ratio: 4.9%
potential support ratio: 20.4% (2015 est.)

Median Age: *total:* 18.9 years
male: 18.8 years
female: 19 years (2015 est.)
country comparison to the world: 202

Population growth rate: 2.47% (2015 est.)
country comparison to the world: 25

Birth rate: 29.98 births/1,000 population (2015 est.)
country comparison to the world: 42

Death rate: 6.28 deaths/1,000 population (2015 est.)
country comparison to the world: 154

Net migration rate: 1 migrant(s)/1,000 population (2015 est.)
country comparison to the world: 63

Urbanization: *urban population:* 34.6% of total population (2015)
rate of urbanization: 4.03% annual rate of change (2010–15 est.)

Major urban Areas—population: SANAA (capital) 2.962 million; Aden 882,000 (2015)

Sex ratio: *at birth:* 1.05 male(s)/female
0–14 years: 1.04 male(s)/female
15–24 years: 1.03 male(s)/female
25–54 years: 1.05 male(s)/female
55–64 years: 0.86 male(s)/female
65 years and over: 0.87 male(s)/female
total Population: 1.03 male(s)/female (2015 est.)

Mother's mean age at first birth: 21.4
Median Age at first birth among women 25–29 (2013)

Maternal mortality rate: 385 deaths/100,000 live births (2015 est.)
country comparison to the world: 57

Infant mortality rate: *total:* 48.93 deaths/1,000 live births
male: 53. 14 deaths/1,000 live births
female: 44. 5 deaths/1,000 live births (2015 est.)

country comparison to the world: 38
Life expectancy at birth: *total population:* 65. 18 years
male: 63.05 years
female: 67. 41 years (2015 est.)
country comparison to the world: 176

Total fertility rate: 3.91 children born/woman (2015 est.)
country comparison to the world: 40

Contraceptive prevalence rate: 27.7% (2006)

Health expenditures: 5.4% of GDP (2013)
country comparison to the world: 124

Physicians density: 0.2 physicians/1,000 population (2010)

Hospital bed density: 0.7 beds/1,000 population (2012)

Drinking water source:
improved:
urban: 72% of population
rural: 46.5% of population
total: 54.9% of population
unimproved:
urban: 28% of population
rural: 53.5% of population
total: 45.1% of population (2012 est.)

Sanitation facility access:
improved:
urban: 92.5% of population
rural: 34.1% of population
total: 53.3% of population
unimproved:
urban: 7.5% of population
rural: 65.9% of population
total: 46.7% of population (2012 est.)

HIV/AIDS—adult prevalence rate: 0.05% (2014 est.)
country comparison to the world: 119

HIV/AIDS—people living with HIV/AIDS: 7,200 (2014 est.)
country comparison to the world: 104

HIV/AIDS—deaths: 300 (2014 est.)
country comparison to the world: 96

Major infectious diseases: *degree of risk:* high
food or waterborne diseases: bacterial diarrhea, hepatitis A, and typhoid fever
vectorborne diseases: dengue fever and malaria
water contact disease: schistosomiasis (2013)

Obesity—adult prevalence rate: 14.2% (2014)
country comparison to the world: 121

Children under the age of 5 years underweight: 39.9% (2013)
country comparison to the world: 3

Education expenditures: 4.6% of GDP (2008)
country comparison to the world: 67

Literacy: *definition:* age 15 and over can read and write
total population: 70.1%
male: 85.1%
female: 55% (2015 est.)

School life expectancy (primary to tertiary education): *total:* 9 years
male: 10 years
female: 8 years (2011)

Child labor—children ages 5–14: *total number:* 1,334,288 percentage: 23% (2006 est.)

Unemployment, youth ages 15–24: *total:* 33.7%
male: 26%
female: 74% (2010 est.)
country comparison to the world: 22

GOVERNMENT

Country name: *conventional long form:* Republic of Yemen
conventional short form: Yemen
local long form: Al Jumhuriyah al Yamaniyah
local short form: Al Yaman
former: Yemen Arab Republic [Yemen (Sanaa) or North Yemen] and People's Democratic Republic of Yemen [Yemen (Aden) or South Yemen]
etymology: name derivation remains unclear but may come from the Arab term "yumn" (happiness) and be related to the region's classical name "Arabia Felix" (Fertile or Happy Arabia); the Romans referred to the rest of the peninsula as "Arabia Deserta" (Deserted Arabia)

Government type: in transition

Capital: *name:* Sanaa

Geographic coordinates: 15 21 N, 44 12 E
time difference: UTC+3 (8 hours ahead of Washington, DC, during Standard Time)

Administrative divisions: 21 governorates (muhafazat, singular—muhafazah) and 1 municipality*; Abyan, 'Adan (Aden), Ad Dali', Al Bayda', Al Hudaydah, Al Jawf, Al Mahrah, Al Mahwit, Amanat al 'Asimah (Sanaa City)*, 'Amran, Arkhabil Suqutra (Socotra Archipelago), Dhamar, Hadramawt, Hajjah, Ibb, Lahij, Ma'rib, Raymah, Sa'dah, San'a' (Sanaa), Shabwah, Ta'izz

Independence: 22 May 1990 (Republic of Yemen was established with the merger of the Yemen Arab Republic [Yemen (Sanaa) or North Yemen] and the Marxist-dominated People's Democratic Republic of Yemen [Yemen (Aden) or South Yemen]); note—previously North Yemen became independent in November 1918 (from the Ottoman Empire) and became a republic with the overthrow of the theocratic Imamate in 1962; South Yemen became independent on 30 November 1967 (from the UK)

National holiday: Unification Day, 22 May (1990)

Constitution: adopted by referendum 16 May 1991 (following unification); amended several times, last in 2009; note -after the National Dialogue ended in January 2015, a presidentially-appointed Constitutional Drafting Committee worked to prepare a new draft constitution that was expected to be put to a National referendum before being adopted; however, the president's resignation in January 2015 and the subsequent conflict interrupted the process (2016)

Legal system: mixed legal system of Islamic law, Napoleonic law, English common law, and customary law

International law organization participation: has not submitted an ICJ jurisdiction declaration; non-party state to the ICCt

Citizenship: *citizenship by birth:* no

citizenship by descent only: the father must be a citizen of Yemen; if the father is unknown, the mother must be a citizen

dual citizenship recognized: no

residency requirement for naturalization: 10 years

Suffrage: 18 years of age; universal

Executive branch: *chief of state:* President Abd Rabuh Mansur HADI (since 21 February 2012); Vice President Mohsinal AHMAR, Gen. (since 3 April 2016)

head of government: Prime Minister Obaid bin DAGHR (since 3 April 2016)

cabinet: appointed by the president

elections/appointments: president directly elected by absolute majority popular vote in 2 rounds if needed for a 7-year term (eligible for a second term); last election held on 21 February 2012 (next election NA); note—a special election held on 21 February 2012 to remove Ali Abdallah SALIH under the terms of a Gulf Cooperation Council-mediated deal during the political crisis of 2011; vice president appointed by the president; prime minister appointed by the president

election results: Abd Rabuh Mansur HADI (GPC) elected as a consensus president with about 50% popular participation; no other candidates

Legislative branch: *description:* bicameral Parliament or Majlis consists of the Shura Council or Majlis Alshoora (111 seats; members appointed by the president; member tenure NA) and the House of Representatives or Majlisal Nuwaab (301 seats; members directly elected in single-seat constituencies by simple majority vote to serve 6-year terms) *elections:* last held on 27 April 2003 (next scheduled for April 2009 but postponed indefinitely) *election results:* House of Representatives percent of vote by party—GPC 58%, Islah 22.6%, YSP 3.8%, Unionist Party 1.9%, other 13.7%; seats by party—GPC 238, Islah 46, YSP 8, Nasserite Unionist Party 3, National Arab Socialist Ba'th Party 2, independent 4

Judicial branch: Highest cou rt(s): Supreme Court (consists of the president of the Court, 2 deputies, and nearly 50 judges; court organized into constitutional, civil, commercial, family, administrative, criminal, military, and appeals scrutiny divisions) *judge selection and term of office:* judges appointed by the Supreme Judicial Council, chaired by the president of the republic and consisting of 10 high-ranking judicial officers; judges appointed for life with mandatory retirement at age 65

subordinate courts: appeal courts; district or first instance courts; commercial courts

Political parties and leaders: Arab Socialist Ba'ath Party

General People's Congress or GPC [Ali Abdallah SALIH]

Nasserite Unionist Popular Organization [Abdallah NU'MAN]

Yemeni Reform Grouping or Islah [Muhammed Abdallah al-YADUMI, Abdul Wahab al-ANSI]

Yemeni Socialist Party or YSP [Dr. Abd al-Rahman Umar al-SAQQAF]

Political pressure groups and leaders: Huthis Muslim Brotherhood Women National Committee

other: conservative tribal groups; southern secessionist groups; al-Qa'ida in the Arabian Peninsula (AQAP)

International organization participation: AFESD, AMF, CAEU, CD, EITI (temporarily suspended), FAO, G-77, IAEA, IBRD, ICAO, ICRM, IDA, IDB, IFAD, IFC, IFRCS, ILO, IMF, IMO, IMSO, Interpol, IOC, IOM, IPU, ISO, ITSO, ITU, ITUC (NGOs), LAS, MIGA, MINURSO, MINUSMA, MONUSCO, NAM, OAS (observer), OIC, OPCW, UN, UNAMID, UNCTAD, UNESCO, UNHCR, UNIDO, UNISFA, UNMIL, UNMIS, UNOCI, UNWTO, UPU, WCO, WFTU (NGOs), WHO, WIPO, WMO, WTO

Diplomatic representation in the US: *chief of mission:* Ambassador Ahmad Awadh BIN MUBARAK (since 3 August 2015)

chancery: 2319 Wyoming Avenue NW, Washington, DC 20008

telephone: [1] (202) 965-4760

FAX: [1] (202) 337-2017

Diplomatic representation from the US: *note:* US embassy operations suspended on 10 February 2015 amid growing violence; in March 2015, a team of US diplomats established the Yemen affairs Unit in Jeddah, Saudi Arabia

chief of mission: Ambassador Matthew H. TUELLER (since 10 June 2014)

embassy: Sa'awan Street, Sanaa

mailing address: P. O. Box 22347, Sanaa

telephone: [967] (1) 755-2000 ext. 2153 or 2266

FAX: [967] (1) 303-182

Flag description: three equal horizontal bands of red (top), white, and black; the band colors derive from the Arab Liberation flag and represent oppression (black), overcome through bloody struggle (red), to be replaced by a bright future (white)

note: similar to the flag of Syria, which has two green stars in the white band, and of Iraq, which has an arabic inscription centered in the white band; also similar to the flag of Egypt, which has a heraldic eagle centered in the white band

National symbol(s): golden eagle; National colors: red, white, black

National anthem: *name:* "al-qumhuriyatu l-muttahida" (United Republic)

lyrics/music: Abdullah Abdulwahab NOA'MAN/ Ayyoab Tarish ABSI

note: adopted 1990; the music first served as the anthem for South Yemen before unification with North Yemen in 1990

ECONOMY

Economy—overview: Yemen is a low-income country that faces difficult long-term challenges to stabilizing and growing its economy, and the current conflict has only exacerbated those issues. The ongoing war has halted Yemen's exports, pressured the currency's exchange rate, accelerated inflation, severely limited food and fuel imports, and caused widespread damage to infrastructure. At least 82% of the population is in need of humanitarian assistance. Prior to the start of the conflict in 2014, Yemen was highly dependent on declining oil resources for revenue. Oil and gas earnings accounted for roughly 25% of GDP and 65% of government revenue. The Yemeni Government regularly faced annual budget shortfalls and has tried to diversify the Yemeni economy through a reform program designed to bolster non-oil sectors of the economy and foreign investment. As part of these reform efforts, Yemen exported its first liquefied Natural gas in October 2009. The international community supported Yemen's efforts toward economic and political reform in part by establishing the Friends of Yemen group. In 2012, the Friends of Yemen pledged nearly $7 billion in assistance to Yemen. In July 2014, the government continued reform efforts by eliminating some fuel subsidies and in August 2014, the IMF approved a three-year, $570 million Extended Credit Facility for Yemen.

However, the conflict that began in 2014 stalled these reform efforts. Rebel Huthi groups have interfered with Ministry of Finance and Central Bank operations and diverted funds for their own use. Yemen's Central Bank reserves, which stood at $5. 2 billion prior to the conflict, currently stand at $1.5 billion. The Central Bank is exposed to approximately $7 billion in overdraft, more than three times the legal limit, directly linked to the Houthis withdrawing $116 million on a monthly basis. The private sector is hemorrhaging, with almost all businesses making substantial layoffs. The Port of Hudaydah, which handles 60% of Yemen's commercial traffic, was damaged in August 2015 as a result of the conflict and is only operating at 50% capacity. Access to food and other critical commodities such as medical equipment is limited across the country due to security issues on the ground. The Social Welfare Fund, a cash transfer program for Yemen's neediest, is no longer operational and has not made any disbursements since late 2014.

Yemen will require significant international assistance during and after the protracted conflict to stabilize its economy. Long-term challenges include a high population growth rate, high unemployment, declining water resources, and severe food scarcity.

GDP (purchasing power parity): $75.54 billion (2015 est.)

$105.1 billion (2014 est.)

$105.3 billion (2013 est.)

note: data are in 2015 US dollars

country comparison to the world: 93

GDP (official exchange rate): $36.85 billion (2015 est.)

GDP—real growth rate: -28.1% (2015 est.)

-0.2% (2014 est.)

4.8% (2013 est.)

country comparison to the world: 225

GDP—per capita (PPP): $2,700 (2015 est.)

$3,800 (2014 est.)

$3,900 (2013 est.)

note: data are in 2015 US dollars
country comparison to the world: 194

Gross National saving: -3.9% of GDP (2015 est.)
6.2% of GDP (2014 est.)
5% of GDP (2013 est.)
country comparison to the world: 173

GDP—composition, by end use:
household consumption: 102.9%
government consumption: 11.7%
investment in fixed capital: 8.9%
investment in inventories: -5.2%
exports of goods and services: 8.5%
imports of good s and services: -26.8% (2015 est.)

GDP—composition, by sector of origin:
agriculture: 19%
industry: 10.6%
services: 70.4% (2015 est.)

Agriculture—products: grain, fruits, vegetables, pulses, qat, coffee, cotton; dairy products, livestock (sheep, goats, cattle, camels), poultry; fish

Industries: crude oil production and petroleum refining; small-scale production of cotton textiles, leather goods; food processing; handicrafts; aluminum products; cement; commercial ship repair; Natural gas production

Industrial production growth rate: -72% (2015 est.)
country comparison to the world: 202

Labor force: 7.328 million (2015 est.)
country comparison to the world: 65

Labor force—by occupation: *note:* most people are employed in agriculture and herding; services, construction, industry, and commerce account for less than one-fourth of the labor force

Unemployment rate: 27% (2014 est.)
35% (2003 est.)
country comparison to the world: 181

Population below poverty line: 54% (2014 est.)

Household income or consumption by percentage share: *lowest:* 10%: 2.6%
highest: 10%: 30.3% (2008 est.)

Distribution of family income—Gini index: 37.9 (2009 est.)
37.3 (1999 est.)
country comparison to the world: 76

Budget: *revenues:* $2.933 billion
expenditures: $5.925 billion (2015 est.)
Taxes and other revenues: 8.4% of GDP (2015 est.)
country comparison to the world: 211

Budget surplus (+) or deficit (–): -8.6% of GDP (2015 est.)
country comparison to the world: 201

Public debt: 93.5% of GDP (2015 est.)
57.2% of GDP (2014 est.)
country comparison to the world: 23

Fiscal year: calendar year

Inflation rate (consumer prices): 30% (2015 est.)
8.2% (2014 est.)
country comparison to the world: 222

Central bank discount rate: NA%

Commercial bank prime lending rate: 25% (31 December 2015 est.)

24% (31 December 2014 est.)
country comparison to the world: 6

Stock of narrow money: $4.388 billion (31 December 2015 est.)
$5.256 billion (31 December 2014 est.)
country comparison to the world: 102

Stock of broad money: $16.02 billion (31 December 2014 est.)
$14.04 billion (31 December 2013 est.)
country comparison to the world: 96

Stock of domestic credit: $8.452 billion (31 December 2015 est.)
$12.78 billion (31 December 2014 est.)
country comparison to the world: 108

Market value of publicly traded shares: $NA

Current account balance: -$2.072 billion (2015 est.)
-$715 million (2014 est.)
country comparison to the world: 145

Exports: $1.416 billion (2015 est.)
$8.291 billion (2014 est.)
country comparison to the world: 151

Exports—commodities: crude oil, coffee, dried and salted fish, liquefied Natural gas

Exports—partners: China 24.5%, UAE 16.5%, South Korea 10%, Saudi Arabia 9.9%, Kuwait 9.1%, India 8.5% (2015)

Imports: $5.491 billion (2015 est.)
$10.19 billion (2014 est.)
country comparison to the world: 122

Imports—commodities: food and live animals, machinery and equipment, chemicals

Imports—partners: UAE 20.9%, China 14.3%, Saudi Arabia 9.8%, Kuwait 7.4%, India 4.6% (2015)

Reserves of foreign exchange and gold: $2.309 billion (31 December 2015 est.)
$4.665 billion (31 December 2014 est.)
country comparison to the world: 117

Debt—external: $7.772 billion (31 December 2014 est.)
$7.671 billion (31 December 2013 est.)
country comparison to the world: 114

Stock of direct foreign investment—at home: $NA

Exchange rates: Yemeni rials (YER) per US dollar—
214.89 (2015 est.)
214.89 (2014 est.)
214.89 (2013 est.)
214.35 (2012 est.)
213.8 (2011 est.)

ENERGY

Electricity—production: 6.185 billion kWh (2012 est.)
country comparison to the world: 112

Electricity—consumption: 3.838 billion kWh (2012 est.)
country comparison to the world: 127

Electricity—exports: 0 kWh (2013 est.)
country comparison to the world: 218

Electricity—imports: 0 kWh (2013 est.)

country comparison to the world: 219

Electricity—installed generating capacity: 1.535 million kW (2012 est.)
country comparison to the world: 116

Electricity—from fossil fuels: 99.9% of total installed capacity (2012 est.)
country comparison to the world: 39

Electricity—from nuclear fuels: 0% of total installed capacity (2012 est.)
country comparison to the world: 212

Electricity—from hydro electric plants: 0% of total installed capacity (2012 est.)
country comparison to the world: 155

Electricity—from other renewable sources: 0.1% of total installed capacity (2012 est.)
country comparison to the world: 118

Crude oil—production: 125,100 bbl/day (2014 est.)
country comparison to the world: 42

Crude oil—exports: 43,000 bbl/day (2014 est.)
country comparison to the world: 49

Crude oil—imports: 0 bbl/day (2012 est.)
country comparison to the world: 85

Crude oil—proved reserves: 3 billion bbl (1 January 2015 est.)
country comparison to the world: 30

Refined petroleum products—production: 27,840 bbl/day (2012 est.)
country comparison to the world: 88

Refined petroleum products—consumption: 134,000 bbl/day (2013 est.)
country comparison to the world: 71

Refined petroleum products—exports: 20,840 bbl/day (2012 est.)
country comparison to the world: 72

Refined petroleum products—imports: 110,600 bbl/day (2012 est.)
country comparison to the world: 47

Natural gas—production: 10.3 billion cu m (2013 est.)
country comparison to the world: 42

Natural gas—consumption: 700 million cu m (2013 est.)
country comparison to the world: 95

Natural gas—exports: 9.6 billion cu m (2013 est.)
country comparison to the world: 21

Natural gas—imports: 0 cu m (2013 est.)
country comparison to the world: 84

Natural gas—proved reserves: 478.5 billion cu m (1 January 2014 est.)
country comparison to the world: 32

Carbon dioxide emission from consumpstion of energy: 21.28 million Mt (2012 est.)
country comparison to the world: 80

COMMUNICATIONS

Telephone—fixed lines: *total subscriptions:* 1.17 million
subscriptions per 100 inhabitants: 4 (2014 est.)
country comparison to the world: 71

Telephones—mobile cellular: *total:* 17.1 million

subscriptions per 100 inhabitants: 66 (2014 est.)
country comparison to the world: 62

Telephone system: *general assessment:* since unification in 1990, efforts have been made to create a National telecommunications network
domestic: the National network consists of microwave radio relay, cable, tropospheric scatter, GSM and CDMA mobile-cellular telephone systems; fixed-line and mobile-cellular teledensity remains low by regional standards
international: country code—967; landing point for the international submarine cable Fiber-Optic Link Around the Globe (FLAG); satellite earth stations—3 Intelsat (2 Indian Ocean and 1 Atlantic Ocean), 1 Intersputnik (Atlantic Ocean region), and 2 Arabsat; microwave radio relay to Saudi Arabia and Djibouti (2006)

Broadcast media: state-run TV with 2 stations; state-run radio with 2 National radio stations and 5 local stations; stations from Oman and Saudi Arabia can be accessed (2007)
Radio broadcast stations: AM 6, FM 1, shortwave 2 (1998)
Television broadcast stations: 3 (including one Egypt-based station that broadcasts in Yemen); plus several repeaters (2007)

Internet country code: .ye

Internet hosts: 33,206 (2012)
country comparison to the world: 105

Internet users: *total:* 5 million
percent of population: 19.1% (2014 est.)
country comparison to the world: 67

TRANSPORTATION

Airports: 57 (2013)
country comparison to the world: 84

Airports—with paved runways: *total:* 17
over 3,047 m: 4
2,438 to 3,047 m: 9
1,524 to 2,437 m: 3
914 to 1,523 m: 1 (2013)

Airports—with unpaved runways: *total:* 40
over 3,047 m: 3
2,438 to 3,047 m: 5
1,524 to 2,437 m: 7
914 to 1,523 m: 16
under 914 m: 9 (2013)

Pipelines: gas 641 km; liquid petroleum gas 22 km; oil 1,370 km (2013)

Roadways: *total:* 71,300 km
paved: 6,200 km
unpaved: 65,100 km (2005)
country comparison to the world: 66

Merchant marine: *total:* 5
by type: chemical tanker 2, petroleum tanker 2, roll on/roll off 1
registered in other countries: 14 (Moldova 4, Panama 4, Sierra Leone 2, Togo 1, unknown 3) (2010)
country comparison to the world: 126

Ports and terminals: *major seaport(s):* Aden, Al Hudaydah, Al Mukalla

Transportation—note: the international Maritime Bureau reports offshore waters in the Gulf of Adenare high risk for piracy; numerous vessels, including commercial shipping and pleasure craft, have been attacked and hijacked both at anchor and while underway; crew, passengers, and cargo are held for ransom; the presence of several Naval task forces in the Gulf of Adenand additional anti-piracy measures on the part of ship operators reduced the incidence of piracy in that body of water

MILITARY AND SECURITY

Military branches: Land Forces, Naval and Coastal Defense Forces (includes Marines), Air and Air Defense Force (al-Quwwat al-Jawwiya al-Yemeniya), Border Guards, Strategic Reserve Forces (2013)

Military service age and obligation: 18 is the legal minimum age for voluntary military service; no conscription; 2-year service obligation (2012)

Military expenditures: 4.02% of GDP (2012)
3.48% of GDP (2011)
4.02% of GDP (2010)
country comparison to the world: 12

Military—note:

TRANSNATIONAL ISSUES

Disputes—international: Saudi Arabia has reinforced its concrete-filled security barrier along sections of the fully demarcated border with Yemen to stem illegal cross-border activities

Refugees and internally displaced persons: *refugees (country of origin):* 13,643 (Ethiopia) (includes asylum seekers) (2015); 253,950 (Somalia) (2016)
IDPs: 2,053,093 (conflict in Sa'ada Governorate; clashes between al-Qa'ida in the Arabian Peninsula and government forces) (2016)

Trafficking in persons: current situation: Yemen is a source and, to a lesser extent, transit and destination country for men, women, and children subjected to forced labor and women and children subjected to sex trafficking; trafficking activities grew in Yemen in 2014, as the country's security situation deteriorated and poverty worsened; armed groups increased their recruitment of Yemeni children as combatants or checkpoint guards, and the Yemeni military and security forces continue to use child soldiers; some other Yemeni children, mostly boys, migrate to Yemeni cities or Saudi Arabia and, less frequently Oman, where they end up as beggars, drug smugglers, prostitutes, or forced laborers in domestic service or small shops; Yemeni children increasingly are also subjected to sex trafficking in country and in Saudi Arabia; tens of thousands of Yemeni migrant workers deported from Saudi Arabia and thousands of Syrian refugees are vulnerable to trafficking; addition ally, Yemen is a destination and transit country for women and children from the Horn of Africa who are looking for work or receive fraudulent job offers in the Gulf states but are subjected to sexual exploitation or forced labor upon arrival;

reports indicate that adults and children are still sold or inherited as slaves in Yemen

tier rating: *Tier 3*—Yemen does not fully comply with the minimum standards for the elimination of trafficking and is not making significant efforts to do so; weak government institutions, corruption, economic problems, security threats, and poor law enforcement capabilities impeded the government's ability to combat human trafficking; not all forms of trafficking are criminalized, and officials continue to conflate trafficking and smuggling; the status of an anti-trafficking law drafted with assistance from an international organization remains unknown following the dissolution of the government in January 2015; the government did not report efforts to investigate, prosecute, or convict anyone of trafficking or slavery offenses, including complicit officials, despite reports of officials willfully ignoring trafficking crimes and using child soldiers in the government's armed forces; the government acknowledged the use of child soldiers and signed a UN action plan to end the practice in 2014 but made no efforts to release child soldiers from the military and provide them with rehabilitative services; authorities failed to identify victims and refer them to protective services; the status of a draft National anti-trafficking strategy remains unknown (2015)

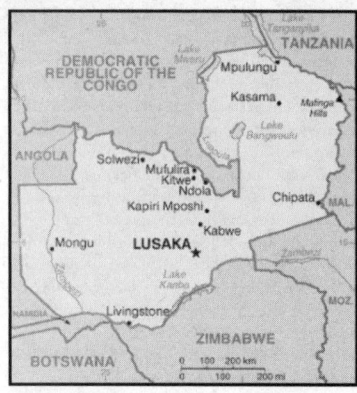

INTRODUCTION

Background: The territory of Northern Rhodesia was administered by the former British South Africa Company from 1891 until it was taken over by the UK in 1923. During the 1920s and 1930s, advances in mining spurred development and immigration. The name was changed to Zambia upon independence in 1964. In the 1980s and 1990s, declining copper prices, economic mismanagement, and a prolonged drought hurt the economy. Elections in 1991 brought an end to one-party rule and propelled the Movement for Multiparty Democracy (MMD) to government. The subsequent vote in 1996, however, saw increasing harassment of opposition parties and abuse of state media and other resources. The election in 2001 was marked by administrative problems, with three parties filing a legal petition challenging the election of ruling party candidate Levy MWANA-WASA. MWANAWASA was reelected in 2006 in an election that was deemed free and fair. Upon his death in August 2008, he was succeeded by his vice president, Rupiah BANDA, who won a special presidential byelection later that year. The MMD and BANDA lost to the Patriotic Front (PF) and Michael SATA in the 2011 general elections. SATA, however, presided over a period of haphazard economic management and attempted to silence opposition to PF policies. SATA died in October 2014 and was succeeded by his vice president, Guy SCOTT, who served as interim president until special elections were held in January 2015. Edgar LUNGU won the presidential by election and will complete SATA's term, which expires in August 2016 when new presidential, as well as parliamentary and local elections, will be held.

GEOGRAPHY

Location: Southern Africa, east of Angola, south of the Democratic Republic of the Congo

Geographic coordinates: 1500 S, 3000 E

Map references: Africa

Area: *total:* 752,618 sq km

land: 743,398 sq km

water: 9,220 sq km

country comparison to the world: 39

Area—comparative: slightly larger than Texas

Land boundaries: *total:* 6,043.15 km

border countries (8): Angola 1,065 km, Botswana 0.15 km, Democratic Republic of the Congo 2,332 km, Malawi 847 km, Mozambique 439 km, Namibia 244 km, Tanzania 353 km, Zimbabwe 763 km

Coastline: 0 km (landlocked)

Maritime claims: none (landlocked)

Climate: tropical; modified by altitude; rainy season (October to April)

Terrain: mostly high plateau with some hills and mountains

Elevation: *mean elevation:* 1,138 m

elevation extremes: *lowest point:* Zambezi river 329 m

highest point: unnamed elevation in Mafinga Hills 2,301 m

Natural resources: copper, cobalt, zinc, lead, coal, emeralds, gold, silver, uranium, hydropower

Land use: *agricultural land:* 31.7%

arable land: 4.8%

permanent crops: 0%

permanent pasture: 26.9%

forest: 66.3%

other: 2% (2011 est.)

Irrigated land: 1,560 sq km (2012)

Total renewable water resources: 105.2 cu km (2011)

Freshwater withdrawal (domestic/industrial/agricultural): *total:* 1.57 cu km/yr (18%/8%/73%)

per capita: 147 cu m/yr (2002)

Natural hazards: periodic drought; tropical storms (November to April)

Environment—current issues: air pollution and resulting acid rain in the mineral extraction and refining region; chemical runoff into watersheds; poaching seriously threatens rhinoceros, elephant, antelope, and large cat populations; deforestation; soil erosion; desertification; lack of adequate water treatment presents human health risks

Environment—international agreements: *party to:* Biodiversity, Climate Change, Climate Change-Kyoto Protocol, Desertification, Endangered Species, Hazardous Wastes, Law of the Sea, Ozone Layer Protection, Wetlands signed, but not ratified: none of the selected agreements

Geography—note: landlocked; the Zambezi forms a Natural riverine boundary with Zimbabwe; Lake Kariba on the Zambia-Zimbabwe border forms the world's largest reservoir by volume (180 cu km; 43 cu mi)

PEOPLE AND SOCIETY

Nationality: *noun:* Zambian(s)

adjective: Zambian

Ethnic groups: Bemba 21%, Tonga 13.6%, Chewa 7.4%, Lozi 5.7%, Nsenga 5.3%, Tumbuka 4.4%, Ngoni 4%, Lala 3.1%, Kaonde 2.9%, Namwanga 2.8%, Lunda (north Western) 2.6%, Mambwe 2.5%, Luvale 2.2%, Lamba 2.1%, Ushi 1.9%, Lenje 1.6%, Bisa 1.6%, Mbunda 1.2%, other 13.8%, unspecified 0.4% (2010 est.)

Languages: Bembe 33.4%, Nyanja 14.7%, Tonga 11.4%, Lozi 5.5%, Chewa 4.5%, Nsenga 2.9%, Tumbuka 2.5%, Lunda (North Western) 1.9%, Kaonde 1.8%, Lala 1.8%, Lamba 1.8%, English (official) 1.7%, Luvale 1.5%, Mambwe 1.3%, Namwanga 1.2%, Lenje 1.1%, Bisa 1%, other 9.7%, unspecified 0.2%

note: Zambia is said to have over 70 languages, although many of these may be considered dialects; all of Zambia's major languages are members of the Bantu family (2010 est.)

Religions: Protestant 75.3%, Roman Catholic 20.2%, other 2.7% (includes Muslim Buddhist, Hindu, and Baha'i), none 1.8% (2010 est.)

Population: 15,066,266

note: estimates for this country explicitly take into account the effects of excess mortality due to AIDS; this can result in lower life expectancy, higher infant mortality, higher death rates, lower population growth rates, and changes in the distribution of population by age and sex than would otherwise be expected (July 2015 est.)

country comparison to the world: 70

Age structure: *0–14 years:* 46.12% (male 3,490,151/female 3,458,035)

15–24 years: 20.02% (male 1,506,925/female 1,509,554)

25–54 years: 28.6% (male 2,171,292/female 2,136,987)

55–64 years: 2.89% (male 204,767/female 230,244)

65 years and over: 2.38% (male 155,179/female 203,132) (2015 est.)

Dependency ratios: *total dependency ratio:* 95.4%

youth dependency ratio: 89.7%

elderly dependency ratio: 5.7%

potential support ratio: 17.6% (2015 est.)

Median age: *total:* 16.7 years

male: 16.6 years

female: 16.8 years (2015 est.)

country comparison to the world: 225

Population growth rate: 2.88% (2015 est.)

country comparison to the world: 11

Birth rate: 42.13 births/1,000 population (2015 est.)

country comparison to the world: 4

Death rate: 12.67 deaths/1,000 population (2015 est.)

country comparison to the world: 21

Net migration rate: -0.68 migrant(s)/1,000 population (2015 est.)

country comparison to the world: 142

Urbanization: *urban Population:* 40.9% of total population (2015)
rate of urbanization: 4.32% annual rate of change (2010–15 est.)

Major urban Areas—population: LUSAKA (capital) 2.179 million (2015)

Sex ratio: *at birth:* 1.03 male(s)/female
0–14 years: 1.01 male(s)/female
15–24 years: 1 male(s)/female
25–54 years: 1.02 male(s)/female
55–64 years: 0.89 male(s)/female
65 years and over: 0.76 male(s)/female
total population: 1 male(s)/female (2015 est.)

Mother's mean age at first birth: 19.3
note: Median Age at first birth among women 20–24 (2013/14 est.)

Maternal mortality rate: 224 deaths/100,000 live births (2015 est.)
country comparison to the world: 26

Infant mortality rate: *total:* 64.72 deaths/1,000 live births
male: 70.19 deaths/1,000 live births
female: 59.09 deaths/1,000 live births (2015 est.)
country comparison to the world: 17

Life expectancy at birth: *total population:* 52.15 years
male: 50.54 years
female: 53.81 years (2015 est.)
country comparison to the world: 216

Total fertility rate: 5.72 children born/woman (2015 est.)
country comparison to the world: 7

Contraceptive prevalence rate: 40.8% (2007)

Health expenditures: 5% of GDP (2013)
country comparison to the world: 95

Physicians density: 0.17 physicians/1,000 population (2012)

Hospital bed density: 2 beds/1,000 population (2010)

Drinking water source: improved:
urban: 85.6% of population
rural: 51.3% of population
total: 65.4% of population
unimproved:
urban: 14.4% of population
rural: 48.7% of population
total: 34.6% of population (2015 est.)

Sanitation facility access:
improved:
urban: 55.6% of population
rural: 35.7% of population
total: 43.9% of population
unimproved:
urban: 44.4% of population
rural: 64.3% of population
total: 56.1% of population (2015 est.)

HIV/AIDS—adult prevalence rate: 12.37% (2014 est.)
country comparison to the world: 7

HIV/AIDS—people living with HIV/AIDS: 1,150,400 (2014 est.)
country comparison to the world: 9

HIV/AIDS—deaths: 18,900 (2014 est.)
country comparison to the world: 16

Major infectious diseases: *degree of risk:* very high
food or waterborne diseases: bacterial and protozoal diarrhea, hepatitis A, and typhoid fever
vectorborne diseases: malaria and dengue fever
water contact disease: schistosomiasis animal contact disease: rabies (2013)

Obesity—adult prevalence rate: 7.2% (2014)
country comparison to the world: 174

Children under the age of 5 years underweight: 14.8% (2014)
country comparison to the world: 49

Education expenditures: 1.1% of GDP (2008)
country comparison to the world: 170

Literacy: *definition:* age 15 and over can read and write English
total population: 63.4%
male: 70.9%
female: 56% (2015 est.)

Child labor—children ages 5–14: *total number:* 1,000,850 percentage: 41%
note: data represent children ages 7–14 (2005 est.)

Unemployment, youth ages 15–24: *total:* 15.2%
male: 14.6%
female: 15.8% (2012 est.)
country comparison to the world: 42

GOVERNMENT

Country name: *conventional long form:* Republic of Zambia
conventional short form: Zambia former: Northern Rhodesia
etymology: name derived from the Zambezi River, which flows through the western part of the country and forms its southern border with neighboring Zimbabwe

Government type: presidential republic

Capital: *name:* Lusaka

Geographic coordinates: 15 25 S, 28 17 E
time difference: UTC+2 (7 hours ahead of Washington, DC, during Standard Time)

Administrative divisions: 10 provinces; Central, Copperbelt, Eastern, Luapula, Lusaka, Muchinga, Northern, North-Western, Southern, Western

Independence: 24 October 1964 (from the UK)

National holiday: Independence Day, 24 October (1964)

Constitution: several previous; latest adopted 24 August 1991, promulgated 30 August 1991; amended 1996, 2015, last in 2016; note—changes to bill of rights scheduled for a referendum concurrent with the August 2016 general elections (2016)

Legal system: mixed legal system of English common law and customary law

International law organization participation: has not submitted an ICJ jurisdiction declaration; accepts ICCt jurisdiction

Citizenship: *citizenship by birth:* yes citizenship by descent: yes

dual citizenship recognized: no
residency requirement for Naturalization: not specified

Suffrage: 18 years of age; universal

Executive branch: *chief of state:* President Edgar LUNGU (since 25 January 2015); Vice President Inonge WINA (since 26 January 2015); note—the president is both chief of state and head of government

head of government: President Edgar LUNGU (since 25 January 2015); Vice President Inonge WINA (since 26 January 2015
cabinet: Cabinet appointed by president from among members of the National Assembly
elections/appointments: president directly elected by absolute majority popular vote in 2 rounds if needed for a 5-year term (eligible for a second term); special presidential election held on 20 January 2015 to complete President SATA's term in office after his death in October 2014 (next to be held on 16 August 2016); note—under constitutional changes in early 2016, the vice president is elected on the same ticket as the president
election results: Edgar LUNGU elected president; percent of vote—Edgar LUNGU (PF) 48.3%, Hakainde HICHILEMA (UPND) 46.7%, other 5%

Legislative branch: *description:* unicameral National Assembly (158 seats; 150 members directly elected in single-seat constituencies by simple majority vote, and 8 appointed by the president; members serve 5-year terms); note—for the 11 August 2016 election, 6 addition al seats will be added
elections: last held on 20 September 2011 (next to be held in 2016); note—35 byelections, prompted by resignation, death, change of party or legal nullification have taken place since September 2011
election results: percent of vote by party—NA; seats by party—PF 60, MMD 55, UPND 28, ADD 1, FDD 1, independent 3, seats not determined 10; note—seats as of March 2016—PF 89, MMD 33, UPND 31, ADD 1, FDD 1, independent 2, other 1

Judicial branch: *highest court(s):* Supreme Court (consists of the chief justice, deputy chief justice, and 7 judges); note—a Constitutional Court was established under 2016 constitutional reforms; court will consist of the court president, vice-president, and 11 judges and is expected to begin operation by mid-2016
judge selection and term of office: Supreme Court and Constitutional Court judges appointed by the president upon the advice of the 9-member Judicial Service Commission—headed by the chief justice, and ratified by the National Assembly; judges normally serve until age 65
subordinate courts: High Court (competence on constitutional issues); Industrial Relations Court; Subordinate Court; magistrate's courts and local courts

Political parties and leaders: Alliance for Democracy and Development or ADD [Charles MILUPI]
Forum for Democracy and Development or FDD [Edith NAWAKWI]

Movement for Multiparty Democracy or MMD [Nevers MUMBA]

Patriotic Front or PF [Edgar LUNGU]

United Party for National Development or UPND [Hakainde HICHILEMA]

International organization participation: ACP, AfDB, AU, C, COMESA, EITI (compliant country), FAO, G-77, IAEA, IBRD, ICAO, ICCt, ICRM, IDA, IFAD, IFC, IFRCS, ILO, IMF, Interpol, IOC, IOM, IPU, ISO (correspondent), ITSO, ITU, ITUC (NGOs), MIGA, MONUSCO, NAM, OPCW, PCA, SADC, UN, UNAMID, UNCTAD, UNESCO, UNHCR, UNIDO, UNISFA, UNMIL, UNMISS, UNOCI, UNWTO, UPU, WCO, WHO, WIPO, WMO, WTO

Diplomatic representation in the US: *chief of mission:* Ambassador Palan MULONDA (since 14 January 2013)

chancery: 2419 Massachusetts Avenue NW, Washington, DC 20008

telephone: [1] (202) 265-9717 through 9719

FAX: [1] (202) 332-0826

Diplomatic representation from the US: *chief of mission:* Ambassador Eric T. SCHULTZ (since 12 December 2014)

embassy: Ibex Hill, Lusaka

mailing address: P. O. Box 31617, Lusaka

telephone: [260] (211) 357-000

FAX: [260]) (211) 357-224

Flag description: green field with a panel of three vertical bands of red (hoist side), black, and orange below a soaring orange eagle, on the outer edge of the flag; green stands for the country's Natural resources and vegetation, red symbolizes the struggle for freedom, black the people of Zambia, and orange the country's mineral wealth; the eagle represents the people's ability to rise above the nation's problems

National symbol(s): African fish eagle; National colors: green, red, black, orange

National anthem: *name:* "Lumbanyeni Zambia" (Stand and Sing of Zambia, Proud and Free)

lyrics/music: multiple/Enoch Mankayi SONTONGA

note: adopted 1964; the melody, from the popular song "God Bless Africa," is the same as that of Tanzania but with different lyrics; the melody is also incorporated into South Africa's anthem

ECONOMY

Economy—overview: Zambia has had one of the world's fastest growing economies for the past ten years, with real GDP growth averaging roughly 6.7% per annum, though growth slowed in 2015 to just over 3%, due to falling copper prices, reduced power generation, and depreciation of the kwacha. Zambia's lack of economic diversification and dependency on copper as its sole major export makes it vulnerable to fluctuations in the world commodities market and prices turned downward in 2015 due to declining demand from China; Zambia was overtaken by the Democratic Republic of Congo as Africa's largest copper producer. Despite recent strong economic growth

and its status as a lower middle-income country, widespread and extreme rural poverty and high unemployment levels remain significant problems, made worse by a high birth rate, a relatively high HIV/AIDS burden, and by market-distorting agricultural and energy policies. Economic policy inconsistency and poor budget execution in recent years has hindered the economy and contributed to weakness in the kwacha, which was Africa's worst performing currency during 2015. Zambia has raised $7 billion from international investors by issuing separate sovereign bonds in September 2012, April 2014, and July 2015, significantly increasing the country's public debt as a share of GDP.

Poor management of water resources has also contributed to a power generation shortage, which has hampered industrial productivity and contributed to an increase in year-on-year inflation to 23% by March 2016. Zambia's currency, the kwacha, also depreciated sharply against the dollar through 2015, before the central bank restricted lending.

GDP (purchasing power parity): $62.71 billion (2015 est.) $60.51 billion (2014 est.) $57.61 billion (2013 est.)

note: data are in 2015 US dollars

country comparison to the world: 103

GDP (official exchange rate): $21.89 billion (2015 est.)

GDP—real growth rate: 3.6% (2015 est.) 5% (2014 est.) 5.1% (2013 est.)

country comparison to the world: 76

GDP—per capita (PPP): $3,900 (2015 est.) $3,800 (2014 est.) $3,800 (2013 est.)

note: data are in 2015 US dollars

country comparison to the world: 177

Gross National saving: 31.1% of GDP (2015 est.) 37.1% of GDP (2014 est.) 33.5% of GDP (2013 est.)

country comparison to the world: 22

GDP—composition, by end use:
household consumption: 52.6%
government consumption: 20.9%

investment in fixed Capital:
25.3% investment in inventories: 1.1%
exports of goods and services: 40.7%
imports of goods and services: -40.6% (2015 est.)

GDP—composition, by sector of origin:
agriculture: 8.6%
industry: 31.3%
services: 60% (2015 est.)

Agriculture—products: corn, sorghum, rice, peanuts, sunflower seeds, vegetables, flowers, tobacco, cotton, sugarcane, cassava (manioc, tapioca), coffee; cattle, goats, pigs, poultry, milk, eggs, hides

Industries: copper mining and processing, emerald mining, construction, foodstuffs, beverages, chemicals, textiles, fertilizer, horticulture

Industrial production growth rate: 2.2% (2015 est.)

country comparison to the world: 107

Labor force: 6.906 million (2015 est.)

country comparison to the world: 66

Labor force—by occupation: *agriculture:* 85%
industry: 6%
services: 9% (2004)

Unemployment rate: 15% (2008 est.) 50% (2000 est.)

country comparison to the world: 152

Population below poverty line: 60.5% (2010 est.)

Household income or consumption by percentage share: *lowest:* 10%: 1.5%
highest: 10%: 47.4% (2010)

Distribution of family income—Gini index: 57.5 (2013) 50.8 (2004)

country comparison to the world: 10

Budget: *revenues:* $3.643 billion
expenditures: $5.189 billion (2015 est.)
Taxes and other revenues: 14.9% of GDP (2015 est.)

country comparison to the world: 193

Budget surplus (+) or deficit (-): -6.3% of GDP (2015 est.)

country comparison to the world: 185

Public debt: 60.3% of GDP (2015 est.) 37.3% of GDP (2014 est.)

country comparison to the world: 62

Fiscal year: calendar year

Inflation rate (consumer prices): 10.1% (2015 est.) 7.8% (2014 est.)

country comparison to the world: 210

Central bank discount rate: 9.1% (31 December 2012) 19% (31 December 2011)

country comparison to the world: 30

Commercial bank prime lending rate: 12.5% (31 December 2015 est.) 11.57% (31 December 2014 est.)

country comparison to the world: 61

Stock of narrow money: $1.137 billion (31 December 2015 est.) $2.118 billion (31 December 2014 est.)

country comparison to the world: 148

Stock of broad money: $5.682 billion (31 December 2014 est.) $5.437 billion (31 December 2013 est.)

country comparison to the world: 125

Stock of domestic credit: $3.111 billion (31 December 2015 est.) $5.006 billion (31 December 2014 est.)

country comparison to the world: 129

Market value of publicly traded shares: $3.004 billion (31 December 2012 est.) $4.009 billion (31 December 2011) $2.817 billion (31 December 2010 est.)

country comparison to the world: 94

Current account balance: -$768 million (2015 est.) $581 million (2014 est.)

country comparison to the world: 111

Exports: $6.316 billion (2015 est.) $10.22 billion (2014 est.)

country comparison to the world: 103

Exports—commodities: copper/cobalt, cobalt, electricity; tobacco, flowers, cotton

Exports—partners: China 25.5%, Democratic Republic of the Congo 13%, South Africa 6.4%, South Korea 4.9%, India 4.3% (2015)

Imports: $6.798 billion (2015 est.) $8.595 billion (2014 est.)

country comparison to the world: 114

Imports—commodities: machinery, transportation equipment, petroleum Products, electricity, fertilizer, foodstuffs, clothing

Imports—partners: South Africa 34.5%, Democratic Republic of the Congo 18.2%, Kenya 9.7%, China 7.2%, India 4.4% (2015)

Reserves of foreign exchange and gold: $2.716 billion (31 December 2015 est.)
$3.078 billion (31 December 2014 est.)
country comparison to the world: 108

Debt—external: $6.73 billion (31 December 2014 est.)
$5.596 billion (31 December 2013 est.)
country comparison to the world: 120

Stock of direct foreign investment—at home: $NA

Stock of direct foreign investment—abroad: $NA

Exchange rates: Zambian kwacha (ZMK) per US dollar -8.7 (2015 est.) 6.2 (2014 est.) 6.2 (2013 est.) 5.1 (2012 est.) 4,860.7 (2011 est.)

ENERGY

Electricity—production: 11.73 billion kWh (2012 est.)
country comparison to the world: 93

Electricity—consumption: 8.327 billion kWh (2012 est.)
country comparison to the world: 97

Electricity—exports: 606 million kWh (2012 est.)
country comparison to the world: 65

Electricity—imports: 13 million kWh (2012 est.)
country comparison to the world: 109

Electricity—installed generating capacity: 1.888 million kW (2012 est.)
country comparison to the world: 108

Electricity—from fossil fuels: 0.4% of total installed capacity (2012 est.)
country comparison to the world: 212

Electricity—fron nuclear fuels: 0% of total installed capacity (2012 est.)
country comparison to the world: 213

Electricity—from hydroelectric plants: 99.6% of total installed capacity (2012 est.)
country comparison to the world: 3

Electricity—from other renewable sources: 0% of total installed capacity (2012 est.)
country comparison to the world: 147

Crude oil—production: 0 bbl/day (2014 est.)
country comparison to the world: 213

Crude oil—exports: 0 bbl/day (2012 est.)
country comparison to the world: 213

Crude oil—imports: 14,340 bbl/day (2012 est.)
country comparison to the world: 73

Crude oil—proved reserves: 0 bbl (1 January 2015 est.)
country comparison to the world: 214

Refined petroleum Products—production: 14,750 bbl/day (2012 est.)
country comparison to the world: 100

Refined petroleum Products—consumption: 18,000 bbl/day (2013 est.)
country comparison to the world: 131

Refined petroleum Products—exports: 1,216 bbl/day (2012 est.)
country comparison to the world: 110

Refined petroleum Products—Imports: 5,765 bbl/day (2012 est.)
country comparison to the world: 156

Natural gas—production: 0 cu m (2013 est.)
country comparison to the world: 151

Natural gas—consumption: 0 cu m (2013 est.)
country comparison to the world: 214

Natural gas—exports: 0 cu m (2013 est.)
country comparison to the world: 214

Natural gas—imports: 0 cu m (2013 est.)
country comparison to the world: 85

Natural gas—proved reserves: 0 cu m (1 January 2014 est.)
country comparison to the world: 211

Carbon dioxide emissions from consumption of energy: 3.054 million Mt (2012 est.)
country comparison to the world: 140

COMMUNICATIONS

Telephones—fixed lines: *total subscriptions:* 110,000 subscriptions per 100 inhabitants: 1 (2014 est.)
country comparison to the world: 144

Telephones—mobile cellular: *total:* 10.1 million *subscriptions per 100 inhabitants:* 69 (2014 est.)
country comparison to the world: 86

Telephone system: *general assessment:* among the best in sub-Saharan Africa
domestic: high-capacity microwave radio relay connects most larger towns and cities; several cellular telephone services in operation and network coverage is improving; domestic satellite system being installed to improve telephone service in rural areas; Internet service is widely available; very small aperture terminal (VSAT) networks are operated by private firms
International: country code—260; satellite earth stations—2 Intelsat (1 Indian Ocean and 1 Atlantic Ocean), 3 owned by Zamtel (2010)

Broadcast media: state-owned Zambia National Broadcasting Corporation (ZNBC) operates 3 TV stations, is the principal local-content provider, and owns about 45% of multi-channel Zambia shares; several private TV stations and multi-channel subscription TV services are available; ZNBC operates 4 radio networks; 64 private radio stations are available (most region ally) and relays of at least 2 international broadcasters — including BBC and Radio France International—are accessible in Lusaka and Kitwe (2015)
Radio broadcast stations: AM 19, FM 5, shortwave 4 (2001)
Television broadcast stations: 9 (2001)

Internet country code: .zm

Internet hosts: 16,571 (2012)
country comparison to the world: 122

Internet users: *total:* 2.3 million
percent of population: 15.4% (2014 est.)
country comparison to the world: 94

TRANSPORTATION

Airports: 88 (2013)
country comparison to the world: 63

Airports—with paved runways: *total:* 8
over 3,047 m: 1
2,438 to 3,047 m: 3
1,524 to 2,437 m: 3
914 to 1,523 m: 1 (2013)

Airports—with unpaved runways: *total:* 80
2,438 to 3,047 m: 1
1,524 to 2,437 m: 5
914 to 1,523 m: 53
under 914 m: 21 (2013)

Pipelines: oil 771 km (2013)

Railways: *total:* 3,126 km
narrow gauge: 3,126 km 1.067-m gauge
note: includes 1,860 km of the Tanzania-Zambia Railway Authority (TAZARA) (2014)
country comparison to the world: 57

Roadways: *total:* 40,454 km
paved: 9,403 km
unpaved: 31,051 km (2005)
country comparison to the world: 86

Waterways: 2,250 km (includes Lake Tanganyika and the Zambezi and Luapula rivers) (2010)
country comparison to the world: 37

Ports and terminals: *river port(s):* Mpulungu (Zambezi)

MILITARY AND SECURITY

Military branches: Zambian Defense Force (ZDF): Zambia Army, Zambia Air Force, Zambia National Service (support organization) (2015)

Military service age and obligation: National registration required at age 16; 18–25 years of age for male and female voluntary military service (16 years of age with parental consent); no conscription; Zambian citizenship required; grade 12 certification required; mandatory HIV testing on enlistment; mandatory retirement for officers at age 65 (Army, Air Force) (2012)

Military expenditures: 1.55% of GDP (2012)
1.59% of GDP (2011)
1.55% of GDP (2010)
country comparison to the world: 59

TRANSNATIONAL ISSUES

Disputes—international: in 2004, Zimbabwe dropped objections to plans between Botswana and Zambia to build a bridge over the Zambezi River, thereby de facto recognizing a short, but not clearly delimited, Botswana-Zambia boundary in the river

Refugees and internally displaced persons: *refugees (country of origin):* 18,598 (Democratic Republic of the Congo) (2014)

Illicit drugs: transshipment point for moderate amounts of methaqualone, small amounts of heroin, and cocaine bound for southern Africa and possibly Europe; a poorly developed financial infrastructure coupled with a government commitment to combating money laundering make it an unattractive venue for money launderers; major consumer of cannabis

ZIMBABWE

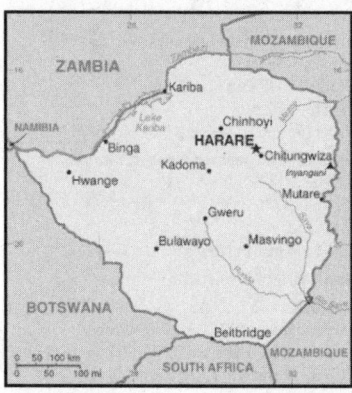

INTRODUCTION

Background: The UK annexed Southern Rhodesia from the former British South Africa Company in 1923. A 1961 constitution was formulated that favored whites in power. In 1965 the government unilaterally declared its independence, but the UK did not recognize the act and demanded more complete voting rights for the black African majority in the country (then called Rhodesia). UN sanctions and a guerrilla uprising finally led to free elections in 1979 and independence (as Zimbabwe) in 1980.Robert MUGABE, the nation's first prime minister, has been the country's only ruler (as president since 1987) and has dominated the country's political system since independence. His chaotic land redistribution campaign, which began in 1997 and intensified after 2000, caused an exodus of white farmers, crippled the economy, and ushered in widespread shortages of basic commodities. Ignoring international condemnation, MUGABE rigged the 2002 presidential election to ensure his reelection.

In April 2005, the capital city of Harare embarked on Operation Restore Order, ostensibly an urban ration alization program, which resulted in the destruction of the homes or businesses of 700,000 mostly poor supporters of the opposition. MUGABE in June 2007 instituted price controls on all basic commodities causing panic buying and leaving store shelves empty for months. General elections held in March 2008 contained irregularities but still amounted to a censure of the ZANU-PF-led government with the opposition winning a majority of seats in parliament. Movement for Democratic Change—Tsvangirai opposition leader Morgan TSVANGIRAI won the most votes in the presidential poll, but not enough to win outright. In the lead up to a run-off election in June 2008, considerable violence against opposition party members led to the withdrawal of TSVANGIR AI from the ballot. Extensive evidence of violence and intimidation resulted in international condemnation of the process.

Difficult negotiations over a power-sharing "government of National unity," in which MUGABE remained president and TSVANGIRAI became prime minister, were finally settled in February 2009, although the leaders failed to agree upon any key outstanding governmental issues. MUGABE was reelected president in June 2013 in balloting that was severely flawed and Internationally condemned. As a prerequisite to holding the election, Zimbabwe enacted a new constitution by referendum, although many provisions in the new constitution have yet to be codified in law.

GEOGRAPHY

Location: Southern Africa, between South Africa and Zambia

Geographic coordinates: 20 00 S, 30 00 E

Map references: Africa

Area: *total:* 390,757 sq km
land: 386,847 sq km
water: 3,910 sq km
country comparison to the world: 61

Area—comparative: slightly larger than Montana

Land boundaries: *total:* 3,229 km
border countries (4): Botswana 834 km, Mozambique 1,402 km, South Africa 230 km, Zambia 763 km

Coastline: 0 km (landlocked)

Maritime claims: none (landlocked)

Climate: tropical; moderated by altitude; rainy season (November to March)

Terrain: mostly high plateau with higher central plateau (high veld); mountains in east

Elevation: *mean elevation:* 961 m

elevation extremes: *lowest point:* junction of the Runde and Save Rivers 162 m
highest point: Inyangani 2,592 m

Natural resources: coal, chromium ore, asbestos, gold, nickel, copper, iron ore, vanadium, lithium, tin, platinum group metals

Land use: *agricultural land:* 42.5%
arable land: 10.9%
permanent crops: 0.3%
permanent pasture: 31.3%
forest: 39.5%
other: 18% (2011 est.)

Irrigated land: 1,740 sq km (2012)

Total renewable water resources: 20 cu km (2011)

Freshwater withdrawal (domestic/industrial/agricultural): *total:* 4.21 cu km/yr (14%/7%/79%) per capita: 333.5 cu m/yr (2002)

Natural hazards: recurring droughts; floods and severe storms are rare

Environment—current issues: deforestation; soil erosion; land degradation; air and water pollution; the black rhinoceros herd—once the largest concentration of the species in the world—has been significantly reduced by poaching; poor mining practices have led to toxic waste and heavy metal pollution

Environment—International agreements: *party to:* Biodiversity, Climate Change, Desertification, Endangered Species, Law of the Sea, Ozone Layer Protection
signed, but not ratified: none of the selected agreements

Geography—note: landlocked; the Zambezi forms a Natural riverine boundary with Zambia; in full flood (February-April) the massive Victoria Falls on the river forms the world's largest curtain of falling water; Lake Kariba on the Zambia-Zimbabwe border forms the world's largest reservoir by volume (180 cu km; 43 cu mi)

PEOPLE AND SOCIETY

Nationality: *noun:* Zimbabwean(s)
adjective: Zimbabwean

Ethnic groups: African 99.4% (predominantly Shon a; Ndebele is the second largest ethnic group), other 0.4%, unspecified 0.2% (2012 est.)

Languages: Shon a (official; most widely spoken), Ndebele (official, second most widely spoken), English (official; traditionally used for official business), 13 minority languages (official; includes Chewa, Chibarwe, Kalanga, Koisan, Nambya, Ndau, Shangani, sign language, Sotho, Tonga, Tswana, Venda, and Xhosa)

Religions: Protestant 75.9% (includes Apostolic 38%, Pentecostal 21.1%, other 16.8%), Roman Catholic 8.4%, other Christian 8.4%, other 1.2% (includes traditional, Muslim), none 6.1% (2011 est.)

Population: 14,229,541
note: estimates for this country explicitly take into account the effects of excess mortality due to AIDS; this can result in lower life expectancy, higher infant mortality, higher death rates, lower population growth rates, and changes in the distribution of population by age and sex than would otherwise be expected (July 2015 est.)
country comparison to the world: 72

Age structure: *0–14 years:* 37.88% (male 2,723,586/female 2,666,624)
15–24 years: 21.65% (male 1,550,518/female 1,530,737)
25–54 years: 33.4% (male 2,485,086/female 2,267,125)
55–64 years: 3.57% (male 184,517/female 324,079)
65 years and over: 3.49% (male 193,928/female 303,341) (2015 est.)

Dependency ratios: *total dependency ratio:* 80.4%
youth dependency ratio: 75%
elderly dependency ratio: 5.3%
potential support ratio: 18.7% (2015 est.)

Median age: *total:* 20.5 years
male: 20.4 years

female: 20.7 years (2015 est.)
country comparison to the world: 188

Population growth rate: 2.21% (2015 est.)
country comparison to the world: 39

Birth rate: 32.26 births/1,000 population (2015 est.)
country comparison to the world: 34

Death rate: 10.13 deaths/1,000 population (2015 est.)
country comparison to the world: 41

Net migration rate: 0 migrant(s)/1,000 population (2015 est.)
country comparison to the world: 77

Urbanization: *urban Population:* 32.4% of total population (2015)
rate of urbanization: 2.3% annual rate of change (2010–15 est.)

Major urban Areas—population: HARARE (capital) 1.501 million (2015)

Sex ratio: *at birth:* 1.03 male(s)/female
0–14 years: 1.02 male(s)/female
15–24 years: 1.01 male(s)/female
25–54 years: 1.1 male(s)/female
55–64 years: 0.57 male(s)/female
65 years and over: 0.64 male(s)/female
total population: 1.01 male(s)/female (2015 est.)
Mother's mean age at first birth: 20.5
note: Median Age at first birth among women 25–29 (2010/11 est.)

Maternal mortality rate: 443 deaths/100,000 live births (2015 est.)
country comparison to the world: 15

Infant mortality rate: *total:* 26.11 deaths/1,000 live births
male: 28.4 deaths/1,000 live births
female: 23.76 deaths/1,000 live births (2015 est.)
country comparison to the world: 69

Life expectancy at birth: *total population:* 57.05 years
male: 56.54 years
female: 57.57 years (2015 est.)
country comparison to the world: 205

Total fertility rate: 3.53 children born/woman (2015 est.)
country comparison to the world: 45

Contraceptive prevalence rate: 58.5% (2010/11)

Physicians density: 0.08 physicians/1,000 population (2011)

Hospital bed density: 1.7 beds/1,000 population (2011)

Drinking water source:
improved:
urban: 97% of population
rural: 67.3% of population
total: 76.9% of population
unimproved:
urban: 3% of popu lation
rural: 32.7% of population
total: 23.1% of population (2015 est.)

Sanitation facility access:
improved:
urban: 49.3% of population

rural: 30.8% of population
total: 36.8% of population
unimproved:
urban: 50.7% of population
rural: 69.2% of population
total: 63.2% of population (2015 est.)

HIV/AIDS—adult prevalence rate: 16.74% (2014 est.)
country comparison to the world: 5

HIV/AIDS—people living with HIV/AIDS: 1,550,300 (2014 est.)
country comparison to the world: 4

HIV/AIDS—deaths: 38,600 (2014 est.)
country comparison to the world: 6

Major infectious diseases: *degree of risk:* high
food or waterborne diseases: bacterial and protozoal diarrhea, hepatitis A, and typhoid fever
vectorborne diseases: malaria and dengue fever
water contact disease: schistosomiasis animal
contact disease: rabies (2013)

Obesity—adult prevalence rate: 8.4% (2014)
country comparison to the world: 143

Children under the age of 5 years underweight: 11.2% (2014)
country comparison to the world: 69

Education expenditures: 2% of GDP (2010)
country comparison to the world: 155

Literacy: *definition:* age 15 and over can read and write English
total population: 86.5%
male: 88.5%
female: 84.6% (2015 est.)

School life expectancy (primary to tertiary education): *total:* 10 years
male: 10 years
female: 10 years (2013)

Unemployment, youth ages 15–24: *total:* 8.7%
male: 7.7%
female: 9.8% (2012 est.)
country comparison to the world: 116

GOVERNMENT

Country name: *conventional long form:* Republic of Zimbabwe
conventional short form: Zimbabwe *form er:* Southern Rhodesia, Rhodesia
etymology: takes its name from the Kingdom of Zimbabwe (13th-15th century) and its capital of Great Zimbabwe, the largest stone structure in precolonial southern Africa

Government type: semi-presidential republic

Capital: *name:* Harare

Geographic coordinates: 1749S, 3102E
time difference: UTC+2 (7 hours ahead of Washington, DC, during Standard Time)

Administrative divisions: 8 provinces and 2 cities* with provincial status; Bulawayo*, Harare*, Manicaland, Mashonaland Central, Mashon aland East, Mashon aland West, Masvingo, Matabeleland North, Matabeleland South, Midlands

Independence: 18 April 1980 (from the UK)

National holiday: Independence Day, 18 April (1980)

Constitution: previous 1965 (at Rhodesian independence), 1979 (Lancaster House Agreement), 1980 (at Zimbabwean independence); latest final draft completed January 2013, approved by referendum 16 March 2013, approved by Parliament 9 May 2013; amended many times in 2013; note— significant amendments proposed in early 2015 (2016)

Legal system: mixed legal system of English common law, Roman-Dutch civil law, and customary law

international law organization participation: has not submitted an ICJ jurisdiction declaration; non-party state to the ICCt

Citizenship: *citizenship by birth:* no
citizenship by descent only: the father must be a citizen of Zimbabwe; in the case of a child born out of wedlock, the mother must be a citizen
dual citizenship recognized: no
residency requirement for naturalization: 5 years

Suffrage: 18 years of age; universal

Executive branch: *chief of state:* Executive President Robert Gabriel MUGABE (since 31 December 1987); Vice Presidents Emmerson Dambudzo MNANGAGWA and Phelekezela MPHOKO (both since 12 December 2014); note—Vice President Joice MUJURU (since 6 December 2004) was dismissed 9 December 2014
head of government: Executive President Robert Gabriel MUGABE (since 31 December 1987); note -following the 31 July 2013 presidential election, the position of prime minister was abolished
cabinet: Cabinet appointed by president, responsible to House of Assembly
elections/appointments: each presidential candidate nominated with a nomination paper signed by at least 10 registered voters (at least 1 candidate from each province) and directly elected by absolute majority popular vote in 2 rounds if needed for a 5-year term (no term limits); election last held on 31 July 2013 (next to be held in 2018); co-vice presidents drawn from party leadership
election results: Robert Gabriel MUGABE reelected president; percent of vote—Robert Gabriel MUGABE (ZANU-PF) 61.1%, Morgan TSVANGIRAI (MDC-T) 34.4%, Welshman NCUBE (MDC-N) 2.7%, other 1.8%; note—the election process was considered flawed and roundly criticized by election monitors and international bodies; both the African Union and the South African Development Community endorsed the results of the election with some concerns

Legislative branch: *description:* bicameral Parliament consists of the Senate (80 seats; 60 members directly elected in multi-seat constituencies—6 seats in each of the 10 provinces—by proportional representation vote, 16 indirectly elected by the region al governing councils, 2 reserved for the National Council Chiefs, and 2 reserved for members with disabilities; members serve 5-year terms) and the House of Assembly (270 seats; 210

members directly elected in single-seat constituencies by simple majority vote and 60 seats reserved for women directly elected by proportional representation vote; members serve 5-year terms)

elections: last held on 31 July 2013 (next to be held in 2018)

election results: Senate—percent of vote by party—NA; seats by party—ZANU-PF 37 MDC-T 21, MDC-N 2, chiefs 18, people with disabilities 2; House of Assembly—percent of vote by party—NA; seats by party—ZANU-PF 197, MDC-T 70, MDC-N 2, independent 1

Judicial branch: *highest court(s):* Supreme Court (consists of the chief justice and 4 judges)

judge selection and term of office: Supreme Court judges appointed by the president upon recommendation of the Judicial Service Commission, an independent body consisting of the chief justice, Public Service Commission chairman, attorney general, and 2–3 members appointed by the president; judges normally serve until age 65 but can elect to serve until age 70

subordinate courts: High Court, region al magistrate courts, and special courts

Political parties and leaders: Freedom Party [Cosmas MPONDA]

Movement for Democratic Change—Ncube or MDC-N [Welshman NCUBE]

Movement for Democratic Change—Renewal or MDC-R [Sekai HOLLAND]; note—has been kicked out of Parliament as of 17 May 2015

Movement for Democratic Change—Tsvangirai or MDC-T [M organ TSVANGIRAI]

Transform Zimbabwe or TZ [Jacob NGARIVHUME]

United Parties [Abel MUZOREWA]

Zimbabwe African National Union-N donga or ZANU-N donga [Wilson KUMBULA]

Zimbabwe African National Union-Patriotic Front or ZANU-PF [Robert Gabriel MUGABE]

Zimbabwe African Peoples Union or ZAPU [Dumiso DABENGWA]

Political pressure groups and leaders: Crisis in Zimbabwe Coalition

National Constitutional Assembly or NCA [Lovemore MADHUKU]

Women of Zimbabwe Arise or WOZA [Jenni WILLIAMS]

Zimbabwe Congress of Trade Unions or ZCTU [Japhet MOYO]

Zimbabwe Lawyers for Human Rights or ZLHR [Irene PETRAS]

International organization participation: ACP, AfDB, AU, COMESA, FAO, G-15, G-77, IAEA, IBRD, ICAO, ICRM, IDA, IFAD, IFC, IFRCS, ILO, IMF, IMO, Interpol, IOC, IOM, IPU, ISO, ITSO, ITU, ITUC (NGOs), MIGA, NAM, OPCW, PCA, SADC, UN, UNAMID, UNCTAD, UNESCO, UNIDO, UNMIL, UNMISS, UNOCI, UNWTO, UPU, WCO, WFTU (NGOs), WHO, WIPO, WMO, WTO

Diplomatic representation in the US: *chief of mission:* Ambassador Ammon MUTEMBWA (since 18 November 2014)

chancery: 1608 New Hampshire Avenue NW, Washington, DC 20009

telephone: [1] (202) 332-7100

FAX: [1] (202) 483-9326

Diplomatic representation from the US: *chief of mission:* Ambassador Harry THOMAS (since 25 February 2016)

embassy: 172 Herbert Chitepo Avenue, Harare

mailing address: P. O. Box 3340, Harare

telephone: [263] (4) 250-593 through 250-594

FAX: [263] (4) 796-488, or 722-618

Flag description: seven equal horizontal bands of green, yellow, red, black, red, yellow, and green with a white isosceles triangle edged in black with its base on the hoist side; a yellow Zimbabwe bird representing the long history of the country is superimposed on a red five-pointed star in the center of the triangle, which symbolizes peace; green represents agriculture, yellow mineral wealth, red the blood shed to achieve independence, and black stands for the native people

National symbol(s): Zimbabwe bird symbol, African fish eagle, flame lily; National colors: green, yellow, red, black, white

National anthem: *name:* "Kalibusiswe Ilizwe leZimbabwe" [Northern Ndebele language] "Simudzai Mureza WeZimbabwe" [Shona] (Blessed Be the Land of Zimbabwe)

lyrics/music: Solomon MUTSWAIRO/Fred Lecture CHANGUNDEGA

note: adopted 1994

ECONOMY

Economy—overview: Zimbabwe's economy depends heavily on its mining and agriculture sectors. Following a decade of contraction from 1998 to 2008, the economy recorded real growth of more than 10% per year in the period 2010–13, before slowing to roughly 3% in 2014 due to poor harvests, low diamond revenues, and decreased investment. Lower mineral prices, infrastructure and regulatory deficiencies, a poor investment climate, a large public and external debt burden, and extremely high government wage expenses impede the country's economic performance.

Until early 2009, the Reserve Bank of Zimbabwe (RBZ) routinely printed money to fund the budget deficit, causing hyperinflation. Dollarization in early 2009—which allowed currencies such as the Botswana pula, the South Africa rand, and the US dollar to be used locally—ended hyperinflation and reduced inflation below 10% per year. The RBZ introduced bond coins denominated in 1,5, 10, and 25 cent increments on a par with the US dollar in December 2014, more than five years after the Zimbabwe dollar was taken out of circulation. In January 2015, as part of the government's effort to boost trade and attract foreign investment, the RBZ announced that the Chinese renmimbi, Indian rupee, Australian dollar, and Japanese yen would be accepted as legal tender in Zimbabwe.

Zimbabwe's government entered a second Staff Monitored Program with the IMF in 2014 and undertook other measures to reengage with international financial institutions. Foreign and domestic investment continues to be hindered by the lack of clarity regarding the government's Indigenization and Economic Empowerment Act. in 2015 the depreciation of the South African rand against the US dollar has led to deflation in Zimbabwe as prices for South African imports decline while the costs of domestic production in US dollars rem ains stable.

GDP (purchasing power parity): $28.1 billion (2015 est.)

$27.69 billion (2014 est.)

$26.66 billion (2013 est.)

note: data are in 2015 US dollars

country comparison to the world: 132

GDP (official exchange rate): $14.27 billion (2015 est.)

GDP—real growth rate: 1.5% (2015 est.)

3.9% (2014 est.)

4.5% (2013 est.)

country comparison to the world: 155

GDP—per capita (PPP): $2,100 (2015 est.)

$2,100 (2014 est.)

$2,000 (2013 est.)

note: data are in 2015 US dollars

country comparison to the world: 202

Gross National saving: -4.3% of GDP (2015 est.)

-5.5% of GDP (2014 est.)

-11% of GDP (2013 est.)

country comparison to the world: 175

GDP—composition, by end use:

household consumption: 68.9%

government consumption: 32.2%

investment in fixed Capital:

22.5% investment in inventories: -0.1%

exports of goods and services: 68.8%

imports of goods and services: -92.3% (2015 est.)

GDP—composition, by sector of origin:

agriculture: 20%

industry: 26%

services: 53.3% (2015 est.)

Agriculture—products: tobacco, corn, cotton, wheat, coffee, sugarcane, peanuts; sheep, goats, pigs

Industries: mining (coal, gold, platinum, copper, nickel, tin, diamonds, clay, numerous metallic and nonmetallic ores), steel; wood products, cement, chemicals, fertilizer, clothing and footwear, foodstuffs, beverages

Industrial production growth rate: 4.2% (2015 est.)

country comparison to the world: 52

Labor force: 5.777 million (2015 est.)

country comparison to the world: 71

Labor force—by occupation: *agriculture:* 66%

industry: 10%

services: 24% (1996)

Unemployment rate: 95% (2009 est.)

80% (2005 est.)

note: figures include unemployment and underemployment; true unemployment is unknown and, under current economic conditions, unknowable

country comparison to the world: 207

Population below poverty line: 72.3% (2012 est.)

Household income or consumption by percentage share: *lowest:* 10%: 2%
highest: 10%: 40.4% (1995)

Distribution of family income—Gini index: 50.1 (2006) 50.1 (1995)
country comparison to the world: 22

Budget: *revenues:* $3.732 billion
expenditures: $4.615 billion (2014)
Taxes and other revenues: 26.8% of GDP (2014)
country comparison to the world: 108

Budget surplus (+) or deficit (-): -6.4% of GDP (2014)
country comparison to the world: 187

Public debt: 205.3% of GDP (2015 est.) 184.1% of GDP (2014 est.)
country comparison to the world: 2

Fiscal year: calendar year

Inflation rate (consumer prices): 0.1% (2015 est.) 1.63% (2014 est.)
country comparison to the world: 53

Central bank discount rate: 7.17% (31 December 2010)
975% (31 December 2007)
country comparison to the world: 45

Commercial bank prime lending rate: 18% (31 December 2015 est.)
22% (31 December 2014 est.)
country comparison to the world: 20

Stock of narrow money: $76.2 billion (31 December 2015 est.)
$41.3 billion (31 December 2014 est.)
note: Zimbabwe's central bank no longer publishes data on monetary aggregates, except for bank deposits, which amounted to $2.1 billion in November 2010; the Zimbabwe dollar stopped circulating in early 2009; since then, the US dollar and South African rand have been the most frequently used currencies; there are no reliable estimates of the amount of foreign currency circulating in Zimbabwe
country comparison to the world: 41

Stock of broad money: $47.64 billion (31 December 2013 est.)
$101.1 billion (31 December 2014 est.)
country comparison to the world: 70

Stock of domestic credit: $9.902 billion (31 December 2015 est.)
$9.474 billion (31 December 2014 est.)
country comparison to the world: 103

Market value of publicly traded shares: $4.073 billion (13 April 2015 est.) $11.82 billion (31 December 2012) $10.9 billion (31 December 2011 est.)
country comparison to the world: 90

Current account balance: -$2.466 billion (2015 est.) -$2.639 billion (2014 est.)
country comparison to the world: 153

Exports: $3.301 billion (2015 est.) $3.263 billion (2014 est.)
country comparison to the world: 127

Exports—commodities: platinum, cotton, tobacco, gold, ferroalloys, textiles/clothing

Exports—partners: China 27.8%, Democratic Republic of the Congo 14%, Botswana 12.5%, South Africa 7.6% (2015)

Imports: $5.207 billion (2015 est.) $5.135 billion (2014 est.)
country comparison to the world: 123

Imports—commodities: machinery and transport equipment, other manufactures, chemicals, fuels, food products

Imports—partners: South Africa 48.1%, China 12.1%, India 5.2%, Zambia 4.6% (2015)

Reserves of foreign exchange and gold: $457 million (31 December 2015 est.)
$448 million (31 December 2014 est.)
country comparison to the world: 152

Debt—external: $9.13 billion (31 December 2014 est.)
$8.193 billion (31 December 2013 est.)
country comparison to the world: 109

Stock of direct foreign investment—at home: $NA

Stock of direct foreign investment—abroad: $NA

Exchange rates: Zimbabwean dollars (ZWD) per US dollar—
NA (2013)
234.25 (2010)
234.25 (2009)
9,686.8 (2007)
note: the dollar was adopted as a legal currency in 2009; since then the Zimbabwean dollar has experienced hyperinflation and is essentially worthless

ENERGY

Electricity—production: 7.736 billion kWh (2012 est.)
country comparison to the world: 104

Electricity—consumption: 6.831 billion kWh (2012 est.)
country comparison to the world: 106

Electricity—exports: 653 million kWh (2012 est.)
country comparison to the world: 63

Electricity—imports: 1.201 billion kWh (2012 est.)
country comparison to the world: 60

Electricity—installed generating capacity: 2.038 million kW (2012 est.)
country comparison to the world: 106

Electricity—from fossil fuels: 63.2% of total installed capacity (2012 est.)
country comparison to the world: 125

Electricity—fron nuclear fuels: 0% of total installed capacity (2012 est.)
country comparison to the world: 214

Electricity—from hydroelectric plants: 36.8% of total installed capacity (2012 est.)
country comparison to the world: 62

Electricity—from other renewable sources: 0% of total installed capacity (2012 est.)
country comparison to the world: 148

Crude oil—production: 0 bbl/day (2014 est.)
country comparison to the world: 214

Crude oil—exports: 0 bbl/day (2012 est.)

country comparison to the world: 214

Crude oil—imports: 0 bbl/day (2012 est.)
country comparison to the world: 86

Crude oil—proved reserves: 0 bbl (1 January 2015 est.)
country comparison to the world: 215

Refined petroleum Products—production: 0 bbl/day (2012 est.)
country comparison to the world: 150

Refined petroleum Products—consumption: 14,000 bbl/day (2013 est.)
country comparison to the world: 145

Refined petroleum Products—exports: 0 bbl/day (2012 est.)
country comparison to the world: 150

Refined petroleum Products—Imports: 14,730 bbl/day (2012 est.)
country comparison to the world: 126

Natural gas—production: 0 cu m (2013 est.)
country comparison to the world: 152

Natural gas—consumption: 0 cu m (2013 est.)
country comparison to the world: 215

Natural gas—exports: 0 cu m (2013 est.)
country comparison to the world: 215

Natural gas—imports: 0 cu m (2013 est.)
country comparison to the world: 86

Natural gas—proved reserves: 0 cu m (1 January 2014 est.)
country comparison to the world: 212

Carbon dioxide emissions from consumption of energy: 10.12 million Mt (2012 est.)
country comparison to the world: 101

COMMUNICATIONS

Telephones—fixed lines: *total subscriptions:* 330,000
subscriptions per 100 inhabitants: 2 (2014 est.)
country comparison to the world: 113

Telephones—mobile cellular: *total:* 11.8 million
subscriptions per 100 inhabitants: 86 (2014 est.)
country comparison to the world: 77

Telephone system: *general assessment:* privatization and competion have driven rapid expansion of telecommunications, particularly cellular voice and mobile broadband, in recent years; continued economic instability and infrastructure limitations, such as reliable power, hinder progress
domestic: consists of microwave radio relay links, open-wire lines, radiotelephone communication stations, fixed wireless local loop installations, fiber optic cable, VSAT terminals, and a substantial mobile-cellular network; Internet connection is most readily available in Harare and major towns; 1 government owned and 3 private cellular providers; 3G and VoIP services are widely available with 4G/LTE service being deployed
International: country code—263; satellite earth stations—2 Intelsat; 5 international digital gateway exchanges; fiber optic connections to neighboring states provide access to international networks via undersea cable (2015)

959

Broadcast media: government owns all local radio and TV stations; foreign shortwave broadcasts and satellite TV are available to those who can afford antennas and receivers; in rural areas, access to TV broadcasts is extremely limited (2007)
Radio broadcast stations: AM 7, FM 20 (plus 17 repeater stations), shortwave 1 (1998)
Television broadcast stations: 16 (1997)

Internet country code: .zw

Internet hosts: 30,615 (2012)
country comparison to the world: 108

Internet users: *total:* 6,759,032
percent of population: 47.5% (2015 est.)
country comparison to the world: 88

TRANSPORTATION

Airports: 196 (2013)
country comparison to the world: 29

Airports—with paved runways: *total:* 17
over 3,047 m: 3
2,438 to 3,047 m: 2
1,524 to 2,437 m: 5
914 to 1,523 m: 7 (2013)

Airports—with unpaved runways: *total:* 179
1,524 to 2,437 m: 3
914 to 1,523 m: 104
under 914 m: 72 (2013)

Pipelines: refined products 270 km (2013)

Railways: *total:* 3,427 km
narrow gauge: 3,427 km 1.067-m gauge (313 km electrified) (2014)
country comparison to the world: 53

Roadways: *total:* 97,267 km
paved: 18,481 km
unpaved: 78,786 km (2002)
country comparison to the world: 47

Waterways: (some navigation possible on Lake Kariba) (2011)

Ports and terminals: *river port(s):* Binga, Kariba (Zambezi)

MILITARY AND SECURITY

Military branches: Zimbabwe Defense Forces (ZDF): Zimbabwe National Army (ZNA), Air Force of Zimbabwe (AFZ) (2012)

Military service age and obligation: 18–24 years of age for voluntary military service; no conscription; women are eligible to serve (2012)

Military expenditures: 2.79% of GDP (2014)
2.64% of GDP (2013)
2.94% of GDP (2012)
2.05% of GDP (2011)
2.94% of GDP (2010)
country comparison to the world: 22

TRANSNATIONAL ISSUES

Disputes—international: Namibia has supported, and in 2004 Zimbabwe dropped objections to, plans between Botswana and Zambia to build a bridge over the Zambezi River, thereby de facto recognizing a short, but not clearly delimited, Botswana-Zambia boundary in the river; South Africa has placed military units to assist police operations along the border of Lesotho, Zimbabwe, and Mozambique to control smuggling, poaching, and illegal migration

Refugees and internally displaced persons: *IDPs:* undetermined (political violence, violence iNAssociation with the 2008 election, human rights violations, land reform, and economic collapse) (2015)
stateless persons: 300,000 (2015)

Trafficking in persons: *current situation:* Zimbabwe is a source, transit, and destination country for men, women, and children subjected to forced labor and sex trafficking; Zimbabwean women and girls from towns bordering South Africa, Mozambique, and Zambia are subjected to forced labor, including domestic servitude, and prostitution catering to long-distance truck drivers; Zimbabwean men, women, and children experience forced labor in agriculture and domestic servitude in rural areas; family members may recruit children and other relatives from rural areas with promises of work or education in cities and towns where they end up in domestic servitude and sex trafficking; Zimbabwean women and men are lured into exploitative labor situations in South Africa and other neighboring countries

tierrating: Tier 3—Zimbabwe does not fully comply with the minimum standards for the elimination of trafficking and is not making significant efforts to do so; the government passed an anti-trafficking law in 2014 defining trafficking in persons as a crime of transportation and failing to capture the key element of the international definition of human trafficking—the purpose of exploitation—which prevents the law from being comprehensive or consistent with the 2000 UN TIP Protocol that Zimbabwe acceded to in 2013; the government did not report on anti-trafficking law enforcement efforts during 2014, and corruption in law enforcement and the judiciary remain a concern; authorities made minimal efforts to identify and protect trafficking victims, relying on NGOs to identify and assist victims; Zimbabwe's 2014 anti-trafficking law required the opening of 10 centers for trafficking victims, but none were established during the year; five existing shelters for vulnerable children and orphans may have accommodated child victims; in January 2015, an inter-ministerial anti-trafficking committee was established, but it is unclear if the committee ever met or initiated any activities (2015)

Illicit drugs: transit point for cannabis and South Asian heroin, mandrax, and methamphetamines en route to South Africa

ABBREVIATIONS

ABEDA	Arab Bank for Economic Development in Africa
ACP Group	African, Caribbean, and Pacific Group of States
ADB	Asian Development Bank
AfDB	African Development Bank
AFESD	Arab Fund for Economic and Social Development
AG	Australia Group
Air Pollution	Convention on Long-Range Transboundary Air Pollution
Air Pollution-Nitrogen Oxides	Protocol to the 1979 Convention on Long-Range Transboundary Air Pollution Concerning the Control of Emissions of Nitrogen Oxides or Their Transboundary Fluxes
Air Pollution-Persistent Organic Pollutants	Protocol to the 1979 Convention on Long-Range Transboundary Air Pollution on Persistent Organic Pollutants
Air Pollution-Sulphur 85	Protocol to the 1979 Convention on Long-Range Transboundary Air Pollution on the Reduction of Sulphur Emissions or Their Transboundary Fluxes by at Least 30%
Air Pollution-Sulphur 94	Protocol to the 1979 Convention on Long-Range Transboundary Air Pollution on Further Reduction of Sulphur Emissions
Air Pollution-Volatile Organic Compounds	Protocol to the 1979 Convention on Long-Range Transboundary Air Pollution Concerning the Control of Emissions of Volatile Organic Compounds or Their Transboundary Fluxes
AMF	Arab Monetary Fund
AMU	Arab Maghreb Union
Antarctic Marine Living Resources	Convention on the Conservation of Antarctic Marine Living Resources
Antarctic Seals	Convention for the Conservation of Antarctic Seals
Antarctic-Environmental Protocol	Protocol on Environmental Protection to the Antarctic Treaty
ANZUS	Australia-New Zealand-United States Security Treaty
AOSIS	Alliance of Small Island States
APEC	Asia-Pacific Economic Cooperation
Arabsat	Arab Satellite Communications Organization
ARF	ASEAN Regional Forum
ASEAN	Association of Southeast Asian Nations
AU	African Union
Autodin	Automatic Digital Network
BA	Baltic Assembly
bbl/day	barrels per day
BCIE	Central American Bank for Economic Integration
BDEAC	Central African States Development Bank
Benelux	Benelux Union
BGN	United States Board on Geographic Names
BIMSTEC	Bay of Bengal Initiative for Multi-sectoral Technical and Economic Cooperation
Biodiversity	Convention on Biological Diversity
BIS	Bank for International Settlements
BRICS	(Brazil, Russia, India, China, and South Africa)
BSEC	Black Sea Economic Cooperation Zone
C	Commonwealth
CD	Community of Democracies
c.i.f.	cost, insurance, and freight
CACM	Central American Common Market
CAEU	Council of Arab Economic Unity
CAN	Andean Community
Caricom	Caribbean Community and Common Market
CB	citizen's band mobile radio communications
CBSS	Council of the Baltic Sea States
CCC	Customs Cooperation Council

CDB	Caribbean Development Bank
CE	Council of Europe
CEI	Central European Initiative
CELAC	Community of Latin America and Caribbean States
CEMA	Council for Mutual Economic Assistance
CEMAC	Economic and Monetary Community of Central Africa
CEPGL	Economic Community of the Great Lakes Countries
CERN	European Organization for Nuclear Research
CIA	Central Intelligence Agency
CICA	Conference of Interaction and Confidence-Building Measures in Asia
CIS	Commonwealth of Independent States
CITES	see Endangered Species
Climate Change	United Nations Framework Convention on Climate Change
Climate Change-Kyoto Protocol	Kyoto Protocol to the United Nations Framework Convention on Climate Change
COCOM	Coordinating Committee on Export Controls
COMESA	Common Market for Eastern and Southern Africa
Comsat	Communications Satellite Corporation
CP	Colombo Plan
CPLP	Comunidade dos Paises de Lingua Portuguesa
CSN	South American Community of Nations became UNASUL—Union of South American Nations
CSTO	Collective Security Treaty Organization
CTBTO	Preparatory Commission for the Nuclear-Test-Ban Treaty Organization
CY	calendar year
D-8	Developing Eight
DC	developed country
DDT	dichloro-diphenyl-trichloro-ethane
Desertification	United Nations Convention to Combat Desertification in Those Countries Experiencing Serious Drought and/or Desertification, Particularly in Africa
DIA	United States Defense Intelligence Agency
DSN	Defense Switched Network
DST	daylight savings time
DWT	deadweight ton
EAC	East African Community
EADB	East African Development Bank
EAEC	Eurasian Economic Community
EAPC	Euro-Atlantic Partnership Council
EAS	East Asia Summit
EBRD	European Bank for Reconstruction and Development
EC	European Community or European Commission
ECA	Economic Commission for Africa
ECB	European Central Bank
ECE	Economic Commission for Europe
ECLAC	Economic Commission for Latin America and the Caribbean
ECO	Economic Cooperation Organization
ECOSOC	Economic and Social Council
ECOWAS	Economic Community of West African States
ECSC	European Coal and Steel Community
EE	Eastern Europe
EEC	European Economic Community
EEZ	exclusive economic zone
EFTA	European Free Trade Association
EIB	European Investment Bank
EITI	Extractive Industry Trnsparency Iniative
EMU	European Monetary Union
Endangered Species	Convention on the International Trade in Endangered Species of Wild Flora and Fauna (CITES)

Entente	Council of the Entente
Environmental Modification	Convention on the Prohibition of Military or Any Other Hostile Use of Environmental Modification Techniques
ESA	European Space Agency
ESCAP	Economic and Social Commission for Asia and the Pacific
ESCWA	Economic and Social Commission for Western Asia
est.	estimate
EU	European Union
Euratom	European Atomic Energy Community
Eutelsat	European Telecommunications Satellite Organization
Ex-Im	Export-Import Bank of the United States
f.o.b.	free on board
FAO	Food and Agriculture Organization
FATF	Financial Action Task Force
FAX	facsimile
FLS	Front Line States
FOC	flags of convenience
FSU	former Soviet Union
FY	fiscal year
FZ	Franc Zone
G-3	Group of 3
G-5	Group of 5
G-6	Group of 6
G-7	Group of 7
G-8	Group of 8
G-9	Group of 9
G-10	Group of 10
G-15	Group of 15
G-11	Group of 11
G-20	Group of 20
G-24	Group of 24
G-77	Group of 77
GATT	General Agreement on Tariffs and Trade; now WTO
GCC	Gulf Cooperation Council
GCN	Global Caribbean Network
GCTU	General Confederation of Trade Unions
GDP	gross domestic product
GMT	Greenwich Mean Time
GNP	gross national product
GRT	gross register ton
GSM	global system for mobile cellular communications
GUAM	Organization for Democracy and Economic Development; acronym for member states— Georgia, Ukraine, Azerbaijan, Moldova
GWP	gross world product
Hazardous Wastes	Basel Convention on the Control of Transboundary Movements of Hazardous Wastes and Their Disposal
HF	high-frequency
HIV/AIDS	human immunodeficiency virus/acquired immune deficiency syndrome
IADB	Inter-American Development Bank
IAEA	International Atomic Energy Agency
IANA	Internet Assigned Numbers Authority
IBRD	International Bank for Reconstruction and Development (World Bank)
ICAO	International Civil Aviation Organization
ICC	International Chamber of Commerce
ICCt	International Criminal Court
ICJ	International Court of Justice (World Court)
ICRC	International Committee of the Red Cross

ICRM	International Red Cross and Red Crescent Movement
ICSID	International Center for Settlement of Investment Disputes
ICTR	International Criminal Tribunal for Rwanda
ICTY	International Criminal Tribunal for the former Yugoslavia
IDA	International Development Association
IDB	Islamic Development Bank
IDP	Internally Displaced Person
IEA	International Energy Agency
IFAD	International Fund for Agricultural Development
IFC	International Finance Corporation
IFRCS	International Federation of Red Cross and Red Crescent Societies
IGAD	Inter-Governmental Authority on Development
IHO	International Hydrographic Organization
ILO	International Labor Organization
IMF	International Monetary Fund
IMO	International Maritime Organization
IMSO	International Mobile Satellite Organization
Inmarsat	International Maritime Satellite Organization
InOC	Indian Ocean Commission
Intelsat	International Telecommunications Satellite Organization
Interpol	International Criminal Police Organization
Intersputnik	International Organization of Space Communications
IOC	International Olympic Committee
IOM	International Organization for Migration
IPU	Inter-Parliamentary Union
ISO	International Organization for Standardization
ISP	Internet Service Provider
ITC	International Trade Center
ITSO	International Telecommunications Satellite Organization
ITU	International Telecommunication Union
ITUC	International Trade Union Confederation, the successor to ICFTU (International Confederation of Free Trade Unions) and the WCL (World Confederation of Labor)
kHz	kilohertz
km	kilometer
kW	kilowatt
kWh	kilowatt-hour
LAES	Latin American and Caribbean Economic System
LAIA	Latin American Integration Association
LAS	League of Arab States
Law of the Sea	United Nations Convention on the Law of the Sea (LOS)
LDC	less developed country
LLDC	least developed country
London Convention	see Marine Dumping
LOS	see Law of the Sea
m	meter
Marecs	Maritime European Communications Satellite
Marine Dumping	Convention on the Prevention of Marine Pollution by Dumping Wastes and Other Matter
Marine Life Conservation	Convention on Fishing and Conservation of Living Resources of the High Seas
MARPOL	see Ship Pollution
Medarabtel	Middle East Telecommunications Project of the International Telecommunications Union
Mercosur	Southern Cone Common Market
MHz	megahertz
MICAH	International Civilian Support Mission in Haiti
MIGA	Multilateral Investment Guarantee Agency
MINURCAT	United Nations Mission in the Central African Republic and Chad

MINURSO	United Nations Mission for the Referendum in Western Sahara
MINUSTAH	United Nations Stabilization Mission in Haiti
MONUSCO	United Nations Organization Stabilization Mission in the Democratic Republic of the Congo
NA	not available
NAFTA	North American Free Trade Agreement
NAM	Nonaligned Movement
NATO	North Atlantic Treaty Organization
NC	Nordic Council
NEA	Nuclear Energy Agency
NEGL	negligible
NGA	National Geospatial-Intelligence Agency
NGO	nongovernmental organization
NIB	Nordic Investment Bank
NIC	newly industrializing country
NIE	newly industrializing economy
NIS	new independent states
nm	nautical mile
NMT	Nordic Mobile Telephone
NSG	Nuclear Suppliers Group
Nuclear Test Ban	Treaty Banning Nuclear Weapons Tests in the Atmosphere, in Outer Space, and Under Water
NZ	New Zealand
OAPEC	Organization of Arab Petroleum Exporting Countries
OAS	Organization of American States
OAU	Organization of African Unity; see African Union
ODA	official development assistance
OECD	Organization for Economic Cooperation and Development
OECS	Organization of Eastern Caribbean States
OHCHR	Office of the United Nations High Commissioner for Human Rights
OIC	Organization of the Islamic Conference
OIF	International Organization of the French-speaking World
OOF	other official flows
OPANAL	Agency for the Prohibition of Nuclear Weapons in Latin America and the Caribbean
OPCW	Organization for the Prohibition of Chemical Weapons
OPEC	Organization of Petroleum Exporting Countries
OSCE	Organization for Security and Cooperation in Europe
Ozone Layer Protection	Montreal Protocol on Substances That Deplete the Ozone Layer
PCA	Permanent Court of Arbitration
PFP	Partnership for Peace
PIF	Pacific Islands Forum
PPP	purchasing power parity
Ramsar	see Wetlands
RG	Rio Group
SAARC	South Asian Association for Regional Cooperation
SACEP	South Asia Co-operative Environment Program
SACU	Southern African Customs Union
SADC	Southern African Development Community
SAFE	South African Far East Cable
SCO	Shanghai Cooperation Organization
SECI	Southeast European Cooperative Initiative
SELEC	Convention of the Southeast European Law Enforcement Centers (successor to SECI)
SHF	super-high-frequency
Ship Pollution	Protocol of 1978 Relating to the International Convention for the Prevention of Pollution From Ships, 1973 (MARPOL)
SICA	Central American Integration System
Sparteca	South Pacific Regional Trade and Economic Cooperation Agreement

SPC	Secretariat of the Pacific Communities
SPF	South Pacific Forum
sq km	square kilometer
sq mi	square mile
TAT	Trans-Atlantic Telephone
TEU	Twenty-Foot Equivalent Unit, a unit of measure for containerized cargo capacity
Tropical Timber 83	International Tropical Timber Agreement, 1983
Tropical Timber 94	International Tropical Timber Agreement, 1994
UAE	United Arab Emirates
UDEAC	Central African Customs and Economic Union
UHF	ultra-high-frequency
UK	United Kingdom
UN	United Nations
UN-AIDS	Joint United Nations Program on HIV/AIDS
UNAMA	United Nations Assistance Mission in Afghanistan
UNAMID	African Union/United Nations Hybrid Operation in Darfur
UNASUR	Union of South American Nations
UNCLOS	United Nations Convention on the Law of the Sea, also know as LOS
UNCTAD	United Nations Conference on Trade and Development
UNDCP	United Nations Drug Control Program
UNDEF	United Nations Democracy Fund
UNDOF	United Nations Disengagement Observer Force
UNDP	United Nations Development Program
UNEP	United Nations Environment Program
UNESCO	United Nations Educational, Scientific, and Cultural Organization
UNFICYP	United Nations Peace-keeping Force in Cyprus
UNFPA	United Nations Population Fund
UN-Habitat	United Nations Center for Human Settlements
UNHCR	United Nations High Commissioner for Refugees
UNICEF	United Nations Children's Fund
UNICRI	United Nations Interregional Crime and Justice Research Institute
UNIDIR	United Nations Institute for Disarmament Research
UNIDO	United Nations Industrial Development Organization
UNIFIL	United Nations Interim Force in Lebanon
UNISFA	United Nations Interim Force for Abyei
UNITAR	United Nations Institute for Training and Research
UNMIK	United Nations Interim Administration Mission in Kosovo
UNMIL	United Nations Mission in Liberia
UNMIS	United Nations Mission in the Sudan
UNMISS	United Nations Mission in South Sudan
UNMIT	United Nations Integrated Mission in Timor-Leste
UNMOGIP	United Nations Military Observer Group in India and Pakistan
UNOCI	United Nations Operation in Cote d'Ivoire
UNODC	United Nations Office of Drugs and Crime
UNOPS	United Nations Office of Project Services
UNRISD	United Nations Research Institute for Social Development
UNRWA	United Nations Relief and Works Agency for Palestine Refugees in the Near East
UNSC	United Nations Security Council
UNSSC	Untied Nations System Staff College
UNTSO	United Nations Truce Supervision Organization
UNU	United Nations University
UNWTO	World Tourism Organization
UPU	Universal Postal Union
US	United States
USSR	Union of Soviet Socialist Republics (Soviet Union); used for information dated before 25 December 1991

UTC	Coordinated Universal Time
UV	ultra violet
VHF	very-high-frequency
VSAT	very small aperture terminal
WADB	West African Development Bank
WAEMU	West African Economic and Monetary Union
WCL	World Confederation of Labor
WCO	World Customs Organization
Wetlands	Convention on Wetlands of International Importance Especially As Waterfowl Habitat
WEU	Western European Union
WFP	World Food Program
WFTU	World Federation of Trade Unions
Whaling	International Convention for the Regulation of Whaling
WHO	World Health Organization
WIPO	World Intellectual Property Organization
WMO	World Meteorological Organization
WP	Warsaw Pact
WTO	World Trade Organization
ZC	Zangger Committee

INTERNATIONAL ORGANIZATIONS AND GROUPS

advanced developing countries
another term for those less developed countries (LDCs) with particularly rapid industrial development; see newly industrializing economies (NIEs)

advanced economies
a term used by the International Monetary FUND (IMF) for the top group in its hierarchy of advanced economies, countries in transition, and developing countries; it includes the following 33 advanced economies: Australia, Austria, Belgium, Canada, Cyprus, Czech Republic, Denmark, Finland, France, Germany, Greece, Hong Kong, Iceland, Ireland, Israel, Italy, Japan, South Korea, Luxembourg, Malta, Netherlands, NZ, Norway, Portugal, Singapore, Slovak Republic, Slovenia, Spain, Sweden, Switzerland, Taiwan, UK, US; note—this group would presumably also cover the following nine smaller countries of Andorra, Bermuda, Faroe Islands, Guernsey, Holy See, Jersey, Liechtenstein, Monaco, and San Marino that are included in the more comprehensive group of "developed countries"

African Development Bank Group (AfDB)
note—regional multilateral development finance institution temporarily located in Tunis, Tunisia; the Bank Group consists of the African Development Bank, the African Development Fund, and the Nigerian Trust Fund
established—10 September 1964
aim—to promote economic development and social progress
regional members—(53) Algeria, Angola, Benin, Botswana, Burkina Faso, Burundi, Cameroon, cabo Verde, Central African Republic, Chad, Comoros, Democratic Republic of the Congo, Republic of the Congo, Cote d'Ivoire, Djibouti, Egypt, Equatorial Guinea, Eritrea, Ethiopia, Gabon, The Gambia, Ghana, Guinea, Guinea-Bissau, Kenya, Lesotho, Liberia, Libya, Madagascar, Malawi, Mali, Mauritania, Mauritius, Morocco, Mozambique, Namibia, Niger, Nigeria, Rwanda, Sao Tome and Principe, Senegal, Seychelles, Sierra Leone, Somalia, South Africa, Sudan, Swaziland, Tanzania, Togo, Tunisia, Uganda, Zambia, Zimbabwe
nonregional members—(25) Argentina, Austria, Belgium, Brazil, Canada, China, Denmark, Finland, France, Germany, India, Italy, Japan, South Korea, Kuwait, Netherlands, Norway, Portugal, Saudi Arabia, Spain, Sweden, Switzerland, UAE (ADF members only), UK, US

African Union (AU)
note—replaces Organization of African Unity (OAU)
established—8 July 2001
aim—to achieve greater unity among African States; to defend states' integrity and independence; to accelerate political, social, and economic integration; to encourage international cooperation; to promote democratic principles and institutions
members—(54) Algeria, Angola, Benin, Botswana, Burkina Faso, Burundi, Cabo Verde, Cameroon, Central African Republic, Chad, Comoros, Democratic Republic of the Congo, Republic of the Congo, Cote d'Ivoire, Djibouti, Egypt, Equatorial Guinea, Eritrea, Ethiopia, Gabon, The Gambia, Ghana, Guinea (suspended), Guinea-Bissau, Kenya, Lesotho, Liberia, Libya, Madagascar, Malawi, Mali, Mauritania, Mauritius, Mozambique, Namibia, Niger, Nigeria, Rwanda, Sahrawi Arab Democratic Republic (Western Sahara), Sao Tome and Principe, Senegal, Seychelles, Sierra Leone, Somalia, South Africa, South Sudan, Sudan, Swaziland, Tanzania, Togo, Tunisia, Uganda, Zambia, Zimbabwe

African Union/United Nations Hybrid Operation in Darfur (UNAMID)
established—31 July 2007
aim—to contribute to the restoration of security conditions which will allow safe humanitarian assistance throughout Darfur, to contribute to the protection of civilian populations under imminent threat of physical attack, to monitor, observe compliance with, and verify the implementation of various ceasefire agreements
members—(47) Bangladesh, Benin, Bolivia, Burkina Faso, Burundi, Cambodia, Cabo Verde, Cameroon, Djibouti, Ecuador, Egypt, Ethiopia, The Gambia, Germany, Ghana, Indonesia, Iran, Jordan, Kenya, South Korea, Kyrgyzstan, Lesotho, Malawi, Malaysia, Mali, Mongolia, Namibia, Nepal, Nigeria, Pakistan, Palau, Peru, Rwanda, Senegal, Sierra Leone, South Africa, Tajikistan, Tanzania, Thailand, Togo, Tunisia, Turkey, Uganda, Yemen, Zambia, Zimbabwe

African, Caribbean, and Pacific Group of States (ACP Group)
established—6 June 1975
aim—to manage their preferential economic and aid relationship with the EU
members—(79) Angola, Antigua and Barbuda, The Bahamas, Barbados, Belize, Benin, Botswana, Burkina Faso, Burundi, Cabo Verde, Cameroon, Central African Republic, Chad, Comoros, Democratic Republic of the Congo, Republic of the Congo, Cook Islands, Cote d'Ivoire, Cuba, Djibouti, Dominica, Dominican Republic, Equatorial Guinea, Eritrea, Ethiopia, Fiji, Gabon, The Gambia, Ghana, Grenada, Guinea, Guinea-Bissau, Guyana, Haiti, Jamaica, Kenya, Kiribati, Lesotho, Liberia, Madagascar, Malawi, Mali, Marshall Islands, Mauritania, Mauritius, Federated States of Micronesia, Mozambique, Namibia, Nauru, Niger, Nigeria, Niue, Palau, Papua New Guinea, Rwanda, Saint Kitts and Nevis, Saint Lucia, Saint Vincent and the Grenadines, Samoa, Sao Tome and Principe, Senegal, Seychelles, Sierra Leone, Solomon Islands, Somalia, South Africa, Sudan, Suriname, Swaziland, Tanzania, Timor-Leste, Togo, Tonga, Trinidad and Tobago, Tuvalu, Uganda, Vanuatu, Zambia, Zimbabwe

Agency for the Prohibition of Nuclear Weapons in Latin America and the Caribbean (OPANAL)
note—acronym from Organismo para la Proscripcion de las Armas Nucleares en la America Latina y el Caribe (OPANAL)
established—14 February 1967 under the Treaty of Tlatelolco; effective—25 April 1969 on the 11th ratification

aim—to encourage the peaceful uses of atomic energy and prohibit nuclear weapons
members—(33) Antigua and Barbuda, Argentina, The Bahamas, Barbados, Belize, Bolivia, Brazil, Chile, Colombia, Costa Rica, Cuba, Dominica, Dominican Republic, Ecuador, El Salvador, Grenada, Guatemala, Guyana, Haiti, Honduras, Jamaica, Mexico, Nicaragua, Panama, Paraguay, Peru, Saint Kitts and Nevis, Saint Lucia, Saint Vincent and the Grenadines, Suriname, Trinidad and Tobago, Uruguay, Venezuela

Alliance of Small Island States (AOSIS)
established—November 1990
aim—to call attention to threats of sea-level rise and coral bleaching to small islands and lowlying coastal developing states from global warming; to emphasize the importance of information and information technology in the process of achieving sustainable development
members—(39) Antigua and Barbuda, The Bahamas, Barbados, Belize, Cabo Verde, Comoros, Cook Islands, Cuba, Dominica, Dominican Republic, Fiji, Grenada, Guinea-Bissau, Guyana, Haiti, Jamaica, Kiribati, Maldives, Marshall Islands, Mauritius, Federated States of Micronesia, Nauru, Niue, Palau, Papua New Guinea, St. Kitts and Nevis, St. Lucia, St. Vincent and the Grenadines, Samoa, Sao Tome and Principe, Seychelles, Singapore, Solomon Islands, Suriname, Timor-Leste, Tonga, Trinidad and Tobago, Tuvalu, Vanuatu
observers—(5) American Samoa, Guam, Netherlands Antilles, Puerto Rico, U.S. Virgin Islands

Andean Community (CAN)
note—formerly known as the Andean Group (AG) and the Andean Common Market (Ancom)
established—26 May 1969; present name established 1 October 1992; effective—16 October 1969
aim—to promote harmonious development through economic integration
members—(4) Bolivia, Colombia, Ecuador, Peru
associate members—(5) Argentina, Brazil, Chile, Paraguay, Uruguay
observers—(1) Spain

Arab Bank for Economic Development in Africa (ABEDA)
note—also known as Banque Arabe de Developpement Economique en Afrique (BADEA)
established—18 February 1974; effective—16 September 1974
aim—to promote economic development
members—(17 plus the Palestine Liberation Organization) Algeria, Bahrain, Egypt, Iraq, Jordan, Kuwait, Lebanon, Libya, Mauritania, Morocco, Oman, Qatar, Saudi Arabia, Sudan, Syria, Tunisia, UAE, Palestine Liberation Organization; note—these are all the members of the Arab League excluding Comoros, Djibouti, Somalia, Yemen

Arab Fund for Economic and Social Development (AFESD)
established—16 May 1968
aim—to promote economic and social development
members—(20 plus the Palestine Liberation Organization) Algeria, Bahrain, Djibouti, Egypt, Iraq, Jordan, Kuwait, Lebanon, Libya, Mauritania, Morocco, Oman, Qatar, Saudi Arabia, Somalia (suspended 1993), Sudan, Syria, Tunisia, UAE, Yemen, Palestine Liberation Organization

Arab Maghreb Union (AMU)
established—17 February 1989
aim—to promote cooperation and integration among the Arab states of northern Africa
members—(5) Algeria, Libya, Mauritania, Morocco, Tunisia

Arab Monetary Fund (AMF)
established—27 April 1976; effective—2 February 1977
aim—to promote Arab cooperation, development, and integration in monetary and economic affairs
members—(21 plus the Palestine Liberation Organization) Algeria, Bahrain, Comoros, Djibouti, Egypt, Iraq, Jordan, Kuwait, Lebanon, Libya, Mauritania, Morocco, Oman, Qatar, Saudi Arabia, Somalia, Sudan, Syria, Tunisia, UAE, Yemen, Palestine Liberation Organization

Arctic Council
established—18 September 1996
aim—to address the common concerns and challenges faced by Arctic governments and the people of the Arctic; to protect the Arctic environment
members—(8) Canada, Denmark (Greenland, Faroe Islands), Finland, Iceland, Norway, Russia, Sweden, US
permanent participants—(6) Aleut International Association, Arctic Athabaskan Council, Gwich'in Council International, Inuit Circumpolar Conference, Russian Association of Indigenous People of the North, Saami Council
observers—(12) China, France, Germany, India, Italy, Japan, South Korea, Netherlands, Poland, Singapore, Spain, UK

ASEAN Regional Forum (ARF)
established—25 July 1994
aim—to foster constructive dialogue and consultation on political and security issues of common interest and concern
members—(27) Australia, Bangladesh, Brunei, Burma, Cambodia, Canada, China, EU, India, Indonesia, Japan, North Korea, South Korea, Laos, Malaysia, Mongolia, NZ, Pakistan, Papua New Guinea, Philippines, Russia, Singapore, Sri Lanka, Thailand, Timor-Leste, US, Vietnam

Asia-Pacific Economic Cooperation (APEC)
established—7 November 1989
aim—to promote trade and investment in the Pacific basin

members—(21) Australia, Brunei, Canada, Chile, China, Hong Kong, Indonesia, Japan, South Korea, Malaysia, Mexico, NZ, Papua New Guinea, Peru, Philippines, Russia, Singapore, Taiwan, Thailand, US, Vietnam
observers—(3) Association of Southeast Asian Nations, Pacific Economic Cooperation Council, Pacific Islands Forum Secretariat

Asian Development Bank (ADB)
established—19 December 1966
aim—to promote regional economic cooperation
members—(48) Afghanistan, Armenia, Australia, Azerbaijan, Bangladesh, Bhutan, Brunei, Burma, Cambodia, China, Cook Islands, Fiji, Georgia, Hong Kong, India, Indonesia, Japan, Kazakhstan, Kiribati, South Korea, Kyrgyzstan, Laos, Malaysia, Maldives, Marshall Islands, Federated States of Micronesia, Mongolia, Nauru, Nepal, NZ, Pakistan, Palau, Papua New Guinea, Philippines, Samoa, Singapore, Solomon Islands, Sri Lanka, Taiwan, Tajikistan, Thailand, Timor- Leste, Tonga, Turkmenistan, Tuvalu, Uzbekistan, Vanuatu, Vietnam
nonregional members—(19) Austria, Belgium, Canada, Denmark, Finland, France, Germany, Ireland, Italy, Luxembourg, Netherlands, Norway, Portugal, Spain, Sweden, Switzerland, Turkey, UK, US

Association of Southeast Asian Nations (ASEAN)
established—8 August 1967
aim—to encourage regional economic, social, and cultural cooperation among the non-Communist countries of Southeast Asia
members—(10) Brunei, Burma, Cambodia, Indonesia, Laos, Malaysia, Philippines, Singapore, Thailand, Vietnam
dialogue partners—(10) Australia, Canada, China, EU, India, Japan, South Korea, NZ, Russia, US
observers—(2) Papua New Guinea, Timor-Leste

Australia Group (AG)
established—June 1985
aim—to consult on and coordinate export controls related to chemical and biological weapons
members—(42) Argentina, Australia, Austria, Belgium, Bulgaria, Canada, Croatia, Cyprus, Czech Republic, Denmark, Estonia, European Commission, Finland, France, Germany, Greece, Hungary, Iceland, Ireland, Italy, Japan, South Korea, Latvia, Lithuania, Luxembourg, Malta, Mexico, Netherlands, NZ, Norway, Poland, Portugal, Romania, Slovakia, Slovenia, Spain, Sweden, Switzerland, Turkey, Ukraine, UK, US

Australia-New Zealand-United States Security Treaty (ANZUS)
established—1 September 1951; effective—29 April 1952
aim—to implement a trilateral mutual security agreement, although the US suspended security obligations to NZ on 11 August 1986; Australia and the US continue to hold annual meetings
members—(3) Australia, NZ, US

Baltic Assembly (BA)
established—12 May 1990
aim—to thoroughly discuss various cooperation issues between Baltic states
members—(3) Estonia, Latvia, Lithuania

Bank for International Settlements (BIS)
established—20 January 1930; effective—17 March 1930
aim—to promote cooperation among central banks in international financial settlements
members—(60) Algeria, Argentina, Australia, Austria, Belgium, Bosnia and Herzegovina, Brazil, Bulgaria, Canada, Chile, China, Colombia, Croatia, Czech Republic, Denmark, European Central Bank, Estonia, Finland, France, Germany, Greece, Hong Kong, Hungary, Iceland, India, Indonesia, Ireland, Israel, Italy, Japan, South Korea, Latvia, Lithuania, Luxembourg, Macedonia, Malaysia, Mexico, Netherlands, NZ, Norway, Peru, Philippines, Poland, Portugal, Romania, Russia, Saudi Arabia, Serbia, Singapore, Slovakia, Slovenia, South Africa, Spain, Sweden, Switzerland, Thailand, Turkey, UAE, UK, US; note—Montenegro has a separate central bank; its links with BIS are currently under review

Bay of Bengal Initiative for Multi-Sectoral Technical and Economic Cooperation (BIMSTEC)
established—June 1997
aim—to foster socio-economic cooperation among members
members—(7) Bangladesh, Bhutan, Burma, India, Nepal, Sri Lanka, Thailand

Benelux Union (Benelux)
note—acronym from Belgium, Netherlands, and Luxembourg; was formerly known as Benelux Economic Union
established—3 February 1958; effective—1 November 1960; changed names 17 June 2008
aim—to develop closer economic and legal cooperation and integration
members—(3) Belgium, Luxembourg, Netherlands

Big Seven
note—membership is the same as the Group of 7
established—1975
aim—to discuss and coordinate major economic policies
members—(7) Big Six (Canada, France, Germany, Italy, Japan, UK) plus the US

Black Sea Economic Cooperation Zone (BSEC)
established—25 June 1992

aim—to enhance regional stability through economic cooperation
members—(12) Albania, Armenia, Azerbaijan, Bulgaria, Georgia, Greece, Moldova, Romania, Russia, Serbia, Turkey, Ukraine; note—Macedonia is in the process of joining
observers—(17) Austria, Belarus, Black Sea Commission, EU, Croatia, Czech Republic, Egypt, Energy Charter Secretariat, France, Germany, International Black Sea Club, Israel, Italy, Poland, Slovakia, Tunisia, US; note—Bosnia and Herzegovina and Slovenia have applied for observer status

BRICS
note—the name of the organization stands for the first letter of each of the five members' names
established—BRIC established 16 June 2009; BRICS established 24 December 2011
aim—to seek common ground in political and economic venues; to achieve peace, security, development, and cooperation; to contribute significantly to the development of humanity and to establish a more equitable world
members—(5) Brazil, Russia, India, China, South Africa

Caribbean Community and Common Market (Caricom)
established—4 July 1973; effective—1 August 1973
aim—to promote economic integration and development, especially among the less developed countries
members—(15) Antigua and Barbuda, The Bahamas, Barbados, Belize, Dominica, Grenada, Guyana, Haiti, Jamaica, Montserrat, Saint Kitts and Nevis, Saint Lucia, Saint Vincent and the Grenadines, Suriname, Trinidad and Tobago
associate members—(5) Anguilla, Bermuda, British Virgin Islands, Cayman Islands, Turks and Caicos Islands
observers—(8) Aruba, Colombia, Curacao, Dominican Republic, Mexico, Puerto Rico, Sint Maarten, Venezuela

Caribbean Development Bank (CDB)
established—18 October 1969; effective—26 January 1970
aim—to promote economic development and cooperation
regional members—(21) Anguilla, Antigua and Barbuda, The Bahamas, Barbados, Belize, British Virgin Islands, Cayman Islands, Colombia, Dominica, Grenada, Guyana, Haiti, Jamaica, Mexico, Montserrat, Saint Kitts and Nevis, Saint Lucia, Saint Vincent and the Grenadines, Trinidad and Tobago, Turks and Caicos Islands, Venezuela
nonregional members—(5) Canada, China, Germany, Italy, UK

Central African Customs and Economic Union (UDEAC)
see *Economic and Monetary Community of Central Africa (CEMAC)*

Central African States Development Bank (BDEAC)
note—acronym from Banque de Developpement des Etats de l'Afrique Centrale
established—3 December 1975
aim—to provide loans for economic development
members—(11) African Development Bank (AfDB), Cameroon, Central African States Bank (BEAC), Central African Republic, Chad, Republic of the Congo, Equatorial Guinea, France, Gabon, Kuwait, Libya

Central American Bank for Economic Integration (BCIE)
note—acronym from Banco Centroamericano de Integracion Economico
established—13 December 1960 signature of Articles of Agreement; 31 May 1961 began operations
aim—to promote economic integration and development
members—(5) Costa Rica, El Salvador, Guatemala, Honduras, Nicaragua
nonregional members—(7) Argentina, Colombia, Dominican Republic, Mexico, Panama, Spain, Taiwan

Central American Common Market (CACM)
established—13 December 1960, collapsed in 1969, reinstated in 1991
aim—to promote establishment of a Central American Common Market
members—(5) Costa Rica, El Salvador, Guatemala, Honduras, Nicaragua

Central American Integration System (SICA)
established—13 December 1991; operational 1 February 1993
aim—to strengthen democracy; to set up a new model of regional security; to promote freedom; to achieve a regional system of welfare and economic and social justice; to attain economic unity and strengthen the area as an economic bloc; to act as a bloc in international matters
members—(7) Belize, Costa Rica, El Salvador, Guatemala, Honduras, Nicaragua, Panama
associated member—(1) Dominican Republic
observers—(15) Argentina, Australia, Brazil, Chile, China, France, Germany, Holy See, Italy, Japan, South Korea, Mexico, Peru, Spain, US

Central European Initiative (CEI)
note—evolved from the Quadrilateral Initiative and the Hexagonal Initiative
established—11 November 1989 as the Quadrilateral Initiative, 27 July 1991 became the Hexagonal Initiative, July 1992 its present name was adopted
aim—to form an economic and political cooperation group for the region between the Adriatic and the Baltic Seas
members—(18) Albania, Austria, Belarus, Bosnia and Herzegovina, Bulgaria, Croatia, Czech Republic, Hungary, Italy, Macedonia, Moldova, Montenegro, Poland, Romania, Serbia, Slovakia, Slovenia, Ukraine

centrally planned economies

a term applied mainly to the traditionally Communist states that looked to the former USSR for leadership; most are now evolving toward more democratic and market-oriented systems; also known formerly as the Second World or as the Communist countries; through the 1980s, this group included Albania, Bulgaria, Cambodia, China, Cuba, Czechoslovakia, German Democratic Republic, Hungary, North Korea, Laos, Mongolia, Poland, Romania, USSR, Vietnam, Yugoslavia, but now is limited to Cuba and North Korea, and less so to China

Collective Security Treaty Organization (CSTO)

established—7 October 2002
aim—to coordinate military and political cooperation, to develop multilateral structures and mechanisms of cooperation for ensuring national security of the member states
members—(7) Armenia, Belarus, Kazakhstan, Kyrgyzstan, Russia, Tajikistan, Uzbekistan

Colombo Plan (CP)

established—May 1950 proposal was adopted; 1 July 1951 commenced full operations
aim—to promote economic and social development in Asia and the Pacific
members—(27) Afghanistan, Australia, Bangladesh, Bhutan, Brunei, Burma, Fiji, India, Indonesia, Iran, Japan, South Korea, Laos, Malaysia, Maldives, Mongolia, Nepal, NZ, Pakistan, Papua New Guinea, Philippines, Saudi Arabia, Singapore, Sri Lanka, Thailand, US, Vietnam

Common Market for Eastern and Southern Africa (COMESA)

note—formerly known as Preferential Trade Area for Eastern and Southern Africa (PTA)
established—treaty signed 5 November 1993; treaty ratified 8 December 1994
aim—recognizing, promoting and protecting fundamental human rights, commitment to the principles of liberty and rule of law, maintaining peace and stability through the promotion and strengthening of good neighborliness, commitment to peaceful settlement of disputes among member states
members—(19) Burundi, Comoros, Democratic Republic of the Congo, Djibouti, Egypt, Eritrea, Ethiopia, Kenya, Libya, Madagascar, Malawi, Mauritius, Rwanda, Seychelles, Sudan, Swaziland, Uganda, Zambia, Zimbabwe

Commonwealth (C)

note—also known as Commonwealth of Nations
established—31 December 1931
aim—to foster multinational cooperation and assistance, as a voluntary association that evolved from the British Empire
members—(53) Antigua and Barbuda, Australia, The Bahamas, Bangladesh, Barbados, Belize, Botswana, Brunei, Cameroon, Canada, Cyprus, Dominica, Fiji (suspended), Ghana, Grenada, Guyana, India, Jamaica, Kenya, Kiribati, Lesotho, Malawi, Malaysia, Maldives, Malta, Mauritius, Mozambique, Namibia, Nauru, NZ, Nigeria, Pakistan (reinstated 2004), Papua New Guinea, Rwanda, Saint Kitts and Nevis, Saint Lucia, Saint Vincent and the Grenadines, Samoa, Seychelles, Sierra Leone, Singapore, Solomon Islands, South Africa, Sri Lanka, Swaziland, Tanzania, Tonga, Trinidad and Tobago, Tuvalu, Uganda, UK, Vanuatu, Zambia; note—on 7 December 2003 Zimbabwe withdrew its membership from the Commonwealth

Commonwealth of Independent States (CIS)

established—8 December 1991; effective—21 December 1991
aim—to coordinate intercommonwealth relations and to provide a mechanism for the orderly dissolution of the USSR
members—(11) Armenia, Azerbaijan, Belarus, Kazakhstan, Kyrgyzstan, Moldova, Russia, Tajikistan, Turkmenistan (unofficial), Ukraine (unofficial), Uzbekistan; note—neither Ukraine as a participating member nor Turkmenistan as an associate member have signed the 1993 CIS charter, although both participate in meetings; Georgia left the organization in August 2009

Communist countries

traditionally the Marxist-Leninist states with authoritarian governments and command economies based on the Soviet model; most of the original and the successor states are no longer Communist; see centrally planned economies

Community of Democracies (CD)

established—27 June 2000
aim—"to respect and uphold core democratic principles and practices" including free and fair elections, freedom of speech and expression, equal access to education, rule of law, and freedom of peaceful assembly
signatories of the Warsaw Declaration—(110) Albania, Algeria, Argentina, Armenia, Australia, Austria, Azerbaijan, Bangladesh, Belgium, Belize, Benin, Bolivia, Bosnia and Herzegovina, Botswana, Brazil, Bulgaria, Burkina Faso, Cabo Verde, Canada, Chile, Colombia, Costa Rica, Croatia, Cyprus, Czech Republic, Denmark, Dominica, Dominican Republic, Ecuador, Egypt, El Salvador, Estonia, Finland, Georgia, Germany, Greece, Guatemala, Guyana, Haiti, Honduras, Hungary, Iceland, India, Indonesia, Ireland, Israel, Italy, Japan, Jordan, Kenya, South Korea, Kuwait, Latvia, Lesotho, Liechtenstein, Lithuania, Luxembourg, Macedonia, Madagascar, Malawi, Mali, Malta, Mauritius, Mexico, Moldova, Monaco, Mongolia, Morocco, Mozambique, Namibia, Nepal, Netherlands, NZ, Nicaragua, Niger, Nigeria, Norway, Panama, Papua New Guinea, Paraguay, Peru, Philippines, Poland, Portugal, Qatar, Romania, Russia, Saint Lucia, Sao Tome and Principe, Senegal, Seychelles, Slovakia, Slovenia, South Africa, Spain, Sri Lanka, Suriname, Sweden, Switzerland, Tanzania, Thailand, Tunisia, Turkey, Ukraine, UK, US, Uruguay, Venezuela, Yemen, Yugoslavia

Community of Latin American and Caribbean States (CELAC)

note—successor to the Rio Group and the Latin America and Caribbean Summit on Integration and Development
established—created 23 February 2010; established July 2011

aim—to deepen the integration within Latin American and to reduce the influence of the US in the politics and economics of that part of the world

members—(33) Antigua and Barbuda, Argentina, The Bahamas, Barbados, Belize, Bolivia, Brazil, Chile, Colombia, Costa Rica, Cuba, Dominica, Dominican Republic, Ecuador, El Salvador, Grenada, Guatemala, Guyana, Haiti, Honduras, Jamaica, Mexico, Nicaragua, Panama, Paraguay, Peru, St. Kitts and Nevis, St. Lucia, St. Vincent and the Grenadines, Suriname, Trinidad and Tobago, Uruguay, Venezuela

Comuinidade dos Paises de Lingua Portuguesa (CPLP)
established—1996
aim—to establish a forum for friendship among Portuguese-speaking nations where Portuguese is an official language
members—(8) Angola, Brazil, Cabo Verde, Guinea-Bissau, Mozambique, Portugal, Sao Tome and Principe, Timor-Leste
associate observers—(3) Equatorial Guinea, Mauritius, Senegal

Conference of Interaction and Confidence-Building Measures in Asia (CICA)
established—proposed 5 October 1992; established 14 September 1999
aim—promoting a multi-national forum for enhancing cooperation towards promoting peace, security, and stability in Asia
members—(23 and the Palestine Liberation Organization) Afghanistan, Azerbaijan, Bahrain, Cambodia, China, Egypt, India, Iraq, Iran, Israel, Jordan, Kazakhstan, Kyrgyzstan, Mongolia, Pakistan, South Korea, Russia, Tajikistan, Thailand, Turkey, UAE, Uzbekistan, Vietnam, and the Palestine Liberation Organization
observers—(13) Bangladesh, Indonesia, Japan, League of Arab States, Malaysia, OSCE, Parliamentary Assembly of the Turkic Speaking Countries, Philippines, Qatar, Sri Lanka, Ukraine, UN, US

Convention of the Southeast European Law Enforcement Center (SELEC)
note—successor to Southeast European Cooperative Initiative (SECI) formed in 1996 to help the Southeast European countries rebuild and stabilize through access to resources
established—7 October 2011
aim—to provide support for Member States and enhance coordination in preventing and combating crime in trans-border activity
members—(13) Albania, Bosnia and Herzegovina, Bulgaria, Croatia, Greece, Hungary, Macedonia, Moldova, Montenegro, Romania, Serbia, Slovenia, Turkey
observers—(15) Austria, Azerbaijan, Belgium, Canada, France, Georgia, Germany, Italy, Japan, The Netherlands, Portugal, Spain, Ukraine, UK, US

Coordinating Committee on Export Controls (COCOM)
established in 1949 to control the export of strategic products and technical data from member countries to proscribed destinations; members were: Australia, Belgium, Canada, Denmark, France, Germany, Greece, Italy, Japan, Luxembourg, Netherlands, Norway, Portugal, Spain, Turkey, UK, US; abolished 31 March 1994; COCOM members established a new organization, the Wassenaar Arrangement, with expanded membership on 12 July 1996 that focuses on nonproliferation export controls as opposed to East-West control of advanced technology

Council for Mutual Economic Assistance (CEMA)
note—also known as CMEA or Comecon
established 25 January 1949 to promote the development of socialist economies and abolished 1 January 1991; members included Afghanistan (observer), Albania (had not participated since 1961 break with USSR), Angola (observer), Bulgaria, Cuba, Czechoslovakia, Ethiopia (observer), GDR, Hungary, Laos (observer), Mongolia, Mozambique (observer), Nicaragua (observer), Poland, Romania, USSR, Vietnam, Yemen (observer), Yugoslavia (associate)

Council of Arab Economic Unity (CAEU)
established—3 June 1957; effective—30 May 1964
aim—to promote economic integration among Arab nations
members—(17 plus the Palestine Liberation Organization) Algeria, Bahrain, Egypt, Iraq, Jordan, Kuwait, Lebanon, Libya, Morocco, Oman, Qatar, Saudi Arabia, Sudan, Syria, Tunisia, UAE, Yemen, Palestine Liberation Organization
candidates—(4) Comoros, Djibouti, Mauritania, Somalia

Council of Europe (CE)
established—5 May 1949; effective—3 August 1949
aim—to promote increased unity and quality of life in Europe
members—(47) Albania, Andorra, Armenia, Austria, Azerbaijan, Belgium, Bosnia and Herzegovina, Bulgaria, Croatia, Cyprus, Czech Republic, Denmark, Estonia, Finland, France, Georgia, Germany, Greece, Hungary, Iceland, Ireland, Italy, Latvia, Liechtenstein, Lithuania, Luxembourg, Macedonia, Malta, Moldova, Monaco, Montenegro, Netherlands, Norway, Poland, Portugal, Romania, Russia, San Marino, Serbia, Slovakia, Slovenia, Spain, Sweden, Switzerland, Turkey, Ukraine, UK
observers—(6) Canada, Holy See, Israel, Japan, Mexico, US

Council of the Baltic Sea States (CBSS)
established—6 March 1992
aim—to promote cooperation among the Baltic Sea states in the areas of aid to new democratic institutions, economic development, humanitarian aid, energy and the environment, cultural programs and education, and transportation and communication
members—(12) Denmark, Estonia, EC, Finland, Germany, Iceland, Latvia, Lithuania, Norway, Poland, Russia, Sweden
observers—(10) Belarus, France, Italy, Netherlands, Romania, Spain, Slovakia, Ukraine, UK, US

Council of the Entente (Entente)
established—29 May 1959
aim—to promote economic, social, and political coordination
members—(5) Benin, Burkina Faso, Cote d'Ivoire, Niger, Togo

countries in transition
a term used by the International Monetary Fund (IMF) for the middle group in its hierarchy of formerly centrally planned economies; IMF statistics include the following 28 countries in transition: Albania, Armenia, Azerbaijan, Belarus, Bosnia and Herzegovina, Bulgaria, Croatia, Czech Republic, Estonia, Georgia, Hungary, Kazakhstan, Kyrgyzstan, Latvia, Lithuania, Macedonia, Moldova, Mongolia, Montenegro, Poland, Romania, Russia, Serbia, Slovakia, Slovenia, Tajikistan, Turkmenistan, Ukraine, Uzbekistan; note—this group is identical to the group traditionally referred to as the "former USSR/Eastern Europe" except for the addition of Mongolia

Customs Cooperation Council (CCC)
note—see World Customs Organization (WCO)

developed countries (DCs)
the top group in the hierarchy of developed countries (DCs), former USSR/Eastern Europe (former USSR/EE), and less developed countries (LDCs); includes the market-oriented economies of the mainly democratic nations in the Organization for Economic Cooperation and Development (OECD), Bermuda, Israel, South Africa, and the European ministates; also known as the First World, high- income countries, the North, industrial countries; generally have a per capita GDP in excess of $15,000 although four OECD countries and South Africa have figures well under $15,000 and eight of the excluded OPEC countries have figures of more than $20,000; the DCs include: Andorra, Australia, Austria, Belgium, Bermuda, Canada, Denmark, Faroe Islands, Finland, France, Germany, Greece, Holy See, Iceland, Ireland, Israel, Italy, Japan, Liechtenstein, Luxembourg, Malta, Monaco, Netherlands, NZ, Norway, Portugal, San Marino, South Africa, Spain, Sweden, Switzerland, Turkey, UK, US; note—similar to the new International Monetary Fund (IMF) term "advanced economies" that adds Hong Kong, South Korea, Singapore, and Taiwan but drops Malta, Mexico, South Africa, and Turkey

developing countries
a term used by the International Monetary Fund (IMF) for the bottom group in its hierarchy of advanced economies, countries in transition, and developing countries; IMF statistics include the following 126 developing countries: Afghanistan, Algeria, Angola, Antigua and Barbuda, Argentina, Aruba, The Bahamas, Bahrain, Bangladesh, Barbados, Belize, Benin, Bhutan, Bolivia, Botswana, Brazil, Burkina Faso, Burma, Burundi, Cambodia, Cabo Verde, Cameroon, Central African Republic, Chad, Chile, China, Colombia, Comoros, Democratic Republic of the Congo, Republic of the Congo, Costa Rica, Cote d'Ivoire, Cyprus, Djibouti, Dominica, Dominican Republic, Ecuador, Egypt, El Salvador, Equatorial Guinea, Ethiopia, Fiji, Gabon, The Gambia, Ghana, Grenada, Guatemala, Guinea, Guinea-Bissau, Guyana, Haiti, Honduras, India, Indonesia, Iran, Iraq, Jamaica, Jordan, Kenya, Kiribati, Kuwait, Laos, Lebanon, Lesotho, Liberia, Libya, Madagascar, Malawi, Malaysia, Maldives, Mali, Malta, Marshall Islands, Mauritania, Mauritius, Mexico, Federated States of Micronesia, Morocco, Mozambique, Namibia, Nepal, Netherlands Antilles, Nicaragua, Niger, Nigeria, Oman, Pakistan, Panama, Papua New Guinea, Paraguay, Peru, Philippines, Qatar, Rwanda, Saint Kitts and Nevis, Saint Lucia, Saint Vincent and the Grenadines, Samoa, Sao Tome and Principe, Saudi Arabia, Senegal, Seychelles, Sierra Leone, Solomon Islands, Somalia, South Africa, Sri Lanka, Sudan, Suriname, Swaziland, Syria, Tanzania, Thailand, Togo, Trinidad and Tobago, Tunisia, Turkey, UAE, Uganda, Uruguay, Vanuatu, Venezuela, Vietnam, Yemen, Zambia, Zimbabwe; note—this category would presumably also cover the following 46 other countries that are traditionally included in the more comprehensive group of "less developed countries": American Samoa, Anguilla, British Virgin Islands, Brunei, Cayman Islands, Christmas Island, Cocos Islands, Cook Islands, Cuba, Eritrea, Falkland Islands, French Guiana, French Polynesia, Gaza Strip, Gibraltar, Greenland, Grenada, Guadeloupe, Guam, Guernsey, Isle of Man, Jersey, North Korea, Macau, Martinique, Mayotte, Montserrat, Nauru, New Caledonia, Niue, Norfolk Island, Northern Mariana Islands, Palau, Pitcairn Islands, Puerto Rico, Reunion, Saint Helena, Ascension, and Tristan da Cunha, Saint Pierre and Miquelon, Tokelau, Tonga, Turks and Caicos Islands, Tuvalu, Virgin Islands, Wallis and Futuna, West Bank, Western Sahara

Developing Eight (D-8)
established—15 June 1997
aim—to improve developing countries' positions in the world economy, diversify and create new opportunities in trade relations, enhance participation in decision-making at the international level, provide better standards of living
member—(8) Bangladesh, Egypt, Indonesia, Iran, Malaysia, Nigeria, Pakistan, Turkey

East African Community (EAC)
note—originally established in 1967, it was disbanded in 1977
established—January 2001
aim—to establish a political and economic union among the countries
members—(5) Burundi, Kenya, Rwanda, Tanzania, Uganda

East African Development Bank (EADB)
established—6 June 1967; effective—1 December 1967
aim—to promote economic development
members—(4) Kenya, Rwanda, Tanzania, Uganda

East Asia Summit (EAS)
established—14 December 2005
aim—to promote cooperation in political and security issues; to promote development, financial stability, energy security, economic integration and growth; to eradicate poverty and narrow the development gap in East Asia, and to promote deeper cultural understanding

members—(18) Australia, Brunei, Burma, Cambodia, China, India, Indonesia, Japan, South Korea, Laos, Malaysia, NZ, Philippines, Russia, Singapore, Thailand, US, Vietnam

Economic and Monetary Community of Central Africa (CEMAC)
note—was formerly the Central African Customs and Economic Union (UDEAC)
established—8 December 1964; effective—1 January 1966
aim—to promote the establishment of a Central African Common Market
members—(7) Cameroon, Central African Republic, Chad, Democratic Republic of the Congo, Equatorial Guinea, Gabon, The Gambia

Economic and Monetary Union (EMU)
note—an integral part of the European Union; also known as the European Economic and Monetary Union
established—1-2 December 1969 (proposed at summit conference of heads of government; 7 February 1992 (Maastricht Treaty signed)
aim—to promote a single market by creating a single currency, the euro; timetable—2 May 1998: European exchange rates fixed for 1 January 1999; 1 January 1999: all banks and stock exchanges begin using euros; 1 January 2002: the euro goes into circulation; 1 July 2002 local currencies no longer accepted
members—(18) Austria, Belgium, Cyprus, Estonia, Finland, France, Germany, Greece, Ireland, Italy, Latvia, Luxembourg, Malta, Netherlands, Portugal, Slovakia, Slovenia, Spain

Economic and Social Council (ECOSOC)
established—26 June 1945; effective—24 October 1945
aim—to coordinate the economic and social work of the UN; includes five regional commissions (Economic Commission for Africa, Economic Commission for Europe, Economic Commission for Latin America and the Caribbean, Economic and Social Commission for Asia and the Pacific, Economic and Social Commission for Western Asia) and nine functional commissions (Commission for Social Development, Commission on Human Rights, Commission on Narcotic Drugs, Commission on the Status of Women, Commission on Population and Development, Statistical Commission, Commission on Science and Technology for Development, Commission on Sustainable Development, and Commission on Crime Prevention and Criminal Justice)
members—(54) selected on a rotating basis from all regions

Economic Community of the Great Lakes Countries (CEPGL)
note—acronym from Communaute Economique des Pays des Grands Lacs
established—20 September 1976
aim—to promote regional economic cooperation and integration
members—(3) Burundi, Democratic Republic of the Congo, Rwanda; note—organization collapsed because of fighting in 1998; reactivated in 2006

Economic Community of West African States (ECOWAS)
established—28 May 1975
aim—to promote regional economic cooperation
members—(15) Benin, Burkina Faso, Cabo Verde, Cote d'Ivoire, The Gambia, Ghana, Guinea, Guinea-Bissau, Liberia, Mali, Niger, Nigeria, Senegal, Sierra Leone, Togo

Economic Cooperation Organization (ECO)
established—27-29 January 1985
aim—to promote regional cooperation in trade, transportation, communications, tourism, cultural affairs, and economic development
members—(10) Afghanistan, Azerbaijan, Iran, Kazakhstan, Kyrgyzstan, Pakistan, Tajikistan, Turkey, Turkmenistan, Uzbekistan

Eurasian Economic Community (EAEC or EurasEC)
note—merged with Central Asian Cooperation Organization (CACO) in 2005
established—May 2001
aim—to create a common economic and energy policy
members—(6) Belarus, Kazakhstan, Kyrgyzstan, Russia, Tajikistan, Uzbekistan
observers—(3) Armenia, Moldova, Ukraine

Euro-Atlantic Partnership Council (EAPC)
note—began as the North Atlantic Cooperation Council (NACC); an extension of NATO
established—8 November 1991; effective—20 December 1991
aim—to discuss cooperation on mutual political and security issues
members—(50) Albania, Armenia, Austria, Azerbaijan, Belarus, Belgium, Bosnia and Herzegovina, Bulgaria, Canada, Croatia, Czech Republic, Denmark, Estonia, Finland, France, Georgia, Germany, Greece, Hungary, Iceland, Ireland, Italy, Kazakhstan, Kyrgyzstan, Latvia, Lithuania, Luxembourg, Macedonia, Malta, Moldova, Montenegro, Netherlands, Norway, Poland, Portugal, Romania, Russia, Serbia, Slovakia, Slovenia, Spain, Sweden, Switzerland, Tajikistan, Turkey, Turkmenistan, Ukraine, UK, US, Uzbekistan

European Bank for Reconstruction and Development (EBRD)
established—8-9 January 1990 (proposals made); 15 April 1991 (bank inaugurated)
aim—to facilitate the transition of seven centrally planned economies in Europe (Bulgaria, former Czechoslovakia, Hungary, Poland, Romania, former USSR, and former Yugoslavia) to market economies by committing 60% of its loans to privatization
members—(66) Albania, Armenia, Australia, Austria, Azerbaijan, Belarus, Belgium, Bosnia and Herzegovina, Bulgaria, Canada, Croatia, Cyprus, Czech Republic, Denmark, Egypt, EU, European Investment Bank (EIB), Estonia, Finland, France, Georgia, Germany, Greece,

Hungary, Iceland, Ireland, Israel, Italy, Japan, Jordan, Kazakhstan, South Korea, Kosovo, Kyrgyzstan, Latvia, Liechtenstein, Lithuania, Luxembourg, Macedonia, Malta, Mexico, Moldova, Mongolia, Montenegro, Morocco, Netherlands, NZ, Norway, Poland, Portugal, Romania, Russia, Serbia, Slovakia, Slovenia, Spain, Sweden, Switzerland, Tajikistan, Tunisia, Turkey, Turkmenistan, Ukraine, UK, US, Uzbekistan

European Central Bank (ECB)
established—1 June 1998
aim—to administer the monetary policy of the EU Eurozone member states
members—(18) Austria, Belgium, Cyprus, Estonia, Finland, France, Germany, Greece, Ireland, Italy, Latvia, Luxembourg, Malta, Netherlands, Portugal, Slovakia, Slovenia, Spain

European Community (or European Communities, EC)
established 8 April 1965 to integrate the European Atomic Energy Community (Euratom), the European Coal and Steel Community (ECSC), the European Economic Community (EEC or Common Market), and to establish a completely integrated common market and an eventual federation of Europe; merged into the European Union (EU) on 7 February 1992; member states at the time of merger were Belgium, Denmark, France, Germany, Greece, Ireland, Italy, Luxembourg, Netherlands, Portugal, Spain, UK

European Free Trade Association (EFTA)
established—4 January 1960; effective—3 May 1960
aim—to promote expansion of free trade
members—(4) Iceland, Liechtenstein, Norway, Switzerland

European Investment Bank (EIB)
established—25 March 1957; effective—1 January 1958
aim—to promote economic development of the EU and its predecessors, the EEC and the EC
members—(28) Austria, Belgium, Bulgaria, Croatia, Cyprus, Czech Republic, Denmark, Estonia, Finland, France, Germany, Greece, Hungary, Ireland, Italy, Latvia, Lithuania, Luxembourg, Malta, Netherlands, Poland, Portugal, Romania, Slovakia, Slovenia, Spain, Sweden, UK

European Organization for Nuclear Research (CERN)
note—acronym retained from the predecessor organization Conseil Europeenne pour la Recherche Nucleaire
established—1 July 1953; effective—29 September 1954
aim—to foster nuclear research for peaceful purposes only
members—(20) Austria, Belgium, Bulgaria, Czech Republic, Denmark, Finland, France, Germany, Greece, Hungary, Italy, Netherlands, Norway, Poland, Portugal, Slovakia, Spain, Sweden, Switzerland, UK
observers—(7) EC, India, Japan, Russia, Turkey, United Nations Educational, Scientific, and Cultural Organization (UNESCO), US

European Space Agency (ESA)
established—31 May 1975
aim—to promote peaceful cooperation in space research and technology
members—(20) Austria, Belgium, Czech Republic, Denmark, Finland, France, Germany, Greece, Ireland, Italy, Luxembourg, Netherlands, Norway, Poland, Portugal, Romania, Spain, Sweden, Switzerland, UK
cooperating states—(3) Estonia, Hungary, Slovenia

European Union (EU)
note—see European Union entry at the end of the "country" listings

Extractive Industry Transparency Initiative (EITI)
established—October 2002 Initiative announced; June 2003 first EITC Plenary Conference
aim—to set a global standard for transparency in the extractive industries in an effort to make natural resources benefit all
stake holders or implementing countries—(17) Australia, Belgium, Canada, Denmark, Finland, France, Germany, Italy, Japan, Netherlands, Norway, Qatar, Spain, Sweden, Switzerland, UK, US
compliant countries—(23) Albania, Azerbaijan, Burkina Faso, Cameroon, Congo, Cote d'Ivoire, Ghana, Iraq, Kazakhstan, Kyrgyzstan, Liberia, Mali, Mauritania, Mongolia, Mozambique, Niger, Nigeria, Peru, Tanzania, Timor-Leste, Togo, Yemen, Zambia; note—Central African Republic is suspended
candidate countries—(13) Afghanistan, Chad, Guatemala, Guinea, Honduras, Indonesia, Philippines, Sao Tome and Principe, Senegal, Solomon Islands, Tajikistan, Trinidad and Tobago, Ukraine; note—Democratic Republic of the Congo, Madagascar, and Sierra Leone are suspended

Financial Action Task Force (FATF)
established—by G-7 Summit in Paris in 1989
aim—to develop and promote policies to combat money laundering and terrorist financing
members—(36) Argentina, Australia, Austria, Belgium, Brazil, Canada, China, Denmark, EC, Finland, France, Germany, Greece, Gulf Cooperation Council, Hong Kong, Iceland, India, Ireland, Italy, Japan, South Korea, Luxembourg, Mexico, Netherlands (Aruba, Curacao, Sint Maarten), NZ, Norway, Portugal, Russia, Singapore, South Africa, Spain, Sweden, Switzerland, Turkey, UK, US

First World
another term for countries with advanced, industrialized economies; this term is fading from use; see developed countries (DCs)

Food and Agriculture Organization (FAO)
established—16 October 1945
aim—to raise living standards and increase availability of agricultural products; a UN specialized agency
members—(195) includes all UN member countries except Liechtenstein (192 total); plus Cook Islands, EU, and Niue
associate members—(2) Faroe Islands, Tokelau

former Soviet Union (FSU)
former term often used to identify as a group the successor nations to the Soviet Union or USSR; this group of 15 countries consists of: Armenia, Azerbaijan, Belarus, Estonia, Georgia, Kazakhstan, Kyrgyzstan, Latvia, Lithuania, Moldova, Russia, Tajikistan, Turkmenistan, Ukraine, Uzbekistan

former USSR/Eastern Europe (former USSR/EE)
the middle group in the hierarchy of developed countries (DCs), former USSR/Eastern Europe (former USSR/EE), and less developed countries (LDCs); these countries are in political and economic transition and may well be grouped differently in the near future; this group of 27 countries consists of: Albania, Armenia, Azerbaijan, Belarus, Bosnia and Herzegovina, Bulgaria, Croatia, Czech Republic, Estonia, Georgia, Hungary, Kazakhstan, Kyrgyzstan, Latvia, Lithuania, Macedonia, Moldova, Poland, Romania, Russia, Slovakia, Slovenia, Tajikistan, Turkmenistan, Ukraine, Uzbekistan, Yugoslavia; this group is identical to the IMF group "countries in transition" except for the IMF's inclusion of Mongolia

Four Dragons
the four small Asian less developed countries (LDCs) that have experienced unusually rapid economic growth; also known as the Four Tigers; this group consists of Hong Kong, South Korea, Singapore, Taiwan; these countries are included in the IMF's "advanced economies" group

Franc Zone (FZ)
note—also known as Conference des Ministres des Finances des Pays de la Zone Franc
established—1964
aim—to form a monetary union among countries whose currencies were linked to the French franc
members—(16) Benin, Burkina Faso, Cameroon, Central African Republic, Chad, Comoros, Republic of the Congo, Cote d'Ivoire, Equatorial Guinea, France, Gabon, Guinea-Bissau, Mali, Niger, Senegal, Togo

Front Line States (FLS)
established to achieve black majority rule in South Africa; has since gone out of existence; members included Angola, Botswana, Mozambique, Namibia, Tanzania, Zambia, Zimbabwe

General Agreement on Tariffs and Trade (GATT)
see the World Trade Organization (WTO)

General Confederation of Trade Unions (GCTU)
established—16 April 1992
aim—to consolidate trade union actions to protect citizens' social and labor rights and interests, to help secure trade unions' rights and guarantees, and to strengthen international trade union solidarity
members—(10) Armenia, Azerbaijan, Belarus, Georgia, Kazakhstan, Kyrgyzstan, Moldova, Russia, Tajikistan, Ukraine

Group of 10 (G-10)
note—also known as the Paris Club; includes the wealthiest members of the IMF who provide most of the money to be loaned and act as the informal steering committee; name persists despite increased membership
established—October 1962
aim—to coordinate credit policy
members—(11) Belgium, Canada, France, Germany, Italy, Japan, Netherlands, Sweden, Switzerland, UK, US
observers—(4) BIS, EC, IMF, OECD

Group of 11 (G-11)
established—2006
aim—to narrow the income gap with the world's richest nations
members—(11) Croatia, Ecuador, El Salvador, Georgia, Honduras, Indonesia, Jordan, Morocco, Pakistan, Paraguay, Sri Lanka

Group of 15 (G-15)
note—byproduct of the Nonaligned Movement; name persists despite increased membership
established—September 1989
aim—to promote economic cooperation among developing nations; to act as the main political organ for the Nonaligned Movement
members—(17) Algeria, Argentina, Brazil, Chile, Egypt, India, Indonesia, Iran, Jamaica, Kenya, Malaysia, Mexico, Nigeria, Senegal, Sri Lanka, Venezuela, Zimbabwe

Group of 20 (G-20)
established—created 1999; inaugurated 15-16 December 1999
aim—to promote open and constructive discussion between industrial and emerging-market countries on any issues related to global economic stability; helps to support growth and development across the globe

members—(20) Argentina, Australia, Brazil, Canada, China, EU, France, Germany, India, Indonesia, Italy, Japan, South Korea, Mexico, Russia, Saudi Arabia, South Africa, Turkey, UK, US

Group of 24 (G-24)
established—1 August 1989
aim—to promote the interests of developing countries in Africa, Asia, and Latin America within the IMF
members—(24) Algeria, Argentina, Brazil, Colombia, Democratic Republic of the Congo, Cote d'Ivoire, Egypt, Ethiopia, Gabon, Ghana, Guatemala, India, Iran, Lebanon, Mexico, Nigeria, Pakistan, Peru, Philippines, South Africa, Sri Lanka, Syria, Trinidad and Tobago, Venezuela
observers—(1) China

Group of 3 (G-3)
established—September 1990
aim—mechanism for policy coordination
members—(2) Colombia, Mexico; note—Panama shows interest in joining

Group of 5 (G-5)
note—with the addition of Italy, Canada, and Russia, it is now known as the Group of 8 or G-8; meanwhile the Group of 5 now refers to Brazil, China, India, Mexico, and South Africa
established—22 September 1985
aim—to coordinate the economic policies of five major noncommunist economic powers
members—(5) France, Germany, Japan, UK, US

Group of 6 (G-6)
also known as Groupe des Six Sur le Desarmement (not to be confused with the Big Six) was established in 22 May 1984 with the aim of achieving nuclear disarmament; its members were Argentina, Greece, India, Mexico, Sweden, Tanzania

Group of 7 (G-7)
note—membership is the same as the Big Seven
established—22 September 1985
aim—to facilitate economic cooperation among the seven major noncommunist economic powers
members—(7) Group of 5 (France, Germany, Japan, UK, US) plus Canada and Italy

Group of 77 (G-77)
established—15 June1964; October 1967 first ministerial meeting
aim—to promote economic cooperation among developing countries; name persists in spite of increased membership
members—(132 plus the Palestine Liberation Organization) Afghanistan, Algeria, Angola, Antigua and Barbuda, Argentina, The Bahamas, Bahrain, Bangladesh, Barbados, Belize, Benin, Bhutan, Bolivia, Bosnia and Herzegovina, Botswana, Brazil, Brunei, Burkina Faso, Burma, Burundi, Cambodia, Cabo Verde, Cameroon, Central African Republic, Chad, Chile, China, Colombia, Comoros, Democratic Republic of the Congo, Republic of the Congo, Costa Rica, Cote d'Ivoire, Cuba, Djibouti, Dominica, Dominican Republic, Ecuador, Egypt, El Salvador, Equatorial Guinea, Eritrea, Ethiopia, Fiji, Gabon, The Gambia, Ghana, Grenada, Guatemala, Guinea, Guinea-Bissau, Guyana, Haiti, Honduras, India, Indonesia, Iran, Iraq, Jamaica, Jordan, Kenya, Kiribati, North Korea, Kuwait, Laos, Lebanon, Lesotho, Liberia, Libya, Madagascar, Malawi, Malaysia, Maldives, Mali, Marshall Islands, Mauritania, Mauritius, Federated States of Micronesia, Mongolia, Morocco, Mozambique, Namibia, Nauru, Nepal, Nicaragua, Niger, Nigeria, Oman, Pakistan, Panama, Papua New Guinea, Paraguay, Peru, Philippines, Qatar, Rwanda, Saint Kitts and Nevis, Saint Lucia, Saint Vincent and the Grenadines, Samoa, Sao Tome and Principe, Saudi Arabia, Senegal, Seychelles, Sierra Leone, Singapore, Solomon Islands, Somalia, South Africa, Sri Lanka, Sudan, Suriname, Swaziland, Syria, Tajikistan, Tanzania, Thailand, Timor-Leste, Togo, Tonga, Trinidad and Tobago, Tunisia, Turkmenistan, Uganda, UAE, Uruguay, Vanuatu, Venezuela, Vietnam, Yemen, Zambia, Zimbabwe, Palestine Liberation Organization

Group of 8 (G-8)
established—October 1975
aim—to facilitate economic cooperation among the developed countries (DCs) that participated in the Conference on International Economic Cooperation (CIEC), held in several sessions between December 1975 and 3 June 1977
members—(8) Canada, EU, France, Germany, Italy, Japan, UK, US

Group of 9 (G-9)
established—NA
aim—to discuss matters of mutual interest on an informal basis
members—(9) Austria, Belgium, Bulgaria, Denmark, Finland, Hungary, Romania, Serbia, Sweden

Gulf Cooperation Council (GCC)
note—also known as the Cooperation Council for the Arab States of the Gulf
established—25 May 1981
aim—to promote regional cooperation in economic, social, political, and military affairs
members—(6) Bahrain, Kuwait, Oman, Qatar, Saudi Arabia, UAE

high income countries
another term for the industrialized countries with high per capita GDPs; see developed countries (DCs)

Indian Ocean Commission (InOC)
established—21 December 1982
aim—to organize and promote regional cooperation in all sectors, especially economic
members—(5) Comoros, France (for Reunion), Madagascar, Mauritius, Seychelles

industrial countries
another term for the developed countries; see developed countries (DCs)

Inter-American Development Bank (IADB)
note—also known as Banco Interamericano de Desarrollo (BID)
established—8 April 1959; effective—30 December 1959
aim—to promote economic and social development in Latin America
members—(48) Argentina, Austria, The Bahamas, Barbados, Belgium, Belize, Bolivia, Brazil, Canada, Chile, China, Colombia, Costa Rica, Croatia, Denmark, Dominican Republic, Ecuador, El Salvador, Finland, France, Germany, Guatemala, Guyana, Haiti, Honduras, Israel, Italy, Jamaica, Japan, South Korea, Mexico, Netherlands, Nicaragua, Norway, Panama, Paraguay, Peru, Portugal, Slovenia, Spain, Suriname, Sweden, Switzerland, Trinidad and Tobago, UK, US, Uruguay, Venezuela

Inter-Governmental Authority on Development (IGAD)
note—formerly known as Inter-Governmental Authority on Drought and Development (IGADD)
established—15-16 January 1986 as the Inter-Governmental Authority on Drought and Development; revitalized—21 March 1996 as the Inter-Governmental Authority on Development
aim—to promote a social, economic, and scientific community among its members
members—(6) Djibouti, Ethiopia, Kenya, Somalia, Sudan, Uganda; note—Eritrea declared its suspension in 2007
partners—(20) Austria, Belgium, Canada, Denmark, EC, France, Germany, Greece, International Organization for Migration, Ireland, Italy, Japan, Netherlands, Norway, Sweden, Switzerland, UK, UN Development Program, US, World Bank

Inter-Parliamentary Union (IPU)
established—1889
aim—fosters contacts among parliamentarians, considers and expresses views of international interest and concern with the purpose of bringing about action by parliaments and parliamentarians, contributes to the defense and promotion of human rights, contributes to better knowledge of representative institutions
members—(162 and the Palestine Liberation Organization) Afghanistan, Albania, Algeria, Andorra, Angola, Argentina, Armenia, Australia, Austria, Azerbaijan, Bahrain, Bangladesh, Belarus, Belgium, Benin, Bhutan, Bolivia, Bosnia and Herzegovina, Botswana, Brazil, Bulgaria, Burkina Faso, Burma, Burundi, Cambodia, Cabo Verde, Cameroon, Canada, Chad, Chile, China, Colombia, Democratic Republic of the Congo, Republic of the Congo, Costa Rica, Cote d'Ivoire, Croatia, Cuba, Cyprus, Czech Republic, Denmark, Djibouti, Dominican Republic, Ecuador, El Salvador, Equatorial Guinea, Estonia, Ethiopia, Finland, France, Gabon, The Gambia, Georgia, Germany, Ghana, Greece, Guatemala, Guinea-Bissau, Haiti, Honduras, Hungary, Iceland, India, Indonesia, Iran, Iraq, Ireland, Israel, Italy, Japan, Jordan, Kazakhstan, Kenya, North Korea, South Korea, Kuwait, Kyrgyzstan, Laos, Latvia, Lebanon, Lesotho, Libya, Liechtenstein, Lithuania, Luxembourg, Macedonia, Malawi, Malaysia, Maldives, Mali, Malta, Mauritania, Mauritius, Mexico, Federated States of Micronesia, Moldova, Monaco, Mongolia, Montenegro, Morocco, Mozambique, Namibia, Nepal, Netherlands, NZ, Nicaragua, Niger, Nigeria, Norway, Oman, Pakistan, Palau, Panama, Papua New Guinea, Paraguay, Peru, Philippines, Poland, Portugal, Qatar, Romania, Russia, Rwanda, Samoa, San Marino, Sao Tome and Principe, Saudi Arabia, Senegal, Serbia, Seychelles, Sierra Leone, Singapore, Slovakia, Slovenia, Somalia, South Africa, South Sudan, Spain, Sri Lanka, Sudan, Suriname, Sweden, Switzerland, Syria, Tanzania, Tajikistan, Thailand, Timor-Leste, Togo, Trinidad and Tobago, Tunisia, Turkey, Uganda, Ukraine, UAE, UK, Uruguay, Venezuela, Vietnam, Yemen, Zambia, Zimbabwe, Palestine Liberation Organization
associate members—(10) Andean Parliament, Central American Parliament, East African Legislative Assembly, European Parliament, Inter-Parliamentary Committee of the West African Economic and Monetary Union, Latin American Parliament, Parliament of the Economic Community of West African States, Parliament of the Economic and Monetary Community of Central Africa, Parliamentary Assembly of the Council of Europe, Transitional Arab Parliament

International Atomic Energy Agency (IAEA)
established—26 October 1956; effective—29 July 1957
aim—to promote peaceful uses of atomic energy
members—(162) Afghanistan, Albania, Algeria, Angola, Argentina, Armenia, Australia, Austria, Azerbaijan, The Bahamas, Bahrain, Bangladesh, Belarus, Belgium, Belize, Benin, Bolivia, Bosnia and Herzegovina, Botswana, Brazil, Brunei, Bulgaria, Burkina Faso, Burma, Burundi, Cabo Verde, Cambodia, Cameroon, Canada, Central African Republic, Chad, Chile, China, Colombia, Democratic Republic of the Congo, Republic of the Congo, Costa Rica, Cote d'Ivoire, Croatia, Cuba, Cyprus, Czech Republic, Denmark, Dominica, Dominican Republic, Ecuador, Egypt, El Salvador, Eritrea, Estonia, Ethiopia, Fiji, Finland, France, Gabon, Georgia, Germany, Ghana, Greece, Guatemala, Haiti, Holy See, Honduras, Hungary, Iceland, India, Indonesia, Iran, Iraq, Ireland, Israel, Italy, Jamaica, Japan, Jordan, Kazakhstan, Kenya, South Korea, Kuwait, Kyrgyzstan, Laos, Latvia, Lebanon, Lesotho, Liberia, Libya, Liechtenstein, Lithuania, Luxembourg, Macedonia, Madagascar, Malawi, Malaysia, Mali, Malta, Marshall Islands, Mauritania, Mauritius, Mexico, Moldova, Monaco, Mongolia, Montenegro, Morocco, Mozambique, Namibia, Nepal, Netherlands, NZ, Nicaragua, Niger, Nigeria, Norway, Oman, Pakistan, Palau, Panama, Papua New Guinea, Paraguay, Peru, Philippines, Poland, Portugal, Qatar, Romania, Russia, Rwanda, San Marino, Saudi Arabia, Senegal, Serbia,

Seychelles, Sierra Leone, Singapore, Slovakia, Slovenia, South Africa, Spain, Sri Lanka, Sudan, Swaziland, Sweden, Switzerland, Syria, Tajikistan, Tanzania, Thailand, Togo, Tonga, Trinidad and Tobago, Tunisia, Turkey, Uganda, Ukraine, UAE, UK, US, Uruguay, Uzbekistan, Venezuela, Vietnam, Yemen, Zambia, Zimbabwe

International Bank for Reconstruction and Development (IBRD)
note—also known as the World Bank
established—22 July 1944; effective—27 December 1945
aim—to provide economic development loans; a UN specialized agency
members—(188) includes all UN member countries except Andorra, Cuba, North Korea, Liechtenstein, Monaco, Nauru; plus Kosovo

International Chamber of Commerce (ICC)
established—1919
aim—to promote free trade and private enterprise and to represent business interests at national and international levels
members—128 plus the Palestine Liberation Organization
countries with national committees—(93 and the Palestine Liberation Organization) Albania, Algeria, Argentina, Australia, Austria, Bahrain, Bangladesh, Belgium, Bolivia, Brazil, Bulgaria, Burkina Faso, Cameroon, Canada, Caribbean, Chile, China, Colombia, Costa Rica, Croatia, Cuba, Cyprus, Czech Republic, Denmark, Dominican Republic, Ecuador, Egypt, El Salvador, Estonia, Finland, France, Georgia, Germany, Ghana, Greece, Guatemala, Hong Kong, Hungary, Iceland, India, Indonesia, Iran, Ireland, Israel, Italy, Japan, Jordan, Kenya, South Korea, Kuwait, Lebanon, Lithuania, Luxembourg, Macao, Madagascar, Malaysia, Mexico, Monaco, Morocco, Netherlands, NZ, Nigeria, Norway, Pakistan, Panama, Philippines, Poland, Portugal, Qatar, Romania, Russia, Saudi Arabia, Senegal, Serbia, Singapore, Slovakia, Slovenia, South Africa, Spain, Sri Lanka, Sweden, Switzerland, Syria, Taiwan, Thailand, Togo, Tunisia, Turkey, Ukraine, UAE, UK, US, Uruguay, Palestine Liberation Organization; note—Peru is restructuring
countries with no national committees having direct members—(35) Afghanistan, Andorra, Armenia, Azerbaijan, Belarus, Bermuda, Bosnia and Herzegovina, Botswana, Democratic Republic of the Congo, Burma, Cote d'Ivoire, Eritrea, Ethiopia, Gibraltar, Haiti, Honduras, Iraq, North Korea, Latvia, Liberia, Macedonia, Malta, Mauritania, Mauritius, Moldova, Mongolia, Montenegro, Mozambique, Oman, Peru, Sudan, Tajikistan, Tanzania, Uganda, Vietnam

International Civil Aviation Organization (ICAO)
established—7 December 1944; effective—4 April 1947
aim—to promote international cooperation in civil aviation; a UN specialized agency
members—(191) includes all UN member countries except Dominica, Liechtenstein, and Tuvalu (190 total); plus Cook Islands

International Civilian Support Mission in Haiti (MICAH)
established 17 December 1999 to promote respect for human rights; members included Argentina, Benin, Canada, France, India, Mali, Niger, Senegal, Togo, Tunisia, US; closed 2001

International Committee of the Red Cross (ICRC)
established—17 February 1863
aim—to provide humanitarian aid in wartime
members—(15-25 individuals) all Swiss nationals

International Court of Justice (ICJ)
also known as the World Court; primary judicial organ of the UN
established—26 June 1945 with the signing of the UN Charter (inaugural sitting of the Court was on 18 April 1946); superseded Permanent Court of International Justice (attached to the League of Nations)
aim—to settle disputes submitted by member states and to provide advice to UN organs and other international agencies
members—(15 judges) elected by the UN General Assembly and Security Council to represent all principal legal systems; judges elected to nine-year terms (eligible for two additional terms); elections held every three years for one-third of the judges
jurisdiction—based on the principle of consent in contentious issues; consent to compulsory jurisdiction is outlined in Statute 36 of the ICJ; states provide declarations of consent to compulsory jurisdiction of the ICJ either with or without reservations (date in parens after each state is when the declaration was deposited with the UN Secretary-General); Haiti, Luxembourg, Nicaragua, and Uruguay deposited declarations with the Permanent Court of International Justice prior to 1945 and these were later transferred to the ICJ)
states accepting compulsory jurisdiction with reservations—(57) Australia (22 March 2002), Barbados (1 August 1980), Belgium (17 June 1958), Botswana (16 March 1970), Bulgaria (21 June 1992), Cambodia (19 September 1957), Canada (10 May 1994), Democratic Republic of the Congo (8 February 1989), Cote d'Ivoire (29 September 2001), Cyprus (3 September 2002), Denmark (10 December 1956), Djibouti (2 September 2005), Egypt (22 July 1957), Estonia (31 October 1991), Finland (25 June 1958), The Gambia (22 June 1966), Germany (30 April 2008), Greece (10 January 1994), Guinea (4 December 1998), Honduras (6 June 1986), Hungary (22 October 1992), India (18 September 1974), Japan (9 July 2007), Kenya (19 April 1965), Lesotho (6 September 2000), Liberia (20 March 1952), Liechtenstein (29 March 1950), Lithuania (26 September 2012), Madagascar (2 July 1992), Malawi (12 December 1966), Malta (2 September 1983), Marshall Islands (23 April 2013), Mauritius (23 September 1968), Mexico (28 October 1947), Netherlands (1 August 1956), New Zealand (23 September 1977), Nicaragua (24 September 1929), Nigeria (30 April 1998), Norway (25 June 1996), Pakistan (13 September 1960), Panama (25 October 1921), Peru (7 July 2003), Philippines (18 January 1972), Poland (25 March 1996), Portugal (25 February 2005), Senegal (2 December 1985), Slovakia (28 May 2004), Somalia (11 April 1963), Spain (20 October 1990), Sudan (2 January 1958), Suriname (31 August 1987), Swaziland (26 May 1969), Sweden (6 April 1957), Switzerland (28 July 1948), Togo (25 October 1979), Uganda (3 October 1963), United Kingdom (5 July 2004)

states accepting compulsory jurisdiction without reservations—(13) Austria (19 May 1971), Cameroon (3 March 1994), Costa Rica (20 February 1973), Dominica (31 March 2006), Dominican Republic (30 September 1924), Georgia (20 June 1995), Guinea-Bissau (7 August 1989), Haiti (4 October 1921), Ireland (15 December 2011), Luxembourg (15 September 1930), Paraguay (25 September 1996), Timor-Leste (21 September 2012), Uruguay (28 January 1921)

International Criminal Court (ICCt)
established—1 July 2002
aim—to hold all individuals and countries accountable to international laws of conduct; to specify international standards of conduct; to provide an important mechanism for implementing these standards; to ensure that perpetrators are brought to justice
members—21 judges (three judges form the Presidency) and six judges each in the Pre-trial, Trial, and Appeals Divisions; judges elected by secret ballot by the Assembly of States Parties to the Rome Statute for nine-year terms (not eligible for reelection) governed by the Statute of the International Criminal Court treaty (or Rome Statute), adopted 17 July 1998 at the UN Conference of Plenipotentiaries in Rome and entered into force 1 July 2002
states accepting jurisdiction—(122) Afghanistan, Albania, Andorra, Antigua and Barbuda, Argentina, Australia, Austria, Bangladesh, Barbados, Belgium, Belize, Benin, Bolivia, Bosnia and Herzegovina, Botswana, Brazil, Bulgaria, Burkina Faso, Burundi, Cambodia, Canada, Cabo Verde, Central African Republic, Chad, Chile, Colombia, Comoros, Cook Islands, Democratic Republic of the Congo, Republic of the Congo, Costa Rica, Cote d'Ivoire, Croatia, Cyprus, Czech Republic, Denmark, Djibouti, Dominica, Dominican Republic, Ecuador, Estonia, Fiji, Finland, France, Gabon, The Gambia, Georgia, Germany, Ghana, Greece, Grenada, Guatemala, Guinea, Guyana, Honduras, Hungary, Iceland, Ireland, Italy, Japan, Jordan, Kenya, South Korea, Latvia, Lesotho, Liberia, Liechtenstein, Lithuania, Luxembourg, Macedonia, Madagascar, Malawi, Maldives, Mali, Malta, Marshall Islands, Mauritius, Mexico, Moldova, Mongolia, Montenegro, Namibia, Nauru, Netherlands, NZ, Niger, Nigeria, Norway, Panama, Paraguay, Peru, Philippines, Poland, Portugal, Romania, Saint Kitts and Nevis, Saint Lucia, Saint Vincent and the Grenadines, Samoa, San Marino, Senegal, Serbia, Seychelles, Sierra Leone, Slovakia, Slovenia, South Africa, Spain, Suriname, Sweden, Switzerland, Tajikistan, Tanzania, Timor-Leste, Trinidad and Tobago, Tunisia, Uganda, UK, Uruguay, Vanuatu, Venezuela, Zambia

International Criminal Police Organization (Interpol)
established—September 1923 set up as the International Criminal Police Commission; 13 June 1956 constitution modified and present name adopted
aim—to promote international cooperation among police authorities in fighting crime
members—(190) Afghanistan, Albania, Algeria, Andorra, Angola, Antigua and Barbuda, Argentina, Armenia, Aruba, Australia, Austria, Azerbaijan, The Bahamas, Bahrain, Bangladesh, Barbados, Belarus, Belgium, Belize, Benin, Bhutan, Bolivia, Bosnia and Herzegovina, Botswana, Brazil, Brunei, Bulgaria, Burkina Faso, Burma, Burundi, Cabo Verde, Cambodia, Cameroon, Canada, Central African Republic, Chad, Chile, China, Colombia, Comoros, Democratic Republic of the Congo, Republic of the Congo, Costa Rica, Cote d'Ivoire, Croatia, Cuba, Curacao, Cyprus, Czech Republic, Denmark, Djibouti, Dominica, Dominican Republic, Ecuador, Egypt, El Salvador, Equatorial Guinea, Eritrea, Estonia, Ethiopia, Fiji, Finland, France, Gabon, The Gambia, Georgia, Germany, Ghana, Greece, Grenada, Guatemala, Guinea, Guinea-Bissau, Guyana, Haiti, Holy See, Honduras, Hungary, Iceland, India, Indonesia, Iran, Iraq, Ireland, Israel, Italy, Jamaica, Japan, Jordan, Kazakhstan, Kenya, South Korea, Kuwait, Kyrgyzstan, Laos, Latvia, Lebanon, Lesotho, Liberia, Libya, Liechtenstein, Lithuania, Luxembourg, Macedonia, Madagascar, Malawi, Malaysia, Maldives, Mali, Malta, Marshall Islands, Mauritania, Mauritius, Mexico, Moldova, Monaco, Mongolia, Montenegro, Morocco, Mozambique, Namibia, Nauru, Nepal, Netherlands, NZ, Nicaragua, Niger, Nigeria, Norway, Oman, Pakistan, Panama, Papua New Guinea, Paraguay, Peru, Philippines, Poland, Portugal, Qatar, Romania, Russia, Rwanda, Saint Kitts and Nevis, Saint Lucia, Saint Vincent and the Grenadines, Samoa, San Marino, Sao Tome and Principe, Saudi Arabia, Senegal, Serbia, Seychelles, Sierra Leone, Singapore, Sint Maarten, Slovakia, Slovenia, Somalia, South Africa, South Sudan, Spain, Sri Lanka, Sudan, Suriname, Swaziland, Sweden, Switzerland, Syria, Tajikistan, Tanzania, Thailand, Timor-Leste, Togo, Tonga, Trinidad and Tobago, Tunisia, Turkey, Turkmenistan, Uganda, Ukraine, UAE, UK, US, Uruguay, Uzbekistan, Venezuela, Vietnam, Yemen, Zambia, Zimbabwe
subbureaus—(11) American Samoa, Anguilla, Bermuda, British Virgin Islands, Cayman Islands, Gibraltar, Hong Kong, Macau, Montserrat, Puerto Rico, Turks and Caicos Islands

International Development Association (IDA)
established—26 January 1960; effective—24 September 1960
aim—to provide economic loans for low-income countries; UN specialized agency and IBRD affiliate
members—(173) Afghanistan, Albania, Algeria, Angola, Argentina, Armenia, Australia, Austria, Azerbaijan, The Bahamas, Bangladesh, Barbados, Belgium, Belize, Benin, Bhutan, Bolivia, Bosnia and Herzegovina, Botswana, Brazil, Burkina Faso, Burma, Burundi, Cabo Verde, Cambodia, Cameroon, Canada, Central African Republic, Chad, Chile, China, Colombia, Comoros, Democratic Republic of the Congo, Republic of the Congo, Costa Rica, Cote d'Ivoire, Croatia, Cyprus, Czech Republic, Denmark, Djibouti, Dominica, Dominican Republic, Ecuador, Egypt, El Salvador, Equatorial Guinea, Eritrea, Estonia, Ethiopia, EU, Fiji, Finland, France, Gabon, The Gambia, Georgia, Germany, Ghana, Greece, Grenada, Guatemala, Guinea, Guinea-Bissau, Guyana, Haiti, Honduras, Hungary, Iceland, India, Indonesia, Iran, Iraq, Ireland, Israel, Italy, Japan, Jordan, Kazakhstan, Kenya, Kiribati, South Korea, Kosovo, Kuwait, Kyrgyzstan, Laos, Latvia, Lebanon, Lesotho, Liberia, Libya, Lithuania, Luxembourg, Macedonia, Madagascar, Malawi, Malaysia, Maldives, Mali, Marshall Islands, Mauritania, Mauritius, Mexico, Federated States of Micronesia, Moldova, Mongolia, Montenegro, Morocco, Mozambique, Nepal, Netherlands, NZ, Nicaragua, Niger, Nigeria, Norway, Oman, Pakistan, Palau, Panama, Papua New Guinea, Paraguay, Peru, Philippines, Poland, Portugal, Russia, Rwanda, Saint Kitts and Nevis, Saint Lucia, Saint Vincent and the Grenadines, Samoa, Sao Tome and Principe, Saudi Arabia, Senegal, Serbia, Sierra Leone, Singapore, Slovakia, Slovenia, Solomon Islands, Somalia, South Africa, South Sudan, Spain, Sri Lanka, Sudan, Swaziland, Sweden, Switzerland, Syria, Tajikistan, Tanzania, Thailand, Timor-Leste, Togo, Tonga, Trinidad and Tobago, Tunisia, Turkey, Tuvalu, Uganda, Ukraine, UAE, UK, US, Uzbekistan, Vanuatu, Vietnam, Yemen, Zambia, Zimbabwe

International Energy Agency (IEA)

established—15 November 1974

aim—to promote cooperation on energy matters, especially emergency oil sharing and relations between oil consumers and oil producers; established by the OECD

members—(29) Australia, Austria, Belgium, Canada, Czech Republic, Denmark, EC, Finland, France, Germany, Greece, Hungary, Ireland, Italy, Japan, South Korea, Luxembourg, Netherlands, NZ, Norway, Poland, Portugal, Slovakia, Spain, Sweden, Switzerland, Turkey, UK, US

International Federation of Red Cross and Red Crescent Societies (IFRCS)

note—formerly known as League of Red Cross and Red Crescent Societies (LORCS)

established—5 May 1919

aim—to organize, coordinate, and direct international relief actions; to promote humanitarian activities; to represent and encourage the development of National Societies; to bring help to victims of armed conflicts, refugees, and displaced people; to reduce the vulnerability of people through development programs

members—(187 plus the Palestine Liberation Organization) Afghanistan, Albania, Algeria, Andorra, Angola, Antigua and Barbuda, Argentina, Armenia, Australia, Austria, Azerbaijan, The Bahamas, Bahrain, Bangladesh, Barbados, Belarus, Belgium, Belize, Benin, Bolivia, Bosnia and Herzegovina, Botswana, Brazil, Brunei, Bulgaria, Burkina Faso, Burma, Burundi, Cabo Verde, Cambodia, Cameroon, Canada, Central African Republic, Chad, Chile, China, Colombia, Comoros, Democratic Republic of the Congo, Republic of the Congo, Cook Islands, Costa Rica, Cote d'Ivoire, Croatia, Cuba, Czech Republic, Denmark, Djibouti, Dominica, Dominican Republic, Ecuador, Egypt, El Salvador, Equatorial Guinea, Estonia, Ethiopia, Fiji, Finland, France, Gabon, The Gambia, Georgia, Germany, Ghana, Greece, Grenada, Guatemala, Guinea, Guinea-Bissau, Guyana, Haiti, Honduras, Hungary, Iceland, India, Indonesia, Iran, Iraq, Ireland, Israel, Italy, Jamaica, Japan, Jordan, Kazakhstan, Kenya, Kiribati, North Korea, South Korea, Kuwait, Kyrgyzstan, Laos, Latvia, Lebanon, Lesotho, Liberia, Libya, Liechtenstein, Lithuania, Luxembourg, Macedonia, Madagascar, Malawi, Malaysia, Maldives, Mali, Malta, Mauritania, Mauritius, Mexico, Federated States of Micronesia, Moldova, Monaco, Mongolia, Montenegro, Morocco, Mozambique, Namibia, Nepal, Netherlands, NZ, Nicaragua, Niger, Nigeria, Norway, Pakistan, Palau, Panama, Papua New Guinea, Paraguay, Peru, Philippines, Poland, Portugal, Qatar, Romania, Russia, Rwanda, Saint Kitts and Nevis, Saint Lucia, Saint Vincent and the Grenadines, Samoa, San Marino, Sao Tome and Principe, Saudi Arabia, Senegal, Serbia, Seychelles, Sierra Leone, Singapore, Slovakia, Slovenia, Solomon Islands, Somalia, South Africa, South Sudan, Spain, Sri Lanka, Sudan, Suriname, Swaziland, Sweden, Switzerland, Syria, Tajikistan, Tanzania, Thailand, Timor-Leste, Togo, Tonga, Trinidad and Tobago, Tunisia, Turkey, Turkmenistan, Uganda, Ukraine, UAE, UK, US, Uruguay, Uzbekistan, Vanuatu, Venezuela, V

observers—(3) Cyprus, Eritrea, and Tuvalu

International Finance Corporation (IFC)

established—25 May 1955; effective—24 July 1956

aim—to support private enterprise in international economic development; a UN specialized agency and IBRD affiliate

members—(183) includes all UN member countries except Andorra, Brunei, Cuba, North Korea, Liechtenstein, Monaco, Nauru, Saint Vincent and the Grenadines, San Marino, Tuvalu; plus Kosovo

International Fund for Agricultural Development (IFAD)

established—November 1974

aim—to promote agricultural development; a UN specialized agency

members—(171)

List A—(23 industrialized aid contributors) Belgium, Canada, Denmark, Estonia, Finland, France, Germany, Greece, Hungary, Iceland, Ireland, Italy, Japan, Luxembourg, Netherlands, NZ, Norway, Portugal, Spain, Sweden, Switzerland, UK, US

List B—(12 petroleum-exporting aid contributors) Algeria, Gabon, Indonesia, Iran, Iraq, Kuwait, Libya, Nigeria, Qatar, Saudi Arabia, UAE, Venezuela

List C—(133 aid recipients) Afghanistan, Albania, Angola, Antigua and Barbuda, Argentina, Armenia, Azerbaijan, The Bahamas, Bangladesh, Barbados, Belize, Benin, Bhutan, Bolivia, Bosnia and Herzegovina, Botswana, Brazil, Burkina Faso, Burma, Burundi, Cabo Verde, Cambodia, Cameroon, Central African Republic, Chad, Chile, China, Colombia, Comoros, Democratic Republic of the Congo, Republic of the Congo, Cook Islands, Costa Rica, Cote d'Ivoire, Croatia, Cuba, Cyprus, Djibouti, Dominica, Dominican Republic, Ecuador, Egypt, El Salvador, Equatorial Guinea, Eritrea, Ethiopia, Fiji, The Gambia, Georgia, Ghana, Grenada, Guatemala, Guinea, Guinea-Bissau, Guyana, Haiti, Honduras, India, Israel, Jamaica, Jordan, Kazakhstan, Kenya, Kiribati, North Korea, South Korea, Kyrgyzstan, Laos, Lebanon, Lesotho, Liberia, Macedonia, Madagascar, Malawi, Malaysia, Maldives, Mali, Malta, Marshall Islands, Mauritania, Mauritius, Mexico, Moldova, Mongolia, Morocco, Mozambique, Namibia, Nauru, Nepal, Nicaragua, Niger, Niue, Oman, Pakistan, Panama, Papua New Guinea, Paraguay, Peru, Philippines, Romania, Rwanda, Saint Kitts and Nevis, Saint Lucia, Saint Vincent and the Grenadines, Samoa, Sao Tome and Principe, Senegal, Seychelles, Sierra Leone, Solomon Islands, Somalia, South Africa, South Sudan, Sri Lanka, Sudan, Suriname, Swaziland, Syria, Tajikistan, Tanzania, Thailand, Timor-Leste, Togo, Tonga, Trinidad and Tobago, Tunisia, Turkey, Tuvalu, Uganda, Uruguay, Uzbekistan, Vanuatu, Vietnam, Yemen, Zambia, Zimbabwe

International Hydrographic Organization (IHO)

note—name changed from International Hydrographic Bureau on 22 September 1970

established—June 1919; effective—June 1921

aim—to train hydrographic surveyors and nautical cartographers to achieve standardization in nautical charts and electronic chart displays; to provide advice on nautical cartography and hydrography; to develop the sciences in the field of hydrography and techniques used for descriptive oceanography

members—(81) Algeria, Argentina, Australia, Bahrain, Bangladesh, Belgium, Brazil, Burma, Cameroon, Canada, Chile, China (including Hong Kong and Macau), Colombia, Democratic Republic of the Congo, Croatia, Cuba, Cyprus, Denmark, Dominican Republic, Ecuador, Egypt, Estonia, Fiji, Finland, France, Germany, Greece, Guatemala, Iceland, India, Indonesia, Iran, Ireland, Italy, Jamaica, Japan, North

Korea, South Korea, Kuwait, Latvia, Malaysia, Mauritius, Mexico, Monaco, Morocco, Mozambique, Netherlands, NZ, Nigeria, Norway, Oman, Pakistan, Papua New Guinea, Peru, Philippines, Poland, Portugal, Qatar, Romania, Russia, Saudi Arabia, Serbia, Singapore, Slovenia, South Africa, Spain, Sri Lanka, Suriname, Sweden, Syria, Thailand, Tonga, Trinidad and Tobago, Tunisia, Turkey, Ukraine, UAE, UK, US, Uruguay, Venezuela; note—members approved but waiting for Instrument of Accession: Bulgaria, Mauritania, Montenegro, Sierra Leone

International Labor Organization (ILO)
established—28 June 1919 set up as part of Treaty of Versailles; 11 April 1919 became operative; 14 December 1946 affiliated with the UN
aim—to deal with world labor issues; a UN specialized agency
members—(185) includes all UN member countries except Andorra, Bhutan, North Korea, Liechtenstein, Federated States of Micronesia, Monaco, Nauru, Tonga; note—includes the following dependencies: Netherlands (Aruba, Curacao, Sint Maarten)

International Maritime Organization (IMO)
note—name changed from Intergovernmental Maritime Consultative Organization (IMCO) on 22 May 1982
established—6 March 1948 set up as the Inter-Governmental Maritime Consultative Organization; effective—17 March 1958
aim—to deal with international maritime affairs; a UN specialized agency
members—(170) includes all UN member countries except Afghanistan, Andorra, Armenia, Belarus, Bhutan, Botswana, Burkina Faso, Burundi, Central African Republic, Chad, Kyrgyzstan, Laos, Lesotho, Liechtenstein, Mali, Federated States of Micronesia, Nauru, Niger, Rwanda, South Sudan, Swaziland, Tajikistan, Uzbekistan, Zambia; and Cook Islands
associate members—(3) Faroe Islands, Hong Kong, Macau

International Mobile Satellite Organization (IMSO)
established—15 April 1999
aim—acts as watchdog over Inmarsat (International Maritime Satellite Organization), a private company, to make sure it follows ICAO standards and recommended practices; plays an active role in the development of international telecommunications policies
members—(98) Algeria, Antigua and Barbuda, Argentina, Australia, The Bahamas, Bahrain, Bangladesh, Belarus, Belgium, Bosnia and Herzegovina, Brazil, Brunei, Bulgaria, Cameroon, Canada, Chile, China, Colombia, Comoros, Cook Islands, Costa Rica, Croatia, Cuba, Cyprus, Czech Republic, Denmark, Egypt, Finland, France, Gabon, Germany, Ghana, Greece, Hungary, Iceland, India, Indonesia, Iran, Iraq, Israel, Italy, Japan, Kenya, North Korea, South Korea, Kuwait, Latvia, Lebanon, Liberia, Libya, Malaysia, Malta, Marshall Islands, Mauritius, Mexico, Monaco, Mongolia, Montenegro, Morocco, Mozambique, Netherlands, NZ, Nigeria, Norway, Oman, Pakistan, Palau, Panama, Peru, Philippines, Poland, Portugal, Qatar, Romania, Russia, Saudi Arabia, Senegal, Serbia, Singapore, Slovakia, South Africa, Spain, Sri Lanka, Sweden, Switzerland, Tanzania, Thailand, Tonga, Tunisia, Turkey, Ukraine, UAE, UK, US, Vanuatu, Venezuela, Vietnam, Yemen

International Monetary Fund (IMF)
established—22 July 1944; effective—27 December 1945
aim—to promote world monetary stability and economic development; a UN specialized agency
members—(188) includes all UN member countries except Andorra, Cuba, North Korea, Liechtenstein, Monaco, Nauru; plus Kosovo; note—includes the following dependencies or areas of special interest: China (Hong Kong and Macau), Netherlands (Aruba, Curacao, Sint Maarten)

International Olympic Committee (IOC)
established—23 June 1894
aim—to promote the Olympic ideals and administer the Olympic games: 2012 Summer Olympics in London, UK; 2014 Winter Olympics in Sochi, Russia
National Olympic Committees—(204 and the Palestine Liberation Organization) Afghanistan, Albania, Algeria, American Samoa, Andorra, Angola, Antigua and Barbuda, Argentina, Armenia, Aruba, Australia, Austria, Azerbaijan, The Bahamas, Bahrain, Bangladesh, Barbados, Belarus, Belgium, Belize, Benin, Bermuda, Bhutan, Bolivia, Bosnia and Herzegovina, Botswana, Brazil, British Virgin Islands, Brunei, Bulgaria, Burkina Faso, Burma, Burundi, Cabo Verde, Cambodia, Cameroon, Canada, Cayman Islands, Central African Republic, Chad, Chile, China, Colombia, Comoros, Democratic Republic of the Congo, Republic of the Congo, Cook Islands, Costa Rica, Cote d'Ivoire, Croatia, Cuba, Cyprus, Czech Republic, Denmark, Djibouti, Dominica, Dominican Republic, Ecuador, Egypt, El Salvador, Equatorial Guinea, Eritrea, Estonia, Ethiopia, Fiji, Finland, France, Gabon, The Gambia, Georgia, Germany, Ghana, Greece, Grenada, Guam, Guatemala, Guinea, Guinea-Bissau, Guyana, Haiti, Honduras, Hong Kong, Hungary, Iceland, India, Indonesia, Iran, Iraq, Ireland, Israel, Italy, Jamaica, Japan, Jordan, Kazakhstan, Kenya, Kiribati, North Korea, South Korea, Kuwait, Kyrgyzstan, Laos, Latvia, Lebanon, Lesotho, Liberia, Libya, Liechtenstein, Lithuania, Luxembourg, Macedonia, Madagascar, Malawi, Malaysia, Maldives, Mali, Malta, Marshall Islands, Mauritania, Mauritius, Mexico, Federated States of Micronesia, Moldova, Monaco, Mongolia, Montenegro, Morocco, Mozambique, Namibia, Nauru, Nepal, Netherlands, NZ, Nicaragua, Niger, Nigeria, Norway, Oman, Pakistan, Palau, Panama, Papua New Guinea, Paraguay, Peru, Philippines, Poland, Portugal, Puerto Rico, Qatar, Romania, Russia, Rwanda, Saint Kitts and Nevis, Saint Lucia, Saint Vincent and the Grenadines, Samoa, San Marino, Sao Tome and Principe, Saudi Arabia, Senegal, Serbia, Seychelles, Sierra Leone, Singapore, Slovakia, Slovenia, Solomon Islands, Somalia, South Africa, Spain, Sri Lanka, Sudan, Suriname, Swaziland, Sweden, Switzerland, Syria, Taiwan, Tajikistan, Tanzania, Thailand, Timor-Leste, Togo, Tonga, Trinidad and Tobago, Tunisia, Turkey, Turkmenistan, Tuvalu, Uganda, Ukraine, UAE, UK, US, Uruguay, Uzbekistan, Vanuatu, Venezuela, Vietnam, Virgin Islands, Yemen, Zambia, Zimbabwe, Palestine Liberation Organization

International Organization for Migration (IOM)

note—established as Provisional Intergovernmental Committee for the Movement of Migrants from Europe; renamed Intergovernmental Committee for European Migration (ICEM) on 15 November 1952; renamed Intergovernmental Committee for Migration (ICM) in November 1980; current name adopted 14 November 1989
established—5 December 1951
aim—to facilitate orderly international emigration and immigration
members—(151) Afghanistan, Albania, Algeria, Angola, Antigua and Barbuda, Argentina, Armenia, Australia, Austria, Azerbaijan, The Bahamas, Bangladesh, Belarus, Belgium, Belize, Benin, Bolivia, Bosnia and Herzegovina, Botswana, Brazil, Bulgaria, Burkina Faso, Burma, Burundi, Cabo Verde, Cambodia, Cameroon, Canada, Central African Republic, Chad, Chile, Colombia, Comoros, Democratic Republic of the Congo, Republic of the Congo, Costa Rica, Cote d'Ivoire, Croatia, Cyprus, Czech Republic, Denmark, Djibouti, Dominican Republic, Ecuador, Egypt, El Salvador, Estonia, Ethiopia, Finland, France, Gabon, The Gambia, Georgia, Germany, Ghana, Greece, Guatemala, Guinea, Guinea-Bissau, Guyana, Haiti, Holy See, Honduras, Hungary, India, Iran, Ireland, Israel, Italy, Jamaica, Japan, Jordan, Kazakhstan, Kenya, South Korea, Kyrgyzstan, Latvia, Lesotho, Liberia, Libya, Lithuania, Luxembourg, Madagascar, Malawi, Maldives, Mali, Malta, Mauritania, Mauritius, Mexico, Federation of Micronesia, Moldova, Mongolia, Montenegro, Morocco, Mozambique, Namibia, Nauru, Nepal, Netherlands, NZ, Nicaragua, Niger, Nigeria, Norway, Pakistan, Panama, Papua New Guinea, Paraguay, Peru, Philippines, Poland, Portugal, Romania, Rwanda, Saint Vincent and the Grenadines, Senegal, Serbia, Seychelles, Sierra Leone, Slovakia, Slovenia, Somalia, South Africa, South Sudan, Spain, Sri Lanka, Sudan, Suriname, Swaziland, Sweden, Switzerland, Tajikistan, Tanzania, Thailand, Timor-Leste, Togo, Trinidad and Tobago, Tunisia, Turkey, Uganda, Ukraine, UK, US, Uruguay, Vanuatu, Venezuela, Vietnam, Yemen, Zambia, Zimbabwe
observers—(12) Bahrain, Bhutan, China, Cuba, Indonesia, Macedonia, Qatar, Russia, San Marino, Sao Tome and Principe, Saudi Arabia, Turkmenistan

International Organization for Standardization (ISO)

established—February 1947
aim—to promote the development of international standards with a view to facilitating international exchange of goods and services and to developing cooperation in the sphere of intellectual, scientific, technological and economic activity
members—(114 national standards organizations) Algeria, Argentina, Armenia, Australia, Austria, Azerbaijan, Bahrain, Bangladesh, Barbados, Belarus, Belgium, Bosnia and Herzegovina, Botswana, Brazil, Bulgaria, Cameroon, Canada, Chile, China, Colombia, Democratic Republic of the Congo, Costa Rica, Cote d'Ivoire, Croatia, Cuba, Cyprus, Czech Republic, Denmark, Ecuador, Egypt, El Salvador, Estonia, Ethiopia, Fiji, Finland, France, Gabon, Germany, Ghana, Greece, Hungary, Iceland, India, Indonesia, Iran, Iraq, Ireland, Israel, Italy, Jamaica, Japan, Jordan, Kazakhstan, Kenya, North Korea, South Korea, Kuwait, Lebanon, Libya, Lithuania, Luxembourg, Macedonia, Malaysia, Mali, Malta, Mauritius, Mexico, Mongolia, Morocco, Namibia, Netherlands, NZ, Nigeria, Norway, Oman, Pakistan, Panama, Peru, Philippines, Poland, Portugal, Qatar, Romania, Russia, Rwanda, Saint Lucia, Saudi Arabia, Senegal, Serbia, Singapore, Slovakia, Slovenia, South Africa, Spain, Sri Lanka, Sudan, Sweden, Switzerland, Syria, Tanzania, Thailand, Trinidad and Tobago, Tunisia, Turkey, Uganda, Ukraine, UAE, UK, US, Uruguay, Uzbekistan, Vietnam, Yemen, Zimbabwe
correspondent members—(45 plus the Palestine Liberation Organization) Afghanistan, Albania, Angola, Benin, Bhutan, Bolivia, Brunei, Burkina Faso, Burma, Burundi, Cambodia, Republic of the Congo, Dominica, Dominican Republic, Eritrea, Gabon, The Gambia, Georgia, Guatemala, Guinea, Guyana, Hong Kong, Kyrgyzstan, Latvia, Lesotho, Liberia, Macau, Madagascar, Malawi, Mauritania, Moldova, Montenegro, Mozambique, Nepal, Nicaragua, Niger, Papua New Guinea, Paraguay, Seychelles, Sierra Leone, Suriname, Swaziland, Tajikistan, Togo, Turkmenistan, Zambia, Palestine Liberation Organization
subscriber members—(4) Antigua and Barbuda, Honduras, Laos, Saint Vincent and the Grenadines

International Organization of the French-speaking World (OIF)

note—name changed from Agency of Cultural and Technical Cooperation (ACCT) in 1997; also known as Organisation Internationale de la Francophonie
established—20 March 1970
aim—founded around a common language to promote and spread the cultures of its members and to reinforce cultural and technical cooperation between them
members—(57) Albania, Andorra, Armenia, Belgium, Benin, Bulgaria, Burkina Faso, Burundi, Cabo Verde, Cambodia, Cameroon, Canada, Canada - New Brunswick, Canada - Quebec, Central African Republic, Chad, Comoros, Democratic Republic of Congo, Republic of Congo, Cote d'Ivoire, Cyprus, Djibouti, Dominica, Egypt, Equatorial Guinea, France, French Community of Belgium, Gabon, Ghana, Greece, Guinea, Guinea-Bissau, Haiti, Laos, Lebanon, Luxembourg, Macedonia, Madagascar, Mali, Mauritania, Mauritius, Moldova, Monaco, Morocco, Niger, Qatar, Romania, Rwanda, Saint Lucia, Sao Tome and Principe, Senegal, Seychelles, Switzerland, Togo, Tunisia, Vanuatu, Vietnam
observers—(20) Austria, Bosnia and Herzegovina, Croatia, Czech Republic, Dominican Republic, Estonia, Georgia, Hungary, Latvia, Lithuania, Montenegro, Mozambique, Poland, Serbia, Slovakia, Slovenia, Thailand, Ukraine, UAE, Uruguay

International Red Cross and Red Crescent Movement (ICRM)

established—1928
aim—to promote worldwide humanitarian aid through the International Committee of the Red Cross (ICRC) in wartime, and International Federation of Red Cross and Red Crescent Societies (IFRCS; formerly League of Red Cross and Red Crescent Societies or LORCS) in peacetime
National Societies—(187 countries and the Palestine Liberation Organization); note—same as membership for International Federation of Red Cross and Red Crescent Societies (IFRCS)

International Telecommunication Satellite Organization (ITSO)

established—August 1964

aim—to act as a watchdog over Intelsat, Ltd., a private company, to make sure it provides on a global and non-discriminatory basis public telecommunication services

members—(150) Afghanistan, Algeria, Angola, Argentina, Armenia, Australia, Austria, Azerbaijan, The Bahamas, Bahrain, Bangladesh, Barbados, Belgium, Benin, Bhutan, Bolivia, Bosnia and Herzegovina, Botswana, Brazil, Brunei, Bulgaria, Burkina Faso, Cabo Verde, Cameroon, Canada, Central African Republic, Chad, Chile, China, Colombia, Comoros, Democratic Republic of the Congo, Republic of the Congo, Costa Rica, Cote d'Ivoire, Croatia, Cuba, Cyprus, Czech Republic, Denmark, Dominican Republic, Ecuador, Egypt, El Salvador, Equatorial Guinea, Estonia, Ethiopia, Fiji, Finland, France, Gabon, The Gambia, Georgia, Germany, Ghana, Greece, Guatemala, Guinea, Guinea-Bissau, Haiti, Holy See, Honduras, Hungary, Iceland, India, Indonesia, Iran, Iraq, Ireland, Israel, Italy, Jamaica, Japan, Jordan, Kazakhstan, Kenya, North Korea, South Korea, Kuwait, Kyrgyzstan, Lebanon, Liechtenstein, Luxembourg, Madagascar, Malawi, Malaysia, Mali, Malta, Mauritania, Mauritius, Mexico, the Federated States of Micronesia, Monaco, Mongolia, Montenegro, Morocco, Mozambique, Namibia, Nepal, Netherlands, NZ, Nicaragua, Niger, Nigeria, Norway, Oman, Pakistan, Panama, Papua New Guinea, Paraguay, Peru, Philippines, Poland, Portugal, Qatar, Romania, Russia, Rwanda, Saudi Arabia, Senegal, Serbia, Singapore, Somalia, South Africa, Spain, Sri Lanka, Sudan, Swaziland, Sweden, Switzerland, Syria, Tajikistan, Tanzania, Thailand, Togo, Trinidad and Tobago, Tunisia, Turkey, Uganda, UAE, UK, US, Uruguay, Uzbekistan, Venezuela, Vietnam, Yemen, Zambia, Zimbabwe

International Telecommunication Union (ITU)

established—17 May 1865 set up as the International Telegraph Union; 9 December 1932 adopted present name; effective—1 January 1934; affiliated with the UN—15 November 1947

aim—to deal with world telecommunications issues; a UN specialized agency

members—(193) includes all UN member countries except Palau (192 total); plus Holy See

International Trade Union Confederation (ITUC)

note—its predecessors were the International Confederation of Free Trade Unions (ICFTU) and the World Confederation of Labor (WCL)

established—3 November 2006

aim—to promote the trade union movement

members—(325 affiliated organizations in 156 countries or territories and the Palestine Liberation Organization as of 2013) Albania, Algeria, Angola, Antigua and Barbuda, Aruba, Argentina, Australia, Austria, Azerbaijan, Bahrain, Bangladesh, Barbados, Belarus, Belgium, Belize, Benin, Bermuda, Bonaire, Bosnia and Herzegovina, Botswana, Brazil, Bulgaria, Burkina Faso, Burma, Burundi, Cabo Verde, Cambodia, Cameroon, Canada, Central African Republic, Chad, Chile, Colombia, Comoros, Democratic Republic of the Congo, Republic of the Congo, Cook Islands, Costa Rica, Cote d'Ivoire, Croatia, Curacao, Cyprus, Czech Republic, Denmark, Djibouti, Dominica, Dominican Republic, Ecuador, El Salvador, Eritrea, Estonia, Ethiopia, Fiji, Finland, France, French Polynesia, Gabon, The Gambia, Georgia, Germany, Ghana, Greece, Grenada, Guatemala, Guinea, Guinea-Bissau, Haiti, Holy See, Honduras, Hong Kong, Hungary, Iceland, India, Indonesia, Ireland, Israel, Italy, Japan, Jordan, Kenya, Kiribati, South Korea, Kosovo, Kuwait, Latvia, Liberia, Liechtenstein, Lithuania, Luxembourg, Macedonia, Madagascar, Malawi, Malaysia, Mali, Malta, Mauritania, Mauritius, Mexico, Moldova, Mongolia, Montenegro, Morocco, Mozambique, Namibia, Nepal, Netherlands, New Caledonia, NZ, Nicaragua, Niger, Nigeria, Norway, Pakistan, Panama, Paraguay, Peru, Philippines, Poland, Portugal, Romania, Russia, Rwanda, Saint Lucia, Samoa, San Marino, Sao Tome and Principe, Senegal, Serbia, Sierra Leone, Singapore, Slovakia, South Africa, Spain, Sri Lanka, Suriname, Swaziland, Sweden, Switzerland, Taiwan, Tanzania, Thailand, Togo, Tonga, Trinidad and Tobago, Tunisia, Turkey, Uganda, Ukraine, UK, US, Vanuatu, Venezuela, Yemen, Zambia, Zimbabwe, and the Palestine Liberation Organization

Islamic Development Bank (IDB)

established—15 December 1973 by declaration of intent; effective—12 August 1974

aim—to promote Islamic economic aid and social development

members—(55 plus the Palestine Liberation Organization) Afghanistan, Albania, Algeria, Azerbaijan, Bahrain, Bangladesh, Benin, Brunei, Burkina Faso, Cameroon, Chad, Comoros, Cote d'Ivoire, Djibouti, Egypt, Gabon, The Gambia, Guinea, Guinea-Bissau, Indonesia, Iran, Iraq, Jordan, Kazakhstan, Kuwait, Kyrgyzstan, Lebanon, Libya, Malaysia, Maldives, Mali, Mauritania, Morocco, Mozambique, Niger, Nigeria, Oman, Pakistan, Qatar, Saudi Arabia, Senegal, Sierra Leone, Somalia, Sudan, Suriname, Syria, Tajikistan, Togo, Tunisia, Turkey, Turkmenistan, Uganda, UAE, Uzbekistan, Yemen, Palestine Liberation Organization

Latin American and Caribbean Economic System (LAES)

note—also known as Sistema Economico Latinoamericana (SELA)

established—17 October 1975

aim—to promote economic and social development through regional cooperation

members—(28) Argentina, the Bahamas, Barbados, Belize, Bolivia, Brazil, Chile, Colombia, Costa Rica, Cuba, Dominican Republic, Ecuador, El Salvador, Grenada, Guatemala, Guyana, Haiti, Honduras, Jamaica, Mexico, Nicaragua, Panama, Paraguay, Peru, Suriname, Trinidad and Tobago, Uruguay, Venezuela

Latin American Integration Association (LAIA)

note—also known as Asociacion Latinoamericana de Integracion (ALADI)

established—12 August 1980; effective—18 March 1981

aim—to promote freer regional trade

members—(14) Argentina, Bolivia, Brazil, Chile, Colombia, Cuba, Ecuador, Mexico, Nicaragua, Panama, Paraguay, Peru, Uruguay, Venezuela *observers*—(29) China, Corporacion Andina de Fomento, Costa Rica, Dominican Republic, EC, El Salvador, Guatemala, Honduras, Inter-American Development Bank, Inter-American Institute for Cooperation on Agriculture, Italy, Japan, South Korea, Latin America Economic System, Nicaragua, Organizacion Panamericana de la Salud, Organizacion Mundial de la Salud, Organization of American States, Pakistan, Portugal, Romania, Russia, San Marino, Secretaria General Iberoamericana, Spain, Switzerland, Ukraine, United Nations Development Program, United Nations Economic Commission for Latin America and the Caribbean

League of Arab States (LAS)
note—also known as Arab League (AL)
established—22 March 1945
aim—to promote economic, social, political, and military cooperation
members—(20 plus the Palestine Liberation Organization) Algeria, Bahrain, Comoros, Djibouti, Egypt, Iraq, Jordan, Kuwait, Lebanon, Libya, Mauritania, Morocco, Oman, Qatar, Saudi Arabia, Somalia, Sudan, Tunisia, UAE, Yemen, Palestine Liberation Organization
observers—(4) Brazil, Eritrea, India, Venezuela

least developed countries (LLDCs)
that subgroup of the less developed countries (LDCs) initially identified by the UN General Assembly in 1971 as having no significant economic growth, per capita GDPs normally less than $1,000, and low literacy rates; also known as the undeveloped countries; the 44 LLDCs are: Afghanistan, Bangladesh, Benin, Bhutan, Burkina Faso, Burma, Burundi, Cambodia, Cameroon, Central African Republic, Chad, Comoros, Democratic Republic of the Congo, Cote d'Ivoire, Equatorial Guinea, Eritrea, Ethiopia, The Gambia, Ghana, Guinea, Guinea-Bissau, Haiti, Kenya, Lesotho, Liberia, Malawi, Mali, Moldova, Mozambique, Nepal, Niger, Rwanda, Sao Tome and Principe, Senegal, Sierra Leone, Somalia, Sudan, Tajikistan, Tanzania, Togo, Tokelau, Tuvalu, Uganda, Zambia

less developed countries (LDCs)
the bottom group in the hierarchy of developed countries (DCs), former USSR/Eastern Europe (former USSR/EE), and less developed countries (LDCs); mainly countries and dependent areas with low levels of output, living standards, and technology; per capita GDPs are generally below $5,000 and often less than $1,500; however, the group also includes a number of countries with high per capita incomes, areas of advanced technology, and rapid rates of growth; includes the advanced developing countries, developing countries, Four Dragons (Four Tigers), least developed countries (LLDCs), low-income countries, middle-income countries, newly industrializing economies (NIEs), the South, Third World, underdeveloped countries, undeveloped countries; the 172 LDCs are: Afghanistan, Algeria, American Samoa, Angola, Anguilla, Antigua and Barbuda, Argentina, Aruba, The Bahamas, Bahrain, Bangladesh, Barbados, Belize, Benin, Bhutan, Bolivia, Botswana, Brazil, British Virgin Islands, Brunei, Burkina Faso, Burma, Burundi, Cabo Verde, Cambodia, Cameroon, Cayman Islands, Central African Republic, Chad, Chile, China, Christmas Island, Cocos Islands, Colombia, Comoros, Democratic Republic of the Congo, Republic of the Congo, Cook Islands, Costa Rica, Cote d'Ivoire, Cyprus, Djibouti, Dominica, Dominican Republic, Ecuador, Egypt, El Salvador, Equatorial Guinea, Eritrea, Ethiopia, Falkland Islands, Fiji, French Guiana, French Polynesia, Gabon, The Gambia, Gaza Strip, Ghana, Gibraltar, Greenland, Grenada, Guadeloupe, Guam, Guatemala, Guernsey, Guinea, Guinea-Bissau, Guyana, Haiti, Honduras, Hong Kong, India, Indonesia, Iran, Iraq, Isle of Man, Jamaica, Jersey, Jordan, Kenya, Kiribati, North Korea, South Korea, Kuwait, Laos, Lebanon, Lesotho, Liberia, Libya, Macau, Madagascar, Malawi, Malaysia, Maldives, Mali, Marshall Islands, Martinique, Mauritania, Mauritius, Mayotte, Federated States of Micronesia, Mongolia, Montserrat, Morocco, Mozambique, Namibia, Nauru, Nepal, Netherlands Antilles, New Caledonia, Nicaragua, Niger, Nigeria, Niue, Norfolk Island, Northern Mariana Islands, Oman, Palau, Pakistan, Panama, Papua New Guinea, Paraguay, Peru, Philippines, Pitcairn Islands, Puerto Rico, Qatar, Reunion, Rwanda, Saint Helena, Ascension, and Tristan da Cunha, Saint Kitts and Nevis, Saint Lucia, Saint Pierre and Miquelon, Saint Vincent and the Grenadines, Samoa, Sao Tome and Principe, Saudi Arabia, Senegal, Seychelles, Sierra Leone, Singapore, Solomon Islands, Somalia, Sri Lanka, Sudan, Suriname, Swaziland, Syria, Taiwan, Tanzania, Thailand, Togo, Tokelau, Tonga, Trinidad and Tobago, Tunisia, Turks and Caicos Islands, Tuvalu, UAE, Uganda, Uruguay, Vanuatu, Venezuela, Vietnam, Virgin Islands, Wallis and Futuna, West Bank, Western Sahara, Yemen, Zambia, Zimbabwe; note—similar to the new International Monetary Fund (IMF) term "developing countries" which adds Malta, Mexico, South Africa, and Turkey but omits in its recently published statistics American Samoa, Anguilla, British Virgin Islands, Brunei, Cayman Islands, Christmas Island, Cocos Islands, Cook Islands, Cuba, Eritrea, Falkland Islands, French Guiana, French Polynesia, Gaza Strip, Gibraltar, Greenland, Grenada, Guadeloupe, Guam, Guernsey, Isle of Man, Jersey, North Korea, Macau, Martinique, Mayotte, Montserrat, Nauru, New Caledonia, Niue, Norfolk Island, Northern Mariana Islands, Palau, Pitcairn Islands, Puerto Rico, Reunion, Saint Helena, Ascension, and Tristan da Cunha, Saint Pierre and Miquelon, Tokelau, Tonga, Turks and Caicos Islands, Tuvalu, Virgin Islands, Wallis and Futuna, West Bank, Western Sahara

low-income countries
another term for those less developed countries with below-average per capita GDPs; see less developed countries (LDCs)

middle-income countries
another term for those less developed countries with above-average per capita GDPs; see less developed countries (LDCs)

Multilateral Investment Guarantee Agency (MIGA)
established—12 April 1988
aim—encourages flow of foreign direct investment among member countries by offering investment insurance, consultation, and negotiation on conditions for foreign investment and technical assistance; a UN specialized agency
members—(179) includes all UN member countries except Andorra, Bhutan, Brunei, Burma, Cuba, Kiribati, North Korea, Liechtenstein, Marshall Islands, Monaco, Nauru, San Marino, Somalia, Tonga, Tuvalu; plus Kosovo

Near Abroad

Russian term for the 14 non-Russian successor states of the USSR, in which 25 million ethnic Russians live and in which Moscow has expressed a strong national security interest; the 14 countries are Armenia, Azerbaijan, Belarus, Estonia, Georgia, Kazakhstan, Kyrgyzstan, Latvia, Lithuania, Moldova, Tajikistan, Turkmenistan, Ukraine, Uzbekistan

new independent states (NIS)

a term referring to all the countries of the FSU except the Baltic countries (Estonia, Latvia, Lithuania)

newly industrializing countries (NICs)

former term for the newly industrializing economies; see newly industrializing economies (NIEs)

newly industrializing economies (NIEs)

that subgroup of the less developed countries (LDCs) that has experienced particularly rapid industrialization of their economies; formerly known as the newly industrializing countries (NICs); also known as advanced developing countries; usually includes the Four Dragons (Hong Kong, South Korea, Singapore, Taiwan), and Brazil

Nonaligned Movement (NAM)

established—1-6 September 1961
aim—to establish political and military cooperation apart from the traditional East or West blocs
members—(119 plus the Palestine Liberation Organization) Afghanistan, Algeria, Angola, Antigua and Barbuda, Azerbaijan, The Bahamas, Bahrain, Bangladesh, Barbados, Belarus, Belize, Benin, Bhutan, Bolivia, Botswana, Brunei, Burkina Faso, Burma, Burundi, Cabo Verde, Cambodia, Cameroon, Central African Republic, Chad, Chile, Colombia, Comoros, Democratic Republic of the Congo, Republic of the Congo, Cote d'Ivoire, Cuba, Djibouti, Dominica, Dominican Republic, Ecuador, Egypt, Equatorial Guinea, Eritrea, Ethiopia, Fiji, Gabon, The Gambia, Ghana, Grenada, Guatemala, Guinea, Guinea-Bissau, Guyana, Haiti, Honduras, India, Indonesia, Iran, Iraq, Jamaica, Jordan, Kenya, North Korea, Kuwait, Laos, Lebanon, Lesotho, Liberia, Libya, Madagascar, Malawi, Malaysia, Maldives, Mali, Mauritania, Mauritius, Mongolia, Morocco, Mozambique, Namibia, Nepal, Nicaragua, Niger, Nigeria, Oman, Pakistan, Panama, Papua New Guinea, Peru, Philippines, Qatar, Rwanda, Saint Kitts and Nevis, Saint Lucia, Saint Vincent and the Grenadines, Sao Tome and Principe, Saudi Arabia, Senegal, Seychelles, Sierra Leone, Singapore, Somalia, South Africa, Sri Lanka, Sudan, Suriname, Swaziland, Syria, Tanzania, Thailand, Timor-Leste, Togo, Trinidad and Tobago, Tunisia, Turkmenistan, Uganda, UAE, Uzbekistan, Vanuatu, Venezuela, Vietnam, Yemen, Zambia, Zimbabwe, Palestine Liberation Organization
observers—(17) Argentina, Armenia, Bosnia and Herzegovina, Brazil, China, Costa Rica, Croatia, El Salvador, Kazakhstan, Kyrgyzstan, Mexico, Montenegro, Paraguay, Serbia, Tajikistan, Ukraine, Uruguay

Nordic Council (NC)

established—16 March 1952; effective—12 February 1953
aim—to promote regional economic, cultural, and environmental cooperation
members—(5) Denmark (including Faroe Islands and Greenland), Finland (including Aland Islands), Iceland, Norway, Sweden
observers—(6) Estonia, Latvia, Lithuania, and the Sami (Lapp) local parliaments of Finland, Norway, and Sweden

Nordic Investment Bank (NIB)

established—4 December 1975; effective—1 June 1976
aim—to promote economic cooperation and development
members—(8) Denmark (including Faroe Islands and Greenland), Estonia, Finland (including Aland Islands), Iceland, Latvia, Lithuania, Norway, Sweden

North

a popular term for the rich industrialized countries generally located in the northern portion of the Northern Hemisphere; the counterpart of the South; see developed countries (DCs)

North American Free Trade Agreement (NAFTA)

established—17 December 1992
aim—to eliminate trade barriers, promote fair competition, increase investment opportunities, provide protection of intellectual property rights, and create procedures to settle disputes
members—(3) Canada, Mexico, US

North Atlantic Treaty Organization (NATO)

established—4 April 1949
aim—to promote mutual defense and cooperation
members—(28) Albania, Belgium, Bulgaria, Canada, Croatia, Czech Republic, Denmark, Estonia, France, Germany, Greece, Hungary, Iceland, Italy, Latvia, Lithuania, Luxembourg, Netherlands, Norway, Poland, Portugal, Romania, Slovakia, Slovenia, Spain, Turkey, UK, US

Nuclear Energy Agency (NEA)

note—also known as OECD Nuclear Energy Agency
established—1 February 1958
aim—to promote the peaceful uses of nuclear energy; associated with OECD

members—(31) Australia, Austria, Belgium, Canada, Czech Republic, Denmark, Finland, France, Germany, Greece, Hungary, Iceland, Ireland, Italy, Japan, South Korea, Luxembourg, Mexico, Netherlands, Norway, Poland, Portugal, Russia, Slovakia, Slovenia, Spain, Sweden, Switzerland, Turkey, UK, US

Nuclear Suppliers Group (NSG)
note—also known as the London Suppliers Group or the London Group
established—1974; effective—1975
aim—to establish guidelines for exports of nuclear materials, processing equipment for uranium enrichment, and technical information to countries of proliferation concern and regions of conflict and instability
members—(48) Argentina, Australia, Austria, Belarus, Belgium, Brazil, Bulgaria, Canada, China, Croatia, Cyprus, Czech Republic, Denmark, Estonia, Finland, France, Germany, Greece, Hungary, Iceland, Ireland, Italy, Japan, Kazakhstan, South Korea, Latvia, Lithuania, Luxembourg, Malta, Mexico, Netherlands, NZ, Norway, Poland, Portugal, Romania, Russia, Serbia, Slovakia, Slovenia, South Africa, Spain, Sweden, Switzerland, Turkey, Ukraine, UK, US
observer—(2) Chairman of the Zangger Committee, European Commission (a policy-planning body for the EU)

Organization for Democracy and Economic Development (GUAM)
note—acronym standing for the member countries, Georgia, Ukraine, Azerbaijan, Moldova; formerly known as GUUAM before Uzbekistan withdrew in 5 May 2005
established—7 June 2001
aim—commits the countries to cooperation and assistance in social and economic development, the strengthening and broadening of trade and economic relations, and the development and effective use of transport and communications, highways, and related infrastructure crossing the boundaries of the member states
members—(4) Azerbaijan, Georgia, Moldova, Ukraine

Organization for Economic Cooperation and Development (OECD)
established—14 December 1960; effective—30 September 1961
aim—to promote economic cooperation and development
members—(34) Australia, Austria, Belgium, Canada, Chile, Czech Republic, Denmark, Estonia, Finland, France, Germany, Greece, Hungary, Iceland, Ireland, Israel, Italy, Japan, South Korea, Luxembourg, Mexico, Netherlands, NZ, Norway, Poland, Portugal, Slovakia, Slovenia, Spain, Sweden, Switzerland, Turkey, UK, US
special member—(1) EC

Organization for Security and Cooperation in Europe (OSCE)
note—formerly the Conference on Security and Cooperation in Europe (CSCE) established 3 July 1975
established—1 January 1995
aim—to foster the implementation of human rights, fundamental freedoms, democracy, and the rule of law; to act as an instrument of early warning, conflict prevention, and crisis management; and to serve as a framework for conventional arms control and confidence building measures
members—(57) Albania, Andorra, Armenia, Austria, Azerbaijan, Belarus, Belgium, Bosnia and Herzegovina, Bulgaria, Canada, Croatia, Cyprus, Czech Republic, Denmark, Estonia, Finland, France, Georgia, Germany, Greece, Holy See, Hungary, Iceland, Ireland, Italy, Kazakhstan, Kyrgyzstan, Latvia, Liechtenstein, Lithuania, Luxembourg, Macedonia, Malta, Moldova, Monaco, Mongolia, Montenegro, Netherlands, Norway, Poland, Portugal, Romania, Russia, San Marino, Serbia, Slovakia, Slovenia, Spain, Sweden, Switzerland, Tajikistan, Turkey, Turkmenistan, Ukraine, UK, US, Uzbekistan
partners for cooperation—(11) Afghanistan, Algeria, Australia, Egypt, Israel, Japan, Jordan, South Korea, Morocco, Thailand, Tunisia

Organization for the Prohibition of Chemical Weapons (OPCW)
established—29 April 1997
aim—to enforce the Convention on the Prohibition of the Development, Production, Stockpiling, and Use of Chemical Weapons and on Their Destruction; to provide a forum for consultation and cooperation among the signatories of the Convention
members (countries that have ratified the Convention)—(190) Afghanistan, Albania, Algeria, Andorra, Antigua and Barbuda, Argentina, Armenia, Australia, Austria, Azerbaijan, The Bahamas, Bahrain, Bangladesh, Barbados, Belarus, Belgium, Belize, Benin, Bhutan, Bolivia, Bosnia and Herzegovina, Botswana, Brazil, Brunei, Bulgaria, Burkina Faso, Burundi, Cabo Verde, Cambodia, Cameroon, Canada, Central African Republic, Chad, Chile, China, Colombia, Comoros, Democratic Republic of the Congo, Republic of the Congo, Cook Islands, Costa Rica, Cote d'Ivoire, Croatia, Cuba, Cyprus, Czech Republic, Denmark, Dominica, Dominican Republic, Djibouti, Ecuador, El Salvador, Equatorial Guinea, Eritrea, Estonia, Ethiopia, Fiji, Finland, France, Gabon, The Gambia, Georgia, Germany, Ghana, Greece, Grenada, Guatemala, Guinea, Guinea-Bissau, Guyana, Haiti, Holy See, Honduras, Hungary, Iceland, India, Indonesia, Iran, Iraq, Ireland, Italy, Jamaica, Japan, Jordan, Kazakhstan, Kenya, Kiribati, South Korea, Kuwait, Kyrgyzstan, Laos, Latvia, Lebanon, Lesotho, Liberia, Libya, Liechtenstein, Lithuania, Luxembourg, Macedonia, Madagascar, Malawi, Malaysia, Maldives, Mali, Malta, Marshall Islands, Mauritania, Mauritius, Mexico, Federated States of Micronesia, Moldova, Monaco, Mongolia, Montenegro, Morocco, Mozambique, Namibia, Nauru, Nepal, Netherlands, NZ, Nicaragua, Niger, Nigeria, Niue, Norway, Oman, Pakistan, Palau, Panama, Papua New Guinea, Paraguay, Peru, Philippines, Poland, Portugal, Qatar, Romania, Russia, Rwanda, Saint Kitts and Nevis, Saint Lucia, Saint Vincent and the Grenadines, Samoa, San Marino, Sao Tome and Principe, Saudi Arabia, Senegal, Serbia, Seychelles, Sierra Leone, Singapore, Slovakia, Slovenia, Solomon Islands, Somalia, South Africa, Spain, Sri Lanka, Sudan, Suriname, Swaziland, Sweden, Switzerland, Syria, Tajikistan, Tanzania, Thailand, Timor-Leste, Togo, Tonga, Trinidad and Tobago, Tunisia, Turkey, Turkmenistan, Tuvalu, Uganda, Ukraine, UAE, UK, US, Uruguay, Uzbekis
signatory states (countries that have signed, but not ratified, the Convention)—(2) Burma, Israel

Organization of African Unity (OAU)
see African Union

Organization of American States (OAS)
established—14 April 1890 as the International Union of American Republics; 30 April 1948 adopted present charter; effective—13 December 1951
aim—to promote regional peace and security as well as economic and social development
members—(35) Antigua and Barbuda, Argentina, The Bahamas, Barbados, Belize, Bolivia, Brazil, Canada, Chile, Colombia, Costa Rica, Cuba (suspended), Dominica, Dominican Republic, Ecuador, El Salvador, Grenada, Guatemala, Guyana, Haiti, Honduras, Jamaica, Mexico, Nicaragua, Panama, Paraguay, Peru, Saint Kitts and Nevis, Saint Lucia, Saint Vincent and the Grenadines, Suriname, Trinidad and Tobago, US, Uruguay, Venezuela
observers—(68) Albania, Algeria, Angola, Armenia, Austria, Azerbaijan, Belgium, Benin, Bosnia and Herzegovina, Bulgaria, China, Croatia, Cyprus, Czech Republic, Denmark, Egypt, Equatorial Guinea, Estonia, EU, Finland, France, Georgia, Germany, Ghana, Greece, Holy See, Hungary, Iceland, India, Ireland, Israel, Italy, Japan, Kazakhstan, South Korea, Latvia, Lebanon, Lithuania, Luxembourg, Macedonia, Malta, Monaco, Morocco, Netherlands, Nigeria, Norway, Pakistan, Philippines, Poland, Portugal, Qatar, Romania, Russia, Saudi Arabia, Serbia, Slovakia, Slovenia, Spain, Sri Lanka, Sweden, Switzerland, Thailand, Tunisia, Turkey, Ukraine, UK, Vanuatu, Yemen

Organization of Arab Petroleum Exporting Countries (OAPEC)
established—9 January 1968
aim—to promote cooperation in the petroleum industry
members—(11) Algeria, Bahrain, Egypt, Iraq, Kuwait, Libya, Qatar, Saudi Arabia, Syria, Tunisia (suspended), UAE

Organization of Eastern Caribbean States (OECS)
established—18 June 1981; effective—4 July 1981
aim—to promote political, economic, and defense cooperation
members—(9) Anguilla, Antigua and Barbuda, British Virgin Islands, Dominica, Grenada, Montserrat, Saint Kitts and Nevis, Saint Lucia, Saint Vincent and the Grenadines

Organization of Islamic Cooperation (OIC)
note—formerly the Organization of the Islamic Conference
established—22-25 September 1969
aim—to promote Islamic solidarity in economic, social, cultural, and political affairs
members—(56 plus the Palestine Liberation Organization) Afghanistan, Albania, Algeria, Azerbaijan, Bahrain, Bangladesh, Benin, Brunei, Burkina Faso, Cameroon, Chad, Comoros, Cote d'Ivoire, Djibouti, Egypt, Gabon, The Gambia, Guinea, Guinea-Bissau, Guyana, Indonesia, Iran, Iraq, Jordan, Kazakhstan, Kuwait, Kyrgyzstan, Lebanon, Libya, Malaysia, Maldives, Mali, Mauritania, Morocco, Mozambique, Niger, Nigeria, Oman, Pakistan, Qatar, Saudi Arabia, Senegal, Sierra Leone, Somalia, Sudan, Suriname, Syria, Tajikistan, Togo, Tunisia, Turkey, Turkmenistan, Uganda, UAE, Uzbekistan, Yemen, Palestine Liberation Organization
observers—(12) AU, Bosnia and Herzegovina, Central African Republic, ECO, LAS, Moro National Liberation Front, NAM, Parliamentary Union of the OIC Member States, Russia, Thailand, Turkish Muslim Community of Kibris, UN

Organization of Petroleum Exporting Countries (OPEC)
established—14 September 1960
aim—to coordinate petroleum policies
members—(12) Algeria, Angola, Ecuador, Iran, Iraq, Kuwait, Libya, Nigeria, Qatar, Saudi Arabia, UAE, Venezuela; note—Indonesia left OPEC in 2008

Pacific Alliance
established—28 April 2011
aim—to reduce trade barriers between member countries, to install visa-free travel, to install a common stock exchange, and to set up joint embassies in some countries
members—(5) Chile, Columbia, Costa Rica, Mexico, Peru
observers—(29) Australia, Canada, China, Dominican Republic, Ecuador, El Salvador , Finland, France, Germany, Guatemala, Honduras, India, Israel, Italy, Japan, Morocco, Netherlands, New Zealand, Panama, Paraguay, Portugal, Singapore, South Korea, Spain, Switzerland, Turkey, United Kingdom, United States, Uruguay

Pacific Community (SPC)
local name of the Secretariat of the Pacific Community

Pacific Islands Forum (PIF)
note—formerly known as South Pacific Forum (SPF)
established—5 August 1971
aim—to promote regional cooperation in political matters
members—(16) Australia, Cook Islands, Fiji, Kiribati, Marshall Islands, Federated States of Micronesia, Nauru, NZ, Niue, Palau, Papua New Guinea, Samoa, Solomon Islands, Tonga, Tuvalu, Vanuatu
associate members—(2) French Polynesia, New Caledonia
partners—(14) Canada, China, EU, France, India, Indonesia, Italy, Japan, South Korea, Malaysia, Philippines, Thailand, UK, US

observers—(12) ACP Group, American Samoa, Asia Development Bank, The Commonwealth, Commonwealth of the Northern Marianas, Guam, Timor-Leste (special observer), Tokelau, UN, Wallis and Futuna, Western and Central Pacific Fisheries Commission, the World Bank

Paris Club

established—1956

aim—to provide a forum for debtor countries to negotiate rescheduling of debt service payments or loans extended by governments or official agencies of participating countries; to help restore normal trade and project finance to debtor countries

members—(19) Australia, Austria, Belgium, Canada, Denmark, Finland, France, Germany, Ireland, Italy, Japan, Netherlands, Norway, Russia, Spain, Sweden, Switzerland, UK, US

associate members—(13) Abu Dhabi, Argentina, Brazil, Israel, South Korea, Kuwait, Mexico, Morocco, NZ, Portugal, South Africa, Trinidad and Tobago, Turkey

Partnership for Peace (PFP)

established—10-11 January 1994

aim—to expand and intensify political and military cooperation throughout Europe, increase stability, diminish threats to peace, and build relationships by promoting the spirit of practical cooperation and commitment to democratic principles that underpin NATO; program under the auspices of NATO

members—(22) Armenia, Austria, Azerbaijan, Belarus, Bosnia and Herzegovina, Finland, Georgia, Ireland, Kazakhstan, Kyrgyzstan, Macedonia, Malta, Moldova, Montenegro, Russia, Serbia, Sweden, Switzerland, Tajikistan, Turkmenistan, Ukraine, Uzbekistan; note—a nation that becomes a member of NATO is no longer a member of PFP

Permanent Court of Arbitration (PCA)

established—29 July 1899

aim—to facilitate the settlement of international disputes

members—(115) Albania, Argentina, Australia, Austria, Bahrain, Bangladesh, Belarus, Belgium, Belize, Benin, Bolivia, Brazil, Bulgaria, Burkina Faso, Cambodia, Cameroon, Canada, Chile, China, Colombia, Democratic Republic of the Congo, Costa Rica, Croatia, Cuba, Cyprus, Czech Republic, Denmark, Dominican Republic, Ecuador, Egypt, El Salvador, Eritrea, Estonia, Ethiopia, Fiji, Finland, France, Germany, Greece, Guatemala, Guyana, Haiti, Honduras, Hungary, Iceland, India, Iran, Iraq, Ireland, Israel, Italy, Japan, Jordan, Kenya, South Korea, Kuwait, Kyrgyzstan, Laos, Latvia, Lebanon, Libya, Liechtenstein, Lithuania, Luxembourg, Macedonia, Madagascar, Malaysia, Malta, Mauritius, Mexico, Montenegro, Morocco, Netherlands, NZ, Nicaragua, Nigeria, Norway, Pakistan, Panama, Paraguay, Peru, Philippines, Poland, Portugal, Qatar, Romania, Russia, Rwanda, Saudi Arabia, Senegal, Serbia, Singapore, Slovakia, Slovenia, South Africa, Spain, Sri Lanka, Sudan, Suriname, Swaziland, Sweden, Switzerland, Thailand, Togo, Turkey, Uganda, Ukraine, UAE, UK, US, Uruguay, Venezuela, Vietnam, Zambia, Zimbabwe

Petrocaribe

established—29 June 2005

aim—to eliminate existing social inequities, to foster high standards of living, to promote effective people's participation in shaping their own destiny

members—(18) Antigua and Barbuda, The Bahamas, Belize, Cuba, Dominica, Dominican Republic, Grenada, Guatemala, Guyana, Haiti, Honduras, Jamaica, Nicaragua, St. Kitts and Nevis, St. Lucia, St. Vincent and the Grenadines, Suriname, Venezuela

Rio Group (RG)

note—formerly known as Grupo de los Ocho, established NA December 1986; composed of the Contadora Group and the Lima Group established in 1988 to consult on regional Latin American issues; its members were Argentina, Belize, Bolivia, Brazil, Chile, Colombia, Costa Rica, Cuba, Dominican Republic, Ecuador, El Salvador, Guatemala, Guyana, Haiti, Honduras, Jamaica (representing CARICOM), Mexico, Nicaragua, Panama, Paraguay, Peru, Uruguay, Venezuela; in 2010 joined with the Caribbean Summit on Integration and Development (CALC) to form the Community of Latin American and Caribbean States (CELAC)

Schengen Convention

established—signed June 1990; effective March 1995

aim—to allow free movement within an area without internal border controls

members—(26) Austria, Belgium, Czech Republic, Denmark, Estonia, Finland, France, Germany, Greece, Hungary, Iceland, Italy, Latvia, Liechtenstein, Lithuania, Luxembourg, Malta, Netherlands, Norway, Poland, Portugal, Slovakia, Slovenia, Spain, Sweden, Switzerland; note- UK and Ireland have not joined; Cyprus will probably join in the near future; Bulgaria and Romania are still not fully implemented

De Facto members (microstates within or between Schengen states)—(5) Andorra, Holy See, Liechtenstein, Monaco, San Marino

Second World

another term for the traditionally Marxist-Leninist states of the USSR and Eastern Europe, with authoritarian governments and command economies based on the Soviet model; the term is fading from use; see centrally planned economies

Secretariat of the Pacific Community (SPC)

established—6 February 1947; effective 29 July 1948

aim—to serve island development in 22 Pacific countries; to develop technical assistance and professional, scientific, and research support; to build planning and management capability *members*—(26) America Samoa, Australia, Cook Islands, Fiji, France, French Polynesia, Guam, Kiribati, Marshall Islands, Federated States of Micronesia, Nauru, New Caledonia, Niue, Northern Mariana Islands, NZ, Palau, Papua New Guinea, Pitcairn Islands, Samoa, Solomon Islands, Tokelau, Tonga, Tuvalu, Vanuatu, US, Wallis and Futuna

Shanghai Cooperation Organization (SCO)
established—15 June 2001
aim—to combat terrorism, extremism, and separatism; to safeguard regional security through mutual trust, disarmament, and cooperative security; and to increase cooperation in political, trade, economic, scientific and technological, cultural, and educational fields
members—(6) China, Kazakhstan, Kyrgyzstan, Russia, Tajikistan, Uzbekistan
dialogue members—(3) Belarus, Sri Lanka Turkey
observers—(5) Afghanistan, India, Iran, Mongolia, Pakistan

socialist countries
in general, countries in which the government owns and plans the use of the major factors of production; note—the term is sometimes used incorrectly as a synonym for Communist countries

South
a popular term for the poorer, less industrialized countries generally located south of the developed countries; the counterpart of the North; see less developed countries (LDCs)

South American Community of Nations (CSN)
established on 9 December 2004; its aim was to coordinate common policies regarding multilateral organizations, to integrate physical infrastructure, and to consolidate the merger of CAN and Mercosur; the members were Argentina, Bolivia, Brazil, Chile, Colombia, Ecuador, Guyana, Paraguay, Peru, Surinam, Uruguay, Venezuela; in 2008 it became Union of South American Nations (UNASUR)

South Asia Co-operative Environment Program (SACEP)
established—January 1983
aim—to promote regional cooperation in South Asia in the field of environment, both natural and human, and on issues of economic and social development; to support conservation and management of natural resources of the region
members—(8) Afghanistan, Bangladesh, Bhutan, India, Maldives, Nepal, Pakistan, Sri Lanka

South Asian Association for Regional Cooperation (SAARC)
established—8 December 1985
aim—to promote economic, social, and cultural cooperation
members—(8) Afghanistan, Bangladesh, Bhutan, India, Maldives, Nepal, Pakistan, Sri Lanka
observers—(9) Australia, Burma, China, EU, Iran, Japan, South Korea, Mauritius, US

South Pacific Forum (SPF)
note—see Pacific Island Forum

South Pacific Regional Trade and Economic Cooperation Agreement (Sparteca)
established—1981
aim—to redress unequal trade relationships of Australia and New Zealand with small island economies in the Pacific region
members—(16) Australia, Cook Islands, Fiji (suspended), Kiribati, Marshall Islands, Federated States of Micronesia, Nauru, NZ, Niue, Palau, Papua New Guinea, Samoa, Solomon Islands, Tonga, Tuvalu, Vanuatu

Southern African Customs Union (SACU)
established—11 December 1969
aim—to promote free trade and cooperation in customs matters
members—(5) Botswana, Lesotho, Namibia, South Africa, Swaziland

Southern African Development Community (SADC)
note—evolved from the Southern African Development Coordination Conference (SADCC)
established—17 August 1992
aim—to promote regional economic development and integration
members—(15) Angola, Botswana, Democratic Republic of the Congo, Lesotho, Madagascar, Malawi, Mauritius, Mozambique, Namibia, Seychelles, South Africa, Swaziland, Tanzania, Zambia, Zimbabwe

Southern Cone Common Market (Mercosur) or Southern Common Market
note—also known as Mercado Comun del Cono Sur (Mercosur)
established—26 March 1991
aim—to increase regional economic cooperation
members—(6) Argentina, Bolivia, Brazil, Paraguay (suspended), Uruguay, Venezuela
associate members—(6) Chile, Colombia, Ecuador, Guyana, Peru, Surinam

Third World
another term for the less developed countries; the term is obsolescent; see less developed countries (LDCs)

underdeveloped countries

refers to those less developed countries with the potential for above-average economic growth; see less developed countries (LDCs)

undeveloped countries

refers to those extremely poor less developed countries (LDCs) with little prospect for economic growth; see least developed countries (LLDCs)

Union Latina

established—15 May 1954; became functional 1983
aim—to project, protect, and promote the common heritage and unifying identities of the Latin, and Latin-influenced, world
members—(36) Andorra, Angola, Bolivia, Brazil, Cabo Verde, Chile, Colombia, Cote d'Ivoire, Costa Rica, Cuba, Dominican Republic, Ecuador, El Salvador, France, Guatemala, Guinea-Bissau, Haiti, Honduras, Italy, Moldova, Monaco, Mozambique, Nicaragua, Panama, Paraguay, Peru, Philippines, Portugal, Romania, San Marino, Sao Tome and Principe, Senegal, Spain, Timor-Leste, Uruguay, Venezuela
observers—(4) Argentina, Holy See, Mexico, Order of Malta

Union of South American Nations (UNASUR—Spanish; UNASUL—Portuguese)

formerly South American Community of Nations (CSN) which terminated on 16 April 2007
established—23 May 2008
aim—to model a community after the European Union which will include a common currency, parliament, passport, and defense policy
members—(12) Argentina, Bolivia, Brazil, Chile, Colombia, Ecuador, Guyana, Paraguay, Peru, Suriname, Uruguay, Venezuela
observers—(2) Mexico, Panama

United Nations (UN)

established—26 June 1945; effective—24 October 1945
aim—to maintain international peace and security and to promote cooperation involving economic, social, cultural, and humanitarian problems
constituent organizations—the UN is composed of six principal organs and numerous subordinate agencies and bodies as follows:
1) Secretariat
2) General Assembly: International Computing Center (ICC), International Trade Center (ITC), Joint United Nations Program on HIV/AIDS (UN-AIDS), Office of the United Nations High Commissioner for Refugees (UNHCR), United Nations Center for Human Settlements (UN-Habitat), United Nations Children's Fund (UNICEF), United Nations Conference on Trade and Development (UNCTAD), United Nations Development Program (UNDP), United Nations Environment Program (UNEP), United Nations Institute for Disarmament Research (UNIDIR), United Nations Institute for Training and Research (UNITAR), United Nations Interregional Crime and Justice Research Institute (UNICRI), United Nations Office on Drugs and Crime (UNODC), United Nations Population Fund (UNFPA), United Nations Office of Project Services (UNOPS), United Nations Relief and Works Agency for Palestine Refugees in the Near East (UNRWA), United Nations Research Institute for Social Development (UNRISD), United Nations System Staff College (UNSSC), United Nations University (UNU), United Nations Women, World Food Program (WFP)
3) Security Council: International Criminal Tribunal for the Former Yugoslavia (ICTY), International Criminal Tribunal for Rwanda (ICTR), United Nations Compensation Commission, United Nations Disengagement Observer Force (UNDOF), African Union/United Nations Hybrid Operation in Darfur (UNAMID), United Nations Assistance Mission in Afghanistan (UNAMA), United Nations Interim Administration Mission in Kosovo (UNMIK), United Nations Interim Force for Abyei (UNIFSA), United Nations Interim Force in Lebanon (UNIFIL), United Nations Mission in Liberia (UNMIL), United Nations Military Observer Group in India and Pakistan (UNMOGIP), United Nations Multidimensional Integrated Stabilization Mission in Mali (MINUSMA), United Nations Operation in Cote d'Ivoire (UNOCI), United Nations Mission for the Referendum in Western Sahara (MINURSO), United Nations Mission in South Sudan (UNMISS), United Nations Organization Stabilization Mission in the Democratic Republic of the Congo (MONUSCO), United Nations Peace-Keeping Force in Cyprus (UNFICYP), United Nations Stabilization Mission in Haiti (MINUSTAH), and United Nations Truce Supervision Organization (UNTSO)
4) Economic and Social Council (ECOSOC): Commission for Social Development, Commission on Crime Prevention and Criminal Justice, Commission on Narcotics Drugs, Commission on Population and Development, Commission on Science and Technology for Development, Commission on Sustainable Development, Commission on the Status of Women, Economic and Social Commission for Asia and the Pacific (ESCAP), Economic and Social Commission for Western Asia (ESCWA), Economic Commission for Africa (ECA), Economic Commission for Europe (ECE), Economic Commission for Latin America and the Caribbean (ECLAC), Statistical Commission, Food and Agriculture Organization of the United Nations (FAO), International Atomic Energy Agency (IAEA), Preparatory Commission for the Nuclear-Test-Ban Treaty Organization (CTBTO), International Bank for Reconstruction and Development (IBRD), International Center for Secretariat of Investment Disputes (ICSID), International Civil Aviation Organization (ICAO), International Development Association (IDA), International Finance Corporation (IFC), International Fund for Agricultural Development (IFAD), International Labor Organization (ILO), International Maritime Organization (IMO), International Monetary Fund (IMF), International Telecommunication Union (ITU), Multilateral Investment Guarantee Agency (MIGA), Statistical Commission, United Nations Educational, Scientific, and Cultural Organization (UNESCO), United Nations Forum on Forests, United Nations Industrial Development Organization (UNIDO), Universal Postal Union (UPU), World Health Organization (WHO), World Intellectual Property Organization (WIPO), World Meteorological Organization (WMO), World Tourism Organization (UNWTO), and World Trade Organization (WTO), Statistical Commission, UN Forum on Forests
5) Trusteeship Council (inactive; no trusteeships at this time)
6) International Court of Justice (ICJ)
UN members—(193) Afghanistan, Albania, Algeria, Andorra, Angola, Antigua and Barbuda, Argentina, Armenia, Australia, Austria, Azerbaijan, The Bahamas, Bahrain, Bangladesh, Barbados, Belarus, Belgium, Belize, Benin, Bhutan, Bolivia, Bosnia and Herzegovina,

Botswana, Brazil, Brunei, Bulgaria, Burkina Faso, Burma, Burundi, Cabo Verde, Cambodia, Cameroon, Canada, Central African Republic, Chad, Chile, China, Colombia, Comoros, Democratic Republic of the Congo, Republic of the Congo, Costa Rica, Cote d'Ivoire, Croatia, Cuba, Cyprus, Czech Republic, Denmark, Djibouti, Dominica, Dominican Republic, Ecuador, Egypt, El Salvador, Equatorial Guinea, Eritrea, Estonia, Ethiopia, Fiji, Finland, France, Gabon, The Gambia, Georgia, Germany, Ghana, Greece, Grenada, Guatemala, Guinea, Guinea-Bissau, Guyana, Haiti, Honduras, Hungary, Iceland, India, Indonesia, Iran, Iraq, Ireland, Israel, Italy, Jamaica, Japan, Jordan, Kazakhstan, Kenya, Kiribati, North Korea, South Korea, Kuwait, Kyrgyzstan, Laos, Latvia, Lebanon, Lesotho, Liberia, Libya, Liechtenstein, Lithuania, Luxembourg, Macedonia, Madagascar, Malawi, Malaysia, Maldives, Mali, Malta, Marshall Islands, Mauritania, Mauritius, Mexico, Federated States of Micronesia, Moldova, Monaco, Mongolia, Montenegro, Morocco, Mozambique, Namibia, Nauru, Nepal, Netherlands, NZ, Nicaragua, Niger, Nigeria, Norway, Oman, Pakistan, Palau, Panama, Papua New Guinea, Paraguay, Peru, Philippines, Poland, Portugal, Qatar, Romania, Russia, Rwanda, Saint Kitts and Nevis, Saint Lucia, Saint Vincent and the Grenadines, Samoa, San Marino, Sao Tome and Principe, Saudi Arabia, Senegal, Serbia, Seychelles, Sierra Leone, Singapore, Slovakia, Slovenia, Solomon Islands, Somalia, South Africa, South Sudan, Spain, Sri Lanka, Sudan, Suriname, Swaziland, Sweden, Switzerland, Syria, Tajikistan, Tanzania, Thailand, Timor-Leste, Togo, Tonga, Trinidad and Tobago, Tunisia, Turkey, Turkmenistan, Tuvalu, Uganda, Ukraine, UAE, UK, US, Uruguay, Uzbekistan, Vanuatu, Venezuela, Vietnam, Yemen, Zambia, Zimbabwe; note—all UN members are represented in the General Assembly
observers—(1 plus the Palestine Liberation Organization) Holy See, Palestine Liberation Organization

United Nations Assistance Mission in Afghanistan (UNAMA)
established—January 2010
aim—to support the government of Afghanistan, in its attempt to improve security, governance, and economic development and regional cooperation; protect civilians and support efforts to support human rights
note—gives civilian support only

United Nations Children's Fund (UNICEF)
note—acronym retained from the predecessor organization, UN International Children's Emergency Fund
established—11 December 1946
aim—to help establish child health and welfare services
executive board members—(36) selected on a rotating basis from all regions

United Nations Conference on Trade and Development (UNCTAD)
established—30 December 1964
aim—to promote international
trade members—(194) all UN members plus Holy See

United Nations Development Program (UNDP)
established—22 November 1965
aim—to provide technical assistance to stimulate economic and social development
members (executive board)—(36) selected on a rotating basis from all regions

United Nations Disengagement Observer Force (UNDOF)
established—31 May 1974
aim—to observe the 1973 Arab-Israeli cease-fire; established by the UN Security Council
members—(6) Fiji, India, Ireland, Nepal, Netherlands, Philippines

United Nations Educational, Scientific, and Cultural Organization (UNESCO)
established—16 November 1945; effective—4 November 1946
aim—to promote cooperation in education, science, and culture
members—(194 plus the Palestine Liberation Organization) includes all UN member countries except Liechtenstein (192 total); plus Cook Islands, Niue, and the Palestine Liberation Organization
associate members—(9) Anguilla, Aruba, British Virgin Islands, Cayman Islands, Curacao, Faroe Islands, Macau, Sint Maarten, Tokelau

United Nations Environment Program (UNEP)
established—15 December 1972
aim—to promote international cooperation on all environmental matters
members—(58) selected on a rotating basis from all regions

United Nations General Assembly
established—26 June 1945; effective—24 October 1945
aim—to function as the primary deliberative organ of the UN
members—(193) all UN members are represented in the General Assembly

United Nations High Commissioner for Refugees (UNHCR)
established—3 December 1949; effective—1 January 1951
aim—to ensure the humanitarian treatment of refugees and find permanent solutions to refugee problems
members (executive committee)—(87) Algeria, Argentina, Australia, Austria, Azerbaijan, Bangladesh, Belgium, Benin, Brazil, Bulgaria, Cameroon, Canada, Chile, China, Colombia, Democratic Republic of the Congo, Republic of the Congo, Costa Rica, Cote d'Ivoire, Croatia, Cyprus, Denmark, Djibouti, Ecuador, Egypt, Estonia, Ethiopia, Finland, France, Germany, Ghana, Greece, Guinea, Holy See,

Hungary, India, Iran, Ireland, Israel, Italy, Japan, Jordan, Kenya, South Korea, Lebanon, Lesotho, Luxembourg, Macedonia, Madagascar, Mexico, Moldova, Montenegro, Morocco, Mozambique, Namibia, Netherlands, NZ, Nicaragua, Nigeria, Norway, Pakistan, Philippines, Poland, Portugal, Romania, Russia, Rwanda, Serbia, Slovenia, Somalia, South Africa, Spain, Sudan, Sweden, Switzerland, Tanzania, Thailand, Togo, Tunisia, Turkey, Turkmenistan, Uganda, UK, US, Venezuela, Yemen, Zambia

United Nations Industrial Development Organization (UNIDO)
established—17 November 1966; effective—1 January 1967
aim—UN specialized agency that promotes industrial development especially among the members
members—(174) includes all UN member countries except Andorra, Antigua and Barbuda, Australia, Brunei, Canada, Estonia, Iceland, Kiribati, Latvia, Liechtenstein, Marshall Islands, Federated States of Micronesia, Nauru, Palau, San Marino, Singapore, Solomon Islands, South Sudan, US

United Nations Institute for Training and Research (UNITAR)
established—11 December 1963 adoption of the resolution establishing the Institute; effective—24 March 1965
aim—to help the UN become more effective through training and research
members (Board of Trustees)—(12) Algeria, Brazil, Republic of the Congo, Guatemala, India, Iran, Jamaica, Nigeria, Norway, Russia, South Africa, Switzerland; note - the UN Secretary General can appoint up to 30 members

United Nations Integrated Mission in Timor-Leste (UNMIT)
established—25 August 2006
aim—to support the Government, to support the electoral process, to ensure the restoration and maintenance of public security
members—(15) Australia, Bangladesh, Brazil, China, Fiji, Japan, India, Malaysia, Nepal, NZ, Pakistan, Philippines, Portugal, Sierra Leone, Singapore

United Nations Interim Administration Mission in Kosovo (UNMIK)
established—10 June 1999
aim—to promote the establishment of substantial autonomy and self-government in Kosovo; to perform basic civilian administrative functions; to support the reconstruction of key infrastructure and humanitarian and disaster relief
note—gives civilian support only; works closely with NATO Kosovo Force (KFOR)

United Nations Interim Force in Lebanon (UNIFIL)
established—19 March 1978
aim—to confirm the withdrawal of Israeli forces, and assist in reestablishing Lebanese authority in southern Lebanon; established by the UN Security Council
members—(37) Armenia, Austria, Bangladesh, Belarus, Belgium, Brazil, Brunei, Cambodia, China, Croatia, Cyprus, El Salvador, Finland, France, Germany, Ghana, Greece, Guatemala, Hungary, India, Indonesia, Ireland, Italy, Kenya, South Korea, Macedonia, Malaysia, Nepal, Nigeria, Qatar, Serbia, Sierra Leone, Slovenia, Spain, Sri Lanka, Tanzania, Turkey

United Nations Interim Security Force for Abyei (UNISFA)
established—27 June 2011
aim—to protect civilians and humanitarian workers in Abyei
members—(28) Benin, Bolivia, Brazil, Burundi, Cambodia, Ecuador, Ethiopia, Ghana, Guatemala, Guinea, India, Mongolia, Namibia, Nepal, Nigeria, Paraguay, Peru, Philippines, Russia, Rwanda, Sierra Leone, Sri Lanka, Tanzania, Ukraine, Uruguay, Yemen, Zambia, Zimbabwe

United Nations Military Observer Group in India and Pakistan (UNMOGIP)
established—24 January 1949
aim—to observe the 1949 India-Pakistan cease-fire; established by the UN Security Council
members—(9) Chile, Croatia, Finland, Italy, South Korea, Philippines, Sweden, Thailand, Uruguay

United Nations Mission for the Referendum in Western Sahara (MINURSO)
established—29 April 1991
aim—to supervise the cease-fire and conduct a referendum in Western Sahara; established by the UN Security Council
members—(30) Argentina, Austria, Bangladesh, Brazil, China, Croatia, Egypt, El Salvador, France, Ghana, Guinea, Honduras, Hungary, Ireland, Italy, South Korea, Malawi, Malaysia, Mongolia, Nepal, Nigeria, Pakistan, Paraguay, Peru, Poland, Russia, Sri Lanka, Togo, Uruguay, Yemen

United Nations Mission in Liberia (UNMIL)
established—19 September 2003
aim—to support the cease-fire agreement and peace process, protect UN facilities and people, support humanitarian activities, and assist in national security reform
members—(43) Bangladesh, Benin, Bolivia, Brazil, Bulgaria, China, Croatia, Denmark, Ecuador, Egypt, El Salvador, Ethiopia, Finland, France, The Gambia, Ghana, Indonesia, Jordan, Kenya, South Korea, Kyrgyzstan, Malaysia, Moldova, Montenegro, Namibia, Nepal, Niger, Nigeria, Pakistan, Paraguay, Peru, Philippines, Poland, Romania, Russia, Senegal, Serbia, Togo, Ukraine, US, Yemen, Zambia, Zimbabwe

United Nations Mission in the Central African Republic and Chad (MINURCAT)

established on 25 September 2007; to create the security and conditions which will to contribute to the protection of refugees, displaced persons, and citizens in danger, to facilitate the provision of humanitarian assistance in eastern Chad and the northeastern Central African Republic, to create favorable conditions for the reconstruction and economic and social development of these areas; members were Bangladesh, Benin, Burkina Faso, Democratic Republic of the Congo, Egypt, Ethiopia, Ghana, Ireland, Kenya, Mali, Mongolia, Namibia, Nepal, Nigeria, Norway, Pakistan, Poland, Russia, Rwanda, Senegal, Serbia, Sri Lanka, Togo, Tunisia, US; MINURCAT was dissolved in December 2010

United Nations Mission in the Republic of South Sudan (UNMISS)

established—8 July 2011
aim—to consolidate peace and security and to establish the conditions in South Sudan which will strengthen its ability to govern effectively and democratically and establish good relations with its neighbors
members—(54) Australia, Bangladesh, Belarus, Benin, Bolivia, Brazil, Cambodia, Canada, China, Denmark, Ecuador, Egypt, El Salvador, Fiji, Germany, Ghana, Guatemala, Guinea, India, Indonesia, Italy, Japan, Jordan, Kenya, South Korea, Kyrgyzstan, Moldova, Mongolia, Namibia, Nepal, Netherlands, NZ, Nigeria, Norway, Papua New Guinea, Paraguay, Peru, Poland, Romania, Russia, Rwanda, Senegal, Sri Lanka, Sweden, Switzerland, Tanzania, Timor-Leste, Togo, Uganda, Ukraine, UK, US, Yemen, Zambia

United Nations Mission in the Sudan (UNMIS)

established in March 2005 to support implementation of the comprehensive Peace Agreement by monitoring and verifying the implementation of the Cease Fire Agreement, by observing and monitoring movements of armed groups, and by helping disarm, demobilizing and reintegrating armed bands; members were Australia, Bangladesh, Belgium, Benin, Bolivia, Brazil, Burkina Faso, Cambodia, Canada, China, Croatia, Denmark, Ecuador, Egypt, El Salvador, Fiji, Finland, Germany, Greece, Guatemala, Guinea, India, Indonesia, Iran, Japan, Jordan, Kenya, Kyrgyzstan, Malaysia, Moldova, Mongolia, Morocco, Namibia, Nepal, Netherland, NZ, Niger, Norway, Pakistan, Paraguay, Peru, Philippines, Poland, Qatar, Romania, Russia, Rwanda, Sierra Leone, Spain, Sweden, Switzerland, Tanzania, Thailand, Turkey, Uganda, Ukraine, UK, Yemen, Zambia, Zimbabwe; UNMIS was dissolved on 9 July 2011

United Nations Multidimensional Integrated Stabilization Mission in Mali, MINUSMA

established—25 April 2013
aim—to support political processes and carry out a number of security-related tasks
members—(36) Bangladesh, Benin, Burkina Faso, Cambodia, Chad, China, Cote d'Ivoire, Denmark, Dominican Republic, Estonia, Finland, France, The Gambia, Germany, Ghana, Guinea, Guinea-Bissau, Italy, Jordan, Kenya, Liberia, Mauritania, Nepal, Netherlands, Niger, Nigeria, Norway, Rwanda, Senegal, Sierra Leone, Sweden, Switzerland, Togo, UK, US, Yemen

United Nations Operation in Cote d'Ivoire (UNOCI)

established—27 February 2004
aim—to facilitate the implementation by the Ivorian parties of the peace agreement signed by them in January 2003
members—(44) Bangladesh, Benin, Bolivia, Brazil, Chad, China, Ecuador, Egypt, El Salvador, Ethiopia, France, The Gambia, Ghana, Guatemala, Guinea, India, Ireland, Jordan, South Korea, Malawi, Moldova, Morocco, Namibia, Nepal, Niger, Nigeria, Pakistan, Paraguay, Peru, Philippines, Poland, Romania, Russia, Senegal, Serbia, Tanzania, Togo, Tunisia, Uganda, Ukraine, Uruguay, Yemen, Zambia, Zimbabwe

United Nations Organization Stabilization Mission in the Democratic Republic of the Congo (MONUSCO)

established—28 May 2010
aim—to protect the civilians; to assist the government in the areas of stabilization and peace consolidation
members—(49) Algeria, Bangladesh, Belgium, Benin, Bolivia, Bosnia and Herzegovina, Burkina Faso, Cameroon, Canada, China, Czech Republic, Egypt, France, Ghana, Guatemala, Guinea, India, Indonesia, Ireland, Jordan, Kenya, Malawi, Malaysia, Mali, Mongolia, Morocco, Nepal, Niger, Nigeria, Pakistan, Paraguay, Peru, Poland, Romania, Russia, Senegal, Serbia, South Africa, Sri Lanka, Sweden, Switzerland, Tanzania, Tunisia, Ukraine, UK, US, Uruguay, Yemen, Zambia

United Nations Peacekeeping Force in Cyprus (UNFICYP)

established—4 March 1964
aim—to serve as a peacekeeping force between Greek Cypriots and Turkish Cypriots in Cyprus; established by the UN Security Council
members—(13) Argentina, Austria, Brazil, Canada, Chile, China, Croatia, Hungary, Paraguay, Serbia, Slovakia, Ukraine, UK

United Nations Population Fund (UNFPA)

note—acronym retained from predecessor organization UN Fund for Population Activities
established—July 1967
aim—to assist both developed and developing countries to deal with their population problems
members (executive board)—(36) selected on a rotating basis from all regions

United Nations Relief and Works Agency for Palestine Refugees in the Near East (UNRWA)

established—8 December 1949
aim—to provide assistance to Palestinian refugees
members (advisory commission)—(25) Australia, Belgium, Canada, Denmark, Egypt, Finland, France, Germany, Ireland, Italy, Japan, Jordan, Kuwait, Lebanon, Luxembourg, Netherlands, Norway, Saudi Arabia, Spain, Sweden, Switzerland, Syria, Turkey, UK, US
observers—(3) EC, LAS, Palestine Liberation Organization

United Nations Research Institute for Social Development (UNRISD)
established—1963
aim—to conduct research into the problems of economic development during different phases of economic growth
members—no country members, but a Board of Directors consisting of a chairman appointed by the UN Secretary General and 10 members confirmed by ECOSOC and a representative of the Secretary General

United Nations Secretariat
established—26 June 1945; effective—24 October 1945
aim—to serve as the primary administrative organ of the UN; a Secretary General is appointed for a five-year term by the General Assembly on the recommendation of the Security Council
members—the UN Secretary General and staff

United Nations Security Council (UNSC)
established—26 June 1945; effective—24 October 1945
aim—to maintain international peace and security
permanent members—(5) China, France, Russia, UK, US
nonpermanent members— (10) elected for two-year terms by the UN General Assembly; Argentina (2013-14), Australia (2013-14), Chad (2014-15), Chile (2014-15), Jordan (2014-15), Lithuania (2014-15), Luxembourg (2013-14), South Korea (2013-14), Nigeria (2014-15), Rwanda (2013-14)

United Nations Truce Supervision Organization (UNTSO)
established—June 1948
aim—to supervise the 1948 Arab-Israeli cease-fire; currently supports timely deployment of reinforcements to other peacekeeping operations in the region as needed; initially established by the UN Security Council
members—(24) Argentina, Australia, Austria, Belgium, Canada, Chile, China, Denmark, Estonia, Finland, France, Ireland, Italy, Nepal, Netherlands, NZ, Norway, Russia, Serbia, Slovakia, Slovenia, Sweden, Switzerland, US

United Nations Trusteeship Council
established on 26 June 1945, effective on 24 October 1945, to supervise the administration of the 11 UN trust territories; members were China, France, Russia, UK, US; it formally suspended operations 1 November 1994 after the Trust Territory of the Pacific Islands (Palau) became the Republic of Palau, a constitutional government in free association with the US; the Trusteeship Council was not dissolved

United Nations University (UNU)
established—3 December 1973
aim—to conduct research in development, welfare, and human survival and to train scholars
members—(16 members of UNU Council and the Rector are appointed by the Secretary General of the United Nations and the Director General of UNESCO)

Universal Postal Union (UPU)
established—9 October 1874, affiliated with the UN 15 November 1947; effective—1 July 1948
aim—to promote international postal cooperation; a UN specialized agency
members—(192) includes all UN member countries except Andorra, Marshall Islands, Federated States of Micronesia, Palau (189 total); plus Aruba, Curacao, and Sint Maarten; and Holy See; and Overseas Territories of the UK; note—includes the following dependencies or areas of special interest: Australia (Norfolk Island), China (Hong Kong, Macau), Denmark (Faroe Islands, Greenland), France (French Guiana, French Polynesia including Clipperton Island, French Southern and Antarctic Lands, Guadeloupe, Martinique, Mayotte, New Caledonia, Reunion, Saint Barthelemy, Saint Martin, Saint Pierre and Miquelon, Scattered Islands [Bassas da India, Europe, Juan de Nova, Glorioso Islands, Tromelin], Wallis and Futuna), Netherlands (Aruba, Curacao, Sint Maarten), NZ (Cook Island, Niue, Tokelau), UK (Guernsey, Isle of Man, Jersey; Anguilla, Bermuda, British Indian Ocean Territory, British Virgin Islands, Cayman Islands, Falkland Islands, Gibraltar, Montserrat, Pitcairn Islands, Saint Helena, Ascension, and Tristan da Cunha, South Georgia and South Sandwich Islands, Turks and Caicos), US (American Samoa, Guam, Northern Mariana Islands, Puerto Rico, Virgin Islands)

Warsaw Pact (WP)
established 14 May 1955 to promote mutual defense; members met 1 July 1991 to dissolve the alliance; member states at the time of dissolution were: Bulgaria, Czechoslovakia, Hungary, Poland, Romania, and the USSR; earlier members included German Democratic Republic (GDR) and Albania

West African Development Bank (WADB)
note—also known as Banque Ouest-Africaine de Developpement (BOAD); is a financial institution of WAEMU
established—14 November 1973
aim—to promote regional economic development and integration
regional members—(8) Benin, Burkina Faso, Cote d'Ivoire, Guinea-Bissau, Mali, Niger, Senegal, Togo

West African Economic and Monetary Union (WAEMU)
note—also known as Union Economique et Monetaire Ouest Africaine (UEMOA)
established—1 August 1994
aim—to increase competitiveness of members' economic markets; to create a common market
members—(8) Benin, Burkina Faso, Cote d'Ivoire, Guinea-Bissau, Mali, Niger, Senegal, Togo

Western European Union (WEU)

established 23 October 1954; effective—6 May 1955; aim to provide mutual defense and to move toward political unification; 10 members: Belgium, France, Germany, Greece, Italy, Luxembourg, Netherlands, Portugal, Spain, UK; 6 associate members: Czech Republic, Hungary, Iceland, Norway, Poland, Turkey; 7 associate partners: Bulgaria, Estonia, Latvia, Lithuania, Romania, Slovakia, Slovenia; 5 observers: Austria, Denmark, Finland, Ireland, Sweden; note—to cease existence completely by June 2011

World Bank Group

includes International Bank for Reconstruction and Development (IBRD), International Development Association (IDA), International Finance Corporation (IFC), and Multilateral Investment Guarantee Agency (MIGA)

World Confederation of Labor (WCL)

established 19 June 1920 as the International Federation of Christian Trade Unions (IFCTU), renamed 4 October 1968; aim was to promote the trade union movement; on 31 October 2006 it merged with the International Confederation of Free Trade Unions (ICFTU) to form the International Trade Union Confederation (ITUC); members were (105 national organizations) Antigua and Barbuda, Argentina, Aruba, Austria, Bangladesh, Belgium, Belize, Benin, Bolivia, Brazil, Bulgaria, Burkina Faso, Cameroon, Canada, Central African Republic, Chad, Chile, Colombia, Democratic Republic of the Congo, Republic of the Congo, Costa Rica, Cote d'Ivoire, Cuba, Cyprus, Czech Republic, Denmark, Dominica, Dominican Republic, Ecuador, El Salvador, France, French Guiana, Gabon, The Gambia, Ghana, Guadeloupe, Guatemala, Guinea, Guyana, Haiti, Honduras, Hong Kong, Hungary, India, Indonesia, Iran, Italy, Japan, Kazakhstan, South Korea, Liberia, Libya, Liechtenstein, Lithuania, Luxembourg, Macedonia, Madagascar, Malawi, Malaysia, Malta, Martinique, Mauritania, Mauritius, Mexico, Morocco, Namibia, Nepal, Netherlands, Nicaragua, Niger, Pakistan, Panama, Paraguay, Peru, Philippines, Poland, Portugal, Puerto Rico, Romania, Rwanda, Saint Lucia, Saint Vincent and the Grenadines, Sao Tome and Principe, Senegal, Serbia, Sierra Leone, Singapore, Slovakia, South Africa, Spain, Sri Lanka, Suriname, Switzerland, Taiwan, Thailand, Togo, Trinidad and Tobago, Ukraine, US, Uruguay, Venezuela, Vietnam, Zambia, Zimbabwe

World Customs Organization (WCO)

note—began as the Customs Cooperation Council (CCC)
established—15 December 1950
aim—to promote international cooperation in customs matters
members—(180) Afghanistan, Albania, Algeria, Andorra, Angola, Argentina, Armenia, Australia, Austria, Azerbaijan, The Bahamas, Bahrain, Bangladesh, Barbados, Belarus, Belgium, Belize, Benin, Bermuda, Bhutan, Bolivia, Bosnia and Herzegovina, Botswana, Brazil, Brunei, Bulgaria, Burkina Faso, Burma, Burundi, Cabo Verde, Cambodia, Cameroon, Canada, Central African Republic, Chad, Chile, China, Colombia, Comoros, Democratic Republic of the Congo, Republic of the Congo, Costa Rica, Cote d'Ivoire, Croatia, Cuba, Curacao, Cyprus, Czech Republic, Denmark, Djibouti, Dominican Republic, EU, Ecuador, Egypt, El Salvador, Eritrea, Estonia, Ethiopia, Fiji, Finland, France, Gabon, The Gambia, Georgia, Germany, Ghana, Greece, Guatemala, Guinea, Guinea-Bissau, Guyana, Haiti, Honduras, Hong Kong, Hungary, Iceland, India, Indonesia, Iran, Iraq, Ireland, Israel, Italy, Jamaica, Japan, Jordan, Kazakhstan, Kenya, South Korea, Kuwait, Kyrgyzstan, Laos, Latvia, Lebanon, Lesotho, Liberia, Libya, Lithuania, Luxembourg, Macau, Macedonia, Madagascar, Malawi, Malaysia, Maldives, Mali, Malta, Mauritania, Mauritius, Mexico, Moldova, Mongolia, Montenegro, Morocco, Mozambique, Namibia, Nepal, Netherlands, NZ, Nicaragua, Niger, Nigeria, Norway, Oman, Pakistan, Panama, Papua New Guinea, Paraguay, Peru, Philippines, Poland, Portugal, Qatar, Romania, Russia, Rwanda, Saint Lucia, Samoa, Sao Tome and Principe, Saudi Arabia, Senegal, Serbia, Seychelles, Sierra Leone, Singapore, Slovakia, Slovenia, Somalia, South Africa, South Sudan, Spain, Sri Lanka, Sudan, Swaziland, Sweden, Switzerland, Syria, Tajikistan, Tanzania, Thailand, Timor-Leste, Togo, Tonga, Trinidad and Tobago, Tunisia, Turkey, Turkmenistan, Uganda, Ukraine, UAE, UK, US, Uruguay, Uzbekistan, Vanuatu, Venezuela, Vietnam, Yemen, Zambia, Zimbabwe

World Federation of Trade Unions (WFTU)

established—3 October 1945
aim—to promote the trade union movement
members—(in 2013 there were 126 participating nations and territories and the Palestine Liberation Organization); (in 2009 there were 125 nations and the Palestine Liberation Organization) Afghanistan, Albania, Angola, Antigua and Barbuda, Argentina, Armenia, Australia, Austria, Azerbaijan, Bahrain, Bangladesh, Barbados, Belarus, Benin, Bolivia, Botswana, Brazil, Bulgaria, Burkina Faso, Cambodia, Cameroon, Canada, Chile, Colombia, Democratic Republic of the Congo, Republic of the Congo, Costa Rica, Cote d'Ivoire, Cuba, Cyprus, Czech Republic, Djibouti, Dominican Republic, Ecuador, Egypt, El Salvador, Eritrea, Ethiopia, Fiji, Finland, France, French Guiana, The Gambia, Ghana, Greece, Guadeloupe, Guatemala, Guinea, Guinea-Bissau, Guyana, Haiti, Honduras, Hungary, India, Indonesia, Iran, Iraq, Jamaica, Japan, Jordan, Kazakhstan, North Korea, Kuwait, Kyrgyzstan, Laos, Lebanon, Lesotho, Liberia, Libya, Madagascar, Malawi, Malaysia, Mali, Martinique, Mauritius, Mexico, Mozambique, Nepal, New Caledonia, NZ, Niger, Nigeria, Oman, Pakistan, Panama, Papua New Guinea, Peru, Philippines, Poland, Portugal, Puerto Rico, Reunion, Romania, Russia, Saint Lucia, Saint Pierre and Miquelon, Saint Vincent and the Grenadines, Saudi Arabia, Senegal, Sierra Leone, Slovakia, Solomon Islands, Somalia, South Africa, Sri Lanka, Sudan, Sweden, Syria, Tajikistan, Tanzania, Thailand, Togo, Trinidad and Tobago, Tunisia, Turkey, Turkmenistan, Uganda, Ukraine, Uruguay, Uzbekistan, Vanuatu, Venezuela, Vietnam, Yemen, Zimbabwe, Palestine Liberation Organization

World Food Program (WFP)

established—24 November 1961
aim—to provide food aid in support of economic development or disaster relief; an ECOSOC organization
members (Executive Board)—(36) selected on a rotating basis from all regions

World Health Organization (WHO)

established—22 July 1946; effective—7 April 1948
aim—to deal with health matters worldwide; a UN specialized agency
members—(194) includes all UN member countries except Liechtenstein (192 total); plus Cook Islands and Niue

World Intellectual Property Organization (WIPO)
established—14 July 1967; effective—26 April 1970
aim—to furnish protection for literary, artistic, and scientific works; a UN specialized agency
members—(185) includes all UN member countries except Marshall Islands, Federated States of Micronesia, Nauru, Palau, Solomon Islands, South Sudan, Timor-Leste, Tuvalu (185 total); plus Holy See

World Meteorological Organization (WMO)
established—11 October 1947; effective—4 April 1951
aim—to sponsor meteorological cooperation; a UN specialized agency
members—(185) includes all UN member countries except Andorra, Equatorial Guinea, Grenada, Liechtenstein, Marshall Islands, Nauru, Palau, Saint Kitts and Nevis, Saint Vincent and the Grenadines, San Marino (183 total); plus Cook Islands and Niue

World Tourism Organization (UNWTO)
established—2 January 1975
aim—to promote tourism as a means of contributing to economic development, international understanding, and peace
members—(156) Afghanistan, Albania, Algeria, Andorra, Angola, Argentina, Armenia, Australia, Austria, Azerbaijan, The Bahamas, Bahrain, Bangladesh, Belarus, Benin, Bhutan, Bolivia, Bosnia and Herzegovina, Botswana, Brazil, Brunei, Bulgaria, Burkina Faso, Burma, Burundi, Cabo Verde, Cambodia, Cameroon, Central African Republic, Chad, Chile, China, Colombia, Democratic Republic of the Congo, Republic of the Congo, Costa Rica, Cote d'Ivoire, Croatia, Cuba, Cyprus, Czech Republic, Djibouti, Dominican Republic, Ecuador, Egypt, El Salvador, Equatorial Guinea, Eritrea, Ethiopia, Fiji, France, Gabon, The Gambia, Georgia, Germany, Ghana, Greece, Guatemala, Guinea, Guinea-Bissau, Haiti, Honduras, Hungary, India, Indonesia, Iran, Iraq, Israel, Italy, Jamaica, Japan, Jordan, Kazakhstan, Kenya, North Korea, South Korea, Kuwait, Kyrgyzstan, Laos, Lebanon, Libya, Lithuania, Macedonia, Madagascar, Malawi, Malaysia, Maldives, Mali, Malta, Mauritania, Mauritius, Mexico, Moldova, Monaco, Mongolia, Montenegro, Morocco, Mozambique, Namibia, Nepal, Netherlands, Nicaragua, Niger, Nigeria, Norway, Oman, Pakistan, Panama, Papua New Guinea, Paraguay, Peru, Philippines, Poland, Portugal, Qatar, Romania, Russia, Rwanda, San Marino, Sao Tome and Principe, Saudi Arabia, Senegal, Serbia, Seychelles, Sierra Leone, Slovakia, Slovenia, South Africa, Spain, Sri Lanka, Sudan, Swaziland, Switzerland, Syria, Tajikistan, Tanzania, Thailand, Timor-Leste, Togo, Trinidad and Tobago, Tunisia, Turkey, Turkmenistan, Uganda, Ukraine, UAE, Uruguay, Uzbekistan, Vanuatu, Venezuela, Vietnam, Yemen, Zambia, Zimbabwe
associate members—(6) Aruba, Flemish Community of Belgium, Hong Kong, Macau, Madeira Islands, Puerto Rico
observers—(1 plus Palestine Liberation Organization) Holy See, Palestine Liberation Organization

World Trade Organization (WTO)
note—succeeded General Agreement on Tariff and Trade (GATT)
established—15 April 1994; effective—1 January 1995
aim—to provide a forum to resolve trade conflicts between members and to carry on negotiations with the goal of further lowering and/or eliminating tariffs and other trade barriers
members—(159) Albania, Angola, Antigua and Barbuda, Argentina, Armenia, Australia, Austria, Bahrain, Bangladesh, Barbados, Belgium, Belize, Benin, Bolivia, Botswana, Brazil, Brunei, Bulgaria, Burkina Faso, Burma, Burundi, Cabo Verde, Cambodia, Cameroon, Canada, Central African Republic, Chad, Chile, China, Colombia, Democratic Republic of the Congo, Republic of the Congo, Costa Rica, Cote d'Ivoire, Croatia, Cuba, Cyprus, Czech Republic, Denmark, Djibouti, Dominica, Dominican Republic, Ecuador, Egypt, El Salvador, Estonia, EU, Fiji, Finland, France, Gabon, The Gambia, Georgia, Germany, Ghana, Greece, Grenada, Guatemala, Guinea, Guinea-Bissau, Guyana, Haiti, Honduras, Hong Kong, Hungary, Iceland, India, Indonesia, Ireland, Israel, Italy, Jamaica, Japan, Jordan, Kenya, South Korea, Kuwait, Kyrgyzstan, Laos, Latvia, Lesotho, Liechtenstein, Lithuania, Luxembourg, Macau, Macedonia, Madagascar, Malawi, Malaysia, Maldives, Mali, Malta, Mauritania, Mauritius, Mexico, Moldova, Mongolia, Montenegro, Morocco, Mozambique, Namibia, Nepal, Netherlands, NZ, Nicaragua, Niger, Nigeria, Norway, Oman, Pakistan, Panama, Papua New Guinea, Paraguay, Peru, Philippines, Poland, Portugal, Qatar, Romania, Russia, Rwanda, Saint Kitts and Nevis, Saint Lucia, Saint Vincent and the Grenadines, Samoa, Saudi Arabia, Senegal, Sierra Leone, Singapore, Slovakia, Slovenia, Solomon Islands, South Africa, Spain, Sri Lanka, Suriname, Swaziland, Sweden, Switzerland, Taiwan, Tajikistan, Tanzania, Thailand, Togo, Tonga, Trinidad and Tobago, Tunisia, Turkey, Uganda, Ukraine, UAE, UK, US, Uruguay, Vanuatu, Venezuela, Vietnam, Zambia, Zimbabwe
observers—(25) Afghanistan, Algeria, Andorra, Azerbaijan, The Bahamas, Belarus, Bhutan, Bosnia and Herzegovina, Comoros, Equatorial Guinea, Ethiopia, Holy See, Iran, Iraq, Kazakhstan, Lebanon, Liberia, Libya, Sao Tome and Principe, Serbia, Seychelles, Sudan, Syria, Uzbekistan, Yemen; note - with the exception of the Holy See, an observer must start accession negotiations within five years of becoming observers

Zangger Committee (ZC)
established—early 1970s
aim—to establish guidelines for the export control provisions of the Nonproliferation of Nuclear Weapons Treaty (NPT)
members—(39) Argentina, Australia, Austria, Belarus, Belgium, Bulgaria, Canada, China, Croatia, Czech Republic, Denmark, Finland, France, Germany, Greece, Hungary, Ireland, Italy, Japan, Kazakhstan, South Korea, Luxembourg, Netherlands, NZ, Norway, Poland, Portugal, Romania, Russia, Slovakia, Slovenia, South Africa, Spain, Sweden, Switzerland, Turkey, Ukraine, UK, US
observers—(1) European Commission

APPENDIX C

SELECTED ENVIRONMENTAL AGREEMENTS

Air Pollution
see Convention on Long-Range Transboundary Air Pollution

Air Pollution-Nitrogen Oxides
see Protocol to the 1979 Convention on Long-Range Transboundary Air Pollution Concerning the Control of Emissions of Nitrogen Oxides or Their Transboundary Fluxes

Air Pollution-Persistent Organic Pollutants
see Protocol to the 1979 Convention on Long-Range Transboundary Air Pollution on Persistent Organic Pollutants

Air Pollution-Sulphur 85
see Protocol to the 1979 Convention on Long-Range Transboundary Air Pollution on the Reduction of Sulphur Emissions or Their Transboundary Fluxes by at least 30%

Air Pollution-Sulphur 94
see Protocol to the 1979 Convention on Long-Range Transboundary Air Pollution on Further Reduction of Sulphur Emissions

Air Pollution-Volatile Organic Compounds
see Protocol to the 1979 Convention on Long-Range Transboundary Air Pollution Concerning the Control of Emissions of Volatile Organic Compounds or Their Transboundary Fluxes

Antarctic—Environmental Protocol
see Protocol on Environmental Protection to the Antarctic Treaty

Antarctic Treaty
opened for signature—1 December 1959
entered into force—23 June 1961
objective—to ensure that Antarctica is used for peaceful purposes only (such as international cooperation in scientific research); to defer the question of territorial claims asserted by some nations and not recognized by others; to provide an international forum for management of the region; applies to land and ice shelves south of 60 degrees south latitude
parties—(50) Argentina, Australia, Austria, Belarus, Belgium, Brazil, Bulgaria, Canada, Chile, China, Colombia, Cuba, Czech Republic, Denmark, Ecuador, Estonia, Finland, France, Germany, Greece, Guatemala, Hungary, India, Italy, Japan, North Korea, South Korea, Malaysia, Monaco, Netherlands, NZ, Norway, Pakistan, Papua New Guinea, Peru, Poland, Portugal, Romania, Russia, Slovakia, South Africa, Spain, Sweden, Switzerland, Turkey, Ukraine, UK, US, Uruguay, Venezuela

Basel Convention on the Control of Transboundary Movements of Hazardous Wastes and Their Disposal
note—abbreviated as Hazardous Wastes
opened for signature—22 March 1989
entered into force—5 May 1992
objective—to reduce transboundary movements of wastes subject to the Convention to a minimum consistent with the environmentally sound and efficient management of such wastes; to minimize the amount and toxicity of wastes generated and ensure their environmentally sound management as closely as possible to the source of generation; and to assist LDCs in environmentally sound management of the hazardous and other wastes they generate
parties—(171) Albania, Algeria, Andorra, Antigua and Barbuda, Argentina, Armenia, Australia, Austria, Azerbaijan, The Bahamas, Bahrain, Bangladesh, Barbados, Belarus, Belgium, Belize, Benin, Bhutan, Bolivia, Bosnia and Herzegovina, Botswana, Brazil, Brunei, Bulgaria, Burkina Faso, Burundi, Cambodia, Cameroon, Canada, Cape Verde, Central African Republic, Chad, Chile, China, Colombia, Comoros, Democratic Republic of the Congo, Republic of the Congo, Cook Islands, Costa Rica, Cote d'Ivoire, Croatia, Cuba, Cyprus, Czech Republic, Denmark, Djibouti, Dominica, Dominican Republic, Ecuador, Egypt, El Salvador, Equatorial Guinea, Eritrea, Estonia, Ethiopia, EU, Finland, France, Gabon, The Gambia, Georgia, Germany, Ghana, Greece, Guatemala, Guinea, Guinea-Bissau, Guyana, Honduras, Hungary, Iceland, India, Indonesia, Iran, Ireland, Israel, Italy, Jamaica, Japan, Jordan, Kazakhstan, Kenya, Kiribati, North Korea, South Korea, Kuwait, Kyrgyzstan, Latvia, Lebanon, Lesotho, Liberia, Libya, Liechtenstein, Lithuania, Luxembourg, Macedonia, Madagascar, Malawi, Malaysia, Maldives, Mali, Malta, Marshall Islands, Mauritania, Mauritius, Mexico, Federated States of Micronesia, Moldova, Monaco, Mongolia, Montenegro, Morocco, Mozambique, Namibia, Nauru, Nepal, Netherlands, NZ, Nicaragua, Niger, Nigeria, Norway, Oman, Pakistan, Panama, Papua New Guinea, Paraguay, Peru, Philippines, Poland, Portugal, Qatar, Romania, Russia, Rwanda, Saint Kitts and Nevis, Saint Lucia, Saint Vincent and the Grenadines, Samoa, Saudi Arabia, Senegal, Serbia, Seychelles, Singapore, Slovakia, Slovenia, South Africa, Spain, Sri Lanka, Sudan, Swaziland, Sweden, Switzerland, Syria, Tanzania, Thailand, Trinidad and Tobago, Tunisia, Turkey, Turkmenistan, Uganda, Ukraine, UAE, UK, Uruguay, Uzbekistan, Venezuela, Vietnam, Yemen, Zambia
countries that have signed, but not yet ratified—(3) Afghanistan, Haiti, US

Biodiversity

999

see Convention on Biological Diversity

Climate Change
see United Nations Framework Convention on Climate Change

Climate Change-Kyoto Protocol
see Kyoto Protocol to the United Nations Framework Convention on Climate Change

Convention for the Conservation of Antarctic Seals
note—abbreviated as Antarctic Seals
opened for signature—1 June 1972
entered into force—11 March 1978
objective—to promote and achieve the protection, scientific study, and rational use of Antarctic seals, and to maintain a satisfactory balance within the ecological system of Antarctica
parties—(16) Argentina, Australia, Belgium, Brazil, Canada, Chile, France, Germany, Italy, Japan, Norway, Poland, Russia, South Africa, UK, US
countries that have signed, but not yet ratified—(1) NZ

Convention on Biological Diversity
note—abbreviated as Biodiversity
opened for signature—5 June 1992
entered into force—29 December 1993
objective—to develop national strategies for the conservation and sustainable use of biological diversity and to address the fair and equitable sharing of benefits arising out of the utilization of genetic resources
parties—(191) Afghanistan, Albania, Algeria, Andorra, Angola, Antigua and Barbuda, Argentina, Armenia, Australia, Austria, Azerbaijan, The Bahamas, Bahrain, Bangladesh, Barbados, Belarus, Belgium, Belize, Benin, Bhutan, Bolivia, Bosnia and Herzegovina, Botswana, Brazil, Brunei, Bulgaria, Burkina Faso, Burma, Burundi, Cambodia, Cameroon, Canada, Cape Verde, Central African Republic, Chad, Chile, China, Colombia, Comoros, Democratic Republic of the Congo, Republic of the Congo, Cook Islands, Costa Rica, Cote d'Ivoire, Croatia, Cuba, Cyprus, Czech Republic, Denmark, Djibouti, Dominica, Dominican Republic, Ecuador, Egypt, El Salvador, Equatorial Guinea, Eritrea, Estonia, Ethiopia, EU, Fiji, Finland, France, Gabon, The Gambia, Georgia, Germany, Ghana, Greece, Grenada, Guatemala, Guinea, Guinea-Bissau, Guyana, Haiti, Honduras, Hungary, Iceland, India, Indonesia, Iran, Iraq, Ireland, Israel, Italy, Jamaica, Japan, Jordan, Kazakhstan, Kenya, Kiribati, North Korea, South Korea, Kuwait, Kyrgyzstan, Laos, Latvia, Lebanon, Lesotho, Liberia, Libya, Liechtenstein, Lithuania, Luxembourg, Macedonia, Madagascar, Malawi, Malaysia, Maldives, Mali, Malta, Marshall Islands, Mauritania, Mauritius, Mexico, Federated States of Micronesia, Moldova, Monaco, Mongolia, Montenegro, Morocco, Mozambique, Namibia, Nauru, Nepal, Netherlands, NZ, Nicaragua, Niger, Nigeria, Niue, Norway, Oman, Pakistan, Palau, Panama, Papua New Guinea, Paraguay, Peru, Philippines, Poland, Portugal, Qatar, Romania, Russia, Rwanda, Saint Kitts and Nevis, Saint Lucia, Saint Vincent and the Grenadines, Samoa, San Marino, Sao Tome and Principe, Saudi Arabia, Senegal, Serbia, Seychelles, Sierra Leone, Singapore, Slovakia, Slovenia, Solomon Islands, Somalia, South Africa, Spain, Sri Lanka, Sudan, Suriname, Swaziland, Sweden, Switzerland, Syria, Tajikistan, Tanzania, Thailand, Timor-Leste, Togo, Tonga, Trinidad and Tobago, Tunisia, Turkey, Turkmenistan, Tuvalu, Uganda, Ukraine, UAE, UK, Uruguay, Uzbekistan, Vanuatu, Venezuela, Vietnam, Yemen, Zambia, Zimbabwe
countries that have signed, but not yet ratified—(1) US

Convention on Fishing and Conservation of Living Resources of the High Seas
note—abbreviated as Marine Life Conservation
opened for signature—29 April 1958
entered into force—20 March 1966
objective—to solve through international cooperation the problems involved in the conservation of living resources of the high seas, considering that because of the development of modern technology some of these resources are in danger of being overexploited
parties—(39) Australia, Belgium, Bosnia and Herzegovina, Burkina Faso, Cambodia, Colombia, Republic of the Congo, Denmark, Dominican Republic, Fiji, Finland, France, Haiti, Jamaica, Kenya, Lesotho, Madagascar, Malawi, Malaysia, Mauritius, Mexico, Montenegro, Netherlands, Nigeria, Portugal, Senegal, Serbia, Sierra Leone, Solomon Islands, South Africa, Spain, Switzerland, Thailand, Tonga, Trinidad and Tobago, Uganda, UK, US, Venezuela
countries that have signed, but not yet ratified—(21) Afghanistan, Argentina, Bolivia, Canada, Costa Rica, Cuba, Ghana, Iceland, Indonesia, Iran, Ireland, Israel, Lebanon, Liberia, Nepal, NZ, Pakistan, Panama, Sri Lanka, Tunisia, Uruguay

Convention on Long-Range Transboundary Air Pollution
note—abbreviated as Air Pollution
opened for signature—13 November 1979
entered into force—16 March 1983
objective—to protect the human environment against air pollution and, as far as possible, to gradually reduce and prevent air pollution, including long-range transboundary air pollution
parties—(51) Albania, Armenia, Austria, Azerbaijan, Belarus, Belgium, Bosnia and Herzegovina, Bulgaria, Canada, Croatia, Cyprus, Czech Republic, Denmark, Estonia, EU, Finland, France, Georgia, Germany, Greece, Hungary, Iceland, Ireland, Italy, Kazakhstan, Kyrgyzstan, Latvia, Liechtenstein, Lithuania, Luxembourg, Macedonia, Malta, Moldova, Monaco, Montenegro, Netherlands, Norway, Poland, Portugal, Romania, Russia, Serbia, Slovakia, Slovenia, Spain, Sweden, Switzerland, Turkey, Ukraine, UK, US
countries that have signed, but not yet ratified—(2) Holy See, San Marino

Convention on Wetlands of International Importance Especially as Waterfowl Habitat (Ramsar)

note—abbreviated as Wetlands
opened for signature—2 February 1971
entered into force—21 December 1975
objective—to stem the progressive encroachment on and loss of wetlands now and in the future
parties—(168) Albania, Algeria, Andorra, Antigua and Barbuda, Argentina, Armenia, Australia, Austria, Azerbaijan, The Bahamas, Bahrain, Bangladesh, Barbados, Belarus, Belgium, Belize, Benin, Bhutan, Bolivia, Bosnia and Herzegovina, Botswana, Brazil, Bulgaria, Burkina Faso, Burma, Burundi, Cambodia, Cameroon, Canada, Cape Verde, Central African Republic, Chad, Chile, China, Colombia, Comoros, Democratic Republic of the Congo, Republic of the Congo, Costa Rica, Cote d'Ivoire, Croatia, Cuba, Cyprus, Czech Republic, Denmark, Djibouti, Dominican Republic, Ecuador, Egypt, El Salvador, Equatorial Guinea, Estonia, Fiji, Finland, France, Gabon, The Gambia, Georgia, Germany, Ghana, Greece, Grenada, Guatemala, Guinea, Guinea-Bissau, Honduras, Hungary, Gambia, Georgia, Germany, Ghana, Greece, Grenada, Guatemala, Guinea, Guinea-Bissau, Honduras, Hungary, Iceland, India, Indonesia, Iran, Iraq, Ireland, Israel, Italy, Jamaica, Japan, Jordan, Kazakhstan, Kenya, Kiribati, South Korea, Kyrgyzstan, Laos, Latvia, Lebanon, Lesotho, Liberia, Libya, Liechtenstein, Lithuania, Luxembourg, Macedonia, Madagascar, Malawi, Malaysia, Mali, Malta, Marshall Islands, Mauritania, Mauritius, Mexico, Moldova, Monaco, Mongolia, Montenegro, Morocco, Mozambique, Namibia, Nepal, Netherlands, NZ, Nicaragua, Niger, Nigeria, Norway, Oman, Pakistan, Palau, Panama, Papua New Guinea, Paraguay, Peru, Philippines, Poland, Portugal, Romania, Russia, Rwanda, Saint Lucia, Samoa, Sao Tome and Principe, Senegal, Serbia, Seychelles, Sierra Leone, Slovakia, Slovenia, South Africa, South Sudan, Spain, Sri Lanka, Sudan, Suriname, Swaziland, Sweden, Switzerland, Syria, Tanzania, Tajikistan, Thailand, Togo, Trinidad and Tobago, Tunisia, Turkey, Turkmenistan, Uganda, Ukraine, UAE, UK, US, Uruguay, Uzbekistan, Venezuela, Vietnam, Yemen, Zambia, Zimbabwe

Convention on the Conservation of Antarctic Marine Living Resources

note—abbreviated as Antarctic-Marine Living Resources
opened for signature—5 May 1980
entered into force—7 April 1982
objective—to safeguard the environment and protect the integrity of the ecosystem of the seas surrounding Antarctica, and to conserve Antarctic marine living resources
parties—(34) Argentina, Australia, Belgium, Brazil, Bulgaria, Canada, Chile, China, Cook Islands, EU, Finland, France, Germany, Greece, India, Italy, Japan, South Korea, Mauritius, Namibia, Netherlands, NZ, Norway, Peru, Poland, Russia, South Africa, Spain, Sweden, Ukraine, UK, US, Uruguay, Vanuatu

Convention on the International Trade in Endangered Species of Wild Flora and Fauna (CITES)

note—abbreviated as Endangered Species
opened for signature—3 March 1973
entered into force—1 July 1975
objective—to protect certain endangered species from overexploitation by means of a system of import/export permits
parties—(179) Afghanistan, Albania, Algeria, Angola, Antigua and Barbuda, Argentina, Armenia, Australia, Austria, Azerbaijan, The Bahamas, Bahrain, Bangladesh, Barbados, Belarus, Belgium, Belize, Benin, Bhutan, Bolivia, Bosnia and Herzegovina, Botswana, Brazil, Brunei, Bulgaria, Burkina Faso, Burma, Burundi, Cambodia, Cameroon, Canada, Cape Verde, Central African Republic, Chad, Chile, China, Colombia, Comoros, Democratic Republic of the Congo, Republic of the Congo, Costa Rica, Cote d'Ivoire, Croatia, Cuba, Cyprus, Czech Republic, Denmark, Djibouti, Dominica, Dominican Republic, Ecuador, Egypt, El Salvador, Equatorial Guinea, Eritrea, Estonia, Ethiopia, Fiji, Finland, France, Gabon, The Gambia, Georgia, Germany, Ghana, Greece, Grenada, Guatemala, Guinea, Guinea-Bissau, Guyana, Honduras, Hungary, Iceland, India, Indonesia, Iran, Ireland, Israel, Italy, Jamaica, Japan, Jordan, Kazakhstan, Kenya, South Korea, Kuwait, Kyrgyzstan, Laos, Latvia, Lebanon, Lesotho, Liberia, Libya, Liechtenstein, Lithuania, Luxembourg, Macedonia, Madagascar, Malawi, Malaysia, Maldives, Mali, Malta, Mauritania, Mauritius, Mexico, Moldova, Monaco, Mongolia, Montenegro, Morocco, Mozambique, Namibia, Nepal, Netherlands, NZ, Nicaragua, Niger, Nigeria, Norway, Oman, Palau, Pakistan, Panama, Papua New Guinea, Paraguay, Peru, Philippines, Poland, Portugal, Qatar, Romania, Russia, Rwanda, Saint Kitts and Nevis, Saint Lucia, Saint Vincent and the Grenadines, Samoa, San Marino, Sao Tome and Principe, Saudi Arabia, Senegal, Serbia, Seychelles, Sierra Leone, Singapore, Slovakia, Slovenia, Solomon Islands, Somalia, South Africa, Spain, Sri Lanka, Sudan, Suriname, Swaziland, Sweden, Switzerland, Syria, Tanzania, Thailand, Togo, Trinidad and Tobago, Tunisia, Turkey, Uganda, Ukraine, UAE, UK, US, Uruguay, Uzbekistan, Vanuatu, Venezuela, Vietnam, Yemen, Zambia, Zimbabwe

Convention on the Prevention of Marine Pollution by Dumping Wastes and Other Matter (London Convention)

note—abbreviated as Marine Dumping
opened for signature—29 December 1972
entered into force—30 August 1975
objective—to promote effective control of all sources of marine pollution and to take all practicable steps to prevent pollution of the sea by dumping and to encourage regional agreements supplementary to the Convention
parties—(87) Afghanistan, Antigua and Barbuda, Argentina, Australia, Azerbaijan, Barbados, Belarus, Belgium, Benin, Bolivia, Brazil, Bulgaria, Canada, Cape Verde, Chile, China, Democratic Republic of the Congo, Costa Rica, Cote d'Ivoire, Croatia, Cuba, Cyprus, Denmark, Dominican Republic, Egypt, Equatorial Guinea, Finland, France, Gabon, Germany, Greece, Guatemala, Haiti, Honduras, Hong Kong (associate member), Hungary, Iceland, Iran, Ireland, Italy, Jamaica, Japan, Jordan, Kenya, Kiribati, South Korea, Libya, Luxembourg, Malta, Mexico, Monaco, Montenegro, Morocco, Nauru, Netherlands, NZ, Nigeria, Norway, Oman, Pakistan, Panama, Papua New Guinea, Peru, Philippines, Poland, Portugal, Russia, Saint Lucia, Saint Vincent and the Grenadines, Serbia, Seychelles, Sierra Leon, Slovenia, Solomon Islands, South Africa, Spain, Suriname, Sweden, Switzerland, Syria, Tanzania, Tonga, Tunisia, Ukraine, UAE, UK, US, Vanuatu
associate members to the London Convention—(2) Faroe Islands, Macau
countries that have signed, but not yet ratified—(3) Chad, Kuwait, Uruguay

Convention on the Prohibition of Military or Any Other Hostile Use of Environmental Modification Techniques

note—abbreviated as Environmental Modification
opened for signature—18 May 1977
entered into force—5 October 1978
objective—to prohibit the military or other hostile use of environmental modification techniques in order to further world peace and trust among nations
parties—(76) Afghanistan, Algeria, Antigua and Barbuda, Argentina, Armenia, Australia, Austria, Bangladesh, Belarus, Belgium, Benin, Brazil, Bulgaria, Canada, Cameroon, Cape Verde, Chile, China, Costa Rica, Cuba, Cyprus, Czech Republic, Denmark, Dominica, Egypt, Estonia, Finland, Germany, Ghana, Greece, Guatemala, Honduras, Hungary, India, Ireland, Italy, Japan, Kazakhstan, North Korea, South Korea, Kuwait, Laos, Lithuania, Malawi, Mauritius, Mongolia, Netherlands, NZ, Nicaragua, Niger, Norway, Pakistan, Panama, Papua New Guinea, Poland, Romania, Russia, Saint Lucia, Saint Vincent and the Grenadines, Sao Tome and Principe, Slovakia, Slovenia, Solomon Islands, Spain, Sri Lanka, Sweden, Switzerland, Tajikistan, Tunisia, Ukraine, UK, US, Uruguay, Uzbekistan, Vietnam, Yemen
countries that have signed, but not yet ratified—(16) Bolivia, Democratic Republic of the Congo, Ethiopia, Holy See, Iceland, Iran, Iraq, Lebanon, Liberia, Luxembourg, Morocco, Portugal, Sierra Leone, Syria, Turkey, Uganda

Desertification

see United Nations Convention to Combat Desertification in those Countries Experiencing Serious Drought and/or Desertification, Particularly in Africa

Endangered Species

see Convention on the International Trade in Endangered Species of Wild Flora and Fauna (CITES)

Environmental Modification

see Convention on the Prohibition of Military or Any Other Hostile Use of Environmental Modification Techniques

Hazardous Wastes

see Basel Convention on the Control of Transboundary Movements of Hazardous Wastes and Their Disposal

International Convention for the Regulation of Whaling

note—abbreviated as Whaling
opened for signature—2 December 1946
entered into force—10 November 1948
objective—to protect all species of whales from overhunting; to establish a system of international regulation for the whale fisheries to ensure proper conservation and development of whale stocks; and to safeguard for future generations the great natural resources represented by whale stocks
parties—(88) Antigua and Barbuda, Argentina, Australia, Austria, Belgium, Belize, Benin, Brazil, Bulgaria, Cambodia, Cameroon, Chile, China, Colombia, Republic of the Congo, Costa Rica, Cote D'Ivoire, Croatia, Cyprus, Czech Republic, Denmark, Dominica, Dominican Republic, Ecuador, Eritrea, Estonia, Finland, France, Gabon, The Gambia, Germany, Ghana, Greece, Grenada, Guatemala, Guinea, Guinea-Bissau, Hungary, Iceland, India, Ireland, Israel, Italy, Japan, Kenya, Kiribati, South Korea, Laos, Lithuania, Luxembourg, Mali, Marshall Islands, Mauritania, Mexico, Monaco, Mongolia, Morocco, Nauru, Netherlands, NZ, Nicaragua, Norway, Oman, Palau, Panama, Peru, Poland, Portugal, Romania, Russia, Saint Kitts and Nevis, Saint Lucia, Saint Vincent and the Grenadines, San Marino, Senegal, Slovakia, Slovenia, Solomon Islands, South Africa, Spain, Suriname, Sweden, Switzerland, Tanzania, Togo, Tuvalu, UK, US, Uruguay

International Tropical Timber Agreement, 1983

note—abbreviated as Tropical Timber 83
opened for signature—18 November 1983
entered into force—1 April 1985; this agreement was superseded by the International Tropical Timber Agreement, 1994
objective—to provide an effective framework for cooperation between tropical timber producers and consumers and to encourage the development of national policies aimed at sustainable utilization and conservation of tropical forests and their genetic resources
parties—(59) Australia, Austria, Belgium, Bolivia, Brazil, Burma, Cambodia, Cameroon, Canada, Central African Republic, China, Colombia, Democratic Republic of the Congo, Republic of the Congo, Cote d'Ivoire, Denmark, Ecuador, Egypt, EU, Fiji, Finland, France, Gabon, Germany, Ghana, Greece, Guatemala, Guyana, Honduras, India, Indonesia, Ireland, Italy, Japan, South Korea, Liberia, Luxembourg, Malaysia, Mexico, Nepal, Netherlands, NZ, Nigeria, Norway, Panama, Papua New Guinea, Peru, Philippines, Portugal, Russia, Spain, Suriname, Sweden, Switzerland, Thailand, Togo, Trinidad and Tobago, UK, US, Vanuatu, Venezuela

International Tropical Timber Agreement, 1994

note—abbreviated as Tropical Timber 94
opened for signature—1 April 1994
entered into force—1 January 1997 (provisional application)
objective—to provide a framework for international cooperation on conservation and sustainable development of tropical timber and enhance the capacity of members to implement a strategy for achieving exports of tropical timber and timber products from sustainably managed sources by the year 2000; to establish a fund to assist tropical timber producers in obtaining the resources necessary to reach this objective
parties—(61) Australia, Austria, Belgium, Bolivia, Brazil, Burma, Cambodia, Cameroon, Canada, Central African Republic, China, Colombia, Democratic Republic of the Congo, Republic of the Congo, Cote d'Ivoire, Denmark, Ecuador, Egypt, EU, Fiji, Finland, France, Gabon, Germany, Ghana, Greece, Guatemala, Guyana, Honduras, India, Indonesia, Ireland, Italy, Japan, South Korea, Liberia, Luxembourg,

Malaysia, Mexico, Nepal, Netherlands, NZ, Nigeria, Norway, Panama, Papua New Guinea, Peru, Philippines, Poland, Portugal, Spain, Suriname, Sweden, Switzerland, Thailand, Togo, Trinidad and Tobago, UK, US, Vanuatu, Venezuela

Kyoto Protocol to the United Nations Framework Convention on Climate Change
note—abbreviated as Climate Change-Kyoto Protocol
opened for signature—16 March 1998
entered into force—23 February 2005
objective—to further reduce greenhouse gas emissions by enhancing the national programs of developed countries aimed at this goal and by establishing percentage reduction targets for the developed countries
parties—(192) Albania, Algeria, Angola, Antigua and Barbuda, Argentina, Armenia, Australia, Austria, Azerbaijan, The Bahamas, Bahrain, Bangladesh, Barbados, Belarus, Belgium, Belize, Benin, Bhutan, Bolivia, Bosnia and Herzegovina, Botswana, Brazil, Brunei, Bulgaria, Burkina Faso, Burma, Burundi, Cambodia, Cameroon, Cape Verde, Central African Republic, Chad, Chile, China, Colombia, Comoros, Democratic Republic of the Congo, Republic of the Congo, Cook Island, Costa Rica, Cote d'Ivoire, Croatia, Cuba, Cyprus, Czech Republic, Denmark, Djibouti, Dominica, Dominican Republic, Ecuador, Egypt, El Salvador, Equatorial Guinea, Eritrea, Estonia, Ethiopia, EU, Fiji, Finland, France, Gabon, The Gambia, Georgia, Germany, Ghana, Greece, Grenada, Guatemala, Guinea, Guinea-Bissau, Guyana, Haiti, Honduras, Hungary, Iceland, India, Indonesia, Iran, Iraq, Ireland, Israel, Italy, Jamaica, Japan, Jordan, Kazakhstan, Kenya, Kiribati, North Korea, South Korea, Kuwait, Kyrgyzstan, Laos, Latvia, Lebanon, Lesotho, Liberia, Libya, Liechtenstein, Lithuania, Luxembourg, Macedonia, Madagascar, Malawi, Malaysia, Maldives, Mali, Malta, Marshall Islands, Mauritania, Mauritius, Mexico, Federated States of Micronesia, Moldova, Monaco, Mongolia, Montenegro, Morocco, Mozambique, Namibia, Nauru, Nepal, Netherlands, NZ, Nicaragua, Niger, Nigeria, Niue, Norway, Oman, Pakistan, Palau, Panama, Papua New Guinea, Paraguay, Peru, Philippines, Poland, Portugal, Qatar, Romania, Russia, Rwanda, Saint Kitts and Nevis, Saint Lucia, Saint Vincent and the Grenadines, Samoa, San Marino, Sao Tome and Principe, Saudi Arabia, Senegal, Serbia, Seychelles, Sierra Leone, Singapore, Slovakia, Slovenia, Solomon Islands, Somalia, South Africa, Spain, Sri Lanka, Sudan, Suriname, Swaziland, Sweden, Switzerland, Syria, Tajikistan, Tanzania, Thailand, Timor-Leste, Togo, Tonga, Trinidad and Tobago, Tunisia, Turkey, Turkmenistan, Tuvalu, Uganda, Ukraine, UAE, UK, Uruguay, Uzbekistan, Vanuatu, Venezuela, Vietnam, Yemen, Zam ia, Zimbabwe
countries that have signed, but not yet ratified—(1) US

Law of the Sea
see United Nations Convention on the Law of the Sea (LOS)

Marine Dumping
see Convention on the Prevention of Marine Pollution by Dumping Wastes and Other Matter (London Convention)

Marine Life Conservation
see Convention on Fishing and Conservation of Living Resources of the High Seas

Montreal Protocol on Substances That Deplete the Ozone Layer
note—abbreviated as Ozone Layer Protection
opened for signature—16 September 1987
entered into force—1 January 1989
objective—to protect the ozone layer by controlling emissions of substances that deplete it
parties—(197) Afghanistan, Albania, Algeria, Andorra, Angola, Antigua and Barbuda, Argentina, Armenia, Australia, Austria, Azerbaijan, The Bahamas, Bahrain, Bangladesh, Barbados, Belarus, Belgium, Belize, Benin, Bhutan, Bolivia, Bosnia and Herzegovina, Botswana, Brazil, Brunei, Bulgaria, Burkina Faso, Burma, Burundi, Cambodia, Cameroon, Canada, Cape Verde, Central African Republic, Chad, Chile, China, Colombia, Comoros, Democratic Republic of the Congo, Republic of the Congo, Cook Islands, Costa Rica, Cote d'Ivoire, Croatia, Cuba, Cyprus, Czech Republic, Denmark, Djibouti, Dominica, Dominican Republic, Ecuador, Egypt, El Salvador, Equatorial Guinea, Eritrea, Estonia, Ethiopia, EU, Fiji, Finland, France, Gabon, The Gambia, Georgia, Germany, Ghana, Greece, Grenada, Guatemala, Guinea, Guinea-Bissau, Guyana, Haiti, Holy See, Honduras, Hungary, Iceland, India, Indonesia, Iran, Iraq, Ireland, Israel, Italy, Jamaica, Japan, Jordan, Kazakhstan, Kenya, Kiribati, North Korea, South Korea, Kuwait, Kyrgyzstan, Laos, Latvia, Lebanon, Lesotho, Liberia, Libya, Liechtenstein, Lithuania, Luxembourg, Macedonia, Madagascar, Malawi, Malaysia, Maldives, Mali, Malta, Marshall Islands, Mauritania, Mauritius, Mexico, Federated States of Micronesia, Moldova, Monaco, Mongolia, Montenegro, Morocco, Mozambique, Namibia, Nauru, Nepal, Netherlands, NZ, Nicaragua, Niger, Nigeria, Niue, Norway, Oman, Pakistan, Palau, Panama, Papua New Guinea, Paraguay, Peru, Philippines, Poland, Portugal, Qatar, Romania, Russia, Rwanda, Saint Kitts and Nevis, Saint Lucia, Saint Vincent and the Grenadines, Samoa, San Marino, Sao Tome and Principe, Saudi Arabia, Senegal, Serbia, Seychelles, Sierra Leone, Singapore, Slovakia, Slovenia, Solomon Islands, Somalia, South Africa, South Sudan, Spain, Sri Lanka, Sudan, Suriname, Swaziland, Sweden, Switzerland, Syria, Tajikistan, Tanzania, Thailand, Timor-Leste, Togo, Tonga, Trinidad and Tobago, Tunisia, Turkey, Turkmenistan, Tuvalu, Uganda, Ukraine, UAE, UK, US, Ur guay, Uzbekistan, Vanuatu, Venezuela, Vietnam, Yemen, Zambia, Zimbabwe

Nuclear Test Ban
see Treaty Banning Nuclear Weapons Tests in the Atmosphere, in Outer Space, and Under Water

Ozone Layer Protection
see Montreal Protocol on Substances That Deplete the Ozone Layer

Protocol of 1978 Relating to the International Convention for the Prevention of Pollution From Ships, 1973 (MARPOL)
note—abbreviated as Ship Pollution
opened for signature—1 June 1978
entered into force—2 October 1983
objective—to modify the International Convention for the Prevention of Pollution from Ships, 1973, including by extending the period of compliance under the Convention by three years
parties—(152) Albania, Algeria, Angola, Antigua and Barbuda, Argentina, Australia, Austria, Azerbaijan, The Bahamas, Bahrain, Bangladesh, Barbados, Belarus, Belgium, Belize, Benin, Bolivia, Brazil, Brunei, Bulgaria, Burma, Cambodia, Canada, Cape Verde, Chile, China, Colombia, Comoros, Republic of Congo, Cote d'Ivoire, Croatia, Cuba, Cyprus, Czech Republic, Denmark, Djibouti, Dominica, Dominican Republic, Ecuador, Egypt, El Salvador, Equatorial Guinea, Estonia, Faroe Islands, Finland, France, Gabon, The Gambia, Georgia, Germany, Ghana, Greece, Guatemala, Guinea, Guyana, Honduras, Hong Kong, Hungary, Iceland, India, Indonesia, Iran, Ireland, Israel, Italy, Jamaica, Japan, Jordan, Kazakhstan, Kenya, Kiribati, North Korea, South Korea, Kuwait, Latvia, Lebanon, Liberia, Lithuania, Luxembourg, Libya, Macau, Madagascar, Malawi, Malaysia, Maldives, Malta, Marshall Islands, Mauritania, Mauritius, Mexico, Moldova, Monaco, Mongolia, Montenegro, Morocco, Mozambique, Namibia, Netherlands, NZ, Nicaragua, Nigeria, Norway, Nuie, Oman, Pakistan, Palau, Panama, Papua New Guinea, Peru, Philippines, Poland, Portugal, Qatar Romania, Russia, Saint Kitts and Nevis, Saint Lucia, Saint Vincent and the Grenadines, Samoa, Sao Tome and Principe, Saudi Arabia, Senegal, Serbia, Seychelles, Sierra Leone, Singapore, Slovakia, Slovenia, Solomon Islands, South Africa, Spain, Sri Lanka, Suriname, Sweden, Switzerland, Syria, Tanzania, Togo, Tonga, Trinidad and Tobago, Tunisia, Turkey, Turkmenistan, Tuvalu, Ukraine, UAE, UK, US, Uruguay, Vanuatu, Venezuela, Vietnam

Protocol on Environmental Protection to the Antarctic Treaty
note—abbreviated as Antarctic-Environmental Protocol
opened for signature—4 October 1991
entered into force—14 January 1998
objective—to provide for comprehensive protection of the Antarctic environment and dependent and associated ecosystems; applies to the area covered by the Antarctic Treaty
consultative parties—(28) Argentina, Australia, Belgium, Brazil, Bulgaria, Chile, China, Ecuador, Finland, France, Germany, India, Italy, Japan, South Korea, Netherlands, NZ, Norway, Peru, Poland, Russia, South Africa, Spain, Sweden, Ukraine, UK, US, Uruguay
non consultative parties—(22) Austria, Belarus, Canada, Colombia, Cuba, Czech Republic, Denmark, Estonia, Greece, Guatemala, Hungary, North Korea, Malaysia, Monaco, Pakistan, Papua New Guinea, Romania, Slovakia, Switzerland, Turkey, Venezuela

Protocol to the 1979 Convention on Long-Range Transboundary Air Pollution Concerning the Control of Emissions of Nitrogen Oxides or Their Transboundary Fluxes
note—abbreviated as Air Pollution-Nitrogen Oxides
opened for signature—31 October 1988
entered into force—14 February 1991
objective—to provide for the control or reduction national of nitrogen oxide emissions and their transboundary fluxes
parties—(35) Albania, Austria, Belarus, Belgium, Bulgaria, Canada, Croatia, Cyprus, Czech Republic, Denmark, Estonia, EU, Finland, France, Germany, Greece, Hungary, Ireland, Italy, Liechtenstein, Lithuania, Luxembourg, Macedonia, Netherlands, Norway, Poland, Russia, Slovakia, Slovenia, Spain, Sweden, Switzerland, Ukraine, UK, US

Protocol to the 1979 Convention on Long-Range Transboundary Air Pollution Concerning the Control of Emissions of Volatile Organic Compounds or Their Transboundary Fluxes
note—abbreviated as Air Pollution-Volatile Organic Compounds
opened for signature—18 November 1991
entered into force—29 September 1997
objective—to provide for the control and reduction of national emissions of volatile organic compounds in order to reduce their transboundary fluxes
parties—(23) (24) Austria, Belgium, Bulgaria, Croatia, Czech Republic, Denmark, Estonia, Finland, France, Germany, Hungary, Italy, Liechtenstein, Lithuania, Luxembourg, Macedonia, Monaco, Netherlands, Norway, Slovakia, Spain, Sweden, Switzerland, UK Sweden, Switzerland, UK
countries that have signed, but not yet ratified—(6) Canada, EU, Greece, Portugal, Ukraine, US

Protocol to the 1979 Convention on Long-Range Transboundary Air Pollution on Further Reduction of Sulphur Emissions
note—abbreviated as Air Pollution-Sulphur 94
opened for signature—14 June 1994
entered into force—5 August 1998
objective—to provide for a further reduction in national sulfur emissions or transboundary fluxes on a regional basis within Europe
parties—(29) Austria, Belgium, Bulgaria, Canada, Croatia, Cyprus, Czech Republic, Denmark, EU, Finland, France, Germany, Greece, Hungary, Ireland, Italy, Liechtenstein, Lithuania, Luxembourg, Macedonia, Monaco, Netherlands, Norway, Slovakia, Slovenia, Spain, Sweden, Switzerland, UK
countries that have signed, but not yet ratified—(3) Poland, Russia, Ukraine

Protocol to the 1979 Convention on Long-Range Transboundary Air Pollution on Persistent Organic Pollutants
note—abbreviated as Air Pollution-Persistent Organic Pollutants
opened for signature—24 June 1998
entered into force—23 October 2003
objective—to provide for the control, reduction, or elimination of discharges, emissions of persistent organic pollutants

parties—(33) Austria, Belgium, Bulgaria, Canada, Croatia, Cyprus, Czech Republic, Denmark, Estonia, EU, Finland, France, Germany, Hungary, Iceland, Italy, Latvia, Liechtenstein, Lithuania, Luxembourg, Macedonia, Moldova, Montenegro, Netherlands, Norway, Romania, Serbia, Slovakia, Slovenia, Spain, Sweden, Switzerland, UK
countries that have signed, but not yet ratified—(8) Armenia, Greece, Ireland, Poland, Portugal, Spain, Ukraine, US

Protocol to the 1979 Convention on Long-Range Transboundary Air Pollution on the Reduction of Sulphur Emissions or Their Transboundary Fluxes by at Least 30%

note—abbreviated as Air Pollution-Sulphur 85
opened for signature—8 July 1985
entered into force—2 September 1987
objective—to provide for national reductions in sulfur emissions or transboundary fluxes by 30% of 1980 emission or transboundary flux levels by no later than 1993
parties—(25) Albania, Austria, Belarus, Belgium, Bulgaria, Canada, Czech Republic, Denmark, Estonia, Finland, France, Germany, Hungary, Italy, Liechtenstein, Lithuania, Luxembourg, Macedonia, Netherlands, Norway, Russia, Slovakia, Sweden, Switzerland, Ukraine

Ship Pollution

see Protocol of 1978 Relating to the International Convention for the Prevention of Pollution From Ships, 1973 (MARPOL)

Treaty Banning Nuclear Weapon Tests in the Atmosphere, in Outer Space, and Under Water

note—abbreviated as Nuclear Test Ban
opened for signature—5 August 1963
entered into force—10 October 1963
objective—to ban nuclear weapons testing in the atmosphere, outer space, or under water
parties—(124) Afghanistan, Antigua and Barbuda, Argentina, Armenia, Australia, Austria, The Bahamas, Bangladesh, Belarus, Belgium, Benin, Bhutan, Bolivia, Bosnia and Herzegovina, Botswana, Brazil, Bulgaria, Burma, Canada, Cape Verde, Central African Republic, Chad, Chile, China, Colombia, Costa Rica, Cote d'Ivoire, Croatia, Cyprus, Czech Republic, Democratic Republic of the Congo, Denmark, Dominican Republic, Ecuador, Egypt, El Salvador, Fiji, Finland, Gabon, The Gambia, Germany, Ghana, Greece, Guatemala, Honduras, Hungary, Iceland, India, Indonesia, Iran, Iraq, Ireland, Israel, Italy, Jamaica, Japan, Jordan, Kenya, South Korea, Kuwait, Laos, Lebanon, Liberia, Libya, Luxembourg, Madagascar, Malawi, Malaysia, Malta, Mauritania, Mauritius, Mexico, Mongolia, Montenegro, Morocco, Nepal, Netherlands, New Zealand, Nicaragua, Niger, Nigeria, Norway, Panama, Pakistan, Papua New Guinea, Peru, Philippines, Poland, Romania, Russia, Rwanda, Samoa, San Marino, Senegal, Serbia, Seychelles, Sierra Leone, Singapore, Slovakia, Slovenia, South Africa, Spain, Sri Lanka, Sudan, Suriname, Swaziland, Sweden, Switzerland, Syria, Tanzania, Thailand, Togo, Tonga, Trinidad and Tobago, Tunisia, Turkey, Uganda, Ukraine, UK, US, Uruguay, Venezuela, Yemen, Zambia
countries that have signed, but not yet ratified—(11) Algeria, Burkina Faso, Burundi, Cameroon, Ethiopia, Haiti, Mali, Paraguay, Portugal, Somalia, Vietnam

Tropical Timber 83

see International Tropical Timber Agreement, 1983

Tropical Timber 94

see International Tropical Timber Agreement, 1994

United Nations Convention on the Law of the Sea (LOS)

note—abbreviated as Law of the Sea
opened for signature—10 December 1982
entered into force—16 November 1994
objective—to provide a comprehensive legal regime for the sea and oceans
parties—(164) Albania, Algeria, Angola, Antigua and Barbuda, Argentina, Armenia, Australia, Austria, The Bahamas, Bahrain, Bangladesh, Barbados, Belarus, Belgium, Belize, Benin, Bolivia, Bosnia and Herzegovina, Botswana, Brazil, Brunei, Bulgaria, Burkina Faso, Burma, Cameroon, Canada, Cape Verde, Chad, Chile, China, Comoros, Democratic Republic of the Congo, Republic of the Congo, Cook Islands, Costa Rica, Cote d'Ivoire, Croatia, Cuba, Cyprus, Czech Republic, Denmark, Djibouti, Dominica, Dominican Republic, Egypt, Equatorial Guinea, Estonia, EU, Fiji, Finland, France, Gabon, The Gambia, Georgia, Germany, Ghana, Greece, Grenada, Guatemala, Guinea, Guinea-Bissau, Guyana, Haiti, Honduras, Hungary, Iceland, India, Indonesia, Iraq, Ireland, Italy, Jamaica, Japan, Jordan, Kenya, Kiribati, South Korea, Kuwait, Laos, Latvia, Lebanon, Lesotho, Liberia, Lithuania, Luxembourg, Macedonia, Madagascar, Malawi, Malaysia, Maldives, Mali, Malta, Marshall Islands, Mauritania, Mauritius, Mexico, Federated States of Micronesia, Moldova, Monaco, Mongolia, Montenegro, Morocco, Mozambique, Namibia, Nauru, Nepal, Netherlands, NZ, Nicaragua, Nigeria, Niue, Norway, Oman, Pakistan, Palau, Panama, Papua New Guinea, Paraguay, Philippines, Poland, Portugal, Qatar, Romania, Russia, Saint Kitts and Nevis, Saint Lucia, Saint Vincent and the Grenadines, Samoa, Sao Tome and Principe, Saudi Arabia, Senegal, Serbia, Seychelles, Sierra Leone, Singapore, Slovakia, Slovenia, Solomon Islands, Somalia, South Africa, Spain, Sri Lanka, Sudan, Suriname, Swaziland, Sweden, Switzerland, Tanzania, Thailand, Timor-Liste, Togo, Tonga, Trinidad and Tobago, Tunisia, Tuvalu, Uganda, Ukraine, UK, Uruguay, Vanuatu, Vietnam, Yemen, Zambia, Zimbabwe
countries that have signed, but not yet ratified—(15) Afghanistan, Bhutan, Burundi, Cambodia, Central African Republic, Colombia, El Salvador, Ethiopia, Iran, North Korea, Libya, Liechtenstein, Niger, Rwanda, UAE

United Nations Convention to Combat Desertification in Those Countries Experiencing Serious Drought and/or Desertification, Particularly in Africa

note—abbreviated as Desertification
opened for signature—14 October 1994
entered into force—26 December 1996
objective—to combat desertification and mitigate the effects of drought through an integrated framework that is consistent with Agenda 21, employing international cooperation and partnership arrangements, and effective action at all levels
parties—(195) Afghanistan, Albania, Algeria, Andorra, Angola, Antigua and Barbuda, Argentina, Armenia, Australia, Austria, Azerbaijan, The Bahamas, Bahrain, Bangladesh, Barbados, Belarus, Belgium, Belize, Benin, Bhutan, Bolivia, Bosnia and Herzegovina, Botswana, Brazil, Brunei, Bulgaria, Burkina Faso, Burma, Burundi, Cambodia, Cameroon, Canada, Cape Verde, Central African

Republic, Chad, Chile, China, Colombia, Comoros, Democratic Republic of the Congo, Republic of the Congo, Cook Islands, Costa Rica, Cote d'Ivoire, Croatia, Cuba, Cyprus, Czech Republic, Denmark, Djibouti, Dominica, Dominican Republic, Ecuador, Egypt, El Salvador, Equatorial Guinea, Eritrea, Estonia, Ethiopia, EU, Fiji, Finland, France, Gabon, The Gambia, Georgia, Germany, Ghana, Greece, Grenada, Guatemala, Guinea, Guinea-Bissau, Guyana, Haiti, Honduras, Hungary, Iceland, India, Indonesia, Iran, Iraq, Ireland, Israel, Italy, Jamaica, Japan, Jordan, Kazakhstan, Kenya, Kiribati, North Korea, South Korea, Kuwait, Kyrgyzstan, Laos, Latvia, Lebanon, Lesotho, Liberia, Libya, Liechtenstein, Lithuania, Luxembourg, Macedonia, Madagascar, Malawi, Malaysia, Maldives, Mali, Malta, Marshall Islands, Mauritania, Mauritius, Mexico, Federated States of Micronesia, Moldova, Monaco, Mongolia, Montenegro, Morocco, Mozambique, Namibia, Nauru, Nepal, Netherlands, NZ, Nicaragua, Niger, Nigeria, Niue, Norway, Oman, Pakistan, Palau, Panama, Papua New Guinea, Paraguay, Peru, Philippines, Poland, Portugal, Qatar, Romania, Russia, Rwanda, Saint Kitts and Nevis, Saint Lucia, Saint Vincent and the Grenadines, Samoa, San Marino, Sao Tome and Principe, Saudi Arabia, Senegal, Serbia, Seychelles, Sierra Leone, Singapore, Slovakia, Slovenia, Solomon Islands, Somalia, South Africa, Spain, Sri Lanka, Sudan, Suriname, Swaziland, Sweden, Switzerland, Syria, Tanzania, Timor-Leste, Togo, Tonga, Trinidad and Tobago, Tunisia, Turkey, Turkmenistan, Tuvalu, Uganda, Ukraine, UAE, UK, US, Uruguay, Uzbekistan Vanu tu, Venezuela, Vietnam, Yemen, Zambia, Zimbabwe

United Nations Framework Convention on Climate Change
note—abbreviated as Climate Change
opened for signature—9 May 1992
entered into force—21 March 1994
objective—to achieve stabilization of greenhouse gas concentrations in the atmosphere at a low enough level to prevent dangerous anthropogenic interference with the climate system
parties—(195) Afghanistan, Albania, Algeria, Andorra, Angola, Antigua and Barbuda, Argentina, Armenia, Australia, Austria, Azerbaijan, The Bahamas, Bahrain, Bangladesh, Barbados, Belarus, Belgium, Belize, Benin, Bhutan, Bolivia, Bosnia and Herzegovina, Botswana, Brazil, Brunei, Bulgaria, Burkina Faso, Burma, Burundi, Cambodia, Cameroon, Canada, Cape Verde, Central African Republic, Chad, Chile, China, Colombia, Comoros, Democratic Republic of the Congo, Republic of the Congo, Cook Islands, Costa Rica, Cote d'Ivoire, Croatia, Cuba, Cyprus, Czech Republic, Denmark, Djibouti, Dominica, Dominican Republic, Ecuador, Egypt, El Salvador, Equatorial Guinea, Eritrea, Estonia, Ethiopia, EU, Fiji, Finland, France, Gabon, The Gambia, Georgia, Germany, Ghana, Greece, Grenada, Guatemala, Guinea, Guinea-Bissau, Guyana, Haiti, Honduras, Hungary, Iceland, India, Indonesia, Iran, Iraq, Ireland, Israel, Italy, Jamaica, Japan, Jordan, Kazakhstan, Kenya, Kiribati, North Korea, South Korea, Kuwait, Kyrgyzstan, Laos, Latvia, Lebanon, Lesotho, Liberia, Libya, Liechtenstein, Lithuania, Luxembourg, Macedonia, Madagascar, Malawi, Malaysia, Maldives, Mali, Malta, Marshall Islands, Mauritania, Mauritius, Mexico, Federated States of Micronesia, Moldova, Monaco, Mongolia, Montenegro, Morocco, Mozambique, Namibia, Nauru, Nepal, Netherlands, NZ, Nicaragua, Niger, Nigeria, Niue, Norway, Oman, Pakistan, Palau, Panama, Papua New Guinea, Paraguay, Peru, Philippines, Poland, Portugal, Qatar, Romania, Russia, Rwanda, Saint Kitts and Nevis, Saint Lucia, Saint Vincent and the Grenadines, Samoa, San Marino, Sao Tome and Principe, Saudi Arabia, Senegal, Serbia, Seychelles, Sierra Leone, Singapore, Slovakia, Slovenia, Solomon Islands, Somalia, South Africa, Spain, Sri Lanka, Sudan, Suriname, Swaziland, Sweden, Switzerland, Syria, Tajikistan, Tanzania, Thailand, Timor-Leste, Togo, Tonga, Trinidad and Tobago, Tunisia, Turkey, Turkmenistan, Tuvalu, Uganda, Ukraine, UAE, UK, US, Uruguay, Uzbekistan, Vanu tu, Venezuela, Vietnam, Yemen, Zambia, Zimbabwe

Wetlands
see Convention on Wetlands of International Importance Especially As Waterfowl Habitat (Ramsar)

Whaling
see International Convention for the Regulation of Whaling

CROSS-REFERENCE LIST OF COUNTRY DATA CODES

GEOPOLITICAL ENTITIES and CODES (formerly FIPS PUB 10-4): FIPS PUB 10-4 was withdrawn by the National Institute of Standards and Technology on September 2, 2008 based on Public Law 104-113 (codified OMB Circular A-119 and the National Technology Transfer and Advancement Act of 1995). The National Geospatial-Intelligence Agency (NGA), as the maintenance authority for FIPS PUB 10-4, has continued to maintain and provide regular updates to its content in a document known as Geopolitical Entities and Codes (GEC) (Formerly FIPS 1PUB 10-4).

ISO 3166: Codes for the Representation of Names of Countries (ISO 3166) is prepared by the International Organization for Standardization. ISO 3166 includes two- and three-character alphabetic codes and three-digit numeric codes that may be needed for activities involving exchange of data with international organizations that have adopted that standard. Except for the numeric codes, ISO 3166 codes have been adopted in the US as FIPS 104-1: American National Standard Codes for the Representation of Names of Countries, Dependencies, and Areas of Special Sovereignty for Information Interchange.

STANAG 1059: Letter Codes for Geographical Entities (8th edition, 2004) is a Standardization Agreement (STANAG) established and maintained by the North Atlantic Treaty Organization (NATO/OTAN) for the purpose of providing a common set of geo-spatial identifiers for countries, territories, and possessions. The 8th edition established trigraph codes for each country based upon the ISO 3166-1 alpha-3 character sets. These codes are used throughout NATO.

Internet: The Internet country code is the two-letter digraph maintained by the International Organization for Standardization (ISO) in the ISO 3166 Alpha-2 list and used by the Internet Assigned Numbers Authority (IANA) to establish country-coded top-level domains (ccTLDs).

Entity	GEC	ISO 3166			Stanag	Internet	Comment
Afghanistan	AF	AF	AFG	004	AFG	.af	
Akrotiri	AX	–	–	–	–	–	
Albania	AL	AL	ALB	008	ALB	.al	
Algeria	AG	DZ	DZA	012	DZA	.dz	
American Samoa	AQ	AS	ASM	016	ASM	.as	
Andorra	AN	AD	AND	020	AND	.ad	
Angola	AO	AO	AGO	024	AGO	.ao	
Anguilla	AV	AI	AIA	660	AIA	.ai	
Antarctica	AY	AQ	ATA	010	ATA	.aq	ISO defines as the territory south of 60 degrees south latitude
Antigua and Barbuda	AC	AG	ATG	028	ATG	.ag	
Argentina	AR	AR	ARG	032	ARG	.ar	
Armenia	AM	AM	ARM	051	ARM	.am	
Aruba	AA	AW	ABW	533	ABW	.aw	
Ashmore and Cartier Islands	AT	–	–	–	AUS	–	ISO includes with Australia
Australia	AS	AU	AUS	036	AUS	.au	ISO includes Ashmore and Cartier Islands, Coral Sea Islands
Austria	AU	AT	AUT	040	AUT	.at	
Azerbaijan	AJ	AZ	AZE	031	AZE	.az	
Bahamas, The	BF	BS	BHS	044	BHS	.bs	
Bahrain	BA	BH	BHR	048	BHR	.bh	
Baker Island	FQ	–	–	–	UMI	–	ISO includes with the US Minor Outlying Islands
Bangladesh	BG	BD	BGD	050	BGD	.bd	
Barbados	BB	BB	BRB	052	BRB	.bb	

Entity	GEC	ISO 3166		Stanag	Internet	Comment
Bassas da India	BS	–	–	–	–	–	administered as part of French Southern and Antarctic Lands; no ISO codes assigned
Belarus	BO	BY	BLR	112	BLR	.by	
Belgium	BE	BE	BEL	056	BEL	.be	
Belize	BH	BZ	BLZ	084	BLZ	.bz	
Benin	BN	BJ	BEN	204	BEN	.bj	
Bermuda	BD	BM	BMU	060	BMU	.bm	
Bhutan	BT	BT	BTN	064	BTN	.bt	
Bolivia	BL	BO	BOL	068	BOL	.bo	
Bosnia and Herzegovina	BK	BA	BIH	070	BIH	.ba	
Botswana	BC	BW	BWA	072	BWA	.bw	
Bouvet Island	BV	BV	BVT	074	BVT	.bv	
Brazil	BR	BR	BRA	076	BRA	.br	
British Indian Ocean Territory	IO	IO	IOT	086	IOT	.io	
British Virgin Islands	VI	VG	VGB	092	VGB	.vg	
Brunei	BX	BN	BRN	096	BRN	.bn	
Bulgaria	BU	BG	BGR	100	BGR	.bg	
Burkina Faso	UV	BF	BFA	854	BFA	.bf	
Burma	BM	MM	MMR	104	MMR	.mm	ISO uses the name Myanmar
Burundi	BY	BI	BDI	108	BDI	.bi	
Cabo Verde	CV	CV	CPV	132	CPV	.cv	
Cambodia	CB	KH	KHM	116	KHM	.kh	
Cameroon	CM	CM	CMR	120	CMR	.cm	
Canada	CA	CA	CAN	124	CAN	.ca	
Cayman Islands	CJ	KY	CYM	136	CYM	.ky	
Central African Republic	CT	CF	CAF	140	CAF	.cf	
Chad	CD	TD	TCD	148	TCD	.td	
Chile	CI	CL	CHL	152	CHL	.cl	
China	CH	CN	CHN	156	CHN	.cn	see also Taiwan
Christmas Island	KT	CX	CXR	162	CXR	.cx	
Clipperton Island	IP	–	–	–	FYP	–	ISO includes with France
Cocos (Keeling) Islands	CK	CC	CCK	166	AUS	.cc	
Colombia	CO	CO	COL	170	COL	.co	
Comoros	CN	KM	COM	174	COM	.km	
Congo, Democratic Republic of the	CG	CD	COD	180	COD	.cd	formerly Zaire
Congo, Republic of the	CF	CG	COG	178	COG	.cg	
Cook Islands	CW	CK	COK	184	COK	.ck	
Coral Sea Islands	CR	–	–	–	AUS	–	ISO includes with Australia

Entity	GEC		ISO 3166		Stanag	Internet	Comment
Costa Rica	CS	CR	CRI	188	CRI	.cr	
Cote d'Ivoire	IV	CI	CIV	384	CIV	.ci	
Croatia	HR	HR	HRV	191	HRV	.hr	
Cuba	CU	CU	CUB	192	CUB	.cu	
Curacao	UC	CW	CUW	531	–	.cw	
Cyprus	CY	CY	CYP	196	CYP	.cy	
Czech Republic	EZ	CZ	CZE	203	CZE	.cz	
Denmark	DA	DK	DNK	208	DNK	.dk	
Dhekelia	DX	–	–	–	–	–	
Djibouti	DJ	DJ	DJI	262	DJI	.dj	
Dominica	DO	DM	DMA	212	DMA	.dm	
Dominican Republic	DR	DO	DOM	214	DOM	.do	
Ecuador	EC	EC	ECU	218	ECU	.ec	
Egypt	EG	EG	EGY	818	EGY	.eg	
El Salvador	ES	SV	SLV	222	SLV	.sv	
Equatorial Guinea	EK	GQ	GNQ	226	GNQ	.gq	
Eritrea	ER	ER	ERI	232	ERI	.er	
Estonia	EN	EE	EST	233	EST	.ee	
Ethiopia	ET	ET	ETH	231	ETH	.et	
Europa Island	EU	–	–	–	–	–	administered as part of French Southern and Antarctic Lands; no ISO codes assigned
Falkland Islands (Islas Malvinas)	FK	FK	FLK	238	FLK	.fk	
Faroe Islands	FO	FO	FRO	234	FRO	.fo	
Fiji	FJ	FJ	FJI	242	FJI	.fj	
Finland	FI	FI	FIN	246	FIN	.fi	
France	FR	FR	FRA	250	FRA	.fr	ISO includes metropolitan France along with the dependencies of Clipperton Island, French Guiana, French Polynesia, French Southern and Antarctic Lands, Guadeloupe, Martinique, Mayotte, New Caledonia, Reunion, Saint Pierre and Miquelon, Wallis and Futuna
France, Metropolitan	–	FX	FXX	249	–	.fx	ISO limits to the European part of France
French Guiana	FG	GF	GUF	254	GUF	.gf	
French Polynesia	FP	PF	PYF	258	PYF	.pf	
French Southern and Antarctic Lands	FS	TF	ATF	260	ATF	.tf	FIPS 10-4 does not include the French-claimed portion of Antarctica (Terre Adelie)
Gabon	GB	GA	GAB	266	GAB	.ga	

Entity	GEC	ISO 3166			Stanag	Internet	Comment
Gambia, The	GA	GM	GMB	270	GMB	.gm	
Gaza Strip	GZ	PS	PSE	275	PSE	.ps	ISO identifies as Occupied Palestinian Territory
Georgia	GG	GE	GEO	268	GEO	.ge	
Germany	GM	DE	DEU	276	DEU	.de	
Ghana	GH	GH	GHA	288	GHA	.gh	
Gibraltar	GI	GI	GIB	292	GIB	.gi	
Glorioso Islands	GO	–	–	–	–	–	administered as part of French Southern and Antarctic Lands; no ISO codes assigned
Greece	GR	GR	GRC	300	GRC	.gr	For its internal communications, the European Union recommends the use of the code EL in lieu of the ISO 3166-2 code of GR
Greenland	GL	GL	GRL	304	GRL	.gl	
Grenada	GJ	GD	GRD	308	GRD	.gd	
Guadeloupe	GP	GP	GLP	312	GLP	.gp	
Guam	GQ	GU	GUM	316	GUM	.gu	
Guatemala	GT	GT	GTM	320	GTM	.gt	
Guernsey	GK	GG	GGY	831	UK	.gg	
Guinea	GV	GN	GIN	324	GIN	.gn	
Guinea-Bissau	PU	GW	GNB	624	GNB	.gw	
Guyana	GY	GY	GUY	328	GUY	.gy	
Haiti	HA	HT	HTI	332	HTI	.ht	
Heard Island and McDonald Islands	HM	HM	HMD	334	HMD	.hm	
Holy See (Vatican City)	VT	VA	VAT	336	VAT	.va	
Honduras	HO	HN	HND	340	HND	.hn	
Hong Kong	HK	HK	HKG	344	HKG	.hk	
Howland Island	HQ	–	–	–	UMI	–	ISO includes with the US Minor Outlying Islands
Hungary	HU	HU	HUN	348	HUN	.hu	
Iceland	IC	IS	ISL	352	ISL	.is	
India	IN	IN	IND	356	IND	.in	
Indonesia	ID	ID	IDN	360	IDN	.id	
Iran	IR	IR	IRN	364	IRN	.ir	
Iraq	IZ	IQ	IRQ	368	IRQ	.iq	
Ireland	EI	IE	IRL	372	IRL	.ie	
Isle of Man	IM	IM	IMN	833	UK	.im	
Israel	IS	IL	ISR	376	ISR	.il	
Italy	IT	IT	ITA	380	ITA	.it	
Jamaica	JM	JM	JAM	388	JAM	.jm	

Entity	GEC	ISO 3166			Stanag	Internet	Comment
Jan Mayen	JN	–	–	–	SJM	–	ISO includes with Svalbard
Japan	JA	JP	JPN	392	JPN	.jp	
Jarvis Island	DQ	–	–	–	UMI	–	ISO includes with the US Minor Outlying Islands
Jersey	JE	JE	JEY	832	UK	.je	
Johnston Atoll	JQ	–	–	–	UMI	–	ISO includes with the US Minor Outlying Islands
Jordan	JO	JO	JOR	400	JOR	.jo	
Juan de Nova Island	JU	–	–	–	–	–	administered as part of French Southern and Antarctic Lands; no ISO codes assigned
Kazakhstan	KZ	KZ	KAZ	398	KAZ	.kz	
Kenya	KE	KE	KEN	404	KEN	.ke	
Kingman Reef	KQ	–	–	–	UMI	–	ISO includes with the US Minor Outlying Islands
Kiribati	KR	KI	KIR	296	KIR	.ki	
Korea, North	KN	KP	PRK	408	PRK	.kp	
Korea, South	KS	KR	KOR	410	KOR	.kr	
Kosovo	KV	XK	XKS	–	–	–	XK and XKS are ISO 3166 user assigned codes; ISO 3166 Maintenace Authority has not assigned codes
Kuwait	KU	KW	KWT	414	KWT	.kw	
Kyrgyzstan	KG	KG	KGZ	417	KGZ	.kg	
Laos	LA	LA	LAO	418	LAO	.la	
Latvia	LG	LV	LVA	428	LVA	.lv	
Lebanon	LE	LB	LBN	422	LBN	.lb	
Lesotho	LT	LS	LSO	426	LSO	.ls	
Liberia	LI	LR	LBR	430	LBR	.lr	
Libya	LY	LY	LBY	434	LBY	.ly	
Liechtenstein	LS	LI	LIE	438	LIE	.li	
Lithuania	LH	LT	LTU	440	LTU	.lt	
Luxembourg	LU	LU	LUX	442	LUX	.lu	
Macau	MC	MO	MAC	446	MAC	.mo	
Macedonia	MK	MK	MKD	807	FYR	.mk	
Madagascar	MA	MG	MDG	450	MDG	.mg	
Malawi	MI	MW	MWI	454	MWI	.mw	
Malaysia	MY	MY	MYS	458	MYS	.my	
Maldives	MV	MV	MDV	462	MDV	.mv	
Mali	ML	ML	MLI	466	MLI	.ml	
Malta	MT	MT	MLT	470	MLT	.mt	
Marshall Islands	RM	MH	MHL	584	MHL	.mh	

Entity	GEC		ISO 3166		Stanag	Internet	Comment
Martinique	MB	MQ	MTQ	474	MTQ	.mq	
Mauritania	MR	MR	MRT	478	MRT	.mr	
Mauritius	MP	MU	MUS	480	MUS	.mu	
Mayotte	MF	YT	MYT	175	FRA	.yt	
Mexico	MX	MX	MEX	484	MEX	.mx	
Micronesia, Federated States of	FM	FM	FSM	583	FSM	.fm	
Midway Islands	MQ	–	–	–	UMI	–	ISO includes with the US Minor Outlying Islands
Moldova	MD	MD	MDA	498	MDA	.md	
Monaco	MN	MC	MCO	492	MCO	.mc	
Mongolia	MG	MN	MNG	496	MNG	.mn	
Montenegro	MJ	ME	MNE	499	MNE	.me	
Montserrat	MH	MS	MSR	500	MSR	.ms	
Morocco	MO	MA	MAR	504	MAR	.ma	
Mozambique	MZ	MZ	MOZ	508	MOZ	.mz	
Myanmar	–	–	–	–	–	–	see Burma
Namibia	WA	NA	NAM	516	NAM	.na	
Nauru	NR	NR	NRU	520	NRU	.nr	
Navassa Island	BQ	–	–	–	UMI	–	ISO includes with the US Minor Outlying Islands
Nepal	NP	NP	NPL	524	NPL	.np	
Netherlands	NL	NL	NLD	528	NLD	.nl	
Netherlands Antilles	NT				ANT	.an	disestablished in October 2010 this entity no longer exists; ISO deleted the codes in December 2010
New Caledonia	NC	NC	NCL	540	NCL	.nc	
New Zealand	NZ	NZ	NZL	554	NZL	.nz	
Nicaragua	NU	NI	NIC	558	NIC	.ni	
Niger	NG	NE	NER	562	NER	.ne	
Nigeria	NI	NG	NGA	566	NGA	.ng	
Niue	NE	NU	NIU	570	NIU	.nu	
Norfolk Island	NF	NF	NFK	574	NFK	.nf	
Northern Mariana Islands	CQ	MP	MNP	580	MNP	.mp	
Norway	NO	NO	NOR	578	NOR	.no	
Oman	MU	OM	OMN	512	OMN	.om	
Pakistan	PK	PK	PAK	586	PAK	.pk	
Palau	PS	PW	PLW	585	PLW	.pw	
Palmyra Atoll	LQ	–	–	–	UMI	–	ISO includes with the US Minor Outlying Islands
Panama	PM	PA	PAN	591	PAN	.pa	

Entity	GEC		ISO 3166		Stanag	Internet	Comment
Papua New Guinea	PP	PG	PNG	598	PNG	.pg	
Paracel Islands	PF	–	–	–	–	–	
Paraguay	PA	PY	PRY	600	PRY	.py	
Peru	PE	PE	PER	604	PER	.pe	
Philippines	RP	PH	PHL	608	PHL	.ph	
Pitcairn Islands	PC	PN	PCN	612	PCN	.pn	
Poland	PL	PL	POL	616	POL	.pl	
Portugal	PO	PT	PRT	620	PRT	.pt	
Puerto Rico	RQ	PR	PRI	630	PRI	.pr	
Qatar	QA	QA	QAT	634	QAT	.qa	
Reunion	RE	RE	REU	638	REU	.re	
Romania	RO	RO	ROU	642	ROU	.ro	
Russia	RS	RU	RUS	643	RUS	.ru	
Rwanda	RW	RW	RWA	646	RWA	.rw	
Saint Barthelemy	TB	BL	BLM	652	–	.bl	ccTLD .fr and .gp may also be used
Saint Helena, Ascension, and Tristan da Cunha	SH	SH	SHN	654	SHN	.sh	includes Saint Helena Island, Ascension Island, and the Tristan da Cunha archipelago
Saint Kitts and Nevis	SC	KN	KNA	659	KNA	.kn	
Saint Lucia	ST	LC	LCA	662	LCA	.lc	
Saint Martin	RN	MF	MAF	663	–	.mf	ccTLD .fr and .gp may also be used
Saint Pierre and Miquelon	SB	PM	SPM	666	SPM	.pm	
Saint Vincent and the Grenadines	VC	VC	VCT	670	VCT	.vc	
Samoa	WS	WS	WSM	882	WSM	.ws	
San Marino	SM	SM	SMR	674	SMR	.sm	
Sao Tome and Principe	TP	ST	STP	678	STP	.st	
Saudi Arabia	SA	SA	SAU	682	SAU	.sa	
Senegal	SG	SN	SEN	686	SEN	.sn	
Serbia	RI	RS	SRB	688	–	.rs	
Seychelles	SE	SC	SYC	690	SYC	.sc	
Sierra Leone	SL	SL	SLE	694	SLE	.sl	
Singapore	SN	SG	SGP	702	SGP	.sg	
Sint Maarten	NN	SX	SXM	534	–	.sx	
Slovakia	LO	SK	SVK	703	SVK	.sk	
Slovenia	SI	SI	SVN	705	SVN	.si	
Solomon Islands	BP	SB	SLB	090	SLB	.sb	
Somalia	SO	SO	SOM	706	SOM	.so	
South Africa	SF	ZA	ZAF	710	ZAF	.za	

Entity	GEC	ISO 3166		Stanag	Internet	Comment
South Georgia and the Islands	SX	GS	SGS	239	SGS	.gs	
South Sudan	OD	SS	SSD	728	–	–	IANA has designated .ss as the ccTLD for South Sudan, however it has not been activated in DNS root zone
Spain	SP	ES	ESP	724	ESP	.es	
Spratly Islands	PG	–	–	–	–	–	
Sri Lanka	CE	LK	LKA	144	LKA	.lk	
Sudan	SU	SD	SDN	729	SDN	.sd	
Suriname	NS	SR	SUR	740	SUR	.sr	
Svalbard	SV	SJ	SJM	744	SJM	.sj	ISO includes Jan Mayen
Swaziland	WZ	SZ	SWZ	748	SWZ	.sz	
Sweden	SW	SE	SWE	752	SWE	.se	
Switzerland	SZ	CH	CHE	756	CHE	.ch	
Syria	SY	SY	SYR	760	SYR	.sy	
Taiwan	TW	TW	TWN	158	TWN	.tw	
Tajikistan	TI	TJ	TJK	762	TJK	.tj	
Tanzania	TZ	TZ	TZA	834	TZA	.tz	
Thailand	TH	TH	THA	764	THA	.th	
Timor-Leste	TT	TL	TLS	626	TLS	.tl	
Togo	TO	TG	TGO	768	TGO	.tg	
Tokelau	TL	TK	TKL	772	TKL	.tk	
Tonga	TN	TO	TON	776	TON	.to	
Trinidad and Tobago	TD	TT	TTO	780	TTO	.tt	
Tromelin Island	TE	–	–	–	–	–	administered as part of French Southern and Antarctic Lands; no ISO codes assigned
Tunisia	TS	TN	TUN	788	TUN	.tn	
Turkey	TU	TR	TUR	792	TUR	.tr	
Turkmenistan	TX	TM	TKM	795	TKM	.tm	
Turks and Caicos Islands	TK	TC	TCA	796	TCA	.tc	
Tuvalu	TV	TV	TUV	798	TUV	.tv	
Uganda	UG	UG	UGA	800	UGA	.ug	
Ukraine	UP	UA	UKR	804	UKR	.ua	
United Arab Emirates	AE	AE	ARE	784	ARE	.ae	
United Kingdom	UK	GB	GBR	826	GBR	.uk	for its internal communications, the European Union recommends the use of the code UK in lieu of the ISO 3166-2 code of GB
United States	US	US	USA	840	USA	.us	

Entity	GEC	ISO 3166		Stanag	Internet	Comment
United States Minor Outlying Islands	–	UM	UMI	581	–	.um	ISO includes Baker Island, Howland Island, Jarvis Island, Johnston Atoll, Kingman Reef, Midway Islands, Navassa Island, Palmyra Atoll, Wake Island
Uruguay	UY	UY	URY	858	URY	.uy	
Uzbekistan	UZ	UZ	UZB	860	UZB	.uz	
Vanuatu	NH	VU	VUT	548	VUT	.vu	
Venezuela	VE	VE	VEN	862	VEN	.ve	
Vietnam	VM	VN	VNM	704	VNM	.vn	
Virgin Islands	VQ	VI	VIR	850	VIR	.vi	
Virgin Islands (UK)	–	–	–	–	–	.vg	see British Virgin Islands
Virgin Islands (US)	–	–	–	–	–	.vi	see Virgin Islands
Wake Island	WQ	–	–	–	UMI	–	ISO includes with the US Minor Outlying Islands
Wallis and Futuna	WF	WF	WLF	876	WLF	.wf	
West Bank	WE	PS	PSE	275	PSE	.ps	ISO identifies as Occupied Palestinian Territory
Western Sahara	WI	EH	ESH	732	ESH	.eh	
Western Samoa	–	–	–	–	–	.ws	see Samoa
World	–	–	–	–	–	–	the Factbook uses the W data code from DIAM 65-18 Geopolitical Data Elements and Related Features, Data Standard No. 3, December 1994, published by the Defense Intelligence Agency
Yemen	YM	YE	YEM	887	YEM	.ye	
Zaire	–	–	–	–	–	–	see Democratic Republic of the Congo
Zambia	ZA	ZM	ZMB	894	ZMB	.zm	
Zimbabwe	ZI	ZW	ZWE	716	ZWE	.zw	

APPENDIX E

CROSS-REFERENCE LIST OF HYDROGRAPHIC DATA CODES

IHO 23-4th: *Limits of Oceans and Seas,* Special Publication 23, Draft 4th Edition 1986, published by the International Hydrographic Bureau of the International Hydrographic Organization.

IHO 23-3rd: *Limits of Oceans and Seas,* Special Publication 23, 3rd Edition 1953, published by the International Hydrographic Organization.

ACIC M 49-1: *Chart of Limits of Seas and Oceans,* revised January 1958, published by the Aeronautical Chart and Information Center (ACIC), United States Air Force.

DIAM 65-18: *Geopolitical Data Elements and Related Features,* Data Standard No. 4, Defense Intelligence Agency Manual 65-18, December 1994, published by the Defense Intelligence Agency. The US Government has not yet adopted a standard for hydrographic codes similar to the Federal Information Processing Standards (FIPS) 10-4 country codes. The names and limits of the following oceans and seas are not always directly comparable because of differences in the customers, needs, and requirements of the individual organizations. Even the number of principal water bodies varies from organization to organization. *Factbook* users, for example, find the Atlantic Ocean and Pacific Ocean entries useful, but none of the following standards include those oceans in their entirety. Nor is there any provision for combining codes or overcodes to aggregate water bodies. The recently delimited Southern Ocean is not included.

Principal Oceans and Seas of the World With Hydrographic Codes by Institution

	IHO 23-4th	IHO 23-3rd*	ACIC M 49-1	DIAM 65-18
Arctic Ocean	9	17	A	5A
Atlantic Ocean	–	–	–	–
Baltic Sea	2	1	B26	7B
Eastern Mediterranean	3.1.2	28 B	–	8E
Indian Ocean	5	45	F	6A
Mediterranean Sea	3.1	28	B11	–
North Atlantic Ocean	1	23	B	1A
North Pacific Ocean	7	57	D	3A
Pacific Ocean	–	–	–	–
South Atlantic Ocean	4	32	C	2A
South China and Eastern Archipelagic Seas	6	49, 48	D18 plus others	3U plus others
South Pacific Ocean	8	61	E	4A
Western Mediterranean	3.1.1	28 A	–	8W

*The letters after the numbers are subdivisions, not footnotes.

CROSS-REFERENCE LIST OF GEOGRAPHIC NAMES

Name	Entry in *The World Factbook*	Latitude (deg min)	Longitude (deg min)
Abidjan (capital)	Cote d'Ivoire	5 19 N	4 02 W
Abkhazia (region)	Georgia	43 00 N	41 00 E
Abu Dhabi (capital)	United Arab Emirates	24 28 N	54 22 E
Abu Musa (island)	Iran	25 52 N	55 03 E
Abuja (capital)	Nigeria	9 12 N	7 11 E
Abyssinia (former name for Ethiopia)	Ethiopia	8 00 N	38 00 E
Acapulco (city)	Mexico	16 51 N	99 55 W
Accra (capital)	Ghana	5 33 N	0 13 W
Adamstown (capital)	Pitcairn Islands	25 04 S	130 05 W
Addis Ababa (capital)	Ethiopia	9 02 N	38 42 E
Adelie Land (claimed by France; also Terre Adelie)	Antarctica	66 30 S	139 00 E
Aden (city)	Yemen	12 46 N	45 01 E
Aden, Gulf of	Indian Ocean	12 30 N	48 00 E
Admiralty Island	United States (Alaska)	57 44 N	134 20 W
Admiralty Islands	Papua New Guinea	2 10 S	147 00 E
Adriatic Sea	Atlantic Ocean	42 30 N	16 00 E
Adygey (region)	Russia	44 30 N	40 10 E
Aegean Islands	Greece	38 00 N	25 00 E
Aegean Sea	Atlantic Ocean	38 30 N	25 00 E
Afars and Issas, French Territory of the (or FTAI; former name for Djibouti)	Djibouti	11 30 N	43 00 E
Afghanestan (local name for Afghanistan)	Afghanistan	33 00 N	65 00 E
Agalega Islands	Mauritius	10 25 S	56 40 E
Agana (city; former name for Hagatna)	Guam	13 28 N	144 45 E
Ajaccio (city)	France (Corsica)	41 55 N	8 44 E
Ajaria (region)	Georgia	41 45 N	42 10 E
Akmola (city; former name for Astana)	Kazakhstan	51 10 N	71 30 E
Aksai Chin (region)	China (de facto), India (claimed)	35 00 N	79 00 E
Al Arabiyah as Suudiyah (local name for Saudi Arabia)	Saudi Arabia	25 00 N	45 00 E
Al Bahrayn (local name for Bahrain)	Bahrain	26 00 N	50 33 E
Al Imarat al Arabiyah al Muttahidah (local name for the United Arab Emirates)	United Arab Emirates	24 00 N	54 00 E
Al Iraq (local name for Iraq)	Iraq	33 00 N	44 00 E
Al Jaza'ir (local name for Algeria)	Algeria	28 00 N	3 00 E
Al Kuwayt (local name for Kuwait)	Kuwait	29 30 N	45 45 E
Al Maghrib (local name for Morocco)	Morocco	32 00 N	5 00 W
Al Urdun (local name for Jordan)	Jordan	31 00 N	36 00 E
Al Yaman (local name for Yemen)	Yemen	15 00 N	48 00 E
Aland Islands	Finland	60 15 N	20 00 E
Alaska (state)	United States	65 00 N	153 00 W

Name	Entry in *The World Factbook*	Latitude (deg min)	Longitude (deg min)
Alaska, Gulf of	Pacific Ocean	58 00 N	145 00 W
Alboran Sea	Atlantic Ocean	36 00 N	2 30 W
Aldabra Islands (Groupe d'Aldabra)	Seychelles	9 25 S	46 22 E
Alderney (island)	Guernsey	49 43 N	2 12 W
Aleutian Islands	United States (Alaska)	52 00 N	176 00 W
Alexander Archipelago (island group)	United States (Alaska)	57 00 N	134 00 W
Alexander Island	Antarctica	71 00 S	70 00 W
Alexandretta (region; former name for Iskenderun)	Turkey	36 34 N	36 08 E
Alexandria (city)	Egypt	31 12 N	29 54 E
Algiers (capital)	Algeria	36 47 N	2 03 E
Alhucemas, Penon de (island group)	Spain	35 13 N	3 53 W
Alma-Ata (city; former name for Almaty)	Kazakhstan	43 15 N	76 57 E
Almaty (former capital)	Kazakhstan	43 15 N	76 57 E
Alofi (capital)	Niue	19 01 S	169 55 W
Alphonse Island	Seychelles	7 01 S	52 45 E
Alsace (region)	France	48 30 N	7 20 E
Amami Strait	Pacific Ocean	28 40 N	129 30 E
Amindivi Islands (former name for Laccadive Islands)	India	11 30 N	72 30 E
Amirante Isles (island group; also Les Amirantes)	Seychelles	6 00 S	53 10 E
Amman (capital)	Jordan	31 57 N	35 56 E
Amsterdam (capital)	Netherlands	52 23 N	4 54 E
Amsterdam Island (Ile Amsterdam)	French Southern and Antarctic Lands	37 52 S	77 32 E
Amundsen Sea	Southern Ocean	72 30 S	112 00 W
Amur River	China, Russia	52 56 N	141 10 E
Amurskiy Liman (strait)	Pacific Ocean	53 00 N	141 30 E
Anadyrskiy Zaliv (gulf)	Pacific Ocean	64 00 N	177 00 E
Anatolia (region)	Turkey	39 00 N	35 00 E
Andaman Islands	India	12 00 N	92 45 E
Andaman Sea	Indian Ocean	10 00 N	95 00 E
Andorra la Vella (capital)	Andorra	42 30 N	1 30 E
Andros (island)	Greece	37 45 N	24 42 E
Andros Island	The Bahamas	24 26 N	77 57 W
Anegada Passage	Atlantic Ocean	18 30 N	63 40 W
Angkor Wat (ruins)	Cambodia	13 26 N	103 50 E
Anglo-Egyptian Sudan (former name for Sudan)	Sudan	15 00 N	30 00 E
Anjouan (island)	Comoros	12 15 S	44 25 E
Ankara (capital)	Turkey	39 56 N	32 52 E
Annobon (island)	Equatorial Guinea	1 25 S	5 36 E
Antananarivo (capital)	Madagascar	18 52 S	47 30 E
Antigua (island)	Antigua and Barbuda	14 34 N	90 44 W
Antipodes Islands	New Zealand	49 41 S	178 43 E
Antwerp (city)	Belgium	51 13 N	4 25 E
Aomen (local Chinese short-form name for Macau)	Macau	22 10 N	113 33 E
Aozou Strip (region)	Chad	22 00 N	18 00 E
Apia (capital)	Samoa	13 50 S	171 44 W

Name	Entry in *The World Factbook*	Latitude (deg min)	Longitude (deg min)
Aqaba, Gulf of	Indian Ocean	29 00 N	34 30 E
Arab, Shatt al (river)	Iran, Iraq	29 57 N	48 34 E
Arabian Sea	Indian Ocean	15 00 N	65 00 E
Arafura Sea	Pacific Ocean	9 00 S	133 00 E
Aral Sea	Kazakhstan, Uzbekistan	45 00 N	60 00 E
Argun River	China, Russia	53 20 N	121 28 E
Aru Sea	Pacific Ocean	6 15 S	135 00 E
As-Sudan (local name for Sudan)	Sudan	15 00 N	30 00 E
Ascension Island	Saint Helena, Ascension, and Tristan da Cunha	7 57 S	14 22 W
Ashgabat, Ashkhabad (capital)	Turkmenistan	37 57 N	58 23 E
Asmara, Asmera (capital)	Eritrea	15 20 N	38 53 E
Assumption Island	Seychelles	9 46 S	46 34 E
Astana (capital; formerly Akmola)	Kazakhstan	51 10 N	71 30 E
Asuncion (capital)	Paraguay	25 16 S	57 40 W
Asuncion Island	Northern Mariana Islands	19 40 N	145 24 E
Atacama (desert)	Chile	23 00 S	70 10 W
Atacama (region)	Chile	24 30 S	69 15 W
Athens (capital)	Greece	37 59 N	23 44 E
Attu Island	United States	52 55 N	172 57 E
Auckland (city)	New Zealand	36 52 S	174 46 E
Auckland Islands	New Zealand	51 00 S	166 30 E
Australes, Iles (island group; also Iles Tubuai)	French Polynesia	23 20 S	151 00 W
Avarua (capital)	Cook Islands	21 12 S	159 46 W
Axel Heiberg Island	Canada	79 30 N	90 00 W
Azad Kashmir (region)	Pakistan	34 30 N	74 00 E
Azarbaycan, Azerbaidzhan (local name for Azerbaijan)	Azerbaijan	40 30 N	47 30 E
Azores (islands)	Portugal	38 30 N	28 00 W
Azov, Sea of	Atlantic Ocean	49 00 N	36 00 E
Bab el Mandeb (strait)	Indian Ocean	12 40 N	43 20 E
Babuyan Channel	Pacific Ocean	18 44 N	121 40 E
Babuyan Islands	Philippines	19 10 N	121 40 E
Baffin Bay	Arctic Ocean	73 00 N	66 00 W
Baffin Island	Canada	68 00 N	70 00 W
Baghdad (capital)	Iraq	33 21 N	44 25 E
Baku (capital; also Baki, Baky)	Azerbaijan	40 23 N	49 51 E
Balabac Strait	Pacific Ocean	7 35 N	117 00 E
Balearic Islands	Spain	39 30 N	3 00 E
Balearic Sea (Iberian Sea)	Atlantic Ocean (Mediterranean Sea)	40 30 N	2 00 E
Bali (island)	Indonesia	8 20 S	115 00 E
Bali Sea	Indian Ocean	7 45 S	115 30 E
Balintang Channel	Pacific Ocean	19 49 N	121 40 E
Balintang Islands	Philippines	19 55 N	122 10 E

Name	Entry in *The World Factbook*	Latitude (deg min)	Longitude (deg min)
Balkan Peninsula	Albania, Bosnia and Herzegovina, Bulgaria, Croatia, Greece, Kosovo, Macedonia, Montenegro, Romania, Serbia, Slovenia, Turkey (European part)	42 00 N	23 00 E
Balleny Islands	Antarctica	67 00 S	163 00 E
Balochistan (region)	Pakistan	28 00 N	63 00 E
Baltic Sea	Atlantic Ocean	57 00 N	19 00 E
Bamako (capital)	Mali	12 39 N	8 00 W
Banaba (Ocean Island)	Kiribati	0 52 S	169 35 E
Banat (region)	Hungary, Romania, Serbia	45 30 N	21 00 E
Banda Sea	Pacific Ocean	5 00 S	128 00 E
Bandar Seri Begawan (capital)	Brunei	4 53 N	114 56 E
Bangka (island)	Indonesia	2 30 S	106 00 E
Bangkok (capital)	Thailand	13 45 N	100 31 E
Bangui (capital)	Central African Republic	4 22 N	18 35 E
Banjul (capital)	The Gambia	13 28 N	16 39 W
Banks Island	Canada	75 15 N	121 30 W
Banks Island	Australia	10 12 S	142 16 E
Banks Islands (Iles Banks)	Vanuatu	14 00 S	167 30 E
Barbuda (island)	Antigua and Barbuda	17 38 N	61 48 W
Barcelona (city)	Spain	41 25 N	2 13 E
Barents Sea	Arctic Ocean	74 00 N	36 00 E
Barranquilla (city)	Colombia	10 59 N	74 48 W
Bashi Channel	Pacific Ocean	22 00 N	121 00 E
Basilan Strait	Pacific Ocean	6 49 N	122 05 E
Basque Provinces	Spain	43 00 N	2 30 W
Bass Strait	Pacific Ocean	39 20 S	145 30 E
Bassas da India	Indian Ocean	21 30 S	39 50 E
Basse-Terre (capital)	France (Guadeloupe)	16 00 N	61 44 W
Basseterre (capital)	Saint Kitts and Nevis	17 18 N	62 43 W
Bastia (city)	France (Corsica)	42 42 N	9 27 E
Basutoland (former name for Lesotho)	Lesotho	29 30 S	28 30 E
Batan Islands	Philippines	20 30 N	121 50 E
Bavaria (region; also Bayern)	Germany	48 30 N	11 30 E
Beagle Channel	Atlantic Ocean	54 53 S	68 10 W
Bear Island (see Bjornoya)	Svalbard	74 26 N	19 05 E
Beaufort Sea	Arctic Ocean	73 00 N	140 00 W
Bechuanaland (former name for Botswana)	Botswana	22 00 S	24 00 E
Beijing (capital)	China	39 56 N	116 24 E
Beirut (capital)	Lebanon	33 53 N	35 30 E
Bekaa Valley	Lebanon	34 00 N	36 05 E
Belau (Palau Islands)	Palau	7 30 N	134 30 E
Belep Islands (Iles Belep)	New Caledonia	19 45 S	163 40 E
Belfast (city)	United Kingdom	54 36 N	5 55 W
Belgian Congo (former name for Democratic Republic of the Congo)	Democratic Republic of the Congo	0 00 N	25 00 E

Name	Entry in *The World Factbook*	Latitude (deg min)	Longitude (deg min)
Belgie, Belgique (local name for Belgium)	Belgium	50 50 N	4 00 E
Belgrade (capital)	Serbia	44 50 N	20 30 E
Belize City	Belize	17 30 N	88 12 W
Belle Isle, Strait of	Atlantic Ocean	51 35 N	56 30 W
Bellingshausen Sea	Southern Ocean	71 00 S	85 00 W
Belmopan (capital)	Belize	17 15 N	88 46 W
Belorussia (former name for Belarus)	Belarus	53 00 N	28 00 E
Benadir (region; former name of Italian Somaliland)	Somalia	4 00 N	46 00 E
Bengal (region)	Bangladesh, India	24 30 N	88 15 E
Bengal, Bay of	Indian Ocean	15 00 N	90 00 E
Berau, Gulf of	Pacific Ocean	2 30 S	132 30 E
Bering Island	Russia	55 00 N	166 30 E
Bering Sea	Pacific Ocean	60 00 N	175 00 W
Bering Strait	Pacific Ocean	65 30 N	169 00 W
Berkner Island	Antarctica	79 30 S	49 30 W
Berlin (capital)	Germany	52 31 N	13 24 E
Berlin, East (former name for eastern sector of Berlin)	Germany	52 30 N	13 33 E
Berlin, West (former name for western sector of Berlin)	Germany	52 30 N	13 20 E
Bern (capital)	Switzerland	46 57 N	7 26 E
Bessarabia (region)	Moldova, Romania, Ukraine	47 00 N	28 30 E
Bharat (local name for India)	India	20 00 N	77 00 E
Bhopal (city)	India	23 16 N	77 24 E
Biafra (region)	Nigeria	5 30 N	7 30 E
Big Diomede Island	Russia	65 46 N	169 06 W
Bijagos, Arquipelago dos (island group)	Guinea-Bissau	11 25 N	16 20 W
Bikini Atoll	Marshall Islands	11 35 N	165 23 E
Bilbao (city)	Spain	43 15 N	2 58 W
Bioko (island)	Equatorial Guinea	3 30 N	8 42 E
Biscay, Bay of	Atlantic Ocean	44 00 N	4 00 W
Bishkek (capital)	Kyrgyzstan	42 54 N	74 36 E
Bishop Rock	United Kingdom	49 52 N	6 27 W
Bismarck Archipelago (island group)	Papua New Guinea	5 00 S	150 00 E
Bismarck Sea	Pacific Ocean	4 00 S	148 00 E
Bissau (capital)	Guinea-Bissau	11 51 N	15 35 W
Bjornoya (Bear Island)	Svalbard	74 26 N	19 05 E
Black Forest (region)	Germany	48 00 N	8 15 E
Black Rock (island)	South Georgia and the South Sandwich Islands	53 39 S	41 48 W
Black Sea	Atlantic Ocean	43 00 N	35 00 E
Bloemfontein (judicial capital)	South Africa	29 12 S	26 07 E
Bo Hai (gulf)	Pacific Ocean	38 00 N	120 00 E
Boa Vista (island)	Cabo Verde	16 05 N	22 50 W
Bogota (capital)	Colombia	4 36 N	74 05 W
Bohemia (region)	Czech Republic	50 00 N	14 30 E
Bombay (city; see Mumbai)	India	18 58 N	72 50 E
Bonaire (island)	Netherlands	12 10 N	68 15 W

Name	Entry in *The World Factbook*	Latitude (deg min)	Longitude (deg min)
Bonifacio, Strait of	Atlantic Ocean (Mediterranean Sea)	41 01 N	14 00 E
Bonin Islands	Japan	27 00 N	142 10 E
Bonn (former capital)	Germany	50 44 N	7 05 E
Bophuthatswana (region; enclave)	South Africa	26 30 S	25 30 E
Bora-Bora (island)	French Polynesia	16 30 S	151 45 W
Bordeaux (city)	France	44 50 N	0 34 W
Borneo (island)	Brunei, Indonesia, Malaysia	0 30 N	114 00 E
Bornholm (island)	Denmark	55 10 N	15 00 E
Bosna i Hercegovina (local name for Bosnia and Herzegovina)	Bosnia and Herzegovina	44 00 N	18 00 E
Bosnia (political region)	Bosnia and Herzegovina	44 00 N	18 00 E
Bosporus (strait)	Atlantic Ocean	41 00 N	29 00 E
Bothnia, Gulf of	Atlantic Ocean	63 00 N	20 00 E
Bougainville (island)	Papua New Guinea	6 00 S	155 00 E
Bougainville Strait	Pacific Ocean	6 40 S	156 10 E
Bounty Islands	New Zealand	47 43 S	174 00 E
Bourbon Island (former name of Reunion)	Reunion	21 06 S	55 36 E
Brasilia (capital)	Brazil	15 47 S	47 55 W
Bratislava (capital)	Slovakia	48 09 N	17 07 E
Brazzaville (capital)	Republic of the Congo	4 16 S	15 17 E
Bridgetown (capital)	Barbados	13 06 N	59 37 W
Brisbane (city)	Australia	27 28 S	153 02 E
Bristol Bay	Pacific Ocean	57 00 N	160 00 W
Bristol Channel	Atlantic Ocean	51 18 N	3 30 W
Britain (see Great Britain)	United Kingdom	54 00 N	2 00 W
British Bechuanaland (region; former name for northwest South Africa)	South Africa	27 30 S	23 30 E
British Central African Protectorate (former name of Nyasaland)	Malawi	13 30 S	34 00 E
British East Africa (former name for British possessions in eastern Africa)	Kenya, Tanzania, Uganda	1 00 N	38 00 E
British Guiana (former name for Guyana)	Guyana	5 00 N	59 00 W
British Honduras (former name for Belize)	Belize	17 15 N	88 45 W
British Solomon Islands (former name for Solomon Islands)	Solomon Islands	8 00 S	159 00 E
British Somaliland (former name for northern Somalia)	Somalia	10 00 N	49 00 E
Brussels (capital)	Belgium	50 50 N	4 20 E
Bubiyan (island)	Kuwait	29 47 N	48 10 E
Bucharest (capital)	Romania	44 26 N	26 06 E
Budapest (capital)	Hungary	47 30 N	19 05 E
Buenos Aires (capital)	Argentina	34 36 S	58 27 W
Bujumbura (capital)	Burundi	3 23 S	29 22 E
Bukovina (region)	Romania, Ukraine	48 00 N	26 00 E
Byelarus (local name for Belarus)	Belarus	53 00 N	28 00 E
Byelorussia (former name for Belarus)	Belarus	53 00 N	28 00 E
Cabinda (province)	Angola	5 33 S	12 12 E
Cabot Strait	Atlantic Ocean	47 20 N	59 30 W
Caicos Islands	Turks and Caicos Islands	21 56 N	71 58 W
Cairo (capital)	Egypt	30 03 N	31 15 E

Name	Entry in *The World Factbook*	Latitude (deg min)	Longitude (deg min)
Calcutta (city)	India	22 32 N	88 21 E
Calgary (city)	Canada	51 02 N	114 04 W
California, Gulf of	Pacific Ocean	28 00 N	112 00 W
Cameroun (local name for Cameroon)	Cameroon	6 00 N	12 00 E
Campbell Island	New Zealand	52 33 S	169 09 E
Campeche, Bay of	Atlantic Ocean (Gulf of Mexico)	20 00 N	94 00 W
Canal Zone (former name for US possessions in Panama)	Panama	9 00 N	79 45 W
Canarias Sea	Atlantic Ocean	28 00 N	16 00 W
Canary Islands	Spain	28 00 N	15 30 W
Canberra (capital)	Australia	35 17 S	149 08 E
Cancun (city)	Mexico	21 10 N	86 50 W
Canton (city; now Guangzhou)	China	23 06 N	113 16 E
Canton Island (Kanton Island)	Kiribati	2 49 S	171 40 W
Cape Juby (region; former name for Southern Morocco)	Morocco	27 53 N	12 58 W
Cape Province (region; former name for Northern, Western, and Eastern Cape Provinces of South Africa)	South Africa	31 30 S	22 30 E
Cape Town (legislative capital)	South Africa	33 57 S	18 25 E
Cape of Good Hope (cape; also alternate name for Cape Province of South Africa)	South Africa	34 15 S	18 20 E
Caracas (capital)	Venezuela	10 30 N	66 56 W
Cargados Carajos Shoals	Mauritius	16 25 S	59 38 E
Caribbean Sea	Atlantic Ocean	15 00 N	73 00 W
Caroline Islands	Federated States of Micronesia, Palau	7 30 N	148 00 E
Carpatho-Ukraine (region; former name for Zakarpattya oblast')	Ukraine	48 22 N	23 32 E
Carpentaria, Gulf of	Pacific Ocean	14 00 S	139 00 E
Casablanca (city)	Morocco	33 35 N	7 34 W
Castries (capital)	Saint Lucia	14 01 N	61 00 W
Catalonia (region)	Spain	42 00 N	2 00 E
Cato Island	Australia	23 15 S	155 32 E
Caucasus (region)	Russia	42 00 N	45 00 E
Cayenne (capital)	French Guiana	4 56 N	52 20 W
Celebes (island)	Indonesia	2 00 S	121 00 E
Celebes Sea	Pacific Ocean	3 00 N	122 00 E
Celtic Sea	Atlantic Ocean	51 00 N	6 30 W
Central African Empire (former name for Central African Republic)	Central African Republic	7 00 N	21 00 E
Ceram (Seram) Sea	Pacific Ocean	2 30 S	129 30 E
Ceska Republika (local name for Czech Republic)	Czech Republic	49 45 N	15 30 E
Ceskoslovensko (former local name for Czechoslovakia)	Czech Republic, Slovakia	49 00 N	17 30 E
Cetinje (capital city)	Montenegro	42 24 N	18 55 E
Ceuta (city)	Spain	35 53 N	5 19 W
Ceylon (former name for Sri Lanka)	Sri Lanka	7 00 N	81 00 E
Chafarinas, Islas (island)	Spain	35 12 N	2 26 W
Chagos Archipelago (Oil Islands)	British Indian Ocean Territory	6 00 S	71 30 E
Challenger Deep (Mariana Trench)	Pacific Ocean	11 22 N	142 36 E

Name	Entry in *The World Factbook*	Latitude (deg min)	Longitude (deg min)
Channel Islands	Guernsey, Jersey	49 20 N	2 20 W
Charlotte Amalie (capital)	Virgin Islands	18 21 N	64 56 W
Chatham Islands	New Zealand	44 00 S	176 30 W
Chechnya (region; also Chechnia)	Russia	43 15 N	45 40 E
Cheju Strait	Pacific Ocean	34 00 N	126 30 E
Cheju-do (island)	Korea, South	33 20 N	126 30 E
Chengdu (city)	China	30 43 N	104 04 E
Chennai (city; also Madras)	India	13 04 N	80 16 E
Chesterfield Islands (Iles Chesterfield)	New Caledonia	19 52 S	158 15 E
Chihli, Gulf of (see Bo Hai)	Pacific Ocean	38 30 N	120 00 E
Chiloe (island)	Chile	42 50 S	74 00 W
China, People's Republic of	China	35 00 N	105 00 E
China, Republic of	Taiwan	23 30 N	121 00 E
Chisinau (capital; also Kishinev)	Moldova	47 00 N	28 50 E
Choiseul (island)	Solomon Islands	7 05 S	121 00 E
Choson (local name for North Korea)	North Korea	40 00 N	127 00 E
Christmas Island (Indian Ocean)	Australia	10 25 S	105 39 E
Christmas Island (Pacific Ocean; also Kiritimati)	Kiribati	1 52 N	157 20 W
Chukchi Sea	Arctic Ocean	69 00 N	171 00 W
Chuuk Islands (Truk Islands)	Federated States of Micronesia	7 25 N	151 47 W
Cilicia (region)	Turkey	36 50 N	34 30 E
Ciskei (enclave)	South Africa	33 00 S	27 00 E
Citta del Vaticano (local name for Vatican City)	Holy See	41 54 N	12 27 E
Cochin China (region)	Vietnam	11 00 N	107 00 E
Coco, Isla del (island)	Costa Rica	5 32 N	87 04 W
Cocos Islands	Cocos (Keeling) Islands	12 30 S	96 50 E
Colombo (capital)	Sri Lanka	6 56 N	79 51 E
Colon, Archipielago de (Galapagos Islands)	Ecuador	0 00 N	90 30 W
Commander Islands (Komandorskiye Ostrova)	Russia	55 00 N	167 00 E
Comores (local name for Comoros)	Comoros	12 10 S	44 15 E
Con Son (islands)	Vietnam	8 43 N	106 36 E
Conakry (capital)	Guinea	9 31 N	13 43 W
Confederatio Helvetica (local name for Switzerland)	Switzerland	47 00 N	8 00 E
Congo (Brazzaville) (former name for Republic of the Congo)	Republic of the Congo	1 00 S	15 00 E
Congo (Leopoldville) (former name for the Democratic Republic of the Congo)	Democratic Republic of the Congo	0 00 N	25 00 E
Constantinople (city; former name for Istanbul)	Turkey	41 01 N	28 58 E
Cook Strait	Pacific Ocean	41 15 S	174 30 E
Copenhagen (capital)	Denmark	55 40 N	12 35 E
Coral Sea	Pacific Ocean	15 00 S	150 00 E
Corfu (island)	Greece	39 40 N	19 45 E
Corinth (region)	Greece	37 56 N	22 56 E
Corisco (island)	Equatorial Guinea	0 55 N	9 19 E
Corn Islands (Islas del Maiz)	Nicaragua	12 15 N	83 00 W
Corocoro Island	Guyana, Venezuela	3 38 N	66 50 W
Corsica (island; also Corse)	France	42 00 N	9 00 E

Name	Entry in *The World Factbook*	Latitude (deg min)	Longitude (deg min)
Cosmoledo Group (island group; also Atoll de Cosmoledo)	Seychelles	9 43 S	47 35 E
Cotonou (former capital)	Benin	6 21 N	2 26 E
Cotopaxi (volcano)	Ecuador	0 39 S	78 26 W
Courantyne River	Guyana, Suriname	5 57 N	57 06 W
Cozumel (island)	Mexico	20 30 N	86 55 W
Crete (island)	Greece	35 15 N	24 45 E
Crimea (region)	Ukraine	45 00 N	34 00 E
Crimean Peninsula	Ukraine	45 00 N	34 00 E
Crooked Island Passage	Atlantic Ocean	22 55 N	74 35 W
Crozet Islands (Iles Crozet)	French Southern and Antarctic Lands	46 30 S	51 00 E
Cyclades (island group)	Greece	37 00 N	25 10 E
Cyrenaica (region)	Libya	31 00 N	22 00 E
Czechoslovakia (former name for the entity that subsequently split into the Czech Republic and Slovakia)	Czech Republic, Slovakia	49 00 N	18 00 E
D'Entrecasteaux Islands	Papua New Guinea	9 30 S	150 40 E
Dagestan (region)	Russia	43 00 N	47 00 E
Dahomey (former name for Benin)	Benin	9 30 N	2 15 E
Daito Islands	Japan	43 00 N	17 00 E
Dakar (capital)	Senegal	14 40 N	17 26 W
Dalmatia (region)	Croatia	43 00 N	17 00 E
Daman (city; also Damao)	India	20 10 N	73 00 E
Damascus (capital)	Syria	33 30 N	36 18 E
Danger Islands (see Pukapuka Atoll)	Cook Islands	10 53 S	165 49 W
Danish Straits	Atlantic Ocean	58 00 N	11 00 E
Danish West Indies (former name for the Virgin Islands)	Virgin Islands	18 20 N	64 50 W
Danmark (local name)	Denmark	56 00 N	10 00 E
Danzig (city; former name for Gdansk)	Poland	54 23 N	18 40 E
Dao Bach Long Vi (island)	Vietnam	20 08 N	107 44 E
Dar es Salaam (capital)	Tanzania	6 48 S	39 17 E
Dardanelles (strait)	Atlantic Ocean	40 15 N	26 25 E
Davis Strait	Atlantic Ocean	67 00 N	57 00 W
Dead Sea	Israel, Jordan, West Bank	32 30 N	35 30 E
Deception Island	Antarctica	62 56 S	60 34 W
Denmark Strait	Atlantic Ocean	67 00 N	24 00 W
Desolation Islands (Isles Kerguelen)	French Southern and Antarctic Lands	49 30 S	69 30 E
Deutschland (local name for Germany)	Germany	51 00 N	9 00 E
Devils Island (Ile du Diable)	French Guiana	5 17 N	52 35 W
Devon Island	Canada	76 00 N	87 00 W
Dhaka (capital)	Bangladesh	23 43 N	90 25 E
Dhivehi Raajje (local name for Maldives)	Maldives	3 15 N	73 00 E
Dhofar (region)	Oman	17 00 N	54 10 E
Diego Garcia (island)	British Indian Ocean Territory	7 20 S	72 25 E
Diego Ramirez (islands)	Chile	56 30 S	68 43 W
Dili (capital)	Timor-Leste	8 35 S	125 36 E
Dilmun (former name for Bahrain)	Bahrain	7 00 N	81 00 E

Name	Entry in *The World Factbook*	Latitude (deg min)	Longitude (deg min)
Diomede Islands	Russia (Big Diomede), United States (Little Diomede)	65 47 N	169 00 W
Diu (region)	India	20 42 N	70 59 E
Djibouti (capital)	Djibouti	11 30 N	43 15 E
Dnieper (river)	Belarus, Russia, Ukraine (Dnyapro, Dnepr, Dnipro)	46 30 N	32 18 E
Dniester (river)	Moldova, Ukraine (Nistru, Dnister)	46 18 N	30 17 E
Dobruja (region)	Bulgaria, Romania	43 30 N	28 00 E
Dodecanese (island group)	Greece	36 00 N	27 05 E
Dodoma (city)	Tanzania	6 11 S	35 45 E
Doha (capital)	Qatar	25 17 N	51 32 E
Donets Basin	Russia, Ukraine	48 15 N	38 30 E
Douala (city)	Cameroon	4 03 N	9 42 E
Douglas (capital)	Man, Isle of	54 09 N	4 28 W
Dover, Strait of	Atlantic Ocean	51 00 N	1 30 E
Drake Passage	Atlantic Ocean, Southern Ocean	60 00 S	60 00 W
Druk Yul (local name for Bhutan)	Bhutan	27 30 N	90 30 E
Dubai, Dubayy (city)	United Arab Emirates	25 18 N	55 18 E
Dublin (capital)	Ireland	53 20 N	6 15 W
Duesseldorf (city)	Germany	51 13 N	6 47 E
Durban (city)	South Africa	29 51 S	31 02 E
Dushanbe (capital)	Tajikistan	38 35 N	68 48 E
Dutch Antilles (former name for the Netherlands Antilles)	Aruba, Curacao, Sint Maarten	12 10 N	68 30 W
Dutch East Indies (former name for Indonesia)	Indonesia	5 00 S	120 00 E
Dutch Guiana (former name for Suriname)	Suriname	4 00 N	56 00 W
Dutch West Indies (former name for the Netherlands Antilles)	Aruba, Curacao, Sint Maarten	12 10 N	68 30 W
Dzungarian Gate (valley)	China, Kazakhstan	45 25 N	82 25 E
East China Sea	Pacific Ocean	30 00 N	126 00 E
East Frisian Islands	Germany	53 44 N	7 25 E
East Germany (German Democratic Republic; former name for eastern portion of Germany)	Germany	52 00 N	13 00 E
East Korea Strait (Eastern Channel or Tsushima Strait)	Pacific Ocean	34 00 N	129 00 E
East Pakistan (former name for Bangladesh)	Bangladesh	24 00 N	90 00 E
East Siberian Sea	Arctic Ocean	74 00 N	166 00 E
Easter Island (Isla de Pascua)	Chile	27 07 S	109 22 W
Eastern Channel (East Korea Strait or Tsushima Strait)	Pacific Ocean	34 00 N	129 00 E
Eastern Samoa (former name for American Samoa)	American Samoa	14 20 S	170 00 W
Edinburgh (city)	United Kingdom	55 57 N	3 11 W
Eesti (local name for Estonia)	Estonia	59 00 N	26 00 E
Eire (local name for Ireland)	Ireland	53 00 N	8 00 W
Elba (island)	Italy	42 46 N	10 17 E
Elemi Triangle (region)	Ethiopia (claimed), Kenya (de facto), Sudan (claimed)	5 00 N	35 30 E
Ellada, Ellas (local name for Greece)	Greece	39 00 N	22 00 E
Ellef Ringnes Island	Canada	78 00 N	103 00 W
Ellesmere Island	Canada	81 00 N	80 00 W

Name	Entry in *The World Factbook*	Latitude (deg min)	Longitude (deg min)
Ellice Islands	Tuvalu	8 00 S	178 00 E
Ellsworth Land (region)	Antarctica	75 00 S	92 00 W
Elobey, Islas de (island group)	Equatorial Guinea	0 59 N	9 33 E
Enderbury Island	Kiribati	3 08 S	171 05 W
Enewetak Atoll (Eniwetok Atoll)	Marshall Islands	11 30 N	162 15 E
England (region)	United Kingdom	52 30 N	1 30 W
English Channel	Atlantic Ocean	50 20 N	1 00 W
Eniwetok Atoll (see Enewetak Atoll)	Marshall Islands	11 30 N	162 15 E
Eolie, Isole (island group)	Italy	38 30 N	15 00 E
Epirus, Northern (region)	Albania, Greece	40 00 N	20 30 E
Episkopi Cantonment (capital)	Akrotiri, Dhekelia	34 40 N	32 51 E
Ertra (local name for Eritrea)	Eritrea	15 00 N	39 00 E
Espana	Spain	40 00 N	4 00 W
Essequibo (region; claimed by Venezuela)	Guyana	6 59 N	58 23 W
Etorofu (island; also Iturup)	Russia (de facto)	44 55 N	147 40 E
Europa Island	Indian Ocean	22 20 S	40 22 E
Farquhar Group (island group; also Atoll de Farquhar)	Seychelles	10 10 S	51 10 E
Fashoda (town; also Kodok)	South Sudan	9 53 N	32 7 E
Fergana Valley	Kyrgyzstan, Tajikistan, Uzbekistan	41 00 N	72 00 E
Fernando Po (island; see Bioko)	Equatorial Guinea	3 30 N	8 42 E
Fernando de Noronha (island group)	Brazil	3 51 S	32 25 W
Filipinas (local name for the Philippines; also Pilipinas)	Philippines	13 00 N	122 00 E
Finland, Gulf of	Atlantic Ocean (Baltic Sea)	60 00 N	27 00 E
Fiume (city; former name for Rijeka)	Croatia	45 19 N	14 25 E
Florence (city)	Italy	43 46 N	11 16 E
Flores (island)	Indonesia	8 45 S	121 00 E
Flores Sea	Pacific Ocean	7 40 S	119 45 E
Florida, Straits of	Atlantic Ocean	25 00 N	79 45 W
Fongafale (largest island of Funafuti)	Tuvalu	8 30 S	179 12 E
Former Soviet Union (FSU)	Armenia, Azerbaijan, Belarus, Estonia, Georgia, Kazakhstan, Kyrgyzstan, Latvia, Lithuania, Moldova, Russia, Tajikistan, Turkmenistan, Ukraine, Uzbekistan		
Formosa (island)	Taiwan	23 30 N	121 00 E
Formosa Strait (see Taiwan Strait)	Pacific Ocean	24 00 N	119 00 E
Foroyar (local name for Faroe Islands)	Faroe Islands	62 00 N	7 00 W
Fort-de-France (capital)	Martinique	14 36 N	61 05 W
Frankfurt am Main (city)	Germany	50 07 N	8 41 E
Franz Josef Land (island group)	Russia	81 00 N	55 00 E
Freetown (capital)	Sierra Leone	8 30 N	13 15 W
French Cameroon (former name for Cameroon)	Cameroon	6 00 N	12 00 E
French Guinea (former name for Guinea)	Guinea	11 00 N	10 00 W
French Indochina (former name for French possessions in southeast Asia)	Cambodia, Laos, Vietnam	15 00 N	107 00 E
French Morocco (former name for Morocco)	Morocco	32 00 N	5 00 W

Name	Entry in *The World Factbook*	Latitude (deg min)	Longitude (deg min)
French Somaliland (former name for Djibouti)	Djibouti	11 30 N	43 00 E
French Sudan (former name for Mali)	Mali	17 00 N	4 00 W
French Territory of the Afars and Issas (or FTAI; former name for Djibouti)	Djibouti	11 30 N	43 00 E
French Togoland (former name for Togo)	Togo	8 00 N	1 10 E
French West Indies (former name for French possessions in the West Indies)	Guadeloupe, Martinique	16 30 N	62 00 W
Friendly Islands	Tonga	20 00 S	175 00 W
Frisian Islands	Denmark, Germany, Netherlands	53 35 N	6 40 E
Frunze (city; former name for Bishkek)	Kyrgyzstan	42 54 N	74 36 E
Funafuti (capital, atoll)	Tuvalu	8 30 S	179 12 E
Fundy, Bay of	Atlantic Ocean	45 00 N	66 00 W
Futuna Islands (Hoorn Islands/Iles de Horne)	Wallis and Futuna	14 19 S	178 05 W
Fyn (island)	Denmark	55 20 N	10 25 E
Gaborone (capital)	Botswana	24 45 S	25 55 E
Galapagos Islands (Archipielago de Colon)	Ecuador	0 00 N	90 30 W
Galicia (region)	Spain	42 45 N	8 10 E
Galicia (region)	Poland, Ukraine	49 30 N	23 00 E
Galilee (region)	Israel	32 54 N	35 20 E
Galleons Passage	Atlantic Ocean	11 00 N	60 55 W
Gambier Islands (Iles Gambier)	French Polynesia	23 09 S	134 58 W
Gaspar Strait	Pacific Ocean	3 00 S	107 00 E
Gdansk (city; formerly Danzig)	Poland	54 23 N	18 40 E
Geneva (city)	Switzerland	46 12 N	6 10 E
Genoa (city)	Italy	44 25 N	8 57 E
George Town (capital)	Cayman Islands	19 20 N	81 23 W
George Town (city)	Malaysia	5 26 N	100 16 E
George Town (city)	The Bahamas	23 30 N	75 46 W
Georgetown (capital)	Guyana	6 48 N	58 10 W
Georgetown (city)	The Gambia	13 30 N	14 47 W
German Democratic Republic (East Germany; former name for eastern portion of Germany)	Germany	52 00 N	13 00 E
German Southwest Africa (former name for Namibia)	Namibia	22 00 S	17 00 E
Germany, Federal Republic of	Germany	51 00 N	9 00 E
Gibraltar (city, peninsula)	Gibraltar	36 11 N	5 22 W
Gibraltar, Strait of	Atlantic Ocean	35 57 N	5 36 W
Gidi Pass	Egypt	30 13 N	33 09 E
Gilbert Islands	Kiribati	1 25 N	173 00 E
Glorioso Islands	Indian Ocean	11 30 S	47 20 E
Goa (state)	India	15 20 N	74 00 E
Gobi (desert)	China, Mongolia	42 30 N	107 00 E
Godthab (capital; also Nuuk)	Greenland	64 11 N	51 44 W
Golan Heights (region)	Syria	33 00 N	35 45 E
Gold Coast (former name for Ghana)	Ghana	8 00 N	2 00 W
Golfo San Jorge (gulf)	Atlantic Ocean	46 00 S	66 00 W
Golfo San Matias (gulf)	Atlantic Ocean	41 30 S	64 00 W

Name	Entry in *The World Factbook*	Latitude (deg min)	Longitude (deg min)
Good Hope, Cape of	South Africa	34 24 S	18 30 E
Goteborg (city)	Sweden	57 43 N	11 58 E
Gotland (island)	Sweden	57 30 N	18 33 E
Gough Island	Saint Helena, Ascension, and Tristan da Cunha	40 20 S	9 55 W
Graham Land (region)	Antarctica	65 00 S	64 00 W
Gran Chaco (region)	Argentina, Paraguay	24 00 S	60 00 W
Grand Bahama (island)	The Bahamas	26 40 N	78 35 W
Grand Banks (fishing ground)	Atlantic Ocean	47 06 N	55 48 W
Grand Cayman (island)	Cayman Islands	19 20 N	81 20 W
Grand Turk (capital; also Cockburn Town)	Turks and Caicos Islands	21 28 N	71 08 W
Great Australian Bight	Indian Ocean	35 00 S	130 00 E
Great Belt (strait; also Store Baelt)	Atlantic Ocean	55 30 N	11 00 E
Great Bitter Lake	Egypt	30 20 N	32 23 E
Great Britain (island)	United Kingdom	54 00 N	2 00 W
Great Channel	Indian Ocean	6 25 N	94 20 E
Great Inagua (island)	The Bahamas	21 00 N	73 20 W
Great Rift Valley	Ethiopia, Kenya	0 30 N	36 00 E
Greater Sunda Islands	Brunei, Indonesia, Malaysia	2 00 S	110 00 E
Green Islands	Papua New Guinea	4 30 S	154 10 E
Greenland Sea	Arctic Ocean	79 00 N	5 00 W
Grenadines, Northern (island group)	Saint Vincent and the Grenadines	13 15 N	61 12 W
Grenadines, Southern (island group)	Grenada	12 07 N	61 40 W
Grytviken (town; on South Georgia)	South Georgia and the South Sandwich Islands	54 15 S	36 45 W
Guadalahara (city)	Mexico	20 40 N	103 24 W
Guadalcanal (island)	Solomon Islands	9 32 S	160 12 E
Guadalupe, Isla de (island)	Mexico	29 11 N	118 17 W
Guangzhou (city; also Canton)	China	23 09 N	113 21 E
Guantanamo Bay (US Naval Base)	Cuba	20 00 N	75 08 W
Guatemala (capital)	Guatemala	14 38 N	90 31 W
Guine-Bissau (local name for Guinea-Bissau)	Guinea-Bissau	12 00 N	15 00 W
Guinea Ecuatorial (local name for Equatorial Guinea)	Equatorial Guinea	2 00 N	10 00 E
Guinea, Gulf of	Atlantic Ocean	3 00 N	2 30 E
Guinee (local name for Guinea)	Guinea	11 00 N	10 00 W
Gustavia (capital)	Saint Barthelemy	17 53 N	62 51 W
Guyane Francaise (local name for French Guiana)	French Guiana	4 00 N	53 00 W
Ha'apai Group (island group)	Tonga	19 42 S	174 29 W
Habomai Islands	Russia (de facto)	43 30 N	146 10 E
Hadhramaut (region)	Yemen	15 00 N	50 00 E
Hagatna (capital; formerly Agana)	Guam	13 28 N	144 45 E
Hague, The (seat of government)	Netherlands	52 05 N	4 18 E
Haifa (city)	Israel	32 50 N	35 00 E
Hainan Dao (island)	China	19 00 N	109 30 E
Haiphong (city)	Vietnam	20 52 N	106 41 E

Name	Entry in *The World Factbook*	Latitude (deg min)	Longitude (deg min)
Hala'ib Triangle (region)	Egypt (claimed), Sudan (de facto)	22 30 N	35 00 E
Halifax (city)	Canada	44 39 N	63 36 W
Halmahera (island)	Indonesia	1 00 N	128 00 E
Halmahera Sea	Pacific Ocean	0 30 S	129 00 E
Hamburg (city)	Germany	53 34 N	9 59 E
Hamilton (capital)	Bermuda	32 17 N	64 46 W
Han-guk (local name for South Korea	South Korea	37 00 N	127 30 E
Hanoi (capital)	Vietnam	21 02 N	105 51 E
Harare (capital)	Zimbabwe	17 50 S	31 03 E
Harvey Islands (former name for Cook Islands)	Cook Islands	21 14 S	159 46 W
Hatay (province)	Turkey	36 30 N	36 15 E
Havana (capital)	Cuba	23 08 N	82 22 W
Hawaii (island)	United States	19 45 N	155 45 W
Hawaiian Islands	United States	21 00 N	157 45 W
Hawar (island)	Bahrain	25 40 N	50 47 E
Hayastan (local name for Armenia)	Armenia	40 00 N	45 00 E
Heard Island	Heard Island and McDonald Islands	53 06 S	73 30 E
Hejaz (region)	Saudi Arabia	24 30 N	38 30 E
Helsinki (capital)	Finland	60 10 N	24 58 E
Herzegovina (political region)	Bosnia and Herzegovina	44 00 N	18 00 E
Hiiumaa (island)	Estonia	58 50 N	22 30 E
Hispaniola (island)	Dominican Republic, Haiti	18 45 N	71 00 W
Ho Chi Minh City (formerly Saigon)	Vietnam	10 45 N	106 40 E
Hokkaido (island)	Japan	44 00 N	143 00 E
Holland (region)	Netherlands	52 30 N	5 45 E
Hong Kong (special administrative region)	Hong Kong	22 15 N	114 10 E
Honiara (capital)	Solomon Islands	9 26 S	159 57 E
Honshu (island)	Japan	36 00 N	138 00 E
Hormuz, Strait of	Indian Ocean	26 34 N	56 15 E
Horn of Africa (region)	Djibouti, Eritrea, Ethiopia, Somalia	8 00 N	48 00 E
Horn, Cape (Cabo de Hornos)	Chile	55 59 S	67 16 W
Horne, Iles de (island group)	Wallis and Futuna	14 19 S	178 05 W
Hrvatska (local name for Croatia)	Croatia	45 10 N	15 30 E
Hudson Bay	Arctic Ocean	60 00 N	86 00 W
Hudson Strait	Arctic Ocean	62 00 N	71 00 W
Hunter Island	New Caledonia, Vanuatu	22 24 S	172 06 E
Iberian Peninsula	Portugal, Spain	40 00 N	5 00 W
Iceland Sea	Arctic Ocean	68 00 N	20 00 W
Ifni (region; former name of part of Spanish West Africa)	Morocco	29 22 N	10 09 W
Inaccessible Island	Saint Helena, Ascension, and Tristan da Cunha	37 17 S	12 40 W
Indochina (region)	Cambodia, Laos, Vietnam	15 00 N	107 00 E
Ingushetia (region)	Russia	43 15 N	45 00 E
Inhambane (region)	Mozambique	22 30 S	34 30 E

Name	Entry in *The World Factbook*	Latitude (deg min)	Longitude (deg min)
Inini (former name for French Guiana)	French Guiana	4 00 N	53 00 W
Inland Sea	Japan	34 20 N	133 30 E
Inner Hebrides (islands)	United Kingdom	56 30 N	6 20 W
Inner Mongolia (region; also Nei Mongol)	China	42 00 N	113 00 E
Ionian Islands	Greece	38 30 N	20 30 E
Ionian Sea	Atlantic Ocean	38 30 N	18 00 E
Irian Jaya (province)	Indonesia	5 00 S	138 00 E
Irish Sea	Atlantic Ocean	53 30 N	5 20 W
Iron Gate (river gorge)	Romania, Serbia	44 41 N	22 31 E
Iskenderun (region; formerly Alexandretta)	Turkey	36 34 N	36 08 E
Islamabad (capital)	Pakistan	33 42 N	73 10 E
Island (local name for Iceland)	Iceland	65 00 N	18 00 W
Islas Malvinas (island group)	Falkland Islands (Islas Malvinas)	51 45 S	59 00 W
Istanbul (city)	Turkey	41 01 N	28 58 E
Istrian Peninsula	Croatia, Slovenia	45 00 N	14 00 E
Italia (local name for Italy)	Italy	42 50 N	12 50 E
Italian East Africa (former name for Italian possessions in eastern Africa)	Eritrea, Ethiopia, Somalia	8 00 N	38 00 E
Italian Somaliland (former name for southern Somalia)	Somalia	10 00 N	49 00 E
Ittihad al-Imarat al-Arabiyah (local name for the United Arab Emirates)	United Arab Emirates	24 00 N	54 00 E
Iturup (island; see Etorofu)	Russia (de facto)	44 55 N	147 40 E
Ityop'iya (local name for Ethiopia)	Ethiopia	8 00 N	38 00 E
Ivory Coast (former name for Cote d'Ivoire)	Cote d'Ivoire	8 00 N	5 00 W
Iwo Jima (island)	Japan	24 47 N	141 20 E
Izmir (region)	Turkey	38 25 N	27 10 E
Jakarta (capital)	Indonesia	6 10 S	106 48 E
James Bay	Arctic Ocean	54 00 N	80 00 W
Jamestown (capital)	Saint Helena, Ascension, and Tristan da Cunha	15 56 S	5 44 W
Jammu (city)	India	32 42 N	74 52 E
Jammu and Kashmir (region)	India, Pakistan	34 00 N	76 00 E
Japan, Sea of	Pacific Ocean	40 00 N	135 00 E
Jars, Plain of	Laos	19 27 N	103 10 E
Java (island)	Indonesia	7 30 S	110 00 E
Java Sea	Pacific Ocean	5 00 S	110 00 E
Jerusalem (capital, proclaimed)	Israel, West Bank	31 47 N	35 14 E
Jiddah, Jeddah (city)	Saudi Arabia	21 30 N	39 12 E
Johannesburg (city)	South Africa	26 15 S	28 00 E
Joseph Bonaparte Gulf	Pacific Ocean	14 00 S	128 45 E
Juan Fernandez, Islas de (island group)	Chile	33 00 S	80 00 W
Juan de Fuca, Strait of	Pacific Ocean	48 18 N	124 00 W
Juan de Nova Island	Indian Ocean	17 03 S	42 45 E
Juba (capital)	South Sudan	04 51 N	31 37 E
Jubal, Strait of	Indian Ocean	27 40 N	33 55 E
Judaea (region)	Israel, West Bank	31 35 N	35 00 E

Name	Entry in *The World Factbook*	Latitude (deg min)	Longitude (deg min)
Jugoslavia, Jugoslavija (local names for Yugoslavia, a former Balkan federation)	Bosnia and Herzegovina, Croatia, Macedonia, Montenegro, Serbia, Slovenia	43 00 N	21 00 E
Jutland (region)	Denmark	56 00 N	9 15 E
Juventud, Isla de la (Isle of Youth)	Cuba	21 40 N	82 50 W
Kabardino-Balkaria (region)	Russia	43 30 N	43 30 E
Kabul (capital)	Afghanistan	34 31 N	69 12 E
Kaduna (city)	Nigeria	10 33 N	7 27 E
Kailas Range	China, India	30 00 N	82 00 E
Kalaallit Nunaat (local name for Greenland)	Greenland	72 00 N	40 00 W
Kalahari (desert)	Botswana, Namibia	24 30 S	21 00 E
Kalimantan (region)	Indonesia	0 00 N	115 00 E
Kaliningrad (region; formerly part of East Prussia)	Russia	54 30 N	21 00 E
Kamaran (island)	Yemen	15 21 N	42 34 E
Kamchatka Peninsula (Poluostrov Kamchatka)	Russia	56 00 N	160 00 E
Kampala (capital)	Uganda	0 19 N	32 25 E
Kampuchea (former name for Cambodia)	Cambodia	13 00 N	105 00 E
Kane Basin (portion of channel)	Arctic Ocean	79 30 N	68 00 W
Kanton Island	Kiribati	2 49 S	171 40 W
Kara Sea	Arctic Ocean	76 00 N	80 00 E
Karachevo-Cherkessia (region)	Russia	43 40 N	41 50 E
Karachi (city)	Pakistan	24 51 N	67 03 E
Karafuto (island; former name for southern Sakhalin Island)	Russia	50 00 N	143 00 E
Karakoram Pass	China, India	35 30 N	77 50 E
Karelia, Kareliya (region)	Finland, Russia	63 15 N	30 48 E
Karelian Isthmus	Russia	60 25 N	30 00 E
Karimata Strait	Pacific Ocean	2 05 S	108 40 E
Kashmir (region)	India, Pakistan	34 00 N	76 00 E
Katanga (region)	Democratic Republic of the Congo	10 00 S	26 00 E
Kathmandu (capital)	Nepal	27 43 N	85 19 E
Kattegat (strait)	Atlantic Ocean	57 00 N	11 00 E
Kauai Channel	Pacific Ocean	21 45 N	158 50 W
Kazakstan (former name for Kazakhstan)	Kazakhstan	48 00 N	68 00 E
Keeling Islands	Cocos (Keeling) Islands	12 30 S	96 50 E
Kerguelen, Iles (island group)	French Southern and Antarctic Lands	49 30 S	69 30 E
Kermadec Islands	New Zealand	29 50 S	178 15 W
Kerulen River	China, Mongolia	48 48 N	117 00 E
Khabarovsk (city)	Russia	48 27 N	135 06 E
Khanka, Lake	China, Russia	45 00 N	132 24 E
Khartoum (capital)	Sudan	15 36 N	32 32 E
Khios (island)	Greece	38 22 N	26 04 E
Khmer Republic (former name for Cambodia)	Cambodia	13 00 N	105 00 E
Khuriya Muriya Islands (Kuria Muria Islands)	Oman	17 30 N	56 00 E
Khyber Pass	Afghanistan, Pakistan	34 05 N	71 10 E
Kibris (Turkish local name for Cyprus)	Cyprus	35 00 N	33 00 E

Name	Entry in *The World Factbook*	Latitude (deg min)	Longitude (deg min)
Kiel Canal (Nord-Ostsee Kanal)	Atlantic Ocean	53 53 N	9 08 E
Kiev (city; former name for Kyiv)	Ukraine	50 26 N	30 31 E
Kigali (capital)	Rwanda	1 57 S	30 04 E
Kingston (capital)	Jamaica	18 00 N	76 48 W
Kingston (capital)	Norfolk Island	29 03 S	167 58 E
Kingstown (capital)	Saint Vincent and the Grenadines	13 09 N	61 14 W
Kinshasa (capital)	Democratic Republic of the Congo	4 18 S	15 18 E
Kipros (Greek local name for Cyprus)	Cyprus	35 00 N	33 00 E
Kirghiziya, Kirgizia (former name for Kyrgyzstan)	Kyrgyzstan	41 00 N	75 00 E
Kirguizstan (local name for Kyrgyzstan)	Kyrgyzstan	41 00 N	75 00 E
Kiritimati (Christmas Island)	Kiribati	1 52 N	157 20 W
Kishinev (see Chisinau)	Moldova	47 00 N	28 50 E
Kithira Strait	Atlantic Ocean	36 00 N	23 00 E
Kobe (city)	Japan	34 41 N	135 10 E
Kodiak Island	United States	57 49 N	152 23 W
Kodok (town; also Fashoda)	South Sudan	9 53 N	32 7 E
Kola Peninsula (Kol'skiy Poluostrov)	Russia	67 20 N	37 00 E
Kolonia (town; former capital; changed to Palikir)	Federated States of Micronesia	6 58 N	158 13 E
Korea Bay	Pacific Ocean	39 00 N	124 00 E
Korea Strait	Pacific Ocean	34 00 N	129 00 E
Korea, Democratic People's Republic of	North Korea	40 00 N	127 00 E
Korea, Republic of	South Korea	37 00 N	127 30 E
Koror (capital)	Palau	7 20 N	134 29 E
Kosovo (region)	Kosovo	42 30 N	21 00 E
Kosrae (island)	Federated States of Micronesia	5 20 N	163 00 E
Kowloon (city)	Hong Kong	22 18 N	114 10 E
Kra, Isthmus of	Burma, Thailand	10 20 N	99 00 E
Krakatoa (volcano)	Indonesia	6 07 S	105 24 E
Krakow (city)	Poland	50 03 N	19 56 E
Kuala Lumpur (capital)	Malaysia	3 10 N	101 42 E
Kunashiri (island; also Kunashir)	Russia (de facto)	44 20 N	146 00 E
Kunlun Mountains	China	36 00 N	84 00 E
Kuril Islands	Russia (de facto)	46 10 N	152 00 E
Kuwait (capital)	Kuwait	29 20 N	47 59 E
Kuznetsk Basin	Russia	54 00 N	86 00 E
Kwajalein Atoll	Marshall Islands	9 05 N	167 20 E
Kyiv (capital)	Ukraine	50 26 N	30 31 E
Kyushu (island)	Japan	33 00 N	131 00 E
La Paz (administrative capital)	Bolivia	16 30 S	68 09 W
La Perouse Strait	Pacific Ocean	45 45 N	142 00 E
Labrador (peninsula, region)	Canada	54 00 N	62 00 W
Labrador Sea	Atlantic Ocean	60 00 N	55 00 W
Laccadive Islands	India	10 00 N	73 00 E
Laccadive Sea	Indian Ocean	7 00 N	76 00 E
Lagos (former capital)	Nigeria	6 27 N	3 24 E

Name	Entry in *The World Factbook*	Latitude (deg min)	Longitude (deg min)
Lahore (city)	Pakistan	31 33 N	74 23 E
Lake Erie	Atlantic Ocean	42 30 N	81 00 W
Lake Huron	Atlantic Ocean	45 00 N	83 00 W
Lake Michigan	Atlantic Ocean	43 30 N	87 30 W
Lake Ontario	Atlantic Ocean	43 30 N	78 00 W
Lake Superior	Atlantic Ocean	48 00 N	88 00 W
Lakshadweep (Laccadive Islands)	India	10 00 N	73 00 E
Lantau Island	Hong Kong	22 15 N	113 55 E
Lao (local name for Laos)	Laos	18 00 N	105 00 E
Laptev Sea	Arctic Ocean	76 00 N	126 00 E
Las Palmas (city)	Spain (Canary Islands)	28 06 N	15 24 W
Latakia (region)	Syria	36 00 N	35 50 E
Latvija (local name for Latvia)	Latvia	57 00 N	25 00 E
Lau Group (island group)	Fiji	18 20 S	178 30 E
Lefkosa (see Nicosia)	Cyprus	35 10 N	33 22 E
Leipzig (city)	Germany	51 21 N	12 23 E
Lemnos (island)	Greece	39 54 N	25 21 E
Leningrad (city; former name for Saint Petersburg)	Russia	59 55 N	30 15 E
Lesser Sunda Islands	Indonesia	9 00 S	120 00 E
Lesvos (island)	Greece	39 15 N	26 15 E
Leyte (island)	Philippines	10 50 N	124 50 E
Liancourt Rocks (claimed by Japan)	South Korea	37 15 N	131 50 E
Liaodong Wan (gulf)	Pacific Ocean	40 30 N	121 20 E
Liban (local name for Lebanon)	Lebanon	33 50 N	36 50 E
Libreville (capital)	Gabon	0 23 N	9 27 E
Lietuva (local name for Lithuania)	Lithuania	56 00 N	24 00 E
Ligurian Sea	Atlantic Ocean	43 30 N	9 00 E
Lilongwe (capital)	Malawi	13 59 S	33 44 E
Lima (capital)	Peru	12 03 S	77 03 W
Lincoln Sea	Arctic Ocean	83 00 N	56 00 W
Line Islands	Jarvis Island, Kingman Reef, Kiribati, Palmyra Atoll	0 05 N	157 00 W
Lion, Gulf of	Atlantic Ocean	43 20 N	4 00 E
Lisbon (capital)	Portugal	38 43 N	9 08 W
Little Belt (strait; also Lille Baelt)	Atlantic Ocean	55 05 N	9 55 E
Ljubljana (capital)	Slovenia	46 03 N	14 31 E
Llanos (region)	Venezuela	8 00 N	68 00 W
Lobamba (city)	Swaziland	26 27 S	31 12 E
Lombok (island)	Indonesia	8 28 S	116 40 E
Lombok Strait	Indian Ocean	8 30 S	115 50 E
Lome (capital)	Togo	6 08 N	1 13 E
London (capital)	United Kingdom	51 30 N	0 10 W
Longyearbyen (capital)	Svalbard	78 13 N	15 33 E
Lord Howe Island	Australia	31 30 S	159 00 E
Lorraine (region)	France	48 42 N	6 11 E
Louisiade Archipelago	Papua New Guinea	11 00 S	153 00 E

Name	Entry in *The World Factbook*	Latitude (deg min)	Longitude (deg min)
Lourenco Marques (city; former name for Maputo)	Mozambique	25 56 S	32 34 E
Loyalty Islands (Iles Loyaute)	New Caledonia	21 00 S	167 00 E
Luanda (capital)	Angola	8 48 S	13 14 E
Lubnan (local name for Lebanon)	Lebanon	33 50 N	36 50 E
Lubumbashi (city)	Democratic Republic of the Congo	11 40 S	27 28 E
Lusaka (capital)	Zambia	15 25 S	28 17 E
Luxembourg (capital)	Luxembourg	49 45 N	6 10 E
Luzon (island)	Philippines	16 00 N	121 00 E
Luzon Strait	Pacific Ocean	20 30 N	121 00 E
Lyakhov Islands	Russia	73 45 N	138 00 E
Macao	Macau	22 10 N	113 33 E
Macau (special administrative region)	China	22 10 N	113 33 E
Macquarie Island	Australia	54 36 S	158 54 E
Madagasikara (local name for Madagascar)	Madagascar	20 00 S	47 00 E
Maddalena, Isola	Italy	41 13 N	09 24 E
Madeira Islands	Portugal	32 40 N	16 45 W
Madras (city; see Chennai)	India	13 04 N	80 16 E
Madrid (capital)	Spain	40 24 N	3 41 W
Magellan, Strait of	Atlantic Ocean	54 00 S	71 00 W
Maghreb (region)	Algeria, Libya, Mauritania, Morocco, Tunisia	34 00 N	3 00 E
Magreb (local name for Morocco)	Morocco	32 00 N	5 00 W
Magyarorszag (local name for Hungary)	Hungary	47 00 N	20 00 E
Mahe Island	Seychelles	4 41 S	55 30 E
Maiz, Islas del (Corn Islands)	Nicaragua	12 15 N	83 00 W
Majorca Island (Isla de Mallorca)	Spain	39 30 N	3 00 E
Majuro (capital)	Marshall Islands	7 05 N	171 08 E
Makassar Strait	Pacific Ocean	2 00 S	117 30 E
Makedonija (local name for Macedonia)	Macedonia	41 50 N	22 00 E
Malabo (capital)	Equatorial Guinea	3 45 N	8 47 E
Malacca, Strait of	Indian Ocean	2 30 N	101 20 E
Malagasy Republic	Madagascar	20 00 S	47 00 E
Malay Archipelago	Brunei, Indonesia, Malaysia, Papua New Guinea, Philippines	2 30 N	120 00 E
Malay Peninsula	Malaysia, Thailand	7 10 N	100 35 E
Male (capital)	Maldives	4 10 N	73 31 E
Mallorca, Isla de (island; also Majorca)	Spain	39 30 N	3 00 E
Malmady (region)	Belgium	50 26 N	6 02 E
Malpelo, Isla de (island)	Colombia	4 00 N	90 30 W
Malta Channel	Atlantic Ocean	56 44 N	26 53 E
Malvinas, Islas (island group)	Falkland Islands (Islas Malvinas)	51 45 S	59 00 W
Mamoutzou (capital)	Mayotte	12 47 S	45 14 E
Managua (capital)	Nicaragua	12 09 N	86 17 W
Manama (capital)	Bahrain	26 13 N	50 35 E

Name	Entry in *The World Factbook*	Latitude (deg min)	Longitude (deg min)
Manchukuo (former state)	China	44 00 N	124 00 E
Manchuria (region)	China	44 00 N	124 00 E
Manila (capital)	Philippines	14 35 N	121 00 E
Manipa Strait	Pacific Ocean	3 20 S	127 23 E
Mannar, Gulf of	Indian Ocean	8 30 N	79 00 E
Manua Islands	American Samoa	14 13 S	169 35 W
Maputo (capital)	Mozambique	25 58 S	32 35 E
Marcus Island (Minami-tori-shima)	Japan	24 16 N	154 00 E
Margarita, Isla (island)	Venezuela	10 00 N	64 00 W
Mariana Islands	Guam, Northern Mariana Islands	16 00 N	145 30 E
Marie Byrd Land (region)	Antarctica	77 00 S	130 00 W
Marigot (capital)	Saint Martin	18 04 N	63 05 W
Marion Island	South Africa	46 51 S	37 52 E
Marmara, Sea of	Atlantic Ocean	40 40 N	28 15 E
Marquesas Islands (Iles Marquises)	French Polynesia	9 00 S	139 30 W
Marseille (city)	France	43 18 N	5 23 E
Martin Vaz, Ilhas (island group)	Brazil	20 30 S	28 51 W
Mas a Tierra (Robinson Crusoe Island)	Chile	33 38 S	78 52 W
Mascarene Islands	Mauritius, Reunion	21 00 S	57 00 E
Maseru (capital)	Lesotho	29 28 S	27 30 E
Mata-Utu (capital)	Wallis and Futuna	13 57 S	171 56 W
Matsu (island)	Taiwan	26 13 N	119 56 E
Matthew Island	New Caledonia, Vanuatu	22 20 S	171 20 E
Mauritanie (local name for Mauritania)	Mauritania	20 00 N	12 00 W
Mazatlan (city)	Mexico	23 13 N	106 25 W
Mbabane (capital)	Swaziland	26 18 S	31 06 E
McDonald Islands	Heard Island and McDonald Islands	53 06 S	73 30 E
Mecca (city)	Saudi Arabia	21 27 N	39 49 E
Mediterranean Sea	Atlantic Ocean	36 00 N	15 00 E
Melbourne (city)	Australia	37 49 S	144 58 E
Melilla (exclave)	Spain	35 19 N	2 58 W
Memel (region)	Lithuania	55 43 N	21 30 E
Mesopotamia (region)	Iraq	33 00 N	44 00 E
Messina, Strait of	Atlantic Ocean	38 15 N	15 35 E
Mexico City (capital)	Mexico	19 24 N	99 09 W
Mexico, Gulf of	Atlantic Ocean	25 00 N	90 00 W
Middle Congo (former name for Republic of the Congo)	Republic of the Congo	1 00 S	15 00 E
Milan (city)	Italy	45 28 N	9 11 E
Milwaukee Deep (Puerto Rico Trench)	Atlantic Ocean	19 55 N	65 27 W
Minami-tori-shima (Marcus Island)	Japan	24 16 N	154 00 E
Mindanao (island)	Philippines	8 00 N	125 00 E
Mindanao Sea	Pacific Ocean	9 15 N	124 30 E
Mindoro (island)	Philippines	12 50 N	121 05 E
Mindoro Strait	Pacific Ocean	12 20 N	120 40 E
Mingrelia (region)	Georgia	42 30 N	41 52 E

Name	Entry in *The World Factbook*	Latitude (deg min)	Longitude (deg min)
Minicoy Island	India	8 17 N	73 02 E
Minorca Island (Isla de Menorca)	Spain	40 00 N	4 00 E
Minsk (capital)	Belarus	53 54 N	27 34 E
Misr (local name for Egypt)	Egypt	27 00 N	30 00 E
Mitla Pass	Egypt	30 02 N	32 54 E
Mocambique (local name for Mozambique)	Mozambique	18 15 S	35 00 E
Mogadishu (capital)	Somalia	2 04 N	45 22 E
Moldavia (region)	Moldova, Romania	47 00 N	29 00 E
Molucca Sea	Pacific Ocean	2 00 N	127 00 E
Moluccas (Spice Islands)	Indonesia	2 00 S	128 00 E
Mombasa (city)	Kenya	4 03 S	39 40 E
Mona Passage	Atlantic Ocean	18 30 N	67 45 W
Monaco (capital)	Monaco	43 44 N	7 25 E
Mongol Uls (local name for Mongolia)	Mongolia	46 00 N	105 00 E
Monrovia (capital)	Liberia	6 18 N	10 47 W
Monterrey (city)	Mexico	25 40 N	100 19 W
Montevideo (capital)	Uruguay	34 53 S	56 11 W
Montreal (city)	Canada	45 31 N	73 34 W
Moravia (region)	Czech Republic	49 30 N	17 00 E
Moravian Gate (pass)	Czech Republic	49 35 N	17 50 E
Moroni (capital)	Comoros	11 41 S	43 16 E
Mortlock Islands (Nomoi Islands)	Federated States of Micronesia	5 30 N	153 40 E
Moscow (capital)	Russia	55 45 N	37 35 E
Mount Pinatubo (volcano)	Philippines	15 08 N	120 21 E
Mozambique Channel	Indian Ocean	19 00 S	41 00 E
Mumbai (city; also Bombay)	India	18 58 N	72 50 E
Munich, Muenchen (city)	Germany	48 08 N	11 35 E
Muritaniyah (local name for Mauritania)	Mauritania	20 00 N	12 00 W
Musandam Peninsula	Oman, United Arab Emirates	26 18 N	56 24 E
Muscat (capital)	Oman	23 37 N	58 35 E
Muscat and Oman (former name for Oman)	Oman	21 00 N	57 00 E
Myanma, Myanmar	Burma	22 00 N	98 00 E
N'Djamena (capital)	Chad	12 07 N	15 03 E
Nagorno-Karabakh (region)	Azerbaijan	40 00 N	46 40 E
Nairobi (capital)	Kenya	1 17 S	36 49 E
Namib (desert)	Namibia	24 00 S	15 00 E
Nampo-shoto (island group)	Japan	30 00 N	140 00 E
Nan Madol (ruins)	Federated States of Micronesia	6 85 N	158 35 E
Naples (city)	Italy	40 51 N	14 15 E
Nassau (capital)	The Bahamas	25 05 N	77 21 W
Natal (region)	South Africa	29 00 S	30 25 E
Natuna Besar Islands	Indonesia	3 30 N	102 30 E
Natuna Sea	Pacific Ocean	3 30 N	108 00 E
Naxcivan (region)	Azerbaijan	39 20 N	45 20 E
Naxos (island)	Greece	37 05 N	25 30 E
Nederland (local name for the Netherlands)	Netherlands	52 30 N	5 45 E

Name	Entry in *The World Factbook*	Latitude (deg min)	Longitude (deg min)
Nederlandse Antillen (local name for the former Netherlands Antilles)	Curacao, Sint Maarten	12 15 N	68 45 W
Negev (region)	Israel	30 30 N	34 55 E
Negros (island)	Philippines	10 00 N	123 00 E
Nejd (region)	Saudi Arabia	24 05 N	45 15 E
Netherlands Antilles (former name of Dutch Caribbean dependencies)	Curacao, Sint Maarten	12 15 N	68 45 W
Netherlands East Indies (former name for Indonesia)	Indonesia	5 00 S	120 00 E
Netherlands Guiana (former name for Suriname)	Suriname	4 00 N	56 00 W
Nevis (island)	Saint Kitts and Nevis	17 09 N	62 35 W
New Britain (island)	Papua New Guinea	6 00 S	150 00 E
New Delhi (capital)	India	28 36 N	77 12 E
New Guinea (island)	Indonesia, Papua New Guinea	5 00 S	140 00 E
New Hebrides (island group)	Vanuatu	16 00 S	167 00 E
New Ireland (island)	Papua New Guinea	3 20 N	152 00 E
New Siberian Islands	Russia	75 00 N	142 00 E
New Territories (mainland region)	Hong Kong	22 24 N	114 10 E
Newfoundland (island, with mainland area, and a province)	Canada	52 00 N	56 00 W
Niamey (capital)	Niger	13 31 N	2 07 E
Nicobar Islands	India	8 00 N	93 30 E
Nicosia (capital; also Lefkosia)	Cyprus	35 10 N	33 22 E
Nightingale Island	Saint Helena, Ascension, and Tristan da Cunha	37 25 S	12 30 W
Nihon, Nippon (local name for Japan)	Japan	36 00 N	138 00 E
Nomoi Islands (Mortlock Islands)	Federated States of Micronesia	5 30 N	153 40 E
Norge (local name for Norway)	Norway	62 00 N	10 00 E
Norman Isles (Channel Islands)	Guernsey, Jersey	49 20 N	2 20 W
North Atlantic Ocean	Atlantic Ocean	30 00 N	45 00 W
North Channel	Atlantic Ocean	55 10 N	5 40 W
North Frisian Islands	Denmark, Germany	54 50 N	8 12 E
North Greenland Sea	Arctic Ocean	78 00 N	5 00 W
North Island	New Zealand	39 00 S	176 00 E
North Ossetia (region)	Russia	43 00 N	44 10 E
North Pacific Ocean	Pacific Ocean	30 00 N	165 00 W
North Sea	Atlantic Ocean	56 00 N	4 00 E
North Vietnam (former name for northern portion of Vietnam)	Vietnam	23 00 N	106 00 E
North Yemen (Yemen Arab Republic; now part of Yemen)	Yemen	15 00 N	44 00 E
Northeast Providence Channel	Atlantic Ocean	25 40 N	77 09 W
Northern Areas	Pakistan	36 0 N	75 0 E
Northern Cyprus (region)	Cyprus	35 15 N	33 44 E
Northern Epirus (region)	Albania, Greece	40 00 N	20 30 E
Northern Grenadines (political region)	Saint Vincent and the Grenadines	12 45 N	61 15 W
Northern Ireland	United Kingdom	54 40 N	6 45 W
Northern Rhodesia (former name for Zambia)	Zambia	15 00 S	30 00 E
Northwest Passages	Arctic Ocean	74 40 N	100 00 W
Norwegian Sea	Atlantic Ocean	66 00 N	6 00 E

Name	Entry in *The World Factbook*	Latitude (deg min)	Longitude (deg min)
Nouakchott (capital)	Mauritania	18 06 N	15 57 W
Noumea (capital)	New Caledonia	22 16 S	166 27 E
Nouvelle-Caledonie (local name for New Caledonia)	New Caledonia	21 30 S	165 30 E
Nouvelles Hebrides (former name for Vanuatu)	Vanuatu	16 00 S	167 00 E
Novaya Zemlya (islands)	Russia	74 00 N	57 00 E
Nubia (region)	Egypt, Sudan	20 30 N	33 00 E
Nuku'alofa (capital)	Tonga	21 08 S	175 12 W
Nunavut (region)	Canada	72 00 N	90 00 W
Nuuk (capital; also Godthab)	Greenland	64 11 N	51 44 W
Nyasaland (former name for Malawi)	Malawi	13 30 S	34 00 E
Nyassa (region)	Mozambique	13 30 S	37 00 E
Oahu (island)	United States (Hawaii)	21 30 N	158 00 W
Ocean Island (Banaba)	Kiribati	0 52 S	169 35 E
Ocean Island (Kure Island)	United States	28 25 N	178 20 W
Oesterreich (local name for Austria)	Austria	47 20 N	13 20 E
Ogaden (region)	Ethiopia, Somalia	7 00 N	46 00 E
Oil Islands (Chagos Archipelago)	British Indian Ocean Territory	6 00 S	71 30 E
Okhotsk, Sea of	Pacific Ocean	53 00 N	150 00 E
Okinawa (island group)	Japan	26 30 N	128 00 E
Oland (island)	Sweden	56 45 N	16 40 E
Oman, Gulf of	Indian Ocean	24 30 N	58 30 E
Ombai Strait	Pacific Ocean	8 30 S	125 00 E
Oran (city)	Algeria	35 43 N	0 43 W
Orange River Colony (region; former name of Free State Province of South Africa)	South Africa	28 20 S	26 40 E
Oranjestad (capital)	Aruba	12 33 N	70 06 W
Oresund (The Sound) (strait)	Atlantic Ocean	55 50 N	12 40 E
Orkney Islands	United Kingdom	59 00 N	3 00 W
Osaka (city)	Japan	34 42 N	135 30 E
Oslo (capital)	Norway	59 55 N	10 45 E
Osumi Strait (Van Diemen Strait)	Pacific Ocean	31 00 N	131 00 E
Otranto, Strait of	Atlantic Ocean	40 00 N	19 00 E
Ottawa (capital)	Canada	45 25 N	75 40 W
Ouagadougou (capital)	Burkina Faso	12 22 N	1 31 W
Outer Hebrides (islands)	United Kingdom	57 45 N	7 00 W
Outer Mongolia (region)	Mongolia	46 00 N	105 00 E
P'yongyang (capital)	North Korea	39 01 N	125 45 E
Pacific Islands, Trust Territory of the (former name of a large area of the western North Pacific Ocean)	Marshall Islands, Federated States of Micronesia, Northern Mariana Islands, Palau	10 00 N	155 00 E
Pagan (island)	Northern Mariana Islands	18 08 N	145 47 E
Pago Pago (capital)	American Samoa	14 16 S	170 42 W
Palawan (island)	Philippines	9 30 N	118 30 E
Palermo (city)	Italy	38 07 N	13 21 E
Palestine (region)	Israel, West Bank	32 00 N	35 15 E
Palikir (capital)	Federated States of Micronesia	6 55 N	158 08 E
Palk Strait	Indian Ocean	10 00 N	79 45 E

Name	Entry in *The World Factbook*	Latitude (deg min)	Longitude (deg min)
Pamirs (mountains)	China, Tajikistan	38 00 N	73 00 E
Pampas (region)	Argentina	35 00 S	63 00 W
Panama (capital)	Panama	8 58 N	79 32 W
Panama Canal	Panama	9 00 N	79 45 W
Panama, Gulf of	Pacific Ocean	8 00 N	79 30 W
Panay (island)	Philippines	11 15 N	122 30 E
Pantelleria, Isola di (island)	Italy	36 47 N	12 00 E
Papeete (capital)	French Polynesia	17 32 S	149 34 W
Paramaribo (capital)	Suriname	5 50 N	55 10 W
Parece Vela (island)	Japan	20 20 N	136 00 E
Paris (capital)	France	48 52 N	2 20 E
Pascua, Isla de (Easter Island)	Chile	27 07 S	109 22 W
Pashtunistan (region)	Afghanistan, Pakistan	32 00 N	69 00 E
Passion, Ile de la (island)	Clipperton Island	10 17 N	109 13 W
Patagonia (region)	Argentina	48 00 S	61 00 W
Peking (see Beijing)	China	39 56 N	116 24 E
Pelagian Islands (Isole Pelagie)	Italy	35 40 N	12 40 E
Peleliu (Beliliou) (island)	Palau	7 01 N	134 15 E
Peloponnese (peninsula)	Greece	37 30 N	22 25 E
Pemba Island	Tanzania	5 20 S	39 45 E
Penang Island	Malaysia	5 23 N	100 15 E
Pentland Firth (channel)	Atlantic Ocean	58 44 N	3 13 W
Perim (island)	Yemen	12 39 N	43 25 E
Perouse Strait, La	Pacific Ocean	44 45 N	142 00 E
Persia (former name for Iran)	Iran	32 00 N	53 00 E
Persian Gulf	Indian Ocean	27 00 N	51 00 E
Perth (city)	Australia	31 56 S	115 50 E
Pescadores (islands)	Taiwan	23 30 N	119 30 E
Peshawar (city)	Pakistan	34 01 N	71 40 E
Peter I Island	Antarctica	68 48 S	90 35 W
Petrograd (city; former name for Saint Petersburg)	Russia	59 55 N	30 15 E
Philip Island	Norfolk Island	29 08 S	167 57 E
Philippine Sea	Pacific Ocean	20 00 N	134 00 E
Philipsburg (capital)	Sint Maarten	18 1 N	63 2 W
Phnom Penh (capital)	Cambodia	11 33 N	104 55 E
Phoenix Islands	Kiribati	3 30 S	172 00 E
Pinatubo, Mount (volcano)	Philippines	15 08 N	120 21 E
Pines, Isle of (island; former name for Isla de la Juventud)	Cuba	21 40 N	82 50 W
Pleasant Island	Nauru	0 32 S	166 55 E
Plymouth (capital)	Montserrat	16 44 N	62 14 W
Podgorica (administrative capital)	Montenegro	42 26 N	19 16 E
Polska (local name)	Poland	52 00 N	20 00 E
Polynesie Francaise (local name for French Polynesia)	French Polynesia	15 00 S	140 00 W
Pomerania (region)	Germany, Poland	53 40 N	15 35 E
Ponape (Pohnpei) (island)	Federated States of Micronesia	6 55 N	158 15 E
Port Louis (capital)	Mauritius	20 10 S	57 30 E

Name	Entry in *The World Factbook*	Latitude (deg min)	Longitude (deg min)
Port Moresby (capital)	Papua New Guinea	9 30 S	147 10 E
Port-Vila (capital)	Vanuatu	17 44 S	168 19 E
Port-au-Prince (capital)	Haiti	18 32 N	72 20 W
Port-of-Spain (capital)	Trinidad and Tobago	10 39 N	61 31 W
Porto-Novo (capital)	Benin	6 29 N	2 37 E
Portuguese East Africa (former name for Mozambique)	Mozambique	18 15 S	35 00 E
Portuguese Guinea (former name for Guinea-Bissau)	Guinea-Bissau	12 00 N	15 00 W
Portuguese Timor (former name for Timor-Leste)	Timor-Leste	9 00 S	126 00 E
Poznan (city)	Poland	52 25 N	16 55 E
Prague (capital)	Czech Republic	50 05 N	14 28 E
Praia (capital)	Cabo Verde	14 55 N	23 31 W
Prathet Thai (local name for Thailand)	Thailand	15 00 N	100 00 E
Pretoria (administrative capital)	South Africa	25 42 S	28 13 E
Prevlaka peninsula	Croatia	42 24 N	18 31 E
Pribilof Islands	United States	57 00 N	170 00 W
Prince Edward Island	Canada	46 20 N	63 20 W
Prince Edward Islands	South Africa	46 35 S	38 00 E
Prince Patrick Island	Canada	76 30 N	119 00 W
Principe (island)	Sao Tome and Principe	1 38 N	7 25 E
Pristina, Prishtina, Prishtine (capital)	Kosovo	42 40 N	21 10 E
Prussia (region)	Germany, Poland, Russia	53 00 N	14 00 E
Pukapuka Atoll	Cook Islands	10 53 S	165 49 W
Punjab (region)	India, Pakistan	30 50 N	73 30 E
Puntland (region)	Somalia	8 21 N	49 08 E
Qazaqstan (local name for Kazakhstan)	Kazakhstan	48 00 N	68 00 E
Qita Ghazzah (local name Gaza Strip)	Gaza Strip	31 25 N	34 20 E
Quebec (city)	Canada	46 48 N	71 15 W
Queen Charlotte Islands	Canada	53 00 N	132 00 W
Queen Elizabeth Islands	Canada	78 00 N	95 00 W
Queen Maud Land (claimed by Norway)	Antarctica	73 30 S	12 00 E
Quemoy (island)	Taiwan	24 27 N	118 23 E
Quito (capital)	Ecuador	0 13 S	78 30 W
Rabat (capital)	Morocco	34 02 N	6 51 W
Ralik Chain (island group)	Marshall Islands	8 00 N	167 00 E
Rangoon (capital; also Yangon)	Burma	16 47 N	96 10 E
Rapa Nui (Easter Island)	Chile	27 07 S	109 22 W
Ratak Chain (island group)	Marshall Islands	9 00 N	171 00 E
Red Sea	Indian Ocean	20 00 N	38 00 E
Redonda (island)	Antigua and Barbuda	16 55 N	62 19 W
Republica Dominicana (local name for Dominican Republic)	Dominican Republic	19 00 N	70 40 W
Republique Centrafricain (local name for Central African Republic)	Central African Republic	7 00 N	21 00 E
Republique Francaise (local name for France)	France	46 00 N	2 00 E
Republique Gabonaise (local name for Gabon)	Gabon	1 00 S	11 45 E
Republique Rwandaise (local name for Rwanda)	Rwanda	2 00 S	30 00 E
Republique Togolaise (local name for Togo)	Togo	8 00 N	1 10 E

Name	Entry in *The World Factbook*	Latitude (deg min)	Longitude (deg min)
Revillagigedo Island	United States (Alaska)	55 35 N	131 06 W
Revillagigedo Islands	Mexico	19 00 N	112 45 W
Reykjavik (capital)	Iceland	64 09 N	21 57 W
Rhodes (island)	Greece	36 10 N	28 00 E
Rhodesia, Northern (former name for Zambia)	Zambia	15 00 S	30 00 E
Rhodesia, Southern (former name for Zimbabwe)	Zimbabwe	20 00 S	30 00 E
Riga (capital)	Latvia	56 57 N	24 06 E
Riga, Gulf of	Atlantic Ocean	57 30 N	23 30 E
Rio Muni (mainland region)	Equatorial Guinea	1 30 N	10 00 E
Rio de Janiero (city)	Brazil	22 55 S	43 17 W
Rio de Oro (region)	Western Sahara	23 45 N	15 45 W
Rio de la Plata (gulf)	Atlantic Ocean	35 00 S	59 00 W
Riyadh (capital)	Saudi Arabia	24 38 N	46 43 E
Road Town (capital)	British Virgin Islands	18 27 N	64 37 W
Robinson Crusoe Island (Mas a Tierra)	Chile	33 38 S	78 52 W
Rocas, Atol das (island)	Brazil	3 51 S	33 49 W
Rockall (island)	United Kingdom	57 35 N	13 48 W
Rodrigues (island)	Mauritius	19 42 S	63 25 E
Rome (capital)	Italy	41 54 N	12 29 E
Roncador Cay (island)	Colombia	13 32 N	80 03 W
Roosevelt Island	Antarctica	79 30 S	162 00 W
Roseau (capital)	Dominica	15 18 N	61 24 W
Ross Dependency (claimed by New Zealand)	Antarctica	80 00 S	180 00 E
Ross Island	Antarctica	81 30 S	175 00 W
Ross Sea	Antarctica, Southern Ocean	76 00 S	175 00 W
Rossiya (local name for Russia)	Russia	60 00 N	100 00 E
Rota (island)	Northern Mariana Islands	14 10 N	145 12 E
Rotuma (island)	Fiji	12 30 S	177 05 E
Ruanda (former name for Rwanda)	Rwanda	2 00 S	30 00 E
Rub al Khali (desert)	Saudi Arabia	19 30 N	49 00 E
Rumelia (region)	Albania, Bulgaria, Macedonia	42 00 N	22 30 E
Ruthenia (region; former name for Carpatho-Ukraine)	Ukraine	48 22 N	23 32 E
Ryukyu Islands	Japan	26 30 N	128 00 E
Saar (region)	Germany	49 25 N	7 00 E
Saaremaa (island)	Estonia	58 25 N	22 30 E
Saba (island)	Netherlands	17 38 N	63 10 W
Sabah (state)	Malaysia	5 20 N	117 10 E
Sable Island	Canada	43 55 N	59 50 W
Safety Islands (Iles du Salut)	French Guiana	5 20 N	52 37 W
Sahara Occidental (former name for Western Sahara)	Western Sahara	24 30 N	13 00 W
Sahel (region)	Burkina Faso, Chad, The Gambia, Guinea- Bissau, Mali, Mauritania, Niger, Senegal	15 00 N	8 00 W
Saigon (city; former name for Ho Chi Minh City)	Vietnam	10 45 N	106 40 E
Saint Brandon (Cargados Carajos Shoals)	Mauritius	16 25 S	59 38 E
Saint Christopher (island)	Saint Kitts and Nevis	17 20 N	62 45 W
Saint Christopher and Nevis	Saint Kitts and Nevis	17 20 N	62 45 W

Name	Entry in *The World Factbook*	Latitude (deg min)	Longitude (deg min)
Saint Eustatius (island)	Netherlands	17 30 N	63 00 W
Saint George's (capital)	Grenada	12 03 N	61 45 W
Saint George's Channel	Atlantic Ocean	52 00 N	6 00 W
Saint Helena Island	Saint Helena, Ascension, and Tristan da Cunha	15 57 S	5 42 W
Saint Helens, Mount (volcano)	United States	46 15 N	122 12 W
Saint Helier (capital)	Jersey	49 12 N	2 07 W
Saint John (city)	Canada (New Brunswick)	45 16 N	66 04 W
Saint John's (capital)	Antigua and Barbuda	17 06 N	61 51 W
Saint Lawrence Island	United States	49 30 N	67 00 W
Saint Lawrence Seaway	Atlantic Ocean	49 15 N	67 00 W
Saint Lawrence, Gulf of	Atlantic Ocean	48 00 N	62 00 W
Saint Paul Island	Canada	47 12 N	60 09 W
Saint Paul Island	United States	57 11 N	170 16 W
Saint Paul Island (Ile Saint-Paul)	French Southern and Antarctic Lands	38 43 S	77 29 E
Saint Peter Port (capital)	Guernsey	49 27 N	2 32 W
Saint Peter and Saint Paul Rocks (Penedos de Sao Pedro e Sao Paulo)	Brazil	0 23 N	29 23 W
Saint Petersburg (city; former capital)	Russia	59 55 N	30 15 E
Saint Thomas (island)	Virgin Islands	18 21 N	64 55 W
Saint Vincent Passage	Atlantic Ocean	13 30 N	61 00 W
Saint-Denis (capital)	Reunion	20 52 S	55 28 E
Saint-Pierre (capital)	Saint Pierre and Miquelon	46 46 N	56 11 W
Saipan (island)	Northern Mariana Islands	15 12 N	145 45 E
Sak'art'velo (local name for Georgia)	Georgia	42 00 N	43 30 E
Sakhalin Island (Ostrov Sakhalin)	Russia	51 00 N	143 00 E
Sakishima Islands	Japan	24 30 N	124 00 E
Sala y Gomez, Isla (island)	Chile	26 28 S	105 00 W
Salisbury (city; former name for Harare)	Zimbabwe	17 50 S	105 00 W
Salzburg (city)	Austria	47 48 N	13 02 E
Samar (island)	Philippines	12 00 N	125 00 E
Samaria (region)	West Bank	32 15 N	35 10 E
Samoa Islands	American Samoa, Samoa	14 00 S	171 00 W
Samos (island)	Greece	37 48 N	26 44 E
San Ambrosio, Isla (island)	Chile	26 21 S	79 52 W
San Andres y Providencia, Archipielago (island group)	Colombia	13 00 N	81 30 W
San Bernardino Strait	Pacific Ocean	12 32 N	124 10 E
San Felix, Isla (island)	Chile	26 17 S	80 05 W
San Jose (capital)	Costa Rica	9 56 N	84 05 W
San Juan (capital)	Puerto Rico	18 28 N	66 07 W
San Marino (capital)	San Marino	43 56 N	12 25 E
San Salvador (capital)	El Salvador	13 42 N	89 12 W
Sanaa (capital)	Yemen	15 21 N	44 12 E
Sandzak (region)	Montenegro, Serbia	43 05 N	19 45 E
Santa Cruz (city)	Bolivia	17 48 S	63 10 W
Santa Cruz Islands	Solomon Islands	11 00 S	166 15 E

Name	Entry in *The World Factbook*	Latitude (deg min)	Longitude (deg min)
Santa Sede (local name for the Holy See)	Holy See	41 54 N	12 27 E
Santiago (capital)	Chile	33 27 S	70 40 W
Santo Antao (island)	Cabo Verde	17 05 N	25 10 W
Santo Domingo (capital)	Dominican Republic	18 28 N	69 54 W
Sao Paulo (city)	Brazil	23 35 S	46 43 W
Sao Pedro e Sao Paulo, Penedos de (rocks)	Brazil	0 23 N	29 23 W
Sao Tiago (island)	Cabo Verde	15 05 N	23 40 W
Sao Tome (island)	Sao Tome and Principe	0 12 N	6 39 E
Sapporo (city)	Japan	43 04 N	141 20 E
Sapudi Strait	Pacific Ocean	7 05 S	114 10 E
Sarajevo (capital)	Bosnia and Herzegovina	43 52 N	18 25 E
Sarawak (state)	Malaysia	2 30 N	113 30 E
Sardinia (island)	Italy	40 00 N	9 00 E
Sargasso Sea (region)	Atlantic Ocean	30 00 N	55 00 W
Sark (island)	Guernsey	49 26 N	2 21 W
Savage Island (former name for Niue)	Niue	19 02 S	169 52 W
Savu Sea	Pacific Ocean	9 30 S	122 00 E
Saxony (region)	Germany	51 00 N	13 00 E
Schleswig-Holstein (region)	Germany	54 31 N	9 33 E
Schweiz (local German name for Switzerland)	Switzerland	47 00 N	8 00 E
Scopus, Mount	Israel, West Bank	31 48 N	35 14 E
Scotia Sea	Atlantic Ocean, Southern Ocean	56 00 S	40 00 W
Scotland (region)	United Kingdom	57 00 N	4 00 W
Scott Island	Antarctica	67 24 S	179 55 W
Senegambia (region; former name of confederation of Senegal and The Gambia)	The Gambia, Senegal	13 50 N	15 25 W
Senyavin Islands	Federated States of Micronesia	6 55 N	158 00 E
Seoul (capital)	South Korea	37 34 N	127 00 E
Serendib (former name for Sri Lanka)	Sri Lanka	7 00 N	81 00 E
Serrana Bank (shoal)	Colombia	14 25 N	80 16 W
Serranilla Bank (shoal)	Colombia	15 51 N	79 46 W
Settlement, The (capital)	Christmas Island	10 25 S	105 43 E
Severnaya Zemlya (island group; also Northland)	Russia	79 30 N	98 00 E
Shaba (region)	Democratic Republic of the Congo	8 00 S	27 00 E
Shag Island	Heard Island and McDonald Islands	53 00 S	72 30 E
Shag Rocks	South Georgia and the South Sandwich Islands	53 33 S	42 02 W
Shanghai (city)	China	31 14 N	121 30 E
Shenyang (city; also Mukden)	China	41 46 N	123 24 E
Shetland Islands	United Kingdom	60 30 N	1 30 W
Shikoku (island)	Japan	33 45 N	133 30 E
Shikotan (island)	Russia (de facto)	43 47 N	146 45 E
Shqiperia (local name for Albania)	Albania	41 00 N	20 00 E
Siam (former name for Thailand)	Thailand	15 00 N	100 00 E

Name	Entry in *The World Factbook*	Latitude (deg min)	Longitude (deg min)
Siberia (region)	Russia	60 00 N	100 00 E
Sibutu Passage	Pacific Ocean	4 50 N	119 35 E
Sicily (island)	Italy	37 30 N	14 00 E
Sicily, Strait of	Atlantic Ocean	37 20 N	11 20 E
Sidra, Gulf of	Atlantic Ocean	31 30 N	18 00 E
Sikkim (state)	India	27 50 N	88 30 E
Silesia (region)	Czech Republic, Germany, Poland	51 00 N	17 00 E
Sinai Peninsula	Egypt	29 30 N	34 00 E
Singapore (capital)	Singapore	1 17 N	103 51 E
Singapore Strait	Pacific Ocean	1 15 N	104 00 E
Sinkiang (autonomous region; also Xinjiang)	China	42 00 N	86 00 E
Sint Eustatius (island)	Netherlands	17 29 N	62 58 W
Sint Maarten (island; also Saint-Martin)	Sint Maarten, Saint Martin	18 04 N	63 04 W
Sjaelland (island)	Denmark	55 30 N	12 00 E
Skagerrak (strait)	Atlantic Ocean	57 45 N	9 00 E
Skopje (capital)	Macedonia	41 59 N	21 26 E
Slavonia (region)	Croatia	45 27 N	18 00 E
Slovenija (local name for Slovenia)	Slovenia	46 00 N	15 00 E
Slovensko (local name for Slovakia)	Slovakia	48 40 N	19 30 E
Smyrna (region; former name for Izmir)	Turkey	38 25 N	27 10 E
Society Islands (Iles de la Societe)	French Polynesia	17 00 S	150 00 W
Socotra (island)	Yemen	12 30 N	54 00 E
Sofia (capital)	Bulgaria	42 41 N	23 19 E
Solomon Islands, northern	Papua New Guinea	6 00 S	155 00 E
Solomon Islands, southern	Solomon Islands	8 00 S	159 00 E
Solomon Sea	Pacific Ocean	8 00 S	153 00 E
Somaliland (region)	Somalia	9 30 N	46 00 E
Somers Islands (former name for Bermuda)	Bermuda	32 20 N	64 45 W
Songkhla (city)	Thailand	7 12 N	100 36 E
Sound, The (strait; also Oresund)	Atlantic Ocean	55 50 N	12 40 E
South Atlantic Ocean	Atlantic Ocean	30 00 S	15 00 W
South China Sea	Pacific Ocean	10 00 N	113 00 E
South Georgia (island)	South Georgia and the South Sandwich Islands	54 15 S	36 45 W
South Island	New Zealand	43 00 S	171 00 E
South Korea	South Korea	37 00 N	127 30 E
South Orkney Islands	Antarctica	61 00 S	45 00 W
South Ossetia (region)	Georgia	42 20 N	44 00 E
South Pacific Ocean	Pacific Ocean	30 00 S	130 00 W
South Sandwich Islands	South Georgia and the South Sandwich Islands	57 45 S	26 30 W
South Shetland Islands	Antarctica	62 00 S	59 00 W
South Tyrol (region)	Italy	46 30 N	10 30 E
South Vietnam (former name for the southern portion of Vietnam)	Vietnam	12 00 N	108 00 E

Name	Entry in *The World Factbook*	Latitude (deg min)	Longitude (deg min)
South Yemen (People's Democratic Republic of Yemen; now part of Yemen)	Yemen	14 00 N	48 00 E
South-West Africa (former name for Namibia)	Namibia	22 00 S	17 00 E
Southern Grenadines (island group)	Grenada	12 20 N	61 30 W
Southern Rhodesia (former name for Zimbabwe)	Zimbabwe	20 00 S	30 00 E
Soviet Union (former name of a large Eurasian empire, roughly coequal with the former Russian Empire)	Armenia, Azerbaijan, Belarus, Estonia, Georgia, Kazakhstan, Kyrgyzstan, Latvia, Lithuania, Moldova, Russia, Tajikistan, Turkmenistan, Ukraine, Uzbekistan		
Spanish Guinea (former name for Equatorial Guinea)	Equatorial Guinea	2 00 N	10 00 E
Spanish Morocco (former name for northern Morocco)	Morocco	32 00 N	7 00 W
Spanish North Africa (exclaves)	Spain (Ceuta, Islas Chafarinas, Melilla, Penon de Alhucemas, Penon de Velez de la Gomera)	35 15 N	4 00 W
Spanish Sahara (former name)	Western Sahara	24 30 N	13 00 W
Spanish West Africa (former name for Ifni and Spanish Sahara)	Morocco, Western Sahara	25 00 N	13 00 W
Spice Islands (Moluccas)	Indonesia	2 00 S	28 00 E
Spitsbergen (island)	Svalbard	78 00 N	20 00 E
Srbija (local name for Serbia)	Serbia	44 00 N	21 00 E
St. John's (city)	Canada (Newfoundland)	47 34 N	52 43 W
Stanley (capital)	Falkland Islands (Islas Malvinas)	51 42 S	57 41 W
Stockholm (capital)	Sweden	59 20 N	18 03 E
Strasbourg (city)	France	48 35 N	7 44 E
Stuttgart (city)	Germany	48 46 N	9 11 E
Sucre (constitutional capital)	Bolivia	19 02 S	65 17 W
Suez Canal	Egypt	29 55 N	32 33 E
Suez, Gulf of	Indian Ocean	28 10 N	33 27 E
Suisse (local French name for Switzerland)	Switzerland	47 00 N	8 00 E
Sulawesi (island; Celebes)	Indonesia	2 00 S	121 00 E
Sulawesi Sea	Pacific Ocean	3 00 N	122 00 E
Sulu Archipelago (island group)	Philippines	6 00 N	121 00 E
Sulu Sea	Pacific Ocean	8 00 N	120 00 E
Sumatra (island)	Indonesia	0 00 N	102 00 E
Sumba (island)	Indonesia	10 00 S	120 00 E
Sumba Strait	Pacific Ocean	9 10 S	120 00 E
Sumbawa (island)	Indonesia	8 30 S	118 00 E
Sunda Islands (Soenda Isles)	Indonesia, Malaysia	2 00 S	110 00 E
Sunda Strait	Indian Ocean	6 00 S	105 45 E
Suomi (local name for Finland)	Finland	64 00 N	26 00 E
Surabaya (city)	Indonesia	7 13 S	112 45 E
Surigao Strait	Pacific Ocean	10 15 N	125 23 E
Surinam (former name for Suriname)	Suriname	4 00 N	56 00 W
Suriyah (local name for Syria)	Syria	35 00 N	38 00 E
Surtsey (volcanic island)	Iceland	63 17 N	20 40 W
Suva (capital)	Fiji	18 08 S	178 25 E

Name	Entry in *The World Factbook*	Latitude (deg min)	Longitude (deg min)
Sverdlovsk (city; also Yekaterinburg)	Russia	56 50 N	60 39 E
Sverige (local name for Sweden)	Sweden	62 00 N	15 00 E
Svizzera (local Italian name for Switzerland)	Switzerland	47 00 N	8 00 E
Swains Island	American Samoa	11 03 S	171 15 W
Swan Islands	Honduras	17 25 S	83 56 W
Sydney (city)	Australia	33 53 S	151 13 E
T'bilisi (capital)	Georgia	41 43 N	44 49 E
Tadzhikistan (former name for Tajikistan)	Tajikistan	39 00 N	71 00 E
Tahiti (island)	French Polynesia	17 37 S	149 27 W
Taipei (capital)	Taiwan	25 03 N	121 30 E
Taiwan Strait	Pacific Ocean	24 00 N	119 00 E
Tallinn (capital)	Estonia	59 25 N	24 45 E
Tanganyika (former name for the mainland portion of Tanzania)	Tanzania	6 00 S	35 00 E
Tangier (city)	Morocco	35 48 N	5 45 W
Tannu-Tuva (region)	Russia	51 25 N	94 45 E
Tarawa (island)	Kiribati	1 25 N	173 00 E
Tartary, Gulf of	Pacific Ocean	50 00 N	141 00 E
Tashkent (capital)	Uzbekistan	41 20 N	69 18 E
Tasman Sea	Pacific Ocean	4 30 S	168 00 E
Tasmania (island)	Australia	43 00 S	147 00 E
Tatar Strait	Pacific Ocean	50 00 N	141 00 E
Taymyr Peninsula (Poluostrov Taymyr)	Russia	76 00 N	104 00 E
Tchad (local name for Chad)	Chad	15 00 N	19 00 E
Tegucigalpa (capital)	Honduras	14 06 N	87 13 W
Tehran (capital)	Iran	35 40 N	51 26 E
Tel Aviv (capital, de facto)	Israel	32 05 N	34 48 E
Teluk Bone (gulf)	Pacific Ocean	4 00 S	120 45 E
Teluk Tomini (gulf)	Pacific Ocean	0 30 S	121 00 E
Terre Adelie (claimed by France; also Adelie Land)	Antarctica	66 30 S	139 00 E
Terres Australes et Antarctiques Francaises (local name for the French Southern and Antarctic Lands)	French Southern and Antarctic Lands	43 00 S	67 00 E
Thailand, Gulf of	Pacific Ocean	10 00 N	101 00 E
The Former Yugoslav Republic of Macedonia	Macedonia	41 50 N	22 00 E
Thessaloniki (city; also Salonika)	Greece	40 38 N	22 57 E
Thimphu (capital)	Bhutan	27 28 N	89 39 E
Thuringia (region)	Germany	51 00 N	11 00 E
Thurston Island	Antarctica	72 20 S	99 00 W
Tiberias, Lake	Israel	32 48 N	35 35 E
Tibet (autonomous region; also Xizang)	China	32 00 N	90 00 E
Tibilisi (see T'bilisi)	Georgia	41 43 N	44 49 E
Tien Shan (mountains)	China, Kyrgyzstan	42 00 N	80 00 E
Tierra del Fuego (island, island group)	Argentina, Chile	54 00 S	69 00 W
Timor (island)	Timor-Leste, Indonesia	9 00 S	125 00 E
Timor Lorosa'e (local name for Timor-Leste)	Timor-Leste	9 00 N	126 00 E
Timor Sea	Pacific Ocean	11 00 S	128 00 E
Tinian (island)	Northern Mariana Islands	15 00 N	145 38 E

Name	Entry in *The World Factbook*	Latitude (deg min)	Longitude (deg min)
Tiran, Strait of	Indian Ocean	28 00 N	34 27 E
Tirana, Tirane (capital)	Albania	41 20 N	19 50 E
Tirol, Tyrol (region)	Austria, Italy	47 00 N	11 00 E
Tobago (island)	Trinidad and Tobago	11 15 N	60 40 W
Tokyo (capital)	Japan	35 42 N	139 46 E
Tonkin, Gulf of	Pacific Ocean	20 00 N	108 00 E
Toronto (city)	Canada	43 40 N	79 23 W
Torres Strait	Pacific Ocean	10 25 S	142 10 E
Torshavn (capital)	Faroe Islands	62 01 N	6 46 W
Toshkent (see Tashkent)	Uzbekistan	41 20 N	69 18 E
Transcarpathia (region; alternate name for Carpatho-Ukraine)	Ukraine	48 22 N	23 32 E
Transjordan (former name for Jordan)	Jordan	31 00 N	36 00 E
Transkei (enclave)	South Africa	32 15 S	28 15 E
Transvaal (region; former name for northeastern South Africa)	South Africa	25 10 S	29 25 E
Transylvania (region)	Romania	46 30 N	24 00 E
Trindade, Ilha de (island)	Brazil	20 31 S	29 20 W
Trinidad (island)	Trinidad and Tobago	10 22 N	61 15 W
Tripoli (capital)	Libya	32 54 N	13 11 E
Tripoli (city)	Lebanon	34 26 N	35 51 E
Tripolitania (region)	Libya	31 00 N	14 00 E
Tristan da Cunha Group (island group)	Saint Helena, Ascension, and Tristan da Cunha	37 15 S	12 30 W
Trobriand Islands	Papua New Guinea	8 38 S	151 04 E
Tromelin Island	Indian Ocean	15 52 S	54 25 E
Trucial Coast (former name for the United Arab Emirates)	United Arab Emirates	24 00 N	54 00 E
Trucial Oman (former name for the United Arab Emirates)	United Arab Emirates	24 00 N	54 00 E
Trucial States (former name for the United Arab Emirates)	United Arab Emirates	24 00 N	54 00 E
Truk Islands (former name for the Chuuk Islands)	Federated States of Micronesia	7 25 N	151 47 E
Tsugaru Strait	Pacific Ocean	41 35 N	141 00 E
Tuamotu Islands (Iles Tuamotu)	French Polynesia	19 00 S	142 00 W
Tubuai Islands (Iles Tubuai)	French Polynesia	23 00 S	150 00 W
Tunb al Kubra (island)	Iran	26 14 N	55 19 E
Tunb as Sughra (island)	Iran	26 14 N	55 09 E
Tunis (capital)	Tunisia	36 48 N	10 11 E
Turin (city)	Italy	45 04 N	7 40 E
Turkish Straits (see Bosporus and Dardenelles)	Atlantic Ocean	40 40 N	28 00 E
Turkiye (local name for Turkey)	Turkey	39 00 N	35 00 E
Turkmenia, Turkmeniya (former name for Turkmenistan)	Turkmenistan	40 00 N	60 00 E
Turks Island Passage	Atlantic Ocean	21 40 N	71 00 W
Tuscany (region)	Italy	43 25 N	11 00 E
Tutuila (island)	American Samoa	14 18 S	170 42 W
Tyrrhenian Sea	Atlantic Ocean	40 00 N	12 00 E
Ubangi-Shari (former name for the Central African Republic	Central African Republic	6 38 N	20 33 E
Ukrayina (local name for Ukraine)	Ukraine	49 00 N	32 00 E
Ulaanbaatar (capital)	Mongolia	47 55 N	106 53 E
Ullung-do (island)	South Korea	37 29 N	130 52 E

Name	Entry in *The World Factbook*	Latitude (deg min)	Longitude (deg min)
Ulster (region)	Ireland, United Kingdom	54 35 N	7 00 W
Uman (local name for Oman)	Oman	21 00 N	57 00 E
Unimak Pass (strait)	Pacific Ocean	54 20 N	164 50 W
Union of Soviet Socialist Republics or USSR (former name of a large Eurasian empire, roughly coequal with the former Russian Empire)	Armenia, Azerbaijan, Belarus, Estonia, Georgia, Kazakhstan, Kyrgyzstan, Latvia, Lithuania, Moldova, Russia, Tajikistan, Turkmenistan, Ukraine, Uzbekistan		
United Arab Republic or UAR (former name for a federation between Egypt and Syria)	Egypt, Syria		
Upper Volta (former name for Burkina Faso)	Burkina Faso	13 00 N	2 00 W
Ural Mountains	Kazakhstan, Russia	60 00 N	60 00 E
Urdunn (local name for Jordan)	Jordan	31 00 N	36 00 E
Urundi (former name for Burundi)	Burundi	3 30 S	30 00 E
Ussuri River	China, Russia	48 28 N	135 02 E
Vaduz (capital)	Liechtenstein	47 09 N	9 31 E
Vakhan (Wakhan Corridor)	Afghanistan	37 00 N	73 00 E
Valletta (capital)	Malta	35 54 N	14 31 E
Valley, The (capital)	Anguilla	18 13 N	63 04 W
Van Diemen Strait (Osumi Strait)	Pacific Ocean	31 00 N	131 00 E
Vancouver (city)	Canada	49 16 N	123 08 W
Vancouver Island	Canada	49 45 N	126 00 W
Vatican City (capital)	Holy See	41 54 N	12 27 E
Velez de la Gomera, Penon de (island)	Spain	35 11 N	4 18 W
Venda (enclave)	South Africa	23 00 S	31 00 E
Verde Island Passage	Pacific Ocean	13 34 N	120 51 E
Victoria (capital)	Seychelles	4 38 S	55 27 E
Victoria (island)	Canada	71 00 N	110 00 W
Victoria Land (region)	Antarctica	72 00 S	155 00 E
Vienna (capital)	Austria	48 12 N	16 22 E
Vientiane (capital)	Laos	17 58 N	102 36 E
Vilnius (capital)	Lithuania	54 41 N	25 19 E
Viti Levu (island)	Fiji	18 00 S	178 00 E
Vladivostok (city)	Russia	43 10 N	131 56 E
Vojvodina (region)	Serbia	45 35 N	20 00 E
Volcano Islands	Japan	25 00 N	141 00 E
Vostok Island	Kiribati	10 06 S	152 23 W
Wake Atoll	Wake Island	19 17 N	166 39 E
Wakhan Corridor (see Vakhan)	Afghanistan	37 00 N	73 00 E
Walachia (region)	Romania	44 45 N	26 05 E
Wales (region)	United Kingdom	52 30 N	3 30 W
Wallis Islands	Wallis and Futuna	13 17 S	176 10 W
Walvis Bay (city; former exclave)	Namibia	22 59 S	14 31 E
Warsaw (capital)	Poland	52 15 N	21 00 E
Washington, DC (capital)	United States	38 53 N	77 02 W
Weddell Sea	Southern Ocean	72 00 S	45 00 W
Wellington (capital)	New Zealand	41 28 S	174 51 E

Name	Entry in *The World Factbook*	Latitude (deg min)	Longitude (deg min)
West Frisian Islands	Netherlands	53 26 N	5 30 E
West Germany (Federal Republic of Germany; former name for western portion of Germany)	Germany	53 22 N	5 20 E
West Island (capital)	Cocos (Keeling) Islands	12 10 S	96 55 E
West Korea Strait (Western Channel)	Pacific Ocean	34 40 N	129 00 E
West Pakistan (former name for present-day Pakistan)	Pakistan	30 00 N	70 00 E
West Siberian Plain	Russia	60 00 N	75 00 E
Western Channel (West Korea Strait)	Pacific Ocean	34 40 N	129 00 E
Western Samoa (former name for Samoa)	Samoa	13 35 S	172 20 W
Wetar Strait	Pacific Ocean	8 20 S	126 30 E
White Sea	Arctic Ocean	65 30 N	38 00 E
Wilkes Land (region)	Antarctica	71 00 S	120 00 E
Willemstad (capital)	Curacao	12 06 N	68 56 W
Windhoek (capital)	Namibia	22 34 S	17 06 E
Windward Passage	Atlantic Ocean	20 00 N	73 50 W
Winnipeg (city)	Canada	49 53 N	97 10 W
Wrangel Island (Ostrov Vrangelya)	Russia	71 14 N	179 36 W
Xianggang (local name for Hong Kong)	Hong Kong	22 15 N	114 10 E
Y'israel (local name for Israel)	Israel	31 30 N	34 45 E
Yaitopya (local name for Ethiopia)	Ethiopia	8 00 N	38 00 E
Yalu River	China, North Korea	39 55 N	124 20 E
Yamoussoukro (capital)	Cote d'Ivoire	6 49 N	5 17 W
Yangon (see Rangoon)	Burma	16 47 N	96 10 E
Yaounde (capital)	Cameroon	3 52 N	11 31 E
Yap Islands	Federated States of Micronesia	9 30 N	138 00 E
Yaren (governmental center)	Nauru	0 32 S	166 55 E
Yekaterinburg (city; formerly Sverdlovsk)	Russia	56 50 N	60 39 E
Yellow Sea	Pacific Ocean	36 00 N	123 00 E
Yemen Arab Republic (also Yemen (Sanaa); former name for northern portion of Yemen)	Yemen	15 00 N	44 00 E
Yemen, People's Democratic Republic of (also Yemen (Aden); former name for southern portion of Yemen)	Yemen	14 00 N	46 00 E
Yerevan (capital)	Armenia	40 11 N	44 30 E
Yokohama (city)	Japan	35 26 N	139 37 E
Youth, Isle of (Isla de la Juventud)	Cuba	21 40 N	82 50 W
Yucatan Channel	Atlantic Ocean	21 45 N	85 45 W
Yucatan Peninsula	Mexico	19 30 N	89 00 W
Yugoslavia (former name for a federation of Serbia and Montenegro)	Montenegro, Serbia	43 00 N	21 00 E
Yugoslavia, Kingdom of (former name for a Balkan federation)	Bosnia and Herzegovina, Croatia, Macedonia, Montenegro, Serbia, Slovenia	43 00 N	19 00 E
Yugoslavia, Socialist Federal Republic of (former name for a Balkan federation)	Bosnia and Herzegovina, Croatia, Macedonia, Montenegro, Serbia, Slovenia	43 00 N	19 00 E
Zagreb (capital)	Croatia	45 48 N	15 58 E
Zaire (former name for the Democratic Republic of the Congo)	Democratic Republic of the Congo	15 00 S	30 00 E
Zakhalinskiy Zaliv (bay)	Pacific Ocean	54 00 N	142 00 E

Name	Entry in *The World Factbook*	Latitude (deg min)	Longitude (deg min)
Zaliv Shelikhova (bay)	Pacific Ocean	60 00 N	157 30 E
Zambezia (region)	Mozambique	16 00 S	37 00 E
Zanzibar (island)	Tanzania	6 10 S	39 11 E
Zhong Guo, Zhonghua (local name for China)	China	35 00 N	105 00 E
Zion, Mount (locale in Jerusalem)	Israel, West Bank	31 46 N	35 14 E
Zurich (city)	Switzerland	47 23 N	8 32 E

WEIGHTS AND MEASURES

Note: At this time, only three countries—Burma, Liberia, and the US—have not adopted the International System of Units (SI, or metric system) as their official system of weights and measures. Although use of the metric system has been sanctioned by law in the US since 1866, it has been slow in displacing the American adaptation of the British Imperial System known as the US Customary System. The US is the only industrialized nation that does not mainly use the metric system in its commercial and standards activities, but there is increasing acceptance in science, medicine, government, and many sectors of industry.

Mathematical Notation

Mathematical Power	Name
10^{18} or 1,000,000,000,000,000,000	one quintillion
10^{15} or 1,000,000,000,000,000	one quadrillion
10^{12} or 1,000,000,000,000	one trillion
10^{9} or 1,000,000,000	one billion
10^{6} or 1,000,000	one million
10^{3} or 1,000	one thousand
10^{2} or 100	one hundred
10^{1} or 10	ten
10^{0} or 1	one
10^{-1} or 0.1	one-tenth
10^{-2} or 0.01	one-hundredth
10^{-3} or 0.001	one-thousandth
10^{-6} or 0.000 001	one-millionth
10^{-9} or 0.000 000 001	one-billionth
10^{-12} or 0.000 000 000 001	one-trillionth
10^{-15} or 0.000 000 000 000 001	one-quadrillionth
10^{-18} or 0.000 000 000 000 000 001	one-quintillionth

Metric Interrelationships

Prefix	Symbol	Length, weight, or capacity
yotta	Y	10^{24}
zetta	Z	10^{21}
exa	E	10^{18}
peta	P	10^{15}
tera	T	10^{12}
giga	G	10^{9}
mega	M	10^{6}
kilo	k	10^{3}
hecto	h	10^{2}
deka	da	10^{1}
basic unit	–	1 meter, 1 gram, 1 liter
deci	d	10^{-1}
centi	c	10^{-2}

milli	m	10^{-3}
micro	u	10^{-6}
nano	n	10^{-9}
pico	p	10^{-12}
femto	f	10^{-15}
atto	a	10^{-18}
zepto	z	10^{-21}
yocto	y	10^{-24}

Conversion Factors

To Convert From	To	Multiply By
acres	ares	40.468 564 224
acres	hectares	0.404 685 642 24
acres	square feet	43,560
acres	square kilometers	0.004 046 856 422 4
acres	square meters	4,046.856 422 4
acres	square miles (statute)	0.001 562 50
acres	square yards	4,840
ares	square meters	100
ares	square yards	119.599
barrels, US beer	gallons	31
barrels, US beer	liters	117.347 77
barrels, US petroleum	gallons (British)	34.97
barrels, US petroleum	gallons (US)	42
barrels, US petroleum	liters	158.987 29
barrels, US proof spirits	gallons	40
barrels, US proof spirits	liters	151.416 47
bushels (US)	bushels (British)	0.968 9
bushels (US)	cubic feet	1.244 456
bushels (US)	cubic inches	2,150.42
bushels (US)	cubic meters	0.035 239 07
bushels (US)	cubic yards	0.046 090 96
bushels (US)	dekaliters	3.523 907
bushels (US)	dry pints	64
bushels (US)	dry quarts	32
bushels (US)	liters	35.239 070 17
bushels (US)	pecks	4
cables	fathoms	120
cables	meters	219.456
cables	yards	240
carat	milligrams	200
centimeters	feet	0.032 808 40
centimeters	inches	0.393 700 8
centimeters	meters	0.01
centimeters	yards	0.010 936 13
centimeters, cubic	cubic inches	0.061 023 744

Conversion Factors

To Convert From	To	Multiply By
centimeters, square	square feet	0.001 076 39
centimeters, square	square inches	0.155 000 31
centimeters, square	square meters	0.000 1
centimeters, square	square yards	0.000 119 599
chains, square surveyor's	ares	4.046 86
chains, square surveyor's	square feet	4,356
chains, surveyor's	feet	66
chains, surveyor's	meters	20.116 8
chains, surveyor's	rods	4
cords of wood	cubic feet	128
cords of wood	cubic meters	3.624 556
cords of wood	cubic yards	4.740 7
cups	liquid ounces (US)	8
cups	liters	0.236 588 2
degrees Celsius	degrees Fahrenheit	multiply by 1.8 and add 32
degrees Fahrenheit	degrees Celsius	subtract 32 and divide by 1.8
dekaliters	bushels	0.283 775 9
dekaliters	cubic feet	0.353 146 7
dekaliters	cubic inches	610.237 4
dekaliters	dry pints	18.161 66
dekaliters	dry quarts	9.080 829 8
dekaliters	liters	10
dekaliters	pecks	1.135 104
drams, avoirdupois	avoirdupois ounces	0.062 55
drams, avoirdupois	grains	27.344
drams, avoirdupois	grams	1.771 845 2
drams, troy	grains	60
drams, troy	grams	3.887 934 6
drams, troy	scruples	3
drams, troy	troy ounces	0.125
drams, liquid (US)	cubic inches	0.226
drams, liquid (US)	liquid drams (British)	1.041
drams, liquid (US)	liquid ounces	0.125
drams, liquid (US)	milliliters	3.696 69
drams, liquid (US)	minims	60
fathoms	feet	6
fathoms	meters	1.828 8
feet	centimeters	30.48
feet	inches	12
feet	kilometers	0.000 304 8
feet	meters	0.304 8
feet	statute miles	0.000 189 39
feet	yards	0.333 333 3
feet, cubic	bushels	0.803 563 95
feet, cubic	cubic decimeters	28.316 847
feet, cubic	cubic inches	1,728

Conversion Factors

To Convert From	To	Multiply By
feet, cubic	cubic meters	0.028 316 846 592
feet, cubic	cubic yards	0.037 037 04
feet, cubic	dry pints	51.428 09
feet, cubic	dry quarts	25.714 05
feet, cubic	gallons	7.480 519
feet, cubic	gills	239.376 6
feet, cubic	liquid ounces	957.506 5
feet, cubic	liquid pints	59.844 16
feet, cubic	liquid quarts	29.922 08
feet, cubic	liters	28.316 846 592
feet, cubic	pecks	3.214 256
feet, square	acres	0.000 022 956 8
feet, square	square centimeters	929.030 4
feet, square	square decimeters	9.290 304
feet, square	square inches	144
feet, square	square meters	0.092 903 04
feet, square	square yards	0.111 111 1
furlongs	feet	660
furlongs	inches	7,920
furlongs	meters	201.168
furlongs	statute miles	0.125
furlongs	yards	220
gallons, liquid (US)	cubic feet	0.133 680 6
gallons, liquid (US)	cubic inches	231
gallons, liquid (US)	cubic meters	0.003 785 411 784
gallons, liquid (US)	cubic yards	0.004 951 13
gallons, liquid (US)	gills (US)	32
gallons, liquid (US)	liquid gallons (British)	0.832 67
gallons, liquid (US)	liquid ounces	128
gallons, liquid (US)	liquid pints	8
gallons, liquid (US)	liquid quarts	4
gallons, liquid (US)	liters	3.785 411 784
gallons, liquid (US)	milliliters	3,785.411 784
gallons, liquid (US)	minims	61,440
gills (US)	centiliters	11.829 4
gills (US)	cubic feet	0.004 177 517
gills (US)	cubic inches	7.218 75
gills (US)	gallons	0.031 25
gills (US)	gills (British)	0.832 67
gills (US)	liquid ounces	4
gills (US)	liquid pints	0.25
gills (US)	liquid quarts	0.125
gills (US)	liters	0.118 294 118 25
gills (US)	milliliters	118.294 118 25
gills (US)	minims	1,920
grains	avoirdupois drams	0.036 571 43

Conversion Factors

To Convert From	To	Multiply By
grains	avoirdupois ounces	0.002 285 71
grains	avoirdupois pounds	0.000 142 86
grains	grams	0.064 798 91
grains	kilograms	0.000 064 798 91
grains	milligrams	64.798 910
grains	pennyweights	0.042
grains	scruples	0.05
grains	troy drams	0.016 6
grains	troy ounces	0.002 083 33
grains	troy pounds	0.000 173 61
grams	avoirdupois drams	0.564 383 39
grams	avoirdupois ounces	0.035 273 961
grams	avoirdupois pounds	0.002 204 622 6
grams	grains	15.432 361
grams	kilograms	0.001
grams	milligrams	1,000
grams	troy ounces	0.032 150 746 6
grams	troy pounds	0.002 679 23
hands (height of horse)	centimeters	10.16
hands (height of horse)	inches	4
hectares	acres	2.471 053 8
hectares	square feet	107,639.1
hectares	square kilometers	0.01
hectares	square meters	10,000
hectares	square miles	0.003 861 02
hectares	square yards	11,959.90
hundredweights, long	avoirdupois pounds	112
hundredweights, long	kilograms	50.802 345
hundredweights, long	long tons	0.05
hundredweights, long	metric tons	0.050 802 345
hundredweights, long	short tons	0.056
hundredweights, short	avoirdupois pounds	100
hundredweights, short	kilograms	45.359 237
hundredweights, short	long tons	0.044 642 86
hundredweights, short	metric tons	0.045 359 237
hundredweights, short	short tons	0.05
inches	centimeters	2.54
inches	feet	0.083 333 33
inches	meters	0.025 4
inches	millimeters	25.4
inches	yards	0.027 777 78
inches, cubic	bushels	0.000 465 025
inches, cubic	cubic centimeters	16.387 064
inches, cubic	cubic feet	0.000 578 703 7
inches, cubic	cubic meters	0.000 016 387 064
inches, cubic	cubic yards	0.000 021 433 47

Conversion Factors To Convert From	To	Multiply By
inches, cubic	dry pints	0.029 761 6
inches, cubic	dry quarts	0.014 880 8
inches, cubic	gallons	0.004 329 0
inches, cubic	gills	0.138 528 1
inches, cubic	liquid ounces	0.554 112 6
inches, cubic	liquid pints	0.034 632 03
inches, cubic	liquid quarts	0.017 316 02
inches, cubic	liters	0.016 387 064
inches, cubic	milliliters	16.387 064
inches, cubic	minims (US)	265.974 0
inches, cubic	pecks	0.001 860 10
inches, square	square centimeters	6.451 600
inches, square	square feet	0.006 944 44
inches, square	square meters	0.000 645 16
inches, square	square yards	0.000 771 605
kilograms	avoirdupois drams	564.383 4
kilograms	avoirdupois ounces	35.273 962
kilograms	avoirdupois pounds	2.204 622 622
kilograms	grains	15,432.36
kilograms	grams	1,000
kilograms	long tons	0.000 984 2
kilograms	metric tons	0.001
kilograms	short hundredweights	0.022 046 23
kilograms	short tons	0.001 102 31
kilograms	troy ounces	32.150 75
kilograms	troy pounds	2.679 229
kilometers	meters	1,000
kilometers	statute miles	0.621 371 192
kilometers, square	acres	247.105 38
kilometers, square	hectares	100
kilometers, square	square meters	1,000,000
kilometers, square	statute miles	0.386 102 16
knots (nautical mi/hr)	kilometers/hour	1.852
knots (nautical mi/hr)	statute miles/hour	1.151
leagues, nautical	kilometers	5.556
leagues, nautical	nautical miles	3
leagues, statute	kilometers	4.828 032
leagues, statute	statute miles	3
links, square surveyor's	square centimeters	404.686
links, square surveyor's	square inches	62.726 4
links, surveyor's	centimeters	20.116 8
links, surveyor's	chains	0.01
links, surveyor's	inches	7.92
liters	bushels	0.028 377 59
liters	cubic feet	0.035 314 67
liters	cubic inches	61.023 74

Conversion Factors

To Convert From	To	Multiply By
liters	cubic meters	0.001
liters	cubic yards	0.001 307 95
liters	dekaliters	0.1
liters	dry pints	1.816 166
liters	dry quarts	0.908 082 98
liters	gallons	0.264 172 052
liters	gills (US)	8.453 506
liters	liquid ounces	33.814 02
liters	liquid pints	2.113 376
liters	liquid quarts	1.056 688 2
liters	milliliters	1,000
liters	pecks	0.113 510 4
meters	centimeters	100
meters	feet	3.280 839 895
meters	inches	39.370 079
meters	kilometers	0.001
meters	millimeters	1,000
meters	statute miles	0.000 621 371
meters	yards	1.093 613 298
meters, cubic	bushels	28.377 59
meters, cubic	cubic feet	35.314 666 7
meters, cubic	cubic inches	61,023.744
meters, cubic	cubic yards	1.307 950 619
meters, cubic	gallons	264.172 05
meters, cubic	liters	1,000
meters, cubic	pecks	113.510 4
meters, square	acres	0.000 247 105 38
meters, square	hectares	0.000 1
meters, square	square centimeters	10,000
meters, square	square feet	10.763 910 4
meters, square	square inches	1,550.003 1
meters, square	square yards	1.195 990 046
microns	meters	0.000 001
microns	inches	0.000 039 4
mils	inches	0.001
mils	millimeters	0.025 4
miles, nautical	kilometers	1.852 0
miles, nautical	statute miles	1.150 779 4
miles, statute	centimeters	160,934.4
miles, statute	feet	5,280
miles, statute	furlongs	8
miles, statute	inches	63,360
miles, statute	kilometers	1.609 344
miles, statute	meters	1,609.344
miles, statute	rods	320
miles, statute	yards	1,760

Conversion Factors

To Convert From	To	Multiply By
miles, square nautical	square kilometers	3.429 904
miles, square nautical	square statute miles	1.325
miles, square statute	acres	640
miles, square statute	hectares	258.998 811 033 6
miles, square statute	sections	1
miles, square statute	square kilometers	2.589 988 110 336
miles, square statute	square nautical miles	0.755 miles
miles, square statute	square rods	102,400
milligrams	grains	0.015 432 358 35
milliliters	cubic inches	0.061 023 744
milliliters	gallons	0.000 264 17
milliliters	gills (US)	0.008 453 5
milliliters	liquid ounces	0.033 814 02
milliliters	liquid pints	0.002 113 4
milliliters	liquid quarts	0.001 056 7
milliliters	liters	0.001
milliliters	minims	16.230 73
millimeters	inches	0.039 370 078 7
minims (US)	cubic inches	0.003 759 77
minims (US)	gills (US)	0.000 520 83
minims (US)	liquid ounces	0.002 083 33
minims (US)	milliliters	0.061 611 52
minims (US)	minims (British)	1.041
ounces, avoirdupois	avoirdupois drams	16
ounces, avoirdupois	avoirdupois pounds	0.062 5
ounces, avoirdupois	grains	437.5
ounces, avoirdupois	grams	28.349 523 125
ounces, avoirdupois	kilograms	0.028 349 523 125
ounces, avoirdupois	troy ounces	0.911 458 3
ounces, avoirdupois	troy pounds	0.075 954 86
ounces, liquid (US)	cubic feet	0.001 044 38
ounces, liquid (US)	centiliters	2.957 35
ounces, liquid (US)	cubic inches	1.804 687 5
ounces, liquid (US)	gallons	0.007 812 5
ounces, liquid (US)	gills (US)	0.25
ounces, liquid (US)	liquid drams	8
ounces, liquid (US)	liquid ounces (British)	1.041
ounces, liquid (US)	liquid pints	0.062 5
ounces, liquid (US)	liquid quarts	0.031 25
ounces, liquid (US)	liters	0.029 573 53
ounces, liquid (US)	milliliters	29.573 529 6
ounces, liquid (US)	minims	480
ounces, troy	avoirdupois drams	17.554 29
ounces, troy	avoirdupois ounces	1.097 143
ounces, troy	avoirdupois pounds	0.068 571 43
ounces, troy	grains	480

Conversion Factors

To Convert From	To	Multiply By
ounces, troy	grams	31.103 476 8
ounces, troy	pennyweights	20
ounces, troy	troy drams	8
ounces, troy	troy pounds	0.083 333 3
paces (US)	centimeters	76.2
paces (US)	inches	30
pecks (US)	bushels	0.25
pecks (US)	cubic feet	0.311 114
pecks (US)	cubic inches	537.605
pecks (US)	cubic meters	0.008 809 77
pecks (US)	cubic yards	0.011 522 74
pecks (US)	dekaliters	0.880 976 75
pecks (US)	dry pints	16
pecks (US)	dry quarts	8
pecks (US)	liters	8.809 767 5
pecks (US)	pecks (British)	0.968 9
pennyweights	grains	24
pennyweights	grams	1.555 173 84
pennyweights	troy ounces	0.05
pints, dry (US)	bushels	0.015 625
pints, dry (US)	cubic feet	0.019 444 63
pints, dry (US)	cubic inches	33.600 312 5
pints, dry (US)	dekaliters	0.055 061 05
pints, dry (US)	dry pints (British)	0.968 9
pints, dry (US)	dry quarts	0.5
pints, dry (US)	liters	0.550 610 47
pints, liquid (US)	cubic feet	0.016 710 07
pints, liquid (US)	cubic inches	28.875
pints, liquid (US)	deciliters	4.731 76
pints, liquid (US)	gallons	0.125
pints, liquid (US)	gills (US)	4
pints, liquid (US)	liquid ounces	16
pints, liquid (US)	liquid pints (British)	0.832 67
pints, liquid (US)	liquid quarts	0.5
pints, liquid (US)	liters	0.473 176 473
pints, liquid (US)	milliliters	473.176 473
pints, liquid (US)	minims	7,680
points (typographical)	inches	0.013 837
points (typographical)	millimeters	0.351 459 8
pounds, avoirdupois	avoirdupois drams	256
pounds, avoirdupois	avoirdupois ounces	16
pounds, avoirdupois	grains	7,000
pounds, avoirdupois	grams	453.592 37
pounds, avoirdupois	kilograms	0.453 592 37
pounds, avoirdupois	long tons	0.000 446 428 6
pounds, avoirdupois	metric tons	0.000 453 592 37

Conversion Factors

To Convert From	To	Multiply By
pounds, avoirdupois	quintals	0.004 535 92
pounds, avoirdupois	short tons	0.000 5
pounds, avoirdupois	troy ounces	14.583 33
pounds, avoirdupois	troy pounds	1.215 278
pounds, troy	avoirdupois drams	210.651 4
pounds, troy	avoirdupois ounces	13.165 71
pounds, troy	avoirdupois pounds	0.822 857 1
pounds, troy	grains	5,760
pounds, troy	grams	373.241 721 6
pounds, troy	kilograms	0.373 241 721 6
pounds, troy	pennyweights	240
pounds, troy	troy ounces	12
quarts, dry (US)	bushels	0.031 25
quarts, dry (US)	cubic feet	0.038 889 25
quarts, dry (US)	cubic inches	67.200 625
quarts, dry (US)	dekaliters	0.110 122 1
quarts, dry (US)	dry pints	2
quarts, dry (US)	dry quarts (British)	0.968 9
quarts, dry (US)	liters	1.101 221
quarts, dry (US)	pecks	0.125
quarts, dry (US)	pints, dry (US)	2
quarts, liquid (US)	cubic feet	0.033 420 14
quarts, liquid (US)	cubic inches	57.75
quarts, liquid (US)	deciliters	9.463 53
quarts, liquid (US)	gallons	0.25
quarts, liquid (US)	gills (US)	8
quarts, liquid (US)	liquid ounces	32
quarts, liquid (US)	liquid pints (US)	2
quarts, liquid (US)	liquid quarts (British)	0.832 67
quarts, liquid (US)	liters	0.946 352 946
quarts, liquid (US)	milliliters	946.352 946
quarts, liquid (US)	minims	15,360
quintals	avoirdupois pounds	220.462 26
quintals	kilograms	100
quintals	metric tons	0.1
rods	feet	16.5
rods	meters	5.029 2
rods	yards	5.5
rods, square	acres	0.006 25
rods, square	square meters	25.292 85
rods, square	square yards	30.25
scruples	grains	20
scruples	grams	1.295 978 2
scruples	troy drams	0.333
sections (US)	square kilometers	2.589 988 1
sections (US)	square statute miles	1

Conversion Factors

To Convert From	To	Multiply By
spans	centimeters	22.86
spans	inches	9
steres	cubic meters	1
steres	cubic yards	1.307 95
tablespoons	milliliters	14.786 76
tablespoons	teaspoons	3
teaspoons	milliliters	4.928 922
teaspoons	tablespoons	0.333 333
ton-miles, long	metric ton-kilometers	1.635 169
ton-miles, short	metric ton-kilometers	1.459 972
tons, gross register	cubic feet of permanently enclosed space	100
tons, gross register	cubic meters of permanently enclosed space	2.831 684 7
tons, long (deadweight)	avoirdupois ounces	35,840
tons, long (deadweight)	avoirdupois pounds	2,240
tons, long (deadweight)	kilograms	1,016.046 909 8
tons, long (deadweight)	long hundredweights	20
tons, long (deadweight)	metric tons	1.016 046 908 8
tons, long (deadweight)	short hundredweights	22.4
tons, long (deadweight)	short tons	1.12
tons, metric	avoirdupois pounds	2,204.623
tons, metric	kilograms	1,000
tons, metric	long hundredweights	19.684 130 3
tons, metric	long tons	0.984 206 5
tons, metric	quintals	10
tons, metric	short hundredweights	22.046 23
tons, metric	short tons	1.102 311 3
tons, metric	troy ounces	32,150.75
tons, net register	cubic feet of permanently enclosed space for cargo and passengers	100
tons, net register	cubic meters of permanently enclosed space for cargo and passengers	2.831 684 7
tons, shipping	cubic feet of permanently enclosed cargo space	42
tons, shipping	cubic meters of permanently enclosed cargo space	1.189 307 574
tons, short	avoirdupois pounds	2,000
tons, short	kilograms	907.184 74
tons, short	long hundredweights	17.857 14
tons, short	long tons	0.892 857 1
tons, short	metric tons	0.907 184 74
tons, short	short hundredweights	20
townships (US)	sections	36
townships (US)	square kilometers	93.239 572
townships (US)	square statute miles	36
miles, square statute	acres	640
miles, square statute	hectares	258.998 811 033 6
miles, square statute	square feet	27,878,400

Conversion Factors

To Convert From	To	Multiply By
miles, square statute	square meters	2,589,988.110 336
miles, square statute	square yards	3,097,600
yards	centimeters	91.44
yards	feet	3
yards	inches	36
yards	meters	0.914 4
yards	miles	0.000 568 18
yards, cubic	bushels	21.696 227
yards, cubic	cubic feet	27
yards, cubic	cubic inches	46,656
yards, cubic	cubic meters	0.764 554 857 984
yards, cubic	gallons	201.974 0
yards, cubic	liters	764.554 857 984
yards, cubic	pecks	86.784 91
yards, square	acres	0.000 206 611 6
yards, square	hectares	0.000 083 612 736
yards, square	square centimeters	8,361.273 6
yards, square	square feet	9
yards, square	square inches	1,296
yards, square	square meters	0.836 127 36
yards, square	square miles	0.000 000 322 830 6

AFRICA

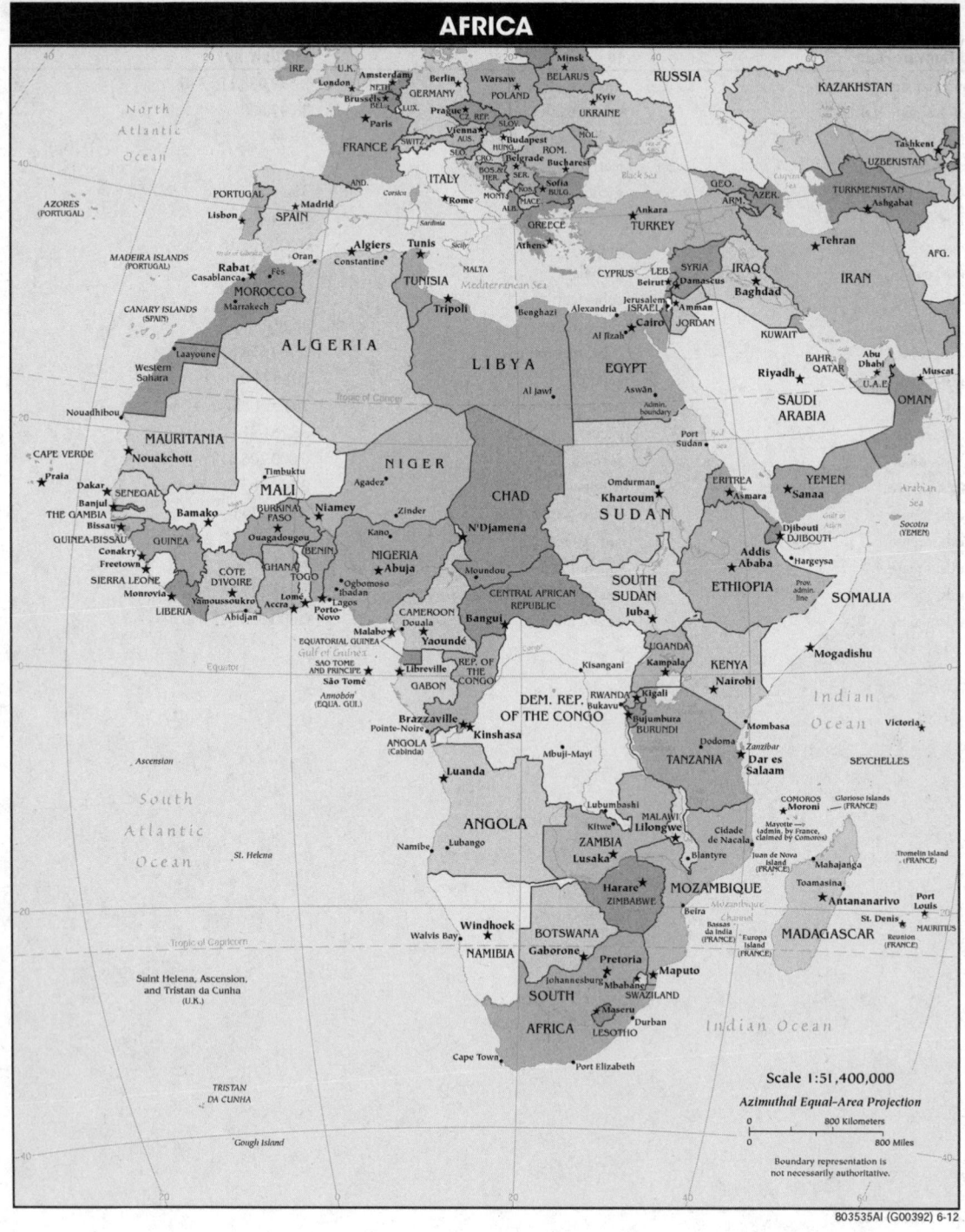

Scale 1:51,400,000

Azimuthal Equal-Area Projection

| 0 | 800 Kilometers |
| 0 | 800 Miles |

Boundary representation is
not necessarily authoritative.

803535AI (G00392) 6-12

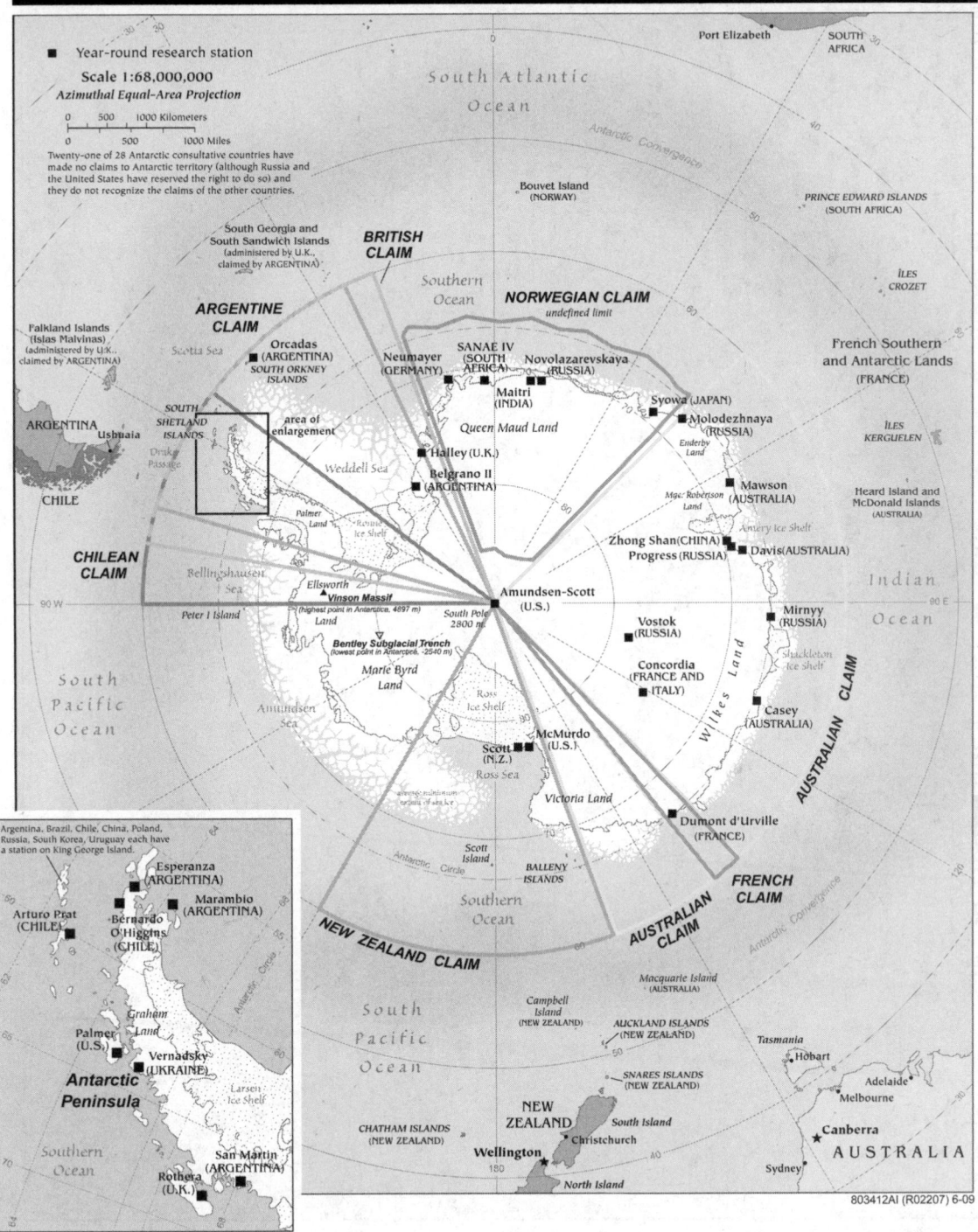

■ Year-round research station

Scale 1:68,000,000
Azimuthal Equal-Area Projection

0   500   1000 Kilometers
0   500   1000 Miles

Twenty-one of 28 Antarctic consultative countries have
made no claims to Antarctic territory (although Russia and
the United States have reserved the right to do so) and
they do not recognize the claims of the other countries.

North Pacific Ocean

Bering Sea

ALEUTIAN ISLANDS

KURIL ISLANDS

occupied by the Soviet Union in 1945; administered by Russia; claimed by Japan.

JAPAN

Sea of Japan

Petropavlovsk-Kamchatskiy

Sea of Okhotsk

Khabarovsk

Kodiak

Bethel

Providodniya

Anadyr'

Magadan

Okhotsk

CHINA

Anchorage

Nome

Bering Strait

Chukchi Sea

Arctic Circle

Oymyakon

Valdez

UNITED STATES

Fairbanks

Peyek

Cherskiy

Yakutsk

Juneau

Whitehorse

Dawson

Verkhoyansk

Prince George

Fort Nelson

Prudhoe Bay

Barrow

Wrangel Island

East Siberian Sea

Tiksi

120°

Inuvik

Beaufort Sea

sea ice extent summer average 2002-2005

NEW SIBERIAN ISLANDS

Laptev Sea

Fort McMurray

Yellowknife

Banks Island

Victoria Island

Cambridge Bay

QUEEN ELIZABETH ISLANDS

Arctic Ocean

80°

SEVERNAYA ZEMLYA

RUSSIA

Churchill

Arviat

Rankin Inlet

90°W

Repulse Bay

Gjoa Haven

Resolute

Ellesmere Island

Noril'sk

Kara Sea

Dikson

Hudson Bay

CANADA

Pond Inlet

Alert

FRANZ JOSEF LAND

90°E

Baffin Island

Qaanaaq (Thule)

Nord

NOVAYA ZEMLYA

Iqaluit

Baffin Bay

Yekaterinburg

Kuujjuaq

Davis Strait

Greenland (DENMARK)

Longyearbyen

Svalbard (NORWAY)

Barents Sea

70°

Perm'

Labrador Sea

Ilulissat (Jakobshavn)

Sisimiut (Holsteinsborg)

Nuuk (Godthåb)

Ittoqqortoormiit (Scoresbysund)

Murmansk

Arkhangel'sk

Kazan'

Samara

Qaqortoq (Julianehåb)

Tasiilaq

Jan Mayen (NORWAY)

Greenland Sea

Bjørnøya (NORWAY)

Nizhniy Novgorod

Moscow

Saratov

Denmark Strait

Norwegian Sea

70°

Volgograd

North Atlantic Ocean

Reykjavík

ICELAND

Arctic Circle

NORWAY

FINLAND

Saint Petersburg

Voronezh

KAZ.

Faroe Islands (DENMARK)

SWEDEN

Helsinki

Tórshavn

SHETLAND ISLANDS

Oslo

Stockholm

Tallinn EST.

Riga LATVIA

Minsk

Kharkiv

Rostov

Krasnodar

Scale 1:39,000,000

Lambert Azimuthal Equal-Area Projection

Dublin IRE.

Belfast

U.K.

Amsterdam

London

Brussels

North Sea

Copenhagen

DENMARK

Berlin

GERMANY

LITH. Vilnius

Kaliningrad RUS.

Warsaw

POLAND

Prague

CZECH REP.

BELARUS

Kyiv

UKRAINE

Chișinău

Black Sea

Baltic Sea

ROMANIA

TURKEY

0   500 Kilometers
0   500 Miles

Scale 1:48,000,000

Azimuthal Equal-Area Projection

0   800 Kilometers

0   800 Miles

Boundary representation is
not necessarily authoritative.

803537AI (G00543) 6-12

EUROPE

Greenland
(DENMARK)

Jan Mayen
(NORWAY)

Greenland
Sea

Denmark
Strait

Norwegian Sea

Barents
Sea

Hammerfest
Tromsø
Murmansk

Kiruna

Arctic Circle

Luleå
Oulu

Reykjavík
ICELAND

NORWAY

FINLAND

SWEDEN

Umeå

Tampere

Trondheim

Gulf
of
Bothnia

Saint Petersburg

RUSSIA

Tórshavn
Faroe Islands
(DENMARK)

SHETLAND
ISLANDS

Bergen

Gävle

Turku
Helsinki

Moscow

Oslo

Stockholm

ÅLAND
ISLANDS

Tallinn
ESTONIA

Rockall
(U.K.)

ORKNEY
ISLANDS

Stavanger

Gotland

Riga

LATVIA

HEBRIDES

Aberdeen

North
Sea

Baltic Sea

LITHUANIA

Vitsyebsk

Smolensk

North
Atlantic
Ocean

Glasgow
Edinburgh

UNITED

Øland

Vilnius

Mahilyow
Minsk

Belfast

Isle
of
Man
(U.K.)

DENMARK
Copenhagen

Malmö

Kaliningrad

RUSSIA

BELARUS

Homyel

Dublin

Leeds

KINGDOM

Liverpool
Manchester

Birmingham

Bornholm

Gdańsk

Hrodna

Brest

Chernihiv

Kyiv

IRELAND

Irish
Sea

Hamburg

Poznań

Warsaw

Cardiff

Celtic
Sea

London

Rotterdam
NETH.

Bremen

Berlin

POLAND

Łódź
Wrocław

Zhytomyr

Lviv

UKRAINE

Guernsey (U.K.)
Jersey (U.K.)

English Channel

Amsterdam

Essen
Cologne
Bonn

Leipzig

Kraków

Vinnytsya

Brussels
Lille
BEL.

GERMANY

Prague

Chernivtsi

Mykolayiv

Paris

Luxembourg
LUX.

Frankfurt

CZECH REPUBLIC

SLOVAKIA

Chişinău

Odesa

Strasbourg

Stuttgart

Brno

Iaşi
MOLDOVA

Nantes

Munich

Bratislava

Budapest

Cluj-
Napoca

Bay of
Biscay

Zürich
Bern
SWITZ.

LIECH.
Vaduz

AUSTRIA

Vienna

HUNGARY

ROMANIA

FRANCE

Geneva

Ljubljana

Zagreb

Bucharest

Constanţa

Lyon

SLOVENIA

Milan

Venice

CROATIA

Belgrade

Varna

Black
Sea

A Coruña

Bordeaux

Turin

Genoa

BOSNIA AND
HERZEGOVINA
Sarajevo

SERBIA

BULGARIA

Bilbao

Toulouse

MONACO

SAN
MARINO

Florence

MONT.
Podgorica

Priština
KOS.
Skopje
MACE.

Sofia

Istanbul

Porto

Zaragoza

Andorra
la Vella
ANDORRA

Marseille

Ligurian
Sea

Corsica

ITALY

Rome

Adriatic
Sea

Tirana

ALB.

Thessaloníki

Bursa

TURKEY

PORTUGAL
Lisbon

Madrid

Barcelona

VATICAN
CITY

Naples

GREECE

Izmir

SPAIN

Valencia

Balearic
Sea

Sardinia

Tyrrhenian
Sea

Athens

Aegean
Sea

Sevilla

BALEARIC
ISLANDS

Cagliari

Ionian
Sea

Rhodes

Gibraltar
(U.K.)

Málaga

Palermo

Mediterranean Sea

Crete

Ceuta
(SPAIN)

Alhorán
Melilla
(SPAIN)

Oran

Sicily

Scale 1:19,300,000
Lambert Conformal Conic Projection,
standard parallels 40°N and 68°N

Rabat
Casablanca

Algiers

Tunis

Valletta
MALTA

0   300 Kilometers

MOROCCO

ALGERIA

TUNISIA

0   300 Miles

803539AI (G00772) 6-12

1069

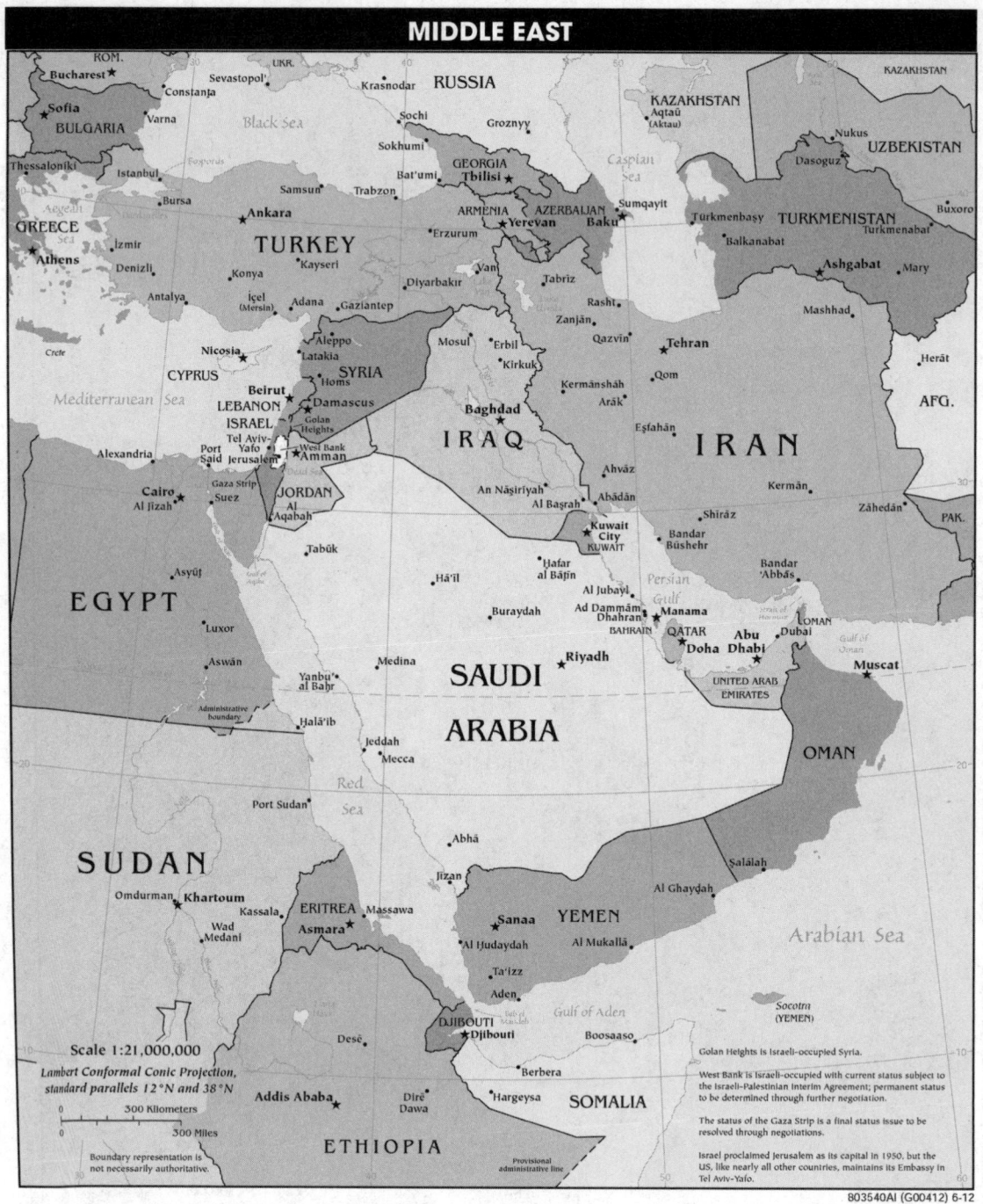

Scale 1:21,000,000

Lambert Conformal Conic Projection,
standard parallels 12°N and 38°N

0   300 Kilometers
0   300 Miles

Boundary representation is
not necessarily authoritative.

Golan Heights is Israeli-occupied Syria.

West Bank is Israeli-occupied with current status subject to
the Israeli-Palestinian Interim Agreement; permanent status
to be determined through further negotiation.

The status of the Gaza Strip is a final status issue to be
resolved through negotiations.

Israel proclaimed Jerusalem as its capital in 1950, but the
US, like nearly all other countries, maintains its Embassy in
Tel Aviv-Yafo.

803540AI (G00412) 6-12

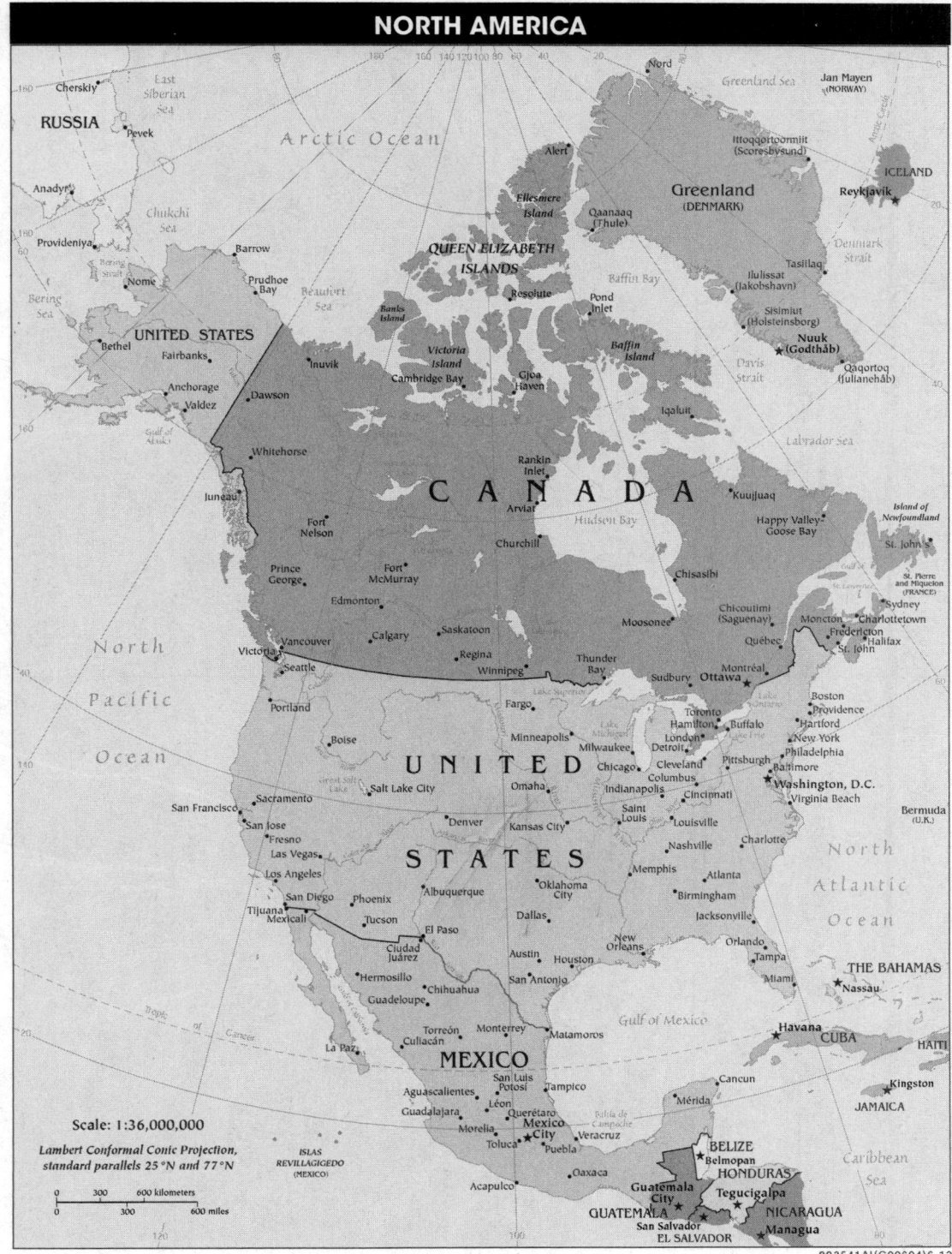

RUSSIA

Cherskiy
Pevek
Anadyr'
Provid:niya
Nome
Bethel

Arctic Ocean

Barrow
Prudhoe
Bay

UNITED STATES

Fairbanks
Anchorage
Valdez
Juneau

Nord
Greenland Sea
Jan Mayen
(NORWAY)

Alert

Ittoqqortoormiit
(Scoresbysund)

ICELAND

Reykjavik

Ellesmere
Island

Greenland
(DENMARK)

Qaanaaq
(Thule)

Tasiilaq

QUEEN ELIZABETH
ISLANDS

Baffin Bay

Ilulissat
(Jakobshavn)

Banks
Island

Resolute

Pond
Inlet

Sisimiut
(Holsteinsborg)

Victoria
Island

Cambridge Bay

Gjoa
Haven

Baffin
Island

Nuuk
(Godthåb)

Qaqortoq
(Julianehåb)

Inuvik

Davis
Strait

Dawson

Iqaluit

Whitehorse

Rankin
Inlet

Labrador Sea

C A N A D A

Arviat

Kuujjuaq

Island of
Newfoundland

Fort
Nelson

Churchill

Hudson Bay

Happy Valley-
Goose Bay

St. John's

Prince
George

Fort
McMurray

Chisasibi

St. Pierre
and Miquelon
(FRANCE)

Edmonton

Chicoutimi
(Saguenay)

Sydney

North

Vancouver

Calgary

Saskatoon

Moosonee

Québec

Moncton
Charlottetown
Fredericton
Halifax
St. John

Pacific

Victoria
Seattle

Regina

Winnipeg

Thunder
Bay

Sudbury

Montréal

Ottawa

Ocean

Portland

Fargo

Lake Superior

Toronto
Hamilton
London
Buffalo

Boston
Providence
Hartford
New York

Boise

Minneapolis

Milwaukee

Detroit

Pittsburgh
Philadelphia

U N I T E D

Chicago
Cleveland
Columbus

Baltimore

Salt Lake City

Omaha

Indianapolis
Cincinnati

Washington, D.C.
Virginia Beach

San Francisco
Sacramento

Denver

Kansas City

Saint
Louis

Louisville

Bermuda
(U.K.)

San Jose
Fresno
Las Vegas

S T A T E S

Nashville

Charlotte

North

Los Angeles

Albuquerque

Oklahoma
City

Memphis

Atlanta

Atlantic

San Diego
Tijuana
Mexicali

Phoenix
Tucson

Dallas

Birmingham

Jacksonville

Ocean

El Paso

Austin

New
Orleans

Orlando

Ciudad
Juárez

Houston

Tampa

Hermosillo

San Antonio

Miami

THE BAHAMAS

Chihuahua

Nassau

Guadeloupe

Gulf of Mexico

Havana

CUBA

La Paz

Torreón
Culiacán

Monterrey

Matamoros

Cancun

Kingston

HAITI

MEXICO

Mérida

JAMAICA

Aguascalientes

San Luis
Potosí

Tampico

Bahía de
Campeche

Guadalajara

León

Querétaro

BELIZE

Morelia

Mexico
City

Veracruz

Belmopan

Toluca

Puebla

Caribbean

Acapulco

Oaxaca

Guatemala
City

HONDURAS

Tegucigalpa

Sea

GUATEMALA

NICARAGUA

San Salvador
EL SALVADOR

Managua

Scale: 1:36,000,000

Lambert Conformal Conic Projection,
standard parallels 25°N and 77°N

ISLAS
REVILLAGIGEDO
(MEXICO)

0   300   600 kilometers
0   300   600 miles

803541AI(G00694)6-12

OCEANIA

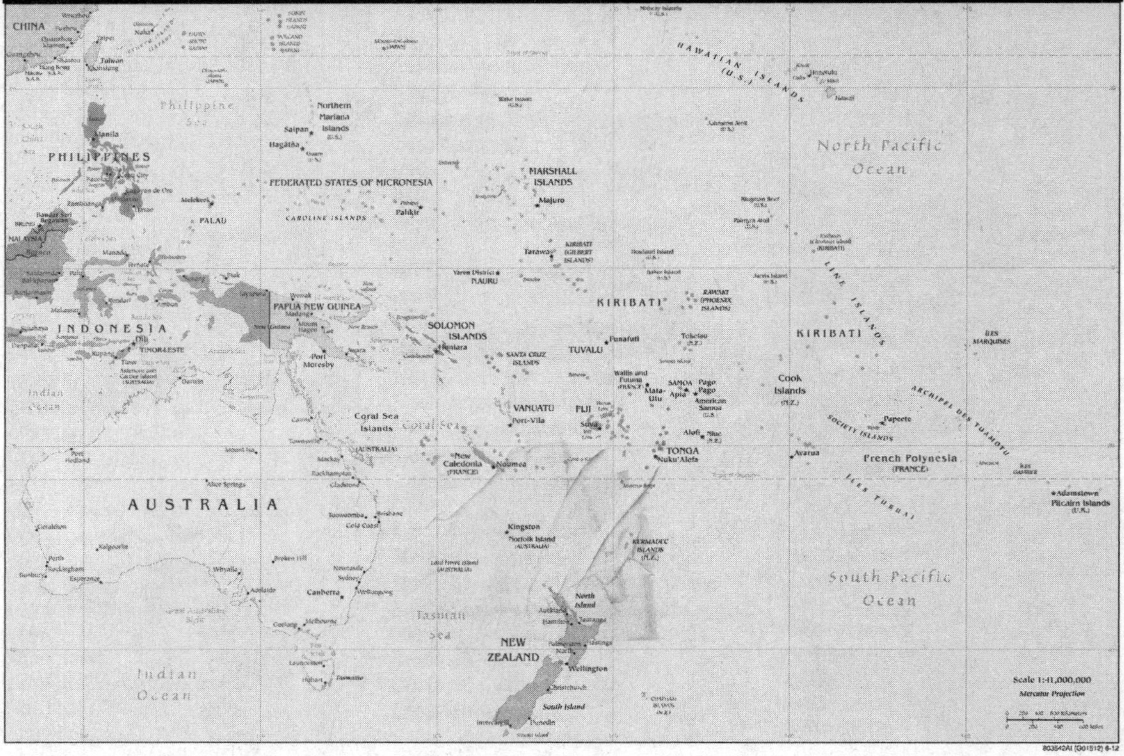

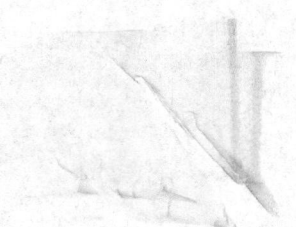

Scale 1:41,000,000
Mercator Projection

PHYSICAL MAP OF THE WORLD

Physical Map of the World, January 2015

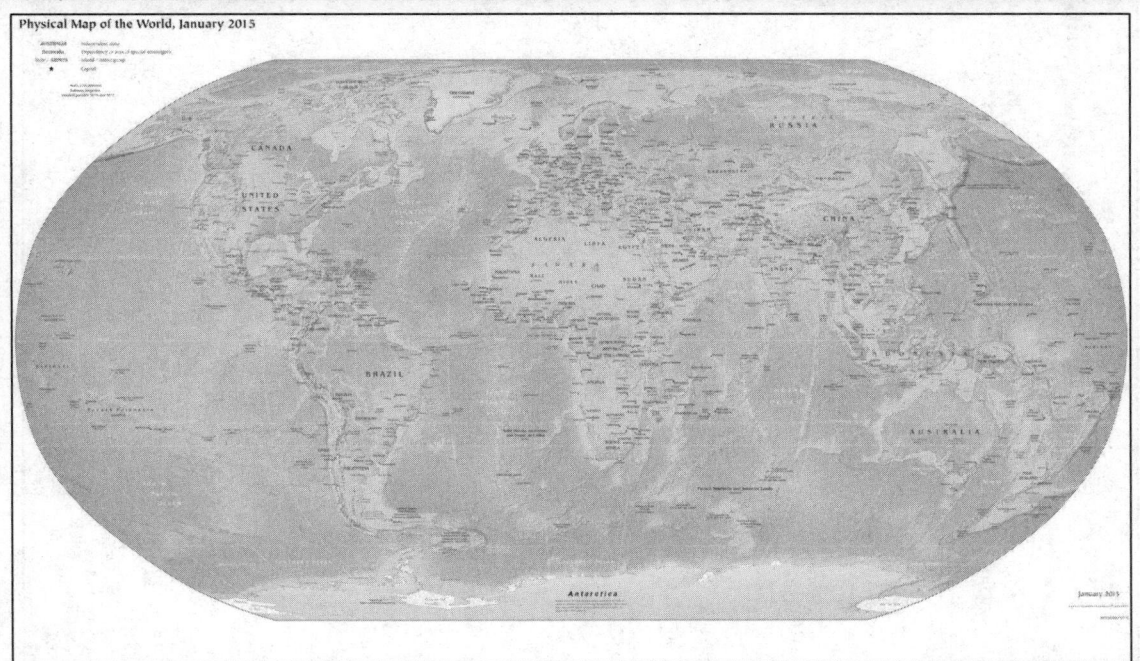

POLITICAL MAP OF THE WORLD

Political Map of the World, January 2015

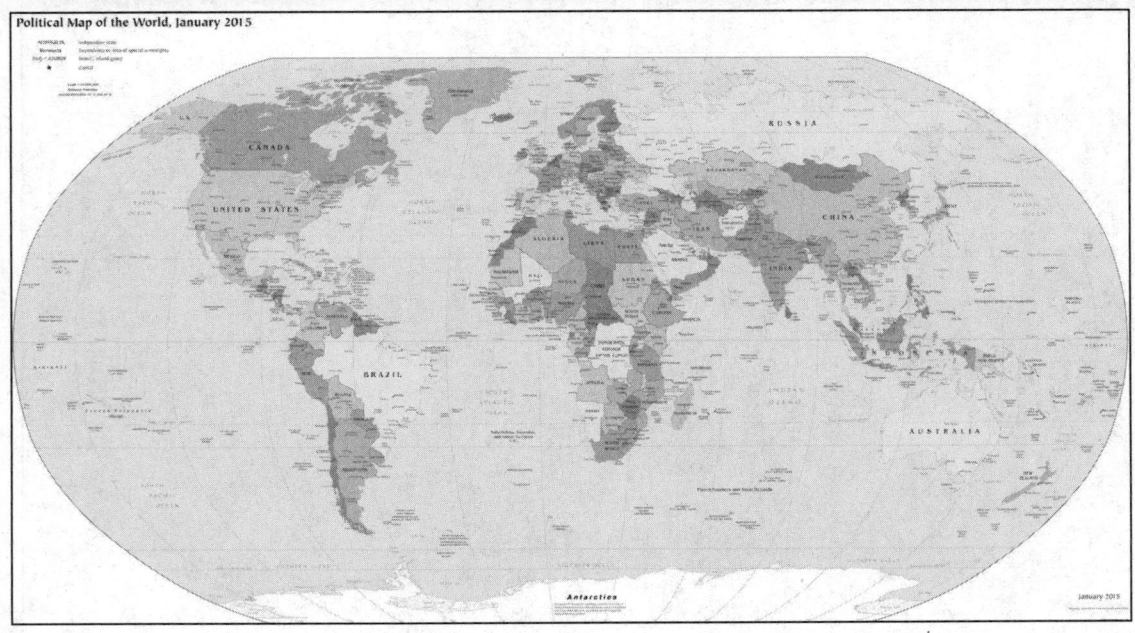

SOUTH AMERICA

Caribbean Sea

HONDURAS
Tegucigalpa
NICARAGUA
Managua
San José
COSTA RICA
PANAMA
Panama City

Isla de Providencia (COLOMBIA)
Isla de San Andrés (COLOMBIA)
Isla de Malpelo (COLOMBIA)

Barranquilla
Cartagena
Maracaibo
Cúcuta
San Cristóbal
Bucaramanga
Medellín
Pereira
Ibagué
Bogotá
Cali

Curaçao (NETH.)
Aruba (NETH.)

Martinique (FRANCE)
ST. LUCIA
ST. VINCENT AND THE GRENADINES
GRENADA
BARBADOS

Valencia
Caracas
Barcelona
Ciudad Guayana

Port of Spain
TRINIDAD AND TOBAGO

VENEZUELA

Georgetown
GUYANA
Paramaribo
SURINAME
Cayenne
French Guiana (FRANCE)

COLOMBIA

Boa Vista

North Atlantic Ocean

Equator

Quito
ECUADOR
Guayaquil
Cuenca

Iquitos

Macapá

Río Negro
Manaus
Santarém
Amazon
Belém
São Luís
Fortaleza

Piura
Chiclayo
Trujillo

Pucallpa
Río Branco
Pôrto Velho

Teresina
Natal
João Pessoa
Recife

South Pacific Ocean

Huánuco
PERU
Huancayo
Lima
Ica
Cusco
Arequipa
Arica
Iquique

Trinidad
La Paz
BOLIVIA
Cochabamba
Sucre Santa Cruz
Potosí

BRAZIL

Brasília

Goiânia
Contagem
Uberlândia
Belo Horizonte
Vitória

Maceió
Aracaju
Salvador

Tropic of Capricorn

Isla San Félix (CHILE)
Isla San Ambrosio (CHILE)

Antofagasta

Campo Grande

PARAGUAY
Asunción

Salta
San Miguel de Tucumán
Resistencia
Ciudad del Este

Londrina
Campinas
São Paulo
Santos
Rio de Janeiro
Curitiba
Joinvile
Florianópolis

ARCHIPIÉLAGO JUAN FERNÁNDEZ (CHILE)

CHILE

Córdoba
Mendoza
Rosario
Santa Fe
Salto
URUGUAY

Porto Alegre

Valparaíso
Santiago

Buenos Aires
La Plata
Montevideo

Concepción
ARGENTINA
Temuco
Bahía Blanca
Mar del Plata

South Atlantic Ocean

Puerto Montt
San Carlos de Bariloche

Comodoro Rivadavia

Scale 1:35,000,000
Azimuthal Equal-Area Projection

0   500 Kilometers
0   500 Miles

Boundary representation is not necessarily authoritative.

Río Gallegos
Punta Arenas
Strait of Magellan
Ushuaia
Cape Horn

Stanley
Falkland Islands (Islas Malvinas)
(administered by U.K., claimed by ARGENTINA)

South Georgia and South Sandwich Islands
(administered by U.K., claimed by ARGENTINA)

803543AI (G00186) 6-12

SOUTHEAST ASIA

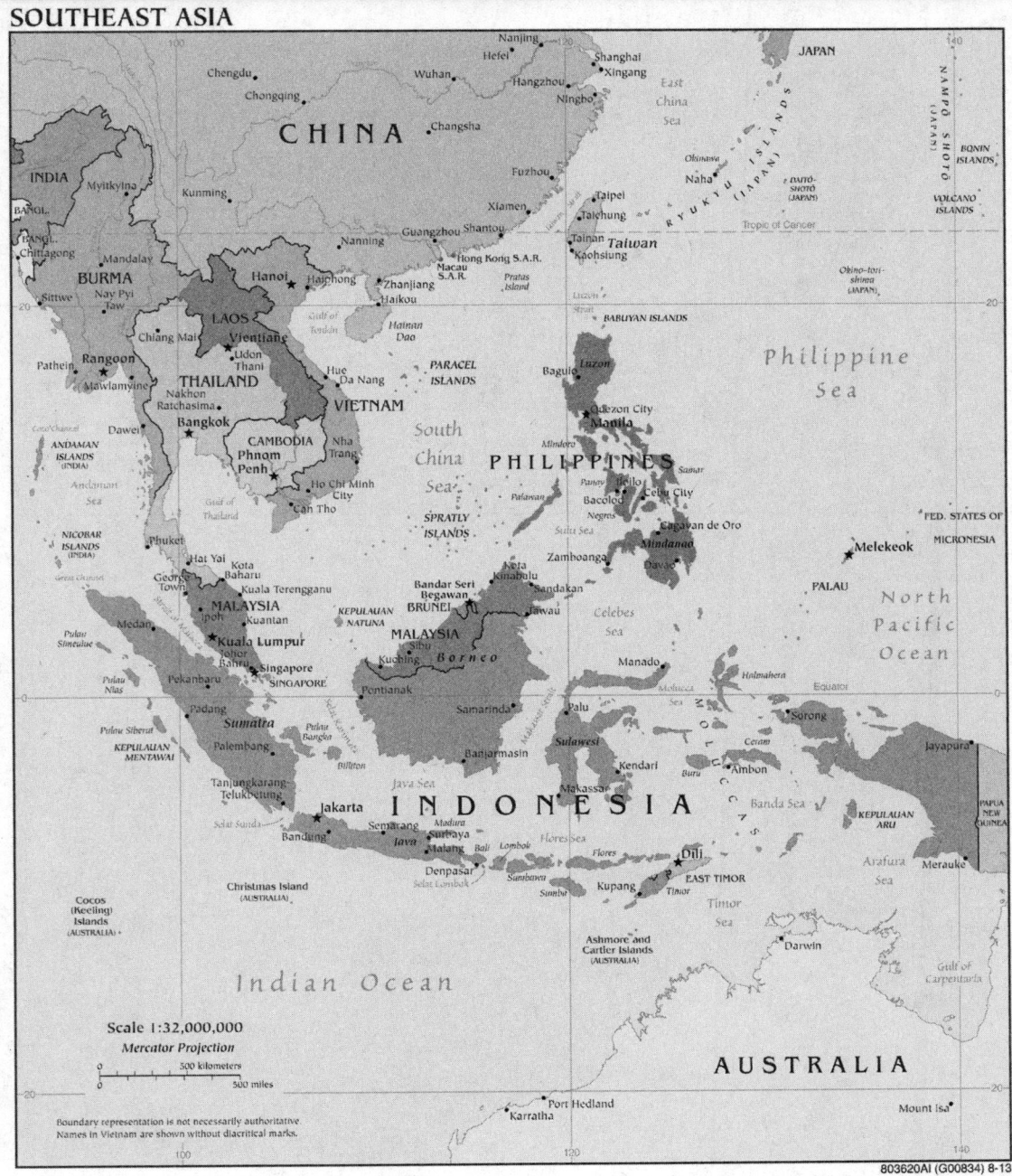

Scale 1:32,000,000
Mercator Projection

0   500 kilometers

0   500 miles

Boundary representation is not necessarily authoritative.
Names in Vietnam are shown without diacritical marks.

803620AI (G00834) 8-13

STANDARD TIME ZONE OF THE WORLD

UNITED STATES

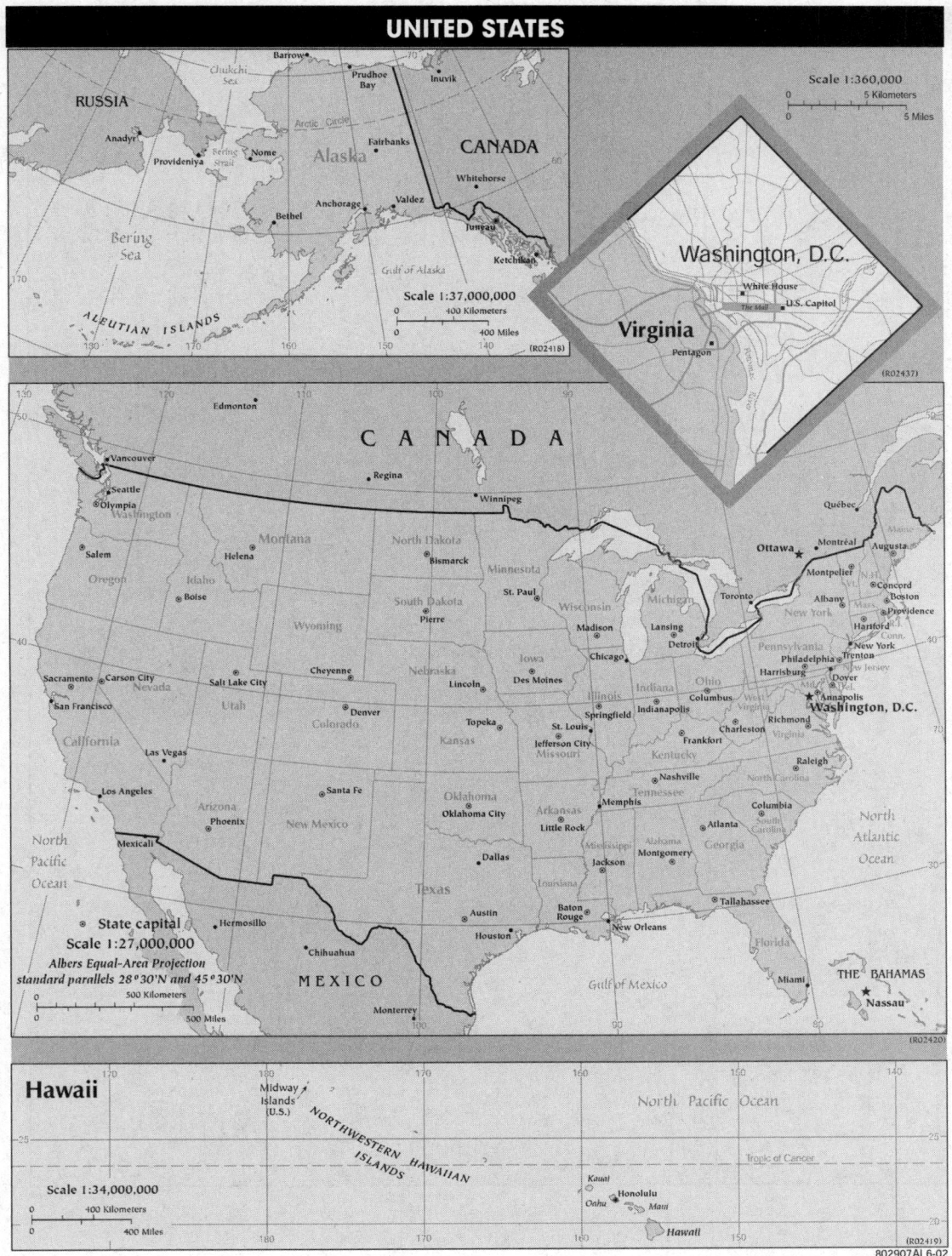

Scale 1:360,000

Washington, D.C.

White House
The Mall
U.S. Capitol

Virginia

Pentagon

(R02437)

RUSSIA

Chukchi Sea

Barrow

Prudhoe Bay

Inuvik

Arctic Circle

Anadyr

Nome

Fairbanks

CANADA

Alaska

Whitehorse

Providyeniya

Bering Strait

Anchorage

Valdez

Bethel

Juneau

Bering Sea

Gulf of Alaska

Ketchikan

ALEUTIAN ISLANDS

Scale 1:37,000,000

400 Kilometers

400 Miles

(R02418)

Edmonton

CANADA

Vancouver

Regina

Winnipeg

Québec

Seattle

Montréal

Augusta

Olympia

Ottawa

Montpelier

Washington

Montana

North Dakota

Minnesota

Salem

Helena

Bismarck

St. Paul

Wisconsin

Michigan

Toronto

New York

Concord

Boston

Providence

Hartford

Oregon

Idaho

South Dakota

Pierre

Madison

Lansing

Albany

Boise

Wyoming

Detroit

Pennsylvania

Philadelphia

Trenton

New York

New Jersey

Sacramento

Carson City

Salt Lake City

Cheyenne

Nebraska

Iowa

Lincoln

Des Moines

Chicago

Indiana

Ohio

Harrisburg

Dover

Washington, D.C.

San Francisco

Nevada

Utah

Denver

Topeka

Springfield

Indianapolis

Columbus

West Virginia

Richmond

Annapolis

California

Las Vegas

Colorado

Kansas

St. Louis

Jefferson City

Frankfort

Charleston

Virginia

Raleigh

Santa Fe

Missouri

Kentucky

North Carolina

Arizona

Phoenix

New Mexico

Oklahoma

Oklahoma City

Memphis

Nashville

Tennessee

Columbia

South Carolina

North Atlantic Ocean

Mexicali

Dallas

Arkansas

Little Rock

Mississippi

Atlanta

Georgia

North Pacific Ocean

Hermosillo

Texas

Austin

Jackson

Alabama

Montgomery

Tallahassee

• State capital

Scale 1:27,000,000

Albers Equal-Area Projection
standard parallels 28°30'N and 45°30'N

500 Kilometers

500 Miles

Chihuahua

MEXICO

Monterrey

Houston

Baton Rouge

New Orleans

Louisiana

Gulf of Mexico

Florida

Miami

THE BAHAMAS

Nassau

(R02420)

Hawaii

Midway Islands (U.S.)

NORTHWESTERN HAWAIIAN ISLANDS

North Pacific Ocean

Tropic of Cancer

Scale 1:34,000,000

400 Kilometers

400 Miles

Kauai

Oahu

Honolulu

Maui

Hawaii

(R02419)

802907AI 6-02

1077

CENTRAL BALKAN REGION